WHO'S
WHO
AMONG

AFRICAN
AMERICANS

ISSN 1081-1400

WHO'S WHO AMONG AFRICAN AMERICANS

11th EDITION

Foreword by
Dr. Mae C. Jemison
Former Astronaut and Founder,
The Jemison Group, Inc.

Edited by
Shirelle Phelps

GALE

DETROIT • LONDON

While every effort has been made to ensure the reliability of the information presented in this publication, Gale Research Inc. does not guarantee the accuracy of the data contained herein. Gale accepts no payment for listing, and inclusion in the publication of any organization, agency, institution, publication, service, or individual does not imply endorsement of the editors or publisher. Errors brought to the attention of the publisher and verified to the satisfaction of the publisher will be corrected in future editions.

Copyright © 1998
Gale Research
835 Penobscot Bldg.
Detroit, MI 48226-4094

ISBN 0-7876-2469-1
ISSN 1081-1400

Printed in the United States of America

10 9 8 7 6 5 4 3 2 1

Who's Who Among African Americans
Advisory Board

William C. Matney, Jr.
Founding Editor, Who's Who among Black Americans
Former Senior Public Affairs Specialist,
U.S. Bureau of the Census

Lerone Bennett, Jr.
Author and Historian
Executive Editor, Ebony

Vivian D. Hewitt
Former Librarian
Carnegie Endowment for International Peace

Jessie Carney Smith
University Librarian
Fisk University

Contents

Foreword

This eleventh edition of *Who's Who Among African Americans* describes the accomplishments of over 20,000 outstanding Americans of African ancestry. Here are women and men who oversee the operation of financial and publishing empires; who mirror human trials and triumphs in the silky warmth of their voice and the staccato of drums; who fought and won desperate wars on urban streets, on rural farms, and who commanded battalions on foreign mine fields; who have committed themselves to educate us and our children; people who urge and help us to find the charitable side of our hearts; folks who paint pictures and fly spaceships; and who design silicon chips that enable the information age. Contained in these pages are the names, work, and achievements of people who offered their lives, energy, and well-being so that we, all Americans and people around the world may wake each morning to pursue our own dreams. They have parlayed extraordinary potential and ordinary talents—physical, intellectual, musical, artistic, and spiritual— through diligence, training, character, perseverance, and the support of others into noteworthy accomplishments and defining moments. These individuals reflect the contributions African Americans have always made to each other, this country, and the world.

I am afraid that some adults will hand this book to a student or child and say, Inside are role models for you." No, they are not role models. Inside this book are images—public figures who represent only the beginning of the myriad possibilities that a student or child is capable of attaining. The adult who gave the child this book, the adult who is with that student daily, is the real role model because that adult is the person from whom the child will learn to cope with successes and failures, respond to challenges, build healthy relationships, and maintain his or her self-esteem. Look in this book to see the promise inside each one of us, and understand that African Americans have always been active in every sphere of human endeavor and created new ones when needed.

Use this book not only as a reference for names to make one proud, but also as a source for themes—new and old, that affect our lives. Find people to invite to conferences and from whom to solicit invaluable opinions. Here are folks to be honored, acknowledged, and awarded; to be recognized as resources for companies, policymaking, education, and entertainment. This is a source to build networks within a specialty or across disciplines. And please, use this book to discover the richness and expertise that are part of the African American community—in traditional fields, current trends, and unprecedented areas.

That, I believe is one of the most important uses of this book—to highlight the vital role that African Americans, right here and now, play in shaping the world's future. Not just the African American future, but that of the whole earth and all of humanity. Issues of concern to the African American community are commonly tied to poverty, housing, teenage pregnancy, violence, crime, racism, and vague notions of political party affiliation. Too often critical themes of world governance, technological development, and human safety are assumed not to be "Black issues" and are deemed unsuitable for prominence in African American leadership and thought. Yet, these very same concerns affect our well-being, the world's future and, therefore, affect our children. In fact, African American communities and leaders are not that narrow. Entries in this book chronicle individuals who are at the forefront of change.

If you look closely in this book, you will see names like Condoleeza Rice, who played an integral role in the United States policy and helped change the face of the former Soviet Union and Eastern Block. As one of the founders of Silicon Graphics, Marc Hannah developed the technology that not only enabled "morphing" special effects in Hollywood movie hits, but also allowed biochemists to manipulate three dimensional images of medicinal molecules. Charles Bolden, a space shuttle pilot and commander, is now one of the highest ranking members of the U.S. Marines. Hazel O'Leary, former secretary of the U.S. Department of Energy, lifted the veil of secrecy on radiation testing by the United States on its citizens and worked tirelessly to ensure that nuclear waste be properly disposed. Ben Carson is undeniably one of the best pediatric neurosurgeons in the world. Marian Wright Edelman, an unwavering spokesperson for the future of all children, has galvanized public attention. The leadership of these individuals affect the entire world.

The technology and information age that we hear of daily is not predetermined. It is being designed by some of the biologist, engineers, software developers, businesspeople, environmentalists, politicians, physicians, and writers that are included in these pages. What is remarkable is not that we have the opportunity to influence these aspects of our lives today, but that throughout our history we have always made contributions despite the obvious and subtle roadblocks that were thrown our way.

What will I do with my copy of *Who's Who Among African Americans*? I am going to keep it ready, next to my pen and paper, computer and telephone, to be prepared for today and the future—to continue our proud tradition of surpassing the leadership challenges of the twentieth and twenty-first centuries.

.

Dr. Mae C. Jemison
Former Astronaut and Founder,
The Jemison Group, Inc.

Introduction

Now in its eleventh edition, *Who's Who Among African Americans* (WWAFA) is your guide to more than 20,000 men and women who have changed today's world and are shaping tomorrow's. The biographical entries you will find on these pages reflect the diversity of African-American achievement by documenting the contributions of leaders in all fields of endeavor. Together these entries make *Who's Who Among African Americans* the most comprehensive publication devoted to recording the accomplishments of African-Americans.

Compilation Methods

The selection of *WWAFA* listees is based primarily on reference value. In order to identify noteworthy new achievers and monitor significant events in the lives of current listees, the editorial staff scans a wide variety of books, magazines, newspapers, and other material on an ongoing basis. Associations, businesses, government offices, and colleges and universities were also contacted for their suggestions. Users, current listees, and members of the *WWAFA* Advisory Board continue to provide their recommendations as well.

These candidates become eligible for inclusion by virtue of positions held through election or appointment to office, notable career achievements, or outstanding community service. Black persons who are not American citizens are considered eligible if they live or work in the United States and contribute significantly to American life. Such broad coverage makes *Who's Who Among African Americans* the logical source for you to consult when gathering facts on a distinguished leader or a favorite celebrity, locating a colleague, contacting an expert, recruiting personnel, or launching a fund-raising effort.

Once this identification process is complete, we make every effort to secure information directly from biographees. Potential new listees receive a questionnaire asking them to furnish the data that forms the basis of an entry. Those candidates whose achievements merit inclusion proceed through the remaining stages of entry compilation.

In an almost simultaneous process, current listees receive copies of their entries from the most recent edition in which they appeared. They then update their biographies as necessary to reflect new career positions, address changes, or recent awards and achievements.

Sometimes potential and current listees decline to furnish biographical data. Recognizing that this does not satisfy your need for comprehensiveness, we have compiled selected entries from a variety of secondary sources to help ensure that the people you want to see in *WWAFA* are indeed listed. These entries are marked by an *asterisk (*)*, indicating that the listees have not personally provided or reviewed the data. But you still benefit from having basic biographical information at your fingertips.

Important Features

To complement its thorough coverage, *Who's Who Among African Americans* uses these important features to help you locate the information you need:

- **Boldface Rubrics** allow quick and easy scanning for specifics on personal data, educational background, career positions, organizational affiliations, honors and awards, special achievements, military service, home address, business address, and telephone number.

- **Obituaries Section** provides you with entries on recently deceased newsworthy African Americans. This section provides a full entry plus date and place of death, when available.

Indexing

Who's Who Among African Americans features two indexes, both of which make quick work of your searches:

- **Geographic Index.** Locate biographees by specific city, state, and country of residence and/or employment. (Only those listees who agree to allow their addresses to be printed in the directory will appear in this index.)

- **Occupation Index.** With more than 150 categories, this index allows you to identify listees working in fields ranging from accounting to zoology.

Acknowledgments

The editors wish to thank the Advisory Board members whose names appear at the front of this volume for their advice and encouragement as we compiled the eleventh edition of *Who's Who Among African Americans*.

We would also like to thank the many individuals and organizations who nominated achievers for consideration in this edition.

Available in Electronic Formats

Diskette/Magnetic Tape. *WWAFA* is available for licensing on magnetic tape or diskette in a fielded format. Either the complete database or a custom selection of entries may be ordered. The database is available for internal data processing and nonpublishing purposes only. For more information, call 800-877-GALE.

Online. *WWAFA* is available online through LEXIS-NEXIS Service as part of the Gale Biographies file.

Suggestions Welcome

Comments and suggestions from users on any aspect of *WWAFA* are cordially invited to write:

The Editor
Who's Who Among African Americans
Gale Research Inc.
835 Penobscot Bldg.
Detroit, Michigan 48226-4094

Key to Biographical Information

[1] MATNEY, WILLIAM C., JR.
[2] Federal official (retired), communications consultant. [3] **Personal**: Born Sep 02, 1924, Bluefield, WV; son of William C Matney Sr and Jane A Matney; widowed; children: Alma, Angelique, William III. [4] **Educ**: Wayne State Univ, 1940-42; Univ of Michigan, BA, 1946. [5] **Career**: The Michigan Chronicle, reporter, sports editor, city editor, mng editor, 1946-61; Detroit News, reporter, writer, 1962-63; WMAQ-NBC, TV and radio reporter, 1963-65; NBC Network Television, correspondent, 1966-72; ABC Network News, correspondent, 1972-78; Who's Who among Black Americans, founding editor, 1974-88, consulting editor, 1988-93; US Bureau of the Census, sr public affairs coord, 1979-93. [6] **Orgs**: Mem, Big Ten Championship Track Team, 1943; pres, Cotillion Club, 1962-63; mem, NAACP, AFTRA; Alpha Phi Alpha; Natl Acad of Television Arts and Sciences. [7] **Honors/Awds**: Natl Achievement Award, Lincoln Univ, 1966; Man of the Year, Intl Pioneers, 1966; Sigma Delta Chi Citation, 1967; Outstanding Achievement Citation (Emmy), Natl Acad of Television Arts and Sciences, 1967; Natl Award, Southern Press Inst, 1976; Hon Dr Jour, Benedict Coll, 1973; Outstanding TV Correspondent, Women in Media, 1977; Outstanding Natl Corres Serv Award, Michigan Minority Business Enterprise Assn, 1977; Natl Advisory Comm, Crisis Magazine, NAACP, 1981-91. [8] **Special Achievements**: First Black exec sec, Michigan State Ath Assn, 1950-61; First Black reporter, Detroit News, 1960-63; First Black network news correspondent, NBC-News, 1965-70; First Black correspondent permanently assigned to the White House, Washington NBC News, 1970-72. [9] **Military Serv**: USAAF, 1943-45. [10] **Business Addr**: Former Sr Public Affairs Specialist, US Bureau of the Census, Washington, DC 20233.

[1]   Name of biographee
[2]   Occupation
[3]   Personal data
[4]   Educational background
[5]   Career information
[6]   Organizational affiliations
[7]   Honors/Awards
[8]   Special Achievements
[9]   Military Service
[10] Home and/or business address and telephone number (at listee's discretion)

Biographees are listed alphabetically by surname. In cases where the surnames are identical, biographees are arranged first by surname, then by first and middle names, and finally by suffixes such as Jr., Sr., or II, III, etc. Surnames beginning with a prefix (such as Du, Mac, or Van), however spaced, are listed alphabetically under the first letter of the prefix and are treated as if there were no space. Other compound surnames, hyphenated names, and names with apostrophes, likewise, are alphabetized as if there were no space or punctuation. Surnames beginning with Saint, Sainte, St., or Ste. appear after names that begin with Sains and before names that begin with Sainu.

Abbreviations Table

AK	Alaska	**MT**	Montana
AL	Alabama	**NC**	North Carolina
Apr	April	**NH**	New Hampshire
AR	Arkansas	**NJ**	New Jersey
Aug	August	**NM**	New Mexico
AZ	Arizona	**Nov**	November
CA	California	**NUL**	National Urban League
CO	Colorado	**NV**	Nevada
CT	Connecticut	**NY**	New York
DC	District of Columbia	**Oct**	October
DE	Delaware	**OH**	Ohio
Dec	December	**OK**	Oklahoma
Feb	February	**OR**	Oregon
FL	Florida	**PA**	Pennsylvania
GA	Georgia	**PR**	Puerto Rico
HI	Hawaii	**PUSH**	People United to Save Humanity
IA	Iowa		
ID	Idaho	**RI**	Rhode Island
IL	Illinois	**SC**	South Carolina
IN	Indiana	**SCLC**	Southern Christian Leadership Conference
Jan	January		
Jul	July	**SD**	South Dakota
Jun	June	**Sep**	September
KS	Kansas	**TN**	Tennessee
KY	Kentucky	**TX**	Texas
LA	Louisiana	**UT**	Utah
MA	Massachusetts	**VA**	Virginia
Mar	March	**VI**	Virgin Islands
MD	Maryland	**VT**	Vermont
ME	Maine	**WA**	Washington
MI	Michigan	**WI**	Wisconsin
MN	Minnesota	**WV**	West Virginia
MO	Missouri	**WY**	Wyoming

Biographies

A

AALIYAH
Vocalist. **Career:** Singer, currently. **Special Achievements:** Albums include: "Age Aint Nuthin' But A Number, 1994; One In A Million, 1996; performed with Gladys Knight at age 11 in Las Vegas. **Business Addr:** Singer, Atlantic Records, 75 Rockefeller Plaza, New York, NY 10019, (212)275-1000.*

AARON, HENRY LOUIS (HANK)
Business executive, professional baseball player (retired). **Personal:** Born Feb 5, 1934, Mobile, AL; son of Pearl Caldwell and Edwin Caldwell; married; children: Gail, Hank, Lary, Gary (dec), Dorenda, Ceci. **Educ:** Josephine Allen Inst, attended 1951. **Career:** Milwaukee Braves, professional baseball player 1954-65; Atlanta Braves, prof baseball player 1966-76; Milwaukee Brewers, vice pres player devel 1975-76; Atlanta Braves, farm system director, 1976-90, vice pres, special asst to the pres, beginning 1990; Henry-Aaron Inc, pres, currently. **Orgs:** Atlanta Braves Bd Dirs; vice pres & dir Player Develop Club; pres No Greater Love 1974-; natl sports chmn Natl Easter Seal Soc 1974; sponsor Hank Aaron Celebrity Bowling Tourn for Sickle Cell Anemia 1972; natl chmn Friends of Fisk for Athletes; state chmn Wisconsin Easter Seals Soc 1975. **Honors/Awds:** Broke Babe Ruth's home run record April 18, 1974; holds 18 major league records; holds 9 National League records; Hall of Fame, 1982; coauthor of autobiography, I Had a Hammer, Harper, 1991. **Business Addr:** Retired Professional Baseball Player, Atlanta Braves, PO Box 4064, Atlanta, GA 30302, (404)559-9006.

ABDELNABY, ALAA
Professional basketball player. **Personal:** Born Jun 24, 1968, Cairo, Egypt. **Educ:** Duke University. **Career:** Portland Trail Blazers, 1990-92; Milwaukee Bucks, 1992; Boston Celtics, 1992-94; Sacramento Kings, 1994-. **Business Addr:** Professional Basketball Player, Sacramento Kings, 1 Sport Pkwy, Sacramento, CA 95814, (916)928-6900.*

ABDUL, RAOUL
Writer, editor, concert singer. **Personal:** Born Nov 7, 1929, Cleveland, OH; son of Beatrice Shreve Abdul and Abdul Hamid. **Educ:** Attended Acad of Mus & Dramatic Art Vienna, Austria; Harvard Summer Sch, additional studies 1966; Salzburg Mozarteum, Salzburg Austria, diploma 1988. **Career:** 3000 Years of Black Poetry, co-editor 1970; Blacks in Classical Music, author 1977; Famous Black Entertainers of Today, author; The Magic of Black Poetry, editor; lieder recitals in Austria, Germany, Holland, Hungary, US & Canada; TV & radio guest appearances; lectr, Kennedy Ctr for the Performing Arts/ Lincoln Ctr for the Performing Arts/Harvard Univ/Atlanta Univ/ Univ of CT/Howard Univ/Columbia; faculty, Harlem Sch of Arts; music critic, Amsterdam News. **Orgs:** Founder Coffee Concerts Series in Harlem; bd mem, NY Singing Teachers Assn 1989-. **Honors/Awds:** Recipient Harold Jackman Meml Com Award 1978; received Key to City of Cleveland from Mayor Ralph Perk 1974; recipient Natl Assn of Negro Musicians Distinguished Serv Award 1974, 1978. **Home Addr:** 360 W 22 St, New York, NY 10011.

ABDUL-JABBAR, KAREEM (LEW ALCINDOR)
Professional basketball player (retired). **Personal:** Born Apr 16, 1947, New York, NY; children: Habiba, Sultana, Kareem, Amir. **Educ:** UCLA, BA 1969. **Career:** Actor, Game of Death, Airplane, The Fish that Saved Pittsburgh, Fletch; TV appearances, Mannix, Different Strokes; NBA Milwaukee Bucks, 1969-75; Los Angeles Lakers, 1975-89. **Orgs:** Pres Cranberry

Records affiliated with MCA. **Honors/Awds:** MVP of NCAA Tournament 3 consecutive years; MVP 6 times; All Star Team 14 times; Rookie of the Yr 1970; Maurice Podoloff Cup 1971-77; author autobiography "Giant Steps" 1984 w/Peter Krobler; received in 1985 The Jackie Robinson Award for Athletics for career accomplishments as the NBA's Most Valuable Player, for achievements as all-time leading scorer, and for leadership of the world-champion LA Lakers; Sports Illustrated Sportsman of the Year 1985; mem 36th & 37th NBA All-Star Teams. **Special Achievements:** NBA Hall of Fame. **Business Addr:** c/o Public Relations Dept, Los Angeles Lakers, PO Box 10, Inglewood, CA 90306, (310)419-3100.*

ABDUL-JABBAR, KARIM
Professional football player. **Personal:** Born Jun 28, 1974, Los Angeles, CA; married Sabria; children: Ibrahim Abdullah. **Educ:** UCLA. **Career:** Miami Dolphins, running back, 1996-. **Business Addr:** Professional Football Player, Miami Dolphins, 2269 NW 199th St, Miami, FL 33056, (305)620-5000.*

ABDUL-KABIR, JAMAL. See WYATT, S. MARTIN, III.

ABDULLAH, LARRY BURLEY
Dentist. **Personal:** Born Apr 17, 1947, Malvern, AR; married Barbara; children: Zakkiyya, Jeffery, Kerry, Larry II, Najla. **Educ:** Univ of AR, BS 1968; Meharry Dental Coll, DDS 1972; Governors State Univ, MHA; Governors State Univ, MHA, 1996. **Career:** Private practice, dentist. **Orgs:** Mem Amer Dental Assoc 1974-, Chicago Dental Soc 1974-, IL Dental Assoc 1974-, Acad of General Dentistry 1974-, Amer Straight Wire Orthodontic Soc 1982-; Health Volunteers Overseas, 1994-. **Honors/Awds:** Fellow, Academy of General Dentistry, 1987. **Business Addr:** Dentist, 7013 S Western Ave, Chicago, IL 60636, (312)476-0600.

ABDULLAH, SHARIF (VAUGHN ALLEN GOODWIN)
Motivational speaker, businessman, philanthropist. **Personal:** Born Jan 1, 1968, Philadelphia, PA; son of Mary Goodwin and Alfred Goodwin; divorced. **Educ:** Temple University, Philadelphia, PA; Morehouse College, Atlanta, GA; Lancaster University; Islamic Teaching Center. **Career:** Temple University, Philadelphia, PA, assistant to the dean of students, 1988-89; American Friends Service Committee, student consultant; Vine Memorial Baptist Church, Philadelphia, PA, youth minister; Morehouse College, DuBois Hall, resident assistant; American Family Financial Services, mortgage financial planner, currently; Ummah International Foundation: A Muslim Investment Group, ceo/founder. **Orgs:** Executive member, Youth Section, Democratic Socialists of America; founder/president, Temple Progressive NAACP, 1988; speechwriter and speaker, Jesse Jackson 1988 Campaign; founder and chairman, Student Coalition of Racial Equality; Martin Luther King International Chaplain Assistants; International Assn of Financial Planning; Islamic Society of North America; Metro-Atlanta Chamber of Commerce; Speakers Bureau; Consumer Credit Counseling Service of Metro Atlanta; Georgia Bankers Assn. **Honors/Awds:** Seniors of Pennsylvania Service Award, Outstanding Service, 1989; Outstanding Scholastic Achievement, 1985; ACTSO Winner, NAACP, 1985-86; Oratorical Contest Winner, Black History Month, 1985; License, National Baptist Convention, 1990; Certificate of Outstanding Service, African Fellowship Fund; Certificate of Achievement, Islamic Teaching Center of ISNA. **Special Achievements:** Contributing author and editor: Towards 2000: Young African-American Males in the 21st Century, 1994. **Business Addr:** Mortgage Financial Planner, American Family Financial Services, 3565 Piedmont Rd, Bldg 3, Ste 715, Atlanta, GA 30305, (404)814-1660.

ABDULLAH, TARIQ HUSAM
Physician. **Personal:** Born Oct 23, 1941, Florala, AL; married Khadijah Marie Cole; children: Eric Merrit, Kyle Bernard Nichols, Keith Freeman Nichols. **Educ:** Lane College, BS, 1962; Emory Univ Medical Center, externship, 1964; Meharry Medical College, MD, 1967. **Career:** Hubbard Hosp, internship, 1968; Washington Univ Med Ctr, resident, 1968-71; Howard University Medical Center, instructor, 1973-74; Natl Inst of Health, resident/capt, 1971-73; Thrash Med Clinic, dir, 1974-82; Akbar Clinic Panama, staff member, 1983-86; Coston & Laton Clinic, dir, 1974-86. **Orgs:** Natl Bd of Medical Examiners States of FL, AL, GA, medical licensures, 1968-; Republic of Guyana, honorable consul, 1978-87; AAAS, 1985-87. **Honors/Awds:** Lane College, alumni award. **Home Addr:** PO Box 458, Paxton, FL 32538. **Business Addr:** 3230 A East 15th St, Panama City, FL 32405.

ABDUL-MALIK, AHMED H.
Musician. **Personal:** Born Jan 30, 1927, Brooklyn, NY; children: Amina, Khadija, Rashida, Halima. **Educ:** New York Univ, BS Music Educ 1969. **Career:** Bd of Educ New York City High School, music teacher 1969-84; New York Univ Div of Music Educ, prof of music 1970-; Brooklyn Coll Dept of African Studies, adjunct prof of African & Middle Eastern music & jazz 1973-; New York Univ, New York, NY, prof of music, 1973-; Numerous appearances as solo bassist or oudist. **Honors/Awds:** Major recordings East Meets West RCA Victor LPM 2015; Spellbound Status Subsidiary Prestige New Jazz 8266; Jazz Sahara Riverside 12287, Eastern Moods of Ahmed Abdul-Malik New Jazz 8298; Playboy "Bassist of the Year", recognition as Innovator in the Meshing of Middle Eastern Musicand Jazz; recognition throughout Middle Eastern countries as Oudist & Bassist; United Nations Org of groups of Eastern music specialists and presentation for Upper Volta Delegation to the UN (The Waldorf Astoria) and the Cameroon Delegation (The Plaza), Oud and Bass under sponsorship of US Dept of State; org/supervision of music groups performing/lecturing throughout Europe & So Amer sponsored by Amer Soc for African Culture. **Business Addr:** Professor of Music, Brooklyn College, Africana Studies, Brooklyn, NY 11210.

ABDUL-MALIK, IBRAHIM
Nutritional consultant, health counselor. **Educ:** CCNY, BS 1952, MA 1954; Harvard Univ, EdD 1971. **Career:** Tchr/asst prin/staff developer 1954-65; Bank St Coll, dir Educ Resources Ctr 1965-68; Harlem Sch NYC, prin 1968-69; New York City Urban Educ, Div Dir 1971-72; New York City Bd of Educ, vice chmn Bd of Examiners 1972-74, educational planner 1974-76, science assoc 1976-79; UNESCO, overseas science advisor 1979-81; curriculum spec coll/univ faculty; faculty; educ counsel; admin; researcher; writer; health counselor & practitioner/nutritional consultant. **Orgs:** Bd dir Harlem Neighborhood Assn; 1968-70; mem Comm Serv Soc; Family Life Educ Comm 1966-70; mem Natl Assn for Bilingual Educ; mem Amer Assn of Sch Personnel Admin; Intl Coun on Educ for Teaching; mem Kappa Delta Pi; Phi Delta Kappa. **Honors/Awds:** Recipient Natl Sci Found Fellow. **Business Addr:** Nutritional Consultant, 131 Livingston St, Brooklyn, NY 11201.

ABDUL-RAHMAN, TAHIRA SADIQA
Realtor. **Personal:** Born Dec 15, 1947, Shreveport, LA; daughter of Estella Martin Moody and Albert Maurice Moody Sr; married Mustafa Abdul-Rahman; children: Jamilla, Zainab, Naeema, Ibn, Ismail. **Educ:** Howard Univ, BA 1968; Howard Univ Sch of Social Work, MSW 1970; Adams Institue of Marketing Shreveport, LA, completed courses required for brokers license, 1990; Baker's Professional Real Estate College, Shreveport, LA, completed courses required for brokers license,

1990. **Career:** New Careers Prog, specialty instructor 1970-71; Parent & Child Ctr, supvr, 1971-72; Morgan Univ, assoc prof, 1972-74; Assoc for Comm Training Inc, dir homemaker prog, 1984-87; The Family Ctr for Assn for Community Training Inc, dir 1987-88; Marak Realty, Shreveport, LA, Realtor/assoc, 1986-90; Tahira & Assoc Realty, Shreveport, LA, Realtor/owner, 1990-. **Orgs:** Pres PTA West Shreveport Elem Sch 1982-84; exec bd mem Dist Parent Teachers Assoc 1984-85; guest columnist The Shreveport Sun 1985-87; vice pres PTA Booker T Washington HS 1986-87; guest speaker Annual Luncheon for the Sr Citizens of the Union Mission Baptist Ch, 1987; steering comm YMCA Annual Awareness Banquet 1986; mem Delta Sigma Theta Sor Inc, Political Action Comm Delta Sigma Theta Sor Inc; president, Booker T Washington High School Alumni Foundation, 1990-; chairperson, fundraiser committee, Natl Assn of Women Business Owners, Shreveport Chapter, 1991-. **Honors/Awds:** Certificate of Appreciation West Shreveport School, annually 1980-87; Honorary Life Mem Louisiana State PTA 1984; Outstanding Leadership Awd West Shreveport School PTA 1984; Outstanding Realtor/Associate, Marak Ralty, 1988; Emerging Young Leader, YWCA Allendale Branch, Shreveport, 1989; Outstanding Service Award, BTW Alumni Foundation, 1990; GRI Designation (Graduate Realtor Institute), 1996; Shreveport African-American Chamber of Commerce, Business Award, Outstanding Leadership as a model Business Leader in Northwest LA, 1995. **Business Addr:** Realtor, Tahira & Associates Realty, 2835 Hollywood Ave, Centrum Office Plz, Ste 380, Shreveport, LA 71108, (318)636-7305.

ABDUL-RAUF, MAHMOUD (CHRIS JACKSON)
Professional basketball player. **Personal:** Born Mar 9, 1969, Gulfport, MS. **Educ:** Louisiana State. **Career:** Denver Nuggets, guard, 1990-96; Sacramento Kings, 1996-. **Honors/Awds:** NBA, Most Improved Player, 1993; NBA, All-Rookie second team, 1991. **Special Achievements:** NBA Draft, First round pick, #3, 1990. **Business Addr:** Professional Basketball Player, Sacramento Kings, One Sports Pkwy, Sacramento, CA 95834, (916)928-6900.*

ABDUL-WAHAD, TARIQ (OLIVIER SAINT-JEAN)
Professional basketball player. **Personal:** Born Nov 3, 1974; son of George Goudet; married Khadijah; children: Amine. **Educ:** San Jose State Univ. **Career:** Sacramento Kings, forward-guard, 1997-. **Business Addr:** Professional Basketball Player, Sacramento Kings, One Sports Parkway, Sacramento, CA 95834, (916)928-6900.*

ABDUR-RAHIM, SHAREEF (JULIUS SHAREEF ABDUR-RAHIM)
Professional basketball player. **Personal:** Born Dec 11, 1976, Marietta, GA. **Educ:** California. **Career:** Vancouver Grizzlies, forward, 1996-. **Honors/Awds:** NBA, All Rookie Team, 1997. **Special Achievements:** NBA Draft, First round pick, #3, 1996. **Business Addr:** Professional Basketball Player, Vancouver Grizzlies, 788 Beatty St, Ste 311, Vancouver, BC, Canada V6B 2M1, (604)688-5867.*

ABDUS-SALAAM, SHEILA
Judge. **Career:** New York State Supreme Court, justice, currently. **Business Addr:** Justice, New York State Supreme Ct, 71 Thomas St, New York, NY 10013, (212)815-0878.

ABE, BENJAMIN OMARA A.
Educator. **Personal:** Born Nov 19, 1943, Gulu, Uganda; married Joan B White; children: Daudi John, Peter Okech. **Educ:** Carleton College, BA, social anthropology, 1968; Washington State University, MA, anthropology, 1970. **Career:** TransWorld Trading Corp, president/chairman of bd, 1974-75; BAS Associates Intl, managing general partner, 1975-; North Seattle Communtiy College, East-African Study Tour Program, director, 1978-, Anthropology Dept, professor, 1970-. **Orgs:** American Anthropology Assn. **Business Addr:** Professor, Dept of Anthropology, North Seattle Community College, 9600 College Way, Seattle, WA 98103.*

ABEBE, RUBY
Civil rights commissioner. **Personal:** Born Apr 19, 1949, Waterloo, IA; children: Yeshi Marie, Tsehay Eugena, Saba DyAnn. **Educ:** University of Iowa, BA 1972. **Career:** Natl Black Republicans, IA state chair 1984-; Governor Branstad Black Adv Bd, ad hoc 1985; Retired Senior Volunteer Program, adv bd 1985; IA Civil Rights Commn, commissioner 1986; citizen advisor to secretary Dept of Agriculture, 1991. **Orgs:** ABC. **Home Addr:** 621 Independence Ave, Waterloo, IA 50703.

ABEL, RENAUL N.
Operations administrator. **Personal:** Born Dec 28, 1940, Philadelphia, PA; son of Revender C Strother Abel and William J Abel; married Patricia Fenner, Aug 24, 1964; children: Sean Abel, Damien Abel. **Educ:** Central State Univ, Wilberforce, OH, BS, Biology, 1962; Ohio State Univ, Columbus, OH, 1972. **Career:** Anheuser-Busch Inc, Newark, NJ, Columbus, OH, asst plant mgr, mgr beer packaging and shipping, mgr packaging, mgr warehouse and shipping, asst mgr industrial relations, coord technical serv for operations dept, quality control laboratory supvr, Tampa, FL, beer packaging and shipping mgr, asst plant mgr, plant mgr, 1965-. **Orgs:** Bd mem, Greater Tampa Urban League, Pinellas County Urban League, Boy Scouts of Amer, Gulf Ridge Council, Hillsborough Community Coll Found; mem, Pebble Creek Civic Assn, Master Brewers Assn, Beer & Beverage Packaging Assn, Boys & Girls Clubs of Amer, Greater Tampa Chamber of Commerce; mentor, Hillsborough Community Coll, Minority Affairs; board member, Tampa Marine Institute, Inc, 1991-; chairman, business retention committee, Greater Tampa Chamber of Commerce Committee 100, 1991-; board member, University of South Florida Institute on Black Life, 1984-; member, minority development council, Greater Tampa Chamber of Commerce, 1991-. **Honors/Awds:** Outstanding Participant, Greater Tampa Urban League, 1987, 1988; Leadership Award, Boy Scouts of Amer, Gulf Ridge Council, 1988; Support Award, Univ of S Florida Inst on Black Life, 1989; Executive of the Year, Greater Florida Minority Development Council, 1990. **Military Serv:** US Army, special weapons instructor, first lieutenant; special weapons detatchment commander. **Business Addr:** Plant Mgr, Anheuser-Busch Inc, 3000 E Busch Blvd, PO Box 9245, Tampa, FL 33674-9245.

ABERCRUMBIE, PAUL ERIC
Educational administrator. **Personal:** Born Jun 14, 1948, Cleveland, OH; son of Margaret Louise Taylor-Nelson; married Claudia Marie Colvard-Abercrumbie, Jun 14, 1987; children: Paul Eric II, Erica Marie. **Educ:** Eastern Kentucky Univ, BA, 1970, MA, 1971; Univ of Cincinnati, PHD, 1987. **Career:** Princeton City School District, advisory specialist, 1971-72; Univ of Cincinnati, resident counselor, 1972-73, special services counselor, 1973-75, dir, ethnic programs and services, 1975-. **Orgs:** Member, Omega Psi Phi Fraternity Inc; bd member, Dr Martin Luther King Jr Coalition; coach, Athletic Assn; member, NAACP; exec bd member, Dr Martin Luther King Jr Coalition 1980-; head basketball coach, BON-PAD Athletic Assn, 1979-; president, National Association of Blacks in Higher Education on Predominantly White Campuses. **Honors/Awds:** Omicron Delta Kappa Honor Soc, Univ of Cincinnati, 1974; Outstanding Young Men of Amer, US Jaycees, 1978, 1980; Dr Martin Luther King Jr Award of Excellence, Alpha Phi Alpha Fraternity Inc, 1980; Graduate Minority Fellows & Scholars, 1984-85; Community Leaders of the World, Amer Biographical Inst, 1985; Golden Key National Honor Society, 1987; Black Educator of the Year, US Peace Corps, 1987; Black Achiever, YMCA, 1989; University Cincinnati, United Black Faculty & Staff Association, Presidental Award of Excellence, 1988; University of Cincinnati Morta Board, Outstanding Faculty Member for a Quarter, 1989, Appreciation Day, 1992, Presented the Key to the City of Cincinnati, 1993. **Business Addr:** Director, Ethnic Programs and Services University of Cincinnati, PO Box 210092, Cincinnati, OH 45221-0092.

ABERNATHY, JAMES R., II. **See Obituaries section.**

ABERNATHY, RALPH DAVID, III
State senator. **Personal:** Born Mar 19, 1959; son of Ralph David Abernathy II; married Annette. **Career:** Georgia General Assembly, state representative, 1988-92, state senator, 1992-. **Business Addr:** State Senator, Georgia General Assembly, State Capitol, Atlanta, GA 30334.

ABERNATHY, RONALD LEE
Basketball coach. **Personal:** Born Dec 13, 1950, Louisville, KY; son of Juanita Abernathy and Ben W Abernathy (deceased). **Educ:** Morehead State Univ, BA Soc 1972; LA State Univ, MA Admin 1979. **Career:** Shawnee HS Louisiana KY, head basketball coach 1972-76; LSU Baton Rouge, asst basketball coach 1976-83, assoc head coach 1983-89; Tennessee State Univ, head basketball coach, 1989-. **Orgs:** Pres S&R Oilfield Serv Co 1981-; mem NABC 1976-; dir, lead singer Gospel Chorus Gr Salem Baptist Church 1954-76; lead singer Young Adult Choir Shiloh Baptist Church 1976-; bd mem Morehead Rec Commiss 1971-72; big brother prog Family Court Baton Rouge LA 1982; head basketball coach Belgium All-Star Team NamurBelgium 1981; exec dir LA Assoc of Basketball Coaches All-Star Game 1981; asst basketball coach Natl Assoc of Basketball Coaches All-Star Game 1982; memLA Pageant Judges & Entertainers Assoc 1983-. **Honors/Awds:** Teacher of the Year Shawnee HS Louisville KY 1976; Louisville Urban League HS Coach of the Year 1976; Runner-up State of KY HS Coach of the Year 1976; Houston Post Top Ten Asst Coaches in Amer 1980; Final Four Basketball Team Philadelphia, PA coach 1981; elected to Blue Book of Outstanding Blacks in LA 1982; host for Sickle Cell Anemia Telethon 1982; Selected as major host for Sickle Cell Anemia Telethon 1983, major campaign speaker for United Way 1983, one of LA's 10 Best Dressed Men 1983, one of LA's Most Eligible Bachelors 1983, Baton Rouge's Most Fashionable Man 1983; Final Four Basketball Team Dallas, TX coach 1986; 1st black appt to full time coaching position LSU; Sporting MagazineRecruiter of the Year in College Basketball. **Business Addr:** Head Basketball Coach, Tennessee State University, 3500 John A Merritt, Nashville, TN 37209.

ABNEY, ROBERT
Educational administrator, consultant, playwright, producer. **Personal:** Born Jul 2, 1949, Washington, DC; son of Willie Mae Carson Abney and Robert Abney Sr; married Stephanie Early, Apr 13, 1974; children: Keisha, Kara. **Educ:** DC Teachers Coll, BS, education psychology, 1972. **Career:** First Georgetown Adv DC, vice pres 1981-82; Windstar, Ltd DC, pres 1981-; Washington DC, advertising consultant 1982-; Creative Connection DC, dirmkts adver 1982-83; DC Public Schools, coord home study program 1987-; Channel 48 Cable TV, Volunteer's Forum, host, independent video producer, 1985-; playwright, 1973. **Orgs:** Clearing house mgr D C Public Lib Comm Info Serv DC 1976-81; chrmn SNEA Human Rel Coun Natl Ed Assn DC 1970-71, consltnt US Dept Comm DC Pub Schl Systm 1983-; pres Amidon Ele PTA 1984-86; mem Internation Platform Assn, Natl Leadership Conf, The Honor Book; bd of dirs Southwest Neighborhood Assembly; board of directors, Southwest House, 1989-90. **Honors/Awds:** Special Award Jaycee's Vlntr Citation 1969, Headstart Vlntr Citation 1977-84, DC Public Schl 1976-84; Award for Artistic Achvmnt 1978; Riggs National Bank Community Achievement Award, 1990, 1991. **Home Addr:** 3346 Erie St SE, Washington, DC 20020. **Business Addr:** Coordinator, DC Public Schools, Home Study Program, 4th & Eye Sts, SW, Washington, DC 20024.

ABRAHAM, CLIFTON EUGENE
Professional football player. **Personal:** Born Dec 9, 1971, Dallas, TX. **Educ:** Florida State. **Career:** Tampa Bay Buccaneers, 1995; Chicago Bears, 1996; Carolina Panthers, 1997-. **Business Addr:** Professional Football Player, Carolina Panthers, 800 Mint St, Ericsson Stadium, Charlotte, NC 28202, (704)358-7000.

ABRAHAM, DONNIE
Professional football player. **Personal:** Born Oct 8, 1973, Orangeburg, SC; married Tunisia; children: Devin Isaiah. **Educ:** East Tennessee State, attended. **Career:** Tampa Bay Buccaneers, defensive back, 1996-. **Business Addr:** Professional Football Player, Tampa Bay Buccaneers, One Buccaneer Place, Tampa, FL 33607, (813)870-2700.

ABRAHAM, SHARON L.
Educational administrator. **Educ:** University of Michigan, BA, 1980, MBA, 1984, PhD, in progress. **Career:** City of Detroit, urban renewal asst, 1980-82; IBM, mktg rep, 1984-87; Ameritech, mgr, 1987-94; Oakland University, dir, 1996-. **Orgs:** National Black MBA Association, 1990-; Better Business Bureau, arbitrator, 1989-94; Head Start Agency, finance comm chair, vice bd chair, 1989-94; Heidelberg Project, volunteer coord, 1995-97; Leadership Detroit XIX, 1997-. **Special Achievements:** State of Michigan Entrepreneurial Training Program, certificate, 1996; Dale Carnegie Course in Human Relations, certificate, 1996. **Home Addr:** 26336 Lathrup Blvd, Lathrup Village, MI 48076.

ABRAHAM, SINCLAIR REGINALD
Educator. **Personal:** Born Jun 6, 1951, Orangeburg, SC; son of Willie Lee Martin Abraham and Theodore Abraham, Sr; married Bessie Bowman; children: Sinclair Reginald Jr, Stephanie Lynette. **Educ:** South Carolina State Coll, BS 1973, MS Ed 1977. **Career:** Bowman School District, asst principal/coach; Orangeburg School District #1, principal, currently. **Orgs:** Mem SC Assoc of School Administrators, SC Assoc of Secondary Sch Principals; bd of dirs SC Coaches Assoc of Woman Sport, SC Basketball Assoc, SC Athletic Coaches Assoc, Natl Teachers Educ Assoc; mem Omega Psi Phi Fraternity; trustee bd Hickory Grove Baptist Church. **Honors/Awds:** Five-time State Coach of the Year for the South Carolina Basketball Assn. **Home Addr:** 1396 Essex Dr, Orangeburg, SC 29115. **Business Addr:** Principal, Orangeburg School District #1, PO Box 158, Springfield, SC 29146.

ABRAHAM, TAJAMA
Professional basketball player. **Personal:** Born Sep 27, 1975. **Educ:** George Washington. **Career:** Sacramento Monarchs, center, 1997; Detroit Shock, 1998-. **Business Addr:** Professional Basketball Player, Detroit Shock, The Palace of Auburn Hills, 2 Championship Dr, Auburn Hills, MI 48326, (248)377-0100.

ABRAHAMS, ANDREW WORDSWORTH
Physician. **Personal:** Born Oct 8, 1936, Kingston, Jamaica. **Educ:** Columbia Univ, BS 1961; NY Med Coll, MD 1966, resident 1972. **Career:** Kings Co Hospital, physician 1973-. **Orgs:** Fndr dir Bedford Stuyvesant Alcoholism Treatment Ctr 1972; med dir Bur of Alcoholism New York City 1970-72; med consult Comm Health Facilities; bd mem NY State Assn of Cncl on Alcoholism Inc 1975; mem NY State Senate Legislative Adv Comm 1976 New York City affiliate Natl Cncl on Alcoholism 1972; lectr consult Natl Cncl on Alcoholism 1972. **Honors/Awds:** Cert of Appreciation Bedford Alcoholism Treatment Ctr NY State Assn of Alcoholism Cncl; New York City AFL-CIO. **Business Addr:** Kings Co Hosp, 1121 Bedford Ave, Brooklyn, NY 11216.

ABRAM, JAMES BAKER, JR.
Educator. **Personal:** Born Dec 5, 1937, Tulsa, OK; married Darlene Sheppard, 1961; children: James B III, Carmelita. **Educ:** Langston University, BS, 1959; Oklahoma State University, MS, 1963, PhD, zoology, 1968. **Career:** Ardmore Douglass HS, science teacher, 1959-62; Maryland State College, Princess Anne, from instructor to associate biology professor, 1963-70; Hampton Institute, from associate professor to professor, 1973-82; Central State University, School of Math & Science, Edmond, OK, assistant dean, 1982-83; Norfolk State Univ, Biology Department, chairman & professor, 1983-88; Dillard Univ, Biology Deptartment, professor, 1988-. **Orgs:** American Society of Parasitologists; American Society of Mammalogists. **Honors/Awds:** Kappa Man of the Year, OK City Alumni Chapter, 1968; Outstanding Teacher of the Year, Univ of Maryland, Eastern Shore, 1969; Eastern Province of Kappa Alpha Psi, Achievement Award, 1970, 1974; Outstanding Educators of America, 1970.

ABRAMS, KEVIN
Professional football player. **Personal:** Born Feb 28, 1974. **Educ:** Syracuse, attended. **Career:** Detroit Lions, defensive back, 1997-. **Business Addr:** Professional Football Player, Detroit Lions, 1200 Featherstone Rd, Pontiac, MI 48342, (248)335-4131.

ABRAMSON, JOHN J., JR.
Government official. **Personal:** Born Aug 26, 1957, Brooklyn, NY; son of Norine Abramson and John J Abramson; divorced; children: John III, Jason, Monae'. **Educ:** University of Delaware, BS, 1979; New Hampshire College, MS, 1991; The Union Institute, pursuing PhD, currently. **Career:** Government of the Virgin Islands, energy director, 1981-87; Legislature of the Virgin Islands, chief of staff, 1987-89, 1991-92, consultant to Senator Judy M Gomez, 1992-94, supervisor of elections, 1995-; Energy Resources International, Caribbean representative, 1988-90; Private Industry Council, instructor, consultant, 1989-90; US Small Business Administration, documents examiner, 1990. **Orgs:** Resource Conservation and Development Council, chairman, 1988-90; VI Tourism Awareness Link, 1988-90; VI Bd of Education, community and parental committee chair, 1986-88; International Basketball Federation, 1986-93; Omega Psi Phi Fraternity, chapter president, 1985-89; VI Department of Health, advisory bd chairman, 1983-84. **Honors/Awds:** Omega Psi Phi Fraternity, Man of the Year, 1983; Distinguished Political Achievement Award, 1985; Terrance Todman Scholarship for International Affairs, 1990; US Small Business Administration, Outstanding Service Award, 1990. **Special Achievements:** Certified Legal Assistant, 1985, Certified Parliamentarian, 1989. **Home Addr:** PO Box 55, Frederiksted, Virgin Islands of the United States 00841-0055, (809)692-9304. **Business Addr:** Election System of the Virgin Islands, PO Box 1499, Lagoon Complex, Kingshill, Virgin Islands of the United States 00851-1499, (809)773-1021.

ABSTON, NATHANIEL, JR.
Clinical psychologist. **Personal:** Born Jul 18, 1952, Mobile, AL; son of Minnie L Abston and Nathaniel Abston Sr; married Elverna McCants; children: Jamila Aziza, Khalid Amir. **Educ:** Univ of So AL, BA 1975, MS 1978; Univ of So MS, PhD 1984. **Career:** Mobile Youth Court, student social worker, 1971-74; Mobile Mental Health Center, counselor 1974-76; Univ of So AL, instructor/prof 1978-; VA Medical Ctr, staff clinical psychologist 1984-. **Orgs:** Officer/mem Alpha Phi Alpha Frat 1974-; mem American Psychological Assn, 1977-; member, Alabama Psychological Assn, 1978-; member, Mississippi Psychological Assn, 1981-; mem Urban League of Mobile 1984-. **Honors/Awds:** Mem Psi Chi Honorary Psychology Club Univ So AL Chap 1975-; USA Rsch Grant Awd Univ of So AL 1978-79; several scientific publications, presentations 1980-. **Business Addr:** Staff Psychologist, VA Medical Center, Psych Serv (116B), Gulfport, MS 39501.

ACKER, DANIEL R.
Chemist. **Personal:** Born Feb 28, 1910, Radford, VA; married Louise Broome; children: Carolyn, Daniel Jr, Nannette. **Educ:** WV State Coll, BS; Univ of MI, MA 1942. **Career:** Williamson, teacher chemistry & physics 1932-42; Sandusky, analytical rsch chemist, group suprv 1942-44; Union Carbide Corp, rsch chemist, group leader 1944-. **Orgs:** Comm mem Erie Co Affirmative Action 1974, Alpha Kappa Boule Sigma Pi Phi; chmn bd, trustees New Covenant United Church Christ; pres NAACP, Housing OpptyMADE Equal; mem Natl Council YMCA, United Fund Buffalo; pres Minority Faculty & Staff Assoc SUNY Buffalo 1984. **Honors/Awds:** Amer Chem Soc Medgar Evers Civil Rights Awd 1975; Buffalo Urban League Evans-Young Awd for Commitment to Human Dignity & Equal Oppty 1976; Bus & Professional Womens Org Awd for Comm Serv 1976; apptd admin of student affairs Cora P Maloney Coll, State Univ of NY Buffalo; YMCA Gold Key Awd 1972; City Buffalo Good Neighbor Awd; Kappa Alpha Psi No Provicne Achievement Awd; Comm Serv Awd Minority Student Org 1974; WV State Coll Alumnus Awd; Natl Conf of Christians & Jews Brotherhood Awd 1981; Inducted into Alpha Kappa Alpha Sor Black Hall of Fame 1983; So Christian Leadership Conf Comm Awd 1984; Amer Affirm Action Assoc Comm Serv Awd 1984. **Business Addr:** Research Chemist, Group Leader, Union Carbide Corp, Mass Spectroscopy Lab, 531 E Ferry St, Buffalo, NY 14214.

ACKERMAN, PATRICIA A.
Educator. **Personal:** Born Feb 6, 1944, Cleveland, OH; daughter of Minnie Ruth Glover Ackerman and Amos Abraham Ackerman (deceased); divorced. **Educ:** Ohio Univ, Athens, OH, BA, English, 1966; Cleveland State Univ, OH, MEd, admin, 1974; Kent State Univ, OH, PhD, admin, 1983. **Career:** Cleveland Bd of Educ, OH, teacher, 1966-72; Beachwood Bd of Educ, OH, teacher, 1972-74; Lima City Schools, OH, dean of girls, 1974-75; Cleveland Heights- Univ Heights Bd of Educ, OH, coord, 1975, high school asst principal, 1975-87, principal Taylor Acad, 1987-. **Orgs:** Past pres, Natl Alliance of Black School Educ, 1987-89; mem, Leadership Cleveland, 1988-89. **Honors/Awds:** George A Bowman Fellowship, Kent State Univ, 1981; Commendation, Intl Assn of Business Communicators, 1982; African-Amer Educ of the Year, African Amer Museum, Cleveland, OH, 1988; Distinguished Alumna, Cleveland State University, 1990; Distinguished Educator, Cleveland State University Black Faculty/Staff, 1991; President's Social Responsibility Award, Kent State University, 1993. **Home Addr:** 5911 Bear Creek Dr, Bedford Heights, OH 44146.

ACKLIN, PAMELA LYN
Educator. **Personal:** Born Mar 24, 1968, Detroit, MI; daughter of Elbert & Bertha Acklin; children: Chaz Vaton. **Educ:** Wayne State University, BS, education, 1992. **Career:** United Parcel Service, clerk, 1989-92; Inkster Public Schools, 2nd grade teacher, 1992-93; Detroit Public Schools, 2nd grade teacher, 1993-. **Orgs:** Big Brothers/Big Sisters, Sister to Sister Organization Mentor Program; Michigan Reading Assn, 1992-94; Wayne County Reading Council, 1992-94. **Honors/Awds:** American Business Women's Assn, scholarship, 1992. **Special Achievements:** Children's Hospital, Christmas party, organizer, 1990.

ACKORD, MARIE MALLORY
Educator. **Personal:** Born Jan 5, 1939, Bronwood, GA; daughter of Lula Perry Mallory and Clarence Mallory; married Ronald A Ackord, Sep 14, 1983; children: Monique Patrice Campbell. **Educ:** Bethune-Cookman Coll, BS, math, 1960; Nova University, Fort Lauderdale FL, MS, 1982. **Career:** North Ft Myers High School, math teacher 1973; Dunbar Middle School, head of math dept & teacher 1970-73; N Ft Myers High School, math teacher 1966-70; Dunbar High School, math teacher 1964-66; Carver High School, Naples FL, 1960-64; sponsor, varsity cheerleading 1976-77; math dept, chairperson; Ft Myers Comm Relations Commin, commr; School Bd of Lee Co, North Fort Myers FL, math teacher, 1983-, human relations specialist, 1980-83. **Orgs:** School Comm Adv Com; NCTM FL Math Teachers; Lee Co Teachers of Math, Delta Sigma Theta Inc; sec Fort Myers Alumnae Chapter Delta Sigma Theta 1975-77; past charter pres, vice pres Ft Myers Alumnae Chapter Delta Sigma Theta; NAACP; advisory bd Dunbar Day Care; Deputy Elections Clerk, Lee County, 1987-; Phi Delta Kappa Education Fraternity; NCNW; treasurer Ft Myers Alumnae Chapter Delta Sigma Theta, 1991-; consumer member, State of Florida, Agency for Health Care Admini, Board of Clinical Social Work, Marriage & Family Therapy and Mental Health Counselor, 1991-98; Sec Caribbean Continental Social Club, bd mem, clavary AME Church. **Honors/Awds:** Nom Lee Co Woman of the Yr 1976-77; Elected Beta Kappa Chi 1960; Zeta Phi Beta Minority Woman of the Year; North Fort Myers High School, Teacher of the Month, 1976, Staff Member of the Mont, Sept. 1990; Certificate of Appreciation from Governor Bob Graham, 1986; Staff Member of the Month, North Fort Myers High School, 1995. **Home Addr:** 1921 SE 8th Street, Fort Myers, FL 33990. **Business Phone:** (813)995-2117.

ACKRIDGE, FLORENCE GATEWARD
Director. **Personal:** Born Jun 14, 1939, Philadelphia, PA; married John C Ackridge; children: Anthony, Antoinette, Angelo. **Educ:** Temple Univ, BSW 1977. **Career:** Norris Brown & Hall, legal sec 1965-68; Rentex Systems, ofc asst 1968-69; Philadelphia Urban Coalition, sec 1969-71; Rebound Med Group, clerical supr 1971-73; YMCA Youth Leadership Inst, prog coord 1973-74; YMCA. **Orgs:** Vol consult Prisoners Rights Cncl; social worker Walton Village; mem Natl Concl for Black Child Develop; Black Social Workers Alliance; W Oak Lane Comm Group; Black & Non-White YMCA; staff Model Legisl Plan Com Model Judicial Plan Com; vol Christian St YMCA Mem Drive. **Honors/Awds:** Recog Vol Serv to Comm Temple Univ; Trophy Outstanding Serv to Youth in Struggle for Peace. **Business Addr:** YMCA, 1421 Arch St, Philadelphia, PA 19102.

ACON, JUNE KAY
Publicist, public relations specialist, producer. **Personal:** Born Apr 9, 1948, Philadelphia, PA; children: Rory Edward. **Educ:** San Diego State Univ, MPA 1971; Univ of Southern CA, Broadcast Mgmt 1980; Los Angeles City Coll, TV Production/Media Law 1982. **Career:** Caltrans State of CA, dir personnel & public information 1971-75; San Diego City Coll, communication instructor/counselor 1975-80; Human Behavior Inst, dir public relations/media relations 1980-85; June Kay Productions Inc, production coord 1985-87. **Orgs:** Mem Women in Communications, Black Women Network, Univ Women 1977-87; exec bd mem Hollywood/Beverly Hills NAACP 1982-87; mem Acad of TV Arts & Sciences, Black Journalists Assn, Black Public Relations Soc; governing bd County Human Relations Commn; mem City's Advisory Bd on Women, Council on Black Amer Affairs, Natl Academic Advisory Assn, New Coalition for Economic and Social Change, United Way Advisory Bd; productions film for tv, art and community serv; exec bd mem Help Public Serv Foundation; drug and aids prevention program for youths; Sickle Cell Anemia Radio-a-Thon 1986-87; producer host TV talk show "June Acon Show". **Honors/Awds:** Service Award United Negro Coll Fund Telethon 1980-85; Media Relations Jesse Jackson Presidential Campaign 1984; Image Award Outstanding Media Relations & Publicity 1984; Media Award 1984 Olympics; Role Model Women of the Year 1985; Help Public Serv Foundation Award Youth "No Dope" film 1987; PBWA Rose Awards Professional Black Women's Alliance 1989; Certificate of Merit for Distinguished Service to the Community 1989. **Business Addr:** Producer/Dir Public Relations, June Kay Productions Inc, 8306 Wilshire Blvd Ste 697, Beverly Hills, CA 90211.

ACREY, AUTRY
Educational administrator. **Personal:** Born Mar 20, 1948, Frederick, OK; son of Mildred Thomas Acrey and William Acrey. **Educ:** Jarvis Christian Coll, BS, education, 1970; Texas Christian Univ, MA 1972; North Texas State Univ, attended. **Career:** Jarvis Christian College, Hawkins, TX instructor of history 1973-76, asst dean 1976-79, asst prof 1976-, assoc dean 1981-89, vice president for academic affairs 1994-. **Orgs:** Dir Consortium on Rsch Training 1974-76; mem/sec Mu Rho Lambda Chapter, Alpha Phi Alpha 1978; dir East TX Rsch Council 1983-84; dir Cooperative Educ 1981-. **Honors/Awds:** Outstanding Teacher, Jarvis Christian College 1975; Outstanding Member, Mu Rho Lambda Chapter, Alpha Phi Alpha 1979. **Home Addr:** 1011 N Francis, Hawkins, TX 75765-0351. **Business Addr:** Vice President of Academic Affairs, Jarvis Christian College, Meyer Science and Mathematics Center, S-23, Hawkins, TX 75765-9989.

ADAIR, ALVIS V.
Educator. **Personal:** Born Jul 19, 1940, Hare Valley, VA; son of Sereta Adair and Eddie Adair (deceased); married Deloris; children: Almaz, Poro. **Educ:** VA State Coll, BS 1962, MS 1964; Univ of MI, PhD 1971; Monrovia Coll Liberia W Africa, LLD 1973. **Career:** Peace Corps, tchr & comm developer 1965-68; Allen Univ, assessor & dir spl experimental progs 1968-69, asst prof 1971, assoc prof 1972, chmn of social rsch 1973, pres 1977-79; Howard Univ, prof & asst to dean for rsch develop, 1979-84; Allen Univ, pres, 1977-79. **Orgs:** Past bd mem Social Work Abstracts; Hillcrest Children Ctr; DC Commn on Aging; State Planning Comm for White House Conf on Families & Aging 1980-81; co-chairperson Assn of Black Psychologists; trustee of St Paul AME Church; Assn of Univ Prof, Social Workers, Black Social Workers, Psychologists; member, chairman, DC Nursing Home Advisory Commission, 1988-90; member, DC Board of Psychology, 1990-. **Honors/Awds:** Outstanding Educator of Amer 1974; Outstanding Young Men of Amer 1974; Outstanding Univ Prof 1972 1974; Serv Awd Fed City Coll Chap Black Social Workers 1974; Honorary Paramount Chief of Loma and Kpelle Chieftain of W Africa 1968; Hon mem Crossroads Africa 1966; Expert Testimonies House Select Comm on Aging & Fed Trade Commn on TV 1978-80; author, Desegregation: The Illusion of Black Progress, University Press of America, 1984. **Business Addr:** Professor, Howard Univ, Sch of Social Work, Washington, DC 20059.

ADAIR, ANDREW A.
Chief executive officer, attorney. **Personal:** Born Aug 5, 1933, Chicago, IL; children: Andrew Jr, Suzanne. **Educ:** Morehouse Coll, BS 1965; Univ Toledo Coll of Law, JD 1969. **Career:** Natl Urban League, assoc dir field oper 1971-72, assoc dir progs 1973-74, dir Mauy Devel Ctr 1975-79, acting gen cnsel 1978-79; dir cntrl region 1979-. **Orgs:** Legal counsel Ctr for Students Rights Dayton 1969-70; mem IN Bar Assn 1971; mem Fed Bar US Dist Ct 1971; mem Natl Bar Assn 1971; sec natl cncl exec dir Natl Urban League 1971-72; mem Amer Bar Assn 1976; natl advisor & cnsel Natl Cncl of Urban League Guilds 1972-79; bd mem Human Rights Commn Dayton 1969-71; bd mem ACLU Dayton Chap 1969-71; bd mem Council of Econ Educ NY 1975-78. **Military Serv:** US Army, cpl, 1953-55; Korean Serv Medal. **Business Addr:** Director, Central Region, Natl Urban League, 36 S Wabash Ave &, Chicago, IL 60603.

ADAIR, GWEN
Sports official. **Career:** Athletic Commission, referee, currently. **Special Achievements:** First African American and only woman referee to officiate a world championship heavyweight bout. **Business Addr:** Referee, Athletic Commission, 1424 Howe Ave, Ste 33, Sacramento, CA 95823, (916)263-2195.

ADAIR, JAMES E.
Educator. **Personal:** married Marjorie P Spellen; children: Andrea Denice, Tonja Michelle. **Educ:** Fort Valley State Coll, BS. **Career:** Adair's Art Gallery Atlanta, dir 1963-64; Barber-Scotia Coll Concord, art instr 1964-66; Parks Jr HS Atlanta, art instr 1967-69; Morris Brown Coll Atlanta, art lectr 1970-. **Honors/Awds:** Executed murals, Ft Valley State Coll 1962, GA Tchrs Educ Assn Bldg Atlanta 1957; Annual Negro Exhibition

1st Place Awd 1969; presented one man show at Miles Coll Birmingham 1962; Fine Arts Gallery Atlanta 1964 1968. **Military Serv:** USNR. **Business Addr:** Art Lecturer, Morris Brown College, Atlanta, GA 30314.

ADAIR, ROBERT A.

Physician. **Personal:** Born Jun 27, 1943, New York, NY; married Ella; children: Kai, Robert A. **Educ:** Univ of PA, BA 1965; Howard Univ Med Sch, MD 1969; Met Hosp, med intern 1970; Dept of Hlth NYC, pub hlth rsdcy 1972; Columbia U, MPH 1972. **Career:** Sydenham Hosp NYC, dir of ambul serv 1972-; New York City Dept of Correc, physic 1971; New York City Dept of Hlth, act dist hlth offcr for Cent Harlem 1970-71; WNBC-TV, med consult co-prod 4 TV films 1971-72; Pub Hlth Nurses of New Pub Hlth Sch syst, spl consult & instr 1971-72; E Harlem Alcoh Anony Assn,spl consult 1970; Narcot Addict & Ven Dis Mt Morr Presb Ch, spl consult 1970-72; Morrisania Yth Ctr & box tm, consult physic 1970-72; Bd Educ Harlem Pub Sch, consult 1970-71; Staten Is Comm Coll, adj prof 1970-; Manhattanville Coll, spl hl. **Orgs:** Tght spl hlth course on stud hlth prob Manhattanville Coll 1972; fell Am Pub Hlth Assn 1969; mem NY Co Med Soc; NY State Med Soc; NY StateMed Soc; Nat Med Assn; Blck Am Med & Dent Assn of Stud; Blck Cauc of Hlth Wkrs; Am Med Assn; med adv bd Found for Rsrch & Educ in SickCell Dis; sec adv counc of Pres Med Bd New York City Hlth & Hosp Corp; bd pres med bd Sydenham Hosp; bd dir Physic For Inc; chmn Hlth Com 10 Blck Men; consult Hlth Dept Englewood NY; admis com Bio-Med Prog City Coll of NY 1973-; mem NAACP; Harlem Alli of May Orgn Task Force; Duke Elling Jazz Soc; elder Mt Morris Unit Presb Ch; sub-area hlth plan body of mod cit; fin com Mt Morris Fed Cred Un; bd trust Mary Holmes Coll; bd trust Harl Interf Couns Svc; mem 1st Aid Com Red Cross Assn; adv counc NY Urban-League Manhat; bd dSherm Terr Corp. **Honors/Awds:** Woodrow Wilson Acad Scholar 1961-65; diplo Nat Med Bd 1970; bd Elig Am Acad of Pub Hlth & Prevent Med 1972; chmn Prevent Med Sect of 1973 Nat Med Conv 1973; auth of sev pub; hon disc 1974. **Business Addr:** 41 W 96th St, New York, NY 10025.

ADAMS, AFESA M.

Educator. **Personal:** Born Feb 20, 1936, Greenwood, MS; daughter of Annie Miller Adams and Eddie Adams; married Allan Nathaniel, Jul 19, 1975; children: Suzanne Bell-Brown, Steven A Bell, David C Bell. **Educ:** Weber State College, BS, 1969; University of Utah, MS, 1973, PhD, 1975. **Career:** University of Florida, asst professor, behavioral studies, 1974-79, acting chair, behavioral studies, 1976-78, assoc professor, psychology, 1976-80; University of Utah, dept of family & consumer studies, chair, 1980-83, assoc vice president, academic affairs, 1984-89, assoc professor, family & consumer studies, adjunct assoc professor, dept of psychology; University of North Florida, College of Arts & Sciences, dean, 1989-93; Professor of Psychology, 1993- currently. **Orgs:** American Psychological Assn; Utah Council on Family Relations; Natl Council of Negro Women Inc; Southeastern Psychological Assn; American Psychological Assn; Gainesville Women's Health Center, board of directors; State of Utah, Divison of Children, Youth & Families Day Care, advisory board, 1980-83; Governor's Committee for Exec Reorganization, 1983-85; Governor's Task Force, study financial barriers to health care, 1983-84, employer sponsored child care, 1984; several publications and papers; Daniel Memorial Institute, Inc, board of directors, 1989; Jacksonville Community Council, Inc; Hubbard House Programs for Spouse Abuse, board of directors, 1992-94; Advocates for a Better Jacksonville, 1989-, Jacksonville Art Museum, bd of dirs, 1990-93; Jacksonville Women's Network, 1989-; Raines High School, advisory council, 1989-; Andrew Jackson High School, accreditation team, 1989-; JCCI Study, Young Black Males, management team, 1989-; Chair, Implementation Community: JCCI Young Black Males Study, 1989-; National Council on Family Relations, 1989-; Popular Culture Association, 1989-; American Association for High Education, 1989-93; JCCI, bd of dirs, 1993-, sec, 1994-95, president elect 1996-97; Leadership Jacksonville Class, 1994; LJ, bd of dirs, 1994-95; Florida Theatre, board of directors, 1994-, vice pres, 1996-; UNF/NW Link: A Service Learning Monitoring Program, 1995-. **Honors/Awds:** Beehive Lodge, Elks, community service award, 1986; Phi Kappa Phi; United Way, Great Salt Lake Area, recognition for community service award, 1986; Hall of Fame, Granite High School, 1987-88; Civil Rights Worker of the Year, NAACP SL Branch, 1988; Featured in State Office of Educational Equity Unit film, Building on a Legacy: Contemporary Pioneering Women, 1988. **Business Addr:** Psychology Department, University of North Florida, St Johns Bluff Rd, S, Jacksonville, FL 32224-2645.

ADAMS, ALBERT W., JR.

Human resources executive. **Personal:** Born Nov 22, 1948, Detroit, MI; son of Goldie I Davis Adams and Albert W Adams, Sr; married Linda; children: Nichole Leahna, Albert III, Melanie Rachel, Kimberly Monet. **Educ:** Harris Tchr Coll St Louis, BA 1970; Harris Tchr Coll, post grad; So IL Univ, MBA 1974. **Career:** City of St Louis, recreation supr 1968-70; St Louis Pub Sch, tchr 1970-71; Magdala Found, counselor 1971-77; Seven-Up Co, personnel asst 1971-74, EEO adminstr 1974-77, mgr employment 1977-79, mgr affirmative action 1979-80, mgr indus relations 1981-83, mgr personnel progs & serv 1983-85, manager personnel operations 1985-89; Citicorp Mortgage Inc Sales Division, asst vice pres human resources 1989-91; Human Resources Lincoln Industrial, vice pres, 1991-95; HR & Quality, vice pres, 1995-. **Orgs:** Corp chmn United Negro Coll Fund 1972; nominated to US Naval Acad 1965; mem ASPA 1971-78; St Louis Indus Relations Assn 1971-78; trustee San Luis Hills subd 1975-78; comm mem at large St Louis Univ Affirmative Action Comm 1975-77; Mo Advsy Comm for Vocational Placement 1980-83; St Louis EEO Group charter mem 1974-76; mem Kappa Alpha Psi; Antioch Baptist Church, St Louis MO; commissioner, St Louis Civil Rights Enforcement Agency, 1988-91; mem board of directors, United Way of St Louis, 1989-92; mem board of directors, Vanderschmidt School, 1989-; development council member, Habitat for Humanity, 1996-; trustee and deacon, Antioch Baptist Church. **Honors/Awds:** Recognition for raising funds for United Negro Coll Fund; Jr Achievement Scholarship 1966. **Home Addr:** 2331 Albion Pl, St Louis, MO 63104.

ADAMS, ALICE OMEGA

Physician. **Personal:** Born Apr 28, 1951, Washington, DC; children: Sharon, Leslie Wilbanks. **Educ:** Univ of the District of Columbia, BS 1974; Howard Univ Grad Sch, PhD 1979; Howard Univ Coll of Medicine, MD 1984. **Career:** Univ of District of Columbia, teaching asst 1972-74; Childrens Hosp Natl Medical Ctr, rsch assoc 1975-77; Howard Univ, grad teaching asst 1976-79, medical student tutor 1978-79; Children's Hospital, medical tech 1977-81; Univ of DC, asst prof 1979-81; Howard Univ Hospital, resident physician internal medicine 1984-85, asst prof neurology 1985-. **Orgs:** Asst prof & course coord Special Academic Programs Univ of DC. **Honors/Awds:** Outstanding Achievement DC Medical Chirolurgical Soc 1983; Outstanding Achievement Howard Univ Dept of Internal medicine 1984; Outstanding Achievement Alpha Omega Alpha Honor Medical Soc 1984. **Business Addr:** Assistant Professor, Howard University Hospital, 2041 Georgia Ave NW, Washington, DC 20001.

ADAMS, ANNE CURRIN

Educator. **Personal:** Born Jun 28, 1942, Hackensack, NJ; daughter of Etta Greer Currin and Charles Colbert Currin; married Thomas E Adams; children: Tracey Anne. **Educ:** Keuka Coll NY, BA 1964; Rutgers Univ Grad Sch of Social Work, MSW 1970; Rutgers Univ, Doctoral studies, education and sociology. **Career:** YWCA, prog dir youth & teen-agers 1964-66; NJ Bureau of Children's Serv, caseworker/activities dir 1966-70; Newark NJ Bd of Educ, sch social worker 1970-72; Newark Coll of Engrg, adminstr asst to EOP dir 1971-72; Rutgers Grad Sch of Social Work, asst prof 1972-86, consultant/trainer in human service delivery, 1986-; Brandels Univ, Ctr for Human Resources, research associate, 1994-. **Orgs:** Shiloh Bapt Ch, Cascade, VA; Natl Coun of Negro Women. **Honors/Awds:** Outstanding Student Award Rutgers GSSW 1969; Excellence in Education Award, Paterson Alumnae Chapter, Delta Sigma Theta Sorority, 1989. **Special Achievements:** Publications: Book Review Intl Social Welfare Journal, 1980; Article "Field Training for Social Work Stuents in Maternal and Child Health", 1978; co-author, "Group Approach to Training Ethnic-Sensitve Practitioners," in C Jacobs and D Bowles, ed. Ethnicity and Race, Critical Concepts in Social Work, National Assn of Social Workers, 1988; co-author "Nourish and Publish: An Academic Women's Self-Help Effort" in Affilia, Journal of Women an Social Work, Vol. 1, #3, Fall, 1986; Co-author "Characteristics and Consequences of a Time-Limited Writing Group in a Academic Setting" in Social Worth With Groups, Vol. 8, #2, 1985. **Business Addr:** Brandels Univ, Ctr for Human Resources, 60 Turner St, Waltham, MA 02254-9110, (617)736-3770.

ADAMS, ARMENTA ESTELLA (ARMENTA ADAMS HUMMINGS)

Concert pianist. **Personal:** Born Jun 27, 1936, Cleveland, OH; daughter of Estella Mitchell Adams and Albert Adams; married Gus Lester Hummings, Feb 1, 1973; children: Amadi, Gus Jr, Martin, Marcus. **Educ:** New England Conservatory, Preparatory Div 1941-53; Juilliard School of Music, MS 1960; Post Graduate Study, London England 1961-63. **Career:** Juilliard School Preparatory Div, piano teacher 1967-69; Harlem School of Music, piano teacher 1968-69; Florida A&M Univ, piano faculty 1965-66; Urban Arts Winston-Salem, artist-in-residence 1983-84; Winston-Salem State Univ, instrumental faculty 1984-85; NC A&T Univ, piano faculty 1987-88. **Orgs:** Extensive concert tours throughout the world US State Dept 1963-67. **Honors/Awds:** First prize Musicians Club of NY 1956; John Hay Whitney grant; Martha Baird Rockefeller grant; First prize Natl Assn of Negro Musicians; Special prize Intl Competition Leeds England; grant Intl Inst of Educ; Freida Loewenthal Eising Award; performance at Univ of Maryland International Piano Festival Great Performer Series 1985.

ADAMS, BENNIE

Professional basketball referee. **Career:** NBA official, currently. **Business Addr:** NBA Official, c/o National Basketball Association (NBA), 645 5th Ave, 15th Fl, New York, NY 10022-5986.

ADAMS, BILLIE MORRIS WRIGHT

Pediatrician, pediatric hematologist. **Personal:** Born in Bluefield, WV; married Frank M Adams; children: Frank M Jr. **Educ:** Fisk Univ, BS 1950; IN Univ, MA 1951; Howard Univ, MD 1960. **Career:** Cook Co Hosp Hekutoen Inst, rotating intern 1960, pediatric residency 1961-63, hematology fellowship 1963-65, rsch assoc hematology dept 1965-67; Martin Luther King Ctr, pediatrician 1967-68; Michael Reese Hosp, Mercy Hosp Med Ctr, attending med staff; Pediatric Hematology Clinic Mercy Hosp, pediatric hematologist, acting bureau chief, currently. **Orgs:** Mem Natl Medical Assoc 1962; mem Pediatric Assn SC; mem Amer Acad of Pediatrics 1963; mem Amer Soc of Hematology 1968; mem Chicago Pediatric Soc; med adv Com Planned Parenthood 1972-75; mem Alpha Gamma Pi 1972; mem Cook Co Physicians Assoc 1974-; mem med adv com Chicago Bd of Health's Child & Maternal Com; mem AMA; mem Chicago Inst of Med; mem operational consult Sickle Cell Comprehensive Ctr Univ of IL Coll of Med; clinical asst prof Deptof Pediatrics Univ of IL Coll of Med; mem Chicago Med Assn; IL State & Med Soc; bd dir Midwest Assn; mem Art Inst of Chicago; mem Lyric Opera Guild; mem Ounce of Prevention Bd, Links Inc, Delta Sigma Theta; mem bd South Side Comm Art Ctr; mem Friends Carter G Woodson Library. **Honors/Awds:** Diplomate Amer Bd of Pediatrics 1964; apptd chairperson State of IL Commn for Sickle Cell Anemia 1972; Alpha GammaPi Honoree 1973; PUSH Woman of the Yr 1975; 1st Congressional Dist Awd in Medicine 1985; United Negro College Fund Star 1986. **Business Addr:** Pediatric Hematologist Dir, Mercy Hospital Pediatric Hematology Clinic, 2011 E 75th St, Chicago, IL 60649.

ADAMS, CAROL LAURENCE

City official, sociologist. **Personal:** Born May 11, 1944, Louisville, KY; divorced; children: Nia Malika Augustine. **Educ:** Fisk Univ, BA 1965; Boston Univ, MA 1966; Union Grad School, PhD 1976. **Career:** Northeastern IL Univ Ctr for Inner City Studies, asst dir 1969-78; The Neighborhood Inst, dir of rsch & plng 1978-81; Loyola Univ, dir Afro-Amer studies, assoc prof sociology beginning 1981; Chicago Housing Authority, dir of resident programs, until 1997; International House of Blues Foundation, executive director, 1997-. **Orgs:** Natl Assn of Blacks in Criminal Justice, African Heritage Studies Assn; Amer Sociological Assn; bd mem Ebony Talent Creative Arts Found, Assn for the Advancement of Creative Musicians; bd of dir Cable Access Corp; Natl Council on Black Studies, IL Council on Black Studies. **Honors/Awds:** Phi Beta Kappa Fisk Univ 1965; George Edmund Hayes Social Sci Awd Fisk Univ 1965; Community Achievement Awd Hubame Assoc; Leadership in Ed Awd YMCA Metropolitan Chicago; Governors Awd in the Arts; Black Business Awd Black Book Directory; Achievement Awd IL Board of Higher Educ. **Home Addr:** 6929 S Crandon #3A, Chicago, IL 60649. **Business Addr:** Executive Director, International House of Blues Foundation, c/o Alexander Tennant, Treas., 114 Mt. Auburn St., Cambridge, MA 02138.

ADAMS, CECIL RAY

Banker. **Personal:** Born Feb 15, 1948, Crockett, TX; son of Verna Davis Adams (deceased) and Leo Adams; married Myra Bliss Adams, Oct 30, 1971; children: Jennifer, Kraig, Andrew. **Educ:** University of North Texas, Denton, TX, BA, Political Science, Economics, 1970; University of Houston, Houston, TX, MS, Accountancy, 1982. **Career:** First City National Bank Houston, TX, vice president, 1973-85, senior vice president, 1985-86; Union Bank, Los Angeles, CA, vice president, 1986-88; Unity National Bank, Houston, TX, president & CEO, 1988-90; Imperial Bank, Costa Mesa, CA, vice president, 1990-95; Community Bank of the Bay, Oakland, CA, president/ceo, 1995-. **Orgs:** Board member, Hester House (Community Center), 1978-80; board member, Houston Sun Literacy Academy, 1988-90; board member, South Central YMCA, 1988-90; board member, Professions & Finance Associates, 1990-93. **Honors/Awds:** Bank of the Year, Black Enterprise Magazine, 1990; Cecil Adams Day, Harris County, TX, 1990; Resolution, City of Houston, 1990; Founders Award, YMCA, 1990. **Military Serv:** US Army, Specialist 4, 1971-73. **Home Addr:** 3359 Daisy Ct., Hayward, CA 94542-2615.

ADAMS, CHARLES GILCHRIST

Clergyman. **Personal:** Born Dec 13, 1936, Detroit, MI; son of Clifton Verdelle Gilchrist Adams (deceased) and Charles Nathaniel Adams; married Agnes Hadley Adams, 1987; children: Tara Hancock Adams-Washington, Charles Christian Adams. **Educ:** Fisk University, Nashville, TN, 1954-56; University of Michigan, Ann Arbor, MI, BA, 1958; Harvard Divinity School, Cambridge, MA, M Div, 1964. **Career:** Concord Baptist Church, Boston, MA, pastor, 1962-69; Hartford Memorial Baptist Church, Detroit, MI, pastor, 1969-. **Orgs:** President, Progressive National Baptist Convention, 1990-94; president, Detroit Branch, NAACP, 1984-86; teacher, Andover Newton Theological Seminary, 1969; lecturer, Boston University School of Theology, 1968-69; president, Black Alumni-Nae Association Harvard Divinity School, 1988-94; World Council of Churches, central comm, 1991, planning comm, 1994; Natl Council of Churches, chair of ecumenical urban strategy comm, 1992; Michigan Chronicle, editorial columnist. **Honors/Awds:** Doctor of Divinity, Morehouse College, 1984; Doctor of Laws, Dillard University, 1985; Doctor of Humanities, University of

Michigan, 1986; Doctor of Humane Letters, Marygrove College, 1985; Doctor of Divinity, Morris College, 1980; Ebony Magazine, 15 Greatest Black Preachers, 1993-94; Top 100 Influential Black Americans, 1990-94; Harvard Divinity School, Rabbi Marvin Katzenstein Award, 1992. **Special Achievements:** Spoke before United Nations, 1989; World Congress of the Baptist World Alliance, Speaker, 1990; Seventh General Assembly of the World Council of Churches, speaker, 1991; Spoke before President Clinton at the White House, 1992. **Business Addr:** Pastor, Hartford Memorial Baptist Church, 18700 James Couzens Hwy, Detroit, MI 48235.

ADAMS, CLARENCE LANCELOT, JR.
Educator, psychologist. **Personal:** Born in New York, NY; son of Ernesta Clarrisa Coppin-Larier Adams and Clarence Lancelot Adams Sr. **Educ:** Yeshiva Univ NYC, EdD 1973; NY Univ, MA 1952; Long Island Univ, BS 1950. **Career:** Private practice, NY State licensed clinical psychologist 1958-; Hunter Coll CUNY, psychologist 1961-64; Bureau of Child Guidance, New York City Bd of Ed, psychologist 1967-68; SEEK Prog, Hunter College CUNY, psychologist, counselor 1968-70; New York City Bd of Ed, research consultant 1970-73; Bronx C of C, CUNY, assoc prof 1973-; Psychology Dept, Pace Univ, NYC, adjunct prof 1981-. **Orgs:** Consultant, Psychol Proj 145 1976-, AMCRO Inc 1977-; comm for educ & mental health, 100 Black Men 1973-; mem Harlem Cultural Council, Natl Assoc Blacks Concerned in Criminal Justice, Coll Publ Agency Prog Comm, US Civil Serv Comm, NY Psychol Assn, Amer Psychol Assn, NY Soc of Clinical Psychol, Assn of Black Psychol, Amer Ortho Psychol Assn, Amer Assn on Mental Def, Amer Soc Gp Psychol, Soc for Study of Gr Tensions, NEA, Professional Staff Congress. **Honors/Awds:** NY Perm Cert School Psychol, 1968; published A Study of Factors Which Affect Academic Success Among SEEK Students; NY Academic Scholarship, 1946; diplomate, Amer Acad of Behaviorial Medicine; Natl Registered Health Provider in Psychol, 1975-; American Orthopsychiatric Association, fellow, 1992. **Military Serv:** US Army. **Business Addr:** Professor, Pace University, 1 Pace Plaza, New York, NY 10038.

ADAMS, CURTIS N.
Dentist. **Personal:** Born Mar 28, 1931, Waycross, GA; married Jean; children: Cheryl, Curtis Jr. **Educ:** SC State Coll, BS 1954; Howard Univ, attended 1958, DDS 1962; Provident Hosp, 1963. **Career:** Private Practice, Baltimore MD 1963-68; Provident Hosp, staff-oral surg 1963-; Rosewood St Hosp, staff 1964-68; Provident Compreh Neigh Hlth Ctr, dental clinical supr 1968-; Work Incentive Prog, lectr 1970-71; Provident Hosp Compl, lectr 1970-71; Private Practice, dentist 1968-. **Orgs:** Mem Amer Dental Assn, Natl Dental Assn, MD Dental Soc, MD St Dental Assn, Alpha Phi Alpha Frat; mem Chi Delta Mu Frat; NW Civic Forum; Model Cities Policy Steering Bd; Provident Hosp Med Staff; bd dir Hlth & Welfare coun of Ctr MD; bd dir Commun Coll Allied Health Fields; chmn Hlth Task Force 1969-71; treas med staff Provident Hosp 1970-73; treas NW Civic Forum 1971-73; pres elect MD Dental Soc 1971-73; pres MD Dental Soc 1971; chmn med audit Provident Hosp Complex; mem patient care com Provident Hosp; mem utiliz com Provident Hosp; mem med exec com Provident Hosp; orgzng com Harbor Nat Bank 1973; MD State Board of Dental Examiner, 1991-95; Northeast Regional board, 1991-; Heritage United Church of Christ, president, 1994-. **Honors/Awds:** Alumnus of the Year, SC State College. **Business Addr:** Adams, Ashford Dental Assoc, 2300 Garrison Blvd, Baltimore, MD 21216.

ADAMS, DAVID, JR.
Clergyman. **Personal:** Born Oct 29, 1927, Monroe, LA; married Virginia Lee Parker (divorced); children: Ronda O, Onie M Brown. **Educ:** Grambling Coll, BS 1950; NLU, Grad Study 1970, Cert 1971; Morgan State Coll, Cert. **Career:** Mineral Springs HS, instr 1950-51; Vet Ed of Ouachita Parish, instr 1951-52; Clark Elem School, instr 1956-67; Reliable Life Ins Co, gen mgr 1967-76; Baptist minister, 1976-. **Orgs:** Mem Doric Lodge 1 AF&AM; deacon Macedonia Bapt Church; big brother 1958-64. **Honors/Awds:** 1st black on Mun Police & Fireman Civ Serv Bd apptd by Mayor 3 yrs term 1973.

ADAMS, DOLLY DESSELLE
Educational administrator. **Personal:** Born Aug 18, Marksville, LA; married Bishop John Hurst Adams; children: Gaye D, Jann Hurst, Madelyn Rose. **Educ:** Southern Univ, BA 1951; Univ of MI, MA 1953; Baylor Univ, EdD 1979. **Career:** Paul Quinn Coll, visiting prof 1973-75; KWTX-TX, producer/host; College Without Walls Prairie View A&M Univ 1973-74; free lance consultant 1975-81; Howard Univ School of Law, visiting lecturer 1981-83; The Links Inc, natl pres; Black Women's Agenda, natl pres, currently. **Orgs:** Vice chmn McLennan Co United Way; consultant White House Conf on Families; bd mem WHMM TV Washington; advisory bd mem African-American Institute NY; organizer & pres Black Women's Consultation Washington; Alpha Kappa Alpha Sor; chair Board of Mgrs YWCA; editor of newsletter Church Women United; consultant & speaker World Federation of Methodist Women; Jack and Jill Clubs of Amer 1980-; supvr Women's Missionary Soc AME Ch 2nd and 10th Districts 1972-80. **Honors/Awds:** Alpha Kappa Mu Honor Soc; Citation of Merit Business & Prof Women's Club 1971; Woman of the Year Paul Quinn College 1980; Distinguished leadership UNCF 1983; 100 Most Influential Black Amers Ebony Mag 1982-85; Distinguished service Africare 1984.

ADAMS, DON L.
Investment adviser. **Personal:** Born Nov 27, 1927, Jonesboro, GA; married Mary Wilson; children: Don Jr, Damar. **Educ:** Northwestern Univ, attended 1970. **Career:** Professional basketball player: San Diego-Houston Rockets, Atlanta Hawks, Detroit Pistons, St Louis Spirits, Buffalo Braves; Cigna Corp, Southfield, MI, investment adviser, currently. **Honors/Awds:** Co-MVP at Northwestern Univ; All-Rookie Team 1971. **Business Addr:** Investment Adviser, Cigna Corporation, 26555 Evergreen, No. 200, Southfield, MI 48076.

ADAMS, EDWARD B.
State external affairs manager. **Personal:** Born Jan 31, 1939, New York, NY; son of Erna C Adams and Clarence L Adams Sr; married Mary Louise; children: Jennifer, Teddy, Michelle. **Educ:** NY Univ, BIE 1959; Brooklyn Polytechnic Inst, grad study; Stanford University, Sloan Fellow, 1974. **Career:** IBM Corp CO, buying mgr, indus engrg mgr, plant mgr, dir of site operations, mgr of external pgms. **Orgs:** Past chmn Austin Urban League; Regent TX State Technical College System; past chmn mem Brackenridge Hospital Bd; chmn past trustees Huston-Tillotson Coll; mem bd of dir TX Research League; past vice chmn govt relations, Greater Austin Chamber of Commerce; mem, Sigma Pi Phi; mem, Urban League; mem, NAACP. **Honors/Awds:** Stanford Sloan Fellow 1973-74; judge TX Women's Hall of Fame; Whitney Young Award, Austin Area Urban League, 1989; Dr Humane Letters, Huston-Tillotson College, 1989. **Business Addr:** Manager External Programs, IBM, 11400 Burnet Rd, Austin, TX 78758.

ADAMS, EDWARD ROBERT
Attorney. **Personal:** Born Nov 1, 1943, Jamaica, NY; son of Anna Mae Nelson. **Educ:** Queens College, BA, 1971; Rutgers University, School of Law, JD, 1977. **Career:** New York State Department of Law, assistant attorney general, 1979-. **Orgs:** NYS Commission on Quality of Care for Mentally Disabled, committee member, 1993-; BRC Human Services Corp., board of directors, 1982-; New York County Lawyers Association, 1980-; National Bar Association, regional representative, 1988-; Metropolitan Bar Association, 1989-; Third World Lawyer's Caucus, 1981-, past chair; Macon B Allan Black Bar Association, 1979-; New York City Community Board 12, chair bylaws committee, 1984-89. **Honors/Awds:** Queens College, two Student Achievement Awards, 1971. **Military Serv:** US Army, Signal Corp, sp-4, 1963-66. **Home Addr:** 100 West 93rd St, Apt 30D, New York, NY 10025.

ADAMS, ELAINE PARKER
Educational administrator. **Educ:** Xavier Univ of LA, BA (cum laude) 1961; LA State U, MS 1966; Univ of Southern CA, PhD 1973; Harvard Univ, Management Development Program 1986, Institute for Educational Management 1989. **Career:** Orleans Parish School System, librarian/tchr 1961-68; Xavier Univ, New Orleans, LA, reference librarian, 1966-67; Grossmont Union HS Dist, dist catalog librarian 1971; Upper St Clair School Dist, librarian 1972-73; Univ of MD, visiting asst prof 1973; Univ So CA Health Sciences Campus, media specialist 1974-75; TX Southern Univ, coord learning resource ctr 1976-80; Getty Oil Co Rsch Ctr, supervisor library service 1980-83; Prairie View A&M Univ, assoc vice pres, acad serv & planning 1983-85, vice pres student affairs 1985-89; Texas Higher Ed. Coord. Bd, asst commissioner, 1989-91; Houston Comm Coll Syst, NE, president, 1991-96, vice chancellor, 1997-. **Orgs:** Various comm assign Amer Library Assn 1970-, Special Libraries Assn 1981-84; chairperson CA Librarians Black Caucus, So Area 1975; rec sec Natl Coalition of 100 Black Women Houston 1984-86; area rep Youth for Understanding Int Student Exch 1979-82; mem Alpha Kappa Alpha Sor 1967-; pres Xavier Univ Alumni Assn 1989-91; various comm assign Natl Assn of Student Personnel Adminis 1986-89; inst rep Prairie View A&M Univ Army ROTC Adv Camp 1986; mem Amer Assn for Higher Educ 1987-; Board Member, Black Caucus, 1989-; Natl Assn of Women Deans, Administrators, and Counselors 1985-; accreditation team mem, Middle States Assn of Colleges and Universities, 1987-91; accreditation team mem, Southern Assn of Colleges and Schools, 1991-; Xavier University, board of trustees, 1990-95; Amer Council on Educ, Commission on Leadership, 1994-96. **Honors/Awds:** Co-editor, Media & The Young Adult, Chicago ALA 1981; Fellow, HEA Title II USC, 1968-71; articles, various journals in librarianship & educ 1970-; contributor Media & the Young Adult Series 1977-84; Marguerite Bougere Award, Deep South Writers & Artists Conf, 1965; Meritorious Service Award, Assn of Black Social Workers of Texas, 1988; Xavier University, Victor J Labat Alumna of the Year, 1992; Louisiana State University, Sch of Lib & Info Science Alumna of the Year, 1992; Makeda Award, Natl Coalition of 100 Black Women, 1993. **Business Addr:** Vice Chancellor, Educational Development, Houston Community College System, PO Box 7849, Houston, TX 77270-7849.

ADAMS, EUGENE BRUCE
Mortician. **Personal:** Born May 6, 1953, Atlanta, GA; son of Eunice Hines Adams and John Wesley Adams (deceased); children: Amari Alexander. **Educ:** Morehouse College, Atlanta, GA, BS, Biology, 1980-82; Gupton Jones College of Mortuary Science, Atlanta, GA, 1974-75; Morehouse College, Atlanta, GA, BA, Business Admin, 1971-74. **Career:** Guyton Bros Funeral Home, co-owner, 1974-78; Sellers Bros Funeral Home, general manager, 1978-84; Williams and Williams Funeral Home, general manager, 1984-86; Speed-Smart Funeral Home, general manager and secretary of corporation, 1986-. **Orgs:** Vice-president, First District Georgia Funeral Service Practictioner Assn, 1986-; president, Georgia Funeral Service Practitioners Association, 1992-; member, National Funeral Directors and Morticians Association, 1975-; member, Kappa Alpha Psi Fraternity Inc, 1973-; member, Epsilon Nu Delta Mortuary Fraternity, 1975-. **Honors/Awds:** Eagle Scout, Boy Scouts of America, 1970; appointed by Governor of GA, Joe Frank Harris, to Georgia State Board of Funeral Service, 1984, pres, 1988-90; appointed by Govenor of GA, George Busbee, to Juvenile Justice Committee, 1980-84. **Business Addr:** General Manager and Secretary, Speed-Smart Funeral Home, Inc, 224 Houston St, Savannah, GA 31401.

ADAMS, EUGENE WILLIAM
Veterinary educator (retired). **Personal:** Born Jan 12, 1920, Guthrie, OK; son of Lucille Evelyn Owens Adams and Clarence Leon Adams; married Myrtle Louise Evans Adams, Jul 25, 1956; children: Eugene W Jr, Clyde, Michael. **Educ:** Wichita State Univ, Wichita, KS, 1938-41; Kansas State University, Manhattan, KS, DVM, 1944; Cornell University, Ithaca, NY, MS, 1957, PhD, 1962. **Career:** US Dept Agriculture, St Louis, MO, public health vet, 1944-51; Ahmadu Bello Univ, Zaria, Nigeria, professor, 1970-72; Tuskegee University, Tuskegee, AL, professor, vice provost, 1951-89 (retired), professor emeritus. **Orgs:** Member, National Resources Research Council, National Institutes of Health, 1974; member, Africa Bureau Steering Comm on Agric Education USAID, Africa Bureau, 1984; member, Advisory Panel, Office Technology Assessment, 1987; chair, Trustee Board Southeast Corsortium Inter Develop 1987-89; member, Board Directors Institute for Alternative Agriculture, 1990. **Honors/Awds:** Distinguished Teaching Award, Vet Med Norden Drug Co, 1956; Board Certification College Veterinary Pathologists, 1964; Veterinary prototype in Nine Black American Doctors, Robert C Hayden & J Harris, Addison-Wesley Publishing Co Boston, 1976; Tuskegee University Distinguished Faculty Achievement Award, 1979; Sigma Xi, Kappa Alpha Psi, Phi Zeta and Phi Boule. **Military Serv:** US Air Force (reserve), Capt, 1949-56. **Home Addr:** 704 Patterson Street, Tuskegee Institute, AL 36088.

ADAMS, EULA L.
Company executive. **Personal:** Born Feb 12, 1950, Tifton, GA; son of Thelma Billington; married Janet C Adams, May 19, 1973; children: Kevin B. **Educ:** Morris Brown Coll, BS, 1972; Harvard Bus School, MBA, 1976. **Career:** Deloitte & Touche, partner, 1972-91; First Data Corp, exec vp & COO, 1991-. **Orgs:** Congressional Black Caucus Foundation, bd mem, treasurer, 1993-; Southern Ed Foundation, bd mem, treasurer, 1988-; Am Inst of CPAs, 1974-; Colorado Society of CPAs, 1991-; Amer Heart Assn, bd mem, treasurer, 1991-93; Denver Zoological Society, bd mem, 1994-; USO of GA, bd mem, treasurer, 1988-91; United Way of CO, bd mem, 1993-. **Honors/Awds:** 100 Black Men of America; Best & Brightest Young Men in America under 35; Ten Outstanding Young Atlantans under 35. **Military Serv:** Georgia Air National Guard, sergeant, 1972-78. **Business Addr:** Exec VP & COO, First Data Corp Merchant Services, 6200 S Quebec, Englewood, CO 80111, (303)488-8354.

ADAMS, EVA W.
Educator. **Personal:** Born Feb 1, 1928, Eutaw, AL; daughter of Mr & Mrs S H Walker; married Willie G Adams. **Educ:** Alabama A&M Univ, BSc 1949; Ohio State Univ, MSc 1955; Pennsylvania State Univ, EdD 1968. **Career:** Univ of DE, assoc prof; AL A&M Univ, prof; DE State Coll Dept Home Econ, prof & chmn. **Orgs:** Amer Home Economics Assn, secretary/treasurer of the Coll and Univ Section; Assn of Home Economics Admin, chairperson, North East Home Economics Admin Section; Council of 1890 Home Economics Admin, past pres; Amer Vocational Educ, past pres, Natl Assn for Teacher Educ in Home Economics; Natl Assn for the Advancement of Colored People; Natl Coalition for Black Devel in Home Economics. **Honors/Awds:** Honorary mem in Future Homemakers of Amer AL 1970; Hon mem in Future Homemakers of Amer DE 1975; Outstanding Achievement by Natl Alumni Normalite Assn 1974 Alabama A & M Univ; Plaque for Outstanding Leadership as President of Delaware Assn for Supervision and Instruction 1986; Plaque for Outstanding Leadership as pres of Delaware Home Economics Assn, 1987; Alumni Achievement Award for Class of 1949, at Commencement, May 1989, by Alabama A & M Univ; Natl Alumni Normalite Assn; mem Alpha Mu Natl Honors Soc; mem Omicron Nu Natl Soc; mem Phi Lambda Theta Honors Soc for Women in Educ; mem Delta Kappa Gamma Natl Teachers Org Professional Org for Women. **Business Addr:** Chairman, Home Econ Dept, DE State College, Box 759, Dover, DE 19901.

ADAMS, FLOYD, JR.
Mayor. **Personal:** Born May 11, 1945, Savannah, GA; son of Floyd Sr and Wilhelmina Adams; children: Kenneth, Khristi. **Career:** Savannah Herald, president of general management, editor; Savannah City Council, councilman, alderman-at-large; Savannah mayor pro tem, mayor, currently. **Special Achievements:** First African-American to be elected mayor of Savannah; first African-American to win alderman-at-large post 1 in his own right; first African-American mayor pro tem of Savannah. **Business Addr:** Mayor, City of Savannah, PO Box 1027, Savannah, GA 31402, (912)651-6444.

ADAMS, FREDERICK G.
Educator. **Personal:** Born Jul 27, 1931, Columbus, OH; married Olivia P Marshall; children: Christie Lynn, Keline Marie, Alexis Jean. **Educ:** OH State Univ, BS 1956, DDS 1960; Yale Univ, MPH 1970. **Career:** State Dept of Hlth Psychiat Hosp for Emotionally Disturbed Children, therapist 1956-60; General Practice, dentist 1960-69; Univ CT, ombudsman 1969-70, spl asst to pres allied health prof devel 1969-72, dean 1972-74, vice pres student affairs & serv 1974-. **Orgs:** Bd dir CT Bank & Trust Corp 1976; bd dir So New England Tel Co 1977; various offices coms Amer Assn of Comm & Jr Colls; mem Amer Dental Assn; Amer Pub Health Assn; Amer Soc of Allied Health Professions; CT Health League; CT Hosp Assn; CT Inst for Health Manpower Resources; CT Pub Health Assn; CT State Dental Assn; CT Adv Com for the Health Scis Rsch Project; Hartford Dental Soc; corporator Hartford Hosp; adv bd Manchester Comm Coll; Natl Dental Assn; New England Bd Higher Educ State Adv Comm Royal Soc of Health England; S Central Comm Coll Adv Cncl; Amer Assn Allied Health Professions; chmn Statewide Hlth Coord Cncl for CT 1977-; pres Urban League of Greater Hartford 1978-80. **Honors/Awds:** Numerous civic, community affiliations; consultantships, honors, publications & writings in field. **Military Serv:** USAF 1951-54. **Business Addr:** Vice Pres Student Afrs & Serv, Univ of CT, Storrs, CT 06268.

ADAMS, GREGORY ALBERT
Attorney. **Personal:** Born Jun 10, 1958, Atlanta, GA; son of Emily E Jackson Adams and Enoch Q Adams, Sr; married Wanda C Adams, Oct 27, 1984. **Educ:** Georgia State Univ, Atlanta, GA, BS, 1981; Univ of Georgia School of Law, Athens, GA, JD, 1983. **Career:** Georgia State Univ, Atlanta, GA, supvr, 1977-81; Inst of Continuing Judicial Educ, Athens, GA, researcher, 1983-84; Dekalb County Solicitor, Decatur, GA, asst solicitor, 1984-87; Dekalb County Dist Atty, Decatur, GA, asst dist atty, 1987-94, Judge, currently. **Orgs:** Bd mem, Decatur-Dekalb Bar Assn, 1988-89; past pres, 1987-88. mem, 1984-, Dekalb Lawyers Assn; past pres, Scarbrough Square Homeowners Assn, 1986, 1987; parliamentarian, Alpha Phi Alpha Fraternity Inc, 1988-90; vice pres, Dekalb Jaycees, 1989-; mem, Alpha Phi Alpha Fraternity Inc, 1980-, Assn of Trial Lawyers of Amer, 1984-88, State Bar of Georgia, 1984-, Dekalb County NAACP, 1987-; DeKalb Bar Assn, pres, 1994-95; Rotary International, 1995-; Leadership DeKalb, bd chmn, 1996; Chief Justice Commission on Professionalism, mem, 1994-. **Honors/Awds:** Service Award, Dekalb Branch NAACP, 1988; Merit Award, Dekalb Lawyers Assn, 1988; Legion of Honor, Dekalb-Atlanta Voters Council, 1988; Outstanding Public Service, Dunwoody Rotary Club, 1990-. **Business Addr:** Judge, 3631 Camp Cir, Decatur, GA 30032, (404)294-2727.

ADAMS, GREGORY KEITH
Meeting planner. **Personal:** Born Apr 9, 1958, Philadelphia, PA. **Educ:** Rutgers Univ, Economics/Business 1977-81. **Career:** Hyatt Hotels Corp, sales mgr 1981-83; Westin Hotels Corp, sales mgr 1983-85; Radisson Corp, asst dir of sales 1985; NAACP, natl conf dir 1985-. **Orgs:** Mem Greater Washington Soc of Assoc Execs, Natl Assoc Exposition Mgrs, Omega Psi Phi Frat, Prince Hall Master Mason; bd mem Natl Coalition of Black Meeting Planners; steering comm Baltimore Black Enterprise Professional Exchange. **Business Addr:** Natl Conference Dir, NAACP, 4805 Mt Hope Dr, Baltimore, MD 21215.

ADAMS, HOWARD GLEN
Educator. **Personal:** Born Mar 28, 1940, Danville, VA; married Eloise Christine Davis; children: Stephanie Glenn. **Educ:** Norfolk State Univ, BS 1964; Virginia State Univ, MS 1970; Syracuse Univ, PhD 1979. **Career:** Norfolk City Pulbic Schools, biology/general science teacher 1964-70; Norfolk State Univ, alumni affairs dir 1970-73; vice pres student affairs 1974-77; National Consortium GEM, executive director, 1978-. **Orgs:** Comm serv bd YMCA 1979-85; bd of trustees Meadville/Lombard Theol Sch 1980-87; corp adv bd Natl Assoc for Equal Oppor in Higher Educ 1981-; consultant Black Collegian Publications 1984-91; Council on Economic Priorities, bd of dirs, 1986-93; Coll Industry Partnership Div, Amer Society for Engineering Educ, bd of dirs, 1988-; US Congressional Task Force on Women, Minorities & the Handicapped in Sci & Tech, 1987-90; Natl Advisory Council for Environmental Tech Transfer, US Environmental Protection Agency, 1988-90; Sci & Engineering Reviw group, Waste Policy Institute, US Dept of Energy, 1990-; Women in Engineering Program Advocates Network, Washington DC, 1990-92; Coll of Engineering, Univ of MI, natl advisory comm, 1992-95. **Honors/Awds:** Natl Teachers of Science Fellowship 1964-65; Natl Alumni Service Awd Norfolk State Alumni 1974; Torch Bearers Awd Natl Society of Black Engineers 1986; Promotion of Higher Educ Award, US Black Engineering Magazine, 1987; Reginald H Jones, Distinguished Service Award, Natl Action Council for Minorities in Engineering, Inc, 1987; Centennial Medallion, Amer Society for Engineering Educ, 1993. **Special Achievements:** Author, Successfully Negotiating the Graduate School Process: A Guide for Minority Students; Mentoring: An Essential Factor in the Doctoral Process for Minority Students; Focusing on the Campus Milieu: A Guide for Enhancing the Graduate School Climate; Making the Grade in Graduate School: Survival Strategy 101. **Business Addr:** National Consortium Minorities in Engineering, Box 537, Notre Dame, IN 46556.

ADAMS, JAMES MALCOLM
Journalist. **Personal:** Born Jan 30, 1954, Pittsburgh, PA; married Barbara Henderson; children: Bryce, Marti. **Educ:** Fisk Univ, Political Sci, Speech & Drama 1975. **Career:** WRFN-FM, news dir 1971-75; WSM-TV, studio camera operator 1971-75; KHOU-TV, news reporter 1975-76; WTTG-TV, news anchor 1976-. **Orgs:** Mem Natl Press Club; mem Natl Acad TV Arts & Sci, Natl Assoc of Black Broadcaster. **Honors/Awds:** 32 Emmy Nominations Natl Acad for TV Arts & Sci 1976-86; Communications Excellence for Black Aduiences NY 1985.

ADAMS, JEAN TUCKER
Appointed government official. **Personal:** Born in Baltimore, MD; children: Stuart Randall, Scott Hamilton. **Educ:** Coppin State Teachers Coll, BS 1958; Univ of MD, MSW 1972. **Career:** Baltimore City, teacher 1958-64; Health & Mental Hygiene Juvenile Serv Admin, asst reg dir 1965-76; Private practice, psychotherapist 1975-; Office of Mayor Baltimore MD, dep dir 1976-80; State House Governors Office, exec asst. **Orgs:** Consult Private Public 1975-; mem Natl Assoc Soc Workers 1975-; legislative adv Exec & Professional Women's Council of MD 1980-; vice pres United Serv Org 1982-; bd mem Sudden Infant Death Syndrome Inst 1983-. **Honors/Awds:** Mayor's Citation Baltimore City 1979; Governor's Citation State of MD 1984; Scroll of Appreciation Wiesbaen Germany Military Comm 1984; Social Worker of the Year Natl Assoc of Soc Workers 1984.

ADAMS, JOHN HURST
Clergyman. **Personal:** Born Nov 27, 1929, Columbia, SC; married Dolly Jacqueline Desselle; children: Gaye Desselle, Jann Hurst, Madelyn Rose. **Educ:** Johnson C Smith Univ, AB 1948; Boston Univ Sch of Theology, STB & STM 1951-52; Attended, Union Theol Sem NYC; Payne Theol Sem, DD 1956; Paul Quinn Coll, HHD 1972; Wilberforce Univ, LLD 1956. **Career:** Payne Theol Sem, prof 1952-56; Paul Quinn Coll Waco, pres 1956-62; First AME Ch Seattle, sr pastor 1962-68; Grant AME Ch LA, sr pastor 1968-72; African Meth Epis Ch, 87th bishop 1972-. **Orgs:** Chmn of bd Paul Quinn Coll 1972-; chmn Commn on Higher Educ AME Ch 1976-; dir Amer Income Life Ins Co 1977-; chmn AME Ch Serv & Devel Agency 1978; dir The Fund for Theol Educ 1976-; vice pres Natl Black United Fund 1977-; chmn The Congress of Natl Black Ch 1978-; dir Interdenominational Theol Ctr 1978-. **Honors/Awds:** Man of the Yr B'nai B'rith Northwest 1964; Man of the Yr Urban League (Seattle & Northwest Area) 1965. **Business Addr:** AME Church, 208 Auburn Ave, NE, Atlanta, GA 30303.

ADAMS, JOHN OSCAR
Attorney, art dealer, lecturer. **Personal:** Born Apr 3, 1937, Chatanooga, TN; son of Queen M Adams and John M Adams. **Educ:** Wayne State Univ, BS 1962; Loyola Univ, JD 1970. **Career:** Detroit Publ School, instr 1962-64; Pasadena City Coll, lecturer 1964-65; IBM LA, mgr, sys engr, instr 1964-70; IBM Corp Hdqtr, attny antitrust 1970-72; US Senate Small bus Comm, minor coun 1972-75; City of Los Angeles, dep city attny 1975-76; Wallace & Wallace, special counsel 1975-80; Adams Industries Inc of CA, president, bd chmn 1978-82; attorney at law 1982-; art dealer 1985-. **Orgs:** Former chairman and mem of bd of dirs Hollywood Chamber of Commerce; bd dirs Hollywood Arts Council; mem Supreme Court, CA, NY, Washington DC Bar Assns; former mem Hollywood Kiwanis. **Honors/Awds:** Special Achievement Awd Los Angeles Urban League 1970; Saturday Review Commen Issue 1975; Men of Achievement; "Future Hope for the US"; author "Notes of an Afro-Saxon.". **Military Serv:** USN So Pacific Fleet 1958-62. **Business Addr:** Partner, Adams & Alexander, 8383 Wilshire Blvd #528, Beverly Hills, CA 90211, (213)966-5533.

ADAMS, JOSEPH LEE, JR.
Educator. **Personal:** Born Jan 5, 1944, Kansas City, MO; son of Thelma V O'Neil Adams and Joseph L Adams Sr; children: Joseph III, Patrick. **Educ:** Univ of MO Kansas City, BA 1970, MA 1971; Washington Univ St Louis, Post Grad 1976-79. **Career:** IBM, data ctr suprv 1968-70; Univ of MO Kansas City, teaching asst 1970-71; University City, councilman, 1974-95, mayor, 1995-; Meramec Comm Coll, assoc prof to prof history 1971-. **Orgs:** Mem So Hist Assn, Natl League Cities; bd of dir MO Mcpl League, St Louis Cty Mcpl League; mem Episcopalian Church, Creve Coeur Democrats; member, Missouri Commission on Intergovernmental Cooperation, 1985-; steering comm on transportation commun, Natl League of Cities 1982-; vice chmn, Transportation and Communication Steering Comm 1988; chairman, Telecommunication Subcommittee of Transportation and Communication, Natl League of Cities, 1991; National League of Cities, board of directors, 1991-93, advisory council, 1993-, vice chair, 1997; bd of dirs, Citizens for Modern Transit, 1994-97; advisory council, Natl League of Cities, 1993. **Military Serv:** USAF sgt 1962-66. **Business Addr:** Professor of History, Meramec Community College, 11333 Big Bend, St Louis, MO 63122.

ADAMS, KATHERINE
Journalist. **Personal:** Born Oct 16, 1952, Pittsburgh, PA; married Herman L Adams Jr (divorced); children: H Dean Adams. **Educ:** Malone Coll, Communications 1970-72; Kent State Univ, Communications 1972-74; Cleveland State Univ, Communications; Wayne State Univ, BA, 1993. **Career:** WJKW-TV Storer Broadcasting, desk asst 1974-75, reporter trainee, prod asst 1976-77, news anchor, reporter, host, 1977-82; WDIV, news anchor, 1982-. **Orgs:** Comm Commn Cleveland Chap NAACP; hostess Focus Black-Pub Serv Prog; mem City of Cleveland Comm Relations Bd; adv bd Salvation Army Hough Multi Purpose Center. **Honors/Awds:** Salute to Black Clevelanders Awd Greater Cleveland Interchurch Cncl 1980. **Business Addr:** News Anchor, WDIV-TV, 550 W Lafayette, Detroit, MI 48231.

ADAMS, KATTIE JOHNSON
Educator. **Personal:** Born Sep 8, 1938, Orlando, FL; married Henry Adams; children: Kathie Jenan. **Educ:** Edward Waters Coll, AA 1959; FL A&M Univ, BS 1961. **Career:** Orange Co School System, teacher 1962-80; Valencia Comm Coll, internship coord 1983-; Orange Co School Bd, elected official 1980-. **Orgs:** Vice chairperson 1980,81,83, chairperson 1982 Orange County Sch Bd; mem State Comm on Black Educ in FL 1985-; mem dist adv comm We Care HRS & Rollins Coll 1985-; nominating bd Citrus Cncl of Girl Scouts 1986-. **Honors/Awds:** Outstanding Contributions to the Field of Educ Alpha Phi Alpha Frat 1981; Educational Leadership Phi Delta Kappa 1981; Outstanding Leadership in Comm Serv Alpha Kappa Alpha Sor 1982; Faith and Devoted Efforts to the Comm Kappa Frat 1982. **Home Addr:** 2500 Lauderdale Court, Orlando, FL 32805. **Business Addr:** Elected Official, Orange County FL Sch Bd, 434 No Tampa Ave, Orlando, FL 32801.

ADAMS, LEHMAN D.
Dentist. **Personal:** Born Feb 19, 1925, Mansfield, LA; married Gloria Estelle Williams; children: Troy S, Traci L. **Educ:** Wilberforce Univ, BS 1945; IN Univ Sch of Dentristry, DDS 1949; IN Univ, grad study 1951. **Career:** Private Practice Indianapolis, dentist. **Orgs:** Mem Natl Dental Assn; Amer Dental Assn, IN Dental Assn, IN Implant Soc, Midwest Soc of Periodontia, Amer Analgesia Soc, Acad of Gen Practice; various other professional orgns; pres WECAN Found; chmn life mem Com NAACP; bd dirs Indianapolis Br NAACP; bd dirs Indianapolis Natl Bus League; treas bd dir OIC; Indianapolis C of C; bd dir Summit Lab 1959-72; bd dir Midwest Natl Bank 1975; mem Alpha Phi Alpha, Chi Delta Mu, Omicron Kappa Upsilon (hon); mem elder Witherspoon Presb Ch. **Honors/Awds:** Freedom Awd NAACP Natl Office 1973; Man of the Yr Alpha Phi Alpha 1958.

ADAMS, LESLIE (HARRISON LESLIE)
Composer. **Personal:** Born Dec 30, 1932, Cleveland, OH; son of Jessie B Manease Adams and Harrison Leslie Adams Sr. **Educ:** Oberlin Coll, BME 1955; Long Beach State Univ, MA 1967; OH State Univ, PhD 1973. **Career:** Univ of KS, assoc prof 1970-79; Yaddo Artist Colony, composer fellow 1980-84, Rockefeller Found 1977; artist in residence, Martha Holden Jennings Found, 1981-83; Cleveland Music School Settlement, resident composer 1982-84; Karamu House, resident composer, 1980-82; Accord Assoc, composer in residence & exec vice pres 1980-92; Haridan Enterprises, president & artist in residence, 1993-97; Creative Arts Inc, pres & composer-in-residence, 1997-. **Orgs:** Amer Composers Alliance 1984-, Phi Kappa Phi 1965-, Phi Kappa Lambda 1972-; Phi Mu Alpha Sinfonia 1973-; Phi Delta Kappa 1974-; American Organists Guild, 1992-. **Honors/Awds:** Cleveland Orchestra Commissioned Composer, 1995; Natl Endowment for the Arts, Washington, DC 1979; Natl Choral Comp Competition Award, New York City 1974; Rockefeller Foundation Fellowship Award 1979; Yaddo Artists Fellowship Award 1980-84; KC Composers Forum winner choral composition competition 1974; compositions Symphony No 1, A Kiss In Xanadu (ballet), Ode to Life (orch), Hymn to Freedom, Piano Concerto, Sonata for Violin & Piano, Sonata for Horn & Piano, Sonata for Cello & Piano, Love Expressions (orch), Five Millay Songs, African American Songs, The Wider View, The Righteous Man-Cantata to the Memory of Dr ML King, Blake (opera); numerous other works for solo and ensemble vocal & instrumental groups; Works Published by American Composers Edition of NY. **Special Achievements:** Works performed by the Cleveland Orchestra, Buffalo Philharmonic, Indianapolis Symphony, Detroit Syphony, Savannah Symphony, Ohio Chamber Orchestra; Robert Page Singers & Orch; Springfield Symphony, Prague Radio Symphony, many others. **Business Addr:** Creative Arts, Inc, 9409 Kempton Ave, Cleveland, OH 44108.

ADAMS, LILLIAN LOUISE T.
Educator. **Personal:** Born Aug 8, 1929, Greenwood, SC; married David H Adams; children: Hannah Iula, David Jr, Debra. **Educ:** Fisk Univ, AB 1951; SC State Coll, MEd 1970. **Career:** Teacher, Gordon HS 1951-53, Lincoln HS 1955-57, Willow Creek Elem 1957-68, Harllee Elem Sch 1968-. **Orgs:** Mem Florence Co Educ Assn; Assn Classroom Tchr; NEA; mem Cumberland United Meth Ch; bd Ministries; chmn Stewardship Commn. **Honors/Awds:** United Meth Woman saved 4th Grade Student's Life; 1st Black Zone Pres Amer Legion Aux; Tchr Month 1974; Dist Tchr Yr 1975. **Business Addr:** Teacher, Harllee Elem Sch, 408 E Pine St, Florence, SC 29501.

ADAMS, LUCINDA WILLIAMS
Educator (retired). **Personal:** Born Aug 10, 1937, Savannah, GA; daughter of Willie M Williams and David Williams; married Floyd Adams, Sep 1959 (deceased); children: Kimberly. **Educ:** Tennessee State University, BS, 1959, MS, 1961; University of Dayton, 1970-79; Ohio State University, 1979-84. **Career:** Dayton Public Schools, teacher, 1960-73, curriculum supervisor, 1975-; Dayton Division of Parks and Recreation, recreation leader, 1968-70. **Orgs:** Alpha Kappa Alpha Sorority, Inc, 1958-; Ohio Association for Health, Physical Education, Recreation, Dance, 1970-; Midwest District Association for Health, Physical Education, Recreation, Dance, 1958-, president, 1990; Ohio Special Olympic Board, 1989-; Phi Delta Kappa, 1979; Dayton Chapter of Ronald McDonald's Charities Board, 1991; American Alliance for Health, Physical Education, Recreation, and Dance, 1983-; University of Dayton Physical Education, advisory board, 1983-. **Honors/Awds:** United States Olympic Gold Medal, 1960; Savannah, Georgia Hall of Fame, 1968; Tennessee State University Hall of Fame, 1983. **Special Achievements:** Co-author, "Standards for Elementary Health Education," 1992; author, "An Olympic Experience," 1988. **Home Addr:** 5049 Coulson Dr, Dayton, OH 45417.

ADAMS, M. ELIZABETH
Educator (retired). **Personal:** Born Mar 12, 1906, Jefferson, TX; daughter of Millie Elizabeth Jones and John S Wilkinson; married William P Adams, Jul 19, 1934 (deceased); children: Amelia, W Patrick. **Educ:** Wiley Coll, BA Math (Cum Laude) 1928; SE State Coll, grad work; attended OK State Univ, OK Univ. **Career:** Teacher, Leesville LA 1928-31, Oak Hill TX 1931-33, Jefferson TX 1933-36, Linden TX 1942-44, Texarkana TX 1944-45, DeKalb TX 1945-48, Hallsville TX 1948-49, Haynesville LA 1950-53, Booker T Washington High School 1953-71, Hugo School System OK retired. **Orgs:** Mem LA Teachers Assn 1928-31, TX State Teachers Assn 1932-36, 1942-49, OK Educ Assn 1953-71, OK Teachers of Math 1953-71, OK Classroom Teachers 1953-71, Natl Educ Assn 1953-71, OK Retired Teachers Assn 1971-, Amer Assn of Retired Persons 1971-; sec Belles Lettres Club; bd dirs Hugo Child Devel Center; sec PAC Com of Hugo Urban Renewal; mem Hugo Chamber of Commerce; Alpha Kappa Sorority Phi Chapter 1926-36; Choctaw Co Black Heritage Club; RSVP Program; Choctaw Co Youth Serv Center (tutor); mem, chp, 1985-87, Choctaw Co Library Bd of Trustees. **Honors/Awds:** Distinguished Achievement, The Natl Caucus & Center on Black Aged, 1988; Serv to Community, Retired Sr Volunteer Program (15 years), 1989; Service as Volunteer Tutor, Choctaw Co Youth Serv Center, 1989.

ADAMS, MARIE ELIZABETH (BETTY PHILLIPS ADAMS)
Foundation executive. **Personal:** Born Apr 9, 1944, Washington, DC; daughter of Mary Ellen Russell Phillips and Charles Willis Phillips III; divorced. **Educ:** Howard Univ, BA; Stanford Univ, Graduate School of Business, MS. **Career:** National Urban League Natl Planning and Eval, dir, vp for admin; Jackie Robinson Foundation, pres/CEO, currently. **Orgs:** Assn of Black Foundation Execs, bd of dir,; Black Leadership Commission on AIDS, bd of dir and exec committee; YWCA of New York City, bd of dir; New York City Off Track Betting, bd of dir; Spelman Corporate Women's Roundtable, bd of dir; Black Exec Exhcange Prog, visiting prof. **Honors/Awds:** Seagrams Vanguard Award; YWCA Academy of Achievers; Rockefeller Foundation Fellowship; Sloan Fellow, Stanford Sloan Program for Execs. **Special Achievements:** National Urban League, Planning System; "Overview: The Status of Affirmative Action," The Urban League Review. **Business Addr:** Pres/CEO, The Jackie Robinson Foundation, 3 W 35th St, New York, NY 10001.

ADAMS, MARTHA E. W.
Organization executive. **Personal:** Born Oct 14, 1938, Dayton, OH; daughter of Elva & Joe Washington; married Ernest H Adams, Dec 27, 1975; children: Bilah Momin, Darnella, Teresa Armstrong. **Career:** Miami Valley Hospital; Dayton Post Office, mail carrier, retired 1973. **Orgs:** Roosevelt Chess Club, president/coordinator/founder, local tournament director, 1982-; Dayton Volunteer Service Reg, 1986-97. **Honors/Awds:** Ellison Senior Center, Certificate of Appreciation, 1983-97. **Special Achievements:** Organized the annual United States Chess Tournaments, 1983-94; Traveled to prisons to teach prisoners how to play chess; Organized and directed prison chess tournaments. **Home Addr:** 1123 Dennison Ave, Dayton, OH 45408.

ADAMS, NELSON EDDY
Association executive. **Personal:** Born Aug 11, 1945, Southport, NC; married Yvonne McKenzie; children: Nelson Demond, Marius Anton. **Educ:** Cape Fear Tech Inst, nondestructive testing 1973, rec admin 1972; Convair Sch for Nondestructive Testing, 1974; Southeastern Comm Coll, police sci 1975; Northwestern Univ, super of police personnel 1976. **Career:** Brown & Root Const Co, quality control inspector 1974; Brunswick Co Sheriff's Dept, jailer-patrolman-sgt-detective 1974-80; Intl Longshoremans Assn, pres. **Orgs:** Mem & steward Mt Carmel AME Church; mem Pythagoras Lodge No 6 F&AM; mem Southport Lions Club; city alderman Southport Bd of Aldermen 2nd 4 yr term; former advisor NAACP Youth Council 1967-69. **Honors/Awds:** Cert of Appreciation pres elect S Brunswick Middle Sch PTO 1982-83; Cert of Appreciation pres S Brunswick Middle Sch PTO 1984. **Home Addr:** 303 W 10th St, Southport, NC 28461. **Business Addr:** President, Intl Longshoremans Assn, PO Box 7, Southport, NC 28461.

ADAMS, OLETA
Vocalist, songwriter. **Personal:** Born in Seattle, WA; married John Cushon, 1996. **Career:** Tears for Fears, Seeds of Love, backup singer, 1989; Circle of One, Singer, 1991; opened tour for Michael Bolton, singer, 1992; Movin On, 1996. **Special Achievements:** Debut album, Circle of One, earned a certified gold record, 1991. **Business Addr:** Singer, Moovin On, c/o Fontana Records, Worldwide Plaza, 825 Eighth Ave, New York, NY 10019, (212)333-8000.

ADAMS, PAUL BROWN
Police lieutenant. **Personal:** Born Jul 9, 1929, Roanoke, VA; married Elaine D Frogg; children: Beverly P Adams, Susan A Hughes, Constance A Reid, Paul B Jr. **Educ:** Attended, Bluefield St Coll. **Career:** Roanoke City Police Dept, patrolman 1955-64, detective 1964-71, chief homicide investigator 1967-71, lieutenant 1973-. **Orgs:** Vice chmn Natl Conf of Minority Police Officers 1971. **Honors/Awds:** Black Business League Award for Achievement in Law Enforcement 1971; Good Neighbor Award, Natl Council of Christians & Jews 1972; Natl Council of Christians & Jews Brotherhood Citation 1983; 1st & only black commanding officer in Roanoke City Police Dept. **Military Serv:** US Army, Corps of Engrs 1950-52. **Business Addr:** Lieutenant, Roanoke City Police Dept, 309 3rd St SW, Roanoke, VA 24011.

ADAMS, QUINTON DOUGLAS. **See Obituaries section.**

ADAMS, RICHARD MELVIN, JR.
Educational administrator. **Personal:** Born May 13, 1951, Pittsburgh, PA; son of J Marion Adams and Richard M Adams Sr; married JoAnn Kirk. **Educ:** Bowdoin Coll, AB Govt & Afro-Amer Studies 1973; Univ of Pittsburgh, Grad Sch of Public & Intl Affairs attended 1974. **Career:** GMAC, field rep 1974-75; Homewood-Brushton Comm Improvement Assoc, field rep 1975-76; Operation Better Block Inc, comm develop specialist 1976-85; Comm Coll of Allegheny County, asst to the exec dean. **Orgs:** Vice chair, Primary Care Health Serv Inc 1978-; bd mem Dist I Pittsburgh Public Schools 1985-; regional vice chair Natl Assoc of Neighborhoods 1985-; bd mem Northeast Region Council of Black Amer Affairs 1985-; bd dirs Amer Assoc of Sch Administrators; mem NAACP, Operation PUSH, TransAfrica; state chairman, PA Natl Rainbow Coalition, 1986-. **Honors/Awds:** Named one of Pittsburgh Press 200 Most Influential Pittsburghers 1983. **Business Addr:** Asst to the Executive Dean, Comm College of Allegheny Co, 1750 Clairton Rd Rt 885, West Mifflin, PA 15122.

ADAMS, ROBERT EUGENE
Educator. **Personal:** Born May 14, 1946, Richmond, VA; son of Thomas S & Daisy Adams; married May 12, 1973; children: Shannon Marie. **Educ:** Norfolk State University, ASD, 1969; Virginia State University, BS, 1972, MEd, 1990. **Career:** Imperial Plaza, assistant food service manager, 1972-73; Marriott Corp, manager of food service, 1973-82; Creative Cuisine, owner/manager, 1982-88; Northern Virginia Community College, instructor for restaurant management program, 1989-90; Virginia State University, instructor, recruiter, 1990-92; Morris Brown College, instructor, director of community service for hospitality administration department, 1992-. **Orgs:** The American Dietetic Association; Council on Hotel, Restaurant & Institutional Education; Omega Psi Phi Fraternity, Psi Alpha Alpha Chapter; International Food Executives Association, secretary; Historical & Predominantly Black Colleges & Univerties. **Honors/Awds:** Marriott Corp, Manager of the Year, 1980; Omega Psi Phi Fraternity Inc, Meritorious Service Award, 1982; IFSEA, Member of the Year, 1996; VA State University, Friend of Human Ecology, 1995; Morris Brown College, Outstanding Contributions to Service, 1996, Learning Program Hospitality Diamonds of the Future, 1994.

ADAMS, ROBERT HUGO
Editor, publisher. **Personal:** Born Dec 6, 1943, Washington, DC; son of Ella Mary Hodge Adams (deceased) and Gerald H Adams (deceased); divorced; children: Tiffany K Adams. **Educ:** Dist of Columbia Teachers Coll, Washington, DC, BS, 1967; Univ of Hawaii, Honolulu, 1971-73. **Career:** Xerox Corp, Honolulu, HI, salesman, 1973-74; KGMB Radio & Television, Honolulu, salesman, writer, 1974-75; H.R. Adams & Assoc, Honolulu, owner, 1975-76; CS Wo Furniture, Honolulu, salesman, 1976-78; Levitts Furniture, Garden City, NY, salesman, 1978-80; New York Amsterdam News, Harlem, NY, acct exec, business editor, 1980-81; Minority Business Review, Hempstead, NY, editor, publisher, 1981-. **Orgs:** Omega Psi Phi Fraternity, 1962-; Assn of Minority Enterprises of New York, 1980-; Natl Minority Business Council, 1981-; Minority Business Enterprise Week Planning Comm, 1984-; Natl Assn of Minority Contractors, 1986-; New York Region Small Business Admin Advisory Council, 1988-; mentor, Small Business Enterprise Center, State Univ of New York at Old Westbury, 1988-; advisor, New York State Science and Technology Program, 1988-; Procurement Task Force, 100 Black Men of Nassau/Suffolk, 1989-; chairman, Street Fair, Celebrate Hempstead 350th Anniversary; Congregational Church of South Hempstead. **Honors/Awds:** Writing Excellence Award, Advertising Club of New York, 1980; Outstanding Journalism Award, Assn of Minority Enterprises of New York, 1983; Regional Minority Advocate of the Year, Minority Business Devel Agency, US Dept of Commerce, 1987; Serv Award, Equal Opportunity Commn of Nassau County, 1988; African Amer Achievement Award, New York Million Dollar Boys Club, 1988; African Amer Award, United New Jersey Minority Business Brain Trust, 1989; began publishing first newspaper dedicated to minority business success, Minority Business Review, 1981; author, "When WBLS Comes to Harlem," article picked up by the New York Times, resulting in funding for the Apollo Theater, 1982; author, articles on White House Conf of Small Business, 1986, articles on African-Americans abused by corporations and agencies, 1988; series of radio interviews, MBR Forum, 1989; Media Award, Natl Minority Bus Council, 1995; Business Advocacy Award, Brooklyn Minority Business Development Center, 1995; Media Advocacy Award, US Dept of Commerce, Minority Business Develop Agency, NY Region, 1995; Cert of Recog, Incorporated Village of Hempstead and the Town of Hempstead, 1995; published book "15 Years of Minority Business Development," 1995. **Military Serv:** US Army, captain, 1968-72. **Business Addr:** Editor and Publisher, Minority Business Review, PO Box 2132, Hempstead, NY 11551-1132.

ADAMS, ROBERT THOMAS
Economist. **Personal:** Born Nov 19, 1913, Griffin, GA; son of Rosa Reid Adams and Robert T Adams; married Marguerite. **Educ:** Amer Univ, MA 1958, BSA 1948. **Career:** Economist, Bur of Labor Statistics, 1947-67; Office of the Undersec for Transportation, 1967-69; US Dept Commerce, chief economic analysis unit, asst sec of transportation, US Dept of Transportation, chief transp econ div, Fed Hwy Admin, 1969-74; acting dir, office prog & policy plng FHWA, consultant, econs & transp 1974-81. **Orgs:** Mem, Amer Soc Traffic & Transp, Photog Soc of Amer, USCG Aux 1972. **Honors/Awds:** Hwy Admin Awd 1974; Group Hon Awd Productivity Div Bur Labor Stat 1967; 2 Star Color Award, PSA. **Military Serv:** US Army, pfc 1941-42.

ADAMS, RONALD, JR.
Social services. **Personal:** Born Oct 15, 1958, The Bronx, NY. **Educ:** Benjamin Franklin HS, Regents Diploma 1976; Wagner Coll, BA Soc Work & Spec Ed 1980; Dale Carnegie, general course business graduate, 1995; Central Labor, peer counseling course, certificate, 1995; Arrive/Eponents, HIV & AIDS Education, certificate, 1996; Addiction Training Center, OASAS, certificate, 1996; Evangelism Eplosion, Gethsemane Baptist Church, Bronx, NY; Department of Health, Community HIV/AIDS Educator Team, certificate, 1996. **Career:** Police Athletic League 25th Precint, asst track coord 1973-74; Dunlevy Milbank Day Care Ctr, sr day camp counselor 1974-75; Gramercy Boys Club, head camp unit leader 1977-79; People Care Inc, head suprv 1981-85; Progressive Home Hlth Serv; sr health care mngr 1985-. **Orgs:** Natl governing council Sigma Phi Rho 1978-; volunteer worker March of Dimes 1980-, Spec Olympics 1981-; Boys Club of Amer 1981-; Evangelism Eplosion Ministry, asst trng, 1996; pres, Men's Fellowship Ministry, 1996; FOCUS, 1995; Prison Ministry, 1995. **Honors/Awds:** Spec Serv Awds Black Concern Wagner Coll 1976-80; Sports Letter Awds Track Team 1976-80; Acad Awd Pre-Freshman Summer Session Wagner Coll 1976; Track Team Capt Wanger Coll 1978-80; Service Awd March of Dimes 1984; 1 of 13 founding mems of Sigma Phi Rho Frat. **Home Addr:** 110 East 177th St, #2E, Bronx, NY 10453.

ADAMS, RUSSELL LEE
Educator. **Personal:** Born Aug 13, 1930, Baltimore, MD; married Eleanor P; children: Sabrina, Russell. **Educ:** Morehouse College, BA, 1952; University of Chicago, MA, 1954, PhD, 1971. **Career:** Fed City College, assoc professor, 1969-71; Howard University, assoc professor, 1971-, chairman, Dept of Afro-American Studies, currently. **Orgs:** Private consultant, Afro-American Studies Career Program In-Serv & Dept, Montgomery County Board of Education; consultant for numerous facilities including: University of Pittsburgh, Center for Deseg, 1976-, Wilmington DE Public Schools, 1977, Newark-New Castle-Marshalton McKean School District, Jackson Public

Schools, 1969-70; lecturer/consultant, US Info Agency, 1977; chairman, committee on status of blacks in profession Amer Pol Sci Assn, 1974-77; NAACP, Curr Eval Pool, Prince Georges County Bd of Ed 1976-. **Honors/Awds:** Author, Great Negroes Past & Present, 1963-69, 1972; Leading American Negroes, 1965; Perceptual Difficulties Dev Pol Sci Varia, Spring 1976; publisher, Black Studies Movement, Assessment Journal of Negro Education, 1977. **Business Addr:** Chairman, Dept of Afro-American Studies, Howard University, 2400 Sixth St NW, Washington, DC 20059-0002.

ADAMS, SAM AARON
Professional football player. **Personal:** Born Jun 13, 1973, Houston, TX; son of Sam Sr. **Educ:** Texas A&M. **Career:** Seattle Seahawks, defensive tackle, 1994-. **Business Addr:** Professional Football Player, Seattle Seahawks, 11220 NE 53rd St, Kirkland, WA 98033, (206)827-9777.

ADAMS, SAMUEL CLIFFORD, JR.
Foreign service officer (retired). **Personal:** Born Aug 15, 1920, Houston, TX; son of Sarah Catherine Roberts and Samuel C Adams; married Evelyn Sheppard Baker. **Educ:** Dept of State Sr Sem for Foreign Policy, post PhD 1965; Syracuse Univ Maxwell School, post PhD 1958; University of London, London School of Economics; School of Oriental & African Studies, post PhD 1957; Univ of Chicago, PhD 1953; Fisk Univ, BA, 1940, MA, 1947. **Career:** Marion Cooperative Center, director, 1947-50; The Univ of Chicago, the Committee on Education, Research and Training in Race Relations, 1951; US Special Technical and Economic Mission to Indo-China, mass education specialist and acting chief of education division, 1952-54; US Operations Mission to Cambodia, chief of education and community development, 1955-57; US International Cooperation Administration, Lagos, Nigeria, chief education advisor, 1958-60; US AID Mission to the Republic of Mali, director, 1961-65; US AID Mission to Morocco, director, 1965-69; United Nations General Assembly, Fifth Special Section, US representative, 1967; AEP to Republic of Niger, US ambassador, 1968-69; US Department of State, Bureau for Africa, asst administrator, 1969-75; Samuel C Adams Jr and Co International, pres, 1976-. **Orgs:** Mem Adv Comm Science, Technol & Devel, Exec Office of Pres 1978, Economic Devel Adv Bd Volta River 1977-78, Subcommittee on Intl Economic Policy Chamber of Commerce US 1977-78, Adv Comm on S Natl Academy of Sci 1979-81; mem International Business Committee, Houston Chamber of Commerce, 1978; mem bd dir Houston World Trade Assn 1980-81; mem bd trustees Fisk Univ 1978-81; mem bd dir Texas Greenhouse Vegetable Growers Assn, TX A&M Univ; mem Houston Committee on Foreign Relations. **Honors/Awds:** William A Jump Award, 1954; Decorated by Prince Sianhouk for Outstanding Service to Cambodian Education, 1956; Arthur S Flemming Award, 1957; King Hassan II, Rabat, Morocco, Cross of the Ouizzan Alouite, 1968; Agency for International Development, Meritorious Unit Citation, 1971, Equal Employment Opportunity Award, 1971, Distinguished Honor Award, 1972; Opportunities Industrialization Center, Ralph Bunche Award, 1972; Rockefeller Public Service Award, 1972; US Department of State, Bureau of African Affairs, Scroll of Appreciation, 1975. **Military Serv:** USAF, priv first class, 1944-46; Certificate of Meritorious Service 1946. **Business Addr:** Consultant, 3226 N MacGregor Way, Houston, TX 77004.

ADAMS, SAMUEL LEVI, SR.
Educator. **Personal:** Born Jan 25, 1926, Waycross, GA; son of Viola Virgil Adams (deceased) and Joe Nathan Adams; married Elenora Willette Grimes; children: Carol W, Bruce L, Samuel L Jr. **Educ:** WV State Coll, BA 1948; Wayne State Univ, AB 1950; Univ of MN, MA 1954; Univ of WI, Russell Sage Fellow Behavioral Sci Writing 1965-66. **Career:** Atlanta Daily World, reporter 1954-56; Des Moines Register, copy editor 1956-57; Gibbs-St Petersburg Jr Coll, dir pub rel 1958-60, part-time teacher 1960-64; St Petersburg Times, reporter 1960-65; So Reg Council Inc, dir res 1965-66; WI St Jour, corr 1966-67; St Petersburg Times, investigative reporter 1967-68; Univ of WI, visiting prof 1968-69; Univ of S FL, asst prof 1969-71; Dem Natl Comm, asst dir Minorities Div & asst pres sec 1970-72; Univ of KS, assoc prof journalism 1972-; Hampton Univ, visiting prof journalism 1982-83; Univ of the Virgin Islands, visiting prof of journalism 1985-87. **Orgs:** Founder, dir Continuing Acad Cultural Enrich Prog 1962-64 (programs won natl Lane Bryant Vol Serv Awards); 1st vice pres Greater St Petersburg Council of Churches 63-65; prog dir div & joint sessions San Diego Conv 1974; Assn Educ Journ Head Minorities Div 1974-75; dir Gannett-AEJ Project for Enrichment of Journalism Educ 1975-80; pres & bd chmn Natl Youth Communication Inc 1977-82; dir The Newspaper Fund's Natl Minority Internship Prog 1979-80; KU Tenure Study Task Force; Task Force Univ Outreach; Minority Affairs Adv Bd; AAUP; co-founder and curator, Ida B Wells Award, 1983-; mem of board of directors and educ resource chmn, Jones Holloway-Bryan Foundation, 1986-; consultant for communications, Amnesty International USA, 1988-. **Honors/Awds:** Regional Award Natl Conf Christians & Jews 1962; Pulitzer Prize Award nominee in journalism 1964-65; Lane Bryant Awards semi-finalist outstanding volunteer service 1966; Russell Sage Fellow Univ of WI 1966-67; Hampton Jr Coll Award 1966; Green Eyeshade Sweepstakes Award Sigma Delta Chi Atlanta 1969; state, local & regional awards, journalism; Award for Distinguished Serv to Journalism NC A&T State Univ 1978; Distinguished Visiting Prof Hampton Univ 1981-82; ''Blackening in the Media,'' in NUL's State of Black America, 1985; ''Highways to Hope,'' in St Pete Times and Hohenburg's The New Front Page, 1965; Partners in Progress Award, National Association of Black Journalists, 1990; NABJ, Lifetime Achievement Award, 1997; United Minority Medi Assn, (UMMA), Distinguished Service to Journalism Award, 1996. **Military Serv:** US Army, field artillery survey & chem warfare specialist 1950-52. **Business Addr:** Associate Professor Journalism, Univ of Kansas, 208 Stauffer-Flint Hall, Lawrence, KS 66045.

ADAMS, SHEILA MARY
Consultant. **Personal:** Born Jun 7, 1947, Chicago, IL; daughter of Delores Lawrence Wasmund and Frank Ricks; married Alvin Adams, Oct 23, 1968; children: Lara, Kristina, Stefani, Susan. **Educ:** De Paul University, Chicago, IL, BA, music, 1979; Office for Ministry Formation, Chicago, IL, lay ministry, 1983. **Career:** Chicago Police Dept, Chicago, IL, junior clerk, 1968-71; US Treasury Dept, Chicago, IL, clerk, 1973-74; Archdiocese of Chicago, IL, elementary teacher, 1979-90, Office for Black Catholic Ministries, executive director 1990-91; Office for ethnic Ministries, 1991-. African-American consultant. **Orgs:** Regional coordinator, National Black Catholic Congress VII, 1990-92; chair, Bishop's National Advisory Council, 1989; member, Bishop's National Advisory Council, 1985-90; chair, Spirituality Committee of the Archdiocesan Pastoral Council, 1986-88; delegate Congress VI, 1987; delegate, National Black Catholic Congress VI, 1987; Congress VII, 1992; Congress VIII, 1996-98; Secretary of the National Association of Black Catholic Administrators, 1996-98. **Honors/Awds:** Archdiocesan Honoree, Fr Augustus Tolton Hon Award, 1997-1988 Sr Thea Bowman Award, 1994. **Business Addr:** African American Consultant, Ethnic Ministries, Archdiocese of Chicago, 155 E Superior St, Chicago, IL 60611.

ADAMS, T. PATTON
Mayor. **Personal:** Born Feb 16, 1943, Columbia, SC; married Jacquelyn Hackett Culbertson; children: Thomas, John, Lucas. **Educ:** Washington and Lee University, BA, 1965; University of South Carolina, JD, 1968. **Career:** Columbia Zoning Board Adjustments, member, 1974-76; City of Columbia, SC, city councilmember, 1976-86, mayor, 1986-. **Orgs:** South Carolina Bar Assn; Richland County Bar Assn; South Carolina Chamber of Commerce; Columbia Visitors and Convention Bureau; American Legion. **Military Serv:** US Army, Lt, 1961-65, Capt, 1969-70; Bronze Star. **Business Addr:** Mayor, City of Columbia, PO Box 147, Columbia, SC 29217.

ADAMS, THEODORE ADOLPHUS, JR.
Business executive. **Personal:** Born Sep 9, 1929, Newark, NJ; married Jeanie Perry; children: Karen, Deborah, Christina, Theodore III. **Educ:** US Army, Eng School, 1961; US Army Command & Gen Staff Coll, 1962; US Army Mgmt Eng Training Agency, 1967; Harvard Univ 1977. **Career:** Unified Ind Inc, pres 1970-. **Orgs:** Exec dir Natl Assoc of Black Mgrs 1972-74; proj mgr Astro Reliability Corp 1969-72; assoc prof Agr Coll of NC 1957-59; dir Natl Assoc of Black Mfrs 1974-76; bd mem Retired Officers Assoc, Intl Business Serv Inc, Natl Minority Purchasing Council 1972-74; life mem Natl Business League; bd of councilors Fed City Coll, Ripon Soc, ASAE, WA Urban League; mem Amer Platform Assoc, Amer Natl Metric Council, bd mem YMCA of Metro WA 1976, District of Columbia Chamber of Commerce 1977, Legion of Merit AUS 1967, 1968, citation Natl Bus League 1974, Small Business Admin 1976; life mem Natl Business League 1977; mem Republican Senatorial Trust, Republican Congressional Leadership Council, Natl Black Leadership Roundtable; co-chmn Legal Defense & Educ Fund. **Honors/Awds:** Spec Serv Awd Natl Assoc of Black Mfrs 1974,76. **Military Serv:** US Army, pvt ltd 1947-69; Vietnamese Medal of Honor 1st Class. **Business Addr:** President, Unified Ind Inc, 6551 Loisdale Court, Ste 400, Springfield, VA 22150.

ADAMS, V. TONI
Business executive. **Personal:** Born Dec 13, 1946, Oakland, CA; married James L Robinson; children: Karla, Doyle, Todd, Vikki. **Educ:** Oxford Univ England, 1976; CA State Univ, MPA 1976; Mills Coll, BA 1968; Golden Gate Univ, DPA. **Career:** UC Berkeley, cont ed spec 1968-77; City of Oakland, spec asst to mayor 1977-84; Natl Assoc of Black & Minority Chamber of Commerce, vice pres of tourism. **Orgs:** Grand juror Alameda Cty superior Court 1973-74; mem bd of dir CA Alcoholism Found 1975-77; mem Alameda Cty Juvenile Delinquency Prevention 1976-78; chief fin officer Builders Mutual Suriety Co 1982-83; adv bd mem Displaced Homemakers Ctr 1983-; bd of dir Oakland Convention Ctr Mgt Inc 1983-. **Honors/Awds:** Outstanding Service to Ed Coll Bounders Oakland 1979; Outstanding Young Women of Amer 1981,83.

ADAMS, VERNA MAY SHOECRAFT
Educational administrator (retired). **Personal:** Born Jul 1, 1928, Toledo, OH; daughter of Ogrietta Lee Shoecraft and John Henry Shoecraft; married Fred Andrew; children: Jacqueline O Redd, Fred A Jr, Douglas F, Cynthia V McBride. **Educ:** St Francis Coll Ft Wayne IN, BS 1962, MS Ed 1964; Ball State Univ Muncie IN, EdD, 1979. **Career:** Ft Wayne Comm Schools, teacher 1961-67; St Francis Coll Ft Wayne IN, instr, lecturer 1964-74; Ft Wayne Comm Schools, guidance couns, consulting teacher 1966-68, elem cons, teacher 1967-71, elem principal 1971-80, dir title I prog 1980-82; dir, Supplemental Instructional Programs, 1982-89. **Orgs:** Former bd of dirs, Parkview Hosp; Fort Wayne Foundation, bd of dirs; Fort Wayne Philharmonic outreach community devel committee; Turner Chapel AME, trustee bd; The Intl Links, Inc; NAACP; Urban League, Phi Delta Kappa Ft Wayne Chapter; National Alliance of Black School Educators; Fort Wayne Alliance Black School Educators, cofounder. **Honors/Awds:** Woman of the Year Ft Wayne Urban League 1964; Woman of the Year Kappa Alpha Psi Ft Wayne Alumni Chap 1976; Verna M. Adams Educational Financial Assistance Program for Excellence in Teacher Education, Lincoln National Bank and Fort Wayne Community Schools, 1989; Zeta Phi Beta, Ft Wayne Chapter, Woman of the Year.

ADAMS, VICTORINE QUILLE
City official. **Personal:** Born Apr 28, Baltimore, MD; married William Adams; children: 1. **Educ:** Morgan State Univ, Coppin State Teachers Coll. **Career:** Health & Welfare Council of Central MD, vp, treas; Woman Power Inc, exec dir 12 yrs; 4th Dist Baltimore MD, city councilwoman. **Orgs:** Past mem House of Del 4th Dist MD Gen Assembly, Archdiocesan Urban Comm Chmn Mun Works; mem United Fund Campaign 1972, Phi Delta Kappa, Sigma Gamma Phi, Iota Phi Lambda, Com for Hist & Archit Preservation, NAACP, YWCA, YMCA, Unite Negro Women; adv com Cultural Progress for Mayor's Ball Cert. **Honors/Awds:** USAF Defense Team Rubensteen's Success Sch; Afro-Amer Citz Awd Woman Power Inc; Serv Awd Natl Sojourner Truth Awd; Zeta Phi Beta's Woman of the Year; Century Club Awd YMCA; Alumni Awd Howard Univ; OES Awd Naomi Grand Chapt. **Business Addr:** City Councilwoman, 4th Dist Baltimore, Holiday St City Hall, Room 523, Baltimore, MD 21202.

ADAMS, YOLANDA
Gospel singer. **Personal:** Born Aug 27, 1961, Houston, TX; married Tim Crawford, 1997. **Educ:** Received teaching degree and certification in Texas; Howard Univ, divinity student, currently. **Career:** Gospel music recording artist, 1987-. **Honors/Awds:** Recorded four albums on the Tribute label that received gospel-industry Stellar awards; Soul Train Music Award for Best Gospel Album for ''More Than a Melody,'' 1995; Grammy nomination, ''Yolanda..Live in Washington,'' 1996. **Special Achievements:** Albums: ''Just as I Am,'' 1987; ''Through the Storm,'' 1991; ''Save the World,'' 1993; ''More Than a Melody,'' 1995; ''Yolanda..Live in Washington,'' 1996. **Business Addr:** Gospel Singer, c/o Mahogany Entertainment, 12201 Pleasant Prospect, Mitchellville, MD 20721.

ADAMS-DUDLEY, LILLY ANNETTE
Educator, consultant. **Personal:** Born Jun 7, 1950, Lochgelley, WV; daughter of Jerlena Paulanne williams Adams and James Alfred Adams Sr; married Jerry Lee Dudley Sr; children: Jerry Jr. **Educ:** Canisius College, BA 1972, MA 1976, MS 1984. **Career:** Hampton City Schools, english teacher 1972-73; Buffalo Public Schools, english teacher 1974-75; Canisius Coll, language arts specialist 1975-78, asst dir 1978-80, writing lab instr 1982-84, reading & study skills instr 1981-, dir COPE office, consultant on self-esteem devel & multiculturalism in workplace. **Orgs:** Policy bd mem Consortium of the Niagara Frontier 1980-; treas & campus rep AJCU Conf on Minority Affairs 1980-81; Buffalo/Rochester regional rep HEOP Professional Org 1980-; mem Amer Assn of Black Women in Higher Educ, Amer Soc for Training & Develop, Amer Assn of Univ Women, Natl Assn of Female Executives; seminar developer and coleader Today's Professional Woman, Developing Attitudes for Success; Self-Esteem and Your Success; Professional Black Women and Success; mem American Soc of Professional and Exec Women 1986-. **Honors/Awds:** Martin Luther King Jr Full Academic Scholarship 1968-72; Canisius Coll Di Gamma Honor Soc 1983; workshop given: Managering the Multicultural Workforce 1989. **Home Addr:** 72 Andover Ave, Buffalo, NY 14215. **Business Addr:** Dir COPE Office, Canisius College, 2001 Main St, Buffalo, NY 14208.

ADDAMS, ROBERT DAVID
Attorney, association executive professor. **Personal:** Born Feb 12, 1957, Chicago, IL. **Educ:** Princeton University, AB, 1978; Columbia University Graduate School of Journalism, MSJ, 1980; Columbia University School of Law, JD, 1982. **Career:** Goodman, Eden, Millender & Bedrosian, associate attorney, 1982-86; National Conference of Black Lawyers, associate director, 1986; City Coll of NY, Revson Prof, 1986-87; Association of Legal Aid Attorneys, executive director, 1986-92; Institute for Mediation and Conflict Resolution, president/chief executive officer, currently; Brooklyn Coll, visiting prof, currently. **Orgs:** National Conference of Black Lawyers, board of directors, 1985-87; Metropolitan Black Bar Association, 1992; State Bar of Michigan, 1982-92; National Lawyers Guild, 1982-86; American Bar Association, 1982-84; National Bar Association, 1982-84; Wolverine Bar Association, 1982-86; NY State Mediation Assn, bd of dirs, 1993-94. **Honors/Awds:** Princeton University Department of Afro-American Studies, Sr Thesis

Prize, 1978; Revson Fellowship City College of New York Center for Legal Education, 1986-87; Brooklyn Coll, Belle Zeller, Visiting Distinguished Professorship, 1994-. **Home Addr:** 137 Central Park North, New York, NY 10026. **Business Phone:** (212)690-5700.

ADDEI, ARTHELLA HARRIS

Educational administrator. **Personal:** Born in St Louis, MO; daughter of Iona L Harris (deceased) and Jesse K Harris (deceased); married Kwabena A Addei MD, Nov 28, 1970; children: D'Asante. **Educ:** Harris Teacher Coll St Louis MO, BA; Columbia Univ NYC, MA; CUNY, MS; Long Island Univ, professional diploma educ admin supervision. **Career:** New Perspectives WWRL Radio NYC, producer & moderator; Essence Magazine, contributing editor; New York City Public Schools, guidance counselor; Manpower Prog NYC, supv counselor; St Louis Public School, tchr; Comm Sch Dist 19 New York City Public Schools, dist supervisor; NY Public School System, principal Ethan Allen Elem School; Department of School Administration, adjunct professor, currently; Queens College, supervisor, currently. **Orgs:** Mem prog chairperson NY State Div for Youth Adv Bd & Youth Serv Action Team; mem Alpha Kappa Alpha Sor; Women's Aux of Nassau Co Med Soc AMA; Women's Auxiliary of National Medical Association, (NMA); mem CSA Council of Supervisors and Administrators, NY City; NYESPA Principals Assoc; member, Mayor's Task Force/Early Childhood, 1989-90. **Honors/Awds:** Awd for Service Recognition Westbury Mothers Group of Westbury Long Island 1974; Community Service, Assn for Study of African-American Life & History, 1974; Honorary Education Fraternity, Kappa Delta Pi, 1962; featured administrator in New York City Board of Education newsletter Impact Star, Winter 1991; Community School District 19, Brooklyn, NY, Administrator of the Year, 1993; Featured Alumnus in the International House World Newsletter, November, 1996. **Home Addr:** 475 Glen Cove Rd, Roslyn, NY 11576. **Business Addr:** Principal, Ethan Allen Elementary School, 970 Vermont St, PS 306, Brooklyn, NY 11207, (718)649-3155.

ADDERLEY, HERB ANTHONY

Professional football player (retired), business executive. **Personal:** Born Jun 8, 1939, Philadelphia, PA; son of Rene White Adderley and Charles Adderley; married Bell; children: Toni. **Educ:** Michigan State Univ, BS, education, 1961. **Career:** Professional football player: Green Bay Packers 1961-69, Dallas Cowboys 1970-72, New England Patriots, Los Angeles Rams 1973, retired; Giant Step Record Co, vp. **Honors/Awds:** Participated in Super Bowl 1967, 1968, 1971; All-Star Game 1963-67; played in Pro Bowl 1963-67; Inducted into Football Hall of Fame 1980. **Military Serv:** US Army, 1962-66.

ADDERLEY, NATHANIEL

Musician, composer. **Personal:** Born Nov 25, 1931, Tampa, FL; married Ann; children: Nat, Alison. **Educ:** FL A&M Univ, AB, BS 1951. **Career:** Lionel Hampton 1954-55, Julian Adderly 1956-67, 1960-75, JJ Johnson 1957-58, Woody Herman 1959, musician; Sermonnette 1956, Jive Samba 1962, composer; Big Man, The Legend of John Henry, co-composer. **Orgs:** Mem Top of Gate 1976. **Military Serv:** US Army, 1951-53. **Business Addr:** 119 W 57th St, New York, NY 10011.

ADDERLY, T. C., JR.

Human resources director. **Personal:** Born Feb 7, 1949, Miami, FL; son of Bertha Dean Adderly and T C Adderly Sr; married Kathy Williamson Adderly; children: Beth, Andrew, Jánine, Ashlee. **Educ:** Miami Dade Community College, Miami, FL, AA, 1980; University of Miami, Miami, FL, Masters, business, 1991. **Career:** Florida Power & Light, Miami, FL, human resources mgr, 1969-91; City of Miami Beach, Miami Beach, FL, human resources director, 1992-. **Orgs:** Member & past vice-chairman, FCAA, 1979-; president, Y's Men International, 1979-83; mentor chairman, Ocean Reef Mentor Program, 1986-91; member, Amigos De Ser, 1983-; scholarship chairman, Miami-Dade Chamber of Commerce, 1981-. **Honors/Awds:** America's Best & Brightest Young Business/Professionals, Dollars & Sense, 1989; Leadership Miami, Greater Miami, Chamber, 1980; Membership Chairman App Award, FCAA, 1990; Black Achiever, FCAA, 1984. **Business Addr:** Human Resoures Director, Human Resources Dept, City of Miami Beach, 1700 Convention Center Dr, Miami Beach, FL 33139.

ADDISON, ADELE

Singer. **Personal:** Born Jul 24, 1925, New York, NY; married Norman Berger. **Educ:** Westminster Choir Coll, BMus, Scholar 1946; Univ of MA, DHV 1963. **Career:** Town Hall NYC, recital debut 1952; US, CAN, Soviet Union, recital tours 1963; Appeared w/New Eng City Ctr Washington Opera Co; orchestral & engagements w/symphonies Boston, Cleveland, NY Philharmonic, Natl, Chgo, Pittsburgh, Indpls, LA, SF; World Premiere performances incl John La Montaigne's Fragments from Song of Songs w/New Haven Symphony 1959, Poulenc's Gloria w/ Boston Symphony 1961, Foss' Time Cycle w/NY Philharmonic 1960; faculty artist Aspen Music Festival 1956; sang role of Bess in Goldwyn's Porgy & Bess 1958; soloist opening concert Philharmonic Hall of Lincoln Ctr 1962; spec interest in German Lieder. **Orgs:** American Academy of Teachers of Singing. **Honors/Awds:** Appeared w/New Eng City Ctr Washington Opera Co; orchestral & engagements w/symphonies Boston, Cleveland , NY Philharmonic, Natl, Chgo, Pittsburgh, Indpls, LA, SF; World Premiere performances incl John La Montaigne's Fragments from Song of Songs w/New Haven Symphony 1959, Poulenc's Gloria w/Boston Symphony 1961, Foss' Time Cycle w/NY Philharmonic 1960; faculty artist Aspen Music Festival 1956; sang role of Bess in Goldwyn's Porgy & Bess 1958; soloist opening concert Philharmonic Hall of Lincoln Ctr 1962; spec interest in German Lieder. **Home Addr:** 98 Riverside Dr, New York, NY 10024.

ADDISON, CAROLINE ELIZABETH

Director/associate professor. **Personal:** Born Nov 14, 1938, Brooklyn, NY; married Wallace O'Kelly Peace; children: Douglas K, Rock P. **Educ:** Bronx Comm Coll, AAS 1964; Long Island Univ, BSN 1972, MS 1974; New York Univ, MPA 1976; Walden Univ, PhD 1978; Wayne State Univ, EdD 1986. **Career:** Passaic County Coll, dir of nursing/allied health prog 1978-80; St Joseph's Coll, dean of faculty 1976-78; VA State Univ, dean/dir nursing 1980-81; Univ of Detroit, dir/chair nursing educ 1981-. **Orgs:** Mem Natl League of Nursing 1964-, Amer Nursing Assoc 1964-, MI Assoc of Colleges of Nursing 1981-; mem MI Holistic Assoc 1983-; mem League of Women Voters 1984-; mem Wellness Network 1986. **Honors/Awds:** "Factors Associate with Educational Success of Black Inner City Nursing Students" Wayne State Univ 1986; "Selected Factors Related to Admission and Retention of Adult Registered Nurses". **Home Addr:** 29264 Franklin Hills Dr, Southfield, MI 48034-1149. **Business Addr:** Director of Academics, University of Phoenix-Michigan Campus, 26999 Central Park Blvd., Suite 100, Southfield, MI 48076.

ADDISON, JAMES DAVID

Business owner, auto parts wholesaler. **Personal:** Born Jan 8, 1949, Shelby, NC; son of Inez Mildred Addison and Jimmie Lee Addison; married Marie Yolene Pierre Addison, Mar 27, 1982; children: Jessica Marie, Jennifer Maureen. **Career:** Addison Auto Parts, president, 1987-. **Business Addr:** President, Addison Auto Parts, 3908 Pennsylvania Ave SE, Washington, DC 20020, (202)581-2900.

ADDISON, RAFAEL

Professional basketball player. **Personal:** Born Jul 22, 1964, Jersey City, NJ. **Educ:** Syracuse Univ. **Career:** Phoenix Suns, 1986-87; Livorno, Italy, 1987-91; New Jersey Nets, 1991-93; Benetton, Italy, 1993-94; Detroit Pistons, 1994-95; Charlotte Hornets, 1995-. **Business Addr:** Professional Basketball Player, Charlotte Hornets, One Hive Dr, Charlotte, NC 28217, (704)357-0252.

ADDISON, TERRY HUNTER, JR.

Educational administrator. **Personal:** Born May 15, 1950, Memphis, TN; son of Carsaunder Goosby Addison and Terry H Addison Sr; married Michele Ann Walker Addison, Mar 9, 1985; children: Terry III, Matthew Kenneth, Amanda Kathryn. **Educ:** Univ of Minnesota-Minneapolis, BA (magna cum laude), 1971, MA, 1973. **Career:** ABC Prog Carleton Coll, instructor 1972; English Dept Macalester Coll, instructor 1972; Minority Programs Augsburg Coll, dir 1972-73; Minneapolis Urban League St Acad, instructor 1979-81; Macalester Coll, coord minority program 1981-84; Univ of Rhode Island, dir minority student serv, beginning 1984, dir, multicultural student services, currently; Multicultural Student Services, dir, 1984-93; Ctr for Non-Violence Couseling Ctr, asst dir, dir, 1993-95; Kent County YMCA, Greater Providence YMCA, assoc exec dir, 1995-97; Intown Providence YMCA, Greater Providence YMCA, exec dir, 1997-. **Orgs:** Board of Directors, Leadership RI; bd of dirs, Sojourner House; mem, Omega Psi Phi Frat Inc, Urban League, NAACP. **Honors/Awds:** Positive Image Award, Minneapolis Urban League, 1984; Henry L Williams Memorial Award, Univ of Minnesota; Awareness Award, 1987, Leadership Award, 1989, USN Recruiting Dist Boston; Leadership Rhode Island, Lambda Class, 1991; Inductee Golden Key National Honor Society, 1992; Inductee Order of Omega National Honor Society, 1992; Leadership RI, David L Sweet Award, 1996. **Military Serv:** USMC, pfc, 1976-77. **Business Addr:** YMCA of Greater Providence, 160 Broad St, Providence, RI 02903, (401)456-0100.

ADDY, TRALANCE OBUAMA

Medical products company executive. **Personal:** Born Aug 24, 1944, Kumasi, Ghana; son of Docea L Baddoo Addy (deceased) and Matthew Biala Addy; married Jo Alison Phears, May 26, 1979; children: Mantse, Miishe, Dwetri, Naakai. **Educ:** Swarthmore Coll, Swarthmore, PA, BA, chemistry, BS, mechanical engineering, 1969; Univ of Massachusetts, Amherst, MA, MSME, PhD, 1974; Harvard Business School, Boston, MA, advanced mgmt program, 1987. **Career:** Scott Paper Co, Philadelphia, PA, sr research project engineer, 1973-76, research scientist, 1976-79, program leader, 1979-80; SURGIKOS Inc, Arlington, TX, dir applied research, 1980-85, dir technological venture devel, 1986-88, vice pres, gen mgr ASP div, 1988-95, president, ASP, 1995-. **Orgs:** Teacher, Upward Bound, 1967-73; mem, Amer Soc of Mechanical Engineers, 1979-; Amer Assn for the Advancement of Science, 1983-, Black/Jewish Dialogue of Dallas, 1986-92; chmn, co-chmn, SURGIKOS United Way Campaign, 1985-86. **Honors/Awds:** First person to receive both BA and BS degrees simultaneously from Swarthmore; Johnson & Johnson Entrepreneurial Achievement Award, 1986; One of 125 Alumni to Watch, Univ of Massachusetts, Amherst, 1988; mem, Sigma Xi; inventor on several patents; author, several publications on nonconventional food resources and production. **Business Addr:** President, ASP, Division of Johnson & Johnson Medical, Inc, 33 Technology Dr, Irvine, CA 92718.

ADEGBILE, GIDEON SUNDAY ADEBISI

Physician/educator. **Personal:** Born May 18, 1941, Iree, Nigeria; son of Sarah and Rev John; children: Lisa, Titilayo, Babalola. **Educ:** Virginia Union Univ, BS (cum laude) 1966; Meharry Med Coll, MD 1971. **Career:** Good Samaritan Hosp, intern 1971-72; Drexel Hlth Ctr, comm health physician 1972-73; PEG Inc, emergency physician 1972-75; Wright State Univ Sch of Med, clinical instr 1975-79; private practice, physician 1973-; Wright State Univ School of Med, asst clinical prof 1979-85, assoc clinical prof 1985-92, clinical professor, 1992-. **Orgs:** Pres Gem City Med Dental & Pharm Soc 1978-80; chmn of bd Dayton Contemp Dance Co 1978-80; chmn Horizon in Med Prog 1978-; trustee Montgomery County Med Soc 1978; bd mem adv mental health bd Good Samaritan Hosp & Health Center 1979-85; chmn Long Term Care Comm Region II Med Review Corp 1979-81; sec Buckeye Med Assn 1980-82; mem House of Delegate of Natl Med Assn 1980-91; chmn Quality Assurance Comm St Elizabeth Med Center 1980-82,84; bd mem Region II Review Corp 1981-84, exec bd mem 1982-84; med dir Christel Manor Nursing Homes; mem AAFP; mem, OAFP; Ohio State Med Association; Natl Med Assn; Montgomery County Med Soc; NAACP; Alpha Phi Alpha Frat; Sigma Pi Phi Frat; Dem Bapt; Miami Valley Racquet Club; bd mem Dayton Area Health Plan 1985-92; med director, DAHP, 1994-, board member, Dayton Area American Red Cross, 1994-; pres Selectmen 1986-87; sec Montgomery County med Soc 1987; chmn Dept of Family Practice GSH & H Ctr, 1987-88; chmn Credentials & Accreditation Comm St Eliz Med Center 1987-88, 1995-96; pres Buckeye Med Assoc 1987-89; chief of staff, St Elizabeth Med Ctr, 1993-94; board member, St Elizabeth Med Ctr, PHO, 1994-. **Honors/Awds:** Cert of Appreciation Christel Manor Nursing Home 1977. **Business Addr:** Clinical Professor, Wright State University, School of Medicine, 4001 Free Pike, Dayton, OH 45416.

ADESUYI, SUNDAY ADENIJI

Educator. **Personal:** Born Jun 27, 1948, Igbajo, Oyo, Nigeria; son of Mary Ojuolape Adesuyi and Jacob Owolabi Adesuyi. **Educ:** Howard Univ, Washington, DC, BS (with Honors), 1974, PhD, 1980. **Career:** Howard Univ, Chem Dept, teaching asst, 1974-75, teaching fellow, 1974-78, instructor, 1978-79; St Paul's Coll, Science & Math Dept, asst prof, 1979-83, prof and chairman, currently; Med Coll of Virginia, Dept of Pharmacology, rsch assoc, 1983-84; St Paul's Coll, interim provost, academic vice pres, acting pres, 1988. **Orgs:** Pres, Graduate Student Assoc, 1976-78; Exec Bd Mem, US Student Assoc, 1977-78; Co-Chmn, St Paul's Subcommittee; Howard Univ's Steering Committee on Self-Study, 1977-79; Coordinator, Science & Math Fair, St Paul's Coll, 1980-82; Member, ACS, 1976-; Coordinator, Annual Project, STEP (Service to Elderly People), Lawrenceville, VA 1981-; Founder & Advisor, Xi Rho Chapter, Phi Beta Sigma, 1983-; Advisor, Science & Math Club, St Paul's Coll, 1984-; Faculty Rep to Bd of Trustees, St Paul's Coll, 1985-88; Advisor, Inter-Fraternal Council, St Paul's Coll 1986-; advisor, Intl Student Assoc, St Paul's Coll, 1986; Member, Presidential Search Committee, St Paul's Coll, 1986; Chmn, Provost SearchCommittee, St Paul's Coll, 1987; Member, Steering Committee, Self-Study, St Paul's Coll, 1987-; Chmn, Institutional purpose Committee, Self-Study, St Paul's Coll, 1987-; Chmn, Athletic Committee, St Paul's Coll, 1988-; Faculty Athletic Chair, CIAA, 1988-; Northern Division, CIAA, vp 1992-94; SACS Visiting Team to Erskine College, 1992; Miles Coll, 1993; Campbellsville Coll, 1994; Berea Coll, 1995. **Honors/Awds:** Teaching Assistantship, Chemistry Dept, Howard Univ, 1974-75; Teaching Fellow, Chemistry Dept, Howard Univ, 1975-78; Most Outstanding Graduate Student, Graduate Student Assoc, Howard Univ, 1978; Presidential Silver Award, Howard Univ Student Assoc, 1978; Appreciation Award, Sophomore class, St Paul's Coll, 1979-80; Student Merit Award, Student Body, St Paul's Coll, 1982, 1983; Most Outstanding Dept Faculty Mem, Science & Math Club, St Paul's Coll, 1982; #1 Supporter Award, Tennis Team, St Paul's Coll, 1982; Appreciation Award, Senior Class, St Paul's Coll, 1983; Presidential Medal for Outstanding Contributions to St Paul's Coll, 1988; Excellence in Academic Advising Award, St Paul's College, 1990; Sears-Roebuck Faculty of the Year, 1990-91; UNCF Distinguished Leadership Award, 1991, Meritorious Service Award, 1992; Sunbelt Video Sports/CIAA Partnership Award, 1993; CIAA Outstanding Service Award, 1994; SPC Athletic Dept, Appreciation Award, 1995. **Home Addr:** PO Box 71, Lawrenceville, VA 23868. **Business Addr:** Professor & Chairman, St Pauls College, Dept of Natural Science and Mathematics, 115 College Dr, Lawrenceville, VA 23868.

ADEWUMI, JONATHAN

Clothing manufacturer. **Personal:** Born Sep 12, 1962, London, England; son of Grace U Adewumi and Jacob O Adewumi. **Educ:** Utica College of Syracuse University, BS, 1986. **Career:** Software Synergy, sales representative, 1986-87; Philon

Inc, sales representative, 1986-87; Ziff Davis Publishing Co, PC magazine sales representative, 1987-91; Nigerian Fabrics & Fashions, owner/CEO, 1990-. **Orgs:** Kappa Alpha Psi Fraternity Inc, 1985; Human Resource Administration District Advisory Council, 1991. **Special Achievements:** Featured in Class Magazine, Februrary 1991; featured in Brides Today, December 1992. **Business Phone:** (718)230-8060.

ADEYIGA, ADEYINKA A.
Educator. **Personal:** Born Jan 20, 1948, Irolu, Nigeria; son of Alhaja Oladunni Apadiya-Osinbowale and Alhaji Adeyiga Osinbowale; married Abidemi Adibi-Adeyiga, Dec 21, 1975; children: Adeleke, Adebunmi, Adetayo. **Educ:** Tennessee Tech Univ, BS, 1974; Univ of Missouri, MS, 1977; Oklahoma State Univ, PhD, 1980. **Career:** Oklahoma State Univ Fluid Properties Research Inc, research asst, 1979-80; EI DuPont DeNemours Co, research engr, 1981-82; Shell Petroleum Devel, reservoir engr, 1982-84; Virginia State Univ, asst prof, 1984-85; Hampton Univ, assoc prof of chem engr, 1985-, head of engrg, 1986-. **Orgs:** Chief consultant, Padson Engineering Co, 1983-84; mem, Engineering Deans Council of HBCU, 1986-; mem, State of Virginia Engineering Dean Council, 1986-; mem, HBCU of ASEE, 1986-; mem, US Dept of Energy Exec Comm HBCU Research 1989-. **Honors/Awds:** Vapor-liquid equil coefficient for acid gas constituents and physical solvents, 1980; equilibrium constants for physical solvents in natural gas, 1980; a manual of chemical engineering labs, 1988; evaluation of onboard hydrogen storage for aircraft, 1989; catalytic gasification of coal chars by non-transition metal catalyst, 1986. **Business Addr:** Head, Department of Engineering, Hampton University, East Queen St, 318 Olin Engineering Building, Hampton, VA 23668.

ADEYIGA, OLANREWAJU MUNIRU
Physician. **Personal:** Born Sep 30, 1949, Irolu, Nigeria; married Mosekunola Omisakin; children: Adebowale, Oladunni, Adeniyi, Temitope. **Educ:** Southern IL Univ Edwardsville, BA 1973, MSc 1975; Howard Univ Coll of Medicine, MD 1979. **Career:** SIP Prog Southern IL Univ, vstg lecturer 1976-77; Howard Univ Hosp, instructor/attending 1985-86; Columbia Hosp for Women, attending 1985-; Washington Hosp Ctr, attending 1985-; Group Health Assoc, physician. **Orgs:** Mem AMA 1976-, ACOG 1986-. **Honors/Awds:** Diplomate Natl Bd of Med Exam 1981, Amer Bd of Ob/Gyn 1986; Fellow Amer Coll of Ob/Gyn 1987. **Business Addr:** Ob/Gyn Dept, 2041 Georgia Ave NW, Washington, DC 20060.

ADIELE, MOSES NKWACHUKWU
Government official. **Personal:** Born Jun 22, 1951, Umuahia, Nigeria; son of Virginia Adiele and Robert Adiele; married Vickie I Eseonu Adiele, Jul 7, 1984; children: Elizabeth, Bobby. **Educ:** Georgia Inst of Tech, BSHS 1976; Howard Univ, MD 1980; Johns Hopkins Univ, MPH 1981; Uniformed Services Univ of the Health Sciences, Bethesda, MD, certificate of completion of the armed forces combat casualty care course, 1990; Academy of Health Sciences, San Antonio, TX, certificate of completion of the officer advanced course, 1990; Fort Leavenworthe, Kansas, Completion of the US Army Command and General Staff Officer Course, 1993. **Career:** Baltimore City Health Dept, public health clinician 1980-81; Howard Univ, medical house officer residency in family practice, 1981-84; Diplomate Nat Bd Med Examiners, Fed Licensure Examiners Med Bd; Richmond City Health Dept, asst dir of public health 1984-86; Virginia State Health Dept, dist health dir 1986-90; Virginia Dept of Medical Assistance Services, Richmond, VA, director of medical support, 1990-. **Orgs:** Pres 1981-84, mem bd of dirs 1984-, Assoc of African Physicians in North Amer; active prof mem Amer & Virginia Assoc of Family Physicians 1982-; mem bd of advisors Intl United Black Fund 1984-; member, Richmond Academy of Medicine, 1986-; member, Richmond Medical Society, 1984-; member, US Military Reserve Officers Association, 1988-; member, Virginia Public Health Association, 1984. **Honors/Awds:** Am Acad Famiy Physicians, fellow; American College of Medical Quality, Fellow; Outstanding Resident Physician Awd 1982, Who Most Exemplifies a Family Physician Awd 1982 (both at Howard Univ Hospital); Mead-Johnson Scientific Presentation Awd 1983; Outstanding Serv Awd Richmond Redevelop and Housing Auth 1984; Outstanding Serv Awd Richmond Area High Blood Pressure Ctr 1985, 1986; Physician Recognition Award, American Med Association, 1984, 1989, 1991; Community Service Achievement, City of Richmond, 1989. **Military Serv:** US Army Reserve, Major, 1989-; Certificate of Achievement, 1988, Army Service Ribbon, 1988, National Defense Service Medal, 1991, Southwest Asia Service Medal, 1991, Army Command Combat Patch, 82nd Airborne Div, 1991. **Business Addr:** Director of Medical Support Services, Virginia Dept of Medical Assistance Services, PO Box 24826, Richmond, VA 23224-2482, (804)786-3820.

ADKINS, CECELIA NABRIT
Church official, business executive. **Personal:** Born Sep 3, 1923, Atlanta, GA; daughter of Augusta Nabrit and James Nabrit Sr. **Educ:** Fisk Univ, BS (summa cum laude), BA, history. **Career:** Sunday School Public Bd of the Natl Baptist Convention USA Inc, first woman to serve as chief accountant 1952, chief fiscal agent (first woman) 1965, first woman to become exec dir, 1975-; J W Adkis Funeral Home, owner. **Orgs:** President, first woman mem exec comm Protestant Church Owned Publishers Assn; mem YWCA Investment Mgmt Comm and Capital Fund Dr Plng comm; mem United Way Bd; mem Educ Comm Nashville C of C, Scholarship Comm for Residents of Nashville Housing Projects; mem Progressive Bapt Church. **Honors/Awds:** Presidential Citation for Exemplary Exp, Natl Assn for Equal Opportunity in Higher Educ, 1979-84; Outstanding Leadership & Serv of the Community, Alpha Kappa Alpha Sor Southeastern Regional Conf 1984; Commr, Nashville Convention Ctr, 1986-87; Honorary Member, Alpha Kappa Alpha Sorority, 1990. **Business Addr:** Executive Dir, Sunday School Publishing Bd, 330 Charlotte Ave, Nashville, TN 37201.

ADKINS, IONA W.
Government official (retired). **Personal:** Born Jul 20, 1925, Charles City Cty, VA; daughter of Luevania M Whitehead and Robert E Whitehead; married Malchi Adkins Sr; children: Barry E Sr, Malchi Jr, Byron M Sr, Mona Adkins-Easley. **Career:** St John Baptist Church, clerk 1955; Charles City Cty VA, clerk, circuit court 1968-88. **Orgs:** Mem exec comm Charles City Branch NAACP 1942-; mem Charles Cty Civic League Inc 1942-, VA Court Clerks Assoc 1970-; mem Charles City Democratic Comm 1974; sec Charles City Fair Comm 1980-; correspondance sec Star of the East Baptist Assoc 25 yrs; mem exec bd VA Assoc of Democratic Elected Officials. **Home Addr:** 3521 Wayside Road, Charles City, VA 23030.

ADKINS, LEROY J.
Law enforcement official (retired). **Personal:** Born Jun 17, 1933, St Louis, MO; son of Fannie E Adkins and Alfred J Adkins; married Glenda J Watt, Jan 19, 1957; children: Kevin L, Alfred J. **Educ:** Forrest Park Community College, AA, 1976; Columbia College, BA, 1978; Webster University, MA, 1979. **Career:** St Louis Police Department, deputy chief, 1958-92; St Louis Airport Police Department, chief, 1992-96. **Orgs:** IACP, 1984-; Missouri Police Chiefs, 1992-; NOBLE, 1976-; Omega Psi Phi, 1980-. **Honors/Awds:** Amer Legion Certificate of Achievement, Outstanding Police Work, 1976; Recipient of ten Letters of Commendations, Chief of Police, Exceptional Performance of Duty; Letter of Commendation from the St Louis Jr Chamber of Commerce, 1968; Letter of Commendations, Grand Jury Assn of St Louis, MO, 1968; Recipient of two Letters of Commendation, Chief of Detectives; Humanitarian Award from the Congress of Racial Equality, St Louis, MO, 1974; Jr Chamber of Commerce Law Enforcement Award, Outstanding Police Officer in Metro St Louis, 1971; St Louis Argus Newspaper Award, Distinguished Public Service, 1982; St Louis Amer Newspaper Salute to Excellence Award, 1992; Annie Malone Children's Home Founders Award, 1992; 4th Ward Advisory Council, Citizenship, 1982; Sumner High School, Hall of Fame, 1994; Noble's Robert Lamb Humanitarian Awd, 1995. **Military Serv:** US Navy, petty officer, 1950-54.

ADKINS, RODNEY C.
Computer company executive. **Personal:** Born Aug 23, 1958, Augusta, GA; son of Archie & Wauneta; married Michelle Collier Adkins, Dec 17, 1983; children: Rodney II, Ryan. **Educ:** Georgia Institute of Technology, BSEE, 1981; Rollins College, BA, 1982; Georgia Institute of Technology, MSEE, 1983. **Career:** IBM, exec asst of dir of planning, 1990-91, exec asst of vp of systems, 1991-92, mgr, ps/2 desktop devel, 1992-93, mgr, mobile computing operations, 1993-94, dir, commercial desktop devel, 1994-95, vp, commercial desktop devel, 1995-96, vp & gen mgr, desktop systems, 1996-. **Orgs:** Kappa Alpha Psi, life mem, 1979-; Micro Channel Developers Assn, chmn, 1994-95, bd of dirs, 1995-96; Natl Soc of Black Engineers, exec sponsor, 1995-98; Southeastern Consortium for Minorities in Engineering, bd of dirs, 1996-98; IBM Academy of Technology, bd of governors, 1996-98. **Honors/Awds:** Professional Achievement in Industry, Black Engineer of the Year, 1996; Georgia Tech, Outstanding Young Engineering Alumni, 1996; Edges Group, A New Generation Leader, 1996. **Special Achievements:** Harvard Business School, program for management development, 1993. **Business Addr:** Vice Pres/General Manager, IBM, 3039 W Cornwallis Rd, Building 203, Research Triangle Park, NC 27709, (919)543-1568.

ADKINS, RUTHERFORD. **See Obituaries section.**

ADOLPH, GERALD STEPHEN
Management consultant. **Personal:** Born Dec 30, 1953, New York, NY. **Educ:** MIT, BS Chem Engrg 1976, BS Mgmt 1976, MS Chem Engrg 1981; Harvard Business School, MBA 1981. **Career:** Polaroid, engr 1976-81; Booz Allen & Hamilton, assoc 1981-83, sr assoc 1983-85, principal 1985-. **Orgs:** Mem Black MBA Assoc; vice chmn 21st Century Political Action Comm; bd of dirs Malcolm-King Coll. **Home Addr:** 203 West 102nd, New York, NY 10025. **Business Addr:** Principal, Booz Allen & Hamilton, 101 Parker Ave 21st Fl, New York, NY 10178.

ADOM, EDWIN NII AMALAI (AKUETE)
Psychiatrist. **Personal:** Born Jan 12, 1941, Accra, Ghana; son of Juliana Adorkor Brown and Isaac Quaye Adom; married Margaret Odarkor Lamptey, May 28, 1977; children: Edwin Nii Nortey Jr, Isaac Michael Nii Nortei. **Educ:** Univ of Pennsylvania, BA 1963; Meharry Medical Coll, MD 1968; Royal Society of Health, FRSH, England, 1974. **Career:** Pennsylvania Hosp, internship 1968-69; Thomas Jefferson Univ, residency 1969-72; West Philadelphia Consortium, staff psychiatrist 1972-; Univ of Penna Sch of Medicine, faculty, clinical asst prof of psychiatry, 1972-; St of PA, cons psychiatrist for Bur of Visually Handicap & Blindness, 1974—, and Bur of Disability Determination, 1975—; Parents Preparing for Parenthood, Philadelphia PA, cons psychiatrist, 1975-76; The Graduate Hosp, Philadelphia, cons psychiatrist, 1976—; St Joseph Hosp, Philadelphia, cons psychiatrist, 1976-80; Stephen Smith Home for the Aged, Philadelphia, cons psychiatrist, 1976-80; Mercy Douglas Human Services Center, Philadelphia, cons psychiatrist, 1977-79; St Ignatius Home for the Aged, Phildelphia, cons psychiatrist, 1978-85; Philadelphia Psychiatric Center, attending psychiatrist, 1987—;Hzon House Rehabilitation Center, Philadelphia, cons psychiatrist, 1987-89; Hosp of the Univ of PA, cons psychiatrist, 1989—; West Philadelphia Community Mental Health Consortium, Philadelphia, PA, medical dir, 1991-. **Orgs:** Mem APA, NMA, MSEP; mem Black Psych of Amer, World Federation of Mental Health, Royal Soc of Health; member, New York Academy of Science, 1987-; member, American Academy of Psychiatry and the Law, 1990-; Amer Society of Clinical Psychooharmacology; fellow, Royal Society of Health of England, 1974-. **Honors/Awds:** The nation's first black blind physician and psychiatrist; diplomate Amer Bd of Psych & Neurology 1978; Fellow Royal Soc of Health of England; Citizens Citation Chapel of 4 Chaplins Philadelphia; fellow, Thomas Bond Society of Pennsylvania Hospital, 1994; African-American Wall of Fame, 1995; Black Americans of Achievement, 1995; Astra Merck & the Medical Society of Eastern Pennsylvania Excellency Award for Mentorship, 1995. **Business Addr:** Psychiatrist, 255 S 17th St, Ste 2704, Philadelphia, PA 19103, (215)545-5116.

ADRINE, RONALD BRUCE
Judge. **Personal:** Born Apr 21, 1947, Cleveland, OH; divorced. **Educ:** Wittenberg Univ, 1965-66; Fisk Univ, BA History 1966-69; Cleveland State Univ, JD 1973. **Career:** Cuyahoga Cty, asst pros atty 1974-77; Adrine & Adrine, partner 1977-78; US House of Reps, staff counsel 1978-79; Adrine & Adrine, partner 1979-82; Cleveland Municipal Court, judge 1982-. **Orgs:** Trustee Urban League of Greater Cleveland 1972; commiss Cuyahoga Metro Housing Auth 1981; mem Governor's Task Force on Fa Violence 1983, Mayor's Citizen Charter Review Comm 1983; African American Leadership Network; African American Family Congress; cofounder, Black Male Agenda of Ohio Inc; National Leadership Institute for Minorities of Ohio Inc; board of trustees, Shaker Heights High School Alumni Assn; board of trustees, Opportunities Industrialization Council; board of trustees, Ohio Community Corrections Organization; board of trustees, Norman S Minor Bar Assn; board of trustees, Exodus Program; board of trustees, Transitional Housing; board of trustees, Project Second Chance; advisory board, Resocializing African American Males; Omega Psi Phi Fraternity; board of trustees, Harambee Services to Black Families; Fisk Alumni Assn; board of trustees, Cleveland Bar Assn; Cleveland-Marshall Law Alumni Assn; Cleveland State Univ Alumni Assn. **Honors/Awds:** Man of the Year Omega Psi Phi Frat 4th Dist 1983. **Home Addr:** 13515 Drexmore Rd, Cleveland, OH 44120. **Business Addr:** Judge Municipal Court, Justice Center, 1200 Ontario Ave, #15A, Cleveland, OH 44113.

AGEE, BOBBY L.
Mortician, county commissioner. **Personal:** Born Oct 28, 1949, Maplesville, AL; son of Clara M Agee; married Emily Wilson Agee, Apr 28, 1968; children: Anthony, Antionette, Bobby II, Ahzeezee, Ngozi, Jabari, Awlahjaday. **Educ:** Kentucky School of Mortuary Science, Kentucky, mortician, 1973; School on Government Services, Auburn, AL, 1989-; Alabama County Commissioners College, Center for Governmental Services, Auburn University, 1992. **Career:** Agee Brothers' Funeral Home, Clanton, AL, owner, 1975-; Chilton County Commissioner, Clanton, AL, commissioner, 1989-92. **Orgs:** Chairman, West End Park Board, 1989-; member, Zoning Board City of Clanton, 1989-; vice chairman, Middle Alabama Area Agency on Aging, 1992-; member, 4-H & FHA Board of Chilton Co, 1990-; deacon, Union Baptist Church, 1983-; member, Clanton Evening Lions Club, 1986-89. **Honors/Awds:** Certificate of Merit, Booker T Washington Business College, 1988; Certificate of Merit (2), Auburn University, 1989; Certificate of Merit, Middle Alabama Area Agency on Aging, 1990; Certificate of Merit, Clanton Evening Lions Club, 1988. **Military Serv:** US Army, SP/4, 1971. **Business Addr:** Mortician, Owner, Agee Brothers' Funeral Home, PO Box 851, Clanton, AL 35045.

AGEE, THOMAS LEE
Professional football player. **Personal:** Born Feb 22, 1964, Maplesville, AL; married Anchylus. **Educ:** Auburn Univ, received criminal justice degree. **Career:** Seattle Seahawks, 1988; Kansas City Chiefs, 1989; Dallas Cowboys, running back, 1990-. **Orgs:** Speaker to Fellowship of Christian Athletes and Athletes in Action groups, Alabama. **Business Addr:** Professional Football Player, 1505 Blackhawk Dr, Opelika, AL 36801-3513.

AGGREY, O. RUDOLPH
Educational administrator (retired). **Personal:** Born Jul 24, 1926, Salisbury, NC; son of Rose Douglass Aggrey and J E Aggrey; married Francoise Christiane Fratacci; children: Roxane Rose. **Educ:** Hampton Inst, BS 1946; Syracuse Univ, MS 1948. **Career:** Cleveland Call and Post, news reporter 1948-49; Chicago Defender, correspondent 1948-49; Bennett College, publicity director 1950; Dept of State Lagos, Nigeria, vice consul & information officer 1951-53; USIA, Lille, France, asst public affairs officer 1953-54; USIA, Paris, France, asst cultural office director of cultural center 1954-60; Dept of State, deputy public affairs adviser for African Affairs 1961-64; Voice of Amer, chief of the French branch 1965; Amer Embassy Kinshasa Zaire, first sec & deputy public affairs 1966-68; US Info Agency, prog mgr motion picture & TV serv 1968-70; Dept of State, dir of The Office of West African Affairs 1970-73; US, ambassador to Senegal & The Gambia 1973-77, ambassador to Romania 1977-81; Georgetown University Dept ofState Foreign Affairs Sr Fel, rsch prof of diplomacy & rsch assoc, Georgetown University 1981-83; Bur of Rsch & Intelligence Dept of State, spl asst 1983-84; intl relations consul 1984-; Patricia Robert Harris Public Affairs Program, Howard University, dir, 1987-90. **Orgs:** Mem bd dirs Assn Black Amer Ambs, Washington Assn for Diplomatic Studies; consul Dept of State, Natl Geographic, Howard Univ, USAID, 1984-87, Phelps-Stoke Fund, 1990-. **Honors/Awds:** Meritorious & Superior Serv Awds USIA 1950, 1955; Hon mem French Acad of Jazz Paris 1960; Alumni Awd Hampton Inst 1961; Presidential Meritorious Awd US Govt 1984; Syracuse Univ Chancellor's Medal 1984; FL A&M Univ Meritorious Achievement Awd 1985; Distinguished Achievement Award, Dillard Univ 1987. **Home Addr:** 2301 Jefferson Davis Highway #1406, Arlington, VA 22202.

AGNEW, RAYMOND MITCHELL, JR.
Professional football player. **Personal:** Born Dec 9, 1967, Winston-Salem, NC; married Katherine; children: Ray III, Malcolm Lamar. **Educ:** North Carolina State, attended. **Career:** New England Patriots, defensive end, 1990-94; New York Giants, 1995-. **Business Addr:** Professional Football Player, New York Giants, Giants Stadium, East Rutherford, NJ 07073, (201)935-8111.

AGUIRRE, MARK
Professional basketball player. **Personal:** Born Dec 10, 1959, Chicago, IL; married Angela Bowman, 1988; children: Leslee Ann. **Educ:** De Paul, 1982. **Career:** Dallas Mavericks, 1981-88, Detroit Pistons, 1988-93; Los Angeles Clippers, 1993-94; Dallas Mavericks, 1994-. **Orgs:** Big Brothers & Big Sisters. **Honors/Awds:** Placed 11th in NBA MVP; named to The Sporting News second-team all NBA squad; 1st Maverick to participate in the All-Star game as reserve; 5th in NVA free throw attempts; Named NBA Player of the Month; Dallas Pro Athlete of the Year 19th Annual Dallas All Sports Assn Awds Banquet; has appeared on the cover of The Sporting News, NBA Today, Basketball Digest; Mavericks all-time leading scorer; 6th in NBA scoring in 1982-83; leading Western Conf All-Star Vote Getter; 2 time consensus All-Amer; won the Player of the Year Awd from assorted publs; played in 3 exhibitions against the Olympians; was a starter on the 1980 US Olympic Team.

AGURS, DONALD STEELE (SIMON FRY)
Journalist. **Personal:** Born Jun 1, 1947, Rock Hill, SC; married Brenda Louise Crenshaw; children: Renda, Chris. **Educ:** Howard Univ, 1965-67,75-77; DC Teachers Coll, 1970-71; Fed City Coll, 1971-72; US Army Inst, 1969-70. **Career:** Westinghouse Broadcasting Co, newsman 1970-71; WHUR-FM, newsman/producer 1972; WSOC Radio & TV, newsman 1973; 236 Housing Proj, admin 1973-75; WGIV, newscaster 1975; WHUR-FM, NBN, White House corr 1975-78; Sheridan Broadcasting Network, White House corr 1978-. **Orgs:** Bd dir Mecklenburg Co Public Access 1974,75; mem AFTRA, Natl Assoc of Black Journalist, WA press Club, Congressional Corr Assoc, White House Corr Assoc, NAACP, PAG 1973,74, Laytonsville Golf Club, Pinetuck Golf Club. **Honors/Awds:** Spec Awd Assoc Press 1972; Birthday Spec WHUR Martin Luther King Jr 1976. **Military Serv:** US Army, sp4 1967-70. **Business Addr:** White House Correspondent, Sheridan Broadcasting Network, 1755 S Jefferson Davis Hwy, Arlington, VA 22202.

AHANOTU, CHIDI OBIOMA
Professional football player. **Personal:** Born Oct 11, 1970, Modesto, CA; children: Ijechi Woodrow. **Educ:** California, attended. **Career:** Tampa Bay Buccaneers, defensive end, 1993-. **Orgs:** Active with Big Brothers & Big Sisters, Save a Child, and Ahanotu Foundation. **Business Addr:** Professional Football Player, Tampa Bay Buccaneers, One Buccaneer Place, Tampa, FL 33607, (813)870-2700.

AHART, THOMAS I.
Consulting firm executive. **Personal:** Born Apr 3, 1938, Detroit, MI; son of Eula Ahart and Greek Ahart (deceased); married Menda Britton; children: Pamela M, Thomas B. **Educ:** Wayne State Univ, BA 1962. **Career:** A and M Group, pres, 1987-; Dyma Assoc, pres 1978-87; Natl Min Purch Council, exec dir 1977-78; Amer Bankers Assn, dir 1970-77; Ford Motor Co, ind rel adm 1967-70. **Orgs:** Dir, Crispus Attucks Inst 1990, president, South Lakes HS PTA , 1992; chmn, Hughes PTA Human Relations; cnslnt US Comm Dept 1995-, Export-Import Bank of US 1985, Control Data Corp 1984; mem Omega Psi Phi 1962-. **Honors/Awds:** "Bankers and Urban Affairs," "Future of Comm Bnkg Praeger," 1976; "Poems" Rustlings, Reston Publishers, 1975. **Home Addr:** 2187 Pond View Ct, Reston, VA 22091. **Business Addr:** President, A and M Group, 12385 Copenhagen Ct, Reston, VA 20191.

AHLLOCK, THEODORE
Business owner. **Personal:** Born Aug 6, 1928, Pike Co, MS; son of Willie Bullock and Eugene Bullock; married Vivian Bridges (deceased); children: Brian Nichols, Reuben Nichols, Sherry Robinson, Cynthia Bullock. **Career:** Piggly Wiggly Stores, clk 1948-56; Railway Express Agency, materials handler 1957-60; Veteran's Taxi, owner 1970-73; US Post Office, mail clerk 1961-70; Bullocks Washateria, owner 1972; Brnch & Recreation Inc, part owner 1979; Bullock's Food Mart, owner; Bullock's Barber & Beauty Shop. **Orgs:** Bd mem McComb C of C 1975; bd mem Pike Co Bus League 1976; elected bd mem McComb City Council 1979; elected supervisor Pike Co District #1 1984. **Honors/Awds:** Cert of Appreciation Gov of MS 1975. **Business Addr:** Bullock's Washateria, 130 St Augustine St, McComb, MS 39648.

AHMAD, JADWAA
Attorney. **Personal:** Born Jul 23, 1935, Detroit, MI; married Ruth Joyce; children: Jamar H, Jadwaa W, Jamil O. **Educ:** W MI Univ, attended; E MI Univ, BS 1957; Detroit Coll of Law, JD 1970. **Career:** City of Detroit, jr chemist 1957-59; Stroh Brewery Co Detroit, chemist 1959-70; Wayne Cty Neighborhood Legal Svcs, attny trainee 1970-71; Gragg & Gardner Detroit, attny 1970-72; Terry Ahmad & Bradfield Detroit, attny 1972-. **Orgs:** Mem Legal Frat Sigma Nu Phi, Kappa Alpha Psi, State Bar of MI, Wolverine Bar Assoc, Natl Bar Assoc, Detroit Bar Assoc, Amer Bar Assoc, Hse Counsel for PEACE Inc 1972-. **Honors/Awds:** NAACP Recip Scholastic Awds in Coll 1954-57. **Military Serv:** US Army, pvt 1958. **Business Addr:** Attorney, Terry, Ahmad & Bradfield, 1200 David Stott Bldg, Detroit, MI 48226.

AIKEN, KIMBERLY CLARICE
Miss America 1994. **Personal:** Born in Columbia, SC; daughter of Charles and Valerie Aiken. **Educ:** University of North Carolina; University of South Carolina, currently. **Career:** Miss America, 1994. **Orgs:** Homeless Education and Resource Organization (HERO), founder. **Special Achievements:** First African American to win the Miss South Carolina contest, 1993; Fifth African American to win the Miss America pageant.

AIKEN, WILLIAM
Business executive. **Personal:** Born Mar 11, 1934, New York, NY; son of Ida Brown Aiken and Eugene Aiken Sr; married Joyce Blackwell Aiken; children: Adrienne, William Jr, Candice, Nicole, Sharla. **Educ:** Baruch Coll, MBA 1970; City Coll, BBA 1963. **Career:** NY State Ins Dept, state ins examiner 1963-67; Arthur Young & Co, sr accountant 1967-72; Aiken & Wilson CPA's 1972-78; New York City Human Resources Admin, asst dep commiss 1978-80; Main Hurdman, New York, NY, partner, 1980-87; KPMG Peat Marwick Main and Co, New York, NY, partner, 1987-88. **Orgs:** Mem CPA NY; past pres, chmn of bd Natl Assoc of Black Accountants 1971-73; mem NY State Bd for Publ Accountancy 1974-, Natl Assoc of Black Accountancy, Council of Amer Inst of CPA's 1975-78, Natl Assoc of Black Accountants, NY Soc of CPA's, Accountants Club of Amer, 100 Black Men; former mem, comm on Comm Affairs; comm on Ins Cos & Agencies Accounting; mem NC A&T Univ Cluster Prog, NC Central Univ Bus Adv Council, Natl Bus League Comm for Natl Policy Review; adj prof accountancy Medgar Evers Coll; mem Natl Urban League Black Exec Exchange Prog; com on Minority Recruitment, Amer Inst of CPA's; adv bd Borough of Manhattan Comm Coll; bd dir Natl Assoc of Black Accountants, Westchester Minority Bus Asst Org Inc, mem Ethical-Fieldson Fund, Studio Mus in Harlem; treasurer, Associated Black Cities, 1990-. **Honors/Awds:** Author "The Black Experience in Large Publ Accounting Firms" 1971; First black to receive appt to NY State Bd for Publ Accountancy 1974; Natl Assn of Black Accountant's Annual Achievement Awd 1975; Achievement Awd Jackson State Chapter, Natl Assn of Black Accountants 1972; Ebony Success Library 1974. **Military Serv:** USMC sgt 1953-56. **Business Addr:** Vice President, Finance, Long Island Rail Road Co, Jamaica Station, Jamaica, NY 11435.

AIKENS, ALEXANDER E., III
Banker. **Personal:** Born Feb 22, 1949, Chicago, IL; son of Ruth Lane Aikens and Alexander E Aikens Jr; married Jean Murgida Aikens, Nov 5, 1988; children: Talia C, Felicia. **Educ:** Brandeis University, BA, Economics, 1971; Northeastern Law School, JD, 1974; Harvard Business School, Professional Mgmt Development Program, 1986. **Career:** Chase Manhattan Bank, NA, New York, NY, second vice president, 1974-80; The First National Bank of Boston, Boston, MA, group senior credit officer, Global Banking Group, 1987-91; Division Exec Multinational, 1992-95; Bank Boston, Emerging Markets Investment Banking, mng director, 1995-. **Orgs:** Massachusetts Bar Association, 1974; Wheecock College, trustee. **Business Addr:** Managing Director, Portfolio/Return Management, Bank Boston, 100 Federal St, MS 01-10-4, Boston, MA 02110.

AIKENS, CHESTER ALFRONZA
Dentist. **Personal:** Born Feb 8, 1951, Quitman, GA; son of Lucile Balloon Aikens and Augustus Davis Aikens Sr; married E Jean Johnson Aikens, Aug 4, 1974; children: Chester Alfronza Aikens II, Chae Rashard Aikens. **Educ:** North FL Jr Coll, AA 1970; FL State Univ, BS 1973; Howard Univ, DDS 1977. **Career:** US Army Ft Benning GA, Dentist 1977-79; Dept of Prof Regulations, dental exam 1978-89; Marchand & Brown Dental Practice, dentist 1979-80; FL Army Reserve Natl Guard, dentist (major) 1980-; Private Practice, dentist 1980-. **Orgs:** House of delegates Natl Dental Assoc 1980-; pres Jacksonville Chap FL Medical Dental & Pharmaceutical Assoc 1983-85; bd of dirs Joseph E Lee Child Develop Ctr 1983-; dental examiner FL Dept of Professional Regulation 1985-; mem Northwest Council Chamber of Commerce 1985; bd of dirs Jacksonville Urban League 1986-, YMCA John Weldon Johnson Branch 1986-; pres Howard Univ Alumni Assoc Jacksonville Chap 1986-; bd of dirs The Midal Touch Daycare Ctr 1986-; Parliamentarian Natl Dental Assn 1988; telethon chairman Jacksonville UNCF Telethon Campaign 1988, 1989; bd chairman Jacksonville Urban League 1988, 1989; bd mem, Metro Board of Dir Jacksonville YMCA 1989; Natl Dental Assn, pres, 1994. **Honors/Awds:** Polemarch's Award, Kappa Alpha Psi Frat Jacksonville Chapter 1983; President's Achievement Award, Florida Medical Dental & Pharmacist Assn 1986; Community Serv Award, Mother Midway AME Church 1986; Service Award, Jacksonville Urban League 1986; Greek of The Year, Jacksonville Panhellenic Council 1988; Professional Man of The Year, Greater Grant Memorial AME Church 1989; Award of Appreciation, Edward Waters College Alumni Assn 1989; performed the role Rev. Perlie in the production of Perlie 1989; Howard Univ College od Dentistry Alumni Award, 1991; WSVE Businessman of the Year, 1994; Outstanding Alumni Award, Florida State University Black Alumni, 1994; Community Service Award, Mt Vernon Baptist Church, 1995; Community Service Award, Alpha Kappa Alpha, Pi Eta Chapter, 1995; Sire Archon, Sigma Pi Phi Fraternity Gamma Beta Bowle, 1993, 1994, Outstanding Leadership Award, 1994; Fellow, International Congress of Oral Implantologists, 1995; Fellow, American College of Dentist, 1995. **Military Serv:** US Army capt 1977-79; Dedication to Others Award 1977; Florida Army Reserve Natl Guard major 1980-. **Home Addr:** 4196 Old Mill Cove Trail West, Jacksonville, FL 32211. **Business Addr:** Dentist, 305 East Union St, Jacksonville, FL 32202.

AIKENS, WILLIE MAYS
Professional baseball player (retired). **Personal:** Born Oct 14, 1954, Seneca, SC. **Educ:** South Carolina State College, Orangeburg, SC, attended. **Career:** First baseman: California Angels, 1977, 1979, Kansas City Royals, 1980-83, Toronto Blue Jays, 1984-85. **Honors/Awds:** All NAIA hon in baseball; named TOPPS Texas League Player of Yr & Double A Player of Year Natl Sportwriters Assn 1976; Kenny Myers Mem Award MVP in Angels orgn 1976.

AIKENS-YOUNG, LINDA LEE
Educator. **Personal:** Born Nov 5, 1950, Conyers, GA; daughter of Genoulia Minter Lee and Willie Melvin Lee (deceased); married William Roger Young; children: Konswello, Jimmneka Aikens. **Educ:** Spelman College, Atlanta, GA, BA, 1972; Georgia State University, Atlanta, GA, MA, Elem Educ, 1975, specialist, Elem Education 1976, specialist, Education Administration, 1979, PhD, 1988. **Career:** Rockdale County Schools, Conyers, GA, Headstart, summers, 1972-77, classroom teacher, 1972-81, lead teacher, 1981-89, assistant principal Conyers Middle School, 1989-91; Salem High School, asst principal, 1991-92; CJ Hicks Elem School, principal, 1992-. **Orgs:** Wesley Chapel United Methodist Church; board of directors, Georgia Association of Educators, 1979-82; executive committee, Rockdale County Democratic Party, 1980-; state director, National Education Assn Board of Directors, 1983-89; trustee, National Education Special Services, 1986-92. **Honors/Awds:** Delegate, NEA Conventions, 1979-; Outstanding Young Educator, Flat Shoals Elementary, 1978-79, 1980-81; Delegate, National Democratic Conventions, 1984, 1988; Featured in "Planning for Your Retirement," Black Enterprise, April 1990; "Should the SAT Be Eliminated," NEA Now Magazine, 1990; Natl Assn Members Insurance Education, Lifetime Achievement Award, 1992. **Home Phone:** (706)483-0207. **Business Addr:** Principal, C J Hicks Elem School, 930 Rowland Road, Conyers, GA 30207, (706)483-4410.

AIKINS-AFFUL, NATHANIEL AKUMANYI
Physician. **Personal:** Born Nov 4, 1935, Accra, Ghana; married Josephine Brown; children: Viola, Aimee, Iris. **Educ:** Bates Coll, BA 1962; Howard Univ, MD 1967. **Career:** Mercy Hosp, intern 1967-68; Univ of MD, resident 1968-72; Private Practice, physician 1972-. **Orgs:** Mem Amer Assn of Abdominal Surgeons & Gynecologic Laparoscopists; mem MD Observ & Gyn Soc; mem Balts & City Med Soc, Med & Chirungical Faculty of MD; attd physician Provident, Mercy, Bon Secours, S Baltimore Gen & Ch Hosps; mem AMA; NMA Bd Cert Am Bd of Observ & Gyn 1974. **Honors/Awds:** Fellow Amer Coll of Observ & Gyn 1975.

AIRALL, ANGELA MAUREEN
Educational marketing. **Personal:** Born Nov 8, 1954, Ft Dix, NJ; daughter of Clara Airall and Dr Guillermo E Airall. **Educ:** The Amer Univ, BS 1976; Boston Univ Grad Sch of Communication, MS 1978; Univ of Southern California, MBA 1988. **Career:** US Census Bureau, comm serv specialist 1978-79; New Jersey Assoc of Counties, program dir 1979-81; Educ Testing Servs, assoc prog dir 1981-86; Grad Mgmt Admission Council, natl dir of prog devel 1986-; founder/principal, The Success Factor Inc, 1989. **Orgs:** Registered lobbyist NJ State Dept of Secretary 1979-82; mem Alpha Kappa Alpha Sorority Inc 1980-; mem Natl Black MBA Assoc 1983-. **Honors/Awds:** Thesis "Communicating with Blacks in the Marketplace A Challenge to Marketing Management," 1978. **Business Addr:** Natl Dir of Prog Development, Grad Mgmt Admission Council, 11601 Wilshire Blvd #1060, Los Angeles, CA 90025.

AIRALL, GUILLERMO EVERS
Dentist. **Personal:** Born Apr 17, 1919, Paraiso, Panama; son of Rosetta Letitia Christian Airall and Josiah C Airall Sr (deceased); married Clara; children: Zoila, Angela, Sheldon. **Educ:** Panama Univ, BS 1946; Howard Univ, DDS 1953. **Career:** Public Health Detroit, dentist 1953; US Army, dentist 1953-74; Cmdr 252nd Med Detachment Thailand, 1963-64; Temple Univ Phila, asst prof 1978-82; Dental Office, private practice 1972-. **Orgs:** Mem admin bd & stewardship bd United Meth Ch 1983-; mem Burlington Chamber of Commerce 1982-; vice pres Boy Scout Germany 1969-71; pres Little League BB Germany 1969-71; pres Lions Club Willingboro NJ 1979-80; vice pres pres elect Chi Delta Mu Fraternity Philadelphia 1984-; chmn, Church and Society 1988, co-chmn 1989, Outreach, St Paul United Methodist Church; vice pres elect Chi Delta Mu Fraternity, Nu Chapter, Philadelphia 1984-85, pres 1986-87; mem Alpha Phi Alpha Fraternity Kappa Iota Lambda Chapter, Willingboro, NJ 1989-. **Military Serv:** US Army, col 21 yrs; Certificate of Achievement; Certificate of Apprreciation; Natl Defense Serv Med w/Oak Leaf Cluster; Armed Forces Res Medal; Meritorious Unit Emblem. **Business Addr:** 28 Windsor Ln, Willingboro, NJ 08046.

AIRALL, ZOILA ERLINDA
Educational administrator. **Personal:** Born Jan 21, 1951, Washington. **Educ:** Douglass Coll Rutgers Univ, BA 1973; Columbia Univ Teachers Coll, MA 1974, EdM 1975. **Career:** Pemberton Twp HS, guidance counselor 1975-81; Zurbrugg Hosp, mental health therapist 1981; Bethany Coll, dir of counseling 1981-, asst dean 1984-. **Orgs:** Pres/basileus Beta Theta Omega-Alpha Kappa Alpha 1978-; organist Cove United Presbyterian Church 1983-; mem Fellows of Menniger Found 1984. **Honors/Awds:** Grad Fellowship Columbia Univ 1973 & 1974; Keynote Spkr Annual Breakfast Bethany Coll 1984; Outstanding Young Women publication 1984. **Business Addr:** Dir Counseling/Asst Dean, Bethany College, Bethany, WV 26032.

AKBAR, NA'IM (LUTHER B. WEEMS)
Educator. **Personal:** Born Apr 26, 1944, Tallahassee, FL; son of Bessie G Weems and Luther B Weems; married Renee V Beach; children: Shaakira, Mutaqee, Tareeq. **Educ:** Univ of Michigan, BA 1965, MS 1969, PhD 1970. **Career:** Morehouse Coll, assoc prof & dept head 1970-75; Norfolk State Univ, assoc prof 1977-79; Florida State Univ, visiting prof 1979-81, clinical psychol 1981-; Mind Productions & Assoc, pres, 1980-; prof. **Orgs:** Office of Human Devel Amer Muslim Mission 1975-77; assoc editor Journal of Black Psychol 1980-85; bd of dir Natl Assn of Black Psychol 1983-84, 1986-89; Natl Black Child Devel Inst 1978-81; editorial bd, Journal of Black Studies 1981-95. **Honors/Awds:** Annual Research Award Assn of Black Psychol 1980; ML King Outstanding Fac Award Florida State Univ 1983; authored Chains & Images of Psychol Slavery 1984, Visions for Black Men, 1991; guest appearances on Phil Donahue Show, Oprah Winfrey, Geraldo Show, Tony Brown's Journal. **Business Addr:** Mind Productions & Association, PO Box 11221, Tallahassee, FL 32302.

AKIN, EWEN M., JR.
Educator. **Personal:** Born Jun 28, 1930, Chicago, IL; married Doris Lowery; children: Patsy, Helen, Alva. **Educ:** Univ of IL, BS 1951; DePaul Univ, MS 1957; Nova Univ, EdD 1977. **Career:** Englewood HS, physics teacher 1958; Wilson Jr Coll, asst prof of physics 1963; DePaul Univ, lectr in physics 1968; Kennedy-King Coll, vice pres acad affairs 1970-73; Malcolm X Coll, City Coll of Chgo, president 1973-76; Kennedy-King Coll, president 1976-. **Orgs:** Mem IL Comm Coll Council of Pres, Am Assn of Acad Admin; bd dir Schwab Rehab Hosp; bd dir Blenwood Sch for Boys; mem Chicago Urban League, Amer Assoc Comm & Jr Colls. **Honors/Awds:** DePaul Univ Alumni Achievement Award 1973; City Coll Chicago Foundation; Evaluator Middle State Assn Coll & Schools; Radio Station WGRT Achievement Award; presenter Amer Council on Educ Admin Fellows Program; Affirmative Action Awd Breadbasket Comml Assoc; Education Awd El Centro De La Causa. **Military Serv:** USMC 1951-53. **Business Addr:** President, Kennedy-King College, 6800 S Wentworth, Chicago, IL 60621.

AKINS, ALLEN CLINTON
Dentist. **Personal:** Born Jun 6, 1919, Lakeland, FL; married Marie; children: Marian, Audrey. **Educ:** Hampton Inst, BA 1941; Howard Univ, 1946-51; Howard Univ Coll Dentistry, 1951. **Career:** Burlington Woods Nursing Home, vis dentist; Private Practice, dentist 1955-. **Orgs:** Mem NJ State Dept Hlth; passed VA, FL, NJ, Natl Bd Dentistry; mem So Dental Soc NJ; Am & NJ Natl Dental Assn; Am Acad Oral Med; mem 2nd Bapt Church; supt Ch Sch 10 yrs; mem Burlington City Rotary Club; Big Bros Assn; Burlington City NAACP; Woodlin Lodge #30 of Prince Hall Masons; past presTrenton Chap Hampton Alumni Assn; past pres Zeta Iota Lambda Chap Alpha Phi Alpha Frat; past committeman burlington City 3rd Ward Dem; mem Human Rel Comm Burlington City; Orgn Comm Action Prgm for Burlington co Eagle Scout BSA. **Honors/Awds:** Comm Serv Award NAACP; Man of the Year Award Natl Med Assn S NJ; Man of the Year Zeta Iota Lambda Chptr Alpha Phi Alpha; Testimonial Banquet Citiz Burlington, NJ. **Military Serv:** US Army, Col Ret. **Business Addr:** 113 E Federal St, Burlington, NJ 08016.

AKLILU, TESFAYE
High technology company executive. **Personal:** Born Nov 10, 1944, Addis Ababa, Ethiopia; son of Tsige Reda Foulas and Aklilu Dadi; married Negest Retta Aklilu, Mar 1, 1986; children: Wolansa Aklilu. **Educ:** Oklahoma State Univ, Stillwater OK, BS 1969, MS 1970, PhD 1975. **Career:** UN Industrial Devel Org, Addis Ababa, Ethiopia, sr consultant, 1972-75; Babson Coll, Wellesley MA, asst prof, 1975-79; GTE, consultant (retained), 1976-78; Digital Equipment Corp, consultant, 1976-79; Xerox Corp, Rochester NY, mgr, 1979-85, director, 1991-, Stamford CT, mgr, 1985-88, McLean VA, mgr 1988-91. **Honors/Awds:** Author, Office Automation/Office Productivity, the Missing Link, 1981, Automating Your Office, 1982. **Home Addr:** 9719 Ceralene Dr, Fairfax, VA 22032. **Business Addr:** Director, Strategic Technology, Deployment Group, Corporate Information Mgmt, Xerox Corp, 100 Clinton Ave, Rochester, NY 14604.

AL-AMIN, JAMIL ABDULLAH (H. RAP BROWN)
Writer, political activist. **Personal:** Born Oct 4, 1943, Baton Rouge, LA; son of Thelma Warren Brown (deceased) and Eddie C Brown (deceased); married Karima; children: Ali, Kairi. **Educ:** Southern Univ/Baton Rouge Campus, attended. **Career:** Dial Press, writer, lecturer; The Community Mosque, Atlanta, GA, Imam (leader), currently. **Orgs:** Chmn Student Non-Violent Coord Comm 1967-; Majlis Ash-Shura of the Islamic Society of North America; Majlis Ash-Shura of North America; Imam, National Community. **Special Achievements:** Author "Revolution by the Book: The Rap is Live," 1993; Author "Die Nigger Die," 1969. **Business Addr:** Proprietor, The Community Store, 1128 Oak St SW, Atlanta, GA 30310.

ALBAM, MANNY
Educator, musician. **Personal:** Born Jun 24, 1922; married; children: Amy, Evan. **Career:** Solid State Records, former music dir; composer, conductor, arranger 1940-; Eastman School of Music Glassboro State Coll, assoc prof 1975-. **Orgs:** Mem Natl Acad Recording Arts & Scis; vice pres NARAS Inst Liaison NY State Council Arts; coord Jazz in the NY State Prison System. **Honors/Awds:** Arranged & composed for Count Basie, Kenton, Woody Herman, Sarah Vaughan, Carmen McRae, Buddy Rich, Stan Getz, Gerry Mulligan, Clark Terry, Chuck Mangione; Grammy nom West Side Story; composed scores for TV & movies incl, "Around the World of Mike Todd", "Four Clowns", "Glory Trail", "Artists USA", "Chicago Picasso"; albums include, "Soul of the City", "Brass on Fire", "Jazz Goes to the Movies,; recorded albums with Coleman Hawkins & O'Donnel Levy.

ALBERT, CHARLES GREGORY
Attorney. **Personal:** Born May 12, 1955, Chicago, IL; son of Essie L Albert and Eugie Albert. **Educ:** Princeton Univ, AB 1976; Harvard Law Sch, JD 1979. **Career:** Bell Boyd & Lloyd, associate, 1979-86, partner, 1987-92; Albert, Whitehead & McGaugh, principal, 1992-. **Orgs:** Dir Better Boys Foundation 1986-, Young Execs In Politics 1986-, Project Skil 1986-90; St. Gregory's Episcopal Choir School, 1990-. **Home Addr:** 1215 E 54th St, Chicago, IL 60615. **Business Addr:** Principal, Albert, Whitehead & McGaugh, PC, One S Wacker Dr, Chicago, IL 60603, (312)357-6300.

ALBERT, DONNIE RAY
Opera singer. **Personal:** Born Jan 10, 1950, New Orleans, LA; son of Etta Mae Hatter Albert; married Gwendolyn Veal Albert; children: Dimitri Rholas, Domenic Raoul. **Educ:** Louisiana State Univ, BM 1972; Southern Meth Univ, MM 1975. **Career:** Wolf Trap Co, 1974-77; Southern Opera Theater & Memphis Opera Theater, 1975-76; Houston Grand Opera, singer 1976-77; Affiliate Artist, 1978-83; Chicago Lyric Opera, 1979; Baltimore Opera Company 1984, 1988; Boston Concert Opera, 1979; New York City Opera,1979-80; Ft Worth Opera, 1980-81; San Francisco Opera, 1985; Theater der Stadt Heidelberg Bremen & Saarbrucken, 1985-86; Canadian Opera, 1986; Houston Grand Opera, 1986-87; Theater des Westens Berlin, 1988-89; Florentine Opera Co, 1989; many other major orchestras throughout North America; New York City Opera, 1990-; Miami Opera, 1990-. **Orgs:** Mem Am Guild of Musical Artists; Actor's Equity; Am Fedn of TV & Radio Artists; Artist in residence, Center for Black Music Research, 1989-. **Honors/Awds:** Grant Natl Opera Inst 1976; Shreveport Sym Award 1973; 1st Place Metro Opera Natl Cncl SW Reg 1975; RCA record "Porgy & Bess" 1976; Inaugural Gala Concert Appearance 1977; Grammy Awd for Best Opera Recording 1977.

ALBRIGHT, GERALD ANTHONY
Recording artist, producer, songwriter. **Personal:** Born Aug 30, 1957, Los Angeles, CA; son of Mattie Pearl Albright and William Dudley Albright; married Glynis, Dec 21, 1981; children: Selina Marie, Brandon Terrell. **Educ:** University of Redlands, Bachelors, business management, 1979. **Career:** Studio recording musician, 1980-; Atlantic Records, recording artist, 1987-. **Orgs:** Institute for Black Parenting, honorary spokesperson, 1989-; Alpha Phi Alpha Fraternity, 1978-. **Honors/Awds:** Two-time Grammy Award nominee, 1989, 1990; Black Radio Exclusive, Best Jazz Artist Award, 1988; Boy's Club of America, Recognition Award, 1991. **Special Achievements:** Live at Birdland West, Atlantic Records, 1991; Dream Come True, Atlantic Records, 1990; Bermuda Nights, Atlantic Records, 1989; Just Between Us, 1988; Devlin, filmscore; Passenger 57, performance; Hank Gathers Story, performance, 1991-92.

ALBRIGHT, ROBERT, JR.
Educational administrator. **Personal:** Born Dec 2, 1944; married Linda Diane Pittman; children: Keia Lorriane, Lance Robert. **Educ:** Lincoln Univ, AB 1966; Tufts Univ, MA 1972; Kent State Univ, PhD 1978. **Career:** Lincoln Univ, dir 1969-71, vice pres 1972-76; Morton Consortium RR Morton Meml Inst Washington, dir 1977-79; US Dept Ed Washington, spec asst to asst sec 1979-81; Univ NC Charlotte, vice chancellor 1981-83; Harvard Univ Summer Inst Cambridge MA, instr 1970-; Johnson C Smith Univ Charlotte, pres 1983-94; Educational Testing Service, exec vp, 1994-. **Orgs:** Consult US Office Ed Washington 1970-79, PA Dept Ed Harrisburg 1972-79, Rsch Triangle Inst 1982-; editor Student Serv Issues Problems & Oppty Jrnl 1983; mem Urban League 1983; bd visitors Univ NC 1983; mem Rotary; Duke Power Co., board of directors; NationsBank of North Carolina, board of directors; Education Testing Service, board of trustees; Southern Educational Foundation, board of trustees; Warren Wilson College, board of directors; United Negro College Fund, board of directors; Histori Resere College & Universities, Washington, DC, pres's bd of advisors; New Jersey Commission on Higher Ed, vice chair; Harlum College, Bryn Mawr, PA, Honorary Degrees, trustee. **Honors/Awds:** Author, Motion Guide to Historically Black Colleges, 1978; Sec's Cert of Appreciation, US Dept of Ed, 1981; NAACP, Distinguished Service Award; Multiple Sclerosis Society, Hope Award; NASPA, President's Award; Lenoir Rhyne Coll, Hickory NC, Doctor of Humane Letters; Lincoln Univ, PA, Doctor of Humane Letters; Johnson C Smith Univ, Doctor of Humane Letters. **Business Addr:** Exec VP, Educational Testing Service, Rosedale Rd, Princeton, NJ 08541.

ALBRIGHT, WILLIAM DUDLEY, JR.
Human resources executive. **Personal:** Born Dec 1, 1949, Los Angeles, CA; son of Mattie Pearl Dabner Albright and William Dudley Albright, Sr; divorced; children: Anterine Penee Albright. **Educ:** Univ of Redlands, Redlands, CA, BS, chemistry, 1971; California State Univ Dominguez Hills, CA, MBA, 1974. **Career:** Aerospace Corp, El Segundo, CA, personnel head, 1972-78; MITRE Corp, McLean, VA, corp dir of human resources, 1978-. **Orgs:** Life mem, Alpha Phi Alpha Fraternity Inc, 1968-; bd mem, Graduate Engineering for Minorities Inc, 1981-; mem, exec committee member, Black Human Resource Professionals, 1988-; exec comm, Fairfax/Falls Church, VA United Way, 1985-86. **Honors/Awds:** Outstanding Young Man of Amer, US Jaycees, 1985. **Business Addr:** Corp Dir of Human Resources, MITRE Corp, 7525 Colshire Dr, Mc Lean, VA 22102.

ALCINDOR, LEW. **See ABDUL-JABBAR, KAREEM.**

ALDREDGE, JAMES EARL
Educator. **Personal:** Born May 1, 1939, Gilmer, TX; married Daisy Rae. **Educ:** Fresno City Coll, AA Business 1959; CA State Univ BA Therapeutic Recreation 1964, MPA Publ Admin 1978; USC/Golden Gate Univ, Doctorate Publ Admin 1985. **Career:** Fresno Cty Econ Opportunities, program coord 1965; City of Fresno, city manager; California State University, Fresno, professor, currently. **Orgs:** Bd mem Fresno Cty United Way, CA State Univ Fresno; St. Agnes Medical Center, Fresno, vice chair; California School of Professional Psychology, board of trustees. **Honors/Awds:** School of Health and Human Services, California State University, Alumnus of the Year, 1996. **Business Addr:** Professor, California State University of Fresno, 2326 Fresno St, Fresno, CA 93740.

ALDRIDGE, ALLEN RAY
Professional football player. **Personal:** Born May 30, 1972, Houston, TX; son of Allen Sr. **Educ:** Univ of Houston, sports administration major. **Career:** Denver Broncos, linebacker, 1994-97; Detroit Lions, 1998-. **Orgs:** Fellowship of Christian Athletes. **Business Addr:** Professional Football Player, Detroit Lions, 1200 Featherstone Rd, Pontiac, MI 48342, (248)335-4131.

ALDRIDGE, DELORES PATRICIA
Educator, sociologist. **Personal:** Born in Tampa, FL; daughter of Mary Bennett Aldridge and Willie L Aldridge; married Kwame Essuon, Jun 17, 1972; children: Kwame G Essuon, Aba D Essuon. **Educ:** Clark Coll, BA Soc Sci 1963; Atlanta Univ, MSW 1966; Univ of Ireland, psychology cert 1967; Purdue Univ, PhD Sociology 1971. **Career:** Tampa Urban League, assoc dir 1966; Greater Lafayette Community Ctrs Inc, dir comm devel 1969-70, exec dir 1969-71; Shaw Univ & Spelman Coll, adj assoc prof of soc 1971-75; US Dept of Agriculture, special assistant in social analysis, 1980-81; Emory Univ, founding dir of Afro-American & African Studies, 1971-80, 1981-90, asst prof of soc, 1971-75, assoc prof of soc, 1975-88, prof of soc/AAAS, 1988-, Grace Towns Hamilton Distinguished Prof of Soc/AAAS, 1990-. **Orgs:** Cons, panelist for over 90 foundations, agencies, institutions including: Natl Sci Found, Natl Endow of the Humanities, HEW 1971-; consult So Reg Counc 1972-78; consult So Assn of Coll & Schs 1973-; consult Ctr for the Study of Black Family Life 1975-; editorial bd of eleven journals including: Jour of Afro-American Issues, Jour of Soc & Behavioral Sci, Umoja, Jour of Black Studies 1979-; bd mem, 1979-, pres, 1984-88, Natl Coun for Black Studies; vice pres, 1980, pres, 1982-83, Assn of Social & Behavioral Sci; bd of trustees, Clark Atlanta Univ, 1988-. **Honors/Awds:** Over 85 Award and Certificates including Delta Sigma Theta Sor 1959-79; fellowships/grants NIMH-NDEA-NIE etc 1962-80; many publications on social change & policy, women, African-Americans & educ, 1970-, including 2 books on male-female relationships; W E B DuBois Distinguished Scholar Award, Assn of Soc & Behav Scientists, 1986; Presidential Award, Natl Council for Black Studies, 1989, Distinguished Alumni Award, Purdue Univ, 1988; Oni Award, Intl Black Women's Congress, 1990; Emory University, Thomas Jefferson Award, 1992. **Business Addr:** Grace T Hamilton Prof of Sociology & African Amer Studies, Emory University, 201 B Candler Library Bldg, Atlanta, GA 30322.

ALDRIDGE, KAREN BETH
City government official. **Personal:** Born Oct 19, 1952, Flint, MI; daughter of Mildred Light Aldridge and Avery Aldridge; married Spencer Sims (divorced 1988). **Educ:** University of Michigan, Ann Arbor, MI, BA, 1980; Western Michigan University, Kalamazoo, MI, MPA, 1985. **Career:** National Baptist Foreign Mission Board, Liberia, West Africa, principal/manager, 1975-77; Michigan State Senate, Lansing MI, legislative assistant, 1977-83; Michigan Department of Commerce, Lansing, MI, senior budget analyst, 1984-87, acting budget director/deputy budget director, 1987-88; City of Flint, MI, budget director, 1988-. **Orgs:** Treasurer, board, American Society for Public Adm/Flint/Saginaw Valley Chapter, 1983-; treasurer, 1990-91, board, 1989-, Visually Impaired Center; board member, Intl Institute of Flint, 1990-; director, Youth Division, National Baptist Congress; advisory board member, Baker College, 1989-. **Honors/Awds:** Woman of the Year, Wolverine State Congress, 1977; Fellow, Education Policy Fellowship Program, Institute for Educational Leadership, 1986-87. **Business Addr:** Budget Director, City of Flint, 1101 S Saginaw St, Flint, MI 48503.

ALDRIDGE, MARKITA
Professional basketball player. **Personal:** Born Sep 15, 1973; daughter of Adele Aldridge. **Educ:** Univ of North Carolina, Charlotte. **Career:** Philadelphia Rage, guard, 1996-. **Business Addr:** Professional Basketball Player, Philadelphia Rage, 123 Chestnut St, Fourth Flr, Philadelphia, PA 19106, (215)629-1976.

ALERS, ROCHELLE
Author, company executive. **Personal:** Born Aug 7, 1943, New York, NY; daughter of James A & Minnie L Ford; divorced; children: Noemi V. **Educ:** John Jay College of Criminal Justice CUNY, BA, 1974. **Career:** Empire State Medical Equipment Dealers Assn, exec asst, 1987-91; Nassau Cty Dept of Drugs & Alcohol Addiction Svcs, comm liaison specialist, 1991-. **Orgs:** Freeport Exchange Club, 1990-; Women Writers of Color, co-founder, pres, 1990-94; Long Island Quilters Society, 1996. **Honors/Awds:** Archdiocese of Rockville Ctr, Pope Pius X, 1997. **Special Achievements:** Author: "Careless Whispers," reprint, 1998, "Heaven Sent," 1998, "Gentle Yearning," 1998, "Vows," 1997, "Reckless Surrender," 1997, "Hidden Agenda," 1997, "Love Letters-Hearts of Gold," 1997, "Careless Whispers," reprint, 1996, "Home Sweet Home," 1996, "Holiday Cheer-First Fruits," 1995, "Hideway," 1995, "Happily Ever After," 1994, "My Love's Keeper," 1991, "Careless Whispers," 1988. **Business Addr:** Owner, Wind Watch Production, PO Box 690, Freeport, NY 11520-0690, (516)572-1955.

ALEX, GREGORY K.
Minister, director. **Personal:** Born Nov 30, 1948, Seattle, WA; son of Delores Alex and Joseph P Alex; married. **Educ:** Univ of Washington, BA, urban planning/architecture, 1971; MA candidate, Theology, 1996. **Career:** HUD Washington DC, urban planner, 1971-; HUD Disaster Recovery Operations Wilkes Barre PA, dir Liason Operation 1972-75; Seattle Housing Authority, dir Target Projects Program 1975-78; A & R Imports Inc, pres 1978-80; Matt Talbot Ministry, Seattle, WA, minister/director, 1985-. **Orgs:** Dir soc planning bd, mem Urban Planning & Architect Consultant, Seattle WA 1970; mem Amer Soc of Planning Officials; Natl Assn of Planners; Interagency Coastal Zone Mgmt Comm; Natl Urban Intern Training Comm; mem Yale Univ Black Enviornmental Studies Team Curriculum Comm; Commissioner for Judo, Goodwill Games, 1988-90. **Honors/Awds:** Sec Outstanding Achievement Award HUD 1972; Outstanding Achievement Award Univ of WA; Black Athletic Alumni Award 1971; Master TKD, Chang Moo Kwan, Seoul, Korea, 1989; Fran Nordstrom Volunteer of the Year, King County Boys and Girls Clubs, 1986; Community Service Award, Downtown Human Services Council, 1986. **Business Addr:** Minister/Director, Matt Talbot Center, 2313 3rd Ave, Seattle, WA 98121-1711, (206)343-0948.

ALEXANDER, A. MELVIN
Dermatologist. **Personal:** Born Feb 4, 1943, Cleveland, OH; son of Grace C Alexander and A Melvin Alexander; married Leslie Gaillard; children: Hollie C, Allison L. **Educ:** Hillsdale Coll, BS 1965; Howard Univ Coll of Medicine, MD 1968. **Career:** US Army Medical Center Okinawa, chief dermatology serv 1972-74; Howard Univ, asst prof 1975-80; Shaw Health Center, dermatology consultant 1977-78; Alexander Dermatology Center, PC senior research associate, dir 1978-. **Orgs:** Consultant Amer Safety Razor Co 1980-82; chmn dermatology section Natl Medial Assoc 1985-87; consultant, United Parcel Service, 1992-; Gillette Research Inst, 1993-; Black Entertainment TV, 1993-. **Honors/Awds:** Upjohn Award for Excellence in Research, Howard Univ; contributor "Conn's Current Therapy," 1983, 1984; author of several published professional articles. **Military Serv:** AUS major 2 yrs. **Home Addr:** 1 East Chase Street, #1010, Baltimore, MD 21202.

ALEXANDER, ALMA DUNCAN
Educator. **Personal:** Born May 13, 1939, New Orleans, LA; married Lorrie; children: Sybil. **Educ:** Dillard Univ, BA 1961; IN Univ, MS 1969. **Career:** Orleans Parish School Bd, teacher 1968-70; IN Univ, intern counseling & guidance of children & foreign born 1969; Univ New Orleans, counselor 1970-71; TX Southern Univ, administrative asst to dean of students . **Orgs:** Mem Am Inst Parliamentarians; natl pres Eta Phi Beta Sor; exec bd mem Natl Cncl Negro Women; mem Amer Assn Univ Women; mem Natl Assn Women Deans, Cnslrs and Adminstrs. **Honors/Awds:** Citation Dept Common Cncl 1977; Awards from City Miami Beach 1976, NAACP 1977. **Business Addr:** Admin Asst to Dean of Student, TX So Univ, PO Box 543, Houston, TX 77004.

ALEXANDER, BENJAMIN HAROLD
Company executive. **Personal:** Born Oct 18, 1921, Roberta, GA; son of Annie Alexander and Manoah Alexander; married Mary E; children: Drew W, Dawn C. **Educ:** Univ of Cincinnati, BA 1943; Bradley Univ, MS 1950; Georgetown Univ, PhD 1957. **Career:** Dept of Agriculture, rsch chemist 1945-62; Walter Reed Army Inst Rsch, chief rsch chemist 1962-67; HEW, health sci admin 1967-74; Chicago State Univ, pres 1974-82; Univ of Dist of Columbia, pres 1982-83; US Dept of Educ, dep asst sec 1983-84; Drew Dawn Enterprises Inc, pres 1984-. **Orgs:** Mem Amer Chem Soc 1945-; fellow Washington Acad of Sci 1957-; rsch prof Amer Univ 1960-94; mem Bradley Univ Bd Trustee 1980-; pres YMCA Trustee Council 1983-; mem Natl Bd Fund for Improvement Post Sec Educ 1985-; president-elect, Washington Academy of Sciences, 1997. **Honors/Awds:** Plaque Best Coll Pres 1978; Hon Doctor of Law 1979; Dr Percy L Julian Awd 1982; Plate of Appreciation 1985; Annual Alumni Achievement Award, Georgetown University, 1974; Distinguished Alumni Award, Bradley University, 1977; Distinguished Alumnus Award, University of Cincinnati, 1983. **Military Serv:** USA tsgt 1945-47; USAR maj 1947-65; 13 commendations, 12 citations 1945-47. **Business Addr:** President, Drew Dawn Enterprises, Inc, 850 Sligo Ave, Ste 602, Silver Spring, MD 20910.

ALEXANDER, BRENT
Professional football player. **Personal:** Born Jul 10, 1970, Gallatin, TN; married Mari; children: Corey. **Educ:** Tennessee State, attended. **Career:** Arizona Cardinals, defensive back, 1994-. **Business Addr:** Professional Football Player, Arizona Cardinals, 8701 S Hardy, Tempe, AZ 85284, (602)379-0101.

ALEXANDER, CHARLES FRED, JR.
Professional fooball player (retired). **Personal:** Born Jul 28, 1957, Galveston, TX; married Yvette; children: Nicole. **Educ:** LSU, 1975-79. **Career:** Cincinnati Bengals, running back/fullback 1979-85. **Honors/Awds:** All-Am at LSU; Only LSU player to ever account for 4000 or more yards in a career.

ALEXANDER, CLIFFORD L., JR.
Management consultant. **Personal:** Born Sep 21, 1933, New York, NY; married Adele Logan; children: Elizabeth, Mark Clifford. **Educ:** Harvard Univ, AB (Cum Laude) 1955; Yale Univ, LLB 1958; Malcolm X Coll, LLD (hon) 1972; Morgan State Univ, LLD (hon) 1972; Wake Forest Univ, LLD (hon) 1978; Univ MD, LLD (hon) 1980; Atlanta Univ, LLD (hon) 1982. **Career:** Ny County, asst to dist atty 1959-61; Manhattanville Hamilton Grange (neighborhood consult proj), exec dir 1961-62; HARYOU Inc, exec dir 1962-63; private practice, atty New York City 1962-63; Natl Security Cncl, staff mem 1963-64; Pres Lyndon Johnson, dep special asst 1964-65, assoc special counsel 1965-66, dep special counsel 1966-67; Equal Employment Opportunity Commn, chmn 1967-69; Arnold & Porter, partner 1969-75; Verner, Liipfert, Bernhard, McPherson & Alexander, partner 1975-76; Dept of the Army, secretary, 1977-80; Alexander & Assoc Inc Washington, pres 1981-; consultant to Major League Baseball, to improve minority hiring practices. **Orgs:** Dir PA Power & Light Co; dir Dreyfus Third Century Fund, Dreyfus Gen Money Market Fund, Dreyfus Common Stock Fund, Dreyfus Govt Sec Fund, Dreyfus Tax Exempt Fund, MCI Corp; adj prof Georgetown Univ; prof Howard Univ; mem Pres's Commn on Income Maint Progs 1967-68; Pres's spl ambassador to the Independence of Swaziland 1968; mem Pres's Commn for Observation Human Rights Yr 1968; bd dirs Mex-Amer Legal Def and Educ Fund; NAACP Legal and Educ Fund; bd overseers Harvard Univ 1969-75; trustee Atlanta Univ; host/co-producer TV prog Cliff Alexander, Black on White 1971-74; mem Amer & DC Bar Assns; dir Equitable Resources, Inc; chairman The Comm for Food & Shelter, Inc; chmn of bd Dance Theatre of Harlem, 1995-. **Honors/Awds:** Named Hon Citizen Kansas City, MO 1965; recip Ames Award Harvard Univ 1955; Frederick Douglass Award 1970; Outstanding Civilian Serv Award Dept Army 1980; Disting Publ Serv Award Dept Def 1981. **Military Serv:** US Army, 1958-59. **Business Addr:** President, Alexander & Assoc Inc, 400 C St NE, Washington, DC 20002.

ALEXANDER, CORNELIA
Government administrator, beauty consultant, public speaker. **Personal:** Born in Winona, MS; daughter of Emma Trotter Thompson and George Thompson; married John Alexander Sr (died 1979); children: Margaret Alexander McLaughlin, John Jr, Leslie B Hardy, Charles, Carl E Hardy, Constance E Hardy Atkins. **Educ:** Vestal Laboratories, Certificate 1969; Youngstown State Univ, Certificate 1977. **Career:** Alexander's Garage, office manager 1959-77; Salem City Hospital, laundry manager 1965-80; Mary Kay Cosmetics, beauty consultant 1979-; NCSC Senior Aide Program, senior aide 1982-83; Salem City Council, 2nd ward city councilwoman 1984-89; public speaker, 1986-; Columbiana County Recorder's Office, deputy recorder 1982-. **Orgs:** Mt Zion AME Church mem 1957-82; mem Salem YWCA 1968-; dir Salem YWCA 1971-75; dem precinct comm 1980-; mem Bus & Professional Women-Lisbon OH 1981-83, Amer Cancer Soc 1982-83, Believer's Christian Fellowship 1982-; Salem YWCA Spec Exec ard 1982-83; spec exec nom comm Salem YWCA 1984-85; bd dir Mobile Meals of Salem 1978-; chmn Fed & State Funding Comm of City Council; served on all 9 council committees (only Democrat); mem Salem Bus & Professional Women Org; Salem Women's Aglow, corresponding secretary, 1992-; Salem Area Habitat Housing for Humanity, board member, vice pres, 1992-; Salem Senior Citizens Organization, advisory board, human services dept, 1991-, vice president, pres; Salem Women's Dem Club, pres; Salem Historical Society, mem; East Liverpool African American History Museum, mem; Columbiana County Community Corrections Planning Board, 1984-. **Honors/Awds:** One of three nominees Chosen as Democrat of the Year, 1985; Columbiana County Senior Citizen of the Year, 1992. **Special Achievements:** First African American to obtain a seat on the City Council of Salem; "Local Heroes/They Made a Difference in 1992," The Vindicator, Jan 3, 1992; Salem News, June 8, 1992; May 17, 1993; Ohio's Heritage, Autumn 1994; Yesteryears, January 14, 1995. **Home Addr:** 189 W Wilson St, Salem, OH 44460.

ALEXANDER, CORY LYNN
Professional basketball player. **Personal:** Born Jun 22, 1973, Waynesboro, VA. **Educ:** Virginia, bachelor's degree in psychology. **Career:** San Antonio Spurs, guard, 1995-98; Denver Nuggets, 1998-. **Business Addr:** Professional Basketball Player, Denver Nuggets, 1635 Clay St, Denver, CO 80204, (303)893-6700.

ALEXANDER, DAWN
Marketing executive. **Personal:** Born Nov 5, 1960, Washington, DC. **Educ:** Oberlin Coll, BA 1982; Harvard Univ JFK Sch of Govt, Certificate 1985; Yale Sch of Mgmt, MPPM 1987. **Career:** Morgan-Stanley, systems analyst 1982-84; Drew-Dawn Enterprises, pres 1984-85; Morgan-Stanley, data ctr oper supv 1984-85; DFS Dorland Worldwide, asst acct exec 1986; Pepsi-Cola Co, asst assoc, sr assoc, mktg mgr 1987-90; Colgate-Palmolive, product mgr, 1990-91; Uniworld Group, account supervisor, 1991-92, vp of management supervisor, 1992-95; Compuserve, sr product mgr, 1995-96, promotions group mgr, 1996-97; IBM, sr product mgr, 1997; Drew Dawn Enterprises, Inc, chair and CEO, 1997; Image Marketing Solutions, Inc, pres. **Orgs:** Alumni admissions rep Oberlin Coll 1982-; mem Natl Black MBA Assoc 1986-; vice pres/dir Drew-Dawn Enterprises 1984-97; dir, Dance Theatre Workshop, 1993-95; chairperson, Oberlin African-American Alumni Group, 1996-; Oberlin Coll Alumni Association, bd mem, 1996-. **Business Addr:** Drew Dawn Enterprises, Inc, 850 Sligo Av, Ste 602, Silver Spring, MD 20910, (301)495-0387.

ALEXANDER, DEANGELO HEATH
Educator, union representative. **Personal:** Born Apr 8, 1966, Hamilton, OH; son of Valinette L Lapsley and James W Renfro Jr. **Educ:** Central State University, BS, education, 1990. **Career:** Simon Kenton Elementary, student teacher, spring 1990; Ferndale School System, substitute teacher; Carter G Woodson Elementary, teacher, 1990-91; Paul Robeson Academy, teacher/union rep, 1991-. **Orgs:** Kappa Alpha Psi Fraternity Inc; National Council Tchrs for English; American Federation of Teachers; Detroit Federation of Teachers; National Education Association; Man to Man, mentor. **Home Addr:** 2030 W Grand River Ave, Loft 4, Detroit, MI 48226, (313)838-5917. **Business Addr:** Teacher/Union Rep, Detroit Board of Education, 13477 Eureka, Paul Robeson African Centered Academy, Detroit, MI 48212, (313)368-6982.

ALEXANDER, DERRICK
Professional football player. **Personal:** Born Nov 3, 1973, Jacksonville, FL. **Educ:** Florida State, attended. **Career:** Minnesota Vikings, defensive end, 1995-. **Business Addr:** Professional Football Player, Minnesota Vikings, 9520 Viking Dr, Eden Prairie, MN 55344, (612)828-6500.

ALEXANDER, DERRICK SCOTT
Professional football player. **Personal:** Born Nov 6, 1971, Detroit, MI. **Educ:** Univ of Michigan, bachelor's degree in sports management. **Career:** Cleveland Browns, wide receiver, 1994-95; Baltimore Ravens, 1996-. **Special Achievements:** 1st round/11th overall NFL draft pick, 1995; Pro Bowl alternate, 1996. **Business Addr:** Professional Football Player, Baltimore Ravens, 11001 Owings Mills Blvd, Owings Mills, MD 21117, (410)654-6200.

ALEXANDER, DOROTHY DEXTER
Educator. **Personal:** Born Jun 17, 1929, Chattaroy, WV; daughter of Georgia Dexter (deceased) and William Dexter (deceased); married Robert D Alexander, May 22, 1956 (deceased); children: Robert D Jr, Doncella Darice. **Educ:** West Virginia State College, Bachelor of Music, 1950; Pikeville College, 1957; Marshall University, 1962; Ohio State University, 1964. **Career:** Mingo County Board of Education, social studies/music teacher, 1950-63; Franklin County Child Welfare Board (Ohio), teacher, 1963-66; Columbus (Ohio) Board of Education, vocal music teacher, 1966-88; Shiloh Baptist Church, minister of music, 1992-. **Orgs:** AKA Sorority, Inc, local vice pres, 1950, 1984, local secretary, music, 1982-92, chairman, awards luncheon, 1983, Great Lakes regional music director, 1990; United Negro College Fund, collector, 1979-88; Aesthetics Social Club, president, 1980-84; Columbus Boychoir, accompanists, 1985-88; Franklin County Child Development Council, community represt, education committee, 1988-92; Lunch Bunch, chairman of scholarship committee, 1991-92; Natl Council of Negro Women, 1989-; Mid-Ohio and Franklin County Health Planning Federation, 1979-80; National Council of Negro Women (NCNW); NAACP; Federated Women's Club; Esther Chap No 3, OES PHA; Friends of the Arts for Community Enrichment. **Honors/Awds:** Columbus Boychoir, Outstanding Accompanists, 1986; Alpha Kappa Alpha Sorority, Inc, Human Service Award, 1988, Leadership, 1983; Trinity Baptist Church, Outstanding Director (Messiah), 1987; Inducted into the Board of Sponsors, Morehouse College, 1995. **Special Achievements:** Local Music Director of Pre-Convention Musical for the 93rd annual Lott Carey National Music Convention, 1989; director of Shiloh-Trinity Baptist Churches Presentation of "Excerpts from Handel's Messiah," 1986-89; collaborated with a Franklin County Committee to develop a reading system for Educable Retarded Children, Library of Congress, 1971; composed hymn for 125th Anniversary of Shiloh Baptist Church "Steadfast Faith.". **Home Addr:** 2187 Liston Ave, Columbus, OH 43207. **Business Phone:** (614)253-7946.

ALEXANDER, DREW W.
Physician, educator. **Personal:** Born Dec 21, 1948, Peoria, IL. **Educ:** Earlham College, BA, 1970; Medical College of Ohio, MD, 1973; Albert Einstein College of Medicine, pediatric training, 1976. **Career:** University of Texas, Health Science Center Dallas, fellow adolescent medicine, 1976-77, asst professor of pediatrics, 1977-; West Dallas Youth Clinic, health team leader, 1977-. **Orgs:** Society for Adolescent Medicine, education committee, 1976-; Dallas Cty Juvenile Detention Clinic, asst medical director, 1977-; consult, Multidisciplinary Adolescent Health Training Project, 1977-; University of Texas Dallas, admissions committee, 1978-, Minority Affairs, coordinator, 1979-; Big Brothers & Big Sisters, volunteer, 1976-; Child Care Assn of Metro Dallas, board member, 1978-. **Business Addr:** Asst Professor, Dept of Pediatrics, University of Texas Southwestern Medical School, 5323 Harry Hines Blvd, Dallas, TX 75235-7200.

ALEXANDER, EDWARD CLEVE
Educator, scientist. **Personal:** Born Nov 20, 1943, Knoxville, TN; son of Gladys Clardy Alexander and Robert W Alexander; married Edwina Carr; children: Everett, Erika, Efrem. **Educ:** City Coll of City Univ of NY, BS 1965; State Univ of NY at Buffalo, PhD 1969. **Career:** IA State Univ, post doctoral fellowship 1969-70; Univ of CA at San Diego, ast prof of chem 1970-78; CA State Univ at Los Angeles, lecturer 1978-82; BOOST Prog San Diego, supervisor dept of math & sci 1982-89; San Diego Mesa College, professor of chem, 1989-, Dept of Chemistry, chair, 1995-, chair of chairs, 1996-. **Orgs:** Consultant NIH, Minority Biomed Support Branch 1974-78, IBM, San Jose, CA 1976; mem bd of dir and exec bd San Diego Urban League 1972-76; Amer Chem Soc 1965-. **Honors/Awds:** Published fourteen research papers in field of Phys & Organic Chem. **Home Addr:** 3381 Lone Jack Rd, Encinitas, CA 92024. **Business Addr:** Chairman, Dept of Chemistry, San Diego Mesa College, 7250 Mesa College Dr, San Diego, CA 92111-4998.

ALEXANDER, ELIJAH ALFRED, III
Professional football player. **Personal:** Born Aug 2, 1970, Fort Worth, TX; married Kimberly; children: Elijah IV. **Educ:** Kansas State, bachelor's degree in accounting. **Career:** Tampa Bay Buccaneers, linebacker, 1992; Denver Broncos, 1993-95; Indianapolis Colts, 1996-. **Orgs:** Helping Young People Excel (HYPE), co-founder. **Business Addr:** Professional Football Player, Indianapolis Colts, PO Box 535000, Indianapolis, IN 46253, (317)297-2658.

ALEXANDER, ERROL D.
Company president. **Personal:** Born Jul 11, 1941, Sandusky, OH; divorced; children: Kay, Doug. **Educ:** Ohio State Univ, BS 1963; Univ of Mich, MBA 1966. **Career:** Bendix Corp, asst proj mgr 1965-70; United Tech Corp, engrg 1968-70; Planned Resource Corp, exec vice pres 1970-71; HCCC Div of Hartford Natl Bank, gen mgr 1970-71; Profiles Rsch & Consult Groups Inc, pres, founder, chmn of bd 1971-. **Orgs:** Adj prof Manchester Comm Coll 1975-80; bd of dir Black Corp Presidents of New England 1976-85, United Way Inc of Gr Hartford 1979-81; pres Urban League 1980; managing dir Bauer Electro Mfg Co 1983-85; dir Task Force for US FAA 1985-86; rsch fellow Univ of Strathclyde 1986-87; post bus grad class chmn Strathclyde Bus School in Scotland 1986; bd dir Catholic Family Serv; mem Tri-Town C of C; Heraldic Coll of Arms. **Honors/Awds:** "How to Be a Corp Expert" Bd Room Mag 1977; "Selecting a Consulting Firm" Black Enteprise Mag 1978; "Devel of FDO Organizations" MOAA Dept of Commerce 1980; "How To Conduct a Perceptional Survey" Manage Mag 1981; conf key note speaker "Delphi Business Forecasting" Univ of NC, "A Profile of Black Executives, Conceptually, Globally and Statistically" Harvard Bus School 1981, 1983; Distinguished Serv Awd, Hartford Area Small Bus Admin 1983. **Business Addr:** President, Chmn of the Board, Profiles Research & Consult Grp, Profiles Corp Bldg, Vernon, CT 06066.

ALEXANDER, ESTELLA CONWILL
Educator, poet. **Personal:** Born Jan 19, 1949, Louisville, KY; children: Patrice Sales, Dominic. **Educ:** Univ of Louisville, BA 1975, MA 1976; Univ of IA, PhD 1984. **Career:** Univ of Iowa, instructor/director of black poetry 1976-79; Grinnell Coll, asst prof 1979-80; KY State Univ, prof of English; poet, currently. **Honors/Awds:** Recording Motion Grace Gospel Recordings 1983; KY Arts Council Grant 1986; Art Grant KY Foundation for Women 1986. **Business Addr:** Professor, Dept of English, CUNY, Hunter College, 695 Park Ave, New York, NY 10021.

ALEXANDER, F. S. JACK
State official. **Personal:** Born Dec 7, 1930, Iola, KS; son of Agnes Marie Stewart and James Floyd Alexander; married Tillie Marie Simon; children: Patricia M, Jack Jr, Stephanie R, Terrell L. **Educ:** Washburn Univ, BA 1954. **Career:** Topeka Bd of Educ, stockroom mgr 1948-51; Goodyear Tire & Rubber Co, quality control 1951-85; City of Topeka, water commn 1973-85; State of KS Oilfield and Environmental Geology, consultant 1985-86, dept of health & environment 1986-90; Governor's Legislative Affairs, 1990-91; Kansas Corp. Commission, commissioner, 1991-96. **Orgs:** On leave ex-com & bd NLC 1975-85; Economic & Comm Devel Comm 1975-85; mem vice pres Topeka United Way Bd 1975-85; pres Topeka Cty Comm 1975-85; trustee St Vail Hospital Bd 1976-85, 1992-; mem State Water Authority 1981-86; ex comm NAACP; past pres KS League of Municipalities 1983-84. **Honors/Awds:** Public Serv Shawnee County Comm Asst 1972-83; Outstanding Public Official Awd Topeka Comm Devel 1976; Awd USA #501 Dir Assoc 1977; Awd Reg 7 Comm Action 1979. **Military Serv:** USN radiomen 2nd class 4 yrs. **Home Addr:** 2509 Fillmore St, Topeka, KS 66611, (913)232-5715.

ALEXANDER, FRITZ W., II
Judge. **Personal:** Born Apr 24, 1926, Apopka, FL; married Beverly J; children: Karen, Kelly Marie, Fritz III. **Educ:** Dartmouth Coll, AB 1947; NY Univ School of Law, LLB; NY Bar 1952; US Supreme Ct & US Circuit Court, Natl Coll of State Judiciary Reno NV, graduate. **Career:** Demov Morris Levin & Hammerling, assoc; Thomas B Dyett, attny 1952-58; Dyett Alexander & Dinkins, founding partner 1958-62, 1963-68; Upper Manhattan Dist Off of the City Ren & Rehab Admin, dist dir 1962-63; NY Urban Coalition, chmn lawyers comm 1968-70; Civil Court 5th Munic Dist, judge 1970-77; Appellate Div, assoc justice 1977-84; NY Court of Appeals, assoc judge 1985-. **Orgs:** Mem Amer & Natl Bar Assoc; founding mem, exec comm Judicial Council of the Natl Bar Assoc; vice pres Assoc of the Bar of the City of NY; former mem Committee on Lectures & Continuing Ed & the Centennial Study on Decentralization of Govt in NYC; mem Metro Black Bar Assoc, NY Bar Assoc, Amer Judicature Soc, Adv Comm of the Ctr for Judicial Conduct Org of the Amer Judicature Soc; trsutee NY Univ Law Ctr Found, dir NY Soc for the Prevention of Cruelty toChildren past pres founding mem Dartmouth Coll Black Alumni Assoc; past pres Harlem Lawyers Assoc; founding mem 100 Black Men Inc; former mem, bd of dir Harlem Neighborhhods Assoc Inc; former dir, exec vice pres United Mutual Life Ins Co; former mem Bd of Mgrs & Treas of United Charities; former mem, bdof dir NY City Mission Soc; hon mem Thrder of the Coif. **Honors/Awds:** Man of the Year Awd Omicron Chap Omega Psi Phi 1981; Achievement Awd of NY Univ Law School Alumni Assn 1982; Golda Meir Award Jewish Lawyer's Guild 1985;William H Hastie Achievement Award Natl Bar Assn Judicial Cncl 1985; Spec Recogn Award Metro Black Bar Assn 1985; Arthur T Vanderbilt Gold Medal Awd NYU Sch of Law 1985; Hope R Stevens Awd NBA Region II Regional Conf 1985; LLD Pace Univ and Long Island Univ. **Military Serv:** USN Reserve 1942-46, 1948-52. **Business Addr:** Associate Judge, NY Court of Appeals, 20 Eagle St, Albany, NY 12207.

ALEXANDER, GARY
Professional basketball player. **Personal:** Born Nov 1, 1969, Jacksonville, FL. **Educ:** Jacksonville Univ. **Career:** Miami Heat, 1993; Elecon Desio, Italy, 1993-94; Cleveland Cavaliers, 1994-. **Business Addr:** Professional Basketball Player, Cleveland Cavaliers, Gund Arena, One Center Ct, Cleveland, OH 44115, (216)659-9100.

ALEXANDER, HARRY TOUSSAINT
Judge (retired). **Personal:** Born Jul 22, 1924, New Orleans, LA; married Beatrice Perkins; children: Normastel Agnes, Harry Jr, Beatrice, Louis. **Educ:** Georgetown Univ School of Law, JD 1952; Xavier Univ, BS 1949. **Career:** Georgetown Univ, rsch asst Cmdr Langdon P Marvin 1951-52; Office of Price Stabilization, atty adv 1952-53; Private practice, attny 1953; US Attny DC, asst 1953-61, spec attny 1961-64, staff asst criminal div 1964-65; US Dept of Justice, attny 1961-66; Superior Ct DC, assoc judge 1966-76; Howard Univ School of Law, adj prof 1970-. **Orgs:** Mem Judicial Conf DC; comm Abolition of Mandatory Capital Punishment DC 1959-62; mem Prob Connected with Mental Exams of the Accused in Criminal Cases Before Trial 1960-63, Cardoza Comm on Judicial Conf, Amer Bar Assoc; mem 1961-65, recording sec 1955-60, WA Bar Assoc; mem Phi Delta Phi Intl Legal Frat, PAlpha Delta Intl Legal Frat; pres NAACP DC 1977, United Natl Bank of WA 1977, Family & Child Serv of WA 1971, Natl Conf of Christians & Jews 1965-70; vchmn BSA 1966, Interreligious Comm on Race Rels 1963-66, Scouters Intl Rep St Gabriels Cath Church 1963-65; mem, 1st natl vice pres 1960-62 Xavier Univ Alumni Assoc; pres NW Boundary Civic Assoc 1958-60; vice pres Natl Fed of Cath Coll Students LA Reg; mem US Natl Students Assoc; pres, vice pres LA-MS-AR Reg1947-48,48-49; treas NAACP YouCouncil New Orleans LA. **Honors/Awds:** Dr Cruezot Awd; Frederick W Shea Awd; Wm H Hastie Awd Natl Conf of Black Lawyers 1976; Outstanding Comm Serv Awd 1975; Outstanding Serv DC C of C;Cert of Degree Strategic Air Command 1973; Martin Luther King Jr Outstanding Serv Awd Howard Univ School of Law 1977; Harry Toussaint Alexander Day DC Council; publ "Appeals in Fed Jurisdiction" NBA 1960, "Curbing Juvenile Delinquency with Adequate Playground Facilities" 1957, "The Nature of Our Heritage" 1950-51, "The Unconstitutionality of Segregation in Ed" 1950-51, "Due Process Required in Revocation of a Conditional Pardon" 1950-51, "The Antislavery Origins of the Fourteenth Amendment", "Convention Coverage" Assoc Negro Press Inc 1947, Xavier Herald 1946-49;TV appearances The Admin of Juv Criminal Justice; radioappearances The Admin of Cinal Juv Justice. **Military Serv:** USN 1943-46.

ALEXANDER, HUBBARD LINDSAY (AXE)
Professional football coach. **Personal:** Born Feb 14, 1939; married Gloria; children: Todd, Chad, Bard. **Educ:** Tennessee State Univ, four years. **Career:** Tennessee State Univ, coach, 1962; high school coach, Memphis, TN, seven seasons; Vanderbilt Univ, assistant coach, six seasons; Univ of Miami, football coach, tight ends, 1979-84, wide receivers, 1985-89; Dallas Cowboys, coach, receivers, 1990-. **Business Addr:** Coach, Receivers, Dallas Cowboys, One Cowboys Pkwy, Irving, TX 75063-4999.

ALEXANDER, JAMES, JR.
Attorney. **Personal:** Born Oct 7, 1945, Charlotte, NC. **Educ:** Columb Coll Columb U, BA 1967; Case West Res U, JD 1970; Nat Coll of Crim Def Lawy, cert 1974. **Career:** Reginal Heber Smith Fellow Cleveland, 1970-72; Hough Area & Devel Corp Cleveland, gen couns 1971-72; Cuyahoga Co, asst co prosec 1972; Tolliver Nimrod & Alexender, atty 1972-75; Hardiman Alexander Buchanan Pittman & Howland Co LPA, atty. **Orgs:** Mem Cleveland Bar Assn, Amer Acad of Trial Layers, Natl Bar Assoc, Cuyahoga Bar Assn, Nat Conf of Blck Lawyers Assn; pres Hough Comm Coun Inc 1972; treas Columbia Univ Clb of Cleve; mem bd of trust Un Torch Svcs; Fedn for Comm Plan Bd; Goodrich Soc Settle Bd; vice pres Legal Aid Soc of Cleve; pres Hough Area Devel Corp. **Honors/Awds:** Recpt 1972 Pres awd; Hough Comm Coun; Martin Luth King awd Case West Res Law Sch 1970.

ALEXANDER, JAMES ARTHUR
Educational administrator. **Personal:** Born Aug 22, 1953, Memphis, TN; son of Katherine Alexander and Calvin Alexander; married Vicki Marshall, Oct 7, 1978. **Educ:** Yale University, BA, 1975, JD, 1978. **Career:** Lord Bissell & Brodk, associate attorney, 1978-84; Chicago State University, executive assistant to president, 1985-86, vp, administration, 1986-89; Illinois State University, vp, business & finance, 1989-93; Governors State Univ, 1993; Administration & Planning, University Park, IL, vp. **Orgs:** ABA; CBA; CCBA; NACUBO; NACUA. **Home Addr:** 8329 S Calumet Ave, Chicago, IL 60619.

ALEXANDER, JAMES BRETT
Staff reporter, journalist. **Personal:** Born Nov 19, 1948, Boston, MA. **Educ:** Northeastern Univ, BA 1971. **Career:** NE Univ Div of Instr Commun The Urban Confrontation, producer, dir 1968; The Christian Sci Monitor Boston, staff writer 1968-71; Random House Inc Lang Arts Div, editorial asst 1972-73; Manhattan Comm Coll, dir publs New York City 1973-74; New York Post, staff reporter, journalist, until 1994. **Orgs:** Mem The Experiment in Intl Living 1969-, The Amer Forum for Intl Study, The Boston Black United Front 1969-70, The Intl Peace Acad 1972-, The Sixth Pan-African Cognress; dir of publ No Amer Reg Ford Found Fellow 1966-69; mem The Experiment in Intl Living 1969. **Honors/Awds:** Martin Luther King Fellow Univ of Denver 1971-72.

ALEXANDER, JOHN STANLEY
Community relations administrator. **Personal:** Born Dec 31, 1944, Charlotte, NC; son of Vernice Moore Alexander and Grady Alexander; married Dana Alston (divorced 1990); children: Rava, Richard, Regina. **Educ:** John C Smith University, Charlotte, NC, BA, 1967; Atlanta University, Atlanta, GA, 1969-70. **Career:** City of Hickory, Hickory, NC, dir, job placement, 1967-68; Youth Programs, Charlotte, NC, dir, 1968-69; Voter Education Project, Atlanta, GA, dir, research, 1971-79; National Conference of Black Mayors, Washington, DC, dir of Washington office, 1979-83; Dillard University, New Orleans, LA, dir, 1986; Entergy, New Orleans, LA, mgr, 1986-. **Orgs:** Member, Atlanta Black United Fund, 1971-73; member, NAACP Energy Committee, 1988-; finance committee, Hotel Dieu Hospital, 1990-; board member, Cities in Schools of New Orleans, 1989-; board member, Boys Club of New Orleans, 1989-. **Honors/Awds:** NAACP Corporate Award, NAACP-National, 1991; NAACP Citizens Award, NAACP-New Orleans, 1990; Appreciation Award, Howard University, 1982; Appreciation Award, National Conference of Black Mayors, 1990; Appreciation Award, New Orleans Public Schools, 1989.

ALEXANDER, JOHN WESLEY, JR.
Educational administrator. **Personal:** Born May 17, 1938, Salem, OH; son of Virgina and John Wesley. **Educ:** Southern CO State Coll, AA 1958; Boston Univ, BS 1961; Bowling Green State Univ, MA 1965; Boston Univ, EdD 1985; California Coast Univ MBA 1985-87, PhD 1987-89. **Career:** Model Cities Coll Consortium, acad dean 1969-70; West African Reg Math Prog, math adv 1970-77; Ed Devel Ctr, consult editor 1977-78; CT Mutual Life Ins Co, acturial analyst 1978-81; The Futures Group, chief statistician, 1981-82; Wentworth Inst of Tech, professor of math, 1982-84, College of Arts & Sciences, dean, 1984-90; University of the District of Columbia, Dept of Mathematics, chairman, 1992-94; National Academy of Sciences, Board on Mathematical Sciences, prog officer, 1995-. **Orgs:** Campaign chairperson, United Combined Health Appeal, CT Mutual Life Ins Co, 1981. **Honors/Awds:** Southern Colorado & Boston Univ, athletic scholarships 1956-60; Bowling Green State Univ, fellowship 1964-65; Boston Univ, assistantship 1977-78; Connecticut Mutual Life Ins Co, Award of Excellence 1981. **Home Addr:** 9739 Country Meadows Lane, Apt 2A, Laurel, MD 20723. **Business Addr:** Program Officer, Natl Academy of Scis, Bd on Math Scis, 2101 Constitution Avenue, NW, Washington, DC 20418.

ALEXANDER, JOSEPH LEE
Physician. **Personal:** Born Oct 29, 1929, Oneonta, AL; married Phyllis L Campbell; children: Arnold Larry. **Educ:** Fisk Univ Nashville, BA 1947-51; Univ of Louisville, MD 1951-55; Harvard Univ, Rsch Fellow Surgery 1967-69; UCLA School of Publ Health, MPH 1977. **Career:** US Army Hosp Ft Hood TX, chief gen surgery 1961-62; 5th Surg Hosp Heidelberg Germany, comdg officer 1962-63; 2nd Gen Hosp Landsthul Germany, asst chief gen surgery 1963-64; Kimbrough Army Hosp Ft Meade MD, chief gen surgery serv 1964-66; Walter Reed Gen Hosp Wash DC, chief organ transplant serv 1969-71; Charles Drew Postgrad Med School, chief surgery 1971-76; UCLA School of Med, prof of surgery 1971-; Private practice Los Angeles, physician 1978-; St Vincent Medical Ctr, chief of surgery 1985-86; Alexander Health Systems Medical Group Inc, pres, currently. **Orgs:** Mem Alpha Phi Alpha, Phi Delta Epsilon Med Frat Univ of Loisville; diplomate Natl Bd of Med Examiners; fellow Amer Coll of Surgeons 1956. **Honors/Awds:** Mem Beta Kappa Chi Hon Sci Soc Fisk Univ, Sigma Upsilon Phi Fisk Univ 1951, Alpha Omega Alpha Hon Med Soc Univ of Louisville 1954, Phi Kappa Phi Honor Soc Univ of Louisville 1955. **Military Serv:** US Army, col 14 yrs; Cert of Achievement 1964; Commendation Medal 1971. **Business Addr:** President, Alexander Health Systems Medical Group Inc, 201 S Alvarado St, Ste 221, Los Angeles, CA 90057.

ALEXANDER, JOSEPHINE
Registered nurse. **Personal:** Born in Tuskegee, AL; daughter of Daisy Menefee Alexander and P Alexander. **Educ:** Tuskegee University, Tuskegee, AL, BSN, 1958; University of California, Los Angeles, CA, MN, 1972. **Career:** Veterans Administration Medical Center, West Los Angeles, CA, staff nurse, 1958-60, nurse manager, 1960-72, psychiatric clinical specialist, 1972-, primary adult care nurse practitioner, 1977-. **Orgs:** Life member, Chi Eta Phi; American Nurses Association; National League of Nursing; member, National Council of Negro Women; historian, 1974-84, first vice president, 1980-84, president, 1985-89, Chi Eta Phi; Sigma Theta Tau Honor Society; ANA Foundation; Black Women Forum. **Honors/Awds:** Outstanding Leadership Award, Chi Eta Pi, Southwest Region, 1987; Outstanding Service Award, Tuskegee University Alumni Association, Los Angeles Chapter, 1988; Black Woman of Achievement Award, NAACP Legal Defense and EDucation Fund, 1989. **Business Addr:** Clinical Nurse Specialist/ Psychiatry, Veterans Administration Medical Center, Brentwood Division, Wilshire and Sawtelle Blvds, Los Angeles, CA 90073.

ALEXANDER, JOYCE LONDON
Judge. **Personal:** daugHter of Edna London and Oscar London. **Educ:** Howard Univ, BA 1969; New England Law School, JD 1972. **Career:** Boston Legal Assistance Project, Reginald Heber Smith community law fellowship 1972-74; Youth Activities Commission, leagl counsel, 1974-75; Tufts Univ, asst professor 1975-76; MA Board of Higher Education, general counsel 1976-79; WBZ-TV Boston, on-camera legal editor 1978-79; US District Court for MA, chief judge, 1979-. **Orgs:** Urban League of Eastern MA, president emeritus 1979-; Nat'l Council of US Magistrates, 1st circuit dir 1984-; MA Black Judges Conference, chairperson 1985-87; Nat'l Bar Assoc Judicial Council, chair 1987-88; City of Boston Youth Activities Commission, legal counsel, 1974-75; Joint Ctr for Political & Economic Studies, Washington DC, board member, 1996. **Honors/Awds:** Northeastern University Law School, honorary doctor of law, 1980; Honorary Doctor of Law, New England Law School, 1985; Northeastern University; Bridgewater Sate College; Suffolk University, 1996; North Carolina Central University, 1996. **Business Addr:** Chief United States Magistrate Judge, US District Court, District of Massachusetts, 90 Devonshire St, Rm 932, Boston, MA 02109.

ALEXANDER, KELLY MILLER, JR.
Funeral director. **Personal:** Born Oct 17, 1948, Charlotte, NC; son of Margaret Alexander and Kelly Alexander; divorced; children: Kelly M III. **Educ:** Univ of NC, AB Polit Sci 1970, MPA 1973. **Career:** NC Personnel Dept, admin intern 1971-72; Charlotte Area Fund, planner 1972-74; Alexander Funeral Home, vice pres, 1973-94, chairman, 1994-. **Orgs:** Exec vice pres US Youth Council 1976-85; past vice pres Natl NAACP; chmn Natl NAACP Economic Develop Fair Share Committee; trustee, NAACP Special Contributions Fund 1985-98; pres, NC NAACP, 1985-97. **Honors/Awds:** UNCF Labor Dept Rsch Grant 1977. **Business Addr:** Chairman, Alexander Funeral Home, PO Box 36468, Charlotte, NC 28236, (704)333-1167.

ALEXANDER, LARRY
Hotel industry executive. **Career:** Westin Hotels and Resorts, 1973-93; Westin Hotel, managing dir, 1993-. **Orgs:** Metropolitan Detroit Convention & Visitors Bureau, exec committee, owners advisory committee, bd of dirs; Michigan Hotel, Motel & Resort Assn, bd of dirs; Greater Detroit Chamber of Commerce. **Special Achievements:** Appointed by Michigan Gov John Engler to the White House Conf on Travel and Tourism, 1995; appointed by Detroit Mayor Dennis Archer to serve on the Detroit Master Plan Task Force, 1994. **Business Addr:** Managing Director, Westin Hotel, Renaissance Center, Detroit, MI 48243, (313)568-8000.

ALEXANDER, LAURENCE BENEDICT
Educator. **Personal:** Born Oct 31, 1959, New Orleans, LA; son of Dorothy Alexander (deceased) and Garland Alexander (deceased); married Veronica Wicker Alexander, Aug 13, 1988; children: Brandon Keith, David Laurence, Tyler Christian. **Educ:** University of New Orleans, BA, 1981; University of Florida, MA, 1983; Tulane University, School of Law, JD, 1987. **Career:** The Times-Picayune, New Orleans, staff writer, 1981; The Houma Courier, staff writer, 1982; The Times Picayune, staff writer, 1982-85; University of New Orleans, director of journalism program, assistant professor of journalism, 1987-88; Temple University, director of news editorial sequence, assistant professor of communications, 1988-91; The Philadelphia Inquirer, summer copy editor, 1989-92; University of Florida, assistant professor of journalism, 1991-94, associate professor and chair of journalism, 1994-. **Orgs:** Assn for Education in Journalism and Mass Communication, 1989-; International Communications Association, 1992-; Society of Professional Journalists, 1989-; Natl Assn of Black Journalists, 1989-; American Bar Association, 1987-; Louisiana State Bar Association, 1987-. **Honors/Awds:** AEJMC Baskett Mosse Award, 1994; AEJMC, AHANA Research Grant, 1990; The Poynter Institute, Selected Teaching Fellow, 1989; Press Club of New Orleans, Deadline News Writing Award, 1985. **Special Achievements:** Works published in: The Tulane Maritime Lawyer, 1987; The Black Law Journal, 1989; Newspaper Research Journal, 1992, 1994, 1995, 1996; Western Journal of Black Studies, 1992; Communications and the Law, 1993, 1996; Journalism Educator, 1994, Notre Dame Journal of Legislation, 1997; Editor and Publisher, 1990, 1993, 1996. **Business Addr:** Professor, University of Florida, 2089 Weimer Hall, Department of Journalism, Gainesville, FL 32611, (352)392-0500.

ALEXANDER, LENORA COLE
Company executive. **Personal:** Born Mar 9, 1935, Buffalo, NY; daughter of Susie Stamper Cole and John L Cole; married Theodore M Alexander Sr. **Educ:** State Univ Coll Buffalo NY, BS 1957; State Univ of New York at Buffalo, MEd 1969, PhD 1974. **Career:** State Univ of New York, rsch asst 1968-69, asst to vice pres for student life 1969-73; The American Univ, vice pres for student life 1973-77; Univ of the District of Columbia, vice pres for student affairs 1978-81; US Dept of Labor, dir women's bureau 1981-86; George Mason Univ, commonwealth vstg prof of public admin 1986-89; LCA and Associates Inc, president, 1989-. **Orgs:** Bd dirs DC Chamber of Commerce 1979-81; US Rep to Working Party on Role of Women in the Econ, Org for Econ Devel & Coop Paris France 1981-86; mem adv comm Women Veterans Affairs US Vet Admin 1983-86; US rep conf Intl Commiss on the Status of Women Cartegena Colombia 1983; conf Vienna Austria 1984; mem US Del to United Nations Decade for Women Conf Nairobi Kenya 1985; bd dirs Jerusalem Intl Forum of Amer Israel Friendship League 1987-89; board of directors, McAuley Institute; board of directors, Foundation for Exceptional Children; member, Defense Advisory Committee for Women in the Services; member, 1989-92; The Girl Friends Inc, 1983-; member, Delta Sigma Theta Sorority, 1976-. **Honors/Awds:** Salute to an Influential Decision Maker Alpha Kappa Alpha Sor Inc 1982; Special Citation Awd Commission for Women's Affairs Office of Governor Puerto Rico 1982; Salute for Contributions Awd Club Twenty Washington 1983; Disting Amer and Humanitarian Coahoma Jr College 1983; Distinguished Alumnus Awd State Univ of NY 1983; Special Proclamation Coahoma Jr Coll 1984; Pauline Weeden Maloney Awd in Natl Trends and Serv The Links Inc Philadelphia 1984; Gratitude for Success Awd Unit Church Usher's League Chicago 1984; Disting Serv Citation Natl Black MBA Assn Inc Washington 1984; Outstanding Women Awd Progressive DC Chaptof Federally Employed Women Washington 1984; Outstanding Political Achievement Awd Natl Assoc of Minority Political Women 1985; Outstanding CareerWoman Awd Alpha Phi Alpha 19 Woman of Achievement Awd Women's City Club of Cleveland 1986. **Home Addr:** 3020 Brandywine St NW, Washington, DC 20008.

ALEXANDER, LOUIS G., SR.
Business executive (retired). **Personal:** Born Feb 14, 1910, Houston, TX; married; children: Louis G III (deceased). **Educ:** Bishop Coll, attended 1927-29; Armour Inst of Tech, attended 1929-33; IL Inst of Tech, attended 1939; Univ of HI, attended 1943. **Career:** Reliable Elec Serv Co, 1933-42; Murray's Superior Prods Co, 1945-47; Circuit Engrg Sales & Serv Co, 1947-49; APTI Inc 1948-52; APEMCO Inc 1952-66; Alexander & Assoc, 1967-68; Amalgamated Trust & Savings Bank, vice pres 1968-86. **Orgs:** Board of directors, Better Boys Found; bd dir Hyde Park Coop Fed Credit Union; bd dir Chicago Chap NAACP; Omega Psi Phi; Natl Tech Assn; Chicago Cncl of Foreign Relations; Amer Veterans Comm. **Honors/Awds:** Author "The New Amer Crisis," The Race for Space; Lawndale Scholarship Fund, Good Guy Award, 1972. **Military Serv:** US Army, 1942-45. **Business Addr:** VP, Louis Alexander & Assoc, PO Box 1086, Chicago, IL 60690.

ALEXANDER, LYDIA LEWIS
Educational administrator. **Personal:** Born Aug 21, 1938, Bessemer, AL; daughter of Flora Laird Lewis and Clinton E Lewis; married Judson T Alexander Sr, Dec 29, 1961 (died 1980); children: Judson T Jr. **Educ:** Talladega College, Talladega, AL, BA, 1958; Indiana University, Bloomington, IN, MAT, 1964; Auburn University, Auburn, AL, EdD, 1972. **Career:** Wenonah High School, Birmingham, AL, English instructor, 1959-66; T A Lawson State Junior College, Birmingham, AL, speech and English instructor, 1966-70; Auburn University, Auburn, AL, assistant professor, school of education, 1972-74; University of Alabama at Birmingham, asst professor, secondary education, 1974-79, asst to vice president, 1980-84, biomed sciences prog dir, 1982-84, dir of general studies, 1984-89, asst dean, 1989-94, associate professor of educational leadership, 1994-. **Orgs:** President, UAB Faculty & Staff Benevolent Fund Council, 1990; president, Birmingham Chapter of The Links Inc, 1988-89; president, Omicron Omega Chapter, Alpha Kappa Alpha Sorority Inc, 1978-82; national president, The Holidays Inc, 1987-91; member, Association for Supervision and Curriculum Development, 1989-; member, American Association of Colleges of Teacher Education, 1989-. **Honors/Awds:** Outstanding Soror in the Southeast Region, Alpha Kappa Alpha, 1988; Soror of the Year, Omicron Omega Chapter, Alpha Kappa Alpha, 1987, 1993; Educator of the Year, UAB Chapter, Omega Psi Phi Fraternity, 1990; Woman of Distinction, Iota Phi Lambda Sorority, Birmingham Chapter, 1979. **Special Achievements:** Co-author, Wearing Purple, 1996. **Home Addr:** 1141 Posey Ave, Bessemer, AL 35023. **Business Addr:** Assoc Prof of Educational Leadership, Sch of Educ, The University of Alabama at Birmingham, EB 210-B, Birmingham, AL 35294-1250.

ALEXANDER, MARCELLUS WINSTON, JR.
Television executive. **Personal:** Born Oct 3, 1951, Austin, TX; son of Juanita Smith Alexander and Marcellus Alexander Sr; married Linda Carter Alexander, Sep 20, 1975; children: Ehrin, Andrea, Marcellus III. **Educ:** Southwest Texas State Univ, San Marcos, TX, BS, 1973. **Career:** American Broadcasting Co, Detroit, MI, general sales manager, 1982-84, vice president & general manager, 1984-86; Silver Star Communications, Detroit, MI, chief operating officer, part owner, 1986; Group W Broadcasting, Philadelphia, PA, station manager, 1987-89; Group W Broadcasting, Baltimore, MD, vice president & general manager, 1989-. **Orgs:** Board member, Baltimore Urban League, 1989-; board member, Advertising Assn of Baltimore, 1989-; board member, Kennedy Institute, 1989-; board member, Advertising & Professional Club, 1989-; member, National Assn of Black Journalists, 1987-. **Honors/Awds:** Distinguished Black Marylander, Towson State Univ, 1991; Humanitarian Award, Juvenile Diabetes Assn, 1991. **Business Addr:** Vice President & General Manager, WJZ-TV Group W Broadcasting, Television Hill, Baltimore, MD 21211.

ALEXANDER, MARGARET WALKER. See WALKER, MARGARET ABIGAIL.

ALEXANDER, MERVIN FRANKLIN
Executive administrator. **Personal:** Born Jul 29, 1938, Clover, SC; children: Mervin F, Michael F. **Educ:** Benedict Coll, 1958-60; New York City Coll, 1960-62; Rutgers Univ MEd 1976; Riden Coll, MPa 1980-. **Career:** Day Care 100, regional admin 1970; Div of Youth & Family Servs, adm of day care oper 1976; Div of Youth & Fam Serv, chief bur of licensing 1977; SpecServ for Children, dir office of dir child care 1978-. **Orgs:** Pres Piscataway Bd of Ed 1979-80; councilman Township of Piscataway 1980-; pres Piscataway Twnshp Council 1985-.

ALEXANDER, OTIS DOUGLAS (SULE)
Musician. **Personal:** Born Jun 1, 1949, Norfolk, VA; son of Vivian Bell-Alexander and Gilbert Alexander. **Educ:** Federal City Coll, Washington, DC, BA Urban Studies 1972; Federal City Coll , Washington, DC MSc, Media Science 1974; Ball State Univ, Muncie, IN, MLS Library Science 1983; Atlanta Univ GA, 1982. **Career:** African Heritage Dancers & Drummers Washington DC, professional dancer 1973-76; Dept of Educ of VI St John, itinerant libr 1976-77; Bur of Libr Mus & Archeol Serv Christiansted St Croix US VI, juvenile serv libr 1977-78; Cuttington Univ Coll Liberia W Africa, asst libr & lectr childrens lit 1978-79; Dept of Educ of VI, info spec 1979-83; Bur of Libr & Mus, head librn 1983-85; St Dunstan's Episcopal School St Croix VI, literature teacher 1985-90; Department of Education of VI, Secondary Music, 1990-98. **Orgs:** Mem Amer Libr Assn 1983-; dir St John Ethnic Theatre 1976-77, Children's Theatre on Isl of St Croix 1977-78; dir, performer Cuttington Cultural Troop West Afr 1978-79; artistic dir St Theatre 1986-97; board of directors, University of DC Alumni Assn 1991-93; Phi Delta Kappa, chapter advisor; American Federation of Teachers; St Croix Federation of Teachers, Local 1826, Omega Psi Phi Fraternity, Inc, life mem. **Honors/Awds:** Publs, "Librarianship in a Developing Nation" Bur of Libr Mus & Archael Servs, "Media-Children-Reading" Personality & Instrl Strat Thesis 1974; publ book reviews "They Came Before Columbus," "The Red Wind," "Where Did I Come From?", "Sturdy Black Bridges," "When Harlem Was In Vogue"; Awds, Fellowship USDOE 1982-83, Scholarship Atlanta Univ 1982; Howard Reed International Scholarship, 1992; The Encyclopedia As An Information Source, A Study of the Usefulness & Objectivity of Selected Encyclopedias as Perceived by School & Public Librarians in Muncie IN 1983; "Arthur Shomburg Alfonso and his Contributions to Black Culture" in St Croix Avis; Virgin Islands and Caribbean Comm, (joint author), 1988; "Writers in the Comm," 1984; author, "Helping Cool Black Males," 1991, "An Unfinished Agenda: Aiding Hispanic Students," 1990, "Education Also Requires Curiosity and Exploration," 1990, VI Daily News; "A Love for the Arts is the Best Lesson We Can Teach Our Youth," 1992; "Teach the Children in A Way In Which They Love Learning," 1995; "Home School and Community Should Help Young Black Males," 1996; "Students Need Community's Help Getting Over Hurdles to Success," 1996. **Military Serv:** USMC Reserve, 1968-69. **Home Addr:** 609 Obendorfer Rd, Norfolk, VA 23523.

ALEXANDER, PAMELA GAYLE
Judge. **Personal:** Born Sep 25, 1952, Minneapolis, MN; daughter of Frances L Smith & Robert W Bellesen; married Albert G Alexander, Jan 16, 1982; children: two. **Educ:** Augsburg Coll, BA, 1970-74; Univ of MN School of Law, JD, 1977. **Career:** First Bank of Minneapolis, trust administrator, 1977-78; Legal Rights Ctr Inc, criminal defense atty, 1978-81; Hennepin County Attorney's Office, Prosecutor-Criminal Div, 1981-83; State of MN, county court judge, 1983-86, district court judge 1986-96, asst chief judge, 1996-. **Orgs:** Charter mem, former vice pres, Minnesota Minority Lawyers Assn, 1977-; trustee, Greater Friendship Missionary Bapt Church, 1980-84; Natl Bar Assn Judicial Council, 1983-; parliamentarian, treas Minneapolis/St Paul Links Inc, 1985-. **Honors/Awds:** Special Recognition Award, Phi Beta Sigma Frat, 1982; Constance B Motley Award, TCBWTC Comm, 1982-83; Community Serv Award, Inner City Youth League, 1983, Loft Teen Ctr, 1983; Distinguished Serv Award, Hennepin Co Attorney's Office, 1983; Community Service Award, Kappa Alpha Psi Fraternity, 1992; BIHA The Comm Award, for dedicated public service to Communities of Color, 1993; Omega Citizen of the Year Award, 10th District, 1993; Chauncey Eskridge Distinguished Barrister Award, SCLC, 1993; NAACP, Freedom Fund Award, Minneappolis Branch, 1993; Mpls Community Coll Humanitarian Award, 1995. **Business Addr:** Asst Chief Judge, State of Minnesota, 1053-C Government Center, Minneapolis, MN 55487.

ALEXANDER, PATRISE
Professional football player. **Personal:** Born Oct 23, 1972. **Educ:** Southwestern Louisiana, attended. **Career:** Washington Redskins, linebacker, 1996-. **Business Addr:** Professional Football Player, Washington Redskins, 13832 Redskin Dr, Herndon, VA 22071, (703)471-9100.

ALEXANDER, PAUL CRAYTON
Physician. **Personal:** Born Aug 5, 1946, Tulsa, OK; children: Vyron. **Educ:** Coll of Pharmacy Howard Univ, BS 1970; Meharry Medical Coll, MD 1974. **Career:** Meharry Medical Sch, asst prof of medicine 1978-85; TN Dept of Corrections, medical consultant 1984-; TN State Penitentiary Hosp, med director, currently. **Orgs:** Mem Amer Heart Assoc 1978-; mem House of Delegates Natl Medical Assoc 1980,81,82,83; pres RF Boyd Medical Soc 1983-85; vice pres Middle TN Div Volunteer State Medical Assoc 1985-. **Honors/Awds:** Chief Coord for Hypertension Patient Educ Grant Meharry Medical Coll Ambulatory Serv 1979-80; 8 publications including "Innovative Chemotherapy (nifedipine and verapamil) in Hereditary Hypertension," w/WJ Crawford, LE Burgess, MT Scott, JM Stinson Lab Ani Sci 1982.

ALEXANDER, PRESTON PAUL, JR.
Personnel director. **Personal:** Born Apr 20, 1952, Bronx, NY; son of Sylvia Alexander and Preston Alexander Sr; children: Drew Philip, Jason Ross. **Educ:** Fairleigh Dickinson Univ, BA, Psychology, 1973, M, Public Admin, 1980. **Career:** Teaneck Volunteer Ambulance Corps, Sunday evening crew chief 1972-; Midlantic Natl Bank/Citizens, internal auditor 1973-74; Fairleigh Dickinson Univ Central Admiss, dir of admission relations 1974-79; Natl Assn of Coll Admission Counselors, vice pres human relations 1978-79; Citibank NA, dir human resources 1979-89; Alexander's Surgical Supply Co, Co-owner 1989-91; Joseph E Seagram & Sons Inc, human resources dir, 1993-. **Orgs:** SHRM. **Honors/Awds:** Outstanding/Distinguished Serv Award, Fairleigh Dickinson Univ, 1978. **Business Addr:** Human Resources Dir, Joseph E Seagram & Sons Inc, 1625 S Congress Ave, Delray Beach, FL 33447.

ALEXANDER, RICHARD C.
Association executive. **Career:** National Guard Assn of the United States, adjutant general, Ohio, pres, currently. **Special Achievements:** First African-American pres of NGAUS. **Business Addr:** President, National Guard Assn of the United States, 1 Massachusetts Ave, NW, Washington, DC 20001, (202)789-0031.

ALEXANDER, ROBERT I.
Social worker. **Personal:** Born Feb 17, 1913; son of Frances Alexander and Israel Alexander; married J L Black; children: Arthur Harris Jr, Claudette E Douglas, Robert A, John Rodney. **Educ:** St Augustine's Coll, BA 1943; Atlanta Univ, MA 1948. **Career:** Buncombe Co NC Welfare Dept, child welfare caseworker 1948-53; Guildord Co NC Welfare Dept, child welfare caseworker 1953-65; A&T Coll Greensboro, soc worker, Project Uplift 1965-66; Meharry Med Coll, chief soc worker, child develop clinic 1966-79. **Orgs:** Diamond Am Bridge Assn 1976-77; coord Preventive Serv Meharry Med Coll Comm 1975-79; candidate 20th Councilman Dist Nashville 1975,79; past scoutmaster & troup committeeman; past prog chmn PTA; past chmn Educ Comm; past pres Nashville Branch NAACP; organizer & past chmn Z Alexander Freedom Fund Ball; past pres, Middle Tennessee Chap, Natl Assn of Soc Work; past area rep, State of Tennessee, Natl Assn of Soc Workers; various comm in connection with Baptist Ch; mem Phi Beta Sigma; past pres Nashville Duplicate Bridge Club; mem Emerald Soc Club; past vice chmn Comm Sch Inc; past mem governance bd, Community Mental Health Ctr, Meharry Med Coll; 19th Dist Representative, Metro Nashville Davidson Co 1979; organized Hadley Senior Center Bridge Club (ABA) Nashville, 1988; general chairman, ABAing National Tournament Nashville, 1989; past pres Men's Bridge Club. **Military Serv:** US Army, 1943-46.

ALEXANDER, ROBIN
Paralegal. **Personal:** Born Dec 6, 1950, Richmond, VA; daughter of Lelia Battle Orange and Robert Alexander. **Educ:** Howard Univ, Washington, DC, 1968-73. **Career:** Stone's Mercantile Agency, Washington, DC, 1969-70; Triple "L" Construction Co, Inc, Pittsburgh, PA/Washington, DC, 1991; Cole Brothers Enterprises, Washington, DC, 1970-; Mabel D Haden Law Office, PC, Washington, DC, legal asst, 1971-; Natl Assn of Black Women Attorneys, Washington, DC, exec asst, 1985-. **Orgs:** Scholarship chairperson, Natl Assn of Black Women Attorneys, 1980-; researcher, legislative comm, 1978, mem, 1977-80, DC Business & Professional Women's Club; mem, Natl Assn of Legal Assistants, 1976-78; sec, DC Automobile Dealers Assn, 1990-; mem The National Democratic Club, 1992. **Honors/Awds:** Service Award, Natl Assn of Black Women Attorneys, 1978, 1980, 1989; Certification, Natl Assn of Legal Assistants, 1977. **Home Addr:** 1936 Fourth St NW, Washington, DC 20001.

ALEXANDER, RONALD ALGERNON
County government official. **Personal:** Born Oct 24, 1950, New Orleans, LA; son of Essie M Alexander and Reginald A Alexander; married Stephanie; children: Regina Ashley. **Educ:** Nicholls State Univ, attended 1968-71. **Career:** Pan Amer World Airways Inc, accountant 1971-78; City of Thibodaux LA, dir mayor's office of fed grants 1978-85; Terrebonne Parish Consolidated Govt, Houma, LA, asst dir, community development programs 1985-89, community development administrator, 1989-93; City of Baton Rouge, LA, asst urban development dir, 1993-. **Orgs:** Chmn, bd of commissioners, City of Thibodaux Housing Authority 1985; regional worshipful master, Region I Prince Hall Grand Lodge of Louisiana, 1987-89; president, Louisiana Chapter of NAHRO, 1995-97; vice president, chair, dir, Southwest Regional Council of NAHRO, 1991-93; member, National Assn of Housing Redevelopment Officials, 1982-. **Honors/Awds:** District #4 Master of the Year, Prince Hall Grand Lodge of Louisiana, 1985; Outstanding Community Service Award, NAACP, 1988; 33 Degree Mason, Ancient Accepted Scottish Rite Freemasonary-Southern Jurisdiction, Prince Hall, 1983; Commander-in-Chief, Pelican Council of Deliberation, 1990; Honorary Lt Governor, State of Louisiana, 1990; HUD, Outstanding Service Award, 1996. **Home Addr:** 2133 78th Ave, Baton Rouge, LA 70807.

ALEXANDER, ROSA M.
Business executive. **Personal:** Born Sep 25, 1928, Dunn, NC; married Nathaniel L Alexander; children: Helen M Vaughan, Amos, Thaddeus, Nathaniel, Nathalin. **Educ:** Harnett HS, diploma 1945. **Career:** Ford Motor Co, cafeteria mgr 1950-70; Norfolk Naval Air Station, electronics 1974-78; A&B Contract Svcs, pres 1978-. **Orgs:** Treas Amer Business Women Assn 1969; bd mem Tidewater Business & Contractors Assn 1978-; mem Norfolk & Chespeake Chamber of Comm 1984. **Honors/Awds:** Outstanding Achievement Chesapeake Men for Progress 1980; Businessperson of the Yr TABCA 1980; Outstanding Business US Dept of Commerce 1983; Citizen of the Yr Lambda Omega Chap 1984; Notable Achievement Norfolk State Univ 1984. **Business Addr:** President, A&B Contract Serv, 3001 Lafayette Blvd, Norfolk, VA 23509.

ALEXANDER, SIDNEY H., JR.
Personnel manager. **Personal:** Born Oct 26, 1919, Pueblo, CO; son of Maggie Levi Levy (deceased) and Sidney H Alexander Sr (deceased); married Ruby R Autry; children: Sidney III, Saundra L Archer, Steven W. **Educ:** Univ of Denver, BA 1949, MSW 1951; Cornell Univ State Sch of Labor & Ind Relations, cert 1966; Kingsborough Comm Coll, cert 1967. **Career:** Lectr & field work supr various Colls & Univs 1953-; Urban League Affiliates in Lincoln NE, Grand Rapids MI, Wichita KS, New Haven CT, exec dir 1953-65; Anti-Poverty Agencies Nassau Co, Harlem, Brooklyn, dir/coord 1965-69; St Philip's Comm Serv Counc, adminstrv officer 1969-70; Newsweek Inc, mgr personnel serv 1970-79; college associate dean, continuing education, 1980-88; consultant, 1988-; college lecturer, 1988-. **Orgs:** Consult US Dept of Labor & HEW 1962; mem NY Personnel Mgmt Assn; mem Natl Urban League; mem NAACP; mem natl Cncl of Negro Women; mem Natl Assn of Soc Workers; mem Omicron Delta Kappa; mem Phi Sigma Iota; Episcopal Diocese of Connecticut, ordained deacon, 1991; Yale New Haven Hospital, volunteer chaplain. **Honors/Awds:** Hon Life Mem KS Congress of Parents & Tchrs. **Military Serv:** USAF sgt 1943-45. **Home Addr:** 14 Collingsdale Dr, Milford, CT 06460.

ALEXANDER, THEODORE MARTIN, SR.
Insurance executive/educator (retired). **Personal:** Born Mar 7, 1909, Montgomery, AL; son of Hattie Hamilton Alexander and James H. Alexander; married Lenora; children: Theodore Martin Jr (dec), Alvia Elizabeth, Dorothy Gwendolyn M. **Educ:** Morehouse Coll, BA Bus Admin (with honors) 1931, LLD 1970. **Career:** Alexander & Co Gen Ins Agency Atlanta, founder 1931-; Howard Univ, adj prof, insurance. **Orgs:** Chmn bd Alexander & Assoc Inc; founder 1951, former exec vice pres Southeastern Fidelity Fire and Casualty Co Ins Co Atlanta; pres treas Univ Plaza Apts Inc; sec/dir exec com Mut Fed Savngs & Loan Assn Atlanta 1932-68; partner Met Atlanta Rapid Transit Authority Ins Mgrs; v chmn Atlanta Univ Cntr Corp; fed jury commr No Dist GA Trustee Atlanta Comm Chest; sec bd trustees Morehouse Coll; bd dirs Butler St YMCA Atlanta 1958; mem Race Rel Comm Intl Comm Del World Council 1961; mem natl bd Citizens Adv Com; chmn Relocation Comm Atlanta Urban Renewal; mem Better Housing Commn; mem Housing Appeal Bd; v chmn Ethics Bd City of Atlanta; mem Natl Citizens' Comm for Community Rel Dept Commerce 1964; mem Adv Comm Met Planning Commn Atlanta; asst treas Atlanta Comm Chest; mem, Atlanta Comm Relationbd mem, Greater Washington Boys Club; member, NAACP. **Special Achievements:** Author, Beyond the Timberline, 1993; The

Demise of Service & the Birth of Greed; Albums include History of the Black Man, The Black Man's Revolt, Power: Black or White. **Business Addr:** President, TM Alexander & Co, Inc, PO Box 76677, Atlanta, GA 30358.

ALEXANDER, THEODORE THOMAS, JR.
Educator, educational administrator. **Personal:** Born Nov 24, 1937, Los Angeles, CA; son of Pauline Bruner Alexander and Thomas Alexander; married Patricia Perry (divorced 1967); children: Theodore Thomas III, Mark Anthony. **Educ:** Los Angeles Community College, Los Angeles, CA, AA, electronics, 1958; California State University, Los Angeles, CA, BA, education, 1960, MA, education, 1964; University of Southern California, Los Angeles, CA, EdD, education, 1975. **Career:** Los Angeles Board of Education, principal, 1971-75, administrative coord, 1975-76, administrative consultant, 1976-77, deputy area administrator, 1977-78, asst dir, 1978-82, asst superintendent, 1982-; University of Southern California, adjunct associate professor, 1971-. **Orgs:** President, Council of Black Administrators, 1983-85; president, Education Alumni Assn, USC, 1980-81; member, board of governors, General Alumni Assn, USC, 1986-89; president, polemarch, Los Angeles Alumni Chapter Kappa Alpha Psi Fraternity, 1986-89; president, Educare Support Group, USC, 1985-86. **Honors/Awds:** USC Ebonics Support Group Outstanding Black Alumni Award, 1984; USC General Alumni Assn Tommy Statue Volunteer Service Award, 1984; National Achievement Award, Lamba Kappa Mu Sorority, 1985; Hilburn Award, Human Relations Award, City of Los Angeles Human Relations Committee, 1969; Award for Contribution to the field of education, The Assn of Black Law Enforcement Executives, 1991; Community Service Award, Kappa Alpha Psi National Award, 1988. **Home Addr:** 4309 Don Carlos Dr, Los Angeles, CA 90008. **Business Addr:** Assistant Superintendent, Los Angeles Board of Education, 450 N Grand, Rm G-353, Los Angeles, CA 90012.

ALEXANDER, VINCENT J.
Publisher, president, CEO. **Personal:** Born Oct 19, 1958, Fort Wayne, IN; son of John Alexander & Dorothy Logan; married Gail Alexander, Feb 1, 1990; children: Vince II, Colin, Gavin. **Educ:** Vincennes Univ, AS, 1979; Indiana State Univ, BS, 1981. **Career:** WMRI-WGOM, announcer/reporter, 1982-85; Chronicle-Tribune, sports writer, 1985-90; The Journal-Gazette, sportswriter, 1990-; High School sports editor, 1990-97; Sports Page Magazine, founder, 1997; It's All Good, Inc, pres, CEO. **Orgs:** Better Business Bureau of NE; South Side Business Association. **Honors/Awds:** APME Sports Writing Contest, 2nd Place, 1996; Recipient, General Salute Alumni Award, Outstanding Graduate of Wayne High School, 1993. **Home Addr:** 1002 Northwood Blvd, Fort Wayne, IN 46805. **Business Addr:** Publisher, The Sports Page, PO Box 5694, Fort Wayne, IN 46895-5694, (219)471-8889.

ALEXANDER, WALTER GILBERT, II
Dentist. **Personal:** Born Jul 6, 1922, Petersburg, VA. **Educ:** Rutgers Univ, BS Mech Engrg 1943; Howard Univ, DDS 1952. **Career:** Douglas Aircraft Co LA, designer 1943; Private Practice S Orange NJ, dentist 1952-. **Orgs:** Mem post-grad dental faculty NJ Coll of Med & Dentistry 1967-; clin asst prof 1969; mem Amer Natl, NJ Dental Assns; Commonwealth, Essex Co Dental Soc; mem Urban League; life mem NAACP; mem NJ St Bd of Dentistry 1972-76; pres NJ St Bd of Dentistry 1976; mem Amer Assn of Dental Examiners; active mem Northeast Regional Bd of Dental Examiners; mem Tau Beta Pi, Omicron Kappa Upsilon; Episcopalian. **Business Addr:** 555 Center St, South Orange, NJ 07079.

ALEXANDER, WARDINE TOWERS
Hospital technical services exec. **Personal:** Born Jul 26, 1955, Birmingham, AL; daughter of Thelma Otey Towers and Ward Towers Jr; married Gregory Bernard Alexander Sr, Sep 6, 1975; children: Gregory Bernard II. **Educ:** Univ of Alabama, Birmingham, AL, BS, 1978. **Career:** American Red Cross, Birmingham, AL, reference lab technologist, 1977-84, asst dir, tech serv, 1984-90, dir hosp serv, 1990-; Hosp/Tech Services, reg mgr, 1994-; American Red Cross Blood Svcs, education manager, currently. **Orgs:** Publicity comm chair, Alpha Kappa Alpha Sorority Inc, 1982-; mem, Amer Assn of Blood Banks, 1977-; mem, AL State Assn of Blood Banks, 1977-; mem, Amer Society of Medical Technologist, 1977-; mem, Amer Society of Clinical Pathologist, 1977-; Al State Assn of Blood Banks, pres, 1994-95. **Honors/Awds:** "Stored Red Cells," Amer Red Cross Publication, 1979. **Home Addr:** 5708 Camden Ave, Birmingham, AL 35228. **Business Phone:** (205)325-4427.

ALEXANDER, WARREN DORNELL
Businessman. **Personal:** Born May 27, 1921, San Antonio, TX; married Mary Catherine Bryant; children: Lawrence, Lynette, Sharon. **Educ:** Omaha Univ, BGE 1958; Iliff Sch of Theology Univ of Denver, postgrad; ordained Meth Min, 1963. **Career:** CO Civil Rights Commn, dep dir 1965-74; Metro Denver Urban Coalition, pres 1975-78; Western First Financial Corp, financial consult 1979-. **Orgs:** Pres NE Park Hill Civic Assn 1964-67; orign mem Skyline Urban Renewal Proj 1965-67; bd dir Rocky Mountain Reg Kidney Found 1967-68; pres Inter-AgyOrgn 1966-67; vice pres CO Conf of Soc Workers 1968-69; co-found/1st bd chmn Denver Fair Housing Ctr 1965-66; chmn Commn of Christian Soc Concerns Park Hill United Meth Ch 1968-69; cand Denver Bd of Educ 1971; chmn bd dir Denver Head Start 1972-74; chmn bd dir Denver Owl Club 1975-76; pres Hubert L "Hooks" Jones Chap Tuskegee Airmen 1976-; St of CO Adv Councl for Vocational Educ 1976-78; dir selective serv St of CO 1978-; Kappa Alpha Psi 1974-. **Honors/Awds:** 1st Annual Martin Luther King Jr Award Outstanding Contb in Field of Civic & Human Rights 1977. **Military Serv:** USAF Maj 1942-46/1948-64.

ALEXANDER, WILLIAM H.
Judge. **Personal:** Born Dec 10, 1930, Macon, GA; children: Jill Marie. **Educ:** Ft Valley State Coll, BS 1951; Univ of MI, JD 1956; Georgetown Univ, LLM, 1961. **Career:** GA House of Rep, state rep 1966-75; City Court of Atlanta, judge 1975-76; Criminal Court of Fulton County, judge 1976-77; State Court of Fulton County, judge 1977-July 1985; Judge, Fulton Superior Court 1985-95; Senior Judge, 1996-. **Orgs:** Mem Amer Bar Assn, Atlanta Bar Assn, Amer Judicature Soc, Lawyers Club of Atlanta,Gate City Bar Assn, Old War Horse Lawyers Club, Natl Bar Assn. **Military Serv:** US Army, 1951-53. **Home Addr:** 4540 Birdie Ln SW, Atlanta, GA 30331. **Business Addr:** Senior Judge, Fulton Superior Court, 136 Pryor St, Atlanta, GA 30303.

ALEXANDER, WILLIAM M., JR.
Business executive. **Personal:** Born Mar 18, 1928, St Louis, MO; married Marlene Crump Alexander, 1978; children: Brian. **Educ:** Univ of IL, BS Mechanical Engineering, 1948. **Career:** Northrop Aircraft Corp, Hawthorne, CA, thermodynamicist, 1948-50; Rockwell International, Downey, CA, mgr, sr project engineer, 1955-68; Golden Oak Inc, pres, gen mgr, 1968-79; G/O Furniture Inc, chmn of the bd, 1979-. **Orgs:** Mem, Amer Soc of Mechanical Engineers; vice pres, Epis City Mission Soc; director, United Way of Los Angeles, 1975-86; director, Natl Assn of Black Manufacturers, 1970-74; member, Kappa Alpha Psi, 1946-. **Honors/Awds:** Special Achievement Award, Natl Urban League, 1948; Achievement Award, Natl Aeronautics & Space Admin, 1968. **Military Serv:** US Army, 1953-55.

ALEXANDER, WILLIE
Professional sports administrator. **Educ:** Alcorn A & M, attended. **Career:** Houston Oilers, defensive back, 1971-79, career consultant, 1981-86, director of player relations, 1987-.

ALEXANDER-WHITING, HARRIETT
Educator. **Personal:** Born in Charlotte, NC; daughter of Mr & Mrs James Alexander, Sr; married Robert W Whiting. **Educ:** Northern IL Univ, BS Educ 1968; Kent State Univ, MA 1970. **Career:** Virginia Regional Medical Prog, asst allied health officer 1971-72; Emory Univ, instructor 1972-74; Alabama Inst for the Deaf & Blind, Talladega Coll, program coord/supervising teacher, 1974-80, asst visiting prof, 1976-79; Gallaudet Univ, speech/lang path & coord of communication unit & lab 1980-84, program supervisor 1985-96, asst dir for support services 1996-. **Orgs:** Mem Amer Speech Language and Hearing Assoc 1971-; bd of trustees AL Assoc of Retarded Citizens 1977-79; mem task group Mayor's Comm on Early Childhood 1987; mem Natl Comm on Deafness Amer Speech Language & Hearing Assoc 1987-90; Conference for Educators & Administrators Serving the Deaf 1992-. **Honors/Awds:** Natl Accreditation Cncl Site Team 1978; Outstanding Young Women of Amer 1979; mem Natl Task Force on Deaf-Blind US Dept of Educ 1979; mem Natl Comm on Develop Disabilities Amer Speech Language and Hearing Assoc 1980-82; mem Middle States Accreditation Team 1983. **Business Addr:** Assistant Director for Support Services, PCNMP, Gallaudet Univ, 800 Florida Ave, Washington, DC 20002.

ALEXANDRE, JOURNEL
Physician. **Personal:** Born Jul 14, 1931, Arcahaie, Haiti; children: Cibe, Colette. **Educ:** Lycee Toussaint Louverture, BS 1952; Univ of Mexico, MD 1960. **Career:** Physician, St Joseph Hosp, Mercy Cath Med Ctr, Montgomery Hosp, Valley Forge Med Ctr; Scarborough Genl Hosp, internship 1960-61; Mercy Douglass Hosp, resid 1961-65; Montgomery Hosp, 1965-66; Private Practice, physician. **Orgs:** Mem PA & Montgomery Co Med Soc 1967; Intl Coll of Surgeons; fellow Amer Coll of Surgeons 1969; diplomate Amer Bd of Surgery 1968. **Business Addr:** 731 W Erie Ave, Philadelphia, PA 19140.

ALEXIS, CARLTON PETER
Educational administrator. **Personal:** Born Jun 29, 1929, Port of Spain, Trinidad and Tobago; married Ogbonia M; children: Carla, Anthony, Lisa. **Educ:** NY Univ, BA 1953; Howard Univ, MD 1957; Haiti, DHC 1972; Georgetown, DSc 1980. **Career:** Walter Reed Army Hosp, intern 1957-58; Bronx VA Hosp, res int med 1961-63; Georgetown Univ Hosp, fellow endocrinology 1963-64; Freedmens Hosp, pres med-dent staff 1968-69; Howard Univ, instr prof med 1964-; Howard Univ, vice pres health affairs 1969-. **Orgs:** Mem Natl Med Assn; Amer Med Assn; Amer Coll Phys; Amer Soc Int med; Assn Acad Hlth Ctr; Med Soc DC; Med Chirurgical soc of DC; chmn GovBd DC Gen Hosp; mem Mayors Task Force on reorg dept of Human Resources DC; mem adv comm to Comm IRS; Mayors Comm on Drug Abuse; mem Ed Bd Jour of Med Edn. **Honors/Awds:** Elected Alpha Omega Alpha; Fellowship Amer Coll of Phys; Outstanding Tchr Howard Univ Coll of Med 1966. **Military Serv:** Med Corps 2nd lt to capt 1956-61. **Business Addr:** Vice President Health Affairs, Howard Univ, 2400 6th St NW, Washington, DC 20059.

ALEXIS, DORIS VIRGINIA
Director. **Personal:** Born Jul 10, 1921, Brooklyn, NY; married Joseph Alexis; children: Neal Howe, Priscilla Rand. **Educ:** Hunter Coll, New York NY, attended, 1946; Univ of California, Los Angeles CA, attended 1960; Univ of California, Davis, Cert of Program Mgmt, 1976. **Career:** California Dept of Motor Vehicles, dep dir, 1975-77, first woman and first career dir 1977-. **Orgs:** Bd trustees Sacramento Safety Cncl (chpt of Natl Safety Cncl) 1978-79; bd dir Amer Assn of Motor Vehicle Admin 1979-; bd dir Sacramento Safety Cncl (chpt Natl Safety Cncl) 1979-; pres bd trustees Commonwealth Equity Trust 1979-; mem Women's Forum 1977-; mem bd dir YWCA 1978-; mem NAACP 1978-; mem Urban League 1978-. **Honors/Awds:** Let planning & implementation DVM Child Care Cntr for children of State Employees 1975; Grand Masters Award MW Prince Hall Grand Lodge F and AM; Honoree Coalition of Women in State Svc; 1st CA Official nominated for membership Women's Forum. **Business Addr:** Dir, CA Dept of Motor Vehicles, 2415 1st Ave, Sacramento, CA 95818.

ALEXIS, MARCUS
Educator. **Personal:** Born Feb 26, 1932, Brooklyn, NY; married Geraldine M. **Educ:** Brooklyn Coll, BA 1953; MI State Univ, MA 1954; Univ of Minnesota, PhD 1959. **Career:** Macalester Coll, asst prof 1957-60; DePaul Univ, assoc prof 1960-62; Univ of Rochester, assoc prof, 1962-70; Univ of CA at Berkeley, vis prof 1969-71; Northwestern Univ, prof econs & urban affairs 1970-85; US Interstate Commerce Commn, commr 1979-81; Northwestern Univ, prof econs & urban affairs 1970-85; Univ of IL at Chicago Coll of Business Admin, dean 1985-90; Northwestern Univ, visiting prof of economics, 1990; J L Kellogg Prof; Federal Reserve Bank of Chicago, deputy chm, 1986-90, chm, 1991; Northwestern Univ, bd of trustees, prof of economics, prof of management & strategy, 1991-. **Orgs:** Pres bd dir Urban League of Rochester 1966-69; mem Natl Bd Amer Mktg Assoc 1968-70; mem chmn Caucus Black Economists 1969-71; com Increasing Supply Minority Economists Amer Econ Assn 1970-73; natl bd dirs PUSH 1972-73; chmn com Status Minorities Prof Amer Econ Assn 1974-80; com Minorities in Sci Natl Rsch Cncl Nat Acads Sci 1975; trustee Macalester Coll 1983-88; mem educ policy bd review, Review of Black Political Economy 1984-; chair economic policy task force Joint Ctr for Political Studies 1985-; trustee Teachers Insurance and Annuity Assoc 1987-; Beta Gamma Sigma; Order Artus; board of economists, Black Enterprise magazine. **Honors/Awds:** Ford Found Fellow, post-doctoral studies, Harvard Univ & MIT 1961-62; Samuel Z Westerfield Disting Achievement Awd Natl Economic Assn 1979; Outstanding Achievement Awd Univ of MN 1981; Caribbean Amer Intercultural Org Scholar Awd 1981; Minority Trucking/Transportation Develop Cncl President's Awd 1981; Chicago Tribune, University Teacher's Honor Roll, 1992. **Business Addr:** Bd of Trustees/Prof, Econ/Mgmt, Northwestern Univ, Leverone Hall, Evanston, IL 60208-2001.

ALFONSO, PEDRO
Business executive. **Personal:** Born Jun 28, 1948, Tampa, FL; son of Florencia Alfonso and Eugenio Alfonso. **Educ:** Brevard Jr Coll, Assoc of Arts 1970; Howard Univ, Business Admin 1973. **Career:** General Electric Co, mktg rep 1973-78; Seymore Systems Inc, consultant 1971-73; IBM Corp, systms engineer 1968-71; Dynamic Concepts Inc, Washington DC, pres 1978-. **Orgs:** Bd mem Washington DC Chamber of Commerce 1982-; chair of the bd, National Capital Area YMCA; Bd mem Leadership Washington 1987-; past pres Washington DC Chamber of Commerce 1990; past pres, Black President's Round Table Assn 1988-89; bd mem Bureau of Rehabilitation; mem, US Small Business Admini, Natl Advisory Council; bd mem National Small Business United; chmn, DC Private Industry Council. **Honors/Awds:** Mayor's appointment Washington DC Citizen's Energy Advsory Comm 1983-; elected Advisory Neighborhood Commissioner 1980-81; Outstanding Entrepreneur of the Year, Natl Black Master of Business Admin Assn 1987; Businessman of The Year Washington DC Chamber of Commerce 1987; Howard Univ Entrepreneur of the Year, 1994; Presidential Apointee, White House Conference on Small Business. **Special Achievements:** Company is ranked #95 on Black Enterprise magazine's 1997 list of Top 100 Black businesses. **Business Addr:** President, Dynamic Concepts Inc, 2176 Wisconsin Ave NW, Washington, DC 20007, (202)944-8787.

ALFORD, BRENDA
Association executive. **Personal:** Born Jan 27, 1947, Atlanta, GA; daughter of Rosette Alford and James Alford. **Educ:** TN State Univ, BS 1969; Univ of Pittsburgh, MSW 1975. **Career:** City of Houston, prog mgr human resources 1975-78; US Dept Health & Human Svcs, public health advisor 1978-83; RABA Inc, exec vice pres 1981-84; Brasman Health and Business Research, pres 1985-; Amer Assn of Black Women Entrepreneurs Inc, natl pres, exec dir 1982-. **Orgs:** Mem Natl Assoc of Social

Workers, Amer Public Health Assoc, treas WA Urban League Guild 1980-82; Silver Spring Chamber of Commerce, Federation of Republican Women, Natl Assn of Small Research Companies. **Honors/Awds:** Fellowship Natl Inst Mental Health Fellowship 1973-75; edited ''Predicted Kilograms Quantities of Medical & Rsch Needs for Controlled Substances'' 1980-81. **Business Addr:** Natl President, Amer Assn Black Women Entrepreneurs, PO Box 13933, Silver Spring, MD 20911-3933.

ALFORD, HAILE LORRAINE
Attorney, lecturer. **Personal:** Born Jul 2, 1949, Brooklyn, NY; children: Julian Alexander Moore, Kaamilah Michelle Moore. **Educ:** Herbert H Lehman, BA 1971; Rutgers Univ School of Law Camden, JD 1976. **Career:** Jr HS, teacher 1971; Wiltwyck School for Boys, teacher 1972-73; Lincoln Univ, adj lecturer 1981-; Hercules Inc, attny 1976-. **Orgs:** Mem ABA Labor Law Sect 1976-, NBA Corp Sect 1976-, PA Bar Assoc 1976-, DE Bar Assoc 1981-. **Business Addr:** Attorney, Hercules Inc, Hercules Plaza, Wilmington, DE 19894.

ALFORD, THOMAS EARL
Librarian. **Personal:** Born Mar 5, 1935, McKeesport, PA; son of Della Slade Alford and Horace Alford; married Kay Alice Taylor Alford, Aug 26, 1962; children: Thomas E Jr, Elaine Kay. **Educ:** Eastern Michigan University, Ypsilanti, MI, BS, 1958; University of Michigan, Ann Arbor, MI, MALS, 1964. **Career:** Mideastern Mich Library Coop, Flint, MI, coordinator, young adult services, 1967-69; Berrien County Library League, Benton Harbor, MI, director, 1969-74; Benton Harbor Public Library, dir, 1969-74; Library Cooperative of Macomb, Mount Clemens, MI, director, 1974-80; Macomb County Library, Mount Clemens, MI, director, 1974-80; Los Angeles Public Library, Los Angeles, CA, asst city librarian, 1980-. **Orgs:** American Library Assn, 1960-; co-chair, Michigan Delegation to White House Conference on Library Info & Services, 1979-80; Michigan Library Association, 1960-80; California Library Assn, 1980-. **Honors/Awds:** Librarian, Library/USA New York World Fair, 1964; Author, chapter, Black Librarian in America, Scarecrow, 1970, What Black Librarians Are Saying, Scarecrow, 1972, Libraries in the Political Process, Scarecrow, 1980. **Military Serv:** US Army, First Lt, 1958-61. **Business Addr:** Assistant City Librarian, Los Angeles Public Library, 630 West Fifth St, Los Angeles, CA 90071.

ALFRED, DEWITT C., JR.
Medical educator, psychiatrist. **Personal:** Born Oct 12, 1937, Chattanooga, TN; son of Dewitt Clinton and O'Teele Eloise (Nichols); married Marion Leticia Bottoms, Aug 22, 1959; children: Leticia O'Teele Alfred Garrick, Dewitt Clinton Alfred III. **Educ:** Morehouse Coll, BS (Cum Laude) 1956; Howard Univ, MD 1960. **Career:** Homer G Philips Hosp St Louis, internship 1960-61; Wash Univ St Louis, asst res psychiatry 1961-62; USAF Reg Hosp, gen med officer, 1962-64; Walter Reed General Hosp, resident psychiatrist, 1964-67; USAF Area Medical Center, asst chief of psychiatry, 1967-68; USAF Regional Hosp, chief psychiatrist, 1968-71; Grady Memorial Hosp, prof of psychiatry, 1971-84; Morehouse School of Medicine, professor, currently. **Orgs:** Mental health admins/dipl Amistrv Legal & Comm Psychiatry Amer Psychiatric Assn 1978; diplomate Am Bd of Psychiatry & Neurology 1970; dir Inpatient Psych & asst chf of psych Malcolm-Grow USAF Area Med Cntr Andrews AFB 1967-68; chmn Dept Mental Hlth USAF Reg Hosp Sheppard AFB TX & REg Consult in Psychiatry USAF Surgeon Gen 1968-71; dir Inpt Psych & Asst supt Psychiatry & Grady Meml Hosp Atlanta, GA 1971-73; staff psychiatrist Emory Univ Clinic & Emory univ Hosp 1971-; Dept of Psychiatry Grady meml Hosp Atlanta 1973-; mem Amer Med Assn; mem Natl Med Assn; fellow Amer Psychiatric Assn 1977; Amer Acad pf Psychiatry & Law; So Psychiatric Assn; past pres Soc USAF Psychiatrists; mem Black Psychiatrists of Amer; trustee GA Psychiatric Assn 1979-82; founding chmn, psychiatry dept, Morehouse School of Medicine, 1984-; director, Morehouse Medical Assocs, 1985-93; National Mental Health Coun, 1992-. **Honors/Awds:** Atlanta Medical Assn, Young MD of the Year, 1976; Mental Health Assn of Metro Atlanta, Public Service Award, 1989; Solomon Carter Fuller Award, 1994. **Business Addr:** Morehouse School of Medicine, 720 Westview Dr SW, Atlanta, GA 30310-1495, (404)756-1440.

ALFRED, RAYFIELD
Firefighter. **Personal:** Born Jul 11, 1939, Ville Plate, LA; married Cynthia A Patterson; children: A LaChelle, Shaun C, Raphael W, Jonathan K. **Educ:** Univ of VA, Certs 1975; Univ of DC, AA 1977, BS 1981; OK State Univ, Certs 1981 & 1983; US Fire Acad, Certs 1983 & 1984. **Career:** Univ of DC, asst professor cardiopulmonary resuscitation 1980-81; DC Fire Dept, fire chief, 1988-93; Consultant, public info officer. **Orgs:** Instructor/trainer Amer Heart Assoc 1977; advisory neighborhood comm DC Govt 1981-84; advisory subcommittee of facilities, bd of trustees Univ of DC 1982-83; udc professional advisory committee Greater SE Comm Hosp 1983-85; emergency cardiac committee Amer Heart Assn 1983-84; Leadership Washington, bd of dirs; Anthony Bowen, YMCA, bd of dirs; DC Street Academy, bd of dirs; Greater DC Cares, chmn of bd; Natl Fire Protection Assn, (NFPA). **Honors/Awds:** Cert of Hon Mention DC Fire Dept 1967; Cert of Appreciation DC Dental Soc/Amer Red Cross 1978-83; Cert of Appreciation Amer Heart Assoc 1982-83; Silver Medal for Valor DC Fire Dept 1984. **Military Serv:** AUS Sergeant/Sp-5 3 years; Hon Discharge 1958-61.

AL-HAFEEZ, HUMZA
Business executive, clergyman. **Personal:** Born Feb 28, 1931, New York, NY; son of Rosa May Danielson-Weir and Asa Mose Weir; children: Rasul, Bismillah, Habib, Wardi, Yuhana, Larry, Don, Mariama, Jacqueline. **Career:** US Justice Dept, comm relations consultant; Lloyd Sealy, asst chief; WWRL, host/comm relations cons; Law & Order, lecturer/TV host 1972-75; Trinity Mission Ch, boxing instr; NYPD, law enforcer 1959-76; WLIB-TV, host ''Our Times''; al-Hafeez Sec & Investigations Serv State of New York and Commonwealth of Virginia, owner/dir/lic private investigator. **Orgs:** Fdr/past pres Natl Soc of Afro-Amer Policemen 1964; editor & chief ''Your Muhammad Speaks''; mem Natl Assn of Chfs of Police; inspector NY State Athletic Commn; minister Muhammad's Temple of Islam Inc; mem Pastoral Care Comm Interfaith Hosp & St John's Hosp; mem Intl Platform Assn; mem Intl Police Congress. **Honors/Awds:** Father of the Year Awd Kinlock Mission for the Blind 1974; Comm Serv Awd City of NY Council of Churches 1975; Natl Black Police Assn Person of the Year 1982; 6 Medals Excell Police Duty NYPD; Marksman Sharpshooter NYPD; many TV and radio appearances; Ebony Success Library 1000 Successful Blacks; Sojourner Truth Rm Prince George's Meml Libr; Appreciation Awd US Penitentiary Terre Haute IN 1986; Service Awd US Penitentiary at Lewisburg 1986; author ''Our Time, Book #1'' The Slanderer 1987. **Business Addr:** Editor-in-Chief, Your Muhammad Speaks Newspaper Serv, 591 Vanderbilt Ave, Brooklyn, NY 11238.

ALI, FATIMA (ANN LOUISE REDMON)
Educational administrator, marriage/family therapist. **Personal:** Born Apr 20, 1925, Indianapolis, IN; daughter of Eugenia Dudley Adams (deceased) and Theophilus Adams (deceased); married LeRoy Redmon (deceased); children: Lydia Ann. **Educ:** Purdue Univ, BS 1946, MS 1960, Ph D 1970; Univ of Pittsburgh, NDEA Summer Fellow 1964. **Career:** Gary IN Public Schools, teacher, counselor, 1948-65; Purdue Univ, asst dir admissions, dir Black Students Affairs 1965-70; Univ of CA Berkeley, assoc coord Afro-Am Studies 1970-71; CA State Univ, Hayward, asst prof of educ psychology 1971-74; Contra Costa County Hosp, clin psych 1971-75; Amer Muslim Mission, natl minister of educ & dir of educ 1974-79; clinical dir Pueblo House 1980-83; Reading Rsch Council Burlingame CA, CEO 1982-; vice pres Davis Research Foundation, 1988-. **Orgs:** Consultant US Dept of Educ 1979, CA State Dept of Public Health 1972-73, CA State Dept of Educ 1972, Contra Costa County CETA Prog 1978, IN St Dept of Public Instr 1978, Jenkins Homes for Disabled Chldrn 1981-82, Oakland, CA Public Lib Adult Literacy Prog 1984; prof educ psy Univ of Santa Barbara, Santa Barbara, CA 1982-; consultant Serene Comm Schools Sacramento, CA 1972-; trustee Benicia, CA Unified School Dist 1973-75; mem Assn for Children With Learning Disabilities, The Common Wealth Club of CA, CA Alliance of Black Educators, Alpha Kappa Alpha Sor, Assn for Humanistic Psychology 1985-; Advisory Council, International Biographical Centre, Cambridge, England, 1988; Deputy Governor and Research Board of Advisors, American Biographical Institute, 1988. **Honors/Awds:** Sabbatical leave Gary IN Public Schools 1959-60; teaching asst Purdue Univ 1959-60; coll student personal internship Purdue Univ 1965-66; NDEA summer fellowship Purdue Univ 1962; EOP summer fellowship Purdue Univ 1966-67; Distinguished Leadership Award, American Biographical Institute, 1987; International Leaders in Achievement Award, International Biographical Centre, Cambridge, England, 1987. **Business Addr:** Chief Executive Officer, Reading Research Council, 1601 Old Bayshore Hwy, Ste 260, Burlingame, CA 94010, (415)692-8990.

ALI, GRACE L.
Business executive. **Personal:** Born May 27, 1952, Georgetown, Guyana; daughter of Victoria Nurse Moore and Joseph Moore; married Oscar Ali, Jun 16, 1973; children: Asgar, Rasheed. **Educ:** Univ of Massachusetts, Amherst, MA, BBA, 1973; Univ of Miami, Miami, FL, MBA, 1987. **Career:** Peat, Marwick, Mitchell, New York, NY, internal analyst, 1973-76; Peat, Marwick, Main, Miami, FL, sr auditor, 1976-79; Air Florida System, Miami, FL, asst controller, 1979-80; Air Florida Europe, London, England, vice pres finance, 1980-83; Univ of Miami, Miami, FL, asst controller, 1983-89; Florida Memorial Coll, Miami, FL, vice pres business and fiscal affairs, 1989-. **Orgs:** Mem, American Institute of CPAs, 1984-; mem, FL Institute of CPAs, 1984-; bd mem, FL Institute of CPAs-South Dade, 1987-, committee chairperson, 1987-89; mem finance committee, United Way of Dade County, 1990-. **Honors/Awds:** CPA, State of Florida, 1984; Service Award, Town of Crawley England, 1983; Outstanding Professional, Phi Beta Sigma, 1983; Outstanding Committee, FICPA-South Dade, 1988, 1989; Service Award, Florida Memorial College, 1990. **Home Addr:** 10920 SW 125 Street, Miami, FL 33176. **Business Addr:** Vice President, Business & Fiscal Affairs, Florida Memorial College, 15800 NW 42nd Ave, Miami, FL 33054.

ALI, KAMAL HASSAN
Educator. **Personal:** Born Sep 3, 1944, Springfield, MA; son of Stella Abrams Bridges-Marshall and Edwin Harold Marshall, Sr; married Ayesha Ali, Apr 1, 1966; children: Ahmed Hassan, Quesiyah Sana'a, Ibrahim Suhnoon. **Educ:** Hunter College, 1963-64; New York Univ, 1964-65; Univ of Massachusetts, Amherst, MEd, 1977, EdD, 1981. **Career:** Human Resources Admin, sr human resource specialist, 1967-71; Harlem East-Harlem Model Cities, project liason, 1971-74; Univ of Massachusetts, Amherst, graduate research and teaching asst, 1974-78; Vantage Consultants, Hartford, CT, training program developer, 1978-79; Westfield State College, dir, minority/bilingual vocational teacher educ programs, 1980-81, dir minority affairs, beginning 1981-, associate dean of academic affairs, currently. **Orgs:** Vice pres, Islamic Soc of Western Massachusetts, 1983-; Dunbar Community Center, chmn, bd of dir, 1984-86, chmn, New Bldg Comm, 1986-. **Honors/Awds:** Producer, host, cable television program ''Coll Journal,'' Springfield, MA, 1983-; public speaking on educ, foreign policy, apartheid, 1984-86; author, ''Islamic Education in the United States: An Overview of Issues, Problems and Possible Approaches,'' 1984, ''The Shariah and Its Implications to Muslim School Planning,'' 1986, Amer Journal of Islamic Social Studies. **Business Addr:** Associate Dean, Academic Affairs, Office of Multicultural Devt, Westfield State College, Western Ave, Westfield, MA 01086.

ALI, MUHAMMAD (CASSIUS MARCELLUS CLAY)
Professional boxer (retired). **Personal:** Born Jan 17, 1942, Louisville, KY; son of Odessa Grady Clay and Marcellus Clay; married Sonji (divorced 1966); children: Maryum, Jamillah, Rasheeda, Muhammad Jr; married Kalilah Tolona, Apr 18, 1967 (divorced 1977); married Yolanda Williams, Nov 1986; children: Hana, Laila, Ahad Amin. **Career:** Professional boxer, 1960-81; Starred in autobiographical film, The Greatest, 1976; appeared in TV movie Freedom Road. **Orgs:** World Community Islam; conducts missionary work, The Nation of Islam. **Honors/Awds:** Light heavyweight champion, AAU, 1959, 1960; winner of 6 Golden Glove Titles in Kentucky; light heavyweight champion, Golden Gloves, 1959; heavyweight champion, Golden Gloves, 1960; gold medal, 1960 Olympics, light heavyweight div; world heavyweight championship 1964-67, 1974-78, 1978-79; honored for long, meritorious service to boxing, BWA, 1985; elected Boxing Hall of Fame, The Ring, 1987; author, The Greatest: My Own Story, 1975; Jim Thorpe Pro Sports Award, Lifetime Achievement Award,1992.

ALI, RASHEEDAH ZIYADAH
Community services administrator. **Personal:** Born Jul 3, 1950, Springfield, IL; daughter of Montez R McIntosh Crawford (deceased) and Zeddie L Crawford; married Rahman Munir Ali, Jun 15, 1970; children: Jamillah, Sakinah, Rahman II. **Educ:** Sangamon State Gerontology Seminars, certificates 1976, 1977, 1978; United Way, counselors training certificate 1986. **Career:** Springfield Fair Housing Coalition, vice pres, pres 1987. **Orgs:** Bd mem Advocates for Health 1986-; adv council mem and bd mem Community Action Agency 1986; volunteer Community Energy Systems 1986, Access to Housing 1986, People for Progress 1986-; chairman of board Imani, Inc 1988-; exec board member Sangamon County Democrat Minority Caucus 1988-; commissioner Springfield Human Relations Commission 1989-. **Honors/Awds:** City of Springfield, Fair Housing Award, 1990; IL Municipal Human Relations Assoc Community Service, Humanitarian Award, 1992.

ALI, RASHIED
Musician. **Personal:** Born Jul 1, 1933, Philadelphia, PA; son of Dorothy Mae Christopher and Randolph Patterson; married Patricia Bea Wyatt; children: Akeela, Annik. **Educ:** Wm Penn Business Inst Phila, attended 1953; Granoff Music School, 1954-55; studied with Philly Joe Jones 1953-55, and Joe Jones 1963-64. **Career:** Played drums with Len Bailey various local groups rock & roll combos; also worked with Bill Dixon, Paul Bley, Sonny Rollins, Archie Shepp, Marion Brown, Sun Ra, New York City 1963-; joined John Coltrane Combo 1965; special concert performances; recorded with A Shepp, John Coltrane, Jackie McLean, Alice Coltrane; 5 recordings as Leader Survival Records; formed own quintet, The Funkyfreeboppers; Ali's Alley Jazz Club, owner. **Special Achievements:** Survival Record & Studio (Recording). **Home Addr:** 77 Greene St, New York, NY 10012.

ALI, SCHAVI MALI
Educator. **Personal:** Born Apr 30, 1948, Detroit, MI; daughter of Margaret Ruis Walton Ross and William Earl Ross, Sr; married Derrick Ali, Apr 19, 1986. **Educ:** Wayne State Univ, Detroit, MI, BA, 1970, MA, 1977; Univ of Michigan, Ann Arbor, MI, PhD, 1989. **Career:** Highland Park High School, Highland Park, MI, English, social studies teacher, 1970-71; Roeper City & Country School, Bloomfield Hills, MI, English teacher, 1973-77; Wayne State Univ, English, Afro-Amer Studies teacher, 1978-89; Oakland Community Coll, Farmington Hills, MI, English teacher, 1989-; Nile Valley Cosmetics, Detroit, MI, CEO, owner, developer, 1990-. **Orgs:** Assn for the Study of Afro-Amer Life and History; Natl Council of Black Studies, 1980-; Phi Delta Kappa, 1982-; mem, bd dir, Afro-Amer Studio Theater, 1983-89; dir, Assn for Human Devel, 1988-; historian

and lecturer, Alkebulan Assn, 1989-; member, Assn for the Study of Classical African Civilization, 1991-. **Honors/Awds:** Outstanding Educ, Woodward Ave Presbyterian Church, 1982; Spirit of Detroit, Detroit City Council, 1984; Outstanding Educ, governor James Blanchard, 1984; Outstanding Community Leader, Phi Beta Sigma Fraternity, 1984; Univ Author Recognition Award, Wayne State Univ, 1987, 1988; author, Growing Together, 1971, Lament for the Sixties, 1981, "Struggling and Surviving," Black Literature Forum, 1982, Moments in Time, 1987, "Claude McKay," Dictionary of Literary Biography, 1984.

ALI, SHAHRAZAD
Writer. **Personal:** Born Feb 5, 1949, Cincinnati, OH; daughter of Lucy Marshall and Harry Levy; married Solomon Ali, 1965 (died 1985); children: twelve. **Educ:** Xavier University, Cincinnati, OH; Georgia State Univ, Atlanta, GA. **Career:** Cincinnati Herald, Call & Post, Cincinnati Enquirer and Hi-Lites Magazine, feature contributing editor, 1966-71; medical transcriptionist, 1977-83; Clark College, assistant to vice president, 1983-85; Civilized Publications, Atlanta, GA, 1985; Ali's Unlimited Accessories, executive assistant, 1986-89; Temple University, PASCEP Program for Independent Publishing, teacher, 1987. **Orgs:** Advisory board member, Ford Recreation Center, Philadelphia, PA, 1988-89; advisory board member, Pennsylvania Board of Probation and Parole, Philadelphia, PA, 1988-89; public relations director, Mayor's Commission on Women, Philadelphia, PA, 1987-88; published author, Moonstone Black Writers Association, Philadelphia, PA, 1987-88. **Honors/Awds:** Alpha Phi Alpha Literary Award, 1987; Mayor's Proclamation for Writing, New Orleans, LA, 1987, Detroit, MI, 1990; Third Place, Top Georgia Authors of Atlanta Public Library, 1985; author, How Not to Eat Pork, 1985; author, The Blackman's Guide to Understanding the Blackwoman, 1990, #1 book on Black Best Selling List for 40 weeks, 1990; The Blackwoman's Guide to Understanding the Blackman, 1992; Blackman's Guide on Tour Video, 1992; Are You Still a Slave?, 1994. **Special Achievements:** Promotional activities include appearances on Donahue, Geraldo, Sally, Montel, Larry King, Jerry Springer, Ricki Laker, Judge for Yourself, Gordon Elliot, Rolonda, Our Voices-BET, Tony Brown's Journal, and numerous others. **Business Addr:** Owner/Director/Writer, Civilized Publications, 2019 S Seventh St, Philadelphia, PA 19148, (215)339-0062.

ALICE, MARY (MARY ALICE SMITH)
Actress. **Career:** Broadway debut No Place to Be Somebaody, Morosco Theatre, 1967; other NYC appearances include A Rat's Mass, 1969, The Duplex, 1972, Miss Julie, 1973, House Party, 1973, Black Sunlight, 1974, Terraces, 1974, Heaven and Hell's Agreement, 1974, In the Deepest Part of Sleep, 1974, Cockfight, 1977, Nongogo, 1978 (Obie award Village Voice 1979), Player #9, Spell #7, NY Shakespeare Festival, 1979, Zooman and the Sign, 1980, Glasshouse, 1984, Take Me Along, 1984, Fences, Goodman Theatre, Chgo, 1986, 46th St Theatre, NYC, 1987 (Antoinette Perry award for best featured actess in a play, Drama Desk award 1987), The Shadow Box, 1994; other theatre appearances include Open Admissions Long Wharf Theatre, New Haven, 1982, A Raisin in the Sun, Yale Repertory, 1984; film debut The Education of Sonny Carson, 1974; other film appearances include Sparkle, 1976, Teachers, 1984, Brat Street, 1984, To Sleep With Anger, 1990, Awakenings, 1990, Bonfire of the Vanities, 1990, A Perfect World, 1992, Life with Mikey, 1993, The Inkwell, 1994; TV films The Sty of the Blind Pig, 1974, Just an Old Sweet Song, 1976, This Man Stands Alone, 1979, Joshua's World, 1980, The Color of Friendship, 1981, The Killing Floor, 1984, Concealed Burmies, 1984, Charlotte Forten's Mission: Experiment on Freedom, 1984, The Women of Brewster Place, 1989, Laurel Avenue, 1993, The Mother, 1994, The Vernon Johns Story, 1994; TV series include: Sanford and Son, 1972, A Different World, 1988-89, I'll Fly Away (Emmy Award, Outstanding Supporting Actress in a Drama Series, 1993), 1991-93. **Orgs:** Mem AFTRA, SAG, Actor's Equity Assn. **Special Achievements:** Tony Award nominee, "Having Our Say: The Delany Sisters' First 100 Years.". **Business Addr:** Writers & Artists Agency, 924 Westwood Blvd, Ste 900, Los Angeles, CA 90024, (310)824-6300.

ALI-JACKSON, KAMIL
Attorney. **Personal:** Born Mar 4, 1959, El Paso, TX; daughter of Ruth & John Ali; married Michael S Jackson, Aug 31, 1985; children: Ross Jackson, Kendall Jackson. **Educ:** Princeton Univ, AB, 1981; Harvard Law School, JD, 1984. **Career:** McCarter & English, associate, 1984-86; Pepper, Hamilton & Scheetz, associate, 1986-90; Merck & Co Inc, director, Corporate Licensing, 1990-. **Orgs:** National Bar Association, 1986-92; Philadelphia Bar Association, 1986-92; Pennsylvania Bar Association, 1986-. **Honors/Awds:** Princeton Univ, Ralph G Treen Memorial Scholarship, 1980. **Special Achievements:** The Experienced Hand, How to Make the Most of an Internship, 1980. **Home Addr:** 143 Hart Avenue, Doylestown, PA 18901.

ALLAIN, LEON GREGORY
Architect. **Personal:** Born Nov 17, 1924, New Orleans, LA; son of Cecile Warnick Allain and George A Allain Sr; married Gloria Grace Dinvaut, Sep 4, 1952; children: Rene'e, Diane. **Educ:** Univ of MI, BArch 1949. **Career:** Parsons, Brinckerhoff, Hall & McDonald, draftsman, 1953-55; Meyer Whitelsey & Glass, 1956; Skidmore, Owings & Merrill, draftsman 1957-58; Miller & Allain, Architects, partner 1958-67; Allain & Assoc Inc, Architects, pres 1967-. **Orgs:** Mem, Amer Inst of Architects, 1965-; Natl Organization of Minority Architects, 1970-; life member, NAACP. **Honors/Awds:** Permanent deacon Roman Catholic Church 1982. **Military Serv:** US Army, first lt, 1943-46. **Business Addr:** President, Allain & Associates Inc, 100 Peachtree St NW, Ste 1930, Atlanta, GA 30303, (404)688-0157.

ALLEN, ALEX JAMES, JR.
Judge. **Personal:** Born Dec 8, 1934, Louise, MS; married Nancy Ann Green; children: Alex III, Michael P, Derek J. **Educ:** Wayne State Univ, BA 1964; Detroit Coll of Law, JD 1969. **Career:** Total Action Against Poverty Med Div, admin asst 1966-68; Comm on Children & Youth for City of Detroit, asst dir 1968-71; Stone Richardson & Allen PC, atty 1971-82; 36th Dist Court Detroit MI, presiding judge. **Orgs:** Mem Omega Psi Phi, NAACP, Founders Soc Detroit Inst of Arts, State Bd of MI, Amer Judges Assoc, MI Dist Judges Assoc; bd of dir MI Black Judge Assoc. **Military Serv:** USAF s/sgt 1954-57. **Home Addr:** 1943 Hyde Park Drive, Detroit, MI 48207. **Business Addr:** Presiding Judge, 36th Judicial Dist, 600 Randolph, OCB, Detroit, MI 48226.

ALLEN, ALEXANDER J.
Business executive. **Personal:** Born Apr 30, 1916, Boston, MA; married Elizabeth V Banks; children: Alexander J III, Leslie M, Sydney K. **Educ:** Wilberforce Univ, BS 1937; Yale Univ, BD 1940; Columbia Univ, MSSW 1942; Wilberforce Univ, D Humanities 1972. **Career:** Baltimore Urban League, exec dir 1944-50; Pittsburgh Urban League, exec dir 1950-60; Philadelphia Counc for Comm Advancement, assoc & dir 1963; NY Urban League, exec dir 1964-66; Natl Urban League NYC, vice pres for prog 1971-. **Orgs:** Pres SW PA Chap natl Assn of Soc Workers 1957-59; pres Natl Assn of Intergroup Rel Officials 1966-67; trustee Wilberforce Univ 1960-; bd mem RegPlan Assn of NY 1965-. **Honors/Awds:** Fellowship Natl Urban League Columbia Univ Sch of Social Work 1940-42; Ann Tanneyhill Award Natl Urban League 1976. **Business Addr:** Vice President For Programming, Natl Urban League, 500 E 62nd St, New York, NY 10021.

ALLEN, ANDREW A.
Dental surgeon. **Personal:** Born Jul 30, 1921, Port Allen, LA. **Educ:** St Augustine Coll, BS 1942; Howard Univ, DDS 1945; Guggenheim Dental Clinic, certificate 1946; Med Field Serv Sch, attended 1951; AF Inst Pathology, cert 1952; NY Univ, post grad studies 1972; Harvard Sch of Den Med, post grad studies 1976; UCLA Sch of Dentistry, post grad studies. **Career:** Self-Employed, dental surgeon. **Orgs:** Pres Chas A George Dental Soc 1948-49; chmn Prog Com Chas A George Dental Soc 1954-64; Gulf State Dental Soc 1954-64; treas Gulf State Dental Soc 1971-; mem Natl Dental Assn; Amer Dental Assn; Houston Dist Dental Soc; TX Dental Assn; Acad of Dental Dentistry; mem St Lukes Epis Ch; NAACP; YMCA; mem Intl Coll of Oral Implantologists 1976; Pres Club Howard Univ 1976; Alpha Phi Alpha; Chi Delta Mu. **Honors/Awds:** Awd of Merit Natl Found for Infantile Paralysis 1958; Cert Awd Howard Univ Dental Alumni Assn 1956. **Military Serv:** US Army pfc 1943-45, capt Dental Corp 1951-56. **Business Addr:** 2916 Southmore, Houston, TX 77004.

ALLEN, ANITA FORD
Business executive, former public administrator. **Personal:** Born in Washington, DC; daughter of Jerlean Reynolds Ford and Leonard G Ford; children: George A Ferguson III, Stephen F Ferguson. **Educ:** Howard Univ, BA (Summa Cum Laude); Univ of Chicago, MA (w/honors); Univ of MA, EdD 1976. **Career:** Dept of Education, mgr 1964-81; Federal Govt, mgr 30 yrs ending 1981; Several Organizations, mgmt consultant 1982; Robt R Moton Meml Inst, pres; Anita F Allen Assocs, pres 1983-. **Orgs:** Apptd by mayor to mem DC Adv Comm on Educ 1985-; mem Metro Baptist Ch Washington; sec exec comm mem Bapt Home of DC 1978-82; vice pres & Pres Dist of Columbia Bd of Educ 1967-72; life mem Delta Sigma Theta Sor; mem bd of dirs DC League of Women Voters 1987-89. **Honors/Awds:** Distinguished public serv awds and/or hon degrees, Prairie View A&M Univ 1976, AL; Broaddus Coll 1976.

ALLEN, BENJAMIN P., III
Financial Advisor. **Personal:** Born Feb 27, 1942, Washington, DC; son of Elizabeth Allen (deceased) and Benjamin Allen (deceased); married Francesca M Winslow; children: Nicole, Camille. **Educ:** Howard Univ, BS 1963; Rutgers Univ MBA 1976. **Career:** Marine Midland Bank, project officer 1970-78, asst branch manager 1978-80, branch manager 1980-84, operations 1985; corporate manager employee relations 1986-87; asst vice pres, branch manager 1987-88; Riggs Bank NA, vice pres, private banking officer 1988-89, vice pres, branch manager, 1990-91, vice pres, regional manager, 1992-97; Prudential Securities, financial advisor, 1997-. **Orgs:** Treas Edges Group Inc 1984-88; mem Urban Bankers Coalition 1984-88; Natl Black MBA Assoc 1984-88; vestry mem St Andrews Church 1985; Washington Urban Bankers Assn, 1988-; treas, Edges Group Inc, Metropolitan Washington D.C. Chapter 1989-; bd of directors, Mentors, Inc, 1989-94. **Honors/Awds:** Black achiever Harlem Branch YMCA 1974. **Military Serv:** USAR-MSC Col (retired); US Army Achievement Award 1983; Meritorious Service Medal 1989, Oak Leaf Cluster, 1994. **Home Addr:** 5451 Ashleigh Rd, Fairfax, VA 22030. **Business Addr:** Vice President, Riggs Bank N.A., PO Box 96758, Washington, DC 20090-6758, (202)506-2736.

ALLEN, BERNESTINE
Federal transportation official. **Personal:** Born Aug 20, 1944, Soperton, GA. **Educ:** Ft Valley State Coll, BS 1967; Northeastern Univ, MA 1968. **Career:** Dept of Labor, Washington, econ analyst 1967; General Elec Co, financial analyst 1968-69; Dept of Transportation, Washington, economist 1969-71; Airport & Airway Cost Allocation Study, economist asst dir 1971-73; Intl Aviation Policy, economist 1973-75; Dept of Transportation, intl transportation specialist 1975-80, senior international transportation specialist, 1980-87, international cooperation division & secertarial chief, .1987-95, international cooperation & trade divison chief, 1995-. **Orgs:** Amer Econ Assn; Amer Fedn Govt Employees 1970-72; Natl Econ Assn; Amer Acad Polit & Social Scis; Bus & Professional Women's League; DC Assn for Retarded Citizens; Delta Sigma Theta Inc pres chap 1966-67, 1972-74; March of Dimes, National Capital Area Chpter, executive committee, 1988-91, chair, budget & finance; board of directors DST Telecommunications Inc, 1976-81; Garfield Home for Sr Citizens; Project Women; Women Ex-Offenders Prog 1973; Natl Council of Negro Women; NAACP; Natl Urban League; National Pan-Hellenic Council Inc, executive board/financial secretary, 1991-95. **Honors/Awds:** Alpha Kappa Mu Natl Honor Soc 1965; Wall St Journal Scholastic Achievement Award 1967; Natl Science Foundation Grant 1967; Dollars and Sense Magazine, Outstanding Service in Government, 1990; Silver Medal for Meritorious Professional Achievement, 1990. **Business Addr:** Chief, International Cooperation and Trade Division, Dept of Transportation, OST/X-25, Room 10302, 400-7th St SW, Washington, DC 20590.

ALLEN, BETTIE JEAN
State government official. **Personal:** Born Oct 21, 1926, Springfield, IL; divorced. **Educ:** Grad, Springfield Coll, Lincoln Coll of Law, Univ of IL, Sangamon State Univ. **Career:** YWCA in Kenya, vol intl div, 1967-68; Springfield Human Rel Commn, exec dir, 1969-70; entrepreneur, 1970-74; Assoc Gen Contr of Illinois, training dir, 1971-72; State of Illinois, Capitol Devel Bd, coord, 1973-. **Orgs:** Past pres NAACP; Serv Bur for Colored Children; supr Zion Bapt Ch Sch; trustee bd mem YWCA 1954-70; bd mem United Way; mem RR Relocation Auth. **Honors/Awds:** Webster Plaque Awd Springfield NAACP 1957; Achievement Awd Urban League 1964; Affirmative Action Awd 1975; Breadbasket Commercial Achiev Awd 1977. **Business Addr:** Coordinator, State of IL, CDB 3rd Fl, Wm G Stratton Bldg, Springfield, IL 62706.

ALLEN, BETTY
Educator, opera singer (retired). **Personal:** Born in Campbell, OH; daughter of Dora Catherine Mitchell Allen and James Corr Allen; married Ritten Edward Lee III, Oct 17, 1953; children: Juliana Catherine Hogue, Anthony Edward. **Educ:** Wilberforce University, attended, 1944-46; Hartford School of Music, certificate, 1952; studied voice under Sarah Peck More, Paul Ulanousky, Carolina Segrera Holden, Zinka Milanov. **Career:** North Carolina School of the Arts, teacher, 1978-87; Curtis Institute of Music, teacher; Manhattan School of Music, trustee, teacher; Harlem School of the Arts, executive director, Voice Dept, chair, 1979-. **Orgs:** NAACP; Hartford Music Club; Metro Opera Guild; Urban League; American Guild Music; Artists Equity; America Museum of Natl History; AFTRA; Silvermine Guild Artists; Jeunesses Musicales; Gioventu Musicales; Unitarian Universalist Women's Federation; Student Sangverein Trondheim; Natl Negro Musicians Assn; board member/executive committee member in numerous organizations including: Carnegie Hall, Natl Foundation for Advancement in the Arts, Arts & Business Council, American Arts Alliance; US Committee for UNICEF, Manhattan School of Music; trustee, Chamber Music Society of Lincoln Center, Children's Storefront, InterSchools Orchestras, Theatre Development Fund. **Honors/Awds:** Ford Foundation Concert Soloist Grantee, 1963-64; Exceptional Achievement Award, Women's Project & Productions, 1988; American Eagle Award, Natl Music Council, 1988; first recipient, ISO Award, InterSchools Orchestras, 1988; Philadelphia Natl Bank Distinguished Artist of the Year, Settlement Music School, 1989; Laurel Leaf Award, American Composers' Alliance, 1989; 15th AnniversaryHarlem Week Award, Harlem Week & the Uptown Chamber of Commerce, 1989; has appeared as soloist with world's leading orchestras & renowned conductors including: Bernstein, Casals, Dorati, Leinsdorf, Maazel, Martinon, Munch, Ormandy, Ozawa, Pritchard, Solti, Steinberg, & Stokowski; regularly appears at the Marlboro, Casals, Tanglewood, & other music festivals. **Business Addr:** President Emeritus, Harlem School of the Arts, 645 St Nicholas Ave, New York, NY 10030.

ALLEN, BILLY R.
Personnel recruiter, consultant. **Personal:** Born Mar 16, 1945, Crossroads, TX; son of Fannie M Allen; married Clare Dicker-

son Allen, Aug 14, 1971; children: Sheldon C, Sean L, Kristy B. **Educ:** University of North Texas, BA, 1968. **Career:** New York Life Insurance, field underwriter, 1970-72; Pitney Bowes, account representative, 1971-73; Minority Search Inc, president, chief executive officer, 1975-. **Orgs:** DFW Airport Board, committee chairman, 1988-; National Recreation & Park Association, vice chairman of the board, 1986-92; Concord Missionary Baptist Church, deacon, 1990-; The Dallas Assembly; The Dallas Black Chamber of Commerce, past president; The Committee of 100, past president; University of North Texas, board of visitors, 1990-; Society of International Business Fellows, 1986-. **Honors/Awds:** The Dallas Black Chamber, Willow Award, 1986; Henderson County Jr College, Outstanding Ex-Student, 1985; National Association of Community Leadership Organizations, Distinguished Leadership Award, 1986; Dallas Chamber of Commerce, Leardership, 1976; YMCA, Achievement, 1984. **Business Addr:** President & CEO, Minority Search Inc, 777 S RL Thronton, Suite 105, Dallas, TX 75203, (214)948-6116.

ALLEN, BLAIR SIDNEY
Educator. **Personal:** Born Aug 7, 1952, Abington, PA; divorced; children: Thageron. **Educ:** PA State Univ, BS Biophysics 1974; Univ of CA at Berkeley, Master Biophysics 1979. **Career:** Presbyterian Univ of PA Med Ctr, rsch teacher 1980-81; Harcum Jr Coll, instr of sci. **Orgs:** Pres Rsch Inst Tech Inc 1978-, Oppty Council of Eastern Montgomery Cty 1980-82; mem NAACP Amber Branch 1984-85. **Honors/Awds:** 1st Prize Chem Montgomery & DE Valley Sci Fairs 1970; Scholarship PA Senatorial Scholarship & Grad 1970-74; Grad Fellowshp Minority Fellowship 1974-79; Fellowship Nato Advance Study Inst 1981; Fellowship Faculty Summer Inst 1983. **Business Addr:** Asst Professor of Science, Harcum Jr Coll, Morris & Montgomery Aves, Bryn Mawr, PA 19010.

ALLEN, BRENDA FOSTER
Educator. **Personal:** Born Jan 24, 1947, Gloucester, VA; married Robert P Allen; children: Tameka D. **Educ:** VA State Univ, BS 1969; NC State Univ, MS 1976, EdD 1985. **Career:** Cornell Univ Coop Extension Service, youth development specialist 1971-72, county 4-H agent 1969; Natl 4-H Foundation Div of Leadership Development, program specialist 1972-75; NC State Univ, School of Educ research asst 1975-76, Div of Student Affairs coord 1976-80, asst dir 1980-83, Office of the Provost coord 1983-85; Agricultural Extension Service program specialist 1985-. **Orgs:** NC State Univ, graduate student's assoc adult education executive board; Natl 4-H Foundation, staff development and training committee, volunteers' forum planning committee; Task Force on Program Development for 4-H volunteers; Natl Teen Leaders' Symposium Planning Committee; American Home Economics Assn; Natl 4-H Assn; Kappa Omicron Phi; Image of NC State Univ Seminars, facilitator 1979-80, task force mem 1978-79; Outstanding Young Women of America, mem 1980; NCSU committe on Recruitment and Retention of Black Students, mem 1982-83; Governor's Conf on Women and the Economy, facilitator 1983; Shaw Univ Seminary Ext Program, teacher 1984-86, Youth Motivation Task Force mem 1985-86; NC Home Economics Ext Program Comm, mem 1983-84; NC 4-H Volunteer Task Force, mem 1986;NC Home Econ Volunt Task Force, mem 1986; mem, Epsilon Sigma Phi, Natl Honorary Extension Fraternity 1989. **Honors/Awds:** Publications, "Making Incentives Work for You" 1976, "Competencies Needed by 4-H Volunteers for the Effective Use of Incentives - A Needs Asessment Study" 1976, "Criteria for Selection, Evaluating or Developing Learning Modules" 1976, "Are Your Reading Habits a Liability?" 1977, "Videotapes Help University Students Learn How to Learn" 1981, "Build Up One Another" 1986, "Women, Builders of Communities and Dreams" 1986, "Rural Minority Women As Community Volunteers" 1986; NC Coordinator, Women and Chronic Disease Teleconference, 1988; received Infant Mortality Grant from United Church of Christ, 1989. **Home Addr:** 2025 Rabbit Run, Raleigh, NC 27603. **Business Addr:** Leadership Development Spec, NC Agricultural Extension Serv, NC State University, Box 7605, Raleigh, NC 27695.

ALLEN, CAROL WARD
Educational administrator. **Career:** Oakland Port Authority, head, until 1993; Laney College, Community Services Office, director, 1993-. **Special Achievements:** First African American female to head the Oakland Port Authority. **Business Addr:** Director of Community Services, Laney College, 900 Sallon St, Oakland, CA 94607, (510)834-5740.

ALLEN, CHARLES CLAYBOURNE
Consultant-urban planning. **Personal:** Born Sep 21, 1935, Newport News, VA; son of Margaret C Allen and John C Allen; married Sallie; children: Charles II, John IV, Sallie Monique. **Educ:** Hampton Inst, BS 1958; Columbia Univ, MSUP 1963. **Career:** Clarke & Rapuano Inc, urban planner 1963-68; Dept of Devel & Planning Gary, dir 1968-74; The Soul City Coll, vice pres gen manager 1974-75; Wendell Campbell Assoc Inc, sr vice pres 1975-88; deputy dir, Depart of Planning and Devel, Newport News, VA, 1988-91, consultant, urban planning, 1991-. **Orgs:** Bd mem, 1979-82, charter mem, Amer Planning Assn 1979-; charter mem Amer Inst of Certified Planners, 1979; bd mem Amer Soc of Planning off 1971-73; mem Amer Inst of Planners 1977-78; chmn joint AIP/ASPO Comm for Min Affairs 1973-78; pres Natl Assn of Planners 1976; Kappa Alpha Psi Fraternity 1955; bd mem Interracial Council for Business Opportunity 1987-96; mem Lambda Alpha; Newport News City Council, 1992-, vice mayor, 1996-. **Honors/Awds:** Dept Head of Yr City of Gary 1973; Outstanding Govt Award Gary Jaycees 1974; Meritorious Serv Award Gary Chapter Frontiers 1974; City Council Resol Gary City County 1974; Outstanding 20 Yr Alumnus Hampton Inst 1978; Outstanding Person DuPage Co NAACP 1978; Award of Achievement, Hampton-Newport News, Alumni Chap, Kappa Alpha Psi Fraternity, 1992; Distinguished Citizen Award, Zeta Lambda Chap, Alpha Phi Alpha Fraternity, 1992. **Military Serv:** US Army, lt 1958-60; USAR capt 1963-66; USANG capt 1966-68. **Business Addr:** Charles C Allen, AICP, 97K-28th Street, Newport News, VA 23607.

ALLEN, CHARLES EDWARD
Real estate investor. **Personal:** Born Feb 22, 1948, Atlanta, GA; son of Ruby Collins Allen Hill and Charles Edward Allen, Sr; married Elizabeth Ann Glover, Jul 6, 1972; children: Charles Phillip, David Kennedy, Rebecca Ann. **Educ:** Morehouse College, Atlanta, GA, BA, 1970; Graduate School of Business, Chicago, IL, MBA, 1972. **Career:** First Natl Bank, Chicago Il; Bank of CA, vice pres & manager, 1976-78; First Bank Natl Assn, pres & COO, 1978-80; United Natl Bank, Washington DC, exec vice pres & CAO, 1980-81; First Ind Natl Bank, pres & CEO, 1981-88; MIG Realty Adv, vice pres & reg manager, beginning 1988; Graimark Realty Advisors In c, pres & CEO, currently. **Orgs:** Bd of dirs, AAA Michigan & Affiliated Insurance Companies; corp dir, Blue Cross/Blue Shield of Michigan; past pres, Natl Bankers Assn; Museum of Afro-American History; trustee, Benedict College; 7th Federal Reserve Bank, Detroit Branch, dir. **Honors/Awds:** Black Achiever's Award 1976; Outstanding Young Men of America, YMCA, 1981, Boy Scouts of Amer, 1984, Alpha Theta GPD Sorority, 1981; Citizen of the Year, Hartford Ave Baptist Church, 1982; Mayor's Award of Merit, 1984; America's Best & Brightest Young Men & Women, 1987; During tenure, First Ind Natl Bank was featured as Bank of the Year, Black Enterprise Magazine; profiled in Minority Business Entrepreneur Magazine. **Business Addr:** President, Graimark Realty Advisors, Inc, 300 River Place, Suite 2050, Detroit, MI 48207.

ALLEN, CLYDE CECIL
Marketing executive. **Personal:** Born Jan 29, 1943, Youngstown, OH; son of Frances Allen and Eugene Allen; married Gayle Thigpen; children: Michael Clyde, Brett Donaldo. **Educ:** Kent State Univ, BA Bio 1965; Rutgers Univ, MA Ind Rel 1977. **Career:** Schering Corp, sr microbiologist 1965-70, personnel admin 1970-72; Ind Comm Ctr, exec dir 1972-74; Johnson & Johnson, sr personnel admin 1974-75, sr comps admin 1975-76, mgr human resource planning 1976-78; M&M Mars Inc, mgr compensation benefits 1978-80; JE Seagrams Inc, corp mgr EEO 1980-83, director of community relations, 1983-87, director of public relations/event marketing, 1987-. **Orgs:** EDGES NY NJ 1972-; Amer Comps Assoc 1976-; chairperson US Comm on Civil Rights 1968-; Employer Assoc NJ 1976-; Port Auth Airport Rev Cncl 1972-74; pres Frontiers Intl Inc 1974-; chairperson Plainfield Econ Dev Comm 1975-; fndr dir Youth Leadership Club Inc 1968-; vice chmn Bd dir Union Co OIC 1973-75; board of directors, Negro Ensemble Co, 1989-92; trustee, Jack & Jill of America Foundation, 1989-92. **Honors/Awds:** Outstanding Serv Awd Frontiers Intl 1978; Malcolm X Awd YLC Inc 1971; Outstanding Serv Awd Elizabeth YMCA 1970; Blackbooks Business & Professional Award, 1989; Community Service Award, President Reagan; Pinnacle Award, Harbor Publishing Co, 1990; Most Outstanding Marketer Award, National Assn of Market Developers, 1987; Still Award, New Jersey Minority Braintrust, 1989; Man of the Year, National Assn of Negro Business and Professional Women, 1986; Outstanding Corporate Executive, Black Pages, 1989. **Business Addr:** Director, Public Relations/Event Marketing, The House of Seagram, Joseph E Seagram & Sons, Inc, 800 3rd St, 10 Fl, New York, NY 10022-7699.

ALLEN, DEBBIE
Actress, singer, dancer. **Personal:** Born Jan 16, 1950, Houston, TX; daughter of Vivian Ayers; married Wim Wilford (divorced); married Norm Nixon; children: Vivian Nicole, Norm Jr. **Educ:** Howard University School of Fine Arts, BA (with honors), speech and drama. **Career:** Actress, dancer, singer, choreographer; plays include: Ti-Jean and His Brothers, 1972; Purlie, 1972; Raisin, 1973; Ain't Misbehavin', 1978; The Illusion and Holiday, 1979; West Side Story, 1980; Louis, 1981; The Song is Kern!, 1981; Parade of Stars Playing the Palace, 1983; Sweet Chartity, 1986; choreographer for TV series Fame, 1982-87; producer and director, A Different World, 1988-93; In the House, 1995-; has appeared in numerous television shows and specials; served as executive producer on the film "Amistad," 1997. **Orgs:** Actors' Equity Association; Screen Actors Guild; American Federation of Television and Radio Artists. **Honors/Awds:** Drama Desk Award, Outstanding Featured Actress in a Musical, West Side Story, 1980; Tony Award nomination, Best Actress, Sweet Charity, 1986. **Special Achievements:** Choreographer for the Academy Awards, 1994, 1995.

ALLEN, DOZIER T., JR.
Trustee. **Personal:** Born Jan 10, 1931, Gary, IN; married Arlene McKinney; children: 4. **Educ:** Los Angeles Jr Coll; Indiana Univ; Valparaiso Univ. **Career:** Allen Ent, vice pres, 1957-67; Northwest Indiana Urban League, field rep, 1968-69; Gary City Council, vice pres, 1970; Gary IN, city councilman-at-large, 1968-72; Dozier T Allen, Jr Ent, pres; Double AA Inc, pres; Lake Shore-Birch Inc, pres; MACH Investors Inc, vp; Downtown Deli-Mart, proprietor; Calumet Township, trustee, 1970-. **Orgs:** Founder & chmn bd dir NW IN Sickle Cell Found 1971-73; mem Natl PTA; Natl Roster of Black Elected Officials; Natl Black Caucus of Local Elected Officials; IN Black Caucus; In Township Trustee Assn; NW IN Urban League; Gary Toastmasters Intl; life mem NAACP Gary Br; charter mem Gary Hum Rel Commn; bd mem Gary Marona House Drug Abuse Inc; chmn IN 1st Congr Democratic Dist 1971; pres Lake County Mental Health Board; mem Amer Pub Welfare Assn; contrib mem Democratic Natl Comm; mem IN Township Trustee Assn; mem Lake County Bd of Edn; mem Gary C of C; mem IN Assn of Commerce & Ind; mem Downtown Gary Merchant's Assn; mem Chancellor's Assoc IN Univ; mem Natl Sheriff's Assn; asst chief Lake County Sheriff's Police Res Unit. **Honors/Awds:** Sponsors Award Gary Greens Pop Warners Football League 1974; Boss of Century Award 1974; Recognition for Comm Serv Gary Pub Sch 1974; Mexican Amer Award 1974; Recipient NAACP Ovington Award; Recipient NAACP Humanitarian Award; incl over 150 additional awards.

ALLEN, EDNA ROWERY
Educational administrator. **Personal:** Born Jul 20, 1938, Carrollton, AL; married Robert H Allen; children: Robin, Dawn, Robert Jr. **Educ:** Lincoln Univ, BS, Business Educ, 1960; Univ of IL, MS, Counselor Educ, 1970; Edwardsville IL, postgraduate work, 1974; McMurray Coll, Dr of Humanities, 1983. **Career:** Rock Jr HS, teacher 1962-70, counselor 1970-71; Bd of Ed Dist 189 E St Louis, Dr of gifted programs 1971-. **Orgs:** Chmn of social action Delta Sigma Theta Sorority Inc 1971-; bd of dirs Natl Assn of Gifted Children 1973-83; bd of dirs E St Louis Public Library 1974-83; bd of trustees State Comm Coll E St Louis 1975-78; pres St Ann's Sodality of St Patrick's Church 1982-; vice pres Concerned Citizens for the Comm 1984-; chmn of social action Top Ladies of Distinction 1984-; chmn Status of Women Comm, Top Ladies of Distinction; mem Phi Delta Kappa. **Honors/Awds:** "Those Who Excel" IL Office of Education 1978; Service Awd State Comm Coll 1978; Merit Awd ML King Jr HS E St Louis 1979; Recognition Awd Delta Sigma Theta Sor Inc 1984; Honorary Doctorate MacMurray Coll Jacksonville IL 1983. **Home Addr:** 664 N 33rd St, East St Louis, IL 62205. **Business Addr:** Director of Gifted Programs, East St Louis Board of Education 189, 1005 State St, East St Louis, IL 62201.

ALLEN, ELBERT E.
Dentist. **Personal:** Born Sep 19, 1921, Shreveport, LA; married Carolyn Sims. **Educ:** Wiley Coll TX, BS 1942; Meharry Med Coll TN, DDS 1945; Acad Gen Dentistry, FAGD 1969. **Career:** Private Practice, dentist. **Orgs:** Fndg mem Pelican State Dental Assn 1946; editor NAA Jour Natl Dental Assn 1950-51; assoc mem Chicago Dental Soc; mem NW LA Dental Assn; LA State Dental Assn; Amer Dental Assn; past finance chmn Pioneer Div BSA 10 yrs; fndg mem & past mem bd dirs Mt Moriah Day Care Ctr & Nursery past 10 yrs numerous other orgns & affiliations; pres Supreme Camp of the Amer Woodmen. **Honors/Awds:** Pierre Fuchared Awd for Outstanding Serv to the Country for Military Serv 1952; first black elected to any elective office since reconstruction days; Liberty Bell Awd, Shreveport Bar Assn 1970; Silver Beaver Awd 1972; Notable Amer Awd 1976-77. **Military Serv:** US Army Reserve Corps 2nd lt 1941-43; AUS pfc 1943-44; USAF capt 1951-53; USAF Reserve 1953-58. **Business Addr:** Dentist, Allens' Dental Clinic, 1004 Sprague St, Shreveport, LA 71101.

ALLEN, ERIC ANDRE
Professional football player. **Personal:** Born Nov 22, 1965, San Diego, CA; married Lynn; children: Eric Austin. **Educ:** Arizona State, bachelor's degree in broadcasting, 1988. **Career:** Philadelphia Eagles, defensive back, 1988-94; New Orleans Saints, 1995-. **Honors/Awds:** Pro Bowl appearances, 1989, 1991, 1992, 1993, 1994, 1995; United Negro College Fund, Eagle of the Year, 1993. **Business Addr:** Professional Football Player, New Orleans Saints, 5800 Airline Hwy, Metairie, LA 70003, (504)733-0255.

ALLEN, ESTHER LOUISA
Army officer/teacher (retired). **Personal:** Born Jan 20, 1912, Raton, NM; daughter of Alice Matilda Woods Allen and John Allen. **Educ:** KC General Hospital School of Nursing, Diploma 1940; Univ of Colorado School of Nursing, BS 1949; Univ of Washington School of Nursing, MS 1958. **Career:** Hubbard Hospital, Meharry Medical College, supervisor operating rooms; San Joaquin County Hosp, Stockton CA, asst supervisor operating rooms 1951-58; Santa Rosa Junior Coll School of Nursing, first and only black instructor 1960-73 (retired). **Orgs:** Mem Retired Officers Assn, Disabled American Veterans, Alpha Kappa Alpha Sor. **Honors/Awds:** Plaque for Outstanding Service to the Cause of Nursing Educ, Alumni of Santa Rosa Jr Coll. **Military Serv:** AUS Nurse Corps 2nd lt 26

months; American Defense Medal, American Campaign Medal, World War II Medal. **Home Addr:** 1604 Elm St, Denver, CO 80220.

ALLEN, EUGENE, JR.

Manufacturing company executive. **Personal:** Born Nov 7, 1937, Chicago, IL; son of Pearl Allen and Eugene Allen Sr; married Ledell Fields, Apr 16, 1961; children: Sheryl, Karla, Nicole, Eugene III. **Educ:** Illinois Institute of Technology, BS, 1970; University of Chicago Graduate School, MBA, 1976. **Career:** Sherwin-Williams Co., paint technologist/chemist, 1963-67; Libby McNeil & Libby, materials mgr/engineer, 1967-69; Avon Products, Inc, division manager, 1969-76; Hub States Corp, senior vp, 1976-79; Clinitemp, Inc, president, 1979-81; Aquamint Laboratories, Inc, president, 1981-; Allen Chemical, Inc, president, 1989-; Consolidated Cleaning Systems, Inc, president, 1990-; Allen Industries, Inc, chairman, president, chief executive officer, 1981-. **Orgs:** Indianapolis Business Development, chairman of the board, 1986-90; Junior Achievement, board member, 1986-96; District Export Council, board member, 1979-91. **Military Serv:** US Army, sgt, 1961-63. **Business Addr:** Chairman, President, Chief Executive Officer, Allen Industries, Inc, 1801 E 30th St, Indianapolis, IN 46218, (317)925-8520.

ALLEN, GEORGE

Educational administrator. **Personal:** Born May 22, 1955, Bay City, TX; son of Grace Allen; married Cathy Hunt; children: Amanda Michele. **Educ:** Attended, Kilgore Coll 1973-75; Stephen F Austin State Univ, BS 1977, MEd 1979. **Career:** Lufkin State School, therapy asst 1977; Lufkin Independent Schools, teacher/coach 1978, asst principal 1979; Youth Opportunity Unlimited, recreation coordinator 1985-86, headmaster 1988-91; Stephen F Austin State Univ, asst football coach 1979-86, asst dir for continuing education, 1990-. **Orgs:** Mem Natl Assn of Collegiate Dirs of Athletics; mem, exec board 1989-90, regional rep 1989-90, Natl Assn of Academic Advisors for Athletics; newsletter committee Texas Assn for Community Service and Continuing Education 1991. **Honors/Awds:** Mr Black SFA Stephen F Austin St Univ; Merit Awd Council of Black Organizations 1980-81. **Business Addr:** Assistant Director, Stephen F Austin State Univ, Continuing Education, PO Box 611, SFA Station, Nacogdoches, TX 75962.

ALLEN, GEORGE MITCHELL

Business executive. **Personal:** Born Nov 14, 1932, Boston, MA; married E Louise Peek, Jun 5, 1954; children: Leslie. **Educ:** Massachusetts Univ, Ext Courses; US Army Career Ext Courses. **Career:** Special Asst to Gov, 1970-74; Commonwealth of MA, dep commr of vet serv; Intergovernmental Relations, notary public 1972; Dept of Army, fed women's prog mgr, equal employment opportunity officer. **Orgs:** Real estate broker; town rep Stoughton MS; past pres Roxbury Med Tech Found 1971-73; external adv bd for Minorities Educ Advancement; MS Coll of Pharmacy 1972-; natl pres African American Veterans; mem NAACP; MS Joint Ctr for Polit Studies; vice pres Blacks in Govt AZ Chapt; NAACP Greater Huachuca Area Branch, president; arbitrator/mediator, AZ Court System. **Military Serv:** US Army, sgt first class, 20 yrs retired; Army Commendation Medal; many serv medals Japan, Korea, Germany; Certificates of Commendation from Military Serv & Comm Agencies. **Business Addr:** President, African American Veterans, PO Box 873, Fort Huachuca, AZ 85613.

ALLEN, GLORIA MARIE

Physician. **Personal:** Born in Washington, DC; daughter of Viola Childs Allen and Archie Allen; married William Henry Toles; children: William Henry III, Allen Wesley. **Educ:** Howard Univ, BS 1947; Howard Univ Med Sch, MD 1951. **Career:** Harlem Hosp, asst attending phys 1954-56; Jamaica Hosp NY, asst attending phys 1963-; Carter Comm Health Ctr, chief of pediatrics 1974-85; private medical practice, 1985-. **Orgs:** Mem Med Soc of the Co of Queens 1964-; sec Empire State Med Assn 1975-; treas/charter mem Susan S McKinney Smith Med Soc 1976-; bd dirs Queens Urban League 1970-; nom comm YMCA of New York City 1974-75; chmn Merrick YM-YWCA Day Care Ctr 1975-77; past president, Omega Wives of Long Island, 1964-; member, Delta Sigma Theta Sorority, 1964-. **Honors/Awds:** Woman's World Awd Bethel Temple 1958; Sr to Youth Comm Queens YWCA 1973; Community Awd Queens Fresh Air Fund 1978; Commnr Commn on the Status of Women New York City apptd Mayor Koch 1979. **Home Addr:** 104-27 192 St, Jamaica, NY 11412. **Business Addr:** Physician, 145-04 97th Ave, Jamaica, NY 11435.

ALLEN, HARRIETTE LOUISE

Educator. **Personal:** Born Oct 24, 1943, Savannah, GA; divorced; children: Tracy Marcette, Heather Lenae. **Educ:** Fisk Univ, BA 1964; Univ of WI, MST 1972; George Peabody Coll for Tchrs Vanderbilt Univ, PhD English Educ 1980. **Career:** S America Columbia, foreign exchange tchr of english 1964-65; Chicago Bd of Educ, spanish resource consult 1965-68; WI State Univ, asst proj dir tutorialprog 1970-72; Fisk Univ, poet-storyteller 1973-; Univ TN, poet-in-residence 1977-79; TN State Univ, asst prof of comm 1979-; State of TN, ambassador of letters 1979-. **Orgs:** Mem Alpha Kappa Alpha; Natl Theatre Assn; Black Theatre Assn SCETC; Natl Assn for Preservation & Perpetuation of Storytelling; Theta Alpha Phi Hon Forensic Frat; GA Soc of Poets; Natl Soc Pub Poets; Originator of Ballad Folk Theatre Art; star Jubas Jubilee Folktale Traveling Ensemble Co; 1st black storyteller at Natl Storytelling Fest Jonesboro TN. **Honors/Awds:** 1st Black to receive Gov Spotlight Awd; 1st Black poet to be read into the Congressional Record; author "Genesis & Jubas Folk Games"; 1st poet to be pub in Attica Rebirth Newspaper of Attica Prison. **Business Addr:** Ambassador of Letters, State of TN, #35 Legislative Plz, Nashville, TN 37219.

ALLEN, HERBERT J.

Educator. **Personal:** Born May 19, 1922, Jersey City, NJ; son of Jeanetta Casey Allen and Benjamin Allen; divorced; children: Deborah. **Educ:** Univ of Cincinnati Teachers Coll, BS 1946; Case Western Reserve Univ, MSSW 1948; Natl Cincinnati Admin/Mgmt Training Prog, Grad. **Career:** Cincinnati Gen Hosp, sr caseworker; Montgomery Cty Child Welfare Bd, suprv 1952-64; Barney Childrens Med Ctr, dir social serv 1964-66; Good Samaritan Hosp, dir soc serv 1966-67; Univ Cincinnati Med Ctr, adj assoc prof, dir soc work 1970-89, asst administrator, human resources, 1990-. **Orgs:** Acad of Cert Soc Workers; past pres OH Valley Chap of Natl Assn of Soc Workers 1972-74; past vice pres OH Council of Chapters of Natl Assn of Soc Workers; past pres Miami Valley Chap Dayton Natl Assn of Social Workers 1969; trustee Central Comm Health Bd of Hamilton Cty Inc 1976-77; chmn Commun Action Commiss 1974-77; Soc Serv Assn of Gr Cincinnati; mem, past pres Child Health Assn; clin instr School of Soc Work OH State Univ; pres Mt Auburn Health Ctr 1975-; Manpower Serv Adv Council of City of Cincinnati 1975-; Cincinnati Gen Hosp Med Audit Comm 1975; mem Coll of Med Expanded Deans Conf 1977; pres OH Valley Chapt; soc dir Hosp Soc Work Depts. **Honors/Awds:** Cert Outstanding Social Worker of the Year Natl Assn of Social Workers 1973; Cert Cincinnati Gen Hosp Empl Arts & Crafts Awd Gold Medal 1973; Cert Leadership Training Prog for Soc Workrs in Mental Health Natl Assn of Social Workers 1974; Cert Rsch Neigh Commun Assn 1975; Cert of Apprec Mt Auburn Comm Council 1975; Cert of Apprec Lincoln Heights Health Ctr Inc 1975; Cert Admin Mgmt Interns Univ of Cincinnati 1975; Cert Cincinnati Gen Hosp Arts & Crafts Harvest & Merit Awd Gold Medal 1975; Cert Natl Inst of Law Enforcement & Criminal Justice (Rape & its Victims) 1977; nominee Social Worker of the Year 1974; nominee Outstanding Citizen Awd 1976; University of Cincinnati Humanitarian Award, 1990; Community Service Award, Kappa Alpha Psi, Cincinnati Alumni Chapter, 1990. **Military Serv:** US Army, t/sgt 1942-45.

ALLEN, JACOB BENJAMIN, III

Vocational rehabilitation counselor. **Personal:** Born Sep 20, 1927, Raleigh, NC; son of Fannie Williams Allen and Jacob Benjamin Allen Jr; married Shirley K Allen, Nov 24, 1961. **Educ:** Shaw University, 1955; Springfield College, graduate certificate, 1962. **Career:** North Carolina Department of Vocational Rehabiliation, Human Resources Department; North Carolina Department of Mental Health; Patterson Ave Branch YMCA; Vocational Evaluation Facility, vocational rehabilitation counselor, currently. **Orgs:** National Black Achievers Association; COBY; Raleigh Mayor's Eastside Neighborhood Task Force; Omega Psi Phi; Shaw University Alumni Association; North Carolina Rehabilitation Counselor Association; AEAONMS Inc, Prince Hall Shrine; Boyer Consistory No 219, past commander in chief; United Supreme Council Ancient and Accepted Scottis Rite of Masonary 33 Degree; Garner Rd Family YMCA, past chairman, executive board, currently; North Carolina State Employees Association; Davie St Presbyterian Church, ruling elder; Kabala Temple No 177, AEANMS, Inc, past potentate. **Special Achievements:** Achieved independent status as a counselor. **Military Serv:** US Army, staff sgt, 1950-52; Korean Service Medal, UN Service Medal. **Business Addr:** Vocational Rehabilitaion Counselor, Vocational Evaluation Facility, Raleigh, NC 27610, (919)733-5407.

ALLEN, JAMES H.

Auditor, real estate. **Personal:** Born Apr 20, 1934, Farmville, VA; married Angelene Elliott; children: James Jr, Anita, Edward. **Educ:** Johnson C Smith Univ, AB 1960; Rutgers State Univ, MBA 1976. **Career:** Progressive Life Ins Co, debit mgr 1960-62; Jet-Heet Creative Mfg, perpetual inventory control clerk 1962-64; Wyssmont Engr Co, asst to ofc mgr 1964-68; Bendix Corp, expeditor 1968-69; State of NJ Div of Taxation, field auditor. **Orgs:** Mem Passaic Cty Bd of Realtors, Amer Soc of Notaries, Fed Govt Accountants Assoc, Natl Assoc of Black Accountants, Natl Assoc of Black MBA's, NatlAssoc of MBA; exec pres Delta Mu Lambda Chap Alpha Phi Alpha; pres Clavary Bapt Church, Fed Credit Union; exec bd mem Paterson Br NAACP; volunteer probation sponsor for Passaic Cty Probation Dept; mem Paterson Financial Aid Corp, Amer Legion Post 268. **Honors/Awds:** Faithful Serv Awd NAACP 1968; Outstanding Alumnus Johnson C Smith Univ Alumni Assoc Reg I 1971; Johnson C Smith Univ Gen Alumni Assoc Dedicated Serv 1973; State of NJ Outstanding Performance Awd 1971.

ALLEN, JAMES TRINTON

Elected official. **Personal:** Born Oct 31, 1924, Michigan, MS; married Magnolia Hudson; children: James Jr, Charles Banks, Sam, Margie Ree Holcomb, Melvin, Helen Ruth Thomas, Auther Wayne. **Career:** Elected official, currently. **Orgs:** Masonic #68, 1979. **Home Addr:** Rt 1 Box 244, Lamar, MS 38642.

ALLEN, JANE ELIZABETH

Psychologist. **Personal:** Born Apr 12, 1945, Bridgeport, CT; daughter of Jane Briscoe Allen and William A Allen; married Jonathan Schiesel; children: Seth Briscoe Schiesel. **Educ:** Barnard College, New York, NY, BA, 1967; Teacher's College, Columbia Univ, New York, NY, MA, 1970; State Univ of New York, Albany, NY, MS, 1980; Saybrook Institute, San Francisco, CA, PhD, 1985. **Career:** JEA Associates, Woodstock, NY, president, 1977-89; Knight-Ridder Inc, Miami, FL, internal consultant, 1989-; Knight-Ridder News Service, Washington, DC, columnist, 1989-; Miami Herald Publishing Co, Miami, FL, columnist, 1989-. **Orgs:** Member, American Psychological Association, 1978-; member, Society of Industrial/Organizational Psychologists, 1980-; member, National Assn of Black Journalists, 1989-; board member, Children's Home Society of South Florida, 1989-. **Honors/Awds:** Beyond Time Management: Organizing the Organization, Addison-Wesley, 1985. **Business Addr:** Columnist, Miami Herald, One Herald Plaza, Miami, FL 33132.

ALLEN, JERRY ORMES, SR.

Attorney. **Personal:** Born Dec 16, 1953, Cleveland, OH; son of Luther Ormes Allen & Netty L Cooper; married Jacqueline L Allen, Oct 10, 1987; children: Danielle Y, Jerry Ormes II. **Educ:** Capital Univ, BA, 1975; Capital Univ Law School, JD, cum laude, 1984; New York Univ Law School, LLM, taxation, 1987. **Career:** Chief Counsel, IRS, staff attorney, 1984-86; Bricker & Eckler, partner, 1987-. **Orgs:** Natl Bar Assn; Amer Bar Assn; Ohio Bar Assn; Columbus Bar Assn; Martin Luther King Arts Complex, bd pres; Columbus Zoo, bd mem; Hospice at Riverside Hosp, bd mem; Greater Columbus Arts Council, bd mem. **Business Addr:** Partner, Bricker & Eckler, Attys at Law, 100 South Third Street, Columbus, OH 43215.

ALLEN, JOHN HENRY

Engineer. **Personal:** Born Jan 16, 1938, Youngstown, OH; married Shirley; children: Kristine, Eric. **Educ:** CA State Univ LA, BS 1964, MSEE 1969; Pepperdine Univ, MBA 1983. **Career:** Packard Bell Electronics, system test tech 1959-61; Lockheed CA Cty, rsch engr 1961-64; Gen Dynamics Pomona Div, dynamics engr 1964-65; Teledyne Systems Co, mem tech staff 1965-66; Systems Integration & Support Ctrs, asst mgr 1966-79; CA State Coll, asst prof 1969-78; Aerojet Electro Systems Azusa CA Co Data Systems Integration Test, mgr. **Orgs:** Sr mem IEEE, EIT CA; second class radio telephone license patents-disclosures, Doppler Oper Test Sets & Dissimilar Metal Anti-Corrosion Ground Stub. **Military Serv:** USN electronics tech 1st class 1955-59. **Business Addr:** Manager, Aerojet Electro Syst Azusa CA, Data Systems Integration Test, Box 296, Azusa, CA 91702.

ALLEN, KAREN

Educator. **Career:** Univ of Maryland at Baltimore School of Nursing, associate prof, division of psychiatry, community health and adult primary care, currently. **Orgs:** National Nurses Society on Addictions, pres; Phi Kappa Phi; Sigma Theta Tau. **Honors/Awds:** Black Student Christian Forum Alumni Leadership Award, Andrews Univ, 1996; Assn for Medical Educ and Research in Substance Abuse, New Investigator/Educator Award, 1995; Univ of IL at Chicago Coll of Nursing, Distinguished Alumna Award, 1995, Dean's Award for Scholary Activity, 1992; Edited Text: "Nursing Care of the Addicted Client," cited as suggested reading in the 1997-98 Joint Comm Comprehensive Accreditation Manual for Behavioral Health Care. **Special Achievements:** First African American president of the National Nurses Society on Addictions. **Business Addr:** Assoc Professor, Dept of Psychiatry, Univ of Maryland at Baltimore School of Nursing, 655 W Lombard St, Baltimore, MD 21201.

ALLEN, LARRY CHRISTOPHER

Professional football player. **Personal:** Born Nov 27, 1971, Los Angeles, CA; married Janelle; children: Jayla, Larry Jr. **Educ:** Sonoma State, attended. **Career:** Dallas Cowboys, guard, 1994-. **Honors/Awds:** Pro Bowl, 1995, 1996. **Business Addr:** Professional Football Player, Dallas Cowboys, One Cowboys Pkwy, Irving, TX 75063, (214)556-9900.

ALLEN, LECESTER L.

Educational administrator. **Personal:** Born Feb 27, 1944, Pickens, AR; son of Joe & Rebecca Allen; married Mattie, Aug 31, 1968; children: Dana Nicole, Aaron Matthew. **Educ:** Wayne State Univ, BS, 1966, pursuing MA. **Career:** Do Re Mi Learning Ctrs & Academy of Detroit Schools, pres/CEO, currently. **Orgs:** Booker T Washington Bus Assn, pres, 1980-82; MI Assn of Childcare Ctrs, pres, 1974-80; Optimist Club of Central Det, pres, 1976-77; Metropolitan YMCA, bd mem/nominating com, 1988-; Don Bosco Home for Boys, pres, 1982-86; United Comm Services, chairman summer funding comm, 1979-82; Citizens for Better Government, co-chair/funding mem, 1982-; MI State Job Training Council, appt by Governor of MI, 1983-85; The Lawton School, president; Charter School Administration Services, president. **Honors/Awds:** Alabama A & M, Outstanding Educator/Businessman, 1995; Success Guide Magazine, Outstanding Educator/Entrepreneur, 1991; Small Business Admin, Advocate of the Year, 1982; Sate of MI, Minority Bus Excellence Award, 1977; City Clerk, City of Detroit, Distinguished Detroit Citizen, 1981. **Special Achievements:** Opened first pre-school computer lab in Detroit, 1983; Served as member of MI Dept of Commerce Minority Business; City of Detroit, Private Industry Council for Job Training, 1982; Special Commendation, Gov William Milliken, MI Conference on Small Businesses, 1981; Conducted workshops for new & prospective child care centers. **Business Addr:** President, CEO, Do Re Mi Learning Centers and Academy of Detroit Schools, 20755 Greenfield Road, Suite 300, Southfield, MI 48075, (810)569-7787.

ALLEN, MARCUS
Educator. **Personal:** Born Mar 2, 1924, Pittsburgh, PA; married Mary; children: Diane. **Educ:** Univ of Pittsburgh, BA 1949; Columbia Univ, MA 1951; Univ of Pittsburgh, PhD 1964. **Career:** Morgan State Univ, teacher 1955-66; Univ of MO, teacher 1966-. **Orgs:** Chmn Dept of Modern Lang; mem Amer Assoc of Teachers of French, Modern Lang Assoc. **Military Serv:** US Army, 1942-46. **Business Addr:** Teacher, Univ of Missouri, 8001 Natural Bridge Road, St Louis, MO 63103.

ALLEN, MARCUS
Professional football player (retired), sports commentator. **Personal:** Born Mar 26, 1960, San Diego, CA; married Kathryn. **Educ:** Univ of Southern California. **Career:** Los Angeles Raiders, running back, 1982-93; Kansas City Chiefs, 1993-98; CBS Sports, commentator, 1998-. **Honors/Awds:** Holds NCAA record for 200 yard rushing games with 11; established 12 NCAA records and tied another; played in Hula Bowl and Olympic Gold Bowl; Walter Camp, Maxwell Club and Football News Awds as Coll Player of the Year; Heisman Trophy winner 1981; set an all time single season rushing record with 2,342 yds; led NFL in scoring as rookie in 1982 with 84 pts in 9 games; Top receiver among AFC backs 3 straight years 1982-84; MVP 1983 Super Bowl; set Super Bowl rushing record with 191 yds; highest scoring non-kicker in NFL with 108 pts 1984; mem Pro Bowl team 5 times; named NFL's MVP by Professional Football Writers Assoc and the Associated Press; Player of the Year by The Sporting News and Football News; Offensive Player of Year by UPI; led NFL in rushing with Raider record 1,759 yds duringurth pro season; most consecutive games, 100 plus yards rushing (9), 1985; Pro Bowl, 1982, 1984, 1985, 1986, 1987, 1993. **Business Addr:** Commentator/Analyst, CBS Sporst, 51 W 52nd St, New York, NY 10019, (212)975-4321.

ALLEN, MARK
Civic leader. **Personal:** Born Mar 18, 1962, Chicago, IL; son of Minor Sr and Ollie Allen; children: Dania, Markus. **Educ:** Western Illinois University, BA, 1986. **Career:** Citizen Action-Midwest Academy, asst to national co-dir, 1986-87; Push for Excellence, project dir-Chicago Office, 1987-88; Jesse Jackson for President '88, natl youth coordinator/natl field staff, 1988; Operation Push, interim chief of staff/special projects coordinator, 1988-89; Chicago Urban League, voter educational/govt relations specialists, 1989-92; Chicago Rehab Network, field coordinator, 1993; Illinois Dept of Human Rights, human rights investigator, 1994-. **Orgs:** Black Leadership Devel Institute, founder/pres, 1989-;Natl Coalition on Black Voter Participation, local coordinator, 1989-; Chicago Urban Policy Institute, 1991; Kappa Alpha Psi Fraternity, 1987; Black elected Officials of Illinois, 1990-; Chicago School Board Nominating Commission, vice chair, 1989-; Task Force for Black Political Empowerment, 1986-. **Honors/Awds:** Monroe Foundation, Community Service Award, 1994; Dollars and Sense Magazine, America's Best and Brightest, 1989; United American Progress Assn, Man of the Year, 1989; Kool Achiever Awards, Chicago Area Finalist, 1990. **Special Achievements:** "Voices of the Electorate," Natl PBS TV Documentary on 92 Presidential Elections; Analyst, Live Broadcast "Front and Center" Chicagoland TV News on Urban Violence, 1994. **Home Phone:** (312)365-7489. **Business Addr:** President, Black Leadership Development Inst, 334 E 37th St, Chicago, IL 60653, (312)723-6275.

ALLEN, MAXINE BOGUES
Educational administrator. **Personal:** Born Jul 31, 1942, Portsmouth, VA; daughter of Essie M Kemp and Raymond A Bogues (deceased); married George Stanley Allen; children: Vanya A Belk. **Educ:** Norfolk State Univ, BS 1966; Hampton Univ, MA 1972; Virginia Polytech Inst & State Univ, EdD 1976. **Career:** Portsmouth City Schools, head of math dept 1966-74; Norfolk State Univ, prof of math 1976-79, dir inst rsch AA/EEO 1980-86, exec asst to pres dir inst rsch 1986-87; associate vice president for academic affairs 1987-; director, institutional research and planning, 1980-. **Orgs:** Mem Alpha Kappa Alpha Sor 1974-; consultant A&T Univ 1978-79; consultant Inst for Services to Educ 1982; bd of trustees Southeastern Univs Rsch Assoc 1984-; pres Suffolk Chap of The Links Inc 1985-92; bd dirs WHRO Educ TV 1986-92; school bd vice chair, Suffolk City 1986-92; member, The Moles, Inc, 1990-. **Honors/Awds:** Math Textbook for Health Science NSU Press 1978; Administrative/Mgmt Grant Title III 1980-96; Presidential Citation, Assn for Equal Opportunity, 1988; Administrator of the Year, Norfolk State Univ, 1996. **Business Addr:** Associate Vice President, Academic Affairs, Director, Institutional Research and Planning, Norfolk State University, 410 Wilson Hall, 2401 Corprew Ave, Norfolk, VA 23504, (757)683-8679.

ALLEN, MINNIE LOUISE
Health insurance. **Personal:** Born Jun 28, 1956, Lilesville, NC. **Educ:** Durham Business Coll, AAS 1976; Attended, NC Central Univ, Univ of SC. **Career:** Duke Power Co, programmer 1977-78; Blue Cross Blue Shield of SC, programmer systems analyst 1978-86; Blue Cross Blue Shield of TN, systems analyst 1986-. **Orgs:** Program chairperson Amer Business Women Las Mujeres Chap 1984; health fair volunteer NAACP. **Honors/Awds:** Woman of the Year Amer Business Women Assoc 1984. **Business Addr:** Systems Analyst, Blue Cross Blue Shield of TN, 730 Chestnut St, Chattanooga, TN 37403.

ALLEN, OTTIS EUGENE, JR.
Educational administrator. **Personal:** Born Feb 2, 1953, Fletcher, NC; son of Georgia Bradley Allen and Eugene Allen (deceased); married Vanessa R Northcutt; children: Dawn, Ottis III, Eboni. **Educ:** Appalachian State Univ, BA 1975, MA 1976; Univ of SC, additional studies in Ed TV; Spartanburg Methodist Coll, additional studies in Computer Science. **Career:** Council on Ministries of the United Methodist Church of SC, field coord 1981; Radio Shack Corp, salesman 1982-; Spartanburg Methodist Coll, dir of audio-visual services, assoc librarian/dir of multimedia services, currently. **Orgs:** Mem SC Library Assn 1977-; mem Piedmont Library Assn 1980-; mem Mt Moriah Baptist Church 1980-; chmn of sound comm Mt Moriah Baptist Church 1983-; mem bd of trustees Mt Moriah Baptist Church 1983-; mem United Way Allocation Comm of Spartanburg 1986-; mem, Epsilon Nu Chapter of Omega Psi Phi Fraternity, 1987-. **Honors/Awds:** Trustee of the Year, Mount Moriah Baptist Church, 1990; Omega Man of the Year, Epsilon Nu Chapter of Omega Psi Phi Fraternity Inc, 1990, 1992. **Home Addr:** 208 Sheffield Dr, Spartanburg, SC 29301. **Business Addr:** Assoc Librarian/Dir of Multimedia Services, Spartanburg Methodist College, 1200 Textile Road, Spartanburg, SC 29301.

ALLEN, PERCY, II
Hospital administrator. **Personal:** Born Apr 7, 1941, New Orleans, LA; son of Esther Anderson Allen and Percy Allen, Sr; married Zennia Marie McKnight; children: Merrily Marie Littlejohn, Percy III. **Educ:** Delgado Trade & Tech Inst, 1965; Oakland Univ Rochester MI, BA Econ 1973; Cornell Univ Grad Sch of Bus & Pub Adminstrn, MPA 1975. **Career:** Gr New Mt Moriah Baptist Church, Detroit, MI, youth director/summer camp founder & director, 1968-73; Chrysler Corporation, Detroit, MI, quality control supervisor, 1968-70; Oakland Univ, Rochester, MI, residence hall director, 1972-73; Cornell Univ, Ithaca, NY, program consultant, 1973-75; Parkview Memorial Hospital, Fort Wayne, IN, asst hospital administrator, beginning 1975; Sinai Hospital, asst administrator; Univ Hospital of Brooklyn, chief executive officer/vice pres for hospital affairs, 1989-. **Orgs:** Exec com NE IN Emergency Med Serv Commn 1977-; mem Emrgcy Med Serv Commn IN Hosp Assn 1978-; mem Counc on Hlth Care Dlvry Sys IN Hosp Assn 1979-; 1st vice pres Ft Wayne Urban Leag 1976-; bd mem Am Cancer Soc 1977-; 1st vice pres Allen Co Oppor Indstrlztn Ctr 1978-; bd mem United Way of Allen Co 1979-; past president, National Assn of Health Service Executives; fellow, American College of Healthcare Executives; program development committee member, Greater New York Hospital Assn; board member, Colony South Brooklyn Houses, Inc. **Honors/Awds:** Outst ldrshp serv Oakland U Rochester MI 1971-73; in apprctn for serv as fdr & dir of smmr cmpng prgm Mt Moriah Bapt Ch Detroit 1973; recog for 1st in empl postn Union Bapt Ch Ft Wayne IN 1976; cert of apprctn Sickle Cell Found 1979. **Military Serv:** US Air Force, E-4, 1959-64. **Business Addr:** Vice Pres for Hospital Affairs, CEO, University Hospital of Brooklyn, SUNY Health Science Center at Brooklyn, 445 Lenox Rd, Al-359, Brooklyn, NY 11203.

ALLEN, PHILIP C.
Internal audit manager. **Personal:** Born Nov 20, 1936, Pittsburgh, PA; son of Vivian A Taylor and Elmer C Allen; divorced; children: Lauretta L, Wanda I, Karl C, Phylis D, Michelle L, Sylvia D, Arthur K, Marlyn L, Tracy, David, Brandy, Philip M. **Educ:** Univ of Pittsburgh, BBA 1958; retail mgmt school 1960; systems engineering school (IBM) 1962; banking mgmt school Brown Univ 1966; Dale Carnegie training 1967; advanced audit school, Inst of Internal Auditors 1972; Univ of Pittsburgh, MEd 1977. **Career:** May Co-Kaufmanns Dept Store, asst buyer 1959-60; IBM Corp, systems engr 1960-65; Dollar Savings Bank, internal auditor 1965-67; PPG Ind, sr EDP auditor 1967-73; Comm Coll of Allegheny Co, director of internal audit 1973-. **Orgs:** Basileus Omega Psi Phi 1962; treas Bidwell Cultural & Training Ctr 1969; treas Pro-Sports Orgn 1975-; chmn US Bond Dr CCAC 1976; vice pres CCAC Credit Union 1977-; bd mem United Way of Amer 1977-; vice chmn Allegheny YMCA 1978-80; mem NAACP, Amer Mgmt Assn, Inst of Internal Auditors, EDP Auditors Found; pres CCAC Credit Union 1984-; bd mem United Negro Coll Fund. **Honors/Awds:** Distinguished Serv Awd United Way 1977-79; Distinguished Serv Awd YMCA 1978-79; Cert Data Processing Auditor CDPA, EDP Auditors Found 1979; certified information systems auditor CISA 1982. **Business Addr:** Director of Internal Audit, Comm Coll of Allegheny County, 800 Allegheny Ave, Pittsburgh, PA 15233.

ALLEN, RAY (WALTER)
Professional basketball player. **Personal:** Born Jul 20, 1975, Merced, CA; children: Tierra. **Educ:** Connecticut. **Career:** Milwaukee Bucks, guard, 1996-. **Honors/Awds:** Big East Player of the Year, 1996; NBA All-Rookie Second Team, 1997. **Special Achievements:** NBA Draft, First round pick, #5, 1996; appeared in starring role, He Got Game, 1998. **Business Addr:** Professional Basketball Player, Milwaukee Bucks, 1001 N 4th St, Bradley Ctr, Milwaukee, WI 53203, (414)227-0500.

ALLEN, ROBERT
Law enforcement official. **Career:** Indianapolis Police Dept, asst police chief, currently. **Business Addr:** Asst Police Chief, Indianapolis Police Dept, 50 N Alabama St, Indianapolis, IN 46204, (317)327-6509.

ALLEN, ROBERT L.
Editor. **Personal:** Born May 29, 1942, Atlanta, GA; son of Sadie Sims Allen and Robert Lee Allen; married Janet Carter, Jun 11, 1995; children: Casey Douglass; married Pamela Parker, Aug 25, 1965 (divorced). **Educ:** Attended Univ of Vienna, 1961-62; Morehouse College, BS, 1963; attended Columbia Univ, 1963-64; New School for Social Research, New York NY, MA, 1967; Univ of California, San Francisco, PhD, 1983. **Career:** Guardian Newsweekly NYC, staff reporter 1967-69; San Jose State Coll, asst prof new coll & black studies dept 1969-72; The Black Scholar Mag, editor; Mills College, Oakland CA, began as lecturer, became asst prof of ethnic studies, 1973-84; Wild Trees Press, gen mgr, 1984-90; The Black Scholar, senior editor, 1990-; African-American & Ethnic Studies, University of California-Berkeley, visiting prof, 1994-. **Orgs:** Pres, Black World Foundation; mem, American Sociological Assn; mem, American Historical and Cultural Society; mem, Association of Black Sociologists; mem, Pacific Sociological Assn; mem, Council for Black Studies; Bay Area Black Journalists. **Honors/Awds:** Author "Black Awakening in Capitalist Amer" Doubleday, 1969, "Reluctant Reformers, The Impact of Racism on Amer Social Reform Movements" Howard Univ Press, 1974; Guggenheim fellowship, 1978; contributor to periodicals; author, The Port Chicago Mutiny, Warner Books, 1989; co-editor Brotherman Ballantine, 1995; Winner American Book Award, 1995. **Business Addr:** Senior Editor, The Black Scholar, PO Box 2869, Oakland, CA 94618.

ALLEN, S. MONIQUE NICOLE
Publisher. **Personal:** Born Dec 20, 1964, New York, NY; daughter of Sallie Tucker-Allen and Charles Allen. **Educ:** Princeton University, Princeton, NJ, AB, 1986. **Career:** Tucker Publications, Inc, Lisle, IL, vice president, 1989-. **Orgs:** The Links, Inc, recording secretary. **Business Addr:** Vice President, Tucker Publications, 5823 Queens Cove, Lisle, IL 60532, (708)969-3809.

ALLEN, SAMUEL WASHINGTON
Poet, educator (retired). **Personal:** Born Dec 9, 1917, Columbus, OH; son of Jewett Washington and Alexander Joseph Allen; divorced; children: Marie-Christine Catherine. **Educ:** Fisk Univ, AB 1938; Harvard Law Sch, JD 1941; New Sch for Soc Rsch, grad study 1946-47; Sorbonne, 1949-50. **Career:** NYC, dep asst dist atty 1946-47; USAF Europe, civilian employment 1951-55; NYC, general practice, 1956-57; TX So Univ, assoc prof 1958-60; Washington, DC, atty 1961-68; Tuskegee Inst, prof 1968-70; Wesleyan Univ, vis prof 1970-71; Boston Univ, prof 1971-81; professor emeritus, 1981-. **Orgs:** Mem, vp, bd dirs So Educ Found Atlanta 1969-76; mem bd dir Afrikan Heritage Inst Roxbury, MA 1974-78; bd New England Museum of African-American History; board mem, Boston Partners in Educ, 1986-91; mem bd of dir, Old South Meeting House, 1994; Commissioner, Massachusetts Historical Commission 1986-92; mem, board of directors, Blackside, Inc, 1988-97. **Honors/Awds:** Elfenbeinzahne (poems) 1956; translated Orphee Noir (Jean Paul Sartre), 1960; public reading and recording of poetry Libr of Congr Wash, DC 1972; NEA Award Poetry 1979; author pen name Paul Vesey, Ivory Tusks & Other Poems 1968; editor Poems from Africa 1973; Paul Vesey's Ledger (poems) 1975; Every Round (poems), 1987. **Military Serv:** US Army, 1st Lt 1942-46. **Home Addr:** 145 Cliff Ave, Winthrop, MA 02152.

ALLEN, SANFORD
Violinist. **Personal:** Born Feb 26, 1939, New York City, NY; married Madhur Jaffrey. **Educ:** Juilliard School of Music, attended; Mannes Coll of Music, attended. **Career:** Livingston Coll of Rutgers Univ, former faculty mem; NY Philharmonic, former violinist; violinist recitals, concerts, solo engagements. **Orgs:** Past adv panel NY Stte Arts Council; recorded Cordero Violin Concerto with Detroit Symphony on Black Composers Series; vchmn, adv comm HS Performing Arts Fed Music Clubs Awd. **Honors/Awds:** Won High Fidelity Mag Koussevitzky Intl Recording Awd 1974.

ALLEN, SHIRLEY JEANNE
Educator. **Personal:** Born Dec 19, 1941, Tyler, TX; daughter of Theressa Carter McDonald and Ralph C Allen; divorced. **Educ:** Talladega Coll, Music 1959-60; Jarvis Christian Coll Hawkins TX, Music 1960-63; Gallaudet Coll Wash DC, BA Eng Lit 1963-66; Howard Univ Wash DC, MA Couns 1969-72; Univ of Rochester, EdD, counseling, 1992. **Career:** Rochester Inst of Tech, assoc prof Gen educ 1973-; Gallaudet Coll Wash DC, couns instr 1967-73; US Peace Corp, clssfctn clk 1964-65; US IRS, ed clk; US Post Ofc, dist clk 1966-67. **Orgs:** Mem Nat Assn of Deaf; mem Conf of Am Instr of Deaf; mem Am Assn of Univ Prof; mem Nat Assn of Women in Education; representative Natl Black Deaf Advocates. **Honors/Awds:** Believed to be the first Black deaf female to earn a doctoral degree, 1992; Quota Internation's, Natl Deaf Woman of the Year, 1993; Inducted into the Jarvis Christian Coll Pioneer Hall of Fame, 1994; CA State Dept of Rehabilitation & Los Angeles Black Deaf Advocates Achievement Award, 1994; Special Achievement Award from Campbell Alumni Assn. **Special Achievements:** Received BA, MA, & EdD after becoming deaf in 1962. **Business Addr:** Associate Professor, Rochester Inst of Technology, One Lomb Memorial Drive, PO Box 9887, Rochester, NY 14623.

ALLEN, STANLEY M.
Airline pilot. **Personal:** Born Dec 6, 1941, Washington, DC; married Josita E Hair; children: Khyron Shane, Kesha Lynette. **Educ:** Howard Univ, BA 1965. **Career:** Eastern Airlines Inc, airline pilot. **Orgs:** Mem Airline Pilots Assoc; co-capt Howard Univ Football 1964; sr class pres Fairmont Hts HS 1960. **Honors/Awds:** MD State High Hurdles Champion 1960. **Military Serv:** USAF capt 1965-70. **Business Addr:** Airline Pilot, Eastern Airlines Inc, Washington Natl Airport, Washington, DC.

ALLEN, TAJE
Professional football player. **Personal:** Born Nov 6, 1973. **Educ:** Univ of Texas, bachelors degree in sports management. **Career:** St Louis Rams, defensive back, 1997-. **Business Addr:** Professional Football Player, St Louis Rams, One Rams Way, St Louis, MO 63045, (314)982-7267.

ALLEN, TERRELL ALLISON, III
Association executive. **Personal:** Born Feb 10, 1959, Washington, DC. **Educ:** Howard Univ, BS Elec Engrg 1982; Univ of Pennsylvania, MBA Finance 1987. **Career:** Eastman Kodak Co, coop educ student 1978-81; Howard Univ, electronics lab asst 1980-82; Commonwealth Edison Co, general engr 1982-85; Coopers & Lybrand,consultant; Wharton Black MBA Assoc, pres. **Orgs:** Vice pres Phi Beta Sigma Frat Inc Alpha Chap 1981-82; comm chmn Chicago Jr Assoc of Commerce and Industry 1982-85; science club dir Chicago Adopt-A-School Program 1982-85. **Honors/Awds:** Outstanding Young Men of Amer 1984; Leadership Awd/Fellowship Johnson & Johnson Family of Companies 1985; Fellowship Consortium for Grad Study in Mgmt 1985. **Business Addr:** c/o Denise McGregor, National Black MBA Association, PO Box 1384, Philadelphia, PA 19105.

ALLEN, TERRY THOMAS, JR.
Professional football player. **Personal:** Born Feb 21, 1968, Commerce, GA; married Annette; children: Shayna, Haley. **Educ:** Clemson, attended. **Career:** Minnesota Vikings, running back, 1991-94; Washington Redskins, 1995-. **Honors/Awds:** Pro Bowl, 1996. **Business Addr:** Professional Football Player, Washington Redskins, 13832 Redskin Dr, Herndon, VA 22071, (703)471-9100.

ALLEN, TREMAYNE
Professional football player. **Personal:** Born Aug 9, 1974. **Educ:** Florida. **Career:** Chicago Bears, tight end, 1997-. **Business Addr:** Professional Football Player, Chicago Bears, 1000 Football Dr, Halas Hall at Conway Park, Lake Forest, IL 60045-4829, (847)295-6600.

ALLEN, TY W.
Transportation company executive. **Personal:** Born Jun 27, 1961, Denver, CO; son of Carleen Matis Allen and Elijah Allen. **Educ:** University of Colorado, Denver, CO, English, political science, 1979-83. **Career:** Burlington Northern Air Freight, sales, 1982-85; C F Air Freight, sales, 1985; Worldwide Air Freight, president, 1985-88; AFI International Forwarding, founder, 1988-. **Business Addr:** Founder, Director, AFI International Forwarding, Inc, Domestic & International Sales & Operations, 4665 Paris St, Ste 100, Denver, CO 80237.

ALLEN, VAN SIZAR
Educational administrator. **Personal:** Born Apr 2, 1926, Edwards, MS; son of Edna Sizar Allen and Van Allen; married Mary Frances Cartwright Allen, Dec 1, 1990; children: Van S Jr, Nathaniel B. **Educ:** Tougaloo Coll, BA 1950; Univ of MI, MS 1952; Yale Univ, Certificate 1955; Univ of NC, MPH 1962, PhD 1969. **Career:** Bennett Coll, assoc prof 1952-68; Guilford Co Anti-Poverty Prog, deputy dir 1966-68; Southern Regional Educ Bd, assoc dir of inst of higher educ opp 1969-71; TACTICS, exec dir 1971-80; Tougaloo Coll, vice pres for acad affrs 1980-85; Paul Quinn Coll, vice pres for acad affairs 1985-87, 1989-90, vice pres/CEO Waco Campus, 1990-; dir of the Central Texas Cancer Network Program 1988-89. **Orgs:** Mem Amer Assoc of Univ Profs, Beta Kappa Chi Scientific Soc, Natl Inst of Science, Amer Assoc for the Advancement of Sci; mem John Hay Whitney Oppor Fellow Org, Phi Delta Kappa Natl Educ Frat; mem NC Comm Develop Assoc, Omega Psi Phi Frat, Sigma Pi Phi Frat; mem NAACP, SOPHE; pres Tougaloo Coll Natl Alumni Assoc 1978-80; chmn Tougaloo Coll Natl Alumni Fundraising Campaign 1980-84. **Honors/Awds:** John Hay Whitney Oppor Fellowship Univ of MI 1950; Natl Science Foundation Scholarship Univ of NC 1960; Centennial Awd for Disting Serv to Tougaloo Coll 1970; Alumnus of the Year Tougaloo Coll 1977; Presidential Citation/NAFFOHE/For exemplary experience that honors Alma Mater, Washington DC 1979; Meritorious Serv TACTICS Prog 1980; Outstanding Serv Awd Greensboro NC Public Housing Auth 1981; Tougaloo Comm Alumni Club Awd 1984; Outstanding Commitment to Strengthening Black Colls & Univs NAFEO 1987; numerous publications and book reviews. **Military Serv:** USN 3rd class petty officer 1944-46; Asiatic Theater Ribbon, Good Conduct Ribbon. **Home Addr:** 225 Garrison St, Waco, TX 76704.

ALLEN, W. GEORGE
Attorney. **Personal:** Born Mar 3, 1936, Sanford, FL; married Enid Meadows; children: Timothy, Frederick, Amy. **Educ:** FL A&M Univ, BA (Hon) Pol Sci 1954; Univ FL Law School, JD 1962. **Career:** FL Human Relations Comm, commiss; Orr & Kaplan Miami, attny 1963; Private practice, attny 1963-. **Orgs:** Commiss FL Ethics Commiss; mem FL FL Adv Commiss, US Civil Rights Comm, Govs prop Rights Study Commun; mem, pres elect 1974-75 Natl Bar Assoc; mem FL Bar Assoc, Broward Cty Bar Assoc, Amer Trial Lawyers Assoc, FL Acad of Trail Lawyers, Broward Crim Defense Assoc, Natl Assoc of Crim Defense Lawyers, NAACP, Alpha Phi Alpha, Elks, YMCA, FL A&M Univ Alumni Assoc, State of FL. **Honors/Awds:** 1st black to finish the Univ of FL; 1st black to work in integrated law firm. **Military Serv:** US Army, 1st lt spec agent CIC 1958-60. **Business Addr:** Attorney, 116 SE 6 Ct, Fort Lauderdale, FL 33301.

ALLEN, WALTER R.
Educator. **Personal:** Born Aug 18, 1930, Allendale, SC; married Mary Clay; children: Walter Jr, Jeffrey, Brian. **Educ:** Claflin College, AB, 1951; Oberlin College, BM, 1957; Western Reserve University, MA, MM, 1960; University of Georgia, EdD, 1974. **Career:** Shoals High School, asst principal; University of Georgia, asst professor; Faulkner State Junior College, Dept of Fine Arts, professor, currently. **Orgs:** Kappa Alpha Psi; Phi Delta Kappa; Kappa Kappa Psi; 32nd Degree Mason; American Psych Assn; Natl Assn of Musicologists; educator, Haile Selassie in Ethiopia; social psychologist, musician & administrator, 100 Percenters Org; Hill First Baptist Church; NAACP; Free Lance Musician. **Honors/Awds:** Kappa Alpha Psi Achievement Award; 100 Percenters Award; Educators Award; Phi Delta Kappa Award; Natl Assn of Musicologists; Kappa Kappa Psi Award. **Military Serv:** US Army, 1951-53. **Business Addr:** Professor, Dept of Fine Arts, Faulkner State Junior College, Bay Minette, AL 36507-2698.

ALLEN, WENDELL
Business consultant. **Personal:** Born Aug 21, 1947, Chattanooga, TN; children: Kristen, Adrienne, Ian. **Educ:** Fisk Univ, BA, 1970; Case Western Reserve Univ School of Law, 1970-72; Eastern MI Univ, MPA, 1987. **Career:** General Motors Corp., Fisher Body Div, conf leader, 1972-73, Hydra-Matic Div, human resources executive, 1976-80; Amer Steel Corp, corp mgr, 1973-75; Paine Webber Jackson & Curtis, stockbroker, 1975-76; City of Ann Arbor, 1st Ward, councilman, 1976-78; Washtenaw County, commissioner, 1978-80; Univ of MI, contracts compliance officer, 1980-81; Catherine McAuley Hlth Systems, executive asst to president, 1980-91; Mercy Hlth Services, public affairs executive, 1991-92; Wendell Allen & Associates, senior associate, 1992-. **Orgs:** Oppty Indust Ctr, board of directors, 1977, Cleveland, secretary, board of directors, 1972-75; Phi Alpha Delta Intl Law Frat; Prince Hall F&AM Masons; Alpha Phi Alpha; Kiwanis Intl; Repub Party; Ann Arbor Chamber of Commerce, board of directors, 1981-82; MI Hospital Assn, legislative cmte, 1984-88; MI Catholic Hlth Assn, legisltve and public policy steering cmte, vice chair, 1986-88; St Andrews Episcopal Ch, vestry mbr, 1987-90; Boy Scouts of America, Wolverine Cncl, Washtenaw Dist Cmsnr, 1988-92, Natl Eagle Scout Assn, 1976-, Woodbadge Assn, 1992; Hlth Care Braintrust of Southeast MI, co-fndr, 1983-; MI Assn of Alcohol and Drug Abuse Counslrs, bd mbr/newsltr editor, 1990-92; MI Coalition of Substance Abuse, legisltve advsr, 1987-; United Community Services of Metro Detroit, Oakland Div, bd mbr, 1991-; MI Communities in Action for Drug-Free Youth, bd mbr, 1990-; MIg Eductn Advsry Cmte, 1991-; MI Coalition for Diabetes Eductn and Minority Hlth, president, 1991-. **Honors/Awds:** MI Department of Public Hlth, Distinguished Dr Martin Luther King Jr, Community Service Award, 1993.

ALLEN, WILLIAM BARCLAY
Educator. **Personal:** Born Mar 18, 1944, Fernandina Beach, FL; son of Rosa Lee Johnson Allen (deceased) and Rev James P Allen; married Susan Ayers Macall; children: Danielle Susan, Bertrand Marc. **Educ:** Pepperdine Coll, BA 1967; Claremont Grad School, MA 1968, PhD 1972. **Career:** Univ de Rouen, lecteur 1970-71; The Amer Univ, asst prof 1971-72; Harvey Mudd Coll, asst prof 1972-76, assoc prof 1976-83; St John's Coll Grad Inst, visiting tutor 1977-; Harvey Mudd Coll, prof of govt, 1983-94; Michigan State University, James Madison College, dean, 1993-. **Orgs:** Mem Claremont Rotary 1980-86; mem pres Claremont Unified School Dist Bd 1981-84; bd mem CA Assembly Fellowship Prog 1982-92; prog dir Liberty Fund Inc1982-89; chmn CA Scholars for Reagan 1984; bd mem LeRoy Boys Home; mem Natl Council for the Humanities, 1984-87; mem Am Pol Sci Assoc, Academie Montesquieu; mem, Chair US Commission on Civil Rights, 1987-92; US Civil Rights Commission, CA State Adv Committee, 1985-87. **Honors/Awds:** Fulbright Fellowship 1970-71; Kellogg Natl Fellow WK Kellogg Found 1984-87; Prix Montesquieu Academic France 1986; Pi Sigma Alpha, Sigma Alpha; LID, Pepperdine University, 1988. **Military Serv:** USATC 1968, Colonel's Orderly. **Business Addr:** Dean, James Madison College, Michigan State Univ, Dean's Office, East Lansing, MI 48825-1205.

ALLEN, WILLIAM DUNCAN
Musician. **Personal:** Born Dec 15, 1906, Portland, OR; son of Lillian Medley Allen (deceased) and William Duncan Allen Sr (deceased). **Educ:** Oberlin Coll, Bachelor of Music 1928; Juilliard School of Music, certificate 1929; Oberlin Coll, master of music 1936; David Mannes School of Music, certificate 1939. **Career:** Howard Univ School of Music, instructor Piano 1929-35; Fisk Univ, assistant prof 1936-43; Talladega Coll, visiting prof of Piano 1980-82. **Orgs:** Pres Golden Gate Branch/Music Tchrs Assn CA 1970-74, Golden Gate Branch/Natl Assn Negro Musicians 1970-74; counselor San Fran Boy's Chorus 1957-62; music dir Jr Bach Fesitval, Berkeley 1956-76; mnstr of music S Berkeley Comm Church 1954-79; ACT-SO NAACP Program; Accompanist ''Art of the Spiritual'' Concert Carnegie Hall 1987, 1988 & 1989; board mem, Stern Gove Festival Assn, San Francisco; board mem, DeBose Natl Piano Competitions, Southern University, Baton Rouge, LA; board member, Center for Black Music Research, Chicago, IL, 1988-. **Honors/Awds:** Doctorate of Music Black Theological School for Urban Studies, Berkeley 1978; 11th Annual Afro-Amer Music Workshop Homage Atlanta Univ Center 1982. **Special Achievements:** 85th birthday was celebrated with a concert in Oakland, California, featuring 24 artist colleagues from all over the United States, 1991. **Home Addr:** 3400 Richmond Parkway Dr, Hilltop Bayview #4009, Richmond, CA 94806-5235.

ALLEN, WILLIAM HENRY
Dentist, educator. **Personal:** Born Jan 27, 1917, New Orleans, LA; son of Victoria Allen and William H Allen; married Martha Mae Mosley (deceased). **Educ:** Tougaloo Coll, AB 1935; Meharry Medical Coll, DDS 1943; Univ of Michigan, Postgraduate 1944. **Career:** Meharry Medical Coll, Nashville TN, instructor 1943-44; School of Dentistry, asst prof dental materials, prosthetics & clinical dentistry 1945-47, acting dean 1946-47, dir, dean, dental educ 1949-50, dean 1950-71, prof prosthetics, dir div dental technology 1947-86; professor emeritus, 1986. **Orgs:** Mem Council Natl Bd Dental Examiners; pres Capitol City Dental Soc 1958-59; mem Pan-TN, Amer, TN, Natl Dental Assoc, Amer Assoc Dental Schools; advisory comm Negro Scholarship Program, Amer Fund for Dental Educ; dental training comm Natl Inst Dental Research 1971-; regional med advisory comm, fellow AAAS; hon mem AL State Dental Soc; mem Amer Assoc Cleft Palate Rehabilitation, Amer Assoc Dental Schools, Nashville Dental Soc, Amer Assoc Endodontists, Kappa Sigma Pi, Kappa Alpha Psi, Omicron Kappa Upsilon, Chi Boul Frat; mem, Dental Materials Group Assoc, Int Assoc Dental Research. **Honors/Awds:** Author of articles to professional journals.

ALLEN, WILLIAM OSCAR
Business executive. **Personal:** Born Nov 29, 1923, Tuscaloosa, AL; married Ruth Jordan; children: Gwendolyn, Renee, William III. **Educ:** Tuskegee Inst, BS 1947; Columbia Univ, Cert 1958; NY Univ School of Publ Admin & Health Svc, MPA 1972. **Career:** Knickerbocker Hosp, admin asst 1963-68, asst exec dir 1968-70; AC Logan Meml Hosp, exec dir 1970-. **Orgs:** Mem Amer Coll of Hosp Admins, Amer Publ Health Assoc, House of Del, Hosp Assoc of NY State, 100 Black Men. **Honors/Awds:** Comm Serv Awd for Health 1972; Outstanding Achievement Awd Assoc PTA Tuscaloosa AL 1974; Outstanding Achievement Awd Tuscaloosa Womens Club 1974. **Business Addr:** Executive Dir, AC Logan Memorial Hospital, 70 Convent Ave, New York, NY 10027.

ALLEN, WILLIE B.
Clergyman. **Personal:** Born Jul 12, 1921, Richmond, VA; son of Susie B Allen and John H Allen; married Ella Sizer; children: 6 sons, 1 daughter. **Educ:** VA Union Univ, attended; Monrovia Coll & Indus Inst West Africa, Hon Doctor of Humane Letters 1984. **Career:** Bethlehem Baptist Church Washington, pastor; Upper Room Baptist Ch Washington, pastor/founder/organizer 1957-. **Orgs:** Mem Progressive Natl Baptist Convention Inc; former pres Baptist Ministers' Conf of Washington & Vicinity; pres Ministers' Youth Advocacy Comm of Metro Police Dept;

founder/first pres North East Center for the Amer Red Cross; former pres Ministerial Alliance of Far North East Washington; former mem Mayor's Advisory Comm on Alcoholism; chaplain Greater Southeast Hospital; chief consultant DC Substance Abuse Partnership Program; mem District of Columbia Armory Bd Stadium Advisory Comm 1989-; president/founder/ organizer Allen House Home for the Elderly District of Columbia, 1990-. **Honors/Awds:** Hon Doctor of Divinity VA Seminary and Coll Lynchburg VA 1985. **Business Addr:** Pastor Emeritus, Upper Room Baptist Church, 60 Burns Street, NE, Washington, DC 20019.

ALLEN, WINSTON EARLE
Business executive. **Personal:** Born May 28, 1933, New York, NY; married Ruby; children: Vaughn, Julie. **Educ:** NY Univ Washington Square Coll of Arts & Sci, BA 1955; City Coll of NY, MA 1958; Fordham Univ, PhD 1971. **Career:** New York City Bd of Educ, teacher of econ 1956-68; Fordham Univ, asst prof 1970-72; George Washington Univ and American University, adj prof mgmt sci dept 1974-75; Creative Investor Serv Inc, pres 1962-; Xerox Corp Educ Planning & Devel, mgr 1972-82; Innovative Health Products, Inc, 1991-. **Orgs:** BD mem, US Comm for UNICEF 1972-82; mem Phi Delta Kappa Professional Frat; Sunrise Rotary of Westport, Connecticut, board of directors; chairman, Westport Conservation Commission, 1989-93; Zoning Board of Appeals, Westport, CT, 1993-; president-elect, Westport Sunrise Rotary, 1997-98. **Honors/Awds:** Fulbright Grant Inst d'Etudes Politques Univ of Paris France 1962; Paul Harris Fellow Awd, Rotary International. **Home Addr:** 4 Burritts Landing, Westport, CT 06880. **Business Phone:** (203)227-4897.

ALLEN, ZULINE GRAY
Public health administrator. **Personal:** Born Feb 10, 1947, Philadelphia, PA; daughter of Gladys & Arthur Sr; divorced; children: Archibald IV, Thomas S. **Educ:** Temple Univ, Sch of Liberal Arts, BA, 1968; Univ of PA, Sch of Social Work, MSW, 1972, doctoral student, 1991; LaSalle Univ, bilingual-bicultural studies, 1990-91. **Career:** American Lung Assn, Philadelphia, program dir, 1975-79; Pottstown Memorial Med Ctr, dir, social work, 1980-86; Albert Einstein Med Ctr, dir, social work, 1987-91; Boston Dept of Health, Hospitals, dir, social work, 1991-. **Orgs:** Natl Assn of Social Workers, MA Chapter; Soc for Social Work Administrators in Health Care of the American Hosp Assn, Eastern PA Chaper; Soc for Hosp Social Work Directors of the Hosp Assn of PA; Soc for Hosp Social Work Admins in Health Care of the Amer Hosp Assn, Natl Org; Parents and Childrens Servs Inc, bd of dirs; Brookside Health Ctr, Urban Youth Connection Prog, adv comm, 1991-; Central Boston Elder Servs, bd of dirs; Roxbury Youthworks, bd of dirs, 1993-; numerous past memberships. **Honors/Awds:** Dollars & Sense Magazine, America's Outstanding Business and Professional Women Award, 1993; Accion Communal Latino Americano de Montgomery County, Norristown, PA, Service Award, 1990; Tri-County Long Term Care Committee, Founder's Award, 1989; Univ of PA, Sch of Social Work, Alumni Achievement Award, 1987; Soc for Hosp Social Work Dirs, Helen B Clark Award, 1987. **Special Achievements:** Presentations: Moderator, "Another Dimension of Domestic Violence," A Forum on Elderly Abuse, Dept of Health and Hosps, 1994; Faculty, "Healthcare Reform," Univ of PA, Sch of Social Work, 1994; Conducted various workshops and seminars, Univ of PA Sch of Social Work, Temple Univ, etc; Publications: "Understanding Cultural Diversity," Discharge Planning Update, 1992; "Effective Communication: Basics to Discharge Planning," Discharge Planning Update, 1992; numerous others; fluent in Spanish. **Business Addr:** Director, Assistant Deputy Commissioner, Boston Dept of Health & Hospitals, 818 Harrison Ave, Boston, MA 02118, (617)534-5458.

ALLEN-JONES, PATRICIA ANN
Journalist. **Personal:** Born Nov 9, 1958, Pittsburg, CA; daughter of Bettye J Allen and William J Allen; married George Wallace Jones Jr, May 25, 1991. **Educ:** California State University, BA, 1981. **Career:** The Neighbor News, reporter, 1981-83; The Suncoast News, reporter, 1983-84; Florida Sentinel Bulletin, reporter, 1984-86; Leesburg Commercial Newspaper, reporter, 1986-88; Sarasota Herald-Tribune Newspaper, reporter, 1988-. **Orgs:** St Martha's Catholic Church, 1988-; Adult Black Achievers, 1992-. **Honors/Awds:** Easter Seal Society of Southwest Florida, Media Award, 1992. **Business Addr:** Journalist, Sarasota Herald-Tribune Newspaper, 801 S Tamiami Trail, Sarasota, FL 34236, (813)957-5167.

ALLEN-NOBLE, ROSIE ELIZABETH
Educational administrator. **Personal:** Born Jun 22, 1938, Americus, GA; daughter of Velma Douglas and Ulysses Grant Allen; married Apr 1963 (divorced); children: Antoinette Celine Noble-Webb. **Educ:** Albany State Coll, BS 1960; Atlanta Univ, MS 1967; Rutgers Univ, MS 1974, DEd, 1991. **Career:** Rutgers Univ, instructor 1970-76; Seton Hall Univ, visiting asst prof 1972-78; Univ of Medicine & Dentistry of NJ, instructor 1972-; Fairleigh Dickinson Univ, asst prof 1974-80; Upsala Coll, dir science enrichment program 1976-; Montclair State Coll, dir health careers program 1979-. **Orgs:** Mem Alpha Kappa Alpha Sorority 1959, Amer Assn of Univ Women 1969-; consultant Univ of Medicine & Dentistry of NJ 1972-; Soroptomist Intl 1974-; mem NJ Chapter of Albany State Coll Alumni Assn 1974, Natl Assn of Medical Minority Educ 1980; consultant/evaluator Univ of CT 1981-83; consultant Hobart William Smith Coll 1983, Long Island Univ 1984, Omicrom Xi Omega 1984; Wichita State Univ 1984; evaluation comm on Higher Educ Middle State Assoc Evaluation Team 1984; mem Natl Assoc Pre-Professional Advisors 1984, Natl Assn of Medical Minority Educ Inc natl treasurer 1984; consultant Univ of Medicine & Dentistry of NJ-school of Health Related Professions 1986-; NE regional director, Nat Assn Med Minority Educators, 1988-90; member, board of directors, National Assn Med Minority Educators, 1990; consultant, Gwynedd-Mercy College, 1987-. **Honors/Awds:** Honor student at all academic levels 1956-; Merit Award for Outstanding Serv, Montclair State Coll 1982; Outstanding Leadership & Serv, Upsala Coll 1982; Natl Science Found Grants; Numerous Fed, State & Private Found Fellowship Grants over the past 20 years; Outstanding Serv Award, Montclair State Coll 1984-85; Merit Award for Outstanding Serv, Montclair State College 1987. **Home Addr:** 364 Orange Rd C5, Montclair, NJ 07042. **Business Addr:** Dir, Health Careers Program, Montclair State College, School of Math & Nat Sciences, Valley Rd and Normal Ave, Richardson Hall Rm 368, Upper Montclair, NJ 07043.

ALLEN-RASHEED, JAMAL RANDY
Judiciary/corrections. **Personal:** Born Dec 15, 1953, Memphis, TN; married Jacquline Carlotte Gipson; children: Randy D. **Educ:** Southern IL Univ Carbondale, BS 1980; Prairie View A&M Univ, MA 1986. **Career:** KEWC-AM/FM Radio, disc jockey/reporter 1975-76; WPHD-NBC TV, news asst 1979-80; Black Observer Newspaper, managing editor 1979-80; WLS-ABC Network, productionengr 1980; Lackland Tailspinner Airforce Pub, reporter 1981; Forward Times Newspaper, asst circulation mgr 1982-83; Sam Houston State Univ/Housing, public relations dir 1983-84; The Martin Luther King Jr Ctr for Nonviolent Social Change Inc, comm develop asst 1984; TX Dept of Corrections, correctional officer 1984-86. **Orgs:** Mem Alpha Epsilon Rho Hon Radio/TV 1978-80; natl bd of dirs 1978-79, natl dir coll bro 1979-80 Alpha Phi Alpha Frat Inc; mem Sigma Delta Chi Prof Journalist 1979-80; publ relations dir Black Affairs Council SI U-C 1979-80; founder/dir The Martin Luther King Jr Inst for Afro-Amer Studies/Soc Change 1985-86; bd of dirs Hillvale Educ Assoc for Substance Abuse 1986-; mem Blacks in Soc, Blacks in Journalism, Blacks in Criminal Justice, 32 Degree Ancient & Accepted Scottish Rite Masonary Prince Hall Affiliation. **Honors/Awds:** Outstanding Serv to Midwest Region Alpha Phi Alpha 1979; Outstanding Serv on Bd of Dirs Alpha Phi Alpha 1979; Outstanding Serv Black Affairs Council SIU-C1980; Certificate for Training in Nonviolent Social Change The Martin Luther King Jr Ctr for Nonviolent Social Change Inc 1984; Intl Disting Young Leaders1987. **Military Serv:** USAF airman 1st class 2 yrs; Basic Training Leadership Awd.

ALLENSWORTH, JERMAINE LAMONT
Professional baseball player. **Personal:** Born Jan 11, 1972, Anderson, IN. **Educ:** Purdue. **Career:** Pittsburgh Pirates, outfielder, 1996-. **Business Addr:** Professional Baseball Player, Pittsburgh Pirates, PO Box 7000, Pittsburgh, PA 15212, (412)323-5000.

ALLEYNE, EDWARD D.
Roman Catholic priest. **Personal:** Born Jun 14, 1928, Brooklyn, NY. **Educ:** Catholic Univ of Amer, BA 1956. **Career:** Mother of the Savior Seminary, instructor 1960-67; various parishes in Diocese of Camden, assoc pastor 1968-84; St Monica's Church, pastor 1984-. **Orgs:** Dir Parkside Catholic Ctr 1971-75; mem Diocesan Bd of Educ 1969-; mem Diocesan Ecumenical Commn 1971-; mem Diocesan Campaign for Human Devel Com 1971-; mem Diocesan Social Justice Commn 1972-; Camden Region Moderator Diocesan PTA 1971-; Financial coord of Consolidated Catholic Sch in City of Camden 1972-75. **Business Addr:** Pastor, St Monica's RC Church, 108 N Pennsylvania Ave, Atlantic City, NJ 08401.

ALLIGOOD, DOUGLASS LACY
Business executive. **Personal:** Born Feb 15, 1934, St Louis, MO; son of Countess M Murphy Alligood and Forest D Alligood; married Linda A Monaco; children: Donna L Johnson, Craig F, Debra L, Douglass L Jr. **Educ:** Bradley Univ Peoria, IL, BFA 1956. **Career:** Seymour, Leatherwood & Cleveland, Inc, Detroit, staff artist/copywriter 1956; Radio Station WCHB, Detroit, MI, merch dir 1959-62; Batten, Barton Durstine & Osborn, Inc Detroit, acct exec 1962-64; Batten, Barton, Durstine & Osborn, Inc, NYC, sr acct exec 1964-71; dir, corp adv RCA Corp, New York 1971-83; pres UniWorld Group, Inc New York, NY 1983-84; senior vice pres, special markets, BBDO Inc 1984-. **Orgs:** Chairman, Health Watch Information & Promotion Svc, 1995-; Dir Adv Council 1976-, Intrnl Film & TV Festival of NY 1983-; mem, Amer Assn of Advertising Agencies EOO Committee 1986-93; speaker, Advertising Educational Foundation 1985-; Ethnic Perspectives Committee, chairman adv council, 1991-93. **Honors/Awds:** Hon degree humane letters King Memorial Coll 1976-; CEBA Advertising Campaign Awards 1980-82; "Five To Watch Award" Amer Women In Radio & TV, Detroit 1964; A P Phillips Lecturer, Univ of Florida 1989; Black Achievers in Industry Harlem Branch YMCA of Greater New York 1990; BBDO Founders Award, 1993; Bradley University Centurion, 1994; 2o Year Service Award, Adv Council, 1996. **Special Achievements:** An Analysis of Hispanic Audience Primetime Network Viewing Preferences, 1993-; An Analysis of Black Audience Primetime Network Viewing Preferences, 1984-; Media Opportunities Newsletter, 1991; Special markets Media Guidebook, 1993; Spindex Media Star, Advertising Age, 1997. **Military Serv:** USAF capt 1956-59. **Business Addr:** Senior Vice President Special Mkts, BBDO New York, 1285 Avenue of the Americas, New York, NY 10019.

ALLISON, FERDINAND V., JR.
Chief executive officer. **Personal:** Born Jan 15, 1923, Emporia, VA; son of Elizabeth R Allison and Ferdinand Vincent Allison Sr (deceased); married E Lavonia Ingram; children: Karen Michele Allison-Davis, Ferdinand Vincent Allison III. **Educ:** Hampton Inst, BS 1948; NYU, MBA 1952. **Career:** Army Air Force, inventory clerk, squadron clerk 1943-46; Hampton Inst, budget clerk 1948-50, invoice auditor 1952-53; Mutual Savings & Loan Assn, dir, pres 1953-, chairman, ceo. **Orgs:** Dir Natl Bus League; dir, past pres, chairman, Durham Bus & Professional Chain, Inc; past dir John Avery Boys Club; mem exec comm, chairman Durham Co Comm on Affairs of Black People; life mem NAACP; mem Omega Psi Phi; mem AS Hunter Lodge 825 F&AM; mem Durham Chap Hampton Inst Natl Alumni; mem Durham C of C; trustee White Rock Bapt Ch; mem Rotary Club of Durham; board of directors, executive committee, Savings and Community Bankers of America; Found for Better Health of Durham; board member NC Alliance Community Financial Inst; dir, exec comm Natl Bus League; trustee White Rock Baptist Church; mem Rotary Club of Durham; past chairman, vchmn Amer League of Financial Insts. **Military Serv:** USAC served 3 years. **Business Addr:** President, Chairman, CEO, Mutual Savings & Loan Assn, 112 W Parrish St PO Box 3827, Durham, NC 27702.

ALLISON, LUTHER. See Obituaries section.

ALLISON, VIVIAN
Consumer affairs executive. **Personal:** Born Aug 27, 1936; widowed; children: one (deceased). **Educ:** Fisk Univ, coursework in sociology, psychology, 1951-53; Wayne County Gen Hosp, medical technology internship, 1958-59; Wayne State Univ, BS, chemistry, 1958. **Career:** Robeson-Tubman Community Development Corp, 1970-79, bd of dirs, 1979-85, chairperson, 1981-85; Office of US Congressman John Conyers, congressional asst, 1980-93; Office of Wayne County Executive William Lucas, exec asst, 1983-86; Michigan Dept of Licensing and Regulation, administrative asst to dir, 1987-90; City of Detroit, Consumer Aff Dept, deputy dir, 1991-. **Orgs:** NAACP; American Medical Technologists; Natl Assn of Black Substance Abuse Workers; Natl Clearinghouses for Licensure, Enforcement and Regulation; Intl Assn of Transportation Regulators; Greenacres-Woodward Civic Assn; Natl, State, 14th District Democratic Party. **Honors/Awds:** President Gerald R Ford, Certificate of Appreciation as Member of the Selective Service System, 1974; Governor William Milliken, Community Service in Substance Abuse, 1972; Mayor of Detroit, Roman Gribbs, Contributions to the Development of Detroit's Substance Abuse Programs, 1971; Congressman John Conyers, Outstanding Community Service, 1969; State Rep Teola Hunter, Mother of the Year, 1990; Detroit City Council, Spirit of Detroit, 1982. **Business Addr:** Consumer Affairs Deputy Director, City of Detroit, 1600 Cadillac Tower, Detroit, MI 48226, (313)224-3508.

ALLISON, W. ANTHONY
Physician, surgeon. **Personal:** Born Oct 10, 1926, Durham, NC; son of Lydia Hammie Allison and Willis F Allison; married Dale Muther; children: Patricia, Vivian, Anita. **Educ:** Morgan State Coll Univ Baltimore MD, BS 1951; Univ of Munich Med Univ Munich Germany, MD 1958. **Career:** Friedman Hosp Howard Univ Med School, emergency room phys & clin instr 1965-67; Mercy Douglass Hosp Phila, attending phys, surg 1967-73; Philadelphia Gen Hosp, attending phys dept rehab med 1967-75; St Josephs Hosp Phila, attending phys, surg 1973-75; VA Ambulatory Care Clinic, acting chief surg serv 1975-79, physician, surgeon; VA Ambulatory Care Clinic, mgmt & care of veteran patients with musculoskeletal conditions, surgeon 1980-. **Orgs:** Mem PA DE Cty Med Soc 1967-72, AMA 1967-72, Natl Med Assoc 1967-, Amer Coll of Sports Med 1977-, NY Natl Acad of Sci, Assoc for Computing Machinery, Amer Professional Practice Assoc; diplomate, Amer Academy of Pain Management, 1988-; mem, Eastern Pennsylvania Medical Society of the Natl Medication Association 1973-; mem, The Computer Society of the IEEE, 1986-. **Honors/Awds:** Awd improved method of titanium dioxide determination in paint pigments US Quartermaster Gen Testing Lab Philadelphia 1952; improved method of determining iron in paint pigments US Quartermaster Gen Testing Lab Philadelphia 1953; Honor Mem Chapel of Four Chaplains 1976; Awarded Cert of Appreciation for Outstanding Dedication to the Disabled Amer Veterans by Chap 4 of Camden County NJ 1981; Citation for Appreciation & Coop of Serv Rendered Awd by Disabled Amer Vets of the Philadelphia Liberty Bell Chap 96 & Aux 1984; Citation of Merit in appreciation for outstanding

service, Disabled Amer Veterans, Delaware County Chapter No 113, 1987; "A Physician's Approach- Designing in Prolog: A Deductive Database of Patient Statistics of Patients with Musculoskeletal Disorders,"proceedings-12th AnnuSymposium on Computer Application in Medical Care, 1988; "Patient Visits: A Survey of Veterans with Musculoskeletal Disorders" VA Practicioner Vol 5, 1988. **Military Serv:** US Army, sgt 1945-46.

ALLS, HOWARD E.
Attorney. **Personal:** Born May 8, 1959, Savannah, GA; son of Alberta Alls; children: Geoffrey, Elise, Slyvia. **Educ:** Savannah State College, BA, Political Science, 1983; Mercer University, JD, 1987. **Career:** Alston & Byrd, PC, law clerk, 1985; Ficholz & Assocs, PC, attorney, 1988-90; Howard E Alls & Assocs, PC, attorney, 1992-. **Orgs:** Savannah Chapter of SCLC, pres, 1983; Natl Board of Dirs of the Southern Christian Leadership Conf, 1984; Phi Gamma Mu, pres, 1981-83; Omega Psi Phi, vp, 1979-80; Savannah State College, SGA Chief Justice, 1982-83; Student Non-violent Coord Com, pres, 1981-82. **Honors/Awds:** Walter E George School of Law, NAACP Legal Defense Fund Award, 1987, Mercer University Merit Scholarship, 1987, Earl Warren Scholarship, 1987; Savannah State College, Dean's List, 1982-83; Porter Scholarship, 1982. **Business Addr:** Attorney, Howard E Alls & Assoc, PC, 24 Drayton Street, The New Realty Building, Ste 703, Savannah, GA 31401, (912)236-2555.

ALLSTON, THOMAS GRAY, III (TIM)
Communications company executive, consultant. **Personal:** Born Jul 13, 1954, Stoneham, MA; son of Zeola Belle (Germany) Allston and Thomas G Allston II. **Educ:** Hampton Inst, BA, English 1977; Hampton University, master's degree, business management, 1994. **Career:** Burson-Marsteller, New York, NY, asst acct executive 1977-78; Hampton Inst/ Univ, asst dir of public relations 1979-85; Hill and Knowlton Inc, account exec 1985-87; Renaissance Comm, vice pres 1987-91; Allston Communications, Inc, Newport News, VA, president/CEO, 1991-; Hampton University, internal consultant, 1991-. **Orgs:** Life mem Alpha Phi Alpha Fraternity Inc 1974-; mem Natl Hampton Alumni Assoc 1977-; mem Public Relations Soc of Amer 1977-, mem Calvary SDA Church, 1973-. **Honors/Awds:** John W Hill Award, Outstanding Communications Achievement, Hill & Knowlton, 1986. **Business Phone:** (804)888-6583.

ALLY, AKBAR F.
Educator. **Personal:** Born Aug 23, 1943, Wismar, Demerara, Guyana; son of Lucille Ward and Beraspratt Ally; married Ellen Mason Ally, Dec 22, 1967; children: Antonius, Kristina. **Educ:** St Lawrence Univ, BA, 1967; Hunter Coll, MA, 1972; Univ of Wisconsin-Milwaukee, PhD, 1981. **Career:** Chase Manhattan Bank, New York, NY, intl adjuster, 1970; Metropolitan Life Ins, New York, NY, claims adjuster, 1970-72; Brooklyn Coll, Brooklyn, NY, lecturer, 1973-75; Bronx Community Coll, New York, NY, lecturer, 1975; Univ of Wisconsin-Milwaukee, Milwaukee, WI, dir/coordinator, 1975-82; Univ of Wisconsin-Madison, Madison, WI, asst dean, 1982-89, asst to vice chancellor, 1989-. **Orgs:** Mem, Caribbean Historical Society, 1972-; mem, NAACP (Madison), 1985-; mem, Madison Urban League, 1985-. **Honors/Awds:** Fulbright Hays Award, US State Dept, 1963-67; New York State Education Scholarship, New York State, 1971-72; Professional Development Certificate, Harvard University, MA, 1991; Professional Development Certificate, University of Wisconsin, Madison, WI, 1986. **Business Addr:** Assistant Vice Chancellor, University of Wisconsin-Madison, 500 Lincoln Dr, Bascom Hall, Ste 121, Madison, WI 53706.

AL-MATEEN, CHERYL SINGLETON
Physician. **Personal:** Born Aug 26, 1959, Washington, DC; daughter of Carole Waters Singleton and Israel Benjamin Singleton; married Kevin Bakeer Al-Mateen; children: Benjamin, Katherine. **Educ:** Howard Univ, Coll of Liberal Arts BS 1981, Coll of Medicine MD 1983. **Career:** Howard Univ Hospital, transitional medicine internship 1983-84; Hahnemann Univ Hospital, psychiatry residency 1984-87; Hahnemann Univ Hospital, Philadelphia, PA, Child Psychiatry Residency 1987-89; Medical College of Virginia, asst prof, 1989-96, assoc prof, 1996-. **Orgs:** Vice pres of administration Howard Univ Coll of Medicine Class of '83' 1982-; editor-in-chief Spectrum APA/NIMH Fellowship Newsletter 1986-87; component member, Amer Psychiatric Assn, 1985-; member, Amer Academy of Child & Adolescent Psychiatry, 1987-. **Honors/Awds:** Service Citation Howard Univ Coll of Medicine Faculty 1983; Amer Psychiatric Assn Natl Inst of Mental Health Fellow Amer Psychiatric Assoc 1985-87. **Business Addr:** Associate Professor, Psychiatry, Medical College of Virginia, Box 980489, Richmond, VA 23298.

AL-MATEEN, K. BAKEER
Physician. **Personal:** Born Aug 31, 1958, Pasadena, CA; son of Margaret Janet Strain Johnson and Eddie Johnson Jr; married Cheryl Singleton; children: Benjamin. **Educ:** Univ of CA Davis, attended 1976-80; Howard Univ Coll of Medicine, MD 1984. **Career:** St Christopher's Hospital, pediatric resident; Medical Coll of Virginia Dept of Neonatology, assistant professor of pediatrics, director of Neonatal ECMO program, currently. **Orgs:** Pres Class of 1984 Howard Univ Coll of Medicine 1983-. **Honors/Awds:** Malcolm X Scholarship Howard Univ Coll of Medicine 1984; Service Citation Howard Univ Coll of Medicine 1984. **Home Addr:** 2212 Turtle Hill Lane, Midlothian, VA 23112.

ALOMAR, ROBERTO
Professional baseball player. **Personal:** Born Feb 5, 1968, Salinas, Puerto Rico; son of Sandy Alomar Sr. **Career:** San Diego Padres, professional baseball player, 1988-91; Toronto Blue Jays, professional baseball player, beginning 1991; Baltimore Orioles, currently. **Honors/Awds:** American League, Gold Glove, 1991. **Business Addr:** Professional Baseball Player, Baltimore Orioles, Oriole Park at Camden Yards, 333 W Camden St, Baltimore, MD 21201, (410)685-9800.

ALOMAR, SANDY
Professional baseball coach. **Personal:** Born Oct 19, 1943, Salinas, Puerto Rico; married Maria Alomar; children: Sandia, Sandy Jr, Roberto. **Career:** Infielder: Milwaukee Braves, 1964-67, New York Mets, 1967-69, California Angels, 1969-74, Texas Rangers, 1974-78; Puerto Rican National Team, coach; San Diego Padres, third base coach, 1986-90; Cleveland Indians, coach, 1990-. **Business Addr:** Coach, Cleveland Indians, 2401 Ontario, Cleveland, OH 44115, (216)420-4200.

ALOMAR, SANDY, JR.
Professional baseball player. **Personal:** Born Jun 18, 1966, Salinas, Puerto Rico; son of Sandy Alomar Sr. **Career:** San Diego Padres, professional baseball player, 1989-90, Cleveland Indians, professional baseball player, 1990-. **Honors/Awds:** Sporting News, Minor League Co-Player of the Year, 1988, Minor League Player of the Year, 1989, American League Rookie Player of the Year, 1990; Pacific Coast League, Player of the Year, 1989; American League, Gold Glove, 1990; Baseball Writers Association of America, American League Rookie of the Year, 1990. **Business Addr:** Professional Baseball Player, Cleveland Indians, Cleveland Municipal Stadium, Cleveland, OH 44114, (216)420-4200.

ALSBROOK, JAMES ELDRIDGE
Educator, columnist. **Personal:** Born Nov 28, 1913, Kansas City, MO; son of Elgeitha Stovall Alsbrook and Irving A Alsbrook. **Educ:** Univ of Kansas, BS, journalism, 1963, MS, journalism, 1964; Univ of Iowa, PhD, mass communication, 1968. **Career:** The Call, sports and theatricals editor; Louisville Courier-Journal, staff writer; Univ of Iowa, journalism teaching asst; Central State Univ, public relations and publications director, journalism and English professor; Ohio Univ, professor of journalism, professor emeritus. **Orgs:** Kansas City NAACP, information dir; Assn for Education in Journalism and Mass Communication; Sigma Delta Chi; Kappa Tau Alpha; American Society of Composers Authors and Publishers. **Special Achievements:** "Minority Report" column appears in about 50 newspapers; feature stories published by AP, UPI, etc; articles in Journalism Quarterly and New Republic; writings appear in Urban Violence in America, Violence and Riots in America, and in dailies including New York Times and Baltimore Sun; First African-American to found, own and operate chain of retail stores in downtown Kansas City, MO, or in downtown Kansas City, Kansas. **Home Addr:** 6844 Gura Rd, Athens, OH 45701, (614)593-8754.

ALSTON, BETTY BRUNER
Educator (retired). **Personal:** Born Jul 5, 1933, Concord, NC; daughter of Ethel Torrence Bruner and Buford Bruner Sr; married Henry Clay Alston; children: Henry Clay Jr, Terry Verice. **Educ:** Barber-Scotia College, BS 1955; A&T State Univ, 1957; Appalachian State Univ, 1969. **Career:** PTA/Odell Elem School, secretary 1979; PTSA/Northwest Middle School, secretary 1980; First United Pres Church, 1981; Northwest High School Booster Club, secretary 1982, vice president 1983; Briarwood, school teacher 1983-93. **Orgs:** Member North Carolina Association of Educators; elder, organist First United Presbyterian Church; board of directors, Stonewall Jackson School, 1988, adv council, 1988, vice chair, 1991, Cabarrus County Board of Educ; second vice pres, Democrat Women's Organization, 1989; Concord/Cabarrus Chamber of Commerce, president's club, 1994; Cabarrus County Board of Education, chairman, 1993-94; Democratic Women, president, 1993; Stonewall Jackson School, advisory council, 1995; Barber-Scotia College, bd of trustees, 1995. **Honors/Awds:** Member Alpha Kappa Alpha; member Cabarrus County School Board; member Northwest HS Board of Directors; Publication-Poem-Teachers' Invitation to Writing 1983; first vice chairperson of the Democratic Party of Cabarrus Co 1985; apptd by Gov Jim Martin to serve on the Cabarrus Co Resource Council of Mt Pleasant Prison Unit 1986; Outstanding Achievement in Educ and Comm Service Omega Psi Phi Frat 1986; Service to the Welfare of the Community West Central Cabarrus Optimist 1986; International Leaders in Achievement, 1989; Distinguished Barber-Scotia Alumni Citation of the Year Award, 1994; Cabarrus Chamber of Commerce, President's Club Member of the Year Award, 1995. **Home Addr:** PO Box 1365, Concord, NC 28026.

ALSTON, DERRICK SAMUEL
Professional basketball player. **Personal:** Born Aug 20, 1972, Bronx, NY. **Educ:** Duquesne Univ. **Career:** Philadelphia 76ers, 1994-. **Business Addr:** Professional Basketball Player, Philadelphia 76ers, PO Box 25040, Philadelphia, PA 19147, (215)339-7600.

ALSTON, FLOYD WILLIAM
Educational administrator. **Personal:** Born Oct 23, 1925, Brooklyn, NY; married Marilyn Deloris Baker; children: Craig E F, Marilyn Suzanne. **Educ:** Temple Univ, BS Business Admin 1970; Fels Inst of State and Local Govnmnt Univ of PA. **Career:** HOPE Development Corp, pres 1968-73; Philadelphia Housing Authry, housing mgr 1958-68; Philadelphia Board of Education, president, currently. **Orgs:** Pres Union Benevolent Assoc Fdn 1979-; pres JM Nursing Serv 1980-85, Philadelphia Housing Dvlmnt Corp 1982; past pres Comm Servc Plng Cncl 1982-84; natl vp, acting exec dir Frontiers Intl Inc 1984-, Philadelphia Tribune Charities 1980-83. **Honors/Awds:** Tribune Charities Chrmn Award Philadelphia Tribune Charities 1983; Don Alexander Award Natl Bankers Assoc 1978; Prentice-Hall article published "Helping Troubled Employees" 1978. **Military Serv:** USMC sgt 1943-46, 1950-51. **Business Addr:** President, Philadelphia Board of Education, 21st and the Parkway, Administration Bldg, Rm 111, Philadelphia, PA 19103, (215)299-7823.

ALSTON, GERALD
Singer. **Personal:** Born Nov 8, 1951, Henderson, NC; son of Geraldine Boyd Alston and John Alston; married Edna Chew Alston, Jun 26, 1982; children: Kyle, Tod M. **Educ:** Kittrell Coll. **Career:** Singer. **Honors/Awds:** Grammy Winner, 1980; Nominee, American Music Award, 1980.

ALSTON, GILBERT C.
Judge. **Personal:** Born Apr 4, 1931, Philadelphia, PA; married Lydia Mary Wold; children: Carl, Anita. **Educ:** UCLA, BA Economics 1959; Univ of S CA, JD Law 1965. **Career:** LA Co Dist Atty, deputy dist atty 1965-67; Hauptman & Alston, private prac 1967-71; LA Mun Court, judge 1971-77; Pasadena Mun Court, judge 1977-80; LA Superior Court, judge 1980-. **Military Serv:** USAF capt fighter pilot 5 1/2 yrs. **Business Addr:** Judge, Superior Court, Los Angeles Co, 300 E Walnut, Pasadena, CA 91101.

ALSTON, HARRY L. **See Obituaries section.**

ALSTON, JAMES L.
Manager. **Personal:** Born Jan 14, 1947, Bronx, NY; children: Lorraine, Jeanette. **Educ:** Loras Coll Dubuque IA, BA Sociol 1970; CCNY, 1972-73; NY Univ, 1975-76. **Career:** Simpson St Devel Assoc Youth Prog, training coord 1970-74; Fox St Relocation Shelter, asst dir 1974-76, dir 1975-76; S Bronx Comm Housing Bronx, dir 1976-80; Sebco Mgmt Co Inc, dir 1980-. **Orgs:** Chmn hsg com Bronx Comm Plng Bd 1971-; bd mem Comm Greening Com 1975-; bd of dirs Natl Assoc of Hsg Mgmt & Owners 1976-79; vchmn Sebco Housing Corp 1971-80; chmn PTA Fin Com St Athanasius 1975-; bd mem Prospect Hosp Adv 1978-. **Honors/Awds:** Cardinal Spellman Youth Awd Archdiocese of NY 1966; John F Kennedy Youth Awd casita Maria/Bronx NY 1974; Cert of Achievement Comm Serv Soc 1976; Spec Cert Awd Comm Plng Bd Bronx Comm Coll 1976. **Business Addr:** Sr Vice Pres, Field Operations, United Negro College Fund, 500 E 62nd St, New York, NY 10021-8386.

ALSTON, KATHY DIANE
Physician. **Personal:** Born Mar 29, 1958, Staten Island, NY. **Educ:** Univ of VA, BA 1980; Howard Univ Coll of Medicine, MD 1984. **Career:** Martin Luther King Genl Hosp, physician. **Orgs:** Mem Assoc of Black Women Physicians 1985-86; dorm council Joint Council of Interns & Residents 1986-87. **Honors/Awds:** Natl Health Serv Corp Scholarship 1980-83. **Home Addr:** 1540 Hunting Ave, Mc Lean, VA 22102-2914. **Business Addr:** Martin L King Genl Hosp, 12021 So Wilmington Ave, Los Angeles, CA 90059.

AL'UQDAH, WILLIAM MUJAHID
Attorney. **Personal:** Born Oct 29, 1953, Cincinnati, OH; son of William Henry Jones, Sr, Helen G Jones; married Deborah, Oct 30, 1976; children: William M Ibn III, Shareefah N, Nadirah A. **Educ:** University of Cincinnati, BS, 1982; Salmon P Chase College of Law, JD, 1987. **Career:** Hamilton County Prosecutors Office, asst district attorney, 1988-94; WCIN 1480 AM Radio, sports dir and on air personality, 1992-; Harmon, Davis and Keys Co, LPA, senior assoc, 1994-96; Lawson and Gaines, attorney, 1996-. **Orgs:** Black Male Coalition, first exec dir, 1988-89; Black Law Student Assn of America, president, 1985-86. **Honors/Awds:** Black Professionals, Scholarship, 1986. **Special Achievements:** The Good, The Bad, and The Ugly, Criminal Justice State of Cincinnati, sponsored by Cincinnati Urban League, 1995; When Going Gets Tough, Central State University Symposium, Welfare Reform, 1982. **Military Serv:** Infantry, Ohio Army Natl Guard, Captain, 1979-, Ohio Commendation Medal 1990.

ALVERANGA, GLANVIN L.
Business executive. **Personal:** Born Feb 20, 1928, New York, NY; married Ramona E Fontany; children: Denise, Glenn. **Educ:** City College of New York, BS, 1958; John Jay Coll of Criminal Justice, New York NY, MA, 1976. **Career:** New York City Police Dept, dep insp, 1955-77; New York City Health & Hosp Corp, dir of security corp, 1977-. **Orgs:** Ed consult New York City Bd of Ed 1977; sec NOBLE 1977; mem 100 Black Men 1978-. **Military Serv:** US Army, corpl 1951-52. **Business Addr:** Dir of Security Corp, Health & Hosp Corp, 125 Worth St, New York, NY 10013.

ALWAN, MANSOUR
Government official. **Personal:** married; children: 5. **Career:** Chesilhurst NJ, mayor, 1975-83, electronic engr, consultant, currently. **Orgs:** Adenu Allah Arabic Assn; Coalition for Youth and Family Development. **Honors/Awds:** Certified Network Administrator. **Business Addr:** Government Official, Burrough of 2nd & Grant Avs, Chesilhurst, NJ 08089.

AMAKER, H. TOMMY
College basketball coach. **Career:** Duke Univ, asst coach, nine years; Seton Hall Univ, head men's basketball coach, 1997-. **Business Addr:** Head Men's Basketball Coach, Seton Hall University, 400 S Orange Ave, South Orange, NJ 07079.

AMAKER, NORMAN CAREY
Attorney, educator. **Personal:** Born Jan 15, 1935, New York, NY; son of Gladys Corley Amaker and Carey Amaker; married Mattie Jeannette Owens, Oct 20, 1962; children: Alicia, Alana, Arthur. **Educ:** Amherst Clg, BA (cum laude) 1956; Columbia U, JD 1959. **Career:** NAACP Legal Def Fund NYC, atty 1960-68, first asst cnsl 1968-71; Nbrh Legal Serv Prog Wash DC, exec dir 1971-73; Rutgers Univ, prof of law 1973-76; Loyola Univ of Chicago Law Sch, prof of law 1976-. **Orgs:** Gen cnsl Natl Comm Agnst Dscrmntn in Housing 1973; vstng prof Rutgers Law Sch Newark, NJ 1973-76; sch bd mem Dist 202 Evanston Twnshp H S 1980-87, pres pro-tem 1983-84; pres Chicago Forum Chicago 1982-83; bd of gov Soc of Am Law Tchrs 1979-87. **Honors/Awds:** IBPOE of W Awd 1965; BALSA Awd 1973; Civil Liberties & Civil Rghts Oceana 1967; Civil Rights and the Reagan Adm, Urban Inst Wash DC 1988. **Military Serv:** USAR 1960-66. **Business Addr:** Professor of Law, Loyola University of Chicago, 1 E Pearson St, 526, Chicago, IL 60611.

AMAN, MOHAMMED M.
Educator, educational administrator. **Personal:** Born Jan 3, 1940, Alexandria, Egypt; son of Fathia Ali al-Maghrabi Aman and Mohammed Aman; married Mary Jo Parker, Sep 15, 1972; children: David. **Educ:** Cairo Univ Egypt, BA (with honors), 1961; Columbia Univ New York NY, MS, 1965; Univ of Pittsburgh, PhD, 1968; New York Univ, postdoctoral studies in Comp Sci, 1970-71. **Career:** Univ of Pittsburgh, research asst, 1965-66; Duquesne Univ Pittsburgh, reference librarian, 1966-68; Pratt Inst NY, asst prof; St Johns Univ NY, asst and assoc prof 1969-73, dir and prof 1973-76; Long Island Univ, Greenvale Long Island NY, dean & prof 1976-79; Univ of Wisconsin-Milwaukee, dean and prof, 1979-. **Orgs:** Info mgmt consultant UNIDO 1978-; UNESCO 1982-, US-AID 1984-96; chmn Intl Relations Comm Amer Lib Assn 1984-86, Assn Lib & Info Sci Ed 1985-86; Amer Soc for Info Science Intl Rel Comm; chair, Intl Issues in Information Special Interest Group; life mem, founding exec bd mem, NAACP 1984-; mem Amer Arab Affairs Council 1983-; mem Egyptian Amer Scholars Assn 1971-; bd member, A Wisconsin African Relief Effort (AWARE), 1986-89; bd member, Wisconsin African Historical Society/Museum, 1988-, member, Audience Development Committee, Milwaukee Art Museum; founder, Milwaukee Leader's Forum. **Honors/Awds:** Beta Phi Mu Intl Lib & Info Sci Honor Soc; author, contributing consultant Intl Library Review, 1969-91, editor-in-chief, Digest of Middle East Studies (DOMES), Arab Serials & Periodicals, 1979, Cataloging & Classification of Non-Western Library Material, 1980, Librarianship in the Third World, 1976, Developing Computer Based Library Sys 1984, Online Access to Database 1984, Information Services 1986; Urban Library Management, 1990; award of appreciation from the Black Caucus of the Amer Library Assn, 1986; Award of Serv, Assn for Library and Information Science Educ, 1988; UNESCO consultant on the Revival of the Alexandrian Library Project, 1988-; John Ames Humphry/OCLC-Forest Press Award for Outstanding Contributions to Intl Librarianship, Amer Library Assn, 1989; Black Caucus of the Amer Library Assn (BCALA), Leadership Award, 1994; the WLA Special Service Award, 1992; Black Caucus of The ALA Award of Excellence, 1995; Prof Kaula Medal & Citation, 1996. **Business Addr:** Dean & Prof, School of Library & Information Science, University of Wisconsin, PO Box 413, Enderis Hall, Milwaukee, WI 53201.

AMARO, RUBEN
Baseball manager. **Personal:** Born Jan 7, 1936, Monterrey, Mexico; married Judy, 1988 (divorced); children: David, Ruben Jr; married Lilia, 1988; children: Luis Alfredo, Ruben Andres. **Career:** Philadelphia Phillies, shortstop 1960; NY Yankees, shortstop 1966-68; California Angels, shortstop, 1969; Philadelphia Phillies, player, coach minor leagues, 1970-71, scout, 1972-74, coordinator, Latin America, asst to Dallas Green, Minor Leagues of Scouting Director, 1974-77, scout of development supervisor, 1977-79, M L coach, 1980-81, scout, 1982-; Chicago Cubs, coach, 1982-87, Caribbean area scout, 1988-; Detroit Tigers, scout, 1989-96; Chicago Cubs, minor league manager, 1996-. **Honors/Awds:** National League Gold Glove, shortstop work, 129 games. **Special Achievements:** Guided Zulia to Venezuelan League title, Caribbean World Series championship when Zulia defeated defending champion Puerto Rico; hit major league career-high in 1964; led Intl League shortstops in double plays with 84 in 1959. **Business Addr:** Minor League Manager, Chicago Cubs, 1060 W Addison St, Chicago, IL 60613.

AMAYA, ASHRAF
Professional basketball player. **Personal:** Born Nov 23, 1971, Oak Park, IL. **Educ:** Southern Illinois. **Career:** CBA: Fort Wayne Fury, 1993-94; Quad City Thunder, 1993-94; NBA: Vancouver Grizzlies, 1995-96; Washington Wizards, 1996-. **Business Addr:** Professional Basketball Player, Washington Wizards, 1 Harry S Truman Dr, Capitol Centre, Landover, MD 20785, (301)773-2255.

AMBEAU, KAREN M.
Marketing manager. **Personal:** Born Jul 4, 1956, Berkeley, CA; daughter of Mildred Anthony Ambeau and Lucien Ambeau; married Michael McClendon, Aug 7, 1983. **Educ:** Tuskegee University, Tuskegee, AL, BSEE, 1981. **Career:** Pacific Gas & Electric, Hayward, CA, acct rep, 1981-. **Orgs:** Member, McGee Avenue Church Educational Aid, 1982-; corresp sect, Delta Sigma Theta Sorority, 1987-89, chairperson/fund-raiser, 1990; member, Business Professional Women's Club, 1987-90. **Honors/Awds:** Outstanding Young Careerist, Business & Professional Womens, 1987. **Business Addr:** Marketing Supervisor, Pacific Gas and Electric Co, 24300 Clawiter Road, Hayward, CA 94545.

AMBERS, MONIQUE
Professional basketball player. **Personal:** Born Dec 21, 1970; daughter of Robert and Linda Ambers. **Educ:** Arizona State, BS in child development. **Career:** Phoenix Mercury, forward, 1997-. **Business Addr:** Professional Basketball Player, Phoenix Mercury, 201 E Jefferson St, Phoenix, AZ 85004, (602)252-9622.

AMBROSE, ASHLEY AVERY
Professional football player. **Personal:** Born Sep 17, 1970, New Orleans, LA; married Monica. **Career:** Indianapolis Colts, defensive end, 1992-95; Cincinnati Bengals, 1996-. **Honors/Awds:** NFL Players Assn, AFC Defensive Back of the Year, 1996. **Business Addr:** Professional Football Player, Cincinnati Bengals, One Bengals Dr, Cincinnati, OH 45202, (513)621-3550.

AMBROSE, ETHEL L.
City official. **Personal:** Born Dec 18, 1930, Perryville, AR; divorced; children: Ethel M Harris, Derek S Brown, Lakeitha Brown. **Educ:** Univ of MI, Licensed Soc Worker 1973; Highland Park Comm Coll, 1975; Southeastern Univ, BS Sociology 1980. **Career:** City of Highland Park, spec asst to mayor 1969-76; Detroit Adult Ed, substitute teacher 1978-79; Diversified Health Ctr, social worker 1979-80; Alpha AnnexNursing Ctr, soc worker 1984-. **Orgs:** Mem Citizen of Interest Scholarship Comm 1967-; life mem Highland Park Caucus Club 1973-; bd pres Wayne Metro Comm Serv Agency 1983-84; mem, trustee Highland Park Bd of Ed/Comm Coll 1983-; pres ACCT Minorities Affairs/Central Region 1984-; mem Natl Political Congress of Black Women 1984.

AMIJI, HATIM M.
Educator. **Personal:** Born Jun 11, 1939, Zanzibar. **Educ:** London, BA (Hons) 1964; Princeton Univ, MA, PhD. **Career:** Univ of MA Dept of History, assoc prof. **Orgs:** Sec gen Zanzibar Youth League 1960; lecturer Trinity Coll Nabingo Uganda 1964; lecturer Princeton Univ 1969-70; rsch assoc Dept of History Univ of Nairobi Kenya 1967-68; lecturer Dept of History & Centre for African Studies Boston Univ 1972; dir African Studies Workshop World Affairs Council Boston 1972; mem Middle Eastern Studies Assoc; fellow E African Acad; mem African Studies Assoc of USA; ed bd Gemini Review; founder mem Pan-African Univ Org. **Honors/Awds:** E African Railways & Harbours Rsch Awd 1963; Rockefeller Found Fellow 1965-67; Princeton Univ Fellow 1969-70; Zanzibar Govt Scholar 1961-64; Superior Merit Awd Univ of MA. **Business Addr:** Associate Professor, Univ of Massachusetts, Dept of History, Harbor Campus Univ of MA, Boston, MA 02125.

AMIN, KARIMA (CAROL ANN AIKEN)
Educator, storyteller. **Personal:** Born Jun 1, 1947, Buffalo, NY; daughter of Bessie Mabry Aiken and Harvey Aiken; children: Abdur Rahman, Takiyah Nur, Sabriyah. **Educ:** St Univ of NY at Buffalo, BA 1969, MEd 1974. **Career:** Buffalo Public Schools, teacher of language arts scndry, 1969-92, multicultural literature specialist, 1992-94; professional storyteller, 1994-. **Orgs:** Special appointments, Natl Cncl of Tchrs of Eng, 1982-86; Natl Comm for Storytelling, 1987-90; Comm for Prsrvtn of Multicultural Lit in Am; bd of dir Afro-Am Hstrcl Asso of Niagara Frontier 1984-86; past treas & sec Taara Zakkiyya Islamic Strhd 1975-; coord Spin-a-Story Tellers of Western NY 1984-; consultant, Project Reach, 1989-; Epic Natl, bd of dirs, 1994-; national advisory bd, MacMillan McGraw-Hill Publishers, 1994-96. **Honors/Awds:** Wm Wells Brown Awd Afro-Am Hstrcl Asso 1984; Tchr of Tomorrow awd Buffalo Bd of Ed 1978; co-author Black Lit for H S Stdnts NCTE 1978; Black Edctrs of the Yr Black Edctrs Asso of Wstrn NY 1977; Awd English Speaking Union of Western NY 1986; Achievement Award, Natl Assn of Negro Business & Professional Women's Clubs, 1994; Apple for the Teacher Award, Iota Phi Lambda Sorority Inc, Beta Phi Chapter, 1994; Alpha Kappa Alpha, Community Service Award, 1997. **Special Achievements:** Co-wrote Black Lit for H S Students, NCTE, 1978; Published: You Can Say That Again!, Galactic Multimedia, 1994; Brer Rabbit, Dorling-Kendersley, 1998. **Home Addr:** 103 Fernhill Ave, Buffalo, NY 14215. **Business Addr:** PO Box 273, Buffalo, NY 14212.

AMORY, REGINALD L.
Engineer, educator. **Personal:** Born Jul 17, 1936, Peekskill, NY; married Marion Rose Boothe; children: Reginald, Susan. **Educ:** New York University, BCE, 1960; Clarkson College, MCE, 1963; Rensselaer Polytechnic Institute, PhD, 1967. **Career:** Throop & Feiden, engineer, 1960-61; Abbott, Jerkt & Co, engineer, 1961-63; RPI, tech asst, 1963-64, instructor, 1965-66; North Carolina A&T University, dean, 1968-74; Northeastern University, Dept of Civil Engineering, asst prof, 1966-68, professor, 1974-. **Orgs:** Consultant to numerous organizations including: GE Co, Natl Science Foundation, B&M Technical Services, US Dept of Energy, Education Development Corp, Natl Academy of Engineering, SC Commission on Higher Education, TN State University, Mobil Oil Co, Robert Charles Assoc; American Society for Engr Education, Project Board, vice president, executive bd; American Society of Civil Engineers; Intl Assn for Bridge & Structural Engineers; Natl Society of Professional Engineers; American Assn for Advancement of Science; bd of trustees, St Augustine's College; advisory bd, Natl Urban League; Sigma Psi Phi. **Honors/Awds:** Excellence Award, NC A&T State University, 1972; Engineer of Distinction, Joint Engineering Council, 1973; Alumni Achievement Award, RPI, 1977; University of Cambridge, visiting scholar, 1983; Alcoa Foundation Professorship, Northeastern University; Natl Science Honor Society. **Business Addr:** Professor, Dept of Civil Engineering, Northeastern University, 360 Huntington Ave, Boston, MA 02115-5096.

AMOS, ETHEL S.
Educator. **Personal:** dauGHter of Edna B Scott and Dunlap Scott; married Clinton D Amos Jr; children: Ednalyn Hurley. **Educ:** Tuskegee Institute, BS, nursing, 1973; Vanderbilt University, MS, nursing, 1981; Texas Woman's University, PhD, 1985. **Career:** Columbus College, associate professor, 1979-87; Tuskegee Institute, associate professor, 1988-89; Dillard University, Division of Nursing, dean, professor, 1991-. **Orgs:** American Nurses' Association, 1979-; Association of Black Nurses, faculty, 1988-. **Home Phone:** (504)254-4852. **Business Addr:** Chair and Professor, Division of Nursing, Dillard University, 2601 Gentilly Blvd, New Orleans, LA 70122.

AMOS, KENT B.
Association executive. **Personal:** Born May 21, 1944, Washington, DC; son of Gladys C Amos and Benjamin F Amos; married Carmen. **Educ:** DE State Coll, BS, 1970. **Career:** Xerox Corp, sales mgr 1975-76, area mgr 1976-77, mgr ISG Affirm Action 1977-78, dir corp affirm action, EEO 1978-82; pres, The Triad Group; Urban Family Inst, pres/founder, currently. **Orgs:** Corp Few 1971-79; bus consultant Congressional Black Caucus 1975-79; Business Policy Review Comm 1977-79; Big Bros 1971-74; Inside/Outside 1972-; Alpha Kappa Mu Natl Hon Soc 1968-69; NAACP; Natl Urban League; Natl Council of Negro Women; Delaware State Coll Alumni Assn; Coolidge High School Alumni Assn; Omega Psi Phi; bd of dirs, Boys and Girls Club of Greater Washington, 1990-; advisory board member, I Have a Dream Foundation, 1990-. **Honors/Awds:** Black History Week Awards, WMAL Radio/TV Station, 1974; Merit Awards for Job Performance, Xerox Corp; President's Sales Recognition Award, Xerox Corp; Chair's Award, Congressional Black Caucus, 1979; awards from DC Public Schools Bd of Educ, Natl Assn for Equal Oppportunity in Higher Educ; Legacy Award, Natl Council of Negro Women; Image Award, NAACP; Whitney Young Award, Urban League; Roy Dykes Memorial Award, Xerox Corp; Citizen of the Year, Omega Psi Phi; Man of the Year, Shiloh Baptist Church; Alumnus of the Century, Delaware State Coll; Alumnus of the Year, Calvin Coolidge High School; Alumnus of the Year, Delaware State Coll; scholarship funds created in his name at Calvin Coolidge High School and Delaware State Coll; Annual Service to Youth Award, Big Brothersof the National Capea, 1990; Thanksgiving Tuesday Award for Distinguished Community Service, Catholic Univ of America & Madison National Bank, 1990. **Military Serv:** US Army, lt, 1964-71; numerous Vietnam Decorations, 1970. **Business Addr:** President, Founder, Urban Family Inst, 1400 16th St, NW, Ste 101, Washington, DC 20036, (202)939-3490.

AMOS, ORIS ELIZABETH CARTER
Educator. **Personal:** Born in Martinsville, VA; daughter of Fannie M Swanson Carter (deceased) and Samuel H Carter (deceased); married Winsom; children: Patsi. **Educ:** VA State Coll, BA 1951; OH State Univ, MA 1963, PhD 1971. **Career:** VA Pub Schools, teacher 1951-55; Columbus OH Pub Sch, teacher 1963-66; OH State Univ, instr 1966-69; Otterbein Coll, asst prof 1971-75; Council for Exceptional Children, pres 1975; Coll of Educ, chmn Human Rel Comm 1975; Wright State Univ, prof of educ 1975-88; educ development consultant, 1988-. **Orgs:** Teachers Adv Comm State of OH 1975; adv Black Students Otterbein Coll 1975; adv bd Miami Valley Reg Res Ctr; adv bd Dayton Area United Cerebral Palsy Professional Serv; adv bd Sinclair Comm Coll Special Educ; Panel of Experts to review proposals St Bd of Educ Columbus, OH 1975; mem Delta Sigma Theta Sorority; Pi Lambda Theta Women's Honorary in Educ; Central Chapel Church Yellow Springs. **Honors/Awds:** Named Outstanding Educator of Yr 1972; Award for Distinguished Comm Serv Delta Sigma Theta Sorority 1972; Special Award Serv to Black Students at Otterbein Coll 1973; Teacher Excellence Award Wright State Univ 1979; Educator of Yr OH Fed Council of Exceptional Children 1982; Coord of Special Educ 1978-87; WSU Trustees Award, 1987; Greene County Hall of Fame for Women, Greene County OH, 1988. **Business Addr:** Prof Emeritus of Education, Wright State Univ, PO Box 416, Yellow Springs, OH 45387.

AMOS, WALLY
Entrepreneur. **Personal:** Born 1937, Tallahasse, FL; married Christine. **Career:** William Morris Agency, mail clerk to exec vice pres, agent for Simon & Garfunkel, The Temptations, The Supremes, the late Marvin Gaye, Dionne Warwick, Patti LaBelle; manager, Franklin Ajaye, Abby Lincoln, Oscar Brown Jr, & numerous other singers & actresses; Famous Amos Chocolate Chip Cookies, owner/pres, 1975-85, vice chairman, 1985-. **Orgs:** Literacy Volunteers of America, natl spokesperson. **Honors/Awds:** HS Diploma & Chef's Hat NY Foods Trade HS; Straw Panama Hat and embroidered Indian pullover shirt corporate symbols added to Business Americana Collection at the Smithsonian's Collection of Advertising History; Excellence Award, President Reagan. **Military Serv:** US Air Force, 4 years.

AMPREY, WALTER G.
Educational administrator. **Personal:** Born Dec 13, 1944, Baltimore, MD; son of Joseph L Sr and Marion A; married Freda Jones; children: Kimberley, Keli. **Educ:** Morgan State College, BA, 1966, MS, history and social science, 1971; John Hopkins Univ, MS, educational administration and supervision, 1977; Temple Univ, PhD, 1984. **Career:** Calverton Jr High School, teacher, 1966-71; Walbrook Sr High School, teacher, 1971, school administrator, 1971-73, asst principal, 1973-78, principal, 1978-84; Greenwood Baltimore County Public Schools, dir, chief negotiator, office of staff relations, 1984-85; Baltimore County Public Schools, assoc supt, division of physical facilities, 1985-90, assoc supt, divison of staff and community relations, 1991, supt, public instruction, 1991-. **Orgs:** Mcpl Employees Credit Union, bd of dirs; National Aquarium, Baltimore, bd of dirs; Baltimore Museum Art, bd of trustees; Northwest Hospital Center, bd of trustees; NEA; Maryland State Teachers Assn; National Assn Black School Exec; Nat Assn Secondary School Administrators; Assn Supervision and Curriculum Developers; American Assn School Administrators; Phi Alpha Theta; Omega Psi Phi, grand keeper of records and seal, 1982-84. **Honors/Awds:** Omega Psi Phi, Omega Man of the Year, 1971. **Business Addr:** Superintendent, Baltimore Public Schools, Education Department, 200 E North Ave Ste 405, Baltimore, MD 21202-5910.

AMPY, FRANKLIN R.
Educator/researcher. **Personal:** Born Jun 22, 1936, Dinwiddie, VA; son of Beatrice Tucker Ampy and Preston Ampy (deceased). **Educ:** Virginia State Coll,Petersburg, VA, BS, 1954-58; Oregon State Univ, Corvallis, OR, MS, PhD 1958-62; Univ of California Post Doctorate 1968-70. **Career:** Amer Univ of Beirut, asst prof, Lebanon, 1962-68; Univ of California, Davis CA, post doctorate 1968-70, Educ Oppor Prog, assoc dean 1970-71; Howard Univ, assoc prof zoology, Washington, DC, 1971-, acting chmn zoology 1973-75, 1984-86; Oregon State Univ, Corvallis, OR, Research Asst 1958-62. **Orgs:** Consultant Natl Inst of Health 1981, 1983; treasure Howard Chapter Amer Assoc Univ Prof 1983-84; evaluator VA Talent Search 1980-; mem Project Thirty, Carnegie Found New York City, comm selected to make recommendation on the improvement of secondary teacher training, profs & admins were selected from 30 inst of higher educ. **Honors/Awds:** Geneticist World Poultry Con Kiev Russia 1966; Faculty Fellow NASA/Ames Moffett Fields CA 1976; Fulbright Nominee Natl Council of Scholars 1984-85. **Business Addr:** Assoc Prof, Department of Zoology, Howard University, 414 College St NW, Washington, DC 20059.

ANDERS, KIMBLE LYNARD
Professional football player. **Personal:** Born Sep 10, 1966, Galveston, TX. **Educ:** Univ of Houston. **Career:** Kansas City Chiefs, running back, 1991-. **Honors/Awds:** Pro Bowl, 1995, 1996. **Business Addr:** Professional Football Player, Kansas City Chiefs, One Arrowhead Dr, Kansas City, MO 64129, (816)924-9300.

ANDERS, RICHARD H.
Educator. **Personal:** Born Jul 29, 1925, Arcadia, FL; son of Nettie Anders and James Anders; married Charlotte King; children: Kenneth, Keith, Rosalind. **Educ:** FL A&M Univ, BS 1947; IN Univ, MS 1963. **Career:** Dunbar HS Ft Myers, athletic dir coach 1947-48; Richardson HS Lake City, 1948-69; Part time city recreation asst, 1968-; Coord summer recreation 1973-74; Columbia HS, supr phys educ health 1973-75, intramural dir 1970-. **Orgs:** 1st vice pres Columbia Educ Assn 1974-75; sec Gateway Serv Unit of FL Educ Assn 1974-75; adv bd N Central FL Phys Educ Clinics 1970-; mem CEA Exec Bd; pres FL A&M Alumni Gateway Chap Lake City 1974-; Polemarch Gainesville Alumni Chap Kappa Alpha Psi Frat 1968-69, 1972-73; keeper records Kappa Alpha Psi 1973-74;mem, president, 1989-91; Lake City Optimist Club; Emerg Med Training Com (EMT); Columbia Co Planning Bd; mem FHSAA Game Ofcls; Versiteers Soc Club; Masonic Fraternal Order Shiloh 619; chorister New Bethel Bapt Ch; president, Columbia County Family Health Center Board of Directors, 1990- Columbia County School Board, chairman, 1988, 1992-. **Honors/Awds:** Football Championships 1947, 1951, 1953, 1959, 1963-65; runner up 1955-56, 1961-62; Coach of Yr Awd 1963, 1966; FL Athletic Coaches Assn Life Mem Awd 1970; FL Interscholastic Coaches Assn Awd 1967; Music Dir Trophy 1974; Versiteers Presidential Award, Versiteers Club, 1987-89; SABO Service Award, Sothern Association of Basketball Official, 1991; Education Achievement Award, NAACP, 1985; Achievement Award, Girl Scout Troop 117, 1989; Kappa Founders Day Award, Kappa Alpha Psi Fraternity, 1991. **Business Addr:** Intramural Dir, Columbia HS, Lake City, FL 32055.

ANDERSON, ABBIE H.
Educational administrator. **Personal:** Born Jun 3, 1928, Terrell, TX; son of Abbie Gill Anderson and James C Anderson; married Frances R Morgan; children: Donna R, Rosalind T, Abbie H Jr, Michael EC. **Educ:** Tuskegee Inst, BS 1953; Lincoln Univ of MO, MEd 1966. **Career:** Brigade exec ofcr; Vietnamese Chf of Reg Forces/Popular Forces, dist sr adv/adv; asst prof military sci; mem gen staff; chief auto weapons sec; marksmanship Unit, co commander; co exec ofcr; rifle platoon leader/weapons & platoon leader; US Army, ret Lt Col sect leader; NY Life Ins Co, ins salesman; Terrell Ind Schl Dist, school bd trustee. **Orgs:** Mem Dallas Assn of Life Underwriters 1971-; pres Amer Heart Assn Kaufman Cnty 1983-85; mem NAACP; treas Tuskegee Alumni Club of Dallas; sch bd mem Terrell Ind Sch Dist; bd mem Rosehill Water Coop; mem Cath Ch; mem Omega Psi Phi Frat; grand knight Father Vincius Council #6887 of the Knights of Columbus; chmn bd Jackson Comm Hosp; bd mem Terrell Comm Hosp. **Honors/Awds:** Rookie of the Year NY Life Ins Co; Recip Bronze Star; Combat Infantryman's Badge; Armed Forces Honor & Medal 1st Class Vietnam; Army Occupational Medal Germany; Natl Def Medal & First Oak Leaf Cluster; Armed Forces Reserve Medal; Vietnam Serv Medal. **Military Serv:** US Army, lt col, over 24 years; Repub of Vietnam Campaign Medal; Meritorious Serv Medal. **Home Addr:** 336 FM 2578, Terrell, TX 75160. **Business Addr:** School Board Trustee, Terrell Ind School Dist, 212 W High St, Terrell, TX 75160.

ANDERSON, AL H., JR.
Entrepreneur. **Personal:** Born May 1, 1942, Winston-Salem, NC; son of Gladys H Anderson and Albert H Anderson Sr; married Jeanette Robbins, Nov 25, 1971; children: April, Albert H. **Educ:** Morehouse College, BS, 1964; Rutgers University, 1970-71. **Career:** C&S National Bank, management trainee, 1967-68; Citizens Trust Bank, vice pres, 1968-70; Entreprises Now, Inc, executive director, 1970-72; Anderson Communications, chief executive officer, 1971-. **Orgs:** Black Public Relations Society, vice pres; African-American Marketing & Media Association; National Association of Market Developers. **Honors/Awds:** Outstanding Agency Award, Honorary Doctorate Degree, AAF. **Special Achievements:** Speaker at numerous seminars, universities and conferences. **Business Addr:** Chief Executive Officer, Anderson Communications, 2245 Godby Rd, Atlanta, GA 30349, (404)766-8000.

ANDERSON, ALFRED ANTHONY
Company executive. **Personal:** Born Aug 4, 1961, Waco, TX. **Educ:** Baylor University, attended. **Career:** Minnesota Vikings, running back, 1984-92; General Nutrition Ctr, owner, 1993-. **Orgs:** Arlington South Rotary Club, Optimist Club; Baylor Alumni Organization. **Honors/Awds:** Played in NFC Championship Game, post-1987 season; NFC Offensive Rookie of the Year, 1984-85. **Business Addr:** 5801 West I20, Ste 340, Arlington, TX 76016.

ANDERSON, AMEL
Educational administrator. **Personal:** Born Nov 17, 1936, Hazelhurst, MS; children: Kurt, Debra, Reynaldo, Terrence, Robert. **Educ:** Jackson State Univ, BS 1962; Univ of Houston, MS 1969; Va Polytechnic Inst & State Uiv, EdD 1976. **Career:** USAF OH, chemist 1969-71; USAF VA Tech & State Univ, asst prof 1971-75; VA Polytechnic Inst State Univ, rsch asst 1975-76; Univ of MD Div of Agricultural & Life Scis, asst to the provost 1976-. **Orgs:** MD Assn of Non-White Concerns in Personnel & Guidance 1980-81; vol instr Receiving Home for Children Washington DC 1977-79; pres Jackson State Univ Alumni Chap 1978-79; pres PTA Happy Acres Elementary School, 1978-80. **Honors/Awds:** Civitan Jackson MS 1960; Graduated w/Honors Jackson State Univ 1962; NSF Fellow Univ of Houston 1967. **Military Serv:** USAF capt 1964-75. **Business Addr:** Assistant Dean, Univ of MD, College of Life Sciences, 1110 Symons Hall, College Park, MD 20742.

ANDERSON, AMELIA VERONICA
Interior designer. **Personal:** Born Mar 13, 1947, New York, NY; daughter of Bernardine Turbee Grissom and Howard A Anderson. **Educ:** Bernard M Baruch Coll, BBA 1969. **Career:** Bloomingdales, dept mgr & personnel rep 1967-74; Essence Magazine, dir sales promotion & merchandising 1974-83; Playboy Enterprises Inc, promotion mgr, Games Magazine, 1983-84, promotion mgr, Playboy Magazine, 1985-87; Mary Gilliatt Interiors Ltd, design asst/office mgr, 1987-88; Anderson-Rooke Designs, partner, 1988-90; AVA Company, owner, 1991-. **Orgs:** Mem Advertising Women of New York; mem, Amer Women Entrepreneurs. **Honors/Awds:** CEBA Award of Excellence, 1980; Outstanding Achievements in Communications, BESI Inc, 1982; CEBA Award of Merit, 1983; CEBA Award of Excellence, 1983. **Business Addr:** Partner, AVA Company, PO Box 6921, New York, NY 10128.

ANDERSON, ANTONIO
Professional football player. **Personal:** Born Jun 4, 1973. **Educ:** Syracuse, attended. **Career:** Dallas Cowboys, defensive tackle, 1997-. **Business Addr:** Professional Football Player, Dallas Cowboys, One Cowboys Pkwy, Irving, TX 75063, (214)556-9900.

ANDERSON, ARNETT ARTIS
Orthodontist. **Personal:** Born Apr 1, 1931, Georgia; married Delores C Perry; children: Angela C, Andrea C. **Educ:** Savannah State Coll, BS 1953; Howard Univ, grad sch 1955-57; Howard Univ, DDS 1962; Univ of MI, MS 1965. **Career:** Inst of Health, nutrition & endocrinology rsch 1956-58; Howard Univ, cardiovascular rsch part-time 1960-62, pedodontics & instr 1962-63; Children's Orthodontic Clinic Livonia MI, dir 1964-65; Howard Univ Coll of Dentistry, assoc prof 1965-69; Private Practice Washington DC, dentist 1966-. **Orgs:** Orthodontic consult for Comm Group Health found St Elizabeth Hosp Washington DC; mem NE Regional Bd of Dental Examiners; DC Bd of Dental Examiners Sec; mem Amer Assn of Orthodontists; Middle Atlantic Soc of Orthodontists; Amer Coll of Dentists; Amer Assn of Dental Examiners; Natl Dental Assn; Amer Dental Assn; Intl Assn of Dental Rsch; Amer Soc of Dentistry for Children; Robt T Freeman Dental Soc; mem SW Neighborhood Assembly; Alpha Phi Alpha Frat. **Honors/Awds:** Best Thesis Awd Univ of MI Sch of Orthodontics, C Edward Martin Awd 1965; 1st Place Intl competition in Dental Rsch Edward H Hetton Awd 1966; Omicron Kappa Upsilon Natl Hon Dental Soc; Sigma Xi Hon Scientific Soc; Beta Kappa Chi; Alpha Kappa Mu. **Military Serv:** US Army. **Business Addr:** 635 G St SW, Washington, DC 20024.

ANDERSON, AVIS OLIVIA
Educator. **Personal:** Born Aug 27, 1949, Vivian, WV; daughter of Naomi T Fails and Harvey Fails; married Weldon Edward Anderson. **Educ:** Bronx Comm Coll, AAS 1970; Herbert H Lehman Coll, BS 1971; Hunter Coll, MS 1973; New York Univ, PhD 1986. **Career:** Bronx Comm Coll, coll lab tech 1971-72; Herbert H Lehman Coll, adjunct instructor 1972-73; LaGuardia Comm Coll, full-time instructor 1973-75, asst/assoc/full professor 1975-. **Orgs:** Mem Morrisania Educ Council 1972-; exec bd mem Business Educ Assoc 1978-; pres Coll Business Educators 1981-82; mem Charismatic Prayer Group 1985-; Conf Coordinator SUNY Office Tech/Secretarial Educators 1986-87; 2nd vice pres Business Educ Assoc 1986-87; past pres Gregg Shorthand Teachers Assoc 1986-87. **Honors/Awds:** Outstanding Administrator Morrisania Educ Council 1980; Service Awd Business Educ Assoc 1987. **Business Addr:** Professor of Business Educ, LaGuardia Community College, 31-10 Thomson Ave, Long Island City, NY 11101.

ANDERSON, BARBARA LOUISE
Library director. **Personal:** Born in San Diego, CA; daughter of Louise Morgan Anderson and Lorenzo Anderson. **Educ:** San Diego State Coll, BS 1954; KS State Tchrs Coll, MS in LS 1955. **Career:** LA Public Library, br young adult librarian 1956-59; San Diego Pub Libr, ref young adult librarian 1959-64; US Army Europe, 1964-69, administrative librarian, Serra Regl Library Systems San Diego, ref proj coord 1969-70; Riverside Pub Library, head of reader serv 1971-74; San Bernardino Co Library, dir 1974-. **Orgs:** Mem Amer, CA Library Assns; mem NAACP; Alpha Delta Chi; bd of directors, YWCA, San Bernardino, 1989-; president, California Society of Librarians, 1974-75; delegate, OCLC, Users Council, 1983-88; delegate, White House Conference on Information Sciences, 1979-; bd of directors, Inland Empire Sumphony, 1982-83. **Honors/Awds:** Citizen of Achievement, San Bernardino League of Women Voters, 1990; Honoree, Black Art and Culture Club of Lake Elsinore, 1988; Blacks in Government, Riverside City College, 1972.

ANDERSON, BARBARA STEWART JENKINS
Pathologist, educator. **Personal:** Born Nov 21, Chicago, IL; daughter of Alyce Walker Stewart and Carlyle F Stewart; married Sidney B Jenkins, Sep 22, 1951 (divorced); children: Kevin C Jenkins, Judith Jenkins Kelly MD, Sharolyn Jenkins Sanders, Marc J Jenkins, Kayla S Jenkins French; married Arthur E Anderson, Sep 30, 1972. **Educ:** Univ of MI, BS 1950; Wayne State Med Sch, MD 1957. **Career:** Wayne Co Hosp, 1966-70; Detroit Genl Hosp, dir of clinical lab; Wayne State Med Sch, assoc prof 1970-, staff pathol; DMC University Labs, admin medical director, Detroit Receiving Hosp, chief of pathology, 1988-. **Orgs:** Mem Wayne Co Med Soc, MI State Med Soc, AMA, Detroit Med Soc, Wolverine Med Soc, Natl Med Soc, Coll of Amer Pathol; Amer Soc of Clinical Pathol; Minority Recruitment Com Wayne Med Sch; Careers Club for HS Students; elected Alpha Omega Alpha 1956. **Honors/Awds:** Alexander McKenzie Campbell Awd 1957. **Business Addr:** Assoc Professor Pathology/ Director of Clinical Labs, Wayne State Medical School/Detroit Receiving Hospital, 4201 St Antoine, Third floor 3E, Detroit, MI 48201.

ANDERSON, BENJAMIN STRATMAN, JR.
Physician. **Personal:** Born Feb 23, 1936, Dothan, AL; son of Lula Sutton Anderson and Benjamin Anderson Sr; married Sandra C Wright, Jun 15, 1962 (died 1995); children: Benjamin III, Kevin, Carita. **Educ:** Fisk Univ, BS 1957; Meharry Medical Coll, MD 1962; Amer Bd of Family Practice, diplomate 1975, recertified 1981, 1987, 1995; Amer Acad of Family Physicians, fellow 1979. **Career:** Polk General Hosp, staff pres 1969-70, 1978-79, 1988-89, 1991-93; GA State Med Assn, exec bd 1973-; Polk Co Bd of Health, mem 1980-; chmn 1985-; GA Bd Human Resources, sec 1972-86; medical director, Brentwood Park Nursing Home, 1988-94; Coosa Valley Residential Substance Abuse Program, dir of medical services, 1989-; Anderson Medical Center, physician, currently. **Orgs:** Vice speaker House of Delegates GA Acad Family Physicians 1975-77; health serv dir Project Headstart Tallatoona EOA Inc 1974-79; consultant & preceptor Polk Co Primary Care Project 1981-83; consultant/advisor Polk Emergency Medical Serv 1979-; life mem Kappa Alpha Psi Frat 1970-; life mem NAACP 1975-; adv council Cedartown City Commission 1970-86; bd dirs of Cedartown Little League 1976-85; Cedartown Comm Relations Council 1986-; Wayside Inn Alcohol & Drug Residential Rehab Prgm, consultant 1986-92; board of directors, Georgia Assoc of Minority Entrepreneurs, 1988-90; member, American Society of Addiction Medicine, 1989-; member, Cedartown Recreation Commission, 1990-; board of advisors, Columbia/Polk General Hospital, 1996-. **Honors/Awds:** Service Award Atlanta Medical Assn 1973; Service Award GA State Medical Assn 1975; President's Award GA County Welfare Assn 1982; Northwest Georgia Minority Business Assoc, Businessman of the Yr 1986; Community Service Commendation, Georgia House of Representatives, 1988; Community Service Award, Polk County NAACP, 1987. **Business Phone:** (770)748-3006.

ANDERSON, BERNADINE M.
Cosmotologist. **Personal:** Born Dec 1, 1942, New York, NY; daughter of Benjamin Tonsler & Sarah Brown; divorced; children: Sherri Bruce, Jacqueline Brown,. **Educ:** New York City Univ, BA in arts, 1963; Brooklyn Coll, BA, 1963. **Career:** Cicely Tyson, head make-up artist, 1979-81; Jane Fonda Movies, 20th Century Fos, personal make-up artist, 1980-84; Stevie Wonder, head make-up artist, 1981-82; Eddie Murphy Movies, Paramount, head make-up artist, 1985-94; Lionel Ritchie, head make-up artist, 1986-87; Laurence Fishburne, Touchtone, personal make-up artist, 1990-93; Angela Basset Movies, Paramount, head of dept, 1994-95. **Orgs:** IASE Local 706, SAG-SEG, 1970-. **Honors/Awds:** Academy Awards, Emmy Nomination, Amen (4 times), 1987-89; Filmmakers Academly, Academy Award Nomination, Best Make-Up, 1990; Black Filmmakers Hall of Fame, Inductee, 1991. **Special Achievements:** Roots, 1976; A Soldiers Story, 1982; Another 48 Hours, 1985; Whats Love Got To Do With It, 1991; Bad Company, 1993. **Business Addr:** Pres, Bernadine M Anderson, Make-Up Artist to the Stars, 4559 Don Richardo Drive, Los Angeles, CA 90008, (213)296-5891.

ANDERSON, BERNARD E.
Government official. **Personal:** Born in Philadelphia, PA; son of Dorothy Gideon Anderson and William Anderson; children: Melinda D, Bernard E II. **Educ:** Livingstone Coll, AB; MI State Univ, MA; Univ of PA, PhD; Shaw Univ, LHD; Livingstone College, LHD. **Career:** US Bureau of Labor Statistics, economist 1964-66; The Rockefeller Foundation, dir social scis 1979-85; Woodrow Wilson School, Princeton Univ, visiting fellow 1985; Wharton School, Univ of PA, asst to full prof 1970-79; Urban Affairs Partnership, managing director; US Dept of Labor, asst secretary, 1993-; The Anderson Group, president; Univ of Maryland, College Park, economics prof. **Orgs:** Mem of bd Philadelphia Urban League 1970-76; mem former pres Natl Economic Assoc 1970-; mem bd NAACP Special Contributions Fund 1976-80; board of directors member, 1977-93, vice chair, 1988-93, MDRC Corp; consultant Ford Foundation 1985-93; mem bd of economists Black Enterprise Magazine 1981-93; mem Natl Commn Jobs & Small Business 1986; member, board of directors, Provident Mutual Life Insurance Co, 1988-; member, 1987-93, chairman, 1990-93, Lincoln University Board of Trustees; Livingstone College, bd of trustees, 1980-94. **Honors/Awds:** Publs Soul in Management with Richard America, Birch Lane Press, 1996; Black Managers in Amer Business 1980, Youth Employment and Public Policy 1981, "Economic Growth and Social Equity," The Changing Amer Economy 1986; keynote speaker dedication of new NAACP Natl Headquarters 1986. **Military Serv:** US Army, nco 2 yrs; Good Conduct Medal. **Business Addr:** Asst Secretary, US Dept of Labor, 200 Constitution Ave NW, Ste S-2321, Washington, DC 20210.

ANDERSON, BETTY KELLER
Journalist, editor. **Personal:** Born Dec 13, 1951, Pineville, LA; daughter of Helen L Keller and Arthur D Keller Sr; divorced; children: Tamara Renee, Travis Randolph. **Educ:** University of New Mexico, Albuquerque, NM, BA, Journalism, 1973. **Career:** Albuquerque Journal, summer intern, 1971; Tacoma News Tribune, reporter/copy editor, 1974-85; Houston Chronicle, copy editor, 1985-86; Seattle Times, copy/design editor, 1986-. **Orgs:** Deputy regional director, Region 10, Natl Assn of Black Journalists, 1990-91; NABJ, regional director, 1991-93; president, Black Journalist Assn of Seattle, 1988-90; supervisor, Editing & Publishing Ministry, Tacoma Christian Center, 1994-. **Honors/Awds:** Fellowship, Editing Program for Minority Journalists, Institute for Journalism Education, 1984. **Business Addr:** Letter/Opinion Page Editor, Editorial Dept, The Seattle Times, PO Box 70, Seattle, WA 98111.

ANDERSON, BRYAN N.
Business executive. **Personal:** Born Jun 18, 1955, New Haven, CT. **Educ:** Univ of Connecticut, grad, 1977. **Career:** Sen Weicker, staff asst; Virgin Islands Legislative Improvement Project, St Thomas, US Virgin Islands, proj dir; former admin asst to chf dep Minority Leaders, Connecticut state senate; former Harlem mayor; Hamden CT, constable, 1973-80; Pace Advertising, coord of client svcs. **Orgs:** Former bd mem State Bd Higher Educ; dist leader Hamden Rep Town Com; mem Hamden Arts Cncl; Hamden League of Women Voters; mem Ripon Soc Natl Governing Bd. **Honors/Awds:** Hamden Outstanding Youth Awd 1971; Comm Involvement Awd Greater New Haven Urban League 1973. **Business Addr:** Coordinator of Client Serv, Pace Advertising, Woodbridge, CT.

ANDERSON, CAREY LAINE, JR.
Architect. **Personal:** Born Jan 12, 1950, Louisville, KY; married Karen Elizabeth White; children: Latrice Elizabeth. **Educ:** Univ of KY, BArch 1973. **Career:** Arrasmith Judd Rapp & Assoc Architects, architect draftsman 1973-77; Robert F Crump Architects, proj architect 1977-78; City of Louisville Pub Works Dept,city architect 1978-79; Larry E Wright & Assocs Architects, asso/project architect 1979-80; Anderson & Assocs Architects, architect 1980-. **Orgs:** Prog chmn Central KY Chap AIA; mem Construction Specification Inst; mem KY Soc of Architects; mem NAACP; mem Phi Beta Sigma Frat Inc. **Honors/Awds:** First Black Architect License KY 1977; first Black Architect to establish architectural firm KY. **Business Addr:** Architect, Anderson & Assoc Architects, 736 S First St, Louisville, KY 40202.

ANDERSON, CARL EDWARD
Judge. **Personal:** Born Jan 8, 1939, Pendleton, SC; son of Wilhelmina Anderson and Amos Anderson; married Etta Humphrey, Feb 26, 1972; children: Carl Wendell. **Educ:** Tri County Tech College, associate's, criminal justice, 1975; South Carolina Criminal Justice Academy. **Career:** Sangamo Electric Co, 1965-70; Anderson County Sheriffs Department, 1970-89; Anderson County Summary Court, chief magistrate, judge, 1989-. **Orgs:** Tri County Judicial Association; South Carolina Summary Court Education Comm; Anderson Junior Assembly Advisory Board; South Carolina Summary Court Association. **Special Achievements:** First black chief magistrate, Anderson County, 1991; first black capt, Anderson Count Sheriff Department, 1988; first black officer, Anderson County Sheriff Department, 1970. **Military Serv:** US Army, lcpl, 1963-65. **Business Addr:** Chief Magistrate, Judge, Anderson County Summary Court, 100 S Main St, Bailes Bldg, Court House Annex, Anderson, SC 29624, (803)260-4156.

ANDERSON, CARL EDWIN
Educational administrator, consultant, federal offical. **Personal:** Born Sep 29, 1934, St Louis, MO; son of Elizabeth Hooper Anderson and Raymond W Anderson; married Ida Bass Anderson, Jun 19, 1954; children: Carl Jr, Rhonda L Anderson-Speight, Sherri Anderson-Cherry. **Educ:** Souther IL Univ, BA 1956, MS 1958; Univ of MD, EdD 1969. **Career:** Howard Univ, dir of student activities 1960-64, assoc dean of students 1964-69, acting dean of students 1969, vice pres for student affairs 1969-90, consultant, 1991-; US House of Representatives, Post Office and Civil Service Committe, professional staff, 1992-95. **Orgs:** Bd of dir Amer Assoc of Univ Admin, Southern IL Univ Found, Howard Univ Found; mem Natl Assoc of Student Personnel Admin, Amer Assn for Counseling & Dev, Natl vice pres for Student Affairs Org; evaluator Middle States Assoc/Sec Schools & Coll; mem Natl Urban League, NAACP; president Kappa Scholarship Fund Inc; Kappa Alpha Psi Frat; Sigma Pi Phi Fraternity (Boule); board of directors, William L Clay Scholarship & Research Fund, 1988-; member, National Association of Personnel Workers; member, Eastern Association of College Deans. **Honors/Awds:** Disting Alumni Achievement Award Southern IL Univ 1972; Lamont Lawson Awd for Outstanding Contrib Kappa Alpha Psi Frat 1984; Serv to Southern IL Univ; Admin of the Year Student Council Howard Univ; Phi Delta Kappa Honor Society in Education; Pi Sigma Alpha Honor Society in Political Science; Psi Chi Honor Society in Psychology; Scott Goodnight Award for Outstanding Performance as a Dean, National Association of Student Personnel Administrators, 1990; John E King Award for Outstanding Contribution to Higher Education, Southern Illinois University, 1990; Omicron Kappa Upsilon Dental Honor Society; Golden Key Honor Society. **Home Addr:** 2100 Yorktown Rd NW, Washington, DC 20012.

ANDERSON, CARLTON LEON
Corporation executive. **Personal:** Born Jan 12, 1942, Ashland, VA. **Educ:** VA State Coll, BA 1963. **Career:** Prudential Ins Co, coll relations consult 1972-73, mgr employment & col rel 1973-74, regl group mr 1974-76, sr group ins consult 1976, mgr group claims 1976-78, dir group claims 1978-83, general mgr 1983-85, dir, DMO, 1985-87, vice pres, group systems, 1987-89; vice pres, administration 1989-. **Orgs:** Bd dir/mem Planned Parenthood Fed of Amer 1980; board of dir/mem, New Jersey Commission on Smoking or Health, 1990. **Honors/Awds:** Outstanding Leader in Bus YM/YWCA Chicago 1977; YM/YWCA Newark 1981, 1987. **Military Serv:** US Army, capt 1963-70; Bronze Star w/Oak Leaf Clusters; Army Commendation w/Oak Leaf Cluster. **Home Addr:** 14 Plymouth Ave, Maplewood, NJ 07040.

ANDERSON, CAROL BYRD
Economist, educator, banker. **Personal:** Born Jun 7, 1941, Kansas City, MO; daughter of Elmira Byrd and Hartwell Byrd; married Dr Winston Anthony; children: Laura Elisabeth, Lea Elmira. **Educ:** Coll of St Teresa, BA 1962; Boston Coll, MA 1964, PhD 1969. **Career:** Bur Labor Statistics, gen economist 1963-64; Fed Reserve Boston, economist 1969-70; First Natl Bank of Chicago, staff officer 1970-75; Howard Univ Wash, DC, assoc prof 1975-76; Fed Reserve Wash, DC, economist/bd of govs 1976-. **Orgs:** Mem Amer Econ Assn 1960-; Natl Econ Assn 1975-; mem Social Econ 1960-; trustee Coll of St Teresa 1975-81. **Honors/Awds:** Woodrow Wilson Scholarship Award 1962; numerous publs 1st Natl Bank of Chicago 1971-73; Award, Chicago Jr C of C 1972. **Business Addr:** Economist/Bd of Govs, Fed Reserve, 20th Constitution Ave NW, Washington, DC 20551.

ANDERSON, CHESTER R.
Educator, designer, consultant. **Personal:** Born Jan 28, 1912, Weir, KS; son of Mary Anderson and Jami Anderson; married Charlene; children: Ercelle Johnson. **Educ:** Univ of Pittsburg, KS, BS 1934; IA State Univ, MS 1949; Central MI Univ, LLD 1977. **Career:** Kansas City, MO Schl System, teacher 1934-68, gen coord voc end 1968-71; Amer Inst of Design & Drafting, consult 1971-. **Orgs:** Pres Ind Art Club & Vocational Educ 1940-50; MO State Disadvantaged and Handicapped Assn pres 1976-77, vice pres 1975-76; mem Pres comm for Disadv & Handicapped Task Force; life mem NAACP; bd of dir Amer Inst for Design and Drafting; chmn awards com Amer Inst for Design and Drafting. **Honors/Awds:** Outstanding Serv Award MO Voc Assn 1977; Outstanding Serv Award MO Cncl for Local Adminstr 1977; Cert of Award Sch of Human Dignity 1977; Alumni Merit Achieve Award Pitts State Univ 1978; Maharishi Award 1980; Award from Friends of KEB Dubois Learning Center; Outstanding Lifetime Contrib to Kansas City, MO from Coca Cola Bottling Co of Mid-Amrica 1984; School Dist of Kansas City Award for Services as Member of Board of Educ 1980-84; Jefferson Award from AmerInst for Publ Serv by WDAFTV Kansas City, 1980; Award for Disting and Devoted Servs to Public Education in MO at 19 Ann Conf for MO School Adminstrs 1980. **Business Addr:** Consultant, MO Correction Dept, Tulsa, OK.

ANDERSON, DARREN HUNTER
Professional football player. **Personal:** Born Jan 11, 1969, Cincinnati, OH; married Robyn. **Educ:** Toledo. **Career:** Tampa Bay Buccaneers, defensive back, 1992; New England Patriots, 1992; Tampa Bay Buccaneers, 1993; Kansas City Chiefs, 1994-. **Business Addr:** Professional Football Player, Kansas City Chiefs, One Arrowhead Dr, Kansas City, MO 64129, (816)924-9300.

ANDERSON, DAVID ATLAS
Educator/administrator. **Personal:** Born Apr 28, 1930, Cincinnati, OH; son of Mary Alice Anderson and Willie David Anderson; married Ruth Joanine; children: David M, Kenwood M, Joanine C. **Educ:** Rochester Inst of Tech, BFA 1960; Syracuse Univ, MA 1962; Union Grad School, PhD 1975. **Career:** Urban League of Rochester, deputy exec dir 1967-70; State Univ of NY Brockport, lecturer Afro-Amer studies; Rochester Inst of Tech, visiting asst prof 1981-, dir parent educ, Rochester City School District. **Orgs:** Assoc Comm Health Univ of Rochester Medical Sch 1970-82; bd mem vice pres Mental Health Assoc 1980-86; lecturer Correctional Institutions at Sonyea and Oatka NY 1983-85; bd of dirs Rochester Museum & Sci Ctr 1986-90; Natl Assn of Black Storytellers, 1988-89. **Honors/Awds:** Community Leadership Awd Urban League of Rochester 1982; Out-

standing Community Serv, Health Assn of Rochester 1984; Distinguished Volunteer, Mental Health Assn Rochester 1986. **Military Serv:** USAF staff sgt 6 yrs. **Business Addr:** Dir Parent Education, Rochester City School District, 131 W Broad St, Rochester, NY 14614.

ANDERSON, DAVID TURPEAU
Judge. **Personal:** Born Aug 9, 1942, Cincinnati, OH; son of Florida Turpeau Anderson and Randall Hudson Anderson; children: David M, Daniel M. **Educ:** University of Cincinnati, BS, 1963; George Washington University, JD, 1972. **Career:** Congressman Robert Taft Jr, congressional staff asst, 1967-69; HUD, assistant for congressional relations, 1970; American Hospital Association, assistant for legislation, 1971-73; Stanley, Durham & Johnson, associate, 1972-76; City of Philadelphia, asst city solicitor, 1976-81; HUD, chief administrative judge, 1981-. **Orgs:** National Press Club; Philadelphia Bar Assn; BCA Judges Assn; Inter-American Bar Assn; Sr Executives Assn. **Home Addr:** PO Box 7304, Washington, DC 20044. **Business Addr:** Chief Administrative Judge, Board of Contract Appeals, U.S. Department of Housing & Urban Development, 451 7th St SW, Rm 2131, Washington, DC 20410, (202)927-5110.

ANDERSON, DEL MARIE
Educational administrator. **Personal:** Born Nov 6, 1937, Vicksburg, MS; daughter of Emma Grissom Williams and James Neely; married E Frederick Anderson, Mar 31, 1967 (divorced 1984). **Educ:** San Diego State University, AB, family and consumer studies, 1965, MSW, 1967; Claremont College, School of Executive Management, 1985. **Career:** San Diego State University, professor, social work; Grossmont College, counselor, dean of counseling; Los Angeles Harbor College, dean of students; Skyline College, vice pres, instruction and student services; San Jose City College, president, currently. **Orgs:** ACCCA, 1986-93; City of San Jose, Project Diversity, chairperson, 1992-94, Urban University Task Force member, 1992-94; Ernesto Galarza Institute, board of directors, 1993. **Honors/Awds:** San Diego State University, Alumna of the Year, 1992; KGO-TV, San Francisco, Profile in Excellence, 1992. **Special Achievements:** Book chapter, author, Cracking the Wall: Women in Management in Higher Education, 1993. **Business Addr:** President, San Jose City College, 2100 Moorpark Ave, San Jose, CA 95128, (408)288-3725.

ANDERSON, DEREK
Professional basketball player. **Personal:** Born Jul 18, 1974. **Educ:** Kentucky, bachelor's degree in pharmacy. **Career:** Cleveland Cavaliers, guard, 1997-. **Business Addr:** Professional Basketball Player, Cleveland Cavaliers, One Center Ct, Cleveland, OH 44115-4001, (216)659-9100.

ANDERSON, DONALD EDWARD
Publishing executive. **Personal:** Born Nov 19, 1938, Los Angeles, CA; son of Valdiar Howard Small and James Anderson; divorced; children: Donald E Jr, Brian Keith. **Educ:** Los Angeles City Coll, 1956-58; UCLA, 1958-59; Western Electronic Inst, 1959-60. **Career:** TRW Systems Group, engineering designer 1958-65; Watts Manufacturing Co, manager 1965-68; Audio-Video Communications, Inc, pres 1968-72; Nat'l Cable TV Assoc, dir govt relations 1973-74; Home Box Office, Inc, sr vp 1974-90; Emerge Communications, Inc, president & CEO 1990-. **Orgs:** Nat'l Broadcasting Club, bd of dir 1973-74; Black United Fund, bd of dir 1974; CA Cable TV Assoc, bd mem 1976-; Walter Kaitz Foundation, past chairman, vice pres and mem of the exec committee 1982-; Los Angeles Urban League, bd of dir 1983-84. **Honors/Awds:** YMCA, named black achiever in business & industry; Participant in Pres Jimmy Carter's Sponsored Prog for Minority Ownership and Control of Media, 1980; Time Inc, Andrew Heiskell awd for distinguished comm serv 1984.

ANDERSON, DONALD L.
Association executive. **Personal:** Born Apr 2, 1932, Pittsburgh, PA; son of Celeste Johnson Anderson and Russell L Anderson Sr. **Educ:** University of Michigan, Ann Arbor, MI, BS, 1953; London School of Economics, London, England, MSc, economics, 1957; University of Michigan Law School, Ann Arbor, MI, JD, 1960. **Career:** Common Pleas Court, Pittsburgh, PA, law clerk, 1961-63; Carlowe University, Pittsburgh, PA, teacher of economics, 1961-63; US House of Representatives Committee on Education & Labor, counsel & general counsel, 1963-66; US House of Representatives Government Operations Committee, legal & monetary affairs sub, 1966-68; National Assn for the Southern Poor, Durham, NC, executive director, 1968-. **Honors/Awds:** Community Leadership Award, 100 Black Men of America Inc; guest lecturer, E. F. Schumaker Society. **Military Serv:** US Army, Infantry, 1st Lieutenant, 1953-55. **Business Addr:** Executive Director, National Association for the Southern Poor, 712A 3rd Street, SW, Washington, DC 20024.

ANDERSON, DOREATHA MADISON
Human resource. **Personal:** Born Apr 3, 1943, Lynchburg, VA; widowed; children: Wanda M Taylor, Rae M Lamar, Raymond B Madison Jr, Doretha L Madison, Octavia D Madison. **Educ:** VA Seminary Coll, BS 1968; VA Union Univ, BA 1984. **Career:** Juvenile Detention Home, youth care worker 1968-82; Bags Unlimited Inc, pres 1982-; NAACP, finance chmn 1982-84; Comm Educ Employment Svcs, prog mgr 1985-86; Youth Development Svcs, prog mgr 1986-. **Orgs:** Mem Diamond Hill Baptist Church 1944-; mem Usher Bd 1975-, Church Aid 1975-; recording sec Daughter Elk Chap 181 IPOEW 1975-82, Eastern Star 1980-82; pres Missionary Circle 1980-; asst treas Variety Garden Club Hill City Chap 1984-; mem Amer Business Women Assoc 1983, United Way 1986, Natl Assoc for Female Exec Inc 1986. **Home Addr:** 2114 Indian Hill Rd, Lynchburg, VA 24503.

ANDERSON, DORIS J.
Educator, counselor. **Personal:** Born Oct 16, 1933, Reagan, TX; married Franklin D Anderson; children: Deborah, Daryl F, Caleb. **Educ:** BA, 1962; MEd, 1966. **Career:** Teacher, 13 yrs; Bastian School, counselor. **Orgs:** Life mem NEA, TSTA; mem TCTA, HTA, APGA, TVGA, ASCA, NVGA, ANWC, TPGA, TACES, HSCA; treas Houston Tchrs Assn 1974-75; pres Houston Sch Counselors Assn 1975; Ct Vol WICS Vol; Sigma Gamma Rho Sor Inc 1962; Phi Delta Kappa 1975; Natl Cncl of Negro Women. **Honors/Awds:** Sigma Woman of Yr 1975; Outstanding Serv Awd Houston Tchrs Assn 1975. **Business Addr:** Counselor, Bastian School, 1415 Southmore Blvd, Houston, TX 77004.

ANDERSON, EDDIE LEE, JR.
Professional football player. **Personal:** Born Jul 22, 1963, Warner Robins, GA. **Educ:** Fort Valley State. **Career:** Seattle Seahawks, defensive back, 1986; Oakland Raiders, 1987-. **Business Addr:** Professional Football Player, Oakland Raiders, 1220 Harbor Bay Pkwy, Alameda, CA 94502, (510)615-1875.

ANDERSON, EDWYNA G.
Attorney (retired). **Personal:** Born Feb 11, 1930, Tulsa, OK; daughter of Jeanne Osby Goodwin and Edward Lawrence Goodwin; divorced; children: Kathie Dones-Carson, Jenni R Dones. **Educ:** Fisk University, BA, 1950; University of Michigan, 1958-59; Detroit College of Law, JD, 1974. **Career:** Oklahoma Eagle Publishing Co, managing editor, vice pres, 1951-53; Kansas State Department of Social Welfare, clerk-typist, 1953-55; Mott Foundation, Flint Board of Education, sociology instructor, 1956-71; Hurley Hospital, social director, counselor, 1956-62; Flint Journal, news reporter, feature writer, 1963-65; Genesee County, Consumer Protection and Economic Crime Division, assistant prosecuting attorney, 1974-78, Prosecuting Attorney's Office, chief, 1978-80, assistant prosecuting attorney, 1980; Michigan Public Service Commission, commissioner, 1980-88; Dusquesne Light Co, general counsel, 1988-94, special counsel to the president, 1994-95. **Orgs:** Bar Associations: American, National, Pennsylvania, Michigan; NAACP; American Civil Liberties Union; board of directors: ONEOK Inc, 1995-, Pennsylvania Electric Association, American Corporate Counsel Association, YWCA of Greater Pittsburgh; numerous others. **Honors/Awds:** Flint New Human Relations Commission, Humanitarian Award, 1982; Sojourner Truth Award, Legislative Citations; numerous others.

ANDERSON, ELIZABETH M.
Accountant, government official. **Personal:** Born Nov 1, Paris, TX; daughter of Emma McClure Mason and Walter Mason; married Rev Harold Anderson, Oct 3, 1941; children: Andrew Anderson, Patricia Anderson Roper, Theresa Anderson Danzy, Portia Anderson Tucker. **Educ:** Draughon Business Coll, 1955-58; Tulsa Univ, 1969-74. **Career:** Oklahoma Tax Commission, Tulsa OK, dir of personnel-supervisor of accounting; Anderson Amusement Corp, Tulsa OK, dir of personnel. **Orgs:** Mem, NAACP Tulsa Chapter, 1949-89; mem, Tulsa Urban League, 1950-89; mem, past pres, Jack & Jill of Amer, Tulsa Chapter, 1952-71, 1984-86; exec bd, Tulsa Pastor's Wives Council; mem, numerous state and city boards & committees; national board, Natl Council of Negro Women, Washington DC; natl council, Assault on Illiteracy, NY City; exec bd, YWCA, Tulsa OK; southern regional dir, Eta Phi Beta Sorority; natl pres, CEO, vice pres, Eta Phi Beta Sorority. **Home Addr:** 1724 Mohawk Blvd, Tulsa, OK 74110.

ANDERSON, ELOISE B. MCMORRIS
Educator. **Personal:** Born Jan 26, Columbus, OH; divorced; children: Juanita B. **Educ:** OH State Univ, BS 1943; Wayne State Univ, MEd 1947, EdD 1973. **Career:** Cleveland Jr High School, teacher 1944-63, exact sci dept head 1963-65; Western High School, Detroit MI, sci dept head 1965-70; Cass Tech High School, Detroit MI, asst principal 1970-; Denby High School, Detroit MI, principal 1983-84; Murray Wright High School, Detroit MI, principal 1984-. **Orgs:** Pres bd dir Detroit Teachers Credit Union; life mem Delta Sigma Theta; past mem bd of dir Afro-Amer Mus Detroit; Bethel AME Church; bd mem met Detroit Alliance of Black School Ed; life mem Natl Sci Teachers Assoc, Natl Alliance Black School Ed; bd dir Wayne State Univ Alumni Assoc; mem Natl & MI Assoc Secondary School Principal, Natl & MI Assoc for Suprv & Curriculum Devel, Professional Womens Network, Org School Admin & Suprv. **Honors/Awds:** Anthony Wayne Awd Wayne State Univ 1979. **Business Addr:** Principal, Murray-Wright HS, 2001 W Warren Ave, Detroit, MI 48208.

ANDERSON, EUGENE
Government official, company executive. **Personal:** Born Mar 9, 1944, Diffee, GA; son of Velma Anderson and Velver Anderson Sr; married Mamie Jewel Sapp, Dec 3, 1966; children: Timothy E, Tamara E, Melanie J. **Educ:** Wichita Tech Inst, radio, telephone communications 1971. **Career:** State of KS, state rep 1973-76; Congressman Dan Glickman, dist aide 1976-78; KS Commiss on Civil Rights, chairperson 1979-83; Black Democratic Caucus of KS, sec 1982-85; Rollin' & Smokin' Bar-B-Que Hut, owner/operator; Kansas Legislature, senator, currently. **Orgs:** Pres Optimist Club of Northeast Wichita 1974-75; treas State Democratic Party KS 1985-87; mem Masonic Lodge, NAACP; ranking minority mem Fed & State Affairs; mem Confirmations Comm, Ed Comm, Public Health & Welfare Comm, Midwestern Conf of the Council of State Govts, Adv Council on Aging, Legislative Ed Planning Comm. **Honors/Awds:** Community Serv Award Police Neighborhood Serv Center 1976; Coach of the Year Award The Salvation Army Biddy Basketball Program 1983. **Military Serv:** AUS sp5 1962-65, Parachutist Badge. **Home Addr:** 1832 N Poplar, Wichita, KS 67214.

ANDERSON, GARRET JOSEPH
Professional baseball player. **Personal:** Born Jun 30, 1972, Los Angeles, CA. **Career:** Anaheim Angels, outfielder, 1994-. **Honors/Awds:** The Sporting News, American League Rookie Player of the Year, 1995. **Business Addr:** Professional Baseball Player, Anaheim Angels, PO Box 2000, Anaheim, CA 92803, (714)937-6700.

ANDERSON, GARY WAYNE
Professional football player. **Personal:** Born Apr 18, 1961, Columbia, MO; married Ollie; children: Antisha, Gary Jr. **Educ:** Arkansas, attended. **Career:** Tampa Bay Bandits (USFL), 1983-85; San Diego Chargers, running back/wide receiver 1983-89; Tampa Bay Buccaneers, running back, beginning 1990; Detroit Lions, currently. **Honors/Awds:** Named MVP in three bowl games during college career; named second team All-USFL by College and Pro Football Newsweekly, 1984; All-Rookie First Team honors from UPI, Football Digest and Pro Football Writers; 1987 Pro Bowl team. **Business Addr:** Professional Football Player, Detroit Lions, 1200 Featherstone Rd, Pontiac, MI 48342.

ANDERSON, GEORGE A.
Business executive. **Personal:** Born Nov 15, 1923, Chicago, IL; married; children: George Jr. **Educ:** Attended, Howard Univ, Roosevelt Univ, Central YMCA Coll in Chicago. **Career:** Draper & Kramer, former branch office mgr; Lake Meadows Apts Chicago, mgr; Draper & Kramer Inc, vice pres. **Orgs:** Mem Chicago Real Estate Bd; Natl Real Estate Bd; Inst of Real Estate mgmt; Apt Bldg Owners & Mgrs Assn; South Side Planning Bd; supports LaRabida Children's Hosp, Jane Dent Home for the Aged. **Business Addr:** Vice President, Draper & Kramer Inc, 500 E 33 St, Chicago, IL 60616.

ANDERSON, GEORGE ALLEN
Attorney. **Personal:** Born Sep 11, 1941, Zanesville, OH; son of Louis B & Cenna M Anderson; married Brenda, Sep 28, 1962; children: Kim, George A Jr. **Educ:** South Carolina State University, BA, 1962, JD, 1965. **Career:** Aiken-Barnwell CAC Inc, ceo, 1966-; Anderson & Associates of Aiken PA, owner, currently. **Orgs:** American Bar Association; National Bar Association; Southeastern Lawyers Association; South Carolina Bar Association; Lower Savannah Council of Governments; Zoning Board of Adjustments, City of Aiken, chairman; Cumberland AME Church, Aiken, South Carolina; Aiken County Bar Association; South Carolina State College Alumni Association. **Honors/Awds:** South Carolina State College School of Law Awd. **Business Addr:** Owner, Anderson & Assocs of Aiken, PA, 302 Park Ave SE, Ste 2, Aiken, SC 29802, (803)648-0797.

ANDERSON, GLADYS PEPPERS
Media specialist (retired). **Personal:** Born May 12, Jacksonville, FL; daughter of Nancy Washington Peppers and Robert Peppers; married James Carl Anderson (divorced 1957); children: James Michael (deceased). **Educ:** Florida A&M University, Tallahassee, FL, AB, 1938; Atlanta University; Hampton University, Hampton, VA, BSLS, 1939; New York University, New York, NY, MA, 1947. **Career:** Lincoln High School, Tallahassee, FL, head librarian, 1939-68; Leon High School, Tallahassee, FL, head media specialist, 1968-78. **Orgs:** Organizer, first president, Florida State Library Assn; member, American Library Assn Council; past vice pres, Council of Negro Women, Tallahassee Chapter; past board member, Florida Assn of Media in Education; charter member, undergraduate and graduate chapter, Delta Sigma Theta Sorority. **Honors/Awds:** Meritorious Achievement in the Field of Education, 1966; Outstanding Secondary Education of America Award, 1974; Plaque, Outstanding Services, Leon High School, 1977; Plaque, Services Rendered, Delta Sigma Theta Sorority, 1977; Certificate, Pioneering in Library Services, Hampton University, 1977. **Home Addr:** 522 Campbell St, Tallahassee, FL 32310.

ANDERSON, GLORIA L.
Educator. **Personal:** Born Nov 5, 1938, Altheimer, AR; daughter of Elsie Foggie Long (deceased) and Charley Long (deceased); divorced; children: Gerald L. **Educ:** AR AM&N Coll, BS 1958; Atlanta Univ, MS 1961; Univ of Chicago, PhD 1968. **Career:** SC State Coll, instr 1961-62; Morehouse Coll, instr 1962-64; Univ of Chicago, teaching & rsch asst 1964-68; SC State Coll, prof summer sch 1967; Lockheed GA Corp, NSF rsch fellow 1981, rsch consultant 1982; Air Force Rocket Propulsion Lab, SCEEE faculty rsch fellow 1984; Morris Brown Coll, assoc prof & chmn 1968-73; Callaway prof & chmn 1973-84; acting vice pres for academic affairs 1984-85, dean of academic affairs 1985-89; UNCF Distinguished Scholar, 1989-90; Fuller E Callaway, professor of chemistry, 1990-; Morris Brown College, interim president, 1992-, dean of science and technology, 1996-; American Institute of Chemists, certified professional chemist, 1992-. **Orgs:** Mem, fellow, American Institute of Chemists, Amer Chem Soc, GA Acad of Sci, NY Acad of Sci, Amer Assn for Advancement of Sci, Natl Sci Tchrs Assn, Amer Assn of Univ Profs, Delta Sigma Theta Sor Inc; Natl Inst of Sci, Atlanta Univ Sci Rsch Inst, Natl Assn of Educ Broadcasters; mem of numerous adv bd comms & special projects; mem NAACP; author of numerous scientific publications; educ consultant US Dept of Educ 1976-88; mem ad hoc tech review group Natl Cancer Inst 1986; NIADA, contract reviewer, 1990-91. **Honors/Awds:** Alpha Kappa Mu Natl Honor Soc; Beta Kappa Chi Sci Honor Soc; Alpha Kappa Mu Honor Trophy Coll All Expense Scholarship Highest Average in Freshman Class 1955; appointed by Pres Nixon mem of bd Corp for Pub Broadcasting 1972; honored by Atlanta Chap AR AM&N Coll Natl Alumni Assn 1973; honored by Atlanta Chap Delta Sigma Theta Sor Inc as one of 25 Atlanta Deltas "Breaking New Ground" 1974; Fellow Mem Amer Biographical Inst 1977; governor's appointee Public Telecommunications Task Force 1980; Atlanta Magazine "Atlanta's Best and Brightest Scientists," 1983; Arkansan of Achievement in Educ 1985; United Negro Coll Fund Distinguished Scholar 1985; NAFEO Natl Alumni Awd 1986; All-Star Excellence in Educ Award, Univ of Arkansas at Pline Bluff Alumni, 1987; 30other honors and awards. **Business Addr:** Interim President, Morris Brown Coll, 643 Martin Luther King Jr Dr, Atlanta, GA 30314.

ANDERSON, GRANVILLE SCOTT
Educational administrator. **Personal:** Born Jul 25, 1947, Honolulu, HI; son of Olga Edna Jones Anderson and Granville P Anderson; married Jennifer Sachie Kato, Sep 13, 1986. **Educ:** Queensborough Comm Coll, AAS, 1971; Ruskin College, Oxford, England, Certificate of Study, 1970; Queens Coll, BA, 1972. **Career:** City Univ, exec asst, 1972-82; CCNY, exec officer, 1982-87; Rsch Found, CUNY proj coordinator, 1987-90; CUNY, Deputy Director of Admissions, 1990-. **Orgs:** Mem Univ Chancellor's Scholarship to Study in the UK 1969-70; Oscar Wilde Speaker's Tour to Belfast, Northern Ireland 1969; administrator CUNY Pamela S Galiber Scholarship Fund 1976-86; mem exec bd Metro Squash Racquets Assoc 1977-80; Sports Management Consultant 1977-; chmn Referees Comm MSRA 1978; pres Queensborough Comm Coll Alumni Assoc 1979-86; squash professional Town Squash Inc 1980-; member, New York Aikido Club, 1990-. **Honors/Awds:** John F Kennedy Award 1968; Nationally ranked amateur squash player US Squash Racquets Assoc.

ANDERSON, GREGORY WAYNE
Professional basketball player. **Personal:** Born Jun 22, 1964, Houston, TX; married Tammie; children: Greg Jr, Geia, Gabrielle, Geremy. **Educ:** Univ of Houston, Houston, TX, 1983-87. **Career:** San Antonio Spurs, center-forward, 1987-89; Milwaukee Bucks, 1989-90; New Jersey Nets, 1991; Denver Nuggets, 1991-92; Phonola Caserta (Italy), 1992-93; Detroit Pistons, 1993-94; Atlanta Hawks, 1994-95; San Antonio Spurs, 1995-97; Atlanta Hawks, 1997-. **Honors/Awds:** NBA All-Rookie Team, 1988. **Business Addr:** Professional Basketball Player, Atlanta Hawks, One CNN Center, Ste 405, Atlanta, GA 30335, (404)827-3800.

ANDERSON, HAROLD A.
Manager. **Personal:** Born Oct 12, 1939, New York, NY; married Alice Campbell; children: Joi, Dwight. **Educ:** Morehouse Coll, 1961-63; Queens Coll, BA 1966; NYU, 1967-69. **Career:** NY Life Ins Co, pub rel asst 1967-69; Interracial Cncl for Bus Oprt, dir pub rel 1969-70; ITT News Serv, writer 1970-74; ITT News & Pub Aff, admin 1974-76; ITT, mgr pub affairs 1977-86; Schomburg Ctr for Rsch in Black Culture NY Public Library, public relations officer 1986-. **Orgs:** Former bd mem Provide Addict Care Today; Rutgers Minority Invest Co; CCBE; Harlem Consumers Educ Cncl Inc; Former mem Natl Urban Affairs Cncl; Pub Rel Soc of Amer; 100 Black Men; OIC NY Tech Adv Com; mem Nigerian/Amer Friendship Soc; visiting prof Natl Urban League Black Exec Exch Prgm Coord; Youth Motivation Task Force Living Witness Prgm; conslt Natl Urban League; Coll Awareness Prgm; Black Achiever ITT 1976; bd mem Harlem YMCA of Greater NY. **Honors/Awds:** Hon YMCA Black Achiever in Indus; Citations US Dept of Treas; Dillard Univ Louise Wise Services' Save our Schlrshp Com; Former prof singer, rec artist& song writer. **Business Addr:** Public Relations Officer, NY Public Library Schomburg Ctr for Rsch in Black Culture, 515 Lenox Ave, New York, NY 10037-1801.

ANDERSON, HELEN LOUISE
Retail executive, consultant. **Personal:** Born Feb 23, 1941, Luxora, AR; daughter of Ruby Lee Evans Nunn and Mack Anderson. **Educ:** Attended, Syracuse Univ, 1959-61, Fashion Inst of Tech 1965-67. **Career:** Eastern Airlines, flight attendant 1965-67; Fashion Barn, exec vice pres 1967-88, Anderson & Associates, pres, 1988-. **Orgs:** Dir, bd member, Fred J Rogers Memorial Foundation; mem, Princess Grace Foundation, Exec Women of NJ, Coalition of 100 Black Women, Cornell Univ Medical Sch Comm for the Benefit of Minority Students, BRAG, Natl Assn of Black Journalists; bd of dirs, Fashion Barn 1987-; bd mem, Support Network Inc. **Honors/Awds:** Twin Award Natl Bd of the YWCA 1986. **Business Addr:** President, Anderson & Associates, Inc, One Lincoln Plaza, Suite 12B, New York, NY 10023.

ANDERSON, HENRY L. N.
Educational administrator. **Personal:** Born May 23, 1934, Ogeechee, GA; son of Louise Burns Lonon Anderson and Egister Lee Anderson; married Agnes Fox Anderson, Feb 14, 1961; children: Brenda Ivelisse, Ileana La Norma, Henry Lee Norman. **Educ:** Earlham College, Richmond, IN, 1953-54; Cheyney University of Pennsylvania, BS, 1954-57; Yale University, MAR, 1957-59; University of California at Los Angeles, EdD, 1969-72. **Career:** Los Angeles County Schools, teacher, 1961-66; Los Angeles Unified Schools District, instructor and administrator, 1967-68; University of California, Los Angeles, director of "Project Upward Bound," 1968-69; Loyola University, Graduate School of Education, assistant professor, 1968-72; California State University, Graduate School of Education, 1972-73; Evaluations & Management International Inc, director, 1971; Windsor University, Los Angeles, CA, vice president, 1973-75; City University Los Angeles, CA, president, 1974-; Fruitarian and Wellness lecturer; financial consultant; real estate developer/entrepreneur; African American Community Trust, CEO. **Orgs:** Yale Club of Southern California; life member, NAACP; life member, UCLA Alumni Association; founder, Organic Wellness Crusade Network; former pres, Phi Delta Kappa. **Honors/Awds:** "You and Race," 1960; "No Use Cryin'," 1961; Revolutionary Urban Teaching, 1973; Helping Hand: 8-Day Diet Programs, 1986; A Guide to Healthy Living, 1990. 4 Honorary Doctorates; Inducted into Hall of Fame, Cheyney University of PA, 1984; Danford Foundation Honoree, "I Dare You" Honor Roll, 1953; produced and hosted an award-winning TV talk show on wellness . **Special Achievements:** Ihre Gesundheit in Ihrer Hand, 1992; Organic Wellness Fasting Technique, 1992; African: Born in America, 1993. **Military Serv:** US Army, Cpl., 1953-60. **Business Addr:** President/Chancellor, City University-Los Angeles, c/o EMI, Inc, 111 N LaBrea Ave, Suite 307, Inglewood, CA 90301, (310)671-0783.

ANDERSON, HOWARD D.
Health agency executive. **Personal:** Born Feb 28, 1936, Lumpkin, GA; son of Lila Anderson and James M Anderson; married Susan Benson. **Educ:** Morehouse College, BA, 1968; University of Iowa School of Law, attended, 1968-69. **Career:** United States Post Office, clerk, 1957-66; Merck, Sharpe & Dohme, sales rep, 1969-70; University of Chicago, staff writer, 1970-72; SCDAI, president, 1972-. **Orgs:** Sickle Cell Disease Assn of America, 2nd vice chair, 1994-95, 3rd vice chair, 1990-91; National Voluntary Health Agencies of Illinois, chairman, 1985-93; Combined Health Appeal, secretary, 1991-; Chicago Regional Blood Program, board member, 1979-84. **Honors/Awds:** Chicago Urban League, Beautiful People Award; Chicago Regional Blood Program; Fred Hampton Scholarship Fund; Black Woman's Hall of Fame Foundation; League of Black Women, 1992. **Military Serv:** Army, sp-4, 1958-60; Letter of Commendation. **Business Addr:** President, Sickle Cell Disease Assn of Illinois, 200 N Michigan Ave, #605, Chicago, IL 60601-5980, (312)663-5700.

ANDERSON, HUBERT, JR. **See Obituaries section.**

ANDERSON, IVY I.
Consultant. **Personal:** Born Nov 18, 1957, Flint, MI; daughter of Willie A Anderson and Eugene Anderson Sr. **Educ:** GMI Engineering & Management Institute, BSME, 1980; The Wharton School, University of Pennsylvania, MBA, 1984. **Career:** AC Spark Plug, GMC, cooperative student engineer in training, 1975-80; Scott Paper Co, process engineer, 1980-82; University of Pennsylvania, management analyst, 1983-84; FMC Corp, planning management, 1984-85, office systems project mgr, 1985-86, planning support mgr, 1987-90, product mgr, 1990-93; Gemini Consulting, consultant, 1993-. **Orgs:** Chicago Chapter, National Black MBA Association, program committee chairman, 1988-90, executive board, 1988-90; Regal Theater Aux Board, strategic planning chair, 1989-90; Project Literacy, tutor, 1987-90; Cosmopolitan Community Church, youth program co-chair, 1987-90; Masterman Middle School, tutor, 1990-93; Salem Baptist Church, trustee, 1992-,literacy program, 1992. **Honors/Awds:** Dollars & Sense Magazine, Tribute for Business Accomplishments, African-American Women, 1991. **Special Achievements:** Toastmasters International, Able Toastmaster, 1985. **Business Addr:** Consultant, Gemini Consulting, 25 Airport Rd, Morristown, NJ 07960, (201)285-9000.

ANDERSON, J. MORRIS
TV producer, publisher, entrepreneur. **Personal:** Born Jul 6, 1936, Greenville, SC; divorced; children: J Morris Jr, Gracelyn, Aleta, Kathy. **Educ:** Amer Univ, BA 1961. **Career:** Miss Black Amer Beauty Pageant, Little Miss Black Amer, Tiny Miss Black Amer, Miss Black Am Teenager, Ms Black Amer, Mrs Black Amer, Miss Third World, founder/exec producer. **Orgs:** Pres Success Seekers Seminar; chmn & fndr Black Amer Radio & TV Network; chmn Miss Black Amer Beauty Ctrs; exec dir Rehab Inst of Amer; fndr J Morris Anderson Assn Investments Stocks & Bonds; mem Omega Psi Phi; bd mem several public orgns. **Honors/Awds:** Author "Recipes for Black Togetherness", "The Seeds of Positivity", "The Secrets of Mind Control" Vol 1-12; received over 50 awds & citations. **Business Addr:** Executive Producer, Ms Black Amer Beauty Pageant, PO Box 25668, Philadelphia, PA 19141.

ANDERSON, JAMES ALAN
Educator. **Personal:** Born Dec 13, 1948, Washington, DC. **Educ:** Villanova Univ, BA 1970; Cornell Univ, PhD 1980. **Career:** Xavier Univ, asst prof of psychology 1976-80, chmn dept of psychology and assoc prof of psychology 1980-83; Indiana Univ of PA, assoc prof of psych 1983-87; prof of psych, 1987-. **Orgs:** Mem Assn of Black Psychologists 1982-, Assn of Black Women in Higher Educ 1983-, Amer Federation of Teachers 1983-; dir Benjamin E Mays Acad of Scholars IUP 1985-; editor Benjamin E Mays Acad of Scholars Monograph Series 1986-; American Psychological Society; National Assn of Developmental Education. **Honors/Awds:** Grant to Develop Rsch Modules in Psychology Natl Sci Foundation 1976; Danforth Fellow 1980; grant Cross-Cultural Rsch Dillard Univ 1982; Rsch Travel Awd Intl Congress of Psychology 1984; Distinguished Black Alumni, Villanova Univ, 1987; Distinguished Black Pennsylvanian, 1988. **Business Addr:** Prof of Psychology, Indiana Univ of PA, Dept of Pyschology, Clark Hall, Indiana, PA 15705.

ANDERSON, JAMES R., JR.
Educator. **Personal:** Born Feb 25, 1922, Brazil, IN; son of Eva Roberts Anderson and James R Anderson; married Fern Gabenez Turner; children: James III, Reginald H, Stephen E, Pamela S, Carla J. **Educ:** Indiana Univ, BS Soc Serv 1952, AM Soc Serv 1954; Michigan School of Public Health, attended 1965-68. **Career:** Indiana State Dept of Public Welfare, child welfare consultant 1954-55; VA Hospital Indianapolis, clinical social worker 1955-60; VA Hosp Dearborn MI, chief inpatient sect social serv 1960-61; Wayne State Univ School of Social Work, asst prof 1961-63, assoc prof 1963-68, University of Washington, assoc prof school of social work, 1968-90, asst to the dean for health scis & coord health care concentration, adj assoc prof health serv school of public health & comm med, assoc prof emeritus, 1991-. **Orgs:** Consultant Multiple Sclerosis Soc King Co 1976-79; mem adv com AMSA Found Interdisciplinary Team Proj 1977-79; consult ID Migrant Health Council 1979-81; mem bd dir, pres, vice pres, Seattle Urban League 1971-73; mem adv com Midwifery Proj Group Health Coop of Puget Sound 1979-82; bd of dirs, Chr Prog Com African American Community Health Network, 1996-. **Military Serv:** AAF t/sgt 1941-45; ETO Ribbon w/9 clusters. **Home Addr:** 4081 224th Ln SE, Apt 203, Issaquah, WA 98029.

ANDERSON, JOE LEWIS, SR.
Personnel relations manager. **Personal:** Born Mar 18, 1948, Washington, GA; son of Veola Cofer Anderson and Leroy Anderson Sr; married Angeles Webb Anderson, Aug 28, 1971; children: Joe L Jr, Jeffrey L, April N. **Educ:** North Carolina A&T State University, Greensboro, NC, BS, Economics, 1966-70. **Career:** Eastman Kodak Co., Walnut Creek, CA, manager of personnel relations, 1970-. **Orgs:** Member, board of directors, Interface Institute, Oakland, CA, 1988-90; advisory board member, Bay Area Urban League, San Francisco, CA, 1988-90; member, Reserve Officers Association, 1970-; member, Omega Psi Phi Fraternity, 1967-; member, Black MBA Association, 1988-. **Military Serv:** US Army, LTC, 1971-73, reserves, 1973-; received Army Commendation Medal. **Business Addr:** Manager, Personnel Relations, Eastman Kodak Co, 350 N Wiget Lane, Walnut Creek, CA 94598.

ANDERSON, JOHN C., JR.
Probation officer (retired), educator. **Personal:** Born Aug 12, 1917, Dwiggins, MS; son of Carrie Hicks Anderson and John C Anderson Sr; married Celestyne L; children: Corrie Reginald. **Educ:** Univ of Toledo, Toldeo OH, AB, 1940; Golden Gate Law Sch, JD, 1953; Univ of California, post doctoral studies. **Career:** Civil Service, LeCarne OH, fed employee, 1941; Golden Gate Mutual Ins Co, 1946-47; Civil Service, Oakland CA, fed employee, 1946-52; Naval Supply Ctr, Oakland CA, 1952-53; Alameda Co Probation Dept, sr dep probation officer, beginning 1953; City College, San Francisco, CA, criminology instructor, 1976-. **Orgs:** Bd trustees Peralta Comm Coll Dist 1971-92; bd trustees Beth Eden Bapt Ch; past pres Beth Eden Housing Inc; mem Omega Psi Phi Frat; mem Monarch #73 Prince Hall Masons; mem Bay Area Urban League; mem Oakland Br NAACP; pres, East Oak Senior Center; commissioner, Council on Aging, City of Oakland, CA, 1994-95; pres, East Oakland Senior Citizens, Inc, 1993-95. **Honors/Awds:** Men of Tomorrow, Oakland Man of Yr Beth Eden Bapt Ch 1962;

Omega Cit of Yr Sigma Iota Chap Omega Psi Phi 1971; Minister's Distinguished Service Award, 1978; Public School Service Award, 20 years, 1991; Western Region, Council of Black American Affairs Award, 1989; Peralto Colleges Foundation Award, 1991; College of Alameda Service Award, 1992; Certificate of Honor and Appreciation, Vista College, 1992; Beth Eden Baptist Church, Honorary Trustee Award, 1992. **Military Serv:** OH NG pvt 1938-40; US Army, m/sgt 1942-46; US Air Force, Tuskegee Airman Award, 1991. **Home Addr:** #9 lMaggiora Ct, Oakland, CA 94605.

ANDERSON, JOSEPH B., JR.
Automobile co. executive. **Career:** General Motors Corp, currently. **Orgs:** Chivas Products, Ltd, chair/CEO.

ANDERSON, JOSEPH F.
Supply company executive. **Personal:** Born Aug 27, 1921, Roanoke, VA; son of Catherine Anderson and Wiley Anderson; married June Emily Thomas, Aug 25, 1946; children: Jeffrey J Sr, Yvonne J. **Educ:** The University of the State of New York, computer programming, 1968. **Career:** US Postal Services, data systems specialist, 1963-76; Antronix Distribution & Supply, Inc, president, 1980-, chmn of the bd of dirs, currently. **Orgs:** Carolinas Minority Supplier Development Councils, Inc, 1983-; Greensboro Chamber of Commerce, 1990-; Woodlea Neighborhood Association, 1982-; Triad Minority Supplier Development Council, 1988-; Metropolitan United Methodist Church: United Methodist Men, Chancel Choir, Male Chorus, former board of trustees member, 1982-. **Honors/Awds:** National Association of Negro Business of Professional Women's Club, Achievement in Minority Business, 1990; Hayes-Taylor YMCA, Support of Services to Young People Gold Club 500, 1992, 1995, 1996; AT&T, MWBE Champion Supplier, 1995. **Business Addr:** President, Antronix Distribution & Supply, Inc, 103-M Creekridge Rd, PO Box 16679, Greensboro, NC 27406, (919)272-0878.

ANDERSON, KATHLEEN WILEY
Government official (retired). **Personal:** Born May 22, 1932, Kansas City, KS; married Harvey L Anderson (deceased); children: Harvey, H Delon, Doryanna. **Educ:** Univ of Kansas, Lawrence KS, BS, 1954, MS, 1955; Univ of Southern California, MPA, 1974; Wharton School, Univ of Pennsylvania, attended 1979. **Career:** Kansas City, hs tchr, 1954-56; Sch for the Deaf, tchr, 1958-63; California Inst for Women, adminstr, 1963-74; Correctional Training Facility, assoc supt act dep supt, 1974-76; California Inst for Women, supt, 1976-80; California Inst for Men, superintendent, retired 1991. **Orgs:** Mem United Black Correctional Workers Assn; CA Black Correctional Coalition; NAACP; Amer Correctional Assn; mem Alpha Kappa Alpha Sor; Eastern Star; Links Inc; guest instructor Simon Fraser Univ Banbury British Columbia, Wharton School; instructor Intl Women in Corrections. **Honors/Awds:** Ombudsman type prog Ford Found Fellowship Fisk Univ, Univ of KS 1948-55; Ina B Temple Fellowship Univ of KS; 1st female correctional administr in male facility; 1st black woman correctional supr 1 in CA; listed Women in Corrections; listed in Book of Honors 1977-87, 2000 Notable Women 1977-87; African-Americans in Criminal Justice, Hall of Fame Inductee. **Home Addr:** 4795 Boyd Ct, Riverside, CA 92507.

ANDERSON, KEISHA
Professional basketball player. **Personal:** Born May 17, 1974. **Educ:** Univ of Wisconsin, attended. **Career:** Colorado Xplosion, guard, 1997-. **Business Addr:** Professional Basketball Player, Colorado Xplosion, 800 Grant St, Ste 410, Denver, CO 80203, (303)832-2225.

ANDERSON, KENNETH RICHARD
Electrical engineer (retired). **Personal:** Born Aug 4, 1936, Philadelphia, PA; son of Dorothy and William; married Dorothy, Apr 17, 1987; children: Pamela, Veronica. **Educ:** Drexel Univ, BSEE 1968; Central MI Univ, MA BA 1975. **Career:** Inselek, mgr test eng 1971-75; Aeroneutronic Ford, super comp engrg 1975-76; RCA Government Systems Div, mgr rel & test 1976-79; Siemens RTL, mgr IC design & test, strategic planning, analysis & design of mfg syst; Widener University, adjunct prof, 1982-. **Orgs:** Bd mem, Willingboro NJ Sch Dist 1971-74; IEEE Computer Society, president, 1988-90, 2nd vice pres chairman, technical activities, 1987, governing bd, 1979-. **Honors/Awds:** Distinguished Service Award US Jaycees 1972; Computer Soc Meritorious Service Awards 1981-85. **Military Serv:** US Army, specialist 4, 2 yrs. **Home Addr:** 158 Camber Lane, Mount Laurel, NJ 08054.

ANDERSON, KENNY
Professional basketball player. **Personal:** Born Oct 9, 1970, Queens, NY; married Tammi; children: Lyric Chanel, Kenni Lauren. **Educ:** Georgia Tech. **Career:** New Jersey Nets, guard, 1991-95; Charlotte Hornets, 1995-96; Portland Blazers, 1996-97; Boston Celtics, 1998-. **Honors/Awds:** NBA All-Star, 1994. **Special Achievements:** NBA Draft, First round pick, #2, 1991. **Business Addr:** Professional Baskteball Player, Boston Celtics, 151 Merrimac St, Boston, MA 02114, (617)523-6050.

ANDERSON, KERNIE L.
Communications company executive. **Personal:** Born Jun 5, 1940, Harrisburg, PA; son of Fannie R Anderson and George P Anderson; married Althmeana C Coachman, Mar 10, 1973; children: Shama. **Educ:** Howard University, 1958-63; University of Maryland, Korean Extension School, 1967. **Career:** WQMR AM/WGAY FM, 1963-68; Ed Winton & Associates, WOCN AM/FM, gen mgr & program director, 1968-76; WWBA AM/FM, consultant & troubleshooter, 1969-75; WCGL AM, gen mgr, 1976-77; KDIA, gen mgr, 1977-81; WBMX AM/FM, gen mgr, 1981-88; WIZF FM, vice pres/gen mgr, 1988-89; WDAS AM/FM, vp/gen mgr, 1989-. **Orgs:** Greater Philadelphia Chamber of Commerce, board of directors; NAACP; National Adoption Center, board of directors; Operation PUSH; Philadelphia Industrial Development Corp; Police Athletic League of Philadelphia; Philadelphia Radio Organization, board of directors; Urban League; Utility Emergency Service Fund, board of directors; ACLU; American Red Cross, Southeastern Pennsylvania Chap; Intl Visitors Council; Natl Adoption Center; Nation Council of Chiristians and Jews; Philadelphia Industrial Development Corp; Police Athletic League; Soul Children of Chicago, Youth Choir; United Way of Southeastern Pennsylvania; Utility Emergency Service Fund. **Military Serv:** US Army, 1966-67. **Business Addr:** Vice Pres, General Manager, WDAS Radio, Beasley Broadcast Group, 23 W City Ave, Bala Cynwyd, PA 19004, (610)617-8500.

ANDERSON, LEON H.
Corporate director. **Personal:** Born Sep 22, 1928, Jacksonville, FL; married Mary T Taylor; children: Lisa, Leon R, Leah, Lori. **Educ:** Morris Coll, BA 1956; Columbia Univ, M Pub Admin 1963. **Career:** Corbett HS, tchr 1956-58; Morris Coll, tchr 1958; Saltertown Elem Sch, prin 1958-61; Morris Coll, Tchr 1958; Saltertown Elem Sch, prin 1958-61; Morris Coll, tchr 1959; Moore Elem Sch, prin 1961-64; Ninth Ave HS, prin 1964-65; Los Pinos Job Corps Ctr Cleveland Natl Forest, dep dir for educ 1964-65; USDA Forest Serv San Fran, educ spec 1965-69; USDA Forest Serv Wash, educ spec 1969-70; USDA MO, liaison ofcr 1970-72; Human Resource Prog USDA,asst dir 1972-74; USDA Human Resources Prog Wash, dir 1974-. **Orgs:** Helped to develop a curriculum of therapeutic educ for a non-profit corp Assn for the Treatment of Troubled & Underachieving Children So CA 1969. **Honors/Awds:** Cum Laude Morris Coll 1953; Superior Serv Awd USDA 1972; Superior Serv Awd Lincoln Univ 1974. **Military Serv:** US Army, cpl, 3 yrs. **Home Addr:** 12320 Millstream dr, Bowie, MD 20715.

ANDERSON, LESLIE BLAKE
Attorney. **Personal:** Born Sep 14, 1966, Port Jefferson, NY; daughter of Andrea & Alphonso Anderson. **Educ:** University of Endinburgh, Scotland, 1985-86; State University of NY - Albany, BA, 1987; Albany Law School, JD, 1990. **Career:** Suffolk County District Attorney, assistant district attorney, district court bureau, 1991-92, case advisory bureau, 1993, major crime bureau, 1993-. **Orgs:** NY District Attorneys Association, 1991-; Boy Scouts of America, Eagle Scout committee, 1993-; Suffolk County Human Rights Commission, commissioner, 1996; Suffolk County Bar Association, 1992-; African-American Advisory Board, congressman Rick Lazio, 1996. **Honors/Awds:** Suffolk County Executive, Advocate Awd, 1996. **Business Addr:** Assistant District Attorney, Suffolk County District Attorney's Office, 200 Center Dr, Arthur Cromarty Criminal Court, Riverhead, NY 11901, (516)852-2454.

ANDERSON, LOUISE PAYNE
Educator (retired), community center director. **Personal:** Born Oct 18, 1923, West Virginia; daughter of Nancy Elizabeth Johnson Payne and Andrew Payne Sr; married William Alexander Anderson, Feb 14, 1946 (deceased); children: Patricia C Petty, Cheryl Oni Plear. **Educ:** Bluefield State Coll, BS 1945; WV Coll, MA; WV Univ, grad study. **Career:** Pentagon, sec 1946; Kanawha County Schools, teacher 1947-85 (retired). **Orgs:** CLk Bethel Bapt Ch 1955-; youth dir Mt Olivet Baptist Youth Assn; Delta Kappa Gamma 1972-; Natl Assn of Univ Women 1973; pres Montgomery Branch NAACP; pres Washington High Alumni Assn 1985-; auditor Mt Olivet Women's Missionary Convention 1983-; Beta Beta Omega Chap Alpha Kappa Alpha Sorority 1943-; counselor West Virginia Baptist State Convention Youth Assn; NAACP, life membership, 1989; Alpha Kappa Alpha Sorority, Inc, life membership; WVA Coalition of Minority Health, mem, 1995. **Honors/Awds:** Kanawha County Teacher of the year, Kanawha Co Bd of Educ, 1982-83; Living the Dream Award, Martin Luther King Commission, 1986; Excellence in Teaching, West Virginia State College, 1982; Community Service Award, Omega Psi Phi Frat, West VA Inst of Tech, 1988; Noell Award, United Teaching Profession, Kanawha Teachers Assn, 1981; Human Relations Award, Mary L Williams Memorial Committee, WV Educ Assn, 1980; Bluefield State High School, Commercial Teacher of the Year, 1957; Kanawha County Education Association, Citation in Recognition of Significant Contribution as Sponsor of East Bank High, FTA; Received Certificate of Honor, Golden Circle Soror for 50 Years of Svc, Alpha Kappa Alpha & Education, July 12, 1994; Ettie Mayham Brown, WVEA Minority Affairs Committee for Community Growth & Contributions, Oct 1, 1993. **Special Achievements:** Delta Sigma Theta, Inc, Charleston Institue Alumnae Chapter; organizer of non profit WHS Community Education Center, currently; serving as president of the WHS Alumni Association, sponsor of the organization supporting the project, grand opening, Nov 11, 1989; Helped to organize a Black Caucus within the West Virginia Education Association, and served as first chairperson, 1972.

ANDERSON, MADELINE
Producer, director. **Personal:** Born in Lancaster, PA; daughter of Nellie Whedbee and William Whedbee; married Ralph Joseph Anderson; children: Adele, Rachel, Laura, Ralph Jr. **Educ:** NY Univ, BA 1956. **Career:** Onyx Prod, pres 1975-; Infinity Factory Educ Devel Ctr, exec producer 1976-77; Children's TV Workshop, supervising editor prod dir 1971-75, TV producer/intl, 1985-87. **Orgs:** Board of trustees, Intern Film Seminars, 1974-77; film panelist, NY State Cncl for the Arts 1975-79; mem Natl Acad TV Arts & Sci; board of Women Make Movies, 1986-88. **Honors/Awds:** Woman of the Yr Sojourner Truth Festival of the Arts 1976; Grand Prize Film ''I Am Somebody'' Media Women 1977; Grants NYSCA WNET Documentary Fund NEA & AFI; producer for ''Al Manaahil'' a literacy series for Arabic children in the Middle East produced by the Children's TV Workshop working in Amman Jordan 1986-; Indie Awd 1985; Lifelong Achievement Awd from AIVF; Gallery of the Greats, Miller Brewing Co, 1991; inducted into the Black Filmmakers Hall of Fame, 1992. **Home Addr:** 83 Sterling St, Brooklyn, NY 11225.

ANDERSON, MARCELLUS J., SR.
Investment company executive. **Personal:** Born Jun 21, 1918, Anderson, SC; son of Edward Anderson; married Ada; children: Sandra Joy, Marcellus Jr. **Educ:** OH State Univ, AB; London Coll of Applied Sci England, doctor humane rel. **Career:** Livingstone Coll, Samuel Huston Coll, Huston-Tillotson Coll, former teacher; Pan TX Mortgage Invest Co Austin, TX, pres, 1978-85; Great National Investment Co, currently. **Orgs:** Pres, board chairman, 1989-, Fedn of Masons of the World; dir comm Natl Bank of Austin; dir United Mortgage Bankers of Amer Inc; president, National Alliance of Black Organizations, 1980-; grand master, MW St Joseph Grand Lodge, 1978-95. **Honors/Awds:** St Andrew General Grand Masonic Congress AF & AM, Distinguished Meritorious Award; The Seven-Up Company, Outstanding Leadership & Community Service Award; Texas State Assn, BCL Citizenship Award; TX Church Ushers & United Political Organizations, Distinguished Service Award; Kappa Alpha Psi Fraternity, Successful Businessman Award; NAACP, Emerson Marcee Award; City Council of Austin TX, Distinguished Service Award; TLOD, Achievement Award; District 13 AF & AM, Outstanding Leadership Award; Austin Area Brotherhood, Businessman of the Year Award. **Business Addr:** President, Great National Investment Co, 3724 Airport Blvd, Austin, TX 78722, (512)478-9802.

ANDERSON, MARJORIE
Public relations director. **Personal:** Born Apr 10, Detroit, MI. **Educ:** Univ of Detroit, BBA. **Career:** US Govt, EEO counselor, staff adv; D-Sace Charm Sch Comm, pub rel; Urban League Youth Assemb, pub rel dir; St Paul's Ch, pub rel dir; Afboney Mod & Fin Sch, pub rel dir; CANAC, pub rel dir. **Orgs:** Bd mem Det Soc for Adv of Cultur & Edn; bd mem Fisher YMCA; pres FEMS for Fisher YMCA; corr secy media coor Det Urban League Guild; Red Cross vol; coord child hops Sickle Cell Anemia prog; columnist Spirit of Det Tarcom Newspaper; bicentennial chmn Det Urban League Guilds Fund Raising Proj; natl historian Gamma Phi Delta Sor Inc; edit in chief past Basileus Delta Nu Chap GPD Sor; youth dir Delta Nu's Rosebud Youth Group; US Govt coord Equal Oppty Day Upward Mobility Race Relat Unit Found Programs. **Honors/Awds:** Comm Serv Award GPD Sor 1976; Comm Serv Award Det Urban League; Most Val Mem Award Urban League Guild 1976; Pres of the Year Gamma Phi Delta 1973; Outstanding Basileus GPD Natl Pres 1974; Bi-Centennial Award Delta Nu's Youth Group 1976.

ANDERSON, MARVA JEAN
County official. **Personal:** Born May 9, 1945, Morrilton, AR; children: Tamikko Afresa Green. **Educ:** Los Angeles Trade Tech Coll, AA 1970; CA State Univ Dominguez Hills, BA 1973; UCLA, MSW 1978. **Career:** Communicative Arts Acad, admin asst 1972-76; Special Serv for Groups, asst dir prog devel 1976-82; YWCA Women Shelter, dir 1982-84; LA Co Dept of Childrens Svcs, special asst 1984-. **Orgs:** Vice pres 1980-81, pres 1982-83, treas 1984-87 Natl Assn of Black Social Workers LA Chapt; natl rep Natl Assn Black Social Workers 1984-87; commmem Image Awds, 1984-86, board mem, 1987, NAACP Hollywood Chap 1984-86; vice pres Jenesse Inc 1986-88; Assn of Black Social Workers of Gr eater Los Angeles, 1976-; Jenesse Domestic Violence Shelter, board member, 1985 -; Lambda Kappa Mu Sorority, 1990-; Black Women's Forum, sponsor, 1990-. **Honors/Awds:** Plaque of Appreciation Assn of Black Social Workers LA 1983; Recognition & Appreciation for Contribution to XXIII Olympics LA Olympic Organizing Comm 1984; Certificate of Commendation LA City Councilman Robert Farrell 1984; Leadership Awd LA Brotherhood Crusade 1985; Plaque of Recognition CA Assn of Black Social Workers 1986. **Business Addr:** Deputy Children's Services Administrator, Los Angeles County Dept of Children and Family Services, 425 Shatto Pl, Rm 603, Los Angeles, CA 90020.

ANDERSON, MARY ELIZABETH
Government official, educator. **Personal:** Born in Andersonville, VA. **Educ:** VA Union Univ, BS; Chicago Coll of Commerce, postgrad; Attended, Amer Univ; US Dept of Agric Grad Sch. **Career:** Office of Educ, fiscal officer 1965-70, women's prog coord 1975-; Union HS, tchr; VA Union Univ Rept Women's Natl Adv Cncl, couns 1976-; HEW, specialist 1970-. **Orgs:** Affiliate Natl Alliance of Black Sch Educs; life mem NAACP, exec bd mem 1975-77; DC Women's Polit Caucus; Friends of Frederick Douglass Mus of AfricanArt; Alpha Kappa Alpha. **Honors/Awds:** Outstanding Serv Awd NAACP 1976; Cit of Apprec NAACP 1974; Spl Cit US Civil Serv Commn 1973; publ "Sex Equality in Educ"; co-author "History of US Ofcof Educ & Fld Svcs". **Business Addr:** Specialist, HEW, DHEW Ofc of Educ, 400 Maryland Ave SW, Washington, DC 20202.

ANDERSON, MICHAEL WAYNE
Public relations manager. **Personal:** Born Feb 24, 1942, Wilmington, DE; married Yvonne Gloria Copeland; children: Kima-Joi Michaele. **Educ:** CA State Univ LA, BS 1973. **Career:** YMCA Youthmobile of Metro Los Angeles, dir 1971-73; A Better Chance Inc, western states reg dir 1973-; Crenshaw Branch YMCA of Metro Los Angeles, exec dir 1975-77; CA FAIR Plan Assn, mgr public affairs 1977-. **Orgs:** Mem CA Arson Prevent Comm 1977-80; epres LA chap Natl Assn of Mkt Developers 1978-80; mem San Francisco Arson Task Force 1979-80; chmn speakers bur Pub Club of LA 1979-80; eligibil com chmn Pub Rel Soc of Amer 1980; rec sec PIRATES 1980; bd dirs Angeles Girl Scout Cncl 1980; pres Toastmasters Intl (WIIS) 1980; mem LA Mayor's Arson Supression Task Force; mem LA Chap NAACP; mem LA Chap Urban League; mem Crenshaw Neighbors. **Honors/Awds:** Cert of Apprec Co of LA 1972; Cert of Apprec City of LA 1974; Cert of Apprec LA Jr C of C 1974; Disting Toastmaster Toastmasters Intl 1977; Speaker's Award Western Ins Information Serv 1978-80. **Military Serv:** US Army, E-4 1964-66. **Business Addr:** Recruitment Coordinator, A Better Chance, Inc, 419 Boylston St, Boston, MA 02116.

ANDERSON, MONROE
Broadcasting company executive. **Personal:** Born Apr 6, 1947, Gary, IN; married Joyce Owens; children: Scott, Kyle. **Educ:** Indiana Univ, BA 1970. **Career:** Chicago Tribune, journalist; Ebony Magazine, asst ed 1972-74; Natl Observer, staffwriter 1970-72; Post-Tribune, 1969; Newsweek Magazine, correspondent, beginning 1968; WBBM-TV, dir of station servs and community affairs, currently. **Orgs:** NABJ, Region V, dir, currently. **Honors/Awds:** AP IL St Award for In-Depth Rptng 1976; Chicago Trib Edward Beck Spcl Award for Outst Invstgtv Rprtng 1976; First Place Inland Press Awd 1977; Jacob Scher Awd for Investigative Reporting 1979; Best Comm Serv Awd UPI 1980; Outstanding Print Journalism Awd Chicago Assoc of Black Journalists 1981; Outstanding Print Journalism Awd DuSable Museum 1982; Outstanding Commentary Chicago Assoc of Black Journalists 1985; NY State Bar Assoc Media Awd 1986. **Business Addr:** Dir, Station Servs & Community Affairs, WBBM-TV, 630 N McClurg Ct, Chicago, IL 60611.

ANDERSON, MOSES B.
Clergyman. **Educ:** St Michael's College, BA (magna cum laude), philosophy, MAT, sociology, 1961; St Edmund Seminary; Xavier University, ThM, 1968. **Career:** Our Lady of Consolation Parish, associate pastor, 1958-59; St Michael College, lecturer, 1959-61; St Catherine, Parish, pastor, 1961-64; St Michael College, associate professor of theology, 1964-71; Xavier University, Notre Dame Seminary, director of religious affairs and associate professor, 1971-81; All Saints Parish, pastor, 1981; Titular Bishop of Vatarba; Detroit, auxiliary bishop 1982-. **Honors/Awds:** St Michael College, Doctor of Humane Letters, 1984; Kansas Neumann College, LLD, 1985; Madonna College, Honorary Doctor of Humanities, 1989. **Special Achievements:** Ordained priest, 1958. **Business Addr:** Archdiocese of Detroit, 1234 Washington Blvd, Detroit, MI 48226.

ANDERSON, NICHOLAS CHARLES
City government official. **Personal:** Born Feb 7, 1953, Charlotte, NC; son of Fannie Mae Moses Anderson and Nicodemus Anderson (deceased); married Darlene Davis (divorced 1990); children: Takecia Kamari, Brandye Nicole, Michelle Darlene; married Marionette, Jun 25, 1994. **Educ:** Wayne State Univ, Detroit, MI, BA, 1981; Central Piedmont Community Coll, Charlotte, NC, 1971-72. **Career:** American Tobacco Co, sales representative, 1974-76, district sales manager, 1976-81; NAACP, youth program director, 1981-83, director Midwest region III, 1983-87; Com Freddie G Burton Jr, legislative aide, 1983-87; Detroit Urban League, president/CEO, 1987-94; City of Detroit, executive director, Department of Human Svcs, 1994-97; Detroit Urban League, president/CEO, 1997-; Detroit Board of Education, 1997-. **Orgs:** WSU Alumni Assn, bd of dirs, pres, 1996-97; Economic Club of Detroit, 1988-; NBD Community Dev Corp, advisory bd, 1990-95; CATCH, bd of dirs, 1991-; Operation ABLE, bd of dirs, 1990-; Michigan Black Caucus, bd of dirs, 1991-96; Michigan Non-Profit Forum, trustee, 1991-; Detroit Compact Community Partners Committee; Detroit Public Schools City-Wide Community Organization. **Honors/Awds:** NAACP, Regional III Service, 1988; Minority Women's Network, Man of the Year, 1992; Board of Police Commissioners, Testimonial Resolution, 1994. **Business Addr:** President/CEO, Detroit Urban League, 208 Mack Ave, Detroit, MI 48202, (313)832-4600.

ANDERSON, NICK (NELISON)
Professional basketball player. **Personal:** Born Jan 20, 1968, Chicago, IL. **Educ:** Univ of Illinois, Champaign, IL, 1986-89. **Career:** Orlando Magic, forward-guard, 1989-. **Honors/Awds:** Rich and Helen DeVos Community Enrichment Award, 1996. **Special Achievements:** NBA Draft, First round pick, #11, 1989. **Business Addr:** Professional Basketball Player, Orlando Magic, 1 Magic Pl, Orlando, FL 32801, (407)649-3200.

ANDERSON, ODDIE
Psychiatric nurse. **Personal:** Born Jan 20, 1937, Detroit, MI; daughter of Annie Suggs Walker Brown and Sam Brown; married Armstead Anderson, Jul 23, 1955; children: Cheryl Anderson-Hunter, Debra Anderson. **Educ:** Highland Park Coll, Detroit, MI, AS, Nursing; Wayne State Univ, Detroit, MI, BA, Gen Studies. **Career:** Herman Kiefer Hospital; Detroit Receiving Hospital; Detroit E Community Mental Health Center, currently. **Orgs:** Pres, Wayne County Partial Hospitalization Program, 1989, Chalmers Jr Block Club; mem, Great Lakes Regional Partial Hospitalization Assn, Amer Assn Partial Hospitalization Inc, United Sisterhood, Detroit Metropolitan District Young People's Dept; assoc, Detroit Black Nurses Assn; youth dir, St James Missionary Baptist Church; chairperson, Detroit E Client Fund Comm. **Honors/Awds:** Heart of Gold, United Found, 1989; Sojourner Truth Award, Natl Assn Negro Business Women, 1989; Special Serv Award, Detroit Bd of Dir, 1989; Community Serv Award, Wayne County Mental Health Bd; Outstanding Serv Award, St James Baptist Church; Outstanding Youth Leader, governor James Blanchard; established "Take a Senior to Dinner" program, 1979; established Detroit chapter of "Just Say No to Drugs," 1988; established scholastic programs to monitor young people's report cards. **Business Addr:** Program Supervisor, Detroit East Community Mental Health Ctr, 9141 E Jefferson, Detroit, MI 48214.

ANDERSON, PATRICIA HEBERT
Community service organizer. **Personal:** Born Aug 28, 1945, Houston, TX; daughter of Emma Jean Pope Hebert and Rev Aldaah Augusta Hebert; married Rev Adolphus Anderson Jr, Jun 28, 1964 (deceased); children: Renee, Reginald, Adolphus III, Ruthalyn, Victor, Albert, Michael, Miriam. **Educ:** TX Southern Univ, 1963; Houston Comm, 1972, 1984; Manpower Business Training, Key Punch Comp, 1974; Gulf Coast Bible Coll, AA Theol, 1975; COGIC, national evangelist prog, 1987; Union Baptist Bible College and Seminary, bachelor of theology, 1992; Arts & Sciences Social Work, TSU, bachelor's degree, 1995; Union Baptist Seminary & Bible Coll, Counseling & Rel Ed, master's degree, 1995; licensed social worker, 1995; Texas Southern Univ, MS, 1997, doctoral student, currently. **Career:** Harris City Democratic Exec Comm, precinct comm, 1976-; Glen Manor Weyburn Pl Civic Cl, pres 1979-; Gulf Coast Comm Serv, sec, bd of dir, 1980; North Forest ISD, sec, bd of dir, 1981; Natl Black Caucus of School Bd, sec, 1982, 1984, bd of dir, 1984; church musician & director 32 yrs; Pleasant Green Bapt Church, active church musician; Star of Faith Grand Chap, OES #55 grand musician; North Forest School Dist, trustee; North Forest School Dist Bd of Educ, pres, 1988-89. **Orgs:** Comm coord, North East Comm Project Fund, 1972; chairwoman, New Hope Baptist Church Missionary Affairs, 1975; pres, Glen Manor Weyburn Pl, 1979-; alternate person, City Commr Jim Fontero, 1980; sec, Gulf Coast Comm, Serv 1981, BATTS Bd of Dir, 1982; admin asst, City Comm EA Squattylyons, 1982; Harris County Black Elected Officials, 1986; bd mem, Evangelistic Bible Days Revival Church; secretary, Natl Caucus of Black School Bd Members, 1986-; Houston Central Young Women Christian Council, 1987-89; bd mem, Greater Park Hill Church of God in Christ Evangelical Bd, 1987-; pres, sewing circle, 1988-, pres, Young Women Christian Council, 1988-, Houston Central District Church of God in Christ; Mt Sinai Grand Lodge, AF&AM, grand matron; Greater Park Hill Church of God In Christ. **Honors/Awds:** Community Serv Awd, City of Houston Mayor Whitmire, 1983; honored by Natl Black Caucus of School Bd Members, 1983; Woman of the Year, New Hope Baptist Church, 1983; Honor Award, Gulf Coast Community Serv, 1983; High Achievement, North East Comm Proj, 1984; Merit of Achievement, Legislative Black Caucus State Rep Harol Dutton, 1986; Mother of the Year, New Hope Baptist Church, 1986; Outstanding Black Elected Official, Wayside Church of Christ, 1986; Juneteenth Freedom Award, NAACP, 1987; National Dean's List, Texas Southern Univ, 1989-90; TSU, Deans List, National, 1993-95; Outstanding Leadership, Board of Education, North Forest ISD, 1992.

ANDERSON, PEARL G.
Governmental administrator. **Personal:** Born Oct 8, 1950, Richmond, VA; daughter of Mabel Fleming Green and Howard H Green Jr; divorced; children: Nicholas. **Educ:** Randolph-Macon Woman's Coll, BA 1972. **Career:** City of Richmond, mgmt intern 1972-73, budget analyst 1973-78, sr budget analyst 1978-82. **Orgs:** Mem Amer Soc for Public Admin; mem Natl Forum for Black Public Admins; bd of Christian educ Fifth St Baptist Church; bd of dirs Young Women's Christian Assn 1973-79; bd of dirs Richmond Supplemental Retirement System 1973-79; mem Intl City Mgmt Assn 1978-82; bd dir Gr Richmond Transit Co. **Honors/Awds:** Four Yr Scholarship at RMWC; Outstanding Jr Major 1971. **Business Addr:** Dir Admin Services, VA Dept of Personnel-Training, 101 N 14th St, Richmond, VA 23219.

ANDERSON, PERRY L.
Law enforcement official. **Career:** Cambridge Police Dept, commissioner, currently. **Orgs:** Natl Organization of Black Law Enforcement Officials, president. **Business Addr:** Commissioner, Cambridge Police Department, 5 Western Ave, Cambridge, MA 02139, (617)349-3377.

ANDERSON, RICHARD CHARLES
Attorney. **Personal:** Born Nov 25, 1945, Vallejo, CA; son of Walter & Margaret Anderson; married Rosalynn Anderson, Jan 26, 1974; children: Walter. **Educ:** Kennedy-King Jr College, AA, 1972; University of Chicago, BA, 1973; Northwestern Univ School of Law, JD, 1977. **Career:** CNA Insurance Co, account exec, 1980-81; Cook County State's Attorney, asst state's attorney, 1981-84; Private Practice, attorney at law, 1984-86, 1995-; Chicago Housing Authority, deputy general counsel, 1986-95. **Orgs:** Volunteers for Housing, chairman, 1971-76. **Special Achievements:** Regenald Heber Smity Community Lawyer Fellowship, 1977; published article, "I Love My Son Walter As He Is," in Exceptional Parent Magazine, 1991; published article, "Walter At 10," in book entitled Uncommon Fathers Reflections on Raising a Child with a Disability, Woodline House, 1995. **Military Serv:** US Army, spec 5, e-5, 1967-69; Purple Heart, 1968.

ANDERSON, RICHARD DARNOLL
Professional football player. **Personal:** Born Sep 13, 1971, Sandy Spring, MD. **Educ:** Penn State Univ, attended. **Career:** New York Jets, running back, 1993-. **Business Addr:** Professional Football Player, New York Jets, 1000 Fulton Ave, Hempstead, NY 11550, (516)560-8100.

ANDERSON, RONALD EDWARD, SR.
Manager. **Personal:** Born Aug 4, 1948, Indianapolis, IN; married Dolores Jean Benson; children: Ronald Jr. **Educ:** TN State Univ, BS 1970; Graduate Work, Univ of Evansville 1976, Central Michigan Univ 1986. **Career:** State Farm Fire & Casualty Ins, admin & tech trainee 1971-72, sr claim rep 1973-75, claim specialist 1975-80, claim supt 1980-85; State Farm Mutual Insurance Co, claim supt 1985-. **Orgs:** Trustee New Hope Bapt Ch Evansville IN 1974-80; bd dir Transit System Evansville 1976-78; bd dir Carver Com Orgn Evansville 1976-80; v pole march Evansville Alumni Chap Kappa Alpha Psi 1977-79; chmn finance com Evansville Black Expos 1979; secty/treas Flint Alumni Chap of Kappa Alpha Psi 1982-86. **Honors/Awds:** Good Neighbor of the Yr Awd IN Regional Office State Farm Ins Co W Lafayette IN 1978. **Military Serv:** US Army Reserves, cpt 6 yrs. **Business Addr:** Claim Superintendent, State Farm Mutual Ins Co, 9121 Oakdale Ave, Northridge, CA 91328.

ANDERSON, RONALD GENE
Professional basketball player. **Personal:** Born Oct 10, 1958, Chicago, IL. **Educ:** Fresno State, 1980-84. **Career:** Cleveland Cavaliers, 1984-85, Indiana Pacers, 1986-88, Philadelphia 76ers, 1988-. **Honors/Awds:** For Cavs' entry in the CA Summer League, led Cavs in scoring with an average of 187 points per game and was only NBA rookie named to league's All-Star team. **Business Addr:** Professional Basketball Player, Philadelphia 76ers, Broad St & Pattison Ave, Spectrum, Philadelphia, PA 19148-5288.

ANDERSON, RUSSELL LLOYD. **See Obituaries section.**

ANDERSON, RUTH BLUFORD
Educator, government official (retired). **Personal:** Born Oct 28, 1921, Braden, OK; daughter of Josie Blocker Knowles and Roy Bluford; married James C Anderson Jr; children: Eugene McKinnis, Carl, Valerie (deceased), Glennis Anderson Mines, Dennis, James Anderson, Keith McKinnis. **Educ:** Lincoln Univ Jeff City, Mo, 1939-41; Univ of CA Berkeley, BA 1946; Columbia Univ NY, MSW 1956; Univ of Chicago, SSA, Summer Inst 1973-71; Smith Coll Northampton, MA, Workshop 1982. **Career:** Black Hawk Co Welfare Dept, dir 1963-67; Wartburg Coll Waverly IA, asst prof soc work 1967-1969; University of Northern Iowa, asst prof soc work 1969-73, assoc prof 1973-86, prof 1986-93; acting head, dept of social work 1988-90; Black Hawk County, board of supervisors 1988-91, chair 1990. **Orgs:** Comm Gov Branstads Long Term Care 1984-; president IA NB St Conf NAACP 1990-; mem bd of dir NE Coun on Substance Abuse 1990; National Assoc of Black Social Workers, 1989; Golden Life mem, Delta Sigma Theta Sorority; North East Iowa AIDS Coalition, 1987. **Honors/Awds:** Women's Hall of Fame 1982; Articles on Blacks and Substance Abuse; Author From Mother's Aid Child to Univ Prof, Auto of Amer Black Woman 1985; Jim Kraft Award, Governor's Conference on Substance Abuse, 1988; Women of Achievement, Networking Together

IX, 1988; Honorary Doctor of Humane Letters, Simpson College, 1990; Social Worker of the Year, Iowa 1991; Great Delta Teacher, 1992; Iowa African-American Hall of Fame Inductee, 1996. **Home Addr:** Box 1692, Waterloo, IA 50704.

ANDERSON, S. A.
Business executive. **Personal:** Born May 31, 1935, Ennis, TX; married Betty; children: Monetta Kaye, Madeline Joyce, Arthur Girard. **Educ:** Prairie View A&M Univ, BS 1956; attended Atlanta Univ, Texas Southern Univ, Univ of Oklahoma. **Career:** Pemberton HS Marshall TX, tchr/coach 1958-69. **Orgs:** Mem Natl Urban League; East Texas Coaches & Officials Assn 1958-69; Amer Soc Pub Admin; TX Assn Comm Action Agencies; chmn NAACP 1970-75; Natl Assn Comm Devel; Natl Comm Action Agency Exec Dir Assn; Assn Black Soc Workers Inc; mem Order of Arrow Boy Scouts of Amer 1962; mem bd dir East Texas Legal Serv Corp; mem Alpha Phi Alpha Frat; SW Baseball Umpires Assn; Amer Assn Retired Persons. **Honors/Awds:** Man of Yr Reg Fellows Club 1970 1975; Natl Sci Found Grants 1960b 1962-64 1967; Excellence Awds East Texas Coaches & Officials Assn 1964 1968; Serv Awd Zeta Phi Beta 1972; Serv Awd Phi Beta Sigma 1971; Serv Awd AKA 1976; Outstanding Ach Awd TX St Conf NAACP 1971. **Military Serv:** US Army, capt 1956-58; Sr Parachutist Badge. **Business Addr:** PO Box 1343, 214 E Houston St, Marshall, TX 75670.

ANDERSON, SHANDON RODRIGUEZ
Professional basketball player. **Personal:** Born Dec 31, 1973, Atlanta, GA; children: Kori. **Educ:** Georgia. **Career:** Utah Jazz, forward, 1996-. **Business Addr:** Professional Basketball Player, Utah Jazz, 301 W South Temple, Salt Lake City, UT 84101-1216, (801)575-7800.

ANDERSON, STEVE
Professional football player. **Personal:** Born May 12, 1970, Monroe, LA. **Educ:** Grambling State, attended. **Career:** New York Jets, wide receiver, 1994; Arizona Cardinals, 1995-. **Business Addr:** Professional Football Player, Arizona Cardinals, 8701 S Hardy, Tempe, AZ 85284, (602)379-0101.

ANDERSON, TALMADGE
Educator (retired), writer. **Personal:** Born Jul 22, 1932, Hazelhurst, GA; son of Viola Lee Baker Anderson; married Cerci Lee (divorced); children: Rose, Ramona, Talmadge, Rhunell, Raul. **Educ:** Savannah State Coll, BS 1953; Atlanta Univ, MBA 1958. **Career:** Lane Coll, chmn dept of bus 1958-59; Allen Univ, asst prof 1959-62; St Augustine's Coll, asst prof/chmn 1963-65; Bethune-Cookman Coll, assoc prof 1966-67; WV Inst of Tech, asst prof 1968-70; Western Journal of Black Studies, founder & editor; Washington State Univ, assoc prof bus admin, dir assoc prof marketing & black studies. **Orgs:** Adv bd mem Employment Security Commn Washington 1975-77; exec bd mem Natl Cncl of Black Studies 1975-; exec cncl mem ASALH 1977-86. **Honors/Awds:** 100 Most Influential Friends Awd Black Journal 1977; Cert of Achievement inst on Africa-Hamline Univ 1978; NW, NCBS Frederick Douglass Scholar Awd 1986. **Military Serv:** US Army, sagt 1953-56.

ANDERSON, THOMAS JEFFERSON
Educator. **Personal:** Born Aug 17, 1928, Coutesville, PA; son of Anita Turpeau Anderson and Thomas J Anderson; married Lois Ann Field; children: T J III, Janet, Anita. **Educ:** West Virginia State College, BM, 1950, D Music, 1984; Pennsylvania State University, MEd, 1951; University of Iowa, PhD, 1958; Holy Cross College, DMA, 1983. **Career:** High Pt City Public School, teacher, 1951-54; West Virginia State College, instructor, 1955-56; Langston University, professor & chairman, 1958-63; Tennessee State University, professor of music, 1963-69; Atlanta Symphony Orchestra, composer-in-residence, 1969-71; Morehouse College, Danforth visiting professor of music, 1971-72; Tufts University, professor of music & chairman, 1972-80, Austin Fletcher professor of music, starting 1976; DeKalb University, Dept of Fine Arts, professor, currently. **Orgs:** Founder/president, Black Music Caucus MENC; board member, Elma Lewis School of Fine Arts, 1975-; advisory bd, Meet The Composer, 1980; chair, Comm of the Status of Minorities, College Music Society, 1976-80; Music Council the Arts & Humanities 1978-81; Harvard Musical Assn, 1976-; St Botolph Club, 1980. **Honors/Awds:** Fellow, MacDowell Colony, 1960-83; fellow, Yhaddo 1970-77; Copley Foundation Award, 1964; Fromm Foundation Award, 1964-71; Phi Beta Kappa, honorary member, 1977; over 50 published compositions; artistic residency, University of Salvador, 1988; 60th Birthday Concert, Videmus, Harvard University, 1989; fellow, John Simon Guggenheim Foundation, 1989; bd mem, Harvard Musical Assn, 1989. **Home Addr:** 34 Grove St, Medford, MA 02155.

ANDERSON, TONY
Insurance company executive. **Personal:** Born Jun 14, 1947, Dillon, SC; son of Mary Agnes Anderson; married Westley A Smith, Oct 22, 1983; children: Christopher, Natasha. **Educ:** Western Connecticut State Coll, Danbury, CT, BA, 1979; Univ of New Haven, West Haven, CT, MBA, 1989. **Career:** Citirust, Bridgeport, CT, securities trader, 1977-80; Equitable Life, New York, NY, vice pres funding operations, 1980-. **Orgs:** NASD, 1977-; dir, Equitable Credit Union, 1988-. **Honors/Awds:** Ford Found Scholar, 1976. **Military Serv:** USAF, E-4, 1965-68.

ANDERSON, TONY
Entertainment executive. **Personal:** Born Oct 29, 1950, Washington, DC; son of Frances & William Anderson; married Antoinette, Dec 5, 1981; children: Angela, William, Nathan, Aja. **Career:** Track Recording Studio, recording engineer, 1971-73; Warner Elektra Atlantic Distribution, mktg coordinator, 1974-75; Jonas Cash Promotions, independent promotion rep, 1975-82; Motown Records, national R&B promotion dir, 1982-85; Arista Records, vp, R&B promotion, 1985-91; Mercury Records, exec vp/gen mgr, 1991-93; Columbia Records, svp/black music, 1993-. **Honors/Awds:** Black Enterprise Magazine, One of the Top 50 Black Entertainment Power Brokers, 1994; International Assn of African American Music, Joe Medlin Contributors Award, 1995; Black Entertainment & Sports Lawyers Assn, Hall of Fame, 1993. **Business Phone:** (212)833-7272.

ANDERSON, VINTON RANDOLPH
Cleric. **Personal:** Born Jul 11, 1927, Somerset, Bermuda; married Vivienne Louise Cholmondeley, 1952; children: Vinton R Jr, Jeffrey Charles, Carlton Lawson, Kenneth Robert. **Educ:** Wilberforce University, BA (with honors); Payne Theological Seminary, MDiv, 1952; Kansas University, MA, philosophy; Yale University Divinity School, continuing education; Urban Training Center for Christian Missions. **Career:** St Mark AME Church, pastor, 1952-53; Brown Chapel AME Church, pastor, 1953-55; St Luke AME Church, Lawrence, pastor, 1955-59; St Paul AME Church, Wichita, pastor, 1959-64; St Paul AME Church, St Louis, pastor, 1964-72; presiding bishop, chief pastor: 9th Episcopal District, Alabama, 1972-76; 3rd Episcopal District, Ohio, West Virginia, West Pennsylvania, 1976-84; Office of Ecumenical Relations and Development, 1984-88; 5th Episcopal District, 14 states including 255 Churches west of the Mississippi River, 1988-. **Orgs:** World Council of Churches, numerous committees and delegations; World Methodist Council, North American Region, first vice pres, executive committee; World Methodist Council and Conference, delegate, 1961-; National Council of Churches, governing board, Faith & Order Commission, chairperson; Congress of National Black Churches, vice pres, charter member; Consultation on Church Union, vice pres; United Methodist Church, General Commission of Christian Unity and Interreligious Concern; Schomburg Center for Research in Black Culture, national advisory board; NAACP, life member; Urban League, St Louis dialogue group. **Honors/Awds:** Ebony Magazine, Religion Award, 1988, 1991; American Black Achievement Awards, 1991; National Association for Equal Opportunity in Higher Education, Distinguished Alumni Honoree, 1988; Honorary Doctorate Degrees: Eden Theological Seminary; Paul Quinn College; Wilberforce University; Payne Theological Seminary; Temple Bible College; Morris Brown College. **Special Achievements:** Developed: church hymnal, The Bicentennial Edition; first AME Book of Worship; established, edited: The Connector; produced, edited: A Syllabus For Celebrating The Bicentennial; numerous articles in publications of the AME Church. **Business Addr:** Presiding Bishop, Fifth Episcopal District, African Methodist Episcopal Church, 4144 Lindell Blvd, Suite 222, St Louis, MO 63108.

ANDERSON, WARREN E.
Company executive. **Career:** The Anderson-Dubose Co, president/general manager, currently. **Orgs:** Young Presidents. **Honors/Awds:** NE Ohio Entrepreneur of Year. **Business Addr:** President/General Manager, Anderson-Dubose Co., 6575 Davis Industrial Pkwy, Solon, OH 44139, (216)248-8800.

ANDERSON, WILLIAM A.
Physician. **Personal:** Born Jul 21, 1921, Atlanta, GA; son of Mary Anderson and Will Anderson; married Joyce McIntosh; children: Serena, Cheryle Posey, William A III. **Educ:** Tuskegee Inst, BA 1942; Univ MI Med Sch, MD 1953. **Career:** Private Practice, dermatologist 1957-; Whitehall Labs NYC, assoc med dir 1965-69; Cornell Univ Med Coll, clin assoc prof of dermatology, currently. **Orgs:** Consul Natl Acad Sci Natl Rsch Cncl 1965; pres Metro Derm Soc NY 1962; pres NJ Dermatological Soc 1963; fellow Amer Acad Dermatology 1959-; mem Natl Med Assn; officer, Essex Co Med Soc of New Jersey, 1989-91. **Honors/Awds:** Rsch Fellow Div Virus Rsch Cornell Univ Med Coll 1957-61; Councilor Essex Co Med Soc NJ 1983-85; author, articles on clinical dermatology, immunology, virology. **Military Serv:** US Army, cpl, 4 yrs; Combat Medical Badge 1945. **Business Addr:** Clinical Assoc Prof of Med, Cornell Univ Medical College, 185 Central Ave, East Orange, NJ 07018.

ANDERSON, WILLIAM A.
Educator. **Personal:** Born May 28, 1937, Akron, OH; children: 1. **Educ:** Ohio State Univ, PhD 1966. **Career:** Kent State Univ, instr 1961-62; Disaster Rsch Ctr Ohio State Univ, rsch asst 1966-69; Minority Fellowship Prog, Amer Sociol Assn, dir 1974-75; AZ State Univ, assoc to full professor 1969-76; National Science Foundation, program director, 1976-. **Orgs:** Mem Natl Acad of Sci Panel on the Pub Policy Implications of Earthquake Prediction 1974-; mem Natl Acad of Sci Ad Hoc Comm on Minorities in the Sci 1975; mem Amer Sociol Assn; Pacific Sociol Assn; co-author of two books. **Business Addr:** Program Director, National Science Foundation, Washington, DC 20550.

ANDERSON, WILLIAM GILCHRIST
Physician, surgeon. **Personal:** Born Dec 12, 1927, Americus, GA; son of John D & Emma G Anderson; married Norma Dixon Anderson, Nov 23, 1946; children: A Laurita Faison, W Gilchrist II, V Jeanita Henson, Frank L, Darnita Dawn Anderson-Hill. **Educ:** Alabama State Coll, BS, 1949; Univ of Osteopathic Medicine, DO, 1956. **Career:** Art Center Clinical Group, staff surgeon, 1967-71; Zieger Clinical Group, attending surgeon, 1971-74; Detroit Surgical Assn, sr attending surgeon & consultant, 1974-84; MI Healthcare Corp, exec vp & chief medical officer, 1984-86; Detroit Osteopathic Hosp, dir, government affairs, 1986-92; Detroit Riverview Hosp, dir medical education, 1992-; Kirksville Coll of Osteopathic Meeicine, assoc dean, 1996-. **Orgs:** YMCA, dir, 1970-; Univ Osteopathic Medicine, dir, 1974-; Citizens Trust bank, dir, 1974-; Wayne County Osteo Assn, dir, 1968-, pres, 1977, exec dir, 1993-; MI Assn of Osteo Physicians, dir, 1975-, pres, 1981; American Osteopathic Assn, delegate, 1980-, trustee, 1981-, pres, 1994-95. **Honors/Awds:** MI State Univ, Patenge Meritorious Service Award, 1982; Ohio Univ, Phillips Meritorious Service Award, 1986, Doctor of Humane Letters, 1990; Univ of New England, Doctor of Humane Letters, 1992; W VA School of Osteo Med, Doctor of Science, 1993; Univ of Osteo Med, Doctor of Humane Letters, 1994. **Special Achievements:** Publications: Abnormal Uterine Bleeding after Tubal Ligation, MI Journal of Osteo Med, 1957; Von Redklinghausen's Disease of the Mesentery, MI Journal of Osteo Med, 1965; Choledocholithiasis After Cholecystectomy, Journal of AOA, 1973; Osteopathic Physician Looks at Quality, DO Magazine, 1984. **Military Serv:** US Navy, petty officer, 1944-46. **Home Addr:** 24535 N Carolina, Southfield, MI 48075. **Business Phone:** (313)499-4202.

ANDERSON, WILLIE AARON
Professional football player. **Personal:** Born Jul 11, 1975, Mobile, AL. **Educ:** Auburn. **Career:** Cincinnati Bengals, tackle, 1996-. **Special Achievements:** NFL Draft, First round pick, #10, 1996. **Business Addr:** Professional Football Player, Cincinnati Bengals, One Bengals Dr, Cincinnati, OH 45202, (513)621-3550.

ANDERSON, WILLIE LEE, JR.
Professional football player. **Personal:** Born Mar 7, 1965, Philadelphia, PA. **Educ:** UCLA, attended. **Career:** Los Angeles Rams, wide receiver, 1988-. **Honors/Awds:** Set NFL record for pass reception yards in a game (336), against New Orleans, 26 Nov 1989; played in NFC Championship Game, post-1989 season. **Business Addr:** Professional Football Player, Los Angeles Rams, 505 N Tustin Ave, Ste 243, Santa Ana, CA 92705-3735.

ANDERSON, WILLIE LLOYD
Professional basketball player. **Personal:** Born Jan 8, 1967, Greenville, SC. **Educ:** Univ of Georgia, Athens, BS, educ, 1988. **Career:** San Antonio Spurs, 1988-95; Toronto Raptors, 1995;, New York Knicks, 1996; Miami Heat, 1996-. **Honors/Awds:** NBA All-Rookie First Team, 1989; member of US Olympic team, 1988. **Special Achievements:** NBA Draft, First round pick, #10, 1988. **Business Addr:** Professional Basketball Player, Miami Heat, 721 NW 1st Ave, Miami Arena, Miami, FL 33136, (305)577-4328.

ANDERSON JANNIERE, IONA LUCILLE
Educator (retired). **Personal:** Born Aug 28, 1919, Brooklyn, NY; daughter of Clarine Ashby and Oliver Ashby; married Ivan Lloyd Janniere, Jun 17, 1988; children: Wendie Anderson Peterson, Robert. **Educ:** Hunter Coll, BA 1942; New York Univ, MA 1959; Heed Univ of FL, PhD 1976; City Univ of New York, Post Doctorate Study 1978-81. **Career:** Bd of Educ New York City, teacher of common branches 1945-69; Bank St College New York City, field rep 1969-70; Brooklyn Coll of CUNY, asst prof of educ 1969-74; City Univ of New York Medgar Evers Coll, assoc prof of educ 1974-85; Manatee Community College, instructor, 1990-97; writer/financial planner; Modern Woodmen Insurance Co. **Orgs:** Education consultant Richmond Coll of CUNY 1973-75; chairperson Northeast Flatbush Comm Coalition 1977; comm rep New York City Planning Bd #17 1978-83; evaluator of Early Childhood Programs for Bd of Educ District #73 1979-80 and District #9 1974-76; consultant on Eng as a Standard Dialect Bd of Educ New York 1983; reading consultant Houghton Mifflin Publishing Co 1983-84; board of directors East New York Development Corp 1984-85; early childhood consultant PS Dist 17 New York 1984-85; financial planner Krueger Assoc North Port FL 1986-87; mem, AAUW (Venice Branch) 1987-; journal committee, Bethune Cookman Chorale Women's Coalition of SW Florida, 1990-; commissioner, Commission on The Status of Women, Florida, 1987-90; Equity by 2000, 1988-; Planning and Zoning Advisory Board of North Port, 1988-91; Charter Board North Port, vice-chair, 1991-97. **Honors/Awds:** Fanny Lou Hamer Awd Medgar Evers Coll 1983; Sojourner Truth Awd Natl Business and Professional Women 1984; Special Awd New York State Tesol 1985; ESL Students in the Mainstream published in Integrative Approaches to ESL Teaching & Learning 1986; Womens Inner Circle of Achievement, 1991; Women of Today, 1992; Women of Change, AAUW, 1991; published many articles, the latest on Ebonics, 1997. **Home Addr:** 5893 Mayberry Ave, North Port, FL 34287.

ANDERSON-TANNER, FREDERICK T., JR.
Educator. **Personal:** Born Feb 17, 1937, Winston-Salem, NC; divorced; children: Allyson-Jenine, Frederick III. **Educ:** Morgan State Univ, BS 1959; Atlanta Univ, MA 1964; VA Poly Inst & State Univ, EdD 1975. **Career:** Kathmandu Nepal, Fulbright scholar prof of English, 1962-63; Bd of Educ Sandersville GA, reading consult 1962; Clark Coll, instructor of English 1963-64; Morehouse Coll, reading specialist, 1965-66; Rosewood State Hosp, adult educ teacher 1966-67; Rosewood School for Retarded Children, vice principal, 1967-69; Coppin State Coll, Loyola Coll, visiting prof 1968; Bowie State Coll, prof 1968-69; Federal City Coll, dep dir skills center, 1969-70; State Dept of Health & Mental Hygiene, principal, 1970-72; Federal City Coll, assoc prof 1972-73; Gov Commn on Structure & Governance of Educ in MD, asst dir 1973-75; Gov of MD, educ aide 1975; Morgan State Univ, assoc prof of educ 1975-. **Orgs:** Life mem Alpha Phi Alpha; Masonic Order; Natl Educ Assn; Natl Cncl Tchrs of English; Cncl for Exceptional Children; Natl Rehab Counseling Assn; Phi Delta Kappa; natl Assn of State Dirs of Spec Educ; Assn for Supervision & Curriculum Devel; MD Consortium for Cooperative Planning in Spec Educ. **Honors/Awds:** Fulbright Scholar to Nepal India, 1962-63; Natl Honor Soc; Exceptional Childrens Leadership Awd 1975; pres Black Caucus of Special Educators; Intl Council for Exceptional Children; 10 Yr Serv Award, State of MD; dissertation A Modified Delphi Study of Political Feasibility of Critical Issues Affecting Educ Reform in MD 1975. **Business Addr:** Assoc Prof, Educ, Morgan State Univ, Coldspring Lane, Baltimore, MD 21207.

ANDREWS, ADELIA SMITH
Business executive. **Personal:** Born Nov 7, 1914, New Orleans, LA; daughter of Adelia Beatty Smith and Christopher Columbus Smith; married Joseph H; children: Yolanda Reed, Joseph Reginald. **Educ:** Professional Secretaries Intl; Certified Professional Secretary 1978. **Career:** Whiteway Cleaners & Dyers, sec 1933-36; State of California, sec 1936-42; Los Angeles County Probation Dept, sec 1942-44; A-Z Steno Serv, sec bookkeeper 1946-49; Los Angeles Urban League, admin asst 1949-53; Watkins Entrepreneurs Inc, admin asst 1953-63; California Museum of Science & Indus, admin asst 1963-84; Caribbean Childrenspace, St Croix US VI, admin asst 1985-. **Orgs:** Bd mem Childrens Dmnsn (Childrens Space) 1979-; project dir CMSI Black Achievement Exhibit 1973-78; mem Assn Women of Pepperdine Univ, Los Angeles Urban League, Professional Secretaries International 1971-; Congress if California Seniors, 1991-. **Honors/Awds:** 25 year pin State of California 1982. **Home Addr:** 754 W 109 Pl, Los Angeles, CA 90044.

ANDREWS, ADOLPHUS
Educational administrator. **Personal:** Born Jan 19, 1943, Tampa, FL; son of Marjorie Andrews and Willie L Andrews; married Ruby Nell Brownlee; children: Adolphus William, Dawn Ingliss. **Educ:** Howard Univ, BA Political Science 1964; Southern IL Univ Edwardsville, MS Political Sci 1970; OH State Univ, PhD Political Science 1982; Harvard Institute for Education Management, graduate, 1995. **Career:** USAF Security Serv, flight commander 1965-67; USAF Scott AFB IL Military Airlift Command, special security officer 1967-70; USAF Squadron Officer School Air Univ Maxwell AFB, AL, section commander/instructor 1970-73; USAF Nakhon Phanom RTAFB Thailand, intelligence analyst dept of defense command briefing officer 1973-74; Sec of the Air Force Legislative Liaison, legislative liaison officer 1975; USAF Acad, instructor/ asst prof Dept of Political Science 1974-76, asst prof/ personnel officer/ dir of Amer & policy studies 1979-81; Office of the Sec of the Air Force,policy analyst/speech writer 1984-85; USAF Acad Prep School, commander 1985-89; executive dir, Budget & Planning, Atlantic Community Coll, 1989-93, dean of Administration and Business Services, currently. **Orgs:** Mem Air Force Assn 1978-; mem Amer Political Science Assn 1978-; mem Natl Conf of Black Political Scientists 1979-; mem Alpha Phi Alpha Fraternity Inc 1980; National Association of College and University Business Officers, 1989-; Society of College and University Planners, 1989-. **Honors/Awds:** Outstanding Chief Business Officer, Community College Business Officers, Northeast Region, 1995-96. **Military Serv:** USAF Col 1964-89; Distinguished Military Graduate ROTC 1964; Outstanding Unit Award Citation USAF 1967 & 1973; Scott AFB Jr Officer of the Month USAF April 1970; USAF Commendation Medal 1970 & 1973, Joint Serv Commendation Medal 1974, Meritorious Service Medal 1984 & 1985; Legion of Merit, 1989. **Home Addr:** 715 E Chip Shot Lane, Absecon, NJ 08201. **Business Addr:** Dean of Administration & Business Services, Atlantic Community College, Mays Landing, NJ 08330-2699, (609)343-5111.

ANDREWS, BENNY
Artist, educator. **Personal:** Born Nov 13, 1930, Madison, GA; son of Viola Perryman Andrews and George C Andrews; married Nene Humphrey, Jun 14, 1986; children: Christopher, Thomas Michael, Julia Rachael. **Educ:** Ft Valley State College, attended, 1948-50; University of Chicago, attended, 1956-58; Chicago Art Institute, BFA, 1958. **Career:** One man show, Kessler Gallery Provincetown, 1960-70; New School for Social Research, instructor, 1965-68; work displayed at numerous galleries including: Studio Museum, 1970, Museum of Modern Art, 1968-71, ACA Gallery, 1972, UMD, 1972, Aronson Midtown Gallery, 1973; Visual Arts Program, Natl Endowment for the Arts, director, 1982-84; Natl Arts Program, director, 1985-; CUNY, Queens College, Dept of Art, assoc professor, 1967-. **Orgs:** Co-chairman, Black Emergency Cultural Coalition, 1969; board director, Children's Art Council. **Honors/Awds:** John Jay Whitney Fellow, 1965-67; New York Council on the Arts, grantee 1971; articles on black art culture in professional journals; NEA, fellowship, 1974; Bellagie Fellow, Rockefeller Foundation, 1987; Painting Fellowship, National Endowment, 1986; Atlanta School of Art, honorary doctorate, 1984. **Military Serv:** US Air Force, s sgt, four years. **Business Addr:** Professor, Dept of Art, CUNY, Queens College, Flushing, NY 11367-1597.

ANDREWS, CARL R.
Association executive (retired). **Personal:** Born Apr 20, 1926, Williamsport, PA; son of Georgie Bannister Andrews and Carl M Andrews; married Jeanette M White, May 1, 1955; children: Carl R Jr, Keith R, Cheryl Y. **Educ:** Lycoming Coll, 1946-48; Howard Univ, 1948-50; Howard Univ School of Social Work, 1951-52; Rutgers Univ, Adj Urban Fellowship Program 1963-64; Yale Univ Drug Dependence Inst, 1971. **Career:** Boys' Clubs of Newark, NJ, club dir 1952-66; Boys' Clubs of Amer Natl Prgm & Training Svc, asst dir 1966-73; Boys' Club Assn of Indianapolis, IN, exec dir 1973-89. **Orgs:** Member: Kiwanis International, IN Juvenile Justice Task Force; elder in Witherspoon Presbyterian Church, Alpha Phi Alpha Fraternity, Exec Service Corps, Boys & Girls Clubs of Indianapolis. **Honors/Awds:** Mem, Natl Scholastic Hon Soc; NJ Afro-Amer Newspaper Award 1959; Man of Wk Award Prudential Ins Co 1966; Midwest Reg Heart & Soul Award 1978; Paul Lemmon Adminstr of Yr Award 1977; past pres award E Orange Comm Day Nursery 1973; Library dedicated in honor Newark, NJ 1982; Kiwanis Club of Indianapolis Career Award 1980; State of Indiana, Sagamore of the Wabash, 1989. **Military Serv:** USN 1944-46. **Home Addr:** 4924 Olympia Dr, Indianapolis, IN 46208.

ANDREWS, CHARLES CLIFTON, JR.
Radio executive. **Personal:** Born Dec 16, 1939, San Antonio, TX; son of Charles Clifton; married Thelma W Andrews; children: Charles III, Michael. **Educ:** Lincoln Univ. **Career:** Inner City Broadcasting Co - SA, pres, 1982-; AfriCom Telecommunications Ltd, scy, bd mem, 1990-. **Business Addr:** President/ General Manager, Inner City Broadcasting Co - SA, 217 Alamo Plz, Ste 200, San Antonio, TX 78205, (210)271-9600.

ANDREWS, EMANUEL CARL
Elected government official. **Personal:** Born Sep 9, 1956, New York, NY. **Educ:** Medgar Evers Coll, BA 1978; Albany State Univ, MA 1981. **Career:** Black & Puerto Rican Caucus NYS Legislature, asst exec dir 1980-81; US Congressman Major Owens, specl asst 1982-84; NY State Assembly, special asst state assembly; Government Relations for the NYS Senate Minority, dir.

ANDREWS, FRAZIER L.
Clergyman. **Personal:** Born May 3, 1933, Mobile, AL; married Lula Tillett. **Educ:** AL State Univ, BS 1955; VA Union Grad Sch of Rel, MDiv 1958; Columbia Pacific Univ, PhD, philosophy, 1993. **Career:** First Baptist Church Hertford NC, pastor 1957-68; First Baptist Ch High Point NC, minister 1968-, Sr pastor, currently; Shaw Univ, teacher. **Orgs:** Treas High Point Ch Hsg Inc; fndr & pres Antil Enterp Inc; mem Head Start Pol Co Bd Guilford Co; mem ESAA Adv Com; High Point City Schs; mem exec bd Model City Comm; former bd mem SCLC; pres Minister's Conf High Point & Vic; chmn High Point Bus Dev Corp; pres Brentwood Shop Ctr; mem Legal Aid Bd & Fam Serv Bur; co-spon London Wood Dev low-mid-inc hsg dev; former mem NC Good Neigh Counc; pres Hertford Movement; stud at Urban Training Cent Chi. **Honors/Awds:** Pastor of Yr Hertford NC 1966; holds sev Hon Degrees; rec'd sev Ford Found Grants. **Business Addr:** Minister, First Baptist Church, 701 E Washington Dr, High Point, NC 27260.

ANDREWS, JAMES E.
Educator/psychologist. **Personal:** Born Aug 6, 1943, Pensacola, FL; son of Emma Andrews and C Andrews; married Pat; children: Lisa, Marcus. **Educ:** Compson Coll, AA, 1970; CA State Dom Hill, BA, 1972; UCLA, MA, 1974; Nova Univ, PhD, 1977. **Career:** Compson Unified Sch, psychologist 1973-75; Pomona Unified Sch, psychologist 1975-79; Psychological Assessment Lab, owner 1977-; Mt San Antonio College, psychologist 1979-. **Orgs:** Pres Southern California Assn of Black Psychologists 1975-76; consultant Dept of Rehabilitation 1975-; consultant CA Poly 1981-. **Honors/Awds:** Published book Theories of Child Observation, 1974; published several articles on children and learning. **Military Serv:** AUS sp/4 2 yrs.

ANDREWS, JAMES EDWARD
Labor union official. **Personal:** Born Sep 29, 1948, Norlina, NC; son of Bettie Hargrove Andrews and Merlin Andrews; married Audrey P Andrews; children: Timothy, Annisha, LaTonya. **Career:** Perfect Packed Product Co, Henderson, NC, 1971-75; NC State AFL-CIO, Raleigh, NC, project outreach dir, 1975-84, acting secretary/treasurer, 1984, sec/treasurer, 1985-, secretary/treasurer, CEO, 1991-. **Orgs:** President, Warren County NAACP, 1971-75; executive board, NC APRI, 1975-; executive committee & board, National APRI, 1978-; regional representative, APRI Southern Region, 1978-. **Military Serv:** US Army, E-5, 1969-70, Purple Heart. **Home Addr:** 1309 Lions Way, Raleigh, NC 27604.

ANDREWS, JAMES F.
Educator. **Personal:** Born Oct 25, 1918, Council, NC; married Dollie Ellison; children: Audrey, Hal. **Educ:** Fagetteville State Univ, BS 1949; NC A&T State Univ, attended 1961. **Career:** Plain View Elementary School, principal. **Orgs:** Pres Bladen Co Tchr Assn; pres Southeastern Schoolmasters Orgn 1975; sec Kappa Rho Chapt, Omega Psi Phi Frat Inc; mem Div of Prin; em Fayetteville State Univ Natl Alumni Assn; mem Lodge #374 Prince Hall F&AM of NC; mem Young Dem of NC. **Business Addr:** Principal, Plain View Elementary School, Rte 1 Box 144, Tar Heel, NC 28392.

ANDREWS, JUDIS R.
Attorney. **Personal:** Born Aug 27, 1941; married Cheryl D. **Educ:** AZ State Univ, JD, 1972. **Career:** AZ Civil Rights Commn, asst dir 1964-67; Phoenix Coll, instr 1967-68; AZ State Univ, adminstrv asst to pres 1968-69; Joshua M Bursh II firm of Cunningham Goodson Tiffany & Weltch, law clerk 1968-69; Private Practice, attorney. **Orgs:** Dir Summer Youth Project Phoenix OIC 1969; dir Spl Serv Maricopa Co Comm Action Prog 1969; spl asst to dir of Housing at AZ State Univ 1969-70; dir Progs & Opers Seattle Oppors Indus Ctr Inc Seattle 1972-73; fndg mem first sec to bd dir Wm F Patterson Lodge IBPOE #447; Civil E Neighborhood Council fndg mem & initial bd mem; Negro Polit Action Assn of AZ State Pres 1966-67; NAACP Youth Pres Pinal Co; CORE chmn vice chmn sec treas; 50 Bus Man Club fndr 1st pres; Omega Psi Phi Frat AZ State Univ Scholarship Comm; mem bd dir AZ State Alumni Assn 1975; mem bd dir AZ Commn on Post Secondary Educ 1974-75. **Honors/Awds:** Scholarship Awd Martin Luther King Ctr for Disadvantaged Youth Seeking Educ Oppors; Negro Polit Action Assn of AZ Man of Yr 1968; 50 Bus Man Club Man of Yr 1967-68.

ANDREWS, MALACHI
Educator, artist, sports researcher. **Personal:** Born Sep 11, 1933, Los Angeles, CA; son of Geneva Downing Smith and William L Smith (stepfather); divorced; children: Kim Andrews Warnette, Sekou Eusi, Atiba Azikwe. **Educ:** Los Angeles City College, AA, 1953; University of Arizona, BA, 1956, MEd, 1961; Louisiana State University, ethnic intl study, Ethnic Kinesiology Research Inst, Ed DE, 1979. **Career:** Barstow Intermed School, teacher, 1959-62; Barstow High School, teacher & coach, 1962-66; Compton High School, art teacher & track coach, 1966-68; consultant, Melanin Healing & Movement of African Centric Sports Life & Health; California State University Hayward, Dept of Kinesiology & Physical Education, assoc professor, 1968-79, professor, 1979-. **Orgs:** Research director, Thomas Ethnic Kinesiology & Sports Research Institute; USOlympic Track Team, member, 1956; KM-WR Science Consortium, bd of directors, vice pres or education, 1988-; bd of directors, Seymour-Smith Inc; Gymnastic Sports Training Director, California Special Olympics, 1987-. **Honors/Awds:** All-Around State Gymnastic Champion, 1955; first Black head track coach at a major university in California; recipient, Professional Art Awards; author, Psychoblackology; author, Six Melanin Dollar Man and Zionic Woman; author, Elastic Communication; author, Color Me Right, Then Frame Me in Motion; co-author, Black Language; particip, 2nd World Black & African Festival of Arts & Culture, Nigeria, 1977. **Military Serv:** US Army, private first class, 1956-58. **Home Addr:** PO Box 4742, Hayward, CA 94540-4742. **Business Addr:** Professor, Dept of Kinesiology/Phys Education, California State University Hayward, 25800 Carlos Bee Blvd, Hayward, CA 94542-3000.

ANDREWS, MAXINE RAMSEUR
Educator. **Personal:** Born in Fayetteville, NC; daughter of Patsy Evans Ramseur; divorced; children: Dr Sabrina Andrews Molden, Gigi, Thurman J III. **Educ:** Fayetteville State Univ, BS 1956; North Carolina Central Univ, MEd 1963; East Carolina Univ EdS 1975; Univ of NC at Greensboro, EdD 1985. **Career:** Cumberland County Schools, teacher 1956-66, school social worker 1966-69; Elizabeth City State Univ, title III coord 1969-71; Fayetteville State Univ, adj prof 1985-; Sincerely Yours Writing & Specialty Svcs, proprietor 1986-; Cumberland County Schools, elem supervisor 1971-84, supervisor secondary educ 1984-90; Fayetteville State University, assistant professor/ coordinator of secondary education, coordinator of educational administration/curriculum/instruction, director, teaching fellows program, currently. **Orgs:** Member, Natl Educ Assoc; member, Assoc for Supervision and Curriculum Div; member, NC Assoc for Educators; member, Phi Delta Kappa; member, NC Assoc of Administrators; member, Delta Sigma Theta Sor; member, NC Historical Preservation Soc; member, Fayetteville State Alumni Assoc; president, 1987-90, secretary, 1988-91, North Carolina Association of Supervision and Curriculum Development; Master of School Administration, Fay State University, coordinator, 1997-. **Honors/Awds:** Distinguished Alumnae Fayetteville State Univ Natl Assoc for Equal Oppor in

Higher Educ 1986. **Business Addr:** School Administration Coordinator, Fayetteville State University, Fayetteville, NC 28301.

ANDREWS, NELSON MONTGOMERY
Statistician. **Personal:** Born Jul 9, 1951, Winston-Salem, NC; son of Frances Andrews and Clem Andrews Sr.; married Sharon Millicent Parrish; children: Elenora, Ava. **Educ:** Johnson C Smith Univ, Physics, Math, 1969-73; Purdue Univ, Statistics, MSD 1977. **Career:** BF Goodrich, statistician 1977-78; Bell Laboratories NJ, statistician 1978-82; Bellcore Comm NJ, statistician 1982-84; GTF Deer Valley AZ, sr org statistician 1985-87; NEC, Mgr, Quality Statistics, presently. **Orgs:** Mem, Phi Beta Sigma Fraternity 1971-; participant Gistault Inst Career Devel Program 1978; career recruiter Bell Labs Bellcore NJ 1980-84; Affirmative Action Educ Career Developer 1982-84; charter mem, Boule, Sigma Pi Phi Fraternity 1986-. **Honors/Awds:** Pres Beta Kappa Chi, Phi Beta Sigma, Johnson C Smith Univ; speaker on statistical abstracts 1986 Joint Statistical Meeting 1986; speaker Intl Communications Meeting Tokyo Japan 1987.

ANDREWS, PHILLIP
Business executive. **Personal:** Born Jun 8, 1963, Hempstead, NY; son of Daphine Andrews and Frank Andrews; married Chriscelle S Seldon; children: Phillip, Chriscelle Seldon II. **Educ:** International Career Institute, paralegal diploma, 1984-85; John Jay College of Criminal Justice, 1986-90. **Career:** New York City Department of Correction, correction officer, 1984-; The Hair Cut Hut, vice pres, 1990-; Envogue I Beauty Salon, co-owner, currently. **Orgs:** One Penny a Day Self Help Movement, chairman, 1991-; Roosevelt Chamber of Commerce, board member, 1992-; Roosevelt Kiwanis Club, board member, 1992-; Majestic Eagles of Long Island, Speaker's Bureau, chairman, 1990-; Black Unity Day Committee, 1990-91; 100 Black Men of Nassau/Suffolk Inc, board of directors; Barber Culture Association of Long Island and Queens, vice pres of cosmetologist; Hempstead NAACP, executive committee; Wet Indian American Chamber of Commerce, board member; Economic Forum Newspaper, editorial board; West Indian American Chamber of Commerce. **Honors/Awds:** Village of Hempstead, First Annual Entrepreneur's Award, 1991; Black Unity Committee, First Annual African-American Entrepreneur Award, 1991; New York City Department of Correction, Excellent Duty, 1992; Operation Get Ahead, Award of Appreciation for Outstanding Contribution, 1992; Roosevelt High School, African-American Human Relations Award, 1991; Black Entrepreneurs Award, 1993; Operation Get Ahead, Award of Appreciation, 1993; Long Island Cares Inc, Certificate of Appreciation, 1993; Nassau County Council of Chambers, Roosevelt Chamber of Commerce, The Haircut Hut Small Businessman of the Year, 1995; New York State Assembly Certificate of Merit, 1995; LI Youth Foundation, Outstanding Youth Advocate Award, 1996. **Special Achievements:** Mind Development Series, poetry, 1990; The Community Reporter, staff writer, 1990-91. **Home Addr:** 38 Virginia Ave, Hempstead, NY 11550.

ANDREWS, RAWLE
Physician. **Personal:** Born Feb 4, 1926, St George's, Grenada; son of Adina Andrews and Lawrence Andrews; married Naomi Cox Andrews, Aug 1963; children: Rawle, Rhetta, Ronald, Rhonda. **Educ:** Hampton Inst, BS (w/Honors) 1956; URIU MI, postgrad 1956-58; Meharry Med Coll, MD 1963. **Career:** LA Co General Hospital, intern 1963-64; Charles R Drew School Houston, school physician 1964; William Jr & Sr High Houston, school physician 1965-67; General Practice Medicine Houston, physician 1964-; Rawle Andrews, MD Clinic Assn, general practitioner; Texas Boxing Commission, ring physician, 1982-86. **Orgs:** Vice pres Acres Home City Council 1969-70, pres 1970-72; mem advisory bd Riverside Natl Bank Houston; pres Houston Med Forum 1970-72; bd dirs Operation Breadbasket; co-chmn task force comm Houston Galveston Area Council 1970-; vice pres trustee Montessori School Houston 1970-71; bd dir So Christian Leadership Conf; Martin Luther King Center; mem AMA, Royal Soc Health; chmn, bd trustees, bd dirs Natl Med Assn; board mem, pres, board of trustees, Eliza Johnson Nursing Home. **Honors/Awds:** Humanitarian Award Antioch Baptist Church, 1969; Physician of the Year, State of Texas Black Caucus, 1989. **Business Addr:** Diplomate, American Bd of Professional Disability Consultant, Andrews Medical Clinic, 7901 W Montgomery Rd, Houston, TX 77088.

ANDREWS, ROSALYN MCPHERSON
Publishing company executive. **Personal:** Born Mar 27, 1953, New Orleans, LA; daughter of James & Lillie McPherson; divorced; children: Jackie Robert Kelley II, Monique Cheri Kelley, Jasmin Renee Andrews. **Educ:** Southern Univ & A & M College, BS, sec ed, 1973; Fairleigh Dickinson Univ, MBA, marketing, 1982. **Career:** Roosevelt Pub Schools, teacher, 1975-76; CBS Inc, editor, 1976-79; McGraw-Hill, editor, 1979-80; Scholastic Inc, product mgr, 1980-83; Time Inc, source mgr, circulation, 1983-85; McPherson Andrews Marketing Inc, president, 1985-92; Time Life Inc, vp & publisher, 1992-. **Orgs:** Natl Assn of Black School Educ; Intl Reading Assn; Natl Cncl for Social Studies; Northern Virginia Urban League, bd mem; Models in Excellence, NASA, NSF, bd mem; Women's Project & Productions, bd mem; The College Board, Task Force mem. **Special Achievements:** Author, Milestones in Science & Mathematics, Facts-on-File, endorsed by AAAS, 1996. **Business Addr:** Vice President, Time Life Inc, 2000 Duke St, Alexandria, VA 22314, (703)838-7494.

ANDREWS, SHARONY S.
Journalist. **Personal:** Born Jan 28, 1967, Miami, FL; daughter of Estela Meyers Andrews and Garcia Andrews. **Educ:** University of Miami, BS, political science/broadcast journalism, 1989. **Career:** The Miami Hearald, reporter, 1989-92; The Detroit Free Press, reporter, 1993-. **Orgs:** South Florida Association of Black Journalists, vice pres of print, 1991-92; Journalism and Women's Symposium (JAWS), 1992-; Alpha Kappa Alpha Sorority, 1986-. **Honors/Awds:** University of Miami, Greater Miami Achievers Goldendrum Scholar, 1985; Society of Professioal Journalists Scholarship, 1985; Alpha Kappa Alpha, Gamma Zeta Omega Chapter, Scholarship, 1985.

ANDREWS, WILLIAM HENRY
Hospital administrator (retired). **Personal:** Born Oct 16, 1919, Wellston, MO; son of Viola Andrews and William H Andrews; married Mildred E Joyce; children: William, Brenda. **Educ:** Lincoln Univ, BS 1941; WA Univ, MHA 1954. **Career:** Homer G Phillips Hospital, asst adminis 1941-52; People's Hospital, administ 1954-55; George W Hubbard Hospital Meharry Med Coll, admin 1955-59; Forest City Hospital, admin 1959-64; Cleveland Metro General Hospital, asst dir, dep dir, dir 1969-81; Kaiser Found Hospital, admin 1981-86 retired; Case Western Reserve University Schools of Medicine and Dentistry, lecturer, currently. **Orgs:** Mem Faculty Hlth Serv Admin Grad Sch OH State Univ; cncl mem Natl Inst Arthritis & Metabolic Diseases 1968-71; mem Physicians Clinic; asst adv com Cuyahoga Comm Coll; personnel adv com & soc serv clearing house com Cleveland Fedn for Comm Plang; Cath Interracial Cncl Cleveland Arthritis Found; trustee Cleveland Hemophilia Found; Hough Norwood Family Hlth Care Prgrm; Commonwealth Fund Fellow 1952; Fellow Amer Coll Hosp Adminstrs; mem WA Univ Alumni Assn; mem Natl Assn Hlth Serv Execs; panel mem OH Hosp Assn; exec com Blood Bank Comm, House Staff Comm, Grtr Cleveland Hosp Assn; mem Kappa Alpha Psi; Rotarian. **Home Addr:** 2960 Ripley Rd, Cleveland, OH 44120.

ANDREWS, WILLIAM L., SR.
Company executive. **Personal:** Born Dec 25, 1955, Thomasville, GA; son of Ethel Lee Glenn and Azell Andrews, Sr; married Lydia Elzy Andrews, Jan 1, 1980; children: William Andrews Jr, Micah Ryan Andrews, Khea D'ana Andrews. **Educ:** Auburn. **Career:** Housing Specialists, executive; Atlanta Falcons, fullback 1979-87; The William Andrews Group Ltd 1987. **Orgs:** Special Olympics; Project CURE for leukemia research; Drug Abuse Programs. **Honors/Awds:** Second player in NFL history to get over 2,000 yards rushing & receiving twice; NFL'S 26th most prolific rusher of all-time in 5 seasons; tied 3rd on Falcons' all-time scoring list with 240 points; named to Pro Bowl for 4 seasons; 12th player in league history to go over 1,000 yds in rookie season; All-NFL 1983; 2nd team All-NFL; Pro Bowl 1979, 1981 & 1983; Falcons' MVP 1980 & 1982; NFL All-Rookie; Falcons' Man of the Year 1983. **Business Addr:** Director, Community Affairs, West Paces Ferry Hospital, 3200 Howelk Mill Road, Atlanta, GA 30327.

ANDREWS, WILLIAM PERNELL
Educator, psychotherapist, administrator. **Personal:** Born Mar 24, 1947, Richmond, VA; son of William & Rena Thompson Andrews; married Michele Evans Andrews, Dec 10, 1983; children: Oronde K, Joshua T, Kayla S. **Educ:** Cambridge College, EdM, 1989; Fielding Institute, PhD, Candidate. **Career:** Boston City Hosp, staff psychologist, narcotics, 1981-83; MA Department of Corrections, clinical coord, psychologist, 1983-92; Roxbury Youth Words Inc, executive director, 1992-93; Dimock Comm Health Ctr, director, family counseling, 1993-95; Northeastern University, assistant director, TDOAAI, 1995-. **Orgs:** American Counselors Association, 1986-92; American Mental Health Counselors Association, 1986-92. **Honors/Awds:** US Chamber of Commerce, Outstanding Young Men In America, 1980. **Special Achievements:** "Treatment of Families in Urban Community," 1995; "Beyond Stereotyping - Historic Media Presentation," 1994; "New Horizons - A Conceptual Model for Treatment," 1992; "Racial/Cultural Issues in Corrections," 1985; "African Philosophical Foundations," 1982. **Military Serv:** US Air Force, technical sgt, 1966-70, 1976-86. **Home Addr:** 18 Curve St, West Newton, MA 02165, (617)244-1095. **Business Phone:** (617)373-4918.

ANDREWS, WILLIAM PHILLIP
Brewing company executive. **Personal:** Born Jan 9, 1938, Kansas City, MO; son of Florence Andrews and William Andrews; married Dolores Caesar, Mar 31, 1961; children: Phillip, Steven, Jeffrey. **Educ:** Lincoln University, Jefferson City, MO, BS, 1961; USFF Fort Sam Houston, San Antonio, TX, 2nd Lt. Comm, 1961. **Career:** Anheuser-Busch Inc, Houston, TX, ethnic sales mgr, 1967-. **Orgs:** Member, Kappa Alpha Psi, 1958-. **Honors/Awds:** Distinguished Service, Lincoln University, Jefferson City, MO, 1989. **Military Serv:** US Army, 1st Lt., 1961-63. **Business Addr:** Ethnic Sales Mgr, Anheuser-Busch Inc, 1800 West Loop S, Suite 1100, Houston, TX 77027.

ANDUJAR, JOAQUIN
Professional baseball player (retired). **Personal:** Born Dec 21, 1952, San Pedro de Macoris, Dominican Republic; married Walkiria; children: Jesse Joaquin. **Career:** Pitcher: Houston Astros, 1976-81, St Louis Cardinals, 1981-85, Oakland Athletics, 1986-87, Houston Astros, 1988.

ANGELL, EDGAR O.
Physician. **Personal:** marrIed Anita Roach; children: Thelma, Sheila. **Educ:** Drake Univ, tchr diploma BA 1950; COMS, DO 1954. **Career:** Jamaica, tchr; Private Practice, Cleveland; Private Practice Jackson TN, physician 1970-. **Orgs:** Mem Amer Osteopathic Assn, OH Osteopath Assn, Cuyahoga Co Osteopathic Assn; TN Osteopathic Assn; mem ACGOP; mem NAACP; mem Civic Action Group of Jackson TN.

ANGELOU, MAYA (MARGUERITE JOHNSON)
Author, poet, playwright. **Personal:** Born Apr 4, 1928, St Louis, MO; daughter of Vivian Baxter Johnson and Bailey Johnson; married Tosh Angelos (divorced); married Paul Du Feu, 1973; children: Guy Johnson. **Career:** Author, poet, playwright, stage and screen producer, director, actress, 1954-; Southern Christian Leadership Conference, coordinator, 1959-60; Arab Observer Egypt, associate editor, 1961-62; University of Ghana, asst administrator, 1963-66; African Review, editor, 1964-66; California State University, Wichita State University, visiting professor; Wake Forest University, Department of Humanities, Reynolds professor of American studies, 1974-. **Orgs:** American Federation of Television & Radio Artists; board of trustees, American Film Institute, 1975-; Directors Guild; Actors' Equity; Women's Pri son Assn. **Honors/Awds:** 32 Honorary Degrees; Pulitzer Prize Nomination, "Just Give Me A Cool Drink of Water 'fore I Diiie," 1972; Tony Award Nomination, "Look Away," 1975; Ladies Home Journal, one of the Women of the Year in Communications, 1976; Emmy Award Nomination, Performance, "Roots," 1977; Distingushed Woman of North Carolina, 1992; Essence Magazine, Woman of the Year, 1992; Horatio Alger Award, 1992; Women In Film, Crystal Award, 1992; American Academy of Achievement, Golden Plate Award, 1990; Horatio Alger Awards Dinner Chairman, 1993; National Society for the Prevention of Cruelty to Children, London, England, NSPCC Maya Angelou CPT and Family Centre, London, England, center dedication, June 20, 1991; NAACP, Image Award, Literary Work, Nonfiction, 1998. **Special Achievements:** Author, works include: I Know Why the Caged Bird Sings, 1970; Just Give Me A Cool Drink of Water 'Fore I Die, 1971; Gather Together in My Name, 1974; Oh Pray My Wings Are Gonna Fit Me Well, 1975; Singin & Swingin & Getting Merry Like Christmas, 1976; And Still I Rise, 1978; The Heart of a Woman, 1981; Shaker, Why Don't You Sing? 1983; All God's Children Need Traveling Shoes, 1986; Mrs Flowers: A Moment of Friendship, 1986; Wouldn't Take Nothing for My Journey Now, Random, 1993; poems: Maya Angelou, 1986; Now Sheba Sings the Song, 1987; I Shall Not Be Moved, Random House, 1990; plays include: Cabraret for Freedom, 1960; The Least of These, 1966; Ajax, 1974; And Still I Rise, 1976; screenplays include: Georgia Georgia, 1972; All Day Long, 1974; PBS-TV Documentaries: "Who Cares About Kids" "Kindred Spirits," KERA-TV, Dallas, TX; "Rainbow In The Clouds," series, host, writer, WTVS-TV, Detroit, MI; "To The Contrary," Maryland Public Television; lecturer: Nancy Hanks Lecture, American Council for the Arts, 1990; contributing writer: "Brewster Place," mini-series, HARPO Productions; panelist: Institute for the Study of Human Systems, Zermatt, Switzerland, 1990; lyricist: "King Now," theatrical project, London, England; has appeared in numerous plays and TV productions as both an actress and singer; wrote and presented a poem for President Clinton's Swearing-In Ceremonies, 1993; Down in the Delta, director. **Business Addr:** Reynolds Professor of American Studies, Wake Forest University, Dept of Humanities, PO Box 7314, Winston-Salem, NC 27109.

ANGLEN, REGINALD CHARLES
Journalist. **Personal:** Born Feb 20, 1952, Cleveland, OH; son of Barbara Anglen and Howard Anglen. **Educ:** Ohio State University, BA, 1989; Columbus Technical Institute, grantsmanship certification. **Career:** Ohio State School for the Blind, public relations director, 1973-75; St Stephen's Community House, caseworker, 1979-85; The Ohio State University, communications specialists, 1989-. **Orgs:** Phi Beta Sigma Fraternity, 1972-; Natl Assn of Black Journalists, 1989-; Columbus Association of Black Journalists, 1989-; Columbus Area Leadership Program. **Honors/Awds:** White House Council on Youth, delegate, 1970; Columbus Citizen Journal, 1 of 10 Outstanding Young Man, 1974; Ohio Jaycees, 1 of 5 Outstanding Ohioans, 1974. **Business Addr:** Communications Specialist, The Ohio State University, 1125 Kinnear Rd, #102, Columbus, OH 43212, (614)292-8423.

ANISE, LADUN OLADUNJOYE E.
Educator. **Personal:** Born Mar 24, 1940. **Educ:** Albion College, BA, 1967; Syracuse Univ, MA 1968, PhD Political Science 1970; Univ of Pittsburgh, MA 1975. **Career:** Syracuse Univ, African Studies-Minority Studies, lecturer 1968-70; Educ Policy & Resource Devel Center, Syracuse Univ, rsch assoc 1969-70; Univ of Pittsburgh, asst prof 1970-75; Univ of Ife Ni-

geria, visiting sr lecturer 1979-83; Hill Dist Catholic School System & Educ Devel Center, Pittsburgh PA, consultant 1972-75; Univ of Pittsburgh, assoc prof 1975-, African Studies Group, coord 1982-88, Black Studies Dept, chmn (summers) 1987, 1989. **Orgs:** Mem Current Issues Comm African Studies Assoc 1968-, Amer Political Science Assoc, Natl Org of Black Political Science, African Heritage Studies Assoc, Natl Acad of Social Science. **Honors/Awds:** ASPAU Achievement & Scholastic Award 1967; Omicron Delta Kappa 1967; Maxwell Fellow 1967-70; Woodrow Wilson Doctoral Fellow 1970; Meritorious Achievement Award Univ of Pittsburgh 1974. **Business Addr:** Associate Professor, Dept of Political Science, Univ of Pittsburgh, 4T25 Forbes Quad, Pittsburgh, PA 15260.

ANTHONY, BERNARD WINSTON
Utility co. director. **Personal:** Born Mar 20, 1945, St Maurice, LA; son of Ica O Wade Anthony and Lee Anthony; married Marion D Sherman Anthony, Nov 28, 1987; children: Alaric B, Timothy W, Corwin S, Shelley D, Christopher M, Dante Harris, Tanesha M Harris. **Educ:** Bakersfield City College, Bakersfield, CA, AA; Fresno City College, Fresno, CA, 1990-92; Merced Coll, 1992-. **Career:** Pacific Gas & Electric Co, Merced CA, dir of gas & electric construction, maintenance & operations, 1965-. **Orgs:** Member, NAACP, Fresno, 1987-; member, tax preparer, Enrolled Agents of America, 1988-; president, Black Employees Assn, Bakersfield, 1983-; teacher, trustee, deacon, coord, dir, St Peter Miss Baptist Church, 1965-; mentor, facilitator, Fresno Unified School District, 1988-; member, Black Employees Assn, Fresno, 1986-; Black Employees Association, Yosemite Division, advisor; mentor & dir, Tassel Program Merced High School District, 1992-. **Honors/Awds:** Community Service Award, Pacific Gas and Electric Co, 1989, 1990; Service Award, Fresno Unified School District, 1989-90. **Home Addr:** 3325 Fathom Ct, Atwater, CA 95301. **Business Addr:** Director of Electric & Gas Construction, Maintenance & Operations, Electric & Gas Transmission & Distribution, 3185 M Street, Merced, CA 95348.

ANTHONY, BRENDA TUCKER
Finance executive. **Personal:** Born Aug 4, Java, VA; daughter of Beulah E Tucker and James P Tucker; married Edward French Anthony, Nov 28. **Educ:** Central State University, BS, 1969; University of Dayton, MBA, 1974. **Career:** NCR Corp, financial analyst, 1969-76; General Motors Corp, accountant, 1976-87; Johnson Energy Company, finance mgr, 1987-90; EFA & Associates Inc, comptroller, 1987-. **Orgs:** Central State University Alumni Association, 1969-; National Black MBA Association, 1970-; National Association of Female Executives, 1973-; Alpha Kappa Alpha, 1967-; NAACP, 1969-; National Council Negro Women, 1974-. **Business Addr:** Comptroller, EFA & Associates, Inc, 3023 Production Court, Dayton, OH 45414-3514, (513)454-5387.

ANTHONY, CLARENCE EDWARD
Business management consultant. **Personal:** Born Oct 10, 1959, Belle Glade, FL; son of Irene and Bill Anthony; children: Reidel V. **Educ:** Palm Beach Jr Coll, AA 1979; FL Atlantic Univ, BA 1981, MPA 1982. **Career:** South FL Water Mgmt Dist, internship rsch asst; Treasure Coast Regional Planning Council, regional planner; Commissioner Ken Adams District V, admin asst; Dept of Equal Opportunity, dir; Palm Beach Co Bd of Commissioners, county commissioner; Anthony & Associates, pres. **Orgs:** Pres, FL Atlantic Univ Alumni Assn; bd of dirs Big Brothers/Big Sisters; mem District IX Mental Health Drug Abuse Planning Council; bd of dirs Leadership Palm Beach County; bd of dirs Hispanic Human Resources, Glades Area Retarded Citizens; mem FL League of Cities Urban Admin Comm; bd of dirs FL Inst of Govt; former pres, founder FAU Black Alumni Assn; mem Omega Psi Phi Fraternity; chmn FL League of Cities Finance and Taxation Comm; bd mem Palm Beach County Area Planning Bd; mayor, South Bay Florida 1984-. **Honors/Awds:** McKnight Foundation Black Doctoral Fellowship; FAU Distinguished Alumnus Awd; Palm Beach Jr Coll Distinguished Alumnus Award; Environmental Growth Mgmt Graduate Fellowship; Phi Theta Kappa Scholarship; Intl Youth in Achievement; 30 Leaders of the Future, Ebony Magazine, 1988. **Home Addr:** 310 SE 4th Ave, PO Box 23, South Bay, FL 33493.

ANTHONY, DAVID HENRY, III
Educator. **Personal:** Born Apr 28, 1952, Brooklyn, NY; son of Carolyn Anthony and David H Anthony Jr; married Allison Anitra Sampson; children: Adey Tabita Frances, Djibril Senay Frederick William. **Educ:** NY Univ, AB 1968-72; Univ of WI-Madison, MA History 1975, DPhil History 1983. **Career:** Fulbright Fellow Dept of State, rsch assoc 1976-77; Univ of Dar es Salaam Tanzania, rsch assoc 1976-77; Clark Univ, visiting prof 1979; Coppin State Coll, instructor of history 1980-84; Univ of Oregon, Eugene, OR, assistant professor of history, 1984-88; Univ of California, Oakes College, Santa Cruz, assistant professor, currently. **Orgs:** Curr spec Madison Metro Sch Dist 1977-78; consul Swahili Anteiro Pietila Helen Winternitz 1980; rsch affiliate Univ of FL Ctr for African studies 1982; visiting prof History Dept Towson State Univ 1982-83; judge Gr Baltimore History Fair 1982-84; mem Phi Alpha Theta 1983-; mem Fulbright Alumni Assn 1981-. **Honors/Awds:** Fulbright Hays Awd Fulbright Found Dept of State 1976-77; President's Humanities Fellowship, University of California, 1990-91. **Business Addr:** Assistant Professor, Oakes College, Univ of California, 1156 High St, Santa Cruz, CA 95064.

ANTHONY, EMORY
Judge. **Career:** Birmingham Municipal Court, judge, 1991-. **Business Addr:** Judge, Municipal Court, City Hall, Room 100, Birmingham, AL 35203, (205)254-2161.

ANTHONY, ERIC TODD
Professional baseball player. **Personal:** Born Nov 8, 1967, San Diego, CA. **Career:** Houston Astros, TX, outfielder, 1989-94; Seattle Mariners, 1994-. **Honors/Awds:** Most Valuable Player, Southern League, 1989. **Business Addr:** Professional Baseball Player, Seattle Mariners, 411 1st Ave S, PO Box 4100, Seattle, WA 98104, (206)628-3555.

ANTHONY, GREGORY C.
Professional basketball player. **Personal:** Born Nov 15, 1967, Las Vegas, NV. **Educ:** Portland; University of Nevada Las Vegas. **Career:** New York Knicks, guard, 1991-95; Vancouver Grizzlies, 1995-97; Seattle Supersonics, 1997-. **Special Achievements:** New York Knicks, first round draft pick, 12th overall, NBA Draft, 1991. **Business Addr:** Professional Basketball Player, Seattle Supersonics, PO Box 900911, Seattle, WA 98109, (206)281-5850.

ANTHONY, JEFFREY CONRAD
Entertainment producer. **Personal:** Born Jun 3, 1949, Washington, DC. **Educ:** Georgetown Univ, BA 1976. **Career:** Natl Endowment for the Arts, sr program specialist 1980-85; Brooklyn Acad of Music, dir comm relations 1985-86; Freelance Consultant, independent production consultant 1986-. **Orgs:** Assoc producer Capital City Jazz Festival Washington DC 1982-85; assoc mem Smithsonian Inst; mem Natl Assoc of Jazz Educators; bd mem New Music Distribution Svcs; assoc mem Mgt Natl Jazz Serv Org 1984-; producer "Dance Africa" Brooklyn NY 1986; assoc producer "Black Family Reunion Celebration," Wash DC, Atlanta GA, Los Angeles CA, Detroit MI 1986-87; producer "1st Annual DIVA Found Awds" Kennedy Center, Wash DC 1987. **Honors/Awds:** Certificate of Merit Outstanding Young Men of Amer 1983; Natl Endowment Arts, Sustained Superior Performance 1984, Special Act & Serv Awd 1984, Certificate of Appreciation 1985. **Military Serv:** USMC sgt E-5 3 1/2 yrs; Silver Star, Bronze Star, Purple Heart (2), Vietnamese Service, Vietman Campaign Medal, Natl Defense Medal, Good Conduct Medal, Vietnamese Cross of Gallantry. **Home Addr:** 221 Clermont Ave 2, Brooklyn, NY 11205.

ANTHONY, LEANDER ALDRICH
Elected government official. **Personal:** Born Sep 21, 1917, St Joseph, LA; married Evelyn Minor; children: Elizabeth, Leander A Jr. **Educ:** Southern Univ, BS; AUS Infantry, 2nd Lt; Tuskegee Inst, Dr's Degree of Veterinary Med. **Career:** Mad Parish Port Comm, chairperson; JTPA-Manpower Ctr, dir; City of Tallulah, mayor 1978-82 1982-86. **Orgs:** Mem North Delta Regional Planning Dist; mem Elks; mem Omega Psi Phi Frat. **Honors/Awds:** Goodwill Ambassador State of LA; Man of the Year-Outstanding Black Omega Psi Phi Frat 1979. **Military Serv:** 93rd Infantry 2nd lt 4 yrs. **Home Addr:** 800 Ethel St, Tallulah, LA 71282. **Business Addr:** Mayor, City of Tallulah, 204 N Cedar, Tallulah, LA 71282.

ANTHONY, REIDEL
Professional football player. **Personal:** Born Oct 20, 1976. **Educ:** Florida, attended. **Career:** Tampa Bay Buccaneers, wide receiver, 1997-. **Special Achievements:** NFL Draft, First round pick, #16, 1997. **Business Addr:** Professional Football Player, Tampa Bay Buccaneers, 1 Buccaneer Pl, Tampa, FL 33607, (813)870-2700.

ANTHONY, WENDELL
Cleric, association executive. **Personal:** Born 1950; divorced; children: two daughters. **Educ:** Wayne State Univ, BA, political science, 1976; Marygrove College, MA, pastoral ministry, 1974. **Career:** Fellowship Chapel, pastor, currently. **Orgs:** NAACP, Detroit Branch, president, 1993-. **Business Addr:** Pastor, Fellowship Chapel, 19555 W Mcnichols, Detroit, MI 48219, (313)538-8695.

ANTHONY-PEREZ, BOBBIE M.
Educator. **Personal:** Born Nov 15, 1923, Macon, GA; daughter of Maude Alice Lockett Cotton (deceased) and Solomon Cotton, Sr (deceased); married Andrew S Perez; children: Freida M Chapman. **Educ:** DePaul U, BS 1953, MS 1954, MA 1975; Univ of IL at Urbana, MS 1959; Univ of Chgo, PhD 1967. **Career:** Chicago Pub Schs, math tchr 1954-68; Univ of Chgo, math consult 1965; Worthington Hurst, psych Head Start 1971-72; Howard U, Inst for Urban Afrs rsrch cood 1977; Chicago St U, acting ccrd for Black Studies 1981; Chicago St Univ, prof of psych 1968-95, coordinator of black studies, 1990-94, prof emeritus, currently. **Orgs:** Local rep, Midwestern Psych Assn 1979-97; Am Ed Rsrch Assn 1980-; chp bus rltns Chatham Avalon Pk Comm Council 1982-; conference presenter Intl Assn for Applied Psychology, 1974, 1982, 1986, 1988, conference presenter Intl Assn for Cross-Cultural Psychology, 1986, 1988, 1990, 1992, 1994; Asian Regional, 1992; communications chair Communications Ingleside Whitfield Parish 1989-91, 1994-96, presenter, United American Progress Assn, 1980-; asst secretary/board member, Chicago Chapter, Assn of Black Psychologists, 1990-92, president, 1995-96; International Congress of Psychology, conference presenter, 1992; Midwestern Educational Research Association, conference presenter, 1989, 1990, 1992; National Council of Teachers of Mathematics, Pi Lambda Theta, Educational Honor Association; Association of Black Psychologists, Midwestern Educational Research Association. **Honors/Awds:** Outstndng comm serv Chicago Area Assn of Black Psyhcs 1983; appreciation serv Yng Adults of Ingleside Whitfield Parish 1984; cert for serv & support 1984, distinguished bd mem 1988, Chatham Bus Assn; many plaques & certificates for services to students and for Black studies teaching & curriculum development; visited all 7 continents in 10 1/2 months to study cultural factors through ethnography; Faculty of the Year Award, Student Government Assn, 1980, 1988, 1990, 1995, Professional Advancement Award, 1989, Faculty Achievement Merit Award, 1986, 1988, 1991, Chicago State Univ; United American Progress, Woman of the Year, 1991-92. **Special Achievements:** Public Education & Public Information, chair, Chatham Avalon Unit of American Cancer Society, 1988-96; publication in the areas of cultural studies, Black American Issues, gender issues, mathematics, spelling, multicultural curricula, test development, 1968-96; editor, Torch Newsletter of the Chatham Avalon Park Comm Council. **Business Addr:** Professor Emeritus of Psychology, Chicago St Univ, 9501 S King Dr, Harold Washington Hall, Rm 328, Chicago, IL 60628.

APEA, JOSEPH BENNET KYEREMATENG
Business executive. **Personal:** Born Aug 19, 1932, Aburi, Ghana; son of Madam Nancy Ofeibea Norman and Nana Esumgyima II Omanhene of Ejisu; married Agnes Johanna Hinson; children: Kathleen Kyerewa, Adwoa Ofeibea, Abena Otwiwa, Akua Nyam. **Educ:** IL Inst of Tech, BSCE 1968; Univ of IL, Arch. **Career:** Westenhoff & Novic Inc, Chgo, civil engr 1961-64; Kaiser Engrs, Chgo, stgruct engr 1964-65; Sargent & Lundy Engrs, Chgo, struct engr 1965-72; Samuels, Apea & Asso, Inc pres 1972-80; Joseph Apea & Assocs, Inc, Consulting Engineers, pres, 1981-86; Apian International Ltd, Chicago, IL, president, 1986-; Cosmic Petroleum, Inc, president, currently. **Orgs:** Mbr Natl Soc Prof Engrs; mem Am Soc Civil Engrs; mem IL Asso Struct Engrs. **Honors/Awds:** Frmwrk for reconstruction Ghana Citizens Org of USA & Canada 1984; positive attitude toward progress The Talking Drums UK 1985; chmn DBE/WBE Adv Cncl IL Dept of Transportation 1986-88. **Business Addr:** President, Cosmic Petroleum, Inc., 112 W. Wacker Dr, LL75, Chicago, IL 60606.

APPLEBY-YOUNG, SADYE PEARL
Educator (retired). **Personal:** Born Dec 18, 1927, Gainesville, GA; married Harding B; children: Sybil Bernadette, Harding G, Angela, Gregory. **Educ:** Tuskegee Inst, BS 1945; Cornell Univ, MS, child devel 1946; GA State Univ, PhD, educ & psychology, 1974. **Career:** Univ of AR Pine Bluff, AR, div dir 1946-57; NC Central Univ Durham, NC, interim div dir 1958-60; Spelman Coll Atlanta, GA, dept chmn 1961-78; Morris Brown Coll, div dir, educ & psychology, 1978-89 (retired). **Orgs:** Mem Alpha Kappa Mu Natl Hon Soc 1943-; sec Pi Lambda Theta Hon Soc 1978; Fac sec, Omicron Delta Kappa Natl Hon Leadership Soc 1983-89; mem St Paul of the Cross Roman Catholic Church; rep, Catholic School Board of Educ; Acad Councils Work Related, Morris Brown Coll. **Honors/Awds:** Moton Scholar Tuskegee Inst Tuskegee, AL 1945, Hon Soc 1943; Alpha Kappa Mu Nat; Frederick Patterson's Winner Oratory Tuskegee Inst 1945; All Expense Fellowship General Educ Bd to Cornell Univ, 1945.

APPLETON, CLEVETTE WILMA
Social worker. **Personal:** Born Jul 22, Louisville, KY; daughter of Wilma Henry Appleton and Cleve Appleton. **Educ:** KY State University, BA 1971; Kent School of Social Work, University of Louisville, MSSW 1974. **Career:** Neighborhood Youth Corp, teacher asst 1966-67; Louisville Free Publ Library, clerk 1968-70; KY Dept of Human Resources, soc worker 1971-73; Metro Soc Serv Dept, student soc worker 1974; Bridgehaven, student soc worker 1974; KY Dept of Human Resources, soc worker grad I 1975-77; River Region Svcs, sr social worker 1977-78; University of Louisville School of Medicine, sr social worker 1978-91; Bryce Hospital, social worker II 1991-92; Indian Rivers Comm Mental Health, Mental Retardation Ctr, asst trainer, 1993. **Orgs:** Council of Nephrology Soc Workers Network 9; Natl Kidney Foundation of Metro Louisville. **Honors/Awds:** Miss Wesley Club, KY State Univ 1971; Maude Ainslie Scholarship 1967; KY Dept for Human Resources, Grad School Stipend 1973; Natl Honor Society of Secondary Schools, 1965. **Business Addr:** 1108 14th Ave, #325, Tuscaloosa, AL 35401-3078, (205)345-6016.

APPLEWHAITE, LEON B.
Attorney. **Personal:** Born Sep 4, 1927, Brooklyn; married Louise J Harley. **Educ:** NY Univ, BA 1948; Brooklyn Law Sch, JD 1951; Brooklyn Univ Law Sch, LLM 1961. **Career:** Social Security Admin, claims authorizer 1955-59; Judge Francis E Riv-

ers, legal sec 1959-63; NY State Comm for Human Rights, field rep; NY State Bd of Mediation, labor arbitrator & mediator 1964-67; NY State Workmen's Comp Bd, assoc coun 1967-68; NY State Pub Empl Relations Bd supervising mediator regional rep. **Orgs:** Mem Assn of Bar of City of NY; Natl Academy of Arbitrators; Indus Relations Rsch Assn; Natl Bar Assn; Amer Arbitration Assn; Soc of Profls in Dispute Resolution. **Military Serv:** US Army, 1952-54. **Business Addr:** Supervising Mediator, NYS Pub Emp Rel Bd, 342 Madison Ave, New York, NY 10017.

ARAMBURO, SOPHIE WATTS
Church officer. **Personal:** Born Nov 23, 1931, New Orleans, LA; daughter of Eugenia Robinson Watts and George Victor Watts; married Alvin Noel Aramburo Sr, Jun 26, 1954; children: Alvin N, Sue A, Anthony J, Sheryl A, Alden G. **Educ:** Xavier University, New Orleans, LA, BA, 1951, Institute for Black Catholic Studies, 1990-91; Tulane University, New Orleans, LA, MEd, 1967. **Career:** Orleans Parish School Board, New Orleans, LA, teacher, 1951-66, rdg specialist, 1967-70, high school rdg teacher, 1970-76, team assoc/proj real, 1976-77; Southern State Univ of Louisiana, New Orleans, rdg lab teacher/asst professor, 1977-85; Archdiocese of New Orleans, LA, exec/assoc director, 1990-. **Orgs:** Past Louisiana State president, past Louisiana State Deputy, past grandlady, financial secretary, Knights of Peter Claver, Ladies Aux Ct 21, 1950-; chair national trends committee, Links Inc, Crescent City Chapter, 1984-; secretary advisory board, Crescent House (Home for Battered Women), 1983-; member, Natl Assn Black Catholic Administrators, 1990-; member of secretariat, Cursillo Movement, New Orleans, 1971-; regional coord, National Black Catholic Congrss-Region V, 1990-. **Honors/Awds:** Pro Ecclesia et Pontifice, Papal Award, 1976; Silver Medal, National Court, LAKPC, 1979; Lady of the Year, New Orleans Central Comm, KPC, 1976; St Louis Medallion, 1994. **Home Addr:** 2126 Amelia St, New Orleans, LA 70115-5802. **Business Addr:** Associate Director, Office for Black Catholics, Archdiocese of New Orleans, 7887 Walmsley Ave, Room 109, New Orleans, LA 70125, (504)861-6207.

ARAUJO, NORMAN
Educator. **Personal:** Born Mar 22, 1933, New Bedford, MA; son of Julia Coracao Araujo and Jose Joao Araujo; widowed. **Educ:** Harvard Coll, AB (Magna Cum Laude, Phi Beta Kappa) 1955; Universite d'Aix-Marseille, Certificat d'etudes litteraires 1956; Harvard Univ, AM 1957, PhD 1962. **Career:** Univ of MA-Amherst, asst prof 1962-64; Boston Coll, asst prof 1964-68, assoc prof 1968-. **Orgs:** Mem Modern Language Assoc of Amer 1976-; chief advisor Cape Verdean News. **Honors/Awds:** Fulbright Fellowship (France); Natl Defense Act Fellowship (Portugal). **Special Achievements:** Book "A study of Cape Verdean Literture," 1966; book "In Search of Eden, Lamartine's Symbols of Despair and Deliverence," 1976; article "Emile Augier," in Magill's Critical Survey of Drama 1986; article, "Theophile Gautier," in Magill's Critical Survey of Literary Therory, 1988; article, "The Language of Business and the Business of Language," in Becque's Les Corbeaux, French Review, 63 (1989), pages 66-77; "Prosaic Licence and the Use of the Literary Past in Daudet's La Chevre de M Seguin," Forum for Modern Language Studies, 27:3, p 195-208, 1991; "Petrus Borel," Dictionary of Literary Biograph, Ed Catharine Savage Brosman, vol 119; Nineteenth-Century French Fiction Writers: Romanticism and Realism, 1800-1860, p 49-61, 1992. **Business Addr:** Assoc Prof Romance Languages, Boston College, 302-C Lyons Hall, Chestnut Hill, MA 02167.

ARBERRY, MORSE, JR.
State assemblyman. **Personal:** Born Mar 1, 1953, Oakland, CA; married Carol I Daniels. **Career:** Nevada State Assembly, Carson City NV, state assemblyman, District 7. **Business Addr:** State Assemblyman, State Capitol, Carson City, NV 89710.

ARBUCKLE, JOHN FINLEY, JR.
Banker. **Personal:** Born Jan 16, 1938, Peoria, IL; son of Florence E Netter Arbuckle and John F Arbuckle Sr; married Janet M Johnson Arbuckle, Feb 7, 1959; children: Elana L Alexander, Andrea D Parker. **Educ:** Bradley University, 1956-58, 1982-85; Life Underwriter Training Council, graduate, 1962; American Bankers Association, Graduate School at University of Oklahoma, 1985. **Career:** Chicago Metropolitan Mutual Assurance, assistant district manager, 1958-66; Metropolitan Life Ins Co, sales consultant, 1966-75; First of America Bank, business lender/vice pres, 1975-97; AT/Investor Service, sr investment analyst, 1997-. **Orgs:** Minority Business Management Conference Board, president, 1990-; Centre for Study, Research and Learning, project manager, 1981-; Florence Crittenton Home, past president, 1980; Phoenix Business Awareness Association, 1992-93; Peoria Area Chamber of Commerce, corporate mem, 1975-; Creve Coeur Club of Peoria, sr mem, 1970-; NAACP, life mem, 1984-; Sons of Union Veterans of the Civil War, 1976-77. **Honors/Awds:** Inducted into African-American Hall of Fame Museum Inc, 1992; Peoria Chamber of Commerce, leadership School, graduate, 1977; Peoria District Met-Life "Man of the Year", 1969. **Special Achievements:** Chairman, American Freedom Train, City of Peoria, 1974-75; Chicago Urban Lie, article on "Negro New Breed," 1962. **Military Serv:** US Air Force ROTC, Bradley University, 1956-58; Precision Drill Team. **Business Addr:** Sr Investment Analyst, AT/Investor Service, 3201 W Richwoods Blvd, Peoria, IL 61604.

ARBUCKLE, PAMELA SUSAN
Dentist. **Personal:** Born Mar 12, 1955, Oakland, CA; daughter of Ruby Arbuckle. **Educ:** Laney College, AS 1975; Univ of CA, AB 1977, BS, DDS 1982, MPP 1984. **Career:** Univ of CA, teaching asst 1982-83; Congressional Rsch Service, policy analyst summer 1983; San Francisco Gen Hosp, staff dentist 1983-91; Alameda Cty Health Care Serv Agency, staff dentist 1983-; Johnson, Bassin & Shaw Inc, consultant, jobs corps health support project, 1987-95; Prison Health Services Inc, 1988-96; San Francisco Community Provider, dental consultant, AIDS project, 1990-93; Humanitas, Inc, Job Corps Health Support Project, consultant, 1996-. **Orgs:** Sec Natl Dental Soc of the Bay Area 1983-84; comm Emeryville Comm Devel Adv Comm 1983-85; mem Alameda Cty Bd of Suprvs Subcomm on Dental Health 1983-85; prog comm mem Bay Area Black Consortium for Quality 1983-85; ed Network for Black Health Prof newsletter 1984-85; bd mem Berkeley Head Start Health Adv Bd 1984-85; vice pres CA Chap Natl Dental Assoc 1985; councilor UC CA Alumni Assoc 1984-87; bd mem City of Berkeley Maternal Child & Adolescent Health Bd 1985-86, Univ of CA Black Alumni Club; mem NAACP 1985; bd mem Holy Names HS Alumnae Bd 1983-. **Honors/Awds:** Williard Fleming Scholarship Univ CA 1979; Regents Scholarship Univ of CA 1978-84; Comm Dentistry Service Awd Univ of CA 1982; Cert of Appreciation SF Area Health Educ Ctr 1984; Rosalie Stern Award for Community Service, University of California, 1990. **Business Addr:** Lead Dentist, Alameda Cty Hlth Care Svs, 470-27th St, Oakland, CA 94612.

ARBUCKLE, RONALD LEE, SR.
Customer engineer (retired), police officer (retired), real estate agent. **Personal:** Born Jul 13, 1945, Newark, NJ; son of Mary Alice White Arbuckle and Robert Lee Arbuckle; married Helena Yvonne Patrick, Sep 9, 1967 (divorced); children: Ronald L Jr. **Educ:** Rutgers Univ, Newark, NJ, 1971-73; AT&T Corporate Schools; Newark Police Academy, NJ Institute of Real Estate. **Career:** Sweet Temptations Lingerie Co, East Orange, NJ, sales, 1986-88; AT&T, Edison, NJ, customer eng, 1963-; Newark Special Police, Newark, NJ, pres, 1971; Maylock Realty Corp, Newark, NJ, sales, 1987-. **Orgs:** Pres, Newark Special Police Assn, 1988-94; pres, Federation of Afro American Police Officers, 1976-; 1st vice pres, Neighborhood Housing Services of Newark, 1988-91; conference chairperson, Natl Black Police Assn, Northeast Region, 1988-92; bd of dirs, Theater of Universal Images, Newark, NJ, 1985-. **Honors/Awds:** Member of the Year, Natl Black Police Assn, Northeast Region, 1985; Member of the Year, Newark Special Police Assn, 1988; Class A Valor Award, Newark Special Police Assn, 1978; Outstanding Service Award, Natl Black Police Assn, Northeast Region, 1990; Rookie of the Year, Sweet Temptations, 1986. **Home Addr:** 21 Porter Ave, Newark, NJ 07102.

ARBURTHA, LEODIES U. **See Obituaries section.**

ARCHAMBEAU, LESTER MILWARD, III
Professional football player. **Personal:** Born Jun 27, 1967, Montville, NJ; married Kathleen; children: Lester IV. **Educ:** Stanford, bachelor's degree in industrial engineering. **Career:** Green Bay Packers, defensive end, 1990-92; Atlanta Falcons, 1993-. **Business Addr:** Professional Football Player, Atlanta Falcons, Two Falcon Place, Suwanee, GA 30174, (404)945-1111.

ARCHER, CHALMERS, JR.
Educational administrator, educator. **Personal:** Born Apr 21, 1938, Tchula, MS; son of Eva Rutharford Archer and Chalmers Archer Sr (deceased). **Educ:** Saints Junior College, Associate, art; Tuskegee Inst, Alabama, BS 1972, MEd 1973; Auburn University, Alabama, PhD 1979; Univ of Alabama, Post Doctorate Certificate, 1979; MIT, Cambridge MA, Certificate 1982. **Career:** Saints Jr College, asst to the pres, 1968-70; Tuskegee Inst, asst vice pres & asst prof 1970-83; Northern Virginia Community College, admin/prof, 1983-; Jackson Advocate, contributing editor. **Orgs:** Natl Assn of Coll Deans, Registrars, and Admissions Officers; Phi Delta Kappa; Kappa Delta Pi; APGA; NAACP; charter mem Kiwanis Intl of Macon Coll; AAUP; AACRAO; Southeastern Assoc of Community Coll; Cooperative Educ; vice pres, Saints Jr Coll Alumni; past bd mem, Natl Consortium for the Recruitment of Black Students from Northern Cities; past chmn, State of Alabama's Steering Comm for Advanced Placement of High School Students; consultant, Department of Education on Retention, 1990-92. **Honors/Awds:** Honorary Doctorate of Letters, Saints Jr Coll, Lexington MS, 1970; Phi Delta Kappa Award for Leadership; Exemplary Research & Program Development, 1981; cited for community contribution; lectured at Cambridge Univ, England, and five major universities on teaching and learning interdisciplinary studies, 1988-89; architect of Comp Counseling Ctr & Weekend College at Tuskegee Inst; Architect of Reading & Language Arts Special Emphasis Curriculum for public schs; developed successful multi-level Educ Alliance to Adv Equal Access with public schs; author of 22 educational & other publications; author, Growing Up Black in Rural Mississippi, Walker & Co, published 1992; Robert F Kennedy Book Awards; The Francis B Simkins Award; Martha Albrand Award; The Sidney Hillman Foundation Award; participated in President-elect Clinton's "A Call for Reunion" Opening Ceremony; President Clinton's Task Force, Americans for Change, charter member; Democratic National Committee; Clinton/Gore Rapid Response Team. **Special Achievements:** Author: Growing Up Black in Rural Mississippi, 1992; On the Shoulders of Giants, 1994; Growing Up With the Green Berets, 1998. **Military Serv:** US Army Green Berets-Airborne; distinction of saving life of first Amer injured in Vietnam, 1957; Attempted to save life of first American killed, Capt Harry H Cramer, United State Special Forces, 1957. **Home Addr:** 7885 Flager Cir, #40, Manassas, VA 22110. **Business Addr:** Professor & Educ Admin, Northern Virginia Community Coll, Manassas Campus, 6901 Sudley Rd, Manassas, VA 22110.

ARCHER, DENNIS WAYNE
Mayor. **Personal:** Born Jan 1, 1942, Detroit, MI; son of Frances Carroll Archer and Ernest James Archer; married Trudy DunCombe, Jun 17, 1967; children: Dennis Wayne Jr, Vincent DunCombe. **Educ:** Wayne State Univ, Detroit MI, 1959-61; Western Michigan Univ, BS, 1965; Detroit Coll of Law, Detroit MI, JD, 1970. **Career:** Gragg & Gardner PC, trial lawyer, 1970-71; Hall Stone Allen & Archer, trial lawyer, 1971-73; Detroit Coll Law, Detroit MI, assoc prof, 1972-78; Charfoos Christensen & Archer, trial lawyer, 1973-85; Wayne State Univ Law School, Detroit MI, adj prof, 1984-85; Michigan Supreme Court, assoc justice, 1986-90; Dickinson, Wright, Moon, Van Dusen & Freeman, partner, 1991-93; City of Detroit, mayor, 1994-. **Orgs:** Life mem, former pres Natl Bar Assn; Amer Bar Assn; Amer Judicature Soc; past pres State Bar of MI; Wolverine Bar Assn; Detroit Bar Assn; fellow, Intl Soc of Barristers; Old Newsboys Goodfellow Fund, 1980-97; bd of dirs, Legal Aid & Defenders Assn of Detroit, 1980-82; Detroit Chamber of Commerce, 1984-85; bd of dirs, Metro Detroit Convention & Visitors Bureau, 1984-87; Alpha Phi Alpha; The Fellows of the Amer Bar Assn; life mem NAACP; bd of trustees Detroit Coll of Law, 1985-88; bd of dirs MI Cancer Foundation, 1985-92; bd of trustees, Olivet Coll, 1991-94; US Conference of Mayors, served on several committees, 1994; Natl Conf of Black Mayors, bd of dirs, 1994; Democratic Conv Platform Comm, cochair, 1996; Natl Conf of Democratic Mayors, pres, 1996; Brading Inst, mem adv bd, 1997; Natl League of Cities, vice-chmn, 1997. **Honors/Awds:** Co-winner Amer Bar Assn Personal Finance Annual Appellate Court Argument 1976; Western MI Univ Distinguished Alumnus Awd 1982; named one of the 100 Most Influential Black Americans by Ebony magazine 1984; publications including "Blackballed — A Case Against Private Clubs" Barrister 1983; cited in Natl Law Journal as one of the 100 most powerful attorneys in the US 1985; Community Serv Awd Detroit Urban Ctr 1985; Distinguished Achievement Awd NAACP Detroit Branch 1985; Probity Merit Awd Quinn Chapel AME Church 1986; Honorary Doctor of Laws Degrees, Western Michigan University, 1987, Detroit College of Law, 1988, University of Detroit School of Law, 1988, John Marshall Law Sch, 1991; Most Respected Judge in Michigan, Michigan Lawyers Weekly, 1990; Gonzaga Univ, 1991; Univ of Mich, 1994; Aquinas Coll, 1996; Marygrove Coll, 1997; Honorary Doctor of Public Svc, Eastern Mich Univ, 1994; Honorary Doctor of Educ, Madonna Univ, 1997; Amer Bar Assoc, Spirit of Excellence Award, 1996. **Business Addr:** Mayor, City of Detroit, 1126 City County Bldg, Detroit, MI 48226, (313)224-3400.

ARCHER, EVA P.
Nurse. **Personal:** Born in Hackensack, NJ; daughter of Jennie Patrick and Richard; widowed; children: Reginald T Jr. **Educ:** Lincoln School for Nursing, RN 1926; NYU, BS 1954. **Career:** Lincoln School for Nursing, operating room nurse 1927-28; New York City Health Dept, public health nurse 1928-69, public schools & prevention; Public School 92 Queens, educ asst 1970-73; Day Care Centers BCL, health advisor 1973-78. **Orgs:** Financial sec & treasurer Bd of Dir Langston Hughes Library Comm 1980-81; pres L I Seetem Natl Council Negro Women; past moderator Corona Congressional Church; past Basilous Delta Clap Lambda Kappa Nu Sorority; pres No Shore Club Business & Professional Assn 1980-84; pres NY Region Fedn of Colored Womens Club 1978-80; financial sec Queens Dist 369 Vet Assn Womens Div; cmdrs Daughters of Isis Aba Bekr Ct Brooklyn. **Honors/Awds:** Long Island Sec Citation for Leadership 1960-75; Ordinance of Eastern Star Serv Award 1961-79; Appreciation Award, No Shore Natl Assn Business & Professional Women 1984; Community Service Award, Natl Council of Negro Women 1987. **Home Addr:** 107 1/2 32nd Ave, East Elmhurst, NY 11369.

ARCHER, JUANITA A.
Physician. **Personal:** Born Nov 3, 1934, Washington, DC; daughter of Anna Blakeney Hinnant and Roy E Hinnant; married Frederick Archer; children: Frederick II. **Educ:** Howard Univ, Washington, DC, BS, 1956, MS, 1958, MD, 1965. **Career:** Freedman's Hospital, intern 1965-66; Howard Univ, resd 1966-68, flw 1970-71, instr 1971-75; Diabetes Investigative Grp, dir; Endocrine Metabolic Lab 1972-; Endocrine & Metabolic Diseases Sect, asst prof of medicine 1975-79, assoc prof medicine 1980-. **Orgs:** Coll of Medicine, admissions comm 1979-, Biohazards Comm 1981-, Comm to Review the Dermatology Dept 1980, mem Spec Awds Comm 1980, Srch Comm for Chmn of the Dept of Comm Health & Family Practice 1982, Rsch Comm 1978; Genl Clinical Rsch Ctr 1982, Alumni Awds Comm 1982; mem DC Med Soc; rsch comm Washington Area

Affiliate of the Amer Diabetes Assn; mem Sigma Xi, Beta Kappa Chi, DC Med Soc, Amer Federation for Clinical Rsch, The Endocrine Soc, NY Acad of Sci, Delta Sigma Theta; mem Genl Clinical Rsch Comm NIH 1976-86; Biohazards & Biosafety Comm Howard U; consultant Arizona Research Council 1986, 1987. **Honors/Awds:** Josiah Macy Faculty Fellow 1974-77; mem Genl Clinical Rsch Ctr Comm Natl Institutes of Health; Physician's Recognition Award 1983-86; numerous publications including, with P Gorden & J Roth, Defect in Insulin Binding to Receptors Clin Invest 55,166-175 1975; with R Knopp, J Olefsky, C R Shuman, ''Clinical Diabetes Update 11'' Upjohn Monograph Jan 1980; Natl Podiatry Medical Award, 1989; Amer Red Cross Award, 1988; Amer Medical Assn Physicians Recognition Award; Moses Wharton Young Research Award, 1988; Public Relations Award, Howard University Hospital, 1990. **Business Addr:** Associate Professor of Medicine, Howard University College of Medicine, Howard University Hospital, 2041 Georgia Ave NW, Washington, DC 20060.

ARCHER, SUSIE COLEMAN
Educator, director. **Personal:** Born Mar 29, 1946, Pembroke, KY; married Dennis Archer. **Educ:** BS, 1968; MA 1969; Vanderbilt Univ, completed all course work for PhD. **Career:** Austin Peay State Univ, supvr women's dormitories 1969-74; Austin Peay State Univ, tchr 1969-75; Univ of MD European Br W Berlin Germany, instr 1975-77; Salt Lake City Sch Dist, supvr of counselors, 1978-80; UT Tech Coll at Salt Lake, dir of regis & admin, 1980-87; assoc univ registrar, Vanderbilt Univ, 1987-. **Orgs:** Mem Altrusa Club 1979; bd dir Travelers Aid Soc 1979-; mem Acad Governance Com; Discrimination & Unfair Grading Practices Comm; Affirmative Action Comm; Com to Revise Promotion & Tenure Policies; Comm Union for Women's Rights; mem Middle TN Educ Assn; mem APSU Women's Club; faculty adv Phi Alpha Theta 1971-72; faculty adv Alpha Mu Gamma; faculty adv Sr Classical League 1973-; faculty adv Circle K; faculty adv Alpha Phi; faculty adv Intl Students Assn; mem, Amer Assn of Collegiate Registrars & Admissions Officers, 1980-; pres, UT Assn of Collegiate & Admissions Officers, 1985-86; Mem, TN Southern Assn of Collegiate Registrars & Admissions Officers, 1987-. **Honors/Awds:** Phi Alpha Theta Outstanding Student in History 1968; Outstanding Student in French 1967; Rene Descartes Medal in French Literature 1968; APSU Grad Assistantship 1968; Alpha Mu Gamma's Scholarship to participate in experiment in Intl Living Vanderbilts Chancellors Fellowship for Grad Study 1972-73. **Business Addr:** Assoc Univ Registrar, Vanderbilt Univ, 242 Alexander Hall, Nashville, TN 37240.

ARCHER, TRUDY DUNCOMBE
Judge. **Personal:** married Dennis W Archer, Jun 17, 1967; children: Dennis Wayne Jr, Vincent DunCombe. **Career:** 36th District Court, judge, currently. **Business Addr:** Judge, 36th District Court, 421 Madison Ave, Detroit, MI 48226, (313)965-8726.

ARCHIBALD, B. MILELE
Attorney. **Personal:** Born Jul 4, 1945, New York, NY; married Faruq Muhammad; children: Nyota. **Educ:** Bronx Comm Coll, AAS, 1968; Hunter Coll, New York NY, BA, 1973; Univ of California, Berkeley, JD, 1976. **Career:** Chief Judge DC Ct of Appeals, law clerk, 1976-77; Fed Trade Comm, Washington DC, staff atty, 1977-78; Overseas Private Investment Corp, spec asst to the pres, 1978-. **Orgs:** Mem Washington DC Bar Assn 1977-; mem Natl Assn of Black Women Attys 1978. **Business Addr:** Special Assistant to President, Overseas Priv Investmt Corp, 1129 20th St NW, Washington, DC 20527.

ARCHIBALD, NATE
Professional basketball player (retired), recreation director. **Personal:** Born Sep 2, 1948. **Educ:** Univ of TX, attended 1970. **Career:** Cincinnati/KC Royals, basketball player 1970-76; NJ Nets, basketball player 1976-77; Buffalo Braves, basketball player 1977-78; professional basketball player, Boston Celtics, 1978-83, Milwaukee Bucks, 1983-84; Harlem Armory Homeless Shelter, recreation director, currently. **Honors/Awds:** Led league in scoring & assists 1972-73; played in All Star Game 5 times; named NBA Comeback Player of Yr 1979-80; Fourth NBA passing 1980-81; inducted National Basketball Hall of Fame, 1991. **Business Addr:** c/o NBA Hall of Fame, PO Box 179, Springfield, MA 01101.

ARCHIE, SHIRLEY FRANKLIN
Association administrator, educator. **Personal:** Born Apr 15, 1944, Philadelphia, PA; married Robert Lewis Archie Jr; children: Keita T, Kweli I. **Educ:** Cheyney State Coll, BA 1966; Howard Univ, grad study 1967-69; Temple Univ, Urban Educ 1979-81. **Career:** DC School System, educator 1967-70; Philadelphia School System, educator 1976-; Temple Univ, instructor 1983-85; Sigler Travel Serv Inc, travel consult 1983-; National Association of Bench & Bar Spouses, natl pres, currently. **Orgs:** Mem Links Inc, Alpha Kappa Alpha, Jack & Jill of Amer, Women's Leaders Team, African-Amer Inst Zimbabwe; bd of dir Girl Scouts of Amer 1982-; bd of trustees Springside School 1982-; commiss Camden Cty Commiss for Women 1983; commiss Philadelphia-Major's Commiss for Women 1985. **Honors/Awds:** Distinguished Serv Award, Girl Scouts of Amer 1982; Commendation for Outstanding Teacher Philadelphia Syst 1982, 1984. **Business Addr:** National President, National Association of Bench & Bar Spouses, Philadelphia, PA 19119.

ARDREY, SAUNDRA CURRY
Educator. **Personal:** Born Aug 26, 1953, Louisville, GA; daughter of Estella Curry and Earle Curry; married William McCarty Ardrey. **Educ:** Winston-Salem State University, BA, 1975; Ohio State University, MA, 1976, PhD, 1983. **Career:** University of North Carolina Chapel Hill, visting lecturer 1979-80; Jefferson Community College, University of Kentucky, instructor, 1980-81; Furman University, asst prof 1983-88; Western Kentucky University, Dept of Government, professor, 1988-, associate professor, 1994-. **Orgs:** American Political Science Assn, 1975-87; Natl Conference of Black Political Science, 1978-; Southern Political Science Assn, 1983-87; American Assn of University Professor, 1983-85; bd mem, Greenville City Urban League, 1983-87; Greenville City United Way, 1983-84; exec comm, Greenville City Democratic Party, 1984-85; pres, Greenville City Young Democrats, 1984-85; pres, Bowling Green NOW; NAACP, Bowling Green Branch, 1990-; Alpha Kappa Alpha Sorority, 1989-. **Honors/Awds:** Western Kentucky University, Outstanding Achievement in Service Award, 1990; Outstanding Paper Awd, National Conference of Black Political Scientists, Annual Conference, 1994; Elections Analyst for Kentucky Public TV, 1995-; campaign consultant, 1995-. **Business Addr:** Professor, Dept of Government, Western Kentucky University, Grise Hall, Bowling Green, KY 42101, (502)745-6106.

ARGRETT, LORETTA COLLINS
Government official. **Personal:** married Vantile E Whitfield; children: Lisa, Brian. **Educ:** Howard Univ, BS, 1958; Institute Fur Organische Chemie, Technische Hochschule; Harvard Law School, JD, 1976. **Career:** US Congress, Joint Committee on Taxation, attorney; Wald, Harkrader and Ross, attorney, partner; Howard Univ School of Law, professor; US Justice Dept, Tax Div, asst attorney general, 1993-. **Orgs:** Harvard Law School, visiting committee mem, 1987-93; American Bar Foundation, fellow, 1993-; District of Columbia Bar, legal ethics committee mem, 1993-97; Univ of Baltimore Law School, Graduate Tax Program, advisory committee mem, 1986-. **Special Achievements:** First African American woman in the history of the Justice Department to hold a position requiring Senate confirmation; first African American member of the staff of the Joint Committee on Taxation of the US Congress. **Business Addr:** Assistant Attorney General, US Justice Department Tax Division, 950 Pennsylvania Ave NW, Rm 4143, Washington, DC 20530, (202)514-2901.

ARGRETTE, JOSEPH
Construction company executive. **Personal:** Born Apr 1, 1931, New York, NY; son of Mariah Tucker Dawson and Joseph Argrette, Jr; married June Parker; children: Kendelle Ruth. **Educ:** Long Island Univ, Brooklyn, NY, BS, MS 1954. **Career:** Riverside Hospital, Bronx, NY, dir vocational counseling; Federal Govt Office of Equal Opportunity, Offic of Inspections, Washington, DC, dir Region 2; Natl Alliance of Businessmen, Washington, DC, dir community relations; Stone Craft Intl, New York, NY, pres; Argrett Enterprises Corp, New York, NY, pres, 1977-. **Orgs:** Dir, vice pres, Natl Assn of Minority Contractors, 1985-89; dir, Gen Bldg Contractors-Assoc Gen Contractor, Assoc Gen Contractors of Amer, 1980-89. **Honors/Awds:** Outstanding Minority Contractor, New York State Dept of Environmental Conservation, 1984; delegate, White House Conf on Small Business, 1986; Outstanding Mem Award, Natl Assn of Minority Contractors, 1987; Distinguished Serv Award, Assn of Minority Enterprises of New York, 1987; Contractor of the Year Award, Westchester Minority Contractors of Westchester, New York, 1988; Boy Scouts of America, Eagle Scout. **Business Addr:** President/CEO, JMA Concrete Construction Co, Inc, 24 Van Siclin Ave, Floral Park, NY 11001, (516)488-0600.

ARKANSAW, TIM
Sculptor, songwriter, playwright, recording artist. **Personal:** Born Oct 18, 1925, Anniston, AL; son of Mattie Grace Hudgons and George Hudgons. **Educ:** City Coll of NY, BA voice-music, minor in business admin 1951. **Career:** Amer Federation of Musicians, musician 1961-85; Atlanta Public Schools, teacher of music 1972; Grady Memorial Hospital, pr admin 1973-74; Atsumhill Enterprises, founder, pres; artist in residence, Georgia Council for the Arts; Fulton County Schools, art teacher; Atsumhill Folklore Studios, artist, currently. **Orgs:** Admin yeoman MSC-LANT Navy Dept Brooklyn 1975-78; volunteer work Dekalb-Rockdale Chap GA 1976-85; comm worker Dekalb-Atlanta Voters Council 1970-85; volunteer worker Economic Opportunity Atlanta 1965-85. **Honors/Awds:** Great Talent Search RCA Records WSB Radio Atlanta 1967; Bronze Jubilee Honoree in Music WPBA Ch 30 Atlanta 1981; composer, Children You're Our Tomorrow, Atlanta Public Schools, 1985; Martin Luther King Jr Community Serv Award, 1986, 1995; State of Georgia, Senate Resolution 149, commending Tim Arkansaw, 1993. **Special Achievements:** Participant, Georgia Arts Day, 1993; ''Folk artist makes clay watermelon a cash crop,'' Atlanta Business Chronicle, p 32A, June 26-July 2, 1992. **Military Serv:** USN chief petty officer 1943. **Home Addr:** 1344 Hardee St, NE, Atlanta, GA 30307.

ARKHURST, JOYCE COOPER
Librarian (retired). **Personal:** Born Oct 20, 1921, Seattle, WA; daughter of Hazel James Cooper and Dr Felix Cooper; married Frederick Arkhurst, Oct 3, 1959; children: Cecile Arkhurst. **Educ:** Univ of Washington, Seattle, BA (cum laude), 1944; Columbia Univ, MLS, 1957. **Career:** New York Public Library, children's librarian, 1947-58; Chicago Public Library, children's librarian, 1967-69; Fieldston School, Bronx, NY, librarian, 1971-74; Elisabeth Irwin School, New York, NY, 1978-83; New York City Bd of Educ, library teacher, 1983. **Orgs:** Delta Sigma Theta Sorority, 1943-; NAACP, 1984-88; Amer Library Assn, 1983-85; Schomburg Corp, 1988-; New York Black Librarians Caucus, 1983-; Countee Cullen Library Support Group, 1988-; American Assoc of University Women, 1991-. **Honors/Awds:** Mortar Board, Sociology Honorary, Univ of Washington, 1944; author, The Adventures of Spider, 1964, More Adventures of Spider, 1971. **Business Addr:** Author, c/o Little Brown & Co, 34 Beacon St, Boston, MA 02116.

ARLENE, HERBERT
Administrator. **Personal:** Born Sep 5, 1917, Harrison, GA; married Emma; children: Herbert, Jr, Clara. **Educ:** Philadelphia Bus Sch, grad. **Career:** Philadelphia 47th Ward, state rep, 1958-66, administrator; State of PA, retired senator, 1966-81. **Orgs:** Exec sec Dem City Com; past chmn Senate Labor & Industry Com; vice chmn Military Affairs & Aeronautics Comm; bd dir Wharton Neighborhood Comm Ctr; Greater Philadelphia Devel Corp; senate chmn Labor & Industry Comm; vice chmn Urban Affairs & Housing; senate comm Appropriations Ins Pub Health & Welfare & RuPes; mem of House 1958-66; senate 1967-80; N Philadelphia Business Men's Assn; Local #10 Laundry & Dry Cleaners Intl Union; AFL; YMCA; NAACP; Odd Fellows; Elks; Tuscan Morning Star #48; Prince Hall Masonic Order; Melchizedek Chap #25; Holy Royal Arch Masons; DeMolay Consistory #1; Ancient Accept Scottish Rite 33rd Degree; Pyramid Temple #1; Promotion Comm AEAO; Nobles of Mystic Shrine Inc; Philadelphia Athletic Club; mem bd dir Wharton NeighborhoodComm Ctr; trst Union AME Ch; Urban Lea; bd dir Temple Mental Health/Mental Retardation No Central Comm Organ Peoples Nghbrhd Med Ctr; bd trste Lincoln Univ, PA Coll ofPodiatric Med, Berean Inst; bd dir Philadelphia Assn for Retarded Citizens; del Model Cities Nghbrhd Council #15; officer Union AME Church; 32 Degree Mason. **Honors/Awds:** First Black Senator in PA; Hon LLD Miller State Coll.

ARMISTEAD, MILTON
Attorney. **Personal:** Born Jun 19, 1947, Indianpolis, IN; son of Margarette Armistead and Mitchell Armistead; children: Jeff, Milton. **Educ:** Pasadena City College, AA 1967; San Jose State College, BA 1969; University of Southern California, MS 1972, JD 1974. **Career:** Private practice, attorney, currently. **Orgs:** Pres, Wiley Manual Law Soc 1979-; correspondent, Sacramento Observer 1981; Calif Trial Lawyers Assn; Defense Rsch Inst 1983; pres, Toastmasters Capital Club 1984; bd dir, Sacramento Claims Assn 1984; vice pres, Sacramento Black Chamber of Commerce 1985-; chmn, Volunteers of America 1985; Black Ins Prof Assn 1985. **Honors/Awds:** Best Speaker Toastmasters 1984; Competent Toastmaster Award 1987; seminar speaker for Sacramento Claims Assn 1988. **Business Addr:** Attorney, Private Practice, 5777 Madison Ave, #630, Sacramento, CA 95841.

ARMOUR, CHRISTOPHER E.
Physician. **Personal:** Born Nov 1, 1959, Columbus, GA; son of Mildred L Armour and John Henry Crowder Armour III; married Jacqueline L, Dec 16, 1984; children: Jonathan R, Kristen M. **Educ:** University of Georgia, BS, 1982; Morehouse School of Medicine, MD, 1987. **Career:** Southwest Hospital, medical resident physician, 1987-90; Smyrna Medfirst, medical director/physician, 1990-94; Aetna Healthways Family Med Ctr, staff physican, 1995-. **Orgs:** American Academy Family Physicians, diplomate, 1990-; Georgia Academy Family Physicians, diplomate, 1990-; National Medical Association, 1991-; Amer Med Assn, 1994. **Special Achievements:** Benchmark Office for Medfirst System Atlanta, 1992. **Home Addr:** 2725 Thornbury Way, College Park, GA 30349. **Business Addr:** Physician, Healthways, 1611 Sands Place, Marietta, GA 30067, (404)916-1690.

ARMSTEAD, CHAPELLE M.
Social worker (retired). **Personal:** Born Aug 12, 1926, Monroe, AL; married; children: Marcia, Helen, Joseph, Dorothy. **Educ:** Morgan State Coll, BS, 1950; Howard Univ, MSW, 1961. **Career:** Baltimore Cty Dept Soc Serv, caseworker, 1955-57, acting supr, 1957-59, stu caseworker, 1959-61, cs supr, 1961-64, dist supr, 1964-67, asst dir for staff services, 1978-85, Maryland Soc Serv Admin, training spec, 1967-70, spec mnl polcy coordn, 1970-73, field supr, 1974-78; Baltimore City Department of Social Services, assist, dir, retired, 1985. **Orgs:** Organizer Women of Augesburg Lutheran Ch; mem bd Lutheran Soc Serv; pres Baltimore Alum Chap Delta Sigma Theta Inc; cordntr Reg Golden Life Membership Eastern Reg, dir, Delta Sigma Theta, 1976-80; mem Blk Admin in Child Welfare; mem NAACP, NCNW, NASW, YWCA. **Honors/Awds:** Delta Sigma Theta, Inc, numerous awards; State of Maryland, Certificates of Merit and Appreciation; Baltimore City Mayor's Certificates of Merit.

ARMSTEAD, JESSIE
Professional football player. **Personal:** Born Oct 26, 1970, Dallas, TX. **Educ:** Miami (Fla.). **Career:** New York Giants, linebacker, 1993-. **Business Addr:** Professional Football Player, New York Giants, Giants Stadium, East Rutherford, NJ 07073, (201)935-8111.

ARMSTEAD, RON E.
Social worker, urban planner. **Personal:** Born Apr 12, 1947, Boston, MA; son of Ruby Smith and Leemon Smith; children: Tod, Kaili, Ronni. **Educ:** Boston Univ Metro Coll, attended 1970-74; Boston State Coll, BA (with honors) 1975-79; Harvard Univ, Graduate School of Design, Certificate 1983; Massachusetts Inst of Technology, Cambridge MA, MCP 1989. **Career:** Teen Educ Center, educ counselor 1970-73; Model Cities Admin, community planner 1970-74; Veterans Center Veterans Admin, readjustment counselor, social worker 1979-87; Amistad Assoc, pres. **Orgs:** Bd of dirs William Joiner Center for the Study of War & Social Consequences; conference issue coordinator Speakers Conf on Vietnam Veterans; co-chmn Natl Black Veterans Working Group; coord Massachusetts Black Veterans Think Tank Group; mem Soc for Traumatic Stress Studies, Natl Assn of Black Social Workers, Assn for the Study of Afro-Amer Life & History 1985-; pres, bd of dirs Veterans Benefits Clearinghouse Inc 1975-85; mem Natl Assn of Social Workers 1980-, Senator John F Kerry's Black Advisory Comm 1989. **Honors/Awds:** Commendation, Veterans Admin 1982; Commendation, Gov Michael L Dukakis 1983; Salute Award, Chelsea Soldiers Home 1986; Fellowship Massachusetts Inst of Technology 1987; Scholarship Award, Massachusetts Inst of Technology 1987; Certificate of Award, Massachusetts Office of Affirmative Action 1989; coordinated Black Veterans Workshops at Congressional Black Caucus Legislative Weekends 1985, 1987, 1988; presented Stress & Trauma Workshops at Natl Assn of Black Social Workers Conferences 1987-89. **Military Serv:** USN E-4 1966-69; Vietnam Campaign Medal, Vietnam Serv Medal with 3/16 Bronze Star, Natl Service Defense Medal. **Home Addr:** 86 Thornton St, Roxbury, MA 02119.

ARMSTEAD, WILBERT EDWARD, JR.
Engineering administrator. **Personal:** Born Jun 23, 1934, Baltimore, MD; son of Mary Josephine Hill Armstead and Wilbert Edward Armstead; married Erma Shirley Cole; children: Barbara E, Valerie, Sheryl J, Joann C, Jeri L Connelly, Angela M Bernard. **Educ:** Johns Hopkins Univ, Bachelor Elect Engr 1955. **Career:** RCA Missile & Surface Radar, assoc mem engr staff 1955-58, mem engr staff 1958-62, sr mem engr staff 1963-74, unit mgr 1974-86; GE, Moorestown, NJ, mgr, 1986-93; Martin Marietta Principal Program, control specialist, 1993-95; Lockheed Martin GES, prog mgr, 1995-. **Orgs:** Mem 1967-79, vice pres 1979, pres 1980-86, Moorestown Township Board of Educ; Moorestown Inprovement Assn, vp & newsletter editor; Burlington Cty Family Svc, mem, bd of trustees; Moorestown Citizens, advisory bd; Low and Moderate Income Housing, mem; Moorestown Zoning Bd, 1st alternate. **Honors/Awds:** Community Serv Club Blue Chips 1975, Ed Comm & Baptist Church Moorestown 1977, NJ State Fed of Colored Women 1981. **Military Serv:** AUS Corp of Engrs 2nd lt; NJ Natl Guard, AABN, 2nd lt. **Home Addr:** 325 Farmdale Rd, Moorestown, NJ 08057.

ARMSTER-WORRILL, CYNTHIA DENISE
Educator, educational administrator. **Personal:** Born Aug 7, 1960, Tokyo, Japan; daughter of Dorothy L Armster and Franksin Armster; married Dr Conrad W Worrill, Mar 7, 1987; children: Sobeenna Armster Worrill. **Educ:** Emporia State Univ, BS 1982, MS 1983. **Career:** Emporia State Univ, job devel coordinator, 1982-83; Northern IL Univ, counselor, minority programs 1983-85; George Williams Coll, dir of academic support 1985; Chicago State Univ, dir of freshmen serv 1986-. **Orgs:** Chairperson Minority Personnel Concerns Comm 1984-85; prog chair 1985-86, membership chair 1986-87 Amer Coll Personnel Assoc; recording sec Alpha Kappa Alpha Sor Inc 1986-87; mem Natl Black United Front 1986-87; YWCA Chmn, Monarch Awards Found, 1989. **Honors/Awds:** Outstanding Black Woman Black Student Union NIU, 1984. **Home Addr:** 7414 S Chappel, 2nd fl, Chicago, IL 60649.

ARMSTRONG, B. J. (BENJAMIN ROY JR.)
Professional basketball player. **Personal:** Born Sep 9, 1967, Detroit, MI; married. **Educ:** Univ of Iowa, Iowa City, IA, 1985-89. **Career:** Chicago Bulls, guard, 1989-95; Golden State Warriors, guard, 1995-97; Charl otte Hornets, guard, 1997-. **Honors/Awds:** NBA Championship, Chicago, 1991-93; NBA All-Star, 1994. **Special Achievements:** NBA Draft, First round pick, #18, 1989. **Business Addr:** Professional Basketball Player, Charlotte Hornets, 100 Hive Dr, Charlotte, NC 28217, (704)357-0252.

ARMSTRONG, BRUCE CHARLES
Professional football player. **Personal:** Born Sep 7, 1965, Miami, FL; married Melinda Yvette; children: Candace Lynne, Nicholas Charles. **Educ:** Louisville, attended. **Career:** New England Patriots, tackle, 1987-. **Honors/Awds:** Pro Bowl, 1990, 1991, 1994, 1995, 1996; 1776 Quarterback Club of New England, Rookie of the Year, 1987. **Business Addr:** Professional Football Player, New England Patriots, 60 Washington St, Foxboro Stadium, Foxboro, MA 02035, (508)543-7911.

ARMSTRONG, DARRELL
Professional basketball player. **Personal:** Born Jun 22, 1968, Gastonia, NC; married Deidra; children: Arkia, Mayliah. **Educ:** Fayettville State. **Career:** Global Basketball Assoc, 1991-92, 1992-93; Capitol Reign Pontiacs (CBA), 1992-93; Atlanta Trojans (USBL), 1992-94; Coren Orense (Spain), 1994-95; Orlando Magic guard, 1995-. **Business Addr:** Professional Basketball Player, Orlando Magic, 1 Magic Pl, Orlando, FL 32801, (407)649-3200.

ARMSTRONG, ERNEST W., SR.
Educator, real estate broker, military chaplain (retired). **Personal:** Born May 1, 1915, Soper, OK; son of Vinnie Armstrong and Giles Armstrong; divorced; children: Earl M Armstrong, Everett W Armstrong. **Educ:** Dillard Univ, AB 1942; Howard Univ, MDiv 1946, MA 1947; Univ Heidelberg Germany, cert 1954; Univ OK, MEd 1969; Santa Barbara Univ, PhD 1974; Prince Georges Community College AA 1979, 1981. **Career:** National YMCA, NY Army-Navy Dept, student sec, 1944-45; Howard Univ Washington DC, chaplain, 1946-48; Shiloh Baptist Church, Washington DC, asst pastor, 1946-48; Savannah State College, college chaplain/asst prof social science, 1948-49; Triton Community College, Reiver Grove IL, counselor/instructor, 1969-70; Enon Baptist Church, Baltimore MD, asst pastor, 1970-71; Catonsville Community College, counselor, 1970-72; Livingstone College, Salisbury NC, counselor, 1972-73; Annapolis MD Senior High School, counselor, 1973-77; real estate broker, 1977-90. **Orgs:** Mem APGA, ACPA, AAMFC, MPGA, MCPA, Indiv Psy Assn DC, Natl Assn Black Psy, Omega Psi Phi Frat, Prince Hall Masons 33rd degree, US Chess Fedn. **Honors/Awds:** Omega Man of the Year Frankfort, Germany/Theta Rho Tau Chap 1962; Mason of the Year 1962 OK Prince Hall Grand Lodge; Licensed Marriage Counselor; Publ Army Chpln in Korea "The Oracle" Omega Psi Phi Frat Inc 1952; Doctoral Dissertation, Psychosocial factors & Academic Success in Black Colleges, Santa Barbara Univ 1974. Distinguished Alumni Award, Dillard Univ 1983; honorary doctorate degree, Faith Grant College, 1995. **Military Serv:** US Army chaplain 1948-69, retired as colonel 1969; received: BSM, KSM; NDSM; NDSM w/st OLC; UNSM, 1O/S Bar: AFRM w/10 year Dev. **Home Addr:** 4046 Hilton Rd, Baltimore, MD 21215-7507, (410)367-5383.

ARMSTRONG, EVELYN WALKER
Research laboratory library director (retired). **Personal:** Born in Philadelphia, PA; daughter of Laurena Walker and Jay D Walker. **Educ:** Howard Univ, BA 1949; Drexel Univ, MSLS 1956; Temple Univ, grad school of bus admin 1976. **Career:** Sharp & Dohme Inc, asst librarian 1950-53, assoc librarian 1953-57, chief librarian 1957-66; Drexel Univ Grad School of Library Sci, adjunct faculty 1963-66; Merck Sharp & Dohme Research Laboratories, mgr library serv 1966-81; Drexel Univ Grad School of Library Sci, visiting lecturer 1975-80; Merck Sharp & Dohme Research Laboratories, dir literature resources center 1981-92. **Orgs:** Mem Adv Comm on Accreditation, Drexel Univ Grad School of Library Sci, 1974-75; mem Adv Comm on Library/Med Curriculum, Montgomery County Community College, 1973-77; membership comm, Special Libraries Assn, 1972-73; mem Professional Studies Comm, 1965-67; chmn Pharm Div, 1963-64; past sec & exec bd mem of Sci Tech Div, Rankin Fund Comm, & Elect & Nom Comm, Special Libraries Council of Philadelphia, 1956-75; past adv bd mem & sec, Special Interest Group/Biol Chem Elect & Nom Comm, Amer Soc for Info Sci, 1965-73; chmn Regis Comm, Montreal Drug Info Assn 1973; conf comm mem, Boston, 1974; mem Div of Chem Info, Amer Chem Soc; steering comm mem Sci Info Subsection, Pharmaceutical Mfrs Assn, 1976-81; adv bd mem Drexel Univ College of Info Studies, 1989-; bd mem Montgomery County Emergency Se 1988-90; Big Sisters of Montgomery County, 1989-; Jenkintown PA Library Board, 1993-. **Honors/Awds:** Co-author "Computer Processing of Clinical Data for a New Drug Application" Drug Info Bulletin 1967; presented paper on Scientific Info Ctr Admin 12th Annual Natl Colloquium on Info Retrieval 1975; participant on panels of various mtgs of Special Libraries Assn, Drug Info Assn, Amer Soc for Info Sci; Black Achievers; Drexel University Centennial, Drexel 100 Honoree, 1992. **Home Phone:** (215)576-0263.

ARMSTRONG, J. NIEL
Educational administrator (retired). **Personal:** Born Jun 17, 1907, Rogersville, TN; son of Elizabeth Wolfe Armstrong and Charley H Armstrong; married Jacquetta Sensabaugh. **Educ:** Swift Mem Jr Coll, AA 1929; NC A&T State Univ, BS 1931; Univ of MI, MS 1939; OH State Univ, Univ of Chicago, Univ of NC at Greensboro, additional study. **Career:** Pruitt Hill Elem School, teacher, principal 1932-33; Jr HS, principal 1933-34; Farmers Union School, principal 1934-37; Langston HS, principal 1937-54; NC A&T State Univ, dir summer school, assoc prof ed 1963-78, acting dean grad school 1965-66. **Orgs:** Mem Exec Comm So Assn Sec School & Coll 1940-55, Phi Delta Kappa 1955-, Natl Soc for Study of Ed 1955-80, Amer Assoc of Suprv & Curr 1956-78; natl dir ed Phi Beta Sigma 1969-75; mem Zoning Comm Greensboro 1970-77, Exec Comm Unied Way 1970-75; chmn Selective Serv Bd #51 1983-. **Honors/Awds:** Pres East TN Teachers Assn 1952-53, NC Assn of Summer Session Dir 1966-67; hon life mem N Amer Assn of Summer Session Dir 1978; Disting Serv Key Triad Chap Phi Delta Kappa 1982-; vice pres N Amer Assn of Summer School Dir. **Home Addr:** 808 Bellaire, Greensboro, NC 27406.

ARMSTRONG, JOAN BERNARD
Judge. **Personal:** Born Feb 15, New Orleans, LA; married Andrew Armstrong; children: David M, Anna K. **Educ:** Xavier Univ, BA 1963; Loyola Univ School of Law, Juris Doctor 1967; Natl College of Juvenile Justice, college certificate 1974. **Career:** Orleans Parish Juvenile Court, judge 1974-84; State of LA Court of Appeal, 4th Circuit, judge 1984-. **Orgs:** Pres Community Relations Council 1972-74; pres LA League of Good Gov't 1972-74; member Visiting Comm Loyola Univ 1980-; charter member Natl Assn of WomenJudges 1981-; trustee Loyola Univ of the South 1984-; Bar Association memberships; served on numerous boards Family Service Society; Amer Red Cross; Legal Aid Bureau; LA Assn for Mental Health; Crisis Care Center. **Honors/Awds:** Outstanding Young Woman New Orleans Jaycees 1974; member Visiting Committee Loyola Law School 1981; trustee Loyola Univ 1984; hon member Alpha Kappa Alpha 1974.

ARMSTRONG, KEVIN
Finance company executive. **Educ:** Rutgers Univ, bachelors degree; Rutgers Univ Law School, JD. **Career:** Prudential Securities, management; Thomson McKinnon Securities, Inc, management; NY Stock Exchange, sr market analyst; National Association of Securities Dealers, sr compliance examiner; First of Michigan Corp, vp, dir of compliances; Fleet Financial Group, svp, functional dir in compliance, 1998-. **Orgs:** NJ State Bar Association; PA State Bar Association; American Bar Association; National Bar Association; Bond Market Association; Securities Industry Association.

ARMSTRONG, MATTHEW JORDAN, JR.
Business administrator. **Personal:** Born Dec 18, 1955, Rocky Mount, NC; son of Sarah Jane McDowell Armstrong and Matthew J Armstrong Sr. **Educ:** Winston-Salem State Univ, Bachelor 1974-78; IA State Univ, Master 1978-. **Career:** Minority Student Affairs IA State Univ, rsch asst 1979-80, sec II 1980-82, sec III 1982, office coord 1982-84, admin asst 1984-85; Univ of Iowa Special Support Serv, outreach counselor 1986-; Univ of Iowa, Outreach Coordinator, 1986-. **Orgs:** Rsch asst history dept IA State Univ 1978-79; asst to pres Mid-Amer Assoc 1979-80; office asst III Minority Student Affairs IA State Univ 1979-; admin asst Spec Serv Prog 1980-; black cultural ctr Liaison/Black Cultural Ctr 1980-. **Honors/Awds:** President's Awd, Mid-Amer Assoc, 1980; 1st Black Male Sec Office Coord & Admin Asst, Certificate of Recognition, MO-KAN-NE Chap of MAEOPP 1981.

ARMSTRONG, REGINALD DONALD, II
Editor. **Personal:** Born Jul 28, 1958, Long Beach, CA; son of Marie Roque Armstrong and Reginald D Armstrong, I; married Sandra Achue Armstrong, Dec 21, 1985; children: Omari Hasan, Sarou Bakila. **Educ:** Univ of California, San Diego, La-Jolla, CA, 1975-77; Morehouse College, Atlanta, GA, 1977; Univ of South Carolina, Columbia, SC, BA, 1979. **Career:** NAACP/Crisis Magazine, Brooklyn, NY, editorial asst, 1983-85; Village Voice, New York, NY, asst editor, 1985-88; Times Mirror/Sports Inc, New York, NY, copy chief, 1988-89; General Media/Omni, asst managing editor, 1989; Emerge Magazine, New York, NY, asst managing editor, 1989-. **Orgs:** Member, Natl Assn of Black Journalists, 1990-.

ARMSTRONG, ROBB
Cartoonist, illustrationist. **Personal:** Born Mar 4, 1962, Wynnefield, PA; son of Dorothy Armstrong (deceased); married Sherry West; children: Tess. **Educ:** Syracuse Univ, BA, art. **Career:** Various ad agencies, art dir; syndicated cartoonist, 1988-; Savannah Coll of Art and Design, 1997. **Orgs:** Syracuse Univ Alumni Bd. **Honors/Awds:** Religious Public Relations Council, Wilbur Award, 1995; Nestle, Men of Courage Award. **Special Achievements:** Created cartoon strip, "Jump Start," 1988-; created strip "Hector," in college; created "Cherry Top;" created line of greeting cards featuring "Jump Start;" appeared along with "Jump Start" characters in "The Fabulous Funnies," CBS; published "Jump Start: A Love Story," 1996; signed four-book deal which published: Drew and the Bub Daddy Showdown, 1996; Drew and the Homeboy Question, 1997; Drew and the Filthy Rich Kid, soon to be published; also lent characters for several public service campaigns, including: American Diabetes Assn's Diabetes Risk Test; American Cancer Soc's Great American Smokeout. **Business Addr:** Cartoonist, "Jump Start", c/o United Media, 200 Madison Ave, New York, NY 10016.

ARMSTRONG, SANDRA BROWN
Judge. **Career:** US District Court-Northern CA, federal judge, 1991-. **Business Addr:** Federal Judge, US District Court-Northern California, 1301 Clay St, Rm 400 S, Oakland, CA 94612-5212.

ARMSTRONG, WILLIAM
Automobile dealer. **Career:** Hollywood Ford Inc, CEO; Armstrong Toyota-Ford-Pontiac-GMC-Buick, pres, currently. **Business Addr:** CEO, Armstrong Toyota-Ford-Pontiac-GMC-Buick, 29330 S Dixie Hwy, Homestead, FL 33030, (305)248-6330.

ARNELLE, HUGH JESSE
Attorney. **Personal:** Born Dec 30, 1933, New Rochelle, NY; son of Lynn Arnelle and Hugh Arnelle; married Carolyn; children: Nicole, Paolo, Michael. **Educ:** PA State Univ, BA 1955; Dickinson School of Law, JD 1962; admitted to practice CA, PA, United States Supreme Court. **Career:** AU State Univ All-Amer Basketball, 1952-54; PA State Univ, honorable mention All-Amer Football 1953-54; NBA Ft Wayne Piston, 1955-56; NFL Baltimore Colts, 1957-58; Dept of Labor, atty 1962-63; Peace Corps, assoc dir 1963-65, dir 1965-66, staff 1966-67; FPC, asst to gen counsel 1967-68; IDEA Inc Chas F Kettering Found 1968-69; Morrison Foerster Holloway, atty 1971-73; US Dist Ct, asst federal public defender, sr partner, 1985-; private practice 1973-85; Arnelle & Hastie, civil litigation & public finance atty, senior partner, 1985-. **Orgs:** Mem Coll of Civil Trial Advocacy 1976; faculty Hastings Law School Criminal Trial Advocacy 1977; mem Hall of Fame NY 1977; commissioner San Francisco Redevelopment Agency 1981-; bd of dir SF Boys Club 1981-; mem Amer Bd of Criminal Trial Lawyers 1982-; exec commissioner, bd of trustees San Francisco World Affairs Council 1983-; bd of trust PA State Univ; PA State Board of Trustees, vice chairman, 1993-; PA State Univ; dir Renaissance Fund PA State Univ; mem Charles Houston Bar Assn; life mem Natl Bar Assn, Bar of PA, CA, Bar of US Supreme Court; diplomate Hastings Law School; mem Natl Panel of Arbit, Amer Trial Lawyers Assn, Westchester County Hall of Fame; National Football Foundation Hall of Fame, 1993; adj prof Hastings Law School Coll of Advocacy; former pres Afro-American Hist Society; board of directors San Francisco Op; bd of dir Bay Area UNICEF; Corporate BoardS, Wells Fargo Bank and Wells Fargo & Co, director, 1991, FPL Groups Inc, director, 1990, Waste Management, Inc, director, 1992, University Governance, Pennsylvania State University Board of Trustees, vice-chairman, 1993.

ARNETTE, DOROTHY DEANNA
Personnel administrator. **Personal:** Born Sep 19, 1942, Welch, WV; married Joseph; children: Kristina Nicole. **Educ:** MI State Univ, BS 1965; Pace Univ, MBA 1979. **Career:** MI Natl Bank, asst branch mgr 1966-68; Metropolitan Life Ins Co, recruiting consult 1968-72; CIBA-GEIGY Corp, dir equal oppty affairs 1974-85; Amer CanCo, dir corp eeo & employ law beginning 1985; CARE, vice pres of human resources, 1991-. **Orgs:** Charter mem Fairfield Cty Chapter Links 1970-78; mem/pres Urban League Guild SW Fairfield Cty 1974-77; charter mem 1979-, pres 1985 Fairfield Cty Alumnae Chap DST; workshop leader legal issues Fairfield Cty Alumnae Chp DST 1981; mem, pres advisory council Coll of New Rochelle 1982-; advisory council Manhattan Ctr for Sci & Math 1983-84.

ARNEZ, NANCY L.
Educator, author (retired). **Personal:** Born Jul 6, 1928, Baltimore, MD; daughter of Ida Barbour Rusk and Emerson Milton Levi; divorced. **Educ:** Morgan State Coll, AB 1949; Columbia Univ, MA 1954, EdD 1958; Harvard Univ, post doctoral 1962; Loyola Coll, 1965. **Career:** Baltimore Pub Sch, English tchr 1949-58, dept head 1958-62; Morgan State Coll, dir student teaching 1962-66; Northeastern IL Univ, assoc prof/asst dir Cntr for Inner City Studies 1966-69, prof/dir Cntr for Inner City Studies 1969-74, co-founder, Cultural Linguistic, Follow Through Early Childhood CICS 1969-74; Howard Univ School of Educ, acting dean 1975, assoc dean 1974-, dept chairperson 1980-86, professor 1986-. **Orgs:** Congress of African People 1968-70; Amer Assn of School Admin 1968-87; Black Child Devel Inst DC 1971-74; Assn of African Historians Chicago 1972; Assn of the Study of Afro-Amer Life & Hist 1972-77; mem African Heritage Studies Assn, bd of dir membership sec 1973-77; Natl Alliance of Black Sch Educators 1973-; Amer Assn of Sch Admin Resolutions Comm 1973-75; African Information Cntr Catalyst Chicago 1973-77; bd of dir DuSable Museum Chicago 1973-74; mem Black Women's Comm Devel Found DC 1974; Amer Assn of Coll Tchrs of Educ 1977; Natl Council of Negro Women 1977; mem Phi Delta Kappa Howard Univ Chap 1974-, editorial bd 1975-78; Journal of Negro Education, editorial bd 1975-80; AASA Professor, editorial bd 1981-84; NABSE Newsbrief, editor 1984-86;mem DC Alliance of Black School Educator984-, pres 1986-88. **Honors/Awds:** Assn of African History Serv Award 1972; Alpha Kappa Alpha Sor Serv Award 1971; Appointed Hon Citizen of Compton, CA 1972; Howard Univ distinguished faculty research awd 1983; 4th place in the international competition for Phi Delta Kappa's biennial awd for outstanding research 1985; 180 publications. **Business Addr:** Retired Professor, Howard University, 2400 6th St, NW, Washington, DC 20059.

ARNOLD, ALTON A., JR.
Educator. **Personal:** Born Aug 10, 1932, Little Rock, AR; married Ramona L Worlds; children: Anita Alton III, David. **Educ:** Philander Smith Coll, BA Psych 1953; Univ of AR, ME Elem Ed 1954; Univ of CA LA, MA School Admin 1972; Univ of LA, EdD Ed Policy & Planning 1976. **Career:** Cty of LA, juvenile hall couns 1955-56; LA Unified School Dist, elem teacher 1956-69; Arnolds Shell Serv Shell Oil Co, owner 1959-65; LA Unified School Dist Div of Career & Continuing Ed 1970-72; LA Unified School Dist, adult school 1972-; Pepperdine Univ, adj prof ed 1975-76; Jordan-Locke Comm Adult School, principal 1976-. **Orgs:** Mem Alpha Phi Alpha Beta Chi Chap 1950, Phi Delta Kappa Ed Soc 1967; chmn, bd of dir LA Cty Model Cities/Model Neighborhood Prog 1972-76, LA Cty Econ Housing Devel Corp 1975-77, So Central Comm Child Care Ctr Inc 1979-80; mem CA State Vocational Educ Comm 1980. **Honors/Awds:** Alpha Kappa Mu Natl Hon Soc 1951; Fellowship Ford Found 1953-54; HEW Fellowship US Dept of HEW 1970-72; Resolution LA Cty 1975; Citizens Part Awd Model Neighborhood Prog LA Cty 1976. **Military Serv:** US Army, pvt 1953-54; Good Conduct Medal; Marksman Medal. **Business Addr:** Principal, Jordan-Locke Comm Adult School, 325 E 11th St, Los Angeles, CA 90061.

ARNOLD, CLARENCE EDWARD, JR.
Educational administrator. **Personal:** Born May 18, 1944, Eastville, VA; son of Nicey Press Arnold and Clarence Edward Arnold Sr; married Katreena Davenport Arnold, Dec 23, 1989; children: Sherri Mignon, Chelsea N Davenport (stepdaughter). **Educ:** VA State Univ, BS 1970, MEd 1973; Howard Univ, 1979; University of Virginia. 1990-. **Career:** Petersburg HS, home-sch coord 1970-71; McGuffy Educ Cntr, tchr 1971-72; 16th Dist Ct Serv Unit, counsl juvenile & domestic rel 1973-74; VA State Univ, tchr educ TV prodn & photog 1977-78; J Sargeant Reynolds Comm Coll, instr/coord audio visual serv dept 1974-80; C E Arnold Photographic Services, free lance photographer, 1980-81; Virginia State Univ, instructor/coordinator mass communications prog, 1981-88; Danville Community College, director, Learning Resource Center, 1988-91; University of Virginia, doctoral internship, 1991-. **Orgs:** Richmond Br NAACP, vice pres 1976-82; VA State Conf NAACP, bd dir 1976-82; mem Black Advisory Council, WTVR TV AM & FM, 1979-83; Assn for Educ Communications & Technology; Virginia Educ Media Assn; Community Coll Assn for Instruction and Technology 1976-80; Virginia Television Representatives in Higher Educ 1976-80; pres, Richmond Media Society, 1986-87; Natl Educ Assn; Virginia Educ Assn; Virginia State Univ Educ Assn 1981-88; Kappa Alpha Psi Frat Inc; member, Virginia Community College Assn, 1988-; member, Virginia Library Assn, 1988-. **Honors/Awds:** R P Daniel Award & Trophy for Outstanding Mil Leadership & Scholastic Achievement in ROTC VA State Univ 1966; Grant NDEA Educ Media Inst for Trainers of Tchrs VA State Univ 1972-73; Black Arts Award for Visual Arts, BOTA, 1981; Chancellor's Fellowship, Virginia Community College System, 1990-91; University of Virginia, Minority Fellowship, 1991-93. **Military Serv:** US Army 1968-70; Reserves, Capt, 1970-79; Recipient Bronze Star/CIB, VietnamCommendation Medal, Vietnam Serv Medal, Natl Defense Serv Medal, Expert Marksman Badge.

ARNOLD, DAVID
Opera singer. **Personal:** Born Dec 30, 1946, Atlanta, GA; son of Mr and Mrs Charles Arnold. **Educ:** IN Univ, BA 1968, MA 1970; New England Conservatory, artist diploma 1974. **Career:** Opera Co Boston, Metropolitan Opera, Boston Symphony, New York City Opera, English Natl Opera, Amer Symphony, San Francisco Opera, American Composer Orchestra conducted by Leonard Bernstein, Atlanta Symphony, Wolf Trap Festival, Baltimore Symphony, Chautauqua Festival, Spoleto Festivals, Nashville Symphony, Tanglewood Festival, Chicago Symphony under Sir Georg Solti, Cincinnati May Festival conducted by James Conlon, Concertgebouw conducted by S Comissiona; Tulsa Opera, Musica Sacra of New York, Boston Baroque, Handel and Haydn Society Boston and the American Symphony New York; opera singer; Metropolitan Opera, baritone singer; leading baritone with the Komische Opera, Berlin. **Honors/Awds:** Met Auditions Winner 1967; Sullivan Found Music Awd 1978; MYC Opera Gold Debut Awd 1980; Recordings include ''Gurrelieder'' on Philips, ''The Magic World'' on Leonarda, ''Full Moon in March'' on CRI; ''Walpurgisnacht'' on Arabesque; ''Beethoven Ninth Symphony,'' ''Mozart Requiem'' on Telarc, and ''Haydn's Lord Nelson Mass'' on Koch Classics; guest appearances at the White House on the occasion of a state dinner honoring Prime Minister Margaret Thatcher, and at musical events for President and Mrs. Clinton. **Business Addr:** c/o Grant House, 309 Wood St, Burlington, NJ 08016.

ARNOLD, ETHEL N.
Business executive. **Personal:** Born Dec 20, 1924, Stillwater, OK; married; children: Nishua Bell, Renay Thigpen, Booker Jr, Myron, Geino. **Educ:** Langston Univ, ICS Business Coll, Assoc; Northwestern Coll, BBA. **Career:** Cleve Cell & Post, news columnist; Picker Corp, tax specialist 1968; Harshaw Chemical, asst tax mgr 1970; Diamond Shamrock, acts asst 1973; OH Cel Pod Med, dir community relations 1976-84; Avant-Garde Models Inc, Modeling School & Agency, owner; R & E, pres & owner. **Orgs:** Natl pres Natl Assn Career Womens Civic Club Inc 1964-88; chm pp Natl Assn Negro Bus Prof Womens Club Cleve 1984-85; chp publicity Radio TV Cnclof Greater Cleve; mem Human Rsrch Comm. **Honors/Awds:** Liberty Bell Awd Mayor of Philadelphia 1972; cong placque awd Univ S House Rep 1977; comm serv awd Ohio Cal Pod Med 1977, Bell Air Civic Club 1978, Mayor of Cleve 1977. **Business Addr:** President, R & E, 14402 Kinsman, Cleveland, OH 44120.

ARNOLD, HASKELL N., JR.
Utility company executive. **Personal:** Born Jul 20, 1945, Savannah, GA; son of Rosalyn J Griffin and Haskell N Arnold Sr; married Linda H Grayson; children: Shaun, Tia. **Educ:** Hampton Inst, BS 1966; Harvard Bus Sch, MBA 1971. **Career:** H G Parks, controller 1972-74; Potomac Elec Power Co, mgr 1974-76; Pub Serv Broadcasting, vice pres 1977-80; MD Pub Serv Comm 1980-84; Commonwealth Tele Ent, controller 1984-85. **Orgs:** Amer Inst of CPA's; MD Assn of CPA's; Harvard Bus Sch Club; Kappa Alpha Psi; chairman, Columbia Housing Corp, 1987. **Military Serv:** US Army, 1st lt 2 yrs. **Business Addr:** Manager, Baltimore Gas & Electric Co, 39 W Lexington St, Baltimore, MD 21203, (410)234-6581.

ARNOLD, HELEN E.
Educational administrator. **Personal:** Born Aug 2, 1924, Burlington, NJ; daughter of Lydia Rebecca Harvey Crandall (deceased) and Samuel Ashley Crandall (deceased); divorced; children: Cathy Dixx, Royal, Mona Diamond, Gale, John, Gary, Carla Anderson, Gerald, Donna. **Educ:** Akron Sch of Cosmetology, 1500 hrs 1957; Black Univ, Pan Africanism 1968; attended Inst of Cultural Affairs-Global Acad, Chicago, IL; other courses, Akron Univ. **Career:** Beautician in self-owned shop 1959-62; Candeub Fleissig & Assoc, interviewer & surveyor 1964; City of Akron, neighborhood advisor; Partnership in small business 1970-73; UNCI, interim dir 1978-79; Community Action Agency, 1978-79; Summit Co Bd of Elections, employee 1982-; Dept of Human Svcs, community relations asst, employee 1985-; Bd of Educ Akron City Sch Dist, member 1978-89, past pres 1984, 1988-89, re-elected 3rd term. **Orgs:** Mem St Philips Episcopal Church 1950-; past mem, bd of dirs, Fallsview Mental Hosp; mem, past pres Akron branch 1970-71, NAACP; mem Summit Co Welfare Adv Bd; past financial officer Akron Summit Tutorial Prog; mem, Natl Assn of Black School Bd Educ, Large City Commn of Ohio School Bd Members, Natl Caucus of Black School Bd Members, Akron Univ Community Leaders Advisory Coucil; vice pres, Ohio Caucus of Black School Bd Members; member, National School Boards Assn, 1984-; member, Ohio School Boards Assn, 1984-; member, Akron Black Elected Officials; member, Akron Alliance of Black School Educators. **Honors/Awds:** Appreciation Awd NAACP 1968; Black Applause Awd Phi Beta Kappa 1983; Certificate from Akron Bd of Educ for Outstanding Serv as pres in 1984; Certificate from Akron Public Schools for Outstanding Serv & Effective Leadership 1985; Good Citizen Awd WHLO; Certificate from State of OH House of Reps for Meritorious Serv as Akron Bd of Educ Pres; articles Akron Reporter Newspaper; letters to editor Akron Beacon Journal; Awd Amer Cancer Soc 1985; Fund Raising Efforts Award Alpha Kappa Alpha 1986; Univ of Akron Awd Black Cultural Ctr 1986; Award from Ohio NABSE, 1987; Award of Appreciation, State of Ohio Welfare Rights Org, 1989; Award of Appreciation, State of Ohio Legislative Div, 1989; Achievement Award, Proclamation State of Ohio; William M Cosgrove Justice Award, Akron Catholic Commission,82; Bootstrap Award, Welfare Rights Organization, 1989. **Home Addr:** 413 Selzer St, Akron, OH 44310. **Business Addr:** Personnel Div Social Worker Liaison Aide, Summit County Dept of Human Services, 47 N Main St, Bldg I, Room 616G, Akron, OH 44310.

ARNOLD, JOHN RUSSELL, JR.
Broadcasting company executive. **Personal:** Born Sep 13, 1954, Detroit, MI; son of John Russell Arnold, Sr & Christene Ford Arnold; married Cheryl Anne Young Arnold, Jul 7, 1984 (divorced); children: John R III. **Educ:** University of Detroit/ Mercy, 1971-75; University of Michigan, currently. **Career:** WABX, disc jockey, 1972-73; WERD, program dir, 1973-74; WCHB, music dir, 1974-87; WFXY, prog dir, 1987-88; WCXI/ WWWW, dj, staff announcer, 1988-89; Barden Cable, advertising sales, 1988-90; WCHB, host & exec producer, 1989-. **Orgs:** Talk Radio Host of America, 1994-; Talkers, 1995-; Black Men, Inc, founder, 1992-; Black Women, Inc, founder, 1992-; Inkster, MI City Planning Commissioner, 1990-94. **Honors/Awds:** BART, Talk Show Host of the Year, Detroit, 1995-97; various keys and proclamations. **Special Achievements:** Youngest Disc Jockey in the World, Major Market, 1969, 1970; President Clinton's Bi-Continent Summit Economic with South Africa, 1996.

ARNOLD, LIONEL A.
Educator. **Personal:** Born Aug 30, 1921, Greenville, PA; son of Gertrude Dowe and J P Arnold. **Educ:** Thiel Coll, AB (Cum Laude) 1943; Anderson Coll, BTh 1943-44; Oberlin Grad Sch, MA BD 1947; Harvard Univ, STM 1955; Drew Univ, PhD 1969. **Career:** LeMoyne-Owen Coll, college pastor, 1947-64, dean, 1964-71; OK State Univ, prof 1971-86, prof emeritus. **Honors/Awds:** Hon Doc Humane Letters, Thiel Coll Greenville, PA 1964. **Home Addr:** 2132 University, Stillwater, OK 74074.

ARNOLD, RALPH M.
Artist, educator. **Personal:** Born Dec 5, 1928, Chicago, IL; son of Bertha Harris Arnold and Roy Arnold. **Educ:** Univ of IL, attended; School of Art Inst of Chgo, attended; Hyde Park Art Ctr, attended; Roosevelt Univ, BA 1955; Art Inst of Chgo, MFA 1977. **Career:** Rockford & Barat Coll, teacher art; Art Inst of Chicago, MFA 1977; Loyola Univ, prof of fine art. **Orgs:** Member, IL Arts Council, 1978-. **Honors/Awds:** Participated in numerous group exhibits; one-man shows; works can be found in many pvt & publ collections; Faculty Member of the Year, Loyola University, 1986. **Military Serv:** US Army, Sgt, 1951-53.

ARNOLD, RUDOLPH P.
Attorney, banker. **Personal:** Born May 24, 1948, Harlem, NY; married Linda J Kelly; children: Preston, Rebecca. **Educ:** Howard Univ, BA 1970; Univ of CT, JD 1975; NY Univ, LLM 1976. **Career:** Aetna Life & Casualty 1971-72; Legal Aid Soc of Hartford Cty, attny 1976-81; Arnold & Hershinson, attny 1982-84; Arnold & Assoc, atty 1985-; Society for Savings Bancorp Inc, chmn, 1991-93. **Orgs:** CT Bar Assn, Hartford Bar Assn; bd of dir, Urban League 1977-79; deputy mayor Hartford City Council 1979-83; bd of dir World Affairs Ctr 1983-88; chmn, Hartford Comm TV 1986-89; bd dir Soc for Savings 1987-93; Natl Bar Assn; Amer Bar Assn; lifetime mem, NAACP; dir, Natl Council for Intl Visitors 1989-92; Hartford Public Library, board of directors, 1994-; National Association Bond Lawyer; Natl Assn Securities Prof. **Honors/Awds:** Publ Intl Lawyer-Law 1974, Natl Bar Assn, 1980-; Hartford County Bar, Pro Bond Award, 1991; Author: What You Should Know About Evictions, 1981. **Business Addr:** Attorney, Arnold & Assoc, 80 Cedar Street, Hartford, CT 06106.

ARNOLD, WALLACE C.
Military officer. **Personal:** Born Jul 27, 1938, Washington, DC; son of Lydia Gibson Arnold and George W Arnold; married Earlene Costner Arnold, Jan 21, 1961; children: Sheila, Stephanie. **Educ:** Hampton Institute, Hampton, VA, BS, industrial education, 1960; George Washington Univ, Washington, DC, MA personnel mgt & admin, 1965; US Army Commmand & Gen Staff College, Ft Leavenworth, KS, 1970-71; Naval War College, Newport, RI, 1976-77. **Career:** US Army, Washington, DC, military asst & executive officer, ofc of the under secretary of the army, 1979-81; US Army, USA Europe, inspector general, VII corps Europe, 1981-82, cdr, 69th air defense artillery brigade, 1982-84, dir/ofcr personnel & admin for Europe, 1984-87; US Army, Fort Bragg, NC, commanding general, 1st ROTC reg, 1987-90; US Army, Fort Monroe, VA, commanding general, ROTC cadet command, 1990-93; US Army, Washington, DC, asst deputy chief of staff for Personnel, currently. **Orgs:** Chairman, Boy Scout District, Boy Scouts of America Council, Raleigh, NC, 1987-90; deacon, Second Baptist Church, Falls Church, VA, 1977-81; chairman, budget committee, Second Baptist Church, Falls Church, VA, 1977-81; president, Northern VA Chapter Nat'l Hampton University Alumni Assn, 1979-81; chairman, European School Council, DOD Dependent Schools System, 1984-87. **Honors/Awds:** Roy Wilkins Meritorious Service Award, NAACP Inc, 1990; Hampton University Outstanding Alumni Award, 1985; Honorary Doctor of Law Degree Campbell University, Buies Creek, NC, 1990. **Military Serv:** US Army, Major General, 1961-; Distinguished Service Medal; Defense Superior Service Medal, Legion of Merit, Bronze Star Medal, Meritorious Service Medal, Parachutist Badge. **Business Addr:** Assistant Deputy Chief of Staff for Personnel, 300 Army Pentagon, Washington, DC 20310-0300.

ARRINGTON, HAROLD MITCHELL
Physician. **Personal:** Born Apr 9, 1947, Detroit, MI; son of Irene Arrington and Robyn Arrington. **Educ:** Adrian Coll, BS 1968; Univ of MI Med Sch, MD 1972; Wayne State Univ Hosps, resident ob/gyn 1972-76; Amer Bd of Obstetrics & Gynecology, diplomate 1978; commercial instrument pilot's license, 1979. **Career:** Army Natl Guard Med Corps, Colonel 1972-; private practice, Ob/Gyn Detroit MI 1976-; Planned Parenthood League Inc, med dir 1976-; Detroit Bd of Educ, med dir 1978-. **Orgs:** Life mem NAACP; mem LPN Adv Comm Detroit, Amer Med Assn, Natl Med Assn; Natl Guard Association of United States; Iota Boule of Sigma Pi Phi, 1988-. **Honors/Awds:** Fellow Amer Coll of Ob/Gyn 1980; Fellow Intl College of Surgeons. **Military Serv:** USNG, Colonel, 207th EVAC HOSP, 1972-; colonel, officer in charge of American personnel, King Fund Military Complex, Dhahrar, Kingdom of Saudia Arabia during Operation Desert Shield/Storm; commander, 207th Evacuation Hospital, Michigan Army National Guard, 1992. **Business Addr:** 3800 Woodard, Ste 502, Detroit, MI 48201.

ARRINGTON, LLOYD M., JR.
Investment executive. **Personal:** Born Dec 12, 1947, Montgomery, AL; son of Annie Arrington and Lloyd Arrington; children: Briana, Bianca. **Educ:** Fisk Univ, BA 1970; Stanford Univ, MBA 1973. **Career:** Bankers Tr NY Corp, asst treasurer 1973-77; Assoc for the Integration of Mgmt, proj dir 1974-75; Pfizer Inc, mgr strategic planning 1978-79; US Small Business Admin, asst adv 1979-81; US Dept of Comm MBDA chief, capital devel 1981-82; Arrington & Co, pres; Economic Development Finance Corp., investment associate, 1988-90, vice pres, 1990-92; president, 1992-; Neighborhood Economic Dev Corp, president, 1990-. **Orgs:** Chm MD Small Business Devel Finance Authority 1986-93; Natl Black MBA Assn; Omega Psi Phi; WA Soc of Investment Analyst. **Honors/Awds:** T J Watson Fellow Fisk Univ 1970-71; C E Merrill Fellow Stanford Univ 1972-73, COGME Fellow 1971-73; J Barlow Schlr Bd of Educ, Redding, CT 1966. **Home Addr:** 1602 Pebble Beach Dr, Mitchellville, MD 20721.

ARRINGTON, MARVIN
City council president. **Career:** City Council, pres, City of Atlanta, GA, currently. **Business Addr:** 68 Mitchell St SW, Atlanta, GA 30335.

ARRINGTON, PAMELA GRAY
Professor. **Personal:** Born Feb 28, 1953, Montgomery, AL; daughter of Mr & Mrs Willis E Gray; married Richard Arrington III; children: Gray, Julian, Justin. **Educ:** Spelman Coll, BA 1974; The Univ of MI, MA 1975; George Mason Univ, DA 1987, PhD, 1993. **Career:** Talladega Coll, counselor 1976-77; Northern VA Comm Coll, counselor 1977-80, coord of affirmative action & grants develop 1980-88; Bowie State Univ, Human Resource Devel, professor 1988-. **Orgs:** Mem ASTD, OD; HRD Professors Network, Washington Metro Area; American Assn of Univ Prof; dir, Natl Retention Project, Amer Assn of State Colleges and Universities, 1993-; Alpha Kappa Alpha Sorority. **Honors/Awds:** Honor Scholarship Spelman Coll 1972-74; Psi Chi Spelman College 1974; Graduate Scholarship Univ of MI 1-74-75; Pi Lambda Theta 1975; Leaders for the 80's FIPSE/Maricopa Colleges 1983; Phi Delta Kappa 1983; Grad Rsch Asst & Scholarship George Mason Univ 1984-86; Faculty Fellow, Dept of Defense, Office of the Secretary of Defense, Civilian Personnel Policy, 1989-91. **Business Addr:** Associate Professor, Bowie State University, Human Resource Devt, Dept of Behavioral Sciences & Human Services, Bowie, MD 20715-9465.

ARRINGTON, RICHARD, JR.
Mayor. **Personal:** Born Oct 19, 1934, Livingston, AL; married; children: Anthony, Kenneth, Kevin, Angela, Erika Lynn. **Educ:** Miles Coll, AB, 1955; Univ of Detroit, MS, 1957; Univ of Oklahoma, PhD, 1966. **Career:** Miles Coll, prof, 1957-63; Univ of Oklahoma, spl instr, 1965-66, prof, 1966-; Univ of Alabama, assoc prof, part-time, 1971-72; Miles Coll, counselor to men, 1962-63, dir summer sch & acting dean, 1966-67, dean of coll academic, 1967-70; Alabama Ctr for Higher Educ, dir, 1970-79; City of Birmingham AL, mayor, 1979-. **Orgs:** Mem Birmingham City Cncl 1971-75; mem Amer Inst of Biol Sci; OK Acad of Sci; Amer Assn for Advancement of Sci; Amer Soc of Zoologists; Phi Sigma Nat Biol Soc; Soc of Sigma Xi; Amer Assn of Coll Deans; mem adv bd Family Counseling Assn of Jefferson Co; mem Alpha Phi Alpha. **Honors/Awds:** Ortenburger Award for Outstanding Work in Biology Univ of OK 1966; Alpha Phi Alpha Man of Yr 1969; Alpha Phi Alpha Achievement Award for Outstanding Comm Serv 1971; Man of Yr Awd AL Fedn of Civic Leagues 1971; Comm Civic Serv Award Druid Hill-Norwood Civic League 1972; Charles A Billups Comm Serv Award 1972; Comm Achievement Award 1972; Distinguished Alumni Award Miles Coll Alumni Assn 1972; Freedom Achievement Award Emancipation Assn 1973; Public Serv Award Birmingham Chapter Delta Sigma Theta 1974; Outstanding Educator Award Friends of Miles Coll 1973; Presidential Commendation Award Miles Coll Alumni Assn 1974; Distinguished Comm Serv Awd Birmingham Oppors Indus 1974. **Business Addr:** Mayor, City of Birmingham, 710 20th St N, Birmingham, AL 35203.

ARRINGTON, WARREN H., JR.
Corporate executive. **Personal:** Born Jul 10, 1948, Raleigh, NC; son of Lois B Arrington and Warren H Arrington; married Annie Hilliard, Aug 4, 1979; children: Janssen, Jamaine, Jarrodd. **Educ:** Livingstone College, BS, math, 1970; Hardbarger Bus Coll, accounting & business, 1979. **Career:** American Safety Products, president/chief executive officer, currently. **Orgs:** Piedmont Minority Supplier Development Council, 1990-91; Minority Business Enterprises Input Committee Executive Board, 1991-; Livingstone College Alumni Association; Touch-A-Teen Foundation of Wake County, director, 1985-; The Greater Raleigh Chamber of Commerce, bd of dirs, 1993-96, vp, small bus bd, 1994-, MCI small bus ctr, advisory bd, 1994-; Touch-A-Teen Foundation of NC, state dir, 1993-; Livingston College and Hood Theological Seminary, bd of trustees, currently. **Honors/Awds:** Piedmont Minority Supplier Development Council, Outstanding New Vendor of the Year, 1987; Carolina Minority Supplier Development Council, Vendor of the Year, 1989; Piedmont Minority Supplier Development Council, Minority Vendor of the Year, 1989; Minority Business Development Center, Supplier/Distributor Firm of the Year, 1991; Durham Business and Professional Chain, Progress Business Award, 1992; Capital City Sertoma Club, Service to Mankind Award, 1990-91; The Greater Raleigh Chamber of Commerce, Centennial Award, 1992, ''1993 Triangle Future 30,'' 1993; Touch-A-Teen Foundation of North Carolina, Outstanding County Director, 1989; Peat Merick Triangle Business Journal, ''1994 Fast Fifty,'' 1994; MBE, Entrepreneur of the Year, Service of the Year, 1996; Triangle, Future 30 award, 1997. **Business Addr:** President/CEO, American Safety Products, 3200 Glen Royal Rd, Ste 105, Raleigh, NC 27612-7419.

ARROYO, MARTINA
Opera & concert singer, educator. **Personal:** Born in New York, NY; daughter of Lucille Washington and Demetrio Arroyo. **Educ:** Hunter College, BA, 1956; pupil of Marinka Gurewich, Mo Martin Rich, Joseph Turnau, Rose Landver; Kathryn Long Course Metro Opera, studies. **Career:** Metropolitan Opera; Vienna State Opera; Paris Opera; Covent Garden, London; Teatro Colon, Buenos Aires; Hamburg Staatsoper; La Scala, Milan; Munich Staatsoper; Berlin Deutsche Opera; Rome Opera; San Francisco, Chicago and all major opera houses; soloist NY, Vienna, Berlin, Royal/London, Paris Philharmonics, San Francisco, Pittsburgh, Philadelphia, Chicago, Cleveland Symphonies; Indiana University Bloomington, School of Music, distinguished professor of music, currently. **Orgs:** Former member, Natl Endowment of Arts; honorary trustee, Carnegie Hall; trustee, Hunter College Foundation. **Honors/Awds:** First soprano in thirty years to sing three opening nights for the Met, 1970, 1971 & 1973; leading role in Aida, Madame Butterfly, Un Ballo in Maschera, Cavalleria Rusticana, La Forza del Destino, Macbeth, Don Giovanni, La Gioconda, Trovatore, one of 4 natl winners, Metro Opera Award & one of the guest contributors, 1959; Hunter College Outstanding Alumna; rec for Columb Lond Ang DGG Phil; Dr Honoris Cause of Human Letters, Hunter College; UCLA, Bowling Green University, Distinguished Visiting Professor. **Business Addr:** Distinguished Professor of Music, School of Music, Indiana University, Bloomington, IN 47405.

ARTERBERY, VIVIAN J.
Corporate secretary. **Educ:** Howard Univ, BA, 1958; Univ of So CA, MLS, 1965. **Career:** Space Tech Laboratories; Aerospace Corp. CA, 1960-79; Rand Corp Santa Monica, library dir, 1979-86, corporate secretary, 1988-; US Natl Commission on Libraries and Information Sciences, executive director, 1986-88. **Orgs:** Consultant US Office of Educ 1974-76; pres Special Libraries Assoc 1984-85; SLA rep Amer Library Assoc/US Dept of Educ Accreditation Project 1985-86; adv bd mem CA Library Assoc Councilor and Univ of So CA Library Sch; Santa Monica YMCA, board of directors; National Conference of Christians and Jews, Santa Monica Chapter, treasurer; Santa Monica YWCA, board of dirs; Santa Monica College Foundation, board of dirs; Salvation Army, advisory board; Links, Inc.

ARTHUR, GEORGE KENNETH
Elected administrator. **Personal:** Born Jun 29, 1933, Buffalo, NY; son of Jayne M Potter and William E Arthur; married Frances Bivens Arthur, Jun 19, 1960; children: George K Jr, Janice M, Hugh. **Educ:** Empire State Coll, Pol Sci 1977. **Career:** Erie Cty Bd of Supervisors, suprv 1964-67; City of Buffalo, councilman 1970-77; city of Buffalo, councilman at large 1978-84, pres of common council 1984-. **Orgs:** Bd of dir Better Bus Bureau, Buffalo Philharmonic Orch, Kleinhans Music Hall, NAACP Life Mem; Jr Warden St John Lodge #16; mem First Shiloh Baptist Church. **Honors/Awds:** Man of the Year The Buffalo Club 1970; Man of the Year Afro Police 1973; Medgar Evers Awd NAACP 1984; Jackie Robinson Awd YMCA 1985. **Military Serv:** AUS corpl 1953-55. **Home Addr:** 154 Roebling Ave, Buffalo, NY 14215. **Business Addr:** President, Buffalo Common Council, Room 1315 City Hall, Buffalo, NY 14202.

ARTIES, LUCY ELVIRA YVONNE
Educator. **Personal:** Born Aug 18, Pittsburgh, PA; daughter of Catherine Lillian Holland Arties (deceased) and William Walter Eugene Arties Jr. **Educ:** Oakwood Coll, Huntsville AL, 1952-53, 1956-58; Univ of the Dist of Columbia, BA 1972; Howard Univ, Washington DC, 1972-74; George Washington Univ, 1983-84; University of the District of Columbia, 1988-89. **Career:** Dept of the Navy, Pers Spec 1964-69; Federal City Coll, Washington DC, staff asst 1969-72; Dept of Housing & Urban Devel, Washington DC, educ specialist 1973-74; Washington DC Public Schools, educator 1974-; Kinder-Care Learning Center, Bowie, MD, teaching, 1991-92. **Orgs:** Mem Oakwood Coll Alumni Assoc 1958-; mem Univ of the Dist of Columbia Alumni Assoc 1981-; mem Washington DC Chamber of Commerce 1985; DC/DECA DC Public Schools 1985; Breath of Life Television Program, Washington Metropolitan Area, sercretary, 1991-; Botsmota Club, chaplain, 1992-. **Honors/Awds:** Mayor of the Dist of Columbia 1981; Certificate of Apprecication, Gov of the State of MD 1982; Graduate School Award, George Washington Univ 1982-83; Meritorious Award, Wilson Sr High School 1982; Certificate of Merit, Spingarn Sr High School 1984; Certificate of Appreciation, McFarland Jr High School, 1988-89; Certificate of Appreciation, District of Columbia Court System, 1987; In Appreciation, Breath of Life SDA Church-10th Anniversary, 1993; Outstanding Art Dedicated Service, Breath of Life SDA Church, Board of Ushers, 1993; Contributions to the Breath of Life Telecast on its 20th Anniversary, Breath of Life Committee, Washington Metropolitan Area, 1994. **Home Addr:** The Doreen, 5950 14th St NW, Washington, DC 20011.

ARTIES, WALTER EUGENE, III
Producer, director, musician. **Personal:** Born Nov 12, 1941, Pittsburgh, PA; married Beverly Ruth Deshay. **Educ:** Faith Coll Birmingham, LHD 1977. **Career:** Walter Arties Chorale LA, dir/arranger 1961-71; Little Richard Gospel Singer Penniman, arranger 1961-63; Webber Button Co, office head 1961-71; Billy Graham Crusades Assn Minneapolis, guest tenor soloist 1971-; KHOF-TV & FM Radio, comm services dir 1971-74; Breath of Life Telecast, prod coord 1974-. **Orgs:** Bd of trustees 7th Day Adventist Radio & TV Film Center Thousand Oaks, CA 1974-; exec com mem N Amer Adv Com Wash, DC; SDA Radio Film Center Thousand Oaks, CA 1974-; bd dir RV Operations Thousand Oaks, CA 1974-; baseball particip LA Dept of Rec Univ SDC Ch LA 1966-67; singing particip World Evangilization Lusanne Switzerland 1974. **Honors/Awds:** Recip Outstanding Music Accomplishment Award Grant Theol Sem Birmingham 1977; Mus Contributions for Singing Award Port Albernia Brit Columbia, Canada 1977; Outstanding Prodn

Coord Award Breath of Life Comm Wash, DC MD Chap 1980. **Business Addr:** Prod/Coordinator, Breath of Life Telecast, 1100 Rancho Conejo Blvd, Newbury Park, CA 91320.

ARTIS, ANTHONY JOEL
Environmental designer. **Personal:** Born Jan 11, 1951, Kokomo, IN; son of Yvonne S Artis and Myrle E Artis; married Iris Rosa; children: Andre Antonio, Claudia Lizet. **Educ:** Miami Univ Oxford OH, B Environ Design 1975. **Career:** Musician/instrumentalist bass guitar various groups in IN & OH 1967-; percussionist, 1990-; various architects in IN & OH, draftsman/designer 1974-79; Artis Environments, owner 1979-; Group "Directions" jazz/fusion 1985-92; Groups: Invisible Art, 1992-; Sancocho, 1994-; Coal Bin Productions, owner, 1992-. **Orgs:** Mem youth advisory council Center for Leadership Devel 1979-; speaker & mem exhibition comm Minorities in Engineering 1979-82; mem Meridian Kessler Neighborhood Assn 1981-; mem Natl Trust for Historic Preservation 1983-; mem volunteer staff Indianapolis City Center 1983-84; mem Indianapolis Chamber of Commerce 1984-; bd dirs Neighborhood Housing Serv of Indianapolis 1985-87; board of directors development corp., Meridian-Kessler Neighborhood Association, 1996-. **Honors/Awds:** Governors Trophy Indianapolis 500 Festival Parade Float Design Team Indiana Black Expo 1982; Black Achiever in Science, Childrens Museum, IN 1989. **Business Addr:** Owner, Artis Environments, 3946 Guilford Ave, Indianapolis, IN 46205.

ARTIS, KATASHA
Professional basketball player. **Personal:** Born Jul 9, 1973. **Educ:** Northeastern, bachelor's degree in criminal justice. **Career:** Charlotte Sting, forward, 1997-. **Business Addr:** Professional Basketball Player, Charlotte Sting, 2709 Water Ridge Pkwy, Ste 400, Charlotte, NC 28217, (704)424-9622.

ARTIS, MYRLE EVERETT
Physician. **Personal:** Born Sep 28, 1924, Kokomo, IN; married Pamela; children: Anthony, Mark. **Educ:** IN Univ, AB 1953; IN Univ Med School, MD 1957. **Career:** Cty Bd of Health, pres; St Joseph Mem Hosp, pres of staff, internship, chief of med; Private practice, physician 1958-. **Orgs:** Mem Howard Cty Med Assoc, IN Med Assoc, AMA, Natl Med Assoc, Amer Acad of Family Practice Fellowships, Bd of Health, St Joseph Mem Hosp Found, Cty Library Adv Comm, C of C; mem dir Forest Park Convalescent Ctr Kokomo In; govt adv comm Sickle Anemia 1979-83, 1983-87; bd of dirs Kokomo Pal Club, Carver Community Ctr. **Military Serv:** US Army, 1943-46. **Business Addr:** 402 S Berkley, PO Box 3067, Kokomo, IN 46901.

ARTISON, RICHARD E.
Law enforcement official. **Personal:** Born Jun 9, 1933, Omaha, NE; married Charleszine; children: Lisa, Richard Jr, Kelli. **Educ:** Drake Univ, Sociol & Psych 1954; Univ of NE Law School, 1954-55; Cornell Univ, Ed for Publ Mgmt 1973-74. **Career:** US Army Counter Intelligence, spec agent 1955-58; Omaha NE Police Dept, police officer 1958-62; US Treas Secret Svc, spec agent 1963-67; Milwaukee Office Secret Svc, spec agent in charge 1974-83; Milwaukee Cty, sheriff 1983-. **Orgs:** Exec bd mem Milwaukee Cty Boy Scouts; bd of dir Boys & Girls Clubs of Greater Milwaukee; past pres Fed Officials Assn; past vice pres Milwaukee Frontiers Intl; Milwaukee Cty Metro Police Chiefs; charter mem Fed Criminal Invest Assoc. **Honors/Awds:** Exemplary Achievement Kappa Alpha Psi; High Quality Awd US Treasury Dept; Wisconsin Attorney General, Law Enforcement Executive of the Year Award, 1992. **Military Serv:** US Army, spec agent, 3 yrs. **Business Addr:** Sheriff, Milwaukee County, 821 W State St, Milwaukee, WI 53233.

ARTISST, ROBERT IRVING
Educator (retired). **Personal:** Born Jul 13, 1932, Washington, DC; children: Tawnya Alicia, Robert Irving II, Kevin Frederick. **Educ:** Howard Univ, BA 1959, MA 1969; Univ of DC, MA 1971. **Career:** Appalacian Reg Comm, public information/visual specialist 1966-71; Urban Inst, dir of pub 1972-71; Natl Assn of Black Manufacturing Inc, exec liaison officer 1972-73; Cooperative Extension Serv WTI, public information & comm coord 1973-76; Univ of Washington DC, assoc prof of media; Mary Mount Univ, professor, currently. **Orgs:** Comm D C Human Rights Comm 1978-84; comm Adv Neighborhood Comm 1975-85; chm of bd DC Capitol Head Start 1983-85; pres Brookland Civic Asso, Inc 1977-84; vice chm Neighborhood Plng Cncl 1976-79; vicepres DC Citizens for Better Pub Ed 1977-84; Democratic Clinton Delegate, adm neighbor commissioner, 1988-. **Honors/Awds:** Edtr/Writer Handbook for Tchrs of Adult 1971-72; spec awd Tchng Youth Operation Rescue 1982-84; spec accmdtn Mayor of the City for Services 1976-77, spec citation 1978-79; Selective Service, board of directors, appointed by President George Bush; President Special Award for Citizen Service, 1993; Special Award by Phi Delta Kappa. **Military Serv:** US Army, 1st lt Univ S 11th Airborne Div 5 yrs Wings/Calvary Star-Airman Star 1954.

ARTOPE, WILLIAM
Advertising executive. **Personal:** Born Apr 2, 1943, New York, NY; son of Warnetta Mays Artope and James Artope; married Linda Young Artope, Nov 2, 1979; children: Westley, Tamara, George, William. **Educ:** New York University, New York, NY; RCA Institute of Technology, electronics. **Career:** Columbia Prep School, teacher, 1965-69; J Walter Thompson, producer, 1970-79; W B Donner & Co, executive producer, 1980-81; DDB Needham, executive producer, 1981-. **Orgs:** Chapter Chief, Nichiren Shoshu Soka Gakkai of America. **Honors/Awds:** Clio Award, 1974; Clio Award, 1979. **Business Addr:** Vice President/Executive Producer, DDB Needham Worldwide Inc, 303 E Wacker Dr, Chicago, IL 60601.

ASANTE, KARIAMU WELSH
Educator, choreographer. **Personal:** Born Sep 22, 1949, Thomasville, NC; daughter of Ruth Hoover and Harvey Farabee; married Molefi K Asante; children: Daahoud, Khumalo. **Educ:** State Univ of NY at Buffalo, BA 1972, MA 1975; New York University, doctorate, arts, 1992. **Career:** Black Dance Workshop, choreographer 1970-77; Center for Positive Thought Buffalo, NY, artistic dir 1971-81; Kariamu & Co, choreographer 1977-84; Natl Dance Co of Zimbabwe Harare, Zimbabwe, artistic dir 1981-83; Temple Univ, prof/choreographer. **Orgs:** Dir Museum of African Amer Art & Antiquities 1978-; editorial bd Journal of Black Studies 1982-; panel mem Buffalo Arts Cncl 1983-85; panel mem NYS Council on the Arts Spec Arts Serv 1984-85; consult Natl Dance Co of Zimbabwe 1984-; dir Institute of African Dance Research & Performance Temple Univ 1985-; Commonwealth of Pennsylvania Council on the Art, dance panel, 1991-93. **Honors/Awds:** Natl Endowment for the Arts Choreography Fellowship 1973; NYS Creative Artist Serv Awd 1974; Choreographer Awd Clark Ctr for the Performing Arts NY 1977; Choreographers Fellowship NYS Creative Artist Serv Awd 1978; Fulbright Scholars Fellowship Harare Zimbabwe 1982-83; Minority Choreographers Fellowship NY State Cncl on the Arts 1984; Pew Fellow, 1996; Guggenheim, 1997; co-editor The African Culture, Rhythms of Unity 1985; Dance Historian Fellowship, Commonwealth of PA Council on the Arts 1988; editor The African Aesthetic: Keeper of the Traditions, Greenwood Press 1989; editor Journal of African Dance 1989. **Special Achievements:** Guest editor, Sage: The Scholarly Journal on Black Women, 1992; author: African Dance; Zimbabwean Dance; Dictionary of African Dance. **Business Addr:** Professor/Choreographer, Temple University, Broad & Montgomery Sts, Philadelphia, PA 19122, (215)204-8626.

ASANTE, MOLEFI KETE (ARTHUR L. SMITH, JR.)
Educator. **Personal:** Born Aug 14, 1942, Valdosta, GA; son of Lillie B Wilkson Smith and Arthur L Smith Sr; married Kariamu Welsh; children: Kasina Eka, Daahoud, Molefi Khumalo. **Educ:** Southwestern Christian Coll, AA 1962; Oklahoma Christian Coll, BA 1964; Pepperdine Univ, MA 1965; UCLA, PhD 1968. **Career:** CA State Polytechnic Coll, instr 1967; CA State Univ Northridge, instr 1968; Purdue Univ, asst prof 1968-69; Pepperdine Univ, visit prof 1969; Univ of CA LA, asst prof 1969-71; CA State Univ, visit prof 1971; Univ of CA LA, dir Center for Afro-Amer Studies 1970-73, assoc prof speech 1971-73; FL State Univ Tallahassee, visit assoc prof 1972; State Univ of NY Buffalo, prof communication dept; Center for Positive Thought Buffalo, curator; Univ of Ibadan, Univ of Nairobi, external examiner 1976-80; Zimbabwe Inst of Mass Communications, fulbright prof; Howard Univ, visiting prof 1979-80; Temple Univ Dept of African-American Studies, prof, currently. **Orgs:** Spec in Black Rhetoric County Probation Dept LA 1969-; bd editors Black Man in Am; editorial assoc "The Speech Teacher"; editor "Journal of Black Studies"; adv bd Black Journal; mem Intl Soc for Gen Semantics; Intl Assn for Symbolic Analysis; Intl Comm Assn; Western Speech Assn; Central State Speech Assn; So Speech Assn; Natl Assn for Dramatic & Speech Arts; ed bds Nigerian Journal of Political Economy, Afrodiaspora, Afrique Histoire, Africa and the World, Urban African Quarterly, Journal of African Civilization; contributing writer for Buffalo Challenger, Philadelphia New Observer, Philadelphia Tribune; UNESCO reviewer for scholarly books 1985; consultant Zimbabwe Ministry of Information and Telecommunications; Intl Scientific Comm of FESPAC 1986-87 Senegal; chairperson, IMHOTEP 1987-; president, Natl Council for Black Studies, 1988-; vice president, African Heritage Studies Assn 1989-. **Special Achievements:** Author of 40 books; consulting editor for books; Christian Ed Guild Writer's Awards 1965; LHD Univ of New Haven 1976; Outstanding Comm Scholar Jackson State Univ 1980; author of The Afrocentric Idea 1987; Afrocentricity, 1987; Kemet, Afrocentricity and Knowledge, 1990; Historical and Cultural Atlas of African-Americans, 1991; African American History: A Journey of Liberation, 1995; Love Dance, 1996; African Intellectual Heritage, 1996; African American Names, 1998. **Business Addr:** Professor, Dept of African-American Studies, Temple University, Gladfelter Hall 025-26, Philadelphia, PA 19122, (215)204-4322.

ASBURY, WILLIAM W.
Educational administrator. **Personal:** Born Feb 22, 1943, Crawfordville, GA; son of Ida B McLendon Asbury (deceased) and William J Asbury (deceased); married Leslee Diane Swift Asbury, Mar 30, 1968; children: Keleigh, Kristin, Kimberly. **Educ:** Kent State University, Kent, OH, Bachelors, 1966, MA, 1973. **Career:** NFL Pittsburgh Steelers, 1966-69; Sanford Rose Assoc, Akron, OH, senior consultant, 1969-70; City of Akron, OH, contract compliance officer, 1970-74; Kent State University, Kent, OH, dir of human resources, 1974-76; Penn State University, University Park, PA, affirmative action officer, 1976-83, exec asst to the president, 1983-85, vice president, 1985-. **Orgs:** Pres 1991-92, exec council secretary, NASULGC Student Affairs Council; American Assn for Higher Education; Natl Assn of Student Personnel Administrators; parlimentarian, Penn Black Conference on Higher Education; member, Forum on Black Affairs, Penn State Univ; honorary member, Natl Residence Hall Honorary; overall chairman, American Cancer Soc for Centre County, 1990-91; bd of directors, past pres 1987-90, Counseling Services, Inc; bd of directors, Centre HomeCare, Inc; board of directors, past pres 1987-89, Quarterback Club; honorary chairman, Penn State 4-H Ambassador Program; member, Univ Club, State College, PA; Penn State Univ Nittany Lions Club; Penn State Univ Basketball Club; life member, Kent State Univ Alumni Assn; past pres, Kiwanis Club of State College; National Urban League,r; NASPA Foundation, board of directors; Special Olympics, bd of dirs. **Honors/Awds:** 4-H Clover Award, Benjamin Rush Award, 1992; Distinguished President Kiwanis Club of State College, 1991; Special Achievement Award, Kent State Alumni Association, 1991; Kent State University Hall of Fame, 1981; Cultural Diversity and Equity Award, PSU Forum on Black Affairs, 1990; Honorary Member, Golden Key National Honor Society, 1983. **Home Addr:** 119 Wildernest Lane, Port Matilda, PA 16870. **Business Phone:** (814)865-0909.

ASH, RICHARD LARRY
Hotel/hospitality executive. **Personal:** Born Mar 23, 1959, Newark, NJ; son of Daisy Pugh Ash and Richard Ash Jr; married Kathy W (divorced 1985); children: Alexandra Erin. **Educ:** Snow College, Ephraim, UT, 1980-83; Rutgers University, Newark, NJ, 1984-85. **Career:** McDonald's Corp, various New Jersey locations, crew person, 1978-80, restaurant mgr, 1983-85; Ana Services, Bedminster, NJ, banquet sized catering mgr, 1985-87; Chelsea Catering, Newark Airport, Newark, NJ, asst food production mgr, 1987-89; Marriott/Host, Newark Airport, Newark, NJ, asst food & beverage mgr, 1989-90; Harrisburg Hilton and Towers, Harrisburg, PA, dir of human resources, 1990-. **Orgs:** Vice pres, National Assn of Black Hospitality Professionals, 1988-; member, National Job Corps Alumni Assn, 1982-. **Honors/Awds:** Silver Hat Award, McDonald's Corp, 1984; numerous national and regional debate awards, 1980-83. **Business Addr:** Director, Human Resources, Harrisburg Hilton and Towers, MHM, Inc, 1 N 2nd St, Harrisburg, PA 17101.

ASHANTI, KEESHA-MARIA
Judge. **Personal:** Born Aug 10, 1948, Mobile, AL; daughter of Cleo M Caldwell. **Educ:** Tuskegee Inst, BS soc 1970; Univ of Southwestern School of Law, JD 1978. **Career:** District Attorney's Office, asst district attorney 1983-86; Metropolitan Court, judge 1987-. **Honors/Awds:** Monroe N Work Awd 1970; Southwestern Univ Sch of Law Certificate of Disting Serv 1977; NAACP Legal Defense and Educ Fund Certificate of Honor. **Home Addr:** PO Box 26524, Albuquerque, NM 87125. **Business Addr:** Judge, Metropolitan Court, PO Box 133, Albuquerque, NM 87103.

ASHBURN, VIVIAN DIANE
Business Executive. **Personal:** Born Oct 7, 1949, Kansas City, KS; daughter of Margaret V Patterson and Alvin M Patterson; married Richard R Ashburn, Jun 30, 1972; children: Aaron Cedric, Joseph Elliott. **Educ:** Ohio State University, BA, industrial relations, 1972; IBM Systems Engineering Institute, 1973-74. **Career:** International Business Machines, systems engineer, 1972-77; Ashburn Pizza dba Domino's, vice pres, 1977-85; Stark Technical College, 1984-88; University of Akron, lecturer, 1990-; VDP Associates Inc, president, 1990-. **Orgs:** Black Data Processing Associates, vice pres, 1986-; Portage Private Industry Council, ch air, program planning, 1985-; Franklin Mills Mediation Council, executive director, 1989-91; W VIZ Radio, board member, 1987-88; Alpha Kappa Alpha Sorority, 1970-; Minority Business Council, Ohio Chapter, 1989-91. **Honors/Awds:** USDA, Minority Contractor of the Year, 1989; IBM Corp., Systems Engineering Symposium, 1977, 1979, National Business Partner, 1990-. **Home Addr:** 305 E Archwood, Akron, OH 44301. **Business Phone:** (216)384-7169.

ASHBY, DOROTHY J.
Musician, composer. **Personal:** Born Aug 6, 1932, Detroit, MI; daughter of Julia Thompson and Wiley Thompson; married John Ashby. **Educ:** Attended, Wayne State Univ. **Career:** Assists youth in developing skills in mus & theater 1957-; WJR, staff harpist 1960-63; WCHD-FM, radio show 1963-68; musicals produced by John Ashby & Wiley Thompson Detroit 1967, Toronto CAN 1968, Detroit 1970, Toronto 1970, Chicago 1971, Detroit 1972; professional harpist/composer. **Orgs:** Mem Amer Harp Soc; currently most recorded contemporary Harpist in world can be heard on virtually all albums of major pop artists, Johnny Mathis, Stevie Wonder, Natalie Cole, Bill Withers, Donald Byrd, Ramsey Lewis, Earth Wind & Fire, Black Byrds, Helen Reddy, Emotions, Jon Lucien, Freddie Hubbard etc; num commercials on radio & tv; mem Natl Acad of Recording Arts & Scis; Black Comm Theatre; Amer Fedn of Mus Local #47; Hollywood Local #5 Detroit; 12 LP Albums.

ASHBY, ERNESTINE ARNOLD
Educator. **Personal:** Born Aug 20, 1928, Washington, DC; widowed; children: Ira Von. **Educ:** Cortez Peters Bus Sch, bus cert 1947; Coppin State Tchrs Coll, BS 1950; Univ of MD, MEd 1967; Walden Univ, PhD candidate. **Career:** Baltimore City Public Schools, teacher 1950-69; Accomack County School System, reading spec 1969-. **Orgs:** Bd dir Emmanuel Christian Comm Sch Fed Credit Union Adv Cncl 1954-57; owner mgr Furniture Excng United Appeal Orgr Comm Chest 1955-57; bd mem YWCA; multi-media specialist 1968-; author co-author num children's stories & poems; mem NEA, VEA, AEA, IRA area chmn NAACP 1976. **Honors/Awds:** Awd in Recog Literary Guild; Cert of Achievement Small Bus Mgmt; Vol Serv Awd PTA.

ASHBY, LUCIUS ANTOINE
Business executive, certified public accountant. **Personal:** Born Feb 1, 1944, Des Moines, IA; son of Ruth M Moore and Lucius A Ashby Sr; married Victoria Lacy; children: Felecia, Armand. **Educ:** Univ of Colorado Denver, BBA 1969; Harvard Univ, SCMP 1982-84. **Career:** Great Western Sugar Co, management trainee program 1968-69; Arthur Andersen & Co sr accountant 1969-72; Ashby Armstrong & Co, managing partner 1973-91; Ashby Jackson, Inc, investor, consultant, chairman of bd, 1991-. **Orgs:** Mbr Amer Inst of CPA's; bd of dir CO Soc of CPAW's Denver Partnerships, Assoc of Black CPA Firms, Ldrshp Denver Assn, Salvation Army 1975-; bd of dirs Downtown Denver Inc; chmn of bd, Colorado Invesco Inc, 1988-. **Honors/Awds:** Rcpnt Barney Ford Eastside Action Mvmnt 1975; entrepreneur award United Negro Coll Fund 1980; achievement award Natl Assn of Black Accountants 1979. **Military Serv:** US Army, sp-5, e-5 1961-64.

ASHBY, REGINALD W.
Business executive. **Personal:** married Ernestine C Arnold; children: Eugene Paula, Iravon. **Educ:** Morgan State Coll, cert bus adminstrn. **Career:** Life Ins Career, 1936-; Universal Life Ins Co Norfolk, agent 1969-. **Orgs:** Mem VFW (1st Black exec offcr dist); pres Accomack Co, VA NAACP; orgn Neighborhood Boys Club Baltimore 1963; Grand Jury Baltimore 1968-69. **Military Serv:** US Army, 1946. **Business Addr:** Agent, Universal Life Ins Co, 2802 Virginia Beach Blvd, Norfolk, VA 23504.

ASHFORD, EVELYN
Amateur athlete. **Personal:** Born 1957; married Ray Washington; children: Raina Ashley Washington. **Educ:** Univ of California at Los Angeles, attended. **Career:** 1976 Summer Olympics, Montreal, Canada, runner; 1984 Summer Olympics, Los Angeles, CA, runner; 1988 Summer Olympics, Seoul, South Korea, runner. **Honors/Awds:** 4 World Cup Titles; 2 Olympic Gold Medals, 1984; Flo Hyman Award, Women's Sport Foundation, 1989; first Black woman to carry the American flag during an Olympic opening ceremony, 1988; Olympic Silver Medal, 1988. **Business Addr:** 818 Plantation Lane, Walnut, CA 91789.

ASHFORD, L. JEROME
Health services executive. **Personal:** Born Aug 7, 1937, Woodville, MS; son of Mazie Iola Moore Ashford and Littleton Perry Ashford; married Alicestine D Miller-Ashford, Sep 6, 1984; children: Wesley Jerome, Maurice Eugene, Dwayne Perry, Jerome. **Educ:** Boston Univ, Boston, MA, BS, 1968; Univ of Southern CA, Los Angeles, CA, MPA, 1979. **Career:** Natl Assn of Community Health Ctrs, Washington, DC, exec dir, 1973-78; US Dept of Health & Human Services, Washington, DC, sr research fellow, 1978-82; IPM Health Plan, Vallejo, CA, pres, 1982-88; Kaiser Permanente/Colorado Region, Denver, CO, health plan mgr, 1988-90; Kaiser Permanente/Southern CA Region, Pasadena, CA, vice pres/health plan mgr, 1990-94. **Orgs:** USC Alumni Assn; Los Angeles March of Dimes, board of directors; NAACP, life mem. **Home Addr:** 3105 Peters Circle, Glendale, CA 91208. **Business Phone:** (818)957-7259.

ASHFORD, LAPLOIS
Association executive. **Personal:** Born Jul 18, 1935, McCool, MS. **Educ:** Univ of Rochester, BA Hist 1957; NY State Univ, MA Soc Studies 1960; Univ of AK, attended. **Career:** Rochester Special Edn, teacher 1960-62; NAACP Youth & Coll Div, natl dirf 1962-65; City of Rochester, dep commr of pub safety 1965-67; Rochester Urban League, exec dir 1967-70; Chicago Urban League, exec dir 1970-72; Natl Urban Coalition, vice pres for Urban Edn. **Orgs:** Mem Natl Educ Assn; Amer Assn of Jr & Comm Colls; Amer Assn of State & Pub Inst of Higher Educ Commr of Schs Rochester 1967-69; pres Bd of EdnRochester 1968-69; chmn Action for Survival Chicago 1970-72; chmn UNCF of DC 1974. **Honors/Awds:** Recip Outstanding Young man of the Year NY State Jaycees 1965; Leroy E Snyder Award for Outstanding Comm Serv Rochester 1967; Richard Allen Award AME Ch1970; Afro-Am Patrolmens League Testimonial Award Chicago 1971; Outstanding Serv Award Natl Urban Coalition 1974. **Military Serv:** US Army, 1957-59. **Business Addr:** Vice Pres for Urban Education, Natl Urban Coalition, 2100 M St NW, Washington, DC 20037.

ASHFORD, NICHOLAS
Singer, songwriter. **Personal:** Born May 4, 1943, Willow Run, MI; married Valerie Simpson; children: Nicole. **Career:** Singer/songwriter. **Special Achievements:** With Valerie Simpson wrote You're All I Need to Get By, Let's Get Stoned, Ain't No Mountain High Enough, Ain't Nothing Like the Real Thing; albums with Valerie Simpson as Ashford and Simpson: Musical Affair, Is It Still Good to Ya, Stay Free, Solid, High Rise, Love or Physical.

ASHHURST, CARMEN
Communications company executive. **Career:** Former filmmaker; former fundraiser; Def Jam Records, president, until 1992; Rush Communications, president, 1992-. **Business Addr:** President, Rush Communications, 652 Broadway, 3rd Fl, New York, NY 10012, (212)941-3825.

ASHLEY, CORLANDERS
Secretary/treasurer. **Personal:** Born May 9, 1951, Cleveland, OH. **Educ:** OH Wesleyan Univ, attended 1969-71; Boston Univ, BS Business Admin 1971-73; Case Western Reserve, cand for MBA 1975. **Career:** ITT Headquarters NY, adm asst 1973-74; Ashley Distributors Inc, officer sec/treas 1975-. **Orgs:** Mem Cleveland Jaycees 1976-; bd mem Fam Bus Assn 1978-; bd trustee Cleveland Bus League 1980-81; Chi Chap treas Kappa Psi Frat 1971-73; mem Councilof Small Enterprises 1975-; mem Univ Serv Inst 1975-; Cert of Particip Univ Serv Inst 1975. **Honors/Awds:** Outstanding Young Men of Amer Jaycees 1979. **Business Addr:** Secretary/Treasurer, Ashley Distributors Inc, 19701 S Miles Rd, Warrensville Heights, OH 44128.

ASHLEY, LILLARD GOVERNOR
Educator. **Personal:** Born May 1, 1909, Boley, OK; married Velma Dolphin; children: Lewis, Lillard Jr. **Educ:** Langston Univ, BS 1933; OK State Univ, MS. **Career:** Bd of Educ Dist I-13. **Orgs:** Past pres Okfuskee Co Educ Assn; sec/treas Co Dem Assn; vice pres State Adv Council to St Bd of Voc & Tech Edn; mem/past pres Central OK Econ Devel Dist; past vice pres SW Reg Alpha Phi Alpha; sec Beta Epsilon Lambda Alpha Phi Alpha; mem OK Educ Assn; mem OK Assn of Sch Adm; treas Masonic Bene Assn Prince Hall Grand Lodge Jurisd of OH; past sec/treas Charity Comm Prince Hall Grand Lodge Jurisd of OK; Sunday Schl supt deacon Antioch Bapt Ch; chrt mem Boley Kiwanis Intl; past sec/treas Boley C of C; mem Okfuskee Co Fair Bd. **Honors/Awds:** Special Recogn in ch 1954; Mason of the year 1968; Selected by Amer Assn of Sch Adm to visit schools in Germany 1973.

ASHMORE, ANDREA LYNN
Corporate communications manager. **Personal:** Born Oct 22, 1954, Chicago, IL; daughter of Wilma Jean Lee Jones and Plato Webster Jones Jr.; married Edward Lane Ashmore (divorced 1983). **Educ:** Cornell College, Mt. Vernon, IA, BA, 1976; Mt. Vernon College, Washington, DC, 1980; Georgetown University, Washington, DC, 1981. **Career:** American College of Nursing Home Administrators, Bethesda, MD, publications supervisor, 1978-81; ASHRAE, Atlanta, GA, assistant editor, 1981-83; Communications Channel, Atlanta, GA, editor, 1983-86; TV Data, Atlanta, GA, editorial manager, 1986-88; Ball Corporation, Mogadore, OH, marketing communications manager, 1988-90; Yokogawa Corporation of America, Newnan, GA, corporate communications manager, 1990-. **Orgs:** Member, Atlanta Association of Black Journalists, 1983-. **Honors/Awds:** Magazine of the Month, Communication Channels Inc, 1985. **Business Addr:** Corporate Communications Manager, Yokogawa Corporation of America, 2 Dart Rd, Newnan, GA 30265.

ASHMORE, DARRYL ALLAN
Professional football player. **Personal:** Born Nov 1, 1969, Peoria, IL. **Educ:** Northwestern, bachelor's degree in business. **Career:** Los Angeles Rams, tackle, 1993-94; St Louis Rams, 1995-96; Washington Redskins, 1997-. **Business Addr:** Professional Football Player, Washington Redskins, 13832 Redskin Dr, Herndon, VA 22071, (703)471-9100.

ASHTON, VIVIAN CHRISTINA R.
Elected official (retired), business executive (retired), political activist. **Personal:** Born Aug 14, 1910, Spokane, WA; daughter of Madeline D Mackingham Reynolds (deceased) and Elijah J Reynolds (deceased); married Lawrence Thomas Ashton (deceased). **Educ:** Washington Lee Coll US Armed Forces, Cert 1945; Berne-Davis Business Coll, Certificate 1948; OH State Univ, Sociology 1948-50; Howard Univ, Sociology 1946-82. **Career:** The Wee-Angels Inc, chmn 1959-85; NOW, lobbyist 1975-76; Advisory Commission 5D DC govt, commiss 1981-85; League of Women Voters, speaker 1983-85. **Orgs:** Mem, Col Charles Young Chap 3 DAV, 1945-95, Prince Hall #5 OES Masonic Order, 1950-95; public relat, Club Intl, 1960-80; chairperson, crime comm, Brookland Civic Assoc, 1980-85; community liaison, DC Comm Humanities Council, 1981; chairperson, Historical Comm ANC-5C, 1981-85; mem, panel comment on Pres Reagan's address to nation, 1981; group leader, Solidarity Club, St Anthony's Church, 1991; NOW. **Honors/Awds:** Letter of Appreciation, Mayor Walter Washington, 1975; Cert of Appreciation, Spingarn Moreland Rsch, 1975; Awd, Active Bicentennial Program, 1976; Cert of Appreciation, DC City Council, 1985; researcher, compiler, presenter, editor, Masonic Historic Landmark Application for Woodlawn Cemetary, 1990-92 (landmark approved, 1992); DC Talent Search, First Place Adult Singer "Summer Time," 1989; MW Prince Hall Grand Masonic Lodge, FAAM-PHA, Wash DC, Humanities Award, 1994; MW Prince Hall Grand Masonic Lodge, FAAM-PHA, Wash DC, Certificate of Appreciation-Exemplary Acts of Service, 1990. **Military Serv:** Sp E-2 personnel serv 1943-45; WAC WWII; WWII Victory Medal, Amer Campaign Med. **Business Addr:** PO Box 4518, Washington, DC 20017.

ASINOR, FREDDIE ANDREW
Association executive. **Personal:** Born Feb 16, 1955, Norwalk, CT; son of Cecilia Benson Asinor and Nicholas Asinor; married Janice Ophelia, May 31, 1981; children: Nicole Leslie, Celia Lynn, Amanda Jayvonne. **Educ:** Newbury School of Journalism, diploma, 1978; Morehouse College, BA, cum laude, 1985; Northwestern Univ, MS, 1986; Atlanta Univ, EdD, 1988. **Career:** AUC Digest, Atlanta, reporter, 1982-83; Morehouse College, Atlanta, pub relations assistant, 1983-85, dir of student activities, 1986-89; Medill News Service, Washington, reporter, 1985-86; Clemson Univ, SC, dir of undergrad academic special projects, beginning 1989; Georgia State Univ, Dept of Communication, vice chairman, 1993; Morehouse School of Medicine, asst residency program dir, 1993, associate residency program dir, 1994-; Morehouse School of Med, asst prof of clinical family med, 1994-; Morehouse School of Med Family Practice Residency Program's Comm Med Ed & Prevention Project, project dir, 1995; Atlanta Minority Access to Higher Education Program Inc, Atlanta, GA, pres/exec dir, currently. **Orgs:** Big Brothers/Big Sisters, Atlanta, 1986; Georgia Council on Child Abuse, Atlanta, 1986; Alpha Phi Alpha. **Honors/Awds:** Fellowship, Time Inc, 1983, 1984; fellowship, Poynter Found, 1983; Cox Acad Excellence Awd, Cox Communications, 1985.

ASKA, JOSEPH
Professional football player. **Personal:** Born Jul 14, 1972, St. Croix, Virgin Islands of the United States; married. **Educ:** Central Oklahoma. **Career:** Oakland Raiders, running back, 1995-. **Business Addr:** Professional Football Player, Oakland Raiders, 1220 Harbor Bay Pkwy, Alameda, CA 94502, (510)615-1875.

ASKEW, BONNY LAMAR
Elected official & business executive. **Personal:** Born Mar 4, 1955, Rome, GA; married Adrianne Denise Smith. **Educ:** US Naval Acad, 1973-75; West GA Coll, BA Political Sci 1977. **Career:** South Rome Comm Assoc, co-founder 1979; 2nd Ward City of Rome, commissioner 1983-84; GA Kraft Co, laborer 1977-; Rome Council on Human Relations, vice chmn. **Orgs:** Mem Thankful Baptist Church; mem S Rome Comm Assoc; mem Starlight Lodge #433 FAAYM; comm mem GA Municipal Assoc Comm Dev 1983-84; comm mem Natl League of Cities Comm Dev 1983-84; mem Natl Black Caucus local elected official 1983-84; mem GA Assoc Black Elected Off 1983-84. **Home Addr:** 503 Cotton Ave, Rome, GA 30161.

ASKEW, VINCENT JEROME
Professional basketball player. **Personal:** Born Feb 28, 1966, Memphis, TN. **Educ:** Memphis State Univ. **Career:** Philadrlphia 76ers, 1987; Savannah Spirits (CBA), 1987-88; Bologna Arimo (Italy), 1988-89; Albany Patroons (CBA), 1988-91; Golden State Warriors, 1990-92; Sacramento Kings, 1992; Seattle Supersonics, 1993-96; Denver Nuggets, 1996-97; Portland Trailblazers, 1997-. **Business Phone:** (503)234-9291.

ASKINS, KEITH BERNARD
Professional basketball player. **Personal:** Born Dec 15, 1967, Athens, AL. **Educ:** Alabama. **Career:** Miami Heat, guard-forward, 1990-. **Business Addr:** Professional Basketball Player, Miami Heat, 721 NW First Ave, Miami Arena, Miami, FL 33136, (305)577-4328.

ASMA, THOMAS M.
Custom artist. **Educ:** Layton Sch of Art, advertising art/design 1966-68; Coll of Lake Co, Liberal Arts 1975; Univ of IL, attended 1975-76. **Career:** Layson Prods, commercial artist 1970-71; Carlson Studios, commercial artist 1971-72; Lake Co Regional Planning Comm, planning tech 1972-73; Lake Co SafetyComm, graphic artist 1973-74; BALL Corp, palletizer genl factory 1976-78; Kitchens of Sara Lee, production sanitation 1978-80; Amer Heritage Indus, customartist 1980-. **Business Addr:** American Heritage Industries, 3400 W Grand Ave, Waukegan, IL 60085.

ASOM, MOSES T.
Scientist. **Personal:** Born Jul 27, 1958, Gboko Benue, Nigeria; son of Lydia Asom and Asom Ikyutor. **Educ:** Univ of DC, BSC, physics (magna cum laude), 1980; Howard Univ, MSC, 1982, PhD, electrical engineering, 1985; University of Pennsylvania, Wharton School, MBA, 1994. **Career:** Univ of DC, Washington, DC, instructor, 1984; Howard Univ, Washington, DC, research asst, 1981-85; AT&T, Bell Laboratories, Murray Hill, NJ, MTS, 1986-89; AT&T Bell Labs, SSTC, 1990-94; AT&T Microeletronics, Asia/Pacific, Japan & South America, mgr,

1994-. **Orgs:** Comm mem, Educ Affairs, Amer Soc for Materials; mem, IEEE, American Physical Soc, Natl Technical Assn, Natl Org for the Advancement of Black Chemists & Chemical Engineers; Materials Research Society; member, American Vacuum Society. **Honors/Awds:** NASA-HBCU, NASA, 1989; Black Engineer of the Year, 1989; published and presented over 70 technical papers and seminars; 2 patents awarded and 3 patents pending. **Business Addr:** Member of Technical Staff, Lightwave Service Research Department, AT&T Bell Laboratories, 9999 Hamilton Blvd, 2A-209, Breinigsville, PA 18031.

ATCHISON, CALVIN O.
Business executive. **Personal:** Born Sep 15, 1920, Millry, AL; married Amanda Rosetta McFadden; children: Antoinette, Calvin, II. **Educ:** AL A&M Coll, BS 1944; Columbia Univ, MA 1949; IN Univ, EdD 1958. **Career:** Charlotte City Schools, school psych 1949-53; TN State Univ, assoc prof 1953-58, prof/coord of graduate studies & rsch 1958-64, prof of psych/asst grad dean 1964-67, acting dir rsch & devel 1968-69, devel officer 1969-72, vice pres for rsch planning & devel 1972-; TN State Univ Found, exec dir 1986-. **Orgs:** Mem Amer Psych Assn, Soc for Study of Projective Techniques, Psy Chi, Nashville Mental Health Assn, Better Bus Bureau of Nashville, Metro Nashville Housing & Urban Devel, Council for the Advancement & Study of Educ. **Honors/Awds:** Danforth Teacher 1956-57; Outstanding Educator 1972-73; Administrator of the Year 1985. **Military Serv:** USN Yeoman 2nd Class 1944-46. **Business Addr:** Executive Dir, TN State Univ Foundation, 3500 John Merritt Blvd, Nashville, TN 37202.

ATCHISON, LEON H.
Business executive. **Personal:** Born Feb 27, 1928, Detroit, MI; son of Rosy Lee Atchison and A R Atchison; children: Aleta, Terrance, Erika. **Educ:** MI State Univ, BA 1960; MI State Univ, MA 1962. **Career:** US Congressman John Conyers, admin asst 1965-71; Univ of Detroit, dir urban studies 1971-74, dir of purchasing 1974-75, dir parks & recreation 1975-79; MI Consol Gas Co, dir civic affairs 1979-. **Orgs:** Bd of gov Wayne State Univ State Wide Election 1970-; central business district board of directors 1981; mem Amer Assn of Blacks in Energy; bd of directors, Greater Detroit Chamber of Commerce, 1987-. **Honors/Awds:** Man of the Year Awd Natl Assn Negro Bus & Professional Women's Clubs 1976; Outstanding Serv Awd United Cerebral Palsy Assoc 1978; Testimonial Resolution Outstanding Publ Serv Detroit City Council 1979; Proclamation, Outstanding Publ Serv Mayor City of Detroit 1979. **Military Serv:** USN 3/c petty ofcr 1945-47; Good Conduct Medal, S Pacific Ribbon. **Business Addr:** Dir of Civic Affairs, Michigan Consolidated Gas Co, 500 Griswold Ave, Detroit, MI 48226.

ATCHISON, LILLIAN ELIZABETH
Educator. **Personal:** Born Jan 27, Meridian, MS; daughter of Danella Gardner Hilliard and Robert W Hilliard; married Guy R Atchison, Feb 5, 1948. **Educ:** Harris-Stowe State College, St Louis, MO, BA; Univ of Illinois, Urbana, IL, MA, ed, 1948; Washington Univ, St Louis, MO, BS, 1968; Univ of Illinois, Urbana, IL, MS, library science, 1971. **Career:** St Louis Board of Education, St Louis, MO, teacher, library consultant, 1966-71; University City School District, University City, MO, librarian (K-12), 1972-. **Orgs:** Board member, Sigma Gamma Rho Sorority, Inc, 1963-65; north central secretary, National Assn of Univ Women, 1953-63; leader, Wyoming Trekkers, Girl Scouts of Greater St Louis, 1973-74; board member, MO Assn of School Librarians, 1985-89; Kappa Delta Pi, Univ of Illinois, 1948; Beta Phi Mu, Univ of Illinois, 1972. **Honors/Awds:** Woman of the Year, Greyhound, 1974; Service Certificate Award, MO Assn of School Librarians; Arts Award, Sigma Gamma Rho Sorority, Inc, 1991; Alpha Zeta Chapter, Iota Phi Lambda Sorority, Inc, Apple for the Teacher Award, 1992; Zeta Sigma Chapter, Sigma Gamma Rho Sorority Inc, Community Service Awards, 1996. **Home Addr:** 3924 San Francisco Court, St Louis, MO 63115, (314)383-7338. **Business Phone:** (314)863-1710.

ATKINS, BRENDA J.
Educational administrator. **Personal:** Born Jan 25, 1954, Washington, DC. **Educ:** Loyola Marymount U, BA 1975; Georgetown Univ Law Ctr, JD 1978. **Career:** Georgetown Univ Law Center, asst dean 1978-; White House Office of Couns to the President, law clerk 1977-78; US Dept of Justice Tax Div, law clerk 1977; Lawy Com for Civil Rights Educ Proj, researcher 1976. **Orgs:** Org pan "Corp Divest in S Afr" 1979, "Palest Debate" 1979; mem ABA Sect on Leg Educ & Interntl Law; mem Nat Conf of Black Lawy; mem Nat Bar Assn. **Honors/Awds:** Managing editor, Am Crim Law Review 1977-78; author, US Tax of For & For Tax Art 1980. **Business Addr:** 1070 S LaBrea Ave, Los Angeles, CA 90019.

ATKINS, C. CLYDE
Judge. **Career:** Federal District Court, Miami, FL, judge, currently. **Business Addr:** Judge, Federal District Court, 301 N Miami Ave, Rm 150, Miami, FL 33128-7788, (305)536-5563.

ATKINS, CARL J.
Musician, arts administrator, consultant. **Personal:** Born Jul 4, 1945, Birmingham, AL; son of Kathryn Watson Woods and James Spencer Atkins; married Deborah Little Atkins, May 17, 1981; children: Kathryn-Louise, Leslie Stevens-Atkins Dowdell. **Educ:** Central State College, Wilberforce, OH, 1962-63; Indiana University, Bloomington, IN, BMus, 1967; New England Conservatory, Boston, MA, MMus, 1975; University of Rochester, Eastman School, Rochester, NY, DMus, 1982. **Career:** Amer Natl Opera Co, Boston, MA, orchestra, 1967-68; New England Conservatory Boston, MA, faculty, 1968-78; Hochstein Music School, Rochester, NY, dean, 1979-81; University of Rochester, Rochester, NY, assistant professor, 1981-84; David Hochstein Memorial Music School, Rochester, NY, president, 1984-91; Rochester Philharmonic Orchestra, Inc, president, CEO, 1991-93; Carl Atkins & Assoc, pres, 1993-; Thelonious Monk Inst of Jazz at New England Conservatory, Boston, MA, dir, 1995-. **Orgs:** Member, Amer Federation of Musicians, 1960-; member, College Band Directors National Assn, 1981-; vice president, 1988-, pres, 1991-93, chairman, 1993-95; Natl Guild Comm Schools of the Arts. **Honors/Awds:** Grant for Research, Black Marching Music, NEA, 1977; Conducting Fellowship, Univ of Rochester Eastman School, 1978; Alabama Jazz Hall of Fame, 1984. **Home Addr:** 32 Whites Ave, No 2206, Watertown, MA 02172-4305. **Business Phone:** (617)262-1120.

ATKINS, CAROLYN VAUGHN
Educator. **Personal:** Born Sep 21, 1930, St Louis, MO; daughter of Eva Merritt Vaughn (deceased) and George Louis Vaughn Sr (deceased); divorced. **Educ:** Fisk Univ Nashville, attended; Morgan State Univ Baltimore, BS 1951; So IL Univ Edwardsville, attended; Washington Univ St Louis, MA 1968; Central Missouri State Univ Warrensburg, MS Criminal Justice 1981; St Louis University, public policy, PhD, 1993 analysis and administration. **Career:** Mental Health Center of St Clair Co, counseling psychologist 1968-72; St Louis City Jail, consultant research eval & planning 1972-73; State Correctional Center for Women, supt 1974-76; Div of Corrections, prog specialist, 1976-77, human relations officer, 1977-78; Div of Probation & Parole Interstate Compact Admin, chmn & dir bd of probation & parole 1978-85; Lincoln University, assoc prof, criminal justice; KLUM 98.9 FM, hostess, Criminal Justice Radiogram. **Orgs:** Mem Amer Corrections Assn, MO Corrections Assn Delegate Assmebly, 1990-92, former sec/pres Acme Art & Culture Club 1964-; bd chmn, Wesley Center-Lincoln University; various offices Union Memorial United Meth Ch 1968-80; mem Psi Chi (scholastic hon psychology) So IL Univ 1969; chmn Soc Action Mental Health St Louis Alumnae Chap 1971-74; pres MO Chap Natl Assoc of Blacks in Criminal Justice 1979-80; MO reclamation coord Delta Sigma Theta Sorority 1990, pres Jefferson City Alumni Chapter 1988-90; elected member, Scholarship and Standards, 1991-95; alternate member Child Abuse and Neglect Review Board, State of Missouri 1988; life member NAACP; adviser, Alpha Theta Chapter, Delta Sigma Theta Sorority, 1988-; Institutional Review Bd, Memorial Hospital, Jefferson City, MO. **Honors/Awds:** Sigma Gamma Rho Comm Serv Award St Louis 1977; Comm Serv Award & Distinguished Women's Tea Union Memorial United Meth Ch St Louis 1978; MO Distinguished Citizen Award Union Memorial United Meth Ch 1979. **Business Addr:** Associate Professor, Criminal Justice, Lincoln University, 313 Founders Hall, 820 Chestnut St, Jefferson City, MO 65101, (314)681-5151.

ATKINS, EDMUND E.
City planner. **Personal:** Born Dec 6, 1944, Winston-Salem, NC; married Vera Clayton; children: Damien. **Educ:** Grinnell Coll, BA, 1966; Univ of Oklahoma, MRCP, 1972. **Career:** San Francisco Redev Agency, asst planner, 1969; Oakland Model Cities, chief physical planner, 1970-71; US Dept HUD, urban planner, 1971-74; City of Berkeley, city planner, 1974-. **Orgs:** Assoc mem Amer Inst Planners; vice pres Natl Assn Planners; pres Bay Area chap New Niagra Movement Demo Club; treas Oakland Citizens Comm for Urban Renewal 1976-; mem Alameda Co Human Serv Cncl 1976-; CA Land Use Taks Force; life mem NAACP; vice pres Youth Council. **Military Serv:** US Army, Reserves 1968-74. **Business Addr:** City Planner, City of Berkeley, 2030 Milvia St, Berkeley, CA 94704.

ATKINS, EDNA R.
Attorney. **Personal:** Born Jan 22, 1945, Sicily Island, LA. **Educ:** Univ of Omaha, BA 1967; Creighton Law School, JD 1970. **Career:** Legal Aid Soc of Omaha, Council Bluffs Inc, staff atty 1970-. **Orgs:** Mem NE State Bar Assoc, Natl Bar Assoc, Amer Bar Assoc, Natl Assoc of Black Women Attny, NAACP 1970; gen counsel CARE Prog Inc 1973-. **Business Addr:** Staff Attorney, Legal Aid Soc of Omaha, Council Bluffs Inc, 1613 Farnam St, Omaha, NE 68102.

ATKINS, FREDD
City commissioner. **Personal:** Born Jun 19, 1952, Sarasota, FL; son of Glossie Atkins; married Luethel Chochran Atkins, Oct 1985 (divorced); children: Carol, Nilaja, Amina, Baraka, Dumaka, Zakia. **Educ:** Manatee Junior College, Bradenton, FL, AA, 1979; University of Southern Florida, Sarasota, FL. **Career:** Storefront Newtown Community Center, Sarasota, FL, assistant director, 1982-85; Genus Enterprises, Inc, Sarasota, FL, director of marketing, 1985-87; City of Sarasota, FL, commissioner, 1985-; Central Life Insurance, Tampa, FL, vice president, 1988-89. **Orgs:** Member, National Black Family Foundation; member, National Forum for Black Administrators; member, NAACP, Sarasota chapter; member, Southwest Florida Regional Planning Council; member, Florida League of Cities. **Honors/Awds:** Political Academic Award, Kappa Alpha Psi, 1987; Martin Luther King Award for Service to Youth, 1988; NAACP Achievement Award, 1988; Human Rights and Achievement Award, Interdenominational Ministerial Alliance, 1988. **Home Addr:** 1598 29th St, Sarasota, FL 34234. **Business Addr:** Commissioner, City of Sarasota, PO Box 1058, Sarasota, FL 34230.

ATKINS, HANNAH DIGGS
State official (retired), educator. **Personal:** Born Nov 1, 1923, Winston-Salem, NC; daughter of Mabel Kennedy Diggs and James T Diggs; married Charles N Atkins, May 24, 1943 (deceased); children: Edmund, Valerie, Charles Jr; married Everett P O'Neal, Jun 1993 (deceased). **Educ:** St Augustine's Coll, Raleigh, NC, BS, 1943; Univ of Chicago Graduate Library School, BLS, 1949; Oklahoma City Univ School of Law, 1963-64; Univ of Oklahoma, MPA, 1989; John F Kennedy School of Govt; Harvard Univ, Program for Sr Exec. **Career:** Winston-Salem Journal/Sentinel, reporter, 1945-48; Atkins High School, French teacher, 1945-48; Meharry Med Coll, biochem res asst, 1948-49; Fisk Univ, reference librarian, 1949-50; Kimberly Park Elem School, school librarian, 1950-51; Oklahoma City Public Library, branch librarian, 1953-56; Oklahoma State Library, reference librarian, 1962-63, chief gen ref div & acting law librarian, 1963-68, instructor of library science, 1967-68; Oklahoma City Univ, instructor of law, 1967; Oklahoma State Rep, 1968-80; US delegate to UN, 35th Gen Assembly, 1980; Oklahoma Dept of Human Serv, asst dir, 1983-87; State of Oklahoma, secretary of state/cabinet secretary of human resources, 1987-91; Univ of Central Oklahoma, prof, 1991-92; Oklahoma State University, professor, 1992-93; University of Oklahoma, professor, 1993. **Orgs:** Former exec bd Sunbeam Home & Family Serv, CAP-NAACP; past pres, Visiting Nurses Assn; Govt Comm on Status of Women; bd mem, Women Exec in State Govt; natl bd member, Trans-Africa; past pres, Oklahoma Chapter of the Amer Soc of Public Admin; former bd mem, Natl Amer Civil Liberties Union, Natl Black Child Devel Inst; founder and pres emeritus, Ntu Art Gallery, Oklahoma City; past chairperson, Oklahoma Advisory Comm of the US Commn on Civil Rights; vice pres, Oklahoma City Chapter of People to People; sec, Oklahoma Sister Cities; member, Executive Comm of the Oklahoma Chapter of UN/USA. **Honors/Awds:** Outstanding Woman of the Year, Oklahoma Soroptomist Intl, 1965; Woman of the Year, Theta Sigma Phi, 1968; Outstanding Soror, Natl Founders Serv Award, Alpha Kappa Alpha Midwest Region; Legislative Conference, Rutgers Univ Eagleton Inst of Politics, 1972; Distinguished Serv Award, Natl Links Inc, 1972; Hibler Award for Distinguished Serv, 1973; Finer Womanhood Award, Zeta Phi Beta; Natl Public Citizen, Natl Assn of Social Work, 1975; Oklahoma Woman's Hall of Fame, 1982; Afro-American Hall of Fame of Oklahoma, 1983; scholar, Aspen Inst; Phi Beta Kappa; Doctor of Humane Letters, Benedict College; Hannah Atkins Endowed Chair in Public Service, Oklahoma State Univ, 1990; Phi Beta Kappan of the Year, Oklahoma Chapter, Phi Beta Kappa,1990; Humanitarian Award, Oklahoma Chapter, National Confere of Christians and Jews, 1990; Distinguished Service to State Government Award, National Governor's Assn; Trailblazers Award, OK Historical Society, 1997; Keeper of the Dream, Ebony Tribune, 1997. **Home Addr:** 6006 N Pennsylvania Ave, Oklahoma City, OK 73112.

ATKINS, JAMES
Professional football player. **Personal:** Born Jan 28, 1970, Amite, LA; married Nicole, May 28, 1995. **Educ:** Southwestern Louisiana. **Career:** Seattle Seahawks, tackle, 1994-. **Business Addr:** Professional Football Player, Seattle Seahawks, 11220 NE 53rd St, Kirkland, WA 98033, (206)827-9777.

ATKINS, MARILYN
Judge. **Career:** 36th District Court, judge, currently.

ATKINS, PERVIS
Business executive. **Personal:** Born Nov 24, 1935, Ruston, LA; son of Mattie and Pervis; children: Gerald, Christine, Gregory, Gayle. **Educ:** NM State Univ, BA 1961. **Career:** LA Rams, WA Redskins, Oakland Raiders, professional football player 1961-68; KIIX, TV sports commentator 1962; Southern California Edison Co, industrial psych 1963-66; asst dir for motion pictures for ABC-TV; Artist Career Mgmt, vice pres; Atkins & Associates, owner, currently. **Orgs:** Mem Pop Warner Football League; adv Concensus All Amer Football 1961; Kwanza, advisory board. **Honors/Awds:** Outstanding Citizen Ruston LA 1961; USO Commendation for Meritorious Serv 1971. **Military Serv:** USMC, sgt 1954-57. **Business Addr:** Owner, Atkins & Associates, 303 S Crescent Heights Blvd, Los Angeles, CA 90048.

ATKINS, RICHARD
Company executive, architect. **Personal:** Born Feb 9, 1949, Stephens, AR; son of Clemmine Ferguson and Robert Atkins; married Diane Williams, Sep 1, 1971; children: Gregory, Gary

R. **Educ:** Forest Park Community College, 1968-71; Washington University, 1969-70; Howard University, B Arch, 1975; Lindenwood College, MBA candidate, 1980-82. **Career:** Stotler, Stagg & Associates, engineer technician II, 1972-74; Gordon H Ball, Inc, engineer technician/draftsman, 1974; Itzig Heine Construction, engineer technician/draftsman, 1974-75; Peckham-Guyton, Inc, architect-in-training, 1975-77; J G Randle & Associates, project architect, 1977-78; Environmental Seven, Ltd, office manager, project architect, 1978-80; TDP/St Louis, Inc, president, owner, architect, 1980-. **Orgs:** NCARB Certificate Holder; National Organization Of Minority Architects; 100 Black Men of St Louis, president, 1994-. **Honors/Awds:** St Louis Public Schools, Career Education Plaque, 1987; Society of American Military Engineers, Sustaining Member, 1988; St Louis County Bldg Code Review Committee, 1990; Boy Scouts of America, Chairman, School Night for Scouting, 1991; 100 Black Men, St Louis Chapter, Man of the Year, 1992. **Business Addr:** President, TDP/St Louis, Inc, 3101 Olive St, St Louis, MO 63103-1212, (314)533-1996.

ATKINS, RUSSELL
Author, composer. **Personal:** Born Feb 25, 1926, Cleveland, OH; son of Mamie Belle Kelley Atkins and Perry Kelly. **Educ:** Cleveland Sch of Art, Schlrshp 1943-44; Cleveland Music Sch Settlement, Pri Schlrshp 1943; Cleveland Inst of Music, 1944-45; Private Music Study, 1950-54. **Career:** Free Lance Mag, editor founder 1950-79; Sutphen Sch of Music, asst to dir 1957-60; Karamu House, writing instr 1973-; OH Poets Assn & Natl Endowment for Arts, writer in schools prog 1973-78. **Orgs:** Speaker, consultant OH Humanities Prog 1978; res workshops lectures Colleges & Univ 1963-78; consultant ETV WVIZ Cleveland 1970-72; mem Ltry Adv Panel OH Arts Council 1973-76; mem Intl Platform Assoc 1976-77; trustee Poets League of Greaster Cleveland 1978; writer-in-residence, Cuyahoga Community College 1973; writer-in residence, East Cleveland Public Library, 1979; writer-in-residence, Univ Circle, Inc., Cleveland Bd of Educ, 1988. **Honors/Awds:** Hon doctorate Cleveland State Univ 1976; orig music theory intro Darmstadt Festival of Avant-garde Music, Germany 1956; ind artists fellowship OH Arts Council 1978; coord council of lit mag Grants 1970-77; invited to Bread Loaf Writers Conf 1956; published poetry books Here In The, Cleveland State Univ Press 1976, Heretofore, Breman Publishers, London England, 1968. **Home Addr:** 6005 Grand Ave, Cleveland, OH 44104.

ATKINS, SAM OILLIE
Urologist. **Personal:** Born Aug 5, 1934, Decatur, AL; married Jeanne Cain; children: Courtland, April Melia. **Educ:** Morehouse Coll Atlanta GA, BS 1957; Howard Univ Med Sch Wash DC, MD 1962. **Career:** Atlanta Med Assoc; pres 1978; Hughes Spalding Comm Hosp, pres med staff 1981-82; GA St Med Assoc, pres elect 1984-86; SW Atlanta Urology Assoc, urologist. **Orgs:** Mem bd of dir Woodward Academy Coll GA 1985-88, Med Assoc of Atlanta; mem adv bd Morehouse Med School; consult Atlanta Southside Comprehnsion Health Ctr; mem Morehouse Coll Alumnae Assoc; mem Alpha Phi Alpha; elder West End Pres Church. **Honors/Awds:** 2nd place winner GA partners Exchange Prog Recife, Raz 1975; listed Outstanding Atlantans 1978-79; Unhearld Citizen Atlanta Omega Chap of Y's Men Intl 1980; Phys of Year Atlanta Med Assoc 1982. **Military Serv:** Army colonel, res 1981- 3 yrs. **Home Addr:** 1021 Flamingo Dr S W, Atlanta, GA 30311.

ATKINS, THOMAS IRVING
Attorney. **Personal:** Born Mar 2, 1939, Elkhart, IN; son of Rev & Mrs N P Atkins; married Sharon Annette Soash (divorced); children: Todd, Thomas Jr, Trena. **Educ:** Indiana Univ, BA 1961; Harvard Univ, MA 1963; Harvard Law School, JD 1969. **Career:** Boston NAACP, exec secretary 1963-65; Boston City Council, Boston city councilman 1968-71; Exec Office Communities & Dev (Governor's Cabinet), secretary 1971-75; NAACP, general counsel 1980-84; attorney, private practice, currently. **Orgs:** ABA; Natl Bar Assn; Massachusetts Bar Assn; bd of dir, Public Broadcasting Serv 1972-74; vice chmn, Federal Reserve Bank of Boston 1980-85; Harvard University, board of overseers. **Honors/Awds:** Honorary PhD Northeastern Univ 1974; Honorary LLD New England School of Law 1982. **Business Addr:** Attorney, 135 Eastern Parkway, #11-B-1, Brooklyn, NY 11238.

ATKINSON, CURTIS L.
State official. **Personal:** Born Sep 12, 1934, Brunswick, GA; son of Mr & Mrs Israel Atkinson; married Dr Melvis Evans. **Educ:** Howard Univ, 1953-54; Fort Valley State Coll, BS 1956; Columbia Univ, 1969. **Career:** Teacher, 1956-69; US Senate, staff 1969-80; State of Georgia, assistant Secretary of State, currently. **Orgs:** Exec comm, Georgia Special Olympics, 1984-85; bd of dir, Georgia Alliance for Children, 1980-; bd of dir, Southeast Regional/SERO/NSSFNS, 1980-; chmn/sec, State's Economic Develop Task Force, 1983-; bd of dir, Fort Valley St Coll Foundation, 1983-; trustee/bd, CME Church; Eta Lambda/Alpha Phi Alpha. **Honors/Awds:** Roy Wilkins Award, Georgia NAACP, 1983; Public Serv Award, Alpha Phi Alpha, 1983; Outstanding Georgian, Fort Valley State Coll, 1984; Community Serv Award, Georgia Council of Deliberation, 1984; Res, Georgia House of Rep, 1983; Res, Georgia State Sen, 1983; City of Atlanta Proc, 1983; Hon from Georgia Young Farmers Assn, 1985; Leadership Award, Metro Atlanta Chap, FVSC Natl Alumni Assn, 1985; Political Leadership Award, Bronner Bros Intl, 1984. **Military Serv:** US Army, 1st Lt, 1951-53. **Business Addr:** Assistant Secretary of State, State of Georgia, State Capitol, Rm 214, Atlanta, GA 30334.

ATKINSON, EUGENIA CALWISE
Administration director. **Personal:** Born Jan 16, 1943, Laurens, SC; married Richard W Atkinson; children: Najuma, W Omari, Akilah, Jamila. **Educ:** Youngstown State Univ, ABA 1971; Hiram College, BA, 1989. **Career:** Hon Natlaniel R Jones Judge US Dist Court, sec 1960-63; Youngstown Sheet Tube Co, suprv sec-steno pool 1969-74; Youngstown Area Com Action Council, admin asst 1974-76, dir WIC prog 1976-79; Western Reserve Transit Auth, pres bd of trustees 1979-; Youngstown Civil Service Comm, chairman; Metro Housing Authority, director of admin, currently. **Orgs:** Youngstown State University, board of trustees, 1989; Ohio MLK Holiday Commission; Scholarship com chmn Youngstown Chap OH Black Womens Leadership Caucus 1977-80; pres YWCA 1981-81; Leadership Warren-Youngstown Alumni Assn; Yo Alumnae Chapter Dqlta Sigma Theta; Natl Afro-Amer Mus Plng Council 1978-80; bd trustee Career Devel Ctr for Women 1979-80; mem Youth Area Urban league, NAACP. **Honors/Awds:** Dedication Commitment Awd Freedom Inc Youngstown OH 1972; Outstanding Admin Performance OH Dept of Health Cols OH 1978; Downtown Improvement Com Serv Youngstown Bd of Trade 1980. **Business Addr:** Director Administration, Metro Housing Authority, 131 W Boardman St, Youngstown, OH 44504.

ATKINSON, GLADYS WHITTED
Government official. **Personal:** Born Dec 8, 1932, Durham, NC; daughter of Gwynetta Riley Whitted and Edmond R Whitted Sr; married Charles N Atkinson (divorced); children: Milan Lucas, Joseph Lucas, Gwynetta Lucas, Allen E Lucas Jr, Cedric Lucas, Lisa, Patrick, Gregory, Cheryl. **Educ:** Attended, Univ of DC 1969, Catholic Univ 1970-71, Department of Agriculture Graduate School, 1970-74. **Career:** US Dept of Agriculture, purchasing agent 1973-77; Natl Inst of Health, supervisory purchasing agent 1977-79; Celebrity Fashion Jewels, regional mgr 1971-81; Atkinson Builders Const Co, vice pres 1981-; Natl Insts of Health, small and disadvantaged business specialist 1979-. **Orgs:** Chairperson NBL Council of Women Business Owners 1984-; bd mem Black Business Alliance Baltimore 1984-; bd mem Natl Business League 1984-; bd mem Charlene Drew Jarvis Council for Women Business Owners Washington DC 1985-; bd mem Divas Foundation 1986-, Minority Business Adv Bd Port Amer MD 1986-; fund raising chairperson, National Assn of Black Procurement Officials 1989. **Honors/Awds:** US Public Health Serv NIH Directors Awd 1983; President Reagan's Outstanding Business Woman Awd 1983; Outstanding Professional and Business Woman Awd Black Business Alliance 1985; Outstanding Serv Awd Blacks in Govt NIH Chap 1986; Superior Performance, NIH 1984; Outstanding Performance, Small Business Administration 1989; Awd of Excellence, NBL Montgomery County, Maryland, 1992; Outstanding Contribution National Association Asian Professional Women, 1992. **Home Addr:** 5655 Columbia Road #203, Columbia, MD 21044.

ATKINSON, LEWIS K.
Physician. **Personal:** Born Nov 3, 1924, Georgetown, SC; married Theresa C; children: 6. **Educ:** Howard Univ, BA 1950, MD 1956. **Career:** WA Hospital Center, attending physician; Howard Univ Hospital, attending physician, instr med 1961-; Private practice, physician. **Orgs:** Mem Med Staff SE Comm Hosp, Natl Med Assoc, Medico-Chirurgical Soc of DC, Amer Soc of Internal Med, So Med Assoc, Howard Univ Med Alumni Assoc, Daniel Hale Williams Reading Club, Natl Symphony Assoc, of Wash DC, Diabetes Assoc, DC Med Soc, NAACP, Friends Museum African Arts, Urban League, Endocrine Society. **Military Serv:** US Army, s/sgt 1943-46. **Business Addr:** 5505 5 St NW, Ste 301, Washington, DC 20011.

ATKINSON, REGINA ELIZABETH
Social worker. **Personal:** Born May 13, 1952, New Haven, CT; daughter of Virginia Louise Atkinson Griffin and Samuel Griffin. **Educ:** Univ of CT, BA 1974; Atlanta Univ, MSW 1978. **Career:** Pal Beach Co Health Dept, medical social worker 1978-81; Glades General Hosp, dir social services; Palm Beach County Community Services-Senior Svcs, case manager, currently. **Orgs:** Mem AHA Soc for Hospital Soc Work Directors, Comm Action Council, Florida Public Health Assn Inc, Glades Area Assn for Retarded Citizens, Natl Assn of Black Social Workers Inc, Natl Assn of Social Workers Inc, The Florida Assn for Health and Social Serv, The Natl Chamber of Commerce for Women Inc, National Association for Female Executives, Area Agency on Aging Advisory Council, NAACP. **Honors/Awds:** American Legion Awd; Whitney Young Fellowship; DHEW Public Health Serv Scholarship. **Home Addr:** 525 1/2 SW 10th St, Belle Glade, FL 33430. **Business Addr:** Case Manager, Palm Beach County Community Services- Senior Services, 2916 State Rd 15, Belle Glade, FL 33430.

ATLAS, JOHN WESLEY
Educator. **Personal:** Born Aug 15, 1941, Lake Providence, LA; married Arthurlean Johnson; children: Mavis, Candace, Jamila, Amina. **Educ:** Grambling Coll, BS 1963; Wayne State Univ, MEd 1968, EdD 1972. **Career:** LA Schools, music teacher 1963-65; Detroit Public Schools, music teacher 1965-67, guidance counselor 1967-70, asst prin 1970-72; Gov State Univ, prof 1972-73; Oakland Univ, assoc prof 1973-. **Orgs:** Mem Amer Personnel & Guidance Assn; mem Assn for Non-White Concerns in Personnel & Guidance; mem Omega Psi Phi Frat; Topical Conf on Career Educ for Handicapped Indiv 1979. **Honors/Awds:** Publ "Consulting, Affecting Change for Minority Students" Jour of Non-White Concerns in Pers & Guidance Wash, DC 1975; publ "Effects of Crystal & Bolles on Vocational Choice" Jour of Emp Counsel Wash, DC 1977; publ "Career Planning Need of Unemployed Minority Persons" Jour of Emp Counseling Wash, DC 1978; book chap "The Role of Counseling & Guidance in Facilitating Career Educ Needs of Handicapped". **Business Addr:** Associate Professor, Oakland Univ, Sch of Human & Educ Serv, Rochester, MI 48309.

ATTAWAY, JOHN DAVID
Educator. **Personal:** Born Jan 30, 1929, Chicago, IL; son of Pearl Holloway Attaway and Allen Attaway Sr; married Paquita Anna Harris. **Educ:** Central State College, BS, 1950; Babson College, MBA, 1956; George Washington University, DBA, 1979. **Career:** US Dept of Commerce, Secretary's Staff, policy analyst, 1970-72; US General Svcs Administration, Office of Civil Rights, executive director, 1973; US Dept of Labor OFCCP, chief policy & procedures, 1984; University of District Columbia, Dept of Business Management, professor, 1984-97; Univ of MD Univ College, professor, 1997-. **Orgs:** President, Attaway Associates, 1978-; chairman, The Dr Chester E Harris Medical Student Fund Inc, 1978-; Sigma Pi Phi, Epsilon Boule, 1985-; Kappa Alpha Psi, 1948-. **Honors/Awds:** Grass Roots Award, Outstanding Civic Work, DC Federation of Civic Assns Inc, 1970; Public Service Award, General Service Administrator, 1976. **Military Serv:** US Army, battalion commander, 3rd Armored Division. **Home Addr:** 3127 Appleton St NW, Washington, DC 20008. **Business Phone:** (301)282-3718.

ATTLES, ALVIN
Sports manager. **Personal:** Born in Newark, NJ; married Wilhemina Rice; children: Alvin III, Erica. **Educ:** NC A&T. **Career:** Golden State Warriors, guard, coach, beginning 1970, general mgr, 1983-89. **Honors/Awds:** Warriors' all-time winningest coach; NBA Championship (1974-75); two division titles (1974-75 & 1975-76); league's best record in 1975-76 (59-26); twice coached the NBA All-Star Western Conf team 1975-76; his 555-516 (518) coaching mark places him sixth among all-time winningest NBA coaches and last season he joined Red Auerbach, Red Holzman, Jack Ramsey, Gene Shue and Dick Motta as the only mentors to coach in 1,000 NBA contests.

ATWATER, STEPHEN DENNIS
Professional football player. **Personal:** Born Oct 28, 1966, Chicago, IL; married Letha; children: Stephen Jr., DiAndre, Paris. **Educ:** Univ of Arkansas, BS, business admin, 1989. **Career:** Denver Broncos, safety, 1989-. **Honors/Awds:** Pro Bowl, 1990-96. **Special Achievements:** Super Bowl championship, 1998. **Business Addr:** Professional Football Player, Denver Broncos, 13655 Broncos Pkwy, Englewood, CO 80112, (303)649-9000.

AUBERT, ALVIN BERNARD
Educator (retired), poet, editor. **Personal:** Born Mar 12, 1930, Lutcher, LA; son of Lucille Roussel Aubert and Albert Aubert; married Bernadine; children: Stephenie, Miriam, Deborah. **Educ:** Southern Univ, BA 1959; Univ of MI, MA 1960. **Career:** Southern Univ, prof 1960-70; Univ of OR, prof, summer 1970; State Univ of NY, prof 1970-79; Wayne State Univ, prof 1979-92, professor Emeritus of English, 1992-. **Orgs:** Book rvr Libr Journ 1972-74; eval NY State Poets in Schls 1974; adv ed Drama & Thr Mag 1973-75; adv ed Black Box 1974-; adv ed Gumbo 1976-78; advised Collaloo 1977-; ed & pub Obsidian, Black Literature in Review 1975-85; mem College Lang Assn; bd of dir Coord Councl for Literary Magazines 1983-86; Black Theatre Network. **Honors/Awds:** Undergrad Liberal Arts Schlrshp 1957-59; Woodrow Wilson Flwshp 1959-60; Schlrshp Bread Loaf Writers Conf 1968; Natl Endowment for the Arts Creative Writing Flwshp Grant 1973, 1981; CCLM Editors Flwshp 1979; poetry books, "Against the Blues" 1972; "Feeling Through" 1975; "New and Selected Poems" 1985; "If Winter Comes: Collected Poems" 1994; "Harlem Wrestler" 1995; play "Home From Harlem," 1986; "Piney Brown" 1996; listed Broadside Authors & Artists; A Directory of Amer Poets; Black Amer Writers Past & Present; Contemporary Poets of the English Lang; The Callaloo Award, Callaloo Magazine, 1988. **Home Addr:** 18234 Parkside Ave, Detroit, MI 48221, (313)345-4790.

AUBESPIN, MERVIN R.
Journalist. **Personal:** Born Jun 30, 1937, Opelousas, LA; son of Blanche Sittig Earsery and Henry Aubespin; divorced; children: Eleska. **Educ:** Tuskegee Inst, BS 1958; IN State Univ, postgrad 1960; Columbia Univ, Spec Minority 1972; Univ of Louisville (KY), postgrad work 1973. **Career:** Courier Jrnl &

Louisville Times, 1st black staff artist 1965-72; Courier Jrnl, reporter 1972-84; Courier Jrnl & Louisville Times, dir of minority recruitment, spec asst to exec editor; The Courier-Journal Newspapers, assoc editor development; Natl Assoc of Black Journalists, pres 1983-85. **Orgs:** Pres, founder Louisville Assoc of Black Comm 1979-80; dir reg 5 Natl Assoc of Black Jrnlst 1979-81; mem Bd of Overseers Bellarmine Coll 1980-81; vice pres Natl Assoc of Black Jrnlst 1981-83; pres Natl Assoc of Black Jrnlst 1983-; mem Minorities Comm Amer Soc of Newspaper Ed 1985; chair Minorities Comm & Human Resource Comm, The Amer Soc & Newspaper Editors; co-chmn Industry Wide Minority Issues Steering Comm 1985-; chmn Ida B Wells Jury 1986-88; Mid America Press Inst, bd mem, 1995; School of Journalism, Howard Univ, Univ of KY, Western KY Univ, bd of advisors; Black Coll Communication Assn, advisory bd. **Honors/Awds:** Leadership Awd West End Catholic Council 1970; Unity Awd Econ Reporting Lincoln Univ 1980; Outstanding Achievement Awd Louisville Branch Natl Assoc of Black Jrnlst 1980; Louisville Man of the Year Awd Louisville Defender Newspaper 1980; Unity Awd Civil Rights Reporting Lincoln Univ 1981; Outstanding Achievement Awd Natl Assn of Black Journalists 1981; Achievement Awd NAACP 1981; Spec Achievement Awd Reporting on the Concerns of Blacks; Leadership Awd Louisville Assoc of Black Communicators 1981; Meritorious Serv Awd Southern Reg Press Inst 1985; Disting Serv Award Inst for Journalism Educ 1985; Recp Mary HDunn Lecturship Univ of IL; Ida B Wells Award, Natl Assn of Black Journalists, 1990; Distinguished Service Award, Assn of Schools of Journalism & Mass Communications, 1991; First Recipient of Mervin Aubespin Award, Black Coll Comm Assn, 1991; Natl Assn of Black Journalist Region VI, Hall of Fame, 1994; E Kentucky Journalism, Hall of Fame, 1995. **Military Serv:** AUS E-4 2 yrs. **Home Addr:** 733 Southwestern Parkway, Louisville, KY 40211. **Business Addr:** Associate Editor, Louisville Courier-Jnl Nwspapr, 525 W Broadway, Louisville, KY 40202.

AUDAIN, LINZ
Educator, attorney, economist, physician. **Personal:** Born Jul 13, 1959, Port-au-Prince, Haiti; son of Georgette Nicoleau Audain and Fenelon B Audain. **Educ:** Southern College, BA, 1979; University of Miami, MBA/MA, 1981; Florida International University, MSM, 1982; University of Chicago, JD, 1987; Duke University, PhD, 1991; Howard University, MD, 1997. **Career:** Various universities, part-time instructor of economics, 1981-86; Hartunian, Futterman & Howard, attorney/associate, 1987-88; Loyola University of Chicago, instructor of economics, 1988-89; Washington College of Law, The American University, assistant/associate professor of law, 1989-95; The Mandate Corporation, CEO, 1992-. **Orgs:** American Bar Association; Illinois Bar Association; National Bar Association; Hispanic National Bar Association; Law & Society Association; American Economics Association; American Society for Law & Medicine; Radio & TV News Director Association; American Law & Economics Association; American Medical Association; Nation Medical Association. **Honors/Awds:** Cocaine Use as an Abdominal Pregnancy Risk Factor, Journal of Nat'l Med Assn forthcoming; Gender and Trauma in the Near-Death Experience: an Epidemiological and Theoretical Analysis, Journal of Near-Death Studies forthcoming; NDE's and a Theory of the Extraneuronal Hyperspace, Journal of Near-Death Studies forthcoming. CLS, Feminism, L & Ec and the Veil of Intellectual Tolerance, Hofstra Law Review; The Economics of Law-Related Labor vs Judicial Careers, American University Law Review, 1992; Of Posner & Newton & Twenty-First Century Laws: an Economic, Loyola Law Review, 1990; Critical Cultural Law & Economics, Indiana Law Journal, 1995; Professor of the Year, American Univ, 1995. **Business Addr:** The Mandate Corp, Ste 252, 4410 Massachusetts Ave, NW, Washington, DC 20016, (202)828-3054.

AUGMON, STACEY ORLANDO
Professional basketball player. **Personal:** Born Aug 1, 1968, Pasadena, CA; son of Vernett. **Educ:** University of Nevada at Las Vegas. **Career:** Atlanta Hawks, forward, 1991-96; Detroit Pistons, 1996; Portland Blazers, 1996-. **Honors/Awds:** Olympic Games, Bronze Medal, US Basketball Team, 1988; NBA All-Rookie first team, 1992. **Special Achievements:** NBA Draft, First round pick, #9, 1991. **Business Addr:** Professional Basketball Player, Portland TrailBlazers, 1 Center Court, Ste 200, Portland, OR 97227, (503)234-9291.

AUGUSTINE, MATTHEW
Company executive. **Career:** Eltrex Industries, CEO, currently. **Special Achievements:** Company is ranked #95 on Black Enterprise's list of Top 100 Industrial/Service Companies, 1993. **Business Addr:** CEO/President, Eltrex Industries, 8 Cairn St, Rochester, NY 14611, (716)464-6260.

AUGUSTUS, FRANKLIN J. P.
Aerobatic air show pilot. **Personal:** Born Mar 6, 1950, New Orleans, LA; son of Annie Cooper Augustus and Henry Augustus, Jr; children: Brandi Augustus. **Educ:** North Carolina State Univ; AUS, Military Police, MPI, CID Narcotic Agent; NCSBI Schools & Conferences. **Career:** Terrebonne Parish Sheriff's Office, reserve deputy, instructor in acad; New Orleans Recreation Dept, LA, head of martial arts dept; Franklin JP Augustus Detective Agency Inc, New Orleans, LA, pres; Orleans Parish Civil Sheriff's Office, reserve duty; Super Air Shows Intl Inc, New Orleans, LA, pres. **Orgs:** Pres, Black Wing Pilots Assn; mem, Experimental Aircraft Assn, New Orleans and Slidell Area Chapters of the Experimental Aircraft Assn, Negro Airmen Intl, Intl Aerobatic Club, Intl Council of Air Shows; charter mem, Cajun Chapter #72 of the Intl Aerobatic Club, Crescent City Aviators; accident prevention counselor, FAA, 1985-. **Honors/Awds:** Aerobatic license, FAA Unlimited Low Level; private license earned 1977; commercial license earned 1978; flight instructor certificate, 1979; certified in scuba, NOSD School, 1977-; Master of Martial Arts; movie stuntman; logged over 8000 flight hours. **Military Serv:** AUS, sergeant. **Business Addr:** Pres, Super Air Shows Intl Inc, PO Box 50181, New Orleans, LA 70115.

AULD, ALBERT MICHAEL
Artist. **Personal:** Born Aug 15, 1943, Kingston, Jamaica; married Rose A; children: Ian, Alexei, Kiros. **Educ:** Howard U, BFA 1962-66, MFA 1978-80. **Career:** Lindo, Norman, Craig & Kummel, designer illustrator 1966-67; Natl Ed Assoc, designer illustrator 1967-73; USDA Graduate School, instructor 1967- Sidwell Friends School, art teacher 1973-77; Dept of Art, Howard Univ, lecturer 1977-82; Duke Ellington School of the Arts, instructor 1982-. **Orgs:** Co-founder dir A & B Assoc Adv 1973-79; co-fndr dir Opus 2 Gallery 1973-77; writer illstrtr for self-syndicated published comic strip 1967-72; freelance Ill designer The Design Co 1977-; cultural chm Caribbean Am Intercutl Org 1975-79; mem Africobra Natl Artists Coop 1977-; mem Intl Sculpture Conf 1983-; mem Natl Art Edctrs Assoc 1984-; mem Artists Equity, Natl Conf of Artists 1986-; mem bd of dirs Fondo del Sol Museum & Cultural Ctr 1986-; Humanities Bd of Fondo del Sol Museum, Wash DC, chairman; Visual Arts Dept, Duke Ellington School of the Arts, past chairman. **Honors/Awds:** Folkloric Article titled Ananesem pub in the Jamarca Journal 1983; article on Africobra Artists Black Collegian 1967-; exhibited widely as a sculptor 1967-; lectured on African Retentions in the Americas Oberlin, Smithsonian Inst, Natl Conf of Artists, NY Univ, Bronx Museum, NBCHs Tony Brown at Daybreak, local & overseas radio networks. **Home Addr:** 1519 Monroe St N W, Washington, DC 20010.

AUSBROOKS, BETH NELSON
Educator. **Personal:** Born May 18, 1930, Philadelphia, PA; daughter of Phoebe Novotny Nelson and David Nelson; children: Dawna Rogers, Gregory Rogers. **Educ:** Howard Univ, Washington, DC, BA, 1952, MA, 1956, PhD, 1971. **Career:** Howard Univ, Washington, DC, associate professor, 1971-72; Univ of N Carolina, Chapel Hill, assoc prof, 1972-74; Univ of Maryland, Baltimore, MD, assoc professor, 1974-75; Univ of District of Columbia, Washington, DC, professor, 1975-. **Orgs:** American Political Science Organization; Council of University Institution of Urban Affairs; American Sociological Association; National Conference of Black Political Scientists, UDC Chapter, Phi Delta Kappa; resident advisory board, District of Columbia Dept of Housing, 1987-; board of directors, Provident Hospital, Baltimore, MD, 1980-83; minority group review committee, National Institute of Mental Health, 1975-79. **Honors/Awds:** Scholar-In-Residence, Fanon Research Center, Martin Luther King Medical School, Los Angeles, CA, 1983. **Business Addr:** Professor, Urban Studies, Univ of the District of Columbia, 4200 Conn Ave, NW, Bldg 48, Room 7204, Washington, DC 20008.

AUSBY, ELLSWORTH AUGUSTUS
Artist, educator. **Personal:** Born Apr 5, 1942, Portsmouth, VA; married Jemillah; children: Amber, Andra, Dawn, Kalif. **Educ:** Pratt Inst, 1960-61; School of Visual Art, BFA 1965. **Career:** School of Visual Arts, instr. **Honors/Awds:** One man shows, Cinque Gallery 1970, Artist House 1973, Soho Ctr for Visual Arts 1975; crit reviews, "Art in Amer", "Barbra Rose", 1970, "Henri Ghent" 1974, "Black Creations" 1972, "The School Weekly News by April Kingsley" 1975, "The Aldrich Museum of Contemp Art, Carles Dyer Dir", "The Soho Weekly News by April Kingsley" 1975; Amer Rep at "FESTAC" 2nd world Black Arts & Cult Festival Lagos Nigeria 1977; Fed Artist Grant CETA Title VI 1978; "Rock Paper Scissors" Port of Auth Publ Works Proj, "Space Odyssey" mural Howard Johnsons Queens Village NY 1980; CAPS Fellowship for Painting NYS Council on the Arts 1980; Exhibit the US Mission to the United Nations 1978; "Universal Units" exhibition at the Afro-Amer Hist & Cultural Mus Philadelphia 1979; "Afro-Amer Abstraction," Long Island NY. **Business Addr:** Instructor, School of Visual Arts, PO Box 15, Brooklyn, NY 11211.

AUSTIN, BOBBY WILLIAM
Educational administrator, author. **Personal:** Born Dec 29, 1944, Bowling Green, KY; son of Mary E Austin and HH Austin Sr; married Joy L Ford; children: Sushama Meredith Cleva, Julian Sanjay Ford, Leah Mary Sajova, Aviana Joy Lalita. **Educ:** Western Kentucky Univ, BA 1966; Fisk Univ, MA 1968; McMaster Univ, PhD 1972; Harvard Univ, Diploma 1986. **Career:** Univ of DC, exec asst to the pres; Georgetown Univ, asst prof 1971-72; Dept of Soc Georgetown summer term, chmn 1972; The Urban League Review Natl Urban League, editor; UDC Bd Vis Team Creative Prod Black Amer Folklore NETA-WASH PBS, pol spec & spec asst; pres Austin & Assoc. **Orgs:** Mem Natl Council for Accrdttn of Tchr Edn; mem Amer Soc Assn; Groves Conf on Marriage & the Family; Alpha Phi Alpha Frat; Natl Cong of Black Professionals; mem VOICE Inc; mem Alphi Phi Omega Natl Serv Fraternity; Peoples Congregational Church; Hannover Project, Germany; Academic Council on the UN Systems; Global Co-Operation for a Better World; UN Assn, DC Chapter. **Honors/Awds:** Author of numerous publications; paper presented at the Assn for the Study of Afro-Amer Life & History New York, 1973; Smithsonian Inst 1976; published Natl Black Opinion ACRA Inc 1977; Kellogg Natl Fellow.

AUSTIN, CARRIE
City official. **Personal:** married Lemuel Austin (died 1994); children: Six. **Career:** Worked on the staffs of state Rep Nelson Rice and 34th ward Democratic committeeman Wilson Frost; US Rep Mel Reynolds, deputy district director of the second Congressional district; City of Chicago, alderman, 34th ward, 1994-. **Business Addr:** Alderman 34th Ward, City of Chicago, 507 W 111th St, Chicago, IL 60628, (312)988-6961.

AUSTIN, DALLAS
Recording co. executive. **Career:** Rowdy Records, pres/CEO, currently. **Special Achievements:** Wrote and produced the following: TLC's "Creep," Madonna's "Secret," Monica's "Don't Take It Personal.".

AUSTIN, ERNEST AUGUSTUS
Physician (retired), educator, health services administrator. **Personal:** Born Nov 26, 1932, Brooklyn, NY; son of Elrica Mildred Davidson Austin and Augustin Austin; married Margaret P Byrd, Aug 24, 1957; children: Vivian, Jean, Alan. **Educ:** St Johns Univ, BS 1953; Howard Univ, MD 1957. **Career:** SUNY, clinical instr surg 1962-69; Fordham Hosp, chief surg 1966-69; Bowman Gray School of Med, asst prof surg 1969-72; Reynolds Meml Hosp, dir of surg 1969-72; Univ of MD School of Med, asst prof surg 1972-79; Provident Hosp, chief of surg 1972-73; Univ of MD Inst for Emerg Med Shock Traum Ctr, chief of surg & traumatology 1974-76, 1978-79; Univ of MD Hosp, dir emergency serv 1977-78; Cooper Med Ctr Camden NJ, chief of traumatology, dir emergency med serv 1979-84; CMDNJ-Rutgers Med School, assoc prof of surgery 1979-84; Prudential Insurance, Horsham, PA, director of medical services, 1989-92, 1994-97; Intracorp, Plymouth Meeting, PA, senior physician advisor, 1992-93. **Orgs:** Founding mem Amer Trauma soc; bd of dir Amer Cancer Soc Forsyth Unit NC; bd dir Natl Found Forsyth-Stokes Chap NC; bd dir Amer Trauma Soc MD Chapt; diplomate Amer Bd of Surg; fellow Amer Coll of Surgeons. **Honors/Awds:** Z Smith Reynolds Found Grant; publ 2 articles in Jrnl of Royal Coll of Surgeons 1975; publ Critical Care Med Jrnl 1979; editorial bd, "Trauma: Clinical Update for Surgeons" Vol 2 1983-86; visiting professor/lecturer at numerous universities & hospitals in US and Canada; "Thoracic Injuries," Camden County Medical Society Bulletin 1982; "Left Atrial Rupture Secondary to Blast Injury," Journal Medical Society of NJ 1985; author and publisher, The Black Amer Stamp Album 1988. **Home Addr:** 3 Hunters Dr, Cherry Hill, NJ 08003.

AUSTIN, ISAAC EDWARD
Professional basketball player. **Personal:** Born Aug 18, 1969, Gridley, CA; married Denise, Dec 24, 1992. **Educ:** Kings River, CA; Arizona State University. **Career:** Utah Jazz, center, 1991-93; Philadelphia 76ers, 1993-96; Miami Heat, 1996-98; Los Angeles Clippers, 1998-. **Business Addr:** Professional Basketball Player, Los Angeles Clippers, 3939 S Figueroa St, Los Angeles Sports Arena, Los Angeles, CA 90037, (213)748-8000.

AUSTIN, JAMES P.
Business executive, appointed official. **Personal:** Born Apr 6, 1900, Jasper, TX; married Teresa Colvin. **Educ:** FL A&M Univ, BS Voc Ed 1947; Amer-Gentlemens Designing School, Cert 1948; Mortgage Bankers Assn of Southwest FL, Cert 1962; Univ of Tampa FL, Cert 1964. **Career:** Austins Tayloring & Clothing, owner/oper 1948-52, 1968-75; Mid-FL Minority Contractors Assn, exec dir 1975-81; JP Austins Real Estate Co, re broker 1981-83; Polk Econ Devel Corp Inc, exec dir 1983-. **Orgs:** Pres NAACP 1954-; commander Amer Legion Post 213 1958-60; treas United Minority Contractors Assn 1975-81; bd chmn Polk Cty Oppty Council Inc 1980-82; bd mem Central FL Reg Planning Council 1982-83; treas FL Fed of CDC 1983-; bd mem FL Small Cities CDBG Adv Bd 1984-. **Honors/Awds:** Loyalty & Dedication NAACP 1968-84; Mary Wolds Case Emperial 25 Club 1979; Citizen of the Year Polk Cty Law Enforcement Assn 1979; commiss City of Lake Wales 1981; vice mayor City of Lake Wales 1984-. **Military Serv:** AUS sgt 3 yrs; Good Conduct, Sharpshooter 1943. **Home Addr:** 602 N Ave, Lake Wales, FL 33853.

AUSTIN, JANYTH YVONNE
Telecommunications company executive. **Personal:** Born Oct 29, 1958, Chicago, IL; daughter of Velmateen Gakins Austin and Willie Austin (deceased). **Educ:** Northwestern Univ, BSIE 1980; IL Inst of Tech, MBA 1986. **Career:** G D Searle & Co, engineering trainee 1977-79; IBT, engr distr serv 1980-83, engr

network planning 1983-84, asst mgr capital recovery 1984-88, product manager, starting 1988; Ameritech Services, Inc, product manager, currently. **Orgs:** Mem Alpha Kappa Alpha 1977-, Inroads Alumni Assn 1980-; mem, bd of dir Inez Harris Scholarship Program, 1984-; asst treasurer Natl Tech Assn 1985-87; treasurer 1987-89, asst secretary 1990-, Chicago Chapter of the Natl Technical Assn; member, bd of directors, Merit Music Program, 1991-. **Honors/Awds:** Up & Coming Black Business & Professional Woman, Dollars & Sense Magazine, 1986. **Business Addr:** Product Mgr, BellSouth Business Systems, Inc., 675 W Peachtree St NE, Fl 28A55, Atlanta, GA 30375.

AUSTIN, JOYCE PHILLIPS
Attorney (retired), church administrator. **Personal:** Born Sep 10, 1923, New York, NY; daughter of Kathleen Miller Phillips and Fitzgerald Phillips; married Rodman W Austin, Mar 20, 1945 (deceased). **Educ:** Hunter College, BA, 1943; Fordham University School of Law, JD, 1945. **Career:** Office of Price Stabilization, attorney advisor, 1951-53; New York State Department of Commerce, executive secretary, Women's Council, 1956-57, assistant deputy commissioner, 1957-59; City of New York, assistant to the mayor, 1959-65; Office of Economic Opportunity, executive assistant to regional director, 1966-68; Sheltering Arms Children's Service, assistant director, 1968-75; Federation of Protestant Welfare Agencies Inc, executive vp, 1975-86. **Orgs:** The Executive Council, Episcopal Church of the United States, 1988-; The General Theological Seminary, trustee; Hunter College School of Social Work, council of advisors; American Bar Association; New York Count Lawyers Association; Fordham Law Alumni Association; NAACP; National Council of Negro Women; Union of Black Episcopalians; The Cosmopolitan Club; The National Arts Club. **Honors/Awds:** Episcopal Diocese of New York, The Bishop's Cross, 1983; Federation of Protestant Welfare Agencies, The Keystone Award, 1986; Hunter College Hall of Fame; The City College (CUNY), The John H Finley Award of the Associate Alumni. **Home Addr:** 510 East 23rd St, New York, NY 10010, (212)674-2903.

AUSTIN, LUCIUS STANLEY
Newspaper editor. **Personal:** Born Jul 3, 1960, Batesville, MS; son of Glennie V Austin Cox and Sherman E Austin Sr (deceased); married Laurie Scott Austin, May 25, 1991; children: Rebekah Hope, Joshua T S. **Educ:** Memphis State Univ, BA, journalism, 1982. **Career:** The Belleville News Democrat, reporter, 1983-84; The St Louis American, city editor, 1984-85; The Kansas City Times, copy editor, 1985-86, makeup editor, 1986-87; The Kansas City Star, assistant bus editor, 1987-. **Orgs:** Alpha Phi Alpha Fraternity Inc, 1980-; Natl Assn of Black Journalist, 1983-; Kansas City Assn of Black Journalist, 1985-; Society of American Bus Editors & Writers, 1992-. **Business Addr:** Assistant Business Editor, The Kansas City Star, 1729 Grand Ave, Kansas City, MO 64108, (816)234-4881.

AUSTIN, MARY JANE
Educational administrator. **Personal:** Born Apr 24, 1935, Orange, NJ; daughter of Louise Margaret Street Greene and George W Greene Jr; married Harry Lester Austin, Dec 21, 1957; children: Sharon Milora, Sherrill Ruth. **Educ:** Newark State Coll, BS 1957; Kean Coll, Grad work 1978; Bank St Coll Parsons School of Design, MS 1983. **Career:** Elizabeth Bd of Educ, layout artist 1973-78; Roosevelt Jr Schools, art consultant 1970-73; Elizabeth Public Schools, art educator 1953-79; William F Halloran Alternative Sch for the Gifted & Talented, art educator 1979-87; Irvington Board of Education, Irvington, NJ, supervisor art education, 1987-. **Orgs:** Arts Educators of New Jersey; Natl Art Educ Assoc 1979-86; The Independent Orders Foresters, associate for supervision and curriculum development; ASCD, 1987-89; treasurer, Citizen Awareness Group/Cranford, 1989-90; chairperson, Women's Day (Celebration of Womanhood), 1989-90; Principal Supervisors Association. **Honors/Awds:** Scholarship Artist Inst Stockton Coll NJ Council of the Arts 1980-81; Art Educ Awd Natl Council of Negro Women Inc 1981; participant Getty Conference Los Angeles Getty Ctr for Art Educ 1987; Governors Awd Governor Teacher Grant NJ State Dept of Educ 1987. **Home Addr:** 15 Wall St, Cranford, NJ 07016.

AUSTIN, PATTI
Singer. **Personal:** Born Aug 10, 1948, California. **Career:** Professional singer, albums include: End of A Rainbow, Havana Candy, Live at the Bottom, Body Language, It's Gonna Be Special, Patti Austin, Getting Away With Murder. **Special Achievements:** Appeared in several television shows, theatre performances, and stage productions; Studio sessions include collaborations with Harry Belafonte, Paul Simon, George Benson, Quincy Jones, Roberta Flack, Steely Dan, numerous others; Duet with James Ingram 'Baby Come to Me' topped the charts at #1 USA, #11 UK along with being the theme song to TV soap opera General Hospital, 1983; "How Do You Keep The Music Playing" from the movie "Best Friends," nominated for best song Oscar. **Business Addr:** Singer, Qwest Records, 3800 Barham Blvd Ste 503, Los Angeles, CA 90068, (213)874-3028.

AUSTIN, RAYMOND
Professional football player. **Personal:** Born Dec 21, 1974. **Educ:** Univ of Tennessee, attended. **Career:** New York Jets, defensive back, 1997-. **Business Addr:** Professional Football Player, New York Jets, 1000 Fulton Ave, Hempstead, NY 11550, (516)560-8100.

AUSTIN, RICHARD H.
Former state official. **Personal:** Born May 6, 1913, Stouts Mountain, AL; son of Lelia Hill Austin and Richard Henry Austin; married Ida Dawson; children: Hazel. **Educ:** Detroit Inst of Technology, BS, 1937; Wayne State Univ, Detroit, MI. **Career:** Certified public accountant, private practice, Detroit, 1941-71; Wayne County Auditor, 1966-70; State of Michigan, Secretary of State, 1971-94. **Orgs:** Amer Inst of Certified Public Accountants; member, National Association of Black Accountants; life mem, MI Assn of Certified Public Accountants; life mem NAACP; vice pres United Way for Southeast Michigan; treasure Comm Found of Southeastern Michigan; Booker T. Washington Business Association; Randolph W Wallace Kidney Research Foundation, Inc; has held numerous positions in political organizations; Commission on Internal Revenue, advisory group, 1965. **Honors/Awds:** Michigan's first African Amer CPA, 1941; Honorary Degrees from Michigan State Univ, Northern Michigan University, Univ of Detroit, Detroit Inst of Tech, Detroit College of Business, Univ of Detroit; Russworm Award for Contributions to Race Relations, National Publishers Association; Distinguished Achievement Award, Michigan Association of CPA's; Distinguished Citizen Award, Michigan State Univ, 1977; Whitney M. Young Award, Boy Scouts of America, 1981; Steering Wheel Award, AAA, 1984; Distinguished Service in Public Sector, Michigan State Chamber of Commerce, 1988; National Public Service Award, American Institute of CPA's; MADD GLADD Award, 1991; Government Leadership Award from Natl Comm Against Drunk Drivers, 1993; Community Service United Way, Max Fisher Award, 1995; Greater Detroit Chamber of Commerce, Richard C Vandusen Award, 1995; numerous others. **Special Achievements:** Longest serving African American statewide elected official in US. **Home Addr:** 3374 Oakman Blvd, Detroit, MI 48238.

AUSTIN, WANDA M.
Engineer. **Personal:** Born Sep 8, New York, NY; daughter of Helen & Murry Pompey; married Wade Austin, Jr. **Educ:** Franklin & Marshall College, BA, 1975; University of Pittsburgh, MS, 1977; University of Southern California, PhD, 1987. **Career:** The Aerospace Corp, general manager, electronic systems div, 1979-. **Orgs:** American Institute of Aeronautics & Astronautics, associate fellow, 1980-; Society of Women Engineers, sr mem, 1979. **Honors/Awds:** Women in Aerospace, Outstanding Achievement, 1996; International Council on Systems Engineering, Svc & Leadership, 1996; Aerospace Corp, Herndon Black Image Awd, 1984; Dollars & Sense, Outstanding Business & Professional, 1993. **Special Achievements:** Austin W & Khoshnevis B, Qualitative Modeling Using Natural Language: An Application in Systems Dynamics; Qualitative Simulation Modeling & Analysis, Springer Verlag, Spring, 1991. **Business Addr:** General Manager, The Aerospace Corp., PO Box 92957, M4/933, Los Angeles, CA 90009, (310)336-6146.

AUTRY, DARNELL
Professional football player. **Personal:** Born Jun 19, 1976. **Educ:** Northwestern. **Career:** Chicago Bears, running back, 1997-. **Business Addr:** Professional Football Player, Chicago Bears, 1000 Football Dr, Halas Hall at Conway Park, Lake Forest, IL 60045-4829, (847)295-6600.

AVANT, CLARENCE
Record company executive. **Career:** Motown Records, chairman, currently. **Orgs:** Polygram, Intl Mgmt Bd. **Honors/Awds:** NAACP Legal Defense and Educational Fund Awards, Lifetime Achievement Award, 1996. **Business Addr:** Chairman, Motown Records, 825 8th Ave, New York, NY 10019, (212)333-8000.

AVENT, EDWIN VERNON
Consumer products company executive. **Personal:** Born Nov 12, 1962, Washington, DC; son of Dollie Avent Fisher and Edward Vernon Hurley. **Educ:** Cornell University, 1980-82; University of Maryland-Eastern Shore, 1983. **Career:** Times Monitor News Magazine, advertising sales mgr, 1984; Career Communications Group, Inc, account executive, 1985-88, director of marketing, 1988-89, director of sales and promotions, 1989-90; UMOJA SASA Products Corp, president/ceo, currently. **Orgs:** Black Professional Men, Inc, co-founder/vice pres, 1991-; Network 2000, chairman of black business development committee, 1992-; Save Another Youth, Inc, board member, 1992-; Kappa Alpha Psi Fraternity, Inc, 1981-. **Honors/Awds:** Baltimore City School System, Mentor's Award, 1990-92. **Home Addr:** 916 Saint Paul St, Baltimore, MD 21202. **Business Addr:** President/Chief Executive Officer, UMOJA SASA Products Corp, PO Box 41410, Baltimore, MD 21203-6401, (410)576-8688.

AVENT, JACQUES MYRON
City official. **Personal:** Born Nov 13, 1940, Washington, DC; son of Virginia Hartwell Avent (deceased) and Charles Alexander Avent Sr; married Loretta Taylor Avent; children: James E. **Educ:** Howard Univ, BS 1963. **Career:** Natl Assoc of Regional Councils, field dir 1969-71; Natl Urban Coalition, asst dir field opers 1971-72; NLC USCM, prog mgr 1972-74; League of CA Cities, spec Proj assoc 1974-75; Human Serv Inst, exec dir 1975; NLC, asst dir mem serv 1976-77, dir office of membership svcs, 1977-86; Security Pacific National Bank, New York, NY, vice president of municipal finance, 1986-88; City of Phoenix, Phoenix, AZ, executive asst to the city council, 1989-90, executive asst to the city manager, 1990-92, deputy city manager, 1992-. **Orgs:** Sec Natl Forum for Black Public Admin 1985; mem Amer Soc for Public Admin 1978-; bd mem Natl Forum for Black Public Admin 1983-. **Honors/Awds:** Urban Exec Program Sloan Sch MIT 1973. **Business Addr:** Deputy City Manager, City of Phoenix, 251 W Washington St, 8th Flr, Phoenix, AZ 85003.

AVERY, BYLLYE Y.
Organization executive. **Career:** National Black Women's Health Project, founder/pres, 1981-91. **Orgs:** Global Fund for Women, bd mem; Intl Women's Health Coalition, bd mem; Boston Women's Health Book Collective, bd mem; Advisory Committee for Kellogg Intl Fellowship Prog, bd mem; Dartmouth Coll, bd of visitors for Tucker foundation; Dana Farber Cancer Advisory Bd. **Honors/Awds:** MacArthur Foundation Fellowship for Social Contribution, 1989; Essence Award for community service, 1989; Academy of Science Institute of Medicine, Gustav O Lienhard Award for the Advancement of Health Care, 1994; recipient of honorary degrees from Thomas Jefferson Univ, State Univ of NY at Binghamton, Gettysburg Coll, and Bowdoin Coll. **Special Achievements:** Co-founder, Gainesville, FL Women's Health Center; co-founder, BIRTHPLACE, an alternative birthing center in Gainesville; author, An Altar of Words: Wisdom, Comfort, and Inspiration for African American Women. **Business Addr:** Founder, National Black Women's Health Project, 1211 Connecticut Ave, NW, Washington, DC 20036, (202)835-0117.

AVERY, CHARLES
Photographer, author. **Personal:** Born Apr 13, 1938, Atlanta, GA; son of Connie Avery and Charles Avery. **Educ:** School of Visual Arts, 1964; Germain School of Photography, 1968; Essex County College, 1974. **Career:** Piscataway Library, sr asst librarian bookmobile, 1988; Piscataway Department Public Works, traffic asst, 1989; author, currently. **Military Serv:** US Army, pfc, 1956-58; Good Conduct Award, June 1958.

AVERY, HERBERT B.
Obstetrician, gynecologist. **Personal:** Born Oct 6, 1933, Columbia County, GA; son of Willie M Avery; married Maunaloa T, Aug 13, 1967; children: Herbert Jr, Randy, Mark, Kenya Sasa, Libra J. **Educ:** UCLA, 1951-56; Howard Univ, BS 1957; Howard Univ Med School, MD 1961. **Career:** Private practice, ob/gyn 1966-; UCLA & USC Schools of Publ Health, guest lect 1971-73; USC School of Med, asst prof; Martin Luther King Hosp, asst clin prof 1973; Leiment Park Hospital, medical director, 1980-82; Lewis & Lewis Marketing Research, vice pres/asst dir, 1987-; California Institute, director of medical education. **Orgs:** Founder, dir Westland Health Serv Inc 1968; founder, chmn Univ Comm Health Serv 1975; founder, dir Amer Sicle Cell Soc Inc 1969; asst dir Ob/Gyn Serv John Wesley Cty Hosp, 1966-68; mem bd dir LA Reg Family Plng Council 1969-72; mem CA Interagency Council on Family Plng 1969-72, Pres Conf on Children & Youth 1972, Alpha Omega Alpha Honor Med Soc 1960-. **Business Addr:** Director of Medical Education, California Institute, 4365 Atlantic Ave, Long Beach, CA 90807.

AVERY, JAMES
Actor. **Career:** Actor, Fresh Prince of Bel Air, 1990-96; Sparks, 1996-.

AVERY, JAMES S.
Oil company executive. **Personal:** Born Mar 24, 1923, Cranford, NJ; son of Martha Ann Jones Avery and John Henry Avery; married Joan Showers; children: Sheryl, James Jr. **Educ:** Columbia University, BA 1948, MA 1949. **Career:** Cranford NJ H S tchr 1949-56; Esso Standard Oil, Humble Oil, comm rel coord 1956-68; Humble Oil, Exxon Co USA, pub rel mgr 1968-71; Exxon Co USA, public affairs mgr, 1971-81, sr pub affairs consultant, retired 1986. **Orgs:** On loan assignment as exec vice pres Council on Municipal Performance 1981-83; vice chmn Natl Campaigns of UNCF 1962-65; vice chmn & chmn Vice Pres Task Force on Youth Motivation 1964-67; natl pres & bd chmn Natl Assn of Market Developers 1964-67; grand basileus Omega Psi Phi Frat Inc 1970-73; vice chmn Amer Pet Insts Offshore Sub-Comm, chmn NY St Pet Council 1978-79; mem of bd of trustees NY & NJ State Councils on Economic Educ 1975-86; vice chmn Philadelphia Reg Intro to Minorities to Engr, 1977-94; bd of trustees NJ State Student Assist Bd; NJ State Educ Opportunity Fund; bd of trustees, Lincoln Univ. **Honors/Awds:** Co-author of the Book of American City Rankings 1983; article on energy devt published by NY State Council for The Social Studies 1978; article on oil decon-

trol published by NY State Council on Econ Educ 1985; several major articles have been published in pamphlet form 1968-72. **Military Serv:** US Army corp 3 yrs. **Home Addr:** 201 Hidden Hollow Ct, Edison, NJ 08820-1054.

AVERY, JEROMYE LEE
Airport superintendent. **Personal:** Born Aug 25, 1949, Dallas, TX; son of Izola Miles Avery and Grady Avery; married Leslie Phillips Avery, Sep 18, 1976; children: Jessica, Daniel, Paul. **Educ:** UCLA, BA, history, 1974; Los Angeles City College, AA, broadcast, 1975. **Career:** Kern County Airports, Bakersfield, CA, operations supervisor, 1983-87; Tuolumne County Airports, Columbia, CA, airports director, 1987-89; City of Fresno, CA, Chandler Airport, superintendent, 1990-. **Orgs:** California Assn of Airport Executives, certified airport executive, 1988-, mem, 1981-91; American Assn of Airport Executives, 1983-91. **Honors/Awds:** Special Commendation, Los Angeles City Fire Department, 1979. **Military Serv:** Naval Reserve; USAF Auxiliary, Civil Air Patrol, Silver Medal of Valor, 1979. **Business Addr:** Superintendent, Fresno Chandler Downtown Airport, City of Fresno Airports Department, 2401 N Ashley Way, Fresno, CA 93727, (209)498-2681.

AVERY-BLAIR, LORRAINE
Banking executive. **Personal:** divoRced; children: Nina, Lanita, Martina. **Career:** First Financial Bank FSB, senior vp, currently. **Orgs:** Woodland Girl Scouts Council, pres, bd of dirs; WI Automated Clearing House, WACHA, pres, bd mem; EFTI/Access 24 Illinois Regional Electronic Funds Network, bd chair; Univ of WI, Stevens Point, bd of visitors; Tyme Regional Electronic Funds Network, adv comm; Zonta, Central WI Chap, pres; United Way Campaign for Portage County, chair; Univ of WI Accountability Measures, governor's task force, 1993-. **Honors/Awds:** Dollars & Sense Magazine, America's Best & Brightest Business Women, 1993.

AWKARD, JULITA CASTRO
Librarian. **Personal:** Born Nov 18, 1929, Manila, Philippines; daughter of Esperanza Basa Castro and Marcos Miranda Castro; married Joseph C Awkard Jr, Apr 7, 1946; children: Jane Marks, Linda Dual, Carol A Neyland. **Educ:** Florida A&M University, College of Education, MED, 1979; Florida State University, School of Library & Information Science, MSLS, 1980, AMD, 1981, PhD, 1990. **Career:** Albany State College, Albany, GA, circulation librarian, 1961; Florida A&M University, Tallahassee, FL, pharmacy librarian, 1962-79, reference librarian, 1979-81, nursing/allied health librarian, 1981-. **Orgs:** Chair, American Library Assn, 1981-82; caucus chair, Florida Library Assn, 1981-82; advisor, Kappa Epsilon Fraternity, 1968-79, 1987-; section council representative, Nursing/Allied Health, Medical Library Assn; library section chair, American Assn of Colleges of Pharmacy, 1974-75. **Honors/Awds:** Alpha Beta Alpha Library Fraternity, 1959; Kappa Delta Pi, 1962; Phi Delta Kappa, 1980; Beta Phi Nu, 1981; Kellogg Fellow, 1972-73. **Business Addr:** Librarian, Coleman Library, Florida A&M University, PO Box 136, Ware/Rhaney Bldg, Tallahassee, FL 32307.

AWKARD, LINDA NANLINE
Attorney. **Personal:** Born Nov 21, 1948, Harrisonburg, VA; daughter of Dr Julita C Awkard and Dr Joseph C Awkard Jr; married Edward C Maddox Jr, Oct 6, 1989; children: Edward C Maddox III. **Educ:** Florida State Univ, BA/BS, chemistry, 1970; Fordham Univ School of Law, JD, 1978, Harvard Law School, graduate certificate, 1982. **Career:** Pan American Airways, international flight attendant, 1970-79; Legal Services Corp, special asst to the pres, 1979-83; Awkard & Associates, owner/pres, 1984-. **Orgs:** American Bar Association, 1979-; National Bar Association, committee member, 1979-; National Business League, 1984-. **Honors/Awds:** National Business League, NBL Merit Citation, 1991. **Special Achievements:** Founder of one of the few minority and female owned law firms in the US specilizing in commercial transactional law with emphasis on financing of automobile, marine vehicle, and commercial real estate development transactions; first female to serve as general counsel of the 93 year-old Natl Bus League; first African-American to graduate from Florida State Univ with a degree in chemistry and mathematics. **Business Addr:** President, Awkard & Associates, Chartered, 1101 30th St NW, Ste 500, Washington, DC 20007, (202)333-2106.

AXAM, JOHN ARTHUR
Consultant, public library service. **Personal:** Born Feb 12, 1930, Cincinnati, OH; married Dolores Ballard, Sep 20, 1958. **Educ:** Cheyney St Univ, BSE 1953; Drexel Univ, MSLS 1958. **Career:** Free Library of Philadelphia, librarian 1958-64, head, stations dept 1964-78, area adm 1978-91. **Orgs:** ALA Cncl Am Lib Assoc 1971-72, various comm 1968; various comm PA Library Assoc 1964-; trustee United Way of So PA 1976-82; lay disciple Haven United Meth Ch 1965-. **Honors/Awds:** Various articles in Library Prof Publications; Chapel of the Four Chaplains Awd; Certificate of Merit, Pennsylvania Library Association, 1988.

AYALA, REGINALD P.
Hospital administrator. **Personal:** Born Sep 7, 1931, Brooklyn, NY; son of Gladys Ayala and Peter Ayala; married R Winifred Covington; children: Kevin, Peter, Terrence, Kathyrn, Gladys, Gail. **Educ:** Michigan State Univ, BA 1954, MBA 1970. **Career:** Harlem Globetrotters, professional basketball player, 1954-55, 1957; Detroit Parks & Rec, instr, 1958-59; Capri Convalescent Home, admin receiver, 1962-65; Kirwood Gen Hosp, 1959-70; Boulevard Gen Hosp, 1970-74; Southwest Detroit Hosp, pres & CEO, 1970-. **Orgs:** Mem State Health Facilities Comm 1976-; fellow Amer Coll of Health Executives 1967, Amer Assn Med Admin 1960-, Hosp Financial Mgmt Assn 1960; past mem Dist II Michigan Hosp Serv Hosp Relations Comm, Natl Assn Health Serv Execs; bd trustees Michigan Hosp Serv; exec comm, assoc serv comm 1970-71 Greater Detroit Area Hosp Council; mem ed comm Greater Detroit Area Hosp Council 1970-71, Michigan Hosp Assn; public relations comm, Adv Comm on Occupational Safety & Health; chmn Personnel Comm, Michigan Cancer Found, House of Delegates, Amer Hosp Assn; chmn Ethics Comm, Amer Coll of Health Executives. **Honors/Awds:** Citizen of the Year, Detroit Med Soc, 1975. **Military Serv:** US Army, lt 1955-57. **Business Addr:** President & CEO, Southwest Detroit Hospital, 2401 20th St, Detroit, MI 48216.

AYCOCK, ANGELA LYNNETTE
Professional basketball player. **Personal:** Born Feb 28, 1973, Dallas, TX; daughter of Charles Williams and Albertine Aycock. **Educ:** Univ of Kansas. **Career:** Seattle Reign, guard, 1996-. **Business Addr:** Professional Basketball Player, Seattle Reign, 400 Mercer St, Ste 408, Seattle, WA 98109, (206)285-5225.

AYERS, GEORGE WALDON, JR.
Dentist. **Personal:** Born Sep 23, 1931, Lake City, FL; married Marjorie; children: Dwayne, Marva, Damian, Donald. **Educ:** FL A&M Univ, BS 1956; Meharry Med Coll School Dentistry, DDS 1966. **Career:** Alachua Cty Health, 1969-70; Sunland Ctr, dental dir 1972-. **Orgs:** Mem Alachua Cty Dental Soc, Central Dist Dental, FL Dental Assoc, Amer Dental Assoc, FL Publ Health Assoc, So Assoc Intl Dentist. **Military Serv:** Sgt 1951-54; capt 1966-68; Serv Medal; Korean War. **Business Addr:** Dental Dir, Sunland Center, PO Box 1150, Waldo Rd, Gainesville, FL 32602.

AYERS, RANDY
Former college basketball coach. **Career:** Ohio State University, basketball coach, until 1997. **Business Addr:** Former Basketball Coach, Ohio State University, 190 North Oval Mall, Columbus, OH 43210.

AYERS, ROY
Musician. **Career:** Vibraphonist, played with Herbie Mann and various LA jazz players in the 60s; formed own group Ubiquity; musician, currently. **Special Achievements:** Evolution: The Polydor Anthology, two-cd compilation, 1995. **Business Addr:** Musician, c/o RCA, 1133 Avenue of the Americas, New York, NY 10036.

AYERS, TIMOTHY F.
Mayor, insurance agent. **Personal:** Born Nov 19, 1958, Springfield, OH; son of Betty R Ayers and Franklin R Ayers; married Lisa J Henry-Ayers, Aug 31, 1985; children: Katheryne ''Lindsay'' Ayers. **Educ:** Capital Univ, Columbus, OH, Political Science, 1977-81. **Career:** Ohio House of Representatives, Columbus, OH, legislative page, 1979, legislative message clerk, 1980-84; Ohio House Campaign Comm, Columbus, OH, 1982; Clark County Community Action Corp, Springfield, OH, 1984-86; City of Springfield, OH, mayor, 1984-; Reach Out for Youth Inc, Springfield, OH, foster care social worker, 1987-; Equitable, Springfield, OH, agent. **Orgs:** Licensed insurance agent, OH; bd mem, Amer Red Cross; mem, Truman-Kennedy Club, Clark County Democratic Exec Comm. **Honors/Awds:** Outstanding Young Man in Amer, 1984, 1985. **Business Addr:** Mayor, City of Springfield, 76 E High St, Springfield, OH 45502.

AYERS-ELLIOTT, CINDY
Financial executive. **Personal:** Born Aug 12, 1956, Ashland, MS; daughter of Annie Mae Ayers Jackson; children: Lagrand, Eric. **Educ:** Rust College, Holly Springs, MS, BA, 1984; University of Massachusetts, Boston, MA, MBA, 1987. **Career:** Senatorial Campaign, Jackson, MS, field coordinator, 1984-85; Governor's Office, Jackson, MS, program specialist, 1985-86, national rural fellow, 1986-87; State Treasurer's Office, Jackson, MS, admininstrative asst, 1987-94; Grigsby Brandford & Co Inc, VP. **Orgs:** Treasurer, Young Democrats of America, 1989-; vice chairperson, board of directors, Mississippi Home Corp, 1989; track delegate, Democratic National Convention, 1988; state coordinator, Presidential Election, 1988; national committee woman, Mississippi Young Democrats, 1986; First Amer bank, chairwoman; Leadership Jackson Class, 1991; Mississippi's First African-American Bank; National Bankers Assn; Mississippi Bankers Assn; NAACP; National Rural Fellow; Delta Foundation, vice chair; Democratic National Convention, natl delegate, 1984-96; Mississippi Home Corp, vice chair, 1990. **Honors/Awds:** Mississippi Head Start, Head Start Association, 1988; National Rural Fellow, National Urban Fellows, New York, 1987; Special Recognition, Mississippi Democratic Party, 1988; Special Recognition, National Bankers Association, 1990; Award of Merit, First American Bank, 1990. **Home Addr:** 4945 South Dr, Jackson, MS 39209, (601)922-8395. **Business Phone:** (601)355-3300.

AYERS-JOHNSON, DARLENE
Government official. **Personal:** Born Feb 28, 1943, Oakland, CA; daughter of Thelma Joseph and Ernest Joseph; married Perry Oliver Johnson, Dec 27, 1981; children: Cynthia Maria Ayers. **Educ:** Holy Names College, 1981-84; Golden Gate University, 1991-. **Career:** Standard Register Company of Oakland, group exec, marketing, 1972-85; Bermuda Business Machines and General Manager, A F Smith Trading Ltd, marketing manager, 1985-88; AMBER Printing Co, chief executive officer and owner, 1989-91; Interagency Support Division, Department of General Services, deputy director, chief deputy director, currently. **Orgs:** Ford's Consumer Appeals Board; Emergency Business Enterprises Commission, appointed by Willie Brown, speaker of house, 1992. **Honors/Awds:** State of California, Woman of the Year Award, 1992; Delegate, Natl Presidential Convention; Federated Republican Women; Postal Commission; numerous others. **Business Addr:** Chief Deputy Director, Interagency Support Div, Dept of General Servs, State of California, 1325 J St, Suite 1910, Sacramento, CA 95814, (916)445-7213.

AYTCH, DONALD MELVIN
Educator. **Personal:** Born Apr 17, 1930, Shreveport, LA; son of Della Aytch and Sullivan Aytch; married C Jean; children: Lynette, Don Jr, Cynthia, Neco, Terri. **Educ:** Grambling State Univ, BS 1954; TX Southern Univ, MA 1969. **Career:** Bethune HS, band dir 1957-68; Southern Univ, chmn 1969-. **Orgs:** Mem Louisiana Educ Assn, Natl Educ Assn, PAP, Natl Assn of Coll Professionals; public official Caddo Parish Police Jury 1966; comm Louisiana State Alcohol Commn 1964; Alpha Kappa Mu Hon Soc; mem Andante Con Expressive, Ark-La-Tex Focus. **Honors/Awds:** First black president of Caddo Parish Police Jury; Honorary Doctorate, Baptist Christian College, 1989. **Military Serv:** US Army, S Sgt E7, 1954-56; received Good Conduct Medal. **Business Addr:** Commissioner, Caddo Parish, District 7, PO Box 19124, Shreveport, LA 71149-0124.

AZIZ, KAREEM A.
Educational administrator. **Personal:** Born Dec 15, 1951, Dayton, OH; married Nini Oseye; children: Jinaki Milele, Atiba Erasto. **Educ:** Central State Univ, BA 1975; Univ of Dayton, M PubAdmin 1976; Morgan State Univ, Doctoral Student 1982-. **Career:** Comprehensive Manpower Ctr, admin asst to exec dir 1975-77; Clark Co Employment & Training Office, coord of comm PSE prog 1977-78; YMCA of Springfield OH, exec dir 1978-80; YMCA of Baltimore MD, exec dir 1980-81; Sojourner Douglass Coll, coord of inst rsch & planning 1981-. **Orgs:** Consultant New Day Assocs 1985; co-chair Natl Communications Comm Natl Black Independent Political Party 1983-. **Honors/Awds:** ''Key Statistics About Minorities in the Dayton Area'' Dayton Human Relations Council 1973. **Home Addr:** 3302 Liberty Heights Ave, Baltimore, MD 21215. **Business Addr:** Coord of Inst Rsch & Planning, Sojourner Douglass Coll, 500 N Caroline St, Baltimore, MD 21205.

AZIZ, SAMIMAH
Book company executive. **Personal:** Born Oct 19, 1960, New York, NY; daughter of Marion Williams Prescott and Larry Prescott. **Educ:** Southeast Missouri State Univ, Cape Girardeau, MO, 1978-80; Howard Univ, Washington, DC, BA, history, 1984; Webster Univ, St Louis, MO, educ program, 1991-. **Career:** Howard Univ Student Assn, Washington, DC, program dir, 1983-84; Natl Archives/Archives Tech, Washington, DC, 1983-84; KITS, Washington, DC, travel consultant/tour guide, 1984, 1985; DC Pretrial Agency, Washington, DC, pretrial officer, 1985-88; Akbars Books-N-Things, St Louis, MO, cost svc mgr/co-owner, 1988-; president, Adventure in Africa Tours, currently. **Orgs:** Mem, Ubiquity, 1983-; mem, Multicultural Publishers Exchange, 1990-; mem, Nation of Islam, 1963-; mem, Africam Am Assn of Book Sellers, Writers & Publishers, 1990-. **Business Addr:** President, Adventure in Africa Tours, 8816 Manchester Rd, Ste 117, St Louis, MO 63144, (314)962-2117.

B

BAAQEE, SUSANNE INEZ
Dentist. **Personal:** Born Nov 24, 1952, Boston, MA; daughter of Inez Sabree and Everett Sabree; married Melvin Bilal; children: Shakir, Aneesah, Mikal. **Educ:** Simmons Coll, BS, 1974; Tufts Dental School, DMD 1978; Harvard School of Dental Implantology, 1987; Simmons Graduate School of Management, MBA, 1995. **Career:** Children's Hospital Med Center, hematology asst, 1972-75; Roxbury Comm Health Clinic, family dentist 1979-81; Harvard Biological Labs, rsch asst 1974; Implant & Family Dental Practice, dentist, 1980-. **Orgs:** Mem,

MA Dental Soc, 1979-; Amer Dental Assn, 1979-; New England Soc Clinical Hypnosis, 1985-; bd mem, Dorchester Counseling Serv, 1983-86; treasurer, Amerislamic EID Assn, 1983-87; vice pres, Mattapan Comm Concern Group, 1984; mem, Amer Acad of Implant Dentistry, 1987-, Massachusetts Women's Dental Society, 1975-; member MAS JID Al Quaran, 1965-. **Honors/Awds:** Girl of the Year Award, 1970; Scholastic Achievement, Natl Honor Soc, 1967-70, Alpha Kappa Alpha 1975-77, Links Soc, 1976-78; HAJJ 1980, 1990. **Business Addr:** Dentist, 1539 Blue Hill Ave, Mattapan, MA 02126.

BABB, VALERIE M.
Educator. **Personal:** Born May 6, 1955, New York, NY; daughter of Dorothy L Babb and Lionel S Duncan. **Educ:** Queens Coll, City Univ of New York, New York, NY, BA, 1977; State Univ of New York at Buffalo, Buffalo NY, MA, 1981, PhD, 1981. **Career:** Georgetown Univ, Washington DC, asst prof, associate professor, currently. **Honors/Awds:** Award for Academic Excellence, Seek Program, City Univ of New York, 1985; MT. Zion United Methodist Church Award for "Black Georgetown Remembered: A Documentary Video," 1989; Book: Ernest Gaines, Twayne/G K Hall, 1991. **Business Addr:** Associate Professor of English, Georgetown University, Department of English, 338 New North, Washington, DC 20057.

BABBS, JUNIOUS C., SR.
Educator. **Personal:** Born Aug 15, 1924, Arkansas; married Bobbie; children: Junious C Jr, Dwayne (deceased), Jade. **Educ:** BS, MS, EdS 1971; EdD 1984. **Career:** Cotton Plant Public Schools, coach, sci teacher, rec dir, principal, supt of school; educational consultant; motivational speaker, 1989-. **Orgs:** Chmn bd trustees Ash Grove Bapt Church; sec ECOEO; mem Cty Health Comm; mem Cty Adv Comm; mem City Council; chmn Finance Comm; mem NEAAA, AEA, State Principals Orgn for Admin; mem NCA State Comm; mem Adv Council on Secondary Ed, Cty Extension Bd; mem dir Cotton Plant Clinic; mem AR State Admin Assn, 32 Deg Mason, NAC; mem bd dir DAD; sec Mental Health Bd; deacon Ash Grove B Church; State Advisory Committee for Chapter II State Bonds & Facility Commission; Chairperson, Woodruff County Local Planning Group, Arkansas Dept of Human Services; mem, bd of directors, Wilber D Mills Ed coop; mem, State Health Committee; Dr Martin Lihing Commission, governor's appointment, 1993; Natl Comm Service Commission, governor's appointment, 1993. **Honors/Awds:** Man of the Year Award 1969, 1973; Coach of the Year 1953, 1956, 1960-62; Biol Teacher Award 1960-61; State Service Chapter I Award, 1990; Service Award, City of Cotton Plant, 1989; Man of the Year Award, American Biographic Institute 1990; Distinguished Service Award, North Arkansas Services, 1994; The JC Babbs Community Ctr, Dedication, 1985. **Home Addr:** 400 Gum St, D-10, Cotton Plant, AR 72036. **Business Addr:** Superintendent, 400 Gum Street, Cotton Plant, AR 72036.

BABER, CEOLA ROSS
Educator. **Personal:** Born Nov 30, 1950, Selma, AL; daughter of Laura Stringer Ross and Frederick Douglas Ross Sr; married Willie L Baber; children: Lorenzo DuBois, Tylisha Marie, Cheickna St Clair. **Educ:** CA State Univ Sacramento, BA 1972; Stanford Univ, MA 1975; Purdue Univ, PhD 1984. **Career:** Sequoia Union HS Dist, teacher 1974-78; Tuskegee Univ, project coord/instructor 1979-80; Purdue Univ, rsch assoc 1980-81, dir/asst prof 1984-89; Univ of North Carolina-Greensboro, School of Education, asst assoc prof 1989-. **Orgs:** American Educational Research Association; National Association of Multicultural Education; National Council for Social Studies; International Reading Association; Phi Delta Kappa; Kappa Delta Pi; Delta Kappa Gamma International Education Society; advisory council, People of America Foundation, 1996-; editorial bd, Theory and Research in Social Education, 1996-; chair, African-American Educators SIG, National Council for the Social Studies, 1996-98; National Bd for Professional Teaching Standards, Advisory Comm on Adverse Impacts, 1996-. **Honors/Awds:** UNCG Alumni Teaching Excellence Awd, Jr Faculty Recipient, 1993; Consortium of Doctors, Distinguished Women of Color Awd, 1991; Invited Faculty Delegate, Congressional Black Caucus Legislative, Weekend Summit '87, Sept 25-26, 1987; Grants: UNC Small Grants School-Based Research Prog, 1992; Project Achieve, Letter of Agreement with Reidsville City Schools, 1991; US Department of Education Demonstration Grant, 1990; NC Humanities Council Grant, 1990; UNCG New Faculty Grant, 1989. **Business Addr:** Associate Professor, Department of Curriculum & Instruction, University of North Carolina-Greensboro, School of Education, PO Box 26171, Greensboro, NC 27402-6171.

BABER, LUCKY LARRY
Educator. **Personal:** Born Apr 16, 1949, Ackerman, MS. **Educ:** Grand Valley State College, BS, 1972; Central Michigan University, MA, 1975; Bowling Green State University, PhD, 1978. **Career:** Saginaw Big Brothers, asst director, 1972-73; Delta College, instructor, 1973-74; Buena Vista High School, teacher, 1974-75; Lincoln University, Dept Soc, asst professor/chairman, 1978-; Goldey Beacon College, College of Arts & Sciences, professor, currently. **Orgs:** Vice chairman, bd of fellows, Center for Studying Soc Welfare and Community Development, 1979-80; chairman, Bowling Green Chapter, Alpha Kappa Delta, 1977-78. **Business Addr:** Professor, College of Arts & Sciences, Goldey Beacon College, 4701 Limestone Rd, Wilmington, DE 19808-1927.

BABERO, BERT BELL
Educator. **Personal:** Born Oct 9, 1918, St Louis, MO; son of Bertha Babero and Andras Babero; married Harriett King; children: Bert Jr, Andras Fanfiero. **Educ:** Univ of Illinois, BS 1949, MS 1950, PhD 1957. **Career:** Artic Health Research Center AK, med parasitologist 1950-55; Ft Valley State Coll, Ga, prof of Zoology 1957-59; Southern Univ, Baton Rouge LA, prof of Zoology 1959-60; F Ed Emergency Sci Skeme, Lagos, Nigeria, lecturer Zoology 1960-62; School of Medicine Univ Baghdad, Iraq, prstlgst 1962-65; Grambling State Univ, prof of Zoology, 1987-89; Univ of NV Las Vegas, prof of Zoology emeritus, 1987-. **Orgs:** Amer Soc of Parasitologists 1951-; Am Mcrscptcl Soc 1951-; Honorary Soc Phi Sigma Biological Soc; Beta Beta Blgc Soc; Helm Soc Wash, 1951-; Wildlife Dis Soc, 1955-. **Honors/Awds:** Comm NV St Equal Rights Comm 1967-68; Alpha Phi Alpha Fraternity 1957-; Sigma Xi Honorary Sci Soc Pres Local Chapter 1966-72; Phi Kappa Phi 1966-; fellow trop med Louisiana State Univ Medical School 1968; council Rep Amer Soc Prstlgsts 1981-85; honorary life mem Rocky Mt Conf Prstlgsts 1982; 100 science publications in Prstlgy in journals of many countries; Hall of Fame DuSable High School Chicago 1985. **Military Serv:** US Army T4 1943-46; 3 overseas serv Bars; Am Cmpgn Medal; Asiatic Pac Cmgn Medal; Bronze Star; Good Conduct Medal; WWII Victory Medal.

BACHUS, MARIE DARSEY
Educator. **Personal:** Born Nov 29, 1940, St Joseph, LA; children: Maurice, Marcia. **Educ:** Grambling State Univ, BS 1964; Southern Univ, ME 1974. **Career:** New Orleans, councilwoman, mayor pro-tem; Mabachus Record & Sweet Shop, owner; teacher. **Orgs:** Mem TEA, LTA, NEA; vice pres Grambling Alumni, PTSA, Athletic Club, Band Booster Club; sec Springfield MBC; dir Com Youth; Waterproof Schools Band Boosters. **Honors/Awds:** Key to City of New Orleans 1975.

BACKSTROM, DON
Investment banker. **Personal:** Born Jun 4, 1941, Los Angeles, CA; son of Julia Carter Backstrom and Walter Backstrom; married Jacquelyn Webster Backstrom, Oct 5, 1969; children: Kellye Dion Backstrom. **Educ:** America Institute of Banking, Los Angeles, CA, certificate, 1965-75; El Camino Community College, Torrance, CA, 1970-75; California State University, Dominguez Hills, CA, 1975-78. **Career:** Bank of America, Los Angeles, CA, bank mgr, 1964-73; Bank of Finance, Los Angeles, CA, bank mgr, 1973-75; Home Bank, Compton, CA, bank mgr, 1975-76; Imperial Bank, Los Angeles, CA, vice pres, 1976-77; Mechanics Bank, bank mgr, 1977-78; State of California, Sacramento, Los Angeles, mgr CAL-VET housing program, 1978-84, California State Treasurer's Office, exec dir CIDFAC, 1984-91; Smith Barney, Harris Upham & Co Inc, vice pres, public finance division, 1991-. **Orgs:** Director, California Statewide Certified Development Corporation, 1988-. **Military Serv:** US Air Force, E-4, 1960-64. **Business Addr:** Vice President, Smith Barney, Harris Upham Co Inc, Public Finance Division, 333 S Grand Ave, 51st Fl, Los Angeles, CA 90071.

BACKUS, BRADLEY
Lawyer. **Personal:** Born Sep 12, 1950, Kings County, NY; son of Bernice Smith Backus and Thomas Backus; married Stephanie George (divorced); children: Crystal Olivia Backus. **Educ:** Lincoln Univ, Oxford, PA, BA, 1972; George Washington Univ, Natl Law Center, JD, 1975. **Career:** Metropolitan Life, New York, NY, advanced underwriting consultant, 1977-80, dir Estate Planning, 1980-82, sr business and estate consultant, 1983-93; Agency Mgr Training, Field Management Training, mgr, Met Life, 1994-. **Orgs:** Pres, Bedford-Stuyvesant Lawyers Assn, 1980-81; bd mem, Bedford-Stuyvesant Community Legal Serv Corp, 1980-89; pres, Metropolitan Black Bar Assn, 1986-89; vice pres, MBBA Scholarship Fund Inc, 1987-; bd mem, Comm for Modern Courts, 1988-; commr, NY State Judicial Commn on Minorities, 1988-90; commr, NY City Korean Veterans Memorial Commn 1988-90; commr, NY State Comm to Improve the Availability of Legal Services, 1988-90; regional director, NBA, 1990-91; National Bar Assn, Region II, reg dir, 1994-; The Legal Aid Society, bd mem, 1988-. **Business Addr:** Advanced Underwriting Consultant/Director, Metropolitan Life Insurance Company, One Madison Avenue, Area 4-H, New York, NY 10010.

BACOATE, MATTHEW, JR.
Business executive. **Personal:** Born Feb 10, 1931, Asheville, NC. **Educ:** Med Adminis Sch, attended 1951; Univ of So CA, USAFI, bus admin 1953-55; Western Carolina Univ, Bus Admin 1970-71; NC State Univ CEU's, 1971-75. **Career:** Asheville Chamber of Commerce, gen mgr; Afran Inc, gen mgr; Asheville Commun Enter Inc, gen mgr 1973-; M Bacoate Disposable's Inc, pres; Western Mtn Scientific Inc, pres, currently. **Orgs:** Fndr & co-chmn Comm of Prog; bd of vis W Carolina Univ; Comm Int & Commit WLOS-TV; bd dir Asheville Chap Amer Red Cross; bd dir Commission Museum of Fire Equip; steering comm, Gov Jim Hunt, 1976-92; adv comm, Sen Robert Morgan, 1974, 1980; Small Bus Adv Cncl 1978; bd dir Gov Western Residence Assn 1978; Priv Indsl Cncl (PIC), 1979, 1988; Employment Security Adv Cncl 1979; Central Asheville Optimist Club 1979; fund for self-devel of People Holston Presbyteria of US; steering comm Martin L King Prayer Break; Daniel Boone Council Boy Scouts of Amer 1978; board member Asheville Area C of C 1981; adv council US Small Bus Admin 1981; chmn bd Victoria Health Care Ctr 1981-; adv committee AB Tech Small Bus 1986; YMI Cultural Center, bd dir, 1987, chairman, 1992; City of Asheville Minority Business Commission, 1989; Buncombe County Sheriffs Transition/Review Comm, 1990; Senator Terry Sanford Adv Comm, 1986; chairman, (Minority) Loan Pool, 1990; board of directors, Pack Place Inc, 1991; North Carolina Sheriff Association, 1991; NC Sml Bus Advocacy Council, 1979; bd of dir, NC Economic Dev, 1977; NC Minority Bus Commission, 1969; Chmn bd, Black Mtn Ctr Foundation, 1994; Chmn Bd, YMI Community Dev Corp, 1992; bd dir, Western NC Regional Economic Dev Commission, 1993; co-founder, Black Bus and Prof League, 1983; Smky Mtn Minority Purchasing Council, 1986; appeal officer, Asheville CitySchools Free Lunch Prog, 1969-95. **Honors/Awds:** Look Mag Recognition, 1970; Appreciation for Svc to the Phalany Frat, Market St YMCA, 1972; Natl Audiance, Exemplifying Accomplishments, documentary "Help" ABC, 1970; Cert of Apprec Asheville Buncombe Tech Inst 1977; White House invitation, Pres Jimmy Carter, 1979; Cert of Recog City of Winston-Salem NC 1980-; Awd Ashville Area C of C Inc 1981; Cert of Recog Western Carolina Univ 1983; Outstanding Serv Inducted into the Chamber of Echoes Central Asheville Optimist 1984; Cert City of Asheville, for service to community, 1988; Asheville Jaycees, Boss of the Year, 1976; Buncombe County Sheriff Department, Outstanding Service Award; Outstanding Svc Recognition, City of Asheville, 1993; Appreciation for Outstanding Leadership, Black Mtn Ctr Foundation, 1995-96; Appreciation for Leadership/Dedication to the Region, Advantage West (WNCREDC), 1993-97. **Military Serv:** Army Med Corps 1951-56. **Business Addr:** President, Western Mtn Scientific, Inc, PO Box 1381, Asheville, NC 28801.

BACON, ALBERT S.
Orthodontist. **Personal:** Born Mar 1, 1942, LaGrange, GA; son of Julia Spain Bacon and Albert Stanley Bacon Sr. **Educ:** Howard Univ, BS 1963, DDS 1967; certified in Orthodontics 1971. **Career:** VA Hosp, staff dentist 1969; private practice 1970; Community Group Health Found, staff dentist 1970; Howard Univ, asst prof 1971; private practice orthodontics 1971-; Dept Comm Dentistry, acting chmn 1972. **Orgs:** Mem Amer/Natl/So MD Dental Assns; Robert T Freeman Dental Soc; Amer Assn Orthodontists; Middle Atlantic Soc Orthodontists; Amer Acad of Group Dental Practice; Chi Delta Mu Frat; Young Adults of Washington; St Albans Soc; Canterbury Club; Howard Univ Alumni Assn. **Business Addr:** West Office Bldg, Ste 308 Landover Mall, Landover, MD 20785.

BACON, BARBARA CRUMPLER
Educational administrator. **Personal:** Born Sep 7, 1943, Youngstown, OH; daughter of Jessie McCray Irby and Robert Crumpler; married Oscar (divorced 1992); children: Robert, Jessica. **Educ:** Youngstown State Univ, BA Sociology 1980; University of Akron School of Law, Akron, OH, 1990-. **Career:** Smithsonian Inst, eeo spec 1972-78; Mahoning Cty Transitional Homes, affirm action consult 1980, instr 1980-81; Youngstown State Univ, asst to the pres for affirm action, 1984-. **Orgs:** Bd mem Assoc Neighborhood Ctrs 1984-92, YWCA 1985-92; mem Links Inc 1985-; bd mem Gateways to Better Living 1985; Design Review Comm; Help Hotline, board member; Burdman Group, board member. **Business Addr:** Asst to the Pres for Affirm Action, Youngstown State Univ, Tod Admin Bldg Rm 209, Youngstown, OH 44555.

BACON, CHARLOTTE MEADE
Educator (retired). **Personal:** Born in Alberta, VA; daughter of Pinkie Manson Meade (deceased) and Ollie Meade (deceased); married Edward D Bacon Jr; children: Judith, Edward P, Susan, Detrick. **Educ:** Hampton Inst, BS (Hon) 1946; Univ of Pittsburgh, MEd 1952. **Career:** Great Aliquippa YWCA, prog comm 1965-72; Aliquippa Ed Assoc, record sec 1969-72; Aliquippa Br of Amer Assoc of Univ Women, corres sec 1971-73; Aliquippa Negro Bus & professional Womens Club, pres 1960-62,63-77; PA State Fed of Negro Womens Clubs, pres 1969-73; Aliquippa School Dist, teacher. **Orgs:** Mem Delta Sigma Theta Sor, Natl Ed Assoc of Retired Teachers, PA St Ed Assoc of Retired Teachers, Triumph Baptist Church, NAACP, World Affairs Council of Pgh; life mem New Sheffield PTA; vchmn Mayors Comm on Civil Rights 1972-77; pres Willing Workers Mission Soc 1988, pres Aliquippa Br Amer Assoc of Univ Women 1977-79; Natl Assoc of Colored Womens Clubs; exec bd 1969-79, chairperson 1990- Black Family and Homeless; ed chrpsn NE Fed of Womens Clubs; chmn Consumer Affairs 1976-80; mem Sewickley Intl Toastmistress Club 1976-82; dir Aliquippa NAACP Creative Dramatics Club 1972-76; mem Sewickley NYPUMProg Comm 1979-82; Black Womens Pol Crusade of Pgh 1987-90; 3rd vice presProg Comm 1979-82; Black Womens Pol Crusade of Pgh 1987-90; 3rd vice pres Aliquippa Elem School PTA 1980-81; communications comm Natl Assoc Negro Bus & Professional Women's Clubs 1985-89; Women's History spkr PA Dept of Educ Speaker's Bureau on Black History Aliquippa Negro Bus & Professional Women's Club 1960-89; mem Penn State Minority Recruitment Comm

1987-91; 1st vice pres Aliquippa NBPW Club 1980-90; second vice pres Aliquippa AAUW 1988-90, Women's History chairperson 1980-90; Adult Literacy Council of Beaver County; recording secretary, Northcentral District NANBPWC 1988-90; exec bd Natl Assn Colored Women's Clubs 1988-; exec bd, Northeastern Federation of Negro Women 1987-; historian Modern Club Aliquippa PA 1987-90; chaplain, Daniel B Mathews Historical Society 1987-89;president Hawthorne Club of Sewickley 1989-; president FFUTURE Associates 1989; Sewickley Community Center, bd of dirs, 1976, 1982, special task force, 1978-83, interim administrator, 1992-. **Honors/Awds:** Woman of the Year Aliquippa NBPW Club 1970; Delta Sigma Theta Comm Involvement Awd 1971; Notable Amer of the Bicent Era 1976; Bict of Intl Biog 1971-76;Sojourner Truth Awd Natl Assoc of NBPW Clubs 1976; PA Woman of the Year Aliquippa Br AAUW 1981; Disting Serv Awd PA State Fed of Negro Womens Clubs Inc 1983; Appreciation Awd Beaver-Castle Girl Scout Cncl 1985; Aliquippa Elem Sch PTA Scholarship Awd 1986; Teacher of the Year Aliquippa Sch Dist 1987; 498 Hardworking Women of PA 1987; Co-Author, Four Drummers, poetry book 1989; Woman of the Year Award Beaver Castle Girl Scout Council 1989; Hall of Fame Award Pennsylvania State Federation of Negro Women 1990; Merit Award Northeastern Federation of Women's Clubs 1990. **Business Addr:** Iterim Administrator, Sewickley Community Center, 15 Chadwick St, Sewickley, PA 15143.

BACON, GLORIA JACKSON
Physician. **Personal:** Born Sep 21, 1937, New Orleans, LA; married Frank C Bacon Jr; children: Constance Jackson, Judith Jackson, Phillip, Geoffrey, Stuart. **Educ:** Xavier Univ, BS 1958; Univ of IL, Sch of Medicine MD 1962, Sch of Public Health MPH 1984. **Career:** Health/Hosp Governing Commn Cook Co, medical dir 1979; The Clinic in Altgeld Inc, founder/dir 1970-82; Provident Hosp and Med Ctr, vp/dev mktg 1985; Clinic Associates of Chicago Ltd, pres 1982-; Metro Care HMO, medical dir 1986-87; Provident Hosp & Med Ctr, pres/medical staff 1985-. **Orgs:** Mem bd of trustees Fisk Univ 1980-85, Gannon/Proctor Commn 1982-83; mem Natl Medical Assoc, The Chicago Network, Tech Adv Comm on School BAsed Adolescent Health Care Prog, Robert Wood Johnson Foundation. **Honors/Awds:** Woman of the Year in Medicine Operation PUSH 1975; Candace Awd Comm of 100 Women 1984; publication "Is Love Ever Enough?" A Finial Press Champaign IL 1987. **Business Addr:** President of Medical Staff, Provident Hosp & Medical Ctr, 500 East 51st St, Chicago, IL 60615.

BACON, RANDALL C.
City official. **Personal:** Born Oct 2, 1937, Youngstown, OH; divorced; children: Randy, Keith, Kevin. **Educ:** Los Angeles City College, AA 1958; CA State Univ, BS 1962; Univ of Southern CA, attended 1962-64; Loyola Law Sch, attended 1964-66. **Career:** Los Angeles County Social Svcs, fiscal officer 1965-69; Los Angeles County Pks & Rec, chief deputy dir 1969-74; Los Angeles County Adm Off, division chief 1974-79; San Diego County, asst chief adm off 1979-81, dir of social serv, beginning 1981; City of Los Angeles, dept of general services, gen mgr, currently. **Orgs:** Black Leadership Council of San Diego; chmn 44th Congressional Dist Adv Bd; past pres, Kappa Alpha Psi Frat, 1985; chmn CA Welfare Directors Assn, 1985; Natl Forum for Black Public Administrators, president. **Honors/Awds:** Published article "A Model Program for all California," Public Welfare Magazine 1986; 1987 Natl Public Serv Awd; Marks of Excellence Award, Forum for Black Public Administrators, 1990.

BACON, ROBERT JOHN, JR.
Psychiatrist. **Personal:** Born Nov 20, 1948, Houston, TX; son of Bernice Bacon and Robert Bacon Sr; married Karen; children: Robyn, Kristen, Angelle. **Educ:** Stanford Univ, BA 1970; Meharry Medical Coll, MD 1975. **Career:** TX Medical Foundation, physician advisor 1982-88; Univ of TX-Houston, clinical asst prof 1984-90; Ben Taub General Hosp, dir of psychiatric emergency serv 1984-88; Baylor Coll of Medicine, asst prof 1984-90; Charter Hospital of Kingwood, clinical director of adult psychiatry, 1989-94; NBA Aftercare Network Team, network provider, 1989-93. **Orgs:** Clinical consultant Harris Co Forensic Treatment Unit 1979-81; Sun Arts. **Business Addr:** Psychiatrist, 5225 Katy Fwy, Ste 105, Houston, TX 77007.

BACON, WILLIAM LOUIS
Surgeon. **Personal:** Born Dec 3, 1936, Austin, TX; son of Louise Bacon and William Bacon; married Donna Marie Harbatis; children: Tyra, William II, Donna, Mary Schroeder, Jesse, Louise, Jonathan, Nicholas. **Educ:** Morehouse Coll, 1956; Meharry Med Coll, 1962. **Career:** Fitzsimons Gen Hosp, intern 1962-63; Ireland Army Hosp, prespec surg 1963-64; Brooke Army Med Ctr, ortho 1964-67; Wash DC, course dir 1972-74; Miami, surg 1975-; private practice, physician. **Orgs:** Cert Amer Bd of Ortho Surg 1970; mem Amer Coll of Surg 1971; Amer Acad of Ortho Surg 1972; guest lecturer Univ of Miami 1976; staff consult Friedman's Hosp & Howard Univ; staff mem Mt Sinai Med Ctr, Cedars of Leb Hosp, Vict Hosp, Jack Mem Hosp; mem bd Cedars of Leb Hosp; mem Dade Co Med Assn, FL Med Soc, Amer Med Assn, Miami Ortho Soc, FL Ortho Soc; recert Amer Bd Ortho Surg 1983; commander 324th Gen Hosp USAR 1983-86. **Honors/Awds:** Merit Serv Med 1970,74; Examiner Amer Bd Ortho Surg 1978-84. **Military Serv:** US Army, 1962-74; US Army Reserves, Col, 1975-; Army Commendation Medal, 1972; Meritorious Service Medal, 1970, 1974; Persian Gulf Medal, 1992. **Business Addr:** Physician, Dept of Orthopedic Surgery, Meharry Medical Coll, 1005 DB Todd Blvd, Nashville, TN 37208.

BADGER, BRENDA JOYCE
Counselor. **Personal:** Born May 10, 1950, Camden, AR; daughter of Lizzie Mae Frazier Hildreth and Woodrow Hildreth; married David Badger, Feb 27, 1982; children: Kreya Jackson, Keith Jackson. **Educ:** Wayne State University, BS, criminal justice, 1982, MA, guidance and counseling, 1987. **Career:** Wayne County Community College, secretary, 1970-92; The Community Informant, editor, columnist, 1988-; "Did You Know?" producer, host, 1990-; Lawrence Technological University, counselor, 1992-; American Counseling Association, Red Cross, disaster mental health counselor/instructor, 1992-. **Orgs:** Spirit, Ambition, Vigor, & Enthusiasm (SAVE), founder, president, 1986-; Juvenile/Teen & Violence Committee, City of Detroit, 1986-; American Counseling Association, 1985-; Association of Marriage and Family Counseling, 1992-; American College Counseling Association, 1992-. **Honors/Awds:** WJLB-FM Radio, Strong Achiever Award, 1991. **Special Achievements:** Author, "Teachers Still Work Miracles," Detroit Free Press, 1984; "Did You Know?" song, 1992; "The Alto," poem, 1993; State Counseling Licensee, 1991; licensed counselor, selected nationwide for training, 1992; Wrote a proposal for a $74,000, the Buddy System, which was approved for funding. **Business Addr:** Counselor/Director, Student Affairs, Lawrence Technological University, 21000 W 10 Mi Rd, CAAC-West Bldg, Southfield, MI 48075-1058, (313)356-0200.

BADGER, LLOYD, JR.
City councilmember. **Personal:** Born May 25, 1950, Hiltonia, GA. **Educ:** Rochester Inst of Techn, Indust Mgmt 1970-72. **Career:** Self-employed salesman; City of Hiltonia, city councilmenber 1983-. **Orgs:** Mem Johnson Grove Baptist Ch, NAACP, Optimist Club, Masons. **Business Addr:** City Councilmember, City of Sylvania, 106 Roberts St., Sylvania, GA 30467.

BADGETT, EDWARD
City manager. **Personal:** Born May 22, 1935, Cleveland, OH; son of Margurite Rogers Lowe and Edward Daniel Badgett; married Erbetine Jackson Badgett, Dec 18, 1955; children: Edward Ronald, Evelyn Denise, Evette Marie. **Educ:** University of Akron, Akron, OH, BA, 1965, MA, 1971. **Career:** City of Flint, Flint, MI, dir, dept of community devel, 1974-77; US Dept of Housing and Urban Development, Kansas City, MO, regional dir, community planning and devel, 1978-80; City of Austin, TX, asst city mgr, 1980-82; City of Berkeley, CA, asst city mgr, 1982-84; City of Commerce, TX, city mgr, 1984-86; City of Forest Hill, TX, city mgr, 1986-. **Orgs:** Board member, Tarrant County Red Cross, 1990-; member, National Forum for Black Public Administrators, 1985-; member, International City Management Assn, 1975-; trustee, Historic Savannah Foundation, 1972-74; trustee, Michigan Beethoven Society Foundation, 1975-77. **Honors/Awds:** Honorary Order of Kentucky Colonels, Commonwealth of Kentucky, 1990; Distinguished Service Award, City of Austin, TX, 1982; Image Award, Phoenix Branch, NAACP, 1978; Image Award, Akron Branch, NAACP, 1968, 1969; Eagle Scout, Cleveland Council, BSA, 1950. **Military Serv:** US Navy, Petty Officer 1st Class, 1953-57; received Korean Presidential Citation. **Business Addr:** City Manager, City of Forest Hill, 6800 Forest Hill Dr, Forest Hill, TX 76140.

BADU, ERYKAH (ERICA WRIGHT)
Vocalist. **Personal:** daugHter of Kolleen Wright; children: Seven. **Educ:** Grambling State Univ. **Career:** Vocalist, currently. **Honors/Awds:** Soul Train Lady of Soul Awards, Best New Artist, Best Album, Best Single, Best Song, 1997; American Music Awards, Favorite New Artist Soul & Rap, Favorite Soul Album, 1998; NAACP Image Awards, Outstanding New Artist, Outstanding Female Artist, 1998; Danish Grammy Awards, Best Internations Newcomer, Best Intl Female Artist, 1998; Soul Train Music Awards, Best R&B/Soul Single-Female, Best R&B/Soul Album-Female, Best R&B/Soul or Rap Album of the Year, Best R&B/Soul or Rap New Artist, 1998; Blockbuster Awards, Favorite Female New Artist, Favorite Female R&B Artist, 1997. **Special Achievements:** Albums include: Baduizm, 1996; Erykah Badu Live, 1997; co-directed "On & On;" "Next Lifetime;" sang duo with D'Angelo, Busta Rhymes, and others; hosted "Soul Train's Lady of Soul Awards;" appeared in Blues Brothers 2000, 1998. **Business Addr:** Singer, c/o Kedar Entertainment, 1755 Broadway, 7th Fl, New York, NY 10019, (212)373-0600.

BAETY, EDWARD L.
Attorney, judge. **Personal:** Born Mar 13, 1944, Jacksonville, FL; married. **Educ:** Morris Brown Coll, BS 1965; Howard Univ Sch of Law, JD 1968. **Career:** Atlant Leg Aid Soc, staff atty 1968-71; Equal Employ Opp Commn, dist coun 1971-72; Hill Jones & Farr, asso coun 1972-74; Hill Jones & Farr, part 1974-76; City of Atl Ct, asso jdg 1976-. **Orgs:** Mem Atl Bar Assn; Gate City Bar Assn; State Bar Assn of GA; Atlan Bus League; Vol Leg Serv Atty (Sat law); pres Atlan Spart Ath Clb; pst vice pres Phi Beta Sigma Frat Inc; Black Consort. **Military Serv:** US Army, spec-5. **Business Addr:** City Court of Atlanta, 104 Trinity Ave SW, Atlanta, GA 30335.

BAGBY, RACHEL L
Composer, writer, performing artist, educator. **Personal:** Born Feb 11, 1956, Philadelphia, PA; daughter of Rachel Edna Samiella Rebecca Jones Bagby and William H Bagby; married Martin Neal Davidson, Oct 3, 1987. **Educ:** North Carolina AT&T State, Greensboro, NC, 1973-74; Univ of Pittsburgh, Pittsburgh PA, BA (summa cum laude), 1977; Stanford Law School, Stanford CA, JD, 1983. **Career:** The Wall Street Journal, San Francisco CA, writer 1979; freelance composer, writer, Stanford CA, 1979-; Philadelphia Community Rehabilation Corp, Philadelphia PA, asst dir, 1980-82; African and American Studies, Stanford Univ, program coord, 1983-85; Comm on Black Performing Arts, Stanford CA, program coord, 1983-85; Martin Luther King Jr, Papers Project, Stanford CA, assoc dir, 1985-; Bobby McFerrin's Voicestra, San Francisco CA, composer, performer, 1989-; pres, Outta the Box Recordings, 1989. **Orgs:** Mem & consultant, Natl Black Women's Health Program, 1986-; co-dir, Woman Earth Inst, 1986-; consultant, CA Arts Council, 1984-86; mem, CA Lawyers for the Arts (formerly Bay Area Lawyers for the Arts), 1982-. **Honors/Awds:** Chancellor's Teaching Fellowship, V of Pitssburgh, 1975; admitted into master class with Bobby McFerrin, Omega Inst, 1988; composed and recorded "Grandmothers' Song," theme for a documentary on Alice Walker; chapters published in anthologies: "A Power of Numbers," Healing the Wounds, 1989, "Daughters of Growing Things," Reweaving the World: The Emergenance of Econfeminish, 1989; composed, recorded and produced anti-racism tape "Reach Across the Lines," on self-owened independent label, 1989.

BAGLEY, GREGORY P.
Engineer (retired). **Personal:** Born Sep 19, 1930, New York, NY; son of Carrie A Bagley and Garrett P Bagley; married Helen Smith; children: Gregory Jr, Carole, John. **Educ:** Johns Hopkins Univ, BES 1958; Adelphi Univ, MS 1969. **Career:** Hazeltine Corp, electrical engr 1958-62; Sperry Gyroscope Cty, sr electrical engr 1962-68; Assoc Univ Brookhaven Natl Lab, rsch engr I 1968-93. **Orgs:** Sec bd deacons Union Baptist Church Hempstead 1962-, Supt ss 1985-96; vice pres Franklin PTA 1972-73; mem bd Park Lake Devel Fund Corp 1970-. **Honors/Awds:** Tau Beta Pi, Eta Kappa Nu Hon Engr Soc. **Military Serv:** USAF a/1c 1950-53. **Home Addr:** 11 Botsford St, Hempstead, NY 11550.

BAGLEY, PETER B. E.
Educator, music conductor. **Personal:** Born May 22, 1935, Yonkers, NY; married Bythema Byrd; children: Margaret R. **Educ:** Crane School of Music, SUNY/Potsdam, BS, 1957; Indiana University, School of Music, MM, chor cond, 1965, DM, chor cond, 1972. **Career:** Greenwich Connecticut Public Schools, vocal music teacher, 1957-61; First Baptist Church, director of music, 1964-66; New Paltz Concert Choir & Chamber Singers, conductor, 1966-; All State Choruses of West Virginia, 1970-71, New Hampshire, 1972, Connecticut, 1976, Vermont, 1978; New England Festival Chorus, guest conductor, 1980; SUNY New Paltz, assoc prof of music 1966-; University of Connecticut, Dept of Music, professor, currently. **Orgs:** American Choral Directors Assn; American Choral Foundation; Music Editor Natl Conference; Music Library Assn; Natl Assn for Afro-American Education; New York State School of Music Assn. **Business Addr:** Professor, Dept of Music, University of Connecticut, U-12, 876 Coventry Rd, Storrs Mansfield, CT 06269-0001.

BAGLEY, STANLEY B.
Chaplain. **Personal:** Born Sep 7, 1935, Trenton, NJ; son of Leomae Walker Bagley (deceased) and Dr Semuel M Bagley (deceased); married Ruth McDowell; children: Bernard, Sharon, Bryant, Brett. **Educ:** Morehouse Coll, BA 1958; Crozer Theol Sem, BD 1961; Ashland Theol Sem, MDiv 1973; Univ of OK, grad study, 1967; Century University, PhD, 1994; Association Mental Health Clergy, certified professional mental health clergy, 1976; Department of VA National Black Chaplin Association, certified clinical chaplain, 1996. **Career:** Galilee Bapt Ch Trenton NJ, asst pastor 1961-65; Calvary Bapt Ch, pastor 1965-67; Bapt Campus Ministry Langston Univ, dir 1967-70; Hough Ch, minister of educ comm 1970-71; VA Medical Center Brecksville OH, chaplain 1971-; Lakeside Bapt Ch E Cleveland OH, pastor 1972-1979. **Orgs:** E Cleveland Ministerial Alliance 1975; Assn of Mental Health Clergy, bd certified chaplain, 1974; Ohio Health Care Chaplains; Amer Protestant Hosp Assn; College of Chaplains; chmn, Evangelism Com Bapt Minister's Conf Cleveland OH; Dept of Metropolitan Ministry Cleveland Baptist Assn; life mem and golden heritage life mem, NAACP; Omega Psi Phi Fraternity Inc; American Association of Christian Counselors; Associations of Christian Marriage Counselors; Dept of Veterans Affairs, Natl Black Chaplains Assn, certified clinical chaplain, 1996. **Honors/Awds:** Christian Leadership Citation Bapt Student Union Langston Univ 1969; Outstanding Young Man, Outstanding Amer Found, 1970; 33 Degree Free Mason; United Supreme Council 33 De-

gree Ancient and Accepted Scottish Rite of Freemasonry Prince Hall Affiliation; loaned executive from VAMC to the Combined Federal Campaign, 1988; Crozer Theological Seminary, Crozer Scholar, 1989, 1995. **Home Addr:** 2361 Traymore Rd, University Heights, OH 44118, (216)932-0085.

BAILER, BONNIE LYNN
Business executive. **Personal:** Born Oct 11, 1946, New York, NY; daughter of Maryelyne Matthews Bailer and Lloyd Harding Bailer; children: Miles Bailer Armstead. **Educ:** Queens Coll of City Univ of NY, BA 1968, MS 1975; Columbia University School of Law, currently. **Career:** Foreign Language Dept, New York City Public School System Jr High School, acting chmn 1970-75; Yellow-Go-Rilla Prod, Ltd, vice pres 1975-77; Manhattan Borough pres campaigns, political campaign admin 1977; NAACP, membership consultant 1978-79; The Talkshop Foreign Language Program for Children, founder & pres 1981-; The Gilbert Jonas Co Inc, professional fund raiser, vice pres 1979-86; United Nations Assn of the USA, dir capital campaign 1986-88; Bailer Studios, artists' agent & professional fund raising consultant 1988-; Jones, Day, Reavis & Pogue, legal intern, 1991-. **Orgs:** Bd member, Morningside Montessori School 1979-82, The Grinnell Housein Defense Corp 1984-; certified building mgr City of NY 1979; press coord Annual Westside Comm Conf 1979-; consultant, Minisink City Mission Soc 1984; giving comm member, Cathedral School 1984-; member, Natl Assn of Female Exec, NAACP, Natl Soc of Fundraising Exec, Women in Financial Devel, Planned Giving Group; member, Black Law Students Assn of Columbia University, 1989-.

BAILEY, AARON DUANE
Professional football player. **Personal:** Born Oct 24, 1971, Ann Arbor, MI. **Educ:** Louisville. **Career:** Indianapolis Colts, wide receiver, 1994-. **Business Addr:** Professional Football Player, Indianapolis Colts, PO Box 535000, Indianapolis, IN 46253, (317)297-2658.

BAILEY, ADRIENNE YVONNE
Foundation administrator, educator. **Personal:** Born Nov 24, 1944, Chicago, IL; daughter of Julia Spalding Bailey and Leroy Bailey. **Educ:** Mundelein Coll, BA 1966; Wayne State Univ, MEd 1968; Northwestern Univ, PhD 1973. **Career:** Chicago Bd of Educ, Deneen Elementary School, teacher Social Studies, English, French, Math 1966-67; So Shore YMCA, Chicago, neighborhood youth corps supvr 1967; Circle Maxwell YMCA, Chicago, program coordinator 1967-68; Detroit Bd of Educ, substitute teacher 1968-69; Gov Office of Human Resources, Chicago, educ coord 1969-71; Northwestern Comm Educ Proj, Northwestern Univ, univ coord 1972-73; Chicago Comm Trust, Chicago, sr staff assoc 1973-81; College Bd NY, vice pres acad affairs 1981-. **Orgs:** Gov Educ Adv Comm 1983-87, Natl Comm on Secondary Schooling for Hispanics 1983-85, Educ & Career Devel Advisory Comm Natl Urban League 1982-, visiting comm Grad School of Educ Harvard Univ 1977-83; advisory panel Phi Delta Kappa Gallup Poll of the Publics Attitudes Toward Public Educ 1984; policy comm School of Educ Northwestern Univ 1983-; bd of trustees Hazen Found, New Haven CT, 1977-87; bd of trustees So Educ Found, Atlanta GA, 1983-; Natl Task Force on State Efforts to Achieve Sex Equity 1980-83, chmn advisory comm Council on Found Internship & Fellowship Program for Minorities & Women 1980-82; adv comm Inst for Educ Finance & Govt Stanford Univ 1980-85; bd of dir Assn of Black Found Exec 1975-87; IL State Bd of Educ 1974-81, pres1978-79; Natl Assn of State Bds of Educ; commiss 1981, steering comm 1974-79, exec comm 1977-75, 1978-79 Educ Commiss of the States; Natl Assessment of Educ Program Policy Comm 1976-80; task force Desegregation Strategies Project 1976-81; bd of dir Council on Foundations 86; META 86; editorial bd, The Kappan (Phi Delta Kappan); Governor's Advisory Comm on Black Affairs, NY, co-chair, Educ sub-Committee 1986-; bd of dir The Negro Ensemble, NY, 1987-; bd of trustees Marymount Coll 1988-89; bd of trustees The Foundation Center 1989-. **Honors/Awds:** Merit Award, NW Alumni Assn 1981; Diamond Jubilee Recognition, Phi Delta Kappa 1981; Certificate of Recognition, Phi Delta Kappa NW Univ Chapter 1980; Salute IL Serv, Federal Savings & Loan Bank 1980; Meritorious Serv Award, Educ Commission of the State NAEP 1980; Human Relations Award, IL Educ Assn 1980; attendance at White House Celebration for the Signing of S210 Creating a Dept of Educ, 1979; Kizzy Award for Outstanding Contributions in Educ 1979; Outstanding Achievement Award in Educ, YWCA of Metro Chicago 1978; Distinguished Serv Award, Ed Commission of the State 1977; 1 of 10 Outstanding Young Citizens Award, Chicago Jaycees 1976; Community Motivation Award HU MA BE Karate Assoc 1975; 1 of 10 Outstanding Young Persons Award, IL Jaycees 1975; 1of 100 Outstanding Black Women in AmAward, Operation PUSH 1975; Commencement Speaker Mundelein Coll 1975; Image Award for Outstanding Contributions in Field of Educ, League of Black Women 1974; Recognition Award, Black Achiever of Indust YMCA of Metro Chicago 1974; TTT Fellowship, Northwestern Univ 1971-73; MDEA Inst in French, Univ of ME 1966; numerous publications including, "Comm Coll Capability Project," IL Bd of Higher Educ 1972, "Citizens in Public Ed in Chicago" Citizen Action in Educ 1976, "Agenda for Action" Educ Leadership 1984; "Top 100 Black Business & Professional Women," Dollars & Sense Magazine, 1985; Special Service Award, Natl Alliance of Black School Educators, 1987. **Home Addr:** 2951 S King Dr Apt 911, Chicago, IL 60616. **Business Addr:** Vice President Acad Affairs, The College Board, 45 Columbus Ave, New York, NY 10023.

BAILEY, AGNES JACKSON
Educator. **Personal:** Born Aug 18, 1931, Dallas, TX; divorced. **Educ:** San Jose State Univ, BA 1951. **Career:** Hanford Joint Union High School, instructor 1954-58; Sacramento Sr High School, instructor 1959-74; California Youth Authority N Reception Center Clinic, math consultant 1967; Valley Area Constrn Opportunity Program, consultant & tutorial specialist 1970-; Sacramento Sr High School, Sacramento City Unified School Dist, counselor 1974-. **Orgs:** Mem CA Tchrs Assn 1954-; life mem Natl Educ Assn 1965; Sacramento City Tchrs Assn; pres Hanford HS Tchrs Assn 1957-58; mem CA Math Cncl 1956-; mem NAACP; Alpha Kappa Alpha; Delta Kappa Gamma Soc for Women in Educ; Amer Assn of Univ Women 1954-69. **Honors/Awds:** First Black hs tchr at Hanford HS 1954; 2nd Black HS tchr in Sac City Unified Sch Dist 1959; honored by Stanford Univ Coll of Engrg 1966; Outstanding Secondary Educator of Amer 1975. **Business Addr:** Counselor, Sacramento Sr HS, 2315 34 St, Sacramento, CA 95817.

BAILEY, ANTOINETTE M.
Aerospace industry executive. **Personal:** Born Oct 4, 1949, St Louis, MO; daughter of Margurie Brown Rollins and Jack D Rollins; married George E Bailey, Jul 10, 1988; children: Dara Braddock, Errin Braddock. **Educ:** Southern IL Univ, Carbondale, IL, BA, 1972; MI State Univ, East Lansing, MI, MA, 1973. **Career:** MI State Univ, East Lansing, MI, graduate asst, 1973-75; East Lansing High School, East Lansing, MI, teacher, 1973-74; Panama Canal Co, Balboa Heights, CZ, EEO specialist investigator, 1976-77; Narcotics Service Council, St Louis, MO, supervisory counselor, 1978-80; MO Div Vocational Rehab, Olivette, MO, sr counselor for the deaf, 1980-84; McDonnell Douglas Corp, St Louis, MO, dir of training & devt, 1984-, vp of community relations, currently. **Orgs:** Urban League of Metropolitan St Louis, board member; Regional Commerce & Growth Association, board member. **Honors/Awds:** Leadership Award, YMCA, 1988; Presenteeism Award 2, McDonnell Douglas, 1986-87; Presenteeism Award 1, McDonnell Douglas, 1985-86; Natl Insts of Mental Health Fellow, 1972-75; Counselor of the Year, MO Natl Rehab Assn, 1983; Leadership St Louis Participant, Class of 1991-92. **Business Addr:** VP, Community Relations, McDonnell Douglas Corp, PO Box 516, Mail Code 1001510, St Louis, MO 63166.

BAILEY, ARTHUR
Government administrator. **Personal:** Born in Wilkinsburg, PA; son of Winifred Townsend Bailey and William Henry Bailey. **Educ:** Pittsburgh Acad, 1947-49; Carnegie Inst of Tech, 1949-55; Dept of Agr Grad Sch Washington DC, 1955-56; Dept of Interior, Mgmt Training Prog 1955-56. **Career:** Dept of Interior Bureau of Mines, admin asst 1956-58, purchasing agent 1958-60; Holmes & Narver Inc, sec 1964-65; NASA Pasadena, CA, contract asst 1966-68; Social Security Admin, claims rep 1968-73, field rep 1974-81, claims rep 1981-93, social insurance specialist, 1993-. **Orgs:** Actor Pittsburgh Playhouse 1958-59; field rep journalist, public speaker Social Security Admin 1974-83; dir of public rel Black Porsche Inc 1976-78; mem, parliamentarian 1979-82, historian 1983-84 BPI 1973-; Porsche Club of America, 1981-; Federal Employees West Credit Union, board of directors, 1986-88, treasurer, board of directors, 1989-90, secretary, board of directors, 1991-92. **Honors/Awds:** Sustained Superior Performance Awd Corps of Engrs 1960-61; Outstanding Performance Awd Social Security Admin Huntington Park CA 1976; Superior Performance Awd Social Security Admin Los Angeles CA 1984; Outstanding Performance Award, Univ Village Office, Los Angeles, CA, Social Security Admin 1988; Public Service Award in Recognition of 40 years of service in the govt of USA, Commr of Social Security, Baltimore, MD, 1988; Social Security Administration, University Village Office, Outstanding Performance Award, 1992, Pittsburgh, PA, Downtown Chorale, singer, tenor, 1949-58; performed 2-3 concerts a year in addition to performances with the Pittsburgh Symphony and Wheeling Symphony Orchestra, the chorale appeared on television and made recordings; Social Security, University Village Office, Los Angeles, CA, Outstanding Performance Award, 1992, 1993. **Military Serv:** USAF sgt 1945-46. **Business Addr:** Social Insurance Rep, Social Security Admin, 1115 W Adams Blvd, Los Angeles, CA 90007.

BAILEY, BOB CARL
Business executive. **Personal:** Born Oct 13, 1935, Colbert Co, AL. **Educ:** Attended AL A&M Univ Huntsville. **Career:** Bailey & Co, owner 1965-; Bailey Used Cars, owner 1969-78; WZZA Radio/Muscle Shoals Broadcasting, owner/pres/gen mgr 1977-. **Orgs:** Chmn, Northwest Alabama Community Development Corp, 1988-. **Military Serv:** US Army, Sgt 1953-56. **Home Phone:** (205)381-6006. **Business Addr:** President/General Manager, WZZA Radio Muscle Shoals Brdcs, 1570 Woodmont Dr, Tuscumbia, AL 35674, (205)381-1862.

BAILEY, CARLTON WILSON
Professional football player. **Personal:** Born Dec 15, 1964, Baltimore, MD. **Educ:** Univ of North Carolina, bachelor's degree in sociology, 1988. **Career:** Buffalo Bills, linebacker, 1988-92; New York Giants, 1993-94; Carolina Panthers, 1995-. **Business Addr:** Professional Football Player, Carolina Panthers, 800 Mint St, Ericsson Stadium, Charlotte, NC 28202, (704)358-7000.

BAILEY, CAROL A.
Air traffic controller. **Career:** Federal Aviation Administration, Detroit Metropolitan Air Traffic Control, supervisory air traffic control specialist, 1991-. **Orgs:** Professional Women Controllers. **Special Achievements:** First African American female supervisory air traffic control specialist at the Detroit Metropolitan Air Traffic Control. **Business Addr:** Supervisory Air Traffic Control Specialist, Detroit Metropolitan Air Traffic Control, Bldg 801, Rm 104, Detroit, MI 48242.

BAILEY, CLARENCE WALTER
Business executive. **Personal:** Born Sep 25, 1933, Longview, TX; married Mavis Lean Blankenship; children: Sherry Lenel Smith. **Educ:** Wiley Clg, BS 1954; Drake Univ, Mstrs 1959. **Career:** Baileys Ins Agency, mgr 1966-. **Orgs:** Life mem Million Dollar Round Table 1973-; dir Oil Belt Asso of Life Underwriters 1967-; sec LISD Sch Bd 1984-; dir Good Shephard Med Ctr 1983-. **Honors/Awds:** Mem Civitan Club 1978-; dir Jr Achvmnt 1984-; Silver Beaver Awd BSA 1980; top ten prod Pres Cncl NWL 1971-; edctn Phi Delta Kappa 1981-; outstndng citizen awd NAACP 1978; Honorary Doctorate Degree, Wiley College, 1995. **Military Serv:** USAF, sgt 1954-57. **Home Addr:** 2307 Lilly St, Longview, TX 75602. **Business Addr:** Divisional Sales Manager, Bailey's Ins Agency, PO Box 7606, Longview, TX 75607.

BAILEY, CURTIS DARNELL
Educator, marketing and commnunications consultant. **Personal:** Born May 21, 1954, Philadelphia, PA; son of Helena Bailey. **Educ:** Temple Univ, BA 1976; Clark/Atlanta Univ, MBA 1978. **Career:** Benton & Bowles Inc, asst account exec 1978-79; Atochem Corp, advertising mgr 1979-84; DuPont Co, marketing communications specialist 1984-87; marketing and communications consultant 1987; Rowan Univ, professor of management/marketing, 1990-93; Eastern College, professor fast-track MBA program, 1997-. **Orgs:** Kappa Alpha Psi Frat 1983-. **Honors/Awds:** Bell Ringer Awd, Best Newsletter Business & Professional Advertising Assns, 1982, 1983; Top Ten Readership Ad Awd Chemical Processing Magazine, 1983, 1985; State of New Jersey, Department of Higher Education, faculty fellowship, 1993. **Home Addr:** 2412 Aspen St, Philadelphia, PA 19130.

BAILEY, D'ARMY
Circuit court judge. **Personal:** Born Nov 29, 1941, Memphis, TN; son of Will Ella Bailey and Walter L Bailey Sr; married Adrienne Marie Leslie; children: Justin, Merritt. **Educ:** Clark Univ, AB 1964; Yale Univ, LLB 1967; Attended, Southern Univ 1959-62, Boston Univ 1964-65. **Career:** Field Found NY, prog adv 1970; City Council Bkly CA, 1971-73; Private Practice, attorney 1970-90; Circuit Court Judge, 1990-. **Orgs:** Staff atty Neighborhood Legal Assts Found 1968-70; natl dir Law Students Civil Rights Rsch Cncl 1967-68; bd dir Vollitine Boys Club 1974-76; Council Legal Ed Prof Resp 1969-70; founder, National Civil Rights Museum, Memphis; Tennessee Historical Commission, 1990-; Tennessee Commission on Humanities 1984-88. **Honors/Awds:** Screen actor, Mystery Train and People Vs. Larry Flynt. **Special Achievements:** Publications: The Role of Race in the Memphis Courts, Washington and Lee Law Review, 1994; Mine Eyes Have Seen, Dr Martin Luther King Jr Final Journey, Towery Press, 1993; Inequities of the Parole System in CA, Howard Univ Law Journal, 1972; Trying to Make it (The Law) Real Compared to What, Univ of Toledo Law Review, 1971; Equal But Separate, Civil Liberties, 1969; Enjoining the Enforcement of the State Criminal Statutes Which Abridge First Amendment Freedoms, Harvard Civil Rights, Civil Liberties Law Review, 1967. **Home Phone:** (901)327-5544. **Business Addr:** Circuit Court Judge, Div VIII, Shelby County Courthouse, 140 Adams Ave, Memphis, TN 38103, (901)576-4022.

BAILEY, DIDI GISELLE
Psychiatrist. **Personal:** Born Mar 14, 1948, New York, NY; daughter of Gertha Jones Smith and William Buster Bailey; divorced; children: Jordan Eleanor Pete. **Educ:** Howard Univ, BS 1968, MD 1972; Howard Univ Hosp, Cert Gen Psych 1975. **Career:** District of Columbia Govt, forensic psychiatrist 1974-79, med consult disability dept 1979-80; State of CA, med consult disability dept 1981-85; Didi G Bailey MD, psychiatrist 1975-. **Orgs:** Mem adv bd, Alameda County Mental Health 1981-89, vice pres, 1987; pres No CA Black Women Physicians Assn 1990-93; counselor Golden State Medical Assn 1990-93; mem exec comm Sinkler Miller State Med Assn, 1991-92; mem Medical Educ and Hospitals Cnl, NMA 1989-. **Honors/Awds:** Commendation, Alameda Co Bd of Supervisors, 1989. **Home Addr:** 4324 Rilea Way, #35, Oakland, CA 94605-3720. **Business Addr:** Psychiatrist, 2700 E 14th St, Oakland, CA 94601-1576, (510)534-0605.

BAILEY, DONN FRITZ
Educational administrator. **Personal:** Born Feb 26, 1932, New Castle, IN; son of Thelma Cottman Bailey and Walter F Bailey; married Andrea June Bess; children: Donna, Marta, Traja. **Educ:** IN Univ, BS 1954, MA 1962; PA State Univ, PhD 1974. **Career:** Chicago Bd of Educ Div of Speech Corr, speech therapist 1954-66; Center for Inner City Studies Chicago, asst dir 1966-68; PA State Univ Speech Comm Dept, research assoc 1968-70; Center for Inner City Studies Chicago, asst dir/asst prof 1970-74, dir/prof 1974-. **Orgs:** Vice pres of trustees Abraham Lincoln Center 1974-; exec dir 1978-80, chm, bd, Natl Black Assn for Speech Lang & Hearing; sec bd of dir Coretta Scott King YWCA 1979-; chmn Comm on Communication Behaviors Amer Speech Lang & Hearing Assn 1976-; chmn, Monitoring Commn for Desegregation Implementation 1985-; chm, brd of dir, Open Lands Project 1987-; chmn 1st Congressional Dist Task Force on Educ 1988-. **Honors/Awds:** Mem Kappa Alpha Psi Frat; Ford Advanced Study Grant Ford Foundation 1969-70. **Military Serv:** US Army, capt 1954-56. **Business Addr:** Director/Professor, Northeastern Illinois Univ, 700 E Oakwood Blvd, Center for Inner City Studies, Chicago, IL 60653.

BAILEY, DORIS JONES
Association executive, social rights activist. **Personal:** Born May 16, 1927, Port Chester, NY; daughter of Alice M Randall Jones and Robert Leon Jones; married Alfred K Bailey, May 31, 1964; children: Alethia Joy Streeter. **Educ:** Immanuel Lutheran College, Associate Degree, education, 1947. **Career:** Department of the Army-Pentagon, clerk; New York State, secretary; BOCES, social worker assistant, administrative assistant. **Orgs:** Port Chester/Rye NAACP, president, 1990-; Immanuel Lutheran College Alumni Association, president, 1985-; Council of Community Service, board member, 1992-; Carver Community Center, board member, 1990-; State University of New York, museum advisory committee member, 1992-. **Home Addr:** 325 King St, Port Chester, NY 10573, (914)937-6613.

BAILEY, DUWAIN
Public administrator. **Personal:** Born May 29, 1957, Chicago, IL; son of Arlena Sanders Bailey and McWillie Bailey; married Jocelyn Kyle Bailey, Jul 16, 1983; children: Branden, Kyle. **Educ:** Southern Illinois University, Carbondale, IL, BA, 1980. **Career:** State of Illinois, Springfield, IL, technical manager/safety projects mgr, 1980-84; State of Illinois, Chicago, IL, technical mgr III/public transportation mgr, 1984-85; City of Chicago, Chicago, IL, senior budget analyst, 1985-87, finance manager, 1987-88, deputy commissioner, 1988-. **Orgs:** Asst financial secretary, Phi Beta Sigma Fraternity-Upsilon Sigma, 1991-; chairman, social action committee, Phi Beta Sigma Fraternity-Upsilon Sigma, 1990-; treasurer, board of directors, National Forum for Black Public Admin, Chicago Chapter, 1989-; South Shore High School College Club, advisor; Apostolic Church of God; Chicago Association of Commerce & Industry Youth Motivation Program, participant. **Honors/Awds:** Spinx Club, Southern Illinois University Honorary Society, 1979; Pan-Hellinic Member of the Year, 1977. **Business Addr:** Deputy Commissioner, General Services, City of Chicago, 510 North Peshtigo Ct, 6th Floor, Chicago, IL 60611.

BAILEY, EUGENE RIDGEWAY
Military/government official (retired), business owner. **Personal:** Born Oct 1, 1938, Painter, VA; son of Alma Cleo Jacobs Bailey and James Hatton Bailey; married Juanita Hicks Bailey, Aug 28, 1961; children: Denise, Duane. **Educ:** Virginia State University, Petersburg, VA, BS, 1960; US International University, San Diego, CA, MA, 1976, DBA, 1986. **Career:** USS Fort Fisher, LSD-40, San Diego, CA, executive officer, 1977-79; Amphibious Squadron, San Diego, CA, chief of staff, 1979-81; USS Racine, LST-1191, Long Beach, CA, commanding officer, 1981-83; Telecommunications, CMD, Washington, DC, division director, 1983-85; USS Juneau, LPD-10, San Diego, CA, commanding officer, 1985-87; Naval Recruiting HDQ, Arlington, VA, deputy, 1987-89; Naval Educ & Training Support Center, San Diego, CA, captain/commanding officer, currently; Eugene R Bailey & Associates, currently. **Orgs:** Member, Greater San Diego Chamber of Commerce, 1989-91; member, National Naval Officers Association, 1977-91; member, California Continuing Military Educators, Assn, 1990-91; board of director, Jackie Robinson, YMCA, San Diego, 1987-91. **Military Serv:** US Navy, Captain, 1961-91; Legion of Merit 1989, Meritorious Service 1987. **Business Addr:** Eugene R Bailey & Associates, 6206 Lake Lucerne Dr, San Diego, CA 92119, (619)463-7671.

BAILEY, GARY
Human service executive. **Personal:** Born Oct 9, 1955, Cleveland, OH; son of Samuel Jr & Lucille Bailey. **Educ:** University School for Boys, 1973; Tufts University, BA, 1977; Boston University, School of Social Work, MSW, 1979. **Career:** Family Svcs of Greater Boston, director of Boston Social Svcs, 1980-93; Parents & Children's Svcs, executive director, 1993-. **Orgs:** AIDS Action Committee Inc, president, 1992-; National Association of Soc Wrks, Washington DC, treasurer, 1994-97; Wang Ctr for Performing Arts, 1994-; Phillips Brooks House Association, Harvard University, 1996. **Honors/Awds:** Fenway Community Health Ctr, Congressman Gerry Studds, Visibility Awd, 1996; Boston University, School of Soc Wrk, Greatest Contribution to Soc Work Prac, 1995; University Mass Gerontology Institute, Community Svc Awd, 1993. **Business Addr:** Executive Director, Parents' & Children's Services, 654 Beacon St, Boston, MA 02215.

BAILEY, GRACIE MASSENBERG
Educator administrator. **Personal:** Born Feb 25, 1936, Waverly, VA; daughter of Maxine Stith Massenberg and Ernest R Massenberg; married Erling Sr (divorced); children: LaYetta B Goldsborough, Erling Jr. **Educ:** VA State Coll, BS 1958; VA State Coll, Elem Ed 1963, Computer Mgmt 1969, MEd 1970; VA Polytechnic Inst and State Univ, DEd 1983. **Career:** VA State Coll, sec 1958-62; Amelia Cty School Bd, teacher 1958-60; Hartford Variable Annuity Life Insurance Co, salesperson 1960-79; Sussex Cty School Bd, teacher 1961-63; Dinwiddie Cty School Bd, business educ teacher 1963-74; Richard Bland Coll, dir of personnel, assoc prof business, asst to pres AA/EEO 1974-, registrar 1986-88, associate provost for student service, 1988-90, associate provost, 1990-. **Orgs:** Mem Sussex Ed Assoc 1961-63; sec Dinwiddie Ed Assoc 1963-74; sec, treas Erling Baily Elect Contr 1966-85; mem & recording sec Amer Bus Women Assoc Dinwiddie Charter Chap 1971-84; mem Amer Assoc of Univ Profs 1974-79; mem Amer Assoc of Affirmative Action 1976-; mem adv cncl Educ Computing for the State of VA 1976-80; mem Coll and Univ Personnel Assoc 1978-; mem & rep Natl & VA Assoc for Women in Higher Ed 1978-; recording sec VA Admissions Cncl on Black Concerns 1984-; mem Human Rights Comm for Hiram Davis Medical Ctr 1986-; mem VA Assoc of Coll Registrars and Admissions Officers, Southern Assoc of Collegiate Registrars & Admissions Officers, Amer Assoc of Collegiate Registrars and Admissions Officers 1986-; vp Budget, Allocation and Fund Raising, UnitedWay Services 1988-89; chairpersonouthside Operations Board, 1990; past chairperson member, Girl Scouts of VA 1991-94; Petersburg Festival Chorus, Inc, board member 1990-. **Honors/Awds:** Salutatorian Sussex Cty Training School 1954; Cert & Plaque of Apprec Future Bus Leaders of Amer 1972-74; Achievement Awds Dinwiddie Ed Assoc 1973-74; Outstanding Ed of Amer 1975. **Business Addr:** Associate Provost, Richard Bland Coll, Route 1 Box 77 A, Petersburg, VA 23805.

BAILEY, HARRY A., JR.
Educator, city official. **Personal:** Born Dec 19, 1932, Fort Pierce, FL; married Mary L; children: Harry III, Larry B. **Educ:** Florida A&M University, BA, 1954; University of Kansas, MA, 1960, PhD, 1964. **Career:** University of Kansas, asst instructor, 1960-62, asst instructor, Western Civilization, 1962-64, instructor, Sociology, 1964; Temple University, asst professor, 1964-68, assoc professor & chairman, Dept of Political Science, 1970-73, professor, Dept of Political Science, 1973-75, professor & direct, Masters Program in Public Administration, 1975-80, chairman, graduate studies, 1985-90. **Orgs:** American Political Science Assn; American Society of Public Administration; Center Study Pres; PA Political Science & Public Administration Assn, 1970-72; vice president, Northeastern Science Assn, 1971-72; president, bd gov, Temple University Faculty Club, 1972-73. **Honors/Awds:** Editor, Negro Politics in America, Charles Merrill Publishers, 1967; co-editor, Ethnic Group Politics, Charles Merrill Publ, 1969; Leonard D White Award Com American Political Science Assn, 1974-75; Pi Sigma Alpha; Danforth Assn, 1975-81; editorial bd, Journal Politics, 1975-76; editor, Classics of the Am Pres, Moore Publishing Co, 1980. **Special Achievements:** Co-editor, The American Presidency, Dorsey Press, 1988; winner, Lindback Distinguished Teaching Award, 1978; winner, Temple University Great Teacher's Award, 1992; co-editor, State & Local Government & Politics, FE Peacock Publishers, 1993; chairman, Civil Service Commission, City of Philadelphia, 1983-91; Zoning Board of Adjustment, City of Philadelphia, 1992-. **Military Serv:** US Army, 2nd lt 1954-55, 1st lt, 1955-57. **Business Addr:** Professor, Dept of Political Science, Temple University, Philadelphia, PA 19122-2585, (215)204-7787.

BAILEY, HENRY
Professional football player. **Personal:** Born Feb 26, 1973. **Educ:** Univ of Nevada-Las Vegas. **Career:** New York Jets, wide receiver, 1996; Denver Broncos, 1997-. **Business Addr:** Professional Football Player, Pittsburgh Steelers, Three Rivers Stadium, 300 Stadium Circle, Pittsburgh, PA 15212, (412)323-1200.

BAILEY, JERRY DEAN
International business executive. **Personal:** Born Sep 4, 1950, Colquitt, GA; son of Wyolene Webb Bailey and Clarence Bailey; married Cheryl Y Gould-Bailey, Aug 30, 1972; children: Jelani N Gould-Bailey, Camilah A Gould-Bailey. **Educ:** Ohio University, Athens, OH, BA (cum laude), 1972; Boston Univ Law School, Boston, MA, JD, 1975; Massachusetts Inst of Technology, Cambridge, MA, MBA, 1979. **Career:** Boston Juvenile Ct, Boston, MA, asst clerk, 1975-77; Hewlett Packard Co, Palo Alto, CA, financial analyst, 1979-81; RJR Nabisco Inc, Winston-Salem, NC, assoc tax counsel, 1981-83; Winston-Salem State Univ, instructor in corp finance, 1982-86; RJR Nabisco Inc, Winston-Salem, NC, intl tax mgr, 1983-87; RJR Nabisco Inc, Atlanta, GA, sr intl tax counsel, 1987-89; World Trade Inst, seminar speaker, 1987-89. **Orgs:** Mem, Massachusetts Bar, 1975-89; area governor, pres, Toastmasters, 1980-89; treasurer, bd mem, Winston-Salem Junior Achievement, 1982-85; chapter pres, Optimist Club, 1984-87; mem, Tax Executives Institute, 1984-89; chmn, Soccer League, East Winston Optimist, 1986-87. **Business Addr:** Dir, Intl Taxes, RJR Nabisco Inc, 300 Galleria Pkwy, Atlanta, GA 30339.

BAILEY, JOSEPH ALEXANDER, II
Physician. **Personal:** Born Jul 22, 1935, Pine Bluff, AR; children: Ryan, Jana, Joseph III, Johathan, Jerad, Jordan. **Educ:** Univ Of MI Ann Arbor, undrgrad 1953-55; Morehouse Clg, BS 1957; Meharry Med Sch, Med Degree 1961. **Career:** Los Angeles Co Hosp, internship 1961-62 hahnemann hosp phil pA, chf res 1964-66; st hosp for crippled children pA, chief res 1966-67; hosp for Joint Diseases NY, NY, sr res 1967-68. **Orgs:** Asso staff & prof San Bernardino Co Gen Hosp; independent med examiner for St of Ca; asso staff St Betnardines Hosp; chief of gen sect Acdmy of Ortho-Neuro Soc. **Honors/Awds:** Flw Med Gen John Hopkins Hosp MA 1968-69; fellow Ortho Sur John Hopkins Hosp Baltimore 1968-69; fellow Am Clg of Surgeons 1971-; diplomate Am Bd ofOrtho Surgeons 1971; listed in best Drs of Am 1979; Comm Ldr Awd from Noteworthy Americans 1978; awd Black Voice News 1985. **Military Serv:** USAF capt 1962-64. **Business Addr:** President, JA Bailey II M D Prof Corp, 399 E Highland Ave #501, San Bernardino, CA 92404.

BAILEY, LAWRENCE R., SR. **See Obituaries section.**

BAILEY, LEE
Communications company executive. **Career:** Disc jockey; Lee Bailey Communications, president, currently. **Business Addr:** President, Lee Bailey Communications, 3151 Cahuenga Blvd W, Suite 200, Los Angeles, CA 90068, (213)969-0011.

BAILEY, LINDA F. (LINDA F. GLOVER)
Government official. **Personal:** Born Oct 1, 1951, Emerson, AR; daughter of Alberta Washington Glover and Edmond Glover; married Fred E Bailey, May 19, 1979; children: Janelle Nicole, Jocelyn Briana. **Educ:** South Arkansas University, Magnolia, AR, BME, 1973; University of Missouri, Kansas City, MO, MPA, 1978. **Career:** Social Security Admin, Kansas City, MO, Social Insurance Claims Examiner, 1973-79; Small Business Admin, Kansas City, MO, equal opportunity officer, 1979-82, business development spec, 1982-90, assistant district director for business dev, 1990-94, chief, economic development team 1, 1994-. **Business Addr:** Assistant District Director for Business Development, Small Business Administration, 323 W 8th St, #501, Room 501, Kansas City, MO 64105-1500.

BAILEY, MONA HUMPHRIES
Educational administrator. **Personal:** Born Dec 14, 1932; married William Peter Bailey; children: Peter Govan, Christopher Evans. **Educ:** FL A&M Univ Tallahassee, BS 1954; OR State Univ Corvalis, MS 1962. **Career:** Meany-Madrona Middle School, Seattle WA, principal, 1970-73; Univ of WA, instructor, 1973-74; Eckstein Middle School, Seattle WA, principal appointee, 1974-75; WA State Supt of Public Instuction, asst supt, 1974-. **Orgs:** Bd dirs Totem Girl Scout Cncl Seattle 1977-; chmn adv com Seattle Oppors Industrialization Ctr 1978; mem adv bd United Negro Coll Fund Inc Seattle1978-; Commn mem Gov's Commn on Criminal Justice 1974-; bd of trustees Pacific Sci Ctr Seattle 1975-; natl pres Delta Sigma Theta 1980. **Honors/Awds:** Disting Serv Field of Educ Inner City Awd Carnation Co 1973-74; Achievement Awd Les Dames Bridge Club Seattle 1974; Disting achievement Serv to Youth Awd The Links Inc 20th Natl Assn Seattle 1976; Disting Comm Serv Awd Benefit Guild Seattle 1978. **Business Addr:** Assistant Superintendent, WA State Supt of Pub Instn, Old Capitol Bldg FB-11, Olympia, WA 98504.

BAILEY, MYRTLE LUCILLE
Business owner. **Personal:** Born Jul 11, 1954, St Louis, MO; daughter of Mildred Turrentine Bailey and George Wendell Bailey; married R Mark Odom, Oct 18, 1986; children: Jared Michael. **Educ:** Dillard University, BA, psychology, 1976; St Louis University, cert applied gerontology, 1977, MA, urban affairs, 1977. **Career:** Central Medical Center, director marketing, 1977-80; Greater St Louis Health Systems Agency, planning associate, 1980-81; Catalyst, consultant, 1981-84; Harris-Stowe College, director public relations, 1984-87; Catalyst Public Relations, Inc, CEO, 1987-. **Orgs:** Paraquad, board of directors, 1992-; City-wide Federation of Republican Women, president, 1992-; Catholic Commission on Housing, board of directors, 1990-; Provident School, board of directors, 1990-; St Louis Convention & Visitors Commission, 1991-; RCGA-St Louis, 1992-; NAACP Executive Committee, 1992-. **Honors/Awds:** St Louis Development Agency, Outstanding Business, 1992; Annie Malone Children's Home, Special Contribution, 1990; Lincoln University Student Gov Association, Participation-YMTF, 1988; Harris-Stowe State College, Appreciation Student Gov, 1987, Dedication & Service Alumni Association, 1987. **Special Achievements:** Silver Microphone Award for "We Wish to Plead Our Own Cause," 1989. **Business Phone:** (314)535-7535.

BAILEY, PHYLLIS ANN
Newspaper copy editor. **Personal:** Born Dec 10, 1957, Long Beach, CA; daughter of Ammie Fusilier Bailey and Norris Bailey. **Educ:** California State University, Long Beach, CA, BA, Journalism, 1981; Graduate School of Journalism, Berkeley, CA, Summer Program for Minority Journalists, 1983. **Career:** Register, Santa Ana, CA, copy clerk, 1980-81; Sentinel, Los Angeles, CA, reporter, 1981-83; Register, Des Moines, IA, reporter, 1983-87; Times, Trenton, NJ, reporter, copy editor, 1987-89; Journal, Milwaukee, WI, copy editor, 1989-. **Orgs:** Secretary, Southern California Assoc of Black Journalists, 1982-83; vice pres, Garden State Association of Black Journalists, 1988-89.

BAILEY, RANDALL CHARLES
Minister, educator. **Personal:** Born May 26, 1947, Malden, MA; son of Lorraine Margolis Bailey and Charles C Bailey; married Dorothy Jean Lewis Bailey, Apr 7, 1973; children: Omari Lewis Bailey, Imani Akilah Bailey. **Educ:** Brandeis Univ, Waltham, MA, BA (cum laude), 1969; Univ of Chicago, IL, AM, Social Serv Admin, 1972; Candler School of Theology, Atlanta, GA, MDiv (cum laude), 1979; Emory Univ, Atlanta, GA, PhD, Religion, 1987. **Career:** PCSAP Loop College, Chicago, IL, dir of educ prog, 1972-1973; Shelby Co Devel Coord Dept, Memphis, TN, assoc dir, 1973; Atlanta Univ School of Social Work, Atlanta, GA, asst prof, 1973-81; First Cong Church, UCC, Atlanta, GA, asst minister, 1980-81; Interdenominational Theological Center, Atlanta, GA, instructor 1981-87, asst prof 1987-90, assoc prof 1990-. **Orgs:** Mem, Black Theology Project, 1986-; co-chair, Afro-Amer Theology & Biblical Hermeneutics Soc of Biblical Lit, 1987-94; co-chair, Unity/Renewal Study, COFO/NCCCUSA, 1988-; mem, Div Educ & Min/NCCCUSA, 1988-91, Bible Translation & Utilization Comm DEM/NCCCUSA, 1988-91, Soc for the Study of Black Religion, 1988-; mem, bd of dir, S DeKalb YMCA. **Honors/Awds:** Distinguished Serv Award, Atlanta Natl Assn of Black Social Workers, 1978; Fellow, Black Doctoral Prog/FTE, 1979-81, 1984-85; ''Litany for Beginning,'' Inauguration of Mayor Andrew Young, 1981; Fellow, United Negro Coll Fund, 1984-85. **Special Achievements:** Author: ''The Redemption of Yhwh: A Literary Critical Function of the Songs of Hannah and David,'' Biblical Interpretation, 1995; ''Is That Any Name for a Nice Hebrew Boy?' - Exodus 2:1-10: The De-Africanization of an Israelite Hero,'' The Recover of Black Presence: An Interdisciplinary Exploration, Abingdon, 1995; ''They're Nothing but Incestuous Bastards: The Polemical Use of Sex and Sexuality in Hebrew Canon Narrative,'' Reading From This Place: Social Location and Biblical Interpretation in the United States, Fortress, 1994; ''And Then They Will Know That I Am YHWH: The P Recasting of the Plague Narratives,'' JITC, 1994; ''What Price Inclusivity?: An Afrocentric Reading of Dangerous Biblical Texts,'' Voices from the Third World, 1994; ''Cobb Clergy's Gay Stance Loses Punch in Biblical Debate,'' Atlanta Journal/Constitution, p F2, June 26, 1994; '' A De-politicized Gospel: Reflections on Galatians 5:22-23,'' Ecumenical Trends, 22 No 1, Jan 1993; ''Doing the Wrong Thing: Male-Female Relationships in the Hebrew Canon,'' We Belong Together: The Churches in Solidarity with Women, Friendship Press, 1992; numerous other publications. **Business Addr:** Assoc Prof of Old Testament and Hebrew, Interdenominational Theological Center, 671 Beckwith St SW, Atlanta, GA 30314.

BAILEY, ROBERT MARTIN LUTHER
Professional football player. **Personal:** Born Sep 3, 1968, Miami, FL; married Wylidra; children: Kharee. **Educ:** Miami (Fla.), BS degree in science. **Career:** Los Angeles Rams, defensive back, 1991-94; Washington Redskins, 1995; Dallas Cowboys, 1995; Miami Dolphins, 1996; Detroit Lions, 1997-. **Orgs:** Save the Earth Foundation, spokesperson. **Business Addr:** Professional Football Player, Detroit Lions, 1200 Featherstone Rd, Pontiac, MI 48342, (248)335-4131.

BAILEY, RONALD W.
Consultant, planner. **Personal:** Born May 21, 1938, Chicago, IL; son of Leona Z Smith Alexander and Claude Bailey; married Florentine Kelly; children: Darlene Bailey, Ronald Jr, Charles. **Educ:** Univ of WI, BS 1962; Northeastern IL Univ, MEd 1972; Univ of MI, Mgmt by Objective 1978; John Marshall Law School, Community Law Cert 1979. **Career:** Dayton YMCA, Dayton, OH, youth program dir, 1964-67; Office of Economic Opportunity, Dayton, OH, exec dir, 1967-70; Chicago Youth Centers, assoc exec dir; Northeastern IL Univ, instr; United Way of Chicago, planner; City of Chicago, child care manager; Cook County IL, manpower planner; United Way of Dade County, sr consultant, program manager, Community Renewal Soc. **Orgs:** Chicago Urban League, 1970-88; co-founder, chairman, Chicago Black Child Develop, 1978-; Black Child Dev Inst Washington, 1978-, Chicago Blacks in Philanthropy, 1984-, Association of Black Fund Raising Execs, 1984-; People United to Save Humanity, 1984-88; Association Black Fundraising Execs, 1986-88; vice pres, Roosevelt PTA; Steering Comm Neighborhood Capitol Budget Group; Chicago Council on Urban Affairs, Chicago Workshop on Economic Dev, Chicago Mgmt Assistance Program; board member, Provident St Mel Development Corp, 1990-; board member, Provident St Mel School, 1990-; Village of Bellwood, IL, board of health; Canaan AME Church, steward; Chicago Area Technical Assistance Providers, board member; LEAD, board member; coord, Black Caucus, Family Resource Coalition, Chicago; mem, Statewide Family Preservation, Statewide Task Forck, IL Dept of Children & Family Services; consultant, IL Dept of Children & Family Services; consultant, Fishers of Men Project, a male mentoring program, Chicago; consultant, Project 2000, Governors State Univ, IL; consultant, Council on Accreditation of Services for Families and Children, Inc. **Honors/Awds:** Superior Supervisor Awd SCOPE 1969-70; Executive of the Year, Chicago Youth Center, 1980. **Military Serv:** AUS Corpl 2 yrs; Good Conduct Medal, Expert Marksman 1962-64. **Home Addr:** 125 Rice Ave, Bellwood, IL 60104, (708)544-5140.

BAILEY, THURL LEE
Professional basketball player. **Personal:** Born Apr 7, 1961, Seat Pleasant, MD. **Educ:** North Carolina State, communications major, 1983. **Career:** Forward: Utah Jazz, 1983-91, Minnesota Timberwolves, 1991-. **Honors/Awds:** Shot 500 or better from the field in 46 games. **Business Addr:** Professional Basketball Player, Minnesota Timmberwolves, 600 First Ave N, Minneapolis, MN 55404.

BAILEY, WELTMAN D., SR.
Dentist. **Personal:** Born Jan 26, 1927, Harveil, MO; married Margaret Barber; children: Sandra, Weltman Jr, Peter, Robert. **Educ:** Univ WI, BS 1950; Meharry Med Coll, DDS 1956; Univ MO, MPA, MPH 1973. **Career:** Staff numerous hosps health centers; Private Practice, dentist 1958-. **Orgs:** Mem Natl, Amer Dental Assns; Amer Pub Health Assn; Amer Soc Pub Adminstrn; Natl Rehab Assn; Amer Assn Hosp Dentists Inc; bd dirs Mid-Amer Comprehensive Health Planning Agency 1970-71; Rehab Inst; Reg Health Welfare Council 1969-70; med adv bd MO Div Family Health 1974-; fellow Royal Soc Health; mem Acad Gen Dentistry; Alpha Phi Alpha Frat; YMCA; Urban League; Bapt trustee 1967-. **Military Serv:** US Army, 1945-47. **Business Addr:** 2514 E 27 St, Kansas City, MO 64127.

BAILEY, WILLIAM H.
Association executive. **Personal:** Born in Detroit, MI; married Anna Porter; children: John Robert, Kimberley Ann. **Educ:** Morehouse Coll, BA, 1947. **Career:** Count Basie Orchestra, featured vocalist, 1946-50; Las Palmas Theatre, Hollywood CA, entertainer, musical comedy, 1950-51; Natl & Intl Supper Club, tours, 1951-54; Moulin Rouge Hotel, producer, production singer, entertainer, 1955; Las Vegas ABC, CBS, PBS Affiliates, TV producer, 1955-65, 1985; Las Vegas Sun, newspaper columnist, 1955-57; First Securities Investment, broker-owner, 1962-72; Sugar Hill Inc, restaurant, lounge manager, retail merchant, 1964-71; Manpower Serv Las Vegas, dir, 1971; New Ventures ''503'', Cert Devel Co & New Ventures Inc, pres, exec dir; NEDCO Inc, pres, exec dir, 1972-. **Orgs:** Mem Las Vegas Bd of Realtors, Ctr for Bus & Econ Rsch, UNLV, Southern NV Econ Devel Council; exec bd mem So NV ''Special Impact Area''; mem OEDP; pres Prospectors; exec bd mem Las Vegas C of C; mem White House Small Bus Conf 1980, 1986, NV Mktg Assoc, SW Equal Oppty Bd, Officers Assoc, NV Minority Purchasing Council, Las Vegas Press Club; exec bd mem NAACP, So Christian Leadership Conf; hon mem NV Assoc of Latin Amers; mem Uptown Kiwanis Club, Alpha Phi Alpha, 33 Degree Mason; exec bd mem Natl Assoc Black & Minority C of C; chmn NV Inst of Bus. **Honors/Awds:** Recipient of over 150 awards from ntl, state, and local gvts, and private sector organizations; ''Bob Bailey Day'' Proclaimed for 30 Yrs Serv in State of NV; National University, Doctor of Humane Letters, 1987. **Business Addr:** Deputy Director, Minority Business Development Agency, US Dept of Commerce, 14th & Constitution Ave NW, Room 5055, Washington, DC 20230.

BAILEY, WILLIAM R.
Business executive. **Personal:** Born Feb 19, 1935, Nashville, TN; son of Annie Bailey and Robert Bailey; children: Michelle Maria. **Educ:** TN St Univ, BS 1956, Grad Stds in guidance. **Career:** Metropolitan Pub Schs, tchr 1960-64; Pres War on Poverty Met Pub Schs, work training coord 1964-66; Metropolitan Life Ins Co, sales mgr 1966- 69; part-time inst TN St Univ 1979-81; Metropolitan Life, sr account executive, 1969-. **Orgs:** Mem Kappa Alpha Psi, TN St Alumni Assoc, Agora Assn Life; Million Dollar Round Table, 1976-; pres Buddies of Nashvl 1980-82; pres Nashville O L I C 1982-84; bd of dir Citizens Savings Bank 1979-; Metro Planning Comm Metro Govt 1979-. **Honors/Awds:** Man of the yr Mt Zion Baptist Ch 1969; citizen of the yr Alpha Phi Alpha Frat 1984. **Military Serv:** UAS sp4 3 yrs. **Home Addr:** 2484 Walker Lane, Nashville, TN 37207. **Business Addr:** Senior Sales Representative, Metropolitan Life Insurance, One Rorton Hills Blvd, Ste 370, Nashville, TN 37212.

BAILEY-THOMAS, SHERYL K.
Audio-visual technician, newspaper executive. **Personal:** Born Jul 29, 1958, Palmer, AK; daughter of Evelyn D Bailey and Algian R Bailey; children: Mykal Jabari Thomas. **Educ:** University of Alaska, AAS, electronics technology, 1978, BA, business mgt, 1988. **Career:** National Weather Service, technician, 1979-80; Multivision Cable TV, audio-visual technician, 1980-85; State of Alaska, audio-visual technician, 1988-; Abram Abraham Productions & Management Inc, president, currently. **Orgs:** UCAAN, organizing committee, founder; BIG, 1990-92. **Special Achievements:** Anchorage Gazette, The African-American Voice of Alaska, associate editor, 1992-93; ''African-American in Alaska,'' a Black Community Booklet and Calendar of Events, publisher, 1990-93; FCC, Radio-Telephone License, 1978. **Business Addr:** CEO, Productions & Mgmt, Abram Abraham Productions and Management Inc, PO Box 201741, Anchorage, AK 99520-1741, (907)344-1554.

BAIN, JOSIE GRAY
Educator. **Personal:** Born in Atlanta, GA; married John C Bain; children: John David. **Educ:** CA State Coll, MA 1954; Univ So CA, grad work; Attended, Immaculate heart Coll. **Career:** LA Unified School Dist, teacher, training teacher, vice principal, principal, acting admin asst, supr prin, coord prin, admin coord asst supr, area supt, supr, assoc supt instr 1946-; UCLA Graduate Division of Educ, principal administrative analyst, currently. **Orgs:** Mem Delta Kappa Gamma, Delta Sigma Theta; Natl Cncl Negro Women; Natl Cncl Adminstr Women in Educ; vice chmn W Reg Bd United Way; exec bd Urban League; Comm Rel Conf So CA; mem Econ & Youth Oppor Agency; Family Serv Agency exec bd; coord Women's Soc Christian Serv. **Honors/Awds:** Educ Awd Natl Cncl Negro Women 1966; Educator of Yr Beta Phi Chap Phi Delta Kappa 1967; Negro Hist Week Achiev Awd Out Authors Study Club 1968; Women of Yr Zeta Phi Beta Natl Hon Soc 1969; Trailblazers Awd Natl Assn Bus & Professional Women 1969; US Congressman Augustus Hawkins Awd 1970; Comm Serv Awd W Div Federated Kings Daughters 1971; Drake Univ conferred Doctor of Humanehetters, 1960. **Business Addr:** Associate Superintendent, LA Unified Sch Dist, 450 N Grand Ave, Los Angeles, CA 90012.

BAIN, LINDA VALERIE
Management consultant. **Personal:** Born Feb 14, 1947, New York, NY; daughter of Helen Boyd Bain and Carlton L Bain; married Samuel Green, Mar 21, 1986. **Educ:** City Coll of NY, BA 1974. **Career:** NYS Dept of Labor, sec 1965-66; New York City Dept of Soc Serv, exec sec 1966-70; Manhattan St Hosp, prog coord 1970-73; Natl Coun of Negro Women's Ctr for Educ & Career Advancement, assoc dir 1973-79; Donchian Mgmt Serv, sr consultant 1980-85; Bain Assoc Inc, pres 1985-. **Orgs:** Mem Amer Soc for Training & Development 1981-; mem Natl & New York Org Develpment Network 1981-; bd of dir, NY Friends of Alvin Ailey 1985; mem Natl Assn of Female Exec 1980-; chairperson, bd of dirs, The Friendly Place, 1989-; mem, Corporate Women's Network; The Books for Kids Foundation, board of directors, 1992-. **Honors/Awds:** Mem & natl vice pres, Natl Coun of Negro Women 1963-; mem, Studio Museum of Harlem 1984-; mem, Coalition of 100 Black Women 1971-; mem, Alvin Ailey Amer Dance Theatre; Mary McLeod Bethune Achievement Award, Natl Coun of Negro Women; mem, NY Urban League. **Business Addr:** President, Bain Associates, Inc, P O Box 20789, New York, NY 10025.

BAIN, RAYMONE KAYE
Sports agent. **Personal:** Born Apr 27, 1954, Augusta, GA; daughter of Rosena L Bain and Raymond K Bain (deceased). **Educ:** Spelman Coll, Atlanta GA, BA Pol Sci, 1976; Georgetown Univ Law Ctr, JD, 1983. **Career:** Asst to pres Jimmy Carter, 1975-80; Exec Ofc of Pres, the White House, spec asst to dir, 1977-81, trnstn asst, 1981; DC Dept Env Svc, lgs pnl anlst, 1982-84; Baskin & Steingut PC, assoc, 1984; Jackson & Bain Inc, spts agt/atty, pres, 1984-85; The Bain Group, sports agents, pres, 1985-. **Orgs:** Delta Sigma Theta Sor, Inc 1973-; executive council, The World Boxing Council, 1986-; chairman, WBC, Retirement and Pensions Council, 1987-; member, North American Boxing Federation, 1988-. **Honors/Awds:** Pi Sigma Alpha Pol Sci Hon Soc; Ebony Mag 1978; 50 Future Blk Ldrs of Am; Citizen of Yr Augusta, GA 1977; Article Written ''On Sports Violence'' 1983; Contributions by Lynn Swann & Marvelous Marvin Hagler.

BAINES, HAROLD DOUGLAS
Professional baseball player. **Personal:** Born Mar 15, 1959, Easton, MD; married Marla Heney; children: Antoinette. **Career:** Outfielder: Chicago White Sox, 1980-89, Texas Rangers, 1989-90, Oakland Athletics, 1990-92, Baltimore Orioles, 1993-. **Orgs:** Chicago White Sox, 1996. **Honors/Awds:** 12th batter in White Sox history to reach double figures in extra base categories in one season; set major league record 22 game-winning RBI; led the AL in homers hit in winning games 18; drove in career high 105 runs at 23, became youngest player White Sox history to crack the 100 RBI barrier; ended longest game (8 hrs 6 min) in history on May 9 when he hit 753rd pitch into ctr field bullpen to give White Sox a 25 inning victory over Milwaukee, bat used sent to Baseball Hall of Fame at Cooperstown NY; homered three times at Minnesota Sept 17; hit 9th Inning sacrifice fly to drive in the run that beat Seattle and clinched the White Sox AL West Div championship the franchise's first title since 1959; American League All-Star Team, 1985, 1986, 1987, 1989. **Business Addr:** Professional Baseball Player, Baltimore Orioles, Oriole Park at Camden Yards, 333 W Camden St, Baltimore, MD 21201.

BAINES, HENRY T.
Company executive. **Career:** Stop Shop and Save, pres/CEO, currently. **Honors/Awds:** Company is #9 on the Black Enterprise List of Top 100 Industrial Companies, 1992. **Business Addr:** President/CEO, Stop Shop & Save Food Markets, 200 S Arlington Ave, Ste 300, Baltimore, MD 21223-2672.

BAINES, TYRONE RANDOLPH
Foundation administrator. **Personal:** Born Feb 22, 1943, Exmore, VA; son of Clarease Dillard Baines and Hilton Baines; married Shereatha; children: Tyrone R II, Tonita. **Educ:** Morgan State Univ, AB 1965; Univ of PA, MSW 1967; Univ of MD, MA 1971, PhD 1972. **Career:** Community Programs Inc, consult 1971-72; MD School Syst, consult 1972; Fed Exec Inst, sr faculty mem 1974-75; NC Central Univ, dir of public admin 1975-78; NC Central Univ, dir of publ admin prog 1979-82; NC Central Univ, Durham, NC, executive assistant to chancellor, 1985-88; W K Kellogg Foundation, Battle Creek, MI, program director, 1988-. **Orgs:** Social worker Children's Serv Inc Philadelphia PA 1967; capt US Army Med Serv Corp 1967-69; consult US Congress House of Rep 1969-70; grad teaching asst Univ of MD 1969-70; personnel relations spec Office of Econ Opport 1970-71; exec council Natl Assoc of Schools of Public Affairs & Admin 1985; bd of trustees Durham Acad, 1986; ed bd Political Sci, Southern Review of Public Admin, 1986; mem Citizens Advisory Comm for Durham Bd of Educ, 1987; bd of dir Natl Inst for Public Mgmt; board of directors, Battle Creek YMCA, 1990-; member, National Forum of Black Public Administrators, 1989-; board of trustees, Mt Zion AME Church, 1989-; member, Omega Psi Phi Fraternity, 1965-. **Honors/Awds:** Conf of Minority Public Admin Natl Awd 175; Fellowship to attend Harvard Univ Inst for Ed Mgmt 1977; Selected to participate in 1977 Phelps-Stokes Fund West Africa Seminar 1977; Selected as an Amer Council on Ed Fellow in Ed Amin 1978; US Dept of Labor Cert of Recognition from Atlanta Reg 1979; Kellogg Natl Fellow Kellogg Found 1982-85. **Military Serv:** AUS capt 1967-69; Superior Performance of Duty Awd 1969; Outstanding Achievement Awd 1969. **Business Addr:** Program Director, Education & Youth, W K Kellogg Foundation, One Michigan Ave East, Battle Creek, MI 49017.

BAIRD, KEITH E.
Educator. **Personal:** Born Jan 20, 1923; children: Diana Baird N'Diaye, Marcia Baird-Johnson. **Educ:** Columbia University, BS, 1952; Union Graduate School, PhD, 1982. **Career:** Hunter College, professor/director, Afro-American studies, 1969-70; Hofstra University, professor of humanities, 1970-73; SUNY at Old Westbury, professor of humanities, 1973-75; SUNY at Buffalo, assoc prof of anthropology, 1975-; Clark Atlanta University, Dept of Social Sciences, professor, currently. **Orgs:** Assoc fellow, Center for Afro-American Studies, Atlanta University, 1973-; SUNY Chancellor's Task Force on Afro Studies, 1984; consult on Gullah Lang, Sea Island Center, 1977; pres emeritus, New York African Studies Assn; assoc ed, Freedomways; ed bd, Journal of Black Studies, African Urban Quarterly. **Honors/Awds:** Travel Seminar Grant, Ford Foundation, 1969; publication, Names from Africa, Johnson Publishing Co, 1972; Summer Scholarship Grant, US GOR Friendship Comm, University of Jena, 1981. **Home Addr:** 2289 Venetian Dr SW, Atlanta, GA 30311-3310. **Business Addr:** Professor, Dept of Social Sciences, Clark Atlanta University, 223 James Brawley SW, Atlanta, GA 30314-4358.

BAITY, GAIL OWENS
Human resources professional. **Personal:** Born May 20, 1952, New York, NY; daughter of Ruth Owens and George A Owens; married Elijah A Baity, Apr 20, 1985; children: Allen J. **Educ:** Spelman Coll, BA Psych 1970-74; Univ of WI Madison, MA Indust Relations 1974-76. **Career:** Corning Consumer Prod Div, prdn suprv 1978; Corning Info Serv Div, personnel dev spec 1978-80; Elmira Coll, instr 1980; Corning R&D Div, personnel suprv 1980-82; Corning Consumer Products Div, personnel suprv 1982-83; Corning Personnel Div, human resource consultant; Corning Glass Works, human resource consultant, 1983-87. **Orgs:** Consult Career Devel Council 1982-; vice pres Soc of Black Professional 1982,86; treas Elmira Corning NAACP 1982-83; mem Soc of Black Profl, Elmira/Corning NAACP; chairperson policy comm Corning Children's Ctr 1986-87; member, Organizational Development Network (ODN), 1988-; member, American Society of Education and Training (ASTD), 1987-; member, National Black MBA Association, 1987-; board member, Career Development Council, 1988-; board member and chair person personnel policy comm, Corning Children's Center, 1986-. **Home Addr:** 39 Forest Hill Dr, Corning, NY 14830-3603. **Business Addr:** Human Resources Consultant, Corning Glass Works, Houghton Park, Corning, NY 14831.

BAKER, ALTHEA
Judge pro tem. **Personal:** Born Dec 24, 1949, San Francisco, CA; daughter of Ethel Ross and Vernon Ross; married Bruce Mitchell, Sep 22, 1990; children: Chase Brendan Mitchell. **Educ:** Pepperdine University, BA, 1970, MA, clinical psychology, 1974; Loyola University, School of Law, JD, 1984. **Career:** Licensed marriage family child therapist, 1976-1984; LA Community Colleges, professor, counseling & psychology, 1975-89; Law Office Althea Baker, attorney, 1984-93; Los Angeles Community Colleges, trustee, 1989-; LA Superior Court, judge pro tem, 1993-. **Orgs:** American Arbitration Association, mediator/arbitrator, 1990-93; Southern California Mediation Association, board member, 1990-92; Pepperdine University Graduate School of Education & Psychology Board, 1990-92; Black Women Lawyers of Los Angeles, 1984-. **Honors/Awds:** Delores Award, Distinguished Service Psychology, Pepperdine University, 1990; California State Bar Association, Outstanding Pro-Bond Service, 1990. **Home Addr:** 1059 Glen Arbor Avenue, Los Angeles, CA 90041. **Business Phone:** (213)254-5014.

BAKER, ANITA
Vocalist, songwriter. **Personal:** Born Jan 26, 1958, Toledo, OH; married Walter Bridgforth, Dec 31, 1988; children: Walter Baker Bridgforth, Edward Carlton Bridgforth. **Career:** Vocalist, several Detroit bars & nightclubs; lead vocalist, Chapter Eight, 1978; receptionist, Detroit law firm; released first solo album, The Songstress, 1983; Rapture album, 1986; performed with singer Al Jarreau, Montreu Jazz Festival in Switzerland, 1988; album, Giving You The Best That I Got, 1988; album, Compositions, 1990; Rhythm of Love, 1994. **Honors/Awds:** NAACP Image Award for Best Female Vocalist and Best Album of the Year; Grammy Awards for best female singer and for best song "Giving You the Best That I Got," 1989; 2 Grammy Awards for Rapture album; hit singles include "I Just Want toBe Your Girl," 1980, "Angel," "Sweet Love," "You Bring Me Joy," "Giving You the Best That I Got," "Talk to Me," "Fairy Tales".

BAKER, BEVERLY POOLE
Attorney. **Personal:** Born Jan 14, 1944, Birmingham, AL; daughter of Minda Ingersoll Poole and Grafton C Poole; married James K Baker, Nov 1968; children: Paige, Paula, Leslie. **Educ:** Univ of Alabama at Birmingham, BA (summa cum laude), 1982; Cumberland School of Law, Birmingham AL, JD, 1985. **Career:** McMillan & Spratling, Birmingham, AL, atty, 1985-86; Haskell Slaughter & Young, Birmingham, AL, atty, 1986-. **Orgs:** American Bar Assn, Standing Committee on Lawyers' Public Service Responsibility; co-chair, Equal Opportunity Committee of the Litigation Section; Natl Bar Assn; Natl Assn of Bond Lawyers; Magic City Bar Assn; Birmingham Bar Assn; Leadership Alabama, board of directors, alumni council; Leadership Birmingham; Jefferson County Medical Examiners Comm; Research Council of Alabama; Cumberland School of Law, advisory board; University of Alabama in Birmingham Leadership Council. **Honors/Awds:** Dean's Award, Univ of Alabama at Birmingham, 1981, 1982; Fellow, Amer Assn of Univ Women, 1984; "Perceptions and Propinquity on Police Patrol," SE Sociological Assn, 1982; "Privacy in a High-Tech World," seminar, 1985; "The Age Discrimination in Employment Act and Termination of the Public Sector Employee," Alabama Bar Inst Seminar, 1989; "Basic Wage and Hour Law in AL," NBI, 1996. **Home Addr:** Blackacre, 224 Cahaba Lake Circle, Helena, AL 35080. **Business Addr:** Atty, Haskell Slaughter & Young, 1901 Sixth Ave N, Ste 1200, Birmingham, AL 35203, (205)251-1000.

BAKER, C. C.
Educational administrator. **Career:** Alabama State University, interim president, currently. **Business Addr:** Interim President, Alabama State University, PO Box 271, Montgomery, AL 36101, (205)293-4100.

BAKER, DARRYL BRENT, SR.
Business executive. **Personal:** Born May 5, 1955, Detroit, MI; son of Mary L Scott Baker and Elliott D Baker Sr; children: Darryl Jr, Donnathon, LaKeisha. **Educ:** General Motors Inst of Tech, attended 1973-75; Mott Community Coll, AS 1983; Univ of MI, 1986-88; Baker College, bachelors in business leadership, currently MBA candidate. **Career:** Stockbroker/financial consultant, currently; General Motors Corp, supervisor 1977-88; First American National Securities, Atlanta GA, investment representative 1988-91; A L Williams Home Mortgage Inc, Atlanta GA, regional mgr 1989-91; General Motors Truck & Bus, machinist, machine repairer 1977-; Baker Financial Services, owner, president, chief executive officer, 1992-. **Orgs:** Owner income tax serv 18 yrs; Ebony and Ivory Enterprises investment consultant serv 9 yrs; cub scout/boy scout leader 5 yrs; dist exec Boy Scouts 1975-77; football/basketball coach Primary School 1981-82; mem Order of the Arrow; mem exec bd NAACP 1987-; exec bd mem, unit chmn UAW Local 659; Flint Neighborhood Coalition, executive board; manager Little League & Pee Wee League Baseball Teams 1987; exec bd mem, The Black Caucus of Genessee Cty; exec bd mem Millionth Man; chmn UAW Black Leadership Caucus, Local 659; Genessee Cty Bd of Canvassers; Vernon Chapel AME Ch; vp DCCS, Inc. **Honors/Awds:** Scouting Wood Badge Awd; Business Award Top Gun, 1989; Life-Accident-Health Insurance License and Securities Investment License 1988; Ex-cell, Home Mortgage License 1989; Sunday School Superintendent at Bethel Victory Tabernacle Church of God in Christ, 1989; Flint Journal, Top 10 Personality of Flint, 1994. **Business Addr:** President, Baker Financial Services, Inc, 601 S Saginaw St, Ste 505, Flint, MI 48502, (810)232-0522.

BAKER, DAVE E.
Educator. **Personal:** Born Jun 18, 1943, Manhattan, KS; married Janice; children: Sherri Ann. **Educ:** Emporia State College, BS, physical education, 1968, MPE, 1969. **Career:** Emporia State College, Physical Education, grad asst, asst baseball coach, 1969; Liberal Community Junior College, head track coach, asst basketball coach, instructor physical education, 1970; Creighton University, instructor physical educ, asst basketball coach, asst baseball coach, 1971-75, head baseball coach, 1972-. **Orgs:** Phi Delta Kappa; NCAA College World Series Games Comm,1972-75. **Business Addr:** Instructor, Athletic Dept, Creighton University, 2500 California St, Omaha, NE 68178.

BAKER, DAVID NATHANIEL, JR.
Musician, composer, educator. **Personal:** Born Dec 21, 1931, Indianapolis, IN; married Lida Margret Belt; children: April Elaine. **Educ:** School of Jazz Lenox, MA, attended; studied trombone with JJ Johnson; IN Univ, BME, MME. **Career:** Performed as soloist with Boston Symphony Evansville, IN Philharmonic; guest conductor Indianapolis Symphony, The Indianapolis Civic Orch, IN Univ Symphony; composed 100 jazz & classical works; performed with Stan Kenton, Lionel Hampton, Wes Montgomery; former mem George Russell Sextet; toured Europe with Quincy Jones 1961; IN Univ Jazz Dept, chmn. **Orgs:** Chmn Natl Endowment for Arts; bd dir natl Music Council; mem AAUP; mem Natl Assn of Negro Musicians. **Honors/Awds:** Author of 64 books on music improvisation; Recipient Dizzy Gillespie Scholarship 1959; Presidential Appointment to "The Natl Council of the Arts"; pres Natl Jazz Serv Org; nom Pulitzer Prize; nom for a Grammy; President's Awd for Disting Teaching IN Univ. **Business Addr:** Chairman, Jazz Department, IN Univ School of Music, Music Annex Room 309, Bloomington, IN 47405.

BAKER, DELBERT WAYNE
Editor. **Personal:** Born Jan 25, 1953, Oakland, CA; son of Amelia A Baker and Paul Thomas Baker; married Susan M Lee Baker; children: David Mathias, Benjamin Joseph, Jonathan Michael. **Educ:** Oakwood Coll, Huntsville, AL, BA (cum laude), 1975; Andrews Univ Seminary, Berrien Springs, MI, MDiv (with honors), 1978; Howard Univ, Washington, DC, PhD, 1992. **Career:** Pastor in MI, VA, OH, 1975-85; Messsage Magazine, Hagerstown, MD, editor-in-chief, 1985-92; Howard University, instructor, 1990-91; consultant, 1990-; Loma Linda University, assistant to the president, director of diversity, associate professor, 1992-. **Orgs:** Bd mem, San Mars Children's Home, 1986-89; bd mem, bd of dir, Oakwood Coll, 1985-; bd mem, Human Relations Council General Conference of Seventh-day Adventist Church, 1987-; Clergy's Black Caucus, 1985-; contributor video, Africa Continent of Explosive Growth, 1987; bd mem, Review & Herald Pub Assn, 1985-; board member, Loma Linda University; chairman, Diversity Advisory Committee. **Honors/Awds:** Alumnus of the Year, Oakwood Coll, 1985; Editorial Journalism Awards, Editors Intl, 1988-90. **Special Achievements:** Author of four books: The Unknown Prophet, 1986; From Exile to Prime Minister, 1988; Profiles of Service, 1990; Communication and Change in Religious Organization, 1992. **Home Addr:** 2141 Hill Ct, Colton, CA 92324. **Business Addr:** Office of Diversity, Loma Linda University, Magan Hall, Rm #103, Loma Linda, CA 92350.

BAKER, DUSTY (JOHNNIE B. JR.)
Professional baseball manager. **Personal:** Born Jun 15, 1949, Riverside, CA; married Harriet; children: Natosha. **Educ:** American River Junior Coll, Sacramento, CA. **Career:** Atlanta Braves, outfielder 1968-76; Los Angeles Dodgers, outfielder 1976-83; San Francisco Giants, outfielder 1984; Oakland Athletics, outfielder/first baseman, 1985-86; Minnesota Twins, 1990; San Francisco Giants, manager, currently. **Honors/Awds:** Sporting News All-Star and Silver Slugger teams 1981; National League All-Star Team 1981, 1982. **Business Addr:** Manager, San Francisco Giants, Candlestick Park, San Francisco, CA 94124.

BAKER, FLOYD EDWARD
Dentist. **Personal:** Born Mar 28, 1920, Auxvasse, MO; married Gertrude Andrews; children: Floyd E Jr, Teressa. **Educ:** Lincoln Univ of MO, BS 1943; Meharry Coll of Dentistry, DDS 1946; Inst for Grad Dentistry, Post-Graduate 1956. **Career:** Mercy Douglas Hosp, staff dentist 1954-74, co-chair oral surgery 1970-74; New Era Dental Society, board member, currently. **Orgs:** Zone vice pres Natl Dental Assn, 1958-80; mem Mt Airy Presbyterian Church, 1964-87; treas Bravo Investment Corp, 1964-87; registrar, Amer Dental Assn, Philadelphia County Dental 1978-85; mem Special Olympics 1983-87. **Honors/Awds:** Forty Year Plaque Omega Psi Phi Frat 1984; Alumni of Year Awd Presidential Citation 1984; Life Membership Pin Amer Dental Assoc 1985. **Military Serv:** US Army Dental Corps, Capt, 1946-48. **Business Addr:** Board Member, New Era Dental Society, 1826 W Girard Ave, Philadelphia, PA 19130.

BAKER, GREGORY D.
Corporate executive. **Personal:** Born Mar 2, 1948, Kansas City, MO; son of Lacy B Baker and Richard A Baker; married Janet L Carlson, Jun 6, 1986; children: Kimberly R, Timothy P, Chad G, Sydney L, Aaron Mitchell. **Educ:** Rockhurst College, BA, 1974; Kansas University, MPA, 1981. **Career:** District of Columbia Refugee State Coordinator; Community Development International Business, mgr; Chamber of Commerce of Greater KC, MO; Kansas City Minority Developer Supplier Council, president; Missouri Gas Energy, vice pres, community leadership; Executive Management & Leadership Consultants, lead team. **Orgs:** KC Consensus, president, 1981; Junior Achievement, vice pres, 1991-; Leukemia Society, board of directors, 1991-; Truman Medical Center, board of directors, 1990-; board

of directors, CORO, MOCSA; board of directors, Citizens Association, Metropolitan Energy Ctr, bd; Metropolitan Comm Coll Trust Fund, bd. **Honors/Awds:** Top 100 Most Influential Black Americans in Kansas City, Missouri, 1994; Up & Comers Award, 1994; Career Focus Magazine, Eagle Leadership Award, 1994. **Special Achievements:** Omni Award Winner, "Project Restart" Vocals, 1992; Emmy Award Winner, Song "Remember Me KC," 1997. **Military Serv:** US Air Force, A 1st Class, 1967-69. **Business Addr:** Vice Pres, Community Leadership, Missouri Gas Energy, Kansas City, MO 64105.

BAKER, GWENDOLYN CALVERT
Organization executive. **Personal:** Born Dec 31, 1931, Ann Arbor, MI; daughter of Viola Lee Calvert and Burgess Edward Calvert; married James Grady Baker (divorced 1978); children: JoAnn, Claudia, James Jr. **Educ:** University of Michigan, Ann Arbor, MI, BS, elementary education, 1964, MA, educ administration, 1968, PhD, education, 1972. **Career:** Ann Arbor Public Schools, Ann Arbor, MI, teacher, 1964-69; University of Michigan, Ann Arbor, MI, assistant/associate professor, 1969-76, director of affirmative action, 1976-78; National Institute of Education, Washington, DC, chief, minorities and women's programs, 1978-81; Bank Street College, New York, NY, vice president and dean of graduate and children's programs, 1981-84; YWCA of the USA, New York, national executive director, 1984-; UNICEF, president, US Committee, beginning 1993; Calvert Baker & Assn, pres, currently. **Orgs:** New York City Board of Education, member, 1986-90, president, 1990; board of directors, Institute for Responsive Education; board of directors, Natl Black Child Development Institute; executive committee, Natl Collaboration for Youth; member, Alpha Kappa Alpha Sorority; member, American Assn for University Administrators; member, American Assn of University Women; member, Natl Alliance of Black School Educators; member, Natl Assn of Women Deans, Administrators and Counselors; member, Natl Black Child Development Institute; member, Natl Council of Negro Women, Inc; member, New York Alliance of Black School Educators; member, Women's City Club of New York. **Honors/Awds:** Honorary Degree, Medgar Evers College of the City of New York, 1990; Honorary Degree Univ of Michigan, 1996; Strength of the City Awards, 1989; Award for Service Advocacy, Coalition of 100 Black Women, 1989; Distinguished Alumna, University of Michigan Education Alumni Society, 1987; Dollars and Sense Award, Salute to America's Top 100 Black Business and Professional Women, 1986; Old Masters Award, Purdue University, 1985; Willystine Goodsell Award, American Educational Research Assn and Women Educators, 1985; Support Network, First Tribute to Excellence in Education Award, 1991. **Special Achievements:** Author, "Multicultural Training for Student Teachers," Journal of Teacher Education, v XXIV, n 4, Winter 1973; "An Educator's Response to the Federal Reserve Bank Study," Today's Education, November/December, 1975. **Business Addr:** President, Calvert Baker & Associates, New York, NY 10128.

BAKER, HENRY W., SR.
Educator. **Personal:** Born Apr 26, 1937, Valdosta, GA; son of Amie Lee Harrell Baker and Herbert Baker; married Rubye Veals, Jan 29, 1969; children: Henry W II, Michael De Leon, Debra Marie, Edith Marie, Brittnye Nicol e. **Educ:** Alcorn State Univ, BS 1964, Grad Study 1983; William Paterson College, MA, 1992. **Career:** Anchorage Jr HS, 1964-67; Natchez MI, tchr & coach phys educ; Eastside HS, Paterson NJ, phys educ tchr & basketball coach 1967-80; Passic Co Coll, Paterson NJ, head basketball coach 1978-83; Eastside HS, head coach girls tennis team coord phys educ, 1983-84; Passaic County Community Coll, Head Basketball Coach, 1979-91; Eastside High School, head track coach (boys), 1988-89, coord of physical education, 1989-91, head coach, boys baskeball & track, 1991-. **Orgs:** Dir Martin Luther King Comm Ctr Paterson 1970-76; founder/dir Black Youth Orgn Paterson 1971-77; pres/past vice pres Passaic Co Planned Parenthood Inc1976-79; vice pres bd of dirs Children Youth Serv Paterson NJ 1986-; vice pres Afrikan Amer Men Interested in Neighborhood Develop Inc 1986-; Brd of dirs Childrens Haven, 1985-89. **Honors/Awds:** Comm Serv Awd Master Barber's Assn Unit 9 1975; Youth Serv Awd New Political Alliance Paterson1975; Basketball Coach of the Yr NY Dailey News 1975; Coach of the Yr Basketball Passaic Co Assn 1976; Coach of the Yr Girls Track Passaic Co Coaches Assn 1977-80; Junior College Coach of the Year 1985-86; Junior College 100 Victory Club Award, Garden State Athletic Conference, 1990. **Business Addr:** Coordinator, Physical Education, Eastside High School, 150 Park Ave, Paterson, NJ 07501.

BAKER, HOUSTON A., JR.
Educator. **Personal:** Born Mar 22, 1943, Louisville, KY; married Charlotte Pierce; children: 1 son. **Educ:** Howard University, BA, 1965; UCLA, MA, 1966, PhD, 1968; University of Edinburgh, Scotland, doctoral work, 1967-68. **Career:** Howard University, instructor, 1966; Yale University, instructor, 1968-69, asst professor, 1969; Center for Advanced Studies, University of Virginia, assoc professor, 1970-73, professor, 1973, director, Dept of Afro-American Studies, beginning 1974; Univ of Pennsylvania, prof of English, currently. **Orgs:** MLA Executive Council; assoc editor, BALE; com on Scholarly Worth, Howard University Press. **Honors/Awds:** Numerous academic awards & honors. **Special Achievements:** Workings of the Spirit: Poetics of Afro-American Women's Writings, 1991. **Business Addr:** Director, Center for the Study of Black Literature and Culture, University of Pennsylvania, 3808 Walnut St, Philadelphia, PA 19104.

BAKER, JAMES E.
Government official. **Personal:** Born Jan 21, 1935, Suffolk, VA. **Educ:** Havenford Coll, BA, 1956; Fletcher Sch of Law and Diplomacy, MA, MALD, 1960. **Career:** Dept of State, Washington DC, frgn serv officer, 1960-80; United Nations, dir spec econ asst prog, 1980-95; Long Island University, adjunct professor, 1995-. **Orgs:** Cncl on Foreign Rltns; Am Foreign Serv Assoc; NAACP. **Honors/Awds:** Carnegie Endowment, sr resrch asst, 1978. **Military Serv:** US Army, E-4 1957-59.

BAKER, KIMBERLEY RENEE
Journalist. **Personal:** Born Sep 26, 1965, Houston, TX; daughter of Diane Denise Randolph Baker and Melvin Lavoisier Baker. **Educ:** University of Texas at Austin, Austin, TX, BA, journalism, 1988. **Career:** Bellaire Texan, Houston, TX, community reporter, 1981-84; Houston Sun, Houston, TX, general assignments intern, 1987; Amarillo Globe-News, Amarillo, TX, lifestyles reporter, 1988-93; City of Austin, media pr mgr; Texas Department of Commerce, community assistance and small business, currently. **Orgs:** Board member, Texas Student Publications, UT-Austin, 1987-88; issue staff, The Daily Texan, UT-Austin, 1984-87; chairwoman communications week, Communications Council, UT-Austin, 1985-88; publicity liaison, Afro-American Culture Committee, UT-Austin, 1984-88; 2nd vice president, Delta Sigma Theta Sorority, UT-Austin, Amarillo, 1987-; member, National Association of Black Journalists, 1987-88, 1990-94; Provisional Class of the Jr League of Amarillo, 1993; Natl Assn of Black Journalists. **Honors/Awds:** Texas Student Publications Board Award, UT-Austin, 1987-88; Plaque for helping the handicapped, Goodwill Industries, 1988-93; Community Service/Reporting, United Way, 1988-93; Honorary Big Sisters, 1st ever recipient of this award, Big Brothers/Big Sisters, 1993-94; Outstanding Alumnus, Delta Sigma Theta Sorority, Amarillo Alumnae, 1993-94; Opportunity Symposium Series Award, Austin, 1992, 1993. **Home Addr:** 5321 Wilmington, Houston, TX 77033. **Business Addr:** Community Assistance & Small Business, Texas Department of Commerce, 1700 N Congress Ave, Austin, TX 78711.

BAKER, LAVOLIA EALY
Insurance broker. **Personal:** Born Nov 11, 1925, Shreveport, LA; married Luchan G Baker; children: Paul, Ronald, Luchan Jr. **Educ:** Contra Costa, AA 1970; UC Berkeley Sch of Bus, attended 1968; Golden Gate Univ, attended 1972-74; Univ of San Francisco, BS, 1998. **Career:** L Baker Ins, owner/mgr 1974, fire & casualty ins broker. **Orgs:** Chairperson Oakland Metro Enterprises; chmn WAPAC; dir San Fran Indep Agents Assn 1975; dir Black Brokers & Agents Assn; vice pres Natl Assn of Negro Bus & Professional Womens Club; pres bd chmn Alpha Phi Alpha Wives Aux; dir Sojourner Truth Housing Corp 1974; life mem NAACP; Bay Area Urban League; mem BOWOPA & E Bay Area Dem Club 1972; fndr The Ch By the Side of the Road 1955. **Honors/Awds:** Bus Woman of the Yr. **Business Addr:** Fire & Casualty Ins Broker, 1230 Fillmore St, San Francisco, CA 94115.

BAKER, MOOREAN ANN
Dentist. **Personal:** Born in Washington, DC; daughter of Nina Baker and Joseph Baker. **Educ:** Howard Univ, BS 1975, DDS 1980; ML King Hosp Los Angeles, Certificate in Pediatric Dentistry 1982. **Career:** Private Practice, pediatric dentist; Howard Univ College of Dentistry, assistant professor, 1982-. **Orgs:** Mem Amer Assoc of Women Dentists 1981-, Amer Acad of Pediatric Dentistry 1981-, Amer Soc of Dentistry for Children 1984-, Robert T Freeman Dental Soc 1983-; member National Dental Association.

BAKER, MYRON TOBIAS
Professional football player. **Personal:** Born Jan 6, 1971, Haughton, LA. **Educ:** Louisiana Tech. **Career:** Chicago Bears, linebacker, 1993-95; Carolina Panthers, 1996-. **Business Addr:** Professional Football Player, Carolina Panthers, 800 Mint St, Ericsson Stadium, Charlotte, NC 28202, (704)358-7000.

BAKER, OSCAR WILSON
Attorney. **Personal:** Born Mar 29, 1911, Bay City, MI; son of Ida Mae Harrison and Oscar William Baker; married Robbie Lee Brooks, Jun 10, 1942; children: Gail, Cheryl Parker, Christine. **Educ:** Univ of MI, AB 1933, LLB 1935. **Career:** Baker, Baker & Selby, sr mem, currently. **Orgs:** Chmn MI State Bar Comm on Civil Liberties 1952-54; mem MI State Bar Comm 1952-75; pres Bay Co Bar 1958; chmn MI State Bar Comm on Equal Justice 1966; Bay Co Bar Assn; MI Bar Assn; MS Civil Rights Voting Proj; MI NAACP; chmn St Legal Redress 1937-39; Bay City Charter Revision Com 1950; chmn mem Bay Co Rec Comm 1952-68; chmn Bay Co Red Cross 1964; pres Citizens League for Low Rent Housing 1951; Gov Comm on Migratory Labor 1966; Alpha Phi Alpha; Sigma Pi Phi; Iota Boule Chpt. **Honors/Awds:** Special Award Bay City NAACP 1973; Saginaw Valley Coll Bd of Fellows 1973; Univ of MI Bd of Visitors 1970; Life Mem 6th Fed Circuit Jud Conf; Natl Lawyers Guild Award 1964-65; Keith Civic Award, Detroit YMCA 1986; Outstanding Achievement Award, University of Michigan Regents, 1988. **Business Addr:** Attorney, Baker and Selby, Attorneys-at-Law, Chemical Bank Bldg, Ste 508, Bay City, MI 48708.

BAKER, ROBERT N.
Transportation company executive. **Personal:** Born Sep 15, 1943, Cleveland, OH; son of Ora Lee Pettit Baker and R C Baker; divorced; children: Schaaron, Brionne. **Educ:** University of Minnesota, extension division. **Career:** Werner Continental Transportation, central dispatcher, 1969-73; Glendenning Motorways, manager of linehaul transportation, 1973-77; Gateway Transportation, manager labor & industrial relations, 1977-82; Regency Air Freight, Inc, co-owner, 1982-83; Baker Motor Freight, Inc, owner, 1983-86; Astro Air Express, Inc, regional vice president, 1986-89; Shippers Air Freight Express, Inc, owner, ceo, 1989-. **Orgs:** Better Business Bureau, Detroit, Michigan, arbitrator, 1986-89; Better Business Bureau, Minnesota, senior arbitrator, 1989-; Amer Bar Assn. **Honors/Awds:** BBB, Minnesota, senior arbitrator, 1990. **Military Serv:** US Army, PFC, 1961-67; Mortar Gunner 81mm, Emer Med Care, Sharpshooter, 5 ton truck. **Business Addr:** CEO, Shippers Air Freight Express, Inc, 119 North 4th St, Ste 404, Minneapolis, MN 55401, (612)339-9093.

BAKER, ROLAND CHARLES
Business executive. **Personal:** Born Aug 12, 1938, Chicago, IL; married Addie Scott; children: Scott, Stephen, Stefanie. **Educ:** Univ of CA, BS Bus Admin 1961; Univ of CA, MBA 1962; CPA licensed in CA 1971; Chartered Life Underwriter; Life Insurance Management Institute, Fellow. **Career:** N Amer Rockwell Corp CA, budget adminstr 1962-64; Ampex Corp Culver City, financial analyst 1964-65; Beneficial Standard Life Ins Co, staff asst/controller 1965-67, mgr corporate acctg 1967-68, asst controller 1968-69, vice pres & controller 1969-71, adminstrv vice pres & controller 1973-75, sr vice pres 1975-77; Colonial Penn Ins Co/Colonial Penn Franklin Ins Co/Colonial Penn Life Ins Co, exec vice pres bd dirs; Colonial Penn Group Inc, sr vice pres 1977-80; The Signature Group, chairman & ceo 1980-. **Orgs:** Mem CA Soc of CPA's/AICPA; bd dir Philadelphia Zool Soc 1979-80; bd dir Fund for an Open Society "OPEN" 1979-; com mem Central Allocations Com United Way Fund 1979-. **Honors/Awds:** Fellow Life Mgmt Inst 1971; CLU Bryn Mawr PA 1976. **Military Serv:** USMCR 1962-67. **Business Addr:** Chairman, Chief Exec Officer, The Signature Group, 200 N Martingale Rd, Schaumburg, IL 60194.

BAKER, SHARON SMITH
Government official. **Personal:** Born Oct 13, 1949, Boston, MA; daughter of Elnora Clark Smith and Howard William Smith; married Donald Baker, May 20, 1972. **Educ:** North Carolina Central University, Durham, NC, BA, 1971; North Carolina Central University Law School, Durham, NC, JD, 1975; Duke University, Durham, NC, 1975. **Career:** Paul C Bland Law Firm, Durham, NC, paralegal, 1978-81; City of Durham, Durham, NC, affirmative action director for CETA, 1979-80, administrative assistant II, 1982-85, assistant to the city manager, 1985-87; Public Technology, Inc, Washington, DC, membership officer, 1987-88; City of Durham, Durham, NC, director of employment & training, 1988-. **Orgs:** Vice President, N.C. Triangle Area Chapter National Forum for Black Public Administrators, 1989-91; member, NAACP, Durham, N.C., 1985-; member, N.C. Black Child Development, 1990-91; North Carolina Job Training Administrators Assn, vice pres, 1992-94; Holy Cross Catholic Church, parish council bd mem, 1989-. **Honors/Awds:** Award of Merit, N.C.C.U. Law School, 1975; Appreciation Award, Durham Human Relations Commission, 1987; Leadership Award, Negro Council of Business and Professional Women, 1983. **Business Addr:** Director, Employment and Training, City of Durham, 401 E. Lakewood Ave, Durham, NC 27707, (919)560-4121.

BAKER, THURBERT E.
Attorney general. **Personal:** Born Dec 16, 1952, Rocky Mount, NC; son of Mary Baker High; married Catherine; children: Jocelyn, Chelsea. **Educ:** University of NC, Political Science; Emory University, School of Law, JD, 1979. **Career:** Georgia House of Representatives; attorney; attorney general, currently. **Orgs:** Georgia Bar Association; Kiwanis. **Business Addr:** Attorney General, Law Department, 40 Capitol Sq, Rm 134, Atlanta, GA 30334, (404)656-3300.

BAKER, VIN (VINCENT LAMONT)
Professional basketball player. **Personal:** Born Nov 23, 1971, Lake Wales, FL; son of James. **Educ:** Hartford. **Career:** Milwaukee Bucks, forward, 1993-97; Seattle SuperSonics, 1997-. **Honors/Awds:** NBA All-Rookie Team, 1994; NBA All-Star, 1995-98. **Special Achievements:** NBA Draft, first round, eighth pick, 1993. **Business Addr:** Professional Basketball Player, Seattle SuperSonics, PO Box 900911, Seattle, WA 98109-4926, (206)281-5850.

BAKER, WILLIE J.
Elected official. **Personal:** Born May 10, 1938, Birmingham, AL; married Barbara Ann Johnson; children: Barbara, Beverly,

Carol Lynn Rance, Christopher, Dindi. **Educ:** Graduated from IBM Computer Specialists, Control Data Corp, Univac Sperry Rand Peripherial Engrg, US Naval Electronics, Naval Nuclear Power Sch, Naval Leadership & Mgmt; Albany State Coll, M Astrophysics 1984; Alexander City JC, grad Magna Cum Laude. **Career:** Baker's Enterprises, pres; Macon Co Dist 1, co commissioner. **Orgs:** Mem Simmons Chapel AME Zion Church; vice pres Tuskegee Chamber of Comm; mem FOP; mem NAACP; mem Pres Council on Physical Fitness; mem AL Forest Farmers; pres Natl Assn of Landowners; mem Natl Assn of Black Co Officials; chmn Health & Human Serv Steering Comm; mem bd of dirs ACCA; pres AL Black Co Commissioners Assoc. **Honors/Awds:** Bestowed Doctorate of Humanities Degree 1971; Young Man of the Year 1972; AL Democratic Conference Black Retail Businessman of the Year 1983; publications "The Dying Universe" 1981; "Cosmology and the Redshift" 1982; "Einsteins Theory of Relativity for the Layman" 1982; part in MGM's film "The Wind and the Lion" released 1974; Outstanding Student of the Year 1983. **Military Serv:** USN data systems tech 1st class 20 yrs; 5 Navy Good Conduct Medals; Natl Defense Medal; Navy Achievement Awd Medal; Navy Chief Master-at-Arms. **Business Addr:** County Commissioner, Macon Co Dist 1, PO Box 179, Tuskegee, AL 36083.

BAKER, WILLIE L., JR.
Labor union officer. **Personal:** Born May 21, 1941, Sanford, FL; son of Ila Jessie Harris Baker and Willie L Baker Sr; married Madeline Dennis, Jan 26, 1966 (deceased); children: Kim, Keith. **Educ:** Univ of Maryland Eastern Shore, Princess Anne, MD, BA, 1965. **Career:** United Food and Commercial Workers, Local 56, Bridgeton, NJ, recording sec, 1974-80, business agent, 1974-85, legislative-South Jersey, 1974-85, vice pres, 1980-85; United Food and Commercial Workers Intl Union, Washington, DC, intl vice pres 1985-, dir, Civil Rights and Community Relations Dept, currently. **Orgs:** Executive vice pres, Coalition of Black Trade Unionists, 1986-; bd mem, Community Serv Comm AFL-CIO, 1986-95; Univ of Maryland Eastern Shore National Alumni Assn, 1987-91; Consumer Federation of America Exec Committee, 1990-95. **Honors/Awds:** Presidential Citation, Natl Assn of Equal Opportunity in Higher Educ, 1981; Alumnus of the Year Award, Univ of Maryland Eastern Shore, 1986. **Business Addr:** Intl Vice Pres and Dir of Civil Rights & Comm Relations Dept, United Food and Commercial Workers Intl Union, 1775 K Street, NW, Washington, DC 20006.

BAKER-KELLY, BEVERLY
Lawyer, educator. **Personal:** Born Nov 2, 1942, Detroit, MI; daughter of Cornelia Lewis Baker and Robert Edwoods Baker; married A.Paul Kelly, Jun 25, 1966; children: Traci Allyce Kelly, Kara Gisele Kelly. **Educ:** Howard Univ, 1961-62; Univ of Mich, BA, 1964; Columbia Univ, MA, 1966, MEd, 1970, School of International Affairs, Certificate of African Studies, 1970, EdD, 1973; Univ of California, Berkeley, JD, 1976; Harvard Univ, MA, 1977, PhD, 1978; Johns Hopkins Univ, 1984-86; London School of Economics, 1991-92. **Career:** Columbia Univ, co-dir of African-American Summer Studies Program, 1970; Univ of Windsor, sociology instructor, 1971-73; Greenberg and Glusker, law clerk, 1974; Dunn and Cruthcer, law clerk, 1975; Legal Aid Society, law clerk, 1976; California State Univ, assoc prof, 1976-82; Mayr, Galle, Weiss-Tessback, und Ben Ibler, Attorneys at Law, stagiaire, 1978-79; UNESCO, stagiaire, 1979-80; Univ of Maryland, US Army Bases, lecturer and facilitator, 1980; Southern Poverty Law Cent, assoc, 1981; Univ of Calif, dir of Academic Support Program, lecturer, 1982-84; Research Management Services, partner and director of Intl Law Div, 1984-86; Focus Intl Consultancy, dir, 1986-93; Private Immigration Law Practice, 1991-93; Howard Univ, visiting assoc prof, 1993-; Golden Gate University, School of Law, 1996, 1997. **Orgs:** Natl Bar Assn, Intl Law Section, Chair, 1994-96; Union Internationale Des Avocats; Boalt Hall Fund for Diversity, VP/Bd of Dir, 1988-91. **Honors/Awds:** Natl Bar Assn, Presidential Award for Outstanding Service, 1992, 1993, 1995. **Special Achievements:** Assoc Ed, California Law Review; Articles Editor, Black Law Journal; Co-author, The African-American Encyclopedia of Education, 1994; A Study of the Degree of Transnationalization of College and Non-College Educated Blacks, Columbia Univ; Housing Conceptions and Satisfactions of Residents in Federally Subsidized Lower-Middle Income Housing, Harvard Univ; "US Immigration: A Wake up Call," Howard Law Journal, 1995; Participant, Fulbright Seminar for Intl Law Professors on McDougal-Lasswell Jurisprudence. **Business Addr:** Attorney, 536 Mission Street, San Francisco, CA 94105-2968.

BAKER-PARKS, SHARON L.
Social worker. **Personal:** Born Jan 18, 1958, New York, NY; daughter of Lee Baker (deceased) and Willie Baker Jr (deceased); married Brainard J Parks; children: Kendra. **Educ:** University of NC at Charlotte, BA, sociology, Afro-Amer & African studies, 1979; Columbia University, School of Social Work, MSW, 1983; Baruch College, School of Continuing Studies, certificate in business, 1986. **Career:** Steinway Child & Family Developmental Center, social worker, 1983-84; South Bronx Mental Hlth Cncl Inc, psychiatric social worker 1984; Bedford Stuyvesant Comm Mental Health Ctr Inc, psychiatric social worker/recreation coord 1985; Victim Serv Agency, casework supervisor 1985-86; Bronx-Lebanon Hosp

Ctr, psychiatric social worker 1986-89; New York City Board of Education, school social worker, 1989-. **Orgs:** NYC Chapter Assn of Black Social Workers, 1981-; chair, Black Caucus Columbia Univ, School of Social Work, 1982-83; corresponding sec, NY Alumnae Chap, Delta Sigma Theta Sorority Inc, 1983-87; chair, social action, mem, 1993-; Delta Sigma Theta Sorority, Inc, 1977-; Assn of Black Educators of NY, ABRNY, 1994-; Natl Assn of Social Workers, NYC Chap, 1981-; Natl Black Child Dev Inst, 1991-; Workshop in Bus Opportunities Alumni Assn, 1985-. **Honors/Awds:** NY State Certification in Social Work (CSW), 1986; NY State School of Social Work, License, NY City School Social Work, License, School Social Work Specialist Credential; Society of 49 (UNCC) 1979; Bertha L Maxwell Award, 1979. **Home Addr:** 880 Colgate Ave #11L, Bronx, NY 10473.

BAKI
Storyteller. **Personal:** Born Oct 13, 1947, Washington, DC; daughter of Bernice Jefferson Ward and Myles Butler; married Ross Anderson (divorced 1982); children: Kawi Scott Anderson, Omar Hakam Anderson. **Educ:** Weist/Barron/Hill, Burbank, CA, 1988; Los Angeles Valley College, North Hollywood, course in voice & diction, 1989. **Career:** Young People's Acting Workshop, Los Angeles, CA, voice & diction coach, 1988-89; producer & director, 1989; Ellaraino & Baki, Storytellers, Los Angeles, CA, storyteller, 1989-. **Business Addr:** Storyteller, Ellaraino & Baki, Storytellers, 8722 Skyline Dr, Los Angeles, CA 90046.

BALDON, JANICE C.
Lecturer. **Personal:** Born Jun 5, 1955, Louisville, KY; daughter of Willana & Virgil Baldon. **Educ:** University of Louisville, Business Science Commerce, 1977; Bellarmine College, masters, business, 1987. **Career:** DuPont Dow Elastomers, office coord, 1978-; University of Louisville, lecturer of economics, 1990-. **Orgs:** National Council Negro Women; Million Man March Community Advisory; Alpha Kappa Alpha; Kentucky Alliance Against Racism/Repression. **Honors/Awds:** National Council of Negro Women, 1994; Black Achievers, 1996. **Special Achievements:** Assisted in establishing higher education in underserved minority area, college in nontraditional locations, 1993.

BALDWIN, CAROLYN H.
Beverage company executive. **Educ:** Fisk University, bachelor's degree; University of Chicago, master's degree. **Career:** Citibank, NA, acct officer, sr acct officer; Coca-Cola Financial Corp, president; Coca-Cola Co, sr financial analyst, treasury specialist, asst treasurer/mgr, Latin Amer treas svcs, pres, financial corp, vp, 1977-. **Orgs:** ReliaStar Financial Corp, dir; Federal Home Loan Bank of Atlanta; Leadership Atlanta, Society of Intl Business Fellows; Audit Executives Assn, exec leadership council; Manufacturers Alliance and Consumer Credit Counseling Svcs; Emory University, bd of visitors. **Special Achievements:** Honored by Black Enterprise magazine as one of the most powerful women executives, 1991. **Business Phone:** (404)676-2121.

BALDWIN, CYNTHIA A.
Judge. **Personal:** Born Feb 8, 1945, McKeesport, PA; daughter of Iona Meriweather Ackron (deceased) and James A Ackron; married Arthur L Baldwin, Jun 17, 1967; children: James A, Crystal A. **Educ:** Pennsylvania State Univ, University Park PA, BA, English, 1966, MA, English, 1974; Duquesne Univ School of Law, Pittsburgh PA, JD, 1980. **Career:** Pennsylvania State Univ, McKeesport PA, asst dean student affairs, 1976-77; Neighborhood Legal Serv, McKeesport PA, staff atty, 1980-81; Office of Attorney Gen, PA, deputy atty gen, 1981-83, atty-in-charge, 1983-86; Palkovitz and Palkovitz, McKeesport PA, atty; Duquesne Univ of Law, Pittsburgh PA, adjunct professor, 1984-86, visiting professor, 1986-87, adjunct professor, 1989-; Allegheny County, Court of Common Pleas, adult/family division, and civil division judge, 1990-. **Orgs:** Exec comm, Homer S Brown Law Assn, 1980-; vice pres, bd of dir, Neighborhood Legal Serv Assn, 1986-88; pres-elect, 1987-88, Penn State Alumni Assn; president 1989-91; bd of dir, Greater Pittsburgh YMCA, 1987-; mem, Allegheny County Bar Assn, 1980-, Greater Pittsburgh Commn on Women, 1987-, Pennsylvania Bar Assn, 1988-, Pennsylvania Bar Assn House of Delegates, 1988-; member, Pennsylvania Commission on Crime and Delinquency. **Honors/Awds:** Distinguished Daughters of Pennsylvania Award, Governor Tom Ridge, 1996; Tribute to Women Award in the Professions, YWCA, 1987; Humanitarian Service Award, Penn State Forum on Black Affairs, 1989; Whitney M Young Jr Service Award, Boy Scouts of America, 1991; Women's Equality Day Recognition Plaque, Greater Pittsburgh Comm on Women, 1990; Inducted into MCK School Hall of Fame, 1990; first black woman elected to the Allegheny County, PA, bench for a ten-year term; first black woman installed as president of Penn State Alumni Assn. **Business Addr:** Judge, 820 City-County Bldg, Pittsburgh, PA 15219.

BALDWIN, GEORGE R.
Attorney. **Personal:** Born Oct 4, 1934, Brunswick, GA; children: Kirk, Goldie. **Educ:** Lincoln Univ, BA Economics 1955; Brooklyn Law Sch, LLB, JD 1964; NYU Law Sch, LLM 1976. **Career:** Private Practice NYC, attorney 1966-67; Danch, Riv-

ers & Baldwin Westbury, NY, partner 1967-71; Legal Aid Soc NYC, atty-in-charge Comm Defender Office 1971-. **Orgs:** Mem Natl Bar Assn; mem Natl Conf of Black Lawyers; mem 100 Black Men Inc; JFK Dem Club; mem Metro AME Church. **Military Serv:** US Army, 1957-59. **Business Addr:** George R Baldwin, PC, 78 Mott St, Ste 300, New York, NY 10013.

BALDWIN, JAMES
Professional baseball player. **Personal:** Born Jul 15, 1971, Southern Pines, NC. **Career:** Chicago White Sox, pitcher, 1995-. **Honors/Awds:** The Sporting News, American League Rookie Pitcher of the Year, 1996. **Business Addr:** Professional Baseball Player, Chicago White Sox, 333 W 35th St, Chicago, IL 60616, (312)924-1000.

BALDWIN, JOHN H.
Business executive. **Personal:** Born Oct 13, 1913, Clinton, MO; married Mae Hayden. **Educ:** Two years college 1941; Phase 1 & 2 Busn Law completed; Real Estate & Appraisal course 1 completed. **Career:** Retired non-professional male model; Swanson's Hallmark, serv mgr. **Orgs:** John R McGruder Masonic AMFM Lodge; NAACP; steward CME ch; elected 1st Black Dist Gov Dist 260 MO Lions Lions Intl 1974; bd of govs MO Lions Eye Tissue Bank Columbia 1977; bd dirs Eye Research Found of MO Inc 1978. **Honors/Awds:** Lion of the Year 1974; Outstanding Dist Gov Award 1975; Outstanding Layman Award 1974. **Military Serv:** US Army, CW0-W4 1941-61 retired; Serv Awards; Good Conduct Medal; Bronze Star; Meritorious Serv Medal.

BALDWIN, LEWIS V.
Minister, educator, author. **Personal:** Born Sep 17, 1949, Camden, AL; son of Flora Bell Baldwin and L V Baldwin; married Jacqueline Loretta Laws-Baldwin, Sep 29, 1979; children: Sheryl Boykin-Robinson. **Educ:** Talladega College, BA, history, 1971; Colgate-Rochester, Bexley Hall, Crozer Seminary, MA, black church studies, 1973, MDiv, theology, 1975; Northwestern University, PhD, history of Christianity, 1980. **Career:** Wooster College, visiting assistant professor of religion, 1981-92; Colgate University, assistant professor of philosophy and religion, 1982-84; visiting assistant professor of church history, 1983-84, Colgate-Rochester Divinity School; Vanderbilt University, assistant professor of religious studies, 1984-90, associate professor, 1991-. **Orgs:** Society for the Study of Black Religion, 1981-; American Academy of Religion, 1981-; American Society of Church History, 1981-; NAACP, 1980-; Southern Christian Leadership Conference, financial supporter, 1986-. **Honors/Awds:** US Jaycees, Outstanding Young Man of America, 1975, 1980, 1985, 1990; American Theological Library Association, Book Award, 1981; Mid-West Publishers' Association, MBA Book Award, 1992. **Special Achievements:** Books published: Freedom is Never Free: A Biographical Profile of E D Nixon Sr, 1992; To Make the Wounded Whole: The Cultural Legacy of M L King Jr, 1992; There is a Balm in Gilead: The Cultural Roots of M L King Jr, 1991; The Mark of a Man: Peter Spencer and the African Union Methodist Tradition, 1987; Invisible Strands in African Methodism: The AUMP and UAME Churches, 1805-1980, 1983; Toward the Beloved Community: Martin Luther King Jr and South Africa, 1995. **Home Addr:** 651 Harpeth Bend Dr, Nashville, TN 37221, (615)646-6524. **Business Phone:** (615)322-6358.

BALDWIN, LOUIS J.
Human resources executive. **Personal:** Born in New York, NY. **Educ:** Ithaca College, Business Admin 1970. **Career:** Ithaca College, asst to the dir of admissions 1970-72; American Arbitration Assoc, asst dir 1972-73; Union Carbide Corp, administrator, recruitment & placement 1974-77; Allied Corporation, supervisor, employee relations 1977-83; Staten Island Cable, manager, human resources 1984-85; Amerada Hess Corp, personnel admin 1985-86; Time Warner Cable, mgr human resources 1986-91; Cablevision of NYC, director, human resources, 1992-. **Orgs:** Advisor Junior Achievement of NY 1976; bd mem Forum to Advance Minorities in Engineering, 1980-82; loaned exec United Way 1982; mem the EDGES Group, Inc 1977-; member NAACP 1978-; mem NY Chapter of Minorities in Cable 1984-; scy/bd mem Harlem Dowling, Westside Childrens and Family Ctr for Servs 1986-; mem NY Urban League 1986-; One Hundred Black Men Inc, 1990-. **Business Addr:** Director, Human Resources, Cablevision of NYC, 930 Soundview Ave, Bronx, NY 10473.

BALDWIN, MITCHELL CARDELL
Systems analyst. **Personal:** Born Aug 22, 1958, Birmingham, AL; son of Ezell Caldwell Barnes and Bernard Baldwin. **Educ:** Jacksonville State University, Jacksonville, AL, BS, computer science, 1980. **Career:** American Intermedial Resources, Birmingham, AL, computer program, 1980-82; Federal Reserve Bank, Birmingham, AL, computer analyst, 1982-84; Alabama Power Company, Birmingham, AL, systems analyst, 1984-; Smart Talk with MCB, pres. **Orgs:** Founder, chairman of the board, CHAMP, Inc, 1989-; education committee, AABE. **Honors/Awds:** 200th Point of Light, President George Bush, 1990; KOOL Achiever finalist, Brown and Williamson, 1990; People Who Make the Difference finalist, Helene Curtis, 1990; Volunteer of the Year, Gov Guy Hart, 1990; Outstanding Community Services, Hayes Middle School PTA, 1990. **Business Addr:** Chairman of the Board, CHAMP, Inc, PO Box 11290, Birmingham, AL 35202-1290.

BALDWIN, OLIVIA MCNAIR
City official. **Personal:** Born Mar 30, 1943, Cleveland, OH; daughter of Carrie Mae Head McNair and Merdic McNair Jr; married Otis L Baldwin, Apr 14, 1962; children: Omar L Baldwin. **Career:** St Lukes Hospital, Cleveland, OH, food service supervisor, 1962-65; Sumby Hospital, River Rouge, MI, purchasing asst, 1965-66; City of Detroit, Detroit, MI, typist, 1970-75, asst market master, 1975-90, market master, 1990-; Amer Bus Womens Assn, vice pres. **Orgs:** Order of the Eastern Star, 1980-; Ways and Means Committee, American Business Womens Association, treasurer, 1990-; second vice president, Local 808-M, SEIU, 1989-. **Honors/Awds:** First female assistant market master, first female market master, City of Detroit, Bureau of Markets; Unity Bap Church, Sr Ursher Bd, Busy Bee. **Business Addr:** Market Master/Bureau of Markets, Finance/Purchasing, City of Detroit, 2934 Russell, Detroit, MI 48207.

BALDWIN, WILHELMINA F.
Educator (retired). **Personal:** Born Aug 27, 1923, Anderson, SC; daughter of Almena Louise Martin Francis (deceased) and Charles Warwick Francis, Sr (deceased); married Bernard Joseph Baldwin Sr, Jun 11, 1945 (died 1968); children: Bernard Jr, Judith Dianne. **Educ:** NC Coll for Negroes, BA 1944; Tuskegee Inst, MEd 1956. **Career:** Boggs Acad, instructor English, social studies, librarian 1944-46; John Andrew Hospital, information officer 1946-47; Cotton Valley School, jr high school instructor 1947-57; Macon County Bd of Educ, principal 1957-63; Maxwell Elementary School, librarian 1963-66; Title I ESEA Remedial Program, pilot reading teacher 1966-67; EPDA Projects, supvr dir reading & libraries 1967-69, dir 1969-70, dir career opportunitiess program 1970-72; Macon County Bd of Educ, educ, dir of Title I ESEA 1978; retired educ. **Orgs:** Member, AL Educ Assn, Natl Educ Assn, Macon County Educ Assn, Amer Library Assn, AL State Reading Assn, Natl Council of Negro Women, NABSE, Phi Delta Kappa Fraternity; elder member, Session Westminster Presbyterian Church; bd of advisors Southern Vocational Coll Natl Sorority of Phi Delta Kappa; mem, Natl Sorority of Phi Delta Kappa Inc Upsilon Chapter; member, vice chair bd of dir, Central Alabama OIC, Montgomery. **Honors/Awds:** Woman of year, Zeta Phi Beta Sor, Inc; Apple for the Teacher Award, Iota Phi Lambda Sor, Inc; Excellence in Teaching Award, Macon Co, Bd of Ed; Excellence in Ed Leadership, Career Opportunities Program; Award for Outstanding Service, DC Wolfe High School; Award for Outstanding Service, Stillman Coll, Bd of Trustees. **Home Addr:** 2006 Colvert St, PO Box 1145, Tuskegee Institute, AL 36087-1145, (205)727-0615.

BALL, BRENDA LOUISE
Health insurance executive. **Personal:** Born May 26, 1951, Springfield, OH; daughter of John W & Virginia L Davis Ball; married Richard Nixon, Jan 2, 1981; children: Majenni Nixon, Johnathan Nixon. **Educ:** Sinclair Comm College, ABA, 1971; Univ of Cincinnati, BBA, 1973; State of MI, CPA, 1975; Univ of Detroit, MBA, 1988. **Career:** Arthur Andersen & Co, senior auditor, 1973-78; Ford Motor Co, financial analyst, 1978-79; Federal-Mogul Corp, bank & pension fund manager, 1979-81, staff controller, 1982-86, internal audit, 1986-88; Blue Cross & Blue Shield of Michigan, vp & controller, 1988-94, vp & deputy treasurer, 1995-96, vp & treas, 1996-. **Orgs:** Financial Executives Inst; Economics America, bd of dirs; Liberty BIDCO, bd of dirs; Richard Austin Scholarship Comm, Wayne State; United Way, Community Services' Community Priority Review Committee; National Assn of Black Accountants; Univ of Detroit-Mercy, bd of dirs; Luella Hannan Memorial Foundation, bd of dirs; Vista Maria, advisory & financial committees; American Hear Assn, women & heart disease committee; Leadership Detroit, trustee. **Honors/Awds:** National Assn of Black Accountants, National & Local Achievement Awards; Wall Street Journal Award; Links, Inc Scholarship; Ford Foundation Scholarship. **Business Addr:** Vice President & Treasurer, Blue Cross/Blue Shield of Michigan, 27000 W Eleven Mile Rd, Ste B378, Southfield, MI 48034, (810)448-8400.

BALL, CLARENCE M., JR.
Nursing home administrator. **Personal:** Born Dec 23, 1949, New Braunfels, TX; son of Clarice Coleman Ball and Clarence Ball; married Charlesetta Owens Ball, Aug 20, 1970; children: Sean Terrell, Kevin Denard, Cherise Montre. **Educ:** Texas A&I University, Kingsville, TX, 1968-70; Southwest Texas State University, San Marcos, TX, BA, 1970-72; North Texas State University, masters degree, 1972-74. **Career:** Vari-Care Inc, Rochester, NY, administrator, 1974-84; Ball Healthcare Inc, Mobile, AL, president, 1983-. **Orgs:** Alabama Nursing Home Association, 1988-; president, American College Nursing Home Administrators, 1982; president, Montgomery Area Council of Nursing Home Administrators, 1980; board member, YMCA, Mobile, AL, 1987-. **Honors/Awds:** Minority Business Service Award, Mobile Minority Business Center, 1990; Community Service Award, Mobile Chapter of NABSW, 1990; Alumnus of the Year Award, North Texas State University, 1989; Small Business of the Month, Mobile Area Chamber of Commerce, 1987; Benefactor of Youth Award, Mobile YMCA, 1990.

BALL, DREXEL BERNARD
Educational administrator. **Personal:** Born Apr 30, 1948, McClellanville, SC; son of Lucille Ball Garrett; married Brenda Petty Ball, Feb 16, 1975; children: Tyler Anderson. **Educ:** Morehouse College, Atlanta, GA, BA, 1972; North Carolina A&T State Univ, Greensboro, NC, MS, 1986. **Career:** Greensboro Daily News, Greensboro, NC, reporter, 1972-82; North Carolina A&T State Univ, Greensboro, NC, asst director of public relations, 1982-89; Delaware State University, Dover, DE, director of public relations, 1989-92, executive assistant to the president, 1992-. **Orgs:** President, Gate City Morehouse Alumni Chapter, 1985-89; member, Sigma Delta Chi, member, National Assn Black Journalist, member, Steering Committee Delaware Chicken Festival, 1991; member PR Specialist, Central Delaware United Way Campaign, 1991; chairman, Dev Committee, Dover Arts Council; co-director, Collage Proj, Dover Art League. **Business Addr:** Executive Assistant to the President, Delaware State University, 1200 N Dupont Hwy, Dover, DE 19901, (302)739-4924.

BALL, JANE LEE
Educator. **Personal:** Born Jun 2, 1930, Springfield, OH; daughter of Luella Simpson Lee and Henry Lee; married Wilfred R Ball, Apr 1, 1958; children: Janet, Carol B Williams, Wendy B Felder, Wilfred Cristan. **Educ:** Wilberforce Univ, Wilberforce OH, 1946-47; Central State Univ, Wilberforce OH, BSEd, 1949; Howard Univ, Washington DC, MA, 1951; Washington Univ, St Louis, MO 1957; Ohio State Univ, Columbus OH, 1967. **Career:** Southern Univ, Baton Rouge LA, instructor, asst prof, 1951-58; Alcorn Coll, Lorman MS, asst prof, 1959-60; Ohio State Univ, Columbus OH, instructor, 1961, 1964-65; North Carolina Central, Durham NC, asst prof, 1963-64; Wilberforce Univ, Wilberforce OH, instructor, asst prof, assoc prof, prof, 1966-; Wiljaba Publishing Co, owner, 1989-91. **Orgs:** AME Church, 1945-; Alpha Kappa Mu Honor Soc, 1948-; Delta Sigma Theta Sorority, 1949-; Coll Language Assn, 1955-; Wilberforce Univ Faculty Assn, 1975-80, 1989-. **Honors/Awds:** Teacher of the Month, 1982, Wilberforce Univ Faculty Merit Award, 1980, 1985, 1991, Wilberforce Univ; co-author, College Writing, 1977; author, articles in Humanist, 1980, Critical Survey of Short Fiction; author, "Virginia Hamilton," "Gordon Parks," in Dictionary of Literary Biography, 1984; The Black Experience Perpetual Calendar, 1989; author, articles on Joan Collins, Anne Rice, Beacham's Popular Fiction in America, 1990; author, articles on Erskine Caldwell, Hamlin Garland, Research Guide/Biog & Criticism, 1985. **Business Addr:** Prof of English, Wilberforce Univ, Walker Center, Wilberforce, OH 45384.

BALL, JERRY LEE
Professional football player, entrepreneur. **Personal:** Born Dec 15, 1964, Beaumont, TX. **Educ:** Southern Methodist Univ. **Career:** Detroit Lions, nose tackle, 1987-93; Cleveland Browns, 1993-94; Oakland Raiders, nose tackle, 1994-96; Minnesota Vikings, nose tackle, 1997-; Ice Box Sportswear, president, currently. **Honors/Awds:** Pro Bowl, 1989. **Business Addr:** Professional Football Player, Minnesota Vikings, 9520 Viking Dr, Eden Prairie, MN 55344, (612)828-6500.

BALL, JOHN CALVIN, SR.
Park policeman (retired). **Personal:** Born Jan 26, 1924, Hyattsville, MD; son of Gladys Wilkerson Ball and Doctor L Ball; married Lola Smith Ball, Dec 28, 1945; children: John Jr, Dillard, Michelle, Patricia. **Educ:** Wilberforce University, Wilberforce, OH, 1941; Ohio Peace Officer Basic Training Program, diploma, 1980. **Career:** City of Canton, Canton, OH, park patrolman, 1975-94. **Orgs:** Hiram Abiff Lodge #72, 1967; FOP McKinley Loge #2; Canton Patrolmen's Assn, 1991; treasurer, Ebony Police Assn of Stark County, 1984; American Legion #204, 1946; VFM 3417, 1946. **Honors/Awds:** Commendation, Police Chief Thomas W Wyatt, 1983; certificate, Criminal Justice Adminstration, National Police Assn, 1987; certificate, Firearms & Explosives Recognition Seminar, Dept of the Treasury, 1983; certificate, Firearms & Explosives Ident & Familiarization, Stark County Police Chiefs Assn, 1983; Resolution, Canton City Council, 1996. **Military Serv:** US Army, PFC, 1942-45; ETO Ribbon, Honorable Discharge, Combat Infantry Badge, Good Conduct Medal, WWII Victory Medal, American Defense Metal. **Home Addr:** 377 Hamilton Ave, Canton, OH 44704.

BALL, RICHARD E.
Educator, legal economist, attorney. **Personal:** Born Jul 18, 1918, Springfield, MA; married Edwinton Raiford. **Educ:** NYU, BS 1946, MBA 1948; Brooklyn Law Sch, LLB 1954, JD 1967. **Career:** New York City Housing Authority; Dept of Welfare; New York City Bd of Educ; St Augustine's Coll, chmn/prof; NC Central Univ, bd trustees/acting pres/business mgr; NAACP, atty/legal editor/counsel/consultant; Episcopal Church, lay reader. **Orgs:** Mem Masons, shriners; Consistory; life mem Alpha Phi Alpha; life mem Amer Natl Bar Assn; NC, MA State Bar Assns; Natl Mgmt Assn; pres Alpha Phi Lambds Chpt. **Honors/Awds:** Candidate for Superior Court Judge. **Business Addr:** Ste 304 Odd Fellows Bldg, Raleigh, NC 27601.

BALL, RICHARD ERWIN
Zoologist. **Personal:** Born Sep 24, 1946, Zanesville, OH; son of Evelyn T Ball; divorced; children: Jennifer Giodano, Michael Ball. **Career:** Paradise Park, operations mgr, 1969-76; Honolulu Zoo, animal keeper I, 1976-88, working foreman II, 1988-90, animal specialist III, 1990-. **Orgs:** American Zoo Assn; Amer Assn of Zoo Keepers; Sierra Club. **Business Addr:** Mammal Specialist/Curator, Honolulu Zoo, 151 Kapahulu Ave, Honolulu, HI 96815, (808)971-7193.

BALL, ROGER
Computer company executive. **Personal:** Born Feb 19, 1961, Ashtabula, OH; son of Helen R Ball and E Peter Ball; married Trenisha G Moore, Mar 19, 1989; children: Demetrius A D, Quinton T. **Educ:** American Bankers Association, bank marketing, 1984; The Ohio State University, BSBA, 1985; Ohio University, MBA, currently. **Career:** Evcor Business Systems, government account manager, 1986-87; TBS, Ohio, national account manager, 1987-88; Dispatch Consumer Service, Inc, account executive, 1988-89; B&B Computer Services, Inc, president, 1986-. **Orgs:** Omega Psi Phi Fraternity Inc, chairman of computer operation, 1981; OSU, Black Alumni Society, treasurer & steering committee, 1991; OSU Advocate, 1991; Adopt a School Program, adopter, 1990. **Honors/Awds:** Columbus City Council, Outstanding Community Service, 1985; Ohio House of Representatives, Community Service, 1986; Ohio State University, Student Leadership, 1985, Pace Setter Award, 1985. **Special Achievements:** Volunteer speaker for OSU Young Scholars Program, 1992. **Business Phone:** (614)447-2100.

BALL, WILFRED R.
Educator (retired). **Personal:** Born Jan 3, 1932, Chicago, IL; son of Mary Sanders Ball and Wilfred Ball Sr; married Jane Lee, Apr 1, 1958; children: Janet, Carol, Wendy, Cris. **Educ:** Morehouse Coll, BS 1952; Atlanta Univ, MS 1955; OH State Univ, PhD 1965. **Career:** Southern Univ, instructor 1955-60; Alcorn Coll, asst prof 1960-61, 1968-69; Knoxville Coll, assoc prof 1969-70; Wilberforce Univ, assoc & prof 1972-, Natural Science Division, chairperson, 1991-96. **Orgs:** Kappa Alpha Psi Fraternity. **Honors/Awds:** NSF Fellowship, 1960-62; mem Beta Kappi Chi Honor Scientific Soc, Beta Beta Beta Biol Soc; President's Awd Outstanding Teacher Wilberforce Univ 1985.

BALL, WILLIAM BATTEN
Attorney, tax law specialist. **Personal:** Born Aug 28, 1928, San Antonio, TX; son of Lillian Edna Young Ball (deceased) and William Henry Ball (deceased); married Charlie Mae Cooper, Nov 9, 1956; children: Jeffrey Christopher, Kathleen Lorraine, William Eric. **Educ:** Woodrow Wilson Jr Coll, Chicago IL, 1944-45; Roosevelt Univ, Chicago IL, BS, Commerce, 1955, MBA, 1960; Chicago Kent Coll of Law of IL Inst of Technology, Chicago IL, JD, 1968. **Career:** IRS, revenue officer 1955-57; Supreme Life Insurance Co, accountant, jr exec 1957-59; State of IL Dept of Labor, auditor 1959; IRS, agent 1959-67, appellate appeals officer 1967-86; management coordinator, 1972-73; attorney, private practice, 1986-. **Orgs:** Member, Chicago & Cook Co Bar Assoc, IL State Bar Assn, Amer Bar Assn, Natl Bar Assn; chmn admin bd St Mark United Meth Ch 1973-77; troop committeeman BSA; member Order of the Arrow Natl Fraternity of Scout Honor Campers; member Order of Brotherhood; life member, Kappa Alpha Psi Fraternity Inc; member, bd of dir, Community Mental Health Council, 1982-87; Chicago Board of Education, mem of: Westcott Local School Council, 1989-93, chairman, Bylaws Committee, Subdistrict 8 Council Representative, 1989-93. **Honors/Awds:** Various Awards & Honors, BSA; Outstanding Performance Award, IRS; master's thesis, "Insurance Co Annual Statement Preparation/Instructions," Roosevelt Univ, 1960. **Special Achievements:** Chicago, School Reform Act, created by Illinois State Legislature. **Military Serv:** US Army, cpl, 1951-53. **Home Addr:** 8355 S Perry Ave, Chicago, IL 60620.

BALLANCE, FRANK WINSTON, JR.
Attorney. **Personal:** Born Feb 15, 1942, Windsor, NC; married Bernadine; children: Garey, Angela, Valery. **Educ:** NCCU, BA 1963, JD 1965. **Career:** SC State Coll, librarian/asst prof 1965-66; prosecuting atty 1966-. **Orgs:** Dir Found Comm Devel 1973-74; chmn Warren Co Bd Educ 1974-76; past pres NC Assn Black Lawyers. **Military Serv:** NC Natl Guard. **Business Addr:** Prosecuting Attorney, 307 W Franklin St, Warrenton, NC 27589.

BALLARD, ALLEN BUTLER, JR.
Educator. **Personal:** Born Nov 1, 1930, Philadelphia, PA; son of Olive Robinson and Allen Ballard; divorced; children: John, Alayna. **Educ:** Kenyon Clg, BA 1952; Harvard Univ, MA, PhD 1961. **Career:** City Coll of NY, asst prof, assoc prof 1961-69; City Univ of NY, dean of faculty 1969-76; professor emeritus, 1986, professor of history, SUNY-Albany, 1986-. **Honors/Awds:** Ford Fndtn, Natl Humanities Cntr, Moton Ctr Grants; Fulbright Schlr; Phi Beta Kappa 1952; Books "The Education of Black Folk" Harper & Row 1974; "One More Days Journey" McGraw-Hill 1984. **Military Serv:** US Army, cpl, 1952-54. **Home Addr:** 15 Cobble Court, Clifton Park, NY 12065.

BALLARD, BILLY RAY
Physician, dentist, educator. **Personal:** Born Aug 15, 1940, Bossier City, LA; married Rose M Carter; children: Rachel, Percy. **Educ:** Southern Univ, BS 1961; Meharry Med Coll, DDS 1965, MD 1980. **Career:** Dept of Oral Path SUNY at Buffalo, asst prof of oral pathology 1971-74; Meharry, assoc prof of pathology 1974-82; assoc prof & chmn of oral pathology 1981-82; UMC, assoc prof dept of oral pathology & radiology 1982-; Univ of MS Med Ctr, assoc prof dept of pathology 1982-; dir minority student affairs1982-. **Orgs:** Lay reader/vestry St Philips Episcopal Church; mem NAACP, Urban League, Amer Acad of Oral Pathology, Amer Assoc of Dental Schools, Amer Assoc of Medical Colls, Amer Dental Soc, Amer Medical Assoc, Amer Soc of Clinical Pathologists, Amer Soc of Cytology, Central MS Medical Soc, Intl Acad of Pathology, Intl Assoc of Dental Rsch, MS Medical and Surgical Assoc; bd of dir MS Div Amer Cancer Soc. **Honors/Awds:** Fellowship NIH Hubbard Hosp Meharry St Univ of NY at Buffalo 1965-67; Fellowship NIH Amer Cancer Soc Buffalo 1967-69; Fellowship NIH NCI Roswell Park Buffalo 1967-70; Fellow Surgical Pathology & Cytopathology 1982-85 Dept of Pathology Univ of MS Medical Ctr; Fellow Amer Soc of Clinical Pathologists 1986-; Fellow Coll of Amer Pathologists 1986-; Bd of Certification, Diplomate Amer Bd of Dentistry, Fellow Amer Bd of Oral Pathology, Diplomate Amer Bd of Oral Pathology, Diplomate Amer Bd of Pathology Anatomic Pathology. **Business Addr:** Minority Student Affairs Dir, Univ of MS Medical Center, 2500 N State St, Jackson, MS 39216.

BALLARD, BRUCE LAINE
Physician, psychiatrist. **Personal:** Born Dec 19, 1939, Waverly Hills, KY; married Eleanor Glynn Cross; children: Tracy, Timothy. **Educ:** Yale Univ, BA 1960; Columbia Univ Coll of Physicians & Surgeons, MD 1964. **Career:** Harlem Hospital Center - Dept of Psychiatry, assoc dir for training 1970-76; New York Hospital-Westchester Div, assoc dir - adult out patient dept 1976-81; Cornell Univ Medical Coll, assoc dean 1981-. **Orgs:** Amer Psychiatric Assn, chmn, selection/advisory comm for APA-NIMH fellowship program, 1974-80; chmn, comm of black psychiatrists, 1982-86. **Honors/Awds:** American Psychiatric Assoc, fellow 1976. **Military Serv:** US Air Force, captain 1968-70, commendation medal 1970. **Business Addr:** Associate Dean, Cornell Univ Med College, 1300 York Ave D-119, New York, NY 10021.

BALLARD, EDWARD HUNTER
Banker. **Personal:** Born Apr 2, 1900, Lexington, KY; married Betty M Smith; children: Leslie Denise, Edward H Jr. **Educ:** KS City, MO Gen Hosp, intern 1926-27; Howard Univ Wash DC, BS, MD. **Career:** Private Pract Birmingham, AL, physician 1927-49; Los Angeles, realtor 1950-64; Bank of Finance Los Angeles, organizer/chmn of bd 1964-, vice pres 1967-retirement. **Orgs:** Bd mem Watts Skill Center 1965-; adv council Dist Atty's Ofc 1965-; Comm Relations Conf So CA 1965-; exec bd Westside Br NAACP 1972-73; commrLos Angeles Co Health Facilities 1972-; bd dir Sickle Cell Disease Research Found 1965-73; chmn bd Men of Tomorrow 1967-69; bd dir Central City Comm Mental Health Center; mem Los Angeles C of C; Urban League; life mem Alpha Phi Alpha; mem AME Ch; Mason; Elks; former bd mem Morningside Hosp edevel-Prog; mem Community Relations conf; former mem United Way; bd life mem NAACP. **Honors/Awds:** Awds from Howard Univ Alumni Assn of So CA; Awds Natl Assoc of Coll Women; Awd Miracle Mile Optimist Club; Awds Jesse M Unrah, Billy Mills, Mayor Tom Bradley, KDAY Radio Station Interdenominational Minister Alliance, Councilman Gilbert Lindsay.

BALLARD, HAROLD STANLEY
Physician. **Personal:** Born Nov 25, 1927, New Orleans, LA; son of Lillie Ballard and Dan Ballard; married Gail; children: Harold Jr, Kevin. **Educ:** Univ of CA, AB; Meharry Med Coll, MD. **Career:** Natl Heart Lung & Blood Inst, cons; Columbia Univ, clinical prof, physician & surgeon; NY VA Hosp, asst chf; physician. **Orgs:** Natl Inst of Health Cncl on Thrombosis; Amer Heart Assn Cert; Amer Bd of Intl Med; Hematology; oncology chmn policy bd Natural History Study of Sickle Cell Anemia. **Honors/Awds:** Publ approx 30 scientific articles. **Business Addr:** Physician, 408 1st Ave, New York, NY 10010.

BALLARD, HOWARD LOUIS
Professional football player. **Personal:** Born Nov 3, 1963, Ashland, AL. **Educ:** Alabama A&M, attended. **Career:** Buffalo Bills, tackle, 1988-93; Seattle Seahawks, 1994-. **Honors/Awds:** Pro Bowl, 1992, 1993. **Business Addr:** Professional Football Player, Seattle Seahawks, 11220 NE 53rd St, Kirkland, WA 98033, (206)827-9777.

BALLARD, JAMES M., JR.
Psychologist. **Personal:** Born May 19, 1938, Petersburg, VA; married Natalie Dandridge; children: Tresa Melinda, James, III. **Educ:** VA State Coll, BS 1963, MS 1964; attended IN Univ, Geo Washington Univ; Univ of MN, PhD Soc Psychol 1971. **Career:** Mid-Level Comm Clinical Psychology Prog, dir; Howard Univ, assoc prof; Univ of Manitoba, assoc prof; Bowie State Coll, first dir of Inst, Rsch & Eval; Crownsville State Hosp, staff psychol; BASS (Behavioral & Soc Sys), founder & pres. **Orgs:** Mem SE Psychol Assn; Amer Educ Research Assn; Assn of Black Psychologists; pres Eta Eta Lambda Chap Alpha Phi Alpha Frat; mem Psi Chi Psychol Hon Soc 1964. **Honors/Awds:** Cited by NAACP for Svc/Inspiration/Support; Cert of Appreciation 1974. **Military Serv:** USAF E-3 1955-59. **Business Addr:** President, BASS Inc, PO Box 43, Arnold, MD 21012.

BALLARD, KATHRYN W.
Federal goverment administrator. **Personal:** Born Jun 10, 1930, Waverly Hills, KY; daughter of Kathryn Wise Ballard (deceased) and Orville L Ballard Sr (deceased). **Educ:** Howard Univ, BS 1951; Univ of MI, MS 1953; Western Reserve Univ, MS 1959; Univ of So CA, PhD 1967. **Career:** Karolinska Institutet, visiting scientist 1968-70; Los Angeles County Heart Assn, sr investigator 1971-74; Univ of Southern CA, asst prof 1971-79; UCLA, assoc research physiologist 1979-82; Univ of Southern CA Cardiovascular Rsch Lab, sr staff rsch assoc 1984-87; Los Angeles, Chiropractic College, Assoc Prof 1982-83; National Heart, Lung and Blood Inst, scientific review administrator, Bethesda, MD 1987-. **Orgs:** Mem Amer Heart Assn 1972-77; sec/treas Med Faculty Assn 1975-77; cncl Microcirculatory Soc 1974-77; faculty mem Med & Paramedical Seminars for HS Students; mem postdoctoral fellowship evaluation panel Natl Rsch Cncl 1977-; mem Faculty Senate 1977; attended several scientific meetings 1971-75; mem AAAS, Amer Physiol Soc, Microcirculatory Soc; elected to council on circulation Amer Heart Assn 1979; mem Arteriosclerosis Hypertension & Lipid Metabolism Adv Comm Natl Heart Lung & Blood Inst 1983-85. **Honors/Awds:** Numerous articles & publns; grant recip NIH 1975-78; Weight Watchers Found Inc 1976-77; Amer Heart Assn 1976-77. **Business Addr:** Scientific Review Administrator, Review Branch, National Heart, Lung, & Blood Institute, NIH, 5333 Westbard Ave, Westwood Bldg, Rm 550, Bethesda, MD 20892.

BALLARD, MYRTLE ETHEL
Employment program manager. **Personal:** Born Apr 20, 1930, Shreveport, LA; daughter of Roxanna Turner Alexander-Gammage and Henry Alexander, Jr; married Thomas A Ballard, Jun 8, 1952; children: Thomas A Ballard, Jr, Roxane R Johnigan, Michael S Ballard, Alexandria Alicia Ballard. **Educ:** Saint Mary's Coll, Moraga CA, BA, Public Mgmt, 1978. **Career:** CA State Employment Devel, Antioch, CA, office mgr, 1967-. **Orgs:** Sec, Intl Assn of Personnel Security, 1971-73; sec, Black Personnel Mgmt Assn, 1972-75; pres, CA State Employees Assn, 1973-75; sec, Moneyworks, 1981-83; bd mem, CA Council on Children & Youth, 1973-75; bd mem, Lincoln Child Center, 1975-; bd chairperson, Sickle Cell Anemia Research & Educ, 1982-84; regional dir, Zeta Phi Beta Sorority, 1986-92; loan exec, United Way, 1988; board member, Lincoln Child Center 1990-, chair, regional exec bd, 1992-; National, 1994-, chair, personnel committee, 1994-. **Honors/Awds:** Certificate of Appreciation, Sickle Cell Anemia Research, 1984; Zeta of the Year, Zeta Phi Beta Sorority, 1986; Those Who Care Award, Zeta Nu Chapter, Zeta Phi Beta, 1987; Noble Citizen, Phi Beta Sigma Fraternity, 1989; Outstanding State Employee of the Year, 1992. **Home Addr:** 2239 Dexter Way, Hayward, CA 94541.

BALLARD, WALTER W.
Dentist (retired), educator. **Personal:** Born Feb 12, 1928, Toledo, OH; son of Edna F and Walter W; married Joanne Marie Brown; children: Patricia Joan, Walter III. **Educ:** Bowling Green State Univ, BA, 1956; Notre Dame Univ, MS, 1961; IN Univ, DDS, 1963. **Career:** CO Univ, asst prof/oper dentist, 1979-80; general practice (retired). **Orgs:** Amer Dental Assn; Natl Dental Assn; Chicago Dental Soc; IN Dental Assn,1963-80; CO Dental Assn 1966-80; pres, trustee, Southeastern CO Dental Assn, 1974-75; chmn, Cncl Jud Affairs, CDA, 1979-84; pres, Pueblo Symphony Assn, 1979; 32nd degree, Worshipful master Eureka #2 PHA F&AM, 1979; shriner, Dentist Amer Soc Forensic Odontology, 1971; Fellow, Pierre Fouchard Soc, 1974; Fellow Acad of Gen Dentistry, 1978; Fellow, Amer Coll of Dentists, 1979; dist gov, 1978-79, intl dir, 1984-86, Lions Club Intl; Kappa Alpha Psi Fraternity. **Honors/Awds:** Ambassador of Goodwill, 1985, Melvin Jones Fellow, 1986, Lions Club Intl; Pueblo Image Award, Pueblo, CO, Chamber of Commerce, 1984; 33 Degree Mason, 1996. **Military Serv:** USNR, lt, 1946-73.

BALLENTINE, KRIM MENELIK
Business executive. **Personal:** Born Oct 22, 1936, St Louis, MO; son of Rose Mae Grimes Ballentine and Habib Dickey Ballentine; married Rosalie Erica Simmonds; children: Taraka T, Jabriel S. **Educ:** Wayne St Univ, BS 1980; Univ of VA Quantico Continuing Educ Prog, Certificate 1980; U of VA, MA, Education Counseling. **Career:** Pinkerton Natl Detective Agency, special investigator 1958-60; St Louis Airport Police, patrolman 1960-66; US Marshals Serv, chf dpty 1966-94 retired; St Thomas-St John Crime Comm, exec dir 1984-85; ICOP Investigations, exec officer 1984-; Minority Business Development Center, business counselor, 1987-88; CBS Affiliate, talk show radio host, 1987-88; University of Virgin Islands, teacher, 1996. **Orgs:** Charter mem Natl Orgn of Black Law-Enforcement Exec; Intl Assn of Chiefs of Police; MO Peace Officers Assn; FBI Acad Assn; Rotary Intl; life member, Disabled Amer Veterans; former Intl Platform Assn; Intl Assn of Law Enforcement Intelligence Analysts; mem Northeast Regional Boy Scout Committee; Virgin Islands Republican Territorial Committee; chairman, Governors Commission on Crime & Violence, Criminal Justice Institute. **Honors/Awds:** Hon mem Mark Twain Society; alum mem Wayne St U; contributing founder Natl Civil Rights Museum & Hall of Fame; Delegate to Republican Convention, 1988; Boy Scouts of America, Order of the Arrow, 1982, Silver Beaver, 1983. **Special Achievements:** Author, Krim's Simplistic Philosophies, Vantage Press Inc. **Military Serv:** USAF & Army Res warrant officer 18 Yrs; National Defense, NCO Development, Reserves Overseas Ribbon, and Army Achievement Medal. **Home Addr:** PO Box 305396, St Thomas, Virgin Islands of the United States 00803, (809)776-0581. **Business Addr:** Chief Executive Officer, ICOP-Investigations, PO Box 305396, St Thomas, Virgin Islands of the United States 00803-5396, (809)776-0581.

BALL-REED, PATRICE M.
State official. **Personal:** Born Sep 16, 1958, Chicago, IL; daughter of Portia & Arthur Ball; married Roy L Reed, Jul 16, 1983; children: Candace, Alexis, William. **Educ:** The John Marshall Law School, JD, 1984. **Career:** Washington, Kennon, Hunter & Samuels, law clerk, 1984-85, associate attorney, 1985-88; Patricia Banks & Associates, independent contractor, 1988-89; Cook County State's Attorney Office, asst state's attorney, 1989-. **Orgs:** IL State Bar Assn, assembly, family section council, women and minority participation committee, Bar Publication bd; Women's Bar Assn; Black Women Lawyer's Assn of Greater Chicago, bd of dirs, treasurer, scholarship foundation; Cook County Bar Assn; Marcy-Newbarry Assn, bd of dirs; John Marshall Alumni Assn, bd of dirs; National Black Prosecutors Association, registered agent, treasurer. **Special Achievements:** Discovery Checklist for child support, Illinois Inst of Continuing Legal Education publication, 1993, 1994. **Business Addr:** Assistant State's Attorney, Cook County State's Attorney Office, 500 Richard J Daley Center, Room 561, Chicago, IL 60602, (312)443-3469.

BALMER, HORACE DALTON, SR.
Professional sports executive. **Personal:** Born May 28, 1939, Norfolk, VA; son of Martha W Balmer; children: Pamela Walker, Horace D Balmer Jr. **Educ:** Norfolk State Univ, 1957-59; Virginia State Univ, 1959-60. **Career:** New York City Police Dept, detective, 1965-85; Natl Basketball Assn, asst dir of security, 1985-86, dir of security, 1986-89, vice pres & dir of security, 1989—. **Orgs:** Mem, Natl Org of Black Law Enforce Execs; mem, Intl Soc of Black Security Execs; mem, Intl Assn of Police Chiefs; mem, New York City Police Dept Guardians Assn; mem, NAACP; Omega Psi Phi. **Honors/Awds:** Guardians Assn, 1985-87; Drug Enforcement Agency, 1986; 8 awards from New York City Police Dept, Elmcor-Youth Org, 1987; Guardian Person of the Year Award, 1990; The Wheelchair Charities, Sports Executive of the Year Award, 1992; New York Chapter of National Organization of Black Law Enforcement, Executives Achievement Award, 1993. **Business Addr:** Vice Pres & Dir of Security, Natl Basketball Assn, 645 Fifth Ave, 15th Fl, New York, NY 10022.

BALTHROPE, JACQUELINE MOREHEAD
Educator. **Personal:** Born Dec 2, Philadelphia, PA; married Robert G Balthrope Sr (deceased); children: Robert G, Jr, Yvonne G, Robin B. **Educ:** Central State Univ, BS (Magna Cum Laude) 1949; Case Western Reserve Univ, MA 1959, hrs on PhD; John Carroll Univ, Bowling Green State Univ, Cleveland State Univ, Kent State, post-grad work. **Career:** Cleveland Call-Post, free-lance writer/columnist; Chicago Defender, free-lance writer/columnist; Pittsburgh Courier Afro-Am, free-lance writer/columnist, 1960-69; Cleveland Public School System, teacher/supvr of student teachers; Cleveland Bd of Educ, Oliver Hazard Perry Elementary School, principal; Consultant, education. **Orgs:** Hon mem Entre Nous Club; mem/ofcr Royal Hearts Bridge Club; The Pair Ables Vol Homes for the Aged & Juvenile; active mem/ofcr Alpha Kappa Alpha Sor 1946-; Delta Kappa Gamma Soc 1972; Eta Phi Beta Sor 1972; Natl Sor of Phi Delta Kappa 1960; Natl Council Negro Women; Cleveland Chap The Carats Inc; Cleveland Squaws; The Jr League; mem local, state, natl Elem Sch Principals; active church worker St John AME Ch; vol Heart, Cancer, March of Dimes; UNICEF; Mental Health; United Negro Coll Fund; Girl Scouts Campaigns; Retarded Child; active mem/ofcr League of Women Voters; NAACP; YWCA; Phillis Wheatley Assn; Forest Hosp; Urban League & Guild; Phi Delta Kappa Natl Frat; organizer of Top Ladies of Distinction; Chums Inc; Project Friendship; Pi Lambda Omega; Amer Assoc ofUniv Women. **Honors/Awds:** Received scholastic, citizenship, civic and religious awards; Cleveland Tchr of the Year; Outstanding Black Women of Cleveland OH; America's Outstanding Community Worker; Natl Honor Soc.

BALTIMORE, RICHARD LEWIS, III
Government official. **Personal:** Born Dec 31, 1947, New York, NY. **Educ:** MacMurray Coll, 1965-67; Geo Washington Univ, BA, 1969; Harvard Law Sch, JD, 1972. **Career:** Dept of State, fgn serv ofcr; US Embassy Lisbon, Portugal, polit/econ ofcr, 1973-75; US Embassy, political officer, Pretoria, S Africa, 1976-79; Dept of State, special asst to the Sec of State, 1979-81;

US Embassy Cairo, Egypt, political officer, 1981-83; US Embassy, Budapest, Hungary, political chief, 1984-87; deputy, dir of Office of Regional Affairs, Bureau of Near East & South Asian Affairs, 1987-90; US Embassy Budapest, dep chief of Mission, Budapest, Hungary, 1990-94; sr political advisor for asst sec for European/Canadian affairs, 1994-95; Sr Seminar, class pres, 1995-96; US Embassy, dep chief of Mission, San Jose, Costa Rica, 1996-. **Honors/Awds:** Salgo Award, Political Reporting, 1986, Group Honor Award, 1997. **Business Addr:** American Embassy, Unit 2501, San Jose 34020, Costa Rica.

BALTIMORE, ROSLYN LOIS
Business executive. **Personal:** Born Dec 17, 1942, New York, NY; daughter of Lois and Richard Baltimore Jr; divorced; children: Richard. **Educ:** Boston Univ, AB, 1964; Harvard Graduate School of Educ, EdM, 1970; Harvard Business School, MBA, 1972. **Career:** Paul Sack Prop, asst devel, 1972-73; Wells Fargo Bank, asst vice pres, 1973-77; RL Baltimore Co, 1977-; Baltimore Mortgage Co Inc, owner, pres, 1989-. **Honors/Awds:** Pres, Handicapped Access Appeals Bd, 1985; bd mem, Reality House W, 1978-; dir, Bay Area Rapid Transit; Business Woman of the Year, Savvy Magazine, 1984; proclamation, Mayor of San Francisco, 1985; Key to the City, Evansville, IN, 1985; honorary mem, Sigma Gamma Rho, 1986. **Business Addr:** President, RL Baltimore Co., PO Box 193422, San Francisco, CA 94119-3422.

BALTON, KIRKWOOD R.
Construction company executive. **Personal:** Born Jun 9, 1935, Birmingham, AL; son of Gertrude Balton and William Balton (deceased); married Juanita Jackson, Jul 13, 1957; children: Adriene Yvette. **Educ:** Miles Coll, BS 1957; Stamford Univ, MBA 1970. **Career:** Bradford's Industrial Insurance Co, bookkeeper, 1957-59; Booker T Washington Insurance Co, bookkeeper, internal auditor, admin asst to pres & vice pres, 1959-73, executive vice pres, mem bd of dir, beginning 1973-, pres, currently; Booker T Senior Washington Broadcasting Services Inc; A G Gaston Construction Co Inc, pres 1988-; Zion Memorial Gardens; New Grace Hill Cemetery; L & K Electric Supply Co LTD. **Orgs:** Bd dir Birmingham Turf Club; Birmingham Area Chamber of Commerce; mem, Our Lady Queen of the Univ Catholic Church; Rotary International; Leadership Birmingham Class of 1986-87; Natl Assn of Black-Owned Broadcasters; Jefferson Club; Alpha Phi Alpha Fraternity bd dir; A G Gaston Boys' Club Inc; pres, Alabama School of Fine Arts Foundation; Metropolitan Development Board; Birmingham Area Council Camp Fire -past pres; Greater Birmingham Convention Bureau; chairman, Natl Camp Fire Inc; Lakeshore Inc and Lakeshore Hospital; Associated Builders & Contractors of Alabama Inc; Colonial Bank; 101 Black Men; AL Assn of Minority Contractors; Leadership AL, 1994-95; President's Advisory Council; Business Council of AL; U-Care Network Inc; Univ of AL at Birmingham, Health Services Foundation; United Way of Central AL Inc. **Business Addr:** President & CEO, Booker T Washington Ins Co, PO Box 697, Birmingham, AL 35201.

BANCROFT, RICHARD ANDERSON
Superior court judge (retired). **Personal:** Born Aug 30, 1918, Albany, NY; son of Anna Anderson Bancroft (deceased) and William E Bancroft (deceased); married Barbara; children: Richard, William, David, Kathleen. **Educ:** Howard Univ, AB 1942, JD 1951; Univ of CA, LLM 1952. **Career:** Private practice, atty 1954-76; State of CA, Superior Court Judge 1976-88; currently active as judge pro tem, arbitrator, referee, special master, mediator and protem judge; lecturer and seminar panel leader, regarding race, gender and disability in and out of judicial system. **Orgs:** Trustee Alameda Co Law Libr; past dir Bay Area Rapid Transit; past bd commissioner SF Permit Appeals Board; past mem CA State Bar Assn; Amer Bar Assn, SF, Contra Costa and Alameda County Bar Assns; Amer Assn of Trial Lawyers; CA Assn of Trial Lawyers; CA Atty for Criminal Justice; past dir Mt Zion Hosp med Cntr; past pres San Francisco NAACP; past sec/treas Community Bd Prog. **Honors/Awds:** Published, "Practice & Procedure Before the Industrial Accident Commn" Univ of California Boalt Hall Law Review 1952; "Mainstreaming, Controversy & Consensus"; "Special Educ -Legal Aspects". **Military Serv:** USMC Sgt 1944-46. **Business Addr:** Jams/Endispute, 100 Pringle Avenue, Ste 700, Walnut Creek, CA 94596.

BANDO, THELMA PREYER
Educator (retired). **Personal:** Born Mar 11, 1919, Philadelphia, PA; daughter of Katherine Person Preyer Perry and Henry J Preyer; married McDonald M Bando, Dec 27, 1947 (deceased). **Educ:** Howard Univ, BA 1935; VA Sem & Coll, LHD; Columbia Univ, MA 1939; Univ of PA, postgrad 1940; Temple Univ, postgrad 1949-55. **Career:** Bishop Coll, chmn Educ Dept 1939-40; Dudley HS, chmn Eng Dept 1940-41; Morgan State Univ, assoc prof 1942-55, dean 1942-77 (retired). **Orgs:** Coll Woman's Assn; Alpha Kappa Alpha; natl pres Chi Delta Mu Wives 1949-53; Governor's Commn on Status of Women; pres Women's Med Auxil Balt, MD; commissioner Baltimore City Commission for Women; pres Philomathian Club; bd mem Pickersgill, Park Ave Lodge; committee member, Baltimore Symphony Orchestra, 1990-; pres, Morgan Univ Bredgettes, 1943-. **Honors/Awds:** Received 2 major proclamations in Balt, MD; At Morgan Univ founder of, Women's Week, Charm Club, Mentor Syst, Coll Canteen; Author Handbook for Coll Res Hall Dir; Author Guide for Off Campus Housing; Author Handbook for Mentors; City Council Award; Morgan State Univ Meritorious Awd; Morgan Heritage Award, Morgan State University, 1991; Recognition Award, Distinguished Service as Pres of the Phelomathians, 1994; Thelma Preyer Bando Lounge was dedecated in the Harper-Lubman Residence Hall, Morgan State Coll, 1994. **Home Addr:** 3506 Callaway Ave, Baltimore, MD 21215.

BANDY, RILEY THOMAS, SR.
Insurance agency director (retired). **Personal:** Born May 14, 1920, Beloit, WI; married Norma H; children: Riley Jr, Larry. **Educ:** Lane Coll, AB 1947. **Career:** Wright Mutual Ins Co, asst vice pres 1981, conserv dir; Great Lakes Ins Co, mgr, assoc agency dir. **Orgs:** Mem, 1960-, pres, 1973-75, Detroit Council of Ins Executives; past vice pres Michigan NAACP; past pres Detroit Lane Coll Alumni; mem, 1961-, chmn trustee bd, 1976-90, Carter Metropolitan CME Church Detroit; mem Alpha Phi Alpha; life mem NAACP. **Honors/Awds:** Outstanding Alumni Award Lane Coll, 1971; elected to Athletic Hall of Fame Lane Coll 1984. **Military Serv:** USAC Sgt. **Home Addr:** 18822 Marx, Detroit, MI 48203.

BANFIELD, ANNE L.
Public relations director. **Personal:** Born May 27, 1925, Detroit, MI; married William J Banfield; children: DuVaughn, Bruce, William Credric. **Educ:** Detroit Inst of Commerce Sec Sci, attended 1945; Wayne State Univ, 1 year; HP Coll, Univ of MI, Wayne Comm Coll. **Career:** US Army Signal Corps, tech sec/chf engr; Dr HM Nuttall, med sec; Julian Rodgers & Julian Perry, legal sec; Anne's Secretarial Svc, self-employed; YWCA, sec to exec dir; Detroit Inst of Commerce, asst admissions ofcr, asst ofc mgr; MI Chronicle, public relations dir. **Orgs:** Bd mem Natl Media Women; bd mem Mayor's Keep Detroit Beautiful Comm; mem Women's Econ Club of Detroit; mem Women's Conf of Concerns; mem Women's Comm United Negro Coll Fund; bd mem Randolph Wallace Kidney Found; Urban League; Natl Tech Assn Auxiliary; Concerned Boaters.

BANFIELD, EDISON H.
Surgeon. **Personal:** Born Jun 25, 1924, Baltimore, MD; married Julia; children: Ava, Yvonne, Stephen, Edison, Jr. **Educ:** Howard Univ, BS (cum laude) 1950, MD 1954. **Career:** Baylor Coll of Med, instr surgery; private practice, physician/surgeon, currently. **Orgs:** Fellow of Amer Coll of Surgeons 1963. **Military Serv:** US Army, cpl, 1943-46. **Business Addr:** Physician, 2914 Blodgett, Houston, TX 77004.

BANKETT, WILLIAM DANIEL
Government official. **Personal:** Born Dec 8, 1930, Oak Grove, VA; son of Edna Weeden Rich and William Daniel Rich; married Evelyn Robinson Bankett, Jun 25, 1955; children: Wendell, Kevin. **Educ:** West Virginia State Coll, Institute WV, BS, 1954; George Washington Univ, Washington DC, 1957-58; Hampton Inst, Hampton VA, 1961; Massachusetts Inst of Technology, Boston MA, certified Urban Exec, 1972. **Career:** Natl Security Agency, Washington DC, 1954-55; Dept of Agriculture, Minneapolis, MN, examiner, 1955-57; Westmoreland County Schools, Oak Grove VA, principal, 1957-62; Prince William County Schools, Manassas VA, principal, 1962-67; Southeast House, Washington DC, exec dir, 1967-68; Southwest Community House, Washington, DC, exec dir, 1968-70; Redevelopment Land Agency, H Street area dir, Dept of Housing & Community Devel, special asst, 1970-; chief exec officer, Dan the Man Mustangs Inc, 1973-. **Orgs:** Vice pres, Elementary Principals Assn, 1960-65; mem, Mayor's Economic Task Force, 1970-78; mem, VOICE, 1970-79; mem, Anacostia Economic Devel Corp, 1970-80,mem, Marlton Swim Assn, 1972-; mem Mustang Club of Amer, 1980-; mem Dept of Housing & Community Devel Assn, 1985-; vice pres at Johnson Alumni Assn 1986-. **Honors/Awds:** Outstanding Mem Award, Amer Cancer Soc, 1985, 1986, 1987; Presidential Award, Amer Cancer Soc, 1988; Platinum Award for going 266% above the quota, DC One Fund, 1988; author, "Schools Without Grades," Virginia Educ Journal, 1967. **Military Serv:** US Army corporal, 1945-47; Good Conduct, Sharp Shooter, 1946.

BANKHEAD, PATRICIA ANN
Educator. **Personal:** Born Dec 30, 1947, Los Angeles, CA. **Educ:** CA State Univ Los Angeles, BS Sociology 1972; Pepperdine Univ, MS School Mgmt 1976; San Jose State Univ, Certificate Aerospace Educ 1983. **Career:** Los Angeles Unified School Dist, elem teacher 1973-76; CA Lutheran Coll, lecturer 1977; Los Angeles Southwest Coll, instructor 1977-80; Los Angeles Unified School Dist, program coord 1977-80; State of CA, mentor/teacher 1984-87. **Orgs:** Sponsor Black Women's Forum Los Angeles 1980-87; mem adv bd United Negro College Fund 1981-87; official hostess City of Los Angeles 1983-87; mem NAACP 1984-87; mem Mentor Adv Bd LA Unified Schools 1984-87, CA Aerospace Assoc 1985-87, Delta Kappa Gamma Intl 1987; mem Natl Cncl of Negro Women 1987. **Honors/Awds:** Black College Fair Black Women's Forum 1981; selected for Public Service TV spot State of CA Dept of Educ 1986; Letter of Appreciation for Serv Supt of Educ State of CA 1986; Certificate of Appreciation Mayor of Los Angeles for 200 service hrs; Letter of Recognition as Master Teacher City of Los Angeles. **Business Addr:** Mentor Teacher State of CA, Los Angeles Unified Sch Dist, 1745 Vineyard Ave, Los Angeles, CA 90019.

BANKS, ANTONIO DONTRAL
Professional football player. **Personal:** Born Mar 12, 1973, Ivor, VA. **Educ:** Virginia Tech, attended. **Career:** Minnesota Vikings, defensive back, 1997-. **Business Addr:** Professional Football Player, Minnesota Vikings, 9520 Viking Dr, Eden Prairie, MN 55344, (612)828-6500.

BANKS, ARTHUR C., JR.
Educator (retired). **Personal:** Born Nov 7, 1915, Columbus, OH; married Bertha Means; children: David, Dannett, Arthur. **Educ:** St John's Univ, BS 1939; NYU, MA 1945; Johns Hopkins Univ, PhD 1949. **Career:** NY Univ, lecturer, 1945; Southern Univ, Baton Rouge LA, instructor, 1945-46; Morehouse Coll, instructor, 1946-47; Fisk Univ, asst prof & lecturer, 1951; NC Coll, asst prof, 1951-54; Morgan State Coll, asst dean, 1954-57; Atlanta Univ, visiting prof, 1958-59; Morehouse Coll, prof, 1959-67; Emory Univ, exchange prof, 1965; Greater Hartford Comm Coll, pres, 1967-85. **Orgs:** Mem Amer Assn Comm & Jr Coll; New England Jr Coll Councl; Amer Polit Sci Assn; New England Polit Sci Assn; numerous comm assignments & organizations. **Honors/Awds:** LLD; Trinity Course, Univ. of Hartford, Eastern Conn. Univ. **Business Addr:** President Emeritus, Greater Hartford Comm College, 61 Woodland St, Hartford, CT 06105.

BANKS, BEATRICE
Business executive. **Personal:** Born Jul 24, 1936, Uniontown, AL; daughter of Mr & Mrs Robert Banks. **Educ:** Wayne State Univ, BS 1963. **Career:** Detroit Bd Educ, tchr 1963; Residential & consumer Serv, advisor 1963-71, asst supvr 1971-72; Detroit Wayne Div Customer Marketing Serv, asst mgr 1972-74, mgr 1974-75, dir marketing serv Detroit Div 1975-79; dir, Customer & Marketing Srrv, Macomb Div, 1979-80; Detroit Edison Co, asst mgr 1980-. **Orgs:** Mem Women's Econ Club, Engrg Soc of Detroit, Greater Detrioit C of C, Project Pride Board, Corp Urban Forum; bd dir Don Bosco Home for Boys, State of Michigan ivil Rights Commission 1979-84. **Honors/Awds:** Headliner Awd Women of Wayne State Univ 1976; YMCA Minority Achievement Awd 1982. **Business Addr:** Asst Mgr, Detroit Edison Co, 2000 Second Ave, Detroit, MI 48221.

BANKS, CARL
Professional football player. **Personal:** Born Aug 29, 1962, Flint, MI. **Educ:** Michigan State Univ, attended. **Career:** New York Giants, 1984-93; Washington Redskins, beginning 1993; Cleveland Br owns, currently. **Honors/Awds:** Post-season play: NFC Championship Game, 1986, NFL Championship Game, 1986, Pro Bowl, 1987. **Business Addr:** Professional Football Player, Cleveland Browns, 80 First Ave, Berea, OH 44017.

BANKS, CARLTON LUTHER
Staff accountant. **Personal:** Born Apr 9, 1958, Bronx, NY; married Creecy Seymore; children: Regina, Attallah. **Educ:** Morgan State Univ, BA 1980; New York Univ, Certificate Direct Marketing 1985; Columbia Univ, MS 1997. **Career:** TroCar Realty Inc, vice pres 1981-85; The Greek Gallery, pres; Talented Tenth Investments Inc, CEO. **Orgs:** Keeper of finance 1987-, mem Omega Psi Phi Frat 1977-, Direct Marketing Club NY 1986-, NAACP 1987-. **Home Addr:** 676 Riverside Dr #10A, New York, NY 10031.

BANKS, CAROLINE LONG
City council member, business executive. **Personal:** Born Oct 30, 1940, McDonough, GA; daughter of Rubye Carolyn Hall Long and Ralph A Long; divorced; children: April Lynn, James H Jr. **Educ:** Clark College, Atlanta GA, BA, 1962; Univ of Hawaii, 1962-63; Georgia S tate Univ, MA, 1973. **Career:** Hawaii Board of Education, English teacher, 1963-64; Atlanta Board of Education, English teacher, 1967-69; Rich's Department Store, from management trainee to manager, corporate credit services, 1973-89; Atlanta City Council, 1980-, public safety committee, finance committee, chair, 1992, committee on council, executive, and community development committees; Minority Training and Assistance Partnerships, Inc, chief executive officer, 1990-. **Orgs:** National League of Cities, 1980-, advisory council, 1990-, board of directors, 1981-; National Black Caucus of Local Elected Officials, 1981-, president, 1992, board of directors, 1981-; National Forum of Black Public Administrators, 1983-; Delta Sigma Theta Sorority Inc, Golden Life Member, 1980-; Georgia Municipal Association, 1980-, board of directors, 1990-92, domestic violence task force, 1990-92; Atlanta League of Women Voters, 1980-; Black Women's Coalition, board of directors, 1980-; Georgia Coalition of Black Women, 1980-; National Purchasing Council; Atlanta Regional Minority Purchasing Council; Atlanta Chamber of Commerce. **Honors/Awds:** Iota Phi Lambda, Bronze Woman of the Year, 1980; Clark College, Outstanding Achievement Award, 1988; Cummings Forsyth Optimist Club and Forsyth County School System, 1987; Human Economic Love Plan of the Atlanta Jamaican Association, Gamma Theta

Chapter, Outstanding Community Awards, 1987; Port-of-Spain People-to-People Exchange, Outstanding Contributions, 1987. **Special Achievements:** First African-American woman appointed to Atlanta City Council, 1980; Democratic National Part Convention delegate, 1984; panelist, National Congress of Black Women, 1989; panelist, Atlanta Historical Society Educational Series: 150 Years of Key Civil Rights Decisions, 1990. **Business Addr:** City Council Member, City of Atlanta, City Hall, 55 Trinity Ave, SW, Ste 2900, Atlanta, GA 30335.

BANKS, CECIL J.
Attorney. **Personal:** Born Sep 27, 1947, Des Moines, IA; married Dr Margot H Banks; children: Kimberly, Imani, Jamaal. **Educ:** Sophia Univ Tokyo, Japan; Duquesene Univ, BA 1970; Univ of Pittsburgh Grad School of Public & Intl Affairs, MPA 1974; Rutgers Univ School of Law, JD 1976. **Career:** McCarter & Enguisir Esq, assoc, 1976; Newark Board of Educ, gen counsel 1978-82; City of Orange, legislative counsel 1980-, city atty 1984; Sills Beck Cummis, Zuckerman Radin Tischman & Epstein,partner 1984-. **Orgs:** Bd trustees United Comm Corp; chmn & founder, Young Lawyer's Com Essex Co Bar Assn; bd dir NAACP; mem Natl Bar Assn, Amer Bar Assn, Natl Assn of Bond Lawyers; bd mem Natl Assn of School Law Attys; bd of dir Community Coop Devel Found Bridgeport CT; Advice & Consent of the US Senate to the bd of dir of the African Development Foundation, pres; Annual Fundraising Luncheon for the Girl Scouts of Essex County, chairman; Unite Hosps Foundation, bd of dirs; The Childrens Hosp for the State of NJ. **Honors/Awds:** Serv Awd United Comm Corp; Serv Awd United Clergy of the Oranges. **Business Addr:** Partner, Sills, Beck, Cummis, Zuckerman, Radin, Tischman & Epstein, 33 Washington, Newark, NJ 07102.

BANKS, CHARLIE
Chief executive officer. **Personal:** Born Aug 11, 1931, Little Rock, AR; son of Lela Ervin Williams and George Banks; married Mary Caster Catherine, Sep 13, 1969; children: Charles, Lamarr, Daphne. **Educ:** Chicago Tech College, Chicago, IL, BSEE, 1953-55; Western State University, Fullerton, CA, Bachelors, Law, 1971-75. **Career:** Rockwell Intl, Downey, CA, engineering, logistics, 1960-75; Rockwell Intl, Pittsburgh, PA, purchasing mgr, 1975-79; Gould, Inc, Rolling Meadows, IL, purch dir, 1979-83; Mitchell S Watkins Assoc, Chicago, IL, vice pres, 1981-83; City of Chicago, Chicago, IL, first deputy PA, 1983-85; Production Dynamics, Chicago, IL, president, 1985-. **Orgs:** Omega Psi Phi, 1959-; member, Amer Mgmt Assn, 1960-75; member, Purch Mgmt Assn, 1975-79. **Honors/Awds:** Black Enterprise Top 100, Black Enterprise Magazine, 1990-91; Chicago Crains, Crains, 1990-91; Booker T Washington Foundation, 1990. **Military Serv:** US Air Force, airman first class, 1949-53. **Business Addr:** President, Chief Executive Officer, Production Dynamics of Chicago, Inc, 455 W North Ave, Chicago, IL 60610.

BANKS, DWAYNE MARTIN
Educator. **Personal:** Born Apr 7, 1961, Newport News, VA. **Educ:** Norfolk State Univ, BS 1985; Old Dominion University, MEd, 1992. **Career:** NEA, technology teacher. **Orgs:** Bd mem SCA 1986-87, PTA 1986-87; Alpha Phi Alpha Fraternity Inc. **Honors/Awds:** Deans List Norfolk State Univ 1985; Assn for Supervision and Curriculum Development, 1992-; Staff Development Council, 1994. **Home Addr:** 604 S Ave, Newport News, VA 23601. **Business Addr:** Teacher, NEA, 4200 Marshall Ave, Newport News, VA 23607.

BANKS, ELLEN
Artist. **Personal:** Born in Boston, MA. **Educ:** MA Coll of Art, BA; School Museum of Fine Arts. **Career:** Dunbarton Galleries, painter/exhibits 1962; Boston Mus Fine Arts 1970; Smith-Mason Gallery 1971; Natl Ctr Afro-Am Artist. **Honors/Awds:** Recipient Prix De Paris 1967. **Business Addr:** 328 Flatbush Ave., Ste 208, Brooklyn, NY 11238.

BANKS, ERNIE (ERNEST)
Baseball coach. **Personal:** Born Jan 31, 1931, Dallas, TX; son of Essie and Eddie; married Marjorie (divorced); children: Jan, Jerry, Joey, Lyndel; married Liz Ellzey, 1997. **Career:** Negro Amer League, 1950-53; Kansas City Monarchs, 1953-54; Chicago Cubs, infielder, 1953-71, first base coach, 1954-; Seaway Natl Bank, exec. **Orgs:** Bd mgr Chicago Met YMCA; bd mem Chicago Transit Auth; bd mem LA Urban League; motivational lecturer. **Honors/Awds:** Author "Mr Cub"; Named Most Valuable Player in Natl League 1958-59; Played in 13 All-Star Games; Named to TX Sports Hall of Fame 1971; Holds Natl Record for grand slam home runs; Inducted into Natl Baseball Hall of Fame 1977. **Military Serv:** US Army.

BANKS, FRED L., JR.
Justice. **Personal:** Born Sep 1, 1942, Jackson, MS; son of Violet Mabery Banks and Fred L Banks; married Pamela Gipson, Jan 28, 1978; children: Rachel, Jonathan, Gabrielle. **Educ:** Howard Univ, BA 1965; Howard Univ Sch of Law, JD 1968. **Career:** Banks, Nichols Attys & Pred, partner, 1968-84; Mississippi House of Rep, rep 1976-85; Banks Owens & Byrd Attys, 1985; 7th Circuit Court Dist of Mississippi, circuit judge 1985-91; Mississippi Supreme Court, justice, 1991-. **Orgs:** Pres State Mutual Fed Savings & Loan Assn 1979-89; mem Mississippi Bd of Bar Admissions 1978-80; mem natl adv comm Educ of Disadvantaged Children 1978-80; mem natl bd of dir NAACP 1982-, Jackson Goodwill Industries 1985-91; Phi Beta Sigma, Beta Gamma Boule. **Honors/Awds:** Numerous civic awards from state and local organizations. **Business Addr:** Justice, Mississippi Supreme Court, Box 290, Jackson, MS 39205.

BANKS, GARNIE
Government official. **Personal:** Born Oct 9, 1932, Elizabeth City, NC; married Alma Billups (deceased); children: Robin Banks, Sandra B Batise. **Educ:** Elizabeth City State Univ, 1959; Coll of Albermarle, 1963; Good Year Trade Work Shop Williamsburg VA, Front End Alignment 1973; Inst of Governor Chapel HillNC, Training 1982. **Career:** Elizabeth City Boys Club, troop-leader 1956-57; Cornerstone Baptist Church, supt of ss 1957-72; Trustee Bd, vice chmn 1971-74; Deacon Bd cornerstone Baptist Church, vice chmn 1979-83; Public Works, vice chmn 1980; Perry Tire Store, alignment mgr; City of Elizabeth NC, city councilman. **Orgs:** Mem Pasquotank Cty ABC Bd 1979-81; Fireman's Relief Fund 1981, New Horizon 1981, Task Force Fair Housing; vice chmn, mem City Councilman Civic Affairs NAACP 1984; chmn Public Works Comm for City Council City of Elizabeth NC. **Honors/Awds:** Man of the Year Cornerstone Baptist Church E City NC 1974; Cert of Honor Omega Psi Phi Frat E City NC 1979; Hunts Dinner Bell Governor Hunt's Dinner Bell Raleigh NC 1980; Men's Day Speaker Cornerstone Baptist Church. **Military Serv:** AUS sgt 2 yrs; Good Conduct 1953-55. **Business Addr:** City Councilman, City of Elizabeth City NC, 1005 N Poindexter St, Elizabeth City, NC 27909.

BANKS, GENE
Basketball player. **Personal:** Born May 15, 1959, Philadelphia, PA; married Belle. **Educ:** Duke Univ, BS 1981. **Career:** San Antonio Spurs, 1982-85, Chicago Bulls, 1986-87, La Crosse Catbirds, 1989-. **Orgs:** Walter Kennedy Citizenship Award 1984. **Honors/Awds:** Season high 28 points with 13 rebounds 1984; 56 games with double points incl 12 with 20 plus led in steals 21 times, 17 in rebounds; 1984 Walter Kennedy Citizenship Award; career high of 568 shooting, 741 at the line, 256 fouls, 105 steals, 23 blocks, all were 1983-84; All-ACC as a senior and All-Amer; ACC rookie of the year and led Duke to NCAA finals.

BANKS, HAYWOOD ELLIOTT
Attorney. **Personal:** Born Dec 3, 1922, Suffolk, VA; son of Rosa Coston Banks and William Henry Banks; married Barbara Farthing, Jun 12, 1946; children: Bobby Darnell, Linda. **Educ:** A&T College of North Carolina, 1939-41; Kentucky State College, 1941-43; St Louis University Law School; Lincoln University School of Law, LLB, 1949. **Career:** Shobe Lunderman and Banks, law partner, 1949-52; Cincinnati Ordinance District, lawyer for the army, 1952-58; National Labor Relations Board, lawyer, 1958-83; private lawyer, labor relations consultant, 1983-. **Orgs:** NAACP, Business and Labor Committee, 1958-; Natl Bar Assn, 1988. **Military Serv:** Medical Corps, Dental Lab Tech, tech grade 5, 1943-46. **Home Addr:** 138-10 Franklin Ave, Apt 11N, Flushing, NY 11355. **Business Phone:** (718)445-4583.

BANKS, J. B.
Government official. **Personal:** Born Mar 13, 1934, Missouri; married Annette. **Educ:** Washington Univ, MA; Attended, Lincoln Univ. **Career:** State of Missouri, rep, 1966-76, senator 1976-. **Orgs:** Pres, All Bank Bankers MO; chmn Urban Affairs & Housing Com Health Welfare Com; mem, Alpha Kappa Phi; deacon, Price Baptist Church. **Honors/Awds:** Man of the Year Award 1974.

BANKS, JAMES ALBERT
Educator, author. **Personal:** Born Sep 24, 1941, Marianna, AR; son of Lula Holt Banks and Matthew Banks; married Cherry Ann McGee; children: Angela Marie, Patricia Ann. **Educ:** Chicago City College, AA, 1963; Chicago State University, BE, 1964; Michigan State University, MA, 1967, PhD, 1969. **Career:** Joilet Illinois Public Schools, teacher, 1965; Francis W Parker School, teacher, 1965-66; University of Michigan, visiting prof of education, summer 1975; The British Academy, UK, visiting lecturer, 1983; Monash University, Australia, visiting prof of education, 1985; University of Washington-Seattle, assoc prof, 1971-73, professor of education, 1973-, chairman, dept of curriculum & instruction, 1982-87, College of Education, professor, currently. **Orgs:** Natl Defense Education Act; Spencer fellow, Natl Academy of Education, 1973-76; Natl fellow, W K Kellogg Foundation, 1980-83; Rockefeller Foundation Fellowship, 1980; bd of dirs, Social Science Education Consortium, 1976-79; bd dir, Assn for Supervision & Curriculum Development, 1976-80; Natl Council for the Social Studies, vice president, 1980, president elect, 1981, president, 1982, bd of dirs, 1980-84. **Honors/Awds:** Golden Key Natl Honor Society, honorary member, 1985; Distinguished Scholar/Researcher on Minority Education, American Education Research Assn, 1986; wrote numerous books including, We Americans, Our History and People, two volumes 1982, Teaching Strategies for the Social Studies, 4th ed, 1990, Multicultural Education in Western Societies, w/James Lynch, 1986, Teaching Strategies for Ethnic Studies, 4th ed, 1987, Multiethnic Education Theory and Practice, 2nd ed 1988, March Toward Freedom: A History of Black Americans, 1978, Multicultural Education: Issues and Prespectives, w/Cherry A McGee Banks, 1989. **Business Addr:** Professor, College of Education, DQ-12, University of Washington, Seattle, WA 98195-0001.

BANKS, JEFFREY
Fashion designer. **Personal:** Born Nov 3, 1953, Washington, DC. **Educ:** Attended Pratt Institute, 1971-73; Parsons School of Design, BA, 1975. **Career:** Ralph Lauren/Polo, design asst to the pres, 1971-73; Calvin Klein/Calvin Klein Ltd, design asst to the pres, 1973-76; Nik-Nik Clothing & Sportswear, designer, 1976-78; Jeffrey Banks Ltd, 1978-; Alixandre, designed furs for men, 1980; Merona Sports, head designer, 1980s; Jeffrey Banks International, 1980-. **Orgs:** Designers Collective; Fashion Institute of Technology, board of directors. **Honors/Awds:** Coty Fashion Critics Award, Special Coty Award, Men's Furs, 1977, Special Coty Award, Menswear, 1982; Harvey's Bristol Cream Tribute to Black Designers, Excellence in Men's Wear Design, 1978-80; Cutty Sark Award, Outstanding US Designer, 1987. **Business Addr:** Owner/Designer, Jeffrey Banks, Ltd., 15 East 26th St, Ste 1811, New York, NY 10010, (212)889-4424.

BANKS, JUNE SKINNER
Speech/language pathologist (retired). **Personal:** Born Jun 5, 1936, Norfolk, VA; daughter of Gaynell Clanton Skinner and Solomon Kermit Skinner; married John L Banks, Jan 27, 1962; children: Junelle Letha. **Educ:** Fisk University, BA, English, 1956; New York University, MA, speech education, 1966; Old Dominion University; Norfolk State University; University of Virginia. **Career:** American Military Secondary School, English Department, chairman, 1968-69; Old Dominion University, instructor, 1969-70; JRE Lee High School, English teacher, 1956-57; Norfolk Public Schools, English teacher, 1957-67, speech/language pathologist, 1967-93, speech eligibility liaison, 1989-93, teacher specialist, 1993-95. **Orgs:** The Links Inc, national member-at-large, 1990-94, Foundation bd, 1990-94; Mt Zion Baptist Church, Norfolk, trustee bd, chairperson, 1993-; Coalition of 100 Black Women, local board of directors, 1992-94; Delta Sigma Theta Sorority Inc, local social action committee, 1991-95; Dejouir Inc, national parlimentarian, 1988-90; The Moles Inc, 1981-94, Norfolk Chapter, vp, 1990-94; The Chums Inc, 1992-, local publicity dir, 1994-96; Amer Speech & Hearing Assn; Speech/Hearing Assn of VA, Multicultural Interest Group, chair, 1994-95; Pinochle Bugs Inc, 1971-. **Honors/Awds:** Iota Phi Lambda Sorority, Apple for the Teacher Award, 1989; The Links Inc, Distinguished Service Award, 1984; Urban League, selected participant, National Urban League Leaders, 1981; National Honor Society, 1952; Dejouir Inc, National Service Award, 1996. **Home Addr:** 1052 Lockwood Ct, Virginia Beach, VA 23464, (757)424-2591.

BANKS, LAURA N.
Educational administrator (retired), former restaurant owner. **Personal:** Born Jun 29, 1921, Tucson, AZ; daughter of Missouri Johnson Nobles and James Nobles; married Jack Leonard Banks, Jun 6, 1950. **Educ:** BS, 1943; MEd, 1966; Univ of AZ, Educ Specialist Degree 1970, EdD 1981. **Career:** Univ of AZ, 5 summers, asst teacher workshops; Cavett Elementary School, elementary teacher 25 yrs, principal 6 yrs; Tucson Public School Dist #1, coord reading programs K-12; MariMac Corp, public relations dir; LNB Enterprises, pres/owner; Jack's Original Bar-B-Q, Tucson, AZ, owner, 1950-. **Orgs:** Coordinator, Neighborhood Youth Corp; lecturer, Peace Corp, Univ AZ; mem Natl Cncl of Women in Admin; TEA, AEA, NEA; past & 1st chp Elem Prin Group; AZ Admin Assn; Natl Assn of Elem Prin; YWCA Natl Bd 1965-76; active on numerous committees in this field; NAACP; Tucson Urban League; Palo Verde Mental Health Found; bd dir Alumni Bd Univ AZ; organizer/pres local chap, past far western reg dir, natl secretary, natl prog chmn, Alpha Kappa Alpha; Natl Council of Negro Women; Model Cities Neighborhood Housing Task Force; pres Council United Way; natl rec sec Links Inc 1974-78; Pima Coll Exec Com for Comm Affairs; Women at the Top; adv bd Resources for Women; hon Soroptomist; bd of dirs Univ of AZ President's Club, Comm Housing Resource Bd; Rotary International; Tucson Rotary Club, 1990-; Coalition of 100 Black Women-San Antonio, TX. **Honors/Awds:** Shriners Award of Excellence in Educ; NAACP Successful Business Awd; Black Economic Devel Certificate of Merit; Women on the Move Recognition YWCA; Pioneer in Educ Award The Links; U.A. Distinguished Citizen Award; YWCA Outstanding Lifetime Achievement Award; Inducted in AZ Restaurant Hall of Fame, 1994. **Home Addr:** 9438 Gray Sage, Helotes, TX 78023, (210)695-3424.

BANKS, LULA F.
City official. **Personal:** Born Feb 23, 1947, Tallahassee, FL; daughter of Elizabeth Gaines Richardson and Harry E Banks, Sr; divorced; children: Felicia A Williams, Deanna M Williams. **Educ:** Tallahassee Comm Coll, FL, AA 1985; Florida State Univ, Tallahassee, FL, BS, 1992; FL A&B M Univ, Tallahassee, FL, 1995-. **Career:** Harris Corp, Melbourne, FL, 1978; Indian River County School Board, Vero Beach, teacher of adult educ, 1978; Brevard County School Board, Melbourne, FL, teacher of adult educ, 1979; Leon County Board of Commis-

sioners and Leon County School Board, Tallahassee, FL, purchasing agent 1980-85, purchasing director 1985-90; City of Tallahassee, purchasing administrator, 1990-. **Orgs:** Exec mem, Small Business Week Committee; mem, Natl Inst of Governmental Purchasing, FL Assn of Govt Purchasing Officers, Amer Soc of Public Admin, COMPA/ASPA; Natl Forum for Black Pub Admin & graduate of Exec Leadership Inst, 1994. **Honors/Awds:** FL Teacher Certificate, VOTECH, 1977; Professional Public Buyer, NIGP, 1984; Professional Manicuring/Pedicuring License, 1989; named Philo of Year, Sigma Gamma Rho, 1981, and 2nd place national runner-up, 1986; WEB DuBoise Honor Society, FL State Univ; FL State Univ Black Alumni. **Business Phone:** (904)891-8280.

BANKS, MANLEY E.
Business executive. **Personal:** Born Oct 12, 1913, Anniston, AL; married Dorothy M Jones; children: Manley E Jr, Jacquelyn A. **Educ:** AL State Univ, BS 1937; Howard Univ, LLB 1949. **Career:** Perry Co Sch Uniontown AL, asst prin coach 1937-42; Afro Cab Co Inc Enterprises, co-fndr vice pres 1946-51; tchr, 1949-52; Banks Bicycle Shop, owner, currently. **Orgs:** Elected chmn City Water & Sewer Bd 1976; 1st Black apptd City Adv Bd; mem ofcr Alpha Phi Alpha Frat Inc; mem Boy Scout Council Exec Bd 20 yrs; elder 1st United Presb Ch; mem legal adv Calhoun County Improvement Assn; NAACP; mem Human Relations Council 1964-70; City Adv Bd Water & Sewer Bd 1965-; Dist Adv Bd Salvation Army 1972-; treas deacon clerk United Ch Christ 1949-69. **Military Serv:** US Army, sgt, 1942-45. **Business Addr:** Owner, Banks Bicycle Shop, 112 W 10 St, Anniston, AL 36201.

BANKS, MARGUERITA C.
Journalist. **Personal:** Born Sep 13, 1946, New York, NY; married Alfred Quarles. **Educ:** Notre Dame Coll Cleveland, BA Engl & Fr Lit 1967. **Career:** Cleveland Press, reporter 1967-69, editor comm page 1969-70; WEWS-TV Scripps Howard Broadcasting, gen assignment reporter & consumer troubleshooter, host "Black on Black" 1970-; WEWS-TV Scripps Howard Brdcstg, co-host Edition Five 1986-. **Orgs:** Exec bd mem Amer Sickle Cell Anemia Assoc 1972-; adv bd mem Notre Dame Coll 1978-; exec bd mem Harambee Serv to Black Children 1979-; past bd trustee Big Bros of Greater Cleveland; past bd trustee Urban League Cleveland; past bd trustee Blacks in Commun, NE YWCA; mem Womens Equity Action League, Sigma Delta Chi; mem & ed Gamma Phi Delta Sor; former ballet & mod dance teacher local art centers; leadership Cleveland Class of '87. **Honors/Awds:** Most Interesting People Cleveland Mag 1979; numerous Comm Serv Awds pamphlet "Buying Used Cars" distrib by City of Cleveland Office of Consumer Affairs; "Punk Kids" series made into film distributed to comm groups by Cuyahoga Cty Juvenile Ct 1979; Notre Dame Coll Woman of the Year 1982; Female Broadcaster of the Year Natl Assn of Career Woman's Civil League 1982; Career Woman of Achievement Awd YWCA of Cleveland 1985; numerous press awds from Press Club of Cleveland and Women in Communications Cleveland Chapt. **Business Addr:** Reporter, Host, WEWS-TV Scripps Howard Brdcstg, 3001 Euclid Ave, Cleveland, OH 44115.

BANKS, MARSHALL D.
Educator, urologist. **Personal:** Born Dec 29, 1940, Richmond, VA; married Kathy; children: Marshall II, Martainn, Matthieu. **Educ:** VA Union Univ, BS 1962; Howard Univ, 1963; Meharry Med Coll, MD 1970; Roswell Park Meml Inst, resd 1972-73; Wayne State Univ, 1975. **Career:** Detroit Rehabilitation Inst, cons; Coll of VA, rsch tech 1963-65; Maggie Walker High School, chem teacher 1964-65; Wayne State Univ, instructor urology 1975-76; Allen Park Veterans Hospital, chief urology 1976-; Wayne State Univ, asst prof 1976-. **Orgs:** Dir urogenital surg Allen Park VA Hosp; mem AMA; candidate Amer Coll surgeon; mem Wayne Cty med Soc, Detroit Surg Soc, Amer Urol Assoc, Natl Med Assoc, MI State Med Soc, Kappa Alpha Psi; surg resd yr Queens Med Ctr 1971-72. **Honors/Awds:** 1st prize essay Buffalo Urol Soc 1973; publ "Topical Instillation of Adriamycin in Treatment of Superficial Bladder Cancer" Jrnl Urol 1977; co-investigator Natl Prostatic Cancer Proj 1978-79.

BANKS, PATRICIA
Attorney. **Personal:** Born Feb 6, 1949, Marianna, AR. **Educ:** Univ IL, BA 1969; Univ WI, JD 1972. **Career:** US Dept of Labor Chicago Region, 1972-73; Leadership Council for Met Open Comms, atty 1973-74; Sears Roebuck & Co, 1974-78; Private Practice, attorney 1978-. **Orgs:** Member of the following Bar Assns: Natl Bar Assn; Cook Co; Chicago; Federal; WI; IL; Delta Sigma Theta Sor. **Honors/Awds:** League of Black Women Awd US Marine Corps 1974; 1 of 10 Outstanding Young Citizens of Chicago-Chicago Jaycees 1977.

BANKS, PAULA A.
Executive Director. **Career:** Amoco Foundation Inc, pres, currently. **Special Achievements:** First African American president of the Amoco Foundation Inc, highest ranking black female in Amoco Corp.

BANKS, PERRY L.
Telecommunications company executive. **Personal:** Born Apr 15, 1955; son of Josie Greer Banks and Walter Banks; married Shirley Banks, Jul 30, 1985; children: Patrice, Chinua. **Educ:** Shaw Business College, Detroit, MI, 1974-76; National Institute of Technology, Detroit, MI, AS, 1981. **Career:** General Telephone AE, Northland, IL, test engineer II, 1981-84; Rotelcom Business Systems, Rochester, NY, technician, 1984-86; The Telecommunications Bank Inc, Rochester, NY, president/CEO, 1986-. **Orgs:** Trustee, Greater Rochester Metro Chamber of Commerce, 1990-92; vice president, Black Business Association Chamber of Commerce, 1991-; member, Greater Rochester Metro Chamber of Commerce, 1989-. **Honors/Awds:** Administrator's Award for Excellence, US Small Business Administration, 1990; Service Award, Minority Enterprise Development Committee, 1990; Special Recognition for Entrepreneurial Spirit and Leadership Committee, 1989; Up & Coming Entrepreneur Award, Minority Enterprise Development Committee, 1988; Superior Performance Certificate, 89th Army Reserve Corp, 1986. **Business Addr:** President & CEO, The Telecommunication Bank Inc, 302 N Goodman St, Rochester, NY 14607.

BANKS, PRISCILLA SNEED
Federal government official. **Personal:** Born Jul 13, 1941, Washington, DC; daughter of Mabel Sneed and Excell Sneed; widowed; children: Monica Banks Greene. **Educ:** Amer Univ. **Career:** Low Income Housing, tech instr; Low Rent Occupancy; US Dept Housing & Urban Devel, task force to desegregate public housing, housing program specialist; Anti-Drug Program for Public Housing; Civil Rights Act of 1964 and Title VIII, 1988. **Orgs:** Mem NAACP; Washington Urban League; Natl Welfare Mothers; NAHRO. **Honors/Awds:** Public Service Awards; Miss HUD 1972; Special Achievement 1975-76 & 1978; Sustained Superior Performance 1969 & 1980; received 2nd highest award given by US Dept of Housing & Urban Devel - the Cert of Merit 1984; Outstanding Performance Awd, numerous times, 1984-. **Special Achievements:** Assumed the role of the Vidor Housing Authority Chairperson and appointed to oversee the Authority's day-to-day operations; On Jan 14, 1994, four months after taking over the complex four black families moved into the all-white project. **Business Addr:** Housing Specialist, US Department of Housing & Urban Development, 451 7th St, Ste 4112, Washington, DC 20410.

BANKS, RICHARD EDWARD
Civil trial lawyer. **Personal:** Born Jan 5, 1960, St Louis, MO; son of Laura M. Gillispie and Vincent A. Banks (deceased); married Jan Forrest Banks, May 23, 1987; children: Jessica Ruth, Richard Edward, Jr. **Educ:** Howard University, Washington, D.C., BBA, 1982; Texas Southern University, Houston, TX, JD, 1986. **Career:** State Farm Insurance Co, St. Louis, MO, claims attorney, 1986-88; Vickers, Moore & Wiest, St. Louis, MO, associate attorney, 1988-89; Banks & Associates, St. Louis, MO, managing partner, 1989-. **Orgs:** Member, Missouri Trial Lawyers Association, 1989-; member, Missouri & Illinois Bar Association, 1988-; member, Bar Association of Metropolitan St. Louis, 1988-; member, Chicago Bar Association, 1989-; member, American & National Bar Association, 1988-; MO Bar Disciplinary Board, 1995-. **Honors/Awds:** 50 Leaders of the Future, Ebony Magazine, 1990; Leaders Conference, Children's Defense Fund, 1990; Judicial Selection Committee, Missouri Bar, 1990; "Forty Under Forty Making A Difference in St Louis," St Louis Magazine, 1991; St Louis Sentinal Newspaper, Outstanding Business Leader Awd, 1996. **Business Addr:** Attorney, Banks & Associates, PC, 8000 Maryland Ave, Ste 1260, St Louis, MO 63105-3752.

BANKS, RICHARD L.
Attorney. **Personal:** Born Nov 22, 1930, Boston, MA; married Catherine Martin; children: 3. **Educ:** Harvard Coll, AB 1951; Harvard Law Sch, LLB 1958. **Career:** Boston Legal Aid Soc, atty 1958-60; Cardozo & Tucker, assoc 1960-69; Boston Lawyers for Housing, dir 1969-71; Unity Bank & Trust Co, conservator 1972-73; Municipal Ct Roxbury Dist Suffolk Co Boston, presiding justice. **Orgs:** Lectr Boston Univ Law Sch; mem MA Bd Educ 1965-72. **Military Serv:** USNR lt 1953-57. **Business Addr:** Presiding Justice, Municipal Ct Roxbury Dist, 85 Warren St, Roxbury, MA 02119.

BANKS, RONALD
Manufacturers representative agency executive. **Personal:** Born Jun 19, 1951, Chicago, IL; son of Geneva Martin Banks and Earl Banks; married Vera D Lott; children: Janel, Lauren. **Educ:** Loyola Univ of Chicago, BA 1973. **Career:** Montgomery Ward Chicago, buyer 1973-82; Sherwin Williams Co Cleveland, buyer 1982-84; Parks/Carver Tripp Cos, regional vice pres 1984-91; Marketing 2000, president, 1991-. **Business Addr:** 1939 Miller Ct, Homewood, IL 60430, (708)922-0391.

BANKS, RONALD TRENTON
Educational administrator, educator. **Personal:** Born Sep 20, 1947, Knoxville, TN; son of Clara Banks and Ralph Banks; children: Rashondra Trenia, Brianna Jene'. **Educ:** Meharry Medical Coll, Certification in Mental Health 1971; Tenn State University, BS 1970; MS 1976. **Career:** Meharry Medical Coll, mental hlth tech trainees, pres 1970-71; Kentucky State Univ, co-chair rotating staff adv bd, vice pres 1983-84, career planning and placement, asst director, currently; Kentucky Tchrs Network, 1984-85 Cooperative Educ Handicap Comm, natl co-chairperson 1985-86. **Orgs:** Kentucky State Police, drug & alcohol consultant 1976; Kentucky School System, consultant 1976-81; Frankfort Comm, dir crisis serv 1977- ; Kentucky St Univ, founder & dir of Dial A Job prog 1978- ; Kappa Alpha Psi 1978; United Way, 1978; YMCA, Sr Citizens, Blind, Juvenile Deliq Mental Health Volunteer 1978; Cooperative Educ Assn of Kentucky, Awards Comm 1988-89; College Placement Assn, Cooperative Educ Assn. **Honors/Awds:** Most Loyal Co-Op Coordinator-KY 1982; Staff Awd KY Student Government KSU 1983; Cooperative Educ Appreciation Awd KSU 1983 & 1984; Most Outstanding Cooperative Educ Coordinator, State of Kentucky 1987; Kentucky Colonel 1987; State "B" Kentucky Racquetball Champion 1997, Kentucky Racquetball Assn 1987; State "B" Senior Runner Up, Kentucky Racquetball Assn 1988; producer, Street Life of Drugs on a College Campus, 1989; Martin Luther King Equality Award, 1992 & 1994; Community Action Council Volunteer of the Year, 1992; Gold Medal Racquetball, State of KY, 1994. **Home Addr:** 177 Winding Way, Frankfort, KY 40601. **Business Addr:** Asst Dir Counseling, Kentucky State Univ, E Main St, Frankfort, KY 40601.

BANKS, SAUNDRA ELIZABETH
Government official. **Personal:** Born May 1, 1948, Baltimore, MD; daughter of Eva Cook Smith and Horace N Smith; married LeRoy Banks. **Educ:** Morgan State Univ, BA 1974; Univ of Baltimore, 1979. **Career:** Baltimore City Schools, teacher 1975-77; WEAA, news reporter 1977-78; Court of Common Pleas, chief clerk 1978-82; Circuit Court Baltimore City, chief clerk 1982-. **Business Addr:** Chief Clerk, Circuit Ct, 111 N Calvert St N, Baltimore, MD 21202.

BANKS, SHARON P.
Attorney, educator. **Personal:** Born Sep 21, 1942, Washington, DC. **Educ:** Morgan State Coll, BA 1964; Howard Univ Law Sch, JD 1967. **Career:** Neighborhood Legal Serv Program, 1967-72; Private Practice, attorney 1972-; Howard Univ, part-time teacher 1969-72, full-time teacher 1972-. **Orgs:** Mem Natl, Amer, DC Bar Assns; Howard Univ Law Alumni Assn; bd dir DC ACIU; Kappa Beta Pi Legal Sor. **Business Addr:** Teacher, Howard Univ, Dept of Pol Sci, 112 Douglass Hall, Washington, DC 20001.

BANKS, TAZEWELL
Educator. **Personal:** Born Jan 7, 1932, Washington, DC; son of Cora Page and Seldon Banks; married Myrtle Marie Trescott; children: Andrea, Gregory, Kelley. **Educ:** Howard Univ, BS Chem 1953; Howard Med Clg, MD 1957. **Career:** Howard Medical Coll, clncl instructor 1966-68, asst prof 1968-71, assoc prof 1971-76, prof Med 1976-. **Orgs:** Bd of dir WA Heart Asso 1983-87; Phi Beta Kappa Howard Univ 1953; Alpha Omega Alpha Howard Medical College 1957. **Honors/Awds:** Chm Stdnt Rsrch Com WA Heart Asso mem Multiple WA Heart Asso Comms 1966-; meritorious serv DC Gen Hosp 1970; Citzns Adv Comm to DC Bar 1972-76; outstndng tchr Stdnt Cncl Awd Howard Med 1977; WA Heart Asso Golden Apple Awd 1983; DC General Hospital; outstanding physician award 1985-86; published over 40 articles on cardiovascular diseases; prsntd over 200 talks on cardiovascular diseases. **Military Serv:** US Army Med Corps capt 1956-61. **Business Addr:** Professor of Medicine, Howard Medical College, Washington DC General Hospital, 1900 Mass Ave, SE, Washington, DC 20003.

BANKS, TONY
Professional football player. **Personal:** Born Apr 5, 1973, San Diego, CA. **Educ:** Michigan State. **Career:** St Louis Rams, quarterback, 1996-. **Business Addr:** Professional Football Player, St Louis Rams, One Rams Way, St Louis, MO 63045, (314)982-7267.

BANKS, TYRA
Model, actress. **Personal:** Born Dec 4, 1973, Los Angeles, CA; daughter of Don Banks and Carolyn London-Johnson. **Career:** Fresh Prince of Bel-Air, actress; Higher Learning, actress; model, currently. **Orgs:** The Center for Children & Families, spokesperson; established the Tyra Banks Scholarship, Immaculate Heart High School (CA). **Special Achievements:** First African-American model on cover of Sports Illustrated, 1997.

BANKS, WALDO R., SR.
Educator, organization executive. **Personal:** Born Mar 30, 1928, Beaumont, TX; married Anice D; children: Monica Diane, Natalie Anice, Waldo R. **Educ:** Bishop Coll, BA 1951; Prairie View Univ, attended 1952; TX So Univ, MA 1957; IN Univ, EdS 1964; Claremont Grad Sch of Educ, PhD 1975. **Career:** S Park IN Sch Dist, psychol consult instr 1952-54; Orange IN Sch Dist, psychol consult instr 1954-56; So Univ, instr couns 1957-58; IN Univ, admins tchr rschr 1958-59; Knoxville Coll, dean dir asst prof adminstrv asst 1959-61; Gary Public Schs, dir fdr operation scholarship 1961-65, dir consult 1961-65; LA Bd of Educ, instr & couns 1965-66; CA St Univ, consult LA City Human Relat Bur asst prof couns dir 1965-67; PACE Proj, professional rschr writer 1967-69; Compton Unified Sch Dist, ad-

minstr & dir 1967-75; UCLA, instr 1971-76; Global Oil Co Inc, pres 1975-77; Imperial Health Ctr Inc, dir 1975-77; Natl Employ Ctr, pres 1975-77; Amer Educ Found, pres 1970-80. **Orgs:** Consult to pres foreign & domestic affairs; consult dept of HEW Dept of Commerce Dept of Defense Dept of the Navy Dept of Labor Amer Soc of Mil History LA; Natl Adv Counc on Educ Profns Devel; mem Harry Walker Inc; Amer Prog Bur Inc; United Nations Spkrs Bur; mem Amer Assn of Coll Registrars &Admissions Officers; Amer Assn of Coll & Univ Deans; Amer Assn of Secondary Sch Prin; Amer Assn of Sch Adminstr; Amer Assn of Univ Profs; AmerColl Personnel Assn; Amer Educ Econ Asst Found; Amer Fed of Tchrs; Amer Jr Coll Assn; Amer Personnel & Guidance Assn; Amer Polit Sci Assn; Amer Sociol Soc; Amer Psychol Assn Boys Club of Amer; BSA; BPOE; CA Assn for Prog Dem; CA Fed of Tchrs; CA Person & Guid Assn; CA St Tchrs Assn; Intl Platform Assn; Masonic Lodge; NAACP; Natl AdvCncl on EPDA; Natl Assn ofter-Grp Relations Ofcls; Natl Cong of Parents & Tchrs; NEA; Natl Urban League; Phi Delta Kappa; So Christian Leadership Conf; YMCA. **Honors/Awds:** Dr Joseph J Rhoads Schlrshp Grant Bishop Coll 1946-50; Adminstrv Rsch Asstshp Grant IN Univ 1957-58; educ grants Claremont Grad Sch of Educ 1972-74; pres USA appointee Natl Adv Cncl on Educ Profns Devel 1972-75; grant Natl Fellowship Fund Atlanta 1974-75; numerous publications, research programs and projects; Natl Professional Serv Citation Pres Ford USA. **Business Addr:** President, International Cougar Corp, 1806 E Turmont St, PH Suite 300, Carson, CA 90746.

BANKS, WILLIAM JASPER, JR.

Physician, educator. **Personal:** Born Jul 4, 1944, Richmond, VA; son of C E Banks and W J Banks. **Educ:** VA Univ, BS 1965; VA Commonwealth Univ, MS 1966; Howard Univ, MD 1970; Univ of Edinburgh McMasters Coll, MA 1986. **Career:** DC Gen Hosp, med officer 1977-, vice pres med staff 1981-82; Howard Univ Hosp, chief orth clinics 1979-; Howard Univ, instr surgery 1977-80, sec div of orth surg, asst prof surgery, beginning 1980, associate prof, currently. **Orgs:** Fellow Amer Coll of Surgeons, Amer Acad of Ortho Surgeons, Intl Coll of Surgeons; mem AMA, DC Med Soc, Southern Med Soc; mem Arlington Hosp Foundation, Intl Oceanographic Foundation; sec Capital City Orth Found; fellow Royal Coll of Surgeons Edinburgh, Natl Geographic Soc Navl Inst; mem Southern Orth Soc, Eastern Orth Soc, Sigma Xi, Amer Assoc for the Advancement of Sci, NY Acad of Sci, Amer Philosophical Soc, Pan Amer Orth Group, Soc of Clinical Investigators. **Honors/Awds:** Honorable Fellow JF Kennedy Library; Community Serv Silver Spring Boys Club; "Complications of Amputatim" Ortho Update Series; Osteoporosis Intl Conf Metabolic Bone Diseases-Rome Spec Citation Southern Poverty Law Center; Osteomyelitis A New Look At An Old Problem Jrnl of Diseases of Children. **Military Serv:** USN rear adm; Legion of Merit, Presidential Citation, Vietnam Medal. **Business Addr:** Associate Professor, Surgery, Howard Univ, 2139 Georgia Ave, NW, Washington, DC 20060.

BANKS, WILLIAM MARON, III

Educator. **Personal:** Born Sep 22, 1943, Thomasville, GA; children: David, Tracey, Trey, Shane. **Educ:** Dillard Univ, B 1963; Univ of KY, Doctorate 1967. **Career:** Attebury Job Corps Center, supr counselor & psychol 1967; Howard Univ, counselor psychol 1967-70, dept chairperson 1972-75; Univ of CA at Berkeley, prof 1970-, provost, 1988-89. **Orgs:** Mem Soc for Psychol Study of Soc Issues; Soc for Study of Soc Problems; Amer Personnel & Guid Assn; chairperson Univ of CA Afro-Amer Studies Consortium 1979-81; Assn of Black Psychologists. **Honors/Awds:** Summer Scholars Awd US Civil Serv Commn; Univ of CA Regents Fellowship; Instructional Improve Grant; num scholarly articles & monographs pub on effects of racial differences in psychotherapy & counseling; American Book Award, 1996. **Special Achievements:** Published "Black Intellectuals.". **Business Addr:** Professor, University of California, African-American Studies, 682 Barrows, Berkeley, CA 94720.

BANKS, WILLIE ANTHONY

Professional baseball player. **Personal:** Born Feb 27, 1969, Jersey City, NJ. **Career:** Minnesota Twins, pitcher, 1991-94; Chicago Cubs, 1994-95; Los Angeles Dodgers, 1995; Florida Marlins, 1995; Philadelphia Phillies, 1995-97; New York Yankees, 1997-. **Business Addr:** Professional Baseball Player, New York Yankees, 161th St and River Ave, Yankee Stadium, Bronx, NY 10451, (718)293-4300.

BANKSTON, ARCHIE M.

Attorney, utility company executive. **Personal:** Born Oct 12, 1937, Memphis, TN; son of Elsie Shaw Bankston and Archie M Bankston, Sr; married Emma Ann DeJan; children: Alice DeJan, Louis Shaw. **Educ:** Fisk Univ, BA 1959; Washington Univ School of Law, LLB 1962; Washington Univ Graduate School of Business Admin, MBA 1964. **Career:** General Foods Corp, asst div counsel 1964-67, product mgr Maxwell House Div 1967-69; Pepsico Inc, asst sec & corp counsel 1969-72; Xerox Corp, div counsel 1972-73; Consolidated Edison Co of NY, sec & asst general counsel 1974-89; sec & assoc general counsel 1989-. **Orgs:** Phi Delta Phi Legal Fraternity 1960-; admitted to practice law NY & MO; former mem Securities Indu Comm; advisory group, NY Chapter, Corporate Practices Commission; former chairman, National Membership Committee; former chmn budget comm, former mem bd of dirs, Amer Soc of Corp Sec Inc 1974-; former pres Stockholder Relat Soc of NY; Amer Bar Assn; NY State Bar Assn; Assn of Black Lawyers of Westchester Co Inc; dir Beth Israel Med Center NYC; former dir Mental Health Assn of Westchester Co; former dir Amer Mgmt Assn; dir, Associated Black Charities; trustee, College of New Rochelle; mem 100 Black Men Inc; Beta Zeta Boule (Sigma Pi Phi Frat); Alpha Phi Alpha Fraternity; pres, Westchester Clubmen Inc. **Honors/Awds:** Recipient Black Achievers in Industry Award Harlem Branch YMCA 1971; Merit Award for Black Exec Exchange Program Natl Urban League 1974; distinguished service commendation award, Mental Health Assn, 1987; 1st Black atty/product mgr Gen Foods 1964-67; 1st Black Sr Exec Officer Consolidated Edison 1974; 1st Black Corp Sec of a major US Co 1974. **Business Addr:** Secretary, Associate General Counsel, Consol Edison Co of NY Inc, 4 Irving Pl, New York, NY 10003.

BANKSTON, CHARLES E.

Automobile dealership executive. **Career:** Village Ford, owner, currently. **Honors/Awds:** Co. is ranked #65 on Black Enterprise magazine's list of top 100 auto dealers, 1992. **Business Phone:** (214)221-2900.

BANKSTON, MICHAEL

Professional football player. **Personal:** Born Mar 12, 1970, East Bernard, TX; married Kimberly; children: Michael Jr., Mikaela. **Educ:** Sam Houston State, bachelor's degree in business management, 1995. **Career:** Arizona Cardinals, defensive end, 1994-. **Business Addr:** Professional Football Player, Arizona Cardinals, 8701 S Hardy, Tempe, AZ 85284, (602)379-0101.

BANNER, MELVIN EDWARD

Educator, author (retired). **Personal:** Born Jul 16, 1914, McDonald, PA; son of Patricia Banner and Clyde Banner; married Patricia Duignan; children: Melvina Banner Ford. **Educ:** Flint Jr Coll, AA 1936; Univ of MI, BA 1948, MA 1952; MI State Univ, grad studies. **Career:** Flint Dept of Recreation, 1934-36; MI Chronicle, Flint, reporter, 1936-38; Chevrolet Motor, 1936-38; Mott Found, adult ed rec 1938-48; Fisher Body, 1939; Buick Motor Div, foundry 1940-50; Bronze Reporter, asst editor, 1940-55; Flint Bd of Educ, tchr 1950-80; Flint Spokesman, editor, 1956-59; Flint Mirror Urban League Circle, editor, 1961-63. **Orgs:** Treas 1966, pres 1971-72 United Teachers of Flint; bd dir 1970-72, exec bd 1971-72 MI Educ Assn; chmn Natl Educ Assn Comm Ed Finance 1971-74; vice pres Economic Crisis Ctr 1984-85; bd mem Comm Serv & Referral Ctr 1984; East Lansing Human Rel Comm 1981-87; chmn Martin Luther King Commemoration 1987; secretary/treasurer, Lake Tahoe Rock and Gem Society, 1989-; Lake Tahoe Gem and Mineral Society, secretary, 1990-91, president, 1991-93; Lake Tahoe Choir, 1992-93. **Honors/Awds:** Heritage Awd Genesee Co Historical & Museum Soc; Liberty Bell Awd Law Day; Distinguished Serv MI, Natl Educ Assn; Big Brother Awd; Outstanding Newsmaker Awd Natl Assn of Media Women 1978; Reg 10 MI Educ Assn Tchr Hall of Fame 1982; Citation MI State House of Rep Tribute; MI State Legislature Senate Concurrent Resolution No 718; US Congressional Cert of Merit Educ & Author; Cert of Appreciation from The People of the City of Flint, Flint Comm Schs, Flint Central Optimist Club Flint, Urban League of Flint; Outstanding Comm Serv Awd from United Fund of Genesee and Lapeer Counties; Cert of Honored Serv State Bd of Educ. **Special Achievements:** Author, "Black Pioneer in Mich" and "Reflections in Black Poetry.". **Home Addr:** PO Box 17035, South Lake Tahoe, CA 96151.

BANNER, WILLIAM AUGUSTUS

Educator (retired). **Personal:** Born Sep 18, 1915, Philadelphia, PA; son of Nannie Beatrice Perry and Zacharias Banner; married Beatrice V Suggs; children: Beatrice Anne, William Perry. **Educ:** PA State Univ, BA 1935; Yale Univ, MDiv 1938; Harvard Univ, MA 1944, PhD (Sheldon Traveling Fellow) 1947. **Career:** Bennett Coll, philosophy instr 1938-43; Howard Univ Sch of Divinity, asst to assoc prof 1945-55, Coll Liberal Arts, assoc prof of philosophy 1955-58, prof, beginning 1958, graduate prof, 1981-85; Yale Univ, visiting prof 1964-65; Univ of Rochester, distinguished visiting prof 1970; Coll Liberal Arts, assoc dean 1971-75; Howard Univ, department of philosophy, chairman 1976-81; Folger Institute, lect 1984-85. **Orgs:** Mem Amer Philos Assn; Natl Humanities Faculty; Guild Scholars of Episcopal Ch; fellow Soc Religion in High Educ; mem Harvard Club. **Honors/Awds:** Doctor of Humane Letters, Howard University, 1988. **Special Achievements:** Author, "Ethics, An Introduction to Moral Philosophy" 1968, "Moral Norms and Moral Order, The Philosophy of Human Affairs" 1981; contributor "Greece, 478-336 BC" a handbook 1982; "The Path of St Augustine," 1996. **Home Addr:** 5719 1 St NW, Washington, DC 20011.

BANNERMAN-RICHTER, GABRIEL

Educator. **Personal:** Born Oct 28, 1931, Oyo, Nigeria; married Jane Harvey-Ewusie; children: Anna, Jessica, Gabriel Jr, Matilda, Elizabeth. **Educ:** CA State Univ, BA 1963-69; CA State Univ, MA 1969-70; Univ of CA Davis, 1970-72. **Career:** Sacramento City Coll, instr 1969-80; Univ of CA Davis, instr 1972-75; Univ of Cape Coast Ghana, vstg assoc prog 1976-77; CA State Univ Sacramento, prof 1969-. **Orgs:** Publ Gabari Publ Co 1982-. **Honors/Awds:** Author "Practice of Witchcraft in Ghana" 1982, "Don't Cry My Baby, Don't Cry" 1984; NEH Scholar NEH Inst Univ of IN 1985; Author "Mmoetia, The Mysterious Dwarfs" 1985. **Home Addr:** 3612 21 Ave, Sacramento, CA 95820. **Business Addr:** Prof, English/Ethnic Studies, California State Univ, 6000 J St, Sacramento, CA 95819.

BANTON, WILLIAM C., II

Brigadier general. **Personal:** Born Nov 9, 1922, Washington, DC. **Educ:** Howard Univ Coll of Liberal Arts & Sci, Howard Univ Coll of Med, mD 1946; Homer G Phillips Hosp, 1946-47; Robert Koch Hosp, 1947-49; USAF Gen Hosp, 1950-52; John Hopkins Univ Sch of Hygiene & Pub Health, 1970; St Louis Univ Schl of Med; USAF Sch of Aviation Med; USPHS; Sch of Aerospace Med; USN Med Sch; Armed Forces Inst of Pathology; Wash Univ Sch of Med; Def Atomic Support Agy; Sch of Awrospace Med; Boston U; Harvard U; Tufts Univ Sch of Med; Indsl Coll of Armed Forces. **Career:** Mitchell Air Force Base NY, med officer of internal med; 2230th AFR Floyd Bennett Naval Air Sta, flight surgeon 1951-52; St Louis Health Div Chest & TB Svc; part-time pvt prac in internal med; 8711th USAFG Hosp Scott Air Vorce Base, comdr & flight surgeon 1954-71; Hq USAF/SG Forrestal Bldg Wash, asst to surgeon gen 1971-; served on short active duty tours in So Vietnam 1968-69; Dept of Comm Health & Med Care St Louis Co MO, dir; St Louis Univ Sch ofMed, holds apptmnts as asst clinical prof of internal med. **Orgs:** Mem Reserve Officer's Assn; Air Force Assn; life mem Alpha Phi Alpha; Chi Delta Mu; Howard Univ Alumni Assn; life mem NAACP; bd dirs Koch Welfare Assn;Friends of City Art Mus of St Louis; Nat Geographic Soc; St Louis Zoo Assn; John Hopkins Univ Alumni Assn; Homer G Phillips Hosp Intern Alumni Assn. **Honors/Awds:** Promoted Brigadier Gen Apr 6 1973; recipient WW II Victory Medal; Am Campaign Medal; Nat Def Serv Medal; Good Conduct Medal; Expert Marksman Medal; Armed Forces Longevity Serv Award; Award Forces Res Medal; S Vietnam Campaitn Medal. **Military Serv:** US Army, 1st lt 1946; USAFR capt 1950.

BAPTISTA, HOWARD

Association executive. **Personal:** Born Nov 24, 1930, Nantucket, MA; married Margarit Von Steiger; children: Mark, Kim, Kevin, Stephan. **Educ:** Bryant Coll, BA 1956; NY Univ, MA 1960. **Career:** Altman's Dept Store, jr exec; New York City Housing Auth, 1959-60; NY Bd Educ, 1960-62; Bedford Redevelop Auth, exec dir. **Orgs:** Vice pres SE Bank & Trust Co; incorporator NB Inst Savs Bank; dir Vol Amer; Comm Council; United Fund; New England Council NAHRO. **Honors/Awds:** Eqalitarian Awd NAACP. **Military Serv:** US Army, cpl.

BAPTISTE, HANSOM PRENTICE, JR.

Educator. **Personal:** Born Jan 18, 1939, Beaumont, TX; married Mirabelle; children: 7. **Educ:** Universaity of California, attended, 1962; University of Notre Dame, attended, 1964; Lamar State College, BS, 1961; Indiana University, MAT, 1966, EdD, 1968. **Career:** Cuero Independent School District, 1961-63; Beaumont Independent School District, teacher, 1963-65; Indiana University, asst professor, 1968-72; University of Houston, Dept of Education Administration, assoc professor, currently. **Orgs:** Many workshops & seminars, 1971-75; Indiana University Alumni Assn; Natl Science Teachers Assn; Natl Congress Parents & Teachers; Phi Delta Kappa. **Honors/Awds:** Education Grant, Career Opportunity Program, 1970-72; Office Education Title III, grant training faculty, doctorate level, 1973-75; Valedictorian Scholarship, 1957-58; Outstanding Teacher Award, 1969-70; Natl Defense Education Act Grant, 1966-68; Natl Science Foundation, Academic Year Grant, 1965-66. **Business Addr:** Dept of Education Administration, University of Houston, Houston, TX 77204-0001.

BARAKA, IMAMU AMIRI (LEROI JONES)

Writer, editor, poet, educator. **Personal:** Born Oct 7, 1934, Newark, NJ; son of Anna Lois Russ Jones and Coyette LeRoi; married Hettie Robinson Cohen, Oct 13, 1958 (divorced 1965); children: Kellie Elisabeth, Lisa Victoria Chapman; married Bibi Amina Baraka, 1966; children: Obalaji Malik Ali, Ras Jua Al Aziz, Shani Isis, Amiri Seku, Ahi Mwenge. **Educ:** Howard Univ, BA, English, 1954; Columbia Univ, MA; attended, Rutgers Univ, 1951-52. **Career:** Yugen Magazine, founder, 1958; New School for Social Research, New York, NY, instructor, 1961-64; writer, 1961-; Univ of Buffalo, visiting professor, 1964; Columbia Univ, visiting professor, fall 1964, 1966-67; Yale Univ, visiting professor, 1977-78; George Washington Univ, visiting professor, 1978-79; State University of New York at Stony Brook, associate professor, 1983-85, professor of Afro American studies, 1985-. **Orgs:** Black Academy of Arts and Letters; secretary general, co-governor, National Black Political Assembly; chairman, Congress of African People; United Brothers; All African Games; Pan African Federation; mem, African Liberation Day Support Commt; Political Prisoners Relief Fund; IFCO Internatl Force. **Honors/Awds:** Plays include: Dutchman and the Slave, 1964; The Toilet, 1964; The Baptism: A Comedy in One Act, 1966; The System of Dante's Hell, 1965; Slaveship, 1967; Arm Yourself, or Harm Yourself! A One-Act Play, 1967; Four Black Revolutionary Plays: All

Praises to the Black Man, 1969; J-E-L-L-O, 1970; What Was the Relationship of the Lone Ranger to the Means of Production: A Play in One Act, 1978; has written numerous plays for the stage. Poetry includes: April 13, 1959; Spring and So Forth, 1960; The Dead Lecturer, 1964; A Poem for Black Hearts, 1967; It's Nation Time 1970; Reggae or Not! Poems, 1982; Jesse Jackson and Black People, 1994; numerous others; Has edited several books and anthologies; Longview Best Essay of the Year Award for Vuba Libre, 1961;John Whitney Foundation Fellowship, 1962bie Award for Dutchman, 1964; Guggenheim Fellowship, 1965-66; National Endowment for the Arts Grant, 1966; Poetry Award, National Endowment for the Arts, 1981; New Jersey Council of the Arts Awsard, 1982; American Book Award, Before Columbus Foundation for Confirmation: An Anthology of African-American Women, 1984; Drama Award, 1985. **Military Serv:** US Air Force, 1954-57. **Business Addr:** Professor, Department of Africana Studies, State University of New York, Stony Brook, NY 11794-4340.

BARAKA, LARRY

Judge. **Career:** Dallas Criminal Court, District 2, judge, currently. **Business Addr:** Judge, ATTN: Alberta Medlin, Criminal District Court #2, Dallas County Courthouse, Dallas, TX 75202, (214)653-5912.

BARANCO, BEVERLY VICTOR, JR.

Dentist. **Personal:** Born in New Orleans, LA; widowed; children: 8. **Educ:** LA State Univ Dental Sch, DDS. **Career:** Private Practice, dental surgery. **Orgs:** Mem 6th Dist Dental Assn; Amer Dental Assn; LA Dental Assn; Pelcn State Dental Soc; pres chmn of bd of dir First Fed Sav & Loan Assn; Baton Rouge; mem Serra Club; Alpha Phi Alpha; Sigma Pi Phi; Chi Delta Mu; bd dir Blndn Home; bd dir Family Coun Serv; chmn bd dir Baranco-Clark YMCA; dir GoodSamaritans; mem Comm for Rehab of Penal Inst State of LA; mem St Agnes Roman Catholic Ch; mem Mayor's Bi-Rcl Comm Rel Comm. **Honors/Awds:** Knights of St Peter Claver Awd; Knights of St Gregory the Great Pope Paul VI; Silver Beaver Awd BSA. **Business Addr:** 1200 6 St, 2191 Main St, Detroit, MI 48226.

BARANCO, GORDON S.

Judge. **Personal:** Born Feb 25, 1948, Oakland, CA; son of Lillian Baranco and Arnold Baranco; married Barbara N Gee; children: Lauren Barbara Gee Baranco, Brandon Michael Gee Baranco. **Educ:** Univ of CA, BA 1969, JD 1972. **Career:** San Francisco, asst dist attny 1974-77; Neighborhood Legal Asst, managing attny 1977-80; Oakland, asst city attny 1980; Oakland Municipal Court, judge 1980-84; Alameda Cty Superior Court, judge, 1984-. **Business Addr:** Judge, Alameda County Superior Court, 1225 Fallon, Oakland, CA 94612.

BARANCO, GREGORY T.

Automobile dealership executive. **Career:** Chief exec, Baranco Lincoln-Mercury Inc, Duluth, GA, Baranco Pontiac-GMC Truck-Subaru Inc, Decatur, GA, Acura of Tallahassee, Tallahassee, FL; Baranco Automotive Group, president, currently. **Honors/Awds:** Auto 100 listing (Baranco's three auto dealerships), Black Enterprise, 1991. **Business Addr:** Pres/CEO, Baranco Automotive Group, 4299 Covington Hwy, Decatur, GA 30035.

BARANCO, RAPHAEL ALVIN

Dentist. **Personal:** Born Nov 19, 1932, Baton Rouge, LA; married Terry Bryant; children: Angela, Rachel, Raphael. **Educ:** Xavier Univ, BS 1956; Meharry Med Coll, DDS 1961. **Career:** Jersey City Med Ctr, intern 1961-62; Meharry Med Coll Nashville, instr Prosthetic dentistry 1963-64; VA Hosp Tuskegee AL, dir clin dentistry 1964-68; Individual Practice, dentistry; 1968-. **Orgs:** Mem Amer Dental Assn; chmn Lafayette Parish Comm Action Cncl 1971; Lafayette Cncl on Human Relations 1968-; Lafayette Parish Sch Bd; Lafayette Parish Cncl of Govt; mem Sheriff's Adv Commn 1968-; bd dirs Tri-Parish Comm Action Agency; United Givers Fund; pres bd dirs Holy Family Sch 1971-; mem NAACP; chmn housing com; C of C; Alpha Phi Alpha; Alpha Phi Omega; Chi Delta Mu. **Military Serv:** US Army, 1953-55. **Business Addr:** 1006 Surrey St, Lafayette, LA 70501.

BARBEE, LLOYD AUGUSTUS

Attorney. **Personal:** Born Aug 17, 1925, Memphis, TN; son of Adlina Gilliam Barbee and Ernest Aaron Barbee; divorced; children: Finn, Daphne, Rustam. **Educ:** LeMoyne Coll, BA 1949; Univ of WI Madison, JD 1956. **Career:** Industrial Commn of WI UC Dept, law examiner I 1957-62; Gov's Comm on Human Rights, legal consul 1959; NAACP, pres 1962-64; Milwaukee United Sch Integration Comm, chmn 1964; WI Legislature, state representative 1965-77; Univ of Wisconsin, Law Sch, teacher 1968-69, 1972; Univ of Wisconsin at Milwaukee, adjunct prof 1976-88; Bronx Community Coll, adjunct prof, 1990-92; private practice, attorney, 1956-. **Orgs:** Mem State Bar of WI 1956-; chmn Enrolled Bills comm 1965-66; mem Comm on Joint Finance 1965-73; chmn Assembly Judiciary Comm 1973-77; mem Comm on Transportation 1969-77; pres/pres emeritus WI Black Lawyers Assn 1965-80; chmn WI Black Elected & Apptd Officials 1972-76; minister Political Empowerment Comm Natl Black Assembly 1973-75; Milwaukee Symphony Orchestra, bd of dirs, 1994-96; Natl Bar Assn; Wisconsin Bar Assn; American Bar Assn. **Honors/Awds:** Milwaukee Man of the Yr Alpha Phi Alpha Frat Inc 1965; Medgar Evers Awd Milwaukee Br NAACP 1969; Outstanding & Continuing Contrib to Milwaukee Black Business Comm 1976; Disting Civil Serv Milwaukee Frontiers 1978; Lawyer Scholar Pub Serv Milwaukee Theological Inst 1978; Serv in Education Law & Govern St Mark AME Church 1979; Outstanding Serv as Law Sch Tchr Univ WI Madison Law Sch 1984; Univ of WI at Milwaukee, Coll of Letters & Sci Amer Studies Dept Faculty Award; Madison West HS, award for outstanding services toward improving civil rights in WI 1986; Wisconsin Black Political and Economic Development Council Award, 1987; Rufus King Education Award, 1989; Wisconsin Assn of Minority Attorneys Award, 1993; Milwaukee Homeless Project Inc, Award, 1993; Milwaukee Times, Black Excellence Award, 1994; Amer Civil Liberties Union, Wisconsin, Lifetime Civil Liberties Achievement Award, 1995; Annual James H Baker Award, 1996; Malcolm X Commemoration Mount Freedom Award, 1997; Dedication of West Barbee St, Milwaukee, WI; Mayor John Norquist Proclamation of Lloyd A Barbee Day, Sept 6, 1997. **Military Serv:** USN, sm 2/c, 3 yrs; Asiatic-Pacific & Victory Medals.

BARBER, HARGROW DEXTER

Oral/maxillofacial surgeon. **Personal:** Born Aug 29, 1956, Alameda, CA; son of Jessie Singleton Barber and Hargrow Dexter Barber Sr; married Kimberly Higgins DDS. **Educ:** Univ of California at Davis, BA 1978; Meharry Medical Coll, DDS 1983; Oral Surgery Residency Highland Hospital 1989. **Career:** Private practice, dentist 1983-85; Highland General Hosp, oral maxillofacial surgeon in residency 1985-89. **Orgs:** Mem Natl Dental Assn 1979-, Amer Acad of Oral Medicine 1983-, CA Dental Assn 1986-, Amer Assn of Oral and Maxillofacial Surgeons 1986-; Amer Dental Society of Anesthesiology 1989-, Maryland State Dental Assn 1988-; Amer Dental Assn 1986-. **Honors/Awds:** Outstanding Achievement Award Amer Acad of Oral Medicine 1983; Honor Scholarship Award Meharry Medical Coll School of Dentistry 1983; Hospital Dentistry Award Meharry Medical Coll 1983; second black person accepted into the Oral and Maxillofacial Residency Program at Highland General Hospital in its fifty year history; Golden State Achievement Award 1988; published "Double Degree Oral Surgeons," Journal of Oral and Maxillofacial Surgery, Oct 1989, and "Orbital Infections," Journal of Oral and Maxillofacial Surgery, Nov 1989. **Business Addr:** Highland General Hospital, Dept of Oral/Maxillofacial Surgery, 1411 E 31st St, Oakland, CA 94602.

BARBER, JAMES W.

Educator. **Personal:** Born Sep 17, 1936, Alexandria, VA; married Doris; children: Laura, Tracy. **Educ:** BS 1964. **Career:** High Meadows CT State Treatment Center, dir of educ & group life; AL Center for Higher Educ, sr group training consultant 1972; So CT State Coll, dir comm & minority affairs. **Orgs:** Consult New York City Bur of Youth Detention 1970, New Haven CT Publ School System 1971-72, State of CT Dept of Children Youth Serv 1975-77; chmn protem Eastern Alliance of Black Counselors 1975; pres Consumer Council So CT Gas Co; adv Org of Afro-Amer students at S CT State Coll; pres Assoc of Black Personnel in Higher Ed CT CHapt; mem High Meadows Child Study & Treatment Ctr; pres New Haven Scholarship Fund Inc; mem NAACP, Urban League, RIF. **Business Addr:** Dir of Comm Min Affairs, So CT State Coll, 501 Casscent St, New Haven, CT 06515.

BARBER, JANICE DENISE

Dentist. **Personal:** Born Nov 6, 1952, Alameda, CA; daughter of Jessie Singleton Barber and Hargrow Barber; married Russell J Frazier. **Educ:** Mills Coll, BA 1974; Meharry Medical Coll Dental Sch, DDS 1979. **Career:** Hubbard Hosp, 1st yr general practice resident 1981, 2nd yr general practice resident 1983, asst instr in hosp dentistry 1981; New York City, assoc dentist 1983-86; Sydenham NFCC/Harlem Hosp, attending dentist 1984-86; Harlem Hosp, clinical floor coord 1985-86; Oakland CA, assoc dentist 1986-; Highland General Hospital, 1990-. **Orgs:** Mem Delta Sigma Theta, Acad of General Dentistry, Amer Dental Assoc. **Honors/Awds:** Employee of the Year Harlem Hosp Dental Clinic 1985; Employee of the Month Harlem Hosp 1985; Harlem Hosp Attending of the Year Dental Clinic 1986; abstract "The Mental Foramen Injection" The NY Journal of Dentistry 1983; "Cosmetic Dentistry" Harlem Hosp Ambulatory Newsletter 1986. **Home Addr:** 2142 66th Ave, Oakland, CA 94621.

BARBER, JESSE B., JR.

Neurosurgeon (retired). **Personal:** Born Jun 22, 1924, Chattanooga, TN; son of Mae F Barber and Jesse Sr; married Constance Bolling; children: Clifton, Jesse III, Charles, Joye. **Educ:** Lincoln Univ, BA; Howard Univ Coll of Medicine, MD 1948. **Career:** Freedmen's Hospital, intern & resident general surgeon, 1948-54; Howard Univ Coll of Med, instructor surgery, pathology 1956-58; McGill Univ Montreal Neurologic Inst, resident, 1958-61; Howard Univ Coll of Med, chief div of neurosurgery 1961-83, prof of surgery/nrs 1964-91, first prof of social medicine 1983-91; District of Columbia General Hospital, chief of NRS, 1983-94, president of medical dental staff, assoc prof of Community Medicine, 1994-. **Orgs:** Founder, dir, Howard Univ Med Stroke Project, 1968-70; co-founder, co-chair, HEAL (Health Equal Access League) DC, 1984-91; mem, Kappa Pi, Alpha Omega Alpha; fellow, Amer Coll of Surgeons; pres, Natl Med Assn, 1978-79; chair, Home Care for Homeless, 1986-90; NE Presbyterian Church, elder; past pres, Medico - Chirorgical Society of DC, 1996-98. **Honors/Awds:** Howard Univ Alumni Fed Award for Meritorious Prof & Comm Serv 1970; Wm Alonzo Warfield Award 1974; Century Award YMCA 1974; Distinguished Serv Award Natl Med Assn, 1974; Outstanding Serv Award HTA 1982-86; Outstanding Serv Award Commn Public Health of DC 1985; Hon DSC Lincoln Univ 1978; Community Service Award: Med Soc of DC 1989, DC Hospital Assn 1988, AFL-CIO 1986, United Black Fund 1988, Howard Univ 1981; 1st Humanitarian CFH of DC 1986; Distinguished Service Award HU Dept of Surgery 1979. **Military Serv:** US Army, pfc 1943-46; US Army, Med Corps capt 1954-56. **Home Addr:** 38 Longfellow St NW, Washington, DC 20011.

BARBER, MICHAEL

Professional football player. **Personal:** Born Nov 9, 1971, Edgemore, SC. **Educ:** Clemson. **Career:** Seattle Seahawks, linebacker, 1995-. **Business Addr:** Professional Football Player, Seattle Seahawks, 11220 NE 53rd St, Kirkland, WA 98033, (206)827-9777.

BARBER, RONDE

Professional football player. **Personal:** Born Apr 7, 1975. **Educ:** Univ of Virginia, bachelor's degree in commerce. **Career:** Tampa Bay Buccaneers, defensive back, 1997-. **Business Addr:** Professional Football Player, Tampa Bay Buccaneers, One Buccaneer Place, Tampa, FL 33607, (813)870-2700.

BARBER, TIKI

Professional football player. **Personal:** Born Apr 7, 1975. **Educ:** Univ of Virginia. **Career:** New York Giants, running back, 1997-. **Business Addr:** Professional Football Player, New York Giants, Giants Stadium, East Rutherford, NJ 07073, (201)935-8111.

BARBER, WILLIAM, JR.

Building service supervisor. **Personal:** Born Jan 4, 1942, Morristown, NJ; married Anita Clayter; children: William III. **Educ:** Univ of NE, BE 1967. **Career:** Town of Morristown, recreational dir; M&M Mars, employment & comm relations rep; No Jersey Morris Catholic HS, 1st black wrestling coach, head track coach, 1967-73; Urban 4H, social comm worker, 1967-73; Morristown Neighborhood House, social rec dir, 1967-; Intl Harvester, sales trainee, school comm worker, social case & guidance counselor, 1967-73; Barber Maintenance Cleaning Contractor, pres; AT&T, mgr bldg operations, mgr public relations, bldg serv supervisor, until 1990; Passaic Tech Voc Educ, intervention instructor, physical health educ instructor; St Clare Riverside Med Ctr, mental health couselor. **Orgs:** Counselor After Care Clinic Drug Rehabilitation Regions Clergy Council; chmn Juvenile Conf Bd; natl bd dir Morristown YMCA 1967-71; recreations commission 1967-69; mem Morris Community Coll 4H EOF, Cty Coll of Morris & St Elizabeth Coll 1969-72; More help bd of dir, scholorship comm Morristown Neighborhood House 1969; TYEFA dances 1972; local TV show "Cable-Whats Happening Now," "Union Baptist Church Program," 1973-; mem Plainfield NAACP 1974, Human Civil Rights Commiss; mem Morristown Kiwanis Club, Morris Cty NAACP 1980; 1st black volunteer fireman in Morristown 1980-; mem Morristown Memorial Hospital; parole bd State of New Jersey 1980; mem Intl Group Friendship Force; 2nd ward councilman, sr mem Town Govt; Market Street Mission Christian Counselling Training; bd of dir forMorris Habitat for Humanity; St Clair Hospi Canes Program, mental health counseling; New Jersey School, Social Workers Council, pres, 1995; Hands Across Morristown; Zeke Harris Science Club; Charlest Menninger Society; Notary Public for NJ. **Honors/Awds:** Jaycees Distinguished Serv Award 1969; Outstanding Citizen 4-H Club Award 1970; Morris County Human Resource Award 1978; NAACP Comm Serv Award; Comm Serv Award for Ike Martin Book of Honors 1987; developed a private library with antique radios. **Special Achievements:** Teacher, General Science and PE Health to special educational students. **Business Addr:** Instructor, Passaic County Technical Institute, 45 Reiwhardt Rd, Wayne, NJ 07470.

BARBER DICKERSON, ORNETTA M.

Marketing executive. **Personal:** Born Mar 14, 1949, St Louis, MO; daughter of Edna Morales and James Ornett Barber; married R Gregg Dickerson, Feb 24, 1990. **Educ:** California State University at Los Angeles, BA, radio and television broadcasting, 1978. **Career:** Greater Los Angeles Community Action Agency, community activist, KHJ Television, Frankly Female, associate producer, 1977-86; Elektra/Asylum Records, National Marketing Research, sr director, 1979-86; WEA, Corp, Black Music Marketing, national director, 1986-87, vice pres, 1987-. **Orgs:** Thurgood Marshall Scholarship Fund, 1990-; Institute for Black Parenting, 1989-; Yes to Jobs Program, 1987-; National Association of Rec Arts & Sciences, 1979-; Avalon Carver Community Center, 1976-; Westminster Neighborhood Association, 1976-; 331 Foundation, 1991-. **Honors/Awds:**

NAACP Legal Defense Fund, Black Woman of Achievement, 1991; Ebony Magazine, Best & Brightest 100 Women in Corporate America, 1990; Jack the Rapper, Original 13 Award, 1990; Black Radio Exclusive, Heritage Award, 1991; Impact Magazine, Women's Networking Award, 1990. **Business Addr:** VP, Warner/Elektra/Atlantic Corp., 111 N Hollywood Way, Burbank, CA 91505, (818)840-6323.

BARBOZA, ANTHONY
Photographer, painter. **Personal:** Born May 10, 1944, New Bedford, MA; son of Anthony & Lillian Barboza; married Laura Carrington, Jul 15, 1985; children: Leticia, Laryssa, Danica, Alexio, Lien. **Career:** Began photographic career with Kamoinge Workshop, under the direction of photographer, Roy DeCarava, 1964; commerical photographer, currently. **Special Achievements:** Art Pubs: Day in the Life of Israel, Viking, 1994; African-Americans, Viking, 1993; Songs of My People, Little Brown, 1992; Flesh & Blood; Picture Project, 1992; Shooting Stars: Stuart, Tabori & Chang, 1992; numerous others; Books: ''Black Borders,'' ''Piano For Days,'' ''Black Book of Lists,'' NYU Press, 1998; Exhibitions: Songs of My People, Time Life Tour, 1990; Cinque Gallery, NY, 1990; Drew Univ, One-Man Show, 1989; numerous others; TV Commercial, Miles Davis Present Van Liquor, It's A Miracle!, Dentsu Advertisting, Dentsu of Japan, 1984; Permanent Collections, Museum of Modern Art; Studio Museum of Harlem; Newark Art Museum; Howard Univ; Orleans Public Library; Univ of Ghana; Univ of Mexico; Lectures & Grants at various schools, 1965-. **Business Addr:** 13-17 Laight St, 3rd Fl, New York, NY 10013, (212)925-7991.

BARBOZA, STEVEN ALAN
Author. **Personal:** Born Jul 20, 1952, New Bedford, MA; son of Lillian Barros Barboza and Anthony Canto Barboza; married Regina Lewis, Aug 8, 1992. **Educ:** Boston University, BA, 1976; Columbia University Gradute School of Journalism, MSJ, 1979. **Career:** Writer, currently. **Special Achievements:** Books include: I Feel Like Dancing, American Jihad: Islam After Malcolm X, Door of No Return, numerous magazine and newspaper articles. **Home Phone:** (212)995-5921.

BARCLAY, CARL ARCHIE
Physician (retired). **Personal:** Born Jul 30, 1922, Nanticoke, MD; married Mae Neece Hodge; children: Carl Archie, Kenneth Dale. **Educ:** Hampton Inst, BS 1942; Howard Univ, MD 1947. **Career:** Hampton Inst, teaching asst 1942-44; Homer G Phillips Hosp, intern St Louis 1947-48; Edwards Mem Hosp OK City, house physician 1948-51; OK City Bd of Ed, school physician 1949-59; OK City, gen practice 1951-79; Guthrie, OK Job Corps Ctr, physician 1971-91. **Orgs:** Pres OK City Med De-Phar Soc 1962-65; pres OK Med Dental & Pharm Assoc 1965-66; chmn Met Outreach Dept Greater OK City YMCA 1971-75; mem OK Cty Med Soc 1971-, OK State Med Assoc 1971-, Amer Med Assoc 1971-; mem Natl Med Assoc; dir, treas, managing officer 1968-86, M-D-P Investment Fund Inc; mem OK City Urban League; life mem NAACP; OK County Medical Society, life member, 1992; OK State Medical Assoc, life member, 1992; American Medical Assoc, life member, 1992; National Medical Assoc, life member, 1992. **Honors/Awds:** Metro Outreach Comm - Greater OK City YMCA, service awd 1975; Greater OK City YMCA Hall of Fame 1977; Eastside Branch-Greater OK City YMCA, outstanding volunteer awd 1979; OK Med Dental & Pharm Assn, life member awd 1983; China Painter, won several ribbons at the state fair of Oklahoma 1983. **Home Addr:** 2813 NE 19th St, Oklahoma City, OK 73111.

BARCLAY, DAVID RONALD
Electronics company executive. **Personal:** Born Aug 28, 1932, Oakland, CA; son of Margaret Barclay and Fred Barclay; married Pauline Brown; children: Steven, Danielle. **Educ:** Los Angeles State College, BA 1961; UCLA Exec Prog, Cert 1982. **Career:** LA Co Bur of Pub Asst, soc case wrkr 1961-64; California Youth Authority, parole agent 1964-66; CA Fair Employment Prct Comm, supervisor, consultant 1967-71; Hughes Aircraft Co head EEO programs 1971, mgr urban afrs 1972-78, dir human resources 1978-87, staff vice pres human resources development, 1987-90; corp vice president workforce diversity 1990-. **Orgs:** National Black Business Roundtable, chair; California Academy of Mathematics & Science, corp advisory committee; Aerospace Industry Equal Opportunity Committee, chair; bd mem, Leadership Education for Asian Pacifics; bd mem, LA Brotherhood Crusade; fmr bd mem, Natl Black United Fund; fmr bd mem, San Fernando Branch NAACP. **Honors/Awds:** Outstanding Alumnus California State Univ - Los Angeles Black Support Group, 1988; John Anson Ford Award, Los Angeles County Commission on Human Relations 1989; Business & Community Leader of the Year, California State University/Black Support Group 1991; Civil Rights Leadership, Southern California Employment Roundtable 1992; Outstanding Alumnus Calif State Univ, LA Black Support Group, 1988; John Anson Ford Award, LA County Commission on Human Relations, 1989; Business & Community Leader of the Year, Calif State Univ, LA Black Support Group, 1991; Corporate Leadership in Community & Education Activities, JUGS, 1991; Civil Rights Leaderships, Southern Calif Employment Roundtable, 1992; Corporate Leadership in Community Programs, Leadership Education for Asian Pacifics, 1993; Alumnus of the Year, California State University, LA, 1996. **Military Serv:** US Army, cp 2 yrs. **Home Addr:** 12638 Remington St, Pacoima, CA 91331. **Business Addr:** Vice President, Workforce Diversity, Hughes Aircraft Co, PO Box 80028, Los Angeles, CA 90080, (310)568-6751.

BARCLAY, ROBIN MARIE (ROBIN BARCLAY DUNCAN)
Health care executive. **Personal:** Born Jan 9, 1956, Detroit, MI; daughter of Carolyn Lowe Barclay and Sydney Barclay; married Thomas Duncan Sr (divorced 1985); children: Thomas Jr. **Educ:** Univ of Michigan, Ann Arbor, MI, BA general studies, 1976; Univ of North Carolina, Chapel Hill NC, MA public health adm, 1978. **Career:** Comprehensive Health Services of Detroit, Detroit, MI, health center administrator, 1979-83; Blue Cross & Blue Shield, Detroit, MI, sr analyst, hospital programs policy, 1983-86; Total Health Care, Detroit, MI, marketing manager, 1986-88; self-employed, Detroit, MI, health care consultant, 1986-88; Southwest Detroit Hospital, Detroit, MI, sr vice president, 1988-90; LifeChoice Quality Health Plan Inc, Detroit, MI, ceo, 1990-. **Orgs:** Member, National Association for the Advancement of Colored People; member, Health Care Marketing Executives; member, Group Health Association of America; member, National Black Caucus; member, Trade Union Leadership Council; member, Univ of Michigan Alumnae; Minority Technology Council of Michigan, director. **Honors/Awds:** Outstanding Achievement in Community Health Care, Detroit Chapter Southern Christian Leadership Council, 1991; Outstanding Civic and Community Contributions, Wall Street Inc, 1991.

BARDEN, DON H.
Real estate developer, cable television executive. **Personal:** Born Dec 20, 1943, Detroit, MI; son of Hortense Hamilton Barden and Milton Barden Sr; married Bella Marshall, May 14, 1988; children: Keenan Barden. **Educ:** Central State Univ, 1963-64. **Career:** Former city councilman, TV show host; The Don H Barden Co, pres; City of Lorain, councilman 1972-75; Don H Barden Co, owner/pres 1976-81; WKYC-TV NBC Cleveland, talk show host 1977-80; Barden Companies Inc, chmn, pres 1981-; Majestic Star Casino, owner, currently. **Orgs:** Pres Urban Action Inc; del White House Conf on Small Business Pres, Lorain Cty Comm Action Agency; exec comm Democratic Party; mem Ed Task Force; dir, Detroit Symphony Orchestra 1986-, Natl Cable TV Assoc IOB 1985-; dir, MI Cable TV Assoc 1987-, dir, First Independence Natl Bank 1987-; dir, Metropolitan Detroit Convention Bureau, 1988-. **Special Achievements:** Company is ranked #18 on Black Enterprise magazine's 1997 list of Top 100 Black businesses. **Business Addr:** President, Chairman, Barden Companies, 400 Renaissance Center, Detroit, MI 48243.

BARDWELL, RUFUS B., III
Business executive. **Personal:** Born Jan 25, 1937, Sylacauga, AL; married Barbara Vidrine; children: Andrea, Rufus IV. **Educ:** Tennessee State Univ, BS, 1960; CCNY, advance studies. **Career:** Tuskegee Inst, intern, 1960-61; Home Ins Co, accountant, 1961; State of NY, tax accountant, 1961-62; IRS, New York NY & Dallas TX, revenue agent, 1962; DHUD, officer bus devel office, 1969-. **Orgs:** Mem Alpha Phi Alpha, Dallas Big Bro Assoc; bd mem Dallas Negro C of C. **Honors/Awds:** US Army, pfc, 1954-56. **Business Addr:** Officer Business Devel Office, DHUD, 1100 Commerce St, Dallas, TX 75202.

BAREFIELD, MORRIS
Educator. **Personal:** Born Aug 15, 1939, Madison, IL; son of Pearlie McClelland and William Barefield; married Lun Ye Crim Barefield, Aug 18, 1963; children: Erik, Myla. **Educ:** So IL Univ, BS 1961, MS 1965. **Career:** Eisenhower HS Blue Island IL, instr 1961-64; Richard HS Oak Lawn IL, instr 1964-66; New Trier East HS, instr 1966-. **Orgs:** Mem, Instructional Affairs Comm Natl Council of Teachers of Math, 1969-72, NEA, IL Educ Assn; treasurer, sec New Trier Educ Assn 1971-74; mem Glencoe Concerned Parents Assn; dir, student prog Rights & Responsibilities New Trier HS 1973-75; guest speaker Natl Council of Teachers of Math, 1972, regional speaker, 1971-72; faculty council pres New Trier HS 1987-88; New Trier Education Association, president, 1993-. **Honors/Awds:** Award for Outstanding Effort in Human Relations IL Educ Assn 1974. **Business Addr:** Instructor, New Trier East High School, 385 Winnetka Ave, Winnetka, IL 60093.

BAREFIELD, OLLIE DELORES
Educational administrator. **Personal:** Born Dec 19, 1930, Teague, TX; married Henry B Barefield Sr; children: John Anthony. **Educ:** Huston-Tillotson Coll, BA (Magna Cum Laude) 1950; Univ of No CO, MA 1966, EdS 1970. **Career:** Teague Independent School Dist, English teacher 1950-55; Bureau of Indian Affairs AZ, Bilingual teacher 1955-60; Denver Public Schools, elementary teacher 1960-70, elementary principal 1970-. **Orgs:** Mem Amer Assoc of Univ Women 1980, Ministers Wives Assoc 1980, Natl Assoc of Elem Principal 1980; bd of dir NAACP Denver 1980; mem Delta Sigma Theta1980, Natl Council of Negro Women Inc 1980; guest lecturer Rocky Mountain Book Festival 1970. **Honors/Awds:** Teacher of the Year Denver Publ School 1969; Woman of the Year Kappa Omega Chi Beauticians Sor 1980. **Business Addr:** Principal, Denver Public School, 2480 Downing St, Denver, CO 80205.

BARFIELD, CLEMENTINE
Organization founder, executive director. **Personal:** Born Aug 19, 1950, Lexington, MS; daughter of Malinda Baugh Chism and Tolbert Chism; married John J Barfield, Apr 4, 1967 (divorced); children: John, Ollie, Malinda, Derick (deceased), Roger. **Educ:** Wayne State Univ, Detroit MI, BS, 1981. **Career:** Save Our Sons and Daughters (SOSAD,) Detroit MI, founder/exec dir. **Orgs:** Mem, Amer Humanics, Wayne State Univ; commr, Detroit City Council-Youth Advisory Commn; bd mem, Project Start; bd mem, Michigan Victim Alliance; mem, Natl Org of Victim Assistance (NOVA). **Honors/Awds:** Community Service Award, Natl Assn Negro Professional and Business Women, 1987; Natl Black Journalist, 1987; Community Service Award, Amer Muslim Community, 1987; Community Service Award, Univ of Detroit, 1987; Black Professionals Award, Michelob Beer, 1988; honorary doctorate degree, Marygrove Coll, Detroit MI, 1988; Victims Advocacy Award, Pres Ronald Reagan, 1988; Special Tributes, City of Detroit/State of Michigan; Status of Women Awards, Top Ladies of Distinction; Public Citizen of the Year Award, Natl Assn of Social Workers, 1989.

BARFIELD, DEBORAH DENISE
Journalist. **Personal:** Born Jul 6, 1963, St Albans, NY; daughter of Carrie Montgomery Barfield and William Barfield. **Educ:** University of Maryland, College Park, MD, BS, College of Journalism, 1985. **Career:** Black Explosion, College Park, MD, reporter, 1983-85; Star-Democrat, Easton, MD, sportswriter, 1985-87; Times Herald Record, Middletown, NY, reporter, 1987-89; Providence Journal-Bulletin, Providence, RI, reporter, 1989-. **Orgs:** Member, National Association of Black Journalists, 1987-; member, Sigma Circle of Omicron Delta Kappa, 1984-; member, Sigma Delta Chi, Society of Professional Journalist, University of Maryland, 1983-85. **Honors/Awds:** Best in Show, ''How Far Have We Come,'' Maryland, Delaware, DC Press Assn, 1985; NAACP Service Awards, 1987, 1988. **Business Addr:** Journalist, Providence Journal-Bulletin, 75 Fountain St, Providence, RI 02902.

BARFIELD, JOHN E.
Company executive. **Personal:** married Betty; children: Jon, Aaron. **Career:** Univ of MI, janitor 1954; Part-Time Janitorial Svc, janitor 1954-69; ITT, mgr; realtor; consult to major corporations; Janitorial Serv 1975; Barfield & Assoc; Barfield Companies, chief exec/pres, 1954-. **Orgs:** Ypsilanti Chamber of Commerce; bd mem Eastern MI Univ Coll of Business. **Honors/Awds:** Jewish Natl Fund, Tree of Life Award, 1992. **Military Serv:** US Army. **Business Phone:** (313)665-2666.

BARFIELD, LEILA MILLFORD
Elected official. **Personal:** Born Jun 16, 1923, Atlanta, GA; daughter of Leila Williams and Eugene Millford; married Quay F Barfield, Jun 19, 1970; children: Jeanne T. Meadows, William C. Terry (deceased). **Educ:** Morris Brown Coll, BA 1952; Atlanta Univ, MA Educ 1962, EdS Reading 1968, EdS Admin 1970. **Career:** Atlanta Public Schools, curriculum coordinator, 1948-70; Lawton Public Schools, team teacher 1971-73; Bishop Elementary School, curriculum coordinator 1970-72; Univ of OK FAA Mgmt Training School, prof of History 1973-7; City of Lawton, councilwoman; Mayor Pro Tempore, formerly. **Orgs:** Clerk, sec Friendship Baptist Church, 1960-70; supvr, teacher, Atlanta Univ, C Morris Brown, Clark & Spelman Coll 1962, 1968; visiting prof Jackson State Coll 1968, 1969; chmn nominating comm, Amer Assn of Univ Women 1970-; facilitator workshops Univ of OK 1971, 1972; chairperson Bd of Family Health Care Serv 1971-73; nominated for 1st lady of Lawton 1972; mem Lawton-Ft Sill Comm Ed Citizens Adv Bd 1974-; sec NAACP 1979-84, Stewardess Bd Barnett Chapel AME Church 1979-; sunday school teacher Barnett Chapel Church 1979-; mem OK Municipal League 1979-; pres Women's Missionary Soc Barnett Chapel AME Church 1980-84; past pres Pan Hellenic Council 1980; exec bd Women in Municipal Govt 1981-; exec sec NAACP 1984; candidate State Legislature 1984; asst sec Usher BdBarnett Chapel 1984-85; mem en Involved in Global Issues Alpha Kappa Alpha Sorority, 1984-85; mem, Lawton Mobile Meals Bd, 1984; Mem, chairperson, sec, Alpha Kappa Sorority, Theta Upsilon Omega Chapter. **Honors/Awds:** Full Scholarship for EdS Reading Ford Found 1968; Twice Outstanding Graduate Soror, Alpha Kappa Alpha 1980, 1984; Omega Citizen of the Year, Psi Upsilon Chapter, 1981, 1983; Consinious Support & Contribution to Comm & NAACP, 1982; Accomplishment in Political Awareness & Involvement Delta Sigma Theta Sorority, 1984; Wrote Proposal for City/County Teachers in Human Relations & Reading. **Home Addr:** 3304 Overland Dr, Lawton, OK 73501.

BARFIELD, QUAY F.
Business executive. **Personal:** Born Aug 3, 1912, Hugo, OK; married Leila M. **Educ:** Langston Univ, BA 1952. **Career:** Fort Sill, Fort Sill, OK, supply supervisor 1955-76. **Orgs:** Member Omega Psi Phi 1952-; trustee bd Barnett Chapel AME Church 1960-81; owner/mgr Barfield's Rentals 1968-; owner/mgr Barfield's Package Store 1970-; bd mem CEDAR 1972-81, Assoc

of S Central OK Govt 1981-, NAACP; mem comm Natl Reclamation Comm Omega Psi Phi 1963-64; chmn 9th Dist Reclamation Comm Omega Psi Phi; 1st vice dist rep 9th Dist Omega Psi Phi 1963-64. **Honors/Awds:** Greatest Master of Ceremony Froggs Civic & Social Club 1960-76; Outstanding Serv Psi Upsilon Chap Omega Psi Phi 1968-69; President Usher Board Barnett Chapel AME Church 1975-80; Best MC of Year Ladies Prog Social & Civic Club 1983; Dedicated Serv as President Natl Dunbar Alumni Assn 1979-83; MC East Side CommClub 1983; Dedicated Serv W Coast Region Cuney Booker T Washington HS Reunion 1984; Man of the Year Psi Upsilon Chaptger Omega Psi Phi; Commendation for Outstanding Performance of duties as supply clerk tactics Combined Amrs Dept USA Artillery & Missile School Ft Sill OK 11962-63. **Military Serv:** Ordnance staff sgt 3 years 10 mo; Good Conduct 1942-46. **Home Addr:** 3304 Overland Dr, Lawton, OK 73501.

BARFIELD, RUFUS L.
Educator. **Personal:** Born Nov 14, 1929, Hickman, KY; married Emma Crawford; children: Rufus Jr, Sheila, Joselyn. **Educ:** KY State U, BA 1952; Univ of KY, MA 1956; Univ of Cinc, EdM 1966; OH State, adv grad wk 1967; Miami U, PhD 1972. **Career:** Rosenwald High School KY, teacher 1952-55; Lincoln Heights Schools OH, teacher 1955-56; Hoffman Schools, Cincinnati OH, teacher 1956-64; Schiel Schools, Cincinnati OH, teacher 1964-66, asst prin 1966-69; Colum Schools, prin 1969; Burton Schools, Cincinnati OH, prin 1969-71; KY State Univ, admin asst to pres 1972-74; Acad Affairs Univ of AR, vice chancellor 1977-78; Acad Affairs KY State Univ, vice pres 1974-77; Bowie State Univ, president, pupil personnel admin, Montgomery Co Public School, currently. **Orgs:** Mem Nat Ed Assn; Am Assn of Sch Admin; Phi Delta Kappa; Nat Orgn on Legal Probl in Ed; Soc of Resrch Admin; ky Coun on Hghr Ed; Commn on Hghr Educ in KY commn on child srvcs; commn on voc ed for hghr ed; commd KY colonel. **Honors/Awds:** Sel as Cit of Day Cincin Radio Sta; awd for merit serv as exec sec YMCA 1964; cert of awd for outstdng serv in Corryville Comm Coun of Cincin 1967; OH Dept of Elem Sch Prin Prof Growth Com; Cincin Sch Comm Assn Task Force; Cincin Hum Rel Aux Com; NDEA fellow OH State Univ Crit Rdng & Child Lit 1967; dem tchr Univ of Cincin Tchr Coll at Schiel Sch 1964-66; invit from chmn Dept of Ed Admin Sch of Ed Miami Univ to ent doct prog&tch cours in innov & ed; apptd KY Coll 1975. **Military Serv:** US Army, 1953-54. **Business Addr:** Pupil Personnel Administration, Montgomery Co Public Schools, Spring Mill Field Office, Silver Spring, MD 20902.

BARGONETTI, JILL
Educator, biologist. **Personal:** married Nicholas Chavarria, 1991; children: Carlo. **Educ:** State Univ of NY at Purchase; NYU, MS, PhD, molecular biology; Columbia Unv, postdoctoral work. **Career:** City Univ of NY (CUNY), Hunter College, biology prof, 1994-, cancer researcher, currently. **Honors/Awds:** Presidential Early Career Award for Scientists and Engineers, 1997. **Business Addr:** Cancer Researcher/Biology Professor, Hunter College, 695 Park Ave, New York, NY 10021, (212)772-4000.

BARHAM, WILBUR STECTSON
Service industry executive. **Personal:** Born in Como, NC; son of Jessie Mae Cowper Barham and Lincoln Barham; married Sonia Arlene Guy Barham, May 16, 1981. **Educ:** North Carolina Central Univ, Durham, NC, BSC, 1977; Univ of Wisconsin, Madison, Madison, WI, MBA, 1980. **Career:** Prudential Insurance Company, Washington, DC, associate investment manager, 1980-83; Kentucky Fried Chicken, Hanover, MD, real estate manager, 1983-88; Cardinal Industries, Glen Burnie, MD, real estate representative, 1988; Host Marriott Services Corp, Bethesda, MD, director, government affairs, 1988-. **Orgs:** Natl Forum for Black Public Administrators; First Baptist Church, Glenarden, MD. **Home Addr:** 1214 Kings Heather Dr, Mitchellville, MD 20721. **Business Addr:** Director, Government Affairs, Host Marriott Services Corp, 6600 Rockledge Dr, Bethesda, MD 20817-1109, (301)380-3768.

BARKER, PAULINE J.
Business executive. **Personal:** Born Apr 30, 1930, Ottawa, KS; daughter of John C Wilson; married Keyton E Barker Jr; children: Sheila K Ewell, Brenda Lynn. **Educ:** Washburn University, AA, business, 1950. **Career:** Web of Thread, president, currently. **Business Addr:** President, Web of Thread Inc, 220 SW 33rd St, Ste 2, Topeka, KS 66611.

BARKER, ROY
Professional football player. **Personal:** Born Feb 14, 1969, New York, NY. **Educ:** North Carolina, bachelor's degree in speech communications. **Career:** Minnesota Vikings, defenisve end, 1992-95; San Francisco 49ers, 1996-. **Business Addr:** Professional Football Player, San Francisco 49ers, 4949 Centennial Blvd, Santa Clara, CA 95054, (415)562-4949.

BARKER, TIMOTHY T.
Educator, coach. **Personal:** Born Feb 3, 1948, Des Moines, IA; son of Barbara J Barker. **Educ:** Simpson Coll, BS 1970. **Career:** Des Moines Public Schools, teacher/coach; Chicago Public Schools, teacher/coach, 1990-91. **Orgs:** Exalted ruler Hawkeye Elks Lodge #160 1976-85; keeper of Peace Omega Psi Phi 1987-; mem Royal Dukes, Monarch Club, Sigma Phi Gamma, YMCA, NAACP, DMEA, SMB. **Honors/Awds:** Youngest Exalted Hawkeye Elks Lodge #160 Ruler in the World.

BARKLEY, CHARLES WADE
Professional basketball player. **Personal:** Born Feb 20, 1963, Leeds, AL; son of Charcey Glenn; married Maureen. **Educ:** Auburn University, attended. **Career:** Philadelphia 76ers, forward, 1985-92, Phoenix Suns, 1992-96; Houston Rockets, 1996-. **Honors/Awds:** NBA Most Valuable Player, 1992-93; NBA All-Star, 1986-97; NBA All-Star MVP, 1991; selected as on of the 50 Greatest Players in NBA History, 1996. **Special Achievements:** US Olympic Basketball team, 1992, 1996; NBA Draft, First round pick, #5, 1984. **Business Addr:** Professional Basketball Player, Houston Rockets, PO Box 272349, Houston, TX 77277, (713)627-0600.

BARKLEY, MARK E.
Government budget officer. **Personal:** Born Oct 2, 1932, Alpine, AL; son of Ruby Bledsoe Barkley and Simon W Stamps Barkley; married Arrie Ann Morton Barkley, Oct 3, 1959. **Educ:** Alabama State Univ, BS 1957; Ohio State Univ, 1960; Atlanta Univ, 1963; Washington Univ, DSC, 1976; Oper Rsch, Computer Sci, Statistics 1967-76. **Career:** AVSCOM Dir for S & CA, mathematician 1969-70; AVSCOM Dir for S&CA & P&P, oper rsch analyst 1970-72; AVSCOM Dir for Plans & Analysis, supr oper rsch analyst 1972-77; AVSCOM BLACK HAWK Proj Mgr, supr oper rsch analyst 1977-86; Program Innovators Inc St Louis, pres, vice pres 1973-; Chm, bd of dires, 1972-. **Orgs:** Mem, Assn for Comp Mchnry 1968-; mem, Oper Rsch Soc of Am 1972-; sec, bd of dirs, Gateway Fed Empls CU 1976-87, chmn, bd of dires, 1987-91; mem, Soc of Logistics Engrs 1977-; mem, Army AVN Assn of Am 1972-; deacon, Antioch Bapt Ch St Louis, MO 1972; mem, Cedar Vly Est Trustees 1983-; mem, Free & Acptd Masons of AL 1960; mem, Beta Kappa Chi Scientific Honor Society, 1956-. **Honors/Awds:** Hnrs grad AL St Univ 1957; Natl Sc Fnd fellow OSU, Columbus, OH; AU, Atlanta, GA 1960; long term training US Air Force & US Army 1967-68, 1975; cdrs awrd for Civ serv TSARCOM St Louis, MO 1983; Excptl Perf Awrd AVSCOM BLACK HAWK Proj Mgr 1984. **Military Serv:** US Army, pfc 1953-55; Armed Forced Exped Mdl Overseas Serv Mdl 1955-54. **Home Addr:** 12412 Cedarmoor Dr, St Louis, MO 63131-3012.

BARKLEY, RUFUS, JR.
Freelance fashion designer & fashion illustrator. **Personal:** Born Jan 11, 1949, New York, NY; son of Sally Virginia Motron and Rufus Barkley, Sr. **Educ:** Parsons School of Design, NY City 1967-70. **Career:** Teal Traina, New York, designer; Oscar de la Renta Intl, asst designer; Geoffrey Beene Bag & Beene Shirt Bazaar, New York City, designer, 1973-74; Mollie Parnis Boutique & Couture New York City, asst designer, 1975-78; Beldoch Industries, New York City, designer Pierre Cardin blouses, 1982-83; Sherry Cassin & Co Ltd, freelance fashion illustrator, currently. **Honors/Awds:** Don Simonelli Crit Awd; JC Penney Sports Awd; participant in The Ebony Fashion Fair 1969-79; "New Face of '72," article in Women's Wear Daily 1972; dress design, Bazaar Magazine, July 1972; "Soul on Seventh Ave," article in Time magazine, Aug 7, 1972; Designer of the Month, Essence Magazine, Nov 1972; dress design, cover of Cosmopolitan magazine, Jan 1973.

BARKSDALE, HUDSON L.
Business executive. **Personal:** Born Jan 28, 1907, Barksdale, SC; married Katie; children: Jeanne Keith, Rev HL. **Educ:** South Carolina State Coll, AB, 1936; Columbia Univ, MA, 1952. **Career:** Private practice, ins. **Orgs:** Pres Palmetto Ed Assoc 1962-64; pres elect Amer Teachers Assoc 1967; pres Spartanburg NAACP; chmn Natl Ed Assoc 1971; mem SC House Rep 1975-, Resolutions Comm; mem ethics comm NEA; mem Parliamentarian Civic League, Alpha Phi Alpha 1929. **Honors/Awds:** Silver Beaver Awd BSA 1960; invited White House Conf Ed; Dossier Natl Ed Assoc Archives; Serv to Mankind Awd S Spartanburg Sertoma 1978; Recog of SvcCity of Spartanburg 1979; Humanitarian Awd Rutledge Coll 1980.

BARKSDALE, LEONARD N., III
Attorney, cleric. **Personal:** Born Nov 11, 1948, Galveston, TX; son of Joan Pendergraff Barksdale and Leonard N Barksdale II; married Gladys Glass Barksdale, Aug 10, 1974; children: Lea N, Anita J. **Educ:** University of Houston, BA, 1971; Thurgood Marshall School of Law, JD, 1974. **Career:** Legal Aid Society of Louisville, attorney, 1974; Houston Legal Foundation, attorney, 1975; Houston Community College, law instructor, 1975-85; private practice of law, senior attorney, 1976-; Fifth Ward Missionary Baptist Church, minister, 1992-; Fifth Ward Missionary Baptist Church, pastor, currently. **Orgs:** State Bar of Texas, 1974-; The National Bar Association, 1975-; Houston Lawyers Association, secretary, 1975-; Omega Psi Phi, 1970-; Central High School Alumni Association, vice pres, 1988-; Phi Alpha Delta, 1974; NAACP, 1990-; Houston Habitat for Humanity, board of directors, 1988-92. **Honors/Awds:** Boys Scouts of America, Eagle Scout, 1964; Reginald Heber Smith Fellow, 1974-75; legal intern, United States Judge Advocate Gen, Pentagon, Washington, DC, 1972; Boy Scouts of America, Leadership Award, 1987; Sigma Gamma Rho Sorority, Men on the Move in the 90's, 1992. **Special Achievements:** Scout show chairman, W L Davis Dist of Boy Scouts of America, 1980-81; continuing legal education lecturer, Gulf Coast Black Women Lawyers Association, 1992; frequent speaker at church, civic and legal functions. **Business Phone:** (713)660-8787.

BARKSDALE, MARY FRANCES
Manager. **Personal:** Born Apr 5, 1934, Richmond, IN; daughter of Mary Ardelia Mitchell Woodson and Charles Woodson; married Wayne Edward Barksdale, Apr 18, 1953; children: Wayne E Jr, Stacey L McCampbell, Vickki A Morgan. **Educ:** Attended, Earlham Coll, 1952-53, Indiana Univ, 1976-81. **Career:** Intl Harvester Co, employment asst, 1969-74, employment supvr, 1974-77, labor relations supvr, 1977-80, human resources mgr, 1981-83; Navistar Intl Corp, compensation & devel mgr, 1984-90, mgr, human resources, 1990-. **Orgs:** Bd mem, Parkview Memorial Hospital, 1971-74, 1976-79, 1985-92, 1995-98; bd of advisors, Indiana Univ, Purdue Univ, 1977-89; bd mem, Urban League, Ft Wayne, 1979-85; The Links Inc, mem, 1979-, pres, 1989-91; bd of school trustees, East Allen County Schools, 1979-92; bd mem, United Way of Allen County, 1983-86; Leadership Fort Wayne, bd mem, 1983-91; Fort Wayne Museum of Art, board member, 1991-93; Local Education Fund, board member, 1989-93; Fort Wayne Medical Foundation, board member, 1992-95. **Honors/Awds:** Commander of the Garrison Award Community Service, Robert E Armstrong Mayor, City of Ft Wayne, 1979; Recognized for Community Service, Kappa Alpha Psi Fraternity, 1981; Community Service to City of Ft Wayne, The Gent's Club, 1983; Humanitarian Award, Fort Wayne Urban League, 1985; Helene Foellinger Award, Outstanding Contributions, 1989; Fort Wayne Rotary, Paul Harris Fellow, 1992. **Home Addr:** 3424 Mono Gene Dr, Fort Wayne, IN 46806. **Business Addr:** Manager, Human Resources, Reliability & Quality, Navistar International Trans Corp, 3033 Wayne Trace, Fort Wayne, IN 46850.

BARKSDALE, RICHARD KENNETH
Educator. **Personal:** Born Oct 31, 1915, Winchester, MA; son of Sara Barksdale and Simon Barksdale; married Mildred W; children: James, Adrienne Simkins, Calvin. **Educ:** Bowdoin Coll, AB 1937; Syracuse Univ, AM 1938; Harvard Univ, PhD 1951; Bowdoin Coll, LHD 1972. **Career:** Southern Univ, instr Eng 1938-39; Tougaloo Coll, head, Eng dept 1939-42; NC Central, grad dean 1949-58; Morehouse Coll, head Eng dept 1958-62; Atlanta Univ, prof Eng & grad dean 1962-71; Univ of IL, assoc grad dean 1975-82, prof emeritus of English 1985. **Orgs:** Mem bd of overseers Bowdoin Coll 1974-86; mem Grad Record Exam Bd ETS 1982-86; mem univ press bd Univ of IL 1982-86; pres Langston Hughes Soc 1981-84. **Honors/Awds:** Phi Beta Kappa Bowdoin Coll 1937; co-editor, Black Writers of Amer, Macmillan 1972; Langston Hughes Poet and His Critics, Amer Library Assn 1977; Langston Hughes Visiting Prof Univ of Kansas-Lawrence 1986; Tallman Visiting Professor, Bowdoin Coll 1986; United Negro College Visiting Prof, Rust College, 1988; Praisesong for Survival, Essays, Univ of IL Press, 1991-. **Military Serv:** Field Artillery 2nd Lt 1943-46.

BARKSDALE HALL, ROLAND C.
Historian. **Personal:** Born Jul 30, 1960, Sharon, PA; son of Anna Steverson Barksdale Hall (deceased) and Clarence Barksdale Hall (deceased); married Drusilla L Sweeney, Nov 22, 1984; children: Rillis Celeste. **Educ:** Univ of Pittsburgh, Pittsburgh, PA, BS, 1983; Univ of Pittsburgh, Pittsburgh, PA, MS, 1984; Duquesne University, Pittsburgh, PA, MA, 1993-. **Career:** Maxima Corp, Rockville, MD, librarian, 1985; Johns Hopkins Univ, Baltimore, MD, reference librarian, 1986-88; book review editor, Journal of the Afro-Amer Historical and Genealogical Soc, 1987-90; Howard Univ, Washington, DC, coord of black health history, 1988-91; Western PA Afro-American Historical and Genealogical Society, executive director, 1991-; Afro-American Historical and Genealogical Society, national vice pres, history, 1993-. **Orgs:** Mem, African Heritage Classroom Concept Comm, Univ of Pittsburgh, 1984; mem, Assn for the Study of Afro-Amer Life and History, 1986-; bd of dir, Afro-Amer Historical and Genealogical Society, 1988-; knight recorder, Prince Hall Knights of Pythagoras, Odell B Matthews Sr Council 11, 1975-82; mem Sphinxmen Club, 1980; bd of dir, Campus Christian Outreach Ministry, 1981; consultant, Bread for the World Educ Fund, 1984; keyworker, Combined Federal Campaign, 1988; I Dream a World, board of directors, 1992-. **Honors/Awds:** Mem, Quill and Scroll, 1979; Certificate of Merit, Grand Council Knights of Pythagoras, 1979; Certificate of Appreciation, Headquarters US Postal Service, 1987; Provost's Scholarship, Univ of Pittsburgh, 1984; Eagle Award, Combined Federal Campaign, 1988; author of "Rent Parties," poem, The Federal Poet, 1987; author of "Tracing Slave Ancestors," Coweta County Genealogical Society Magazine, 1987, author of "Staying a Little Ahead," Journal of the Afro-Amer Historical & Genealogical Society, 1987; author of Memories of PaSam, The Write Age, 1989; author of "Breast Cancer: Lighting Does Strike Twice," Sisters Magazine, 1989; author of "Our Harps Hang on the Willows," poem, Crisis Magazine. **Military Serv:** US Army Reserves, spec fourth class, 1982-88; received Dept of the Army Certificate of Achievement, 1984. **Business Addr:** Executive Director, Western Pennsylvania African-American Historical and Genealogical Society, 1307 Pointview St, Pittsburgh, PA 15206.

BARLOW, REGGIE DEVON
Professional football player. **Personal:** Born Jan 22, 1973, Montgomery, AL. **Educ:** Alabama State, attended. **Career:** Jacksonville Jaguars, wide receiver, 1996-. **Business Addr:** Professional Football Player, Jacksonville Jaguars, One Stadium Place, Jacksonville, FL 32202, (904)633-6000.

BARLOW, WILLIAM B.
Educator. **Personal:** Born Feb 25, 1943, Fort Rucker, AL; son of Dorothy Goodman Barlow and John Earl Barlow; divorced. **Educ:** San Francisco State University, BA, 1968; University of California at Santa Cruz, MA, 1974, PhD, 1983. **Career:** Mount Vernon College, assistant professor, 1976-80; Howard University, professor, 1980-. **Orgs:** Union of Democratic Communication, steering committee, 1977-; International Association for Study of Popular Music, steering committee, 1989-; International Association for Mass Communication Research, 1986-. **Honors/Awds:** Schomburg, NEH Fellowship, 1991-92; University of Mississippi, NEH Fellowship, 1986. **Special Achievements:** From Cakewalks to Concert Halls, 1992; co-author with Jan Dates, Split Image: African-Americans in the Mass Media, 1990; Looking Up at Down: The Emergence of Blues Culture, 1989. **Military Serv:** US Army, sp-4, 1964-66. **Home Addr:** 19 E Curtis Ave, Alexandria, VA 22301, (703)519-7894. **Business Addr:** Professor of Communications, Howard University, School of Communications, Department of Radio/TV/Film, Washington, DC 20059, (202)806-7927.

BARNARD-BAILEY, WANDA ARLENE
Clinical social worker. **Personal:** Born Jan 29, 1962, Norfolk, VA; daughter of Wilhelmina Phillips Barnard and James Webster Barnard; married Kevin Bernard Bailey, Feb 15, 1992. **Educ:** University of North Carolina, Chapel Hill, BA, 1984, MSW, 1986. **Career:** Albemarle Home Care, hospice social worker/coordinator, 1986-87; Currituck Co Bd of Education, alcohol/drug & dropout prevention coordinator, 1987-92; Navy Family Advocacy Program, clinical social worker, 1992-. **Orgs:** Delta Sigma Theta Sorority, delteen co-chairperson, 1981-; National Association of Social Workers, 1984-; NC Dropout Prevention Association, board of directors, 1987-92; NC School Social Work Association, 1987-92; Albemarle Home Care Hospice, board of directors, 1988-92; Albemarle Hopeline, board of directors, 1991-92; American Cancer Society, board of directors, 1988-92. **Honors/Awds:** Currituck Co Schools, Volunteer Award, 1988-91. **Home Addr:** 1301 Channing Way, Chesapeake, VA 23322-4607, (804)548-1456. **Business Addr:** Clinical Social Worker, Navy Family Advocacy Program, 6500 Hampton Blvd, Norfolk, VA 23508, (804)444-2230.

BARNES, ANNE T.
Business executive. **Personal:** Born Mar 10, 1940, Pitt Co, NC; children: Darryl, Anita. **Educ:** Corrine Brooks Hair Design Inst, diploma cosmetology 1957-58; Natl Beauty Culturist League Inc, BA Masters 1965, 1969; Norfolk State Univ, BA 1964; VA Union Univ Sch of Theology, certification 1979; Gulf Coast Seminary, Bachelor of Theology 1985. **Career:** LaBaron Hairstyling Salon, stylist 1958-61; Bett's Hairstyling Salon, stylist 1961-67; Anne's Beauty Acad, pres 1975-; Anne Barnes, Inc, pres 1967-. **Orgs:** Bd of dirs Tidewater Tele Adv Council; assoc min Garretts Comm Church; bd of dirs 100 Black Women Coalition; bd mem United Christian Front for Brotherhood; bd mem Hal Jackson Talented Teen; mem Natl Beauty Culturists League 1959-; bd mem Church St Merchant Assoc 1982-; bd mem Natl Teachers Educ Council 1983-. **Honors/Awds:** Businessperson of the Year TABCA Norfolk; Awd of merit STOIC Norfolk 1981; Outstanding Citizen Awd Iota Phi Lambda Sor Inc 1984; Black Businesswoman of the Year Norfolk Journal & Guide Nwsp 1984; Outstanding Businessperson of the Year WRAP radio station Norfolk 1984. **Home Addr:** 1506 Covel St, Norfolk, VA 23523-1808. **Business Addr:** President, Anne Barnes Inc, 722 Chapel St, Norfolk, VA 23504.

BARNES, BOISEY O.
Educator, cardiologist. **Personal:** Born May 16, 1943, Wilson, NC; married Bernadine. **Educ:** Johnson C Smith Univ, BS 1964; Howard Univ, MD 1968. **Career:** Howard Univ Hospital, dir noninvasive echocardiography lab 1974-77; Howard Univ Hospital Cardiac Clinic, dir 1976-77; Howard Univ Hospital, asst prof med; Shaw E Corp; Boisey O Barnes, pres; Private Practice, cardiologist. **Orgs:** Professional educ com Amer Heart Assn 1977; lectr AHA 1975-77; past keeper records & seals Omega Psi Phi Frat 1975-77; pres Beta Kappa Chi Hon Soc 1963-64; mem Amer Inst Ultrasound 1975-77; Amer Soc Echocardiography 1977; adv bd Anacostia Congress Hghts Sect Red Cross 1977; mem DC Med Soc Diplomate Amer Bd Intl Med 1972. **Honors/Awds:** Hon Mention Dept Prize Intl Med & Pediatrics Howard Univ 1968; develpr Echocardiography Lab Howard Univ 1973-74; Outstanding Young Men Amer 1970; publ "Echocardiographics Findings in Endocarditis in Heroin Addicts" Amer Journ Card 1977; "Echocardiography Abstracts, Echocardiography in Hypertensive Patients" "Echocardiography in Amyloidosis". **Business Addr:** 413 G St SW, Washington, DC 20024.

BARNES, DELORISE CREECY
Educator, consultant. **Personal:** Born Apr 2, 1947, Hertford, NC; daughter of Easter Lillian Creecy and William O Creecy; married James M Barnes, Jun 8, 1968; children: Victor, Timothy, Stephen, Jonathan. **Educ:** Livingstone Coll, BS (high honors) 1965-69; Univ of TN, MS 1970, EdD Vocational Tech Ed 1978; UT Knoxville-US Office of Educ Fellowship 1975-76. **Career:** Creecy's Poultry Farm, owner 1962-65; Oak Ridge Public Health & Welfare Dept, analyst/surveyor summer 1965; Oak Ridge Schools, adult ed instr 1973-76; Eureka Ctr Roane Co Schools, head office admin 1970-75; Roane State Comm Coll, prof of business, currently. **Orgs:** Mem and advisor, Phi Beta Lambda RSCC 1976-; appt by Gov of TN mem, sec TN Commiss for Human Devel 1977-79; consult Univ of TN's Ctr for Govt Training 1980-87, Knoxville Prof Sec Intl 1983-87, Oak Ridge Schools 1983-88, Martin Marietta Energy Syst Inc 1984-; pres Alpha Kappa Alpha Xi Iota Omega; chmn-organized Homework Hot Lines in Oak Ridge Schools 1986-87; mem Natl Bus Ed Assoc 1969-, Amer Bus Comm Assoc, Delta Pi Epsilon, resource person Youth Enrichment Ctr; bd of dir Big Brother/Big Sisters 1985-88; secretary, Crown Monarch, auxillary of Girls Club 1988-; legislative liaison chmn, Tennessee Business Educ Association 1988-; pres, Tennessee Chap of the Amer Assn of Women in Community Colleges; 1st vp, Monarch Inc, an auxiliary of Girls Inc. **Honors/Awds:** USOE grant UT Knoxville 1975-77; UT grant for a model office 1976; 6 articles in major publs between 1979-84; led a round table discussion at NBEA conv; Dedicated Professional, Phi Beta Lambda, RSCC chapter 1988; Publication Award, The Writing Center, RSCC 1989; "Mobilizing for the Minority Teacher Educ Shortage" in The Balance Sheet, South-Western Publishing 1988; numerous other articles; conducted communication workshops for industry; presented papers at Amer Business Communication Association, South East and Midwestern regionals 1989; Leadership Award, AKA Sorority Inc, 1990; pres, Oak Ridge Chap of AKA Sorority, 1990-92; Business & Prof Women's Organization, Oak Business Businesswoman of the Year Award, 1989; Consortium of Doctors Honoree, Georgia Univ System, 1991. **Business Addr:** Professor of Business, Roane State Community College, Patton Lane, Harriman, TN 37748.

BARNES, DIANE
Police officer. **Personal:** Born Jul 4, 1961, Ridgeland, SC; daughter of Sally Mae Barnes Stevenson and Leroy Stevenson; children: Trameka Lashond Wade. **Educ:** Miami Dade Community College North, Miami, FL, criminal justice; Nova Southeastern Univ, elementary education, 1996. **Career:** Johnson Model City Insurance, Miami, Fl, insurance underwriter, 1977-79; Metro-Dade Police Dept, Miami, Fl, loan servicing clerk, 1979-80, police record specialist, 1981; City of Miami Police Dept, Miami, FL, communication oper, 1981-84, police officer, 1984-. **Orgs:** Head of Organization Newsletter, Miami Community Police Benevolent Association, 1985-; executive board member, Miami Community Police Benevolent Association, 1985-; pass president, Miami Community Police Benevolent Association, 1985; member, National Black Police Association, 1985-; member, Florida Women in Law Enforcement, 1990-. **Honors/Awds:** President's Award, Miami Comm Police Bene Assn, 1990-91; Community Service, People United to Lead Struggle, 1990; Training Advisor Award, Basic Law Enforcement Classes, 1987-89. **Business Addr:** Police Officer, Training Coordinator, City of Miami, Police Department, 400 NW 2 Ave, 3rd Floor, Miami, FL 33128.

BARNES, ERNIE, JR.
Artist. **Personal:** Born Jul 15, 1938, Durham, NC; married Bernadine C Gradney, Dec 1984; children: Deidre, Michael, Sean, Erin, Paige. **Educ:** North Carolina College, BA 1960. **Career:** San Diego Chargers, football player 1960-63; Denver Broncos, football player 1964-65; Amer Football League, official artist 1966; The Company of Art, artist/founder/pres 1970-. **Orgs:** Screen Actors Guild; National Football League Players Association. **Honors/Awds:** United States Sports Academy, Sports Artist of the Year, 1985; Museum of African American Art, Los Angeles, Honoree, 1988; North Carolina Central University, Honorary DFA, 1990. **Special Achievements:** "The Beauty of the Ghetto Exhibit" 1974; one-man exhibitions held at Grand Central Art Galleries in NY, McKenzie Gallery in Los Angeles, Agra Gallery in Washington DC; Heritage Gallery in Los Angeles; works are part of numerous important private collections; official artist of the XXIIIrd Olympiad, Los Angeles, CA, 1984; From Pads to Palette, WRS Publishing, 1994. **Business Addr:** The Company Art, 8613 Sherwood Dr, West Hollywood, CA 90069, (310)652-3034.

BARNES, FANNIE BURRELL
Librarian. **Personal:** Born in New Orleans, LA; married Richard Alexander Barnes; children: Erica Arnetta, Maria Monique. **Educ:** Dillard Univ, AB 1945; Atlanta Univ, MS 1950. **Career:** Gilbert Acad New Orleans, tchr Engl 1945-49; Atlanta Univ, asst libr summer 1950, 1957-61, 1967; Claflin Coll Orangeburg, SC, head libr 1950-54; tchr children's lit, 1957-; Atlanta Pub Libr Bookmobile, children's libr summer 1961; Clark Coll Atlanta, head libr 1954-. **Orgs:** Mem ALA, NEA, NAACP, Alpha Kappa Alpha. **Business Addr:** Head Librarian, Clark College, 240 Chestnut St SW, Atlanta, GA 30314.

BARNES, IRALINE G.
Utility company executive. **Personal:** Born Oct 6, Springfield, MA; daughter of Mary Clemons Green and Reuben Green; married James Barnes; children: Monica, Jason. **Educ:** Howard University, Washington, DC, BA, 1969; University of Michigan, Ann Arbor, MI, JD, 1972. **Career:** Superior Court of DC, Washington, DC, law clerk, 1972-73; Dept of Justice, Civil Div, Washington, DC, trial attorney, 1973-75; US Attorney's Office, Washington, DC, asst US attorney, 1975-78; Dept of Interior, Washington, DC, admin appeals judge, 1978-80; Superior Court of DC, Washington, DC, associate judge, 1980-90, sr judge, 1990, 1994. **Orgs:** Chairman, Providence Hospital Citizens' Board, 1989-; member, Washington Bar, DC Bar, 1980-; member, National Association of Women Judges, 1985-; Washington National Cathedral Chap; National Cathedral School Brd; Greater Washington Brd of Trade, Regional Affairs Committee; Maryland/DC Utilities Association Brd; National Women's Law Ctr Brd; Greater Washington Boys & Girls Clubs Brd; outside director, Century National Bank; director, National Academy of Sciences, National Research Council; DC Mayor's Commission on Violence Against Women. **Honors/Awds:** Leaders of the 80's, Black Enterprise, 1980; Woman of the Year, Glamour Magazine, 1981; Distinguished Alumni Citation of the Year, Howard University, 1990. **Business Addr:** Vice Pres, Corporate Relations Department, Potomac Electric Power Co., 1900 Pennsylvania Ave NW, Ste 504, Washington, DC 20068.

BARNES, JOHN B., SR.
Pedodontist. **Personal:** Born Jan 15, 1922, New Iberia, LA; married Audra M Guyton; children: Audra Yvonne, John B Jr. **Educ:** Meharry Med Coll, DDS 1952; LaSalle Ext Univ, LLB 1965. **Career:** Pedodontist, currently. **Orgs:** Mem Amer Dental Assoc; Amer Soc Dentistry Children; Intl Acad Orthodontics Town Hall CA; Morehouse Alumni Assoc; bd dir Wesley Social Serv Ctr. **Military Serv:** USAF Dental Bd Corp capt. **Business Addr:** 12060 S Central Ave, Los Angeles, CA 90059.

BARNES, JOHNNIE
Professional football player. **Career:** San Diego Chargers, professional football player, 1992-. **Business Addr:** Professional Football Player, San Diego Chargers, Jack Murphy Stadium, 9449 Friars Rd, San Diego, CA 92108, (619)280-2111.

BARNES, JOSEPH NATHAN
Attorney. **Personal:** Born Nov 29, 1950, Hermondale, MO; son of Lillie Mae Barnes and John Wesley Barnes; children: Julius. **Educ:** Ibadan Univ Nigeria, Certificate in Intl Economics 1971; Antioch Coll, BA Finance & Commerce 1973; Univ of PA, MBA 1977; Univ of PA Sch of Law, JD1977. **Career:** Spearman & Sterling, assoc atty 1977-81; Zimet Haines Moss & Friedman, assoc atty 1981-82; Barnes & Williams, partner 1982-85; Barnes & Darby, partner, beginning 1985; Barnes, McGhee, Neal, Poston & Segue, founding partner, currently. **Orgs:** Mem Natl Bar Assoc 1981-87; dir Black Entertainment & Sports Lawyers Assoc 1983-88; bd mem Urban League Manhattan Branch 1985-87; mem Metro Black Bar Assoc 1986-87, Natl Assoc of Securities Profls 1986-87; NY chmn telethon United Negro Coll Fund 1986, 1987, 1988; mem NAACP. **Honors/Awds:** Rockefeller Grant 1968,73; Natl Fellowship Foundation Fellow 1973,74; First Black NY Law firm listed in Dir of Municipal Bond Dealers 1987. **Home Addr:** 150 West End Ave #19M, New York, NY 10023. **Business Addr:** Founding Partner, Barnes, McGhee, Neal, Poston & Segue, 888 7th Ave #1809, New York, NY 10019-3201, (212)944-1095.

BARNES, KAREN MICHELLE
Television executive. **Personal:** Born in Yokahama, Japan. **Educ:** Fordham Law School, JD, 1977. **Career:** Jim Henson Productions, director business affairs, 1981-85, vice pres production, 1985-89; Fox Kids Network, senior vp programming, 1990-91, exec vp; 20th Century Fox Home Entertainment, exec vp, currently. **Orgs:** Environmental Defense Fund, board of directors, 1997. **Honors/Awds:** University of Georgia, Peabody Award, 1993; National Education Association, NEA, 1992, 1994; Parents Choice Award, 1991. **Business Addr:** Exec VP, 20th Cent Fox Home Entertainment, P.O. Box 900, Beverly Hills, CA 90213.

BARNES, MARTIN G.
Mayor. **Personal:** Born Mar 5, 1948, Paterson, NJ; married Diane Judith Grant; children: Gregory, Antoinette, Marcus. **Educ:** Seton Hall Univ, BS Edn. **Career:** Sterling Drug Co, sales & mgr 1968-72; HUD Target Proj Prog, coord dir 1975-77; Barnes Assoc Bus Mgmt Cons, pres 1975-; RP Vivino Esq, priv investigator 1975-; Passaic Co Dept Youth Svc, dir 1977-79; City of Paterson, council president, 1991-92; Hackensack Meadowlands Development Comission, director of administration, 1990-94; elected City Council president, 1991-92; mayor, currently. **Honors/Awds:** Outstanding Young Man Concerned Citizens of Paterson 1976; Hon Mem Bros in Blue 1976; Man of the Year Tombrock Coll 1977. **Business Addr:** Mayor, City of Paterson, 155 Market St, Paterson, NJ 07505.

BARNES, MATTHEW MOLENA, JR.
Program manager (retired), community organization executive. **Personal:** Born Jan 28, 1933, Homer, LA; son of Addie Mae Moore Barnes and Matthew Molena Barnes Sr; married Clara Mae Lee Barnes, Dec 3, 1958 (died 1990); children: Danette LaTrise Barnes Perry. **Educ:** 4 yr apprenticeship; Comm Coll, 2 yrs; mgmt & job related courses; class D credential for teaching certain vocational subjects. **Career:** Mare Island Naval Shipyard, marine machinist 1951-55, machinist 1955-63, foreman machinist 1963-64, equipment spl 1964-65, engrg tech methods & standards 1965-66, foreman machinist 1966-73, engrg tech prev maint 1973-81, program manager 1981-88 (retired); Greater Richmond Community Devt Corp, pres, currently. **Orgs:** Mem Mare Island Supr Assn; Supr Toastmasters Club; pres Richmond Br NAACP; past vice pres Northern Area Conf NAACP; mem choir bd stewarts Davis Chapel CME Ch; past Sunday Sch tchr; past supt Sunday Sch; past chmn Scholarship Com Davis Chapel CME Ch; Richmond City Human Rel Speakers' Bur; chmn bd Richmond City Youth Serv Bur; mem Shipyard Commander's Equal Employment Opp Adv Com; pres The Original 21'ers Club; officer CA State Conf NAACP; staff mem state assembly mem Bob Campbell. **Honors/Awds:** First Black Supv Mare Island Naval Shipyard. **Military Serv:** US Army, 2 years; Army Reserve 21 years, master sergeant. **Business Addr:** President, Greater Richmond Community Development Corp, 334-11th St, Richmond, CA 94801.

BARNES, N. KURT
Business executive. **Personal:** Born Jan 11, 1947, Washington, DC; son of Doris Boyd Barnes and Norman H Barnes. **Educ:** Yale Coll, BA 1968; Harvard Univ, MA, ABD, 1973. **Career:** Rand Corp, assoc economist 1968-73; Fortune Magazine, assoc editor 1973-75; Time Inc, financial analyst 1975-77; Inco Limited, financial analyst, dir investor relations, pres Inco Investment Management 1977-; chmn Marquest Investment Counsel Ltd, 1989-91. **Orgs:** Treas Hale Found 1974-; mem, Friends of Legal Defense Fund. **Honors/Awds:** John Hay Whitney Fellow 1970-71; Harvard Graduate Prize Fellowship 1971-73. **Home Addr:** 1 Sherman Square, New York, NY 10023. **Business Addr:** President, Inco Investment Management, Inco Limited, 1 New York Plaza, New York, NY 10004.

BARNES, PAUL DOUGLAS
Government official. **Personal:** Born Dec 20, 1946, Henderson, TN; married Faye L. Rainey; children: Richard, Michael. **Educ:** Lane Coll, BS, 1968; Univ of Southern California, MPA, 1977. **Career:** Soc Sec Administration, claims rep, 1968-70, admin ofcr, 1970-73, prog analyst, 1973-77, area dir, 1977-79, regional commissioner, 1990-96; Deputy Commissioner for Human Resources, currently. **Orgs:** American Society for Public Administration; Omega Psi Phi; NAACP. **Honors/Awds:** Special Achievement Award 1971, 1974; Superior Perf Award 1975-92; Leadrship Award from Social Security Adm, 1992; Meritorious Service Award from President Bush, 1992; Distinguished Executive Award from President Clinton, 1995; Federal Executive of the Year, 1997. **Business Addr:** Deputy Commissioner for Human Resources, Social Security Administration, 6401 Security Boulevard Ste 200 Altmeyer Building, Baltimore, MD 21235.

BARNES, RONALD LEWIS
Public transportation executive. **Personal:** Born May 2, 1951, Farmville, NC; son of Carlillia Bethea Barnes; married Dannie Edwina barnes, Aug 28, 1976; children: Tiffany Monique Barnes. **Educ:** NC A & T State Univ, BS, Economics, Sociology, 1972; Trinity Univ, MS, Urban Studies, 1974. **Career:** ATE Manageament Service Co, Inc, assoc, 1973-74; Greater Lynchburg Transit Co, dir of mktg, pre & plan, 1974-76; B'ham & Jefferson Cty Transit Authority, asst resident mgr, 1976-80; Transit Mgmt of Wayne & Oakland Ctys, Inc, gen mgr, 1980-81; Western Reserve Transit Authority, exec dir, gen mgr, 1981; Madison Metro Transit, gen mgr, 1982-88; Gr Cleve Regional Transit Authority, deputy gen mgr, 1989-. **Orgs:** Conference of Minority Transit Officials, bd mem; American Public Transit Assn Scholarship Fdn, bd of dirs; Western Reserve Historical Society, bd mem; Greater Cleve Council Boy Scouts of America, bd of dirs; Black Professionals Assn Charitable Fdn, pres; Natl Forum for Black Public Administrators; Blacks In Management; Professionals on the Move, dir/pr. **Honors/Awds:** United Negro Coll Fund, Distinguished Service Citation, 1979; ATE, President Award, 1987; Conference of Minority Transit Officials, Executive of the Year, 1992; Dollars & Sense Magazine, America's Best & Brightest Business & Professional Men Award, 1993; NC A & T State Univ Alumni, Distinguished Service Award, 1994. **Business Addr:** Deputy General Mgr, Greater Cleveland Regional Transit Authority, 615 Superior Ave, W, Frank J Lausche State Office Bldg, 11th Fl, Cleveland, OH 44113, (216)566-5096.

BARNES, STEPHEN DARRYL
Lawyer. **Personal:** Born May 29, 1953, Los Angeles, CA; son of Marian E Barnes and John J Barnes. **Educ:** Univ of Southern California, BA 1978; Harvard Law School, JD 1981. **Career:** Covington & Burling, assoc 1981-86; Weissmann Wolff et al, assoc 1986-87; Strange & Nelson, partner, 1987-89; Bloom, Hergott, Cook, Diemer & Klein, partner, 1989-. **Orgs:** Mem Local Spiritual Assembly Baha'i Faith 1981-. **Business Addr:** Partner, Bloom, Hergott, Cook, Diemer & Klein, 150 Rodeo Dr, Beverly Hills, CA 90212.

BARNES, THOMAS
Mayor. **Personal:** Born Apr 23, 1936, Mark Tree, AR; son of Thelma Louise Brooks and Ollie Garfield; married Francis Jean Carroll; children: Paul Matthew. **Educ:** Purdue Univ, BS, 1958; DePaul Univ, JD, 1972; US Army Command and General Staff College. **Career:** City of Gary, IN, mayor, 1988-; private practice, attorney, Gary, IN, 1972-88. **Orgs:** Life member, NAACP; founding member, James G. Kimbrough Law Association; life member, Reserve Officers Association; AMVETS; Lions Clubs International, Dunes Chapter; hon bd of dirs, Brother's Keeper; mem, St Monica-Luke Cath Church; Alpha Phi Alpha. **Military Serv:** US Amry Res, Col, JAGC; Meritorious Service Medal, 1985. **Business Addr:** Mayor, City of Gary, 1345 Bigger St., Gary, IN 46404-1839.

BARNES, VIVIAN LEIGH
Government official. **Personal:** Born Aug 9, 1946, Wilkinson, WV; daughter of Margaret Lawson Anderson and James Wilder; married Leroy P Barnes, Mar 9, 1974; children: Charles Pershon, Jamila Kali, Nathifa Oni. **Educ:** Delta Coll; Saginaw Valley State Univ, BA, sociology, communications, 1996. **Career:** Greater Omaha Comm Action Youth Prog, asst dir 1969-71; Oppty Indust Ctr, exec sec 1974-76; Delta Coll, Univ Ctr, admin sec 1977-79; Buena Vista Charter Twp, twp clerk 1980-90, trustee, 1991-92. **Orgs:** Exec bd mem Saginaw Cty Dem Party 1980-, vice chair, MI Dem Black Caucus 1980-; alt delegate MI Dem State Central 1980-; commissioner, MI Economic & Social Opportunities Commission; bd mem, Saginaw County Community Action Agency. **Honors/Awds:** Community Service Delta Coll Black Honors Awd 1983. **Home Addr:** 151 Barbara Lane, Saginaw, MI 48601-9469.

BARNES, WILLIAM L.
Attorney. **Personal:** Born Nov 28, 1936, Benton Harbor, MI; married Patricia Jean; children: Barbara. **Educ:** LA City Coll, AA 1962; Van Norman Univ, BS 1965; USC Los Angeles CA, JD 1969. **Career:** Litton Sys, analyst 1963-65; Northrop Corp, buyer & contracts admin 1965-69; workmen's comp splst, 1969-71; Fibre-Therm, gen cnsl/vp; Barnes & Grant, atty 1971-. **Orgs:** Mem Natl Bar Assn, Amer Bar Assn, Nu Beta Epsilon Natl Law, Amer Trial Lawyers Assn, CA Lawyers for Criminal Justice, LA Trial Lawyers Assn, Kappa Alpha Psi; Shriners, Free Mason Scottish Rite. **Honors/Awds:** Scholarship Balwin-Wallace Coll 1953. **Military Serv:** USAF s/sgt, maj co-pilot B-47E (SAC) 1957; Outstanding Crew Chief 1955. **Business Addr:** 111 N LaBrea Ave, Inglewood, CA 90301.

BARNES, WILLIE R.
Attorney. **Personal:** Born Dec 9, 1931, Dallas, TX; married Barbara Bailey; children: Michael, Sandra; Traci, Wendi, Brandi. **Educ:** UCLA, BA, political science, 1953; UCLA School of Law, JD, 1959. **Career:** State of California, Dept of Corps, various attorney positions, 1960-68, supvr corps counsel 1968-70, asst commr, 1970-75, commr of corps, 1975-79; UCLA Alumni Assn, general counsel, dir, 1983-86; Manatt Phelps Rothenberg & Phillips, sr partner, 1979-88; Wyman Bautzer, Kuchel & Silbert, sr partner, 1989-91; Katten, Muchin, Zavis & Weitzman, sr partner, 1991-92; Musick, Peeler & Garrett, sr partner, 1992-. **Orgs:** Exec comm, Business & Corps Sec 1970-86; vp, dir UCLA Law Alumni Assn 1973; Comm Real Estate Franchises Mutual Funds; chmn SEC Liasion Comm 1974-78; chmn Real Estate Investment Comm 1974-78; president Midwest Securities Commission Assn 1978-79; 1st vice pres N Amer Securities Administration Assn 1978-79; comanaging ed, CA Bus Law Reporter 1983; exec comm Corp & Commercial Law Sec, Beverly Hills Bar Assn; board of governors Century City Bar Assn, 1982-84; vice chmn, Comm on Corp; vice chmn, Oil Investment Comm; active leadership in directing the Securities Reg Prog of CA; vice chair, exec committee Business Law Sec, California State Bar, 1983-86; Corp Banking & Bus Law, Fed Regulation of Securities, Commodities, Franchises & State RegulationCommitties, Amer Bar Assn; chmn, bd of trustees, Wilshire United Methodist Church986-91; chmn Knox Keene Health Care Service Plan Comm 1976-79; chmn Leveraged Real Estate Task Force 1985-86; CA Senate Commission on Corporate Governance; Independent Commission to Review the Los Angeles Police Dept; advsry bd Institute of Corporate Counsel. **Honors/Awds:** Practicing Law Institute, Certificate of Appreciation, 1973; UCLA Law School, Alumnus of the Year, 1976; California State Senate & Assembly, Resolutions of Commendation, 1979. **Special Achievements:** Major role in developing uniform standards for real estate progs on nationwide basis; Acknowledged expert in real estate & oil & gas securities. **Military Serv:** US Army, pfc, 1954-56. **Business Addr:** Senior Partner, Musick, Peeler & Garrett, One Wilshire Blvd, Ste 2000, Los Angeles, CA 90017.

BARNES, WILSON EDWARD
Military. **Personal:** Born Jun 9, 1938, Richmond, VA; son of Ora Henderson; married Barbara Jones; children: Kaye, Lynette, Kimberly. **Educ:** VA State Univ, BS Biology 1960, MS 1971; Univ of Southern California, Doctoral Studies. **Career:** AUS 18th Battalion 4th Training, commander 1976-78; Richmond Recruiting Battalion, commander 1978-80; Area IV First ROTC Region, commander 1982-84; Headquarters Dept of the Army ROTC Study Group, dir 1984-86; US Central Command, Deputy J-1 1986-88. **Orgs:** Member Association AUS; Virginia St Univ Alumni Assoc, NAACP; Retired Officer's Assn; Urban League. **Military Serv:** AUS col 28 yrs; ARCOM; Bronze Star; Meritorious Service Medal; Defense Meritorious Service Medal.

BARNES, YOLANDA L.
State assistant attorney general. **Personal:** Born Aug 15, 1961, Cleveland, OH; daughter of Henrietta & Ellis Clancy; married James A Barnes, Dec 24, 1985; children: Alayna. **Educ:** Cleveland State University, BA (cum laude), 1983; Cleveland Marshall College of Law, JD, 1987. **Career:** Ohio Bureau of Worker's Compensation; Industrial Commission of Ohio; Ohio Attorney General's Office, asst attorney general, currently. **Orgs:** Ohio State Bar Assn, workers' compensation committee. **Honors/Awds:** Lloyd O Brown Scholarship, 1986. **Special Achievements:** Defense litigation, jury trials; appellate practice; mediation, negotiation. **Business Addr:** Assistant Attorney General, Ohio Attorney General's Office, 101 East Town Street, 3rd Fl, Columbus, OH 43215-5148, (614)466-6696.

BARNETT, ALVA P.
Educator. **Personal:** Born May 4, 1947, Jacksonville, FL. **Educ:** Bethune-Cookman Coll, BA 1969; Univ of Pittsburgh, MSW 1971, MPH 1978, PhD 1981. **Career:** North Central Comm MH-MR Ctr Crisis Ctr, asst adm dir 1971-72, soc work supervisor 1970-75; admin dir 1972-75; dir consultant social serv 1975-76; Univ of NE at Omaha, asst prof of social work. **Orgs:** Rsch consultant & prog evaluator Maternal & Child Health County Hlth Dept Pgh PA, United Methodist Comm Ctrs Inc; bd of dirs Social Settlement Assoc of Omaha 1982-; Chas Drew Health ctr 1986-, Head Start Child Develop Corp 1986-. **Honors/Awds:** Listed in Dictionary of Intl Biography 1983; Visiting Scholar Quantitative Methods in Social Rsch Univ of MI Ann Arbor 1984; 2 book chapters and 2 articles published. **Business Addr:** Professor, Dept of Social Work, University of Nebraska at Omaha, Omaha, NE 68182-0001.

BARNETT, CARL L., SR.
Automobile dealer. **Career:** Gulf Freeway Pontiac GMC Truck, chief executive officer, currently. **Special Achievements:** Company ranked #34 on Black Enterprise's list of top 100 auto dealers, 1994. **Business Addr:** CEO, Gulf Freeway Pontiac GMC Truck, 11205 Gulf Fwy., Houston, TX 77034, (713)946-9009.

BARNETT, ETHEL S.
Government official. **Personal:** Born Mar 7, 1929, Macon, GA; widowed; children: Prentis Earl Vinson. **Educ:** Pioneer Busn Sch, attended 1947-50; attended Cheyney State Coll. **Career:** Supreme Lib Life Ins Co, ins agent 1954-55; City of Philadelphia Police Dept, officer 1961-71; Amer Found for Negro Affairs (AFNA), natr dir resource devel 1972; Commonwealth of PA, civil serv commr. **Orgs:** Bd dir Women for Greater Philadelphia 1978-; consult PECO Elec Co 1979-; 1st Black reg dir PA Fedn of Dem Women; natl dir Educ Dept (IBPOE of W) 1978-; mem Intl Personnel Mgr Assn; (IPMA); PUSH; Elks; NAACP; natl Assn Female Execs. **Honors/Awds:** Comm Serv Award N Philadelphia Chap NAACP 1973; Humanitarian Award Bell Tel Co of PA 1976; Outstanding Woman of the Year Bright Hope Bapt Ch 1977; Patriots Bowl City of Philadelphia 1980. **Business Addr:** Civil Service Commissioner, Commonwealth of PA, 320 S Office Bldg, Harrisburg, PA 17120.

BARNETT, ETTA MOTEN
Concert artist. **Personal:** Born Nov 5, 1901, Weimar, TX; daughter of Ida Norman Moten and Freeman Moten; married Claude A Barnett (deceased); children: Sue Ish, Etta Traylor, Gladys Brooks. **Educ:** Univ of KS, Music B 1931; Northwestern Univ Sch of Speech, further study 1949-50; Atlanta Univ Spelman Coll, Dr Hum Letters 1980-83. **Career:** Feature acting in Broadway plays and motion pictures, 1933-36; Concert artist toured US & South Amer 1934-42; actress/singer starring role as Bess in "Porgy & Bess" 1942-45. **Orgs:** Co-owner Afro-Arts Bazaar 1950; vol work Intl Women's Decade Conferences 1975-85; mem Women's Decade Conference Nairobi 1985; mem Delta Sigma Theta Int Women's Conf Nassau 1987; mem Bd of Women Univ of Chicago; mem The African American Inst; mem the African Dia Intl Visitors Center; The Du Sable Museum; bd mem Alpha Kappa Alpha Sor; women's bds Univ of Chicago, Lyric Opera, The Field Museum, The Links Inc, Black Women's Agenda, Amer Assoc of Univ Women. **Honors/Awds:** Honorary Doctorate Northeastern IL Univ 1981, Atlanta Univ 1983, Spelman Coll 1985, Univ of IL 1987; portrait commissioned by Alma Mater Univ of KS to be hung among Outstanding Alumnae in library on campus 1987. **Home Addr:** 3619 Martin Luther King Dr, Chicago, IL 60653.

BARNETT, EVELYN BROOKS
Educator. **Personal:** Born Jun 4, 1945, Washington, DC; divorced; children: Nia Brooks. **Educ:** Univ of WI Milw, BA (with honors); Howard Univ, MA 1974; Univ of Rochester, PhD (pending) 1981. **Career:** Milwaukee School System, high school teacher 1969-72; Howard Univ, Moorland-Spingarn Research Center, manuscript rsch assoc 1974-75; Joint Center for Polit Studies, rsch consultant 1977-80; Simmons Coll, instruc-

tor 1979-80; Natl Council for Negro Women Bethune Proj, consultant 1979; Dartmouth Coll, asst prof 1980-; Harvard Univ Women's Studies Prog Div, resource assoc 1980-81; Harvard Univ WEB DuBois Inst for Afro-Amer Rsch, grad fellow. **Orgs:** Mem Alpha kappa Alpha Sorority; mem Natl Council of Negro Women; mem Assn for Study of Afro-Am Life & Hist; mem Amer Hist Assn. **Honors/Awds:** Phi Alpha Theta Hist Honor Soc Univ of WI 1969; Kappa Delta Pi Educ Honor Soc Univ of WI 1969; Ford Fellowship for Grad Study Hist Dept Howard Univ 1972-74; Grad Fellowship Natl Fellowship Fund Atlanta, GA 1975-78; WEB DuBois Fellow Harvard Univ 1979-80; Author of "Changing Family Portrait of Afro-Am Slaves"; "Nannie Burroughs & Educ of Black Women"; "Class Rising but Race Remains". **Business Addr:** Graduate Fellow, Harvard Univ, Canaday Hall B, Cambridge, MA 02139.

BARNETT, FRED LEE, JR.
Professional football player. **Personal:** Born Jun 17, 1966, Shelby, MS. **Career:** Philadelphia Eagles, professional football player, 1990-. **Business Addr:** Professional Football Player, Philadelphia Eagles, 3501 S Broad St, Philadelphia, PA 19148, (215)463-2500.

BARNETT, LORNA
Chiropractor. **Personal:** Born Sep 5, 1951, Trinidad, Trinidad and Tobago; daughter of Theodora J Barnett; children: Ki Joy, Sophia, Angelika Morris. **Educ:** Brooklyn College, 1970-78; Pratt Inst, 1986-87; New York Chiropractic Coll, DC, 1991. **Career:** New York Telephone, supervisor, computer operations, until 1982; Self-employed, massage therapist, 1984-, chiropractor. **Orgs:** NYZS; NY Chiropractic Council. **Business Addr:** Chiropractor, 862 Union St, Ste 22, Brooklyn, NY 11215.

BARNETT, ROBERT
Government official. **Personal:** Born Apr 21, 1938, Fayetteville, GA; son of R C Hightower Barnett and Robert Barnett; married Bessie Pearl Burch Barnett, Nov 7, 1964; children: Robert Terrance. **Educ:** Morris Brown Coll, BA 1961; GA State Univ, MA pending (Deans List). **Career:** Atlanta Housing Auth, adminstrv intern 1966-67, bus relocation adv 1967-69, proj coord 1969-71, asst dir of redevel 1971-75, dir of redevel 1975-; HUD, Atlanta, GA, regional rehabilitation mgmt officer, 1981-. **Orgs:** Basketball & football referee So Conf Ofcl Assn 1965-; mem Natl Assn Housing & Redevel Ofcls 1966-; mem Resurgens 1971-; vice chmn Salvation Army Adv Cncl 1974-; mem Leadership Atlanta 1978-; first vice pres West Manor Elementary Sch PTA 1979-; bd of trustees, Morris Brown Coll, 1989-; pres Morris Brown Coll Athletic Foundation, 1985-; pres, Capitol City Officials Assn, 1980-. **Honors/Awds:** Ford Fellow Scholarship GA State Univ 1970; Annual Housing Awd Interfaith Inc Atlanta 1976; Cert of Appreciation for Outstanding Perf Atlanta Housing Auth 1977; Hall of Fame inductee Morris Brown Coll TAY Club 1978; Federal Employee of the Year, Civic & Community Services, Federal Executive Bd, 1989; Atlanta Univ Center Hall of Fame, Extra Point Club, Inc, 1990. **Military Serv:** US Army, cpl; Cert for Outstanding Serv & Achievements 1964. **Home Addr:** 3317 Spreading Oak Dr SW, Atlanta, GA 30311.

BARNETT, SAMUEL B.
Educator (retired). **Personal:** Born May 5, 1931, Philadelphia, PA; son of Jennie and Solomon; married Dorothy; children: Diane, Avonna, Christopher, Samuel, Donna, Betty. **Educ:** Temple Univ, AA, BS; Kean Coll, MA; Rutgers Univ, EdD candidate; Univ PA, Fels Institute; Woodrow Wilson Sch Princeton Univ, Southeastern Univ, PhD 1979. **Career:** City of Philadelphia PA, police officer 1957-62; Philadelphia Area Delinquent Youth Program, project dir 1965-67; Germantown Settlement, Philadelphia, PA, youth work counselor, 1965-68; State of PA, parole officer 1967-68; Social Learning Lab Educ Testing Serv, prof assoc res div 1968-82; Veterans Administration, Philadelphia, PA, benefits counselor, 1985-86. **Orgs:** Mem Amer Personnel & Guidance Assn; Amer Soc Criminology; Natl Council on Measurement in Educ; Natl Assn Blacks in Criminal Justice System; bd dirs Timberlake Camp Charities Inc. **Honors/Awds:** City of Phila, Chamber of Commerce Award, Pop Warner All-Amer Football Player, 1950; City of Phila, Police Dept Commemdation for Bravery, 1959, Badge & Key Award, 1959; Gtn Comm Council Award, Outstanding Service to Youth, 1967. **Military Serv:** US Army, 1946-49, R A, Korea, 1951-53; Paratrooper Badge; Combat Infantrymans Badge; Serveral other military Awards. **Business Addr:** Retired Prof, Assoc Res Div, Soc Learning Lab Educ Testing Service, Rosedale Rd, Princeton, NJ 08540.

BARNETT, TEDDY
Accountant. **Personal:** Born Mar 12, 1948, Freeport, NY; married Carol Ann Grier; children: Joell Carol, Jason Theodore, Jordan Dai. **Educ:** Boston Univ, BS 1970. **Career:** Price Waterhouse & Co, sr accountant 1970-75; Bedford Stuyvesant Restoration Corp, dir intl audit 1976-78, dir fin admin 1978-79, vice pres fin & admin 1980-81, exec vice pres 1981-82, pres 1982-. **Orgs:** Bd dirs Enock Star Restoration Housing Devel Fund Inc; mem Stearns Park Civic Assn; mem Natl Assn Accountants; mem Natl Assn Black Accountants; bddir Brooklyn Arts Council, Amer Red Cross in Greater NY Brooklyn Chapt. **Honors/Awds:** Black Achievers in Industry Awd 1974; Key Woman of Amer Achievement Awd 1984. **Business Addr:** President, Bedford Stuyvesant Restoration, 1368 Fulton St, Brooklyn, NY 11216.

BARNETT, WILLIAM
Business owner. **Personal:** Born Nov 29, 1917; married Edywna T. **Educ:** YMCA Coll, law enforcement; Correspondence Sch, elec engrg. **Career:** Midwest Security Agency Inc Bd, pres; Chicago Police Dept, policeman; Cook Co Sheriff's Dept, sheriff's police; Chicago Sewer Dept, sewer insp; New 2nd Ward Regular Dem Orgn, alderman & committeeman. **Orgs:** Mem Ada S McKinnley Settlement House; exec dir 35th St Bus Men's Assn; mem 21st & 2nd Police Dist Steering Comm. **Business Addr:** President, Midwest Security Agency Inc, 3430 S Prairie Ave, Chicago, IL 60616.

BARNEY, CLARENCE LYLE
Business executive. **Personal:** Born Sep 19, 1934, New Orleans, LA; married Marie Dude Porter; children: Keith, Shawn. **Educ:** So Univ, BS 1957; KS State, attended 1958; Tulane Univ, MSW 1970; MIT, rsch fellow 1973. **Career:** Franklin Co Welfare Dept Columbus OH, caseworker 1959; Magnolia HS Vacherie LA, tchr 1960; So Univ & Loyola Univ, instr 1964-75; US Equal Employment Oppor Commn, compliance officer 1966; Notre Dame Seminary & Dominican Coll, instr 1970; Urban League of Greater New Orleans Inc, pres, currently. **Orgs:** Consultant/lecturer on various organizations and univs; Tulane Univ Bd of Visitors; New Orleans Chap Natl Assn of SW; Chamber of Commerce; Louisiana State Univ Board, chmn. **Honors/Awds:** "Housing Discrimination in New Orleans," 1969; "Leadership & Decision Making in New Orleans," 1969; "A Process for the Econ Devel of Black Ghetto Areas in the Urban South," 1973. **Military Serv:** US Army, 1957-59. **Business Addr:** President/ CEO, C. Lyle Barney Distributors and C. Lyle Barney Consulting, 1600 Canal St, New Orleans, LA 70122.

BARNEY, LEMUEL JACKSON (LEM)
Professional football player (retired). **Personal:** Born Sep 8, 1945, Gulfport, MS; married Martha; children: Latrece. **Educ:** Jackson State University, BS, 1967. **Career:** Detroit Lions, cornerback, 1967-77; Black Entertainment Television, sports analyst, 1992; MichCon, community activities specialist, until 1993. **Honors/Awds:** Elected to Pro Football Hall of Fame, inducted, Aug 1, 1992; elected to Afro-American Sports Hall of Fame, inducted, March 2, 1992. **Special Achievements:** Warner-Lambert Celebrity Super Bowl Classic, golfer, 1992.

BARNEY, WILLIE J.
Business executive. **Personal:** Born Oct 10, 1927, Parkdale, AR; married Hazel Willis; children: Ronald, Reginald, Raymond, Reynaldo. **Career:** WISEC of C, pres/founder 1967-70; Consol Record Distrib, pres 1968-; Pyramid Intl, pres 1953-66; Barney's Records Inc, pres, 1953-96. **Orgs:** Sr warden Masons Masonic Chicago 1959-69; mem marketing & com Black Music Assn 1978-; mem Westside Bus Assn 1973-75; treas Operation Brotherhood 1979-. **Honors/Awds:** Businessman Awd FORUM 1975; Serv Awd Lu Palmer Found & Fernwood Meth Ch 1976; Serv Awd CBS Records 1978. **Military Serv:** US Army, pvt. **Business Addr:** President, Barney's Records Inc, 3145 W. Roosevelt Rd., Chicago, IL 60612-3939.

BARNHILL, HELEN IPHIGENIA
Business executive. **Personal:** Born Nov 10, 1937, Ponce de Leon, FL; daughter of Faustana Ponds and Willie Ponds; divorced; children: Carmen, Jerdie, Althea, Stanley, Hilliary, Kelli, Dana. **Educ:** Marquette U, 1966; Lakeland Coll, hon dr of human letters 1975. **Career:** Milwaukee Urban League, caseworker 1962-65; Housing & Publ Accommodations State of WI, coord 1965-70; Proj Equality of WI, dir 1970-73; Barnhill-Hayes Inc, pres 1973-. **Orgs:** Bd trst Lakeland Coll; bd dir Better Bus Bur of Milw; corp mem United Way of Gtr Milw; bd dir Froedtert Memorial Lutheran Hosp, Hevi-Haul Intl, Competitive WI, WI MESBIC, Ind Bus Assn of WI; bd of trust Carroll Coll; Personnel-Indust Relations Assn of WI, Plymouth United Church of Christ; bd of governor, Mt. Mary Coll; bd Milwaukee Minority Chamber of Commerce. **Honors/Awds:** B'Nai Brith Interfaith Awd Comm Serv 1969; Freedom of Residence Awd 1966; Outstanding Bus Achiev Awd WI Womens Polit Caucus 1976; YWCA Bus Ldr Awd 1977; WI Conf United Church of Christ 1977; WI Chap ASPA 1980; Midwest Region Soroptimist Intl 1982; Mary McLeod Bethune Awd WI Black Republican Council 1985; WI Assn for Sickle Cell Anemia 1985; Sales & Marketing Exec of Milwaukee 1985; St Francis Children's Center 1985.

BARNWELL, HENRY LEE
Clergyman. **Personal:** Born Aug 14, 1934, Blountstown, FL; married Shelie Yvonne Whiley; children: Aubrey, Cassandra, Timothy, Darlene. **Educ:** Univ of MD, attended; AZ Coll of the Bible, BA 1978; St Stephens Coll, MS 1979; Carolina Christian Univ, Doctorate of Ministry 1984. **Career:** USAF, flight examiner 1954-70, recruiter 1971-74; Maricopa Cty Personnel, admin aide 1977-80; 1st new Life Missionary Baptist, clergyman. **Orgs:** Chmn Evangelism Bd Area I AB PSW 1970-83; exec bd mem Phoenix AZ PUSH Inc 1979-; chaplain Juvenile Dept of Corrections 1980-; exec bd mem Phoenix OIC1980-; moderator Area I Amer Baptist Pacific SW 1984-; pres Interdenominational Ministerial Alliance 1984-; reg dir Natl Evangelism Movement 1984-; religious adv council Maricopa Cty Sheriff Dept 1984-. **Honors/Awds:** Community Serv Awd Williamsfield Air Force Base 1975-78; Hon Citizen of Tucson City of Tucson 1980; Outstanding Citizen Awd Citizens of Phoenix 1982; Appreciation Awd 82nd Flying Training Wing 1984. **Military Serv:** USAF E-7 sgt 20 yrs; Airmans Medal, Air Force Commendation. **Home Addr:** 11633 N 49th Dr, Glendale, AZ 85304. **Business Addr:** 1st New Life Missionary Bapt, 1902 W roeser Rd, Phoenix, AZ 85041.

BARON, NEVILLE A.
Physician. **Personal:** Born Sep 14, 1933, New York, NY; married Cave-Marie Alix; children: Neilda, Collette, Marc, Rodney. **Educ:** The OH State Univ, BSc 1955; Howard Univ Medical Sch, MD 1961; Howard Univ Serv Dist of Columbia Genl Hosp, rotating internship 1961-62. **Career:** Univ of MD Eastern Shore Div, medical dir 1962-68; Campbell Soup Inc, medical dir/consultant 1965-68; Univ of PA, residency training prog academic ophthalmology 1968; Univ of NJ Coll of Medicine, resident training prog clinical and surgical ophthalmology 1968-71; Warner Lambert Co, consultant/ophthalmology 1972-75; Private Practice, general ophthalmology 1972-85; Riverside Genl Hosp, chief of ophthamic dept 1976-85, chief of medical staff 1979-83; Westchester Ophthalmic Inst, clinical prof 1987-. **Orgs:** Mem Contemporary Oculoplastic Soc 1978-; pres The Continual Medical Ed Assoc of NJ 1982; pres NJ Chap Natl Medical Assoc 1985; clinical consultant Cooper Labs Inc 1987, Alergan Labs Inc 1987, Eye Technology Inc 1987. **Honors/Awds:** Physician of the Yr Hudson Co NJ 1985; Howard Alumni Disting Accomplishment Awd 1985; mem China-Amer Scientific and Cultural Foundation 1986; 5 publications including "Ocular Chromophores-Topically Applies," (a new product for a newly-recognized ophthalmic need), Liquid Sunglasses 1986; NIH, Fellowship-Oculaplastic Surgery, The Manhattan Eye & Ear Hosp, 1971-72. **Military Serv:** AUS ROTC OH State Univ completed w/Honors 1955, commissioned 2nd lt Chemical Corps 1955, officer Chemical Corps 1955-57; Honorable Discharge Medical Corps Reserves 1969. **Home Addr:** 146 Sandpiper Key, Secaucus, NJ 07094.

BARR, LEROY
Police official. **Personal:** Born Jul 1, 1936, New York, NY; married Virginia; children: Denise, LeRoy Jr, Nicole. **Educ:** John Jay Coll, AA, 1970, BS, 1971; New York Univ, MA, 1973. **Career:** Youth House for Girls, couns 1959-64; New York City Bd of Educ, tchr 1971-73; Brooklyn Coll, couns 1973; New York City Police Dept, supr. **Orgs:** 100 Black Men; Assn of Black Psychologists; Amer Personnel & Guid Assn; Amer Acad for Professional Law Enforce; dir sec Black Family & marriage Couns Inc 1976-. **Military Serv:** Sgt 1954-57. **Business Addr:** Supervisor, New York City Police Department, One Police Plaza, New York, NY 10038.

BARRETT, ANDREW
Federal agency administrator. **Personal:** Born in Rome, GA. **Educ:** Roosevelt Univ; Loyola Univ, MA; DePaul Univ, JD. **Career:** NCCJ, assoc dir, 1971-75; NAACP, Chicago Branch, exec dir, 1975-79; IL Law Enforcement Commission, dir ops, 1979-80; IL Dept of Commerce, asst dir, 1980-89; IL Commerce Commission, commissioner, beginning 1989; Federal Communications Commission, commissioner, currently. **Business Addr:** Associate, Edelman Public Relations Worldwide, 1420 K Street NW, 10th Floor, Washington, DC 20005.

BARRETT, IRIS LOUISE KILLIAN
Human resources executive. **Personal:** Born Aug 28, 1962, Hickory, NC; daughter of Dorothy Booker Killian and James C Killian. **Educ:** Univ of NC at Chapel Hill, BSPH (Summa Cum Laude) 1984; Duke Univ, MBA 1986. **Career:** Amer Medical Intl, summer associate 1985; Siecor Corp, training specialist 1986-88, production supervisor, 1988-89, supervisor training dept telecommunications cable plant, 1989-92, quality & education manager, 1992-97, staffing and development, manager, 1997-. **Orgs:** Grace Pentecostal Holiness Church, 1994-; American Business Women's Association, 1990-94; Econo Force, bd mem, 1994-; Catawba Valley Community College, trustee, 1995; Chamber of Commerce, bd mem, 1995-; LEAD Advisory Board, 1986-. **Honors/Awds:** Graduate Fellowship Duke Univ Fuqua Sch of Business 1984-86; Wildacres Leadership Initiative Friday Fellow, (1997-99); Wesleyan Univ, hon doctorate, 1996, Dartmouth Coll, hon doctorate, 1997. **Business Addr:** Manager, Staffing & Development, Siecor Corporation, 489 Siecor Park, Hickory, NC 28603.

BARRETT, JACQUELYN H.
Sheriff. **Personal:** dauGHter of Cornelius Harrison Sr (deceased) and Ocie P Harrison; divorced; children: Kimberly, Alan. **Educ:** Beaver College, criminal justice; Clark-Atlanta Univ, master's degree, sociology. **Career:** Georgia Peace Officer Standards & Training Council, 10 years; Fulton County Public Training Safety Center, 5 years; Fulton County, sheriff, 1992-. **Honors/Awds:** Turner Broadcasting System, Trumpet Award, 1998. **Special Achievements:** The nation's first Afri-

can-American female sheriff, Fulton County, 1992. **Business Addr:** Sheriff, Fulton County, 185 Central Ave, Atlanta, GA 30303, (404)730-5100.

BARRETT, JAMES A.
Association representative. **Personal:** Born Dec 2, 1932, Cleveland, OH; married Edith Ransby; children: Zina, Jurena. **Educ:** Attended, Kent State Univ, Cleveland State Univ. **Career:** City of E Cleveland, aptd city commnr 1969 elected 1970-72; E Cleveland Civil Svc, aptd commnr 1972-76; E Cleveland Pub Library, aptd trustee 1974-80; Blue Cross of NE OH, rep labor affairs. **Orgs:** Trustee E Cleveland PA, 1974; former bd mem E Cleveland YMCA 1972-73; mem E Cleveland Cits Adv Commn 1968-69; past pres Chamber-Mayfair Pres League. **Business Addr:** Representative Labor Affairs, Blue Cross of NE OH, 2066 E Ninth St, Cleveland, OH 44112.

BARRETT, MATTHEW ANDERSON
Business executive. **Personal:** Born Nov 13, 1947, Roanoke, VA. **Educ:** VA Commonwealth Univ, BS Bus Admin 1974. **Career:** Univ Ford Motor Co, salesman 1969-70; Standard Drug Stores Inc, asst mgr 1970-72; VA Commonwealth Univ, computer programmer 1972-76; Seminary Walk Unit Owners Association, president, 1986-89; 3M Co, account rep, currently. **Orgs:** Speaker Richmond Public Schools Speakers Bureau 1970-74; big brother Big Brothers Richmond 1970-75; treas Huntington Club Condominiums 1980-84; mem aircraft Owners & Pilots Assoc 1981-; scuba diver NAUI 1982-; Seminary Walk Condominium Association, pres, 1986-90. **Honors/Awds:** Salesman of the Year, 3M Co 1979, 1980; $100,000 Prod Awd 3M Co 1979; Sales, Salesman of the Year, 1987; Apogee Award, 3M Co 1989. **Home Addr:** 53 Skyhill Rd #304, Alexandria, VA 22314. **Business Addr:** Account Representative, 3 M Company, 1101-15th St NW, Washington, DC 20005.

BARRETT, RICHARD O.
Engineer (retired). **Personal:** Born Mar 4, 1923; son of Johanna Barrett and Marcus Barrett; married Vinella P; children: Richard Jr, Adrienne, Arlene, Yvonne. **Educ:** Milwaukee Sch of Engrg, BA 1943, BSEE 1954; Univ of WI, MSEE 1955. **Career:** Kingston Tech School, instr 1946-50; Stearns Elec Corp, rsch engr 1955-59; Honeywell, devel engr 1959-65, systems analyst 1965-67, sr engr 1967-72, supr engrg. **Orgs:** Mem St Louis Park Rotary; registered professional engr MN; mem MN Soc of Professional Engrs 1966-72; pres Industry Section MN Soc of Professional Engrs 1969-75; corp bd mem Milwaukee School of Engrg 1979; commr Maplewood Planning Commn; mem bd dir St Paul Urban League; pres Minds for Prog Inc; pres Monitors (civic group); dir So MN 4-H Group. **Honors/Awds:** NW Orient Airlines Outstanding Serv Awd 1971; Good Neighbor Awd WCCO Radio Northwest Ford Dealers; Engr of the Yr MN Soc of Professional Engrs 1970; Comm Serv Awd Honeywell 1976; Monitor of the Yr Civic Awd Monitor's Club 1977; Milwaukee Sch of Engrg Outstanding Alumnus Awd Class of 1954 granted 1984.

BARRETT, RONALD KEITH
Psychologist, educator. **Personal:** Born Aug 17, 1948, Brooklyn, NY; son of Dorothy and Cyril. **Educ:** Morgan State Univ Baltimore, BS 1970; Univ of Pittsburgh, MS 1974, PhD 1977. **Career:** CA State Univ Dominguez Hills, asst prof psychology 1977-78; Loyola Marymount Univ Los Angeles, prof, Psychology 1978-. **Orgs:** Association of Death Education and Counseling; International Association of Trauma Counselors; International Work Group on Death, Dying & Bereavement; mem, Assn of Black Psychologists; mem, Am Psychological Assn. **Honors/Awds:** Elected Psi Chi Natl Honor Soc, Psychology 1969; Optimist Club, Man of the Year, 1991; numerous scholarly publications and citations. **Business Addr:** Professor of Psychology, Loyola Marymount University, Department of Psychology, Los Angeles, CA 90045.

BARRETT, SHERMAN L.
Educator. **Personal:** Born Aug 15, 1945, Charleston, SC; children: Larry. **Educ:** Aurora Clg, BAE 1963-67; Adelphi U, 1966; UWM Milwaukee, 1975-83. **Career:** MTEA, ngtns 1969-72; WEA, crdntls 1970-72; NEA, del 1970-72; Black Teachers Org Milwaukee & Natl, vice pres 1970-72; Milwaukee Public Schools, teacher. **Orgs:** Dist dir A L Williams 1985; plygrnd/ctr dir Milwaukee Rcrtn 1967-81. **Honors/Awds:** Coach/bsktbl 6th Graders/on own 1972-85. **Home Addr:** 1628 W Capitol Dr, Milwaukee, WI 53206.

BARRETT, WALTER CARLIN, JR.
Roman Catholic priest. **Personal:** Born Sep 30, 1947, Richmond, VA; son of Elizabeth Norrell Barrett and Walter Carlin Barrett, Sr. **Educ:** St John Vianney Seminary, diploma; St Mary's Seminary Coll, Catonsville MD, BA, Philosophy; St Mary's Seminary & Univ, Baltimore MD, MDiv, Theology. **Career:** Roman Catholic Diocese of Richmond, priest 1975-; St Mary's Catholic Church, assoc pastor, 1975-77; St Gerard's Catholic Church, Roanoke VA, pastor 1977-85; Basilica of St Mary, Norfolk VA, rector, 1985-97. **Orgs:** Member, NAACP, Natl Black Catholic Clergy Caucus, Black Catholic Commn, Black Catholic Clergy Conf; appointed to Diocesan Pastoral Council, Diocesan Priest Council; founder Richmond Black Catholic Caucus 1971-74; Exec Comm of Priests Council. **Honors/Awds:** Winner Diocese/Deanery Public Speaking Contest Richmond Area 1965; Recognized for Outstanding Serv & Dedication by the Black Catholic Commn of the Roman Catholic Diocese of Richmond 1985; Consultor to the Bishop of Richmond, Roman Catholic Diocese, 1990-95; Appointed Consultor to the Bishop of Richmond 1995-2000; Pope John Paul II named St Mary's a Minor Basilica, 1991; only predominately African-American Roman Catholic Church in US with this distinction; Named "Prelate of Honor," or Rev Monsignor, by Pope John Paul II, 1996. **Business Addr:** Rector, Basilica of St Mary, 1000 Holt St, Norfolk, VA 23504.

BARRON, REGINALD
Automobile dealership executive. **Career:** Barron Chevrolet-Geo Inc, Danvers, MA, chief executive. **Honors/Awds:** Auto 100, Barron Chevrolet-Geo, Black Enterprise, 1991. **Business Addr:** CEO, Barron Chevrolet-Geo, Inc, 90 Andover, Danvers, MA 01923.

BARRON, WENDELL
Automobile dealer. **Career:** Campus Ford Inc, Okemos MI, chief executive, currently. **Business Addr:** Chief Executive, Campus Ford Inc, 1880 W Grand River, Okemos, MI 48864.

BARROS, DANA BRUCE
Professional basketball player. **Personal:** Born Apr 13, 1967, Boston, MA; married Veronica; children: Jordan. **Educ:** Boston College, Boston, MA, 1985-89. **Career:** Seattle Supersonics, guard, 1989-93; Philadelphia 76ers, 1993-95; Boston Celtics, 1995-. **Honors/Awds:** NBA Most Improved Player, 1995. **Special Achievements:** NBA Draft, First round pick, #16, 1989. **Business Addr:** Professional Basketball Player, Boston Celtics, 151 Merrimac St, 5th Fl, Boston, MA 02114, (617)523-6050.

BARROW, DENISE
Real estate executive. **Personal:** Born Feb 3, 1943, New York, NY; daughter of Hazel Barrow and Henry Barrow. **Educ:** Lebanon Hosp School of Nursing, LPN 1959-60; Bronx Comm Coll, 1963-65; Eastern Airlines Flight Attendant School, 1967; St Peters Coll, 1971-72; Queens Coll, 1979-80; Professional School of Bus, 1984. **Career:** Dr Eugene T Quash, nurse, med asst 1961-66; Eastern Airlines Inc, flight attendant 1967-86, inflight sup; Kennedy Kramer Inc, sales rep, 1984-87; Kenedy & Kenedy Inc, sales & marketing exec, 1988; Riverfront Realty Corp, sales rep, 1989-91; Lank-Friedherz Properties, sales rep, 1991-; Remax Fortune Properties, broker, sales assoc, 1995-. **Orgs:** Bd mem Crotona Morrisania Civic Assoc 1964-67; mem League of Woman Voters 1964-67, Natl Coalescense of Flight Attendants 1983-86, Natl Board of Realtors 1986-, Natl Urban League 1986-, Teaneck Englewood & Vicinity Club of Natl Assoc of negro Bus & Professional Women 1987-; NY Coalition of 100 Black Women 1988. **Honors/Awds:** Cert of Serv Awd United Negro Coll Fund. **Business Addr:** Broker/Sales Assoc, Remax Fortune Properties, 474 Sylvan, Englewood Cliffs, NJ 07632.

BARROW, JOE LOUIS, JR.
Golf company executive. **Personal:** Born May 28, 1947, Mexico City, Mexico; son of Joe Louis & Marva Spaulding; married Susan. **Educ:** University of Denver, BA, 1968. **Career:** United Bank of Denver, trust officer, asst vp, 1968-76; US Dept of Energy, Office of Commercialization Conservation, Solar Energy, dir, 1978-81; Wood Bros, vp of corp mktg, 1981-82, vp regional mktg dir, 1982-85; Ronald H Brown, dir of special projects, sr advisor; IZZO Systems, pres, CEO, currently. **Orgs:** IZZO Systems, Inc, bd mem; IZZO Ltd, UK, bd mem; Franklin & Eleanor Roosevelt Inst, bd mem; Planned Parenthood of the Rocky Mountains, bd mem; National Golf Foundation, bd mem, Colorado Golf Association, bd mem; American Junior Golf Association, be mem; Planned Parenthood Federation of America; Mile High United Way; University of Denver, bd of fellows; Colorado Health Facilities Finance Authority; Urban League of Colorado; Big Brothers of Metro Denver; Piton Foundation Community Dev Project; Denver Metro Chamber of Commerce. **Special Achievements:** Published, "Joe Louis: 50 Years An American Hero," McGraw-Hill, 1988. **Business Addr:** President/COO, IZZO Systems, Inc, 12364 W Alameda Pkwy, Unit M, Lakewood, CO 80228, (303)988-2886.

BARROW, LIONEL CEON, JR.
Business executive. **Personal:** Born Dec 17, 1926, New York, NY; son of Wilhelmina Brookins and Lionel C Barrow Sr; married Carmen (divorced); children: Brenda, Rhonda, Aurea Nellie, K Erin, Leah Estrada. **Educ:** Morehouse Coll, BA 1948; Univ of WI, MA 1958, PhD 1960. **Career:** Foote Cone & Belding Adv Agency NY, vice pres assoc rsch dir 1968-71; Univ of WI, prof mass comm & Afro-Amer studies 1971-75, chmn 1974-75; Howard Univ, dean sch of comm 1975-85; prof 1975-86; The Barrow Information Group, pres 1986. **Orgs:** Pres Journalism Council Inc 1970-79; mem adv bd Journalism Quarterly; consl Black Media; life mem NAACP; mem Natl Assn of Black Journalists, Capital Press Club; Sigma Delta Chi, Assn for Educ in Journalism and Mass Communications; secretary, Elected Advocates, Maryland Conference on Small Business, 1987-89. **Honors/Awds:** Chancellor's Awd, Distinguished Serv in Journalism, Univ of WI, 1971; publ "New Uses of Covariance Analysis" Journal of Advertising Rsch 1967; "Towards a Code of Ethics for Blacks in the Newsroom" Black Journal Review 1976; "History of the Black Press" Black Press Handbook 1977; author of "The Japanese: Are They Giving Us 'The Business'," Crisis, 1988; "Factors Related to Attention to the First Kennedy-Nixon Debate," Journal of Broadcasting, 1965. **Military Serv:** US Army, 1945-47 & 1950-53; Combat Infantry Badge, Korean Service Medal with five Battle Stars, 1951.

BARROW, MICHEAL CALVIN
Professional football player. **Personal:** Born Apr 19, 1970, Homestead, FL. **Educ:** Miami (Fla.), bachelor's degree in accounting, 1992. **Career:** Houston Oilers, linebacker, 1993-96; Carolina Panthers, 1997-. **Business Addr:** Professional Football Player, Carolina Panthers, 800 Mint St, Ericsson Stadium, Charlotte, NC 28202, (704)358-7000.

BARROW, WILLIE T.
Association executive. **Personal:** Born Dec 7, 1924, Burton, TX; married Clyde Barrow; children: Keith (deceased). **Educ:** Warner Sch of Theol Portland, OR; Moody Bible Sch Chicago, IL; Univ of Monrovia, Monrovia, Liberia, DD. **Career:** First Black Church of God Portland, OR, organizer; Vernon Pk Church of God, assoc min/bd trustees; Rev Jackson Pres Campaign, natl dep campaign & road mgr; Operation PUSH, Chicago, IL, chairman of the board. **Orgs:** Bd dir Malcolm X College 1976; commr Intl Women's Year 1978; mem Natl World Peace Cncl; chairperson IL Chap Natl Polit Congr of Black Women; mem Natl Cncl of Negro Women 1945; mem Natl Urban League 1943; Natl Political Congress of Black Women, 1st vice chair; Doctors Hosp of Hyde Park, bd of dir. **Honors/Awds:** Human Serv Award Chicago Firefighters; Woman of the Year City of Chicago 1969; Image Award League of Black Women 1972; Bennett College, Doctor of Humane Letters, 1991; Southern California School of Ministry, Doctor of Divinity, 1992. **Business Addr:** President, Operation Push, 930 E 50th St, Chicago, IL 60615.

BARROWS, BRYAN H., III
Educational administrator. **Personal:** Born May 21, 1952, Bryan, TX; son of Mable Dolores Sadberry Barrows and Bryan H Barrows Jr; married Delia De la Cerda Barrows, Sep 5, 1992; children: Jerry, Gerald, Pat, Marshal, Michelle. **Educ:** Texas A&I, BA, 1974, MA, 1976; Del Mar College, AA, 1972. **Career:** HIALCO, OIC Inc, counselor, off mgr, EEO director, pub inf director, 1979-81; Amoco Production Co, administrative analyst, 1981-85; Chemical Dependency Unit, public information director, 1984-85; City of CC, counselor, 1985; Nueces County MHMR, assistant personnel director & staff dev director, 1985-86; Del Mar College, asst professor of communications, 1985-92; Prairie View A&M University, public information director, 1992-. **Orgs:** NAACP, 1990-91; Speech Comm Association, 1985-91; International Comm Assn, 1985-92; Coastal Bend Public Relations Assn, comm chair, 1984-92; Spectrum Committee, Channel 16 PBS, 1989-91; Del Mar Communications Club, founder/sponser, 1987-91. **Honors/Awds:** National Institute of Staff Dev, National Award for Teaching Excellence, 1991; US Jaycees, Outstanding Young Men of America, 1983, 1988; CC Chamber of Commerce, Leadership Corpus Christi Graduate Cert, 1978; Del Mar College Student Body, East Campus Teacher of the Year, 1989, 1990; Houston Defender Newspaper, Houston Defender Editorial Achievement Award, 1986. **Special Achievements:** Star Film Festival; Excellence in Local TV Award—presented by CC Arts Council to Spectrum TV Show KEDT; presented the Austin Metropolitan Business Resource Center's "Men of Valor" award; US-Philippine Military Award for Merit, 1973; Okinawa Marine Command Commendation, 1973; Plaque for Meritorious Service to US Command, Japan/US Naval Group. **Home Addr:** 7711 Ashton, Houston, TX 77095. **Business Addr:** Director of Public Information, Prairie View A&M University, PO Box 4129, LO Evans Rm 104, Prairie View, TX 77446-4129, (409)857-2117.

BARRY, MARION SHEPILOV, JR.
Mayor. **Personal:** Born Mar 6, 1936, Itta Bena, MS; son of Mattie Barry and Marion S. Barry; married Effi Slaughter Barry, 1978 (divorced 1992); children: Marion Christopher; married Cora Lavonne Masters, 1993. **Educ:** LeMoyne Coll, BS 1958; Fisk Univ, MS 1960; Univ of KS, postgrad 1960-61; Univ of TN, postgrad 1961-64. **Career:** Pride Inc, dir of operations, 1967; Pride Economic Enterprises, co-founder, chair, dir, 1968; Washington DC School Board, mem, 1971-74; Washington City Council, mem-at-large, 1975; Washington, DC, mayor 1979-90, city councilman, 1992-94; City of Washington, DC, mayor, 1994-. **Orgs:** Pres Washington DC Bd of Educ 1972-; first natl chmn SNCC; mem Third World Coalition Against the War; mem Alpha Phi Alpha Frat; pres Natl Conf of Black Mayors. **Business Addr:** Mayor, City of Washington, DC, District Building, 14th & E Sts, Washington, DC 20004.

BARTEE, KIMERA ANOTCHI
Professional baseball player. **Personal:** Born Jul 21, 1972, Omaha, NE. **Educ:** Creighton. **Career:** Detroit Tigers, outfielder, 1996-. **Business Addr:** Professional Baseball Player, Detroit Tigers, 2121 Trumbull St, Detroit, MI 48216, (313)962-4000.

BARTELLE, TALMADGE LOUIS. **See Obituaries section.**

BARTHELEMY, SIDNEY JOHN
Former mayor. **Personal:** Born Mar 17, 1942, New Orleans, LA; son of Ruth Fernandez Barthelemy and Lionel Barthelemy; married Michaele Thibodeaux Barthelemy, 1968; children: Cherrie, Bridget, Sidney Jr. **Educ:** Epiphany Apostolic Jr Coll, attended 1960-63; St Joseph Seminary, BA 1967; Tulane Univ, MSW 1971. **Career:** Admin asst, 1967-68, asst dir, 1969, Total Community Action; guidance counselor, interim dir, Adult Basic Educ Program, 1968-69; asst dir, New Careers Program, 1969; dir, 1969-71, dir social serv, 1971-72, Parent-Child Center; coord, Labor Educ Advancement Program, Urban League, 1969-72; dir, City of New Orleans Welfare Dept, 1972-74; assoc prof of sociology, Xavier Univ, 1974-86; state senator, Louisiana Legislature, 1974-78; councilman-at-large, New Orleans City Council, 1978-86; mayor, city of New Orleans, 1986-93; pres, Natl Assn of Regional Coun, 1987-88; vice chmn for voter registration, Democratic Natl Party, 1988-89; second vice pres, Natl League of Cites, 1988-; pres, Louisiana Conf of Mayors, 1989-93; adjunct prof, Kennedy School ofGovt, Tulane Univ School of Public Health, U of New Orleans Coll of Educ. **Orgs:** Vice pres, Comm Org Urban Politics; member, Orleans Parish Democratic Exec Comm; chmn, Youth Assistance Council; bd dir, Central City Fed Credit Union, Family Serv Soc, St Bernard Neighborhood Comm Ctr, Comm Serv Ctr; member, City Park Commn, Democratic Natl Comm, Labor Educ Advancement Program, Louisiana Conf of Mayors, Louisiana Municipal Assn, Mississippi-Louisiana-Alabama Transit Commn, NAACP, Natl Assn of Black Mayors, Natl Assn of County Officials, Natl Assn of Regional Councils, Natl Black Councils/Local Elected Officials, Natl Inst of Educ, New Orleans Assn of Black Social Workers, US Conf of Mayors; first vice pres, 1989-90, pres, 1990, Natl League of Cities. **Honors/Awds:** Purple Knight Award Best All Around Student, 1960; Outstanding Alumnus of Tulane Univ, Social Worker of the Year, Louisiana Chapter of the Natl Assn of Social Workers, 1987; Amer Freedom Award, Third Baptist Church of Chicago, 1987; Amer Spirit Award, US Air Force Recruiting Serv, 1989; Daniel E. Byrd New Orleans NAACP Award, 1990. **Business Addr:** Former Mayor, City of New Orleans, 1300 Perdido St, Rm 2E10, City Hall, New Orleans, LA 70112.

BARTHWELL, JACK CLINTON, III
Brewery executive. **Personal:** Born Oct 16, 1950, Detroit, MI; son of Catherine McCree Barthwell and Jack C Barthwell, Jr. **Educ:** Trinity Coll, Hartford CT, BA, 1972; Univ of Michigan Law School, Ann Arbor MI JD, 1976. **Career:** US House Comm on the District of Columbia, Washington DC, staff counsel, 1976-78; Hon Charles C Diggs, Jr, US House of Representatives, chief of staff, 1977-80; Hon George W Crockett, Jr, US House of Representatives, chief of staff, 1980-83; The Stroh Brewery Co, Detroit MI, dir, 1984-87, vice pres corporate communications & govt affairs, 1987-. **Orgs:** Mem of bd, Children's Museum Friends; mem bd Diversified Youth Serv Inc; mem bd, Project Pride-Detroit Chamber of Commerce; mem of govt & educ comm, New Detroit; mem, State Bar of Michigan, 1976-; mem, District of Columbia Bar, 1978-; mem, Eastern District of Michigan (Federal), 1980-, mem, NAACP. **Honors/Awds:** Fellow, Thomas J Watson Found, 1972. **Business Addr:** Vice President of University Relations, Wayne State University, 4148 Fab, 656 West Kirby, Detroit, MI 48202.

BARTLEY, TALMADGE O.
Deputy officer, coordinator. **Personal:** Born Dec 5, 1920, Arcadia, FL; married Louise; children: Katye, Ardlin. **Educ:** US Intl Univ, BA, MA, PhD. **Career:** Free lanceTV writer "One Eye One"; Marine Corps Base, auto mech to foreman 1949-67; Marine Corps Base, comm relat spec & human relat ofcr 1967-71; CommEduc Vol Serv Prog, coord 1971-; Naval Ocean Sys Ctr, deputy equal employ oppor ofcr/coord. **Orgs:** Mem Inter Serv Task Force 1970; mem num ofcs, coms, social orgns. **Honors/Awds:** Outstanding Deputy EEO Ofcr in NMC Chf of Naval material 1974; Navy Superior Civilian Serv Medal; num citations awds honors. **Military Serv:** USMC. **Business Addr:** Deputy Equal Employ Oppor Ofcr, Naval Ocean Sys Center, Naval Electronics Lab Ctr, San Diego, CA 92152.

BARTLEY, WILLIAM RAYMOND
Physician. **Personal:** Born Dec 9, 1944, Daytona Beach, FL; married Freddye; children: Diallo, Rashida. **Educ:** Knoxville Coll, BA 1968; Meharry Med Coll, attended 1975. **Career:** Equal Oppor Agency, staff; Little Rock VA Hosp, Lee Co Co-op Clinic, part time staff; Erlanger Hosp, intern 1975; USAF Sch Aerospace Med, 1976; USAF, flight surgeon. **Orgs:** Mem Little League Sports. **Honors/Awds:** Natl Med Flwsp Awd 1970-72; Winn-Dixie Flwsp 1972; Jessie Noyles-Smith Ob-Gyn Fellowship 1973-74. **Military Serv:** USAF capt 1976-. **Business Addr:** Flight Surgeon, USAF Hosp, Little Rock, Jacksonville, AR 72076.

BARTON, RHONDA L.
Engineer. **Personal:** Born Dec 10, 1966, Wilmington, DE; daughter of Olive Barton and Lyndon Barton. **Educ:** Howard University, Washington, DC, BS, mechanical engineering, 1989. **Career:** Pacific Gas & Electric Co, San Francisco, CA, gas distribution engr, 1989-. **Orgs:** Mem, Natl Society of Black Engineers Alumni Extension, 1989-; mem, Pacific Coast Gas Assn, 1991-. **Business Addr:** Gas Distribution Engineer, Pacific Gas & Electric Co, 2180 Harrison St, 3rd Floor, San Francisco, CA 94110.

BARTON, WAYNE DARRELL
Law enforcement official. **Personal:** Born Feb 21, 1961, Fort Lauderdale, FL; son of Burnett Barton and Willie Barton; children: Tarsheka D, Sharque. **Educ:** Palm Beach Junior College, attended, 1991-92. **Career:** Boca Raton Police Department, police aide, 1980-81, police officer, 1981-. **Orgs:** Board member: Salvation Army, March of Dimes, Child Watch, Visions 2002, Boca Raton Jaycees; founding member: I Have a Dream Foundation, Law Day Foundation; numerous others. **Honors/Awds:** Attorney General for the State of Florida, Meritorious Award, 1988; Boca Raton Rotary Club, Officer of the Year Award, 1988; Alabama Governor, Certificate of Appreciation, 1989; Vision Magazine, Unsung Hero Award, 1991; St Paul AME Church, Outstanding Community Service Award, 1992; National Exchange Club, Book of Golden Deeds Award, 1992; numerous others. **Business Addr:** Police Officer, Boca Raton Police Department, 100 NW Boca Raton Blvd, Boca Raton, FL 33432, (407)338-1238.

BARTOW, JEROME EDWARD
Business executive (retired). **Personal:** Born in Orange, NJ; married Louise Tolson; children: Sharon B Mitchell, Jerome E Bartow Jr. **Educ:** VA St Univ, AB 1951; Columbia Univ, MA 1955, EdD 1968. **Career:** Various institutions of higher educ, 1955-64; NY Tele Co, various 1965-69; ITT World Headquarters, mgr exec placement 1969-74, dir employee rel opers 1974-77, dir personnel/industrial rel 1977-79, dir admin bsns systms & comm grp 1979; Hartford Ins Grp, senior vice pres & dir admin 1979-95. **Orgs:** Chm exec adv comm BEEP Natl Urban League 1980-93; past mem bd of trus Natl Urbn League; past mem bd of rgnts Univ of Hartford; past mem bd of visitors Univ of CT; founding charter mem, bd of directors Exec Leadership Council. **Honors/Awds:** Cert of Merit VA St Univ 1983; Cert of Merit Ft Valley State College 1981; Honorary Doctor of Humane Letters, Virginia State University, 1991-; Natl Urban League McGannon Award 1987; Whitney M. Young, Jr. Medallion 1994; Executive Leadership Council Heritage Award 1996. **Military Serv:** US Army, lt 1951-53.

BARZEY, RAYMOND CLIFFORD, II
Attorney. **Personal:** Born Jun 25, New York, NY; son of Elva Waters Barzey and Raymond C Barzey. **Educ:** City Coll City Univ of NYC, BA 1967; Atlanta Univ, MS 1968; State Univ NY, MA 1970; NY Univ, PhD 1980; Seton Hall, JD, 1983. **Career:** Sterns Dept Store, asst buyer 1965-67; MN Mining & Mfg, production analyst 1968-71; Urban Develop Corp, assoc economist 1971-73; Housing Devel Corp, asst to exec dir 1974; Urban Devel Corp, assoc economist 1975; Harlem Urban Devel Corp, dir commercial devel 1976; Co of LA, sr budget analyst; City Univ of NY, Baruch College, NYC, adjunct asst prof, 1981-87; NYC office of Economic Development, 1982; NJ Deputy Attorney General, 1983-. **Orgs:** Mem Amer Assn of Univ Profs; Amer Econ Assn; Amer Inst of Planners; Amer Library Assn; Amer Soc of Planning Officials; Natl Assn of Housing & Redevelopment Officials; Natl Econ Assn Amnesty Intl; Hospital Audience Inc; Natl Trust for Historic Preservation; Natl Urban League; 100 Black Men Inc; Amer Bar Assn, NJ Bar Assn; Assn of City of New York; New York County Lawyers Assn. **Honors/Awds:** Intl Student Com Deans List Atlanta Univ 1968; Martin Luther King Scholarship NY Univ 1975-77. **Home Addr:** 65 W 90th St, New York, NY 10024.

BASEY, OVETTA T.
Educator (retired). **Personal:** Born Mar 31, 1920, Birmingham, AL; married Robert Julian Basey; children: Robert Aulmon. **Educ:** KY State Univ, AB 1945; Univ of KY, MA 1960; Univ of KY, post grad studies. **Career:** Hazard Bd of Educ KY, classroom teacher 1937-80. **Orgs:** Grand Worthy Matron; Cecelia Dunlap Grand Chap KY Jurisdiction; KY Educ Assn bd dir 1974-78; commr KEA Human Relations Commn 1972-; chmn bd trustees Cecelia Dunlap Grant Chap 1975; Jurisprudence Com Cecilia Dunlap Grand Chap 1962-; mem Hazard City Planning & Zoning Commn; HEA; UKREA; KEA; NEA; Mayor'sadv com 1968-72; KY Area Devel Dist Human Resources Comm 1972-74; Commissioned a KY Col 1967. **Honors/Awds:** Lucy Harth Smith, Atwood S Welson Award for Civil & Human Rights in Education by KY ED Assn.

BASHFUL, EMMETT W.
Educational administrator (retired). **Personal:** Born Mar 12, 1917, New Roads, LA; son of Mary Walker Bashful and Charles Bashful; married Juanita Jones, Aug 16, 1941; children: Cornell J Nugent. **Educ:** So Univ Baton Rouge, BS 1940; Univ IL Urbana, MA 1947, PhD 1955. **Career:** Allen Parish Schools, LA, teacher, 1940-41; Keystone Insurance Company, assistant manager, 1941-42; Florida A&M Univ, professor, 1948-58, head, political science department, 1950-58; Southern Univ, Baton Rouge, LA, professor, 1958-59; Southern Univ, New Orleans, LA, dean, 1959-69, vice president, 1969-77, chancellor, 1977-87. **Orgs:** Bd mem, Metropolitan Area Comm; bd mem, World Trade Ctr; adv bd, Goodwill Ind; bd of dir, Comm on Alcoholism of Greater New Orleans United Way Agency; bd mem, New Orleans Chapter, Natl Conf of Christians & Jews; bd dir Frey Fndtn. **Honors/Awds:** Award, 10 Outstanding Citizens of New Orleans, Institute for Human Understanding, 1978; recpnt Volunteer Activist Award, 1976; recpnt, Silver Beaver Award, Boy Scouts of America, 1967; author, The Florida Supreme Court, A Study in Judicial Selection, 1958. **Military Serv:** US Army, 1st Lt, 1942-46. **Home Addr:** 5808 Lafaye St, New Orleans, LA 70122.

BASKERVILLE, CHARLES ALEXANDER
Educator. **Personal:** Born Aug 19, 1928, Queens, NY; son of Annie M Allen Baskerville and Charles H Baskerville; married Susan; children: Mark, Shawn, Charles, Thomas. **Educ:** The City Coll, BS 1953; NYU, MS 1958, PhD 1965. **Career:** NY State Dept of Transportation, 1953-65; McFarland-Johnson, soils engr 1967; Madigan-Hyland Engr, sr soils engr 1968; The City Coll, prof 1965-70, dean School of General Studies 1970-79, professor emeritus 1982; US Geological Survey, project Geologist Geologic Risk Assessment Branch 1979-90; Central Connecticut State Univ, prof 1990-, department chairman, 1992-94. **Orgs:** Mem Natl Advisory Comm on Minority Participant in Earth Science & Mineral Engr US Dept Interior 1972-75; Assn of Engr Geo 1973, Tech Session subcomm for Natl AEG Convention 1976, chmn Marliave Scholarship Com 1976-77; Natl Science Found, Advisory Committee on Earth Sciences 1989-91; Minority Graduate Fellowship Program 1979-80; mem Geological Soc of Washington; panelist Natl Science Found Graduate Fellowship Program; mem Sigma Xi; mem US Natl Comm on Tunnelling Technology Natl Acad of Engrg Natl Rsch Council, chmn Educ and Training Subcommittee; consultant: IBM, Madigan Hyland Praeger Cavanaugh Waterbury, 1969,St Raymond's Cemetery, 1970-76, Consolidated Edison Co, Eastmore Construction Co, New York City Corp Council; mem New York Academy of Sciences; fellow Geological Society of AmericAd Hoc Committee on Minorities in the Geosciences, chm Committee on Committees, E B Burwell Awards Committee, representative, US National Committee on tunneling technology, 1991-; NY State Dept of Transportation construction project expert witness; NY State Dept of Law expert witness. **Honors/Awds:** 125th Anniversary Medal, The City Coll; Founders Day Award, NYU; Award for Excellence in Engineering Geology, Natl Consortium for Black Professional Development; Black Achievers in Science, Museum of Science and Industry, Chicago, IL; US delegate to the Beijing Intl Colloquium on Tunneling and Underground Works, B eijing, People's Republic of China, 1984; presented & published numerous scientific papers; guest lecturer to schools & colleges; commonwealth visiting professor, George Mason Univ, Fairfax VA, 1987-89. **Business Addr:** Professor, Physics and Earth Sciences Dept, Central Connecticut State Univ, 1615 Stanley St, New Britain, CT 06050.

BASKERVILLE, PEARL
Educator. **Personal:** Born Dec 9, 1929, New Bedford, MA; married Walden A Baskerville; children: Jill Louise, Jodi Ann, Judson Alan, Jinx Elaine. **Educ:** William Penn Coll, BA 1951; Western Mi Univ, MA 1953. **Career:** Neighborhood Youth Corps Counselor, 1966-67; Western Michigan Univ, instructor basic studies program 1962-65, counselor, instructor, asst prof coll of genl studies & MartinLuther King program 1967-74, asst prof, counselor, coll of genl studies 1974-. **Orgs:** Founder/chairperson vice chairperson Western MI Univ Black Caucus 1969-75; professional vol to many civic orgns including League of Women Voters; YWCA; Human Relations Council; Amer Assn of Univ Women; NAACP; asst Operation Out-Reach Prog Kalamazoo; admin asst prog coord MI Independent Colleges Oppor Prog; pres Kalamazoo YWCA. **Business Addr:** Asst Prof/Counselor, Western Michigan University, Coll of Gen Studies, 2090 Friedmann, Kalamazoo, MI 49008.

BASKERVILLE, PENELOPE ANNE
Personnel administrator. **Personal:** Born Jul 9, 1946, South Orange, NJ; daughter of Yolanda Reaves Baskerville and Robert L Baskerville; divorced; children: Dylan Craig, Ailey Yolanda. **Educ:** Brown Univ, BA 1968. **Career:** NJ Div on Civil Rights, field rep 1975-77; NJ Dept of Public Advocate Office of Citizen Complaints, field rep 1977-80; Princeton Univ, personnel admin 1980-86; Peterson's Guides Inc, personnel mgr 1986-89; Rider Coll, benefits manager, 1989-. **Orgs:** Mem Brown Univ Alumni Schools Comm 1971-; pres Bd of Trustees Princeton Nursery School 1977-82; mem Intergovernmental Drug Comm; Corner House 1982-; mem Bd of Ed Princeton Reg Schools 1982-85, ET Byrd Scholarship Fund 1983-; mem bd of trustees Princeton YWCA 1985-. **Home Addr:** 210 Birch Ave, Princeton, NJ 08542. **Business Addr:** Benefits Manager, Rider College, Lawrenceville Road, Lawrenceville, NJ 08648.

BASKERVILLE, RANDOLPH
Attorney. **Personal:** Born Jul 22, 1949, Henderson, NC; married Sarah McLean; children: Latoyia, Nathan. **Educ:** Fayetteville State Univ, BS 1971; NC A&T State Univ, MS 1972; NC Central Univ School of Law, JD 1976. **Career:** Admin Office of the Courts, asst da 1979-84; Dept of Social Svcs, staff atty 1985-86; pvt practice, 1985-. **Orgs:** Mem NC Bar Assoc 1977-, Natl Bar Assoc 1977-; dir YMCA 1984-85, Amer Cancer Soc 1984-; pres Charles Williamson Bar Assoc 1985-86; dir NCNB

Bank 1985-; dir C of C 1986-. **Honors/Awds:** Outstanding Young Dem Young Dem of Vance Cty 1983; Contribs to Planning of YMCA Henderson/Vance YMCA 1983; Outstanding Contribs to Ninth Dist Ninth Judicial Dist Bar 1984; Outstanding Contribs to Black Comm Vance Cty Black Leadership Caucus 1984. **Business Addr:** Attorney, PO Box 2224, Henderson, NC 27536.

BASKERVILLE, SAMUEL J., JR.
Physician. **Personal:** Born Mar 2, 1933, Charleston, WV; son of Geraldine Baskerville and Samuel Baskerville Sr. **Educ:** Howard Univ Wash, DC, BS 1953; Meharry Med Coll, MD 1958. **Career:** Detroit Receiving Hosp, intern 1958-59; Kern County General Hospital, res internal med 1959-62, chief res internal med 1961-62; Mercy Hosp Bakersfield CA 1984-, chief of staff 1973, bd of dirs 1979-81, 1986-90. **Orgs:** Bd of dirs Kern Cty Med Soc 1964-67, CA Med Assoc 1964-, Amer Medical Assoc 1964-, Natl Medical Assoc 1967-, Amer Soc Internal Med 1968-; pres 1987 Kern Cty Medical Soc; Omega Psi Phi Fraternity; Kern County Sheriff's Advisory Council 1988-90. **Honors/Awds:** Civil Serv Cmnsn Kern Cnty 1969-77; Kern County Heart Assn 1991-. **Military Serv:** USAF Med Corps capt 1962-64. **Business Addr:** 5000 Physicians Blvd, Bakersfield, CA 93301.

BASKETT, KENNETH GERALD
Educator (retired). **Personal:** Born Nov 18, 1942, Kansas City, MO; son of Rosella Kelly King and W. Cletus Baskett; divorced; children: Charmel, Adrienne, Tiffany. **Educ:** Tuskegee Inst, BS Accounting 1970-72; Alabama A&M, MS Personnel Mgt 1972-75; Command and Gen Staff Coll, Masters 1979. **Career:** AL A&M Univ, asst prof 1972-75; Lincoln Univ, prof 1982-85; Lt Col USA Retired; educator. **Orgs:** Bd mem Optimist Club Jeff City 1982-85; Atlanta City Country Club; mem Alpha Phi Alpha Fraternity, 1989; president, Pi Gamma Lambda Chapter, Alpha Phi Alpha Fraternity, Inc. **Honors/Awds:** Numerous awds for combat service Vietnam 1968-69; #1 Bus Major Tuskegee Inst 1970-72, graduated with honors. **Military Serv:** AUS infantry Lt col 22 yrs; Air Medal, Bronze Star, 3 Meritorious Service Awards 1966-86; captain/company commander, Vietnam 1968-69; Retired 1986. **Home Addr:** 4584 Jamerson Forest, Marietta, GA 30066.

BASKETTE, ERNEST E., JR.
Association executive. **Personal:** Born Apr 24, 1944, Lumpkin, GA; son of Julia Williams Baskette and Ernest E Baskette; married Stephanie R Bush-Baskette; children: Damien B Baskette. **Educ:** City College-CUNY, New York, NY, BA, 1972; Hunter College, New York, NY, Master's of Urban Planning, 1974. **Career:** Town of Islip, Islip, NY, urban planner, 1974-75; City of New Rochelle, New Rochelle, NY, urban planner, 1975-77; NHS of Newark, Newark, NJ, exec dir, 1977-80; Neighborhood Housing Services of America, Oakland, CA, vice pres, 1980-. **Orgs:** Board member, SEW/Lorraine Hansbury Theatre, 1985-87. **Military Serv:** US Air Force, 1961-65. **Home Addr:** 80 Lakeshore Ct, Richmond, CA 94804, (510)237-2748. **Business Phone:** (510)287-4204.

BASKIN, ANDREW LEWIS
Educational administrator. **Personal:** Born Feb 28, 1951, Maryville, TN; son of Eloise Baskin and Jimmy Baskin; married Symerdar Lavern Capehart; children: Thalethia Elois, Thameka La Cape. **Educ:** Berea Coll, BA Hist 1972; VA Tech, MA Am Hist 1975. **Career:** Ferrum Coll, asst prof 1975-83; Berea Coll, dir of Blk Cultural Center, 1983-. **Orgs:** Phi Alpha Theta 1975-; bd dir Mt Maternal Health League 1984-; treasurer Council of So Mts 1983-84; bd dir Berea Coll Credit Union 1985; editor, SCAASI's journal ''The Griot'' 1986-; bd of directors, Kentucky Humanities Council, 1990-; bd of education, Berea Independent School System, chairperson, 1991-; Kentucky Humanities Council, chairperson of bd of dirs, 1995; Boran Independent School System, bd of ed, 1991-, chairperson, 1992-94; Kentucky African Amer Heritage Commission, 1994-; Kentucky River Foothills Dev Corp, chair bd of dirs, 1994-. **Honors/Awds:** Hurt Faculty Achievment Award, Ferrum Coll 1976; James B St Award, Amer Hist, Berea Coll 1972. **Business Addr:** Dir of Black Cultural Center, Berea Coll, CPO 134, Berea, KY 40404.

BASKIN, YVONNE E.
Events planner. **Personal:** Born Mar 19, 1951, Birmingham, AL; daughter of Lois Sanderson Elem and Edward Elem (deceased); divorced 1989; children: Damien, Dana, Danielle. **Educ:** Stillman College, Tuscaloosa, AL, BA, 1973. **Career:** Greater Birmingham Convention and Visitors Bureau, Birmingham, AL, director of membership, 1977-89, 1989-91, director of tourism, 1977-89; EVENTions by VON, Birmingham, AL, president, 1990-. **Orgs:** Leadership Birmingham, 1990; Science Center Board; Community Relations Committee, Goals for Birmingham, 1989; Sister City Commission, City of Birmingham; Transportation Review Board, City of Birmingham; board of directors, Festival Arts, 1988; City of Birmingham Master Plan Committee, women's network, director of community affairs & development, city stages; Birmingham Southern College President's Advisory Council; board of directors, Academy of Fine Arts, 1989; Children's Hospital Foundation Guild; board of trustees, State of Alabama Ballet; National Forum for Black Public Administrators; Young Men's Business Club; Alabama Jazz Hall of Fame Board, 1989-90; Birmingham Area Council, Boy Scouts of America; Birmingham Repertory Theater Advisory Council; Birmingham Civil Rights Institute Public Relations Committee. **Honors/Awds:** PAT Award (Performance, Ability, and Teamwork), The Alabama Travel Council, 1984; Outstanding Career Accomplishments Nomination, Business and Professional Women's Club, 1987; Governor Guy Hunt's Alabama Reunion Award, 1989; Race Relations Award, Westminster Presbyterian Church, 1989; Meritorious Service Award, United Negro College Fund, 1989. **Business Addr:** President, EVENTions by VON, 920 Ninth Ct W, Birmingham, AL 35204-3427.

BASKINS, LEWIS C.
Business executive, dentist. **Personal:** Born Jul 16, 1932, Springfield, AR; married Amanda J; children: Duane, Brian, Kevin, Holli. **Educ:** AR AM & N Coll, BS 1956; Univ IL, DDS 1961. **Career:** Fuller Products Co, vice pres; Dentist. **Orgs:** Pres Chicago Chap AR AM & N Alumni; mem Amer, Chicago, Lincoln Dental Soc; Omega Psi Phi Frat; mem Mt Zion Bapt Ch. **Military Serv:** AUS sp3 1953-55. **Business Addr:** 6906 S Halsted St, Chicago, IL 60621.

BASRI, GIBOR BROITMAN
Educator, scientist. **Personal:** Born May 3, 1951, New York, NY; married Jessica. **Educ:** Stanford Univ, BS, 1973; Univ of CO, PhD 1979. **Career:** Univ of CO, rsch asst 1974-79; Univ CA, postdoctoral fellow 1979-82, asst prof 1982-88; Univ of California Berkeley, assoc prof 1988-94, prof, 1994-. **Orgs:** Mem Amer Astronomical Soc 1979; mem Intl Astronomical Union 1984; mem Astronomical Soc of the Pacific 1984. **Honors/Awds:** Chancellors Fellow Univ of CA 1979-81; several articles Astrophysical Journal 1979-. **Business Addr:** University of California, Astronomy Dept, Berkeley, CA 94720.

BASS, FLOYD L.
Educator. **Personal:** Born Aug 11, 1921, Sullivan, IN; married Hazel B Huddleston; children: Floyd L Jr, Eileen C, Marc C, Lisa C Ealum. **Educ:** Indiana State Univ, BS 1948, MS 1950; Univ of CO-Boulder, EdD 1960. **Career:** LeMoyne Coll, dean 1960-63; AL State Univ, dean 1963-64; CCNY, admin intern w/pres 1964-65; NC Central Univ, prof of educ 1965-68; The Univ of CT, prof of educ 1968-. **Orgs:** Dir The Ctr for Black Studies Univ of CT 1969-; pres Northeastern Chap CT Affiliate ADA 1982-84; pres Willimantic Rotary Club 1983-85; grand historian Grand Encampment Knights Templar 1985,87; pres CT Order of High Priesthood 1985,86; accreditation team mem NCATE 1983,84,85,86,87. **Honors/Awds:** Ellis L Phillips Fellow; UNCF Fellow; John Jay Whitney Fellow; Thirty third Degree United Supreme Council AASR Freemasonry PHA Inc 1987. **Military Serv:** USN 3rd class petty officer 1945-46.

BASS, HERBERT H.
Educator. **Personal:** Born Dec 26, 1929, Warsaw, NC; married Carrie L Ruff; children: Lori. **Educ:** Shaw Univ, BA 1955; Antioch Univ, MEd Counseling 1972; Union Grad, PhD 1980. **Career:** Supreme Liberty Life Co, insurance agent 1956; Philadelphia School Dist, teacher 1957; City of Philadelphia, gang control worker 1959; PA Dept of Public Assistance, social worker 1960; Philadelphia Dept of Welfare, recreation supvr 1960; Philadelphia School Dist, counselor speciall educ 1961; Leeds & Northrup Co, coord of counseling (indsl) 1968-. **Orgs:** Consult Provident Life Ins Co 1965; vice chmn/trustee New Bethlehem Bapt Ch 1960-; commr Boy Scouts of Amer 1963-; mem Council for Exceptional Children; mem NAACP; mem YMCA. **Business Addr:** Coordinator of Counseling, Leeds & Northrup Co, Sumneytown Pike, North Wales, PA 19454.

BASS, JOSEPH FRANK
Administrator. **Personal:** Born Jan 10, 1938, Phenix City, AL; married Jenean Brantley; children: Terence, Steven, Sandra. **Educ:** Hartnell Coll, AA 1958; Carnegie-Mellon Univ, Cert in Transp 1972; Univ of Santa Clara, Cert in Mgmt 1977. **Career:** City of Salinas, engineering draftsman, 1958; City of San Jose, civil engr, 1962, sr civil engr, 1967, prin civil engr/head of transp planning, 1975-, dir dept of traffic, 1980-. **Orgs:** Regis civil engr CA 1966; mem Inst of Traffic Engrs 1970; mem Amer Pub Works Assn 1975; regis traffic engr CA 1977; mem NAACP 1980; mem BlackCoalition of Local Govt Empl 1980; mem No CA Cncl of Black Professional Engrs 1980. **Honors/Awds:** Recip of Federal Grant to attend ''Professional Program in Urban Transp'' Carnegie-Mellon Univ 1972. **Business Addr:** Director, Dept of Traffic, City of San Jose, 801 N First St, San Jose, CA 95110.

BASS, KEVIN CHARLES
Professional baseball player. **Personal:** Born May 12, 1959, Redwood City, CA; married Elaine; children: Garrett Charles, April Brittany, Justin Charles. **Career:** Milwaukee Brewers, outfielder 1981-82; Houston Astros, outfielder 1982-89; San Francisco Giants, outfielder, 1990-94; Houston Astros, 1994-. **Honors/Awds:** Led the Astros in pinch hits in 1981 (13) and 1983 (11); National League All-Star Team, 1986; National League, record for switch hitters who have homered the most from both sides of the plate in one game, 1992; 4th in National League Hitting 311, 1986; 5th in National League Hits, 1986; finished 7th in the League in MVP voting that year, 1986. **Business Addr:** Profesional Baseball Player, Houston Astros, PO Box 288, Houston, TX 77001, (713)799-9500.

BASS, LEONARD CHANNING
Physician. **Personal:** Born Jul 23, 1941, Live Oak, FL; married Janet. **Educ:** Meharry Med Coll, MD 1966; Genessee Hosp, intern 1967. **Career:** Private Practice, physician 1969-. **Orgs:** Mem FL Med Dent & Pharm Assn; Nat Med Assn; FL Med Assn; Broward Co Med Assn; pres FL State Med Assn; mem Am Heart & Assn; vice pres 1976; Fla board of Medicine, 1982-86. **Honors/Awds:** Life mem, Alpha Phi Alpha Frat; Distinguished Serv Award Medical Dental & Pharmacy Assn, 1977; co-chmn, professional conf Amer Heart Assn 1976; one year, Vietnam Commendation Medal, USAF. **Military Serv:** USAF MC capt 1967-69. **Business Addr:** Physician, 2323 NW 19th St, Suite 3, Fort Lauderdale, FL 33311.

BASS, MARSHALL BRENT
Business executive. **Personal:** Born in Goldsboro, NC; son of Estella Bass and Marshall Bass; married Celestine Pate Bass; children: Brenda, Marsha. **Educ:** Univ of MD College Park, BS. **Career:** US Army, officer 1945-68; RJ Reynolds Tobacco Co, mgr personnel develop 1968-70; RJ Reynolds Industries, corporate mgr 1970-76, corporate dir 1976-82, vice pres 1982-; sr vice pres, 1986-91, RJR Nabisco, retired sr vp, 1991; Marshall B Bass & Associates, president, currently. **Orgs:** Bd of dirs Piedmont Federal Savings & Loan Assn; former mem Natl Comm on Working Women; former bd of dirs Winston-Salem/Forsyth Co YMCA; indus adv council Natl Newspaper Publishers Assn; bd of visitors NC Central Univ; chmn bd of dirs Winston-Salem State Univ Found; former mem bd of trustees NC A&T State Univ; mem Phi Beta Sigma Fraternity Inc; mem Gamma Kappa Boule Sigma Pi Phi; sr warden St Stephen's Episcopal Church; lay leader chalice bearer Episcopal Diocese of NC; Board of Trustees NAACP Spec Contribution Fund; chmn, bd of trustees St Augustines Coll, Raleigh; chmn Advisory Bd Consortuim, Graduate Studies in Management; bd of dirs Piedmont Triad Horizon; br of trustees, Vorhees College. **Honors/Awds:** Blackbook Natl Outstanding Business & Professional Award 1984; Several Honorary Degrees: Doctor of Civil Law, St Augustines Raleigh; Doctor of Humane Letters, Florida A&M Tallahasse FL; Doctor of Divinity, TN School of Religion, Detroit MI Division; LLD, Dr of Humane Letters, NC Central Univ, St Augustine Coll, Raleigh, NC, King Memorial Coll, Columbia, SC, Livingston Coll, Salisbury NC, Winston Salem State Univ. **Military Serv:** AUS chief of army promotions 23 yrs; Legion of Merit; 3 Commendation Medals; Purple Heart; Combat Infantryman's Badge. **Business Addr:** President, Marshall Bass & Assoc, 1324 Ashley Square, PO Box 24338, Winston-Salem, NC 27114-4538.

BASSARD, YVONNE BROOKS
Administrator. **Personal:** Born Oct 27, 1937, Oakland, CA; married Edward Lee Jr; children: Edward Lee Jr, Margot Denise Walton, Daryl Lamont, Alicia Yvonne. **Educ:** Patten Bible Coll, BS Theology 1973; St Stephens Coll, MA Health Sci 1975, PhD 1978. **Career:** Parks AFB Hosp, nurse 1956-57; Eden Hosp Castro Valley, CA, nurse 1960-62; St Rose Hosp Hayward, CA, nurse 1962-63; Patten Sch of Religion, sch nurse 1976-; Bassard Rehab Hosp, owner/adminst/nurse 1963-. **Orgs:** Mem Amer Coll of Nursing Home Adminstrs 1976-; mem Lic Voc Norses League 1977-; mem Consumer on Aging Comm CA Assn of Health Fac 1978-80; mem Smithsonian Inst. **Honors/Awds:** Heart Award Patten Bible Coll 1969. **Business Addr:** Administrator, Bassard Conval Hospital, Inc, 3269 D St, Hayward, CA 94541.

BASSETT, ANGELA
Actress. **Personal:** daugHter of Betty; married Courtney Vance, 1997. **Educ:** Yale University. **Career:** Actress; films include: City of Hope; Boyz N the Hood, 1992; Malcolm X, 1992; The Jacksons, 1992; Passion Fish; What's Love Got to Do With It?, 1993; Waiting to Exhale, 1995; Contact, 1997; How Stella Got Her Groove Back; plays include: Joe Turner's Come and Gone, Macbeth. **Business Addr:** Actress, c/o Ambrosio Mortimer, 165 West 46th, Ste 1214, New York, NY 10036, (212)719-1677.

BASSETT, DENNIS
Imaging company executive. **Personal:** Born Dec 12, 1947, Gary, IN; son of Ruby Bassett and Leonard Bassett Sr; married Carmen Johnson, Dec 30, 1969; children: Dennis LaShun, Dawn Lashae. **Educ:** Knoxville College, BA, English, 1970. **Career:** Eastman Kodak, Washington DC, sales mgr, 1980, Chicago IL, district sales mgr, 1982, Rochester NY, program director, worldwide training, 1985, 1st black staff assistant to sr vice pres, 1986, Mid Atlantic, regional sales mgr, 1987, Restructuring Project, project leader, 1989, director intercultural development programs, 1990-94; Bausch & Lomb Corp, regional director, 1994, vice president, field sales, conact lens division, 1995. **Orgs:** Network Northstar, Black Networking Org Ek, president, 1992; Kappa Alpha Psi, Rochester Chapter, board of directors. **Honors/Awds:** Kappa Alpha Psi, Alumni Chapter, Man of the Year, 1992. **Business Phone:** (716)338-8780.

BATAILLE, JACQUES ALBERT
Physician. **Personal:** Born Jul 11, 1926. **Educ:** Faculty Med Haiti, MD 1953. **Career:** Provident Hosp, jr asst 1955-56; Homer G Phillips Hosp, 1956-57; Cumberland Hosp, resd 1957-58; Albert Einstein Med Coll, 1958-59; Port-Au-Prince, private pract 1960-69; Muscatatuck State Hosp, staff physician 1971-73, med dir 1974; Private Practice, physician 1974-77; Sharon Gen Hosp, 1974-. **Orgs:** Mem AMA; NAACP; Shenango Valley C of C; Mercer Co Heart Assn; PA med Soc; mem Smithsonian Inst. **Honors/Awds:** Sharon Gen Hosp Continuing Educ Award AMA; Amer Citiz 1973. **Business Addr:** Sharon General Hospital, 755 Division, Sharon, PA 16146.

BATCHELOR, ASBURY COLLINS
Business executive. **Personal:** Born Nov 26, 1929, Leggett, NC; married William Ethel Stephen; children: Marlon Diane Whitehead. **Educ:** A&T Univ Greensboro, NC, attended 1954-56; NC Central Univ Durham, NC, attended 1957; AUS Intelligence Sch, grad 1958. **Career:** NC Mutual Life Ins Co, agent 1957-61, sales mgr 1961-80; Western Dist Union, dir of training 1970-; Rocky Mount Devel Corp, sec 1973-; NC Mutual Life InsCo, asst to agency dir 1980-. **Orgs:** Past chmn/treas Rocky Mount Opport Industrializ Cntr 1974-; mem Amer Legion Post #323 1965; chmn pub rel Big Brothers/Big Sisters 1978; mem Rocky Mount Rotary Club 1979. **Honors/Awds:** Man of the Year Award Mt Lebanon Masonic Lodge 1960; Staff Manager of the Year NC Mutual Life Ins Co 1963; Appreciation Award Coastal Plain Heart Fund Assn1968; Citation for Meritorious Serv Amer Legion Post #323 1979. **Military Serv:** AUS 1st Sgt 27 years; Good Conduct Medal 1953. **Business Addr:** Assist to Agency Dir, NC Mutual Life Ins Co, Mutual Plaza, Durham, NC 27701.

BATEMAN, CELESTE
Cultural affairs supervisor. **Personal:** Born Sep 1, 1956, Newark, NJ; daughter of Elma Thornton Bateman and William Bateman; married Carter Mangan, May 10, 1986; children: Jamil, Carter Jr. **Educ:** Rutgers Univ, BA 1978. **Career:** New Community Corp, Newark, NJ, program director, 1978-79; Port Authority of New York & New Jersey, secretary, 1981-84; The Newark Museum, Newark, NJ, program coordinator, 1984-87; City of Newark, Division of Recreation/Cultural Affairs, Newark, NJ, cultural affairs supervisor, 1987-97; Celeste Bateman & Associates, pres, currently. **Orgs:** Mem Alpha Psi Omega, 1978, Alpha Epsilon Rho, 1978; selection comm mem Newark Black Film Festival 1984-87; mem Friends of Newark Symphony Hall 1985-88; mem adv cncl Newark Symphony Hall 1987-89; ex-officio member Newark Festival of People; member, Arts for America 1987-96; board of directors, WBGO-FM Jazz Radio, 1989-95; member, Association of American Cultures, 1987-90 member, Association of Performing Arts Presenters 1984-87; board of directors, Newark Jazz Festival, 1991-; exec dir, Newark Arts Council, 1991; board mem, Governors School, NJ, 1991-92. **Business Addr:** Supervisor, Cultural Affairs, City of Newark, Division of Recreation/Cultural Affairs, 94 William St, 2nd Fl, Newark, NJ 07102, (201)733-4301.

BATEMAN, PAUL E.
Attorney. **Personal:** Born Feb 28, 1956, Highland Park, IL; son of Tyree & Joel Bateman; married Sylvia L Bateman, Aug 19, 1978; children: Paul Jr, Philip, Preston. **Educ:** Illinois State University, BS, 1976; University of Michigan, JD, 1980. **Career:** National Labor Relations Board, trial attorney, 1980-84; Friedman & Koven, associate, 1984-86; Sachnoff & Weaver, shareholder, 1986-93; Burke, Warren & MacKay, shareholder, 1993-. **Orgs:** American Bar Association, 1980-; University of Michigan Black Law Alumni, regional liasion, 1991-; Civic Federation of Chicago, advisory board, 1989-; Boy Scouts of America, cubmaster, 1992-. **Special Achievements:** Illinois Institute of Continuing Legal Education, Age Discrimination, 1996; Investigations, Testing & Privacy, 1990. **Business Addr:** Partner, Burke, Warren & MacKay, PC, 330 N Wabash, 22nd Fl, Chicago, IL 60611.

BATES, ALONZO W.
Association executive. **Personal:** Born Oct 7, 1939, Detroit, MI. **Educ:** Alabama State Univ, BS, 1964; Wayne State Univ, grad study. **Career:** Chrysler Corp, mgmt trainee, 1964-66, labor rel rep, 1966-68, training adv, 1968-70, prog analyst, 1971-72; Dept Corrections, prog analyst; Detroit Dept Parks & Recreation, dir, 1993-; Rainbow Commission for Fairness in Athletics, regional director, currently. **Orgs:** Chmn, Region 8 Bd of Educ; Central Bd of Educ, Detroit Public Schools; exec dir, Civil Rights, Southern Christian Leadership Conf; delegate, Natl School Bd conf; chmn of the bd, Detroit Chapter, Operation PUSH; Omega Psi Phi. **Honors/Awds:** Trophy, Eastlake Baptist Church, Operation PUSH; Certificate of Merit, NAACP. **Business Addr:** Regional Director, Rainbow Commission for Fairness in Athletics, 14320 Camden, Detroit, MI 48213.

BATES, ARTHUR VERDI
Attorney (retired). **Personal:** Born Jan 16, 1916, New Haven, CT; son of Beulah Hay Bates and Arthur D Bates; married Ruthann Brennan Bates (deceased); children: Jean, Arthur Jr. **Educ:** Lincoln U, BA 1937; Howard Univ Sch of Law, JD 1940; Brooklyn Law Sch, L LM 1956. **Career:** Private prct, atty 1948-67; The Legal Aid Scty, sr fmly law spclst retired 1986; currently, legal consultant to various orgs and comm groups; Musician, 1933-. **Orgs:** Vice Chairman of Bd, Brooklyn Legal Srvcs Corp, 1977-; cnsltnt Cntrl Brooklyn Coordng Cncl 1975-; pst pres Lincoln Civic Assn 1971-75. **Military Serv:** AUS, 1st lt, 4 1/2 yrs; Brnz Star Mdl, Cmbt Inf Bdg 1945.

BATES, BARBARA ANN
Fashion designer, business executive. **Personal:** chilDren: two sons. **Career:** Corporate secretary, until 1986; BAB Designs, founder, president, 1986-. **Special Achievements:** Has designed clothes for Oprah Winfrey, Hammer, Whitney Houston, the Winans, Isiah Thomas, and other celebrities. **Business Addr:** President, BAB Designs, 1130 S Wabash, Ste 401, Chicago, IL 60605, (312)427-0284.

BATES, CLAYTON WILSON, JR.
Educator. **Personal:** Born Sep 5, 1932, New York, NY; son of Arline Bates and Clayton Bates; married Priscilla Suzanne Baly; children: Katherine Arline, Christopher Thomas, Naomi Elizabeth. **Educ:** Manhattan Coll, BEE 1954; Brooklyn Polytech Inst, MEE 1956; Harvard Univ, ME 1960; Washington Univ, PhD Physics 1966. **Career:** RCA, elect engr 1955; Ford Inst Co, 1955; Sylvania, phys 1955-57; AVCO, phys 1960; Varian Assoc, sr rsch engr 1966-72; Princeton Univ, vstg fellow 1978-79; Stanford Univ, assoc prof 1972-77, prof 1977-. **Orgs:** Fellow Amer Physical Soc 1982; Optical Soc of Amer; sr mem IEEE 1980; AAAS, AAUP, Soc of Photo-Optical Instr Engrs, Sigma Xi, Eta Kappa Nu, Sigma Pi Sigma, Amer Ceramic Soc; chmn Affirm Action Comm of School of Engr Stanford Univ; fac adv Soc of Black Scientists & Engrs Stanford Univ; resident fellow Black Theme House Stanford Univ 1973-76; past mem bd of dir Jr Achievement; past mem Natl Acad of Sci Eval Panel; mem adv panel on metall & matls Natl Sci Found; vstg prof Univ of London 1968; professional model Demeter Agency San Francisco. **Honors/Awds:** Sabbatical Awd Varian Assoc 1968; publ 100 articles sci jrnls, 75 presentations sci meetings; Distinguished Engineer, Tau Beta Pi, 1976. **Business Addr:** Professor, Stanford Univ, Dept of Material Science, Peterson 550J, Stanford, CA 94305-2205.

BATES, DAISY
Publisher (retired), civil rights activist. **Personal:** marrled L. C. Bates (deceased). **Career:** Worked with underprivileged people in the Office of Economic Opportunity Training Prog; Arkansas State Press, past publisher/owner; published book, The Long Shadow of Little Rock, 1962. **Orgs:** NAACP, former state pres; Mitchllnille OEO Self Help Proj, founder. **Honors/Awds:** Univ of AR, honorary degree 1984; Washington Univ, honorary degree 1984; NAACP, Spingarn Medal 1958. **Business Addr:** 221 W 2nd St, Ste 608, Little Rock, AR 72201.

BATES, GEORGE ALBERT
Attorney, consultant, mediator. **Personal:** Born May 30, 1954, Charolttesville, VA; son of Otto L & Lucy H Bates. **Educ:** Princeton Univ, BA, 1976; Univ of VA, JD, 1980; Mediate Tech, Inc, General Mediation Cert, 1994. **Career:** Princeton Univ Food Service, asst mgr, 1972-76; Univ of VA, grad asst track coach, 1976-80; State Farm Ins Co, automobile liability underwriter, 1976-77; US Dept of Labor, law clerk-judge Roy P Smith, 1980-81; Univ of VA, assoc dean/off afro-amer affairs, 1987; General Counsel North Amer Van Lines, norcross trans, 1990-94; Law Office of George A Bates, sole proprietor, 1983-; EEO/Diversity consultant, mediator. **Orgs:** Alpha Phi Alpha Fraternity, 1977-; Central VA Minority Bus Assn, 1987-; Old Dominion Bar Assn, past bd mem, 1985-; Cooperative Extension Srvc Bd VA State Univ, 1985-; Albemarle Co, NAACP, 1981-; UVA Black Law Alumni Assn, president, 1985-96. **Honors/Awds:** Princeton Univ, Co-Captain Track Team, 1976; Track Team Keene-Fitzpatrick Award, 1975; Heptagonal Track Meet All-Ivy, Triple Jump, 1975; NJ State College Champion Triple Jump Winner, 1973-76; Univ of VA Office of Afro-Amer, Affairs Warrior Award, 1987; Saint Paul's College, Humanitarian Service Award, 1988; VA State Univ, Cooperative Extension Service, Humanitarian Service Award, 1987. **Special Achievements:** Started the Richard J Bates Scholarship Fund at Saint Paul's College in Lawrenceville, VA, 1988; Organized the first legal advocacy workshop for the Old Dominion Bar Assn, 1988; Organized the first Employment Law Seminar for the NAACP, 1993; Co-editor w/Prof Kenneth R Redden, "Punitive Damages" Michie Co, 1980; Journalist for five local newspapers & manuscript in progress on "The History of Bid Whist"; mem of the Ministerial Training Program, Charlottesville Church of Christ-Worldwide Bible Way, 1997. **Business Addr:** Attorney, Law Office of George A Bates, 644 Maxfield Rd., Keswick, VA 22947, (804)979-3260.

BATES, LIONEL RAY, SR.
Commercial diver. **Personal:** Born Oct 21, 1955, New Orleans, LA; married Karen M; children: Nicole M, Lionel R Jr. **Educ:** Commercial Dive Ctr, air/mixed gas 1979. **Career:** Anatole's Garage, auto mechanic 1965-78; Sub-Sea Intl, tender 1979-80, commercial diver. **Orgs:** Bible student & minister Inst Divine Metaphysical Rsch Inc 1980-. **Honors/Awds:** 1st Black to Graduate from Commercial Dive Ctr 1979; People & Places Ebony Magazine Jan 1984; 1st Black to do saturation diving to depth of 450 ft 1985. **Business Addr:** Subsea Intl, 131 S Robertson, New Orleans, LA 70112.

BATES, LOUISE REBECCA
Business executive. **Personal:** Born Sep 16, 1932, Cairo, IL. **Educ:** Wilson Jr Coll, AA 1957. **Career:** Gold Blatt Bros Inc, clerk, buyer 1952-75; Evans Inc, buyer 1976-77; Louise Bates Jewelry Store, pres, mgr, owner, currently. **Orgs:** Mem NAACP, Operation Breadbasket, Urban League, WTTW TV, United Negro Coll Fund; mem, pres Jr Hostess Council & Ed of newsletter USO; vol work Better Boys Found hostess Kup's Purple Heart Cruises; vol work & guest lectr Audy Juvenile Home Prog & Chicago Public School. **Honors/Awds:** Woman of the Day 1975; Citation of Merit in REcog of Outstanding Contrib to Comm WAIT Radio St; Cert of Leadership Hon Leadership of Women in Economic Cultural & Civic Life of the Metro Chicago Comm, YWCA of Chicago 1972; Nathan Awd for Outstanding Buyer of the Year Goldblatts 1975. **Business Addr:** President, Louise Bates Jewelry Store, 24 W Madison St, Chicago, IL 60602.

BATES, MARIO DONIEL
Professional football player. **Personal:** Born Jan 16, 1973, Tucson, AZ. **Educ:** Arizona State. **Career:** New Orleans Saints, running back, 1994-. **Business Addr:** Professional Football Player, New Orleans Saints, 5800 Airline Hwy, Metairie, LA 70003, (504)733-0255.

BATES, MICHAEL
Professional football player. **Personal:** Born Dec 19, 1969, Tucson, AZ; married Kethera. **Educ:** Arizona. **Career:** Seattle Seahawks, wide receiver, 1993-94; Cleveland Browns, 1995; Carolina Panthers, 1996-. **Honors/Awds:** Pro Bowl, 1996. **Business Addr:** Professional Football Player, Carolina Panthers, 800 Mint St, Ericsson Stadium, Charlotte, NC 28202, (704)358-7000.

BATES, NATHANIEL RUBIN
City Official. **Personal:** Born Sep 9, 1931, Cason, TX; son of Viola Hill; married Shirley Adams; children: Michael, Gale, Larry, Steven. **Educ:** San Francisco State Coll, BA 1963; CA State-Hayward, teachers certificate, 1975. **Career:** City of Richmond, councilman 1967-, mayor 1971-72, vice mayor 1975-76, mayor 1976-77, unit supervisor probation dept Alameda Co, beginning 1977-retired; State Senator Dan Boatwright, Contra Costa County, CA, field representative. **Orgs:** Pres E Bay Div League of CA Cities; vice chmn Human Resources Comm; chmn Contra Costa Co Mayors Conf; mem Richmond Port Auth 1976-, Richmond Housing Auth 1976-; Richmond Redevel Commn 1976-; mem bd of dir Natl League of Cities; bd of dir League of CA Cities; Black Probation & Parole Assn; Natl Black Elected Officials Adv Bd; mem Natl Council on Alcoholism for Contra Costa Co; Regional Council on Criminal Justice; Bay Area Sewage Serv Agency 1973-; mem adv bd Mt Diablo Cncl Boys Scouts of Amer, Camp Fire Girls, Richmond Boys Club; pres Richmond Democratic Club 1986-89; bd of dir El Sobrante Girls Club 1986-89; West County YMCA 1986-89; Salesian Boys Club 1986-87; mem, US Conference of Mayors, 1972-74; mem, Natl Black Conf League Elected Officials; mem, Citizen Civic Club. **Honors/Awds:** Father of the Year, Easter Hill Doris Cluster, 1988; Richmond Democratic Club Honors, 1990; Bethel Temple POA Church Honors, 1990; Resolution Honors, Senator Dan Boatwright, 1983, 1988, 1990; Resolution Honors, Assemblyman Bob Campbell, 1983, 1988, 1990. **Home Phone:** (510)222-1101. **Business Addr:** City Council Member, City of Richmond, City Hall, Richmond, CA 94804, (510)620-6513.

BATES, PERCY
Educator, educational administrator. **Personal:** Born Jul 8, 1932, Pensacola, FL; son of Gladys Travis Graves and Percy Bates; married Cheryl Proctor, Sep 12, 1962; children: Allison, Nathan. **Educ:** Central Michigan University, Mt Pleasant, MI, BS, 1958; Wayne State University, Detroit, MI, MA, 1961; University of Michigan, Ann Arbor, MI, PhD, 1968. **Career:** University of Michigan, Ann Arbor, MI, associate professor and chairperson, 1969-73, assistant dean, 1973-80; US Department of Education, Washington, DC, deputy assistant secretary/director, 1980-81; University of Michigan, Ann Arbor, MI, division director, 1984-87, professor, 1968-, director, 1987-. **Orgs:** Chair, National Alliance of Black School Educ; member, Technical Assistance to Parent Programs, 1986-; co-chair, TAPP Select Committee, 1986-; member, chair, Perry Nursery School, 1987-. **Honors/Awds:** President's Service Award, NABSE, 1983. **Military Serv:** US Army, Corporal, 1952-54. **Business Addr:** Director, Programs for Educational Opportunity, University of Michigan, 601 E University, 1005 School of Education, Ann Arbor, MI 48109-1259.

BATES, ROBERT E., JR.
Manufacturing manager. **Personal:** Born Oct 12, 1934, Washington, DC; son of Alice M Bates and Robert E Bates Sr; married Gracia M Hillman; children: Dawne E Bates Collier, Brandon R, Hillman M. **Educ:** Univ of IL, AB 1955. **Career:** US Census Bureau, statistician 1958-69; US Office of Economic Opportunity, mgmt info analyst 1967-69; Senator Edward Kennedy, legislative aide 1969-77; Mobil Oil Corp, mgr govt relations. **Orgs:** Bd mem United Black Fund; bd mem NAACP Energy Comm; bd mem Big Brothers of DC; mem NY Stock Exchange Fee Arbitration Bd; mem Amer Petroleum Inst; mem Chem Mfgrs Assn; Amer Assn of Blacks in Energy, bd of dirs. **Military Serv:** AUS 1st lt 1955-58.

BATES, VALENTINO TRAVIS
Company executive, engineer, cleric. **Personal:** Born May 6, 1955, Shreveport, LA; married Connie Denise Bates, Nov 24, 1979; children: Lateef Akin, Takesha Monique, Valencia Coniah, Janna Marlene. **Educ:** University of Missouri-Rolla, BSCE, 1976, MSCE, 1978. **Career:** Black & Veatch, engineer, 1974-77; CH2M Hill, design coordinator, 1978-86; Khafra Engineering Consultants, president, 1986-. **Orgs:** Chi Epsilon, president, 1976-; Tau Beta Pi, 1976-; Order of the Engineer, 1976-; Water Pollution Control Federation, 1976-; American Public Works Assn, 1986-; Alpha Epsilon Pi, 1976-77. **Honors/Awds:** Chi Npsilon, Outstanding Civil Engineering Student, 1976; Alpha Epsilon Pi, Outstanding Undergraduate, 1976, Knight of St Patrick, 1977; Rockhurst High School, "R" Award, 1973. **Special Achievements:** Founder, Khafra Engineering Consultants, 1986. **Business Phone:** (404)525-2120.

BATES, WILLIAM J.
Corporate architect. **Personal:** Born Oct 5, 1952, Canonsburg, PA; son of Laura Ethel Andersen Bates and George C Bates; married Margaret M McDermott, Oct 27, 1977; children: Meaghan A, Owen P, Nora K. **Educ:** Univ of Notre Dame, Notre Dame IN, BA 1975. **Career:** Shields Construction Co, Pittsburgh PA, designer, 1975; Celento & Edison Architects, Pittsburgh PA, intern architect, 1976, partner, 1978-84; Selck Minnerly Group, Inc, Pittsburgh, PA, project architect, 1976-78; Westinghouse Electric Corp, Pittsburgh PA, consultant, 1984-88, design mgr, 1988-93; PNC Bank, Pittsburgh PA, vice pres, 1993-95; Fore Systems Inc, Pittsburgh PA, director of real estate & facilities, 1995-. **Orgs:** Pres, Pittsburgh Architects Woskshop, 1980-85; mem, Partnerships in Educ Speakers Bureau, 1980; founder, Allegheny Trails Architectural Career Explorer Post, 1983; pres, Pittsburgh chapter Amer Inst of Architects, 1987; president, Pennsylvania Soc of Architects, 1991; chmn, Minority Resource Committee Amer Inst of Architects, 1990; mem, Allegheny County Airport Devel Commn, 1989-91; Leadership Pittsburgh, 1989; organizer of International Remaking Cities Conference, with HRH Prince Charles, UK, 1988. **Business Addr:** Director/Real Estate & Facilities, FORE Systems, Inc, 174 Thornhill Rd, Warrendale, PA 15086.

BATES, WILLIE EARL
Business executive. **Personal:** Born Feb 19, 1940, Shaw, MS; son of Magnolia Gossett Bates; married JoEllen; children: Roman Earl II, Patrice Simone. **Educ:** TN State Univ, BS 1963. **Career:** Universal Life Ins Co, salesman, asst mgr, dist mgr, asst vp, dir of ordinary marketing. **Orgs:** Mem Capital Investment Club, Met Bapt Church, Omega Psi Phi; chmn, bd of directors, Goodwill Boys Club, 1989-91; vice basileus, Omega Epsilon Phi Chapter, 1989-91; bd of directors, Junior Achievement, 1984-91. **Honors/Awds:** Manager of the Year 1968; Cox Trophy Natl Ins Assoc 1969; Omega Man of the Year, Omega Psi Phi, 1989. **Business Addr:** Director of Ordinary Marketing, Universal Life Insurance Co, 480 Linden Ave, Memphis, TN 38126.

BATES-PARKER, LINDA
Educator. **Personal:** Born Feb 23, 1944, Cincinnati, OH; married Breland K; children: Robbin, Brandon. **Educ:** Univ of Dayton, BS Eng 1965, grad teaching assistantship 1968; Univ of Cincinnati, MA English 1970. **Career:** Procter & Gamble, market research 1966-67; Shillito's Dept Store, training coord 1968-70; Univ of Cincinnati, head counselor, asst to dean 1970-75, asst to Vice Provost for Student Affairs 1975-76, assoc dir of career planning & placement 1975-81, assoc vice provost 1981-. **Orgs:** Pres consulting firm BCW Inc 1977-; bd mem Black Career Women's Resource Center 1983-; bd mem Cincinnati Local Devel Corp bd mem WCET Educ TV 1973-74; women's com Cincinnati Symphony Orch; mem Midwest Coll Placement Assn; past pres Jr Alliance for Soc/Civic Action; mem United Black Faculty & Staff Assn; mem Assn of Women Adminstrs; mem Middle Mgrs Assn; (UC) President's Commn on Domestic Affairs 1975; commentator OH Valley Kool Jazz Festival 1975; coord Professional Devel Sem for Black Women 1977; mem Cincinnati Charter Bd Com 1980-81; mem Mayor's Comm Relations Comm 1980; mem comm Chest Eval Comm 1980; hon mem Soc of Black Engineers 1980; mem Amer Personnel & Guidance Assn 1980-81; natl presentations APGA Atlanta/ACPA Boston/Coll Placement Counc; memACPA/AASPA Chicago. **Honors/Awds:** YWCA Career Woman of Achievement Award 1982; Women in Communications Advocate Award 1982; Cincinnati Enquirer Woman of the Year 1983; cover story Elancee Magazine Sept 1984; Ethelrie Harper Awd Cincinnati Human Relations Commn1984; Top 100 Black Business and Professional Women in Amer Dollars and Sense Magazine 1985. **Business Addr:** Associate Vice Provost, Univ of Cincinnati, Office of Vice Provost Student Affairs, Mail Code 159, Cincinnati, OH 45221.

BATH, PATRICIA E.
Physician, ophthalmologist. **Personal:** Born Nov 4, 1942, New York, NY. **Educ:** Hunter Coll NY, BA Chem 1964; Howard Univ Med Coll, MD 1968. **Career:** Sydenham Hosp of NYC, asst surg 1973; Flower & Fifth Ave Hosp NYC, asst surg 1973; Metro Surg NYC, asst surg 1973-74; NY Med Coll Dept of Ophthalmol, clinical instr 1973-74; UCLA Cntr for Health Sciences, asst attending 1974-; UCLA Sch of Med, assist prof opthal 1974-; Charles R Drew Postgrad Med Sch, asst prof of opthalmol 1974-, assist prof of surg 1974-; Martin L King Jr Gen Hosp LA, dir clin serv & asst chf Div of Ophthal 1974-; Univ of Nigeria Med Sch, visit prof surg 1976-; Jules Stein Eye Inst Dept Ophthal, prog dir ophthalmic asst 1977-; Charles R Drew Postgrad MedSch LA, asst prof dept of comm med intl health sect. **Orgs:** Consult & chf ophthalmol Mercy Hosp Abak, Nigeria 1977; White House consult Natl & Intl Blindness Prevention Prog USA 1977-78; consult & rapporteur Onchocerciasis Sect 1st Gen Assemb of the Intl Agency for Prev of Blindness Oxford 1978; consult & rapporteur Prim Eye Care Sect WHO Meeting on Tech & Operatnl Approaches to the Prevent of Blindness Asilomar 1978; consult Fed Drug Admin Ophthalmic Devices Panel 1979-; mem Med Soc of Co of NY; mem Amer Med Assn 1973-75; mem Natl Med Assn 1973-; mem Amer Soc of Contemp Ophthalmol 1974-; mem Amer Pub Health Assn 1975-; mem Intl Agency for the Preven of Blindness 1975-; mem Soc of Eye Surg Intl Eye Found 1976-; fellow Amer Coll of Surgeons 1976-; fellow Amer Acad of Ophthalmology & Otolaryngology 1976-;SciFound 1959. **Honors/Awds:** Scholarship Alpha Kappa Alpha Sor 1965; NIH Fellowship 1965; NIMH Fellowship 1965; NIMH Fellow 1966; Fellowship Dept of HEW Childrens' Bur 1967; NIH Fellowship Dept of Ophthal Howard Univ 1968; Outstanding Student in Endocrinology Dept med Howard Univ 1968; Outstanding Student in Pulmonary Diseases (Payne Laurey) Dept of Med 1968; Outstanding Student in Ophthalmology (Edwin J Watson) Prize Dept of Surg 1968; Med Educ for Natl Def Prize for Outstanding Comm Serv Poor People's Campaign Wash, DC 1968; many publns 7 scientific papers. **Business Addr:** Assistant Professor, Charles R Drew Postgrad Med Sc, 12021 S Wilmington Ave, Los Angeles, CA 90059.

BATHER, PAUL CHARLES
Elected official, businessman. **Personal:** Born Jun 30, 1947, Brooklyn, NY; son of Regina Bather and Charles Bather; married Coretta Waddell, Jun 7, 1969; children: Amir, Omar. **Educ:** Fairfield Univ, Fairfield CT, BA, 1968; City Univ of New York, New York NY, MSW, 1970; Univ of Louisville, Louisville KY, MBA, 1980. **Career:** Jefferson County, Louisville KY, treasurer, 1981-86; WJYL Radio, Louisville KY, gen mgr, 1986-88; gen partner, Louisville Communications, 1988-; limited partner, Louisville Radio, 1988-; The Bather Group, Louisville KY, pres, 1988-; City of Louisville, Louisville KY, alderman; Best Bet Magazine, Louisville, KY, pres; Bank of Louisville, vice pres, 1990-. **Orgs:** Chmn, Economic Devel Comm, chmn Affirmative Action Comm; mem bd of dir, Downtown Devel Corp; life mem, Louisville NAACP; mem, Louisville Chamber of Commerce. **Honors/Awds:** Eubank Tucker Award for Courage of Conviction, NAACP, 1984; Natl Alumnus of the Year, Amer Center for Intl Leadership, 1986; Outstanding Achievement, Kentucky Alliance Against Racism, 1988. **Business Addr:** Alderman, City of Louisville, 601 W Jefferson St, Louisville, KY 40202.

BATINE, RAFAEL
Attorney. **Personal:** Born Jul 20, 1947, Santurce, PR; married Patricia Estelle Pryde; children: Rafael Pablo. **Educ:** St John's Univ Coll Bus Admin, BS 1969; St John's Univ Sch of Law, JD 1974. **Career:** Westbury Pub Sch NY, math tchr, 1969-73; Covington Howard Hagood & Holland NY, law clerk, 1973-74; Queens Dist Attys Office, asst dist atty, 1974-75; Rutledge Holmes Willis Batine & Kellam NY, pvt law practice, 1975-78; Georgia Office of Fair Employment, gen counsel, 1978-79; US Dept of Labor, atty, sr trial atty, currently. **Orgs:** Admitted to practice law GA 1983, NY 1975, US Supreme Ct 1977. **Honors/Awds:** Martin Luther King Scholarship St John's Univ Sch of Law 1971-74. **Business Addr:** Senior Trial Attorney, US Department of Labor, Solicitor's Office, 1371 Peach Tree St NE, Atlanta, GA 30309.

BATISTE, EDNA E.
Registered nurse, health programs administrator (retired). **Personal:** Born Aug 28, 1931, Detroit, MI; daughter of LuWilla McDaniel Woody and James Woody; married Walter D Batiste (divorced); children: Lisa, Duane, Anthony. **Educ:** Wayne State Univ, BS 1955; Univ of MI, MPH 1972. **Career:** Detroit Dept Health, staff nurse 1954-63, suprv publ health nurse 1963-66, publ health nurse, dist suprv 1966-68, school health nursing consult 1968-70, asst dir, 1970-78, dir of family primary care div, 1978-93. **Orgs:** Mem Wayne State Coll Nursing Alumni, Univ of MI Alumni Assoc, Wayne State Univ Alumni, Chi Eta Phi, Delta Sigma Theta; NAACP; bd member, Detroit Cental City Community Mental Health Bd, 1985-90; bd mem Traveler's Aid Society 1990-92; bd mem Detroit Compact Project Taft School, 1990-93; Chi Eta Phi, chairman, Taft Middle School Careers Club; bd member Detroit ARC; bd member, Cerreguiers, Inc. **Honors/Awds:** Contemporary African-American Nurse, Chi Eta Phi Sorority, 1991; Received Key to the City of Detroit upon retirement; Spirit of Detroit Award; Chi Eta Phi Sorority, Honored Nurse Award.

BATISTE, KIM (KIMOTHY EMIL)
Professional baseball player. **Personal:** Born Mar 15, 1968, New Orleans, LA. **Career:** Philadelphia Phillies, professional baseball player, 1991-. **Business Addr:** Professional Baseball Player, Philadelphia Phillies, PO Box 7575, Philadelphia, PA 19101, (215)463-6000.

BATISTE, MARY VIRGINIA
Hairstylist, instructor. **Personal:** Born Jul 31, 1925, Alexandria, LA; children: Lela Virginia. **Educ:** US Small Business Assoc, Management 1971; Univ of CA at Los Angeles, Vocational 1975, Educ/Voc 1977; Natl Beauty Culturists League; DEduc 1980. **Career:** CA State Bd of Cosmetology, examiner (first black) 1960-68; LA Unified School Dist, teacher 1975-87; Pacific Coast State Cosmetology Assoc, pres 1984-87; Natl Beauty Culturists League, asst dir educ 1985-87; Los Angeles Community College, district teacher, 1975-; self-employed, state license notary public, 1991-. **Orgs:** Educ consultant Summit Laboratories Deluxal Lect 1963-71; owner-oper Batiste Hair Modules Chain LA 1962-87; mem Mayor Tom Bradley Commn on Youth & Aged 1977-79; basileus Alpha Lambda Chap Theta Nu Sigma Sor 1979-81; first woman mem trustee bd Lewis Metropolitan CME Church 1981-87; mem bd of dirs NBCL Natl Inst 1984-87. **Honors/Awds:** Madame CJ Walker NBCL Natl Awd 1978; Citation by State Assembly US Congress 1978; Woman of the Year Theta Nu Sigma Sor 1980; recipient of numerous first place trophies, awards, certificates, honors; Distinguished Service Award, Pacific Coast State Cosmetology Assn, 1988; Resolution-Outstanding Contribution-Achievements, Los Angeles County Board of Supervisors, 1989. **Home Addr:** 9246 So Hobart Blvd, Los Angeles, CA 90047.

BATSON, RUTH MARION
Foundation executive, educator. **Personal:** Born in Boston, MA; daughter of Cassandra Watson and Joel Watson; children: Cassandra Way, Susan, Dorothy Owusu. **Educ:** Boston Univ Psychology Dept, 1967; Univ MA Amherst, Masters Degree Candidate, 1972-73; Boston Univ School Educ, MEd 1976. **Career:** Commonwealth of MA, commr MA comm against discrimination 1963-66; Metro Council for Educ Opportunity, asst dir & ex dir 1966-70; BU Sch of Med Div of Psychiatry, dir consultant & ex 1970-75, dir school desegregation rsch project 1975-81, coordinator clinical task force 1981-; BU Sch of Med Div of Psychiatry, assoc prof 1986; Museum of Afro Amer History, pres and dir, 1987-90; founder, tres, Ruth M Batson Educational Foundation. **Orgs:** Bd mem New Englnd T V Corp 1978-; edtrl bd & mem WNEV-TV Ch 7 1978-; bd trustees MA General Hospital 1979-, Boston City Hospital 1970-76, Citizens Training Grp Boston Juvenile Court 1979-; mem corp MA General Hospital 1979-; co-chairperson NAACP Natl Convention, 1982; life mem exec bd NE Reg Conf NAACP; co-chair Natl Adv Comm Documentary Series Eyes on the Prize 1985-; mem, bd of trustees, Tougaloo Coll. **Honors/Awds:** Appreciation Citation, Boston Branch NAACP 1982; M L King Awrd M L King Memorial Breakfast 1981; M Cass Black Achievement Award Black Achievers 1979; Woman 76 Awd Boston YWCA, 1976; Comm Contribution Citation Prince Hall Grand Lodge Boston 1976; Action for Boston Comm Devel Award 1985; Outstanding Commitment to Higher Educ Roxbury North Dorchester Area Planning Action Council Inc 1986; Visionary Leadership Wellesley Met Co Program, 1986; Honorary Degrees: Simmons Coll, Salem State & Bridge Water State Coll, Williams Coll, Northeastern Univ; Anne Roe Award, Harvard Univ School of Educ, 1990. **Home Addr:** 250 Cambridge St, Apt 701, Boston, MA 02114.

BATTEAST, MARGARET W. **See Obituaries section.**

BATTEAST, ROBERT V.
Business executive. **Personal:** Born 1931, Rosetta, MS. **Educ:** IN Univ, attended. **Career:** South Bend Devel Corp, vp; Batteast Constr Co Inc, pres. **Orgs:** Dir 1st South Bank. **Business Addr:** President, Batteast Construction Co Inc, 430 LaSalle Ave, South Bend, IN 46617.

BATTEN, GRACE RUTH
Clergywoman. **Personal:** Born Mar 22, 1943, Harbeson, DE; children: Earl William Jr. **Educ:** Delaware Tech & Comm Coll, AAS 1976; Burke Bible Coll, BTh 1977; Wilmington Coll, BS 1986. **Career:** Adult Educ Satellite Prog, administrator 1979-; Natl Youth Conf, educ chairperson 1980-84; Mt Sinai Farm Develop Comm, chairperson 1985-87; Mount Zion Holy Church Inc, pastor/president admin, currently; Mt Zion Bible Institute, Milton, DE, founder, dir, 1988-. **Orgs:** Life mem Natl Council of Negro Women 1977-; bd mem Delaware Assoc of A&C Educ 1982-; councilwoman/sec Milton Town Council (first black) 1982-; mem Amer Soc of Notaries 1985-; vice chairperson Sussex Co Red Cross 1985-; mem Natl Assoc for Female Execs 1986-; bd mem People Place II Counciling Ctr 1986-; 1st black vice mayor, Milton Town Council, 1991-. **Honors/Awds:** Big Sister of the Year Sussex Co Branch of BB/BS 1981; Outstanding Citizen Awd Milton Chamber of Commerce 1983; Certificate of Appreciation Vica of Sussex Voc Tech Ctr 1986. **Home Addr:** 111 Orchard St, Milton, DE 19968. **Business Addr:** Pastor/President Admin, Mount Zion Holy Church Inc, 325 Front St, Milton, DE 19968.

BATTEN, TONY
Director, producer. **Personal:** Born in New York, NY; son of Olga Batten and Edward Batten. **Educ:** City College of NY, attended 1954-57; Univ of Xalapa Mexico, attended 1960-61; San Francisco Art Inst, attended 1961-62; San Francisco State Coll, BA 1967; Univ of CA, Berkeley, attended 1967-68. **Career:**

Freelance photographer: Liberator, Trans-Action, San Francisco Magazine, Ramparts, Bohemia Magazine, NY Times-Sun Magazine, Washington Post, Wilson Library Bulletin 1961-69; films for TV: E Africa Ends & Beginning 1969; Black Journal, mng editor 1968-70; Minnesota Fats 1968; Karate Discipline & Dance 1967; The Toughest Labor Game in Town 1971; Bedlam in the Jails, special reports 1970; Ch 2 News, prod 1970-71; The 51st State, reporter 1971-73; Who Runs Newark? 1971; Ain't Gonna Eat My Mind 1972; The 1st Natl Black Political Convention 1973; Interface, exec prod & host 1974-76; A Prof of Paul Robeson 1975; Eubie Blake Long As You Live 1975; Guilty Until Proven Innocent 1975; Crisis in Paradise 1974; Bad Times on Gold Mountain 1974; ABC News Closeup 1977-79; T Batten Prod, pres/ceo, 1970-; Commerical, Documentary and Industrial Films, producer, director, 1970-95. **Orgs:** Chmn, NE Reg Natl Assn of Black Media Prod 1969; NY Acad of TV Arts & Science; Intl Center for Photo; Dir Guild of Amer; Amer Fed of TV & Radio Artists; Writers Guild of Amer. **Honors/Awds:** Awarded Emmy, Ain't Gonna Eat My Mind 1972; 1st prize, Documentary Black Filmmakers Hall of Fame 1976; 1st prize, Documentary Natl Assn of Black Media Women 1976; included in permanent collections NY Schomburg Collection of Negro Arts & Letters 1976; Intl Center for Photo 1976; Columbia Univ School of Journalism, Dupont Award 1972, 1978 for ABC News Closeup "New Religions, Holiness or Heresy". **Business Addr:** President, Tony Batten Production, 409 Edgecombe Ave, New York, NY 10032.

BATTIE, TONY (DEMETRIUS ANTONIO)
Professional basketball player. **Personal:** Born Feb 11, 1976. **Educ:** Texas Tech. **Career:** Denver Nuggets, center-forward, 1997-. **Business Addr:** Professional Basketball Player, Denver Nuggets, 1635 Clay St, Denver, CO 80204, (303)893-6700.

BATTIES, PAUL TERRY
Physician. **Personal:** Born Jul 22, 1941, Indianapolis, IN. **Educ:** IN Univ, AB 1962; IN Sch of Med, MD 1965. **Career:** Detroit General Hosp, internship, 1965-66; Wayne State Univ, resident internal med, 1966-69, chief med resident, 1969; Univ of KY Cardiology Fellowship, 1971-73; physician private practice. **Orgs:** Association of Black Cardiologists, founding mem, 1974, board of directors, 1983-87; Marion Co Heart Association, past bod; Hypertension Comm, past chmn; Kappa Alpha Psi Frat, mem; Univ United Meth Ch; Indiana Society of Int Med, pres, 1990; American Heart Association; American Med Association; Aesculapian Med Society, pres, 1982-84; IN State Med Assn; NAACP, life mem. **Honors/Awds:** Elected to Fellowship in American College of Cardiology, 1995; Distinguished Citizens Awd, IN, 1976; 2 Cardiac Transplant Patients. **Military Serv:** USAF Maj 1969-71. **Business Addr:** 1633 N Capitol Ave, Ste 510, Indianapolis, IN 46202.

BATTISTE, AUDREY ELAYNE QUICK
Librarian, administrator. **Personal:** Born Aug 24, 1944, Norfolk, VA; daughter of Geneva Shokes Quick and Oscar S Quick Jr; married Eugene Wilson Tyler (divorced 1986); married Auggeretto Battiste. **Educ:** South Carolina State Univ, Orangeburg, SC, BS, 1965; John Carroll University, Cleveland Heights, OH, 1965-66; University of Oklahoma, Norman, OK, 1965; Atlanta University, Atlanta, GA, MSLS, 1968. **Career:** Department of Welfare, Bronx, NY, caseworker, 1966-67; Bristol Myers Research Labs, E Syracuse, NY, librarian, 1968-70; Atlanta Public Library, Atlanta, GA, librarian, 1972-74; South Carolina State College, Orangeburg, SC, instructor, 1975; Atlanta-Fulton Public Library, Atlanta, GA, library administrator, 1977-90; Fulton County Superior Court, Atlanta, GA, project dir, 1990-97; Library Human Resources, Atlanta-Fulton Public Library, mgr, 1997-. **Orgs:** Natl pres 1989-93, national vp 1986-89, South Carolina State Univ Natl Alumni Assn; pres, bd of dirs, Atlanta Council for International Programs, 1987-89; treas, bd of dirs, ACIP, 1985-87; chair, nominations committee 1985-90, chair, prof development committee 1984-86, Black Caucus ALA; Board of Directors, South Carolina State University Education Foundation, 1989-; African-American Family History Association. **Honors/Awds:** Bulldog Award, SCSU Alumni Association. **Home Addr:** 1421 S Gordon St SW, Atlanta, GA 30310. **Business Addr:** Manager, Library Human Resources, Atlanta-Fulton Public Library, 1 Margaret Mitchell Sq, SW, Atlanta, GA 30303.

BATTLE, BERNARD J., SR.
Savings & loan executive. **Personal:** Born Jun 26, 1927, Memphis, TN; son of Lenora Tolbert Battle and Lewis Battle (deceased); married Corinne Stewart Battle, Nov 4, 1985; children: Maureen B Prillerman, Aaron S Battle, B J Battle, Jr, Edwin L Battle, Michelle T Battle. **Educ:** Pioneer Inst, Philadelphia PA, diploma, 1951; A & T State Univ, Greensboro NC, Advance (Special); Guilford Coll, Greensboro NC; Amer Savings & Loan League, certificate Mgmt Training, 1972. **Career:** Palmer Memorial Inst, Sedalia NC, business mgr, 1951-62; Amer Federal Savings & Loan Assn, Greensboro NC, CEO/pres, 1962-. **Orgs:** Treasurer, 1962-84, pres, 1984-88, NAACP, Greensboro branch; treasurer, NAACP, State Conf, 1963-84; asst treasurer, NAACP, Natl Office, 1979-85; mem, NAACP bd of dir, 1982-88; pres, mem exec comm, Greensboro Citizens Assn, 1964-; mem, Greensboro Political Action Comm, 1965-; former vice chmn Greensboro War Memorial Coliseum Commn, 1979-88. **Honors/Awds:** Serv Award, NC State NAACP, 1972; Serv Award, Greensboro Branch NAACP, 1972; Man of the Year, Region V NAACP, 1976; Man of the Year, Greensboro Young Men's Club, 1976; certificate, Youth Service Corp, Greensboro Branch, 1984; Man of the Year, Greensboro Branch NAACP, 1989; Welterweight (amateur) Boxing Champion, Middle-Eastern Serv Conf while in US Army, Fort Meyers VA, 1987. **Military Serv:** AUS, seargent, 1945-48; Marksman Medal, Peace Medal.

BATTLE, CHARLES E.
Business executive. **Personal:** Born Aug 26, 1953, Shreveport, LA; married Sharon; children: Keisha L, Freadda C, Christin' Elisha, John M, Mikayla D. **Educ:** CO Univ, 1970-71; Grambling, 1971-74; Coll for Financial Planning, 1982-83. **Career:** John Hancock Life Ins Co, ins agent 1975-76; Profesco of CO, owner 1977-82; Battle & Co Financial Planner, owner 1983-. **Orgs:** Mem NALU, CALU, DALU 1976-, ICFP 1982-; comm head CAMU 1982-; mem IAFP 1983-; bd mem Aurora Mental Health 1983-. **Business Addr:** President, Battle & Company, 6825 Tennessee Ave. #600, Denver, CO 80224-1606, (303)377-3909.

BATTLE, GLORIA JEAN
County government official. **Personal:** Born May 23, 1950, Deerfield Beach, FL; daughter of Joyce Thompson-Battle and Eugene Battle. **Educ:** Bennett Coll, Greensboro NC, BA, 1972; Howard Univ, Washington DC, MUS, 1976; Florida State Univ, Tallahassee FL, 1985-. **Career:** Social Systems Intervention, Washington DC, research analyst, 1973-76; Mark Battle Assoc, Washington DC, consultant, 1976; Child Advocacy Inc, Ft Lauderdale, FL, planner, 1977-79; Florida International Univ, Miami FL, dir, 1979-80; Broward County Govt, Ft Lauderdale FL, dir human relations div, 1981-. **Orgs:** Pres, Natl Assn of Human Rights Workers, 1981-, pres Deerfield Child Devel Center, 1981-82; first vice pres, NAACP, North Broward Chapter, 1984-85; mem, Intl Assn of Human Rights Officials, 1981-; mem, Community Housing Resource Bd, 1983-86; mem Forum for Black Public Admin, 1984-. **Honors/Awds:** Davison-Foreman Scholarship, Bennett Coll, 1971; NIMH Fellowship, NIMH, Howard Univ, 1973; McKnight Fellowship, McKnight Found, 1985; Global Woman of the 80s, Charmettes, 1987; Liberty Bell Award, Broward County Bar Assn, 1989. **Business Addr:** Dir, Broward County Human Rights Div, 115 S Andrews Ave, A 640, Fort Lauderdale, FL 33301.

BATTLE, JACQUELINE
Mortgage banker. **Personal:** Born Sep 7, 1962, Columbus, GA; daughter of Myrtis Mahone Porter; married Gregory Battle, Nov 26, 1982; children: Gregory II, James. **Educ:** Columbus College, Columbus, GA, 1980-82; Tuskegee Institute, Tuskegee, AL, 1983-84. **Career:** Atlantic Mortgage, Columbus, GA, loan officer, 1983-84; First American South, Columbus, GA, manager, 1984-85; Money Express, Columbus, GA, president, 1985-. **Orgs:** American Business Women's Association; Coordinator of Business Women's Commission; clerk, Seventh-day Adventist Church; director, Children of Praise. **Honors/Awds:** Future Leader of America, Ebony Magazine, Nov 1989; leader of teen support group; Million Dollar Club member. **Business Addr:** President, Money Express Inc, 2310 N Lumpkin Rd, Columbus, GA 31903.

BATTLE, JOE TURNER
Elected government official. **Personal:** Born Aug 25, 1941, Atlanta, TX; married Barbara L; children: Joe D, Kim C. **Educ:** Dept of Defense Race Relations Inst, Cert 1975; CA State Univ Dominguez Hill, BS Bus Admin 1985. **Career:** Officer Training School Ft Sill, staff instr 1967-68; Schweinfurt Germany, equal oppty ed nco 1975-77; Lynnwood Unified School Dist, pres school bd mem 1983-85. **Orgs:** Chairperson, mem Lynnwood School Site Council 1980; mem Lynnwood USD Adv Council 1980-81; mem South Central Area Adv Council Catholic Youth Org 1981-85; pta legislative rep Lynwood PTA Council 1983-84; mem Cerritos Area Trustees Assoc 1981-85. **Military Serv:** AUS sgt 1st class; 21 yrs; Bronze Star, Meritorious Serv Medal, Combat Infantry Badge, 3 Commend Medals, 5 Campaign Stars Vietnam, Vietnam Cross Galantry. **Business Addr:** School Board Member, Lynwood Unified Sch Dist, 11331 Plaza, Lynwood, CA 90262.

BATTLE, JOHN SIDNEY
Professional basketball player. **Personal:** Born Nov 9, 1962, Washington, DC; married Regina Belle; children: Sydni Milan, Tiy, Jayln. **Educ:** Rutgers Univ, New Brunswick, NJ, 1981-85. **Career:** Guard: Atlanta Hawks, 1985-91, Cleveland Cavaliers, 1991-. **Business Addr:** Professional Basketball Player, Cleveland Cavaliers, Gund Arena, One Center Ct, Cleveland, OH 44115.

BATTLE, KATHLEEN
Opera singer. **Personal:** Born Aug 13, 1948, Portsmouth, OH. **Educ:** University of Cincinnati College-Conservatory, BA, 1970, MA, 1971. **Career:** Made professional debut at the invitation of Thomas Schippens appearing in Brahms "Requium" at Cincinnati May Festival, 1972; regular guest soprano with orchestras in New York, Chicago, Boston, Philadelphia, Cleveland, Paris and Be rlin and at major opera houses including the Metropolitan, Paris, Vienna and the Royal Opera/Covent Garden; has appeared in major festivals, including Festival of Two Worlds, Spoleto, Italy. **Honors/Awds:** Honorary doctorate degrees, Westminster Choir Coll, Coll Conservatory of Music Univ of Cincinnati, 1983; Natl Achievement Scholarship; numerous awards and Grammy nominations, including one for Salzburg Recital; Natl Coalition of 100 Black Women, Candace Award, 1992. **Business Addr:** Opera Singer, c/o Herbert Breslin Agency, 119 W 57th St, New York, NY 10019.

BATTLE, MARK G.
Association executive, educator. **Personal:** Born Jul 28, 1924, Bridgeton, NJ; son of Mary Noble Battle (deceased) and Edward M. Battle (deceased); children: Erica, Kewana, Marcus. **Educ:** Univ of Rochester, BA 1948; Case Western Reserve, MSSA 1950; Kings Pt Federal Exec Inst, Certificate, Federal Program Mgmt, 1966. **Career:** Lower North Center, Chicago, 1952-60; Franklin Settlement, Detroit MI, exec dir 1960-64; Bureau of Work Training Program USDOL, admin 1964-69; Mark Battle Assoc, chm bd dir 1969-83; Howard Univ School of Social Work, prof & chmn 1971-85; Natl Assn of Social Workers, exec dir 1984-92; University of Maryland at Baltimore, visiting professor currently. **Orgs:** Mem House of Delegates CSWE; mem Amer Soc of Public Admin 1968-; Amer Public Welfare Assn 1975-85; Natl Urban League 20 yrs; mem bd dir Washington Council Agency 1981-85; life mem Natl Conf Social Welfare; National Non-Profit Risk Mgmt Inst Bd, 1990; Council of Intl Programs, bd of directors; admin Bureau of Work Traing Programs, USDOL 1964-69. **Honors/Awds:** James M Yard Brotherhood Award NCCJ 1957; Distinguished Alumni Award Case Western Reserve SASS 1986; The Presidents Award NASW 1989. **Military Serv:** USNR amm 3/C; USN V12 midshipman 1943-46. **Home Addr:** 10604 Woodbine Rd, Beltsville, MD 20705. **Business Addr:** Visiting Professor, University of Maryland at Baltimore, 525 W Redwood St, Baltimore, MD 21201.

BATTLE, MAURICE TAZWELL
Church administrator. **Personal:** Born Aug 7, 1927, Oberlin, OH; son of Anne Evelyn McClellan Battle and Turner R Battle; married Esther Coleman Battle, Jun 7, 1948; children: Carla M, Maurice T Jr, Renee E, Michael C. **Educ:** Oakwood College, Huntsville Al, BA, 1948; Union Theological Seminary, Birmingham, AL, LLD, 1974. **Career:** Sierra Leone Mission of Seventh-day Adventists, Sierra Leone, West Africa, president, 1958-59; West African Union of Seventh-day Adventists, Accra, Ghana, West Africa, departmental director, 1959-66; Northern European Division of Seventh-day Aventists, Watford, Herts, England, departmental director, 1966-70; General Conference of Seventh-day Adventists, Washington, DC, assoc dept director, 1970-75; Afro-Mideast Division of Seventh-day Adventists, Beirut, Lebanon, secretary, 1975-77; General Conference of Seventh-day Adventists, Silver Spring, MD, associate secretary, 1977-. **Orgs:** Member of board of directors, Rotary Club of Silver Spring, 1988-; treasurer, Rotary Club of Silver Spring, 1990-. **Honors/Awds:** Special Award for Service to Humanity (in Africa); Author, Your Friends the Adventists, 1960. **Business Addr:** Associate Secretary, Secretariat, General Conference of Seventh-day Adventists, 12501 Old Columbia Pike, Silver Spring, MD 20904.

BATTLE, THOMAS CORNELL
Librarian, administrator. **Personal:** Born Mar 19, 1946, Washington, DC; son of Lenora Thomas Battle and Thomas Oscar Battle; divorced; children: Brima Omar, Idrissa Saville, Mensah Lukman. **Educ:** Howard Univ, BA 1969; Univ of MD, MLS 1971; George Washington Univ, PhD 1982. **Career:** Fed City Coll, Sr Media Intern 1969-71; DC Public Library, readers advisor 1971; MSRC, ref librarian 1972-74; Sierra Leone Lib Bd, exchange librarian 1972-73; Howard Univ, Moorland Spingarn Rsch Ctr, curator of manuscripts 1974-86, dir 1986-. **Orgs:** Councillor-at-large 1980-83, treas 1983-85; African Amer Museum Assoc; bd mem museum of the City of Washington 1978, 1981-90; chair task force on minorities Soc of Amer Archivists 1982-86; bd mem Washington DC Natl History Day 1983-85; exec bd Black Caucus of the Amer Library Assn 1980-92; chair nominating comm, chair, African & Caribbean Task Force Black Caucus of the Amer Library Assn 1980-82; bd mem DC Library Assn 1978-80; consul Natl Park Serv 1983-85; mem Amer Library Assn; mem Mid-Atlantic Regional Archives Conf; field reviewer & panelist Natl Endowment for the Humanities 1976-; bylaws comm Metro Washington Caucus of Black Librarians 1982-83; prog comm 1986, nominating comm 1987 Mid-Atlantic Regional Archives Conf; prog comm Soc of Amer Archivists 1987. **Honors/Awds:** Title IIB Higher Educ Act Fellowship 1970-71; Beta Phi Mu Iota Chap 1971; Certified Archivist, Academy of Certified Archivists, 1989; author of: "Howard University: Heritage and Horizons," Academic Affairs Bulletin, Howard University, v. 2, no. 1, February 1977; "Research Centers Document the Black Experience," History News, February 1981; "Behind the Marble Mask," The Wilson Quarterly, New Year's 1989. **Business Addr:** Dir, Moorland-Spingarn Research Center, Howard University, 500 Howard Place NW, Washington, DC 20059.

BATTLE, TURNER CHARLES, III
Association administrator, educator. **Personal:** Born Mar 13, 1926, Oberlin, OH; son of Annie Evelyn McClellan and Turner Battle; married Carmen H Gonzalez Castellanos; children: Anne E McAndrew, Turner IV, Conchita, Carmen. **Educ:** Oakwood Coll, BA 1950; Temple Univ, MFA 1958; Columbia Univ, 1960; New York Univ, 1970; Columbia Pacific Univ, 1984; Wiley Coll, HHD, 1986. **Career:** Oakwood Coll, instructor 1946-50; US Navy Dept, auditor/acct 1950-55; Philadelphia School Dist, teacher 1955-66; Elmira Coll, asst prof 1966-68; Moore Coll of Art, assoc prof 1968-71; La Salle Coll, dir of special programs, 1969; Higher Educ Coalition, exec dir 1969-71; NYU, assoc prof 1970-72; Westmnstr Choir Coll, assoc prof 1971-74; United Negro Coll Fund, Inc, asst exec dir, corp sec, 1974-94; Educational Development Service, pres, currently. **Orgs:** Oakwood Coll Alumni Assn; Temple Univ Alumni Assn; visiting comm of educ Metro Museum of Art; mem Amer Soc of Assoc Exec, Sierra Club, Amer Museum of Natl History, Smithsonian Inst, Amer Assn Higher Educ; Phi Delta Kappa. **Home Addr:** 175 Adams St, Apt 7G, Brooklyn, NY 11201. **Business Addr:** President, Educational Development Service, 1519 W Turner St, Allentown, PA 18102.

BAUDUIT, HAROLD S.
Attorney. **Personal:** Born Aug 27, 1930, New Orleans, LA; children: Lianne, Cheryl. **Educ:** US Naval Acad, BS Engrg 1956; Univ of CO, MA Economics, MS Mgmt, JD Law. **Career:** Univ of CO, atty faculty, 1972-76, instr bus law 1969-76, Economics & Black Studies, assistant professor law practice, 1983-. **Honors/Awds:** Sigma Iota Epsilon Hon Mgmt Frat Univ CO 1969-72; Martin Luther King Jr Fellow; Woodrow Wilson Natl Fellowship Found 1969-71. **Military Serv:** USAF capt retired 1956-69.

BAUGH, EDNA Y.
Attorney. **Personal:** Born Aug 22, 1948, Orange, NJ; daughter of George W & Pauline E Baugh. **Educ:** Hartwick Coll, BA, 1970; Vermont Law School, JD, 1983. **Career:** City of East Orange, corp trial counsel, 1986-94; Medvin & Elberg, attorney, 1988-. **Orgs:** Natl Bar Assn, 1986-; Garden State Bar Assn, 1986-; Essex-Newark Legal Services, bd secy, 1993-; Girl Scout Council of Greater Essex and Hudson Counties, 1986-, pres, 1995-; Essex County College Board of Trustees, 1997-. **Honors/Awds:** Vermont Law School, Alumni Assn Award, 1983; Hartwick Coll, Outstanding Alumna Award, 1993. **Business Addr:** Attorney, Medvin & Elberg, 1 Gateway Center, Newark, NJ 07102, (201)642-1300.

BAUGH, FLORENCE ELLEN
Agency administrator. **Personal:** Born Feb 2, 1935, Beaver Dam, KY; daughter of Glendora Fant Birch and William C Jackson; married Dallas A Baugh, Aug 31, 1953 (deceased); children: Delandria, Dallas, Christopher, Orville, Lynne. **Educ:** Millard Fillmore Coll at SUNY, BA; Empire State College. **Career:** Comm Action Org, Erie Co, comm aide 1965-70; YWCA, dir racial justice public affairs 1971-72; Comm Action Org, Erie Co, dir, neighborhood servs dept 1972-, New Venture Housing Inc, manager, 1990-. **Orgs:** Trustee Sheehan Mem Emer Hosp 1974-86, D'Youville Coll 1979-; Buffalo Bd Educ 1973-89; dir pres Ellicott Houses Inc 1978-; Univ Buffalo CAC 1982-; bd mem We NY Art Inst 1981-, Cncl of Grt City Sch Bds, sec treasurer 1978-89; Governor's appointee to 4th Dist Judicial Review Comm; Providence Bapt Church, organist, clerk, trustee; Pres, Council of Great City Schools, 1988-89; president, State University of Buffalo CAC; board member, EPIC; Erie County Department of Social Services Advisory Board, commissioner, 1991; Concerned Citizens Against Violence Coalition, 1991; Irene Bellamy Scholarship Fund, co-chair, 1986-; National Black Child Development Institute, 1989-; National Caucus & Center on Black Aged, Inc, 1990-; National Museum of Women in the Arts, 1991-; State University of Buffalo Community Advisory Council, 1989-91; EPIC National Board of Directors, 1989-92; Certified Housing Counselor, 1995; Certified Community Action Professional, 1995; Villa Marie College, board of trustees, 1995; City of Buffalo, Enterprise Zone, appointed by Mayor Masiello, board of directors, 1995. **Honors/Awds:** Afro-American Policeman's Assn Comm Serv Award, 1972; Buffalo Chapter Negro Business & Professional Women Comm Serv Award 1973; Black Educators Assoc Educ Serv Awd 1974; Citizen of Yr Buffalo Evening News 1975; Natl Org PUSH, Woman of the Year 1975; Buffalo Urban League Family Life Award 1976; Pres Distinguisheed Medal, Buffalo St Teacher Coll 1978; Univ Alumni Award Univ of Buffalo 1982; Natl Conf of Christians & Jews Educ Award 1982; Medal of Excellence, NY State Univ, Bd of Regents 1984; Week of the Young Child, honorary chmn; Delta Kappa Gamma, Vernie Mulholland Friend of Ed Award 1986; St Univ Syst of NY St, Distinguished citizen awd 1986; Empire State Fed of Women's Clubs Comm Serv Award; honorary doctorate degrees: Canisius College, 1976; Medaille College, 1989; YMCA Community Service Award, 1989. **Special Achievements:** Appointed by Governor Cuomo to New York State School & Business Alliance, 1986-; Conducted numerous Training Sessions as Representative of the State CSBG for New York Board of Directors; Conducted Training Seminar for State of South Carolina Department of Social Services; Conducted Training Seminar for Little Rock, Arkansas Public School Parents; Participated as a Member of the Long Range Committee for People Inc, 1990; Canisius College Sports Committee; Appointed by the Honorable Michael A Telesca, Chief Judge, United States District Court, to the Merit Selection Committee to interview and recommend a candidate for the position of US Magistrate Judge for the Western District of New York, 1994. **Home Addr:** 45 Woodward Ave, Buffalo, NY 14214. **Business Addr:** Director, Neighborhood Service, Community Action Organization of Erie County Inc, 70 Harvard Pl, Buffalo, NY 14209.

BAUGH, JOYCE A.
Educator. **Personal:** Born Jul 19, 1959, Charleston, SC; daughter of Ella Jones Baugh and Jeff Baugh; married Roger D Hatch, Nov 23, 1989. **Educ:** Clemson University, Clemson, SC, BA, 1981; Kent State University, Kent, OH, MA, 1983, PhD, 1989. **Career:** Kent State University, Kent, OH, grad asst, 1982-83, teaching fellow, 1984-88; Central Michigan University, Mt Pleasant, MI, asst prof, 1988-94; assoc prof, 1994-; chairperson, Dept of Political Science, 1995-. **Orgs:** Member, secretary, Women's Aid Service, 1990-; secretary, Midwest Women's Caucus for Political Science, 1990-91; member, Affirmative Action Council, Central Michigan University, 1990-95; Affirmative Action Council, co-chair, 1992-94; Central Michigan University Faculty Association, board of directors, 1991-95. **Honors/Awds:** Harry S Truman Scholarship, Truman Foundation, 4 year scholarship, 1979. **Home Addr:** 414 S Arnold, Mount Pleasant, MI 48858, (517)773-2589. **Business Addr:** Associate Professor & Chairperson, Central Michigan University, Department of Political Science, Anspach Hall 247, Mount Pleasant, MI 48859, (517)774-3442.

BAUGH, LYNNETTE
Utilities company executive. **Personal:** Born Feb 22, 1949, Charleston, WV. **Educ:** West Virginia State Coll, BA, 1971; Univ of Pittsburgh, MPA, 1972. **Career:** City of Chicago Pub Works Dept, planning analyst, 1973-74; Illinois Dept of Local Govt Affairs, area rep, 1974-76; Illinois Dept of Local Govt Affairs, area supr, 1976-77; Tacoma Intergovtl Affairs Office, dir, 1977; City of Tacoma Comm Devel Dept, asst dir, 1978-; Dept of Public Utilities, mgmt analyst, 1984-89, asst dir, customer finance and administrative services, 1989-. **Orgs:** Mem Title 9 Sex Equity Adv Com 1978-81; bd mem Pierce Co Growth Policy Assn 1977-81; exec com & Vice Pres NAHRO Puget Sound Chap of NAHRO 1979-81; bd mem Tacom Urban League 1978-82; mem NAACP 1978-; mem, vice pres Tacoma Alumnae Chap Delta Sigma Theta Sor 1979-81; mem Delta Sigma Theta Sor 1968-; mem Altrusa Intl 1981-, Kiwannianne 1984-86, APPA Committee on Performance Management, Women in Govt 1984-89, Accounting Advisory Comm; member Tacoma Rotary Club 1990-; vice chairman 1989-91, chairman 1991-93, APPA Performance Management Com. **Honors/Awds:** RK Mellon Fellowship 1972; named Washington Potential Black Leader for the 1980's Northwest Conf of Black Pub Officials. **Business Addr:** Assistant Director, CFAS, Tacoma Public Utilities, PO Box 11007, Tacoma, WA 98411.

BAULDOCK, GERALD
Chemical engineer, author, publisher. **Personal:** Born Aug 5, 1957, Trenton, NJ; son of Ora Bauldock and Dalbert Bauldock. **Educ:** Bucknell Univ, Lewisburg, PA, BS, chemical engineering, 1979; Villanova Univ, Philadelphia, PA, MS, chemical engineering, 1986. **Career:** Rohm & Haas, Bristol, PA, process engineer, 1979-90; B-Dock Press, Willingboro, NJ, president, currently; Sybron Chemicals, Birmingham, NJ, senior process engineer, currently. **Honors/Awds:** Achievement Award, Optimist Club of Philadelphia, 1990; Achievement Award, Business Women of Atlantic City, 1990; Villanova University, The Carl T Humphrey Memorial Award, 1992. **Business Addr:** President, B-Dock Press, Box 8, Willingboro, NJ 08046.

BAUTISTA, DANNY
Professional baseball player. **Personal:** Born May 24, 1972, Santo Domingo, Dominican Republic. **Career:** Detroit Tigers, outfielder, 1993-96; Atlanta Braves, 1996-. **Business Addr:** Professional Baseball Player, Atlanta Braves, 521 Capitol Ave SW, Atlanta, GA 30312, (404)522-7630.

BAXTER, ALBERT JAMES, II
Government official, attorney. **Personal:** Born Jun 22, 1935, Marshall, TX. **Educ:** TN State Univ, BA 1956; TX So Univ, MA 1963, JD 1966; Attended, Univ of Denver Sch of Law, Univ of Madrid. **Career:** TX Southern Univ, instructor; FCC, attorney 1966-69, atty-advisor 1970-72, legal asst Comm Benjamin L Hooks 1972-76, asst chief cable TV bureau 1976-82; MA Media Bureau, 1982-85; Communications Consultant, 1985-. **Orgs:** Mem ABA, Fed Bar Assn, TX Bar Assn, DC Bar Assn; mem Omega Psi Phi Frat; Sigma Rho Sigma; Cedar Lane Theatre Group; part-time interior design consultant, Jarmon & Baxter. **Honors/Awds:** Amer Law Student Assn Silver Medal 1966; winner of 3 Amer Jurisprudence Awds; starring roles "In White America", "The Fire Bugs". **Military Serv:** USAF 1956-60.

BAXTER, BELGIUM NATHAN. **See Obituaries section.**

BAXTER, CHARLES F., JR.
Physician. **Personal:** Born Apr 23, 1959, Brooklyn, NY; son of Bernice Kinand Baxter and Charles F Baxter Sr. **Educ:** City College of NY, BS Chemistry 1981; Meharry Medical Coll, MD 1986. **Career:** Coll of Physicians & Surgeons of Columbia Univ, assoc fellow of surgery 1986-; Columbia Univ Coll of Physicians and Surgeons, surgical resident; Harlem Hospital Ctr, surgical resident, 1986-92; Sloan-Kettering Memorial Hospital, New York, NY, surgical president oncology, 1989; McHarry Medical College, visting instructor, dept of anatomy, 1990; Portsmouth Naval Hospital, staff general surgeon, 1990-94; USS George Washington, ship surgeon, 1992-94; United States Naval Hospital, Yokosuka, Japan, staff general surgeon, 1995-. **Orgs:** Mem Amer Medical Assoc, Amer Chem Soc, The New York Acad of Sciences; Association of Military Surgeons for the United States; American College of Surgeons, Candidate Group; Medical Society of New York State; American Association of Clinical Chemists; National Naval Officers Association; National Naval Institute. **Honors/Awds:** Minority Biomedical Studies Program CUNY Grant NIH 1979-81; Baskerville Chemistry Awd City Coll of New York 1981; Navy Commendation Medal, 1994. **Military Serv:** Navy, Medical Corp, LCDR, 1990-. **Business Addr:** Staff General Surgeon, USNH-Yokosuka, PSC 475, Box 1882, Yokosuka 96350-1620, Japan.

BAXTER, FREDERICK DENARD
Professional football player. **Personal:** Born Jun 14, 1971, Brundidge, AL. **Educ:** Auburn. **Career:** New York Jets, tight end, 1993-. **Business Addr:** Professional Football Player, New York Jets, 1000 Fulton Ave, Hempstead, NY 11550, (516)560-8100.

BAXTER, WENDY MARIE
Judge. **Personal:** Born Jul 25, 1952, Detroit, MI; married David Ford Cartwright Jr; children: Samantha. **Educ:** Eastern MI Univ, BBA 1973; Univ of Detroit School of Law, JD 1978. **Career:** General Motors, oil lease analyst 1977; Wayne Cty Criminal Bond, investigator 1978; Recorder's Court, court docket admin 1979; State Appellate Defender's Office, attny 1980; Private practice, attny 1982; 36th Dist Court, judge; Recorder's Court, Detroit, judge, currently. **Orgs:** Bd of dirs, Wolverine Bar Assn, 1981; attorney, private practice, beginning 1982; judge 36th Dist Court; rules & forms committeewoman, Dist Judges Assn, 1982; 7th dist program dir, Natl Assn of Women Judges, 1985; life mem, NAACP; Natl Bar Assn; MI Assn of Black Judges; State Bar of MI; Jim Dandies Ski Club. **Honors/Awds:** Spirit of Detroit Detroit City Council 1981; Adoptive Parent Detroit Public School 1985. **Business Addr:** Judge, Recorder's Court, 1441 St Antoine, Detroit, MI 48226.

BAYE, LAWRENCE JAMES J.
Educator. **Personal:** Born Oct 10, 1933, Houston, TX; son of Bernice Margrett Navy and Frank Claude Baye; children: Elizabeth Lenoa, Ursula Frances. **Educ:** TX So U, BS, 1956, MS 1957; Univ of TX Austin, PhD Chem 1963; University of Tx, Austin, Post Dctrl Rsrch 1964; Univ of TN Knoxville, Post Dctrl Rsrch 1966. **Career:** TX Southern Univ Houston, asst prof Chemistry 1961-64; Knoxville Coll TN, assc prof dept head Chemistry 1964-67; Huston-Tillotson Coll Austin, TX, prof Chemistry 1967-. **Orgs:** Am Chem Scty; Scty of Sigma Xi; Beta Kappa Chi; Natl Org Prof Adv of Black Chemsts/Chem Eng 1980-; Blck Ctzns Task Force 1978-; Phi Beta Sigma Frat 1955-. **Honors/Awds:** Rcpnt Robt A Welch Fndtn Rsrch Grnts; author 14 pblctns in Jour Am Chem Soc & other Major Chem Jrnls 1956-; NASA Grant for Fluorocarbon Polymer Research, 1995-97. **Business Addr:** Professor of Chemistry, Huston-Tillotson Coll, 900 Chicon St, Austin, TX 78702, (512)505-3109.

BAYLESS, PAUL CLIFTON
Educational administrator. **Personal:** Born Nov 25, 1935, West Mansfield, OH. **Educ:** OH State Univ Coll of Engrg, BIE (summa cum laude) 1966; OH State Univ, MSc 1970; Purdue Univ, post grad work. **Career:** Purdue Univ, facilities planning analyst 1966-74, assoc coord for space 1974-78, dir affirmative action 1978-. **Orgs:** Bd dirs Capsulated Systems Inc Yellow Springs OH 1974-; chmn Intl Assn 1975-77; facilities consult JF Blakesley & Assoc; mem Amer Assn for Advancement Sci 1977-; mem, 1977-, pres, 1988-90 Amer Assn for Affirmative Action; mem Natl Tech Assn 1978-; Phi Eta Sigma; OH State Univ 1955; Alpha Pi Mu (Indus Engr Hon) OH State Univ 1965; Tau Beta Pi (Engr Hon) OH State Univ 1966; Phi Kappa Phi Purdue Univ 1973. **Military Serv:** USNG capt 1957-66.

BAYLOR, DON EDWARD
Professional baseball manager. **Personal:** Born Jun 28, 1949, Austin, TX; son of Lillian Brown Baylor and George Baylor; married Rebecca Giles Baylor, Dec 12, 1987; children: Don Jr. **Educ:** Miami Dade Junior College; Blinn Junior College. **Career:** Baltimore Orioles, 1970-75; Oakland A's, 1976; California Angels, 1977-82; New York Yankees, 1983-85; Boston Red Sox 1986-87; Minnesota Twins, 1987; Oakland A's, 1988; Milwaukee Brewers, hitting coach, 1990-91; St Louis Cardinals, hitting coach, 1992; Colorado Rockies, manager, 1993-. **Orgs:** Raised money for Cystic Fibrosis Foundation, 1979-. **Honors/Awds:** Sporting News Minor League Player of the Year, 1970; America League Most Valuable Player and the Sporting News

Player of the Year, 1979 three-time mem of The Sporting New American League Silver Slugger Team; mem, 1979 American League All-Star team; Roberto Clemente Award (presented to "the player who best exemplifies the game of baseball on and off the field"), 1985; American League career record for being hit by a pitch (267 times) and the American League career record for being hit by a pitch the most times in a single season (35); career totals of 338 homeruns, 1,276 RBI's and 285 stolen bases; played in seven American League Championship Series and holds LCS record for most consecutive game with at least one hit (12); played in World Series in his final three seasons with Boston, 1986; Minnesota, 1987; aOakland, 1988, hitting .385 and a homerun in the 1987 series to help the Twins win the World Championship; Baseball Writers of America, National League Manager of the Year, 1995. **Special Achievements:** Don Baylor, Nothing But the Truth: A Baseball Life, with Claire Smith, 1989. **Business Addr:** General Manager, Colorado Rockies, Coors Field, 2001 Blake St, Denver, CO 80205.

BAYLOR, ELGIN
Athletic administrator. **Personal:** Born Sep 1934; married Elaine; children: Krystle. **Educ:** Idaho, attended; Seattle Univ, attended. **Career:** Minneapolis Lakers, player 1958; New Orleans Jazz, asst coach 1974-77, coach 1978-79; Los Angeles Clippers, exec vp & gen mgr 1986-. **Honors/Awds:** NBA's seventh all-time leading scorer; Rookie of the Year 1959; Co-MVP of the All-Star Game; Holds number of records for the most points scored in championship series, most field goals, most points in one half; Seventh Highest single-game point total in NBA History; mem Basketball Hall of Fame 1976. **Business Addr:** Executive VP & General Manager, Los Angeles Clippers, Los Angeles Memorial Sports Arena, 3939 S Figueroa St, Los Angeles, CA 90037.

BAYLOR, EMMETT ROBERT, JR.
City official. **Personal:** Born Oct 18, 1933, New York, NY; son of Emmett and Lilliam Baylor (both deceased); married Margaret, Mar 1, 1937; children: Kathryn R, Gladys E, Emmett R III, Steven G. **Educ:** Wayne County Community College, public administration; Mercy College, public adiminstration, 1991. **Career:** Maidenform Inc, sales representative, 1963-75; Metropolitan Life Insurance, representative, 1975-79; City of Detroit, director of Detroit house of correction, 1977-85; Michigan Department of Corrections, warden/deputy warden, 1985-93; City of Detroit, executive assistant to the Mayor, currently. **Orgs:** Wardens & Superintendents of North America, 1985-93; American Correctional Association, 1985-93; American Jail Association, 1985-93; Michigan Correctional Association, 1985-93; Detroit Chapter, TransAfrica, 1970-; Founder Society, Detroit Institute of Arts, 1970-; NAACP; The Association, 1968-. **Honors/Awds:** Corinthian Baptist Church, Unsung Hero in Community, 1994; MDL 21 Visionaries and Architect Award, 1993; Michigan Correctional Prison Manangement Leadership Award, 1991; St. Scholatica/Benedictine High School, Dedication Award, 1983; Metropolitan Life Insurance, Outstanding Accomplishment, 1976. **Home Phone:** (313)835-1154. **Business Addr:** Executive Assistant to the Mayor/Director, Public Safety, City of Detroit, 2 Woodward Avenue, 1126 City County Building, Detroit, MI 48226, (313)224-3465.

BAYLOR, MARGARET
City official. **Career:** 36th District Court, magistrate, currently. **Business Addr:** Magistrate, 36th District Court, 421 Madison Ave, Detroit, MI 48226, (313)965-5025.

BAYLOR, SOLOMON
Judge (retired). **Personal:** Born Apr 25, 1922, King William, VA; son of Ida Baylor and John Baylor; married Dr Ernestein Walker; children: Michael J, Michelle J Miles. **Educ:** Coppin St Coll, 1939-42; Univ of MD, LLB 1951; Natl Judicial Coll, Cert 1977 & 1979. **Career:** Mayor & City Council, asst city solicitor 1963-67, bd municipal & zoning appeals 1968-70; State of MD, judge dist ct 1970-78; Sup Bench of Baltimore City, assoc judge, 1978-86; US District Court for Maryland, land commissioner; Baltimore City Community Relations Commission, hearing officer. **Orgs:** Mem Natl Bar Assn; mem Monumental City Bar Assn; mem MD State Bar Assn; mem Engrg Soc of Baltimore Inc; mem Citizens Plan & Housing Assn; golden heritage, life member, NAACP. **Honors/Awds:** Cert of Recogn Sunday Sch Bapt Training Union of MD; Cert of Recogn of Serv Enon Bapt Ch; Cert Greater Univ of MD Fund; Citation of Recogn Baltimore Area Counc Boy Scouts of Amer; Golden Heritage Citation NAACP; Citation Minority Scholarship & Leadership Guild Univ of MD for Outstanding Contribution Commitment & Generous Support 1986; Salute from Centennial United Methodist Church 1986. **Military Serv:** AUS Corpl 1943-46; Good Conduct Medal WWII Victory Ribbon Battle of Normandy 1943-46; Citation 272nd Quartermaster Battalion & 4086 Quartermaster Co Vets for Unselfish Dedication & Devotion 1983.

BAYNE, HENRY G.
Microbiologist (retired), Episcopal priest. **Personal:** Born Dec 2, 1925, New York, NY; son of Muriel Undine Walke and Henry Godwin Bayne; married Gloria Loftin; children: Steven, Lisa, Gordon. **Educ:** Brooklyn Coll, BA 1949, MA 1954. **Career:** Fellow in Biology, 1951-53; Brooklyn Coll, sanitarian 1953-55; New York City Dept of Health, bacteriologist 1955; St Mark's Episcopal Ch, assoc pastor 1963-95; Mission of the Holy Spirit Episcopal Ch, vicar 1968-82; Western Regional Rsch Ctr Agr Rsch Serv, rsch microbiologist 1955-87; St Augustine's Episcopal Church, Oakland, CA, interim pastor, 1989-90; St Cyrian's Episcopal Church, San Francisco, CA, interim rector, 1990-91; St John's Episcopal Church, Montclair, interim pastor, 1992; St Cuthbert's Episcopal Church, interim rector, 1994-95; St John's Episcopal Church, interim rector, 1996; All Soul's Parish, Berkeley CA, associate, 1996-. **Orgs:** Standing Com Diocese of CA 1978-82, pres 1981-82; chmn Epis Diocese of CA Comm on Interracial & Ethnic Affairs 1977-79; mem Amer Soc for Microbiology; Amer Soc of Plant Physiologists; AAAS; mem Alpha Phi Omega; Episcopal Conf of the Deaf; bd mem, E Bay Counseling & Referral Agency for Deaf 1969-72; bd mem St Dorothy's Rest Assn 1966-70; mem bd Alzheimer's Disease and Related Disorders 1982-85; Diocese of California, secretary of convention, 1992-; standing committee, Diocese of CA, 1995-. **Honors/Awds:** Harold Ramger Awd E Bay Counseling Agency for the Deaf 1973. **Military Serv:** US Army, 1944-46. **Business Addr:** Pastoral Associate, All Soul's Episcopal Church, 2220 Cedar St, Berkeley, CA 94709.

BAZIL, RONALD
Educator. **Personal:** Born Mar 10, 1937, Brooklyn; married Bonnie; children: Lance, Tami. **Educ:** Springfield Coll, BS 1958; Brooklyn Coll, MS 1964. **Career:** United States Military Acad, coach; Adelphi Univ, dir of intercoll athel 1972-; assoc dean of students 1970-72; dean of mem 1969-70; asst dean of student 1968-69; Health Educ, teacher 1959-68. **Orgs:** Mem exec council ECAC; pres exec council ICA; mem Concerned Cit of Westbury; NCAA Men's & Women's Track and Field Committee, 1994. **Honors/Awds:** Indoor coach of yr USTFF 1974; Cross Country Coach of the Year, Dist II, 1993. **Military Serv:** US Army, reserve sp4, 1958-63. **Business Addr:** United States Military Acad, ODIA, West Point, NY 10996.

BAZILE, LEO
Public administrator. **Career:** Council District 7, Oakland, CA, council member. **Business Addr:** 1 City Hall Plaza, Oakland, CA 94612.

BEACH, MICHAEL
Actor. **Personal:** marrIed Tracey; children: four. **Career:** Actor, currently. **Special Achievements:** Appeared in: Streets of Gold, 1986; Lean On Me; One False Move; White Man's Burden; Waiting to Exhale, 1995; A Family Thing, 1996; Soul Food, 1997; "ER," recurring character, currently.

BEACH, WALTER G., II
Business executive. **Personal:** Born Jul 23, Cataula, GA; married Marian C; children: Pennie, Pamela, Walter III, Bradford. **Educ:** Univ of WI, BS Educ 1975; Marquette Univ Law Colloquium 1974-75; Univ of WI Law Sch, addtl studies. **Career:** Restaurant owner, 1963-64; news director; spec agent insurance; acting asst mgr dept store; Channel 18 (TV), news reporter 1974; WAWA AM & FM Radio, news & pub affairs dir. **Orgs:** Past pres local NAACP; chmn State Polit Action; pres/founder The New Image Concept Inc; pres Criminal Justice Assn Univ of WI; mem chmn NAACP; mem State Police Examining Bd;TV producer/v chmn Soc of Black Drama Heritage Inc; co-founder Com of Twenty-One; managing ed Harambee Newspaper; adv mgr Milwaukee Torch Newspaper; feature writer Echo Mag; mem steering com Model Cities; mem Midtown Kiwanis Club; Sickle Cell Anemia Found. **Honors/Awds:** Man of the Year 1971; Youth Image Maker 1973; Congress Award 1974. **Military Serv:** US Army; USN; Natl Guard. **Business Addr:** News & Public Affairs Dir, WAWA AM & FM Radio, PO Box 2385, Milwaukee, WI 53212.

BEACHEM, CONSTANCE
Librarian, educator. **Personal:** Born Jul 16, 1921, Washington, DC; children: Novert, Wimberly, William Wimberly, Ellen McKee, Emmanuel Humphries, Lincoln Beachem, Connie J. **Educ:** AZ State Univ, BA 1964, MA 1966. **Career:** Phoenix Elementary School Dist, librarian 1964-. **Orgs:** Exec com AZ Educ Assn 1975-; bd dir NEA 1979-82; comm const NEA By-laws-Rules 1979-84; mem AZ Educ Assn 1962-; mem Alpha Kappa Sor; mem NAACP; pres Cath Family & Comm Serv Diocese Phoenix 1978-80; mem Human Devel Counsel; dep registrar AZ Libr Assn. **Business Addr:** Librarian, Dunbar School, 125 E Lincoln St, Phoenix, AZ 85004-2539.

BEADY, CHARLES H., JR.
Educational administrator. **Career:** Piney Woods Country Life School, pres, currently. **Special Achievements:** President of one of six historically black boarding schools remaining in US.

BEAL, BERNARD
Investment banker. **Educ:** Carleton College; Stanford University School of Business, MBA. **Career:** Shearson Lehman Hutton Inc, Municipal and Corporate Finance Division, senior vice president; MR Beal & Co, owner, founder, 1988-. **Special Achievements:** Listed as one of 25 "Hottest Blacks on Wall Street" and company ranked third on BE Investment Bank list, Black Enterprise, 1992. **Business Addr:** Owner, M R Beal & Co, 565 5th Ave, Apt 8, New York, NY 10017-2424, (212)983-3930.

BEAL, JACQUELINE JEAN
Banker. **Personal:** Born Mar 6, 1960, Jamaica, NY; divorced. **Educ:** DePaul Univ, BS 1982. **Career:** Amer Natl Bank, office occupations student 1977-78; The Northern Trust Co, inroads intern 1978-82, sr mktg rep 1981-84, financial serv officer/territorial mgr 1985-. **Orgs:** Grad chap mem Delta Sigma Theta Sor 1982-; policy setting bd mem Alumni Rep Inroads Inc 1983-87; mem Chicago Urban Bankers Assoc 1987-, Chicago League of Black Women 1987-; alumna Inroads Alumni Assoc 1987-; bd representative, Natl Inroads Alumni Assn. **Honors/Awds:** Inroads Alumni Period Awd Inroads Inc 1985; Chicago's Up and Coming Black Business & Professional Women Awd Dollars & Sense magazine 1986. **Business Addr:** Second Vice President, Cash Management Sales, Northern Trust Company, 125 S Wacker, Chicago, IL 60675.

BEAL, LISA SUZANNE
Trade association executive. **Personal:** Born Sep 2, 1963, Paris, France; daughter of Francis Yates & James Thomas Beal. **Educ:** Hampton University, BS, 1987. **Career:** Geo Recource Consultants, info specialist, 1990-92; Amer Trucking Assn, environmental specialist, 1992-95; Hazardous Waste Mgmt Assn, mgr, transportation & safety, 1995-96; Interstate Natural Gas Assn of Amer, dir of environmental affairs, 1996-. **Business Addr:** Director, Interstate Natural Gas Association of America, 10 G St NE, Ste 700, Washington, DC 20004, (202)216-5935.

BEAL BAGNERIS, MICHELE CHRISTINE (MICHELE BAGNERIS)
Attorney. **Personal:** Born Mar 7, 1959, Los Angeles, CA; daughter of Rohelia Beal and M Meredith Beal; married Jules S Bagneris III, Aug 30, 1986; children: Monet Christine, Jules S IV, Mariana. **Educ:** Stanford University, AB, 1980; Boalt Hall School of Law, University California, Berkeley, JD, 1983. **Career:** City of Monrovia, CA, city attorney, 1992-; Richards Watson & Gershon, attorney, 1983-92, partner, 1992-. **Orgs:** San Fernando Legal Services Corp, board mem, 1989-; LA City Attorney's Criminal Justice Panel, 1991-; Langston Bar Association; Black Women Lawyers of Los Angeles; State Bar Committee on Human Rights, 1987-90; Los Angeles Urban League Board of Directors, assistant secretary, 1985-91; AME Church, S California Conference Women's Missionary Society, director of missionary education, 1992-93. **Special Achievements:** Stanford University, international political economy participant, 1979. **Business Addr:** Richards, Watson & Gershon, 333 S Hope St, 38th Fl, Los Angeles, CA 90071, (213)626-8484.

BEAMON, ARTHUR LEON
Attorney. **Personal:** Born Aug 21, 1942, Stantonsburg, NC; son of Sidney I & Pauline N Beamon; divorced; children: Tanika J, Alexis L. **Educ:** US Air Force Academy, BS, 1965; George Washington University, MA, 1970; University of Chicago Law School, JD, 1972; Harvard University Prog of Instruction for Lawyers, Cert, 1981. **Career:** FDIC, atty, 1972-78, sr atty, 1978-80, counsel, 1980-84, asst gen counsel, 1984-89, assoc gen counsel, 1989-. **Orgs:** Tuckerman Station Condominium Assn, elected bd mem, treas, 1996-; Ad Hoc Homeowners Assn Comm, rep, 1997-; Saint Mark Presbyterian Church, outreach comm; District of Columbia Bar Assn; Maryland Bar Assn; National Bar Assn. **Honors/Awds:** Sustained Superior Performance Awards, 1980-97; Annual Performance Bonus Awards, 1989-97.

BEAMON, ROBERT A.
Communications company executive. **Personal:** Born Aug 1946, New York, NY; son of Naomi Brown Beamon; married Milana Walter Beamon, 1994; children: Deanna. **Educ:** Adelphi University, BS, Cultural Anthropology, 1972. **Career:** Youth Svcs/Metro-Dade, director, 1982-95; Bob Beamon Communications Inc, president, 1995-; artist and neckwear designer, 1996-. **Orgs:** South Florida Inner City Games Inc, chairman, 1994-96; US Olympic Committee Alumni, president, 1996-; Orange Bowl Committee, 1994-; Jackson Memorial Children's Foundation, 1995-. **Honors/Awds:** NCAA Long Jump/Triple Jump Champion, 1967; Olympic Long Jump Record, Still Standing, 1968; International Olympic Committee, Gold Medal, 1968; US Olympic Committee, Hall of Fame, 1992; Miami Children's Hospital, Humanitarian, 1995; UNESCO, Humanitarian, 1996; Xerox, Golden Olympian, 1996. **Special Achievements:** Motivational Speaker, 1972-; Children's Advocate, 1972-; Executive Policy Maker, Creative & Business, 1982-; Olympian Producer. **Business Addr:** President, Bob Beamon Communications Inc, 7355 NW 41st St, 2nd Fl, Miami, FL 33166, (305)470-6262.

BEAMON, TERESA KRISTINE NKENGE ZOLA. See ZOLA, NKENGE.

BEAN, BOBBY GENE
Educator, librarian. **Personal:** Born Jan 15, 1951, Houlka, MS; son of Mary Bess Bean and Dan Bean; married Mattie Marie Kitchen Bean, Aug 25, 1974; children: Bobby Gene II. **Educ:** Southeast Missouri State University, BSE, 1974; Southern Illinois University, MSE, 1979, EDS, 1981; Lael University, EDD,1983; Atlanta University, MSLS, 1987; Interdenominational Theological Center, MDiv, 1989; Univ of Sarasota, EDD,

candidate, 1998. **Career:** Sikeston Public School, high school librarian assistant, 1972-73; East St Louis Public School, 6th grade teacher, 1974-82, junior high math teacher, 1982-83, junior high librarian, 1983-87; Atlanta Public School, John Hope Elementary, media specialist, 1988-; Atlanta University Center, R W Woodruff Library, reference librarian, 1988-; Interdenominational Theology Center, instructor, 1992-. **Orgs:** ITC, Dean's List, 1988-89; United Negro College Fund Scholarship, 1989; Theta Phi, 1989; Atlanta University, Beta Phi Mu Library Science Honor Fraternity, 1987; American Library Assn; Georgia Library Assn; American Assn of School Librarians; Georgia Chaplain Assn. **Special Achievements:** American Biographical Institute, Research Board Advisor, 1990; Those Who Excel, School Media Service, Honorable Mention, 1987; ABI, Distinguished Leadership Award. **Business Addr:** Media Specialist, Atlanta Public School, 112 Blvd NE, John Hope Elementary, Atlanta, GA 30312.

BEAN, WALTER DEMPSEY

Educational administrator (retired). **Personal:** Born Oct 16, 1912, Midway, KY; son of Lula G Rollins Bean and James Ennis Bean; married Minnie Peck, Jan 2, 1982; children: Kenneth, Patricia Jenkins. **Educ:** Kentucky State Univ, BS 1935; Butler Univ, MS 1954, Masters plus 30 hrs, 1960. **Career:** Indianapolis Public Schools, teacher 1935-56, asst principal & principal 1957-66, supvr personnel accounting 1966-68, supvr elementary teacher placement 1968-71, coord recruitment placement teacher personnel 1971-78. **Orgs:** First black & charter mem Phi Delta Kappa Fraternity Butler Univ 1956; 2nd black mem USA Amer Assn of School Personnel Admin 1966-78; various offices Assn of School, Coll & Univ Staff IN 1971-78; NAACP 1938-; life mem Kappa Alpha Psi Fraternity 1935-; advisory comm Red Cross Indianapolis Chapter 1961-66; mem Medicare Splmnt Advisory Group Blue Cross Blue Shield IN 1983-; Advisory Comm United Methodist Church 1970-75. **Honors/Awds:** Annual Achievement Award, Kappa Alpha Psi Fraternity Indianapolis Alumni 1966; 1st Black Teacher Recruiter, Indianapolis Public School & IN Admin 1968; 2nd Black Teacher Recruiter, US Amer Assn of School Personnel 1968; IN Dist Citizen Award, Black Bicentennial Comm 1976; Certificate of Achievement Award, Kentucky State Univ Indianapolis Alumni 1981; IN Chamber of Commerce and Center for Leadership Development, Inc, Lifetime Achievement Award 1986; Kentucky State Univ Alumni Assn, selected one of 100 outstanding alumni 1986. **Home Addr:** Meridian Towers East, 25 E 40th St, Apt 3K, Indianapolis, IN 46205.

BEANE, DOROTHEA ANNETTE

Educator. **Personal:** Born Mar 30, 1952, Plainfield, NJ; daughter of Mary Beane and Floyd Beane. **Educ:** Spelman College, 1971-72; Drew University, BA, 1974; Rutgers-Newark College of Law, JD, 1977. **Career:** US Department of Justice, Civil Division, Torts Branch, trial attorney, 1977-81; Law Firm of Robinson and Geraldo, associate attorney, 1981-82; US Department of Justice, assistant US attorney; Stetson University College of Law, assistant professor, 1990-. **Orgs:** American Bar Association, 1990-; Black Law Students Association, faculty advisor, 1990-; Sarasota County American Inns of Court, academic master, 1990-; Association of American Law School, house of representatives, 1991; Stetson University Senate, representative, 1992-; American College of Legal Medicine, 1992-. **Honors/Awds:** US Department of Justice, Attorney General's Special Achievement Award, 1986; Women's Singles Table Tennis Championship of Jacksonville, FL, 1988-89; US Marshal's Service Letter of Appreciation, 1990; US Postal Service Letter of Appreciation, 1990. **Home Addr:** 7912 Sailboat Key Blvd, South Pasadena, FL 33707, (813)367-8138.

BEANE, PATRICIA JEAN

Educator. **Personal:** Born Jan 13, 1944, Massillon, OH; married Frank Llewellyn; children: Frank Clarence II, Adam Tyler. **Educ:** Ashland Coll OH, BS 1966. **Career:** Akron City Schools, teacher 1966-67; Massillon City Schools, teacher 1967-. **Orgs:** Mem Doris L Allen Minority Caucus 1984; mem Massillon Business & Professional Women 1977-80; mem Massillon Youth Ctr Bd of Trustees 1984; mem NEA 1966-76, 1979-; mem OH Educ Assn 1966-76, 1979-; mem E Cent OH Tchrs Assn 1966-76, 1979-; mem Massilon Educ Assn 1966-76, 1979-; mem Akron Symphony Chorus 1966-67; mem Canton Civic Opera Chorus 1969-79; sec bd of trustees Massillon YWCA 1972-76; mem Massillon Bus & Professional Women 1977-; mem OH Assn of Colored Women's Clubs 1978-; mem Natl Assn of Colored Women's Clubs 1978-; mem regional & local women's clubs. **Honors/Awds:** Guest soloist w/various choirs. **Business Addr:** Teacher, Massillon City School, 724 Walnut St, Massillon, OH 44646.

BEANE, ROBERT HUBERT

County government official. **Personal:** Born Mar 4, 1947, New York, NY; son of Lorraine Braithwaite and Sidney Beane; divorced; children: Craig J. **Educ:** Fordham Univ College at Lincoln Center, BA 1974, Fordham Univ Grad School of Social Service, MSW 1976. **Career:** Mt Vernon Community Action Group; Westchester Comm Opportunity Prog, exec dir 1970-73; Westchester Urban Coalition, program dir 1973-74; Alcohelp Program, research & evaluation specialist 1974-76; Westchester County, program specialist 1976, Dept of Mental Health, center administrator 1976-79, asst to commissioner 1979-83, dir community service 1983-. **Orgs:** Comm for Protection of Human Subj NY Med Coll, mem 1980-; City of Yonkers Board of Education, trustee 1983-93, vice president 1988-90, president, 1992-93, 1995-97. **Honors/Awds:** Alpha Sigma Lambda 1974; Woodrow Wilson Foundation, MLK fellow 1975 & 1976; Community Service Award, NAACP, 1991. **Military Serv:** USAF, AFC. **Home Addr:** 412-13 North Broadway, Yonkers, NY 10701. **Business Addr:** Director, Community Service, Westchester County, Dept of Community Mental Health, 112 E Post Rd, White Plains, NY 10601.

BEARD, BUTCH (ALFRED JR.)

Professional basketball coach. **Personal:** Born May 4, 1947, Hardinburg, KY. **Educ:** Louisville Coll, 1969. **Career:** Atlanta Hawks, professional basketball player, 1969-70; Seattle Supersonics, professional basketball player, 1972-73; Golden State Warriors, professional basketball player, 1973-74; Cleveland Cavaliers, professional basketball player, 1971-72, 1975-76; New York Knicks, professional basketball player, 1975-78, asst coach, 1978-82, broadcaster, 1982-87; Atlanta Hawks, broadcaster, 1987-88; New Jersey Nets, asst coach, 1988-90; Howard Univ, head coach, 1990-94; New Jersey Nets, head coach, 1994-96; Dallas Mavericks, asst coach, 1996-. **Honors/Awds:** Floor leader playing in all 82 games and averaging approx 13 pts per game when Golden State Warriors won world championship 1974; NBA All-Star Game 1972. **Business Addr:** Assistant Coach, Dallas Mavericks, Reunion Arena, 777 Sports St, Dallas, TX 75207, (214)988-0117.

BEARD, CHARLES JULIAN

Attorney. **Personal:** Born Dec 24, 1943, Detroit, MI; son of Ethel Coveney Beard and James F Beard; married Vivian Cromwell Beard, Aug 11, 1990. **Educ:** Harvard Coll, AB 1966; Law School, JD 1969. **Career:** Boston Model City Program, asst admin comm serv 1970-74; Foley, Hoag & Eliot, associate 1974-78, partner 1979-. **Orgs:** Commissioner, Massachusetts CATV Commission, 1972-76; mem Gov's Judicial Nom Comm 1976-79; mem Commonwealth Housing Found 1975-90; chmn bd trust Dr SC Fuller Comm; mem Mental Health Corp 1975-80; 2nd vice pres Boston NAACP 1976-79; dir Broadcast Capital Fund, Washington DC 1979-92; trust Roxbury Comm Coll found 1985-; trust The Partnership Inc 1986-; dir Blue Cross of MA Inc 1986-; trustee Emerson Coll 1987-; trustee Boston Community Access and Programming Foundation 1981-89; Phillips Academy, alumni trustee, 1992-96. **Business Addr:** Partner, Foley, Hoag & Eliot LLP, One Post Office Square, Boston, MA 02109.

BEARD, ISRAEL

Educational administrator (retired). **Personal:** Born Jun 27, 1932, Cairo, IL; daughter of Emma Willis Beard and George Beard; married Gwendolyn Etherly, Aug 18, 1962; children: Lori L. **Educ:** Lane Coll, BA 1958; Univ of WI-Milwaukee, MS 1973; Nova Univ, EdD 1980. **Career:** State Voc Training School, counselor 1958-59; Stigall HS, teacher 1959-61; Story School, teacher 1961-68; Opportunities Indust, dir 1968-69; Milwaukee Area Tech Coll, prof 1969-87; MATC, Milwaukee, WI, program coord, 1987-92. **Orgs:** Pres Kappa Alpha Psi Frat 1968-70; pres Milwaukee Frontiers Intl 1975-78; sire archon, Sigma Pi Phi, 1995-96; broker United Realty Co; mem Amer Vocational Assoc, WI Vocational Assoc; treas bd of dirs Child Comprehensive Day Care; member, State Advisory Council-Literacy, 1991-; member, Governor Task Force Literacy 2000, 1987-88; bd mem Board of Attorney for Professional Responsibility. **Honors/Awds:** Presidential Awd Frontiers Intl 1976,77; Meritorious Awd Lane Coll 1981; Disting men of Milwaukee Top Ladies of Distinction 1986; Community Service Award, Career Youth Development, 1988-89; Teacher of the Year, International Student Organization, 1988; Honorary Member, House of Rep Award, Congressman Bone, TN, 1987. **Military Serv:** AUS enlisted ranks, honorably discharged, 1952-55. **Home Addr:** 9619 W Beechwood, Milwaukee, WI 53224, (414)353-2127. **Business Addr:** Retired Program Coordinator, Basic Skills, Milwaukee Area Tech College, 700 W State St, Ste 214, Milwaukee, WI 53224.

BEARD, JAMES WILLIAM, JR.

Attorney, educator. **Personal:** Born Sep 16, 1941, Chillicothe, OH; married Gail LaVerne Rivers; children: James III, Ryan Jamail, Kevin Jarrard. **Educ:** Hardin-Simmons Univ, BS 1967; TX So Univ, JD 1973; Univ of TX, LLM 1976. **Career:** Thurgood Marshall Law School, TX Southern Univ, assoc prof of law, assoc dean for academic affairs & programs, dir fed tax clinic. **Orgs:** Mem Amer Bar Assn, State Bar of TX; bd of govs Natl Bar Assn; chmn Sect of Taxation NBA; mem NAACP; past trust Houston Legal Found. **Honors/Awds:** Outstanding Young Amer for 1977. **Military Serv:** USAF A/2c 1959-63. **Business Addr:** Assoc Prof Law/Dean Acad Aff, Thurgood Marshall Law Sch, TX Southern University, 3100 Cleburne, Houston, TX 77004.

BEARD, LILLIAN MCLEAN

Physician. **Personal:** Born in New York, NY; daughter of Woodie McLean and John Wilson; married DeLawrence Beard. **Educ:** Howard University, College of Liberal Arts, BS, 1965, College of Medicine, MD, 1970; Children's Hospital, Natl Medical Center, pediatric internship, residency, fellowship 1970-73. **Career:** Children's Hospital, Natl Medical Center, Child Development, director, consultant, 1973-75; George Washington University, School of Medicine, Dept of Pediatrics, associate clinical professor, 1982-; private practice, pediatrician, 1973-; child and adolescent health consultant; Good Housekeeping Magazine, ''Ask Dr Beard'' column, authored, 1989-95, contributing editor; Carnation Nutritional Products, communications consultant, 1991-. **Orgs:** American Academy of Pediatrics, media spokesperson; Natl Medical Assn; American Medical Women's Assn; Medical Society of District of Columbia; Links Inc; Girl Friends. **Honors/Awds:** Amer Med Assn, 5 awards; Outstanding Young Women For the Yr, 1979; Diplomate, National Board of Medical Examiners; Diplomate, American Board of Pediatrics; American Medical Association, Physician Recognition Awards; National Medical Association, Hall of Fame Award, 1994; National Association for Equal Opportunity in Higher Education, Distinguished Alumni Leadership Award. **Business Addr:** Associate Professor, Child Health, George Washington University, 5505 5th St NW, Washington, DC 20011, (202)882-5437.

BEARD, MARTIN LUTHER

Physician, educator. **Personal:** Born Jul 15, 1926, Forrest Co, MS; married Delores; children: Myrna, Martin Jr. **Educ:** Tougaloo Coll, BS 1953; Meharry Med Coll, MD 1960. **Career:** Kate B Reynolds Meml Hosp, intern 1960-61, resident 1961-64; Minneapolis VA Hosp, fellow 1964-67; MI State Univ, asst clinical prof 1967-; Private Practice, physician. **Orgs:** Dipl Amer Bd Surgery; fellow Amer Coll Surgeons; mem Optimist; Omega Psi Phi. **Honors/Awds:** First Place Honor Award Excellence in Med Writing Bd MN Med 1969. **Business Addr:** Assistant Clinical Professor, MI State University, 4250 N Saginaw, Flint, MI 48505.

BEARD, MONTGOMERY, JR.

Real estate broker, career placement counselor. **Personal:** Born May 8, 1932, Brownsville, TN; son of Hellen G Snipes Beard and Montgomery Beard Sr; married Lou Etta Outlaw, Jun 2, 1957; children: Valencia Monetta, Helen Veronica, Michael Keith, Montgomery III. **Educ:** TN State Univ, BS 1960, MS 1960. **Career:** Maury County Bd Educ, dir guidance & counseling 1959-64; Jewish Vocational Svc, counseling supvr 1964-68; Kansas City Reg Council for Higher Educ, dir student affairs 1968-69; Educ Projects Inc, exec assn, 1969-70; Natl Planning Assn, sr rsch assoc 1970-72; Intl Mgmt Resources Inc, vice pres 1973-76; Beard Enterprises Inc, CEO, 1976-; Agent LTD, CEO, 1989-. **Orgs:** Amer Personnel & Guidance Assn; Amer Vocational Assn; chmn bd commrs Housing Auth Prince Georges Co 1972-76; candidate House of Delegates State MD Legislature 26th dist; chmn Zoning Comm; pres Millwood-Waterford Civic Assn 1975-77; Phi Beta Sigma Fraternity Inc; PTA; Upper Room Baptist Church; former com Boy Scouts; founder past pres Prince Georges Black Rep Club; former mem State Central Com Rep Party; past vice pres So Prince George Rep Club; mem, Young Reps;bd of dirs, Prince Georges County Public Schools, Occupational Skills Foun d, 1987-; board of directors, Center for Community Development of Prince George's County, 1989-; Center for Counseling Education, Research and Training Center, chairperson, board of directors, 1992-. **Honors/Awds:** Montgomery Beard, Jr Founder's Award, Prince George, Black Republican Council, 1990-, awarded annually. **Military Serv:** USN, 1951-55. **Home Addr:** 510 Millwheel St, Capitol Heights, MD 20743. **Business Addr:** President, CEO, Beard Enterprises Inc, 510 Millwheel St, Capitol Heights, MD 20743.

BEARD, VIRGINIA H.

Psychologist. **Personal:** Born Sep 9, 1941, St Louis, MO; daughter of Lula L Spicer and Monroe C Harrison; married Otis C Beard; children: Bostic Charles, Bonji Lucille. **Educ:** Harris Tchrs Coll, BA Educ 1964; So IL U, MS Guidnc 1968; St Louis U, PhD Cnslr Educ 1974. **Career:** St Louis Public Schools, teacher 1964-68; Univ City Public Schools, counselor 1968-72; St Louis Juvenile Center, behavioral counselor 1974-76; SLU Medical School, comm coord 1976-77; King Fanon Mental Health Center, acting dir 1977-78; Center Urban Living, exec dir 1978-80; Yeatman Univ Sarah Mental Health Center, dir psychological services; Clayton School Dist, special assistant to superintendent; private practice, St Louis, MO, psychologist, 1981-. **Orgs:** Thrpst Professional Counseling Grp 1984-; Am Psych Assn 1977-; Am Counseling Assn, 1985-; bd dir Annie Malone Chldrns Hm 1977-84; North City Am Cncr Scty 1983-87; Conf on Educ 1980-87; Alpha Kappa Alpha. **Honors/Awds:** Ford Fndtn Flw St Louis Univ Dctrl Stdy 1972-73; Gerontolgy Flw St Louis Univ Inst Appld Grntlgy 1973-74; Flw Ldrshp St Louis 1984-85; Co-author Cnslng Enhancing Well Being in Later Yrs 1982; president of board, Hopewell Center 1990-93. **Home Addr:** 890 Berick Dr, St Louis, MO 63132. **Business Addr:** Psychologist, 4144 Lindell, Suite 315, St Louis, MO 63108.

BEASLEY, AARON BRUCE

Professional football player. **Personal:** Born Jul 7, 1973, Pottstown, PA. **Educ:** West Virginia, attended. **Career:** Jacksonville Jaguars, defensive back, 1996-. **Business Addr:** Professional Football Player, Jacksonville Jaguars, One Stadium Place, Jacksonville, FL 32202, (904)633-6000.

BEASLEY, ANNE VICKERS. See Obituaries section.

BEASLEY, ANNIE RUTH
Educator (retired), city official. **Personal:** Born Oct 6, 1928, Nashville, NC; daughter of Lillie Alston Beasley and Lucious Beasley. **Educ:** Shaw Univ Raleigh, BA 1949; NC Central Univ, MA 1954-58. **Career:** Civil Service, file clerk 1951-53; S Nash Sr High, teacher, 1956-90; councilwoman, Town of Sharpsburg NC 1981-83; mayor, Town of Sharpsburg NC 1983-89, 1991-. **Honors/Awds:** Leader of Amer Secondary Educ 1972; Teacher of the Year Nash Co Teachers NC 1973-74; Human Relations Awd Nash Co Teachers NC 1978-79. **Home Addr:** PO Box 636, Sharpsburg, NC 27878. **Business Addr:** Mayor, Town of Sharpsburg, City Hall, Sharpsburg, NC 27878.

BEASLEY, ARLENE A. (PHOEBE)
Artist, business executive. **Personal:** Born Jun 3, 1943, Cleveland, OH; divorced. **Educ:** OH Univ, BA 1965; Kent State Univ, grad 1967-69. **Career:** Cleveland Bd of Edn, tchr 1965-69; Sage Publications, artist 1969-70; KFI/KOST Radio, acct exec 1970-. **Orgs:** Savannah College of Art and Design, bd of trustees; New Regal Theater, Chicago, advisory bd; Museum of African-American Art, board of directors president, honorary bd of trustees; California State University, Long Beach, curriculum advisory bd; Private Industry Council, county commissioner. **Honors/Awds:** American Women in Radio & TV, Merit Award, 1975, Achievement Award, Genii Award; Los Angeles Sentinel, Woman of the Year, 1989; NAACP Legal Defense and Educational Fund, Black Women of Achievement Award, 1991. **Special Achievements:** First African-American female president, American Women in Radio & TV, 1977-78; "Clinton Inaugural" artwork, has been accorded the coveted Presidential Seal, Clinton presented prints of this work to Ambassadors of the Diplomatic Corps at a formal ceremony at Georgetown University; only artist to twice receive the Presidential Seal; selected to design the prestigious International Tennis Trophy and Medal, 1984 Summer Olympic Games; named Official Artist, 1987 Los Angeles Marathon; chosen to design the national poster, Sickle Cell Disease Campaign; commissioned: 20th Anniversary of Essence Magazine, artwork, poster, 1990; Inauguration of former President Bush, artwork, official poster, 1989; "Morning Glory," Paramount Television pilot, artwork, 1989; Oprah Winfrey, series of lithographs, and paintings based on television mini-series "The Womof Brewster Place"; artist, private collections for: Andre and Linda Johnson-Rice, Robert and Nancy Daly, Joel andMarlene Chaseman, Attorney Tyrone Brown, Attorney Reginald Govan, Edward and Bettiann Gardner, William and Carol Sutton-Lewis, Maya Angelou, Anita Baker, Gordon Parks, Oprah Winfrey, numerous others; numerous institutional collections, one-woman exhibits and group exhibitions. **Business Addr:** Artist, 610 S Ardmore, Los Angeles, CA 90005.

BEASLEY, CORA THOMAS
Educator. **Personal:** Born Apr 16, 1945, Oktaha, OK; daughter of Mr and Mrs Clarence Weldon Thomas; married Billy G Beasley, Aug 16, 1968. **Educ:** Langston Univ, BS, 1967; Northeastern OK State, MED, 1980. **Career:** Idabell (Riverside) Schools, instructor, 1967-68; Muskogee Public Schools, instructor, 1969-. **Orgs:** Alpha Kappa Alpha Sor, sec, 1970-80; Natl Sorority of Phi Delta Kappa, financial sec, 1985; Muskogee Ed Assn, treasurer, 1980; Goodwill Industries, sec, 1984; OK Ed Assn, 1967-; Natl Ed Assn; OK State Home Assn, 1967-; OK Baptist State Conv (collate dist), president, 1991. **Honors/Awds:** Zeta Phi Beta, All Greek, 1990. **Home Addr:** 1303 S. 38th St., Muskogee, OK 74401, (918)683-5277.

BEASLEY, DANIEL L.
County tax collector (retired). **Personal:** Born Mar 22, 1910, Tuskegee, AL; son of Hilliard Beasley and Lakey Beasley; married; children: Faye B Scott. **Educ:** Tuskegee Inst, BS, 1937. **Career:** Rosenwald Jr HS, Preston GA, prin, 1937-40; Farm Security Administ Linden, AL, 1940-42; Vet Administrn, clerk, 1946-68; Macon Co, county commr, 1971-75; Macon County, tax collector, 1977-88. **Orgs:** Pres Tuskegee Branch NAACP; mem Tuskegee Civic Assn. **Honors/Awds:** Tuskegee's Man of Yr Award 1962. **Military Serv:** AUS 1942-43.

BEASLEY, DAVE, JR.
Military official. **Personal:** Born Nov 4, 1949, Shreveport, LA; son of Dave and Emma Beasley; married Gean Lynette, Aug 28, 1971; children: David, Damon. **Educ:** Grambling State Univ, BA, 1971; Pepperdine Univ, MA, 1976. **Career:** United States Marine Corps, lieutenant colonel, 1973-. **Orgs:** Natl Naval Officer Assn, vp, DC chapter, 1981-; Retired Officer Assn, 1990-. **Military Serv:** US Marine Corps, Lieutenant Colonel, 1973-; Natl Def Medal, Meritorious Service Medal (2). **Business Phone:** (202)433-3840.

BEASLEY, EDWARD, III
City manager. **Personal:** Born in Omaha, NE; son of Bessie Chandler Beasley and Edward Beasley Jr. **Educ:** Pittsburgh State Univ, Pittsburgh PA, 1976-77; Loyola Univ, BA, Political Science, 1980; Univ of Missouri, Kansas City MO, MPA, 1983; Pioneer Community Coll, Kansas City MO, 1984. **Career:** Jolly Walsh & Gordon, Kansas City MO, legal clerk, 1982-84; Federal Govt, Washington DC, aid to Senator Thomas Eagleton, 1983; City of Kansas City, Kansas City MO, mgmt trainee, 1984-85; City of Flagstaff, Flagstaff AZ, admin asst to city mgr, 1985-88; City of Eloy, Eloy, AZ, city mgr, 1988-. **Orgs:** Mem, bd of dir, Amer Cancer Soc, Pinal County AZ; bd mem, United Way of Northern Arizona, 1988, bd mem, Center Against Domestic Violence, 1988; bd mem, Impact Crisis Funding, 1988; mem, Intl City Managers Assn. **Honors/Awds:** 30 Leaders of the Future, Ebony Magazine, 1988. **Business Addr:** City Mgr, City of Eloy, 628 N Main St, Eloy, AZ 85231.

BEASLEY, EULA DANIEL
Educator. **Personal:** Born Sep 16, 1958, Oxford, NC; daughter of Helen Pettiford Daniel and Benjamin Daniel III; married Robert Beasley, Jun 25, 1983; children: Lydia, Benjamin. **Educ:** Univ of North Carolina, Chapel Hill, NC, BS, pharmacy, 1981; Doctor of Pharmacy, 1983. **Career:** Orange-Chatham Comprehensive Health Svcs, Carrboro, NC, project pharmacist, 1983-84; Univ of NC, Chapel Hill, NC, clinical asst, prof, 1983-84; Washington Hospital Ctr, Washington, DC, clinical pharmacist, 1984-85, 1987-, clinical svcs mgr, 1990-; Howard Univ, Coll of Pharmacy, Washington, DC, asst prof, 1985-. **Orgs:** Faculty rep, Student Information Network, 1986-89; mem, Am Society Hospital Pharmacists, 1981-; mem, DC Society of Hospital Pharmacists, 1985-. **Honors/Awds:** "Sickle Cell Anemia" in Pharmacotherapy, co-author with C Curry; A Pathophysiologic Approach, CT: Appleton & Lang, 2nd edition, 1992; Rho Chi Pharmacy Honor Society, 1980; Phi Lambda Sigma Pharmacy Leadership Society, 1978; Natl Achievement Scholar 1976, James M Johnston Scholar, 1976. **Business Addr:** Asst Prof, Howard University, College of Pharmacy, 2300 4th Street, NW, Washington, DC 20059.

BEASLEY, JESSE C.
Optometrist. **Personal:** Born Mar 11, 1929, Marshall, TX; married Ruth Adella Evans; children: Jesse II, Joseph, Janice. **Educ:** LA City Coll, AA Ophthalmic Optics 1952; LA Coll of Optometry, OD 1956; Univ of CA, MPH 1971. **Career:** Assoc Pract, 1957; Private Practice, optometrist 1957-. **Orgs:** Passed state bd & lic as reg optometrist State of CA 1956; mem LA Co Optom Soc; pres-elect 1975 CA Optom Assn; Amer Optom Assn; elected to Fellow of Amer Acad of Optom 1969; mem Amer Pub Health Assn; chmn Comm Health Div 1973-74; chmn Div of Pub Health Optom 1972-73; Amer Optom Com of the Urban Optom 1969-70; Com on Urban Optom 1970-71; COA Bd of Trustees 1971; CA Optom Assn 1967; pres CA Optometric Assn 1976-77; pres Optom Vision Care Council 1968; chmn Comp Health Planning Com of So CA Optom Socs 1968; mem LA Co Optom Soc; mem Optom cosn in planning Optom; sec S Cntrl Multipurpose Health Serv Cntr 1976; proposal writer Optom Particip 1967; staff optom OEO Health Cntr 1968; mem Exec Com of med Staff Organ 1968; cond Free Vision Care Clinic in Jamaicagave RX glasses to indigent persons68; compl independ Med Records Abstract of Watts Health Cntr under contr to Geomet Inc 1971. **Honors/Awds:** Has published & presented many papers on optometry; appointed to CA State Bd of Optometry by Gov Edmund G Brown Jr 1978-86; elected bd pres CA State Bd Optometry 1982,84. **Military Serv:** USAAF Corp Sgt 1946-49. **Business Addr:** Physician, Manchester Optometric Center, 130 W Manchester Ave, Los Angeles, CA 90003.

BEASLEY, PAUL LEE
Educational administrator. **Personal:** Born Jan 10, 1950, East Point, GA; married Pamela Simmons; children: Deanna Estella, Erin Michelle. **Educ:** Earlham Coll, BA 1972; Trenton State Coll, MEd 1973, Univ of Tennessee, EdD 1988. **Career:** Trenton State Coll, dormitory dir 1973-74; Emory Univ Upward Bound, dir 1974-75; US Office of Educ, educ program specialist 1975-78; Univ of TN Chattanooga, dir special serv 1978-89; Univ of South Carolina TRIO director 1989-. **Orgs:** State rep SE Assn Educ Oppor Prog Personnel 1979-; com chmn TN Assn of Spl Prog 1978-; usher/bd mem First Bapt Ch Chattanooga 1979-; mem Toastmasters Intl 1979-; president SAEOPP 1989-91. **Honors/Awds:** Outstanding Young Men of Amer 1979; Award for Disting Serv SE Assn Educ Oppor Prog Personnel 1977; Outstanding Upward Bounder US Ofc of Educ 1976. **Business Addr:** Dir of TRIO Programs, BTW Auditorium, USC, Columbia, SC 29208.

BEASLEY, ULYSSES CHRISTIAN, JR.
Attorney. **Personal:** Born Jan 14, 1928, Arkansas City, AR; married Rose Jeanette Cole; children: Gayle, Mark, Erika. **Educ:** Fresno City Coll, attended 1949-51; Fresno State Coll, attended 1951-53; San Francisco Law Sch, 1959-65. **Career:** Co of Fresno Welfare Dept, soc worker 1953-54; Fresno Police Dept, police officer 1954-59; Welfare Dept Contra Costa Co, soc worker 1959; State of CA, investigator 1959-66; Dist Atty Office Santa Clara Co, deputy dist atty 1966-. **Orgs:** Vp NAACP San Jose Br; bd dir Santa Clara Youth Village; mem Black Lawyers Assn. **Military Serv:** USN 3rd Class Petty Officer 1945-48; Good Conduct Medal. **Business Addr:** Deputy District Attorney, Dist Atty Santa Clara County, 70 W Hedding St, San Jose, CA 95110.

BEASLEY, VICTOR MARIO
Paralegal. **Personal:** Born Feb 13, 1956, Atlanta, GA; son of Mary L Ferguson Beasley and Willie J Beasley; married Linda Kaye Randolph; children: Cea Janay. **Educ:** Morehouse Coll, BA 1979; Attended, GA Inst of Tech 1974-75, GA State Coll of Law 1984-85. **Career:** City of Atlanta Planning Bureau, planning asst 1977-78; Atlanta Bureau of Corrections, sgt/officer 1980-83; Atlanta Municipal Court, clerk/bailiff 1983-85; Atlanta Public Defender's Office, researcher/investigator 1985-; SOAR Songs, Inc, Douglasville, OH, president 1989-; State of Georgia Board of Pardons and Paroles, parole officer 1991. **Orgs:** Region I mem Morehouse Coll Alumni Assoc 1985; publisher, songwriter, Broadcast Music, Inc 1989-. **Honors/Awds:** Scholarship Atlanta Fellows and Interns 1977-78. **Home Addr:** 6794 Alexander Parkway, Douglasville, GA 30135-3581. **Business Addr:** Parole Officer, Georgia State Board of Pardons and Paroles, 8687 Hospital Drive, Douglasville, GA 30134.

BEASON, KENNETH GARRETT
Cleric. **Personal:** Born Dec 22, 1942, Columbus, OH; son of Helen Beason and Carl Beason; married Carol Bradley, Dec 19, 1981; children: Susan, Jeff, Bram, Joy. **Educ:** Ohio State University, attended, 1960-63; University of Nebraska, BS, 1969; Northwestern University, MDiv, 1972; Boston Theological Institute, attended, 1972-73. **Career:** St John, St James, rector, 1972-74; US Air Force, chaplain, Episcopal priest, 1974-. **Orgs:** Air Force Association, 1974-; Union of Black Episcopalians, 1974-; National Board of Theological Education, 1971-74; National Board of Examination Chaplins, 1972-74. **Special Achievements:** Published: The Life of A Jones, 1972. **Military Serv:** US Air Force, col, 1963-67, 1974-. **Business Addr:** Chaplain, Colonel, US Air Force, Randolph AFB, HQ ATC/HC, Randolph A F B, TX 78150, (210)652-2026.

BEATTY, CHARLES EUGENE, SR.
Educational administrator (retired). **Personal:** Born Apr 24, 1909, Asheville, NC; son of Nellie Beatty and Monroe Beatty; married Evelyn Douglas, Sep 27, 1935; children: Mary Louise Shorter, Charlotte Jordan, Charles Jr. **Educ:** Eastern Mich Univ, BS 1934; Univ of Mich, MA Ed 1962. **Career:** Ypsilanti Public Schools, teacher 1935-40, elementary principal 1940-74, school board mem 1975-87 (retired). **Orgs:** Chairman Selective Service Comm 1965-75; president Boys Club of Ypsilanti 1966-74; president Eastern Mich Univ Alumni Assoc 1969-70; vice president Ypsilanti Board of Education 1977-78. **Honors/Awds:** Outstanding Elem Principal Elem Principal Assoc Region II 1974; EMU Athletic Hall of Fame 1976; EMU Alumni Distinguished Service Award 1982; Univ of Pennsylvania Honored for 50th year winning 400 M Hurd 3 years in a row 1983; Michigan Education Hall of Fame 1985; co-founder internationally known LC Perry Pre-School Ypsilanti, MI 1962. **Home Addr:** 119 Hawkins St, Ypsilanti, MI 48197.

BEATTY, MARTIN CLARKE
Educator. **Personal:** Born Nov 9, New Haven, CT; son of Eunice Clarke Beatty and Raszue Willis Beatty; married Barbara Conger Beatty, Jun 9, 1990. **Educ:** Middlebury Coll, Middlebury, VT, BA, art history, 1984. **Career:** Trinity Coll, Hartford, CT, graduate fellow, 1985-87; Middlebury Coll, Middlebury, VT, asst prof, 1987-. **Orgs:** Minority Issues Group, 1989-; faculty advisor, Middlebury Coll Activities Bd, 1987-1988; African-American Alliance, Commons Faculty Affiliate; Community Relations Advisor on Sexual Harassment. **Business Addr:** Coach, Athletics, Middlebury College, Middlebury, VT 05753.

BEATTY, OTTO, JR.
Attorney, state representative. **Personal:** Born Jan 26, 1940, Columbus, OH; son of Myrna Beatty and Otto Beatty Sr; divorced; children: Otto III, Laurel. **Educ:** Howard University, Washington, DC, BA, business administration, 1961; Ohio State University, Columbus, OH, JD, 1965. **Career:** Ohio House of Representatives, state representative, 1980-; Beatty & Roseboro, Columbus, OH, founder/senior partner, currently. **Orgs:** American Arbitration Assn; American Bar Assn; American Trial Lawyers Assn; Black Elected Democrats of Ohio; Columbus Area Black Elected Officials; Ohio State Consumer Education Assn; Natl Bar Assn; NAACP; Operation PUSH; Natl Conference of Black Lawyers, Columbus Chapter; Columbus Apartment Assn; Chamber of Commerce; Hunger Task Force of Ohio; Ohio Alliance of Black School Educators; Natl Black Programming Consortium; Black Chamber of Commerce; Columbus Assn of Black Journalists; Ohio Assn of Real Estate Brokers; Eastern Union Missionary Baptist Assn. **Honors/Awds:** Citizens for Jesse Jackson Special Achievement Award; Outstanding Leadership Award, Columbus State Community College; Outstanding Service, Family Missionary Baptist Church; Outstanding Services Award, Franklin County Children's Services; 10 Outstanding Young Men Award, Junior Chamber of Commerce of Ohio; Meritorious Service Award, The Ohio Academy of Trial Lawyers; Community Service Award, Ohio Minority Businesses; Certificate of Appreciation for Dedicated Services, Upward Bound Program; Outstanding Legislator Award; Outstanding Local Trial Bar Association, Continuing Legal Education; Outstanding Worksites Award; "Damages in Soft Tissue Cases," Ohio Academy of Trial Lawyers; "Judgments under Ohio Tort Reform Law," "Proving

Damages after Tort Reform,'' Ohio Legal Center. **Business Addr:** Attorney, Beatty & Roseboro Co., LPA, 233 S High St, Suite 300, Columbus, OH 43205.

BEATTY, OZELL KAKASKUS
Educational administrator (retired). **Personal:** Born Mar 1, 1921, Newberry, SC; son of Mamie Counts Beatty and William Beatty; married Ellestine Dillard Beatty, Sep 15, 1942; children: Bryan E. **Educ:** Livingstone Coll, BS 1943; Columbia Univ, MA 1949; Indiana Univ, NC State Univ, Natl Science Foundation Rsch Fellow; Livingstone College, Salisbury, NC, LLD, 1987. **Career:** Salisbury City Council NC, mem city council 1967-77; Livingstone Coll, prof of Biology, 1949-71; govtl relations officer 1971-78; City of Salisbury NC, mayor pro tem 1971-73, 1973-75; Office of the Governor Raleigh NC, deputy dir office of local govt advocacy 1978-85; President of Livingstone College, 1987-89 (retired). **Orgs:** Mem Alpha Kappa Mu Honor Soc, NAACP, Omega Psi Phi Frat, NC Black Leadership Caucus. **Honors/Awds:** Livingstone Coll Alumni Meritious Serv Awd 1977; Salisbury-Rowan Negro Civic League Comm Meritorious Serv Awd 1978; Eastside and Westside Comm Meritorious Serv Awd 1978; Livingstone Coll Meritorious Serv Awd 1978; Inter-Greek Council Meritorious Serv Awd 1978; Livingstone Coll Distinguished Serv Award, 1979; NC Black Elected Municipal Officials Org Distinguished Serv Award 1984; Centennial Award, United Way of Wake County, 1987; Citizen of Year, Salisbury Civitan Club, 1988; President's Service Award, Trustees of Livingstone College, 1989. **Military Serv:** AUS Medical Corps tech sgt 2 1/2 years; Asian Theater, Good Conduct, Overseas Service. **Home Addr:** 4700 Scollay Court, Raleigh, NC 27609.

BEATTY, PEARL
Elected official. **Personal:** Born Oct 3, 1935, Connellsville, PA. **Educ:** Shaw Univ, BA (Cum Laude) Publ Admin; Vale School of Ins, Dipl Ins Corp Syst, Risk Mgmt. **Career:** Career Oriented Program for Employment, office mgr, exec sec; Urban League of NJ, exec sec; Ins Fund Commiss City of Newark, risk mgr. **Orgs:** Bd mem Natl Assoc of Cty Officials, Natl Assoc of Black Cty Officials, Natl Employment Steering Comm; mem 1984 Dem Platform Comm; bd mem, pres NJ Assoc of Counties; mem Essex Cty Women's Avd Bd, Essex Cty Correctional Adv Bd; chairperson Newark Housing Auth; mem Govt Risk & Ins Mgrs; pres NJ State Publ Welfare Bd. **Honors/Awds:** Achievement Awd Newark Tenent Council; Sec Appreciation Awd Kenneth A Gibson Civic Assoc; Woman of the Year Awd South Ward Boys Club, Bronze Shieds Inc;Merit Awd Essex Cty Dem Women; Leadership Awd NJ Assoc of Housing & Redevel; Citation of Appreciaiton Amer Legion Guyton Callahan #152; Outstanding Leadership Awd CAHACO Inc; Pol Serv Awd Natl Council of Negro Women; Apprec Awd Essex Cty Coll; Essex Cty Admin Code Adoption Awd Cty of Essex; Positive Image Awd Positive Image Inc; Outstanding Citizen Awd Jerome D Greco Civic Assoc; Freeholder of the Year Central Parent Council 1984; Proclamation Pearl Beatty Day Nam 16 1985 Cty of Essex; Disting Serv Awd Natl Assoc of Black Cty Officials; Community Serv Awds Essex Cty Police Dept, Frontiers, Sickle Cell Ed& Serv Found, Women's Political Cus of NJ; Kappa Alpha Psi, 22nd Delegation, High Park Gardens, Leaguers Inc, Essex Cty Freeholders, Allen Church. **Business Addr:** Essex Co, 465 Martin Luther King Blvd, Newark, NJ 07102.

BEATTY, ROBERT L.
Business executive. **Personal:** Born Sep 10, 1939, Turin, GA; married Marion L Bearden; children: Tara Patrice. **Educ:** Univ of MD, BA Marketing 1961; Northwood Inst, Spl Diploma Mktg 1969. **Career:** WB Doner & Co Advertising Detroit, audio/vis dir 1965-72; Grey Advertising NY & Detroit, acct supr 1972-75; Ross Roy Inc Advertising Detroit, vp/acct supr 1975-. **Orgs:** Mem Adcraft Club of Detroit 1970-; exec bd com mem NAaCP Detroit Br 1977-; adv bd chmn MI Cancer Found 1978-; com mem New Detroit Inc 1978-. **Honors/Awds:** CLIO Award (advt award equiv to movie industry's Oscar) Natl CLIO Adv Com 1978. **Military Serv:** AUS Sgt 1958-61; Good Conduct European Command Award. **Business Addr:** Vice Pres/Acct Supr, Ross Roy Inc Advertising, 2751 E Jefferson, Detroit, MI 48204.

BEATTY-BROWN, FLORENCE R.
Educator. **Personal:** Born Dec 6, 1912, Cairo, IL; daughter of Mary Alice Titus and Webster Barton Beatty Sr; married Robert Duane Brown Sr (divorced); children: Robert Duane Jr. **Educ:** Fisk Univ, AB (cum laude) 1933; Univ of IL Urbana IL, MA 1936, MS 1939, PhD 1951; Columbia Univ, Post Grad Work 1940-41; WA Univ, Post Grad Work 1954, 1966, 1967; Georgetown University, 1964; St Louis Community College Forest Park, AAS 1977; Mitchell College of Advanced Educ, Bathurst Australia, 1986. **Career:** Fayetteville State Teachers Coll, prof soc sci 1936-45; Lincoln Univ, prof soc sci 1945-47; Harris-Stowe Teachers Coll, Stowe Coll, prof soc sci 1949-60; Gen Bd of Ed Tuskegee Inst AL, guest prof, consult 1952-55; US Dept of State Liberia W AFrica, ed spec US Agency of Intl Devel 1960-63; Barnes/Jewish Hosp School of Nursing, assoc prof sociology 1964; Mark Twain Summer Inst Clayton MO, prof behavioral sci 1965-68; freelance writer; St Louis Comm Coll Meramec, chmn behavioral/social sci 1963-83, professor emerita, 1983-. **Orgs:** Proposal writing Natl Endowment for the Humanities 1980-82; consult & eval No Central Accrediting Assn of Inst of Higher Learning 1971-74; mem St Louis Writers Guild 1984-; chmn Book Review Discussion Club St Louis MO 1980; sec, bd mem Urban League of St Louis 1960-; consult Natl Sci Found, NCAA 1970-77; mem US Div of Laubach Literacy Intl; bd dir Intl Educ Consortium; So Conference on Afro, American Studies, 1983; member, St Louis Junior College Non-Certificated Retirement Plan Committee, 1988; Community Leaders of America, ABI, 14th Edition, 1992; Community Roundtable Search Community for President of St Louis Community College at Meramec, 1992. **Honors/Awds:** Natl Awd for 7 years commun serv Urban League of St Louis; Pub Mem/Foreign Selection Bd Dept of State Wash DC 1972; grant Natl Endowment for the Humanities 1979-81; Most Outstanding Instructor at Meramec Comm Coll Phi Theta Kappa Hon Soc 1980; Recognition Cert Amer Assn of Univ Women; Australian Bicentennial: The Secrets are Out, The Crisis, 1988; Alumna for the Decade, Fisk Univ, 1989; American Biographical Institute, Commemorative Gold Medal of Honor for Outstanding Achievements and Dedication to Personal and Professional Goals, October 1991; served as CORP Volunteer in St Louis County, Missouri Department of Human Services, 1991-1992. **Business Addr:** Professor Emeritus, St Louis Community College at Meramec, 11333 Big Bend Blvd, Kirkwood, MO 63122.

BEAUBIEN, GEORGE H.
Executive director. **Personal:** Born Nov 10, 1937, Hempstead, NY; married Lois Ann Lowe; children: Jacqueline II. **Educ:** Compton Coll, AA 1956; Pepperdine Coll, BA 1958. **Career:** Golden State Mut Life Ins Co, staff mgr, 1960-64; IBM Corp, legal mktg rep, 1964-65, mktg mgr, 1965-71; Self-Employed, gen ins agency all lines of ins, 1971-76; Mayor's Office, Small Bus Asst, exec dir, 1976-85; A & S Resources Inc, pres, 1985-. **Orgs:** Dir/pres Alpha Phi Alpha Frat; dir LA fire Dept Recruitment Prog; consult natl Bank United Fund Wash, DC/Norfolk, VA; chmn of bd LA Brotherhood Crusade 1968; pres New Frontier Dem Club 1969; pres LA bd of Fire Commr 1973-77. **Honors/Awds:** Resolution of Appreciation LA City Council; Top Rookie Salesman of Year IBM corp 1971; Cert of Accomplish IBM Corp 1972-74; Exec of the Year LA Brotherhood Crusade 1976. **Business Addr:** Pres, A & S Resources Inc, 4943 McConnell Ave, Ste O, Los Angeles, CA 90066.

BEAUCHAMP, PATRICK L.
Beer distributor. **Career:** Beauchamp Distributing Co, Compton CA, chief executive. **Business Addr:** Chief Executive, Beauchamp Distributing Co, 1911 S Santa Fe Ave, Compton, CA 90221.

BEAUFORD, FRED
Publisher. **Personal:** Born Nov 11, 1940, Neptune, NJ; children: Danielle, Fred, Tama, Alexis. **Educ:** NY Univ, BS 1971. **Career:** Black Creation, editor, founder 1969-73; Neworld Mag, editor, publisher 1974-81; Univ of So CA, sr lecturer 1977-81; Univ of CA Berkeley, vstg prof 1981-84; The Crisis Mag, editor 1985-; State Univ of New York-Old Westbury, asst prof, American studies, 1990-. **Honors/Awds:** Cert of Serv Inst of Afro-Amer Affairs NYU 1972; Outstanding Serv CA Conf of the Arts 1979. **Military Serv:** AUS pfc 1958-60.

BEAUVAIS, GARCELLE
Actress. **Personal:** divoRced; children: Oliver. **Career:** Models Inc, television series, actress; The Jamie Foxx Show, television series, actress, currently. **Business Phone:** (310)278-8070.

BEAVER, JOSEPH T., JR.
Author, publisher. **Personal:** Born Sep 22, 1922, Cincinnati, OH; son of Eva Beaver and Joseph Beaver; married Helen Mae Greene; children: Joseph T III, James Paul, Northe Lejana Olague, Wendla Tarascana Helene Coonan. **Educ:** Univ of Cincinnati, liberal arts 1940-41; Univ WI Ext, economics 1947; Univ Teuerife Spain, economic geography 1951; Foreign Serv Inst, languages labor confs public speech consular officers courses 1954, 1960-61, 1964-68, sr exec seminar course 1967; College of the Desert Palm Desert CA, journalism, micro-macro economics 1978-79. **Career:** US foreign service, 26 years (retired); foreign service consular officer, retired; Spanish interpreter; Intl Review of Third World Culture & Issues, publisher/editor. **Orgs:** Life mem NAACP; bd mem Western States Black Rsch Ctr; bd mem Coachella Economic Develop Corp; Palm Springs Chamber of Commerce; Citizens for Freedom; affirmative action ofcr Coalicion Politica de la Raza; DEMAND; founder Friends of Jesse Jackson Coalition 1985; exec dir Black Historical & Cultural Soc of Coachella Valley; lectured on foreign policy Africa & Latin America; chmn Martin Luther King Commemoration Comm Palm Springs; pres Jesse Jackson Demo Club of Coachella Valley; College of Desert Advisory Committee; Education Alert Committee; Coachella Valley African American Chamber of Commerce; Greater Palm Springs Hispanic Chamber of Commerce, honorary mem; Coll of the Desert Extended Opportunity Program Services, EOPS, co-chair; Coll of the Desert Diversity Task Force; Black Amer Cinema Society, bd of dirs; Desert Sun, editorial bd; Palm Springs Convention Ctr, bd of dirs; Friends of Cuba, Coachella Valley Branch, organizer; Coachella Valleywide Kwanzaa Celebration Ceremonies, co-pres, 1993-94; Cabazon Indian Cultural Ctr, bd of dirs, 1996; ''Que Nuevas'' Newspaper, advisory bd, 1997. **Honors/Awds:** Meritorious Honor Awd 1965; Trophy for Editorial Excellence in Journalism Coll of Desert CA 1978; author/columnist US & Abroad; author ''Africa In Perspective,'' ''The Best Neighbor''; named Exec Dir Black Historical and Cultural Soc of the Coachella Valley Palm Springs, CA 1984; Certificate of Appreciation for Significant Serv to the Comm and in observation of Black History month County of Riverside; recipient, Buffalo Soldiers Trophy, Edwards A F Base 1991; First Corechella Valley Hispanic Recognition Award, 1997; Kwanzaa Plaque, 1998; International Film Festival Trophy, 1998. **Military Serv:** USMC sgt 1943-46. **Business Addr:** Publisher/Editor, Intl Review of 3rd World Cul, PO Box 1785, Palm Springs, CA 92263.

BEAVERS, NATHAN HOWARD, JR.
Clergyman, business executive. **Personal:** Born Aug 6, 1928, Alexander City, AL; married Velma C; children: Vincent, Norman, Stephany, Rhonda, Lyrica. **Educ:** Howard Univ Sch of Law, JD 1952, addtl studies; Hamma Sch of Theol, MDiv, PhD cand 1975-. **Career:** General Practice, civil & criminal law 1955-62; OH Eagle Newspaper, 1963-65; Cleveland, real est devel/gen contr/cons 1966-71; FHA St Univ of Coll Buffalo, lectr Natl Acad of Sci 1969; Affil Contractors of Amer Inc, fdr & natl exec dir 1971-; Faith Bapt Ch Springfield, co-pastor 1974-. **Orgs:** Past pres Soc of Registered Contractors 1968-70; mem Sigma Delta Tau Legal Frat 1951; fdr & 1st pres Omicron Lambda Alpha Chap 1950; pres Beta Chap 1949; fdr & 1st pres Zeta Delta Lambda Chap Alpha Phi Alpha Frat Inc 1957; mem Prince Hall Masons, Shriners, Knights of Pythias, Elks, Amer Legion; chrtr mem Frontiers Intl; bd of dir YMCA; Nutrition for the Elderly; Planned Parenthood 1975; con World Bank 1973; consult Urban League 1973-75. **Honors/Awds:** Outstanding Contrib to Minority Econ Devel State of OH 1977; Outst Serv to Contractors Mayor Roger Baker 1976; Outst Serv Affiliate Contractors of Amer 1971-72; Outst Businessman of the Yr Urban League 1969; 1st & Outst FHA Multi-Fam Housing Proj HUD 1968. **Military Serv:** USAF Cpt 1955. **Business Addr:** Faith Bapt Church, 328 W Clark St, Springfield, OH 45506.

BEAVERS, ROBERT M., JR.
Restaurant industry executive. **Personal:** Born 1944; married; children: 4. **Educ:** George Washington University, Washington & Jefferson Coll, BS, electrical engineering. **Career:** McDonald's Corp, Oakbrook, IL, entire career with McDonald's, beginning 1963, senior vice president; mem of bd of dirs, currently. **Orgs:** Nicor Inc, Chicago, Zoological Assn, bd of dirs; Hinsdale Hosp, visiting trustee, NC A&T Coll, bd of advisors; Howard Univ School of Business. **Honors/Awds:** Numerous Awards.

BECK, ANGEL CARTER
Syndicated columnist. **Personal:** Born Aug 18, 1951, Omaha, NE; daughter of Aleane Fitz & James Carter; divorced; children: Jaman, Angel Marie, Frank. **Educ:** Frederick Douglas Creative Arts Ctr; University of Nebraska-Omaha, BS, 1975. **Career:** Oakland Tribune, sports writer, 1986-87; Cap Cities/ABC Internship-Print, general assistant reporter, 1988-90; Bronx Net Cable, TV New York, sports reporter, 1995-; WNET-TV, New York, talk show host, 1991-92; Stamford Public Schools, teacher young mothers, currently; Tribune Media Svcs, syndicated columnist, currently. **Orgs:** WCBS-TV, New York, Sharing the Dream, community mem; YMCA, Stamford, membership board; Norwalk Community College, Norwalk, advisory community; New Haven Association of Black Journalists, former president, 1989-90; Adolescent Treatment Project, Fortworth TX, community mem, 1988-89. **Special Achievements:** Author: ''How to Play Bid Whist''; Syndicated Columnist of 1st Bid Whist Column in the Nation; First African-American female to have a games column. **Home Phone:** (203)973-0151. **Business Addr:** National Syndicated Columnist, Tribune Media Svcs, 435 N Michigan Ave, Chicago, IL 60611, 800-245-6536.

BECK, ARTHELLO, JR.
Artist. **Personal:** Born Jul 17, 1941, Dallas, TX; son of Millie Beck and Arthello Beck Sr; married Mae Johnson Beck; children: Mashariki Akiba, Hodari Amin. **Career:** Free-lance artist; Arthello's Gallery, owner; Mountain View College, art instructor, 1979; Choat Paint Store, art instructor, 1981. **Orgs:** National Conference of Artists, Southwest Black Artists Guild. **Honors/Awds:** One of 8 leading artists in Southwest 1964; Special Merit Award State Fair of TX 1974; 2nd Place Southwestern Ceramic Show 1974; 1st Place Black Art Exhibit Fort Worth 1972; Received Fine Arts Award Com of 100 Dallas, TX 1975; Certificate of Recognition, Elite News, 1976; 3rd Place, Temple Emanuel Annual Art Show, 1976. **Special Achievements:** Art Shows: YWCA's Libraries; Midtown Fine Arts League, 1979; Texas Southern University, 1985; numerous others. **Business Addr:** Artist, Owner, Arthello's Art Gallery, 1922 S Beckley, Dallas, TX 75224.

BECK, CLARK E.
Consultant, educator, educational administrator (retired). **Personal:** Born Apr 6, 1929, Marion, IN; son of Mildred Lois Pettiford Beck and Frederick Douglas Beck; divorced; children:

Clark E II, Angela. **Educ:** Virginia Union University, Richmond, VA, BS, Math, 1951; University of Cincinnati, Cincinnati, OH, ME, Engineering, 1955, MS, Engineering, 1969. **Career:** Air Force Systems Command, aerospace engineer, 1955-85; Central State Univ, assoc prof, 1985-87; Wright State Univ, asst dean, 1987-93; CEBEC Associates, consultant, 1993-. **Orgs:** President, Ohio Society of Professional Engineers, 1973-74; president, Engineers Club of Dayton, 1990-91; president, Affiliate Societies Council, 1985-88; charter president, Mad River Optimist Club, 1975-77; president, Kidney Foundation of Miami Valley, 1985-87; National Management Association, (Life Member); American Society for Engineering Education; Engineering and Science Hall of Fame; Engineering and Science Foundation; trustee, Dayton City Plan Board, University of Cincinnati Foundation, 1989-. **Honors/Awds:** Elected Fellow, Society for Technical Communications, 1991; Distinguished Alumnus, University of Cincinnati, 1981; Uncommon Man Award, Ohio Society of Professional Engineers, 1983, 1990; Outstanding Engineer, Engineers Foundation of Dayton, 1967, 1981; Elected Fellow, American Society of Mechanical Engineers, Tau Beta Pi.

BECK, HERSHELL P.
Elected official. **Personal:** Born Dec 19, 1940, Carthage, TX; married Ida Mae Reese; children: Lorengo Raoul, Jackie Deshun. **Educ:** Tyler Barber Coll, 1960. **Career:** Poney League, coach 1977-83; Boy Scouts, leader 1977-85; Planning & Zoning Commiss, mem 1978-80; Human Devel Corp, bd mem 1980-84; City of Carthage, mayor pro tem. **Orgs:** Commisss city of Carthage TX 1980-; mem Turner Alumni Assoc 1980-; exec bd Turner Alumni Assoc 1980-; mayor pro tem City of Carthage TX 1983-; bd mem Devel Block Grant Review Comm 1983-; bd mem East TX Region Community 1984-. **Honors/Awds:** Plaque HUDCO 1980; Cert Governor of TX 1984. **Home Addr:** 402 Highland, Carthage, TX 75633.

BECK, ROSWELL NATHANIEL
Physician. **Personal:** Born in Georgetown, SC; married Barbara; children: Roswell Jr, MD, Janice, Celeste. **Educ:** Fisk Univ, AB 1934; Meharry Med Coll, MD 1944. **Career:** Private practice, physician 1944-51, 1953-. **Orgs:** Mem Natl Med Assoc, So Med Assoc, Inter-Co Med Assoc; advisory mem SC Reg Med Program; mem SC Comm Alcohol & Drug Abuse; bd of visitors Med Univ of SC 1979; mem Mt Zion AME Church, Omega Psi Phi; chmn 6th Congressional Dist Voter Educ Project; past mem, advisory Group Title I on Higher Educ; chmn Florence Comm on Comm Affairs; past mem SC Comm Human Relations, NAACP. **Honors/Awds:** Outstanding Community Service, Zeta Phi Beta Inc, 1972-73; Service Award, Masjid Muhammed of Florence SC, 1977; Leadership in Political Affairs, EC BDO Inc, 1980; Trustee of the Medical Univ at Charleston, 1983-88. **Military Serv:** USMC capt 1951-53; Bronze Star. **Business Addr:** 403 N Dargan St, Florence, SC 29501.

BECK, SAUL L.
Government official. **Personal:** Born Jul 11, 1928, Greenwood, MS; married Elaine; children: 5. **Educ:** Attended, Chicago Tech Coll. **Career:** City Councilman, 1964-72; East Chicago Heights IL, mayor, 1973-, city councilman, 1991-95. **Orgs:** Mem Intl Brotherhood Elec Workers; mem IL Bd of Comm & Econ Develop; past bd mem Prairie State Jr Coll; educ counselor mem Natl Conf Black Mayors 1976; pres IL Chap of Natl Conf of Black Mayors; del Dem Natl Conv NY 1980; bd of dir IL Municipal League; NBC LEO; NAACP; PUSH. **Honors/Awds:** Appreciation Awd Order of Eastern Star; Humanitarian Awd Flwsp for Action; Comm Serv Awd CEDA. **Business Addr:** Mayor, East Chicago Heights, 1501 E 13th Pl, Chicago Heights, IL 60411.

BECK, THOMAS ARTHUR, III
Physician, educator. **Personal:** Born Mar 4, 1929, Birmingham, AL; children: Cynthia, Stephen, Thomas IV. **Educ:** University of Nebraska, BA, 1952; University of Nebraska College of Medicine, MD, 1961. **Career:** University of Southern California School of Medicine, asst clinical professor; Temple University School of Medicine, Dept of Nephrology, professor, currently. **Orgs:** Chairman, Dept OB-GYN, David M Brotman Memorial Hospital; American Medical Assn; Natl Medical Assn; California Medical Assn; Los Angeles Co Medical Assn; American Public Health Assn; American Fertility Society; American Geriatrics Society; Kappa Alpha Psi; bd certified OB-GYN, 1968. **Honors/Awds:** Medical Student Fellow Natl Foundation. **Military Serv:** US Air Force, captain, 1956.

BECKER, ADOLPH ERIC
Educational administrator. **Personal:** Born Mar 16, 1925, East Rutherford, NJ; married Dorothy; children: Linda, Adolph II. **Educ:** Univ So CA, BA 1952, MS 1956. **Career:** Jordan Locke Comm Adult School, principal 1974-77; Watts Branch NAACP, Paramed Occupational Center, 1st on site admin 1977; Abram Friedman Occupation Center, principal 1977-83; Crenshaw-Dorsey Community Ad School, principal 1983-90; chairperson, Youth Intervention Program Family Preservation Agency, 1992-. **Orgs:** Mem Alpha Phi Alpha Frat 1950; mem Nat Assn Pub Continuing & Adult Educ 1958-74; mem Crenshaw Neighbors Inc 1964-; co-founder, owner, dir, producer, with wife, Dorothy, Argo Center Cultural Arts 1969-74; chmn Adult HS Com of Nat Assn Pub 1975-77; dir Nat Council of Urban Adminstrs Adult Educ 1975-; chmn Curr Council LA City Schs 1976-77; Phi Delta Kappa 1977-; charter mem vice pres and prog chmn, Watts Willowbrook Rotary Club Intl Inc; mem Adult Sch Prins Assn & Guid Council LA; chmn Scope & Sequence Com Curriculum Council LA City Schools; comm rep, Policy Planning Council, LA County Headstart Grantee Prog, 1994-; mem research & evaluation comm, LA County Headstart, 1994-; chairperson Academic Comm, LA County Probation Dept. **Honors/Awds:** Recipient Nat Med Assn Found Inc Award 1972; Co-Recipient Bahai Human Rights Award 1972; Best Principal of the Year Award Watts Star Review News 1975; Community Service Award, LA Urban League, 1984; Principal of the Year Award, Youth Intervention Program, 1988; Certificate of Appreciation, LA County Probation Dept, 1994. **Military Serv:** AUS Transp Corps WWII, Europe 1943-45. **Business Addr:** Youth Intervention Program, 4625 Crenshaw Blvd, Los Angeles, CA 90043.

BECKER-SLATON, NELLIE FRANCES
Author, educator. **Personal:** Born Aug 31, 1921, Providence, RI; daughter of Nell Frances Occomy Becker and Leslie Earle Becker; married William H Slaton, Sep 27, 1950; children: Glenn, Shell, Baxter. **Educ:** NY Univ, BS Occup Therapy 1946; CA State Clge at Los Angeles, Tchrs Credential 1952; Pepperdine Univ, MA 1975; Claremont Grad Schl, PhD 1988. **Career:** Hines VA Hosp in Chicago IL, Sawtelle VA Hosp in Los Angeles CA, occup therapist 1947-50; CA Eagle, family edit 1948-51; Pittsburgh Courier, contrib writer 1951-52; LA Unified Sch Dist Reg D, multicultural adult educ tchr 1972-77; Frances Blend School for Visually Handicapped, sci coord 1973-75; Westminster Elem Sch, multicultural coord 1978-79; Walgrove Elem Sch and Charnock Elem Sch, intgrtn coord 1979-80; LA Unified Sch Dist, educ prof writer; Westminster Elementary, 1980-. **Orgs:** Dir Comm Sci Workshops 1960-69; former pres Intl Scribbles West 1960-65; Chap 587 Council for Excep Children; former bd mem LA Reading Assn; Amer Folklore Soc; LA CA Genealogical Soc; EDUCARE; Linguistics Soc of Amer; Alpha Kappa Alpha Sor; co-founder Doctoral Support Group 1982; mem Western Folklore Soc, NAPPS and SCCLYP; Afro-Amer Genealogical Soc of Southern California; Los Angeles Urban League; co-founder, pres Association of Pan African Doctoral Scholars 1981-92; Daughters of American Revolution; Hollywood Chapter of California, 1996 . **Honors/Awds:** Resolution comm work LA City Cncl 1985; Women of the Year LA Sentinel Newspaper 1962; author writers award Our Authors Study Club 1966; comm work Natl Assc for coll Women; Sci Authors Radio Station KDAY 1965; comm work Westminster Presb 1973; Senate Resolution State of California 1990; author Bacteria and Viruses Prentice Hall; author On My Own Harcourt Brace-Jovanovich. **Home Addr:** 2409 S Carmona Ave, Los Angeles, CA 90016.

BECKETT, CHARLES CAMPBELL
Government employee. **Personal:** Born Jan 23, 1912, Philadelphia, PA; married Rubye L Rush; children: Sydney Ann. **Career:** VA, psychiatric soc worker 1939; Booker T Washington Comm Center Hamilton, OH, exec dir 1940-42; Washington Urban Leageu, exec dir 1947-50; Publ Housing Adm Philadelphia Field Office, exec dir racial rel officer 1950-51; Pub Housing Adm Washington, DC, dep dir racial relations 1951-58; SW Demonstration Proj Washington, DC, exec dir 1958-60; Dept of HUD Reg II, reg dir relocation div 1961-71, regional relocation adv 1971-. **Orgs:** Ordained elder AME Ch; mem natl Assn of Housing & Redevel Officials; Natl Assn of Intergroup Rel Officials; Amer Acad of Pol & Soc Sci; past pres Urban League of Phila; bd mem Philadelphia Council for Comm Advancement; bd mem Philadelphia Fellowship House; bd mem Citizens Com on Publ Edn; bd mem PA Citizens Council; mem Human Services Task Force Philadelphia Poverty Program. **Honors/Awds:** Recip of Citations from DC Fedn of Civic Assns; Interdenominational Ministers All; Urban League of Phila; Tioga Meth Ch; Disting Serv Award HUD 1971; Author of several published articles. **Business Addr:** Regional Relocation Advisory, Dept HUD Reg III, 6 & Walnut Streets, Curtin Building, Philadelphia, PA 19106.

BECKETT, EVETTE OLGA
Marketing executive. **Personal:** Born Sep 1, 1956, Glen Cove, NY; daughter of Ollie Leone Hall Beckett and Arthur Dean Beckett (deceased); married J Barrington Jackson. **Educ:** Tufts Univ, BA 1978; Columbia Univ Graduate School of Business, MBA 1981. **Career:** Random House Inc, production asst 1978-79; Bankers Trust Co, corp lending officer 1981-82; Avon Products Inc, merchandising planner, 1982-84, assistant merchandising manager 1984-85, merchanding manager, 1985-86, manager of fragrance marketing 1986-89; director of fragrance marketing 1989-1992; general manager, Speciality Gift Business, 1992-. **Orgs:** Mem Natl Assoc of Female Execs 1986-87; bd mem Coalition of Black Professional Orgs 1986-87; mem Cosmetic Exec Women 1987; program chair NY Chap Natl Black MBA Assoc 1987; vice president operations, National Black MBA Assn, New York Chapter, 1987-88; board of directors, Children House, 1988-; program chmn, 100 Black Women of Long Island, 1987-; board of directors, 100 Black Women of Long Island 1990-; board of directors, Glen Cove Boys and Girls Club 1990-. **Honors/Awds:** Billie Holiday Performing Arts Awd Tufts Univ 1978; Outstanding Volunteer Awd Avon Products Inc 1984; Top 100 Black Business & Professional Women, Dollars & Sense Magazine, 1988; Black Achievers Award, Harlem YMCA 1989; Crain's NY Business 40 People Under 40 to Watch in the 1990's; On The Move, Fortune Magazine, 1990; Essence Magazine 10 Corporate Women, 1991; Marketer of the Month Sales & Marketing Management, 1991.

BECKETT, JUSTIN F.
Organization executive. **Personal:** Born Apr 5, 1963, Boston, MA; son of Eleanor Beckett and Herbert Beckett. **Educ:** Duke University, BA, political science/history, 1985. **Career:** E F Hutton, account executive, 1985-86; NCM Capital Management Group, Inc, executive vice pres, beginning 1986; New Africa Advisors, president/chief executive officer, 1992-. **Orgs:** Elizabeth City State University, trustee, 1992-94; National Minority Suppliers Development Council, advocacy committee, 1989-93; National Investment Managers Association, secretary/treasurer, 1988-92; National Association of Securities Professionals, 1988-; Southern University of New Orleans, adjunct professor, 1989-92; Duke University Black Alumni Connection, 1990-. **Honors/Awds:** Atlanta Coast Confernce, ACC Honor Roll, 1985; Academic All Conference Football Team, 1985; National Minority MBA, Assn Ron Brown Award, 1997. **Business Addr:** President, New Africa Advisors, 103 W Main, Durham, NC 27701, (919)688-0620.

BECKETT, SYDNEY A.
Educator. **Personal:** Born Nov 20, 1943, Philadelphia, PA. **Educ:** Temple Univ, BA 1965, MEd 1967. **Career:** Philadelphia School Dist, elementary teacher 1965-66; IBM, mktg support representative 1967-73; PA Comm on Status of Women, commr appointed by Governor 1972-; EI Dupont, training & devel 1974-. **Orgs:** Bd trustees Temple Univ 1974; bd dir Alumni Assn 1967; bd dir SW Belmont YWCA 1970; Amer Soc Training & Devel 1974; Phi Delta Gamma; mem AAUW 1977; mem Delta Sigma Theta Sor 1962. **Honors/Awds:** Outstanding Woman of Yr Temple Univ 1970; Comm Serv Award IBM 1970-72; Dale Carnegie Inst 2 awards; Sr Recong Award of Pres & Faculty; Outstanding Sr Templar Yearbook; Greek Woman of Yr Temple Univ; Volunteer Serv Award; Treble Clef Alumnae Award; Campbell AME Ch Testimonial Dinner. **Business Addr:** Training & Devel, EI Dupont, Concord Pl Webster Bldg, Wilmington, DE 19898.

BECKFORD, ORVILLE
Automobile dealer. **Career:** Orville Beckford Ford-Mercury Inc, chief executive officer, currently. **Business Addr:** CEO, Orville Beckford Ford-Mercury Inc., 6400 W Hwy 90, Milton, FL 32570, (904)623-2234.

BECKFORD, TYSON
Model. **Personal:** Born in Bronx, NY. **Career:** Bethann Hardison/Bethann Management Co Inc, model, currently. **Honors/Awds:** People Magazine, 50 Most Beautiful People in the World, 1995; VH-1, Hottest Male Model, 1995. **Special Achievements:** First African American to be featured with Ralph Lauren/Polo. **Business Addr:** Model, c/o Bethann Management, 36 N Moore St, New York, NY 10013-2438.

BECKHAM, BARRY EARL
Educator and author. **Personal:** Born Mar 19, 1944, Philadelphia, PA; son of Mildred Williams Beckham and Clarence Beckham; married Betty Louise Hope, Feb 19, 1966 (divorced 1977); children: Brian Elliott, Bonnie Lorine; married Geraldine Lynne Palmer, 1979. **Educ:** Brown Univ, AB, 1966; attended law school at Columbia Univ. **Career:** Chase Manhattan Bank, New York, NY, public relations consultant, 1966-67, urban affairs assoc, 1969-70; Natl Council of YMCAs, New York City, public relations assoc, 1967-68; Western Electric Co, New York City, public relations assoc, 1968-69; Brown Univ, Providence RI, visiting lecturer, 1970-72, asst prof, 1972-78, assoc prof English beginning 1979, dir of graduate creative writing program, beginning 1980; visiting prof at Univ of Wyoming, 1972; mem of literature panel, Rhode Island Council on the Arts, 1980-; Beckham Publishing Group, currently. **Orgs:** Exec bd, PEN, 1970-71; bd editors, Brown Alumni Monthly 1975-; Authors Guild. **Honors/Awds:** Author of books, including My Main Mother, 1969, Runner Mack, 1972, and Double Dunk, 1981; author of play, Garvey Lives! 1972; author of periodical publications, including, "Listen to the Black Graduate, You Might Learn Something," Esquire, 1969, "Ladies and Gentlemen, No Salt-Water Taffy Today," Brown Alumni Monthly, 1970, and "Why It Is Right to Write," Brown Alumni Monthly, 1978. **Business Addr:** Beckham Publications Group, PO Box 4066, Silver Spring, MD 20914.

BECKHAM, EDGAR FREDERICK
Philanthropic foundation program officer. **Personal:** Born Aug 5, 1933, Hartford, CT; son of Willabelle Hollinshed Beckham and Walter Henry Beckham; married Ria Haertl; children: Frederick H. **Educ:** Wesleyan Univ, BA (with honors) 1958; Yale Univ, MA 1959. **Career:** Wesleyan Univ, Instructor, German 1961-66, dir language lab 1963-66, 1967-74, lecturer in German 1967-, assoc provost 1969-73, dean of coll 1973-90; Ford Foundation, program officer, 1990-96, coord campus diversity initia-

tive, 1996-. **Orgs:** Comm on Institutions of Higher Educ 1981-84; dir Sentry Bank for Savings 1985-90; secty, bd trustees Vermont Academy; Democratic Town Comm, 1980-90; bd of consultant Natl Endowment for Humanities 1975-84; corporator Liberty Bank for Savings 1977-82; bd of dir Middlesex Memorial Hospital 1976-90, chmn 1983-85; bd dirs Rockfall Corp 1978-86, chmn 1985-86; chmn CT Humanities Council 1978-80; pres CT Housing Investment Fund 1981-83; bd trustees CT Public Broadcasting, 1980-, chairman 1989-92; board of directors Assoc of Amer Colls 1987-90; chmn board of directors Coll Venture Consortium, 1985-90; Connecticut State Board of Education, chairman, 1993-95; chmn board of directors Donna Wood Foundation, 1991-. **Honors/Awds:** Wesleyan University, Raymond E Baldwin Award, 1991. **Military Serv:** US Army sp-3 1954-57. **Business Addr:** Coordinator, Campus Diversity Initiative, The Ford Foundation, 320 E 43rd St, New York, NY 10017.

BECKHAM, WILLIAM J., JR.
Government official. **Personal:** Born Nov 7, 1940, Cincinnati, OH; married Mattie. **Educ:** Detroit Inst Tech, 1960; Wayne State Univ, 1962, Cert, 1973; American Univ of Maryland, 1966. **Career:** Transport, dep sec 1979-; Ford Mtr Co, treas transp dept 1978-79; US Dept Treas, asst sec 1977-78; Dtrt MI, dep mayor dir myr's elct's trans dir eql oppt subcom hs educ & lbr com 1973-77; US Sntr P Hart, staff asst 1971-72, admin aide 1966-70, aide cmpgn asst 1965-66; US Cptl Plc, ofcr 1962-64. **Honors/Awds:** Metro Dtrt Tch Ftbl Leag All Str Awd 1975, 1976; Over 30 Leag Bsktbl Awd City Dtrt 1975, 1976; Mayor-elect Sem on Urban Prblms 1973; plaque Fcs onDtrt Sem 1973; Butzel Ctr Recog of Serv Rndrd Comm & Hlth Life Devel 1974.

BECKLES, BENITA HARRIS
Insurance company executive. **Personal:** Born Feb 21, 1950, Chicago, IL; daughter of Felicia Mason Williams and Benjamin Harris; married Lionel L Beckles, Jun 27, 1981; children: Lionel E, Jefferson. **Educ:** Hampton University, BA, 1971; George Washington University, MA, 1977. **Career:** US Air Force, military personnel officer, 1972-80; AAA of Michigan, Dearborn, MI, personnel administrator, 1981-92, branch coordinator, 1992-; Potential Plus, human potential consultant, 1996-. **Orgs:** Tuskegee Airmen, Inc; Delta Sigma Theta Sorority, Inkster Alumni Chapter. **Honors/Awds:** White House Fellowship, regional finalist. **Military Serv:** US Air Force, squadron commander, lt colonel, 1981-; received Joint Service Commendation Medal, 1980; Meritorious Service Medal, 1990. **Home Addr:** 18810 Alhambra, Lathrup Village, MI 48076.

BECKLES, IAN HAROLD
Professional football player. **Personal:** Born Jul 20, 1967, Montreal, Canada;married Dayle; children: Zayna, Marques. **Educ:** Indiana, attended. **Career:** Tampa Bay Buccaneers, guard, 1990-96; Philadelphia Eagles, 1997-. **Business Addr:** Professional Football Player, Philadelphia Eagles, 3501 S Broad St, Philadelphia, PA 19148, (215)463-2500.

BECKLEY, DAVID LENARD
College president. **Personal:** Born Mar 21, 1946, Shannon, MS; married Gemma Douglass; children: Jacqueline, Lisa. **Educ:** Rust Coll, BA 1967; Univ of MS, MEd 1975; Univ of MS, PhD 1986. **Career:** Rust Coll, purchasing agent 1968-69; US Army, public relations 1969-71; Rust Coll, dir public relations 1967-77, dir of devel 1977-81, interim provost 1984, dir advancement, beginning 1984; Wiley College, president, 1987-93; Rust College, president, currently. **Orgs:** Consultant, Un Negro Coll Fund Lilly Endwmnt, 1981-84; bd dir, Holly Spgs MS Chamber of Comm, 1980-86; sec, Indust Devel Auth of Marshall Cty, 1985-87. **Honors/Awds:** Kappan Yr Phi Delta Kappa Educ Frat 1984; Omega Man Yr Omega Psi Phi Frat Phi Rho Chptr 1983. **Military Serv:** AUS E-5 2 yrs; Army Commdtn Vietnam Srvc Corp 1967-71. **Home Addr:** PO Box 481, Holly Springs, MS 38635.

BECOTE, FOHLIETTE W.
Banking officer. **Personal:** Born Dec 28, 1958, Burgaw, NC; daughter of Ola Mae Williams Williams and Arlander Williams; married Lawen J Becote II, Aug 28, 1988. **Educ:** University of North Carolina, Chapel Hill, NC, BA, 1981; North Carolina Central University, Durham, NC, MBA, 1985. **Career:** North Carolina Central Univ, Durham, NC, graduate assistant, 1983-84; Mechanics & Farmers Bank, Durham, NC, Analysis Clerk, 1983-84, assistant to the comptroller, 1984-85, assistant comptroller, 1985-87, AVP/assistant comptroller, 1987-88, vice president/comptroller, 1988-96, senior vice president/ comptroller, 1996-. **Orgs:** Member, Leadership Durham Alumni Assn, 1990-; secretary, Bankers Education Society Inc, 1987-88; treasurer, member, Salvation Army Advisory Board, 1985-88; treasurer, Durham Child Advocacy Commission, 1987-88; member, National Association of Accountants, 1986-90. **Honors/Awds:** 100 Most Promising Black Women in Corporate America, Ebony, 1991; YWCA Women of Achievement Award, YWCA, 1985. **Business Addr:** Vice President/ Comptroller, Mechanics and Farmers Bank, 116 W Parrish St, Durham, NC 27701.

BECTON, JULIUS WESLEY, JR.
Educational administrator. **Personal:** Born Jun 29, 1926, Bryn Mawr, PA; married Louise; children: Shirley McKenzie, Karen Johnson, Joyce Best, Renee Strickland, J Wesley III. **Educ:** Prairie View A&M Coll, BS Math 1960; Univ MD, MA Econ 1967; Natl War Coll, 1970. **Career:** 1st Cavalry Div, cmdng gen 1975-76; US Army Oper Test & Eval Agncy, cmdng gen 1976-78; VII US Corps, cmdng gen 1978-81; USA Trngng Dctrn Comd, deputy cmdng gen & the Army inspctr of training 1981-83; Agency for Inl Dev, Ofc of Frgn Disaster Asst, dir 1984-85; Federal Emergency Mgmt Agency, dir 1985-89; Prairie View A & M Univ, president, 1989-94; DC Public Schools, superintendent, 1996-. **Orgs:** Dir Natl Assn of Unfrmd Serv 1969-71; mem Knight of Malta 1973-; The Ret Ofcrs Assn 1983-85; Fairfax Cnty Red Cross 1983-84; vice pres US Armor Assn 1982-91; USO World Bd of Governors 1985-90; bd of governors American Red Cross 1986-90; Hazard Reduction Recovery Center, a United Nations Collaborative Center, senior faculty fellow; bd of dir, Illinois Tool Works Inc; Southern Regional Education Board, board of directors; Defense Equal Opportunity Management Institute, board of visitors; Fund for the Improvement of Post-Secondary Education Board; Commission on Colleges of the Southern Association of Colleges and Schools; National Association for Equal Oopportunity in Higher Education, board of directors; First Cavalry Division Association, board of governors; Marine Spill Response Corp., board of directors; Right Choices, editorial advisory board; Boy Scouts of America, Sam Houston Area Council, board of directors; Resolution Trust, advisory board; Metters Industries, board of advisors; National Communication Systems, advisory board; Wackenhut Corp, bd of dirs; Gen Dynamics, bd of dirs; vicechair Assn of U.S. Army; George C. Marshall Foundation Bd of Trustees; The Citadel bd of visitors, advisory council. **Honors/Awds:** Top Hat Awd Courier Inc 1973; Dist Grad Prairie View A & M Univ 1975; Rock of Yr Rocks Inc 1983; G E Rush Awd Natl Bar Assn 1984; Dist Honor Awd Agency for Intl Develop 1986; Honorary Degrees: Huston-Tillotson, 1982, Muhlenberg College, 1988, Prairie View A&M Univ, 1994, The Citadel, 1997. **Military Serv:** USA lt gen 39 Yrs; DSM, SS 2, LOM 2, DFC, BSN 2, AM 4, PH 2, ACM 2, Knights Cmdrs Cross FRG.

BECTON, RUDOLPH
Barber shop owner. **Personal:** Born May 21, 1930, Eureka, NC; married Annie Veronia Wilson; children: Karen L. **Educ:** Green County Training School Diploma 1950; Harris Barber Coll Diploma 1956; Sampson Tech Inst Certificate 1979; NC Argrcultural Extension Certificate 1984. **Career:** UNC Chapel Hill, emergency medical serv 1976 & 1978; James Sprunt Inst, communications police & patrol 1978; Winston Salem State Univ, hair styling & cutting techniques 1979; James Sprunt Tech Coll, fire apparatus & hose practice 1983; Becton Barber Shop, owner/operator, currently. **Orgs:** President Magnolia Civic League 1967-; committee member Farmer's Home Admin 1970-73 & 1977-80; town commissioner Town of Magnolia 1974-; volunteer fireman/rescue Town of Magnolia 1977-; board member Duplin & Sampson Mental Health 1978-; mayor protem Town of Magnolia 1979-; board member Magnolia Fire Dept & pres Dupenza. **Honors/Awds:** Trailblazer Boy Scouts of Amer, 1968; Humanitarian Magnolia Civic League, 1968-73; Human Relations Duplin Co Good Neighbor Council 1973; Distinguished Citizen Crouton III Boy Scouts of Am 1979. **Military Serv:** AUS PFC two years The Quartermaster Corps (cooking); Honorable Discharge; Good Conduct Medal; Two Battle Stars. **Home Addr:** PO Box 86, Magnolia, NC 28453.

BEDELL, FREDERICK DELANO
Educational administrator. **Personal:** Born Apr 13, 1934, New York, NY; married Gail Smith; children: Karin, Kevin, Keith. **Educ:** NYU, BS 1957, MA 1965; Univ of MA, EdD 1984. **Career:** Rockaway Beach, chief lifeguard 1953-56; White Plains Public Schools, 1957-68, asst prin 1968-69, assistant superintendent for Pupil Services, 1984-; Bd of Coop Educ Serv, prin 1969-76; NY State Div for Youth, dir educ 1983-84; NY State Dept of Corrections, asst comm and dir of Correctional Industries 1983-84; Del-K Educational Consultant Services, president, currently. **Orgs:** Chmn Equal Oppr in Educ Com White Plains Tchr Assn 1966-68; deputy mayor & village trust Ossining 1973-76; v chmn Ossining Urban Revewal Bd 1973-76; presentations Severely Handicapped 1974; Intl Conv 1974; vice pres Cage Teen Ctr; bd mem St Mary's in the Field Sch; sec-treas bd of dir High Meadow Coop; Cub Scout Master Pack 104; life mem NY State Congress of Parents & Tchrs. **Honors/Awds:** Jaycees Award. **Business Addr:** President, Del-K Educational Consultant Services, 8 Rolling Brook Dr, Clifton Park, NY 12065.

BEDFORD, WILLIAM
Professional basketball player. **Personal:** Born Dec 14, 1963, Memphis, TN. **Educ:** Memphis State Univ, Memphis, TN, 1983-86. **Career:** Phoenix Suns, 1986-87; Detroit Pistons, 1987-92; San Antonio Spurs, 1992; Oklahoma Calvary, 1993-. **Honors/Awds:** Member of NBA Championship Team, 1990. **Business Addr:** Basketball Player, Oklahoma Cavalry, 100 W Sheridan, Oklahoma City, OK 73102.

BEECH, HARVEY ELLIOTT
Attorney. **Personal:** Born Mar 22, 1924, Kinston, NC; married Eloise Crowder; children: Pamela Michelle, Harvey Elliott Jr. **Educ:** Morehouse Coll, BA 1944; Univ of NC, LLB 1952. **Career:** Durham NC, practiced law 1952-; Kinston NC, practiced law 1953-; Beech & Pollock, partner/law firm 1966-. **Orgs:** Past vice pres Southeastern Lawyer's Assn; mem Amer Bar Assn, Amer Judicature Soc, NC State Bar, Natl Bar Assn, Amer Trial Lawyers Assn; approved atty for, Lawyer's Title Ins Corp, Chicago Title Ins Corp, First Title Ins Co, US Dept of Agriculture, Farmers Home Adminstrn; vice pres Lenoir Good Neighbor Cncl; bd dirs Lenoir Co United Fund; bd dirs Lamp Inc; mem bd of commnrs Neuse River Economic Develop Commn; pres Lenoir Co Adv Cnc to theCommn; vice pres Eastern Cncl of Comm Affairs; mem NC State Adv Comm on Public Educ; mem State Evaluation Comm on Tchrs Educ; mem State Govt Reorganization Commn; jr warden St Augustine Episcopal Ch; mem exec cncl & finance comm, mem cnslting comm Episcopal Dioscese of East Carolina; bd dirs Wachovia Bank & Trust Co; mem NCOrganized Crime Prevention Cn life mem legal advisor NAACP; mem bd trustees Pitt Co Memorial Hosp Inc; mem bd trustees E Carolina Univ; bd dirs secty-treas World-Wide Marketing Inc; chmn budget & finance comm E Carolina Univ; mem Univ NC at Chapel Hill Bd Vis. **Honors/Awds:** One of three original Honorees named to Adkin Sr HS Hall of Fame Inc 1969. **Business Addr:** Attorney, Beech & Pollock, 308 South Queen St, Kinston, NC 28501.

BEHRMANN, SERGE T.
Business executive. **Personal:** Born Jun 9, 1937, Port-au-Prince; married; children: Rachelle, Daphne, Serge J, Alex, Sophia. **Educ:** Coll Simon Bolivar 1955; Brooklyn Tech; WI Univ, structural fab engrg 1972-73; Purdue Univ, structural fab engrg 1973-74. **Career:** Feinstein Iron Works, 1959-66; Behrmann Iron Works, structural fabricator. **Orgs:** Pres Ferrum Realty Corp. **Business Addr:** Structural Fabricator, Behrmann Iron Works Inc, 832 Dean St, Brooklyn, NY 11238.

BELAFONTE, HARRY
Singer, actor, producer, activist. **Personal:** Born Mar 1, 1927, New York, NY; son of Malvene Love Wright and Harold George Belafonte Sr; married Julie Robinson; children: Adrienne, Shari, David, Gina. **Educ:** Manhattan New School for Social Research Dramatic Workshop, 1946-48. **Career:** Broadway appearances: Almanac 1953, Three for Tonight 1955; films: Bright Road 1952, Carmen Jones 1954, Island in the Sun 1957, The World, the Flesh and the Devil 1958, Odds Against Tomorrow 1959, The Angel Levine 1969, Buck & the Preacher 1971, Uptown Saturday Night 1974; White Man's Burden, 1995; television specials: producer TV Specials, A Time of Laughter 1967, Harry and Lena 1969; Tonight with Belafonte 1960; producer, Strolling Twenties TV, co-producer Beat St, 1984; recording artist with RCA 1954-73; numerous recordings, including Paradise in Gazankulu, 1988; concert performances in Cuba, Jamaica, Europe, Australia, New Zealand, United States 1983; Belafonte Enterprises, pres. **Honors/Awds:** Tony Awd 1953; Emmy Awd 1960; Martin Luther King Jr Nonviolent Peace Prize, 1982; 1985 Recipient ABAA Music Award for efforts to aid African famine victims and for conceiving and giving leadership to USA for Africa, producing the album and video, "We Are the World"; Grammy Awd 1985; Honorary Doctor of Humanities, Park College, 1968; Honorary Doctor of Arts, New School of Social Research, 1968; Honorary Doctorate, Spelman College, 1990; Natl Medal of Arts Award, White House, 1994. **Military Serv:** US Navy, 1943-45.

BELAFONTE, SHARI (SHARI BELAFONTE HARPER)
Actress, model. **Personal:** Born Aug 22, 1954, New York, NY; daughter of Harry Belafonte; married Robert Harper, 1977 (divorced 1988). **Educ:** Hampshire Coll; Carnegie-Mellon University, BFA, 1976. **Career:** Hanna Barbera Productions, publicist assistant; fashion model; Hotel, television series, actress, 1983-88; numerous appearances in motion pictures, television shows, commercials, and movies. **Special Achievements:** Appeared on more than 200 magazine covers; guest appearances: Love Boat, Hart to Hart, Matt Houston, Code Red, numerous others. **Business Phone:** (213)462-7274.

BELARDO DE O'NEAL, LILLIANA
Senator. **Personal:** Born Jan 11, 1944, Christiansted, Virgin Islands of the United States; daughter of Paula Mendez Agosto and Gil Belardo Sanes; married Humberto O'Neal, Jan 30, 1986; children: Carlos Gill Ortiz. **Educ:** Inter-Amer Univ, BA 1963; Univ of MI, MSW 1969; CA State Univ; NY Univ Puerto Rico Extension; University of Miami, doctoral study. **Career:** Dept of Social Welfare social worker 1964, probation worker 1970; Dept of Dept of Social Welfare Girls Training School dir 1971; State of CA youth authority worker 1975; Dept of Ed school guidance counsellor 1976; Legislature of the Virgin Islands legislator 1981-. **Orgs:** Mem, bd of dirs, Amer Red Cross, St Croix Chapt; mem, League of Women Voters; St Croix Lioness Club; Assn of Social Workers, Business & Professional Women. **Military Serv:** US Army, Natl Guard, captain, 5 years; dir, Selective Serv for US Virgin Islands. **Home Addr:** PO Box 3383, Christiansted, St Croix, Virgin Islands of the United States 00820. **Business Addr:** Senator, 18th Legislature, Virgin Islands Legislature, Christiansted, St Croix, Virgin Islands of the United States 00822.

BELCHER, JACQUELINE
Educational administrator. **Career:** Minneapolis Community College, pres; DeKalb College, pres, currently. **Special Achievements:** First African American woman to head a University System of Georgia institution. **Business Addr:** President, DeKalb College, 3251 Panthersville Rd, Decatur, GA 30034.

BELCHER, LEON H.
Educator. **Personal:** Born Aug 8, 1930, Mineral Springs, AR; married Mary S Randall; children: 2 sons. **Educ:** BS, 1955; MS, 1957; PhD, 1961; Post-doctoral Research Fellow, ETS, Princeton NJ, 1966-67; LSU, further study; University of Wisconsin, further study. **Career:** State of Arkansas, teacher, junior high school counselor, 1955-60; Alabama A&M University, Dean of Students, professor, 1961-66; Princeton University, research psychologist, 1966-67; Texas Southern University, director of testing, dir of Inst Research, professor, 1967-71, professor, Dept of Psychology & Guidance, currently. **Orgs:** American Psychological Assn; American Personnel & Guidance Assn; American Educational Research Assn; American College Personnel Assn; editorial bd, College Student Personnel Journal; editiorial bd, Assn of Inst Research; licensed psychologist, Texas State Board of Examiners; Cultural Affairs Committee, Houston Chamber of Commerce; Houston Council of BSA. **Honors/Awds:** Recipient, Wall Street Journal Student Award, 1955; Alpha Kappa Mu, 1955; Phi Delta Kappa, 1960; HEW, Post Doctoral Research Fellowship Award, 1966. **Military Serv:** US Army, 1952-54. **Business Addr:** Professor, Dept of Psychology & Guidance, Texas Southern University, 3100 Cleburne St, Houston, TX 77004-4501.

BELCHER, MARGARET L.
Business executive. **Personal:** Born May 11, 1922, Dallas, GA; married Ralph C Belcher; children: Brenda Vernelle. **Educ:** Carpenters Busn Sch, 1951; LaSalle's Sch of Accounting; Columbus Coll. **Career:** Afro-Am Life Ins Co, cashier 1951-62; ABC Bookkeeping Serv, bookkeeper 1962-65; Belcher's Bookkeeping Serv, owner 1965-. **Orgs:** Bd dir YMCA 1962-; Amer Cancer Soc 1963-73; Goodwill Ind 1970-74; NAACP 1958-; Comm Cntr Inc 1958-; Columbus-Phenix City Club of Negro Bus & Professional Women various offices 1959-71; Continent Soc Inc 1970-; mem Metro-Columbus Urban League 1971-; past sec/mem Council on Human Rel 1961-; mem Columbus Manpower Planning Cncl 1973-; GA State Empl Planning Cncl 1974-; UN Assn 1970-72; pres bd dir Metro Colls Urban League 1975-77; Iota Phi Lambda; Alpha Phi Alpha. **Honors/Awds:** Woman of the Yr Iota Phi Lambda 1960; Woman of Yr Alpha Phi Alpha; Sojourner Truth Award 1963; Meritorious Award GA Conf NAACP 1965; Merit Award Pres L B Johnson 1968; Red Triangle Award YMCA 1969. **Business Addr:** Belcher's Bookkeeping Service, 1323 1/2 Broadway, Columbus, GA 31901.

BELCHER, NATHANIEL L.
Attorney. **Personal:** Born Aug 17, 1929, Plymouth, NC; married Estelle Thorpe. **Educ:** NC Central Univ, AB 1952, LLB 1958, JD 1971. **Career:** CJ Gates, assoc atty 1958-61; Law Firm Bumpass & Belcher, 1961-67; Law Firm Bumpass, Belcher & Avant, 1967-; sole practitioner, 1976-. **Orgs:** Mem, George White Bar Assn, NC State Bar, Natl Bar Assn, Amer Bar Assn, Durham Busn & Professional Chain, Durham Chamber of Commerce, Omega Psi Phi Frat, 1950-; John Avery Boy's Club; NAACP 1948; trustee White Rock Baptist Church. **Military Serv:** AUS 1952-55. **Business Addr:** Attorney at Law, 1015 Red Oak Ave, Durham, NC 27707.

BELL, ALBERTA SAFFELL
Publisher. **Personal:** Born Sep 25, 1944, Knoxville, TN; daughter of Mildred J Saffell and Alfred J Saffell Sr; married C Gordon Bell, Oct 25, 1985 (deceased); children: Tiffany M, C Gordon II. **Educ:** Tennessee State University, BS, 1966, MS, 1968; Howard University, DDS, 1976. **Career:** Nashville Public Schools; United States Army, major, Dental Corp; The Gardner News, vice pres, 1989-92, publisher/president, 1992-. **Orgs:** Montachunett Girl Scout, board member, 1990-; The Gardner Museum, trustee, 1989-; Citchburg State University, trustee, 1991-; Massachusetts Newspapers/Publishers, 1992-; Heritage State Park Friends, vice pres, 1988-; Greater Gardner Chamber of Commerce. **Military Serv:** US Army, major, 1976-86. **Business Addr:** President/Publisher, The Gardner News, 309 Central St, PO Box 340, Gardner, MA 01440, (508)632-8000.

BELL, CARL COMPTON
Psychiatrist. **Personal:** Born Oct 28, 1947, Chicago, IL; son of Pearl Debnam Bell and William Yancey Bell Jr; married Tyra Taylor; children: Briatta, William. **Educ:** Univ of IL Chicago Circle, BS Biology 1967; Meharry Medical Coll, MD 1971; IL State Psychiatric Inst Chicago, psychiatric residency 1974. **Career:** Matthew Walker Comp Health Center, Meharry Medical College, biostatistician, 1970-72; Illinois Dept of Mental Health, resident physician, 1971-74; private practice, psychiatrist, 1972-; Chicago Med Sch, clinical instr of psych, 1975; Jackson Park Hospital, consultant 1972-74, Psychiatric Emergency Serv Prog, dir 1976-77, assoc dir, div of behaviorial & psychodynamic med 1979-80; Human Correctional & Serv Inst, staff psychiatrist 1977-78; Chatham Avalon Mental Health Ctr, staff psychiatrist 1977-79; Chicago Bd of Educ, staff psychiatrist 1977-79; Community Mental Health Council, day treatment ctr, staff psychiatrist 1977-79, med dir 1982-87, president/CEO, 1987-; Univ of IL, Sch of Med, prof, clinical psych, 1983-; WVON-AM, Chicago, IL, radio talk show host, 1987-88; WJPC-FM, The Black Couch, radio talk show, 1992-93; Univ of Il School of Public Health, prof, 1995. **Orgs:** Amer-Indian Asian-Pacific Am/Black & Hispanic Core Mental Health Discipline Adv Comm, Howard Univ Sch of Social Work 1980-83; National Commission on Correctional Health Care, board of directors, 1983, chairman of the board, 1992; chmn Natl Medical Assn Sect on Psych 1985-86; bd of dir Amer Assn of Community Mental Health Center Psychiatrists 1985-89;diplomate, bd examiner, American Board Psychiatry & Neurology; Shorei Goju Karate soc-Rank 6th Degree Black Belt; Black Belt Med Soc of Physicians Martial Arts Assn; sec, treasurer, Natl Council Community Mental Health Ctr 1986-87; fellow, 1986, comm black psychiatrists, 1988-91, chm, Black Caucus, 1990-93, Amer Psychiatric Assn; Amer Coll of Psych, 1987; bd of dirs, IL Council against Handgun Violence, 1990-; co-investigator, African-American Youth Project, Univ of Il School of Public Health, 1994-. **Honors/Awds:** Goldberger Fellowship 1969; Citation of Merit, Disabled Amer Veterans 1971; Mosby Scholarship Book Award, Scholastic Excellence in Medicine, Meharry Medical Coll 1971; Falk Fellowship, Amer Psychiatric Assn to participate on Council of Natl Affairs 1972, 1973; Plaque, IL Shaolin Karate & Kung-Fu Assn 1975; Certificate of Appreciation, Chatham-Avalon Community Mental Health Ctr 1979; Gamma TN Chap Alpha Omega Alpha1980; Scholastic Achievement Award, Chicago Chap, Natl Assn of Black Social Workers 1980; creator & producer of animation "Book Worm," PBS 1984; Monarch Award for Medicine, Alpha Kappa Alpha 1986; Ellen Quinn Memorial Award for Outstanding Individual Achievement in Community Mental Health 1986; editorial bds: Jour of the Natl Med Assn, 1986-87, Jour Hospital & Community Psychiy, 1990-97, Jour Prison & Jail Health, 1990-94, Community Mental Jour, 1989-; Social Action Award, Chicago Chap Black Social Workers, 1988; Mental Health Award, Englewood Community Health Org, 1988; EY Williams Distiguished Sr Clinical Scholar Award, Section on Psychiatry & Behavioral Sciences of the National Medical Assn, 1992; American Association of Community Psychiatrists' Annual Award of Excellence in Community Mental Health, 1992; Outstanding Young Doctor Award, Dollars & Sense Magazine, 1991; Alumnus of the Year, Meharry Medical College 20 Year Reunion, 1991; appointed to the Editorial Board, Journal Health Care to the Poor and Underserved, 1991. **Military Serv:** USNR Lt Commander 1975-76. **Business Addr:** President/CEO, Community Mental Health Council, 8704 S Constance, Chicago, IL 60617, (312)734-4033.

BELL, CHARLES A.
Investment banker. **Career:** Charles A Bell Securities Corp, chief executive officer, currently. **Special Achievements:** Company listed #7 on Black Enterprise's list of top investment banks, 1994. **Business Addr:** CEO, Charles A Bell Securities Corp, 44 Montgomery St, Ste 960, San Francisco, CA 94104-2804, (415)433-0270.

BELL, CHARLES SMITH
Educator. **Personal:** Born May 21, 1934, Capeville, VA; son of Martha Robinson Bell and James A Bell Sr; married Sallie Annette Parker; children: Charlette LaVonne, Mia Sallie, Angel Monique. **Educ:** VA Union University, BS, biology 1954-57, 1970; Old Dominion University 1972; Norfolk State University. **Career:** Northampton County School Board, teacher 1960-90; Northampton County Board of Supervisors, Eastville Magisterial Dist, teacher. **Orgs:** Exec bd, Northampton Cty Branch NAACP 1960-85; Northampton Cty Voter's League 1960-85; Northampton Ed Assoc 1960-85; VA Ed Assn 1960-85; Natl Ed Assn 1960-85; Eastern Shore VA & MD Baptist Assn 1960-85; Dist Dep, Grand MW Prince Hall Masons Inc 1960-85; master, chmn bd of deacons, 1st Baptist Church Capeville VA 1960-85; chmn, scholarship comm, Club Chautauqua 1961-85; chaplain, Northampton Cty Bd of Suprvs 1982-85; chairman, Accomack-Northampton County Planning District Commission 1990-. **Honors/Awds:** Teacher of the Year, Northampton High School 1980, 1981, 1982. **Military Serv:** US Army, staff sgt, 1957-59; Soldier of the Month, Presidents Medal of Honor. **Home Addr:** PO Box 554, Eastville, VA 23347.

BELL, DARRYL
Actor. **Career:** Actor, A Different World, Homeboys In Outer Space, currently. **Business Addr:** Actor, The Gage Group, 9255 Sunset Blvd, Ste 515, Los Angeles, CA 90069, (310)859-8777.

BELL, DENNIS PHILIP. See Obituaries section.

BELL, DEREK NATHANIEL
Professional baseball player. **Personal:** Born Dec 11, 1968, Tampa, FL. **Career:** Toronto Blue Jays, outfielder, 1991-93; San Diego Padres, 1993-96; Houston Astros, 1996-. **Business Addr:** Professional Baseball Player, Houston Astros, PO Box 288, Houston, TX 77001-0288, (713)799-9500.

BELL, DERRICK ALBERT, JR.
Educator. **Personal:** Born Nov 6, 1930, Pittsburgh, PA; son of Ada Bell and Derrick Bell; married Jewel Hairston Bell (deceased); children: Derrick III, Douglass, Carter; married Janet Dewart, Jun 1992. **Educ:** Duquesne Univ, AB, 1952; University of Pittsburgh Law School, LLB. **Career:** US Dept of Justice, 1957-59; Pittsburgh Branch NAACP, exec sec 1959-60; NAACP Legal Defense & Educ Fund, staff atty 1960-66; Dept of Health Educ & Welfare, deputy asst to sec for civil rights 1966-68; Western Center on Law & Poverty, dir 1968-69; Harvard Law School, lecturer on law 1969, prof 1971-80; Univ of OR Law School, dean 1981-85; Harvard Law School, prof of law 1986-92; New York Univ, visiting law prof, 1992-. **Orgs:** Mem of Bar in DC, PA, NY, CA, US Supreme Ct, US Courts of Appeals for 4th, 5th, 6th, 8th, & 10th circuits & several Fed Dist Courts. **Special Achievements:** Author: Afrolantica Legacies, 1988; Gospel Choirs, Psalms of Survival in an Alien Land Called Home, 1996; Confronting Authority: Reflections of an Ardent Protester, 1994; Race, Racism and American Law, third ed, 1992; And We Are Not Saved, The Elusive Quest for Racial Justice, 1987; Faces at the Bottom of the Well: The Permanence of Racism, 1992; editor, Shades of Brown, New Perspectives on School Desegregation. **Military Serv:** USAF 1952-54. **Business Addr:** Visiting Professor of Law, New York University, Law School, 40 Washington Square S, New York, NY 10012.

BELL, DIANA LYNNE
Marketing executive. **Personal:** Born Apr 1, 1952, Baltimore, MD; daughter of Mary E Hendershott Bell and Chester Bell. **Educ:** MI State Univ, BS 1973; Atlanta Univ, MBA 1975. **Career:** Hewlett Packard Co, rsch & devel engr 1975-80, marketing engr 1980-81, product support mgr 1982-84, product mktg mgr 1984-86, program mgr for vertical mkts 1987; product support mgr, 1988-90, marketing manager, 1990-. **Orgs:** Instructor Junior Achievement Project Business 1984; regional coord HP United Way Campaign 1984; pres Women's League Church by the Side of the Rd 1985-86; pres Natl Black MBA Assoc SF Chap 1987-88; volunteer for Amer Heart Assn, OaklandEnsemble Theater; bd of trustees, Church by the Side of the Road, 1989; national board member, National Black MBA Association, 1990-92. **Honors/Awds:** Catalyst Awd Interracial Council for Business Oppor 1975; Outstanding Young Women of Amer 1984; MBA of the Year Award, San Francisco Chapter National Black MBA Assn, 1987. **Business Addr:** Marketing Manager, Hewlett-Packard Co, 5301 Stevens Creek Blvd, Santa Clara, CA 95052.

BELL, DORIS E.
Educator, educational administrator, nurse. **Personal:** Born Nov 25, 1938, Oak Ridge, MO; daughter of Oma A Wilson and James W Lenox; married Charles A Bell, Aug 31, 1963 (deceased). **Educ:** Harris Teacher's College, AA, 1957; Homer G Phillips Hospital School of Nursing, diploma, 1960; Washington University, BSN, 1963, MSN, 1965; St Louis University, PhD, 1979. **Career:** Barnes Hospital, staff nurse, 1960-63; St Luke Hospital, staff nurse, 1963; Missouri Baptist Hospital, staff nurse, 1964-65; Kansas Neurological Institute, director, nursing inservice, 1965-69; Marymont College, psychiatric nurse instructor, 1967-68; Research Hospital, mental health coordinator, 1969-70; SIUE School of Nursing, psychiatric nurse instructor, 1970-72, instructor, coordinator, psychiatric mental health nursing, 1972-73, assistant professor, 1973-81, associate professor, 1981-88, professor, nursing, 1988-, chairperson of area II nursing; St Louis University Medical School, visiting faculty, 1981-; East Central Community College, instructor, 1981-. **Orgs:** American Association of Personnel and Guidance; American Association of University Professors; American Nurses' Association; National League for Nursing; Sigma Phi Omega; Black Nurses' Association; Missouri Nurses' Association; Sigma Theta Tau, Delta Lambda Chapter; Association of Black Faculty in Higher Education; numerous others. **Honors/Awds:** Vernice E Walter Award, Outstanding Student in Gerontology, 1985; Illinois Committee on Black Concerns in Higher Education, Academic Administration, Fellow, 1985-86; Homer G Phillips School of Nursing, Outstanding Alumni, 1987; Project GAIN, Certificate of Appreciation, 1989; Illinois Student Nurses Board of Directors, Award, 1989; numerous others. **Special Achievements:** Author: "Elderly Abuse," 1986; "Primary Prevention in Psychiatric-Mental Health Nursing," 1987; "Psychiatric Nursing Review," Missouri Nurses League Nursing State Board and Review Manual, 1989; numerous others. **Military Serv:** US Air Force, major, 1973-85. **Business Addr:** Professor of Nursing, Chairperson of Area II, School of Nursing, Southern Illinois University at Edwardsville, Bldg 3, #2318, Edwardsville, IL 62025, (618)692-3960.

BELL, EDNA TALBERT
Government official. **Personal:** Born Mar 9, 1944, Detroit, MI; daughter of Edna Rush Talbert and Theodore Talbert Sr; children: Alisha, Sonja. **Educ:** Wayne State University, BS, education, 1989. **Career:** Michigan Bell Phone Co, mgr; Wayne County Government, Wayne County Commissioner, currently. **Orgs:** Southeastern Michigan Council of Government, chairman, environmental task force; National Association of Counties, vice chair economic, vice chair sustainable leadership team, president-elect; National Organization of Black County Officials; Boscoe Home for Boys, board of directors; Renais-

sance West Community Mental Health, board of directors; National Alliance of Black Educators; National Association of Negro Business Professional Women; Optimist Club of Central Detroit; Metro Detroit YWCA, board of directors. **Honors/Awds:** National Caucus of Black School Board Members, 1990-91; Optimist New Club Building Committee Award, 1991-92; Detroit Street Law Project Award, 1991; New Detroit, Inc, 1991; Detroit Public School Region 3 Board Award, 1980-82; Receipient of President's Point of Light, 1996. **Special Achievements:** Congressional Black Caucus Foundation's 22nd Annual Legislative Conference, 1992. **Business Addr:** Wayne County Commissioner, Wayne County Commission, 600 Randolph, Ste 443, Detroit, MI 48226, (313)224-0936.

BELL, ELDRIN A.
Law enforcement official. **Personal:** childDren: Ashley, Terry, Michael, Allyson, Justin. **Educ:** Morris Brown College, Atlanta, GA; Georgia State; Atlanta University. **Career:** Atlanta Police Department, chief of police, 1990-. **Business Addr:** Chief of Police, City of Atlanta, 675 Ponce De Leon Ave, Atlanta, GA 30308.

BELL, ELMER A.
Executive director. **Personal:** Born Nov 17, 1941, Gurdon, AR; married Jo Ann Miller; children: Elmer II. **Educ:** Univ of AR, BS 1964. **Career:** Univ of AR, counselor 1964; Pine Bluff Pub Sch, tchr; Ofc of Econ Oppor Pine Bluff, field rep, asst dir, exec dir. **Orgs:** Licensed professional funeral dir; bd mem bd sec Housing Develop Corp of AR Inc; mem Royal Knight Soc; life mem Kappa Alpha Psi Frat keeper of records; St John Meth Ch; bd dir Amer Red Cross; bd mem Big Bros of Amer. **Honors/Awds:** Cert of Merit AR OEO Training Sch; Volt Tech Inst; Development Assoc Inc; Comm Serv Awd 1974. **Business Addr:** Executive Dir, Office of Economic Oppor, 200 E 8 Ave, City Hall, Pine Bluff, AR 71601.

BELL, EVERETT THOMAS
Clergyman, mayor. **Personal:** Born Jun 26, 1909, Winona, TX; son of Julia Bell and Walter Bell; married Edith Glaspie; children: Joe Everett, John F, Elayne Dedman. **Educ:** Butler Coll, attended 1936-38; TX Coll, sales course 1938-39. **Career:** Universal Life Ins Co, salesman 1938-48; Benevolent Life, mgr 1955-66; clergyman 1965-; Afro-Am Life Ins Co LA, state supr 1972-74; Easton, TX, mayor. **Orgs:** Co-opener Universal Life Ins Co State of CA 1949; co-opener Afro-Am Life Ins Co of FL in State of LA 1972; rebuilt one church/pastored two/ currently building another church; mem NAACP 1938-; mem Natl Negro Council Los Angeles 1946. **Honors/Awds:** Recipient Numerous Awards Natl Assn of Ins; Increase Bonus & Awards Benevolent Life 4 years.

BELL, FELIX C.
Educator. **Personal:** Born Jan 4, 1936, Senatobia, MS; married Eunice; children: Lolita, Kelvin, Jennifer, Kenneth. **Educ:** Atlanta Univ, MS 1970; MS Indust Coll, BA 1958. **Career:** Tute Cty High School, instructor; Rust Coll, instructor. **Orgs:** Chmn dept Tute Cty HS 1967-70; pres Tate Cty Teacher Assoc 1968-70; chmn Tate Cty Leadership Assoc; mem Loyal Dem Party 1974-75; sr deacon Paradise Ch; mem Omega Psi Phi; master Mason Lodge 9 1958-75. **Honors/Awds:** Runner Up Teacher Year Rust Coll 1975. **Business Addr:** Instructor, Rust College, PO Box 121, Holly Springs, MS 38635.

BELL, GEORGE
Public administrator. **Personal:** Born Mar 12, Pittsburgh, PA; children: George Jr, Christian, Kofi. **Educ:** Cheyney State Coll, BS; Univ Detroit, MA. **Career:** Friends Select Sch Phila, tchr; Philadelphia Pub Schs, tchr; Harvou-Act Inc NYC, acting dir after sch study prog; United Ch of Christ, asst to dir & prog coord commn for racial justice; Shaw Coll, chmn div of social sciences; Mayor City of Detroit, exec asst. **Orgs:** Dir Child/ Family Ctr City of Detroit; chmn Reg One Bd of Educ City of Detroit; pres Central Bd of Educ City of Detroit; chmn bd of trustees Wayne Co Comm Coll.

BELL, GEORGE ANTONIO
Professional baseball player. **Personal:** Born Oct 21, 1959, San Pedros de Macoris, Dominican Republic; married Marie Louisa Beguero; children: Christopher, George Jr. **Career:** Toronto Blue Jays, outfielder, 1981, 1983-90; Chicago Cubs, outfielder, 1991-. **Honors/Awds:** Named Labatt's Blue MVP; Blue Jays Minor League Player of Month for June 1983; named Most Valuable Player of the American League; American League Most Valuable Player, Baseball Writers Assn of America, 1987; American League All-Star Team, 1987, 1990. **Business Addr:** Professional Baseball Player, Chicago Cubs, 1060 Addison St W, Wrigley Field, Chicago, IL 60613-4397.

BELL, H. B.
Educator. **Personal:** Born Apr 13, 1938, LaRue, TX; married Susie Alice Davis; children: Diedrae Carron, Dionica Britte. **Educ:** Prairie View A&M Univ, BA 1961, MEd 1967; East TX State Univ, EdD 1981. **Career:** Rust Coll, asst dean of men engrg tchr 1961-63; Dallas Independent Sch Dist, teacher sr high english 1963-68, asst principal 1968-73, educ planner 1973-74, dir teacher educ ctr 1974-76, deputy assoc supt personnel develop 1976-78, deputy assoc supt special funds acquisition and monitoring 1978-82, asst supt subdistrict II 1982-85, asst supt elem instruction 1985-. **Orgs:** Mem TX Educ Agency Eval Team evaluating The Univ of TX at Austin's Prog 1977; presented paper Competency-Based Teacher Educ in Dallas Assoc of Teacher Educators Conf Atlanta GA 1977; mem Southern Assoc Eval Team LG Pinkston HS 1977; adjunct prof East TX State Univ Dept of Admin and Supervision 1985,86; mem Dallas Sch Admin Assoc, Natl Assoc of Secondary Sch Principals, Natl Cncl of Teachers of English, Young Men's Christian Assoc Mooreland Branch, NAACP Dallas Branch, Alpha Phi Alpha Frat; bd of dirs Alpha Merit Group, Woodstream Property Assoc; mem Natl Assoc of Admin of State and Federal EducProgs, Amer Assoc of Sch Administrators. **Honors/Awds:** Disting Alumnus Prairie View A&M Univ 1977; Outstanding Urban Educator for the Dallas Independent Sch Dist 1982; Disting Alumnus East TX State Univ 1983; Outstanding Admin Leadership in Educ Dallas Independent Sch Dist 1984; Outstanding Black Texan's Awd TX House of Rep Austin 1987; 5 publications. **Home Addr:** 6626 Harvest Glen, Dallas, TX 75248. **Business Addr:** Asst Supt, Elem Instruction, Dallas Independent School District, 3700 Ross Ave, Box 7, Dallas, TX 75204.

BELL, HAROLD KEVIN
Radio sportscaster, talk show host. **Personal:** Born May 21, 1939, Washington, DC; son of Mattie Bell and Alfred Bell; married Hatti Thomas, Nov 28, 1968. **Educ:** Winston-Salem State University, 1959-63. **Career:** United Planning Organization, 1964-66; DC Recreation Department, Roving Leader Program, 1966-69; Department of Defense, sports and recreation specialist, 1969-71; Project Build, job placement specialist, 1971-74; WOOK Radio, sportscaster and talk show host, 1974-78; Anheuser-Bush, marketing and sports representative, 1978-80; Nike Shoes, sports promotions representative, 1980-82; WUST Radio, sports director and talk show host, 1986-94; WINX Radio, sportscaster and talk show host, currently; H B Sports & Marketing, president, currently. **Orgs:** Kids In Trouble, president & founder, 1986-; National Jr Tennis League, board member, 1982; SE Youth Development Program, consultant, 1979; NAACP, media coordinator, 1976; United Negro College Fund, consultant/celebrity fund raiser, 1980; Send A Kid To Camp, coordinator, 1970; Sonny Hill/John Chaney Summer League, board member, 1984; DC School System Community Task Force, board member, 1988. **Honors/Awds:** Cited in Congressional Record by Rep Louis Stokes, 1975; Washington Magazine, Washingtonian of the Year, 1980; President of the United States, Cited for Work with the Youth, 1970; Department of Defense, founder of First Half Way House, 1971; Phi Delta Kappa, Howard University, Community Person of the Year, 1988; Image Award, Pioneering/San Francisco, 1995. **Special Achievements:** Hillcrest Children's Center Saturday Program, founder, 1969; founder of first halfway house for juvenile delinquents on a military base, "Bolling Boys Base" 1971; First African-American to host and produce own radio sports talk show in Washington, DC, 1974; First to host and produce own TV sports special on NBC affiliate WRC-TV4, 1975; first sports media personality to create a media roundtable to discuss current issues in the sports world, by inviting radio, TV, and print media personalities to participate on "Inside Sports," once monthly; cited in Congressional record by Sen Bob Dole, 1994. **Business Addr:** President, H B Sports & Marketing Inc, 1325 W St, NW, Ste 318, Washington, DC 20019, (202)234-1077.

BELL, HUBERT THOMAS, JR.
Government official. **Personal:** Born Jul 9, 1942, Mobile, AL; son of Theresa Thomas Bell (deceased) and Hubert Thomas Bell Sr.; married Satwant Kaur Bell, Aug 9, 1975; children: Naydja Maya, Nileah Shanti, Anthony Anand, Andrew Amrit. **Educ:** Alabama State University, Montgomery, AL, BS, 1965. **Career:** US Secret Service, Washington, DC, assistant director, office of protective operations, executive director for diversity management, currently; Nuclear Regulatory Commission (NRC), inspector general, currently. **Orgs:** National president, National Organization of Black Law Enforcement Executives, 1994-95; Fraternal Order of Police, 1991, president, VA chap, Region II, vice pres, 1977-; member, IACP, 1988-; mem, Kappa Alpha Psi Fraternity, 1963-; Natl Ctr for Missing and Exploited Children, bd of dirs. **Home Addr:** 5906 Reservoir Heights Ave, Alexandria, VA 22311.

BELL, JAMES A.
Educational administrator (retired). **Personal:** Born in Charleston, SC; married Sidney Silver; children: J Yvonne. **Educ:** Hampton Univ, BS 1951; NY Univ, MA 1961. **Career:** Hampton Univ, asst prof 1952-70, dir career planning & placement 1970-94. **Orgs:** Mem Amer Soc for Engineering Educ; pres VA College Placement Assn 1980-81; bd of dirs Southern Coll Placement Assn 1980-82; exec bd Episcopal Diocese of So VA 1984-86. **Honors/Awds:** Certificate VA Coll Placement Assn 1975 & 1981; certificate Alpha Phi Alpha Frat 1980; certificate Natl Aeronautics & Space Admin 1980; certificate Southern Coll Placement Assn 1981. **Military Serv:** AUS corpl 1943-46; European Service 2 Stars; Good Conduct Medal; WWII Victory Medal.

BELL, JAMES EDWARD
Physician, radiologist. **Personal:** Born Aug 31, 1926, Baltimore, MD. **Educ:** Virginia Union Univ, BS 1951; Howard Univ Sch of Medicine, MD 1957. **Career:** Jewish Hospital Cincinnati, intern 1957-58; Veteran Hospital Ctr Milwaukee, radiology resident 1958-60; Univ of Chicago Hospital, radiology resident 1960-61; Marquette Univ Medical Sch, radiology instructor 1961-63; Marquette Univ Med Sch, radiology asst prof 1963-66, radiology assoc prof 1966-70, acting chmn radiology dept 1966-68; Univ of MD Medical School, radiology assoc prof 1970-; Radiology Imaging Assocs, pres. **Orgs:** Vice pres bd dir Baltimore City Medical Soc 1977-81; pres MD Radiological Soc 1981-83; chmn Public Relations Comm State Medical Soc 1983-. **Honors/Awds:** Fellowship Awd Amer Coll of Radiology 1982; Alumni of Baltimore Howard Univ Baltimore Chap 1982; Baltimore Alumni VA Univ Baltimore Chap 1983. **Military Serv:** USAF staff sgt 3 yrs. **Business Addr:** President, Radiology Imaging Assocs, 2200 Garrison Blvd, Baltimore, MD 21216.

BELL, JAMES H.
Consultant. **Personal:** Born Mar 21, 1916, Alabama; widowed; children: Thomas M, Minnie Ann Walker. **Educ:** BA. **Career:** Cleveland City Counil, dean 18 yrs; real estate bus cons. **Orgs:** Dir Cedar Imp corp Inc, Welfare Fed; mem NAACP, Settlement Houses Assoc; dir, grand master Scottish Rite Masons; trustee St Phillips Luth Church. **Business Addr:** Real Estate Bus Consultant, 2226 E 55th St, Cleveland, OH 44103.

BELL, JAMES L., JR.
Civil engineer (retired). **Personal:** Born Aug 4, 1921, Buffalo, NY; son of Madie G Nelson Bell (deceased) and James L Bell Sr (deceased); married Jessal Holland Bell, Jun 1957 (divorced); children: James L III. **Educ:** Howard Univ, BSCE 1954; Univ of Buffalo, Cert of Mechanical Engrg 1949; Dept of Transportation Wash DC, certified bridge inspector 1973. **Career:** TVA, retired civil engr div power operations 1954-63, mech engr & asst mech maint supvr Widows Creek Steam Plant 1963-64, prin civil engr divisnl oil spill prevention & control coord 1964-67; TVA Office of Power, chief bridge inspector, 1967-82. **Orgs:** Chattanooga Engr Club; chmn Fellowship Com; Order of the Engr; Equal Empl Oppor; United Way Committee chmn TVA Engrs Assn; Amer Soc Civil Engr Chattanooga Br TN Valley Sect past president; Amer Concrete Inst; Physiography Judge Chattanooga Area Regional Sci & Engineering Fair; engrg career guid couns Chattanooga HS; chmn Credit Com & bd of dirs Chattanooga TVA Employees Fed Credit Union; TVA Chattanooga Comm Relations Com; past keeper of records & seals 5th dist Omega Psi Phi Frat Inc; past basileus Kappa Iota Chap Omega Psi Phi Frat Inc; Dist Commr Cherokee Area Cncl Boy Scouts of Amer; chmn Planning Com; Chattanooga Br NAACP; bd dir Chattanooga Hamilton Co Speech & Hearing Ctr & chmn Indsl Audiology Com; Ruling Elder Renaissance Presb Ch; past pres Chattanooga Chapter Pan-Hellenic Council Inc; Boy Scout Adv; Alpha Phi Omega Frat Boy Scouts of Amer; past dist commr Cherokee Area Counc; mem-at-large; Merit Badge Couns; Chrmn Vet Committee Chattanooga NAACP; mem, Chattanooga Area Urban League; board of directors, and Bd sec, Chattanooga, Hamilton County Air Pollution Control Bureau; board member, Interfaith Elderly Assistance Agency, 1989-; Chattanooga Afro-American Museum; Chattanooga Senior Neighbors; bd member, Chattanooga Memorial Society. **Honors/Awds:** Silver Beaver Awd Arrowhead Honor Commsrs Key Awd Order of the Arrow; 35 yr Vet Awd; People-to-People Award from National Engineer Week Committee, 1984; Citation Plaque, Chattanooga State Technical Community College, 1977; Service Recognition Plaque, Fairview Presbyterian Church, 1987; Recognition Plaque, Alpha Phi Omega Fraternity, 1978; Recognition/Certificate, Chattanooga Branch, ASCE, 1984. **Military Serv:** AUS, capt, 1942-46; South-West Pacific Campaign, Philippine Liberation, World War II Victory, Asiatic-Pacific Campaign with one star, Army of Occupation. **Home Addr:** 606 Mooremont Terr, Chattanooga, TN 37411-2924.

BELL, JAMES MILTON. See Obituaries section.

BELL, JANET SHARON
Financial aid officer. **Personal:** Born Jun 27, 1947, Chicago, IL; divorced; children: Lenny. **Educ:** Chicago State Univ, BS Educ 1972; IL State Univ, MS Educ 1978. **Career:** Chicago Public Schools, teacher 1972-74; State Farm Insurance, coord 1974-76; IL State Univ, academic advisor 1981, counselor w/ special serv program 1981-86, asst coord minority student serv 1986-88, asst dir, financial aid office 1988-. **Orgs:** IL Assn of Educ Oppor Program Personnel 1977-86; Mid-Amer Assn of Educ Oppor Program Personnel 1981-; vice pres Assn of Black Academic Employees 1985-87, 1990-; Midwest Assn of Student Financial Aid Administrators; chairperson, community relations committee, Illinois Assn of Financial Aid Administrators, 1990-92; Illinois Council for College Attendance, Professional Development Committee, co-chair, 1992-. **Business Addr:** Assistant Director, Illinois State University, 2320 Fiancial Aid Office, 231 Fell Hall, Normal, IL 61761-6901.

BELL, JIMMY
Educator. **Personal:** Born Jan 4, 1944, Indianola, MS; married Clara Mcgee; children: Sonya, Arlinda, Meredith, Rasheda. **Educ:** MS Vly St U, BS 1966; MS St U, MA/ABD 1969; NY St Univ Albany, 1978. **Career:** Jackson State Univ, prof dept of criminal justice, criminal justice coord 1972-80, asst prof 1970; Lexington Bks DC Health, writer 1977-79. **Orgs:** Dir of rsrch Proj SCAN Indnl MS 1969; consult Nat Inst of Law Enforc 1975-77; consult IT&T 1970; consult lectr Jcksn Plc Dept 1974-80; chmn Dept of Sclgy MS Vly St Univ 1969; chmn Blck Caucus So Sclgcl Soc 1973; exec com mem Nat Assn of Blcks in Crmnl Jstc 1973-76. **Honors/Awds:** Nat Fellow Nat Inst of Mtl Hlth 1966-70; 1st Blck Recip of MA Dgr MS St Univ 1968; Prsnlty of the So 1977; Otstndng Yng Men of Am Nom 1979. **Business Addr:** Chairman, Jackson State University, Department of Criminal Justice, 1400 Lynch St, Jackson, MS 39217.

BELL, JOSEPH CURTIS
Executive director. **Personal:** Born Mar 23, 1933, Huntington, WV. **Educ:** St Johns Univ, BA 1956; St Maur's Theol Sem, MA 1961; Conception Coll, Cert Pastoral Affairs 1962. **Career:** St Maur Prep School, asst hdmstr 1962-65; St Maur Theol Library, admin 1965-67; USAF, chaplain 1967-70; Holy Cross Church, pastor 1970-72; St Maurs Theol Sem, assoc prof 1972-73; Resurrection School, principal 1973-76; Office of Black Ministry, exec dir 1976-. **Orgs:** Chrpsn Park Duvalle Serv Ctr 1971-73; founder, exec dir Fredrick Douglass Inst 1971-73; chief couns Manpower Unlimited Youth Prog, USAF Acad 1971. **Honors/Awds:** Young Gifted & Black Comm Awd KY 1970. **Military Serv:** USAF capt 1967-70.

BELL, JOSEPH N.
Business executive. **Personal:** Born Aug 15, 1948, Wilmington, NC; married Carolyn. **Educ:** Shaw U, BS 1970; Univ of GA; Armstrng St Coll; Am Inst of Bnkng; BSA. **Career:** Shaw U, hd lncch 1970; Cntrl Trst Co, sr ana 1971; Crvr St Bk, exec vp. **Orgs:** Dir Svnnh Area C of C; dir Svnnh Bus Leag; dir Svnnh Trbn; mem Am Cncr Soc; Grnbr Chldrn Cntr; Cit Adv Com Chthm Urban Trans; Chthm Co Assn Rtrd Chldrn; Svnnh Area Mnrty Cntrctrs; Better Bus Bureau; NAACP; Omega Psi Phi Frat; dcn tst Cnnrs Temp Bapt Ch. **Honors/Awds:** Man Yr Shaw Univ 1969. **Business Addr:** Carver State Bank, PO Box 2769, Savannah, GA 31498.

BELL, KARL I.
Commercial lender. **Personal:** Born Jan 29, 1960, Atlanta, GA; son of Henry & Naomi Bell; married Pamela, Nov 19, 1989; children: Alexis, Kristina, Cameron. **Educ:** Morehouse Coll, BA, 1981; Univ of Wisconsin-Madison, MBA, 1983. **Career:** Lockhead, Georgia Co, 1981; IBM Corp, 1982; NBD Bank, 1983-. **Orgs:** Urban Bankers Forum, pres, 1994-; Detroit Economic Devt Task Force, 1994-95; Morehouse Alumni Assn, Detroit, dir, 1988-90; Southfield Symphony Orchestra, bd of dirs, 1987-88. **Honors/Awds:** Consortium for Graduate School Study, Fellowship, 1981; Trust Co Bank, Student of the Year, 1981; National Assn of Urban Bankers, Banking School Fellowship, 1994. **Business Addr:** Vice President, NBD Bank, 611 Woodward Ave, Detroit, MI 48226, (313)225-3368.

BELL, KATIE ROBERSON
College professor. **Personal:** Born Jun 14, 1936, Birmingham, AL; daughter of Blanche Davis and Alex Roberson; married Leroy Bell Jr; children: Cheryl Kaye, Mada Carol, Janel E, Janet E. **Educ:** AL State Coll, BS 1956, EdS 1977; Wayne State Univ, MSLA 1973; Univ of AL, PhD 1982. **Career:** Tuskegee Inst HS, librarian 1956-59; Parker HS, asst librarian 1959-70, librarian 1970-73; AL State Univ, asst ref lib 1973-74, coord of user serv 1974-75, coord lib educ 1975-; So AL Reg Inserv Educ Ctr, dir 1985; AL State Univ, prof of lib educ 1985-. **Orgs:** Consultant ESAA Task Force ASU & Mobile Sch System 1979-82; Comm Tutorial Prog/Links Inc 1982-84; evaluator Natl Council for the Accreditation of Teacher Educ 1983-; bd mem pres elect AL Instructional Media Assoc 1984-; counselor Nu Epsilon Chap Kappa Delta Pi 1984-; evaluator S Assn of Schs & Colls 1985-; bd mem Montgomery Comm Council of the United Way 1985-; area director, The Links, Inc., southern area director, 1991-94. **Honors/Awds:** Cert of Honor Birmingham Classroom Teachers Assoc 1970; Educator of the Year Area of Instructional Leadership/ Univ of AL 1981; Identification of Activities in Staff Capstone Journal 1982; Development Progs for Secondary Educ Teachers. **Home Addr:** 3651 Goode St, Montgomery, AL 36105. **Business Addr:** Prof of Library Educ, Alabama State University, 915 S Jackson St, Montgomery, AL 36195.

BELL, KENNETH M.
Educator. **Personal:** Born Apr 17, 1941, Bayboro, NC; married Geraldine P; children: Kenneth Jr, Sonji, Marcel. **Educ:** Livingstone Coll, AB 1964; NC State Univ, NC Central Univ, Grad Study; Duke Univ, MEd 1975. **Career:** NC Manpower Devel Corp Bayboro, dep dir; Pamlico Jr High School, teacher, social studies, school guidance counselor; Ashley Associates, general partner; Mt Shiloh Baptist Church, New Bern, NC, minister, 1990-. **Orgs:** Past pres Local NC Teachers Assoc 1966; mem NC Ed Assoc, Assoc of Classroom Teachers, NEA, Local NAACP Chap 1964-; elected alderman Town of Bayboro NC 1969-73; founder Cty Youtharama Prog 1966; dir Local ABC-TV Gospel Music Show 1972-73; org 1st pres Agency Serv Council 3 Cty Areas 1970; elected Democratic Party Nominee for Pamlico County Board of County Commissioners, 1982; Pamlico Co Voter League, chairman of executive board, 1974-. **Honors/Awds:** 1st black elected in Pamlico Cty as town alderman 1969; recog in Pamlico Cty Centen Cele Yearbook as one of most outstanding blacks in Pamlico Cty; vice pres Centennial Celeb for Pamlico Cty 1972; audition for Dick Cavett Show 1971. **Business Addr:** Guidance Counselor, Pamlico Jr High School, Bayboro, NC 28515.

BELL, LAWRENCE A., III
City official. **Career:** Baltimore City Council, pres, currently. **Business Addr:** President, Baltimore City Council, Baltimore City Hall, Rm 400, 100 N Holliday St, Baltimore, MD 21202.

BELL, LAWRENCE F.
Business owner. **Personal:** Born Dec 1, 1958, Philadelphia, PA; son of Marian Green and Furman Bell. **Educ:** Temple University, PA, BBA, 1979; Wharton School, University of Pennsylvania, MBA, 1989. **Career:** Mellon Bank, senior auditor, 1979-81; PPG Industries, senior auditor, 1981-87; IU International, audit supervisor, 1987-88; Wharton School, senior consultant, 1988-89; Bell and Associates, owner, 1989-; Pepsi Cola, finance mgr, 1991-94. **Orgs:** Treasurer, Uptown Community Resource Center, 1987-; mgr, West Philadelphia Enterprise Center, 1989-, partnership, 1995; treasurer, West Philadelphia Neighborhood Enterprise Center, 1990-. **Honors/Awds:** Black Accountant's Entreprenuer of the Year, 1991. **Business Addr:** Owner, Bell and Associates, West Philadelphia Enterprise Center, 4601 Market St, Ste 4000, Philadelphia, PA 19139.

BELL, LEON
Cleric, moderator. **Personal:** Born Jul 14, 1930, Liberty, MS. **Educ:** MS Bapt Sem, ThB 1957; Jackson State Univ, BS 1959; Wheaton Coll, pursued graduate studies, 1963, 1965, 1966; Univ of Southern Mississippi, MS, counseling and English, 1969; Univ of Southern Mississippi, postgraduate studies in English and writing. **Career:** Springhill Priestly Chap Fairview Bapt Church, Pilgrim Br Bapt Church, Monticello First Bapt, pastor 1954-68; Mississippi Baptist Seminary, state dir of vacation Bible schools, 1958-59; MS Bapt Sem, dean of central center, 1959-67; Jackson State Univ, chpln 1965-69, dir student actvts 1967-69, relig advsr, instr 1969-75; Jackson Dist Mission Bapt Assoc, moderator, 1976-82; Hyde Park Bapt Churches, pastor, 1967-91; New Mount Zion Baptist Church, pastor, 1969-; Bell's Robes and Worship Aids, proprietor and manager; Mississippi Baptist Congress of Christian Educ, instructor in Bible history. **Orgs:** Chmn Jackson Bicent City-wide Simultan Reviv 1976; org Bell's All-Faith Lit Supplies 1975; chmn Curriculum Com for Convert Natchez Jr Coll into 4 yrs Bible Coll 1976; moderat Jackson Dist Mission Bapt Assoc 1976-82, 1994-96; mem Jackson Mnstrl Allian; bd mem MS Bapt Sem; 1st vp, Gen Bapt State Conv of MS; Dir of Youth Oratorical/ Musical Contest, Gen Missionary Bapt State Conv of Mississippi, 1993-; Asst Dir of Oratorical Contest, Natl Baptist Conv, USA Inc, 1980-94; VFW; NAACP; Masons; Smithsonian Inst; board member, Southern Christian Leadership Conference, Jackson MS chapter, 1995-; Metropolitan Ministerial Fellowship of Jackson MS, instructor of homiletics, 1996-. **Honors/ Awds:** Ambass Life Mag 1966; Mississippi Baptist Seminary, Honorary DDiv, 1973; Jackson Mississippi Chapter of the National Business League, Most Outstanding Minister in Community Affairs, 1985. **Special Achievements:** Author/publisher, Top Notch Introductory Essays for all Occasions, 1983 (revised 1987); Program Outlines for Special Occasions in the Church, 1987. **Military Serv:** US Army, 1952-54. **Home Addr:** 4322 Beacon Pl, Jackson, MS 39213.

BELL, MARILYN LENORA
Accountant. **Personal:** Born Apr 12, 1943, New York, NY; daughter of Audrey Cheatham Bell and Dr Stephen A Bell; children: Felicia Gray. **Educ:** City Coll of NY Baruch School of Business, BBA 1966. **Career:** Brooklyn Coll of Business Enterprises, accountant 1966-68; Lucas Tucker & Co, auditor 1968-69; Harlem Commonwealth Council Inc, comptroller 1969-, sec treasurer 1971-; Commonwealth Holding Co Inc, comptroller 1970-, sec treasurer; Richards Consultants LTD, financial consultant 1988-89. **Orgs:** Treasurer United Black Political Action Comm; bd of dirs Magna Media; mem Pyramid Tennis Assn Inc 1976-; treasurer Dowdy Family Found 1979-; mem Coalition of 100 Black Women 1979-; mem Natl Council of Negro Women 1980-; bd of dir Freedom Natl Bank of NY, 1985-87.

BELL, MELVYN CLARENCE
Business executive. **Personal:** Born Dec 13, 1944, Los Angeles, CA; married Eliza Ann Johnson. **Educ:** CA State Univ at LA, BS 1971; Univ of So CA, MBA 1973. **Career:** KFOX Radio Inc, co-owner/vice pres 1979-; Security Pacific Natl Bank, vice pres 1971-. **Orgs:** Mem Univ S CA MBA Assn 1973; mem Natl Assn of Black MBA's 1976; mem Kappa Alpha Psi Frat 1969-; mem NAACP 1974-; mem LA Urban League 1977-; mem LA Black Businessmen's Assn 1979-; bd dirs LA So Area Boys Club 1979-; pres Kappa Alpha Psi Frat Upsilon Chap LA 1970-71. **Military Serv:** USN yeoman 3rd 1966-68. **Business Addr:** Vice President, Security Pacific Natl Bank, 33 S Hope St, Los Angeles, CA 90071.

BELL, MYRON COREY
Professional football player. **Personal:** Born Sep 15, 1971, Toledo, OH; children: Myron Corey Jr. **Educ:** Michigan State Univ. **Career:** Pittsburgh Steelers, defensive back, 1994-. **Business Addr:** Professional Football Player, Pittsburgh Steelers, Three Rivers Stadium, 300 Stadium Circle, Pittsburgh, PA 15212, (412)323-1200.

BELL, NAPOLEON A.
Attorney. **Personal:** Born Jun 17, 1927, Dublin, GA; son of Ethel L Bell and Arthur L Bell; married Dorothy J Lyman; children: Kayethel, Napoleon II. **Educ:** Mt Union Coll, BA 1951; Western Reserve Univ Law Sch, LLB 1954. **Career:** Industrial Commn of OH, att examiner 1955-58, commissioner, 1989-91; Bd of Tax Appeals, chmn 1971-74; Beneficial Acceptance Corp, pres & chmn bd; Bell White Saunders & Smallwood, atty 1958-; Governor, Columbus, OH, counsel to governor, 1988-89. **Orgs:** Bd dir Columbus Area C of C 1970-73; bd dir Mt Union Coll; bd dir Columbus Urban League treas 1965-66, pres 1969-72; United Negro College Fund state chmn 1972; Columbus Bar Assn; spl counsel Att Gen State of OH 1972-74; bd dir Central OH Boy Scouts; life mem NAACP; chmn Concerned Cit for Columbus Com 1969;5th Ward Comm 1963; Franklin Co Dem exec com 1965; Dem Party Structure & Delegate Selection Com 1969; Dem State exec com 1971. **Honors/Awds:** Awd of Merit OH Legal Ctr; Kappa Alpha Psi Man of Yr Awd 1964; Awd of Merit Mahoning Co Youth Club 1964; Awd of Merit United Negro Coll Fund; Seminar on Workmen's Compensation OH Legal Ctr; Mt Union Coll Alumni Chair Awd 1967; Gov Community Serv Awd 1974; NCAA Silver Anniversary Honoree Coll Athletic's Top 10 1976. **Military Serv:** AUS 1946-47.

BELL, NGOZI O.
Technology company executive. **Personal:** Born May 10, 1967, Enugu, Nigeria; daughter of Chief & Mrs E Obikwerc; married Durane A Bell, 1991; children: Yamira, Zaneta. **Educ:** University of Portharcourt, BS, physics, electronics, 1988; Fadrihaaym, Florida State University, College of Engineering, MS elec engineering, 1992. **Career:** FAMU/FSU, College of Engineering, research asst, 1990-92; RW Beck, consulting engineer, 1993-95; Lucent Technologies, design engineer, 1995-97; AT&T Bell Labs; Lucent Technologies, market manager, 1997-. **Orgs:** Zita Sigma Honor Society, 1984-88; Natl Assn of Physics Students, vp, 1985-86, pres, 1986-88; School Involv of Lucent Tech, chair, 1996-97; Lucent Diversity Committee, co-chair, 1997-; The Camp Place, Allentown, bd mem, 1997-. **Honors/Awds:** UNCF, Region Br of Dirs, Appreciation Award, 1997. **Special Achievements:** Technical publication of "10 Points to Ponder on Echo Cancellation in Communications System Design," December 1998; International Fashion Designer, fashion shows, October 1997, December 1997, 1994. **Business Addr:** Market Manager, Lucent Technologies Inc, 555 Union Blvd, Allentown, PA 18103, (610)712-6281.

BELL, PAUL, JR.
Chemist. **Personal:** Born Sep 21, 1921, Lineville, AL; married Ruth Twyman; children: 6. **Educ:** Wilberforce Univ, BS 1947; Univ of Pgh, MS 1950; Grad Studies, Univ of Pgh, George Washington Univ. **Career:** Univ of Pgh, rsch assoc 1952-57; VA Hosp Martinsburg WV, biologist 1957-63; VA Hosp Aspinwall PA, histochemist 1963-67; VA Hosp Pgh, chemist 1967-. **Orgs:** Mem Phi Sigma; Sigma Xi; Soc of Experimental Biology & Med; Amer Assn of Clinical Chemist; polemark Kappa Alpha Psi; organized Charlestown Martinsburg WV chap NAACP. **Honors/Awds:** Kappa Man of Yr 1971; Superior Performance Awd VA Hosp 1966 1971 1973; recognition for over 30 publs in med & chem rsch. **Military Serv:** AUS 1943-46. **Business Addr:** VA Hospital, University Dr, Pittsburgh, PA 15240.

BELL, RALEIGH BERTON
Business executive. **Personal:** Born Dec 7, 1915, Clearwater, FL; son of Lillian Hocker Bell and Raleigh B. Bell, Sr.; married Ruth Nelson; children: Deveraux B, Sidney B. **Educ:** Pinellas Indus Inst, graduated 1932; Edward Walters Coll, attended 2 yrs; Harlem School of Music, attended 1935-36. **Career:** 2357 Restaurant Corp, general mgr 1964-69; Centerfield Rest Corp, general mgr 1968-70; Jocks Rest Corp, general mgr 1971-72; Beveruth Rest Corp, pres 1973-85; Fairway Sports Inc, pres 1975-85; The Professional V Unlimited, pres; Sidney Bell Associates, consultant 1980-85; Bell Enterprises, pres. **Orgs:** Pres Harlem Citizens Comm 1977-85; pres trustee bd Cosmopolitan AME Church, 1979-87; 1st vice pres The Xmas Tree in Harlem Comm 1980-84; pres Floggers Golf & Tennis Club NYC, 1987; chmn Public Relations & Fund Raising Boys of Yesteryear Inc; bd mem Harlem Serv Center of The Amer Red Cross Harlem House of Commons; mem, Sickle Cell Disease Found of Greater NY; bd mem Community Bd #10; pres Boys of Yesteryear 1985-87; bd mem Comm Bd #10 New York City 1987; Pres, Christmas Tree in Harlem, 1987-present; mem, bd of dirs, Uptown Chamber of Comm, 1986-89; mem, bd of dirs, Harlem Week Inc, 1986-91. **Honors/Awds:** Comm Serv Award, Amer Red Cross 1976,81; Communityman of the Year Boys of Yesteryear 1980; Baldwin E Sharpe Mem Award Xmas Tree in Harlem Comm 1983; Comm Serv Award Cosmopolitan AME Church 1983; Comm Serv Award Harlem Week 1984; Commu-

nity Serv Award Central Harlem Senior Citizens Coalition 1986; Comm Citation, Manhattan Borough Pres, 1986; Harlem Community Serv Award, 1987; Lifetime Service Award, Harlem Interagency Council for the Aging, 1988. **Home Addr:** 2541 7 Ave, Apt 21D, New York, NY 10039. **Business Addr:** President, Bell Enterprises, 2351 7 Ave, New York, NY 10030.

BELL, RICKY
Vocalist. **Career:** New Edition, singer; Bell, Biv, DeVoe, singer, 1990-. **Special Achievements:** Debut album, Poison, reached Billboard's Top Ten, 1990. **Business Addr:** Singer, Bell Biv Devoe, c/o MCA Records, 70 Universal City Plaza, Universal City, CA 91608, (818)777-4000.

BELL, RICKY
Professional football player. **Personal:** Born Oct 2, 1974. **Educ:** North Carolina State, attended. **Career:** Jacksonville Jaguars, defensive back, 1996; Chicago Bears, 1997-. **Business Addr:** Professional Football Player, Chicago Bears, 1000 Football Dr, Halas Hall at Conway Park, Lake Forest, IL 60045-4829, (847)295-6600.

BELL, ROBERT L.
Psychologist, educator. **Personal:** Born May 10, 1934, Bastrop, TX; married Mattye M; children: Allison E, Millicent P. **Educ:** TX So Univ, BA 1953; Univ of TX, MA 1955, PhD 1961; Univ TX Sch Pub Health, MPH 1980. **Career:** VA Hospital Waco, clinical psychologist 1961-66; Baylor Univ, adj prof psychology 1965-66; VA Hospital, psychologist 1966-72; Rice Univ, consultant 1970-72; VA Hospital Houston Drug Abuse Prog, asst dir 1970-72; TX Southern Univ, assoc prof 1972; Riverside General Hospital Drug Abuse Program, psychologist 1972; Counseling Center Vassar Coll, clinical psychologist 1972-73; Rice Univ Houston, dir of student advising & prof psychology 1973-79; Rice Univ Houston, adj prof 1979-80; Private Practice, clinical psychol. **Orgs:** Mem Assn of Black Psychologists; Amer Psychological Assn; SW Psychological Assn; TX Psychological Assn; Houston Psychological Assn; Amer Group Psychotherapy Assn; Houston Group Psychotherapy Soc; SW Inst for Personal & Organizational Devel; NTL Inst of Applied Behavioral Scis; mem Alpha Phi Alpha Frat Inc; Prof Adv Com Ethnic Arts Ctr Hope Devel Inc. **Honors/Awds:** Sup Perf Awd Vets Adminstrn 1964; Special Serv Perf Awd Vets Adminstrn 1968; Amer Psychological Assn cattell Fund Awd for Rsch Related to Psychol Consultation 1969; Outstanding Alumnus Awd TX So Univ 1972. **Business Addr:** Clinical Psychologist, Medical Towers, Ste 1598, Houston, TX 77030.

BELL, ROBERT MACK
Judge. **Personal:** Born Jul 6, 1943, Rocky Mount, NC. **Educ:** Morgan State Coll, attended 1966; Harvard Law Sch, JD 1969. **Career:** Piper & Marbury, assoc 1969-74; Dist Ct of MD, judge 1975-. **Orgs:** Bd dir Villa Julie Coll; bd of dir Legal Aid Bureau; grader MD St Bar Examiners 1973-75; bd dir Afro Amer Newspaper 1973-74; bd dir Neighborhood Adolescent & Young Adult Drug Prog Inc 1974-75; Grievance Comm exec comm chmn memshp comm Baltimore City Bar Assn; MD State Bar Assn; chmn mem Bar Assn 1971-72; Bail Bond Commn 1973-77. **Honors/Awds:** Dist Perf & Accompl Awd Morgan Alumni 1975; Distinctive Achiev Awd Phi Alpha Theta 1976; Comm Serv Awd Hiram Grand Lodge AF & AM 1976. **Business Addr:** Chief judge, Maryland Court of Appeals, 634 Courthouse, East, 111 N Calvert St, Baltimore, MD 21202.

BELL, ROBERT WESLEY
Building contractor. **Personal:** Born Apr 10, 1918, Bethlehem, GA; married Louvenia Smith. **Educ:** Welders & Mechanic School, 1940. **Career:** Afro-Amer Life Ins Co, agent 1955-75; State of GA, selective serv 1972-, 1st black dist commander of Amer Legion 1973-74, 1st black chmn of children & youth div of Amer Legion 1974-80; Economic Opportunity of Atlanta, mem of fin comm 1980-84; Buford city Schools, elected mem of bd of ed 1981-85; People'sBank of Buford, 1st black mem of bd of dir 1983-85; Bell Brothers Constr Co, part owner; Buford City Schools, vice chmn bd of ed. **Orgs:** Mem deacon bd Poplar Hill Baptist Church 1940-85; church clerk Poplar Hill Baptist Church 1950-85; supt of Sunday School Poplar Hill Baptist Church 1950-85;asst clerk Hopewell Baptist Assoc 1974-85; staff mem Boys State Amer Legion 1976-85; appt mem Planning & Zoning City of Buford 1979-85; chmn Boy Scouts State of GA 1980-82; mem Gwinnett Clean & Beautiful Citizens Bd Gwinnett Cty 1980-83; amer chmn Amer Legion State of GA 1982-85. **Honors/Awds:** Natl Achievement Awd Natl Amer Legion 1966; Man of the Year Buford Comm Org 1974; Gwinnett Clean & Beautiful Awd Gwinnett Cty Citizens Bd 1980. **Military Serv:** AUS master sgt 1943-46; Asiatic Pacific Serv Medal, World War II Victory Medal, Amer Serv Medal, European-African Middle East Serv Medal 2 Bronze Stars. **Business Addr:** Vice Chairman, Buford City Schools, 201 Roberts St, Buford, GA 30518.

BELL, ROSALIND NANETTE
Marketing executive. **Personal:** Born Dec 1, 1958, Panama City, FL; daughter of Bettye Price Bell and Stanley J Bell; married Jacob R Miles III, Oct 25, 1986. **Educ:** Washington University, BSBA, 1980; Northwestern, Kellogg School of Management, MM, 1981. **Career:** Dow Chemical, Merrell Dow Pharmaceutical, sales, assistant production mgr, 1981-84; Kraft Foods, Dairy Group, assistant production mgr, associate production mgr, 1984-86; Pillsbury Company, associate production mgr, pizza new product development, 1986-88; Gillette, Lustrasilk Division, associate product mgr, product mgr, senior product mgr, acting director, 1988-91; Cultural Manager, Exchange Gallery, managing director, 1991; Pillsbury Co, senior marketing mgr, 1991-95, group mktg, 1996-97; Six Flags Inc, vice pres of mktg, 1997-. **Orgs:** Junior League, Minneapolis; National Association of Black MBA's 1981-87; Minneapolis/St Paul Chapter of the Links, 1993-; Ordway Theater Advisory Committee; board of directors, Family & Children's Service; board of directors, Hennpin Unit of The American Cancer Society. **Honors/Awds:** Gillette/Lustrasilk Division, Most Valuable Team Member, 1990; CEBA, Award of Distinction, 1992, Three Awards of Merit, 1992, Two Awards of Merit, 1989. **Home Addr:** 3416 Hightimber Dr, Grapevine, TX 76051-6334.

BELL, ROSEANN P.
Educator. **Personal:** Born May 2, 1945, Atlanta, GA; divorced; children: William David. **Educ:** Howard University, BA, 1966; Emory University, MA (cum laude), 1970, PhD (cum laude), 1974. **Career:** US Civil Service Commission, typist, 1964-66; Atlanta Public School System, instructor, 1966-70; various/part-time teaching positions; freelance editor of education manuscripts, 1970-; Spelman College, asst professor, 1970-; Atlanta Voice Newspaper, columnist, 1971; Cornell University, Afro-American Studies Dept, asst professor; University of Mississippi, Dept of English, professor, currently. **Honors/Awds:** Author of numerous published articles; Emory University, scholarship winner, 1968-70; Natl Institute of Humanities Fellowship, 1971-73; Natl Fellowships Fund Fellowship, Ford Foundation, 1973-74. **Business Addr:** Professor, Dept of English, University of Mississippi, University, MS 38677-9701.

BELL, ROUZEBERRY
Dentist. **Personal:** Born Jul 13, 1934, Pittsburgh, PA; married Alice McGhee; children: Cheryl, Karen, Jeffrey. **Educ:** Univ of Pitts, BS, pharmacy, 1959; Howard U, DDS 1970. **Career:** Pvt Prac, dentist 1973-; KW Clement Family Care Ctr, dental dir 1975-; Hough Norwood Family Care Ctr, staff dentist 1971-75; St Lukes Hosp, intern 1970-71; WA Hosp Ctr, pharmacist 1966-70; Univ Hosp of Cleveland, 1959-66. **Orgs:** Mem Forest City Dental Soc 1970-; Dept of Comm Dentistry Case Western Res Univ 1975-; bd of dir Forest City Dental Indep Prac Assn 1976-; Clevland Dental Soc; mem OH St Dental Assn; Nat Dental Assn; Am Dental Assn; Buckeye St Dental Association; mem Big Bros of Am 1966-; American Cancer Society, Cuyahoga County Unit, board of directors, medical advisory committee, 1991. **Honors/Awds:** Flwsp Dept of Anesthesiology St Luke's Hosp 1971. **Military Serv:** USN hospitalman 3rd class 1952-55. **Business Addr:** Severance Medical Arts Bldg, 5 Severance Circle, Ste 413, Cleveland, OH 44118-1513.

BELL, S. AARON
Educator. **Personal:** Born Apr 24, 1924, Muskogee, OK; married Delores Orton; children: Pamela Lightsy, Aaron Wilson, Robin V. **Educ:** Xavier Univ, BA Music 1938; New York Univ, MA Music 1951; Columbia Univ, MEd Music 1976, DEd Cmpstn 1977. **Career:** Duke Ellington Orchestra, arranger-bassist 1958-64; NBC NY, studio musician 1960-62; La Mama Theatre, res composer 1964-68; Essex County Coll, coll prof 1969-, chmn, music dept, 1979-. **Orgs:** Bassist pianist cndctr Schubert Theatre Org 1964-70; res cmpsr R B Allen Theatre 1980-84; mem ASCAP 1955-85, Blck Caucus of NEA 1980-85, Natl Acad of the Arts 1975-85, Natl Scty of Lit Arts 1976-85. **Honors/Awds:** Pnlst NY St Art Comm 1980, NJ Endwmt 1982, Jackie Robinson Fndtn Comm 1984; Ford Flwshp Columbia Univ 1975-76; Obie Nom Theatre Awd for Cmpstn New York City 1979; Outstndng Comm Srvc UNICEF Newark Chptr 1984; Documentated at Smithsonian Institute in Oral History of Duke Ellington, 1990. **Military Serv:** USN mscn 1st cl 1942-46. **Home Addr:** 444 S Columbus Ave, Mount Vernon, NY 10553. **Business Addr:** Chairman, Music Department, Essex County College, 303 High St, Newark, NJ 07103.

BELL, SANDRA WATSON
Company executive. **Personal:** Born May 30, 1955, San Francisco, CA; daughter of Adell Rogers Watson; married Phillip Bell; children: Phillip Jr, Lauren. **Educ:** San Jose State Univ, San Jose, CA, BS, Business Administration, 1976. **Career:** Fairchild, Mountain View, CA, mgr, sys s/w, 1976-83; Masstor Systems, Santa Clara, CA, vp of human resources, admin, data ctr, 1983-. **Honors/Awds:** Executive Program for Smaller Companies, Stanford University, Graduate School of Business.

BELL, SHEILA TRICE
Attorney. **Personal:** Born Aug 25, 1949, Pittsburgh, PA; daughter of Mildred Moore Trice and William Benjamin Trice; married Howard W Bell Jr, Jun 7, 1971; children: Mayet Maria, Annora Alicia, William Howard. **Educ:** Wellesley Coll, BA 1971; Harvard Law Sch, JD 1974. **Career:** Pine Manor Jr Coll, faculty mem 1972-74; Hutchins & Wheeler, assoc lawyer 1973-77; Private Legal Practice, attorney 1977-79; Fisk Univ, univ counsel 1979-83; Northern KY Univ, acting univ counsel/affirmative action officer 1984-85, univ legal counsel 1985-. **Orgs:** Bd mem Family and Children's Services Nashville TN 1981-83; The Links Inc Cincinnati Chap, mem 1984-, vp 1986-89; mem Jack and Jill Inc Cincinnati Chap 1984-90; mem MA, TN, KY Bars, Amer Bar Assns; mem US Dist Courts of MA, the Middle Dist of TN and the Eastern Dist of KY, US Court of Appeals for the Sixth Circuit; bd mem Natl Assn of Coll and Univ Attys 1985-88; bd mem The Program for Cincinnati 1986-88; bd mem, Bethesda Hospital, Inc, 1990-. **Honors/Awds:** Equal Rights Amendment Commn for the Commonwealth of MA 1976; editorial bd The Journal of College and University Law 1982-83; Mayor's Special Task Force on Union Station Nashville TN 1982-83; publication ''Protection and Enforcement of College and University Trademarks'' co-author w/ Martin F Majestic in the Journal of College and Univ Law, Vol 10, No 1 1983-84; YWCA Career Woman of Achievement, YWCA, Cincinnati, OH, 1988. **Home Addr:** 800 McCeney Ave, Silver Spring, MD 20901-1453. **Business Addr:** Univ Legal Counsel, Northern Kentucky Univ, 834 Administrative Ctr, Highland Heights, KY 41076.

BELL, THEODORE JOSHUA, II
Escrow accountant. **Personal:** Born Jan 8, 1961, Berkeley, CA; son of Beverly Russ Bell and Theodore J Bell. **Educ:** St Mary's Coll of CA, BA 1983; CA Sch of Arts & Crafts, attended 1983-84; Heald Business Coll of Oakland, Career Business diploma 1985; Berkeley School of Computer Graphics, 1989-. **Career:** Marriott Boykin Corp, graphic illustrator/banquet waiter 1981-85; Equitec Financial Group, accountant 1985-88; First American Title Inc, escrow accountant; McCue Systems Inc, product support analyst, 1994-. **Orgs:** Donator/supporter St Mary's Coll Alumni 1983-; illustrator/volunteer Work of Love Program 1984-85; mem admin Heald Coll Business Club 1985; mem adv viewer Kron TV Adv Bd 1985-; mem supporter Natl Urban League 1986-; organizer, developer, TBELL Visual, 1988-; facilitator, speaker, Excel Net Customer First Program, 1990-. **Honors/Awds:** Berkeley Marriott Employee of the Year Awd 1984; Commitment to Excellence Equitec Awd 1986; Customer First Award, First American Title, 1990; Investment in Excellence Award, Equitec Financial Group, 1986; 100 Steps Award, First American Title, 1990. **Home Addr:** 2777 Park St, Berkeley, CA 94702. **Business Addr:** Product Support Analyst, McCue Systems Inc, 111 Anza Blvd, Ste 310, Burlingame, CA 94010.

BELL, THERON J.
Government official. **Personal:** Born Jun 2, 1931, Junction City, KS; married Sonya M Brown; children: Kirk, Mark, Joy Pinell, Kimberly Good, Margo Goldsboro, Michele Brown. **Educ:** Wayne State Univ, 1949-51. **Career:** CA Office of Economic Opportunity, dir 1967-69; Volt Info Sci, dir govt relations 1969-70; Chrysler Motors Corp, exec, 1970-72; Action Agency, various exec 1972-81; Minority Business Devel Agency, US Dept of Commerce, deputy dir, 1981-89; Virginia Dept of Labor & Industry, commissioner, 1994; Walcoff & Associates, business development manager, 1992-94; US Department of the Interior, Office of Surface Mining, asst to director, 1989-91. **Orgs:** Mem CA Assoc for Health & Welfare 1967-69, CA Job Training & Placement Council 1968-69, Erie Cty NY Environ Mgmt Council 1970-71, Alexandria VA Human Rights Commiss, Fed Interagency Comm on Fed Activities for Alcohol Abuse & Alcoholism, Alexandria VA Republican City Comm, CA Republican State Central Comm; life mem Republican Natl Comm; mem Alexandria VA Republican City Comm; Navy League of the US, American Legion, dir Fredrick Douglass Coalition. **Honors/Awds:** Top Producer for One Year, consistently among the top producers for the co North Amer Life & Casualty Co San Francisco. **Military Serv:** AUS pvt 8 mo. **Home Addr:** 3907 Foxfield Ter, Richmond, VA 23233-1018. **Business Addr:** Commissioner, Virginia Dept of Labor & Industry, 13 S 13th St, Richmond, VA 23219.

BELL, THOM R.
Songwriter. **Personal:** Born Jan 27, 1943, Philadelphia, PA; married Sybell; children: Cybell, Mark, Thom Jr. **Career:** Chubby Checker, band leader 1962-65; Cameo Pkwy Records, a&r man musician 1966-68; arranger/songwriter/producer 1968-80; Gamble Huff & Bell, mng partner. **Orgs:** Pres Mighty Three Music; mem AFM; opr Thom Bell Songwriter Workshop. **Honors/Awds:** Ten BMI Awds; 2 Grammy nominations; 45 Gold Albums & 45's; 1 Grammy; 2 Number One Producers Awds; 2 Bus Awds Billboard Mag; 2 Number One Songwriter Awds Billboard Magazine; 2 Number One Producers Awds NATRA. **Business Addr:** Producer, Philadelphia Intl Records, 309 S Broad St, Philadelphia, PA 19107.

BELL, TOM, JR.
Lobbyist, educator. **Personal:** Born Oct 2, 1941, Gilbertown, AL; son of Lular Mae Bell and Tom Bell; married Judith Pullin Bell, Jul 7, 1962; children: Victor Thomas, Vaughn Edward, Vernon Christopher. **Career:** American Steel Foundry, union time study, 1959-76; United Steel Workers, casual staff, 1976-77; Ohio AFL-CIO, director, compensation and civil rights, 1977-. **Orgs:** Bureau of Worker's Compensation, Labor-Government-Management Committee, 1980-92; Industrial Commission Advisory Committee, 1990-; Ohio Supreme Court, Continuing Legal Education Committee, 1989-91; Christ Memorial Baptist Church, trustee, chairman, 1989-90; United

Steelworkers Local 2211, president, 1976-77; Alliance AFL-CIO Central Labor Council, president, 1975-77. **Honors/Awds:** Coalition of Black Trade Unionist, Labor Award, 1991; A Philip Randolph Institute, Exemplary Service Award, 1990; Ohio Rehabiliation Association, Organizational Award, 1990; Cantell Elks Past Exalted Ruler, Elk of the Year, 1977. **Business Addr:** Director, Compensation and Civil Rights, Ohio AFL-CIO, 271 E State St, Columbus, OH 43215, (614)224-8271.

BELL, TOMMY LEE, III
Chief executive. **Personal:** Born Dec 3, 1948, Meridian, MS; son of Roselyn Wilson Bell and Tommie Bell, Jr; married Christiana C Attenson Bell, Oct 28, 1983; children: Antoine, Antanille. **Educ:** Middleton Atten Center, Meridian MS; Glenville, Cleveland, OH. **Career:** TL Bell Power Clean, Inc, Cleveland OH, pres. **Orgs:** Vice pres, bd of trustees, Universal Church, 1984; pres, Successeeds, Inc, 1985-89; first vice pres, Martin Luther King Memorial Fund, 1988-89. **Honors/Awds:** Outstanding Service Achiever, Cleveland Heights High School, 1978; Certificate of Achievement, MSMC Corp, 1986.

BELL, TRAVERS J., SR.
Chocolate manufacturer. **Career:** Cocoline Chocolate Co Inc, Brooklyn NY, chief executive. **Business Addr:** Chief Executive, Cocoline Chocolate Co Inc, 689 Myrtle Ave, Brooklyn, NY 11205.

BELL, TRENTON GRANDVILLE
Human resources executive. **Personal:** Born Jun 13, 1924, Troy, OH; son of Elverta Moton Bell and Harry Bell; married Marjorie Douglas Bell; children: Herbert A, Daryl, Linda Chavis, Linda Coleman, Sonja, Gordon G, Norman Foster. **Educ:** FL A&M Tallahasee, 1942-44. **Career:** Hobart Bros Co, mgr, human resources devel, 1950-. **Orgs:** St pres, IBPOE Elks 1960-69; pres Am Lung Assn 1978-; bd dir Lincoln Ctr; Troy Rec; Salvation Army 1969-; mem Bd of Elections Miami Cnty; chmn Miami County Democratic Party 1983-84; sec Ohio St Democratic Chmns Assn 1984; general mgr Grdn Mnr Housing Authority; mem bd of Health; pres, Troy Employment Svcs. **Honors/Awds:** Serv to Mankind, Sertoma Club, 1981; Hon mem, Alpha Mu Sigma 1981; Key to City, Cleveland OH St Assn Elks; Key to City Youngstown, OH St Assn Elks. **Military Serv:** AUS T/5 2 yrs. **Home Addr:** 1605 Henley Rd, Troy, OH 45373.

BELL, VICTORY
Alderman, business executive. **Personal:** Born Mar 7, 1934, Durant, MS; son of Gladys Thompson Parker and Bea Bell; married Carol Banks, Nov 21, 1981; children: Jeffrey, Gregory, Victor, Michele McAlister, Caryle Farrar, Bradley Farrar. **Career:** Illinois Bell, Rockford, IL, installer tech, 1953-70, asst mgr, 1956-86 (retired); alderman, 1971-; Cwans Corp, Rockford, IL, pres, 1986-. **Orgs:** Mayor's appt Econ Devel Commn C of C; IL Statewide Black Caucus, region coordinator, 1990-; bd mem, Winnebago County Health Dept, 1990-; bd mem, Southwest Ideas for Today and Tomorrow (SWIFTT), 1990-; mem Plgrm Bapt Ch; Rckfrd Ctzn Adv Bd for Sch; chmn Cncl Sub Comm on Soc Serv Prog. **Honors/Awds:** Man of yr recogn Natl Cncl Negro Wmn 1975; man of the yr Pltcl Chrstn Union Bapt Ch 1976; pnlst 1st Stwd Mnrty Conf for St of IL Sprngfld; del Pres Carter Nat Dem Conv 1980; Sr Alderman of Year Allen Chapel (AME) 1989; Continuing the Dream Human Resource Dept (Rockford) 1988; Rockford Set Aside Ordinance Minority Statewide Contractors 1987. **Business Addr:** Owner, President, Cwams Corp, Inc, 1220 Rock, Rockford, IL 61101.

BELL, WARREN, JR.
Journalist. **Personal:** Born Jun 18, 1951, New Orleans, LA; divorced; children: Kristina Marie. **Educ:** Yale Univ, BA 1973. **Career:** WTNH-TV, reporter; WBAL-TV, reporter 1973-74; WDSU-TV, news anchorman. **Orgs:** Bd mem Big Brothers of New Orleans; bd mem Amer Fedn TV/Radio Artists; vice pres New Orleans Blacks in Communications; NABJ, Region VII, dir, currently. **Home Addr:** 716 Pauger St, New Orleans, LA 70122.

BELL, WILHEMENIA
Educator. **Personal:** Born Jul 19, 1954, Detroit, MI; daughter of Julia Sanders Bell and William Bell; married Robert Foster, Dec 31, 1988. **Educ:** Shaw Coll at Detroit, BA 1975; Univ of MI, BA 1975, MA 1978. **Career:** City of Detroit Elections Commission, voting poll supervisor, 1972-80; National Bank of Detroit, computer operator, 1974-75; Michigan Institute for Child Development, teacher, 1976-77; Ypsilanti Public Schools, teacher, 1976-77; Detroit Public Schools, elementary teacher, 1977-80; Shaw College at Detroit, instructor, 1979-82; Mich Department of Corrections, teacher, 1980-. **Orgs:** Club & district officer Toastmasters Intl 1981-; officer-steward St John CME Church 1981-; mem Corrections Educ Assoc 1984-, MI Reading Assoc 1985-; co-founder & coord Young Women's Sor 1985-; founder/organizer Cooley High Speakers Bureau 1986-; member, Detroit Reading Assn; member, American Corrections Assn; member, Michigan Corrections Ass; member, National Assn of Female Executives; member, University of Michigan Alumni Assn. **Honors/Awds:** Appreciation Awd 1984, Competent Toastmasters Awd 1984, Accomplished Toastmaters Awd 1985 all from Toastmasters Intl.

BELL, WILLIAM A.
City council president. **Career:** City Council President, Birmingham, AL. **Business Addr:** City Hall, 710 North 20th St, Birmingham, AL 35203.

BELL, WILLIAM AUGUSTUS, II. See Obituaries section.

BELL, WILLIAM CHARLES
Attorney. **Personal:** Born Dec 28, 1945, Detroit, MI; married Jean Osbay; children: Michael Humbles. **Educ:** Golden Gate Univ, BA 1973; Hastings Coll of Law, JD 1976. **Career:** San Francisco Co Jail Legal Assistance, atty 1978; Law Offices of William C Bell, pvt practice 1978-79; Bell Realty, real estate broker 1978; Holland & Bell, atty/partner 1979-. **Orgs:** Treas Wm H Hastie Bar Assn; mem bd dirs San Francisco Neighborhood Legal Assistance Found 1979-; bd dirs Charles Houston Bar Assn 1979. **Honors/Awds:** Outstanding Young Man of Amer 1980. **Business Addr:** Attorney, Holland & Bell, 390 Hayes St Ste 2, San Francisco, CA 94102.

BELL, WILLIAM JERRY
Government employee (retired), consultant. **Personal:** Born Apr 18, 1934, Chicago, IL; son of Kathlyn Bell and William Bell. **Educ:** Roosevelt Univ, BS Commrc 1958; Univ of IL; Univ of Chgo, PA. **Career:** IL Bur of Budget, sr budget analyst, 1969-72; IL Dept of Labor, mgmt specialist, 1972-75, financial rsch, 1975-79, asst comm unemployment insurance; IDES, document control mgr, 1980-92; Chicago Clustar, consultant, currently. **Orgs:** Bell & Assoc Insurance Agency, 1970-83; consultant Small Business Assn, 1968-69; bd mem, Southside Comm Art Ctr 1985; adv Univ of IL Sch of Art & Dsgn 1981-83; founder/chmn bd, Talent Asst Pgm 1976-77; board of directors, Citizenship Education Fund; Operation PUSH, Illinois Association of Minority Employees. **Business Addr:** The Chicago Clustar, 140 S Dearborn St, Ste 1710, Chicago, IL 60603.

BELL, WILLIAM MCKINLEY
Legal services administrator (retired). **Personal:** Born Aug 31, 1926, Grand Rapids, MI; son of Mentie N Moore Bell (deceased) and William M Bell (deceased); married Patsy Ann Kelley, Oct 1, 1955. **Educ:** Univ of Michigan, AB 1948, MBA 1954. **Career:** Johnson Publishing Co, salesman/merchandising rep 1956-57; William M Bell & Associates, president 1958-75; Equal Employment Opportunity Comm, consultant 1975-76; Bold Concepts, Inc, president 1976-82; US Navy, staff asst sec 1982-87; Legal Serv Corp, legislative asst to dir. **Orgs:** Member Omega Psi Phi Fraternity 1947; member Univ of Michigan School of Business Alumni Assoc 1982; member Shiloh Baptist Church 1986-. **Honors/Awds:** Optimist of the Year, Optimist Club, Renaissance Chapter 1981; special tribute State of Michigan 1981. **Military Serv:** Us Army, 1950-52. **Home Addr:** 1515 S Jefferson Davis Hwy, Arlington, VA 22202.

BELL, WILLIAM VAUGHN
Senior engineer. **Personal:** Born Jan 3, 1941, Washington, DC; son of Willie M Vaughn Mullen and William B Bell (deceased); married Judith Chatters; children: William V II, Tiffany A, Anjanee N, Kristen V. **Educ:** Howard Univ, BSEE, 1961; NY Univ, MSEE, 1968. **Career:** Martin Marietta Corp, jr engr 1961; US Army Electronics Command, proj engr 1963-68; IBM Corp, mgr 1968-83, tech asst 1983-, electrical engrg, elect engr mgr 1985-, service engineer, retired, 1996. **Orgs:** Mem IEEE 1961-; pres bd of dir UDI/CDC 1970-83; bd of dir NC School of Sci & math 1979-; cty commiss Durham Cty Bd of Commiss 1972-; chmn of bd Durham Cty Bd of Commiss 1982-; dir Durham Chamber of Commerce 1982-; bd of trustees, Durham County Hospital Corp 1984-; advisory bd, Duke Univ Hospital 1987-. **Honors/Awds:** Community Serv Awd, State of NC 1981; Outstanding Citizen, Durham Committee on the Affairs of Blacks 1985; Community Serv Awd, Durham Chap Kappa Alpha Psi 1985; Outstanding Alumnus, Howard Univ Club of Research Triangle Pk 1985; Outstanding Citizen Award, Omega Psi Phi, Durham NC 1986; Alumni Award for Distinguished Post-Graduate Achievement, Howard Univ 1988; Service to Mankind Award, James E Shephard Sertoma Club 1989. **Military Serv:** AUS Signal Corp 1st lt 2 1/2 yrs 1961-63. **Home Addr:** 1003 Huntsman Dr, Durham, NC 27713, (919)544-5597. **Business Phone:** (919)544-4597.

BELL, WINSTON ALONZO
Pianist, educator. **Personal:** Born Mar 24, 1930, Winchester, KY; son of Margaret Hansbro Bell and Edward C Bell; married Marlita Peyton; children: Taimia Danielle, Chase. **Educ:** St Louis Institute of Music, St Louis, MO, 1947; Fisk Univ, BA 1951; Univ of Michigan, MusM 1955; Columbia Univ, EdD 1963; General Theol Seminary, StB 1964; studied at Cincinnati Conservatory of Music, Wells Theol Coll Wells England, Oxford Univ, Catholic Univ, UCLA, Univ of Louisville. **Career:** NY City School System, teacher 1955-60; Elizabeth City State Univ NC, instructor in piano 1953-55; Music Studio Nyack NY, pianist/teacher 1955-60; St Augustine Chapel NYC, curate 1963-64; St James the Less Jamaica NY, rector 1964-71; Executive Enterprises, Winsont-Salem, NC, founder/CEO, 1984. Winston-Salem State Univ NC, chmn dept of music 1972-; real estate broker 1981-. **Orgs:** Organist Holy Family Catholic Church; bd of dir Winston-Salem Symphony, Piedmont Opera Society; mem Suzuki Assoc of Amer, MENC, Phi Mu Alpha Sinfonia, Omega Psi Phi Frat, Coll Music Soc; member, Reynolda House Chamber Music Society; member, Knights of Columbus; member, One Hundred Black Men. **Honors/Awds:** Rockefeller Theol Fellowship Fisk Univ; Honor Graduate, Piano Recitals Winchester KY, Louisville, Washington, San Juan, New York, Norfolk, Virginia Beach, Winston-Salem, St Louis, Ft Knox, Santo Domingo, Elizabeth City, London, Oxford, Paris, Heidelberg, Rome, Brussels. **Military Serv:** US Army, spl serv pfc 1951-53. **Business Addr:** Chairman, Dept of Music, Winston-Salem State Univ, Columbia Heights, Winston-Salem, NC 27101.

BELL, YVONNE LOLA (LOLA)
Restaurateur. **Personal:** Born Dec 25, 1953, New York, NY; daughter of Gladys Greene Bell and Henry Bell. **Career:** Flowers by Yvonne, owner/mgr, 1980-84; Pesca Restaurant, manager, 1981-84; Ribbons & Rolls, owner/mgr, 1982-84; Lola Restaurant, owner/mgr, 1985-91, LolaBelle Restaurant, owner/manager, 1992-1994. **Special Achievements:** Working on opening a restaurant, Lalola; starting a television cooking talk show, "Lunch with Lola". **Business Addr:** Owner, Manager, LolaBelle Restaurant, 206 E 63rd St, New York, NY 10021.

BELLAMY, ANGELA ROBINSON
City government official. **Personal:** Born Nov 25, 1952, Miami, FL; daughter of Helen Peavy Robinson and Leon Giddings Robinson; married Gregory Derek Bellamy, Dec 23, 1978; children: Gregory Robinson Bellamy, Evan Matthew Robinson Bellamy. **Educ:** Fisk Univ, Nashville TN, BA, 1974; Vanderbilt Univ, Owen Grad Schof Mgmt, Nashville TN, MBA, 1976; Harvard Univ, John F Kennedy Sch of Govt, Program for Sr Executives in State and Local Govt, 1986; National Forum for Black Administrators Exec Leadership Inst, certificate, 1991. **Career:** City of Miami, admin asst, 1976-77, persnl ofcr, 1977-78, sr persnl ofcr, 1978-79, prsnl supr hum res, 1979, asst to city mgr, 1979-81, asst dir hum res, 1981-84, dir, pers mgmt, 1984-, asst city mgr, 1988-. **Orgs:** Sec 1978, vice pres 1979 IPMA S FL Chapt; co-ch host comm IPMA Intl Conf 1983-84; area coord FL Pub Persnl Assn 1984-85; Delta Sigma Theta, Dade County Alumnae Chapter, president, 1991-93; Natl Forum Black Pub Admin; chair IPMA Human Rights Comm 1985-86; mem IPMA Nomination Comm 1987; member, Society for Human Resource Management; member, Personnel Assn of Greater Miami; member, International Foundation of Employee Benefit Plans; member, American Management Assn; member, International City Management Assn. **Honors/Awds:** Awd for Outstanding Achievement Personnel Assoc of Greater Miami 1987; Greater Miami, Outstanding and Most Influential Blacks, 1986. **Business Addr:** Assistant City Manager, City of Miami, 3500 Pan American Dr, 2nd Fl, Miami, FL 33133.

BELLAMY, BILL
Comedian. **Personal:** Born 1968, Newark, NJ. **Educ:** Rutgers Univ, BS, economics, 1988. **Career:** Tobacco sales rep; MTV Jams, deejay; television appearances include: Martin, Russell Simmons' Def Comedy Jam; film appearances include: Who's The Man?; Love Jones; starring role, How to Be a Player, 1997. **Business Addr:** Host, MTV Jams, c/o MTV, 1515 Broadway, New York, NY 10036, (212)258-8000.

BELLAMY, EVERETT
Educational administrator, educator. **Personal:** Born Dec 29, 1949, Chicago, IL; son of Emma M Bellamy and William T Bellamy; divorced. **Educ:** University of Wisconsin, BS, 1972, MS, 1974; Cleveland State University, JD, 1980; Cleveland-Marshall College of Law. **Career:** University of Wisconsin, graduate assistant; Cleveland State University, coordinator of student activities; Charles Hamilton Houston Pre-Law Institute, instructor and assistant executive director; Georgetown University Law Center, assistant dean, adjunct professor. **Orgs:** National Bar Association, 1986-; American Bar Association, 1984-; National Conference of Black Lawyers, DC Chapter, chairperson, 1981-83; Phi Alpha Delta Law Fraternity International, 1980-. **Honors/Awds:** Honors Cert, Montgomery County, MD, 1996. **Special Achievements:** "The Status of the African American Law Professors," 1990; "Academic Enhancement and Counseling Programs," 1991; Where We Stand: African American Law Professors Demographies, 1992. **Home Addr:** 10612 Woodsdale Dr, Silver Spring, MD 20901, (301)593-8099. **Business Addr:** Assistant Dean & Adjunct Professor of Law, Georgetown University Law Center, 600 New Jersey Ave, Ste 304, Washington, DC 20001, (202)662-9039.

BELLAMY, IVORY GANDY
Educator. **Personal:** Born Feb 21, 1952, Tuscaloosa, AL; daughter of Mr & Mrs Iverson Gandy Sr; married Kenneth Bellamy; children: Cinnamon, Cecily. **Educ:** Stillman College, BA 1974; Florida International University (Miami), further studies; Nova University. **Career:** Dade Co Public Schools, instr 1978-79; Miami Dade Comm Coll, prog coord 1979-85; Univ of Miami, program dir for Minority Admissions 1985-89; Fayette County Schools, teacher 1990-. **Orgs:** Southern Assn for Ad-

missions Counselors (SACAC); Rainbow House, board of directors, 1991-. **Honors/Awds:** Alpha Kappa Mu. **Business Addr:** English Teacher, Flat Rock Middle School, 325 Jenkins Rd, Tyrone, GA 30290.

BELLAMY, JAY
Professional football player. **Personal:** Born Jul 8, 1972, Perth Amboy, NJ. **Educ:** Rutgers. **Career:** Seattle Seahawks, defensive back, 1994-. **Business Addr:** Professional Football Player, Seattle Seahawks, 11220 NE 53rd St, Kirkland, WA 98033, (206)827-9777.

BELLAMY, VERDELLE B.
Nursing administrator. **Personal:** Born Mar 15, 1928, Birmingham, AL; daughter of Gladys Stovall Brim and Zephry Brim; married Monroe Bellamy, Mar 17, 1950; children: Michael B. **Educ:** Tuskegee University, BS, 1958; Emory University, Atlanta GA, MSN, 1963; Georgia State University, Atlanta GA, certificate in community gerontology leadership, 1984. **Career:** Tuskegee University, Tuskegee Institute AL, clinical associate, 1957-58; Grady Memorial Hospital School of Nursing, Atlanta GA, instructor, 1958-62; VA Medical Center, Atlanta GA, coordinator and supervisor, 1963-82, associate chief of nursing, 1983-; Georgia State University, member of board of counselors, gerontology, 1985-. **Orgs:** American Nurses' Association; National League of Nursing; American Cancer Society; state coordinator on the black family, National Council of Negro Women, 1987-89; NAACP; National Parliamentarian Association; board of directors, Georgia Nurses' Association, 1971-74; Georgia League of Nursing; charter member, Century Club, American Nurses Foundation, 1983; Emory University Alumni Assn; Tuskegee University Alumni Assn; Top Ladies of Distinction; board of directors, 1980-, natl secretary, 1984-86, vice president, 1986-, Nurses Organization of Veterans Administration; Supreme Basileus, Chi Eta Phi, 1973-77; Sigma Theta Tau; national executive board, 1979-86, 1988-, natl secretary, 1988-, Delta Sigma Theta; national secretary,Delta Theta Sigma Sorority, Inc, 1988-92; charter member, Thousandair Club, NAACP, 1991. **Honors/Awds:** Outstanding Service Award, American Nurses Assn, 1973; Mary McLeod Bethune Illuminated Scroll, Natl Council for Negro Women, 1976; Distinguished Ludie Andrew Service Award, Natl Grady Nurses' Conclave, 1977; Human Rights Award, American Nurses Assn, 1977; Natl Medical Assn and Natl Council of Negro Women service award, 1979; US Congressional Record for achievement, 1980; Distinguished Tuskegee Institute Alumni Merit Award, 1981; NAACP ''Unsung Heroine'' Award, 1981; Excellence in Health Care Professions Award, 1983, special achievement and community service award, 1984, Black Nurses Assn; Mary Mahoney Award, American Nurses' Assn; Distinguished Alumni Citation of the Year Award, Natl Assn for Equal Opportunity in Higher Education, 1985; NAACP FreedomHall of Fame Award, 1986; Veterans Admstration Leadership Award, 1988; Federal Employee of the Year Award, 1988; America's Top 100 Black Business and Professional Women, Dollars and Sense Magazine, 1988; Amer Academy of Nursing, Fellow, 1993; Ludie Andrew's Award, Georgia Nurses Assn, 1995. **Home Addr:** 1824 Tiger Flowers Dr NW, Atlanta, GA 30314.

BELLAMY, WALTER
Professional Basketball Player (retired). **Personal:** Born Jul 24, 1939, New Bern, NC; son of Theo Jones Bellamy and Walter Bellamy Sr; married Helen Ragland; children: Derrin. **Educ:** Indiana Univ, BS 1961. **Career:** NBA, Chicago Packers, 1961-63, Baltimore Bullets, 1963-65, NY Knicks, 1965-69, Atlanta Hawks, 1970-74. **Orgs:** NBA Player Rep 1971-74; vice pres, Natl Basketball Players Assn 1972-74; Senate Doorkeep GA General Assembly 1977-81; Atlanta Police Athletic League; Alpha Phi Omega Serv Fraternity; mem Alpha Phi Alpha Fraternity; IN Univ Alumni Club Advisory Bd; bd dirs SW YMCA; mem Atlanta Urban League; bd mem SCLC; NAACP memb drive; founder & first pres Men of Tomorrow Inc; trustee Shaw Temple AME Zion Ch; bd mem Southwest Youth Business Organiz; president, Campbellton-Cascade Ysmen Intl; br of trustee, Gate City Nursey; bd of trustee, Friends of Southwest Hospital. **Honors/Awds:** NBA Rookie of the Year 1961-62; Atlanta Hawks MVP 1971-72; Atlanta Salutes Walt Bellamy 1974; Became 9th NBA Player to reach 20,000 point career mark; All-Amer mem, 1960 Olympic Basketball Team; Hall of Fame, United States Olympic, 1984; Hall of Fame, Indiana University, 1984; Hall of Fame, North Carolina Sports, 1984; Basketball Hall of Fame, 1993. **Business Addr:** Public Affairs, 2343 Campbellton Rd, Atlanta, GA 30311.

BELLE, ALBERT JOJUAN
Professional baseball player. **Personal:** Born Aug 25, 1966, Shreveport, LA; son of Carrie Jean Giles Belle and Albert Sylvester Belle. **Educ:** Louisiana State Univ; Cleveland State. **Career:** Cleveland Indians, outfielder, 1992-97; Chicago White Sox, 1997-. **Business Addr:** Professional Baseball Player, Chicago White Sox, 333 W 35th St, Chicago, IL 60616, (312)924-1000.

BELLE, CHARLES E.
Company executive. **Personal:** Born Sep 2, 1940, Chicago, IL; children: Cynthia Maureen, Charles Escobar. **Educ:** Roosevelt Univ, BSBA 1963; Harvard Grad Sch of Bsns, MBA 1973. **Career:** Drexel Burnham Lambert, Inc, asst vice pres 1973-80; A G Edwards & Sons, Inc, investment broker; Prudential Bache Securities, Inc, vice pres and investment mgmt advisor, 1989-. **Orgs:** Business editor Natl Newspaper Publishing Assn Washington, DC 1973-; professional lecturer, Golden Gate Univ San Francisco 1975-; chmn Mayors Adv Comm for Community Devel of SF 1983-85; board of directors, San Francisco Convention and Vistors Bureau; mem bd of gov, The National Conference of Christians and Jews, Northern California Region. **Honors/Awds:** Journalist, Natl Endowment for the humanities 1979; Econ for journalist, Brookings Inst, 1978; COGME Fellowship, Harvard Univ 1971-73; John Ryan Motoring Press Association, Best Column, 1993, 1994. **Home Addr:** 270 Francisco St, San Francisco, CA 94133.

BELLE, JOHN OTIS
Educator. **Personal:** Born Jun 8, 1922, Fort Worth, TX; married Joe Helen Hall. **Educ:** Huston-Tillotson Coll, BA 1948; Our Lady of the Lake, MEd 1956; Attended, Univ of TX. **Career:** Rosewood Elementary School, teacher 1948-56; Sims Elementary School, prin 1956-72; Austin Independent School Dist, asst dir 1972-. **Orgs:** Mem TX Assn of Supv & Curclm Devel; TX Assn for Gifted Children; TX Elem & Prin Assn; TX State Tchrs Assn; Natl Elem Prin Assn; NEA; Austin Assn of Pub Sch Adminstr; Kiwanis Intl; mem Natl PTA Commn reg vice pres TX Cong of PTA; bd mem Austin Energy Commn; mem Curclm Adv Com KLRN-TV; NAACP; Austin Urban League; bd dir Austin Sym Soc; trustee Ebenezer Bapt Ch; adv bd Progm for Teenage Parents; mem Omega Psi Phi Frat; Phi Delta Kappa EducFrat; exec comm Huston Tillotson Coll Alumni Assn; life mem Natl & TX PTA. **Honors/Awds:** Disting Serv Awd Jack & Jill of Amer; Outstanding Accomplishment in Educ; Zeta Phi Beta Sor; Disting Serv Awd Delta Sigma Theta Sor; Cert of Appreciation Child & Family Serv Awd of Amer; Sch Dist Officials. **Military Serv:** AUS sgt 1943-46. **Business Addr:** Assistant Dir, Austin Independent School Dist, 1607 Pennsylvania Ave, Austin, TX 78702.

BELLE, REGINA
Vocalist. **Personal:** Born Jul 17, 1963, Englewood, NJ; daughter of Lois Belle and Eugene Belle; married John Battle, Sep 1991; children: Sydni Milan, Tiy Chreigna, Jayln Nuri, Nyla; married John Battle, Sep 1991. **Educ:** Manhattan School of Music, opera and classical music; Rutgers University, accounting and history. **Career:** Recording artist, singer: toured with, The Manhattans, back-up singer; toured with, Peabo Bryson, Frankie Beverly, Maze; solo recording artist, Columbia Records, 1987-; albums include: All By Myself, 1987; Stay With Me, 1989; Better Together: The Duet Album, 1992; Passion, 1993; Reachin' Back, 1995. **Honors/Awds:** American Music Awards, nomination, Best R&B Female Singer, 1991; headliner, Avery Fisher Hall, New York.

BELLEGARDE-SMITH, PATRICK
Educator. **Personal:** Born Aug 8, 1947, Spokane, WA. **Educ:** Syracuse Univ, BA 1968; The Amer Univ, MA, PhD 1977. **Career:** Howard Univ Dept of Romance Languages, lecturer 1977; Bradley Univ Inst of Intl Studies, assoc prof 1978-86; The Univ of WI-Milwaukee, prof of Dept of Africology, 1986-. **Orgs:** Amer Association of University Professors; African Studies Association, Association of Caribbean Studies; National Council for Black Studies; National Conf of Black Political Scientists; Association of Caribbean Historians; Latin Amer Studies Assn. **Honors/Awds:** Numerous publications including, ''In the Shadow of Powers, Dantes Bellegarde in Haitian Social Thought'' Atlantic Highlands, Humanities Press 1985; ''Haiti: The Breached Citadel,'' Westview Press 1990; ''The Spirit, The Myth, The Reality: Vodou in Haitian Development,'' Univ Press of Florida, 1998. **Business Addr:** Professor Dept of Africology, University of Wisconsin, PO Box 413, Milwaukee, WI 53201, (414)229-4155.

BELLINGER, GEORGE M.
Company executive. **Personal:** Born Aug 18, 1932, Brooklyn, NY; son of Wilhelmena Joyner Bellinger and Richard Eugene Bellinger; married Barbara P; children: George, Randy, Rudolph, Patricia, Monique, Melanie. **Educ:** New Haven Coll, attended; Amos Tuck Business School at Dartmouth. **Career:** Bar-Pat Mfg Co Inc Bridgeport, founder 1970, pres & CEO, currently. **Orgs:** Mem Metro Business Assoc; dir Bridgeport Hospital; dir Business Resource Center CT; dir Bridgeport Economic Devel Corp; Connecticut Afro-American Historical Society, president; Martin Luther King, Jr Commission, chairman; Bridgeport Public Educ Fund, dir; Governor's High Technology Bd; Gov Partnership for a Safe Workplace; chairman, Regional Youth Substance Abuse Project of United Way of Eastern Fairfield County. **Honors/Awds:** Rotary Club, Bridgeport Service Above Self Award; United Way Fairfield County, Outstanding Citizen Award; Sacred Heart University, Volunteerism Award; Connecticut Small Business Council, Small Business Person of the Year. **Military Serv:** USAF 1949-53.

BELLINGER, HAROLD
State government official. **Personal:** Born Mar 28, 1951, New York, NY. **Educ:** SUNY Farmingdale, AAS 1972; Rochester Inst of Technology, BS Social Work 1974; Univ of Pittsburgh, Masters of Public & Intl Affairs 1975; NY State Exec Chamber/NYS Affirmative Action Programs, Certificate of Completion 1982. **Career:** Legislative Commission on Expenditure Review, sr assoc 1976-79; NY State Senate Finance Comm/Minority, legislative budget analyst 1979-81; NY State Dept of Corrections, business affairs & contract compliance mgr 1981-82; New York State Correctional Industries, industries asst dir of marketing sales 1982-84; Economic Oppor Commn of Nassau County, asst dir YOU project 1984-85; State Univ of NY, asst to the pres affirmative action 1985-. **Orgs:** Mem Assoc of Minority Business Enterprises 1981-82; mem Albany Chamber of Commerce 1981-82; course instructor NYS Budget Process in sponsoring w/AL 1982; mem United Nations Assoc of the USA/Mid-Long Island Chap 1986. **Honors/Awds:** City of Rochester Urban Fellowship Awd 1973-74; Univ of Pittsburgh Grad Student Awd Public and Intl Affairs Fellowship 1974-75; Ford Foundation UndergradScholarship Awd; State Univ of NY Office of Special Programs 1977. **Business Addr:** Asst to the President, SUNY at Farmingdale, Ste 235 Administration Bldg, Melville Rd, Farmingdale, NY 11735.

BELLINGER, LUTHER GARIC
Corporate director. **Personal:** Born Apr 24, 1933, Blackville, SC; divorced; children: Luther Garic Jr. **Educ:** John C Smith Univ, BS 1955; Notre Dame Univ, MA 1965; Teamers Sch of Religion, DHL (hon) 1968; Universal Bible Inst, PhD (hon) 1978. **Career:** Edgefield SC, teacher 1959; Mecklenburg School System Charlotte NC, teacher 1959-63; South Bend IN Comm School Corp, teacher 1963-65; Bendix Corp Detroit, mgr EEO program, 1965-70; MI Lutheran Coll, part-time counselor 1968-69; McDonnell Douglas Corp, corporate dir EEO program 1969-. **Orgs:** Co-fndr & mem St Louis EEO Group 1972-; bd dirs United Negro Coll Fund 1972-75; bd dir Loretto Hilton Repetory Theater 1977-; sec MO Health Educ Facilities Auth 1978-80. **Honors/Awds:** Scholarship Natl Sci Found 1961-63; author ''A Guide to Slang'' 1963; co-author primer for parents ''An Internationally Circulated Tabloid on Modern Mathematics'' 1964; Disting Serv Awd Commonwealth of VA Gov Linwood Holton 1970. **Military Serv:** AUS spec 4th class 1956-58. **Business Addr:** Corporate Dir, McDonnell Douglas Corp, Equal Employment Opportunity Program, PO Box 516, St Louis, MO 63166.

BELLINGER, MARY ANNE (BIBI MSHONAJI)
Clergyman, educational administrator. **Personal:** Born Jul 16, 1939, Cincinnati, OH; daughter of Mary Jane Banks Allen and George W Allen; divorced; children: Georgiana, Teresa Lynn, Lawrence Wesley, Maurice, Sheila Renee Kinnard. **Educ:** Andover Newton Theological School, Boston MA, MDiv, 1981; Bentley Coll of Accounting and Finance, Waltham MA, attended 1 1/2 years. **Career:** Wellesley Coll, Wellesley MA, asst chaplain, 1975-80; Andover Newton Theological School, Boston MA, adjunct faculty, 1978-80; Big Bethel AME Church, Atlanta GA, assoc pastor, 1984-85; Grady Memorial Hospital, Atlanta GA, chaplain intern 1986-87; St. Stephens AME Church, Scottsdale, GA, pastor, 1985-87; Newberry Chapel AME Church, Atlanta GA, pastor, 1987-89; The Atlanta Voice Newspaper, Atlanta GA, columnist/editor 1988-89; JASONJAZ Creations/God's Business, founder, dir, 1988-90; elected Atlanta Board of Education, vice president/at large representative, 1989-93; Think About This Inc, Atlanta, GA, pres, 1994; VISION House Inc, group home, founder, dir, 1987-; ordained Baptist clergyman, 1980; ordained intinerant elder AME church, 1984; substitute teacher, Atlanta Public Schools, 1994-96; Black Women in Church & Society, adm asst, 1997-; Interdenominational Theological Ctr, Atlanta, GA, project coordinator, 1997-. **Orgs:** Sec, The Racial Justice Working Group of the Natl Council of Churches, 1988-92; SE regional vice pres, Partners in Ecumenism of the Natl Council of Churches 1984-90; mem, board of dir, Christian Council of Metropolitan Atlanta, 1987-91; faculty mem, first Year Class, AME Church Ministerial Preparation, 1987-89; NAACP Atlanta Chapter; chairperson, Ecumenical Celebrations/Church Women United, 1987-88; mem, The Georgia Network Against Domestic Violence, 1988-89; mem, The Concerned Black Clergy of Atlanta; chairperson, Racial Justice Working Group, National Council Churches Sea Islands Committee, Daufuskie Island, 1989-92; secy, bd of dirs, Exodus, Atlanta Cities in Schools; advisory comm, Success by Six Atl United Way, 1990-94; Atlanta Fulton Commission on Children & Youth, 1990-; Hearts for Youth Salute, judge, organizing committee, 1990-96; Beulah Baptist Church Gospel Choir Parlementarian; asst minister, Beulah Bapt Church, Vine City. **Honors/Awds:** Black Women In Ministry, Boston Ecumenical Commn, 1980; Boston YMCA Black Achiever Award, Boston YMCA, 1980; Salute to Women of the Clergy, Eta Phi Beta Sorority, Gamma Theta Chapter, 1988; sermons and articles published in The AME Christian Recorder; sermon published in Those Preachin' Women Vol I, 1985; ministerial delegate to Cuba, 1987, The People's Republic of Angola, Africa 1988; testified before The United Nations Committee Against Apartheid, 1989; Woman of the Year, Religion Iota Phi Lambda Sorority, 1991; Seventh Seat Update, Newsletter, Self Written & Published Quarterly, 1990-92; Published Poems ''Expressions..Volume 1,'' 1991. **Home Addr:** 63 Peyton Pl SW, Atlanta, GA 30311-1608.

BELLINY, DANIEL S.
Business executive. **Personal:** Born May 24, 1915, Jacksonville, FL; married Ella Walker. **Educ:** Wilberforce Univ, BS 1936; Univ of Chicago, JD 1948. **Career:** IL Div of Unemployment Compensation IL Dept of Labor, employment interviewer, dep claims reviewer dept III, hearing referee & supr, 1st asst chief appeals sect 1940-. **Orgs:** Gen sec Cook Co Bar Assn 1968-; Natl Bar Assn; Chicago Bar Assn; NAACP; Operation PUSH. **Honors/Awds:** Meritorious Serv Awd Cook Co Bar Assn 1973; 1st Black Vol Officer Candidate WWII 1942; 1st Black Hearings Referee IL Div of Unemployment Compensation Benefit Appeals. **Military Serv:** AUS 2nd lt 1942-45. **Business Addr:** 1st Asst Chief Appeals Sect, IL Dept of Labor, IL Div Unemploy Compensation, 6326 Cottage Grove Ave, Chicago, IL 60637.

BELL-SCOTT, PATRICIA
Educator, writer, editor. **Personal:** Born Dec 20, 1950, Chattanooga, TN; daughter of Dorothy Graves Wilbanks and Louis Wilbanks; married Arvin U. **Educ:** Univ of TN Knoxville, BS 1972; MS 1973; PhD 1976; JFK School of Govt Harvard Univ, Post Doctoral Fellow 1979-80. **Career:** MIT, asst equal oppty officer 1982-84; Wellesley Coll Center for Rsch on Women, rsch assoc 1980-84; Pub Policy Prog JFK Sch of Govt Harvard, fellow & rsrch asso 1979-; Child & Fam Stud Univ of TN, asst dir black stud & asst prof 1976-79; Child & Fam Stud Univ of TN, instructor 1974-76; University of Connecticut School of Family Studies, associate professor, 1985-91; University of Georgia Department of Child and Family Studies, Women's Studies Program and Psychology Department, professor, 1991-. **Orgs:** Consult Women's Prog Off of Educ 1978; natl exec bd Nat Assn for Women Deans Adminstr & Counslrs 1978-80; consult Nat Adv Com on Black Higher Educ 1979; chrwoman AWA (Black Women's Comm Com) 1975-77; bd Black Comm Devel Inc Knoxville 1975-77; soc action com Delta Sigma Theta Knoxville Alumnae Chap 1977-78; vice pres, for assoc relations National Association for Women Deans & Admins 1980-82; co-founder SAGE, A Scholarly Jrnl of Black Women 1984; ed bd Jrnl of Negro Educ 1983-, Women of Power, A Jrnl of Feminism & Power 1984; guest ed Psychology of Women Quarterly, new Directions for Women 1982-83, Jrnl of the Natl Assn for Women Deans & Admins 1979-81; co-convener, Coordinating Council, National Women's Studies Association, 1977-78; College Express Foundation, board member, 1989-; National Council on Family Relations, Family Action Section,y-treasurer, 1974-76, chair, nominating committee, 1991-92. **Honors/Awds:** Cit for Outstndg Serv UTK Chap of Mortar Bd 1977; Regl Finlst White House Fellow Prog 1977-78; author over 25 arts and four books; Disting Educ in CT Awd CT Chap of the Coalition of 100 Black Women 1986; Fourth Curriculum Matls Awd Women Educators 1983; Awd for Outstanding Contribution to Feminist Scholarship Nat Inst for Women of Color 1982; Cited for Outstanding Serv to the Univ of TN Knoxville Black Students Association 1978; Citation of Outstanding Contribution to the Psychology of Black Women, Div 35, American Psychological Assn 1988; Esther Lloyd-Jones Distinguished Service Award of the National Assn for Women Deans, Administrators, & Counselors 1989; Guest Co-Editor, Special Issue on Black Adolescents, Journal of Adolescent Research, 1989; Association of Black Women Historians, Letitia Woods Brown Memorial Book Prize, 1992; National Association of Women in Education, Ethnic Women's Caucus, Women of Achievement Award, 1992; Arch of Achievement Alumnae Award, University of Tennessee, 1994; Cited at 20th Anniversary of the Wellesley College Center for Research on Women, 1995. **Business Addr:** Professor, Department of Child and Family Development, University of Georgia, Dawson Hall, Athens, GA 30602.

BELMEAR, HORACE EDWARD
Educational administrator (retired). **Personal:** Born Dec 12, 1916, Bardstown, KY; son of Julia and Horace; married Geraldine; children: Dianne, Derrick, Michael, Tracy. **Educ:** WV State Coll, BA 1940; WV Univ, MS 1948; Postgrad, Univ of IL, Univ of Pgh. **Career:** Dunbar High School, teacher/coach 1946-55; AUS Missile Sect, dir of educ 1964-69; Allegheny County Community Coll, dir of admissions 1969-71; WV Univ, admissions officer/black student advisor 1971-93. **Orgs:** Omega Psi Phi Frat; NAACP; mem Human Relat Bd of Fairmont WV; chmn Affirmative Action Comm WV Univ. **Honors/Awds:** West VA Univ School of Physical Education, Hall of Fame; Outstanding Service to West VA Univ Students, President's African Amer Visiting Committee, Annual Horace & Geraldine Belmearr New Student & Faculty Reception; West Virginia State College National ''W'' Club Hall of Fame. **Military Serv:** USN spec 1st class. **Home Addr:** 892 Vandalia Road, Morgantown, WV 26505.

BELSER, JASON DAKS
Professional football player. **Personal:** Born May 28, 1970, Kansas City, MO. **Educ:** Oklahoma. **Career:** Indianapolis Colts, defensive back, 1992-. **Honors/Awds:** NFL Players Assn, Unsung Hero Award, 1996. **Business Addr:** Professional Football Player, Indianapolis Colts, PO Box 535000, Indianapolis, IN 46253, (317)297-2658.

BELSON, JERRY
Regional director. **Personal:** Born Mar 1, 1949, Lafayetta, LA; son of Joseph & Elrose Belson; married JoAnn St Clair, Apr 25, 1970; children: Dedrick, Abayomi, Farisa, Aisha, Jonathan. **Educ:** Southern University, BA, 1970; Sulross State University, BS, 1983. **Career:** Amistad National Recreation Area, district ranger, 1973-85; Tuskegee Inst NHS, superintendent, 1985-87; National Park Service, Ft Frederica National Monument, superintendent, 1987-89, MLK National Historic Site, superintendent, 1989-91, Yosemite National Park, deputy superintendent, 1991-94, Southern Arizona Group, general superintendent, 1994-95, Atlanta, deputy regional dir, 1995-96, regional dir, 1996-. **Orgs:** Atlanta Convention & Visitors Bureau, bd of dirs, 1992-95; Atlanta Olympic Committee, bd of dirs, 1995-96; Trust for Public Land, bd mem, 1990-92; Roundtable Associates, bd mem, 1996-98; National Association of Interpreters, bd of dirs, 1992-. **Honors/Awds:** National Park Service, Meritorious Service, 1995. **Military Serv:** US Airforce, ssgt, E-5, 1970-74.

BELTON, C. RONALD
Investor (retired). **Personal:** Born Aug 28, 1948, Jacksonville, FL; son of Bettye Ruth Taylor Belton and Clarence A Belton Jr. **Educ:** Hampton Inst, BA 1970. **Career:** Jacksonville Urban League, assoc dir 1970-76; Tucker Brothers, mortgage broker 1972-; Merrill Lynch Inc, senior financial consultant 1976-96. **Orgs:** Chmn of the bd Jacksonville Urban League 1983-84; life mem NAACP; mem Natl Eagle Scout Assn; chmn, Jacksonville Downtown Development Authority 1987-90; mem, Board of Governors, Jacksonville Chamber of Commerce 1988-91; bd mem, Jacksonville Symphony Assn 1988-91; mem, Advisory Board, Univ of North Florida School of Business 1988-91; member, finance committee, Jacksonville Community Foundation, 1990-92, bd member, 1994-98; Sigma Pi Phi Fraternity; State Brd of Community Colleges. **Home Addr:** PO Box 923, Jacksonville, FL 32201.

BELTON, HOWARD G.
Director, educator. **Personal:** Born Mar 22, 1934, Muskogee, OK; son of Jonella Belton and Louis Belton; married Ann Rempson; children: Consandra Denise, Sheryl Anne. **Educ:** MI State Univ, BA, MS. **Career:** Michigan Dept of Social Services, case worker 1960-64; Lansing MI School Dist, teacher 1964-69; Michigan Educ Assn, human relations consultant 1969-72; Natl Educ Assn, organizational specialist 1972-73, dir employee relations 1973-85, director internal operations, 1985-. **Orgs:** Mem NAACP; Chicago Chap Operation PUSH; Urban League, Project Equality. **Honors/Awds:** Lansing MI Jaycees Outstanding Tchr Awd. **Business Addr:** Director, Internal Operations, NEA, 1201 16 St NW, Washington, DC 20036.

BELTON, ROBERT
Attorney, educator. **Personal:** Born Sep 19, 1935, High Point, NC; son of Mary L Belton and Daniel Belton; married Joyce B Martin; children: R Keith, Alaina Yvonne. **Educ:** Univ of CT, BA 1961; Boston Univ, JD 1965. **Career:** NAACP, Legal Defense & Educ Fund Inc, civil rights atty asst counsel; 1965-70; Chambers Stein & Ferguson Charlotte NC, atty 1970-75; Vanderbilt Univ School of Law, dir fair employment clinical law program 1975-77, assoc prof of law 1977-82; prof of law, 1982-; visiting prof of law, Harvard Law School, 1986-87; UNC School of Law, Chapel Hill NC, visiting prof of law 1990-91; NCCU Law School, Charles Hamilton Houston Distinguished Visiting Professor, 1997. **Orgs:** American Association of Law Schools, executive committee, 1991-1994; Consultant TN Commn for Human Devel 1976-; editoral bd Class Action Reports 1978-89; consult Equal Employment Opportunity Commn Trial Advocacy Training Programs 1979-; consultant Pres Reorganization Proj Civil Rights 1978; consultant Office of Fed Contracts Compliance Programs Dept of Labor 1979-80; NC Assn of Black Lawyers; Amer Bar Assn; TN Bar Assn, NBA; Amer Law Institute, 1996-. **Honors/Awds:** Awarded NC Legal Defense Fund Dinner Comm Plaque for successful litigation in area of employment discrimination 1973; counsel for plaintiffs in Harris v Forklift Sys, 1993; Griggs v. Duke Power Co., 401 US 424 (1971); Albemarle Paper Co vs. Moody, 422 US 405 (1975); published, Remedies in Employment Discrimination Law, Wiley, 1992; Discrimination in Employment (west pub. 1986); ''Mr Justice Marshall and the Sociology of Affirmative Action'' 1989; Reflections on Affirmative Action after Johnson and Paradise, 1988. **Business Addr:** Professor of Law, Vanderbilt School of Law, Nashville, TN 37240.

BELTON, SHARON SAYLES
City official. **Personal:** Born 1951, Minnesota; married Steven Belton; children: three. **Educ:** Macalester Coll. **Career:** MN Dept of Corrections, parole officer; MN Program for Victims of Sexual Assault, asst dir; Minneapolis City Council, council member; City of Minneapolis, mayor, currently. **Orgs:** Minneapolis Youth Coordinating Bd; Bd of Estimates and Taxation; Heritage Bd; MN Minority Lawyers Assn; Harriet Tubman Shelter for Battered Women, past pres; Natl Coalition Against Sexual Assault, past pres; Metropolitan Task Force on Developmental Disabilities; Minneapolis Youth Diversion Prog, bd mem; MN Women Elected Officials; Children's Theater and Turning Point. **Special Achievements:** Author of resolution passed by Minneapolis City Council mandating the divestment of city funds in South Africa. **Business Addr:** Mayor, City of Minneapolis, 350 S 5th St, City Hall, Rm 127, Minneapolis, MN 55415, (612)673-2100.

BELTON, Y. MARC
Company executive. **Educ:** Dartmouth Coll, bachelor's degree, economics and environmental studies, 1981; Univ of Pennsylvania, Wharton School of Business, MBA, marketing and finance, 1983. **Career:** General Mills, beginning 1983, vp, beginning 1991, pres, Snack Products Div, currently. **Business Addr:** Pres, Snacks Products Division, General Mills Inc, 1 General Mills Blvd, Minneapolis, MN 55426, (612)540-2311.

BEMBERY, CHESTER ALLEN, JR.
Clergyman. **Personal:** Born Sep 3, 1955, Camden, NJ; son of Mary J Bembery and Chester A Bembery Sr; married Denice M Cooks Bembery, Jul 22, 1978. **Educ:** Deliverance Bible Institute; Soul Searchers School of Bible Training; TEIA School of Ministry. **Career:** Rutgers University, building and grounds maintenance, 1975-76; Cooper Hospital, University Medical Center, head account examiner, 1976-90; Soul Searchers Ministries, vice pres, 1979-. **Orgs:** Billy Graham Association, conference crusade planning board, 1991-; JDT Ministries, oversea's coordinator, 1991-.

BEMBRY, LAWRENCE
Government official. **Personal:** Born Nov 29, 1946, Columbus, OH; son of Richard Bembry & Willie B Matthews Bembry; married Carol Flax Bembry, Oct 14, 1985; children: Steve Lakin, Lisa Lee Steptoe, Ross Lakin, Laura Jean. **Educ:** Amer International College, BS, industrial management, 1967; Univ of Delewa re, 1972-73; Lewis and Clark Univ, 1990-91. **Career:** US Merit Systems Protection Board, admin dir, 1979-82; US Equal Employment Opportunity Comm, admin management dir, 1982-85; Dept of Agriculture, assoc equal opportunity dir, 1985-86, dir, 1986-89, deputy regional forester, 1989-91, natural resources program dir, 1991-94; Bureau of Land Management, service center dir, 1994-. **Orgs:** Tau Epsilon Phi Fraternity, 1963-; B'nai B'rith, 1982-93; Hebrew Education Alliance; HEAR Now, chief financial officer, 1994-. **Honors/Awds:** Presidential Rank Awards, 1986, 1988, 1989. **Business Addr:** Special Asst to the Deputy Director, US Bureau of Land Management, PO Box 25047, Denver Federal Center, Bldg 41, Denver, CO 80225-0047, (303)236-6452.

BEMPONG, MAXWELL A.
Educator. **Personal:** Born Sep 14, 1938, Oda, Ghana; married Jacqueline B; children: Jeffrey Eugene, Kwabena Alexander. **Educ:** Michigan State University, BS, MS, PhD, 1967. **Career:** Journal of Basic & Applied Sciences, Natl Institute of Science Transactions, editor-in-chief; Norfolk State University, Dept of Biology, director of biomedical research, professor, currently. **Orgs:** American Genetic Assn; American College of Toxicology; American Assn for Advancement of Science; Environmental Mutagen Society; Torrey Botanical Club; Natl Institute of Science; Sigma Xi; Beta Kappa Chi; Alpha Pi Zi; clinical consultant, Tidewater Center for Sickle-Cell Anemia. **Honors/Awds:** Michigan State University Research Assistantship, 1965-67; Phelps-Stokes Foundation Fellowship, 1962-64; Cocoa Marketing Board Fellowship, 1964-67; University of Nevada Reno, teaching fellow, 1970. **Business Addr:** Director of Biomedical Research, Dept of Biology, Norfolk State University, 2401 Corprew Ave, Norfolk, VA 23504-3907.

BENDER, BARBARA A.
Entrepreneur. **Personal:** Born Nov 12, 1939, Milwaukee, WI; daughter of Elizabeth Crape and Frank Brown; divorced; children: Lisa, Jason. **Educ:** Cardinal Stritch, Milwaukee, WI, MS, business 1987. **Career:** Admissions examiner; Milwaukee County Dept of Public Welfare, adoption social worker; Univ of WI, asst dir of instr support/experimental program in higher edn, dir of financial aid; Milwaukee Metro Sewerage Dist, Milwaukee, WI, sec of dist, 1978-88; Bab Inc, Milwaukee, WI, pres/CEO, 1990. **Orgs:** Mem Natl Adv council Amer Coll Testing & Svcs; Natl Task Force for Student Aid Problems; bd dir Curative Workshop of Milwaukee; pres bd dir Finan & Debt Counseling Svc; mem Midwest Assn of Student Financial Aid Administrators; mem WI Assn of Student Finan Aid Adminstrs; mem Delta Sigma Theta; Eta Phi Beta; NAACP; Fam Serv of Milwaukee; co-chair, Small Business Coalition of Wisconsin, 1991-92; bd member, Greater Milwaukee Bridge Assn, 1989-92; Wisconsin Minority Contractors' Assocaition; Catholic Social Services; Milwaukee Task Force on Solid Waste. **Home Addr:** 4237 N 19 St, Milwaukee, WI 53209.

BENEFIELD, MICHAEL MAURICE, JR.
County official. **Personal:** Born Jan 22, 1968, Washington, DC. **Educ:** University of North Carolina at Chapel Hill, BA, 1990. **Career:** US Senator William V Roth Jr, staff assistant, 1990-91; New Castle County Chamber of Commerce, mgr of city/state government relations, 1991-. **Orgs:** Christina Educational Endowment Fund, board of directors, 1992. **Business Addr:** Manager, City/State Govt Relations, New Castle County Chamber of Commerce, PO Box 11247, Ste 201, Bldg 3, Wilmington, DE 19850-1247, (302)737-4343.

BENHAM, ROBERT
Judge. **Personal:** Born Sep 25, 1946, Cartersville, GA; son of Jessie Benham and Clarence Benham; married Nell Dodson; children: Corey Brevard, Austin Tyler. **Educ:** Tuskegee Univ, BS 1967; Univ of GA, JD 1970; Univ of VA, LLM, 1990. **Career:** State of Georgia, spec asst atty gen 1978-84; Georgia Court of Appeals, judge, 1984-89; GA Supreme Court, judge, 1989-. **Orgs:** Cartersville Bar Assn, president 1981-82; GA Conf of Black Lawyers, vice pres; Federal Defender Prog, board mem 1983-84; Amer Judicature Soc, mem; Cartersville Chamber of Commerce, bd of dirs, 1976; Coosa Valley APDC, bd chm, 1978; Georgia Historical Soc, mem. **Honors/Awds:** Dent Awd Georgia Assn of Black Elected Officials 1986; outstanding service Cartersville Bar Assn 1984; first black appointed to Georgia State Court of Appeals, 1984; first black named to Georgia Supreme Court, 1989. **Military Serv:** AUS reserve Capt 1970-77. **Business Addr:** Judge, Supreme Court of Georgia, Judicial Bldg, Room 402, Atlanta, GA 30334.

BENJAMIN, ARTHUR, JR.
Business executive. **Personal:** Born Feb 8, 1938, Wagener, SC; married Dorothy Carrington; children: Lisa Simone, Cecily Lyn, Stacy Elisabeth. **Educ:** Natl Bsns Coll, Jr Acct Cert 1955; TN St Univ, BS 1959; Univ of CO, 1960; NY Univ, 1963-64. **Career:** Franklin Book Pgms, sr acct 1962-67; Amer Home Prod Corp, asst comptroller 1967-68; Whitehall Labs, asst treas 1968-72; ITT, sen fncl anlyst 1972-77; Wallace & Wallace Ent, vice pres & cmptrlr 1977-82; Unity Brdcstng Ntwrk, vice pres fnc. **Orgs:** Chmn bd Queensborough Scty for Prevention of Cruelty to Children 1981-83; pres Jamaica Serv Program for Older Adults 1979-81. **Honors/Awds:** Blck Achvrs Harlem Branch YMCA 1978; Awrd of Hon TN St Univ Sch Bsns 1978. **Military Serv:** AUS spec 4 3 Yrs. **Home Addr:** 115-101 222nd St, Cambria Heights, NY 11411.

BENJAMIN, DONALD S.
Communication arts and cultural research analyst. **Personal:** Born Feb 13, 1938, New Orleans, LA; married Tritobia Hayes; children: Zalika Aminah, Aminah Liani, Anwar Saleh. **Educ:** So Univ, BS 1961; Howard Univ, MFA 1972. **Career:** US Army Engineer Sch, artist/illustration 1961-63; Bailey's Cross Roads, asst art dir 1964-67; Defense Comm Agy, illustrator 1964-67; Naval Observatory, audio-visual specialist 1967; PTAI/CDC S Vietnam, consultant 1967-69; free-lance writer/artist/cons 1969-71; Comm Control Experimental Sch, coordinator 1973; Washington Tech Inst, research coordinator 1974-75; James Mason's University, Black Studies Program, media/research associate, 1980-81; Donald Benjamin Artist Diversified & Association, free-lance visual communication arts consultant and culturalist, 1982-87; Saints Missionary Foundation, director, Memorial Rebirth Program, currently. **Orgs:** National Consortium for Multi-Ethnic Studies and Cultural Exchange, co-founder, director; Diva Foundation, executive in charge of production; Lemeul Penn Center Consortium for Training and Production, founder, 1988-90; Wheel-in-Wheel Summer Youth Program, activity director. **Special Achievements:** Artist, exhibitions include: Tribute to Caribbean Independence Martin Luther King Library, Wash, DC, 1977; Madam's Organ Gallery Exhibition Adams Morgan Comm 1977; 1st Annual Kappa Alpha Psi Scholarship Benefit 1977; Black Caucus Annex Exhibit of Washington Area Artists 1975-77; Project director EXPO '76; Compared to What Inc 1974; assisted research that resulted in the placement of the first slave memorial in America which was located at Mount Vernon, home of George Washington; conducting research to isolate, identify and give high profile to 100 Black Historical sites in the south-eastern quadrant of the United States of America; provides guidance and support to reestablish the 1936 National Memorial to the Progress of the Colored Race in America and the Rebirth of Elder light foot Solomon Michaux; research efforts resulted in the placementan historical marker in the National Colonial Parkway, at Williamsburg opposite Jamestown Island. **Business Addr:** Project Director, Saints Missionary Foundation, 1307 Irvin St NW, Washington, DC 20010.

BENJAMIN, MONICA G.
Health care administrator. **Personal:** Born Feb 27, 1947, New York, NY; daughter of Gloria Delapenha Gittens and Milton Gittens; married Delvin E Benjamin (divorced 1983); children: Delvin L, Nyla M. **Educ:** Pace College, BA, 1968; University of Vermont, MA in teaching, 1976; University of Connecticut, MSW, 1982. **Career:** Concord Academy, Concord, MA, teacher and counselor, 1972-76; Choate Rosemary Hall, Wallingford, CT, teacher and counselor, 1976-80; Greater Bridgeport Community Mental Health Center, director of inpatient alcohol rehabilitation program, 1980-85; New York City Transit Authority, assistant vice president of medical services, 1985-89; Bronx Municipal Hospital Center, director of occupational health and safety, 1989-91; Health and Hospitals Corp, executive assistant to president, 1991-92; Kings County Hospital Center, senior associate director, adult emergency services, 1993-. **Orgs:** American Public Health Association; National Forum for Black Public Administrators; National Association for Female Executives; New York State Governor Mario Cuomo's Anti Drug Abuse Council. **Business Addr:** Senior Associate, Adult Emergency Services, Kings County Hospital Center, 451 Clarkson Ave, Brooklyn, NY 11203.

BENJAMIN, REGINA M.
Physician. **Personal:** Born Oct 26, 1956, Mobile, AL; daughter of Clarence & Millie Benjamin. **Educ:** Xavier University, BS chemistry, 1979; Moorehouse School of Medicine, 1979-82; University of AL, Birmingham, MD, 1984; Medical Center of Central GA, Macon GA, Residency, 1984-87; Tulane University, New Orleans LA, MBA, 1991. **Career:** Bayou La Batre Rural Health Clinic, physician, 1990-. **Orgs:** Mobile County Med Society, pres, board of directors, 1997; Board of Health, Mobile County Health Department, bd mem, 1992-97; Governor's Health Care Reform Task Force, 1994-95; Governor's Commission on Aging, past vice chair, 1994-95; American Medical Association, bd of trustees, 1995-; Council on Graduate Medical Education, 1997; Clinical Laboratory Improvement, advisory committee, 1994-; AL Bd of Censors MASA, bd of med examiners, bd of public health, 1992-97. **Honors/Awds:** Kellogg-National Fellow, Leadership Development, 1993-96; Time Magazine, 50 Future Leaders Age 40 & Under, 1994; New York Times, Angel in a White Coat, 1995; ABC World News Tonight with Peter Jennings, Person of the Week, 1995; CBS This Morning, Woman of the Year, 1996. **Special Achievements:** National Forum, The Phi Kappa Phi Journal, "Feeling Poorly: The Troubling Verdict on Poverty & Health Care in America", Summer 1996. **Business Addr:** Physician, Bayou La Batre Rural Health Clinic, PC, 13823 Shell Belt Rd, Bayou La Batre, AL 36509, (334)824-4985.

BENJAMIN, RONALD
Accountant, auditor. **Personal:** Born Dec 31, 1941, New York, NY; married Carmen E Hodge; children: Nicolle, Danielle, Christopher. **Educ:** Bernard M Baruch Coll, MBA 1974; Pace Coll, BBA 1968; Bronx Comm Coll, AAS 1966. **Career:** Main LaFrentz & Co CPA's, sr acct 1968-71; Union Camp Corp, sr auditor 1971-74; Ross Stewart & Benjamin PC CPA's, dir 1974-. **Orgs:** CPA 1971; mem Amer Inst of CPA; NY St Soc of CPA; NJ Soc of CPA; co-fdr Natl Assn of Black Accountants; adjunct prof Hostos Comm Coll; William Patterson & Essex Co Coll. **Military Serv:** USAF e-3 1960-64. **Business Addr:** Dir, Ross Stewart & Benjamin, 666 5th Ave, New York, NY 10019.

BENJAMIN, ROSE MARY
City official. **Personal:** Born Apr 28, 1933, Pueblo, CO; married Orville B Benjamin; children: Darryl Kevin, Darwin Craig, Duane Carter, Benjamin. **Career:** Inglewood Unified Bd of Ed, pres 1982; Southern CA Reg Occupation, clerk 1983, vice pres 1984; CA Urban Assoc School Dist, sec exec bd 1985; Inglewood School Bd, vp. **Orgs:** Mem local chmn Coaltition Black School Bd 1983-84; dist chairperson coalition Advocating Reform in Ed 1984; sec exec March of Dimes Bd of Dir 1984; march of dimes rep Inglewood Council PTA 1984; bd of dir Centinela Child Guidance Clinic 1984; comm mem CA School Bd Hall of Fame Awd 1985. **Honors/Awds:** Salute to Women Mornigside News Advertiser 1970; Martin Luther King Awd Holy Faith Episcopal Church 1970; Community Contrib Inglewood Neighbors 1973; Commendation Centinela & Professional Business Women 1983; Hon Serv CA Congress PTA 1985. **Home Addr:** 8711 3rd Ave, Inglewood, CA 90305. **Business Addr:** Vice President, Inglewood School Board, 401 S Inglewood Ave, Inglewood, CA 90301.

BENJAMIN, TRITOBIA HAYES
Educator, art historian, educational administrator. **Personal:** Born Oct 22, 1944, Brinkley, AR; married Donald S Benjamin; children: Zalika Aminah, Aminah Liani, Anwar Salih. **Educ:** Howard University, BA, 1968, MA, 1970; University of Maryland College Park, PhD, 1991. **Career:** Georgetown University, instructor, 1970; Howard University, instructor, 1970-73, Cafritz guest lecturer, 1978; Afro-American Institute, guest curator African Artists in America; Howard University, Art Dept, assistant professor, 1973-77, associate professor, 1977-93, professor, 1993-, associate dean, Gallery of Art, College of Fine Arts, director, currently. **Orgs:** National Conference of Artists; College Art Association; Smithsonian National Associates; Studio Museum, Harlem; National Museum of American Art. **Honors/Awds:** Recipient, Natl Endowment for the Humanities, Fellowships-in-Residence for College Teachers, 1975-76, Fellowship for Faculty of Historically Black Colleges & Universities, NEH, 1984-85; Spencer Foundation Research Award, Howard University School of Education, 1975-77; honorary member, Eta Phi Sigma, 1986; United Negro College Fund, PEW Humanities Fellowship Grant, humanities Fellowship Program for Private Black Colleges, 1986-87; Howard University, Office of the VP for Academic Affairs, Faculty Research Grant in the Social Sciences, Humanities, and Education, 1988-89. **Special Achievements:** Author, works include: "Color, Structure, Design: The Artistic Expressions of Lois Mailou Jones," The International Review of African-American Arts, 1991; biographies on: "Selma Hortense Burke, American Sculptor," and "Lois Mailou Jones, American Painter," Black Women in America, An Historical Encyclopedia, Brooklyn, New York: Carlson Publishing Inc, 1992; biography on: "Annie EA Walker, Painter," Dictionary of American Negro Biography, New York: WW Norton Publishing, 1993; cultural consultant, Washington-Moscow Cultural Exchange, Moscow, Russia, 1989; 2 summer publications: Haitian Art Newsletter, Africa Reports Magazine; The Life & Art of Lois Mailou Jones, San Francisco: Pomegranate Artbooks, 1994. **Business Addr:** Associate Dean, College of Arts & Sciences, Div of Fine Arts, Howard University, 2455 Sixth St NW, Washington, DC 20059-0002.

BENNETT, AL
Automobile dealer. **Personal:** married Yvonne. **Career:** Al Bennett Inc, Flint MI, chief executive. **Business Addr:** Chief Executive, Al Bennett Ford Inc, 6206 Kings Crown Rd, Grand Blanc, MI 48439.

BENNETT, ARTHUR T.
Judge. **Personal:** Born Feb 3, 1933, Corapeake, NC; married Josephine Adams. **Educ:** Norfolk State Coll, Cert 1957; Howard Univ, BA 1959; Howard Univ Sch of Law, LLB 1963; Univ of Houston Natl Coll of District Atty, grad 1972. **Career:** BL Hooks, AW Willis Jr, RB Sugarmon Jr & IH Murphy Memphis, TN, assoc atty 1963-65; Natl Coll of Dist Atty, faculty adv 1973; Shelby Co, TN Gen Sessions Ct, judge 1976; Shelby Co, TN Criminal Ct, judge, currently. **Orgs:** Mem Memphis & Shelby Co Bar Assns, Natl Bar Assn; legal dir & exec bd mem Natl United Law Enforcement Officers Assn; mem NAACP; mem bd dirsMemphis Branch NAACP; mem Memphis Chptr Assn for the Study of Afro-Amer Life & History; mem Title XX State Adv Councl Dept of Human Svcs; mem Natl Dist Atty Assn. **Honors/Awds:** King of Cotton Makers Jubilee Memphis 1974; Natl Historical Honor Soc Phi Alpha Theta 1959; Natl Forensic Honor Soc Tau Kappa Alpha 1959. **Military Serv:** AUS 1953-55. **Business Addr:** Judge, Shelby County, 201 Poplar Ave, Memphis, TN 38103.

BENNETT, BESSYE WARREN
Attorney. **Personal:** Born Aug 16, 1938, Prairie View, TX; daughter of Juanita McBroom Warren and Samuel Enders Warren (deceased); married Dr John H Bennett, Jun 12, 1958; children: Vera Elizabeth, John Stephen, Margaret Elaine. **Educ:** Radcliffe Coll, BA (cum laude) 1958; Trinity Coll, MA 1967; Univ of CT Law Sch, JD 1973. **Career:** Psychiatric Residency Program, research sec 1958-59; Hartford Pub Schools, tchr 1964-69; Hartford Coll for Women, administ asst to pres 1970; Soc for Savings, assoc counsel/mgr equal oppty programs, asst vice pres 1973-83; Ct St Employees Retirement Comm, gen counsel 1983-84; Town of Bloomfield, dep town atty 1985-91; private practice, atty 1983-; Law Offices of Bessye W Bennett, principal, 1990-95. **Orgs:** Mem Am/CT/Hartford Bar Assns 1974-; mem Hartford Assn of Women Attys 1977-84; mem Natl Assn of Bank Women 1978-84; former pres Hartford League of Women Voters 1970-71; dir Univ of CT Law Sch Alumni Bd 1978-80; chmn CT Sr Civil Serv Bd 1980-87; chair Hartford Women's Network 1980-81; former trustee CT Women's Legal & Educ Fund, 1974-76; past co-chmn & bd mem allocations comm United Way of Hartford; past pres George W Crawford Law Assoc; trust Hartford Symphony Orchestra 1983-; trustee Hartford College for Women 1993-; secretary Univ of Connecticut Law School Foundation 1990-91; dir Connecticut Natural Gas Corp, 1986-; corporator, Hartford Public Library, 1980-; director, The New Samaritan Corp, 1992-; director, The Trust Company of CT, 1992-; director, Children in Placement, 1990-95; Governor's Task Force on Sexual Violence, 1992; Attorney General's Blue Ribbon Committee on Permanency for Children, 1992; trustee, Greater Hartford Rehabilitation Center, 1992-95; chairman, Commission on Victim Services, 1992-93; trustee, YMCA, Knox Foundation, 1996-. **Honors/Awds:** Women in Bus Awd Salvation Army 1975; Women in Bus Awd YWCA 1983; Honoree Balsa Univ of Connecticut Law School 1989; Today Award, George W Crawford Law Association, 1996; Hartford Children 1st Initative, director, 1996-. **Business Addr:** Principal, Law Offices of Bessye W Bennett, 11 Mountain Ave, Ste 305, Bloomfield, CT 06002.

BENNETT, CHARLES JAMES, JR.
Community relations manager. **Personal:** Born Aug 17, 1956, Shreveport, LA; son of Emma M Fountain Bennett and Charles Bennett Sr. **Educ:** Wiley College, Marshall, TX, BA, education. **Career:** Coors Brewing Co, Golden, CO, field manager, 1979-. **Orgs:** Board of directors, Brass Foundation, 1989-; recruitment committee, Chicago Urban League, 1989-; Coors African-American Association, board of directors; NAACP, South Side Branch, committee member. **Honors/Awds:** America's Best & Brightest Business and Professional Men, Dollars & Sense Magazine, 1989; Achievement in Business and Professional Excellence, Being Single Magazine Pinnacle Award, 1988; Coors Scholarship of Excellence Program for Minority Students; Chicago "Race for Literacy" Campaign for Chicago Public Schools.

BENNETT, COLLIN B.
Business executive. **Personal:** Born Jun 8, 1931, St Andrew; married Winifred Tate; children: Michael, Adlia, Collin Jr, Sharon, Lisa, Dawn Colleen. **Educ:** Attended Bus Coll Univ of CT Sch of Ins. **Career:** Justice of the peace; human relation commr; Collin Bennett Real Estate & Ins Agency, owner/pres. **Orgs:** Mem Metro Water Bur; adv bd Salvation Army; chmn Comm Renewal Team of Gr Hartford; vice pres Redevel Agency for City of Hartford; former bd mem Urban League of Gr Hartford; former pres Barbour Sch PTA; councilman City of Hartford; chmn Housing & Planning & Governing Comm 8

years; regent Univ of Hartford; mem Electoral Coll; C of C of Gr Hartford; bd dir CT Savings & Loan Assn; Gr Hartford Bd of Realtors; Indpt Mutual Ins Agents; area prop mgr US Dept of Housing & Urban Devel; developer; sr warden St Monica's Epis Ch; vice pres St Monica's Day Care Entr; mem Visitors & Conv Bur of Greater Hartford; bd mem Mt Sinai Hosp. **Honors/Awds:** W Indian Comm Award; Council of Negro Women Award; Humanitarian Award City of Hartford; mem Natl Bd of Realtors; recip Order of Distinction (one of highest honors bestowed) Govt of Jamaica, West Indies Outstanding Serv Rendered to Nationals abroad & surrounding areas. **Business Addr:** President, Collin Bennett Real Est/Ins, 1229 Albany Ave, Hartford, CT 06112.

BENNETT, CORNELIUS O'LANDA
Professional football player. **Personal:** Born Aug 25, 1965, Birmingham, AL; son of Lino Bennett. **Educ:** Univ of Alabama. **Career:** Buffalo Bills, linebacker, 1987-95; Atlanta Falcons, 1996-. **Special Achievements:** Vince Lombardi Trophy; Super Bowl, 1990-93; Pro Bowl, 1988, 1990-93, 1995. **Business Addr:** Professional Football Player, Atlanta Falcons, 2 Falcon Pl, Suwanee, GA 30174, (404)945-1111.

BENNETT, COURTNEY AJAYE
Educator. **Personal:** Born Nov 17, 1959, New York City, NY. **Educ:** HS of Music & Art, diploma/music 1972-76; Wagner Coll, BS 1980. **Career:** Health Ins Plan of Greater NY, marketing rep 1983; Ralph Bunch School, science coord/teacher 1983-. **Orgs:** Partner/oper JBR Discount Corp; pres/founder Sigma Phi Rho Frat 1978-80; bd of dirs Sigma Phi Rho Frat 1978-; advisor Sigma Phi Rho Frat 1981-; mem 100 Young Black Men 1985. **Honors/Awds:** Wagner Coll Parker scholarship Music scholarship 1977 & 1978; Outstanding Young Man of America US Jaycees 1982; Outstanding service Sigma Phi Rho Frat 1983. **Home Addr:** 50 West 132nd St, New York, NY 10037.

BENNETT, DAINA T.
Author, educational materials distributor. **Educ:** Southwest Texas State, journalism. **Career:** Daina Bennett, Distributor, Chelsea House, Scholastic Publishing, Educational Materials, Distributor, owner, currently. **Orgs:** African-American Parent Council, co-chair, 1987-91; African-American Community Improvement Foundation, chair, 1991-92; Country Doctor, board member, 1991-92. **Special Achievements:** State of Washington, designed & implemented multiculture materials program, 1989; Seattle School District, multiculture materials, 1992. **Business Addr:** Distributor, Educational Materials, Distributor, PO Box 80832, Seattle, WA 98108, (206)763-1036.

BENNETT, DEBORAH MINOR
Consultant. **Personal:** Born Aug 13, 1951, Long Branch, NJ; daughter of Caroline Minor and Leonard Minor. **Educ:** Montclair State Coll, BA 1973, MA 1976; NYU, Doctoral candidate. **Career:** Neptune Sr HS, humanities instructor 1974-75; Webster Hall Res Hall Montclair State, dir 1975-76; Upward Bound, dir 1976-78; Stevens Tech Enrichment Pgm, dir 1978-83; Chicago Area Pre-Coll Engineering Pgm (CAPCEP), exec dir; The Right Source: An Information Network, pres, currently. **Orgs:** Bd mem/treas Assn for Equality & Excell in Edn; bd mem NJ Assn of Black Educators; bd mem Educ Oppor Fund Dir Assn; elected to steering comm formed NAMEPA, elected natl sec; mem Nat Assn of Pre-Coll Dir; mem Assn for Supr & Curr Devel (ASCD); mem The Coalition to Keep the School Open, Bd, Illinois Fair Schools Coalition, Blacks in Devel, President-Partners for Profit (investment club), Youth on the move for Christ; Chicago Institute for Urban Poverty, vice chairman, women employed. **Honors/Awds:** Named to Congressman Haye's Educ Leg Adv Cncl; published article, "Case for Retention Programs"; Served on educ comm Commission on The Status of Women IL; Published Article, "Overcoming Barriers"-Winning The Retention Battle, NSBE Journal, Dec 85/Jan 86. **Business Addr:** PO Box 811462, Chicago, IL 60681.

BENNETT, DEBRA QUINETTE
Editor. **Personal:** Born Feb 10, 1958, New York, NY. **Educ:** Wagner Coll, BA English (dean's list) 1980. **Career:** Assn of Ship Brokers & Agents, asst exec dir 1980; Newsweek Magazine, researcher/reporter 1981-82; Mamaroneck Daily Times, reporter 1981; Scientific American Magazine, proofreader/copy editor. **Orgs:** Managing editor Sigma Phi Rho Frat Newsletter 1981-; sunday sch teacher Grace Episcopal Church 1984-; Zeta Phi Beta Sor Inc (mem & Finer Womanhood Comm mem). **Honors/Awds:** Dean's List Wagner Coll 1980; Zeta Lady Awd for Scholarship & Serv Zeta Tau Alpha Frat Delta Epsilon Chap 1980. **Business Addr:** Scientific American Magazine, 415 Madison Ave, New York, NY 10017.

BENNETT, DELORES
Community activist. **Personal:** Born Nov 23, Clarksville, TN; daughter of Carrie B Barbee-Caudle (deceased) and Will Henry Caudle (deceased); married Eugene Bennett Sr, Oct 12, 1951; children: Ronda J Bennett, Eugene Bennett Jr, Mary Bennett-King, Esther M Bennett. **Career:** Wayne County, Michigan, Wayne County commr, 1978-82. **Orgs:** Bd of trustees, Henry Ford Hospital; chairperson of by-laws committee, Detroit Health Dept Substance Abuse Advisory Council; bd of dir, United Community Serv; lifetime mem, NAACP; bd of assembly, United Found; mem, Detroit Recreation Partners; founder/dir Northend Youth Improvement Council, 1964-. **Honors/Awds:** Annual Adopt a Child for Christmas Program, 1965-; Resolution of Service, Detroit Bd of Educ, 1982; Proclamation of Dolores Bennett Day, Mayor of City of Detroit, 1982; MI State Senate Resolution, MI State Senate, 1982; Jefferson Award, Amer Inst for Public Serv, 1987; Michiganian of the Year, The Detroit News, 1988; Northend Youth Improvement Council (NEYIC), Mental Health Clothing Drive; Operation Green Thumb (NEYIC); Jobs for Youth Conf (NEYIC); NEYIC Youth Against Drugs; America's Award Hero, Positive Thinking, 1990; WWJ Radio 95 Citizen, WWJ Radio, 1990.

BENNETT, DONNELL
Professional football player. **Personal:** Born Sep 14, 1972, Fort Lauderdale, FL. **Educ:** Miami (Fla.). **Career:** Kansas City Chiefs, running back, 1994-. **Business Addr:** Professional Football Player, Kansas City Chiefs, One Arrowhead Dr, Kansas City, MO 64129, (816)924-9300.

BENNETT, EDGAR
Professional football player. **Personal:** Born Feb 15, 1969, Jacksonville, FL; children: Edgar IV. **Educ:** Florida State, bachelor's degree in political science. **Career:** Green Bay Packers, running back, 1992-. **Business Addr:** Professional Football Player, Green Bay Packers, 1265 Lombardi Ave, Green Bay, WI 54304, (414)494-2351.

BENNETT, GEORGE P.
Deputy chief police department. **Personal:** Born Jun 22, 1927, Detroit, MI; married Tommie; children: George, Gary. **Educ:** Completed Criminal Justice Inst Mgmt Trng; attended Wayne State Univ; grad Southern Police Inst. **Career:** Detroit Police Dept, served in all sworn ranks; currently deputy chief. **Orgs:** Instrum in initiating & devel Wayne Co Comm Coll Law Enforcement Adminst 1969; mem Intl Assn of Chiefs of Police; Wayne Co Comm Coll Law Enforcement Adv Com; founding mem Natl Assn of Black Police Officers; founding mem Guardians (Black Police Officers) of MI; founding mem/mem Mayor's Steering Comon reorgn of Detroit City Govt; mem New Detroit Drug Abuse Comm; bd dir Univ of Detroit HS; mem Fitzgerald Comm Council. **Honors/Awds:** MI State Legisl Award for Outstanding Police Service; Award Natl Black Police Officers Assn; Major Contrib in field of Law Enforcement; Natl Bapt Conv Service Award; Annual Fitzgerald Club Outstanding Service Award; presented paper on Police Comm Relations to Natl Conf of Christians & Jews MI State Univ. **Business Addr:** Deputy Chief, Detroit Police Dept, 1300 Beaubien, Detroit, MI 48226.

BENNETT, IVY H.
Marketing executive. **Personal:** Born Oct 30, 1951, Waterbury, CT. **Educ:** Hampton Univ, BA, 1973; Univ of Michigan, Ann Arbor, MPH, 1975; Harvard Business School, MBA, 1982. **Career:** Quaker Oats Co, brand mktg assoc, 1982-84; Kraft Foods, mktg brand mgr, various brand mktg positions, 1984-89; Allstate Insurance Co, asst vice pres of mktg, 1989-. **Special Achievements:** Charted Property Casualty Underwriter, CPCW, insurance designation, 1995. **Business Addr:** Asst VP/Mktg, Allstate Insurance Co, 2775 Sanders Rd, Ste F-4, Northbrook, IL 60062, (847)402-5690.

BENNETT, JOYCE ANNETTE
Research assistant. **Personal:** Born Apr 18, 1941, Columbia, NC; daughter of Henry & Polly Bryant; married Robert L Bennett, Oct 6, 1960; children: Roderick, Roberta, Rhonda J Banks, Juancara, Robert, Chet. **Educ:** Washington Technical Institute, AA, accounting, 1974; Univ of the District of Columbia, BBA, accounting, 1989. **Career:** Raleigh Haberdasher, accounting technician, 1970-72; Riggs National Bank, bank teller, 1972-73; Federal Reserve Board, statistical asst, 1973-79, senior statistical asst, 1979-94, research asst, 1994-; Bennett Beauty Inst Inc, School of Cosmetology, Barbering and Manicuring, owner, currently. **Orgs:** Greater Mount Calvary Holy Church, chair, trustee bd, 1985-; Women of Virture, 1992-; Pastor's Aid, 1985-. **Business Addr:** Research Assistant, Bd of Governors of the Federal Reserve Board, 20th & C Sts, NW, B2219-A, Washington, DC 20551.

BENNETT, LERONE, JR.
Editor, author, historian. **Personal:** Born Oct 19, 1928, Clarksdale, MS; son of Alma Reed Bennett (deceased) and Lerone Bennett Sr; married Gloria Sylvester, 1956; children: Alma Joy, Constance, Courtney, Lerone III. **Educ:** Morehouse Coll, AB, 1949. **Career:** Atlanta Daily World, reporter 1949-52, city editor 1952-53; Jet, Chicago, assoc editor 1953; Ebony, Chicago, assoc editor 1954-57, senior editor, 1958-87, exec editor, 1987-; Northwestern Univ, visiting prof history 1968-69. **Orgs:** Sigma Delta Chi; Kappa Alpha Psi; Phi Beta Kappa; trustee, Chicago Historical Society, Morehouse Coll, Columbia Coll. **Honors/Awds:** Author, "Before the Mayflower: A History of Black America, 1619-1964"; "The Negro Mood" 1964; "What Manner of Man: A Biography of Martin Luther King Jr" 1964; "Confrontation, Black and White" 1965; "Black Power USA" 1968; "The Challenge of Blackness" 1972, plus many more; Patron Saints Awd, Soc Midland Authors 1965; Book of Yr Awd, Capital Press Club 1963; AAAL Acad Inst Lit Awd 1978; Hon Dr of Letters, Morris Brown Univ 1985, SC Univ 1986, Boston Univ 1987; Honorary Degrees: Morehouse Coll, DLetters, 1966; Wilberforce Univ, DHum, 1977; Marquette Univ, DLitt, 1979; Voorhees Coll, DLitt, 1981; Morgan State Univ, DLitt, 1981; Univ of IL, LHD, 1980; Lincoln Coll, LHD, 1980; Dillard Univ, LHD, 1980; named to President Clinton's Committee on the Arts and Humanities; Turner Broadcasting System, Trumpet Award, 1998. **Special Achievements:** Advisory board member of the publication, Who's Who among African Americans. **Military Serv:** US Army, 1st sgt, 1951-52. **Business Addr:** Executive Editor, Ebony, Johnson Publishing Co, 820 S Michigan Ave, Chicago, IL 60605.

BENNETT, LONNIE M.
Automobile dealer. **Career:** Roundtree Cadillac-Olds Co, Inc, CEO, currently. **Business Addr:** CEO, Rountree Cadillac-Olds Co Inc, PO Box 52038, Shreveport, LA 71135, (318)798-7250.

BENNETT, MARIAN C.
Attorney; government official. **Educ:** Radcliffe College, honors history; University of Pennsylvania Law School. **Career:** National Labor Relations Board, investigator, staff attorney; US Department of Energy, various positions; Office of the Inspector General, senior attorney; United States Information Agency, inspector general, currently. **Special Achievements:** First African American inspector general of the US Information Agency, 1994. **Business Addr:** Inspector General, US Information Agency, 301 4th St. SW, Washington, DC 20547, (202)619-4006.

BENNETT, MARIO MARCELL
Professional basketball player. **Personal:** Born Aug 1, 1973, Denton, TX. **Educ:** Arizona State Univ. **Career:** Phoenix Suns, forward, 1995-96; Los Angeles Lakers, 1997-. **Business Addr:** Professional Basketball Player, Los Angeles Lakers, PO Box 10, Inglewood, CA 90306, (310)419-3100.

BENNETT, MARION D.
Clergyman, legislator. **Personal:** Born May 31, 1936, Greenville, SC; married Gwendolyn; children: Marion Jr, Karen. **Educ:** Morris Brown Coll, AB; Interdenom Theol Center, MDiv; studied at Univ of NV, Atlanta Univ, Switzerland Ecumenical Inst. **Career:** Zion United Meth Ch Las Vegas, NV, pastor. **Orgs:** Mem NV Legislature; bd dir Black Meth for Ch Renewal; chmn Health & Welfare Comm; mem Legislative Functions & Rules Comm; pres Las Vegas Br NAACP; 1963-67, 1971-73, vice pres 1967-69, treas 1969; chmn bd dir Operation Independence 1969-71; treas Econ Bd of Clark Co,NV 1969; dem. **Business Addr:** Pastor, Zion United Methodist Church, 1911 Goldhill Ave, Las Vegas, NV 89106.

BENNETT, MAYBELLE TAYLOR
Urban planner. **Personal:** Born Oct 19, 1949, Washington, DC; daughter of Ruby Elizabeth Mills Taylor and Raymond Bernard Taylor; married Robert Alvin Bennett, Apr 17, 1971 (divorced); children: Rebeccah Leah. **Educ:** Vassar Coll, Poughkeepsie NY, AB (cum laude), 1970; Columbia Univ, New York NY, MSUP, 1972. **Career:** Lagos State Devel & Property Corp, Lagos, Nigeria, town planning officer, 1972-75; Joint Center for Political Studies, Washington DC, project mgr, 1975-78; Working Group for Community Devel Reform, dir of research, 1978-81; Natl Comm Against Discrimination in Housing, asst dir of program serv, 1982-84; District of Columbia Zoning Commn, chairperson, 1997-98; Coalition on Human Needs, dir of research, 1984-91; Howard University, Office of the President, assistant for community relations and planning, 1991-; Howard University Comm Assoc, dir, 1996-. **Orgs:** Mem, Alpha Kappa Alpha Sorority, 1968; mem, Eckankar, 1994; mem, Lambda Alpha Land Economics Soc, 1986-; Leadership Washington, 1991-. **Honors/Awds:** Maryland Vassar Club Scholarship, Maryland Vassar Club, 1966; Carnegie-Mellon Fellowship for Graduate Studies, Carnegie-Mellon Found, 1970-71; HUD Work-Study Fellowship for Graduate Study, US Dept HUD, 1971-72; William Kinne Fellows Travel Fellowship, Columbia Univ School of Architecture, 1972; author, Community Development Versus Poor Peoples' Needs: Tension in CDBG, 1981, Citizen-Monitoring-A How-To Manual: Controlling Community Resources through Grass Roots Research & Action, 1981, Private Sector Support for Fair Housing: A Guide, 1983, Block Grants: Beyond the Rhetoric, An Assessment of the Last Four Years, 1986, 1987, Block Grants: Missing the Target, An Overview of Findings, 1987. **Home Addr:** 2806 2nd St, SE, Washington, DC 20032.

BENNETT, PATRICIA A.
Administrative judge. **Personal:** divoRced; children: Shandra Elaine. **Educ:** Coll of Guam Agana GU, 1960-61; Riverside City Coll CA, 1967-70; Univ of CA, BA 1973, with honors, Hastings Coll of Law San Francisco, CA, 1973-76. **Career:** State of OH Dept of Finance, asst supr payroll div 1962-66; UCR Computing Ctr, prin clk 1967-71; Stanislaus Co Dist Atty's Office, legal researcher 1974; State of CA Dept of Water Resources, legal researcher 1975; Contra Costa Co Dist Atty's

Office Martinez, CA, law clerk 1976-77; State Pub Utilities Comm, attorney, 1978-88; administrative law judge, 1988-. **Orgs:** Urban League Guild 1970; UC Riverside Student Council 1971-72; volunteer San Francisco Co Legal Asst Prog San Bruno CA 1973; Council of Legal Educ Opport Scholarship 1973-76; San Francisco International Visitors, volunteer, 1980-83; Polit Sci Intern, Assemblyman Walter Ingalls Sacramento, CA 1973; Natl Dist Atty's Assn Intern 1974; Charles Houston Bar Assn 1976-; Natl Bar Assn 1979-. **Business Addr:** ALJ, California Public Utilities Comm, 505 Van Ness Avenue, Rm 5117, San Francisco, CA 94102, (415)703-2271.

BENNETT, PATRICIA W.
Educator. **Personal:** Born Aug 31, 1953, Forest, MS; daughter of Velma Watkins and J C Watkins. **Educ:** Tougaloo College, BA, 1975; Mississippi College School of Law, JD, 1979. **Career:** Small Business Administration, attorney, 1979-80; Mississippi Attorney General, special asst attorney general, 1980-82; District Attorney of Hinds County, asst district attorney, 1982-87; US Attorney, asst US attorney, 1987-89; Mississippi College School of Law, professor, currently. **Orgs:** Smith Robertson Museum Board, 1992; Central Mississippi Legal Services Corp Board, secretary, 1989-; YMCA Board of Directors, 1991-; Mississippi Board of Bar Commissioners, commissioner, 1992. **Honors/Awds:** Women for Progress, Woman Achiever, 1988. **Military Serv:** US Army Reserves, captain, 1984-92; several certificates and medals during six year tenure. **Business Addr:** Professor, Mississippi College School of Law, 151 E Griffith St, Jackson, MS 39201, (601)944-1950.

BENNETT, ROBERT A.
Educator, author, cleric. **Personal:** Born Jan 11, 1933, Baltimore, MD; son of Irene Julie Harris (deceased) and Robert Bennett (deceased); married Marceline M Donaldson; children: Elise Frazier, Mark, Malica Aronowitz, Ann, Michelle Aronowitz, Jacqueline Aronowitz. **Educ:** Kenyon Coll, AB (magna cum laude) 1954; Gen Theo Seminary NYC, STB 1958, STM 1966; Harvard Univ, PhD 1974. **Career:** Episcopal Diocese of Maryland, ordained priest, 1959; Episcopal Theo School/Divinity School, instructor/asst prof, 1965-74, prof, 1974-94; Interdnmntnl Theo Center, Atlanta, visiting prof, 1973-77; Boston Univ School of Theology, visiting prof, 1975, 1982; Princeton Theo Seminary, visiting prof, 1975, 1983, 1986; Harvard Divinity School, visiting prof, 1976; Hebrew Univ, Jerusalem, Israel, fld arch stf supr, 1984; Episcopal Divinity Sch, prof Old Tstmt, 1974-94. **Orgs:** Trustee bd mem Interdenmntnl Theo Ctr, Atlanta 1973-77; vice-chr Stndng Litrgcl Commsn Episcopal Chrch 1982-; mem lctnry comm Natl Cncl Churchs of Chrst1982-; mem fnl slctn comm Fund for Theo Educ 1984-. **Honors/Awds:** Phi Beta Kappa Kenyon Coll 1953; Fulbright Schlr Univ Copenhagen, Denmark 1954-55; Vstng Rsrch Schlr Am Rsrch Ctr Cairo, Egypt 1979-80; Rsrch Schlr Univ Khartoum, Sudan 1980; Fld Stf Tel Dor, Israel Hebrew Univ 1984. **Special Achievements:** Author "The Book of Zephaniah," The New Interpreter's Bible, vol 7, Abington Press, 1996; "Africa," Oxford Companion to the Bible, Oxford U Press, 1993; "Black Experience and the Bible," African American Religious Studies, Duke U Press, 1989; "The Bible for Today's Church," Seabury Press, 1979; "Black Episcopalians," The Episcopal Diocese of Massachusetts 1784-1984, 1984. **Home Addr:** PO Box 380367, Cambridge, MA 02238-0367.

BENNETT, TOMMY
Professional football player. **Personal:** Born Feb 19, 1973. **Educ:** UCLA, attended. **Career:** Arizona Cardinals, defensive back, 1996-. **Business Addr:** Professional Football Player, Arizona Cardinals, 8701 S Hardy, Tempe, AZ 85284, (602)379-0101.

BENNETT, TONY LYDELL
Professional football player. **Personal:** Born Jul 1, 1967, Alligator, MS. **Educ:** Mississippi. **Career:** Green Bay Packers, defensive end, 1990-93; Indianapolis Colts, 1994-. **Business Addr:** Professional Football Player, Indianapolis Colts, PO Box535000, Indianapolis, IN 46253, (317)297-2658.

BENNETT, WILLIAM DONALD
Educator. **Personal:** Born Feb 19, 1939, Buffalo, NY; married Joyce Marie Echols; children: Craig, Jennifer. **Educ:** Canisius Coll, BS 1961, MA 1967. **Career:** E High School, teacher, 1962-73, basketball coach, 1967, 1968, 1972, asst prin evening school, 1968-70, coord 1973-76; SUNY, instructor 1974-; Canisius Coll, instructor 1975-; E High School, principal 1976-. **Orgs:** Consortium com Canisius Coll 1977; pres 1060 Elmwood Ave Inc 1977; bd dir Buffalo Boys Town 1977; vice pres Black Tchrs Assn 1972; mem Di Gamma HonSoc 1973; pres Buffalo Secdr Prin Assn 1977. **Honors/Awds:** Martin Luther King Citz Awd 1977; varsity basketbl & track Canisius Coll 1957-61. **Military Serv:** AUSR capt 1962-68. **Business Addr:** Principal, East High School, 820 Northampton, Buffalo, NY 14211.

BENNETT, WILLIAM RONALD
Educational administrator. **Personal:** Born Jan 1, 1935, Parkersburg, WV; son of Pearl C Bennett and William D Bennett; married Sarah L Clarkson; children: Denise Renee, Diane Elizabeth, Douglas Eugene. **Educ:** Hampton Univ, BS 1956; John Carroll Univ, MEd 1972. **Career:** Cleveland Clnc, rsch tech 1960-62; Cleveland Bd Educ, sch admin 1962-72; Cleveland St Univ, dir, financial aid 1972-. **Orgs:** Pres, Natl Assn Student Financial Aid Admin, 1984-85; dir, Inroads N E Ohio Inc 1983-; treasurer, Inner City Renewal Soc, 1985; trustee Antioch Baptist Church 1985-88; pres Friendly Town Inc 1983-; mem CEEB Comm Pre Coll Guidance & Counseling, 1984-. **Honors/Awds:** Article published NASFAA Journal; Man of Year, Alpha Phi Alpha Fraternity, 1982, 1986, 1988; NASFAA Distinguished Services Award-NASFAA Alan Purdy Distinguished Service Award Department of Education-Region V-Regional Citation. **Business Addr:** Dir of Financial Aid, Cleveland State Univ, 1983 E 24th St, Cleveland, OH 44115.

BENNETT-ALEXANDER, DAWN DEJUANA
Educator, lawyer. **Personal:** Born Jan 2, 1951, Washington, DC; daughter of Ann Pearl Frances Liles Bennett and William H Bennett Sr; divorced; children: Jenniffer Dawn Bennett Alexander, Anne Alexis Bennett Alexander, Tess Alexandra Bennett Harrison. **Educ:** The Defiance College, 1968-70; Federal City College, BA, 1972; Howard University, School of Law, JD, 1975. **Career:** The DC Court of Appeals, law clerk to Honorable Julia Cooper Mack, 1975-76; The White House Domestic Council, assistant to associate director & counsel, 1976-77; US Federal Trade Commission, law clerk, 1977-78; Antioch School of Law, instructor, 1979-80; Federal Labor Relations Authority, attorney, advisor, 1981-82; University of North Florida, associate professor of business & employment law, 1982-87; University of Georgia, associate professor legal studies, 1988-. **Orgs:** Southeastern Academy of Legal Studies in Business, president, 1992-93; American Academy of Legal Studies in Business, co-chair, Employment Law Section, 1992-94; Georgia Political Action Committee PAC, 1993-94; National Council of Negro Women, 1983-; National Organization for Women, 1985-; treasurer, GA Now, 1993-95; DC Bar, 1979-; Friends of Athens Creative Theater, board member, 1990; Consumer Credit Counseling Services of NE Florida, board member, 1983-84; Girls Clubs of Jacksonville, Inc, board member, 1983-85. **Honors/Awds:** Selig Foundation, Selig Fellowship for Excellence in Research & Teaching, 1992; Terry Foundation, Terry Fellowship for Excellence in Research & Teaching, 1991; Consortium on Multi-Party Dispute Resolution, Seed Grant Award, 1992; Beta Gamma Sigma National Honor Society, selection to membership, 1992; McKnight Foundation, Florida Endowment Fund, McKnight Jr Faculty Award, Fellowship, 1984. **Special Achievements:** Employment Law for Business, Irwin Pub, 1995; The Legal, Ethical & Regulatory Environment of Business, South-Western Pub, 1996; "Hostile Environment Sexual Harassment: A Clearer View," Labor Law Journal, vol 42, no 3, p 131-143, March 1991; "The State of Affirmative Action in Employment: A Post Stotts Retrospective," American Business Law Journal, vol 27/4, p 565-597, winter 1990; "Sexual Harassment in the Office," Personnel Administrator, vol 33, no 6, p 174-88, June 1988. **Business Addr:** Professor, University of Georgia, 202 Brooks Hall, Terry College of Business, Athens, GA 30602-6255, (706)542-4290.

BENNETTE, CONNIE E.
Editor. **Personal:** Born Sep 9, 1951, Georgia. **Educ:** Savannah State Coll Savanna, GA, BS 1973. **Career:** Coll TV News & Radio News Series Savannah, narrator/dir; The Medium Newspaper, reporter 1971-72; Univ of WA, supvr journalism interns; Tacoma True Citizen,editor; Tiloben Publ Co, vp; Mgt Bd YWCA, suvp hs newspapers; ABC News Seattle, monthly reporter 1974-. **Honors/Awds:** Awards at Savannah State Coll, Alfred E Kennicker Journ Award; Columbia Sch of Journalism Award; Dean's List Recipient; Recip for Outstanding Scholastic Achievement; Med Newspaper Awards; Natl Newspapers Publishers Assn Merit Award for "Best New Story of 1974" 1975; Garfield HS Outstanding Publicity Award; Comm Serv Award; Unsung Heroine Honorable Mention Award. **Business Addr:** Editor, PO Box 22047, Seattle, WA 98122.

BENNING, EMMA BOWMAN
Educator (retired). **Personal:** Born Oct 5, 1928, Columbus, GA; daughter of Tinella Bowman and Ralph Bowman; married Calvin C Benning, 1946; children: Sheryl Ann Benning, Nathaniel A, Dr Eric A. **Educ:** Cleveland State Univ, Cleveland OH, BS, MEd; Case Western Reserve Univ, Cleveland OH; Kent State Univ, Kent OH; LaSalle Univ, Mandeville, LA, PhD. **Career:** Cleveland Public Schools, Cleveland OH, principal, Benjamin Franklin Elementary, 1975-77, principal, planner, 1979, dir, elementary schools, 1979-80, cluster dir, 1980-85, area supt, 1985-87, asst supt curriculum & instruction, 1987-90. **Orgs:** Trustee, board of directors, Children's Serv, 1969-; pres, Karamu House Board of Directors, 1976-80; first vice pres, Jack & Jill of Amer Found, 1977-85, natl pres, 1985-96; mem Shaker Heights; Human Relations commission, 1991-96; pres, Ludlow Community Assn, 1979-80; mem Delta Sigma Theta; mem, Natl Sorority of Phi Delta Kappa; mem, The Links Inc; St James AME Church. **Honors/Awds:** Outstanding AME Woman of the Year; Good Neighbor Award; Outstanding Contributions to Jack & Jill of Amer Found; Outstanding Achievement Award, Cleveland Public Schools; author, Early Learning Laboratory Curriculum Guide, Early Childhood Education Guide Supplement, Education Program Guide for Inner City and EMR Children, Parent Guide, Get Into the Equation, Amer Assoc for the Advancement of Science; City of Cleveland, Good Neighbor Award. **Special Achievements:** Community Hero Torch Bearer for the 1996 Olympic Torch Relay; Curricula Guides for major subject areas, Cleveland Public Schools; Education Fellow, Educ Policy Fellowship Program; Author, Early Learning Laboratory Curriculum Guide; Early Childhood Educ Guide Supplement; Educ Program Guide for Inner City and EMR Children; Parent Guide, Getting Into The Equation, Amer Assn for the Advancement of Science. **Home Addr:** 3143 Ludlow Rd, Shaker Heights, OH 44120.

BENOIT, DAVID
Professional basketball player. **Personal:** Born May 9, 1968, Lafayette, LA; married Aline; children: Deseree, David Jr. **Educ:** Tyler Junior College; Alabama. **Career:** Utah Jazz, forward, 1991-96; New Jersey Nets, 1996-98; Orlando Magic, 1998-. **Business Addr:** Professional Basketball Player, Orlando Magic, PO Box 76, Orlando, FL 32801, (407)649-3200.

BENOIT, EDITH B.
Director of nursing. **Personal:** Born Mar 7, 1918, New York, NY; married Elliot Benoit; children: Barbara, Lloyd. **Educ:** Hunter Coll, AB 1938; Harlem Hosp Sch of Nursing, RN 1942; Tchrs Coll Columbia Univ, MA 1945, professional dipolma 1959. **Career:** Harlem Hosp, instr/supr/asst supt nurses 1942-51; VA Hosp Brooklyn, NY, supr/instr/asst chf nurse rsch & coord 1951-64; VA Hosp East Orange, NJ, assoc chf nursing serv for educ 1964-65; VA Hosp Bronx, NY, asst chf nursing serv 1965-67; Harlem Hosp NY,NY, dir nursing serv 1967-. **Orgs:** Chmn NY State Assn Comm to Study the Nurse Practice Act 1970; asst prof Columbia Univ 1967-; adj asst prof Pace Univ 1973-; bd dirs Natl League for Nursing; mem Open Curric Comm NLN 1972; mem Amer Nurses Assn 1942; Hunter Coll Alumnae Assn; mem bd dir Natl League for Nursing 1973-77; bd mgrsMinisink Town House New York City Mission Soc 1972-77. **Business Addr:** Dir Nursing Serv Sch of Nurs, Harlem Hospital, 506 Lenox Ave, New York, NY 10037.

BENSON, DARREN
Professional football player. **Personal:** Born Aug 25, 1974, Memphis, TN. **Educ:** Trinity Valley Community College, attended. **Career:** Dallas Cowboys, defensive tackle, 1995-. **Business Addr:** Professional Football Player, Dallas Cowboys, One Cowboys Pkwy, Irving, TX 75063, (214)556-9900.

BENSON, GEORGE
Guitarist, singer, composer. **Personal:** Born Mar 22, 1943, Pittsburgh, PA; married Johnnie; children: Keith Givens (deceased), Robert, Marcus, Christopher, George Jr, Stephen. **Career:** Composed score for film The Greatest; album Breezin' is largest-selling jazz album of all time; Warner Bros Records, guitarist, performer, singer, composer, currently. **Honors/Awds:** Grammy Award for Record of the Year for This Masquerade; Grammy Award for Best Record of Year 1977; Grammy Award for Best Instrumental Performance, also for Best Engineered Recording 1977; Grammy Awd for Best Pop Instrumental Performance 1984; Grammy Award, Best R&B Male Vocal Performance, 1980; Grammy Award, Best R&B Instrumental, 1980; Grammy Award, Best Jazz Vocal Performance, 1980; Grammy Award, Best Pop Instrumental, 1983; Multi-platinum Album: Breezin'; Platinum Albums: Give Me the Night, In Flight, Weekend in LA; Gold Albums: 20/20, In Your Eyes, Livin Inside Your Love, The George Benson Collection, Collaboration; Honorary Doctorates in Music, Berklee School of Music, Morris Brown College. **Business Addr:** Guitarist, c/o Ken Fritz Management, 648 N Robertson Blvd, Los Angeles, CA 90069.

BENSON, GILBERT
Counselor, administrator. **Personal:** Born Nov 1, 1930, Paterson, NJ; son of Hattie Benson and Walter Benson; widowed; children: Michelle, Gilda. **Educ:** Howard Univ Wash, DC, BS; Wm Paterson Coll Wayne, NJ, MA. **Career:** Family Planning Adm Youth Serv, welfare caseworker/youth worker 1960-74; Passaic Community Comm Coll, EOF counselor/admin; Council on Problems of Living, counselor/administrator; Bergen County Shelter for the Homeless, supervisor; Paterson Board of Education, Eastside HS, Paterson, NJ, counselor, currently. **Orgs:** Past chmn Paterson NAACP; past affirm action chmn NJ State NAACP; chmn Paterson Coalition of Media Changes; chmn Passaic Co Citizens Vs Passaic Co Vocational Sch Bd; NOW Theatre of Paterson, NJ; mem Black Male Caucus of Paterson, NJ; member, Omega Psi Phi Fraternity, 1985-; delegate assembly member, National Education Assn, 1987-90; past chmn, Greater Paterson Arts Council. **Honors/Awds:** Comm Service Award NAACP 1973; Community Leader of America Award 1969; Passaic Co College Merit Award 1978; Salute to Black Men & Women Duke Ellington Award for the Arts, 1985; Counseling Service Award, Passaic County College, 1976; Administrator's Merit Award, Passaic County College, 1978; JFK High School Award for Contribution to the Arts, 1990. **Military Serv:** US Army Reserves, Captain, 1956-58. **Home Addr:** 515 Eleventh Ave, Paterson, NJ 07514.

BENSON, HAYWARD J., JR.
County official, educational administrator. **Personal:** Born Aug 29, 1936, Mt Dora, FL; son of Emily Smith Benson and Hayward J Benson Sr; married Mattie Jo Alexander; children: Stephan, Cameron. **Educ:** FL A&M Univ, BS Elem Ed 1958; Univ of AZ, MS Educ 1965; Univ of FL, Cert Admin & Suprv 1968; FL Atlantic Univ, EdD 1984. **Career:** Broward Cty School Bd, dir office of comp planning for equal opport 1975-77; Nova Univ, adj prof part time; Broward Cty School Bd, admin asst to supt of schools 1977-83; Broward Cty Govt, dir public serv dept 1983-. **Orgs:** Mem Florida Assn for Health & Soc Serv, Broward Cty Human Relations div, State Univ System EEO Adv Comm Bd of Regents, Democratic Exec Comm; mem, bd of dir, Areawide Council on Aging, Amer Red Cross; chmn, bd of dir, Nova Univ Clinic; pres Florida Assn Comm Relations Prof, vice pres Natl Alliance of Black School Educ. **Honors/Awds:** BCTA Teacher of the Year Awd 1966; BCTA Distinguished Serv Awd 1967; Certificate of Recognition Awd School Bd Broward Cty 1971; FEA Human Relations Awd 1972; LINKS Project Pioneer in Community Serv Awd 1975; Numerous other awds & citations for professional and community serv. **Military Serv:** AUS capt 1959-65. **Home Addr:** 4410 NW 67 Terr, Lauderhill, FL 33319.

BENSON, JAMES RUSSELL
Educator, administrator. **Personal:** Born Jan 19, 1933, Marks, MS; son of Tressie V Benson and Escar Benson; married Madgeolyn Warren; children: Barry Ray, Agnela Davis. **Educ:** AL State Univ, BS 1963; Claremont Grad Coll, MA 1972, PhD 1977. **Career:** Radio Station WRMA Montgomery AL, news dir 1960-63; Urban League, dir teen post 1963-64; Lincoln High School, human relations dir 1964-66; Gow-Dow Experience, pres 1968-; Pomona Unified Sch Dist, dir of music; Palomares Jr High School, vice principal. **Orgs:** Bd of dirs JoAnn Concert Dance Corp 1984-85; bd of dirs NAACP 1986-87; dir MESA 1986-87; chairman, ACT-CO/Academic Excellence Program, 1989-91; National Alliance of Black School Educators, policy development in public education. **Honors/Awds:** Teacher of the Year Pomona Unified Sch Dist 1982-84; Langston Hughes Art Awd NAACP Pomona 1985; Bravo Awd LA Music Ctr 1985-86; Contemporary African-American Achievement Award, Pomona Alliance of Black School Educators, 1990. **Military Serv:** AUS Sp4 2 yrs; High Honor Trainee. **Business Addr:** Vice Principal, Palomares Junior High School, 800 So Gary Ave, Pomona, CA 91767.

BENSON, LILLIAN
Motion picture editor. **Career:** Film editor, currently; films include: The Promised Land, 1990; Eyes on the Prize. **Orgs:** American Cinema Editors. **Honors/Awds:** The Promised Land, Emmy Nomination, News & Documentary, 1990. **Special Achievements:** First African-American woman elected to the American Cinema Editors Assn, 1991. **Business Addr:** Member, American Cinema Editors, 1041 N Formosa Ave, West Hollywood, CA 90046, (213)850-2900.

BENSON, RUBIN AUTHOR
Publication designer, educator, graphic artist. **Personal:** Born Feb 8, 1946, Philadelphia, PA; son of Mable S Skinner and Calvin Benson; married Janet Wicks, Jul 10, 1978; children: Rubin, Heather, Badeerah. **Educ:** Cheyney Univ, Cheyney PA, BS, 1969; Univ of Pennsylvania, Philadelphia PA, 1971; Parsons School of Design, New York NY, 1972. **Career:** Philadelphia School Dist, Philadelphia PA, graphic arts teacher, 1969-; Philadelphia Intl Records, art dir, 1982-84; First Impressions Design Group, Philadelphia, PA pres. **Orgs:** Judge, CEBA Awards, 1980-. **Honors/Awds:** Award of Distinction, CEBA, 1983, 1984, 1985; Award of Excellence, CEBA, 1986. **Business Addr:** Pres, First Impressions Design Group, 4920 Hazel Ave, Philadelphia, PA 19143, (215)472-1660.

BENSON, SHARON MARIE
Administrator. **Personal:** Born Apr 20, 1959, Chicago, IL. **Educ:** IL State Univ, BS 1981, MS 1983. **Career:** IL State Univ, rsch asst 1982-83; Goodwill Industries, vocational coord 1983-84; Operations Training Inst, job skills developer 1984-85; SAMCOR Dev Corp, administrator small business ctr. **Orgs:** Business consultant Westside Small Business Dev Ctr 1985-; mem MED Week Steering Comm 1985-; mem Chicago Assoc of Neighborhood Dev 1986-; mem Task Force on Small Business Needs 1986. **Home Addr:** 7918 South Escanaba, Chicago, IL 60617. **Business Addr:** Administrator Small Bus Ctr, SAMCOR Development Corp, 4 North Cicero Avenue, Ste 38, Chicago, IL 60644.

BENSON, WANDA MILLER
Publisher. **Personal:** Born Jul 15, 1956, Washington, DC; daughter of Rosetta & William Miller; married Steve Benson, Jul 15, 1986; children: Brandon, Connor. **Educ:** Tennessee State University, BA, 1980. **Career:** IRS, union representative, 1975-86; Contempra Brides, publisher, 1986-. **Orgs:** NAACP, personnel committee, 1995-96. **Business Addr:** Publisher, Contempora Brides, 1818 Morena St, Nashville, TN 37208, (615)321-3268.

BENTLEY, HERBERT DEAN
Business executive. **Personal:** Born Jan 29, 1940, DeSoto, MO; married Judy Ann Lazard; children: Herbert, Karthryn, Karyn. **Educ:** Harris Teachers Coll, AA 1958; So IL Univ, BS 1966; Amer Management Assn, Cert in Systems Design 1972. **Career:** New Age Fed Savings & Loan Assn, mng officer. **Orgs:** Pres PAS Mgmt Systems Inc; mem bd dir Gateway Natl Bank 1973-; mem bd dir New Age Fed Svngs & Loan Assn 1974-; bd dir Natl Assn of Black Accountants 1974-75; past officer bd mem Natl Assn of Black Accountants 1975-; mem bd dir Interracial Councl of Bus Oppty 1974-; mem bd dir Cntr Med Ctr 1976-; mem bd dir Christian Med Cntr 1976-; mem bd dir Oppty Indsln Cntr 1976-; mem bd dir Minority Bus Forum Assn 1976-; St Louis Tax Task Force for Congress of the US 1977. **Honors/Awds:** Public Service Award Small Business Admin 1977. **Business Addr:** Managing Officer, New Age Fed Savings & Loan, 1401 N Kings Highway, St Louis, MO 63113.

BENTON, GEORGE A.
President. **Personal:** Born May 15, 1933, Philadelphia, PA; married Mildred Hogans; children: Anthony, Ondra. **Career:** Pro boxer 1949-70; Smokin' Joe Frazier, boxing trainer. **Honors/Awds:** Outstanding Coach Award; Inducted in PA Hall of Fame 1979. **Military Serv:** AUS Pfc served 2 years 14th Div Korea 1957. **Business Addr:** President, Hardknocks, Inc, 2830 N Bailey St, Philadelphia, PA 19132.

BENTON, JAMES WILBERT, JR.
Attorney. **Personal:** Born Sep 16, 1944, Norfolk, VA; son of Annie Scott Benton and James W Benton (deceased); children (previous marriage): Laverne Aisha; married Marrianne H. Ruppmann. **Educ:** Temple Univ, AB 1966; Univ of VA Law Sch, JD 1970. **Career:** Hill Tucker & Marsh attorneys, Richmond, VA, partner, 1970-85; Court of Appeals of VA, Richmond VA, judge, 1985-. **Orgs:** Former bd mem, Friends Assn for Children; bd mem, VA ACLU; mem, VA State Educ Asst Authority; mem NAACP; former bd mem, Neighborhood Legal Aid Soc; former mem Richmond Traffic Safety Comm; former bd mem, VA Educ Loan Authority; bd mem, VA Arts Comm; bd mem, VA Center for the Performing Arts. **Business Addr:** Judge, Court of Appeals of Virginia, 101 N Eighth St, Richmond, VA 23219.

BENTON, LEONARD D.
Association executive. **Personal:** Born Jul 1, 1939, Chickasha, OK; married Barbara Y Pointer; children: Quincy L. **Educ:** Grambling Coll, BS 1961; IL Wesleyan Univ, MS 1964; Univ of Pittsburgh, MPA 1975. **Career:** Pub Schools Shreveport, LA & Chicago, instr 1961-65; Urban League, assoc dir 1967-69; Urban League Job Center, dir 1969-70; Southern Regional Office National Urban League, dir, 1986-88; Urban League of OK City, pres, currently. **Orgs:** Chmn Natl Balck Luth Lay Comm; exec sec Coalition for Civil Leadership OK city; polemarch Kappa Alpha Psi Frat; gen mgr SW Urban Devel Corp;sec Council of Exec Dirs So Region; Natl Urban League; chmn Soc Ministry OK Dist Luth Ch. **Honors/Awds:** Natl Sci Found 1962-64; Serv to Mankind Award Seroma Club Okla City 1975. **Business Addr:** President, Urban League of OK City, 3017 N Martin Luther King Ave, Oklahoma City, OK 73111.

BENTON, NELKANE O.
Business executive. **Personal:** Born Jun 15, 1935, New York City, NY; married Thomas J Hill; children: Donna M. **Career:** KABC & KLOS Radio, dir pub affairs; Bing Crosby, pub rel/record promo; STEPInc, counselor; NKB Prod of Hollywood, exec dir; KABC-AM/KLOS-FM Am Broadcasting Corp, dir comm rel/dir ombudsman ser; Director of Community Relations for KABC Talk radio, KLOS FM, KMPC 710. **Orgs:** Mem KABC Radio Edn; bd mem, bd dir Consumer Credit Counsl of LA; bd dir LA Beautiful, Community Resources Development; mem Pacific Bell Consumer Adv Panel, Southern CA Gas Go Black Adv Panel. **Honors/Awds:** Unity Award for Human Rel 1974; Mayor's Award Public Serv 1974; Outstanding Awds President Carter, Senator Alan Cranston, Supv Kenneth Hahn, State Senator Nate Holden 1976; Outstanding Employee Amer Broadcasting Co, Los Angeles Mayor Tom Bradley 1977,78; LA County Media Volunteer Award, 1990; United Way Media Award for Public Service, 1989-90; The National Broadcasting Assn Award for Outstanding Community Relations, Crystal Award, 1989-90; American Cancer Society, Community Relations Award, 1993-94. **Business Addr:** Dir of Community Relation, Radio KABC-AM KLOS FM, 3321 S LaCienega, Los Angeles, CA 90016.

BENTON, PHYLLIS CLORA
Entrepreneur. **Personal:** Born Dec 4, 1947, Portland, OR; daughter of Theresa & William T Benton, Sr. **Educ:** Portland State University, BS, 1970, MSW, 1972, Certificate Black Studies, 1974. **Career:** State of Oregon, Children's Services Div, social worker, 1976-77; US DHSS Social Security Administration, claims rep, 1977-80, Office for Civil Rights, investigator, 1980-84, Office of Child Support Enforcement, prog specialist, 1984-93; Midnight Ramble Video, owner, 1992-. **Business Addr:** Owner, Midnight Ramble Video, PO Box 11522, Portland, OR 97211-0522, (503)287-0319.

BENYARD, WILLIAM B., JR.
Senior systems programmer. **Personal:** Born Nov 6, 1948, Detroit, MI; son of Frances Wilcher Tidwell and Willie B. Benyard; married Regenia Christine Powell, Aug 4, 1984; children: Erica, Brian, Clarence, Ian. **Educ:** Delta College, University Center, MI, 1978; Wayne State University, Detroit, MI; Indiana University, South Bend, IN. **Career:** Dow Chemical USA, Midland, MI, operations analyst, 1974-80; American Natural Service Co, Detroit, MI, production control analyst; Michigan Consolidated Gas Co, Detroit, MI, programmer analyst, 1980-82; A.M. General Corporation, South Bend, IN, MIS analyst, 1982-85; Genesis Information Systems, Akron, OH, independent contractor, 1985; Premark International Food Equipment Group, Troy, OH, senior MIS analyst, 1986-87; Advanced Programming Resolutions, Inc, Dublin, OH, MIS consultant, 1987-88; Dayton Board of Education, Dayton, OH, senior systems programmer/operations facilitator, Senior Principal Computer Analyst, Metters Industries; Bil Gen Group, Real Estate Investments and Marketing & Distribution, partner, 1988-. **Orgs:** National recording secretary, Black Data Processing Associates, 1982-86; founder, Dayton Chapter, Black Data Processing Associates, 1988-90; president, Princeton Park Neighborhood Association, 1989-; NAACP, Dayton Chapter, 1984; Equity Lodge, 121 PHFAU, 1990. **Honors/Awds:** Founders Award, Black Data Processing Associates, 1989. **Home Addr:** 800 Glensdel Dr, Dayton, OH 45427-2734, (513)268-6473. **Business Addr:** Senior Principal Computer Systems Analyst, Metters Industries, Inc, 5200 Springfield Pike, Ste 300, Dayton, OH 45431-1255, (513)253-3697.

BERAKI, NAILAH G.
Massage therapist. **Personal:** Born Jun 17, 1957, New York, NY; daughter of Ina L Green; divorced; children: Omar Jackson. **Educ:** San Diego State College, BA psychology, 1981; Mueller's College of Wholistic Medicine, 1987; Lehman College, BS health education, 1997. **Career:** Muwasi Wholistic, massage therapist, currently. **Orgs:** International Massage Association; International Reflexology Association; National Black Iridologist Association; Association Rebirthers International; Society of Public Health Educators, Greater New York Chapter; National Acupuncture Detox Assoc. **Home Addr:** PO Box 585, Bronx, NY 10475.

BERGER, NATHANIEL
Architect. **Personal:** marrIed Lady Washington-Berger. **Educ:** Carnegie Mellon Univ, bachelor's degree in architecture. **Career:** JMGR Inc, partner, currently. **Special Achievements:** First African American to be named a partner with JMGR Inc, the oldest architectural and engineering design firm in Memphis.

BERHE, ANNETTE TONEY
Librarian. **Personal:** Born Aug 21, Batesville, MS; daughter of Adelle Toliver Cole and Roland Cole. **Educ:** Jackson State University, Jackson, MS, BS, 1974; Atlanta University, Atlanta, GA, MLS, 1979. **Career:** Quitman County Public Schools, Marks, MS, teacher, 1974-77; Lemoyne-Owen College, Memphis, TN, librarian, 1979-. **Orgs:** Board member, Young Women Christian Association, 1982-90; tutor, Memphis Literacy Council, 1982-86; member, treasurer, Les Gemmes Inc, 1989-; member, American Library Association, 1987-; member, Tennessee Library Association, 1986-. **Honors/Awds:** Archival Training Institute, National Historical Publications and Record Commission, 1982. **Home Addr:** 4189 Kenosha, Memphis, TN 38118.

BERKLEY, CONSTANCE E. GRESHAM
Poet, educator. **Personal:** Born Nov 12, 1931, Washington, DC; children: Robert, Richard. **Educ:** Columbia University, BA, 1971, MA, 1972; New York University, Dept of Near Eastern Language & Literature, PhD, 1979. **Career:** Fordham University, Black Drama, 1971-72; Vassar College, literature lecturer, 1972-75; Ramapo College, African literature, 1976; Fordham University, asst professor, African/Afro-American & Islamic literature, starting 1979; Vassar College, Studies Program, lecturer of Africana Studies, currently. **Orgs:** Harlem Writer's Guild, 1961-; NEC Dramatists Workshop Affiliate, 1969-; New York State Council of the Arts, lecturer; Intl Poetry Society; Assn Study Afro-American Life & History; Middle Eastern Studies Assn; bd dir, Natl Council of Soviet American Friendship, 1968; African Literature Assn; New York African Studies Assn; contributing editor, American Dialog, 1967; guest lecturer, ''Islam in Africa,'' CBS/NYU Sunrise Semester Program, ''1400 Years of Islam,'' 1980; guest lecturer, New School for Social Research, 1980-81. **Honors/Awds:** Poetry published in several anthologies; Black American Writers Past & Present; Fisk University, Biography of Living Black Writers. **Special Achievements:** One of the founders of the Sudan Studies Assn, 1981; Editor of the SSA Newsletter; Specialist in the literature of the famous Sudanese writer, Tayeb Salih; Invited participant in special tribute to Tayeb Salih at Asilah's 17th Season in Asilah Morocco, 1994; Fulbright Lecturer at Ahfad Univ for Women, Omdurman, Sudan, 1990; Author of numerous articles concerning Sudanese literature. **Business Addr:** Lecturer, Program in Africana Studies, Vassar College, 124 Raymond Ave, Poughkeepsie, NY 12601-6121.

BERKLEY, THOMAS LUCIUS
Attorney. **Personal:** Born Aug 9, 1915, DuQuoin, IL; married Velda Maureen; children: Theon King, Gail, Miriam. **Educ:** Fullerton Jr Coll, AA 1936; UCLA, BS 1938; Univ of CA Hastings School of Law, JD 1943. **Career:** Post Newspaper, publr; CA State World Trade Commiss, commiss; Private practice, attny. **Orgs:** Mem Alameda Cty Bar Assoc, CA State Bar Assoc, Amer Bar Assoc, Assoc of Trial Lawyers of Amer; mem Commiss of the Port of Oakland; mem bd dir Childrens Hosp Found, SF World Trade Club, SF Commonwealth Club, NAACP; past dir Oakland Unified School Dist; past mem, bd dir Oakland C of C; former regent John F Kennedy Univ; former mem adv council School of Bus Admin. **Military Serv:** AUS 2nd lt 1943-46. **Business Addr:** Attorney, 630 20th St, Oakland, CA 94612.

BERNARD, CANUTE CLIVE
Physician. **Personal:** Born Jan 1, 1924, Costa Rica; married Daisy; children: Canute Jr, Carmen, Sonja, Arthur, Gregory. **Educ:** Pharmacist Coll, degree pharmacist 1945; Howard Univ, BS 1949; NY Univ, MS 1951; Geneva Sch Med Univ Geneva, MD 1956. **Career:** Surgeon, Genl Practice; Jamaica Hosp, Queens Hosp Ctr, Harlem Hosp, Jamaica C of C, Health Systems Agency, NY State Workmen's Compensation Bd. **Orgs:** Third vice pres Natl Med Assn 1977-; bd of trustees Natl Med Assn; dir Med Bureau of NYS Workers Compensation Bd; bd secty/mem exec od Hlth Systems Agency; sec HSA Bd; mem HSA Exec Bd; mem Queens Clinical Soc NYC; past mem Chetto Med Prog; past pres Gamma Rho Sigma; past sec Queen's GGen Hosp; past pres Harlem Hosp; past v chmn Com Interns & Resd City NY; past chmn Pub Info Com MOTF for CHP; adv cncl York Coll; bd adv cnclQueen's Urban League; mem NY State Health Planning Commn; Boro Pres's Cncl; mem CHPA Ad Hoc Task Force; v chmn Queens Med Hlth Prog; bd mem Friends York Coll; mem Queens United Dem Polit Club; S Jamaica Restoration Corp Bd; tstee Queens Med Sch; Queens Park Assn; mem Charter Revision Commn City NY 1977. **Business Addr:** Surgeon, 107-60 Sutphin Blvd, Jamaica, NY 11435.

BERNARD, HAROLD O.
Educator, physician. **Personal:** Born Jan 5, 1938; married Clara; children: Harold, Emily, Warren. **Educ:** St Mary's College, attended, 1955; University of Manitoba, attended, 1956-68; Fisk University, attended, 1958-60; Meharry Medical College, attended, 1964. **Career:** Hubbard Hospital, intern, 1964-65, resident, 1965-68; Emory University, Dept of OB-GYN, associate, 1968-71; Meharry Medical College, asst professor, currently. **Orgs:** American Board Ob-Gyn, fellow, American College Ob-Gyn; Morgagni Society; consultant, Maternal & Infant Care Project, Grady Hospital; Maternal & Child Health Family Planning, Meharry Medical College; Natl Medical Assn; RF Boyd Medical Society; Vol State Medical Assn; Atlanta Medical Society; Georgia State Medical Assn; Tennessee State Medical Foundation; YMCA, Century Club. **Honors/Awds:** Beta Kappa Chi; Alpha Omega Alpha; Professor of the Year, 1975. **Business Addr:** Professor, Meharry Medical College, School of Medicine, Dept OB/GYN, 1005 Dr B D Todd Blvd, Nashville, TN 37208-3501.

BERNARD, JASON. See Obituaries section.

BERNARD, LOUIS JOSEPH
Surgeon, educator. **Personal:** Born Aug 19, 1925, LaPlace, LA; son of Jeanne Vinet Bernard (deceased) and Edward Bernard (deceased); married Lois Jeanette McDonald Bernard, Feb 1, 1976; children: Marie Antonia Bernard Jenkins, Phyllis Elaine Bernard Robison May. **Educ:** Dillard Univ, BA (magna cum laude), 1946; Meharry Med Coll, MD 1950. **Career:** Hubbard Hospital Nashville, intern 1950-51, resident 1954-56, 1957-58; Memorial Center NYC, resident 1956-57; Practice, med spec in surg, Oklahoma City OK, 1959-69, Nashville 1969-; Meharry Medical Coll, interim dean 1987-, School of Medicine, dean, 1987-90; Health Services, vice pres, 1988-90; Drew/Meharry/Morehouse Consortium Cancer Center, dir, 1990-96. **Orgs:** Nat'l Cancer Inst Rsch Fellow 1953-54; Amer Cancer Soc Clin Fellow 1958-59; bd dir TN Div Amer Cancer Soc; clin asst prof surg Univ of OK 1959-69; assoc prof vice chair surg dept Meharry Med Coll 1969-73, prof chmn surg dept 1973-87, assoc dean Sch of Med 1974-81; fellow Amer Coll of Surgeons; fellow Southeastern Surgical Congress; mem Nashville Acad Med; TN & Natl Med Assn; mem Soc of Surgical Oncologists; OK Surgical Assn; OK City Surgical Assn; Commn on Cancer Amer Coll of Surgeons 1974-84; Alpha Omega Alpha; Alpha Phi Alpha; Sigma Pi Phi; TN Div Amer Cancer Society, president, 1987-88. **Honors/Awds:** AMCA Soc, St George Award, 1985; Distinguished Professor of Surgery Emeritus, 1990; Louis J Bernard Neighbors for Life Award, 1992; Humanitarian Award, Natl American Cancer Soc, 1993; Margaret Edwards, Hay Award, AACE, 1996. **Military Serv:** US Army, 1st lt, 1951-53. **Home Addr:** 156 Queen's Ln, Nashville, TN 37218.

BERNARD, MICHELLE DENISE
Attorney. **Personal:** Born Jul 30, 1963, Washington, DC; daughter of Nesta Hyacinth Grant Bernard and Milton D. Bernard. **Educ:** Spelman College, Atlanta, GA, 1981-82; Howard University, Washington, D.C., BA, 1985; Georgetown University Law Ctr., Washington, D.C., JD, 1988. **Career:** Washington, Perito & Dubuc, Washington, D.C., attorney, 1988-. **Orgs:** Member, American Bar Association, 1988-; member, National Foundation for Black Public Administrators, 1990-; member, Maryland Chamber of Commerce, 1990-. **Honors/Awds:** Georgetown University Law Center Award for outstanding contribution to the Law Center Academic Program, 1988.

BERNARD, NESTA HYACINTH
Educational administrator. **Personal:** Born Sep 29; daughter of Edith Eliza Henry Grant and Charles Reginald Grant; married Milton Desmond Bernard, Dec 22, 1962; children: Michelle, Nicole, Andrea, Desmond. **Educ:** Howard University, Washington, DC, BA, 1975; University of Maryland, College Park, MD, MS, 1977. **Career:** United Planning Organization, chief, new programs branch; Howard University, Washington, DC, director of alumni affairs. **Orgs:** Member, National Assn Fundraising Executives, 1983-; executive secretary, Howard Univ Alumni Assn, 1982-; member, Alpha Kappa Alpha Sorority, member, Girlfriends; Links, Inc. **Honors/Awds:** Distinguished Service in the field of Development, Howard University, 1983; Distinguished Service, United Planning Org, 1977-79; Distinguished Service, National Assn for Blacks in Higher Education, 1990. **Business Addr:** Director of Alumni Affairs, Howard University, 2400-6th St NW, Washington, DC 20059.

BERNARD, SHARON ELAINE
Banker. **Personal:** Born Apr 19, 1943, Detroit, MI; daughter of Dorothea Bernard and John Bernard; children: Cylenthia, Sharon Gayle. **Educ:** Univ of AR Sch of Law, BSL, JD 1969. **Career:** Self-employed, attorney 1970-74; Michigan Natl Bank, various mgmt positions, vice pres 1975-. **Orgs:** Mem Kappa Beta Pi Legal Sor 1968-, Women's Economic Club 1975-; police commissioner Detroit Police Dept 1979-84; chairperson Children's Trust Fund 1982-88, Detroit Urban League Bd 1984-89; pres, Neighborhood Service Organization Board 1987-; dir, National Committee, Prevention of Child Abuse Board 1984-; dir, vice pres, United Way, SE Michigan Board, 1988-; dir, vice chair, United Community Services Board, 1989-; dir, vice chair, Ennis Center for Children Board, 1987-; member, Michigan Family Planning Advisory Board, 1990-. **Honors/Awds:** Minority Achiever in Industry Awd YMCA 1980; Spirit of Detroit City Council of Detroit 1984; Humanitarian of the Yr Optimist Youth Foundation 1986; Outstanding Volunteer MI Natl Bank 1987; Kool Achiever Award Nominee, Brown & Williamson 1988; Michigan 150 First Lady Award, State of Michigan 1988; Volunteer Services Award, Central Region, National Urban League, 1990; First Black Female Law Graduate Award, Black Law Students Assn, University of Arkansas, 1989; Outstanding Leadership Award, Detroit Urban League, 1989. **Business Addr:** Vice President, Michigan Natl Bank, PO Box 9065, Farmington Hills, MI 48333-9065, (810)473-3371.

BERNOUDY, MONIQUE ROCHELLE
Educator. **Personal:** Born May 18, 1960, Detroit, MI; daughter of Benjamin Joseph & Cynthia Bernoudy. **Educ:** Univ of MI; Spelman Coll, BA, 1983; Northern IL Univ, MS Ed, 1992. **Career:** Northern IL Univ, asst dir, admin asst, 1984-86; Northern IL Univ, Coll of Bus, academic counselor, 1987-92; Valparaiso Univ, Student Affairs, dir of multicultural programs, 1992-. **Orgs:** Advisory Council for Multiracial Concerns, 1992-; Campus Coordinating Comm, Sexual Harassment & Assault, co-chair, 1994; Campus Parking Comm, 1992-94; Coordinating Comm, Campus Diversity, 1992-; "Diversity Plan," development comm, 1994; Heritage Festival, coord comm, 1992-; Intercultural Studies Comm, 1992-; Judiciary Bd Hearing Panel, 1994; Knight Foundation, advisory comm, 1992-; Martin Luther King Day Observance, planning comm, 1992-; Porter County Comm Corrections Comm, 1992-; Racial Harassment Advocate, 1994-; Intercultural Comm, student senate, 1994-; Town & Gown Comm, 1992-94; Valparaiso Univ, alumni bd, 1993-, alumni bd multiracial sub-comm, 1993-, guild, 1994-; Week of Challenge Coord Comm, 1994; West Side High School Partnership Coord Comm, co-chair, 1992-; William Randlph Hearst Scholarship Comm, 1994-; Goshen Coll, Lilly Foundation Grant, evaluator, 1994-95; Indiana Coalition of Blacks in Higher Education, 1993-; Mid-America Assn Educational Opportunity Program Personnel, 1994-. **Special Achievements:** Residence Hall Presentation, Brandt Hall, Valparaiso Univ, Encouraging Cross-Cultural Learning, 1995; Indiana Corrections Conference, Radisson Hotel at Star Plaza, Women & Minorities in Corrections, 1994; Enhancing Minority Attainment IV Conference, Indiana Univ, We're All in This Together: Comm Partnerships that Work, 1994; Urban School Conference, Confronting Racist Attitudes, 1994; Orientation Assistants Training Presentation, Soup, Salad and the Main Course, 1994; Athletic Directors Consortium Presentation, Achieving Diversity, 1994; Physical Plant Employees Workshop, Racism in the Workplace, 1993; Harvesting Your Potential, ACU-I Region 9 Conference, Crayon Campus: Valuing Diversity, 1993. **Home Addr:** 3900 W 95th, #304, Evergreen Park, IL 60642. **Business Addr:** Dir, Multicultural Programs, Valparaiso Univ, Kretzmann Hall, Multicultural Programs, Valparaiso, IN 46383, (219)464-5400.

BERNSTEIN, MARGARET ESTHER
Newspaper editor. **Personal:** Born Nov 23, 1959, Los Angeles, CA; daughter of Alice Collum Bernstein and Morris Bernstein; married C Randolph Keller, Feb 16, 1991. **Educ:** University of Southern California, BA, print journalism, 1993. **Career:** Wave Newspapers, Los Angeles, CA, staff writer, 1981-84; Herald-Dispatch, Huntington, WV, feature writer, 1984-87; Tucson Citizen, Tucson, AR, asst city editor, 1987-89; Plain Dealer, Cleveland, OH, feature writer/columnist, 1989-92, editor, women's section, 1992-. **Orgs:** Board member, Black Journalists Assn of Southern Cal, 1982-84; founder/president, Tri-State Black Media Assn, 1986-87; committee chair, Cleveland Chapter, National Assn of Black Journalists, 1989-; member, Delta Sigma Theta Sorority, 1981-; member, Catholic Big Sisters of Cleveland, 1989-. **Honors/Awds:** Project Editor for "Tucson's Tapestry of Cultures," a 1988-89 newspaper series that received: Sweepstakes Award & 1st Place for In Depth News, Arizona Associated Press, and 3rd Place, Staff Enterprise Award, Best of Gannett Competition; Ohio Excellence in Journalism Awards, First Place, Column-writing, 1992; Cleveland Services for Independent Living, Best in Media Award, 1992. **Business Addr:** Editor, Women's Section, The Plain Dealer, 1801 Superior St NE, Cleveland, OH 44114.

BERNSTINE, DANIEL O.
Attorney, educator. **Personal:** Born Sep 7, 1947, Berkeley, CA; children: Quincy, Justin. **Educ:** Univ of CA, BA 1969; NW Univ Sch of Law, JD 1972; Univ of WI Law Sch, LLM 1975. **Career:** US Dept of Labor, staff atty 1972-73; Univ of WI Law Sch, teaching fellow 1974-75; Howard Univ Law Sch, asst prof 1975-78; Howard Univ, asst vice pres for legal affairs, 1984-87, general counsel, 1987-1990; Univ of WI Law Sch, prof, 1978-97, dean, 1990-97; Portland State University, president, currently. **Honors/Awds:** Various publications. **Business Addr:** President, Portland State University, PO Box 751, Portland, OR 97207, (503)725-2376.

BERNSTINE, ROD EARL
Professional football player. **Personal:** Born Feb 8, 1965, Fairfield, CA; married Stephanie Kay Smith, Feb 9, 1991; children: Payton Chanel, Roderick Earl Jr. **Educ:** Texas A & M Univ, attended. **Career:** San Diego Chargers, tight end, 1987-93; Denver Broncos, 1993-95.

BERRY, ARCHIE PAUL
Business executive. **Personal:** Born Nov 2, 1935, Akron, OH; married Sheila Yvonne Robinson; children: Troy Paul, Trent Anthony. **Educ:** Univ Akron, BSEE 1963; Kent State Univ, MBA 1979. **Career:** Akron Standard Mold, elec engr 1963-64; IBM, systems engr 1964-65, market rep 1965-69, instr EXEC Educ 1969-71, instr mgr 1971, mgr info serv 1971-73, mgr computer serv 1973-76, mgr 1976-77, mgr castings & spl prods 1977-79, mgr prod educ. **Orgs:** Vice pres bus & finance Alpha Phi Alpha Homes Inc; NAACP; Urban League; Alpha Phi Alpha; vis prof Urban League's BEEP Prog; trustee Akron Regional DevelBd. **Honors/Awds:** Man of Yr Alpha 1976; Four 100 Percent Sales Club Awds IBM 1966-69; Golden Cir Sales Awd IBM 1968. **Military Serv:** USAF a/1c 1954-57. **Business Addr:** Manager of Prod Educ & Training, Babcock & Wilcox, 20 S Van Buren Ave, Barberton, OH 44203.

BERRY, BENJAMIN DONALDSON
Educational administrator, educator. **Personal:** Born Dec 22, 1939, Washington, DC; son of Otis Holley Berry and Benjamin D Berry Sr; married Linda Baker; children: Richard, Kathleen, Thena, Akuba. **Educ:** Morehouse College, BA, 1962; Harvard Divinity School, STB, 1966; Case-Western Reserve University, PhD, 1977. **Career:** Plymouth UCC, pastor, 1966-68; Tampa Inner City Parish, director, 1968-70; University of South Florida, Afro-American Studies, director, 1969-70; Heidelberg College, American Studies, asst professor, 1970-74; College of Wooster, Black Studies, director, 1974-78; Skidmore College, Minority Affairs, director; Prairie View A&M, Dept of Social & Political Sciences, Honors College, professor, currently. **Orgs:** Board of director, Natl American Studies Faculty, 1974-78; Board of Education, 1981-; consultant, Berry Associates. **Honors/Awds:** Merrill Scholar, Morehouse College, 1961; Rockefeller Fellow, Harvard Divinity, 1962-66; Danforth Associate, Heidelberg College, 1972; Mellon Visiting Scholar, Skidmore College, 1978; Morehouse College, Phi Beta Kappa, 1987, Jesse Ball du Pont, Visiting Scholar, 1992. **Home Addr:** 14522 Cypress Ridge Dr, Cypress, TX 77429. **Business Addr:** Professor, Dept of Social & Political Sciences, Prairie View A&M University, PO Box 519, Prairie View, TX 77446-0519.

BERRY, BERT
Professional football player. **Personal:** Born Aug 15, 1975, Houston, TX. **Educ:** Notre Dame. **Career:** Indianapolis Colts, linebacker, 1997-. **Business Addr:** Professional Football Player, Indianapolis Colts, PO Box 535000, Indianapolis, IN 46253, (317)297-2658.

BERRY, CHARLES F., JR.
Audit assoc. **Personal:** Born May 15, 1964, Detroit, MI; son of Charles F Sr & Edna J Berry; married D Lynn Berry, May 30, 1992. **Educ:** Univ of MI-Ann Arbor, bachelors, 1987. **Career:**

Citizens Trust Bank & Trust, bank teller, 1986-87; Plante & Moran CPA's, auditor, 1987-. **Orgs:** Toastmasters International, past pres, 1991-93; Volunteer Income Tax Assistance, tax preparer, 1987-92; Natl Assn of Black Accountants, 1987-; American Institute of Certified Public Accountants, 1988-; MI Assn of Certified Public Accountants, 1987-; United Way Health & Human Services Allocation Committee, 1994-. **Honors/Awds:** Detroit Chamber of Commerce, Leadership Detroit Graduate, 1994. **Business Addr:** Audit Associate, Plante & Moran CPA's, 27400 Northwestern Hwy, Southfield, MI 48034, (810)827-0387.

BERRY, CHUCK (CHARLES EDWARD ANDERSON BERRY)
Singer/composer. **Personal:** Born Oct 18, 1926, St Louis, MO; son of Martha Bell Banks Barry and Henry William Berry; married Themetta (Toddy) Suggs, Oct 28, 1948; children: Four. **Career:** Singer/songwriter. Sir John's Trio, guitarist, 1952; solo recording artist, 1955-. **Honors/Awds:** Hit singles include: Maybelline, 1955; Roll Over Beethoven, 1956; Too Much Monkey Business/Brown Eyed Handsome Man, 1956; School Day (Ring Ring Goes the Bell), 1957; Rock and Roll Music, 1957; Sweet Little Sixteen, 1958; Johnny B Goode/Around and Around, 1958; Caraol, 1958; Sweet Little Rock and Roller, 1958; Little Queenie/Almost Grown, 1959; Memphis/Back in the USA, 1959; Nadine, 1964; No Particular Place to Go, 1964; My Ding-a-Ling, 1972; numerous albums; appeared in several movies (Hail Hail Rock and Roll autobiograhical) and TV shows. Triple Award for having the number one record on the R&B, Country/Western, and Pop Charts for Maybelline, Billboard Magazine, 1955; Best R&B Singer, Blues Unlimited, 1973; National Music Award, American Music Conference, 1976;Grammy Award for Lifetimchievement, 1984; inductee into Rock and Roll Hall of Fame, 1986; Lifetime Achievement Award, Guitar Player Magazine, 1987; Hollywood Walk of Fame, 1987. **Business Addr:** Berry Park, 691 Buckner Rd, Wentzville, MO 63385.

BERRY, FREDRICK JOSEPH
Educator. **Personal:** Born May 29, 1940, Jacksonville, IL; married Quereda Ann Harris; children: Anthony, Frederick Jr. **Educ:** Roosevelt Univ, 1961; Southern IL Univ, BMus 1962, MMus 1964; Stanford Univ, 1966-69. **Career:** S IL Univ Lab School, super of music 1964; Chicago Public School System, instructor 1964-66; Stanford Univ, asst dir of bands 1966-69; Coll of San Mateo, dir of jazz ensembles 1972-88; Stanford Univ, Jazz Ensembles, dir, 1989-; Nueva Learning Center, Hills Borough, CA, brass specialist, 1984-. **Orgs:** Mem Amer Fed of Musicians 1956-95; mem San Fran 49ers Band 1970-85; Amer Fed of Teachers 1970-; vice pres Amer Fed of Music Local 6 Credit Union 1973; mem CA Teachers Assn 1975-85; pres Berry Enterprises & Music Serv 1980-95; mem CA Music Educ Assn 1980-. **Honors/Awds:** Guest soloist Oakland Symphony 1971; contractor Black Filmmakers Hall of Fame 1978-93; mem Golden Gate Theatre Orchestra 1982-90; musical dir Black Film Makers Hall of Fame 1983. **Business Addr:** Professor of Music, College of San Mateo, 1700 W Hillsdale Blvd, San Mateo, CA 94402.

BERRY, GEMERAL E., JR.
Magazine publisher. **Personal:** Born Aug 9, 1948, San Antonio, TX; son of Gemeral E & Leotha O Berry, Sr; married Elaine Berry, Dec 29, 1973; children: Gemeral III. **Educ:** University of North Texas, BA, 1974. **Career:** Our Texas Magazine, publisher, 1990-; University of North Texas, adjunct professor of journalism, 1996-. **Orgs:** Dallas Black Chamber of Commerce; Acres Home Citizens Chamber of Commerce; Ft Worth Metropolitan Chamber; Midland Black Chamber of Entreprenuers, Midland, DFW/ABC Journalists; Dallas Ft Worth/Association of Black Journalists. **Honors/Awds:** Texas NAACP, Torchbearer, 1996; DFW/ABC Journalistm Excellence, 1996; University of North Texas, Outstanding Area Journalist, 1995; Press Club of Dallas, Certificate of Excellence, 1996, Katie, Journalism Excellence, 1993. **Special Achievements:** Certificate of Participation, Howard University, 1990. **Military Serv:** USAF, sgt, 1966-70. **Business Addr:** Publisher, Out Texas Magazine, PO Box 4463, Dallas, TX 75208, (214)946-5315.

BERRY, GORDON L.
Educator, author, lecturer. **Personal:** son Of Gertrude Berry and Marcus Berry; married G Juanita Berry; children: Gordon Jr, Steven, Cheryl. **Educ:** Central State Univ, BS 1955; Univ of WI, MS 1961; Marquette Univ, EdD 1969. **Career:** Milwaukee Tech Coll, counseling psychologist; Marquette Univ, asst to academic vice pres; UCLA, asst dean 1970-76, prof 1976-. **Orgs:** Natl Assoc of Sch Psychologists 1970-; Phi Delta Kappa; Bd of Los Angeles Film Teachers Assn; mem Amer Psychological Assn; American Psychological Society; Academy of Television Arts & Sciences Foundation, board member. **Honors/Awds:** Ralph Metcalfe Chair Lecturer; The Academy of Television Arts & Sciences. **Military Serv:** AUS capt 1955-57. **Business Addr:** Professor, UCLA, School of Education, 405 Hilgard Ave, #2018 Moore Hall, Los Angeles, CA 90024.

BERRY, HALLE M.
Actress. **Personal:** Born Aug 14, 1967, Cleveland, OH; daughter of Judy Berry; married David Justice, Jan 1, 1993 (divorced 1996). **Educ:** Cleveland State University. **Career:** Actress: "Living Dolls," tv show, lead, 1988-89; Jungle Fever, feature film, co-star lead, 1989; Strictly Business, feature film, lead, 1990-91; "Knot's Landing", tv series, guest lead, 1991; The Last Boy Scout, feature film, co-star role, 1991; "Queen," tv miniseries, lead, 1992; Boomerang, feature film, co-star role, 1992; The Flintstones, co-star role, 1994; Losing Isaiah, 1994; Executive Decision, 1996; Race the Sun, 1996; BAPS, 1997; Bullworth, 1998; The Wedding, 1998; Why Do Fools Fall in Love, 1998. **Orgs:** Juvenile Diabetes Association, spokesperson; Children Outreach, spokesperson; Revlon, model. **Honors/Awds:** Miss Teen Ohio; Miss Teen All America; Runner Up to Miss USA; nominated Best New Comer by the Women's Hollywood Press; Nominated Best Actress by The Image Awards. **Business Addr:** Actress, c/o Gage Group, 9255 Sunset Blvd, Ste 215, Los Angeles, CA 90069, (310)859-8777.

BERRY, JAY (JEROME)
Sports reporter. **Personal:** Born Aug 5, 1950, Tulsa; married Claudia; children: Carla Michelle, Kristen Lynette, Kayla Renee'. **Educ:** Univ WY; Tulsa U; Bishop Coll. **Career:** Gulf Oil Co, 1970-73; KTUL TV, news reporter sportscaster 1973-74; KPRC TV Houston, news reporter, sportscaster 1974-79; WLS-TV, sportscaster 1979-82; WXYZ-TV Detroit, 1982-, sports reporter, currently. **Orgs:** NAACP; mem Black Communicators; co-chair Black United Fund. **Honors/Awds:** Best Sportscaster in TX Assoc Press 1977; Best Feature in TX United Press Intl 1977; Outstanding Achievement "UPI" Sports Feature MI 1984; Emmy nom "When the Cheering Stops," 1984. **Business Addr:** Sports Reporter, WXYZ, PO Box 789, Southfield, MI 48037.

BERRY, LATIN
Professional football player. **Personal:** Born Jan 13, 1967, Lakeview Terrace, CA. **Educ:** Univ of Oregon, 1985-89. **Career:** Los Angeles Rams, cornerback, 1990-92; Cleveland Browns, 1992-93; Green Bay Packers, 1993-. **Orgs:** LA Jets; MS Volunteer; Kappa Alpha Psi Fraternity. **Honors/Awds:** Multicultural Leadership Award. **Business Addr:** Professional Football Player, Green Bay Packers, 1265 Lombardi Ave, Green Bay, WI 54304.

BERRY, LEE ROY, JR.
Educator. **Personal:** Born Nov 5, 1943, Lake Placid, FL; married Elizabeth Ann Hostetler; children: Joseph Jonathan, Malinda Elizabeth, Anne Hostetler. **Educ:** Eastern Mennonite College, BA, 1966; University of Notre Dame, PhD, 1976; Indiana University Bloomington, School of Law, JD, 1984. **Career:** Cleveland Public Schools, teacher, 1966-68; Goshen College, professor, 1969-79, leader, study serv trimester, 1979-80, Dept of History & Government, associate professor, 1980-. **Orgs:** General Board, Mennonite Ch; chairman, High Aim Committee, member, Relief & Service Committee, Mennonite Board of Missions; Peace Sect, Mennonite Central Committee. **Honors/Awds:** John Hay Whitney Fellow, 1970-71; Natl Fellowships Fund Felow, 1975-76. **Business Addr:** Associate Professor, Dept of History & Government, Goshen College, S Main St, Goshen, IN 46526-4795.

BERRY, LEMUEL, JR.
Educator. **Personal:** Born Oct 11, 1946, Oneonta, NY; children: Lemuel III, Cyrus James. **Educ:** Livingstone College, BA, 1969; University of Iowa, MA, 1970, PhD, 1973. **Career:** Sabin Elementary School, 1971; Southeastern Junior High School, 1972; Fayetteville State University, instructor of weekend coll in serv teachers, 1975-76, chairman, Division of Humanities, 1973-75, chairman, Dept of Music, 1973-76; Langston University, chairman, Dept of Music, 1976-83, chairman, Dept of Music & Art, 1981-83; Alabama State University, dean, School of Music, assoc professor, School of Music, 1983-86; Mercy College, chairman/professor, Dept of Music & Fine Arts; Virginia State Unviersity, Dean of Humanities and Social Scieces, currently; Memphis State Univ, Dept of Music, chairperson, 1988-90. **Orgs:** Kappa Kappa Psi, natl president, 1983-85; Research Assn of Minority Professors, natl president, 1983-86; bd of trustees, Assn of Concert Bands, 1984-85; bd of trustees, Southern Conference of Afro-American Studies, 1983-87; counicl member, Council for Research in Music Education, 1978-; Oklahoma Arts Assn, 1982-84; North Central Teacher Certification, 1982-84; state chairperson, Natl Black Music Collequium, 1979-80; Alabama Jazz Education Assn, 1984-; reviewer, American Choral Directors Assn, 1984-; board mem, The Richmond Symphony, Petersburg Music Festival, The Richmond Ballet, 1990-; Southern Conference for African Studies, president, 1992-93; Natl Assn of African Amer Studies, founder, exec dir, 1992-. **Honors/Awds:** German Academic Research Scholarship, 1979; Outstanding Educator, 1975; Natl Endowment of the Humanities, grant recipient, 1985. **Business Addr:** Dean, School of Humanities, Virginia State University, Petersburg, VA 23803.

BERRY, LEROY
Educator (retired). **Personal:** Born Oct 20, 1920, Birmingham, AL; son of Lubertha Foster (deceased) and Lester Berry; married Ruth Brothers Berry, Jul 28, 1949; children: Lorenzo Armstead. **Educ:** Western Reserve Univ, Cleveland OH, 1946; UCLA-USC, Los Angeles, CA; UCLA, Los Angeles CA, BA, Sociology, 1957; CA State Univ, Los Angeles CA, MA, Elementary Teaching, 1961, MA, Elementary Admin, 1962, MA, Counseling, 1976. **Career:** Dept of Water & Power, Los Angeles CA, electr tester, 1948-54; Los Angeles Unified School Dist, Los Angeles CA, teacher 1957-77, substitute principal 1969-72, counselor 1977-80, teacher advisor 1980-82; coordinator, precinct comm, Tom Bradley city council and mayoral campaigns, 1980-88. **Orgs:** Mem, Kappa Alpha Psi Fraternity; life mem, NAACP; mem, Urban League, S Christian Lead Corp, Crenshaw Neighbors; alumni life mem Univ of CA at LA, 1958-; pres Leimert Democratic Club, 1958-61; asst dist rep, CA Democratic Council, 1964-66; southern cred chmn, CA Democratic Council 1964-66; vice pres reg II CA Democratic Council 1966-68; representative, Democratic County Committee, 1967-71; representative, State Democratic Committee 1967-73. **Honors/Awds:** Appointed commr of Environmental Quality Bd, 1976, commr of Human Relations Comm, 1983, by mayor and city of Los Angeles. **Military Serv:** AUS 54th Coast Artill, corporal 1941-44; US Air Corps, radio technician, 1944-45; marksman, sharpshooter, good conduct medal. **Home Addr:** 3801 Welland Ave, Los Angeles, CA 90008.

BERRY, MARY FRANCES
Educator. **Personal:** Born Feb 17, 1938, Nashville, TN; daughter of Frances Southall Berry and George F Berry. **Educ:** Howard University, BA, 1961, MA, 1962; University of Michigan, PhD, 1966, JD, 1970. **Career:** Howard University, teaching fellow, American history, 1962-63; University of Michigan, teaching asst, 1965-66, asst professor, Dept of History, 1966-68, assoc professor, 1968-70; University of Maryland, assoc professor, 1969-76; University of Colorado, Afro-American Studies, acting director, 1970-72, director, 1972-74, provost, Division of Behavioral Social Science, 1974, chancellor, 1976-77, professor, Dept of History, 1976-80; US Dept HEW, asst secretary for education, 1977-80; US Commission on Civil Rights, commissioner & vice chairman 1980-; Howard University, professor, Dept of History & Law, 1980-87; University of Pennsylvania, Geraldine R Segal Professor of American Social Thought, 1987-. **Orgs:** DC Bar Assn, 1972; consultant to curator of education, Natl Portrait Gallery, Smithsonian Institution; consultant, Office Policy Planning, HUD; bd mem, Afro-American Bicentennial Corp; chairman, Maryland Commission Afro-American/Indian History Culture, 1974; exec bd member, Organization of American Historians, 1974-77; exec bd, Assn Study of Afro-American Life History, 1973-76; American Historical Assn; Organization of American Historians; American Bar Assn; Natl Bar Assn; natl panel of advisors, University of Mid-America; Tuskegee Institute, bd of trustees; bd of dirs, DC Chapter, ARC. **Honors/Awds:** Civil War Round Table Fellowship Award, 1965-66; author, Black Resistance/White Law: A History of Constitutional Racism in America, 1971; Why ERA Failed: Women's Rights & the Amending Process of the Constitution, 1986; assoc editor, Journal of Negro History, 1974-; honorary degrees, University of Akron, 1977, Benedict College, 1979, Grambling State University, 1979, Bethune-Cookman Coll, 1980, Clark College, 1980, Oberlin College, 1983, Langston University, 1983, Haverford College, 1984, Colby College, 1986, DePaul University, 1987; Rosa Parks Award, Southern Christian Leadership Conference; Ebony Magazine, Black Achievement Award; Ms Magazine, Woman of the Year 1986. **Business Addr:** Professor, Dept of History, University of Pennsylvania, Philadelphia, PA 19104.

BERRY, ONDRA LAMON
Police officer. **Personal:** Born Oct 3, 1958, Evansville, IN; son of Ethel Gibson Kuykendall and Charles Berry; married Margo Curry, Aug 14, 1980; children: Jarel. **Educ:** University of Evansville, Evansville, IN, BA, education, 1980; University of Nevada-Reno, Reno, NV, MPA, 1996. **Career:** Reno Police Department, Reno, NV, lieutenant, deputy chief, currently. **Orgs:** Past president, Northern Nevada Black Cultural Awareness Society; vice chair, United Way of Nevada, 1991-97; state appointment by governor, State Job Training Council, 1989-93. **Honors/Awds:** Outstanding Law Enforcement Officer, Reno Jaycees, 1989-90. **Military Serv:** Air National Guard, captain, 1986-; Achievement Medal, 1989; Air Man of Year for Nevada, 1989; Outstanding Airman of Year for United States, 1989. **Business Addr:** Deputy Chief, Reno Police Department, 455 E Second, Reno, NV 89505.

BERRY, PAUL LAWRENCE
Reporter. **Personal:** Born Feb 15, 1944, Detroit, MI; married Marilyn; children: Karen. **Educ:** Attended, USAF Def Info Sch, Basic Med Sch, Basic Dental Sch. **Career:** WXYZ-TV, staff rep & co-anchor 1969-72; WMAL-TV, anchor st rep & mod 1972-75; WMAL-TV, st rep mod & co-anchor 1975-; Amer Black Forum, panelist; Paul Berry's WA, weekend anchor & host. **Orgs:** Wash DC Mayors Ad Hock Comm on Criminal Justice; DC Fed 524 Coun for Except Child; Sigma Delta Chi Prof Journ Soc; bd of dir Amer Digest Disease Assn; Lion Club of Wash DC. **Honors/Awds:** Broadcasters Awd Chesapeake Assoc Press 1976; Metro Wash Mass Media Awd Amer Assoc of Univ Women 1976; Comm Awd MI Chap SCLC; Comm Serv Awd 1974;Comm Serv Awd Unit Cit Inc 1975; Media Awd Cap Press Club 1975; Natl Cap Area Health Assn Awd 1974; Outstanding Cit Awd MMEOC Assn 1976; Dept Comm Serv Awd Amer Amvets DC 1974; Comm Serv Awd Rap Inc 1976. **Military Serv:** USAF staff sgt 1961-69. **Business Addr:**

Weekend Anchorman, c/o WJLA-TV Channel 7, 4461 Connecticut Avenue NW, Washington, DC 20008.

BERRY, PHILIP ALFONSO
Consumer products company executive. **Personal:** Born Jan 28, 1950, New York, NY; married Karen Bryan; children: Kiel, Maya. **Educ:** Manhattan Comm Coll, AA 1971; Queens Coll CUNY, BA 1973; Columbia Univ Sch of Social Work, MS 1975; Xavier Univ of Cincinnati, MBA 1983. **Career:** Urban League of Westchester NY, dir 1975-78; Procter & Gamble, industrial relations mgr 1978-86; Digital Equipment Corp, human resources consultant 1986-; Triboro Bridge & Tunnel Authority, NY, vp, human resources 1988-90; Colgate-Palmolive, vice pres Human Resources International. **Orgs:** EDGES, membership committee, 1990-; National Association Social Workers, chair, industrial social work, 1989-; NY State chmn Assoc of Black Social Workers 1975-78; fndr/pres Housing & Neighborhood Develop Inst 1976-78; pres The Delta Group & Berry Assoc Consulting 1983-; bd mem Cincinnati Comm Action Agency 1985-86; dean of pledges Alpha Phi Alpha Frat Alumni Chap 1986; mem Amer Soc for Training & Develop, World Future Soc; pres Black Student Union Queens Coll, Black Student Caucus Columbia Univ; Natl Foreign Trade Council, mem; Columbia Univ Alumni Board, representative. **Honors/Awds:** Ford Foundation Fellowship; Mayor's Proclamation "Philip Berry Day" Mt Vernon NY 1978. **Home Addr:** 7 Rutgers Pl, Upper Montclair, NJ 07043. **Business Addr:** Vice Pres, Human Resources International, Colgate-Palmolive Corp., 300 Park Ave, 13K, New York, NY 10022, (212)310-2947.

BERRY, THEODORE M.
Attorney (retired). **Personal:** Born Nov 8, 1905, Maysville, KY; married Johnnie M Newton; children: 3. **Educ:** Univ Cincinnati, AB 1928, LLB 1931. **Career:** Cincinnati City Council, council mem 1950-57; OEO, asst dir 1965-69; City of Cincinnati, mayor 1972-75; Tobias & Kraus, atty; Coll of Law Univ of Cincinnati, adj prof 1976-78; NAACP, interim gen counsel 1979-80. **Orgs:** Mem Amer, OH, DC Cincinnati, Sup Ct Bar Assns; dir Cedar Grove Homestead Assn; trustee Cincinnati Better Housing League & Family Svc; Natl Dem Pol Comm; counsel West End Dev Corp; dir Southern OH Bank 1973-84; president, trustee Cincinnati Southern Railway 1977-; mem Lawyer's Del to China-Sponsor, Citizen Ambassador People to People Prog 1987. **Honors/Awds:** Hon LLD Univ Cincinnati 1968; Humanitarian Awd ACTION 1973; bro chmn Natl Conf Christians & Jews 1973; Outstanding Citizen Awd Omega Psi Phi 1974; Natl Conf Christ & Jews Awd 1977; Hebrew Union Coll Doctor of Humane Letters 1979; NAACP Wm R Ming Advocacy Awd 1979; Disting Alumni Awd UC Coll of Law 1982; Cincinnati C of C Great Living Cincinnatian Awd 1984; Wm Howard Taft Americanism Award, Anti-Defamation League, 1990; Community Service Award, Ohio Black Male Coalition, 1991; Community Service Award, A Philip Randolph Institute, 1991; Ohio Bar Foundation, 50 Year Public Service Award, 1993; Certificate of Excellence Awd, Tuskegee Airmen, 1996. **Business Addr:** Keys & Simpkinson, 36 East 4th St, Ste 1304, Cincinnati, OH 45202.

BERRY, WELDON H.
Attorney. **Personal:** Born Jan 4, Dallas, TX; married Lurlene Barnes. **Educ:** TX Coll, AB 1941; TX So Univ Sch Law, LLB 1952. **Career:** Private practice, law. **Military Serv:** USAF 2nd lt 1941-43. **Business Addr:** Attorney, 711 Main St, Houston, TX 77002.

BERRYMAN, MACON M.
Lecturer (retired). **Personal:** Born Feb 17, 1908, Lexington, KY; married Dortha Hackett; children: James Henry. **Educ:** Lincoln Univ PA, BA 1931; Atlanta Univ Sch of Social Work, MA 1933; Lincoln Univ PA, DCL 1967. **Career:** Casework Supr, investigator 1933-34; Burlington Co Emergency Relief Admin, dist adminstr 1934-36; NY State Training Sch for Boys, parole ofcr 1936-45; Sunnycrest Farm for Boys, exec dir 1945-50; Dept of Social Welfare, St Thomas VI, dir child welfare 1950-58; Social Welfare, actg commr 1958-59, ret commr 1959-74; Div of Social Sci Coll Of VI, guest lectr 1974-77; Retired. **Orgs:** Mem Nat Assn of Social Workers 1938-; fellow Acad of Cert Social Workers 1960-; Nat Cncl of State Pub Welfare Admin 1959-74; Nat & Intl Conf of Scl Wrk 1936-; Am Pub Wlfr Assn 1950-; mem bd of dir St Thomas & St John Chpt; ARC 1957-; mem Bd Dirs, St Thomas United Way 1959-85; chmn Bd of Dirs 1976-78; treas St Thomas Fed Credit & Union 1954-59; Civil Def Dir Welfare Disaster Serv 1958-74; consult VA Youth Commn 1950-59; VI Aging Commn 1959-74; mem Bd Dirs VI Cncl Boy Scouts 1964-; organizer & pres VI Chap Lincoln Univ Alumni Assn 1964-67; mem Alpha Phi Alpha Frat; Masonic Lodge; Episcopalian pres St Thomas Rotary Club 1966-67; sec Dist 404 Rotary Club 1978-79; founder St Thomas Rotary Club II 1979. **Honors/Awds:** Citation for Distinguished Serv as Chmn; bd mem St Thomas, St John Chap ARC 1965; Citation in Recog of Outstanding Achievement in Serving Human Needs of Comm; St Thomas United Way 1957 & 1979; Citation in Apprec for interest in Serv to Youth of Comm; VI Cncl Boy & Scouts 1965; Silver Beaver 1969; Reg Cncl Boy Scouts Silver Antelope 1972; citation St Thomas USO 1966; citation St Thomas Women's League 1966; citation PR Cancer League 1966, 1967, 1972, 1974; citation Am Bicentennial Res Inst 1974; awarded Paul Harris Fellow 1980; Life Achievement Award, Macon M Berryman Life Achievement Award Scholarship Fund, Rotary Club of St Thomas, 1990; Resolution for outstanding contribution and service to VI community, legislature of VI, 1990; citation for outstanding and dedicated service to the pee of VI, Amer Red Cross, St Thomas, St John Chap, 1990; Award of Excellence for Outstanding Achievements and Leadership in the Service of Humanity, Alpha Phi Alpha Frat, Theta Epsilon Chap, 1990. **Home Addr:** PO Box 3892, St Thomas, Virgin Islands of the United States 00801.

BERRYMAN, MATILENE S.
Attorney. **Personal:** Born in Prince Edward Co, VA; divorced; children: D'Michele, Sherrill Diane Miller. **Educ:** Attended, Bluefield State Univ WV; Howard Univ, attended 1945-46; Attended, PA State, UCLA, George Washington 1957-65; Amer Univ Washington DC, BMath 1957; Howard Univ Washington DC, JD 1973; Univ of RI, M Marine Affairs 1979. **Career:** US Naval Oceanographic Office Suitland, physical oceanographer 1955-63, oceanographer instructor 1963-68; Exec Office of Pres & Defense Documen Center, Alexandria VA, physical science admin 1968-70; Consortium for DC, dir marine science 1973-76; Univ of Washington DC, prof of marine science 1970-. **Orgs:** Chmn Enviromental Sci Dept Univ of DC 1971-78; financial sec Natl Assn of Black Women Atty 1975-; visiting prof Purdue Univ; mem PA State Bar 1974-; mem DC Bar 1975-; trustee Shiloh Bapt Ch Washington DC; bd dir DC Mental Health. **Honors/Awds:** Nominated vice pres Marine Tech Soc 1978-79; Outstanding Serv to Marine Sci & Law Natl Assn of Black Women Atty 1978. **Business Addr:** Prof of Marine Sci, Univ of DC, Van Ness Campus, 4200 Connecticut Ave NW, Washington, DC 20008.

BESSENT, HATTIE
Educator. **Personal:** Born Dec 26, 1926, Jacksonville, FL. **Educ:** FL A&M U, BS 1959; Nurs Educ IN U, MS 1962; Univ of FL, Intrnshp 1975, EdD 1970; Univ of FL Nurs Coll; Mtl Hlth Cnslt, Dipl 1971. **Career:** Vanderbuilt Univ School of Nursing, assoc dean grad affairs prof 1976-, prof psychist 1974-75; Univ of FL, psychol fnd teaching rsch 1971-76; Tulane Univ, consultant 1970-71; FL A&M Univ, asst prof psychist nurs 1962-67. **Orgs:** Am Educ Rsch Assn; Am Nurs' Assn; Am Pgtn Soc; Assn for Supvsn & Curr Devel; FL Nurs Assn; Nat Leag for Nurs; Delta Sigma Theta Sor; Alch Co Mtl Hlth Assn; Gnsvl Hum Relat Bd Sigma Theta Tau; Phi Lambda Theta; Phi Delta Kappa. **Honors/Awds:** Career Tchrs Grant. **Business Addr:** Deputy Executive Dir, American Nursing Assoc, 1030 15th St NW #716, Washington, DC 20005.

BESSON, PAUL SMITH
Attorney. **Personal:** Born May 11, 1953, New York, NY; son of Patricia Smith Besson and Frederick A. Besson. **Educ:** Cornell Univ, BS labor relations 1975, MBA marketing/finance 1976; Northwestern Univ, JD 1980; Georgetown University Law Center, LLM, 1995. **Career:** Cummins Engine Co, market planning analyst 1976-77; Jewel Companies, Inc, labor relations counsel 1980-82, mgr personnel/labor relations 1982-83; NBC, Inc, mgr labor relations, 1984-88, dir employee relations, 1988-. **Orgs:** Mem Amer, IL, Chicago, DC Bar Assn; mem IL, NY, & DC Bars; bd of dir Cornell Club Assn 1982; pres Cornell Black Alumni Assn Chicago 1982-83; contributing writer Black Enterprise Magazine; Amer Arbitration Assn panel commercial arbitrations; hearing officer, Civil Serv Commn IL; bd of dir ABE Credit Union; pres, Cornell Black Alumni Assn, Washington, DC, 1989-91; Capital Press Club; Washington Association of Black Journalists; mediator, US District Court, Dist of Columbia. **Business Addr:** Dir, Employee Relations, NBC Inc, 4001 Nebraska Ave, NW, Washington, DC 20024.

BEST, JENNINGS H.
Attorney. **Personal:** Born Aug 5, 1925, Jacksonville, FL; married Elizabeth Blake; children: Valorie. **Educ:** JD, 1956. **Career:** Knights of Pythias Jurisdic of FL, grand atty. **Orgs:** Mem DW Perkins Bar Assn; Natl Bar Assn; mem Phi Beta Sigma Frat. **Military Serv:** AUS WW II 1944-46; Korean War 1950-52. **Business Addr:** Grand Attorney, Knights of Pythias, 3410 N Myrtle Ave, Jacksonville, FL 32209.

BEST, JOHN T.
Federal government official, analyst, counselor. **Personal:** Born Jan 24, 1936, Philadelphia, PA; son of Mary Eliza Best and John Thomas Best; married Mary Anna Grady; children: Toussaint, Johanna, Johnathan, Kevin, Deborah, Lydia Timmons. **Educ:** Henry George School of Social Science, New York, certificate, 1969-72; LaSalle University Institute, accounting, certificates, 1970-72; Community Coll of Philadelphia, AGS 1972; Rutgers Univ, BA 1974; Univ of Pennsylvania, MCP 1976; attended Philadelphia Govt Training Inst 1972; Rutgers Univ, labor management, 1980; Amer Mgmt Assn, management studies, 1984; Franklin Inst, computer training, 1984; Morris Arboretum, landscape design certificate, 1987; Rosemont College, Holistic Health, certificate, 1989. **Career:** Best Associates, urban planner 1976-; City of Philadelphia, City Planner II, 1980-81; USPS, supervisor 1981-; Radio, communicator, 1996-. **Orgs:** Amer Planning Assn 1976-90; Society for the Advancement of Mgmt 1981-90; Amer Mgmt Assn 1981-91; comm mem United Way 1981-91; life mem Amer Legion Post 292; life mem 101st Airborne Assn; life mem NAACP; mem Philaxis Soc; Prince Hall Affiliation, Lemuel Googins #129 Philadelphia; life member, Dobbins Alumni Assn, 1990-; mem Comm Coll of Philadelphia Alumni Assn; mem Rutgers Univ, African Amer Alumni Assn; life member, National Caucus and Center on Black Aged, Inc. **Honors/Awds:** Certificate of Awd USPO GPO Philadelphia PA 1972-75; Certificate of Appreciation, Motivation Counselor Philadelphia Prisons Philadelphia PA 1976; Certificate of Recognition, Basic Reading Tutor Ctr for Literacy Philadelphia 1978; Certificate of Appreciation Probation Counselor Camden Co NJ 1979; Certificate of Appreciation, United Way of Southeastern Pennsylvania, 1988; Commendation, Sales Promotion and Merchandising Specialist, USPS, 1990; Certificate of Appreciation, AARP, 1988; Philadelphia Processing and Distribution Center, USPS, certificate of appreciation; Certificate of Appreciation, Willow Grove Air Station USAF, 1994. **Military Serv:** AUS Airborne; Parachutists Badge, Natl Defense Medal 1954-57.

BEST, PRINCE ALBERT, JR.
Educational administration (retired). **Personal:** Born Feb 2, 1938, Goldsboro, NC; married Ernestine Flowers; children: Bryon, Selina, Gary. **Educ:** A&T State Univ, BS Music 1959; East Carolina Univ, MA Ed 1971. **Career:** Johnston Cty Public School, band dir 1960-67; New Bern City Schools, band dir 1967-70; Goldsboro HS, counselor 1970-71; Johnston Tech Coll, counselor 1971-74; Wayne Comm Coll, admin 1974-, dean of human devel svcs, 1992. **Orgs:** Mem Alpha Phi Alpha 1957-, NAACP 1960-; bd of dir Alpha Arms Apts 1967-; bd mem Goldsboro Bd of Ed 1976-; mem Wayne Cty Pol Action Comm 1976-; bd of dir NC Employment & Training 1978-; chmn Goldsboro Bd of Ed 1984-; NC Employment & Training Assn, vp, 1988-90. **Honors/Awds:** Outstanding Citizen Awd Dillard HS Alumni Assoc 1984; Father of the Year, 1992; Employee of the Year, 1992; NAACP, Outstanding Service, 1986; Chamber of Commerce, Outstanding Service, 1993. **Business Addr:** Dean of Human Devel Serv, Wayne Comm Coll, Caller Box 8002, Goldsboro, NC 27533-8002.

BEST, SHEILA DIANE
Physician. **Personal:** Born Feb 23, 1956, Sacramento, CA; daughter of Elizabeth Best and Eddie Best. **Educ:** Univ of CA Riverside, BA Biology 1978; Howard Univ Coll of Medicine, MD 1982. **Career:** Howard Univ Hosp, intern 1982-83, resident 1983-85; Independent Contractor, emergency medicine physician 1985-. **Orgs:** Mem Emergency Medicine Residents Assoc 1984-85, Amer Coll of Emergency Physicians 1985-, Action Alliance of Black Managers 1986-. **Business Addr:** Emergency Medical Physician, 651 W Marion Rd, Mount Gilead, OH 43338.

BEST, TRAVIS ERIC
Professional basketball player. **Personal:** Born Jul 12, 1972, Springfield, MA. **Educ:** Georgia Tech. **Career:** Indiana Pacers, guard, 1995-. **Business Addr:** Professional Basketball Player, Indiana Pacers, 300 E Market St, Indianapolis, IN 46204, (317)263-2100.

BEST, WILLIAM ANDREW
Pastor. **Personal:** Born Sep 17, 1949, Newburgh, NY; married Sharon Gerald; children: Cleveland, Andrew, Stephany, Shawn. **Educ:** Revelation Bible Institute, Certificate, 1973; Mt St Mary Coll, BA, 1975; Western Conn State Coll, 1981. **Career:** Middletown Minority Ministerial Alliance, pres, 1984-87; Church of God in Christ, regional pres, 1986-91; Inner Faith Council, vice pres, 1986-87; YMCA, board member, 1987-; Church of God In Christ, National Pastor's and Elder Council, secretary, 1993-; Catskill District Church of God in Christ, 2nd Ecclesiastical Jurisdiction, district superintendent, 1994-. **Orgs:** Mem Kiwanis 1986-87, NAACP; pres Middletown State Ctr 1985-86. **Honors/Awds:** Certificate of Honor City of Middletown 1983; Citation State of NY Assembly 1985. **Business Addr:** Pastor, St James Church of God In Christ, 137-139 Linden Ave, Middletown, NY 10940.

BEST, WILLIE ARMSTER
Accounting executive. **Personal:** Born Dec 30, 1954, LaGrange, NC; married Joanne Loretta Jones. **Educ:** NC Central Univ, BA 1973-77; Amer Univ, MPA 1979-81. **Career:** Roanoke Chowan Reg Housing Auth & Redevel Commiss, finance officer 1982-84; Natural Resources & Commun Devel, finance contracts & labor stds monitor. **Orgs:** Basileus Omega Psi Phi Frat Inc 1981-; sec Delta Lodge 436 Prince Hall 1981-; Roanoke-Chowan Consistory 276 1983-; mem Amer Soc for Public Admin 1984-85; Rosfelt Pasha Temple 175 1985-. **Honors/Awds:** Serv Awd Prince Hall Mason Delta Lodge 436 1982.

BETHEA, EDWIN AYERS
Educational administrator. **Personal:** Born May 15, 1931, Birmingham, AL; son of Marzetta Bethea and Monroe Bethea; divorced. **Educ:** Knoxville Coll, BA 1953; Howard Univ, MSW 1962. **Career:** United Planning Orgn, comm organizer 1966-68; Youth Enterprises Inc, exec dir 1968-70; Volunteers for Intl Tech Ctr, dir/regional dir 1970-72; GA Tech Rsch Inst, sr rsch assoc/project dir 1972-86; assoc director, Office of Minority

Business Development, 1987-88, director, 1989-; University of Georgia, Small Business Development Center; Hudson Strategic Group, partner/assoc, currently. **Orgs:** Mem Southern Industrial Council 1974-, GA Industrial Developers Assn 1974-; mem GA Tech Centennial Comm 1986. **Honors/Awds:** Outstanding Contribution White House Conf of Small Business 1980; Certificate of Honor Mayor of Cleveland Contrib to Small Business 1984. **Military Serv:** AUS pfc 1953-55; Korean Medal, Overseas Tour of Duty Medal. **Home Addr:** 50 Inwood Circle NE, Atlanta, GA 30309. **Business Addr:** Partner/Associate, Hudson Strategic Group, 1882 Princeton Ave, Atlanta, GA 30307-3519.

BETHEA, GREGORY AUSTIN
Assistant city manager. **Personal:** Born Sep 18, 1952, Hamlet, NC; son of Annie Austin Bethea and Thomas J Bethea; married Hope Stelter Bethea, Aug 21, 1983; children: Ryan Stelter, Austin Cox. **Educ:** North Carolina Central Univ, Durham NC, BA, 1974. **Career:** Forsyth County, Forsyth County NC, asst to mgr, sr asst to mgr, intergovernmental relations & budget analysis, 1975-84; United Way, Forsyth County NC, deputy dir, 1984-85; City of Durham, Durham NC, asst city mgr, 1985-. **Honors/Awds:** Edwin McGill Award, Univ of North Carolina Inst of Govt, 1980. **Business Addr:** Asst City Mgr, City of Durham, 101 City Hall Plaza, Durham, NC 27701.

BETHEL, JESSE MONCELL, SR.
Insurance agent, chemist (retired). **Personal:** Born Jul 8, 1922, New York, NY; son of Ethel Williams (deceased) and Jesse M Bethel; married Claudia M Nichols, May 22, 1944; children: Marilyn Bethel-McAllister, Jesse M, Jr, Veronica Bethel-Johnson. **Educ:** Huston-Tillotson Coll, Austin, TX, BS Chemistry 1944; UC Berkeley Graduate School. **Career:** Mare Island Naval Shipyard, analytical chemist 1944-61, nuclear chemist 1961-68, research chemist, 1968-73; State Farm Insurance, agent 1974-89. **Orgs:** Board of dir Vallejo Salvation Army; member NAACP; member Council of Navy League of US; member Vallejo Chamber of Commerce; member Friendship Baptist Church; board of directors Cal Coalition for Fair School Finance; past pres & board of directors Vallejo City Unified School Board 1969-85; past president Cal School Boards Assn 1976; member Alpha Phi Alpha Fraternity for 50 years; member Navy City Elks Lodge IBPOE of W. **Honors/Awds:** Vallejo Citizen of the Year Omega Psi Phi Fraternity 1974; Man of the Year Western Region Alpha Phi Alpha 1976; Award Natl Caucas of Black School Board members 1977; Award NAACP Vallejo Branch 1982; new high school named "Jesse M Bethel High School," Vallejo City Unified School District, 1991. **Home Addr:** 315 Pepper Drive, Vallejo, CA 94589.

BETHEL, KATHLEEN EVONNE
Librarian. **Personal:** Born Aug 4, 1953, Washington, DC; daughter of Helen Evonne Roy Bethel and Frederick Errington Bethel. **Educ:** Elmhurst College, Elmhurst, IL, BA, 1975; Rosary College, River Forest, IL, MALS, 1977; Northwestern University, Evanston, IL, MA, 1989. **Career:** Newberry Library, Chicago, IL, receptionist, 1975-77; Maywood Public Library, Maywood, IL, branch librarian, 1977-78; Johnson Publishing Co, Chicago, IL, asst librarian, 1978-82; Northwestern University, Evanston, IL, African-American studies librarian, 1982-. **Orgs:** DuSable Museum of African American History, bd of trustees, 1994-; Member, Assn for the Study of Afro-American Life and History, 1985-; member, NAACP, 1983-; member, Black Caucus of the American Library Assn, 1978-; member, American Library Assn, 1976-. **Honors/Awds:** Scholarship, National Bridge Assn, 1971. **Business Addr:** African-American Studies Librarian, University Library, Northwestern University, 1935 Sheridan Rd, Evanston, IL 60208-2300.

BETHEL, LEONARD LESLIE
Educator. **Personal:** Born Feb 5, 1939, Philadelphia, PA; married Veronica Bynum; children: Amiel Wren, Kama Lynn. **Educ:** Lincoln Univ, BA 1961; Johnson C Smith Univ Sch of Theology, MDiv 1964; New Brunswick Theological Sem, MA 1971; Rutgers Univ, DEd 1975. **Career:** Washington United Presbyterian Church, pastor 1964-67; Lincoln Univ, asst chaplain & dir counseling 1967-79; Bethel Presbyterian Church, pastor 1982-92; Rutgers Univ Dept Africana Studies, faculty & staff 1969-, assoc prof 1980-. **Orgs:** Mem Bd of Trustees Rutgers Prep Sch 1971-84; fellow Rutgers Coll Rutgers Univ 1980-; mem Amer Assn Univ Profs Rutgers Univ 1980-; mem board of directors Plainfield Branch, Union County Coll, 1980-86; mem Frontiers Intl 1980-; mem Presbytery of Elizabeth 1982-; bd of trustees, Bloomfield Coll, 1980-86; bd of trustees, Lincoln Univ, 1996-; bd of dirs, VCC, 1980-87. **Honors/Awds:** Phi Delta Kappa Rutgers Univ 1975; Paul Robeson Faculty Awd Rutgers Univ 1978; NAFEO Pres Citation Lincoln Univ 1981; Woodrow Wilson Fellow Princeton Univ 1984; published with Fred Johnson, Advancement Through Service: A History of the Frontiers International. **Special Achievements:** Co-author, Advancement Through Service: A History of The Frontiers International, Lanham, University Press of America, 1991, Plainfield's African American: Northern Slavery to Church Freedom, University Press of America, 1997; author, Educating African Leaders: Missionism in America, Edwin Mellon Press, 1997. **Home Addr:** 146 Parkside Rd, Plainfield, NJ 07060. **Business Addr:** Assoc Prof, Dept of Africana Studies, Rutgers University, Beck Hall #112, New Brunswick, NJ 08903.

BETTIS, ANNE KATHERINE
Market manager. **Personal:** Born Jun 16, 1949, Newark, NJ. **Educ:** Jersey City State Coll, BA 1972; Columbia Univ, MBA 1979. **Career:** Avon Products Inc, sr editor 1973-77; AT&T, acct exec 1979-82, natl acct mgr 1983-85, staff mgr 1985-. **Orgs:** Pres 8th Irving Park Condominium Assoc 1984-; mem Calvary Baptist Church, Natl Black MBA Assoc. **Honors/Awds:** Achiever's Club AT&T 1982-84. **Home Addr:** 83 Boston St, Newark, NJ 07103.

BETTIS, JEROME ABRAM
Professional football player. **Personal:** Born Feb 16, 1972, Detroit, MI. **Educ:** Notre Dame Univ. **Career:** Los Angeles Rams, running back, 1993-94; St. Louis Rams, 1995; Pittsburgh Steelers, 1996-. **Honors/Awds:** NFL Rookie of the Year, 1993; Pro Bowl, 1993, 1994, 1996; NFL Alumni, Running Back of the Year, 1996. **Business Addr:** Professional Football Player, Pittsburgh Steelers, Three Rivers Stadium, 300 Stadium Ctr, Pittsburgh, PA 15212, (412)323-1200.

BETTS, SHERI ELAINE
Organization executive. **Personal:** Born Nov 11, 1958, St Louis, MO; daughter of Patsy Betts and Herman Betts; married Victor Peaks (divorced 1990). **Educ:** Washington University, St Louis, MO, BSBA, 1980; UCLA, Los Angeles, CA, MBA, 1988. **Career:** Arthur Andersen, Los Angeles, CA, staff accountant, 1980-83; Xerox, Woodland Hills, CA, account rep, 1983-86; Pepsi Cola, Irvine, CA, asst marketing mgr, 1988-89; Inroads, Los Angeles, CA, managing dir, 1989-. **Orgs:** Vice president of student services, Natl Assn of Black Accountants, 1982-83; member, Natl Assn of MKF Developers, 1988-85; member, Natl Black MBA Assn, 1986-; executive adviser, Junior Achievement, 1982-83. **Honors/Awds:** Outstanding Member Award, Natl Assn of Black Accountants, 1982; Top Sales/Co Award, Junior Achievement, 1982; Scholarship, Natl Black MBA Assn, 1986-88.

BETTY, WARREN RANDALL
Physician. **Personal:** Born Apr 21, 1931, Chicago, IL; son of E C Brewington and A L Lucas; married Judy A Austermiller, Nov 25, 1988; children: Lisa C, Michael W. **Educ:** Indiana Univ, AB 1954; Indiana Univ School of Medicine, MD 1959. **Career:** Richmond Co Prof Standard Review Organ, treasurer & bd of dir 1979-84; Health Ins Plan of Greater NY, mem bd of dir 1983-92, 1993-; Group Council Mutual Ins Co, mem bd of dir 1983-; Island Peer Review Organ, treasurer & bd of dir 1984-; Staten Island Med Group, medical dir, 1981-. **Orgs:** Vice pres Richmond Cnty Med Soc 1983-84; asst clinical prof of pediatrics Albert Einstein Coll of Medicine NY 1965-; mem advisory bd, Staten Island Urban League 1982-90; mem Reg Advisory Council of The State Div of Human Rights; Professional Med Conduct, bd, 1994-. **Honors/Awds:** Recipient Black Achiever Award Harlem Branch YMCA 1982; Governors Commission on Hospital Information Data. **Military Serv:** USAF airman 2 c 1952-55. **Business Addr:** Medical Dir, Staten Island Med Group, 4771 Hylan Blvd, Staten Island, NY 10312.

BEVERLY, BENJAMIN FRANKLIN
Automobile dealer. **Personal:** Born Feb 27, 1938, Detroit, MI; son of Dr. Benjamin F Beverly II and Viola Suggs Beverly; married; children: Benjamin F IV, Adrienne Beverly Collins. **Educ:** Univ of Detroit, BBA, Finance, 1973. **Career:** Bank of America, computer operator, 1960-62; Crocker Citizens National Bank, customer service representative, 1962-66; Bank of the Commonwealth, vice president, 1966-72; General Motors Corp, assistant director of urban affairs, 1973-88; Taylor Automotive Group, salesman, 1988-90; Magic Valley Ford-Mercury, president, 1990-91; Buffalo Ford-Mercury, president, 1991-92; Delta Automotive Group, pres/CEO, 1993-95; Greenville Olds-Cadillac, Inc, pres/CEO, 1996-. **Orgs:** NAACP, life member, 1974-; Greenville Chamber of Commerce, 1994-; Greenville Rotary, 1994-; Greenville United Way, board member, 1994-; 100 Black Men of the Delta, 1994-; National Association of Minority Auto Dealers, 1994-; Kappa Alpha Psi Fraternity, 1957-; 32 AEAONMS, 1986-. **Honors/Awds:** Urban Bankers Forum, Founders Award, 1979; YMCA of Metropolitan Detroit, Minority Achiever in Industry, 1983; Minority Women Network, Man of the Year Award, 1985; Black Enterprise, Professional Exchange Forum, 1987; NAACP, Detroit Chapter, Recognition Award, 1989. **Military Serv:** US Army, spec 5, 1959-62. **Business Addr:** Pres/CEO, Greenville Olds-Cadillac Inc, 2730 Laurens Rd, Greenville, SC 29606, (864)288-8900.

BEVERLY, CREIGS C.
Educator, social worker, educational administrator. **Personal:** Born Sep 5, 1942, Selma, AL; married Olivia D Beverly; children: Cheryl, Creigs Jr. **Educ:** Morehouse College, BA, 1963; Atlanta University, MSW, 1965; University of Wisconsin, PhD, 1972. **Career:** University of Ghana, professor, 1983-84, acting coordinator, 1984; Atlanta University, School of Social Work, professor, 1974-83, dean, 1984-86, vice president and provost, 1986-87, Social & Behavioral Science, senior professor, starting 1987; Wayne State University, School of Social Work, professor, 1988-; Center for African Life & Development, post doctorate training, 1984. **Orgs:** Special asst to the mayor, Carnegie Foundation Fellow, 1976-77; board of directors, Council of Intl Programs, 1985; Natl Assn of Black Elected Officials; Natl Assn of Social Workers; Natl Assn of Black Social Workers; CSWE; ACSW; planning commission, City of Detroit, 1988-; National Council on Black Alcoholism, 1980-82; NAACP. **Honors/Awds:** Achievement & Contribution Plaque, City of Atlanta, 1977; Fulbright Scholar, West Africa, 1983, 1984; Atlanta University, Distinguished Alumni Citation Award, NAFEO, 1980; Distinguished Youth Service Award, State of Oklahoma, 1986; Martin L King Visiting Scholar, Wayne State University, 1987-88; NASW Social Worker of the Year, 1992; NABSW Distinguished Service Award, 1992; Spirit of Detroit Award, 1991; NABSW Student Chapter, Distinguished Teaching Award, 1991. **Special Achievements:** Author: Theory and Reality, 1986; Social Development and African Development 1984; Black Men in Prison, 1990-92; Alcoholism in the Black Community, 1976, 1982, 1990, 1992; Beyond Survival, 1992; Characteristics of Progressive Social Workers, 1992; Of Utmost Good Faith, 1992; Schools as Communities in Communities, 1992; WSU Distinguished Faculty, 1993; Card for All Mothers, 1993; Card for All Fathers, 1994; Black on Black Crime: Compensation for Idomatic Purposeslessness, 1997. **Business Addr:** Professor, School of Social Work, Wayne State University, 4756 Cass Ave, Thompson Home, Detroit, MI 48201.

BEVERLY, FRANKIE
Musician. **Career:** Frankie Beverly and Maze, lead singer, 1977-. **Honors/Awds:** Record albums: Maze Featuring Frankie Beverly, 1977, Golden Time of Day, 1978, Inspiration, 1979, Joy and Pain, 1980, Live in New Orleans, 1980, We Are One, 1983; 6 Gold Albums. **Business Addr:** Singer, c/o Capitol Records Inc, 1750 N Vine St, Hollywood, CA 90028.

BEVERLY, WILLIAM C., JR.
Attorney. **Personal:** Born Jan 23, 1943, Los Angeles, CA; married Mona Birkelund. **Educ:** Pepperdine Coll, BA 1965; SW Univ Sch Law, JD 1969. **Career:** Los Angeles Superior Court, judge; DPSS, soc wrkr & supvr 1965-70; Private Practice Law, attorney 1970-. **Orgs:** Mem CA & Long Beach Bar Assns; Langston Law Club; co-chmn Mil Law Panel 1971; instr Bus Law CA State Univ Long Beach; mem Langston Bar Assn; vice pres LA Co Commn on Human Relations. **Business Addr:** Judge, Los Angeles Superior Court, 111 N Hill St, Los Angeles, CA 90012.

BEXLEY, DONALD T. See Obituaries section.

BEYER, TROY
Actress. **Personal:** Born 1964; daughter of Hannan Wells Parks and Jerrold Beyer; children: one. **Educ:** CUNY, performing arts; UCLA, political science. **Career:** Actress, currently; television appearances include: Sesame Street; Dynasty; Knots Landing; Uncle Tom's Cabin; Falcon Crest, Fame, Fortune & Romance; The Colbys, 1986; film appearances include: The Five Heartbeats; The White Girl, 1989; Rooftops, 1989; Disorderlies, 1987. **Business Addr:** Actress, c/o William Morris Agency, 151 El Camino Dr, Beverly Hills, CA 90212, (310)274-7451.

BIAGAS, EDWARD D.
Automobile dealer. **Personal:** Born Oct 24, 1948, Lake Charles, LA; son of Veda Orsot Biagas and Alvin J Biagas; married Lillie Belton Biagas, Aug 7, 1969; children: Edwin Jr, Shelley, Kevin. **Career:** Cities Service Oil, Lake Charles, LA, shift operator, 1972-75; Radford Buick, Lake Charles, LA, salesman, mgr, 1975-81. **Orgs:** Bd mem, YMCA, 1986-, Chamber of Commerce, 1987-, Northern Ches County Nurses Assn, 1987-; chmn, PEP Comm, General Motors, 1988-; Minority Advisory Council, General Motors, 1989-. **Military Serv:** US Army E-5, 1969-71. **Business Addr:** President, Biagas Pontiac-Buick, Inc, PO Box 4357, Troy, MI 48099-4357.

BIAKABUTUKA, TIM (TSHIMANGA)
Professional football player. **Personal:** Born Jan 24, 1974. **Educ:** Univ of Michigan. **Career:** Carolina Panthers, running back, 1996-. **Business Addr:** Professional Football Player, Carolina Panthers, Ericsson Stadium, 800 Mint St, Charlotte, NC 28202, (704)358-7000.

BIASSEY, EARLE LAMBERT
Physician. **Personal:** Born Jan 20, 1920, New Brunswick, NJ; son of Lillian Craig and Earl Henry Biassey; married Marie Davis; children: Sharon, Earle Jr, Eric, Sandra. **Educ:** Upsala Coll, BS 1943; Howard Univ School of Medicine, MD 1947; Jersey City Medical Center, internship 1947-48, resident 1948-50; VA Hospital, 1950-51; Univ of MI Univ Hospital Ann Arbor, 1951-53; Horace Racham Graduate School, MS 1953. **Career:** Mental Hygiene Clinic, chief 1955-60; Park City Hospital, attending staff, 1957-; Woodfield Children's Home, psychiatric consultant 1957-62; Bridgeport Hospital, assoc attending 1959-67, sr attending chief psychiatric dept 1968-76; Elmont Psychiatric Institute, courtesy stff, 1969-75; Weslyen Univ, psychiatric consultant 1970-; Whiting Forensic Inst, Middletown CT, psychiatric consultant 1976-; sr attending physician; St Vincent Hospital. **Orgs:** Mem Amer Psychiatric Assn

1950-, fellow 1969-; life fellow Amer Acad of Psychoanalysis 1966-; mem Soc of Medical Psychoanalysts; Fairfield Co Medical Soc; CT Medical Soc; Mental Hygiene Assn of Greater Bridgeport; mem Mental Health Council Com for Comm Mental Health Center; Stratford Rotary Club; Omega Psi Phi Fraternity; advisory bd Bridgeport Mental Health Center 1975; pres Fairfield Co Litchfield Chap CT Psychiatric Assn 1971; sec 1970-71, treasurer 1974-77 CT Psychiatric Assn; bd mem Bridgeport YMCA 1967-72; mem Com on Acad Educ Amer Psychiatric Assn 1971-74; Com on Social Issues Amer Acad of Psychoanalysis, chairman, Black Rock Congressional Church; chancellor Soc of Med Psychoanalysts 1969-74; chmn Professional Advisory Com Bridgeport Mental HealthAssn; psychiatric consultant Bridgep Educ System 1969-76; med adv bd Elmcrest Psychiatric Inst 1969-75; consultant Mental Health Serv & Afro-Amer Inst Wesleyan Univ 1971- ; Whiting Forensic Inst 1976-; mem Christian Med Soc 1971-; licensed NY, NJ, CT; life fellow Amer Psychiatric Assn 1984-. **Honors/Awds:** Daniel Griffin Award, Bridgeport Mental Health Assn. **Military Serv:** US Army, capt, 1953-55. **Business Addr:** Psychiatric Consultant, Whiting Forensic Institute, 3200 Main St, Middletown, CT 06457.

BIBB, T. CLIFFORD
Educator. **Personal:** Born Oct 29, 1938, Montgomery, AL; son of Alma Bibb and Bennie Bibb; children: Tura Concetta. **Educ:** AL State Univ, BS 1960, MEd 1961; Northwestern Univ, PhD 1973. **Career:** Rust Coll, chair English dept 1961-65; Daniel Payne Coll, chair English dept 1965-67; Miles Coll, English coord 1967-71; Northwestern Univ, English supr 1971-72; AL State Univ, chair advancement studies and dir four year plus curriculum prog. **Orgs:** Dir upward prog Northwestern Univ 1972-73; commiss, composition NCTE 1973-76; sec Peterson-Bibb Lodge 762 1974-; fac adv Alpha Phi Alpha 1981-; exec comm NCTE 1983-88; exec sec & bd mem Central Montgomery Optimists 1984-86; desoto commiss State of AL 1986-95; National Council of Teachers of Eng, 1991-93; newsletter editor, AL Assn for Dev Ed, 1992-95; table leader (ETS), Ed Testing Service for APT/ENG, 1994-; Alabama State Council on The Arts, 1992-; NAT Council of Ed Opportunity Assn, 1992-. **Honors/Awds:** Choir Dir/Singer in "The Long Walk Home", starring Whoopi Goldbert & Sissy Spacek. **Home Addr:** 5933 Provost Ave, Montgomery, AL 36116, (205)288-1554. **Business Phone:** (334)293-4328.

BIBBS, PATRICIA
College basketball coach. **Career:** Grambling State Univ, head women's basketball coach, currently. **Business Addr:** Head Coach, Women's Basketball, Grambling State University, 100 Main St, Grambling, LA 71245, (318)274-2435.

BIBBY, DEIRDRE L.
Museum administrator. **Personal:** Born Jun 9, 1951, Pittsburgh, PA. **Educ:** MA Coll of Art, BFA 1974; City Coll of the City Univ of NY, MA candidate 1981-83; Museum Management Inst, graduate. **Career:** Ile-Ife Museum, dir/curator 1974-76; Afro-American Historical & Cultural Museum, curator 1977-81; Mid-Atlantic Consortium, visual arts coordinator; The Studio Museum of Harlem, assoc curator, 1981-85; Schomburg Center for Rsch in Black Culture, Art and Artifacts Division, head, 1985-91; Museum of African-American Art, executive director, curator; Wadsworth Atheneum, curator of African-American art, currently. **Orgs:** African-American Museums Assn 1978-; co-chair Women's Caucus for Art 1985; Natl Conf of Artists 1978-; Amistad Foundation, exec dir. **Special Achievements:** First African-American to hold full-time curatorial post in a major New England museum. **Business Addr:** Curator African-American Art, Wadsworth Atheneum, 600 Main St, Hartford, CT 06103.

BIBLO, MARY
Librarian. **Personal:** Born Dec 31, 1927, East Chicago, IN; daughter of Flora Chandler Davidson and James Davidson; married Herbert D Biblo, Aug 27, 1950; children: Lisa, David. **Educ:** Roosevelt University, Chicago IL, BS, 1966; Rosary College, River Forest IL, MLS, 1970; Teachers College, Columbia University, 1984-85. **Career:** South Chicago Community Hospital School of Nursing, Chicago IL, medical librarian, 1966-67; Chicago Board of Education, Chicago IL, school librarian, 1967-70; University of Chicago Laboratory Schools, Chicago IL, librarian, 1970—. **Orgs:** American Library Assn; past president, Children's Reading Round Table; Natl Caucus of Black Librarians; Natl Assn of Independent Schools; vice chair, minority affairs committee, IL State Board of Education, 1988-90; International Federation of Library Assns, chair, IFLA's Round Table on Women's Issues; American Assn of School Librarians; intellectural freedom round table, social responsibility round table, IL Library Assn; IL Assn for Media in Education. **Honors/Awds:** Klingenstein fellow, Columbia University, 1984-85; master teacher, University of Chicago Laboratory School, 1985. **Business Addr:** Librarian, University of Chicago Laboratory Schools, 1362 East 59th St, 101 High School, Chicago, IL 60637.

BICKERSTAFF, BERNARD TYRONE, SR.
Professional basketball coach. **Personal:** Born Feb 11, 1944, Benham, KY; married Eugenia King Bickerstaff, Jul 22, 1967; children: Tim, Robin, Cydni, Bernard, John Blair. **Educ:** Univ of San Diego, BS, 1968. **Career:** Univ of San Diego, asst basketball coach; Wash Bullets, asst coach & scout 1974-85; Seattle SuperSonics, head coach, 1985-90; Denver Nuggets, general manager, 1990-96, pres, 1996-97; Washington Wizards, head coach, 1997-. **Orgs:** conducted a sucessful summer basketball camp in Baltimore, MD; coached National Puerto Rican team in the Caribbean tour & won the Championship in 1976; vice pres, NBA Coaches Assn, 1980-90. **Honors/Awds:** Turned down offer to play for the Harlem Globetrotters; youngest asst coach in the Natl Basketball Assn; 3 conf Championships & one NBA title; NBA Coach of the Year, Sporting News, 1987. **Business Addr:** Head Coach, Washington Wizards, 1 Harry S. Truman Dr., USAir Arena, Landover, MD 20785, (301)622-3865.

BICKHAM, L. B.
Educator. **Personal:** Born Mar 2, 1923, New Orleans, LA; married Dorothy B; children: Luzine Jr, Nedra E. **Educ:** Univ MI, BBA 1945, MBA 1947; Univ TX, PhD 1965. **Career:** Dillard Univ, instructor 1949; Watchtower Life Insurance Co, sec 1950; TX Southern Univ, instructor 1952; TX Soutern Univ School of Business, dean 1969-. **Orgs:** Mem Amer Mktg Assn; bd dirs Std Savs & Loan Assn; TX So Fin; St Eliz Hosp Found. **Military Serv:** AAC 1943-45. **Business Addr:** Professor, TX Southern University, 3201 Cleburne St, Houston, TX 77021.

BIDDLE, STANTON F.
Library administrator. **Personal:** Born Sep 16, 1943, Cuba, NY; son of Imogene M Peterson Biddle and Christopher F Biddle. **Educ:** Howard University, Washington, DC, BA, 1965; Atlanta University, Atlanta, GA, master of library science, 1966; New York University, New York, NY, master of public administration, 1973; University of California, Berkeley, CA, doctor of library and information studies, 1988. **Career:** The New York Public Library Schomburg Research Center, New York, NY, reference librarian, archivist, 1967-73; Howard University Libraries, Washington, DC, associate dir, 1973-76; State University of New York-Buffalo, associate dir of libraries, 1979-84; Baruch College City University of New York, chief librarian, 1984-88; City University of New York Central Office, asst dean of libraries, 1988-89; Baruch College CUNY, admin services librarian, 1989-. **Orgs:** Board of trustee, Black Caucus of American Library Assn 1976-82, 1989-91; president, Schomburg Collection of Black Literature, History and Art, 1988-90; chair, Afro-American Studies Librarians' Section, Assn of College and Research Libraries, 1991-92; correspondent secretary, City University African American Network, 1990-93; treasurer, New York Black Librarians Caucus, 1990-94; President, Black Caucus of the American Library Assn, 1994-96; President, Library Assn of the City Univ of New York, 1992-94. **Honors/Awds:** Library Management Intern, Council on Library Resources, 1976-77; ACRL Doctorate Fellowship in Librarianship, University of California, 1977; William Wells Brown Award, Afro-American Historical Assn, Buffalo, NY, 1984. **Home Addr:** 195 Adams St, #11-H, Brooklyn, NY 11201.

BIENIEMY, ERIC
Professional football player. **Personal:** Born Aug 15, 1969, New Orleans, LA; married Mia; children: Eric III. **Educ:** Univ of Colorado, attended. **Career:** San Diego Chargers, running back, 1991-94; Cincinnati Bengals, 1995-. **Honors/Awds:** NFL Players Assn, Bengals Unsung Hero, 1996. **Business Addr:** Professional Football Player, Cincinnati Bengals, One Bengals Dr, Cincinnati, OH 45202, (513)621-3550.

BIGBY YOUNG, BETTY
Educational administrator. **Personal:** Born Nov 8, New York, NY; daughter of Dorothy Bigby and Lucius Bigby; married Haskell I Young; children: Haskell I II (Chato), Jessica Melissa Bigby. **Educ:** City Univ of NY Brooklyn Coll, BA 1970, MS 1972; Nova Univ, EdD, 1987. **Career:** Dept of State Foreign Serv Corps, admin asst foreign serv staff 1959-67; Office of the Mayor NYC, comm relations specialist 1968-71; CUNY Brooklyn Coll, dir model city TV training prog 1972-73; Model City Prog, comm relations specialist 1974-77; FL Intl Univ, dir univ relations & devel 1977-83; dir academic support prog l983-89; Florida Memorial College, dir AIDS & drug abuse prevention program, 1990-92; coordinator, Dewitt Wallace, Reader's Digest Fund: Pathways to Teaching Careers Program, 1992-. **Orgs:** Founder/counselor, Phi Eta Chapter KDP, FMC, 1995-; mem Natl Assn of Female Executives 1984-89; Intl Platform Assn; Kappa Delta Pi Intl Honor Soc in Educ 1980-; founder/counselor Omicron Theta Chap KDP FIU 1981-89; lifetime mem Alpha Epsilon Rho Radio TV Frat; Amer Assn of Univ Women; KDP Intl Honor Soc constitution/bylaws chairperson 1982-84; Amer Council on Educ; Southeast Dist Liaison for Minority Affairs PRSA; YWCA Women's Network; Mental Health Assn 1981-82; FL State Sickle Cell Found Inc 1978-; White House Conf on Arts Testimony Congressional Hearing 1978; bd mem Art in Public Places Trust; pres Scott Lake Elem Sch PTA, Parkview Elem, Greynolds Park Elem; Congress of Black Scholars Dade Co 1982; radio talk show host WMBM Miami 1981-82; FIU Black Student Union Advisor founder 1978-89; South FL Center for theFine Arts; natl mem Smitnian Assn; mem Public Relations Soc of Amer, Council for Advancement and Support of Educ 1978-80; chief advisor Florida Black Student Assn Inc 1988-89; president Dade County Sickle Cell Foundation 1980-82, 1992-94; board member DCPS Magnet Advisory Committee; board member Center for Haitian Studies. **Honors/Awds:** Community Service Award, Natl Congress of Parents and Teachers, 1989; Dr B B Young, Dr C McIntosh Scholarship, Florida Sickle Cell Assn, currently; Outstanding Admin, FIU North Campus, 1985; Dr B B Young BSU Leadership Honor Roll, FIU North Campus, currently; Parkway Elementary School, Outstanding Service Award; Scott Lake Elementary School, Outstanding Service Award, 1990; Florida African-American Student Association, Exemplary Leadership, 1990; Florida Memorial College, Outstanding Service Award, 1996, 1997. **Business Addr:** Coordinator, Dewitt Wallace, Reader's Digest Fund: Pathways to Teaching Career Program, Florida Memorial College, 15800 NW 42nd Ave, Miami, FL 33054, (305)626-3680.

BIGGERS, SAMUEL LORING, JR.
Neurological surgeon. **Personal:** Born Nov 6, 1935, Crockett, TX; son of Nelia J Martinez Biggers and Samuel L Biggers Sr; married Florestine A Robinson; children: Samuel L III, Shaun Denise, Sanford Leon. **Educ:** Dillard U, AB (cum laude) 1956; Univ of TX Galveston, MD (cum laude) 1961. **Career:** Univ of TX Grad Sch, rsrch & teaching asst 1957-58; Orange Cnty Gen Hosp, intern 1961-62; USAF Med Corp, capt 1962-64; Univ of Southern CA Med, instructor clinical 1964-70; Los Angeles Cnty USC Med Cntr, asst prof clinical 1970-85; Charles R Drew Med Sch, professor, neuroscience, 1993-; Charles R Drew Medical Sch Martin Luther King Jr Hosp, vice chmn dept of neurological surgery; California Medical Ctr, vice pres medical staff; Samuel L Bigger & John J Holly Inc Neurological Surgery, pres; California Medical Center, Los Angeles, chief of surgery, 1989-. **Orgs:** Pres Samuel L Biggers, John J Holly MD Inc 1974-; Kappa Alpha Psi; Alpha Kappa Mu; Alpha Omega Alpha; Sigma Pi Phi; bd of trustees CA Medical Ctr; board of directors, CMCLA Foundation, 1990-; board of directors, Unihealth America Foundation, 1990-; Dipolmate American Board of Neurological Surgery, 1970; American Assn of Neurological Surgeons. **Honors/Awds:** Alumnus of the Year Dillard Univ 1985; Humanitarian of Year, California Medical Center, 1992; Distinguished Physician Award, Minority Health Institute, 1994. **Military Serv:** USAF Capt 1962-64. **Business Addr:** President, SL Biggers/JJ Holly Inc, 1414 S Grand Avenue, Los Angeles, CA 90015.

BIGGINS, J. VERONICA
Government official. **Personal:** marrIed Franklin; children: Two daughters. **Educ:** Spelman College; Georgia State University, master's degree in education. **Career:** Citizens and Southern Georgia Corp., director of human resources; NationsBank Corp, executive vice president; The White House, director of presidential personnel, vice ch US delegation to UN Women's confab in Beijing. **Orgs:** Atlanta Life Insurance Company, board member; Atlanta-Fulton County Recreation Authority, board member; Atlanta AIDS Walk, co-chair, 1991. **Business Phone:** (202)456-6676.

BIGGS, CYNTHIA DEMARI
Songwriter. **Personal:** Born Oct 2, 1953, St Pauls, NC. **Educ:** Lincoln Univ Oxfrd PA, 1972; Temple Univ Phila, BA Commu 1975. **Career:** Philadelphia Intl Records, songwriter producer 1975-; Philadelphia Bd of Educ, substitute teacher 1975-77; The New Observer Newspaper, staff reporter 1974-78; Stlmnt Music Sch Madrigal Singers Philadelphia, vocalist 1969-71; Lincoln Univ Concert Choir, vocalist 1971-72; Ted Wortham Singers, composer vocalist 1972-. **Orgs:** Mem Sigma Delta Chi Nat Hon Soc 1970. **Honors/Awds:** Amer Legion Awd for Girls, Amer Legion Soc Philadelphia Chap 1968; 1st Recip of the Art Peters Meml Scholarship for Journalism Philadelphia Inquirer Newspaper 1974; nominee Outstanding Young Woman of Amer, Outstanding Young Woman of Amer 1977-78. **Business Addr:** Cindex Publishing, Inc, PO Box 18829, Philadelphia, PA 19119.

BIGGS, RICHARD LEE
Director of training. **Personal:** Born Jan 16, 1949, Dyersburg, TN; divorced. **Educ:** TN State Univ, BS Biol 1971. **Career:** Questor Corp, mgmt coord 1974-81; Dyersburg Fabrics Inc, asst personnel dir 1981-; Dyer County, commissioner. **Orgs:** Mem Dyer Co Ed Comm 1978-86; clerk & trustee Tabernacle Baptist Church 1979-; advisor Dyersburg State Comm Coll Tech Dept 1980-84; chmn of bd Dyersburg Elect Syst 1980-; mem Dyer Co Budget Comm 1980-86; dir Private Ind Council 1983-86, West TN Investment Corp 1983-; dir C of C; pres elect Dyer County C of C 1988-89; bd mem Habitat For Humanity; bd mem Lifeline Blood Program; bd mem United Way of Dyer Co. **Honors/Awds:** Eligible Bachelor Ebony Mag 1980. **Home Addr:** 409 Reynolds Ave, Dyersburg, TN 38024.

BIGGS, SHIRLEY ANN
Educator. **Personal:** Born Mar 9, 1938, Richmond, VA; daughter of Jennie Hill and Richard B Hill; married Charles F Biggs; children: Charles F Jr, Cheryl A. **Educ:** Duquesne U, BEd 1960; Univ of SC, MEd 1972; Univ of Pittsburgh, EdD 1977. **Career:** Pittsburgh Public School, teacher, 1961-68; Benedict Coll, instructor, 1968-72, reading specialist consultant, 1972-; Univ of Pittsburgh, faculty in school of educ, 1974-, asso prof, asst dean for student affairs 1986-, director of affirmative ac-

tion, minority affairs, 1989-. **Orgs:** Coord Summer Communications Skills Project 1963-66; pres Gerald A Yoakam Reading Cncl 1978-79; chmn research div Pittsburgh Literacy Coalition 1984-; mem Intl Reading Assoc 1973-; mem Nat Reading Conference; director of research Coalition for the Advancement of Literacy Pittsburgh, 1985-; chair College Reading Improvement Group, International Reading Association, 1990-; chair, Pittsburgh Peace Institute, 1997-. **Honors/Awds:** Co-author Reading to Achieve, Strategies for Adult Coll 1983; co-author Students Self Questioning and Summarizing 1984; honored for literacy research activities by the Pittsburgh City Council 1986; editor Innovative Learning Strategies, 1989-90; Intl Reading Assn, 1989-90. **Special Achievements:** Author, "The Plight of Black Males in American Schools: Separation May not be the Answer," "Building on Strengths: Closing the Literacy Gap," "African American Adult Reading Performance: Progress in the Face of Problem;" editor, Forum for Reading. **Business Addr:** Director, Affirmative Action and Minority Affairs, School of Education, Univ of Pittsburgh, 5TO1 Forbes Quandrangle, Pittsburgh, PA 15260.

BIGHAM, RETA LACY
Information specialist, research assistant. **Personal:** Born Jan 7, 1949, Augusta, GA; daughter of Ruth Jefferson Lacy and Joseph Tolbertte Lacy; married Bruce W Bigham (divorced 1988). **Educ:** Morris Brown College, Atlanta, GA, BS, 1969; Atlanta University, Atlanta, GA, MSLS, 1970. **Career:** Morris Brown College, Jordan-Thomas Library, Atlanta, GA, cataloger, 1970-79; Atlanta University, Trevor Arnett Library, Atlanta, GA, head, tech services, 1979-82; Atlanta University Center, Inc, Robert W Woodruff Library, Atlanta, GA, dir, tech services, 1982-87; Interdenominational Theol Center, Atlanta, GA, research asst, 1987-. **Orgs:** American Library Assn, 1970-; vice pres, dean of pledgees, Gamma Zeta Chapter, Delta Sigma Theta Sorority, 1968-69; Beta Phi Mu, International Library Science Honor Society, 1970-; National Council of Negro Women, 1990-. **Honors/Awds:** Cum Laude Graduate, Morris Brown College, 1969; Ford Foundation Fellow, Atlanta University School of Library Science, 1969-70; Mellon Association of College and Research Libraries Intern, 1976-77. **Business Addr:** Research Assistant to Endowed Faculty Chairs, Research Dept, Interdenominational Theological Center, 671 Beckwith St SW, Atlanta, GA 30314.

BILLINGS, SISTER CORA MARIE
Clergywoman. **Personal:** Born Feb 11, 1939, Philadelphia, PA; daughter of Ethel Lorraine Lee Billings and Jesse Anthony Billings. **Educ:** Gwynedd Mercy Coll, Gwynedd, PA, 1957-63; Villanova Univ, Philadelphia, PA, BA, Humanities, 1967; St Charles Borromed Seminary, Philadelphia, PA, Min Rel Studies, 1970-74. **Career:** Natl Black Sisters' Conference, Philadelphia, PA, exec directress, 1977-79; Cardinal Krol, Philadelphia, PA, directress of Mariama, 1979-80; religion teacher at WPCGHS, 1970-79; Bishop Walter F Sullivan, Richmond, VA, campus minister of VSU, 1981-90; directress, Office for Black Catholics, 1984-, pastoral coordinator, 1990-. **Orgs:** Canon Law Society of America, 1974-; chair of Black-Hispanic Caucus, 1986-; ed & e comm, Urban League, 1987-; pres, Natl Black Sisters Conference, 1975-77; mem, Catholic Campus Ministry Assn, 1981-. **Honors/Awds:** Appreciation Mayor-Bicentennial Celebration, Mayor of Philadelphia, PA, 1976; Appreciation as President, Natl Black Sisters' Conference, 1985; Religious Service Award, St Martin De Porres Society, 1987; Outstanding Woman Award, YWCA of Richmond, 1990; Bishop Walter F Sullivan Serra Award, 1990; Distinguished Catholic School Graduate Award, 1992. **Special Achievements:** Inducted West Catholic Hall of Fame, 1994. **Home Addr:** Parish, 1301 Victor St, Richmond, VA 23222-3997. **Business Addr:** Directress, Office for Black Catholics, 811 Cathedral Place, Richmond, VA 23220-4801.

BILLINGS, EARL WILLIAM
Actor. **Personal:** Born Jul 4, 1945, Cleveland, OH; son of Willie Mae Billings; divorced. **Educ:** Karamu House Theater, 1955-63; Cuyahoga Community College, 1963. **Career:** Cleveland Summer Arts Festive, project director, 1967; Karamu Theatre, director performing arts, 1968-70; Arkansas Arts Center, director performing arts, 1970-73; Free Southern Theater, artistic director, 1973-76; New Orleans Public Schools, artist-in-resident, 1976; actor, 1976-. **Orgs:** Screen Actors Guild; Actors Equity Association; American Federation of Television and Radio Artist; Academy of Motion Picture Arts and Sciences. **Special Achievements:** Film appearances: One False Move, National Top Ten List Film, 1992; Stakeout, National Blockbuster Hit Fillm, 1988; stared in eleven television movies; guest stared in seventy television episodics; television series, "What's Happening," role of Rob, 1976-79, "New Attitude," 1990, "South Central," 1993. **Military Serv:** US Navy, 1965-67. **Business Addr:** Actor, Borinstein Oreck Bogart Agency, 8271 Melrose Ave, #110, Los Angeles, CA 90046, (213)658-7500.

BILLINGSLEA, EDGAR D.
Educator. **Personal:** Born Jun 16, 1910, Canton, GA; married Anne Miller; children: Anne Beletta. **Educ:** Tuskegee Inst, BS 1938; Atlanta Univ, MA 1953; West GA Coll Univ GA, grad study. **Career:** Various high schools in GA, principal since

1938; Project Headstart, dir 1964-69; Adult Night School, instructor 1973-74; Polk Sch Dist, coord E Polk County Vocational Educ Program 1970-75. **Orgs:** Mem PAE, GAE, NEA, Guid Div of GVA, AVA; pres GIA Dist 1 1963; chmn bd dir Tallatoona Econ Oppor Auth Inc 1972; pres Amer Cancer Soc E Polk Co1969-75; mem Natl All Black Educ 1973-75; sec Sarah D Murphy Home Inc 1970-74; deacon Friendship Bapt Ch 1974 (mem sr usher bd, mem hospitality Com, sunday sch tchr); apptd to gov's staff by Hon Jimmy Carter 1971. **Honors/Awds:** Hon LLD 1974. **Business Addr:** Coordinator Voc Educ Prog, Polk School District, 60 Hill St, Rockmart, GA 30153.

BILLINGSLEA, MONROE L.
Dentist, author. **Personal:** Born Aug 3, 1933, West Palm Beach, FL; divorced; children: Brent, Christa. **Educ:** Howard Univ Sch of Dentistry, grad 1963. **Career:** Coney Island Hosp Brooklyn, intern oral surgery 1963-64; Minot AFB ND, chief oral surgery 1964-65; Self-employed, dentist LA 1965-. **Orgs:** Mem NAACP, SCLC, Kendrin Mental Health. **Honors/Awds:** Educational Achievement Awd USAF 1954; author "Smoking & How to Stop", "Better Health Through Preventive Dentistry & Nutrition". **Military Serv:** USAF capt 1965-67. **Business Addr:** 8500 S Figueroa #3, Los Angeles, CA 90003.

BILLINGSLEY, ANDREW
Educator, educational administrator. **Personal:** Born Mar 20, 1926, Marion, AL; married Amy; children: Angela, Bonita. **Educ:** Hampton Univ, 1947-49; Grinnell College, AB, political science, 1951; Boston University, MS, social work, 1956; University of Michigan, MS, sociology, 1960; Brandeis University, PhD, social welfare, 1964. **Career:** Res Asst Massachusetts Society for the Prevention of Cruelty to Children, social worker, 1960-63; University of California, asst dean of students, 1964-65, assoc professor of social welfare, 1964-68, asst chancellor of academic affairs, 1968-70; Howard Univ, vice president, 1970-75; Metro Applied Research Center, Natl Urban League NYC, fellow, 1968; Morgan State University, president, 1975-84; University of Maryland, professor of Sociology & Afro-American studies, 1985-87, professor/chairman, Dept Family Studies; visiting scholar in residence, adjunct prof of Sociology, Spelman Coll, 1992-95; Journal of Negro Educ, Journal of Family Issues, editorial bd, 1987-. **Orgs:** Editorial board, Journal of Afro-American Studies, 1969-; editorial board, Black Scholar, 1970-75; board member, Shiloh Bapt Church, Washington DC; Joint Center for Political Studies, DC, 1972-75; Assn Black Sociologists, ASA; Natl Assn of Black Social Workers; chairman, Family Section, ASA, 1972-73; chairman, Committee on Management, Howard University Press, 1972-74; chairman of advisory board, Journal of Abstracts; Natl Assn of Social Workers, chairman, 1973; Assn of Black Sociologists; Natl Council on Family Relations, Groves Conference on Marriage and the Family. **Honors/Awds:** 1st Bienneal Research Award, Natl Assn of Social Workers, 1964; Social Science Fellowship, Metro Applied Research Center, 1968; The Michael Schwerner Memorial Award, 1969; Grinnell College, honoarary DHL, 1971; Afro-American Families & Comm Service, 1st Natl Leadership Award, 1972; Howard University Science Institute, Appreciation Award, 1974; recipient, Natl Council of Black Child Development, Appreciation Award, 1974; Mercy College, honorary DHL, 1982; author, Black Families in White America, 1968; co-author, Children of the Storm Black Children & American Child Welfare, 1972; author, Black Families and the Struggle for Survival, Friendship Press, 1974; American Sociological Assn, Dubois Johnson Frazier Award, 1992; Assn of Black Sociologist, Distinguished Scholar Award, 1991; Natl Council on Family Relations, Matie Peters Award, 1990. **Special Achievements:** Author, Climbing Jacob's Ladder: The Enduring Legacy of African American Families, 1993. **Military Serv:** US Army, Quartermaster Corps, personnel sgt, 1944-46. **Business Addr:** Professor & Chairman, Dept of Family Studies, University of Maryland, College Park, MD 20742-0001.

BILLINGSLEY, ORZELL, JR.
Judge. **Personal:** Born Oct 23, 1924, Birmingham, AL; married Geselda. **Educ:** Tldg Coll, BA, 1946; Howard Univ, LLB, 1950. **Career:** Recorder's Ct, jdg; Roosevelt City AL, frmr mncpl jdg; pvt prac, atty; gen counsel, AL cities, co-orgn; Roosevelt City, fndr, 1967; civil rights Atty, 1968. **Orgs:** Orgn Afro Cntrctrs Assn of AL; consult corps Crdt Unions Coop; mem dem exec com of Jfrsn Co; bd dir AL St Conf of NAACP; bd dir Jfrsn Co Com for Econ Opp. **Business Addr:** Maonic Temple Building, 1630 Fourth Ave, Birmingham, AL 35203.

BILLINGSLEY, RAY C.
Artist, writer, cartoonist. **Personal:** Born Jul 25, 1957, Wake Forest, NC; son of Laura Dunn Billingsley and Henry Billingsley. **Educ:** School of Visual Arts, New York, NY, BFA, 1979. **Career:** Crazy Magazine, New York, NY, humorous artist, writer, 1975-79; Ebony Magazine, Chicago, IL, freelance cartoonist, 1979-87; Disney Productions, Orlando, FL, animator, 1979-80; United Feature Syndicate, syndicated cartoonist, 1980-82; freelance jobs (layouts, advertising, magazine illustration, fashion), 1982-88; King Features Syndicate, New York, NY, syndicated cartoonist, 1988-. **Orgs:** National Cartoonist's Society; International Museum of Cartoon Art. **Honors/Awds:** Pioneer of Excellence, The World Institute of Black Communi-

cations, 1988; Award of Recognition, Detroit City Council, 1989. **Special Achievements:** Started Oct 1969, at age 12, with "KIDS Magazine". Possibly first Black artist to become professional at such a young age. Creator of comic strip "Curtis", King Features, the most popular minority comic strip in history. First Black artist to have a second comic strip published; Author of Curtis and Twist and Shout, Ballantine Books. **Business Addr:** Syndicated Cartoonist, King Features Syndicate, 216 E 45th St, 4th Floor, New York, NY 10017.

BILLINGSLY, MARILYN MAXWELL
Medical administrator, internist, pediatrician. **Personal:** Born in St Louis, MO; daughter of Warren & Willie Mae Maxwell; married Dwight Bilingsly, 1988. **Educ:** St Louis University, BA, Biology, 1977, MD, 1981. **Career:** St Louis University, assistant professor, 1985-92; People's Health Ctrs, medical director, 1992-. **Orgs:** National Medical Association, 1995-; Mound City Medical Forum, local branch, 1985-, president, 1994-95; American Academy of Pediatrics, 1985-; American College of Physicians, 1985-; Focus on the Family Physicians Resource Council, 1994-; Christian Medical & Dental Society, 1995-; Medical Institute for Sexual Health, advisory bd, 1995-. **Honors/Awds:** Health Care for the Homeless Coalition, Volunteer of the Year, 1989; Salvation Army, Medical Fellowship Member of the Year, 1993; National Health Svcs Corps, Public Health Svcs Physician Awd for Excellence, 1995; Sigma Gamma Rho George Washington Carver Distinguished Svc Awd, 1996; Missouri Conference of the AME Church, Research & Status of Black Women Awd, 1996. **Special Achievements:** Provides a free clinic in a homeless shelter, 1986-; Postponing Sexual Involvement Program for Teens, 1995-. **Business Addr:** Medical Director, People's Health Centers, 5701 Delamar Blvd, St Louis, MO 63112, (314)367-7848.

BILLINGTON, CLYDE, JR.
State representative (retired). **Personal:** Born Aug 29, 1934, Hartford, CT; married Malora W; children: Mark, Christal, Courtney. **Educ:** Lincoln Univ, BA; Attended, Connecticut Univ, Maryland Univ. **Career:** Pratt & Whitney Aircraft, chem engr 1961-65; State of CT, state rep, 1969-80; Clyde Billington Real Estate & Liquor Merchants Inc CT, owner/operator 1965-. **Orgs:** Area broker for US Dept HUD; mem Hartford Bd Realtors 1967-74; pres N Hartford Prop Owners Assn; pres Oakland Civic Assn; bd dir Businessmen's Assn; bd dir Pioneer Budget Corp; mem Amer Chem Soc; mem NAACP; mem Urban League; dir Gr Hartford Conv & Vis Bur; treas Dem Town Com; mem of othercivic & professional organizations. **Honors/Awds:** Voted 1 of 1,000 Most Successful Black Businessmen Ebony Mag. **Military Serv:** AUS SPP 1959-61. **Business Addr:** Clyde Billington Real Estate, 919 Albany Ave, Hartford, CT 06112.

BILLOPS, CAMILLE J.
Artist, filmmaker. **Personal:** Born Aug 12, 1933, Los Angeles, CA; daughter of Alma Gilmore and Lucious Billops; married James Hatch; children: Christa Victoria. **Educ:** LA City Coll, AA 1955; LA State Coll, BA 1960; City Coll, MFA 1973. **Career:** NY Times, Amsterdam News, Newsweek, art articles; numerous exhibits US & abroad; Hatch-Billops Coll, co-founder; The Afro-Amer Bellwether Press NY, editor 1975-76; Rutgers Univ, City Coll City Univ NY, artist, art educator, lecturer, filmmaker; Rutgers Univ at Newark, instructor of art, 1975-87; co-director & producer, with James Hatch: Older Women and Love, Finding Christa (1992 Sundance, Grand Jury Prize), KKK Boutique Ain't Just Rednecks, A String of Pearls. **Orgs:** Former mem Natl Conf Artists 1972; Natl Conf Art Teachers; NY Women in Film; pres/admin, Hatch-Billops Collection, 1975-. **Honors/Awds:** Huntington Hartford Found Fellowship 1963; MacDowell Fellowship 1975; author "The Harlem Book of the Dead" with James Van der Zee & Owen Dodson; film: Suzanne Suzanne, New Directors/New Films, 1983, Museum of Modern Art, Ch 13, Independent Focus; Finding Christa, New Directors New Films, Museum of Modern Art, Ch 13, POV; News Directors/New Films; grants for film: NY State Council on the Arts, 1987, 1988; NYSCA and NY Foundation for the Arts, 1989; Rockerfeller Foundation 1991; NEA, 1994. **Home Addr:** 491 Broadway, 7th Fl, New York, NY 10012.

BILLS, JOHNNY BERNARD
Physician. **Personal:** Born Oct 3, 1949, Hickory Valley, TN; married Hilda M; children: Jacqueline; Melissa; Johnny III. **Educ:** Ashland High School Ashland, MS, Diploma 1967; Memphis State Univ, adv chemistry courses 1970; Rust College Holly Springs, MS, BS chem math 1971; Univ of Miss Medical Sch Jacksonm MS, MD 1977. **Career:** Ashland High School, mathematic teacher 1971-72; Rust College, lab technician 1972-73; University Hospital, intern 1977-78; Jefferson County Hospital, staff physician 1978-79; Madison, Yazoo, Leake Family Health Center, consultant physician 1979-80; Hospital Emergency Room, physician (several hospitals) 1977-; Bills Medical Clinic, medical dir 1980-. **Orgs:** Phi Beta Sigma Fraternity, member 1968-; American Medical Association, member 1977-; Jackson Medical Society, member 1977-; Mississippi Medical and Surgical Assoc,(secretary 1983-85) 1977-; Southern Medical Assoc, member 1980-; Methodist Hospital, Lexington, MS, chairman of infection control 1981-; Chamber of Commerse, member 1983-; mem NAACP, Jackson YMCA,

New Hope Baptist Ch, Jackson Rust Coll Club, Baptist Haiti mission, World Concern. **Honors/Awds:** Rust College, academic achievement award, science student of year 1971; Alpha Beta Mu Honor Society 1967-71; Friend of Children Citation-World Concern, United League of Holmes C Citation, member 1983. **Home Addr:** 140 Fairfield Dr, Jackson, MS 39206. **Business Addr:** Medical Dir, Bills Medical Clinic, 115 China St PO Drawer 119, Lexington, MS 39095.

BILLUE, ZANA
Business executive. **Personal:** Born Feb 5, 1964, Brooklyn, NY; daughter of Erma Billue & Windsor Rhoden. **Educ:** Temple Univ, BA, 1986; The Culinary Inst of America, AOS, 1993. **Career:** Nestle USA, recipe development specialist, 1996-; Zana Cakes, owner, 1997-. **Orgs:** Retail Baker's Assn, 1998; United Way Services-Greater Cleveland, comm mem, 1997-; Harvest for Hunger, comm mem. **Home Addr:** 3020 S Moreland Blvd, Cleveland, OH 44120.

BILLUPS, CHAUNCEY
Professional basketball player. **Personal:** Born Sep 25, 1976. **Educ:** University of Colorado. **Career:** Boston Celtics, guard, 1997-98; Toronto Raptors, 1998-. **Business Addr:** Professional Basketball Player, Toronto Raptors, 150 York St, Ste 110, Toronto, ON, Canada M5H 3S5, (416)214-2255.

BILLUPS, FLORENCE W.
Educator. **Personal:** Born Jan 16, 1921, St Louis; married Kenneth; children: Kathleen, Karla, Karyl, Ken Jr. **Educ:** Stowe Tchrs Coll, BA 1941; Northwestern Univ, MA 1945. **Career:** Teacher, 1941-. **Orgs:** Mem MO State Tchrs Assn; past pres Assn Childhood Educ Intl Reading Assn; mem YWCA, NAACP, Urban League, Iota Phi Lambda Sor; past pres St Louis Music Assn; Top Ladies Distinction. **Honors/Awds:** Woman Achievement St Louis Globe Dem 1974; Woman Yr Iota Phi Lambda St Louis Chap 1973; Woman Yr Regional 1974. **Business Addr:** Teacher, Hamilton Br 3 Sch, 450 Des Peres, St Louis, MO 63131.

BILLUPS, MATTIE LOU
Elected official. **Personal:** Born Mar 5, 1935, Bixby, OK; married Vernon S Billups Sr; children: Jacci Love, Jocelyn Palmer, Vernon Jr, Ricci Evans, Reginald Evans, Cheryl Lee, Robyn Evans, Murphy, Debi Cayasso, Beverly, Lesa Singleton. **Educ:** BTW High School, 1954. **Career:** Branding Iron Saddle Club, treas 1972-85; Wagoner Cty Democratic Women, vice pres 1983-85. **Orgs:** Mem Church of Christ 1967-; treas Red Bird Park Fund 1977-80. **Honors/Awds:** Most Outstanding Mayor for Black Mayors OK Conf of Black Mayor 1984. **Home Addr:** 679 S Market, Redbird, OK 74458. **Business Addr:** Mayor, Town of Red Bird, PO Box 222, Redbird, OK 74458.

BILLUPS, MYLES E., SR.
Union official. **Personal:** Born Sep 25, 1926, Norfolk, VA; married Dorothy Vaughan; children: Darlene, Michael, Carolyn, Jean, Myles, Jr, Dorothy, Alma C. **Career:** ILA Lgl 1248, rec sec 1955; Pt of Hmptn Rds, de dist cncl 1961, vice pres dist cncl tst mrtm assn ILA wlfr pnsn fund sfty dir orgn 1967, pres lcl 1970-, pres dist cncl 1967-; Intl Lngshrmn's Assn AFL-CIO, intl vice pres 1975; Bethany Baptist Church, assoc pastor, currently. **Orgs:** Vp mem bd VA Pt Athrty 1971-74; orgn bd dirs Atlntc Nat Bank; Prince Hall Mason; chmn bd dcns Bethl Bapt Ch; bd dirs Hlth Wlfr & Plng Cncl; Chld & Fmly Svcs; adv bd Estrn VA Med Sch; vice pres Tdwtr Chap Cystic Fbrss Soc; bd dirs Bnt Coll. **Special Achievements:** Ordained a Baptist minister, 1986.

BINFORD, HENRY C.
Educator. **Personal:** Born May 2, 1944, Berea, OH; son of Dorothy Johnston Binford and Henry F Binford; married Janet Cyrwus. **Educ:** Harvard Univ, AB 1966, PhD 1973; Univ of Sussex England, MA 1967. **Career:** Northwestern Univ, asst prof 1973-79, assoc prof 1979-. **Orgs:** Dir Business and Professional People for the Public Interest 1985-; mem Sigma Pi Phi 1985-; editorial board, Chicago Reporter, 1988-. **Honors/Awds:** Author, The First Suburbs, Univ of Chicago Press, 1985. **Business Addr:** Assoc Prof of History, Northwestern University, History Dept, Evanston, IL 60208.

BING, DAVE
Business executive, professional basketball player (retired). **Personal:** Born Nov 29, 1943, Washington, DC; children: Cassaundra, Bridgett, Aleisha. **Educ:** Syracuse Univ, grad 1966. **Career:** Detroit Pistons, 1966-74, Washington Bullets, 1975-77, Boston Celtics, 1977-78; The Bing Group, owner, currently. **Orgs:** Standard Federal Bank, board of directors, 1997-. **Honors/Awds:** Named to first team NBA All Star 1967-68 1970-71; Rookie of the Yr 1967; All Amer Career at Syracuse Univ; leading scorer in Syracuse Univ History; All Star 6 times. **Business Addr:** Chairman/CEO, The Bing Group, 1200 Woodland Ave, Detroit, MI 48211.

BING, RUBELL M.
Librarian. **Personal:** Born Jan 6, 1938, Rocky Mount, NC; daughter of Alberta Green Moody and Lonnie Moody; married Alex Bing Sr, Jan 7, 1961; children: Bonita, Tovoia, Yvonne, Alex J. **Career:** St Francis DeSales School, librarian, 1977-. **Orgs:** Member, DC Board of Election and Ethics, 1984-; board member, Bettie Benjamin Scholarship Funds, 1984-87. **Honors/Awds:** Girl Scout Council Award 1974; William R Spaulding Award Council of Washington DC 1981; Washington DC PTA Lifetime Membership 1975; ANC-5B Commissioners' Plaque for Outstanding Community Serv 1985-86; Dictionary of Intl Biography.

BINGHAM, REBECCA JOSEPHINE
Educator, librarian. **Personal:** Born Jul 14, 1928, Indianapolis, IN; married Walter D Bingham; children: Gail Elaine Simmons, Louis Edward Simmons. **Educ:** IN Univ, BS 1950; Univ Tulsa, MA 1961; IN Univ, MLS 1969. **Career:** Alcorn A&M Coll, asst librarian, 1950-51; Tuskegee Inst, serials librarian, 1952-55; Jarvis Christian Coll, acting librarian, 1955-57; Indianapolis Public Library, librarian school serv dept, 1957; Tulsa Jr High School, librarian, 1960-62; Russell Jr High School, English teacher 1962-63; Jackson Jr High School, librarian, 1963-66; Louisville Public Schools, supvr library serv ,1966-70, dir of media serv 1970-75; KY Public Schools, dir media serv Jefferson County 1975-. **Orgs:** Mem Alumni Bd Grad Library Sch; chmn Amer Assn of Sch Librns; Amer Sch Counselors Assn; Joint Media Com; mem KY Govs State Adv Coun on Libraries 1971-73; mem AA5L Natl Libry Week Com; Coun of Amer Libry Assn 1972-; ALA Com on Planning 1973-; vice pres pres-elect Alumni Assn of Grad Libry Sch 1973-74; KY Libry Assn Legislative Com 1973-74; sec treas So E Regional Libry Assn Resources & Tech Serv Div 1973-75; exec bd Amer Libry Assn 1974-78; pres Alumni Bd Grad Libry Sch 1974-75; chmn Amer Assn of Sch Librns/Ency Britannica Sch Libry Media Prog of Yr Awds; selec com exec bd KY Assn for Sprvn & Curriculum Develop 1976-77; KY Sch Supt Adv Counc for Suprvn 1977-; adv com for Bro-Dart Elem Sch Lib Collection 1975-77, Britannica Jr 1975-76, World Book 1977-79,White House Conf on Libraries & Irmation Serv 1978-79; pres Amer Assoc of School Librarians 1979-80; Louisville Jefferson Co Health & Welfare Cncl Bd Dirs; pres Southeastern Library Assoc 1984-86, Jefferson Co School of Administrators 1985-86. **Honors/Awds:** Tangley Oaks Fellowship 1967; Beta Phi Lib Sci Hon; Outstanding Sch Librn KY Libry Trustees 1969; published article KY 1974 edition Amer Educator Ency;contrib 1974 edition Comptons Ency critical reviewer; Louise Maxwell Awd Outstanding Achievement field of Lib Sci Gra Lib Sch IN Univ; YWCA Woman of the Year Louisville 1978. **Business Addr:** Dir Media Services, Jefferson City Board of Educ, 3001 Crittenden Dr, Louisville, KY 40209-1104.

BINNS, SILAS ODELL
Physician. **Personal:** Born Nov 18, 1920, Newport News, VA; married Marion Edwina Calloway; children: D'Jaris, Claudette, Silas Jr, Darlene, Vincent. **Educ:** VA Union Univ, BS 1942; Howard Univ, MD 1945; Homer G Phillips Hosp, intern 1945-46, asst res 1946-47, asst res urol 1947-48, res urol 1948-49. **Career:** Homer G Phillips Hosp, 1949-50; Hampton Genl Hosp, Whittaker Meml Hosp, urologist; Norfolk Richmond Comm Hosps, urological cons; JW Binns Corp, pres; Self-employed, urologist. **Orgs:** Mem Natl Medical Assn 1950; Peninsula Med Soc 1950-; Old Dominion Med Soc 1950-; NY Acad of Sci 1956-; Tidewater Urol Assn 1964-; Hampton Med Soc 1969-; VA Med Assn 1969-; Amer Urol Assn 1970-; AMA 1970-; Alpha Phi Alpha Frat; NAACP. **Honors/Awds:** First black urologist VA 1950; appt Med Malpractice Rev Panel Supreme Ct of VA 1976. **Military Serv:** AUS 1943-45. **Business Addr:** Urologist, 2901 Chestnut Ave, Newport News, VA 23607.

BINS, MILTON
Consultant. **Personal:** Born Dec 11, 1934, Hazlehurst, MS; son of Elizabeth Middleton Bins and John Bins; married Adrienne O King; children: Gregory Milton, Randall S Jackson. **Educ:** Univ of IL, BS 1953-56; IL Inst of Tech, 1957-59; Univ of IL, BS 1960; Chicago State U, MS 1966; Univ of PA, MS 1972. **Career:** Chicago Bd of Educ, high school math teacher, 1960-66; Harcourt Brace Jovanovich, textbook salesman and urban education consultant, 1966-69; Cncl of The Great City Sch, senior associate 1974-81; appointee White House Initiative on Historically Black Coll and Univ, US Dept of Edn, exec dir, 1981-82; Cncl of The Great City Sch, deputy executive director, 1982-91; Community Vision, Inc, vice pres of education, 1994. **Orgs:** Corporate dir John F Small Advertising Agency, Washington Office 1973-74; mem Alpha Phi Alpha Frat 1973-; member, Cncl of 100 Black Republican Leaders 1974-; chmn Council of 100 1986-89, 1991-; chmn & CEO, Douglass Policy Inst; life member, National Alliance of Black School Educators, 1986-; life member, Africare, 1984-; life member, America-Israel Friendship League, 1987-; appointee, President George Bush's Advisory Board on Historically Black Colleges and Universities, 1990-93. **Honors/Awds:** Apptd by Sec of Commerce Malcolm Baldrige to serve a three year term on the 1990 Census Adv Comm, reappointed by secretary of commerce, Barbara H Franklin to a two year term through 1993; apptd to Natl Advisory Coun Electric Power Research Inst, 1997-2001. **Home Addr:** 10454 Sparkle Ct, Orlando, FL 32836, (407)363-1916.

BIRCH, ADOLPHO A., JR.
Judge. **Educ:** Lincoln Univ, 1950-52; Howard Univ, BA, 1956, JD, 1956. **Career:** Private law practice, 1958-69; Meharry Medical Coll, adjunct prof of legal medicine, 1959-69; Davidson County, asst public defender, 1964-66, asst district attorney general, 1966-69; Davidson County Part 1, Court of General Sessions, judge, 1969-78; Fisk Univ, lecturer in law, 1970-72; Tennessee State Univ, lecturer in law, 1970-72; Criminal Court of Davidson County, Div III, judge, 1978-87; Tennessee Court of Criminal Appeals, assoc judge, 1987-93; Supreme Court of Tennessee, justice, chief justice, currently; Nashville School of Law, instructor in law, currently. **Special Achievements:** First African American General Sessions Court judge in the state of Tennessee; only the second African American to serve on the Tennessee Supreme Court; first African American Chief Justice to the Tennessee Supreme Court. **Business Addr:** Chief Justice, Tennessee Supreme Court, 304 Supreme Court Bldg, Nashville, TN 37219, (615)741-6750.

BIRCH, WILLIE
Artist. **Personal:** Born Nov 26, 1942, New Orleans, LA; son of Wilson & Anna Birch; children: Christopher, Postelle, Ama, Freedom. **Educ:** Southern University, BA, 1969; Maryland Institute, College of Art, MFA, 1973. **Career:** Bowie State College, teacher, 1973; Henry St Settlement, teacher, 1980; Guggenheim Museum, teacher, 1981; Hunter College, teacher, 1988-96, artist, currently. **Orgs:** Luise Ross Gallery, New York; Arthur Roger Gallery, New Orleans. **Honors/Awds:** Municipal Collaborative Project, Downtown Winston-Salem, 1995; NYC Metro Transit Authority, Arts for Transit, Philadelphia Intl Airport, 1994; John Simon Guggenheim, Memorial Foundation Fellowship, 1993; Lila Wallace, Reader's Digest, Intl Artists Fellowship, 1992; NY State, Council on the Arts, Natl Endowment for the Arts, Visual Artist Fellowship, 1989-90; NY Foundation for the Arts, Artist's Fellowship Award, painting, 1986; Natl Endowment for the Arts, Visual Artist Fellowship Grant, sculpture, 1984-85; Artist in Residence, The Studio Museum in Harlem, 1977-78. **Special Achievements:** Selected solo exhibitions: Wilmington, DE, Delaware Ctr for the Contemporary Arts, 1998; NY, NY, Luise Ross Gallery, "In Search of Heroes?" part 1, 1996; Chicago, IL, Satori Fine Art, "Not Just a Pretty Picture: Urban American Portraits," 1996; Philadelphia, PA, Philadelphia Art Alliance, 1990; Miami, FL, Miami-Dade Library, 1984; Baltimore MD, Art Works Gallery, 1975; Philadelphia, PA, Gallery Joe, "Intimate Objects," 1997-98; Washington, DC, Smith-Mason Gallery, 1973; numerous others. **Military Serv:** Air Force, airman 1st class, 1962-65.

BIRCHETTE, WILLIAM ASHBY, III
Educational administrator. **Personal:** Born May 9, 1942, Newport News, VA; children: Stacy Olivia, William Ashby IV. **Educ:** St Augustine's College, BA 1964; VA State Univ, MEd 1973; Univ of VA, EdD 1982. **Career:** Wilson City Public Schools; Delaware Tech & Community College; Banneker Jr HS, principal, DC Public Schools; Hampton Univ, instructor; asst to reg supt, DC Public Schools; Magruder Middle School, principal 1983-87; Reservoir Middle School, principal 1988-90; Vasguard Middle School, VA Dept of Education, principal, 1989; Southern Vance High School, Vance County Schools, principal, 1990-92; Isle of Wight County Schools, assistant superintendent for instruction, 1992-97. **Orgs:** Phi Delta Kappa; ASCD; Natl Comm Educ Assn; VA Comm Educ Assn; advisory bd Hampton Roads Boys Club; bd of directors Youth Programs-Mall Tennis Club; Omega Psi Phi; member NAACP; pres Peninsula Council of Urban League; pres, PTPA; An Achievable Dream, bd of dirs. **Honors/Awds:** Outstanding Leadership Awd 1978; Citizen Involvement in Education 1980; Charles Stewart Mott Fellow 1980; Education Fellow Univ of VA; Principal, Vanguard Middle School, VA Dept of Education 1987; Author, "Guidelines for Middle Schools in Virginia," (VASSP Journal) 1988; Contributions (Executive Educator) 1988; Twenty-Five Outstanding High Schools, NC Dept of Ed, principal, 1991. **Home Addr:** 802 Shamrock Drive, Fredericksburg, VA 22407.

BIRCHETTE-PIERCE, CHERYL L.
Physician. **Personal:** Born Sep 25, 1945, New Orleans, LA; married Samuel H Pierce II; children: Samuel Howard. **Educ:** Spelman Coll, AB 1968; Meharry Medical Coll, MD 1972; Harvard Univ, MPH 1980. **Career:** Joslin Clinic, patient mgmt/instruction 1972-75; Lahey Clinic NE Deaconess Hospital, intern resident 1972-75; Peter Bent Brigham Hospital, ambulatory care doctor 1973-74; Harvard Univ Medical Sch, instructor in medicine 1973-80; NE Baptist Hospital, critical care cpr physician coord 1975-78; Roxbury Dental Medical Group, medical dir 1976-80; McLean Hospital, consultant internal medicine 1976-80; MIT-HMO Cambridge MA, dir health screening physician provider 1981-86; Private Practice, clinician. **Orgs:** Television/conference/health workshop appearances varied health issues 1974-; attending physician US Olympic Team Pan Amer Games 1975; sec house of delegates 3rd vice pres Natl Medical Assoc 1983-85, 1986-; work group participant Health Policy Agenda AMA 1985-86; mem Amer Public Health Assoc. **Honors/Awds:** Merrill Scholarship Study & Travel Faculte de Medicine Univ of Geneva Switzerland 1966-67; Outstanding Young Women in Amer 1973; US Dept of Health Human Serv Fellowship 1980-81; Keynote/Founder's Day Speaker Delta Sigma

Theta 1981. **Home Addr:** 407 Washington St #1, Brookline, MA 02146. **Business Addr:** 91 Parker Hill Ave, Boston, MA 02120.

BIRRU, MULUGETTA
City administrator. **Personal:** Born Sep 30, 1946, Tig-Ray, Ethiopia; son of Birru Sibhat and Mizan Berbe; married Elizabeth Birru, 1974; children: Elizabeth, Mehret, Rahel. **Educ:** Addis Ababa Univ, BA, Mgt/accounting, 1970; Syracuse Univ, MA, Economics, 1975, MBA, business and intl finance, 1974; Univ of Pittsburgh, PhD, public and intl affairs, 1991. **Career:** Agricultural and Ind devel Bank (Ethiopia), senior project and research officer, 1970-75; Ethopian Beverage Corp, mgr planning and bus devel, 1975-78; Natl Chemicals Corp, general mgr and CEO, 1978-80; Seminole Econ Dev Corp, vp and dir business devel, 1980-83; Homewood-Brushton RDC, exec dir, 1983-92; Urban Redevelopment Authority of Pittsburgh, exec dir, 1992-. **Orgs:** Pittsburgh Downtown Partnership, board member, 1993-; Pittsburgh Partnership for Neighborhood Devel, board member, 1992-; I Have A Dream Foundation, board member, 1993-; Carnegie Mellon Univ; Heinz School of Public Policy and Mgt, adjunct professor, 1993-. **Honors/Awds:** Verex, 1994 Pittsburgh Man of the Year, 1995; Dollars and Sense, Best and Brightest Business and Prof Men, 1993; Small Business Assn Eastern Region Financial Services of the Year, 1990; City of Pittsburgh, Bus recruitment/real estate devel/serv, 1990; Pa Chamber, Financial Services Award, 1989. **Special Achievements:** Publication in part of An Incentive Scheme for Industrial Labor Force in Ethiopia; Communication, Participation, Development, PhD Dissertation, 1991.

BIRTHA, JESSIE M.
Librarian (retired). **Personal:** Born Feb 5, 1920, Norfolk, VA; married Herbert M Birtha; children: Rachel Roxanne Eitches, Rebecca Lucille. **Educ:** Hampton Inst, BS 1940; Drexel Univ, MLS 1962. **Career:** Penn School St Helena Island SC, secondary school teacher 1941-42; Norfolk, elementary school teacher 1942-46; Antioch Grade School, children's literature instructor, adjunct faculty Philadelphia Center, 1975-76; Free Library of Philadelphia, br librarian 1959-80. **Orgs:** Amer Library Assn; PA Library Assn; Publisher's consul for McGraw Hill Lang Arts Prog Am Lang Today 1974. **Honors/Awds:** Articles published, PLA Bulletin, Top of News, McCann & Woodward-The Black Am in Books for Children, 1972, Josey & Shockley Handbook of Black Librarianship, 1977, Jessie Carney Smith, Images of Blacks in American Culture, 1987; Free Library Citation as Supvr of Year 1973; Chapel of Four Chaplains Legion of Hon Awd for Outstanding Work with Minority Children 1979.

BISAMUNYU, JEANETTE
Marketing executive. **Personal:** Born in Kabale, Uganda; daughter of Irene Rosemary Bisamunyu and Eli Nathan Bisamunyu. **Educ:** Makerere University, Kampala, Uganda, B commerce, transferred in 1981; Talladega College, BA, 1983; Atlanta University, MBA, 1985. **Career:** Talladega College, student tutor, 1981-83; Equitable Life Assurance Society, management intern, 1982; Atlanta University, graduate assistant, 1984-85; Citicorp Acceptance Co, management intern, 1984; US West, mgr, 1985-91; Environmental Educational Solutions, general manager, 1991-. **Orgs:** National Association of Female Executives, 1991-; American Association of University Women, 1991-; Omaha Women's Chamber of Commerce, 1991-; Vision of HOPE Program, mentor, 1988-; Nebraskans for Peace, co-chair of the board, 1988-; Church of the Resurrection, organist & choir director, 1991-; Dale Carnegie Communications Course, graduate assistant, 1987; Toastmasters International, vice pres, 1985-90. **Honors/Awds:** Alpha Chi, 1983; Certificate of Honor for Student with Highest GPA in Business, 1983; Beta Gamma Sigma, 1985. **Special Achievements:** Nebraska Music Olympics, piano performance, gold trophy, 1988, 1989, 1991, bronze medal, 1990; Makerere University, interhall tennis champion, 1979-80; Uganda Junior Tennis Champion, 1978. **Business Addr:** PO Box 662, New York, NY 10268-0662.

BISHOP, ALFRED A.
Consultant. **Personal:** Born May 10, 1923, Philadelphia, PA; son of Samuel and Rose; divorced; children: Janet L. **Educ:** Univ of PA, BS, chemical eng, 1950; Univ of Pgh, MS, chemical eng, 1965; Carnegie Mellon Univ, PhD, mechanical eng, 1974. **Career:** Naval Rsch, engineer, 1950-52; Fischer & Porter Co, engineer, mgr, 1952-56; Westinghouse Corp, engineer, 1956-65, mgr, reactor safety, thermal & hydraulic design & devel, 1965-70; Westinghouse Corp Nuclear Energy, consulting engineer 1970-85; BB Nuclear Energy Consultants, partner 1974-; Univ of Pittsburgh, research prof, 1970-74, assoc prof, chemical engineering, dir, nuclear engineering program, 1974-80, full prof, 1981-85, prof emeritus, 1985-. **Orgs:** Lectr Carnegie Mellon Univ 1967-69; engr consult Westinghouse Advanced Reactors Div 1970-85; member, AICAE 1960-, ASME, AWS, ASEE; author of numerous publ in field of nuclear engrg heat transfer & fluid mechanics; mem bd dir PA Youth Ctrs 1973-; mem bd dir United Fund 1969-73; sr life master Amer Bridge Assn. **Honors/Awds:** Natl Sci Found Awd 1975; Scholarships Rutgers & Lincoln Univ 1942; DuPont Rsch Awd 1971; Non-Newtonian Research, NSF, 1981-84. **Military Serv:** US Army, T/4, 92nd div, signal corps, 1943-46; three battle stars. **Home Addr:** 50 Belmont Ave, Bala Cynwyd, PA 19004.

BISHOP, BLAINE ELWOOD
Professional football player. **Personal:** Born Jul 24, 1970, Indianapolis, IN. **Educ:** Ball State, BS in insurance. **Career:** Houston Oilers, defensive back, 1993-96; Tennessee Oilers, 1997-. **Honors/Awds:** Pro Bowl appearances, 1995, 1996. **Business Addr:** Professional Football Player, Tennessee Oilers, c/o Baptist Sports Park, 7640 H 70-5, Nashville, TN 37221.

BISHOP, CECIL
Clergyman. **Personal:** Born May 12, 1930, Pittsburgh, PA; married Wilhelma. **Educ:** Knoxville Coll, BA 1954; Howard Univ Sch of Religion, BD 1958; Wesley Theol Sem, STM 1960. **Career:** Ordained deacon 1955; elder 1957; Clinton AME Zion Ch, pastor 1957-60; Trinity AME Zion Church Greensboro NC, pastor 1960-. **Orgs:** Dir AME Zion Ch's Div of Preaching Ministries Dept of Evangelism; mem bd of Homes Missions; mem NC State Adv Com of US Commn on Civil Rights; chmn Greensboro Housing Authority. **Business Addr:** Bishop, 2663 Oakmeade Dr, Charlotte, NC 28270-9743.

BISHOP, CLARENCE
Assistant supervisor. **Personal:** Born Feb 19, 1959, Selma, AL; married Caroly. **Educ:** Wayne College, BA 1980, M Spec Educ 1985. **Career:** Lake Park Day Care Ctr, counselor 1977-78; Mission of the Immaculate Virgin Group Home, sr counselor 1978-79, child care worker 1980-81; Wagner Coll, asst lead teacher 1980; NY State Division for Youth, asst supervisor 1982-; Sigma Phi Rho, founder. **Orgs:** Organized Lake View Park Basketball League for teenagers; founder/regional dir/advisor Sigma Phi Rho Frat; business mgr Natl Governors Council Sigma Phi Rho; mem Honorary Society of Art, Catholic Youth Organization Basketball League, Rutgers Univ Pro-Basketball League. **Honors/Awds:** NY State Div for Youth's Regional Dir Awd for Academic Excellence and Career Development; Founders Achievement Awd Sigma Phi Rho Frat. **Business Addr:** c/o Mark Johnson, Sigma Phi Rho, 720 E 216, Bronx, NY 10467.

BISHOP, DAVID RUDOLPH
Dentist. **Personal:** Born Aug 20, 1924; married Joan; children: Robyn, Celeste, David. **Educ:** Howard Univ, BS 1954, DDS 1958. **Career:** Howard Univ, instructor 1958-61; Self-Employed, DDS. **Orgs:** Mem pres Robert T Freeman Dental Soc 1972-74, sec 1968-69; mem Peer Review Comm DC Dental Soc 1972-75; dir Dental Serv Corp 1970-77; mem House of Del Natl Dental Assn 1972; pres DC Bd of Dental Examiners 1980; mem DC Health Planning Adv Com 1971-76; mem Task Force for Effective Health Care Delivery System DC 1973; mem "Hill-Burton" subcomm on hosp cert & need; mem State Adv Bd to Control Health Fees 1973; chmn adv bd United Natl Bank 1977; mem adv comm Armstrong HS Spec Educ Prog 1972-73; fellow Royal Soc of Health 1974; mem Robert T Freeman Dental Soc; mem ADA; NDA; Acad of Gen Dentistry; Chi Delta Mu Professional Frat; Amer Assn of Dental Examiners; mem DC Bd of Dental Examiners 1976; mem NE US Bd of Dental Examiners 1977; mem Pierre Fauchard Acad ofDentistry 1981; fellow Amer Coll oentistry 1984; pres DC Delta Dental Corp 1985; fellow, International College of Dentist 1989-. **Honors/Awds:** Howard Dental Alumni Awd for Distinguished Serv to Profn & Comm 1979; DC Govt Certificate of Appreciation for Outstanding Performance as chmn & mem Bd of Dental Examiners 1983. **Business Addr:** Dr of Dental Surgery, 2608 Sherman Ave NW, Washington, DC 20001.

BISHOP, JAMES, JR.
County official. **Personal:** Born Jan 7, 1930, Humboldt, TN; married Ruby L Dickenson; children: James Gerald, Kathy L. **Educ:** Attended, Univ of MI Ext Svc, Lewis Bus Coll. **Career:** Ford Motor Co, elected sec coke ovens blast furnace unit 1957-59, elected pres UAW 1959-73; UAW Natl Negotiation Com, elected 1961; Wayne Co Labor Relations Bd, dir secty. **Orgs:** Sec bd dir Rouge Employees Credit Union 1969; sec Van Dyke 100 Club; mem NAACP; Trade Union Leadership Council; mem Democratic Party of MI; delegate Intl Confederation of Free Trade Unionists UAW European Conf 1964. **Military Serv:** AUS corpl 1953-55. **Business Addr:** Director-Secretary, Wayne Co Labor Relations Bd, 728 City Co Bldg, Detroit, MI 48226.

BISHOP, RONALD L.
County official. **Personal:** Born Apr 24, 1949, Lewisburg, TN; son of Erma L Bishop and David D Bishop; married Sharon Wooten, Jul 7, 1973; children: Jennifer, Meredith. **Educ:** Fisk University, BS, health and physical education, 1970; Tennessee State University, completed course work for masters, 1971. **Career:** Tennessee Department of Correction, associate warden of security, 1976-79, director of rehabilitative services, 1979-80, director of institutional programs, 1980-83, director of special programs, 1983, assistant to the commissioner, 1983, deputy commissioner, 1983-85; Tennessee Board of Paroles, chairman of parole board, 1986-87, board member, 1988-90; Shelby County Government, Division of Correction, director, 1990-94, chief, currently. **Orgs:** Free the Children, board of directors, 1991-94; Leadership Memphis Class, 1992; United Way, Shelby County Group, chairman, 1992; NACO, justice and public safety steering cmte, 1991-95; Tennessee Legislative Comm, Tennessee sentencing cmsn, 1987; City Mayor WW Herenton, Transition Team, criminal justice comm, 1991, Mayor's Black-on-Black Crime Task Force, 1992. **Honors/Awds:** NABCJ, Jonathan Jasper Wright Award, 1992. **Special Achievements:** Author: "Shelby County Inmate Training Emphasizes Local Labor Market," Large Jail Network Bulletin, 1992. **Business Addr:** Chief, Dept of Corrections, Jefferson County, 730 W Main St, Ste 300, Louisville, KY 40202, (502)574-2167.

BISHOP, SANFORD D., JR.
Congressman, attorney. **Personal:** Born Feb 4, 1947. **Educ:** Morehouse College, BA; Emory University, JD. **Career:** Civil rights attorney; Georgia State House of Representatives, 1977-91; Georgia State Senate, 1991-92; US House of Representatives, Congressman, 1992-. **Orgs:** Eagle Scout; 32nd Degree Mason; Shriner; Sigma Pi Phi Fraternity; Kappa Alpha Psi Fraternity; Urban League; Congressional Black Caucus; Blue Dog Democratic Conservative Coalition in the House; State Bar of Georgia; Alabama State Bar; American Bar Association; National Bar Association. **Honors/Awds:** Georgia Trend Magazine, 100 Most Influential Georgians, 1997; Columbus Men's Progressive Club, Man of the Year Award; Southern Center for Studies in Public Policy, Top 10 List of Georgia State Legislators; Georgia Informer, 50 Most Influential Black Men in Georgia. **Business Addr:** Congressman, US House of Representatives, 1433 Longworth HOB, Washington, DC 20515, (202)225-3631.

BISHOP, SHERRE WHITNEY (SHERRE MILLER)
Publicist, writer. **Personal:** Born Sep 2, 1958, Nashville, TN; daughter of Carrie Pillow and Christian Lytle; married Joseph Bishop, Apr 22, 1989; children: Joseph Bishop Jr. **Educ:** Tennessee State University, BS, communication, theatre, 1982, MA, English, 1994. **Career:** WPTF-TV, news reporter, 1984-89; Meharry Medical College, media specialist, 1989-91; Black Entertainment Television, freelance reporter, 1989-94; Tennessee State University, producer/public information officer, 1991-94; WVOL Radio, producer/talk show host, 1992-94; WLAC-TV, talk show host, 1993-94; Nashville Airport Authority, public affairs manager, 1994-. **Orgs:** International Association of Business Communicators, board member, 1994-; Save Our Black Female Adolescents Project, committee member, 1995-; Nashville Area Chamber of Commerce, committee member, 1994-; Mayor's Transportation Workshop, committee member, 1994-. **Honors/Awds:** Bethlehem Center, Volunteer Service Award, 1991; CASE District III, Scholarship Award, 1991; Nashville Peace Officers Association, Raymond Black Service Award, 1993; Society of Professional Journalists, Journalistic Achievement Award, 1995. **Special Achievements:** Author: "Auntie Grace," entered Essence Magazine writing contest, 1993; playwright: How I Got Over, staged at two area churches, 1991; actor: lead role, Purlie, 1991.

BISHOP, VERISSA RENE
Law enforcement official. **Personal:** Born Nov 22, 1954, Houston, TX; daughter of Julia Lee Bishop (deceased). **Educ:** Texas Southern University, BA, 1987. **Career:** Foley's Department Store, Houston, TX, receptionist/beauty operator, 1973-75; Houston Police Department, Houston, TX, clerk in dispatchers division, 1975-78, police officer, 1978-90, sergeant of police 1990-. **Orgs:** Board member, secretary, Afro-American Police Officers League; financial secretary, secretary, board member, National Black Police Association; YWCA; Phi Beta Lambda; City Wide Beauticians, member Christian Hope Baptist Church, NAACP. **Honors/Awds:** Member of Year, Afro-American Police Officers League; Member of Year, National Black Police Assn, southern region, outstanding member 1990. **Home Addr:** 3829 Wichita, Houston, TX 77004. **Business Addr:** Sergeant, Houston Police Department, 61 Riesner, Houston, TX 77001.

BISPHAM, FRANK L.
Retired government administrator. **Personal:** Born Nov 2, 1924, Cambridge, MA; married Annie Larkins; children: Francine Harris, Gail Murphy, Jo-Ann Duke, Eric. **Educ:** Lowell Inst Sch at MIT Cambridge, Engrg diploma 1965. **Career:** Office of Minority Business US Dept of Commerce, project officer 1970-78; Mattapan Enterprises, partner 1971-; NAACP Boston Branch, exec bd mem 1971-; Natl Business League, regional vice pres 1976-; Minority Business Develop Agency US Dept of Commerce, project officer 1978-82; Suffolk Univ, adv bd mem sch of mgmt 1986-; US Small Business Admin, asst regional administrator 1982-88; retired. **Orgs:** Mem Greater Boston Chamber of Commerce 1980-; vice chmn of bd Youth Business Initiative Prog 1985-. **Honors/Awds:** Outstanding Civic Serv Boston Branch NAACP 1973; Outstanding Achievement Awd Natl Business League 1975; Citizern of the Year Awd Omega Psi Phi Frat 1979; Comm Serv Awd Boston Urban bankers Forum 1982; Community Fellows Program at MIT, 1988-89; Community Fellows Program, Community Service Award 1990; Massachusetts Black Caucus, Distinguish Service Award, 1994; The Black Corporate Presidents of New England, Outstanding Achievement Award. **Military Serv:** USMC nco 31 months. **Home Addr:** 52 Violet St, Boston, MA 02126.

BISWAS, PROSANTO K.
Educator. **Personal:** Born Mar 1, 1934, Calcutta; married Joan; children: Shila. **Educ:** University of Calcutta, BS, 1958; University of Missouri, MS, 1959, PhD, 1962. **Career:** University

of Missouri, research associate, 1961; Tuskegee Realty, president; Tuskegee University, Tuskegee Institute Campus, Dept of Agriculture, professor of plant and soil science, 1962-. **Orgs:** Macon County, Board of Education, chairman. **Business Addr:** Professor, Dept of Agriculture, Tuskegee University, Tuskegee Institute Campus, Tuskegee Institute, AL 36088-1634.

BIVENS, SHELIA RENEEA
Nurse. **Personal:** Born Jul 10, 1954, Pine Bluff, AR; daughter of Myrtle Jones Ervin King and Leon J King; widowed; children: Cory, Ronnie, Ronniesha. **Educ:** Univ of AR Fayetteville, A 1974; Univ of AMS Coll of Nursing, BSN 1977, MNSC, 1982. **Career:** Dr C E Hyman, nurse practitioner 1977-81; Jefferson Regional Medical Ctr, charge nurse 1981-83; Univ of AMS Univ Hosp, staff nurse 1983-89, charge nurse 1989-; Arkansas Cares, ob-gyn nurse/practitioner, currently. **Orgs:** AR State Nurses Assoc 1977-; sec Little Rock Branch NAACP 1983-84, state sec 1984-; chap pianist 19 Electa Chap #5 OES 1984; AR Black Nurses Assoc 1987; Arkansas Perinatal Assoc 1987; Sigma Theta Tau Nursing Honor Society 1989-; National Perinatal Association; Napare. **Honors/Awds:** Outstanding Youth Awd Livingstone Coll Genl Educ of AME Zion Church 1970; Outstanding Serv Awd OES Electa Chap #5 1983; Five Year Service Award, UAMS 1989; Outstanding Black Employee of the Month UAMS 1989; NAACOG Certifications in Obstetrics. **Home Addr:** 54 Saxony Circle, Little Rock, AR 72209.

BIVINS, EDWARD BYRON
Business executive. **Personal:** Born May 11, 1929, Birmingham, AL; married Sarah Felton; children: Cheryl Ann, Janet Yvette. **Educ:** Tuskegee Inst, BS 1951; OH State Univ, MA 1955; So IL Univ, Tuskegee Inst, further study 1961-63 summer. **Career:** Savannah State Coll, coll tchr 1955-64; Oppors Indus Ctr Philadelphia 1964-68; OIC Natl Inst, training dir, branch dir, natl dir of educ & trng, reg dir; Midwest Rsch Inst, sr staff 1968-69; Urban Coalition of Greater KC, exec dir 1969-70; Hallmark Cards Inc, dir of urban & minority affairs 1970-. **Orgs:** Mem C of C Small Bus Affairs Comm 1974-75; President's adv coun on Minority Bus Enterprise; MO State Dept of Educ Adv Comm; Bus Resources Ctr bdchmn 1974-75; mem KC MO Bd of Police Commr 1973-77; KC Region Manpower Council chmn; Downtown Kiwanis Club of KC; United Comm Serv treas; Children's Mercy Hosp bd; Greater KC Housing Inc secty; Family & Chidlren Serv Bd. **Honors/Awds:** Kiwanian of Yr 1972-73; Kappa Alpha Psi Achievement awd Middlewestern Province 1973; Kappa Man of Yr KC Alumni Chap 1973; author of several publs. **Military Serv:** AUS 1952-54. **Business Addr:** Dir of Urban & Minority Affrs, Hallmark Cards Inc, 25 Mc Gee Trafficway, Kansas City, MO 64141.

BIVINS, OLLIE B., JR.
Judge. **Personal:** Born Jul 7, 1923, Americus, GA; married Julia T Hawkins; children: Ollie B III. **Educ:** Fisk Univ, AB 1950; Boston Univ Sch of Law, LLB 1953. **Career:** Atty Dudley Mallory, assoc 7 yrs; Flint MI, atty 1954; Genesee Co Pros, trial atty 1965, chief trial atty 1966-68; Municipal Court, aptd judge 1968; 68th Dist Flint, judge 1969; Dist Judge, elected 1971 8 yr term; Circuit Judge, aptd 1972; MI Ct of Appeals, judge 1976. **Orgs:** Bd dirs Genesee Co Legal Aid Soc; bd dirs Genesee Co Bar Assn; mem State of MI & Amer Bar Assn; past assoc mem Frat Order of Police; mem N Amer Judges Assn; MI Dist Judges Assn; Amer Judicatur Soc; lectr Dist Judges Seminary; served as Circuit Judge Circuit Ct of Genesee Co; served as Judge Detroit Recorders Ct; mem Kappa Alpha Psi Frat; Phi Delta Phi Legal Frat; Frontiers of Amer exec com Tall Pine Coun BSA; charter mem Y's Men's Club of Flint; past mem Sierra Club; bd dirs Cath Social Svcs; mem Knights of Columbus; hon chmn March of Dimes Walk-A-Thon 1972; bd dirs March of Dimes. **Military Serv:** USN WW II. **Business Addr:** Judge, MI Ct of Appeals, 7th Judicial Court, 900 S Saginaw, Flint, MI 48502.

BLACK, BARBARA ROBINSON
Educational administrator. **Personal:** Born Aug 6, 1936, West Chester, PA; daughter of Isabelle Johnson Robinson and George I Robinson; married Samuel Hassell Sr; children: Samuel H Jr, Chad R. **Educ:** Cheyney State Coll, BS 1959; Kean Coll NJ, MA 1970; Cheyney State Coll, post graduate admin, 1971. **Career:** Rahway Sch Dist, tchr/counselor 1963-68; NJ State Dept, counselor/writer for black studies 1968; W Chester State Coll, asst prof black hist 1970-72, coord/counselor act 101 1972-79, asst dean of student devel/coord of Greek life/student orgs 1979-. **Orgs:** Dir first prog Rahway NJ Comm Head Start 1968; counseling Chester PA Sch Dist 1972; treas BOLD Inc 1978; bd of dirs Friends Shelter for Girls 1970; charter mem Local Alpha Kappa Alpha Sor 1972; charter mem Local Twigs Inc 1973; founder/pres, Frederick Douglass Society, 1984-; trustee board, OTC, 1986-. **Honors/Awds:** Delta Kappa Gamma Intl Hon Soc 1979; NJ State HS Hist NJ State Bd 1968; Tchr of the Yr Awd Rahway NJ; cons/writer Black History Elem/HS Unit Rahway NJ 1969; Rahway Civic Assn Awd Rahway NJ 1970; Act 101 Faculty Awd W Chester PA 1978; Outstanding Serv Awd West Chester State Acad Devel Prog 1979. **Business Addr:** Asst Dean of Student Devel, West Chester State Coll, 204 Sykes Student Union Bldg, West Chester, PA 19383.

BLACK, BILLY CHARLESTON
Educational administrator. **Personal:** Born Feb 1, 1937, Beatrice, AL; married Helen Ruth Jeenings; children: James Edward, Marla Jeaninne. **Educ:** Tuskegee Inst, BS 1960; IA State Univ, MS 1962, PhD 1964. **Career:** Tuskegee Inst, lab instructor 1959-60; IA State Univ, rsch asst 1960-64; Albany State Coll, prof of chem 1964-; chmn dept of chem & physics 1966-80, chmn div of sci & math 1969-70, chmn div of arts & scis 1970-80, interim asst to the dean for academic affairs 1979-80, acting pres 1980-81, pres 1981-. **Orgs:** Consul Natl Sci Foundation 1966-; consul Natl Inst of Health 1966-; have served in the following capacities at Albany State Coll of GA coord Inst of Tech; prog dir Campus Action Prog; prog dir Natl Sci Found; proj dir NSF Grant; proj dir Natl Heart Inst; prog dir Interdisciplinary Biomedical Sci Rsch Prog; site development advocate Phelps-Stokes Albany State Coll Project; health develop advocate Phelps-Stokes Albany State Coll Project on Health Awareness; mem Albany State Coll Graduate Studies Council 1974-80; mem Amer Assn for the Advancement of Sci; mem Gamma Sigma Delta; mem Soc of Sigma Xi; mem IA Acad of Sci; mem Phi Lambda Upsilon; mem Amer Assn of Clinical Chemists; mem Amer Chem Soc; mem Amer Oil Chemists Soc; mem Amer Instof Chemists; mem GA Acad of Sci;mem Inst of Food Technoists; mem basileus Omega Psi Phi Frat 1980-; chmn bd of stewards Hines Memorial CME Church;chmn Council of Presidents SIAC 1984-; mem Natl Service Comm Amer Assoc of State Colls & Univs, NCAA President's Commn 1987-91. **Honors/Awds:** Amer Inst of Chemists Awd; Black Georgian of the Yr Awd 1980; 9 publications including "The Separation of Glycerides by Liquid-Liquid Column Partition Chromatography" Journal of Amer Oil Chemists Soc 1963; "The Isolation of Phosphatides by Dielectrophoresis" Journal of the IA Acad of Scis 1964. **Business Addr:** President, Albany State Coll, 504 College Dr, Albany, GA 31705.

BLACK, CHARLES E.
Pilot. **Personal:** Born Apr 2, 1943, Bainbridge, GA; divorced; children: Harriet, Michael. **Educ:** Purdue Univ, BS 1964; GA State Univ, MS 1976. **Career:** Eastern Airlines Inc, pilot. **Orgs:** Mem Alpha Phi Alpha Frat 1961-65; Amer Soc of Pub Adminstrn 1971; mem Orgn of Blk Airline Pilots; coord SW Atlanta Comprehensive Comm Planning Workshops 1974. **Honors/Awds:** Ford Fellow GA State Univ, 1971-73; Best All Around Student Washington HS 1960; Natl Honor Soc 1960. **Military Serv:** USAF capt pilot b-52 1967-71; Air Medal with 2 Oak Leaf Clusters USAF 1970. **Business Addr:** Eastern Airlines Inc, Flight Operations, Hartsfield Intl Airport, Atlanta, GA 30354.

BLACK, CHARLIE J.
Educator, author and business consultant. **Personal:** Born Apr 19, 1934, Beatrice, AL; son of Mattie E Black (deseased) and Napolean Black (deceased); married Lola P; children: Lisa Yvonne, La Sonja Ann. **Educ:** AL State Univ, BS Sec Ed 1956; Tuskegee Inst, 39 Sh Sc Ed 1959-60; Atlanta Univ, 24 Sh Sc Ed 1962-66; ACIC, St Louis, MO, certificate, cartography, George Washington University, Washington, DC, ed administration, 1968-69; Southeastern Univ, MBPA Business Govt Relations 1978; UDC, Washington, DC, math, 1978-79; Catholic Univ, Doctorial Stud Educ Admin 1979-80. **Career:** RR Moton High School, band dir 1956-58; Harrison High School, band dir & math teacher 1958-62; Atlanta Public Schools, Atlanta GA, math teacher 1962-63; Aero Chart & Info Center, cartographer 1963-65; US Army Educ Center, educ advisor 1965-66; St Louis Public Schools, St Louis MO, math teacher 1966; US Navy Publication Div, educ specialist 1966-67; Tracor Inc, technical writer 1967-68; Ogden Technology Lab, program dir 1968-71; Equitable Life Assurance Soc of US, ins rep 1972-73; Southern Aid Life Insurance Co, dist mgr 1973-75; DC Public Schools, math teacher 1976-79; C J Black Enterprises, Washington, DC, president, 1979-; Montgomery County Public School, math teacher 1981-84; The Washington Provider, publisher, editor, 1984-. **Orgs:** Pres Brightwood Comm Assn 1974-80; comm chrmn DC Fed of Civic Assn 1974-80; vice pres Horizontes Investment Club 1976-78; mem Assn of MBA Executives 1981-85; pres West Elementry School PTA 1971-73; mem, Washington Teachers Union, 1976-80; chmn Georgia Ave Corridor Comm Devel Corp 1978-81; mem Intl Platform Assn 1989-; member, US Golf Assn, 1990-91; member, International Platform Assn, 1990-91; Democratic Senatorial Campaign Committee Task Force, 1993-; American Airlines Admirals Club, 1980-84; Concord Coalition, 1994-. **Honors/Awds:** Fellowship Natl Science Found 1959-60; 2 sales awards Equitable Life WA Dist Agency 1972; 2 service awards DC Chapter AL State Alumni Assn 1970-73; outstanding male DC Federation of Civic Assoc 1977; outstanding PTA pres DC Congress of Parents and Teachers 1973; author, Meeting the Mathematical Needs of Students in a Georgia Secondary School, 1971; author, After the Fact, 20/20 Hindsight, 1988; author, column, Upward Mobility, 1971-; Outstanding Father, DCFCA, 1995. **Home Addr:** 6435 13th St NW, Washington, DC 20012. **Business Addr:** President, C J Black Enterprises, 6435 13th St NW, Washington, DC 20012-2959.

BLACK, DANIEL L., JR.
Government official. **Personal:** Born Sep 16, 1945, Sheldon, SC; son of Susie Black and Daniel Black; married Mary Lemmon; children: Carlita. **Educ:** SC State College, BA (summa cum laude) 1971; Univ of SC, MBA 1975. **Career:** IRS, Jacksonville, exam group mgr 1976-78, Atlanta, sr regional analyst 1980-81, exam branch chief 1981-82, Oklahoma City, chief appeals office 1983-85, Greensboro Dist asst district director; Laguna Niguel Dist, asst district dir; Springfield district dir. **Orgs:** Life mem Omega Psi Phi Frat 1978-; mem Amer Inst of CPA's 1977-86; mem FL Inst of CPA's 1977-; mem Sr Executives Assn 1985-; Beta Alpha Psi Accounting Fraternity; Alpha Kappa Mu Natl Honor Soc. **Honors/Awds:** Distinguished Alumni Awd 1985. **Military Serv:** AUS specialist E-4 1963-66; Good Conduct Medal; Vietnam Service and Defense Medal. **Business Addr:** CPA, District Dir, IRS-Springfield District, 320 W Washington St, Springfield, IL 62701.

BLACK, DAVID EUGENE, SR.
Educator. **Personal:** Born Nov 9, 1940, Columbus, OH; son of Alberta L Black and James E Black; married Marie Robinson, Oct 5, 1962; children: David E Jr, Monika L. **Educ:** Central State University, BS, education, 1964; Xavier University, Masters, educational administrator, 1974. **Career:** Columbus Public Schools, Columbus Alternative High School, assistant principal, currently. **Orgs:** National Alliance of Black School Educators, 1992; Ohio Association of Secondary School Administrators, 1992; National Association of Secondary School Administrator, 1992; Columbus Administration Association, 1992; Central State Alumni Association, Columbus Branch, past president, 1991-92; Lenden Community Alliance, 1992; Columbus Public School, Multi-Cultured Steering Committee, 1992. **Honors/Awds:** Columbus Public School, Outstanding Educator Apple Award, 1992; Upward Bound, Outstanding Administrator, 1980. **Business Phone:** (614)365-6006.

BLACK, DON GENE
Public relations consultant. **Personal:** Born Sep 6, 1945, Chicago, IL; son of Inez Franklin-Davidson and Uster Black; married Glenda Camp Black, Aug 14, 1966; children: Donerik, Shronda. **Educ:** Sinclair Comm Coll, A 1967; Wright State Univ, BA 1970. **Career:** Dayton Express News, dir public relations 1967-68; Monsanto Rsch Corp, mktg 1968-70; Don Black Assoc Inc, pres 1970-77; Multi-Western Co, pres 1977-. **Orgs:** Bd mem Urban Youth Assn 1976-81; pres OH Assoc of Blk PR/Adv/Mktg Co 1983-85; pres Dayton Chap Natl Business League 1983-86; advisory board, Goodwill Industries. **Honors/Awds:** Achievement Awd Dayton Public School 1985; free lance writer; Community Service Award, US Air Force, 1987; Presidents Award, National Business League, 1989; Martin Luther King Coordination Award, 1990; Success Guide Award, WROV Radio Award, 1995; MLK President's Award, 1995. **Special Achievements:** Publisher: Dayton Weekly News. **Business Addr:** President/Senior Consultant, Multi-Western Public Relations/Marketing, 15 East Fourth St, Suite 601, Dayton, OH 45402, (513)223-8060.

BLACK, FRANK S.
Educational administrator. **Personal:** Born Feb 3, 1941, Detroit, MI; son of Zella Fisher Black and Frank Black; married Ruby S Lindsey, Mar 16, 1973; children: Piper L, Jason B. **Educ:** Central State Univ Wilberforce OH, BS (cum laude) 1967; OH State Univ, MA 1969, PhD 1972. **Career:** Columbus OH Public Schools, eval asst, 1969-71; OH State Univ, project dir, adjunct asst prof, 1972-73; TX Southern Univ, assoc prof, dir institutional rsch, 1973-77, assoc prof of educ, 1973-78; Murray State Univ, assistant dean, 1978-84; Univ of Southern FL at Ft Myers, assoc dean for acad affairs 1984-85; Jackson State Univ, vice pres academic affairs 1985-87; Univ of Tennessee at Martin, vice chancellor for academic affairs, 1988-94; Univ of TN at Martin, prof of educ, 1995-. **Orgs:** Mem Amer Ed Rsch Assn 1971-75; mem exec comm Assn for Inst Rsch 1977-79; mem Amer Assn of Coll of Teacher Ed 1979, Murray KY Human Rights Comm 1979-; adv bd WKMS Univ Radio Sta 1979-; adv bd W KY Reg Mental Health & Retarded Bd 1979; Phi Delta Kappa 1974-; Phi Kappa Phi, 1988-; Mid-South Educ Research Assn, 1995; Amer Assn of Schools, Colleges & Universities, 1994. **Honors/Awds:** Grad Fellow Soc OH State Univ 1967-69; Friend of Nursing Award, TN Nurses Assn, District 10, 1994; Alpha Kappa Alpha Award, AKA Sorority Inc, UTM Chapter, Outstanding Achievement, 1994; Greek Man of the Year, Univ of TN, 1997. **Military Serv:** AUS sp4 1958-61. **Business Addr:** Professor of Education, University of Tennessee at Martin, Dept of Educational Studies, Martin, TN 38238-5021.

BLACK, FREDERICK HARRISON
Business executive. **Personal:** Born Nov 11, 1921, Des Moines, IA; son of Mr & Mrs F H Black; married Kay Browne; children: Joan Jackson, Lorna, Jai, Crystal. **Educ:** Fisk Univ, BS Eng Physics 1949; USC, Los Angeles, CA, MS, physics, 1952; Pepperdine Univ, MBA 1972; Univ of MA, DEd Personel 1975. **Career:** USN, consultant to chief of naval personnel; President's Domestic Council, consultant; General Electric Co, missile project engr, marketing rep in Washington DC, corporate mgr EEO/safety & security; Watts Indus Park, exec dir; FH Black & Assocs, mng partner. **Orgs:** Diplomat Amer Personnel Soc; bd pres TRY US; mem bd ICBO; trustee Fisk Univ; published several articles; board chairman, Myerhoff Fund, 1990-; vice president, National Minority Jr Golf Scholarship Assn, 1988-; board of directors, The Arts Council of Richmond Inc,

1990-. **Military Serv:** AUS 2nd lt 3 1/2 yrs. **Business Addr:** Managing Partner, FH Black & Assocs, 1377 K St, Washington, DC 20005.

BLACK, GAIL

Business executive. **Personal:** Born Aug 29, 1950, Klamath Falls, OR; married Carl B Bowles; children: Amil Christopher Bowles, Teri Ruth Bowles. **Educ:** Portland State Univ, attended 1970-71; Portland OIC, cert legal sec 1977. **Career:** Union Pac RR Co Law Dept, litigation specialist 1977-; Clairon Defender Newspaper, asst editor & pub 1970-. **Orgs:** Bd mem Knockout Industries Inc 1971-; exec bd charter mem Tenth Ave Irregulars Chap Toastmasters Intl Inc 1979-; dir Jimmy Bang-Bang Walker Youth Found 1969-; chmn Albina Rose Festival float com 4 prize winning floats Portland Rose Festival Parade 1969-71; asst to Albina area coord United Good Neighbors 1970-73; United Way rep Union Pac RR Co 1979-80; parent adv com mem NE Christian Sch 1980-. **Honors/Awds:** Dean's List Portland State Univ 1970-71. **Business Addr:** Asst Editor & Publisher, Clairon Defender Newspaper, 319 NE Wygant St, Portland, OR 97211.

BLACK, JAMES TILLMAN

Dentist. **Personal:** Born Feb 19, 1935, Guthrie, OK; married Joyce Toran; children: James Jr, Jeanine. **Educ:** TN State Univ, BS 1955; Michael Reese Sch of Medical Tech, attended 1956; Central State Univ, MA 1960; Loyola Univ Sch of Dentistry, attended 1964. **Career:** Private Practice, dentist. **Orgs:** Ofcr LA Dental Soc 1977; LA Co Pub Health Serv 1964-71; mem NAACP; mem Amer Dental Assn; LA Dental Soc; Angel City Dental Soc; Kappa Alpha PsiFrat; Xi Psi Phi Dental Frat. **Honors/Awds:** Publ "Dentistry in a Headstart Program" 1972; "Changes in Dental Concepts" 1976. **Military Serv:** AUS spec 3 1956-58. **Business Addr:** 3015 Crenshaw Blvd, Los Angeles, CA 90016.

BLACK, JOSEPH

Business executive. **Personal:** Born Feb 8, 1924, Plainfield, NJ; son of Martha Black and Joseph Black Sr; divorced; children: Joseph F, Martha J. **Educ:** Morgan State Coll, BS 1950; Shaw Coll at Detroit, Dr Humane Letters 1974; Central State Univ, Dr of Law, 1979; Miles Coll, Dr of Letters, 1982; Morgan State Univ, Dr of Public Works 1983. **Career:** Baltimore Elite Giants, Negro Natl League, pitcher 1944-50; Cuba, Venezuela, Santo Domingo, pitcher 1947-51; Washington Senators Cincinnati Reds, Brooklyn Dodgers, pitcher 1952-57; Plainfield NJ, teacher 1957-63; special markets rep 1962-64; dir special markets 1964-67; Greyhound Lines, vice pres, special markets 1967-69; Greyhound Corp, vice president, 1969-87; Jay Bee & Associates, pres, currently. **Orgs:** Bd of trustees Jackie Robinson Found; Natl Assn of Market Devel, pres, 1967-68, chmn bd 1968-69, 1972-73; bd of trustees Natl Assn for Sickle Cell Disease; bd of trustees Miles Coll; advisory panel US Census Bureau 1978-82; bd of directors, Baseball Assistant Team. **Honors/Awds:** Natl League Rookie of Year Brooklyn Dodgers 1952; New Jersey Sports Hall of Fame 1972; Morgan St Univ Hall of Fame 1972; Black Athletes Hall of Fame 1974; "Ain't Nobody Better Than You" Autobiography 1983; Central Intercollegiate Athletics Assn 1986; Mid-Eastern Athletic Conf 1986; Martin Luther King Jr Distinguished Serv Award, 1987. **Military Serv:** US Army, 1943-46. **Business Addr:** President, Jay Bee & Associates, 3116 E Shea Blvd, Phoenix, AZ 85028.

BLACK, KEITH

Physician. **Personal:** Born in Tuskegee, AL. **Educ:** Univ of MI, undergrad degree, medical training. **Career:** UCLA Medical Center; UCLA, prof of neurosurgery; Cedars-Sinai Medical Center, Neurosurgical Institute, head, currently. **Special Achievements:** Published more than 100 scientific articles. **Business Addr:** Head, Neurological Institute, Cedars-Sinai Medical Center, 8700 Beverly Blvd, Los Angeles, CA 90048-1804.

BLACK, LEE ROY

Law enforcement administrator. **Personal:** Born Jul 29, 1937, Oakland, MS; married Christine Gray; children: Lori Lynette, Colette Marie, Angela Denise, Lee Roy Jr. **Educ:** Univ of IL Navy Pier, 1956-58; Roosevelt Univ, BA History 1962; Loyola Univ School of Law, 1969-70; OH State Univ, Fellow NPEL 1972-74; Union Grad School, PhD 1976. **Career:** Cook Cty Dept of Public Aid, caseworker 1953-62; Juv Ct of Cook Cty, probation officer 1963-67, suprv prob officer 1966-67; Chicago Dept Human Resources DiDiv Correctional Svcs, unit dir Lawndale-Garfield Corrections Unit 1967-70, asst dir 1967-70; UECU, dir Correctional Educ Prog 1970-72; Tchr Corps Youth Adv Prog US Off of Ed; field liaison rep 1975-76; UECU, spvsr 1975-76; IN Univ Dept of Forensic St, vstg asst prof 1975-76; St of IN Dept of Corr, dir Div Class & Treat 1976-77; St of WI Dept Hlth & Soc Serv, deputy admin Div of Corr 1977-81; St of MO Dept Cor & Human Res, dir 1981-. **Orgs:** Pres Midwest Assoc of Corrections Admin; bd of governors Amer Corrections Assoc; mem Natl Alliance for Shaping Safer Cities, NAACP, Natl Urban League,Alpha Phi Alpha, Natl Assoc of Blacks in Criminal Justics; chmn corrections subcommittee MO Governors Commiss on Crime; chmn/prog cncl ACA Natl Conf 1986. **Honors/Awds:** Outstanding Achievers Awd MO Black Leg Caucus; Great Guy Awd for promoting youth leadership WGRT Radio Station Chicago IL; Fellow Natl Prog for Ed Leadership; Grad Scholarship Union for Experimenting Coll & Univ to Union Grad School Yellow Springs OH; Image Awd for Outstanding Contrib to Youth Career Youth Devel Milwaukee WI; many publ incl "Perspectives in Community Corrections" Under grant from Law Enforcement Asst Admin Washington DC 1975. **Business Addr:** Dir, MO Dept Correct & Human Resour, 2729 Plaza Dr, PO Box 236, Jefferson City, MO 65102.

BLACK, LEONA R.

States attorney, administrative director. **Personal:** Born Jan 5, 1924, Galveston, TX. **Educ:** Prairie View Coll, attended; Roosevelt Univ, attended; Chicago Univ, attended; DePaul Univ, attended. **Career:** Cook Cty Dept of Public Aid, file clerk, finance clerk, head file clerk, office mgr, Chicago US Post Office, clerk supvr; Intl Harvester Co, equipment expeditor; AA Rayner Alderman 6th Ward, alderman's sec, admin asst; AR Langford Alderman 16th Ward, alderman's sec, admin asst; Donald Page Moore, polit org; State's Attorney of Cook County, political coordinator for Bernard Carrey; Fraud & Consumer Complaint Div Cook Cty, appt admin chief 1972; Cook County States Attorney Office, dir victim/witness asst proj 1974-. **Orgs:** Ombudsman States Atty Office; political activist, Natl Delegate 1972; lobbyist, Local Cty State for Consumer Protection Judicial Reform; advocate for, Criminal Justice, Consumerism, Judicial Reform, Child Abuse, Drug Abuse, Alcoholism; youth gr dir, founder, org SCAPY; bd of dir Natl Org of Victim Assn, 1976. **Honors/Awds:** Set up Consumer Fraud classes within City Coll. **Business Addr:** Dir Victim/Witness Asst, Cook Cty States Attny Office, 2600 S California Ave, Chicago, IL 60608.

BLACK, LUCIUS, SR.

State representative. **Personal:** married Mildred Black; children: Urey Rufus, Lucius Jr, Don Keith. **Educ:** Alabama State Univ, BS; Columbia Univ, MA. **Career:** Sumter County School System, teacher; York Citizens Federal Credit Union, manager/treasurer; Alabama House of Representatives, District 67, representative, 1985-94; District 71, 1995. **Orgs:** Natl Conf of State Legislators; SCLC; NBCSL; NAACP; AL New South Coalition. **Honors/Awds:** Appreciation Plaques & Awards, various organizations. **Business Addr:** State Representative, District 71, PO Box 284, York, AL 36925.

BLACK, MALCOLM MAZIQUE (MIKE BLACK)

Educator, musician. **Personal:** Born Nov 28, 1937, Vicksburg, MS; son of Henriette Grace Smith Black and Fred Bell Black; married Emma Kern Black; children: Varen Delois, Karen Barron. **Educ:** Jackson State Univ, BME 1959; Univ of WI, MME 1967; Nova Univ, EdD 1975. **Career:** FL & MS HS, band dir 1959-69; FL Assn of Collegiate Registrars & Admission Officers, vice pres 1979; Broward Community Coll, registrar, dir of admissions 1969-79, dir of Jazz Studies & Bands, currently; as a musician has performed with Patti Page, Sam Cooke, Marilyn McCoo, Billy Davis, and others. **Orgs:** Member, Placement Comm Amer Assn Collegiate Registrars & Admission Officers 1975, FL Veterans Advisory Council 1975, FL School Relations Comm 1975; vice pres FL Assn Coll Registrars & Admission Officers 1977; bd mem Broward County Housing Authority Advisory Bd 1978, Sunshine State Bank, Sistrunk Historical Festival Comm; American Federation of Musicians; Music Educators Natl Conference; Natl Assn of Jazz Educators; Kiwanis Club. **Honors/Awds:** Plaque, FL Assn Coll Registrars & Admission Officers 1979; recognition as Broward County Black Pioneer, Links Inc 1980; plaque, 25 Years of Serv Omega Psi Phi Frat 1981; plaques, Sistrunk Historical Festival Comm 1981-85; Outstanding Florida Citizen, governor of Florida, 1986; Good Neighbor Award, Miami Herald Newspaper, 1986; Sharps & Flats to Freedom exhibit, Chicago, 1988. **Home Addr:** 2991 NW 24th Ave, Fort Lauderdale, FL 33311. **Business Addr:** Dir of Jazz Studies/Bands, Broward Comm College, 3501 SW Davie Rd, Fort Lauderdale, FL 33314, (305)475-6731.

BLACK, MIKE. See BLACK, MALCOLM MAZIQUE.

BLACK, ROSA WALSTON

Urban planner, educator. **Personal:** Born in Moyock, NC; children: Adrienne Vernice. **Educ:** Norfolk State Coll, BS; Univ of VA, M Urban Planning. **Career:** Hampton Public School, teacher 1964-66; Portsmouth Public School, teacher 1966-70, suprv teacher 1967-68; Concentrated Employment Program, consultant, 1968-69; Central VA Comprehensive Health Planning Comm, researcher & statistician 1970-71; Charlotte Model Neighborhood Comm, dir of planning 1972; Baltimore Model Cities Program, consultant 1972; Dept of Devel & Planning, Gary IN, asst dir, 1973; Seat Pleasant MD, former city planning consultant; Antioch Coll, former chmn dept of health serv admin; City of Seat Pleasant, asst city admin. **Orgs:** mem, Amer Soc of Planning Officials, Natl Negro Business & Professional Womens Club, NAACP, Delta Sigma Theta. **Business Addr:** Walston Research Inc, 1145 19th St, NW, Suite 717, Washington, DC 20036.

BLACK, VERONICA CORRELL

Human resources executive. **Personal:** Born Oct 30, 1946, Winston-Salem, NC; daughter of Beatrice Moore Correll and Vance A Correll (deceased); married Isiah A Black Jr; children: Braswell, Sandra B. **Educ:** Livingstone College, Salisbury, NC, BA, 1969; American Bankers Assoc, Washington, DC, human resources certificate, 1984; University of North Carolina, Chapel Hill, NC, young exec program, 1987; Duke University, Sr Management Dev Prog, 1996. **Career:** Wachovia Bank & Trust Co, Winston-Salem, NC, senior vice president, group executive, personnel, 1969-. **Orgs:** Personnel committee member 1986-, personnel committee chairman 1987-89, board member 1985-89, YWCA; regional vice president, Bankers Educational Society, 1981-86; chairman, Career Services Advisory Committee, Winston-Salem State University, 1989-. **Honors/Awds:** Leadership Award, Winston-Salem State co-op office, 1986; received the 1992 Positive Image Award from the Minority Recruiter Newspaper. **Home Addr:** 3400 Del Rio Ct, Winston-Salem, NC 27105. **Business Addr:** Sr Vice Pres, Human Resources Department, Wachovia Bank & Trust Co., 100 N Main St, Mail Code 37074, Winston-Salem, NC 27105.

BLACK, WALTER KERRIGAN

Attorney. **Personal:** Born Jan 27, 1915, Birmingham, AL; married Dorothy E Wickliffe. **Educ:** Univ of IL, AB; John Marshall Law School, JD 1952. **Career:** McCoy & Black, partner 1952-59; Robbins IL, village atty 1952-69, E Chicago Heights IL, village atty 1952-59; McCoy, Ming & Leighton, partner 1959-64, 1965-77; Mitchell Hall Jones & Black PC, principal. **Orgs:** Gen counsel, Fuller Prod Co, 1968; gen counsel, Boyer Intl Lab Inc, 1968; sec & gen counsel, LaCade Prod Co, 1972; sec, dir, Lawndale Pkg Corp, 1974; hearing exam, IL Fair Practice Comm; panel arbitrator, Amer Arbitration Assn; mem gov bd, Cook County Legal Asst Found; co-counsel, Hon Richard Gordon Hatcher, 1967, 1971. **Business Addr:** Principal, Mitchell, Hall, Jones & Black, 134 S La Salle St, Chicago, IL 60603.

BLACK, WALTER WELDON, JR.

Business executive. **Personal:** married Clairdean E Riley; children: Walter III. **Educ:** Morgan State Coll, BS 1958; Amer Univ Law School, 1960-62. **Career:** Prudential Ins Co of Amer, spec agent; NAACP Spec Contrib Fund, urban prog dir 1968-69; Pinkett-Brown-Black Assoc, chmn bd 1969-72; Howard Univ, mkt rsch analyst 1972-76; Alaska Assoc Inc, Flennaugh Reliable Svcs, supt 1976-. **Orgs:** Pres MD State Conf of Br NAACP 1973-; dir of MD State Conf of NAACP 1965-68; vice pres DC Chap Morgan State Coll Alumni Assoc 1966-67; mem Alpha Phi Alpha. **Honors/Awds:** Meritorious Serv Awd MD State Conf of Br NAACP 1973. **Military Serv:** US Army, 1st lt 1963-64.

BLACK, WILLA

Businesswoman. **Personal:** Born Jul 11, 1915, Cheraw, SC; married Luke; children: Margaret Buchan, Carolyn Smith, Carolyn Black. **Career:** Billie's Wholesale Distr, pres, owner 1946-. **Orgs:** Dist org Negro Bus & Professional Womens Club Inc; adv 4-H Club; mem Urban League, NAACP, Natl Council of Negro Women Inc. **Honors/Awds:** Jobber of the Year OH Beautician Assoc 1957; Bus Woman of the Year Iota Phi Lambda 1967; N Central Gov Awd Negro Bus & Professional Women Club 1973; Ollie Porter Gold Awd (nat high awd) Negro Bus & Professional Women Club 1973; Spec Apprec Awd Youngstown Negro Bus & Professional Women Clubs Inc 1974; Youngstown Black Bus Women 1976. **Business Addr:** President, Billie's Wholesale Distr, 533 W LaClede Ave, Youngstown, OH 44511.

BLACKBURN, BENJAMIN ALLAN, II

Prosthodontist. **Personal:** Born Jun 10, 1940, Jackson, MS; married Sara Driver; children: Kellye, Benjamin III, Leigh. **Educ:** Morehouse Coll, BS 1961; Meharry Med Coll, DDS 1965; Sydenham Hosp, intern 1966; NY Univ, Cert Prosthodontics 1968. **Career:** Private practice, prosthodontist. **Orgs:** Fellow Amer Coll of Prosthodontist; mem Amer Prosthodontist Soc, SE Acad of Prosthodontist, Kappa Alpha Psi, NAACP, Urban League; diplomate Amer Bd Prosthodontists. **Honors/Awds:** Hon Fellow GA Dental Assoc. **Military Serv:** US Army, Dental Reserve maj. **Business Addr:** 75 Piedmont Ave NE, Atlanta, GA 30303.

BLACKBURN, CHARLES MILIGAN, II

Corporate executive. **Personal:** Born Nov 4, 1937, Florence, AL; son of Dovie E Blackburn and Charles M Blackburn; married Jun 12, 1965; children: Mary L, Charles M. III, Mark E. **Educ:** Alabama A&M University, BS, 1960. **Career:** Commerce Bank, director; Sigma Systems Inc, president, currently. **Orgs:** Packaging Machinery Manufacturers Institute; Prince Georges County Community College; Queen Anne School Board. **Honors/Awds:** Outstanding Black Businessman, State of Maryland. **Special Achievements:** PMMI, Board of Directors. **Military Serv:** US Army, SP, 1960-64. **Business Addr:** President, CEO, Sigma Systems, Inc, 231 Westhampton Pl, Capitol Heights, MD 20743, (301)336-7000.

BLACKMAN, ROLANDO ANTONIO
Professional basketball player. **Personal:** Born Feb 26, 1959, Panama City, Panama; married Tamara; children: Valarie, Brittany, Briana. **Educ:** Kansas State, marketing and soc, 1981. **Career:** Dallas Mavericks, 1981-92, New York Knicks, 1992-94. **Orgs:** Community: Dallas Independent School District; Big Brothers and Big Sisters; Special Olympics; Muscular Dystrophy Assn; Children's Medical Center of Dallas; Just Say No Foundation; Summer Basketball Camp for youths. **Honors/Awds:** Second all-time leading scorer, Dallas Mavericks; 3-time NBA All Star; Most Popular Maverick Basketball Player; team captain; bi-weekly radio show in Dallas; Olympic team member, mens basketball, 1980; Pro Athlete of the Year 1986-87; 46 points, 20 of 21 fts (club records for makes and attempts) on 1/5/83 vs San Antonio in Reunion, scored 22 in the first quarter. **Business Addr:** Former Professional Basketball Player, New York Knicks, 2 Pennsylvania Plaza, New York, NY 10121.

BLACKMON, ANTHONY WAYNE
Business executive. **Personal:** Born Feb 13, 1957, Newark, NJ; son of Bettye Blackmon; children: Terry, Johanna. **Educ:** Cornell Univ, NY SSILR, BS 1979; LaSalle Law School, JD, 1996. **Career:** WTKO Ithaca NY, broadcaster 1976-79; Meadowlands Sports Complex NJ, asst dir matrix opers 1976-79; Hollywood Park Racetrack, dir matrix oper 1979-; Blackmon Enterprises, pres, consult 1981-. **Orgs:** Mem Urban League, NAACP, Black Businessmans Assn of LA, LA Better Bus Arbitrator; BBB of America, arbitrator; certified assoc, Amer Bar Assn; Maricopa County Sheriffs Exec Posse. **Honors/Awds:** Youngest & only black dir Matrix Oper Hollywood Park Racetrack. **Business Addr:** President, TBE Office Business Services, 8405 W Sells Dr, Phoenix, AZ 85037, (602)849-6841.

BLACKMON, BARBARA ANITA (BARBARA ANITA MARTIN)
State senator, attorney. **Personal:** Born Dec 7, 1955, Jackson, MS; daughter of Willie T Martin and Julious Martin Sr; married Edward Blackmon Jr, Sep 27, 1986; children: Madison Edward, Bradford Jerome. **Educ:** Jackson State University, BS, 1975; University of Alabama, MBA, 1976; University of Santa Clara Law School, 1978-79; University of Mississippi Law School, JD, 1981; New York University, LLM, taxation, 1982. **Career:** Hinds Junior College, instructor, 1976-78; Bristol-Myers Co., associate tax attorney, 1982-83; Banks & Nichols, associate, 1983-84; Barbara Martin Blackmon PC, attorney-at-law, 1984-87; Blackmon, Blackmon & Evans, partner, 1987-; State of Mississippi, Mississippi State Senate, senator, 1992-. **Orgs:** American Bar Association; Association of Trial Lawyers of America; Magnolia Bar Association; Mississippi Bar Association; Natl Bar Assn; New York State Bar Association; Mississippi Research Consortium; JSU Development Foundation. **Honors/Awds:** National Association for Equal Opportunity in Higher Education, Distinguished Alumni Citation of the Year, 1992; Medgar Evers Faces of Courage Award, 1992; Special Executive Business Partner Award, 1991; Constance Baker Motley Award, 1981. **Business Addr:** State Senator, Mississippi State Senate, State of Mississippi, 907 W Peace St, PO Box 105, Canton, MS 39046.

BLACKMON, EDWARD, JR.
Attorney. **Personal:** Born Jul 21, 1947, Canton, MS; son of Mollie Blackmon and Edward Blackmon Jr; married Barbara Martin Blackmon; children: Madison, Bradford, Janessa. **Educ:** Tougaloo Coll, BA, political sci 1967-70; George Washington Univ, JD, 1970-73. **Career:** N MS Rural Legal Serv, staff atty 1973-74; Blackmon & Smith, partner 1974-; Blackmon, Blackmon & Evans, partner, currently. **Orgs:** State rep, MS House of Rep, 1979, 1984-. **Honors/Awds:** NAACP, Medgar Evers Medallion Award, outstanding services to the community, 1992; Magnolia Bar Association, R Jesse Brown Award, 1990-91; Canton Branch NAACP, Outstanding Service Award, 1991; Magnolia Bar Association, special award for outstanding leadership and service as president, 1984-85; Tougaloo College, numerous awards. **Business Addr:** Representative, Mississippi State Legislature, PO Box 105, Canton, MS 39046.

BLACKMON, JOYCE MCANULTY
Utility company executive. **Personal:** Born Nov 25, 1937, Memphis, TN; daughter of Evelyn Simons & Samuel McAnulty (both dedeased); married Lawrence Burnett Blackmon Sr, Dec 21, 1956 (died 1985); children: Lawrence B Jr, David G. **Educ:** Memphis State University, Memphis, TN, BS, 1966, master of education, 1970. **Career:** Memphis City Schools, Memphis, TN, teacher, guidance co, 1959-79; Memphis Light, Gas and Water, Memphis, TN, sr vice president, administration & support, 1979-. **Orgs:** President, Memphis Chapter, The Links, Inc, 1990-92; board of trustees, Tougaloo College, 1986-92; board of directors, Mid South Public Communications Foundation, WKN TV and FM, 1990-; graduate, former board member, Leadership Memphis, class of 1981; Memphis Rotary, 1988-; Alpha Kappa Alpha Sorority, 1956-. **Honors/Awds:** Contempora, Coping with a Crisis Award, Contempora Magazine, 1991; Prominent Black Woman, Memphis State Chapter of Alpha Kappa Alpha, 1990; Dedicated Service Award, Memphis in May International Festival, Inc, 1990; Distinguished Service Award, NAACP, Memphis Chapter, 1982; Dedicated Service Award, Lemoyne-Owen College, UNCF drive and annual fund drive, 1990; president elect, Memphis In May International Festival Inc, 1993; Child Advocacy Bd, 1995. **Business Addr:** Sr Vice President, Administration and Support, Memphis Light, Gas and Water, 220 S Main, Memphis, TN 38103.

BLACKMON, MOSETTA WHITAKER
Corporation executive. **Personal:** Born Jan 2, 1950, Homestead, PA; daughter of Elgurtha Spruill Whitaker and Garvis Whitaker; married Michael George Blackmon, Oct 19, 1975; children: Jason B., Jacqueline Renee, Jenelle Laraine. **Educ:** University of Pittsburgh, Pittsburgh, PA, BA, 1970; American University, Washington, DC, MS, 1986. **Career:** Comsat Corp, Washington, DC, job analyst, 1974-76, employment manager, 1977-79; Marriott Corp, Bethesda, MD, senior compensation analyst, 1979-80; Mitre Corp, McLean, VA, employment manager, 1980-96; Mitretek Sys, Inc, dir human resources, 1996-. **Orgs:** American Compensation Association, 1975-89; Washington Technical Personnel Forum, 1975-; Prince Georges County PTA, 1986-94; board of advisors, US Black Engineer Magazine, 1988-90; Black Human Resources Professionals, 1988-95; Alpha Kappa Alpha. **Honors/Awds:** Certified compensation professional, American Compensation Association, 1983; Outstanding Recruiter, Career Communications Group, 1988. **Business Addr:** Director, Human Resources, Mitretek Systems, Inc, 7525 Colshire Dr, Mc Lean, VA 22102.

BLACKMON, ROBERT JAMES
Professional football player. **Personal:** Born May 12, 1967, Bay City, TX; married Gayle; children: Kyrsten Nicole, Kierra Denise. **Educ:** Baylor. **Career:** Seattle Seahawks, defensive back, 1990-96; Indianapolis Colts, 1997-. **Business Addr:** Professional Football Player, Indianapolis Colts, PO Box 535000, Indianapolis, IN 46253, (317)297-2658.

BLACKSHEAR, JEFFERY
Professional football player. **Personal:** Born Mar 29, 1969, Fort Pierce, FL. **Educ:** Northeast Louisiana. **Career:** Seattle Seahawks, guard, 1993-95; Baltimore Ravens, guard, 1996-. **Business Addr:** Professional Football Player, Baltimore Ravens, 11001 Owings Mills Blvd, Owings Mills, MD 21117, (410)654-6200.

BLACKSHEAR, JULIAN W., JR.
Attorney. **Personal:** Born Jul 9, 1941, Chattanooga, TN; married Margaret Ann; children: Jeffrey. **Educ:** Morehouse Coll, BA 1963; Univ of TN Coll of Law, JD 1970. **Career:** NAACP Legal Defense & Ed Fund NY, coop civil rights attny 1970-; State Sen Avon N Williams Jr NASHVILLE TN, attny in gen prac law 1970-74; Petway Blackshear Hagwood & Thompson Law Firm, attny. **Orgs:** Mem Natl Bar Assoc, Amer Bar Assoc, Amer Trial Lawyers Assoc, TN Trial Lawyers Assoc, Delta Theta Phi, Natl Legal Aid & Defender Assoc; bd mem Nashville Urban League, Grace Eaton Day Care Ctr; supt Sunday School, John Calvin Presbyterian Church; sec Tau lambda. **Honors/Awds:** Listed in Outstanding Young Amers 1974, Outstanding Amer of Southeast 1974; Individual Appellate Arguement Awd Univ of TN Coll of Law 1970; Outstanding Achievement Awd Freedom Found Valley Forge 1968; Individual Moot Ct Competition Awd Univ of TC Coll of Law 1970. **Military Serv:** USAF sgt 1965-68.

BLACKSHEAR, WILLIAM
Businessman. **Personal:** Born Jun 1, 1935, Marianna, FL; married Betty Jean Booze; children: Bruce, Angelia, Edwina, Jeffery, Jacquline, Sylvia. **Educ:** State of FL, Educ Cert 1963; Gen Elec Employ Educ, 1969. **Career:** Gen Elec Co, 1958-70; Wkly Challenger News, 1968-; Black Gold Inc, mgr. **Orgs:** Mem consult Black Media Inc; VAC; C of C; Black Gold of FL Inc; scout ldr 1950-53; pres PTA 1960-63; pres and founder, Home Improvement Commn 1961-67; pres, founder, HOPE 1965-67; pres and founder, Lincoln Nursery Assn 1961-67; elec city commn (1st black); pres and founder SE Black Pub Assn Inc 1978; v chmn OIC of Suncoast; adv Youth of Amer NAACP; Urban League; Southern Poverty Associate; Dem FL. **Honors/Awds:** Citation Gen Elec Stud Guid Prog 1970; Citation Outstanding Efforts for Human Rights Ridgcrest Improv Assn 1966; Outstanding Comm Serv The Le Cercle Des Jeunes Femmes 1965; Key to City Pensacola FL 1979; Key to City Ft Lauderdale 1977; 29 year service weekly challenger newspaper. **Military Serv:** AUS staff sgt 1955-62. **Business Addr:** Manager, Black Gold Inc and Tri-County Challenger, 2500 9th St S, St Petersburg, FL 33705.

BLACKWELL, ARTHUR BRENDHAL, III
County commissioner, fire department executive. **Personal:** Born Jun 10, 1953, Detroit, MI; son of Florrie Love Willis Blackwell and Robert Brendhal Blackwell; married Zenobia Weaver, Oct 19, 1985; children: Mosii Mays Blackwell, Robert Brendhal Blackwell, II. **Educ:** North Carolina A&T Univ, Greensboro, NC, BA, political science, 1976. **Career:** Detroit Bank & Trust, Detroit, MI, asst branch mgr, 1978-79; 1980 Census, Detroit, MI, dir field oper, 1980; Wayne County Bd of Commr, Detroit, MI, commr, 1980-82, 1987-, chairman, 1989-94; Blackwell & Assoc, Detroit, MI, owner, 1983-86; Mayor Young's Re-election Campaign, Detroit, MI, headquarters coord, 1985; Detroit Fire Dept, Detroit, MI, community admin coord, 1986-; Wayne County Board. **Orgs:** Chmn, Detroit/Wayne County Port Authority, 1988-; mem Natl Org of Black City Officials; Michigan Assn of County Officials, Detroit Windsor Port Corp, 1988-, mem First Congressional Dist Democratic Party; mem Michigan Democratic Party, City Resident Comm, The Young Alliance; member, National League of Counties; member, Local Development Finance Authority; member, Kids In Need of Direction; member, Highland Park Caucus Club; member, New Detroit Inc, Governmental Affairs Committee; member, Wayne County Retirement Board. **Honors/Awds:** Father/Son Outstanding Achievement Award, Northern YMCA, 1981; Certificate of Appreciation, Wayne County Bd of Commr, 1982; Outstanding Performance for Oboe Solo in Quarter State Music Competition, 1969. **Business Addr:** Wayne County Bd of Commr, 600 Randolph, Suite 450, Detroit, MI 48226.

BLACKWELL, DAVID HAROLD
Educator. **Personal:** Born Apr 24, 1919, Centralia, IL; married Ann; children: 8. **Educ:** Univ IL, AB 1938, AM 1938, PhD 1941; Honorary DSc, Univ of IL 1965, MI State Univ 1968, So IL Univ 1970. **Career:** Inst Advanced Study Princeton Univ, Post-doctoral Fellow 1941-42; Southern Univ, instructor 1942-43; Clark Coll, instructor 1943-44; Howard Univ, asst prof 1944-54, chmn dept statistics 1957-61; Univ of CA Berkeley, prof statistics 1954-. **Orgs:** Pres Inst Math Stat 1955, AAAS, Amer Math Soc; Rosenwald Fellow Inst Advanced Study Princeton Univ 1941-42; rsch fellow Brown Univ 1943; fellow InstMath Statistics 1947; mem Natl Acad Sci 1965; faculty rsch lecturer Univ of CA 1971. **Business Addr:** Professor Statistics, Univ of California, Berkeley, CA 94720.

BLACKWELL, FAIGER MEGREA
Educational administrator. **Personal:** Born Dec 14, 1955, Reidsville, NC; divorced; children: Alexdria. **Educ:** Winston-Salem State, 1974-76; UNC Chapel Hill, BS. **Career:** Jones Cross Baptist Church, chmn, trustee 1975-; NC Long Term Care Facilities, vice pres 1976-; Caswell NAACP; Caswell Cty Voters League, pres 1976; Caswell NAACP, bd mem 1978-. **Orgs:** Founder Blackwell Bros Florist 1974-; pres Blackwell Rest Home Inc 1976-; bd mem Wiz 4-H Club 1979-, Caswell Cty Planning Bd 1980-; pres Dogwood Forest Rest Home Inc 1980-. **Honors/Awds:** Martin Luther King Jr Awd Caswell Sportsman Club; Leader of the Year NC Long Term Care; Outstanding Serv NC Long Term Care; Outstanding Serv Caswell Cty School Bd.

BLACKWELL, FAYE BROWN
Educator, government official. **Personal:** Born May 10, 1942, Monroe, LA; married Fred Blackwell. **Educ:** Southern Univ, BA 1964. **Career:** Calcasiew Fed of Teachers 1978-82; Coalition for Comm Prog, pres of bd of dir 1983-85; Calcasiew Dem Assoc, pres 1984-85; Lake Charles City Council, vice pres 1984-85; Lake Charles City Council, council mem dist B, currently; KZWA-FM radio station, owner, mgr, currently. **Orgs:** Owner, oper Faye Brown Rental Inc 1968-85; pres Brown Enterprises P Monse LA 1978-85; sec Independent Invert Corp 1980-85; mem Women League of Voters, NAACP, Top Ladies of Distinction, Natl Assoc of Univ Women. **Honors/Awds:** Community Serv Zeta Sor; Ed Exal Natl Assn for Univ Women; Woman of the Year, Martin L King Found, Los Angeles Municipal, School Los Angeles Municipal Assn. **Business Addr:** Council Member, Lake Charles City Council, Lake Charles, LA 70601.

BLACKWELL, HARVEL E.
Educator. **Personal:** Born Sep 25, 1937, Hulbert, OK; son of Lavada Blackwell and R B Blackwell; children: Carmella C, Howard E. **Educ:** Compton Coll, AA 1959; CA State Univ of Los Angeles, BA 1961; Univ of Southern CA, MS 1963, PhD 1968. **Career:** Southern Assoc of Coll & School, consultant 1970-; Inst for Serv to Educ, consultant, 1970-75; National Science Foundation, proposal review; Lovanium Univ, visiting prof; JSC NASA Lockhead Corp & Others, consultant 1975-85; Abstract Subj Realism & Portrait, artist; Texas Southern Univ, prof of Physics, 1970-; BSA Service, Scientific and Engineering Consultants, pres, 1982-. **Orgs:** Bd of dir United Cerebal Palsy Gulf Coast 1978-80; mem Nat Tech Assn; mem Nat Society of Black Physicists; board of directors, K-RAM Corp, 1980-84. **Honors/Awds:** Grants Nat Sci Found & NASA; monographs Introd to Orbital Flight Planning, Lectures in The Natural Sciences; publications in Aerospace Engineering, Atomic and Molecular Physics, Optics, Plasma Physics, Educators.

BLACKWELL, J. KENNETH
State treasurer. **Personal:** Born Feb 28, 1948, Cincinnati, OH; married Rosa E; children: K Anika, Rahshann K, Kristin S. **Educ:** Xavier Univ, BS 1970, MEd 1971, MBA 20 hrs; Harvard Univ, Prog for Sr Execs in State and Local Govts 1981. **Career:** Cincinnati Bd of Ed, teacher, coach 1971; Model Cities for Comm School Assoc, ed & consult 1973; Afro-Amer Studies Univ of Cincinnati, teacher; Xavier Univ, Univ & Urban Affairs, instr, dir; Cincinnati City Council, mem 1977-; Community Relations, assoc vice pres 1980-; City of Cincinnati, vice mayor 1977-78, mayor 1979-80, vice mayor 1985-87; Cincinnati Employees Retirement System, vice chair, 1988; US Dept

of Housing & Urban Development, deputy under secretary, 1989; United Nations Human Rights Comm, UNHRC, confirmed at the rank of ambassador, US representative, 1991; State of Ohio, treasurer, currently; Certified Government Financial Manager, 1997. **Orgs:** Chm Local Legislators Comm 1978-79; vchmn Transportation Comm 1979-80; mem Cable TV Task Force; mem Intl Econ Devel Task Force; steering comm Commission on Cities in the 1980's; co-chmn Labor Relations Adv Comm Natl League of Cities; mem, bd trust Public Tech Inc; state & local govt bd of advisors John F Kennedy School of Govt Harvard Univ; adv comm, bd of dirs, Amer Council of Young Political Leaders; mem Jerusalem Comm; bd mem Natl Leg Conf on Arson; mem Rotary Intl, Cincinnati Fine Arts, Inst Bd, Cincinnati Opera; trustee Birthright of Cincinnati Inc; bd mem Gr Cincinnati Coalition of People with Disabilities; Fifth Third Bancorp of Cincinnati, bd of dirs, 1993; Fifth Third Bank of Cincinnati, bd of dirs, 1993; Physicians for Human Rights, bd of dirs, 1993; Greater Cincinnati Council on World Affairs, bd of dirs, 1993; International Republican Institute, bd of dirs, 1993; Congressional Human Rights Foundation, bd of dirs, 1993; Council on Foreign Relations, New York, NY, mem, 1994; Natl Assn of State Treasurers; Natl Assn of State Auditors, Comptrollers & Treasurers; Natl Assn of Securities Professionals; National Commission on Economic Growth & Tax Reform; Greater Cincinnati Urban Bankers Association; Xavier University, bd of trustees; Wilmington College, bd of trustees; Wilberforce University, bd of trustees; Cincinnati Technical College, bd of trustees; Grant/Riverside Hospitals, board of directors, National Taxpayers Union of Ohio, board member; Government Accounting Standards Board, task force mem; National Coalition of Black and Jewish Americas, bd of governors; Washington Legal Foundation, bd of advisors; Underground Railroad Foundation Inc, chmn, policy bd; John M. Ashbrook Center for Public Affairs, Ashland Univ, mem, bd of advisors, 1997; Pension & Public Funds Committee, Ntl Assoc of State Auditors, Comptrollers & Treasurers, chmn, 1997; US Dept of Labor Advisory Council on Employee Welfare and Pension Benefit Plans, mem, 1997; National Taxpayers Union, mem, bd of directors. **Honors/Awds:** Hon JD Wilberforce Univ 1980; Wilberforce Univ, Honorary Degrees, 1980; HUD Public Leadership Fellow Harvard Univ 1981; Gordon Chase Meml Fellow Harvard Univ 1981; The Aspen Institute, Fellow, 1984; Cincinnati Technical Coll, Honorary Degree, 1987; Salzburg Seminar, Austria, Fellow, 1988; Republican candidate for congress, 1990; Franklin Pierce Coll, Honorary Degree, 1992; Urban Morgan Institute for Human Rights, Univ of Cincinnati, Senior Fellow, 1992; Heritage Foundation, Washington DC, Senior Fellow & Domestic Policy Analyst, 1992; Recipient of Xavier Univ Distinguished Alumnus Award, 1992; School of Advanced International Studies at Johns Hopkins University, Fellowship Award; US State Department, Superior Honor Award, 1993; US Small Business Administration Advocacy Award, 1995; Martin Luther King DreamKeeper Award, 1996; NAACP Public Service Award, 1996; Ashbrook Center's Thomas A. Van Meter Scholarship Award for Outstanding Conservative Leadership, 1997; President's Award, Natl Assoc of State Auditors, Comptrollers & Treasurers, 1996. **Business Addr:** 30 East Broad Street, 9th Fl, Columbus, OH 43266-0421.

BLACKWELL, LUCIEN E.
US representative. **Personal:** Born Aug 1, 1931, Whitset, PA; married Jannie; children: 4. **Educ:** St Josephs Coll, attended. **Career:** Intl Longshoremens Assoc Local 1332, bus agt; PA House of Reps 188 Dist; Dist 3 City of Philadelphia, councilmember; State of Philadelphia, US rep, 1992-. **Orgs:** Port Coord Council of Port Coord Council of Philadelphia, Dist Council Port of Philadelphia; committeeman, chmn labor comm 46th Ward; instr Supreme Council of Cadets of Amer; org Neighborhood Youth Council; Pyramid Temple No 1, Demolay Consistory No 1. **Honors/Awds:** Novice Diamond Belt Championship, amateur boxer, 1949; Light Middleweight Title, US Army 25th Infantry Div Korea 1953. **Military Serv:** US Army. **Business Addr:** Representative, Pennsylvania, United States House of Representatives, 2454 Rayburn HOB, Washington, DC 20515.

BLACKWELL, MILFORD
Neurologist. **Personal:** Born Apr 2, 1921, Chicago, IL; son of Nellie Blackwell and Govornor Blackwell; children: Peter. **Educ:** So IL Univ, BE 1943; Meharry Med Coll, MD 1948. **Career:** Harlem Hospital NYC, rotating intern, 1948-49; VA Hospital, Tuskegee AL, resident, 1949-50; Cushing VA Hospital, Framingham MA, resident, 1950-51; VA Hospital, Newington CT, resident, 1951-52; IN Univ Medical Center Indianapolis, resident, 1952-53; Natl Hospital, London England, resident, 1954, 1956-57; Bellevue Hospital NYC, clinical assoc visiting neurologist; Harlem Hospital NYC, assoc visiting psych; Sydenham Hosp NYC, assoc visiting neuro-psych; Knickerbocker Bracie Sq Hospital NYC, courtesy staff; New York City Speech Rehabilitation Inst, Spencer-Chapin Adoptin Serv NYC, McMahon Memorial Shelter NYC, staff mem; NY Univ Med Coll, clinical instructor neurology, 1960-. **Orgs:** Consult neurologist Sydenham Hosp, Ken Garden Hosp NY, NY Foundling Hosp, Edwin Gould Found for Children; consult child psych Soc for Seaman's Children SI Foster Home Care Unit New York City Dept Social Svc; consult psych & neurology NY State Athletic Comm; panel psych NY State Dept Social Svc; comm Blind Vocational Rehab Serv Bur; disability determinations NY State Dept Social Svc; diplomate in psych, neurology, neurology with spec competence in child neurology Amer Bd Psych & Neurology; mem AMA, Amer Psych Assoc, Amer Epilepsy Soc, Amer Inst Hypnosis, NY State, NY Cty Med Soc; pres Neurol Disease Found 1966-. **Military Serv:** USAF capt 1954-56. **Business Addr:** 828 Homestead Turnpike, Franklin Square, NY 11010.

BLACKWELL, PATRICIA A.
Business executive. **Personal:** Born in Metropolis, IL; daughter of Minnie Allen Blackwell and Phinis N Blackwell. **Educ:** Southern Illinois Univ-Carbondale, 1962-65, BA 1992; Southern Illinois Univ-Edwardsville, 1966-67; Howard Univ Small Business Development Center, 1983-84. **Career:** Natl Urban League, WA Bureau, administrative asst 1971-72; John Dingle Associates, Inc, Washington rep/lobbyist 1972-73; E H White and Company, Inc, director, east coast operations 1973-74; Unified Industries Incorporated, program manager 1974-84; PA Blackwell & Associates, Inc, president 1984-. **Orgs:** Consultant DC Democratic Committee 1974; vice-president SIMBA Associates, Inc-Fund Raiser 1978-80; board member Regional Purchasing Council of VA 1978-; member Natl Conference of Minority Transportation Officials 1983-; member Natl Forum for Black Public Administrators 1984-; member Natl Assn of Female Executives 1984-; tutor Operation Rescue-Washington Urban League 1984-; mem Women's Transportation Seminar 1987; mem Natl Coalition of Black Meeting Planners. **Honors/Awds:** Citation of Recognition Governor's Office-State of VA 1978; Certificate of Appreciation Virginia State Office of Minority Business Enterprise 1979; nominated Outstanding Young Women of America 1984. **Home Addr:** 4236 W Pine Blvd, Saint Louis, MO 63108.

BLACKWELL, RANDOLPH TALMADGE
Administrative executive. **Personal:** Born Mar 10, 1927, Greensboro, NC; married Elizabeth Knox; children: Blanche. **Educ:** North Carolina Univ, BS Sociology 1949; Howard Univ, JD 1953; Amer Univ, Grad Study; Syracuse Univ, Grad Study. **Career:** Winston-Salem Teacher Coll NC, assoc prof of social sci 1953-54; AL A&M Coll Huntsville, assoc prof of econ 1954-63; Voter Ed Proj Inc Atlanta, field dir 1963-65; SCLC Atlanta, prog dir 1964-66; So Rural Action Atlanta, dir 1966-76; OMBE Wash DC, dir 1977-79; Ofc of Minority Enterprise Prog Devel Dept of Commerce, dir 1979-. **Orgs:** Lecturer MIT, Fed Exec Inst, Urban Training Ctr for Christian Mission Chgo; partic 3 White House Conf & 2 Natl Task Forces 1964; bd mem So Growth Policy 1965, Martin Luther King Jr Ctr for Social Change. **Honors/Awds:** Cert of Merit HEW Dept of Commerce Dept of Labor 1973; Peace Prize Martin Luther King Jr Ctr for Social Change 1976; Equal Justice Awd Natl Bar Assoc 1978; Man of the Year Awd Natl Assoc of Minority CPA Forms 1978. **Military Serv:** AUS pvt 1st class 1944-45. **Business Addr:** Dir, Dept of Commerce, 275 Peachtree St NE Ste 150, Atlanta, GA 30303.

BLACKWELL, ROBERT B.
Consultant. **Personal:** Born Nov 4, 1924, Meridian, MS; son of Dr & Mrs Arthur B Blackwell; married Florrie Love Willis; children: Brenda B Mims, June Blackwell-Hatcher, Arthur Blackwell, Bobbi Blackwell. **Educ:** Howard Univ, BA 1949; Detroit Coll of Law, 1965-68. **Career:** UAW, AFL-CIO, pres, local 889, 1955-62; City of Highland Park, city police & fire commissioner, 1958-63; Michigan Labor Relations Bd, exec dir, 1962-67; City of Highland Park, city councilman, 1963-67, mayor, 1967-75; US Dept of Labor, special assistant under secretary, 1975-76; US Aid, Senate Dept, consultant, 1976-78; City of Highland Park, mayor 1968-72, 1980-88; Wayne County, commissioner, currently. **Orgs:** life mem, Golden Heritage mem NAACP; Urban League; Kappa Alpha Psi Fraternity; Guardsmen, Boys Club of Amer; board of directors, Natl League of Cities; chmn, labor comm, Michigan Municipal League; trustee, US Conference of Mayors; vice chair, Wayne County Commissioner 3rd District Committee on Roads, Airports, and Public Service. **Honors/Awds:** Alumni of the Year, Howard Univ; Man of the Year, Little Rock Baptist Church; founder & first sr chmn, Natl Black Caucus of Local Elected Officers. **Special Achievements:** First full-time elected African-American mayor in Michigan. **Military Serv:** AUS, master sgt, 1942-48; Purple Heart. **Home Addr:** 133 Massachusetts, Highland Park, MI 48203.

BLACKWELL, UNITA
Former government official. **Career:** City of Mayersville, MS, mayor, 1976-93. **Orgs:** National Conference of Black Mayors, president, currently. **Honors/Awds:** MacArthur Fellow, 1992. **Special Achievements:** Instrumental in persuading federal government to fund a 20-unit housing development in Mayersville and give the town a new fire truck. **Business Addr:** Mayor, City of Mayersville, PO Box 162, Mayersville, MS 39113, (601)873-4281.

BLACKWELL, WILLIE
Food service manager, literacy coordinator. **Personal:** Born Dec 1, 1954, St Louis, MO; son of Flora Lee Williams Blackwell and Willie Blackwell Jr.; married Kathy Loman Blackwell, 1981; children: Lamont Blackwell, Crystal Blackwell, April Blackwell. **Educ:** Morris Brown College, Atlanta, GA, BS, 1977. **Career:** Dobbs International Service, Atlanta, GA, production supervisor, 1977-84, relief manager, 1984-88, hot food manager, 1988-, literacy coordinator, currently. **Orgs:** Board member, Georgia Literacy Coalition, currently; advisory board member, Southside High School, Atlanta, GA, currently. **Honors/Awds:** Letter of Encouragement for Literacy, Mrs. Barbara Bush, 1990; has been featured on CNN, the Atlanta Journal Constitution, and CBN Family Channel for involvement with literacy programs. **Business Addr:** Literacy Coordinator, Dobbs International Service, 1669 Phoenix Pkwy, Suite 204, College Park, GA 30349.

BLACKWELL-HATCHER, JUNE E.
Judge. **Personal:** daugHter of Robert Blackwell; married Jim Hatcher; children: two daughters. **Educ:** Syracuse University, BA, psychology, 1974; American University, JD, 1979. **Career:** Wayne State University, admission counselor, recruiter, 1974-76; legal intern, various agencies, 1977-79; Office of Appeals and Review, Dept of Employment Services, hearing and appeals examiner, 1979-80, chief of dept, 1981-83; Midwest Legal Services, director of operations, 1984-88; private practice, attorney, 1988-92; Wayne County Probate Court, Estates Division, judge, 1992-. **Orgs:** Natl Bar Assn; Michigan Bar Assn; Wolverine Bar Assn; Women Lawyers Assn; Meals on Wheels, volunteer; president, Association of Black Judges of Michigan; co-chair, Adopt-A-School Committee, Association of Black Judges of Michigan. **Honors/Awds:** Woman of the Year, National Political Congress of Black Women, 1995; Golden Gavel Award, Wayne County Probate Bar Association, 1996. **Special Achievements:** Author, ''Law on Your Side,'' monthly column, appeared in over 250 labor publications throughout the US. **Business Addr:** Judge, Wayne County Probate Court, 1319 City-County Bldg, Detroit, MI 48226, (313)224-5676.

BLACKWOOD, RONALD A.
Mayor (retired). **Personal:** Born Jan 19, 1926, Kingston, Jamaica; married Ann; children: Helen Marie. **Educ:** Kingston Tech School, 1944; Kingston Commercial Coll, 1946; Westchester Comm Coll, attended; Elizabeth Seton Coll, Grad; Iona Coll New Rochelle NY, BBAMgmt. **Career:** Mount Vernon, NY, mayor, 1985-95; Westchester Co Bd of Supervisors; Mt Vernon City Council. **Orgs:** Life mem NAACP; National Conference of Christians and Jews, board of directors; Mental Health Association of Westchester, Inc; United Way of Westchester/Putnam; Boy Scouts of America-Westchester Putnam Council; Rotary Club of Mount Vernon; Progressive Lodge No 64 AFM; All Islands Association; Westchester 2000 Board of Directors; Omega Psi Phi Fraternity; Portuguese American Club (honorary member). **Special Achievements:** First African American to be elected mayor in NY state.

BLACQUE, TAUREAN
Actor. **Personal:** Born in Newark, NJ; divorced 1966; children: adopted 8 boys, 3 girls. **Educ:** Amer Musical and Dramatic Acad. **Career:** Made Broadway debut in The River Niger; also appeared in We Interrupt This Program; appeared with various Negro Ensemble Co productions; appearances on TV shows include Backstairs at the White House 1979 (miniseries), Hill St Blues (series regular) The $520 an Hour Dream 1980, Generations; films include House Calls; Generations, tv series, until 1990.

BLADES, BENNIE (HORATIO BENEDICT)
Professional football player. **Personal:** Born Sep 3, 1966, Fort Lauderdale, FL; children: Horatio Jr, Ashley, Amber, Jaylen, Bianca. **Educ:** Univ of Miami (FL), attended. **Career:** Detroit Lions, safety, 1988-96; Seattle Seahawks, 1997-. **Honors/Awds:** Pro Bowl, 1991. **Business Addr:** Professional Football Player, Seattle Seahawks, 11220 NE 53rd St, Kirkland, WA 98033, (206)827-9777.

BLADES, BRIAN KEITH
Professional football player. **Personal:** Born Jul 24, 1965, Fort Lauderdale, FL. **Educ:** Univ of Miami (FL), attended. **Career:** Seattle Seahawks, wide receiver, 1988-. **Honors/Awds:** Played in Pro Bowl, post-1989 season. **Business Addr:** Professional Football Player, Seattle Seahawks, 11220 NE 53rd St, Kirkland, WA 98033, (206)827-9777.

BLADE-TIGGENS, DENISE PATRICIA
Attorney. **Personal:** Born Dec 16, 1957, Chicago, IL; daughter of Mary Lucille Blade and Marshall Blade; married Willie Tiggens Jr, Apr 4, 1981. **Educ:** Southern Illinois University, BS, 1978; Chicago State University, MS, 1979; John Marshall Law School, JD, 1989. **Career:** Volunteers of America, counselor, 1978-79; Department of Justice, correctional officer, 1979-81; Cook County Juvenile Services, caseworker, 1981-82; Chicago Police Department, police officer, 1982-90; Hyatt Legal Services, attorney, 1990-91; D Blade-Tiggens & Associates, partner, 1992-. **Orgs:** United Citizens Community Organization, consultant, 1980-; American Bar Association, 1986-; Illinois Bar Association, 1986-; Chicago Bar Association, 1986-; Phi Delta Phi, 1987-. **Honors/Awds:** International Legal Fraternity, Phi Delta Phi, Scholastic Achievement Award, 1987. **Business Addr:** Partner, D Blade-Tiggens & Associates, 17027 Meadowcrest, Lockport, IL 60441, (815)462-1212.

BLAIR, CHARLES MICHAEL
Newspaper owner, philanthropy administrator. **Personal:** Born Aug 5, 1947, Indianapolis, IN; married Margo Mills Blair; children: Michael A, Tchad K. **Educ:** Oberlin Coll, AB Communications 1970; Kean Coll, MA Stdnt & Personnel Admin 1972. **Career:** Lilly Endowment Inc, program evaluator 1973, asso pgm officer 1975, pgm officer 1977, senior pgm officer 1981-; President & Owner, Grand Slam Inc and Interlace Marketing Inc 1986-91; Sports, entertainment & Mgmt Consultants; Indianapolis Recorder Newspaper, co-owner, vice pres, president, currently. **Orgs:** Chmn Assoc of Black Found Exec 1980-83; founder & bd mem Madame CJ Walker Bldg Restoration Project 1979-; consult Fund Raising to Numerous Organ 1977- ;chmn bd Blair Communications Indep Prod 1979-; bd of dir Big Bro Big Sisters Intl 1982-; bd of dir & Founder Youth Works Inc 1979-; Bd of dir & founder Ind Black Expo Found 1984-; Founder and Vice Chairman Bussiness Opportunities Systems, Inc, Vice Chairman Flanner Hous Inc Founder & president Youth Works, Inc. **Honors/Awds:** Martin Luther King Award North Ward Cntr Newark NJ 1982; producer writer 5 Stage Plays, Middle Passage, Songs for Creator 1979-; Honored Spec Advocate for Girls Girls Club of Am New York City 1979; Community Service Award Center for Leadership Devel Indianapolis 1984; roastee Indianapolis Links 1983. **Special Achievements:** Executive producer of documentary film ''Facing the Facade.''. **Business Addr:** President, Indianapolis Recorder Newspaper, 2901 N Tacoma Ave, Indianapolis, IN 46218.

BLAIR, CHESTER LAUGHTON ELLISON
Attorney, association executive. **Personal:** Born Jul 2, 1928, Corsicana, TX; married Judith K; children: Gregory, Bradford, Jefferson, Jan, Brent, Judy-Lee. **Educ:** Chicago Teachers Coll, BEd 1952; John Marshall Law School, JD 1959. **Career:** Chicago Publ School, teacher, 1952-54, 1956-59; private practice, attorney, 1959-; 7th Congress dist of IL, legal counselor 1974-78; Blair & Cole, founding partner 1974-. **Orgs:** Chicago Bar Association, president, 1989-; Cook County Bar Association, president, 1978; Illinois Trial Lawyers Association; Association of Trial Lawyers of America; American Bar Association, Tort and Insurance Practice Section; Attorney Registration & Disciplinary Commission, review board, 1978-84, chairman, 1984-89; Illinois Supreme Court Committee on Professional Standards, 1977-84; Illinois Institute of Continuing Legal Education, board of directors, 1988-91; Chicago Bar Association, 1985-87. **Honors/Awds:** Black Awareness Awd Coll of St Thomas Min Prog 1977; Cook County Bar Association, Earl H Wright Award, 1989; guest instructor, National College of Advocacy, Advanced Trial Practice, 1991; guest speaker, National Association of Bar Executives Annual Meeting, 1990. **Special Achievements:** Author, Chapter 13, ''Return of the Verdict,'' ICCLE Illinois Civil Practice Series, 1988, 1992. **Military Serv:** AUS spec 1st class 1954-56. **Business Addr:** Attorney, 310 S Michigan Ave, #2700, Chicago, IL 60604.

BLAIR, CURTIS
Professional basketball player. **Career:** Houston Rockets, professional basketball player, 1992-. **Business Addr:** Professional Basketball Player, Houston Rockets, PO Box 272349, Houston, TX 77277, (713)627-0600.

BLAIR, GEORGE ELLIS, JR.
Foundation executive, publisher. **Personal:** Born May 5, 1932, Braddock, PA; son of Edith Madden Cowans and George E Blair, Sr; married Eleanor Ann Blair, Sep 29, 1956; children: Cheryl Ann, Stephanie Rene Warner. **Educ:** Indiana Univ, BS, 1954; Adelphia Univ, Garden City, NY, MS, 1959; St John's Univ, Jamaica, NY, PhD, 1959-63. **Career:** Indiana Public Schools, teacher, 1953-54; Rockville Ctr Public Schools, teacher, guidance counselor, administrator, 1956-66; Drug Prevention, Treatment and Rehabilitation Program, consultant, 1965-; Roslyn Public Schools, asst supt for special programs, 1965-66; NY State Dept of Educ, asst commissioner for innovations in education, 1966-70, assoc commissioner for urban ed, 1970-72; ordained minister, 1970-; Long Island Univ, vice pres for planning and development, 1972-75; US Steel Companies of America, arbitrator, 1975-; CUNY, Borough of Manhattan Community Coll, NYC Educational Opportunity Ctr, dean of education, and dir, 1975-77; State Univ of NY, asst vice chancellor for special programs, 1977-78, assoc chancellor for special programs, 1978-79, deputy to the chancellor for special programs, 1979-82, executive asst to the chancellor, 1982-89; Black World Championship Rodeo, founder/pres, 1989-1993; Ascent Foundation, pres, 1993-. **Orgs:** New York City Riding Academy, chairman, bd of dirs; NYC Rikers Island Correctional Facility, Community Advisory Committee, chairman; Ascent Publishing Co, chairman, bd of dirs; Human Affairs Research Ctr, pres, bd of dirs; Urban Ctr for Research and Communications, pres, chairman bd of dirs; Summit Transportation, chairman, bd of dirs; Summit Farms, chairman, bd of dirs; Camp Pioneer, chairman, bd of dirs. **Honors/Awds:** NYC Dept of Parks and Recreation, Light of the World Awards. **Special Achievements:** Editor, Indiana News; editor-in-chief, Ascent Magazine, Harlem Week Magazine, Tennis Classic Magazine, Metropolitan Profile Magazine, Black New Yorker Magazine. **Military Serv:** US Army, First Lt, 1954-61. **Business Addr:** Publisher and Editor-in-Chief, The Black New Yorker Magazine, 156 Fifth Ave, Suite 812, New York, NY 10010.

BLAIR, JAMES H.
Business executive. **Personal:** Born Oct 6, 1926, Pittsburgh, PA; married Murleen M; children: Keith J, Steven M. **Educ:** Univ of Pittsburgh, BA 1950; Rutgers Univ, MA 1971, Doctoral Candidate 1971-72. **Career:** Essex Cty Probation Dept Newark NJ, sr probation officer 1953-64; United Comm Corp, comm action dir 1965-66, prog dir 1966-67; Ofc of Tech Asst Dept of Comm Affairs Trenton NJ, dir 1967-69; NJ Div on Civil Rights Newark, dir 1968; JH Blair Assoc, pres 1977-; Fair Housing Equal Oppty Dept of Housing & Urban Devel Wash DC, asst sec; MI Dept of Civil Rights, exec dir; MI Comm on Criminal Justice, commiss 1972-. **Orgs:** Mme bd dir NJ State C of C 1972-74; chmn Intl Assoc of Ofcl Human Rights Agys 1970-71; commiss NJ State Prof Occup License Study Comm 1970-71; mem State Adv Council Inst of Mgmt & Labor Rel Rutgers Univ 1969-73; mem bd dir Montclair NJ YMCA 1960-64,69-72; mem Gov Council on Urban Affairs NJ 1968-69; mem Kappa Alpha Psi 1947-, Frontiers Intl 1966-, NAACP. **Honors/Awds:** Humanitarian Awd Montclair Br 1973; Outstanding Contribs Awd 1975 MI Civil Rights Comm; Kappa Alpha Psi Achievement Awd 1969. **Military Serv:** USAAC 1944-47. **Business Addr:** Commissioner, MI Commiss on Criminal Justice, 3625 Stonewall Court, Atlanta, GA 30339.

BLAIR, LACY GORDON
Physician. **Personal:** Born Oct 10, 1937, Lynchburg, VA; son of Sara Williams Blair and Lacy Blair. **Educ:** Hampton Inst, BS 1959; Meharry Med Coll, MD 1969. **Career:** Military Svc, lab tech 1961-64; Private practice, physician. **Orgs:** Writer, intl traveler; student of Ethiopia's History and The Hebrews; National Medical Association; United African Movement.

BLAIZE, MAVIS. **See THOMPSON, MAVIS SARAH.**

BLAKE, ALPHONSO R.
Clergyman. **Personal:** Born Apr 23, 1935, Charleston, SC; married Doris Jackson; children: Sybil Renee, Alphonso Jr. **Educ:** Amer Bapt Theol Sem, BA 1961. **Career:** WPAZ Radio, religious dir; Concentrated Employment Prog, counselor; Westwood Bapt Church Nashville, pastor; Morris St Baptist Church, pastor. **Orgs:** Pres Bapt Ministers Conf Charles Co; past pres, treas Charles Cty SS&BTU Congress; chmn exec com Charles Cty Bapt Assoc; past pres Charles Cty NAACP; trustee Charleston Cty School Dist, Morris Coll, Sumpter SC; chaplain Charleston Cty Jail. **Honors/Awds:** NAACP Outstanding Freedom Fighter Citation; Omega Psi Phi Frat Scroll of Honor; Charles Cty Adult Ed Prog Citation. **Military Serv:** AUS 1954-56. **Business Addr:** Pastor, Morris St Baptist Church, Charleston, SC 29403.

BLAKE, CARL LEROY
Administrator, concert pianist. **Personal:** Born Sep 25, 1951, Liberty, MO; son of Hazel Roberson Blake and Rev William Louis Blake. **Educ:** Boston University, Boston, MA, bachelor of music, magna cum laude, 1973; San Jose State University, San Jose, CA, MA, music, 1976; Cornell University, Ithaca, NY, doctor of musical arts, 1988. **Career:** City of San Jose, Fine Arts Commission, San Jose, CA, music specialist, 1977-78; Bishop College, Dallas, TX, chrm, music dept, asst prof of music, 1978-79; Ohio University, Athens, OH, music lecturer, 1980-84; Music & Arts Institute, San Francisco, CA, music instructor, 1988-89; Pennsylvania State University, University Park, PA, asst dean, College of Arts and Arch, assoc dir & asst prof of music, 1989-. **Orgs:** Member, Natl Music Honor Society, Pi Kappa Lambda, 1973-; member, American Matthay Association, 1988-. **Honors/Awds:** Marian Anderson Young Artist Award, Today's Artists Concerts, Inc, San Francisco, CA, 1978; Carnegie Recital Hall debut presented by Today's Artists Concerts, Inc, 1986; grant for foreign study abroad with Pierre Sancan, Paris Conservatory of Music, 1980-81; Harold C Case Scholar, Honors Award in Piano Performance, Boston University, 1972. **Special Achievements:** Weill Recital, 1986, 1992, 1996; Artistic Ambassador to Brazil, Caribbean Islands, and Central and South America, 1996; Artist in Residence Hereen State Pedagogical University in St. Petersburg, Russia, 1997. **Business Addr:** Associate Dir & Associate Prof of Music, Institute for the Arts & Humanistic Studies, The Pennsylvania State University, Ihlseng Cottage, University Park, PA 16802-1703.

BLAKE, CARLTON HUGH
Psychiatrist. **Personal:** Born Apr 11, 1934, San Fernando, Trinidad and Tobago; son of Thelma Marshall Carty and Fitzevans Blake; married Carmelita, Oct 16, 1976; children: David. **Educ:** Fatima Coll, Sr Cambridge Cert Grade 1; Queens Univ, MB, BCh, BaO 1960; NY School of Psychiatry, Cert Psych 1964. **Career:** Albert Einstein Coll, asst clinical prof 1969-71; Sound View-Throgs Neck Comm Mental Health Ctr, asst dir 1969-71; Sunrise Psychiatric Clinic, suprv psychiatrist 1971-75; Roosevelt Mental Health Ctr, comm psychiatrist 1972-74, med dir 1974-79; private practice, psychiatrist 1964-; Freeport School Dist, psychiatric consult 1974-89; Nassau Ctr for Developmentally Disabled, med dir 1985-89; Mercy Hosp, psychiatrist 1973-, attending 1971-; Nassau Co, Dept of Drug & Alcohol Abuse, Roosevelt, NY, consultant, 1988-89; med Mercy Hospital, Psychiatric Dept, Rockville Centre NY 1973-; Woodhull Med Associates, New York, NY, director of education and training, 1990-. **Orgs:** Mem NY Soc of Acupuncture for Physicians & Dentists, NY State Qualified Psych 1968-, NY State Qualified Acupuncturist 1975-; mem bd of vis Suffolk Devel Ctr 1976-83, NY Cty Med Soc, Nassau Psych Soc, FRSH; faculty State Univ Stoney Brook; mem NMA, FAPA; diplomate Amer Bd of Psych & Neurol 1976-. **Honors/Awds:** Many publications. **Home Addr:** 343 Washington Ave, Roosevelt, NY 11575. **Business Addr:** PO Box 327, Farmingdale, NY 11735-0327.

BLAKE, ELIAS, JR.
Educational administrator. **Personal:** Born Dec 13, 1929, Brunswick, GA; married Mona Williams; children: Michael, Elias Ayinde. **Educ:** Paine Coll, BA 1951; Howard U, MA 1954; Univ of IL, PhD 1960. **Career:** Inst for Serv to Educ, dir of upward bound 1967-66, dir of evaluation 1969-67, pres 1969-77; Clark Coll, pres, beginning 1977; Howard Univ, dir, Higher Educ Policy Research, currently. **Honors/Awds:** Outstanding tchr Coll of Liberal Arts Howard Univ 1964; meritorious achievement TN State Univ 1981; distinguished serv OH State Univ 1983; Honorary Doctorate, Paine College 1985; Documentary Film ''The Story of One'' 1986; Distinguished Achievement Awd Southern Univ 1986; Honors of the Southeastern Assn of Educational Opp Program Personnel 1985.

BLAKE, J. HERMAN
Educator. **Personal:** Born Mar 15, 1934, Mt Vernon, NY; son of Lylace Michael Blake and J Henry Blake; married Maria W Brown; children: Vanessa E, Lylace Y, Audrey RA, Denise L, L Sidney Nathaniel. **Educ:** NY Univ, BA 1960; Univ CA, MA 1965, PhD 1973. **Career:** Univ CA, asst prof 1966-70, assoc prof 1970-74; UCSC, prof 1974-84; Oakes Coll UCSC, founding provost 1972-84; Tougaloo Coll, pres 1984-87. **Orgs:** Mem Amer Sociol Assn, Population Assn of Amer, Pacific Sociol Assn; bd trustee Save the Children Fedn; bd trustee Penn Comm Serv Fellowships Woodrow Wilson 1960, John Hay Whitney 1963; mem Population Council 1964; Danforth Found 1964; Rockefeller Found 1965; Ford Found 1970. **Honors/Awds:** Coauthor ''Revolutionary Suicide'' 1973; named among Top 100 Emerging Young Leaders in Higher Educ Amer Council of Educ 1978. **Business Addr:** Professor, Swarthmore College, Department of Sociology, Swarthmore, PA 19081.

BLAKE, J. PAUL
Public relations executive, educator. **Personal:** Born Mar 31, 1950, Neptune, NJ; son of Shirley Blake. **Educ:** Drake Univ, BA 1972. **Career:** University of Minnesota, assistant director of university relations 1976-83, assistant to vice president for student development, 1983-86; Pandamonium, pres 1986-88; Seattle University, assistant vice president and director of public relations, Communications Department, instructor, currently. **Orgs:** Bd of trustees Council for Advancement and Support of Educ 1982-84, 1992-94; pres MN Press Club 1988; bd of dir US China Peoples Friendship Assoc MN Chapt. **Honors/Awds:** Volunteer Serv Awd, Minneapolis Urban League, 1977; Good Neighbor Awd, WCCO-AM Radio, 1982; Outstanding Service Award, University of Minnesota, 1984; Positive Image Award, Minneapolis Urban League, 1984. **Business Addr:** Asst VP/Dir, PR/Instructor, Comm Dept, Seattle University, Seattle, WA 98122.

BLAKE, JAMES G.
Minister, executive director. **Personal:** Born Dec 4, 1944, Charleston, SC. **Educ:** Morehouse Coll, AB 1965; Boston Univ School of Theol, MTh 1968. **Career:** Gov of RI, spec asst 1968; Interfaith City-Wide Coord Com NYC, exec dir 1968-71; Union AME Church Little Rock, pastor 1971-72; Sen Hubert Humphrey, natl field coord 1972; SC Comm For Farm Workers Inc, exec dir. **Orgs:** Mem, natl vice pres NAACP; mem Selec Comm, US Youth Council; del World Assembly of Youth Leige Belgium 1970; del The World Council of Chs 1975; coord The Del of Black Religious Ldrs to Republic of China 1976; del 1st Pan African Youth Festival Tunis Tunisia 1972. **Business Addr:** Pastor, Gr Zion AME Church, 134 Meeting St, PO 861, Charleston, SC 29402.

BLAKE, JEFF
Professional football player. **Personal:** Born Dec 4, 1970, Daytona Beach, FL; son of Emory Blake; married Lewanna; children: Emory, Torre, Trey. **Educ:** East Carolina. **Career:** Cincinnati Bengals, 1994-; New York Jets, 1992-94. **Special Achievements:** Pro Bowl, 1995; one of nine African-American quarterbacks, largest number in NFL history, 1997. **Business Addr:** Professional football player, Cincinnati Bengals, One Bengals Dr, Cincinnati, OH 45202, (513)621-3550.

BLAKE, JOHN
Football coach. **Personal:** married Freda. **Career:** Dallas Cowboys, asst coach; Univ of Oklahoma, head coach, 1996-. **Business Addr:** Head Coach, Football, University of Oklahoma, 180 W Brooks, Rm E8, Norman, OK 73019.

BLAKE, MILTON JAMES
Labor/industrial relations manager. **Personal:** Born Nov 11, 1934, Chicago, IL; married Beverly Marlene Skyles; children:

Milton J Jr (dec), Robin. **Educ:** Bradley Univ Peoria IL, BS Indust Arts 1957. **Career:** AUS Active & Res, infantry officer 1955-; Chicago Police Dept , human rel officer 1961-65; Continental Can Co, suprv indust rel 1966-72; Whittaker Metals,div mgr indust rel 1972-74; Gulf & Western Energy Products Group, group mgr employee rel 1974-78; Bunker Ramo Corp, corp mgr eeo & compliance mgmt 1979-; Amphenol Co, dir salary admin, org plnng & devel 1982-. **Orgs:** Mem indust rel adv comm Univ of WI 1971-; consult EEO, Gulf & Western 1979; youth adv St James Luthern Church 1961-66; mem Oak Brook Assoc of Commerce & Indust 1979-; mem Chicago Urban Affairs Council 1982; mem bd of dir Chicago Childrens Choir 1980; mem Alpha Phi Alpha, Alpha Phi Omega, Phi Mu Alpha. **Honors/Awds:** Hon Mention Chicago Police Dept 1961; ;author "Supervisory Awareness Program" Continental Can Co 1969; vstg instr Affirm Action Prog Univ of WI 1977; Publ Affirm Action Prog Bunker Ramo Corp 1979; Good Conduct Medal AUS 1957. **Military Serv:** AUS lt col 30 yrs; Armed Forces Reserve Medal 1976. **Business Addr:** Dir Salary Administrator, Amphenol Co, 900 Commerce Dr, Oak Brook, IL 60521.

BLAKE, PEGGY JONES
Librarian. **Personal:** Born Jan 26, 1946, Georgetown, GA; daughter of Carrie Griggs Jones and David Jones; married. **Educ:** Tuskegee University, Tuskegee, AL, BS, 1968; University of Michigan, Ann Arbor, MI, AMLS, 1974. **Career:** National Library of Medicine, Bethesda, MD, librarian, 1974-87; Morehouse School of Medicine, Library, Atlanta, GA, AHEC librarian, 1987-89; National Agricultural Library, Beltsville, MD, ARS coordinator, 1989-96, special asst to the dir, 1996-. **Orgs:** American Library Assn, 1974-76, 1989-; Medical Library Assn, 1974-87; United States Agricultural Information Network, 1989-; Black Caucus of the American Library Association, 1990-; Associates of the National Agricultural Library, 1989-; Tuskegee University Alumni Assn, 1976-. **Honors/Awds:** Post-Graduate Intern Library Associate, National Library of Medicine, 1980-81; Scholarship Award, Special Library Assn, 1972; Certification-Medical Librarian, Medical Library Assn, 1975-86. **Business Addr:** Special Assistant to the Director, Office of Director, National Agricultural Library, 10301 Baltimore Blvd, Rm 100, Beltsville, MD 20705.

BLAKE, WENDELL OWEN
Physician. **Personal:** Born Aug 9, 1940, Bartow, FL; married Mildred; children: Wendi, Michael. **Educ:** Howard Univ, BS 1961; Meharry Med Coll, MD 1967. **Career:** Good Samaritan Hosp, intern 1967-68; Meharry Med Coll, resident 1968-72; Surg Oncology, fellow; Roswell Park Meml Inst, physician 1974-75; Private Practice, physician genl surgeon. **Orgs:** Soc of Abdominal Surgeons; FL Med Assn, Polk Co Med Assn of FL, natl Med Assn, FL Med Dental & Pharm Assn; staff mem Lakeland Regional Med Ctr, chief Genl Surgery, 1984; polemarch Lakeland Alumni Chapt; diplomate Amer Bd of Surgery; Kappa Alpha Psi Fraternity, national chairman, life membership committee; Boys and Girls Club of Lakeland, Florida, president, board of directors, 1993. **Honors/Awds:** Awd for Achievement in recog meritorious performance of duty US Kenner Army Hosp 1972-74; publ "Thyroid Surgery at Hubbard Hosp" Jour Natl Med Assn;"The Changing Picture of Carcinoma of the Lung" Jour Natl Med Assn; Fellow Southeastern Surgical Congress; Polk County, Florida, School Board Award Recipient, 1991. **Military Serv:** AUS mc major 1972-74. **Business Addr:** 505 Martin L King Jr, Lakeland, FL 33801.

BLAKELY, ALLISON
Educator, author. **Personal:** son Of Alice Blakely and Ed Walton; married Shirley Ann Reynolds Blakely, Jul 5, 1968; children: Shantel Lynn, Andrei. **Educ:** Oregon State Colege, Corvallis, OR, 1958-60; University of Oregon, Eugene, OR, BA, 1962; Univ of California, Berkeley, CA, MA, 1964, PhD, 1971. **Career:** US Army Active Duty, 1966-68; Stanford University, Stanford, CA, instructor, 1970-71; Howard University, Washington, DC, assistant professor, 1971-77, associate professor, 1977-87, professor, 1987-. **Orgs:** Chair, Scholarly Worth Committee, Howard University Press, 1989-; member, Committee on Qualifications, Phi Beta Kappa Society, 1991-97; American Historical Association, Association for the Advancement of Slavic Studies, World History Association; Phi Beta Kappa, Governing Senate, 1994-2000. **Honors/Awds:** Author, Russia and the Negro: Blacks in Russian History and Thought, Howard U Pr, 1986; Recipient of the American Book Award, 1988; Fulbright-Hays Research Fellowship, 1985-86; Andrew Mellon Fellow, Aspen Institute for the Humanities, 1976-77; Woodrow Wilson Fellow, Woodrow Wilson Foundation, 1962-63. **Special Achievements:** Author, Blacks in the Dutch World: the Evolution of Racial Imagery in a Modern Society, Indiana U Pr, 1994. **Military Serv:** Military Intelligence, Captain, 1966-68; Bronze Star, Purple Heart, 1968. **Home Addr:** 1 Sunnyside Road, Silver Spring, MD 20910. **Business Addr:** Professor, Dept of History, Howard University, Washington, DC 20059.

BLAKELY, CAROLYN
Educational administrator. **Career:** University of Arkansas, Pine Bluff, former interim chancellor, Honors College, dean, currently. **Orgs:** Natl Collegiate Honors Council, 1980-; Natl Council of Teachers of English, 1980-; Southern Regional Honors Council, 1980-, president, 1991; National Association of African-American Honors Programs, past president. **Honors/Awds:** Top 100 Women in Arkansas; Distingushed Alumnus-UAPB. **Business Addr:** Dean, Honors College, University of Arkansas, Pine Bluff, 1200 N University Dr, Pine Bluff, AR 71601, (501)543-8065.

BLAKELY, CHARLES
Educational administrator. **Personal:** Born Jan 31, 1951, Batesville, MS; son of Edna Blakely and Willie Blakely (deceased); widowed. **Educ:** Coahoma Jr Coll, AA 1972; Jackson State Univ, BS 1975; attended MS State Univ one semester 1973, Delta State Univ two semesters 1981-82, Univ of MS one semester 1984. **Career:** Jackson State Univ, student admin clerk 1974-75; North Panola Vocational High School, substitute teacher 1975-78; Northwest Jr Coll Greenhill Elementary School, adult basic educ instructor 1981-88; Inst of Comm Serv, licensed social worker 1988-; North Panola Consolidated School Dist I, pres school bd 1989-90, secretary, 1991; Panola Co, school attendance officer, counselor, 1989-; St Francis Behavior Center, counselor/consultant; Path Finder, youth counselor; North Panola High School, Continuing Education Dept, site supervisor, 1992-. **Orgs:** Member, Cavalette Social Club; pres, Sardis Panola County Voters League 1980-88; asst supt of Sunday school, Miles Chapel CME Church 1982-; bd member, MACE affiliate local bd for continued educ 1983-85; bd member Selective Serv Local Draft Bd representing Panola County 1981-93; bd mem, Democratic Exec Comm for Panola County 1984-93; pres, North Panola School Bd of Educ 1989-90; member, Stewart Bd; member, part time Sunday school teacher, member of choir, Miles Chapel CME Church, school board member, 1980-92, selective service board member, 1981-. **Honors/Awds:** Certificate in recognition of noteworthy performance of serv MS United for Progress to the Black Comm 1980-81; certificate award Outstanding Serv in the Community NAACP 1982; outstanding serv and dedication and cooperation in the community Panola County Voter League Inc 1982; staff of the year, Inst of Community Serv Headstart Program, 1989; Outstanding School Board Award for Svc Rendered, 1990; Certified Master Addiction Counselor, 1996-; Certified Criminal Justice Specialist, 1996-. **Home Addr:** 19324 Hwy 51, Sardis, MS 38666. **Business Addr:** School Attendance Officer/Counselor, PO Box 141, Sardis, MS 38666.

BLAKELY, EDWARD JAMES
Educator. **Personal:** Born Apr 21, 1938, San Bernardino, CA; son of Josephine Carter and Edward Blakely; married Maaike van der Slessen; children: Pieta, Brette. **Educ:** San Bernardino Valley Coll, AA 1958; Univ of CA, BA 1960, MA 1964; Pasadena Coll, MA 1967; Univ of CA, PhD 1971. **Career:** UCLA Ext, training dir 1966-68; Western Comm Action Training Inc, exec dir 1968-70; US State Dept, special asst to asst sec 1970-71; Univ of Pittsburgh, asst to chancellor 1971-74; Univ of CA, dean, asst vice pres 1977-84, professor 1976-. **Orgs:** Consult US Agcy Intl Devel, United Nations & others; bd dir YMCA 1972-74; NAACP Pittsburgh 1972-74; Comm Devel Soc of Am 1976-; Intl Soc of Educ Planners 1977-. **Honors/Awds:** All League Football & Basketball 1953-56; Young Man Yr San Bernardino 1955, 1958; hon mention Small Coll Coast Football 1959; Scholar Athlete Award Univ of CA 1959; Most Inspirational Player UC 1959; Coro Found Fellow 1960; Sgt Shriver Rural Serv Award 1968; NAACP Comm Serv Award 1970; Civic Serv Award Richmond, CA 1984; author of over 20 articles & 3 books on comm planning & devel; received 125th Anniversary Professor Award, 1992; Hall of Fame Athlete, 1991; San Francisco Foundation Award for Service to the Bay Area, 1991. **Military Serv:** USAF 1st Lt 1961-64; Outstanding Ofcr Training 1961. **Business Addr:** Professor, University of California, Dept of City & Regional Planning, Berkeley, CA 94720.

BLAKELY, RONALD EUGENE
Government official. **Personal:** Born Feb 22, 1952, Spartanburg, SC; son of Melba Foster Blakely and Lonnie William Blakely Jr; divorced. **Educ:** Tuskegee Univ, BA; Pepperdine Univ, MA, 1980. **Career:** US Army, recruiting officer, 1975-76, personnel officer, 1976-78, human relations officer, 1978-80, equal emp specialist, 1980-82, equal emp officer, 1983-87; US Environmental Protection Agency, equal employment mgr, currently. **Orgs:** NAACP; SCLC; Masonic Org; MLK Federal Holiday Committee, 1988; Historically Black Colleges & Universities, interagency liaison, 1988-; Blacks in Government, Region XI, vice pres, 1981-83; National Guard Assn, 1980-. **Military Serv:** US Army, Captain, 1975-80; Meritorious Service Medal; Point Service Commendation. **Business Addr:** Equal Employment Manager, US Environmenta Protection Agency, Office of Civil Rights, 401 M St SW, Room 206 WT (A-105), Washington, DC 20460-0001.

BLAKELY, WILLIAM H., JR.
Executive search consultant. **Personal:** Born Feb 12, 1927, Warren, OH; son of Romelia Blakely and William Blakely Sr; married Marcelle Wallace; children: Donna, Glenn. **Educ:** NC A&T Univ, BS Sociology & History (w/honors) 1952; Rutgers Univ, postgrad. **Career:** Staff Univ Settlement NYC, mem 1952-62; Lillian Wald Recreation Rooms Settlement NYC, evening dir 1963-64; Urban League Skills Bank Newark, dir 1964-67; Engelhard Industries Newark, industrial relations rep 1967-74; Engelhard Mineral & Chem Corp Iselin NJ, corp mgr personnel; Phibro-Salomon Inc NYC, corp mgr employee relations 1981-85; WR Lazard & Co Inc, consultant 1985; Sandia Machine Co, consultant 1986; Salomon Inc, consultant 1986; Salomon Bros, consultant 1987; Radd Maintenance & Supply Co, pres 1987; H C Smith Ltd, senior assoc 1988, managing director, chemical and technical areas, 1991-; Strategic Financial Systems, consultant 1989; Ty Blake Ltd, chairman, executive search consultant, 1992-. **Orgs:** Mem NJ Corps Comm United Negro Coll Fund; bd dirs past pres Urban League Essex Co 1968-75; mem chancellor's council NC A&T Univ; mem pres The EDGES Group Inc staff pres's office 1984-85; mem Newark Comm Affairs Group Businessmen Century Club of YMCA; trustee Kessler Inst Rehab; bd dirs Interracial Council Business Oppor, Better Business Bureau Project Pride, Harlem Br YMCA, Black Achievers; pres bd dirs Urban Leaguers Inc; vice pres West Kenney Jr HS Scholarship Fund; commr juries Essex Co 1968-75; mem exec comm NCCJ; mem Natl Urban League Grand St Boys Assn C of C; mem Sigma Rho Sigma, Omega Psi Phi; bd of dirs General Machine Co 1985, Radd Maintenance & Supply Co 1986. **Honors/Awds:** Achievement Awd Frontiersman Amer 1974; Awd Human & Civil Rights Assn NJ 1976; Awd Black Achievers in Industry 1976; Project Pride 1979; FOCUS Awd 1979; Awd United Comm Corp Union Co Urban League; NC A&T Univ Alumni Awd 1978; named to Athletic Hall of Fame 1978; Humanitarian Awd Essex Co Urban League Guild 1980; NCCJ Awd 1981; Larrie Stalk's Civic Assn Awd 1981; Black Achievers in Industry Awd 1975; Chmn's Plaque Congressional Black Caucus Found Inc 1982; NAACP Corporate Awd of Achievement 1986; Congressional Black Caucus 1986; Service Award, NAACP Oranges and Maplewood New Jersey 1988; Champion of Change, Anti Defamation League Award, 1997. **Business Addr:** Generalist, Tyblake Ltd, 6 N Cobane Terr, West Orange, NJ 07052.

BLAKEY, WILLIAM A.
Attorney. **Personal:** Born Sep 1, 1943, Louisville, KY. **Educ:** Knoxville Coll, BA 1965; Howard Univ Sch of Law, JD 1968; Georgetown Law Ctr, pursuing LLM. **Career:** Sen Daniel Brewster, exec asst/spl asst 1965-68; Dept of HUD, atty adv 1968-69; Natl Urban Coalition, exec asst to vice pres for field opers 1969-70; Transcentury Corp, vice pres sr assoc 1970-71; AL Nellum & Asssoc, sr assoc 1971-72; US Commn on Civil Rights, spl asst to staff dir 1972-74; KY Comm on Human Rights, lgl spclst/atty 1976-77; DHEW, dep asst sec for legis 1977-80; US Commn on Civil Rights, dir congressional Liaison 1974-. **Orgs:** Consult Neighborhood Consumer Information Ctr 1968; instr in Common Legal Problems Control Data Corp 1969 1971; mem KY, WA, Amer Natl Bar Assns; Omega PsiPhi Frat; Phi Alpha Delta Law Frat; Sen Waeden St Stephen Incarnation Episcopal; mem bd Louisville Br NAACP Legal Aid Soc of Louisville 1976-77; The Inner Voices Inc; chmn The Minority & Legislative Educ Proj chmn 1979-80; Natl Bar Assn 1975; Congressional Action Fund 1970-72. **Honors/Awds:** Omega Psi Phi Dist Scholar 1965; Alpha Kappa Mu & Phi Alpha Theta Hon Soc. **Business Addr:** Senior Legislative Assistant, Senator Paul Simon, 462 Dirksen Senate Office Bldg, Washington, DC 20510.

BLALOCK, MARION W.
Educational director. **Personal:** Born Dec 18, 1947, East Chicago, IN; married Roger; children: Erin Juliane. **Educ:** Purdue Univ, BA 1969, MS 1973. **Career:** Parker Career Ctr, employment counselor 1970; Family Serv of Metro Detroit, family caseworker 1970-71; Purdue Univ, grad teaching asst 1971-73, asst dean of students 1974-75, dir mep and academic advisor freshman engrg 1975-. **Orgs:** Faculty advisor and mem natl adv bd Natl Soc of Black Engrs; mem Natl Assoc of Minority Engrg Program Administrators, Amer Soc for Engrg Educ, Black Colls Develop Comm; vice chair of steering comm Purdue Black Alumnmi Organization; bd dirs Tippecanoe Area Planned Parenthood Assoc 1985-88. **Honors/Awds:** Dean M Beverly Stone Awd 1982; Hon member Golden Key Natl Honor Soc; Vincent M Bendix Minorities in Engrg Awd Amer Soc of Engrg Educ 1983; Reginald H Jones Disting Serv Awd Natl Action Council for Minorities in Engrg 1984; President's Affirmative Action Awd Purdue Univ 1985; Best Teacher Awd Dept of Freshman Engrg Purdue Univ 1985, 86; Outstanding Advisor of the Natl Adv Bd Natl Soc of Black Engrs 1986; Helen B Schleman Awd 1986; Hon member Iron Key; Hon member Natl Soc of Black Engrs Purdue Chapt. **Business Addr:** Dir Minority Engrg, Purdue Univ, Room 211 ENAD Bldg, West Lafayette, IN 47907.

BLANC, ERIC ANTHONY-HAWKINS
Events coordinator. **Personal:** Born Jun 10, 1969, New Orleans, LA; son of Rosa Hawkins and Stephen Blanc; married Dori, Jun 13, 1992; children: Kendal. **Educ:** Florida State Univ, BS, Marketing, 1991. **Career:** Copitech Corp, marketing consultant, 1991-92; Thunderdome, events coord, 1992-93; Tampa Convention Center, sr events coord, 1993-. **Orgs:** Florida Classic Assn, host committee chair, 1994-; NAACP, 1991-94; NAACP Youth Council, advisor, 1991-94; Omega Psi Phi Fraternity Inc. **Business Addr:** Senior Events Coord, Tampa, FL, Convention Facilities/Tampa Convention Center, 333 S Franklin St, Event Services Dept, Tampa, FL 33602, (813)274-7760.

BLANCHET, WALDO WILLIE E.
Educator (retired). **Personal:** Born Aug 6, 1910, New Orleans, LA; married Josephine Lavizzo; children: Geri Therese, Waldo E Jr. **Educ:** Talladega Coll, AB 1931; Univ of MI, MS 1936, PhD 1946. **Career:** Fort Valley N & I Sch, sci tchr 1932-35, dean 1936-39; Fort Valley State Coll, prof physical sci & adm dean 1939-66, pres 1966-73, pres emeritus, 1973-. **Honors/Awds:** Consultant to sci tchrs Adv Cncl on Educ of Disadvantaged Children 1970-72; sci research & sci teaching fellowship Atlanta Univ 1931-32; fellowship Genl Educ Bd Univ of MI 1935-36, 1938-39; Phi Kappa Phi Hon Scholastic Soc; Phi Delta Kappa Univ of MI; pres Natl Assn of Research in Sci Teaching 1957; Sci Educ Magazine Award; NARST Award. **Home Addr:** 508 Camelot Dr, College Park, GA 30349.

BLAND, ARTHUR H.
Government employee. **Personal:** Born Dec 1, 1923, Milledgeville, GA; married Valerie Howard; children: Deborah, Stephanie, Angela. **Educ:** Ohio State Univ, BS, 1950; Central Michigan Univ, grad study; Attended, Industrial Coll of Armed Forces, Air War Coll. **Career:** Dept of Defense, entire career has been within defense dept presently systems mgr. **Orgs:** Mem Amer Logistics Assn; bd mem Comm Serv Corp; mem adv bd Columbus Parks & Recreation; mem adv bd Columbus Metro Parks Dist Adv Bd; bd mem Central Comm House. **Honors/Awds:** Meritorious Civilian Serv Awd 1968; Ten Outstanding Personnel Defense Constr Supply Ctr 1972 1975; inventor hand computer 1968. **Military Serv:** USAC flight officer. **Business Addr:** Systems Manager, Dept of Defense, 3990 E Broad St, Columbus, OH 43215.

BLAND, BOBBY BLUE (ROBERT CALVIN)
Vocalist. **Personal:** Born Jan 27, 1930, Rosemark, TN. **Career:** Member of the Miniatures musical group, 1949; chauffeur of musical artist B B King, 1950; formed Beale Streeters musical group, 1951; began playing with Junior Parker, 1958; touring and recording with arranger Joe Scott and guitarist Wayne Bennett, 1958-68; Scott and Bennett leave Bland and he tours with Ernie Fields Orchestra, 1968-71; signed with Malaco Records, 1985. **Honors/Awds:** Nominated for Grammy Award for "Get Your Money Where You Spend Your Time," 1989; inducted into the Rock & Roll Hall of Fame, 1991. **Special Achievements:** Single recordings include: "Farther on up the Road," 1957, "I Pity the Fool," 1961, "That's the Way Love Is," 1963, "Stormy Mondy," "Turn On Your Lovelight," "Get Your Money Where You Spend Your Time," "Ain't No Heart in the City"; albums include: " His California Album," "Dreamer," "Members Only," "Midnight Run," "I Pity the Fool: The Duke Recordings.". **Military Serv:** US Army, 1952-55. **Business Addr:** Vocalist, c/o Malaco Records, PO Box 9287, 3023 Northside Dr, Jackson, MS 39206.

BLAND, EDWARD
Producer. **Personal:** Born in Chicago, IL; divorced; children: Edward, Robert, Stefanie. **Career:** "Cry of Jazz", co-produced directed film 1959; composed many serious chamber works, articles in film culuture 1960; Mus of Modern Art, mus consult 1968-74; Brooklyn Acad of Music, mus consult 1973-75; innumerable mus scores for documentary & educ films; arranging and/or producing of record dates for Al Hirt Dizzy Gillespie, Lionel Hampton, Hesitations, Clark Terry, James Moody, Elvin Jones, Big Mama Thornton; Vanguard Records, exec producer. **Orgs:** Mus of Modern Arts Newsletter 1968. **Military Serv:** USN 18 months. **Business Addr:** Welk Record Group, 1299 Ocean Ave, Suite 800, Santa Monica, CA 90401.

BLAND, HEYWARD
Business executive. **Personal:** Born Oct 17, 1918, Tillatoba, MS; married Maemell Fuller; children: Patricia, Ronald (dec). **Educ:** Shiloh Seventh-Day Adventist Acad, attended 1937. **Career:** Furniture Dealer, Chicago 1943-48; Real Estate Investor, 1948-; Shore Motel Corp, pres; 37th & Indiana Ave Bldg Inc, pres; Pacific Coast Bank, pres chmn bd. **Orgs:** Precinct capt 2nd Ward Dem Orgn 1962-68; co-sponsor Little League 1969 1970; mem bd dirs Girls' Club of San Diego 1974-; bd dirs PUSH Orgn of San Diego; organizer Pacific Coast Bank San Diego. **Honors/Awds:** Honored as Business Man of Yr Women's Club of San Diego. **Business Addr:** Chairman of the Board, Pacific Coast Bank, 5540 S Shore Dr, Chicago, IL 60637.

BLAND, ROBERT ARTHUR
Government official. **Personal:** Born Jan 26, 1938, Petersburg, VA; married Shirley Thweatt; children: Angela Rene, Lael Gregory. **Educ:** Univ of VA, BSEE 1959; CA State Univ, MA 1975; Nova Univ, EdD 1979. **Career:** Naval Weapons Ctr, proj engr 1959-71; Oxnard Comm Coll, counselor 1976-77, instr 1977-; Aquarius Portrait Photography, photographer 1983-; Naval Ship Weapons System Engrg Station, div head. **Orgs:** Instr Oxnard Comm Coll 1977-; mem Commiss on Ministry for Episcopal Diocease of Los Angeles 1980-; mem v chmn Ventura Cty Affirmative Action Advisory Comm 1982-; photographer Aquarius Portrait Photography 1983-; vestry St Patricks Episcopal Church 1985-. **Honors/Awds:** First black undergrad to attend and/or grad from Univ of VA 1959. **Home Addr:** 3915 Crown Haven Ct, Newbury Park, CA 91320.

BLANDEN, LEE ERNEST
Educational administration. **Personal:** Born Sep 16, 1942, Arcadia, FL; divorced; children: Teresa, Toni, Yvonne, Curtis. **Educ:** Voorhees Jr Coll Denmark SC, AA 1962; Lane Coll Jackson TN, BA Elem Ed 1965; Univ of IL Urbana, MEd Admin & Suprv 1970, Post Grad Study Ed Admin & Suprv; Eastern IL Univ Charleston, Admin & School Law; IL Assoc of School Bd, Negotiations & School Law. **Career:** Gen Devel Corp summers 1958-60; Voorhees Jr Coll Denmark SC, maintenance 1960-62; Wildwood Linen Supply Wildwood NJ, laborer summers 1963-65; Lane Coll Jackson TN, library asst, asst varsity coach 1965-70; Danville Dist 118, elem teacher, asst principal 1965-70; Elementary Bldg, principal 1970-74; Danville Area Comm Coll, part time adult educ faculty 1970-74, dir of personnel 1974-80, asst to the pres, dean of student serv. **Orgs:** Mem Alpha Phi Alpha Frat Inc, Omicron Lambda Beta, Danville United Fund, Amer Soc for Personnel Admin; bd of dir, chairperson Laura Lee Fellowship House; trsutee bd, sanctuary choir, Second Baptist Church; ed admin Danville Rotary Intl; personnel mgr comm Danville Chamber of Comm; past master & sec Corinthian Lodge 31 F&AM; bd of dir Ctr for Children Svcs; bd of dir, treas Vermilion Cty Opportunities Indust Ctr Inc; bell ringer Salvation Army; school bd mem Danville Comm Consol School Dist 118 Bd Policy Revisions; chief negotiator Bd of Ed; consult & speaker Natl School Bd Annual Convention; attended several workshops. **Honors/Awds:** Outstanding Educator of Midwest; Top 100 Administrators in North Amer 1980; Cited for Cost Containment Related to Personnel Absences. **Home Addr:** 4 W Bluff, Danville, IL 61832. **Business Addr:** Assistant to President/Dean, Danville Area Comm Coll, 2000 E Main St, Danville, IL 61832.

BLANDING, LARRY
State representative, real estate associate. **Personal:** Born Aug 29, 1953, Sumter, SC; son of Rosa Lee Williams Blanding and Junius Blanding Sr (deceased); married Peggy Ann Mack, Dec 24, 1977; children: Dreylan Dre'Neka. **Educ:** Claflin Coll, BA 1975; SC State Coll, MEd 1977; SC School of Real Estate 1988. **Career:** United Way of Jacksonville, campaign assoc 1975; United Way Richland & Lexington Cty, acting dir comm planning 1976; SC State Coll, head resident 1976-77; SC House of Representatives, state rep 1976-; Univ of South Carolina, guest lecturer 1983; Realty World Colonial-Moses, sales associate 1987-. **Orgs:** Mem Natl Caucus Black Leg 1976-; bd dir Sumter Learning Devel Center 1977-82; State dir, 1979-83, chm, 1990-, Natl Real Estate Comm; Phi Beta Sigma; mem Sumter Public Awareness Assoc 1977-; mem NAACP, Hon Soc, Pi Gamma Mu Iota Chapter Orangesburg SC; chmn SC Leg Black Caucus; mem St Paul Lodge 8, CC Johnson Consistory 136, Cario Temple 125; bd mem Sumter County Devel Bd 1983-; comm mem Southern Legislative Conference 1986-; bd mem Sumter Chamber of Commerce 1986-; mem Local, State & Natl Bd of Realtors 1987-; inspector general USCAAR 33rd degree Masons 1986-. **Honors/Awds:** Sigma Man of the Year Phi Beta Sigma Fraternity Inc 1977; Man of the Year Claflin Coll 1975; Citizen of the Year Omega Psi Phi Fraternity Gamma Iota Chapter 1976; One of Fifty Future Leaders of Amer Ebony Magazine 1978; Alumni Award, Claflin Coll 1987; Family Pioneer, Williams Family Reunion Comm 1989. **Business Addr:** State Representative, State of South Carolina, Blatt Building, 432-B, Pendleton St, Columbia, SC 29201.

BLANFORD, COLVIN
Clergyman. **Personal:** Born Feb 6, 1938, Dallas, TX; son of Hattie Ellen Colvin Blanford and John Hardee Blanford; married Margaret Ann Tyrrell; children: Colvin II, Christopher. **Educ:** San Francisco State Coll, BA 1960; Berkeley Bapt Div Sch, BD 1963; So CA Sch Theol, RelD 1969. **Career:** Third Baptist Church San Francisco, youth & asst minister 1956-63; Cosmopolitan Baptist Church San Francisco, pastor 1963-70; San Francisco Youth Guidance Ctr, prot chaplain 1963-70; Brooks House of Christian Serv Hammond IN, exec dir 1970-73; North Baptist Theol Sem, adj prof 1974-; First Baptist Church Gary IN, pastor 1973-81; Christ Baptist Church, organizing pastor 1981-. **Orgs:** Mem bd dir Morehouse School of Religion 1976-; Baptist Ministers Conf 1973-; Interfaith Clergy Council 1973-; bd mem, Gary NAACP 1986-; life mem NAACP 1980-. **Honors/Awds:** Youth of Yr San Francisco Sun Reporter 1958; sermon publ in Outstanding Black Sermons by Judson Press 1976; represented the Baptist denomination as a participant in the Baptist-Lutheran dialogue on the meaning of baptism 1981; acclaimed by Dollars & Sense Magazine as one of the outstanding black ministers in Amer 1981; preaching missions to Liberia, Malawi, Swaziland, Republic of South Africa 1985, 1987, 1989. **Business Addr:** Pastor, Christ Baptist Church, 4700 E 7th Ave, Gary, IN 46403.

BLANKENSHIP, EDDIE L.
City official. **Personal:** Born Jan 22, 1925, Roanake, AL; married Mary L Bates; children: Donald E, Deborah J. **Educ:** Booker T Washington Jr Coll, AAD 1949; Miles Coll, BS 1960; Southwestern Univ BS 1983. **Career:** US Postal Svc, mail handler 1953; US Dept of Commerce/Minority Bus Dev, ed & training spec 1973; Mayor's Office, spec admin asst 1976; US Dept of Commerce/Minority Bus Dev, dist officer 1983; City of Birmingham, city councillor. **Orgs:** Officer Minority Bus Opportunity; bd pres JCCEO, Urban Impact Inc; bd mem Pratt City Devel Corp. **Honors/Awds:** Outstanding Supervisor Birmingham Urban League; Cert of Apprec Metropolitan Bus Assoc; Superior Accomplishment US Postal Svcs; Man of the Year Birmingham Sales Assoc. **Military Serv:** AUS T/5 3 yrs. **Home Addr:** 1928 Center St South, Birmingham, AL 35205. **Business Addr:** City Councilman, City of Birmingham, 710 N 20th St, Birmingham, AL 35203.

BLANKENSHIP, GLENN RAYFORD
Government official. **Personal:** Born Aug 11, 1948, Memphis, TN; son of Geraldine Walton Blankenship and Elbert Blankenship; married Zita R Jackson; children: Maia, Rayford. **Educ:** Amer Univ Wash Semester Prog, 1968-69; LeMoyne-Owen College, BA 1970; Graduate Study in Public Administration, Syracuse Univ 1971, Univ of WI 1973, Univ of CO 1976. **Career:** US Dept of Housing & Urban Development, program analyst, community development representative, equal opportunity specialist 1971-74; Federal Energy Admin, regional equal oppor officer 1974-77; US Dept of Energy, regional equal oppor spec 1977-79; USDA Forest Service, regional eeo/affirmative action mgr 1979-89; USDA Forest Service, Historically Black Colls & Univs, national program manager, currently. **Orgs:** Life mem, Kappa Alpha Psi; life mem, NAACP; pres, Atlanta Chap Natl Alumni Assn LeMoyne-Owen College 1984-89; registered football official, Capitol City Officials Assn 1985-89; conference coord, Sons of Allen-Atlanta/No Georgia 6th Episcopal District AME Church 1985-89; trustee, Flipper Temple AME Church 1986-89; trustee, First AME Church-Gaithersburg 1990-91; secretary, Sons of Allen, 1992-, First AME Church 1989-. **Honors/Awds:** Certificate of appreciation, Natl Alliance of Business 1983; Golden Parade of Alumni, LeMoyne-Owen Coll Class of 86, 1985; certificate of appreciation, Martin Luther King Jr Ctr for Nonviolent Social Change Inc 1986; certificate of merit, USDA Forest Service 1986; Presidential Citation, NAFEO Disting Alumni 1987; director's award, Jacobs Creek Job Corps Center 1987; outstanding service award, J C Williams Usher Board 1988; distinguished leadership award, Sons of Allen-Atlanta North Georgia Conference 1989; certificate of appreciation, George Washington Natl Forest 1991; USDA Honor Awards, 1993-95. **Home Addr:** PO Box 19803, Birmingham, AL 35219. **Business Phone:** (202)205-0497.

BLANKS, DELILAH B.
Educator. **Personal:** Born Apr 5, 1936, Acme, NC; married Eddie W Blanks; children: Sherri Ann, Rhonda Fay. **Educ:** Shaw University, AB, English/social studies, 1957; E Carolina University, AB, library science, 1965; University of North Carolina, MSW, 1972, PhD in progress, 1974-. **Career:** Wake County Board of Education, teacher/librarian, 1963-67; Whiteville City Schools, teacher of English, 1960-62; Brunswick County Board of Education, teacher/librarian, 1963-67; Neighborhood Youth Corps, counselor, 1967-68; Bladen County Dept of Social Services, child welfare worker, 1968-71; North Carolina State Dept of Social Services, community development specialist I, 1971-72; University of North Carolina, asst professor, sociology/social work, 1972-. **Orgs:** Income tax consultant, 1957-; notary public, 1957-; Natl Assn of Social Workers, 1974-; Natl Council on Social Work Educ, 1974-; Delta Sigma Theta; chair, Arcadia Bd of Town Councilmen; NAACP; 1st vice chair, Bladen Co Dem Exec Com;Bladen Co Improvement Assn; bd mem, Wilmington New Hanover Headstart Inc; bd mem, NC Comm for a Two Party System, 1974. **Honors/Awds:** Bladen County, Citizen of the Year, 1968; North Carolina Senclander of the Month, 1974. **Business Addr:** Professor, Dept of Sociology & Anthropology, University of North Carolina at Wilmington, 601 S College Rd, Wilmington, NC 28403-3201.

BLANKS, WILHELMINA E.
Government employee. **Personal:** Born Nov 10, 1905, Decatur, AL; married Walter T Blanks; children: Wilhelmina Balla, Muriel Inniss. **Educ:** Atlanta Univ, AB 1927; Attended, Loyola Univ, Northwestern Sch of Journalism, Univ Chicago. **Career:** Prairie View State Coll, tchr 1927-29; Cook Co Dept of Public Aid, 1936-74, asst dist office supr 1974-. **Orgs:** Organizer MI Ave Adult Educ Ctr 1965-; mem Tutoring Project for Mothers Univ of Chicago; mem Social Serv Guild of St Edmund's Episcopal Ch 1950-; bd mem City Asso of Women's Bd of Art Inst of Chicago; vice pres South Side Comm Art Ctr Chicago; mem Bravo Chap Lyric Opera Chicago; mem PUSH, NAACP, Chicago Urban League; vice pres Amer Friends of Liberia; mem Citizens Com Du Sable Museum of African Amer Hist; freelance writer. **Honors/Awds:** Awd for Achievement in Public Welfare Intl Travelers Assn; 1972; Disting Serv Awd Dedication to Devel of Art in Blk Comm S Side Comm Art Ctr 1970. **Business Addr:** Asst Dist Office Supr, Dept of Public Aid, 300 W Pershing Rd, Chicago, IL 60609.

BLANTON, DAIN
Sports figure. **Career:** Association of Volleyball Professionals, professional volleyball player, currently. **Honors/Awds:** Won the $300,000 Miller Lite/AVP Hermosa Beach Grand Slam. **Special Achievements:** Is the first and only African American on the Association of Volleyball Professionals Tour. **Business Addr:** Pro Volleyball Player, Association of Volleyball Professionals Tour, 330 Washington Blvd, 6th Fl, Ste 600, Marina del Rey, CA 90292-5147, (310)577-0775.

BLANTON, JAMES B., III
Association executive. **Personal:** Born Feb 6, 1949, Knoxville, TN; son of Martha Luckey Blanton and James B Blanton Jr; married Emily DeVoi Besley, Dec 25, 1977; children: Joseph, Sidney, James IV. **Educ:** Knoxville Coll, BS Commerce 1971; Univ of TN, MBA. **Career:** Alpha Phi Alpha Frat Inc, exec dir 1977. **Orgs:** Asst exec sec Alpha Phi Alpha Frat Inc; dir of office serv TVA Knoxville 1966-73; asst state dir of TN Alpha Phi Alpha 1970-73; asst chief accountant US Postal Serv Knoxville 1971-73; dir of finances Our Voice Magazine Knoxville 1970-72; mem Amer Accounting Assn; life mem Alpha Phi Alpha; mem Pi Omega Pi; Phi Beta Lambda; Young Democrats of Amer; US Jaycees; Urban League; YMCA; Knoxville Coll Alumni Assn; bd dirs Alpha Phi Alpha; mem Prince Hall Masons North Star Lodge #1 F&AM; life mem Knoxville Coll Natl Alumni Assn; Prince Hall Shriner Arabic Temple; Order of Eastern Stars; Western Consistory AASR of Freemasonry; United Supreme Council AASR Thirty Third Degree Mason; past potentate Imperial Council AEAONMS Inc;Holy Royal Arch Masons-Oriental; past master North Star F&AM; appt to bd adv American Biographical Inst 1986; bd of dir Alpha Phi Alpha, bd dir Building Foundation; Natl Pan Hellenic Council Exec Committee. **Honors/Awds:** Alpha Kappa Mu Natl Hon Soc; Bro of the Yr Award; Alpha Mu Lambda Chap; Alpha Phi Alpha 1975; Mary E Gilbert Scholarship Award for Grad Study 1972; MWPH Grand Lodge of IL-Grand Master's Award 1982; Clarence Clinkscales Award North Star Lodge 1985; Outstanding Young Men of America 1981 & 1985; Appreciation Award Chicago Society of Children & Families bd of dir 1985; Outstanding Serv Award Black Media Inc 1986; Alpha Phi Alpha Presidential Award 1988.

BLANTON, RICKY
Professional basketball player. **Career:** Pheonix Suns, 1990-. **Business Addr:** Professional Basketball Player, Phoenix Suns, PO Box 1369, Phoenix, AZ 85001-1369.

BLASSINGAME, JOHN W.
Educator, editor. **Personal:** Born Mar 23, 1940, Covington, GA. **Educ:** Ft Valley State College, BA, 1960; Howard University, MA, 1961; Yale University, PhD, 1971. **Career:** Yale University, lecturer, 1970-71, asst professor, 1971-72, acting chairman, Afro-American Studies Dept, 1971-72, assoc professor, 1972-74, History Dept, professor, 1974-. **Orgs:** Phi Alpha Theta; Assn Behavioral Social Sciences; Assn Study Afro-American Life & History; Southern & American Historical Assn, 1974-; orgn, American Historian; contributing editor, Black Scholar, 1971-; adv bd, Afro-American Bicentennial Corp, 1971-; bd, Centre Internationale de Recherches Africaines, 1971-; American Historical Assn, rev bd, 1972-73; ed bd, Reviews of American History, 1973-; Journal of Negro History, 1973-; executive council, Assn for the Study Afro-American Life & History, 1973-; chairman, program com, Organization of American Historians, 1974. **Honors/Awds:** Author of various books, essays and articles. **Business Addr:** Professor, Dept of History, PO Box 1504a, Yale University, New Haven, CT 06520.

BLAYLOCK, ENID V.
Educator. **Personal:** Born Jan 24, 1925; married Lorenzo Blaylock; children: Andre, Dellis. **Educ:** Loma Linda Univ, BSRN 1953; UCLA, MS 1959; Univ of So CA, PhD 1966. **Career:** White Memorial Hospital & St Vincent Hosp LA, staff nurse 1953-59; LA City School Dist, health supvr 1960-66; Inst for Intercultural Educ, dir 1974-; CA State Univ, assoc prof educ Psychology 1966-. **Orgs:** Lecturer UCLA Med Media Network 1969-; consult Vet Adminstrn Hosp 1970-74; Human Awareness Training Orange Co Personnel 1974; mem Professional Adv Bd Charles Drew Post Grad Med Sch 1973-; sec treas Assn of Black Coll Faculty & Staff of So CA 1972-; mem Women in Educ Leadership; Hon Assn for Women in Educ1970-. **Honors/Awds:** Citation Distinguished Serv SDA So CA Conf Sch 1965; Ed Assn of Black Coll Faculty & Staff of So CA Newsletter 1972-74; author of article on drug abuse. **Business Addr:** Assoc Prof Educ Psychol, CA State Univ, 6101 E 7th St, Long Beach, CA 90840.

BLAYLOCK, MOOKIE (DARON OSHAY)
Professional basketball player. **Personal:** Born Mar 20, 1967, Garland, TX; married Janelle; children: Zachary, Daron Jr. **Educ:** Midland College, 1985-87; Univ of Oklahoma, 1987-89. **Career:** New Jersey Nets, guard, 1989-92, Atlanta Hawks, 1992-. **Honors/Awds:** NBA All-Star, 1994. **Business Addr:** Professional Basketball Player, Atlanta Hawks, 1 CNN Center, Ste 405, Atlanta, GA 30335, (404)827-3800.

BLAYLOCK, RONALD
Financial services company executive. **Educ:** Georgetown University, graduate; New York University, MBA. **Career:** Citibank, capital markets, until 1986; PaineWebber Group, Inc, salesperson, beginning 1986; Utendahl Capital Partners, exec vp, 1992-; Blaylock & Partners LP, founder, 1993-. **Honors/Awds:** PaineWebber Group, Inc, top salesperson, 1991; Black Enterprise magazine, one of the 25 Hottest Blacks on Wall Street, 1992. **Special Achievements:** Co. became the first minority firm to co-manage a Federal Home Loan Mortgage Corp deal. **Business Addr:** Founder, Blaylock & Partners LP, 609 5th Ave, New York, NY 10017, (212)715-6600.

BLAYTON-TAYLOR, BETTY
Business executive, artist, arts administrator. **Personal:** Born Jul 10, 1937, Newport News, VA; daughter of Alleyne Houser Blayton and James Blain Blayton; married. **Educ:** Syracuse U, BFA 1959; City Coll; Art Student's League; Brooklyn Museum Sch. **Career:** Major exhibits 1959-; St Thomas, Virgin Island, art tchr 1959-60; City of New York, recreation leader 1960-64; Haryou Art/Graphics & Plastics, art supr 1964-67; The Children's Art Carnival, exec dir 1969, pres 1972-89; New York City Board of Education, consultant 1977-. **Orgs:** Bd mem The Arts & Bus Council 1978-; bd mem The Printmakers Workshop 1975-; founding mem The Studio Museum in Harlem 1965-77, mem bd Major Exhibit 1959-84; mem Commn for Cultural Affairs 1979-89; professional prof City Coll/Elem Ed Dept 1974; mem Nat Guild Sch 1982-; consult NYS Bd of Educ 1977-; Natl Black Child Development Institute 1980-. **Honors/Awds:** Empire State Woman of the Yr in the Arts NYS Governor's Award 1984; Artist in Residence Tougoloo Coll MS 1982; Artist in Residence Norfolk State Coll VA 1980; Artist in Residence Fisk Univ TN 1978; Making Thoughts Become, publication 1978; Black Women in the Arts Award, Governor of New York 1988. **Home Addr:** 2001 Creston Ave, Bronx, NY 10453. **Business Addr:** President, The Children's Art Carnival, 62 Hamilton Terr, New York, NY 10031.

BLEDSOE, CAROLYN E. LEWIS
Government planner. **Personal:** Born Jan 31, 1946, Richmond, VA; married Rev Earl L Bledsoe; children: Katrina L, Tanya N. **Educ:** VA State Univ, AB 1968, 36 hours towards MA degree. **Career:** King William Co Public Schools, teacher 1968-69; Richmond Public Schools, teacher 1969-71; Dept Developmental Progs, rsch analyst 1972-80; City Government,sr planner 1980-. **Orgs:** Vp bd of dirs Commonwealth Girl Scout Cncl of VA Inc 1976-84; 1979-81; secty/treas Northern VA Baptist Ministers' Wives 1981-83; chair scholarship comm the VA State Assn of Ministers' Wives 1981-84. **Home Addr:** 711 Wadsworth Drive, Richmond, VA 23236. **Business Addr:** Senior Planner, Dept Planning & Development, 900 E Broad St Rm 500, Richmond, VA 23219.

BLEDSOE, JAMES L.
City official. **Personal:** Born Dec 1, 1947, Tuskegee, AL; son of Ada M Randle Bledsoe Jackson and Willie James Bledsoe; married Clara A Fisher, Jun 14, 1975; children: Patrice Bledsoe. **Educ:** Univ of West Florida, Pensacola, FL, BS, Marketing, 1972, MPA, 1974. **Career:** Dept of Budget, City of Miami, chief mgmt analyst, 1978-86; Dept of Solid Waste, City of Miami, asst to the dir, 1986; Dept of Solid Waste, City of Miami, asst dir, 1987; Dept of Budget, City of Miami, asst dir, 1988. **Orgs:** Mem, Amer Soc for Public Admin, 1978-, Natl Forum for Black Public Admin, 1982-, Amer Public Works Assn, 1986-; bd mem, Selective Serv System, 1987-.

BLEDSOE, MELVIN
Business executive. **Personal:** Born Jun 5, 1955, Memphis, TN; son of Estell Bledsoe; married Linda Ann Bledsoe, Jun 20, 1976; children: Monica, Carlos. **Educ:** Milwaukee Area Technical Coll, 1978-80. **Career:** Graceland Tours, supervisor over shuttle bus, 1982-83; Grayline Tours, operation mgr, 1983-87; Blues City Sightseeing Tours of Memphis, pres, currently. **Orgs:** Memphis Convention Visitor Ctr, bd mem, 1992; Downtown Memphis Redevelopment Committee, 1993. **Honors/Awds:** Black Bus Assn, Nominated for Best New Business Award, 1989-90, Nominated for Most Outstanding Black Business in Memphis Award, 1992. **Special Achievements:** Recognized by the Local Jr Achievement of Greater Memphis for Applied Economics Project Bus & Bus Basics; several local natl international publications. **Business Addr:** President, Blues City Sightseeing Tours of Memphis, 164 Union Ave, Ste 100, Memphis, TN 38103, (901)522-9229.

BLEDSOE, TEMPESTT
Actress. **Personal:** daugHter of Wilma Bledsoe. **Educ:** New York Univ. **Career:** The Cosby Show, actress, until 1992. **Honors/Awds:** National Merit Scholarship finalist; Clarence Muse Youth Award, 1992.

BLEDSOE, WILLIAM
Judge, educational administrator. **Educ:** Olivet College, 1952. **Career:** City of Highland Park, 30th District Court, municipal judge, currently. **Orgs:** Olivet College, board of trustees. **Business Addr:** Judge, 30th District Court, 28 Gerald Ave, Highland Park, MI 48203, (313)252-0241.

BLIGE, MARY J.
Vocalist. **Personal:** Born 1970?, Bronx, NY; daughter of Cora. **Career:** Vocalist, currently; recordings include: "I'll Do For You," featured on single for Father MC, 1991; Changes, duet on single from Christopher William's album; "One Night Stand," featured on single for Father MC; What's the 411?, debut album, 1992; My Life, album, 1994; Share My World, album, 1996; television: The Jamie Foxx Show. **Business Addr:** Vocalist, MCA/Uptown Records, c/o Maria Kleinman, Natl Director of Publicity, 70 Universal City Plaza, Universal City, CA 91608, (818)777-8918.

BLOCK, CAROLYN B.
Psychologist. **Personal:** Born Sep 7, 1942, New Orleans. **Educ:** Xavier Univ, BS, 1963; Boston Univ, MS 1965, MA 1968, PhD 1971. **Career:** Private Practice, psychologist, 1977-; KQED-TV, content consult 1977-80; Fmly & Chld Crss Serv Mt Zion Hosp San Francisco, dir 1972-74; Children Youth Serv Wstsd Comm Mental Health Cntr, dir 1974-77; Center Univ of CA, psychological counseling 1970-72; Wstsd Mental Health Center, psychologist consultant, 1972-; Private Practice San Francisco, psychologist, 19773-. **Orgs:** Lecturer, Psychology Dept, Univ of CA 1973-; mem, Natl Assn of Black Psychologist, 1970-; San Francisco Red Cross; Am Psychology Assn 1972-; bd mem, San Francisco Com on Children's TV 1973-. **Business Addr:** 1947 Divisadero St #2, San Francisco, CA 94115.

BLOCK, LESLIE S.
Management consulting executive. **Educ:** University of Pittsburgh, BA, political science, 1974, MPA, 1977, PhD, higher education administration, 1982. **Career:** Leslie S Block and Associates, founder, president, 1985-; National-Louis Univ, adjunct graduate faculty; Spertus Coll, visiting graduate faculty; Northwestern Univ, visiting scholar, 1986-93. **Orgs:** Human Relations Commission, Youngstown, Ohio, mayoral appointee, 1974-76; Citizens Information Services of IL, bd of dir, 1990; Evanston Township High School, Booster Club, exec bd, 1993-2000, PTSA, Legislation Committee, chr, 1997-2000. **Honors/Awds:** Omicron Delta Kappa, 1973; Outstanding Young Man of America, 1988; Dollar & Sense, Outstanding Entrepreneur Award, 1991, America's Best & Brightest Hall of Fame, 1994. **Special Achievements:** Coordinated, directed and implemented the first year of the Chicago School- to-Work Opportunities System partnership; conceived and instituted the North Chicago Community Unit School District 187's Partners in Progress Program; developed pre-college science/mathematic cooperative programs promulgated by the US Dept of Labor, Secretary's Commission on Achieving Necessary Skills; conducted several workshops on Public-Private Educational Partnerships; provided expert advice and commentary on several television and radio programs. **Business Addr:** Founder/President, Leslie S Block & Associates, 8612 Monticello Ave, Skokie, IL 60076-2350.

BLOCKER, HELEN POWELL
Accountant, volunteer (retired). **Personal:** Born Aug 15, 1923, Cape Charles, VA; married Adolphus; children: Preston, Kevin. **Educ:** City Coll of NY, 1946; NY U, 1966; Pace Univ NYC, BPS 1983. **Career:** Mt Calvary Child Care Cntr, accountant 1953-78; Shiloh Baptist Ch, youth dir 1962-66; New York City Bd of Edn, family asst 1965-73; Scribner's Publishing, acctnt 1984; Shiloh Baptist Ch, dir of training; Department of Veterans Affairs 306, program clerk-adjudication, until 1994. **Orgs:** Tax cnslr aide AARP 1985-90; mem Inst of Internal Auditors 1982-; mem Nat Assn of Black Acctnts 1982-; exec bd Natl Council of Negro Women Inc 1980-91; sec Comm Planning Bd 8 Yrs; personnel chrmn Hunts Point Multi-Service Cntr 1992-; personnel chair, Montefiore Medical Center Advisory Bd 1978-89; sponsoring board, South Bronx Mental Health Council currently, vice chair bd, 1993-; Shiloh Baptist Church, Board of Christian Education, chair, board of trustees, vice chair; vice chair, Hunts Point Multi-Svcs Corp.; dir Senior Citizens Program, seasoned; coordinator Community Breakfast For the Homeless, Shiloh Bapt Ch; scy South Bronx Housekeeper Vendor Program Bd. **Honors/Awds:** 23 yr Achievement Nat Cncl of Negro Women Inc 1997; 100 yr Serv New York City Mission Soc Cadet Corps 1974; Black History #1 Sch Dist #7 Bronx 1974; Serv to Youth Shiloh Baptist Ch Sch 1981; Bronx NANBP Women's Club, Sojourner Truth Natl Awd 1986; Mary McLeod Bethune Award, Bronx Life Member's Guild, Natl Council of Negro Women, 1992. **Home Addr:** 700 E 156th St, Bronx, NY 10455.

BLOCKSON, CHARLES L.
Educator. **Personal:** Born Dec 16, 1933, Norristown, PA; son of Annie Parker Blockson and Charles E Blockson; children: Noelle. **Educ:** Pennsylvania State University, 1956. **Career:** PA Blk History Committee, dir 1976-; Historical Soc of PA, bd mem 1976-83; PA Afro-Amer Hist Bd, dir 1976-; Governor's Heritage Pgm, governor's commissioner 1983-; Temple Univ Charles L Blockson Afro-Am Collection, curator. **Orgs:** Mem NAACP 1974-; cncl mem PA State Univ Alumni Cncl 1982-; committee mem Temple Univ Centennial Committee 1983-; mem Urban League of PA; mem NAACP; mem Montgomery Cnty of PA Bicentennial Committee 1982-83. **Honors/Awds:** PA St Quarterback Award PA State Quarterback Club 1984; PA Black History Book 1975; Blk Genealogy Book 1977; Alumni Fellow Awd Penn State Univ 1979; Underground Railroad in PA 1980; Cover Story for Nat Geographic Mag "The Underground Railroad" 1984, "People of the Sea Island" 1987; The Underground Railroad First Person Narratives Book 1987; Lifetime Achievement Awd Before Columbus Foundation 1987; Villanova University, Hon Degree Educ, 1979; Lincoln University, Hon Degree, 1987; Hon Degree, Holy Family College, 1995. **Special Achievements:** Publications: Philadelphia State Historical Marker Guide, 1992; Hippocrene Guide: The Underground Railroad, 1994; Chairperson: National Park Service; Underground Railroad Sites Study, 1990-1995; Mem The American Antiquarian Society, 1996; Mem The Grolier Club, 1996; African American Storytellers, 1st Life Time Award,

1996. **Military Serv:** AUS 1957-55. **Business Addr:** Curator, Temple Univ, Broad & Berks St, Sullivan Hall, Philadelphia, PA 19122.

BLOOMFIELD, RANDALL D.
Physician. **Personal:** Born in New York, NY; married; children: 2. **Educ:** CCNY, BS 1949; Downstate Med Ctr, MD 1953. **Career:** Kings City Hospital, intern, surgeon 1953-54; Obs/Gyn, resident 1954-58; Kings City Hosp, Private practice, physician. **Orgs:** Brooklyn-Cumberland Med Ctr; AMA; Kings Cty Med Soc; fellow Amer Coll OB/GYN; mem Amer Coll Surg, Brooklyn Gyn Soc, NY Obs Soc, Natl Med Assoc; diplomate Amer Bd OB/GYN. **Honors/Awds:** Cert Gynecol Oncology; Frank Babbot Awd. **Military Serv:** AUS WWII 1943. **Business Addr:** Physician, Kings County Hosp, 451 Clarkson Ave, Brooklyn, NY 11203.

BLOUIN, ROSE LOUISE
Educator, photographer. **Personal:** Born Dec 13, 1948, Chicago, IL; daughter of Louise Blouin and Paul Blouin; children: Kimaada, Bakari. **Educ:** Univ of IL Chicago, BA 1971; Chicago State Univ, MA 1983. **Career:** Photographer, 1980-; Chicago State Univ, Center for Women's Identity Studies, staff associate, 1980-83, lecturer in English Composition 1983-87; City of Harvey IL, public relations director, 1984-86; Third World Press, assoc editor, 1983-89; Columbia College Chicago, English prof, currently; specializes in teaching African-American and metaphysicl literature, meditation, and writing. **Orgs:** Public relations consultant Inst of Positive Educ, African-Amer Book Ctr, Speak Up!, Communication Ctr Inc 1983-; freelance photography, Amer Airlines, Mary Thompson Hospital, Citizen Newspapers, various artists & arts organizations. **Honors/Awds:** Co-author, Experiencing Your Identity, Developmental Materials, 1982; Best Photography Awd Milwaukee Inner City Art Fair 1985; Purchase Award Museum of Sci & Industry "Black Creativity Exhibit" 1986; Purchase Award DuSable Museum of Afro-Amer History Art Fair 1986; traveling exhibit Roots, A Contemporary Inspiration, Evanston Art Center 1986-88; juried exhibit acceptance Atlanta Life Ins Natl Art Exhibit 1987; JB Speed Art Museum Louisville KY 1987; Put Your Message Here, The Randolph Street Gallery; The Art of Jazz, Chicago Jazz Festival, 1987-89; Rhythms, Axis Photo Gallery, 1987; Saphyre and Crystals: African American Women Artists, South Side Community Art Center, 1987, 1990; photos have appeared in Say That The River Turns: The Impact of Gwendolyn Brooks, 1987; Killing Memory, Seeg Ancestors, 1987; The Chicago Musicale, 1986; Menagerie, 1986, 1987; Citizen Newspaper. **Home Addr:** 8236 So Michigan Ave, Chicago, IL 60619. **Business Addr:** English Inst, Columbia College, 600 S Michigan Ave, Chicago, IL 60605.

BLOUNT, CHARLOTTE RENEE
Journalist. **Personal:** Born Mar 2, 1952, Washington, DC. **Educ:** Catholic Univ Scholastic Journalism Inst, attended 1967; OH Univ, attended 1970-72; Amer Univ Washington DC, BA Journalism 1974, grad courses 1975-76. **Career:** WOUB-FM Athens OH, reporter/announcer 1971-72; Washington DC Voice & Visions Prods, freelance talent 1973-; WOOK-FM Washington, reporter/announcer 1973-74; WILD Boston, reporter/announcer 1974; Securities & Exchange Commn, writer 1974-75; George Washington Univ, assoc prof 1978-; Mutual Black Network, White House/state dept corres. **Orgs:** Mem Zeta Phi Beta Sor Beta Zeta Chap Washington. **Honors/Awds:** Nominated Most Outstanding Young Woman 1976; Newswoman of the Yr Natl Assn of TV & Radio Artists 1976; Young Career Woman DC Natl Fed of Bus & Professional Women 1976; Nat Pub Relations Dir Zeta Phi Beta 1976-78. **Business Addr:** Correspondent, Mutual Black Network, 1755 Jefferson Davis Hwy, Arlington, VA 22202.

BLOUNT, CLARENCE W.
State senator, educational administrator. **Personal:** Born Apr 20, 1921, South Creek, NC; son of Lottie Tillery Blount and Charles J. Blount; married Edith Gordine; children: Michael, Edward, Mark. **Educ:** Morgan State Univ, BA, 1950; Georgetown Univ, 1954-58; Johns Hopkins Univ, MLA, 1965. **Career:** Baltimore City Public Schools, educator, 1950-69; Morgan State College, lecturer, 1969; Community College of Baltimore, executive assistant to the president, currently; Maryland State Senate, senator, 1971-. **Orgs:** Mem, National Education Association, Public School Administrators and Supervisors Association, Urban League, NAACP, National Conference of Christians and Jews. **Honors/Awds:** Comm Serv Awd Druid Hill YMCA 1969; Citizenship Awd Modawmin Merchants Assn; 1970; Merit Awd Zeta Phi Beta, Phi Beta Sigma; Citizenship Awd Alpha Phi Alpha 1974; Man of the Year Award, National Conference of Christians and Jews, 1976. **Military Serv:** US Army, 1st Lt, 1942-46.

BLOUNT, CORIE KASOUN
Professional basketball player. **Personal:** Born Jan 4, 1969, Monrovia, CA. **Educ:** Rancho Santiago Comm Coll, CA; Univ of Cincinnati. **Career:** Chicago Bulls, forward, 1993-95; Los Angeles Lakers, 1995-. **Business Addr:** Professional Basketball Player, Los Angeles Lakers, PO Box 10, Inglewood, CA 90306, (213)419-3100.

BLOUNT, LARRY ELISHA
Educator. **Personal:** Born May 17, 1950, Vidalia, GA; son of Magdalean Jones Blount and Elisha Blount; married Sandra Grace Smith Blount, Jul 31, 1971; children: Carlene Michelle Tuggle, Kendra Michelle, Erin Nichole. **Educ:** Univ of MI, BA pol sci 1972; Univ of Cincinnati Sch of Law, JD 1975; Columbia Univ Sch of Law, LLM 1976. **Career:** Self-employed attorney, 1976-; Univ of Georgia, asst law prof, 1976-79, assoc law prof, professor, currently. **Orgs:** President, Clarke County NAACP, 1988-; board member, Georgia Association of Minority Entrepreneurs, 1985-. **Honors/Awds:** Order of the Coif, 1980, Gold Key Honor Society, 1990, University of Georgia School of Law. **Business Addr:** Professor, University of Georgia School of Law, Athens, GA 30602.

BLOUNT, MELVIN CORNELL (MEL)
Community service leader. **Personal:** Born Apr 10, 1948, Vidalia, GA; married Leslie; children: Tanisia, Norris. **Educ:** Southern Univ Baton Rouge, Grad 1970. **Career:** Pittsburgh Steelers, professional football player 1976-84; NFL, dir player relations 1984-; Cobb Creek Farms, owner/oper; Mel Blount Youth Home Inc, founder; Mel Blount Cellular Phone Co, owner/oper. **Orgs:** Mem bd dirs Pgh Childrens Museum; mem policy Cncl Natl Ctr for Youth & their Families; mem bd dir Amer Red Cross; rep Red Cross on visit to Mauritania N Africa factfinding expedition; mem Paint Horse Assn, Amer Quarter Horse Assn, Natl Cutting Horse Assn. **Honors/Awds:** NFL League Leader in Interceptions 1975; named MVP Pittsburgh Steelers 1975; NFL Player of the Yr 1975; MVP Pro Bowl 1976. **Business Addr:** Head, Mel Blount Youth Home, RD 1, Box 90, Claysville, PA 15323.

BLOUNT, WILBUR CLANTON
Educator. **Personal:** Born Feb 5, 1929, Columbus, OH; married Elsie M; children: Elizabeth, Jacquelyn, Angela, Wilbur. **Educ:** OH State Univ, BSc 1951, Grad Sch 1952, Coll of Medicine MD 1959. **Career:** Bur of Educ Rsch OSU, rsch assoc 1951-52; USAF Biodynamic Branch Aerospace Med Field Lab NM, rsch develop officer 1954-56; Radio Isotope OSU, chemist 1958-59; Inst Rsch in Vision OSU, rsch assoc 1964; Univ of KY Med Ctr, asst prof dir retinal serv 1971-77; Ophthalmologist. **Orgs:** Mem Acad of Medicine of Columbus & Franklin Co; assoc fellow Aerospace Med Assn 1969; life mem Air Force Assn; mem Amer Acad of Ophthalmology; mem Amer Assn for Med Systems Informatics; mem Amer Assn of Ophthalmology; fellow Amer Coll of Surgeons 1973; mem Amer Diabetes Assn; mem Amer Intra-Ocular Implant Soc; mem AMA; mem Assn of Military Surgeons of the US; mem bd trustees Central OH Diabetes Assn; mem Civil Aviation Med Assn; mem Columbus Ophthalmology & Otolaryngology Soc; mem Natl Med Assn; mem OH Ophthalmological Soc; mem Ophthalmic Photographers Soc; mem Order of Hipprocates The OH State Univ Coll of Medicine Med Alumni Soc; mem Pan Amer Assn of Ophthalmologists; life mem Reserve Officers Assn; mem Soc of Military Ophthalmologists; mem Soc of USAFFlight Surgeons, USAF Clinical Seons; life mem OH State Univ Alumni Assn; mem Pres's Club OH State Univ; mem military affairscomm Tuskegee Airmen Inc OH Chapt; mem bd trustees Vision Ctr of Central OH. **Honors/Awds:** Disting Military Student OH State Univ Air Force Reserve Training Corps 1950; Disting Military Grad OH State Univ Air Force Reserve Training Corps 1951; Citation for Distinguished Achievement conferred by OH State Univ Office of Minority Affairs 1984. **Military Serv:** USAF 1st lt air rsch develop command 1954-56; USAF Reserves & Air Natl Guard col oang 20 yrs. **Business Addr:** 300 East Town St, Columbus, OH 43215.

BLOW, SARAH PARSONS
Nursing director (retired). **Personal:** Born Sep 14, 1921, Kennett Square, PA; daughter of Celia Nora Carey Parsons (deceased) and Boston Parsons (deceased); married John Thomas Blow (deceased); children: Roxine Louise, Michael Warren. **Educ:** St Johns Univ, BS 1955; Col Univ, MA 1958. **Career:** Kings Cty Hosp Ctr, asst dir nursing 1966-68; Provident Clin Neighbor Health Ctr, dir nursing 1968-70; Concord Nursing Home, admiss 1972-74; Kings Cty Hosp Ctr, dir of patient serv 1977; White House Conf on Aging, gov appt delegate 1982. **Orgs:** Mem Amer Nurses Assn 1948; founder, past pres Womens League of Sci & Med Inc 1960-75; lic nrsg home adm NY 1972; delegate UN for Natl Assn of Negro Bus & Professional Womens Clubs Inc 1973; sec Brooklyn Assn for Mental Health 1976; bd mem Marcus Garvey Nursing Home 1978; natl chmn Freedmens Nurses Alumni Clubs Reunion 1979; trustee Concord Baptist Church Brooklyn; bd mem Brooklyn Civic Council. **Honors/Awds:** 1st prize NY NAACP Top Memshp Writer 1963; Brooklyn Disting Citizens Awd 1973; Prof Awd 1974; Comm Awd 1974; Humanitarian Awd 1975; Sojourner Truth Awd 1978; Comm Serv Awd 1979; Apprec Awd for Outstanding Comm Partic & Leadership 1984; Apprec Awd from Shirley Chisholm Cultural Inst for Children Inc 1984; Humanitarian Awd (Alpha Cosmetologists) 1986; "A Black Woman Who Makes It Happen," Natl Council of Negro Woman Queens Section, 1989; (non government) delegate to the United Nations for the Natl Assn of Negro Business and Professional Women Clubs Inc, 1988-. **Home Addr:** 312 Brooklyn Ave, Brooklyn, NY 11213.

BLUDSON-FRANCIS, VERNETT MICHELLE
Banker. **Personal:** Born Feb 18, 1951, New York, NY; daughter of Alfreda Peace Bludson and William Benjamin Bludson; married Robert Francis Sr, Aug 15, 1981; children: Robert Jr. **Educ:** New York Univ, New York NY, BS, 1973, MPA, 1976. **Career:** Morgan Guaranty Trust, New York NY, mgmt trainee, 1973-75; Citibank, NA, New York, NY, vice pres, 1975-; Natl Minority/Women's Vendor Program, Citibank, NA, New York, NY vice pres & dir, 1977-. **Orgs:** Natl Urban Affairs Council, 1984-; Natl Minority Business Council, 1986-; Coalition of 100 Black Women; YW/YMCA Day Care Centers Inc, 1986-; National Forum for Black Public Administrators; NAACP; UBC; Black Achievers in Industry Alumni Assn; Images-Wall Street Chapter; Cornell Univ Cooperative Extension Program; Natl Assn of Women Business Owners; New York State Dept of Economic Development/Minority and Women's Division. **Honors/Awds:** Black Achievers, Citibank/Harlem YMCA, 1984; Those Who Make A Difference, Natl Urban Affairs Council, 1985; Minority Advocate of the Year, US Dept of Commerce MBDA Regional Office, 1985; Mary McLeod Bethune Award, Natl Council of Negro Women, 1986; Public Private-Sector Award, US Dept of Housing and Urban Development, 1986; Banker of the Year, Urban Bankers Coalition, 1987; Woman of the Year, Harlem YMCA, 1987; Cecelia Cabiness Saunders Award, New Harlem YMCA, 1987; Top 100 Black Business & Professional Women, Dollars & Sense Magazine, 1988; co-sponsor, Executive Banking programs with NMBC, 1983, 1984, 1985, Executive Banking Program with Westchester Minority Contractors Assn, 1986; Career Exploration summer internship program with Hunter Coll & Coalition of 100 Black Women, 1986; co-host, First Annual BAI Alumni Fundraiser, 1986; chair, NUAC Student Development Dinner, 1988; sponsor, Department of Defense Symposium for the Vendor Input Committee, 1988. **Business Addr:** Vice Pres, Citibank/Citicorp, 1 Court Square, 10th fl, Long Island City, NY 11101.

BLUE, DANIEL TERRY, JR.
Attorney, state representative. **Personal:** Born Apr 18, 1949, Lumberton, NC; son of Allene Morris Blue and Daniel T Blue Sr; married Edna Earle Smith Blue, Jan 26, 1972; children: Daniel Terry III, Kanika, Dhamian. **Educ:** North Carolina Central Univ, Durham, NC, BS, mathematics, 1970; Duke University, Durham, NC, JD, 1973. **Career:** Sanford, Adams, McCullough and Beard, Attys at Law, Raleigh, NC, 1973-76; Thigpen, Blue, Stephens and Fellers, Raleigh, NC, managing partner, 1976-; North Carolina House of Representatives, District 21 representative, speaker of the house, 1991-95. **Orgs:** Elder, Davie Street Presbyterian Church; member, Alpha Phi Alpha Fraternity Inc; member, North Carolina and American Bar Associations; mem, Wautauga Club, Kiwanis Club; mem, bd of dirs, First Union National Bank of NC; trustee, Duke Univ; pres-elect, National Conference of State Legislature, 1997; chair, Clinton/Gore Campaign for NC; bd of visitors, Duke Law School. **Honors/Awds:** First black speaker of the North Carolina House of Representatives; first black speaker of a Southern legislature since Reconstruction; Outstanding Legislator Award, North Carolina Association of Trial Lawyers, 1985; Outstanding Legislature Award, North Carolina Association of Black Lawyers, 1985; Martin Luther King Jr Service Award, North Carolina General Baptist State Convention, 1991; Citizen of the Year Award: Alpha Phi Alpha, Omega Psi Phi, Kappa Alpha Psi, Phi Beta Sigma, Alpha Kappa Alpha, Delta Sigma Theta, Zeta Phi Beta, Sigma Gamma Rho, 1977-91; Adam Clayton Powell Award; Robert F Kennedy-Jacob Jaritz Award; National 4-H Alumni Award; Friend of the Working People, NC AFL-CIO; Outstanding Black Men Award; recipient of eight honorary degrees. **Business Addr:** Attorney, Thigpen, Blue, Stephens and Fellers, PO Box 1730, Raleigh, NC 27602.

BLUE, VIDA, JR.
Sports executive. **Personal:** Born Jul 28, 1949, Mansfield, LA; son of Sallie A Henderson Blue and Vida Rochelle Blue Sr; children: Alexis Lee, Valerie Augusta, Sallie Augusta, Evelyn Diane. **Educ:** Southern Univ Shreveport LA, attended. **Career:** Burlington, pitcher, 1968; Birmingham, pitcher, 1969; Oakland, pitcher, 1969; Iowa, pitcher, 1970; Oakland Athletics, pitcher, 1970-77; Kansas City Royals, pitcher, 1982-83; San Francisco Giants rep, 1978-81, 1985-; Vida Blue Baseball Camp, Pleasanton, CA, founder. **Honors/Awds:** Led Amer League in shutouts with 8 in 1971; Named Amer League Pitcher of the Year by The Sporting News 1971; Named Amer League Most Valuable Player by Baseball Writers' Assoc of Amer 1971; Won Amer League Cy Young Memorial Awd 1971; Named lefthanded pitcher on The Sporting News Amer League All-Star Team 1971; Named to Amer League All-Star Team 1977; Named Lefthanded pitcher on The Sporting News Natl League All-Star Team 1978; Named Natl League Pitcher of the Year by The Sporting News 1978; Named to Natl League All-Star Team 1980. **Business Addr:** Founder, Vida Blue Baseball Camp, PO Box 1449, Pleasanton, CA 94566.

BLUFORD, GRADY L.
Personnel director. **Personal:** Born May 21, 1930, Flint, MI; son of Atha Smyers Bluford and William Bluford; married Harriet Trosper Bluford, Nov 14, 1959; children: Michelle, Brent. **Educ:** Morningside Coll, BS, 1958; University of South Dakota, MA, guidance and counseling, 1974; Covington Theological

Seminary, master's of bible ministry, master's of christian counseling, doctor's of bible ministry; medical technologist training. **Career:** St Luke's Med Ctr, med tech; Goodwill Ind Wall St Mission, vice pres of personnel, bd of dir; pastor, Westside Church of Christ. **Orgs:** Secretary, Sioux and Youth Symphony; committee, Children's Miracle Network Telethon; NAACP; advisory board, Adult Basic Education, state level; appointed by the governor, Commission for Continuing Legal Education for Lawyers, state level. **Honors/Awds:** Outstanding Young Man Award Jr Chamber of Commerce, 1965; past pres, Iowa Rehabilitation, 1989-90; pres, Suburban Rotary Club. **Business Addr:** Dir of Personnel, Goodwill Industries, 3100 West 4th St, Sioux City, IA 51103.

BLUFORD, GUION STEWART, JR.
Astronaut (retired), company executive. **Personal:** Born Nov 22, 1942, Philadelphia, PA; son of Lolita Bluford and Guion Bluford; married Linda Tull; children: Guion Stewart III, James Trevor. **Educ:** Pennsylvania State Univ, BS, 1964; Williams Air Force Base, Arizona, pilot training, 1964; Squadron Officers School, 1971; Air Force Inst of Technology, MS, 1974, PhD, 1978; Univ of Houston, Clear Lake, MBA, 1987. **Career:** USAF F-4C pilot, Vietnam; instructor pilot, standardization/evaluation officer, asst flight commander, Sheppard Air Force Base, Texas, 1967; staff devel engineer, chief of aerodynamics & airframe branch, Wright-Patterson Air Force Base, Ohio, 1974-78; NASA astronaut, 1979-93; mission specialist, STS-8 Orbiter Challenger, August 1983; mission specialist, STS 61-A Orbiter Challenger, October 1985; point of contact for generic Spacelab systems and experiments, payload safety, orbitor systems, and flight software issues, Astronaut Office, 1987; assigned technical duties, Astronaut Office; mission specialist, STS-39 Orbiter Discovery, April 1991; mission specialist STS-53, Orbiter Discovery, December 1992; NYMA Inc, vp/gen mgr, 1993-. **Orgs:** Fellow, Amer Inst of Aeronautics and Astronautics; Natl Research Council's Aeronautics & Space Engineering Bd; bd of dirs, Natl Inventors Hall of Fame; NASA Alumni League; Tau Beta Pi; Natl Technical Assn; Tuskegee Airmen. **Honors/Awds:** Leadership Award, Phi Delta Kappa, 1962; Distinguished Natl Scientist Award, Natl Soc of Black Engineers, 1979; two NASA Group Achievement Awards, 1980, 1981; Distinguished Alumni Award, 1983, Alumni Fellow Award, 1986, Pennsylvania State Univ Alumni Assn; NASA Space Flight Medal, 1983, 1985, 1991, 1992; Ebony Black Achievement Award, 1983; Image Award, NAACP, 1983; Distinguished Service Medal, State of Pennsylvania, 1984; Whitney Young Memorial Award, New York City Urban League; NASA Exceptional Service Medal, 1992; NASA Distinguished Svc Medal, 1994; honorary doctorate degrees from Florida A&M Univ, Texas Southern Univ, Virginia State Univ, Morgan State Univ, Stevens Inst of Technology, Tuskegee Inst, Bowie State Coll, Thomas Jefferson Univ, Chicago State Univ, Georgian Ct Coll, Drexel Univ; Kent State Univ; logged 688 hours in space, 1995; numerous others. **Special Achievements:** First African American to fly in space, STS-8, the eighth flight of the Space Shuttle; first African American to return to space, STS-61A, the 22nd flight of the Space Shuttle, STS-39; the 40th flight of the Space Shuttle, and STS-53, the 52nd flight of the Space Shuttle; Intl Space Hall of Fame, inductee, 1997. **Military Serv:** USAF, col, 1965-93; distinguished Air Force ROTC graduate, 1964; Natl Defense Serv Medal, 1965; Vietnam Campaign Medal, 1967; Vietnam Cross of Gallantry with Palm, 1967; Vietnam Serv Medal, 1967; ten Air Force Medals, 1967; Air Force Outstanding Unit Awards, 1967, 1970, 1972; German Air Force Aviation Badge, Federal Republic of West Germany, 1969; T-38 Instructor Pilot of the Month, 1970; Air Training Command Outstanding Flight Safety Award, 1970; Air Force Commendation Medal, 1972; Mervin E Gross Award, Air Force Inst of Technology, 1974; Air Force Meritorious Serv Award, 1978; USAF Command Pilot Astronaut Wings, 1983; Defense Superior Serv Medal, 1984; Defense Meritorious Service Medal, 1989, 1992, 1993; Air Force Legion of Merit, 1994. **Business Addr:** NYMA Inc, 2001 Aerospace Pkwy, Brook Park, OH 44142.

BLUFORD, JAMES F.
Insurance agent. **Personal:** Born Sep 6, 1943, Ontario;son of Francis J Bluford & Dorysse G Bluford; married Elaine Bluford, Jan 25, 1990; children: James Francis, Sherice S, Nataki Monique, Eric Christopher (stepson). **Educ:** Wayne County Committee College, Arts, 1972. **Career:** Allstate Insurance Co, sr acct agent, currently. **Business Addr:** Senior Account Agent, Allstate Insurance Co, 5836 Wayne Rd, Westland, MI 48185, (313)722-0700.

BLUNDEN, JERALDYNE K.
Performing artist. **Personal:** Born Dec 10, 1940, Dayton, OH; daughter of Elijah (deceased) & Winifred Kilborn; married Charles C, Oct 15, 1959; children: Debra Lynne Blunden-Diggs, Derek Charles. **Career:** Wilberforce Univ, dance instructor, 1966-72; Sinclair College, dance instructor, 1970-77; Wright State Univ, dance instructor, 1978-81; self-employed, founder-artistic dir, 1959-; Dayton Contemporary Dance Co, founder-artistic dir, 1968-. **Orgs:** Dance USA, bd member, 1991-; Intl Assn of Blacks in Dance, bd member, 1991-; Ohio Dance, advisory bd member, 1980-89; Regional Dance America, life, honorary member, 1973-90. **Honors/Awds:** Univ of Dayton, Honorary Doctor of Fine Arts, 1990; MacArthur Foundation, MacArthur Fellowship, 1994; Ohio Anna Library Assn, Citation in Dance, 1994; Natl Council of Christians & Jews, Award, 1990; Ohio Arts Council, Certificate of Achievement, 1988; Ohio Dance, Outstanding Achievement Award, 1989; Wright State Univ, Honorary Doctor of Humane Letters. **Business Addr:** Founder/Artistic Director, Dayton Contemporary Dance Co, 126 North Main St, Metropolitan Arts Center, Ste 200, Dayton, OH 45402, (513)228-3232.

BLUNT, MADELYNE BOWEN
Publisher. **Personal:** Born Apr 7, Providence, RI; daughter of Ora Jackson Davis and William Mansfield Davis; married Leon Battle, Oct 19, 1981 (deceased); children: Rolanda Elizabeth. **Educ:** Numerous special courses; Bryant Business Coll, RI; Case Western Reserve, Mgmt. **Career:** US Dept of Justice, traveling cons-media relations conf planner comm relations dept; Cleveland Call-Post, 1st full-time advertising sales woman 1959-60; Thomas J Davis Agency, admin asst; Kaiser WKBF-TV,TV producer 1968; Hurray for Black Women, prod, founder; Clubdate magazine, pres, owner, publisher. **Orgs:** Mem, NAMD, NHFL, NAACP; special program coordinator ''Com of Concern'' United Pastors Assn; program producer ''Devel of Consumer Conf'', ''Hurray for Black Women'' founder; Leadership Cleveland. **Honors/Awds:** Recognition for Documentary ''Black Peace'' 1968; Business Woman of the Year, CSU 1975; Black Woman of the Year City Council 1979; Award of Excellence Cty Commiss 1979; Gov Business Award 1980; Key to the City Mayor of Omaha NE Media Conf Race Relations; AKA Award; Top Ladies of Distinction Award Serv Comm 1982; Business Award Black Media 1983; Leadership Cleveland 1985 as one of cities Most Valuable Resources; Outstanding Business Contribution media award United Way Sources 1986; Award for Outstanding Contribution WJMO Business 1986; Rosa Parks Award, Pioneer in Business, 1989; Cleveland Roundtable, Congressman Louis Stokes 21st Congressional Caucus Award, Outstanding Business, 1989.

BLUNT, ROGER RECKLING
Construction company executive. **Personal:** Born Oct 12, 1930, Providence, RI; son of Bertha Reckling Blunt and Harry Weeden; married DeRosette Yvonne Hendricks; children: Roger Jr, Jennifer Mari, Amy Elizabeth, Jonathan Hendricks. **Educ:** USMA West Point, NY, BS 1956; MA Inst of Tech, MS 1962, MS 1962. **Career:** US Army Corps of Engr, officer 1956-69; Harbridge House Intl, senior asso 1969-71; Tyroc Construction Corp, CEO chmn 1971-; Blunt Enterprises Inc, CEO chrmn 1974-; Blunt & Evans Consulting Engr, managing partner 1979-84; Essex Construction Corp, chmn of bd, CEO 1985-. **Orgs:** Dir Potomac Electric Power Co 1984-; dir Greater WA Bd of Trade 1985-; dir Univ of MD Foundation; dir Greater Washington Rsch Ctr; mem Natl & DC Socs of Professional Engrs; mem Amer Soc of Civil Engrs; director, United Educators Insurance Risk Retention Group Inc, 1990-; dir, The Acacia Group. **Honors/Awds:** Comm serv Junior Citizens Corps Inc 1985; Reg Prof Engr Dist of Columbia 1963; Business Leadership Greater Washington Business Ctr 1976,78; Reg Prof Engr NY State 1981; Distinguished Serv Awd Natl Asphalt Pavement Assn 1984; Whitney Young Award, Boys Scouts of America. **Military Serv:** US Army Reserves major genl 1983; received Distinguished Service Medal, 1986. **Business Addr:** Chairman of the Board, CEO, Essex Construction Corp., 6432 Bock Rd, Oxon Hill, MD 20745-3001.

BLYE, CECIL A., SR.
Attorney. **Personal:** Born Nov 10, 1927, Gainesville, FL; son of Janie Blye and Richard Blye; married Alice; children: Cecilia, Cecil Jr, Steven. **Educ:** Attended Clark Coll, Northwestern Univ, Univ of Louisville. **Career:** The Louisville Defender, editor 1958-68; Blye & Webb, sr partner 1972-79; Blye, Blye & Blye, attorney 1987-. **Orgs:** Mem Amer, KY, Louisville Bar Assns; gen counsel KY Elks; Louisville-Jefferson Co Fedn Tchrs & Amer Postal Workers Union; Louisville Br mem Alpha Phi Alpha Frat; chmn Louisville NAACP Legal Redress Com. **Military Serv:** AUS 1st lt 1952-54. **Business Addr:** Attorney, 310 W Liberty St, Ste 412, Louisville, KY 40202.

BOAGS, CHARLES D.
Judge (retired). **Personal:** Born Jul 31, 1929, Brooklyn, NY; divorced; children: Lisa M, Martin R, Sarah E. **Educ:** Long Island Univ, BA 1951; Brooklyn Law School, LLB 1956. **Career:** Los Angeles Public Defender's Office, prel hearing dep 1958-61, supr ct trial dep 1961-71, Compton Mun Ct, dep in charge 1971-72; Cen Surpv Ct Trials Div, asst chief 1972-79; Beverly Hills Municipal Ct, judge 1979-90. **Orgs:** Mem, pres adv comm SW Commun Coll 1974; mem Langston Law Club 1958-84, NAPP 1970-77; bd dir Ctr Study Racial & soc Issues 1970-77, CA State Bar Comm, Corr Facilities 1973-77, CA Bd Leg Spec 1973-77, Black Stud Psych Assoc 1969,70; adm NY State Bar 1956, CA State Bar 1958. **Honors/Awds:** Cert Sp Crim Law 1973; Publ, Lectr, Vol Consult Cert of Apprec Awd Black Caucus Faculty, Admin & Staff Univ CA San Diego 1972; Cert of Apprec LA Cty Dist Attny's Youth Adv Bd 1973; Cert of Apprec Teem Post Youth Info Ctr 1974-76; Cert of Apprec Legal Aid Found of LA 1974; Trial Lawyer of the Year Langston Law Club 1975. **Military Serv:** USMC 1951-53. **Business Addr:** PO Box 65768, Los Angeles, CA 90065-6768.

BOARDLEY, CURTESTINE MAY
Federal official. **Personal:** Born Dec 3, 1943, Sandersville, GA; daughter of Zena Reaves May and William N. May; married James E Boardley, Jul 27, 1968; children: Angela B, Zena Y. **Educ:** Tuskegee Inst, BS 1965, MEd 1967. **Career:** Tuskegee Inst, admin asst to dean of women 1966-67; Howard Univ, residence counselor 1967-68; Public Sch of DC, counselor 1968; Vocational Rehab Admin of DC, vocational rehab counselor & acting coord counselor 1968-70; Fed Comm Commn, employee counselor 1970-73, EEO dir 1973-76; Civil Serv Commn, Office of Fed EEO 1976-79; US Office of Personnel Mgmt, EEO specialist & mgr, Office of Affirmative Employ Progs, 1979-83; Strayer Coll, Washington DC, instructor, 1987, 1989, mgr, personnel mgmt training div, 1983-95; US Dept of Agriculture, program management analyst, 1995-. **Orgs:** American Counseling Assn; mem, Ebenezer AME Church, 1987-; charter member, vp, Fort Washington Charter Chapter, Amer Business Women's Assn, 1986-; mem, The Group, Washington DC Metropolitan Area, 1981-; Delta Sigma Theta, 1992-. **Honors/Awds:** Participant in Natl Student YWCA Latin Amer Seminar to Chile & Peru, 1965; US Office of Personnel Mgmt, Meritorious Performance Award, 1985; Directors Award, 1990, Special Act Award, 1991, Sustained Superior Performance, 1992. **Home Addr:** 2902 Kingsway Rd, Fort Washington, MD 20744.

BOATMAN, MICHAEL
Actor. **Personal:** marrIed; children: Jordan. **Career:** Actor, currently. **Special Achievements:** Appeared in Peacemker, 1997; ''Spin city,'' ABC, 1996-.

BOATWRIGHT, CHRISTOPHER. **See Obituaries section.**

BOATWRIGHT, JOSEPH WELDON
Physician. **Personal:** Born Jan 4, 1949, Richmond, VA; married Evelyn Donella Durham; children: Joseph Weldon IV. **Educ:** Davis & Elkins Coll, BS 1970; Univ of VA Sch of Med, MD 1974; Med Coll of VA Grad Sch of Med Edn, residency 1978. **Career:** Private Practice, pediatrician. **Orgs:** Mem active staff St Mary's Hosp; mem active staff Richmond Meml Hosp; clinical instr Med Coll of VA; mem N Chamberlayne Civic Assn. **Honors/Awds:** Hon Scholarship Davis & Elkins Coll 1966; Scholarship Univ of VA 1970. **Home Addr:** 8321 Futham Ct, Richmond, VA 23227.

BOBBITT, LEROY
Attorney. **Personal:** Born Nov 1, 1943, Jackson, MS; son of Susie Bobbitt and Leroy Bobbitt; married Andrea; children: Dawn, Antoinette. **Educ:** MI State Univ, BA 1966; Stanford Univ Sch of Law, JD 1969. **Career:** Paul, Weiss, Rifkind, Wharton & Garrison, attorney 1970-74; Loeb & Loeb, attorney 1974, partner 1980-. **Orgs:** Mem State Bar of CA, Los Angeles Co Bar Assn, Amer Bar Assn; mem Los Angeles Copyright Soc, Black Entertainment & Sports Lawyers Assn. **Business Addr:** Attorney, Loeb & Loeb, 10100 Santa Monica Blvd, #2200, Los Angeles, CA 90067.

BOBINO, RITA FLORENCIA
Educational administrator, psychologist. **Personal:** Born Jun 18, 1934, San Francisco, CA; daughter of Urania Prince Cummings (deceased) and Arthur E Cummings (deceased); married Felix Joseph Bobino Jr; children: Sharelle Denice Hagg, Michael J, Mario K, Mauricio J, Malaika J. **Educ:** Laney Coll, AA 1973; Coll of the Holy Names, BS 1975; CA State Univ Hayward, MS 1977; The Wright Inst, PhD 1985. **Career:** Oakland Poverty Prog, 1960-71; Children Hosp Alameda Cty, dir women infants & childen's prog WIC 1973-76; Berkeley Mental Health Youth Prog, mental health worker 1976-77; San Francisco Streetwork Prog, counselor 1977-80; Oakland Unified Schools Youth Diversion Prog for HS, Cities in Schools dir 1980-84; Oakland Unified School Sr High, counselor, family therapist; on call-sexual assault therapist Highland Emergency Hospital Oakland; private practice in Oakland; Oakland Unified Schools Farwest High School, principal TSA, 1987-88; Oakland Unified Schools, Elmhurst Middle School, administrative assistant principal, Elmhurst Middle School, principal, 1995; Contra Costa College, instructor, Psychology of African American Women, 1994; motivational speaker on male/female relationships and personal empowerment, currently. **Orgs:** Co-founder, dir BWAMU 1976-, Relationship Strategy 1978-; mem Bay Area Black Psych 1979; NAACP 1983-85, Juvenile Hall Diversion Program Lucy King; mem Alpha Nu Omega Chap Alpha Kappa Alpha; Oakland Black Educators; member, Oakland Educ Assn 1980-; licensed marriage family therapist, California, 1980-; American Federation of School Administrators, AFL-CIO. **Honors/Awds:** Social Science Honor Soc Pi Gamma Mu 1975; ''Self-Concept of Black Students Who Have Failed'' masters thesis; ''African Amer Fathers & Daughters'' doctoral dissertation completed; Alpha Kappa Alpha Sorority 63rd Far Western Regional, The Charlene V Carodine Unique Professional Achievement Award, 1992. **Home Addr:** 3833 Elston Ave, Oakland, CA 94602. **Business Phone:** (510)569-3267.

BOBO, ORLANDO
Professional football player. **Personal:** Born Feb 9, 1974; children: Xavier, Anneshia, Kristen. **Educ:** Northeast Louisiana, attended. **Career:** Minnesota Vikings, guard, 1997-. **Business Addr:** Professional Football Player, Minnesota Vikings, 9520 Viking Dr, Eden Prairie, MN 55344, (612)828-6500.

BOBONIS, REGIS DARROW, JR.
Broadcasting company executive. **Personal:** Born Dec 8, 1960, Pittsburgh, PA; son of Regis and Hurley BoBonis. **Educ:** Marquette Univ, BA, 1983. **Career:** Hearst Broadcasting, desk assistant, 1983-85, night assignment editor, 1985-88, day assignment editor, 1988-89, assignment manager, 1989-91, managing editor, 1991-. **Business Addr:** Managing Editor, WTAE-TV Hearst Broadcasting, 400 Ardmore Blvd., Pittsburgh, PA 15221, (412)244-4514.

BOCAGE, RONALD J.
Insurance company corporate counsel. **Personal:** Born Mar 18, 1946, New Orleans, LA; son of Eva Charles Bocage and Charles L Bocage; married Myrna DeGruy Bocage, Aug 16, 1969. **Educ:** Univ of New Orleans, New Orleans LA, BA, 1968; Harvard Law School, Cambridge MA, JD, 1972. **Career:** Mintz, Levin, Cohn, Ferris, Glovsky & Popeo, Boston MA, 1972-74; John Hancock Mutual Life Insurance Co, Boston MA, atty, 1974-79, asst counsel, 1979-83, assoc counsel, 1983-86, sr assoc counsel, 1986, second vice pres & counsel, 1986-88, vice pres & counsel, 1988-. **Orgs:** Mem, Amer Bar Assn (Corporate Section), 1972-; mem, Massachusetts Black Lawyers Assn, 1976-; mem Assn of Life Insurance Counsel, 1986-. **Military Serv:** US Army Reserve, E-7 (staff sergeant), 1969-75. **Business Addr:** Vice Pres/Counsel, John Hancock Mutual Life Ins Co., John Hancock Pl, T-55, PO Box 111, Boston, MA 02117, (617)572-8050.

BODDEN, WENDELL N.
Business executive. **Personal:** Born Mar 8, 1930, New York, NY; married Natalie; children: Mark, Wendell Jr, Ingrid. **Educ:** Attended, CW Post Coll, Armed Forces Inst. **Career:** Grumman Aerospace Corp, asst group leader & designer of structural systems 1966-68, dir cooperative educ & hS work/study progs 1968-74, mgr continuing educ sect 1974-. **Orgs:** Past vice pres Natl Cooperative Educ Assn 1973-74; chmn educ com NAACP Long Island; mem Wyandawch Devel Corp; Belmont Lake Civic Assn; Afro-Amer Rep; NY State Citz Adv Cncl on Occupational Educ 1975-; Nassau/Suffolk United Way Allocations Panel 1975-.

BODDIE, ALGERNON OWENS
Contractor. **Personal:** Born Apr 3, 1933, Demopolis, AL; married Velma Fitzmon. **Educ:** Tuskegee Inst AL, BS Indust Ed 1954. **Career:** St Judes Ed Inst Montgomery AL, teacher 1954-55; Boddie's Bldg Constr Inc, proprietor & estimator 1963-70; FHA Seattle, consult fee insp 1969-71; Tacoma Comm Devel, consult 1976-77; Boddie's Bldg Constr Inc, pres 1970-85. **Orgs:** Mem Tacoma Bldg & Fire Code Appeals Bd 1969-76; mem Tacoma Chap Assoc Gen Contractors of Amer 1974-85; pres Tacoma Publ Library Bd of Trustees 1978-79. **Honors/Awds:** Comm Coop Awd Tacoma Publ Schools Div of Vocational Rehab 1971. **Business Addr:** President, Boddie's Bldg Construction Inc, 2102 S 12th St, Tacoma, WA 98405.

BODDIE, ARTHUR WALKER
Physician. **Personal:** Born Apr 21, 1910, Forsyth, GA; son of Luetta Sams Boddie and William Fisher Boddie; married Denise K Gray MD; children: Arthur W Jr. **Educ:** Atlanta Univ, AB 1931; Meharry Med Coll, MD 1935. **Career:** Physician, currently. **Orgs:** Mem Kappa Alpha Psi 1933; mem Acad of Family Practice 1949, MI State Med Soc 1949, Natl Med Assn, Amer Soc of Abdominal Surgeons 1960, Pan Amer Med Assn 1968; exec comm Acad of Family Practice 1973-77; mem Plymouth Congr Church; life mem NAACP; examiner Selective Service; co-founder Detroit Med & Surg Ctr; chairman of the board, NMA, 1958-65; member, Royal Academy of Physicians. **Honors/Awds:** Citation Pres Roosevelt, Truman, Harper Grace Hosp, St Joseph Meml Hosp, Detroit Meml Hosp; fellow Amer Acad of Family Med. **Home Addr:** 1991 W Boston Blvd, Detroit, MI 48206. **Business Addr:** Physician, 15831 Mack Ave, Detroit, MI 48214.

BODDIE, DANIEL W.
Attorney. **Personal:** Born Feb 10, 1922, New Rochelle, NY; married Annie Virginia Wise. **Educ:** VA Union U, AB 1953; Cornell Law Sch, JD 1949. **Career:** Corp Counsel City of New Rochelle, 2nd asst; Law Sec; City Judge; Privat Practice. **Orgs:** Pres New Rochelle Bar Assn 1972; past chmn New Rochelle Hsng Auth; past legal & counsel NAACP; mem Omega Psi Phi; trustee Bethesda Bapt Ch. **Military Serv:** AUS m/sgt 1945. **Business Addr:** 515 North Ave, New Rochelle, NY.

BODDIE, GWENDOLYN M.
Educator. **Personal:** Born Aug 4, 1957, Columbus, GA. **Educ:** Mercer Univ, BA 1979; Tuskegee Inst, MEd 1981. **Career:** Tuskegee Area Health Educ Ctr, program coord 1981-83; Booker Washington Comm Ctr, program coord 1983; Atlanta Jr Coll, counselor 1983-85; Southern Univ, dir student recruitment 1985-. **Orgs:** Mem United Way 1983. **Honors/Awds:** Kappa Delta Pi Lambda Delta 1980. **Business Addr:** Dir Student Recruitment, Southern University, PO Box 9399, Baton Rouge, LA 70813.

BODDIE, LEWIS F., SR.
Physician (retired). **Personal:** Born Apr 4, 1913, Forsyth, GA; son of Luetta T Sams Boddie and William F Boddie; married Marian Bernice Claytor; children: Roberta, Lewis Jr, Bernice, Pamela, Kenneth, Margaret, Fredda. **Educ:** Morehouse Coll, AB, 1933; Meharry Coll, MD, 1938; Homer G Phillips Hospital, St Louis, MO, internship and residency, 1938-42. **Career:** Physician and surgeon, private practice until 1993. **Orgs:** Diplomate Natl Bd 1941, Amer Bd Obstetrics & Gynecology 1949; fellow Amer Coll Surgeons 1950; Amer Coll Obstetrics & Gynecology 1949; chmn 1968-70, vice chmn 1965-67, Dept OB/Gyn; consult staff Queen of Angels Hosp; clinical asst prof Univ of So CA; dir, sec Vernbro Med Corp 1952-89; dir State Bd Childrens Home Soc of CA 1952-88; pres Children's Home Soc 1968-70; dir Child Welfare League of Amer 1969-75; mem adv comm LA Welfare Planning Council 1958-61; mem Priorities Committee and Allocations Committee, United Way of Los Angeles 1985-95. **Honors/Awds:** Citation, LA Cty Bd Supvr; Resolution of Appreciation, LA City Council, 1958; Physician of the Year, Queen of Angels Hospital, 1987. **Home Addr:** 1215 S Gramercy Pl, Los Angeles, CA 90019.

BODRICK, LEONARD EUGENE
Educator. **Personal:** Born May 17, 1953, Orangeburg, SC; married Sharon Trice; children: Jabari Talib, Nia Imani. **Educ:** Johnson C Smith Univ, BA (Cum Laude) 1976; Univ of Pittsburgh, MPIA Pub Admin 1979; Univ of NC-Chapel Hill, PhD Prog 1980-83. **Career:** Three Rivers Youth Inc, staff counselor 1978-79; Southern Ctr Rural & Urban Develop, training dir 1979-80; Educ Oppor Ctr Roxboro NC, outreach coun 1983-85; Johnson C Smith Univ, dir upward bound prog. **Orgs:** Mem TransAfrica 1977-; finance chair 1985-87, conference chair 1987, NC Southern Area rep 1987-89 NC Council of Educ Oppor Progs; mem Amer Soc of Public Administrators, Conference of Minority Public Administrators; founding mem UNCF Inter-Alumni Chapt; founding mem managing editor GSPIA Journal; founding mem Exec Council Black Grad and Professional Student Caucus; mem Charlotte Council for Children, NAACP, SCLC, Charlotte Drop-Out Prevention Collaborative. **Honors/Awds:** Horne Scholarship 1973; Babcock Scholarship 1974; Pre-Doctoral Fellowship 1976; Training Grant 1977; founding member/managing editor Univ of Pittsburgh GSPIA 1979; Teaching Assistantship UNC Chapel Hill 1981-82; Outstanding Young Men of Amer 1982. **Home Addr:** 2500 Eastway Dr, Charlotte, NC 28205. **Business Addr:** Dir Upward Bound Program, Johnson C Smith University, 100 Beatties Ford Rd, Charlotte, NC 28216.

BOFILL, ANGELA
Singer. **Personal:** Born May 2, 1954, Bronx, NY. **Educ:** Hartt College of Music, 1972-73; Manhattan School of Music, Mus B, 1976. **Career:** Singer in night clubs, cabarets; recording artist, 1979-. **Honors/Awds:** Most Promising New Female Vocalist, Latin New York Magazine, 1979; #1 Female Jazz Artist, Cashbox, 1979; #5 Female Vocalist, Cashbox.

BOGGAN, DANIEL, JR.
Association executive. **Personal:** Born Dec 9, 1945, Albion, MI; son of Ruthie Jean Crum Boggan and Daniel Boggan Sr; married Jacqueline Ann Beal Boggan, Oct 4, 1977; children: DeVone, Daniel III, Dhanthan, Alike. **Educ:** Albion Coll, BA 1967; Univ of MI, MSW 1968. **Career:** Starr Commonwealth for Boys, clinical supv 1968-70; Jackson MI, asst city mgr 1970-72; Flint MI, dep city mgr 1972-74, city mgr 1974-76; Portland OR, dir mgmt serv 1976-78; San Diego CA, asst cty admin 1978-79; Essex Cty NJ, cty admin 1979-82; Berkeley CA, city mgr 1982-86; Univ of CA Berkeley, assoc vice chancellor business and admin serv 1986, acting vice chancellor business and admin serv 1986-87, vice chancellor business and admin serv, beginning 1987; Natl Collegiate Athletic Assn, Education Service Division, head, 1994-96, chief operating officer, 1996-. **Orgs:** Chmn Alameda Cty Mgrs Assn 1984-85; chmn committee on minorities & women League of CA Cities 1985-; board member, Clorox Corp, 1990-; board member, Coro Foundation, 1990; board member, Oakland Chapter, 1985-, pres, 1990-, National Forum for Black Public Administrators; life member, NAACP; Carolina Freight Corp, bd mem, 1995; Payless Shoe Source, bd mem. **Honors/Awds:** Outstanding Public Administrator, 1975, Chapter Service Award, 1986, Marks of Excellence Award, 1987, NFBPA; Youth Leadership Award, 1965; Albion College, Outstanding Alumnus Award, 1991; UC Berkeley Citation, 1994. **Business Addr:** Chief Operating Officer, Natl Collegiate Athletic Assn, 6201 College Blvd, Shawnee Mission, KS 66211.

BOGGS, NATHANIEL
Educator & educational administrator. **Personal:** Born Dec 19, 1926, Anniston, AL; children: Paula, Cornell, Lynette, Andy. **Educ:** Howard Univ, BS 1951, MS 1955, PhD 1963; UCLA, Post Doc 1969-70. **Career:** 155 AGF Band Grafenwohr Germany, dir 1946; Walter Reed, physiologist 1956-59; Natl Inst of Science, eastern reg vice pres 1970-71; Beta Beta Beta Biological Soc, sponsor 1971-73; Coll of Sci & Tech, dean vsu 1972-74, dean famu 1974-76; AL State Univ the Graduate School, interim dean asu 1984-. **Orgs:** Vstg prof zoology UCLA 1969-70; pres Nu Lambda Chap Alpha Phi Alpha Frat 1970-71; editor-in-chief Beta Kappa Chi Bulletin 1972-74. **Honors/Awds:** Plaque Consortium for Black Prof Develop for Excellence in Biological Life and Marine Sciences 1977; trophy 1st place Strikes & Spares Bowling League 1983. **Military Serv:** AUS corpl 2 yrs; Good Conduct Medal; ETO Medal; Expert Rifleman. **Home Addr:** 4060 Strathmore Dr, Montgomery, AL 36116. **Business Addr:** Prof Biol-University College, Alabama State University, 915 S Jackson St, Montgomery, AL 36195.

BOGHASSIAN, SKUNDER
Educator, artist. **Personal:** Born Jul 22, 1937, Addis Ababa, Ethiopia; divorced; children: Aida Maryam, Edward Addissou. **Educ:** St Martins School of Art, London, 1955-57; Ecole des Beaux Arts, Paris, visiting artist, 1959-60; La Grande Chaumiere, Paris, 1961-62. **Career:** Howard University, College of Fine Arts, assoc professor to full professor, 1971-; one man show, Trisolini Gallery, Ohio University, lecturer, 1980; Atlanta Center for Black Art, instructor in painting, 1970-71; Addis Abada Fine Arts School, Ethiopia, instructor in painting & design, 1966-69. **Orgs:** Participant, Afro-American Studies Dept, Harvard University, 1974; chairman, selectioncommittee, Exhibition of Contemporary African Art, Howard University, 1975; external examiner, Makerere University, Kampala Uganda, 1976; African Art Today, African American Institute, show, New York City, 1974; Field Mus, Contemporary Arts Festival, Chicago, group show, 1974. **Honors/Awds:** Invited Participant, 2nd Cultural Moussem, Asilah Morocco, 1979; 1st prize, Contemporary African Painters, Munich Germany, 1967; His Majesty Haile Selassie I & 1st Prize, Natl Contribution in the Field of Art, Addis Abada Ethiopia, 1967; 1st prize, Black Artist, Atlanta University, 1970; commissioned to design a stamp, Combat Racism, UN, New York City, 1977. **Business Addr:** Professor, Dept of Art, Howard University, 2400 Sixth St NW, Washington, DC 20059-0002.

BOGLE, ROBERT W.
Newspaper publishing executive. **Career:** Philadelphia Tribune, publisher, president, currently. **Orgs:** National Newspaper Publishers Association, president, 1991-. **Business Addr:** President, Philadelphia Tribune, 524-526 S 16th St, Philadelphia, PA 19146, (215)843-4050.

BOGUES, LEON FRANKLIN
Association executive. **Personal:** Born Nov 8, 1926, New York, NY; married Dorothy Johnson, 1947; children: Norma, Leon Jr. **Educ:** Long Island Univ, AB 1952. **Career:** Dept Soc Svcs, soc investigator, 1951-53; Magistrate Ct, 1953; Domestic Relations Ct, 1954-59; Bronx Supreme Ct, 1954-59; NY City Dept of Probation, senior probation officer, 1959-80; New York State Senate, senator 29th dist, 1980-86; Harlem Urban Development Corp, vice chairman, currently. **Orgs:** Vice pres bd dir W Side C of C 1975-77; exec bd mem Mid-Man NAACP 1975; chmn Polit Action Comm 1975; 1st vice chmn Comm Planning Bd 1977; chmn Comm Planning Bd; chmn bd of trustees Welfare Fund Probation Officers Assn NYC.

BOGUES, TYRONE (MUGGSY)
Professional basketball player. **Personal:** Born Jan 9, 1965, Baltimore, MD. **Educ:** Wake Forest Univ, Winston-Salem, NC, 1983-87. **Career:** Washington Bullets, 1987-88; Charlotte Hornets, 1988-. **Business Addr:** Professional Basketball Player, Charlotte Hornets, Hives Dr, Charlotte, NC 28217.

BOGUS, HOUSTON, JR.
Physician. **Personal:** Born Sep 10, 1951, Knoxville, TN; son of Louise Bogus and Houston Bogus; married Dorris Loretta Gray; children: Alisha Dione, Houston III, Alyson Gray. **Educ:** Univ of TN, BA 1973; Meharry Medical Coll, MD 1979. **Career:** United States Army, intern internal medicine 1979-80, resident internal medicine 1980-82, staff internist/chief of emergency serv 1982-83, fellow in gastroenterology 1983-85, staff internist/gastroenterologist 1985-90; Kaiser Permanente, gastroenterologist, currently. **Orgs:** Mem Omega Psi Phi Frat 1976-. **Honors/Awds:** Mem Alpha Omega Alpha Honor Medical Soc Meharry Chap 1979-. **Military Serv:** AUS major 10 yrs; Army Commendation Medal 1983. **Home Addr:** 3105 San Simeon Way, Plano, TX 75023-1311. **Business Addr:** Staff Member, Dept of Gastroenterology, Kaiser Permanente, 12606 Greenville Ave, Dallas, TX 75243.

BOGUS, SDIANE ADAMZ (S. DIANE)
Educator, poet, publisher. **Personal:** Born Jan 22, 1946, Chicago, IL; married T Nelson Gilbert, Apr 1, 1989. **Educ:** Stillman Coll Tuscaloosa AL, BA 1968; Syracuse Univ Syracuse NY, MA 1969; Miami Univ Oxford OH, PhD 1988; Univ of Hawaii, PhD, parapsychology, 1998. **Career:** LA Southwest Coll, instructor 1976-81; Miami U, instructor 1981-84; WIM Publications, author 1971-, founder 1979-, publisher; California State University, Stanislaus Turlock, CA, professor of American literature, 1986-90; DeAnza College, Cupertino, CA, instructor,

1990-. **Orgs:** Mem Delta Sigma Theta Sorority 1965-; mem Nat Tchrs of Engl 1981-; mem Feminist Writer's Guild 1980-; mem COSMEP Independent Publishers 1975-; board member, Multicultural Publishers Exchange, 1989-92. **Honors/Awds:** Honored by Art & Music Dept Trenton Public Lib 1983; works adapted into CA State Univ Archives 1982; nominated for Pulitzer Prize, Sapphire's Sampler 1982; nominated for Lambda Literary Award for The Chant of the Women of Magdalena; Black Writer's Award from Peninsula Book Club, 1992; Woman of Achievement Award, 1997. **Business Addr:** Publisher, WIM Publications, PO Box 2087, Cupertino, CA 95015.

BOHANNAN-SHEPPARD, BARBARA
City official. **Personal:** Born Jun 15, 1950, Ornancock, VA; daughter of Mary Sue Chandler and Robert Harry Lee (deceased). **Educ:** Delaware County Community College. **Career:** BB Educational Training and Children's Services, owner, currently; City of Chester, mayor, currently. **Orgs:** National Political Congress of Black Women, honorary chairwoman; Conference of Mayors; Natl Council of Negro Women; NAACP. **Honors/Awds:** Peace and Justice Award, 1991. **Business Addr:** Mayor, City of Chester, Municipal Bldg, 5th & Welsh Sts, Chester, PA 19013, (215)447-7723.

BOHANNON, ETDRICK
Professional basketball player. **Personal:** Born May 29, 1973. **Educ:** Auburn-Montgomery. **Career:** Indiana Pacers, forward, 1997-. **Business Addr:** Professional Basketball Player, Indiana Pacers, 300 E Market St, Indianapolis, IN 46204, (317)263-2100.

BOL, MANUTE
Professional basketball player. **Educ:** Cleveland State Univ, 1984. **Career:** Center, Washington Bullets, 1986-88, Golden State Warriors, 1989-90, Philadelphia 76ers, 1990-. **Business Addr:** Professional Basketball Player, Philadelphia 76ers, Veterans Stadium, Philadelphia, PA 19179-0001.

BOLDEN, BETTY A.
Personnel administrator. **Personal:** Born Dec 24, 1944, St Louis, MO. **Educ:** Univ of Illinois, BA, 1965; DePaul Univ, MA, 1969. **Career:** US Dept of Labor, dep dir prsnl, exec asst 1976-78, supr prsnl mgmt spec 1975-76; US Civil Serv Commn Wash, DC, prsnl mgmt spclst 1973-75; US Postal Serv Chicago/Wash DC, prsnl mgmt spclst 1968-75; US Civl Serv Commn Chicago, career intern 1967. **Orgs:** Mem prsnl com Delta Sigma Theta 1979-81. **Business Addr:** Special Asst to Asso Adm, Small Business Adm, 1441 L St NW Room 602, Washington, DC 20416.

BOLDEN, CHARLES E.
Union representative. **Personal:** Born Feb 12, 1941, Alabama; son of Ernestine Bolden and Charles H Bolden; married Diane Nation; children: Charles R, Marva L. **Educ:** AL State U, BS 1966; LaSalle Ext U, LLB 1975; University of Phoenix, Denver, CO, MA, arts management, 1984. **Career:** Nat Educ Assn Chicago, fld rep 1968-70; Nat Educ Assn Denver, orgnzng team coord 1970-74; National Education Association, Washington, DC, manager of shared staffing program, 1974-76; National Education Association, Denver, CO, organizational specialist, 1976-. **Orgs:** Orgnzr Publ Sch Tchrs for Collective Bargaining 1968-; chmn Ft & Madison IA Hum Rel Comm 1967-68; orgnzd Human Rgts Ordinance Cmpgn; Sigma Rho Sigma, Omega Psi Phi Frat; mem bd dirs Am Civil Libs Union PG Co MD 1975; vice pres PTA Ft Washington Forest Elem Sch 1975. **Honors/Awds:** Tchr Advocate Awrd Compton CA 1973; Outstanding Service Award, United Faculty of Florida, 1984; Appreciation of Service Award, Oklahoma Education Association, 1989; Friend of Education Award, Wyoming Education Assn, 1994. **Business Addr:** Organizational Specialist, National Education Association, One Tabor Center, 1200 17th St, #620, Denver, CO 80202.

BOLDEN, CHARLES FRANK, JR.
Astronaut. **Personal:** Born Aug 19, 1946, Columbia, SC; son of Ethel Bolden and Charles Bolden (deceased); married Alexis "Jackie"; children: Anthony Che, Kelly M. **Educ:** US Naval Acad, BSEE, 1968; Univ of Southern CA, MS, systems mgmt 1977. **Career:** NASA, astronaut candidate 1980-81, systems devel grp work on tile repair, SRB launch over pressure, launch debris prevention, shuttle autoland devel, astronaut office liaison for STS displays and controls, flight data file group, astronaut office safety officer, space shuttle software/hardware testing and verification at shuttle avionics integration lab, tech asst to the dir of flight crew opers, chief of safety div; Johnson Space Ctr, special asst to dir, pilot on STS 61-C Jan 12-18, 1986; pilot for STS-31 Hubble Space Telescope mission, Apr 24-29, 1990; commander for STS-45 (Atlas-1) mission, March 24-April 2, 1992; commander for STS-60, first joint Russian/American Space Shuttle Mission, Feb 3-11, 1994; has logged 680 hours in space. **Orgs:** Mem Marine Corps Assn, Montford Point Marine Assn, US Naval Inst; lifetime mem Naval Acad Alumni Assn, Univ of So CA General Alumni Assn; Omega Psi Phi. **Honors/Awds:** Univ of So CA Outstanding Alumni Awd 1982; Natl Tech Assn Hon Fellow 1983; Hon Doctor of Science from Univ of So Carolina, 1984; Hon DHL Winthrop Coll 1986; Hon DHL, Johnson C Smith Univ, 1990. **Military Serv:** US Marine Corps, Brig Gen Select; Defense Superior Service Medal; Legion of Merit; Distinguished Flying Cross; Defense Meritorious Service Medal; The Air Medal; Strike/Flight Medal.

BOLDEN, DOROTHY LEE
Business executive. **Personal:** Born Oct 13, 1920, Atlanta; married Abram Thompson Sr; children: Frank, Avon Butts, Dorothy Ingram, Altenmiece Knight, Abram, Anthony. **Career:** Natl Domestic Inc, pres, founder. **Orgs:** Dir Training Prog & Employment Agency 1968; contrib Ms Magazine, Essence Magazine, Atlanta Magazine; apptd to sec HEW Washington 1975; Commn on the Status of Women 1975; vice pres City NDP; vice pres Black Women Coalition of Atlanta; bd dir NAACP; mem Fulton County Democrats, legal aid & exec bd; mem Citizens Trust Bank Adv Bd. **Honors/Awds:** Recip Atlanta Inquirer Mayors Awrd 1970; Wigo Adv Cncl Comm Action Awrd 1971-72; Wigo Basic Comm Awrd 1973; Econ Opportunity Atlanta Nghbrhd 1973; Omega Psi Phi Frat outstndng Comm Serv Awrd 1973; Black Womens Intl Awrd 1975; Concerned Citizens Awrd 1975. **Business Addr:** Founder & Dir, Natl Domestic Workers Union, 52 Fairlee St NW, Atlanta, GA 30303.

BOLDEN, FRANK AUGUSTUS
Attorney, business executive. **Personal:** Born Aug 7, 1942, Albany, GA; son of Geraldine Bolden and Augustus Bolden; married Carol Penelope Parsons; children: Brian, Ian. **Educ:** Univ of VT, BA 1963; Columbia Univ Grad Sch of Bus, MBA 1972; Columbia Univ Sch of Law, JD 1972. **Career:** Columbia Univ, asst football coach 1971; Inst for Educ Devel, consult 1972; Cahill Gordon & Reindel, assoc 1972-75; Johnson & Johnson, atty 1975, intl atty 1976-85, sec 1984-86, vice pres corp staff 1986, vice pres headquarters services, corp staff, 1994. **Orgs:** Dir Raritan Credit Union 1976-78; dir Winsor Minerals Inc 1976-87; dir Western Sources Inc 1979-87; dir Healthcare Products Nigeria Ltd, 1978; dir Chicopee 1980; dir Inst Mediation & Conflict Resolution 1972-90; adv Consortium of Met Law Sch 1972-73; sponsor Sponsors for Educ Opportunity 1973; dir NJ Assn on Corrections 1980-88; trustee 1983-, vice chmn 1989-93, chmn 1993-95, Union County Coll; vice pres NJ State Opera 1984-; mem NJ Commission on Pay Equity 1984; mem NBA; board of trustee, vice chmn, 1993-94, chmn 1994-96; Overlook Hospital, Summit, NJ, 1990-96; member, Black Leadership Council, 1988-; board of trustees, City Market, Inc, New Brunswick, NJ, 1988-; Crossroads Theatre, Inc, New Brunswick, NJ, board of trustees, 1989-94, president, 1992-94; member, Florida A&M School of Business Advisory Committee, 1986-90; University of Vermont Business School, advisory committee, 1992; University of Vermont, board of trustees, 1994-; chm, 1997-; The National Conference of Christians and Jews, board of governors 1991-, executive committee, 1992-; bd of trustees, Atlantic Health Systems, 1996-. **Honors/Awds:** Martin Luther King Jr Fellowship Woodrow Wilson Found 1969-72; COGME Fellow 1970-72; Charles Evans Hughes Fellow 1971-72; Distinguished Service Award, 1984; Outstanding Service Award, National Conference, 1984; Freedom Fund Award, Perth Amboy NAACP, 1995; Distinguished Service Award, NJ State Opera, 1996; City News 100 Most Influential, NJ 1996. **Military Serv:** AUS capt 1963-69. **Business Addr:** Vice President/Headquarters Service Corp Staff, Johnson & Johnson, One Johnson & Johnson Plaza, New Brunswick, NJ 08933.

BOLDEN, J. TABER, III
Television station executive (retired). **Personal:** Born Apr 26, 1926, Cleveland, OH; son of Lois Waller Bolden and J Taber Bolden; married Barbara A Williams; children: Lynn Ellen, Joseph Taber IV. **Educ:** Springfield Jr Coll, 1946-47; Boston Univ, AB Psych 1950; Springfield Coll, MEd Guidance & Personnel 1953; Temple Univ, OD prog 1958-60. **Career:** Dept of Army Ordinance Corp Springfield MA, training officer (civilian) 1950-55; RCA Camden, training splst 1955-61; RCA Aerospace Systems Burlington MA, mgr, training & serv 1961-65; RCA Corp Staff Camden, admin training design & appl 1965-67; NBC NY, dir mgmt devel (OD) 1967-72; NBC Wash DC, dir personnel 1972-73; WRC-TV Wash DC, station mgr 1973-77; NBC-TV Stations Div, New York NY, vice pres station affairs 1977-85. **Orgs:** Mem OD Org Devel Network 1963-77; vchmn Amer Soc of Trng; dir OD Div 1970-71; mem Natl Broadcasters Club 1975-79; exec comm Amer Friends Serv Comm 1959-61; exec comm Wash DC C of C 1974-79; trustee Natl Acad of TV Arts & Sci 1975-77; trustee Springfield Coll Springfield MA 1977-; pres Wash Jr Achievement 1978-79; 1st black dir, mgr, station mgr NBC; mem Alpha Epsilon Rho 1973. **Honors/Awds:** Outstanding Achievement Awd 1st Black TV Station Mgr of Major Network by Capital Press Club 1976; Hallmark Awd for Outstanding Serv Jr Achievement of Metro WA 1977, 1979. **Military Serv:** USN aircraft torpedo man 3/c 1944-46; WWII Pin, Pacific Theatre Pin 1944-46. **Business Addr:** Retired Vice President Station Affairs, NBC-TV Stations, 30 Rockefeller Plaza, New York, NY 10020.

BOLDEN, JAMES LEE
Business executive. **Personal:** Born Jun 14, 1936, Quitman, MS; married Margaret P Hardaway; children: James Jr, Sherry, Margery, Jeffery. **Educ:** Topeka State Hosp, Cert 1959; LUCT Training Inst, Cert 1976; Washburn Univ, 1978. **Career:** Little Jim's Trucking Co, gen contractor 1958-71; Bolden Radio & TV Repair, mgr, owner 1958-66; Little Jim's Garage, mgr, owner 1969-; Four M Devel Co Inc, pres 1970-; Mid-Central Ins Cons, owner, gen agt 1974-; Mid-Amer Aviation Inc, pres. **Orgs:** Treas Mt Carmel Missionary Bapt Church 1966-; bd treas Black Econ Council of Topeka 1979-; chmn supervisory comm The Capital City Credit Union 1979-; bd mem Household Tech 1978-, Local Devel Corp 1979-; chmn membership comm NAACP 1979-; lecturer Enroute & Terminal ATC Procedures Oper Rain Check USA Dept of Trans Fed Aviation Admin 1980. **Honors/Awds:** Cert of Appreciation KS State Conf of Br of NAACP 1979. **Business Addr:** President, Mid-Amer Aviation Inc, 1800 Harrison, Topeka, KS 66612.

BOLDEN, JOHN HENRY
Educator. **Personal:** Born Jan 10, 1922, River Junction, FL; married Bertha M Johnson; children: Richard. **Educ:** FL Meml Coll, BS; FL A&M Univ, MS, MEd; IN Univ, EdS, EdD. **Career:** IN Univ, rsch asst; Cheyney State Coll, dean of teachers; Duval Co, area dir; FL State Univ, assoc prof. **Orgs:** Pres Bolden's Coll of Music Inc; pres Bolden's Chorale Music Assn Inc; Bolden's BCM Educ & Labor Relations Ctr Inc; editor BCM Press; dir Bolden's Concert Choral; mem Amer Assn of Sch Admins; mem Phi Delta Kappa, Delta Kappa Pi, Natl Urban League, NAACP; Bolden's Academic Symposium Black Students Can Make It. **Honors/Awds:** Nathan W Collier Meritorious Serv Awd; AASA-NASE Acad Prof Devel Awd Designing & Instructional Mgmt System, A Systematic Approach to Sch Mgmt; publications, "A Competency-Based Clinical Supervisory Module for Observing & Evaluating Teaching Performance"; "A Special Report, The Effective Mgmt Team"; "GettingEffective Results through School-Based Mgmt"; "Increasing the Effective of Personnel Mgmt in Educ"; "Balden's Songs of Faith"; "The Singing Black Church"; "A Cultural Resource and Songs of Jordan"; "Is Competency Testing the Black Students a Dilemma or an Opportunity" Select Issues & Answers; "Black Students are Achieving Excellence in Academic Achievement, Model Programs that made it Happen". **Business Addr:** Associate Professor, FL State Univ, Rm 113 Stone Blvd, Tallahassee, FL 32306.

BOLDEN, JURAN
Professional football player. **Personal:** Born Jun 27, 1974, Tampa, FL. **Educ:** Mississippi Delta CC. **Career:** Atlanta Falcons, defensive back, 1996-. **Business Addr:** Professional Football Player, Atlanta Falcons, Two Falcon Place, Suwanee, GA 30174, (404)945-1111.

BOLDEN, RAYMOND A.
Attorney. **Personal:** Born Dec 17, 1933, Chicago, IL; children: Kathryn, Alan, Joseph. **Educ:** Univ of IL, BS, LLB 1961. **Career:** Intelligence Div US Treas Dept, agt 1961-64; Will County, asst state atty 1964-68; Private Practice, atty. **Orgs:** Mem Natl & Will Cnty Bar Assns; pres Natl Blk Lwyrs Conf Joliet Br NAACP 1964-68; bd dirs Joliet-Will Cnty Comm Action Agency 1967-73; mem Will Cnty Legal Asst Prgm; chmn High Crime Redctn Comm Joliet 1975. **Honors/Awds:** Distinguished Citizens Serv Awrd Black Student Union Lewis Univ 1975; awrd NAACP 1968. **Military Serv:** USAF s/sgt 1953-57. **Business Addr:** 81 N Chicago St, Joliet, IL.

BOLDEN, THEODORE E.
Educator (retired). **Personal:** Born Apr 19, 1920, Middleburg, VA; son of Mary Elizabeth Jackson Bolden and Theodore Donald Bolden; married Dorothy M Forde (deceased). **Educ:** Lincoln U, AB 1941; Meharry Med Coll, DDS 1947; Univ IL, MS 1951, PhD 1958; Lincoln Univ, LLD (hon) 1981. **Career:** School of Dentistry, Meharry Med Coll, instructor, operative dentistry, pedodontics, periodontics 1948-49, spec lecturer 1956, prof dentistry, chmn oral path 1962-69, dir research 1962-73, assoc dean 1967-74; Univ of IL School of Dentistry, instr pathology 1955-57, lecturer postgrad studies 1956; Seton Hall Coll of Med & Dentistry, dentistry 1957-60; Med Ctr, attending pathology 1958-62, assoc prof oral diagnosis, pathology 1960-62; George W Hubbard Hosp Nashville TN, attending med & dental staff 1962-78; Univ of Med & Dentistry of NJ, dean 1977-78, acting chmn gen & oral path 1979-80, prof gen & oral path 1977-90 retired. **Orgs:** Trustee, adv Amer Fund for Dental Health 1978-85; exec comm Amer Assn for Cancer Educ, 1977-78; chmn Dental, Amer Assn for Cancer Educ, 1976-77; chmn, rsch comm Acad of Dentistry for Children Natl Dental Assn 1974; pres, Nashville Sect Amer Assn of Dental Rsch; subcomm Curriculum Planning of Comm on Curriculum & Sched School of Dentistry 1972; councilor-at-large Amer Assn of Dental Schools 1971; chmn standing comm Alumni Assn Meharry Med Coll 1970-73; vchmn 1969-70, chmn 1970-71 Amer Assn of Dental Schools; sec, treas, George W Hubbard Hosp Med & Dental Staff 1968-70; rsch comm 1980-81, 1983-84, admission comm minority sub-comm 1980-82 Univ of Med & Dentistry of NJ; co-chmn Montclair NJ Resd Crusade Amer Cancer Soc 1980-82; vice pres Newark Unit NJDiv Amer Cancer Soc Inc, 1983; editoQuarterly Natl Serv, 1975-82; consultant, VAH, Tuskegee, AL, 1958-90, Brooklyn, NY, 1977-90; trustee, Amer Fund for Dentalhealth, 1978-86; chmn of bd, Newark Unit Amer Cancer Soc, 1984-85; trustee, Neighborhood Council, Montclair, NJ. **Honors/Awds:** Capital City Dental Soc & Pan-TN Dental Assn Plaque 1977; Dentists of the

Year Awd Natl Dental Assn Inc 1977; Boss of the Year Plaque School of Dentistry Meharry Med Coll 1977; Serv to Community as Dean Plaque Natl Council of Negro Women 1978; Plaque The Univ of CT Carter G Woodson Collquim 1979; Outstanding Contribs Plaque CT Black Caucus Dentist 1979; Cert of Apprec for Serv 1979; PATCH Awd of Excellence to Theodore E Bolden DDS, PhD, FICD for Excellence & Attainable Goal of CMDNJ-NJDS, #1 Patch 1979; over 200 scientific publications including 10 books. **Military Serv:** AUS sgt/1st lt DC 1943-44. **Home Addr:** 29 Montague Pl, Montclair, NJ 07042.

BOLDEN, VERONICA MARIE

Personnel administrator. **Personal:** Born May 19, 1952, Brooklyn, NY; daughter of Ruth Mae Greene and Arthur Greene; married Fred A Bolden Jr, Jun 17, 1995; children: Jamal C, Jeron A. **Educ:** New York City Community College, AAS, 1972; University of Rochester, BA, 1975; University of Cincinnati, MEd, 1976. **Career:** Ohio Valley Goodwill Rehabilitation, program manager/vocational evaluator, 1976-78; Citizen's Committee on Youth, intake assessment specialist, 1978-81; University of Cincinnati, coordinator, student employment, 1981-89; Hamilton County Board of Mental Retardation, associate director, personnel services, 1989-. **Orgs:** International Association for Personnel Women, 1989-; Ohio Association for Female Executives, 1990-; Ohio Association of School Personnel Administrators, 1989-; Ohio Association of County Boards of Mental Retardation, 1990-; Midwest Association of Student Employment Administrators, vice pres, 1987-88, member-at-large, 1986-87, membership chairperson, 1987-88, minority concerns chairperson, 1987-89; Ohio State Representative for Student Employment Administrators, 1986-89, Student Employment Administrators Nominations Committee Chairperson, 1986-87; Black Career Women, 1981-; Shroder JHS, PTA vp, 1991-92; North Avondale Montessori School, PTA membership chairperson, 1989-90. **Honors/Awds:** Midwest Association of Student Employment Administrators, Leadership Recognition Award, 1988; YMCA Black Achiever, 1990; Jaycees, Outstanding Young Men/Women of America, 1988; University of Cincinnati, Dedicated Service Award, 1986. **Special Achievements:** Article written and published in response to the Campus Advisor, Black Collegian Magazine, Sept/Oct 1988. **Business Addr:** Associate Director, Personnel Services, Hamilton County Board of Mental Retardation, 4370 Malsbary Rd, Ste 200, Cincinnati, OH 45242, (513)794-3300.

BOLDEN, WILEY SPEIGHTS

Educator (retired). **Personal:** Born Dec 18, 1918, Birmingham, AL; son of Gertrude Mildred Speights Bolden and Wiley Lee Bolden Jr; married Willie Creagh Miller, Sep 13, 1945; children: Millicent Ann, Lisa B Monette, Lelia E Bolden, Wiley Miller, Madeliene Ann. **Educ:** Alabama State University, Montgomery AL, BS, 1939, further study, 1940; Atlanta University, Atlanta GA, 1941; Columbia University, Teachers College, New York NY, MA, 1947, EdD, 1957. **Career:** Shelby County Board of Education, Montevallo AL, principal of Almont Junior High, 1939-42; Mobile County Board of Education, Mobile AL, teacher, 1943-44; Clark College, Atlanta GA, associate professor of psychology, 1948-57, professor of psychology and chairman of department of education and psychology, 1957-63, dean of faculty and instruction, 1963-67; licensed psychologist, State of Georgia, 1962-; Southeastern Regional Educational Laboratory, Atlanta GA, associate director for research, 1967-69; Georgia State University, Atlanta GA, professor of educational foundations, 1970-87; Georgia State University, professor of emeritus of educational foundations, 1987; Savannah State College, Savannah GA, acting president, 1988-89; Morris Brown College, Atlanta GA, acting vice pres for academic affairs, 1993-94. **Orgs:** Coordinator of research, Phelps-Stakes Fund, Cooperative Pre-freshman Programs, Atlanta University Center and Dillard University, 1959-63; study director, Tuskegee University Role & Scope Study, Academy for Educational Development, 1969-70; consultant, 1971-76, board of directors, 1978-82, United Board for College Development; board of directors, 1971-73, co-chairman of education committee, 1980-82, life member, 1980-, Atlanta chapter NAACP; member, Education Task Force, Atlanta Chamber of Commerce, 1972-76; member, Fulton County Grand Jurors Association, 1973-76; vice pres for special projects and associate director of Title III, Advanced Institutional Development Project, 1975-77, university associates, board of directors, 1977-83, president, 1978-82, Southern Education Foundation; member of board, 1978-90, president, 1983-85, Georgia State Board of Examiners of Psychologists; member, Governor's Advisory Committee on Mental Health and Mental Retardation, 1980-83; member, advisory committee on education and career development, National Urban League, 1982-91; life membership, American Psychological Association; life membership, Southeastern Psychological Association; fellow, American Association of State Psychology Boards, 1990. **Honors/Awds:** Salutatorian of graduating class, Alabama State University, 1939; General Education Board fellow in clinical psychology, Teachers College, Columbia University, 1953-54; Phi Delta Kappa; Kappa Delta Pi; National Science Foundation science faculty fellowship, 1963-64; Roger C Smith Service Award, American Association of State Psychology Boards, 1988; Black Georgian of the Year Award, (in education) The State Committee on the Life and History of Black Georgians, 1989. **Military Serv:** US Army, 1944-46; received Good Conduct Medal, 1945. **Home Addr:** 975 Veltre Circle, Atlanta, GA 30311.

BOLDRIDGE, GEORGE

Sales executive. **Personal:** Born Apr 15, 1947, Atchison, KS; son of Decima Boldridge and Adrian Boldridge Sr; married Cynthia Davis Boldridge, Jun 5, 1971; children: Eva, Tamara. **Educ:** Benedictine College, BA. **Career:** Hallmark, district sales manager, currently.

BOLEN, DAVID B.

Consultant. **Personal:** Born Dec 23, 1927, Heflin, LA; married Betty L Gayden; children: Cynthia, Myra White, David B Jr. **Educ:** National War College; University of Colorado, BS, MS, 1950; Harvard University, MPA, 1960. **Career:** American Embassy, Monrovia, Liberia, admin asst, 1950-52; Amer Embassy, Karachi, Pakistan, economic asst, 1952-55; US Dept of State, intl economist at Japan-Korea desk, 1955-56, Afghanistan Desk Officer, 1957-59; Amer Embassy, Accra, Ghana, chief of economic section, 1960-62; staff asst to Asst Secretary of State for Africa, 1962-64; officer in charge, Nigerian affairs, 1964-66; Amer Embassy, Bonn, West Germany, economic counselor, 1967-72; Amer Embassy, Belgrade, Yugoslavia, economic/commercial counselor, 1972-74; ambassador to Botswana, Lesotho, and Swaziland, 1974-76; deputy asst Secretary of State for Africa, 1976-77; American Embassy, East Berlin, East Germany, ambassador to German Democratic Republic, 1977-80; E I Du Pont de Nemours & Co Inc, Wilmington, DE, assoc dir of intl affs, 1981-89; consultant, 1989-. **Orgs:** Mem, Foreign Serv Assn, 1950-; mem, Natl War College Alumni Assn, 1967-; mem, Amer Council on Germany, 1980-; vice pres/dir, Wilmington World Affairs Council, 1981-; dir, Wilmington Trust Co, 1981-; mem, Wilmington Club, 1982-; mem, Rodney Square Club, 1983-; trustee, Univ of Delaware, 1983-; dir, Urban Fund (USA), South Africa, 1987-; mem, Delaware Council on Economic Educ, 1987-; trustee, Med Ctr of Delaware, 1987-. **Honors/Awds:** Member, US Olympic Team, London, 1948; fourth place winner, 400 Meters, Olympic Games, 1948; Robert S. Russell Memorial Awards, 1948; Dave Bolen Olympic Award, University of Colorado, 1948; elected to Hall of Honor, University of Colorado, 1969; Norlin Distinguished Alumni Award, University of Colorado, 1969; superior honor award for outstanding and imaginative performance, Department of State, 1972-73; Department of Commerce Certificate for sustained superior performance, 1974; Alumnus of the Century Award, University of Colorado, 1977; Distinguished Alumni Service Award, University of Colorado, 1983.

BOLLES, A. LYNN

Anthropologist, professor. **Personal:** Born Dec 4, 1949, Passaic, NJ; daughter of Augusta Beebe Bolles and George Bolles (deceased); married Dr James Walsh, Feb 9, 1980; children: Shane Bolles Walsh, Robeson James Walsh. **Educ:** Syracuse University, Syracuse NY, AB, 1971; Rutgers University, New Brunswick NJ, MA, 1978, PhD, 1981. **Career:** Rutgers University, Livingston College, New Brunswick NJ, lecturer and teaching assistant, 1976-78, course coordinator for women's studies program, 1977; Bowdoin College, Brunswick ME, assistant professor, 1980-86, associate professor of anthropology, 1986-89, director of Afro-American studies program, 1980-89, Univ of Maryland, College Park, associate professor of women's studies, 1989-95, prof of women's studies, 1995-. **Orgs:** Assn Black Anthropologist, president, 1983-84, secretary-treasurer, 1988-91, program chair, Assn of Feminist Anthropologists, 1989-92; board of directors, Assn for Women in Development, 1984-86; Caribbean Studies Assn, executive council, 1992-95, pres, 1997-98; American Ethnological Society, councillor, 1993-96; Latin American Studies Assn; National Council for Black Studies; Organization of Black Women Historians; Northeast Anthropological As sn; Maine Commission on Women, Maine Humanities Council, 1983; editorial bo ard, Feminist Studies; editorial and advisory board, Urban Anthropology; Alpha Kappa Alpha, Iota Lambda Omega. **Honors/Awds:** Race Unity Day Award for Bowdoin Afro-American studies program, Spiritual Assembly of the Baha'is, 1983; Black History Maker of Maine Award, Augusta Black Community, 1984; Martin Luther King, Jr, Community Service Award, ME NAACP, 1988; numerous research grants; Syracuse University, chancellor's citation for excellence in education, 1989; Society for Applied Anthropology, fellow; Univ of Maryland Coll Park, Outstanding Minority Faculty member of the Year, 1994. **Home Addr:** 3104 Bold Ruler Ct, Bowie, MD 20721-1281. **Business Addr:** Prof, Women's Studies, University of Maryland College Park, 2101 Woods Hall, College Park, MD 20742.

BOLLING, BRUCE C.

Company executive. **Career:** Massachusetts Alliance for Small Contractors, Inc, exec director, currently. **Home Addr:** 64 Harold Street, Roxbury, MA 02119. **Business Phone:** (617)457-5680.

BOLLING, CAROL NICHOLSON

Human resources manager. **Personal:** Born Jan 28, 1952, Jamaica, NY; daughter of Miriam Nicholson and Paris Nicholson Jr; married Bruce Bolling, Jan 27, 1980. **Educ:** State University of New York, BS, liberal arts, 1974. **Career:** The Gillette Co, group leader, collections, 1976-78, group leader, customer servie, 1978, assistant supervisor, sales administration, 1978-80, suv, records management, 1980-81, personnel recruiter, 1981-83, affirmative action administrator, 1983-84, senior personnel representative, 1984-86, corporate manager of employee relations, 1986-87; WCVB-TV, human resources manager, 1987-. **Orgs:** Visiting Nurses Association, board of directors, 1992-; Coalition of 100 Black Women, board of directors, 1991-; Greater Boston Broadcasters Minority Search Group, board of directors, 1991-; Endowment for Children in Crisis, board of directors, 1990-; Advertising Club of Boston Charitable Trust Fund, board of directors, 1988-; MSPCC, board of directors, 1988-89; Greater Boston Young Men's Christian AssociationA, board of directors, 1988-89; Roxbury Comprehensive Health Center, board of directors, 1987-89; Robert F Kennedy Action Corp, board of directors, 1987-89; Big Sisters Association, board of directors, 1985-88; Black Achievers Association, board of directors, 1984-86. **Honors/Awds:** Boston Jaycees, Young Leaders Award, 1986; YMCA, Black Achiever Award, 1980. **Business Addr:** Human Resources Manager, WCVB-TV, 5 TV Pl, Needham, MA 02192, (617)433-4060.

BOLLING, DEBORAH A.

Filmmaker, business executive. **Personal:** Born Jun 18, 1957, New York, NY; daughter of Daisy Alston Bolling and David Bolling. **Educ:** SUNY Old Westbury, New York, NY, BA, 1979. **Career:** Freelancer, video/filmmaker, currently. **Orgs:** Member, Black Filmmakers Foundation, 1989-; member, Women Makes Movies, 1990-. **Honors/Awds:** Award of Excellence, "Portraits in Black," CEBA, 1990; Production of the Decade, "Two Dollars and a Dream," Black Filmmaker Foundation, 1989; Best Documentary, "Two Dollars and a Dream," National Association of Black Journalists, 1988. **Home Addr:** 159-00 Riverside Dr, New York, NY 10032.

BOLTON, JULIAN TAYLOR

City commissioner, telecommunications executive. **Personal:** Born Oct 28, 1949, Memphis, TN; married Joyce Walker; children: Julian II, Jared Walker. **Educ:** Rhodes Coll, BA 1971; Memphis State Univ, MA 1973. **Career:** New Theatre South Ensemble, producer, dir 1978-; Bell System, systems design cons, telecommun; Shelby Cty Commiss, commissioner. **Orgs:** Producer New Theatre South Ensemble 1977-80; mem Memphis Black Arts Council 1981-; bd of dir Shelby Cty Comm Serv Admin 1982-; review comm Memphis Arts Council 1985. **Honors/Awds:** Producer, Dir of over 40 theatrical productions 1968-80; Fellowship Recipient consortium for Grad Study in Bus for Blacks 1971. **Business Addr:** Commissioner, Shelby Co Dist 2, 160 N Mid Amer Mall, Memphis, TN 38103.

BOLTON, LINDA BURNES

Association executive. **Career:** Past president, National Black Nurses Association. **Orgs:** NBNA, AWA. **Honors/Awds:** Fellow, Am Academy of Nursing. **Business Addr:** President, National Black Nurses Association, Inc, PO Box 1823, Washington, DC 20013-1823, (202)855-5191.

BOLTON, WANDA E.

Cosmetologist. **Personal:** Born Jul 14, 1914, Guthrie, OK; daughter of Martha Capers Woods and Columbus Woods. **Educ:** Pittsburgh State Teachers Seminar, Certificate, 1963-64; Univ of MO Seminar, Certificate, 1964-65; Lincoln Univ, Cosmetology 3 1/2 yrs. **Career:** KC School Dist, instructor; Madame CJ Walker Mfg Co, cosmetology instructor; Prairie View Coll, Prairie View TX, cons-dean 1965-70; State Bd Cosmetology, state bd inspector, 1959-66: State Bd of Examiners, 1984-. **Orgs:** Mem, pres State Bd Dept Consumer Affairs, Cosmetology 1975-; practical testing; mem, Natl State Bds of Cosmetology, Cosmetology Accrediting Comm, Washington DC 1977-; mem Natl Interstate Council, Natl State Bds Cosmetology 1975-; mem Assn of Cosmetologists; mem OIC 1978-. **Honors/Awds:** Recipient Beautician of Year Award 1971; Citizenship Award, 1973. **Business Addr:** Cosmetologist, Missouri School District, 1215 E Truman Rd, Kansas City, MO 64106.

BOLTON-HOLIFIELD, RUTHIE (ALICE)

Professional basketball player. **Personal:** Born May 25, 1967; daughter of Rev. Linwood and Leola Bolton; married Mark Holifield, 1991. **Educ:** Auburn, bachelor's degree in exercise physiology. **Career:** Visby (Sweden), guard, 1989-90; Tungstrum (Hungary), 1991-92; Erreti Faenza (Italy), 1992-95; Galatsaray (Turkey), 1996-97; Sacramento Monarchs, 1997-. **Honors/Awds:** USA Basketball Female Player of the Year, 1991; US Olympic Basketball Team, Gold Medal, 1996; All-WNBA First Team, 1997. **Military Serv:** US Army Reserves, first lieutenant. **Business Addr:** Professional Basketball Player, Sacramento Monarchs, One Sports Parkway, Sacramento, CA 95834, (916)928-3650.

BOMMER, MINNIE L.

Community services professional. **Personal:** Born Feb 3, 1940, Covington, TN; daughter of Eula Ray Maclin Burrell and Malcolm Yarbrough; married John Samuel Bommer Sr, Dec 24, 1957; children: Monica, Gina, John Jr. **Educ:** Univ of TN, continued educ 1976, 1983, 1984; TN State Univ, 1982; Spelman, 1983; Memphis State Univ, BPS, 1991; University of California at Davis, Rural Leadership Development Institute, 1989; Antioch University, MA, 1993. **Career:** Tipton Cty Hosp, LPN 1968-73; Tipton Cty Human Svcs, elig counselor 1974-82; City of Covington, alderwoman (1st Black & 1st female to serve elected 1983); Douglas Health Clinic, maternal infant health outreach worker until 1985; Children & Family Services, founder, dir, currently. **Orgs:** 8th Congressional Representative on State Board of Education, 1990-97; Chmn Tipton Cty Library Bd 1983-85; 1st vice pres TN State NAACP; mem Natl Black Women's Political Caucus, TN Women in Government; Rural West TN African American Affairs Council, chm 1985-; delegate, National Democratic Convention 1988; bd of directors, Tipton County Chamber of Commerce 1986-96; bd of directors, Tennessee Housing Development Agency 1988-91; Tenn representative, Lower Mississippi Delta Center, 1990-; life member, NAACP, 1990; board member, Community Resource Group, 1985-91; Dyensbung State Advisory Committee. **Honors/Awds:** Mother of Year Canaan Church Group 1976; Delegate to White House Cont on Families State & Natl; served on Resolution Advance Drafting Comm NAACP 1985; Tennessee Women on the Move, Tennessee Political Caucus 1987; Distinguished Service Award, Tennessee Black Caucus State Legislators 1988; National Volunteer, Thousand Point of Light, 1989; TN Advocates for Children Pioneer Award 1995. **Business Addr:** Agency Director, Children & Family Services Inc, James O Naifeh Building, 412 Alston St PO Box 845, Covington, TN 38019, (901)476-2364.

BONAPARTE, LOIS ANN
Social worker. **Personal:** Born Mar 17, 1941, New York, NY; daughter of Floree Wilson Graves and Randolph Graves; married Charles Bonaparte Jr (died 1976); children: C Scott Bonaparte. **Educ:** Social Welfare, Garden City, BSW, 1980; Social Work, Garden City, MSW, 1988. **Career:** Family Service Assn, Hempstead, NY, social worker, 1973-79; A Holly Patterson Geriatric Center, Uniondale, NY, dir of senior citizen center, 1979-92. **Orgs:** Advisory council, Ministry for Black Catholics, 1989-; advisory council, St Anthony's Guidance Counsel, 1990-; chairperson, Committee for the Commemoration of African-American History, 1984-92; former recording corresponding secretary, Long Island Senior Citizen Directors Association, 1987-88; member, National Assn of Social Workers, 1979-; member, New York State Conference for the Aging, Inc, 1979-92. **Honors/Awds:** Ebony Vanguard Enrichment Award, Committee for the Commendation of African-American History; nominee, Dr Martin Luther King Jr Award, Nassau County, 1991; originated, produced, an annual African-American history program, 8 years, county-wide. **Special Achievements:** Certified Social Worker, 1989; School Social Worker, 1994. **Home Addr:** 254 Long Beach Rd, Hempstead, NY 11550.

BONAPARTE, NORTON NATHANIEL, JR.
City manager, management educator. **Personal:** Born Apr 10, 1953, New York, NY; son of Beryl Grant Bonaparte and Norton N. Bonaparte, Sr.; married Santa Orcasitas Bonaparte, Jul 1, 1978; children: Akia, Nathaniel. **Educ:** Worcester Polytechnic Institute, Worcester, MA, BS, 1975; Cornell University, Ithaca, NY, MPA, 1977. **Career:** City of Grand Rapids, Michigan, assistant to city manager, 1977-81; American Soc for Public Admin, dir of prog devt, 1981-83; Inst for Govt Servs, govt consultant, 1984-87; East Coast Migrant Head Start Project, asst dir, 1987-88; Auto Cleaning Service, gen mgr/owner, 1988; City of Glenarden, city manager, 1988-95; National-Louis University, McLean, VA, senior instructor, 1989; Township of Willingboro, township mgr, 1995-. **Orgs:** President, City & Town Administrators Dept, Maryland Municipal League, 1991; pres, Maryland City and County Management Assn, 1992; member, International City Management Association; member, National Forum for Black Public Administrators; bd of dirs, Burlington County Red Cross Chapter; mem, Burlington County Chamber of Commerce. **Honors/Awds:** Fellow, International City Management Association, 1978; Fellow, Council for Opportunity in Graduate Management Education, 1978. **Business Addr:** Township Manager, Township of Willingboro, Municipal Complex, 1 Salem Rd, Willingboro, NJ 08046.

BONAPARTE, TONY HILLARY
Educational administrator. **Personal:** Born Jun 13, 1939; son of Myra Bonaparte and Norman Bonaparte; married Sueli Fugita; children: Yvette. **Educ:** St John's Univ, BBA 1963, MBA 1964; NY Univ, PhD 1967. **Career:** St John's Univ, asst prof 1964-68; Business Intl Corp, rsch assoc, mgmt syst 1968-70; Rapan Rsch Corp, exec dir 1970-73; Pace Univ, vice pres, dean, prof of intl bus 1968-85; Bentley Coll, vice pres for acad affairs/provost. **Orgs:** Dir Robert Schalkenbach Found 1975-, World Trade Inst Port Arthur 1977-, Brazil-Interpart Cabaatia Brazil 1979-; pres Middle Atlantic Assoc of Bus Admin1981-82, Fulbright Alumni Assoc 1983-84; chmn Intl Affairs Comm of the Amer Assembly 1983-; dir Assoc Black Charities 1983-. **Honors/Awds:** Fellow Amer Assoc for the Adv of Sci 1969; Fulbright Sr Prof College Liberia 1973-74; Vstg Prof Univ of Strathdyde Univ of Edinburgh 1977; Co-Editor of book Peter Drucker Contribs to Bus Enterprise 1978; Hon DHL Southeastern Univ.

BOND, ALAN D.
Insurance/real estate consultant. **Personal:** Born Jul 16, 1945, Jefferson City, TN; son of Edna Coleman Bond and Frederick D Bond (deceased); married Claudette Davis; children: Melinda Ann, Clayton Alan. **Educ:** Central State Univ, BS Bus Admin 1967, post degree studies in law, business & financial planning. **Career:** Detroit Pub Sch, instr part time; Ford Motor Co, prod planning & inven cont spec 1968-69; Control Data Corp, mat supr 1969-70; Xerox Corp, 1970-71; City of Detroit, police dept 1971-73; Chrysler Corp, prod systems & matl control specialist 1973-75; Equitable Life Assurance Soc of US & other companies, insurance broker 1975-; Detroit Edison Co, corp ins & real estate admin 1978-86; Estate Enhancements, insurance & real estate consultant, owner 1986-. **Orgs:** Mem Natl Assn of Life Underwriters 1975-; trustee New Prospect Bapt Ch 1970-; mem Alpha Phi Alpha Frat 1963-; life mem NAACP 1984-. **Honors/Awds:** Elected delegate Wayne Co Convention of Precinct Delegates 1972-; Hon Grad Natl Sales Develop Prog Xerox Corp 1970; participant Electric Passenger Car Promotion Prog 1982-83; numerous Public Serv Recog Awds; Cambridge Univ England, Men of Achievement Directory; Ford Motor Community Service Award; Spirit of Detroit Awardee, various other awards. **Business Addr:** A&W Root Beer/Food at Wayne State University Center, PO Box 32990, Detroit, MI 48232.

BOND, CECIL WALTON, JR.
Businessman. **Personal:** Born Dec 30, 1937, Chester, PA; son of Frinjela P Bond and Cecil W Bond Sr; married Linette H Bond, Oct 10, 1986; children: Tracy, Cecil III, Devon, Denzel. **Educ:** Morgan State Univ, BS; Wharton Graduate School, two year mgmt program. **Career:** Central PA Natl Bank, vice pres, 1970-80; Southeastern PA Transportation Authority, dir of civil rights, assistant general manager, revenue operations, 1994-96, assistant general manager, satety & security, currently. **Orgs:** Urban Bankers Coalition; bd mem, Comm Accounts; bd mem, Greater Philadelphia Comm Devel Corp; Greater Philadelphia Venture Capital Corp; National Forum for Black Public Administrators; Philadelphia Orchestra's Cultural Diversity Initiative; Philadelphia YMCA, Adult Reading Program; American Public Transportation Association, Minority Affairs Committee, chairman. **Honors/Awds:** Greater Philadelphia Chamber of Commerce, Minority Business Advocate Award, 1989. **Military Serv:** US Army Military Police, major, 1961-70. **Business Addr:** 1234 Market St, Philadelphia, PA 19107.

BOND, GEORGE CLEMENT
Educator, educational administrator. **Personal:** Born Nov 16, 1936, Knoxville, TN; son of Ruth Clement and J Max Bond; married Murray; children: Matthew, Rebecca, Jonathan, Sarah. **Educ:** Boston U, BA 1959; London Sch of Econ London U, MA 1961, PhD 1968. **Career:** Univ of East Anglia England, asst lecturer 1966-68; Columbia U, asst prof 1969-74; Tchrs Coll Columbia U, prof 1975-; School of International and Public Affairs Columbia University, director, Institute of African Studies 1988-. **Honors/Awds:** Fellow Woodrow Wilson Cntr for Inter Scholars DC 1981-82; mem Inst for Advanced Studies, Princeton 1983-84; books "The Politics of Change in a Zambian Community" Univ Chicago 1976; bond African Christianity Acad Press 1979; Social Stratification and Educ in Africa 1981; Social Construction of the Past, editor, 1994; AIDS in Africa and the Carribbean, Westview, 1997. **Business Addr:** Professor of Anthropology, Tchrs Coll Columbia Univ, Box 10 Teachers College, Columbia Univ, New York, NY 10027.

BOND, GLADYS B.
Business executive. **Personal:** Born Aug 26, 1914, Windsor, NC; married George L. **Educ:** Temple Univ Sch of Liberal Arts; Craig Sch of Beauty Culture, grad. **Career:** Gladys Dress & Beauty Shop, owner 1946-67; Bond Hotel, Philadelphia proprietor, 1976-88. **Orgs:** Dir The Center, A Place to Learn 1970-; pres Philadelphia Philos 10 yrs; past 3rd vice pres Bus & Professional Women of Phila; The Cotillion Soc; The Heritage House; City of Philadelphia Commn on Human Rels; The Chapel of Four Chplns; The Greater Philadelphia Press Wmn 1960-61; Unity Frankford Grocery Co; Pepsi Cola Co; Club Cornucopia; natl producer Miss All-Am Teenager Pageant; Block Captain. **Honors/Awds:** The Tribune Chautier Ann Awrd The Gratz HS; Chapel of Four Chaplains Leadership Award; Phila Philos Appreciation Award; OIC Certification of Appreciation. **Business Addr:** c/o Jacqueline Bond, 2235 North 19th St, Philadelphia, PA 19132.

BOND, HOWARD H.
Consulting firm executive. **Personal:** Born Jan 24, 1938, Stanford, KY; son of Edna G Coleman Bond and Frederick D Bond; married Ruby L Thomas, Jan 24, 1970; children: Sherman, Howard, Jr, Anita Warr, John, James, Edward, Alicia. **Educ:** Eastern Michigan Univ, Ypsilanti MI, BS, 1965; Pace Univ, New York NY, MBA, 1974. **Career:** US Govt, Detroit MI, 1959-65; Ford Motor Co, Detroit MI, labor supvr, 1965-68; Gen Electric Co, Cincinnati OH, personnel mgr, 1968-69; Xerox Corp, Chicago IL, personnel dir, 1969-75; Playboy Enterprises Inc, Chicago IL, vice pres, 1975-77; Executech Consultants Inc, Cincinnati OH, pres, 1977-, corporate dir, 1977-89; Ariel Capital Mgmt Inc, corporate dir, 1983-89; Advent Bio Products, corporate dir, 1983-89. **Orgs:** mem, planning bd, United Way; mem, Cincinnati Bd of Educ, 1988-89; mem, Salvation Army, mem, Red Cross, Urban League of Greater Cincinnati, mem, Transafrica, mem, Kappa Alpha Psi, mem, Aleikum Temple. **Honors/Awds:** Developed/implemented Xerox AA/EEO Strategies for Excellence, 1969; Special Recognition, Crusade of Mercy, 1976; Bd Mem of the Year, Lake County Urban League, 1976; Role Model, Cincinnati Friends of Amistad Inc, 1987; Black Business & Professional Award, Quinn Chapel AME Church, 1987; Achievers Award, Robert A Taft High School, 1988. **Military Serv:** US Army, sergeant, 1953-58; Soldier of the Month, three times. **Home Addr:** 4040 Beechwood Ave, Cincinnati, OH 45229. **Business Addr:** Pres, Executech Consultants Inc, 35 E Seventh St, Suite 714, Cincinnati, OH 45202.

BOND, JAMES ARTHUR
Educator (retired). **Personal:** Born Jul 11, 1917, Orangeburg, SC; married Ann Nordstrom; children: Sarah Louise. **Educ:** Johnson C Smith Univ, BS 1938; KS Univ, MA 1942; Chicago Univ, PhD 1961. **Career:** Central Acad, math teacher, 1938-40; Langston Univ, Biology instructor, 1946-48; Chicago Univ & IL Univ School of Pharmacy, asst in zoology 1954-56; IL Univ, instr in biology, 1957-61, asst prof 1961-70, assoc prof 1971, asst dean liberal arts & sciences, 1974; LAS, asst dean 1977-88. **Orgs:** Ecology Soc of Amer; Amer Assn for Adv of Sci; Amer Soc of Zoology; Soc for Study of Evolution; Amer Inst of Biosciences; Biometric Soc of Amer; Soc for Genl Syst Res; Natl Assn Sci Teachers; Assn Field Museum; Assoc Smithsonian Inst; Art Inst of Chicago; Shedd Aquarium Soc; Contemporary Art Museum; DuSable Museum Soc of Sigma Xi; John M Prather Fellow, Chicago Univ, 1953. **Honors/Awds:** Soc of Sigma Xi; John M Prather Fellow Chicago Univ 1953; Fellow of AAAS 1965. **Military Serv:** US Army, 1942-46, 1952-53.

BOND, JAMES G.
Politician. **Personal:** Born Nov 11, 1944, Fort Valley, GA. **Career:** City Hall of Atlanta, politician, currently. **Orgs:** Chairman, Public Safety Com 1977; bd of dir, Atlanta Legal Aid; Atlanta City Council 1973; chairman, Com on Atlanta City Council 1975-76; chairman, Labor Education Advancement Project 1974; bd of resources, Highlander Center; advisory bd, Natl Conference on Alternative State & Local Public Policies; Voter Educucation Project Fellow 1973; southeastern dir, Youth Citizenshp Fund 1972. **Business Addr:** Politician, City Hall of Atlanta, Atlanta, GA 30303.

BOND, JAMES MAX, JR.
Architect. **Personal:** Born Jul 17, 1935, Louisville, KY; son of Ruth Elizabeth Clement Bond and J Max Bond; married Jean Davis Carey; children: Carey Julian, Ruth Marian. **Educ:** Harvard Coll, BA (magna cum laude), Phi Beta Kappa, 1955; Harvard Grad Sch of Design, March 1958. **Career:** Ghana Natl Construction Corp, architect 1964-65; Univ of Sci & Tech Ghana, instructor 1965-67; Architect's Renewal Comm Harlem, exec dir 1967-68; Grad Sch of Arch & Plng Columbia Univ, asst prof to prof & chmn 1970-85; Bond Ryder James Arch PC, partner 1969-90; City Coll/CUNY Sch of Environ Studies, dean/prof 1985-91; Davis, Brody, Bond LLP Architects, partner, currently. **Orgs:** Commr New York City Planning Commn 1980-87; bd mem Studio Museum in Harlem 1984-; Municipal Arts Soc 1986-88; mem Natl Orgn of Minority Architects; elected mem, Amer Academy of Arts and Sciences, 1996. **Honors/Awds:** Schomburg Center for Research in Black Culture, Harlem, New York 1980; Martin Luther King, Jr Center and Memorial, Atlanta Georgia, architect, 1980-82; Award of Excellence, Atlanta Urban Design Commission for Martin Luther King, Jr Center and Memorial 1982; Harry B Rutkins Memorial Awd AIA 1983; Whitney M Young Jr Citation Awd AIA 1987; Civil Rights Institute, Birmingham, AL, Design, 1990; Honorary, Doctor of Humane Letters, New Jersey Institute of Technology, 1994; Fellow, American Institute of Architects, 1995. **Business Addr:** Partner, Davis, Brody, Bond LLP Architects, 315 Hudson St, New York, NY 10031.

BOND, JOHN PERCY, III
Government official. **Personal:** Born Dec 23, 1937, Washington, DC; married Eleanor Sawyer; children: Philip Sawyer, Johnna Carol. **Educ:** Morgan State Univ, AB 1965; Wake Forest Univ Babcock Grad Sch of Mgmt, MBA 1975. **Career:** City of Winston-Salem NC, deputy city mgr 1971-78; City of Miami FL, asst city mgr 1978-79; City of Petersburg, city mgr 1979-84; Hillsborough Co FL, deputy county admin 1984; Durham Co NC, county mgr 1985-. **Orgs:** Past vice pres Intl City Mgmt Assoc; commr Commn on Accreditation and Law Enforcement Agencies; mem Amer Soc of Public Administrators; mem exec bd Natl Forum for Black Public Admins; president, Natl Forum for Black Public Administrators; Natl Advisory Council for Environmental Technology Transfer (EPA). **Military Serv:** AUS capt 1960-67; Bronze Star. **Business Addr:** County Manager, Durham County Government, 201 E Main St, Durham, NC 27701.

BOND, JULIAN (HORACE JULIAN)
Educator, former government official. **Personal:** Born Jan 14, 1940, Nashville, TN; son of Julia Louise Washington Bond and Horace Mann Bond; married Alice Clopton (divorced); children: Phyllis Jane, Horace Mann, Michael Julian, Jeffrey Alvin, Julia Louise; married Pamela Sue Horowitz, 1990. **Educ:** Morehouse Coll, BA 1971. **Career:** Georgia House & Senate, mem, 1965-86; The American University, distinguished visiting prof, 1991-; University of Virginia, Dept of History, prof, 1990-; Harvard University, Dept of Afro-American Studies, visiting professor, 1989; Drexel Univ, prof of History & Politics, 1988-89; America's Black Forum, syndicated television

news show, host, beginning 1980; Student Nonviolent Coordinating Comm, 1960-65; Atlanta Inquirer, managing editor, 1964. **Orgs:** Pres, Atlanta NAACP, 1974-89; mem, Natl NAACP Bd. **Honors/Awds:** Pappas Fellow, Univ of Pennsylvania, 1989. **Home Addr:** 5435 41st Pl, NW, Washington, DC 20015. **Business Phone:** (202)244-1213.

BOND, LESLIE FEE
Physician. **Personal:** Born Feb 20, 1928, Louisville, KY; married Anita; children: Leslie Jr, Erik, Candace. **Educ:** Univ IL, AB 1948; Meharry Med Coll, MD 1952; Am Coll Surgeons. **Career:** Metro Med & Hlth Serv Inc, pres; Washington Univ GI Endoscopy; asst clinical surg; Homer G Phillips Hosp, flw, resd, intern 1951-58. **Orgs:** Flw Am Coll & Surgeons; Intl Coll Surgeons; Soc Abdominal Surgeons; mem AMA; Natl Med Assn; St Louis Surg Soc; MO Surg Soc; pres Mound City Med Soc; MO-Pan Med Soc; Homer G Phillips Int Alumni Assn; St Louis Med Soc Cncl; sec chf staff Christian Hosp; mem Kappa Alpha Psi; Chi Delta Mu; Sigma Pi Phi; Frontiers Intl; fndr bd mem Gateway Natl Bank St Louis MO; tst Central Bapt Ch; choir mem Central Bapt Ch; team physician Country Day HS Ftbl Team; mem Page Park YMCA Bd. **Honors/Awds:** Over 20 med articles publ. **Business Addr:** 3400 N Kingshighway, St Louis, MO 63115.

BOND, LLOYD
Educator, scientist. **Personal:** Born Nov 17, 1941, Brownsville, TN. **Educ:** Hillsdale College, BS, 1960-64; Johns Hopkins University, MA, 1975, PhD, 1976. **Career:** General Motors, personnel representative, 1966-72; University of Pittsburgh, Dept of Psych, asst professor, 1976-82, Learning R & D Center, assoc professor, sr scientist, starting 1982; University of North Carolina at Greensboro, Educational Research Methodology, professor, currently. **Orgs:** NAS Committee on Math Assesment, 1990-; NAE Panel on State NAEP, 1990-; bd of trustees, The College Board, 1984-88. **Honors/Awds:** Phi Beta Kappa, 1977; APA, Post Doctoral Fellow, American Psych Assn, 1982; Spencer Fellow, Natl Academy of Education, 1980-83; Fellow, APA, 1990. **Military Serv:** US Army, sgt, 1965-67. **Business Addr:** Professor, Educational Research Methodology, University of North Carolina at Greensboro, 1000 Spring Garden, Greensboro, NC 27412-0001.

BOND, LOUIS GRANT
Educator. **Personal:** Born Jan 6, 1947, Baltimore, MD; children: Jordan, Meredith. **Educ:** Boston Univ, BA 1958; Harvard Univ, MTS 1972; Boston Coll, MEd, EdD 1974; CA Western Univ, PhD 1977. **Career:** Boston Univ, lecturer, instructor, 1969-; Educ Devel Social Studies, dir, parent educ, teacher trainer, curriculum developer, 1972-74; St Andres United Meth Church, pastor, 1973-; J LU-ROB Enterprises Inc, pres; B&R Corrugated Container Corp & B&R World Oil, pres, chmn of the bd. **Orgs:** Mem Black Meth for Church Renewal, Natl Assoc of Black School Admins, Amer Assoc of Jr & Comm Colls, Assoc of Black Psychologist, Amer Assoc of Gen Liberal Studies, Phi Beta Kappa, Harvard Univ Fac Club, NAACP. **Honors/Awds:** Wm H Lemell Scholarship 1964; Martin Luther King Jr Grant 1970; Rockefeller Found Awd 1972; Fulbright Scholarship 1973; Hatcher Scholarship 1974. **Business Addr:** President, Chmn of the Bd, B&R Corrugated Container Corp, Box 753, Millbury, MA 01527.

BOND, MICHAEL JULIAN
City official. **Personal:** Born 1966; son of Julian Bond. **Career:** Atlanta City Council, councilman, 1994-. **Orgs:** St James Lodge #4, Prince Hall affiliate; Empowerment Bd; GABEO; Georgia Municipal Assn, Atlanta NAACP. **Business Addr:** City Councilman, Atlanta City Council, 55 Trinity Ave, SW, Atlanta, GA 30335, (404)330-6000.

BOND, OLLIE P.
Educator, librarian. **Personal:** Born Nov 23, 1925, Lewiston, NC; daughter of Olive Outlaw Peele (deceased) and Bethlehem Peele (deceased); married John B Bond Jr, Jul 6, 1962. **Educ:** Shaw University, Raleigh, NC, AB, 1946; North Carolina Central University, Durham, NC, MSLS, 1958; Rutgers, the State University, New Brunswick, NJ, workshops, institutes; Norfolk State College; University of Georgia, Athens, GA; Appalachian State University, Boone, NC; East Carolina University, Greenville, NC. **Career:** Bertie County Board of Education, Windsor, NC, elementary and high school teacher, 1946-53, school librarian, 1954-79 (retired). **Orgs:** North Carolina Assn, 1952-88; member, American Library Assn, 1969-91; ALA, 1969-; life member, NAACP, 1950-; member, North Carolina Assn of Educators, 1948-; member, North Carolina Assn of Retired Personnel, 1986-; president, Bertie County Retired School Personnel, 1990-92; Mt Olive Baptist Church; Club Starlite, secretary; Lewiston Light Chapter, Order of the Eastern Star, past matron. **Honors/Awds:** Dedicated Service, Bertie County Assn of Educators, 1979; Service Award, Club Starlite, 1987; Achievement Award, Mt Olive Baptist Church, 1982; Community Service, Manson Mortuary, 1987; Service Award, Bertie County Board of Health, 1986; first black woman elected to board of commissioners, Lewiston-Woodville, NC, 1981; received the Governor's Volunteer Service Award, 1983; Half Century Award, Shaw Univ, 1996. **Home Addr:** 109 Grange, Lewiston Woodville, NC 27849.

BOND, WILBERT, SR.
Federal government official (retired), business executive. **Personal:** Born Oct 21, 1925, Brownsville, TN; son of Ethel Anderson Bond and Hobson Bond; married LaVerne Love Bond, Aug 24, 1946; children: Loretta, Wilbert Jr, Cordia, Thomas. **Educ:** Fisk University, Nashville, TN, BA, 1950; Middle Tennessee State Univ, MA, 1965. **Career:** Murfreesboro Schools, Murfressoboro, TN, music inst, 1950-68; US Navy, Millington, TN, equal employment, 1968-90; Bond Training & Consulting Service, Memphis, TN, president, currently. **Orgs:** President, NAACP (state), 1978-; Leadership Memphis, 1982; Fair board member. **Honors/Awds:** Outstanding Federal Employee, 1987; Superior Civilian Serice Award, 1990. **Military Serv:** US Navy, 1943-46; Asiastic Pacific, American Defence Ribbons, US Navy Reserve, 1947-85. **Home Addr:** 25 E Norwood Ave, Memphis, TN 38109. **Business Addr:** Owner, Bond Training & Consulting Service, 25 E Norwood Ave, Memphis, TN 38109.

BONDS, BARRY LAMAR
Professional baseball player. **Personal:** Born Jul 24, 1964, Riverside, CA; son of Bobby Bonds; married Sun Bonds (divorced); children: Nikolai, Shikari. **Educ:** Arizona State Univ, Tempe, AZ, attended. **Career:** Pittsburgh Pirates, outfielder, 1986-92; San Francisco Giants, 1993-. **Honors/Awds:** National League Most Valuable Player, Baseball Writers' Association of America, 1990, 1992. **Business Addr:** Professional Baseball Player, San Francisco Giants, 3 Com Park, San Francisco, CA 94124.

BONDS, KEVIN GREGG
Fiscal operations manager. **Personal:** Born Mar 3, 1961, Lansing, MI; son of Anita Taylor & Solomon Bonds Jr. **Educ:** Community College of Air Force, AAS, 1990; National Univ, BBA, 1990. **Career:** US Air Force, personnel technician, 1981-90; Wisconsin Physician's Service, claims supervisor, 1990-91; Wisconsin Dept of Devt, fiscal operations mgr, 1991-. **Orgs:** African American Ethnic Academy Inc, treasurer, 1993-; Wisconsin Community Fund, treasurer, 1994-; Dane County: bd supervisor, 1994-, Affirmative Action Commission, commissioner, 1992-, Personnel/Finance Committee, supervisor, 1994-, Housing Authority, commissioner, 1994-; So Madison Neighborhood Center, treasurer, 1993-94. **Honors/Awds:** Dollar's & Sense Magazine, America's Best & Brightest, 1993; Mother's of Simpson Street, Outstanding African-American Role Model, 1994. **Special Achievements:** Depicting African-American History & Sites, 1995. **Military Serv:** US Air Force, staff sergeant, 1981-90; Outstanding Airmen, 1983; Commendation Medal, 1985; Meritorious Medal, 1990. **Home Addr:** 1002 E Sunnyvale Lane, Madison, WI 53713. **Business Addr:** Fiscal Operations Mgr, Wisconsin Dept of Devt, Division of Tourism, PO Box 7970, Madison, WI 53707.

BONE, WINSTON S.
Clergyman. **Personal:** Born Apr 7, 1932, New Amsterdam, Guyana; married Faye Alma O'Bryan; children: Alma Lorraine Bone Constable, Brian Winston. **Educ:** InterAm Univ of PR, BA (summa cum laude) 1958; Waterloo Luth Sem, grad 1961. **Career:** Met NY Synod Evangelical Luth Ch in Am, asst to bishop 1973-; Incarnation Luth Ch Queens, pastor 1968-73; Christ Luth Ch Brooklyn, pastor 1966-68; Luth Ch in Guyana, pres 1966; Ebenezer Luth Ch New Amsterdam Guyana, pastor 1961-66. **Orgs:** Chmn Admn Cncl Luth Ch in Guyana 1965-66; mem Mgmt Com Div for Professional Ldrshp 1972-80; bd of trustees Wagner Coll Staten Island NY 1969; bd of dir Luth Theol Sem at Gettysburg 1977-; chmn S Queens Luth Parish 1970-73; bd of dir Seamen & Intl House NY 1970-73. **Business Addr:** Lutheran Church in America, 390 Park Ave, S, New York, NY 10016.

BONES, RICKY (RICARDO)
Professional baseball player. **Personal:** Born Apr 7, 1969, Salinas, Puerto Rico. **Career:** San Diego Padres, professional baseball player; Milwaukee Brewers, professional baseball player, currently. **Business Addr:** Professional Baseball Player, Milwaukee Brewers, Milwaukee County Stadium, Milwaukee, WI 53214, (414)933-4114.

BONEY, J. DON
University executive. **Personal:** Born Mar 28, 1928, Calvert, TX; married Peggy; children: 3. **Educ:** Prairie View A&M Coll, BS 1948; Univ of TX, MEd 1957, EdD 1964. **Career:** Univ of Houston Downtown Coll, chancellor, 1975; Houston Community Coll System, pres, 1973-75; Houston Independent School Dist, chief of instr, 1971-72; Coll of Educ Univ of Houston, assoc dean of graduate studies, 1970-71; Univ of Houston, assoc prof of educ Psych, 1967-69. **Orgs:** Dir Project Upward Bound Univ of IL 1966-67; asso prof of educ Psych Univ of IL 1964-67; dir of testng Port Arthur Indpndnt Sch Dist 1959-64; coord of Guidance Temple Pub Sch 1956-59, tchr 1948-56; TX Pub Sch Mem, Am & Houston Psych Assn; Nat Training Lab Mem, Adv Educ Com, C of C, Houston; adv com Hope Cntr for Youth Houston; adv com Goodwill Indstrs Houston. **Honors/Awds:** Outstndng Alumnus Awrd Prairie View A&M Coll 1966 & 1970; meritorious serv awd Bd of Educ Houston Indpndnt Sch Dist 1972; outstndng Educator Awrd Houston C of C 1972; Educ Awrd, & Cncl of Negro Wmn 1972; Distingshd TX Awrd Charles A George Dntl Soc 1973; Excellence in Educ Awrd Citizens for GoodSch 1973; Outstanding Educator Awrd Prairie View A&M Coll 1972; Distingshd Edctr Awrd Sigma Gamma Rho 1974. **Business Addr:** 1 Main Plaza, Houston, TX 77002.

BONHAM, VENCE L., JR.
Attorney. **Educ:** Michigan State University, James Madison College, East Lansing, MI, BA (with honors), post graduate studies 1978-79; Ohio State Univ, Columbus, OH, JD, 1982. **Career:** US District Court for Southern District of Ohio, Columbus, OH, student judicial clerk, 1981-82; UAW Legal Services Plan, Lansing, MI, staff attorney, 1983-84; Eastern Michigan University, Ypsilanti, MI, human resources associate, 1984-85, university attorney, 1984-87; Michigan State University, East Lansing, MI, assistant general counsel, 1987-89, associate general counsel, 1989-. **Orgs:** Board member, National Association of College and University Attorneys; member, The Michigan Minority Health Advisory Committee, 1990-92; member, Michigan State Bar; member, National Health Lawyers Association; member, American Society of Law and Medicine; member, American Bar Association; member, Michigan Society of Hospital Lawyers; member, Phi Delta Kappa Fraternity; member, Detroit Area Hospital Counsels Group; board member, Impressions 5 Michigan Science Museum; board member, Lansing Area Boys and Girls Club. **Honors/Awds:** Author of: ''Liability Issues Concerning Faculty and Staff: Academic Advising and Defamation in Context of Academic Evaluation,'' Am I Liable?: Faculty, Staff and Institutional Liability in the College and University Setting, 1989; ''Health Law Update,'' Journal of the College of Human Medicine, 1990-. **Business Addr:** Associate General Counsel, Michigan State University, 407 Administration Building, East Lansing, MI 48824.

BONILLA, BOBBY (ROBERTO MARTIN ANTONIO)
Professional baseball player. **Personal:** Born Feb 23, 1963, New York, NY. **Educ:** New York Technical College, Westbury, NY. **Career:** Chicago White Sox, infielder, 1986; Pittsburgh Pirates, infielder/outfielder, 1986-91; New York Mets, 1992-95; Baltimore Orioles, 1995-96; Florida Marlins, 1997-. **Business Addr:** Professional Baseball Player, Florida Marlins, Pro Player Stadium, NW 199th St, Miami, FL 33169, (305)356-5848.

BONNER, ALICE A.
Judge, attorney. **Personal:** Born Apr 11, 1941, New Orleans; married Al; children: Yvonne, Bernard, Lamont. **Educ:** TX So U, BA 1963, JD 1966; Natl Coll Judiciary, grad; Am Acad Jud Edn, grad. **Career:** 80th Civil Dist Ct State of TX, judge 1979-; Co Criminal Ct at Law #6, judge 1977-78; Mun Ct Houston, judge 1974-77; Law Firm Bonner & Bonner, pvt prctnr family law spclst 1967-77. **Orgs:** Mem State Bd of Spclztn 1975; mem com on increase of female jvnl ofndrs 1967; mem pltfrm com State Dem Conv 1974; orgnzr-fndr-actng pres Black Women Lwyrs Assn 1975; bd mem Judicial Cncl Natl Bar Assn 1975-76; mem bd of govs Natl Bar Assn 1974-77; bd mem Houston Lwyrs Assn 1978; mem com for the indigent State Bar of TX 1980; dem cand for judicials races 1974 1978 1980; life mem Natl Assn of Negro Bus & Professional Women Inc, Phi Alpha Delta Legal Frat, Bapt Sisterhd of TX, City Wide Beauticians of Houston, Natl Cncl Negro Women, Blue Triangle Br YWCA, Women of Achvmnt; mem Eta Phi Beta Bus & Professional Sor; mem NAACP; coord Natl & Cncl Negro Women, Natl Med Assn, Natl Immnztn Prgm; numerous other civic & comm assns. **Honors/Awds:** 1st Black Woman Judge Houston & Harris Co TX; 1st Black Civil Dist Ct TX; 1st Black Woman to win a country-wide election Harris Co TX succeeded to Co Criminal Ct Dem Primary 1978; Am Jrsprdnc Awrds Wills & Decedents Estates & Family Law TX So Univ 1966; Atty of Year Tom Kato Models 1974; Bethune AchvrNatl Cncl Negro Women 1975; Cited Most Influential Black Woman in Houston Focus Mag 1978; Founders Awrd Black Women Lwyrs 1978; Outstndng Serv Mainland Br NAACP 1979; Black Hist Commemoration Philadelphia Bapt Ch 1979; Black Women Lwyrs Achvmnt Awrd 1979. **Business Addr:** 80th Civil Dist Ct, 301 Fannin St Room 212 A, Houston, TX 77002.

BONNER, ALICE CAROL
Foundation executive, journalist. **Personal:** Born Dec 24, 1948, Dinwiddie, VA; daughter of Doletha Edwards Bonner and James R. Bonner; married Leon Dash Jr (divorced 1982); children: Destiny Kloi Dash. **Educ:** Howard University, Washington, D.C., BA, 1971; Columbia University, New York, NY, Certificate, 1972; Harvard University, Cambridge, MA, Nieman Fellowship, 1977-78. **Career:** The Washington Post, Washington, DC, reporter, editor, 1970-85; USA Today, Arlington, VA, editor, 1985-86; Gannett Co Inc, Arlington, VA, journalism recruiter, 1986-89; Gannett Foundation, Arlington, VA, director of education programs, 1990-. **Orgs:** Board member, Youth Communication, 1990-; board member, Community of Hope, 1986-; member, National Association of Black Journalists, 1980-; member, Association Education in Journalism & Mass Communication, 1986-; summer program director, Institute for Journalism Education, 1986. **Home Addr:** 3800 Powell Ln, Falls Church, VA 22041. **Business Addr:** Director, Journalism Education, The Freedom Forum, 1101 Wilson Blvd, Arlington, VA 22209.

BONNER, ANTHONY
Professional basketball player. **Personal:** Born Jun 8, 1968, St Louis, MO. **Educ:** St Louis Univ, St Louis, MO, 1986-90. **Career:** Sacramento Kings, 1990-93; New York Knicks, 1993-. **Business Addr:** Professional Basketball Player, New York Knicks, 2 Pennsylvania Plaza, New York, NY 10121, (212)465-6000.

BONNER, BESTER DAVIS
Educational administration. **Personal:** Born in Mobile, AL; married Wardell; children: Shawn Patrick, Matthew Wardell. **Educ:** AL State Coll Montgomery, BS 1959; Syracuse Univ NY, MSLS 1965; Univ of AL Tuscaloosa, further study. **Career:** Div of Educ Miles Co, chairperson, 1978-; Miles Coll, Birmingham AL, admin asst to pres 1974-78; AL A&M Univ Huntsville, asst prof Library media, 1969-79; Jacksonville State Univ Lab School AL, head librarian, 1965-69; Lane Elementary School, Birmingham AL, librarian & teacher of Literature, 1964-65; Westside High School, Talladega AL, librarian, 1959-64. **Orgs:** Mem Pub Rels Com AL Instrctnl Media Assn 1970-71; pres Dist AL Instrctnl Media Assn 1971-72; chrprsn Ecumenical Com Ch Women 1971-74; mem Am Lbry Assn 1972-74; del World Meth Conf Dublin Ireland 1976; vice chr AL State Ethics Commn 1977-81; exec bd Womens Missionary Cncl CME Ch; mem Kappa Delta Pi Ed Honor Soc; mem Thirgood CME Ch Birmingham AL Youth Adv Cncl Bd of Christian Edn; mem Alpha Kappa Alpha & Sor Mini-Grant for AV Rsrch pt 1 AL Cntr for Higher Educ 1974. **Honors/Awds:** Author ''Multimedia approach to Teaching & Learning'' Birmingham News 1975; Mini-Grant for AV Rsrch Pt 2, AL Cntr Hghr Educ 1976; Citation UNCF 1977 1979; Lilly Endowmnt Fclty Imprvmnt Grant to study for PhD UNCF NY 1978; Citation (Womens Seminar) Miles Coll Comm Serv Awrds Zeta Phi Beta Sor Inc Birmingham 1980; Family Awrd (Outstndng tchr) Miles Coll 1980; Editor/Informer (Newsltr) CME Ch 5th Episcopal Dist; Rsrch Grant to Write Dissertation AL Cntr for the dev of Hghr Educ 1980. **Business Addr:** Miles Coll, 5500 Ave G, Birmingham, AL 35208.

BONNER, DELLA M.
Educator (retired). **Personal:** Born Nov 25, 1929, Red Oak, IA; married Arnett Jackson. **Educ:** Omaha U, BS 1961; Univ of NE at Omaha, MS 1969. **Career:** Omaha Public School teacher, 1962-68; Dir, Greater Omaha Comm Action Inc, 1968-70; instructor, 1970-73; asst prof of Educ, Creighton Univ 1973-90. **Orgs:** chairperson, 1977, 1979, 1981, 1984 team mem, 1973, 1976 Natl Council for Accreditation of Teacher Educ; evaluator, Omaha Public School in Self-Study of Sr High School, 1970; counseling & guidance Jr HS 1971, Social Studies; chairperson, Human Rights Com NE Personnel & Guidance Assn 1972-74; faculty advisor, Coll of Arts & Sci 1970; exec faculty, 1972-73; Univ Com on Status of Women 1972-75; bd trustees Joint Conf Comm, 1973-74; Task Force on Resident Hall Life 1973-75; educ rep Boys Town Urban Prog Adv Bd 1980-, bd dir Urban League of NE 1964-72; chairperson Educ Task Force; recording sec Scholarship Com; bd dir Eastern NE Mental Health Assn 1969-74; Volunteer Bureau of United Community Serv, exec committee 1969-71; vice pres & mem Girls Club of Omaha Board 1973-77; chairperson, Natl Trends & Serv Comm, Omaha Chapter of Links Inc; special advisory Comm, NE Educ TV Commn, 1971-72; Omaha Home for Girls study Comm for UCS, 1974; Charter pres, Omaha Chapter Jack & Jill Of Amer Inc, 1970-71. **Honors/Awds:** Candidate for Outstanding Young Educator Award, Nominee for Woman of Year, Omaha Women's Political Caucus Business & Professional Category 1974; vice chairperson, US Dist Ct Judges 10-mem Interracial Com 1975-76; Phi Delta Kappa 1976-90; Distinguished Faculty Service Award, Creighton Univ, 1991.

BONNER, ELLIS
Health care company executive. **Career:** Comprehensive Health Services Inc, president, CEO, currently. **Honors/Awds:** Group Health Association of America, Man of the Decade in managed health care, 1991. **Business Addr:** President/Chief Executive Officer, Comprehensive Health Services Inc, 6500 John C Lodge, Detroit, MI 48202, (313)875-4200.

BONNER, MARY WINSTEAD
Educator. **Personal:** Born Apr 20, 1924, Nash Co, NC; daughter of Mason Ann Whitted and Charles Edward Winstead; married Thomas E Bonner, Aug 9, 1956. **Educ:** St Pauls University, BS (cum laude) 1946, LhD, 1979; VA State University, MS 1952; New York Univ 1953-67; Southern Univ 1953, 1954; OK State Univ, EdD 1968; Univ of KS, Post Doct 1974; Univ of California Berkeley 1974; Instde Fililogia Satillo Mexico, further study 1984. **Career:** Greensville Cty VA, instr 1946-52; So Univ, instr 1952-57; St Louis Publ Schools, instr 1957-64; OK State Univ, grad asst 1965-66; USC, vstg prof 1968; Norfolk State Coll, vstg prof 1971-73; Emporia State Univ, professor, professor emeritus 1986. **Orgs:** Mem Sigma Gamma Rho, Amer Assn of Univ Women, Natl Council of Negro Women, natl Spanish Hon Soc, Sigma Delta Pi 1979, International Platform Assn, Panel of American Women, KS Children's Service League, Retired Teachers Assn; asst dir, ast district coordinator 1989-90, editor state newsletter 1991-92, Hospital Auxiliaries of Kansas; secretary, Emporia Retired Teachers Assn 1988-89; bd of dirs, Societas Docta; mem, Lyon County Board of Corrections 1990-91; mem, Lyon County Planning Committee 1991-92. **Honors/Awds:** European Tour England, Belgium, Holland, Germany, France, Switzerland 1983; tour of Soviet Union & Warsaw Poland 1974, Spain 1976, Mexico 1979, Venezuela 1981, Caribbean 1986; Hall of Fame Sigma Gamma Rho; Cert of Achievement in Spanish Emporia State Univ 1978; languages Spanish, French, Russian; Outstanding Aluma St Pauls Coll 1979, 1984; creation of Bonner-Bonner Lecture Series, Emporia State Univ; Emporia State Univ, Ruth Schillinger Award, 1998. **Home Addr:** 2314 Sunset Lake Dr, Emporia, KS 66801-5369.

BONNER, THEOPHULIS W.
District manager. **Personal:** Born Jul 25, 1917, Warm Springs, GA; married Blanche. **Educ:** Ft Valley State Clge, AB 1943. **Career:** Atlanta Life Ins Co, dist sales mgr. **Orgs:** Mem sch bd 1972-; mem LUTC 1966; Liami mgmt 1968; LUTC Health 1971; mem NAACP. **Military Serv:** Amvets s/sgt 1943-46. **Business Addr:** 1008 State St, Box 837, Waycross, GA 31501.

BONTEMPS, JACQUELINE MARIE FONVIELLE
Educator, artist. **Personal:** Born in Savannah, GA; daughter of Mattie Louise Davis Fonvielle and William Earl Fonvielle; married Arna Alexander Bontemps, Jul 5, 69 ; children: Traci, Arna, Fanon. **Educ:** Fisk University, BA, 1964, MA, 1971; Illinois State University, EdD, 1976. **Career:** Lane College, chair, 1966-68; Jackson Parks & Recreation, supervisor, 1968; South Side Community Center, director, 1969; Fisk University, Dept of Art, administrative asst, 1971; Tennessee State University, Dept of Art, instructor, 1972-73; University of Tennessee, Dept of Art, instructor, 1972-73, lecturer, 1973; Illinois State University, College of Fine Arts, asst to director, 1975-76, administrative asst, 1976-77, asst professor of art, 1976-78, assoc professor of art, 1978-84; Hampton University, Department of Art, assoc professor, dept chair, 1984-. **Orgs:** Trustee, American Assn of Museums; American Assn for Higher Education; American Council for the Arts; American Film Institute; American Assn of University Professors; Assn of Teacher Educators; committee member, Intl Council of Museums; Natl Council for Black Studies; Delta Sigma Theta; Phi Delta Kappa; natl arts research specialist, 1978-86, director for arts, 1982-84, natl secretary, 1988-90, The Links; Council of Arts Administrators of Virginia Higher Education, 1984-89; Inaugural Natl Blacks Art Festival, natl blue ribbon panel member, 1987-88; bd of directors, Cultural Alliance of Greater Hampton Roads, 1987-91. **Honors/Awds:** Curator/director of exhibit, Forever Free: Art by African-American Women, 1862-1980, 1981-82; Pacesetter Award, Illinois Bd of Education, 1981; certificate of special participation for community efforts, Illinois State University, 1982; Women in the Arts honoree, Virginia Natl Organization for Women, 1986; selected as one of America's Top 100 Black Business & Professional Women, Dollars and Sense Mag, 1986; curator/director of exhibit, Choosing: An Exhibit of Changing Perspectives in Modern Art & Art Criticism by Black Americans, 1925-1985, 1986-87. **Home Addr:** No 1 Johnson Ct, Hampton, VA 23669.

BOOKER, ANNE M.
Public relations executive. **Personal:** Born Feb 28, Spartanburg, SC; daughter of Tallulah Jane Tanner and Claude C Booker. **Educ:** Michigan State Univ, B 1973, M 1986. **Career:** Ford Motor Co, electronic media specialist 1977-78, corporate news rep 1978-82, publications editor 1982-84, senior producer 1984-86, public affairs assoc 1986-88; assistant manager beginning 1988, manager currently. **Orgs:** Mem Public Relations Soc of Amer 1978-; Women in Communications 1978-; Natl Black MBA Assn 1983-; life mem NAACP; mem St. Philip AME, Atlanta; Amer Women in Radio-TV; Press Club 1978-. **Honors/Awds:** Achiever in Industry YMCA Detroit; Aftra Golden Mike Awd; Kappa Tau Alpha Grad Journalism Honor Soc. **Business Addr:** Manager, Ford Motor Company, Southeast Region Public Affairs, 245 Peachtree Center, Ste 2204, Atlanta, GA 30303.

BOOKER, CARL GRANGER, SR.
Fire marshal. **Personal:** Born Aug 16, 1928, Brooklyn, NY; married Jacqueline Mayo; children: Carl G Jr, Adele Williams, Wendy. **Educ:** Hampton Ins Univ 1948-50; Springfield Comm Coll MA 1977; US Fire Acad, MD 1979,80,82; Dartmouth, Yale, Quinsingamond Comm coll, structured coursesof more than 180 hrs. **Career:** City of Hartford CT Fire Dept, firefighter 1958-66, driver-pump oper 1966-67, fire prevention inspector 1967-68, fire prevention lt 1969-79, fire prevention capt/dep fire marshal 1979-81, acting fire marshal 1981-82, appointed fire marshal/fire prevention chief 1982-. **Orgs:** Bd of dir 1972-74, pres 1973, Child Guidance Clinic; pres Phoenix Soc Firefighters 1972-74; legislative rep CT Fire Marshals Assoc 1982-84; mem New England Assoc of Fire Marshals 1983-85; bd of dir Child & Family Serv 1983-; bd of dir Capitol Reg Assoc of Fire Marshals 1982-84; bd of dir Friends of Keney Park Golf Links 1984-85. **Honors/Awds:** Front Page Weekly Reader 1972; Firefighter of the Year Phoenix Soc Firefighters 1972,76; Disting Serv Awd Radio WRCH 1975; Community Awd Makalia Temple 172CT 1983; Cert of Apprec US Consumer Products Comm Washington DC 1984. **Military Serv:** AUS Infantry s-4 record spec 2 yrs. **Business Addr:** Hartford Fire Department, 275 Pearl St, Hartford, CT 06103.

BOOKER, CLIFFORD R.
Pediatrician. **Personal:** Born Nov 20, 1926, Liverpool, OH; son of Cassie Marie Abbitt and Christopher C Booker; children: Claudia, Tina, Cliff. **Educ:** Howard Univ, BS 1949, MD 1955. **Career:** Howard Univ Med Sch, asst prof, tchr 1960-65; Georgetown Univ, clinical asst prof; Washington DC Govt, medical officer, 1987-. **Orgs:** Mem DC Med Soc; Kappa Pi Med Hon Soc; mem Med-Clie Soc; adv bd DC Med. **Honors/Awds:** Research Award Sickle Cell Anemia. **Military Serv:** USAAC 1945-47.

BOOKER, CORLISS VONCILLE
Educator. **Personal:** Born Jun 22, 1954, Stuttgart, Germany; daughter of Curtis & Vera Wrenn; divorced; children: Andrea Voncille, Gorman Lasure. **Educ:** John Tyler Community College, AAS, 1982; Virginia Commonwealth University, BSN, 1989, MPH, 1998. **Career:** Veteran's Administration, staff nurse, 1982-91; Virginia Commonwealth Univ, RN liaison, 1992-94, project dir, 1995-, asst prof, 1996-. **Orgs:** State Board of Social Services, vice chair, 1994-; YWCA, scy, bd mem, 1994-; American Nurses Association, 1982-; Oncology Nursing Society, 1996-; Black Education Association, vice pres, 1997-; National Black Nurses Association, 1994-. **Honors/Awds:** Governor George Allen, Governor's Group Collaboration Award, 1997; VA Health Care Foundation, Unsung Heroes Award, 1996; VA Commonwealth Univ, Black Achievers Award, 1995; American Cancer Society, Minority Student Fellowship, 1989; Free Press Newspaper, Personality of the Week, 1997. **Special Achievements:** Has spoken before numerous groups and has published several articles. **Home Addr:** 3620 Mineola Dr, Chester, VA 23831, (804)796-1907. **Business Addr:** Assistant Professor, Virginia Commonwealth University, Department Family Practice, 1200 E Broad St, PO Box 980251, Richmond, VA 23298-0251, (804)828-6056.

BOOKER, GARVALL H.
Dentist. **Personal:** Born Apr 26, 1925, Washington, DC; married Doris L Wethers; children: Garvall III, Clifford, David. **Educ:** Sarah Lawrence Coll, BA 1949; Dental Coll Howard Univ, DDS 1954; Sydenham Hosp NYC, resident 1954-56. **Career:** Speedwell Serv for Children, dir dentistry 1964-78; private practice, dentist 1956-. **Orgs:** Mem Amer & Dental Assn 1956-; mem NY Acad of Mem Amer Dental Assn 1956-; mem past pres Upper Manhattan Rotary Club 1968-; mem AAAS 1970; alumnae/trustee Sarah Lawrence Coll 1975-78; Paul Harris Fellow of Rotary Fnd Upper Manhattan Rotary Club 1975; adv council mem Harlem-Dowling Children's Serv 1979-; mem NY Acad of Sci 1980; mem Sigma Pi Phi Frat Zeta Boule, Reveille Club. **Military Serv:** AUS t-3 1943-46; Bronze Star; Purple Heart; 3 Battle Stars 1945.

BOOKER, JAMES AVERY, JR.
Physician, general surgeon. **Personal:** Born May 26, 1936, Richmond, VA; son of Thelma and James; married Rita Tezeno; children: James III, Karla, Michael, JaRita. **Educ:** Hampton Univ, BS, 1957; Med Coll of Virginia School of Dentistry, DDS, 1961; Howard Univ, Coll of Med, MD, 1968. **Career:** General surgeon, private practice, 1976-; Oakland CA, city physician, 1976-77; USAF Hospital, Mather AFB, CA surgeon, 1974-76, chief of general surgery, 1975-76; internship & residency, 1968-74; Washington, DC; general dental practice, 1963-68; Armed Forces Entrance & Exam Sta, surgical consultant, 1971-78; Univ of California at Davis School of Med, preceptor principles of physical diagnosis, 1974-76. **Orgs:** Past natl pres, Student Natl Med Assn, 1967-68; life mem, Alpha Phi Alpha Fraternity, 1955-; mem, Chi Delta Mu Med Fraternity, 1958-; Sinkler-Miller Med Assn component Golden State Med Assn & Natl Med Assn, 1977-; mem, Alameda-Contra Costa Med Assn; Component CA Med Assn, 1971-; Diplomate Natl Bd of Dental Examiners 1961; Natl Bd Med Examiners, 1969-; Amer Bd of Surgery Inc, 1976, 1985; Amer Bd of Quality Assurance & Utilization Review Physicians, 1988; Fellow, Intl Coll of Surgeons, 1980; Fellow, Amer Coll of Surgeons, 1983; Fellow, Amer Coll of Utilization Review Physicians, 1989-; Fellow, Southwestern Surgical Congress, 1989-; Chmn, Dept of Surgery, Memorial Hospital, San Leandro, CA, 1985-88; member, American College of Physician Executives, 1989-. **Honors/Awds:** Virginia Dental License granted on basis of class standing, 1961; Appointed City Physician, Oakland, CA, 1976. **Military Serv:** Colonel, US Air Force Reserves, 1985-; Mobilization Augmentee to Commander, David Grant Med Center, Travis Air Force Base, CA, 1986-; Air Force Commendation Medal, 1988.

BOOKER, JAMES E.
Business executive. **Personal:** Born Jul 16, 1926, Riverhead, NY; married Jean Williams; children: James, Jr. **Educ:** Hampton Inst, 1943-44; Howard Univ, AB 1947; NYU & New Sch for Social Research, special courses; Armed Forces Information Sch & AUS Psychol Warfare Sch. **Career:** NY Amsterdam News, columnist & political editor 18 years; James E Booker Consultants (corporate & civil rights consultants), pres. **Orgs:** Chief Information Consult Nat Adv Commn on Civil Disorders; consult & dir of information 1966 White House Conf on Civil Rights; organized first natl conf of black elected officials in Chicago 1968; consult Dem Presidential campaigns 1968, 1972; consult NY State Commn on Human Rights; consult research

specialist NY State Joint Legislative Commn. **Honors/Awds:** Lecturer on numerous occasions. **Home Addr:** 10 W 135 St, New York, NY 10037.

BOOKER, JOHN, III
Business executive. **Personal:** Born Dec 28, 1947, Augusta, GA. **Educ:** Paine Clge, His mjr 1969; NC Cntrl Univ Law Schl, LLB 1974; Univ of RI, Cert Mgmt 1980. **Career:** Amperex Electronic Corp N Amer Philips Co, asst persnl mgr 1980-; Speidel Div of Textron, employ mgr/Urban affairs coord 1977-80; Cntr Savannah & River Area EOA Inc, equal opport ofc 1976-77; Augusta Human Rel Commn, EEOC investigator/ Field rep 1975-76; Atty John D Watkins, legal asst 1974-75. **Orgs:** Woonsocket C of C, act mem 1980; NAACP act mem 1980; co rep local minority & civil org 1980. **Military Serv:** AUS e-4 1970-72. **Business Addr:** Manager, Employee Relations, Amperex Electronic Corp, Div of North American Philips, One Providence Pike, Slatersville, RI 02876.

BOOKER, JOHNNIE BROOKS
Government official. **Personal:** Born Jul 31, 1941, Forsyth, GA; daughter of Lillian B Graves & Willie F Brooks (deceased); divorced; children: Sylvester Courtney III. **Educ:** Hampton Institute, BS, 1961; Atlanta Univ School of Social Work, MSW, 1969. **Career:** Los Angeles Comm Redevelopment Agency, 1969-73; Western Regional Office National Urban League, assistant regional dir, 1974-76; National Urban League-Washington Operations, assistant dir, 1977-78; Federal Home Loan Bank Bd, dir of consumer affairs, 1978-89; Dept of Housing & Urban Devt, deputy assistant sec, 1989-91; Resolution Trust Corp, vp, 1991-. **Orgs:** Amer Society for Public Adm; Women in Housing & Finance; Women of Washington; Washington Urban League; NAACP; Delta Sigma Theta Sorority; The Links, Inc, Capital City Chapter, chair, membership committee; National Black Child Devt Inst; Metropolitan AME Church. **Honors/Awds:** Dryades Savings Bank, Bd Resolution, 1994; City of Kansas City, Missouri-Proclamation, 1994; Minority Asset Recovery Contractors Assn, 1994; National Bankers Assn, 1994; National Assn of Black Accountants, 1993; Dollar & Sense Magazine, 1990. **Special Achievements:** Created unprecedented RTC contracting & investor opportunities for minorities and women; author and publisher of an informational booklet entitled, Fair Housing: It's Your Right; developed a system to detect discrimination in lending patterns and practices of regulated savings & loan assns. **Home Addr:** 1703 Leighton Wood Lane, Silver Spring, MD 20910, (301)565-5115. **Business Addr:** VP, Division of Minority and Women's Programs, Resolution Trust Corp, 801 17th Street, NW, Washington, DC 20434, (202)416-6925.

BOOKER, KAREN
Professional basketball player. **Personal:** Born Apr 10, 1965. **Educ:** Vanderbilt Univ, bachelor's degree in economics. **Career:** Utah Starzz, center, 1997-. **Honors/Awds:** Dr. Jim Robbins Award, 1987. **Special Achievements:** First woman to win the Dr. Jim Robbins Award. **Business Addr:** Professional Basketball Player, Utah Starzz, 301 West South Temple, Salt Lake City, UT 84101, (801)355-3865.

BOOKER, LORETTA LOVE
Venture capital company executive. **Personal:** Born May 16, 1951, Chicago, IL; daughter of Lois Orr Love and Andrew E Love; married. **Educ:** Howard Univ, BS 1972; Univ of Chicago, MBA 1983. **Career:** Sears Roebuck & Co, programmer 1972-74, office mgr 1974-78, consumer rsch serv mgr 1978-80, survey consultant 1980-81; Continental Bank, commercial lending 1981-83, coll relations 1983-84; Kraft Inc, corporate recruiter; Apple Computer, Inc, Cupertino, CA, staffing consultant, 1988-89, coll relations consultant, 1989-90, compensation specialist, 1990-93, prog mgr, 1993-94; Sega of America, hr mgr, 1994-95; Softbank Forums, hr dir, 1995-97; Merlin Venture Partners, principal, 1997-. **Orgs:** Mem Natl Black MBA Assn 1980-94; mem Minority Economic Resources Corp Council 1984-89; seminar dir Werner Erhard & Assn 1985-87; vice pres 1987, Career Mgmt Comm Univ of Chicago Women's Business Group mem; sec/treas and bd of dirs Northern Cook Co Private Industry Cncl 1986-89; mem 1989-, pres, 1990-91, Delta Sigma Theta Soroity Inc, Palo Alto/Bay Area Alumnae. **Home Addr:** 1269 Poplar Ave, #206, Sunnyvale, CA 94086-8620.

BOOKER, MICHAEL
Professional football player. **Educ:** Nebraska. **Career:** Atlanta Falcons, 1997-. **Special Achievements:** NFL Draft, First round pick, #11, 1997. **Business Addr:** Professional Football Player, Atlanta Falcons, Two Falcon Place, Suwanee, GA 30174, (404)945-1111.

BOOKER, ROBERT JOSEPH
Executive director. **Personal:** Born Apr 14, 1935, Knoxville, TN; son of Lillian Allen (deceased) and Willie Edward Booker (deceased). **Educ:** Knoxville Coll, BS Educ 1962. **Career:** Chattanooga TN Pub Schools, teacher 1962-64; State of TN, elected mem of Legislature (3 terms) 1966-72; Mayor of Knoxville, TN, admin asst 1972-74; Stroh Brewery Co, Detroit, MI, market devel mgr 1974-77; Beck Cultural Exchange Ctr, exec dir 1978-84; City of Knoxville, personnel dir 1984-88; Knoxville Journal, weekly columnist, 1987-92; Beck Cultural Exchange Center, executive director, 1988-. **Orgs:** Mem Phi Beta Sigma Frat; NAACP; VFW; American Legion; Martin Luther King Commemoration Commission; Knoxville College Historian. **Honors/Awds:** Bronze Man of the Year, 1990; Martin L King, Distinguished Service Award, 1994. **Special Achievements:** Author of: "200 Years of Black Culture in Knoxville, Tennessee, 1791-1991;" "And There Was Light! The 120 Year History of Knoxville College 1875-1995.". **Military Serv:** US Army, 1954-57. **Home Addr:** 2621 Parkview Ave, Knoxville, TN 37914. **Business Addr:** Executive Director, Beck Cultural Exchange Ctr Inc, 1927 Dandridge Ave, Knoxville, TN 37915.

BOOKER, SIMEON S.
Journalist. **Personal:** Born Aug 27, 1918, Baltimore, MD; son of Roberta Warring and Simeon Booker Sr; divorced; children: Simeon, Jr, James, Theresa. **Educ:** VA Union Univ, BA 1942; Cleveland Coll, attended 1950; Harvard Univ, 1950. **Career:** Johnson Co Inc, bureau chief, 1955-; Jet Magazine, columnist; Washington Post, 1952-54; Westinghouse Broadcasting Co, radio commentator. **Honors/Awds:** Publ "Man's King Taylor Black Mem", "Washington's Speaker's Office"; visited Africa with Pres Nixon 1957, US Attorney General Kennedy 1962, vice pres Humphrey 1968; Nieman Fellowship Journalism Harvard Univ 1950; Washington Association of Black Journalists, Career Achievement Award, 1993. **Business Addr:** Bureau Chief, DC Office, Jet Magazine, 1750 Pennsylvania Ave, NW, Ste 1301, Washington, DC 20006.

BOOKER, TERESA HILLARY CLARKE
Real estate investment banker. **Personal:** Born Feb 8, 1963, Los Angeles, CA; daughter of Audrey Millicent Clarke; married Walter K. Booker, Jun 3, 1989. **Educ:** Harvard College, Cambridge, MA, AB, 1984; Harvard Business School, Boston, MA, MBA, 1989; Harvard Law School, Cambridge, MA, JD, 1989. **Career:** Goldman, Sachs & Co., New York, NY, associate, 1989-. **Orgs:** Board of Trustees, Episcopal Chaplaincy at Harvard, 1988-. **Honors/Awds:** Williston & Competition, Harvard Law School, 1985.

BOOKER, VAUGHAN P. L.
Cleric. **Personal:** Born Sep 17, 1942, Philadelphia, PA; son of Mary E Booker and Lorenzo S Booker; married Portia A McClellan Booker, Jun 30, 1979; children: Kimberly Nichole, Manuel B McClellan. **Educ:** Villanova University, BA, 1978; Virginia Theological Seminary, MDiv, 1992. **Career:** Xerox Corp, account executive, 1981-87; Sprint Communications, major account rep, 1987-89; Meade Memorial Episcopal Church, rector, currently. **Orgs:** Protestant Correctional Chaplain's Association, 1975-80; Offender Aid and Restoration, board member, 1980-87; Virginia CURE, board member; George Washington National Bank, board of advisors; Omega Psi Phi, mem. **Honors/Awds:** Alpha Sigma Lambda, 1977; Xerox Corp, President's Club, 1981. **Business Addr:** Rector, Meade Memorial Episcopal Church, 322 N Alfred St, Alexandria, VA 22314, (703)549-1334.

BOOKER, VAUGHN JAMEL
Professional football player. **Personal:** Born Feb 24, 1968, Cincinnati, OH; married Sheila; children: Vaughn Jr, Breana, DeVaughn. **Educ:** Univ of Cincinnati. **Career:** Kansas City Chiefs, defensive end, 1994-. **Business Addr:** Professional Football Player, Kansas City Chiefs, One Arrowhead Dr, Kansas City, MO 64129, (816)924-9300.

BOOKER, VENERABLE FRANCIS
Banker. **Personal:** Born Sep 23, 1920, Great Bend, KS; son of Ora Ramsey and Venerable O Booker; married. **Educ:** Attended Portland State University. **Career:** Real estate broker; Amer State Bank, President and CEO, currently chief exec, president, chairman of the board. **Military Serv:** AUS corpl, 1942-46. **Business Addr:** Chief Executive, President, Chairman of the board, Amer State Bank, 2737 NE Union Ave, Portland, OR 97212.

BOOKERT, CHARLES C.
Physician (retired). **Personal:** Born Aug 8, 1918, Cottonwood, AL; married Mabel Berneice; children: Lisa. **Educ:** Morris Brown Coll, BS; Meharry Med Coll, MD 1945. **Career:** Private practice, physician. **Orgs:** Pres Natl Med Assoc 1977-78, HSA Western PA; ed com Amer Acad Family Pract; past pres Gateway Med Group, McKeesport Acad of Med, Keystone State Med Soc; bd dir Allegheny Bd of Amer Cancer Soc; staff McKeesport Hosp Family Prac Dept; bd dir Allegheny Cty Comprehensive Health Care Com, Allegheny Rgnl Health Com, Allegheny Smoke Control, Allegheny Cty Med Soc, Med Soc of PA; ret mem Med Dept Westinghouse Elec Corp; mem Chi Delta Med, Phi Beta Sigma, Imperial Benevolent Proctective Order of Elks of World, Prince Hall Mason; trustee Mt Olive Bapt Ch; mem Rho Boule Sigma Pi 1977; del Dem Natl Conv. **Honors/Awds:** Outstanding Alumnus Morris Brown Coll 1971; Athlete Hall of Fame 1974; Black Achiever OES 1974; Contemporary Black Leaders Yale Univ Press 1974; Hon Serv to Afro-Amer Youth in Ed Sears Roebuck Corp 1973; Hon Serv Gaetway Med Grp Keystone State Med Soc 1974-; recipient Family Dr of the Year Awd NMA 1974; Honored McKeesport Br of NAACP 1977; Chi Delta Mu Frat for Serv to Black Youth 1978; Health Rsch Serv Found 1979; Clairton Br of NAACP 1979; Cert of Appreciation NMA 1979; Hand in Hand, Dr Martin Luther King's Citizens award, 1983; GRAC&A, Humanitarian Award, 1984; National Medical Association, Meritorius Service Award, 1986; Tay Club, special recognition, 1986; Atlanta University, Sports Hall of Fame, 1988; Renaissance Magazine, Black Trail Blazer, 1988; Pennsylvania State Baptist Convention, Civic Award,1; National Medical Association, Community Service Award, 1989. **Military Serv:** AUS pfc 1943-45; Med Corp capt 1953-55.

BOON, INA M.
Association executive. **Personal:** Born Jan 6, 1927, St Louis, MO; daughter of Clarence Boon and Lovie Boon; divorced. **Educ:** Oakwood Acad Huntsville AL, Grad; Natl Bus Inst; Tucker's Bus Clge; Washington Univ; WIU. **Career:** NAACP, dir Region IV 1973-, life mbrshp field dir 1968-73; St Louis Br NAACP, admin secr 1962-68; US Army Transp Corp & US Dept of Labor, former employee. **Orgs:** Mem St Louis Chap Natl Council of Negro Women; Natl Professional Women's Club; mem MO Univ adv coun; bd mem St Louis Minority Econ Dev Agcy; secr St Louis Mental Health Assn; 2nd vice pres Top Ladies of Distinction Inc; vice pres St Louis Chpt; vpv Natl Financial Secr; organizer, cardinal chapter, Top Ladies of Distinction, 1987; chairman, board of directors, St Louis Comprehensive Health Center, 1983-87. **Honors/Awds:** Top Ladies of Distinction Inc Award for Distg Srv; St Louis Argus Newspaper Cancer Soc, St Louis Black Firefighters Inst of Racial Equality; Sigma Gamma Rho Sor; Kansas City KS Br NAACP; Kansas City MO Br NAACP & St Louis Globe Dem; Woman of Ach in Social Welfare 1970; Distg Srv Award Union Meml United Meth Ch 1977; Humanitarian Award; Human Dev Corp 1976; Outstanding Ldrshp & Admin Abilities 1973; 1990 Director of the Year Award, Women Action Crusaders & the National Resource Center. **Business Addr:** NAACP, 1408 N Kingshighway Blvd, St Louis, MO 63113.

BOONE, ALEXANDRIA
Co. executive. **Personal:** Born May 15, 1947, Cleveland, OH; daughter of Aria Johnson and Alex Johnson Sr; children: Aria. **Educ:** Case Western Reserve University, MS, organization development and analysis, 1981; Weatherheed School of Mgmt; Dartmouth College, Amos Tuck School of Business Administration, 1987-91. **Career:** GAP Productions, Inc, president & CEO, 1984-. **Orgs:** Black Professinals Charitable Foundation, president. **Honors/Awds:** City of Cleveland, Minority Entrepreneur of the Year, 1988; Mayor of Cleveland, Alexandria B Boone Day, 1988; State of Ohio, Minority Business Advocate of the Year, 1989; CBS This Morning, National Network Program; Business Woman of the Year, 1989. **Special Achievements:** MBE Profiles Magazine, 1991, 1992; Reflections Magazine, 1991, 1992. **Business Addr:** President & Chief Executive Officer, Gap Productions, Inc, 5000 Euclid Ave, Ste 400, Cleveland, OH 44103, (216)391-4300.

BOONE, CAROL MARIE
Government official. **Personal:** Born Nov 22, 1945, Pensacola, FL; daughter of Clarice Thompson Butler and Benjamin J Butler; married Dr Robert L Boone, Sep 28, 1974; children: Carlotta, Robert Jr. **Educ:** Fisk Univ, BA 1966; Univ of Chicago, MA 1968; Vanderbilt Univ, EdD 1982. **Career:** IL Children's Home & Aid Soc, adoption counselor 1968-69; Dede Wallace Mental Health Ctr, branch dir 1970-80; TN State Dept of Mental Health, state employee assistance prog dir 1982-. **Orgs:** Mem Alpha Kappa Alpha Sor 1965-; mem Natl Assn of Social Workers Nashville 1969-; mem, treas 1978- The Links Inc Hendersonville Chap 1976-; mem, sec 1977-; bd of dirs First Baptist Church Capitol Hill Homes Inc; mem, finan sec 1986-87 Jack and Jill of Amer Nashville Chap 1982-; mem Natl Assn of Employee Assistance Professionals 1982-. **Honors/Awds:** Social Worker of the Year Awd Middle TN Chap NASW 1977; Outstanding Professional Student Awd Vanderbilt Univ 1982; Outstanding Employee of the Year Awd TN Dept Mental Health 1986; Outstanding Service to the Tennessee Employee Assistance Program, 1992, 1994, 1997. **Home Addr:** 320 Chicksaw Trail, Goodlettsville, TN 37072. **Business Addr:** Dir Employee Assistance Prog, Tennessee State Government, Andrew Jackson Bldg, Ste 1400, 500 Deaderick St, Nashville, TN 37243.

BOONE, CLARENCE DONALD
Educational administrator. **Personal:** Born Nov 23, 1939, Jackson, TN; married Louise May; children: Terrance A Beard, Torrance. **Educ:** Lane Coll, BS 1961; Memphis State Univ, MEd 1977. **Career:** NAACP, treas 1957; Alpha Phi Alpha, mem 1959; United Teaching Prof, mem 1961; United Way, bd of dir 1980; West High School, principal. **Orgs:** Mem Ambulance Authority 1973, Cty Commn 1977, YMCA 1980; bd of dir Headstart 1980-83; mem JEA; bd of dir Lane Coll Natl Youth Sports. **Honors/Awds:** Serv Awd Madison Cty Ambulance 1973-77; Alumni Awd Lane Coll 1978; Serv Awd State of Tennesse 1978; Educator of the Year Phi Delta Kappa 1984. **Home Addr:** 26 Brooks Dr, Jackson, TN 38301.

BOONE, CLARENCE WAYNE
Physician. **Personal:** Born Aug 27, 1931, Bryan, TX; son of Mae Frances Martin Marion and Elmo Boone; married Blanche Ollie Lane, Dec 18, 1954; children: Terrie, Clarence W Jr, Brian K. **Educ:** IN Univ, AB 1953; IN Univ Schl Med, MD 1956. **Career:** Gary Medical Specialists, Inc, pres, 1969-; Phys pvt prac 1964-; Homer G Phillips Hosp, resd 1957-61, internship 1956-57; Planned Parenthood Assc, med dir. **Orgs:** Mem Great Lakes Reg Med Adv Com Planned Parenthood Assn World Population 1974-; staff phys Meth Hosp of Gary; St Mary Med Ctr; pres Gary Med Specl Inc 1968-; mem Kappa Alpha Psi 1950-; Amer Coll of Ob/Gyn 1964-; Natl Med Assn 1967-; Homer G Phillips Alumni Assn; Assn of Planned Parenthood Phys; Assn of American Gyn Laparoscopists; Amer Ferility Soc Diplomat Amer Bd Ob/gyn 1964; trustee Indiana Univ Fdn, 1990-; rep Exec Council, 1983-; bd mem Neal-Marshall Committee, 1980-; Indiana Univ Alumni Assn. **Military Serv:** USAF capt 1961-64. **Home Addr:** 2386 W 20th Ave, Gary, IN 46404. **Business Addr:** 2200 Grant St, Gary, IN 46404.

BOONE, CLINTON CALDWELL
Government official, cleric. **Personal:** Born Feb 23, 1922, Monrovia, Liberia; son of Rachel Boone and Dr Clinton C Boone; married Evelyn Rowland Boone; children: Evelyn, Clinton III. **Educ:** Houghton Coll, AB 1942; CW Post Center, MA 1973; Eastern Seminary; VA Union Univ. **Career:** Union Baptist Church, Hempstead NY, pastor 1957-; Copiague Public School Mem, teacher; Town of Hempstead, Hempstead NY, commr 1982-; former teacher 29 years VA, NC, NY. **Orgs:** Mem Alpha Phi Alpha Fraternity 1940; VA Union; bd of dir Natl Baptist Convention Inc, Hempstead Chamber of Commerce; pres Hempstead Community Development Comm, Park Lake Housing Develoment; mem 100 Black Men; Man of Year Hempstead Chamber of Commerce 1987. **Honors/Awds:** CIAA Boxing Champion 1940; Unispan Award Hofstra Univ 1974. **Business Addr:** Commissioner, Town of Hempstead, 50 Front St, Hempstead, NY 11550.

BOONE, ELWOOD BERNARD, JR.
Urologist. **Personal:** Born May 7, 1943, Petersburg, VA; son of Dr & Mrs Elwood B Boone Sr; married Carol Fraser; children: Elwood III, Melanie. **Educ:** Phillips Academy, 1961; Colgate Univ, AB 1965; Meharry Med Coll, MD 1969; Med Coll VA, internship 1970, surgery resident 1972, urology resident 1975. **Career:** Med Coll VA, clinical instr 1975-; Richmond Meml Hosp, staff physician 1975-. **Orgs:** Amer Bd of Urology 1977; Omega Psi Phi 1967; Richmond Med Soc; Old Dominion Med Soc; Natl Med Soc; Richmond Urological Soc; Richmond Acad of Med; Med Soc of VA; Fellow Surgery Amer Cancer Soc 1973-74; natl pres Student natl Med Assn 1968-69; mem VA Urological Soc; Fellow Amer Coll of Surgeons 1979; pres Old Dominion Medical Soc 1981-82; chief of surgery Richmond Memorial Hosp 1985,86. **Honors/Awds:** Certified Amer Bd of Urology 1977. **Military Serv:** USAR capt 1971-77. **Business Addr:** President, Elwood B Boone Jr MD PC, 700 W Grace St, #204, Richmond, VA 23220-4119.

BOONE, FREDERICK OLIVER
Pilot. **Personal:** Born Jan 21, 1941, Baltimore, MD; married Penny Etienne; children: Vanessa, Frederick III, Kimberly, Sean, Shannon. **Educ:** Morgan State College, BS 1961. **Career:** Delta Airlines, flight engr 1969-70, 1st ofc 1970-79, capt 1980-86, capt/flight instructor and evaluator (B727) 1986-91, chief instructor, pilot, 1992-. **Orgs:** Mem Airline Pilots Assc; Mem Black Airline Pilots, sec org 1976-; So Christian Ldrshp Conf 1977. **Honors/Awds:** Air Medal USN; Achv Award Wall St Journal. **Military Serv:** US Navy, lt cmdr, Vietnam. **Business Addr:** Delta Airlines, General Offices, Hartsfield International Airport, Dept 052, Atlanta, GA 30320.

BOONE, RAYMOND HAROLD, SR.
Founder, editor, publisher. **Personal:** Born Feb 2, 1938, Suffolk, VA; married Jean Patterson; children: Regina, Raymond Jr. **Educ:** Norfolk St Coll, 1955-57; Boston Univ, BS 1960; Howard Univ, MA 1985. **Career:** Suffolk, VA News-Herald, reporter 1955-57; Boston Chronicle, city editor 1958-60; Tuskegee Inst, deputy dir, public info 1960-61; White House, Afro-Amer reporter 1964-65; Richmond Afro-Amer, ed 1965-81; Afro-Amer Co, editor/vice pres, 1976-81; Howard Univ, visiting prof in Journalism 1981-83, lecturer, 1983-88, assoc prof, 1988-91; Paradigm Communications, Inc, founder, pres, CEO, 1991-; Richmond Free Press, founder, editor and publisher, 1991-. **Orgs:** Life mem, NAACP; Kappa Alpha Psi; Sigma Delta Chi Professional Journalism Society; Governor's Ethics Commission; National Association of Guardsmen Inc; bd of dirs, Metropolitan Richmond Chamber of Commerce, Metropolitan Richmond and Visitors Bureau. **Honors/Awds:** Carl Murphy Comm Serv Award NNPA; 1st Place Robt Abbott Editorial Writing Award 1974, 1976; Distinguished Serv Award VA NAACP 1974; Unity Award for Pol Rpt Lincoln (MO) Univ 1975; Humanitarian of the Year Award Metro Richmond Business League 1976; VA State Coll Media Achievement Award 1976; Pulitzer Prize Juror 1978-79; Outstanding Suffolkian Morgan Memorial Library Suffolk, VA 1980; Metro Baltimore YMCA Outstanding Serv Award, 1986-87; Poynter Inst for Media Studies Award for Outstanding Teaching in Journalism, 1988; Big Shoulders Award, 1992; Delver Woman's Club Award, 1992; Metropolitan Business Award, 1995; Natl Newspaper Publishers Assn, Comm Svc Awd, 1996; Oliver W Hill, Citizen of the Year Awd, 1996; Richmond NAACP, Economic Empowerment Awd, 1997. **Business Phone:** (804)644-0496.

BOONE, ROBERT FRANKLIN
Financial services company executive. **Personal:** Born Feb 9, 1949, West Point, GA; son of Frankie Morgan Boone (deceased) and Robert Boone; divorced 1981. **Educ:** Franklin University, Columbus, OH, BBA, 1976; Ohio State University, Columbus, OH; Central Michigan University, Mt. Pleasant, MI, MA, 1978. **Career:** Miller Brewing Company, Milwaukee, WI, supervisor of special programs, 1979-84; ITT Financial Corporation, Minneapolis, MN, manager of corporate human resources, 1984-86; IDS/American Express Financial Corporation, Minneapolis, MN, director of staffing, 1987-91; Mall of America, director human resources and administration, 1991-. **Honors/Awds:** YMCA, Black Achievers, 1990. **Military Serv:** US Army, 1968-71; received Bronze Star, Army Commendation Medal, Good Conduct Medal. **Business Addr:** Dir of Staffing, Human Resources Dept, IDS/American Express Financial Corp., IDS Tower 10, T7/112, Minneapolis, MN 55402.

BOONE, RONALD BRUCE
Professional basketball player (retired). **Personal:** Born Sep 6, 1946, Oklahoma City, OK. **Educ:** Iowa Western Community College, Clarinda, IA, attended; Idaho State Univ, Poacatello, ID, attended. **Career:** Kansas City Kings, 1976-78; Los Angeles Lakers, 1978-79; Utah Jazz, 1980-81. **Honors/Awds:** Set professional basketball record by playing in 1,041 consecutive games.

BOONE, ZOLA ERNEST
Educational administrator. **Personal:** Born Oct 16, 1937, Wisner, LA; daughter of Zola Amond Ernest and Jesse Ernest; married Arthur I Boone; children: Monica, Denise, Ivan. **Educ:** Mt St Mary's, BA, 1957; MI State Univ, MS, 1970, PhD, 1972; Inst for Educ Mgmt Harvard Univ, Cert 1975. **Career:** Bowie State Univ, Bowie MD, dir of institute for diversity and multicultural affairs, 1996-; Bowie State Foundation, Bowie, MD, executive director, 1984-; Bowie State University, Bowie, MD, vice pres for planning and development, 1984-88, vice pres for development and university relations, 1988-96; US Department of Education, Washington, DC, policy fellow, 1981-82; American Council on Education, fellow, 1978; consultant, 1982-84; SDIP Coord Morgan State Univ, special asst to pres, 1979-80; Morgan St Univ, dir center for curriculum improvement, 1976-79; Coppin State Coll, special asst to vice pres, 1975-76, prof, dept chairperson, 1973-75; Coppin State Coll, honors prog advisor, 1972-73; Michigan State Univ, 1970-71; Baltimore Public Schools, teacher, dept chmn, 1962-69. **Orgs:** Maryland Assn for Higher Education, 1984-; Amer Assn for Higher Education, 1976-77, 1984-; Society for College and University Planners, 1984-; Council for the Advancement and Support of Education, 1984-; Assn for Supv & Curr Dev 1972-77; consult Curr Dev; Phi Kappa Phi; Delta Sigma Theta; pres The Links Inc 1977-78; Howard Co Dem Coalition; ACE/NID Planning Council, 1984-; Mid-Atlantic Regional Council (SCOP), 1989-; Prince Georges Coalition of 100 Black Women; Natl Political Congress of Black Women; Prince Georges County, Delta Sigma Theta Sorority; Maryland Natl Capital Park & Planning Comm & Prince George's County Planning Bd, commissioner. **Honors/Awds:** Ford Fellow MI State Univ 1971-72; Outst Serv Award Adult Educ Coppin State Clge 1975; ACE Fellow 1978-79; Case Commission on Philanthropy, 1996-97; BSU Foundation, Legacy of Excellence Award, 1993. **Business Addr:** Director, Bowie State University, Institute for Diversity & Multicultural Affairs, Jericho Park Rd, Bowie, MD 20715.

BOONIEH, OBI ANTHONY
Writers bureau chief executive. **Personal:** Born Jun 27, 1957, Onitsha, Nigeria; married Neka Carmenta White; children: Amechi. **Educ:** Morgan State Univ, BA 1983; Northeastern Univ Sch of Law, JD 1986. **Career:** African Relief Fund, pres 1982-84; First WRiters Bureau Inc, managing editor 1986-. **Orgs:** Dir Mangrover & Co Ltd 1979-; mem Big Brothers & Sisters of Central MD 1980-83; dir African Relief Fund 1984-85; consultant/dir Culture Port Inc 1986-; mem NAACP, Phi Alpha Delta; dir Intl Pollution Control Corp 1986-. **Honors/Awds:** Published article "Improving the Lot of Farmers," 1975; published book "A Stubborn Fate," ISBN#O-89260-146-9. **Business Addr:** Managing Editor, First Writers Bureau Inc, 819 E Fayette St, Baltimore, MD 21202.

BOOTH, CHARLES E.
Clergyman. **Personal:** Born Feb 4, 1947, Baltimore, MD. **Educ:** United Theological Seminary, DMin, 1990; Howard Univ, BA 1969; Eastern Bapt Theol Sem, MDiv 1973. **Career:** Mt Olivet Bapt Church, Columbus, OH, pastor, 1978-; St Paul's Bapt Ch West Chester PA, pastor 1970-78. **Orgs:** Progressive Nat Bapt Convention; American Bapt Churches. **Honors/Awds:** Ebony Mag, Honor Roll of Great Preachers, Nov 1993; Sermons: "When a Hunch Pays Off," Outstanding Black Sermons, vol III, published by Judson Press; "The Blessings of Unanswered Prayer and Spirituality," published by Judson Press; Meditation: "A Blessed Joy," From One Brother to Another: Voices of African-American Men, published by Judson Press. **Business Addr:** Mt Olivet Baptist Church, 428 E Main Street, Columbus, OH 43215.

BOOTH, KEITH
Professional basketball player. **Personal:** Born Oct 9, 1974. **Educ:** Maryland. **Career:** Chicago Bulls, forward, 1997-. **Business Addr:** Professional Basketball Player, Chicago Bulls, 1901 W Madison St, Chicago, IL 60612, (312)455-4000.

BOOTH, LAVAUGHN VENCHAEL
Clergyman. **Personal:** Born Jan 7, 1919, Collins, MS; son of Mamie Powell Booth and Frederick Douglas Booth; married Georgia Anna Morris (deceased); children: Lavaughn V Jr, William D, Anna M Metwally, Georgia A Leeper, Paul; married Yvette Livers. **Educ:** Alcorn State Univ MS, AB 1940; Howard Univ Sch of Religion, BD 1943; Univ of Chicago Div Sch, MA 1945; Wilberforce U, LHD 1964; Morehouse Coll, DD 1967; Central State Univ, Wilberforce, OH, 1967; Univ of Cincinnati, LHD 1989. **Career:** First Bapt Warrenton VA, pastor 1943; First Bapt of Gary IN, pastor 1944-52; Zion Baptist of Cinci OH, pastor 1952-84; Univ of Cinci, first black bd mem 1968-; Baptist World Alliance, vice pres 1970-75; Prog Nat Bapt Conv, founder & former pres 1971-74; Hamilton Co State Bnk, founder & chrmn 1980; Olivet Bapt Cinci OH, pastor & founder 1984-. **Orgs:** Spec sec Am Bible Soc; first exec sec Prog Nat Bapt Conv 1964-69; founder of "Martin Luther King, Jr Sunday" 1972; founding mem Chan 12 TV Dialogue Panel 1965-; founder & chrmn Cinci OIC 1966-71; chrmn & org Cinci Black Bank 1974; mem bd of dir Martin Luther King Jr Center; mem bd of mgmt Amer Bible Soc. **Honors/Awds:** Cert of Merit Cinci NAACP 1963; Disting Serv Award Churches of Detroit 1968; PNBC Founders Award Prog Nat Bapt Conv 1971; Operation PUSH Award of Excellence 1974; Ebony's Success Library 1974; One of 200 Greater Cincinnatians, Greater Cincinnati Bicentennial Commission, Inc, 1988; First to Make a Lasting Difference, Star Bank, 1989; Outstanding Educator, Applause, 1991. **Home Addr:** 2300 Larkfield Drive, Cincinnati, OH 45237-1502.

BOOTH, LE-QUITA
Administrator. **Personal:** Born Oct 7, 1946, Columbus, GA; daughter of Hilda Reese and Joseph Reese; married Lester Booth; children: Joseph. **Educ:** Columbus College, BS 1972; MBA 1977; Univ of Georgia Athens, EdD 1987. **Career:** Natl Bank & Trust, Commercial Officer 1974-77; Small Business Administration, Disaster Loan Spec 1977-78; Small Business Devel Ctr Univ of GA, Associate Dir 1978-; The National Science Center Foundation, assistant to the president for Educ 1988-. **Orgs:** Natl Business League, Board of Dir & Reg Vice Pres 1983-85; Georgia Assoc of Minority Entrepreneurs 1981-85; International Council for Small Business, Vice Pres for Minority Small Business 1984-86. **Honors/Awds:** Wall St Journal, Award for Achievement 1972; Small Business Administration, Minority Advocate of the Year 1982; University of Georgia, Public Service Extension Award; International Council for Small Business Fellow 1986. **Home Addr:** 609 Zeron Drive, Columbus, GA 31907. **Business Addr:** The National Science Center Foundation, PO Box 1648, 127 Seventh Street, Augusta, GA 30903.

BOOTH, WILLIAM H.
Attorney. **Personal:** Born Aug 12, 1922, Jamaica, NY; son of Mabel Booth and William H Booth; married Suzanne Potter; children: Gini, Jeffrey, Ronald. **Educ:** Queen's Coll, BA 1946; NY Univ Law Sch, LLB 1950, LLM 1954. **Career:** New York City Human Rights Commn, chmn 1966-69; New York City Criminal Court, judge 1969-76; NY State Supreme Court, justice 1976-82; Flamhaft, Levy, Kamins, Hirsch & Booth, partner 1982-87; Queens County, attorney (limited practice), currently. **Orgs:** Dir 100 Black Men of NY Inc; president Amer Comm on Africa; dir Jamaica Serv Prog for Older Adults servicing 14 senior centers and core area of 70,000 senior citizens; pres 24-00 Ericsson St Block Assn; mem Intl Comm to Invest the Crimes of the Chilean Junta; chairman New York City Sickle Cell Found; board of directors Proctor-Hopson Post of the Veterans of Foreign Affairs; Queens Co Bar Assn; Metropolitan Black Bar Assn; board member/assistant treasurer Medgar Evers Found; Jamaica Br NAACP; charter Judicial Cncl of the Natl Bar Assn; Governor's Commn on Voluntary Enterprise; NYS Human rights Adv Cncl; Coalition for a Just New York; Adv Bd CUNY Law Sch Queens, NY; chairman New York CityBoard of Correction. **Honors/Awds:** Recipient of over 100 awards for public service; lecturer at numerous colleges and universities. **Military Serv:** AUS Corp of Engineers M/Sgt served 4 yrs. **Home Addr:** 2301 Kings Crest Rd., Kissimmee, FL 34744-6244. **Business Addr:** Attorney, 25-74 98th St, East Elmhurst, NY 11369.

BOOZER, EMERSON, JR.
Recreation administrator. **Personal:** Born Jul 4, 1943, Augusta, GA; son of Classie Mae Boozer and Emerson Boozer; married Enez Yevette Bowins; children: 1. **Educ:** Univ of MD Eastern Shore, BS 1966. **Career:** CBS-TV, football analyst, 1976-77; New York Jets, football player 1966-76; WLIB Radio, announcer 1971-74; Long Island Cablevision, sports analyst college & hs football games; town of Huntington, NY, parks and

recreation director, exec asst to supvr, currently. **Orgs:** Mem Police Athletic League; mem Natl Football League Players Assn. **Honors/Awds:** Actors Guild Meth Named Rookie of Year, Pittsburgh Courier 1966; All-Amer 1964-65; Outstanding Small Coll Athlete, Washington Pigskin Club, 1965; Named to Amer Football League All-Star Team 1966-68; AFC Scoring Touchdowns Champ 1972; Inductee, The Honors Court, Georgia Sports Hall of Fame 1991. **Home Addr:** 25 Windham Dr, Huntington Station, NY 11746.

BORDEN, HAROLD F., JR.
Artist. **Personal:** Born Feb 3, 1942, New Orleans; married Barbara Sullivan; children: Tony, Tina. **Educ:** LA City Clge, studied drawing under Norman Schwab; Trade Tech Clge LA, studied design; Otis Art Inst LA, studied drawing Charles White; sculpture under Racul Desota. **Career:** Krasne Co, designed jewelry 1969-71; Contemporary Crafts LA, exhibited 1972; H Borden Studios, master jeweler, sculptor artist owner. **Orgs:** Org Jua-Agr Ctr LA; mem Black Artists & Craftsman Guild LA; mem Amer Guild Craftsman; worked with Robert Nevis & Toshi Enami; worked with Thomas Green; bd mem Jua; design consult Black Artists & Craftsman Guild of LA. **Honors/Awds:** Spec ach award Dept Recreation & Parks City LA 1972; participation award City of LA Day in the Park 1974. **Business Addr:** 1255 1/2 S Cochran Ave, Los Angeles, CA.

BORDERS, FLORENCE EDWARDS
Certified archivist. **Personal:** Born Feb 24, 1924, New Iberia, LA; daughter of Julia Gray Edwards and Sylvanus Edwards; married James Buchanan Borders (died 1959); children: James Buchanan IV, Sylvanus Edwards Borders, Thais Borders Adams. **Educ:** Southern University, Baton Rouge, LA, BA, 1945; Rosary College, School of Library Science, River Forest, IL, BA, Library Science, 1947, MA, Library Science, 1966; Louisiana State University, Baton Rouge, LA, Post Master's Fellow, 1967-68. **Career:** University of Chicago, Chicago, IL, library asst, 1946; Bethune-Cookman College, Daytona Beach, FL, asst librarian, 1947-58; Tennessee State University, Nashville, TN, cataloger, 1958-59; Grambling State University, Grambling, LA, head, technical services, 1959-70; Amistad Research Center, Tulane University, New Orleans, LA, senior and ref archivist, 1970-89; Southern University at New Orleans, Center for African and African American Studies, New Orleans, LA, archivist, 1989-. **Orgs:** Founder, director, Chicory Society of Afro-Louisiana History and Culture, 1986-; past president, Our Lady of Lourdes Parish Council, 1986-87; past president, Greater New Orleans Archivists, 1987-88; vice president, Our Lady of Lourdes Parish School Board, 1990-91; nominating committee, Academy of Certified Archivists, 1990-91; block captain, Mayoral Campaign, 1990; member, Society of American Archivists, Society of Southwest Archivists, Coalition of 100 Black Women, American Library Association, Louisiana Archives and Mss Association, League of Good Government, Zeta Phi Beta Sorority. **Honors/Awds:** Certificate of Merit, Phi Beta Sigma Fraternity, 1969; Certificate of Recognition, Black Chorale, 1986; Certificate of Appreciation, Equal Opportunity Advisory Council, 1986; Unsung Heroes Plaque, Crescent City Chapter of Links, 1987; trophy, Louisiana World Exposition, Afro-American Pavilion, 1984; Callaloo Award, University of Virginia, 1988; "Vital as a Heartbeat Award," Urban League, 1988; trophy, Calvary CME Church, 1988. **Business Addr:** Archivist, Southern University at New Orleans, Center for African and African American Studies, 6400 Press Dr, Library, New Orleans, LA 70122.

BORDERS, MICHAEL G.
Educator, artist. **Personal:** Born Oct 17, 1946, Hartford, CT; son of Marjorie Davis Borders and Thomas L Borders; married Sharon Armwood, Feb 4, 1984; children: Nicholas M A Borders. **Educ:** Fisk Univ, BA 1968; Howard Univ, MFA 1970; attended Skowhegan School of Painting & Sculpture. **Career:** Fisk Univ, instructor 1970-71; Fox Middle School, math teacher 1971-72; S Arsenal Neighborhood Devel Sch, artist in residence 1974-78; Greater Hartford Comm Coll, art history instructor 1978; Freelance Artist, 1978-. **Orgs:** First Ann Fine Arts Exhibit 1968; First Annual Congreg Art Show 1968; Student Exhibit 1968; Student Exhibit Skowhegan School of Painting & Sculpture; One-Man Show Central Michigan Univ 1970; Joint Faculty Exhibit Fisk, Vanderbilt, Peabody 1971; display in lobby Phoenix Mutual Life Ins Co 1974; Unitarian Meeting-house Hartford 1974; artist in residence Weaver HS 1973-74; lectr Loomis-Chaffee Prep Sch 1973; Lectr Trinity Coll 1973; portrait painter; works placed in local Washington galleries; billboard painter; Fisk Univ homecoming brochure covers 1967-68. **Honors/Awds:** Two-man Show Natl Cntr for Afro-Amer Artists 1975; mural displayed in Hartford titled "Genesis of Capital City" (largest mural in New England - first permanent monument by Black Amer in Hartford); 18-month trip to Africa, Asia & Europe 1976-77; CT State Panorama of Business & Indus 1980; two mural panels City Hall, Hartford (2nd permanent monument by Black Amer in Hartford) 1980-85; three murals AETNA Insurance Co, Hartford, 1989; four murals AI Prince Regional Vocational Tech School, Hartford 1989; many conceptual paintings and portraits.

BORGES, LYNNE MACFARLANE
Consumer goods company executive. **Personal:** Born Oct 27, 1952, Middletown, OH; daughter of Charma Jordan MacFarlane and Victor MacFarlane, Sr; married Francisco L Borges, May 28, 1988; children: Ryan Elliot Jones. **Educ:** Wesleyan Univ, BA Govt 1975. **Career:** Aetna Life & Casualty, mgr 1975-79; CT General Life Ins, asst dir 1979-82; CIGNA, dir 1982-85; Heublein Inc, dir 1985-. **Orgs:** Corporate adv comm Natl Assn for Equal Oppor in Higher Educ 1983-; bd dirs CT Black Women's Educ/Rsch Foundation 1985-; Council of Bd Chairs, Nat'l Urban League, president, 1992-; women's exec comm mem Greater Hartford Chamber of Commerce 1986-; past chm of bd Greater Hartford Urban League 1989-; bd of trustees Mark Twain Memorial; Child & Family Services, board of directors, 1991-; incorporator, Institute for Living, 1990-. **Honors/Awds:** State of CT Young Career Woman Bus/Prof Women's Federation 1979; Mary McLeod Bethune Awd Natl Council of Negro Women 1981; Outstanding CT Women of the Decade 1987. **Business Addr:** Dir, Human Resources/Planning Devt, Heublein Inc, 330 New Park Ave, Hartford, CT 06142.

BOROM, LAWRENCE H.
Social service administrator. **Personal:** Born Feb 28, 1937, Youngstown, OH; son of Cora Mildred Lewis Borom and Clarence H Russell; married Betty J Fontaine, Nov 29, 1963; children: Martin Antoine Borom. **Educ:** Youngstown State Univ, Youngstown, OH, BS in educ, 1954-58; Mankato State Coll, Mankato, MN, MA urban studies, 1970-71. **Career:** Cleveland Public Schools, Cleveland, OH, elementary teacher, 1962-63; St Paul Urban League, St Paul, MN, employment & educ dir, 1963-66; MN Governor's Human Rights Commn, exec dir, 1966-67; St Paul Urban League, commn, exec dir, 1967-74; Natl Urban League, New York City, NY, dir community devel, 1974-76; Urban League of Metropolitan Denver, Denver, CO, pres/CEO, 1976-. **Orgs:** Mem, Kappa Alpha Psi Fraternity, 1956-; mem, Advisory Comm Denver Mayor's Black Advisory Comm, 1985-; mem, pres, CO Black Roundtable, 1988-; mem, Advisory Comm, "A World of Differene" Project, 1988-; mem, bd of dir, CO African/Carribean Trade Office, 1989-. **Honors/Awds:** Esquire Award, Esquire Club, 1984; Distinguished Service Award, UNCF, 1985; Distinguished Service Award, CO Civil Rights Commn, 1987. **Military Serv:** US Army, Sp4. 1959-62. **Home Addr:** 355 S Oliver Way, Denver, CO 80224.

BORUM, REGINA A.
Educational administrator. **Personal:** Born Jul 28, 1938, Dayton, OH; daughter of Vivien L Hayes Prear and Robert Cortney Prear; married Butler Borum, Oct 14, 1957; children: Joy Louise Middleton, Mark Randall, M Rodney. **Educ:** Capital Univ, Columbus OH, BA, 1984; Union Graduate School, Cincinnati OH, doctoral work, 1988-. **Career:** Wright State Univ, admin asst to dean, 1975-79, asst to vice pres for health affairs, 1979-81, dir of univ & community events, 1981-88, dir of conf & continuing educ, beginning 1988; Greene County Convention and Visitors Bureau, vp, beginning 1987; Portland State Univ, dir of corp and foundation relations, exec dir of development, currently. **Orgs:** Comm mem, YWCA Promotions and Publicity Comm, 1974-; mem, Dayton Urban League, 1979-; mem, NAACP, 1979-; bd mem, Meeting Planners Intl, 1980-, volunteer, Miami Valley Literacy Council, 1981-; mem, Amer Soc for Training & Devel, 1982; mem, Amer Assn for Univ Women, 1984; mem, United Way Allocations Comm, 1985-; Natl Coalition of Black Meeting Planners, 1986-. **Honors/Awds:** Outstanding Volunteer, United Way, 1985; Serv Award, United Negro Coll Fund, 1985; Appreciation Award, Miami Valley Literacy Council, 1987; Appreciation Award, Delta Sigma Theta Sorority, 1988; Meeting Planner of the Year, Meeting Planners Intl, Ohio Valley Chapter, 1989. **Business Addr:** Exec Dir, Development, Portland State Univ, 724 SW Harrison St, Portland, OR 97201.

BOSCHULTE, ALFRED F.
Telecommunications executive. **Personal:** Born Sep 18, 1942, St Thomas, Virgin Islands of the United States; married Kita. **Educ:** City College of New York, BSME; City University of New York, MS, engineering. **Career:** New York Telephone, 1964-76; AT&T, director, cross industries, 1982; Pacific Bell, vice pres, external affairs, 1983-87; NYNEX Service Company, vice pres, carrier services, 1987-90; NYNEX Corporation, vice pres, marketing, NYNEX Mobile Communications, president, 1990-; TomCom LP, president. **Orgs:** Institute of Electrical & Electronic Engineers; INROADS, Westchester & Fairfield counties, chairman of the board; Junior Achievement, board of directors; Clark University, board of trustees; Boys & Girls Clubs of America, board of trustees; Cellular Telecommunications Industry Assn, vice chairman; United Way, board of directors. **Business Addr:** President, TomCom LP, 2000 Corporate Drive, Orangeburg, NY 10962, (914)365-7899.

BOSCHULTE, JOSEPH CLEMENT
Physician. **Personal:** Born Feb 5, 1931, Tortola Britich, VI; married Rubina; children: Cheryl, Jualenda, Joseph. **Educ:** City Coll NY, BS 1954; Hwrd Univ Coll Med, 1958; Frdmn Hosp, Intern 1959, Resd 1967. **Career:** Pvt Prac, physcn 1972-; B Wash DC, chf inptnt serv area 1969-72. **Orgs:** Chmn Dept Psychtry Crtr SE Comm Hosp 1972-, mem 1968-; sr atdg psychtrst WA Hosp Ctr 1968-76; mem Prnc Grg's Hosp 1968-75; mem Am Psycht Assn; WA Psycht Soc; AMA. **Honors/Awds:** DC Med Soc Flwsp Grant Nat Inst Mtl Hlth 1964-67. **Military Serv:** AUS MC gen med of cr capt 1960.

BOSLEY, FREEMAN ROBERTSON, JR.
Former mayor. **Personal:** Born Jul 20, 1954, St Louis, MO. **Educ:** St Louis Univ, Urban Affairs 1976, Pol Sci 1976, JD 1979. **Career:** Legal Serv of Eastern MO, staff atty 1979-81; Bussey & Jordan, assoc 1982-83; supreme Court Judiciary, clerk of the circuit court beginning 1983; City of St Louis, mayor, 1993-96. **Orgs:** Mound City Bar Assn, 1980, Metro Bar Assn, 1980, Bd of Jury Commissioners; Child Support Commission, commissioner, 1985-.

BOSLEY, THAD (THADDIS)
Professional baseball player. **Personal:** Born Sep 17, 1956, Oceanside, CA; married Cherry Sanders. **Educ:** Mira Costa Community College, Oceanside, CA, attended. **Career:** Outfielder: California Angels, 1977, Chicago White Sox, 1978-80, Milwaukee Brewers, 1981, Seattle Mariners, 1982, Chicago Cubs, 1983-86, Kansas City Royals, 1987-88, Texas Rangers, 1989-90. **Honors/Awds:** Named the CA League's Player of the Year in 1976; recorded a gospel contemporary album entitled "Pick Up the Pieces"; working on book of poems for children.

BOST, FRED M.
City official. **Personal:** Born Mar 12, 1938, Monroe, NC; married Sara B; children: Sybil, Olantunji, Kimberly. **Educ:** Bloomfield Coll, BS 1976; Cook Coll, Enviro-Health/Law 1979. **Career:** Elizabeth NJ Bd of Educ, chmn of title I 1970-72; Dept of Prop & Maint, asst mgr 1976-79; Township of Irvington, comm on drugs 1977-79; Essex Co, comm of youth/rehab comm 1977-80; ABC of Irvington, comm chmn 1982-84; Township of Irvington, councilman 1980-. **Orgs:** Pres of the Fred Bost Civic Assn 1975-81; rep for the Bureau of Indian Affairs 1976-78; public relations rep data processing 1977-79; pres East Ward CivicAssn 1979-81. **Honors/Awds:** Concerned Citizen Awd PBA of Irvington 1980. **Military Serv:** AUS sgt 2 yrs. **Business Addr:** Councilmember, City of Irvington, 749 15th Ave, Irvington, NJ 07111.

BOSTIC, JAMES EDWARD, JR.
Director, scientist. **Personal:** Born Jun 24, 1947, Marlboro Co, SC; married Edith A Howard; children: James E III, Scott H. **Educ:** Clemson Univ, BS 1969, PhD 1972. **Career:** Clemson Univ, doctor flw 1969-72, graduate resident counselor 1969-72; Amer Enka & Rsch Corp, sr rsch science, 1972; Dept of Agriculture, special asst to sec of agriculture 1972-73, dep asst sec of agriculture 1973-77; Riegel Text Corp, corp regulat dir tech analyst, 1977-81, convenience products div 1981-85; Georgia Pacific, general mgr. **Orgs:** Mem Assn of Text Chem & Color; amer Chem Soc; Phi Psi Fraternity; Blue Key Natl Hnr Frat; Natl Acad of Engr 1975-76; bd trustees US Dept of Agriculture Graduate School 1976-77; mem Pres Commin on White House Fellowship Region Panel 1975-78; FFA Hnr Amer Farmer Deg 1976; council mem Clemson Univ Graduate School 1971-72; mem US Dept of Commerce Mgmt Labor Textile Advisory Com 1978-85; vice chmn & chmn SC Commn on Higher Educ 1978-83; chmn & mem Career Found Bd of Trustees 1978-; mem President's Commn on White House Fellowships 1981-; mem Clemson Univ, Bd of Trustees 1983-. **Honors/Awds:** Ford Found Doc Fellowship for Black Students 1969-70; first black awarded PhD Clemson Univ; White House Fellow 1972-73; Distinguished Serv Award Greenville Jaycees 1979; Outstanding Public Servant of Year Award 1983 SC Assoc of Minorities for Public Administration. **Military Serv:** USAR 2nd lt 1971-77. **Business Addr:** Executive, Pope & Talbot Inc, 8 Amlajack Blvd, Newnan, GA 30265-1010.

BOSTIC, LEE H.
Attorney. **Personal:** Born Apr 17, 1935, Brooklyn, NY; married Gayle Spaulding; children: Lisa, Staci, Lee. **Educ:** Morgan State Coll, AB 1957; Boston Univ Law School, LLB 1962. **Career:** Allstate Ins Co, claims adj 1964; Solomon Z Ferziger NYC, assoc atty 1964-65; Queens Co, asst dist atty 1966; private practice attorney 1967-. **Orgs:** Mem NY and Queens Co Bar Assocs; mem NAACP; male committeeman 29 AD Reg Rep Club Queens Co; mem NYS Bar Assoc, Macon B Allen Black Bar Assoc; bd of dirs Jr Academy League Inc. **Military Serv:** AUS 1st lt 1957-59.

BOSTIC, VIOLA W.
Association executive. **Personal:** Born Oct 24, 1941, New York, NY; daughter of Peter Williams & Doris Andrews; married Raphael, Apr 24, 1965; children: Raphael William, Ebony Leigh. **Educ:** City College of NY, BA, 1963; City University of NY, MA, 1965; University of PA, MS, 1992. **Career:** Morgan State University, instructor, 1967-68; Burlington County College, instructor, 1969-70; The Courier Post, reporter, 1973-74; Rohm & Haas Company, mgr of marketing services, 1974-93; Big Brothers/Big Sisters of America, asst natl exec dir, 1994-. **Orgs:** Moorestown Visiting Nurse Assn, vice chair, 1984-; Philadelphia Salvation Army, advisory chair, 1976-; Contact 609, chair, community relations, 1993-94; Philadelphia Urban Coalition, chair emeritus, Education Task Force; National Assn of Media Women, Philadelphia, pres, 1982-85; Public

Relations Society of America, 1995-; The National Assembly Public Relations; Marketing Professionals, 1994-; Male Advocacy Network, 1996-. **Honors/Awds:** Ford/Gannett Foundations, Michele Club Fellowship, 1973; Bd Member of the Year, MVNA, 1993; National Urban League, BEEP Award, 1990; Salvation Army Advisory Council Award, 1985; National Assn of Media Women, 1983. **Business Addr:** Asst Natl Exec Dir, Big Brother/Big Sisters of America, 230 N 13th St, Philadelphia, PA 19107-0394, (215)567-7000.

BOSTON, ARCHIE, JR.
Art director, designer, educator. **Personal:** Born Jan 18, 1943, Clewiston, FL; married Juanita; children: Michael, Jennifer. **Educ:** CA Inst of the Arts, BFA 1965; Univ of So CA, MLA 1977. **Career:** Hixon & Jorgensen Inc, art dir 1965-66; Boston & Boston Design, partner 1966-68; Carson Roberts Inc, art dir 1968; Botsford Ketchum Inc, art dir 1968-77;CA State Univ, assoc prof 1977; Design Concepts, pres 1977-78. **Orgs:** Judge num award shows 1965-; pres Art Dir Club of LA 1973; mem Mt Sinai Bapt Church; bd of govs Art Dir Club of LA 1974-; com chmn Graphic Arts Bicent Black Achvmt Exhibit; instr Art Ctr Coll of Design 1976-77; instr CA State Univ 1971; inst CA Inst of the Arts 1966-68; NY Art Dir; San Fran & LA Art Dir Club Show; Type Dir & Aiga Show; Comncn Arts & Art Dir Mag Show; Graphis Annual & Typomondus 20. **Honors/Awds:** Intl Exp of "Best Graphics of the 20th Century". **Military Serv:** AUSR 1st Lt 1965-71. **Home Addr:** 5707 Aladdin St, Los Angeles, CA 90008.

BOSTON, GEORGE DAVID
Dentist, educator. **Personal:** Born Nov 1, 1923, Columbus, OH; son of Iola Adelaide Benson and Samuel David Boston; married Johanna Heidinger; children: George Jr (dec), Donald, Darryl (dec). **Educ:** OSU, BA 1949, DDS 1952. **Career:** Columbus State Hosp Dental Clinic, chief 1952-58; priv pract 1953-; OH State Univ, asst prof 1957-84. **Orgs:** Mem Columbus Dental Soc; OH Dental Assn; Amer Dental Assn; Natl Dental Assn; partner Rosbos Leasing Aircraft Lessor, pilot; mem Omega Psi Phi Frat; Sigma Pi Phi Frat; Cavaliers Inc; Big Bros; bd dirs Beneficial Accept Corp; mem NAACP; mem Natl Dent Honor Soc Omicron Kappa Upsilon; trustee bd mem Isabel Ridgway Nursing Center; mem Flying Dentists Assn; Tuskegee Airmen. **Military Serv:** AUS 1st Lt QMC 1943-47.

BOSTON, GRETHA
Actress. **Career:** Stage performer. **Honors/Awds:** Tony Award, Featured actress in a musical, Showboat, 1995. **Business Addr:** Stage Performer, c/o Ambrosio Mortimer & Associates, 165 W 46th St, New York, NY 10036, (212)719-1677.

BOSTON, HORACE OSCAR
Dentist. **Personal:** Born Jul 27, 1934, Clarksville, TX; married Iola. **Educ:** Southern Univ, BS 1955; TX So Univ; Univ OK; Univ NM; Washington Univ, DDS; Meharry Med Coll, School of Dentistry 1973. **Career:** Private practice, dentist; Wiley Coll, former asst prof biology; former high school science teacher; Midwestern Univ, former asst prof; several nursing homes, cons; WF & Evening Lions Club. **Orgs:** Mem YMCA; past bd dir Eastside Girls Clb; former commr Wichita Falls Housing Authority; former vice pres Wichita Dist Dental Soc; Gulf States Dental Assoc; former mem TX Dental Assn; mem Kappa Alpha Psi Frat; former member, City Council, City of Wichita Falls. **Honors/Awds:** NSF, Grant. **Special Achievements:** Publications include: "Prognathism: a Review of the Lit," 1972. **Military Serv:** USAR capt 1955-73. **Business Addr:** 1709 10th, Wichita Falls, TX 76301.

BOSTON, MCKINLEY, JR.
Educational administrator. **Personal:** Born Nov 5, 1945, Elizabeth City, NC; son of Lenora and McKinley; married Magellia McIntyre, Jan 11, 1969; children: Lance, Kimberly. **Educ:** University of Minnesota, 1964-68; Montclair State College, BA, 1973, MA, 1973; New York University, EdD, 1987. **Career:** New York Giants, professional football player, 1968-71; B C Lions, Canadian football player, 1971-73; Monclair State College, director of student services, 1974-85; Kean College, director of athletics, 1985-88; University of Rhode Island, director of athletics, 1988-91; University of Minnesota, director of athletics, 1991-96, vp for student devt and athletics, 1996-. **Orgs:** Minneapolis Boy Scouts, board of trustees, currently; Methodist Hospital Foundation, board of trustees, currently; Rhode Island Statewide Task Force Anti Drug Coalition, 1989; Atlantic 10 Conference, vice pres, 1991; Eastern Collegiate Athletic Association Council, 1990-91; New England Association of School & College Accreditation, 1989-. **Honors/Awds:** Montclair State College, Watson Honors Award, Outstanding Alumni Award, 1991; National Ethic Fellow, 1990; Harvard University, Visiting Scholar, 1991-92; NIRSA Journal, Editor. **Special Achievements:** University of Michigan, A Survey of Volunteerism in Low Income; Evolution of Intramural Program from Athletics to Physical Education to Student Activities, 1978; Institutional Racism: What is it?, 1980; Who's Boss Student Activities Program, 1981. **Business Addr:** VP, Student Devt & Athletics, University of Minnesota, 226 Bierman Bldg, 516 15th Ave SE, Minneapolis, MN 55455, (612)625-3361.

BOSTON, RALPH
Television broadcasting executive. **Personal:** Born May 9, 1939, Laurel, MS; son of Eulalia Lott Boston and Peter Boston; divorced; children: Kenneth Todd, Stephen Keith. **Educ:** TN State Univ, BS, Grad Work. **Career:** Univ of Tennessee Knoxville, asst dean of students 1968-75; TV commentator, 1969; ESPN-TV, commentator 1978-85; Integon Insurance Corp, sales; South Central Bell Adv Systems, acct exec; WKXT-TV Knoxville, gen partner, 1988-92, limited partner, 1992-; Ericsson-General Electric, major account manager, 1992-. **Orgs:** Capt Natl Track & Field Team 1960-68; mem Olympic Teams 1960-68; lecturer throughout US 1968-; field judge Special Olympics for East TN. **Honors/Awds:** Broke Jesse Owen's 25 Yr Long Jump Record 1960; Gold Medal Rome Olympics 1960; titlist NCAA 1960; athlete of Yr N Am 1961; Helms Hall of Fame 1962; Silver Medal Tokyo Olympics 1964; Olympic Bronze Medal Mexico City 1968; world long jump record; TN Sports Hall of Fame 1970; Natl Track & Field Hall of Fame 1974; US Track & Field Hall of Fame 1975; first black inducted MS Sports Hall of Fame 1977; had parks named in his honor, Laurel, MS 1978; first man to jump 26 ft indoors, 27 ft outdoors; solo 2nd Pl Team Championship NAIA Track Championship; Greatest Long Jumper of the Century 1979; All Time All Star Indoor Track & Field Hall of Fame 1982; Knoxville Sports Hall of Fame 1982; Mobile Oil Corp Track and Field Hall of Fame 1983; TN State Univ Athletic Hall of Fame1983;Olympic Hall of Fame85; NCAA Silver Anniversary Awd, 1985.

BOSWELL, ARNITA J.
Educator. **Personal:** Born Apr 19; married Dr Paul P; children: Bonnie B. **Educ:** KY State Clg, BS Home Ec; Atlanta U, MSW; Columbia Univ Sch of Soc Work, Adv Cert Social Work; CO State U, Adv Ed. **Career:** Social Service Admin Univ of Chicago, assoc prof; Lincoln Inst KY, asst dean of students; Eastman Kodak, asst personnel dir; ARC Munich Germany, asst & clb dir, asst program dir; Family Serv ARC Chicago, sr case worker; Gov Hospital NYC, psychiatric social worker, medical social worker; Family Serv Bureau Unities Charities Chicago, case worker. **Orgs:** Lectr Roosevelt U; lectr Geo Williams Clg; sch soc worker ford found & bd of ed Greater Cities Improvement Proj Chgo; dir Soc Serv Proj Head Start Chgo; acting dir Soc Serv Proj Head Start Wash DC; dir Human Rights Ofc of econ Opp Region IV Chgo; spec cnslr Minority Stdnts Univ of Chicago Under-grad; dir Pub Welfare Curr Dev Proj; assc field work prof Grad Sch & of Soc Serv Admn Univ of Chgo; given many speeches & papers at various Seminars,Insts, Workshops, Radio, TV; consul for Organizing & Dev Soc Serv in Head Start at HI, PR, VI, MS, Appalachian & Spnsh Spkng Comm; chmn Training forDay Care White Hse Conf for Children 1971; cochmn of Women's Div ChgoDr Martin Luther King in Solidarity Day Celebration Soldiers Field; consul First Unitarian Ch Chgo; mem numerousLocal, Spec Local, Me & Natl Com; consul HEW, OEO Poverty Comm Human Rights HUD & Metro Hsng & Plng Cnsl of Chgo. **Honors/Awds:** Recip hon Alpha Gamma Pi for Professional Escellence in Soc Work, Soc Work Educ & Comm Svc; outstndg contribution to Comm Chgo; contrbtn to Youth Awrd, Phi Beta Sigma Frat; outstndg city awrd for Comm Serv Com of 100; outstndg alumni awrd KY State Clg; outstndg serv awrd OEO Work with Proj Head Start & Civil Rights; outstndg region prfmnc awrd OEO Chgo; faculty awrd Black Stdnts Univ of Chicago Work with all Stdnts; 1 of 6 outstndg women in Chicago YWCA HumanRelations Work; black child dev int for Involvement in Action & Progs Retlating to Early Childhood Ed; intrl traveler's awrd Work in Germany, Guam, Jamica, PR, VI, HI Legislativeley in Afrcn Afrs; great gal of day WGRT; natl inst of hlth awrd & spec contrbtn to Sickle Cell Disease Adv Com.

BOSWELL, ARTHUR W.
Association executive. **Personal:** Born Jul 28, 1909, Jersey City; married Vivian S. **Educ:** Howard Univ, AB, 1932; Columbia Univ, AM Dept Pub Law, Grad, 1935. **Career:** Dept HUD, rlty speclst 1950-75; Vet HS Jersey City, ret tchr 1948-50; Freno CA Newport RI, uso dir 1941-48; Dumber Comm League Sprngfld & MA, exec asst 1939-40; Xavier Univ New Orleans, athletic dir 1932-34. **Orgs:** Active mem AOA Frat 1930-; flw Acad of Pol Sci NYC; flw Am Acad Pol & Soc Sci Phila; exec com Local Br NAACP; tchr Adult Bible Class Mt Zion ofGermantown Stdnt of Dr Ralph Bunche. **Honors/Awds:** Achvmnt awrd Alpha Sigma Howard U; masters thesis the Pol Theories & Policies of Negroes in Congress During Reconstruction.

BOSWELL, BENNIE, JR.
Bank executive. **Personal:** Born May 4, 1948, Danville, VA; son of Edith B Williams and Bennie Boswell Sr (deceased); married Helen Thomas. **Educ:** Williams Coll MA, BA (cum laude) 1970. **Career:** Western Reserve Acad Hudson, OH, instr 1970-73; Williams Coll, asst dir of admissions 1973-75; A Better Chance Inc, assoc dir student affairs 1975; Wachovia Corporation, 1976, sr vice pres/mgr community affairs, currently. **Orgs:** Mem Amer Soc of Personnel Admins; mem black Exec Exch Prog; former mem ASTD; former pres, Natl Assn of Bank Affirmative Action Directors; mem NAACP; former bd chmn Fellowship Home of Winston-Salem; former adv bd mem Duke Univ LEAD Prog; former mem exec comm Williams Coll Alumni Soc; consultant in Atlanta Adopt-A-Student program; Atlanta Chapter of the American Institute of Banking, board member; alumni admissions rep, Williams College; bd mem, Georgia American Institute of Banking; vice pres, The Bridge; chmn-elect, The Atlanta Children's Shelter; bd mem, Georgia Partnership for Excellence in Education; asst trea, The Atlanta Urban League; bd mem, Camp Best Friends; bd mem, Families First; bd mem, Research Atlanta; bd mem, Piedmont Park Conservancy; bd mem, Project READ; bd mem, Metro Atlanta Private Industry Council; mem, Annual Fund Comm of Northwest Georgia Council of Girl Scouts; mem, United Way Foundations Comm. **Honors/Awds:** Francis Session Meml Fellowship Williams Coll 1970; Lehman Scholar Williams Coll 1967; Natl Achieve Scholar Natl Merit Found 1966. **Business Addr:** Senior Vice Pres, Personnel, Wachovia Bank of Georgia, 191 Peachtree St NE, Atlanta, GA 30303.

BOTHUEL, ETHEL C. S.
University administrator. **Personal:** Born Mar 18, 1941, Charleston, SC; children: Charles E Smith II, Arnold ASmith, Marvin II. **Educ:** Atlantic Business College, Certificate 1958-60; Howard Univ, BA 1981. **Career:** Gallaudet Univ, asst to pres 1974-79; Self-employed, consultant 1979-, real estate assoc; George Washington Univ, dir eeo 1980-. **Orgs:** Mem Campbell AME Church 1961-; charter mem Washington Metro Area Affirmative Action Assoc 1980-; American Assn for Affirmative Action; Assn of Black Women in Higher Education; consultant Georgetown Univ 1980, Trinity College 1981, Natl Legal Aid & Defender Assoc 1982; real estate assoc Mt Vernon Realty Co Inc 1984-; mem NAACP; dir of choirs, Mathews Memorial Baptist Church 1981-. **Honors/Awds:** Recognition Awd Gallaudet Comm Relations Council 1980; Appreciation Awd Federal Bureau of Investigation 1984; Outstanding Dedicated Serv Awds Campbell AME Church, Matthews Memorial Baptist Church 1979-85. **Business Addr:** Dir Equal Opportunity, George Washington Univ, 2121 Eye St NW Rice Hall, Washington, DC 20052.

BOUIE, MERCELINE
Educator. **Personal:** Born Oct 18, 1929, St Louis, MO; daughter of Mr & Mrs Ray C Morris; married Harry J Bouie; children: Ray Anthony, Pamela Sue. **Educ:** Lincoln Univ, BA, Behavioral Sci, Physical Education, Health, 1953; Webster Univ, BA, Social Behavioral Science, 1972; MA, Social & Behavioral Science, 1973; Open Univ, PhD, Education, Social Behavorial Science, 1976. **Career:** St Louis Archdiocese Parochial School System, elementary & high school physical education/health teacher, 1958-64; Venice, IL School System, dept chmn, physical education & health teacher, 1964-68; Wheeler State School, dept head, young adults, 1968-74; St Louis Bd of Education, resource specialist, 1974-82, St Louis Public Schools, conductor of workshops, 1979-83; psychological examiner, 1982-83, learning disabled specialist, 1985-. **Orgs:** Member, AAUW; Exceptional child specialist counselor, Bouies Learning Center, 1978-85; 2nd Vice Pres, Learning Disability Assn, 1976-79; Advisor, Missouri Learning Disability Assn, 1976-80; Member, St Louis Assn of Retarded Children, 1979-; Mem, Intl Platform Assn, 1976-; Grand-lady, Ladies Aux Peter Claver, 1979-82; Pro-life Committee, Our Lady of Good Counsel Parish; Advisory Bd, Human Rights Office of the Archdiocese; Judge, Intl Platform Assn Convention, Washington, DC, 1987; Advisor, State Rep of the 56th District; Chairperson, High Expectation, Effective & Efficient Schools, Soldan HS; Pres, Mt Carmel School Bd, 1989-93; Vice Pres, chairperson, Webster Univ Alumni Bd of Directors 1989-92; Coordinator, Soldan Parent's Organization, 1989-93; charter member, World Foundation of Succful Women, 1991. **Honors/Awds:** Speaker's Award, Intl Platform Assn, 1979; Committee Leadership, Amer Assn Univ Women, 1977; Fourth Degree Award, Peter Claver, 1981; Special Education Award, Civic Liberty Assn, 1982; Oryx Press, Directory of Speakers, 1981, 1982; Community Leadership Award, 27th Ward Alderman; Amer Assn of Poetry Award, 1986; St Louis Symphony Ladies Assn Award, 1986; Article in North County Journal; published Poem of Life, 1989, Parent Involvement, 1976, Workbook, K-4, 1977; Distinguished Alumni Award, Webster Univ Bd, 1991; Dictionary of Education, Cambridge, England, 1990. **Special Achievements:** Coordinator Drug Free School (TREND) at Cleveland NJROTC High School, 1992; Coord, Intership Program, The Right to be Proud program. **Home Addr:** 1039 Melvin Ave, St Louis, MO 63137.

BOUIE, PRESTON L.
Assistant fire chief (retired). **Personal:** Born Jan 22, 1926, St Louis, MO; son of Emma Reed Bouie and Vennie Bouie; married Stella M Mosby Bouie, Nov 3, 1946; children: Sylvia N Saddler, Sheila N Sledge. **Educ:** Vashon High School, 1944. **Career:** St Louis Fire Dept, private 1952-63, fire capt 1963-76, battalion fire chief 1976-78, deputy fire chief 1978-83, asst fire chief. **Orgs:** Trustee Washington Metropolitan AME Zion Church 1980-. **Honors/Awds:** Inducted into Vashon High School Hall of Fame, Vashon Hall of Fame Comm 1989. **Military Serv:** US Navy AMMC 3rd class 2 years. **Home Addr:** PO Box 771195, St Louis, MO 63177-2195.

BOUIE, SIMON PINCKNEY
Clergyman. **Personal:** Born Oct 3, 1939, Columbia, SC; married Willie Omia Jamison; children: Erich, Harold. **Educ:** Allen Univ, BA 1962; Interdenomination Ctr, BD 1966; SC State

Hosp, clinical ct 1968. **Career:** Metro AME Church, sr minister; Warwick Sch for Boys, first Black Chaplain 1972-74; Mother Bethel AME Church, sr minister. **Orgs:** Chairperson Salute to the Schomburg Ctr for Rsch in Black Culture, The Salute to Harlem Hosp, the Bethel Day Cae Center, the Ministerial Interfaith Assn Health Comm, The Harlem Civic Welfare Assn Comm Bd, NY AME Ministerial Alliance Social Action Comm, North Central Hospital Day; mem trustee bd of the NYAnnual Conference of the AME Church; mem 100 Black Men Inc; mem Alpha Phi Alpha Frat; NY Chap of the NAACP; bd of dirs NY City Council of Churches; NY Branch of the YMCA; Comm for the Soc for the Family of the Man Awd; mem Bd of NY State Council of Churches; pres Prince Hall Masons; pres HarlemCouncil; pres Richard Allen Ctr on Life. **Honors/Awds:** NY Conf Outstanding Awd 1972; Lionel Hampton Awd 1975; Citizen of the Yr Awd Bi-Centennial 1976; Suffolk Day Care Awd 1978; Metro AME Church Outstanding Awd 1980; Distinguished Health & Hospital Corp Awd of NY 1980; first Disting Citizen Awd for North General Hospital 1982; DD Degree Interdenominational Theological Center 1982; DH Degree Monrovia College Monrovia W Africa 1984. **Home Addr:** 1135 Barringer St, Philadelphia, PA 19119. **Business Addr:** Senior Minister, Mother Bethel Ame Church, 419 Richard Allen Ave, Philadelphia, PA 19147.

BOUIE, TONY VANDERSON

Professional football player. **Personal:** Born Aug 7, 1972, New Orleans, LA. **Educ:** Univ of Arizona, BA in media arts, master's degree in language, reading, and culture. **Career:** Tampa Bay Buccaneers, defensive back, 1995-. **Business Addr:** Professional Football Player, Tampa Bay Buccaneers, One Buccaneer Place, Tampa, FL 33607, (813)870-2700.

BOUKNIGHT, REYNARD RONALD

Educator. **Personal:** Born Dec 14, 1946, Washington, DC; son of Johnnie Bell DeWalt Bouknight and Lue Dennis Bouknight; married LaClaire Green Bouknight, Mar 21, 1971; children: Tendai, Omari, Reynard II. **Educ:** Howard University, Washington, D.C., BS, 1968; Michigan State University, E. Lansing, MI, PhD, 1974, MD, 1975; Case Western Reserve University, Cleveland, Ohio, Internal Med. Residency, 1976-79. **Career:** Hough-Norwood Clinic, Cleveland, OH, chief of medicine, 1979-80; Michigan State University, E. Lansing, MI, asst. professor, 1980-85, asst. dean, 1983-; associate professor, 1985-. **Orgs:** Fellow, American College of Physicians, 1987-; vice-chairperson of Quality Intervention Committee, Michigan Peer Review Organization, 1987-93; member, Michigan State Medical Society, 1983-90; member, American Public Health Association, 1987-92. **Honors/Awds:** Alpha Omega Alpha Honor Medical Society, 1988; Phi Beta Kappa, 1968; Fellow, American College of Physicians, 1990; Young Investigator's Award, National Institute of Allergy and Infectious Diseases, 1978; Fellowship, National Science Foundation, 1968. **Business Addr:** Assistant Dean, Michigan State University, College of Human Medicine, 220 D Life Sciences, East Lansing, MI 48824-1317, (517)355-9633.

BOULDES, CHARLENE

Accountant. **Personal:** Born May 5, 1945, Brooklyn, NY; children: Anthony, Christi, Minde. **Educ:** Univ of Albuquerque, BSBA Accounting (Dean's List) 1981, BSBA Public Admin 1982; UNM, M Art 1983. **Career:** Grad Assistant UNM, researcher 1983; City/Co Task Force, financial advisor 1984-85; Univ of NM, acct supervisor; US Forest Service, accountant, 1988. **Orgs:** Natl Assn of Public Accountants, Univ of Albuquerque 1981; Amer Soc for Public Admin Univ NM 1982; graduate asst Univ NM Public Admin 1982-84; pres elect Civitan Intl 1984-85; mem NAACP 1951-, NAACP Youth Sponsor 1982-. **Honors/Awds:** Scholarship Univ of Albuquerque, 1981; Phi Alpha Alpha Natl Honor Soc Univ NM, 1984; Outstanding Graduate Student Univ NM Public Admin 1984.

BOULWARE, FAY D.

Educator (retired), writer. **Personal:** daugHter of Fay Hendley Davis (deceased) and William R Davis (deceased); children: William H. **Educ:** Hunter Coll CUNY, BA; Teachers Coll Columbia Univ, MA, Prof Diploma. **Career:** Teachers Coll Columbia Univ, assoc in admissions 1960-64; Institute for Dev Stds New York Med Coll, adminstr coord/inst 1964-66; Inst for Devel Studies New York Univ, dir of adminstrn and research scientist 1966-71; Educ Studies Prgm Wesleyan Univ, lecturer 1971-75; African Am Inst Wesleyan Univ, dir 1971-75; Emmaline Productions, hist & literary researcher 1982; Merrill Lynch Pierce Fenner & Smith, prof writer 1983-92; Chuckles Prod, dir story devel & research 1983-90. **Orgs:** Consultant NY City Bd of Educ 1971-92; consultant Acad Adv Bd Wesleyan Univ 1971-75; consultant to the Bd of Educ: Middletown, CT 1972-73, Lansing, MI 1971, Atlanta GA 1971, Charlotte, NC 1969-71, Model Cities, Pittsburgh, PA 1969, Univ Of Hawaii 1967, Virgin Isls Day Sch, St Croix, VI 1965. **Honors/Awds:** Wesleyan Univ, Black Alumni Honoree, 1993; Wesleyan Master Teacher, 1972, 1973, 1974. **Home Addr:** 25 W 132nd St Apt 9P, New York, NY 10037.

BOULWARE, PATRICIA A.

Educational administrator. **Personal:** Born Jan 29, 1949, Washington, DC; daughter of Carrie Robbins Boulware and Etheridge H Boulware; children: Kenyatta. **Educ:** Washington Tech Inst, AA 1974; Univ of the District of Columbia, BA 1980. **Career:** United Cerebral Palsy Assoc, legislative analyst 1978-79, rsch asst 1980-81; Amer Assn for the Advancement of Sci, project asst 1981-82, program asst 1982-83, program assoc 1984-88; Tuskegee University, Federal Relations Office, assistant director 1989-. **Orgs:** Chair AAAS Subcommittee on Day Care/Child Develop 1985-88; mem Natl Black Child Develop Inst, Federation of Organizations for Professional Women, Amer Mgmt Assn; development educ advocate Natl Council of Negro Women; mem NAACP; member, United House of Prayer for all People; volunteer, Washington Area Council on Alcoholism and Drug Abuse 1988-. **Honors/Awds:** Numerous publications including "Impact of Child Abuse on Neurological Disabilities," 1979, "Equity and Excellence Compatible Goals," (edited, et al) 1984, "Science, Technology and Women, A World Perspective," (edited, et al) 1985; Kappa Delta Pi; Model City Scholarship.

BOULWARE, PETER

Professional football player. **Educ:** Florida State. **Career:** Baltimore Ravens, 1997-. **Special Achievements:** NFL Draft, First round pick, #4, 1997. **Business Addr:** Professional Football Player, Baltimore Ravens, 200 St. Paul Pl, Ste 2400, Baltimore, MD 21202, (410)547-8100.

BOULWARE, WILLIAM H.

Television writer, producer. **Personal:** Born Jun 10, 1949, New York, NY; son of Fay Davis Boulware and Henry Boulware; married Brenda Cheek, Dec 22, 1984; children: Austin, Cody. **Educ:** Boston University, Boston, MA, MS, Film, 1979; University of North Carolina, Chapel Hill, NC, MS, city planning, 1976; Wesleyan University, Middletown, CT, BA, psychology/sociology, 1971. **Career:** Syracuse University, Syracuse, NY, associate director of admissions, 1971-74; Witt-Thomas-Harris Prod, Los Angeles, CA, writer, 1982-84; Chuckles Prod, Los Angeles, CA, president, 1984-. **Orgs:** Member, Black Writer's Committee, 1979-84.

BOURGEOIS, ADAM

Attorney. **Personal:** Born May 12, 1929, Chicago, IL; son of Mary Lou Bourgeois and Prescott Bourgeois; married Grace J Van Atta (divorced); children: Adam Jr, Yolande, Michael. **Educ:** Xavier Univ, New Orleans, LA, 1946-48; Loyola Univ, Chicago, IL, JD, 1951. **Career:** Adam Bourgeois, atty 1971-; OH State U, prof 1969-71; Human Res Gov's Ofc IL, exec dir 1968-69; W Coast Area Urban Coalition, exec dir 1968; Model Cities Mayor's Ofc St Louis, exec dir 1966-68; JOBS Proj Chicago & YMCA, admnstr 1962-65; Chgo, atty 1951-62. **Orgs:** Member, Chicago Bar Assn; member, Cook County Bar Assn.

BOURNE, BEAL VERNON, II

Funeral director. **Personal:** Born Mar 29, 1950, Pulaski, VA; son of Ruth Miller Bourne and Theadore Bourne; married Peggy Sharlotte Wright; children: Troy, Maurice, John. **Educ:** Univ of MD, Cert History Major 1972; KY School of Mortuary Sci, diploma 1972-73; State of TN Funeral Dir & Embalmer, License 1972-74. **Career:** Amway, distributor 1973-80; Allen-Bourne-Cash Insurance Agency, part owner; Jarnigan & Son Mortuary, asst mgr 1973-75, mgr, dir, embalmer 1975-, owner 1986-. **Orgs:** Bd of dir Knoxville Big Brothers 1973-84; mem Knoxville United Way; Natl & State FD&M Assoc 1974; life mem DAV 1974; Christian Funeral Dir 1975; mem CC Russell Masonic Lodge 262 1976; dir of ed James E Derricks Elks Lodge 1977; Joe Jones Council 1978; mem Epsilon Nu Delta Mortuary Frat 1980; Lennon-Seney United Meth Church Fin & Trustee Bd 1980; mem Aux Knox Cty Sheriff Dept 1980, Knoxville Epileptic Found 1982; past pres & vice pres Chilchowee PTA 1982-84; bd of dir YMCA & YWCA 1982-85; mem E Knox Optimist Club 1983; vice pres 1983-84, pres 1984-85 E TN Funeral Dir; licensed ins agent State of TN 1984; Keblah Temple 78 Shriner 1984; mem House of Rep 1984-85, Natl Funeral Dir 1984-85; mem East Knoxville Advisory Bd. **Honors/Awds:** UT Faculty Club 1980; Cert of Outstanding Serv Knoxville Big Brothers 1981; Notary State of TN 1982; Cert of Merit Knoxville YMVA 1983; Congressional VIP Card Natl Rep Comm 1983-84; Silver People to People Medic Blood Bank 1984; KY Col State of KY Col 1984; Colonel Aide De Camp, State of TN 1984; Saturday Night Gospel, Community Service Award, 1988; City of Knoxville, Service Award, 1988. **Military Serv:** AUS sgt E-5 3 yrs; Cert of Apprec, Cert of Achievement 1972. **Home Addr:** 3002 Woodbine Ave, Knoxville, TN 37914. **Business Addr:** Owner, Jarnigan & Son Mortuary, 2823 McCall Ave NE, Knoxville, TN 37914.

BOURNE, JUDITH LOUISE

Attorney. **Personal:** Born Jul 2, 1945, New York City, NY; daughter of Gwendolyn Samuel Bourne and St Clair T Bourne. **Educ:** Cornell Univ, BA 1966; NY Univ Law Sch, JD 1972, LLM Intl Law 1974. **Career:** NY Univ Clinic for Learning, comm asst 1966-67; New York City Human Resources Admin, special asst to the admin 1967-68; New York City Neighborhood Youth Corps, special consultant to dir for summer progs 1968; Bd for Fundamental Educ, prog assoc admin liaison to tech training 1968-69; Natl Council on Crime & Deliquency, legal intern 1970-71; NY State Spec Commn on Attica, ed staff 1972; NY Univ Sch of Continuing Educ, instr 1973; Emergency Land Fund, SC state coord 1974; private practice, SC atty 1974-77; Office of Fed Public Defender, asst federal public defender 1977-81; private practice, atty St Thomas US VI 1982-. **Orgs:** Junior fellow NY Univ Ctr for Intl Studies 1972-73; mem, natl co-chair 1976-79 Natl Conf of Black Lawyers 1973-; mem Intl Affairs Task Force SC State Dir 1973-76; chairperson Political Affairs Task Force 1979-80; mem VI Bar Assn; mem Almeric L Christian Lawyers Assn; mem Caribbean Develop Coalition; chair Virgin Islands Anti-Apartheid Comm 1985-; secretary, Virgin Islands Bar Assn 1983, treasurer 1984, secretary 1985, mem board of governers, 1987; member, International Commission of Inquiry into the Crimes of the Racist & Apartheid Regimes of Southern Africa, 1976-90; bd mem, United Way of St Thomas and St John, 1987-91; board of directors, Barbados Assn of St Thomas-St John, 1995-97; pres, Interfaith Coalition of St Thomas/St John, 1996-97; pres, United Nations Assn of the Virgin Islands. **Honors/Awds:** Outstanding Young Women of America, 1976. **Business Addr:** Attorney, PO Box 6458, St Thomas, Virgin Islands of the United States 00801, (809)776-8487.

BOUTTE, ALVIN J.

Company executive. **Personal:** Born Oct 10, 1929, Lake Charles, LA; married; children: four. **Educ:** Xavier Univ, BS 1951. **Career:** Independent Drug Stores, pres 1956-64; Independence Bank, co-founder/vchmn 1964-70, CEO, chm, 1970-; Drexel National Bank, chief executive; Indecorp Inc, pres/CEO, currently. **Orgs:** Pres 79th St med corp; bd mem Johnson Prods Co; bd mem BBB; bd gov's Urban Gateways; bd trustees Marion Bus Coll; bd mem Rehab Inst Chicago; Chicago State Univ Found; Jr Achievement; YMCA; Operation PUSH; past pres Small Business Admin; bd mem Chicago Bd Educ 1969-74. **Honors/Awds:** Man of the Year, Chicago Urban League, 1971, Chicago Econ Dev Corp, 1971; Industrial/Service 100, Banks, Black Enterprise, 1990. **Military Serv:** AUS Capt.

BOUTTE, ERNEST JOHN

Utility company executive. **Personal:** Born Aug 18, 1943, Salinas, CA; son of Rose Ann Broussard Boutte and Joseph Adbon Boutte; married Eleanor Rojas Boutte, Feb 6, 1963; children: Mark Joseph, Marlo Shay. **Educ:** Hartnell College, Salinas, CA, AS, electrical eng, 1973; Fresno State University, Fresno, CA, ind tech, 1978-83; University of San Francisco, San Francisco, CA, BS, bus management, 1983; University of Idaho, Moscow, ID, graduate, exec degree program, management, economics, 1989. **Career:** Pacific Gas & Electric Co, division gen mgr, 1965-. **Orgs:** Assoc member, American Blacks in Energy, 1988-; member, Pacific Coast Employee Assn, 1965-; assoc member, Pacific Coast Electrical Assn, 1978-; assoc member, American Management Assn, 1983-. **Honors/Awds:** Honorarium Lifetime Member, Hispanic Employee Assn, 1985; Honorarium Lifetime Member, Black Employee Assn, 1991. **Military Serv:** US Navy, Petty Officer, 2nd Class, 1962-65; Vietnam Service Award Medal. **Business Addr:** Division General Manager, Pacific Gas & Electric, Sacramento Valley Region, 158 Peabody Rd, Vacaville, CA 95687-4729.

BOUTTE, MARC ANTHONY

Professional football player. **Personal:** Born Jul 26, 1969, Lake Charles, LA; married Tananjalyn. **Educ:** Louisiana State, attended. **Career:** Los Angeles Rams, defensive tackle, 1992-93; Washington Redskins, 1994-. **Business Addr:** Professional Football Player, Washington Redskins, 13832 Redskin Dr, Herndon, VA 22071, (703)471-9100.

BOWDEN, JOSEPH TARROD

Professional football player. **Personal:** Born Feb 25, 1970, Dallas, TX. **Educ:** Univ of Oklahoma, attended. **Career:** Houston Oilers, linebacker, 1992-96; Tennessee Oilers, 1997-. **Business Addr:** Professional Football Player, Tennessee Oilers, c/o Baptist Sports Park, 7640 H 70-5, Nashville, TN 37221.

BOWDEN, MARION A.

Association executive. **Career:** Blacks in Government, president, currently. **Business Addr:** President, Blacks in Government, 1820 11th St NW, Washington, DC 20001-5015, (202)667-3280.

BOWDOIN, ROBERT E.

Business executive. **Personal:** Born May 4, 1929, Los Angeles, CA; married Joan; children: Kimberly J, Robert G, Wendy M. **Educ:** UCLA, BS 1951. **Career:** Pasadena Redevel Agy, dep adminstr tech serv redevel mgr; Bowdin Neal & Weathers, fdr; Fairway Escrow Co LA, co-owner mgr; Watts Svngs & Loan, real estate appraiser, loan officer, escrow officer; Family Savings & Loan Assoc, pres & ceo. **Orgs:** Bd mem United Way; Ginge Inc; Nat Archt Engr Firm; mem Brthrhd Crusade; past mem Altadna Lib Bd; bd mem CA Svngs & Loan Leag; mem Amer Savings& Loan League, US Savings & Loan League. **Business Addr:** President & CEO, Family Savings & Loan Assoc, 3683 Crenshaw Blvd, Los Angeles, CA 90016.

BOWE, RIDDICK

Professional boxer. **Personal:** Born 1967; married; children: 3. **Career:** Heavyweight boxer, currently. **Honors/Awds:** WBO

Heavyweight Champion of the World, 1992, 1995. **Special Achievements:** Guest appearance on ''The Fresh Prince of Bel Air,''; Giant Steps Award. **Business Addr:** Heavyweight Boxer, c/o Rock Newman Enterprises, 36 Channing St NW, Washington, DC 20001, (202)332-1868.

BOWEN, BLANNIE EVANS
Educator. **Personal:** Born Apr 26, 1953, Wilmington, NC; son of Beulah Mae Bryant Bowen and Herman Thomas Bowen; married Cathy Faulcon Bowen, Jun 18, 1977; children: Marcus, Douglas. **Educ:** North Carolina A&T State University, Greensboro, NC, BS, 1974, MS, 1976; Ohio State University, Columbus, OH, PhD, 1980. **Career:** Mississippi State University, Mississippi State, MS, asst, assoc professor, 1980-85; Ohio State University, Columbus, OH, assoc professor, 1985-88; Pennsylvania State University, University Park, PA, Rumberger chair of Agriculture, 1988-, associate dean, The Graduate School, 1996-. **Orgs:** University representative, National Council for Agricultural Education, 1990-92; editor, Agricultural Education Magazine, 1986-88; editorial board, Journal of Applied Communications, 1990-92; editorial board, Journal of Vocational and Technical Education, 1990-95; national secretary, Minorities in Agriculture and Related Sciences, 1990-91. **Honors/Awds:** Distinguished Alumni of the Year, National Association for Equal Opportunity in Higher Education, 1990; Outstanding Service Award, Omicron Tau Theta Professional Society, Penn State Chapter, 1990; Outstanding Research Paper, Eastern Agricultural Education Research Conference, 1989; Service Award, Natl Agricultural Communicators of Tomorrow Organization, 1987-88; Outstanding Young Member, American Association of Teacher Educators in Agriculture, 1985. H.O. Sargent Award, National FFA Organization, 1997. **Business Addr:** Professor, Agricultural and Extension Education Dept, Pennsylvania State University, 323 Ag Administration Bldg, University Park, PA 16802, (814)863-7850.

BOWEN, BRUCE
Professional basketball player. **Personal:** Born Jun 14, 1971. **Educ:** Fullerton College. **Career:** Miami Heat, forward, 1996-97; Boston Celtics, 1997-. **Business Addr:** Professional Basketball Player, Boston Celtics, 151 Merrimac St, Boston, MA 02114, (617)523-3030.

BOWEN, CLOTILDE DENT
US Army psychiatrist (retired). **Personal:** Born Mar 20, 1923, Chicago, IL; daughter of Clotilde Tynes Dent (deceased) and William M. Dent (deceased); divorced. **Educ:** OH State Univ, BA 1943; OH State Univ Med Sch, MD 1947; Harlem Hosp, intern 1947-48; NYC, residency in TB 1948-49; NY State, Fellowship in TB 1950; Albany Vets Admin Hosp, residency 1959-62; Amer Bd of Psychiatry & Neurology, diplomate certified in psychiatry 1966. **Career:** Priv general pract, Harlem, 1950-55; Army Captain, major, Valley Forge General Hospital, 1955-59; Active Reserve, 1959-67, VA Hosp, psych 1962-67; Veterans Admin, Roseburg, OR, chief of psychiatry, 1964-67, US Army, Tripler Hosp, chief of psychiatric services, 1967-68; OCHAMPUS, chief of patient services division and psych consultant 1968-70; US Army Vietnam, neuropsych consult 1970-71; Fitzsimons Army Med Ctr, chief dept of psych 1971-74; HSC Region V Area, consult 1971-74; Univ of CO Sch of Med, assoc clin prof of psych 1971-85; US Probation Office Denver, psych consult 1973-85; Tripler Army Med Ctr, chief dept of psych 1974-75; Univ of HI, clin assoc prof 1974-75; Dept of Clinics Fitzsimons Army Med Ctr, liaison psych 1976-77; US Army, Hawley Army Medical Clinic, Ft Benjamin Harrison, IN, commander, 1977-78; Fitzsimons Army Med Ctr, chief dept of primary care, 1979-83; psychiatric consulant, Joint Commission on Accrediation of Healthcare Orgs, 1985-92; Veterans Affairs Medical Ctr, Cheyenne, WY, chief of psychiatry, 1987-90; Veterans Affairs Medical Ctr, Denver, CO, staff psychiatrist, 1990-96; private practice, currently; Denver VAMC Clinic. **Orgs:** Fellow, Amer Psychiatric Assn; Central Neuropsychiatric Assn; Alpha Epsilon Iota; Reserve Officers Assn; Colorado Psychiatric Soc; Oregon Psychiatric Assn; Historical Archives Colorado Med Soc; exec mem, Natl Endowment for the Humanities; APA Cncl on Emerging Issues; fellow, Acad of Psychosomatic Medicine; Intl Soc for Electrotherapy; Natl Medical Assn; Fellow, Menninger Found; Assn of Military Surgeons of the US; Joint Review Comm on Paramedic Standards; Amer Med Assn; Natl Assn of VA Chiefs of Psychiatry, 1989-90. **Honors/Awds:** Scholarship for Achievement Delta Sigma Theta Sor 1945; Cert of Commendation Veterans Admin 1966; Natl Achievement Awd of Natl Assn of Negro Business & Professional Women's Clubs Inc 1969; Woman of the Yr Denver Business & Professional Women's Club 1972; OH State Medical Alumni Achievement Awd 1972; DeHaven-Hinkson Awd by the Natl Medical Assn 1972; Distinguished Awardee at 5th Annual Grad Sch Visitation Day OH State Univ 1975; Hall of Champions Champion Jr HS; Fellow Acad of Psychosomatic Medicine 1978; Fellow Amer Psychiatric Assn 1981; numerous publs; president's 300 Commencement Award OH State Univ, June 1987; Distinguished Black Alumni Award OSU Student Natl Medical Assn 1987; first Black woman to graduate from OSU Medical School and residency in psychiatry at Albany VA and Albany Med Center Hospitals; United Negro College Fund Eminent Scholar, 1990. **Military Serv:** US Army, captain-colonel, 30 yrs; first Black female MD Colonel US Army; Bronze Star, 1971; Legion of Merit, for Service in Vietnam, 1971; Meritorious Service Medal, 1974. **Home Addr:** 1020 Tari Dr, Colorado Springs, CO 80921.

BOWEN, ERVA J.
Sociologist (retired). **Personal:** Born Oct 12, 1919, Winfield, KS; daughter of Mr & Mrs D W Walker; married John R Bowen; children: Randy, John H, Gary. **Educ:** Southwestern College, Teacher's Certificate, 1941; Univ of California at Berkeley, Certificate, Social Service, 1961. **Career:** Santa Cruz City Welfare Dept, social worker, 1958-72 (retired); Senior Outreach Counselor, Family Service Assn, 1989-. **Orgs:** Member, Del Assembly, California School Bd Assn, 1979-81; pres, Santa Cruz City Schools Bd of Ed, 1976-77; mem, Santa Cruz Housing Advisory Committee, 1974-76; member, Citizen's Planning Advisory Committee, 1972; chmn, Santa Cruz Workable Program Committee, 1969-70; mem, Santa Cruz City Committee on Status of Women, 1973-75; California Social Workers Organization; California Alphi Phi Sigma Alpha; mem, bd of dir, YWCA, 1960-64, 1974-75; Santa Cruz Branch, NAACP, pres, 1962-66, 1968-70, secretary, 1960-68, vice pres, 1968-74; pres, Santa Cruz Church Women United, 1980-83; pres, District 28 Amer Legion Auxiliary Dept of California, 1984-85; member, Salvation Army Advisory Bd, 1986-; secretary and membership chairman, Senior's Council (Area Agency on Aging) Santa Cruz and San Benito Counties. S.C. County Affirmative Action Comm; Ch. of Internaffairs Sub Comm; Elected to Santo Cruz City Schools Board of Education, 1973, Reelected, 1979. **Honors/Awds:** NAACP Freedom Award, 1974; Women of Achievement, BPWC, 1974.

BOWEN, RAYMOND C.
Educational administrator. **Personal:** Born Sep 19, 1934, New Haven, CT; married Joan; children: Raymond C III, Rebecca M, Ruth J, Rachel R. **Educ:** Univ of Connecticut, BA, 1956, PhD, 1966; Univ of New Mexico, MS 1962. **Career:** Community College of Baltimore, vice pres of academic affairs and student affairs, 1975-82; Shelby State Community College, pres, 1982-89; LaGuardia Community College, president, 1989-. **Orgs:** Mem ACE, AACC 1981; bd dirs SACJC 1985; bd trustees Leadership Memphis 1985; bd dirs United Way 1985; vice chmn bd of dirs Bio-Medical Rsch Zone 1985. **Honors/Awds:** Outstanding Educator in Pub Higher Educ Memphis Bd of Educ 1982. **Military Serv:** US Army, Sgt 1956-59. **Business Addr:** President, LaGuardia Community College, 31-10 Thomson Ave, Long Island City, NY 11101.

BOWEN, RICHARD, JR.
Business executive, educator. **Personal:** Born Apr 20, 1942, Colp, IL; son of Helen Bowen and Richard Bowen; married Cleatia B Rafe; children: Gerald, Chantel. **Educ:** VTI Southern IL Univ, AA 1966; Southern IL Univ, BS 1969; Purdue Univ, MS 1971. **Career:** Restaurant Bar, owner 1964-71; Purdue Univ, teaching asst 1969-71; Lincoln Land Comm Coll, prof 1971-78, div chmn 1978-, business, public & human svcs chair, currently; Pillsbury Mills, mgmt consult 1973-75; real estate sales 1985. **Orgs:** Leader Boy Scout Adv Bd 1978-80; sec Chrysler Customer Satisfaction Bd 1980-87; training officer, Small Business Admin, 1982-85; suprv comm 1984-85; vp Sangamon School Credit Union; prog chmn Breakfast Optimist Club 1985; Frontiers International Springfield Club. **Military Serv:** AUS E-4, 2 yrs. **Business Addr:** Department Chairman, Lincoln Land Community College, Shepherd Rd, Springfield, IL 62708.

BOWEN, WILLIAM F.
State senator (retired). **Personal:** Born Jan 30, 1929, Cincinnati, OH; married Sharon LaMarr; children: Linda, Kevin, William II, Terrance, Nikol, Gina, Shawnda; married Sharon L Bowen. **Educ:** Attended, Xavier Univ. **Career:** Ohio House of Rep, state rep, 1966-70; State of OH, state senator, past chmn Senate Finance Comm, ranking minority mem of Senate Finance Comm, chairman, Commission on African-American Males, 1970-. **Orgs:** Past pres Cincinnati Br NAACP Hamilton Co Black Caucus; exec comm Dem Party Soc Serv Adv Council; mem Avondale Comm Council; Natl Conf of State Legislators; Outs Freshman Rep 107th Gen Assembly Mental Health Assn; Ohio Commission on African American Males, organizer & chmn, 1988-. **Honors/Awds:** John F Kennedy Pub Serv Awd OH League of Young Dem; Outstanding Leadership 107th Gen Assembly; 1st Annual Awd OH Nursing Homes Assn for Outstanding Comm Svc; Cincinnati Ins Bd Outstanding Contrib during 108th Gen Assembly; NAACP Awd Outstanding & Dedicated Svcs; Black Excellence Awd PUSH; Cert of Recognition & Appreciation VIVA; resolution by 111th Gen Assembly Outstanding Contrib; Pioneer Awd Res Home for Mentally Retarded Hamilton Co; Pub Serv Awd OH Pub Trans Assn; Man of Yr Awd OH Pub Transit Assn; Ann Leadership Awd Concerned Citizens of OH; Ldrshp Awd All African Student Faculty Union OH State Univ; Ohio Democratic Party, Myrtle Shoemaker Award, 1995. **Business Addr:** 7162 Reading Rd, Ste 725, Hillcrest Tower, Cincinnati, OH 45237.

BOWENS, GREGORY JOHN
Government official. **Personal:** Born Jan 7, 1965, Detroit, MI; son of Italee M Bowens; married Jeannine P Bowens, Jul 2, 1994; children: Langston. **Educ:** Morehouse College, attended, 1984-87; Wayne State Univ, 1992. **Career:** Automotive News, special correspondent, 1990-91; Detroit Free Press, reporter, 1991; Business Week Magazine, special correspondent, 1991-93; Congressional Quarterly Magazine, reporter, 1993-94; Flint Journal, reporter, 1994-95; Detroit News, reporter, 1995; Detroit Housing Commission, consultant-media relations, 1996. **Orgs:** National Association of Black Journalists, treas, 1993-97, sgt at arms, 1997-. **Honors/Awds:** Detroit Press Club, News Deputy Reporting Award, 1991; McGraw Hill, Publishing Award for Story of the Month, 1992; Congressional Quarterly, Best Story Award for Special Section, 1994. **Special Achievements:** First reporter to publish article on America's return to family cars. **Military Serv:** US Navy, E-4, 1987-89, Sea Service Ribbon; Development Ribbon. **Business Addr:** Assistant to the Mayor, Media Relations, Mayor's Office, 1126 City County Bldg, Detroit, MI 48204, (313)224-4589.

BOWENS, JOHNNY WESLEY
Educational administrator. **Personal:** Born Jun 2, 1946, Jacksonville, FL; married Monica Darlene Lewis; children: Torrence, Derick, Omari. **Educ:** Dillard Univ, BA 1968; Univ of AZ, MEd 1973; Union Institute, PhD 1977. **Career:** Pima Community Coll, dir student activities 1970-86, coord financial aid 1986-. **Orgs:** Allocation chair Tucson United Way 1985-; 1st vice pres Tucson Branch NAACP 1985-87.

BOWENS, TIM
Professional football player. **Personal:** Born Feb 7, 1973, Okolona, MS; children: Camrin Deion. **Educ:** Mississippi. **Career:** Miami Dolphins, defensive tackle, 1994-. **Honors/Awds:** Named NFL Defensive Rookie of the Year by the Associated Press and Pro Football Weekly, 1994. **Business Addr:** Professional Football Player, Miami Dolphins, 2269 NW 199th St, Miami, FL 33056, (305)620-5000.

BOWER, BEVERLY LYNNE
Educator, librarian, educational administrator. **Personal:** Born Sep 10, 1951, Washington, DC; daughter of Bettylou Calloway Johnson and James T Johnson; married Jack R Bower Jr. **Educ:** Univ of KS, BS Ed 1973; Emporia State Univ, MLS 1980; Florida State University, Tallahassee, FL, PhD, 1992. **Career:** Lansing Jr High School, reading teacher 1973-74; Chillicothe HS, French/English teacher 1974-75; Dept of Defense Dependent Schools, French/English teacher 1975-80; Pensacola Jr Coll, librarian 1980-84; Pensacola Jr Coll, dir lrc serv 1985-92; University of SC, College of Education, asst professor, 1993-96; Florida State Univ, College of Education, asst profes sor, 1997-. **Orgs:** Sec West FL Library Assn 1981-83; mem ALA-JMRT Minorities Recruitment Comm 1982-83, FL Library Assn, community college caucus chair/chair-elect 1986-88; FL Assn of Comm Coll, regional dir 1987; chapter president, Florida Assn of Community Colleges, 1988; bd of directors, YWCA Pensacola, 1989-91; AAWCC, founding chapter president; AAWCC, 1990-; ASHE, 1991-. **Honors/Awds:** Natl Achievement Scholar; Leaders Program, Amer Assn of Women in Community & Junior Colleges, 1989; Florida State University Fellowship, 1990-91; USC Mortar Board Outstanding Teacher Award, 1994. **Business Addr:** Assistant Professor, College of Education, Florida State University, Tallahassee, FL 32306.

BOWERS, MIRION PERRY
Physician. **Personal:** Born Aug 25, 1935, Bascom, FL; married Geraldine Janis Nixon; children: Jasmine Anusha, Mirion Perry Jr, Jarvis Andrew, Jeryl Anthony. **Educ:** FL A&M Univ Tallahassee, BA 1957; Meharry Med Coll Nashville, MD 1963. **Career:** AUS Gen Hosp Frankfurt Germany, chief otolaryngology svc; UCLA School of Med, asst prof dept of surgery (head-neck) 1972-73; Martin Luther King Jr Gen Hosp Div of Otolaryngology Charles R Drew Post Grad Med School, asst prof & chief 1972-73; UCLA School of Med, asst clinical prof dept of head-neck surgery, 1973-; Private practice, physician; USC School of Med, dept of otolaryngology, head & neck, clinical profile; pres & CEO, Good Samaritan Hospital, Los Angeles, CA, 1992-96. **Orgs:** Mem Taunus Med Soc Frankfurt Germany 1969-72; fellow Amer Acad of Ophthalmology & Otolaryngology 1970-, Amer Coll of Surgeons 1972-; mem Amer Med Assn 1972-, Natl Med Assn 1973-, Charles R Drew Med Soc 1973-, Amer Council of Otolaryngology; mem bd of dir Los Angeles Chap Amer Cancer Soc; mem Los Angeles Cty Med Assn; chmn otolaryngology sect California Medical Center 1982-85; chmn otolaryngology 1976-, secretary/treasurer medical staff 1976-, secretary operating rm comm 1986-, mem bd of trustees 1989-, mem exec comm 1989-, The Hosp of the Good Samaritan; bd of dirs, Florida A&M Foundation, 1989-; bd of dirs, City National Bank, Beverly Hills, CA, 1994-; bd of dirs, Braille Institute, CA, 1995-. **Honors/Awds:** Soc of the Upper Tenth, Meharry Medical Coll; numerous publications. **Military Serv:** AUS Med Corps lt col 1963-72.

BOWIE, LARRY
Professional football player. **Personal:** Born Mar 21, 1973. **Educ:** Univ of Georgia, attended. **Career:** Washington Redskins, running back, 1996-. **Business Addr:** Professional Football Player, Washington Redskins, 13832 Redskin Dr, Herndon, VA 22071, (703)471-9100.

BOWIE, OLIVER WENDELL
Certified public accountant. **Personal:** Born Jun 25, 1947, Detroit, MI; son of Ulvene Shaw; married Penelope Ann Jackson; children: Stephanie, Traci, Oliver II. **Educ:** Eastern MI Univ, BBA 1972; Elon College, MBA, 1994. **Career:** Michigan Dept of Treasury, revenue agent 1970-73; Coopers & Lybrand, sr accountant 1973-75; Natl Bank of Detroit, audit mgr 1975-77; Wayne County Community Coll, dir of accounting 1977-79; Garrett Sullivan Davenport Bowie & Grant, vice pres 1980-88; sole proprietor 1988-94, pres, 1994-. **Orgs:** Mem Amer Inst of CPA's 1975-, MI Assoc of CPA's 1975-, NC Assoc of CPA's 1985-, Greensboro W-S HP Airport Auth 1985-; treasurer, president, Triad Sickle Cell Foundation 1985-; pres Trial Natl Assoc of Black Accountants 1986-; chmn L Richardson Hosp 1986-; Greensboro Branch NAACP, treasurer, 1993-. **Honors/Awds:** Certificates of Appreciation Natl Assoc of Black Accts 1977, IRS 1985; City of Greensboro, 1992; Hayes YMCA, 1985, 1986, 1992; Urban League, professor, 1985-. **Business Addr:** CPA, Box 22052, Greensboro, NC 27420.

BOWIE, WALTER C.
Educator. **Personal:** Born Jun 29, 1925, Kansas City, KS; married Cornelia Morris; children: Carolyn Brown, Colleen Wells, Sybil K. **Educ:** KS State U, DVM 1947; Cornell U, MS 1955, PhD 1960. **Career:** Vet Med Ti, instr 1947; Head Dept of Physiology Sch of Vet Med Tuskegee Inst, 1960-71; Vet Admn Hosp Tuskegee, AL, rsrch 1965; Howard U, vis prof 1965-90; Univ Al Med Ctr, vis prof 1967-75; Sch Vet Med Tuskegee Inst, assc dean 1971-72; Sch of Vet Med Tuskegee Inst, dean 1972-90; Dept of Physiology Cornell U, adj prof 1972-73; Univ Al Med Ctr, vis Head Dept of Physio Sch of Vet Med Tuskegee Inst, assoc prof; Physio & Nicotine, consultant, currently. **Orgs:** Mem Deans Adv Cncl Va Hosp 1972-80; consult Inst of Med NAS 1972-74; mem Commn on Hum Resources Nat Rsrch Cncl 1975-79; Mem Comm on Vet Med Sci Nat Rsrch Cncl 1975-76; mem bd dir AL Heart Assc 1972-76; pres Am Soc Vet Physio & Pharmacologists 1966-67; sec World Soc Vet Physio & Pharm; chmn Cncl of Deans AAVMC 1977; consult Hlth Profn Ed Sec DHEW; consult Ford Motor Co S Africa 1974; adv screening com Cncl for Intl Exchange of Schlr Wash 1976-79; deleg Am Heart Assc 1970-72; deleg World Soc of Vet Physio & Pharms Paris 1968; rsrch Sec Ofc Am Vet Med Assc mem com Am Physio Soc 1970-73; consult NIH Arlington 1968-70; Sigman Xi; Phi Kappa Phi; Am Vet Assc; AL Vet Med Assc; mem Primate Rsrch Ctr Adv Com NIH 1972-76. **Honors/Awds:** Prncpl invstgtr of following grnts, Pentose Metabolism in the Ruminant 1956-57, Further Stud on Absorp & Util of Pentose Sugar in Ruminants PHS 1956-57, The Cerebrospinal Fluid of Dogs, Its Physio Diag & Prognostic Eval Mark & L Morris Found 1961-62, Mechanisms of Infection & Immunity In Listeriosis NIH 1961-64, Movement of the Mitral Valve NIH 1964-72; Doctor of Science Degree, Kansas State University, 1984. **Military Serv:** AUS 1st lt. **Business Addr:** Prof, School of Veternary Medicine, Tuskegee Institute, AL 36088.

BOWIE, WILLETTE
Human resources executive. **Personal:** Born Jul 24, 1949, Memphis, TN; daughter of John & Callie Jenkins. **Educ:** Alverno College, BA, 1984; Cardinal Stritch College, MS, 1996. **Career:** Northwestern Mutual Life, employee relations specialist, 1983-91, employee relations officer, 1991-95, dir employee relations, 1995-. **Orgs:** NAACP Membership Comm, Milwaukee Branch, 1997-; Financial Svcs Group, 1983-; Human Resources Management Assn, 1983-; Top Ladies of Distinction, 1986-; Alpha Kappa Alpha Sorority, 1986-; Zonta Club of Milwaukee, 1991-; Eta Phi Beta Sorority, 1986-. **Honors/Awds:** The Milwaukee Times Weekly Newspaper, Black Excellence Award, 1998; Girl Scouts of Milwaukee Area, Inc, Marion Chester Read Leadership Award, 1998. **Business Addr:** Director, Employee Relations, Northwestern Mutual Life Ins Co, 720 E Wisconsin Ave, Milwaukee, WI 53202, (414)299-7120.

BOWLES, BARBARA LANDERS
Business executive. **Personal:** Born Sep 17, 1947, Nashville, TN; married Earl S Bowles; children: Terrence Earl. **Educ:** Fisk Univ, BA 1968; Univ of Chicago, MBA 1971; CFA Designation, 1977. **Career:** First Natl Bank of Chicago, trust officer 1974-77, avp 1977-80, vice pres 1980-81; Beatrice Companies, avp 1981-84; Dart & Kraft Inc, vice pres 1984-; The Kenwood Group, pres, currently. **Orgs:** Pres Chicago Fisk Alumni Assn 1983-85; Alpha Kappa Alpha Sorority; bd mem Childrens Memorial Hosp of Chicago, Black & Decker Corp; bd of dirs Hyde Park Bank. **Honors/Awds:** Top 100 Black Business & Prof Women Black Book Delta Sigma Jul-Aug 1985. **Business Addr:** President, The Kenwood Group, 10 S La Salle St, Ste 3610, Chicago, IL 60603-1002.

BOWLES, HOWARD ROOSEVELT
City manager. **Personal:** Born Oct 14, 1932, Roselle, NJ. **Career:** Parson Inst; Seton Hall Univ City Home Delivery WA Post, mgr; Baltimore News-Am, city mgr; Newark Evening News, dist mgr; Various Clg, auto salesman, sales mgr asst panel rep. **Orgs:** Mem Interstate Circulation Mgrs Assc. **Honors/Awds:** Art awrd 32nd Degree Mason Prince Hall F&AM; mgmt & prodn awards. **Military Serv:** AUS sgt 1952-55. **Business Addr:** 1150 15th St NW, Washington, DC 20017.

BOWLES, JAMES HAROLD, SR.
Physician. **Personal:** Born Jun 12, 1921, Goochland, VA; married Aretha Melton; children: Ruth Quarles, Jacqueline B Dandridge, James Jr. **Educ:** Virginia Union University, BS 1948; Meharry Medical School, MD 1952. **Career:** Private practice, family practitioner, currently. **Orgs:** President, Goochland Recreational Center 1961-81, vice pres, 1981-; vice chairman, Goodland Cty Bd of Supervisors; Goochland NAACP; exec bd, Virginia Assn of Counties; treasurer, Goochland Voters League; Goochland Democratic Comm; vice pres, bd of dir, Citizen Development Corp; Hazardous Waste Siting Comm of Virginia; American Legion; Goochland Cty Social Services Board; bd of dir, Goochland Branch Red Cross; Caledonia Lodge 240 F&AM PHA; Alpha Phi Alpha; pres, trustee bd, Emmaus Baptist Church; teacher, Intermediate Sunday School Class. **Honors/Awds:** Outstanding Leadership, American Red Cross 1969; Valuable Citizen, GoochlandNAACP 1978; Outstanding Service, Goochland Recreational Center 1979; Appreciation, Beulah Baptist Sunday School Convention 1979; Recognition Negro Emancipation Organization, Louisa & Adjacent Counties 1979; Appreciation, American Heart Assn Virginia Affiliate 1982. **Military Serv:** US Army, private 1944-46. **Business Addr:** Family Practitioner, 2884 Sandy Hook Rd, Sandy Hook, VA 23153.

BOWLES, JOYCE GERMAINE
Educator, educational administrator. **Personal:** Born May 16, 1942, Washington, DC; daughter of Mary Gaines and Harvey Johnson; married Robert L Bowles Jr, Jan 1982; children: Lee Robert. **Educ:** University of Evansville, BSN, 1964; University of Maryland, Baltimore, MSN, 1972, College Park, PhD, 1978. **Career:** Army Nurse Corps, progressive leadership positions in nursing, 1962-84; Bowie State University, Department of Nursing, chairperson, 1985-94, professor of nursing, currently. **Orgs:** National League for Nursing, 1974-; Maryland League for Nursing, District 6, first vp, 1989-91; Chi Eta Phi Nursing Sorority, Alpha Chapter, 1972-; Top Ladies of Distinction, Potomac Chapter, president, 1988-92; Sigma Theta Tau Nursing Society, Pi Chapter, 1974-; Association of Black Nursing Faculty, pres, 1996-98, nominating committee chair, souvenir program book chair, 1993; Journal ABNF, review board, 1992-. **Honors/Awds:** Kellog Foundation, FACE Fellow, 1992-; American Nurses Association, Nursing Administration, advanced certification, 1986-. **Military Serv:** US Army Nurse Corp, 1962-84; Army Commendation Medal, 1968, Meritorious Service Medal w/ 2 Oak Leaf Clusters, Legion of Merit, 1984, Bronze Star Medal, 1968, Daughters of American Revolution, ANC of the Year, 1982. **Home Addr:** 9 Potomac School Ct, Potomac, MD 20854. **Business Phone:** (301)464-7824.

BOWMAN, EARL W., JR.
Educator (retired). **Personal:** Born Feb 7, 1927, Minneapolis, MN; son of Edith Bowman and Earl Bowman; married Jacqueline; children: Wayne, Scott. **Educ:** Macalester Coll, BA 1950, MEd 1971. **Career:** Anoka MN, physical therapist, 1950-52; Phyllis Wheatley Settlement House, boys work dir, 1952-55; Minneapolis Public Schools, history teacher, coach of football/basketball/track, jr high principal, 1955-69; Macalester Coll, asst to pres, dir of devel, 1969-78; dean of students, 1973-77, vice president for student affairs, 1977-78; Minneapolis Community Coll, vice pres external affairs, pres, 1980-90. **Orgs:** Mem Mayor's Commn on Human Devel 1967-68; Assn of Afro-Amer Educators 1968-; Natl Alliance for Black Grad Level Educ 1970; bd mem Minneapolis Urban Coalition 1971; bd mem Gr Minneapolis Metro Housing Corp 1972; mem Natl Alliance of Black Sch Educators; pres mgmt com Exchange Inc; mem adv bd Lake St Office Northwestern Natl Bank; brd of trustees, St Peters AME Church brd mpls United Way, Brd TCOIC; brd Phyllis Wheatley Settlement House. **Honors/Awds:** Bush Found Summer Fellow Inst for Educ Mgr Harvard Univ 1976; Recip Student Athlete Award 1950; Disting Alumni Citation 1968; Serv Award MN Track Coaches Assn 1975; Pres Award for Physical Fitness Prog; Outstanding Citizen Award Minneapolis Urban League 1986-90; Governor's Education Award State of MN 1990; Honorary Doctorate of Humane Letters Macalester College 1990. **Military Serv:** United States Military Academy, Cavalry Detachment 1946-47. **Home Addr:** 4909 5 Ave S, Minneapolis, MN 55409.

BOWMAN, JACQUELYNNE JEANETTE
Attorney. **Personal:** Born Dec 4, 1955, Chicago, IL; married David Rentsch; children: Atticus David Bowman Rentsch. **Educ:** Univ of Chicago, BA 1976; Antioch Univ Sch of Law, JD 1979. **Career:** West TN Legal Svcs, staff attorney 1979-84; Greater Boston Legal Svcs, sr attorney 1984-87, managing attorney 1987-92;MLRI, attorney, 1992-. **Orgs:** Mem Amer Bar Assoc 1979-, Natl Conf of Black Lawyers 1980-, Battered Women's Working Group 1984-93; volunteer Project Impact 1984-93; mem MA Bar Assoc 1986-, Boston Bar Assoc 1986-; subcomm chairperson Gov Comm on Foster Care 1986-89; Supreme Judicial Court Gender Bias Comm, task force on dometic violence, 1992-94, juvenile justice comm, 1992-94; Governor's Comm on Domestic Violence, 1993-; Bd of MA, advocacy ctr, 1994-. **Honors/Awds:** Silver Key Awd ABA-LSD 1979; Certificate of Appreciation EACH 1982-84; George Edmund Haynes Fellow Natl Urban League 1982-83; Public Service Award, Project Impact 1985, 1986. **Business Addr:** Attorney, Family & Children's Legal Issues, MA Law Reform Inst, Inc, 99 Chauncy St, Boston, MA 02111.

BOWMAN, JAMES E., JR.
Pathologist, geneticist, educator. **Personal:** Born Feb 5, 1923, Washington, DC; son of Dorothy Bowman and James Bowman; married Barbara Frances Taylor; children: Valerie June. **Educ:** Howard Univ, BS 1943; Howard Med School, MD 1943-46; Freedmens Hosp, internship 1946-47; St Lukes Hosp, resd pathology 1947-50. **Career:** Provient Hosp, Chicago, chmn path, 1950-53; Nemezee Hosp, Shiraz, Iran, chmn path, 1955-61; Shiraz Med School, Shiraz, Iran, prof of path, chr, 1959-61; Univ of Chicago, asst prof, med dir blood bank, 1962-67, assoc prof, 1967-72, prof med & pathology, dir of labs 1971-81, comm on genetics, 1972-; Comprehensive Sickle Cell Center Univ of Chicago, dir, 1973-84; The Univ of Chicago, Pritzker School of Medicine, department of pathology, prof emeritus of pathology medicine, committee on genetics, currently; Center for Clinical Med Ethics, Committee on African and African American Studies, senior scholar. **Orgs:** Ethical, legal and social issues, working group; Natl Human Genome Program, NIH; monitoring board, NHLBI, NIH; Bone Marrow Transplentation Sickle Cell Disease & Thalassemia; Amer Soc Human Genetics, AAAS; consultant, Fed Gov Nigeria, 1985; consultant, Med Corps Laboratories, Defense Forces, United Arab Emirates 1987; Ministry of Health, Islamic Repubic of Iran, consultant, 1992. **Honors/Awds:** Sr fellow, Kaiser Family Found Center for Advance Study in the Behavioral Science, Stanford, CA, 1981-82; fellow, Hastings Ctr of NY, 1979-; fellow, Coll of Amer Pathologists, Amer Soc Clin Path, Royal Soc Tropical Med & Hygiene; Author 90 scientific publ in field of human genetics; Spec Rsch Fellow Galton Lab Univ Coll London 1961-62; edited book ''Dist & Evol of Hemoglobin and Globin Loci;'' mem Alpha Omega Alpha, Sigma Xi, Amer Bd of Path Anat and Clin Path; author, with Robert F Murray, Genetic Variation and Disorders in Peoples of African Origin, Johns Hopkins University Press, 1990. **Military Serv:** AUS pfc 1943-46; AUS capt 1953-55. **Business Addr:** Professor Emeritus of Pathology, The University of Chicago, 5841 Maryland Ave, Chicago, IL 60637.

BOWMAN, JANET WILSON
Educational administrator. **Personal:** Born in Charleston, WV; daughter of Roberta Wilson and Earl Wilson; married Richard Bowman; children: Karen McAfee, M Earl McAfee, Chris, Cheryl, Patricia. **Educ:** Tuskegee Inst, BS, MS; Univ of CA at Berkeley, PhD, 1973; Postgraduate, Univ of Oregon, California State Univ, San Diego. **Career:** Merritt Coll, professor; Univ of California, seismologist, 1960-73; Carnegie Found, Consultant, 1972-73; Diablo Valley Coll, Admin, 1973-85; Compton Coll, administrator, 1986-94; Ashville YWCA, Exec Dir, currently. **Orgs:** Org bd mem, Meridian Natl Bank, 1979; mem, Tuskegee Alumni Assn; UNCF InterAlumni Council; United Way Program Evaluator; mem, Black Women's Leadership Group; MOSTE, Women on Target; bd of dirs, Memorial Mission Foundation; Kiwanis International. **Honors/Awds:** George Washington Carver Fellowship; NSF Scholarship; Graduate Student Assistantship, Univ of California, Berkeley; Certificate of Appreciation, Business Club, 1988; Certificate of Commendation, Compton Coll Bd of Trustees, 1988; America's Black Colleges, author. **Home Addr:** 24 Bevlyn Dr, Asheville, NC 28803. **Business Addr:** Executive Director, YWCA, Asheville, NC 28803.

BOWMAN, JOSEPH E., JR.
Technology specialist, educational administrator. **Personal:** Born May 22, 1950, Brooklyn, NY; son of Violetta Bowman and Joseph Bowman Sr.; married Etwin Mapp Bowman, Mar 27, 1987; children: Amber, Alicia. **Educ:** State Univ of NY, BA 1972; Nat Tchr Corp, MA 1975, MLS 1974; Teachers College, Columbia University, New York, NY, MEd, 1984, MA, 1985, EdD, 1991. **Career:** Teachers College, Columbia University, New York, NY, project director, 1982-, coordinator, 1985-, instructor, 1985-; director, Center for Urban Youth and Technology, currently; Olympic Village XIII Winter Games Lake Placid, fclty mgr/prod/dir/supr of entrmnt, 1979-80; Schenectady Access Cable Cncl Channel 16 NY, location mgr, 1979; Hamilton Hill Arts & Craft Ctr Schenectady NY, instr, 1978-79; Siciliano Studio Schenectady, NY, photographer's asst, 1978-79; WMHT TV, asst prod/dir, 1977-78; WMHT Channel 17 Pub Afrs Div, asst prod, 1975-77; Hamilton Hill Arts & Crafts Ctr, dir audio visual serv, 1974-75; Educ Oppor Pgm Stdnt Assn State Univ of NY, telecommunications instr, 1975; held various positions in the radio broadcast and television industries; teacher. **Orgs:** Consultant, Girl Scouts of America, 1990-; trainer, Boys Scouts of America, 1986-90. **Honors/Awds:** Outstndg Achvment Awrd Schenectady Chptr NAACP 1975; Pride in Heritage Awrd for Acad Achvmnt & Multi-Media Spclst; Theta Chap of Nat Sor Phi Delta Kappa 1978; awrd Intrnl Platform Soc 1980; Outstanding Educational Achievement, Kappa Delta Pi, 1988. **Home Addr:** PO Box 203, 1234 St John's Pl, Brooklyn, NY 11213. **Business Addr:** Director CUYT/IUMC, Teachers College, Columbia University, PO Box 228, 525 W 120 St, 345 Macy, New York, NY 10027.

BOWMAN, PHILLIP JESS
Psychologist, educator. **Personal:** Born Feb 18, 1948, Kensett, AR; married Jacqueline E Creed; children: Phillip, Frederick Dubois. **Educ:** No AZ U, BS Psychology/Industrial Tech 1970; Univ of MI, ed S/MA (Prsnl Serv/Cnslng) 1971-74, phD/MA (Soc Psychology) 1975-77. **Career:** Inst for Soc Rsrch, asst

prof of psychology/research scientist; Inst for Soc Research Univ of Michigan, research investigator, 1977-78; Delta Coll, instructor, 1973-77, counselor 1971-73; Northern AZ Unic, fin aid admin, 1969-70. **Orgs:** Dir Post-doctoral Training Pgm in Survey Rsrch 1978-80; faculty mem Ctr for Afro-am & Afrcn Studies 1978; consult pub Hlth Serv 1980; mem Assc of Black Psychologists; mem Am Psychological Assc; steering com mem Annual Conf on Ethnicity & Mental Hlth; study dir Natl Survey of Black Am Rsrch Pgm Inst for Soc Rsrch Univ of MI. **Honors/Awds:** Post doctoral cert; Joint Inst for Labor & Indsl Relations Univ of MI/Wayne State Univ 1977; What Is Black Psychology? Jour, of Contemporary Psychology 1980; Toward a Dual Labor Market Approach to Black on Black Homicide Pub Hlth Rprts 1980.

BOWMAN, WILLIAM ALTON
Military official (retired). **Personal:** Born Dec 15, 1933, Fayetteville, NC; son of Rebecca L Johnson (deceased) & William H Bowman; married Sylvia I. (deceased); children: Carol, William A Jr (deceased), Arthur E, Susan Okediadi (deceased), Brenda Jones. **Career:** Misle Imports (Auto), svc writer, 1976-77; State Department Roads, mechanic, 1977; Toms Car Care, mechanic, 1977-78; US Postal Svc, letter carrier, 1978-79, fleet manager, 1979-90; Budget Rent A Car, shuttle driver, part time, 1994-. **Orgs:** American Legion, post commander, 1995-96, district 15 commander, 1996-98; 40 & 8 Voiture 103, box car chairman, star chr, 1994-; Disabled Veterans, store board member, 1993-; Air Force Sergeants, 1976; Air Force Association, 1963; Vietnam Veterans, active mem, 1995; National Association Fed Ret, 1990; VA Hospital, volunteer-patient visitor, 1994. **Honors/Awds:** American Legion, Admiral Nebraska Navy, 1996. **Military Serv:** US Air Force, t/sgt, 1954-76; VSM 1968, RVCM, 1968, AFCM W/10LC, 1968, 1971, 1972. **Home Addr:** 2134 S 48th St, Lincoln, NE 68506-5507, (402)489-6447.

BOWMAN, WILLIAM MCKINLEY, SR.
Clergyman. **Personal:** Born Feb 7, 1914, St George, SC; son of Erline Windham (deceased) and Joseph Bowman (deceased); married Annie Mae Jones (deceased); children: William Jr, Audrey Marie, Joseph Augustus, Beverley Elaine. **Educ:** Morris Coll, AB & DD 1938. **Career:** Granger Baptist Ch Elloree, pastor 1938-46; Mt Carmel Bapt Church Cameron, pastor 1942-46; St Paul Baptist Ch Orangeburg, pastor 1946-49; WOIC Radio, religious dir 1952-72; Friendship Baptist Church, pastor 1960-86; Second Nazareth Baptist Church Columbia SC, pastor 1949-. **Orgs:** Pres Gethsemane Sunday Sch Cong Columbia; secty/treas Interracial Bapt Ministers Union Columbia; dir Pub Relations Black Baptist of SC; past pres Columbia Br of NAACP; past chmn Richland Lexington OEO; past pres Columbia Ministers Assn; past pres Interdenom Ministerial Alliance of Columbia; mem vice chairman Richland Co Dist Sch Bd 1979-; past vice chmn of Richland Co Democratic Party; sec Morris Coll Bd of trustees; co-founder and dir of WOIC ra dio system; past pres Columbia Ministers Assc; chmn Richland Cty Bd of Ed, Dist rict 1; treas of Ward 19 Democratic prty. **Home Addr:** 2012 Hydrick St, Columbia, SC 29203.

BOWMAN-WEBB, LOETTA
Systems analyst. **Personal:** Born Dec 16, 1956, Fort Worth, TX; married Carl Webb. **Educ:** TX Wesleyan Coll, BBA 1979; Univ of TX at Arlington; Tarrant Co Jr Coll. **Career:** City of Ft Worth, admin asst I 1980-81, admin intern 1981-82, admin asst II 1982-85, admin asst III 1985-. **Orgs:** Mem Urban Mgmt Assts of N TX 1981-; prog comm Conf of Minority Public Admins 1981-; mem Natl Forum for Black Public Admins 1984-. **Business Addr:** Admininistrative Asst III, City of Ft Worth, 1800 University, Fort Worth, TX 76107.

BOWNES, FABIEN
Professional football player. **Personal:** Born Feb 29, 1972, Aurora, IL. **Educ:** Western Illinois, attended. **Career:** Chicago Bears, wide receiver, 1995-. **Business Addr:** Professional Football Player, Chicago Bears, 1000 Football Dr, Halas Hall at Conway Park, Lake Forest, IL 60045-4829, (847)295-6600.

BOWRON, ELJAY B.
Government official. **Personal:** Born in Detroit, MI; married Sandy; children: one son. **Educ:** Michigan State Univ, bachelor's degree, criminal justice. **Career:** Detroit Police Dept, officer, 1973; US Secret Service, various positions, beginning 1974, director, 1993-. **Orgs:** Intl Assn of Chiefs of Police. **Honors/Awds:** Numerous commendations and awards for outstanding service. **Business Addr:** Director, US Secret Service, 1800 G St, Ste 800 NW, Washington, DC 20500, (202)435-5700.

BOWSER, BENJAMIN PAUL
Educator, research director. **Personal:** Born Aug 20, 1946, New York, NY; son of Nathalia Earle Bowser and Benjamin Bowser; married K Deborah Whittle; children: Paul. **Educ:** Franklin & Marshall Coll, BA 1969; Cornell Univ, PhD 1976. **Career:** SUNY Binghampton, asst prof, sociology 1973-75; Cornell Univ, asst dean grad school 1975-82; Western Interstate Commiss for Higher Ed, dir minority ed 1982-83; Univ of Santa Clara, dir black student resources; Stanford Univ, asst to dir, 1983-85; California State University at Hayward, asst to prof of sociology, 1985-; Bayview Hunter's Point Foundation, San Francisco, CA, research director, 1990-91. **Orgs:** Assoc ed Sage Race Relations Abstracts 1981-; rsch assoc Soc for the Study of Contemporary Soc Problem 1980-82; consult Western Interstate Commiss for Higher Ed 1981-83; mem Committee on Applied Sociology Amer Sociological Assn 1985-87; Assn of Black Sociologists; bd dir Glide Memorial Methodist Church, American Social Health Association, Durham, NC. **Honors/Awds:** Co-Editor ''Impacts of Racism on White Amers'' 1981, 1995; ''Census Data for Small Areas of NY City 1910-60'' 1981; editor, Black Male Adolescents, 1991; Confronting Diversity Issues on Campus, 1993; Toward the Multicultural Univ, 1995; Racism and Anti-Racism in World Perspective, 1995; Impacts of Racism on White Americans, 1996; numerous research grants; California Faculty Field Institute, Fellow, 1992-93; Outstanding Professor, California State Univ at Hayward, 1996. **Business Addr:** Prof, Sociology/Social Services, California State University at Hayward, Hayward, CA 94542.

BOWSER, HAMILTON VICTOR, SR.
Construction company executive. **Personal:** Born Sep 20, 1928, East Orange, NJ; son of Louise Pateman Bowser and Edward T Bowser; married Merle Charlotte Moses; children: Hamilton V Jr, Rebecca Louise, Jennifer Lynn. **Educ:** NJ Inst of Tech, BS Civil Eng 1952, MS Civil Eng 1956; Mass Inst of Tech Grad Sch Civil Eng 1954; Licensed professional engr in NJ, NY, PA. **Career:** Porter Urguhart Eng, structural eng 1954-55; Louis Berger Assocs, sr bridge eng 1955-57; PARCO Inc, sr structural eng 1957-59; Engineers Inc, v pres 1959-69; Evanbow Construction Co, pres 1969-. **Orgs:** Chairman bd Assoc Minority Contractors of Amer 1980-82; bd of dir Natl Assoc of Minority Contractors beginning 1984, president, 1988-89; pres Natl Soc of Prof Eng Essex Chapter 1966-68; bd of dir, treasurer, Reg Plan Assoc of NY, NJ, CT 1981-; trustee & treas Essex County Coll 1971-74; bd chmn Orange YMCA Comm of Mgmt; life mem, Amer Soc of Civil Engrs; mem Prof Engrs in Construction Div of NSPE; mem Amer Concrete Inst; NJ Governors Council for Minority Business Develop, NJ United Minority Business Brain Trust; chmn Mayor's Task Force for Economic Develop of Newark NJ; rep Cty Solid Waste Disposal Commn; rep to White House Conf on Small Business; NJIT Adv Council on Civil and Environ Engrg; trustee New Jersey Institute of Technology, 1989-; vice chairman, New Jersey Governors Study Commission on Discrimination in Public Procurement; Regional Alliance for Small Contractors of New York and New Jersey, vice chair; NAMC Liaison Comm to the US Corporate Surety Bond Industry, chairman. **Honors/Awds:** Fellow Amer Soc of Civil Eng 1969; Natl Advocate Award for minority and small bus dev US Small Bus Admin 1984; Outstanding Alumnus Award NJ Inst of Tech 1985; NY Regional Contractor of the Year 1985 US Dept of Commerce; Outstanding Mem Awds of Natl Assn of Minority Contractors and NJ United Minority Business Brain Trust; NJIT Alumni Athletic Hall of Fame for Fencing; business included as one of Black Enterprise's Top 100 Service Firms 1988. **Military Serv:** USMC pfc 2 yrs; USAFR captain 14 years. **Business Addr:** President, Evanbow Constuction Co Inc, 67 Sanford St, East Orange, NJ 07018, (973)674-1250.

BOWSER, JAMES A.
Educator. **Personal:** Born Nov 11, 1913, Norfolk, VA; married Margaret Smith; children: Barbara B Miller. **Educ:** Virginia State College, BS, 1935; Pennsylvania State University, MEd, 1952, DEd, 1960. **Career:** High school teacher, 1936-37; Orange Virginia High School, principal, 1936-42; Norfolk State College, instructor of building construction, 1947-54, vocational industrial teacher/trainer, 1954-60, industrial education professor, director of Junior College Division, 1960-, director of training, 1962-64, chairman, Div of Industrial Education & Technology, starting 1967; Hocking Tech College, director of development, currently. **Orgs:** Project director, US Office of Education, 1966; co-dir, Project D-054, US Dept of Labor; bd dir, Norfolk Chamber of Commerce, 1971-74; Norfolk Housing Development Corp; vice-chairman, Mayor's Committee of Job Opportunity for Youth; bd dir, Tidewater Minority Contractors Assn, 1971-74; bd dir, United Communities Fund; chairman, Plans & Program Com; Virginia Advisory Com on Vocational Education; adv com, 1202 Commission Virginia State Council of Higher Education, 1975; Comm on Specialized Personnel, US Dept of Labor, 1964-69. **Military Serv:** US Army, captain, 1942-46, 1950-52. **Home Addr:** 2912 Hollister Ave, Norfolk, VA 23504.

BOWSER, KYLE D.
Television producer. **Personal:** marrIed Yvette Lee Bowser. **Educ:** Ohio Univ, BS, 1980; Widener Univ School of Law, JD, 1991. **Career:** Supreme Court of Pennsylvania, law clerk, 1989; NBC Business Affairs, law clerk, 1990; Bowser, Weaver, & Cousounis, law clerk, 1991; Fox, Inc, creative associate, 1991-92; Fox Broadcasting Company, manager of current programing, 1992-93; HBO Independant Productions, dir of creative affairs, 1993-94; RES ISPA Media Inc, pres, currently. **Orgs:** Black Entertainment and Sports Lawyers Association; Black Filmmakers Assoc; National Assoc of Minorities in Cable. **Special Achievements:** Television Program, ''Trial by Jury,'' exec producer, 1995; ''Midnight Mac'' with Bernie Mac.

BOWSER, MCEVA R.
Educator (retired). **Personal:** Born Nov 22, 1922, Elizabeth City, NC; daughter of Rosa Lillian Stewart Roach and Ivy Hillard Roach; married Barrington H Bowser, Apr 12, 1952 (deceased); children: Angela, Barrington Jr. **Educ:** Elizabeth City State U, BS 1944; VA Commonwealth U, MEd 1970. **Career:** Richmond VA Public Schools, curriculum specialist, elementary consultant, teacher; Sussex Co & Louisa Co, teacher (retired). **Orgs:** Pres Richmond Med Aux 1956-58; pres Richmond Club of Chi Delta Mu Wives 1966-68; natl vice pres Chi Delta Mu Wives 1970-72; mem REA, YEA, NEA, ASCD; pres Richmond Chptr Jack & Jill of Am 1964-66; past bd dir Jack & Jill of Am Found 1968-70; treas Richmond Chap Links Inc 1977-79; v-chrmn Regional Reading Commn 1977-; past pres Women of St Philip's Episcopal Ch 1964-68; mem Alpha Kappa Alpha Maymont Civic League; president, Richmond Chapter Links 1981-83; Parliamentarian, Auxiliary to Medical Society 1980-90; Parliamentarian, Richmond Chapter Links 1985-87; School Bd, City of Richmond, 1994. **Honors/Awds:** Outstndg serv awrd Jack & Jill of Am Found 1972. **Home Addr:** 1807 Hampton St, Richmond, VA 23220.

BOWSER, ROBERT LOUIS
Business executive. **Personal:** Born Dec 13, 1935, E Orange, NJ; son of Louise E Pateman Bowser (deceased) and Edward T Bowser Sr (deceased); married Marilyn K Ward Bowser, Dec 30, 1989; children: David, Lisa K Ward, Leslie J Ward. **Educ:** Newark Coll of Engr, BSCE 1958; Northwestern Univ, Certificate 1961; NYU, Certificate 1963. **Career:** City of Newark, city planner 1958-60; Town of Montclair traffic engr 1960-65; structural engr 1965-68; Bowser Engrs & Assoc, vice pres 1968-82; City of East Orange NJ, dir of public works 1986-91; Robert L Bowser Assoc, owner 1982-; Newark Board of Education, principal engineer, 1991-; City of East Orange NJ, elected mayor, 1998-. **Orgs:** Inst of Traffic Engr 1959-65; Natl Soc of Professional Engrs 1963; NJ Soc of Professional Engrs 1963; Land Surveyors Functional Sect NJ 1969; Licensed Professional Land Surveyor NJ 1969; Am Congress of Surveying & Mapping 1970; Licensed Professional Planner NJ 1973; NJ Planners Association, 1978-; vice chmn E Orange Rent Level Bd 1975-76; commr/fdr Essex Co Touch Football League 1975-; pres Natl Assn Builders & Contractors NJ 1976; Public Works Assn 1986-; NJ Society of Professional Planners 1976-; bd of dirs, Girl Scout Council, 1989-93; National Council of Economic Development 1987; adjunct prof, Essex County College 1985-89; member, East Orange Planning Board, clerk, 1986-91; East Orange Kiwanis Club, 1990, pres, 1994; member, East Orange Lions Club, 1989, pres, 1995; Rutgers Urban Gardening Program, advisory Board, 1990-, chairman, 1992-; Citizens Advisory Bd, Orange Hosp Ctr, 1994-; Natl Minority Contractors Assn, 1994-; REAP Investment Corp, bd mem, 1995. **Honors/Awds:** Black Heritage Award, City of East Orange, 1989; Director of Public Works Commendation, City Council of East Orange, 1991. **Military Serv:** USCG Reserve 1960-66. **Business Addr:** Mayor, City of East Orange, 44 City Hall Plz, East Orange, NJ 07019.

BOWSER, VIVIAN ROY
Educator. **Personal:** Born Mar 24, 1926, Weimar, TX; married Jesse Hugh. **Educ:** Prairie View A&M U, BS; TX So U, Cert; Univ of NM, Cert. **Career:** Houston Independent School Dist, teacher. **Orgs:** Pres Houston Class Tchrs Assc; pres Cent TX Dist Tchrs Assc; pres-elect Tchrs St Assc of TX; pres TX Class Tchrs Assc; pr & r com & legis com TX St Tchrs & Assc; pres Houston Alumnae, Delta Sigma Theta Inc; mem exec com NEA Tchrs Professional Pract Commn 1974-79; US Nat Commn to UNESCO 1974-78; gov commn on Early Child Ed 1974; Professional Pract Commn 1972-74; life mem YMCA, TX Women's Polit Caucus; life mem Natl Cncl Negro Women; golden life mem Delta Sigma Theta; Houston Tchrs Assc; TX Class Tchrs Assc; Dist IV TSTA; TX St Tchrs Assc; NEA. **Honors/Awds:** Outst contrib in ed TX Legis 1973, 75; human rel awrd TX Class Tchrs 1976; Trailblazer in Educ SW Reg Delta Sigma Theta 1976.

BOWSER, YVETTE LEE
Television executive. **Personal:** marrIed Kyle D. Bowser. **Career:** ''Living Single'', creator, executive producer, currently. **Business Addr:** Executive Producer, c/o Warner Bros., 4000 Warner Blvd, Burbank, CA 91522, (818)954-7579.

BOX, CHARLES
Mayor. **Personal:** Born 1951. **Educ:** Graduated from Univ of Michigan Law School. **Career:** Mayor of Rockford, IL. **Business Addr:** Mayor, City Hall, 425 East State St, Rockford, IL 61104.

BOYCE, CHARLES N.
Business executive. **Personal:** Born Jun 9, 1935, Detroit, MI; married Delma Cunningham; children: Terralyn, Tracy, Charles, LaShawn. **Educ:** Attended, Wayne State Univ 1955-62, Univ of MI Grad School of Business 1981. **Career:** MI Bell Telephone, comm oper asst 1966-69, order unit mgr 1969-71, dist commer mgr 1971-76, gen customer relations mgr 1976-78, dir of public affairs 1979-83, asst vice pres of urban affairs 1983-. **Orgs:** Alternate for bd of trustees, New Detroit Inc, 1972-75, 1978-; bd of dir, Assn of Black Bus & Engrg Students,

1973-; commr, Detroit Housing Commn, 1976-; bd of dir, 1978-, 1st vice pres, 1985-86, NAACP Detroit; bd of dir, MI League for Human Serv, 1979-; mem, Soc of Consumer Affairs in Bus, 1979-; mem, Million Dollar Club, NAACP, Detroit, 1978 & 1979; bd dir, Inner City Bus Improvement Forum, 1987-89; mem, African-Amer Heritage Assn, Booker T Washington Bus Assn, Bus Policy Review Council, Corp Urban Forum, Detroit Area Pre-Coll Engrg Prog; bd dir, Black Family Devel Inc, Concerned Citizens Council, Jazz Devel Workshop, March of Dimes SE MI Chapt, Neighborhood Serv Org. **Honors/Awds:** Outstanding Serv Awd Oakland Co Urban League 1974; Serv Awd NAACP Detroit 1979; Outstanding Citizen Serv Awd Detroit Housing Commn 1979; Minority Achievers in Industry Awd YMCA 1980; "E" for Excellence in Marketing Awd AT&T 1982; Anthony Wayne Awd for Leadership Wayne State Univ 1983. **Business Addr:** Asst Vice President, MI Bell Telephone Co, 444 Michigan Ave, Detroit, MI 48226.

BOYCE, JOHN G.
Educator. **Personal:** Born May 6, 1935; married Erma; children: Mindora, Jane. **Educ:** Univ British Columbia, MD 1962; Columbia U, MSc 1971. **Career:** State Univ of New York, prof of Obstetrics & Gynecology; chairman, department of Obstetrics & Gynecology, Health Science Center at Brooklyn, currently. **Orgs:** Mem, Kings Co NY State Amer & Natl Med Assn; Am Coll Ob/Gyn; Soc Gynecologic & Oncologists. **Honors/Awds:** Certified special Competence Gynecologic Oncology 1974; The New York Obstetrical Society, president. **Business Addr:** Prof of OB-GYN, State Univ of NY, 450 Clarkson Ave, Brooklyn, NY 11203.

BOYCE, JOSEPH NELSON
Journalist. **Personal:** Born Apr 18, 1937, New Orleans, LA; son of Sadie Nelson Boyce and John B Boyce; married Carol Hill Boyce, Dec 21, 1968; children: Beverly, Leslie, Nelson, Joel. **Educ:** Roosevelt University, Chicago, IL, 1955-63; John Marshall Law School, Chicago, IL, 1963-65. **Career:** Chicago Police Dept, Chicago, IL, patrolman, 1961-66; Chicago Tribune, Chicago, IL, reporter, 1966-70; Time Magazine, New York, NY, correspondent, bureau chief, 1970-87; The Wall Street Journal, New York, NY, senior editor, 1987-. **Orgs:** Member, Natl Assn of Black Journalists, currently; life member, NAACP; member, CORE, 1967-70; visiting faculty, Summer Program for Minority Journalist, 1986-89; lecturer: Stanford University, University of Kansas, South Carolina State, University of California, Berkeley, San Francisco State, Howard University, Bradley University; member, American Federation of Musicians, 1955-. **Honors/Awds:** Time Inc Fellow, Duke University, 1983; Lincoln University Award for Educational Reporting, 1976; Black Achiever, Metropolitan YMCA of New York, 1976; lectured at Poynter Institute, 1992. **Military Serv:** US Naval Reserve, PO 2nd class, 1954-62. **Business Addr:** Journalist, The Wall Street Journal, 200 Liberty St, New York, NY 10281, (212)416-2205.

BOYCE, LAURA E.
Corporate communications management trainee. **Personal:** Born Apr 9, 1962, Brooklyn, NY; daughter of Edwyna Clarke Boyce and Luther W Boyce. **Educ:** Vassar College, Poughkeepsie, NY, BA, 1983. **Career:** Group W's Newsfeed Network, Philadelphia, PA, assoc producer, 1984-87; National Assoc of Black Journalists, Reston, VA, program director, 1988-90; Scott Paper Co, Philadelphia, PA, corporate communicating representative, 1990-. **Orgs:** Co-chair of community service committee, Urban League Young Professionals, 1991-; vice president broadcast, Philadelphia Assn of Black Journalists, 1987; volunteeer, Big Brother, Big Sister of Philadelphia, 1985-88; steering committee member, African-American Alumnae of Vassar College, 1985-89.

BOYCE, ROBERT
Educational administrator. **Career:** Detroit Bd of Educ, pres, currently. **Business Phone:** (313)494-1010.

BOYCE, WILLIAM M.
Personnel administrator. **Personal:** Born Jul 9, 1928, Brooklyn, NY; son of Darnley and Luddie; married Alice M Billingsley; children: David C, Lynne M. **Educ:** Brooklyn Clg, AAS 1957; City Clg of NY, AAS 1962, BBA 1965; Fairleigh Dickinson U, MBA 1976. **Career:** Kings Co Hosp Ctr, dir of prsnl 1974-81; Muhlenberg Hospital, vice pres human resources, 1981-85; Yonkers General Hospital, director human resources, 1987-89; Boyce Consulting Group, president, currently; Passaic County Community College, dir, human resources/labor relations, 1990-. **Orgs:** Dir manpower task force New Urban & Coalition 1970-74; dir Ft Greene Neighborhood Manpower Cntr 1966-70; chmn Brooklyn Hlth Manpower Consortium 1975-77; mem Assn of MBA Exec 1975-; mem NY Assn of Hosp Persnl Admn 1977-. **Honors/Awds:** Recipient of German Occupancy Medal AUS. **Military Serv:** AUS pvt II 1951-53. **Home Addr:** 33 Elk Ave, New Rochelle, NY 10804.

BOYD, BARBARA JEAN
Librarian. **Personal:** Born Jul 14, 1954, Monroe, LA; daughter of Ora Lee Renfro Robinson (deceased) and Rube Robinson; married Willian Boyd, Jun 25; children: Chaundra, Cameron, Chelsea. **Educ:** University of Wisconsin, Eau Claire, Eau Claire, WI; University of Wisconsin, Oshkosh, Oshkosh, WI, BS, 1979; University of Wisconsin, Milwaukee, Milwaukee, WI, MLIS, 1989. **Career:** Heritage Bank, Milwaukee, WI, clerk, 1979-80; City of Milwaukee-Legislative Reference Bureau, Milwaukee, WI, LTA, 1980-89, librarian, 1989-91; Houston Public Library, Johnson Branch, manager; Houston Public Library, Collier Regional, librarian, 1991-. **Orgs:** Member, American Library Assn 1987-; member, Special Libraries Assn, 1987-89; member, Wisconsin Black Librarian Network, 1987-91; Special Libraries Association, positive action program for minority groups stipend; Texas Library Assn, 1995-; mem, Black Caucus of ALA, 1987-. **Honors/Awds:** Library Career Training Fellowship UWM-School of Library and Information Science, 1987-88. **Business Addr:** Librarian, Houston Public Library, Collier Regional, 6200 Pinemont, Houston, TX 77092.

BOYD, BARBARA P. See Obituaries section.

BOYD, CHARLES FLYNN
Educational administrator. **Personal:** Born May 13, 1938, Pensacola, FL; married Marie Moore; children: Marie Therese, Carla, Charles Jr. **Educ:** TX Southern Univ, BS 1956; FL A&M Univ MS 1964; Univ of OK, PhD Philosophy 1972. **Career:** School Dist of Escambia Co, sci teacher 1959-64, asst principal of hs 1964-70; Univ of OK, financial aide counselor 1970, secondary school principal 1971-78; School Dist of Escambia Co, dir fed proj 1972-. **Orgs:** Suburban West Rotary Club 1972-80; Pensacola Metro YMCA 1973-80; PJC Bd of Trustees 1981-; chmn Cert of Need Comm Northwest FL Comprehensive; Kappa Alpha Psi Frat; Phi Delta Kappa; Intl Reading Assn. **Home Addr:** 3370 Bayou Blvd, Pensacola, FL 32503. **Business Addr:** ECIA Chapter 1 Office, 1403 W Cross St, Pensacola, FL 32501-1251.

BOYD, DELORES ROSETTA
Attorney. **Personal:** Born Apr 24, 1950, Ramer, AL. **Educ:** Univ of AL, BA 1972; Univ of VA, JD 1975. **Career:** Judge John C Godbold, law clerk to Federal Judge, US Ct of Appeals 5th Circuit; US Ct of Appeals 11th Circuit, chief judge 1975-76; Mandell & Boyd, partner, 1976-92, solo practice, 1992-. **Orgs:** AL State Bar Bd of Bar Examiners, bar examiner 1979-83. **Honors/Awds:** "The New Women in Court," Time Magazine, May 30, 1983. **Home Addr:** 3 N Anton Dr, Montgomery, AL 36105. **Business Addr:** Attorney, 639 Marth St, Cottage Hill Historic, Montgomery, AL 36103.

BOYD, DORIS REGINA
Planning director. **Personal:** Born Jan 17, 1952, Birmingham, AL; daughter of Joy Williams Boyd and Joseph L Boyd Sr; children: Dayo Z. **Educ:** University of Denver, Denver, CO, 1969; Colorado Women's College, Denver, CO, 1969-70; Stephens College, Columbia, MO, BA, 1975; Northeastern University, Boston, 1988-89. **Career:** Senator Ruby Simmonds, St Thomas, Virgin Islands, public relations aide, 1981; WBNB-TV, St Thomas, Virgin Islands, new reporter/anchor, 1981-83; The Daily News, St Thomas, Virgin Islands, news reporter, 1983-85; The Boston Herald, Boston, MA, news reporter, 1985-86; New England Telephone, Boston, MA, public relations manager, 1986-89; NYNEX Corp, White Plains, NY, staff dir, issues mgmt, 1989-; Freddie Mac, currently. **Orgs:** Business & artistic director, Virgin Islands Folkloric Co, 1982-83; president, Virgin Islands Association, 1983-85; member, National Association of Black Journalists, 1984-; choreographer, Miss Virgin Islands Universe Pageant, 1985; editor, NYNEX Minority Management Association Newsletters, 1987-90. **Honors/Awds:** MMA Achievement Award, NYNEX Minority Mgmt Assn, 1990; Well Done Award, Gannett Co Inc, 1984, 1985; Corporate Recycling Program Director, NYNEX Corporation, 1990-91; Excellence Award, Virgin Islands Advertising Club, 1983.

BOYD, EDDIE L.
Educator. **Personal:** Born May 7, 1939, Canton, MS; son of Mattie Pierce (deceased) and Wesley Boyd; married Carolyn Smith Boyd, Apr 3, 1973; children: Erik R, Rankin. **Educ:** University of California, San Francisco, CA, PharmD, 1970; University of Michigan, Ann Arbor, MI, MS, 1989. **Career:** University of California, San Francisco, CA, asst clinical professor, 1970-71; University of Michigan, College of Pharmacy, Ann Arbor, MI, assoc professor, 1971-; Xavier University, College of Pharmacy, New Orleans, LA, assoc dean, 1991-. **Orgs:** Member, American Pharmaceutical Assn, 1970-; member, National Pharmaceutical Assn, 1975-; member, American Society of Hospital Pharmacists, 1989-; member, American Assn of Colleges of Pharmacy, 1989-; member, Alpha Phi Alpha, 1974-. **Honors/Awds:** Bowl of Hygeia, School of Pharmacy, University of California, San Francisco, CA, 1970-. **Military Serv:** US Air Force, Airman 2nd Class, 1956-60.

BOYD, EVELYN SHIPPS
Educator (retired). **Personal:** Born Aug 4, Birmingham, AL; daughter of Geneva White Shipps and Perry Shipps; married Gilbert M, Nov 28, 1948. **Educ:** Baldwin-Wallace Coll, BMusEd (cum laude) 1959; Cleveland Inst of Music, Master of Music Honor Grad 1970. **Career:** Cleveland Pub Schs, secretary 1942-55, teacher 1959-71; Cuyahoga Comm Coll, asst prof music 1971-81, dept head performing arts 1977-81; Cleveland Inst of Music, teacher 1970-76, retired. **Orgs:** OH Music Teachers Assn 27 years, Music Educ Natl Conf 1961-; tape recorder for Cleveland Soc for Blind 1984-; chaplain staff univ hospitals volunteer, 1992-; Cleveland Clinic Foundation, ombudsman office volunteer, 1993-. **Honors/Awds:** Besse Award for teaching excellence Cuyahoga Com Coll 1980; alumini merit award Baldwin-Wallace Coll 1983; award for 2000 hours volunteer Univ Hosp SICU Unit 1987; Pi Kappa Lambda Music Honor Soc Cleveland Inst of Music; Baldwin-Walla Mu Phi Music Honor Sorority Dayton C Miller Honor Soc; Elizabeth Downes Award (Volunteer Award of Year) University Hospitals 1989. **Home Addr:** 3942 E 123rd St, Cleveland, OH 44105.

BOYD, GEORGE ARTHUR
Scientist. **Personal:** Born Mar 7, 1928, Washington, NC. **Educ:** St Augustine Coll, BS; Amer Univ 1956-57; US Dept of Agriculture Grad Sch 1957; US Office of Personnel Mgmt Exec Inst, 1980, 1982. **Career:** US Naval Oceanographic Office, physical scientist, physical science tech 1956-57; Defense Mapping Agency, retired chief equal oppor officer. **Orgs:** Mem Sigma Xi the Scientific Rsch Soc 1972-; pres Mt Olivet Heights Citizens Assn 1975-; chairperson Gallaudet Coll Comm Relations Council 1977-; DC Federation of Civil Assns Inc 1981-; mem bd of associates St Augustine Coll 1982-; chairperson Advisory Neighborhood Commission 5B 1995-. **Honors/Awds:** Publication co-author "Oceanographic Atlas of the North Atlantic Ocean" 1965; Awd of Commendation Pres of the US 1970; resolution Bd of Trustees GallaudetColl 1981; Disting Alumni Awd Natl Assn for Equal Oppor of Higher Educ 1985. **Military Serv:** US Army, AUS, pfc 2 yrs. **Home Addr:** 1264 Owen Place NE, Washington, DC 20002.

BOYD, GWENDOLYN VIOLA
Chief of police. **Personal:** Born Jun 4, 1954, Sneads, FL; daughter of Vera Mae & Willie C Mathis; children: Sherhonda, Lakeesha. **Educ:** Miami Dade Community Coll, AA, 1974; Biscayne Coll, BA, 1980; Florida Intl Univ, MPA, 1982, EDd, 1997. **Career:** City of Miami Police Dept, police major, 1974-97; City of Prichard Police Dept, chief of police, 1997-. **Orgs:** Natl Organization of Black Law Enforcement Executives, editor; Intl Assn of Women Police; Intl Assn of Chiefs of Police; Amer Soc of Training & Dev; AL Assn of Chiefs of Police; Natl Assn of Negro Bus & Professional Women's Club; United Way of Amer; Mobile County Chiefs of Police Assn. **Honors/Awds:** Sojourner Truth, 1991. **Special Achievements:** Research on Male vs Female Police Officers' Job Performance, published in fall issue of Women Police Magazine; Human Resource Dev Conf, Atlanta, presenter, 1997. **Business Addr:** Chief of Police, Prichard Police Department, 216 E Prichard Ave, Prichard, AL 36610, (334)452-7900.

BOYD, JOSEPH L.
Educational administrator. **Personal:** Born Dec 20, 1947, Columbia, SC; son of Mr & Mrs Frank Boyd; married Nellie Brown; children: Joseph Christopher, Michael Steven, Adrienne Kerise. **Educ:** Univ of SC, BS 1969, MAcctg 1976, PhD 1977. **Career:** Johnson C Smith Univ, instructor 1972-74; Univ of SC, asst prof 1976-77; Univ of IL, asst prof 1977-78; NC A&T State Univ, assoc prof 1978-83; Norfolk State Univ, dean, school of business 1983-. **Orgs:** Mem Beta Alpha Psi, Beta Gamma Sigma, Omicron Delta Kappa, Amer Inst of CPA, Amer Acct Assn, NC Assn of CPA, SC Assn of CPA, Natl Assn of Accts, Natl Assn of Black Accts, Amer Tax Assn, Ins Selling Practices Comm, Curriculum Comm, Cluster Task Force, IRS Advisory Group; Amer Arbitration Assn. **Honors/Awds:** Haskins & Sells Found Fac Fellow 1975; Doctoral Consortium Univ of SC Rep 1976; Amer Acctg Assoc Fellow 1976; Speaker on Unreasonable Compensation Amer Acct Assoc Meeting Portland OR 1977; Moderator of the Session on Tax Rsch Amer Acct Assoc Boston MA 1980; Grants from Alexander Grant & Co 1980, 1981, Deloitte Haskins & Sells 1980, 1981, Monsanto 1980, 1981, Standard Oil of OH 1982; Co-Chmn NC Ed Colloquium 1982; Program Chmn Acct Ed & Practitioners' Forum 1983; Faculty Internship Deloitte Haskins & Sells Intl Acctg Firm 1983; AICPA Faculty Summer Seminar on Teaching of Taxation; Instr Lambers CPA Review Course, Small Business Mgmt Seminar, IL Tax & Acctg Update; Consulting Speaker Devel of the Acct Currciulum at Livingstone Coll; Mem Advisor Council fortheComm of IRS; Publications in Tax Adviser, Oil & Gas Tax Quarterly, Taxes-The Tax Magazine, Prentice-Hall Tax Ideas Service, 1978, 1979, 1983. **Business Addr:** Dean, School of Business, Norfolk State Univ, 2401 Corprew Ave, Norfolk, VA 23504.

BOYD, JULIA A.
Psychotherapist, author. **Personal:** Born Apr 21, 1949, Camden, NJ; daughter of Joseph & Lavada Conyers; divorced; children: Michael Alan Boyd Jr. **Educ:** Antioch University, BA, 1982; Pacific Lutheran University, MEd, 1985; Seattle University, 1991. **Career:** Pierce County Rape Relief, executive director, 1985-86; Group Health Cooperative, psychotherapist, 1986-. **Orgs:** Arts Commission, King County, 1986-89; Domestic Abuse Women's Network, board member, 1983-85; Washington Sexual Assault Committee, Statewide Committee, 1984-86. **Honors/Awds:** 100 Black Women, Jersey Chap, Afri-

can-American Women's Achievement, 1994; African-American Women Forum, Western Washington State University, 1994. **Special Achievements:** Books: In the Co. of My Sisters; Black Women & Self-Esteem, Dutton, 1993; Girlfriend to Girlfriend; Everyday Wisdom & Affirmations from the Sister Circle, Dutton, 1995; Embracing the Fire: Sisters Talk About Sex and Relationships, Dutton, 1997.

BOYD, LOUISE YVONNE
Software systems engineer. **Personal:** Born Jul 24, 1959, Newburgh, NY; daughter of Louise Yvonne Lewis Boyd and Charles Carter Boyd (deceased). **Educ:** University of Florida, Gainesville, FL, BS, 1981. **Career:** NASA, Kennedy Space Center, FL, engineer software systems, 1982-; Brevard Community College, Cocoa, FL, adjunct professor, 1984-88. **Orgs:** President, National Technical Assn, Space Coast Chapter, 1987-89; region III director, National Technical Assn, 1989-91; space coast division governor, Toastmasters International, 1990-91; vice-president, Space Coast Section Society of Women Engineers, 1990-91; founder, chairman of board, Sweet Inc, 1990-; Toastmasters International-District 47, lt governor of marketing, 1991-92, treasurer, governor of education, 1992-93; NASA Kennedy Management Association, treasurer, 1991-92. **Honors/Awds:** 100 Black Science Achievers, Chicago Museum of Science and Industry, 1989; 30 Leaders of the Future, Ebony Magazine, 1989; Crystal Pyramid Award, Brevard Alumnae Chapter Delta Sigma Theta Inc, 1990; Distinguished Toastmaster, Toastmasters International, 1990; Mathematician Individual Technical Achiever Award, NTA Greater Houston Chapter; Distinguished District Award, Toastmasters International, 1992; Excellence In Marketing Award, Toastmasters International, 1992; NASA Points of Light Award, 1992. **Business Addr:** Software Systems Engineeer, LPS Software Engineering, NASA, TE-LPS-21, Kennedy Space Center, Orlando, FL 32899.

BOYD, MARVIN
Banker. **Career:** Gulf Federal Bank, pres/CEO, currently. **Business Addr:** Pres/CEO, Gulf Federal Bank, 901 Springhill Ave, Mobile, AL 36604, (334)433-2671.

BOYD, MELBA JOYCE
Author, educator. **Personal:** Born Apr 2, 1950, Detroit, MI; daughter of Dorothy Wynn and John Percy Boyd; divorced; children: John Percy III, Maya Wynn. **Educ:** Western Michigan University, BA, English, 1971, MA, English, 1972; University of Michigan-Ann Arbor, Doctor of Arts, English, 1979. **Career:** Cass Technical High School, teacher, 1972-73; University of Michigan, graduate assistant, 1978; Broadside Press, assistant editor, 1972-77, 1980-82; Wayne County Community College, instructor, 1972-82; University of Iowa, assistant professor, 1982-88; Ohio State University, associate professor, 1988-89; University of Michigan, director, Afro-American studies, 1989-. **Orgs:** Association Studies Associate, 1982-; German Association of American Studies, 1982-87; Alpha Kappa Alpha Sorority Inc, 1968-71. **Honors/Awds:** University of Michigan, Faculty Research Grant, 1991; Society of the Culturally Concerned, Culture Award, 1990; Ohio State University, Research and Publication Award, 1989; Fulbright Commission, Senior Fulbright Lecturer-Germany, 1983-84; Michigan Council for the Arts, Individual Artists Award, 1980. **Special Achievements:** The Inventory of Black Roses, Detroit, Pasts Tents Press, poetry, 1989; Lied fur Maya/Song for May, Germany, WURF Verlag Press, poetry, 1989; Thirteen Frozen Flamingoes, Germany, Die Certel Press, poetry, 1984; Song for Maya, Detroit, Broadside Press, 1983; Cats Eyes and Dead Wood, Detroit, Fallen Angel Press, poetry, 1978. **Business Addr:** Director, African-American Studies, University of Michigan, Flint, 364 CROB, Flint, MI 48502, (313)762-3353.

BOYD, MURIEL ISABEL BELTON
Educational administrator, librarian (retired). **Personal:** Born Feb 18, 1910, Haughton, LA; daughter of Lula Isabel Tyler Belton (deceased) and Sank Beranger Belton (deceased); married Charles Henry Boyd, Jun 24, 1940 (deceased); children: Dawud Abdus Salaam. **Educ:** Southern University, Baton Rouge, LA, BA, 1932; Columbia University School of Library Science, New York, NY, MLS, 1950. **Career:** Lincoln Parish Schools, Ruston, LA, teacher, 1932-37; Caddo Parish School Board, Shreveport, LA, school supervisor, 1937-41, teacher, 1941-50, librarian, 1950-70. **Orgs:** Life member, National Educational Assn; chairman, librarians division, Louisiana Education Assn; life member, committee of administration, YWCA Allendale Branch; charter member, Shreveport National Council of Negro Women; coordinator, administrative division, National Baptist Congress of Education; life member, Southern University Alumni Assn. **Honors/Awds:** Shreveport Times Educator of the Year, Caddo Education Assn, 1970; featured in The Shreveport Sun, 1970; featured in The Shreveport Journal, 1988; featured in The Shreveport Times, 1989; featured on KEEL-Radio, 1990; Woman of the Year, Zeta Phi Beta, 1964.

BOYD, ROBERT NATHANIEL, III
Dentist. **Personal:** Born Jan 31, 1928, Orange, NJ; son of Kathleen Olton Boyd and Robert N Boyd Jr; divorced; children: Robert Brian, Judith Karen, David Nelthropp. **Educ:** Rutgers Univ, BS 1949; NY Univ Coll of Dentistry, DDS 1954. **Career:** NYU Coll of Dentistry, assoc prof dentl materials 1969-83, admissions comm 1969-83, asst dir admissions 1976-83; Dental Materials Group Ltd, vice pres 1983; Boyd Int Industries Inc, pres. **Orgs:** Fund raiser minority students NYU Coll of Dent; adv Natl Cncl of Negro Women 1979-83; mem Intl Assn of Dental Rsch, Amer Dental Assn, Essex Co Dental Soc, NJ State Dental Soc; panelist Natl Black Sci Students Organiz Conf 1970; consult LD Caulk 1970; consult Vicon Corp 1971; panelist Workshop Grad Oppty for Minority Students Loeb Center 1976; adv comm for Implementation of Task Force 1976; dir Minority Student Recruitment 1972-83; asst in devel of NYU poster and brochure for recruit of disadvantaged students. **Honors/Awds:** Senior Prize Amer Soc of Dentistry for Children 1954; Senior Prize Amer Acad of Dental Med 1954; Omicron Kappa Upsilon NYU Coll Dentistry Hon Soc 1954; 1st in class Dental Med; 1st in class Children's Dentistry, NYU Coll of Dentistry; guestspeaker NYU Coll of Dentistry Alumni Assn Alumni Meeting and Dean's Day 1970; publications incl, with L Colin and GE Kaufman, A Survey of "Resin Systems for Dentistry" Abstract of Papers M25 - JD Res 42nd Gen Meeting IADR March 1964; Radio Broadcasts WLIB, WABC-AM, WNBC-AM, WNEW-TV 1973; Dental Forum White Plains NY 1975-76; NY Univ Continuing Dental Educ Instructor 1975; speaker CT State Dental Assoc 1977; Essayist Greater NY Dental Meeting, 1981, 1983, 1985; speaker, Commonwealth Dental Soc, Alpha Omega Study Club, North Bronx Central Hospital. **Special Achievements:** US Patent #3,503,128, Dental Filling Comosition, 1970. **Military Serv:** USAF Capt Dental Corps 1954-56. **Business Addr:** President, Boyd Int Industries Inc, 2100 Millburn Avenue, Maplewood, NJ 07040.

BOYD, ROZELLE
Educator. **Personal:** Born Apr 24, 1934, Indianapolis, IN. **Educ:** Butler Univ, BA 1957; Ind Univ, MA 1964. **Career:** Marion Cty Dept of Public Welfare, caseworker 1957; Indianapolis Public Schs, teacher-counselor 1957-68; IN Univ, asst/assoc dean 1968-81; IN Univ, dir univ div 1981-. **Orgs:** Indianapolis City councilman 1966-; Democratic Natl Committeeman; minority leader Indianapolis City Council; chmn Indianapolis Black Political Caucus. **Honors/Awds:** Lily Fellow 1957; Freedom's Found Awd. **Home Addr:** 2527 E 35th, Indianapolis, IN 46218. **Business Addr:** Director, University Division, Indiana University, Maxwell Hall 104 IU, Bloomington, IN 47401.

BOYD, TERRY A.
Human resources director, consulting firm executive. **Personal:** Born in Cleveland, OH. **Educ:** Defiance College, BS, 1978; Ohio State University, Masters, 1981, PhD, 1993. **Career:** Human Resources Inc, assistant director, 1981-82; Franklin County Children Services, child welfare worker III, 1982-84; City of Columbus, administrator of youth services bureau, 1984-87, executive assistant to director of human services, 1987-89; administrator, community services, 1989-90, administrator, OMB, 1990-91; US Health Corp, director, human resources, 1991-. **Orgs:** Franklin County ADAMH Board, board of trustees, 1992-; Franklin County Children Services Board, board of trustees, 1989-92; FCCS Citizens Advisory Council, president, 1985-92; Ohio's Children Defense Fund, board member, 1986-92; Alliance for Cooperative Justice, board member, 1985-89; Jobs for Columbus Graduates, board member, 1991-92; COTA Transportation Task Force, 1988-89; United Way Campaign, cabinet member, 1992; ADAMH, board of trustees, treasurer; Columbus Metropolitan Library Board. **Honors/Awds:** Franklin County Commissioners, Service of Merit, 1992; FCCS, Distinguished Service Award, 1992. **Special Achievements:** Changing Attitudes: An Anti-Drug Abuse Policy, 1989. **Business Addr:** Director, Human Resources, US Health Corp., 3555 Olentangy River Rd, Ste 400, Columbus, OH 43214, (614)566-5902.

BOYD, THEOPHILUS B., III
Business executive. **Personal:** Born May 15, 1947, Nashville, TN; married Yvette Duke; children: LaDonna Yvette, Shalae Shantel, T B Boyd IV, Justin Marriell. **Educ:** TN State Univ, BBA 1969; Shreveport Bible Coll, D Divinity 1980; Easonian Baptist Seminary, D Letters 1983. **Career:** Citizens Realty & Develop Co, pres 1982; Citizens Sav & Dev Co, president 1982-; Meharry Med Coll, vice chair, board of directors, 1982-; Natl Baptist Pub Bd, president and ceo; Citizens Bank, chairman board of directors. **Orgs:** Mem bd of dirs March of Dimes TN Chapt; commnr human develop State of TN; bd of dirs Nashville Tech Institute; 100 Black Men of Middle Tennessee Inc, president; 100 Black Men of America Inc, past vice pres of finance & treasurer; United Negro College Fund Telethon, past Middle Tennessee chairman; First Union Bank, board of directors. **Honors/Awds:** Mem bd of governors Chamber of Commerce; March of Dimes, Man of the Year; life mem Kappa Alpha Psi Fraternity Inc; mem Chi Boule of Sigma Pi Phi Frat; Best Dressed of Nashville. **Business Addr:** President, Natl Baptist Pub Bd, 6717 Centennial Blvd, Nashville, TN 37209.

BOYD, THOMAS
Human resources director. **Personal:** Born Apr 6, 1942, Philadelphia, PA; son of Thelma Archie Boyd and John Boyd; married Gwendolyn Lee, Dec 14, 1988. **Educ:** Temple Univ, BA, 1970. **Career:** Remington Rand Inc, mgr, personnel, 1979; Computer Sciences Corp, mgr, equal employment opportunity, 1979-81; US Dept of the Navy, consultant, 1981-84; Hahneman Univ, mgr of employment, 1984-88; Syracuse Univ, director, employment practices, 1988-. **Orgs:** Consultant Navy Dept, 1981-; consultant, Natl Guard Bureau, 1984-. **Home Addr:** 126 Jamesville Ave H5, Syracuse, NY 13210. **Business Addr:** Syracuse Univ, Office of Human Resources, Skytop Office Bldg, Syracuse, NY 13244.

BOYD, WILHEMINA Y.
Organization executive. **Personal:** Born Sep 13, 1942, Baltimore, MD; daughter of Erma L Moore & William Woodley; married Raymond D Boyd, Apr 4, 1965; children: Adam & Jason. **Educ:** Morgan State University, Baltimore, MD, BS, 1964; St Mary's University, San Antonio, TX, MS, 1991. **Career:** Dept of Defense/Heidelberg, Ger, preschool dir/high school teacher, 1978-80, Ft Hood Texas, youth activities/director, 1981-83; City of San Antonio, TX, parks and recreation, special activities supv, 1983-85, events coordinator, 1985-87, convention facilities/facilities mgr, 1987-91; City of Kansas City, MO, convention and entertainment ctrs/exec dir, 1992-93; City of Tampa, FL, convention center/executive director, 1993-. **Orgs:** Suncoast Girl Scout Council, Inc, board of directors, 1994-; Natl Forum for Black Public Administrators, 1993-; Intl Assn of Auditorium Managers, bd of trustees. **Business Addr:** Director, Tampa, Florida, Convention Facilities/Tampa Convention Center, 333 S. Franklin St., Tampa, FL 33602, (813)274-8441.

BOYD, WILLIAM STEWART
Attorney & accountant. **Personal:** Born Mar 29, 1952, Chicago, IL. **Educ:** Univ of IL, BS Accounting 1974; Northern IL Univ Coll of Law, JD 1981. **Career:** Legal Assistance Found of Chicago, clerk 1979; Boyd & Grant, clerk 1978-81; Arthur Anderson & Co, sr staff accountant 1974-77, 1981-83; Boyd & Boyd Ltd, attorney 1983-. **Orgs:** Bd of dirs Grant Park Recreation Assn; mem Young Executives in Politics; mem Natl Business League 1974; mem Amer Bar Assn 1981; mem Cook Co Bar Assn 1981; bd of dirs NIA Comprehensive Ctr Inc 1984. **Home Addr:** 436 W 100th Pl, Chicago, IL 60610.

BOYD-CLINKSCALES, MARY ELIZABETH
Church executive. **Personal:** Born Aug 26, 1918, Haddocks, GA; daughter of Hattie Johnson Range and Charlie Range, Sr.; married William F Clinkscales; children: Barbara Boyd Collins, Gerald F, Carl T. **Educ:** Talladega Coll AL, BA 1936-40; Wayne State Univ Detroit, MI, MA 1956; Univ of Michigan, Ann Arbor, MI, 1968; Christian Theological Seminary, Indianapolis, IN DM program, 1989-90. **Career:** Lawrence N HS Indianpolis, IN, educator 1975-; Detroit Bd of Educ, educator (retired) 1982; Indiana Association of Church of God, senior adult minister; Indiana Ministries, Carmel, IN, director, 1987-. **Orgs:** Curriculum coordinator, Natl Assn of the Church of God 1964-; 1st black woman exec Natl Commn on Soc Concerns 1971-; life mem NAACP Indpls, IN 1979-; adv bd mem WFYI Channel 20 Indianapolis 1979-; pres/founder of Indiana Chap Ex-POSE (Ex-partners of Service Men and Women for Equality) 1980-; sec state bd of Christian Educ 1986-; editorial asst for Indiana Ministries publ Indianapolis IN 1986-; board member, Interfaith Fellowship on Religion and Aging, 1987-91; board member, 1988-91, senior vice pres/coordinatorm, 1990-92, Indiana Federation of Older Hoosiers. **Honors/Awds:** Maurice Endwright Award for Distinguished Activity and Service, Indiana Federation of Older Hoosiers, 1990. **Home Addr:** 6726 Cricklewood Rd, Indianapolis, IN 46220.

BOYD-FOY, MARY LOUISE
Company executive. **Personal:** Born Jun 30, 1936, Memphis, TN; daughter of Mamie E Grey-Boyd (deceased) and Ivory Boyd (deceased); married James Arthur Foy. **Educ:** Columbia Univ NY, BA 1977; Boston University, School of Social Work, certified contract compliance administrator, 1989. **Career:** United Negro Coll Fund Inc, public info asst 1956-60; Foreign Policy Assoc, public info asst 1960-70; Columbia Univ Urban Center, office mgr 1971-73, asst to exec dean sch of engrg 1973-77, exec asst to vice pres personnel admin 1977-78; International Paper Co, rep northeastern sales accts 1978-80; Ebasco Serv Inc, coord legislative affairs 1980-86, corporate mgr subcontract compliance 1986-. **Orgs:** Coalition of 100 Black Women 1980-; founding mem, former vice pres Natl Assoc of Univ Women Long Island NY Branch; past loyal lady, ruler Order of the Golden Circle, Long Island Assembly No 20, 1984, 1992; founder, past matron Emerald Chapter No 81 Order of Eastern Star, Prince Hall Affiliation 1986-; Daughters of Isis Abu-Bekr Court No 74, Prince Hall Affiliation 1986-; adv bd United Negro Coll Fund Inc, Queens, NY Branch, 1986-; ad bd United Negro Fund Inc 1986-, Assn of Minority Enterprises of NY 1986-; past national chairman, bd of dirs, Amer Assn of Blacks in Energy, 1990-92. **Honors/Awds:** Natl Assn of Univ Women, Woman of the Year, 1984, Long Island Branch, Hilda A Davis Award, 1991; Outstanding Woman of New York State, NY Senate, 1984; Outstanding Service Certificate, United Negro Coll Fund Inc, 1984, Distinguished Service Plaque, 1985-86; Recognition Awd; Appreciation Awd, Concerned Women of Jersey City Inc, 1986; Registry of Distinguished Citizens, Queens, NY, Inductee, 1989; Outstanding Service

Award, Assn of Minority Enterprises of NY, 1988; Appreciation Award, US Dept of Commerce, 1989; National Women of Achievement Award, 1992. **Home Addr:** 117-20 232nd St, Cambria Heights, NY 11411. **Business Addr:** Corporate Mgr/EEO Subcontract Compliance, Ebasco Services, Inc, 2 World Trade Center, New York, NY 10048.

BOYER, HORACE CLARENCE
Educator. **Personal:** Born Jul 28, 1935, Winter Park, FL; married Gloria Bernice Blue. **Educ:** Bethune-Cookman College, BA, 1957; Eastman School of Music, University of Rochester, MA, 1964, PhD, 1973. **Career:** Monroe High School, instructor 1957-58; Poinsett Elementary School, instructor, 1960-63; Albany State College, asst professor, 1964-65; University of Central Florida, asst professor, 1972-73; University of Massachusetts Amherst, Dept of Music, professor, 1973-. **Orgs:** Vice Pres, A Better Chance, 1980-82; editorial board, Black Music Research Journal, 1980-83; vice president, Gospel Music Assn, 1983-84. **Honors/Awds:** Ford Foundation Fellow, Eastman School of Music, 1969-72; curator, Natl Museum of American History, Smithsonian, 1985-86; United Negro College Fund, Distinguished Scholar-at-Large, Fisk University, 1986-87. **Military Serv:** US Army, sp-4, 1958-60. **Home Addr:** 92 Grantwood Dr, Amherst, MA 01002. **Business Addr:** Professor, Dept of Music, University of Massachusetts at Amherst, Amherst, MA 01003-0041.

BOYER, JAMES B.
Educator. **Personal:** Born Apr 3, 1934, Winter Park, FL; married Edna Medlock. **Educ:** Bethune-Cookman College, BS, 1956; Florida A&M University, MEd, 1964; Ohio State University, PhD, 1969. **Career:** Florida A&M University, teacher, admin visiting professor, 1969; University of Houston, asst professor, 1969-71; Kansas State University, assoc professor, 1971-, College of Education, curriculum instruction, currently. **Orgs:** Director, Institute on Multi-Cultural Studies; Assn Afro-American Life & History; Assn for Supr/Curric; Natl Alliance of Black Education; Council on Interracial Books for Children; NAACP; Phi Delta Kappa; Natl Assn for Multicultural Education; Human Rel Bd; consulting editor, publs articles in field. **Honors/Awds:** Kelsey Pharr Award, 1956; Teacher of Year, 1957; Outstanding Churchman, 1965, 1969; Danforth Assn, 1972. **Military Serv:** US Army, 1957-59. **Business Addr:** Curriculum Instruction, Kansas State University, Bluemont Hall, Manhattan, KS 66506-5310.

BOYER, MARCUS AURELIUS
Business executive. **Personal:** Born Jul 10, 1945, Vado, NM; married Doris Ann Young; children: Malcolm. **Educ:** WA Univ, MBA 1972; Univ of NM, BA 1967. **Career:** Small Bus Admin, trainee 1967-68, econ dev asst 1970, loan offcr 1971; Marine Midland Bank, asst ofcr 1973-74, ofcr 1974-76, asst vice prec ofcr 1976-77; Bank of Amer, vice president, sr account officer, 1977-87; Resolution Trust Co, Atlanta, GA, managing agent, oversight cluster mgr, 1990-. **Orgs:** Bd mem Natl Black MBA Assn 1973-76; pres NY Chap Natl Black MBA Assn 1975-76; NAACP; Assn of MBA Exec Fellowship; Consortium for Grad Study in Mgmt 1970. **Honors/Awds:** Black Achiev in Ind Awd YMCA 1975. **Military Serv:** AUS sgt E-5. **Home Addr:** 55 Collinwood Road, Maplewood, NJ 07040.

BOYER, SPENCER H.
Educator. **Personal:** Born Sep 23, 1938, West Chester, PA; married. **Educ:** Howard University, BS, 1960; George Washington University Law School, LlB, 1965; Harvard Law School, LlM, 1966. **Career:** US Dept of Commerce, patenter, examiner, 1964-65; University of Florida, College of Law, visiting professor, 1968; Howard University, School of Law, professor, currently. **Orgs:** Director, Atlanta Legal Education Opportunity Program, summers 1971, 1972; director, Mid-Atlantic Legal Education Opportunity Program, summer 1970; Natl Bar Assn; DC Bar Assn; American Council on Education Committee; Natl Academy of Science Publishers; consult attorney, CHANGE, 1967; com cit, Participation Model Cities, 1967-68; City Wide Natl Capitol Housing Authority, 1967-69; asst dev, HUMP; Assn of American Law Scholls, Committee on Minority Students; American Trial Lawyers Assn. **Honors/Awds:** Outstanding professor award, 1973-74; Paul L Diggs Award; outstanding professor, 1972-73; Student Bar Assn Award, Howard University Law School, 1970-71.

BOYKIN, A. WADE, JR.
Educator. **Personal:** Born Feb 7, 1947, Detroit, MI; married Jacquelyn M Starks; children: A Wade III, Curtis. **Educ:** Hampton Institute, BA (magna cum laude), 1968; University of Michigan, MS, 1970, PhD, 1972. **Career:** Hampton Institute, psychology lab student supervisor, 1967-68; Cornell University, asst to assoc professor, 1972-80; Rockefeller University, adjunct assoc professor, 1976-77; Howard University, Dept of Psychology, professor, 1980-. **Orgs:** Selection panel, Natl Science Foundation, Graduate Fellowship Program; NIMH Psychological Sciences Fellowship, Review Board, Mental Retardation Research Committee, 1983-; dir of research, CULS, University of Michigan, 1971-72; race relations consultant, Mental Hygiene Science Division, Ft Sam Houston, 1971; Natl Assn of Black Psychologists; co-founder, planning committee member, Empirical Research Conference in Black Psychology, 1974-; Journal of Black Psycholgy, assoc editor, 1978-81, editorial bd, 1974-; advisory committe on testing, NAACP, 1981-; American Psychological Assn, 1980-; Omega Psi Phi. **Honors/Awds:** Third District Scholar of Year, Basileus of Year, Omega Psi Phi, 1967-68; fellow, Rockefeller University, 1976-; Alpha Kappa Mu; fellow, Center for Advanced Study in the Behavioral Sciences, 1978-79; Spencer Fellow, Natl Academy of Education, 1978-81; scholar-in-residence, Millersville University, 1985; co-editor, Res Directory of Psychologists, 1979. **Military Serv:** US Army, Medical Service Corps, 1st lt, 1971. **Business Addr:** Professor, Dept of Psychology, Howard University, 2400 Sixth St NW, Washington, DC 20059-0002.

BOYKIN, JOEL S.
Dentist. **Personal:** Born Jul 23, 1926, Birmingham, AL; son of Juliett Watson Boykin and Joel Allen Boykin; divorced; children: Stephan, George, Joels, Jr, Lisa Boykin Bolden, Kristina, Joel Allen. **Educ:** Morehouse Coll, BS 1948; Atlanta Univ, MS 1952; Meharry Med Coll, DDS 1956. **Career:** Dentist; Bullock County School System, teacher 1949-50; St Clair Co School System, 1949; Birmingham Public School System, 1948. **Orgs:** Mem Jefferson Co Dental Study Club, Nat Dental Assn, AL Dental Assn, Amer Dental Assn; past pres AL Dental Soc; soc mem Alpha Phi Alpha; deacon, 16th St Baptist Church. **Military Serv:** AUS sgt 1945-46. **Business Addr:** 2723 29th Ave N, Birmingham, AL 35207.

BOYKIN, WILLIE
Educator. **Personal:** Born Nov 7, 1916, Camden, SC; married Mable Violet Reese. **Educ:** Morris Coll Sumter SC, BA 1942; Atlanta U, MA 1956. **Career:** City of Marion SC, coucilman; Marion School Dist #1, teacher 1951-; Mullins School Dist #2, teacher 1949-50. **Orgs:** Mem NEA 1952-80; mem SCEA 1952-80; pres Marion Co Educ & Assn 1972-74; pares Beta Alpha Sigma Chap Phi Beta Sigma Frat Inc 1975-79. **Military Serv:** AUS s/sgt 1944 Good Conduct Medal & ETO Ribbon.

BOYKINS, ERNEST A.
Educator. **Personal:** Born Oct 5, 1931, Vicksburg, MS; son of Georgia Boykins and Ernest Boykins; married Beverly Malveaux; children: Darryl, Rhea, Constance, Karen. **Educ:** Xavier U, BS 1953; TX So U, MS 1958; Cell Biology Univ of CT, 1960; MI State U, PhD 1964. **Career:** Pine Grove, Hattiesburg, MS, counselor, 1989-; Univ of Southen Mississippi, Hattiesburg, MS, assoc prof, 1981-88; MS Valley State Univ, pres, beginning 1971; Alcorn A&M Coll, div of arts & sci, 1970-71, prof, 1964-71; Michigan State Univ, instructor, 1964; Alcorn A&M Coll, instructor, 1959-61, acting head of Science Dept, 1958-59, instructor, 1954-57. **Orgs:** Mem Am Cncl on Educ 1954-57; Am Inst of Biological Sci; AAAS; Nat Cncl on Higher Edn; MS Conservation Educ Adv Cncl; Assn of SE Biologist; AmAssn for Higher Edn; mem Sigma Xi Scientific Hnr Soc; Nat Collegiate Hnrs Cncl; Phi Delta Kappa; Beta Kappa Chi; Omega Psi Phi; Alpha Kappa Mu; has had consult positions & com assignments on numerous com & Commns including MS Select Com for Higher Educ 1973; Spl Health Career Oppor Prog Cons; Delta Cncl BSA exec bd 1973; Greenwood-Leflore Co C of & C 1974; Leflore Co United Givers Inc bd Mem 1974; Post secondary Educ Bd 1974.

BOYLAND, DORIAN SCOTT
Automobile dealer. **Personal:** Born Jan 6, 1955, Chicago, IL; son of Alice Jones and William Boyland; married Denise A Wells Boyland, Apr 5, 1990; children: Shannon, Richard, Adriane. **Educ:** Univ of Wisconsin, Oshkosh, WI, BA, business, 1976. **Career:** Pittsburgh Pirates, professional baseball player, 1976-83; Ron Tonkin-Dodge, Gladstone, OR, owner/general mgr, 1985-86; Gresham Dodge Inc, Gresham OR, president/general mgr, 1986-; Boyland Preperties, pres, 1995-; Boyland Insurance Group, pres, 1996-; Boyland Auto Group, Inc, pres, 1996-. **Orgs:** Chairman, Performance 20 Groups, 1988-; board member, United Negro College Fund, 1990-, Portland Urban League, 1989-, Oregon Arbitration Board, 1990-; Alpha Phi Alpha Fraternity Inc, 1974; Dodge Denter Council. **Honors/Awds:** Nation's Largest Black Businesses, Black Enterprise, 1989-90; MLK Business Leadership Award, State of Oregon, 1990; Urban League Award, Portland Urban League, 1990; Gold Medal Award, Special Olympics, 1989-90; Hall of Fame, Univ of Wisconsin, 1987; Top 100 Black Business Award, Black Enterprise, 1988-90; Top 100 Black Business Awards Black Enterprise, 1988-92. **Special Achievements:** Company is ranked #87 on Black Enterprise magazine's 1997 list of Top 100 Black businesses. **Business Addr:** President, Gresham Dodge Inc, 855 NE Burnside, Gresham, OR 97030.

BOYLE, JIM
Basketball coach. **Career:** Widener Univ, coach, 1971; St Joseph Univ, assistant coach, 1973-81, head coach, 1981-90. **Honors/Awds:** Coach of the Year, Atlantic 10 Conference, 1986.

BOYNTON, ASA TERRELL, SR.
Educational administrator. **Personal:** Born May 20, 1945, Griffin, GA; son of Estell and Willie; married Evelyn Josephine Jordan; children: Asa Terrell Jr, Aaron Vernard, Antoine Debue. **Educ:** Fort Valley State Coll, BS Bus Admin 1967; Univ of GA, MA Public Admin 1973. **Career:** Public Safety Div, St Petersburg, chief community relations 1973; Public Safety Div, Univ of Georgia, assoc dir, 1978, dir of public safety. **Orgs:** Past pres, Assoc of Campus Law Enforcement Admin, 1976; pres, Alpha Phi Alpha Fraternity, Eta Iota Lambda, 1977; mem, Athens Rotary Club, 1983-; past pres, Athens Breakfast Optimist Club, 1984. **Honors/Awds:** Man of the Year, Alpha Phi Alpha, Eta Iota Lambda Chap, 1978; Mem of the Year, Georgia Assn of Campus Law Enforcement Admin, 1984. **Military Serv:** AUS sgt, 2 years; Soldier of the Month, Dec 1968. **Home Addr:** 470 Millstone Circle, Athens, GA 30605. **Business Addr:** Dir of Public Safety, University of Georgia, Public Safety Division, Athens, GA 30602.

BOZE, U. LAWRENCE
Association executive. **Career:** National Bar Assoc, pres, currently. **Business Addr:** President, National Bar Association, 1225 11th St, NW, Washington, DC 20001, (202)842-3900.

BOZEMAN, BRUCE L.
Attorney. **Personal:** Born Jan 21, 1944, Philadelphia, PA; son of Hammie Winston Bozeman and Herman H Bozeman; married Patricia Johnson; children: Herman, Leslie, Patrick, Holly. **Educ:** VA Union Univ, BA 1965; Howard Univ School of Law, JD 1968; NY Univ School of Law, LLM 1975. **Career:** Maxwell House Div GFC, asst counsel 1969-71, Birds Eye div couns 1971-73, beverage & breakfast foods div couns 1973-78, dir consumer affairs, asst gen couns, 1978-81; Norton Simon Inc, asst gen counsel 1981-83; private practice, atty; Bozeman & Trott, LLP, partner; Bruce L Bozeman, PC, president, Westchester Fina ncial Group, Ltd, president. **Orgs:** Mem Natl Bar Assn, Amer Bar Assn, NY Bar Assn, Westchester Cty Bar Assn, Assn of Black Lawyers of Westchester Cty, Bar of DC 1968, NY 1969, US Ct of Appeals 1969, US Supreme Ct 1978; former mem Grievance Comm Westchester Cty Bar Assn; chmn Black Dems of Westchester Cty; adjunct prof of law: CUNY Law School at Queens College, Pace University, School of Law, Iona College. **Business Addr:** Attorney, 6 Gramatan Ave, Mount Vernon, NY 10550.

BOZEMAN, MAGGIE SIMMONS
Educator. **Personal:** Born Jul 24, 1929, Dancy, AL; married Clarence Eric. **Educ:** AL St Univ Montgomery, BS 1951; IA St U, M 1953. **Career:** Tuskegee Inst AL, instructor, 1966; admin supvr headstart, 1965; Pickens County Bd of Educ, prin, 1950, Carrollton AL, elementary teacher, 1947. **Orgs:** Resolution Com AL Educ Assn AEA 1947-80; conv com /screening com AL Educ Assn 1947-80; steering com AKA Sor IWY; pres NAACP Aliceville Carrollton Br 1968-80; AL Dem conf coord Polit Black Caucus of AL ADC 1960-80. **Honors/Awds:** Relgional Awd NAACP Atlanta 1968 75; Martin Luther King Jr Dream Awd AL Polit Black Caucus Montgomery ADC 1980; Minority People Cncl Epes AL 1980.

BRABSON, HOWARD V.
Educator. **Personal:** Born Sep 18, 1925, Knoxville, TN; son of Fannie R Burrough Brabson and Alfred L Jones, Jr; married Rudiene Houston, Sep 13, 1952 (divorced). **Educ:** Coll of Ozarks, BS 1956; Catholic Univ, Nath Catholic School of Social Serv, MSW 1962, DSW 1975. **Career:** Cedar Knoll School, asst supt 1958-62; Boys Industrial School Lancaster, admin vocational ed 1962-63; OH Youth Comm, dep commissioner 1963-65; VISTA Training Ctr, Univ of MD, asst proj dir 1965-66; VISTA E Eastern Region Washington DC, field supvr 1966-67; Great Lakes Region VISTA, prog mgr 1967-69; Univ of MI, prof of social work 1969-91, prof emeritus, 1991-. **Orgs:** Community org consultant Neighborhood Groups 1965-; mem NABSW 1968-; chmn of bd Prog Mgmt & Devel Inc 1969-; Org MI Assoc BSW 1970; vice pres of OIC bd ACSW; VISTA training consultant Control Syst Rsch 1971-73; mem NABSW natl conf chmn 1973-74, vice pres 1974-76, pres 1978-82; pres emeritius 1982-. **Honors/Awds:** Catholic Univ Fellow DSW 1970-71; Humanitarian Awd Willow Run Adversary Club 1977; Certificate of Appreciation for Outstanding Serv Univ of Toledo; Certificate of Appreciation NC ABSW 1979; Outstanding Comm Serv Awd MI ABSW 1979; Comm Serv Awd KY ABSW 1980; Distinguished Serv Awd Albany NY ABSW 1980; United Fund Special Awd; Faculty Recognition Awd Univ of MI 1981; author Job Satisfaction, Job Stress & Coping Among African-Amer Human Service Workers 1989. **Military Serv:** AUS capt 1946-58; Commendation Ribbon. **Business Addr:** Professor Emeritus of Social Work, Univ of Michigan, 1065 Frieze Bldg, Rm 4097, Ann Arbor, MI 48109.

BRACEY, HENRY J.
Educator. **Personal:** Born Jan 31, 1949, Grand Rapids, MI; son of Sheba M Davis Bracey and Joe Bracey; married; children: Anton J, Candice G, Kwando A, Lisa K. **Educ:** Western MI Univ, BS 1971; Univ of SC, MEd 1981. **Career:** SC Personnel and Guidance Assoc, mem exec council 1982; SC Sch Counselors Assoc, mem publicity comm 1982; SC Assoc of Non-White Concerns, pres and bdmem 1982; Southeastern Assoc of Educ Oppor Prog, personnel mgr 1983; Midlands Tech Coll, counselor. **Orgs:** Public relations dir Ms Black Columbia Pageant 1980-82; bd mem Columbia Youth Council 1982-84; bd mem Brothers and Sisters 1984-86; vice pres Coll Place Comm Council 1985-87; mem SC Tech Educ Assoc 1986-87; mem

Southern Regional Council on Black Amer Affairs 1986-87; mem Omega Psi Phi; pres Heritage Comm Productions; student involvement coord Southern Regional Cncl on Black Amer Affairs Conf 1986; pres, Kuumba Circle 1988; pres, Eau Claire Comm Council; Eau Claire Development Corp; Ujamaa A Concern Group of Men; NAACP; Ascac Assn for the study of Classical African Civilizations; South Carolina Conference, Shalom Zone Ministries; pres, mem, Francis Burns United Methodist Church; staff council pres, Midlands Technical College; advisory bd, Columbia Citizens; PTA pres, Alcorn Middle Sch, CA Johnson HS. **Honors/Awds:** Published numerous articles on Cross-Cultural Counseling 1979-; Outstanding Young Men of Amer 1980; Outstanding Service Awd Ms Black Columbia Pageant 1980-82; designed and published Cross-Cultural Counseling Model 1980; Citizen of the Week (WOIC) 1981; Recognition Awd South Carolina Personnel and Guidance Assoc; Columbia Citizens Advisory Committee, Comm Development Appreciation Award. **Home Addr:** 5016 Colonial Dr, Columbia, SC 29203. **Business Addr:** Counselor, Midland Tech College, PO Box 2408, Columbia, SC 29202.

BRACEY, JOHN HENRY, JR.
Educator. **Personal:** Born Jul 17, 1941, Chicago, IL; son of Helen Harris Bracey; married Ingrid Babb, Dec 19, 1975; children: Kali, Bryan, John Peter. **Educ:** Howard Univ, attended; Roosevelt Univ, BA 1964; Northwestern Univ, NDEA Fellow ABD 1969. **Career:** Northeastern IL State Coll, lecturer 1969; Northern IL Univ, lecturer, hist 1969-71; Univ of Rochester, asst prof hist 1971-72; Univ of MA, chmn Afro-Amer studies 1974-79; Univ of MA, assoc prof Afro-Amer studies 1972-. **Orgs:** Assn for the Study of Afro-American Life & History; Org of American Historians, life member, nominating comm, 1978-79; Phi Alpha Theta; Social Sciene History Association. **Special Achievements:** Published 11 books, numerous articles, reviews on various aspects of the history & culture of Afro-Americans. **Business Addr:** Associate Professor, Univ of Massachusetts, WEB Du Bois Dept Afro-American Studies, Amherst, MA 01002.

BRACEY, WILLIAM RUBIN
Chief of patrol. **Personal:** Born May 11, 1920, Brooklyn, NY; married Louise Alleyne; children: Frances Kirton, William Jr, Gary. **Educ:** Delehanty Inst, 1962; John Jay Coll of Criminal Just, 1966; Military Police Sch, compl Civil Disturbances Orientation Course 1973. **Career:** New York City Police Dept, asst chief 1977-79, dep chief 1973-77, inspector 1973, dep inspector 1972-73, capt 1970-72, lt 1959-70, sgt 195459, Patrolman 1945-54. **Orgs:** Past pres Guardians Assn of NY Police Dept; sec Nat Organ of Black Law Enforcement Exec; mem Intl Assn of Chiefs of Police; mem Captains Endowment Assn New York City Police Dept; mem St George Assn of New York City Police Dept. **Honors/Awds:** Holder of 8 Police Dept Recognitions Awds for Otstndng Police Action in Field; recipient Unit Citation 1972; ltr of commendation from Police Comm New York City for outstanding contribution to success of Operation Sail & Bicent Celebration 1976. **Military Serv:** AUS corpl 1943-45. **Business Addr:** 1 Police Plaza, New York, NY 10007.

BRACEY, WILLIE EARL
Attorney, educational administrator. **Personal:** Born Dec 21, 1950, Jackson, MS; son of Alvaretta Bracey and Dudley Bracey; married Dianne Fullenwilder, Aug 15, 1987. **Educ:** Wright Jr Coll, AA 1970; Mt Senario Coll, BS 1973; Eastern IL Univ, MS 1976; Southern IL Univ, JD 1979. **Career:** Southern IL Univ, law clerk 1978-79; Southern IL Univ Ctr for Basic Skill, instr 1977-78; Southern IL Univ Law School, rsch asst 1977-78; Notre Dame Law School, teaching asst 1977; Western IL Univ, dir, student legal serv, 1979-, asst vice pres for student affairs support servs; adj prof, college student personnel grad program, 1987-. **Orgs:** Mem NAACP, 1979-, ATLA 1979-, ABA 1979-, IBA 1979-, McDonough City Bar Assn 1979-, Natl Assn of Student Personnel Admin 1987-; faculty mem Blue Key Honor Soc; Housing Commissoner, McDonough County Housing Authority, appointment ends 1998. **Business Addr:** Assistant Vice President, Western Illinois Univ, One University Circle, Macomb, IL 61455.

BRACKENS, TONY
Professional football player. **Personal:** Born Dec 26, 1974, Fairfield, TX. **Educ:** Univ of Texas, attended. **Career:** Jacksonville Jaguars, defensive end, 1996-. **Business Addr:** Professional Football Player, Jacksonville Jaguars, One Stadium Place, Jacksonville, FL 32202, (904)633-6000.

BRACY, URSULA J.
Public health nurse (retired). **Personal:** Born in Lake Charles, LA; daughter of Evelyn Simpson Johnson and John J Johnson; married Jackson Bracy (deceased). **Educ:** St Louis Univ, BS 1951; So Univ, 1928. **Career:** VNA of Greater St Louis, supvr 1951-73, staff nurse 1934-51; St Louis Chapter ARC; instr 1934. **Orgs:** Mem ANA 1946-; charter mem Nat League for Nursing 1952-; mem St Louis Univ Nursing Alumni 1951-; mem Lane Tabernacle CME Ch 1937; mem bd Vis Nurses Assn of Greater St Louis 1974-83; mem bd dir Annie Malone Childrens Home 1955-80; mem Sigma Theta Tau Natl Honor Soc of Nursing; attended several sessions Intl Council Of Nurses Congress various parts of world; rep Bi-state Chap ARC Melbourne Australia 1961; delegate, World Methodist Conf, Nairobi, Kenya, July 1986. **Honors/Awds:** Cited for 25 yrs Vol Serv; Bi-state Chapters ARC 1976; Plaque for 25 Yrs Dist Serv Annie Malone Childrens Home 1978; mem, Annie Malone Childrens Home Bd, 1955-80; mem, Sigma Theta Tau Intl Soc of Nursing Scholarship; life mem, bd of dir of The VNA of greater St Louis; Woman of Achievement Award, St Louis Globe Dem Newspaper, 1978; Making a Difference Award, Annie Malone Children's Home, 1990; Attended International Council of Nurses Congress, Seoul, Korea, June 1989. **Special Achievements:** First African American to be named an honorary life mem of the Visiting Nurses Assn Board of Directors. **Home Addr:** 4120 W Belle Pl, St Louis, MO 63108.

BRADBERRY, RICHARD PAUL
Library director. **Personal:** Born Dec 6, 1951, Florala, AL; son of Nettie Ruth Hightower Bradberry and Sam Bradberry. **Educ:** Alabama State University, Montgomery, AL, BS, 1973; Atlanta University, Atlanta, GA, MSLS, 1974; University of Michigan, Ann Arbor, MI, PhD, 1988. **Career:** Auburn University, Auburn, AL, humanities librarian, 1974-76; Langston University, Langston, OK, director/librarian/chair librarian science dept, 1976-83; Lake Erie College, Painesville, OH, director of the library, 1983-84; University of Connecticut, W Hartford, CT, director of libraries, 1984-89; Delaware State College, Dover, DE, director of college libraries, 1989-. **Orgs:** Member, American Library Association, 1984-; member, Association for Library& Information Science Education, 1988-; member, Delaware Library Association, 1990-; member, American Association for Higher Education, 1990-; treasurer, 1890 Land-Grant Library Directors Assn, 1989-. **Honors/Awds:** Education Professions Development Act Grant, US Government, 1973; Oklahoma State Regents Doctoral Study Grant, State of Oklahoma, 1980, 1981; Title II-B Fellowship, University of Michigan, 1980, 1981. **Home Addr:** 1300 S Farmview Dr H-31, Dover, DE 19901. **Business Addr:** Diector of College Libraries, William C Jason Library-Learning Center, Delaware State College, 1200 N DuPont Highway, Dover, DE 19901.

BRADDOCK, CAROL T.
Business executive. **Personal:** Born Sep 7, 1942, Hamilton, OH; daughter of Rev and Mrs Carlace A Tipton; married Robert L; children: Ryan Lawrence, Lauren Patricia-Tipton. **Educ:** Univ of Cincinnati, BA 1965, MA 1976; IN U, grad key 1980. **Career:** Banking-financial consultant, currently; Fed Home Loan Bank of Cincinnati, vice pres comm investment officer 1978-85, asst vice pres 1978, exec asst 1975; Fed Home Bank Bd, urban prog Coord 1973; Taft Broadcasting, prod coord 1972; McAlpins Dept Store , buyer 1969; Vogue Care Coll, instr 1971; Coll of Mt St Joseph, lectr 1973; Neighborhood Reinvestment Corp, consult 1974. **Orgs:** Trustee, National Trust for Historic Preservation ; Junior League Sustainee; Founder & past pres Womens Alliance 1966; exec comm mem WCET-TV Pub TV 1972-79; pres Minority Bus Devel Coalition 1980; Queen City Beauty, Cincinnati Enquirer 1973. **Honors/Awds:** Otstndng Serv Awd Urban Reinvestment Task Force 1975; Black Achievers Awd YMCA 1978; Outstanding Career Woman 1983.

BRADDOCK, MARILYN EUGENIA
Educator, dentist, prosthodontist. **Personal:** Born Apr 25, 1955, Washington, DC; daughter of Rita H Glover-Braddock and Ernest L Braddock. **Educ:** Marquette Univ, BS 1977; Meharry Medical Coll, DDS 1982; University of North Carolina at Chapel Hill, prosthetic denistry and research fellow, 1989-92; UNC-CH, MS, Oral Biology Immunology, 1993. **Career:** Cook County Hospital, GPR, 1982-83; US Navy Dental Corps, 1983-86; private practice, dentist, 1986-89; Meharry Medical College, School of Dentistry, Dept of Prosthodontics, asst professor, 1992-95; COR US Navy Dental Corps, USS John F Kennedy (CV-67), 1995-. **Orgs:** Delta Sigma Theta Sor Inc; American Dental Assn; Federal Services Assn, American College of Prosthodontics. **Honors/Awds:** Periodontology Fellowship US Navy Dental Corps 1985-86; National Institutes of Health National Service Fellowship Award 1991-92. **Military Serv:** US Navy, 1983-86, 1995-, Navy Recruiting Command, Campus Liason Officer, Nashville TN. **Business Addr:** CDR, 455 John F Kennedy (CV-67), Dental Department, FPO-AA, Nashville, TN 34095-2800.

BRADEN, EVERETTE ARNOLD
Judge. **Personal:** Born Nov 3, 1932, Chicago, IL; son of Bernice Braden and Zedrick Braden; married Mary Jeanette Hemphill; children: Marilynne. **Educ:** Herzl Jr Coll, 1952; Northwestern Univ, BS 1954; John Marshall Law School, LLB 1961, JD 1969. **Career:** Cook Cty Dept Public Aid, caseworker 1961-66, property & ins consult 1966-69; Cook Cty Publ Defender Office, trial attny 1969-76, suprvising trial attny 1976-77; Circuit Ct of Cook Cty, assoc judge 1977-78; circuit judge, 1978-94; Illinois Appellate Court, justice, 1994-96, circuit judge, 1996-. **Orgs:** Mem Phi Alpha Delta Law, Natl Bar Assoc, IL State Bar Assoc, Chicago Bar Assoc, Meth Bar Assoc; past board of directors IL Judges Assoc; mem Kappa Alpha Psi; past president, John Marshall Law School Alumni Assoc; charter fellow The IL Bar Found. **Honors/Awds:** Golden Key Awd S Shore Valley Comm Assoc; We Can Inc Awd; Black Gavel Awd for Outstanding Judge Black Lawyers Network 1984; Awd of Merit IL Judges Assoc; Disting Serv Awd John Marshall Law School Alumni Assoc, IL Judicial Council; Illinois Judicial Council, Kenneth E Wilson Award. **Military Serv:** US Army, sp-4, 1955-58; Distinguished Service Award. **Business Addr:** Circuit Judge, Richard J. Daley Center, Chicago, IL 60602.

BRADEN, HENRY E., IV
Attorney. **Personal:** Born Aug 24, 1944, New Orleans, LA; married Michele Bordenave; children: Heidi E, Remi A, Henry E V. **Educ:** Le Moyne Coll, BS 1965; Loyola Univ Sch of Law, JD 1975. **Career:** New Orleans Hometown Plan Urban League of New Orleans, author & dir 1974; Labor Educ & Advancement Prog, Total Community Action Inc, dir On-the-Job Training & Prog; Neighborhood Youth Corps Out of Sch Prog TCA Inc, dir 1966; LA Div of Employment Security, coord Huricane Betsy Disaster Relief Proj 1965; City ofNew Orleans, past dir Ofc of Manpower & Economic Devel ; Murray, Murray, Ellis & Braden, atty private practice. **Orgs:** Dem Nat Committeeman St of LA; Mem exec com Dem Natl Com Mem Met Area Com; LA Manpower Adv Com; columnist Op-ed; Page New Orleans States; exec vice pres Community Orgn for Urban Politics; New Orleans Industrial Devel Bd one of 3 blacks on LA Dem State Central Com; former pres St Augustines HS Alumni Assn; dir Building Dr St Augustines HS. **Home Addr:** 2453 Esplanade Ave, New Orleans, LA 70119.

BRADFIELD, CLARENCE MCKINLEY
Attorney. **Personal:** Born Jul 5, 1942, Vaughns, MS; married Linda; children: Clark, Carmen. **Educ:** Wayne State Univ, BS 1964; Detroit Coll of Law, JD 1970. **Career:** Dept of Justice, asst US atty 1971-72; Clarence M Bradfield PC, private practice. **Orgs:** Wolverine Bar Assoc 1970-; vice pres Northwest Deroit Optimist Club. **Business Addr:** Attorney, 2100 Cadillac Tower, Detroit, MI 48226.

BRADFORD, ARCHIE J.
Educator, administrator (retired). **Personal:** Born Feb 6, 1931, Ripley, TN; son of Mildred Bradford and Archie Bradford; married Mariejo Harris; children: Kyle, Kevin. **Educ:** So IL U, BA 1960; Ball St U, MA Guidance & Counseling 1965; Univ of Notre Dame completed course work Pub Sch Adm 1974; St Marys Coll, internship business 1966. **Career:** Univ of Notre Dame, dir of Upward Bound; South Bend Schools, elementary school counselor, 1961-69; Hodges Park Elementary School, prin, 1959-60; South Bend Community Schools, dir of Human Resources, 1975-80, principal, 1980-. **Orgs:** Mem Am Personnel & Guidance Assn 1962-; Am Sch Counselors Assn 1962-61; Am Assn of Non-white Concerns 1971-; mem Mayors Commn on Educ 1972-74; St Joseph Co Urban Coalition Bd 1972-; vice pres Urban Coalition 1974-; chmn Coalition Educ Task Force 1972-; Evaluation & Allocation Div of United Way 1974-; Rotary Club. **Honors/Awds:** Reclip Kappa Alpha Psi Fidelity Awd; Outstanding Service Award, MAAEOPP; O C Carmichael Award, Boy's Club.. **Military Serv:** AUS corpl 1950-53; USAC A1c 1953-57.

BRADFORD, ARVINE M.
Educator. **Personal:** Born Feb 20, 1915, Harriman, TN; married. **Educ:** Univ of Pittsburgh, AB 1941; Fisk U, MA 1943; Harvard U, pub hlth cert 1944; Howard U;; MD 1949. **Career:** Howard Univ, assoc prof; Georgetown Univ, Certified Am Coll OB-GYN, assoc prof 1964; private practice 1959-74. **Orgs:** Mem Am Coll OB-GYN 1965; Amm Med Assn; Nat Med & Assn; Chi Delta Mu; NAACP; Urban League; Mayors Com on Ageing; mem DC Gen Hosp adv com; mem Alpha Phi Alpha Frat Sig Skin Club. **Business Addr:** 1718 7 St NW, Washington, DC 20001.

BRADFORD, CHARLES EDWARD
Clergyman. **Personal:** Born Jul 12, 1925, Washington, DC; married Ethel Lee McKenzie; children: Sharon Louise Lewis, Charles Edward Jr, Dwight Lyman. **Educ:** Oakwood Coll Huntsville AL, BA 1946; Andrews U, Berrien Springs MI;; DD 1978. **Career:** NA GenConf of Seventh-Day Adventists;; Vice Pres 1979-, asso sec 1970-79; Lake Region Conf of Seventh-day Adventists pres 1961-70; LA/TX/MON/NY, Pastor 1945-61. **Orgs:** Trustee Oakwood Coll/Andrews Univ 1961; trustee Loma Linda Univ 1979. **Business Addr:** 6840 Eastern Ave NW, Washington, DC 20012.

BRADFORD, EQUILLA FORREST
Educational administrator. **Personal:** Born Apr 11, 1931, Birmingham, AL; married William Lewis. **Educ:** Wayne State UDetroit, BS 1954, M 1963; MI State Univ East Lansing, PhD 1972. **Career:** Westwood Community School Dist, supt of schools, 1979-, exec asst supt, 1974-77, asst supt personnel, 1971-74; McNair Elementary School, Westwood School Dist, prin, 1968-71; McNair & Daly Elementary Schools, Westwood School Dist, art teacher, 1966-68, teacher, 1955-66; Michigan Assn for Individually Guided Educ, Consult, 1970-; Eastern MI Univ, instructor/lecturer, 1979-; Wayne State Univ Detroit, consultant, 1979-. **Orgs:** Mem Alpha Kappa Alpha Sor Inc 1954-; mem Am Assn for Sch Adm 1968-; mem Detroit Econ Club 1979-; mem St Paul AME Ch Educator of Yr, Delta Sigma Theta Sor 1979. **Honors/Awds:** Dist educator Nat Sor of Phi Delta Kappa Inc 1980 , Woman of Year; Alpha Kappa Alpha Sor Inc Inc Eta Iota Omega & Chap 1980. **Business Addr:** 25913 Annapolis, Inkster, MI 48141.

BRADFORD, GARY C.
Copy editor. **Personal:** Born May 4, 1956, Pittsburgh, PA; son of Glenrose Beatrice Fields Bradford and Frank M Bradford. **Educ:** Univ of Pittsburgh, Pittsburgh, PA, BA, writing, 1979; Temple University, Philadelphia, PA, MA, journalism, 1983. **Career:** WHCR-FM, New York City, NY, volunteer host/producer, 1988-89; Pittsburgh Press, Pittsburgh, PA, reporter, 1979-81; Philadelphia Daily News, Philadelphia, PA, copy editing intern, 1982; In Pittsburgh, Pittsburgh, PA, associate editor, 1985; New York Times, New York, NY, copy editor-metropolitan desk, 1985-. **Orgs:** Member, New York Association of Black Journalists, 1986-; member, 100 Black Men, 1991-; member, Duke Ellington Society, 1990-. **Honors/Awds:** Publisher's Award Headline Writing, New York Times, 1987, 1988. **Business Addr:** Copy Editor, Metropolitan News, New York Times, 229 W 43rd St, 3rd Floor, New York, NY 10036.

BRADFORD, JAMES EDWARD
Accountant. **Personal:** Born Jun 27, 1943, Jonesboro, LA; married Mae Lean Calahan; children: Roderick, Berkita, D'Andra. **Educ:** Grambling State Univ, BS 1965; Wayne State Univ, summer 1966. **Career:** Sabine Parish School Bd, teacher 1965-66; Bienville Parish School Bd, teacher 1966-70; Continental Group, accountant 1970-76, super; Independent ConsultantsInc, pres 1980-85; Bradco Sales, pres 1984-85; Stone Container Corp, super of accounting. **Orgs:** Bd chmn Pine Belt CAA 1979-85; bd chmn, Jackson Council on Aging 1980-85; bd mem North Delta Regional Planning Comm 1983-85. **Honors/Awds:** Outstanding Young Men of America Jaycees 1975; Outstanding Blacks in LA 1982. **Home Addr:** 709 Leon Drive, Jonesboro, LA 71251.

BRADFORD, MARTINA LEWIS
Telecommunications executive. **Personal:** Born Sep 14, 1952, Washington, DC; daughter of Alma Ashton and Martin Lewis; married William Bradford, Dec 24, 1982; children: Sydney. **Educ:** Amer Univ, BA, 1973; Duke Univ, JD, 1975. **Career:** Interstate Commerce Div Finance Div, Washington, DC, atty, 1976-78; Comm on Appropriations, US House of Representatives, Washington, DC, counsel, 1978-81; Interstate Commerce Comm, Washington, DC, chief of staff to vice chmn, 1981-83; AT&T Legal Dept, New York, NY, atty, 1983-85; AT&T Corp Public Affairs, Washington, DC, atty, 1985-88; AT&T External Affairs, New York, NY, vice pres, 1988-; corporate legal intern, Southern Railways, Inc, 1974-; adjunct prof, Amer Univ School of Law, 1982-. **Orgs:** Minority counsel, US House of Representatives, 1978-79, minority counsel, US Senate, 1979-80; founding vice pres, Women's Transportation Seminar, 1978; mem, Dist of Columbia Bar, 1976, Maryland Bar, 1983-, Women's Bar Assn, 1989; bd mem, INROADS Inc, 1989. **Honors/Awds:** Deans List, Amer Univ, 1971-73; Scholastic Honorary, Economics, Amer Univ, 1973. **Business Addr:** VP, Federal Govt Affairs, AT&T, 32 Avenue of the Americas, Room 2604, New York, NY 10013.

BRADFORD, STEVE
Councilman. **Career:** Congresswoman Juanita Millender-McDonald's Office, district dir; Gardena City Council, 1997-. **Special Achievements:** First African American Council member in Gardena, CA's history; Youngest Council member to serve in city's history.

BRADFORD-EATON, ZEE
Advertising executive. **Personal:** Born Oct 10, 1953, Atlanta, GA; daughter of Betty Anthony Davis Harden and William Henry Davis; married Maynard Eaton, Dec 28, 1991; children: Quentin Eugene Bradford Jr, Qiana Yvonne Bradford. **Educ:** Morris Brown Coll, 1971-75. **Career:** QZ Enterprises Inc, public relations dir 1979-83; First Class Inc, public relations dir 1983-84, exec vice pres 1984-. **Orgs:** 1st Black Pres Shaker Welcome Wagon 1980-81; steering comm Mayor's Task Force on Educ 1984-; bd member Amer Diabetes Assn 1984-; steering comm Black Public Relations Soc 1984-; min affairs comm Public Relations Soc of Amer 1985-86; pr comm Atlanta Assoc of Black Journalists 1985-86; adv bd Martin Luther King Jr Center for Social Change 1985-86; prog dir Jack & Jill of America 1985-86; activities chmn Girl Scouts of Amer 1985-87; youth activities chmn Providence Baptist Church 1985-;prog dir Collier Heights Elem School, PTA, Grade Parent 1985-89; publicity rel comm Amer Heart Assoc 1986-87; commiss A Reginald Eaves Blue Ribbon Task Force on Strenghthening the Black Amer Family 1986-87; econ devel task force Natl Conf of Black Mayors 1986-; mem UNCF, Natl Forum of Public Admins 1986-87;c United Way's Media Devel, 1987; chmn SME 1987; comm YWCA Salute to Women of Achievement, 1987; Journalist, Jack & Jill of America, Atlanta Chapter, 1990-92; vice president, Inman Middle School PTA, 1991-92; Fulton County Roundtable on Children, comissioner, Nancy Boxill, 1990- ; Atlantic Historical Society, 1990-; Registered Lobbyist in the State of Georgia, 1989-; executive board member, Leadership Atlanta, 1989-92; board member, Atlanta Chapter of Ronald McDonald Children's Charities, 1989-; public relations committee chairman, Coalition of 100 Black Women of Atlanta, 1990-; board member, Charlee, 1990-. **Honors/Awds:** Congressional Tribute US Congress 1981; Civic Awd United Way 1981; council resolution Cleveland City Council 1981; Cert of Merit Atlanta Assn of Black Journalists 1984; Collier Heights PTA 1985,86; Girl Scouts of Amer 1986; Leadership Atlanta 1986-87; NFL/AFL-CIO Community Serv Awd; Americans Best & Brightest Business & Professional Men & Women, Dollars & Sense Magazine, 1991; One of Ten Outstanding Atlantans, Outstanding Atlantans Inc, 1989; steeting committee, Nelson Mandela's First Atlanta Visit, 1990.

BRADLEY, ANDREW THOMAS, SR.
Counselor. **Personal:** Born Jan 4, 1948, Johnstown, PA; married Annice Bernetta Edwards; children: Andrew T Jr, Elizabeth Lorine, James Christopher. **Educ:** Shaw Univ Raleigh, BA (Magna Cum Laude) 1975; Univ of DC, MA 1982. **Career:** Seacap Inc, mainstream suprv 1968-69; Neuse-Trent Manpower Devel Corp, instr, counselor 1970-72; Craven Comm Coll, instr, counselor 1972-75; Neuse River Council of Govts, reg admin 1975-77; Natl Ctr on Black Aged Inc, dir, crises rsch 1977-81; Bradley Assoc, consult 1981-84; Family & Children Svcs, psychotherapist; Harrisburg Area Comm Coll, counselor acad found. **Orgs:** Trainer Spec Training on Abuse & Neglect of Children & Adults; consult Mgmt Awareness Training; presentor Needs & Problems of the Minority Aged, Practical Approcahes to Providing Social & Health Serv to the Rural Elderly; pastoral counseling Faith Temple First Born Church; teahing, suprv Crisis Intervention Counseling; chairperson Crime Prevention Task Force; mem Natl Assoc of Victim Witness Asst, Natl Assoc of Black Soc Workers, Natl Ctr & Caucus on Black Aged Inc, Natl Council on Aging, Amer Mental Health Counselors Assoc, Amer Assoc for Counseling & Devel, Harrisburg Area Hospice; bonds comm Harrisburg Human Relations Commiss; bd mem WIZZ Calbe FM 1005 Radio. **Honors/Awds:** Outstanding Young Man in Amer Natl Jaycees; Graduate Scholarship Inst of Geontology Univ of the Dist of Columbia. **Military Serv:** USAR sp4 6 yrs. **Home Addr:** 2152 N Sixth St, Harrisburg, PA 17110. **Business Addr:** Counselor, Milton Hershey School, PO Box 830, Hershey, PA 17033-0830.

BRADLEY, DAVID HENRY, JR.
Educator, writer. **Personal:** Born Sep 7, 1950, Bedford, PA; son of Harriette Jackson Bradley and Rev David Bradley (deceased). **Educ:** Univ of PA, BA 1972; Univ London, MA 1974. **Career:** JB Lippincott Co, asst editor 1974-76; Univ of PA, visiting lecturer 1975-76; Temple Univ, visiting lecturer 1976-77, asst prof 1977-82, assoc prof 1982-89, prof 1989-96; Colgate Prof of Humanities, 1988; Dist Found Prof of Literature, Univ of N Carolina, Wilmington; MIT, visiting prof 1989. **Orgs:** Member, Writers Guild of America, East; Author's Guild; PEN. **Honors/Awds:** PEN/Faulkner Award, 1982; Amer Book Award nominee, 1983; Acad Award Amer Inst of Arts and Letters, 1992; Guggenheim Fellowship, 1989; NEA Fellowship, 1991; articles in Esquire, New York Times, Redbook, The Southern Review, Transition; author of novels, South Street, 1975, The Chaneysville Incident, 1981. **Business Addr:** PO Box 12681, La Jolla, CA 92039.

BRADLEY, EDWARD R.
Television journalist. **Personal:** Born Jan 22, 1941, Philadelphia, PA; son of Gladys Bradley and Edward R Bradley; married 1964 (divorced). **Educ:** Cheyney State College, BS, education, 1964. **Career:** Elementary school teacher, 1964; WDAS, newscaster, 1963-67; WCBS Radio, journalist, 1967-71; CBS, stringer in Paris, France, 1971, correspondent in Indochina, 1972-74, 1975, White House correspondent, 1974-78, CBS Sunday Night News, anchor, 1976-81, CBS Reports, principal correspondent, 1978-81, 60 Minutes, correspondent, 1981-, Street Stories, host, 1992-. **Honors/Awds:** WDAS-FM, Distinguished Commentator Award, New York Chapter, Natl Assn of Media Women, 1975; Assn of Black Journalists Award, 1977; George Polk Journalism Award, 1980; Emmy Awards for broadcast journalism, three in 1979, one for ''Blacks in America,'' one for ''The Boat People,'' two in 1983, one for ''Lena,'' with 60 Minutes Team, 1985, 1986; Alfred I duPont-Columbia University Award for broadcast journalism, ''Blacks in America: With All Deliberate Speed,'' 1978, 1980; George Foster Peabody Broadcasting Award, 1979; NCAA Anniversary Award, 1989; Emmy for ''Made in China'' on 60 Minutes, 1992; Nation Press Foundation, Sol Taischoff Award, 1993; Robert F Kennedy Journalism Award Grand Prize and Television First Prize, 1996. **Business Addr:** Correspondent, 60 Minutes, CBS News, 524 W 57th St, New York, NY 10019.

BRADLEY, HILBERT L.
Attorney. **Personal:** Born Jan 18, 1920, Repton, AL. **Educ:** Valparaiso Law Sch, Jd, LlB 1950. **Career:** Pvt Pract Atty; Div of Air Pollution, dep pros atty, corp counsel atty. **Orgs:** Made Documentary for Fed Gov on Role of a Witness; involved, prepared, filed & litigated several landmark civil rights cases; IN mem Thurgood Marshall Law Assn; Nat Black Bar Assn; life mem NAACP; mem IN Il Supreme Ct of US Bars. **Military Serv:** AUS pvt 1947. **Business Addr:** Lawyer, 2148 W 11 Ave, Gary, IN 46404.

BRADLEY, J. ROBERT
Music director. **Personal:** Born Sep 11, 1920, Memphis, TN. **Educ:** Trinity Coll London Eng, Mus 1955. **Career:** Bapt Conv USA Inc, Music Dir Sun Sch Publ Bd Nat; Nat Bap Training Union Bd, dir mus 1935; Nat Sun Sch & BTU Cong Nat Bap Conv USA Inc, intern famous rel concert artist. **Honors/Awds:** Iron Ship Awd 1960, highest awd from Korea; Albert Schweitzer Gold Medal 1970; London Knight Grand Comm Monrovia Lib 1974, highest awd from Rep of Liberia. **Business Addr:** 330 Charlotte Ave, Nashville, TN 37201.

BRADLEY, JACK CARTER
Musician (retired). **Personal:** Born Mar 14, 1919, Moline, IL; son of Eva Melissa Carter Bradley and Earl Russell Bradley. **Educ:** Univ of Denver, AB 1941; Army Bandleaders School, 1946; Univ of Denver, BMus 1948, MMus 1949. **Career:** Violinist, Denver Jr Symphony, 1928-32, Denver Civic Symphony, 1937-41, Denver Symphony, 1940-41, 1946-49, Corpus Christi Symphony, 1967-, Beaumont Symphony, 1968; prof, 1949-84, chmn of Music Dept, 1965-84, Texas Southern Univ; co-composer, co-conductor, soundtrack for NETV series People are Taught to be Different, 1950s & 1960s; first violinist, dir, New Horizon String Quartet, Houston; Texas South Univ, Houston, TX. **Orgs:** Member, Music Educ Natl Conf, Amer String Teachers Assn, Amer Assn of Univ Prof, Texas Assn of Coll Teachers, Amer Federation of Musicians, Amer Chamber Music Society, Kappa Kappa Psi Band Fraternity, Phi Beta Sigma Honorary Physical Educ Fraternity, Texas Assn of Music Schools, Coll Music Soc, Texas Fine Arts Commn, Kappa Alpha Psi, YMCA, Lutheran Campus Council for Houston, Jr Chamber of Commerce Denver, Houston Chamber of Commerce Cultural Affairs Comm, Ebony Tennis Club, Fondren Tennis Club, Houston Tennis Assn, Memorial Park Tennis Club, US Tennis Assn, Houston Ski Jammers, Houston Bicentennial Comm, Tabernacle Baptist Church, Moline IL; Zion Baptist Church Denver CO; Augustana Lutheran Church Houston TX; past dir, Texas Music Educ Assn; bd of dir, Houston Friends of Music; member advisory council, Miller Theater; bd of dir, Houston Youth Symphony, bd of trustees, Theatre Under the Stars; board of directors, Int Inst of Education, 1990-; bd Houston Ebony Opera Guild. **Honors/Awds:** Certificate of Recognition, Natl Urban League, 1948; Natl Assn of Negro Musicians, 1964; first black as a regular member of a professional Amer symphony; recognition as a major black contributor in Colorado, Denver Public Library, 1972; recognition as a pioneer in professional symphony, Music Assistance Fund, 1988. **Military Serv:** USNA warrant officer 1941-46. **Home Addr:** 3316 Rosedale, Houston, TX 77004.

BRADLEY, JAMES GEORGE
Administrator. **Personal:** Born Sep 17, 1940, Cleveland, OH; married Lela; children: Wyette, James, Candace, Jason. **Educ:** UNM, BEd 1963; Univ of Utah, MBA 1973 PhD 1977. **Career:** Human Resources, manpower dev spec 1979; Clearfield Job Corps, dir 1970; Detroit Manpower Center, dir 1976-77; USDA, civil rights 1986. **Orgs:** Advisory Board Special Ed 1983; NAACP, pres 1985. **Honors/Awds:** Alb Police Dept, special ser. **Home Addr:** 6013 Unitas Ct, NW, Albuquerque, NM 87114.

BRADLEY, JAMES HOWARD, JR.
Business executive. **Personal:** Born Nov 26, 1936, Detroit, MI; married Juanita E Bass; children: Vanessa, Angela. **Educ:** MI State Univ, BA 1959; Univ of MI, Grad Work. **Career:** Central Foundry Div Gen Motors Corp, budget analyst 1962-69; Gen Motors Corp, sr financial analyst 1969-70; Jim Bradley Pontiac-Cadillac-GMC Inc, pres 1973-; Saturn of Ann Arbor, owner, president, currently. **Orgs:** Dir City of Ann Arbor Econ Devel Corp 1987-; pres, bd of dir Ann Arbor Comm Center 1979-; dir of exec bd Boy Scouts of Amer Wolverine Council 1980; life mem NAACP; Kappa Alpha Psi, life member; Sigma Phi Pi Fraternity, member. **Military Serv:** AUS, e-4, 6 months. **Business Addr:** President, Jim Bradley Pontiac-Cadillac, 3500 Jackson Rd, Ann Arbor, MI 48103.

BRADLEY, JAMES MONROE, JR.
Clergyman. **Personal:** Born Aug 15, 1934, Mayesville, SC; married Nellie Chambers; children: James, III, Rosemary. **Educ:** Claflin Coll, AB 1956; Gammon Theo Sem;; BD 1959; Drew Theo Sem adv study. **Career:** Trinity United Meth Ch Orangeburg SC, minister 1974-; Emmanuel Ch Sumter NC 1970-74; Orangeburg Dist, dist supt 1964-70; Spartanburg, minister 1962-63; Cheraw, 1960-61; W Camden, 1958-60; Aiken, 1956-58. **Orgs:** Ordained Elder 1959; full connecltion 1958; ordained Deacon 1957; mem SC Conf United Meth Ch On Trial 1955; mem NAACP; Phi Beta Sigma; Mason Past vp; NAACP; mem Sumter Co Bd Educ 1971-73; mem bd dirs Sumter Co Rehab Cntr; delegate World Meth MtngLondon 1966, followed by 9 week tour of Europe.

BRADLEY, JEFFREY
Nursery school teacher. **Personal:** Born Jun 24, 1963, Bronx, NY; son of Beatrice Stevens Bradley and Harry Bradley (deceased). **Educ:** Laguardia Community College, AS, 1985; Hunter College. **Career:** Merricats Nursery School, teacher currently. **Orgs:** Assistant Staff Member to other programs, Association to Benefit Children, 1989-91; Aid, Variety House, 1990-91. **Honors/Awds:** Reebok Human Rights Award Winner, 1990. **Business Addr:** Merricats Nursery School, Association to Benefit Children, 316 E 88th St, New York, NY 10128.

BRADLEY, JESSE J., JR.
Labor official (retired). **Personal:** Born Jul 7, 1929, Hope, AR; son of Fannie Bradley and Jesse Bradley; married Marie A Saunders; children: Shawn P, Gregory J. **Educ:** BA Economics 1968; Grad Work Urban Affairs; Central Michigan Univ, Mt Pleasant, MI, MA, 1977. **Career:** Dept Trans Fed Aviation Admin, equal employment opp splst; Bendix Corp, purchasing agent/asst minority bus coord 1971-74, prod planner 1968-71; USPost Ofc, postal clerk 1956-68, chmn adv com 1974; Mid-Am Minority Bus Expos, exec dir 1973-74; Dept of Labor, Office of Contract Compliance, operations manager, district dir, 1991-94. **Orgs:** Complied/published minority bus dir Bendix Corp; Black Econ Union Dept of Trans Fed Aviation Admin; mem NAACP; Freedom Fund Com 1973-74; parliamentarian Phi Beta Sigma Frat 1974; sw regnl chaplain Phi Beta Sigma Frat 1972-74; Department of Labor/Office of Federal Contract Compliance Program, assistance district director, 1987-89, operations manager, 1989-. **Honors/Awds:** Special Recog Awards Mid-Am Minority Bus Exposition 1974, Ldrshp Awrd 1973, Recog Award 1972; Outstand Serv Award SW Region Phi Beta Sigma Frat 1974; Comm Ldrs of Am Award 1973; Special Achievement Award, 1983, Investigator of the Year, 1986, Director's Award for Excellence, 1987, Department of Labor/Office of Federal Contract Compliance Program. **Military Serv:** AUS pvt 1951-53. **Home Addr:** 14408 Wilshire Circle, Grandview, MO 64030.

BRADLEY, JESSIE MARY
Educational administrator. **Personal:** Born Oct 20, Little Rock, AR; daughter of Ophelia Washington Godley and Jesse Alexander Godley; married William O Bradley, Jun 28, 1953; children: Edwin Geory Bradley. **Educ:** Oakwood, BA 1948; So CT St Univ, BS 1956, MS 1960; Univ of CT, PhD 1973. **Career:** NE Acad, tchr 1948-53; New Haven, tchr 1956-58; So CT St Coll, instr 1958-67; New Haven Bd of Edn, prin 1967-73, Dir 1973-77, asst supt 1977-86; Connecticut State Dept of Education, consultant, 1987-. **Orgs:** Chamber of Commerce Educ Com; Phi Delta Kappa; Pi Lambda Theta; Am Assn of Sch Adminstr; Am Assn of Univ Women; Nat Cncl of Adminstrv Women in Educ dir So CT Chap Am Red Cross; dir Easter Seal Goodwill Ind Rehab Ctr; consultant day care nursery; World Cncl for Curr & Inst; Inter Reading Assn Am Temperance Soc; Intl Quota Club; Arts Coun of Grtr New Haven; CT Assn for Bilingual Bicult Edn; Grtr CT Coun for Open Edn; pres Oakwood Coll Alumni Assn; Urban League; NAACP; United Way; New Haven Jewish Ctr; New Haven Human Rel Coun; Assn of Super & Curr Devel; Nat Coun of Negro Women; sponsor United Negro Club 1976; bd of governors, Univ of New Haven 1987-; trustee, Mt Zion SDA Church; dir, Bank of Boston, 1977-92; dir, Harris & Tucker Day School. **Honors/Awds:** Educ Award Omega Psi Phi 1976; serv awd Oakwood Coll Unit Stud Move 1976; educ awd Gr New Haven Bvs & Professional Assn 1975; serv awd New Haven Headstart 1975; Educ Award Pampered Lady Inc 1973; serv awd Harriet Tubman 1972; achiev awd Nat Fed Kings Dau 1970; career adv awd NAACP 1970; serv awd Oakwood Coll Alumni Assn 1970; Outstanding Comm Serv Award Order of E Star 1970; Distinguished Alumni, Natl Assn for Equal Opportunity in Higher Education 1984; Outstanding Black Educator, Connecticut Historical Society 1984; An Analysis of Bilingual Education Programs (Spanish & English) for Pre-ad Children in Six CT Cities 1973; Ford Foundation Fellow 1977; Friendship Force Ambassador, East & West Germany 1978; Travel Grant, Israel, 1979; Sister CitiesExchange (Ed), Avignon France 1982. **Home Addr:** Oakwood College, Box 92, Huntsville, AL 35894-0001.

BRADLEY, LONDON M., JR.
Executive administrator. **Personal:** Born Mar 3, 1943, Chestnut, LA; son of Inez Bradley and London Bradley Sr; married Olivia Woodfork; children: London, Byron, Bradley. **Educ:** Southern Univ, BS 1964. **Career:** Parks & Recreation Dept KC, MO, recreation dir 1968-69; Bendix Corp, personnel interviewer 1969-71. **Orgs:** Master mason MW Prince Hall Grand Lodge 1963; mem NAACP 1976; referee Big Ten Basketball Conf 1977; Sunday school teacher Second Baptist Church 1984. **Military Serv:** USAF s/sgt 4 yrs. **Business Addr:** Assistant Vice President, Allstate Ins Co, 51 W Higgins Rd, South Barrington, IL 60010.

BRADLEY, MELISSA LYNN
Organization executive. **Personal:** Born Jan 14, 1968, Newark, NJ; daughter of Joan Bradley. **Educ:** Georgetown University, BS, 1989; American University, MBA, 1993. **Career:** Sallie Mae, finance mktg specialist, 1989-91; Bradley Dev Inc, founder/president, 1990-92; TEDI, founder/president, 1991-. **Orgs:** Who Cares, board member, 1996-; Mentors Inc, board member, 1995-; Back on the Block Foundation, 1995-. **Honors/Awds:** Do Something Brick Award Winner, 1996. **Business Addr:** Founder/President, The Entrepreneurial Devt Institute (TEDI), 2025 I St, NW, Ste 1114, Washington, DC 20006, (202)822-8334.

BRADLEY, MELVIN LEROY
Corporate consultant. **Personal:** Born Jan 6, 1938, Texarkana, TX; son of S T Bradley and David Ella Bradley; married Ruth A Terry; children: Cheryl, Eric, Jacquelyn, Tracey. **Educ:** LA City Coll, attended 1955; Compton Coll, attended 1965; Pepperdine Univ, BS 1973. **Career:** Real estate broker 1960-63; LA Co, dep sheriff 1963-69; State of CA, staff assistant gov's office 1970-73; State of CA, asst to Gov Reagan mem gov's sr staff participant in cabinet meetings 1973-75; Charles R Drew Postgrad Med Sch LA, dir pub rel; United Airlines, asst to vice pres 1977-81; President of the US White House, sr policy advisor 1981-82, spl asst to pres 1982-89; Garth & Bradley Associates, president, 1989-. **Orgs:** Mem Kiwanis Club; Toastmasters of Amer Inc; mem Natl Urban League, NAACP. **Honors/Awds:** Awd for Outstanding Contrib City of Los Angeles; Awded Mayor's Key to City Riverside CA; Awd for Contrib in Field of Comm Relations Compton CA; Comm Serv Awd Co of Los Angeles; Shaw Univ, Bishop Coll, Hon Dr of Laws; Disting Alumnus Awd Langston Univ.

BRADLEY, PHIL POOLE
Professional baseball player. **Personal:** Born Mar 11, 1959, Bloomington, IN; married Ramona; children: Megan, Curt. **Educ:** Univ of Missouri, BS, 1982. **Career:** Outfielder: Seattle Mariners, 1983-87, Philadelphia Phillies, 1988, Baltimore Orioles, 1989-90, Chicago White Sox, outfielder, 1990, Montreal Expos, until 1992. **Honors/Awds:** Was selected by CA League managers as ''Best Defensive Outfielder''; Mid-Season All-Star Team, 1985; Post-Season Sporting News All-Star Team, 1985; American League All-Star Team, 1985. **Home Addr:** 3601 Southern Hills Dr, Columbia, MO 65203.

BRADLEY, ROBERTA PALM
Public utility executive. **Personal:** Born Jan 23, 1947, Frederick, MD; daughter of Pauline Hurde Palm and Robert Palm; married Timothy Bradley, May 4, 1985. **Educ:** Morgan State University, Baltimore, MD, 1969; Harvard University School of Business, Cambridge, MA, program for management development, 1991. **Career:** Howard University, Washington, DC, editor, 1972-75; Hoffman Education Systems, El Monte, CA, senior editor, 1975-76; Pacific Gas & Electric Co, Vallejo, Ca, division manager, 1976-. **Orgs:** Board of directors, Vallejo Chambers of Commerce, 1990-95; board of directors, Vallejo Salvation Army, 1990-93; board of directors, Silverado Boy Scout Coucil, 1989-92; member, board of directors, United Way, vice president, Fund-raising 1990-92; co-chair, Vallejo Renaissance 2000 Forum, 1990-91. **Honors/Awds:** Woman of the Year Certificate, B'nai Brith, 1990.

BRADLEY, ROOSEVELT, JR.
Cleric. **Personal:** Born Aug 29, 1934, Memphis, TN; son of Roosevelt Sr & Katie Bradley; married Barbara J, Jan 19, 1955; children: Tommy, Michael, Glenda Turner, Kenneth, Sybil, Kevin. **Educ:** New York Preparatory Serv, diploma, 1973; Urban Baptist Bible Institute, teacher training certificate, 1974; Urban Baptist College, School of Religious Studies, BEd, 1974, DDiv, 1982. **Career:** Truelight Baptist Church, pastor, 1971-. **Orgs:** Prospect District Association, moderator, 1985-. **Honors/Awds:** Wayne County Board of Commissioner, Certificate of Appreciation, 1980; City of Detroit, Spirit of Detroit Award, 1981; Urban Bible Institute, Imperial Award, 1983; Detroit City Council, Award of Recognition, 1992. **Home Addr:** 5457 Baldwin, Detroit, MI 48213, (313)924-5105. **Business Addr:** Reverend, Truelight Baptist Church, 2504 Beniteau, Detroit, MI 48214.

BRADLEY, TOM
Mayor (retired). **Personal:** Born Dec 29, 1917, Calvert, TX; married Ethel Arnold; children: Lorraine, Phyllis. **Educ:** Univ of California, Los Angeles, attended. **Career:** LA Police Dept, 1940-62; Private law practice, 1961-63; LA 10th Dist, councilman 1963-73; Los Angeles CA, mayor 1973-93; Brobeck, Phleger & Harrison, senior counsel, 1993-. **Orgs:** CA State Bar Assn, Natl League of Cities, Southern CA Assn of Govts; founding past pres Natl Assoc of Reg Councils; mem Pres Fords Natl Comm on Productivity & Work Quality, Amer Cancer Soc of LA Cty, Greater LA Urban Coalition, LA World Affairs Council, United Nations Assoc of LA, Urban League of LA, Natl Energy Adv Council; founding mem Black Achievers Comm, NAACP; past natl pres Kappa Alpha Psi; bd dir natl Urban Fellows; numerous others. **Honors/Awds:** Newsmaker of the Year Awd, Natl Assoc of Media Women 1974; Los Amigos De La Humanidad School of Soc Work Univ of So CA 1974; Alumnus of the Year Univ ofCA 1974; Thurgood Marshall Awd; Sword of the Haganah of State of Israel Israeli Ambassador Simcha Dinitz 1974; David Ben Gurion Awd for Outstanding Achievement 1974; NAACP Legal Defense & Ed Fund Dinner 1975; MEDIC Intl Humanitarian Awd 1978; CORO Found Awd 1978; Awd of Merit Natl Council of Negro Women Inc 1978; John F Kennedy Fellowship Awd New Zealand Govt 1978; 1983 Equal Justice Awds Dinner honoring Mayor Bardley 1983; City Employee of the Year 1983; Magnin Awd Rabbi Edgar F Magnin 1984; NAACP Spingarn Medal 1985; Hon Doct of Law Degrees, Brandeis Univ, Oral Roberts Univ, Pepperdine Univ, Wilberforce Univ, WhittierColl, Yale Univ, v of South Carolina, Princeton Univ, Busan Natl Univ, Korea, Southwestern Univ, Antioch Univ, North Carolina Central Univ, California Lutheran Coll, Loyola Marymount Univ; Hon Doct of Philosophy Degree Humanity Rsch Ctr of Beverly Hills. **Business Addr:** Senior Counsel, Brobeck, Phleger & Harrison, 550 South Hope Street, Suite 2100, Los Angeles, CA 90071-2604.

BRADLEY, VANESA JONES
Judge. **Career:** 36th District Court, judge, currently. **Business Addr:** Judge, 36th District Court, 421 Madison Ave, Detroit, MI 48226, (313)965-8708.

BRADLEY, WALTER THOMAS, JR.
Editor. **Personal:** Born Oct 2, 1925, Midway, KY; son of Sarah J Craig Bradley and Walter T Bradley, Sr; married Mollie Priscilla McFarland; children: Walter T III, Harry S. **Educ:** Sprayberry Acad of Electronics, attended 1946-50; AUS Sch of Engrg, attended 1948-50; Univ of KY, attended 1984-85. **Career:** US Civil Service, electronic tech 1950-77; Lex Blue Grass Army Depot, electronics inspector 1950-77; KY Bapt UCLC, exec sec 1970-78; Star Gazer Gr Chap OES KY, p editor 1972-79; PH Conf of Gr Chap OES, southeast region rep 1976-; KY Mapping Div, draftsman 1978-80; Masonic Herald PHGL of KY, editor-in-chief 1979-; CCFC MW Prince Hall Grand Lodge F&AM KY, rw grand sec 1980-88. **Orgs:** Mem trustee Pilgrim Bapt Church 1936-86; mem PH Conf of Gr Chap OES 1973-; councilman Midway City Govt 1977-; Honorary Grand Master, MW Prince Hall Grand Lodge, 1986-; vice pres Midway Lions Club 1986-; mem Immanuel Bapt Church 1986-; mem Royal Arch Masons PHA KY, Royal & Select Masters R&SM Ohio, Knights Templars KT KY, Scottish Rite of Freemasonry KY PHA, TIM, William H Steward Council R&SM 1987-, PM & sec Lone Star Lodge 19 F&AM KY; Rt Ill Grand Recorder, M ILL Prince Hall Grand Council, 1989-; Phylaxis Soc, pres chap of editors, 1984-. **Honors/Awds:** Grand Worthy Patron Grand Chap OES PHA KY 1973-75; Coronated 33 Degree Scottish Rite Mason United Supreme Cncl SJ 1981; Certificate of Merit Phylaxis Soc1983; Medal of Excellence Phylaxis Soc 1984; Fellow Phylaxis Soc 1985; 100 Influential Black Masons of Amer; Hon Grand Sec MW Prince Hall Grand Lodge F&AM Dist of Columbia 1981-; Grand Master MW Prince Hall Grand Lodge F&AM of KY 1986-; author, Prince Hall Founder of Free Masonry among Black Men of America, 1988; Matthew A Henson Man on top of the world, 1989; Deacon Immanuel Baptist Church, 1989-; President Midway Lions Club, 1989-90. **Military Serv:** AUS pfc 1948-50; Engrg Sch graduate 1949. **Home Addr:** 215 E Walnut St, PO Box 749, Midway, KY 40347.

BRADLEY, WAYNE W.
Police officer. **Personal:** Born Aug 20, 1948; married. **Educ:** Wayne State Univ; BA, 1972. **Career:** Detroit Police Dept, police officer 1970-; Cass Corridor Safety for Sr Proj, proj Dir 1974-75; Wayne Co Community Coll, instr 1972-; Western Reserve Fin Services Corp, sales rep 1973-; Sears Roebuck & Co, security 1973-74; Philco Ford Corp, accounts receivable & payable 1968-69; MI Consolidated Gas Co, collecltion rep 1969-70. **Orgs:** Appointed Notary Pub Co of Wayne MI 1974; mem Kappa Alpha Phi Frat; mem Trade Union Ldrshp Coun; second vice pres Nat Pan Helenic Coun; mem NAACP; coach 12th precinct bsbl team; coach Presentation Cath Sch Ftbl Team; mem 1st Precinct Comm Relations Assn; bd mem editorial bd & Community Reporter Newspaper; mem Detroit Police Officers Assn; police Officers Assn of MI; Guardians of MI; Concerned Police Officers for Equal Justice. **Honors/Awds:** Recipient Military Order of Purple Heart Civilian Awd 1971; Detroit Police Dept Wound Bar 1971; Detroit Police Dept Highest Awd; Medal of Valor 1971; 12th Precinct Outstanding Service Awd 1972; Detroit Police Dept Citation 1972; listed in Leaders in Black Am. **Business Addr:** 3165 Second Ave, Detroit, MI 48201.

BRADLEY, WILLIAM B.
Educator. **Personal:** Born Nov 28, 1926, Rushville, IN; married Pearle E Poole; children: William, Philip, Annette, Catherine. **Educ:** Indiana University, BPE, 1949, MPE, 1955, PED, 1959. **Career:** Western Illinois University, Department of Physical Education, professor, coordinator, sport management internship program, 1970-; Virginia State University, Dept of Athletics & Physical Education, director, 1964-70; Southern University, Dept of Physical Education, professor/chairman, 1960-64; Fayetteville State University, Department of Physical Education, professor/chairman, 1959-60; Indiana University, p.e. dir, 1957, School of HPER, graduate asst, 1958-59; Sumner High School, coach physical education, 1955-58. **Orgs:** American Alliance for Health, Physical Education & Recreation; Illinois Assn for Health PE & Recreation; Virginia Assn for Health, PE & Recreation; American Assn of University Professors; Phi Epsilon Kappa; Phi Delta Kappa; Indiana Alumni Assn; ''I'' Mens Assn of Indiana University; consultant, Natl Youth Sports Program Pres Council on Physical Fitness & Sports, 1970-79; bd mem, McDonough Co, YMCA, 1970-73; US Olympic Baseball Committee, 1972; US Olympic Weightlifting Committee, 1968. **Honors/Awds:** Alpha Phi Alpha, Quarter Century Club Award, Illinois Assn for Health, PE & Recreation, 1975; cert of appreciation, McDonough Co American Legion, 1972; certificate of achievement, Virginia State College, 1970; CIAA Baseball Coach of Year, 1968; author of article, ''The Effects of Velocity & Repetition of Motion on the Development of Isokinetic Strength of the Quadriceps Muscle Group''. **Military Serv:** US Army, 1st lt, 1950-53. **Business Addr:** Professor, Department of Physical Education, Western Illinois University, 900 W Adams St, Macomb, IL 61455-1328.

BRADSHAW, DORIS MARION
Educational administrator (retired). **Personal:** Born Sep 23, 1928, Freeman, WV; daughter of Roberta Merchant and Fred Merchant; married Virgil Alanda Bradshaw; children: Victoria Lee, Gary Dwayne, Eric Alanda, Barry Douglas. **Educ:** Concord Coll, BS Early Childhood Educ 1976; WV Coll of Grad Studies, MA Early Childhood Educ 1985. **Career:** Raleigh Co, volun Head Start 1966; RCCAA Head Start Prog, head start teach 1967-69, head start teacher asst dir 1969-70, head start dir. **Orgs:** 2nd vice pres WV Head Start Dirs Assn 1970-; mem WV Comm on Children & Youth 1981-; consul Head Start Review Team for the Educ & Admin portion of the Head Start Prog 1983-; mem bd of dirs Region III Head Start Assoc 1984-. **Home Addr:** 121 Sour St, Beckley, WV 25801.

BRADSHAW, GERALD HAYWOOD
Business executive. **Personal:** Born Dec 13, 1934, Larned, KS; married Wylma Louise Thompson; children: Kim Elaine, Gerri Lynn, Douglas Haywood. **Educ:** KS State Teachers Coll, 1952-56; Univ of CO, BS; Amer Savings & Loan Inst Denver, Hours on Master. **Career:** Equity Savings & Loan Assoc Denver, auditor, appraiser 1958-67; Denver Urb Renew Auth, real estate dir 1960-71; CO Springs Urb Renew Effort, exec dir 1971-76; GH Bradshaw & Assoc, pres 1976-. **Orgs:** Past pres CO Chap Natl Assoc of Housing & Redevel Officials; sr mem Natl Assoc of Review Appraisors; broker Real Estate CO, mem bd dir Urban League of Pikes Peak Region; mem Downtown Rotary Club of CO Springs; former mem El Paso Comm Coll Site Selection Comm; former sec Denver Oppty; former chmn bd of adv comm Columbine Elem School US. **Honors/Awds:** Pres Cert of Awd Serving on Sel Serv Bd. **Business Addr:** President, GH Bradshaw & Assoc, PO Box 9744, Colorado Springs, CO 80932.

BRADSHAW, LAWRENCE A.
Educator. **Personal:** Born Sep 23, 1932, Philadelphia, PA; married Mary Ellen Osgood. **Educ:** Shippensburg State College, BS (with honors), MEd; Bucknell University, graduate studies; University of Vermont; Ball State University; The American University, doctoral studies. **Career:** Shippensburg Area Junior High School, teacher, 1961-62; Shippensburg Area Senior High School, teacher of English & humanities, 1962-69; Shippensburg State College, asst dean of admissions, 1970-72, Academic Affairs Office, asst to vice president, 1972-73, asst to president, 1974-75, Dept of English, assoc professor, currently. **Orgs:** Phi Delta Kappa; American Guild of Organists; Natl Council of Teacher of English; College English Assn; Pennsylvania Council of English Teachers; American Assn of University Administrators; Pennsylvania State Education Assn; Natl Education Assn; Kiwanis Club of Chambersburg PA; bd dir, United Fund of Chambersburg PA; bd dir, Franklin County Sunday School Assn; trustee, Chambersburg Hospital; 1st president, Canterbury Club, Shippensburg State College; 1st president, American Field Serv; Comm Concerts Assn, vestryman & organist, St Andrews Episcopal Church. **Honors/Awds:** Rockefeller Fellowship for University Administration, 1973-74; Outstanding Educator of America, 1974-75. **Military Serv:** US Army, sgt major, 1953-55. **Business Addr:** Associate Professor, Dept of English, Shippensburg University, Shippensburg, PA 17257-2299.

BRADSHAW, WAYNE-KENT
Financial executive. **Career:** Founders Savings and Loan Assoc, chief exec; Family Savings bank, CEO, currently.

BRADTKE, MARK
Professional basketball player. **Personal:** Born Sep 27, 1968. **Educ:** Redcliffe. **Career:** Philadelphia 76ers, 1996-. **Business Addr:** Professional Basketball Player, Philadelphia 76ers, Broad St & Pattison Ave, Veterans Stadium, Philadelphia, PA 19148, (215)339-7600.

BRADY, CHARLES A.
Attorney. **Personal:** Born May 1, 1945, Palestine, TX; son of Leona V Brady and Thomas F Brady Sr; married Ida A Powell; children: Kimberly, Charles A Jr. **Educ:** Coe College, AB 1967; Howard Univ Sch of Law, JD 1970. **Career:** McDaniel Burton & Brady, attorney 1971-82; Charles A Brady & Assoc, attorney 1982-. **Orgs:** Sub instr Bus Law Federal City Coll; active in litigation of employment discrimination cases treas Inner-City & Investment Assn Inc; mem several Forensic & Legal Frat & Assns. **Business Addr:** Attorney, Charles A Brady & Associates, 1343 Pennsylvania Ave SE, Washington, DC 20003.

BRADY, DONNY
Professional football player. **Personal:** Born Nov 26, 1973, North Bellmore, NY. **Educ:** Univ of Wisconsin, attended. **Career:** Baltimore Ravens, defensive back, 1996-. **Business Addr:** Professional Football Player, Baltimore Ravens, 11001 Owings Mills Blvd, Owings Mills, MD 21117, (410)654-6200.

BRADY, JULIO A.
Elected official. **Personal:** Born Aug 23, 1942, St Thomas, Virgin Islands of the United States; married Maria de Freitas; children: Julie, Andrew. **Educ:** Catholic Univ of Puerto Rico, BA English Philosophy 1964; New York Law School, JD 1969. **Career:** NY Legal Aid Soc, public defender 1969-71; District of the Virgin Islands, asst US attorney 1971-73, US attorney 1974-78; Federal Programs Office, coordinator 1979-82; Govt of the Virgin Islands, lt governor 1983-. **Orgs:** Pres Virgin Islands Bar Assn; co-chairman United Way Campaign; state chairman Democratic Party of the Virgin Islands. **Honors/Awds:** Amer Juris Prudence Awd for Excellence in Criminal Law New York Law School 1969. **Business Addr:** Lieutenant Governor, Government of the VI, PO Box 450, St Thomas, Virgin Islands of the United States 00801.

BRAGG, JOSEPH L.
Reporter, journalist. **Personal:** Born Jul 6, 1937, Jackson, NC; married Barbara Brandom. **Educ:** Georgetown Univ Sch of Foreign Serv Diplo & Consular Affairs; Career Acad Sch of Famous Broadcasters 1967; City Univ NY, BA 1976. **Career:** WHN News City Hall Bureau Chief WHN Radio Storer Radio Inc, news rptr; McGovern & Nixon Pres Campaign, covered/pictures 1972; Carter & Ford Pres Campaign, covered 1976; Mutual Black Network, newsman; Mutual Broadcasting Sys, newscaster 1971; Nat Acad of TV Arts & Sci, journalist/mem 1974. **Orgs:** NY Chap Jonathan Davis Consistory #1 32 Deg AASR of Free Masonry So Juris Wash, DC; mem Black Cits for Fair Media 1971; pres Inner Circle; pres NY Press Club. **Honors/Awds:** Top 100 Polit Writers in NY State. **Military Serv:** AUS pvt 1957. **Business Addr:** 400 Park Ave, New York, NY 10017.

BRAGG, ROBERT HENRY
Educator. **Personal:** Born Aug 11, 1919, Jacksonville, FL; son of Lilly Camille McFarland Bragg and Robert Henry Bragg; divorced; children: Robert III, Pamela. **Educ:** Illinois Inst of Tech, Chicago IL, BS 1949, MS 1951, PhD 1960. **Career:** Lockheed Rsch Lab, mgr phys metallurgy 1961-69; IL Inst of Tech Research Institute, sr physicist 1956-61; Portland Cement & Assn, assoc physicist 1951-56; University of California, Lawrence Berkeley Lab, principal investigator 1969-, prof, Dept of Math Sci 1969-87, dept chair, 1978-81, prof emeritus, 1987-; Fulbright Scholar, Nigeria, 1992-93. **Orgs:** Life mem, NAACP; mem Amer Phys Soc; Amer Ceramic Soc; Amer Inst Metal Engr; Amer Carbon Soc; Amer Cryst Assn; AAUP; AAAS; Sigma Xi; Sigma Pi Sigma; Tau Beta Pi; Siemens-Allis, consultant; Natl Science Found, consultant; Natl Research Council, consultant; NASA, consultant; Lockheed Missiles & Space Co, consultant; faculty sponsor Black Engineering & Science Students Assn 1969-; mem Natl Technical Assn 1978-; mem, Northern California Council of Black Professional Engineers, 1969-; advisory committee, Division of Materials Research, National Science Foundation, 1982-88; program dir, Division of Materials Sciences, Office of Energy Research, Dept of Energy, 1981-82; evaluation panel, Research Associates Program, National Research Council, 1984-; evaluation panel, Fulbright CIES, Africa Program, 1994-. **Honors/Awds:** Published articles in technical journals & books; distinguished ser award AIME 1972, ACS 1982, NCCBPE 1985. **Military Serv:** AUS 2nd lt 1942-46. **Business Addr:** Robert H. Bragg & Associates, 2 Admiral Dr, #373, Emeryville, CA 94608, (510)655-6283.

BRAGG, ROBERT LLOYD
Educator. **Personal:** Born Nov 3, 1916, Jackson, MS; son of Anna A Smith Bragg and Jubie Barton Bragg Sr. **Educ:** FL A&M Univ, BS 1936; Boston Univ, MA 1938; Columbia Univ, MD 1952; Harvard School of Publ Health, MPH 1955. **Career:** Human Rel Serv of Wellesley Inc, dir 1963-73; MA Genl Hosp, coord comm mental health training prog 1965-73; Harvard Med School MA Genl Hosp, asst prof 1970-73; Univ of Miami School of Med, assoc dean spec proj 1976-, dir 1974-, prof of psych 1979-. **Orgs:** Mem Amer Psych Assn, Dade County Med Assn, S FL Psych Soc, Behavioral Sci Inst of Miami Inc; Florida Medical Assn; Natl Medical Assn; Florida Medical; Dental Pharmaceutical Assn; Black Psychiatrists of America. **Honors/Awds:** Distinguished Alumnus Awd FL A&M Univ 1964. **Military Serv:** Med Adm Corps capt 1941-46.

BRAILEY, TROY
State legislator. **Personal:** Born Aug 26, 1916, Lynchburg, SC; married Chessie; children: Alice Faye Toriente, Norman. **Educ:** New York University. **Career:** Maryland House of Delegates, state legislator, currently. **Orgs:** Maryland House of Delegates; former rep, Brotherhood Sleeping Car Porters; vice-chairman, Baltimore Delegate to House; chairman, March on Washington 1963; former chairman, Baltimore Chapter American Labor Council. **Honors/Awds:** Honored, Unsung Hero, Maryland Chapter American Labor Council 1965; 1st Black named to one of city's two leadership positions 1970. **Business Addr:** State Legislator, House of Delegates, 2405 Baker St, Baltimore, MD 21216.

BRAILSFORD, MARVIN D.
Company Executive. **Personal:** Born Jan 31, 1939, Burkeville, TX; son of Geneva Vivian Brailsford and Artie Brailsford; married June Evelyn Samuel, Dec 23, 1960; children: Marvin D Jr, Keith A, Cynthia R. **Educ:** Prairie View A & M University, BS, 1959; Iowa State University, MS, 1966. **Career:** US Army, 60th ordnance group, commanding officer, 1982-84, 59th ordnance brigade, commanding general, 1984-87, armament munitions & chemical command, commanding general, 1987-90, materiel command, deputy commanding general, 1990-92; Metters Industries Inc, president, 1992-95; Brailsford Group, CEO/president, 1995-96; Kaiser-Hill, senior vp, 1996-. **Orgs:** Association of US Army, chapter president, 1984-87; American Defense Preparedness Association, executive committee, 1978-; United Way, executive board, 1989; Educate the Children Foundation, bd of dirs, 1994-; Geo Mason Univ, Bus School, bd of advisors, 1993-96; Illinois Tool Works Inc, board of directors, 1996-; TRESP Associates Inc, board of directors, 1996-; Strategic Resources Inc, board of directors, 1996-. **Honors/Awds:** Chamber of Commerce, Boss of the Year, 1969. **Military Serv:** US Army, 1959-92; Defense Superior Service Award, Distinguished Service Medal; Legion of Merit, Bronze Star, Army Commendation Medal, Parachute Badge, Army Staff ID Badge. **Business Addr:** Senior VP, Kaiser-Hill Co., Rocky Flats Enviormental Technology Site, PO Box 464, Golden, CO 80402, (303)966-3221.

BRAITHWAITE, GORDON L.
Business executive. **Personal:** Born in Atlantic City, NJ. **Educ:** Hunter Coll; UCLA; Santa Monica Jr Coll; Herbert Berghof Acting Studios. **Career:** Natl Endowment for the Arts, dir/office of special projects; City of NY Dept Cultural Affairs, pgm spcl. **Orgs:** Mem adv com Comm Gallery Brooklyn Mus 1970-72; 100 Black Men Inc; NAACP. **Business Addr:** C/O Nat Endowment for the Arts, Washington, DC 20506.

BRAITHWAITE, MARK WINSTON
Dentist. **Personal:** Born Jul 15, 1954, New York, NY; son of Grace C Braithwaite and David N Braithwaite; married Carlene V; children: Mark II. **Educ:** Bowdoin Coll, BA Biology 1976; Columbia Univ, attended 1977; State Univ of NY at Buffalo Sch of Dental Medicine, DDS 1982; Columbia Univ, School of Dental and Oral Surgery, Post graduate periodontics, 1993; Columbia Univ, Grad School of Arts & Sciences, MA, dental science, 1995. **Career:** Private Practice Assoc, dentist/general practitioner 1983-85; NY City Dept of Health Bureau of Dentistry, general practitioner dentist 1984-87; Joint Diseases North Genl Hosp, general practitioner dentist 1985-90; Sydenham Hosp Neighborhood Family Care Ctr, attending dentist 1987-90; Harlem Hosp Ctr, attending dentist 1987-. **Orgs:** License/certification Northeast Regional Dental Boards 1982, Natl Dental Boards 1982; licensed in NY, MD, Washington DC; mem Natl Dental Assn, Natl Soc of Dental Practitioners, Dental Health Serv Corp; mem Harlem Dental Soc, SUNY at Buffalo Sch of Dental Medicine Alumni Assn; mem Amer Dental Assn. **Honors/Awds:** Special Academic Achievement Periodontology 1981-82; Attending of the Year, Harlem Hospital 1988-89; Fellowship in Cell & Molecular Biology in the Laboratory of Tumor Biology & Connective Tissue Research, 1993-. **Home Addr:** 159 Midwood St, Brooklyn, NY 11225.

BRAMBLE, PETER W. D.
Author, cleric. **Personal:** Born Jul 24, 1945, Harris, Montserrat, West Indies; son of Margaret B Bramble and Charles William Bramble; married Jocelyn Cheryl Nanton, Dec 28, 1972; children: Jocelyn Cara, Peter David. **Educ:** Codrington College, Barbados, LTh, 1970; Yale Divinity School, MA, religion, 1972, STM, 1974; University of Connecticut, Storrs, PhD, 1976. **Career:** School teacher, 1962-66; parish priest, 1972-73; University of Connecticut, teaching assistant and lecturer, 1974-76; St Katherine's Episcopal, rector, 1976-; Morgan, St Mary's and Western Maryland, univ lecturer, 1978-. **Orgs:** Caribbean/African-American Dialogue, executive committee, 1992-; Governor's Commission on Homelessness, 1982-86; National Institute of Health, animal care committee, 1980-; Baltimore Public Schools, community outreach committee, 1988-, committee on Afro-Centric curriculum; Overcome Institute for Black Institution Development, founder. **Honors/Awds:** Junior Academy of Letters, Living Legend in Religion, 1990; Iota Phi Lambda Sorority, Living Maker of History Award, 1992; Congressional Service Award, 1986; Caribbean American InterCultural Organization, Values Award, 1991; Eco-Fun Project, Leadership and Commitment to Children, 1992. **Special Achievements:** The Overcome: A Black Passover, Fairfax, Baltimore, 1989; Baltimore Times, "Rites for Overcome," Baltimore, 1990. **Home Addr:** 1800 Madison Ave, Baltimore, MD 21217, (410)728-8137.

BRAME, WALTER MELVYN
Association executive. **Personal:** Born Mar 21, 1946, Henderson, NC; son of Rosetta Jeffreys Brame (deceased) and Walter Brame; married Veronica Watford, Jul 19, 1969; children: Kenyatta, Abayomi, William, Tamika. **Educ:** North Carolina Central Univ, North Carolina, BA, 1968; Wayne State Univ, Detroit, MI, MA, 1973; Atlanta Univ, Atlanta, GA, 1984; Western Michigan Univ, Kalamazoo, MI, EdD, 1989. **Career:** Found for Community Devel, Durham, NC, dir, 1968-69; Univ of Maryland, Washington, DC, training officer, 1969; Wayne County Community Coll, Detroit, MI, Comm Coord, 1973-74; Detroit Urban League, Detroit, MI, dept dir, 1974-79; Grand Rapids Urban League, Grand Rapids, MI, pres/CEO, 1979-. **Orgs:** Mem, Grand Rapids Rotary Club, 1980-; founding mem, Comm for Representative Govt, 1982-; bd mem, Grand Rapids Area Transit Authority, 1985-; founder & chairperson, Grand

Rapids Voter Coalition, 1985-; bd mem, St Marys Health Care Corp, 1987-, Kent County Defenders Office, 1987-; Grand Rapids Area Employment & Training Council, 1988-; board of directors; Project Rehab. **Honors/Awds:** Distinguished Humanitarian, True Light Baptist Church, 1988; Phyllis Scott Activist, Grand Rapids GIANTS Comm, 1988; Man of the Year, Madison Park School, 1986; fellowship, Atlanta Univ, 1984; Excellence in Serv, US Dept of HUD, 1981; author, Competencies Needed by a Chief Exec Officer of a Local Urban League, 1989, A System of Accountability and Control, 1989, Required Reading for Educ Blacks, 1988, The Role of the Pres and Chairperson of the Bd, 1986; Service in Urban Affairs, Grand Rapids NAACP, 1991. **Military Serv:** USAF, sergeant, 1969-73; Air Force Commendation Medal for Outstanding Achievement in Human Relations.

BRAMWELL, FITZGERALD BURTON
Educational administrator, chemist. **Personal:** Born May 16, 1945, Brooklyn, NY; son of Lula Burton Bramwell and Fitzgerald Bramwell; married Charlott Burns; children: Fitzgerald, Elizabeth, Jill, Christopher. **Educ:** Columbia Coll, BA 1966; Univ of MI, MS 1967, PhD 1970. **Career:** Esso Rsch & Engineering, rsch chemist 1970-71; Brooklyn College, asst prof chemistry, 1971-72, deputy chairman graduate studies, 1981-84, acting dean graduate studies and research, 1989-90, dean of graduate studies and research, 1990-95, prof emeritus, 1995; CUNY Doctoral Faculty, asst prof chemistry, 1972-74, associate prof chemistry, 1975-79, prof chemistry, 1980-95; Univ of Kentucky, prof biochemistry, 1995-, prof chemistry, 1995-, vice pres research and graduate studies, 1995-. **Orgs:** National Institute of General Medical Sciences Advisory Council 1989; Southeastern Universities Research Assn, board of trustees, 1995-; Univ of Kentucky Research Foundation, executive director, 1995-; American Chemical Society, 1966-; American Physical Society, 1967-95; Sigma Xi, 1971-; New York Academy of Sciences, 1971-; American Institute of Chemists and Chemical Engineers, 1988-; American Assn for the Advancement of Science, 1996-; Kentucky Academy of Sciences, 1996-. **Honors/Awds:** IAESTE Intl Exchange Fellow 1966; Phi Lambda Upsilon 1967; Phillips Petroleum Fellow 1968; Allied Chem Fellow 1969; numerous rsch grants prof publications and textbooks 1970-; Sigma Xi Hon Rsch organ 1971; Natl Science Found Faculty Devel Grant 1977-78; Fellow of the Acad of Science & Human of the City Univ of NY 1980; National Black Science Students Organization, Professor of the Year Award, 1985, 1989, Distinguished Service Award, 1993, 1995; Fellow of Amer Inst of Chemists, 1988; Brooklyn College Graduate Students Organization, Distinguished Service Award, 1994, 1995; TRACC City College of New York, Distinguished Service Award, 1995; Brooklyn Subsection of the American Chemical Society, Distinguished Service Award, 1995; University of Michigan, Department of Chemistry Alumni Excellence Award, 1996. **Special Achievements:** Co-author: Investigations in General Chemistry Quantitative Techniques and Basic Principles, 1977; Instructor's Guide for Basic Laboratory Principles in General Chemistry with Quantitative Techniques, 1990; Basic Laboratory Principles in General Chemistry with Quantitative Techniques, 1990; 6 books, 30 articles, 250 abstracts and presentations in the areas of physical chemistry and chemical education. **Business Addr:** Vice President for Research and Graduate Studies, University of Kentucky, 207 Administration Bldg, Lexington, KY 40506-0032.

BRAMWELL, HENRY
Judge. **Personal:** Born Sep 3, 1919, Brooklyn, NY; son of Florence and Henry; married Ishbel W. **Educ:** Brooklyn Law School, LLB 1948; Brooklyn Coll, LLD (Hon) 1979. **Career:** US Atty Office, asst atty 1953-61; NY State Rent Comm, assoc attny 1961-63; Civil Ct City NY, judge 1969-75; US Dist, judge 1975-. **Orgs:** Mem Natl Fed NY, Amer & Brooklyn Bar Assoc; mem bd of trustees Brooklyn Law School 1979; Federal Judges Association, founding member. **Military Serv:** Sgt 1941-45. **Business Addr:** District Judge, US Courthouse, Brooklyn, NY 11201.

BRAMWELL, PATRICIA ANN
Social worker. **Personal:** Born May 17, 1941, Brooklyn, NY; daughter of Miriam June Campbell Bramwell and Arthur L Bramwell. **Educ:** Ctrl State Univ, BA 1965; Fordham Univ Sch of Social Svcs, MSW 1969; Hofstra Univ, Cert of Managerial Studies & Labor Relations 1980; Para Legal Cert; Certificate Mediation Arbitration. **Career:** The Society for Seamen's Children, Foster Home Care 1966-70; E NY Mntl Health Clinic, grp therapy 1977; The City Coll SEEK Prog, psychol couns, asst professor. **Orgs:** Cert State Soc Worker; vice chairperson Comm Sch Bd Dist 16 1975-77; asst sec Chama Day Care Ctr 1974-76; Life mem Natl Council of Negro Women; bd of dir, first vice pres, Fordham Univ Sch of Social Serv Alumni Assn; Brooklyn Community Planning Bd #3; Community Bd Kings County Hosp; vice pres, bd of directors, New Horizons Adult Education Program, 1989-97; City College Sexual Harassment Panel; vice president, City College Chapter Professional Staff Congress Union, Commissioner; NY City Human Rights Commission. **Business Addr:** Prof, Dept of Counseling & Student Support Services, City College of the City Univ of New York, 138th St and Convent Ave, NAC 5/226, New York, NY 10031.

BRANCH, ANDRE JOSE
Educator. **Personal:** Born May 12, 1959, Valhalla, NY; son of Virginia Ment Smith Branch and Millard Branch. **Educ:** Warnborough Coll, Oxford, England, 1978; Institute of Holy Land Studies, Jerusalem, Israel, 1979; The King's Coll, Briarcliff, NY, BA, 1981; Fayetteville State Univ, Fayetteville, NC, teacher's certificate, 1985; North Carolina, State Univ, Raleigh, NC, MEd, 1989. **Career:** CMML Sec School, Nigeria, W Africa, teacher, 1981-82; New Hanover County School, Wilmington, NC, teacher, 1983-84; City of Wilmington, Wilmington, NC, counselor, 1986; Wake County Public Schools, Raleigh, NC, teacher, 1987-89; North Carolina State Univ, Raleigh, NC, counselor intern, 1988-89; Whitworth Coll, Spokane, WA, dir, multiethnic student affairs, 1989-. **Orgs:** Mem, Amer Assn of Counseling & Dev, 1989-; mem, Amer College Personnel Assn, 1989-; mem, NAACP, 1989-; mem, Black Education Assn of Spokane, 1989-; mem, Washington Comm on Minority Affairs, 1989-. **Honors/Awds:** Fdr, Northwest Assn of AHANA Professionals, 1989; designed and instituted the Natl Students of Color Symposium/Orientation, 1990; designed and provided the Cross-Cultural Awareness for Action Seminar, 1990.

BRANCH, B. LAWRENCE
Personnel administrator. **Personal:** Born Sep 13, 1937, New York, NY; married Elva C; children: Erica Danielle, Gabrielle Angelique. **Educ:** Univ of IL, 1956-59; S IL U, BS 1960-61. **Career:** Merck & Co Inc, dir equal employment affairs 1972-, asst to vice pres personnel 1968-72, employment supr 1966-68; Chesebrough-Ponds Inc, wage & salary analyst1964-66; Traveler's Ins Co, underwriter 1963-64; EEO Cornell Univ Sch of Ind & Labor Rel, prof 1972-; Nat Urban League BEEP Pgm, vist prof 1972-. **Orgs:** Bd mem Cncl of Concerned Black Exec 1968-70; bd mem Assn for Integration of Mgmt 1970-74; bd cochmn Interracial Cncl for Bus Oppor NY 1973-78. **Business Addr:** Director Equal Employment Affairs, Merck & Company, PO Box 2000, Rahway, NJ 07065.

BRANCH, DOROTHY L.
Clergywoman. **Personal:** Born Feb 4, 1912, Chicago, IL; daughter of Nettie Sutton; married Lemmie. **Educ:** N Baptist Theological Seminary, ThB; Northwestern Univ & Garrett Biblical Inst, MA; Divinity School Univ of Chicago, Scholarship Awardee; Burton Theological Seminary, ThD. **Career:** Commonwealth Comm Church, founder/pastor 1946-; Douglas Park Devel Corp, pres 1968-; Bd 508 Eight City Coll of Chicago, trustee 1967-; Rehabilitation Serv Public Asst, psychologist; Cook County Rehabilitation Servs, supvr; Inst Juvenile Research, counselor. **Orgs:** Co-founder Funeral Dir Wives Assn; pres Gr Lawndale Conservation; mem Gov Walker's Task Force; chmn Lawndale Residents Urban Renewal 1954-75; vice pres Citizen Housing Commn Chicago 1969-75; bd dir Scars YMCA 1963-; mem Council Religious Leaders Chicago Urban League 1970-75. **Honors/Awds:** The Intl Yr of the Woman Citation Israeli Parliament for bringing 21 Goodwill pilgrims to Palestine after 6 day war 1967; liquidated $228,000 debt on Lanon Stone Church property 1964-74. **Business Addr:** Commonwealth Comm Church, 140 W 81st St, Chicago, IL 60620.

BRANCH, ELDRIDGE STANLEY
Clergyman. **Personal:** Born Oct 29, 1906, Houston, TX; married Delcenia Mangum. **Educ:** Conroe Coll, AB 1928, BTh 1931, PD 1936. **Career:** Natl Bapt Foreign Mission Natl Baptist Conv of Amer, sec 1949-75; Fourth Mission Baptist Ch, pastor. **Orgs:** Exec edtr Globe Advoc Newsp; sec Foreign Mission Bapt Gen Conv of TX; vice pres bd dir Stand Sav Assn; YMCA; bd mem Conroe Coll; NAACP; bd trust Bishop Coll; 3 hous proj in TX. **Honors/Awds:** Hon degree Bishop Coll. **Business Addr:** Pastor, Fourth Mission Baptist Ch, PO Box 8147, Houston, TX 77004.

BRANCH, G. MURRAY
Clergyman, educator (retired). **Personal:** Born Apr 18, 1914, Prince Edward Co, VA; son of Annie Pearl Clark and George M Branch; married; children (previous marriage): Dianne Everett Branch Nunnally. **Educ:** VA Union U, BS 1938; Andover Newton Theol Sch, BD 1941; Drew U, AM 1946; Hebrew Union Coll, further grad study 1951-52; additional grad study at Drew Univ 1952-53, 1958-59, 1962-63. **Career:** First Baptist Church, Madison NJ, pastor, 1941-44; Natl Student Coun YMCA, field sec, 1944-47; Morehouse Coll, asst to assoc prof, 1947-59; Interdenominational Theology Center, assoc prof, 1959-79, prof emeritus, 1979-; Morehouse School of Religion Interdenominational Theology Center, dir, 1963-66; Dexter Ave Baptist Church, Montgomery AL, pastor, 1966-72; Extension Dept ITC, dir, 1972-75; Dexter Ave King Memorial Baptist Church Montgomery, pastor, 1978-89; Intl Theological Ctr, prof emeritus of Old Testament. **Orgs:** President Morris Co, NJ NAACP 1942-44; mem Soc of Biblical Lit; Am Acad of Religion; Am Sch of Oriental Research; Soc for Values in Higher Edn; Friendship Bapt Church Atlanta GA 1947-; Kent Fellowship 1952; Soc for Scientific Study of Religion; Atlanta Brd of Educ Area I Adv Com 1954-57; vice polemarch Kappa Alpha Psi Frat Atlanta Alumni Chapt 1955-58; vice pres Comm of Southern Churchmen 1962-65; adv comm west side branch Butler St YMCA Atlanta 1963-66; bd dir Cleveland YMCA Montgomery Al 1969-72; bd dir Koinonia Partners Inc Americus GA 1971-77; DD Honorary Benedict Coll Columbia SC 1973; bd dir, Metro-Montgomery YMCA 1980-89; bd dir Metro-Montgomery NAACP, 1979-89, life mem; Habitat for Humanity, 1st vp, bd of dirs, 1977-80; bd dir, Habitat for Humanity International, 1989-92; Church Relations Committee US Holocaust Memorial Council, Washington, DC, 1990-92. **Honors/Awds:** Ford Foundation Fellowship for the Advancement of Education, 1951-52; Kent Fellow, 1952; Theta Phi (International Theol Hon Society), 1973; DD Benedict College, Columbia SC, Hon, 1973; Montgy Cnty, AL Bar Association, Liberty Bell Awd, 1989. **Home Addr:** 1485 S Gordon St SW, Atlanta, GA 30310-2331.

BRANCH, GEORGE
City councilman. **Personal:** Born Oct 20, 1928, Seaboard, NC. **Educ:** ICBO Rutgers, business administration course, 1970; Rutgers University, sociology, vocabulary improvement, urban studies, 1967-68; St Peters College, BS, urban policy. **Career:** City Council of Newark, council member, currently. **Orgs:** Dir, Project Pride; bd mem, Newark Board of Education; founder/supt, Parents Students Forum; promoter, Boxing Match Maker; Professional Trainers for Boxers; executive board, NAACP, 15 yrs; pres, W Dist Comm, Precinct Council; United Comm Corp; New Jersey Transit Advisory Comm. **Honors/Awds:** Outstanding Service to Youth of Newark Award, Queen of Angels Church 1970; Civic Award, Comm Partic, Beta Chap, Theta Nu Sigma 1970; Man of the Year Award, Central Ward Boys Club 1973; Outstanding Achievement Award, Essex Cty of Black Churchmen 1974; Alpha Phi Kappa, Man of the Year, 1992; Irvington, NJ mayor, Community Service Award, 1992. **Military Serv:** US Natl Guard, corporal, 2 years. **Home Addr:** 85 Boston St, Newark, NJ 07103. **Business Addr:** Councilmember, City Council of Newark, 920 Broad St, Newark, NJ 07102.

BRANCH, GERALDINE BURTON
Physician. **Personal:** Born Oct 20, 1908, Savannah, GA; daughter of Agusta Freeman and Joseph Burton; married Robert Henry; children: Elizabeth Doggette, Robert Henry III. **Educ:** Hunter Coll, BA 1931; NY Med Coll, MD 1936; UCLA, MPH 1961. **Career:** Private practice, physician ob/gyn 1938-53; LA Dept of Health Svcs, dist health officer 1964-71, reg dir health serv 1971-74; USC, assoc clinical prof comm med 1966; Watts Health Found Inc, dir preventive health serv 1976-78, med dir, medical consultant, currently. **Orgs:** Bd of govs LA Co Med Assn 1966-70; bd of dir Am Lung Assn 1970-76; pres Federated Kings Daughters Clubs 1966-70; mem Nat Med Assn 1968; Walter Gray Crump Fellowship NY Med Coll 1932-36. **Honors/Awds:** UCSB, Healing Hands Award, 1992; King-Drew Medical, Academic Boosters Award, 1992. **Special Achievements:** Author, "Study of Gonorrhea in Infants & Children," Public Health Reports, 1964; "Study of Use of Neighborhood Aides in Control of a Diphtheria Outbreak," 1966; "Study of Use of Non-Physicians in HB Control," Preventive Med, 1977; "Study of the Adult-Day-Health-Care Center of the Watts Health Foundation," paper presented to the ASA, 1990; "Study of the Problems Concerning the Care of the Alzheimer's patient," paper presented to the Alzheimer's Society, 1992. **Business Addr:** Medical Consultant, Geriatrics & Homebound, Watts Health Foundation, 2620 Industry Way, Lynwood, CA 90262.

BRANCH, HARRISON
Educator, artist. **Personal:** Born Jun 6, 1947, New York, NY; son of Marguerite Williams Branch and Harrison Branch Sr; married Jacqueline Susan Hyde; children: Harrison III, Alexander Hyde, Olivia Marguerite Elizabeth. **Educ:** SF Art Inst, BFA 1970; Yale Univ Sch of Art, MFA 1972. **Career:** OR State Univ, asst prof art 1972-77; Owens Valley Photograph Workshop 1978-86; OR State Univ, assoc prof/prof art 1977-84, professor of art 1984-. **Orgs:** Guest lectr & photographer, Univ of Bridgeport 1970-71. **Honors/Awds:** Recip, Alice Kimball Travelling Fellowship Yale Univ Sch of Art 1972; Research Grant, OR State Found 1974; Research Grant, OR State Univ Grad Sch 1976-77; published photographs in Think Black, Bruce Publishing Co, NY, 1969, and in An Illustrated Bio-Bibliography of Black Photographers, 1980-88, Garland Publishing Co, NY; photographs in collections of Intl Museum of Photography at George Eastman House, Rochester, NY, and Bibliotheque Nationale, Paris, France. **Home Addr:** 1104 N W 29th St, Corvallis, OR 97330. **Business Addr:** Professor of Art/Photography, Oregon State Univ, Dept Art, Corvallis, OR 97331.

BRANCH, OTIS LINWOOD
Educational administrator. **Personal:** Born Sep 7, 1943, Norfolk, VA. **Educ:** Chicago Conservatory Coll, MusB 1966; Chicago Mus Coll of Roosevelt Univ, MusM 1974. **Career:** LaGrange Park (N) Public Schools, chmn music dept, 1970-; Chicago Conservatory Coll, dean admissions & records, 1979-82; Bremen High School, Midlothian IL, dir choral music & humanities, 1970-. **Orgs:** Curriculum writer State Bd of Educ Elem Mus IL; curriculum writer State Bd of Educ Allied Arts IL; evaluator N Central Assn and State Bd of Educ IL Music Educator's Natl Conf; Natl Educ Assn; Humanities Educators Assn;. **Business Addr:** Dir Choral Music/Humanities, Bremen High School, 15203 S Pulaski Rd, Midlothian, IL 60445.

BRANCH, WILLIAM BLACKWELL
Playwright, producer, professor. **Personal:** Born Sep 11, 1927, New Haven, CT; son of Iola Douglas Branch and James Matthew Branch; divorced; children: Rochelle Ellen. **Educ:** Northwestern U, BS 1949; Columbia U, MFA 1958; Columbia U, Postgrad Study 1958-59; Yale Univ Resident Fellow, 1965-66. **Career:** Theatre TV & Motion Pictures, playwright 1951-; The Jackie Robinson Column in NY Post and Syndication, co-author 1958-60; Channel 13 Educ TV NYC, staff writer/producer 1962-64; Columbia Sch of Arts, assoc in film 1968-69; Universal Studios, screenwriter 1968-69; NBC News, producer 1972-73; William Branch Assocs, pres 1973-; Univ of Maryland, vstg prof 1979-82; Luce Fellow Williams Coll 1983; Cornell Univ, prof 1985-94; Univ of California, regents lectr 1985; William Paterson College, visiting distinguished professor, 1994-96. **Orgs:** New York City Bd of Educ, consult 1975-77; consult Ford Foundation Office of Communications 1976; natl adv bd Ctr for the Book Library of Congress 1979-83; treasurer, Natl Conference on African American Theatre 1987-91; National Advisory Board, WEB DuBois Foundation, 1987-. **Honors/Awds:** Hannah B Del Vecchio Awd Columbia 1958; Robert E Sherwood Awd for Light in the Southern Sky 1958; Blue Ribbon Awd for Still a Brother: Inside the Negro Middle Class, Amer Film Festival 1969; author ''Fifty Steps Toward Freedom'' 1959; works include (theatre) A Medal for Willie 1951, In Splendid Error 1954, A Wreath for Udomo 1960, To Follow the Phoenix 1960, Baccalaureate 1975; TV, Light in the Southern Sky 1958; Still a Brother, 1969 (Emmy Award nominee); documentary TV series Afro American Perspectives 1974-83; exec producer Black Perspective on the News, Pub Broadcasting System 1978-79; A Letter from Booker T 1987; screen, ''Together for Days'' 1971; American Book Award for Black Thunder 1992; John Simon Guggenheim Fellowship 1959-60; American Broadcasting Co. Fellowship Yale University 1965-66; National Conference of Christians & Jews Citations for Light in the Southern Sky 1958 and A Letter from Booker T 1988. **Special Achievements:** Editor, author, Black Thunder: An Anthology of Contemporary African-American Drama, 1992; editor, author, Crosswinds: An Anthology of Black Dramatists in the Diaspora, 1993. **Military Serv:** AUS 1951-53. **Business Addr:** President, William Branch Associates, 53 Cortlandt Ave, New Rochelle, NY 10801.

BRANCH, WILLIAM MCKINLEY
Judge (retired), cleric. **Personal:** Born May 10, 1918, Forkland, AL; married Alberta; children: William, Thaddeus, Patricia, Alberta, Malcolm, Vivian, Wanda. **Educ:** Selma U, AB 1944; Union Theol Sch Selma U, DD, LLD 1976; AL State U, BS 1956. **Career:** Eberneezer Bapt Ch, pastor. **Orgs:** Probate judge/chmn Greene Co Commn; co-chmn/past pres Greene Co Educ Assn; past chmn Greene Co Housing Auth; co-chmn Greene Co Dem Exec Com 1976-77; bd dir Greene Co Hlth Svc; mem Nat Assn Co Commr; AL Probate Judge's Assn; Assn Co Commn; Mental Hlth Assn AL; mem NACO Transp Steering Comm; chmn Rural Transp Comm; AL Law Enforcement Planning Agency State Supervisory Bd; mem State-Wide Hlth Cncl AL; mem Lt Gov Staff; Christian Valley Bapt Ch. **Honors/Awds:** Cert of Merit Birmingham Urban League Guild; Cert Recog Fed Greene Co Empl; Leadership Award Augurn Univ Exten Svc; Distgsd Serv Award Greene Co Urban League; Award Outstand Courage S Polit Arena; Hon Lt Col Aide de Camp; Cert Apprctn TN Tombigee Waterway. **Home Addr:** Rt 1 Box 1375, Forkland, AL 36740.

BRANCHE, GILBERT M.
Government official. **Personal:** Born Mar 16, 1932, Philadelphia, PA; son of Wilma M Brown Branche and Merwin E Branche; married Jean Overton; children: Andrea, Dolores, Kelle; children: Quincy, Nickkiiah. **Educ:** Univ of PA, B of Political Sci 1968; PA State Police Exec Devel Course, Cert 1974; FBI Academy, Cert 1975. **Career:** Philadelphia Police Dept, policeman, sgt, lieutenant, captain 1957-74; Philadelphia Dist Atty Office, dep chief co detective 1970-74; Philadelphia Police Dept, inspector 1974-78; Philadelphia Dist Atty Office, chief co detective beginning 1978; Deputy Sec of Fraud and Abuse Investigation & Recovery for Commonwealth of PA; National Organization of Black Law Enforcement Executives, asst exec dir, currently. **Orgs:** Bd dir, vice pres Safe St 1968-80; police consult Assn Consult Wash, DC 1972-77; pres Blacks in Blue 1974-76; pres Natl Orgn of Black Law Enforce Exec 1979-; commr Standard & Accred of Police 1979-; past pres Circle NOBLE 1983-; Free & Accepted Mason. **Honors/Awds:** Meritorious Serv Award Philadelphia City Council 1968; Man of the Year Award Voice Pub 1978; Humanitarian Award Chapel of Four Chaplains 1979; Distinguished Career Award Co Detective Assn of PA 1980; Humanitarian Awd Natl Orgn of Black Law Enforcement Exec 1983; Trail Blazer in Law Enforcement Awds State of PA 1985; James Reaves Man of the Year Awd 1986; inducted into PA Policeman Hall of Fame, International Police 1988. **Military Serv:** USAF, s/sgt, 1951-55; Good Conduct Medal; Korean Serv Medal. **Business Addr:** Assistant Executive Director, National Organization of Black Law Enforment Executives, 4609 Pinecrest Office Park Dr, Ste F, Alexandria, VA 22312-1442.

BRANCHE, WILLIAM C., JR.
Scientist. **Personal:** Born Sep 5, 1934, Washington, DC; son of Frances Branche and William C Branche Sr; married Eloise; children: Christine, Michael, Marc. **Educ:** OH Wesleyan Univ, BA 1956; George Washington Univ, MS 1959; Cath Univ of Amer, PhD 1969. **Career:** Dept of Microbiology, virologist 1958-61; Gastroenteritis Stud Sec, chief 1961-68; Niesseria Meningitis Stud Sec, chief 1968-72; Walter Reed Army Inst of Rsch, safety officer div of comm dis & immun 1971-, safety officer dept of bact dis 1971-76; Inf Dis Serv Lab, chief 1972-76; USAMRD Ad Hoc Comm on Bact & Myopic Dis, asst proj dir 1974-; Walter Reed Army Inst of Rsch, health sci admin 1976-78; NIH Bacteriology & Mycology SS Div of Rsch Grant, health sci admin & scientific review administration, 1979-. **Orgs:** Mem Equal Employment Opportunity Council Walter Reed Army Med Ctr 1969-, Walter Reed Army Inst of Rsch Inc Awd Comm 1969-73, Walter Reed Army Inst of Rsch Ed Bd 1969-; vp, bd of dir Pointer Ridge Swim & Rac, Club 1971-76; asst prof Fed City Coll & Natl Inst of Rsch Camp 1971-76; chmn Walter Reed Army Inst of Rsch Inc Awd Comm 1973-; mem bd of dir South Bowie Boys & Girls Club 1976-80; pres, bd of dir Pointer Ridge Swim & Rac Club 1976; mem Amer Soc of Microbiology; ASM Membership Committee, 1980-90; ASM Manpower Committee, 1989-; ASM Bd of Ed, 1993; Sigma Xi, Amer Wildlife Soc; Staff Training in Extramural Programs Committee (STEP) NIH 1985-88. **Honors/Awds:** 1st black Teaching Assistant George Washington Univ 1956-58; Rsch Grant USN George Washington School of Med 1956-58; Citizen of the Year Awd Kiwanas Club of Bowie 1980; publ numerous articles; NIH Merit Award 1989. **Business Addr:** Health Sci Admin, Exec Sec, Natl Inst of Health, Division of Research Grants, Bethesda, MD 20892.

BRANCH RICHARDS, GERMAINE GAIL
Educator, counselor. **Personal:** Born Apr 25, Philadelphia, PA; daughter of Germaine Lopez Jackson Branch and Earl Joseph Branch; children: Kwadjo. **Educ:** Interamerican University of Puerto Rico, attended; Bennett College, BA 1969; Montclair State Coll, MA 1971; Ohio State Univ, PhD 1984. **Career:** Orange, NJ Bd of Educ, teacher 1969-71; Guilford Co NC Neighborhood Youth Corps, ed specialist 1971-73; OH Dominican Coll Upward Bound, assoc dir 1973-77; Ohio State Univ, grad admin assoc 1978-82; OH Bd of Regents, rsch assoc 1980; Ohio State Univ, dir minority assistance program 1982-89; director, Medpath College of Medicine, Ohio State University, 1989-91; Palm Beach County Schools, counselor, 1994-; Palm Beach Community College, Lynn University, Nova Southeastern University, adjunct professor, 1991-94. **Orgs:** Mem Amer Personnel & Guidance Assn 1978-; mem Natl Assn of Women Deans & Counselors 1978-; adv bd mem OSU Upward Bound 1979-91; team sec Mifflin Youth Assn 1985-89; mem Natl Assn Student Personnel Admin 1985-; consultant State of OH 1986; mem Northwest Coll Placement Assn 1986; mem, Assn for the Study of Classical African Civilizations 1986-; mem, Assn of Black Psychologists 1985-, vice pres, 1988-89; Palm Beach County Counseling Association. **Honors/Awds:** Conference Presentation, Black Student Development, An Africentric Perspective 1988. **Home Addr:** 177 Bobwhite Rd, Royal Palm Beach, FL 33411-1734.

BRAND, DOLLAR. See IBRAHIM, ABDULLAH.

BRANDFORD, NAPOLEON, III
Business executive. **Personal:** Born Feb 23, 1952, East Chicago, IN; son of Cora Lee Brandford; married Sharon Delores Bush. **Educ:** Purdue Univ, BA 1974; Univ of S Calif, MPA 1978. **Career:** Union Carbide-Linde Air Div, summer intern 1970; Standard Oil of Indiana, Summer intern 1971-74; Pacific Telephone, asst transportation coordinator 1976-78; Dade County Finance Dept, asst finance dir 1978-82; Shearson Lehman Bros, Inc, vice president-public finance ; Grigsby, Brandford Inc, dir, investment banking division, vice-chairman; Siebert Brandford Shank Inc, co-owner, currently. **Orgs:** Member Natl Forum of Black Public Administrators 1983-; executive secretary Builders Mutual Surety Co 1984-85; board member Urban Economic Development Corporation 1984-; committee member Mayor's Advisory Committee for International Trade and Foreign Investment Program 1985-; National Assn of Securities Professionals, 1987; University of Southern California Alumni Assn, 1985; board of directors, Alta Bates Medical Center; trustee, San Jose Museum of Modern Art; member, National Black MBAs; interim deputy treasurer/chief financial officer, California Health Care Foundation. **Honors/Awds:** Basketball Hall of Fame East Chicago Roosevelt 1975; Employee Suggestion Award Dade Cty Manager's Office 1981; Recipient Leadership Miami Alumni Assn 1982; Ebony Magazine, Young Tycoons, 1988; Carnation, Men of Courage, 1990. **Business Addr:** Chairman, Siebert Brandford Shank, Inc, 220 Sansome St, 15th Fl, San Francisco, CA 94104.

BRANDON, BARBARA
Cartoonist. **Personal:** Born in Long Island, NY; daughter of Brumsic Brandon Jr. **Career:** Universal Press, syndicated cartoonist, Where I'm Coming From, comic strip, 1991-. **Special Achievements:** First African-American woman to be syndicated in more than 50 newspapers nationwide for the Where I'm Coming From comic strip. **Business Addr:** Cartoonist, c/o Universal Press, 10 Park Lane, Providence, RI 02907-3124, (401)944-2700.

BRANDON, CARL RAY
Therapist. **Personal:** Born Nov 15, 1953, Port Gibson, MS; son of Marjorie Williams Brandon and Alonzo Brandon; married Debra Cynthoria Kiwa, Jun 2, 1984; children: Ashlea. **Educ:** Alcorn State Univ, BS 1976; Alcorn State Univ, MS 1984; additional studies, Univ of Southern Mississippi, Alcorn State Univ. **Career:** Claiborne Cty Public Schools, counselor 1977-84; Southwest Mental Health Complex, case mgr II 1984-88, therapist 1988-; Thompson Funeral Home, Port Gibson MS funeral dir, 1971-. **Orgs:** Mem MS Assoc of Ed 1977-, MS Counseling Assn 1981-, MS Deputy Sheriffs Assn 1982-, MS Assn of Constable 1984-; Sunday school teacher, bd of deacon China Grove MB Church Port Gibson MS; Grand Gulf State Park, Port Gibson MS, bd of dirs 1988; State of Mississippi, Certified Hunter Safety, instructor 1981. **Honors/Awds:** Charlie Griffin, member of Congress, Citizenship Award. **Home Addr:** Rte 01 Box 138, Port Gibson, MS 39150.

BRANDON, DAVID SHERROD
Professional football player. **Personal:** Born Feb 9, 1965, Memphis, TN; married Zondra; children: Xzavian. **Educ:** Memphis. **Career:** San Diego Chargers, linebacker, 1987-90, 1995; Cleveland Browns, 1991-93; Seattle Seahawks, 1993-94; Atlanta Falcons, 1996-. **Business Addr:** Professional Football Player, Atlanta Falcons, Two Falcon Place, Suwanee, GA 30174, (404)945-1111.

BRANDON, TERRELL (THOMAS TERRELL)
Professional basketball player. **Personal:** Born May 20, 1970, Portland, OR; son of Charlotte. **Educ:** Univ of Oregon. **Career:** Cleveland Cavaliers, guard, 1991-97; Milwaukee Bucks, 1997-. **Honors/Awds:** NBA All-Rookie Second Team, 1992; NBA Sportsmanship Award, 1997. **Business Addr:** Professional Basketball Player, Milwaukee Bucks, 1001 N Fourth St, Bradley Center, Milwaukee, WI 53203, (414)227-0500.

BRANDT, LILLIAN B.
Business executive. **Personal:** Born Jul 4, 1919, New York, NY; married George W Sr. **Educ:** City Coll NY. **Career:** James Daugherty Ltd, partner/vp/sec; Teal Traing Inc, 2 1/2 yrs; Sam Friedlander Inc, 27 yrs; Capri Frocks Inc, 2 yrs; Ben Reig Inc, 1 yr. **Orgs:** Mem Fashion Sales Guild; mem Fashion Cncl of NY Inc.

BRANDY (BRANDY RAYANA NORWOOD)
Vocalist, actress. **Personal:** Born Feb 11, 1979, McComb, MS; daughter of Willie Sr & Sonja Norwood. **Career:** Television: Thea; Moesha, currently; Cinderella, 1997; vocalist, self-titled album, 1994; Never Say Never, 1998; films: I Still Know. **Special Achievements:** Platinum debut album: ''Brandy''; song ''Baby'' climbed to no 5 on Billboard's pop charts. **Business Addr:** Vocalist, ''Brandy'', c/o Atlantic Recordings, 1290 Avenue of the Americas, New York, NY 10104, (212)275-2000.

BRANGMAN, H. ALAN
Educational administrator. **Personal:** Born Apr 20, 1952, Hamilton, Bermuda; son of Carolyn I Brangman and Oliver G Brangman Jr; married Patricia A Brangman, Sep 3, 1988; children: Jacob, Jessica, Alaina. **Educ:** Cornell University, BArch, 1976; Harvard GSD, Business School, certificate, 1984; Wharton School of Business, real estate primer certificate, 1985. **Career:** RTKL Associates, Inc, project director, manager, 1977-83; The Oliver Carr Co, director of DC development, 1983-91; NEA-Design Arts Program, deputy director, 1991-94; Georgetown Univ, dir of facilities planning and project mgt, 1994-96, university architect, currently; City of Falls Church, mayor, 1996-. **Orgs:** Urban Land Institute, 1990-91; American Institute of Architects, 1992-; Planning Commission City of Falls Church, 1992-94, Amer Planning Assn, 1992-94. **Honors/Awds:** Lambda Alpha Intl (Real Estate Honor Society); City Council Falls Church, 1994-98; Licensed architect state of Maryland. **Special Achievements:** Alternative Careers in Architecture, AIA Video, 1990. **Business Addr:** Georgetown Univ, University Architect, Main Campus, Office of the Exec VP, 650 Bunn Intercultural Center, Washington, DC 20057, (202)687-8366.

BRANHAM, GEORGE, III
Professional bowler. **Personal:** Born Nov 21, 1962, Detroit, MI; son of Betty Ogletree Branham and George William Francis Branham II; married Jacquelyne Phend Branham, Sep 15, 1990. **Career:** Professional bowler, currently. **Orgs:** Member, Professional Bowlers Assn, 1984-. **Honors/Awds:** Southern California Junior Bowler of the Year 1983; first Black to win a Professional Bowlers Assn Tournament; Brunswick Memorial World Open, 1986, AC/Delco Classic, Professional Bowlers Assn Tournaments, 1987; Baltimore Open, 1993; Firestone Tournament of Champions, 1993; First Black to win a triple crown event. **Business Addr:** Professional Bowler, c/o Professional Bowlers Assn, 1720 Merriman Road, Akron, OH 44313.

BRANKER, JULIAN MICHAEL
Automobile dealer. **Career:** Mike Branker Buick Inc, Lincoln NE, chief executive. **Business Addr:** Chief Executive, Mike Branker Buick - Hyundai, 421 N 48th St, P O Box 30184, Lincoln, NE 68503.

BRANNEN, JAMES H., III
Pilot. **Personal:** Born Dec 25, 1940, Queens, NY; married; children: Keree, Myia, Christopher. **Educ:** Northrop Inst Tech, BS Aero Engrng 1964; Univ Baltimore Law Sch, JD 1975. **Career:** CT Legislature, mem 1973-75; US Patent Office, 1966-67; United Airlines, pilot flight mgr. **Orgs:** Cand US Sen Rep Party 1974; Rep Study Com, CT; bd dir Colchester Montessori Children's House 1973-; mem Rep Town Com 1972-; Jaycees 1972-. **Business Addr:** SFOFO, United Airlines, San Francisco Intnl Airport, San Francisco, CA 94128.

BRANNON, JAMES R.
Insurance company executive. **Personal:** Born Feb 26, 1943, Texarkana, TX; son of Ellen Brannon and James Brannon; married Dorothy Williams; children: Sherrilyn C, Deanna E. **Educ:** NC A&T State Univ, BS, Business Administration, 1967; Harvard Univ Grad School of Business Admin Program for Mgmt Devel, certificate 1975. **Career:** Liberty Mutual Insurance Co, business lines underwriter 1967-68, mgr Roxbury keypunch training center, 1968-69, commercial underwriter 1969-71, coordinator, equal employment 1971-78, asst vice pres, employee relations 1978-. **Orgs:** Mem, NAACP 1967-, A&T State Univ Alumni Assn 1967-, Harvard Business School Assoc of Boston 1976, Natl Urban League Boston 1980-; bd mem Freedom House Boston 1984-; comm mem Lexington Fair Housing 1985-; Lena Park Community Center; board member, Lexington Metco Scholarship Committee. **Honors/Awds:** Numerous articles written on career planning, preparation Black Collegian magazine. **Home Addr:** 380 Lowell St, Lexington, MA 02173, (617)863-2035. **Business Phone:** (617)861-8758.

BRANSFORD, PARIS
Surgeon. **Personal:** Born Jan 1, 1930, Huntsville, AL; married Gladys Toney; children: Paris, Toni, Traci. **Educ:** TN St U, BS 1956; Mhry Med Coll, MD 1963. **Career:** Priv Prac, surgeon; NASA Hntsvl AL, res chem mssl prog; N Cntrl Gen Hosp, bd dirs chf of staff 1973-75; Rvrsd Gen Hosp, chf of emrgncy rm 1972-. **Orgs:** Vp sec Hstn Med Frm 1973-76; pres Med Asso Almd Med Sqr 1973-; mem Alpha Phi Alpha Frat; YMCA; NAACP; Harris Co Med Assn; Am Med Assn; TX Med Assn; Am Soc of Abdmnl Srgry; lectr Srs for Am Cncr Soc. **Honors/Awds:** Recip serv to Chap Comm Delta Theta Lambda Chpts Alpha Phi Alpha Frat Inc 1971; cit of apprec Kappa Psi Phrmctcl Frat Serv to Comm 1975. **Military Serv:** USAF 1950-53. **Business Addr:** 6911 Almeda Rd, Ste 101, Houston, TX 77021.

BRANSON, HERMAN RUSSELL. See Obituaries section.

BRANTLEY, CLIFFORD (CLIFF)
Professional baseball player. **Personal:** Born Apr 12, 1968, Staten Island, NY. **Career:** Philadelphia Phillies, 1991-. **Business Addr:** Professional Baseball Player, Philadelphia Phillies, PO Box 7575, Philadelphia, PA 19101, (215)463-6000.

BRANTLEY, DANIEL
Educator. **Personal:** Born Apr 15, 1944, Savannah, GA; son of Mary Robinson Brantley; married Flossie Connor Brantley, Dec 9, 1948; children: Daniel Jr, Noicole, Jonathan, Adam. **Educ:** Savannah State College, Savannah, GA, BS, 1967; Savannah/Armstrong State Colleges, Savannah, GA, MEd, 1974; Howard University, Washington, DC, PhD, 1979. **Career:** West Georgia College, Carrollton, GA, assistant professor, 1979-82; Univ of Iowa, Iowa City, IA, assistant professor, 1982-83; Dillard University, New Orleans, LA, assistant professor, 1983-86; Univ of the Virgin Islands, St Thomas, VI, assistant professor, 1986-87; Savannah State College, Savannah, GA, associate professor, 1987-89; Alabama State University, Montgomery, Al, associate professor, 1989-. **Orgs:** Director, member, Capitol City Civitan Club, Montgomery, 1989-; member, Phi Alpha Theta History Honor Society, 1972-76; member, Pi Sigma Alpha, Political Science Honor Society, 1977-79; member, Carpi Community Film Society Inc, 1990-91 ; member, Le Club Francais de Alabama State University, 1991. **Honors/Awds:** Dissertation Fellowship, Howard Univ, 1978; Research Award, Learning Resources Committee, 1980; Graduate Fellowship, Ford Foundation, Awards, Howard Univ, 1976-78; Author, Aiding Black American Communities, Journal of State Government, 1988, Postal Administration in the Caribbean, The Griot, Southern Conference on Afro-American Studies Inc, 1990. **Home Addr:** 2112 E 43rd St, Savannah, GA 31404.

BRANTON, LEO, JR.
Attorney. **Personal:** Born Feb 17, 1922, Pine Bluff, AR; married Geri. **Educ:** TN St U, BS 1942; Nrthwstrn U, JD 1949. **Career:** Pvt Prac LA, atty 1949-; Angela Davis, prtcptd in scsfl def 1972; Hlywd Entrtnrs, rprsntd as atty; Communists, rprsntd as atty; Poor Blcks Rblnin Watts, atty 1965; Blck Pnthr Prty, def mem in civ rights actvsts arstd in the so. **Orgs:** Mem ACLU; NAACP; St Bar of CA; Wilshire Bar Assn; J M Langston Law Club. **Honors/Awds:** Recpt outsdng contrib to fld Crmnl Ltgtn Awd 1972; Lwyr of Yr 1974; Trl Lwyr of Yr J M Langston Bar Assn 1973. **Business Addr:** Attorney at Law, 3460 Wilshire Blvd, Ste 410, Los Angeles, CA 90010.

BRASEY, HENRY L.
Educator. **Personal:** Born Nov 25, 1937, Cincinnati, OH; married Anna; children: Darrell, Jenifer. **Educ:** BS 1972; IBM Corp, Cert. **Career:** U Univ of Cincinnati, asst dir of computer serv/adjunct asst prof of engineering analysis; Regional Computer City of Cincinnati, programming proj leader; Full House Inc, pres; Withrow HS Data Processing Prog, curriculum adv. **Orgs:** Mem Assn for Computing Machinery; mem Kennedy Heights Comm Cncl; Ken-Sil Athletic Club; Pleasant Ridge PTA. **Business Addr:** Director, Acad Computer Ser, University of Cincinnati, Mail Location 149, Cincinnati, OH 45221.

BRASHEAR, BERLAIND LEANDER
Judge. **Personal:** Born Apr 18, 1934, Dallas, TX; married Johnnie Mae Blanton; children: Rhonda Elaine, John Henry, Bradley Nathaniel. **Educ:** Prairie View Coll A & M, 1962; TX Southern Univ Sch of Law 1967. **Career:** Dallas Legal Svc, staff atty 1968; private practice 1969-75; municipal judge 1975-77; cnty criminal judge 1977-. **Orgs:** TX Bar Assn; Dallas Cty Bar Assn; TX Judges Assn; Am Judge Assn; bd of dir Operation PUSH; Negro Chamber of Commerce; Nat Bar Assn; bd of dir WestDallas Community Cntrs. **Honors/Awds:** Am Acad of Judicial Edn; Negro Chamber of Commerce; J L Turner Legal Assn. **Military Serv:** USMC pfc good conduct medal 1954-57. **Business Addr:** Judge, Cnty Criminal Court #6, 600 Commerce, Dallas, TX 75202.

BRASHEAR, DONALD
Professional hockey player. **Personal:** Born Jan 7, 1972, Bedford, IN. **Career:** Montreal Canadians, 1992-96; Vancouver Canucks, left wing, 1996-. **Business Addr:** Professional Hockey Player, Vancouver Canucks, 800 Griffin Way, Vancouver, BC, Canada V6B 6G1, (604)899-4600.

BRASS, REGINALD STEPHEN
Association executive. **Personal:** Born Sep 6, 1958, Los Angeles, CA; son of Ernest Brass & Mildred Jackson; divorced; children: Stephen Reginald II. **Career:** Bodyguard; Saint Anne's Maternity House, teacher/counselor; Mini House, teacher/counselor; My Child Says Daddy, founder/pres, 1991-. **Orgs:** Pregnant Minor Task Force of the Sex Equity Commission of the LAUSD; Maranatha Community Church; Los Angeles County, family advisor bd, child support. **Honors/Awds:** Honorable Gwen Moore, Community Architect Award, 1994; California Dept of Social Services, Director's Award, 1994; Yvonne Brathwaite Burke, Commendation, 1994; St Stephen's Educational Bible College, Honorary Doctor of Letters, 1996. **Business Addr:** Founder, My Child Says Daddy, 3856 Martin Luther King Jr Blvd, Ste 204, Los Angeles, CA 90008, (213)296-8816.

BRASWELL, PALMIRA
Educator. **Personal:** Born Mar 23, 1928, Macon, GA. **Educ:** Fort Valley State Coll, AB 1950; Teachers College Columbia Univ, MA 1959; Univ of GA, EdS 1969; Principals Ctr Harvard Univ, attended 1985. **Career:** Bibb Co Bd of Educ and NY Bd of Educ, teacher 1950-64; Bibb Co Bd of Educ, dir instructional materials ctr 1965-74, curriculum dir 1977-83, dir staff development 1983-. **Orgs:** Past mem Civil Service Bd City of Macon 1976-79; past basileus Epsilon Omega Omega-Alpha Kappa Alpha 1979-83; past mem Booker T Washington Comm Ctr 1979-83; mem curriculum council Mercer Univ Medical School 1979-80; past mem Middle GA Chap Amer Red Cross 1980-84; state sec Professional Assoc of GA Educators;pres Middle Georgia Chap Phi Delta Kappa 1986-. **Honors/Awds:** 1st Black female radio announcer City of Macon GA station WBML 1956-58; Teacher of the Yr BS Ingram Elem Sch 1976; 1 of 20 Most Influential Women in Middle GA NAACP Macon Chap 1981; Disting Alumni Awd, Presidential Citation Natl Assoc in Higher Educ for Equal Oppor 1986. **Home Addr:** 3016 Paige Dr, Macon, GA 31211. **Business Addr:** Director, Staff Development, Bibb County Bd of Educ, 2064 Vineville Ave, P O Box 6157, Macon, GA 31213.

BRAUGHER, ANDRE
Actor. **Personal:** married Amy Brabson; children: Michael. **Educ:** Stanford Univ, BA; Juilliard School, MFA. **Career:** Actor, currently. **Special Achievements:** TV include: ''Homicide: Life on the Street,'' 1993-98; ''The Tuskegee Airmen,'' HBO; ''Everybody Has To Shoot the Picture,'' HBO; ''Murder in Mississippi,'' NBC; ''The Court-Martial of Jackie Robinson;'' Films include: Glory, Primal Fear, Get On The Bus; Theatre include: ''Henry V,'' ''King John,'' NY Shakespeare Festival; ''Othello,'' Folger Shakespeare Festival; ''The Way Of The World,'' ''Richard II,'' ''Measure for Measure,'' ''Twelfth Night,'' ''Coriolanus,'' Joseph Papp Public Theater. **Business Addr:** Actor, c/o NBC Television, 30 Rockefeller Plaza, New York, NY 10112.

BRAXTON, EDWARD KENNETH
Priest, educator, theologian, author. **Personal:** Born Jun 28, 1944, Chicago, IL; son of Mr & Mrs Cullen L. Braxton, Sr. **Educ:** BA, 1966; MA, 1968; M, Div, 1969; STB, 1968; PhD, 1975; STD, 1976; Univ of Chicago, Postdoctoral Fellowship. **Career:** Harvard Univ, 1976-77; Notre Dame Univ, visiting prof, 1977-78; Diocese of Cleveland, chancellor for theological affairs & personal theology; Archdiocese ofWashington, DC, chancellor for theological affairs, 1978-81; Rome North Amer Coll, scholar in residence, 1982-83; Univ of Chicago, Catholic Student Center, dir; William H Sadlier Inc, official theological cons; 1988 winter school lecturer, South Africa. **Orgs:** Mem, Amer Acad of Religion; Catholic Theological Soc of Amer; Black Catholic Clergy Caucus; Catholic Bishop's Committee on Liturgy & Doctrine; bd of dir, St Mary of the Lake Seminary, Chicago; keynote speaker, 43 Intl Eucharistic Congress, Nairobi, Kenya; theological advisor to bishops of Africa & Madagascan, 1984; del, writer & speaker for Historic Natl Black Catholic Congress, Washington, DC 1987. **Honors/Awds:** Published, The Wisdom Comm; numerous articles on Catholic Theological Religion; forthcoming book, One Holy Catholic and Apostolic: Essays for the Community of Faith.

BRAXTON, HARRIET E.
Elected official. **Personal:** Born Jul 18, 1926, Charlotte, NC; married Paul A Braxton; children: Paula E Arp, Rosemary L Smith, Harriet A Price, Regina B Mitchell, Julia L, Diana A, Paul M. **Educ:** William Penn HS, Cert Housing Inspectors 1970, Cert HAAC 1972; Latestart Uptown Sr Citizens, Cert 1982. **Career:** Mechanicsburg Naval Depot, clerk typist 1945-49; PA Dept of Revenue, addressograph op 1961-63; City of Harrisburg, housing inspector 1968-71; Harrisburg Housing Authority, housing coun/res ad 1972-73; City of Harrisburg, councilwoman appointed 1982, elected 1983-; Capital Cty Ret Cntr Inc, by-laws comm mem. **Orgs:** Comm chair Uptown Civic Assoc 1963-73; dir Harrisburg Opportunity Bd 1963-65; neighborhood aide Harrisburg Opportunity Program 1965-67; mem Mayor's Advisory Comm 1966-68; bookmobile asst Harrisburg Public Library 1967; inspector of elections Tenth Ward Second Precinct 1975-80; judge of elect 10th ward 2nd precinct 1980; bd mem YWCA 1977; bd mem YMCA 1968; mem of Our Lady of Blessed Sacrament Ch; mem OLBS School PTA. **Honors/Awds:** Braxton Playground Uptown Civic Assoc & City 1965; Merit of Honor Sixth St Uptown Revit Eff 1978-85, Amer Red Cross 1977; Faces & Places Harrisburg Historical Soc 1984; Banneker Tennis Champion 1940; 2nd Place Winner AAU Basketball; 1st Natl Medal Set Baseball throw Fager Field (235 ft) Harrisburg, PA; Capt Soccer Team William Penn HS 1943. **Home Addr:** 2142 N 7th St, Harrisburg, PA 17110. **Business Addr:** Councilwoman, Harrisburg City Council, City Government Center, Harrisburg, PA 17101.

BRAXTON, JANICE LAWRENCE
Professional basketball player. **Personal:** Born Jun 7, 1962; married Steve Braxton. **Educ:** Louisiana Tech, attended. **Career:** Cleveland Rockers, center, 1997-. **Honors/Awds:** Pan Am Games Basketball Team, Gold Medal, 1983; World Championship Basketball Team, Silver Medal, 1983; US Olympic Basketball Team, Gold Medal, 1984. **Business Addr:** Professional Basketball Player, Cleveland Rockers, One Center Ct, Cleveland, OH 44115, (216)263-7625.

BRAXTON, JOHN LEDGER
Judge. **Personal:** Born Feb 6, 1945, Philadelphia, PA. **Educ:** PA State Univ, BS 1966; Howard Univ School of Law, JD 1971. **Career:** Wolf, Block Schorr & Solis-Cohen, assoc 1971-73; Braxton, Johnson & Kopanski, partner 1973-76; Blue Cross of Greater Philadelphia, assoc counsel 1976-78; Asst Dist Atty, chief 1978-81; Court of Common Pleas, judge; Phoenix Management Services, vice pres, currently. **Orgs:** Bd mem Fellowship Commission 1978-85; vice pres Child Psychiatry Center St Christopher's 1976-85; bd mem Judicial Council Natl Bar 1984-85; bd mem Philadelphia Citywide Devel Corp 1981-85; pres Homemaker Serv of the Metropolitan Area; Philadelphia Council Boy Scouts of Amer; National Bar Association, Judical Council, chairman, 1992-93. **Honors/Awds:** State of Black Philadelphia Philadelphia Urban League 1984; Outstanding Alumnus Howard Univ; Boy Scouts of America, Phila Council, Silver Beaver. **Military Serv:** AUS 1st lt 1966-68; bronze star with 1st oak cluster 1968. **Business Addr:** Vice President, Phoenix Management Services, Inc, 110 Chadds Ford Commons, Chadds Ford, PA 19317, (610)358-4700.

BRAXTON, TONI
Vocalist. **Personal:** Born 1968; daughter of Evelyn Braxton and Rev. Michael Braxton. **Career:** Vocalist; self-titled album, 1993; Secrets, 1996. **Business Addr:** Singer, c/o Laface Records, 6 W 57th St, New York, NY 10019.

BRAXTON, TYRONE SCOTT
Professional football player. **Personal:** Born Dec 17, 1964, Madison, WI; married Elizabeth. **Educ:** North Dakota State. **Career:** Denver Broncos, defensive back, 1987-93, 1995-; Miami Dolphins, 1994. **Honors/Awds:** NFL Players Assn, Unsung Hero, 1996; Pro Bowl, 1996; Mackey Award, 1997. **Business Addr:** Professional Football Player, Denver Broncos, 13655 Broncos Pkwy, Englewood, CO 80112, (303)649-9000.

BRAY, LEROY, SR.
Engineer. **Personal:** Born Aug 1, 1950, Norwich, CT; son of Beatrice Bray and Luther Bray; married Patricia Baldwin, Dec 17, 1983; children: Anthony, Desiree, Marquita, Tiffany, Leroy Jr. **Educ:** Howard Univ, BSEE, 1973; Central Michigan Univ,

MBM, 1980. **Career:** Owens Corning Fiberglass, process electrical engineeer, 1973-76; Ford Motor Company, maintenance supervisor, 1976-80; General Motors, manufacturing engineer, 1980-87; Ford Motor Company, automotive safety program manager, 1987-. **Orgs:** American Society for Quality Control, senior member, 1989-. **Honors/Awds:** American Society for Quality Control, Certified Quality Engineer, 1989; American Society for Quality Control, Certified Quality Auditor, 1990. **Business Addr:** Automotive Safety Program Manager, Ford Motor Co, 330 Town Center Dr, Fairlane Plaza South, Ste 400, Dearborn, MI 48126, (313)594-9772.

BRAYNON, EDWARD J., JR.
Dentist (retired). **Personal:** Born Jan 15, 1928, Miami, FL; son of May Dell Jackson Braynon and Edward J Braynon; married Ann Carey; children: Edward III, Keith. **Educ:** Howard Univ, BS 1949, DDS 1954. **Career:** USAF, dental officer 1954-56; private practice, dentist 1956-87; Family Health Center Inc, chief of dental serv 1981-87, vice president of supplemental services, 1987-96. **Orgs:** Past pres Dade Cnty Acad of Med 1962-63; past pres Dade Cnty Dental Soc 1970-72; grand baseileus Omega Psi Phi Frat Inc 1976-79. **Honors/Awds:** Outstanding serv to the community and profession, Howard Univ Washington DC 1976; "Dr E J Braynon, Jr Day" City of Miami, FL 1976; Key to City Columbus, GA 1973; Key to City Fayetville, NC 1976; Key to City Spartanberg, SC 1977; Key to Dade County, FL 1976; One of the 100 Most Influential Black Americans, Ebony Magazine, 1977-79; Honorary Citizen of Louisville KY, Louisville KY, 1977; Honorary Citizen of New Orleans, LA, New Orleans, LA, 1977; Distinguished Service, Florida Dental Association, 1990. **Military Serv:** USAF capt 1954-56. **Home Addr:** 2271 NE 191st St, North Miami Beach, FL 33180.

BRAZIER, WILLIAM H.
Editor, publisher. **Personal:** Born Aug 1, 1922, Xenia, OH; son of Phyllis Brazier and William Brazier; married Alice Marie; children: Tony, Michele. **Educ:** Wilberforce, BS 1952; Teacher's Coll, MS, 1958; Bank St Coll Grad School, 1970-72; Hofstra Univ Grad School, 1975. **Career:** "Big Payoff," "Strike It Rich" shows, TV prod asst 1952-54; NY Amsterdam News, advertising rep 1953-56; New York City Bd of Educ Higher Horizons Proj, dir audio-visual instructional serv 1964-66; New York City Public School, admin 1984 retired; Long Island Weekly Voice, editor, publisher, founder; Long Island Voice Associates, president, currently. **Orgs:** Former vice chmn, public relations, Omega Psi Phi; dir public relations, 2nd Dist, Omega Psi Phi; editor, publisher Omegan Newspaper & Q-2 Monthly; bd dir, cofounder, Banneker Business Devel Corp; charter mem, Long Island Black Business & Professional Men's Assn; steering comm, Harlem Teacher Assn, Suffolk County CORE, LI Black Assembly, NAACP; mem, Bethel AME Church, Huntington NY; former lecturer, adv commun, CW Post Coll Black Studies Prog; commun adv, Stony Brook State Univ Black Studies Prog; producer, Stony Brook Black World Newspaper; life mem, Disabled Amer Vets; former natl dir of public relations, Omega Psi Phi Frat Inc; mem editorial bd, The Oracle Magazine; bd dir, Suffolk County Black History Museum Assn; trustee, Breezy Point Yacht Club, Wilberforce U Alumni Assn, Huntington NAACP; executive bd, LI African American Leadership Council. **Honors/Awds:** Omega Man of the Year LI, Omega Psi Phi, Chi Rho Chapter, 1974, 1985; Second District and Natl Omega Man of the Year 1986; Wilberforce University Hall of Fame Inductee, 1996. **Military Serv:** AUS, Asiatic Pacific Theater 1943-45. **Business Addr:** President, Long Island Voice Associates, PO Box 751, Amityville, NY 11701.

BRAZIL, ERNEST L.
Attorney. **Personal:** Born Dec 16, 1943, Louisville, KY; married Rosemarie Yule. **Educ:** OH State U, BA 1965; Harvard Law Sch, JD 1974. **Career:** Brae Corp, gen counsel/sec; Heller Ehrman White & McAuliffe Law Firm, asso atty 1974-77. **Orgs:** Asso mem Am Bar Assn; mem Am Soc of Corp Secretaries; mem Nat Bar Assn; mem Harvard Club; mem Barristers Club; mem Airplane Owners & Pilots Assn. **Honors/Awds:** Martin Luther King Fellowship 1971; 2nd Place Award for Prose 1st Chap of "For Those In Peril" San Fran Bar Assn Creative Writing Contest. **Military Serv:** USN lt 1966-71.

BRAZIL, ROBERT D.
Educator. **Personal:** Born Mar 19, 1939, Memphis; divorced; children: Patrice, Alan. **Educ:** Chicago Tchrs Coll, BEd 1960; DePaul U, MEd 1965. **Career:** Chicago, tchr 1960; Tesla Sch, prin 1966; Headstart, prin 1966-67; US Dept Juctice, Midwest educ cnsltnt 1967; Parkside Sch, prin 1971; HEW Office Edn, non fed pnlst 1974-75; Parker HS, prin 1975. **Orgs:** Mem Kappa Alpha Psi Frat; adj prof educ McGaw Grad Sch; Natl Coll Educ Past vol S Side Comm Com; mem Beatrice Caffrey Youth Svc; Betty Boys Found; Marillac Comm House;O. **Business Addr:** Parker High School, 6800 Stewart, Chicago, IL 60621.

BRAZINGTON, ANDREW PAUL
Dentist. **Personal:** Born Jun 21, 1918, Philadelphia, PA; married Mabel Coffey; children: Andrew P. **Educ:** Howard Univ DC, BS 1949, DDS 1957. **Career:** Philadelphia Dept of Hlth, clin dntst; Private Practice, dntst New Era Dntl Soc Phila, dntst 1971-. **Orgs:** Philadelphia Cnty Dntl Soc 1958-; PA Dntl Assn 1958-; Am Dntl Assn 1958-; treas vice pres Chrstn St & Y'S Mem Club; mem Olde Philadelphia Club; mem Med Com Cncrnd wth Civ Rgts; bd of mgrs Chrstn St YMCA 1973-; mem NAACP. **Honors/Awds:** Omega Psi Phi Spec Serv Awrd Am Cancer Soc 1969; Serv Hon YMCA Philadelphia 1973-75. **Military Serv:** AUS 1st lt 1941-46. **Business Addr:** 5051 Chestnut St, Philadelphia, PA 19139.

BRAZLEY, MICHAEL DUWAIN
Architect. **Personal:** Born Apr 6, 1951, Louisville, KY; son of Gwendolyn Brazley and William Brazley; married Vallejo Miller, Apr 24, 1982; children: Erin, Katelyn. **Educ:** University of Kentucky, School of Architecture; Howard University, School of Architecture, BAr, 1978; University of Louisville, School of Urban and Public Affairs, urban infrastructure and environmental analysis, currently. **Career:** Federal Railroad Administration, Department of Transportation, MOM - PROVIDENCE, RI, project mgr, 1979; City of Louisville, streetscape designer; Kentucky Air National Guard Airplane Hangar, architect; Eastern High School, renovator; Louisville and Jefferson County Metropolitan Sewer District, storm water drainage master plan implementation; Standiford Field Airport, Air Natl Guard civil engineer, drainage, roadway and utility design; First Baptist Church, renovator; Mt Olive Missionary Baptist Church, designer; Greater Good Hope Baptist Church, designer; Brazley & Brazley, architect, currently. **Orgs:** American Institute of Architects; Kentucky Society of Architects; Construction Specification Institute; Urban Land Institute; American Planning Association; Kentuckiana Minority Supplier Development Council; Louisville Third Century; Kentucky African-American Museum Council, board member; Kentuckiana Regional Planning and Development Agency, mobility task force; YMCA; Louisville's Urban League; NAACP; University of Louisville, Black Engineers and Technicians Association, advisory board; Howard University Alumni Association; Wesley Community House, board of directors. **Honors/Awds:** KMSDC MED Awards, Professional Service Firm of the Year, 1992; Louisville/Jefferson Co Office for Economic Development, Minority Business Development, Emerging Minority Enterprise Award, 1992; Louisville Minority Business Development Center, Minority Service Firm of the Year, 1992. **Business Addr:** President/CEO, Architect, Brazley & Brazley Inc, 2246 Frankfort Ave, Louisville, KY 40206, (502)587-8080.

BREAUX, TIMOTHY
Professional basketball player. **Personal:** Born Sep 19, 1970, Baton Rouge, LA. **Educ:** Univ of Wyoming. **Career:** Milwaukee Bucks, forward, 1997-. **Business Addr:** Professional Basketball Player, Milwaukee Bucks, 1001 N Fourth St, Bradley Center, Milwaukee, WI 53203, (414)227-0500.

BRECKENRIDGE, FRANKLIN E.
Attorney (retired). **Personal:** marrIed Cora Smith, Jun 13, 1964; children: Lejene, Franklin Jr, Emma Estel. **Educ:** IN U, BS 1963, JD 1968. **Career:** Kokomo-Center Township Consolidated Schools, tchr 1963-65; Indianapolis Pre- Schools Inc, tchr 1965-66; IN Dept Revenue, admin supr corporate income tax 1966-68; private practice, 1968-73; Bayer Corp., asst sec, associate council, 1973-96. **Orgs:** Mem Elkhart City Bar Assn, Indiana Bar Assn, Amer Bar Assn; Alpha Phi Alpha Social Frat; mem Phi Delta Phi Legal Frat; numerous offices and committees NAACP; pres IN State Conf of Brs NAACP; mem Natl Bar Assn; Dem Precinct Com for Eklhart Co 1975-. **Honors/Awds:** Numerous NAACP Awards. **Home Addr:** 54653 Briarwood Dr, Elkhart, IN 46514.

BRECKENRIDGE, JACKIE B.
Labor union official. **Personal:** Born Sep 10, 1941, Okolona, MS; son of Winfred Broyles (deceased) and Cole Breckenridge; married Eva Smith Breckenridge, Feb 26, 1983; children: Michael, Winifred, Jackie Jr, Anthony. **Educ:** Okolona Coll, Okolona, MS, AA, Math/Chemistry, 1961; Jackson St Coll, Jackson, MS, Math, 1961-62; Olive Harvey Coll, Chicago, IL, AA, Business Admn, 1973; Governor St Univ, University Park, IL, Public Admin, 1973-74. **Career:** Chicago Transit Authority, money handler; Amalgamated Transit Union Local 24, board mem/1st vp, 1984; Amalgamated Transit Union (International Office), general exec bd mem/intl vp, 1984-. **Orgs:** Mem, PUSH, mem, NAACP, vice pres, Chicago Chapter/State Chapter, A Philip Randolph Institute; Coalition Black Trade Unionists; pastmaster, Mt Hebron #29, Prince Hall Lodge. **Military Serv:** Army, pfc, 1964-66.

BRECKENRIDGE, JOHN L.
Attorney, accountant. **Personal:** Born Jun 12, 1913, Maysville, KY; married Eddye M DeFoor. **Educ:** Youngstown State U, BS Bus Admin 1952, LLB 1958, JD 1969; Natl Coll of Advocacy, ATLA 1974. **Career:** Gen of OH, spcl cnsl atty 1971-; Private Practice, atty 1958-; reg pub accnt 1960-; pub accnt 1948-60. **Orgs:** Mem Am Arbtrtn Assn; The Assn of Trial Lwyrs of Am; OH State Bar Assn; Natl Assn of Crmnl Def Lwyrs; Trumbull Co Bar Assn; Mahoning Co Bar Assn; Nat Bar Assn; The AmS Judicature Soc Life mem NAACP. **Honors/Awds:** Alpha Tau Gamma Hon Accnt Frat 1952; recip Bancroft Whitney Law Sch Awrd 1955; Meritorious Serv Awrd United Negro Coll Fund 1959; Warren Rotary Club Cert 1960; Kiwanis Club of Warren Cert 1961; Omega Psi Phi 4th Dist Man of Yr 1964; Urban League Comm Serv Awrd 1974. **Military Serv:** AUS 1st sgt 1942-45. **Business Addr:** 279 Second St, Warren, OH.

BREDA, MALCOLM J.
Educator. **Personal:** Born Aug 14, 1934, Alexandria, LA. **Educ:** Xavier University of Louisiana, BS, 1956; University of Indiana, MMEd, 1962; University of Southern Mississippi, PhD, 1975. **Career:** NO Archdiocesan Music Programs, lecturer & cons; Alabama A&M University, instructor/asst professor, 1956-64; Boys Town NE, organist, pianist-in-residence, 1964-67; St John Preparatory School NO LA, director of choral activities, 1967-73; Xavier University of Louisiana, Dept of Music, professor, chairman, 1967-. **Orgs:** Alpha Kappa Mu; Phi Mu Alpha; Music Educators Natl Conference; American Guild of Organists; Afro-American Music Opportunities Assn; Natl Assn of School of Music. **Honors/Awds:** Sister M Cornelia Jubilee Award, 1952; Mother Agatha Ryan Award, 1956; ISSP Summer Fellowship, Harvard University, 1968; Natl Fellow, 1973-75. **Military Serv:** US Army, sp-4, 1956-58. **Business Addr:** Professor/Chairman, Dept of Music, Xavier University of Louisiana, 7325 Palmetto St, New Orleans, LA 70125-1056.

BREEDEN, JAMES PLEASANT
Educator. **Personal:** Born Oct 14, 1934, Minneapolis, MN; son of Florence Beatrice Thomas Breeden and Pleasant George Breeden; children: Margaret, Johanna, Frederick, Paul. **Educ:** Dartmouth Coll, BA 1956; Union Theological Seminary NYC, MDiv 1960; Harvard Grad Sch of Educ, EdD 1972. **Career:** Canon St Paul's Cathedral Episc Diocese of MA, 1963-65; Comm on Religion & Race Natl Council of Churches, asst dir, 1965-67; Comm on Church & Race MA Council of Churches, dir 1967-69; Harvard Grad Sch of Educ, assoc prof 1972-76; Univ of Das Salaam Tanzania, prof in ed 1973-75; Boston Public Schs, sr officer planning policy 1978-82; Ctr for Law & Ed, dir 1983-84; Dartmouth Coll, dean Wm Jewett Tucker Found 1984-. **Honors/Awds:** Annual Award MA Soc Worker Assn 1964; The Young Men of Boston Boston Jr Chamber of Commerce 1965; Alper Award Civil Liberties Union MA 1978. **Business Addr:** Dean, Wm Jewett Tucker Foundation, Dartmouth College, 6154 S Fairbanks, Hanover, NH 03755.

BREEDING, CARL L.
Educator, civil rights activist (retired). **Personal:** Born Aug 30, 1932, Indianapolis, IN; son of Derotha Helen Breeding and Otto E Breeding; divorced; children: Loveeta Louise Smith, Tara Lynne Mobley, Andre Lynn, Chad Lamont. **Educ:** Indianapolis Univ, AB 1955; MI State Univ, MA 1970. **Career:** Summer Youth Oppor Prog, coord 1971-72, 1974; Jackson MI Public Schools, algebra teacher 1960-88. **Orgs:** MI State Conf of NAACP 2nd vice pres 1969-70, 1st vice pres 1970-71, pres 1971-; pres MI State NAACP 1971-; candidate for mayor Jackson 1971; chmn Region II Comm Action Agency 1978; NAACP, natl bd of directors 1982-; vice pres Natl NAACP 1986-; Jackson Educ Assn Legis Com; elected mem of Rep Assembly; MI Educ Assn; life mem Natl Educ Assn; life mem NAACP; mem Jackson Br Exec Comm; bd dir vice chmn Jackson-Hillsdale Area EOC; mem exec comm Summer Youth Oppor Adv Council; MI Dem Black Caucus; bd mem Jackson Co Legal Aid Soc; Notary Public; past mem Jackson Jaycees; former mem Jackson Human Relations Commn; adv comm Jackson Citizens Sch Bd; selective serv system Local Bd #39 & McCulloch Sch PTA; appointed chmn, Jackson County Friend of The Court Citizen Advisory Committee, 1997; elected to the Jackson Michigan City Council, selected as Mayor protem, 1997. **Honors/Awds:** Outstanding Young Educator 1965; rec Resolution of Tribute from MI Legislature; Outstanding NAACP State Conference President, 1989. **Military Serv:** US Army, 1956-57. **Business Addr:** Retired Educator, PO Box 361, Jackson, MI 49204.

BREMBY, RODERICK LEMAR
City official. **Personal:** Born Feb 4, 1960, Eufaula, AL; son of Margaret J Robinson-Johnson and Johnny B Bremby; married April Lynne Harris Bremby, Jun 19, 1982; children: Rachel, Arielle. **Educ:** Univ of Kansas, Lawrence KS, BA, 1982, MPA, 1984. **Career:** City of Fort Worth, Fort Worth TX, mgmt intern, 1983-84, admin analyst I, 1984-85, admin analyst II, 1985, admin analyst III, 1985-86, asst to city mgr, 1986-90; City of Lawrence, Lawrence, KS, assistant city manager, 1990-. **Orgs:** Assoc mem, Intl City Mgmt Assn, 1983-; pres, Urban Mgmt Asst of N Texas, 1986; mem, City of Fort Worth Juneteenth Planning Comm, 1986-; mem, City of Forth Worth MLK Planning Comm, 1986-; mem, Leadership Fort Worth, 1987-; pres, 1989-, sec, 1986-89, Natl Forum for Black Public Admin, N Texas Chapter; member, Forum Fort Worth, 1988-90; vice president, NFBPA Council of Presidents, 1990-; member, Pi Sigma Alpha, 1984. **Honors/Awds:** Outstanding Young Man of Amer, YMCA, 1983, 1986; R Scott Brooks Memorial Award, Univ of Kansas, 1984; author, "Voice Processing Applications in the City of Fort Worth," Town & City Magazine, 1988. **Home Addr:** 1022 Ohio, Lawrence, KS 66044. **Business Addr:** Assistant City Manager, City of Lawrence, 6 E 6th St, Lawrence, KS 66044.

BREMER, CHARLES E.
Educator, administrator. **Personal:** Born Sep 12, 1941, New Orleans, LA; married Jocelyn. **Educ:** OH Univ BS govt & hist 1965; Kent State Univ, Certified vocational guidance & counselor, 1965; Southern IL Univ/Rutgers Univ, graduate of labor internship 1978. **Career:** A Philip Randolph Educ Fund/YEP, natl dir 1978-; RTP Inc-Manpower Training & Devel, dep exec dir 1968-74; So IL U, tchr/cnslr 1967; OH State Dept of Labor, voc guid couns 1966; Cleveland Publ Schs, tchr 1965; Contini & Riffs Retails Bus, pres 1974-78. **Orgs:** Bd mediation Inst for Mediation & Conflict Resolution 1971-; chmn schlrshp com WC Handy Schlrshp Club 1975-; bd finance Workers Defense League 1979-. **Honors/Awds:** Clg schlrshp OH Univ 1960-65; Meritorious Awrd Cleveland Br RTP Inc 1974; Serv Awrd Minority Bus Ent Ctr Anchorage AK 1979. **Business Addr:** Assistant Dir, Inter Union of Electronics, Soc Act Dept, 1126 Sixteenth St NW, Washington, DC 20036.

BRENSON, VERDEL LEE
Clergyman. **Personal:** Born Feb 28, 1925, Cumberland City, TN; married Quintine Hayes; children: Beverly Elaine, Verdella Rene. **Educ:** Natl Bapt Sem, 1946. **Career:** Bryant Temple AME Los Angeles, pastor 1968; Brown Memorial AME Pasadena, pastor 1955-68; Price Chapel AME Los Angeles, pastor 1952-55; St Paul AMEImperial Valley, pastor; 1st AME Pomona, pastor 1948-51; St Mathew AME Clarksville, pastor 1946-47. **Orgs:** Past pres Intrdnmntnl Mnstrs Alliance for Pasadena & Vicinity 1960-62; del to AME Gen Conf 1968 & 1972; mem AME Minstrl Alliance of Los Angeles &vicinity; Los Angeles Br NAACP. **Honors/Awds:** Cited for comm ldrshp Los Angeles Cnclmn Robert Farrell 1974. **Business Addr:** 2525 W Vernon Ave, Los Angeles, CA 90008.

BRENT, DAVID L.
Government official. **Personal:** Born Jun 27, 1929, Forrest City, AR; married Estella Bryant; children: David Jr, Patricia, Mary, William, Jeanne. **Educ:** Blackstone Coll of Law, LLB 1966; Missouri Univ, 1963-66; Kansas State Univ, 1966; Moody Bible Inst, 1954-57. **Career:** MO Dept of Mntl Hlth, chf hmn rel ofcr 1971-; St Louis Civil Rgts Law Enfcmnt & Agy, EEOC proj dir 1969-71; Aetna Life Ins Co, consult 1967-69; Washington DC, soc serv rep 1966-67; Prog Bapt Ch, mnstr 1957. **Orgs:** Bible tchr, orgn devel human rel communctns Affirmative Action Plng; Mgmt Principles & Practices; mem NAACP; MO Black Ldrshp Assn Inc; Am Mgmt Assn; US Civil Serv League; Gov Cncl on Affrmtv Action; MO Orgn Devel Network; bd dir MBLA Pub Prsnl Mgmt Awrd 1976; consult exec order on Fair Empmt Pracs 1973. **Honors/Awds:** Human Rels Recg Awrd 1970. **Military Serv:** USAF 1948-52. **Business Addr:** 2002 Missouri Blvd, Jefferson City, MO 65101.

BREWER, ALVIN L.
Physician. **Personal:** Born Nov 8, 1946, Chicago, IL. **Educ:** Triton Coll, AA (hon) 1970; Univ of IL Chicago Circle Campus, BA 1972; attended Univ of IL Med Ctr; Rush Univ Presbyterian St Luke Med Ctr, MD 1979. **Career:** St Mary's Hosp, chief dept of emer med 1985; So MS State Hosp Laurel MS, chief dept of emer med 1985-86, hosp med dir 1986; Hughes Spalding Med Ctr, dir of emer med 1987-; Morehouse School of Med, asst prof. **Orgs:** mem, dir, editor Progressive Sec mag 1985-; contrib editor Functional Human Anatomy; mem Toastmasters, Optimist Intl. **Honors/Awds:** Ford Found Scholarship Triton Coll 1970; Natl Med Fellowship 1975. **Military Serv:** USAF sgt 1965-68. **Home Addr:** 5642 Southern Pine Court, Stone Mountain, GA 30087. **Business Addr:** Asst Prof, Morehouse School of Medicine, 720 Westview Dr, SW, Atlanta, GA 30310-1458.

BREWER, CURTIS
Legal services corporation executive. **Personal:** Born Sep 18, 1925, Cambridge, MA; son of Ethyl Myra Whitaker and Nathaniel Albert Brewer; married Bettie Anne Foster; children: Zakia Al-Ghuiyy, Geri Jefferson, Scott. **Educ:** New Sch for Social Research, BA 1956; NY Univ Sch of Public Admin & Social Svc, 1957-61; Brooklyn Law Sch, JD 1974. **Career:** Community Serv Assoc, dir 1955-60; Self-employed, private ombudsman 1960-67; Untapped Resources Inc, exec dir 1964-74; NY Med Coll Neuropsychology Lab,administrator 1968-70; Untapped Resources Inc, exec dir & genl cnsl 1974-. **Orgs:** Mem natl advisory cncl Architectural & Transp Barriers Compliance Bd Dept of HEW 1977-78; mem bd of dir Nat Cntr for Law & the Handicapped 1975-77; mem advisory cncl Barnard Coll 1980-; mem advisory cncl In-Touch Radio Network 1979-; mem advisory cncl New York City Opera 1980-; mem, American Bar Assn 1975-; mem, New York City Bar Assn 1975-; mem bd of dirs, Fiduciary Insurance Co of America 1988-; mem, Manhattan Borough President's Adv Committee on the Disabled 1986-; mem, Natl Rehabilitation Assn 1976-. **Honors/Awds:** Inductee Nat Hall of Fame for Persons with Disabilities 1983; Handicapped Am of the Yr Pres Comm Emplymnt of Handicapped 1980; Humanitarian Award R Kirzon Group for Handicapped Chldrn 1976; life mem NAACP 1974; Thurgood Marshall Award NY Trial Lawyers Assn 1972.

BREWER, DAVID L., III
Naval officer. **Personal:** Born May 19, 1946, Farmville, VA; son of David & Mildred Brewer; married Richardene B Brewer, Jul 15, 1978; children: Stacey M. **Educ:** Prairie View A & M Univ, BS, 1970; US Naval War Coll, MA, 1993. **Career:** US Navy various positions on ships, 1970-80, USS Okinawa (LPH 3), engineer officer, 1980-82, USS Fresno (LST 1182), exec officer, 1982-84, USS Bristol County (LST 1198), commanding officer, 1986-88, special asst to the chief of naval operations, 1988-90, USS MT Whitney (LCC 20), commanding officer, 1991-93, US Naval Forces Marianas, commander, 1994-. **Orgs:** New St Mark Free Methodist, Orlando FL, 1960-; Alpha Phi Alpha Fraternity, 1969-; Prairie View Natl Alumni Assn, life mem, 1970-; Natl Naval Officer's Assn, chapter pres, life mem, 1974-; Church of the Redeemer, Washington DC, 1986-; Young Adults of Redeemer, pres, 1988-92; Surface Navy Assn, 1988-; US NAval Institute, 1989-. **Honors/Awds:** NAACP, Crispus Attucks Memorial Award, 1990; Natl Naval Officers Assn, Chapter of the Year, 1990. **Special Achievements:** Developed & Inaugurated Youth Empowerment Programs: Super Saturday Scholars Program, 1989; Opening Pathways to Infinite Opportunities Now (Option), 1990. **Military Serv:** US Navy, rear adm, 1970-; Legion of Merit, 1992; Meritorious Service Medal, 1988 & 1990. **Business Addr:** Rear Admiral, Commander, US Naval Forces Marianas, PSC 489, Box 7, FPO AP.

BREWER, GREGORY ALAN
Researcher. **Personal:** Born Feb 3, 1968, Denver, CO; son of Riley & Aileen Brewer. **Educ:** Morehouse Coll, BS, physics, 1990; UCLA, 1990-. **Career:** UCLA, researcher, 1991-. **Orgs:** NSBE, 1986-; IEEE, 1993-; Phi Beta Kappa, 1990-. **Honors/Awds:** UCLA, GAAD Project 88 Fellowship, 1990. **Home Addr:** 2568 Birch St, Denver, CO 80207-3133. **Business Addr:** Student/Researcher, UCLA, 405 Hilgard Ave, Engineering IV, Los Angeles, CA 90024.

BREWER, MOSES
Company executive. **Personal:** Born Mar 12, 1947; married. **Educ:** Northeastern Jr Coll Sterling CO, 1966-67; Univ of Denver, BA 1967-71; Univ of Denver, MA 1975. **Career:** Baseball program for Denver boys, dir, 1969; St Anne's Elementary School, teacher, 1970; City Auditor's Office, coordinator of microfilm, 1969-71; Univ of Denver, coordinator recreational activities, 1971-72; Univ of Denver, asst dean of student life, 1972-73; Denver Univ, univ consultant-at-large, 1973-; Adolph Coors Co, asst natl program mgr; Denver Public Schools, consultant, 1974-75; Adolph Coors Co, asst natl prog mgr, currently. **Orgs:** Mem All-Regional 9 Basketball Team 1966-67; mem Nat Assn Student Personnel Adminstr; mem Natl Speech Communication Assn; mem Pi Kappa Alpha Frat; United Negro Coll Fund; Black Caucus; Black Alumni Assn Univ of Denver; Western Regional Ombudsman Assn; Natl Scholarship Serv & Funds for Negro Students. **Honors/Awds:** Outstanding Athlete Award 1968; Outstanding Faculty Admin Award 1974; Outstanding Personality Awd. **Business Addr:** Assistant National Program Mgr, Adolph Coors Company, 311 10th St #NH420, Golden, CO 80401.

BREWER, ROSE MARIE
Sociologist/educator. **Personal:** Born Oct 30, 1947, Tulsa, OK; daughter of Cloviece Brewer and Wilson Brewer; married Walter Griffin; children: Sundiata Brewer Griffin. **Educ:** Northeastern State Coll, BA 1969; Indiana Univ, MA 1971, PhD 1976; Univ of Chicago, Post-Doctoral studies 1981-83. **Career:** Rice Univ, vstg lecturer 1976; Univ of TX, asst prof 1977-80, 1983-86; Univ of Chicago, post-doctoral fellow 1981-83; Univ of MN, asst prof 1986-. **Orgs:** Bd dirs, vice pres, pres elect Big Brothers/Big Sisters Austin 1984-; bd dirs Soc for the Study of Social Problems 1985-88; council mem Section on Racial & Ethnic Minorities 1985-88; comm mem Amer Sociological Socl 1986-87; chair Comm on Status of Racial and Ethnic Minorities Assoc 1986-87; vice president, Society for the Study of Social Problems, 1991-92; board of director, Midwest Sociological Society, 1990-92; Committee on Freedom of Teaching and Research, ASA, 1989-91; Afro-American & African Studies, chair, 1992-; CIC Leadership Fellow, 1993-94; Oakland Private Industry Council, exec bd mem, 1994; Contra Costa Private Industrial Council, exec bd mem, 1995-. **Honors/Awds:** Ford Foundation Fellow 1972-73; NIMH Post-Doctoral Rsch Fellow 1981-83; articles "Black/White Racial Inequality," Humanities and Society 6 1980; "On Reproducing Racial Inequality," Humanities in Society 6 1983; plus many other articles; Bush Sabbitacal Award, Univ of Minnesota, 1990-91; Multicultural Lectureship Award, Univ of North Texas, 1990; Center for the Study of Women and Society Award, Univ of Oregon, 1990; CIC Leadership Fellow, 1993-94; Wiepking Distinguished Visiting Professor, Miami University of Ohio, 1996. **Business Addr:** Morse Alumni, Distinguished Professor of African Studies, University of Minnesota, 808 Social Science Bldg, Minneapolis, MN 55455.

BREWER, WEBSTER L.
Judge. **Personal:** Born May 11, 1935, Clarksville, TN; son of Margie Brodie Brewer and Marvin Brewer; married Patricia Freeman; children: Elaine, Pamela, Webster Jr. **Educ:** IN U, BS 1957; IN Univ Sch of Law, JD. **Career:** Marion Co Superior Court #2, judge 1975-; Brewer Budnick & Sosin, mng lawyer private practice 1970-75; Indianapolis Lawyers Commn, exec dir 1968-70; United Dist Court for So Dist of IN, probation ofcr 1964-68; US Bur of Prisons, parole ofcr 1960-64; Marion Co Juv Ct, probation ofcr 1958-60; Marion Co Welfare Dept, caseworker 1957-58. **Orgs:** Mem Am Bar Assn; Indianapolis Bar Assn; IN St Bar Assn; Natl Bar Assn; past natl ofcr Phi Alpha Delta Legal Frat Group Leader Christamore Settlement House 1958-60; Juvenile Ct Adv Comm 1960-64; chmn of bd NAACP 1963-64; chmn Labor & Industry Comm Indianapolis Chap NAACP 1964-66; bd mem Forward Inc 1968-70; bd mem Indianapolis Legal Serv Orgn 1970-75; bd mem trustees & chmn Ways & Means Comm Bethel AME Ch 1973-; bd mem Marion Co Child Guidance Clinic 1973-; bd mem Marion Co Youth & Serv Bur 1974-76; bd mem Indianapolis Family Serv Agency 1977-; instr IN Univ Sch of Law seminar 1970; participated in numerous seminars spons by IN Judicial Study Ctr; special proj dir IN Judicial Study Ctr preparing Bench Book for IN judges on facilities avail at various IN penalinstitutions; mem Kappa Alphsi Frat; Trinity Lodge #18; F&AM, PHA; mem Sigma Pi Phi Fraternity 1971. **Business Addr:** 443 City County Bldg, Indianapolis, IN 46204.

BREWINGTON, DONALD EUGENE
Cleric. **Personal:** Born Aug 29, 1954, San Antonio, TX; son of Margie M Bradley and James B Bradley. **Educ:** Sam Houston State University, BA, educ, 1977; Interdenominational Theological Center, MDiv, 1986. **Career:** Greater Corinth Baptist Church, minister of youth/outreach, 1986-89; Ernest T Dixon United Methodist Church, pastor, 1989-92; Huston-Tillotson College, college chaplain, campus minister, 1992-. **Orgs:** Texas Council of Churches, 1992-; Wesley Foundation Partnership Ministries, 1992-; United Church of Christ Bd of Higher Education, 1992-, Southwest Texas Conference, 1992-; Church World Service, Walk for Hunger, 1992-; Huston-Tillotson College Gospel Choir, sponsor, 1992-; Huston-Tillotson College Concert Choir, 1992-. **Business Addr:** Campus Minister, Huston-Tillotson College, 900 Chicon St, King-Seabrook, Austin, TX 78702, (512)505-3054.

BREWINGTON, RUDOLPH W.
Reporter. **Personal:** Born Nov 2, 1946, New York City, NY. **Educ:** Federal City Coll, MA (cum laude) 1973, grad study. **Career:** WRC/NBC Radio News Wash DC, reporter 1975-; WWDC Radio, news reporter edtr 1971-75; WOOK Radio, news dir 1970-71; WUST Radio, news reptr 1969-70; Washington, DC, bus operator 1969; Natl Syndctd TV Prgm "America's Black Forum", rsrch dir/pnlst 1978-79; Natl Syndctd Radio Prgm "The Black Agenda Reprts", pres/exec prod 1979-80; Asso Prsnl Inc Washington DC, dir pub rels 1980; USNR, pub afrs ofcr 1980. **Honors/Awds:** Recipient Robt F Kennedy Jrnlsm Awrd Citation for ""Diagnosis, Desperate, A Report on Minority Hlth Care"" 1973; APHA Ray Bruner Sci Writing Fellowshp 1974. **Military Serv:** USMC corpl e-4 1964-68. **Business Addr:** 4001 Nebraska Ave NW, Washington, DC 20016.

BREWINGTON, THOMAS E., JR.
Ophthalmologist. **Personal:** Born Oct 12, 1943, Dunn, NC; married Janice; children: Kathryne, Mitchelle, Tracy, Brea. **Educ:** Morehouse Coll, BS 1975; Meharry Med Coll, MD 1969; HG Phillips Hosp, intern 1969-70, resd 1970-73. **Career:** Prvt Practice, opthlmlgst 1976-; EENT Clinic AUS, chf 1973-75. **Orgs:** Diplmt Am Bd Ophthlmlgy; flw Am Acad & Ophth; mem Natl Med Assn; NC State Med Soc; Guilford Co Med Soc; Greensboro Acad Med; Greensboro Med Soc; Old N State Med Soc Exec bd Guilford Co Easter Seal Soc; mem Phi Beta Sigma Frat. **Military Serv:** AUS maj 1973-75; recpt Commendation Medal. **Business Addr:** PO Box 20346, Greensboro, NC 27420, (919)272-5628.

BREWSTER, LUTHER GEORGE
Airine company maintenance manager. **Personal:** Born Dec 16, 1942, Manhattan, NY; son of Alethia Samuels and Donald F. Brewster; married Theresa Maria Smart, May 8, 1965; children: Maria, Luther Jr., Renee. **Educ:** Bronx Community College, Bronx NY, 1965-72; College of Aeronautics, Queens NY, AAS, 1974; Lehman College, Bronx NY, 1980-87; North Central College, Naperville IL, 1988-; Olivet Nazarene University, Kankakee, IL, bachelor's degree, applied science & mgt, 1995. **Career:** Pratt & Whitney Aircraft, Hartford CT, engine mechanic, 1964; Pan American, New York NY, aircraft & engine mechanic, 1965-77; Seaboard World Airlines, Frankfurt, West Germany, maintenance rep, 1977; American Airlines, Chicago IL, division mgr aircraft maintenance, 1977-87; American Airlines, Chicago, IL, division mgr of aircraft maintenance, 1987-95, managing dir, eastern division aircraft maintenance, 1995-. **Orgs:** Institute for Certification of Engineering Tech, Aviation Maintenance Foundation, American Management Association; Mt Sinai Hospital, board of directors. **Honors/Awds:** Honored by official resolution of Boston City Council, 1986; certificate of merit, youth motivation program, CACI, 1987-88. **Military Serv:** US Air Force, technical sergeant, 1960-64; good conduct medal, expeditionary medal, outstanding unit award. **Business Addr:** American Airlines, MD 4050, Miami Intl Airport, Miami, FL 33299-7990, (305)526-1311.

BREWTON, BUTLER E.
Educator (retired), poet. **Personal:** Born Feb 7, 1935, Spartanburg, SC; son of J M Brewton and W O Brewton; married Blanca Brewton; children: Seneca, Monica, Catrina. **Educ:** Benedict, BA 1956; Montclair State, MA 1970; Rutgers, PhD 1978. **Career:** Montclair State Coll, assoc prof, English, 1970-. **Orgs:** Consultant, McGraw Hill Intl Press 1972; poet NJ State Council on the Arts 1970-76; speaker NCTE Kansas City 1978; writer book "South and Border States" The Literary Guide to the US; "Richard Wrights Thematic Treatment of Women" ERIC; Modern Century Encyclopedia, editor. **Honors/Awds:** NDEA fellow SC State Coll 1965; poems: Tramp, Lady of the Evening, 5 PM, Discovered, Pattern, Barren, Southbound, Idol, Yesterday Hangs, The Custodial Hour, Democracy, The Kiss, For A Reprieve, Peach Orchard, Full Measure, At the General Store, We Children, 1992, Grandpa's, 1992, "Rafters," 1992, article: "A Diploma Must Mean What It's Supposed to Mean," New York Times 1986; speaker, NCTE. **Special Achievements:** 1st prize winner of Essence Magazine poetry contest 1993. **Military Serv:** USAF A/2. **Business Addr:** Associate Professor of English, Emeritus, Montclair State College, English Department, Upper Montclair, NJ 07043.

BRICE, EUGENE CLAY
Government official (retired). **Personal:** Born Jun 18, 1929, Morristown, TN; son of Elizabeth Moore Brice (deceased) and Henry Brice (deceased); married Vert (deceased); children: Eugene II, Alan, Alesia. **Educ:** Morristown Jr Coll, 1949; MD State Coll, 1950. **Career:** US Govt, 1955-84; Wright-Patterson AFB, data processing 1964-69, computer supv 1969-77, mgr 1977-retired 1984. **Orgs:** Vp Springfield OH Frontiers Intl 1972-75; bd dir Springfield OH Urban League 1974-76; dist treas N Central Dist 1975-82; trustee Rose Devel Corp 1975-; mem Springfield OH Bd of Realtors 1975-80; pres Springfield OH Frontiers Intl 1976; vice pres Rose Devel Corp 1979-. **Honors/Awds:** Player No 1 Football Team MD State Coll 1949; Wright-Patterson AFB Mgr of the Month 1975; Springfield OH Frontiersman of the Year 1978; contestant, Wheel of Fortune game show, 1985. **Military Serv:** AUS 1951-53. **Home Addr:** 1862 S Wittenberg, Springfield, OH 45506.

BRICE, PERCY A., JR.
Professional musician. **Personal:** Born Mar 25, 1923, New York City, NY; married Pearl Minott. **Educ:** Music Sch, 4 yrs; Kingsborough Comm Coll, attended, 1986. **Career:** Luis Russell Orch, 1944; Benny Carter Orch, 1945-46; Mercer Ellington, 1947; Eddie Vinson, 1947-51; Tiny Grimes Show Group, 1951-52; Harlems Savoy Bathroom with Lucky Thompson's 8-piece & Group; Billy Taylor Trio, 1954-56; George Shearing Quintet, 1956-58; Carmen McRae Sarah Vaughn, 1959-61; Harry Belafonte Troupe 1961-68; New Sound, leader plyng lounge circts around metro area. **Orgs:** Taught drums 1969-71; mem Masonic Order 1949-; Famous Friendly 50 Club. **Honors/Awds:** Harlem Dist champ in table tennis. **Special Achievements:** Played in, conducted musical "Bubblin' Brown Sugar," Broadway musical "Eubie;" played in "Ain't Misbehavin'," "Ghost Cafe.".

BRIDGEFORTH, ARTHUR MAC, JR.
Business reporter. **Personal:** Born Sep 18, 1965, Pittsburgh, PA; son of Gwendolyn Holland Bridgeforth and Arthur Mac Bridgeforth Sr. **Educ:** Michigan State University, East Lansing, MI, BA, journalism, 1988. **Career:** Crain's Detroit Business, Detroit, MI, editorial assistant, 1988-89; The Ann Arbor News, Ann Arbor, MI, business reporter, 1989-. **Orgs:** Detroit Chapter, National Association of Black Journalists, 1988-; National Association of Black Journalist, 1989-; Michigan State University Alumni Association, 1988-. **Home Addr:** 19511 Greenfield #3, Detroit, MI 48235.

BRIDGEMAN, DEXTER ADRIAN
Communications company executive. **Personal:** Born Jan 5, 1961, Grenada, West Indies; son of Donald E Bridgeman & Phylis Alexander; divorced. **Educ:** Hofstra University, BS, political science, 1984; SUNY at Stonybrook, 1984-85. **Career:** Ivac Corp, GE Medical Systems, Motorola C&E, Velobind Inc, Allnet Communications, sales executive, 1985-93; Bradford Communications Group, Ltd, pres/COO, 1993-. **Orgs:** Opportunities Industrialization Centers of America, bd mem; National Youth Development Prog, corporate advisory council; National Inner City Leadership Council, advisory bd; YACT, advisory bd; Alpha Phi Alpha Fraternity, Inc; Concerned Black Men of America; Outstanding Young Men of America, 1996. **Home Phone:** (914)668-4525.

BRIDGEMAN, DONALD EARL
Mortgage banker, human resources administrator. **Personal:** Born Mar 14, 1939, Grenville, Grenada; son of Madonna Theresa Hall-Bridgeman and Julien Anthony Bridgeman; married Dr Rosemary Malcolm; children: Winston, Selwyn, Joie, Edelyne. **Educ:** Erdiston Teachers Coll, AA Educ 1960; Howard Univ, BSc 1968; Northwestern Univ, Cert Mortg Banker 1973; Southeastern Univ, MBPA (w/Honors) 1976. **Career:** Foundation for Coop Housing, dir Hsg Spec Inst 1969-72; Howard Univ, dir Ctr for Housing and Real Estate 1975-77; US Dept of Housing & Urban Develop, employee develop spec 1977-84; Prince George's County Govt, deputy personnel officer, 1984-91; SWAADA Imports, pres, 1988-; The MBA Group, pres, 1991-. **Orgs:** United Way Health and Welfare Cncl Washington DC 1965-76; co-founder of CHANGE Federal Credit Union Washington DC; co-founder Natl Assoc of Housing Specialists 1971; conf dir Joint Annual Minority Housing Conf 1974-80; consultant, Winston-Salem State Univ, Southern Univ, Texas Southern Univ, Temple Univ, on develop of housing mgmt curricula 1975-77; pres Housing Specialists Inst 1977-81 & 1993-; pres, Local Government Personnel Assn of the Baltimore-Washington Metro Area 1986-91; pres, Caribbean Council of Prince George's Co, MD, 1989-; vice pres, Council of Caribbean Organizations, Washington, DC, 1991-93; Natl Forum for Black Public Administrators, 1990-; Southern Maryland Business League, 1991-. **Honors/Awds:** Samuel E Sessions Award Natl Assn of Housing Specialists Housing Specialists Inst 1975; Realist of the Year Award Washington Real Estate Brokers Assn 1976; Personnelist of the Year, Intl Personnel Mgnt Assn, Eastern Region 1989; Intl Exchange Fellow to England's SOCPO, Intl Personnel Mgmt Assn-US, 1987; Special Achievement Award, Local Govt Personnel Assn of Baltimore-Washington, 1991. **Home Addr:** 600 Dwyer Pl, Largo, MD 20772, (301)336-8326. **Business Addr:** President, The MBA Group, 9200 Basil Court, Suite 210, Landover, MD 20784, (301)925-7900.

BRIDGEMAN, JUNIOR (ULYSSES LEE)
Professional basketball player. **Personal:** Born Sep 17, 1953, East Chicago, IL; married Doris; children: Justin, Ryan. **Educ:** Louisville, Psychology 1975. **Career:** Milwaukee Bucks, 1976-84, 1987; Los Angeles Clippers, 1985-86. **Honors/Awds:** Earned Acad and Athletic All-Amer honors in Sr year Univ of LA; in Sr year named Most Valuable Player MO Valley Conf.

BRIDGES, ALVIN LEROY
Physician. **Personal:** Born Jun 6, 1925, Dayton, OH; son of Essie Bridges and Cornelius Bridges; married Lois; children: Alvin Jr, Keith, Lori, Cornelius. **Educ:** Univ Dayton, BS 1948; Meharry Med Coll, MD 1952; Kansas City Genl Hosp, intern 1952-53; Univ Cincinnati VA Hosp, resd 1953-54. **Career:** Community Hosp Alderson IN, chief of staff 1984; Private Practice, physician 1954-. **Orgs:** Charter diplomate Amer Bd Family Practice; recertified Amer Bd of Family Practice 1977, 1984; charter fellow Amer Acad Family Physicians; mem Intl SocIntl Medicine; Amer Acad Family Physicians; Natl Med Assn; life mem NAACP; Alpha Phi Alpha Frat. **Military Serv:** US Army, T5; 1943-46; Combat Ingantry Badge, 1944. **Business Addr:** Physician, 1302 S Madison Ave, Anderson, IN 46016.

BRIDGES, BILL
Professional basketball player (retired). **Personal:** Born Apr 4, 1939, Hobbs, NM. **Educ:** Univ of Kansas, Lawrence, KS, attended. **Career:** St Louis Hawks, 1962-68; Atlanta Hawks, 1968-71; Philadelphia Phillies, 1971-72; Los Angeles Lakers, 1972-74; Golden State Warriors, 1975. **Honors/Awds:** NBA All-Star Game, 1967, 1968, 1970.

BRIDGES, JAMES WILSON
Physician. **Personal:** Born Feb 16, 1935, Valdosta, GA; son of Ora Lee Bridges and Leslie Bridges; married Earnestine Bryant; children: Sabrina, Lloyd, Mark. **Educ:** Central State Coll, BS 1956; Meharry Medical Coll, MD 1960; Hmr G Phillips Hospital, intern 1961, chief resident 1966; Univ Miami, resident 1967. **Career:** Private practice, physician; Univ Miami, clinical asst prof; Cedars of Lebanon Health Care Center, chief; Christian Hospital, chief, currently. **Orgs:** Diplomate, Amer Bd of Obstetrics & Gynecology, 1969; bd of trustees, Christian Hospital, 1973-76; bd dir, Florida Div Amer Cancer Soc, 1972-77, Florida Physicians Ins Rec, 1985, Florida Physicians Ins Co, Florida Political Action Comm; chmn, Florida Div United Cancer Task Force, 1975-77; member, Beta Beta Lambda Chapter, Alpha Phi Alpha, NAACP, Comm Minority Affairs Univ of Miami School of Medicine; Florida Bd of Medicine, 1996-97; pres-elect, Dade County Medical Society, 1997; pres, Dade County Medical Society, 1998-99. **Honors/Awds:** Fellow Amer Coll of Obstetrics & Gynecolgy 1970; scholarship Florida State Medical Coll 1959-60. **Military Serv:** AUS medical corps captain 1961-63. **Business Addr:** Physician, 1190 NW 95th St, Ste 110, Miami, FL 33150-2064.

BRIDGES, LEON
Architect, business executive. **Personal:** Born Aug 18, 1932, Los Angeles, CA; son of Agnes Zenobia Johnson Bridges and James Alonzo Bridges; married Eloise Avonne Jones; children: Vanessa Joy, Elise Gay, Leon Jr, Elliott Reynolds. **Educ:** Univ of Washington, BArch, 1959; Urban Syst, post grad studies; Loyola College of MD, MBA, 1984. **Career:** Intern asst city planner 1956; Leon Bridges Arch, owner 1963-66; Bridges/Burke Arch & Planners, partner 1966-72; The Archl Research Collabor Inc, partner 1976-; The Leon Bridges Co, owner 1972-87; TLBC Incorporated, president 1989-; The Leon Bridges Chartered, president, currently. **Orgs:** Exec Comm Planned Parenthood/World Population, 1968-74; Visit prof Hampton Inst 1971, 1973, 1975; visit prof Prairie View A&M 1972; particip Tuskegee Inst Comm Arch Design Charette sponsored by Endowment of the Arts 1971; mem Guild for Religious Architecture; panelist Mental Health Center Design sponsored by AIA and Natl Inst of Mental Health; mem AIA; mem Natl Urban League; mem MD State Arts Council 1980-; bd dir Lutheran Hosp 1980-; bd dir MD Minority Contractors Assn 1981; chmn Morgan State Univ Urban Dev Comm 1981; bd dir Roland Park Place 1981; bd of advisors Univ of Knoxville TN 1981-; bd dir School for the Deaf 1981; bd of dirs The Amer Inst of Architects 1984-86; Middle Atlantic Region Dir of The Amer Inst of Architects 1984-86; pres, Natl Org Minority Architects, 1980; assoc prof Morgan State Univ 1985-88; vice pres The Amer Inst of Architects 1987-. **Honors/Awds:** Honor Award The Amer Soc of Landscape Architects 1980; The Black Pages Award Recogn for Outstanding Contrib to the Economic Health of Minority Enterprise in Baltimore 1981; Merit Award The Amer Inst of Architects in Wash, DC; Recogn for Outstanding Contribution for Restoration of the Baltimore Pennsylvania Station 1981; Design Excellence Award Natl Org of Minority Architects of the Baltimore/Penn Station 1983; Design Excellence Award The Amer Inst of Architects Baltimore Chap Baltimore Penn Station 1985; Design Excellence Award NOMA Lexington Market Subway Station 1985; Grand Conceptor Award Amer Consulting Engrs Council Ft McHenry Tunnel East Ventilation Building & Opers Control Bldg 1986; Baltimore City Council Presidential Citation, 1995; Baltimore City Mayor's Citation, 1995; Maryland State Legislature Official Citation, 1995; State of Maryland Governor's Citation, 1995; Natl Citation Design Excellence Seattle Urban Design, 1971. **Military Serv:** US Army Corpl 1952-54. **Business Addr:** President, TLBC Incorporated, 805 E Fayette St, Baltimore, MD 21202-4012.

BRIDGES, ROCHELLE MARIE
Journalist. **Personal:** Born Nov 23, 1954, Gary, IN; daughter of Carolyn Louise Bridges and Johnnie James Bridges. **Educ:** Southern Illinois University, BS, radio and television/news, 1977; Marquette University, screenplay writing, 1985. **Career:** WISN-TV, reporter, producer, 1977-86; WJZ-TV, reporter, 1986-88; Black Entertainment TV, 1988-89; Maryland Public TV, 1988-89; WSVN-TV, "Inside Report," correspondent, 1989-90, morning anchor, reporter, 1991-; Fox-TV, "Personalities," correspondent, 1990-91. **Orgs:** Natl Assn of Black Journalists; National Academy Television Arts & Science. **Honors/Awds:** Natl Academy of Television Arts & Sciences, Emmy Award, Individual Achievement, 1991; Natl Assn of Black Journalists, Best News Special, 1988; United Press International, Best News Feature; Milwaukee Press Club, Community Welfare Award, 1985. **Special Achievements:** Jaycees, Congress Outstanding Individuals, 1984. **Business Addr:** Anchor, Reporter, WSVN-TV, 1401 79th St Causeway, Northbay Village, Miami, FL 33141, (305)756-2518.

BRIDGEWATER, ALBERT LOUIS
Government official, scientist. **Personal:** Born Nov 22, 1941, Houston, TX; son of Rita Narcisse Bridgewater and Albert Bridgewater; married Juanita Edington (divorced); children: Ramesi, Akin. **Educ:** Columbia Univ, PhD 1972, MA 1967; Univ of CA, BA 1963. **Career:** Univ of CA, postdoctoral fellow 1970-73; Elem Particle Physics, asst prof officer 1973-74; Howard Univ, prof 1974-75; Natl Science Foundation, staff asst 1973-76, special asst 1976-86, acting asst dir for AAEO/NSF 1983-85, deputy assistant director, AAEO/NSF 1981-86, sr staff assoc 1986-. **Orgs:** Mem, Amer Physical Soc; Amer Geophysical Union; mem advisory board, LBL/SSU/AGMFF Science Consortium 1986-88. **Honors/Awds:** Order of Golden Bear; Peace Corp volunteer, West Cameroon, 1963-65. **Business Addr:** Senior Staff Associate, National Science Foundation, 1800 G St, NW, Washington, DC 20550.

BRIDGEWATER, DEE DEE
Vocalist. **Personal:** married Cecil Bridgewater (divorced). **Career:** Vocalist. Has recorded numerous albums including Just Family, 1978, and Dear Ella, 1997. **Special Achievements:** Played Glinda the Good Witch in The Wiz, on Broadway, 1975. **Business Addr:** Vocalist, c/o Verve Records, 825 Eighth Ave, 26th Floor, New York, NY 10019, (212)333-8000.

BRIDGEWATER, HERBERT JEREMIAH, JR.
Sales agent, educator, radio/tv talk show host. **Personal:** Born Jul 3, 1942, Atlanta, GA; son of Mary Sallie Clark Bridgewater Hughes and Herbert Bridgewater (deceased). **Educ:** Clark Coll, BA, Business Admin, 1968; Atlanta Univ, 1968; Univ of Georgia, Inst of Govt & Center for Continuing Educ, 1978; Atlanta Area Technical School, Certificate of Completion, 1980; Federal Law Enforcement Training Center, 1980; Spelman Coll Inst for Continuing Educ, 1984. **Career:** Atlanta Public School Syst, teacher, Business & English Commun, 1964-67; Atlanta Housing Authority, relocation & family serv consultant, 1967-70; Federal Trade Commn, consumer protection specialist, dir of public affairs 1970-83; Bridgewaters Personnel Service, owner, 1971-75; Confrontation, host, 1974-; Atlanta Area Tech School, teacher 1978-; Bridging the Gap, host, 1981-; Clark Coll, assoc prof 1983-; Delta Airlines Inc, customer sales & serv 1984-; Atlanta Daily World Newspaper, columnist, Unsung Heroes, Facts for Consumers, currently. **Orgs:** Bd mem, GA Chapter, Epilepsy Found of Amer, Mid-Atlanta Unit Amer Cancer Soc; bd chmn, Atlanta Dance Theatre; task force Just Us Theater; founding mem, Intl Assn for African Heritage & Black Identity; Atlanta Jr Chamber of Commerce, Big Brothers

Council of Atlanta, Natl Urban League, United Negro Coll Fund; City of Atlanta Water and Sewer Appeals Board, currently; Martin Luther King Center for Non-Violent Social Change; Martin Luther King Ecumenical Holiday Committee. **Honors/Awds:** Received natl acclaim after successfully obtaining & delivering to the US Congress over 10,000 signatures of registered GA voters which were secured in 4 days in support of House of Reps Resolution to refrain former GA Gov Lester Maddox from passing out racially symbolized objects on the US House Capital ground 1969; individually won the struggle to have Black Coll athletic scores aired on TV stations in GA 1966; assisted the City of Atlanta & Consumer Affairs Office in preparing proposed Consumer Protection Ordinance for the City of Atlanta, ordinance currently in existence; Distinguished Supporter Top Star Awd,Natl Assn of Black Journalists, 1983; Dr Herbert J Bridgewater Jr Day in Atlanta Proclaimed by Mayor Andrew Young, 1982; Meritorious Serv Award, GA Chap, Epilepsy Found of Amer981, 1985; Outstanding Serv Award, Amer Red Cross, 1981; Outstanding Serv, Atlanta Fed Exec Bd Minority Business Opportunity Comm, 1981; Disting & Dedicated Serv Award, Greater Travelers Rest Baptist Church, Decatur, GA, 1981; Outstanding Comm Serv Award, SW Career Counsel; Best Talk Show Host on Radio, Atlanta Chapterof the National Assn of Black Journalist, 1983; Outstanding Service Award, Martin Luther King, Jr. Center for Social Change, 1984; Dr. Herbert J. Bridgewater, Jr. Day, State of Georgia, 1985; Congressional Achievement Award, Congressman Wyche Fowler, 1985; Outstanding Communication Silver Voice Award, Bronner Brothers Intl Beauty & Trade Show Convention, 1989; host/master of ceromonies of numerous pageants. **Business Addr:** Modeling Management, PO Box 310272, Atlanta, GA 30331.

BRIDGEWATER, PAUL
Public administration. **Educ:** Saginaw Valley Coll, BA 1975. **Career:** Saginaw Bd of Educ, career advisor 1971; Poverty Peoples Alliance, outreach worker 1972-74; Opportunities Industrialization Ctr of Metro Saginaw, counselor 1974-75; Saginaw County Comm Action Committee, comm developer 1975-77; MI State Univ Cooperative Ext Svcs, ext 4-H youth agent 1977-80; Mayor Young's Farm-A-Lot Program, field coord 1980; Detroit Area Agency on Aging, supervisor 1980-. **Orgs:** Chairperson Comm for the Black Art Festival; mem MI State Fair Agriculture Comm; mem Optimist Intl Club of Central Detroit; mem Natl Caucus and Concernsfor the Black Aged; natl bd mem NCBA; mem Mayor Young's Hunger and Malnutrition Task Force; mem Leadership Detroit VII; mem Chamber of Commerce. **Honors/Awds:** Outstanding Young Men of Amer Jaycees 1981; Special recognition MI House and Senate for "Outstanding Serv to the Comm"; delegate MI White House Conference on Aging. **Business Addr:** Supervisor, Detroit Area Agency on Aging, 3110 Book Building, 1249 Washington Blvd, Detroit, MI 48226.

BRIDGFORTH, WALTER, JR.
Developer. **Personal:** Born in Detroit, MI; married Anita Baker, Dec 31, 1988; children: Walter Baker, Edward Carlton. **Educ:** Western Michigan Univ, degree in finance, 1979. **Career:** IBM, salesman, 1979-89; self-employed manager of residential properties; Bridgforth Development, developer, currently. **Business Addr:** Developer, Bridgforth Development, 13845 Nine Mile Rd, Warren, MI 48089, (810)778-3038.

BRIDWELL, HERBERT H.
Education administrator. **Personal:** Born Aug 23, 1928, Jonesboro, TN; married Cue Tribble. **Educ:** TN State A&I Univ Nashville, BS 1951; TC Columbia Univ NY, MS 1955; IN Univ, 1960-61; GA State Univ, FL A&M Univ, attended. **Career:** Twin Lake High School, Palm Beach City School Dist, teacher, principal sec dir, 1959-85; Palm Beach City School Dist, area supt north. **Orgs:** Pres Palm Beach Cty Principals Assoc 1975-76; bd dir Boy Scouts, YMCA, Rotary, Project Rescue 1975; chmn plng bd City of West Palm Beach 1979-81; chmnCity of West Palm Beach Plng Bd 1979-81; mem Urban League, NAACP 1960-85. **Honors/Awds:** Omega Man of the Year Kappa Upsilon Chap Omega Psi Phi Inc West Palm Beach FL 1963. **Military Serv:** AUS m/sgt 1951-53; Bronze Star 1952. **Home Addr:** 318 S Chillingworth Dr, West Palm Beach, FL 33409.

BRIEVE-MARTIN, ILA CORRINNA
Educator. **Personal:** Born Mar 20, 1939, Newark, NJ; married Robert H Dean. **Educ:** Bloomfield College, BA, 1964; Rutgers University, Graduate School of Education, EdM, 1972, EdD 1975. **Career:** Central High School, Spanish teacher, 1964-67, title I coordinator, 1967-70; US Dept of Justice, Comm Relations Dept, consultant, 1968-70; Rutgers University Grad School of Education, asst professor, 1970-74; Virginia Commonwealth University Richmond, asst education dean, 1975-80; Virginia State University, assoc professor, Dept of Education Leadership, starting 1984; University of the District of Columbia, dean of education, currently. **Orgs:** Vice president, Business and Professional Women, 1967-69; bd of dirs, Richmond Area Programs for Minorities in Engineering, 1977-; bd of dirs, Greater Richmond Transit Co, 1978-80; Phi Delta Kappa, 1973-. **Honors/Awds:** University of Alabama, fellowship, 1979; Richmond Parent Teacher Assn, OutstandingEducator Award; various publications in area of creative dynamics. **Business Addr:** Dean of Education, University of the District of Columbia, 4200 Connecticut Ave NW, Washington, DC 20008-1174.

BRIGANCE, O.J.
Professional football player. **Personal:** Born Sep 29, 1969; married Chanda. **Educ:** Rice, BA in managerial studies. **Career:** Miami Dolphins, linebacker, 1996-. **Business Addr:** Professional Football Player, Miami Dolphins, 2269 NW 199th St, Miami, FL 33056, (305)620-5000.

BRIGGINS, CHARLES E.
Educator. **Personal:** Born Nov 6, 1930, Helena, AL; married Mary Jones; children: Charles, Anthony, Tonya. **Educ:** AL A&M U, BS 1956, MS 1961. **Career:** Huntsville City Schools, diversifiedd occupations coord; Huntsville AL, vctnl T&I coord, 1971; Decatur City Schools, teacher coord, 1958-71; KY State Coll, instructor, 1956-68. **Orgs:** Mem AL Educ Ass; AL Vocational Assn; Am Vocational Assn 1958; mem Alpha Phi Alpha; RE Nelms Elks Lodge #977; Masn; VFW; Am Legion. **Military Serv:** AUS sgt 1951-54. **Business Addr:** SR Butler HS, 2401 Homes Ave, Huntsville, AL.

BRIGGS, GREG
Professional football player. **Career:** Dallas Cowboys, 1992-. **Business Addr:** Professional Football Player, Dallas Cowboys, 1 Cowboys Pkwy, Irving, TX 75063, (214)556-9900.

BRIGGS-GRAVES, ANASA
Senior producer, director of black ethnic affairs. **Personal:** Born in Loma Linda, CA. **Educ:** Univ of CA Riverside, 1968-70; Univ of CA Santa Barbara, BA Drama 1986; San Diego State Univ, Masters pending. **Career:** SD Unified School Dist, drama consult 1976-78; Grad School for Urban Resources, staff consultant 1977-78; Mozaic Repertory Theator, actress 1978-79; Barbizon School of Modeling, TV acting instr 1979; San Diego State Univ KPBS-TV, producer black ethnic affairs. **Orgs:** Pres San Diego Assoc of Black Journalists; chairperson exec bd, exec bd SD Black Leadership Council; Natl Med Assn; bd of dir Comprehensive Health Ctr; United Way Contact Team; SD County Human Relations Commission Advisory Bd for Media; regional dir, Natl Assn of Black Journalists 1987-89; bd of governors San Diego Chapter, Natl Acad of Television Arts & Sciences 1988-89; bd mem San Diego Opera 1989-91; bd mem Mayor's Black Advisor Bd 1986-89; bd mem Study Commn on Black Affairs 1985-89. **Honors/Awds:** Achievement Nancy Wilson Found 1983; Bronze Medal Intl Film & TV Fest of NY 1983; Excellence in Journalism San Diego Chap NAACP 1984; Emmy Nominee Producer Category San Diego 1984; Old Glove Theater Best Supporting Actress in Lead Role 1975-76; 2nd Runner Up Miss San Diego; fellow Media Inst USC Mid Summer Inst in Broadcast Mgmt for Minorities 1982; fellow CA Public Broadcasting Commiss Mgmt Training 1983; SD Pres Club Best Documentary 1986; Natl Assn of Black Journalists1986; Best TV Feature Annual Award; Emmy 1986; Emmy nominee for Religious Program "The Spiritual Legacy of the Gospel" Emmy nominee for Entertainment Program " Water of your Bath".

BRIGHAM, FREDDIE M.
Banker. **Personal:** Born Mar 23, 1947, Minneapolis, MN; daughter of Fred W & Mary L Lewis; divorced; children: Matthew W, Michael F, Jaime M. **Educ:** Metropolitan Community College, 1979-82; National Univ, 1987-88. **Career:** The Pillsbury Co, exec sec to promotion dir, 1973-84; Bank of America Nevada, exec sec to controller, 1988-93, mgr of information processing, 1993-. **Orgs:** North Las Vegas Literacy Council, 1990-92. **Special Achievements:** Volunteer tutor; aspiring fiction writer. **Business Addr:** Manager of Information Processing, Bank of America Nevada, PO Box 98600, Unit 7932, Las Vegas, NV 89193-8600, (702)654-8149.

BRIGHT, ALFRED LEE
Artist, educator. **Personal:** Born Jan 9, 1940, Youngstown, OH; son of Elizabeth Lockhart Daniels Bright and Henry Bright; married Virginia Deanne Newell; children: Leslie, Alfred Jr, Nichole, Steven. **Educ:** Youngstown U, BS 1964; Kent St U, MA 1965. **Career:** Youngstown State Univ, distinguished prof of art, 1965-, dir black studies program, 1970-87. **Orgs:** Alpha Phi Alpha Fraternity; St Dept of Edn, Advisory Com on the Arts; exec mem OH Arts Council; Natl Humanities Faculty; pres, Youngstown Area Arts Council, 1979-80; exec bd, Ohio Arts Council, governor's appointment, 1973-78; Phi Kappa Phi; Phi Beta Delta; The Golden Key National Honor Society. **Honors/Awds:** Numerous solo exhibitions; pvt colls, perm colls dev, "Total Walk-In Environmental Rooms", 1st & hon ment award Butler Art Inst, Youngstown 1967; best of show Haber-Gall 1966; 1st & 2nd awards, oils Village Cntr Fine Art Exhib, Niles OH 1964-67; consult Nat Humanities Faculty 1977-; Best of Show Butler Inst of Amer Art 1984; 1st place AAA Exhibit Butler Inst of Amer Art 1985 & 1994; Solo exhibitions: Cincinnati Art Museum, 1991; Beachwood Museum, 1992; Malcolm Brown Gallery, 1990; painted with live jazz music: Art Blakey and Winton Marsalis, 1980, Jimmy Owens, 1985; Butler Inst of Amer Art, 1985; Roanoke Museum of Fine Arts, 1986; Harmon-Meek Gallery, Naples, FL, 1986, 1991; Cleveland Playhouse Bolton Gallery, solo exhibitions, 1990; fellowship, Canton Museum of Art, Ann Arundel Community College, 1990; aid to individual artist, Ohio Arts Council, 1980; Outstanding Graduate Achiever, National Junior Achievement, Inc, 1975; Distinguished Professor Award, Youngstown State University, 1980, 1985-96; The Ohio House of Representatives, Art Educator of the Year, 1992; The Harmon & Harriet Kelly Collection of African American Art (San Antonio, Texas). **Special Achievements:** Coauthor, An Interdisciplinary Introduction to Black Studies, Kendal-Hunt Publishing, 1978. **Business Addr:** Professor of Art, Youngstown State University, 410 Wick Ave, Youngstown, OH 44555.

BRIGHT, HERBERT L., SR.
Corporate executive. **Personal:** Born Aug 20, 1941, Shelbyville, TN; son of Alvirleen Buchanan and Henry H Bright; married Dzifa Killings, Jun 6, 1992; children: Troy, Sonja, Yolanda, Herbert Jr, Kristi, Kenji Horton. **Educ:** Thornton Junior College, Harvey, IL; Seton Hall University, South Orange, NJ; Graduate Institute of Bible Studies, Lynchburg, VA; Shiloh Theological Seminary, Stafford, VA, doctor of divinity. **Career:** Nabisco Brands, Inc, general clerk, 1963-65, operations manager, 1968-72, assistant accounting office manager, 1972-73, personnel policies specialist, 1973-75, corporate equal opportunity manager, 1975-79, senior manager of personnel services, 1979-83, director of personnel practices, 1983-87, director of personnel services, 1987-89; dir of minority affairs & business development, 1989-; Faith Tabernacle Church, Faith Tabernacle Outreach Ministries, Inc, sr pastor, founder, presiding bishop; Bright Light Comm Service, Inc, chair/CEO. **Orgs:** President, board of directors, Nabisco Brands Employee Credit Union; member, corporate advisory council, NAACP ACT-SO, Opportunities Industrialization Centers of America, Tom Skinner Associates' Industry and Labor Council; member, National Urban League Commerce and Industry Council, American Society for Personnel Administration, Union County Urban League Board, Virginia Union University Cluster, Howard University Cluster, Felician College Business Advisory Board; Life mem, NAACP; charter mem, National Urban League; 100 Black Men of NJ; board of directors, Carter Woodson Foundation; board of directors, National Black United Fund; board of directors, NJ Black United Fund; board of directors, Plainfield Teen Parenting Program. **Honors/Awds:** Whitney M Young, Jr, Memorial Award, Morris County Urban League, 1985; national honoree, Afro-American History Award, 1987; Morris County NAACP Community Service Award; National Association of Marketing Developers Herbert H Wright Award; numerous others. **Military Serv:** US Army, 1963-66. **Business Addr:** Faith Tabernacle Church, 1032 South Ave, Ste 219, Plainfield, NJ 07062.

BRIGHT, JEAN MARIE
Educator, writer. **Personal:** Born Sep 23, 1915, Rutherfordton, NC; daughter of Wollie Lynch Bright and John W Bright, Sr. **Educ:** North Carolina Agricultural and Technical State Univ, Greensboro NC, BS, 1939; Columbia Univ, New York, NY, MA, 1953. **Career:** North Carolina Agricultural and Technical State Univ, Greensboro NC, prof of English, l951-78; lecturer, North Carolina Humanities Comm, 1977-79. **Orgs:** Mem, African Literature Assn; mem, Coll Language Assn; pres, Bright Forest Enterprises, Inc, l980-89. **Honors/Awds:** Co-editor, Images of the Negro in Amer, 1965; co-editor, Voices from the Black Experience, l972. **Home Addr:** 1008 S Benbow Rd, Greensboro, NC 27406.

BRIGHT, KIRK
Convention executive. **Personal:** Born Jan 25, 1943, Louisville, KY; son of Lois S Bright; married Shela, Oct 31, 1992; children: Greg, Yvette, Brett, Yvonne. **Educ:** Howard Univ, attended. **Career:** IBM, customer engineer, 1966-71; Bright's Dist Co, pres, 1971-89; Louisville Convention and Visitors Bureau, convention sales mgr, 1990-. **Honors/Awds:** Sales Marketing Exec, Distinguished Sales Award, 1992; YMCA, Black Achiever, 1995; Conv Bureau, Employee of the Year/ 1997; Louisville Defender Newspaper & Anheuser-Busch, Inc, "Doing My Job Award," 1997. **Military Serv:** US Air Force, Staff Sergeant, 1962-66.

BRIGHT, WILLIE S.
Executive search consultant. **Personal:** Born Feb 7, 1934, Houston, TX; son of Ovida Y Johnson and Willie S Bright; married Mildred Ball, Jun 4, 1960; children: Develous A, Nicole O. **Educ:** Tuskegee Inst, Tuskegee AL, 1951-53; Texas Southern Univ, Houston TX, BA, 1955, MEd, 1964. **Career:** Houston Independent School Dist, Houston TX, teacher, 1959-66; Crescent Found, Houston TX, counselor, 1966-67; Concentrated Employment Program, Houston TX, training officer, 1967-68; Forera Southeastern Inc, Houston TX, dir, 1968-71; The Urban Placement Serv, Houston TX, owner, 1971-. **Orgs:** Vice polemarch, bd mem, Kappa Alpha Psi, Houston Alumni 1954-; mem, Natl Assn of Personnel Consultants, 1971-; vice pres, dir, Houston Area Assn of Personnel Consultants, 1971-; bd of dir, Mental Health Assn of Houston, Harris County, 1974-80, mem, Univ Oaks Civic Club, 1979-; life mem, Kappa Alpha Psi, 1974; mem, Kiwanis Intl, Houston Metropolitan Chapter, 1985-; expert witness, Office of Hearing and Appeal, SSA,

1975-80; bd mem, Citizens for Good School, 1976-78; mem, Natl Assn of Market Developers, Houston Chapter, 1978; vice chmn, PPR Comm, Mt Vernon United Methodist Church, 1989; member, Houston Area Pan Hellenic Council 1986-. **Honors/Awds:** Goodwill Ambassador Award, City of Houston, 1975; Meritorious Service Award, City of Houston, 1976; Certificate of Appreciation, Houston Area Private Employment Assn, 1977; Certified Public Consultant, 1978; Trailblazer Award, Kappa Alpha Psi, Houston Chapter, 1983; Certificate of Appreciation, Ensemble Theatre, 1987; Certificate of Appreciation, Edison Middle School Career Awareness 1990; Certificate of Recognition, Houston Area Pan Hellenic Council 1990-. **Military Serv:** US Army, E-4, 1956-58. **Business Addr:** Owner, Mgr, The Urban Placement Service, 602 Sawyer St, #460, Houston, TX 77077-7510.

BRIMM, CHARLES EDWIN
Physician. **Personal:** Born May 22, 1924; married Edith Mapp; children: Charles Jr, Linda Jean. **Educ:** South Jersey Law School, 1947-48; Ottawa Univ, BS 1951; Ottawa Univ Med School, MD 1955. **Career:** Hahnemann Hosp, teaching 1974-; Family Practice, specialist 1975; Coll of Med & Dentistry of NJ, teaching 1977; Family Practice Hahnemann Hosp, instr 1978-79; General Practice, physician 1956-. **Orgs:** Mem BPUM 1978; founder Concept House Drug Rehab Settlement 1970; mem Camden Cty Heart Assoc; bd of trustees Camden Cty Coll; life mem NAACP; booster club Camden HS; mem Natl Med Assoc; consult Cooper Med Ctr, Dept of Neurology & Psychiatry, Dept of Intl Med, Dept of Family Practice. **Honors/Awds:** Publ "Use of Fluplenazine Decanoate in Managing PCP Intoxication"; Physician of the Year Camden Cty Med Soc 1971; Diplomate of Bd, 1974, Elected an affiliate 1979 Royal Soc of Med by Queen of England 1979; Postgrad Med Rsch Awd 1979. **Military Serv:** AUS chem warfare quartermaster 1943-46. **Business Addr:** Councilmember-at-Large, PO Box 127, Collingswood, NJ 08108-0217.

BRIMMER, ANDREW F.
Economist. **Personal:** Born Sep 13, 1926, Newellton, LA; married Doris Millicent Scott; children: Esther Diane. **Educ:** Univ of Washington, BA, 1950, MA, 1951; Univ of Bombay, India, 1951-52; Harvarvard Univ, PhD, 1957. **Career:** Fed Res Bank NYC, economist 1955-58; MI State Univ, asst prof 1958-61; Wharton Sch Finance & Commerce Univ of PA, asst prof 1961-66; Dept Commerce Washington, dep asst sec 1963-65, asst sec for econ affairs 1965-66; Fed Reserve Bd, member 1966-74; Grad Sch Bus Admin Harvard Univ, Thomas Henry Carroll Ford Found vis prof 1974-76; Brimmer & Co Inc, pres 1976-. **Orgs:** Bd govs/v chmn Commodity Exch Inc; dir Bank of Amer, Amer Security Bank, Intl Harvester Co, United Air Lines, Du Pont Co, Gannett Co Inc; mem Fed Res Central Banking Mission to Sudan 1957; consult SEC 1962-63; mem Trilateral Commn; chmn bd trustees Tuskegee Inst Com for Econ Devel; mem vis com NYU; co-chmn Interracial Cncl for Bus Oppty; mem Amer Econ Assn; Amer Fin Assn; Assn for Study Afro-Amer Life and History (pres 1970-73); mem Natl Economists Club, Cncl on Foreign Relations, Amer Statis Assn; bd of dirs, Mercedes-Benz of North America, 1990-. **Honors/Awds:** Fulbright fellow, Univ of Bombay, India, 1951-52; author, "Survey of Mutual Funds Investors" 1963; "Life Insurance Companies in Capital Market" 1962; "Economic Development, International and African Perspectives" 1976; contrib, articles to professional journals; named Govt Man of the Year Natl Bus League 1963; recip Arthur S Flemming Award 1966; Russwurm Award 1966; Capital Press Club Award 1966; Golden Plate Award Amer Acad Achieve 1967; Alumnus Summa Laude Dignatus Univ Wash Alumni Assn 1972; Natl Honoree Beta Gamma Sigma 1971; Horatio Alger Award 1974; Equal Oppty Award Natl Urban League 1974; One Hundred Black Men and NY Urban Coalition Award 1975; numerous honorary degrees. **Business Addr:** President, Brimmer & Company, Inc, 4400 MacArthur Blvd NW, Washington, DC 20007.

BRINKLEY, CHARLES H., SR.
Educator (retired). **Personal:** Born Nov 13, 1942, Gallatin, TN; son of Ellen and Hutch; married Gloria Johnson; children: Katrena, Angela, Charles II. **Educ:** Mississippi Vally State Univ, BS, MS; Tennessee Technical Univ, Additional Study; Tennessee State Univ, MA, Education, 1989; 30 additional semester hours. **Career:** TPSEA Unit, Tennessee Prep School, Past Pres; Taft Youth Center, Principal, 1968-70; St Training School, Dept of Correctionss, Indianola, MS, Teacher, 1967; Sumner County Election Commission, 1983-89, Chmn, 1985. **Orgs:** Local Rep, TPS Education Assn, Middle TN Council B S Assn; Mem, Tennessee Sheriff's Assn; past Vice Chmn, General Ct Committee, 1975-77; Deputy Sheriff Command, 1975; life mem, pres, NAACP Gallatin Branch, 1996; Member, C of C, 1975; Notary Public at large, State of Tennessee, 1975-78; Mem, NEA, MTEA, TEA, TPSEA; Deacon, 1975-, Chmn, Deacon's Bd, 1985-, First Baptist Church. **Honors/Awds:** Outstanding Service Presidential Award, TPS Education Assn, 1972; NSF Fellowship Grant, 1968; Outstanding Service Award, NAACP, 1989, 1996. **Business Addr:** 1200 Foster Ave, Nashville, TN 37211.

BRINKLEY, NORMAN, JR.
Educational administrator. **Personal:** Born Jul 7, 1931, Edenton, NC; son of Adell Brinkley and Norman Brinkley; married Pearl A Rozier; children: Franklin, Cassandra, Norman T, Carmellia, Christa A. **Educ:** NC Agr & Tech Coll, BS 1950-54; NC Agr & Tech State U, MS 1973-74. **Career:** MS Valley State Univ, dean of students, 1970-; Lincoln Univ, Lincoln PA, activity dir & comm coord, 1969-70; Child Care Serv Media PA, social worker, 1965- 69; Children Serv Inc, Philadelphia PA, caseworker, 1963-64; State Of PA, youth supvr, 1961-63; City of Philadelphia, youth counselor, 1959-61; MS NASPA, state dir, 1979-80. **Orgs:** Mem Voters League 1970-80; mem MS Student Personnel Adminstrn 1970-80; officer M W Stringer Grand Lodge F & AM 1976-80. **Honors/Awds:** Recipient Comm Relations Award Univ of MS 1971; adminstrs for Developing Insts Award Univ of WI 1972-73; Supervisory Leadership Skills Award So IL Univ 1975. **Military Serv:** USAF 2nd lt 1955-58. **Business Addr:** Dean of Student Affairs, Mississippi Valley State Univ, Box 1239, Itta Bena, MS 38941.

BRINN, CHAUNCEY J.
Education administrator. **Personal:** Born Mar 21, 1932, Kalamazoo, MI; married Elizabeth L. **Educ:** BA 1963; MA 1975. **Career:** Western Michigan Univ, dir acad affairs & minority student affairs, asst to vice pres, 1971-, Special Prog Office of Student Financial Aids, coord, 1968-71, banking, branch mgr, minority recruitment, 1965-68; IBM Corp, admin, minority recruitment, 1963-65; Industry, chem lab tech, 1956-58; Assn of Western MI Univ, chem lab tech, resrch, past vice pres 1954-56. **Orgs:** Mem minority caucus Midwest Assn of Stdnt Fin Aid Admin 1971; mem Nat Assn of African Am Educators; Kalamazoo Co Prsnl & Gdnc Assn; MI Prsnl & Gdnc Assn; dir Region XI MI Stdnt Fin Aid Assn 1969-70; chmn Minority Affairs Com, MI Student Fin Aid Assn 1970-71; mem Midwest Assn of Std Fin Aid Admin 1969; del, exec bd natl assn, fin aid admin dir Kalamazoo Comm Serv Cncl 1961-62; dir Citizens Teen 1960-62; dir Kalamazoo Jaycees 1964-66; dir Otsego-plainwell Jaycees 1966-67; chmn Grtr No Dist Explr Scouts 1967; Kalamazoo Chap NAACP 1965; chrmn Mar of Dime 1966; consult Civil Rights Commn Migrant Lbr 1969; mem MI Alliance of Black Educs 1976; state Pres, mem MI Assn for Non White Concerns; adv Affrm Act Bus & Ind 1972-75; Men of Achievement 1976. **Honors/Awds:** Author publ "Going to College Costs Money". **Military Serv:** USN 2d cl petty off 1950-54. **Business Addr:** Western MI Univ, Adminstration Bldg, Kalamazoo, MI 49008.

BRISBANE, SAMUEL CHESTER
Physician (retired). **Personal:** Born Aug 8, 1914, Jacksonville, FL; married Martha Shields. **Educ:** Lincoln Univ PA, BA 1937; Howard Univ Med Coll, 1949. **Career:** Columbia Univ Coll of Physicians & Surgeons, asst clinical prof anes 1963; Harlem Hosp Cntr, asso dir dept of anes 1963, attndng anesthesiolgst 1950;220 W 139 St, gen Prac 1950-. **Orgs:** Mem Nat Med Assn; mem Am Soc of Anesthesiolgsts AMA; past pres Manhattan Grdsmn Inc; mem Alpha Phi Alpha Frat; Sigma Pi Phi Fraternity. **Honors/Awds:** Alpha Phi Alpha Frat Humanitarian Award; John Hunter Mem Camp Fund 1975; Humanitarian & Civic Award; Boys of Yesteryear Inc 1978. **Military Serv:** AUS pvt 1943. **Business Addr:** 506 Lenox Ave, New York, NY 10037.

BRISBY, VINCENT COLE
Professional football player. **Personal:** Born Jan 25, 1971, Lake Charles, LA; children: Donovan Herbert. **Educ:** Northeast Louisiana, attended. **Career:** New England Patriots, wide receiver, 1993-. **Orgs:** Phi Beta Sigma. **Business Addr:** Professional Football Player, New England Patriots, 60 Washington St, Foxboro Stadium, Foxboro, MA 02035, (508)543-7911.

BRISCO, GAYLE
Realtor. **Personal:** Born in Suffolk, VA; divorced; children: One. **Educ:** Hampton Univ, bachelor's degree in psychology; Univ of Maryland, master's degree in social work. **Career:** Otis Warren & Co, currently. **Orgs:** Greater Baltimore Board of Realtors, pres. **Special Achievements:** First African American woman to be elected president of the Greater Baltimore Board of Realtors.

BRISCOE, EDWARD GANS
Physician. **Personal:** Born Nov 18, 1937, Glenridge, NJ; son of Evelyn M Van Dunk and Gans H Briscoe; married Agatha Donatto, Jan 23, 1976; children: Valerie R Washington, Kurt G, Pamela Y Morant, Keith E, Deidre A, Allison M. **Educ:** Howard Univ, BS 1959, MD 1963. **Career:** Howard Univ Dept of Surgery, chief div of anesthesia 1971-74; Martin Luther King Jr General Hosp, assoc prof of anesthesiology 1974-75; West Adams Comm Hosp, staff anesthesiologist 1975-76; Charles R Drew Postgrad Sch, assoc prof of anesthesiology 1976-77; Westside Comm Hosp of Long Beach, chief of anesthesia 1977; private practice, family medicine 1977-79; Hilo Medical Group, family practice 1979-82; Family Practice Treatment of Chronic Pain, 1982-87; Department of Health, US Virgin Islands, territorial medical director of emergency medical services, 1987-90; Tripler Army Medical Center, Honolulu, HI, civilian physician specialist, 1990-. **Orgs:** Mem Amer Assn of Family Practice, Natl Medical Assn, Hawaii Federation of Physicians & Dentists, mem St Thomas-St John Medical Society 1988-; bd mem, Partners for Health, US Virgin Islands, 1989-. **Honors/Awds:** Author "Diary of a Short Timer in Vietnam" 1970; Fellow Amer Coll of Anesthesiologists; Assoc Examiner Amer Coll of Anesthesiologists, Amer Bd of Anesthesiology; 11 papers presented including "Pain Control in an Isolated Clinical Environment," presented to annual meeting Golden State Medical Soc Honolulu, HI 1984. **Military Serv:** USN lt cmdr 5 yrs; Vietnam Serv Medal, Combat Action Medal, Letter of Commendation, Navy Unit Citation.

BRISCOE, HATTIE RUTH ELAM
Attorney. **Personal:** Born Nov 13, 1916, Shreveport, LA; daughter of Clora Beatrice Burton Elam and Willie Perry Elam; married William M Briscoe, Oct 12, 1940 (died 1987). **Educ:** Wiley Coll, BA 1937; Prairie View Coll, MS 1951; St Mary's Law Schl, LLB 1956, JD, 1970. **Career:** Pvt Prac, atty 1956-; Kelly Air Base, clk, typist 1952-56; Briscoe Beauty Salon, beauty operator 1941-45; Booker Wash & Schl, tchr 1937-41. **Orgs:** Mem, past pres Delta Sigma Theta Sor 1937-; mem NAACP 1945-; mem TX St Bar Assn 1956-; mem Am Bar Assn 1956-; mem Nat Assn of Def Lawyers 1964-; mem Nat Assn of Black Women Attys 1975-; member, National Bar Assn, 1965-; member, San Antonio Black Lawyers Assn; past president, Friday Evening Bridge Club. **Honors/Awds:** Hist Achvmt Award, Smart Set Soc Clb 1960; Civic Achvmt Award; Royal Dukes & his Ct 1962; supr achvmt in law Delta Sigma Theta Sor 1975; model comm ldr Miss Black San Antonio Bd 1975; One of 30 Texas "Women of Courage," Bishop College, 1985; one of 100 women honored at the Sixth Biennial Texas Black Women's Conference, 1986; featured at the Institute of Texan Cultures, 1976; St Mary's University, Distinguished Alumna Award, 1992; Hattie Elam Briscoe Scholarship Fund, 1993. **Business Addr:** Attorney, 1416 E Commerce St, #202, San Antonio, TX 78202.

BRISCOE, LEONARD E.
Corporation executive. **Personal:** Born May 22, 1940, Ft Worth, TX; married Rosita; children: Edward, Rosanna. **Educ:** Pepperdine U, MBA 1975; Univ TX, Currently Studying PhD. **Career:** Expediters, pres; NAMCON, Briscoe-morrison, real est; Briscoe Consultant Serv, Rolling Hills Bldg & Devel, Universal Financial Corp, Interntl Mortgage Corp, exec v p; Real & Est Broker 1960-. **Orgs:** Local State & Nat Real Est Brokers Assns; mem Local State & Nat Home Bldrs Assns, Ft Worth City Cncl 1971-75; Nat League Cities; Ft Worth Comm Devel Cncl; pres Assn Mayors Cnclmn & Commrs. **Business Addr:** 2016 Evans Ave, Fort Worth, TX.

BRISCOE, SIDNEY EDWARD, JR. **See Obituaries section.**

BRISCO-HOOKS, VALERIE
Track and field athlete. **Personal:** Born Jul 6, 1960, Greenwood, MS; married Alvin Hooks; children: Alvin. **Educ:** Long Beach Community Coll; California State Univ, Northridge. **Career:** Athletic Congress Natl Championships, 1984; Olympic Games, Los Angeles 1984, Seoul, Korea 1988; UCLA Invitational, 1984; Bruce Jenner Meet, San Jose CA, 1984; European Track Circuit, 1984, 1985; Millrose Games, 1985; Sunkist Invitational, Los Angeles, 1985; Times-Herald Invitational, Dallas, Texas, 1985; LA Times-Kodak Games, Inglewood, CA, 1985. **Honors/Awds:** 3 Gold Medals, 1984 Olympics, Los Angeles; Silver Medal, 1988 Olympics, Seoul, Korea; ranked #6 in world 400 meters, ranked #2 in US 400 meters, ranked #4 in US 200 meters, Track & Field News, 1988; Outstanding Mother's Award, Natl Mother's Day Comm, 1986; co-chairperson, Minnie Riperton Cancer Week, 1986, 1987; 1st female asked to compete in Australia's Stalwell Gift Race, 1987.

BRISKER, LAWRENCE
Educational administrator. **Personal:** Born Oct 5, 1934, St Louis, MO; married Flossie Richmond. **Educ:** So IL U, BA 1959; Univ of NM, MA 1966; Case-Western Res U, PhD 1976. **Career:** Cuyahoga Community Coll, dean student life unit, 1978-, special asst to the chancellor, 1977-78, coord student assistance program, 1976-77; Cleveland Municipal Court, chief deputy clerk, 1975-76; OH Bell Telephone Co Cleveland, employment supvr & traffic mgr, 1964-70; Cleveland Public School System, teacher, 1962-64. **Orgs:** Bd mem Glen Oak Pvt Sch for Girls 1968-; mem Citizen's League 1978-; bd dir Cleveland Pub Radio 1979-; bd trustees Cleveland TB & Respiratory Fed 1966; mem Urban League's Emplymnt & Econs Com 1968; mem United Area Citizens Agency 1979-. **Honors/Awds:** Spinix awrd So IL Univ 1958; Phi Delta Kappa Univ of NM 1960; natl defense ed act flwshp Case-Western Res Univ 1970; ahs flwshp awrd Case-Western Res Univ 1972. **Military Serv:** AUS e-4 1958-60. **Business Addr:** Cuyahoga Community College, 2900 Community College Ave, Cleveland, OH 44115.

BRISTOW, CLINTON, JR.
Educator. **Personal:** Born Mar 15, 1949, Montgomery, AL; son of Betty Colvin Bristow and T C Bristow; married Joyce Moore Bristow, Jan 1, 1975; children: Maya. **Educ:** Northwestern University, Evanston, IL, BS, 1971, JD, 1974, PhD, 1977; Gover-

nors State University, University Park, IL, MBA, 1984. **Career:** Roosevelt University, Chicago, IL, professor, 1976-79; Olive-Harvey College, Chicago, IL, vice-president, 1979-81; Chicago State University, Chicago, IL, professor, chairperson, dean, 1981-. **Orgs:** President, Chicago Bd of Education, 1990-; vice-chairman, North Region, Illinois Committee on Black Concerns in Higher Education, 1987-; member, board of directors, Council of Great City Schools, 1990-; member, board of directors, National Consortium for Educational Access, 1987-. **Honors/Awds:** Legal Opportunity Scholarship Awardee, Northwestern Univ, 1971; Urban Affairs Fellow, Northwestern Univ, 1976; Top Ladies of Distinction Role Model, TLOD Inc, 1987; Outstanding Educator Award, City of Chicago, Department of Human Services, 1991. **Business Addr:** President, Alcorn State Univ, 1000 ASU Dr, #359, Lorman, MS 39096.

BRISTOW, LONNIE R.

Physician. **Personal:** Born Apr 6, 1930, New York, NY; son of Rev Lonnie H & Vivian W Bristow; married Marily H Bristow, Oct 18, 1961; children: Robert E, MD, Elizabeth E. **Educ:** Coll of the City of NY, BS, 1953; NY Univ, Coll of Med, MD, 1957; Internship, San Francisco City & County Hosp, 1957-58; Residency, Internal Med, USVA Hosp, San Francisco, 1958-60; Francis Delafield Hosp, Columbia Univ Service, 1960; USVA Hosp, Bronx, 1961; Residency, occupation med, Univ of CA, San Francisco School of Med, 1979-81. **Career:** Private Practice, internist, currently. **Orgs:** East Bay Society of Internal Med, pres, 1969; Comm on Office Lab Assessment, exec comm sect, 1989-91; Joint Comm on the Accreditation of Healthcare Organizations, commissioner, 1990-92; Amer Coll of Physicians, fellow, master, 1977, 1995; Federated Council of Internal Med, 1976-78; Natl Med Veterans Society; Amer Society of Internal Med, pres, 1981-82; CA Society of Internal Med, pres, 1976; CA Med Assn; Alameda-Contra Costa Med Assn, 1968-; Amer Med Assn, bd of trustees, 1985-, chair, 1993-94, pres elect, 1994-95, pres, 1995-96. **Honors/Awds:** Inst of Med, 1977-; Parket Health Memorial Lecturer, 1982; CA Society of IM, CA Most Distinguished Internist, 1990; Morehouse School of Medicine, Honorary Degree, 1994; Wayne State University School of Medicine, Honorary Degree, 1995; City College of the City University of New York, Honorary Degree, 1995; Contra Costa Bd of Supervisors, Contra Costa Humanitarian of the Year, 1989. **Special Achievements:** Presidential appointment to serve as chair, board of regents, Uniformed Services University of the Health Sciences, 1996-; Board Certification, Am Bd of Internal Med, 1969; Contributing editor of The Internist; Emeritus Member Editorial Advisory Board of Medical World News; Publications: "The Myth of Sickle Cell Trait," medical opinion, The Western Journal of Med, p 77-82 & 121, July 1974; "Shared Sacrifice-The AMA Leadership Response to the Health Sec Act" JAMA, p 271 & 786, Mar 9, 1994; "Mine Eyes Have Seen," Journal of the AMA, p 261, 284-285, Jan 13, 1989. **Business Addr:** Immediate Past President, American Medical Association, 515 N State St, Office Services, 16th Fl, Chicago, IL 60610, (312)464-4469.

BRITT, L. D.

Trauma surgeon. **Personal:** Born Jun 28, 1951, Suffolk, VA; son of Mrs Claretta White Britt. **Educ:** University of Virginia, BA, 1972; Harvard, Med School, MD, 1977; Harvard School of Public Health, MPH, 1977. **Career:** University of Illinois, dept of surgery, clinical instr, 1983-85; Bethany Hosp, active staff, asst dir of emergency medicine, 1984-85; Maryland Inst of Emergency Medical Svcs Systems, chief admin surgical fellow, 1985-86; Eastern VA Med School, asst prof of surgery, 1986-89, chief div of trama & critical care, 1987-97, assoc prof of surgery, 1989-93; Henry Ford prof and vice chair, dept of surgery, 1993-95; Edward Brickhouse, chair, dept of surgery, 1994-; Sentara Norfolk Gen Hosp, Shock Trauma Ctr, asst med dir, 1986-87, med dir, 1987-97, Dept of Surgery, chief, 1997-. **Orgs:** Served on numerous committees and boards including: Senate Joint Subcommittee on EMS personnel training & retention, 1988-91; EMS, advisory bd, 1988-94; Norfolk State Univ, bd of visitors, 1988-96, rector, 1994-96; Univ of VA, bd of mgrs, 1993-; Boy Scouts of Amer, exec bd mem, 1989-; Sentara Hth System, bd of trustees, 1992-94; Amer Bd of Surgery, assoc examiner, 1997-; Amer Coll of Surgeons, natl comm on trauma, 1996-; Assoc of Prog Dirs in Surgery, bd of dirs, 1996-; Pan Amer Trauma Soc, bd of mgrs; Scientific Research Soc; Alpha Omega Alpha Honor Society. **Honors/Awds:** Eastern VA Med School, Sir William Oster Award, Outstanding Attending Physician of the Year, 1988-89, 1992-97; State Council of Higher Education, Outstanding Faculty Award, 1994; NAACP, Man of the Year, 1996; Emmy Award, 1994; ML King Award, Outstanding Achievement and Community Svc, 1997. **Special Achievements:** Royal Society of Medicine in England, fellow; American Assoc for the Surgery of Trauma, fellow; Amer Coll of Critical Care Medicine, fellow; visiting prof, Howard Univ of VA, St Louis Univ; received numerous research grants; published many articles for journals; given countless presentations. **Business Addr:** Brickhouse Professor & Chairman, Eastern Virginia Medical School, Department of Surgery, 825 Fairfax Ave, Norfolk, VA 23507-1912, (757)446-8950.

BRITT, PAUL D., JR.

Educational administrator. **Personal:** Born Feb 3, 1951, Franklin, VA; married Priscilla Harding; children: Pauleatha Clara, Taene Renita. **Educ:** Norfolk State Univ, BA Social Service 1970-74; VA State Univ, M Educ Admin 1980-84. **Career:** Southampton Co Schools, teacher/coach 1975-79; Franklin City Schools, teacher/coach/social studies dept chmn 1979-84; Smithfield HS, asst principal 1984-. **Orgs:** Deacon First Baptist Church Franklin 1979-; councilmember Franklin City Council 1982-. **Business Addr:** Asst Prin & Mem City Council, Smithfield High School, Rt4 Box 115, Smithfield, VA 23430.

BRITTAIN, BRADLEY BERNARD, JR.

Engineer, editor. **Personal:** Born Mar 22, 1948, Arlington, VA; married Lenora C Robinson Freeman; children: Kandakai Freeman, Kini Freeman, Zina Freeman. **Educ:** Attended, Howard Univ. **Career:** ABC Inc, engr editor newsfilm editor apprentice film editor desk asst 1972-; freelance photographer 1976-77; American Broadcasting Co, engr. **Orgs:** Life mem NAACP; Natl Rifle Assn; mem Natl Geog Soc; Radio & TV Corr Assn; Friends Natl Zoo; Natl Capital Velo Club; Assn Corcoran; mem Natl Acad TV Arts & Sci 1983-84-85; mem White House News Photographer Assn 1983-85; mem Capitol Hill Correspondents Assoc 1978-; public relations comm Northern Virginia Gun Club 1983-85; mem Smithsonian Resident Associates 1978-. **Honors/Awds:** Achievement in TV Awd CEBA 1982-83. **Home Addr:** PO Box 2486, Fairfax, VA 22031. **Business Addr:** Engineer, American Broadcasting Co, 1717 DeSales St NW, Washington, DC 20036.

BRITTON, ELIZABETH

Professional registered nurse. **Personal:** Born Jul 18, 1930, Gary, IN; children: Darryl T Gillespie, Tamara A Gillespie, John G Gillespie, Lisa M Roach, Anthony L, Alycyn M. **Educ:** Mayfair-Chicago City Coll, AA 1969; Purdue Univ, BSN 1974; Portland State Univ, MS 1982. **Career:** Chicago Maternity Ctr, nursing serv admin 1970-73; Beverly Learning Ctr, health educ instructor 1972-74; Univ of OR Health Scis Ctr Sch of Nursing, instructor 1976-81; OR Health Scis Univ Office of Minority Student Affairs, asst prof 1981-. **Orgs:** Pres Willamette Valley Racial Minorities Consortium; mem Natl Assoc of Medical Minority Educators; bd dirs North Portland Nurse Practioner Comm Health Clinic; anti-basileus Alpha Kappa Alpha Sor Zeta Sigma Omega; mem Oregon Alliance of Black School Educators; bd of dirs, Oregon Donor Program 1988-; mem, The Link's Inc, Portland Chapter 1988. **Honors/Awds:** Natl Honor Soc of Nursing Sigma Theta Tau 1976; Special Contribution to Indian Educ 1981, 82, 83; Certificate of Appreciation Ctr for Black Studies Portland State Univ 1983; Outstanding AKA Woman, Zeta Sigma Omega Chapter 1986. **Business Addr:** Director, International & Ethnic Affairs, Oregon Health Sciences Univ, 3181 SW Sam Jackson Park Rd, Portland, OR 97201.

BRITTON, JOHN H., JR.

Public relations executive. **Personal:** Born Jul 21, 1937, Nashville, TN; son of Martha Marie Parrish Britton and Rev John Henry Britton Sr; married Betty J Thompson, Jul 21, 1959; children: John III. **Educ:** Drake Univ, BA 1958; Syracuse Univ, MS 1962. **Career:** Atlanta Daily World, reporter 1958-62; Jet Mag, assoc editor asst mng ed 1962-66; US Civil Rights Commn, asst info officer 1966-67; Civil Rights Doc Proj Washington, assoc dir 1967-68; Jet Mag, mng editor 1968-71; Motown Rec Corp Detroit & LA, pub rel mgr 1971-73; Joint Center for Political Studies, pubilc affairs director, 1973-76; Encore Mag, columnist 1974-75; The Washington Post, public relations mgr, 1976-78; Univ of DC, public affairs dir, 1978-97; Bowie State Univ, public relations dir, 1997-. **Orgs:** Black Public Relation Society of Washington, National Advisory Committee, Natl Black Media Coalition; life member, NAACP. **Honors/Awds:** NNPA Merit Awd 1971. **Business Addr:** Director of Public Relations, Bowie State University, 14000 Jericho Park Rd, Bowie, MD 20715.

BRITTON, THEODORE R., JR.

Federal official (retired). **Personal:** Born Oct 17, 1925, North Augusta, SC; son of Bessie B Cook Britton and Theodore R Britton Sr; married Vernell Elizabeth Stewart, Feb 22, 1980; children: Theodore (deceased), Renee, Warren, Sharon, Darwin. **Educ:** New York Univ, BS, 1952. **Career:** Amer Baptist Mgmt Corp, pres 1966-71; HUD, act asst sec for rsch & tech 1973; ambassador Barbados & Grenada 1974-77; Special Representative to Associated States of the Caribbean 1974-77; United Mutual Life Ins Co of NY, pres & chief exec officer 1978-79; mgmt consul 1979-80; D Parke Gibson Intl Ltd, senior consultant, 1979-; Logical Tech Serv Corp, exec vice pres & secty; HUD, asst to sec for international affairs, 1981-89, NY, deputy regional administrator, 1983-84, Newark, manager, 1990-92. **Orgs:** Chmn New York City Urban Renewal mgmt Corp 1968-71; vice chmn Sector Grp Urban Env Orgn for Econ Coop & Devel 1971-74, 1981-84, chmn, 1985-87; deacon, trustee Riverside Church in NYC 1965-77; chair US/China Agreement on Housing 1981-89; vice chmn, 1982-84, chairman, 1985-87; OECD Group on Urban Affairs; dir Riverside Broadcasting Corp; Inst Real Estate Mgmt; Natl Assn Realtors; Amer Baptist Rep; bd of dirs Freedom Natl Bank 1978; exec scy US Agreement on Housing & Urban Develop with Canada Mexico & USSR. **Honors/Awds:** HUD, Distinguished Service Award, 1989; University of Bridgeport Black Law School Student Assn, Thurgood Marshall Award 1990; Institute of Real Estate Management, J Wallace Paleton Award, 1987. **Military Serv:** US Marine Corps Reserves, sgt, 1944-46, 1948-51; American Theater, Asiatic Pac Theater, WW II Victory Medal, Korean War Medal. **Home Addr:** 310 Somerlane Pl, Avondale Estates, GA 30002.

BROACH, S. ELIZABETH JOHNSON

Educational administrator, consultant. **Personal:** Born in Little Rock, AR; daughter of Iris Addie Johnson and Nelvia Johnson; married Hughes M Broach; children: Jacqueline Johnson Moore, David M Johnson, Anita M. **Educ:** Dunbar Jr Coll, Tchrs Cert 1940; Philander Smith Coll, BA Music Ed 1950; Univ of AR, MS Sec Ed 1953; CA State Univ at Hayward, Ed Psychology 1974. **Career:** Little Rock & Pulaski County Public Sch, music instructor 1955-65; SFUSD, music specialist 1967-69; Pelton Jr High Sch, dean of women 1969-70, asst principal 1970-72; Ben Franklin Jr High Sch, asst principal 1973-74; Wilson High Sch, asst principal 1975-77; McAteer High Sch, asst principal 1984-78; San Fran Unified Sch Dist, admin consultant; Beebe Memorial Cathedral. **Orgs:** Organist Beebe Meth Ch 1967-85; organist European Tour Voices of Beebe 1982; Natl Business & Prof Women; dir instructor Creative Arts Center San Fran; music dir Mt Pleasant Baptist Church Little Rock, AR; Natl Assn of Negro Musicians 1984-85; epistoleus Sigma Gamma Rho Sor; Phi Delta Kappa Ed 1978; Natl Council of Negro Women; educ comm NAACP 1984-85; Oakland Symphony Guild; founding board Oakland East Bay Symphony, 1988-; organist, National CME Women's Missionary Copuncil, 1987-. **Honors/Awds:** Diagnostic Counseling Learning Center SFUSD 1973; Commendation Merit Letter Bay Area Rapid Transit; Certificate of Merit CA Conf 9th Episcopal Dist; organ performance Bristol England, Chippenham Methodist Church, Wesley Chapel, London England; Outstanding Bay Area Organist, Natl Assn of Black Musicians. **Home Addr:** 7615 Hanson Dr, Oakland, CA 94605.

BROADNAX, MELVIN F.

Educator. **Personal:** Born Oct 21, 1929, Seaboard, NC; married Ruth Bracey. **Educ:** Shaw U, BA 1963; A&T State U, MS 1963; Shaw U, LlD 1972. **Career:** Northampton Bd of Educ, teacher; Seaboard NC, town commr. **Orgs:** Mem Kappa Frat; deacon & trustee of Ch mem NAACP; NEA. **Honors/Awds:** Ncta selected prsnlty of So 1969; kappa man of yr 1974. **Military Serv:** AUS sgt Korean War.

BROADNAX, WALTER DOYCE

Government official. **Personal:** Born Oct 21, 1944, Starcity, AR; son of Mary L; married Angel LaVerne Wheelock; children: Andrea Alyce. **Educ:** Washburn University, BA, 1967; Kansas University, MPA, 1969; Syracuse University, The Maxwell School of Citizenship & Public Affairs, PhD, 1975. **Career:** The Federal Executive Institute, professor, public administration, 1976-79; State of Kansas, Services to Children, Youth & Adults, director, 1979-80; U.S. Department of Health, Education & Welfare, Health & Human Services, principal deputy asst secretary, 1980-81; The Brookings Institution, The Advanced Study Program, sr staff member, 1981; Harvard University, JFK School of Government, Public Management & Public Policy, lecturer, 1981-87; NYK State Civil Service Commission, commissioner, president, 1987-90; Center for Governmental Research, Inc, president, 1990-93; US Dept of Health & Human Services, deputy secretary, 1993-. **Orgs:** Key Corp, board of directors, board member; National Civic League, board of directors, board member; Center for the Study of the States, advisory committee, CASE Commission, Phase II; State Advisory Council; National Commission on the American State & Local Public Service; New York State Commission on Cost Control; Rochester General Hospital, board of directors, board member. **Honors/Awds:** Auburn University, Gordon Sherman lecture, master of public administration, 1991; National Academy of Public Administration, fellow, 1988; Woodrow Wilson National Fellowship Foundation, National Advisory Commission, 1989; State University at Albany, Rockefeller College, John E Burton lecture, recipient of John E Burton Award & Rockefeller College Medallion, 1989. **Special Achievements:** Visiting lecturer, University of Texas, LBJ School of Public Affairs, 1989; Eminent Public Administrator Lecturer, Cleveland State University, College of Urban Affairs, 1989; National Commission on Innovations in State & Local Government, Ford Foundation, Howard University, 1987-89; South Africa Program, Harvard University, 1992; Transition Team Leader, President-Elect Bill Clinton Transition Team, 1992. **Business Addr:** Deputy Secretary, US Dept of Health & Human Services, 200 Independence Ave SW, Rm 614G, Washington, DC 20201.

BROADWATER, TOMMIE, JR.

Business owner. **Personal:** Born Jun 9, 1942, Washington, DC; married Lillian; children: Tommie III, Tanya, Jackie, Anita. **Educ:** Southern Univ; Prince Georges Comm Coll. **Career:** MD State, senator 1974-78; Broadwater Bonding Corp, owner; Prince Georges Comm Bank, vice pres 1976-77; Ebony Inn, owner 1974. **Orgs:** Cnclmn City of Glenarden 1967-73; Pince Georges C of C; tres MD Legislators Black Caucus; bD dir Prince George Comm Bank; bd dir PAR-LOT Entrprs Glenarden Boys Clb; spnsr Chapel Oaks Fire Dept Baseball Team; 25th Alliance Civic Grp; NAACP; Sr Citizens Adv Cncl. **Honors/Awds:** Outst alumni awrd Fairmont Hts Sch 1976; outst leader in Prince Georges Co Civic Grps 1977. **Business Addr:** 5611 Landover Rd, Hyattsville, MD 20784.

BROCK, ANNETTE
Educational administrator. **Career:** Savannah State College, pres, currently. **Business Addr:** President, Savannah State College, Office of the President, PO Box 20449, Savannah, GA 31404, (912)356-2186.

BROCK, GERALD
Judge. **Personal:** Born Aug 23, 1932, Hamtramck, MI; married Jacqueline B Holmes. **Educ:** Eastern MI Univ, BS 1953; Detroit College of Law, LLB 1961. **Career:** Flint Public Schools, teacher 1953-57; Wayne County Training Sch, teacher 1957-61; Private Practice, attorney 1961-81; 36th District Court, judge 1982-. **Business Addr:** Judge, 36th District Court, 421 Madison, Detroit, MI 48226.

BROCK, LOUIS CLARK
Coach, professional baseball player (retired), business executive. **Personal:** Born Jun 18, 1939, El Dorado, AR; divorced; children: Wanda, Lou Jr. **Educ:** So Univ Baton Rouge LA, attended. **Career:** Chicago Cubs, outfielder 1961-64; St Louis Cardinals 1964-79; Brock World St Louis, business exec, 1980-; Montreal Expos, baserunning coach, 1993-. **Honors/Awds:** Led NL in at bats (689) runs scored (113) stolen bases (52) 1967; 1st in NL in doubles (46) triples (14) stolen bases (62) 1968; led Cardinals in batting (.298) at bats (655) hits (195) doubles (33) triples (10) stolen bases (53) 1969; led Cardinals in runs scored (114) & 2nd in doubles (29) & hits (202) 1970; led Cardinals in doubles (37) & major league in runs scored (126) 1971; 118 stolen bases 1974; Jackie Robinson Awrd Ebony Mag 1975; Roberto Clemente Awrd 1975; B'nai B'rith Brotherhood Awrd; Man of Yr St Louis Jaycees; inducted into Natl Baseball Hall of Fame 1985; mem Natl League All-Star Team 1967, 1971, 1972, 1974, 1975; Player of the Year Sporting News 1974; mem World Series Championship Team: St Louis Cardinals1964, 1967; held stolen base record (938), major league, 14 years.

BROCKETT, CHARLES A.
Educator. **Personal:** Born Jan 24, 1937, Princess Anne Co, VA; married Annette Lee; children: Troy Christopher. **Educ:** VA State Clg, BS 1961; Old Dominion U, MS 1972; Norfolk State Clg Univ of VA. **Career:** Booker T Washington High School, Norfolk VA, asst prin, asst football coach, 1963-67, Biology teacher, 1963-70; Lake Taylor High School, Norfolk VA, 1979-86; Norview High School, asst principal, 1986-. **Orgs:** Mem Natl Assc of Sec Principals; Secondary Principal Assc of Norfolk; VA Assc of Secondary Prin; vice pres Dist L Prin Assc; natl bd mem Natl Black United Fund; pres Black United Fund of Tidewater; Kappa Alpha Psi; Chesapeake Men for Progress; Chesapeake Forward; civic reg dir Kappa Alpha Psi Guide Right Pgm; Eastern Reg pres Kappa Alpha Psi. **Honors/Awds:** Outstanding Serv Awd Kappa Alpha Psi; Outstanding Community Serv Awd 1973; Outstanding Community Serv 1986. **Military Serv:** AUS sp 4 1961-63. **Business Addr:** Asst Principal, Granby High School, 7101 Granby St, Norfolk, VA 23505.

BROCKINGTON, DONELLA P.
Company executive. **Personal:** Born Nov 8, 1952, Washington, DC; daughter of Harriet Brown Brockington and Josiah Armstrong Brockington. **Educ:** Clark Univ, BA Math & Psych 1973; Howard Univ School of Ed, MEd Guidance Counseling 1974, M Urban Sys Eng 1976. **Career:** Health Sys Agency of N VA, sr health sys analyst 1976-80; DC Govt Office of the City Admin, sr oper analyst 1981-85; DC Govt Dept of Admin Serv, deputy real prop admin 1985-87, assoc dir for real property 1987-88; Lockheed Datacom, vice pres for natl mktg 1988-91; Lockheed Martin IMS, Washington, DC, vice pres, marketing, 1991-96, regional vice pres, 1996-. **Orgs:** Coord McKinley High School Alumni Orgn 1980; sec Capital Ballet Guild Inc 1982; mem Natl Forum for Black Public Admin 1984-; mem Natl Assn of Female Executives 1986-; sec, Girl Scout Council of the Nation's Capital, 1993-96, first vice pres, 1996-. **Honors/Awds:** Distinguished Public Serv Awd DC Govt 1982; 1989 Salute to African-American Business & Professional Women, Dollars & Sense Magazine 1989. **Business Addr:** Regional Vice President, Lockheed Martin IMS, 1133 15th St NW, Ste 1100, Washington, DC 20005.

BROCKINGTON, EUGENE ALFONZO
Financial administrator. **Personal:** Born Jun 21, 1931, Darien, GA; married Mable M; children: Eugene Jr, Karyn L. **Educ:** Comm Coll of Philadelphia 1967-68. **Career:** DeMarco Printer Philadelphia, printing press oper 1951; Amer Fiber-Velop Co Collingdale PA, printing press oper 1954; Jones & Johnson Soft Ice Co, salesman 1956; US Postal Serv Philadelphia, postal source data tech 1958; Natl Alliance of Postal & Fed Employees, treas, comptroller, data proc mgr 1976-. **Orgs:** Fin sec NAPFE 1966; scoutmaster Boy Scouts of Amer Philadelphia Council 1968; lay leader Sayre Meml United Meth Church Philadelphia 1969; football coach Philadelphia Police Athl League 1969; treas bd of dir NAPFE Fed Credit Union Washington DC 1977; treas bd of dir NAPFE Housing Corp Wash DC 1979. **Honors/Awds:** Legion of Merit Chapel of the Four Chaplins Philadelphia 1969; Merit Serv Awd Dist Five NAPFE 1973. **Military Serv:** AUS corpl 2 yrs. **Business Addr:** Data Systems, Natl Alliance of Post/Fed Empl, 1628 11th St, NW, Washington, DC 20001.

BROGDEN, ROBERT, JR.
President, retail sales co. **Personal:** Born Feb 13, 1958, Rosewell, NM; son of Robert Sr & Billie; married Kathy Brogden, Feb 1989; children: Robert III, Anna. **Career:** Auto Dealership, sales mgr, 1982-92; GM, 1992-93; Robert Brogden's Olathe, Pontiac-Buick-GMC, Inc, owner/dealer, 1993-. **Orgs:** Olathe Chamber of Commerce, bd of dirs, 1995-. **Business Addr:** President, Robert Brogden Olathe, Pontiac-Buick-GMC Inc, 1500 E Santa Fe St, Olathe, KS 66061-3643, (913)782-1500.

BROKAW, CAROL ANN
Attorney, business executive. **Personal:** Born Nov 14, 1946, Somerville, NJ; daughter of Annis Bryant Brokaw (deceased) and Thomas Brokaw. **Educ:** Cedar Crest Coll Allentown PA, BA 1968; Georgetown Law Ctr Washington DC, JD 1971; Hastings Coll of Law San Francisco, cert trial advocacy 1978. **Career:** Natl Labor Relations Bd Washington DC & Newark NJ, atty/labor 1971-73; Capital Cities/ABC Co NYC, atty/labor 1973-79, assoc dir labor relations 1979-81, genl atty labor relations 1981-90, sr general attorney 1990-. **Orgs:** Mem Women's Natl Dem Club 1972-, DC Bar Assn 1972-; mem Cedar Crest Coll Alumnae Bd 1977-80; mgmt mem Membership & Finance Com Labor & Employment Law Sect Amer Bar Assn 1978-; participant Black Exec Exchange Prog Natl Urban League 1979; founder Plainfield Tutorial Project; bd mem, Theotworks USA, 1989-. **Honors/Awds:** Black Achiever in Industry Awd Harlem Branch of the YMCA of Greater NY Amer Broadcasting Co 1986; Mary Bethune Award, Natl Council of Negro Women, 1988. **Business Addr:** VP, Ad, Sales Admin & Operations, ABC Distributing Co, 77 W 66th St, New York, NY 10023.

BROMERY, KEITH MARCEL
Broadcast journalist. **Personal:** Born Sep 19, 1948, Washington, DC; son of Cecile Trescott Bromery and Randolph Wilson Bromery; married Susan Stanger Bromery, May 7, 1983; children: Marc Russell. **Educ:** Washington Journalism Center, Washington, DC, certificate, 1972; University of Massachusetts, Amherst, MA, BA, 1972. **Career:** Chicago Daily News, Chicago, IL, reporter, 1972-75; CBS News, New York, NY, writer, 1975-77; WBBM-AM Radio, Chicago, IL, anchor/reporter, 1977-83; WMAQ-TV, Chicago, IL, writer/reporter, 1983-84; WLS-TV, Chicago, IL, reporter, 1984-. **Orgs:** Member, National Association of Black Journalists, 1987-; member, Chicago Association of Black Journalists, 1987-; member, Society of Professional Journalists, 1983-; writer/member, Chicago Headline Club, 1983-. **Business Addr:** Reporter, WLS-TV, 190 N State St, Chicago, IL 60601.

BROMERY, RANDOLPH WILSON
Geophysicist, educator. **Personal:** Born Jan 18, 1926, Cumberland, MD; son of Edith E and Lawrence R; married Cecile Trescott; children: Keith M, Carol Ann Thompson, Dennis R, David T, Christopher J. **Educ:** Univ of MI, 1944-46; Howard Univ, BS Math 1956; The American Univ DC, MS Geology & Geophysics 1962; The Johns Hopkins Univ, PhD Geology 1968. **Career:** US Geological Survey, exploration geophysicist 1948-67; Univ of MA, prof geophys & dept chmn 1968-70, vice chancellor 1970-71, chancellor 1971-79, commonwealth prof of geophysics; Westfield State College, acting pres 1988-90; Weston Geophysical Intl Corp, pres, 1981-83; Geoscience Engineering Corp, pres 1983-; Massachusetts Board of Regents, interim chancellor, 1990-; Springfield College, president, 1992-, commonwealth professor emeritus, 1992-. **Orgs:** Mem bd of dirs Exxon Corp, NYNEX Corp, Singer Co; Chemical Bank, Chase Manhattan Bank, John Hancock Mutual Life Insurance Co; trustee, Johns Hopkins University. **Honors/Awds:** Gillman Fellow Johns Hopkins Univ 1965-67; Dr of Laws HON Hokkaido Univ Japan 1976; Dr of Sci Frostburg State Coll MD 1972; Dr of Humane Letters Univ of MA 1979; Dr of Educ Western New England Coll MA 1972; Doctor of Humane Letters, Bentley College, 1993; Doctor of Humanities, Springfield College, 1993; Distinguished Alumni, Howard Univ and John Hopkins Univ; Honorary Alumnus, Univ of Massachusetts; President, Geological Society of America 1990; Dr. Public Service Westfield State College; Dr. Public Service North Adams State College. **Military Serv:** USAF 3 medals. **Home Addr:** 75 Cherry Ln, Amherst, MA 01002. **Business Addr:** President, Springfield College, Springfield, MA 01109.

BRONNER, BERNARD
Publisher. **Career:** Upscale Communications Inc, publisher, currently; Bronner Brothers, pres, currently. **Special Achievements:** Listed in Black Enterprise's Top 100 industrial service companies, 1996.

BRONSON, FRED JAMES
Dentist, pastor. **Personal:** Born Jan 10, 1935, Cincinnati, OH; son of Rev & Mrs William Bronson; married Barbara Dobbins; children: Fred Jr, Mark, Stefanie, Shellie, Shawn, Sharon. **Educ:** Miami Univ Oxford OH, BA 1958; Howard Univ Washington DC, DDS 1962. **Career:** Cincinnati Dental Soc, chrmn peer review 1979-81, pres 1982, vice pres 1980, pres elect 1981; Temple Ch of Christ Written in Heaven, pastor 1984; Private Practice & Temple Church of Christ Written In Heaven, dentist & minister. **Orgs:** Delegate Ohio Dental Assn 1978-, mem 1963-; mem Nat Dental Assn 1962-, delegate & trustee 1962; instructor KY Dental Coll 1973-76; fellow, Intl Coll of Dentists, 1978, AmerColl of Dentists, 1983; mem, Alpha Phi Alpha 1957; chmn, Dentist Concerned for Dentists, 1980; Pierre Fauchard Academy, 1988. **Honors/Awds:** Distinguished Serv Residents of Lincoln Heights, OH 1969. **Business Addr:** Private Practice, 4935 Paddock Rd, Cincinnati, OH 45237.

BRONSON, OSWALD P., SR.
Educational administrator. **Personal:** Born Jul 19, 1927, Sanford, FL; son of Flora Hollingshed Bronson and Uriah Perry Bronson; married Helen Carolyn Williams, Jun 8, 1952; children: Josephine Suzette, Flora Helen, Oswald Perry Jr. **Educ:** Bethune-Cookman College, BS, 1950; Gammon Theological Seminary, BD (summa cum laude), 1959; Northwestern Univ, PhD, 1965; St Paul's College, Lawrenceville, DD. **Career:** Pastor, 1950-66; Interdenominational Theological Center, Atlanta, GA, vice president, 1966-68, president, 1968-75; Bethune-Cookman College, president, 1975-. **Orgs:** United Negro College Fund; American Assn of Theological Schools; Florida Assn of Colleges and Universities; NAACP; Volusia County School Board; Florida Governor's Advisory Council on Productivity; exec committee, Southern Regional Education Board; advisory committee, Florida Sickle Cell Foundation; board of directors: Institute of Black World, Wesley Community Center, Martin Luther King Center for Social Change, American Red Cross, United Way, National Assn for Equal Opportunity in Higher Education, United Methodist Committee on Relief. **Honors/Awds:** Alumni Awards, Gammon Theological Seminary, Bethune-Cookman College; Crusade Scholar; United Negro College Fund Award. **Business Addr:** President, Bethune-Cookman College, Office of the President, 640 Mary McLeod Bethune Blvd, Daytona Beach, FL 32114-3099, (904)252-8667.

BRONSON, ZACK
Professional football player. **Personal:** Born Jan 28, 1974. **Educ:** McNeese State. **Career:** San Francisco 49ers, defensive back, 1997-. **Business Addr:** Professional Football Player, San Francisco 49ers, 4949 Centennial Blvd, Santa Clara, CA 95054, (415)562-4949.

BRONZ, LOIS GOUGIS TAPLIN
Councilwoman, educator. **Personal:** Born Aug 21, 1927, New Orleans, LA; daughter of Elise Cousin and Alex Gougis; married Charles Bronz; children: Edgar, Francine Shorts, Shelly. **Educ:** Xavier Univ, BA 1942; LA State Univ, 1954; Wayne State Univ, MEd 1961; Houston Tillotson Coll, 1962; Coll of New Rochelle, 1974. **Career:** US Treasury Dept, proofreader 1950-51; Orleans Parrish School Bd, classroom teacher 1952-61; Xavier Univ, instru math, recruitment, job placement 1961-67; Natl Merit Comm, consult 1965-67; Civil Serv Commiss, personnel consult 1966; Manhattanville Coll, coll adv 1968-73; Greenburgh Central 7 Sch Dist, teacher 1968-82; Town of Greenburgh, councilwoman 1975-91, former deputy supervisor; Town of Greenburgh, Councilwoman, 1975-81; Westchester County Legislator, 1994-; Westchester Cty Bd, vice-chair, cty legislator. **Orgs:** Founder League of Good Gov New Orleans LA, GROUP; League of Women Voters Greenburgh NY, Greenburgh Housing Council, Community Facility Comm, Woodhill Neighborhood Assoc, Xavier Univ Admiss Comm, Xavier Univ Admin Council, Inter-Alumni Council United Negro Coll Fund, Eds for Johnson & Humphrey, Black Dems of Westchester Cty, Afro-Amer Found, Greenburgh Dem Party; co-chrpsn Westchester Womens Council; vice pres Greenburgh Central #7 PTA; vol United Way of Westchester; bd of dir CO House Greenburgh, Union Child Day Care Ctr, Westchester Coalition; pres, bd of dir Westchester Comm Oppty Prog; life mem White Plains-Greenburgh NAACP; tutor Westchester Cty Penitentary; instr, rel ed Sacred Heart Church Hartsdale; vol Friends of Children's VillageDobbes Ferry; treas Greenburgh Teachers Assoc Ware Bd; charter & exec mem Westchester Black Womens Political Caucus; pres Xavier Univ Natl Alumni Assoc; Childrens Village Dobbs Ferry, bd mem; Child Care Council of Westchester, v chair; Legal Awareness for Women, bd mem; NAACP, life mem; Alpha Kappa Alpha, charter mem of Pi Iota Omega chapter. **Honors/Awds:** Panelist 1st NY State Womens Meeting; co-ord Westchester Womens Recog Day; panelist Panel of Amer Women; Natl Assoc of Negro Bus & Professional Womens Club Awareness Awd; Black Democrats of Westchester Political Awareness Awd; Westchester Black Women's Political Caucus Awd; Westchester Advocate Newspaper Achievement Awd; dir Minority Task Force on Womens Issues, Minority Task Force Contractors Conf; revived & dir Human Rights Commiss; conducted meetings throughout the town & village of Greenburgh Saturday Listening Posts; established Sr Citizens Info Ctr; publ handbook/dir of info for sr citizens; obtained fed funds & established sr legal serv prog; mem Gray Panthers Task Force on Social Security; initiated & completed census of Greenburghs Elderly; Woman of the Year, Westchester Count1990; NY state women's political caucus awd; Westchester Black Lawyers Assn, community service awd; National Association of Social Workers, Public Official of the Year, New York State Chapter; Westchester Chapter of National Association of Social Workers, Public Official of the Year. **Home Addr:** 282 Old Tarrytown Rd, White Plains, NY 10603.

BROOKE, EDWARD WILLIAM
Attorney. **Personal:** Born Oct 26, 1919, Washington, DC; son of Helen Seldon Brooke and Edward W Brooke; married Edward; children: 3. **Educ:** Howard Univ, BS, ML, BL 1940; Boston Univ Law School, LLB, 1948, LLM, 1950. **Career:** Law practice, beginning 1950; Commonwealth of MA, attny gen 1963-67; US Senate, senator 1967-79; Csaplar & Bok, Boston, counsel 1979-; O'Connor & Hannan, Wash DC, partner 1979-; Bear & Stearns, NY, ltd partner 1979-. **Orgs:** Chmn Boston Fin Comm 1961-62; mem Natl Council of BSA, Natl Bd of Boys Clubs of Amer, Amer Bar Assn, Massachusetts Bar Assn, Boston Bar Assn, AMVETS; chmn of bd The Opera Co of Boston Inc; chm bd of dirs Boston Bank Commerce; mem Spingarn Medal Commn; bd of dir Meditrust Inc Boston, Grumman Corp Bethpage NY; public mem Administrative Conf of the US; bd of dirs Washington Performing Arts Soc; chair National Low-Income Housing Coalition 1979-. **Honors/Awds:** Spingarn Medal NAACP 1967; Charles Evans Hughes Awd Natl Conf of Christians & Jews 1967; Distinguished Serv Awd AMVETS, 1952; 30 hon deg from various coll & univ; fellow, American Bar Assn, American Academy of Arts & Sciences; Republican nominee, Commonwealth of Massachusetts, secretary of state, 1960; when elected in 1967, first black to serve in US Senate since 1881. **Military Serv:** AUS capt, 1942-45; Bronze Star. **Business Addr:** 2500 Virginia Ave, NW, Ste 301-S, Washington, DC 20037.

BROOKER, MOE ALBERT
Educator, artist. **Personal:** Born Sep 24, 1940, Philadelphia, PA; son of Lumisher Campbell Brooker and Mack Henry Brooker; married Cheryl McClenney Brooker, Sep 28, 1985; children: Musa, Misha. **Educ:** PA Acad of Fine Art, Cert 1963; Tyler Sch of Fine Art Temple U, BFA 1970, MFA 1972. **Career:** Cleveland Inst of Art, assoc prof, 1975-85; Tyler School of Fine Art, guest lecturer, 1975; Univ of NC, assoc prof, 1974; Univ of VA, asst prof, 1973; Tyler School of Fine Art, instructor, 1972, teacher asst drawing, 1971; Penna Acad of Art, Philadelphia, PA, professor, 1985-. **Orgs:** Bd mem New Orgn for Visual Arts 1978-; 1st Prize May Show Cleveland Mus of Art 1978; juror painting & drawing Scottsdale Ctr for the Arts AZ 1980; panelist OH Cncl of the Arts 1980; Mayor's Comm of the Arts, City of Philadelphia 1985-; Pennsylvania Council of the Arts, State of Pennsylvania 1985-87; Fine Arts Comm of the Pennsylvania Convention Center, 1990-. **Honors/Awds:** Individual Artist Fellowship, State of Pennsylvania, 1988; Artist Giant to China, City of Philadelphia/China, 1987; Cleveland Arts Fellowship, Women's Comm of Cleveland, 1985. **Military Serv:** AUS sp/4 1963-65. **Home Addr:** 6221 Greene St, Philadelphia, PA 19144.

BROOKES, BERNARD L.
Health care executive. **Personal:** Born Oct 1, 1950; married Glenda F Funderburg; children: Darrilyn. **Educ:** Berklee Coll of Music, BM 1978; Boston Univ Grad Sch, MA 1980, PhD 1983; Boston Univ Sch of Mgmt, MBA 1985. **Career:** McLean Hospital, psychology intern 1981-82, psychologist/unit dir 1982-85; MA Dept Mental Health, dir clinical serv 1985-86; New Medico Assoc Inc, deputy dir of operations 1986-87; Basic Health Mgmt Inc, CEO. **Orgs:** Mem Amer Psychological Assoc 1984-, Natl Black MBA Assoc 1986-, MA Psychological Assoc 1986-; corp dir Douglas A Thom Clinic 1986-91; consultant MA Dept Mental Health 1986-87. **Honors/Awds:** Martin Luther King Fellow Boston Univ 1979-81; Clinical Fellow Harvard medical Sch 1981-82; instructor in psychology Harvard Medical Sch 1983-90. **Business Addr:** CEO, Basic Health Management Inc, 2 Park Plaza, Boston, MA 02116.

BROOKS, A. RUSSELL
Educator (retired). **Personal:** Born May 19, 1906, Montgomery, AL; son of Eliza Brooks and John Randolph Brooks; married Sara Tucker; children: Dwight. **Educ:** Morehouse Coll, BA 1931; Univ of WI, MA 1934; Univ of Edinburgh, 1938-39; Univ of WI, PhD 1958. **Career:** NC A&T Coll, chmn English dept 1934-44; Morehouse Coll, assoc prof of English 1946-60; KY State Coll, chmn Engl dept emeritus 1960-72. **Orgs:** Advisory editor CLA Journal; mem Modern Language Assn; mem Nat Cncl of Tchrs of Engl; mem Coll Language Assn. **Honors/Awds:** Author of book "James Boswell" Twayne Publishers 1971; mem KY Arts Commission 1965-68; Outstanding Service Award College Language Association 1990. **Home Addr:** 415 College Park Dr, Frankfort, KY 40601.

BROOKS, ALVIN LEE
Government official. **Personal:** Born May 3, 1932, North Little Rock, AR; married Carol Rich Brooks, Aug 23, 1950; children: Ronall, Estelle, Carrie, Diane, Rosalind, Tameisha. **Educ:** Univ MO Kansas City, BA Hist & Govt 1959, MA Sociology 1973. **Career:** Kansas City Police Dept, detective & police officer; Kansas City Sch Dist, home sch coord 1964-66; Neighborhood Youth Corp of Cath Diocese of Kansas City St Joseph, dir out of school proj 1966-67; Kansas City, coord pub info & com interpr 1967-68; Human Relations Dept Kansas City, dir 1968-73, 1980-; City of Kansas City MO, asst city mgr 1973-80. **Orgs:** Mem past vice pres Bd of Regents Ctr MO State Univ 1975-82; chmn MO Commn on Human Rights 1975-82; chmn MO Black Leadership Assn 1979-82; National Assn of Human Rights Workers 1968-; International Assn of Official Human Rights Agencies 1969-; convenor, Ad Hoc Group Against Crime 1977; vice pres, Prime Heal Inc (HMO) 1987. **Honors/Awds:** Man of the Yr Ivanhoe Club 1969; Outstanding Citizen of the Yr Beta Omega Chap Omega Psi Phi 1972; Outstanding Citizen of the Yr Young Progressives 1973; Alumni Achievement Awd Univ of MO at Kansas City 1975; Kansas City Tomorrow 1988; Natl Conference of Christians & Jews (NCCJ) 1989; recognized by former Drug Czar, William Bennet, as being one of the nation's " . . .frontline soldiers in our war against drugs;" honored by President George Bush in November, 1989, for his work with Ad Hoc; President's National Drug Advisory Council, 1989-92. **Business Addr:** President, Ad Hoc Group Against Crime, 3330 Trooost, Kansas City, MO 64109.

BROOKS, ARKLES CLARENCE, JR.
Salesman. **Personal:** Born Aug 25, 1943, Detroit, MI; married Sarah L; children: Arkles III, Ira David, Alice Ruth, Sharon Louise. **Educ:** Southern IL Univ, BA 1967; Wayne State Univ, MA 1976. **Career:** Natl Bank of Detroit, asst branch mgr 1968-70; Aetna Life & Casualty, career agent 1970-72; Detroit Bd of Educ, math, science teacher 1971-73; The Upjohn Co, hospital sales specialist 1973-; Allstate Insurance, Southfield, MI, sales assoc, 1987-. **Orgs:** Member, Wayne County Notary Public 1968-, Natl Assoc of Life Underwriters 1970-; pres, Varsity Club Inc 1971-; corp treasurer, 1972-, assoc pastor, 1985-, exec vice pres, 1989-, Gospel Chapel of Detroit Inc. **Home Addr:** 30436 Embassy Dr, Beverly Hills, MI 48025.

BROOKS, AVERY
Educator, actor, director. **Personal:** Born in Evansville, IN; son of Eva Lydia Crawford Brooks and Samuel Leon Brooks; married Vicki Lenora; children: Ayana, Cabral, Asante. **Educ:** Indiana Univ; Oberlin College; Rutgers Univ, New Brunswick NJ, BA, MFA. **Career:** Rutgers Univ, assoc prof of theater; staged reading of Lord Byron's Manfred New England Convervatory's 1986 festival Music With Words; starred in Solomon Northrup's Odyssey PBS 1984; appeared as "Hawk" in TV series Spenser: For Hire; star of own ABC-TV series A Man Called Hawk; title role in opera, "X: The Life and Times of Malcolm X"; lead role, Robeson; lead role in "Othello," Folger Shakespeare Theater; appears as Captain Sisko in TV series Star Trek: Deep Space Nine. **Honors/Awds:** Received ACE Award nomination for portrayal of Uncle Tom in "Uncle Tom's Cabin.".

BROOKS, BARRETT
Professional football player. **Personal:** Born May 5, 1972, St Louis, MO; married Sonji, May 7, 1997; children: Romel. **Educ:** Kansas State, attended. **Career:** Philadelphia Eagles, tackle, 1995-. **Business Addr:** Professional Football Player, Philadelphia Eagles, 3501 S Broad St, Philadelphia, PA 19148, (215)463-2500.

BROOKS, BERNARD E.
Management consultant. **Personal:** Born Jul 8, 1935, Camden, SC; son of Bertha Brooks and James Brooks; married Julia D Lyons, May 7, 1988; children: Bernard II, Sharon, Karen, Susan, Theresa. **Educ:** Brooklyn Coll, AAS Accounting 1964; Fairleigh Dickinson Univ, BS Accounting 1973; Pace Univ, MS Mgmt 1978. **Career:** Chase Manhattan Bank, systems planning officer 1968-69; Trans World Airlines, dir data serv admin 1969-70; Arthur Young & Co, principal 1970-74; AT&T, mktg mgr 1974-78; Arthur Young & Co, partner, 1978-85; PA Exec Search, vice pres; MSL Intl Ltd, vice pres; Kearney Executive Search, vice pres; Bernard E Brooks & Associates, Inc, president, currently. **Orgs:** Councilman Twp of Teaneck 1978-82; trustee St Vincents Hosp & Med Ctr 1982-88; mayor Twp of Teaneck 1982-88; NJ Supreme Court District Ethics Committee II-B, 1991-93; board of directors, Spartanburg Area Chamber of Commerce, 1996-. **Honors/Awds:** Publ Intro to Telecomm, 1978; Man of the Year, New Jersey Chap Negro Business & Professional Women, 1979. **Military Serv:** USAF staff sgt 1952-56. **Home Addr:** 314 Meathward Circle, Moore, SC 29369-9027. **Business Phone:** (864)948-1005.

BROOKS, BERNARD W.
Artist. **Personal:** Born Sep 6, 1939, Alexandria, VA; married. **Educ:** Univ of MD, 1958-60; Philadelphia Mus Clg of Art, 1960-61; Corcoran Gallery Sch of Art, 1961-62; Howard U, 1962-65. **Career:** A&B Assc Washington, DC, assc dir; Howard Univ Clg of Dentistry , artist islstr; Opus 2 Galleries, assc dir. **Orgs:** Pblctn artist Am Chem Soc & Washington, DC; asst art dir Van Heusen Shirt Co; asst advertising mgr Grand Union Food Co Inc Landover, MD; tech illstr Atlantic Research Corp Alexandria, VA; silk screen tech Grand Union Food Co Landover, MD; ownr dir Bernard W Brooks Studio; vice pres DC Art Assc; WashingtonWatercolour Assc; pub rel dir Natl Conf of Artists; art exhibited Georgetown Graphics Gallery. **Honors/Awds:** 1st prize D/C Rec Outdoor Art Show 1971; 2nd prize Montgomery Mall Outdoor Art Show 1972; 1st prize George F Muth Awrd Howard Univ 1962; 2nd prize Howard Univ 1963; num profnl exhibtns; collections; Radio-tV Presentations . **Military Serv:** USAR pfc. **Business Addr:** 2315 M St NW, Washington, DC 20037.

BROOKS, BUCKY (WILLIAM ELDRIDGE BROOKS, JR)
Professional football player. **Personal:** Born Jan 22, 1971, Raleigh, NC. **Educ:** North Carolina, bachelor's degree in speech communications, 1994. **Career:** Buffalo Bills, defensive back, 1994; Jacksonville Jaguars, 1996-97; Green Bay Packers, 1996-97; Kansas City Chiefs, 1997-. **Business Addr:** Professional Football Player, Kansas City Chiefs, One Arrowhead Dr, Kansas City, MO 64129, (816)924-9300.

BROOKS, CARL
Utility company executive. **Personal:** Born Aug 1, 1949, Philadelphia, PA; son of Sarah Lee Williams Brooks and Nathaniel Brooks; married Drena Hastings Brooks, Oct 6, 1973; children: Tarik, Karima. **Educ:** Hampton Univ, Hampton, VA, BS, 1971; Southern Illinois Univ, Edwardsville, IL, MBA, 1976; Univ of Iowa, Iowa City, IA, executive develop program, 1982; Dartmouth College, Hanover, NH, Tuck Executive Program, 1990. **Career:** Jersey Central Power & Light Co, Morristown, NJ, corporate manager, contracts, 1977-86, Allenhurst, NJ, division director, shore division, 1986-90; GPU Service Corp, Parsippany, NJ, vice president, materials & services, 1980-96; GPU Generation, Inc, vice pres/finance and administration; GPU Energy, Human & Technical Resources, vp, currently. **Orgs:** National Executive Leadership Council; executive bd, bd of dirs, National Minority Supplier Development Council; chmn of corporate fund-raising, United Way, 1986-90; Leadership New Jersey; chmn, African Relief Fund, Red Cross, 1986-90; bd of dirs, Red Bank Chamber of Commerce, 1986-; YMCA, 1986-; Franklin Little League, 1987-. **Honors/Awds:** Leadership New Jersey, Partnership for New Jersey, 1989; Outstanding Alumni Award, Benjamin Franklin High School, 1989; Outstanding Scholar, Beta Gamma Sigma, 1978; Nice Guy Award, Asbury Park Press, 1990; National Eagle Leadership Award, 1997.

BROOKS, CAROL LORRAINE
Government official. **Personal:** Born Nov 23, 1955, Brooklyn, NY. **Educ:** Univ of VT, BA 1977; Rutgers Univ, postgrad studies 1977-79; School for Intl Training, Eschange Student to Mexico 1975; Recipient of the Walter Russell Scholarship 1977. **Career:** CBS News Inc, project coord 1978-81; NJ Office of the Governor, special asst 1981-85; NJ Dept of Environ Protection, administrator 1985-. **Orgs:** Bd of dir Family Serv Assoc of Trenton/Hopewell Valley 1983-; commn mem NJ Martin Luther King Jr Commemorative Commn 1985-; mem Urban League Guild of Metropolitan Trenton 1986-. **Honors/Awds:** 100 Young Women of Promise Good Housekeeping Magazine 1985; Employ Serv Awd 5 yrs NJ State Govt 1987; Outstanding Young Women of Amer 1986. **Home Addr:** 15 Winthrop Rd, Lawrenceville, NJ 08648. **Business Addr:** Administrator, NJ Environ Protection, 440 E State St, Trenton, NJ 08625.

BROOKS, CAROLYN BRANCH
Educator, educational administrator. **Personal:** Born Jul 8, 1946, Richmond, VA; daughter of Shirley Booker Branch and Charles W Branch; married Henry M Brooks, Sep 28, 1965; children: Charles T, Marcellus L, Alexis J, Toni A. **Educ:** Tuskegee Univ, Tuskegee AL, BS, 1968, MS, 1971; Ohio State Univ, Columbus OH, PhD, 1977. **Career:** Bullock County Bd of Educ, Union Springs AL, science teacher, 1968-69; Macon County Bd of Educ, Tuskegee AL, science teacher, 1971-72; VA Hospital, Tuskegee AL, research technician, 1972-73; Ohio State Univ, Columbus OH, graduate teaching asst, 1975-77; Kentucky State Univ, Frankfort KY, principal investigator & program dir, 1978-81; Univ of Maryland Eastern Shore, Princess Anne MD, asst prof, 1981-87, associate professor, 1987-96, professor, 1996-, departmental chair, 1992, School of Agricultural and Natural Sciences, dean, currently. **Orgs:** Mem, advisory bd, treasurer 1989-90, mem, Salvation Army Youth Club Council; NAACP; National Assn Univ Women; MANRRS (Minorities in Agriculture, Natural Resources, Related Services), American Society for Microbiology, Multiple Sclerosis Council, 1994-95. **Honors/Awds:** Outstanding Serv Award, Silhouettes of Kappa Alpha Psi, 1980; First Place Award, Competitive Paper Presentation, Seventh Biennial Research Symposium HBCU, 1987; Outstanding Faculty Award for Research, School of Agricultural Sciences, 1987-88; Chancellor's Research Scholar Award, 1988; Woman of the Year Award, Maryland Eastern Shore Branch of the Natl Assn of Univ Women, 1988; First Annual White House Initiative Faculty Award for Excellence in Science and Technology, 1988; speaker, "Symposium on Biotechnology," Alabama A&M Univ, 1988; visiting scientist, Hampton Univ, 1989; USDA Peer Review panelist, USDA Natl Needs Fellowship Program, 1989; author, articles for scientific journals, Tropical Agriculture, Journal of Invertebrate Pathology, others; researcher, Togo & Senegal, West Africa, 1984, 1985, Caoon, West Africa, 1988; Outstanding Educator Award, Maryland Assn for Higher Education, 1990; Faculty Award for Excellence and Achievement, UMES Alumni Assn. **Business Addr:** Office of the Pres, Univ of Maryland Eastern Shore, J T Williams Hall, Princess Anne, MD 21853.

BROOKS, CHARLOTTE KENDRICK
Educator, consultant. **Personal:** Born Jun 5, 1918, Washington, DC; daughter of Ruby Moyse Kendrick and Swan Kendrick;

married Walter Henderson Brooks; children: Walter (deceased), Joseph Kendrick. **Educ:** Howard Univ, AB (Magna Cum Laude) 1939; NY Univ, MA 1954; Walden Univ, PhD 1976. **Career:** Baltimore Public Schools, teacher 1939-42; Wash DC Public Schools, teacher 1942-61; DC Public Schools, supvr 1961-73; The Amer Univ, asst prof, dir of commun studies 1974-78; DC Heath Public Co, natl lang arts cons; Brooks Assoc, consult in ed. **Orgs:** Bd of dir Southwest House 10 yrs; chmn Youth Task Force of SW Assembly 1983-84; trustee Rsch Found NCTE 1980-81; mem Commn on the English Language NCTE 1980-81; comm Verbally Gifted & Talented NCTE 1978-81; coordinator, American Art in the Classroom, Smithsonian's Nat Museum of American Art, 1995-98. **Honors/Awds:** Alpha Kappa Alpha Awd for undergrad studies; Eugene & Agnes Meyer Grant 1958; Fulbright Exchange Grant 1960-61; Coll Entrance Exam Bd Grant 1962; Winifred Cullis Lecture Fellowship 1963, 1964; Gulbenkian Grant 1968; Ford Grant 1972; NCTE Black Caucus Awd 1975; Cullis/Mair Lecture Fellowship 1980; author, "Tapping Potential, English & Language Arts for the Black Learner," CK Brooks; editor, African Rhythms, 1985; author, Communicating, DC Heath Publ Co, 1973; author, They Can Learn English, Wadsworth Publ Co, 1972; Dist Black Women Ed BISA 1986; named Dist Black Women and Photo & Bio on 1985 BISA Calendar; NCTE Dist Svc Award, 1985; SW Comm Svc Award, 1995; Published: A Brooks Chronicle, 1989, The Kendrick Kin, 1993, Remembering, 1994, A Small Brooks Book, 1996. **Business Addr:** Consultant in Education, Brooks Associates, 472 M St, SW, Washington, DC 20024.

BROOKS, CHRISTINE D.
Educator, public administrator. **Personal:** Born May 1, Laurinburg, NC; daughter of Evelyn Pate Dockery (deceased) and William Dockery; married Donald Brooks. **Educ:** Tchrs Coll Columbia Univ, Masters 1971; FL State Univ, PhD 1976. **Career:** FL A&M Univ, asst prof & chairperson bus educ 1974-76; Fayetteville State Univ, assoc prof & chairperson bus educ 1976-77, special consul 1978; State of FL Dept of Educ, educational; consultant II 1978-79; FL Dept of Labor & Employment Security, asst dir of administrative serv 1979-80, chief of workers' compensation rehab 1980-86; Office of Policy & Planning DC Government, deputy dir 1986-. **Orgs:** Mem Natl Rehab Assn; mem Intl Assn of Personnel in Employment Security; mem Adult Educ Assn of USA; mem Natl Bus Educ Assn; mem Southern Bus Educ Assn; mem Intl Soc of Bus Educators; mem Amer Vocational Assn; mem FL Adult Educ Assn; mem Natl Rehab Adminstrn Assn; mem FL Assn for Health & Social Svcs; natl bd mem Natl Assn of Black Adult Educators; state bd mem FL State Assn of Rehab Nurses; mem Phi Gamma Mu, Delta Pi Epsilon, Pi Omega Pi; mem EEO Comm City of Tallahassee; mem NAACP; mem Zonta Intl, FL Women's Network; mem AKA Women's Sor; mem Tallahassee Urban League; mem Southern Christian Leadership Conf; mem League of Women Voters; exec dir & fndr Intl League of Black Voters Tallahassee FL 1981. **Honors/Awds:** Kenyan Govt Serv Awd 1977; The Amer Educ Registry 1979; The Amer Govtl Registry 1979; NAACP Annual Serv Awd at the FL State Meeting 1978.

BROOKS, CLYDE HENRY
Personnel administrator, industrial relations manager. **Personal:** Born Sep 5, 1941, Danville, IL; son of Venie Brooks and George Brooks. **Educ:** Western IL Univ McComb, BS 1958, MS. **Career:** Chicago Metro Chap So Christian Ldrshp Conf, pres 1972-. **Orgs:** Dir Natl EEO & Employee Relations Blue Cross/Blue Shield Assn 1973-; assc & exec dir/ manpower dir Cook County Office of Equal Opportunity Inc Chicago 1968-73; area dir Cook County Office of Equal Opportunity Inc Chicago 1966-67; dir Sears Roebuck Comm Coop Proj Chicago 1965-66; supr Dept of Ed JOBS Proj Chicago 1964-65; employment cnsl Il State Employment Serv Chicago 1964; cnsl Crane HS Chicago 1964; neighborhood worker Chicago Comm on Youth Welfare Ch 1961-64; probation ofcr Juvenile Ct of Cook Co Chicago 1959-61; tchr Wendel Phillips Evening Sch 1959-65; cnsl Marillac Settlement House 1963-66; cnsl Scott Foreman Pub Co 1969-; cnsl Il Drug Abuse Pgm 1969-71; vis prof Harper Clg 1970-77; pres bd chmn BRASS (Behavior Research in Action in the Social Sci)Chicago 1969-71; chmn Ed Labs IElk Grove Vlg, IL 1969-71; tchr St Mary of the Lake Sem Mundelein, IL 1965; field work instr Univ of Chicago 1972-; chairman & CEO, Minority Economic Resourses Corp 1972-; mem Chicago C of C & Inds 1973-; mem Il State C of C 1973-; Illinois Parole Bd, 1993-. **Honors/Awds:** Pub "Rockwell Garden Comm Appraisal Study"; Chicago authority pub "Midwest Comm Teenage Study"; pub "The Negro in Amer". **Business Addr:** Minority Economic Resources Corporation, 2570 E Devon, Des Plaines, IL 60018.

BROOKS, DAISY M. ANDERSON
Day care provider. **Personal:** chilDren: Yolanda Denise, Wadell Jr, Cassandra Annette. **Educ:** Natl Inst of Practical Nursing, Chicago, Practical Nurses Training; Northwestern Med School, Chicago, Training in Med Tech; Pacific Western University, MA, Human Resources Dev; Faith Grant College, EdD. **Career:** Tots & Toddlers Day Care Ctr Inc 2 Waukegan, IL, co-owner; Daisy's Nursery, co-owner/exec dir; Victory Meml Hosp, med tech; Phys & Surg Lab Waukegan, IL, supvry med tech. **Orgs:** Past pres N Chicago Dist 64 Band Parents Assc; Worthy Matron Order of Eastern Star 1974; ofcr Golden Cir 59; mem deaconess Shiloh Bapt Ch; past pres Music Dept; mem N Chicago Br NAACP; past pres Progressive Comm Organ of N Chgo; past sec Cntrl Grade Sch PTA; past treas N Chicago Black Caucas; bd dir Altrusa Intrl Clb/Day Care Crisis Cncl for State of IL; mem Citizen Adv Com Lake Co Area Voc Ctr (Child Care Sub Com) N Chicago HS Voc Adv Com; past vice pres N Chicago Great Lakes VA C of C; vice pres Day Care Crisis Cncl for State of IL/Citizens Adv Com N Chicago Comm Block Dev; chprsn Schlrshp Com; mem Mt Sinai Bapt Ch. **Honors/Awds:** Business Person of the Year; Citizen of the Year; Humanitarian of the Year.

BROOKS, DANA DEMARCO
Educator. **Personal:** Born Aug 1, 1951, Hagerstown, MD. **Educ:** Hagerstown Junior College, Hagerstown, MD, AA, 1971; Towson State College, Towson, MD, BS, 1973; West Virginia University, Morgantown, West VA, MS, 1976, EdD, 1979. **Career:** West Virginia University, Morgantown, West VA, instructor, 1978-79, assistant professor, 1979-83, associate professor, 1983-88, associate dean, 1987-, acting dean, 1988, 1992-, professor, 1988-, dean, 1992-. **Orgs:** President 1983-84, chairperson of exhibits, 1988-, chairperson of social justice, 1989-, West Virginia Association of Health, Physical Education, Recreation, Dance, 1983-84; vice president, Midwest District, Health, Physical Education, Recreation, Dance, 1987-88, rep to bd of dirs, 1996-. **Honors/Awds:** Outstanding Teacher of the Year, West Virginia University, 1979-83, 1986-87; Honor Award, West Virginia Association, Health, Physical Education, Recreation, Dance, 1985; Young Professional Award, Midwest District, Health, Physical Education, Recreation, Dance, 1982; West Virginia University Social Justice Award, 1992; Ray O Duncan Award, West Virginia Assocation of Health, Physical Education, Recreation, Dance, 1991; Rev Dr Martin Luther King Jr, Achievement Award, 1997; Hagersfoam Jr Coll, 50th Anniverary Outstanding Alumnus. **Business Addr:** Dean, School of Physical Education, West Virginia University, 257 Coliseum, Morgantown, WV 26506-6116, (304)293-3295.

BROOKS, DERRICK
Professional football player. **Personal:** Born Apr 18, 1973, Pensacola, FL. **Educ:** Florida State, BA in business communications. **Career:** Tampa Bay Buccaneers, linebacker, 1995-. **Special Achievements:** 1st round/28th overall NFL draft pick, 1995. **Business Addr:** Professional Football Player, Tampa Bay Buccaneers, 1 Buccaneer Pl, Tampa, FL 33607, (813)870-2700.

BROOKS, DON LOCELLUS
Business executive. **Personal:** Born Oct 21, 1953, Galveston, TX; married Charlotte; children: Eric, Don Jr, Chris. **Educ:** Galveston Coll, AA Mid Mgmt 1975; Univ of Houston, BS Mktg/Mgmt 1977; Univ of TX Austin, Finance Leadership 1976-78. **Career:** Guaranty Fed Savings & Loans, mgmt trainee 1976-78, reg savings coord 1978-80, asst vice pres 1980-81, vice pres savings 1981-. **Orgs:** Bd of trustees Galveston Park Bd 1982-; bd of dir Family Serv Ctr 1984-85; mem United Way Inc of Galveston 1984-85, Legislative Comm Galveston 1984-; council rep City of Galveston 1984-; chairperson Fiscal Auditing & Insurance Comm City of Galveston Park Bd of Trustees 1984-85; city council ex-officio Galveston Park Bd of Trustees 1984-85. **Honors/Awds:** Two Pres Awd Cert Galveston Coll, 1973; Recipient of Hon Mention Mid-Mgmt Student Awd 1973; Two Deans Awd Certs Galveston Coll 1974; Founder of Galveston Coll Key Club 1975; Highest Vote Getter Galveston City Council (4,013 votes)1984-85; Elected to Exec Comm United Way Inc of Galveston 1985. **Home Addr:** 5506 Ave P, Galveston, TX 77550. **Business Addr:** Vice President, Branch Manager, Guaranty Fed Savings & Loan, 2121 Market St, Galveston, TX 77550.

BROOKS, DUNBAR
Corporation manager. **Personal:** Born Oct 11, 1950, Baltimore, MD; son of Mable Brooks and Ernest Blackwell; married Edythe E Mason Brooks, Jun 8, 1977; children: Tracey Young, Gary Young, Cheryl. **Educ:** Community College of Baltimore, AA, urban development, 1975; Morgan State University, BS, urban studies, 1976; University of Baltimore, MPA, 1978; Johns Hopkins University, postgraduate courses, 1979. **Career:** US Department of Transportation, mail and file clerk, 1973-74; Baltimore Regional Council of Governments, manager, census and small area data, info systems planner, land use and housing planner, 1975-92; Baltimore Metropolitan Council, manager, census and small area data, sr demographer, 1992-. **Orgs:** Baltimore County, Bd of Ed, pres, 1997-; Selective Service System, Local Draft Board 36, Baltimore County, MD, 1994-; Maryland State Boards of Education Association, National School Boards Association, federal relation network chairperson, 1992-; Baltimore County Board of Education, school board member, 1989-; Turner Station Development Corp, chairman of the board, 1980-; Dundalk-Sparrows Point NAACP, president, 1978-. **Honors/Awds:** Baltimore County NAACP, Distinguished Service Award, 1987; Human Resources Development Agency of Baltimore County, Distinguished Service Award, 1985. **Military Serv:** US Army, sp 4c, 1970-73; Vietnam Meritorious Award 2nd Oak Leaf Cluster. **Home Addr:** 102 East Ave, Dundalk, MD 21222, (410)282-6905. **Business Addr:** Manager, Census and Small Area Data Section, Baltimore Metropolitan Council, Old Greyhound Bldg, 601 N Howard St, Baltimore, MD 21201, (410)333-1750.

BROOKS, FABIENNE
Law enforcement official. **Personal:** daugHter of Vyola Wood; married Herbert Brooks. **Educ:** FBI Academy, graduate. **Career:** King County Police Dept, officer, sergeant, lieutenant, captain, currently. **Special Achievements:** First African American woman to be promoted to the ranks of sergeant and lieutenant with the King County Police Dept; First African American officer with the King County Police Dept to attend the FBI Academy; first female to head a major investigations section; Atlantic Fellow in Public Policy (London, England), 1996. **Business Addr:** Captain, King County Police Dept, 516 3rd Ave, Seattle, WA 98104, (206)296-3311.

BROOKS, FRANK B.
Business executive. **Career:** Chicago Economic Development Corp, pres; BFG Inc, founder/pres; Golden West Foods, CEO, currently. **Special Achievements:** Company ranked 39 of 100 top industrial service companies, Black Enterprise, 1992. **Business Addr:** CEO, Golden West Foods, 311 S Wacker Dr, 45th Fl, Chicago, IL 60606.

BROOKS, GWENDOLYN
Author, lecturer. **Personal:** Born Jun 7, 1917, Topeka, KS; daughter of David Anderson Brooks and Keziah Corinne Wims Brooks; married Henry Lowington Blakely, Sep 17, 1939; children: Henry Lowington Blakely III, Nora Brooks Blakely. **Educ:** Wilson Jr Coll, Chicago, 1936. **Career:** Poet, novelist, lecturer; publicity dir, NAACP Youth Council, Chicago, 1937-38; taught poetry at numerous coll and univ; distinguished prof of the arts, City Coll of the City Univ of New York, 1971. **Orgs:** Bd member, Inst Positive Educ, Amer Acad of Arts and Letters, member, Society of Midland Authors Chicago, Illinois Arts Council; Caxton Club. **Honors/Awds:** Grant in literature, Natl Inst of Arts and Letters, 1946; Award for Creative Writing, Amer Acad of Arts and Letters, 1946; two Guggenheim fellowships, Found, 1946, 1947; Eunice Tietjens Memorial Prize, Poetry magazine, 1949; Pulitzer Prize in poetry (for book Annie Allen), 1950; Kuumba Liberation Award; Robert F. Ferguson Memorial Award, Friends of Literature, 1964; Thormod Monsen Literature Award, 1964; Anisfield-Wolf Award, 1968; named Poet Laureate of Illinois, 1968-; honored for outstanding achievement in letters, Black Academy of Arts and Letters, 1971; Shelley Memorial Award, 1976; poetry consultant to the Library of Congress, 1985-86; more than 70 honorary degrees from univ and coll; inductee, Natl Womens' Hall of Fame; Essence Award; Frost Medal, Poetry Soc of Amer; lifetime Achievement Award, Natl Endowment for the Arts, 1989; published works include A Street in Bronzeville, 1945; Annie Allen, 1949; In the Mecca, 1968; Bronzeville Boys and Girls, 1956; and Maud Martha 1953; The Bean Eaters 1960; In the Mecca, 1968; Report from Part One, 1972; Gottschalk and the Grand Tarantelle, 1988; Mayor Harold Washington, 1983; Barat College, Rose Duchesne Society Achievement Award, 1992; Winnie, 1989; Blacks, 1987-91; Aiken-Taylor Award, Sewanee Review, 1992; The Near-Johannesburg Boy, 1987; Primer for Blacks, 1980; Children Coming Home, 1991; Report from Part Two, 1996; Natl Book Foundation, Medal, Distinguished Contribution to American Letters, 1994; National Endowment for the Humanities, Jefferson Lectureship, 1994; National Medal of Arts, 1995; Smithsonian Living Portrait, 1995; Lincoln Laureateship, 1997. **Home Addr:** PO Box 19355, Chicago, IL 60619.

BROOKS, HARRY W., JR.
Business executive. **Personal:** Born May 17, 1928, Indianapolis, IN; son of Nora E Brooks and Harry W Brooks, Sr; married June Hezekiah, Nov 24, 1985; children: Harry W III, Wayne L, Craig E. **Educ:** Univ of Oklahoma, Norman, MA; Univ of Nebraska, Omaha, BGE; attended US Army War Coll, Carlysle, PA; Stanford Graduate School of Business. **Career:** US Army, private to major general, 1947-76, commanding general 25th Infantry Division, Hawaii, 1974-76; Amfac, Inc, senior vice pres and public affairs dir, 1978-82, exec vice pres and chmn of Horticulture group, 1982-84; Advanced Consumer Marketing Corp, chmn and chief exec officer, 1985-; Gurney Seed and Nursery Corp, chmn and chief exec, 1985-90; Gurney Wholesale Inc, chmn and chief exec, 1985-90; Western Computer Group, Inc, chmn and chief exec, 1985-90. **Orgs:** Trustee, Freedom Forum, 1976-; dir, Occupational Medical Corp of America, 1985-96; trustee, San Mateo Easter Seals, 1988-89; director, San Francisco Opera, 1988-92. **Honors/Awds:** Distinguished Service Medal, 1976, Legion of Merit, 1970, Vietnamese Cross of Gallantry, 1967, Bronze Star 1967, all from US Army; Leonard H Carter Award, NAACP, Region I, 1988. **Home Addr:** 14 Parrott Ct, San Mateo, CA 94402. **Business Addr:** Chairman, Brooks Intl, 370 San Bruno Ave W, Ste E, San Bruno, CA 94066.

BROOKS, HENRY MARCELLUS
Educational administrator. **Personal:** Born Oct 16, 1942, Tuskegee, AL; son of Ruth Jackson Brooks and Ewing Tipton Brooks (deceased); married Carolyn D Branch, Sep 28, 1965; children: Charles Tipton, Marcellus Leander, Alexis Janine,

Toni Andrea. **Educ:** Tuskegee Univ, Tuskegee, AL, BS, 1965, MEd, 1966; Ohio State Univ, Columbus, OH, PhD, 1975. **Career:** Auburn Univ, Union Spring, AL, extension farm agent, 1967-73; Kentucky State Univ, Frankfort, KY, extension specialist, 1975-80; UMES, Princess Anne, MD, extension admin, 1980-; Univ of Maryland Coll Pk, College Park, MD. **Orgs:** Grammateus, Sigma Pi Phi, 1984-; polemarch, Kappa Alpha Psi, 1987-89. **Honors/Awds:** University of Maryland, Eastern Shore President's Award for Community Service, 1992; President of Delegte Assembly Mid-Eastern Athletic Conference, 1992. **Home Addr:** 1906 Kipling, Salisbury, MD 21801. **Business Addr:** Extension Admin, Univ of Maryland Eastern Shore, Richard Henson Ctr, Rm 2122, Princess Anne, MD 21853.

BROOKS, HUNTER O.
Educator. **Personal:** Born Sep 1, 1929, Bluefield, WV; married Barbara Boudreaux; children: Hunter, II, Christopher. **Educ:** WV State Clge, BA; WV Univ, MA. **Career:** TX Southern Univ, asst prof History. **Orgs:** Mem Natl Council Soc Studies; Assn Study Negro Life & Hist; Oral Hist Assn. **Honors/Awds:** 2000 Men Ach Carnegie Flwshp 1966; mem Phi Alpha Theta; Sigma Rho Sigma Pubs Man & Civilization 1963; Black Ldrshp Amer 1973; Discovering Black Amer 1973. **Military Serv:** AUS 1951-53. **Business Addr:** TX Southern Univ, Houston, TX 77004.

BROOKS, ISRAEL, JR.
Law enforcement official. **Career:** District of South Carolina, US marshal, currently. **Honors/Awds:** National Public Service Award, 1995. **Special Achievements:** First African American state trooper in the South Carolina Highway Patrol. **Business Addr:** US Marshal, District of South Carolina, 1845 Assembly St, Rm B31, US Court House, Columbia, SC 29202.

BROOKS, JAMES ROBERT
Professional football player. **Personal:** Born Dec 28, 1958, Warner Robins, GA; married Simone Renee; children: James Darnell, Tianna Renee. **Educ:** Auburn Univ. **Career:** Running back: San Diego Chargers, 1981-83, Cincinnati Bengals, 1984-92, Cleveland Browns, 1992, Tampa Bay Buccaneers, 1992-. **Honors/Awds:** Led the NFL in total yards, rushing, receiving, punt & kickoff returns 1981-82; All-American at Auburn; High Sch All-American on Natl Champion Warner-Robins, Georgia team; All Pro; played in Pro Bowl, 1986, 1988, 1989. **Business Addr:** Professional Football Player, Tampa Bay Buccaneers, 1 Buccaneer Pl, Tampa, FL 33607.

BROOKS, JAMES TAYLOR
Military officer. **Personal:** Born Mar 3, 1945, Memphis, TN; son of Rev Booker T & Elizabeth P Brooks; married Jacqueline D Brooks, Apr 11, 1969; children: Bryant O, Brandi C, Kamaroon A. **Educ:** Memphis University, BS, 1976. **Career:** Firestone Tire & Rubber Co, production supervisor, 1968-83; Albright Chemical Co, sales manager, 1983-86; Michigan Air National Guard, recruiting & retention superintendant, 1986-. **Orgs:** National Guard Association of Michigan, 1986-; Tuskegee Airmen (Detroit Chap), 1995-; NCOA Graduate Association, 1983-; Wade A McCree Jr Scholarshop Program, 1990-; Big Brother & Big Sister, 1994-; Cummings St Baptist Church, 1989-; NAACP. **Honors/Awds:** Wade A McCree Jr Scholarship Program, Svc Awd, 1995. **Military Serv:** Michigan Air National Guard, smsgt, 1986-; Airmen of the Year, TN, 1985.

BROOKS, JANICE WILLENA
Outreach counselor. **Personal:** Born Nov 6, 1946, Warrenton, GA; daughter of Rebie Wellington-Brooks and Willie C Brooks. **Educ:** New York University, New York, NY, BS, 1974; University of Phoenix, Phoenix, AZ, MAM, 1988. **Career:** NYC Board of Education, New York, NY, speech therapist, 1974-75; Roosevelt School District #66, Phoenix, AZ, speech therapist, 1976-79; ASU-EOC, Phoenix, AZ, counselor II, 1979-. **Honors/Awds:** Black Students Union, 1991; Appreciation Award, Dept of Corrections, 1985; Appreciation Award, Career Component of MCCD, 1982.

BROOKS, JOHN S.
Engineering manager. **Personal:** Born Mar 4, 1951, Greenwood, MS; son of John J & Bernice Brooks; married Barbara E Brooks, Jul 27, 1973; children: Jason S. **Educ:** ITT Technical Institute, Associates, electrical engineering technology, 1971; Indiana Wesleyan University, BS, business management, 1992; Anderson University, MBA, 1996. **Career:** JS Brooks Realty owner; Delphi-E, production worker, 1969-71, lab technician, 1972-83, supervisor engineering labs, 1983-87, manager product engineering labs, 1987-88, supervisor switch engineering, 1988-91, mgr, switch engineering, 1992, test, facility mgr, 1992-. **Orgs:** Anderson Zion Baptist Church, 1962-; Wilson Boys & Girls Club, bd chmn, 1994-96; Indiana Area Council, Boys & Girls Clubs of America, council pres, 1997-; Junior Achievement of Madison County, bd mem, 1996-; St Johns Hosp, quality committee mem, 1996-; Anderson Community Bank, bd mem, dir, 1995-; Peerless Lodge #32 Masonic, past master, 1980-; Prince Hall Grand Lodge of Indiana, scholarship committee, 1984-; NAACP, life mem, 1983-; Natl Area Council Comm; Boys & Girls Clubs of America, rep for IN & KY, 1997. **Honors/Awds:** US Patent Office, US patent # 4,481,925, 1984; Prince Hall Grand Lodge of Indiana, Worshipful Master of the Year, 1984. **Home Addr:** 840 N Madison Ave, Anderson, IN 46011-1206.

BROOKS, JOYCE RENEE WARD
Systems analyst. **Personal:** Born Sep 9, 1952, Kansas City, MO; married John L Brooks; children: Carmen, Leah. **Educ:** Washington Univ, BS Bus Admin 1974. **Career:** Mobil Oil Corp, programmer/analyst 1972-73; Southwestern Bell Tele Co, acctg office supv 1974-78, acctg mgr 1978-80, asst staff mgr 1980-85, systems analyst 1985-. **Home Addr:** 12844 Stoneridge, Florissant, MO 63033.

BROOKS, LEO AUSTIN
Military. **Personal:** Born Aug 9, 1932, Washington, DC; married Naomi Ethel Lewis; children: Leo Jr, Vincent Keith, Marquita Karen. **Educ:** VA St U, BS Instrmntl Mus Educ 1954; Cent St Univ Wilbeforce OH, Bus Adminstrn addtnl study 1960-62; George Wash Univ Wash DC, MS in Fin Mgmt 1964-66. **Career:** AUS Troop Sprt Agency Ft Lee VA, comdg gen 1978-; 13th Corps Sprt Cmmnd Ft Hood TX, comdg ofcr 1976-78; Sacramento Army Depot, cmdg ofcr 1974-76; Hdqrs Dept of the Army Wash DC, congrsnl coord 1967-70; Joint Chfs of Staff Wash DC, Cambodian desk ofcr 1972-74. **Orgs:** Bd dir United Urban Leag Sacramento CA 1974-76; bd dir Gr Sacramento United Way 1974-76; bd dir United Serv Auto Assn (Usaa) 1978-; chmn bd of Advis Jesuit HS Sacramento CA 1974-76; past master Acacia Lodge #32 Prince Hall F&A Masons VA 1967-; pres Cntrl VA Chap Fed Exec Assn 1979-. **Honors/Awds:** Fam of yr Freedom Found Vly Forge PA 1980; recip Legion of Merit; 2 Oakleaf Clusters; Bronze Star; Meritorious Serv Medal; Army Commndtn Medal, AUS. **Military Serv:** AUS brig gen 1954-. **Business Addr:** Hdqrts-Department of the Army, (DAPE-GO), Room 2E 749, The Pentagon, Washington, DC 20310.

BROOKS, LEROY
Government official. **Career:** Lowndes County, MS, bd of supervisors, currently. **Business Addr:** Bd of Supervisors, Lowndes County, PO Box 1364, Columbus, MS 39703, (601)329-5871.

BROOKS, MACEY
Professional football player. **Personal:** Born Feb 2, 1975. **Educ:** James Madison, attended. **Career:** Dallas Cowboys, wide receiver, 1997-. **Business Addr:** Professional Football Player, Dallas Cowboys, One Cowboys Pkwy, Irving, TX 75063, (214)556-9900.

BROOKS, MARCELLUS
Educator. **Personal:** Born Jun 24, 1941, Senatobia, MS; married Lula M; children: Marcellus Vaughn Brooks. **Educ:** Fisk University, BA, 1964; New York University & University of Madrid, MA, 1965; Vanderbilt University, post graduate work; University of Ilinois; University of Tennessee. **Career:** Fisk University, Dept of Foreign Languages, asst professor/ instructor of Spanish, 1965-. **Orgs:** Sigma Delta Pi; Alpha Mu Gamma; Alpha Phi Alpha; Modern Language Assn of Tennessee for Language Assn, Ford Foundation Grant, University of Illinois, 1968-69; College Language Assn. **Business Addr:** Assistant Professor, Dept of Foreign Languages, Fisk University, Nashville, TN 37203.

BROOKS, MARION JACKSON
Physician. **Personal:** Born Feb 15, 1920, Ft Worth, TX; married Marie Louise Norris; children: Marian Bryant, Carol Eleanor Stroughter, Roy ChArles, Clearence Jackson, Marie Anne. **Educ:** Prairie View A&M Clge, BS 1940; Howard Univ, MD 1951. **Career:** Freedmen's Hosp Wash, intern 1951-52; Ft Worth, gen prac med 1952-; St Joseph Hosp, mem staff; Harris Hosp, mem staff; All Saints Hosp, mem staff;Great Liberty Life Ins Co Dallas, dir; Neighborhood Action Inc, pres 1967-68. **Orgs:** Chmn Sickle Cell Anemia Assc TX; mem Ft Worth City Park & Recreation Bd 1963-67; Ft Worth Symphony Assc; Comm Action Agcy; Ft Worth-Tarrant Co; bddir Tarrant Co Prec Workers Coun; dir Eto TX Council Alpha Phi Alpha; Mason Shriner. **Military Serv:** AUS 1st lt 1942-47. **Business Addr:** 2200 Evans Ave, Fort Worth, TX 76104.

BROOKS, NORMAN LEON
Educational administrator. **Personal:** Born Feb 21, 1932, Port Chester, NY; son of Marion Harrell and William Brooks; married Barbara EmmeLuth. **Educ:** State Univ of NY Potsdam Crane Schl of Music, BS 1954; Tchrs Clge Columbia Univ, MA 1961; NY Univ, A & Sup Cert 1976. **Career:** Music Education, Manhattanville College, adjunct lecturer, 1997; City Schl Dist of New Rochelle, supr mus educ 1969-; New Rochelle HS, choral instr 1967-69; New Rochelle Pub Schl, vocal & gen mus instr 1958-67; Port Chester Pub Schl, instr 1954-58. **Orgs:** Choirmaster & organist St Peter's Episcopal Ch Port Chester 1958-70; asst conductor NY Collegiate Chorale 1970-73; prog chrmn Keynote Fund Com New Rochelle Library 1978-79; vestryman St Peter's Episcopal Church Peekskill 1987-; mem Phi Mu Alpha Sinfonia Hon Music Frat; president, Westchester-county School Music Association, 1990-92; vice president, New Rochelle Rotary Club, 1991-93, pres, 1993-94; chairman, ministries committee, St Peter's Episcopal Church, Peekskill, 1991-. **Honors/Awds:** Guest conductor Westchester Co Sch Mus Assc 1976-80; conductor & artistic dir New Rochelle Chorale 1979-; guest pianist Benefit Concert for CommCh 1980; guest Pianist Stars over Port Chester 1980; NYSSMA Chairperson for Multi-Cultural Awareness Comm 1982, 83; Leadership in Music Education, Black Music Caucus of the Menc, 1989; Contributions to Music Education in New Rochelle, Bethesda Baptist Church, 1990; Rotary Paul Harris Fellow, 1997. **Business Addr:** District Supervisor Music Ed, New Rochelle School Dist, 265 Clove Rd, New Rochelle, NY 10801.

BROOKS, NORWARD J.
City comptroller. **Personal:** Born Sep 10, 1934, New Iberia, LA; son of Ivory Brooks and Cleo Spencer Brooks; married Violet Caldwell; children: Norward Jr, Cleoanna, David Eric Spencer. **Educ:** Southern Univ, BS 1955; Seattle Univ, MBA, 1971; Univ of WA, PhD, 1989. **Career:** The Boeing Co Seattle, various positions 1959-69; United Inner City Dev Fnd, exec dir, 1969-70; King Co Govt Seattle, dir records & elections dept 1970-73; Washington State Employment Sec Dept, commr 1973-77; Univ of Washington, dir admin data proc 1977-81; Model Capitol Corp, pres 1979-; Washington State Employment Security Dept, commissioner 1981-85; City of Seattle, comptroller; Seattle University, adjunct professor, 1988-; Seattle Vocational Institute, director, 1995-. **Orgs:** Past pres Council for Minority Bus Enterprises in Washington State 1969-70; past pres Seattle Econ Oppor Bd Inc 1971-72; mem Govt Adv Council on Voc Educ; chmn Washington Occupational Info Consortium; trustee Washington State Assc of Co Officials 1971-72; co-chmn Washington State Co Auditors' Educ Com 1971-72; past pres Intl Thunderbird Little League Assc; past chrmn Minority Bus Dev Com Seattle Chamber of Commerce; past mem King Co Boys Club Bd Dir; past Mem United Way; mem bd dir Natl Conf of Christians & Jews; mem 1st AME Ch; Alpha Phi Alpha; pres, National Black Caucus, Govern Financial Officers Assn, 1990-; pres, Black Elected and Appointed Officials, Region X, 1986-; regional pres, Blacks in Government, 1982-85; mem, US Commission on Civil Rights Western Region, 1992-. **Honors/Awds:** Magna Cum Laude Southern Univ 1955; Golden Acorn Award Newport Hills PTA 1971; Urban League, Affirmative Action Award 1985; Employment Security Administrator of the Year 1985; One of 100 Outstanding Alumni, Seattle University, 1991. **Military Serv:** AUS 1st lt 1955-59; WA NG capt 1961-65. **Business Addr:** Executive Director, Seattle Vocational Institute, 2120 S Jackson St, Seattle, WA 98144.

BROOKS, PATRICK, JR.
Educator. **Personal:** Born Jun 8, 1944, Newark, NJ; son of Ethel Fields Brooks and Patrick Brooks Sr; widowed; children: Lisa M. Ware, Chrisham, Patrick III. **Educ:** Lane College, Jackson, TN, AB, 1963-67; Texas Southern University, Houston, MEd, 1967-70; University of Minnesota, advanced studies; New York University, NY, advanced studies; Jersey City State University, NJ, MA; Trenton State, Trenton, NJ, advanced studies; Lydon State, Lydonville, VT, advanced studies. **Career:** Wildwood Consolidate Schools, Wildwood, NJ, crisis intervention counselor; New York Housing Authority, NY, assistant district supervisor; Essex County College, Newark, NJ, instructor of sociology and counselor; Kentucky State University, Frankfort, KY, director of student activities; Texas Southern University, Houston, assistant resident hall director and counselor; Houston Urban League, Houston, TX, assistant administrator; Coach: girls cross country, basketball, boys track, wrestling; Rutgers University, NJ, regional workshop director and counselor for vocational education, 1982-. **Orgs:** New Jersey Professional Counselor Association; New Jersey Career Counselor Association; New Jersey Counselors for Non-White Concerns; Cape May County, county committeeman;Students Against Drunk Driving, county advisor; New Jersey Youth Correctional Board, trustee; County Mental Health Advocate Board; County Prosecutors; Superintendent's Task Force on Drug and Alcohol Abuse; South Jersey Coaches Association; New Jersey Career Counselor Association, executive board; New Jersey Correctional Board of Trustees for Penal Youth Prisons; County Mental Health, Drug, and Alcohol Board; County Prosecutor's County Superintendent of School's Alliance on Drug Abuse; Mayor's Council on Drug Abuse; Advisory Council, social services. **Honors/Awds:** New Jersey Counselors Association for Non-White Concern, 1989; City Streets Road Improvement, Commissioner, 1987; Wildwood Historical Society, Commissioner, 1988; Certifications: Students Personal Services, Alcohol Drug Counselor, Administration Supervision, pending. **Business Addr:** Wildwood School District, Wildwood, NJ 08260.

BROOKS, PAULINE C.
Information systems executive. **Career:** Management Technology Inc, CEO, currently. **Special Achievements:** Company is ranked #68 on Black Enterprise magazine's 1997 list of Top 100 Black businesses. **Business Phone:** (301)868-1880.

BROOKS, PHILLIP DANIEL
Business executive. **Personal:** Born Mar 2, 1946, Charlottesville, VA. **Educ:** Norfolk State Coll, BA 1969; VA Commonwealth Univ, MA 1971. **Career:** Norfolk Comm Hospital, admin 1971-, asst admins 1971. **Orgs:** Mem bd dir Blue Cross Blue Shield VA; Tidewater Hospital Council; Amer Hosp Assn; VA Hospital Assn, Amer Coll of Hospital Admin; Natl Assn of Health Serv Execs Mem; Tidewater Regional Political Assn;

United Comm Fund Allocation Liaison Team 1977; chmn advisory com Hal Jackson's Miss US Talented Teen Pageant. **Honors/Awds:** Award of Recognition Norfolk Comm 1976;, Health Mgmt Achievement Award Natl Assn of Health Serv Execs 1976. **Business Addr:** 2539 Corprew Ave, Norfolk, VA 23504.

BROOKS, RICHARD LEONARD
Educator, city official. **Personal:** Born Sep 15, 1934, Meridian, MS; son of Arlena H. Brooks and Joe C. Brooks; married Essie Stewart, May 8, 1967; children: Richard Jr, Gloria R. Watt, Randy, Fredrich, Ronald Maurice, Carolyn. **Educ:** Tougaloo Coll, BA 1958; Jackson State Univ, cont study 1960; Lane Coll Jackson, cont study 1978; MS State Univ, cont studies 1981. **Career:** Teacher, Noxubee County High School, 1964-; boy leader, Explorer Post 110 Macon MS, 1973-83; Noxubee County Comm of Concern, bd of dir, 1980-83; Child Comm Devel Day Care Ctr, bd of dir, 1980-82; chmn, Admin Bd St Paul United Meth, 1980-83; city alderman, Macon, MS, 1981-. **Orgs:** Mem Gamma Rho Chap of Kappa Alpha Psi 1956-58, Metro Lodge 551 IBPIE 1968, Grant Lodge 123 NW Stringer Grand F&AM 1980; pres, Noxubee Ebony Performing Arts Assn Inc, 1981-; commr, Desota Trail, 1989-. **Honors/Awds:** Letter of Commendation Pushmataha Area Council Boy Scouts of Amer 1977; Youth Leadership MS Youth & Govt Affairs 1977, 1978, 1979; Appreciation Award Noxubee Comm Concern Inc 1979-80; numerous other awards Boy Scouts of Amer. **Home Addr:** 205 S Washington St, Macon, MS 39341.

BROOKS, ROBERT DARREN
Professional football player. **Personal:** Born Jun 23, 1970, Greenwood, SC. **Educ:** South Carolina, bachelor's degree in retailing. **Career:** Green Bay Packers, wide receiver, 1992-; Shoo-in 4 Life Records Inc, president, currently. **Business Addr:** Professional Football Player, Green Bay Packers, 1265 Lombardi Ave, Green Bay, WI 54304, (414)494-2351.

BROOKS, RODNEY ALAN, SR.
Newspaper journalist. **Personal:** Born May 29, 1953, Baltimore, MD; son of Mattie Bell Crosson Brooks and William F Brooks; married Sheila Smith Brooks, Aug 1, 1989; children: Rodney Alan Jr, Tahira, Andre. **Educ:** Cornell University, Ithaca, NY, BS, 1974. **Career:** Ithaca Journal, Ithaca, NY, reporter, 1974-77; Asheville Citizen-Times, Asheville, NC, business editor, 1977-80; The Bulletin, Philadelphia, financial writer, 1980-81; Philadelphia Inquirer, Philadelphia, PA, asst business, editor, asst city editor, reporter, 1981-85; USA Today, Arlington, VA, deputy managing editor/Money; 1985-. **Orgs:** Board of Directors, National Association of Black Journalists, College Park, MD, treasurer/chairman of strategic planning committee, 1994-; co-founder/chairman, NABJ Business Writers Task Force, 1989-93; board of governors, Society of American Business Editors & Writers, 1993-96; board of directors, Multi-Cultural Management Progarm, University of Missouri;board of directors, National Association of Minority Media Executives, 1990-93, treasurer, 1991-93; chairman, Strategic Planning Committee, 1994; City of New Carrollton Advisory Planning Committee, 1990-93; board of directors, Pisgah Chapter, March of Dimes, 1978-81; board of directors, Tompkins County Library, University of Alumni Association, Cornell Club of Washington DC. **Honors/Awds:** Inroads Baltimore, Outstanding Contributions, 1994; Greater Ithaca Activities Center, Outstanding Contributions. **Business Addr:** Deputy Managing Editor/Money, USA Today, 1000 Wilson Blvd, Arlington, VA 22229.

BROOKS, RODNEY NORMAN
Social service executive. **Personal:** Born Jun 6, 1954, Asbury Park, NJ; married Mary Jane Carroll; children: Sheena Monique, Anneka LeChelle. **Educ:** Bowling Green State Univ, BS Secondary Education 1976; Kent State Univ, 1981; Atlanta Univ, 1984. **Career:** Massillon Bd of Educ, sub teacher 1977-78; Supreme Life Ins Co, debit mgr 1977-78; Canton Urban League Inc, project dir 1978-83; Massillon Urban League, pres/chief exec officer. **Orgs:** Grand recording sec Buckeye Grand Lodge IF & AMM 1983-; directorship Planned Parenthood of Stark Co 1984-; directorship Westcare Mental Health Ctr 1984-; directorship Social Planning Council/United Way of West Stark 1984-; worshipful master Simpson Lodge #1 IF & AMM 1985. **Honors/Awds:** Whitney M Young Jr Fellow NUL Inc/Atlanta Univ 1984. **Business Addr:** Grand Rapids Urban League, 745 Eastern Ave, SE, Grand Rapids, MI 49503.

BROOKS, ROSEMARY BITTINGS
Educator, publisher. **Personal:** Born Jan 2, 1951, East Orange, NJ; daughter of Ethel Fields Brooks and Patrick Brooks; divorced; children: Haven Michael, Ebony Mekia. **Educ:** Claflin Univ, BA 1971; Seton Hall Univ, MA 1976; Kean Coll, Communication Certification 1978; Rutger's Union, MA Physical Fitness Specialist 1983. **Career:** East Orange Drug Center, substance abuse counselor 1975; Essex Valley School/The Bridge West, dir 1981-82; Second Chance Counseling Center, dir 1982-83; NJ Black Caucus of Legislators, lobbyist 1984-87; Irvington Board of Educ, Educator/History, 1984-; NJ Chapter Parents for Joint Custody, lobbyist 1985-87; Essex Co Fitness Program, specialist 1986-87; Irvington HS NJ Law & Psychology, instructor of history 1985-87; "Staying Fit" Exercise Program NJ Network, host, dir 1984-86; NJ Careers Council Irvington High, coordinator 1986-87; Irvington Bd of Educ, dir of history & law; Person to Person Greeting Cards, pres, writer, 1988-, guidance counselor, 1994-. **Orgs:** Educ comm chmn SOMAC Comm Council 1979-86; mem Governor's Council on Educ 1982-87; mem NJ State Bd of Lobbyists 1982-87, NJ State Bd of Fitness Specialist 1984-87; project chmn Maplewood PTA 1985-86; mem, treas Irvington Awareness Council 1986-87; dir Afro-History Soc Irvington HS 1983-87; writer/consultant, Sands Casino Atlantic City NJ, 1988-89; writer/consultant, Planned Parenthood NJ, 1988-89; Minority Committee chairman local and state NJ; State Instructional Committee, NJEA; Guidance Counselor Irvington School District; Adolescent Justice & Anti-Violence, appointee to the governor's comm; State Bd of Educ, State of NJ, lobbyist. **Honors/Awds:** NAACP Award of Merit/Outstanding Educator 1980-81; creator/dir first black fitness program on cable in NJ/NY 1983-85; Citation for Excellence in Programming NJ State Assembly 1984; TV and radio appearances; feature writer Essence Magazine 1982-87, Focus Magazine 1984-87; choreographer "The Wiz" NJ Theatre Irvington 1986-87; Career Council Award for Outstanding Participation 1986-87; Person to Person Cards were recognized for its contributions to health, 1988-89; Author, NJ Legislation Anti-Violence Program for Adolescents; Feature Guest, A for Kids TV Specials. **Home Addr:** 95 Parker Ave, Maplewood, NJ 07040.

BROOKS, ROY LAVON
Educator. **Personal:** Born Mar 7, 1950, New Haven, CT; married Penny Feller; children: Whitney. **Educ:** University of Connecticut, BA (magna cum laude), 1972; Yale University, JD, 1975. **Career:** United States District Court, law clerk, 1975-77; Yale Law Journal, editor, 1975; Cravath, Swaine, & Moore, corporate attorney, 1977-79; University of San Diego, School of Law, professor, starting 1979; University of Minnesota, School of Law, professor, currently. **Orgs:** Heartland Human Relations Assn, board of directors, 1984-86; NAACP San Diego Chapter, board of directors, 1987. **Honors/Awds:** Author of numerous publications including: Foreign Currency Translations, 1980; Small Business Financing, 1981; Affirmative Action in Law Teaching, 1982. **Business Addr:** Professor, School of Law, University of Minnesota, 285 Law Center, Minneapolis, MN 55455-0100.

BROOKS, SHEILA DEAN
Entrepreneur, broadcast journalist. **Personal:** Born Jun 24, 1956, Kansas City, MO; daughter of Gussie Mae Dean Smith and Stanley Benjamin Smith (deceased); married Rodney Alan Brooks Sr, Aug 1, 1988; children: Andre Timothy. **Educ:** University of Washington, Seattle, WA, BA, broadcast journalism, 1978; Seattle University, Seattle, WA, 1978-80; Howard University, MA, 1998. **Career:** KCTS-TV, Seattle, WA, reporter/producer, 1978-81; KREM-TV, Spokane, WA, reporter/anchor, 1981-83; KAMU-TV/FM, College Station, TX, news director/anchor, 1984-85; The Dallas Morning News, Dallas, TX, executive management program, 1985-88; Vanita Productions, Baltimore, MD, senior producer, 1988-89; WTTG-TV Channel 5, Washington, DC, executive producer, 1989-90; SRB Productions Inc, Washington, DC, president/CEO, 1988-. **Orgs:** Natl Assn of Black Journalists, executive board officer/secretary, 1986-91, chairwoman, internship committee, 1990-91, chairwoman, scholarship committee, 1987-90; board of directors, Archbishop Carroll High School, 1990-95; board of directors, New Carrollton Cablevision Inc, 1990-92; National Association of Women Business Owners, Washington, DC, executive bd/president-elect, 1996-97, board of directors, 1994-, pres, 1997; The National Academy of Television Arts & Sciences, NATAS-DC, bd of governors, 1996-; Maryland/District of Columbia Minority Supplier Development Council, executive bd officer, 1994-; Women in Film & Video, Washington, DC Chapter, board of directors, 1994-96, advisory bd, 1996-. **Honors/Awds:** First Place CEBA Award of Excellence, Best Documentary in the Country, CEBA—World Institute of Communications Inc, New York, 1990; Emmy Award Nomination, Best Local Documentary, National Academy of Television Arts and Sciences, Washington, DC, 1990; Emmy Award Nomination, Best Local Information-Oriented Show, National Academy of Television Arts and Sciences, Washington, DC, 1990; 1st Place (RTNDA) Regional Award, Radio-Television News Director's Association, Washington, DC, 1990; Honorable Mention NABJ Award, Natl Assn of Black Journalists, 1990; Emmy Awards 1979, 1980; Texas Assn of Broadcasters Radio Award, 1984; Maryland/District of Columbia Minority Supplier Development Council, Supplier of the Year, 1995; Telly Awards, 1995 (2), 1996 (2). **Military Serv:** US Navy Reserve, E-4, 1976-78. **Business Addr:** President/CEO, SRB Productions, Inc, 1511 K St NW, Ste 1157, Washington, DC 20005.

BROOKS, SIDNEY JOSEPH
Manager. **Personal:** Born Mar 17, 1935, St Genevieve, MO; married Geraldine Lois Cooper; children: Joey, Mike, Alison, Brett. **Career:** San Diego Chargers, equip mgr; BSA, asst cub master 1962-64; Am Jr Bowling Cong, hd coach 1966-68. **Orgs:** Mem Holy Name Soc 1965-68; panel mem Pre-Cane Conf 1966-68; hd coach Young Amer League Ftbl 1968-71; SOCSY & Awards Com 1968-71; chief judge CO Annual HS Indoor Easter Races 1969-71; protocol NCAA Ice Hockey Champships; asst track coach Corpus Christi Schl 1969-71; mem Rule Com Jr Parochial Annual Track& Field Meet 1969-71; dir 1st El Paso Co Amateur Athletic Union 1969-71; coord Rocky Mt AAU Track & Field Jr Oly Meet 1969; judge Green Thumb Com 1969; commr Amateur Athletic Union 1969-71; chrmn Natl AAU Jr Oly Chmpshp 1969-70; parish cncl mem AF Acad Parish 1970; dir Danang Field Day for Vietnamese Boys & Girls 1972. **Honors/Awds:** Ourstdng active duty Airman of Year 1st AFR Region 1964; outstdng supply supr Alaskan Communications Region 1966; outstdng noncommn ofc of quarter AlaskanCommcn Reg 1967; oursdng sr NCO of Year USAF Acad 1969; outstdng Airman of USAF 1970; outsdng Young Men of Amer 1970; PACAF outstdng Airman of the Year 1972; Serv to mankind award Rocky Mt Sertoma Claub 1972. **Military Serv:** USAF sr m/Sgt 1953-73. **Business Addr:** San Diego Chargers, PO Box 20666, San Diego, CA 92120.

BROOKS, SUZANNE R.
Educational administrator. **Personal:** Born Jan 20, 1941, Philadelphia, PA; daughter of Rayetta Ortiga and John Lemon. **Educ:** LaSalle University, Philadelphia, PA, BS, Education/English, 1975; Washington State University, Pullman, WA, MA, English, 1979, advanced language studies, summers 1979, 1981; University of Nevada-Reno, graduate courses, summers 1982, 1983; Penn State University, University Park, PA, doctoral program, 1985-. **Career:** Philadelphia Police Dept, Philadelphia, PA, policewoman, 1968-72; Philadelphia High School for Girls, Philadelphia, PA, teaching practicum, 1974; Pennsylvania Advancement School, Philadelphia, PA, volunteer teacher, 1975; Washington State University, Pullman, WA, teaching apprentice, 1975-76, research asst, 1978-79, teaching asst, 1978-79, graduate asst, 1978-79, GED instructor, 1980, bi-lingual ESL instructor, 1980-81, dir of science support services, 1979-82; University of Nevada Reno, affirmative action officer, 1982-84; Penn State University, Philadelphia, PA, affirmative action officer, 1984-89; Sign Language Systems, co-owner & educational design/development specialist, 1986-;California State University, Sacramento, CA, director of Multi-Cultural Center, 1990-. **Orgs:** Member, Planning Committee, Center for Women Policy Studies; Natl Assn of Business & Professional Women, State College Chapter; Natinal Council of Negro Women; Natl Assn for Women Deans, Administrators, and Counselors; College & University Personnel Assn; board mem, Natl Institute for Women of Color; chair, Foundations Committee, State College Business and Professional Women's Assn; Affirmative Action Committee, Democratic Party of Centre County. **Honors/Awds:** Andrew V. Kozak Fellowship, Penn State University Chapter, Phi Delta Kappa; Danforth Fellowship; McShain Award, LaSalle College; Alpha Epsilon Honor Society, LaSalle College; Humbert Humphrey Scholarship, Cheyney State College; author/presentor, "Adult Education Programs: Addresssing Cross-Cultural Concerns," American Assn for Adult & Continuing Education Conference, 1987; author/presentor, "Image and Women of Color," American Imagery Conference, 1986; author with A. Hernandez, "Moving Mountains—Past, Present and Future: The Role of Women of Color in the American Political System," Natl Institute for Women of Color, 1984; author, "Life Through the Ivy," Essence, 1975; author and presentor of numerous other articles and publications. **Business Addr:** Director, Multi-Cultural Center, California State University, Sacramento, 6000 J St Library 1010, Sacramento, CA 95819-6095.

BROOKS, THEODORE ROOSEVELT, JR.
Physician, educator. **Personal:** Born Aug 2, 1930, Jackson, MS; married Yolande Stovall; children: Leslie, Naida, Blair, Angelle. **Educ:** Tougaloo Coll, BS summa cum laude 1951; Howard U, MD 1955; USC, MS Ed 1981, MS Gero 1983. **Career:** Private Med Practice, 1956-; Charles Drew Med Sch, prof family practice, geriatric medicine, primary care, gerontology 1978-. **Orgs:** Pres Amada Ent Corp; pres Amalgamated Devel Assn 1980-87; pres TRB Corp 1984-87; AMA; NMA; Kappi Pi; Sigma Pi Phi; NAACP; Alpha Phi Alpha; diplomate Amer Bd of Fam Practice; Alpha Omega Alpha; Fellow Amer Acad of Fam Physicians; Amer Coll Of Medicine; Amer Coll of Gen Practice; Soc of Teachers of Fam Med; bd of dir PSA Martin Luther King Hosp LA CA; bd of dir Ambassador East Develpmnt Inc; bd of dir Allied Diversified Inc; bd of dir Omaha Inc; bd of dir Allied Inc; bd of dir Hypertensive Council of Los Angeles; physician's asst supervisor bd of medical quality assurance; physician's asst examining committee. **Honors/Awds:** Most Outstanding Clinical Faculty, Drew/UCLA Medical School, 1993, 1994; Certificate of Added Qualification in Geriatric Medicine. **Military Serv:** USAF capt 1956-58. **Business Addr:** Professor, Drew Medical School, 3701 Stocker St 104, Los Angeles, CA 90008.

BROOKS, TODD FREDERICK
Physician. **Personal:** Born Sep 1, 1954, New York, NY; son of Effie C Brooks and Delaney Brooks. **Educ:** Drew Univ, BA 1976; Meharry Medical Coll, MD 1980; Univ of TN Health Science, Post Doctorate 1980-84. **Career:** Univ of TN, clinical instructor 1984-; Private Practice, ob/gyn 1984-; Memphis Health Ctr, consultant, 1984-. **Orgs:** Mem Bluff City Medical Soc, Univ of TN Ob/Gyn Soc, chairman; fund raiser Boy Scouts of Amer. **Honors/Awds:** Publ "Perinatal Outcome," Journal of Ob/Gyn 1984. **Business Addr:** 1211 Union Ave Suite 495, Memphis, TN 38104, (901)276-4895.

BROOKS, TYRONE L.
State representative. **Personal:** Born Oct 10, 1945, Warrenton, GA; son of Ruby Cody Brooks and Mose Brooks; children: Tyrone Jr, Nahede Teresa. **Career:** Tyrone Brooks & Associates, natl president, 1973-; Universal Humanities and Visions of Literacy, founder, chairman, currently; African American Business Systems, president; Georgia State House of Representatives, District 54, state representative, 1981-. **Orgs:** Georgia's Legislative Black Caucus; Southern Christian Leadership Conference, former natl field dir; NAACP; American Civil Liberties Union; Gate City Bar Assn, advisory bd; Georgia Assn of Black Elected Officials, pres, 1993. **Honors/Awds:** NAACP, Roy Wilkins Award, 1984, Hall of Fame, 1986; Civil Rights Award, 1990; Inducted to NAACP Hall of Fame; Presidents Award, SCLC, 1990. **Business Addr:** State Representative, House of Representatives, State Capitol, Ste 511, Legislative Offices, Atlanta, GA 30334, (404)656-6372.

BROOKS, W. WEBSTER
Educator. **Personal:** Born May 25, Orangeburg Co, SC; married McPhine Jenkins; children: Carl Edward, Sallie Belita, Lenior Lamar, Wanda Yvonne, Lisa Latanya. **Educ:** SC State Clge, BS 1949, MS 1954; Cornell Univ, attnd 1956; FL State Univ 1968; Univ of SC 1974. **Career:** Jackson High School, Camden SC, Industrial Arts teacher, asst prin, coach, 1949-51; West Lee School, supt, 1952-57; West Lee Primary School, prin, 1958-; Rembert Educ dir of head start, 1968-70. **Orgs:** Mem SCEA; mem NEA; mem NEASP; mem SCASA; mem SCAPS Adult Educ; SCEA Standing Com PEA; PEA House of Delegates SCEA Delegates Assemble; Lee Co Educ Assc Chmn; Civic Educ of Six Congr Dist; pres Lee Co Educ Assc 1972-74; mem exec comm Mbrshp Chrmn Lee Co SCASA; discussion ldr NEASP 1973; legislative comm SCASA; immediate past pres LCEA; mem LCEA-SCEA Pace; chmn Civic Educ Com; mem Voter League; chmn Bi-racial Comm mem Jerusalem Bapt Ch; Deacon supt Clerk, Clerk of Lynches River Union; pres Brotherhood; secr Brotherhood Sumpter Assc; mem Kappa Alpha Psi; pres LCC of State Clge Alumni Assc; mem Sandy Bluff Lodge 44 Ashland Consistory 246 Crescent Temple 148; Delegate to NEA Conv; Chamber of Commerce of Bishopville SC. **Honors/Awds:** Plaque highest percentage mbrshp in SC Educ Assc 1974. **Military Serv:** USN 1943-45. **Business Addr:** Rt 1 Box 360, Rembert, SC.

BROOKS, WADELL, SR.
Personnel administrator (retired). **Personal:** Born Jan 20, 1933, Lexington, MS; married Daisy Anderson; children: Yolanda, Wadell Jr, Cassandra. **Educ:** Illinois State Normal Univ, BS, Business Educ 1957; Northern Illinois Univ, 1958. **Career:** Public Works Ctr Naval Base, Great Lakes, IL, deputy equal employment opportunity ofcr 1979-90; dir housing assignment/referral 1970-79; VA Hosp educ therapist, 1957-68; Naval Training Ctr, Great Lakes Naval Base, educ specialist 1968-70. **Orgs:** Pres Tots & Toddlers Day Care Ctr Inc 1974-; pres Amer Assn for Rehab Therapy Inc 1970; sec/treas Daisy's Nursery Infant & Resource Developmental Center, 1988; past master Rufus Mitchell Lodge 107 1972; pres NAACP N Chicago Br 1976-80; bd dir, Navy League, Lake Co Urban League; life mem NAACP 1979; bd dir Great Lakes Credit Union Naval Base Great Lakes IL 1980-90; Lake County Race Unity Task Force, chmn, 1993-; First Midwest bank Community Reinvestment Council, 1995-; North Chicago Chamber of Commerce, board of directors; Natl Alumni Assn Faith Grant College, pres, 1996. **Honors/Awds:** Superior Perf Award VA Hosp 1967; Superior Perf Award Rufus Mitchell Lodge 107 1975; Non-Fed Contrib Award Pub Works Ctr Great Lakes IL 1979; Superior Achievement Award, We Do Care Organization, Chicago, 1990; Faith Grant Colorado Alumnus of the Year, 1996. **Military Serv:** AUS spec/4 1954-55.

BROOKS, WILLIAM C.
Business executive. **Educ:** Long Island Univ, BA; Univ of OK, MBA; Harvard Business Schools, advanced mgmt prog grad 1985. **Career:** Several Federal Govt positions in Office of Mgmt & Budget in the Exec Office of the Pres, Dept of Defense, Dept of Labor, Dept of Air Force; General Motors Corp, 1978-89, group dir of personnel; Dept of Labor, Employment Standards Admin, 1989-90; General Motors Corp, vp, comm and urban affairs, 1993-. **Orgs:** General Motors Dey Exec to Fl A & M, mem; Nat'l Inst of Ed Advisory Panel on Employability, mem; 70001 Training & Employment; chairman, bd dir; Nat'lCoalition on Black Voter Particitpation, Inc, bd dir; OH State Univ Nat'l Center for Research and Vocational Ed; mem advisory bd; State of Ohio's Public Employment Advisory & Counseling, mem; Boy Scouts of American, dist chairman; Louisiana-Pacific Corp, bd of dir. **Honors/Awds:** Articles Published in the Personnel Administrator, the Nat'l Training Lab Jornal on Social Change, and The Black Collegian; Awarded the Nat'l Assoc of Negro Bus and Prof Women's Ombudsman Appreciation Awd, 1979; CETA, bridge builders award 1979; Nat'l BLack MBA Assoc, outstanding MBA of the year award 1980; Awarded the 70001 Ltd Pathfinder Award 1981. **Business Addr:** Chairman, Entech Human Resources, 363 W. Big Beaver Rd., Troy, MI 48084.

BROOKS, WILLIAM P.
Hospital administrator. **Personal:** Born Nov 19, 1934, Newkirk, OK; son of Mr & Mrs Carl F Brooks Sr; married Sue Jean Johnson; children: Barry P, Leslie J Lykes, Terryl D Abington, William R, Virgil A. **Educ:** Friends Univ Wichita KS, 1952-53; Wichita Univ, 1967. **Career:** Winfield State Hosp Training Ctr, laundry worker 1957, vocational teacher 1961, vocational training suprv 1966, unit b 1970, unit dir, admin officer I 1977-87 special asst to supt 1987-95, supt, 1995-. **Orgs:** Youth comm Winfield Kiwanis Club 1972-; pres Winfield Quarterback Club 1974; adv comm Conley Cty Comm Coll & Voc Tech School 1975-; city plnng commiss City of Winfield 1978-; mem Winfield Police Reserve 1984-. **Honors/Awds:** Disting Serv Awd Winfield Jaycees 1967; Outstanding Young Man KS State Jaycees 1967; Illustrious Potentate Emith Temple #30 Wichita 1975. **Business Addr:** Superintendent, Winfield State Hosp & Training Ctr, N College, Winfield, KS 67156.

BROOME, PERSHING. See Obituaries section.

BROOMES, LLOYD RUDY
Psychiatrist. **Personal:** Born Feb 2, 1936; married Lauvenia Alleyne, Jun 2, 1963; children: Lloyda, Melissa. **Educ:** Shell Tech School, 1950-55; Oakwood Coll, BA 1961; Loma Linda Univ, MD 1966. **Career:** Camarillo State Hospital, staff psychiatrist 1969-71; Meharry Alcohol Drug Abuse Program, asst prof 1972-89; Meharry Comm Mental Health Center, dir clinical serv; Nashville, private practice 1973-86; Tennessee Dept of MH & MR, A & D Division, asst commissioner 1988-89; Alvin C York VA Medical Center, Psychiatry Services, chief 1987-88; Madison Hospital, Department of Psychiatry, chief 1978-80; Carl Vinson VA Medical Center, psychiatry services chief, 1989-. **Orgs:** Mem, Amer Psych Assn; mem Georgia Psychiatric Physicians Assn; mem Gov Advisory Commn Alcohol & Drugs, 1972-76; Black Adventist Med Dent Assn; exec vice pres, Lupus Found of Amer, Nashville Chapter 1986-89; American College of Physician Executives, 1991. **Honors/Awds:** Gold Medal Award Shell Tech School 1955; Fellow, Amer Psychiatric Assn, 1985; Amer Bd of Psychiatry & Neurology, Diplomate in Psychiatry, 1981. **Military Serv:** Civilian Work Program 1969-71. **Business Addr:** Chief, Psychiatry Svc, Mental Health Svc Line Manager, Carl Vinson Veterans Admin Med Ctr, Dublin, GA 31021.

BROOMFIELD, MARY ELIZABETH
Educational administrator. **Personal:** Born Apr 4, 1935, Helena, AR; daughter of Elizabeth Mitchell Hatcher and Walter Broomfield. **Educ:** IL State Normal Univ, BA El Educ 1956; Roosevelt Univ, MA 1963; Univ of Chicago, Chicago, IL, postgrad. **Career:** Chicago Board of Education, Chicago, IL, assistant superintendent of Equal Opportunity, currently; NE IL Univ Residential Schl for Boys & Girls, supt 1973-, prin/Supt 1971-73; Bousfield Soc Adj Sch, asst dir 1969-70; Motley Soc Adj Schl, asst princ 1966-69. **Orgs:** Mem Phi Delta Kappa; mem Samuel B Stratton Prin Assc; Delta Kappa Gamma; Assc of Secondary Schl Prin; Natl Council of Juvenile Justice; mem Council on Comm Svc; League of Black Women; member, National Assn of Black School Educators. **Honors/Awds:** Superior Service Award, City of Chicago, 1989; Outstanding Service, Bureau of Foreign Languages, 1988; Outstanding Leadership, Operation PUSH, 1990.

BROSSETTE, ALVIN, JR.
Educator. **Personal:** Born May 16, 1942, Montgomery, LA; married Delores Gipson; children: Derrie, Alicia, Kathy. **Educ:** Grambling State Univ, BS El Educ 1962; Northwestern State Univ, MEd Admin 1970; Western MI Univ, EdD Educ Ldrshp 1975. **Career:** Wilmer-Hutchins Independent School Dist, gen supt, 1980-; Prairie View A&M Univ TX, dept head Coll of Educ Curriculum & Instr, 1976-80; Northwestern State Univ Los Angeles, asst prof Dept CI Coll of Educ, 1975-76; Kalamazoo Publlic Schools MI, program coord/(R&D), 1974-75; Grant Parish Public Schools, Colfax LA, asst prin/teacher, 1967-73; Winn Parish Public Schools, Winnfield LA, teacher, 1962-67. **Orgs:** Mem Natl Assc for Curriculum Dev 1976-; mem/Tchr ctn adv bd Prairie View A&M Univ TX 1979-; consult N Forest ISD Houston 1979-; mem Phi Beta Sigma 1968-; mem Phi Delta Kappa 1975-; mem Amer Assc of Sch Admin 1980-; pres Grant Parish Educ Assc 1972-73. **Honors/Awds:** Flwshp-Grant Western MI Univ 1973-75. **Business Addr:** 3820 E & Illinois Ave, Dallas, TX 75216.

BROTHERS, TONY
Professional basketball referee. **Career:** NBA official, currently. **Business Addr:** NBA Official, c/o National Basketball Association (NBA), 645 5th Ave, 15th Fl, New York, NY 10022-5986.

BROUGHTON, CHRISTOPHER LEON
Actor, magician. **Personal:** Born Mar 4, 1964, Detroit, MI; son of Theo Faye McCord-Broughton and Ronald Leon Broughton. **Educ:** Mercy Coll of Detroit, attended, 1984. **Career:** Magician, actor, Los Angeles CA, 1976-; comedian; inventor of magical props; writer, currently. **Orgs:** Intl Brotherhood of Magicians, 1984-; Mystics, 1976-89; SAG, 1984-; AFTRA, 1984-; ICAP, 1988-. **Honors/Awds:** Intl Brotherhood of Magicians Award (the world's greatest magician), was the first black to win this award, 1989; created a magical illusion to be marketed, 1989. **Home Addr:** 10458 Westover, Detroit, MI 48204.

BROUHARD, DEBORAH TALIAFERRO
Educator. **Personal:** Born Jul 7, 1949, Springfield, MA; daughter of Julia Beatrice Addison Taliaferro and Ernest Carter Taliaferro; married John Forrest Brouhard, Jul 1, 1972; children: Benjamin Forrest, Rebecca Julia. **Educ:** McGill University, Montreal, Canada, 1970; Aurora University, Aurora, IL, BA, 1971; Indiana University, Bloomington, IN, MSED, 1978. **Career:** Aurora East High School, East Aurora, IL, teacher, 1971-73; Miami University, Oxford, OH, coord special services, 1981-83; Arizona State University, Tempe, AZ, counselor, 1985-. **Orgs:** Board member, Potentials Unlimited, 1991; Mid-American Assn of Educational Opp Programs, 1981-84. **Honors/Awds:** Leadership Award, Phoenix Black Women's Task Force, 1990; Affirmative Action Award, Arizona State University, 1990. **Business Addr:** Counselor, Faculty Associate, Arizona State University, Counseling and Consultation, Education Dept, Student Services Bldg B325, Tempe, AZ 85287-1112, (602)965-6060.

BROUSSARD, ARNOLD ANTHONY
Administrator. **Personal:** Born Sep 26, 1947, New Orleans, LA; married Venita Lorraine Thomas; children: Danielle Lorraine, Darryl Anthony. **Educ:** Tulane Univ, BA Soc 1965-69; Wharton Sch Univ of PA, MBA acct oper research 1969-71. **Career:** City of New Orleans, exec asst to Mayor's Ofc 1978-; J Ray McDermott & Co Inc, fin planning analyst 1975-78; Arthur Andersen & Co, sr consult 1971-75. **Orgs:** Co-coord Jr Achvmnt 1975-77; bd dir New Orleans Area Bayou River Health Sys Agcy 1975-78; mem Natl Assc of Black Acct 1976-. **Business Addr:** 1300 Perdido St, New Orleans, LA 70112.

BROUSSARD, CATHERINE DIANNE
Greeting card producer. **Personal:** Born Oct 8, 1955, Tachikawa, Japan; daughter of Earline Hickman Broussard and Leon Broussard Jr. **Educ:** Golden Gate University, San Francisco, CA, BS, Marketing, 1981. **Career:** Economics Resources Corp, Los Angeles, CA, exec asst, 1982-83; Century Freeway Committee, Los Angeles, CA, public relations, 1983-87; Heritage Unlimited, Berkeley, CA, owner, 1989-. **Orgs:** Member, public relations, planning committee, Big Sisters of Los Angeles, 1986-87.

BROUSSARD, CHERYL DENISE
Investment adviser. **Personal:** Born Sep 25, 1955, Phoenix, AZ; daughter of Gwendolyn J Reid and Theodore Douglas; married John B Broussard, Jun 27, 1981; children: J Hasan. **Educ:** Creighton University, 1973-75; Loyola University, BS, 1977. **Career:** Dean Witter Reynolds, Inc, investment advisor; Broussard/Douglas, Inc, principal/chief investment advisor, currently. **Orgs:** National Association of Negro Business and Professional Women, Economic Development Committee. **Honors/Awds:** Minorities and Women in Business Magazine, voted one of ten Woman Who Made a Difference, 1992. **Special Achievements:** Author: The Black Woman's Guide to Financial Independence: Money Management Strategies for the 1990s; Sister CEO: The Black Woman's Guide to Starting Your Own Business. **Business Addr:** Principal/Chief Investment Advisor, Broussard/Douglas, Inc, 3871 Piedmont Ave, Ste 365, Oakland, CA 94611, (510)482-5129.

BROUSSARD, STEVEN
Professional football player. **Personal:** Born Feb 22, 1967, Los Angeles, CA; married Monique, Feb 22, 1991; children: Talin. **Educ:** Washington State. **Career:** Atlanta Falcons, running back, 1990-93; Cincinnati Bengals, 1994; Seattle Seahawks, 1995-. **Business Addr:** Professional Football Player, Seattle Seahawks, 11220 NE 53rd St, Kirkland, WA 98033, (206)827-9777.

BROUSSARD, VERNON
Educator. **Personal:** Born Jan 30, 1934, Shreveport, LA; son of Verdie Brannon Broussard and Leon Broussard; married Ida Mae Macias, Aug 8, 1982; children: Peggy Anne, Tona Collette, Vernon Jr, Gena Cecil. **Educ:** Southern Univ Baton Rouge, BS 1955; CA State Univ San Jose 1966; MI State Univ, PhD 1971. **Career:** University of Phoenix, inst of math, 1997; School of Educ Univ of Southern CA, assoc dean program devel & operations 1978; Schooll of Educ Univ of Southern CA, assoc prof 1977-78; CA State Dept of Educ, chief bureau & of program devel 1971-77; Unified School Dist, asst supt 1968-71; Stockton Unified School Dist, math supvr 1966-68; Stockton Unified School Dist, classroom teacher 1958-66; Chicago Pub School, Lansing MI, and California Test Bureaus; planning consultant 1966-71; World Congress of Comparative Educ Soc London England/Mexico City, Vancouver BC, presenter/chmn 1977. **Orgs:** Life mem NAACP 1978-; guest seminar lecturer Nat Inst of Ed 1978; Alpha Kappa Mu, Southern Univ Baton Rouge 1955; Presidential Appointment (President Reagan), mem, The Natl Advisory Council on Vocational and Technical Educ 1982-85. **Honors/Awds:** Published various articles 1963-; Natl Sci Found Fellow; NSF Math Washington DC 1965-66; Pres List MI State Univ 1977; State of Kuwait Invitation, Lecture/Tour of the Educational System, 1987. **Military Serv:** AUS major 1955-63. **Business Addr:** University Pk, Los Angeles, CA 90007.

BROWDER, ANNE ELNA
Business executive. **Personal:** Born Mar 18, 1935, Vernon, AL; daughter of Mary E. and Eddie; divorced. **Educ:** LaSalle Ext; Roosevelt U.niv. **Career:** NBC News, Chicago, Production Talent Mgmt, 1960-73; TV News Inc, Office Mgr, 1973-75; The Tobacco Inst, Asst to Pres, Natl Spokesperson, Tobacco Industry, 1976-86; The Exec Television Workshop, assoc, 1988-94; The Institute of Karmic Guidance, admin asst, 1990-. **Orgs:** NAACP.

BROWN, A. DAVID
Personnel and labor relations executive. **Personal:** Born Aug 4, 1942, Morristown, NJ; son of Muriel Kyse Brown and Arthur D Brown, Sr; married Joan Currie, Jun 22, 1980. **Educ:** Monmouth Coll, West Long Branch NJ, BS, 1965. **Career:** Bamberger's New Jersey, Newark NJ, personnel exec, 1968-71, admin, personnel, 1974, vice pres, 1975; R H Macy & Co Inc, New York NY, vice pres, personnel, 1981, sr vice pres, personnel & labor relations, 1983-, bd of dir, 1987. **Orgs:** Mem, Black Retail Action Group. **Military Serv:** US Army Natl Guard, specialist fifth class, 1965-71. **Business Addr:** Sr Vice Pres, R H Macy and Co Inc, 151 W 34th St, New York, NY 10001.

BROWN, A. SUE
Administrator. **Personal:** Born Jun 28, 1946, Lauderdale, MS. **Educ:** Bloomfield Coll, BS 1968; Rutgers Univ Grad Sch of Social Work, MSW 1969; Univ of PA, cert mgmt by objectives 1979; Harvard Univ Sch of Pub Hlth, Cert 1980. **Career:** Urban League-Essex Co Newark, dir health 1969-73; Coll Medicine and Dentistry Newark, health planner 1973-75; Newark Comprehensive Health Service Plan, acting asst dir then dir 1973-75; Martland Hosp Coll Medicine and Dentistry Newark, acting exec dir 1975-77; Coll Univ Hosp, Univ Med and Dentistry NJ, 1977-83; Inst Medicine Natl Acad Scis Office Congressman Richard Gephardt Washington, fellow 1983-; District of Columbia Government Commission on Social Svcs, deputy commissioner, 1993-94, acting commissioner, commission on Health Care Finance, 1994-96, deputy dir, Dept of Human Svcs, 1996-97, acting commissioner, Commission on Social Svcs, 1997-. **Orgs:** Mem adv com Commn Pub Gen Hosps 1977; lectr NJ Med Sch Newark 1979-; mem acute care com Regional Health Planning Council 1980-82; mem NJ Comprehensive Health Planning Council; mem adv com Region II Health Services Mental Health Admin Comprehensive Health Planning; mem Amer Pub Health Assn; founding mem Natl Assn Pub Gen Hosps; mem Assn for Children of NJ; mem NAACP; mem Natl Council Negro Women; mem 100 Women for Integrity in Govt Baptist; Assn Am Med Colls (del); Amer Coll Hosp Adminstrs. **Honors/Awds:** Scholar Scholarship Educ and Def Fund 1964-69; Citizenship Awd Bloomfield Coll 1968; Community Service Awd Natl Council Negro Women 1978; Leadership in Health Services Awd Leaguers 1978; named Woman of Achievement Essex County Coll 1979. **Business Addr:** 645 H Street, NE, Washington, DC 20020.

BROWN, ABNER BERTRAND
Insurance representative. **Personal:** Born Jan 20, 1942, DeQuincy, LA; married Genevieve Mallet; children: Abner B Jr, Alvin D. **Educ:** Southern Univ, BA 1964; TX Southern Univ, MEd 1972, MA 1974. **Career:** TX Southern Univ, instructor 1975-77; Family Serv Ctr, marriage & family counselor 1973-83; State Farm Ins Co, insurance agent 1983-. **Orgs:** Past pres Scenicwood Civic Club 1975-77; pres North Forest ISD 1983-85; mem Amer Assn of Marriage & Family Counselors 1975-. **Military Serv:** AUS sp4 2 yrs; Good Conduct Medal; Vietnam ERA. **Home Addr:** 10500 Caxton, Houston, TX 77016.

BROWN, ADRIAN DEMOND
Professional baseball player. **Personal:** Born Feb 27, 1974, McComb, MS. **Career:** Pittsburgh Pirates, outfielder, 1997-. **Business Addr:** Professional Baseball Player, Pittsburgh Pirates, PO Box 7000, Pittsburgh, PA 15212, (412)323-5000.

BROWN, AGNES MARIE
College administrator (retired). **Personal:** Born Oct 13, 1933, North Holston, VA; daughter of Lonnie Johnson Broady and Frank Broady; married Robert Brown, Sep 19, 1960; children: Agnes, Robin. **Educ:** Virginia Union University, Richmond, VA, BS, 1955; Bowie State University, Bowie, MD, MEd, 1977. **Career:** Bowie State Univ, Bowie, MD, secretary to president, 1955-67, program coordinator, assistant director federal program, 1970-78, director of federal programs, 1978-92. **Orgs:** Member, Bowie State University Women's Assn, 1985; member, Bowie State University Alumni Assn, 1978; member, National Assn of Title III Admin, 1978-.

BROWN, ALEX
Brick mason (retired). **Personal:** Born Jun 9, 1913, Rose Hill, NC; son of Margie Carr (deceased); married Sarah Boney Brown, Apr 16, 1935; children: Gwendolyn West (deceased), Doretta B Bridgers. **Career:** US Federal Govt Camp LeJeune, NC, foreman, 35 yrs. **Orgs:** Board member, Duplin Gen Hosp; board member, James Sprunt Technical College; pres, Coastal Growers Duplin Co; treasurer, Conference of Black Mayors; chairman, deacon board, New Christian Baptist Church; board member, Legal Services and Good Neighbor Council. **Honors/Awds:** Appreciation, Dedication, James Sprunt Community College; Outstanding and Dedicated Service, NC Conference of Black Mayors, Inc; 50 years of service, church choir; Leadership, Southern States Cooperative, Inc; Devotion/Dedication Award, Duplin Co Jury Commission; Service Award, Masonic Lodge.

BROWN, ALVIN MONTERO
Physician. **Personal:** Born Jul 9, 1924, Prince George Co, VA; son of Lillian Brown and Fitzhugh Lee Brown. **Educ:** Morgan State Coll, BS 1941-45; Columbia U, MA 1947; NYU, 1953-54; Meharry Med Coll, MD 1960. **Career:** Chester Co Hosp, intern 1960-61; Phil Gen Hosp, 1962-63; NY Med Coll, resident 1963-65; NY Med Coll, asst prof 1970-71; Emory U, 1969-70; Sinai Hosp Baltimore, staff psychiatrist 1966-69; VA Hosp, asst chf 1965-66; NY Med Coll, resident physician 1963-65; Mt Carmel Mercy Hosp, physician 1972-85; MeHarry Medical College, Nashville Tennessee, consultant physical medicine and rehabilitation 1987-. **Orgs:** Mem Natl Med Assn; AMA; Amer Congress Physical Med & Rehab; Amer Acad Physical Med & Rehab; Amer Coll Sports Med; pres MI Acad Physical Med & Rehab 1979-80; MI Rheumatism Soc; bd dir MI Kenny Rehab Found 1972-; MI Rheumatism Soc; staff mem Meharry Med Coll 1965-69; Howard Univ 1967-69; Univ MD 1967-69; Emory Univ 1969-70; NY Med Coll 1970-; Wayne State Univ 1973-; consultant Rehab Med VA Hosp 1969-; Metro Soc Crippled Children & Adults 1972-; bd tst Neuromuscular Inst 1973-; mem adv bd Comprehensive Health Ctr 1974-; bd dir Met Home Health Care Serv 1976-; clinical rep Wayne State Univ 1975-; sec/treas MI Acad Physical Med & Rehab 1975-; mem MI State Bd Physical Therapy Reg 1977. **Business Addr:** Physician, 5121 Woodland Hills Drive, Brentwood, TN 37027.

BROWN, ALYCE DOSS
Educator. **Personal:** Born in Tuscaloosa, AL; daughter of Julia Doss and John A Doss (deceased); married Lelton C; children: Ouida, Kimberly. **Educ:** Tuskegee Inst, BS 1956; Med Coll of GA, MSN 1975; Nova Univ, doctor of education, 1993. **Career:** Mt Sinai Hosp, charge nurse 1956-57; Colbert County Hosp, charge nurse 1957-73; TVA, industrial nurse 1966-67; Univ of North AL, asst prof 1973-93, assoc prof of nursing, 1993-. **Orgs:** Mem Amer Nurses Assn; mem Natl League for Nurses; vice chairperson Human Rights Comm Alabama State Nurses Assn; pres Muscle Shoals Chap Tuskegee Alumni Assn 1985; dir Christian educ North Central Alabama Conf CME Church; dir of youth WK Huntsville Dist of the CME Church; member University of North Alabama Nursing Honor Society; mem, League of Women Voters; board of trustees, Colbert County-Northwest Alabama Health Care Authority; Chi Eta Phi Nursing Sorority. **Honors/Awds:** Phi Kappa Phi Hon Soc Chap 132 UNA 1977-; Lillian Holland Harvey Awd 1986-87; Martin Luther King Jr Human Relations Award, Alpha Phi Alpha Fraternity, 1987; Shoals Area Woman of the Year, Shoals Council of Women's Organizations, 1988-89. **Business Addr:** Associate Prof of Nursing, Univ of North Alabama, Box 5223, Florence, AL 35630.

BROWN, AMOS CLEOPHILUS
Clergyman. **Personal:** Born Feb 20, 1941, Jackson, MS; son of Louetta Bell Robinson-Brown and Charlie Daniel Brown Sr (deceased); married Jane Evangeline Smith; children: Amos Cleophilus Jr, David Josephus, Kizzie Maria. **Educ:** Morehouse Coll, BA 1964; Crozer Seminary, MDiv 1968; VA Seminary & Coll, DD 1984; United Theological Seminary; Doctor of Ministry, 1990. **Career:** NAACP, field sec 1960-62; St Paul Bapt Church Westchester PA, pastor 1965-70; Pilgrim Baptist St Paul MN, pastor 1970-76; Third Baptist San Francisco CA, pastor 1976-. **Orgs:** Pres MS Youth Council NAACP 1956-59, Hi-Y Clubs MS 1958-59; natl chmn NAACP Youth Dept 1960-62; chmn Amer Baptist Black Caucus 1972-80, chmn, Natl Baptist Civil Rights Comm 1982-; mem Comm Coll Gov Bd 1982-88; founding mem bd Black Amer Resp to African Crisis 1984; life member, NAACP; mem San Francisco City County Board of Supervisors, 1996-. **Honors/Awds:** Outstanding Young Man of Amer Jr Chamber of Commerce 1974-76; Martin Luther King Jr Ministerial Awd Colgate-Rochester Div School 1984; Man of the Yr San Francisco Business & Professional Women Inc 1985. **Home Addr:** 111 Lunado Way, San Francisco, CA 94127. **Business Addr:** Pastor, Third Baptist Church, 1399 McAllister, San Francisco, CA 94115.

BROWN, ANDREW J.
Clergyman. **Personal:** Born Nov 20, 1922, Duncan, MS; married Rosa Lee Nicholson. **Educ:** Bishop Coll; Moody Bible Inst; Butler U; Natchez, MS, Hon DD; Cntrl Theological Sem, DD; Urban Training Cntr Christ Mission Chgo; Wesylan Theol Sem (ch devel & mgmnt). **Career:** St John Missionary Bapt Ch, pastor 33 yrs. **Orgs:** Past pres NAACP; IN Ministerial Alliance; bd mem IN Comm Serv Cncl; Intl Christ Univ Japan; IN Urban League; pres IN Chap SCLC; reg vice pres Nat SCLC. **Honors/Awds:** Disting Man of the Yr. **Military Serv:** AUS tch sgt & acting chpln 1942-46. **Business Addr:** St John's Missionary Church, 1701 Martindale Ave, Indianapolis, IN 46202.

BROWN, ANGELA YVETTE
Journalist. **Personal:** Born Jul 4, 1964, Sacramento, CA; daughter of Ernestine Rose Hatchette Brown and Clinton Edward Brown. **Educ:** Florida State University, Tallahassee, FL, BA, Communication, 1986. **Career:** WPEC-TV, West Palm Beach, FL, production asst, 1987; WEVU-TV, Ft Myers, FL, TV news reporter, 1987-89; WCBD-TV, Charleston, SC, TV news reporter, 1989-. **Orgs:** Vice President, Broadcast SC Coastal Assn Black Journalists, 1989-; member, Natl Assn of Black Journalists, 1988-; member, Alpha Kappa Alpha Sorority, 1985-. **Honors/Awds:** Emmy, Best Newscast, Natl Academy of Television Arts & Sciences, 1989; SCC Assn Black Journalists, Founding Member, 1989; SCCAB Mentors Program, Founder, 1989. **Business Addr:** Reporter, News Department, WCBD-TV, 210 W Coleman Blvd, Mount Pleasant, SC 29464.

BROWN, ANNIE CARNELIA
Real estate investor. **Personal:** Born Jul 19, 1928, Switchback, WV; daughter of Rufus & Rozena Manns; married Samuel Leo Brown, Aug 2, 1997 (deceased); children: Samuel Jr, Carnelia Ann, Susan Leona, Reginald Lee. **Educ:** Wayne St Univ, BA 1976, Theology diploma, 1987; Wayne Cty Comm Coll, AA, 1992. **Career:** Investor. **Orgs:** Operation Get Down, 1969-72; Harambee House, 1969-72; Positive Images, 1989-. **Honors/Awds:** Ford Good Citizens Award, 1971; Wayne Cty Comm Coll, Recognition Award for Community Svc, 1973; Hon Doct of Divinity, SJ Williams School of Rel, 1991; Urban Bible Coll, Distinguished Clergy Award, 1995; Governor's Honor Roll of Volunteers, 1996.

BROWN, ANNIE GIBSON
Tax assessor & collector. **Personal:** Born Aug 12, 1944, Lexington, MS; married Charles. **Educ:** S IL U; MS Valley St Univ 1966. **Career:** Holmes Co, tax assessor/collector 1976-; pub official dep 1971-75; bookkeeper 1969-71; sec 1966-69; preschool tchr 1966. **Orgs:** PTSA Order of E Star Daughter of Elks; Assessor-Collectors Assn State & Nat; vice pres MS Hlth Serv Agency. **Business Addr:** PO Box 449, Lexington, MS 39095.

BROWN, ANTHONY
Professional football player. **Personal:** Born Nov 6, 1972, Okinawa, Japan. **Educ:** Utah. **Career:** Cincinnati Bengals, tackle, 1995-. **Business Addr:** Professional Football Player, Cincinnati Bengals, One Bengals Dr, Cincinnati, OH 45202, (513)621-3550.

BROWN, ARNOLD E.
Business management consultant. **Personal:** Born Apr 21, 1932, Englewood, NJ; son of Hortense Melle Stubbs and John Scott Brown Jr; married Lydia Barbara White, Jun 25, 1955; children: Crystal L Brown, Beverly M Brown-Fitzhugh, Dale E Brown-Davis, Arnold E Brown II. **Educ:** Bowling Green State Univ, BA 1954; Rutgers Univ Sch of Law, JD 1957. **Career:** Self-employed atty, Englewood NJ, 1957-86; Brown & Associates Consultants Inc, Englewood NJ, pres mgmt consultant firm 1986-; Alpha Communications, Inc, a discount long distance telecommunications company, president, 1992-. **Orgs:** Mem Gen Assembly NJ 1965-66; former pres Bergen Co Urban League; NAACP Bergen Co; bd mem Adv Comm Salvation Army Bergen Co; mem and former pres Kappa Theta Lambda Chap Alpha Phi Alpha Frat Inc; pres African American Business Enterprise Council of Northern New Jersey, Inc 1986-; bd mem The Applied Technology Center, Bergen Community Coll 1988-. **Home Addr:** 383 Knickerbocker Rd, Englewood, NJ 07631.

BROWN, ATLANTA THOMAS
Librarian (retired). **Personal:** Born Oct 30, 1931, Bennettsville, SC; daughter of Alice Reid Thomas and Julius A Thomas; married Samuel E Brown, Jan 30, 1965; children: Dale. **Educ:** South Carolina State University at Orangeburg, BS, 1953; University of Wisconsin at Madison, MLS, 1963. **Career:** Columbia City Schools, librarian, 1953-58; Richmond City Schools, librarian, 1958-63; Wilmington City Schools, librarian, 1963-82; Christina School District, librarian, district chair for library media, 1982-90. **Orgs:** Delaware Library Association, president, 1984-85; Delaware Association for Supervision and Curriculum Development, president, 1988-89; American Library Association, national library week committee, 1984-88; Delaware Coalition for Literacy, founder, charter member, 1985-; American Association of University Women, Millcreek Hundred Branch, charter member; American Association of School Librarians, legislative committee, public relations committees, 1984-86; New Castle County Library Advisory Board, 1982-89; Board of Directors: Ingleside Homes; Chesapeake Center: Speer Trust Commission; National Association of University Women, Wilmington Branch, president, 1994-; New Castle Presbytery, moderator, 1994-; Volunteers Against Adolescent Pregnancy; Delta Sigma Theta Sorority; National Council of Negro Women, Wilmington Section, charter member; Gander Hill Prison, volunteer librarian, 1994; Presbyterian Church, general assembly council, 1996-. **Honors/Awds:** Delaware Governor, State Advisory Council on Libraries, Appointee, 1971-75, 1983-89, State's White House Conference on Libraries, Appointee, 1990; NAACP, Wilmington Branch, Membership Award, 1979; Wilmington City Schools, Librarian of

the Year, 1970; Phi Delta Kappa; Delta Kappa Gamma Society International; Church of our Savior, Community Service Award, 1994; Amer Assn of Univ Women's Educational Foundation, Eleanor Roosevelt Fund, Recipient of a named gift Award $500, Millcreek Hundred Branch, 1996. **Special Achievements:** Tech Trends, Nov/Dec 1986; Delaware Library Association Bulletin, Winter 1986. **Home Addr:** 4502 Pickwick Dr, Wilmington, DE 19808, (302)998-0803.

BROWN, BARBARA ANN
City official & photographer. **Personal:** Born Aug 17, 1949, Lynchburg, VA. **Educ:** Phillips Bus College, AA 1967; Cortez W Peters Bus College, AA 1971. **Career:** Bur of Natl Affairs, Inc, Data Entry Operator 1971-; New York Institute of Photography, student 1983-. **Orgs:** Member/recording sect'y Mayfair Mansions Res Coun 1971-; member 6th District Police-Citizens Advisory Council 1979-; correspondeng sect'y Marshall Hghts Comm Development Organ, Inc 1983-; member Citizens Advisory Comm DC Bar 1984-; member Professional Photographers of America, Inc 1985. **Honors/Awds:** Outstanding Community Service ANC7A-Wash DC 1978-81; For Women Only Moorland-Spingarn Rsch 1983-; For Black Women Photographers Howard Univ Wash DC 1984. **Business Addr:** Chairperson, Adv Neighborhood Commission, 650 Anacostia Ave NE, Washington, DC 20019.

BROWN, BARBARA MAHONE
Educator, poet. **Personal:** Born Feb 27, 1944, Chicago, IL; daughter of Anne Savage Mahone and Loniel Atticus Mahone; married Rex Michael Brown, Nov 24, 1978; children: Letta McBain, Aisha, Imani. **Educ:** Fisk University, Nashville, TN, 1962-65; Washington State Univ, Pullman, WA, BA, 1968; University of Chicago, Chicago, IL, MBA, 1975; Stanford Univ, Stanford, CA, PhD, 1988. **Career:** Burrell Advertising, Chicago, IL, copy supervisor, 1970-73; First National Bank, Chicago, IL, advertising manager, 1975; National Broadcasting Co, New York, NY, director of planning, 1975-77; Clark College, Atlanta, GA, assoc professor of business administration, 1978-84; Univ Texas at Austin, Austin, TX, assoc professor of communication, 1988-90; San Jose State Univ, San Jose, CA, assoc professor of marketing, 1990-. **Orgs:** Board mem, Kids in Common, San Jose, CA, 1997-; trustee, Hillbrook School, Los Gatos CA, 1995-; board member, American Cancer Society Austin, TX Chapter, 1989-90; member, Society for Research in Child Development, 1987-; member, International Communication Assoc, 1987-; steering committee, U N Mid-Decade of Women, SE Regional Conference, 1980; advisory task force, Atlanta City Council Finance Committee, 1981-82; member, Organization of Black American Culture, OBAC, 1969-75. **Honors/Awds:** Founding faculty, The Fielding Institute, ODE Master's Degree program; Teacher-Scholar, San Jose State University, 1993-94; Author, "Advertising Influences on Youth", Journal of Communication Inquiry, 1990; Broadcasting: The Next Ten Years, NBC Corporate Planning, New York City, 1977; Sugarfields: Poems, Broadside Press, Detroit, MI, 1970; Writer-Researcher, "The Black Family", WMAQ-TV, Chicago, IL, 1973. **Business Addr:** Associate Professor, Marketing/QS School of Business, San Jose State University, Business Tower 750, San Jose, CA 95192-0069.

BROWN, BARRI ANNE
Anthropologist. **Personal:** Born Jan 2, 1961, New York, NY; married Kevin Moore. **Educ:** Johns Hopkins Univ, BA Biology 1982; New School for Social Rsch, MA Medical Anthropology (Hon) 1986. **Career:** Dialectical Anthropology (journal), managing editor 1984-; New School for Social Research, dept of anthropology. **Orgs:** Mem Alpha Chi Sigma Professional Chemistry Fraternity 1979-82; mem Amer Anthropological Assoc 1985-. **Honors/Awds:** Publication "The Production of Culture," published in Dialectical Anthropology Vol 10 1986.

BROWN, BEATRICE S.
Educator. **Personal:** Born Jul 14, 1950, Louisville, KY; daughter of Irene Brown and Thomas J Brown, Sr. **Educ:** Addis Ababa Univ, psychology, Ethiopia, 1990-; Cornell Univ, Cooperative Nutrition Program, PhD Doctoral/Elected Research Visiting Faculty Member, certificate, 1991; Postgraduate Ctr for Mental Health, New York, certificate, 1995. **Career:** City Coll, City Univ, NY, adjunct prof, 1990-; Upper Manhattan Mental Health Ctr, children day treatment unit dir, 1989-91; Jewish Board of Family & Children Svcs, residential treatment facility girls unit dir, 1994-; Central Brooklyn Coordinating Council Inc, mental health unit psychologist, 1997-. **Orgs:** BSB Wholistic Psychological Center, Inc, founder, dir, CEO, 1997. **Honors/Awds:** American Psychological Assn, Full Membership Status, 1995; Black Psychologists Assn, 1998. **Business Addr:** PO Box 172, Mt Vernon, NY 10552.

BROWN, BENJAMIN LEONARD
City government official. **Personal:** Born Sep 19, 1929, Baltimore, MD; divorced; children: Roslyn B Montgomery, Johanne R. **Educ:** Lincoln Univ, PA, BA, 1951; Univ of Maryland Sch of Law, LLD, 1959. **Career:** State of MD, atty private pract 1960-71; Baltimore City, deputy states atty 1971-73; Dist Court of MD, judge 1973-74; City of Baltimore, city solicitor 1974-. **Orgs:** Pres Nat Inst Muni Law Ofcrs 1983-84, bd of dir 1975-; gen cnsl Municipal Employees Credit Union of Balto City 1975-; gen cnsl MD Credit Union InsCorp 1975-; bd of dir Ideal S & L Assn 1979-; bd of dir Provident Hosp, Inc 1976-85; vice pres Baltimore City Bar Found, Inc 1982-; mem Baltimore City, MD State Nat & Monumental Bar Assns 1960-. **Honors/Awds:** Outstanding City Atty Nat Inst of Mun Law Ofcrs 1976; Outstanding Citizen Award Frederick Douglass High Sch Alumni 1979; Man of the Yr St Francis Acad1980; Cert of Appreciation Minority Bus Oppor; numerous articles & seminar presentations Committee of the Fed Exec Bd 1979-81. **Military Serv:** AUS corporal 1951-53; leadership, combat support 1951-52. **Business Addr:** City Solicitor, Baltimore City, 100 N Holliday St, City Hall Ste 101, Baltimore, MD 21202.

BROWN, BERNICE BAYNES
Educational administrator. **Personal:** Born Jun 19, 1935, Pittsburgh, PA; daughter of Henrietta Hodges Baynes and Howard Baynes; married James Brown, May 4, 1963; children: Kiyeseni Anu. **Educ:** Carnegie Mellon U, BFA 1957; Univ of Pittsburgh, MEd 1964. **Career:** Pittsburgh Public Sch, art tchr 1957-64; Carlow Coll, lecturer 1964-67; Bay Area Urban League, educ specIst 1967-68; San Fran Coll for Women, asst prof 1968-73; Lone Mountain Coll, dean of students 1973-76; The San Fran Found, program exec 1977-86; The Clorox Co, foundation administrator, 1990-91; City College of San Francisco, dean of faculty & staff development, 1991-93, educational consultant; City Coll of SF Campus, dean, 1993-. **Orgs:** Assn of Black Educ Exec; Women & Found Corporate Philanthropy; trustee San Fran Bar Assn Found; trustee Sch of the Sacred Heart; bd mem Found for Community Serv Cable TV; quarterly chairperson, board member, Commonwealth Club of CA; State Adv Comm on Black Affairs; board member, High/Scope Educational Research Foundation; board mem, Urban Economic Development Corporation, Pediatric Council, University of California, San Francisco; bd mem, Howard Thurman Educ Trust. **Honors/Awds:** Visiting Scholar Stanford Univ Stanford CA; Citizens Scholarship Foundation of America, Milestone Award; YWCA, New Generation Leadership Award. **Business Addr:** City Collge of San Francisco, 1800 Oakdale Avenue, San Francisco, CA 94124, (415)550-4347.

BROWN, BERNICE H.
Podiatrist. **Personal:** Born Aug 23, 1907, Ronceverte, WV; widowed. **Educ:** Bluefield State Coll; OH Coll Podiatric Med. **Career:** Private Pract, podiatrist. **Orgs:** Mem 4-H Club Extension Agr Housewife; act prof Negro Bus & Professional Women Assn; treas Altrusa Intl; mem Eta Phi Beta Sor; mem Civic Antioch Bapt Ch;NAACP; Urban League; Fifty-Plus Club. **Honors/Awds:** Appreciation Award Bus & Professional Club 1972. **Business Addr:** 7916 Cedar Ave, Cleveland, OH 44103.

BROWN, BERTRAND JAMES
Educational administrator. **Career:** New York City, Community School Dist 5, supt of schools, currently. **Business Addr:** Superintendent of Schools, Community School District 5, New York City, 433 W 123rd St, New York, NY 10023, (718)769-7533.

BROWN, BETTYE JEAN (BETTYE JEAN CRAWLEY)
Organizing specialist. **Personal:** Born Jan 30, 1955, Hazlehurst, GA. **Educ:** FL State Univ, BS 1976,77; GA Southwestern Coll, MEd 1983. **Career:** Jeff Davis County Bd of Educ, educator 1977-85; South GA Coll, instructor 1983; GA Assoc of Educators, uni serv dir 1985; Richmond County Assn of Educators, executive director. **Orgs:** Founder/coord Student Involvement for Black Unity 1978-85; coord Upward Bound Prog 1981-85; pres Jeff Davis Co Assn of Educators 1982-84; sec NAACP 1984; pres Jeff Davis County Clients Council 1984-88; coord Non-Urban Organizing Project 1986-; vice pres Amer Assn of Univ Women; worthy matron Order of Eastern Star; conf coord Natl Black Staff Network; mem Natl Educ Assn, Natl Council of Social Studies; vice pres Delta Sigma Theta; mem Negro Business & Professional Women; mem Bulloch 2000 Comm; sec State Human Relations Comm; monitor GA Housing Coalition Comm Develop Block Grant Prog; designed & coord progs for Amer Educ Week, World Food Day, Martin Luther King Day, Natl Teacher Day, Black History Month, Y-Club Week, Model Comm, Miss Ebony Pageant; publicspkr; Jeff Davis Co ReapportionmeComm. **Honors/Awds:** Outstanding Serv in Community Clients Council 1985; Outstanding Teacher Y Clubs Model United Nations Club 1985; Dedicated Service NAACP 1986; Outstanding Service Washington Co Assn of Educators 1986; Friend of Education Award, Washington County Association of Educators, 1989. **Home Addr:** 2652 Corning St, Hephzibah, GA 30815-9196. **Business Addr:** Executive Director, Richmond County Association of Educators, 2652 Corning St, Hephzibah, GA 30815-9196.

BROWN, BOBBY
Singer, songwriter. **Personal:** Born 1966, Boston, MA; married Whitney Houston, Jul 18, 1992; children: Bobbi Kristina Houston Brown. **Career:** Member of the singing group, New Edition, 1980-86; solo performer, 1986-; Albums: "King of Stage," 1987, "Don't Be Cruel," 1988, "Bobby," 1992; "Forever," 1998; Ghostbusters II Motion Picture Soundtrack, 1990. **Honors/Awds:** Album "Don't Be Cruel" hit number 1 on the charts, with 5 top singles, 1989. **Special Achievements:** Had four Top 5 singles, "Don't be Cruel," "Roni," "My Perogative," and "Every Little Step"; second solo album, "Don't be Cruel" hit number 1 on the charts, 1989. **Business Addr:** c/o MCA Records, 70 Universal City Plaza, Universal City, CA 91608.

BROWN, BOOKER T.
Personnel manager. **Personal:** Born Aug 10, 1950, Macon, MS. **Educ:** Forest Park Comm Coll, undergrad 1969-71; Boise St U, BSEd 1971-73. **Career:** Morrison-Knudsen Intl Co Inc, dir of recreation; ID 1st Nat Bank, loan ofcr 4 yrs. **Orgs:** Mem Optimist Club; MCU Sports Softball Team. **Honors/Awds:** Dean List Award Boise St Univ 1973; article publ in Today's Psychology 1973; Outstanding Athlete of Amer Award 1973; Most Valuable Player Basketball 1970-71 & 1971-72. **Business Addr:** Personnel Manager, Morrison-Knudson Corporation, PO Box 73, Boise, ID 83702.

BROWN, BRIAN A.
Company executive. **Personal:** Born Jul 7, 1952, Yonkers, NY; son of Demetra A Brown and William T Brown Sr (deceased); married Lorrie L Frost, 1994. **Educ:** Boston University, BA, sociology, 1976, SPC, mass comm, 1977. **Career:** Black Enterprise Magazine, director promotions, 1977-81; AT&T, industry consultant, 1980-84; IBM/ROLM, district sales director, 1984-86; Wang Labs/Intecom, vp sales, 1984-86; Promotion Marketing of America, president, 1986-. **Orgs:** 100 Black Children Inc, chairman, 1992-; Advisory Committee, NY Urban League, board member, 1992-; 100 Black Men, 1991-; Broadway Cares, Equity Fights AIDS, exec bd, 1994. **Business Addr:** President, Promotion Marketing of American, Inc, 27 W 20th St, Ste 900, New York, NY 10011, (212)633-2900.

BROWN, BUCK
Cartoonist. **Personal:** Born Feb 3, 1936, Morrison, TN; married Mary Ellen Steverson; children: Robert, Tracy Elizabeth. **Educ:** Wilson Jr Coll Chgo, AA 1962; Univ of IL, BFA 1966. **Career:** Chicago Transit Auth, bus driver 1958-63; Playboy Esquire Cavalier Tuesday Rogue Rudder & True, cartoonist 1961-. **Orgs:** Pres/founder Fat Chance Prodns Ltd; mem VP's Task Force on Youth Motivation 1968-70; mem Mag Chicago Jr C of C 1970. **Military Serv:** USAF 1955-58. **Business Addr:** c/o Playboy Magazine, 680 N Lakeshore, Chicago, IL 60611.

BROWN, BYRD R.
Attorney. **Personal:** Born Jul 26, 1929, Pittsburgh, PA; son of Wilhelmina Byrd Brown and Homer S Brown; married Barbara D Brown, Jul 13, 1987; children: Patricia Brown Stephens, Cortlyn Wilhelmina Brown. **Educ:** Yale U, BA 1951, LLB 1954. **Career:** Am Bar Assn, mem; Nat Bar Assn; Allegheny Cnty Bar Assn; Acad of Trial Lawyers of Allegheny Cnty, mem; Allegheny Cnty Bar Assn/U of Pittsburgh/Widener University Law School/Trial Advocacy, faculty mem; Lawyers Advisory Committee, former mem; US Court of Appeals for the 3rd Circuit; Disciplinary Bd of Supreme Court of PA, mem, former chair; Law Offices of Byrd R Brown, senior partner/atty at law, currently. **Orgs:** Elected to bd Pittsburgh Branch NAACP Cerca 1957; elected pres Pittsburgh NAACP Cerca 1958; pres Pittsburgh NAACP 13 yrs; founder United Negro Protest Committee; spokesman Black Construction Coalition; bd of dir Am for Democratic Action; bd of dir Centre Avenue YMCA; bd of dir Visiting Nurses Assn; charter mem Mayor's Commission on Human Resources/Community Action Pittsburgh, Inc; mem of bd Pittsburgh Brnch NAACP/AM for Democratic Action; member, distribution committee, Pittsburgh Foundation. **Military Serv:** AUS sp 2 1954-56. **Business Addr:** Senior Partner Atty at Law, Law Offices of Byrd R Brown, Homer S Brown Building, 515 Court Pl, Pittsburgh, PA 15219.

BROWN, BYRON WILLIAM
Government official. **Personal:** Born Sep 24, 1958, New York, NY; son of Clarice Kirnon Brown and Byron Brown; married Michelle Austin Brown, May 25, 1990; children: Byron William II. **Educ:** State University of New York, College at Buffalo, NY, BA, journalism & political science, 1983, MS (in progress), 1989-. **Career:** City of Buffalo, Council President's Office, Buffalo, NY, executive secretary to council pres, 1984-86; Erie County Legislature Chairman's Office, Buffalo, NY, news secretary/executive assistant, 1986-88; State of New York Deputy Speaker's Office, Buffalo, NY, director of public relations, 1986-88; County of Erie, Division of Equal Employment Opportunity, Buffalo, NY, director, 1988-. **Orgs:** Vice president, board of directors, St Augustine's Center, 1989-; member, Western New York Public Broadcasting Board of Trustee, 1990-; assistant scout leader, Boy Scouts of America, Troop #84, 1991-; mentor, Buffalo Public School #38 Chamber of Commerce, 1991-; member, Rho Lambda Chapter Alpha Phi Alpha Fraternity, 1984-; judge, ACT-SO, NAACP, 1989-. **Honors/Awds:** Martin Luther King, Jr Award, Alpha Phi Alpha Fraternity, 1984; Selected to Participate in Leadership Buffalo, Buffalo Chamber of Commerce, 1988; Black Achiever in Industry, 1490 Enterprises Inc, 1988; Selected for Ebony Magazine Article "30 Leaders of the Future", Ebony Magazine, 1989; Selected for Business Study Exchange in Central America, Rotary International, 1990. **Business Addr:** Director, Div of Equal Employment Opportunity, County of Erie, 95 Franklin St, Room 278, Buffalo, NY 14202.

BROWN, CALVIN ANDERSON, JR.
Physician (retired). **Personal:** Born Sep 13, 1931, Athens, GA; son of C A Brown Sr; married Joy San Walker; children: Joi-Sanne, SannaGai. **Educ:** Morehouse Coll, BBS 1952; Meharry Med Coll, MD 1958. **Career:** Hubbard Hosp Nashville, intern 1958-59; specialized family practice 1959; Atlanta Southside Comprehensive Health Ctr, dir 1968; Pineview Convalescent Ctr Atlanta, med dir 1968-74; Holy Family Hosp, Hughes Spalding Hosp Atlanta, mem staff; Martin Luther King Jr Nursing Ctr, chief of staff 1971-73; Fulton County Jails, chief physician 1971-83; Atlanta City Jail, chief physician 1980-85; Hughes Spalding Hosp Atlanta, dir of emergency room 1984-86. **Orgs:** Pres Natl Alumni Assn Morehouse Coll 1962-72; trustee Morehouse Coll 1969-89; vchmn, bd trustees Morehouse Medical School, 1975-89; asst prof preventive med Emory Univ Med School 1968-69; mem Task Force on Cardiovascular Disease Hypertension & Diabetes GA Reg Med Prog 1971; mem Atlanta Med Assoc; mem Alpha Phi Alpha 1975; vice chmn bd of trustees Morehouse Coll 1975-89; pres Kappa Boule of Sigma Pi Phi Frat 1983-84. **Honors/Awds:** Honorary Doctor of Science, Morehouse Coll 1987. **Special Achievements:** First African American on the faculty of Emory Medical School, 1968. **Military Serv:** AUS 1952-54. **Business Addr:** 1123 R D Abernathy Blvd SW, Atlanta, GA 30310.

BROWN, CARL ANTHONY
Company executive. **Personal:** Born Apr 29, 1930, Philadelphia, PA; son of Louise Somers West and Percy Brown; married Kathleen Smith, Mar 10, 1956; children: William C Brown, Carl A Brown, Jr, Michael Brown. **Educ:** Temple Univ, Philadelphia, PA, AB, Math, 1955, MA, Math, 1957, MA, Physics, 1960, doctoral studies, 1960-66. **Career:** Keystone Computer Assoc Inc, Ft Washington, PA, gen mgr div; Onyx Enterprises Inc, Palisades Park, NJ, pres, 1968-69; Kappa Systems Inc, Paoli, PA, program mgr, 1969-71; Amer Technical Assistance Corp, McLean, VA, pres, 1971-74; JRB Assoc Inc, McLean, VA, vice pres, 1974-76; Mandex Inc, Springfield, VA, CEO, 1976-. **Orgs:** Past president, Black Presidents' Roundtable Assn 1979-.

BROWN, CAROL ANN
Educator. **Personal:** Born Jan 25, 1952, Ann Arbor, MI; married Marcellus B Brown; children: Brandon, Marc, Adam. **Educ:** Univ of MI, bachelors 1974, masters 1975. **Career:** Ann Arbor Public Schls, instrumental music instr 1974-75; Joliet Public Schls, coordinator of music 1975-82; Augustana College, asst dean of student services 1982-. **Orgs:** Visiting Nurse Homemaker Assoc, bd of directors 1985-; Delta Sigma Theta, Inc Moline Davenport Alumnae, president 1985-, member 1972-; Sounds of Peace Ensemble, member 1984-; Zonta Interntl, member 1983-. **Honors/Awds:** Outstanding Serv Awd Delta Sigma Theta, Inc 1985; Apprecian Awd Black Student Union, Augustana Coll 1983-85, Joliet Band Parents Assoc 1982, Joliet OrchParents Assoc 1982; Honorary Membership Ladies of Vital Essence Club 1984; Outstanding Service Awd Parent Teacher Assoc 1980. **Business Addr:** Asst Dean of Student Services, Augustana College, Founders Hall 115, Rock Island, IL 61201.

BROWN, CAROLYN M.
Purchasing agent. **Personal:** Born Oct 12, 1948, Seattle, WA; divorced; children: Cesha, Channelle, Clifton. **Educ:** Anderson Coll, BA major speech educ, sociology, minor educ 1970; Ball State Univ, MA speech educ, Commun 1976; Univ of Berkeley, grad work educ; numerous educ & training seminars. **Career:** Indianapolis Publ School, teacher 1970-71; Delco Remy, clerk 1971, secy 1971-72, supv 1972-75, buyer 1975-83, sr buyer 1983-86, genl supv central stores 1986-. **Orgs:** Mem IN Reg Minority Purchasing Council 4 yrs; bd mem Natl Minority Supplier Devel Council 3 yrs; bd mem Channel 49; chairperson Telesale 2 yrs; TV personality 2 yrs; mem Women of the Church of God 3 yrs; alumni dir Anderson Coll 2 yrs; mem Ball State Alumni Assoc 5 yrs; capt Telethon Night Drive 3 yrs; mem The Christian Center, Alpha Kappa Alpha, Alpha Psi Omega; mayoral appointed educ comm Blue Ribbon; mem Madison County Fine Arts Council, Urban League of Madison County 9 yrs; bd dir United Way 6 yrs, United Cerebral Palsy 4 yrs; mem NAACP 7 yrs; mem Natl Republican Comm, Career Guild Assoc 4 yrs, Amer Business Women of Amer 5 yrs; dir Youth Choir 10 yrs; Sunday School teacher 12 yrs; mem Kodiakanal/Woodstock Found 15 yrs; mrm Smithsonian Assoc 2 yrs; fellow, sponsorAnderson Coll; memship drive person Community Concert Series 3 yrs; mem IN Black Expo Inc 2 yrs; sponsor Theada Club of Anderson Coll 2 yrs; judge Black Ball State Pageant 3 yrs; Jr Miss of Madison County 2 times. **Honors/Awds:** Sequentennial Queen 3rd Place; William B Harper Awd for Outstanding Community Serv to Madison County; Outstanding Young Woman of Amer 3 times; Outstanding Black of Amer 2 times; Outstanding Elementary Teacher of Amer; President's Awd Urban League of Madison County; Outstanding Conference Leader-NAACP Natl Convention in Anderson IN; Outstanding Lady of the Day AME Church Anderson IN; nom for Professional Achievers Awd; IN Reg Minority Supplier Development Council Achievement Awd; Natl Supplier of the Year Buyer Recognition Awd. **Business Addr:** General Supervisor, Delco Remy Div of Gen Motors, 2401 Columbus Ave, Anderson, IN 46012.

BROWN, CAROLYN THOMPSON
Library administrator. **Personal:** Born May 18, 1943, Brooklyn, NY; daughter of Frank & Martha Thompson; divorced; children: Christopher Leslie, Michael Arthur Brown. **Educ:** Cornell University, BA, 1965, MA, 1968; The American University, PhD, 1978. **Career:** Howard University, asst prof, dept of english, 1978-84, assoc prof, English Dept, 1984-91, assoc dean for the Humanities, 1988-90; Library of Congress, dir of Educational Services, 1990-92, assoc librarian for cultural affairs, 1992-. **Orgs:** Amer Library Assn, agency representative, 1990-; Assn for Asian Studies. **Honors/Awds:** Cornell University, Cornell Natl Fellowship, 1961-65; Natl Defence Foreign Language, 1965-67; The American University, Graduate Honor Fellowship, 1975-78; Howard University, Faculty Research Grant, 1980, 1986. **Special Achievements:** Writer, Dramatic Production "Goin' Home," 1981. **Business Addr:** Associate Librarian, Cultural Affairs, Library of Congress, 101 Independence Ave., SE, LM 605, Washington, DC 20540-8000, (202)707-1551.

BROWN, CARROLL ELIZABETH
Appointed official, business executive. **Personal:** Born Aug 31, 1942, Ft Worth, TX; married Ralph Theodore Brown Sr; children: Ralph Jr, Erik, Shawn. **Educ:** Seattle Univ, 1960-63. **Career:** WADS Radio "Breakfast for Two," radio talk show hostess, 1976; TRW-Geometric Tool, personal asst, 1978-81; Capital Temporaries Inc, placement mgr, 1980-84; Shubert Theater, group sales assoc and community relations liaison, 1984-85; Connecticut Business Institute, placement director, 1985; Stone Academy, placement director, 1986-90; New Haven Convention & Visitors Bureau, director of visitors services and administration, 1990-91; Legislative Asst to the Labor Committee, 1992-93; Spokeswoman for Chief Quiet Hawk of the Paugussett Indian Tribe, temporary/part-time, 1993-94. **Orgs:** City of West Haven, bd of finance, 1992-; Connecticut State NAACP, 1st vice president, 1991-; Citizens Television Board of Directors, Personnel Committee, 1991-; American Natl Bank Advisory Bd, 1991-; Peabody Museum, board of dirs, 1990-91; Yale-New Haven Hospital Annual Appeal Committee, 1990-; Inner-City Advertiser, advisory bd, 1990-; 1st Vice President of the Greater New Haven NAACP, 1990-; 2nd Vice President of the Connecticut State NAACP, 1987-91; YWCA Board of Director, 1987-89; YWCA Ballroom Restoration Committee, 1987-89; West Haven High Parents Club, 1987-88; Founder/President of the West Haven Black Coalition, Inc, 1986-. **Honors/Awds:** Nominee Jefferson Awd Community Serv 1975; Mrs Connecticut Second Runner-Up 1983; Outstanding Volunteer of the Year Bridgeport Public School System 1982-85; Omega Psi Phi Fraternity, District Citizen of the Year Award, 1994, Local Citizen of the Year Award, 1993; Elm City Business and Professional Women's Assn, Community Service Award, 1993; Connecticut State NAACP, Benjamin L Hooks Outstanding Leadership Award, 1992; Dixwell United Church of Christ, Outstanding Member Award, 1990; Professional and Business Assn of Greater New Haven, Civic/Community Service Award, 1988; Nominated for Jefferson Awards, 1987; West Haven High School, Black Family Achievement Award, 1985.

BROWN, CARRYE BURLEY
Federal official. **Personal:** Born in Palestine, TX; married Larry; children: Two. **Career:** US Fire Administration, administrator, currently. **Special Achievements:** First woman and the first African American to head the US Fire Administration. **Business Addr:** Administrator, US Fire Administration, 16825 S Seton Ave, Emmitsburg, MD 21727.

BROWN, CHADWICK EVERETT
Professional football player. **Personal:** Born Jul 12, 1970, Pasadena, CA; married Kristin, Jun 11, 1994; children: Amani. **Educ:** Colorado, degree in marketing. **Career:** Pittsburgh Steelers, linebacker, 1993-96; Seattle Seahawks, 1997-; Pro Exotics, owner. **Business Addr:** Professional Football Player, Seattle Seahawks, 11220 NE 53rd St, Kirkland, WA 98033, (206)827-9777.

BROWN, CHARLES EDWARD
Educator, research scientist. **Personal:** Born Sep 7, 1948, Buckingham, VA; son of Gretchen H Jackson Brown and Warren G H Brown; married Sadie Banks Brown, Dec 5, 1970; children: Karen Denise, Carla Denette. **Educ:** Virginia State University, Petersburg, VA, BS, geology, 1971; The Pennsylvania State University, State College, PA, MS, geology, 1974, PhD, 1976. **Career:** Chevron Oil, USA, exploration geologist, 1976-78; Virginia State University, Petersburg, VA, assistant professor, 1978-80; US Geological Society, Reston, VA, research hydrologist, 1980-; George Mason University, Fairfax, VA, commonwealth professor, 1988-90. **Orgs:** Member, Society of Exploration Geophysicists, 1985-; member, Geological Society of America, 1980-; member, American Geophysical Union, 1985-; member, National Association of Black Geologists and Geophysicists, 1983-. **Honors/Awds:** Phi Kappa Phi Honor Society, Pennsylvania State University, 1974. **Home Addr:** 15094 Wetherburn Dr., Centreville, VA 22020. **Business Addr:** Hydrologist, Water Resources Div, US Geological Survey, Dept of the Interior, Mail Stop 431, National Center, Reston, VA 22091.

BROWN, CHARLES SUMNER
Clergyman. **Personal:** Born Sep 18, 1937, Plant City, FL; married Joan Marie Steed; children: Charles Jr, Gene Mitchell. **Educ:** Morehouse Coll, AB 1956; United Theol Seminary, MDiv (Cum Laude) 1962; Boston Univ Sch of Theol, ThD 1973. **Career:** Wright-Patterson Air Force Base, mathematician fluid dynamics rsch branch 1956-59; Sheldon St Congregation Church Providence, pastor 1964-66; Ebenezer Bapt Ch Boston, interim pastor 1966-67; United Theol Seminary, prof of church & soc 1968-79; Yale Univ Divinity Sch, assoc prof of practical theol (w/tenure) 1979-83; Bethel Baptist Ch, pastor. **Orgs:** Sec The Soc for the Study of Black Religion 1978-; voluntary assoc prof Dept of Medicine in Soc Wright State Univ Med Sch 1984-; bd mem United Wayof Greater Dayton 1984-, Family Serv Assoc 1984-, Dayton Council on World Affairs 1985-, Dayton Art Institute 1986-; pres Metro Churches United 1986-; moderator Western Union Bapt Dist Assoc 1986-. **Honors/Awds:** Ford Foundation Early Admission Scholarship to Morehouse Coll; Protestant Fellowship Awd Fund for Theol Educ 1961-62; Presbyterian Grad Fellowship United Presby Church USA 1966-67; ATS Basic Rsch Grant for Theol Sch 1975-76; mem Kappa Alpha Psi Frat, Sigma Pi Phi Boule. **Home Addr:** 625 Ridgedale Rd, Dayton, OH 45406. **Business Addr:** Pastor, Bethel Baptist Church, 401 South Summit St, Dayton, OH 45407.

BROWN, CHARLIE
City official. **Personal:** Born Mar 8, 1938, Williston, SC; son of Ruth A Hickson Brown and Charlie Brown Jr. **Educ:** Cheyney State College, BS; Indiana University-Northwest, MPA, 1982. **Career:** Gary IN Public Schools, teacher, 1961-68; Gary Youth Services Bureau, dir until 1983; General Assembly, state representative, 1983-95; City of Gary, Gary IN, affirmative action officer and risk manager, 1988; Gary Comm Mental Health Center, CEO, 1993; consultant, currently. **Orgs:** Mem bd of dir, National Civil Rights Museum and Hall of Fame. **Home Addr:** 9439 Lake Shore Dr, Gary, IN 46403.

BROWN, CHAUNCEY I., JR.
Housing director (retired). **Personal:** Born Oct 8, 1928, Paterson, NJ; married Betty; children: Cheryl, Porchia, Chauncey III, Clifford W. **Educ:** Electronic Tech Inst, Los Angeles, 1952; Rutgers Univ, 1971; NJ Public Serv Inst, 1972; William Paterson Coll. **Career:** City of Paterson, dir of community serv, 1968-70, Action Now dir 1970-75, dep dir & CETA 1976-78, dep dir of housing 1978-85. **Orgs:** Co committeeman Dem Orgin of Passaic Co; scout m Troop #23 First AME Zion Ch; founder & pres SECA Orgin; Sgt of arms Rotary of Paterson; numerous others mem, Oldtimer's Assn; bd of dirs Boy's Club; hon mem Bros in Blue Paterson Police Dept; mem, Paterson Catholic School. **Honors/Awds:** Special Award for Community Serv Oldtimer's Assn; Coaches Award, & Oldtimer's Jr Football League; Dedication to Youth Award, CETA Summer Program, 1976-77; honors by numerous religious & community assns. **Military Serv:** USN, MMM 3/C, 2 Yrs. **Home Addr:** 570 11th Ave, Paterson, NJ 07514.

BROWN, CHRIS (JOHN CHRISTOPHER)
Professional baseball player (retired). **Personal:** Born Aug 15, 1961, Jackson, MS; children: John Jr. **Career:** San Francisco Giants, infielder, 1984-87; San Diego Padres, infielder, 1987-88; Detroit Tigers, infielder, 1989. **Honors/Awds:** Led all NL third basemen with a .971 fielding percentage 1985; named to the Topps and Baseball Digest's All Rookie Squads 1985; National League All-Star Team, 1986. **Home Addr:** 5015 Brighton Ave, Los Angeles, CA 90062.

BROWN, CHRISTOPHER C.
Judge. **Personal:** Born Nov 20, 1938, Pontiac, MI; son of Ardelia Christopher Brown and Arthur Patrick Brown; married Lillian Jean Twitty, Jun 19, 1966; children: Alesa Bailey, Tice Christopher Brown. **Educ:** Wayne State Univ, BA 1962; Detroit Coll of Law, JD 1966. **Career:** Private practice, attorney 1966-73; 50th Dist Ct City of Pontiac, judge 1973-. **Orgs:** Mem NAACP, Urban League, Amer Bar Assn; MI Bar Assn; Wolverine Bar Assn; Oakland Bar Assn; Natl Bar Assn. **Business Addr:** Judge, 50th Judicial Dist, 70 N Saginaw St, Pontiac, MI 48342.

BROWN, CHUCKY (CLARENCE)
Professional basketball player. **Personal:** Born Feb 29, 1968, New York, NY. **Educ:** North Carolina State Univ. **Career:** Cleveland Cavaliers, forward, 1989-91; Los Angeles Lakers, 1991-92; New Jersey Nets, 1992-93; Dallas Mavericks, 1993; Panna Firenze (Italy), 1992-93; Grand Rapid Hoops (CBA), 1993-94; Yakima Sun Kings (CBA), 1994-95; Houston Rockets, 1995-96; Phoenix Suns, 1996; Milwaukee Bucks, 1996-97; Atlanta Hawks, 1997-. **Special Achievements:** NBA, Championship, 1995; CBA, All-League first team, 1995. **Business Addr:** Professional Basketball Player, Atlanta Hawks, One CNN Center, Ste 405, Atlanta, GA 30335, (404)827-3800.

BROWN, CINDY
Professional basketball player. **Personal:** Born Mar 16, 1965. **Educ:** Long Beach State. **Career:** Sidis Ancona (Italy), forward, 1987-88; Toshiba Yana Gi Cho (Japan), 1988-92; Faenza

Errieti Club (Italy), 1992-94; Elitzur Holon (Israel), 1994-96; US Valenciennes Orchies (France); Detroit Shock, 1998-. **Special Achievements:** Won a gold medal with the US Olympic Basketball Team, 1988. **Business Addr:** Professional Basketball Player, Detroit Shock, The Palace of Auburn Hills, 2 Championship Dr, Auburn Hills, MI 48326, (248)377-0100.

BROWN, CLARENCE WILLIAM
Personnel administrator (retired). **Personal:** Born Mar 8, 1933, Lakewood, NJ; son of Madeline Bishop Brown and William Brown; married Alberta L Hardy; children: Patricia, Valerie F. **Educ:** New Mexico Western Coll, Cert Admin, 1951; Rutgers Univ, Cert Bd of Educ, 1969; Univ of Arizona, Tucson, Cert Early Child Educ, 1970. **Career:** Naval Air Engineering Ctr, dep equal employment oppor, retired, 1989. **Orgs:** Chmn Citizens Adv Bd Lakewood Housing Auth 1960-66; chmn Better Community Assn of Lakewood 1960-64; pres Ocean Co Chap of NAACP 1961-66; cent Jersey Youth Adv NJ State NAACP 1963-65; chmn Lakewood Econ Action Pgm 1966-76; bd of dir Ocean Co Econ Action Now Inc 1967-72; vice pres Lakewood Bd of Educ 1969-76; mem EOF Bd Georgian Ct Coll 1974-76; adv bd Ocean Co Coll 1976-; v chmn & mem Lakewood Comm Sch Bd; mem Naval Civilian Admin Assn. **Honors/Awds:** Man of the Yr Negro Bus & Professional Womens Assn 1971; Man of the Yr Lakewood C of C 1973; Meritorious Serv Award Lakewood Bd of Educ 1976; Outstand Serv & Contrib Lakewood Econ Action Pgm Inc 1976; 1st Black Elected to Bd of Educ in Ocean Co Lakewood, NJ. **Military Serv:** USAF A/2c 1951-55; Meritorious Civilian Service Award, Dept of the Navy 1989. **Home Addr:** 932 Somerset Ave, Lakewood, NJ 08701.

BROWN, CLARICE ERNESTINE
Accountant (retired). **Personal:** Born Jun 8, 1929, Toledo, OH; daughter of Margaret Durham (deceased) and Robert Durham (deceased); married Bud Luther Brown; children: Gregory, Babette Jackson, Jocelyn. **Educ:** Roosevelt Univ, BS Business Admin 1965; DePaul Univ, attended; Cortez Business Coll, attended. **Career:** US Treasury IRS, internal revenue agent 1960-84; Iota Phi Lambda Sorority Inc, past natl pres. **Orgs:** Leader, 1st vice pres of bd 1977-73, pres 1977-81; Girl Scouts 1964-81; pres 1973-71, parliamentarian 1985, Alpha Beta Chap Iota Phi Lambda; natl pres Iota Phi Lambda 1981-83; natl finance sec Top Ladies of Distinction 1985-88; mem NAACP, Oper PUSH 1985; court 142 jr daughter counselor, counselor for Catholic girls 7-18 Knights of St Peter Claver Ladies Aux 1985. **Honors/Awds:** Fed Employee of the Year 1967; Outstanding Women St Columbanus 1972; St Anne's Medal 1973; Mother of the Year 1974; Volunteer of the Year; nominee for Aldermans Awd 1982; Cardinals Awd Parish Awd 1983; honoree Alpha Gamma Pi; citations from WAIT & WBEE; Albert Gallatin Awd Treasury Dept US Govt; Mary McCleod Bethune National Council of Negro Women, Pacesetter Award, 1992. **Home Addr:** 9134 S Lowe Ave, Chicago, IL 60620.

BROWN, CLARK S.
Business executive. **Personal:** Born in Roanoke, VA; married Macie E; children: Clark Jr, John T. **Educ:** City Coll NY, attending; Renouard Coll of Embalming NY, 1930. **Career:** Real estate broker; Clark S Brown & Sons Funeral Home, pres. **Orgs:** Mem Most Worshipful Grand Lodge Prince Hall Masons, ABC Bd of NC; former mem, bd trustees NC Central Univ; bd mem Central Orphanage of NC, Salvation Army, Retail Merchants Assoc; former vchmn Dem Party of Forsyth Cty NC; former chmn Civil Preparedness Adv Council; bd trustees Shaw Univ Raleigh; bd trustees, Winston Salem State Univ; former bd, Governors Univ, NC. **Business Addr:** President, Clark S Brown & Sons Funeral, 727 N Patterson Ave, Winston-Salem, NC 27101.

BROWN, CLAUDELL, JR.
Association executive. **Personal:** Born Jun 8, 1949, Jackson, TN; married Linda Ruth Brogden. **Educ:** Lane Coll, BA. **Career:** Happy Children Multi-Svc, Center, Happy Children Day-Care, Inc, dir; Tipton Co Sch Sys, tchr 5th Grade 1974; Lane Coll, french tutor; WH Jones, prof;Bur of Comm & Relations, teen counselor 1969-71; Lane Coll, tutor, English, French Black Literature. **Orgs:** Upward Bound Proj, 1969-70; vp, Shelby Co Dem Voters Council; Precinct 40-2, 1974; bd dirs, Mid-South Med Cntrs Council, 1973; bd dirs, Memphis-Shelby Co Legal Serv Assn, 1973; comm adv com, Memphis-Shelby Co Legal Serv Assn 1973; Chelsea Comm coord com, 1972; Memphis Comm Singers, Inc; Nat Social Workers of Am, 1972; soc serv coord, dep dir Memphis-Shelby Co Comm Action Agency; Chelsea Nghbrhd Serv Cntr, 1972; Prog Rep, US Dept of Health, St Louis, 1971; Memphis Chpt, Lane Coll Alumni Assn, 1971; Basileus, Theta Iota Chap of Omega Psi Phi, Frat Inc, 1973-74; aptd to Pres & Adv Com to Slective Serv Bd of Tn, Operation PUSH, 1972; mem NAACP; Concert Choir; Pre-Alumni Club; Student Christian Assn; French Club; Social Sci Club; Student Tribune. **Business Addr:** 709 Keel Ave, Memphis, TN.

BROWN, CLIFFORD ANTHONY
Business executive, educational administrator. **Personal:** Born Sep 9, 1951, Danville, KY; son of Elizabeth Brown and Frank Brown; married Mary Margaret; children: John C Pollock, Marilyn F, Clifford A Jr, Jason T. **Educ:** Northwood Inst, Assoc in Bus Mgmt 1971; Eastern MI Univ, BBA Accounting 1973. **Career:** Arthur Young & Co, audit staff/sr 1973-78, audit mgr 1979-82; Widger Chem Corp, vice-pres finance 1982-83, exec vice-pres 1983-84; Arthur Young & Co, principal, 1987-90; CAB Industries, Inc, pres 1984-86, 1990-; Detroit Public School System, Office of Internal Audit, director, currently. **Orgs:** Past President Detroit Chap Natl Assn of Black Accountants 1979-81; dir tech affairs National Association Black Accountants 1982; dir long range planning National Association Black Accountants 1984; cert pub accountant State of MI 1975-; membership comm MI Association of Certified Public Accountant 1975-; mem Amer Inst of Certified Public Accountant, 1975-; chmn Downtown Detroit YMCA 1989-91; national dir, National Association of Black Accountants 1982-; Macomb Comm Coll Accounting Curriculum Advisory Comm 1983-; natl dir Natl Assoc of Black Accts, responsible for professional chap admin; chairman, Downtown Detroit YMCA, 1990-91; executive committee member, finance chairperson, Diversified Youth Services, 1990-91; Michigan Minority Business Development Council, finance committee, 1989; Franklin Wright Settlements, treasurer, 1990. **Honors/Awds:** College of Business, honors student, 1972, 1973; Outstanding member Natl Assn of Black Accountants 1982; achievement awd Natl Assn of Black Accountants 1983; minority achievers awd Detroit Metropolitan YMCA 1984. **Business Addr:** President, CAB Industries Inc, 15400 Gratiot, Detroit, MI 48205.

BROWN, CLIFTON GEORGE
Journalist. **Personal:** Born Sep 3, 1959, Philadelphia, PA; son of Maurita Robinson Brown and George Alexander Brown; married Carolyn Martin Brown (divorced 1987); children: Ashley Georgia, Alexander William; married Delores Jones Brown, 1991. **Educ:** Howard University, Washington, DC, 1977-79; Temple University, Philadelphia, PA, 1979-81. **Career:** Boca Raton News, Boca Raton, FL, sportswriter, 1981-83; Detroit Free Press, Detroit, MI, sportswriter, 1983-88; New York Times, New York, NY, sportswriter, 1988-. **Orgs:** Member, National Association of Black Journalists, 1983-. **Honors/Awds:** Second Place Feature Writing, Florida Sports Writer's Association, 1983. **Business Addr:** Sports Writer, The New York Times, 229 W 43rd St, 4th Floor, New York, NY 10036.

BROWN, CONELLA COULTER
Educator (retired). **Personal:** Born Sep 26, 1925, Kansas City, MO; daughter of Carrie Davis Coulter and Charles P Coulter; married Arnold A Brown, Mar 25, 1956. **Educ:** Kansas City Conservatory of Mus, 1949; Univ of Missouri, BA 1953; Case Western Reserve University, MA 1961; Lincoln University; Ohio University; Cleveland State University; Bowling Green State University. **Career:** Ford Fnd Proj, coor in area of curr devel 1963-64; Cleveland Pub Sch, Cleveland OH, social studies teacher 1954-63, asst principal, Rawlings Jr HS, 1964-65, asst supervisor, office of human relations, 1965-66, admin asst to supt ofc of hum rel 1966-72, asst supt 1972-80. **Orgs:** Former mem adv com Sch of Dent; mem vis com stud afrs Cs Wstrn Rsrv U; Delta Kappa Gamma; Am Assn of Sch Admin; Nat Assn for Supv & Curr Devel; bd dir Chrstn Chldrn Fund; bd tst Free Med Clin of Gtr Clvlnd; NAACP; Delta Sigma Theta; Urban Leag of Gtr Clvlnd; mem, trust St James AME Church; hon mem, Phi Delta Kappa; Advisory Board, Accord Associates Inc, 1980-. **Honors/Awds:** Professional Awd for Leadership in Educ Cleveland Bus & Professional Women 1973; Outstanding Achievement Awd in Educ Cuyahoga Comm Coll 1973; Hon Life Mem Cleveland Council of Parent Teacher Assn 1974; 1st Woman Asst Supt of major OH School Dist; 1st Pres Awd Urban League of Greater Cleveland; Distinguished Educator Award, St James AME Church; ''Conella Coulter Brown Day,'' City of Cleveland, and Tribute from US Rep Louis Stokes, March 5, 1989.

BROWN, CONSTANCE CHARLENE
Government official. **Personal:** Born Jun 12, 1939, Chicago, IL; daughter of Myrtle V Jones Porter-King and Charles W Porter; married Leon Paul Brown, Nov 21, 1959 (died 1984); children: Paul Gerard, Donna Elise, Venita Charlene. **Educ:** National Louis University, Evanston, IL, BA (with honors), 1985. **Career:** Municipal Tuberculosis (Sanitarium), Chicago, IL, clerk, 1963-65; Dept of Water, Chicago, IL, principal clerk, 1965-70; Dept of Housing, Chicago, IL, asst commissioner, 1970-. **Orgs:** Member, Altrusa Club of Chicago, IL, Inc, Altrusa International, Inc, 1990; pledgee, Iota Phi Lambda Sorority, Alpha Beta Chapter, 1991; member, National Assn of Females Executives, 1990; member, National Assn of Housing & Redevelopment Officials, 1985. **Business Addr:** Assistant Commissioner, City of Chicago-Dept of Housing, 318 S Michigan St, 6th Fl, Chicago, IL 60604.

BROWN, CONSTANCE YOUNG
Educator. **Personal:** Born Aug 4, 1933, Leonardtown, MD. **Educ:** Morgan State Coll, BS (cum laude) 1955; Univ of MD, MEd 1960, Masters plus 60 1973. **Career:** Western Placement Serv Bd of Educ, Baltimore County, mgr, 1974-; Bd of Educ Baltimore County, data processing instructor, 1971-74, distributive educ teacher & coord, 1969-71, business educ teacher, 1955-69. **Orgs:** Mem TABCO; mem MSTA; mem NEA; mem MVA; former sec/treas MADECA; pres Anne Arundel Co Br NAACP 1973-76, treas 1977-; 1st vice pres MD St Conf NAACP 1974-; basileus Delta Pi Omega Chap Alpha Kappa Alpha Sor 1977-80; Corresponding sec Southgate Comm Assn 1973-; anti-basileus Delta Pi Omega Chap Alpha Kappa Alpha Sor 1974-76; life mem NAACP; mem Nat Nom Com NAACP 1980. **Honors/Awds:** DAR Award Citizenship 1950; Trustee & Senatoral Schlrshp Morgan State Coll; Plaque Who's Who in Human Resources; Dr Carl Murphy Award MD State Conf of BrNAACP 1974; NAACP Award Anne Arundel Co Br 1977; Hon 1st Women's Conf NY Naacp 1980; certs Gov of MD Mayor of Annapolis/Anne Arundel Co Exec.

BROWN, CORNELL DESMOND
Professional football player. **Personal:** Born Mar 15, 1975; son of Reuben Sr and Oglessa. **Educ:** Virginia Tech, attended. **Career:** Baltimore Ravens, linebacker, 1997-. **Business Addr:** Professional Football Player, Baltimore Ravens, 11001 Owings Mills Blvd, Owings Mills, MD 21117, (410)654-6200.

BROWN, CORRINE
Congresswoman. **Personal:** Born Nov 11, 1946, Jacksonville, FL; married Shantrel. **Educ:** Florida A&M University, BS, 1969; University of Florida, EdS, 1974. **Career:** Edward Waters College, University of Florida, educator; Florida House of Representatives, district 17, state rep, 1983-92; United States House of Representatives, 3rd district, Florida, rep, 1993-. **Orgs:** United States House of Representatives Committees: Public Works and Tranportation, Veterans' Affairs; Sigma Gamma Rho; Phi Delta Kappa. **Special Achievements:** National Democratic Convention, delegate, 1988. **Business Addr:** Representative, US House of Representatives, 1037 Longworth House Office Bldg, Washington, DC 20515-0903, (202)225-0123.

BROWN, CORWIN ALAN
Professional football player. **Personal:** Born Apr 25, 1970, Chicago, IL. **Educ:** Univ of Michigan, attended. **Career:** New England Patriots, defensive back, 1993-96; New England Patriots, 1997-. **Business Addr:** Professional Football Player, New York Jets, 1000 Fulton Ave, Hempstead, NY 11550, (516)560-8100.

BROWN, COSTELLO L.
Educator. **Personal:** Born Oct 16, 1942, Mebane, NC; married Florida; children: Eric, Ninita. **Educ:** Hampton Inst, BS 1963; IA State U, MS 1966, PhD 1968; Univ of IL, Postdoctoral 1969. **Career:** CA State Univ, asst prof, 1969-72, assoc prof, 1972-77, prof of Chemistry, 1977-; Univ of GA, visiting prof, 1972-; CA Inst of Technology, visiting fac assoc, 1975. **Orgs:** Mem S CA Section Am Chem Soc; exec com Sigma Xi Hon Soc; Am Chem Soc. **Honors/Awds:** Woodrow Wilson Fellow 1963; Nat Inst Hlth Postdoctoral Fellowship 1969; NIH Marc Fellowship & Career Devel Award 1975. **Business Addr:** Director, Natl Science Foundation, Career Access Program, 1800 G St, NW, Washington, DC 20550.

BROWN, COURTNEY COLERIDGE
Director. **Personal:** Born Jul 29, 1924, New York, NY; married; children: Beverly, Courtney Jr. **Educ:** Shaw U, BA 1954. **Career:** NY State Div of Human Rights, dir, reg dir, 1968-76; Urban League, asst exec dir, 1965-66, coord, 1966-68; Sarco Co, dept mgr, 1944-65; Graduate School of Social Work, asst prof; NY Univ, instructor; NY State Dept of Educ, counselor; Oral History USA, dir. **Orgs:** Clerk St Phillips Prot Epis Ch; vice pres St Phillips Housing Corp; mem Interparish Cncl; bd of dir Grace Episc Sch; mem Child Study Well Met Inc; Children's Prepartory Entr Prog; past pres Dunbar Tenants League; past owner The Negro World; past owner Harlem Daily; past editor Brown Mag. **Business Addr:** 2 World Trade Ctr, New York, NY 10047.

BROWN, CRAIG VINCENT
Educator. **Personal:** Born Jul 22, 1943, St Louis, MO; son of Laura Daniels Brown and Portia Brown. **Educ:** MacMurray Coll, Jacksonville IL, BA 1963; Illinois State Univ, Normal IL, MA 1969; Harris-Stowe State Coll, attended; St Louis Univ, attended. **Career:** St Louis Public Schools, teacher special educ 1968-72; City of St Louis, psychologist 1972-75; Univ of Missouri, Fontbonne Coll, Harris-Stowe State Coll, Forest Park Community Coll, Greenville Coll, adjunct faculty, special educ & psychologist 1971-87; Inst of Black Studies, research project coord 1978-80; Washington Univ, research assoc, project coord; Bellefontaine Rehabilitation Center, psychologist 1987-90; St Louis Job Corps Center, mental health consultant 1988-90; Muskegon Community College, instructor, currently. **Orgs:** Bd dir West End Community Conf 1968-80; Assn of Black Psychologists 1972-93; American Psychological Association, 1992-93; Assn for The Educ of Young Children 1974-87; vice chmn Advisory Comm on Special Needs Adoptions, Missouri Div of Family Serv St Louis 1975-80; governor-at-large (intl exec comm) Council for Exceptional Children 1980-83; life mem, past natl pres Black Caucus of Special Educators; Black Child Devel Inst 1980-93; sec Eastern Region Advisory Comm, Comprehensive Psychiatric Serv Dept of Mental Health State of Missouri 1986-89. **Honors/Awds:** Co-author, Johnson Brown Harris & Lewis ''Manual of Black Parenting'' Educ St Louis Inst of Black Studies 1980.

BROWN, D. JOAN
Insurance company executive. **Personal:** daugHter of Doris M Rhodes and Duplain W Rhodes III. **Career:** Rhodes Mutual Life Insurance Co of Alabama, Mobile, AL, chief executive, currently; Rhodes Life Insurance Co of Louisiana, New Orleans, LA, chief executive; National Service Industrial Life Insurance Co, chief executive. **Honors/Awds:** Industrial/Service 100, Insurance, Ntl Service Industrial Life Ins Co, Rhodes Life Ins Co of LA, Rhodes Mutual Life Ins Co of AL, Black Enterprise, 1990. **Business Addr:** Chief Executive, Rhodes Mutual Life Insurance Company of Alabama, 402 Dr Martin Luther King Jr Ave, Mobile, AL 36603.

BROWN, DALLAS C., JR.
Military officer. **Personal:** Born Aug 21, 1932, New Orleans, LA; son of Rita S Taylor Brown and Dallas C Brown; married Elizabeth T; children: Dallas C III, Leonard G, Jan B, Karen L, Barbara A. **Educ:** WV State Coll, BA History/Pol Sci, Distinguished Grad, 1954; Defense Language Institute, Distinguished Grad, 1965-66; IN U, MA Gov't 1967; US Army Command & General Staff Coll, 1967-68; US Army Russian Inst, 1968-70; US Naval War Coll, Dist Grad 1973-74. **Career:** 519th Military Intelligence Battallion, Vietnam, commander, 1970-71; US Army Field Statn Berlin Ger, commander 1977-78; USA FORSCOM Atlanta, GA, deputy chief of staff/intelligence 1978-80; Defense Intelligence Agency Wash, DC, deputy vice dir 1979-80; US Army War Coll Carlisle, PA, deputy commandant, 1980-84; WV State Coll, assoc prof of history, 1984-96 (retired). **Orgs:** Mem Alpha Phi Alpha 1951-, Natl Eagle Scout Assn 1978-, Assn of US Army 1978-; chmn Greater Atlanta Armed Forces Day 1979; constituent, US Army War Coll Found 1981-; Am Assn of Univ Prof 1984-; mem Upsilon Boule Sigma Pi Phi 1984-97; Alpha Lambda Boule, 1998-; Pi Sigma Theta Natl Political Sci Hon Soc 1985-, Phi Alpha Theta Natl Historical Soc 1985-, Rotary Club Intl 1987-97; mem, Anvil Club, 1989-97. **Honors/Awds:** Contributing author "Soviet Views on War and Peace," NDU 1982; WV State Coll Alumnus of the Yr 1978; WV State Coll ROTC Hall of Fame 1980; board of advisors, West Virginia State College, 1990-91; West Virginia Higher Education Advisory Board, 1992. **Military Serv:** US Army, brigadier general, 1954-84; DSSM; MSM 2 OLC; JSCM; ACM; master parachutist; air crewman; first African-American general officer in the field of military intelligence. **Home Addr:** 17 Devant Dr East, Bluffton, SC 29910-4537.

BROWN, DEBRIA M.
Educator, opera singer. **Personal:** Born Oct 26, 1936, New Orleans, LA; daughter of Eunice Theriot Brown and Bennet Grandison Brown. **Educ:** Xavier University, New Orleans, LA, BS, music education; Manhattan School, New York, NY; conservatories: Aspen, Tanglewood, Zurich, Switzerland, private study, Vienna, Austria, Rome, Italy. **Career:** New Orleans Symphony, 1989-91; Houston Grand Opera, 1990-91; Miami Opera, 1990-91; San Diego Opera, 1990-91; Vienna Volkstheater, 1990-91; University of Houston, artist-in-residence, prof of vocal music, currently. **Honors/Awds:** Received numerous awards and citations: the American Whitney, Rockefeller, Metropolitan Opera; Honorary Professorship, Rheinhardt Seminar, Vienna, Austria. **Home Addr:** 1637 N Tonti St, New Orleans, LA 70119.

BROWN, DEE (DECOVAN KADELL)
Professional basketball player. **Personal:** Born Nov 29, 1968, Jacksonville, FL; married Tammy; children: Alexis Kiah, Alyssa Milan. **Educ:** Jacksonville Univ, Jacksonville, FL, 1986-90. **Career:** Boston Celtics, guard, 1990-98; Toronto Raptors, 1998-. **Honors/Awds:** NBA All-Rookie Team, 1991; won the NBA Slam-Dunk Competition during All-Star Weekend, 1991. **Business Addr:** Professional Basketball Player, Toronto Raptors, 150 York St, Ste 110, Toronto, ON, Canada M5H 3S5, (416)214-2255.

BROWN, DELORES ELAINE
Clergywoman, author, humanitarian. **Personal:** Born Dec 10, 1945, Wildwood, FL; daughter of Mary Lee Robinson and William Levy Robinson Sr; married Marshall L; children: Mare DeShall. **Educ:** FL A&M Univ Tallahasee FL, pre-eng 1962-64; Tuskegee University, BSEE 1965-67. **Career:** Gen Elec/US Atomic Energy Commission, assoc engr 1967-68; FL Power Corp St Petersburg, FL, assoc engr 1968-70; Honeywell Aerospace Inc St Petersburg, FL, assoc engr 1971-75; E-Systems ECI Div St Petersburg, FL, quality engr 1975-78; Sperry Univac Clearwater, FL, engr; publisher/minister, Lakeview Presbyterian Church 1990-. **Orgs:** Soc of Women Engrs 1973-75; Soc of Quality Cntrl 1975-77; mem Tuskegee Alumni Assn 1980-; Project Attack, Lakeview Presbyterian Church 1990-; Republican Natl Committee 1992-; American Institute for Cancer Research; The Rutherford Institute; The Natl Heart Foundation; Help Hospitalized Veterans; Habitat for Humanity International. **Honors/Awds:** EA Grant Award; Electronic Excellence Award, Tuskegee Inst AL 1966; Most Promising Female Engineering Student Award, Sch of Engineering Tuskegee Inst 1966; 1st female to grad from Tuskegee Inst in Engineering 1967; Woman of the Year 1991 by the American Biographical Institute; author, The Story of Salvation, 1990; Republican Presidential Legion of Merit, 1992-95; The Presidential Trust. **Home Addr:** 2630 Queen St South, St Petersburg, FL 33712.

BROWN, DELORIS A.
Attorney. **Personal:** Born Aug 16, Los Angeles, CA; children: Nitobi. **Educ:** CA State Univ, BA 1964; Univ of So CA, MA 1970; Peoples College of Law, JD 1978. **Career:** Peace Corps Brazil, volunteer 1964-67; attorney-at-law, currently. **Business Addr:** Attorney, 1605 W Olympic Blvd, 9th Fl, Los Angeles, CA 90015.

BROWN, DENISE J.
Record company executive, attorney. **Career:** Mayer, Katz, Kaber, Leibowitz & Roberts, attorney; Warner Brothers Records, sr vice pres of black music division, currently. **Business Addr:** Senior VP, Black Music Div, Warner Brothers Records, 3300 Warner Blvd, Burbank, CA 91505.

BROWN, DENISE SHARON
Caseworker. **Personal:** Born Aug 2, 1957, Manhattan, NY; daughter of Geraldine Brown (deceased) and James Brown. **Educ:** North Carolina A&T State University, Greensboro, NC, BS, 1982. **Career:** New York City/HRA/CWA, Jamaica, NY, caseworker, 1988-, notary public, 1989-. **Orgs:** Member, Ministry to Catholics of African Ancestry, 1983-; member, National Black Child Development Institute, 1990-; Parish Outreach, 1995-; Prison ministry, 1994-96. **Home Addr:** 182 Long Beach Rd, Hempstead, NY 11550-7310.

BROWN, DEREK DARNELL
Professional football player. **Personal:** Born Apr 15, 1971, Banning, CA. **Educ:** University of Nebraska. **Career:** New Orleans Saints, running back, 1993-. **Business Addr:** Professional Football Player, New Orleans Saints, 5800 Airline Hwy, Metairie, LA 70003, (504)733-0255.

BROWN, DEREK VERNON
Professional football player. **Personal:** Born Mar 31, 1970, Fairfax, VA. **Educ:** Univ of Notre Dame, bachelor's degree in marketing, 1992. **Career:** New York Giants, tight end, 1992-94; Jacksonville Jaguars, 1996-. **Honors/Awds:** Ed Block Courage Award, 1996. **Business Addr:** Professional Football Player, Jacksonville Jaguars, One Stadium Place, Jacksonville, FL 32202, (904)633-6000.

BROWN, DIANA JOHNSON
Police sergeant. **Personal:** Born Jan 25, 1951, Dania, FL; daughter of Enith Gloria Johnson Mulkey and Walter Rolle; married Sherman Leon Brown, Mar 28, 1987; children: Shantel Ramsey, Laquantas. **Educ:** Broward Community Coll, Davie FL, Associate Science, 1983; Florida Atlantic Univ, Boca Raton FL, 1975-84. **Career:** Broward Community Coll, Davie FL, clerk-typist, admission clerk, sec to registrar, 1970-74; FAU-FIU Joint Center, Ft Lauderdale FL, clerk-typist, 1974-77; Broward County Sheriff's Office, Ft Lauderdale FL, corrections officer, 1977-79; City of Pompano Beach, Pompano Beach FL, police officer 1979-88, sergeant, 1988-. **Orgs:** Mem, Fraternal Order of Police, 1979-; mem 1983-, secretary for State of Florida, 1983-85, Natl Organization of Black Law Enforcement Executives; mem, 1984-, financial secretary for southern region, 1986-, Natl Black Police Assn; pres, Broward County Law Enforcement Organization, 1980-; mem, Police Benevolent Assn, 1983-; mem, steering committee, Preventing Crime in the Black Community, 4th Annual Conf; member, Business & Professional Women's Association of Pompano Beach, 1992-; president, Ely High School Choral Parent's Association, 1990-; Pres, Natl Black Police Assn, Southern Region, 1993-96. **Honors/Awds:** Officer of the Month, City of Pompano Beach, 1982. **Military Serv:** US Army Reserves, SSgt, 1976-, Sgt First Class, 1990; Humanitarian Award 1980, Army Reserve Component Achievement Medal, 1981, 1992. **Business Addr:** Sergeant, City of Pompano Beach Police Department, 100 SW 3rd Street, Pompano Beach, FL 33060, (305)786-4221.

BROWN, DORIS
Educator. **Career:** Brown's Restaurant Servers Academy, pres, currently; State Wage Deviation Board, currently.

BROWN, DOROTHY LAVANIA
Physician, educator. **Personal:** Born Jan 7, 1919, Philadelphia, PA; daughter of Lola Redmon and Samuel Redmon; children: Lola D, Kevin Edward. **Educ:** Bennett Coll, BA 1941; Meharvy Med Coll, MD 1948; Fellow of Am Coll of Surgeons, FACS 1959; Russell Sage Coll, Hon DSc 1972. **Career:** Riverside Hosp, former chief of surgery 1960-83; Meharry Med Coll, clinical prof of surgery. **Orgs:** Mem Metro Bd Health Nashville TN; mem Natl Med Assn; consultant HEW Natl Inst of Health 1980-82; former rep TN State Legislature 85th General Assembly 1966-68; mem Negro Business & Professional Womens Club; life mem NAACP; mem Delta Sigma Theta. **Honors/Awds:** Dorothy L Brown Bldg Meharry Med Coll Nashville TN 1970; Natl Sojourner Truth Award Nashville TN 1973; Amer Heritage & Freedom Fowler Historic Gallery, Chicago, IL 1979; Blazing Torch Award Inter Min Alli 1981; Certificate of Merit Music City BPW Nashville TN 1984; Bennett College, Honorary Doctor of Humane Letters, 1987; Cumberland University, Honorary Doctor of Humanities, 1988; Induction to YWCA Academy for Women of Achievement, 1992; Carnegie Human Relations Award, 1993; Haratio Alger Award, 1994; Honorary Doctor of Humane Letters, Boston Univ, Commencement Boston Univ, 1994. **Home Addr:** 3109 John A Merritt Blvd, Nashville, TN 37209.

BROWN, DWAYNE MARC
Attorney, state government official. **Personal:** Born Mar 16, 1962, Indianapolis, IN; son of Hattie Ligon Brown and Jimmy Emitt Brown; married Autumn Brooks Brown, Jul 7, 1984; children: James-Marc, Kristin. **Educ:** Morehouse College, Atlanta, GA, BA, cum laude, 1984; Columbia University, School of Law, New York, NY, JD, 1987. **Career:** Board of Governors Federal Reserve System, Washington, Dc, staf attorney, 1987-89; Counsel to Secretary of State, Joe Hossett, Indianapolis, IN, counsel, 1985-90; Bingham, Summons, Welsh & Spilman, Indianapolis, IN, associate, 1990; Supreme, Appellate, and Tax Court of Indiana, Indianapolis, IN, clerk, 1990-. **Orgs:** Member, NAACP, 1990. **Honors/Awds:** Certificate of Achievement, Negro Counsel of Women, Indianapolis, 1991; Certificate of Achievement, Van Buren Baptist Church, Gary, 1991; Trail Blazer Award, Fitzgerald's Business Exchange, 1991; Community Player, Dr Mozel Sanders Award, Indianapolis, 1991. **Business Addr:** Clerk of the Supreme, Appellate & Tax Courts, State of Indiana, 217 State House, Indianapolis, IN 46204.

BROWN, EDDIE C.
Investment counselor. **Personal:** Born Nov 26, 1940, Apopka, FL; son of Annis M Brown; married Sylvia Thurston; children: Tonya Yvonne, Jennifer Lynn. **Educ:** Howard Univ, BSEE 1961; NYU, MSEE 1968; IN Univ, MBA 1970; CFA 1979; CIC 1979. **Career:** T Rowe Price Assoc Inc, investment counselor 1973-83; Irwin Mgmt Co, investment manager, 1970-73; IBM, engineer, 1963-68; Brown Capital Mgmt Inc, pres 1983-. **Orgs:** Commissioner, Maryland Public Broadcasting; Baltimore Security Analysts Soc; Financial Analysts Fed; panelist Wall St Week; dir Community Foundation of Greater Baltimore; dean's advisory council member, Indiana Univ School of Business. **Honors/Awds:** Fellowship Grant Consortium for Grad Study in Mgmt 1968. **Military Serv:** AUS 1st lt 1961-63. **Business Addr:** President, Brown Capital Mgmt, Inc, 809 Cathedral St, Baltimore, MD 21201.

BROWN, EDWARD LYNN
Clergyman. **Personal:** Born Apr 2, 1936, Madison Co, TN; married Gladys D Stephens; children: Alonzo, Cheronda. **Educ:** Lane College, BS 1960; Interdenominational Theology Center, MDiv 1963; Miles College, Honorary Doctoral Degree 1979. **Career:** Christian Methodist Episcopal Church, minister, currently. **Orgs:** Gen sec, Bd of Pub Serv, General Education Bd, Christian Methodist Episcopal Church; Long Range & Planning Commission, Commn Pension; rep, World Methodist Conference on Evangelism, Jerusalem 1974; bd dir, OIC; bd dir, Memphis NAACP; exec bd, Natl OIC; bd dir, Memphis Urban League; Intl Society Theta Phi; bd mem, Orange Mound Community Action Agency; Orange Mound Consolidated Civic Club; dean, S Memphis District Leadership Training School; bd mem, Memphis Community Education Project; bd chairman, Orange Mound & Creative Involvement Program; Memphis & Shelby Co Welfare Commission; pres, CME Min Alliance; vice pres, Memphis Min Assn. **Honors/Awds:** Outstanding Service, Memphis NAACP 1973; Outstand Communtiy Service, Memphis Urban League 1973; Service to City of Memphis, Certification of Merit, Mayor Wyeth Chandler 1971; serv gen asst commn, Mayor Wyeth Chandler 1971; Big "S" Citation, City Memphis Co Commn 1972; Outstanding Religious Leader, Alpha Kappa Alpha 1973; Outstand Community Service, UMCAP; Certificate of Appreciation, Community Action Agency 1970. **Business Addr:** Minister, 531 South Parkway E, Memphis, TN 38106.

BROWN, EDWIN C., JR.
Attorney. **Personal:** Born Sep 20, 1935, Washington, DC; son of Pearl W Brown and Edwin C Brown Sr; married Martha; children: 3. **Educ:** Howard Univ, BA 1957, LLB 1960. **Career:** Office US Atty Pres's Comm on Crime, asst US atty 1965; Brown Brown & Watkins, atty 1966-. **Military Serv:** AUS, 1st lieutenant, honor graduate, Officer Candidate School.

BROWN, EFFIE MAYHAN JONES
Educator. **Personal:** Born Apr 8, 1922, Penhook, VA; widowed; children: Ethel Jaqueline, Ristina Etelle, Harry Alva III. **Educ:** Bluefield St Coll, BS 1954; Marshall Univ, MA 1964; West Virginia Univ, grad study; Univ of Virginia; Georgetown Univ; Coll of Grad Studies. **Career:** Preston Elementary School, Wade Elementary School, kindergarten teacher, 1970-71; Stinson Elementary School, asst principal guidance, 1958-69; Mercer County Schools, teacher, currently. **Orgs:** Life mem NEA; West Virginia Educ Assn; 1st black woman pres Mercer Co Assn of Classroom Tchrs 1972-74; mem bd dir Mt Zion Baptist Church; church clerk, Mt Zion Baptist Church; pres Auxiliary Conv; finance sec West Virginia Baptist Congress of Christian Educ; bd mem Mercer Co Adv Comm 1970-73; mem bd dir United Way; chmn Mary C Reed Scholarship Fund; chmn Bible Auxiliary Club; mem Alpha Kappa Alpha, Phi Delta Kappa Frat for Educators Bluefield Virginia Chap. **Honors/Awds:** Recipient Outstanding Elem Tchr of Amer Award 1974; author of This Twig We Bend: A Handbook for Parents and Faculty Handbook & Student Tchr Guide.

BROWN, ELLEN ROCHELLE
Broadcasting company executive. **Personal:** Born Mar 10, 1949, Denton, TX; daughter of Earlene Punch Brown and John Henry Brown. **Educ:** Broadcast & Film Arts, So Melth U, BFA 1971; Columbia U, cert 1972. **Career:** KDFW-TV, Dallas: educ reporter, 1978-80; producer/host, ''Insights,'' 1980-86; minority affairs dir, exec producer, 1986-; WROC-TV, anchor Noon News, 1975-78; NBC News, NY, researcher, 1973-75; KERA-TV, Dallas, reporter, 1971-72. **Honors/Awds:** Journalism Fellow, Columbia Univ, 1972; Alfred I DuPont Award for Journalism, KDFW-TV, 1979; TX Sch Bell Award, Dallas, 1979; Dallas Sch Admin Award, Dallas Sch Distict, 1979. **Business Addr:** Minority Affairs Director, KDFW-TV, 400 N Griffin, Dallas, TX 75202.

BROWN, EMIL QUINCY
Professional baseball player. **Personal:** Born Dec 29, 1974, Chicago, IL. **Educ:** Indian River Community College. **Career:** Pittsburgh Pirates, outfielder, 1997-. **Business Addr:** Professional Baseball Player, Pittsburgh Pirates, PO Box 7000, Pittsburgh, PA 15212, (412)323-5000.

BROWN, EMMA JEAN MITCHELL
Educator (retired). **Personal:** Born Jun 1, 1939, Marshall, TX; daughter of Elvia Washington Mitchell and Johnnie D Mitchell; divorced; children: Charles S Jr, Gene Mitchell. **Educ:** Bishop College, BS, 1961; University of Massachusetts, MEd, 1966; Boston University, attended, 1966; Howard University, attended, 1984; Miami University, attended, 1985; University of Dayton, attended, 1988; PhD in Theology, 1997. **Career:** Kansas City Schools, teacher, 1961-62; Boston/Needham Public Schools, language arts specialist, 1964-67; Sinclair Comm College, lecturer, 1970-73; Wright State University, lecturer, 1970-75; University of Ibadan, Nigeria, West Africa, lecturer, 1975-76; Dayton Public Schools, teacher, 1978-86, supervisor of community arts, 1986-88; international evangelist/missionary, 1989-. **Orgs:** Concerned Educators of Black Students, president, 1988-; Miami Valley Affairs Organization, 1975-90; Zeta Sorority Inc, 1958-; Urban League Guild, 1975-85; National Council of Negro Women, 1975-90. **Honors/Awds:** Miami Valley Affairs Organization, City of Dayton Medallion; Colonel White High School, Teacher of the Month. **Special Achievements:** Author: Come Sit at My Table: An African Cookbook, 1985, Custodial Procedure Guide, 1978; writer: poetry, African Network, 1985; articles: ABC's of Education, 1980, Nigerian-English Studies Journal, 1980; dissertation: Paul's Affirmation of Women in the Ministry. **Home Addr:** 473 Marathon Ave, Dayton, OH 45406, (513)275-9133.

BROWN, EMMETT EARL
Housing administrator (retired). **Personal:** Born Jan 30, 1932, Chicago, IL; son of Julia H Knox and Joseph E Brown; widowed; children: Paula Davis, Patricia E, Emmett E Jr, Cecilia B, Alan C. **Educ:** Pepperdine Univ, 1979; California Cst Univ, BS. **Career:** SEIU AFL-CIO Local 660, bus agent; Central & West Basin Water Replenishment Dist, dir; Peoples Housing of Rogers Park, dir of community organizing; Emmett Brown & Assoc, labor consultant. **Military Serv:** USAF A1/C 1950-53. **Home Addr:** 1550 N Lake Shore Dr, #22F, Chicago, IL 60610.

BROWN, ERNEST DOUGLAS, JR.
Educator. **Personal:** Born Jul 6, 1947, New Britain, CT; son of Alberta Coleman & Ernest Brown; married Susan Revotskie, Sep 25, 1973; children: Rafael, Kalafya, Maceo, Naima. **Educ:** Harvard Univ, BA, philosophy, 1969; UCLA, PhD Candidate, art history, 1970-71; Univ of Washington, Phd, ethnomusicology program, 1984. **Career:** Seattle Art Commission, Neighborhood Arts Program, coord, 1978-80; Cornish Institute for the Allied Arts, faculty mem, 1981-82; Northeastern Univ, asst prof, 1984-87; Harvard Univ, Andrew Mellon, faculty fellow, 1990-91; Williams College, assoc prof, 1988-. **Orgs:** Society for Ethnomusicology, 1985-; African Studies Association, 1986-. **Honors/Awds:** Council for the International Exchange of Scholars, Fulbright Program, Research Fellow, 1986; Andrew Mellon Foundation, Andrew Mellon Teaching Fellowship, Harvard Univ, 1990. **Special Achievements:** Co-director, Kusika and the Zambezi Marimba Band, 1989-; National Council of Negro Women, photography commission, Seattle, 1981; King County Arts Commission, photograph purchased, 1983; ''Lozi,'' NY: Rosen Publishing Co, 1998; ''Turn Up the Volume!'' The Drama Review, Carnival Issue, 1998. **Business Addr:** Professor, Department of Music, Williams College, 54 Chapin Hall Dr, Bernhard Music Ctr, Williamstown, MA 01267, (413)597-3266.

BROWN, EVELYN
City official. **Personal:** Born May 15, 1930, Tifton, GA; married Macon (deceased). **Educ:** Atkinson Cty HS Pearson GA, attended. **Career:** Cafeteria aide; Evelyn Spiritual Hour Radio Station WRMU FM, hostess 15 yrs; MCity of Alliance, councilwoman 1984-85. **Orgs:** Mem Gospel Announcer's Guild of Amer, Inc 1975; mem Democratic Exec Comm 1981; mem Christian Update TV 1985; mem Democratic Party 5 years. **Honors/Awds:** First Black Councilwoman Nails of Thounder Soc Club 1984; Queen for a Day Comm Churches 1976; gospel announcer Gospel Music Workshop of Amer 1978; Woman ofthe Year Altrusic Club 1980.

BROWN, EVELYN DREWERY
Educational administrator. **Personal:** Born Oct 29, 1935, Haddock, GA; daughter of Ada Tatum Drewery and Bennie Drewery; divorced; children: Clinton O, Toni A. **Educ:** Morris Brown Coll, BS 1957; Atlanta U, MA 1969, further studies 1975. **Career:** Econ Opportunity Atlanta, program dir; Atlanta Public Schools, dept chairperson & teacher, 1964-70; Economic Opportunity Atlanta, head start dir, 1965-69; Richmond County Bd of Educ, teacher, 1962-64; Columbia County Bd of Educ, teacher, 1957-62; coordinator, After School Project, Metro Atlanta Boys and Girls Club; Mayor's Office of Community Affairs/Youth Svcs, administrator, currently. **Orgs:** Mem GA Assn of Edctrs; mem Nat Assn for Children Under Six; consult & task force mem Parent & Child Centers; Nat 1st vice pres Zeta Phi Beta Sor 1978; pres Better Infant Birth/March of Dimes 1978-80; sec organizations & communications, The Women's Missionary Cncl 1980-; dir, Overseas Mission, chm, Joint Bd of Finance, pres, Women's Missionary Society, CME Church. **Honors/Awds:** Comm Serv Awd, Zeta Phi Beta Sor Morris Brown; Outstanding Serv Awd in Edn; Zeta of Yr Awd; Outstanding Serv in Field of Religion, Holsey Temple CME Ch Atlanta. **Home Addr:** 1349 Aniwaka Ave SW, Atlanta, GA 30311. **Business Addr:** Administrator, Mayor's Office of Community Affairs/Youth Services, 55 Trinity Ave, SW, Atlanta, GA 30335.

BROWN, EWART F., JR.
Physician. **Personal:** Born May 17, 1946; son of Helene A Darrell Brown and Ewart A Brown; married Priscilla Murray Brown, Sep 5, 1987; children: Kevin, Ewart III, Donovan. **Educ:** Howard Univ, Washington, DC, BS, 1968, MD, 1972; UCLA, Los Angeles CA, MPH, 1977. **Career:** Vermont-Century Medical Clinic, Los Angeles, CA, medical director, 1974-. **Orgs:** Trustee, Howard University, 1990-; trustee, Drew University of Medicine & Science, 1989-92; chairman of the board, Bermuda Times, 1987-. **Honors/Awds:** Service to Howard University, 1968, 1972; Pacesetter Award, Los Angeles Chapter, NAACP, 1985. **Business Addr:** Medical Director, Vermont-Century Medical Clinic, 10024 S Vermont Ave, Los Angeles, CA 90044.

BROWN, FANNIE E. GARRETT
Educator (retired). **Personal:** Born Aug 21, 1924, Jackson, MS; daughter of Bessie Willing Garrett and Edward P Garrett; married William H Brown; children: William E, Kevin C, Mary Devra McMullen. **Educ:** St Mary's Infirmary, Nursing Diploma 1946; Holy Names College, BS Nursing Ed 1969; San Francisco State Univ, MS Health Sci 1972; Nova Univ, Ed Doctorate 1978. **Career:** St Mary's Infirmary operating rm surgical nurse 1946-47; St Mary's Hosp, med/surgical staff nurse 1947-48; Providence Hosp, med/surgical staff nurse 1948-49; Joel E Lewis MD, office nurse 1950-51; Providence Hospital, desk charge nurse 1952-54, nursery staff nurse 1955-62; Kaiser-Permanente Hosp, pediatric clinic staff nurse 1962; Providence Hospital-Peralta Hospital-Sam Merritt Hospital, private duty nurse 1963-67; Richmond Unified Schools, school public health nurse 1969-72; City Coll of San Francisco, nursing instructor & supervisor inservice health educ 1972-78. **Orgs:** Nursing adv bd mem City Coll of San Francisco 1979-; guest lecturer City College, Diablo Valley Community Coll, San Francisco State Univ 1979-83; exec bd mem Family Aid to Catholic Educ 1980-86; former bd mem Mercy Retirement & Skill Nursing Facility 1984-90; mem Oakland Bd of Realtors 1980-; mem Registered Nurses Alumni Assn Holy Names Coll; mem Amer Public Health Assn; mem CA Teachers Assn; mem Amer Assn Univ Women; program vice pres Oakland/Piedmont Amer Assn Univ Women; pres Holy Names College of Nursing Alumni Chapter 1989-90; Sigma Theta Tau, Nu Xi Charter-at-Large; Summit Medical Center, board member/vice chair, Health Education Advisory Committee; chair of Community Service, Chi Eta Phi Sorority, Inc., Omicron Phi Chapter, 1997. **Honors/Awds:** Traineeship HEW 1969-70; Improving the Applicant Selection Process of the Nursing Prog at City Coll of San Francisco, a doctoral dissertation 1978; publication ''Juvenile Prostitution, A Nursing Perspective'' Journal of Psychiatric Nursing & Mental Health Serv 1980; Distinguished Alumni Award, Natl Assn for Equal Opportunity in Higher Educ 1989; ''Leadership America'' Participant, Foundation for Women Resources 1989; member East Bay Nursing Honor Society 1989-; Sigma Theta Tau International Nursing Honor Society, Award for Excellence in Nursing Practice/Scholarship/Leadership, 1994; Holy Names College, Alumni of the Year Award, 1995. **Home Addr:** 5340 Broadway Terrace, #508, Oakland, CA 94618.

BROWN, FLOYD A.
Announcer. **Personal:** Born Nov 5, 1930, Dallas, TX; married Mary E Stephens; children: Floyd Keith, Diane Faye. **Educ:** Northwestern Sch of Bus; Radio Inst of Chicago 1951. **Career:** WGN TV, staff announcer, personality on radio 1971-; NBC-WMAQ Chgo, prgm mgr announcer 1965-71; WYNR-WNUS Radio Chgo, 1962-65; WRMN, announcer chief engr prgm dir asst Mgr 1951-62. **Orgs:** Bd dir 1st Fed Savings & Loan; dir bd dir Selected Funds; Selected Am Selected Spec Mutual Funds & Selected Spec Money Mrt Fund; co-owner, pub rel & advertising Firm Rotary Intnl; bd dir YMCA; bd dir Fox Valley Council; Boy Scouts of Am; NAACP; Urban League; Elgin C of C; bd dir Larkin Home for Children Family Svcs; chmn bd deacons Elgin 1st Cong Ch; mem Elgin Citizens adv com Mental Health Assn. **Military Serv:** AUS sgt 1953-55. **Business Addr:** 2501 Bradley Pl, Chicago, IL 60618.

BROWN, FOXY
Rapper. **Career:** Rapper, currently. **Special Achievements:** Albums include: Ill Na Na; part of group, The Firm, with Nas, AZ; albums include: The Firm, 1997; rapped on ''I Shot Ya,'' with LL Cool J; ''Touch Me, Tease Me,'' with Case; ''No One Else,'' with Total, lil Kim, and Da Brat; ''You're Makin' Me High,'' with Toni Braxton. **Business Addr:** Rapper, Def Jam Recordings Group Inc., 160 Varick St, 12th Fl, New York, NY 10013, (212)229-5200.

BROWN, FRANCHOT A.
Attorney. **Personal:** Born Jul 11, 1943, Columbia, SC; son of Sara D Brown and Rupert A Brown; children: Brian S Brown. **Educ:** Howard Univ, Washington DC, BA 1965; Univ of South Carolina Law School, Columbia SC, JD 1969; Univ of Pennsylvania, Reginald Heber Smith Comm Lawyer 1969. **Career:** Legal Aid Serv Agency Columbia, 1969-72; private law practice, 1972-73; Columbia SC Magistrate, 1973-76; Franchot A Brown & Assoc, lawyer 1976-; Brown & Stanley, sr partner, 1976-90; The Law Offices of Franchot A Brown, 1990-. **Orgs:** Bd SC Blue Cross-Blue Shield; bd Greater Columbia Chamber of Comm; bd Victory Savings Bank; bd mem Drug Response Op; vocational rehab Midlands Center for Retarded Children; chmn Citizens Advisory Comm for Community Devel for the City of Columbia, SC 1975-; The Mens Resource Center, Columbia, SC, 1990-. **Business Addr:** Senior Partner, Law Offices of Franchot A Brown, PO Box 543, Columbia, SC 29202.

BROWN, FRANK
Educator. **Personal:** Born May 1, 1935, Gallian, AL; son of Ora Lomax Brown and Thomas Brown; married Joan Drake; children: Frank G, Monica J. **Educ:** AL State Univ, BS 1957; OR State Univ, MS 1962; Univ of CA at Berkeley, MA 1969, PhD 1970; Harvard University, Institute for Educational Management, fellow, 1988. **Career:** NY State Commiss on Ed, assoc dir, 1970-72; Urban Inst CCNY, dir 1971-72; Cora P Maloney Coll SUNY Buffalo, dir 1974-77; SUNY Buffalo, prof 1972-83; Univ of NC Chapel Hill, School of Ed, dean 1983-90; Institute for Research in Social Science, Chapel Hill, NC, dir, educational research policy studies project, 1990-; Cary C Boshamer, professor of education, 1990-; University of California, Berkeley, CA, visiting scholar, 1990-91. **Orgs:** Rho Lambda Chapter of Alpha Phi Alpha Fraternity, Buffalo, New York, president, 1977-78; Western New York Black Educators Association and the National Urban Education Conference, co-founder, 1975-83; State University of New York at Buffalo; Black Faculty Association, co-founder, 1972; Buffalo Urban League, board of directors, 1978-81; Langston Hughes Institute-Black Cultural Center for Western New York and Buffalo, board of directors, 1978-83; Buffalo School Desegregation Case, Federal District of Western New York, consultant and researcher, 1976-83; vice pres Div A of American Ed Research Assn 1986-88; bd of dirs, American Assn of Colleges of Teacher Education 1988-92; board of directors, National Organization for Legal Problems in Education, 1990-93. **Honors/Awds:** Grad Fellowship OR State Univ 1961-62; Grad Fellowship Univ of CA Berkeley 1968-70; Rockefeller Found Scholars Awd 1979-80; Langston Hughes Inst Award, Outstanding Service & Leadership; SUNY Buffalo Special Award, Achievement in Research, Teaching & Service; Tar Heel of the Week, Raleigh News & Observer; Amer Educ Research Assn Award, Dedicated Service & Leadership; numerours other awards; Publ 5 books, monographs & 90 articles; Fellow, Harvard Univ Institute for Educational Management 1988; Book Series Editor, Educational Excellence, Diversity, and Equity, Corwin Press, 1991-. **Military Serv:** AUS spec 1958-60. **Home Addr:** 6523 Huntingridge Rd, Chapel Hill, NC 27514, (919)489-0757. **Business Phone:** (919)962-2522.

BROWN, FRANK LEWIS
Police chief. **Personal:** Born Jul 30, 1945, Fayetteville, GA; son of Jeff & Annie Brown; married Hazel Brown. **Career:** East Point Police Department, patrolman, 1967-74, sergeant, 1974-79, lieutenant, 1979-84, captain, 1984-90, major, 1990-96, chief, 1996-. **Orgs:** Kiwans Club, president, 1995; FBI National Academy, 1990; Georgia Chiefs Association, 1996; National Organization of Black Law Enforcement Executives, 1994; International Association of Chiefs of Police, 1996. **Honors/Awds:** Officer of the Year, 1975; TRDC, Man of the Year Award, 1990. **Special Achievements:** First Black chief of police in East Point, GA. **Military Serv:** US Air Force. **Business Addr:** Police Chief, East Point Police Department, 2727 East Point St, East Point, GA 30344, (404)765-1104.

BROWN, FREDDIEMAE EUGENIA
Library administrator. **Personal:** Born Oct 16, 1928, Racine, WI; daughter of Eunice Doss Bowman and Fred Bowman. **Educ:** Fisk Univ, Nashville, TN, BA, 1955; Univ of MI, Ann Arbor, MI, AMLS, 1959, PhD, 1973-79. **Career:** Detroit Public Library, asst dir branch serv, 1970-73, pre-prof, librarian I, II, III, chief of div, chief of dept 1956-70; Dept of Library Science Wayne State Univ, asst prof 1973-82; Houston Public Library, regional branch librarian, 1982-89, asst chief, branch services, 1989-, chief, branch services, 1992-. **Orgs:** Mem Am Library

Assn; Texas Lib Assn 1982-; Fisk Univ Alumni Assn; Wayne State Univ School of Lib Sci Alumni Assn 1982-; Univ of Mich School of Library Science Alumni Assn 1979-; Amer Library Assn 1986-; Public Library Assn/ALA 1983-; Univ of Mich Alumni Assn. **Honors/Awds:** Librarian-in-residence, Univ of IA, 1974. **Home Phone:** (281)461-3750. **Business Addr:** Chief, Branch Services, Houston Public Library, 500 McKinney, Houston, TX 77002, (713)247-2227.

BROWN, GARY LEROY
Professional football player. **Personal:** Born Jul 1, 1969, Williamsport, PA. **Educ:** Penn State, majored in rehabilitation education. **Career:** Houston Oilers, running back, 1991-95; San Diego Chargers, 1997-. **Business Addr:** Professional Football Player, San Diego Chargers, Qualcomm Stadium, 9449 Friars Rd, San Diego, CA 92108, (619)280-2111.

BROWN, GARY W.
Engineer. **Personal:** Born Nov 7, 1944, Lawrenceburg, KY; married Wanda Johnson. **Educ:** Lincoln Inst; United Electronics Inst, 1964. **Career:** Intl Bus Machines, gen systems field engr vice-chmn. **Orgs:** KY Black Caucus 1973; city cnclmn Lawrenceburg KY 1974-; little league commn bsbl 1975; mem NAACP. **Military Serv:** USN radarman 2nd class 1965-69. **Business Addr:** 1733 Harrodsburg Rd, Lexington, KY 40501.

BROWN, GATES (WILLIAM JAMES)
Professional baseball coach (retired). **Personal:** Born May 2, 1939, Crestline, OH; married Norma; children: Pamela, William Jr. **Career:** Detroit Tigers, outfielder, 1963-75, coach, 1978-84. **Honors/Awds:** Hit home run as pinch hitter 1st time at bat in majors 1963; played in World Series 1968; played in AL Championship Series 1972; Freedom Found Awd 1973; est AL record most hits for a pinch hitter lifetime (107) & most home runs by a pinch hitter lifetime 16; Batting Coach for the 1984 World Champion Detroit Tigers; African-American Hall of Fame. **Business Addr:** Tiger Stadium, 2121 Trumbull, Detroit, MI 48216.

BROWN, GEOFFREY FRANKLIN
Journalist. **Personal:** Born Oct 30, 1952, Pittsburgh, PA; son of George F & Helen V Brown; married Alice Clark Brown; children: Geoffrey F Jr, Christina. **Educ:** Bowdoin College, BA, 1974. **Career:** Pittsburgh Press, general assignment reporter, 1974-75, 1977-78; Jet Magazine, assistant editor, mng editor, features editor, 1975-77, 1978-80; Chicago Tribune, copy editor, natl-foreign news editor, suburban bureau chief, entertainment editor, 1980-. **Business Addr:** Entertainment Editor, Chicago Tribune, 435 N Michigan Ave, 5th Fl, Chicago, IL 60611, (312)222-3482.

BROWN, GEORGE HENRY, JR.
Judge. **Personal:** Born Jul 16, 1939, Memphis, TN; married Margaret Solomon; children: Laurita, George III. **Educ:** FL A&M, BS 1960; Howard Univ Sch of Law, 1967. **Career:** AA Latting, atty 1967-70; Equal Emp Opp Comm, dep dir 1969-70; Legal Serv Assoc, exec dir 1970-73; Brown & Evans Law Firm, atty 1973-; Shelby County Circuit Court, judge 1983-. **Orgs:** Chmn Memphis Bd of Ed 1974; mem ABA; mem NBA; mem Memphis & Shelby Cnty Bar Assn; comr Memphis Bd of Edn; vice-chrmn Steering Comm NSBA; trustee Lane Coll; trustee memphis Acad of Arts; mem bd of dir Memphis Chap Natl Bus League; bd of dir Memphis Chap NAACP; vice pres & bd mem Beale St Hist Found; mem Vollentine & Evergreen Comm Assn. **Military Serv:** USAR Capt. **Business Addr:** Shelby County Circuit Court, 161 Jefferson Ave, Memphis, TN 38103.

BROWN, GEORGE HOUSTON
Clergyman. **Personal:** Born Oct 15, 1916, Finchburg, AL; son of Annie D Brown and A D Brown; married Amanda S; children: Marian Payne, LaVerne Bruce, Gwendolyn A Rothchild. **Educ:** AL State Univ, BS 1953, MEd 1968; Inter-Baptist Theological Sem, DD 1967; Selma Univ, LLD 1982. **Career:** Free Mission Dist Congress, congress dean 1955-75; Coneuch-Monroe Community Action, bd member 1950-77; Monroe County Mental Health, bd member 1972-80; Tom Bigbee Regional Commission, bd member 1973-89. **Orgs:** Pres Monroe County-Ministerial Assn 1965-70; first vice-moderator Bethlehem No 2 Dist Assn 1963-85; congress dean Bethlehem No 2 Congress 1970-85; member Independent Order Universal Brotherhood 1936-; member Blue Lodge Masons 1940-; member Order of the Eastern Star 1941-; member Enoch Consistory No 222 1960-; mem of Jericho of Alabama 1961-; mem of the Monroe County Board of Educ 1980-; mem United Supreme Council, 33 degree A&ASR 1988. **Honors/Awds:** Moderator's Award for Service, East Star District, 1990; Award as Dean of Christian Edu Service, Bethelhem #2 Dist Association, 1988; Recognition for being 1st black elected to high office in Monroe County, AL, 1980. **Business Addr:** Moderator, East Star Dist Assn, 4620 Turnbull Rd, Beatrice, AL 36425.

BROWN, GEORGE L.
Business executive. **Personal:** Born Jul 1, 1926, Lawrence, KS; son of Alberta Watson Brown and George L Brown Sr; married Modeen; children: Gail, Cindy, Kim, Laura. **Educ:** Univ KS, BS 1950; Univ CO, grad work 1959; Harvard Univ Business Sch, grad work. **Career:** CO House of Reps, 1955; State of CO, state senator 1956-74, lt gov 1975-79; Grumman Ecosystems, vice pres of mktg 1979; Grumman Energy Systems, sr vice pres of business devel 1979-81; Grumman Corp, vice pres Washington office 1981-; Denver Post, Denver CO, writer/editor, 1950-65; Denver Housing authority, asst dir, 1965-69. **Orgs:** Mem Legislatlures Joint Budget Comm 8 yrs; instr Univ CO; instr Univ Denver, Metro St Coll; 1st exec dir Metro Denver Urban Coalition 1969; chmn 1974 Gallup Poll Educ Survey; chmn St Legislative Comm, Senates St Affairs & Finance Comm, Dem Caucus; Natl Policy Council of US Dept of HEW; mem Exec Comm SW Regional Council of Natl Assn of Housing & Redevel Officials; chmn Citizens Adv Council for Denver's Model City Prog; mem Gov Coord Com on Implementation of Mental Health & Mental Retardation Planning; mem Dem Natl Comm; chmn Black Caucus of Dem Natl Comm; mem exec comm Natl Conf of Lt Govs; mem Natl Panel of Natl Acad of Pub Admin Found Neighborhood-Oriented Metro Govt Study; Natl Task Force for Secondary Educ Reform; Nutrition Adv Bd for CO Soc Serv Dept; chmnNatl Urban Coalition Steer Comm; bd dirs World Trade Ctr Washington; McLean VA Orchestra Bd; mem Bocle Fraternity; brd of trustees Davis and Elkins Coll, W. VA, 1988-. **Honors/Awds:** Denver Met Br NAACP Exceptional Man Awd 1972; CO Black Caucus Achievement Awd 1972; Kappa Alpha Psi Achievement Cong Awd 1974; Adam Clayton Powell Awd Polit Achievement Cong Black Caucus 1975; George Brown Urban Journalism Scholarship Est 1976; numerous other honors and awds. **Business Addr:** Vice President, Grumman Corporation, 1000 Wilson Blvd, Ste 2100, Arlington, VA 22209.

BROWN, GEORGE PHILIP
Physician. **Personal:** Born Feb 8, 1920, Arlington, VA; married Phyllis Glazer; children: George Sabree, Rodney, Craig. **Educ:** Howard Univ, BS 1940; Howard Univ Coll of Med, MD 1944. **Career:** Mark Twain School, school psychiatrist 1971-72; Inst for Children, supt 1972; Private practice, physician 1947-. **Orgs:** Diplomate Amer Bd Pediatrics 1953, Amer Bd Neurology & Psychiatry 1962. **Military Serv:** USAF capt 1951-53. **Business Addr:** 11065 Little Patuxent Pkwy, Ste 112, Columbia, MD 21045.

BROWN, GEORGIA W.
Educational administrator. **Personal:** Born Oct 1, 1934, St Francisville, LA; daughter of Mary Jones Calvin and Edward Watts; married Ollie J, Aug 23, 1958; children: Pamel Karen, Oliver Joseph. **Educ:** Southern Univ, BA 1957; LA State Univ, MS 1969. **Career:** Southern Univ, asst serials librarian 1957, serials librarian 1962-69, jr div librarian 1969-72, coordinator of readers serv 1972-75, acting dir of libraries 1975-76, dir of libraries 1976-. **Orgs:** Mem LA Library Assoc; chmn Acad Section LLA 1979-80; mem Amer Library Assoc, Southwestern Library Assoc, SW Rsch Center & Museum for Study of African Amer Life & Culture, Phi Delta Kappa, Advisory Council for Graduate School of Library Science LA State Univ; co-chmn Baton Rouge Bicentennial Comm 1974-76; chmn So Univ Bicentennial Comm 1974-76; mem Mayor-Pres Comm of the Needs of Women 1977-, Arts & Humanities Council, YWCA; Gov's comm of one hundred State of LA 1986-; LA Centseptequinary Commission; mem, East Baton Rouge Parish Library, Board of Control. **Honors/Awds:** Public Service Award Baton Rouge Bicentennial Comm 1976; Public Serv Award Mayor-Pres City of Baton Rouge 1976; Serv Award Southern Univ 1976. **Business Addr:** Dir of Libraries, Southern Univ Baton Rouge, Baton Rouge, LA 70813.

BROWN, GILBERT DAVID, III
Account executive. **Personal:** Born Jul 22, 1949, Philadelphia, PA; son of Rosalie Gaynor Allen and Gilbert David Brown Jr; married Edythe MacFarlane Brown, Jul 5, 1980; children: Gilbert David IV, Courtney Nicole. **Educ:** PA State Univ, BS, business administration, 1973; Pepperdine Univ, MBA, 1983. **Career:** Gillette Co, territory sales rep, 1973-74; Inglewood Meat Co, sales manager, 1974-79; Scott Paper Co, sr sales rep, 1979-84; Paxton Patterson, region manager, 1984-87; McBee Looseleaf Binders Co, account executive, 1987-88; AT&T, General Business Systems, account manager, 1988-91, Commercial Markets, account executive, 1991-92; Pacific Bell, Major Business, account executive, 1992-97; Consumer Market Group, mgr, 1997-. **Orgs:** Kappa Alpha Psi Fraternity Inc, life mem, 1969-, Los Angeles Alumni Ch, polemarch, 1990-93; Alliance of Black Telecommunication Employees, fundraising committee, chairman, 1990-91, professional networking comm, 1991; PA State Univ, alumni recruiter, 1987-95; Young Black Scholars Program, mentor, 1986-; Big Ten Club of Southern California, 1991-; MAARK, advisory board member, 1992-; Professional Communications Association, 1992-; Pepperdine Alumni Association, life mem, 1983-; Penn State Alumni Association, life mem, 1985-; Kappa Achievement Fund Inc, pres, 1994. **Honors/Awds:** Epsilon Pi Tau Fraternity, 1986. **Home Addr:** 741 W 39th St, #3, San Pedro, CA 90731, (310)547-0105.

BROWN, GILBERT JESSE
Professional football player. **Personal:** Born Feb 22, 1971, Farmington, MI; children: Jamal. **Educ:** Kansas, attended. **Career:** Green Bay Packers, defensive tackle, 1993-. **Business Addr:** Professional Football Player, Green Bay Packers, 1265 Lombardi Ave, Green Bay, WI 54304, (414)494-2351.

BROWN, GLENN ARTHUR
Health care executive. **Personal:** Born Jan 27, 1953, Fort Knox, KY. **Educ:** Harvard Univ, AB, 1975; Wharton School Univ of Pennsylvania, MBA, 1980; Univ of Pennsylvania, School of Dental Medicine, DMD, 1982. **Career:** Ambulatory Health Care Consult, mng partner, 1980-83; About Your Smile, PC, pres, 1983-. **Orgs:** Treasurer, Walnut Hill Comm Devel Corp, 1986-90; vice pres, West Philadelphia NAACP, 1989-91; vice pres, Philadelphia Chapter, Natl Black MBA Assn 1989-90; bd mem, Lutheran Children & Family Services 1989-96; bd mem, Greater Philadelphia Health Action 1989-92; National Dental Association; Chess Penn Community Health Ctr, bd mem, 1993-95; African Amer Chamber of Commerce, Philadelphia, charter bd mem, 1993-; advisory committee, Philadelphia Barristers Assn, 1996-97; A Better Chance in Lowe, menon bd, 1996-, treas, 1997-. **Business Addr:** President, About Your Smile, 6772 Market St, Upper Darby, PA 19082-2432, (610)734-0666.

BROWN, GREGGORY LEE
Clergyman. **Personal:** Born Sep 14, 1953, Indianapolis, IN; son of Bettie J. Palmer Brown and Harold S. Brown Sr.; married Beverly Whiteside Brown, Sep 6, 1975. **Educ:** Indiana University, Bloomington, IN, BA, 1971-76; Union Theological Seminary, New York, NY, master of divinity, 1978-80. **Career:** Jarvis Christian College, Hawkins, TX, associate professor, 1979-80; St. Albans Congregational Church, Queens, NY, associate pastor, 1980-81; Springfield Garden Presbyterian Church, Queens, NY, pastor, 1981-85; New Jersey Citizen Action, Hackensack, NJ, regional organizer, 1986-87; Black Tennis and Sports Foundation, New York, NY, executive director, 1987-; Featherbed Lane Presbyterian Church, Bronx, NY, interim pastor, 1988-90; Randall Memorial Presbyterian Church, New York, NY, interim pastor, 1991-. **Orgs:** Chairman, Youth March for Jobs, 1977-79; vice-chairman, Queens Committee, United Negro College Fund, 1984-86; chairman, St. Albans Resource Center, 1980-81; president, Black caucus, Union Theological Seminary, 1978-79; life member, NAACP, 1983. **Honors/Awds:** Merit Award, NAACP, 1980; Coach of the Year, New York City Presbytery, 1983.

BROWN, H. RAP. **See AL-AMIN, JAMIL ABDULLAH.**

BROWN, HANNAH M.
Airline industry executive. **Personal:** Born Jun 23, 1939, Stamps, AR; daughter of Eliza Gardner Junior and Joseph Brown; divorced; children: Juanita LaKay Brown. **Educ:** University of Nevada, Las Vegas, NV; San Mateo College, San Mateo, CA. **Career:** Larry's Music Bar, Las Vegas, NV, salesperson/mgr; Delta Air Lines/Western Air Lines, various positions, 1968-89, regional mgr, 1989-. **Honors/Awds:** NAACP Legal Defense Fund's Black Women of America, 1988; YWCA's Salute to Women of Achievement, 1990; 100 of the Most Promising Black People in America, Ebony Magazine, 1991; Kizzy Award; Dollars and Sense, 1991. **Business Addr:** Regional Manager, Delta Air Lines Inc, Dept 104/ATG, Hartsfield International Airport, Atlanta, GA 30320.

BROWN, HARRIETT BALTIMORE
Educator (retired). **Personal:** Born Sep 13, 1911, Glendale, MD; daughter of Emily Lewis Baltimore and Richard L Baltimore; married Frank C Brown, Dec 27, 1934 (deceased); children: Yvonne, Betty. **Educ:** Hunter College, New York, NY, BS, 1933; Columbia Library School, New York, NY, BLS, 1937. **Career:** New York Public Library, 1934-41; public school teacher, 1941-56; Board of Education, district libraries, 1956-60, supervision of 600 schools, 1960-62; Bd of Educ, bureau of libraries, New York, sup of elementary libraries, 1962-69; Ocean Hill, Brownsville, supervisor of libraries, 1969-73; Ethical Culture, New York, NY, librarian, 1973-76. **Orgs:** President of board, Council of Interracial Books for Children, 1987-91, member, 1967-90; board, Project Rebound, NAACP, 1980-91; board of trustees, Schomburg Library Corp, 1983-88; director, St Philips Elementary Teacher, 1940-55; Coretta Scott King award comm, ALA, 1960-91. **Home Addr:** 382 Central Park, W, New York, NY 10025.

BROWN, HAZEL EVELYN
Association executive. **Personal:** Born Sep 3, 1940, Eden, NC; daughter of Mary Sue Hairston Brown and Joseph Brown (deceased). **Educ:** Russell's Business School, Winston-Salem, NC, Certificate Sec, 1960; Winston-Salem State Univ, Winston-Salem, NC, BA Business Admin, 1977-82; Babcock Center Wake Forest Univ, Winston-Salem, NC, Certificate Mgmt Devel, 1978; NC Central Univ, Durham, NC, Certificate Counsel & Interviewing, 1982; A&T State Univ, Greensboro, NC, MS Adult Educ, 1983-85. **Career:** Winston-Salem Urban League, Winston-Salem, NC, vice pres, 1961-. **Orgs:** Mem, NAACP, 1972-; mem, Mt Zion Baptist Church, 1972-; mem, Winston-Salem State Alumni Assn, 1982-; mem, Up and Coming Investment, 1986-; pres, Natl Women of Achievement/

Clemmons Chapter, 1987-; mem, Delta Sigma Theta Sorority, 1988-; mem, Housing Resource (Bd of Realtors), 1988-; mem, Urban Arts of Arts Council, 1988-; mem, Benton Convention Center Coliseum Comm, 1987-. **Honors/Awds:** Girl Friday, Urban League Guild, 1970; Service Award, NAACP, 1987; Leadership Award, Winston-Salem Urban League, 1988. **Business Addr:** Vice Pres, Winston-Salem Urban League, 201 W Fifth St, Winston-Salem, NC 27101.

BROWN, HELEN E.
Judge. **Personal:** Born Oct 10, Detroit, MI. **Educ:** Wayne State University, BA, 1972, School of Law, JD, 1979. **Career:** Wayne Cty Circuit Court, judge, currently. **Business Addr:** Judge, Wayne County Circuit Ct, 1821 City County Bldg, Detroit, MI 48226.

BROWN, HENRY H.
Business executive (retired). **Personal:** chilDren: 4. **Educ:** Attended, Xavier Univ New Orleans; Texas Southern Univ, Graduate. **Career:** Howard Univ School of Business and Industry, adjunct prof; Anheuser-Busch Inc, vice pres, sr vice pres, mktg develop and affairs, 30 years (retired 1994). **Orgs:** Developed Great Kings and Queens of Africa 1975; Anheuser-Busch's ambassador to major leading natl orgs; chmn Natl Business Policy Review; past imperial Potentate Prince Hall Shriners; also serves on several civic and comm org bds; mem Public Relations Soc of Amer, American Mgmt Assoc, Amer Mktg Assoc, NAMD, St Louis Ambassador and mem Royal Vagabonds. **Honors/Awds:** Disting Awd 1982 World's Fair in Knoxville; Adolphus Awd for Excellence Anheuser-Busch; Disting Amer Awd & 1985 Professional Business Leadership Awd Dollars and Sense Magazine; Omega Man of the Year 1983 St Louis; Corporate Man of the Year NAACP; Marketeer of the Year NAMD; Par Excellence Awd Shielf Foundation; Daniel W Bowles Awd Alpha Phi Alpha; James Weldon Johnson Awd Phi Beta Sigma; Brotherhood Awd Chicago Conf of Human Relations; Disting Pioneer Awd Amer Black Artists; Corporate Executor Natl Assoc of Univ Women; Golden Palm Awd Harris Stowe State; Disting Alumni Awd TX Southern Univ; also various citations from the Links, Jack and Jill, and several municipalities for outstanding supportive svcs. **Business Addr:** Former Senior Vice President-Marketing, Anheuser-Busch, Inc, One Busch Place, St Louis, MO 63118.

BROWN, HERBERT R.
Insurance executive. **Personal:** Born May 20, 1940, Ashville, NC; children: Cheryl, Adrian, Janice. **Educ:** Intl Data Proc Inst, Cert 1961-62; Univ of Cincinnati 1967-69. **Career:** Western Southern Life, computer systems mgmt 1963-78, community affairs/personnel 1978-. **Orgs:** Consult Manpower Training Programs Inc 1978-82; mem & past pres Cincinnati Bd of Ed 1978-; trustee OH School Bds Assoc 1979-; mem Articulation Commiss OH Coll & Secondary Schools 1981-82; vice pres Community Chest United Way 1982-; pres OH Caucus of Black School Bd Mems 1983-; assoc staff dir Greater Cincinnati Found 1983-; bd of dir Amer Red Cross of Cincinnati 1983-; vice pres Private Industry Council of Cincinnati 1983-; pres Natl Caucus of Black School Bd Mems1985. **Honors/Awds:** Outstanding Comm Serv Awd Community Chest of Cincinnati 1976; Jefferson Awd for Public Serv The Amer Inst Public Serv 1979; Leadership Awd Community Chest of Cincinnati 1981; Citizen of the Year Omega Psi Phi Cincinnati 1982. **Military Serv:** AUS sgt E-5 1958-61. **Home Addr:** 2550 Hackberry, Cincinnati, OH 45206. **Business Addr:** Community Affairs Coord, Western Southern Life, 400 Broadway, Cincinnati, OH 45202.

BROWN, HERMAN
Educator. **Personal:** Born Jul 25, 1922, East Orange, NJ; son of Mr & Mrs Harold Brown; divorced. **Educ:** Morgan State College, BS, 1947; New York University, 1949; University of Michigan, MS, 1952; Harvard University, 1955; Washington School of Psychiatry, 1957; Washington Teacher College, 1958; George Washington University, 1958; Washington State University; VA College & Seminary, DHum, 1969; Catholic University of America, PhD, 1972; Hamilton State University, EdD, 1973; Stanton University, Doctorr of Letters, 1975; Washington Saturday College, DHL. **Career:** University of District of Columbia, dean/director, evening school, currently; Washington DC Teachers College, dean, assoc professor, 1970-75, acting dean, professor, 1976; Fed City College, assoc provost, assoc professor, 1975-76; Howard Univ, lecturer, 1970-75; Howard University, instructor, 1960-70; Southern University, asst professor, 1958-63; Lincoln University, assoc professor, 1956; Morris College, research consultant, 1951; Maryland State Teachers College, 1951-58; Bennett College, visiting professor, 1949-51; A&T College, 1948-51. **Orgs:** Natl Education Assn; American Assn of University Professorss; Assn for Supervision & Curriculum Development; Harvard Teachers Assn; American Assn of School Administrators; American Psychol Assn; American Personnel & Guid Assn; Assn for Childhood Education Intl; Education Leadership Council of America Inc; LA Education Assn; Natl History Society; DC Psychol Assn; Natl Alliance of Black School Educators; Black Child Devel Inst Inc; Assn for Study of Afro-American Life & History Inc; Assn for Innovation in Higher Education; Natl Capital Personnel & Guidance Assn; American Heritage Studies Assn; Litton ScienceIndus Inc; Omega Psi; Bachelor Benedict Club; Washington Urban League Inc; Sigma Xi; Phi Eta Sigma; Kappa Delta Pi. **Honors/Awds:** Numerous honors, achievements, appointments, publications; Alumnus of Year Award, Torch Club, Morgan State University, 1979; editorial/advisory bd, Journal of Negro Education; 33 Degree Mason. **Military Serv:** US Army, I&E officer, 1942-46. **Business Addr:** Dean/Director of Evening School, University of District of Columbia, 4200 Connecticut Ave NW, Washington, DC 20008-1174.

BROWN, HEZEKIAH
Educator. **Personal:** Born Jul 29, 1923, Monticello, MS; married Rosa L S. **Educ:** Tuskegee Inst, BS 1950; TN A&I St U, MS 1958; Delta St U, Educ Spec or AAA Cert 1973. **Career:** Simmons High School, group guidance instructor, 1970-75; Carver Elementary School, prin, 1963-70; Simmons High School, teacher, 1951-63; Eutaula, teacher, 1950-51. **Orgs:** Past & treas Sunflower Co Tchrs Assn; chaplain VFW Post 9732 1955-75; Dept chaplain Dept of MS 1974-75; mem Adv Bd CHP; bd of alderman; vice pres Washington Tchrs Assn 1970-75; mem Washington Co Solid Waste Com; VFW; MS Tchrs Assn; MS Vocational Guidance Assn; Alpha Phi Alpha; MS Municipal Assn; AVA; Military Order of Cooties SS #13. **Honors/Awds:** Tchr Awd MS State 1975; life memshp VFW Post #9732. **Military Serv:** AUS sgt 1943-46.

BROWN, HOYT C.
City administrator. **Personal:** Born Nov 1, 1920, Andersonville, GA; married Marjorie Harmon; children: James F, Beatrice C. **Educ:** So U, 1941; Compton JC, 1949; IN Univ NW Campus, 1969. **Career:** City of Gary, adminstr engr ofc bldg 1979-, baliff City Ct 1977-79; Lake Co IN, Justice of Peace, Dem 1962-77; Gary, IN, first black City Zoning & Adminstr 1960, first black City Chief Draftsman 1958; Crown Point, first black Chief Draftsman 1952; Lake Co, juvenile probation ofc 1951. **Orgs:** Pres IN St Assn of Justices of Peace; mem Mason IBOPE; Lake City Elks; Knights of Phythias; IN Black Caucus; Club Future; Steel Dust; Ol' Timers; NAACP; FAB; MADA; Kappa Alpha Psi; Brotherhood of Sleeping Car Porter; Laison of FEPC. **Business Addr:** 401 Broadway, Gary, IN.

BROWN, INEZ M.
Government official. **Career:** Office of US Senator Don Riegle, MI, various positions, 21 years, senior policy advisor on urban affairs, beginning 1989; US Small Busines Admin, regional advocate reg 5, currently. **Orgs:** Genessee County, MI, Economic Development Commission, bd of dir; Bishop Airport Authority; Univ of Michigan, citizen advisory bd; Genessee Economic Revitalization Agency, advisor; Flint, MI, Mayor Woodrow Stanley, Urban Investment Plan, advisor. **Business Addr:** Regional Advocate, Region 5, US Small Business Administration, 1156 15th St. NW, Ste 510, Washington, DC 20005, (202)639-8500.

BROWN, IRMA JEAN
Attorney. **Personal:** Born May 17, 1948, Los Angeles, CA. **Educ:** Marymount Coll, 1970. **Career:** LA Co Pub Defenders Office, law clerk 1973; CA Assoc of Black Lawyers, secty; Greater Watts Justice Ctr Legal Aid Foundation of LA, law clerk, staff atty; Hudson Sndz & Brown, law firm partner; Los Angeles County Municipal Ct, judge. **Orgs:** Pres LA Negro Bus & Professional Wmns Club 1965-66; vice pres So Chap Blck Wmn Lwyrs Assn of CA 1975-76, pres 1976-77; sgt at arms JM Langston Bar Assn 1976-77; LA Co Bar Assn; CA Attys for Crmnl Jstc; treas Nat Conf of Blck Lwyrs 1976-77; Nat Bar Assn; Delta Sigma Theta Sor; Urban Leag; NAACP; Jrdn H S Almn Assn; New Frntr Dem Club; trustee First African Methodist Episcopal Church of Los Angeles; mem 100 Black Women of Los Angeles, Natl Assoc of Women Judges, CA Judges Assoc. **Honors/Awds:** Grnt Schlrsh Lgl Educ Oppty 1970-73; Delta Sigma Theta Schlrsh 1970; So CA Gas Co Schlrsh 1970; publ The Minor & The Juv Ct Lgl Aid Found of LA 1975; Certificates of Recognition for Achievement US Congress, CA Senate, City of Compton, Carson-Lynwood, Los Agneles County.

BROWN, JACQUELINE D.
Educator, orthodontist. **Personal:** Born Oct 27, 1957, Nashville, TN; daughter of Birdie Faulkner Brown and James H Brown, DDS. **Educ:** Brandeis Univ, Waltham, MA, BA, 1979; Meharry Medical Coll, Nashville, TN, DDS, 1983; Univ of Michigan, Ann Arbor, MI, MS, 1985. **Career:** Howard Univ Dept of Orthodontics, Washington, DC, asst prof, 1985-; private practice, Silver Springs, MD, 1986-; Howard Univ School of Dentistry, Advanced Gen Dentistry Program, consultant, 1986-; Howard Univ School of Dentistry, Gen Practice Residency Program, attending physician, 1986-. **Orgs:** Amer Assn of Orthodontists, 1983-; Intl Assn of Dental Research, 1983-; Middle Atlantic Soc of Orthodontists, 1983-; Omicron Kappa Upsilon Dental Honor Soc, 1983-; Metropolitan Washington Study Club, 1983-; Amer Assn of Women Dentists, 1987-. **Honors/Awds:** Univ of Michigan Merit Fellowship, 1983, 1984; Patterson Dental Supply Award, 1983; William H Allen Award, 1983; Certificate of Appreciation, Howard Univ Coll of Dentistry Advanced Gen Dentistry Program, 1988; author, abstract, "The Development of the Oxytalan Fiber System of the Mouse Periodontal Ligament," IADR meeting, 1986.

BROWN, JAMES
Sportscaster. **Career:** WTEM Radio, talk show host; CBS Sports, sportscaster, currently. **Business Addr:** Sports Commentator, CBS Sports, 51 W. 52nd St., New York, NY 10019, (212)925-4321.

BROWN, JAMES
Entertainer. **Personal:** Born Jun 17, 1934, Augusta, GA; son of Susie and Joseph Brown; married Adrianne Brown; children: Deanna, Terry, Daryl, Venisha, Yamma. **Career:** Leader musical group Famous Flames, now solo performer; recordings include Original Disco Man, Please Please Please, Hot on the One, Poppa's Got a Brand New Bag; JB Broadcasting Ltd, pres 1968-; James Brown Network, pres 1968-. **Orgs:** Chmn bd James Brown Productions, James Brown Entertainment, and Man's World Augusta; his organizations include two recording companies, two real estate int & three radio stations. **Honors/Awds:** Known as "Godfather of Soul" & Soul Brother #1; 44 Gold Records; Grammy Awd 1965, 1986; appeared in 3 films and in television and theatre productions; recorded first hit song 1956; received Humanitarian Award, Music & Perform Arts Lodge of B'nai B'rith New York City 1969; one of first ten musicians inducted into Rock n Roll Hall of Fame; hit songs include Don't Be A Dropout; Say It Loud, I'm Black and I'm Proud; I'm Real; Gravity; Reality; author of Autobiography James Brown, The Godfather of Soul; American Music Award, Award of Merit, 1992. **Business Addr:** c/o The New James Brown Enterprises, 1217 West Medical Park Road, Augusta, GA 30901.

BROWN, JAMES E.
Dental surgeon. **Personal:** Born Feb 3, 1923, Holly Hill, SC; married Sarah L Burgess. **Educ:** SC St Coll, BvS 1947; Howard U, DDS 1952. **Career:** Self Employed Dental Surgeon. **Orgs:** Mem Am Dental Assn; SC Dental Assn; Costal Dist Dental Soc; Palmetto Med Dental & Pharmaceutical Assn (pres 1967-68); pres Charleston Co Med Assn;dental staff McClellan Banks Mem Hosp; bd dir Franklin C Fetter Comprehensive Hlth Ctr; past pres Owis Whist Club; Owls Whist Club; treas Athenians Club; Omega Psi Phi; treas St Paul AME Ch; sec treas Midland Park Dem Precinct; mem Tri Dent C of C; chmn Task Force for Quality Edn; mem Charter Commn Charleston Co Consult Govt; Rotary Club of Charleston SC. **Honors/Awds:** Recipient 2 Bronze Stars; honored as outstanding Black Professional Coll of Charleston 1975. **Military Serv:** USAF t/4; 3 yrs. **Business Addr:** 34 Morris St, Charleston, SC 29403.

BROWN, JAMES H.
Business executive. **Personal:** Born Mar 16, 1935, Wake Co, NC; married Geraldine G; children: Deborah C, James H, Jr. **Career:** Raleigh Funeral Home, asst funeral dir 1955-57; Salesman, auto 1957-58; 1st Natl Bank, bank mess 1958-59; Wash Terr Apts, apt supt 1958-59; J W Winters & Co, real estate sales mgr 1961-66; Brown Realty Co, pres 1966-. **Orgs:** Chmn Political Action Comm; NAACP; Raleigh Citizens Assn; Raleigh C of C; precinct chmn Wake Co Democratic Party; chmn trustee bd, chmn bldg comm, chmn finance comm compl chrg of 300,00000 ch Ldc United Church of Chrst 1972-73; Chmn Mayoral Campaign. **Honors/Awds:** 1st Black Mayor Elected in City of Raleigh 1973.

BROWN, JAMES HARVEY (SAC)
Dentist, educator. **Personal:** Born Aug 30, 1924, Malcom, AL; son of Alice Woodyard Brown Ross and Charlie Myles Brown; married Birdie Faulkner-Brown, Jun 1, 1946; children: Albert, Alice, Jacqueline, Renee, James Jr. **Educ:** Alabama A&M University, Normal, AL, BS, 1946; Meharry Medical College, Nashville, TN, DDS, 1952; Tennessee State University, Nashville, TN, MS, zoology, 1961, MEd, education administration, 1964. **Career:** Meharry Medical College, School of Dentistry, Nashville, TN, associate professor, 1952-; private practice, 1955-; Riverside Hospital, dental staff, 1958-78; Tennessee State University Student Health Service, Nashville, TN, assistant to the director, 1958-64, director, 1964-69; Clover Bottom Hospital and School, clinical supervisory of dental students, 1964-72; George W. Hubbard Hospital of Meharry Medical College, Nashville, TN, dental staff, 1952-, secretary-treasurer, 1968-; Hospital Dental Service, Meharry-Hubbard Hospital, Nashville,TN, director, 1964-81; Veterans Administration Hosptial, Nashville, TN and Murfreesboro, TN, consultant, 1968-81. **Orgs:** Alpha Phi Alpha, 1949; charter member, American Assn of Hospital Dentists; Capital City Dental Society; Pan-Tennessee Dental Assn; Natl Dental Assn; Nashville Dental Society; Tennessee State Dental Assn; American Dental Assn; Nashville Academy of Medicine; Davidson County Medical Society; Frontiers, Inc; Tennessee State Medical Assn; American Assn of Dental Schools, Council of Hospitals, Sections on Hospital Dentists, Oral Surgery, Anesthesia, and Operative Dentistry; fellow, American Academy of General Dentistry, 1977; American Academy of Operative Dentistry; American Assn of Tension Control; diplomate, National Board of Dental Examiners, 1955. **Honors/Awds:** President's Award, Meharry Medical College, 1977; Award for Excellence with Students, Pre-Alumni Assn of Meharry College, 1982; Omicron Kappa Upsilon Honor Dental Soc, 1959; author, "The Effect of Calcium Blood Levels in Strontum Fed Rats," "A Program for the Development of a Department of Hospital Dentistry," "The

Predictive Value of the Manual Section of the Dental Aptitude Test on Clinical Performance of Third and Fourth Dental Students at Maharry Medical College''; subject of book, Educating Black Doctors - A History of Meharry Medical College by James Summerville, 1983; subject of article, ''A Father and His Six Children Make Medicine Their Way of Life,'' Ebony Magazine, July, 1988. **Military Serv:** US Army, 11th Airborne Division, Dental Medical Corps, 1st Lt, 1953-55. **Home Addr:** 4208 Enchanted Ct, Nashville, TN 37218.

BROWN, JAMES LAMONT
Professional football player. **Personal:** Born Nov 30, 1970, Philadelphia, PA; children: Semaj. **Educ:** Virginia State. **Career:** New York Jets, tackle, 1993-95; Miami Dolphins, 1996-. **Business Addr:** Professional Football Player, Miami Dolphins, 2269 NW 199th St, Miami, FL 33056, (305)620-5000.

BROWN, JAMES MARION
City official. **Personal:** Born Jul 30, 1952, Holdenville, OK; son of Carrie Mae Knox Brown and Clearnce Brown Jr; married Clarice M Brown (divorced); children: James Jr, Tiffany. **Educ:** East Central Univ, Ada, OK, BS; 12 hours on Masters. **Career:** McAlester High School, teacher 1977-; City of McAlester, Councilmember, 1982-86, 1988-. **Orgs:** Member, Special Service Board for State of Oklahoma Teachers, 1977-81; Member, Board of Directors, State of Oklahoma Teachers Convention Committee, 1977-81; Trustee, McAlester Health Authority, 1982-86; Trustee, McAlester Economic Devel Service, 1982-86; Member, Black Elected Officials, 1982-86; Board Member, Public Works Board, McAlester, Oklahoma; Appointed Member, Oklahoma Human Rights Commission, 1984; Board Member, McAlester Boy's Club, 1984-86; 1st black vice mayor, City, 1990-92. **Honors/Awds:** Awarded Highest Grade Point Average of Alpha Phi Alpha, 1975; Member, Oklahoma Municipal League, 1982-86; Member, McAlester Youth Shelter, 1984; Member, State Attorney General Advisory Commission, 1985; Gov Committee Physical Fitness; NAACP Man of the Year Award, 1988-89. **Home Addr:** 1208 North G St, McAlester, OK 74501. **Business Addr:** Councilman, City of McAlester, 1 Buffalo Drive, McAlester, OK 74501.

BROWN, JAMES MONROE
General chairman. **Personal:** Born Jun 28, 1928, Pulaski, TN; son of Theola Brown and John Brown; married Ann McKissack. **Career:** Abraham McKissack Sr Citizens Homes Inc, chmn of the bd, pres; TN Voters Council, gen chmn; bd TN Black Leadership Round Table; Queen Ann Funeral Home, owner. **Orgs:** Mem Elks Lodge 1489; trustee State Coord TN Voters Council; mem TN Delegation Dem Natl Conventions 1968-72-76; former chmn Giles Co Dem; mem Campbell AME Church; former mem Consumer Affairs Comm So Bell Telephone for State of TN 1980-82. **Honors/Awds:** Man of Yr Giles & Lawrence Cos 1968; Man of Yr Elks Lodge #1489 1973; Elks Man of the Year Giles Co 1985; Invited to the White House by President Carter, 1978. **Military Serv:** USN 1944-46, 1951-55. **Business Addr:** General Chairman, Tennessee Voters Council, 410 N 1st St, Pulaski, TN 38478.

BROWN, JAMIE
Professional football player. **Personal:** Born Apr 24, 1972, Miami, FL; son of Jimmie Brown and Jeannie Blunt. **Educ:** Florida A&M. **Career:** Denver Broncos, tackle, 1995-. **Special Achievements:** Selected in the 4th round/121st overall pick in the 1995 NFL Draft. **Business Addr:** Professional Football Player, Denver Broncos, 13655 Broncos Pkwy, Englewood, CO 80112, (303)649-9000.

BROWN, JAMIE EARL S., JR. (JAMES)
Lawyer, business executive. **Personal:** Born Dec 31, 1940, New York, NY; son of Josephine & Jamie Brown Sr; married Daisy Gore Brown, Aug 13, 1968; children: Michael, Mark, Martin. **Educ:** Northern Michigan Univ, BS, 1970; State Univ of New York at Buffalo, School of Law, JD, 1973. **Career:** Kings County Dist Attorney, law investigator, asst dist atty, 1973-75; Dept of Health Educ & Welfare, attorney advisor, 1975-83; J Earl Brown Realty Corp, pres, 1983-89; State Senator Andrew Jenkins, chief legislative asst, 1989-92; J Earl Brown & Associates, PC, law, real estate, 1992-. **Orgs:** Ancient Free & Accepted Masons, King Solomon Lodge #5, 32nd Degree; Natl Bar Assn; Phi Alpha Delta Legal Frat; New York State Bar Assn; Omega Psi Phi Frat; NAACP; One Hundred Black Men of New York; Amer Bar Assn. **Honors/Awds:** Dept of Health and Human Services, Performance Outstanding Service Award, 1981; Natl Assn, Each One Teach One, Outstanding Comm Citizen, 1990. **Special Achievements:** Conference of Black Art Collectors, Panel Organizer; Fluent in language of Fante, Ghanian, mainly Western & Central Africa. **Business Addr:** President, J Earl Brown Associates Ltd, PO Box 48007, Philadelphia, PA 19144.

BROWN, JANICE ROGERS
Judge. **Personal:** widoWed; children (previous marriage): Nathan Allan; married Dewey Parker. **Educ:** California State Univ, bachelor's degree, 1974; UCLA, JD, 1977. **Career:** California Dept of Justice, deputy attorney general, 1979-87; California Business, Transportation and Housing Agency, deputy secretary/general counsel, 1987-91; Governor Pete Wilson, legal affairs secretary, 1991-94; California Court of Appeals, associate justice, 1994-96; California Supreme Court, justice, 1996-. **Special Achievements:** First African American woman to serve on the California Supreme Court. **Business Addr:** Judge, California Supreme Court, 302 SE Street, South Tower, 9th Fl, San Francisco, CA 94107.

BROWN, JARVIS ARDEL
Professional baseball player. **Personal:** Born Mar 26, 1967, Waukegan, IL. **Educ:** Triton. **Career:** Minnesota Twins, outfielder, 1991-. **Business Addr:** Professional Baseball Player, Minnesota Twins, 501 Chicago Ave S, Minneapolis, MN 55415, (612)375-1366.

BROWN, JASPER C., JR.
Attorney. **Personal:** Born Mar 27, 1946, Columbia, SC; married Sandra Cox; children: Leslie, Douglass, Jasper David. **Educ:** Hampton Inst, BS 1969; Cath Univ Columbus Sch of Law;; JD 1974. **Career:** NLRB Div of Advice, staff atty 1974-77; Gen Electric Co, prodn Mgr 1969-71. **Orgs:** Mem Nat Bar Assn 1974-; mem PA Bar Assn 1974-; mem NC Assn of Black Lawyers 1977-. **Honors/Awds:** Opportunity fellow Council on Legal Educ Opportunity Scholarship Fund Washington DC 1971-74; Earl Warren fellow Earl Warren Found Scholarship Fund NY 1973. **Business Addr:** Natl Labor Relations Board, 241 N Main St, Ste 447, Winston-Salem, NC 27101.

BROWN, J.B. (JAMES HAROLD)
Professional football player. **Personal:** Born Jan 5, 1967, Washington, DC; married Renee; children: Leia Paris Roberts, Michael, Janee Keanna. **Educ:** Univ of Maryland. **Career:** Miami Dolphins, defensive back, 1989-96; Pittsburgh Steelers, 1997-. **Business Addr:** Professional Football Player, Pittsburgh Steelers, Three Rivers Stadium, 300 Stadium Circle, Pittsburgh, PA 15212, (412)323-1200.

BROWN, JEFFREY LEMONTE
Clergyman. **Personal:** Born Dec 22, 1961, Anchorage, AK; son of Geraldine G Brown and Jesse L Brown; married Lesley A Mosley; children: Rayna Adair Brown. **Educ:** East Stroudsburg Univ, BA 1982; Indiana Univ PA, MEd 1984; Andover Newton Theol Sch, MDiv 1987. **Career:** Amer Baptist Churches Inc, rep gen bd 1987-91; Union Baptist Church, senior pastor. **Orgs:** Student body pres 1981-82, black caucus pres 1980-81 East Stroudsburg Univ; student exec officer 1985-86, mem racism/sexism task force 1986-87 Andover Newton Theol Sch; corresponding secretary, United Baptist Convention of Massachusetts, Rhode Island, & New Hampshire 1988-; bd mem, Dept of Church and Society, Amer Baptist Churches of Massachusetts 1988-90; bd mem, Board of Ministry, Harvard Univ 1989-92; president, Cambridge Black Pastors Conference, 1991-; board of directors, Cambridge Economic Opportunity Committee, 1990-. **Honors/Awds:** Jonathan Edwards Honor Soc Andover Newton Theol Sch 1985-87; Student Leadership Awd East Stroudsburg Univ 1982; Outstanding Achievement Awd PA EEO-Act 101 1986; Kelsey Merit Scholar Andover Newton Theol Sch 1986-87. **Home Addr:** 184 Raymond Street, Cambridge, MA 02140.

BROWN, JESSE
Former government official. **Career:** Disabled American Veterans, executive director; US Department of Veteran Affairs, secretary, 1992-97. **Business Addr:** Former Secretary, US Dept of Veterans Affairs, 810 Vermont Ave NW, Washington, DC 20420, (202)233-4010.

BROWN, JIM (JAMES NATHANIEL)
Actor. **Personal:** Born Feb 17, 1936, St Simons Island, GA; son of Theresa Brown and Swinton Brown; married Sue Jones, 1958 (divorced); children: Kim, Kevin, Jim. **Educ:** Syracuse Univ, BA, economics, 1957. **Career:** Cleveland Browns, fullback, 1957-65; film actor; Amer-I-can, founder, currently. **Honors/Awds:** Jim Thorpe Trophy, 1958, 1965; Player of the Year, 1958, 1963, 1965; Hickoc Belt Athlete of Year, 1964; All American, 1956; Hall of Fame, 1971; named to every All-Star Team, 1963; 2nd on all-time rushing list; greatest distance gained in one season; films include: The Dirty Dozen; Fingers; Ice Station Zebra; I'm Gonna Git You Sucka; Kid Vengenance; One Down, Two to Go; 100 Rifles; Pacific Thunder; Take a Hard Ride; numerous TV Appearances; author, Off My Chest, 1964 and recent autobiography; creator of innovative program to help young men leave street gangs. **Special Achievements:** Appointed by California Assembly Speaker, Willie L Brown Jr to the Commission on the Status of African American Males, 1994.

BROWN, JOAN P. (ABENA)
Foundation executive. **Personal:** Born in Chicago, IL; daughter of Lueola Reed and Rufus Phillips; divorced. **Educ:** Roosevelt U, BA 1950; Univ of Chicago, MA 1963; Honorary Doctorate, Humane Letters, Chicago State University, 1993. **Career:** YWCA of Metropolitan Chicago, area dir 1963-65, consult human rel 1965-70, dir of program serv 1970-82; ETA Creative Arts Found, pres 1982-. **Orgs:** Pres Black Theatre Alliance Chicago IL 1978-84; pres Midwest Theatre Alliance 1982-86; chmn City Arts Policy Committee 1985-90; mem/chmn Sub Committee on Pgm Mayor's Dept of Cultural Affairs 1985-; mem Interdisciplinary Panel Natl Endowment for the Arts; Access Committee, IL; Arts Council vice pres, president, 1991-93; Women's Bd, Chicago Urban League and vice chair, Muntu Dance Theatre. **Honors/Awds:** Paul Robeson Award, Black Theatre Alliance of Chicago 1978; Governor's Award in the Arts IL 1981; monograph Politics of/and Black Theatre 1979; producer ETA Mainstage Prod 1983-; dir ''Shango Diaspora,'' ''Witness a Voice Anthology When the Wind Blows'' 1981-; ''Passenger Past Midnight,'' In Americas 100 Top Bus & Prof Women, Dollars & Sense Magazine, Hazel Joan Bryant Award, Midwest African Amer Theatre Alliance, 1988; Black Rose Award, Legue of Black Women, 1988; Finalist Kool Achiever Award, 1988; Outstanding Achievement Award, Young Executives in Politics, 1987; Outstanding Business Award, Iota Phi Lambda, Chicago, 1990; Award of Excellence, Arts & Theatre, National Hook Up Black Women, Chicago chapter, 1990; Garvey, Muhammed, King Culture Award, Majestic Eagles, 1990; City of Chicago, eted to Women's Hall of Fame, 1992; Chicago State University, honorary doctorate of humane letters, 1993; Arts Entrepreneurial Awd, Columbia College of Chicago, 1995. **Home Addr:** 7637 S Bennett St, Chicago, IL 60649. **Business Addr:** Co-Founder, President/Producer, ETA Creative Arts Found, 7558 S South Chicago Ave, Chicago, IL 60619.

BROWN, JOEANNA HURSTON
Consultant/trainer. **Personal:** Born Apr 22, 1939, Auburn, AL; daughter of Lelia Mae Brown Mims and Walter Lee Hurston; married Austin I Brown, Aug 1955 (divorced 1970); children: Deborah, Michael, Suzanne, Neleta, Anthony, Venita. **Educ:** Coll of St Rose, Albany, NY, BA, 1974; American Univ, Washington, DC, MS, 1989; Fielding Institute, Santa Barbara, CA, Doctoral Candidate. **Career:** NY State Cable TV Commissioner, Albany, NY, asst municipal cable TV consultant, 1976-78; NY State Div of Budget, Albany, NY, director professional staffing & career development, 1978-1990; J Hurston Associates, Albany, NY, pres, 1990-; Full Spectrum Inc, co-founder, 1990-; State University of NY, Rockefeller College Center for Women in Government, director of Public Policy Leadership Programs, 1992-. **Orgs:** Co-fndr, Capital Toastmasters; Albany Upstate Blacks in Govt, pres; ex comm mem, NY State Affirmative Action Advisory Council; bd mem, Albany Chapter 100 Black Women; mem, Ctr for Women in Govt, Advisory Comm on Minority Women Issues. **Honors/Awds:** Outstanding Contribution, NY State Affirmative Action Adv Council, 1990; Outstanding Service, NY State Affirmative Action Advisory Council Women's Comm, 1988; Hal Kellner Award, American Univ/Natl Training Lab, 1989. **Business Addr:** President, J Hurston Associates, PO Box 6816, Albany, NY 12206-0816, (518)427-8540.

BROWN, JOHN, JR.
Automobile dealer. **Career:** East Tulsa Dodge Inc, pres, currently. **Orgs:** Kappa Alpha Psi Fraternity Inc; American Red Cross, board of directors; Metropolitan Tulsa Chamber of Commerce, board of directors; Metropolitan Tulsa Urban League, board of directors. **Honors/Awds:** Tulsa Chapter NAACP Freedom Fund Award, 1997. **Business Addr:** President, East Tulsa Dodge Inc, 4627 S Memorial Dr, Tulsa, OK 74145.

BROWN, JOHN ANDREW
Educator, educational administrator. **Personal:** Born Jul 17, 1945, Birmingham, AL; son of Elmira Kelsey-Brown (deceased) and Kalop Todd Brown (deceased); married Phyllis Dean Windham, Jul 17, 1993. **Educ:** Daniel Payne College, AA, 1965; Columbia University, 1966; Dartmouth College, 1966; Miles College, BA, 1967; Yale University Divinity School, MDiv, 1970, STM, 1972. **Career:** Yale Univ Divinity Sch, assoc prof 1970-73; Trinity Coll Hartford, asst prof rel/dir ICS prog 1973-76; CT Coll New London, vstg prof rel 1974-75;The Coll of New Rochelle at NY, theol sem adj prof rel 1980-; Audrey Cohen College, prof/adm, 1979-93, adjunct prof of business ethics, 1988-93, special asst to the vice pres/dir of staff development, 1991-93; Miles Coll, adjunct prof of history, 1994-; Lawson State Community Coll, adjunct prof of history, philosophy and religion, 1994-; Univ of Alabama at Birmingham, consultant, 1994. **Orgs:** Consultant Trinity Coll 1973, Manchester Comm Coll1976; educ admin Bronx Extension Site-Coll for Human Serv 1986-; mem NY Urban League, Alpha Phi Alpha,NAACP, ASALH, Yale Alumni Associates of Afro-Americans, AAUP. **Honors/Awds:** Carnegie Fellowship Columbia Univ 1966; Richard Allen Awd; Rockefeller Protestant Fellowship Theological Education 1967-70; Oliver E Daggett Prize Yale Corp 1969; Research Fellowship Yale Univ 1971-72; mem Pi Gamma Mu; Fellowship UTS Black Econ Develop Fund 1976; Biog sketch in Yale Univ 1985 Alumni Directory; The College of New Rochelle, Ten Years of Outstanding Teaching and Contributions to the College, 1989, Award for Fourteen Years of Outstanding Teaching and Service to the College, 1993; Audrey Cohen College, Crystal Award, 1991; Phi Theta Kappa Inc, Alpha Epsilon Gama Chapter, Award for Outstanding Service, 1996. **Business Addr:** Professor, Social Science Dept, Lawson State Community College, 3060 Wilson Rd, Birmingham, AL 35221.

BROWN, JOHN BAKER, JR.
Journalist. **Personal:** Born Sep 28, 1947, Akron, OH; son of Wanda Elaine Mason Brown and John Baker Brown Sr; children: Drew M J. **Educ:** University of Akron, BS (with honors), education, 1971, MA, communications, 1976. **Career:** Western Reserve Academy, Upward Bound Program, Akron Public Schools, University of Akron, mass media communications, human relations, English comp, African-American history, educator, 1970-75; Babcock & Wilcox Co, writing & graphic services, supervisor, 1976-79; AT&T, Cincinnati and New Jersey, various positions, 1979-85; Cohn & Wolfe, account supervisor, 1987-88; writer and editor for following companies: Coca-Cola Co, AT&T, Joint Ctr for Political & Economic Studies, Georgia's Fulton County Government, Clark Atlanta University, Morehouse College, H J Russell & Co, Jones Worley Design, Atlanta Bd of Educ; The Atlanta Tribune, "Introspect," former editor, columnist. **Orgs:** Atlanta Urban ministry, newsletter editor; Atlanta Ballethnic Dance Co, bd of directors; United Negro College Fund, former pro bono public relations counsel; Southeast UNICEF, former pro bono public relations counsel; Black Public Relations Society, Atlanta Chapter, past president; Interassociation Council for Public Relations, co-founder; Intl Television Assn, former regional director. **Business Addr:** Freelance Writer, 1505 Fieldgreen Overlook, Stone Mountain, GA 30088.

BROWN, JOHN C., JR.
Business executive. **Personal:** Born Jun 9, 1939, Camden, NJ; married Gloria Brown; children: Jay, Ernie. **Educ:** Univ of Syracuse, BA 1962; Univ of Pittsburgh, attended 1972-74; Stonier Grad Sch of Banking, grad degree banking 1980. **Career:** Pittsburgh Nat Bank Oakland, dist mgr dist X 1980; Pittsburgh Nat Bank Oakland, vice pres 1979; Pittsburgh & Nat Bank Oakland, asst vice pres 1978; Pittsburgh Nat Bank Oakland, mgr Oakland ofc 1977; Pittsburgh Nat Bank Oakland, comm banking ofc 1974; Pittsburgh Nat Bank, credit analyst 1970-74; Cleveland Browns, professional football 1962-66; Math & English, tchr & counselor 1962-63; Firestone Tire & Rubber Co, franchise with Paul Warfield 1964; Pittsburgh Steelers, professional football 1966-72. **Orgs:** Bd of dir United Way YMCA; treas Nat Multiple Sclerosis Soc; mem NAACP; mem Rotary Oakland. **Business Addr:** Pittsburgh Natl Bank, 4022 5th Ave, Pittsburgh, PA 15213.

BROWN, JOHN E.
Security services company executive. **Personal:** Born Jul 2, 1948, Columbia, SC; son of Naomi Burrell Brown and John Brown Jr; married Jessie Gwendolyn Reardon, Jul 10, 1975; children: Michael, Roderick, Geoffrey. **Educ:** Palmer Junior College, 1970-71; Columbia Business College, AA, business administration & traffic management, 1979. **Career:** Richland County Sheriff's Department, deputy, 1971-72; South Carolina Highway Patrol, patrolman, 1972-85; Am-Pro Protective Agency, president, chief executive officer, 1982-93, chairman, 1993-97; hazard waste business. **Orgs:** Richland County's Business Round Table for the Governor's Initiative for Work Force Excellence; American Legion, board of directors; United Way of the Midlands, board of directors; Palmetto Boys State, steering committee; Gillcreek Baptist Church, board of directors; Branch Banking & Trust, corporate advisory board; South Carolina State Museum, board of directors; Columbia Urban League; Blue Ribbon Comm; United Black Fund; Comm of 100 Black Men; Columbia Bus Network Assn; Chamber of Commerce Comm of 100; SC Legislative Black Caucus Corp Roundtable; Palmetto Dockside Gaming Assn, advisory comm; Entrepreneur of the Year Judging Comm, Bd of Governors, Capital City Club; SC Chat, Entrepreneur of the Year Inst. **Honors/Awds:** SC Conference of Branches of the NAACP, Corp Award, 1994; Outstanding Achievement Award, Honoree of the SC Black Hall of Fame, 1994; Flour Daniel Contractor Recognition Award, 1994; Inducted to Entrepreneur of the Year Hall of Fame, 1993; SC Entrepreneur of the Year, Non-Financial Svcs, 1993; Natl Urban League, Ruth Standish Baldwin, Eugene Kinckle Jones, Volunteer Svcs Award, 1993; Columbia Urban League, VC Summer Corporate Award, 1992; SC Conference of Branches of the NAACP, Corporate Award, 1992; US Small Business Administration, Administrator's Award for Excellence, 1989, Minority Small Businessman of the Year Award, 1988; 8(a) Contractor of the Year, 1988; Natl Finalist for Federal Sub-Contractor of the Year, 1988; District One Highway patrolman of the Year, 1980; Governor of South Carolina, Order of Palmetto, 1978. **Special Achievements:** Inc 500's listing of #164 of top 500 companies, 1992, listing as #257 of the top 500 companies, 1990, 1991. **Military Serv:** US Army, sgt, 1968-71; Bronze Star, National Defense Service, Expert Rifleman, Vietnam Service, Good Conduct. **Business Addr:** Chairman/CEO, Am-Pro Protective Agency Inc, PO Box 23829, Columbia, SC 29224.

BROWN, JOHN MITCHELL, SR.
General officer (retired), military history expert. **Personal:** Born Dec 11, 1929, Vicksburg, MS; son of Ernestine Foster Brown and Joeddie Fred Brown; married Louise Yvonne Dorsey, Dec 14, 1963; children: Ronald Quinton, Jan Michelle, John Mitchell, Jay Michael. **Educ:** West Point, US Military Academy, BS, Eng, 1955; Syracuse Univ, MBA, 1964; Univ of Houston, 1978. **Career:** US Army, 1955-88: Combat Duty Republic of South Vietnam; Asst Secretary of the General Staff to Chief of Staff Army, 1970-71; Battalion Commander, 8th Infantry Div, 1971-73; Sr Exec to Comptroller of the Army, 1973-77; Commander, 3rd Brigade, 2nd Div, Korea, 1976-77; Asst Commander, 2nd Infantry Div, Korea, 1979-80; Deputy Chief of Staff, Material Plans, Programs & Budget; Office of Army Rsch, Devel & Procurement, 1980-83; Comptroller, US Army Forces Command, 1983-85; Deputy Commander, III Corps & Fort Hood Texas; MBA Analytics, currently. **Orgs:** NAACP, Veteran of Foreign Wars, American Legion, Council of 100, Chamber of Commerce, National Urban League; American Defense Preparedness Association; Minority Development Legal Fund; National Association of Minority Business; Association of US Army; Masons. **Honors/Awds:** Distinguished Service Medal, Two Meritorious Service Awards; Three Army Commendations, 1955-; Published Defense Econ Analysis in Defense, Econ Analysis in the Army, 1969; City of Atlanta and State of Georgia Proclamation Designating June 19, 1985 as "John M. Brown Day". **Military Serv:** AUS, 1955-88. **Business Addr:** President/CEO, MBA, Incorporated, PO Box 1368, Upper Marlboro, MD 20773.

BROWN, JOHN OLLIS
Physician. **Personal:** Born Oct 23, 1922, Colbert, OK; son of Sala Brown and Edward Brown; married Marie Louise Faulkner; children: John, Jr, William E, Gala Munnings, Lawrence F. **Educ:** Univ of WI, 1939-43; Menarry Med Coll, MD 1950; VA Hosp Tuskesee, AL, residency 1951-55. **Career:** Cedars of Lebanon Hosp, physician; Jackson Mem Hosp, physician; Christian Hosp, physician. **Orgs:** Bd of dir Capital Bank 1976-80; trustee 1979-80, pres 1986, Nat Med Assn 1979-80; mem Dade Co Med Assn; mem Am Med Assn; mem FL Med Assn; life mem NAACP; mem Sigma Pi Phi; mem Omega Psi Phi. **Military Serv:** Inf 1st Lt 1943-46; Recipient Purple Heart & Oak Leaf Cluster Inf 1945. **Business Addr:** Physician, 1001 NW 54th St, Miami, FL 33127.

BROWN, JOHN SCOTT
Architect. **Personal:** Born Oct 4, 1930, Englewood, NJ; son of Melle Hortense Stubbs Brown (deceased) and John Scott Brown (deceased); married Brenda Lawson (deceased); children: Leigh Melle, Courtney Hughes, John. **Educ:** Howard U, BArch 1965, Master ofc City Planning 1975. **Career:** IRS Dept of Treas, chief A & E sec; Reg Griffith Asso, sr arch urban planner 1974-78; United & Plan Org, dir office of prgm Dev 1973-74; Concept Design Div United Plan Org, head 1971-73; WA Plan Wrkshp Planner Met WA Planning & Housing Assn, dir 1969-71; Constrn Specs Inst, asst tech dir 1966-69; NAV FAC Dept of Navy, arch plan 1965-66; IRS Dept of Treas, chief building services section 1985-88, technical advisor 1988-. **Orgs:** Reg arch DC; mem Am Inst of Arch; mem Am Inst of Planners; Nat Assn of Comm Dev Pres bd of Commr Mayor Highland Beach Inc Anne Arundel Cty MD 1977-79; 1st vice pres bd dir Friends of Nat Zoo 1969-; mem DC Urban League; Howard Univ Alumni Assn HUDC Alumni Club; Nat Conf of Christians & Jews. **Honors/Awds:** Ford Found Fellowship for Grad Study 1970-71. **Military Serv:** AUS corpl 1952-54. **Home Addr:** 4225 17th St NW, Washington, DC 20011. **Business Addr:** Technical Advisor, Internal Revenue Service/Dept of Treasury, 1111 Constitution Ave NW IGC 6326, Washington, DC 20224.

BROWN, JOSEPH CLIFTON
Museum administrator. **Personal:** Born Oct 15, 1908, Jackson, MS; married Rubye L Threlkeld; children: Velma, Thelma, Selma, Reuben M, Edwin, Edna. **Career:** Dusable Museum of African Am, adminstr; Taylor Voc Agr HS, prin 1934-40; Picayune HS, prin 1941; Oxford Training Schl, instr 1943-45; WPA, instr 1944; Processing Bureau Employment Security & Sec State of IL, oper Data Processing 1945-75; Dusable Museum of Afro-am History, admin staff mem 1970-77. **Orgs:** Mem Phi Beta Sigma Frat 1932; contributor to MS Black Educ Jrnl 1941-42; opr Data Processing 1946; chm Creative Writers Forum 1946-48; lay ldr Christ UM 1963-77. **Honors/Awds:** Humanitarian Awd Christ Ch 1976. **Home Addr:** 6518 S Aberdeen St, Chicago, IL 60621.

BROWN, JOSEPH DAVIDSON, SR.
City administrator, law enforcement official (retired). **Personal:** Born Dec 27, 1929, St Joseph, LA; son of Mary Deon Brown and Mitchell Brown; married Cleola Morris; children: Ann Marie Clayton, Mitchell George, Ollie Mae Neely, Joseph Davidson Jr, Joyce Lavel Davis, Claude Ernest. **Educ:** Eswege Germany School, mechanic 1951; Tyler Barber Coll, barber 1954; Triton Coll, supervision 1978. **Career:** Central Area Park Dist, police officer 1976-79, comm 1979-; Second Baptist Church, deacon 1984-; Village of Maywood, public works 1962-, director, deputy marshal, 1992-97; Maywood Park District, police officer, 1992-97. **Orgs:** Mason Pride of Tensas #99 1954-. **Honors/Awds:** Village of Maywood Code Enforcement Marshal; Natural Hazards Recovery Course (Inland); Emergency Mgmt Inst Emmitsburg MD; Police Law Enforcement Training, Central Area Park District Police Dept, 1981; Fundamentals of Water Supply Operation, State of Illinois Environmental Protection Agency, 1977; Fred Hampton Scholarship Image Award, 1979. **Military Serv:** AUS corp 1948-52. **Home Addr:** 223 South 12th Ave, Maywood, IL 60153. **Business Addr:** Dir of Public Works, Public Works of Maywood, One Madison Plaza, Maywood, IL 60153.

BROWN, JOSEPH SAMUEL
Government official. **Personal:** Born Dec 3, 1943, New York, NY; son of Ruby Reid and Austin Samuel Brown; married Beverly Mallory-Brown, May 18, 1968 (divorced 1988); children: Jamal Hassan, Kareem Saladin, Paul Emmanuel. **Educ:** Elizabeth City State Univ, Elizabeth City, NC, BS, 1966; North Carolina Central Univ, Durham, NC, MS, 1968. **Career:** NY City Bd of Education Harlem High School, principal, 1975-77; NYC Dept of General Services, New York, NY, administrative staff analyst, 1977-79; NYC Dept of Econ Dev Minority Business Dev Office, New York, NY, dir, 1979-85; Darryl E Greene & Assoc, New York, NY, managing dir, 1985-88; Monroe County Dept of Affirmative Action/HR, Rochester, NY, dir, 1988-. **Orgs:** Mem, Baden Street Center Advisory Bd, 1988-; mem, Montgomery Neighborhood Ctr Bd of Dir, 1988-; mem, ACLU Genesee Valley Chapter Bd of Dir, 1988-; mem, NYS Human Rights Comm Advisory Council, 1988-; mem, East House Bd of Dir, 1988; mem Rochester/Monroe County Private Industry, 1991-; mem, Omega Psi Phi Fraternity, 1965-; mem, Austin Stewart Professional Society, 1988-; mem, Rochester/Monroe County Council on Disabled Persons, 1991-; mem, Am Assn for Affirmative Action, 1991-. **Honors/Awds:** Outstanding Young Men in America, US Jaycees, 1979; Certificate of Appreciation NYC Bd of Ed, Open Doors Prog, 1980-84; Certificate of Appreciation, Jr. Achievement, 1973; Assemblyman Louis Nine Citizenship Award, NY State Assembly, 1971; Certificate of Recognition, Natl Alliance of Businessmen, 1972, 1973. **Home Addr:** 385 Columbia Ave, Rochester, NY 14611.

BROWN, JOYCE
Educational administrator. **Personal:** Born Aug 2, 1937, Lagrange, GA; daughter of Nellie Kate Harris Storey and Willis Storey; married Randolph F Brown; children: Randette J, Randolph J, Ronda J, Randal J. **Educ:** OH State Univ, 1956-58; Sinclair Coll, 1958-59. **Career:** Citibank NA, asst mgr/FISG foreign exchange 1975-80, mgr/FMG/treasurer serv 1980-83, mgr/NABG/CSD/treasurer serv foreign exchange 1983-; Hempstead Public School Board, pres; Citibank/Citicorp, New York, asst vice pres, 1983-; NY State School School Board Assn, dir bd devel NYC community school bd improvement project, 1989-. **Orgs:** Chmn Advisory Com on Minority Affairs NY State School Bds Assn; mem bd dir Alliance Counselor for Drug & Alcohol Abuse; mem bd dir Natl Caucus of Black School Bd Members; mem Natl Business & Professional Womens Clubs Inc; pres, mem Hempstead School Bd, 1981-86; mem, Natl Alliance of Black School Educators, 1984-; exec vice pres, Natl Caucus Black School Board Members, 1986-87; chairperson, Governmental Affairs, Natl Assn of Black Business and Professional Women's Clubs, 1987-; mem, 100 Black Women Inc, 1987-; pres, Hempstead Civic Assn, 1987-88; chairperson Hempstead Educ Committee, 1988-; life mem, NAACP; NY State School Bds Assn, supt search consultant, 1992; Natl Alliance of Black School Educators' Policy Commission, co-chair, 1991. **Honors/Awds:** Outstanding Service Award, 100 Black Men, 1984; Legislative Citation, Ohio State Assembly, 1984; Outstanding Service, Hempstead School District, 1986; Legislative Citation, New York State Assembly, 1989; Legislative Citation, Nassau County Elective, 1989. **Home Addr:** 254 Rhodes Ave, Hempstead, NY 11550. **Business Addr:** New York State School Boards Association, 119 Washington Avenue, Albany, NY 12210.

BROWN, JOYCE F.
Educational administrator, psychologist. **Personal:** Born Jul 7, 1946, New York, NY; daughter of Joyce Cappie Brown and Robert E Brown; married H Carl McCall, Aug 13, 1983. **Educ:** Marymount Coll, Tarrytown, NY, BA, 1968; New York Univ, New York, NY, MA, 1970, PhD, 1980. **Career:** City Univ of NY-Central Office, New York, NY, univ dean, 1983-1987, vice chancellor, 1987-90, professor of clinical psychology, 1994-; City Univ of NY-Baruch Coll, New York, NY, acting pres, 1990-; NYC, Public & Community Affairs, deputy mayor. **Orgs:** NYC Outward Bound, Central Park Conservancy, director; Marymont College, trustee; Boys Harbor Inc, director, 1987-. **Honors/Awds:** Institute for Educational Management, Harvard Univ, 1990; Current Crisis Recent Trends-Final Report, Task Force on the Black Family, 1987.

BROWN, JULIUS J.
Real estate agent, educator, city official. **Personal:** Born Feb 17, 1907, Oak City, NC; married Roberta Lassiter; children: Robert D, Julia, Sherrian. **Educ:** A&T St U, BS 1937. **Career:** Self employed Real Estate Salesman; Mitchell Co Training Sch, prin tchr agr; Pitt Co Training Sch, tchr Agr; S Ayden Sch, tchr Agr; Ayden-Grift Sch, tchr Agr. **Orgs:** Pitt Co NC Precinct Chmn; Mason; mem Kappa Alpha Psi Frat; Knights of Pythian; NACW; NEA; commnr Town of Ayden 1968-95, mayor protem 1974; mem Mid E Exec Com 1970-74; mem Mideast Manpower & Finance Com 1974-; mem of Finance & Exec Com. **Honors/Awds:** Recip Cert of Merit Pitt Co Schs; Cert of Appreciation in Occupational Educ at Ayden-Grifton HS; cert of Appreciation Agr & Educ 30 yrs faithful serv NC Vocational Tchrs Assn; cert of Appreciation otstndng serv Mt Olive Bapt Ch 1970; Cert Meritorious Serv Pitt Co United Fund 1972; Achvmnt Awd Pitt Co Br of NAACP 1972; Certt of Merit A&T St Univ Dept of Vo-ag 1975. **Business Addr:** PO Box 126, 218 W 3 St, Ayden, NC 28513.

BROWN, JULIUS RAY
Educational administrator. **Personal:** Born Feb 18, 1940, Birmingham, AL; son of Clessie Brown and Sam Brown; married Betty Jean; children: Laura, Kenyen. **Educ:** Wayne State Univ, BA 1963, MEd 1971; Univ of MI, PhD 1973. **Career:** Project Equality of MI, exec dir 1969-71; Univ of MI, regional dir 1971-76; Wayne County Comm Coll, regional dean 1976-83; Comm Coll of Allegheny Co, vice pres exec dean 1983-89; Wallace Community College, Selma, president 1989-. **Orgs:** Mem bd dirs Northside Chamber of Commerce 1984-; mem bd dirs Local Govt Acad 1985-; mem bd dirs St John's Hospital 1985-; program officer President's Roundtable AACJC 1986; mem Natl Convention Comm Church of Our Lord Jesus Christ 1986. **Honors/Awds:** State of MI Legislative Tribute 1981; Principals & Educators Awd BTWBA 1981; Outstanding Higher Education Administrator Award, Pennsylvania 1988; County of Allegheny, Resolution of Recognition. **Business Addr:** President, Wallace Community College Selma, 3000 Rangeline Rd, Selma, AL 36702-1049.

BROWN, JURUTHA
Government administrator. **Personal:** Born Apr 11, 1950, San Diego, CA; daughter of Bertha Brown and Fred Brown. **Educ:** Occidental College, BS 1972; UCLA, Cert Executive Mgmt Program 1988; Pepperdine University, MBA, 1991. **Career:** Work included test devel, selection rsch, classification prior to 1984; City of Los Angeles, chief police and fire selection div 1984-87, chief workers' compensation div, 1987-92, chief of administrative services, 1992-95, personnel director, 1996-97, dir of public safety employment, 1997-. **Orgs:** Treas/sec Personnel Testing Council of So CA 1982/1984; chair, human rts comm Intl Personnel Mgmt Assoc 1985; mem bd dirs IPMA Assesment Cncl 1984-87, pres, vice pres, treas Western Regional Intergovt Personnel Assessment Council 1985-87; mem Natl Forum for Black Public Admin 1984-; pres Black Alumni of Occidental Coll; frequent speaker on test devel & test rsch, police recruitment. **Business Addr:** Personnel Director, City of Los Angeles, 700 E Temple St, Rm 305, Los Angeles, CA 90012.

BROWN, JUSTINE THOMAS
Mayor, educator. **Personal:** Born May 12, 1938, Guyton, GA; daughter of Marie Easley-Gadson Thomas and J W H Thomas Sr; married Willie Brown, Jul 27, 1961; children: Rahn Andre, Willie Antjuan, Jatavia Anreka. **Educ:** Savannah State College, Savannah GA, BS, 1959; Georgia Southern College, Statesboro GA, 1989. **Career:** Screven County Board of Education, Sylvania GA, teacher, 1959-; mayor of City of Oliver GA, 1988-. **Orgs:** Member, National Association of Educators, member, National Conference of Black Mayors; member, Alpha Kappa Alpha Sorority; member, Georgia Association of Educators; life mem, Georgia Municipal Association; dir, United Way of Screven County; dir, Economic Opportunity Authority. **Honors/Awds:** Educator of the Year Award, Screven County Rotary Club, 1988; First Black Mayor Award, City of Oliver GA, 1988; Screven County, Outstanding Citizen; Outstanding Service, Sylvania-Screven County Recreation Board Award. **Home Addr:** PO Box 82, Oliver, GA 30449. **Business Addr:** Mayor, City of Oliver, PO Box 221, Oliver, GA 30449.

BROWN, KENNETH S.
Educator, pharmacist. **Personal:** Born Jul 3, 1917, Macon; son of Mollie Brown and Jessie Brown; married Lillian Loving; children: Kevin Sylvester. **Educ:** Coll of Pharmacy, BS; Howard U, 1955. **Career:** Rohm & Haas Chemical Co PA, control analytical chemist; Private Practice, pharmacy; PA, lecturer on dangers of drug abuse, jr high school students & parents, 1958-69; Pharmacy School & Temple Univ, clinical instructor. **Orgs:** Pharmacy coord & consult for Temple Univ Comprehensive Health Serv Prog; mem Nat Pharm Assn; mem Am Pharm Assn; mem Nat Pres; Chi Delta Mu Med Frat; elected mem, democratic exec comm, Fourth Ward, Seventeenth Division, 1990-94. **Military Serv:** AUS 1943-46.

BROWN, L. DON
Senior vp operations and tech. **Personal:** Born Jul 15, 1945, Horatio, AR; son of Snowie Brown and Tommie Brown; married Inez Wyatt Brown, May 4, 1968; children: Daria Akilah, Ellynn Donisha, Dalila Jinelle. **Educ:** Univ of Arkansas, Pine Bluff, AR, BS, 1966; Univ of Southwest Missouri, Springfield MO, 1971-72; Kutztown Univ, Kutztown PA, 1973-74; Univ of Penn, Philadelphia PA, 1987; Harvard Univ, Cambridge MA, 1987. **Career:** Howard County, Mineral Springs AR, instructor, 1966-68; State of Arkansas, Texarkana AR, job interviewer, 1968-69; Kraft Inc, Springfield MO, food technologist, 1971-72; Lehigh Valley, PA, gensupt, 1972-79; Glenview, IL, plant mgr, 1979-85, Kraft USA, vice pres production KUSA, 1985-89; Kraft General Foods, White Plains, NY, vice pres, manufacturing, GFUSA, 1989-91, vp, operations, Canada, 1991-94, exec vp, manufacturing; Adolph Coors Co, sr vp, operations and technology, currently. **Orgs:** Amer Mgmt Assn, 1972; Productivity Assn, 1975; NAACP, 1978-84; Urban League, 1978-84; head of Industrial Div, United Way, Dallas TX, 1984; Executive Leadership Council, 1990-; Assn of 100 Black Men, 1989-93; Alumax Inc, bd of dirs, 1994-. **Honors/Awds:** Outstanding Black Achievement, Chicago YMCA, 1980; Kraft Achievement Award, Kraft, Inc, 1982. **Military Serv:** US Army, Spec 5, 1968-70, Commendation Medal-Vietnam Service. **Business Addr:** Sr Vice Pres, Operations and Technology, Adolph Coors Co, PO Box 4030, Golden, CO 80401-0030, (303)279-6565.

BROWN, LARRY
Professional football player. **Personal:** Born Nov 30, 1969, Miami, FL; married; children: one. **Educ:** Texas Christian Univ, degree in criminal justice. **Career:** Dallas Cowboys, cornerback, 1992-95; Oakland Raiders, cornerback, 1996-. **Honors/Awds:** Super Bowl XXX, Most Valuable Player, 1995. **Business Addr:** Professional Football Player, Oakland Raiders, 1220 Harbor Bay Pkwy, Alameda, CA 94502, (510)615-1875.

BROWN, LARRY T.
Automobile dealership executive. **Personal:** Born Apr 21, 1947, Inkster, MI; son of Mattie Lewis Brown and Nander Brown; married Angelina Caldwell Brown, Aug 28, 1971. **Educ:** Wayne County Comm College, Detroit, MI, AA, 1971; Wayne State Univ, Detroit MI, BA, 1973; Central Michigan Univ, Mount Pleasant, MI, MA, 1979. **Career:** Ford Motor Co, Dearborn, MI, market mgr, 1969-85; Landmark Ford, Niles, IL, president, 1991; Ottawa Ford Lincoln, Mercury, Inc, Ottawa, IL, president, 1985-. **Orgs:** Member, board member, Black Ford Lincoln/Mercury Dealers Assn, 1985-; member, Natl Auto Dealers Assn, 1985-; member, Ottawa Rotary, 1986-88; member, Ottawa Chamber of Commerce, 1985-90; Black Ford Lincoln/Mercury Dealers Association, president, 1992-93; National Automobile Minority Dealers Association, president, 1993-94. **Honors/Awds:** Push Capital Spirit Award, 1992. **Military Serv:** US Air Force, Sgt, 1965-69. **Business Addr:** President, Ottawa Ford Lincoln/Mercury, Inc, 4001 N Columbus, Ottawa, IL 61350.

BROWN, LAWRENCE E.
Business executive. **Personal:** Born Jan 28, 1947. **Educ:** Bryant Coll, BS 1969; Bentley Coll, Masters of Taxation 1979. **Career:** Peat Mawrick Mitchell & Co, supervising sr acctnt 1970-75; Lawrence E Brown CPA;s, owner/principal 1975-. **Orgs:** Pres chmn bd dir S Providence Fed Credit Union 1971-; dir Bryant Coll Alumni Assn 1974-; treas Irreproachable Beneficial Assn 1976-; treas dir Accountants for Pub Interest of RI 1975-; treas dir RI Minority Bus Assn 1977-; city councilman Providence 1971-75; asst treas Providence Dem Com 1975-; mem RI Soc of CPA's & Amer Inst of CPA's; mem Phi Beta Sigma; bd dir Bannister House 1976-; mem RI Black Heritage Soc 1976-; co-chmn Natl Black Caucusof Local Elected Officials 1972-74; dir Oppty Indsln Ctr of RI 1970-74; dir Comm Workshops of RI Inc 1974-76; dir Headstart Adv Bd 1971-73; dir Challenge House Inc 1971-74; mem Urban League of RI; mem NAACP. **Honors/Awds:** First Black CPA in RI 1972; 2nd Black City Councilman in Providence; S Providence Comm Serv Awd 1972. **Military Serv:** USMC 1969-75. **Business Addr:** Lawrence C Brown CPA's, 42 Weybosset St, 5th Floor, Providence, RI 02903.

BROWN, LAWRENCE S., JR.
Physician. **Personal:** Born Dec 4, 1949, Brooklyn, NY; son of Lawrence & Mae Rose; divorced. **Educ:** Brooklyn College, BA, 1976; Columbia Univ, School of Public Health, MPH, 1979; New York Univ, School of Medicine, MD, 1979. **Career:** Addiction Research & Treatment Corp, sr vp, 1979-; Natl Football League, medical advisor, 1990-; Columbia Univ, assist clinical prof of medicine, 1986-. **Orgs:** American Public Health Assn, 1977-; Amer Society of Internal Medicine, 1980-; Amer College of Physicians, 1980-; Amer Diabetes Assn, 1989-; Amer Society of Addiction Medicine, 1992-; College on Problems of Drug Dependency, fellow, 1993-. **Special Achievements:** Over 30 peer-reviewed articles; Over 10 book chapters. **Military Serv:** US Army, spec-4; Bronze Star. **Business Addr:** Senior VP, Addiction Research & Treatment Corp, 22 Chapel Street, Brooklyn, NY 11201, (718)260-2915.

BROWN, LEANDER A.
Radio communications executive. **Personal:** Born Jul 1, 1959, Chicago, IL; son of JoAhn Weaver Brown-Nash and Leander A Brown Jr; married Betty Catlett Brown, Mar 11, 1989. **Educ:** Fisk University, Nashville, TN, BS, 1982. **Career:** City of Harvey, Harvey, IL, employment coordinator, 1983-85; Tri-Associates, Chicago, IL, associate, 1985-86; Payne Financial Service, Chicago, IL, financial consultant, 1986-88; B & H Radio Co., Harvey, IL, president, 1988-. **Honors/Awds:** America's Best & Brightest, Dollars & Sense, 1989; Minority Business of the Month, Minority Entrepreneur, 1990; Business Profile, Chicago Defender, 1991.

BROWN, LEE PATRICK
Government official. **Personal:** Born Oct 4, 1937, Wewoka, OK; son of Zelma Edwards Brown and Andrew Brown; married Yvonne C Streets, Jul 14, 1959; children: Patrick, Torri, Robyn, Jenna. **Educ:** Fresno State University, BS, 1960; San Jose State University, MS, 1964; University of California Berkeley, Masters, criminology, 1968, Doctorate, criminology, 1970. **Career:** San Jose CA, police officer, 1960-68; Portland State University, professor, 1968-72; Howard University, professor, 1972-75; Multnomah County OR, sheriff 1975-76, dir of justice serv 1976-78; Atlanta GA, public safety commissioner, 1978-82; Houston Police Dept, police chief, 1982-90; New York City Police Dept, police commissioner, 1990-92; Texas Souuthern University, instructor, 1992; Office of Natl Drug Control Policy, dir, cabinet member, 1993-95; Rice University, sociology professor, 1996-97; City of Houston, mayor, 1997-. **Orgs:** Pres Intl Assoc of Chiefs of Police 1990-91, Natl Org of Black Law Enforcement Exec 1984; mem Police Exec Rsch Forum, Harvard Univ Exec Session on the Police 1985, chmn Natl Minority Adv Council on Criminal Justice 1976-81; dir, Houston Rotary Club; NAACP; bd mem, The Forum Club of Houston; dir, Houston Boy Scouts of Amer; dir, Natl Black Child Devel Inst; dir, Houston Area Urban League; mem, Natl Advisory Commn on Criminal Justice Standards & Goals, Washington DC; mem, Natl Commn on Higher Educ for Police, Washington DC; task force mem, Natl Center for Missing & Exploited Children; advisory bd, Natl Inst Against Prejudice & Violence. **Honors/Awds:** Honorary Doctorate FL Intl Univ 1982; Honorary Doctorate, Portland State Univ, 1990-; Law Enforcement of the Year Awd Natl Black Police Officers Assn 1982; Criminal Justice Professional Awd Natl Assn of Blacks in Criminal Justice 1984; Hon Doct John Jay Coll of Criminal Justice 1985; Mgr of the Year Award, Natl Mgmt Assn, 1986; Communicator of the Year Award, Washington News Service, 1986; Robert Lamb Jr Humanitarian Award, Natl Org of Black Law Enforcement Execs, 1987; August Vollmer Award, Amer Soc of Criminology, 1988; Natl Public Service Award, Amer Soc for Public Admin & the Natl Acad of Public Admin, 1989; co-author of 1 book, editor of 3 books & author of numerous articles & book chapters. **Special Achievements:** First African American mayor of Houston. **Business Addr:** Mayor, City of Houston, Office of the Mayor, City Hall Annex, 901 Bagby St, Houston, TX 77001.

BROWN, LEO C., JR.
Clergyman, association executive. **Personal:** Born Jun 17, 1942, Washington, DC; son of Mildred Vera Brown (deceased) and Leo Charles Brown Sr (deceased); married Barbara DeLespine; children: Debbie Jones, Fred Ross, Angela Ross, Wayne Brown, Charles Ross, Steve Ross, Renee Brown, Anthony Brown, Phillip Brown, Daniel Brown, Jimmy, Cindy. **Educ:** Seattle Comm Coll, Apprenticeship Cement Mason 1966-69; Tacoma Comm Coll, Bus & Psych 1972-73; Evergreen State Coll, BA 1974-77; Amer Bapt Sem of the West, MMA 1980-81; Hardy Theological Institute of Seattle WA, DD 1988. **Career:** Local 528 Cement Mason, cement mason 1964-72; True Vine Comm COGIC, pastor 1975-; Progress House Assoc, exec dir 1972-. **Orgs:** Pres Tacoma Ministerial Alliance 1982-; founder, pres True vine Multi-Serv Ctr 1979-; bd mem Family Broadcasting Station 1979-; vice pres United Brotherhood Fellowship 1977-; founder & pres True Vine Sr Citizen Ctr 1980-; co-founder, dir 1st Minority Christian Summer Camp 1965-; founder, dir Emmanuel Temple Prison Ministry McNeil Island WA 1968; vice pres Metro Devel Council 1973-75; chaplain Tacoma Fire Dept 1975-79; Taoma Urban Policy, bd mem 1979; Intl Halfway House Assoc; Amer Corrections Assoc, NAACP, Tacoma Urban League, Kiwanis Club, Prince Hall Masons, Acad of Criminal Justice Soc; bd mem United Way, Fellowship of Reconciliation A; mem Amer Correctional Assoc, Govs Public Safety Adv Group for State of WA; commissioner, State of Washington HousingFinance Commission 1985-. **Honors/Awds:** Key to the City Mayors Office City of Tacoma 1977; Serv to Manking Awd Sertoma Club 1978; Nominee & runner-up for Rockefeller Found Humanity Awd 1979; Disting Citizens Awd Tacoma Urban League 1983; Newsmaker of Tomorrow Awd Time Mag 1983; Rev Leo C Brown Jr Day City of Tacoma Cty of Pierce & State of WA 1982; Disting Citizen Awd WA State Senate & Office of Lt Gov 1984; Doctor of Divinity, Hardy Theological Institute of Seattle 1988. **Military Serv:** US Army, sp4, 1961-64. **Business Addr:** Executive Dir, Progress House Assn, PO Box 5373, Tacoma, WA 98415.

BROWN, LEROY
Educational administrator (retired), funeral director. **Personal:** Born Dec 10, 1936, Buckner, AR; son of Pearlie Brown and Odis Brown; married Dorothy Jean Hughey; children: Johnny Otis, Cinini Yvette, Titian Valencia, Leviano Regatte. **Educ:** Univ of Ar Pine Bluff, BS Chem; E TX State U, MA. **Career:** Lewisville Sch Dist, middle sch prin 1978-; City of Buckner, mayor 1975-78; Lewisville Sch Dist, asst prin & math 1972-77; Lewisville Sch Dist, Foster HS prin 1970-71; Lewisville Sch Dist, Sci & Math tchr 1960-69; mayor & judge City of Buckner, 1975-78; alderman, City of Buckner, 1980-90, 1994; asst prin, math, Lewisville School Dist High School, 1983-90; A O Smith Funeral Home, funeral director, 1990-; Re-elected as Alderman, City of Buckner, 1994, 1996; Appointed Justice of the Peace, District IV; Lafayette County Arkansas, Gov Bill Clinton, 1990. **Orgs:** Mem AR Educ Assn 1960-80; mem Nat Educ Assn 1970-80; vice pres Lafayette Co Alumni Assn 1977-80; mem St John Bapt Ch Buckner 1948-80; mem NAACP Buckner Hpt 1968-80; sr warden Rose of Sharon Lodge 1978-80; justice of the peace 1990, fair bd mem 1990, quorum court mem 1990, Lafayette County, AR; bd mem, Southwest Arkansas Development Council. **Honors/Awds:** Best School Award, Red River Vo-Tech School, 1981, 1982; recently appointed by Governor and President elect Bill Clinton to the state of Arkansas Criminal Detention Facilities Committee, 1991; re-elected as Alder-

man of the city of Buclener, 1992, fair board member, 1992. **Business Addr:** Funeral Director, A O Smith Funeral Home, 413 E Main St, Stamps, AR 71860.

BROWN, LEROY BRADFORD
Physician. **Personal:** Born Jun 5, 1929, Detroit, MI; married Ola Augusta Watkins; children: Leroy, Rene, Rita. **Educ:** SC State Coll, BS 1954; Howard U, MD 1958. **Career:** Fresno County General Hospital, intern, 1958-59; Internal Med, resident, 1959-62; Prac Medicine, specializing in internal medicine, 1962-; Mercy Hospital, staff mem, 1962-; City of Sacramento, city physician, 1958-71; Medical Examiner, aviation, 1966-; UC Davis Medical School, clinic instr 1977. **Orgs:** Mem Am Ca & Sacramento Co Med Assns;am ca & sacramento co Socs Internal Med; dir Sacramento Co Heart Assn mem Notomas Union Sch Bd 1971-75; mem Ch of God. **Business Addr:** 3031 G St, Sacramento, CA 95816.

BROWN, LEROY RONALD
Educational administrator. **Personal:** Born Dec 18, 1949, Wadmalaw Island, SC; married Eva Elizabeth Choice; children: Tamyka M, Stephan L, Krystine V. **Educ:** Benedict Coll, BS 1971; Univ of OK, EdM 1973; New York Univ, EdD 1982. **Career:** New York Univ, research assoc 1978-80; Denmark Tech Coll, dean of continuing educ 1980-82; Morristown Coll, exec vice pres & dean of coll 1982-83; Midlands Technical Coll, beginning 1983, vice pres, student development services; Florida Memorial College, vice pres, student development and enrollment management, currently. **Orgs:** Mem AACD, NASDA, AAHE; sec of bd of dirs United Black Fund 1984-; mem bd of dirs Southern Region Council of Black Affairs 1985-; mem Columbia Comm Relations Council 1986; mem Leadership Columbia 1986. **Honors/Awds:** Presidential Citation NAFEO 1985; Citation Southern Council on Black Affairs 1985; Outstanding Administrator Midlands Tech Coll 1985. **Home Addr:** 225 Meadowlake Dr, Columbia, SC 29203. **Business Addr:** Vice Pres, Student Development & Enrollment Management, Florida Memorial College, 15800 NW 42nd Ave, Miami, FL 33054.

BROWN, LEROY THOMAS
Educator. **Personal:** Born Aug 8, 1922, Atlantic City, NJ. **Educ:** SUNY, AA 1949; UCLA, BA 1954, MA 1957; Stanford Univ, PhD 1970. **Career:** Veterans Admin Hospital, med tech, 1954-65; UCLA, sr rsch tech, 1957-65; Pasadena High School, teacher, 1963-65; Foothill Jr Coll, instructor, 1965-67; SUNY, asst prof Anatomy, 1970-75; Univ WI Medical School, assoc prof Anatomy, 1975-82, asst dean, 1975-82; Univ WI Madison, asst vice chancellor, 1975-79; Drew Medical School, visiting prof, 1979-. **Orgs:** Mem NIH Scientific Prog Comm 1982-85; bd dir MARC Prog Drew Med School 1983-85; mem Amer Assoc of Anatomists 1970-85; officer communications US CoastGuard Aux 1984-85; vstg rsch fellow Univ WI 1969-70; guest scientists Brookhaven Natl Labs 1970-75, Univ WI Med School 1969-70; mem Soc Electron Microscopists 1971, SUNY Faculty Sub-com on Expanding Ed Oppty 1974-75; chmn SUNY Stony Brook Pres's Com on Equal Oppty; exec com Faculty Senate Partic 1stCong Black Profls in Higher Ed 1972. **Military Serv:** US Army, quartermaster, 1942-44. **Home Addr:** PO Box 241951, Los Angeles, CA 90024. **Business Addr:** Visiting Professor, Drew Medical School, 1621 E 120th St, Mail Point 27, Los Angeles, CA 90059.

BROWN, LES
Motivational speaker, author. **Personal:** Born in Miami, FL; married Gladys Knight, Aug 29, 1995 (divorced 1997); children: six. **Career:** Les Brown Unlimited, Detroit, MI, president, currently; Featured host of own talk show, 1993-. **Special Achievements:** First African-American to win the National Speakers Association's Council of Peers Award for Excellence; Books: Live Your Dreams; It's Not Over Until You Win!, Simon & Schuster, 1997. **Business Phone:** (313)961-1962.

BROWN, LESTER J.
Government official. **Personal:** Born Aug 24, 1942, New York, NY; son of Earlean Price Brown and James Brown; divorced; children: Natalie Milligan, Omar A, Lesondra E. **Educ:** Lincoln Univ, BA 1966; Attended, Fel's Inst of State & Local Govt 1969; State Univ of NY at Albany 1973; Antioch Coll New England Ctr, MEd Mgmt & Org 1978. **Career:** Philadelphia Model Cities Prog, manpower planner 1967-68; Philadelphia Sch Dist, teacher 1968-70; Schenectady Co Comm Coll, sr counselor 1970-76; New York State Div for Youth, resource & reimbursement agent, 1977-79, prog mgmt specialist 1979-89; New York State Division for Youth, contract compliance specialist, 1989-. **Orgs:** New York State Electric and Gas, consumer panel mem, 1991-; mem economic develop & employment committee Broome Co Urban League; mem, allocation panel Broome Co United Way; life mem Omega Psi Phi Frat Inc; mem, Lincoln Univ Alumni Assoc; pres Price Brown Family Reunion Org; vice chmn, NYS Div for Youth Affirmative Action Adv Comm; Broome County NAACP; Prince Hall Masonic. **Honors/Awds:** District Service Omega Psi Phi Frat 1980-83. **Home Addr:** 3706 Coventry Lane, East Greenbush, NY 12061-2327. **Business Addr:** Program Management Specialist, New York State for Youth, 52 Washington Street, Rensselaer, NY 12144.

BROWN, LEWIS FRANK
Attorney. **Personal:** Born Aug 4, 1929, Cleveland, MS; son of Lula Brown and Frank Brown; married Dorothy Jean Fitzerald; children: Lewis Gene, Orville Frank. **Educ:** Vallejo Jr Coll, AA 1955; San Francisco State Univ, BA 1957; Lincoln Univ Law Sch, DJ 1964. **Career:** Vallejo Unified Sch Dist, educator 1957-64; CA Greenleigh Assn, asst dir 1964-65, dir 1965-66; Health Educ & Welfare, private consultant 1966-69; Member Amer Arbitration Assn, arbitrator 1972-; Brown & Bradley, att at law 1978-. **Orgs:** Elected Solano County Demo Central Committeeman 1959-66; Vallejo City Planning Commission 1963-65; Vallejo City Councilman 1965-69; Vallejo City Vice-Mayor 1967-69; golden heritage life mem NAACP; 173rd life mem NBA. **Honors/Awds:** Northern California First Jurisdiction Service Award of Church of God In Christ, 1982; Distinguished Record CA State Senate & Assembly Resolution Commending Lewis F Brown 1982; Civic Leader Award 1982; City of Vallejo Legal Commendation Award Dist Atty of Solano Cnty 1982; Resolution of Commendation, Jones County, Mississippi Board of Supervisors 1988; Resolution of Commendation, City Council of Laurel Mississippi 1988. **Special Achievements:** Vallejo City Council named street Lewis Brown Road, July 1995. **Military Serv:** AUS pfc 1951-53. **Business Addr:** Attorney, Brown & Bradley, 538 Georgia St, Vallejo, CA 94590.

BROWN, LILLIE RICHARD
Nutritionist. **Personal:** Born Feb 25, 1946, Opelousas, LA; daughter of Hester De Jean Richard and John Richard Sr; married Charles J Brown, Apr 20, 1968; children: Jeffrey Andre. **Educ:** Southern University, BS, 1968; Howard University, MS, 1972; Command & General Staff College, diploma, 1989; Early Childhood Education, certification. **Career:** DC Public Schools, nutritionist, 1972-96; DC National Guard, dietitian, 1977-96; Howard Univ, asst prof of nutritional sciences, 1997-; State of MD, Department of Corrections, dietitian, 1998-. **Orgs:** American Dietetic Association, 1971-; American Heart Association, 1986-; Delta Sigma Theta, 1974-. **Honors/Awds:** Army Commendation Medal, 1990. **Special Achievements:** The Manual of Clinical Dietetics, assisted with writing, 1992. **Military Serv:** Army National Guard. **Home Addr:** 2006 Forestdale Dr, Silver Spring, MD 20903, (301)439-3933.

BROWN, LINDA JENKINS
Government official. **Personal:** Born Nov 8, 1946, Baltimore, MD; married Charles Edward Brown II; children: Charles Edward III. **Educ:** Morgan State Univ, BS 1971; Univ of Baltimore, MPA 1980. **Career:** Baltimore County Bd of Educ, elem sch teacher 1971-73; Dept of Defense Ft Holabird MD, equal employ oppor specialist 1973-75; Federal Highway Administration, equal oppor spec 1975-78, regional compliance officer 1978-80, deputy chief int eeo div 1980-84, chief, intl eeo div 1984-, historically black colls and univs and univs coord 1985-. **Orgs:** Basileus Zeta Phi Beta Sor Inc Alpha Zeta Chap 1982-84; adv bd mem Natl Festival of Black Storytelling 1983-86; charter mem Assoc of Black Storytellers 1983-; mem NAACP 1983-; 2nd vice pres Howard Cornish Chap Morgan State Univ Alumni 1984-; adv bd mem US Office of Personnel Mgmt EEO Curriculum 1984-; presidential adv council mem Morgan State Univ 1985-; adv bd mem Atlanta Univ Career Placement 1986-; asst boule marshal Zeta Phi Beta Sor Inc 1986-88. **Honors/Awds:** Outstanding Women of Amer 1984; Outstanding Woman Awd Federally Employed Women 1984; Zeta of the Year Zeta Phi Beta Sor Inc Alpha Zeta Chap 1985; Secretary's Awd for Merit Achievement US Dept of Transportation 1985; Disting Alumni Awd Natl Assoc for EO in Higher Educ 1986. **Home Addr:** 2401 Poplar Dr, Baltimore, MD 21207. **Business Addr:** Chief, Internal EEO Div, Federal Highway Administration, 400 7th St SW, Washington, DC 20590.

BROWN, LLOYD
Social service director. **Personal:** Born Jul 5, 1938, St Louis, MO; son of Veldia B Sproling Brown Stinson and Charles W Brown Sr; married Johnnie Mae Irvin; children: Marvin, Etoy, Rosalinda, Lloyd Jr, Donna, Tanya. **Educ:** Forest Park Coll, AA 1974; Northeast MO State Univ, BS 1976; Urban Development & the Black Community, So Illinois University, Certificate, 1970; Community Organizing Parks College, Certificate, 1970. **Career:** Tandy Area Council, youth counselor 1974-76; Wellston School Dist, dep gen mgr 1976-81; Intl Revenue Svc, tax rep 1982-83; Human Devel Corp, branch mgr 1983-91; Alpha Redevelopment Corp, executive manager, 1991-94; The ABC Infants, Inc, & Child Care, co-owner; Lucas Heights Village, exec manager, 1994-. **Orgs:** Community worker, VISTA (Volunteers in Service to America) 1972-74; Natl Assn of Housing & Redevel 1982-; MO Assn of Housing & Redevel 1982-; chmn Wellston Housing Bd of Commissioners 1982-; Wellston Land clearance for Redevel Bd of Commission 1982-; vice pres Wellston Bd of Ed 1983, 1986, 1989, 1992-; MO State School Bd Association 1983; Natl School Bd Association 1983-; Welston City Council, elected 1985. **Honors/Awds:** Special Service Awd Mathew Dicky Boys Club 1968; Creator Writer & Performer The Messingers Inc 1969; Co-Founder Black Library of St Louis 1971; Student Service Awd Forest Park Coll 1972, 1973, 1974; Community Serv Awd Human Devel Corp 1972; Resolution-Outstanding School Board Member, Missouri State Legislature 1987; Youth Service Award, Providence Schools, St Louis, MO, 1985, 1986, 1987. **Military Serv:** USAF airman 2nd class 1957-61. **Home Addr:** 4313 Cranford Dr, Pasadena Hills, MO 63121. **Business Phone:** (314)534-1361.

BROWN, LLOYD LOUIS
Writer. **Personal:** Born Apr 3, 1913, St Paul, MN; son of Ralph & Magdalen; married Lily, Jun 7, 1937; children: Linda, Bonnie. **Career:** New Masses, managing editor, 1945-48; Masses & Mainstream, managing editor, 1948-52; Author, currently. **Special Achievements:** Author, Novel, Iron City; Co-Author, Here I Stand, Paul Robeson; Author, Biography, THe Young Paul Robeson. **Military Serv:** US Air Force, staff sergeant, 1942-45. **Home Addr:** 156-20 Riverside Dr West, Apt 16-I, New York, NY 10032.

BROWN, LOMAS, JR.
Professional football player. **Personal:** Born Mar 30, 1963, Miami, FL; son of Grace and Lomas Brown Sr; married Dolores; children: Antoinette, Ashley, Adrienne. **Educ:** Univ of Florida, bachelor's degree in public recreation, 1996. **Career:** Detroit Lions, offensive tackle, 1985-95; Arizona Cardinals, 1996-. **Honors/Awds:** NFL Extra Effort Award, 1991; Pro Bowl alternate, 1988, 1989; Pro Bowl, 1991, 1992, 1993, 1994, 1995, 1996. **Business Addr:** Professional Football Player, Arizona Cardinals, 8701 S Hardy, Tempe, AZ 85284, (602)379-0101.

BROWN, LOUIS SYLVESTER
City government official. **Personal:** Born Oct 11, 1930, Navassa, NC; son of Mr & Mrs Claus Brown; married Ruby Moore; children: Yvonne, Yvette, Roderick, Valorie. **Educ:** Tyler Barber Coll, Barber 1959. **Career:** NAACP, bd of dir 1970-; Brunswick Cty Hosp, bd of dir 1975-81; Sencland, bd of dir 1978-85; Apri Inst, bd of dir 1979-; Town of Navassa, NC, mayor, currently. **Orgs:** Masonic Pride of Navassa Lodge 1965-85; noble Habid Temple 1970-85; v chmn Recreation bd 1975-; member, Navassa Community Lion Club. **Honors/Awds:** Organized the first Black Men's Lion Club in North Carolina, 1989; organized the first Black Women's Lion Club in North Carolina, 1990. **Military Serv:** AUS corpl 2 yrs. **Home Addr:** 220 Broadway, Navassa, NC 28404.

BROWN, LUCILLE M.
Educational administrator. **Career:** Richmond Public Schools, VA, superintendent, currently. **Business Addr:** Superintendent, Richmond Public Schools, 301 N 9th St, Richmond, VA 23219, (804)225-2020.

BROWN, MALCOLM MCCLEOD
Educator, artist. **Personal:** Born Aug 19, 1931, Crozet, VA; son of Dorothy Brown and Franklin Brown; married Ernestine Turner, 1964; children: Malcolm, Jeffrey, Rhonda. **Educ:** VA State Coll, BS 1956; Case Western Reserve Univ, MA 1969. **Career:** OH, internationally exhibited & acclaimed watercolorist; Shaker Heights Schools, art teacher, 1969-. **Orgs:** Mem Am Watercolor Soc; work shown museums & Colls throughout US under auspices AWS, Watercolor USA & Mainstreams Intl traveling exhibitions & represented numerous pvt collections; work viewed internationally through CA Watercolor Soc & Am Embassy, Nat exhibitions, Am Watercolor Soc, Nat Acad Design, Butter Inst Am Art, Watercolor USA, CA Watercolor Soc, Mainstreams Internat; Shaker Heights bd educ Evening Faculty Clev Inst Art; mem OH Watercolor Soc, NAACP, Urban League, Friends of Karama, Clev Museum Art, Nat Conf Artists, CA Watercolor Soc, Omega Psi Am Watercolor Soc 1973. **Honors/Awds:** Larry Quackenbush Award 1980; Purchase Award Watercolor USA 1974; First Prize Watercolor VA Beach Boardwalk Show 1971-74; Second Prize Watercolor Canton Art Inst 1971; Henry O Tanner & Award Nat Exhbn Black Artists 1972; Award Excellence Mainstreams Intl 1970; award in Rocky Mt Nat Watermedia Exhib in Golden CO 1975; work featured Mag Art Review; Ohio Watercolor Soc Award, 1984, 1985. **Military Serv:** First lt 1956-59. **Business Addr:** Malcolm Brown Gallery, 20100 Chagrin Blvd, Shaker Heights, OH 44122.

BROWN, MARCUS JAMES
Professional basketball player. **Personal:** Born Apr 3, 1974, West Memphis, AR. **Educ:** Murray State. **Career:** Portland Trail Blazers, guard, 1996-97; Vancouver Grizzlies, 1997-. **Business Addr:** Professional Basketball Player, Vancouver Grizzlies, 788 Beatty St, Ste 311, Vancouver, BC, Canada V6B 2M1, (604)688-5867.

BROWN, MARGERY WHEELER
Author, illustrator, educator (retired). **Personal:** Born in Durham, NC; daughter of Margaret Hervey Wheeler and John Leonidas Wheeler; married Richard E Brown, Dec 22, 1936 (deceased); children: Janice Brown Carden. **Educ:** Spelman Coll, Atlanta, GA, BA, 1932; Ohio State Univ, special art student, 1932-34, 1935. **Career:** Hillside High School, Durham, NC, art instructor, 1934-35; Washington High, Atlanta, GA, art instructor, 1935-37; Spelman Coll, Atlanta, GA, art instructor, 1943-46; Newark Public School System, NJ, art instructor, 1948-74; author/illustrator. **Honors/Awds:** Author, illustrator, That

Ruby, 1969, Animals Made by Me, 1970, The Second Stone, 1974, Yesterday I Climbed a Mountain, 1976, No Jon, No Jon, No!, 1981; illustrator, Old Crackfoot, 1965, I'm Glad I'm Me, 1971; author, Book of Colors, Book of Shapes, 1991.

BROWN, MARJORIE M.
Postal official. **Educ:** Edward Waters College; Duke Univ; Emory Univ; Univ of Virginia. **Career:** US Postal Service, Atlanta, GA, postmaster, currently. **Special Achievements:** Atlanta's first female postmaster. **Business Addr:** Postmaster, US Postal Service, 3900 Crown Rd SW, Rm 219, Atlanta, GA 30304.

BROWN, MARSHA J.
Physician. **Personal:** Born Oct 27, 1949, Baltimore, MD; daughter of Bernice C Brown and Elwood L Brown; married Ray Brodie Jr MD; children: Bradley Ray, Sean Elwooa. **Educ:** Howard Univ, BS 1971; Univ of Maryland, MD 1975. **Career:** Mercy Hospital, internal medicine residency; Baltimore City Police and Fire Dept, physician; deputy chief physician Private Practice, physician internal medicine. **Orgs:** Adv bd Central MD Comm Sickle Cell Anemia; bd of dir LM Carroll Home for the Aged, LM Carroll Nursing Home; Girl Scouts of Amer Teenage Pregnancy Task Force; medical consultant Glass & Assocs Mental Health, Baltimore City Police Dept; Baltimore City Civil Serv Commissioner 1982-; mem Bd Eligible Internal Medicine, Monumental City Medical Assocs, MD medical & faculty for the State of MD, Natl Medical Assoc, Baltimore City Chapter Links Inc, Alpha Kappa Alpha Sor. **Honors/Awds:** Outstanding Young Women of Alpha Kappa Alpha Sorority 1980; Citizens Serv Recognition Award for Comm Serv 1986; Natl Assn Negro Women Humanitarian Award, 1986; Physician Baltimore City Police & Fire Departments, Deputy Chief. **Business Addr:** 301 St Paul Place, Mercy Medical Ctr, Baltimore, MD 21217, (410)244-8383.

BROWN, MARSHALL CARSON
Educator (retired). **Personal:** Born Dec 13, 1918, Washington, DC; son of Louise Brown and Frederick Brown; married Clara Kersey Jackson (deceased); children: Clara Jones, Marshall Jr, Alice Joye. **Educ:** VA State U, BS 1940; Columbia U, MA 1947; NY U, 6th yr Cert 1954-60. **Career:** Armstrong High Sch Richmond VA, tchr/coach 1942-49; VA Dept of Educ of all Black Sch, supr 1949-53; Plainfield High Sch NJ, tchr coach 1954-63; US Dept of State to Nigeria, track consult 1963-64; Essex Community College, Newark, NJ, chair physical education dept, 1964-85; US Dept of State to Iraq, track consultant 1967; US Dept of State Sri Lanka, basketball consult 1967; US Dept of State Trinidad, track consult 1972; chmn coach of phy ed/track coach 1968-84. **Orgs:** Pres Plainfield NAACP 1967-69; chmn Labor & Industry Committee 1969-71; chmn Minorities Action Comm 1966-69; mem exec committee Am Comm on Africa 1968-. **Honors/Awds:** Track Coach of the Yr NJ 1960; 5 book reviews for Freedomways 1978; 1st Black Track Coach in NJ High Sch & Coll 1954; 1st Black Teacher in Plainfield, NJ History 1954. **Military Serv:** AUS sgt 1944-45. **Home Addr:** 1406 E Front St, Plainfield, NJ 07062.

BROWN, MARVA Y.
Educational administrator. **Personal:** Born Aug 25, 1936, Charleston, SC. **Educ:** SC State Coll, BS bus adminstrn 1958; Univ of WA, MEd rehab couns 1970. **Career:** Servs for Handicapped Students Edmonds Community Coll, Lynwood WA, counselor, coordinator, 1971-; Poland Spring ME Job Corp Center, sr counselor, 1966-68; State of CT Welfare Dept/Health Dept, case worker/med & social worker, 1962-66; Park City Hospital, Bridgeport CT, asst bookkeeper, 1959-62; Berkley Training High School, Monks Corner SC, business educ instructor, 1958-59. **Orgs:** Mem NEA 1971; mem WA State Human Rights Commn 1977; mem Gov's Commn on Employment of the Handicapped 1977; mem Nat Assn Sex Educators & Couns 1975; mem Snohomish Co Alcoholic Commn 1978. **Honors/Awds:** Del The White House Conf on Handicapped Individuals Wash DC 1977. **Business Addr:** 20000 68th Avenue, Lynnwood, WA 98036.

BROWN, MARY BOYKIN
Nurse instructor. **Personal:** Born Feb 1, 1942, Sampson Cty, NC; married Franklin Der Brown; children: Franklin Jr, Franita Dawn. **Educ:** Winston-Salem State Univ, BS Nursing 1963; Long Island Univ, MS Comm Mental Health 1978. **Career:** Long Island Jewish Med Ctr, instr inservice ed 1966-70; Harlem Hosp Ctr NY, instr school of nursing 1970-74; Midway Nursing Home, coord inservice ed 1974-75; Mary Gran Nursing Ctr Clinton NC, dir inservice ed 1975-76; Sampson Community Coll Clinton NC, instr school of nursing 1976-, chairman of nursing programs, 1989-. **Orgs:** Mem Amer Nurses Assoc 1964-, Natl League of Nursing 1964-, NC Nurses Assoc Dist 14 1976-, Council of Assoc Degree Nursing 1976-; teacher beginners class St Stephen AME Zion Church 1976-84; chmn, sec Four Cty Med Ctr Bd of Dir 1981-85; police commiss Garland Town Bd 1983-; vice pres Browns Cleaners & Laundromat 1985-; appointed to legislative commission on nursing, 1989; elected to Sampson County Board of Education, 1990; Sampson County School Bd, chairman, 1994. **Honors/Awds:** Outstanding Young Women Outstanding Young Women of Amer 1977; Most Outstanding 4-H Leader Sampson Cty 4-H Clinton NC 1977-78; Outstanding 4-H Volunteer NC Gov Raleigh NC 1980; Cert of Apprec Sampson Cty Voters League 1981; Excellence in Teaching Award, finalist, Depart of Comm Colleges, 1993; Alpha Kappa Alpha Inc, Rho Omega Omega Chap, Educator of the Year, 1995. **Home Addr:** PO Box 296, Garland, NC 28441.

BROWN, MARY KATHERINE
Environmental administrator. **Personal:** Born Oct 14, 1948, Vicksburg, MS; daughter of Macie Little Brown and Elijah Brown. **Educ:** Tuskegee Inst, BS Social Science 1971, MEd Stu Personnel 1972; Jackson State Univ, MPA Public Policy & Admin 1982-85. **Career:** MS Employment Svcs, employment counselor 1972-73; Alabama A&M Univ, dir new women's residence hall 1973-74; Jackson State Univ, coord special serv 1974-82; Comm Housing Resources, dir 1982-84; Hinds Co Bd of Supervisors, comm and economic develop specialist; Mississippi Bureau of Pollution Control, compliance officer, 1989-. **Orgs:** Treas 1977-78, vice pres 1978-80 Jackson Urban League Guild; charter mem Vicksburg Chap Delta Sigma Theta Sor 1978; sec MS Assn of Educ Oppor Progs Personnel 1979-80; pres MS Caucus on Conseumerism 1979-81; treas Assn for Public Policy & Admin 1982-84; bd of dirs Jackson Urban League 1984-87; comm chairperson United Negro College Fund 1986; chmn of bd of directors, Jackson Community Housing and Resources Board, 1987-89. **Honors/Awds:** Kappa Delta Pi & Phi Delta Kappa Honor Socs 1972; Cert of Appreciation Tampa Urban League 1978; Outstanding Serv Plaque Jackson State Univ Upward Bound Program 1980; Outstanding Serv Plaque Jackson State Univ Coronation Comm 1981; HUD Fellowship Jackson State Univ Dept Housing & Urban Develop 1982-84. **Home Addr:** 530 Riley Rd., Vicksburg, MS 39180-8122.

BROWN, MAXINE J. CHILDRESS
Elected official. **Personal:** Born Aug 13, 1943, Washington, DC; married James E Brown; children: Scot, Nikki, Kimberly. **Educ:** Springfield Coll, BS 1971; Univ of MA, MEd 1973. **Career:** Rochester Inst of Tech, asst prof 1973-74; State Coll Geneseo NY, asst prof, spec ed, dir learning disabilities 1975-78; People Helping People, dir 1978-80; City of Rochester Dept of Rec & Comm Svcs, dir of publ rel 1980-83; City of Rochester, councilwoman. **Orgs:** Natl cert interpreter for the deaf Amer Sign Lang 1970-85; vp, bd of dir Puerto Rican Youth Devel 1982-; mem adv bd, chmn ed comm NY State Div of Human Rights 1984-; mem & city council rep, adv bd Monroe Cty Office for the Aging 1984-; mem adv bd Ctr for Ed Devel; vp, bd of visitors State Ag & Indust School at Indust; mem bd of dir Prog for Rochester to Interest Students in Sci & Math; mem, former pres Metro Women's Network; chairperson Arts Reach Arts for Greater Rochester; bd of dir Rochester Area Multiple Sclerosis; mem Urban Ad Hoc Comm Home Econ Monroe Cty Coop Ext. **Honors/Awds:** Nominated by Gov Carey & Approved by State Sen for Bd of Visitors State Ag & Indust School at Indust; 12 Publ including ''About Time Mag'', ''Improving Police/Black Comm Relations'', ''A Not So Ordinary Man'', ''A Study Skills Program for the Hearing Impared Student'' Volta Review Alexander Graham Bell Jrnl; Politician of the Year Eureka Lodge Awd 1984. **Home Addr:** 222 Chili Ave, Rochester, NY 14611. **Business Addr:** City Councilwoman, City of Rochester, 30 Church St, Rochester, NY 14614.

BROWN, MICHAEL
Professional basketball player. **Personal:** Born Jul 19, 1963, Newark, NJ. **Educ:** George Washington Univ. **Career:** Chicago Bulls, 1986-88; Utah Jazz, 1988-93; Minnesota Timberwolves, 1993-. **Business Addr:** Professional Basketball Player, Minnesota Timberwolves, 600 First Ave, N, Minneapolis, MN 55403, (612)337-3865.

BROWN, MICHAEL DEWAYNE
Educator. **Personal:** Born Dec 18, 1954, Franklin, VA; son of Lola B Brown and Albert L Brown. **Educ:** Hampton University, Hampton, VA, BS, 1977; University of Virginia, Charlottsville, VA, continuing education; George Mason University, Fairfax, VA, master's degree, 1991. **Career:** Alexandria City Schools, teacher, 1977-93, lead teacher, 1993-94; Amideast, consultant, assistant principal, 1994-97. **Orgs:** Member, Kappa Delta Pi, 1990-; member, Phi Delta Kappa, 1990-; grade level chairperson, school, 1988-92; member, Educational Technology Com, 1990-; member, Strategic Planning Task Force, 1989; member, Superintendents Teacher Advisory Council, 1988-91; Middle School Steering Committee; VA Educational Comuting Association; Concerned Black Men Inc of NOVA; Assn for Sueprvision and Curriculum Development. **Honors/Awds:** Grant Study Skills, Chapter 2, 1990; Educator's Book of Forms, copyrighted work, 1989; Washington Post Grants in Education, 1991-93. **Home Addr:** 3147 Martha Custis Dr, Alexandria, VA 22302. **Business Phone:** (703)706-4400.

BROWN, MILBERT ORLANDO
Journalist. **Personal:** Born Aug 12, 1956, Gary, IN; son of Mary Blanchard Brown and Milbert Brown, Sr. **Educ:** Ball State Univ, Muncie, IN, BS, journalism, 1978; Ohio Univ, Athens, OH, MA, photo-communication, 1982. **Career:** Washington Post, Washington, DC, photojournalist, 1982; self-employed/freelance photographer, midwestern-based, 1983-86; Wilberforce Univ, Wilberforce, OH, instructor of mass media, 1986-87; Patuxent Publishing Newspapers, Columbia, MD, photojournalist, 1987-89; Boston Globe, Boston, MA, photojournalist, 1990-91; Chicago Tribune, Chicago, IL, picture editor, 1991-. **Orgs:** Omega Psi Phi Fraternity, 1976-; Natl Assn of Black Journalists, 1981-; Natl Press Photographers Assn, 1974-. **Honors/Awds:** 1st Place Sports Picture, Boston Press Photographers Assn, 1991; 1st Place & Best of Show for Spot News, Maryland & Delaware/DC Press Assn, 1988; Lecture-''Photography & Aesthetic Awareness,'' Morris Brown Coll, 1987; Two/Man Show & Lecture, Grambling State Coll, 1987; Natl Assn of Black Journalists, 1992; Chicago Association of Black Journalists, Award of Excellence for essay ''Pieces of Ebony,'' 1992; Natl Assn of Black Journalists & Coca Cola, USA Photo ''Shoot Out'' winner, 1992, 1993; Natl Ass of Black Journalists, Journalism Award, Outstanding Coverage of the Black Condition, photography, 1992, 1994; Lecture & Exhibition, ''Pieces of Ebony,'' Photo Exhibit, Dillard Univ, 1994, Morgan State Univ, 1995; Chicago Press Photographers Assn, 1st place winner, portrait/personality, 1993. **Business Addr:** Photojournalist, Chicago Tribune, 425 N Michigan Ave, Chicago, IL 60611-4041.

BROWN, MILTON F.
Educational administrator. **Personal:** Born Apr 29, 1943, Rochester, NY; divorced; children: Damien. **Educ:** SUNY Oswego, BS 1965; Columbia Univ Teachers Coll, MA 1973; EdD 1983. **Career:** Natl Inst of Ed, Educ Policy Fellow 1978-79; New York City Board of Ed, Asst Sup 1979-80; NY State Educ Dept, Dir 1980-82; NJ Dept of Higher Ed/Academic Affrs, Dir 1982-85; Malcolm X College, Chicago, IL, president, currently. **Orgs:** Independent Consultant 1975-83; IUME Teachers Coll, Sr Research Assoc 1977-78; US Dept of Educ, Consultant 1975-83; vice pres Task Force on Youth Employment 1979-80; vice pres Mondale's Task Force on Youth Employment 1979-80. **Honors/Awds:** George Wash Univ, Inst for Ed Leadership Ed Policy Fellow 1978-79; Teachers College Columbus Univ, Heft Fellow 1972-73. **Military Serv:** USMCR, L/Corporal. **Business Addr:** President, Malcolm X College (Chicago City College), 1900 West Van Buren, Chicago, IL 60612.

BROWN, MORGAN CORNELIUS
Sociologist, educational administrator. **Personal:** Born Jul 26, 1916, Macon, GA; son of Ida Moore Brown and Morgan Cornelius Brown; married Anne L Boles; children: Morgan C III, Andrea E. **Educ:** Paine Coll, BA 1937; OH State Univ, MA 1950, PhD 1954; Harvard Univ, post-doctoral research 1968-69. **Career:** So Univ, prof sociology 1954-60, chmn sociology dept 1960-68; Bridgewater State Coll, prof & chmn sociology dept 1969, dir & dean behavioral sciences div 1972-. **Orgs:** Mem NAACP; Urban League; Am Sociologists Assn; Eastern & MA Sociologists Assns; Alpha Kappa Delta; Pi Gamma Mu; Psi Chi; Alpha Phi Alpha; Christian Methodist Episcopal Church. **Honors/Awds:** Research awards & grants NSF; Ford Found; Milton Fund; US Dept HEW. **Military Serv:** US Army, 1st Lt 1942-45; Bronze Star Award in Pisa, Italy 1945. **Home Addr:** 25 Elder Ave, Yeadon, PA 19050.

BROWN, MORSE L.
County extension director. **Personal:** Born Oct 10, 1943, Oakland, MS; son of Fannie J Moore Brown and Stephen Brown; married Arma George Brown, Aug 30, 1980; children: Khary Dia. **Educ:** Alcorn State University, Lorman, MS, BS, 1965. **Career:** US Soil Conservation Service, Claremont, NH, soil conservationist, 1965-67, Milford, NH, soil conservationist, 1967-71, Nashua, NH, West Branch, MI, dist conservationist, 1971-73, Muskegon, MI, dist conservationist, 1973-82, Ann Arbor, MI, dist conservationist, 1982-85; Michigan State University Cooperative Extension Service, Ann Arbor, MI, county ext director, 1985-88, Detroit, MI, county ext director, 1988-. **Orgs:** Regional director, Alpha Phi Alpha, Fraternity, 1975-82; president, Alpha Phi Alpha, Fraternity Theta Zeta Lambda, 1988-90; chairman, Brown Chapel Building Committee, 1986-88; regional director, Soil Conservation Society America, 1983-84. **Honors/Awds:** Appreciation for Service, Soil Conservation Society, 1985; Appreciation for Service, Washtenaw County, 1988; Resolution of Appreciation Department Heads, Washtenaw County, 1988; Commendation Award, 1990; Alpha Man of Year, Theta Zeta Lambda Chapter, 1991; Resolution of App Washtenaw County, Board of Commissioners Washtenaw County, 1988; Dairy Herd Imp Assoc Washtenaw County, 1988; President's Citation, MI Assoc Ext Agents, 1992; Achievement Award, Natl Assoc of Extension Atents, 1994. **Military Serv:** US Army Reserves, ssgt, 1966-72. **Business Addr:** County Extension Director, MSU Cooperative Extension Service, Michigan State University, 640 Temple, 6th Fl, Detroit, MI 48201.

BROWN, MORTIMER
Clinical psychologist. **Personal:** Born Feb 20, 1924, New York, NY; married Marilyn Green; children: Frank, Mark. **Educ:** Vanderbilt Univ, Nashville, PhD, 1961; City Coll of NY, BS, 1949. **Career:** IL Dept Mental Health, Springfield, IL, asst dir, 1961-69; FL State Univ, Tallahassee, prof, psychology, 1969-73; Florida Mental Health Inst, 1973-78; Independent Practice, 1978-96; St Leo Coll, adj prof of Psych, 1977-; Univ of Sarasota, adj prof of Psych, Tampa Bay Campus, 1998-. **Orgs:** Vari-

ous bd, comm, councils, Am Psychological Assn; Am Black Psychological Assn; bd, various Comm Southeastern Psychological Assn; bd & comm mem, Florida Psych Assn, pres, 1980, 1981. **Honors/Awds:** DP, Bedford Univ, 1960. **Military Serv:** USAF, 1942-46.

BROWN, NANCY COFIELD
Administrator. **Personal:** Born Jul 25, 1932; married David; children: David, Stephen, Philip. **Educ:** Pratt Inst, Grad 1954. **Career:** Trudy Rogers Co, asst designer 1955-57; Family & Child Svc, coord 1974-77; Town of Greenwich, dir comm dev 1978-. **Orgs:** Corp, dir CT Womens's Bk 1974-78; grants consult Town of Greenwich 1977; consult Affirmative Act Town of Greenwich 1977; dir Urban League of SW Fairfield CT 1970-74; mem Links-Fairfield CT 1980; trustee Stanford Found 1980; mem CT Housing Fin Authority; Hartwick College, trustee, 1990. **Honors/Awds:** 10 outstndng women BRAVO Award; YMCA 1979. **Business Addr:** Dir Community Development, Town Hall, 101 Field Pt Rd, Greenwich, CT 06830.

BROWN, NORMAN E.
Scientist, business executive. **Personal:** Born Feb 20, 1935, Cleveland, OH; married Mary Lee Tyus; children: Karen, Dianne, Pamela, David, Robert. **Educ:** Western Res Univ Cleveland OH, BA biology 1959; Univ of MN Minneapolis, MS biochem 1970. **Career:** Western Reserve Univ, rsch assoc 1957-64; Univ of MN, resch assoc; Hoffman-LaRoche Inc, asst sci II 1969-71, assoc sci 1971-73, mgr equal oppor 1973-78, asst dir equal oppor 1978-86; Tampa Bay Regional Planning Council, assoc housing planner 1986-. **Orgs:** Mem Edges Inc 1975-80; pres bd of trustees United Way Plainfield 1978-; vice pres bd of trustees United Way Union Co 1978-; pres 1984-85, mem Plainfield NJ School Bd 1982-85. **Honors/Awds:** Black Achivers in Ind Award; YMCA Harlem Br; YNew York City 1974. **Business Addr:** Associate Planner, Tampa Bay Regional Plng Cncl, 9455 Koger Blvd, St Petersburg, FL 33712.

BROWN, O. GILBERT
Educational administrator. **Personal:** Born Jun 12, 1954, Proctor, AR; son of Zelner & Mable Brown; children: Jacqueline, Jordan. **Educ:** University of Kansas, BS, 1976; Emporia State University, MS, 1984; Miami University-Oxford, Ohio, MS, 1986; Indiana University-Bloomington, EdD, 1992. **Career:** Indiana University-Bloomington, coord, 1986-91; Earlham College, associate dean, 1992-93; Indiana University, Indianapolis, director of residence life, 1993-95; Indiana University School of Education, director of student svcs, asst dean for education, student svcs, currently. **Orgs:** National Association of Student Personnel Administrators, 1984-; American College Personnel Association. **Special Achievements:** Helping African-American Students Attend College, 1997; Debunking the Myth: Stories About African-American College Students.

BROWN, OLA M.
Educator. **Personal:** Born Apr 7, 1941, Albany, GA; daughter of Georgia Butler Johnson and Willie L Johnson (deceased). **Educ:** Albany State Coll, BS 1961; Univ of GA, MEd 1972, EdS 1973, EdD 1974. **Career:** Thomas County Schools, Thomasville GA, teacher, 1961-67; Dougherty County Schools, Albany GA, teacher, 1967-71; Univ of GA Athens, grad asst, 1972-74; Valdosta State Coll GA, prof of educ 1974-91; Dept Head, Early Childhood and Reading Education, 1980-90; dept head, professor emerita, currently. **Orgs:** Mem Phi Delta Kappa Educ Frat 1975-; recording sec GA Council of Intl Reading Assn 1977-79; treas GA Assn of Higher Educ (GAE Affl) 1977-80; mem Amer Assn of Univ Prof 1977-80; vice pres 1979-80, pres 1980-81 GA Council of Intl Reading Assn; state coordinator Intl Reading Assn 1988-91. **Honors/Awds:** Educ Instr of Yr Student GA Assn of Educ (VSC) 1975; WH Dennis Meml Awd Albany State Coll 1976; Ira E Aaron Reading Awd S Central GA Council of IRA 1977. **Home Addr:** 2503 N Oak St, Valdosta, GA 31602.

BROWN, ORAL LEE
Real estate broker, restaurant owner. **Personal:** Born Feb 14, 1945, Batesville, MS; daughter of Nezzie Anna Bivins-Vaughn and Walter Bivins; married Joseph Brown, Mar 6, 1969; children: Lynn Channel Mitchell, Phyllis Bivins Brown. **Educ:** Laney College, Oakland, CA, AA, 1979; Anthony School of Real Estate, Oakland, CA, broker certificate, 1979; University of San Francisco, San Francisco, CA, BS, 1983. **Career:** Lynn Beauty Lounge, Oakland, CA, cosmetologist, 1963-69; Blue Cross Ins, Oakland, Ca, supervisor/mgr, 1969-83; Nationwide Realty, Oakland, CA, owner/broker, 1983-; Cobbler's Restaurant, owner, 1992-. **Orgs:** Founder, Oral Lee Brown Foundation, 1987-; president, Elmhurst Business & Professional Organization, 1990-; chairperson, Community Housing Resource Board, 1988-; board of directors, Associate Real Property Brokers, 1987-; commissioner, Alameda County Assessment Appeal Board, 1987-. **Honors/Awds:** Super Hero, Oakland A, 1988; Community Award, San Francisco Foundation, 1989; Resolution, City of Oakland, 1990; Excel, Operation Push, 1989; Community/Education, New York Club, 1989. **Business Addr:** Real Estate Broker, Nationwide Realty, TPI Corp, 9331 E 14th St, Oakland, CA 94603.

BROWN, ORLANDO CLAUDE
Professional football player. **Personal:** Born Dec 12, 1970, Washington, DC; children: Orlando Jr. **Educ:** South Carolina State, attended. **Career:** Cleveland Browns, tackle, 1994-95; Baltimore Ravens, tackle, 1996-. **Business Addr:** Professional Football Player, Baltimore Ravens, 11001 Owings Mills Blvd, Owings Mills, MD 21117, (410)654-6200.

BROWN, OTHA N., JR.
Educational administrator. **Personal:** Born Jul 19, 1931, DeQueen, AR; son of Elizabeth Gossitt and Otha Brown; married L Evelyn Permenter; children: Darrick Othaniel, Leland Kendrick. **Educ:** Central State Univ OH, BS (Cum Laude) 1952; OH State Univ Law School, 1955; Univ of CT, MA 1956; Univ of Bridgeport, Prof Diploma-Admin 1959; NY Univ, Cert Counseling 1965; Springfield Coll, Mass Cert Counseling 1966; Queens Coll NY, Cert in Counseling 1967; Boston Univ, Cert of Counseling 1969. **Career:** Wooster Jr HS Stratford CT, English & soc studies 1957-60; Rippowam HS Stamford CT, counselor 1961-83; Stamford HS, 1983-90; City of Norwalk, city councilman 1963-69, 1977-81; CT Gen Assembly, legislator 1966-72; 2nd Taxing Dist City of Norwalk, commissioner 1981-, chmn, beginning 1982; Fairfield Cablevision, vp; Biebel Travel Agency, vice pres; licensed notary, real estate broker; 2nd Taxing Dist Water Dept, chair, 1982-; Amer Water Works Assn (AWWA) International Affairs Comm, 1992-; Sub Comm Tech Info, chair, 1994-; Univ of Connecticut, dir, 1994-98. **Orgs:** Regional dir Alpha Phi Alpha 1969-79; mem Amer Personnel & Guidance Assn, Amer School Counselors Assn, Natl & State Educ Assn, Phi Alpha Theta, Kappa Delta Pi; mem Dem Town Comm 1972-74; sec bd of trustees Univ of CT 1975-93; founder & pres Norwalk Area Improvement League Inc 1978-; founder & pres Greater Norwalk Black Democratic Club & Coalition 1976-; pres & dep mayor Norwalk Comm Council 1980; bd dir, vice pres Fairfield Cablevision; founder & pres Southern CT United Black Fund 1983-; co-chmn Jesse Jackson for Pres Norwalk 1984; pres Connecticut State Federation of Black Democratic Clubs Inc 1972-76; State Task Force on Justice & the Courts, 1987-89. **Honors/Awds:** Man of the Year Alpha Phi Alpha 1969; Distinguished Serv Awd 1981; Past Pres Awd CT State Fed of Black Democrats 1979; Citizen of the Year Omega Psi Phi 1970; Young Man of the Year Jaycees 1967; NAACP Leadership Awd 1970; Univ Medal, Univ of Conn, 1994; publications include ''School Counselors, A New Role & Image'' Connecticut Teacher Magazine 1972, Remembering: A Book of Poetry 1977, ''Political Blackout'' Connecticut Magazine 1979, ''Fighting Apartheid UCONN Makes the Decision to Divest'' The Stamford Advocate Viewpoint 1986, ''Thoughts on Education'' Sphinx Magazine, Vol 74 No 4, Alpha Phi Alpha Fraternity 1988; Politics & Service Award, Prince Hall Grand Chapter, Order of Eastern Star, State of Connecticut 1987; Official Citation, City of Hartford 1989; Honorary Alumnus, Langston Univ, 1968; Achievement Hall of Fame, Central State Univ, 1996. **Military Serv:** US Army, psychological warfare officer 1952-54. **Business Addr:** Director, Univ of Connecticut, Waterbury, CT 06710.

BROWN, P. J. (COLLIER BROWN, JR.)
Professional basketball player. **Personal:** Born Oct 14, 1969, Detroit, MI; married Dee; children: Briana. **Educ:** Louisiana Tech. **Career:** Panionios (Greece), center, 1992-93; New Jersey Nets, 1993-96; Miami Heat, 1996-. **Honors/Awds:** J. Walter Kennedy Citizenship Award, 1996-97. **Business Addr:** Professional Basketball Player, Miami Heat, 721 NW 1st Ave, Miami Arena, Miami, FL 33136, (305)577-4328.

BROWN, PAUL, JR.
Manager. **Personal:** Born Oct 10, 1926, Chicago, IL; married Jean Pace. **Career:** Kicks & Co Chicago, mus lyrics & book writer 1961. **Honors/Awds:** Appeared in Village Vanguard 1961; Apollo Theater 1961; Carnegie Hall 1962; Bule Angel 1962; Hungry I 1962; Crescendo 1962; Berns Stockholm 1963; & Waldorf Asteria 1963; Cool Elephand London Eng 1965; one-man shows Prince Charels Theater London 1963; Mus Box Theater Los Angeles 1964; Gramercy Arts Tehater New York City 1965; producer dir Joy '66, Happy Medium Theater; Summer in the City Harper Theater; Alley Theater; In de Beginin' 1977; composer Dat Der 1960; Brown Baby 1960; Work Song 1960; The Sanke 1963; Muffled Drums 1965; series host 13 Prog Pub TV Series ''From Jumpstreet A Story of Black Music'' WETA Wash DC; present mem Author's League Am. **Business Addr:** Solid State Div, Route 202, Somerville, NJ 08876.

BROWN, PAUL E. X.
Business executive. **Personal:** Born Dec 20, 1910, Weir, MS; married Verna. **Educ:** Univ of MN, 1933; Columbia Coll, Moody Bible Inst. **Career:** Natl Assn of Market Devel Inc, exec dir 1985; Atlanta Coca-Cola Bottling Co, 1962-75; Radio WAOK, news public affairs dir, 1958-62; GA Edition, Pittsburgh Courier, ed, mgr; Radio Station WERD, program dir, announcer. **Orgs:** past pres, Atlanta Chapter, Natl Assn Market Devel; sr consultant, Triangle Assn, Inc chmn Adv Council; prince Hall mason Atlanta Emp Vol Merit Emp Assn; Shriner; Elk; Frontiers Int; Phi Beta Sigma; Imperial Dir; public relations Shriners; public Shriners Quarterly; radio nwscstr The Pyramid 1946; bd mem, George Washington Carver Boys Club; bd mem Goodwill Industries of Atlanta; Enterprises Now Inc; sec Pledging Found; past pres Adelphi Clb; mem DeLeg Assembly United Way; mem Task Force on Youth Motivation; NAB. **Business Addr:** 201 Ashby St NW, Ste 306, Atlanta, GA 30314.

BROWN, PAUL L.
Educator (retired). **Personal:** Born Feb 18, 1919, Anderson, SC; married Lorene S Byron; children: Pauletta B, Gloria J, Nanola K. **Educ:** Knoxville Coll, BS 1941, PhD 1955; Univ of IL, MS 1948. **Career:** Atlanta Univ, prof of Biology, 1978-; Clark Coll, dean of fac & instr, 1974-78; Natl Science Found, program mgr, 1974, 1963-64; Norfolk State Coll, chmn, natl science & math, 1958-74; FL A&M Univ, prof of biology, 1958-59; Southern Univ, instructor of biology, 1948-58; Atlanta Univ School of Arts & Science, dean 1982-87. **Orgs:** Consult & sr prog Assoc Inst of Serv to Educ Soc of Sigma Xi; mem Beta Beta, Phi Sigma, Betta Kappa Chi, Phi Beta Sigma, Natl Inst of Sci, Am Zoologists, IL & VA Acad of Sci, Inst of Biol Sci, Am Micro Soc J Hay Whitney Flwshp, Am Med Assoc Flwshp. **Honors/Awds:** Published in American Midland Natl & other learned journals. **Military Serv:** US Army, European theater of oprtns 1942-45. **Business Addr:** Retired Dean, Atlanta Univ, 223 James P Brawley Dr, Atlanta, GA 30314.

BROWN, PAULA EVIE
Educator. **Educ:** Loyola University, BS, BA, 1973; Purdue University, MSM, 1976; Harvard University, EdM, 1980; Northern Illinois University, EdD, 1990. **Career:** Neighborhood Youth Corps, recruiter, 1973-74; Purdue University, instructor, 1974-76; RR Donnelley & Sons, pricing estimator, 1976-79; Chicago & Northwestern Co, HRD administrator, 1981-82; Northern Illinois University, instructor, 1984-88; F Webb Starks, Inc, business developer, 1989-90; Central Michigan University, professor, 1990-. **Orgs:** Black Alumni Council, NIU, 1991-; National Congress of Black Faculty, 1992-; Research Association of Minority Professors, 1992-; Association for Business Communication, 1991-; National Michigan Business Education Association, 1991-; Delta Pi Epsilon, 1991-; Phi Delta Kappa, 1980-; Beta Gamma Sigma, 1973-. **Honors/Awds:** Delta Pi Epsilon, Doctoral Research Award, 1992; Woodson Fellowship, Awardee, Recipient for Minorities, 1984-87; Chicago Junior Association of C&I, Nominee 10 Outstanding Chicagoans, 1982. **Special Achievements:** Publication based on award-winning dissertation, 1992; participant in a nationally recognized entrepreneurship program, 1987; first black to win doctoral research award from DPE, 1992. **Business Addr:** Professor, Central Michigan University, College of Business, Dept of OIS, Grawn Hall #305, Mount Pleasant, MI 48859, (517)774-5900.

BROWN, PHILIP RAYFIELD, III
Clergyman, association executive. **Personal:** Born Oct 7, 1917, New Orleans, LA; married Bertha Duckett; children: Philip IV, Eleanor Miller, Norma West, James. **Educ:** Xavier U, BA; Union Theol Sem, MTH; United Theol Sem, DD. **Career:** US Postal Service, letter carrier, inspector; Pleasant Grove Bapt Ch, pastor 1948-59; Travelers Rest Bapt Ch, pastor 1959; Calvary Missionary Bapt Ch, pastor 1959-. **Orgs:** Exec dir Ouachita Multi-Purpose Comm Action Program 1966; pres Monroe NAACP 1961-63; pres LA Sunday Sch Conv 1969-; instr Nat Sunday Sch Cong 1943-. **Honors/Awds:** Highest City Award New Orleans 1957; Man of Yr Monroe 1970, 1974; Humanitarian of Yr 1972. **Business Addr:** Calvary Miss Bapt Church, 201 S 9th St, West Monroe, LA 71291.

BROWN, PRISCILLA
Marketing executive. **Personal:** Born Aug 14, 1957, Albuquerque, NM; daughter of Marta Gabre-Tsadick and Demeke Tekle-Wold. **Educ:** San Francisco State University, San Francisco, CA, journalism/finance, 1980. **Career:** KQED-TV, San Francisco, CA, field news producer, 1979-81; Sutro & Co, San Francisco, CA, stockbroker 1981-82; Paine Webber, Chicago, IL, stockbroker, 1982-86; Equitable Life-Marvin Rotter Agency, Northbrook, IL, director of marketing, 1986-91; Lincoln Natl Investment Management Co, Fort Wayne, IN, vice president & director, marketing, 1991-. **Orgs:** Director, Chicago Office, Project Mercy, 1984-86. **Honors/Awds:** Chicago's Up & Coming, Dollars & Sense Magazine, 1989. **Business Addr:** Vice President & Director, Sales & Marketing, Lincoln Natl Investment Management Co, 1300 S Clinton St, Box 1110, Fort Wayne, IN 46825.

BROWN, RALPH H.
Administrative law judge. **Personal:** Born Dec 13, 1919, Petersburg, VA; son of Lillian Brown and William H Brown; married Ollie M Brown; children: James A, Ralph K, Steven H, Leland M. **Educ:** St. Augustine Coll; Franklin Univ Law, Capital Univ, Columbus, LLB, JD. **Career:** Postal clerk; pvt law practice OH; attorney; examiner PUCO OH; Bur Hearings & Appeals DHEW SSA, admin law judge. **Orgs:** Mem Alpha Phi Alpha Frat; mem St Phillips Episc Church; mem Columbus Civil Rights Assn; mem Amer, Natl Bar Assns; Robert B Ellist Law Club. **Military Serv:** USAF 1943-46, 1962, 1968. **Business Addr:** DHEW SSA, 50 W Broad St, Room 17, Columbus, OH 43215.

BROWN, RANDY
Professional basketball player. **Personal:** Born May 22, 1968, Chicago, IL; married Katrina; children: Justin, Janel. **Educ:** Houston; New Mexico State. **Career:** Sacramento Kings, guard, 1991-95; Chicago Bulls, 1995-. **Business Addr:** Professional Basketball Player, Chicago Bulls, 1901 W Madison St, Chicago, IL 60612-2459, (312)455-4000.

BROWN, RAY, JR.
Professional football player. **Personal:** Born Dec 12, 1962, Marion, AR; married Ashley; children: Lentisha, Tyler, Andrea, Miriam. **Educ:** Arkansas State, attended. **Career:** St Louis Cardinals, guard, 1986-87; Washington Redskins, 1989-95; San Francisco 49ers, 1996-. **Business Addr:** Professional Football Player, San Francisco 49ers, 4949 Centennial Blvd, Santa Clara, CA 95054, (415)562-4949.

BROWN, RAYMOND MADISON
Business executive, construction group. **Personal:** Born Jan 12, 1949, Fort Worth, TX; son of Lutiel V Houston and Raymond E Brown; married Linda, May 17, 1974; children: Derek, Christopher. **Educ:** W Texas State, BA 1971. **Career:** Life of GA, ins underwriter; Waldo Shirt Co, NY, sales rep; New Orleans Sts, professional 1977-; Atlanta Falcons, def sfty 1971-77; Real Estate Broker 1980-; Brown Boy II Properties Inc, constr co pres 1984-. **Orgs:** Mem, Omega Psi Phi Frat. **Honors/Awds:** Author of one novel. **Business Addr:** Pres, Brown Boy II, Properties Inc, 4936 Lake Fjord Pass, Marietta, GA 30068, (404)642-1316.

BROWN, REGGIE
Professional football player. **Personal:** Born Jun 26, 1973, Detroit, MI. **Educ:** Fresno State. **Career:** Seattle Seahawks, running back, 1996-. **Business Addr:** Professional Football Player, Seattle Seahawks, 11220 NE 53rd St, Kirkland, WA 98033, (206)827-9777.

BROWN, REGINALD DEWAYNE
Writer/producer/director. **Personal:** Born Mar 14, 1952, Memphis, TN; son of Clarence & Nadolyn; married Robin Viva Brown, Feb 16, 1980; children: Brian Alexander, Brittany Nicole. **Educ:** University of California, Irvine, BA-drama, 1974; San Francisco State University, MA-film, 1979. **Career:** Reginald Brown Productions, writer, producer, dir, 1981-; Children's Defense Fund, Beat the Odds Celebration, producer, 1996-97; Central City Productions, Inc, writer, 1991-94; Sam Riddle Productions, Inc, writer, segment dir, 1987-91; Dick Clark Productions, Inc, writer, assoc producer, 1985-87. **Orgs:** Directors of Guild of America, AASC, event chair, 1994-; Writers Guild of America, West, vice chair, black writers committee, 1991-. **Honors/Awds:** TV Lab/WNET Thirteen Independent Filmmakers Grant, 1981; American Film Institute, Independent Filmmakers Grant, 1978. **Home Addr:** 13691 Gavina Ave, #465, Sylmar, CA 91342, (818)364-9993. **Business Phone:** (818)364-1983.

BROWN, REGINALD ROYCE, SR.
Law enforcement officer. **Personal:** Born Mar 18, 1946, Baton Rouge, LA; son of Theresa Mae Bell Brown; married Charlotte Ann Henderson Brown, Feb 22, 1975; children: Reginald Jr, Tashera Patrice, D'Laniger Royce. **Educ:** Southern Univ, NA, 1965. **Career:** 13th Amendment Band, pub relation dir & mgr; Governor's Office on Consumer Protection, program supr 1972-73; So Univ Baton Rouge LA, Centex dir 1972-75, asst to bus mgr 1973-; City Councilman Jospeh A Delpit, aide; Hon State & Sen of LA 1975; E Baton Rouge Sheriffs Office, admin asst, 1975-; Reginald Brown & Assocs Inc, pres, 1972-. **Orgs:** Baranco Clark YMCA, honorary member, chairman of the board; honorary mem NAACP; bd council of First Time Offenders; East Baton Rouge Civil Def Rescue Unit; mem, Natl Sheriffs Assn, 1972-; pres, Holiday Helpers of Baton Rouge Inc, 1987-; pres, Scotlandville Beautification Committee, 1989-; board member, Baton Rouge Green, 1991; Baton Rouge Detox Bd, secretary; Mayor's Anti Drug and Crime Task Force. **Honors/Awds:** Martin Luther King Award, Shady Grove Baptist Church, 1987; Honorary mayor Baton Rouge 1974; award Recognition for Outstanding Serv to So Univ Student Body 1974; outstanding award for Contrib to So Univ Marching Band 1974; award for Serv & Contbns to Sickle Cell Anemia Found & Retarded Childred Assn 1974; cmpgn coord 1st blk Woman Councilwoman in Baton Rouge, LA; awards for outstanding serv to Baranco Clark YMCA 1972; award of appreciation for serv & contbns to S Baton Rouge Neighborhood Serv Center 1971; Distinguished Officer of the Year, Blacks in Law Enforcement, 1990; Award of Distinction, Alpha Kappaha, 1989; Outstanding Black Achiever Award, YMCA; selected as Outstanding Humantarian Award, Baton Rouge Human Relations Council; Outstanding Law Enforcement Officer, 1990; Honored at the White House in Rose Garden, Outstanding Law Enforcement Officer by Pres Clinton & Atty General Janet Reno, 1994; Golden Deeds Award, Baton Rouge, LA, 1997; numerous other awards and letters of accomendations. **Business Addr:** Major, East Baton Rouge Sheriff's Office, PO Box 881, Baton Rouge, LA 70821.

BROWN, RENEE
Sports administrator. **Career:** Women's Basketball, asst coach: Univ of Kansas, Stanford Univ, San Jose State Univ; USA Basketball Women's Natl Team, asst coach to Tara VanDerveer, 1995-96; USA Women's Olympic Team, staff, 1996; WNBA, dir of player personnel, 1996-. **Business Addr:** Director of Player Personnel, WNBA, 645 Fifth Ave., New York, NY 10022.

BROWN, REUBEN
Professional football player. **Personal:** Born Feb 13, 1974. **Educ:** University of Pittsburgh. **Career:** Buffalo Bills, guard, 1995-. **Honors/Awds:** Pro Bowl, 1996. **Special Achievements:** Selected in the 1st round/14th overall pick in the 1995 NFL Draft. **Business Addr:** Professional Football Player, Buffalo Bills, 1 Bills Dr, Orchard Park, NY 14127, (716)648-1800.

BROWN, REUBEN D.
Business executive. **Personal:** Born Aug 11, 1948, Detroit, MI; son of Richard & Josephine Brown; divorced; children: Rochelle, E Aminata, Reuben Brandon. **Educ:** Lawrence Technological Univ, BSIM, 1982; Univ of Michigan, cum laude, MBA, 1984. **Career:** General Motors Corp, construction mgr, 1973-84; Rohm & Haas Co, financial analyst mgr, 1984-91; American Express Financial Advisors Inc, financial advisor, 1991-. **Orgs:** International Child Resource Institute, bd mem, 1996-; A Better Chance, bd mem, 1989-91; Black Business Students Organization, corporate relations chair, 1982-84; Univ of Michigan Steering Comm, 1982-84. **Honors/Awds:** American Express Fin Adv, advanced advisor, 1993. **Special Achievements:** Co-authored publication "Senior Counsel, Financial & Legal Strategies Age 50 & Beyond.". **Business Addr:** Advanced Advisor, American Express Financial Advisors Inc, 255 Shoreline Dr, Ste 500, Redwood City, CA 94065, (650)593-9170.

BROWN, RICHARD EARL
Librarian (retired). **Personal:** Born Apr 1, 1922, Oakland, CA; son of Linnie M Coleman (deceased) and John S Brown (deceased). **Educ:** Univ of San Fran, BS 1960. **Career:** Oakland Public Lib, jr librarian 1951-60, sr librarian 1960-67; Berkeley Public Lib, dir of adult serv 1967-72, acting dir 1972-73, asst dir 1973-83. **Orgs:** Dir of bd Oakland Municipal Civil Serv Assn; bd of dir Berkeley Municipal Credit Union 1973-81. **Home Addr:** 6363 Christie Ave #716, Emeryville, CA 94608.

BROWN, RICHARD OSBORNE
Physician. **Personal:** Born May 20, 1930, Detroit, MI; son of Flossie Eva Osborne Brown and Richard Wells Brown; married Martha Evelyn McGregor, Oct 6, 1973; children: Richard D, Kevin M, Vincent, Tiffany D. **Educ:** Wayne U, BA 1953; Howard Univ Med Sch, MD 1959; Homer G Phillips Hosp, Ophth Residency 1962-65. **Career:** Ophthalmology, private prac 1967-94; Southwest Detroit Hosp, active med staff; Samaritan Hlth Cntr, active med staff; Kirwood Gen Hosp, chief of staff 1974-76; New Center Hosp, active med staff; courtesy staff physician; courtesy med staff, Riverview Hospital 1987-. **Orgs:** Pres Detroit Med Soc 1978-80; pres Wolverine Med Soc 1982-; 2nd vice pres Natl Med Assn 1981-83, 1st vice pres 1983-85, bd of trustees 1985-91; Alpha Phi Alpha Frat; life mem NAACP 1971. **Military Serv:** AUS 1953-55. **Home Addr:** 22854 Newport, Southfield, MI 48075, (313)355-3648.

BROWN, ROBERT, JR.
Government official (retired), criminal justice consultant. **Personal:** Born Mar 23, 1936, Lansing, MI; son of Georgia L Dean Brown and Robert Brown Sr; married Joy G Tunstall. **Educ:** MI State Univ, BA social work 1958. **Career:** MI Dept of Corrections, prison counselor 1961-62, parole officer 1962-67, dep warden 1967-70, dep dir 1970-84, dir 1984-91. **Orgs:** Life mem Alpha Phi alpha 1955-, NAACP; exec bd mem Youth Devel Corp 1978-; pres 1984, life mem MI Correctional Assoc; vice pres 1985-86, treasurer 1986-89, pres 1989-91, Midwest Assoc of Correctional Admin; exec bd mem 1986-, vice pres 1989-91, Chief Okemos Council Boy Scouts of Amer; vice pres, Assn of State Correctional Administrators, 1989-91; exec comm, American Correctional Assn, 1988-90; Sigma Pi Phi Fraternity, Alpha Chi Boule, 1988-. **Honors/Awds:** Black Achievers Awd Phi Beta Sigma 1986; Boy Scouts of America, Whitney Young Service Award; Silver Beaver Award; Amer Correctional Assn, ER Cass Award; Lansing Ed Advancement Foundation, Distinguised Alumni Award; MI State Univ, Black Alumni Inc, Distinguished Alumni Award. **Military Serv:** USAF capt 1958-60, 1962. **Home Addr:** 1912 Kuerbitz Dr, Lansing, MI 48906, (517)323-1183.

BROWN, ROBERT CEPHAS, SR.
Master watch maker, diamond appraiser. **Personal:** Born Dec 9, 1925, Meridian, MS; married Ranola Hubbard; children: Robert Cephas Jr, Ranola LaVohn, Michelle Lynette, Rochelle La Kaye. **Educ:** Attended Van Slyke Sch of Horology (watchmaking); attended Gemological Inst of America. **Career:** Brown's Jewelers, owner/inventor/master watchmaker/diamond appraiser 1950-. **Orgs:** Mem Downtown Merchant's Assn; vice pres Vallejo Revitilization Assn; mem Charter Review Com of Vallejo; mem NAACP. **Military Serv:** AUS pfc 1944-46. **Business Addr:** Brown's Jewelers, 316 Georgia St, Vallejo, CA 94590.

BROWN, ROBERT J., III
Educator. **Personal:** Born May 31, 1919, Norfolk; married Blanche Randall; children: Jeanne, Catherine, Marcia. **Educ:** Hampton Inst, BS 1939; Howard Univ, MS 1941, MS, MIT, MD, 1945. **Career:** Union Baystate Chemical Corp, chemist, 1943-46; Dept of Medicine, Howard Univ, asst prof, 1959-60; Veterans Benefits Office, medical officer, 1960-61; Howard Univ, fellow & Psychiatry, 1961-66; Howard Univ, asst prof, 1966; Clinical Operations Area B Community Mental Health Center, pres, asst dir, 1972-. **Orgs:** Pvt practice mem Am Psychiatric Assn 1966-; mem Med Soc Dist Columbia 1966-; mem Am Assn Advancement Sci Present Position DC Civil Servic. **Honors/Awds:** Research Steric Hindrance & Enolization Acetylenic Precursors Vitamin A 1939-45; Theoretical Biology 1950; USNR LT JG MC 1955-56; LT 1956-57. **Business Addr:** Acting Dir, Howard University Hospital, 2041 Georgia Ave NW, Washington, DC 20060.

BROWN, ROBERT JOE
Consulting firm chief executive. **Personal:** Born Feb 26, 1935, High Point, NC; married Sallie J Walker, Sep 15. **Educ:** Virginia Union Univ; North Carolina A&T State Univ. **Career:** High Point Police Dept, law enforcement officer, 1956-58; US Dept of Treasury, Fed Bureau of Narcotics, agent, 1958-60; B & C Assocs Inc, founder, 1960-68; The White House, special asst to the president, 1968-73; B & C Assocs Inc, chmn, pres, CEO, 1973-. **Orgs:** Operation PUSH Inc, board of directors; MLK Center for Social Change, board of directors; First Union Corp, board of directors; Sonoco, board of dir; Duke Power, board of dir; So Furniture Club; NAACP, life mem; The Wisemen; Arthur W Page Soc; United Natl Bank, board of directors; numerous others. **Honors/Awds:** Junior Chamber of Commerce Distinguished Service, Outstanding Young Man in America; Natl Med Assn, Achievement Award; Alpha Phi Alpha, Natl Merit Award; OIC , Natl Exec Branch Govt Award; Honorary Chief, Sioux Indian Nation; Horatio Alger Assn, Distinguished American Award; Small Business Administration, Lifetime Achievement Award; SCLC, Drum Major for Justice Award; Honorary Degrees: North Carolina A & T State Univ, LHD; Tarkio College, LHD; Clark College, LHD; High Point Coll, LLD; Daniel Payne College, LLD; Shaw Univ, LLD; Florida Memorial Coll, LLD; Malcolm X Coll, LLD. **Business Addr:** President, CEO, B & C Associates Inc, 808 Greensboro Rd, High Point, NC 27260, (910)884-0744.

BROWN, ROBERT LEE
Mayor. **Personal:** Born Jul 31, 1947, Wetumpka, AL; son of Annie Pearl Moore Brown and Samuel Bernard Brown; married Donna Holland; children: Remington. **Educ:** Central Connecticut State, Britain CT, BA Mathematics, Rutgers Law School, Newark NJ, JD. **Career:** Washington DC, counsel, 1973-76; Dept of Public Advocate, Newark NJ, asst deputy public defender; City of East Orange, corp counsel, 1980-81; Brown & Manns, Newark NJ, lawyer, 1981-83; Law Officers of Robert L Brown, Newark NJ, lawyer, 1984-; City of Orange NJ, mayor, 1984-; Comm on Judiciary, House of Rep, US Congress; Rutger's Univ, Newark NJ, mathematics instructor. **Orgs:** New Jersey Trial Lawyers Assn; New Jersey Bar Assn; Natl Criminal Defense; Amer Bar Assn; Criminal Trial Lawyers of New Jersey; Essex County Bar Assn; Roscoe Pound Found; NAACP; Omega Psi Phi. **Honors/Awds:** Outstanding Contributions in Govt, Hillside Valley Presbyterian Church, 1988; Natl Trubute to Black Heritage, Prince Hall Grand Lodge Masons; Congratulations Award, Alif Muhammad Productions, 1988; Resolution of Congratulations, East Orange City Council, 1988; featured in Jet Magazine, Newark Star-Ledger, Orange Transcript, Greater News Perspectus. **Business Addr:** Mayor, City of Orange Township, 29 N Day St, Orange, NJ 07050.

BROWN, ROBIN R.
Public relations executive. **Personal:** Born May 19, Pulaski, TN; son of Robert Brown; married Betty Miller. **Educ:** Eastern MI Univ, attended; Univ of Louisville, attended. **Career:** WSPD-TV Storer Broadcasting Co, reporter, anchor 1969-72; KMOX-TV Columbia Broadcasting Syst, reporter, anchor 1972-73; WAVE-TV Orion Broadcasting, investigative reporter 1973-78; WDIA Radio Viacom Intl, dir news & publ affairs 1978-83; RKO Gen WHBQ-TV, assignments editor; Brown Communication, Memphis, TN, manager/writer/producer, 1985-87; Regan Henry Broadcasting Co, Memphis, TN, news anchor, 1987-89; Memphis Housing Authority, Memphis, TN, director of public relations, 1989-. **Orgs:** Past pres Memphis Black Arts Alliance 1983-84; v chmn Bd of Governors Memphis Health Ctr 1984-85; mem NAACP, Ctr for Southern Folklore, Natl Assoc of Black Journalists, KY Col; board of directors, Boys Club, 1989-. **Honors/Awds:** Spec Awd Promoting Ethnic History Shelby County Historic Commiss 1981; Martin Luther King Awd Natl Assoc of Black Journalist 1982; Innovative Programming Award, Neighborhood Watch, 1991. **Military Serv:** US Navy. **Business Addr:** Public Relations Director, Memphis Housing Authority, 700 Adams Ave, Memphis, TN 38105.

BROWN, RODERICK
Automotive manager. **Personal:** Born Apr 22, 1952, Newport News, VA; son of Clara L Brown and Robert Brown, Sr; divorced; children: Roderick F Brown. **Educ:** Norfolk State Univ,

BSEE 1975; Univ of MI, Grad Study in Elec Engineering 1984; Univ of Detroit, MEM, 1986, MBA, 1988. **Career:** NASA, rsch asst 1974; Atomic Energy Commn Fermi Natl Accelerator Lab, rsch asst 1974; Caterpillar Tractor Co, tech writer 1975, training instructor 1977; Caterpillar Tractor Co Field Serv Operations, asst to div mgr 1978; Caterpillar Tractor Co Serv Engineering Div, asst staff engr 1978; Ford Motor Co Product Develop Dept, prod develop engr 1979; Ford Motor Co Advanced Vehicle Pkg Control and Design Dept, product design engr 1983; Ford Motor Co Medium and Large Car FWD Design Engrg Dept, product design engr, 1985; Ford Motor Co Car Product Planning, product planning analyst, 1986; Siemens automotive manager, Program Development, Strategic Planning, 1990-. **Orgs:** Mem Phi Beta Sigma Fraternity Inc 1976-; speaker Local Career Programs 1976-; mem Natl Tech Assoc 1979-; mem Soc of Automotive Engrs Detroit 1980-, SAE Public Affairs Comm 1980-82, Natl Black MBA Assoc Detroit 1980-; speaker Detroit Area Pre-Coll Engrg Program 1980-; mem Engrg Soc of Detroit 1980-82; mem bd of trustees Metro Detroit Science and Engrg Coalition 1980-83; co-coordinator First Annual Detroit Technical and Business Career Conf 1980; financial coordinator 53rd Annual NTA Convention 1981. **Honors/Awds:** Mem Beta Kappa Chi Natl Scientific Honor Soc 1975-; Outstanding Achievement Award Natl Technical Assoc 1986. **Military Serv:** Army ROTC 1975-76.

BROWN, RODGER L., JR.
Real estate mgmt. **Personal:** Born Aug 15, 1955, Petersburg, VA. **Educ:** Boston Coll, BA 1977; MIT, 1980-82. **Career:** IBM, marketing rep 1977-79; Sittler Assoc, consult 1979-80; United South End/Lower Roxbury Devel Corp, proj mgr 1980-83; Greater Boston Community Devel, proj mgr 1983-86; Cruz Devel Co, devel proj mgr 1986, vice pres, currently; Mintz, Levin, Cohn, Rerries Glousky & Popeo, sr professional; Winn Development Co, Inc, sr vp, currently. **Orgs:** Mem MA Minority Devel Assoc, Builder Assoc of Greater Boston, Citizens Housing & Planning Assoc. **Honors/Awds:** US Dept of Housing & Urban Devel Minority Fellowship 1982. **Business Addr:** Sr Vice President, Winn Development, 6 Famelil Hall Marketplace, Boston, MA 02119.

BROWN, RODNEY W.
Construction company executive. **Personal:** son Of Elise Brown and Sidney Brown. **Career:** Shelly's of Delaware Inc, Wilmington, DE, chief executive. **Business Addr:** Chief Executive, Shelly's of Delaware Inc, 610 W Eighth, Wilmington, DE 19801.

BROWN, ROGER. See Obituaries section.

BROWN, ROLAND O.
Director (retired). **Personal:** Born Jun 28, 1929, Brazoria, TX; married. **Educ:** Bishop Coll, BS 1950; Univ of So CA, MS 1957. **Career:** HISD, dir, hlth & phys edn, cntrl admin 1971-; Lockhart Elem, elem prin 1968-71; J Will Jones Elem, elem prin 1967-68; Doris Miller Elem, elem prin 1964-67. **Orgs:** Mem Am Alliance for Hlth Phys & Educ & Rec; TX Assn for Hlth Phys Educ & Rec; city & co dirs Health & Phys Edn; HPA; TSTA; NEA; mem adv bd BSA 1968-70; mem, bd dirs Houston Tennis Assn 1968-73; commnr SE Div of Youth Tennis League 1968-71; tchr Sunday Sch; exec dir Nat Jr Tennis League1971-73; Hiram Clarke Civic Clb; mem TX ALL Star Ftbl Team, Angel Bowl LA CA 1947. **Honors/Awds:** Recip JJ Sampson Award; cntrbtn to youth tennis Houston Tennis Assn 1971; citation, serv rendered Nat Alumni Fund Camp Bishop Coll 1972. **Military Serv:** AUS pfc 1951-53.

BROWN, RONALD EDWARD
Educator. **Personal:** Born May 5, 1952, Springfield, IL; son of Pearl Brown; married Lillie Sloan, Aug 24, 1974; children: Khari, Katura. **Educ:** Lincoln Land Community College, Springfield, IL, AA, 1972; Southern Illinois University, Carbondale, IL, BA, 1974; University of Michigan, Ann Arbor, MI, MA, 1976, PhD, 1984. **Career:** Eastern Michigan Univ, Ypsilanti, MI, associate professor, 1985-. **Orgs:** Member, American Political Science Association, 1984-; member, National Association of Black Political Scientists, 1984-; assistant superintendent, Sunday School Bethel AME Church, 1987-. **Honors/Awds:** Research Grant, Social Science Research Council, 1991-92; Research Grant, National Science Foundation, 1989-91; Research Grant, National Institute of Aging, 1988-90. **Business Addr:** Associate Professor, Political Science, Eastern Michigan University, 601 Pray-Harrold Hall, Ypsilanti, MI 48197.

BROWN, RONALD PAUL
Educational administrator, educator. **Personal:** Born Mar 19, 1938, Ravenna, OH; son of Agnes L Ervin Brown and Paul L Brown; married Joyce Anita Jones; children: Todd Mason, Lisa Kay, Paula Marie. **Educ:** Univ of Akron, BS, history & govt, 1967, MS, counseling & guidance, 1969, PhD, counselor educ, 1974. **Career:** Univ of Akron, coord of dev serv & student adv 1969-74; Cuyahoga Co Bd of Mental Retardation, dir of habilitation serv 1974-80; Co of Summit, admin asst 1981-84; Kent State Univ, asst to the dean for minority & women affairs 1984-87; Kent State Univ Ashtabula Campus, asst dean and asst prof of counselor educ 1987-92, assistant professor of Pan African studies/director of multicultural affairs, 1992-. **Orgs:** Univ of Akron Alumni Council 1978-81; bd of trustees Cuyahoga Valley Mental Health 1982-84; Natl Cert Counselor Natl Bd for Certified Couns Inc 1984; bd of trustees St Paul AME Church 1978-; Alpha Phi Alpha, 1982-; board of directors Alpha Homes Inc 1982-; chap sec Natl Old Timers Inc 1984-87; treasurers Black Alumni Assoc 1987-; vice pres, Comm Action Council Ashtabula OH; adv board member Ashtabula Salvation Army; dir Community Resource Economic Comm Ashtabula, Home Safe Inc, bd of trustees 1990, adv bd, 1992; Private Industry Council Advisory Board, 1990, vice pres, Jobs for Ohio's Graduates, president, 1992; Goodwill Industries, bd of advisors. **Honors/Awds:** Chmn of the Educ Comm Eta Tau Lambda 1982-84; Outstanding Serv Awd Eta Tau Lambda 1983; "The Joys and Pain of Brotherhood: A Neophyte Expressed Himself" Alpha Newsletter 1983; chairman Univ of Akron's Black Alumni 1984; Key to the City of Ashtabula Ohio, 1990; Developed African American Speaker Series, Ashtabula Campus, 1990. **Special Achievements:** Developed: African-American Speaker Series, Ashtabula Campus, 1990; Multi Ethnic Cultural Association, MECA, for students, 1991; initiated annual Black History Program at Kent Ashtabula, Multicultural Speaker Series, 1993. **Military Serv:** US Army sp4 1961-63. **Home Addr:** 951 Kickapoo Ave, Akron, OH 44305. **Business Addr:** Assistant Professor/Director of Multicultural Affairs, Kent State Univ, Ashtabula Campus, 3325 W 13th St, Ashtabula, OH 44004.

BROWN, ROOSEVELT H., JR.
Professional football scout. **Personal:** Born Oct 20, 1932, Charlottesville, VA; married Linda. **Educ:** Morgan St Coll, BS. **Career:** NY Giants, played with 13 yrs, coached offensive line 5 yrs, scout 1985, Mid-west & Big 10 Coll. **Orgs:** Elks, Sholoh Lodge 1964-. **Honors/Awds:** 8 times pro football all-pro Helms Hall of Fame; 10 times Pro-Bowl; Pro Football Hall of Fame; Drafted by the New York Giants, 1953; NFL Offensive Lineman of the Year, 1956; Morgan State College, Hall of Fame, 1974; Helm, Hall of Fame; Maryland Hall of Fame, 1975; Pro Football Hall of Fame, 1975; Virginia Hall of Fame, 1979; Ohio Hall of Fame, 1991; New York Sports Museum, Hall of Fame, 1992; New Jersey, Hall of Fame, 1994; NFL 75th Year All Pro Team & All Roster Team, 1994. **Business Addr:** New York Giants, Giants Stadium, East Rutherford, NJ 07073.

BROWN, ROSCOE C., JR.
Educational administrator. **Personal:** Born Mar 9, 1922, Washington, DC; divorced; children: Doris, Diane, Dennis, Donald. **Educ:** Springfield Coll MA, BS; New York Univ, MA, PhD. **Career:** Bronx Community College, president, currently. **Orgs:** Inst of Afro-American Affairs, dir; One Hundred Black Men, pres. **Honors/Awds:** Host of weekly TV series, Black Arts and weekly radio series, Soul of Reason; co-host, WCBS-TV program, Black Letters; co-host, WNBC-TV, A Black Perspective; co-editor, Negro Almanac, 1967; co-author, Classical Studies on Physical Activity, 1968; co-author, New Perspectives of Man in Action, 1969; co-author, Black Culture Quib, 1971, 1973; author of more than 50 articles on education, black studies, sports, and physical education and physical fitness; Distinguished Alumni Award, Springfield College, 1973, New York Univ, 1973; Emmy Award, 1973; honorary member, American Alliance for Health, Physical Education, Recreation, and Dance; recipient, Bronx Museum's Education Award, 1990. **Military Serv:** US Air Force, 1943-45; Distinguished Flying Cross; Air Medal. **Business Addr:** Director of Urban Education Institute, City University of New York-Graduate Center, 420 Lexington Ave, Room 1539, New York, NY 10036.

BROWN, ROSE DENISE
Banker. **Personal:** Born in Chicago, IL; daughter of Maggie Williams and Willie Brown. **Educ:** Cornell College, BS, 1979. **Career:** Account administrator/section mgr; documentation specialist; documentation supervisor; loan documentation coordinator; collateral analyst; job analyst; Continental Bank, operations officer, currently. **Orgs:** National Association of Urban Bankers; Continental Bank Foundation, board member; Commerical Finance Association, Midwest Chapter. **Special Achievements:** "Speaking of People," Ebony, July 1992. **Business Addr:** Operations Officer, Continental Bank, 231 S LaSalle St, Business Credit Group, 12th Fl, Chicago, IL 60697.

BROWN, ROY HERSHEL
Educator. **Personal:** Born Aug 2, 1924, Jamaica; married Lilly Berlinger; children: Geraldine, Lawrence, Christopher, Anthony, Andrew. **Educ:** Fordham Coll, BS 1945-59; Univ Zurich Med Sch, MD 1950-56; NY Dip Med Lic, 1960; Dip Phys Med & Rehab, 1971. **Career:** Total Health HMO, senior vp, currently; Jamaica Hosp, dept of rehab med 1985; PM&R, diplomate, asst prof 1968-; Office of Voc Rehab, consult 1975-; Private Prac, 1960-66. **Orgs:** Mem, bd trustee The Barlow Sch; Suffolk Co Med Soc; Nat Med Assn; Am Acad of Physical Med & Rehab; AAAS; NY Soc of PMYR; Am Geriatrics Soc. **Honors/Awds:** Publ "Innovative Aspect of Stroke Prgm In Ghetto" 1971, "The Role of Med Sch in a Ghetto Population" 1971. **Business Addr:** Sr Vice President, Total Health HMO, 1010 Northern Blvd, Great Neck, NY 11021.

BROWN, RUBY EDMONIA
Psychologist. **Personal:** Born Sep 5, 1943, Pittsburghq, PA; married Ephriam Wolfolk Jr; children: Kenneth, Kevin, Keith. **Educ:** Univ of CO, BA 1976-81; Univ of OR, MS 1981-82; Univ of OR, PhD 1982-87; Woodburn Comm Mental Health Ctr, Psych Intern 1985-86. **Career:** Pikes Peak Mental Health Ctr, mental health therapist 1976-81; Univ of OR, teaching asst, instr 1981-85; Woodburn Comm Mental Health Ctr, intern, psych 1985-. **Orgs:** Mem Phi Betta Kappa Hon Soc 1981-, Amer Psych Assoc 1984-; assoc mem Center for the Study of Women 1985-. **Honors/Awds:** Minority Fellow Amer Psychological Assoc 1981-84; Grad Teaching Fellow Univ of OR 1981-85; Alumni & Friend Student of the Year Univ of CO 1981; Rsch Grant Center for the Study of Women Univ of OR 1987; Jane Grant Dissertation Fellowship Univ of OR 1987. **Business Addr:** Psychologist, Woodburn Comm Mental Health, 3340 Woodburn Rd, Annandale, VA 22003.

BROWN, RUBYE GOLSBY
Educator. **Personal:** Born Aug 20, 1923, Birmingham, AL; daughter of Augusta B Blalock Johnson (deceased) and Clifford Golsby (deceased); married Robert L Brown, Jan 2, 1947; children: Harlean, Charles, Louis, Carson, Gloria, Robin, Debbie. **Educ:** Youngstown State Univ, BA, 1953, MD, 1981. **Career:** Ft Leonard-Wood, dept head PX, 1959-60; Ft Leonard-Wood, substitute teacher, 1960-61; Renanos' Jewelry, 1st black credit mgr 1962-64; Mahoning County Treasurer, dept treasurer, 1965-77; Princeton School, teacher, 1977; Youngstown Public School, Youngstown, OH, school teacher, 1977-90; Round Rock Independent School District, Round Rock, TX, high school teacher, 1991-. **Orgs:** 2nd vice pres trustee exec bd Internal Mgmt Project Review; bd trustee Educ Opportunity Youngstown; vice-chmn Consumer Protect Agency, mem NAACP; mem Urban League; past vice pres Comm Action Agy; mem Cavelle Club; mem bd dirs Negro Bus & Prof Club; bd mem State Health Dept OH 1980; com Planning & Devel State Health Dept; chr mem CAC; 1st black trustee Health Sys Agency E OH Valley; mem Nat Cncl of Negro Women; exec comm mem Dem party; precinct & committeewoman 5m; ran for mem Youngstown Bd Educ 1977; pres, Mahoning County Court-Watch; mem, police task force; member, American University Women, 1981-; committee member, State Health Board, 1979-88; Red Cross, nurse. **Honors/Awds:** Only Black 19th dist del Pres Carter; Certificate for Community Involvement & Volunteer Work, Junior Civic League 1986; apptd by Gov Richard Celeste to State Health Bd of Columbus, OH 1986; Community Service, Congressman Carney Award. **Home Addr:** 11623 B Argonne Forest Trail, Austin, TX 78759-2216.

BROWN, RUSHIA
Professional basketball player. **Personal:** Born May 5, 1972. **Educ:** Furman, bachelor's degree in sociology. **Career:** Cleveland Rockers, forward-center, 1997-. **Business Addr:** Professional Basketball Player, Cleveland Rockers, One Center Ct, Cleveland, OH 44115, (216)263-7625.

BROWN, RUTH
Singer. **Career:** Album: RB=Ruth Brown. **Honors/Awds:** Grammy Award nomination; nominated for three W.C. Handy Awards; Women in Music, Touchstone Award.

BROWN, SHARON MARJORIE REVELS
Media executive. **Personal:** Born Sep 26, 1938, Detroit, MI. **Educ:** Fisk U, 1953-57; Wayne State U, BA 1957-60; Coll of Edn, post-degree work 1960-61; MI Bd of Pub Instrn, Teaching Cert 1961; Wayne State U, 1966. **Career:** WXYZ-TV, comm rel dir 1974-; WKBD-TV, news & pub affairs sv 1972-74; Detroit Pub Sch Hutchins Jr HS, instr 1961-70; Univ of MI, resources Ctr Coord1970-71; Univ of MI, educ field consult 1969-70; Hutchins Jr HS, tchr coord 1964-65. **Orgs:** Bd dir Nat Cncl on Alcholism; mem Homes for Black Children; mem educ Com New Detroit Inc mem Urban Affairs Forum; mem Greater Detroit C of C; mem Keep Detroit Beautiful Com; mem Publicity Com United Negro Coll Fund; mem Women's Advertising Club; mem Am Women in Radio & TV; host "Ethnit-City"; chpn Publicity Com Afro-Am Mus of Detroit; publicity com Freedom Fund Dinner NAACP 1977; mem Alpha Epsilon Rho; mem MI Speech Assn; mem v Arious other professional orgns. **Honors/Awds:** Frat sweetheart Kappa Alpha & Psi 1958-59; 3rd pl winner scholarship contest Miss Marracci Beauty-Talent Pageant Shriners.

BROWN, SHERMAN L.
Business executive. **Personal:** Born Nov 18, 1943, Portland, OR; son of Bennie Brown (deceased); married Mable J; children: Sherman Jr, Stephen, Stanton. **Educ:** BS, 1966; MSW, 1968. **Career:** St Elizabeth Hosp, psychiatric social worker 1966-67; Comm Action Agency, urban planner 1966-68; James Weldon Johnson Comm Ctr, prog dir 1968-70; Chase Manhattan Bank, vice pres 1970-80; MCAP Group Ltd, pres, currently. **Orgs:** Bd mem United Neighborhood Houses; bd mem Settlement Housing Fund; founder & bd mem Queens Youth Fedn NY; Bankers Urban Affairs Com, Kappa Alpha Psi Frat; chmn bd dir Neighborhood Housing Serv Jamaica Inc; bd mem S Jamaica Restoration Devel Corp; vice pres bd Bronx River Comm Ctr; bd mem Natl Scholarship Serv Fund for Negro Students; mem Univ S Civ Rights Comm; chmn bd Queens Urban

League; bd mem NAHRO Washington DC; bd mem Natl Housing Conf Bd Washington DC; bd mem United Black Men of Queens Co; mem Natl Assn of Redevelopment Officials; chmn bd Queens Co Overall Econ Devel Corp. **Honors/Awds:** Black Achiever in Industry Award Harlem YMCA, 1973; Professional Serv Award NY Chamber of Commerce, 1973; instr in Urban Econ Amer Inst of Banking; lectr for Banks on Corporate Social Responsibility; lectr Medgar Evers Coll. **Home Addr:** 85-23 Edgerton Blvd, Jamaica, NY 11432. **Business Addr:** President, MCAP Group Ltd, 89-50 164th St, Ste 2B, Citibank Bldg, Jamaica, NY 11432.

BROWN, SHIRLEY ANN VINING
Educator. **Personal:** Born in Monroe, MI; daughter of Annie Vining and Elmer Vining; married Charles Lester; children: Caryn, Sandra, Garret. **Educ:** Univ of MI, AB 1958, MSW 1969, MS 1972, PhD 1975. **Career:** MI Public Sch, teacher 1965; Ann Arbor Public Sch, social worker 1969-1970; Univ of MD, assoc prof 1975-; Nat'l Acad of Sci, proj dir 1986-87; Educational Testing Service, senior research scientist 1989-. **Orgs:** Proj dir Youth Enrichment Program Inc; The Compact for Faculty Diversity; AAAS; AERA; Meyerhoff National Advisory Board. **Honors/Awds:** Community Service Award, Foundation for Black Educational and Cultural Achievement, 1988. **Home Addr:** 5448 Newgrange Garth, Columbia, MD 21045.

BROWN, SIMON F.
Educational administrator. **Personal:** Born Sep 17, 1952, Norristown, PA; son of Lessie Forbes Brown and Albert Brown; married LaVerne Ransom Brown, Mar 17, 1972; children: LaSia, Kevin. **Educ:** Goshen College, Goshen, BA, Communications, 1974; University of Houston, Houston, TX, MA, Higher Education Administration, 1986. **Career:** Elkhart County Employment & Training Admin, Elkhart, IN, coordinator of operations, 1974-77; St Joseph Hospital, Houston, TX, manager, AA/EEO employee relations, 1977-79; University of Houston, Houston, TX, assistant to president for affirmative action/EEO, 1979-89; University of Medicine & Dentistry, Newark, NJ, associate vice president, AA/EEO, 1989-. **Orgs:** Executive committee member, secretary, Ensemble Theatre Company, 1989; member, Newark Museum Council, 1990; member, American Association of Affirmative Action, 1975. **Business Addr:** Associate Vice President, Affirmative Action and Equal Opportunity, University of Medicine and Dentistry, 30 Bergen St ADMC 208, Newark, NJ 07107-3000.

BROWN, STANLEY DONOVAN
Elected official. **Personal:** Born Feb 4, 1933, Washington, DC; married Helen Hampton; children: Kevin, Kimberly, Karla. **Educ:** Southeastern Univ, BS, BA 1962; Amer Univ, Grad 1968. **Career:** Dept of the Army, supr, computer spec 32 years; Office of the Secretary of Defense, spec programs dir 1984-; Town of Glenarden, mayor. **Orgs:** Councilman Town of Glenarden 1967-73; chmn Glenarden Housing Authority 1974-75; councilman Town of Glenarden 1975-78, mayor 1983-. **Honors/Awds:** Recognition of Civic Involvement MD House of Delegates 1978; Cert of Appreciation Boys Scouts of Amer 1980; Outstanding Loaned Exec CFC Dept of Army 1984, 11985; Citizen of the Year Omega Psi Phi Frat 1984. **Military Serv:** USN quartermaster 2nd class 4 years; Korean Conflict Medal, Good Conduct Medal 1957. **Home Addr:** 7916 Grant Drive, Glenarden, MD 20706. **Business Addr:** Mayor, Town of Glenarden, 8600 Glenarden Pkwy, Glenarden, MD 20706.

BROWN, THOMAS EDISON, JR.
Public safety director. **Personal:** Born Aug 22, 1952, Atlanta, GA; son of Rosa B Branham Brown and Thomas E Brown, Sr; married Yolanda Smith Brown, Sep 22, 1978; children: Brittany Joy, Justin Thomas. **Educ:** DeKalb Community Coll, Clarkston, GA, Emergency Medical Serv, 1978, Fire Science, 1980; Brenau Professional Coll, Gainesville, GA. **Career:** Atlanta Fire Bureau, Atlanta, GA, deputy fire chief, 1972-85; DeKalb County Public Safety, Decatur, GA, fire chief, 1985-90; DeKalb County, GA, director of public safety, 1990-. **Orgs:** Intl Assn of Fire Chiefs, 1983-; Natl Fire Protection Assn, 1985-; Intl Assn of Black Professional Firefighters, 1986-; Natl Forum of Black Public Admin, 1986-; 100 Black Men of Atlanta, 1988-; South Decatur Kiwanis, 1988-; International Assn of Chiefs of Police, 1990-; National Organization of Black Law Enforcement Executives, 1990-. **Honors/Awds:** Outstanding Alumnus, DeKalb Community Coll, 1986; Outstanding Serv Award, Toney Gardens Civic Assn, 1986. **Business Addr:** Director, DeKalb County Public Safety, 3630 Camp Cir, Decatur, GA 30032.

BROWN, TIMOTHY DONELL
Professional football player. **Personal:** Born Jul 22, 1966, Dallas, TX. **Educ:** Univ of Notre Dame, bachelor's degree in sociology. **Career:** Los Angeles Raiders, wide receiver, 1988-94; Oakland Raiders, wide receiver, 1995-. **Honors/Awds:** Established NFL record: most yards gained (2,317) by rookie in one season, 1988; Sporting News NFL All-Star Team, kick returner, 1988; Pro Bowl, 1988, 1991, 1993, 1994, 1995. **Business Addr:** Professional Football Player, Oakland Raiders, 1220 Harbor Bay Pkwy, Alameda, CA 94502, (510)615-1875.

BROWN, TODD C.
Food company executive. **Career:** Kraft Foods, executive vice pres/gen mgr of beverage and dessert division, currently.

BROWN, TOMMIE FLORENCE
Educator. **Personal:** Born Jun 25, 1934, Rome, GA. **Educ:** Dillard University, BS (cum laude), 1957; Atlanta University School of Social Work, 1957; Washington University St Louis, MSW, 1964; Columbia University, DSW, 1984. **Career:** Tennessee Dept of Public Welfare, child welfare worker, 1957-64, case worker, supervisor/director training, 1954-71; University of Tennessee at Chatanooga, asst professor sociology, 1971-73, director human services, 1977-82, SOCW & project director, dept head, 1977-82, associate professor, 1982-; Tennessee House of Representatives, 1992-. **Orgs:** Natl Assn of Social Workers, natl sec, 1972-74; bd mem, Chattanooga Psych Center, 1982-; Chattanooga Branch, NAACP, 1964-; bd mem, Chattanooga Model Cities Program, 1969-73; elected commissioner, Chattanooga/Hamilton Metro Charter; League of Women Voters, 1968-70; steering committee, Urban Forum, 1980-81. **Honors/Awds:** Woman of the Year Award, Alpha Kappa Alpha, Pi Omega Chapter, 1968-69; Social Worker of the Year, SE Tennessee Chapter, Natl Assn of Social Workers, 1970; Natl Social Worker of the Year, Natl Assn of Social Workers Inc, 1970; Tommie Brown Day, City of Chattanooga, 1970; Distinguished Alumni Award, Washington University, St Louis, 1971. **Business Addr:** Professor, Social and Community Service, University of Tennessee Chattanooga, 615 McCallie Ave, Chattanooga, TN 37403-2504.

BROWN, TONY (WILLIAM ANTHONY)
TV executive producer, educator, filmmaker, columnist. **Personal:** Born Apr 11, 1933, Charleston, WV; divorced. **Educ:** Wayne State U, BA 1959; Wayne State U, MSW 1961; Univ of MI, LLD 1975. **Career:** Black Journal Nat Educ TV, exec producer; The Detroit Courier, city ed; numerous mag, pub & ed; var TV shows, host & moderator; Howard Univ Sch of Communications, first dean prof & founder; Howard U, communications Conf; Cntrl Wash State U, vis prof; Tony Brown Productions, founder/pres, 1977-; Tony Brown's Journal, exec producer/host, 1978-. **Orgs:** Founder/pres, Video Duplication Center, 1986; Founder/chmn, Buy Freedom Comm, 1985; Nat Assn of Black Media Producers; Nat Assn Of Black TV & Film Producers; bd of govnrs Nat Commnct Cncl; mem Adv Bd Nat Cncl for Black Studies; chmn of bd WHUR-FM radio 1971-74; bd mem Nat Cntr of Afro-AM Artists; Nat Black United Fund; mem Communications Com of Nat Inst of Mental Health; bd of dirs, Assn for the Study of Afro-Amer Life & History; bd of dirs, Natl Business League; bd of dirs, Harvard Found. **Honors/Awds:** Living Legends In Black, 1976; Black Am Ref Book, 1976; Natl Urban League Pub Serv Award 1977; Intl Key Women Of Am Award 1977; 100 Most Influential Black Am Ebony Mag; Top 50 Nat Black & Newsmakers of Yr 1974; Natl Newspaper Pub Assn; Operation PUSH Communicator for Freedom Awd 1973; Frederick Douglass Liberation Award; Solomon Fuller Award, Amer Psychiatric Assn, 1989; Community Service Award, Black Psychologists, 1988; Special Image Award, Beverly Hills/Hollywood NAACP; producer/dir, The White Girl (motion picture), 1989. **Military Serv:** US Army, corporal, 1953-55. **Business Addr:** Pres, Tony Brown Productions Inc, 1501 Broadway, Suite 2014, New York, NY 10036.

BROWN, TONY
Professional basketball player. **Personal:** Born Jul 29, 1960, Chicago, IL. **Educ:** AR Univ, 1982. **Career:** Indiana Pacers, 1985, Chicago Bulls, 1986, New Jersey Nets, 1987, Houston Rockets, 1989, Milwaukee Bucks, 1989-90, Los Angeles Lakers, 1990-. **Orgs:** Invited to the Midwest Summer League.

BROWN, TONY
Communications company executive. **Personal:** Born Mar 1961, Phoenix, AZ; married Janet Brown, Mar 1990; children: 2. **Educ:** Arizona State University, Tempe, AZ, 1978-79, 1981-82; Northern Arizona University, Flagstaff AZ, 1979-81. **Career:** Circles Records, Phoenix, AZ, asst mgr, 1981-82; KUKQ AM Radio, Tempe, AZ, promotions dir, 1982-85; Best Entertainment & Recreation, Phoenix, AZ, consultant, 1982-92; Marshall, Brown & Associates, Phoenix, AZ, consultant, 1982-92; American Multi-Cinema, Inc, Phoenix, AZ, manager, 1985-88; Phoenix Suns Pro Basketball, Phoenix, AZ, community relations director, 1990-91; Targeted Media Communications, Inc, president, 1992-. **Orgs:** Board member, Volunteer Center of Arizona, 1990-92; committee chair, Public Relations Society of America, 1991; Black Theatre Troupe, board mem, 1991-96; American Heart Assn of Arizona, board member, 1991-93. **Honors/Awds:** Co Received NAACP Image Awd, Maricopa County NAACP, 1996. **Special Achievements:** Arizona's Black Pages, publisher, 1986-. **Business Addr:** President, Targeted Media Communications, Inc, 2601 N 3rd St, Ste 102, PO Box 63701, Phoenix, AZ 85082, (602)230-8161.

BROWN, TYRONE W.
Musician, composer, educator. **Personal:** Born Feb 1, 1940, Philadelphia, PA; son of Rebecca Brown and Colbert Brown. **Educ:** Berklee Sch of Music, Certificate in Arranging & Composition. **Career:** Pep's Show Bar, house bassist 1964-69; History of Jazz Lecture & Concert Tours, staff bassist 1968-71; Audi Prodns TV Commercial Prodns & Louisvle, staff bassist 1970-72; Il State U, instr for jazz 1971; Brigham Young U, instr for jazz 1972; Bellermine Coll, instr for jazz 1975; Model Cities Cultural Arts Program, taught composition, advanced harmony & theory, improvisation & bass 1972-74. **Orgs:** Aptd dir Music Dept Model Cities Cultural Arts Program 1974; owner publ Nirvana Music Co; formerly with Grover Washington Jr, Catalyst, Billy Paul, Lou Rawls, Pat Martino, Sonny Fortune, Johnny Coles and Johnny Hartman Currently touring and recording with Max Roach. **Honors/Awds:** 35 recorded albums; 2 gold albums; placed first Fred Miles Publ of Musicians Poll 1974; 22 albums to date.

BROWN, VERNON E.
Business executive. **Personal:** Born Jun 15, 1943, Merced, CA; married Shirley; children: Sara, Kim. **Educ:** BA, Bus & Econ 1973. **Career:** R & B, booked shows 1963; Golden State Mutual Life Ins Co, agt; Emmy Ins Agy; Continental Assurance Co, gen agt; Copley News Service, newspaper columnist. **Orgs:** Pres Am News Svc, World-wide Syndicate, 1975; pres Flain Co; Samson Fi Am Comm Property Devel, Inc; pres Vernon E Brown Mgmt & Consult Ltd; past mem Co Tax Assessment Tax Appeal Bd;pres, past treas, co-founder So Ca Minister Vanguard; nominee for congress 35th Cong Dist 1972. **Honors/Awds:** Authored Constitutional Amendment Tax Relief On Dwellings-Retired & Disabled Owners 1974; appointed first black gen agt in Amby a major life ins co 1969. **Business Addr:** P O Box 8865, Los Angeles, CA 90008.

BROWN, VIRGIL E., JR.
Judge. **Personal:** son Of Lurtissia Brown and Virgil E Brown; married JoAnn. **Educ:** Case Inst of Tech, BS Physics 1968; Cleveland State Univ, JD-cum laude 1974. **Career:** Gen Elec, engr; Cleveland Growth Assn, consultant; Cleveland Business League, chairman; Shaker Heights Municipal Court, judge, currently. **Orgs:** Commissioner Ohio's Minority Financing Board; Ohio Business League. **Honors/Awds:** Negro Womens Business & Professional Association, Businessman of the Year Award, 1992. **Home Addr:** 2136 Noble Road, Cleveland, OH 44112.

BROWN, WALTER E.
Business executive. **Personal:** Born Mar 4, 1931, St Thomas, Virgin Islands of the United States; son of Geraldine James Brown and Arthur Brown; married Cheryl Ann Johnson, Dec 31, 1985; children: Walter E, Cheryl R, Jason Walter. **Educ:** CCNY, BBA 1958, MBA 1961; NY Univ, MPA 1972; Union Grad Sch OH, PhD 1978. **Career:** Shriro Inc NY, admin asst 1956-58; Dept of Health Govt of VI St Croix, admin 1962-71; NENA Comprehensive Health Serv Ctr, 1971-87; NY Univ HEOP, 1980-83; Hunter Coll School of Health Sciences CUNY, adjunct asst prof. **Orgs:** Lecturer Coll of VI St Croix Campus 1967-69, Univ of Cincinnati Community Health Prog 1973, Columbia Univ Sch of Continuing Educ 1973-75; mem Natl Assn of Health Serv Exec; mem Amer Pub Health Assn; Speaker of the House of Del Natl Assn of Neighborhood Health Ctrs 1972-74; pres Natl Assn of Neighborhood Health Ctrs 1974-75; pres Natl Assn of Neighborhood Health Ctr, 1975-76; pres Public Health Assn of NYC 1986-87; editorial consultant, Journal of Public Health Policy; mem Committee on Ambulatory Care Amer Hospital Assn 1972-74; hon trustee NY Infirmary Beekman Downtown Hospital NY 1980-87. **Honors/Awds:** 1st Morris De Castro Fellow Govt of VI St Thomas 1970; Certificate of Appreciation for Outstanding Contribution to & Promotion of Community Health Metro Boston Consumer Health Council Inc 1975; Natl Assn of Neighborhood Health Centers Inc, Past Pres Award, 1976; Public Health Assn of New York City, Past Pres Award, 1988. **Military Serv:** AUS sgt e-5 1956-58. **Business Addr:** Pres, Commercial Security Services Ltd, Inc., PO Box 21, EG Station, St. Thomas, Virgin Islands of the United States 00804.

BROWN, WARREN ALOYSIUS
Journalist. **Personal:** Born Jan 17, 1948, New Orleans, LA; married Maryanne; children: Tony, Binta Niambi, Kafi Drexel. **Educ:** Xavier Univ of LA, BA 1969; Columbia Univ of New York, MSJ 1970. **Career:** Washington Post, natl labor writer 1976, business writer/auto columnist, currently; Philadelphia Inquirer, city reporter/state rep 1972-76; Jet Magazine, assoc editor/educ & politics 1971-72; New Orleans States-Item, city reporter 1970-71; New York Times, natl news desk aide 1969-70; Garden City, Long Island NY, intern reporter 1969. **Orgs:** Regular panelist Am Black Forum 1979; mem Xavier Univ Alumni Assn 1969. **Honors/Awds:** Katharine Drexel Award Xavier Univ of LA 1969; NY Times Fellow NY Times 1969-70; LA/MS AP Award LA/MS Asso Press 1971; Duke Univ Fellow Wash Post 1978. **Business Addr:** Business writer/Auto columnist, The Washington Post, 1150 15th St, NW, Washington, DC 20071.

BROWN, WARREN HENRY, JR.
Educator, journalist, diplomat, behavior scientist. **Personal:** Born Jul 29, 1905, Jackson, TN; son of Ada L Temple Brown and Warren H Brown Sr; married Mattie Pearle Julian. **Educ:** Univ of WI, 1928; NY U, BS 1935; New Sch of Social Research, PHD 1941. **Career:** Council for Democracy in NY, assist dir, 1940s; Amer Assn of State Coll & Univ, consultant,

1974-78; Graduate Faculty Bowie State Univ, prof of urban affairs, 1972-75; Dept of Sociology, Catholic Univ of Amer, adjunct assoc prof, 1971-72; US Govt Counselor of Cultural Affairs, foreign serv officer, 1960-70; City Coll of NY Univ, asst prof, 1947-60; Amer Univ at Cairo Egypt, Fulbright prof, 1955-56; Broadcast Music Inc NYC, research consult 1956-57; UNESCO Mission to Syria, diplomat 1957-58. **Orgs:** Mem Mayor's Com on Puerto Rican Affairs New York City 1949-53; bd of dir Am Civil Liberties Union 1949-60; del Welfare & Health Council of New York City 1950-55; board of directors, Westchester Urban League. **Honors/Awds:** Research grant Martha Chamberlin Found 1954; Dist Serv Award Yale 1962; commendation for social serv Ministry of Health Guatemala 1963; Meritorious Medal of Honor Dept of State US Govt 1965; Gold Plaque awarded by Counsel of Health and Social Work of Guatamala, 1963. **Special Achievements:** The Social Impact of the Black Press was published in 1994, by Carlton Press Corp of New York, NY. **Home Addr:** 2440 Virginia Ave NW, D506, Washington, DC 20037.

BROWN, WESLEY ANTHONY
Navy civil engineer corps (retired). **Personal:** Born Apr 3, 1927, Baltimore, MD; son of Rosetta Shepherd Brown and William Brown; married Crystal M; children: Willetta West, Carol Jackson, Wesley Jr, Gary. **Educ:** US Naval Acad, BSME 1949; Rensselaer Polytechnic Inst, MCE 1951. **Career:** Navy Civil Engr Corps Officer, public works officer-in-charge of construction 1949-69; NY State Univ Construction Fund, project mgr 1969-74; NY State Dorm Authority, project mgr 1974-76; Howard Univ Office of Univ Planning, facilities master planner 1976-88. **Orgs:** Chmn/CEO Natl Business Consultants Inc 1984-88; alumni trustee US Naval Acad 1986-88; life mem Alpha Phi Alpha Frat; Natl Naval Officers Assn, Naval Acad Alumni Assoc, Assoc for the Study of Negro Life and History; mem Naval Inst, Navy League, Sigma Pi Phi Frat; US Service Academies Nominations Board, DC delgate. **Honors/Awds:** "The First Negro Graduate of Annapolis Tells His Story" Saturday Evening Post 1949; article "Eleven Men of West Point" Negro History Bulletin. **Military Serv:** USN lt commander 20 yrs; Antarctic Service, Amer Theatre, Korean Serv World War II Victory, Sec of the Navy Commendation for Achievement Medal 1949-69. **Home Addr:** 6101 16th St NW #805, Washington, DC 20011.

BROWN, WILLARD L.
Attorney. **Personal:** Born Jun 9, 1911, Boston, MA; married Juanita. **Educ:** WV State Coll, BA 1932; Boston U, JD 1935, LLM 1936. **Career:** Pvt Practice, atty; Pub Serv Commn State of WV, adminstr law judge; NAACP, state legal adv 1941; Elks, state legal adv 1949; City of Charleston, councilman 1947-54; Grand Lodge, Prince Hall Masons, past grand counselor 1958-66. **Orgs:** Past potentate of Shriners, Charleston; past mem Charleston Human Relations Commn; past basileus Gamma Chap Boston, Omega Psi Phi; past basileus Xi Alpha Chap Charleston, Omega Psi Phi; past mem State Adv B D Dept of Employment Security; pres Charleston Br NAACP 1950-66; mem Charleston Bus & Professional Mem's Club; coordinator Civil Rights Conf 1964. **Honors/Awds:** Recipient TG Nutter Civil Rights Award, 1970; citizen of year Omega Psi Phi 1950; citation Women's Improvement League 1954; Omega Man of Year 1961. **Business Addr:** 426 Shrewsbury at Lewis St, Ste 201 Brown Bldg, Charleston, WV.

BROWN, WILLIAM, JR.
Physician, surgeon. **Personal:** Born Feb 5, 1935, New Haven; son of Viola P Brown and William Brown Sr; married Sarah Robinson; children: Kirsten, Kecia, Kollette, Karlton. **Educ:** Univ CT, BA 1957; Howard Univ Coll Med, MD 1961. **Career:** Prvt prac; DC Ge Hosp, internship 1961-62; Crownsville State Mental Hosp, resident psychiatry 1962-63; Dept Family Prac & Howard U, asst clinical prof 1972; St Eliz Hospital, general medical officer, 1965. **Orgs:** Chi Delt Mu 1960; DC Med Soc; Beta Sigma Gamma; natl bd Nat Med Assn 1965; diplomate of am bd Of Family Practice 1971-; Medical Chirurgical Society of DC; Amer Academy of Family Physicians. **Honors/Awds:** Fellow, American Academy of Family Physicians. **Military Serv:** AUS capt 1963-65. **Business Addr:** 1210 Mapleview, Washington, DC 20020.

BROWN, WILLIAM CRAWFORD
Educator (retired). **Personal:** Born Jun 3, 1925, Ruthville, VA; married Dr Jessie Lemon. **Educ:** Hampton Inst, BS 1950; New York Univ, MA 1952, EdD 1960; William & Mary Coll, Postgraduate courses, Marketing & Admin. **Career:** DuPont, 1945-47; Hampton Inst, 1947-50; Baltimore Public Schools, 1951-52; Newport News VA Public Schools, 1952-55; Hampton Univ, 1955-65; Prairie View Univ, 1965-66; Hampton Univ, retired prof of mktg 1966-94. **Orgs:** Grad sch prof (part-time) George Washington Univ; dir Project STEP Celanese Corp 1967-74; dir Small Business Ctr Hampton Univ 1973-78; consultant Peninsula Chamber of Commerce, Mayor's Comm on Consumerism, Natl Business League, Southern and Amer Mktg Assoc; life mem NAACP; mem Alpha Phi Alpha, Sigma PiPhi (Boule); mem Hampton Heritage Foundation; bd of dir Hampton Univ Credit Union, Amer Mktg Assoc, Common Cause, Natl Business League, Kiwanis Clubs of Amer. **Honors/Awds:** Distinguished Scholarship Award, New York Univ 1962; mem Kappa Delta Pi, Phi Delta Kappa, Phi Beta Lambda; IBM Summer Internship Award 1978; Lindback Distinguished Teaching Award, Hampton Univ 1986. **Military Serv:** AUS Airforce Engrs sgt 1943-45. **Business Addr:** Professor Emeritus of Marketing, Hampton University, Hampton, VA 23668.

BROWN, WILLIAM CREWS
Educational administrator. **Personal:** Born Feb 28, 1920, Greenwood, SC; married Margaret Elizabeth Curry. **Educ:** Allen U, BS 1942, LLD 1979; NY U, MA 1947, EdD 1960. **Career:** Higher Educ Opportunity, dir Inst Present; Fayetteville State Univ, vice chancellor acad affairs/prof of Educ, 1973-75; Higher Educ Opportunity, assoc dir, instructor, 1972; Barber-Scotia Coll, interim pres, 1971-72, dean of coll, 1967-71; SC State Coll, assoc prof/ prof & chmn dept of Health & Physical Educ, 1950-67. **Orgs:** Consult acad affairs United Negro Coll Fund 1971; mem educ adv com, US Mdl Dist Ct Macon GA 1973; mem natl adv com Inst for Socio-Tech Problems Jackson St Univ 1980; cons, state Agcys for Higher Educ Mem bd of control Allen Univ Columbia SC 1960-80; state dir Fellowsh For the Am Sch Health Assn 1960-67; mem exec com Charlotte Area Educ Consortium 1969-72; mem bd of & dirs United Serv Fund Fyttvl 1974-75; mem adv council Project Read DeKalb Co GA1977; mem adv com Allied Health Professions Spl Project Grant for Minority Recruitment & Retention 1977; chmn bd of trustees DeKalb Co Library System 1978. **Honors/Awds:** Am Serv Medal/EAME Serv Medal/Good Conduct Medal/3 Bronze Stars/WWII Victory Medal AUS; Fellow Am Sch Health Assn 1961; cert of appreciation Bd of Co Commrs of Cumberland Co NC 1975; presidential Citation Nat Assn for Equal Opportunity in Higher Educ 1979. **Military Serv:** AUS staff sgt 1943-45. **Business Addr:** Southern Regional Education Bo, 130 6th St NW, Atlanta, GA 30313.

BROWN, WILLIAM F. See Obituaries section.

BROWN, WILLIAM H.
Educational administrator, consultant. **Personal:** Born Oct 20, 1935, Washington, DC; son of Wilhelmina Brown and Charles H Brown; married Dolores L Arthur; children: DeNaye D. **Educ:** Morgan State U, BS 1957; Springfield Coll, MS 1958; Catholic U, PhD 1976. **Career:** Morgan State Coll, instructor, 1960-61; Baltimore Public Schools, teacher, 1961; DC Public Schools, teacher, counselor, 1962-68; Cardozo High School, asst prin, 1968-69; Washington DC Public Schools, coord youth serv, 1969-71; Spingarn High School, prin, 1971-77; Washington DC Public Schools, asst supt, 1977-88, deputy supt, 1988, vice supt, 1989, interim supt, 1990-91, consultant 1991-. **Orgs:** Notary public Washington, DC 1976-; mem Am Soc of Notaries; mem Nat Alliance of Black Sch Educators 1982-; mem Nat Assn of Secondary Sch Prin 1970-; life mem DC Parent Tchr Assn; mem NAACP; vice pres Capital Children's Museum; cnslr Neighborhood Youth Corps 1967. **Honors/Awds:** Mem Omega Psi Phi; vice pres Phi Delta Kappa Am Univ Chpt; mem Hall of Fame Morgan State Univ Baltimore 1976; mem Hall of Fame Cardozo High Sch Washington DC 1978. **Military Serv:** AUS 1958-60. **Business Addr:** Consultant, 3630 Cousin's Dr, Landover, MD 20785.

BROWN, WILLIAM H., III
Attorney. **Personal:** Born Jan 19, 1928, Philadelphia, PA; son of Ethel L Washington Brown and William H Brown Jr; married D June Hairston, Jul 29, 1975; children: Michele Denise, Jeanne Marie. **Educ:** Temple Univ, BS, 1952; Univ of PA Law School, JD, 1955. **Career:** Schnader, Harrison, Segal & Lewis, partner, attorney, 1974-; Norris, Brown & Hall, partner, 1964-68; Norris, Green, Harris & Brown, partner, 1962-64; Norris, Schmidt, Green, Harris & Higginbotham, assoc, 1956-62; EEOC, chmn, 1969-73; EEOC, commr, 1968-69; Deputy Dist Attorney, chief of frauds, 1968; chmn, Philadelphia Special Investigation Commn, 1985-86. **Orgs:** Bd of dir, United Parcel Serv, 1983-; mem, Regional Bd of Dir, First PA Banking & Trust Co, 1968-73; co-chair, bd dir, mem exec comm, Lawyers Comm for Civil Rights Under Law; founding mem, World Association of Lawyers; permanent mem, 3rd Cir Judicial Conference; mem, Alpha Phi Alpha; Philadelphia, Am Fed & PA Bar Assn; life member, Nat Bar Assn; Am Arbitration Association; Am Law Inst; Inter-Am Bar Assn; mem, Commn on Higher Educ, Middle States Association of Coll; mem, National Sr Citizen's Law Center; faculty mem, Natl Inst Trial Advocacy, 1980-; faculty mem, Practicing Law Inst, 1970-85; pres, mem, bd of dir, National Black Child Devel Institute, 1986-; mem, bd of dir, Community Legal Services; board of directors, NAACP Legal Defense & Educ Fund; fellow, American Bar Foundation; member, board of directors, Philadelphia Diagnostic and Rehabilitation Center; National Senior Citizens Law Center, board of directors, 1988-94. **Honors/Awds:** Award of Recognition, Alpha Phi Alpha, 1969; Handbook of Modern Personnel Admin, 1972; author of numerous articles; Philadelphia NAACP President's Award; Fidelity Award, Philadelphia Bar Assn, 1990; Legal Defense & Education Fund, Judge William H Haste Award, 1992; American Heart Association, Dr Edward S Cooper Award, 1995; The Urban League of Philadelphia, Whitney M Young Jr, Leadership Award, 1996; Lawyers' Committeefor Civil Rights Under Law, The Whitney North Seymoure Award, 1996. **Military Serv:** USAF, 1946-48; World War II Victory Medal. **Business Addr:** Attorney at Law, Partner, Schnader Harrison Segal Lewis, 1600 Market St Ste 3600, Philadelphia, PA 19103.

BROWN, WILLIAM J.
Association executive (retired). **Personal:** Born May 17, 1917, Harrisburg, PA; widowed; children: Natalie Renee, Andrea Delores. **Educ:** West Virginia State College, BA, 1942; Northwestern University, MA, 1947; Advanced Credit Work, George Williams College, July 1953. **Career:** Talladega Coll, dean of men 1947-51; William A Hunton Br YMCA, exec sec 1951-56; Detroit Urban League, vocational serv asst 1956-61; S Bend Urban League, exec dir 1961-64; Hartford & TTT Prog, dir 1970; Urban League of Greater Hartford, exec dir 1964-69, 1971-83; New York City and Boroughs Urban Leagues, interim pres, 1984; Urban League of Eastern Mass (Boston area), interim pres, 1988; Hartford Neighborhood Centers, Inc, interim exec dir, 1993-. **Orgs:** Connecticut Commission on Human Rights and Opportunities, commissioner; Natl Executives Service Corps, consultant; SNET Corps Company, advisory bd; Social Workers Conference of Connecticut; Free and Accepted Masons; Omega Psi Phi Fraternity; Metropolitan AME Zion Church; Bloomfield State Bank, bank dir; Later Security Bank-Then Union Trust Bank; Junior Achievement, bd of dirs; Mental Health Assn of Connecticut; American Red Cross of Connecticut; Greater Hartford Senior Citizens Council; Mt Sinai Hospital, incorporator; Hartford Hospital, incorporator; Hartford Club; Salvation Army Board Member Emeritus. **Honors/Awds:** Tau Iota Chapter, Omega Psi Phi Fraternity, Omega Man of the Year; Greater Hartford Rotary, Rotrian of the Year; Natl Council of Christians and Jews, Human Relations Award; Briarwood College, Honorary Doctorate of Human Relations; University of Hartford, Honorary Doctorate of Laws; Natl Urban League Whitney M Young Jr, Commemorative Award, 1992; United Way of the Capital Area, Community Services Award, 1993; A Founding member of Board High Noon (Social/Civic) Political Award, 1993. **Military Serv:** US Army, 1942-46; warrant officer jr.

BROWN, WILLIAM MCKINLEY, JR.
Public health administrator (retired). **Personal:** Born Jan 24, 1926, Chicago, IL; son of Judith Mitchell Brown and William M Brown Sr; married Gloria G; children: William III, Joseph, Timothy, Anthony. **Educ:** Roosevelt Coll, BS 1950; Meharry Med Coll, MD 1955; Univ MI, MPH 1959; internship gen prac Sacramento Co Hosp 1955-57; pub health resident LA 1962-64. **Career:** Milwaukee WI, public health physician 1959-62; LA, dist health officer 1964-70; consul CA State Dept 1970-75; Pasadena CA, health officer 1970-75; assoc clinical prof Univ So CA Med Sch, 1970-76; Drug Treatment Prog, med dir 1975-; Charles R Drew Postgrad Medical Sch, asst prof comm medicine; Hubert H Humphrey Comp Health Ctr, medical public hlth officer, 1978-92. **Orgs:** El Monte Kiwanis Club 1966-68; Urban Health Conf MI State Univ 1971; trustee US Conf City Health Officers 1971-75; bd dir Pasadena Child Health Found 1973-76; sec treas CA Acad of Preventive Med 1971-73, pres 1975; bd of dir High Blood Pressure Council LA; bd dirs Casa Las Amigas; adv bd El Santos Nino Social Serv Ctr; adv bd Child Health and Disability Prog South Area; bd of dir Amer Cancer Soc San Gabriel Valley Unit; Foothill Free Clinic; Mental Health Assn of Pasadena; Pasadena Council on Alcoholism; Pasadena Humane Soc; Pasadena Lung Assn; Wesley Social Serv Ctr; Visiting Nurses Assn; diplomate Amer Bd of Preventive Med; fellow Amer Coll of Preventive Med; fellow Amer Pub Health Assn; commr City of El Monte Sister City; article Public Health Report 6; Black Caucus Health Workers, APHA Founder. **Military Serv:** USNR phm 3/c 1944-46. **Home Addr:** 37418 Festival Dr, Palm Desert, CA 92211.

BROWN, WILLIAM ROCKY, III
Elected official, clergyman. **Personal:** Born Oct 10, 1955, Chester, PA; son of Gwendolyn Carraway Brown and William Brown Jr (deceased); married Lorraine Baa Brown, Mar 23, 1991; children: Catrina J. **Educ:** Cheyney State Univ, BA Pol Sci 1977; Martin Luther King Jr Ctr, Course in Non-Violence 1978-80; Eastern Baptist Seminary, MA Religion 1983; Jameson Christian Coll, DDiv 1986. **Career:** Chester-Upland School Dist, substitute teacher 1978-81; Calvary Baptist Church, asst pastor 1979-; State of PA, notary public 1980-; PA Legislature Dist 159, asst state rep 1982-83; First Baptist Church of Bernardtown Coatesville PA, pastor; City of Chester, city controller, Law Enforcement Planning Commission, St Thomas, VI, special asst, currently. **Orgs:** Founder, pres Chester Black Expo 1979-; exec bd Black Ministers Conf 1979-; exec bd Chester Branch NAACP 1979-; vice pres Chester Comm Improvement Project 1981-; pres Bill Dandridge Art Gallery 1982-; exec bd Kiwanis Club of Chester 1984-. **Honors/Awds:** Columnist What's Happening Now Newspaper 1978-; Outstanding Young Man US Jaycees 1984; Johnson Freedom Awd Chester Branch NAACP 1984; Outstanding Alumni Natl Assn for Equal Opportunity in Higher Educ 1985. **Home Addr:** PO Box 642, St Thomas, Virgin Islands of the United States 00804. **Business Addr:** Special Assistant, Drug & Crime Prevention Program, Law Enforcement Planning Commission, Office of the Governor, 116 & 164 Subbase, St Thomas, Virgin Islands of the United States 00801.

BROWN, WILLIAM T.
Theater administrator, educator, scenic designer (retired). **Personal:** Born Mar 11, 1929, Washington, DC; son of Henrietta Brown and William Brown; married Alfredine Parham; children: Camilla Parham, Darrell, Kevin; married Frances Farmer.

Educ: Howard Univ, BA 1951; Western Reserve Univ, MFA 1954. **Career:** Theatre Dept Univ of MD Baltimore Co, assoc prof & chmn 1970-75, 1982-94; assoc prof drama, Howard Univ 1959-70, & dept chmn 1967-70; Theatre Univ of Leeds, visiting prof 1975; Theatre Univ of Ibadan Nigeria, sr lecturer & consultant 1963-65; Karamu Theatre Cleveland, tech dir 1951-59, retired, June 1997. **Orgs:** Mem, East Central Theatre Conference; mem, American Theatre of Higher Education; mem, Maryland State Arts Council 1988-91; mem, Howard County Artistic Review Panel 1987-94; Shakespeare Theatre Assn of America, 1993-95; theatre review panel, Pennsylvania Council of the Arts, 1993-94; board of directors, Columba Candlelight Society. **Honors/Awds:** Gold Medallion Award of Excellence in Theatre Amoco Oil Co 1971; Hines-Brooks Award of Excellence in Theatre Howard Univ 1961; Distinguished Program Award, Maryland Assn of Higher Education 1988; creation of Traveling Stage Shakespeare On Wheels 1985. **Home Addr:** 8499 Spring Showers Way, Ellicott City, MD 21043-6058.

BROWN, WILLIAM T.
Scientist. **Personal:** Born Jun 11, 1947, Columbus, MS; divorced; children: Kesha. **Educ:** Dillard Univ, BS (cum laude) 1969; Univ of NM, MS, PhD 1984. **Career:** Los Alamos Sci Lab, tech staff physicist 1969-73; Sandia Natl Lab, tech staff physicist 1974-. **Orgs:** Bd dir Natl Technical Assoc 1983-; mem Natl Black Child Development Inst; pres bd dir Albuquerque Montessori Soc 1975-77; bd dir mem Natl Consortium for Black Professional Development 1976-79; mem Amer Physical Soc 1977-; mem AAAS 1978-; mem NAACP 1976-; mem NM Acad of Sci 1975-; mem Soc of Black Physicists 1978-; mem Natl Tech Assn 1979-. **Business Addr:** Technical Staff Physicist, Sandia Natl Lab, Box 5800 Div 1533, Albuquerque, NM 87185.

BROWN, WILLIE
Former college football coach. **Personal:** Born in Yazoo City, MS; married Elizabeth; children: Three. **Educ:** Grambling Univ, attended. **Career:** Defensive back: Denver Broncos, , 1963-66; Oakland Raiders, 1967-78, defensive back coach; California State University at Long Beach, head football coach, until 1992. **Honors/Awds:** Inducted, Professional Football Hall of Fame, 1984.

BROWN, WILLIE B.
State representative. **Personal:** Born Jun 18, 1940, Anderson, SC. **Educ:** SC State Coll, attended. **Career:** State of New Jersey, assemblyman, dist 29, 1973-; real estate investment bus exec, currently. **Orgs:** National parliamentarian, Natl Black Caucus State Legislators; consultant and advisor, co-founder, South Ward New Dem Club; life mem, NAACP; Wainwright Tri Block Assn; Coun State Governments; Grand Masonic Cong; AF & AM. **Honors/Awds:** Legislator of the Year, Natl Black Caucus of State Legislators, 1983; co-recipient, $10,000 contribution from Anheuser-Busch at annual conf, Natl Black Caucus of State Leg, 1989. **Business Addr:** Minority Leader, General Assembly, New Jersey State House, Trenton, NJ 08625.

BROWN, WILLIE L., JR.
Former state assemblyman/speaker. **Personal:** Born Mar 20, 1934, Mineola, TX; son of Minnie Brown and Willie L Brown Sr; married Blanche Vitero; children: Susan, Robin, Michael. **Educ:** CA State Univ San Francisco, BA 1955; Hastings Coll of Law, JD 1958. **Career:** Brown, Dearman & Smith, partner 1959-; California State Assembly, state representative, 1964-95, speaker, 1980-95. **Orgs:** Mem Assembly Com on Efficiency & Cost Control Elect & Reapportionment Govt Admin; Governor's Commn on Aging; mem Joint Comm on Master Plan for Higher Edn; Legislative Budget; Legis Space Needs Legis Audit; v chmn Select Com on Health Manpower; mem Select Com Deep Water Ports; co-chairperson CA Delegation to Natl Dem Conv 1972; co-chmn CA Delegation to Natl Black Polit Conv 1972; CA rep Credentials Com Dem Conv 1968; bd mem Natl Planned Parenthood Assn; Fellow of Amer Assembly; mem NAACP, League of Women Voters; adv bd mem CA & Tomorrow; honorary lifetime mem ILWU Local #10; San Francisco Planning & Urban Renewal Assn; Sunset Parkside Educ & Action Com; Fillmore Merchants Improvement Assn; Planning Assn for Richmond; Hight Ashbury Neighborhood Council; San Francisco Aid Retarded ChildreChinese for Affirmative Action. **Honors/Awds:** Outstanding Freshman Legislator Press Award 1965; Man of the Year Sun Reporter Newspaper 1963; Children's Lobby Award Outstanding Legislative Efforts 1974; Leader of the Future Time Magazine 1974. **Business Addr:** Mayor, City of San Francisco, San Francisco, CA.

BROWN, WILLIS, JR.
Retired educator. **Personal:** Born Dec 15, 1924, Charleston, SC; son of Evelyn Kirlow Brown and Rev Willis Brown; married Bertha Adams Brown, Nov 25, 1950; children: Angela C Brown, Alford. **Educ:** Benedict Coll, BS. **Career:** Science tchr 1953-79. **Orgs:** Referee Camden Co GA Juvenile CT; charter mem treas mgr Camden Co Comm Fed Credit Union; dir & past pres GA Science Teacher Assn Inc; mem CADRE-100; charter mem Epsilon chap of Omega Psi & Phi; Lambda Tau Grad chap keeper of records & seals; Prince Hall 33 Degree Mason; v chmn Zoning & Planning Commn; co-chmn Camden Co Comm Chest Dr; Coastal Area Planning & Develop Adv Council on Planning; grand secretary Most Worshipful Prince Hall Grand Lodge F&AM of Georgia; deputy of the Orient Georgia's All 32 Degree - 33 Degree Prince Hall Masons of Georgia. **Honors/Awds:** Tchr of yr Camden Co teachers; cited by Am Nat Red Cross & GA Vet Serv. **Home Addr:** PO Box 475, Woodbine, GA 31569.

BROWN, YOLANDA
Business executive. **Personal:** Born May 10, 1946, Taclobam Leyte, Philippines; children: Jo Ann, Yolanda, Charles, Joe L Jr. **Educ:** Pace Univ, BBA (cum laude) 1972-76; Amer Inst of Banking, certificate 1976; New York Credit Inst, credit analysis certificate 1976; Columbia Univ, MBA (honors) 1980. **Career:** Xerox Corp, admin asst to pres 1967-69, credit & mgmt trainee 1976-77; Manufacturers Hanover Trust, marketing officer 1977-80; First Interstate Bank LA, asst vice pres marketing 1980-81; Union Bank LA, vice pres marketing. **Orgs:** Mem, Women in Finance, 1976; vice pres & sec, Urban Bankers Coalition of New York, 1977-78; bd mem Natl Assn of Urban Bankers, 1978; mem, Amer Marketing Assn, 1979-; comm chairperson, Urban Bankers Coalition of LA, 1981-; mem, Southern California Jr Ice Hockey League, 1982-; mem, Wilson High School Football Boosters, 1982-; counselor/facilitator, St John Vianney Youth Group, 1984-; mem, Bank Marketing Assn, 1984-. **Honors/Awds:** Natl Honor Soc, Pace Univ, 1976; Pace & Columbia Univ Scholarships, 1974-80; Outstanding Trainee, Manufacturers Hanover Trust, 1976; Discretionary Award, Union Bank, 1984.

BROWN, ZORA KRAMER
Association executive. **Personal:** Born Mar 20, 1949, Holdenville, OK; daughter of Helen Holden Brown and Willie Brown; divorced. **Educ:** Oklahoma State University, BS, 1969. **Career:** Pharmaceutical Manufacturers Association, secretary, 1969-70; Ford Motor Co., secretary, 1970-76; The White House, administrative assistant, 1976-77; US House Majority Leader, staff assistant, 1977; Federal Communications Commission, assistant director, public affairs, 1977-86; Broadcast Capital Fund Inc, public affairs director, 1989-91; Breast Cancer Resource Committee, chairperson, currently; Broadcast Capital Fund, vice president & chief operating officer, 1995-. **Orgs:** Natl Cancer Advisory Board, 1991-98; President's Cancer Panel, Special Commission on Breast Cancer, 1992-94; District of Columbia Cancer Consortium, 1989-, chairperson, 1993-; Breast Health Institute, Philadelphia, PA, board member, 1992; Susan G Komen Breast Cancer Foundation, board member, 1992. **Honors/Awds:** Washington Association of Black Journalists, Marilyn Trish Robinson Community Service Award, 1992; Susan G Komen Foundation, Community Service Award, 1992; National Cancer Institute, Cancer Control Service Award, 1991; National Women's Health Resource Center, Breast Awareness Award, 1991; Auxiliary to Veterans of Foreign Wars, Community Service Award, 1992. **Special Achievements:** First African-American woman appointed to the National Cancer Advisory Board; founder, Breast Cancer Resource Committee, Cancer Awareness Program Services. **Business Addr:** Chair, Breast Cancer Resource Committee, 1765 N St NW, Ste 100, Washington, DC 20036, (202)463-8040.

BROWNE, ERNEST C., JR.
Former councilman. **Personal:** Born Dec 26, 1925, Detroit, MI; married Evelyn Virginia James. **Educ:** Wayne State U, BS 1967; Program for Urban Exec MIT, grad 1969. **Career:** Detroit Health Dept, pub health sanatarian 1949-64; Detroit Budget Bur, govt budget analyst 1965-69; Mayor's Task Force on Police Recruiting & Hiring, Detroit, staff dir 1968; Detroit, councilman 1970-75. **Orgs:** Pres MI Municipal League; chmn MI Municipal League Humasn Resources Com 1973-74; vice-chmn Revenue & Finance Com; Nat League of Cities; regional dir Nat Black Caucus of Local Elected Officials; vice pres Detroit Area Coun BSA; vice pres United Found; chmn Black Historic Site Com of Detroit Historic Museum; trustee Starr Commonwealth for Boys; MI adv comm on Criminal Justice & Law Enforcement. **Honors/Awds:** Rec Silver Beaver Award, BSA 1960; Two Grand Awards, Employee Award Bd Detroit 1966. **Military Serv:** USAAF. **Business Addr:** 1340 City Co Bldg, Detroit, MI 48226.

BROWNE, JERRY
Professional baseball player. **Personal:** Born Feb 13, 1966, St Croix, Virgin Islands of the United States. **Career:** Infielder: Texas Rangers, 1986-88, Cleveland Indians, 1988-92, Oakland A's, 1992-. **Business Addr:** Professional Baseball Player, Texas Rangers, 1000 Ballpark Way, Arlington, TX 76011, (817)273-5222.

BROWNE, LEE F.
Educator, chemist. **Personal:** Born Dec 18, 1922, High Point, NC; son of Lula Winchester and Lee Browne; married Dorothy G; children: Gail, Daryl, Adriene, Scott (deceased). **Educ:** Storer Coll, HS 1940, AA 1942; WVA State Coll, BS 1944; University of Pennsylvania, Navy V-7 Prog, 1946-47; UCLA, 1946-49; NYU, Doctoral Prog 1955. **Career:** UCLA, teaching fellow 1946-49; Tuskegee Inst, instr 1948-49; Knoxville Coll, div chmn 1950-51; Valley Jr Coll, chem instr 1952-56; Pasadena Schools, sci consult & chem 1964-68; Caltech, lecturer, dir 1969-90, lecturer/emeritus, 1989-90. **Orgs:** Mem ACS, AAAS, AAUP, NSTA, NOBCCHE Natl Assoc of Curriculum Spec, CCTA, Kappa Alpha Psi, Phi Sigma Biol Soc, Phi Delta Kappa Ed Hon Soc; bd of dir Pasadena Hall of Sci, Science Activities Mag, NACME Inc 1980-, Pasadena Boys Club 1981, NAMEPA Minority Engrg Prog 1980-; accred team WASA 1970; vice chmn, chmn MESA 1978. **Honors/Awds:** LA Cty Sci & Engrg Soc Teachers Awd 1968; ACS HS Chem Contest Teacher of #1 Team & #1 Student 1968, 1969; Industry & Educ Council Teacher of the Year 1968; Amer Chem Soc Teacher of the Year 1970; Raymond Pitts Human Rel Awd Pasadena Star News 1970-76; CA Congress of Parent & Teachers Serv Awd 1970; Citizen of the Year 1980; Phi Delta Kappa Edu Honorary 1971; Nominee to Pasadena Bd of Ed 1971; founder & ed Pasadena Eagle newspaper 1968-73; publ "Developing Skills for Coping" 1977, "Midpoint vs Endpoint" 1980; elected to Amer Inst of Chemists 1986. **Military Serv:** USN v-7 cadet 1945-46. **Home Addr:** 871 W Ventura St, Altadena, CA 91001. **Business Addr:** Lecturer/Emeritus, Dir of Secondary School Relations, Caltech, 104-6 Caltech, Pasadena, CA 91125.

BROWNE, ROBERT SPAN
Economist. **Personal:** Born Aug 17, 1924, Chicago, IL; son of Julia Barksdale Patterson (deceased) and William H Browne Jr (deceased); married Huoi Nguyen Browne, Apr 1956; children: Hoa, Mai, Alexi, Marshall. **Educ:** Univ of IL, BA Hon in Econ 1944; Univ of Chicago IL, MBA 1947; City Univ of NY, 1964-67. **Career:** Dillard Univ, instructor, 1947-49; Chicago Urban League, program director, 1950-53; Intl Cooperation Admin, pgm ofcr 1955-61; Phelps-Stokes Fund, project director, 1963-65; Fairleigh Dickinson U, prof 1965-70; Black Eco Research Cntr, pres 1969-80; African Devel Fund, exec dir 1980-82; Howard U, sr research fellow 1982-85; Subcommittee on Domestic Monetary Policy, staff dir 1986; Subcommittee on Interntl Development, Finance, Trade and Monetary Policy, staff director, 1987-91; Howard University, resident scholar, 1992-94, international economic consultant, 1994-. **Orgs:** Bd mem Saxon Industries 1975-80; bd mem Harlem Commonwealth Cncl 1974-80; bd mem, Calvert New Africa Fund, 1995-; pres The 21st Century Found 1972-; chrmn Emergency Land Fund 1972-82; mem Eco Advisory Panel to Congressional Budget Off 1975-80; mem Governor's Commn on Welfare Mgmnt NJ 1976-80; New York Governor Cuomo Commission on Trade and Competitiveness, 1986-88; mem Cncl on Foreign Relations 1976-; mem US Assn for the Club of Rome 1976-. **Honors/Awds:** The Amistad Award NY Friends of Amistad 1984; co-author The Lagos Plan vs The Berg Report, 1984, The Social Scene, 1972. **Military Serv:** USAF sgt 1944-46. **Home Addr:** 214 Tryon Ave, Teaneck, NJ 07666.

BROWNE, ROSCOE LEE
Actor, writer, director. **Personal:** Born 1925, Woodbury, NJ. **Educ:** Lincoln Univ; Middlebury College; Columbia Univ. **Career:** Actor, writer, director; Films include: The Connection, 1962; The Cool World, 1964; The Comedians, 1967; Uptight, 1968; Topaz, 1969; The Liberation of L.B. Jones, 1970; The Cowboys, 1972; The World's Greatest Athlete, 1973; Superfly, 1973; Black Like Me, 1974; Uptown Saturday Night, 1974; Logan's Run, 1976; Twilight's Last Gleaming, 1977; The Fifth Door; The Haunting of Harrington House; King; Legal Eagles; Unknown Powers; Jumping Jack Flash; numerous stage appearances since 1952 including: Julius Caesar, 1956; The Blacks, 1961; King Lear, 1962; The Winter's Tale, 1963; The Man Who Came to Dinner, 1966; The Dream on Monkey Mountain, 1970; A Hand Is on the Gate, 1976-77; My One and Only, 1983; has appeared in many television movies and as guest star in continuing series including Space,num PI, Barney Miller, Soap, and The Cosby Show. **Orgs:** Actor's Equity; Screen Actors Guild; American Federation of Television and Radio Artists. **Honors/Awds:** Obie Award, Best Actor for Benito Cereno, 1965; Best Actor Los Angeles Drama Critics Award for The Dream on Monkey Mountain, 1970; Black Filmmakers Hall of Fame, 1977; 1000 yd indoors track champion, Amateur Athletic Union 1949, 1951; named All-American athlete twice; Emmy Award, Best Actor in a Drama or Comedy Show, The Cosby Show, 1986.

BROWNE, VINCENT J.
Educational administrator. **Personal:** Born Jul 21, 1917, Washington, DC; married. **Educ:** Howard U, AB 1938; Harvard U, AM 1941; PhD 1946. **Career:** Carnegie Corp, research asst, 1939-40; Howard Univ, Washington DC, Political Science instructor, 1941-42, asst prof, 1946-59, assoc prof, 1950-61, asst to pres, 1955-64, prof 1961-; dir affairs scholars & programs, 1964-67, civil rights document project dir & Fund for Advanced Educ dir, 1968-70, Coll Liberal Arts, dean, 1968-71. **Orgs:** Spl asst field relations Fed Civil Def Adminstrn 1951-53, consult 1954-55; pres's commn Vet Benefits 1955-56; mem Polit Sci Assn. **Honors/Awds:** Soc Pub Adminstrn Contrib article to professional publs. **Military Serv:** AUS 1941-46. **Business Addr:** 3915 24 St NE, Washington, DC 20018.

BROWNE, VINCENT JEFFERSON, JR.
Marketing/sales account executive. **Personal:** Born Mar 8, 1953, Washington, DC; son of Frances Raymond Browne and

Vincent J Browne; married Matrice W. **Educ:** Brown Univ, BA 1975; Columbia Univ, MBA 1977. **Career:** Consolidated Rail Corp, mktg analyst 1977-78, business develop analyst 1978-86, account exec 1986-. **Orgs:** Mem Natl Black MBA Assoc 1982-, Assoc of MBA Execs 1986-.

BROWNER, JOEY MATTHEW
Professional football player. **Personal:** Born May 15, 1960, Warren, OH; married Valeria. **Educ:** USC, public admin. **Career:** Safety: Minnesota Vikings, 1983-92, Tampa Bay Buccaneers, 1992-. **Orgs:** NEL Boys & Girls Club of AK Camp "87", camp confident Celebrity Tournament; Vikings Charity Basketball. **Honors/Awds:** Selected first team All PAC 10; UPI All Coast; College Pro Football Newsweekly second-team All-Amer; AP third-team All-Amer; USC's MVP; captain of team in Japan Bowl, 1983; MVP on Defense Vikings, 1985; Pro Bowl teams, 1985-90. **Business Addr:** Professional Football Player, Tampa Bay Buccaneers, 1 Buccaneer Pl, Tampa, FL 33607.

BROWNER, ROSS
Professional athlete (retired), realtor. **Personal:** Born Mar 22, 1954, Warren, OH; son of Julia Geraldine Cook Browner and Jimmie Lee Browner Sr; married Shayla Simpson Browner, Jun 14, 1986; children: Rylan Ross. **Educ:** Attended, Notre Dame. **Career:** Cincinnati Bengals, professional football defensive lineman 1978-87; Green Bay Packers, professional football defensive lineman 1987; Coldwell Banker, Cincinnati OH, realtor 1989-; Browner Productions Inc, CEO, 1995-. **Orgs:** Sister City. **Honors/Awds:** All-Amer Notre Dame; winner of Outland & Lombardi Trophies Notre Dame; Bengal MVP Bengal Fans 1978; HS All-Amer; Robert W Maxwell Trophy 1978. **Business Addr:** CEO, Browner Productions Inc, 1135 Flamingo Dr SW, Atlanta, GA 30311, (404)758-7900.

BROWN-FRANCISCO, TERESA ELAINE
State official, political activist. **Personal:** Born Feb 25, 1960, Oklahoma, OK; daughter of Mary McMullen Brown and Herman Brown; married Andre Francisco, Nov 25, 1989; children: Aaron Geoffrey (deceased), Addam Michael. **Educ:** Phillips University, Enid, OK, 1978-80; Oklahoma City University, Oklahoma City, OK, BA, 1983. **Career:** KOCO-TV, Oklahoma City, OK, associate news producer, 1984-86; Bellmon for Governor, Campaign, Oklahoma City, OK, assistant press secretary, 1986; Bellmon for Governor, Inaugural Committee, Oklahoma City, OK, press secretary, 1986-87; Office of the Governor, Oklahoma City, OK, assistant to the governor for social services & ethnic affairs, 1987-91; Total Concept Consultants, Inc, entrepreneur, 1992; Marketing & Visual Communications, public relations. **Orgs:** Board of directors, Urban League of Greater Oklahoma City, 1987-91; board of directors, Metropolitan Fair Housing Council, 1987-; advisory committee, co-chairman, The Casey Family Program, 1990-94; board of directors, Institute for Child Advocacy, 1988-91; board of directors, Oklahoma City University Alumni Association, 1991-95. **Honors/Awds:** Executive Leadership Institute, National Forum for Black Public Adminstrators, 1989-90; US Delegate, World Youth Forum, Helsinki, Finland, American Center for International Leadership, 1990; 50 Future Leaders in America, Featured Article by Ebony Magazine, 1990; Developer, Martin Luther King, Jr. State of Excellence Scholarship Award, 1988; Developer, Oklahoma Youth in Education and Service, 1990. **Business Addr:** President, Total Concept Consultants, Inc, 9230 N Penn Pl, Ste 187, Oklahoma City, OK 73120.

BROWN-GUILLORY, ELIZABETH
Playwright, educator. **Personal:** Born Jun 20, 1954, Lake Charles, LA; daughter of Marjorie Savoie Brown and Leo Brown; married Lucius M Guillory, Aug 6, 1983; children: Lucia Elizabeth. **Educ:** University of Southwestern Louisiana, BA, English, 1975, MA, English, 1977; Florida State University, PhD, English, 1980. **Career:** University of South Carolina, Spartanburg, assistant professor of English, 1980-82; Dillard University, assistant professor of English, 1982-88; University of Houston, associate professor of English, 1988-. **Orgs:** Southern Conference on Afro-American Studies, Inc; College Language Association; South Central Modern Language Association; Modern Language Association; International Women's Writing Guild; National Council of Black Studies; Conference of College Teachers of English of Texas; Black Theater Network; Association for Theatre in Higher Education. **Honors/Awds:** Sigma Tau Delta, Outstanding Professor, 1991; UH Humanities and Fine Arts Additional Increment Committee Award; Young Black Achievers of Houston Award; Louisiana state wide competition, First Place Playwriting Award, 1985; The City of New Orleans Playwriting Award, 1983; Florida State University, Research Fellowship, 1979; numerous grants and other awards. **Special Achievements:** Editor: Wines in the Wilderness: Plays by African-American Women from the Harlem Renaissance to the Present, 1990; Editor: Women of Color: Mother-Daughter Relationships in 20th Century Literature, 1996; Author: Their Place on the Stage: Black Women Playwrights in America, 1988; playwright: Mam Phyllis, Snapshots of Broken Dolls, 1987; Bayou Relics, 1983; numerous others. **Business Addr:** Professor, English, University of Houston, 4800 Calhoun Rd, Houston, TX 77204-3012, (713)743-2976.

BROWN-HARRIS, ANN
Banking official. **Personal:** Born Dec 5, 1955, Tallahassee, FL; daughter of Carrie M Ware & Junilus A Brown (deceased); married Walter D Harris Jr, Jul 28, 1984; children: Geoffrey D Harris. **Educ:** FL A&M Univ, BS, business administration, 1977. **Career:** Human Resources Clearing House, fiscal officer, 1977-79; Suntrust Bank of Central FL, vice pres, 1979-. **Orgs:** Central Fl Urban bankers, exec officer, bd mem, 1983-; City of Orlando, municipal planning bd, bd mem, 1991; Natl Assn of Urban bankers, southern regional rep, 1991-93; City of Orlando Downtown Dev Bd, bd mem, 1991-; City of Orlando, mayors transition team, 1992; Office of the Governor, FL Commission on African American Affairs, commissioner, 1993-. **Honors/Awds:** Central FL Urban Banker, Outstanding Service Award, 1985, 1986, 1988, 1990 & 1994; Orlando Business Journal, Up & domer in Financial Services, 1991; Dollars & Sense Magazine, Outstanding Business & Professional Award, 1992; US Dept of Commerce, Minority Retailer of the Year, 1993. **Business Addr:** VP, Suntrust Bank of Central Florida, 200 S Orange Ave, Mail Code 0-1035, Tower 3, Orlando, FL 32801, (407)237-6745.

BROWNING, GRAINGER
Educator. **Personal:** Born Nov 5, 1917, Weldon, NC; son of Emma Browning and James Henry Browning; married Esther Merriman; children: Grainger, Jr, Cornelia Aida. **Educ:** Shaw U, AB 1939; Boston U, MA 1945, PhD 1962. **Career:** A&T Coll, instr 1947-49; MA Inst Tech, 1952-53; Johnson C Smith U, asst prof 1954-58; United So Educ Settlements, community organizer 1958-62; Hampton Inst, asso prof 1961-66; Fitchburg State Coll, prof retired 1986. **Orgs:** Mem Mayor's Citizens Adv Comm 1964-66; pres NAACP Fitchburg 1968, exec comm 1969; bd of dirs Fitchburg Planning Bd 1969-; faculty senate Fitchburg State Coll 1969; mem Am Univ Profs; Am Sociological Assn; pres MA Sociological Assn 1971-72; bd dirs United Comm Serv 1973-; MICAH Housing Corp; MA Common Cause; Worcester N Savings Bank Corp 1977-; chmn educ com NAACP 1978-; bd dir Montachusett Opportunity Council 1979-; Omega Psi Phi Frat, Iota Chi Chpt; chmn Nat Achvmt Eek Celebration; pres Men's Fellowship Union Baptist Church Cambridge MA 1987. **Honors/Awds:** Book of Golden Deeds Award, Exchange Club of Fitchburg 1969; Dist Serv Award, Fitchburg State Coll 1979; Omega Man of the Yr, Omega Psi Phi Frat Iota Chi Chap 1980,85; Pioneer Awd Massachusetts Sociological Assoc 1986; Martin Luther King Jr Human Relations Award, Massachusetts Teachers Assn 1982.

BROWNING, JOHN
Professional football player. **Personal:** Born Sep 30, 1973, Miami, FL. **Educ:** Univ of West Virginia. **Career:** Kansas City Chiefs, defensive end, 1996-. **Business Addr:** Professional Football Player, Kansas City Chiefs, One Arrowhead Dr, Kansas City, MO 64129, (816)924-9300.

BROWNLEE, DENNIS J.
Business executive. **Career:** Advance Inc, CEO, currently. **Honors/Awds:** Company is #91 on the Black Enterprise 100 list of top industrial companies. **Business Addr:** CEO, Advance Inc, 2200 Wilson Blvd, Ste 700, Arlington, VA 22201, (703)358-9100.

BROWNLEE, GERALDINE DANIELS
Educator. **Personal:** Born in E Chicago, IN; daughter of Nellie Cossey Daniels and Jerry Daniels; married Brady Brownlee, Aug 4, 1957. **Educ:** West VA State Coll, BA (cum laude) 1947; Univ of IL, grad 1949-50; Univ of MI, grad 1950; Chicago Teachers Coll, grad 1955; Univ of Chicago, MST 1967, PhD 1975; IN Univ, post-doctoral study, american council on education, fellow, 1978-79. **Career:** Cook Co IL, Dept of Pub Welfare, adv caseworker 1950-55; Chicago Public Sch, elem sch teacher 1955-66; Univ of Chicago, staff assoc 1968-70; University of Chicago, Ford Found Training & Placement Prog, coord 1969-70; University of Chicago, asst dir trainer of tchr trainers prog 1970-71; Univ of IL, Coll of Educ, asst dean, asst prof 1971-74; Park Forest IL Sch Dist, dir title VII proj 1975-76; Univ of IL, associate professor emerita, 1990; DePaul University, Urban Teacher Corps, director, office of provost, specail asst, 1990-91. **Orgs:** Consul US Off of Educ; consul Pk Forest Sch Dist 163; Amer Educ Res Assn; Natl Soc for the Study of Educ; Amer Assn for Higher Educ; Alpha Kappa Alpha; Amer Assn of Univ Women; Links Inc; Education Network; International vice pres Pi Lambda Theta Honor Assn for Professionals in Educ; Assn for Supervision and Curriculum Devel, 1988-89; Assn of Teacher Educ; 1982-88; chairperson, Chicago Urban League Education Advisory Comm, 1983-90; bd of dirs, Chicago Urban League, 1984-90; Chicago United Way Allocations, comm, 1992-97; Metropolitan Chicago YWCA, bd of dirs, vice pres, 1991-97. **Honors/Awds:** Fifteenth Annual Distinguished Research Award, from Assn of Teacher Educators: The Role of Teacher Career Stages and Professional Develop Practices in Determining Rewards and Incentives in Teaching 1987; Beautiful People Award, Chicago Urban League, 1989; Outstanding Achievement Award in the Field of Education, YWCA of Metropolitan Chicago, 1990. **Special Achievements:** Publications: "Parent-Teacher Contacts and Students Learning, A Research Report" (with Iverson & Walberg) in The Journal of Educ Rsch 1981; "Characteristics of Teacher Leaders" Educational Horizons, 1979; reprint in the Practising Administrator (Australia) 1980; "Teachers Who Can, Lead" in Alpha Delta Kappan, 1980; "Research & Evaluation of Alternative Programs for High School Truants," 1988, 1989. **Home Addr:** 6937 S Crandon Ave, Chicago, IL 60649.

BROWNLEE, JACK M.
TV operations manager. **Personal:** Born Jul 24, 1940, St Louis, MO; son of Johnny and Clifford; married Martha Diaz, May 23, 1987; children: Bryan, Michael, Gabriel. **Educ:** San Diego City, grad; San Diego St Coll, grad. **Career:** KFMB TV, dir 1972-73, TV oper mgr, 1973-75, prod supr, 1975-95, program coord, 1995-; Starburst Broadcasting, co-owner, vp, 1990-. **Orgs:** Bd of Governors, Natl Assn of Television Arts & Sciences 1984-85. **Honors/Awds:** Upper Level Div Scholarship Award; 1st black dir & 1st black on KFMB TV mng staff; Emmy Award, best entertainment show, Natl Assn of Television Arts & Sciences 1983. **Military Serv:** USMC 1959-64. **Business Addr:** Program Coordinator, Midwest Broadcasting, KFMB-TV, San Diego, CA 92111, (619)571-8888.

BROWNLEE, LESTER HARRISON-PIERCE MACDOUGALL
Educator. **Personal:** Born Apr 25, 1915, Wakefield, RI; son of Rosa Adele Latimer Brownlee (deceased) and Rev Leonidas Brownlee (deceased); married Priscilla Ruth MacDougall, Jul 5, 1987; children: Laird, Raymond, Curtis M, Gerick. **Educ:** Univ of WI Madison WI, 1937-40; Medill Sch of Journalism NU, BSJ 1947, MSJ 1948. **Career:** Ebony Magazine, assoc editor 1946; self-employed, commercial photographer 1947; Chicago Defender, feature writer & adv mgr 1948-50; Chicago Daily News, 1st black news reporter 1950-52, 1953; Chain of Newspapers, Texas, Teacher, TX S U, mgr 1953; Chicago's Am, feature writer 1958-64; Radio Station WBEE, 1st news dir 1964; WLS-TV, 1st black TV reporter 1964; Urban Affairs, editor 1969; WLS-TV, 1st black TV exec 1972-75; Chicago Bd of Educ, media rel 1975-79; WSSD, mgr 1979-80; Chicago IL Fair Plan Assn, public relations advisor 1968-79; Columbia Coll, prof of journalism. **Orgs:** Jury All-Amer Cities 1975; founder Evanston Urban League 1961-63; vice chmn IL Commn on Human Relations 1962-74; vice chmn Governor's Insurance Advisory Bd 1974-76; pres Dewey Day Care Center 1975; bd of dir Evanston Mental Health Assn 1976; 1st Black pres, The Headline Club, Chicago Chapter, Society of Professional Journalists, Sigma Delta Chi. **Honors/Awds:** Man of Yr Lincoln Univ 1952; feature photographer Sigma Delta Chi 1947; Stick-o-Type Award Chicago Newspaper Guild 1952; Emmy Natl Acad TV Arts & Sci 1975; Outstanding Achievement Cook County Bd of Educ; Natl Alliance of Business 1974; Chicago Journalism Hall of Fame, 1993. **Military Serv:** US Army, USNG, lt col; Bronze Star; Legion of Merit; Croce di Guerra, 1945. **Home Addr:** 537 Judson Ave, Evanston, IL 60202-3085. **Business Addr:** Professor of Journalism, Columbia College, 600 S Michigan Ave, Chicago, IL 60605-1996.

BROWNLEE, VIVIAN APLIN
Business executive. **Personal:** Born Sep 17, 1946, Haines City, FL; daughter of Willie Mae Edge Aplin and John Alfred Aplin; married Dennis James Brownlee, Nov 29, 1975; children: Lauren Denise, Stephen James. **Educ:** OH Univ, BS 1968. **Career:** WEWS-TV, interviewer 1974-77; NY Times, Cleveland stringer; The Plain Dealer, suburban reporter, fed court reporter, gen assign reporter, spec reporting teams, subs suburban edit & assign edit, assoc edit, edit writer 1969-78; San Diego Union, asst city editor 1978-79; Dist Weekly/The Washington Post, editor 1979-81, natl staff 1982-86; Advance Inc, Arlington, VA, executive vice pres, 1986-. **Orgs:** Regional dir & exec bd mem Natl Assn of Black Journ; mem bd of adv Cleve Chap of Amer Arbit Assn, ESEA, Title IV-C Comm Proj Cleveland Bd of Educ; steward Amer Newspaper Guild. **Business Addr:** Executive Vice President, Media, Advance Inc, 2200 Wilson Blvd, Arlington, VA 22201.

BROWNLEE, WYATT CHINA
Referee. **Personal:** Born Mar 18, 1909, Hodges, SC; married Emma Roundtree (deceased); children: Wyatt Q. **Educ:** Fenn Coll, 1937-40; John Marshall Law Sch, LLB 1940-44; Cleveland Marshall Law Sch, doc of law conferred 1968. **Career:** Cleveland Eviction Ct, referee, Small Claims Ct, Traffic Ct 1977; private practice, probate, currently. **Orgs:** Mem Judicial Cncl of NBA; asst law dir Cleveland 1973-77; asst Atty & Gen OH 1964-70; past pres Gamma Alpha Sigma Chap of Phi Beta Sigma Frat Inc; 1st pres, orgnzr Jr br NAACP; past exalted ruler of King Tut Lodge #389; asst grand legal adv IBPOE of W; asst st legal adv; St Asn of Elks; advto reg SSS Local Bd #23. **Honors/Awds:** Mem various Bar Assns; outstsvc; legal prof & comm Cleveland Bar Assn; saluted by TA-WA-SI Schlrshp Clb; hon by Zeta Phi Beta Sor; inducted into the Hall of Fame, Natl Bar Assn, 1986. **Business Addr:** Attorney, 1276 W Third St, Ste 218, Cleveland, OH 44113.

BROWN-NASH, JOAHN WEAVER
Educator, businesswoman. **Personal:** Born Nov 27, 1935, Kansas City, KS; daughter of Edna Jones Weaver (deceased) and Theron Adveature Weaver (deceased); married Monroe Chester Nash, Feb 14, 1981; children: Leander III, Brandon, Dwayne, Monte. **Educ:** Fisk University, BA, 1957; Chicago State Uni-

versity, M Ed, 1964; University of Chicago, IL, attended; University of San Francisco, PhD. **Career:** Chicago Public Schools, master teacher, 1962, co-director, Summer Institutes, 1966-67; director, Demonstration Center for Gifted Children, 1966-68; consultant, In-Service Training, 1967-68; Eastern Illinois Development & Service Unit, title III training specialist, 1968-69; Chicago State University, Chicago, IL, instructor, 1969-71; Prescription Learning Corporation, director of research & staff development, 1972-75; Governor's State University, University Park, IL, professor, 1972, assistant dean, 1973-77; Educational Leadership Institute, Chicago, IL, 1976; Prescription Learning Corporation, Chicago, IL, executive vice-president, 1976-87; Jostens Learning Corporation, senior vice president, 1987-94; B & H Radio Communications, Inc, Harvey, IL, chmn of the bd, 1988, CEO, 1994. **Orgs:** The Links Inc, national chapter establishment officer, 1988-90, central area director, 1991-94, natl vp, 1994-; member, American Association of School Administrators; member, American Association of Supervisors & Curriculum Directors; member, Illinois Personnel and Guidance Association; member, National Alliance of Black School Educators; foundation trustee, National Association for the Education of Young Children; member, National Association of Gifted Children; member, Phi Delta Kappa Society; Delta Sigma Theta Sorority, delta leadership academy. **Honors/Awds:** Woodson-Delong Fund, outstanding educator, 1982; Recognition & Appreciation Awd-Academic Olympics, Chicago Public Schls 1982; Outstanding Educator, Chicago Alliance of Black School Educators 1983; Charles D Moody Distinguished Serv, Natl Alliance of Black School Educators 1984; Bethune-Tubman Truth Award, Black Women's Hall of Fame Foundation, Revlon 1989; Dare to Be Great Award, Illinois Women Administrators 1988; Educational Excellence Award, Ohio State House of Representatives 1989; Outstanding Achievement Award, Chicago Area Alliance of Black School Educators, 1989; Distinguished Community Service Award of the Decade, Alpha Kappa Alpha Sorority, 1990; Septima Clark Award for Excellence in Education, Southern Christian Leadership Conference, 1990; National Committee for School Desegregation, disguished service award, 1992; Black Colleges Committee, outstanding service award, 1992; National Council on Educating Black Children, outstanding leadership in education award, 1992; League of Black Women, Black Rose Award, 1994. **Home Addr:** 30 E Dells Way, Harvey, IL 60426.

BROWNRIDGE, J. PAUL

Government official. **Personal:** Born Jun 10, 1945, Macon, MS; son of Arna M Moore Brownridge and James Brownridge; married (Dr) Rose M; children: 4. **Educ:** Jackson State Univ, Jackson MS, 1966-68; Univ of Akron, BS 1970, JD 1974; Indiana Univ, master's degree 1980; Harvard Univ, senior executives program 1987. **Career:** Goodyear Tire & Rubber Co, accountant 1971-73; Container Corp of Amer, tax attorney 1973-78; Clark Equip Co, tax attorney 1978-80; Phillips Petroleum, sr tax attorney 1980-82; Ideal Basic Industries, tax counsel 1982-84; City & County of Denver, deputy mgr of revenue 1984-86; City of Grand Rapids, treasurer 1986-88; City of Chicago, dir of revenue 1988-. **Orgs:** Bd mem Junior Achievement 1978-80; commissioner Denver's Commn on Aging 1984-86; chmn Denver's Tuition Reimbursement Prog 1984-86; mentor Colorado Alliance of Business 1985-86; chmn, Central Support Sub-cabinet mem, Executive Comm & Financial Policy Comm, City of Chicago. **Honors/Awds:** Proclamation recipient for Outstanding Service Mayor of Denver 1986; Leadership Certificate US Postal Service 1987; elected to the Executive Bd of Government Finance Officers Assn of United States & Canada. **Military Serv:** AUS sp4 3 yrs; various commendation medals Vietnam Vet 1963-66. **Business Addr:** Director of Revenue, City of Chicago, 121 N LaSalle, Room 107, Chicago, IL 60602.

BROWN-WRIGHT, MARJORIE

Educator, home economist, social worker. **Personal:** Born Jan 1, 1935, Little Rock, AR. **Educ:** DePaul U, PHB 1956; Univ Il, MSW 1961; Tulane U, Advanced Stud Cert 1970; Or St U, PHD 1976. **Career:** St Elizabeth High School Chicago, 1956-57; Univ of Chicago, proj sec, 1957-58; IL Div Child Welfare Servs, child welfare worker, 1958-60; Champaign IL Public Schools, school & social worker, 1960-61; Lawndale Neighborhood Services Chicago, social group worker, 1962-63; Cook County Dept of Public Welfare, various social work, 1958-66; Univ OK, asst prof Social Work, 1966-70; Community Serv Univ of OR, asst prof, 1970-77; Community Devel & Human Rel Serv Consult Mass Media & Minority Group Rel Conf Tulsa US Dept Justice, presently consultant, 1970; Tulsa Model Cities Prog, social planning team committeewoman, 1968-71. **Orgs:** Nat bd mem & western reg campus coord Sigma Gamma Rho 1974-76; asso ed aurora mag Sigma Gamma Rho 1967-76; pres Lane Dist Nat & Assn Social Wrkrs 1971-72; governor's appointee state chairperson OR Community Coorinated Child Care Council 1974-77; pres Lane Co OR Child Care Council 1973-74; bd mem UN Assn Tulsa 1970-71. **Honors/Awds:** OR Social Wrkr of Yr 1973; Outstanding Young Women in Am 1965; grad study scholarship awards Cook Co Il 1959-61; cen reg scholarship awardee Sigma Gamma Rho 1955; citation mayor Tulsa Contrib Model Cities Prgm 1970; Hall of Fame Educ Award Sigma Gamma Rho 1974; outstanding Human Serv Profs Am 1974; Vol Serv Awd OR Community Coord Child Care Counc 1975. **Business Addr:** 20 Brae Burn Dr, Eugene, OR 97405.

BRUCE, ANTOINETTE JOHNSON

Educator, association administrator. **Personal:** Born Sep 20, 1917, Roanoke, VA; daughter of Louise Willis Johnson and Samuel Johnson; married James Bruce, Apr 10, 1948 (deceased); children: Mercedes L James. **Educ:** Virginia State College, BS, 1939; University of Virginia, MS, 1973. **Career:** Roanoke Teachers Association, treasurer; Literacy Volunteers of America, teacher. **Orgs:** Church Women United, president, 1988-90; General Missionary Society, president, 1980-90; National Organization Pinochle Bugs Social & Civic Club, past executive secretary, 1955-59; Pinochle Bugs, Inc, Roanoke Chapter, 1980-85; President's Council, Roanoke Valley, treasurer, 1985-. **Honors/Awds:** High St Baptist Church, Woman of the Year, 1985. **Special Achievements:** One of the founders of the National Organization of Pinochle Bugs Social and Civic Club, Inc, first black national society club in SW Virginia. **Home Addr:** 1320 Eighth St NW, Roanoke, VA 24016, (703)344-0242.

BRUCE, AUNDRAY

Professional football player. **Personal:** Born Apr 30, 1966, Montgomery, AL. **Educ:** Auburn. **Career:** Atlanta Falcons, defensive end, 1988-91; Los Angeles Raiders, 1992-94; Oakland Raiders, 1995-. **Business Addr:** Professional Football Player, Oakland Raiders, 1220 Harbor Bay Pkwy, Alameda, CA 94502, (510)615-1875.

BRUCE, CAROL PITT

Federal government employee. **Personal:** Born Dec 25, 1941, Elkton, MD; daughter of Elizabeth J Sawyer and Ralph A Pitt; married Don Franklin; children: Donna E Bowie, Keith, Kirk. **Educ:** Morgan State Univ, BA 1964, MBA 1979. **Career:** Hartford Co Dept Social Svcs, asst dir income maint 1975-77; US Army 8th Inf Div ADAPCP, clinical supv 1977-79; US Army Civilian Personnel Ofc Ft Polk, personnel staffing spec 1981-84; US Army Civilian Personnel Ft Geo G Meade, chief tech serv 1984-85; Chemical Rsch Engrg & Dev Ctr Aberdeen Proving Ground, chief alcohol drug control/ea office 1985-. **Orgs:** Mem Exec Bd Baltimore Urban League 1976-79; me Natl Assoc Female Execs; mem Harford County Alumnae Chapter, Delta Sigma Theta Inc 1988-; Youth Program Dir, St. James AME Church 1987-. **Home Addr:** 525 Oak St, Aberdeen, MD 21001. **Business Addr:** Chief Alcohol Drug Control Ofc, Chem Rsch Engrg & Dev Ctr, Aberdeen Proving Ground, Aberdeen, MD 21001.

BRUCE, ISAAC ISIDORE

Professional football player. **Personal:** Born Nov 10, 1972, Fort Lauderdale, FL. **Educ:** Memphis. **Career:** St Louis Rams, wide receiver, 1995-. **Business Addr:** Professional Football Player, St Louis Rams, One Rams Way, St Louis, MO 63045, (314)982-7267.

BRUCE, JAMES C.

Educator. **Personal:** Born Jul 15, 1929, Washington, DC; divorced; children: James C, Jr, Jason W. **Educ:** Howard U, AB 1952, MA 1968; Univ Of Chicago, PhD 1963. **Career:** SC State Coll, German instructor, 1956-57; Univ of Chicago, German instructor, 1961-64, asst prof of German, 1964-69, assoc prof German, 1969-89, assoc prof emeritus, 1989-; Soka Univ, Japan, prof of English, 1989-. **Orgs:** Mem Mod Lang Assn Of Am; sec Am Assn of Tchrs of German 1974; Midwest Mod Lang Assn; Literarische Gesellschaft Chicago; mem IL Commn Human Rel 1971-73. **Honors/Awds:** Fulbright Fellowship Univ of Frankfurt am Main, Germany 1960-61; Inland Steel Fac Fellowship Univ of Chicago 1965. **Military Serv:** US Army, sp5, 1953-55. **Business Addr:** Faculty of Letters, Soka University, Dept of English Literature, 1-236 Tangi-cho Hachioji, Tokyo 192, Japan.

BRUCE, KENNETH E.

Attorney. **Personal:** Born Jul 20, 1921, New York, NY; son of Matthew and Eulalie Bruce; married Rosalia Maria Bruce; children: Vassallo Bruce. **Educ:** CCNY, BA 1945; Columbia Law School, 1946; Fordham Law School, LLD 1950. **Career:** Human Resources Admin of NYC, legal and resource consultant, 1950-82; State of NY, Bureau of Immigration Appeals, state certificate, certified social worker 1950; solo practitioner, atty at law, currently. **Orgs:** 18B Panel, criminal defesnse attorney; Lawyers Trail Assn; Amer Bar Assn; Westchester Bar; Natl Bar Assn; Bronx Bar; Black Lawyers of Westchester; Natl Bar of Black Lawyers; former senior arbitrator of Amer Arbitration Assn. **Honors/Awds:** Physical Handicapped Man of The Yr Awarded by Bronx Women of Bronx Commnty 1982. **Special Achievements:** Admitted to practice: in New York state; Washington, DC, 1951; before the Bureau of Immigration Appeals, 1952; Southern and Eastern Districts of the US Federal Court, 2nd Circuit, 1958; before the Supreme Court, United States of America, 1958. **Military Serv:** USNG 1938. **Business Addr:** Attorney, Solo Practitioner, 44 Livingston Rd, Scarsdale, NY 10583, (914)723-1576.

BRUCE, PRESTON, JR.

Government official. **Personal:** Born Sep 10, 1936, Washington, DC; married Kellene Margot Underdown; children: Preston III, Kellene Elaine. **Educ:** Lyndon State Coll, BS 1958; Univ of Massachusetts, EdD 1972. **Career:** Readsboro School, principal 1959-63; Office of Econ Opp admin asst dir 1964-67; Head Start, dir exec asst 1968-69; Office of Child Devel, dir 4-c prog 1969-71; Univ of MA, asst to chancellor 1971-74; Office of Child Devel, dir daycare 1974-83; ACYF-DHHS, dir NCCAN 1983-84; USDHEW/ACYF-CB dep dir Office of Families. **Orgs:** Mem Lion's Club 1958-63; mem Jaycees 1969-71; mem, vestry mem St Mark's Church 1971-74; board of dir Day Care Council of Amer 1975-83; board of dir Capitol Ballet Guild 1978-80; board of dir District of Columbia O/C 1978-82; chmn Howard Univ School of S/W Vstg Comm 1979-. **Honors/Awds:** Professional baseball pitcher Pittsburgh Pirates 1958; horace mann lecturer Univ of MA 1971-72; disting alumnus Lyndon State Coll 1973; Athlete's Hall of Fame Lyndon State Coll 1985. **Home Addr:** 10341 Maypole Way, Columbia, MD 21044.

BRUIN, JOHN. **See BRUTUS, DENNIS VINCENT.**

BRUMMER, CHAUNCEY EUGENE

Attorney. **Personal:** Born Nov 22, 1948, Louisville, KY; married Isabelle J Carpenter; children: Christopher, Craig. **Educ:** Howard U, BA; Univ of KY, JD. **Career:** Louisville & Nashville RR Co, atty; Louisville Legal Aid, comm educ dir 1973-74; Reginald Heber Smith Fellow, Louisville Legal Aid Society. **Orgs:** Mem KY Bar Assn; Louisville Bar Assn; Nat Bar Assn Explorer advr; Law Explorer Post -#922 1974-; pres Shawnee HS Alumni Assn; mem Alpha Phi Omega. **Honors/Awds:** Nat Serv Frat Pres Award 1976; The Big E Award 1976; Outst Alumnus Award, Shawnee HS 1975. **Military Serv:** AUSR 1970-76. **Business Addr:** 908 W Broadway, Louisville, KY 40203.

BRUNDIDGE, NANCY CORINNE

Educational administrator (retired). **Personal:** Born Sep 27, 1920, Louisville, MS; daughter of Roberta May Thompson (deceased) and Elijah Thompson (deceased); married Roy Lee Brundidge (died 1987); children: Carlita J Nickson, Adrienne E Brundidge. **Educ:** IN Univ Gary IN, AA Soc & Ed 1956; Roosevelt Univ Chicago IL, BA Sociology & Psychology 1960, MA Urban Sociology 1973; Drug Ed Training Resource Ctr Cert 1974; Northwest IN Reg Addiction Authority, Cert 1974. **Career:** Cook Cty Dept Public Aid, suprv 1, caseworker 1,2 1960-69; Gary School Corp, school social worker 1970-71; IN State Employment, work incentive spec 1971-73; Hammond Public Schools, social worker & legal attendance 1973-86; Hammond School City, cert drug cons, social worker/suprv 1974-86; retired. **Orgs:** Mem Calvary Baptist Church 1938-; fin sec Amer West Indian Assoc Inc 1969-; mem Hammond Public Schools 1973-; legislative comm Northwest IN Council of Social Workers & Attendance Officers 1975-; coord Christmas cheer Salvation Army 1976-; past bd chairperson, exec bd mem Bethany Child Care & Devel Ctr 1976-; annual sci fair judge Purdue Univ Reg Sci Fair 1977-; reporter, mem Univ Women Calumet Area Branch 1978-; coord Thanksgiving baskets Lake Cty Econ Opport Council 1979-; assoc mem Bethel Temple Church 1981-; prog comm Adv Bd of Salvation Army 1982-; co-sponsor class 1986 Hammond HS 1982-86; mem, Lake County Coordinating Alliance for Drug Abuse; volunteer social work, drug consultant serving churches, community organizations, civic org & clubs, families. **Honors/Awds:** Bd of Governors Roosevelt Univ Chicago IL 1958-60; Cert of Achievement Lake Area United Way 1980; Guest Lecturer & Resource Person IN Univ Gary Ctr 1980-81; Baptist Woman of the Month Natl Baptist Voice 1981; Cert of Achievement Voluntary Action Ctr 1981; Nom for Florence O Alexander Ed Awd 1981; Cert of Recognition Bethany Child Care Ctr 1982; Dedication to mankind Salvation Army 1982; Cert of Merit IN Dept of Public Instr 1983; Outstanding Serv to Ed School City of Hammond 1983; IN Social worker of the Year State of IN 1984; Candidate Midwest Reg Social Worker for 1985 Award 1984. **Home Addr:** 137 Porter St, Gary, IN 46406.

BRUNER, VAN B., JR.

Architect, educational administrator. **Personal:** Born May 22, 1931, Washington, DC; married Lillian E Almond; children: Scott V. **Educ:** Univ of MI, BS 1954; Drexel Evening Coll, BS 1965. **Career:** Spring Garden Coll Dept of Architecture, dept chmn 1965-72, 1979-81; Natl Org of Minority Architects, charter mem 1972-; Amer Inst of Architecture, former natl vice pres 1972-74; private practice, architect 1968-. **Orgs:** Former mem NJ Hotel & Multiple Dwelling Health & Safety Bd 1971-; elder Philadelphia Evangelistic Ctr; field rep Full Gospel Businessmens Fellowship Intl. **Honors/Awds:** Hall of Fame (track) Woodbury HS NJ; Whitney Young Awd The Amer Inst of Arch 1975; Fellow (FAIA) The Amer Inst of Arch 1979. **Military Serv:** USAF capt 3 yrs. **Business Addr:** Architect, 506 W Park Blvd, Haddonfield, NJ 08033.

BRUNSON, DAVID

Educator, sports official. **Personal:** Born Aug 22, 1929, Ridgeway, SC; son of Rose Belton Peete and Avan Brunson. **Educ:** University of District of Columbia, AS (high honors), public administration, corrections, 1976, BA, social rehab welfare, gerontology, 1978, MA, adult ed, gerontology, 1980. **Career:** Metropolitan Police Department, Washington, DC, patrolman officer, 1962-89. **Orgs:** MW Prince Hall Grand Lodge

DC, Inc, mw grand master, 1989-90; Association of Retired Policeman, DC, Inc; American Association of Adult & Continuing Education; International Senior Citizens Association; United States of America Track and Field (USATF), Potomac Valley Association, certified official track & field; American Association of Retired Persons; Association for Retarded Citizens DC, Inc; University of DC Alumni Association, life membership; University of DC Institute of Gerontology; National Caucus/Center for Black Aged. **Honors/Awds:** University of DC, Natl Deans List, 1976-78; NAACP, Golden Heritage, Life member, 1989-; AEAONMS Inc (Shriners), Honorary Past Potentate, 1980, Honorary Past Imperial Potentate, 1989; AASR, SJ USA, Grand Inspector General 33rd Degree United Supreme Council, 1989. **Military Serv:** US Army, E4, 1958-64; Expert Rifleman, Parachutist School 1959; Parartrooper, 101st Airborne Div, 187th Infantry.

BRUNSON, DEBORA BRADLEY
Educator. **Personal:** Born Apr 15, 1952, Orangeburg, SC; daughter of Blanche Williams Bradley and Louis Bradley; married John Edward Brunson II, Dec 18, 1971 (divorced 1987); children: Courtenay De'Von, Jon Emerson. **Educ:** South Carolina State College, Orangeburg, SC, BS, 1973, MEd, 1974, EdD, 1990. **Career:** Orangeburg City Schools, Orangeburg, SC, teacher, 1973-82, counselor, 1982-86, principal apprentice, 1986-87, counselor, 1987-; principal, currently. **Orgs:** Member, SC Assn for Counseling/Development, 1982-; member, NAACP, 1980-; deputy registrar, Orangeburg County, secretary, Orangeburg County Tourism Advisory Board, 1986-; member, Delta Sigma Theta Sorority, Inc, 1971-; member, SC Education Assn, National Ed Assn, 1973-; Phi Delta Kappa, Board of Higher Education and Campus Ministry, United Methodist Church, Vice president. Association of Supervision and Curriculum Development; SC Association of School Administrators. **Home Addr:** PO Box 1986, Orangeburg, SC 29116.

BRUNSON, DOROTHY EDWARDS
Business executive. **Personal:** Born Mar 13, 1938, Glennsville, GA; children: Edward Ross, Daniel James. **Educ:** State University of New York, BS. **Career:** Sonderling Broadcasting Corp, general mgr, 1963-73; WWRL, New York, asst general mgr, 1969; Inner City Broadcasting Corp, vice pres, general mgr, 1973-79; WEBB Radio Baltimore, owner, 1979-; Brunson Communications Inc, president, CEO, currently. **Orgs:** Former board member: Institute for Mediation & Conflict Resolution, First Women's Bank, United Way of New York, BEDCO, United Way of Central Maryland, John Hopkins Metro Center, Kennedy Institute for Handicapped Children, Greater Baltimore Committee, Foundation for Minorities in Media; part of founding board, Legal Mutual Liability Insurance Society of Maryland Inc, 1988-89; advisory board, Enterprise Foundation, 1992-; Maryland Small Business Finance Development Authority, 1988-; Maryland Venture Trust, 1990-. **Honors/Awds:** Business Woman of the Year, Business & Professional Women's Club of Baltimore; National Convention Distinguished Service Award, Blacks in Government, 1988; Small Business Media Advocate of the Year, United States Small Business Administration, 1988; Wilmington North Carolina Sickle Cell Association Award, 1987; Lifetime Membership Recognition Award, NAACP, 1989; Women Hall of Fame Award, Baltimore City Commission, 1989; American Women Entrepreneur Development Recognition, 1988-90; numerous other awards. **Special Achievements:** First African-American female to co-own an advertising agency on Madison Ave, New York City. **Business Addr:** President, CEO, Brunson Communications, Inc, 3000 Druid Park Dr, Baltimore, MD 21215.

BRUNSON, FRANK
Electrical engineer. **Personal:** Born Jan 20, 1957, Cincinnati, OH; son of Arthur Lee Brunson and Robert Stokes; married Melony E White Brunson, Aug 24, 1985; children: Chanel D'Lynne, Frank Aaron, Jordan Tyler. **Educ:** Otterbein College, 1975-76; University of Dayton, BSEE, 1980. **Career:** Columbus Southern Power Co, electrical engineer, 1980-83, distribution engineer, 1983-87, sr distribution engineer, 1987-91, sr electrical engineer, 1991-. **Orgs:** NSBE, 1981-; NSPE, 1982-; YMCA, Black Achievers Program, Steering Committee, 1992-. **Home Addr:** 3954 Sleaford Ave, Gahanna, OH 43230, (614)475-1029. **Business Addr:** Senior Electrical Engineer, Columbus Southern Power Co, 215 N Front St, Columbus, OH 43230, (614)464-7240.

BRUNT, SAMUEL JAY
Financial administrator. **Personal:** Born Jan 14, 1961, Baltimore, MD. **Educ:** Howard Univ, BA 1979-83; Univ of Baltimore, MPA 1983-. **Career:** Comm Coll of Baltimore, admin asst, instr 1983-84; Balitmore Fed Financial, new accounts, investment clerk 1984-85; MD State Legislature, fiscal rschr 1984 interim & 1985 leg session. **Orgs:** Mem Natl Forum for Black Public Admin 1984-; advisor Youth Ministry Trinity Baptist Church 1984-; supt Trinity Baptist Church School 1985. **Honors/Awds:** HUD Fellow-Baltimore Reg Plnng Council 1983-; Contestant 1983 Natl Pi Alpha Alpha Manuscript competition for Public Admin Literature; Delegate 4th Natl Model OAU at Howard Univ 1983; Recommended for profile in new natl publ Black Profiles. **Business Addr:** ATTN: Lu Ann, University of Baltimore Alumni, 1304 St Paul St, Baltimore, MD 21202.

BRUTON, BERTRAM A.
Architect. **Personal:** Born May 18, 1931, Jacksonville, FL; son of Lula C Bruton and George W Bruton; married Dorothy Garcia; children: Michelle Yvette, Sabra Lee. **Educ:** Howard Univ, BArch 1953. **Career:** Paul Rader AIA, job capt 1956-58; James H Johnson AIA, job capt 1958-59; Donald R Roark Denver, assoc arch 1959-61; Bertram A Bruton & Assoc, arch 1961-. **Orgs:** Mem AIA, NCARB, Natl Organ of Black Arch; Mitchell Sixty-Six Asso Devel; dir Salvation Army; dir Community Credit Union; mem CO State Bd of Examiners of Architects; mem Kappa Alpha Psi; mem Sigma Pi Phi. **Honors/Awds:** Awd of Merit AIA; Achievement Awd Kappa Alpha Psi; Denver Man of Yr 1974 and 1984; Barney Ford Awd. **Military Serv:** USAF 1st lt 1953-56. **Business Addr:** Architect (Principal), Bertram A Bruton & Associates, Architects, 2001 York St, Denver, CO 80205, (303)358-4314.

BRUTUS, DENNIS VINCENT (JOHN BRUIN)
University educator. **Personal:** Born Nov 28, 1924, Harare, Zimbabwe; son of May Jaggers Brutus and Francis Henry Brutus; married Margaret Winifred Bloemetjie, May 14, 1950; children: Jacinta, Marc, Julian, Antony, Justina, Cornelia, Gregory, Paula. **Educ:** Fort Hare Univ, South Africa, BA 1947; Witwatersrand Univ, Johannesburg, South Africa, 1962-63. **Career:** Univ of Denver, Denver CO, visiting prof of English, 1970; Northwestern Univ, Evanston IL, prof of English, 1971-85; Univ of Texas, Austin TX, visiting prof of English, African & African-Amer studies research, 1974-75; Amherst Coll, Amherst MA, visiting prof of English 1982-83; Dartmouth Coll, Hanover NH, visiting prof of African & African Amer studies 1983; Swarthmore Coll, Swarthmore PA, Cornell chair, 1985-86; Univ of Pittsburgh, Pittsburgh PA, prof of African literature & chmn dept of black community educ research & devel, 1986-; University of Colorado, English Department, Distinguished Visiting Humanist, currently. **Orgs:** Pres, South African Non-Racial Olympic Comm (San Roc), 1963-; founding mem, Troubadour Press, 1970-; vice pres, Union of Writers of the African Peoples, 1974-75; founding chair, African Literature Assn, 1975-; mem, Intl Jury Books Abroad Award, 1976; chmn, Africa Network, 1984-; advisory bd mem, African Arts Fund, 1985-; bd mem, Nicaragua Cultural Alliance, 1987-; advisory bd mem, Amer Poetry Center, 1988-; mem, Advisory Comm, Natl Coalition to Abolish the Death Penalty, 1989; coordinator, Union of Writers of the African Peoples, 1986-; program dir, Program on African Writers in Africa and the Diaspora, 1988-. **Honors/Awds:** Mbari Prize for Poetry in Africa, Mbari Press, 1963; Sirens, Knuckles, Boots, 1963; Thoughts Abroad, John Bruin (pseudonym), TX, 1970; A Simple Lust, 1972; Stubborn Hope, 1978; Doctor of Humane Letters, Worcester State Coll, Worcester MA, 1985; Doctor of Humane Letters, Univ of Massacussets, Amherst, MA, 1985; Langston Hughes Medallion, City Univ of New York, 1986; Paul Robeson Award for Artistic Excellence, Political Consciousness and Integrity, 1989; Airs & Tributes, 1989; Doctor of Laws, Northeastern Univ, Boston, MA, 1990. **Home Addr:** 2132 Bluebell Ave, Boulder, CO 80302. **Business Addr:** Distinguished Visiting Humanist, English Dept, Campus Box 226, University of Colorado, Boulder, CO 80309-0339.

BRYAN, ADELBERT M.
Government official, police officer (retired). **Personal:** Born Aug 21, 1943, Frederiksted, Virgin Islands of the United States; son of Wilmot E Bryan and Anesta Samuel Bryan; married Jerilyn CO Ovesen; children: Lecia, Adelbert (deceased), Scheniqua, Lori, Andrea, Lyrhea, Mia. **Educ:** College of VI, AA Police Sci & Admin 1975; FBI Acad, grad 1978; BS, 1988. **Career:** St Croix Police Dept, police officer, 1966-72, sergeant, 1972-74, captain, 1977-86; US Virgin Islands, senator, 1982-. **Orgs:** Chmn Econ Develop & Affairs Comm 15th Legislature; chmn Educ Comm 16th Legislature; mem Olympic Shooting Team; delegate to 3rd & 4th Constitutional Conventions. **Honors/Awds:** Medal of Honor Natl Police Awd; Policeman of the Year; 1st degree Karate Black Belt. **Military Serv:** US Army, 1961-63. **Home Addr:** PO Box D, Christiansted, St Croix, Virgin Islands of the United States 00820.

BRYAN, CURTIS
College president. **Personal:** son Of Betty L Bryan and Rev Alfred H Bryan. **Educ:** Elizabeth City State Univ, BS, 1960; Temple Univ, MEd, 1968; New York Univ, PhD (summa cum laude), 1977. **Career:** Delaware State Coll, assistant academy dean; Fayetteville State Univ, head div of ed and human dev; director of teacher education; Virginia State Univ, executive vp; vp for admin, interim president; Denmark Technical Coll, president, 1986-. **Orgs:** Mem Assoc of the United States Army, Natl Assoc for Higher Educ; AACJC commission on Small Colleges; Bamberg County Economic Development Commission. **Honors/Awds:** New York Univ Educ Fellow; mem Kappa Delta Pi Honor Soc, Phi Delta Kappa, Sigma Rho Sigma; publications ''Quality Control in Higher Education,'' 1973, ''Faculty Personnel, Perspectives on the Academic Freedom,'' 1976. **Business Addr:** President, Denmark Technical College, PO Box 327, Denmark, SC 29042.

BRYAN, DAVID EVERETT, JR.
Attorney. **Personal:** Born Sep 30, 1947, New York, NY; married Jacqueline Alice Weaver. **Educ:** St Johns Univ, BBA, 1965-70; St Johns Univ, School of Law, JD, 1972-75. **Career:** New York City Metro Council, NAACP, exec sec, 1978; US Securities & Exchange Commn, trial atty, 1975-77; SE Queens Comm Corp, asst exec dir, 1971-72; Westvaco Corp, admin asst, 1970-71. **Orgs:** mem, past pres, Kappa Alpha Psi, 1966; mem, past pres, Jamaica Branch, NAACP 1970; pres, Jamaica Branch, NAACP Employment Devel Program, 1975-76; mem, Macon B Allen Black Bar Assn, 1975; bd of dir, Carter Community Health Centre, 1978. **Honors/Awds:** Martin Luther King Jr Scholarship, St John's Univ School of Law, 1972; Thurgood Marshall Award, NY State Trial Lawyers Assn, 1975; Merit Award, St Albans Chamber of Commerce, 1978; Professional Award, Natl Assn of Negro Business & Professional Women's Clubs, Laureltono Club, 1979; Black & Puerto Rican, Caucus, NY State Legislature, Outstanding Achievement Award, 1981; Jamaica Branch, NAACP, Freedom Fund Award, 1983. **Home Addr:** 114-80 179 Street, Jamaica, NY 11434.

BRYAN, FLIZE A.
Physician. **Personal:** daugHter of Mr and Mrs H Bryan; children: Sylvia. **Educ:** Univ of W Indies, Nursing 1956; Tuskegee Inst, BSC 1967; Pomona Coll, Diploma 1968; Howard Univ Med Sch, MD 1972. **Career:** Hlth Dept, nurse 1956-58; Beth Israel Hosp NYC, nurse 1958-60; Pvt Duty, RN 1960-66; Sydenham Hosp NY, surgeon 1977-; Met Hosp NY Med Coll, clinical instr surg 1979-; Sydenham & Hosp NY, dir emerg room 1980-; SNFCC Harlem Hosp, surgeon 1980-; Brooklyn Hospital, staff. **Orgs:** Mem Comm Bd New York City 1984-; delegate Doctors Cncl Union 1980-; mem Susan McKinley Assn 1983; Episcopal Women St Marks Church. **Business Addr:** Surgeon, Sydenham NFCC, 215 W 125th St, New York, NY 10027.

BRYAN, JESSE A.
Educational administrator, educator (retired). **Personal:** Born Jun 15, 1939, Red Springs, NC; son of Laney Osaka Smith Bryan Ward (deceased) and Felix F Bryan (deceased); married Virgie D Daniels Bryan, Sep 26, 1964; children: Tami, Jason. **Educ:** Johnson C Smith Univ, Undergrad Degree 1964; Univ of GA, Grad Studies 1964; Temple Univ, MEd 1968; Univ of Toledo, PhD 1977. **Career:** Admissions Glassboro State Coll, numerous positions & assoc dir 1969-70; Student Field Experience Office Univ of Toledo, admin asst 1970-71; Univ of Toledo, dir upward bound 1971-73; Bloomsburg Univ, dir center for acad devel 1973-87, dir, Dept of Dev Instr, beginning 1987, retired. **Orgs:** Mem Kappa Alpha Psi Fraternity 1961-; mem Phi Delta Kappa 1972-; dir Act 101 Program 1973-; mem Act 101 Exec Comm 1973-83; Black Conf on Higher Educ 1973-; mem Western Reg of Act 101 1978-; mem Kiwanis Intl 1979-; pres Equal Educ Oppor Program 1980-. **Honors/Awds:** Special Recognition Ed Opportunity Ctr, Ctr for Acad Devel; Two Advisory Awards Third World Cultural Soc; Advisory Award Kappa Alpha Psi Lambda Alpha; Vol Leader Awd Young Men's Christian Assoc; special award from former students. **Military Serv:** USN fire control tech 1956-60. **Home Addr:** 375 Hillside Drive, Wonderview, Bloomsburg, PA 17815. **Business Addr:** Professor Emeritus, Department of Developmental Instruction, Bloomsburg University, Waller Administration Bldg Room #14, Bloomsburg, PA 17815.

BRYANT, ANDREA PAIR
Attorney. **Personal:** Born Jul 19, 1942, Baltimore, MD; daughter of Mamie Savoy Pair (deceased) and James M Pair, MD (deceased); married Melvin W Bryant, Oct 19, 1968; children: James Burnett West, Michael David. **Educ:** Morgan State, BS Physics (high honor) 1965; Fulbright Fellowship Karlsruhe Germany 1965-66; Georgetown Univ Law Center, JD 1978. **Career:** IBM Corp, programmer 1967-73, programmer/instructor 1973-74, patent atty in training 1974-78, patent atty 1978-92; TX Resource Conservation Comm, deputy off of public interest counsel, 1993-96; Attorney, private practice, 1996-. **Orgs:** Sec Natl Bar Assn Bd 1988-; bd Legal Aid Soc of Central TX 1985-; Austin Black Lawyers Assn; bd mem Paramount Theatre for the Performing Arts 1989-; Travis County Bar Assn, bd, 1994-; Austin Symphony Orchestra, bd, 1993-; Amer Bar Assn, State Bar of Texas; The Links Inc, Western Area Intl Trends & Services, chair, 1993-95, Round Rock Chap, pres, 1994-96; Natl Consortium for African Amer Children; NAACP, life mem; Delta Sigma Theta Sorority, golden life mem. **Honors/Awds:** Leadership Austin Class 1983-84; Leadership Texas, 1991; Leadership America, 1996; Austin Arts Commission, 1997-98; Outstanding Achievement, Travis City, Women Lawyers Assn, 1997. **Home Addr:** 5202 Vista West Cove, Austin, TX 78731.

BRYANT, ANDREW DANIEL
Architect. **Personal:** Born Dec 27, 1929, Washington, DC; son of Ellen Jones Bryant and Andrew D Bryant; married Elsie Weaver, Sep 18, 1961; children: Andrew D. **Educ:** Howard University, BAr, 1953. **Career:** Bryant Associates, PC, president, owner, currently. **Orgs:** America Institute of Architect, past director; National Association of Minority Architects; DC Chamber of Commerce, past president, 1989-90; DC Architectural Registration Board, past president, 1976. **Honors/Awds:** Howard University, Tuition Scholarship, 1949-52. **Special Achievements:** Architectural Design Awards; The Gettysburg Elderly Bldg, Washington DC, DC Housing Industry; Singapore Embassy, Metropolitan Home Builders Association; Addi-

son Plaza Shopping Center, Cornerstone Award, Maryland Building Association. **Military Serv:** US Air Force, 1st Lt, 1953-55; Good Conduct Metal. **Business Addr:** President and Owner, Bryant Associates PC, 1420 N St NW, 100 Towne Terrace E, Washington, DC 20005, (202)232-5192.

BRYANT, ANTHONY
Electrical engineer. **Personal:** Born Aug 27, 1963, San Francisco, CA; son of Mary A Newt Bryant and Soloman Bryant Jr. **Educ:** San Diego State University, San Diego, CA, BSEE, 1987. **Career:** Navy Public Works Center, San Diego, CA, electrical engineer, 1984-87; Motorola GEG, Inc, Phoenix, AZ, electrical engineer, 1987-89; Pacific Gas & Electric, San Francisco, CA, electrical engineer, 1989-93; San Francisco Energy Company, AES Corp, San Francisco CA, electrical engineer, 1994-. **Orgs:** Administrative director, National Society of Black Engineers, region IV alumni 1991-; Arizona Council of Black Engineers & Scientist, programs director, 1991-93, member 1987-89; member, San Diego Council of Black Engineers & Scientist, 1985-87; vice pres 1985-86, treasurer 1984-85, member 1983, San Diego State University National Society of Black Engineers. **Honors/Awds:** NACME Scholarship, NACME, 1986-84; Service Recognition, San Diego State NSBE, 1989. **Business Addr:** Business Manager, San Francisco Energy Co., 44 Montgomery St, Ste 3450, San Francisco, CA 94124.

BRYANT, ANXIOUS E.
Educator, broker. **Personal:** Born Jan 18, 1938, Nashville, TN; married Christie Tanner; children: Karen, Karl. **Educ:** State University Nashville, BS, 1959; Memphis State University, MS, 1970. **Career:** Memphis One Inc Realtors, affiliate broker, 1980-; State Tech Inst Memphis, associate professor, 1979-; Thompson & Miller Architects, architectural technician, 1978-79; Gassner Nathan Partners, architectural technician, 1977; Jones & Thompson Architects, architectural technician, 1973; Carver High School, teacher, 1959-70; Rust College, part-time lecturer, 1980-. **Orgs:** Chairman of examination board, Shelby Co Plumbing Dept, 1977-. **Business Addr:** Professor, Dept of Engineering Technology, State Tech Institute Memphis, 5983 Macon Cove, Memphis, TN 38134-7642.

BRYANT, BUNYAN I.
Educator. **Personal:** Born Mar 6, 1935, Little Rock, AR; son of Christalee Bryant; married Jean Carlberg, Jan 16, 1993. **Educ:** Eastern MI Univ, BS, 1958; Univ of MI, Social Work, MSW, 1965; Univ of MI, Education, PhD, 1970. **Career:** Univ of MI, School of Natural Resources & Environment, prof. **Orgs:** League of Conservation, bd mem; USEPA Clean Air Act, advisory comm. **Honors/Awds:** MLK Dreamkeeper Award, Distinguished Leadership to the Environmental Justice Movement Award; Environmental Justice Advisory Council, Recognition Award. **Special Achievements:** Author/editor, Environmental Justice: Issues, Policies & Solutions, 1995; Race & the Indicence of Environmental Hazards, Westview Press, Baulder, 1992. **Military Serv:** National Guard, specialist, 1960-66.

BRYANT, CARL
Company executive. **Educ:** Univ of MD-College Park, PhD, counseling and student development. **Career:** Center for Creative Leadership, vp of technology, 1998-. **Special Achievements:** First African American vice pres of technology at Center for Creative Leadership. **Business Addr:** Vice President of Technology, Center For Creative Leadership, 1 Leadership Place, Greensboro, NC 27438, (910)545-3740.

BRYANT, CASTELL VAUGHN
Educational administrator. **Personal:** Born in Jasper, FL; daughter of Bessie Mae Vaughn and Joseph Vaughn; married Leonard Bryant Jr; children: Kathi Merdenia, Craig Leonard. **Educ:** Fl A&M U, BS; Fl A&M U, MS; Nova U, EdD. **Career:** Miami-Dade Community Coll, dean of student services, 1978-, assoc dean of acad support, coordinator of curriculum/Job Placement STP Grant 1974-78; Dade County Public School System, teacher; FL A & M Univ, 1964-74. **Orgs:** Council on Black Am Affairs; Family Christian Assn of America; Metro-Dade Art in Public Places; Metro-Dade Addiction Board; Delta Sigma Theta Sorority, Inc. **Business Addr:** Dean of Students, Miami Dade Community College, 300 NE 2nd Ave, Miami, FL 33132.

BRYANT, CLARENCE
Judge. **Personal:** Born Jun 13, 1928, Lewisville, AR; son of Lucy Faulkner Bryant and Jehugh Bryant; married Doris L Hearns (deceased); children: Nelson T, Kevan L. **Educ:** Roosevelt Coll, BA 1953; Chicago Kent Coll of Law (ITT), LLB 1956, JD 1969. **Career:** Circuit Court of Cook Co IL, elected circuit court judge 1982, assoc appointed judge 1976-; Wash Kennon Bryant & Hunter, atty partner 1960-76; Wash & Durham, atty assoc 1956-60. **Orgs:** Only African American among first 9 mem Review Bd IL Atty Diciplinary System 1973-76; 1st vice pres Cook Co Bar Assn 1970-72; pres Cook Co Bar Assn 1973-74; mem Jud Council NBA 1976-. **Honors/Awds:** Meritorious Serv Award Cook Co Bar Assn 1972. **Military Serv:** US Army, lt, 4 years. **Business Addr:** Circuit Judge, Circuit Court of Cook County, Br 38-727 E 111th Street, Chicago, IL 60628.

BRYANT, CLARENCE W.
Government official (retired). **Personal:** Born May 22, 1931, Clarendon, AR; son of Blonnell Guyden Bray and Clarence Bryant; married Annie Laure Aldridge; children: Carolyn, Antonette, Sibyl, Johanna. **Educ:** City Coll of San Francisco, 1949-50; City Coll of San Francisco, AS Elect 1976; CA State Univ San Fran, BA Design & Industry 1979, MA DAI/Transp 1981. **Career:** Maintenance Engrg Br Los Angeles CA, elect tech, installation 1958-60; Western Reg San Francisco AF Sector Field Office, SFIA, elect tech, commun 1960-68, Elect tech, radar 1974, elect tech 1974-78, elect tech regular relief 1978-79; Fed Aviation Admin of DOT, Washington, DC, suprv elect egr mgr 1979-88, branch mgr, 1988-90 (retired). **Orgs:** Mem San Fran Black Catholic Caucus 1972, Mayors Comm on Crime 1968-71, Arch-Bishops Campaign for Hum Devel 1969-72, Black Leadership Forum of San Francisco; exec bd Catholic Soc Svc, Top Flight Golf Club. **Honors/Awds:** Awd of Achievement CA State Assembly 1968; Awd OMICA 1968; num tech awd FAA. **Military Serv:** USAF a/1c 1950-54.

BRYANT, CONNIE L.
Labor union official (retired). **Personal:** Born Dec 26, 1936, Brooklyn, NY; daughter of Viola Barnes Bryant (deceased) and Charles Bryant (deceased); married Alonzo Anderson (deceased); children: Bradley C. **Educ:** Empire State Labor College, New York, NY; Cornell Univ, Extennsion, New York, NY. **Career:** New York City Dept of Transportation, New York, NY, various, 1963-83; Communications Workers of America, Washington, DC, intl vice pres, 1983-89, Cleveland, OH, staff rep, 1989-91. **Orgs:** 2nd vice president, Coalition of Black Trade Unionist, 1986-; chair, Labor Ad Hoc Committee National Council Negro Women; board of directors, Industrial Relations Council of Goals; executive board, A Philip Randolph Institute, 1985-89. **Honors/Awds:** Special Women's Award Natl Black Caucus of State Legislative Labor, Round Table, 1989; Women Achievers, New York, NY, 1987; New York City, Dept of Transportation Administrator and Trainer, 1981; various other awards from local organizations.

BRYANT, CUNNINGHAM C.
Major general. **Personal:** Born Aug 8, 1921, Clifton, VA. **Educ:** Howard U, 1940-43; Infantry Officer Candidate Sch, 1944; Food Serv Sch, mess mgmt course 1947; Infantry Ofcr Asso, basic course 1948; Engr Ofcr Asso,advanced course 1956; Command & Gen Staff Coll, sr ofcr civil disturbance orientation course 1968; Nat War Coll, def strategy sem 1969. **Career:** Active Duty, 1943, 2nd Lt 1944-Major General Feb 1975; DC Nat Guard, commanding gen 1974-; DC Guard, adj gen 1968-74; various other posts. **Orgs:** Mem Nat Guard Assn of US & DC; Assn of AUS; The Adjs Gen Assn. **Honors/Awds:** Recipient of Bronze Star Medal; Army Commendation Medal; Purple Heart Medal; Army of Occupation Medal (Germany); WW II Victory Medal; Nat Def Serv Medal; European-African-Middle Eastern Campaign Medal with 2 stars; Am Campaign Medal; Combat Infantry Badge; 1st federally recognized black gen officer in Nat Guard. **Military Serv:** USNG gen ofcr. **Business Addr:** DC Nat Guard, Washington, DC.

BRYANT, DONNIE L.
Financial administrator. **Personal:** Born Dec 20, 1942, Detroit, MI. **Educ:** Walsh Inst of Accountancy, attended 1960-63; Wayne State Univ, BA 1970; Univ of MI, MPublic Policy 1972. **Career:** Public Admin Staff, staff assoc 1973-77; Neighborhood Reinvestment Corp, dir of finance & admin 1977-83; Govt of DC, deputy to the city admin. **Orgs:** Mem Intl City Mgmt Assn 1972-; mem Natl Assn of Black Public Admins 1984-. **Honors/Awds:** Graduate Fellowship US Dept of Housing/Intl City Mgmt Assn 1971-72. **Home Addr:** 2400 41st St NW #313, Washington, DC 20007. **Business Addr:** Deputy To City Administrator, District of Columbia, 1350 Pennsylvania Ave NW, Washington, DC 20004.

BRYANT, EDWARD JOE, III
Aircraft power plant specialist. **Personal:** Born Sep 19, 1947, Shreveport, LA; son of Ester Lee (Harper) Bryant and Moses B Bryant; married Bettye Jeane Gordon, Nov 1981; children: Lorie, Khristopher, Elizabeth. **Educ:** Palmer College, Associate 1975; Baptist College, Bachelors 1978; Air Natl Guard & Air Reserve Academy, graduate 1972; Propulison Branch Management, Chanute IL. **Career:** USAF, jet specialist 1965-69; Sperry-Rand Corp, maintenance engr 1969-72; Dept of Defense, aircraft powerplant specialist 1972-; Federal Civil Service Employee, 1972-; North Charleston SC, counselor 1978-89. **Orgs:** Air reserve tech 1969-86; chmn of legal NAACP 1975-86; mem Air Force Assn SC Personnel & Guidance Assn 1978-80; counselor, guidance School System 1978-79; legal chmn NAACP 1980-86; legal staff, North Charleston Citizen Advisory Council 1986-87; State Legal Redress Committee NAACP 1988-89; local chaptr, Air Force Assn. **Honors/Awds:** Sustained Superior Performance Awd 1983; South Carolina NAACP, Best Legal Activities & Staff 1986-87; Superior Performance Award (civil service) 1989; Black Heritage Certificates 1983-1988. **Military Serv:** USAF, sgt 4 yrs; Good Conduct Medal; Meritorious Service Medal; Vietnam Ribbon Oversea Service Medal. **Business Addr:** President, North Charleston SC NAACP, PO Box 41891, Charleston, SC 29423.

BRYANT, FAYE B.
Educator. **Personal:** Born Mar 15, 1937, Houston, TX. **Educ:** Howard Univ, BA 1958; Univ of Houston, MEd 1967. **Career:** Houston Independent Sch Dist, tchr 1960-67, Title I counselor 1967-70; Houston Met YWCA, prog dir 1968-69; Bellaire Sr HS, counselor 1970-75; QIE, HISD field inf coord 1975; Supt for Instruction, prog admin 1976; Office of Supt for Inst, assoc dir 1977; Magnet Sch Prog, asst supt 1978; Magnet Sch Prog & Alternate Educ, assoc supt 1982, asst supt enrichment programs 1987; Houston Independent School Dist, deputy supt, personnel serv 1988-89, deputy superintendent, school operation, 1989-92, deputy superintendent, district planning, accountability and technoloy, currently. **Orgs:** Mem Houston Professional Admins & Assn for Supervision of Curriculum Devel (local, state, natl); pres Houston Personnel & Guidance Assn 1975-76; 1974 Task Force on Human Concerns TX Personnel & Guidance Assn; chap senator Houston Met YWCA 1970-74; bd dirs Com of Admin of Blue Triangle Br; natl past pres Top Ladies of Distinct 1975, pres Houston Chap 1973-74; south central regional dir Alpha Kappa Alpha Sor 1968-72; vice pres Alpha Kappa Alpha Sor 1978; natl pres Alpha Kappa Alpha Sor 1982-86; mem NAACP 1982-86; mem Links Inc; mem NCNW Court of Calanthe; Houston C of C; bd mem Natl Negro College Fund; bd mem, natl chmn Assault on Illiteracy; mem Black Leadership Roundtable, Coalition of 100 Black Women. **Honors/Awds:** Young Educator Awd Finalist 1967; TX Personnel & Guidance Assn Cert of Appreciation in Recog of Commitment & Serv to Statewide Enchancement of Counseling; TX Personnel & Guidance Assn Outstanding Counselor Awd 1975; 100 Most Influential Black Americans Ebony Magazine 1983-86; Community Serv Awd TX Southern Univ's Bd of Regents; Outstanding Alumni Achievement Award, Howard Univ 1987. **Home Addr:** 3215 Milburn St, Houston, TX 77021, (713)747-1344. **Business Phone:** (713)892-6070.

BRYANT, FRANKLYN
Association executive. **Career:** National Alliance of Black Salesmen and Saleswomen, president, currently. **Business Addr:** President, National Alliance of Black Salesmen & Saleswomen, PO Box 2814, New York, NY 10027-8817, (212)409-4925.

BRYANT, HENRY C.
Pathologist (retired). **Personal:** Born Feb 21, 1915, Birmingham, AL; married Barbara; children: Henry, Lisa. **Educ:** Talledega Coll, BA 1936; Univ MI, MD 1940, MS 19478 PhD 1949. **Career:** Physicians Clinical Lab Co, dir pres; Univ MI, rsrch asst, rsrch asso, instr, lectr. **Orgs:** Dir St Joseph Mercy Hosp 1958-64; dir Peoples Comm Hosp 1958-64; dir Merrywood Hosp, Herrick Meml Hosp 1958-82; Washtenew Co MI State Med Soc 1949; AMA 1949-; Nat Med Assn 1949-; NY Acad of Scis 1948-; Am Soc of Clinical Pathologists; MI Soc of Pathologists 1949-; MI Assn of Profs 1976-; NAACP 1945; fellow College of American Pathologists. **Military Serv:** USAR 1941-48. **Home Addr:** 3780 Tremont Lane, Ann Arbor, MI 48105-3023.

BRYANT, HUBERT HALE
Attorney. **Personal:** Born Jan 4, 1931, Tulsa, OK; son of Curlie Beatrice Marshall Bryant and Roscoe Conkling Bryant; married Elnora Roberson, Oct 25, 1952; children: Cheryl Denise Bryant Hopkins, Tara Kay Bryant-Walker. **Educ:** Fisk Univ, BA 1952; Howard Univ Law Sch, LLB 1956. **Career:** Private law practice 1956-61, 1986-; City of Tulsa, OK, asst city prosecutor 1961-63, city prosecutor 1963-67; ND OK, asst US atty 1967-77; ND OK Dept of Justice, US atty 1977-81; City of Tulsa OK, municipal court judge 1984-86. **Orgs:** Trustee First Baptist Church N Tulsa 1970-75, 1995-; Tulsa Urban League bd 1962-64, mem 1964-; archon Sigma Pi Phi Alpha Theta Boule; exec bd Tulsa Branch NAACP; Alpha Phi Alpha; National Set Club. **Honors/Awds:** Outstanding Alumni Howard Univ Sch of Law 1981; Outstanding Citizen Tulsa Branch NAACP 1981; Outstanding Citizen Masons 1978; Mason of Yr Masons 1963; Alpha Kappa Alpha Sorority Inc, Alpha Chi Omega Chapter, Image Award - Outstanding Community Service, 1988; National Bar Assn, Hall of Fame, 1997. **Business Addr:** Attorney, 2623 North Peoria, Tulsa, OK 74106.

BRYANT, ISAAC RUTLEDGE
Consultant. **Personal:** Born Nov 4, 1914, Lawnside, NJ; married AnnaMae Jones; children: Isaac R Jr, Wayne R Esq, Mark K. **Educ:** Attended Temple Univ Phila; US Army Officer Candid Sch Camp Lee VA. **Career:** Borough of Lawnside NJ, dist clerk & bus mang 1938-42; Lawnside NJ Sch Dist, dist clerk & bus mgr 1938-42; IRS, US Treas Dept 1942-74; Borough of Lawnside, adminis aide; Self Employed, consultant, currently. **Orgs:** Pres of trustees & dir Camden Co YMCA 30 yrs; trustee United Way; pres Lawnside NJ Bd of Educ; life mem NAACP; mem adv council Camden Co NJ Employment & training Ctr; pres bd of trustees Mt Zion UM Church; chmn supervy comm Lawnside Fed Cred Union; chmn admin bd Mt Zion UM Church; dir Lawnside Cultural Comm; dir Lawnside Comm Ctr Inc; past mem bd of dir State of NJ Educ Oppor Fund and the Camden Co Comm Coll; past grand sr warden PrinceHall Grand Lodge F&AM State of NJ, past master Hiram Lodge No 5 F&AM. **Honors/Awds:** The Youth of Mt Zion UM Church 1969; YMCA Man of the Yr Camden Co 1973; Gallatin Awd US Dept of Treas 1975. **Military Serv:** US Army, 1st lt, 1942-45.

BRYANT, JEFF DWIGHT
Professional football player. **Personal:** Born May 22, 1960, Atlanta, GA. **Educ:** Clemson Univ, attended. **Career:** Seattle Seahwaks, defensive end, 1982-. **Honors/Awds:** Played in AFC Championship Game, post-1983 season. **Business Addr:** Professional Football Player, Seattle Seahawks, 11220 NE 53rd St, Kirkland, WA 98033-7595.

BRYANT, JENKINS, JR.
State official. **Personal:** married Sadie Jean; children: Cynthia Desadier. **Educ:** Univ of Alabama, AA; Tuskegee Inst, MS, MEd. **Career:** Sunshine High School, Newbern, AL, principal, retired, 1992; state of Alabama, state representative, dist 68, 1983-. **Orgs:** Mason (33nd degree); Amer Farm Bureau; Amer Soc Computer Dealers; Natl Education Assn; Health Care Exhibitors Assn; Nat Assn Secondary School Principals; Mt Valley AME Zion Church, currently. **Business Addr:** 9313 Colgate St, Indianapolis, IN 46268-1216.

BRYANT, JEROME BENJAMIN
Physician. **Personal:** Born Aug 29, 1916, Adel, GA; married Lois. **Educ:** Talladega Coll, AA 1939; Meharry Med Coll, MD 1943; FL Inst Tech, MS 1977. **Career:** US Army, chief physical exam, surg, 1957-77; physician. **Orgs:** GA Med Assn; Assn Mil Surgeons; Alpha Phi Alpha Frat; 32nd degree Mason. **Honors/Awds:** Outstanding Commendation Award, Dir Gen Korean Nat RR 1969; Legion Merit Award 1977. **Military Serv:** US Army, Col, 1957-77. **Business Addr:** Ft Benning, Columbus, GA 31905.

BRYANT, JESSE A.
Business executive. **Personal:** Born Aug 27, 1922, Supply, NC; married Eva Mae Fullwood; children: four. **Career:** Sec Intl Longshoremans Assn; NAACP, president. **Orgs:** Pres Cedar Grove Br NAACP; vice pres SENC Land Chap of A Phillips Randolph Inst; mem exec bd Brunswick Co Cit Assn. **Honors/Awds:** Twice crowned as the Most Outstanding Small Branch NAACP President in NC; crowned once as Mr NAACP of NC.

BRYANT, JOHN G.
Cleric, educator. **Personal:** Born Apr 13, 1944, Lawnside, NJ; son of Colleen Farmer and J Granville Bryant. **Educ:** Golden Gate University, BA, 1972; Rutgers University, MEd, 1976; The General Theological Seminary, MDiv, 1985; St George's College, certificate in Biblical studies, 1990. **Career:** Camden Board of Education, teacher of mathematics, 1970-77; Camden Board of Education, program supervisor, 1977-82; Episcopal Diocese of New Jersey, seminarian, 1982-85; St Mary's Episcopal Church, priest/vicar, 1985-; Atlantic Community College, assistant professor of mathematics, 1987-. **Orgs:** Atlantic County March of Dimes, HPAC Board, 1990-; South Jersey Chapter, National Conference of Christians and Jews, 1987-; National Education Association, 1987-; Kappa Delta Pi Honor Society, 1975-, past president; Alpha Phi Alpha Fraternity Inc, Alpha Theta Lambda Chapter, 1991-; Atlantic County Community Mediator, 1992-; Pleasantville Board of Education, 1996-; Partnership for a Healthy Community, 1996. **Honors/Awds:** Camden County Probation Department, Service, 1973; Camden City Board of Education, Service, 1982; Diocese of NJ, Youth Service, 1988; City of Pleasantville NJ, Community Service, 1988; Atlantic Community College, Community Service, 1989; NJ Senate Resolution, Faithful Ministry to Community, 1996. **Home Addr:** 114 W Bayview Ave, Pleasantville, NJ 08232. **Business Addr:** The Reverend, St Mary Episcopal Church, 118 W Bayview Ave, Pleasantville, NJ 08232, (609)646-1604.

BRYANT, JOHN RICHARD
Clergyman. **Personal:** Born Jun 8, 1943, Baltimore, MD; son of Edith and Harrison; married Cecila Williams; children: Jamal, Thema. **Educ:** Morgan State Coll, AB; Boston Univ Sch of Theol, ThM, MDiv 1970; Colgate Rochester Div Sch, DMin 1975. **Career:** Preached on five continents; guest lecturer to various colleges & universities 1970-72; Peace Corps Liberia, teacher; Boston Urban League, comm organizer; St Paul AME Church, pastor; Bethel AME Church, Baltimore, MD, former pastor; AME Church, 14th Episcopal Dist, Monrovia, Liberia, bishop, beginning 1988, 10th Episcopal Dist, state of Texas, bishop, 1991-. **Orgs:** Bd mem Natl Comm of Black Churchmen; Natl Council of Churches; Black Ecumenical Commn; World Methodist Council on Evangelism; bd mem Ecumenical Inst. **Honors/Awds:** Springfield Outstanding Churchman Award Boston Jaycees; Outstanding Leader Award Winkey Studios; Man of the Year Award; contributed to Pastor's Manual and four other books; honored by Vanguard Organization, Delta Sorority; Boston Univ School Theology Outstanding Alumni Awd; honorary doctorate degrees: Virginia Seminary at Lynchburg, Wilberforce Univ, Payne Seminary. **Business Addr:** Bishop, 10th Episcopal Dist, AME Church, 4347 Hampton Rd, Ste 245, Dallas, TX 75232.

BRYANT, JUNIOR (EDWARD E. BRYANT, JR.)
Professional football player. **Personal:** Born Jan 16, 1971, Omaha, NE. **Educ:** University of Notre Dame, attended. **Career:** San Francisco 49ers, defensive end, 1995-. **Business Addr:** Professional Football Player, San Francisco 49ers, 4949 Centennial Blvd, Santa Clara, CA 95054, (415)562-4949.

BRYANT, KATHRYN ANN
Banker. **Personal:** Born Feb 25, 1949, Detroit, MI; daughter of Mary Avery Bryant and Amos V Bryant. **Educ:** University of Michigan, BA, political science, 1971; Wayne State University, MA, radio, tv & film, 1979. **Career:** City of Detroit, 1972-77, City Council, administrative assistant to Councilman Kenneth Cockrel, 1978-81, Cable Commission, deputy director, 1982-88, Board of Assessors, assessor, 1988; Warner Cable Communications, Inc, director government and community relations, 1988-91; Comerica Inc, vice pres, civic affairs, 1991-. **Orgs:** Michigan Metro Girl Scout Council, board member, 1992-96; Fair Housing Center of Metro Detroit, board member, 1991-; Arab American Center for Economic Social Services, board member, 1992-; Project Pride, treasurer/board member, 1991-93; National Association of Minorities in Cable, board member/membership chair, 1990-91; National Association of Telecommunication Officers & Advisers, board member, 1986-88. **Honors/Awds:** Fair Housing Center of Metro Detroit, Distinguished Services, 1992. **Business Addr:** VP, Civic Affairs, Comerica Inc, PO Box 75000, Detroit, MI 48275-3352.

BRYANT, KOBE B.
Professional basketball player. **Personal:** Born Aug 23, 1978, Philadelphia, PA; son of Joe 'Jelly Bean' Bryant. **Career:** Los Angeles Lakers, guard, 1996-. **Honors/Awds:** NBA All-Star, 1998. **Special Achievements:** NBA Draft, First round pick, #13, 1996; youngest player ever selected for the All-Star game. **Business Addr:** Professional Basketball Player, Los Angeles Lakers, PO Box 10, Inglewood, CA 90305, (213)419-3100.

BRYANT, LEON SERLE
Counselor. **Personal:** Born Jun 22, 1949, Akron, OH; son of Daisy Bryant and Clyde H Bryant; children: Cillicia N. **Educ:** Arizona State University, BA, 1974, MEd, 1991. **Career:** Department of Correction, State of Arizona, correctional officer, 1974-75; Phoenix Urban League, manpower specialist, 1975-78; Arizona State, career specialist senior, 1978-. **Orgs:** Omega Psi Phi, 1971-; Phoenix Job Corp, business advisory committee, 1988-; National Society of Experiential Education, 1989-; Arizona Career Development Association, vp of programs, currently. **Honors/Awds:** Arizona Career Development Assn, VP Programs. **Home Phone:** (602)491-3879. **Business Addr:** Career Specialist Senior, Arizona State University, Career Services, SSV C359, Tempe, AZ 85287-1312, (602)965-2350.

BRYANT, MARK
Professional basketball player. **Personal:** Born Apr 25, 1965; married Shelley, 1989. **Educ:** Seton Hall. **Career:** Portland TrailBlazers, forward-center, 1988-95; Houston Rockets, 1995-96; Phoenix Suns, 1996-. **Business Addr:** Professional Basketball Player, Phoenix Suns, PO Box 515, Phoenix, AZ 85001, (602)379-7867.

BRYANT, N. Z., JR.
Insurance agent/executive. **Personal:** Born Oct 25, 1949, Jackson, MS; son of Christeen M Bryant and N Z Bryant Sr. **Educ:** Western Michigan University, BS, 1971, MA, 1972; University of Michigan, 1974. **Career:** Oakland University, instructor, 1972-74; Detroit College of Business, faculty, academic coordinator, 1974-76; Pontiac Schools, teacher, 1976-79; Equitable Life Insurance Co., agent, 1979-93; Patterson-Bryant Associates Inc, senior vp, 1982-. **Orgs:** Greater Detroit Area Life Underwriters Association, 1980-93; NAACP, Oakland County Branch, trustee, 1984-86, treasurer, 1989-90; Pontiac Area Urban League, finance committee, 1990-91; Pontiac Optimist Club, charter president, 1983-84, vice pres, 1984-85; Million Dollar Round Table, qualifying member, 1989; Positive People of Pontiac, president, 1982-83. **Honors/Awds:** City of Pontiac, Young Man of the Year, 1985; Equitable Life Insurance Co., President's Cabinet, 1988-89; Western Michigan University & Alumni Association, Wall of Distinction, 1992. **Special Achievements:** Author: "Investing in the 90's," 1992. **Business Addr:** Senior VP, Patterson-Bryant Associates, Inc, 755 W Big Beaver, Ste 518, Troy, MI 48084, (248)244-1353.

BRYANT, NAPOLEON ADEBOLA, JR.
Educator. **Personal:** Born Feb 22, 1929, Cincinnati, OH; son of Katie Smith and Napoleon Bryant; married Ernestine C, Jul 15, 1950; children: Karen, Derek, Brian, David. **Educ:** Univ of Cincinnati, BS 1959; IN Univ, MAT, 1967, EdD 1970, NDEA Fellow, 1968-70. **Career:** Cincinnati Public Schs, teacher; Xavier Univ, science resource teacher, prof of educ, 1970-, dir, secondary educ, 1974-79, asst vice pres, student devel, 1984-86; NSF, pre-coll teacher devel projects, 1974-79, dir of minority affairs, 1984-86; Natl Sci Teacher Assn, dir, multicultural sci educ, 1990-93. **Orgs:** OH Council of Elementary School Int; chmn Com for Local Arrngmnts; Rollman Psychist Hosp 1976-78; former basileus, Omega Psi Phi, Beta Iota Chap, 1965-; life mem NAACP; Natl Sci Teachers Assn; consultant on Elem & Secondary Sci Educ for school & publishing firms; co-organizer & participant Caribbean Regional Orgn of Assn of Sci Educators Barbados WI 1979; hon life mem Assn of Sci Teachers of Jamaica 1979; ordained deacon Episcopal 1984; bd of dir Harriet Beecher Stowe Preservation Comm, William Procter Conf Centers;Danforth Fellow 1983; sci cons, sci adv comm State of OH; charter mem, Assn of Multicultural Sci Educ, 1990-; mem, Assn of Supervision & Curriculum Development, 1988-. **Honors/Awds:** "For What Have You Toiled?" Pride Mag, July 1978; "Non-Formal Teacher Educ in Sci," Sci Educ for Prog: A Caribbean Perspective, Oct 1980; "About Films," Jour of Geological Educ, 1982; "Sons, Daughters Where Are Your Books," Jour of Coll Sci Teaching, Mar/Apr 1988; "Hurricane Gilbert," Science & Children, Sept 1989; Omega Man of the Year, Omega Psi Phi, 1973; Nation Builders Awd, 1984, Faculty Support Award, 1991, Black Student Assn, Xavier Univ; Keynote Speaker Annual ASTJ Conf Jamaica WI 1986. **Business Addr:** Professor of Education, Xavier University, Department of Education, 3800 Victory Parkway, Cincinnati, OH 45207.

BRYANT, PRESTON
Educator. **Personal:** Born Aug 8, 1938, Chicago; married Sandra; children: Carolyn, Beverly. **Educ:** Chicago Tchrs Coll, BEd 1961; Roosevelt U, MA 1963; Nova U, EdD 1978. **Career:** Teacher, 1961-63; master teacher, 1963-67; Madison School, asst prin, acting prin 1968-70; EF Dunne Elementary School, prin 1971-73; George Henry Corliss High School, prin 1974-77; Chicago Bd of Educ, supt 1977-; Chicago Teachers Coll, instructor 1975; Union Graduate School, prof 1979; Gov State Univ, instructor 1980; District 10 Chicago IL, supt 1977-. **Orgs:** Mem Samuel B Stratton Educ Assn; IL Assn for Supr & Curriculum Dev; Chicago Prins Assn; Nat Assn Secondary Sch Prins; bd of dir George Howland Adminstrs Assn, former vp; Roosevelt Univ Alumni Assn; bd mem Roosevelt Univ Bd Govs; Roosevelt Educ Alumni Div; Citizens Schs Com; mem Nat Alliance of Black Sch Educators; mem advis counc Olive Harvey Coll Dept of Nursing; Nat Assn Black Sch Edntrs; NAACP; PUSH; Phi Delta Kappa; mem Zion Evangelical Luth Ch, mem bd educ; mem Forum Civic Orgn. **Honors/Awds:** Sch & community award 1974; outst serv in educ Edward F Dunne Sch Comm 1974; educators award Operation PUSH 1977; outst educators award Dr Roger's BelleTone Ensemble 1977. **Business Addr:** 1830 S Keeler Ave, Chicago, IL 60623.

BRYANT, R. KELLY, JR.
Business executive (retired). **Personal:** Born Sep 22, 1917, Rocky Mount, NC; son of Maggie Poole Bryant and R Kelly Bryant; married Artelia Tennesse Bryant, Aug 26, 1945; children: Robert Kelly Bryant III, Sandra Artelia. **Educ:** Hampton Inst, BS, 1940; North Carolina Central University, 1941-42. **Career:** Peoples Building and Loan Association, bookkeeper, 1940; Mutual Savings and Loan, bookkeeper, 1941-44; North Carolina Mutual Life Insurance Company, Ordinary Department, chief clerk, 1944-56, manager, 1956-60, assistant secretary, 1965-81. **Orgs:** Durham Chamber of Commerce; pres Chain Investment Corp; bd dir, Goodwill Industries Inc, 1968-76; bd dir, Vol Serv Bur Inc; chmn, Sch Improvement Com-Burton Sch PTA, 1968-; chmn, Educ Com-Durham Human Relations Commn, 1968-; adv bd, Emergency Sch Assistance Act Prog-Operation Breakthrough Inc, 1972-77; sec, AS Hunter Lodge #825 Free & Accepted Masons & First Worshipful Master, 1961-; registrar, Burton Sch Voting Precinct #3, 1951-; scoutmaster, Boy Scout Troop 187, 1951-; educ com, Durham Com on Negro Affairs; Nat & Durham Chap Nat Hampton Alumni Assn; treas, NC Region; trustee, auditing com, White Rock Baptist Church. **Honors/Awds:** Man of Yr, Durham Housewives League, 1958; NC Hamptonian of Yr, 1957; Silver Beaver Award; Alumni Merit Award, Nat Hampton Alumni Assn, 1969; Appreciation for Serv Award, AS Hunter Lodge No 825 Free & Accepted Masons, 1974; Most Outstanding Sec9 AS Hunter Lodge No 825 Free & Accptd Masons, 1976; Spl Cert for 8 Yrs Serv on Durham Human Relations Commn, Durham City Council, 1977; Appreciation for Serv Award, Nat Hampton Alumni Assn, 1979; Plaque for 38 yrs of service, Durham Business and Professional Chain, 1981; NAACP Freedom Fund Dinner Award, 1987.

BRYANT, REGINA LYNN
Educator. **Personal:** Born Dec 1, 1950, Memphis, TN; daughter of Mrs Dorothy Scruggs-Bryant and Al C Bryant. **Educ:** TN State Univ, BA Foreign Lang 1974; Atlanta Univ, MBA Finance 1980. **Career:** IBM, marketing rep 1976-77; Amer Telephone & Telegraph, mgmt develop prog 1980-82; Comptroller of the Currency, asst natl bank examiner 1983-84; Credit Bureau Inc/Equifax Inc, financial analyst 1984-88; Gorby Reeves, Moraitakis & Whiteman, Atlanta, GA, legal administrator, 1988-92; Atlanta Public Schools, foreign language instructor, 1993-. **Orgs:** Mem Alpha Kappa Alpha Sor Inc 1971-; 2nd vice pres academics Natl Black MBA Assoc 1980-83; business consultant Jr Achievement of Greater Atlanta 1981-; pres Sch of Business Admin Assoc Atlanta Univ 1983-85; chairperson finance comm St Anthony's Catholic Church 1984-86; asst treas Animalife Inc 1984-86; youth motivator Merit Employment Assoc 1985-; chairperson St Anthony's Night Shelter Fund Raising Comm 1986. **Honors/Awds:** Exxon Fellowship 1979; Outstanding Serv Awd Natl Black MBA Assoc 1982; Outstanding Young Women of Amer 1985. **Home Addr:** 3106 Arbor Gates Dr, Atlanta, GA 30324. **Business Addr:** Atlanta Public Schools, 210 Pryor St, SW, Atlanta, GA 30324.

BRYANT, ROBERT E.
Public speaker, attorney. **Personal:** Born Feb 1, 1910, Chattanooga, TN; son of Jennie Anna Bryant and William E Bryant; children: three. **Educ:** YMCA Coll, AB 1938; Kent Coll of

Law, LLB 1941, JD 1969; Roosevelt Univ, MPA 1979. **Career:** Chicago Br NAACP, spec counsel 1941-46; Fed Dist Ct Chgo, practice law 1941-; Cook Cty IL, asst states attny 1953-55; IL State Fair Emp Practices Com, hearing officer 1962-64; IL Sec of State, hearing officer 1964-66; Legal Serv Bur War on Poverty Carbondale, org, dir 1966-67; Tabernacle Comm Hosp & Health Ctr, hosp admin, gen counsel 1972-76; workshop leader in industry. **Orgs:** Mem, Tabernacle Missionary Bapt Church; mem Cook Cty Bar Assoc, Natl Bar Assoc, Amer Bar Assoc; author, "How to Grip and Hold Attention in Public Speaking". **Honors/Awds:** Man of the Year, Special Counsel, NAACP, Pittsburgh Courier, 1946. **Business Addr:** Attorney, 60 E 36 Pl, Ste 408, Chicago, IL 60653.

BRYANT, RUSSELL PHILIP, JR.
Company owner. **Personal:** Born Dec 11, 1949, Waterloo, IA; son of Selena Bryant and Russell Bryant Sr; married Linda Allen, Jan 16, 1982; children: Ian, Russell III, Julian. **Educ:** Ellsworth Jr College, AA, marketing, 1969; Grand Valley State, BS, business administration, 1974; Colorado University, currently attending. **Career:** Chrysler Financial Credit, sales rep, 1974-76; Petro Energy International, president, 1976-79; PB Steel Inc, principal, owner, 1979-82; John Phillips Printing, Inc, principal, owner, 1982-. **Orgs:** Minority Enterprise Inc of Colorado, board of director, 1992-93; Colorado Assn of Commerce & Industry, 1992-94; Mullen High School, board of director, 1992-93; Kid's Against Drugs, board of director, 1992-95; Greater Denver Chamber of Commerce, board of directors. **Honors/Awds:** Public Service, 1990 MBE/WBE Supplier of the Year, 1990; MEI, Service Company of the Year, 1992; Denver Post/Greater Denver Chamber, Minority Business, 1990-91; Rocky Mt Regional Minorty Purchasing, Minority Supplier, 1986; Southwest Business Development, 1989; Entrepreneur of the Year, Ernest & Young, 1996. **Special Achievements:** Part owner of largest black-owned printing company in the Western US. **Home Addr:** 17835 E Powers Dr, Aurora, CO 80015-3092. **Business Phone:** 800-676-4520.

BRYANT, T. J.
Physician. **Personal:** Born Dec 28, 1934, Wellston, OK; son of Minnie Bryant; married Rosie L; children: Daryl, Gregory, Cynthia. **Educ:** AR Univ, BS 1957; Kansas Univ Med Schl, MD 1963; KUMC Menorah, Residency Training 1964-67. **Career:** Jackson County Med Soc, sec 1973-75; UMKC Sch of Med, assoc prof 1977-; UMKC Sch of Med, docent 1974-79; Dept of Med Bapt Med Center, chmn 1980-82; Dept of Med, Menorah Med Center, vice chmn 1980-; Menorah Medical Center, board of directors 1989; Missouri Board of Healing Arts 1989. **Orgs:** Mem MO State Med Assn 1963-, Jackson County Med Soc 1963-, Amer Coll of Gastroenterology 1972-, Amer Soc of Internal Med 1970-, NAACP Urban League 1980-81, Greater Kansas City Chamber of Commerce 1978-; American Medical Association; Metropolitan Medical Society of Kansas City, Missouri; Greater Kansas City Southwest Clinical Society; Kansas City Medical Society; Associate Clinical Professor, UMKC School of Medicine; Appointed to the Misssouri State Board of Healing Arts and Served as a member from, 1989, chairman, 1992-93; Member Board of Directors, Menorah Medical Center; Chairman of Internal Medicine Department, 1982-83, bd of dirs, Baptist Medical Center, currently. **Military Serv:** USAAF a1c 1959-65. **Business Addr:** Physician, 2525 East Meyer Blvd, Kansas City, MO 64132.

BRYANT, TERESENA WISE
City official, educational administrator. **Personal:** Born Jan 19, 1940, St Petersburg, FL; daughter of Mattie Lee Cooksey Gardner and Mose Gardner (deceased); divorced; children: Donna Kaye Drayton. **Educ:** Florida A&M Univ, BS, 1962; Howard Univ, Certificate of Completion Program Evaluation & Craftsmanship, 1976; NYU, MPA, 1977; Man Coll, counseling psych; Fordham Univ, Urban Educ Supervision & Administration, post graduate studies, 1989-; St Petersburg Junior Coll, AA, 1960. **Career:** NYC, admin positions, 1974-81; State Senator, Bronx City NY, legislative asst, comm liaison, 1978-83; Office of the Mayor, New York City Youth Bureau, asst exec dir, 1981-83; NY State Tempy Comm to revise the SS Laws, contract mgr, sr program analyst, 1983-; St Senator, Jos L Galiber, campaign mgr, 1978-; Office of the Mayor, New York City Youth Bureau, dir of planning; campaign mgr, Robert Johnson, first black district attorney in NY state, 1988; special asst to Bronx City Central Board 1987-90; New York State Senator, Bronx, NY, legislative stat/evaluator, 1990-92; City Affairs Liaison, admin mgr, 1992-. **Orgs:** Alpha Kappa Alpha, Tau Omega, 1975-; coordinator of Comm of Bronx Blacks 1977-; under legislative leadership of Sen Joseph L Galiber responsible for securing of additional minority councilman & a black assembly seat in Bronx Co redistricting lines; chairperson/founder, Bronx Center for Program Serv Youth, 1981-; bd of dir, PR Representative, Urban League Bronx Aux Chap, 1982-; Florida A&M Univ Alumni, Amer Assn of Univ Women, NY City Managerial Employees Assn, NAACP, Amer Soc for Public Admin, Natl Forum of Black Public Admin, Natl Assn for Female Exec, William Inst CME Church, Council of Concerned Black Exec, NY Univ Alumni NY Chapter; Former women advisor, NYC Youth Bureau; member, Women Business Owners of New York; member, Bronx Black Assn of Educators; Natl Council of Negro Women (East Bronx); Bronx Political Women's Caucus. **Honors/Awds:** Certificate for Contribution, Time, New York City, Central Labor Rehabilitation Council, 1978-83; SAVE, Dept of Labor Serv Award, 1981-83; Outstanding Civic Leadership Bronx Unity Democratic Club, 1981; Woman of the Year Morrisania Ed Council 1981; Service Award, Bronx Center for Program Service, 1982-84; Community Serv Award Each One Teach One 1983; Outstanding Service & Dedication to the Youth of Our Community, Mid Brooklyn Health Society, 1983; Distinguished Service Award, New York State Assn of Black & Public Relation Legislators, 1989; Presidential Advisory Award, Bronx Council Boy Scouts of America, 1990; Community Service Award, East Bronx Chapter, NAACP, 1989. **Home Addr:** 950 Evergreen Ave Apt 16M, Bronx, NY 10473. **Business Addr:** Legislative Stat/Evaluator/Researcher, State Senator Joseph L Galiber, Community District Office, 1 Fordham Plaza, Bronx, NY 10458.

BRYANT, WAYNE R.
Attorney. **Personal:** Born Nov 7, 1947, Camden, NJ; son of Anna Mae Bryant and Isaac R Bryant Sr; divorced; children: Wayne Richard Jr. **Educ:** Howard Univ, BA 1969; Rutgers Univ Sch of Law, JD 1972. **Career:** Transportation & Communications Comm, vice chmn 1982-84, chmn 1984-, majority leader, 1990-91; Independent Authorities & Commun Comm, mem 1982-84, vice chmn 1984-; State of NJ, assemblyman dist 5 1982-95; Camden Co Council on Economic Oppor, solicitor 1982-; Borough of Somerdale, spec solicitor 1983-; Juvenile Resource Center, solicitor 1983-; Borough of Lawnside, bond counsel 1984-, solicitor 1984-; Camden Co Housing Auth, solicitor 1985-97; Borough of Chesilhurst, spec solicitor 1985-; Zeller and Bryant, general partner, 1974-; NJ State Senate, senator, 1995-; Twnp of Deptford, Planning Bd, solicitor, 1996-. **Orgs:** Natl Black Caucus of State Legislators; NJ Conference of Minority Trans Officials; mem US Supreme Court, US Court of Appeals for the Third Circuit Court of Appeals DC, Supreme Ct of NJ, US Dist Court for the District of NJ; life mem, NAACP; mem Educ Oppor Fund Comm Adv Bd Rutgers Univ; mem Lawnside Educ Assn; chmn Co State & Local Govts United Way Campaign of Camden Co; NJ State Democratic Platform Comm. **Honors/Awds:** Recognition Award, Natl Political Congress of Black Women; Disting Serv Awd Camden Co Bd of Chosen Freeholders; Disting Serv Awd Camden Co Planning Bd; Awd of Merit NJ Co Trans Assn; Legislative Committment Awd Educ Improvement Ctr S Jersey Region; Outstanding Achievement Awd, Lawnside Bd of Educ; Awd of Merit Assn of Parking Authorities State of NJ; Comm Serv Awd Gloucester Co Black Political Caucus; Comm Serv Awd, Grace Temple Baptist Church; Comm Serv Awd, YMCA Camden Co; Mt Pisgah Man of the Year; Comm Serv Awd First Regular Democratic Club of Lawnside; Outstanding Serv to the Comm Brotherhood of Sheriff & Corrections Officers; Outstanding Serv Award, Good Neighbor Award, Juvenile Resource Ctr; Cert of Appreciation Camden City Skills Ctr; OutstandingCommitment to Human Serv Alternats for Women Now Camden Co; Outstanding Serv to the Community Cert of Appreciation Awd Camden Comm Serv Ctr; adv bd Music Festival Rutgers; Hairston Clan Comm Serv Awd; Natl Business League Awd Disting Serv Awd Haddon Heights HS Afro-Amer Cultural Club; Citizen of the Year Alpha Phi Alpha Frat Inc Nu Iota Chapt; NJ Assn of Counties Achievement Awd; Cooper Hospital/Medical Ctr Outstanding Legislator; Honorary Doctorate of Laws Degree, Howard University, 1991; Arthur Armitage Distinguished Alumni Award for 1992, Rutgers University School of Law. **Business Addr:** Senate Member District 5, 200 N. 5th Street, Camden, NJ 08102.

BRYANT, WILLA COWARD
Educator (retired). **Personal:** Born Nov 21, 1919, Durham, NC; daughter of Willa Courtney King Coward and Owen Ward Coward; married Harry Lee Bryant, Jun 6, 1942 (deceased); children: Dr Mona Maree Bryant-Shanklin. **Educ:** NC Central Univ, AB 1951; Temple Univ, MEd 1961; Duke Univ, EdD 1970. **Career:** Durham City Schools, teacher 1954-61; NC Central Univ, asst prof ed 1961-69, adjunct prof ed 1990-94; Livingstone Coll, chairperson, div of ed & psych 1970-83. **Orgs:** Consult Coop School Improvement Prog 1964-66; pres Alpha Tau Chap of Kappa Delta Pi at Duke Univ, 1969-70; Triangle Reading Assoc 1970-72; NC Assoc of Coll for Teacher Ed 1980-81; mem Bd of Ed Durham City Schools 1984-92. **Honors/Awds:** Southern Fellowship Found 1968-70; "Two Divergent Approaches to Teaching Reading" Amer Rsch Assoc 1970; "Crucial Issues in Reading" Views on Elementary Reading 1973; Phelps Stokes Scholar 1975; mem Phi Delta Kappa Fraternity Carolina Chap 1987. **Home Addr:** 302 E Pilot St, Durham, NC 27707.

BRYANT, WILLIAM ARNETT, JR.
Physician. **Personal:** Born Dec 31, 1942, Birmingham, AL; married Hidla R Timpson; children: Kristen, Lamont. **Educ:** Clark Coll Atlanta, BA 1964; State Univ NY at Buffalo Sch of Medicine, MD 1975. **Career:** Pvt Practice of Pediatrics, physician 1979-; Univ of MD Hosp Dept of Pediatrics, intern/Resident/Chief Resident 1975-79; Buffao Med Sch, med student & SUNY 1971-75; Erie Cty Health Dept Buffalo, lab supr 1969-71; Erie Co Health Dept Buffalo, vd epidemiologist 1967-69; Provident Hosp Baltimore MD, asst chief of pediatrics 1980-. **Orgs:** Mem Nat Med Assn 1975-; Peace Corps Vol US Govt 1964-66; mem Chi Delta Mu Health Prof Frat 1977-; pres Baltimore Clark Coll Club 1979-. **Business Addr:** 1532 Havenwood Rd, Baltimore, MD 21218.

BRYANT, WILLIAM BENSON
Federal judge. **Personal:** Born Sep 18, 1911, Wetumpka, AL; married Astaire A Gonzalez; children: Astaire, William B. **Educ:** Howard U, AB 1932, LLB 1936. **Career:** DC Asst US Atty, 1951-54; Houston, Bryant & Gardner, partner 1954-65; US Dist Judge DC, 1965-; Howard U, law prof 1965-. **Orgs:** Sec, Bd Educ DC; mem Amer Bar Assn. **Honors/Awds:** First black chief US District Court Judge. **Military Serv:** US Army, Lt Col, 1943-47. **Business Addr:** Sr US District Judge, US District Court, US Courthouse, 3rd & Constitution Ave NW, Washington, DC 20001.

BRYANT, WILLIAM HENRY, JR.
Flight instructor. **Personal:** Born Feb 10, 1963, Garfield Heights, OH; son of Ruth Earle Bishop-Bryant and William Henry Bryant Sr; married Myra Williams Bryant, Feb 10, 1990; children: Kyle J W Bryant. **Educ:** Kent State Univ, AAS 1984; Pacific-Western Univ, BS 1987; ETI Technical Institute, Engineering Design, Professional Diploma 1989; Embry-Riddle Aeronautical University, attending. **Career:** US Army C Co 101 Aviation Battalion 101st Abn Div, crew engr, 1986-; Cleveland Rebar, cost estimator, 1989-; Veteran's Administration, Cleveland, OH, records mgr, 1989-; Aquatech, Inc, Cleveland, OH, design engineer, 1989-90; Tower Company, Solon, Ohio, computer aided design administrator, 1990-94; Swagelok Co, tool design engineer, currently; Cleveland Flight Training, instructor & charter pilot currently; Swagelok Corporate Aviation Department, 1999-. **Orgs:** Sec Amer Inst of Aero & Astronautics 1982-86; mem Aircraft Owners & Pilots Assoc 1982-; vice pres Phi Beta Sigma Frat; Epsilon, Epsilon chapter, 1984-85; mem Soc of Manufacturing Engrs 1984-; jr deacon Starlight Baptist Church 1984-; mem Future Aviation Profls of Amer 1986-; vice president, Phi Beta Sigma Fraternity, Gamma Alpha Sigma Chapter 1989-; Organization of Black Airline Pilots, 1995-; F&AM Lodge Ecclesiastes, #120, Prince Hall, Cleveland OH, 1996-; National Association of Flight Instructors, 1995; Tuskegee Airmen, Inc, North Coast Chap, 1993-; Civil Air Patrol, 1996-. **Military Serv:** US Army, Warrant Officer, 1988-90; Ohio Natl Guard, OCS cadet; received Letter of Commendation 101st Airborne 1986; Letter of Commendation 5th Group Special Forces 1986; 101st Aviation Battalion Achievement Award 1986; Letter of Commendation Task Force 16Oth, 1987; Good Conduct Ribbon, 1987; Army Commendation Award 1987; Army Achievement Award 3rd Armored Division 1988; Overseas Ribbon 1988. **Home Addr:** 1195 Waldo Way, Twinsburg, OH 44087, (330)963-0419. **Business Phone:** (440)248-4600.

BRYANT, WILLIAM JESSE
Dentist, educator. **Personal:** Born Apr 8, 1935, Jacksonville, FL; son of Katie Bryant Brown; married Taunya Marie Golden Bryant, Feb 22, 1979; children: Kiwanis Linda, William, Deron, Vincent, Michael, Kimberly, Zachary, Jessica. **Educ:** FL A&M U, BA 1960; AZ State U, 1962; Meharry Med Coll, DDS 1967; Boston U, Cert Orthodontics 1970; Boston U, ScD 1971. **Career:** N Eastern U, chmn assoc prof 1972; FL A&M, rsch asst 1961-63; NE U, instr 1969-71; Whittier Dental Clinic, orthodontist 1970-72; Chicago, chmn 1971-72; pvt practice 1970; Roxbury Comprehensive Community Health Ctr, dental dir 1971-78; Boston U, asst prof 1971-74; Boston U, assoc prof 1974; WPFL Stuart FL, private practice 1986. **Orgs:** Exec bd mem Roxbury Med Tech Inst 1972-74; dental consult HEW Boston 1974; exec bd mem United Way 1976; exec bd mem NAACP 1976; Commonwealth Dental Soc of Greater Boston; Am Assn of Orthodontists; NE Soc of Orthodontists; Internatl Assn for Dental Rsrch; Am Dental Assn; Nat Dental Assn; MA Dental Assn; Capital City Dental Soc; Nashville TN FL TN MA GA State Dental Bds; Am Soc of Dentistry for Children; Am Anesthesiology Assn; Soc of the Upper 10th; Alpha Phi Alpha; Guardsmen Inc; NAACP; exec bd mem Health Planning Council of Boston; Pub Health Council; bd dir United Way; bd mem Big Brother Inc Boston; bd member, St Michael's School Stuart FL; fellow, International College Craniomandibular Orthopedics. **Honors/Awds:** Numerous awards & publications. **Business Addr:** 204 West Ocean Blvd, Stuart, FL 34994.

BRYANT-ELLIS, PAULA D.
Financial executive. **Personal:** Born Jan 20, 1962, Youngstown, OH; daughter of James F Bryant, Eugene and Joetta Ross; married Wendell R Ellis, Aug 1, 1981; children: Wendell R Jr. **Educ:** Concordia Lutheran College, BA, Accounting, Business Mgt, Double Major, 1992. **Career:** KOTV-6, accountant, 1991-92; Bank of Oklahoma, NA/private banking officer, 1992-. **Orgs:** Natl Assn of Black Accountants, 1992-93; Natl Assn of Black Accountants, Western Region, student conference chairperson, 1993. **Business Addr:** Private Banking Officer, Bank of Oklahoma, N.A., 2021 South Lewis, Ste 200, Tulsa, OK 74105, (918)748-7231.

BRYANT-MITCHELL, RUTH HARRIET
Business executive, librarian. **Personal:** Born Jun 28, 1943, Birmingham, AL; daughter of Ora Ardell Knight Bryant and Harrison Armstead Bryant; married Ronald J Mitchell, Dec 3, 1966 (divorced); children: Sydney Adele Mitchell. **Educ:** Attended, Hunter Coll NY. **Career:** City Hospital at Elmhurst, asst librarian 1964-65; Chem Construction Corp, asst librarian 1965-67; St Vincent's Hospital, asst librarian 1967-69; Ford

Found, editorial & rsch asst 1969-71; Public Information & Research Library, dir 1971-79; Bedford Stuyvesant Restrant Corp, asst to pres for public relations 1979-80; Magnolia Tree Earth Center of Bedford Stuyvesant Inc, exec dir 1980-82; Brooklyn Acad of Music, dir of comm relations 1983-85; Natl Park Serv Gateway Natl Rec Area, coop activities specialist 1985-86; Bedford-Stuyvesant Early Childhood Devel Center, asst dir 1986-87. **Orgs:** Mem Soc for Preservation of Weeksville & Bedford-Stuyvesant History; mem Brownstoners of Bedford Stuyvesant; adv council Medgar Evers Coll School of Continuing Educ; adv council Empire State Coll; mem Bedford-Stuyvesant Jaycees; chairperson bd dir Bedford-Stuyvesant Early Childhood Devel Center; bd mem Jubilation Dance Co; mem 1st Family Theatre Co; dir HTUR Acting Co, Lionesses of Bedford-Stuyvesant. **Home Addr:** 4 Herkimer Ct, Brooklyn, NY 11216.

BRYANT-REID, JOHANNE
Corporate human resources, executive. **Personal:** Born Mar 11, 1949, Farmington, WV; daughter of Jessie L Scruggs Bryant and Leslie Bryant; divorced. **Educ:** West Virginia Univ, BS 1971. **Career:** Ran Assoc, gen mgr/recruiter 1971-78; Merrill Lynch, exec recruitment mgr 1978-81, vice pres corporate human resources 1981-89, human resources director, Merrill Lynch & Co 1989-. **Orgs:** Amer Soc of Personnel Admin 1983-, Employment Mgrs Assoc 1984-, EDGES 1985-; mem adv bd Natl Council Negro Women 1985-, Black World Championship Rodeo 1985-; Executive bd mem Borough of Manhattan; Community Coll; bd mem James Robert Braxton Scholarship Fund; board of directors West Virginia University Foundation, Inc. **Honors/Awds:** Black Achievers Awd YWCA 1981. **Business Addr:** Director, Human Resources, Merrill Lynch, World Financial Center, South Tower, 11th Fl., New York, NY 10080-6111.

BRYCE, HERRINGTON J.
Insurance executive, economist. **Personal:** married Beverly J Gaustad; children: Marisa Jeanine, Shauna Celestina, Herrington Simon. **Educ:** Mankato State Univ, BA 1957-60; Syracuse Univ, PhD 1960-66; Amer Coll, CLU 1984-85, ChFC 1984-85. **Career:** Natl Planning Assoc, economist 1966-67; Clark Univ, faculty 1967-69; Urban Inst, sr economist 1969-70; Brookings Institution, fellow 1970-71; MIT, faculty 1972-73; Joint Center for Political Studies, dir of rsch 1973-76; Harvard Univ, fellow 1978; Academy for State & Local Govt, vice pres 1978-80; Natl Policy Inst 1980-85; Carlogh Corp/Coll of William and Mary, prof of business 1986-. **Orgs:** Natl Assn of Corporate Directors; American Society of CLU & CFC. **Honors/Awds:** Honorary Citizen City of Atlanta 1975; Minority Admin of Yr Conf of Minority Public Admins 1976; Honorary Citizen City of New Orleans 1976; Distinguished Alumnus Mankato State Univ 1982. **Special Achievements:** Author of books on nonprofits and regional economics. **Business Addr:** Professor, School of Business Admin, College of William & Mary, Williamsburg, VA 23185.

BRYCE-LAPORTE, ROY SIMON
Sociologist, educator. **Personal:** Born Sep 7, 1933; son of Myra C Laporte and Simon J Bryce; divorced; children: Camila, Robertino, Rene. **Educ:** Panama Canal Coll, AA, 1954; Univ of Nebraska-Lincoln, BS in Educ, 1960, social science, Romance Lang, MA sociology & education; Univ Puerto Rico, Adv Cert, 1963; UCLA, PhD, sociology (w/honors), 1968; Yale Law School, MSL, 1985. **Career:** Hunter Coll, CUNY, asst prof soc, 1968-69; Yale Univ, director of African-American St program; assoc prof of sociology, 1969-72; Natl Inst of Mental Health, visiting sci, 1971-72; Smithsonian Inst, dir, research sociologist, 1972-82; Univ of Pennsylvania, visiting prof, 1974-; Howard Univ, guest prof, 1975-; Catholic Univ of Amer, dept of anthropology; Research Inst Immigration Ethnics Studies Inc, dir, pres, research cons, 1983-86; Guest Curator, Schomburg Center for Research in Black Culture, 1985-86; Prof of Sociology, Graduate Center & Dir, The center on Immigrant and Population Studies, Coll of Staten Island, City Univ of New York, 1986-88; Colgate University, John D & Catherine T MacArthur, professor of sociology/director of Africana and Latin American Studies, 1989-94; visiting Neilson prof, sociology, Smith College, 1994; John D, prof of sociology, currently. **Orgs:** Bd of dir, Caucus Black Sociologists, Amer Acad of Polit & Soc Scis; sec gen I Cong of Black Culture in the Americas Cali Colombia, 1979; chmn, Frazier-Johnson-Dubois Awds Comm Amer Soc Assn, 1978-79; Alpha Kappa Delta, Pi Gamma Mu, Phi Delta Kappa, Mu Epsilon Nu, Phi Sigma Iota, Alpha Phi Alpha; adv bd, US Census Adv & Race Ancestry Minorities; Yale Law Schl Assn & Yale Club, Washington, DC; bd of mgr, Seamen's Children's Soc; advisory bd, Schomburg's Afro-Amer Scholar Comm; college accreditation comm/dean's advisory bds, Picker Gallery and Office of Undergraduate Studies, Colgate Univ; nominee, nomination comm, Amer Sociological Assn; chr, academic advisory bd, WADABAGE editorial bd, Caribbean Res Ctr, Medgar Evers Coll, CUNY; advisory bds for research and publication proj, Anacostia Museum, African Voices Proj, Museum of Man & Nat History, Smithsonian Inst; advisory bd, Caribbean Archival Research Proj, Schomburg Ctr. **Honors/Awds:** City Council, Dist of Columbia, 1984, Mayor's Award, 1982, Yale Alumni Assn 1975, Intl Public Relations Assn, 1984; Sociologist, 1978-79; editor, "New Immigration Vols I & II," Transaction Books, 1980; School Contrib Award Caribbean Amer Int Cultural Org, 1981; Mayor's Award for Contrib to the Arts, Washington, 1981; Achievement by Panamanians Award Dedicators Inc New York City, 1982; Arturo Griffith Award Afro Latino Inst Washington, DC, 1983; Recog Resolutions of 1984, City Council of Dist of Columbia, 1984; adv bd, Cimarron Journal Carib Stud Assocs, City Univ of New York, 1984; "Inequality & the Black Experience, Some Intl Dimensions" special issue"Journal of Black Studies"; sr editor, RIIES on New Caribbean Immigrations; Recognition Afro-Amer Studies Yale Alumni of Afro-Amer Inc; Gelman Serv Awd Eastern Sociological Soc; charter fellow Woodrow Wilson Intl Center; "Man of the Year Award," Panamanian Council of New York, 1986; Guest Curator of special exhibition on "Give Me Your Tired, Your Poor?"; Voluntary Black Immigration to the US, Schomburg Center, New York; Centennial of Statue of Liberty, 1986; Colgate University Quincentenary Comm, chair, 1992. **Business Addr:** Professor of Sociology, Colgate University, Dept of Sociology, 13 Oak Dr, Hamilton, NY 13346-1398.

BRYSON, CHERYL BLACKWELL
Attorney. **Personal:** Born May 28, 1950, Baltimore, MD; daughter of Connie Blackwell and Clarence D Blackwell; married James Bryson; children: Bradley, Blake. **Educ:** Morgan State University, BS (magna cum laude), 1972; Ohio State University, College of Law, JD, 1972. **Career:** Ohio State University, College of Law, associate editor of law journal, 1976; Friedman & Koven, labor law associate, 1976-80; Katten, Muchin & Zavis, partner/associate, 1980-86; City of Chicago, deputy corporate counsel, 1986-89; Bell, Boyd & Lloyd, partner, labor & employment law, 1989-92; Rivkin, Radler & Kremer, partner, 1992-. **Orgs:** Loyola University of Chicago, Institute of IDL Relations, board of advisors; IIT Chicago, Kent College of Law, Public Sector Labor Law Conference Board; YWCA of Metropolitan Chicago, board member; The Neighborhood Institute Dev Corp, board member. **Honors/Awds:** Financial Independence Institute, Outstanding Achievement Award, 1987; Chicago Public Schools, Academic Olympics Appreciation, 1989. **Special Achievements:** Author: "Racial Prejudice," Ohio State Law Journal, 1976; "Unfair Labor Practices," The IICLE Labor Law Handbook, 1984; "Sexual Harasssment," Employee Relations Law Journal, 1990; "Health Care Cost Containment," Illinois Public Employee Relations Report, 1990. **Business Addr:** Partner, Rivkin, Radler & Kremer, 30 N LaSalle St, Ste 4300, Chicago, IL 60602, (312)899-0227.

BRYSON, PEABO
Vocalist. **Personal:** Born Apr 13, 1951, Greenville, SC. **Career:** Al Freeman and the Upsetters, singer, 1965; Moses Dillard and the TexTown Display, 1968-73; solo albums and songs: Peabo, "Underground Music," "I Can Make It Better," numerous others; duet with Natalie Cole, "We're the Best of Friends;" duet with Roberta Flack, "Tonight I Celebrate My Love," numerous others. **Special Achievements:** Duet with Roberta Flack produced nine gold albums with songs reaching top ten lists in US and UK. **Business Phone:** (212)975-4321.

BRYSON, RALPH J.
Educator. **Personal:** Born Sep 10, 1922, Cincinnati, OH; son of Annie Davis Bryson and Ralph Bryson. **Educ:** Univ Cincinnati, BS 1947; Univ Cincinnati, MS 1950; OH State Univ, PhD 1953. **Career:** So Univ, instr English 1949; Miles Coll, instr English 1949-50; AL State Univ, associate prof English 1953-62; prof & dept head 1962-75, chmn div of humanities 1975-77, prof of English 1977-; Univ of AL, adjunct prof 1987. **Orgs:** Pres Assn Coll English Tchrs AL; AL Council Tchrs English Exec Bd; Nat Council Tchrs English; Modern Language Assn; S Atlantic MLA; Coll Language Assn; Conf Coll Composition & Communication; Phi Delta Kappa; Lectr Author & Consult; Kappa Alpha Psi; Editor Column Books & Such; chmn Nat Achievement Commn; officer, mem Province Bd Dir; Am Bridge Assn; chmn exec bd & sectional vice pres, Montgomery Seminar Arts; bd of trustees, Museum Fine Arts Assn; Alabama Writers' Forum, bd of dirs. **Honors/Awds:** Dexter Ave King Memorial Baptist Church; Outstanding Journalistic Contributions & Achievement Kappa Alpha Psi; Outstanding Men of Yr & Montgomery; Cited Outstanding OH State Univ Graduate in They Came & They Conquered; Bryson Endowed Scholarships Established at University Cin'ti & Ohio State University, 1995; 56th Recipient of the Elder Watson Diggs Award; 72nd Grand Chapter Meetings, Kappa Alpha Psi, 1995. **Military Serv:** US Army, 1942-45; European Theater of Operations 1943-45. **Business Addr:** Professor of English, Alabama State University, 915 S Jackson St, Montgomery, AL 36101-0271.

BRYSON, SEYMOUR L.
Educational administrator. **Personal:** Born Sep 8, 1937, Quincy, IL; son of Claudine Jackson; married Marjorie; children: Robin, Todd, Keri. **Educ:** Southern IL Univ Carbondale, BA Sociology 1959; MS, Rehabilitation Counseling 1961, PhD Educ Psychology, 1972. **Career:** St Louis State Hospital, rehabilitation counselor 1961-65; Breckinridge Job Corps Center, admin 1965-69; Devel Skills Program, dir 1969-72; Rehabilitation Inst SIU, asst prof 1972-75, assoc prof 1975-84, prof 1984; SIU, Coll of Human Resources, assoc dean 1977-78, 1980-84, interim dean 1978-80, 1984, dean, 1984-88, asst to the pres, 1988-90, exec asst to the pres, 1990-. **Orgs:** Gov appointee Dept of Rehabilitation Serv Advisory Council 1980, State Use Commission 1983-; chmn Racism Comm Amer Rehabilitation Counseling Assn 1972-74; senate Amer Rehabilitation Counseling Assoc Delegate to the Amer Personnel & Guidance Assoc in Personnel & Guidance 1976-78; pres IL Assn of Non-White Concerns 1984-85; mem Amer Assoc of Univ Admin, Assoc of Non-White Concerns, Amer Rehabilitation Counseling Assoc; bd dir Jackson Cty Comm Mental Health Center 1974-82; chmn, bd dir Jackson Cty Comm Mental Health Center 1980-82; Jackson County 708 Bd 1986-; bd dir, Res-Care, 1989-. **Honors/Awds:** Phi Kappa Phi Natl Hon Soc 1972-; Rsch Award Assn of Non-White Concerns, 1976; Special Award for Distinguished Serv ICBC-1985; NAACP Image Award for Education, Carbondale Branch, 1988; Southern Illinois Univ Hall of Fame, 1977; Quincy High Hall of Fame, 1989. **Business Addr:** Executive Asst to the President, Southern Illinois Univ, Coll of Human Resources, Carbondale, IL 62901.

BUCHANAN, CALVIN D. (BUCK)
State official. **Personal:** married Donna Nee Conner. **Educ:** Univ of Mississippi, BA, JD. **Career:** US Army, judge advocate; Northern District of MS, asst US attorney, 1990-97; US attorney, Northern District Miss., 1997-. **Orgs:** Miss. State Bar; Magnolia Bar Ass'n; Second M.B. Church Univ. Alumni Ass'n. **Honors/Awds:** Army ROTC Scholarship; Law School Scholarship; Honorable Discharge: US Army. **Special Achievements:** First African American to serve as US attorney in the state of Mississippi. **Business Addr:** US Attorney, US Attorney's Office, PO Drawer 886, Oxford, MS 38655.

BUCHANAN, RAYMOND LOUIS
Professional football player. **Personal:** Born Sep 29, 1971, Chicago, IL; married Sheree; children: Destinee, Ray Jr. **Educ:** Louisville. **Career:** Indianapolis Colts, defensive back, 1993-96; Atlanta Falcons, 1997-. **Business Addr:** Professional Football Player, Atlanta Falcons, Two Falcon Place, Suwanee, GA 30174, (404)945-1111.

BUCK, IVORY M., JR.
Educational administrator (retired). **Personal:** Born Dec 25, 1928, Woodbury, NJ; married Ernestine; children: L'Tanya Ivy, Ivory Melvin III. **Educ:** William Penn Bus Inst, Certificate Business Ad 1954-56; Glassboro State Coll, BA 1960, MA 1968. **Career:** Public Schools Deptford NJ, teacher 1958-64; Johnstone Training Rsch Ctr, teacher 1960-62; Jr High Sch Deptford, dir guidance 1964-68; Glassboro State Coll, asst registrar 1968-71; Gloucester Co Coll, counselor 1969-72; Glassboro State Coll, asst dir advisement ctr, until 1994. **Orgs:** mem, Kappa Alpha Psi, Phi Delta Kappa Frat; Grand Master Prince Hall Free & Accepted Masons for NJ 1977-79; elected White House Conf for Library Serv 1978; alumni treas, Glassboro State Coll Bd of Dirs 1979; mem Evaluation Team for Sec ondary Educ 1980; sec gen Prince Hall Scottish Rite Masons 33 Degrees 1983; sec of bd of dirs Fitzwater Housing Project 1985; natl elected officer Prince Hall Shriners 1980-; bd dir Camden Co YMCA; Berlin bd Jr Chamber of Commerce; chairperson for Inclusion, Black Studies Monroe Township Public Schools; mem, NAACP, Elks. **Honors/Awds:** Leadership Awd Marabash Museum New Egypt NJ 1978; Legion of Honor Awd for Leadership/Serv Shriners 1980; Distinguished Alumni Awd Glassboro State Coll 1981; The Chapel of Four Chaplains Awd Philadelphia PA 1964, 1984; Honorary Police Captain, Capitol Heights Maryland, Commissioned Kentucky Colonel, Recipient Seagram Vanguard Award; Mayor City, Valdosta GA, proclaimed March 27, 1993, Ivory M Buck Jr Day. **Military Serv:** USAF s/sgt 4 yrs; Airman of the Month; Good Conduct Medal; Eastern Theatre & Korean Medals.

BUCK, JUDITH BROOKS
Educator. **Personal:** Born Mar 3, 1949, Norfolk, VA; daughter of Mr & Mrs George A Brooks, Sr; married Henry Buck Jr; children: Kimberly, Michael Henry. **Educ:** Bennett Coll Greensboro NC, BA 1967-71; Univ of VA, M Educ 1986; Further study at: Norfolk State Univ, Old Dominion Univ, Hampton Univ, Alabama A&M Univ, Univ of AL. **Career:** Council for Exceptional Children, info spec 1972; Fairfax Cty Bd of Ed, learning disabilities teacher 1972-74; Harford Cty Bd of Ed, crisis resource teacher 1974-76; Norfolk Public Schools, child devel spec 1976-77; USAF, child care ctr, preschool dir 1978-80; Norfolk Public Schools, learning disabilities teacher 1980-81; Huntsville Public School, alternative prog coord 1981-83; Norfolk Public Schools, spec ed teacher 1983-86; Huntsville City Schools, spec educ area specialist; Huntsville City Schools, principal; Challenger Middle School, principal. **Orgs:** Mem Shiloh Baptist Church 1959-, Delta Sigma Theta 1968-, Natl VA Ed Assoc 1976; mem Fed Women's Clubs of Amer 1984-85; assoc mem First Baptist Church, 1986; secretary/board of directors, Huntsville/Madison County Daycare Assn, 1991-; member, National Assn of Elementary School Principals, 1988-; member, National Assn of Secondary School Principals, 1986-. **Honors/Awds:** Received scholarships for undergrad studies Bennett Coll 1967-71; Article publ Slow Learner Workshop Mag 1976; Ruth Hindman Fellowship, Ruth Hindman Foundation, 1989. **Business Addr:** Challenger Middle School, 13555 Chaney Thompson Rd, Huntsville, AL 35803.

BUCK, VERNON ASHLEY, JR.
Educational consultant. **Personal:** Born Jan 10, 1920, Atlanta, GA; son of Glennie Eula Kirk Buck and Vernon A Buck; married Eutrilla Graham (deceased); children: Vernon III, Rudolph, Cheryl. **Educ:** Morehouse Coll, BA 1935-39; NY Univ, MS 1948; State Univ of NY at Albany, 1957-74. **Career:** W Charlotte High Charlotte, NC, math teacher & coord of distrib educ program 1946-48; Carver Jr Coll, dir chief adminstrative officer 1948-51, chairman math dept 1953-57; Hackett Jr High Albany, math teacher 1957-68; State Univ of NY at Albany, dir chief adminstr for EOP 1971-85 (retired); Veruch Co, Albany, pres, 1987-. **Orgs:** Inst systems analyst & designer/proj dir/vp Learning Techn Inc Albany 1968-71; mem natl Soc for Performance & Instr; NY State United Univ Profl; Rotary Intl; adj prof SUNYA School of Educ 1971-74; adj prof SUNYA Afr & Afro-Am Studies 1975-; mem adv comm 1982-, chmn adv comm 1986-87 Capital Dist Educ Oppors Prog; mem adv bd LaSalle School for Boys 1986-90; adjunct board member, Child's Hospital Nurshing Home, 1990-; member, Fort Orange Club, 1984-. **Honors/Awds:** Proposal Reader Advanced Inst Develop Prog US Dept of Health Educ and Welfare, Office of Educ, Bureau of Higher and Continuing Educ 1978-82; "The MarketValue Approach to Property Appraisal" NY Bd of Equal & Assess 1972; co-author "Basic Spelling Skills" revised ed McGraw-Hill 1980; author of training system, SICON, Mich Heart Assn, 1972. **Military Serv:** US Army, capt, 1942-46, 1951-52; Org/Training Officer, 1943-46; post-info & educ officer, Ft Stewart, GA, 1951-52.

BUCKHALTER, EMERSON R.
Physician. **Personal:** Born Nov 10, 1954, El Monte, CA; married Veretta Boyd; children: Monica. **Educ:** Univ of CA Los Angeles, BA 1976; Howard Univ Coll of Medicine, MD 1980. **Career:** Hawthorne Comm Med Group, physician 1983-86; St Francis Care Med Group, physician 1986-. **Orgs:** Mem Amer Medical Assoc 1980-. **Honors/Awds:** Alpha Omega Alpha Honor Med Soc 1979; Natl Medical Fellowships; Henry J Kaiser Foundation Merit Scholar 1980. **Home Addr:** 5936 Croft Ave, Los Angeles, CA 90056. **Business Addr:** Physician, 3680 E Imperial Hwy, Lynwood, CA 90262, (213)631-2900.

BUCKHANAN, DOROTHY WILSON
Marketing manager. **Personal:** Born Jul 12, 1958, Sumter, SC; daughter of Ida Gregg; married Walt A Buckhanan, Aug 22, 1987. **Educ:** Benedict Coll Columbia SC, BS Business 1980; Atlanta Univ Grad School of Bus, MBA 1982. **Career:** Xerox Corp, mktg asst 1982-84; SC Johnson & Son Inc, prod mgr 1984-. **Orgs:** Mem Amer Mktg Assn 1980-, Toastmaster's Intl 1980-82, Natl Black MBA Assn 1984-; vice president fundraising chmn, corresponding sec Alpha Kappa Alpha 1984-87; vice president Top Ladies of Distinction Inc 1985-88. **Honors/ Awds:** Outstanding Undergrad Awd Alpha Kappa Alpha 1979; Natl Deans List Atlanta Univ 1980-82; Exec Scholarship Fellow Atlanta Univ 1982-84; Employee Recognition Awd Xerox Corp 1983; Distinguished Alumni Awd Benedict Coll 1987; Service Award, Alpha Kappa Alpha, 1988; Outstanding Speaker Award, Dale Carnegie Institute, 1989. **Home Addr:** 7331 W Marine Dr, Milwaukee, WI 53223. **Business Addr:** Product Manager Consumer Prod, SC Johnson & Son Inc, 1525 Howe St, Racine, WI 53403.

BUCKLEY, CURTIS LADONN
Professional football player. **Personal:** Born Sep 25, 1970, Oakdale, CA; married Shanna; children: Chloe, Ciara. **Educ:** East Texas State, attended. **Career:** Tampa Bay Buccaneers, defensive back, 1993-95; San Francisco 49ers, 1996-. **Honors/ Awds:** Pro Bowl alternate, 1995, 1996. **Business Addr:** Professional Football Player, San Francisco 49ers, 4949 Centennial Blvd, Santa Clara, CA 95054, (415)562-4949.

BUCKLEY, GAIL LUMET
Writer. **Personal:** Born Dec 21, 1937, Pittsburgh, PA; daughter of Lena Horne Hagton and Louis Jones; married Kevin P Buckley, Oct 1, 1983; children: Amy Lumet, Jenny Lumet. **Educ:** Radcliff Coll, Cambridge, MA, BA, 1959. **Career:** Writer, currently. **Honors/Awds:** Author of The Hornes: An American Family, 1986; Doctor of Letters, Univ of Southern IN, 1987. **Business Addr:** c/o Lynn Nesbit, 598 Madison Ave, New York, NY 10128.

BUCKLEY, MARCUS WAYNE
Professional football player. **Personal:** Born Feb 3, 1971, Fort Worth, TX. **Educ:** Texas A&M, attended. **Career:** New York Giants, linebacker, 1993-. **Business Addr:** Professional Football Player, New York Giants, Giants Stadium, East Rutherford, NJ 07073, (201)935-8111.

BUCKLEY, TERRELL
Professional football player. **Personal:** Born Jun 7, 1971, Pascagoula, MS; married Denise; children: Sherrell. **Educ:** Florida State. **Career:** Green Bay Packers, defensive back, 1992-94; Miami Dolphins, 1995-. **Business Addr:** Professional Football Player, Miami Dolphins, 2269 NW 199th St, Miami, FL 33056, (305)620-5000.

BUCKLEY, VICTORIA (VIKKI)
Government Official. **Personal:** Born Nov 2, 1947, Denver, CO; daughter of Charles and Rubye Buckley; married T R Newsome, Dec 30, 1994; children: Ian Charles, JeVon Franklyn, Kahlin DeLaney. **Educ:** Sieble School of Drafting/Engineering, associate's degree, 1968; CU, 1969. **Career:** Humble Oil, draftsperson, 1969-70; Opportunities Industrialization, director, 1971-73; Public Service Careers, office manager, 1973-74; Colorado Secretary of State Office, administrative officer, 1974-94, secretary of state, 1994-; motivational speaker. **Orgs:** Stand Up for Kids, director, 1993-; Feed the Homeless, volunteer drr, 1994; Kids Voting, honorary chair; Natl Assn of Secretaries of State; Natl Ad Hoc Committee on Notary Publics, chair; Natl Voter Registration Committee, co-chair; Nine Healthcare, bd mem. **Honors/Awds:** Received numerous "Breaking Through the Glass Awards;" Natl Federation of Black Business Women, Political Award; Black America Political Achievement Award, 1997, Vision in Politics Award, 1996. **Special Achievements:** First African American Republican secretary of state in Colorado; active participant in Feed-the-Homeless programs; appeared on television and radio programs. **Business Addr:** Secretary of State, Colorado Department of State, 1560 Broadway, Ste 200, Denver, CO 80202, (303)894-2204.

BUCKNER, JAMES L.
Dentist, business executive. **Personal:** Born Jul 29, 1934, Vicksburg, MS; son of Florice Williams Buckner and Dr. Clarence E. Buckner; children: JaSaun, Justina Jordan. **Educ:** Univ of Illinois, BSD, 1957, DDS, 1959. **Career:** Private practice, dentist. **Orgs:** pres, Lincoln Dental Soc, 1965-66; sec, bd of dir, Natl Dental Assn, 1966-67; bd of advisors, Supreme Life Insurance Co, 1970-; trustee, WTTW, Channel 11, 1970-74, City Coll of Chicago 1971-76; chmn Chicago Dental Soc Comm on Public Aid 1971-80; vice chmn, Chicago Econ Devel Corp, 1972-75; mem, Pres Council on Minority Business Enterprise, 1972-75; Gov Walkers Public Health Transition Task Force, 1972-73; bd of adv, Midwest Sickle Cell Anemia Inc, 1972-; trustee, Univ of IL Dental Alumni Assn, 1973-75; co-chmn, Chicago United, 1973-75; mem, Illinois Dental Soc, Amer Dental Soc, Leg Interest Comm of IL Dentists, IL Dental Serv Corp, IL Dept of Public Aid Dental Adv Comm; pres, Chicago Urban League, 1973-76; chmn, Chicago Financial Devel Corp,1973-76; chmn, Council of Natl Urban League P', 1975-76; pres, Trains & Boats & Planes Inc 1978-92; The Foodbasket Inc, 1981, 1988-; mem, Amer Soc of Travel Agents; vice pres, Seaway Commun Inc, 1978-85; founder, mem bd of dir, Seaway Natl Bank, 1965-86; chairman, Seaway Comm Inc, 1985-; chairman, the Push Foundation, 1987-; vice chmn, Illinois Serv Fed Savings & Loan, 1988-. **Honors/Awds:** 10 Outstanding Young Men Award, South End Jaycees 1965; Certificate of Achievement, Amer Inst of Banking, 1965, Natl Dental Assn, 1966; Plaque For Outstanding Contributions to Ed Jensen School, 1970; Certificate of Appreciation, Chicago Area Council of Boy Scouts, 1970; Community Serv Award, Big Buddies Youth Serv Inc, 1971; Man of the Year Award, Chicago Urban League, 1972; Certificate of Appreciation, Commonwealth Church, 1972; Certificate of Recognition, Council of Natl Urban League Pres', 1977; Outstanding Achievement Award, Women's Div, Chicago Urban League, 1985. **Business Addr:** President, The Food Basket, Inc, Chicago, IL 60619.

BUCKNER, MARY ALICE
Attorney. **Personal:** Born Mar 3, 1948, Columbus, GA. **Educ:** Mercer Univ, BA 1970; attended Emory Univ; Mercer Univ, JD 1973. **Career:** Randall & Turner Attys at Law, law clerk 1971; Bishop & Hudlin Attys at Law, law clerk 1973-75, assoc 1975-78; Troy State Univ, part-time instr 1977-79; Recorders Court (Pro Tem), judge 1984; GA Dept of Educl, regional hearing officer 1984; Bishop & Buckner Attys at Law, atty & partner 1978-. **Orgs:** Bd mem AJ McClung Br YMCA 1974-; bd mem Muscogee Co Chap ARC 1976-; mem Delta Sigma Theta Inc. **Honors/Awds:** Natl Merit Semi-Finalist 1966; Rockefeller Scholarship 1966-70; Emory Univ Pre-Law Prog Field Found of NY 1970-71; Herbert Lehman Educ Fund Fellowship 1971-72; Lt Col Aid De Camp Gov's Staff 1976. **Business Addr:** Attorney, 1214 First Ave Commerce Bldg, Ste 370, Columbus, GA 31902.

BUCKNER, QUINN
Professional basketball player (retired), former professional basketball coach. **Personal:** Born 1954. **Educ:** Indiana University. **Career:** Guard: Milwaukee Bucks, 1977-82, Boston Celtics, 1983-85, Indiana Pacers, 1986; NBC Television, NBA telecasts, analyst, until 1993; Dallas Mavericks, head coach, 1993-94. **Special Achievements:** Member of the NBA Championship team, Boston Celtics, 1984. **Business Addr:** Former Head Coach, Dallas Mavericks, Reunion Arena, 777 Sports St, Dallas, TX 75207, (214)998-0117.

BUCKNER, WILLIAM PAT, JR.
Educator. **Personal:** Born Oct 5, 1929, Brazil, IN; son of Mary E. Patton and W.P. Buckner Sr.; married Irene Smith; children: Lawrence, Douglas. **Educ:** DePauw Univ, AB, 1950; Indiana Univ, MS, 1954, HSD, 1969. **Career:** Southern University, New Orleans, LA, Department of Health, Physical Education and Recreation, associate professor and chair, 1959-70; Eastern Michigan University, Ypsilanti, MI, Department of Health, Physical Education, and Recreation, associate professor and health coordinator, 1970-71; Prairie View A&M University, Prairie View, TX, Department of Health, Physical Education, and Recreation, professor and department head, 1971-72; University of Houston, Department of Health and Human Performance, professor and health coordinator, 1972-; Baylor College of Medicine, Houston, TX, adjunct professor, 1987-. **Orgs:** Mem, Assn for the Advancement of Health Ed, 1955-, Family Life Council of TX 1977-, Natl Forum for Death Ed & Couns 1977-; grief couns Life Threatening & Illness Alliance 1972-; adv bd ENCORE Gr Houston YWCA 1978-; constitution comm for the Natl Soc for Allied Health Professions; mem exec council Southern Dist, Amer Alliance for the Advancement of Health Ed; mem Univ of Houston Univ Park Faculty Promo & Tenure Comm, Task Force for the Recruitment & Retention of Minority Students. **Honors/Awds:** Fellow, Royal Health Society, 1969; Scholar, Danforth Foundation, 1972; Faculty Excellence Award, University of Houston, 1990; Presidential Citation Award, Assn for the Advancement of Health Education, 1991. **Military Serv:** USMC 1951-53. **Business Addr:** Professor of Health Science and Allied Health, Department of Health and Human Performance, University of Houston, Central Campus, Houston, TX 77204-5331.

BUCKNEY, EDWARD L.
Director. **Personal:** Born Feb 28, 1929, Keokuk, IA; children: Edwin Darryl (dec). **Educ:** Columbia Coll, BA 1957; IL Inst Tech, MP Admin 1970. **Career:** Chicago Police Capt Assoc, appt date 1954, sgt 1963, lt 1965, capt 1968, dist comdr 1970, asst dep supt 1974, watch comdr 1979, dir of training 1983-. **Orgs:** Sec Chicago Police Capt Assoc 1972-74. **Military Serv:** AUS corpl 1951-53. **Business Addr:** Dir of Training, Chicago Police Assoc, 1121 State St, Chicago, IL 60605.

BUCKSON, TONI YVONNE
Transportation administration. **Personal:** Born Jun 5, 1949, Baltimore, MD; married James Buckson Jr. **Educ:** Coppin State Coll, BS 1971; Univ of Baltimore, MS 1978; Northeastern Univ, certificate 1985; Atlanta Univ, certificate 1985. **Career:** Mayor and City Council of Baltimore, CATV task force manager 1979-81; Natl Aquarium in Baltimore, group events coord 1981-82; Mass Transit Administration, ridesharing dir 1982-86; MD Trasportation Authority, ass't admin bridges 1986-. **Orgs:** Goucher Coll, cirriculum advisor 1975-78; Jr League of MD, board mem 1978-80; Natl Information Center on Volunteerism, trainer 1979-81; MD Food Bank, boardmem 1979-81; Future Homemakers of America, board mem 1980-81; Girl Scouts of Central MD, board mem 1982-84. **Honors/Awds:** Girl Scouts of Central America; service award 1984; MD Dept of Transportation, affirmative action award 1984; Outstanding Young Women in America 1985; Natl Assoc for Equal Opportunity in Higher Education, presidential citation 1986. **Home Addr:** Six Tallow Court, Baltimore, MD 21207. **Business Addr:** Asst Administrator, Bridges, MD Transportation Authority, PO Box 9088, Dundalk, MD 21222.

BUDD, WAYNE ANTHONY
Federal official. **Personal:** Born in Springfield, MA. **Educ:** Boston College, AB (cum laude), 1963; Wayne State University, JD, 1967. **Career:** Ford Motor Co, industrial relations position; private practice, attorney, 1963-; Budd, Wiley and Richlin, senior partner; Commonwealth of Massachusetts, asst attorney general; Boston College School of Law, former lecturer; City of Boston, asst corporate counsel; District of Massachusetts, United States attorney, 1989-92; United States Justice Dept, associate United States attorney general, 1992-. **Orgs:** United States Attorneys Advisory Committee to the Attorney General, vice chairman; Boston College, trustee; Massachusetts Civil Service Commission, chairman, 1972-89; Massachusetts Bar Association; Massachusetts Black Lawyers Association. **Honors/Awds:** Anti-Defamation League of B'nai B'rith, Salmanson Human Relations Award; Boston Edison Co., Outstanding Achievement Award. **Special Achievements:** First African-American attorney to be appointed associate United States attorney general; headed the federal investigation into the beating of Rodney King, 1992. **Business Addr:** Associate Attorney General, United States Justice Department, Executive Office for United States Attorneys, 1107 J W McCormack Post Office & US Courthouse, Boston, MA 02109, (617)223-9400.

BUFFONG, ERIC ARNOLD
Physician. **Personal:** Born May 11, 1951, Oranjestad, Aruba, Netherlands; married Gail Helena LaBorde; children: Erica, Nicole, Alicia, Gabrielle. **Educ:** Manhattan Coll, 1969-73; Howard Univ, MD 1977. **Career:** Harlem Hosp Cntr NY, resident & chief resident, Ob-Gyn, 1977-81, president house staff 1980-81; Albert Einstein Coll, of Medicine, fellow in reproductive endocrinology 1981-83, assoc prof dept gyn 1983-84; private practice 1984-; Onslow Women's Health Center, senior partner, currently. **Orgs:** Board eligible Reproductive Endocrinology 1983; mem Amer Coll of Ob-Gyn 1986,87; diplomate/bd certified FACOG; mem Amer and Natl Medical Assocs; mem Old North State Medical Soc; chairman region III National Medical Assn 1989-92; Trustee-National Medican Association, 1993. **Honors/Awds:** Board of dir NCNB of Jacksonville, NC 1986-; Eastern Area Sickle Cell Assoc board of dir 1986-; performed the Vaginal Delivery of Quadruplets 1985; presented first eight

cases of Laparoscopic Vaginal Hysterectomy in the world, First North American/South American Congress of Gynecologic Endoscopy Dallas, TX 1988; Doctor of the Year Old North State Medical Society 1989. **Business Addr:** Senior Partner, Onslow Women's Health Ctr, 237 White St, PO Box 1354, Jacksonville, NC 28541.

BUFORD, DAMON JACKSON
Professional baseball player. **Personal:** Born Jun 12, 1970, Baltimore, MD. **Educ:** Southern California. **Career:** Baltimore Orioles, outfielder, 1993-95; New York Mets, 1995; Texas Rangers, 1996-97; Boston Red Sox, 1998-. **Business Addr:** Professional Baseball Player, Boston Red Sox, Fenway Park, 24 Yawkey Way, Boston, MA 02215, (617)267-9440.

BUFORD, JAMES HENRY
Association executive. **Personal:** Born Jun 2, 1944, St Louis, MO; son of Myrtle Margaret Brown Buford and James Buford; married Helen Joyce Freeman, Jun 23, 1967; children: James H Jr, Jason. **Educ:** Forest Park Community Coll, AA Business Admin; Elizabethtown Coll, Elizabethtown PA, BA Human Serv Admin. **Career:** Smith, Kline & French, St Louis MO, regional mktg representative, 1972-75; St Louis Community Coll, St Louis MO, program coord, 1975-76; 70001 Ltd, St Louis MO, vice pres, 1976-80; Intl Mgmt & Devel Group LTD, Washington DC, sr vice pres, 1980-81, St Louis MO, exec vice pres, 1981-85; Urban League of Metropolitan St Louis MO, pres/CEO, 1985-. **Orgs:** Mem, NAACP; bd mem, Leadership St Louis, 1985-88; mem exec comm, Blue Cross/Blue Shield, 1986-; exec bd, Boy Scouts, 1986-; mem bd of dir, St Louis Comunity Coll Building Corp, 1986-; chairman bd of regents, Harris Stowe State Coll, 1989; chair nominating comm, Sigma Pi Phi, 1988; mem, Personnel Advisory Comm, President George Bush, 1989-. **Honors/Awds:** Order of the 1st State, Governor of Delaware, 1981; Humanitarian Award, Kappa Alpha Psi-St Louis, 1984; Professionalism Award, Kappa Alpha Psi-St Louis, 1986. **Business Addr:** President/CEO, Urban League of Metropolitan St Louis, 3701 Grandel Square, St Louis, MO 63108, (314)289-0328.

BUFORD, WILLIAM M., III
Manufacturing executive. **Career:** Reliant Industries Inc, chief executive, currently. **Special Achievements:** Company is ranked #30 on Black Enterprise magazine's 1997 list of Top 100 Black businesses. **Business Addr:** President, Reliant Industries Inc/Reliant Bolt, 5025 W 73rd, Bedford Park, IL 60638, (708)496-2930.

BUGG, GEORGE WENDELL
Physician. **Personal:** Born Jun 17, 1935, Nashville, TN; children: George Jr, Michael Stanley, Kevin Gregory, Kisha Monique. **Educ:** TN State Univ, BS 1958; Meharry Med Coll, MD 1962. **Career:** Self Employed, genl surgeon; Dept of Social Services, medical consultant, 1989-. **Orgs:** Chmn Cecil C Hinton Comm Ctr 1969-72; chmn W Fresno Fed of Neighborhood Ctrs 1972; chmn Comm Serv Amer Heart Assn 1972; pres Daniel H Williams Med Forum 1974-77; mem AMA, CMA, NMA, Surveyors, JCAH, Alpha Phi Alpha Inc, Fresno-Madera Med Found; mem Comm Cncl on Black Educ Affairs. **Honors/Awds:** AMA Physicians Recognition Awd 1969; ACE Award, Dec 1993. **Military Serv:** AUS med corps maj 1967-69.

BUGG, JAMES NELSON
Dentist. **Personal:** Born Jul 11, 1904, Savannah, GA; married Janie G. **Educ:** Meharry Med Col, DDS 1930. **Career:** Nat Dental; Old N State Dental; AOA Frat; Meharry Alumni. **Orgs:** Passed GA NC & NY State Dental Boards. **Honors/Awds:** Meharry Med TE 50 Yrs 1980; Old North State Dental 50 Yrs 1980; Meharry Medical Coll 55 Year Plaque 1985; life membership Old North State Dental Society, Natl Dental Assoc.

BUGG, MAYME CAROL
Attorney. **Personal:** Born Apr 18, 1945, Portsmouth, VA; daughter of Mayme P Bugg and George W. **Educ:** Fisk Univ, BA Sociology 1966; George W Brown Sch of Social Work Washington Univ, MSW 1968; Cleveland State Univ, JD 1977. **Career:** Oberlin Coll, educ prog dir 1969-70; Cleveland City Hall, city planner 1970-71; Cuyahoga Comm Coll, asst to dept head 1971-74; Comm Action Against Addiction, court liaison 1976-77; United Labor Agy, proj dir 1977-79; Cuyahoga Co Juvenile Ct, referee 1979-. **Orgs:** Mem League Park Neighborhood Ctr 1979-84; bd mem Harambee Serv to Black Families 1979-84, adv, comm 1985-; bd mem Citizens League of Greater Cleveland 1980-84; bd mem NAACP 1980-84; mem Drop-Out Prevention Comm, Cleveland Bd of Educ 1981-; Fisk Univ Cleveland Alumni Club 1983-; mem Cuyahoga Co Bar Assn 1983; bd mem Project Friendship 1983-88; mem Assn of Blacks in the Juvenile Justice System 1979-84; Leadership Cleveland (Class of 1983); Alpha Kappa Alpha Sor; graduate of United Way Serv Ldrshp Development Prog 1986; African-Amer Family Congress 1986-; Norman S Minor Bar Assn 1986-88; member, visiting committee, Case Western Reserve U Law School, 1986-; member, advisory committee, Fenn Educational Fund, 1987-94; board member/first vice pres, Harambee: Services to Black Families, 1989-92. **Honors/Awds:** Office of Economic Oppor Scholarship Washington Univ 1967; Cert of Recog Natl Assn of Black Social Workers 1979; Cleveland Chapter, Tots & Teens leadership awd 1986; Board Member Emeritus, Project Friendship Big Sister Program, 1991; United Way Serv Leadership Devel Steering Comm, 1994-; United Way Serv Allocations/Panel 1985-88. **Home Addr:** 4421 Granada Blvd, Apt 515, Warrensville Heights, OH 44128.

BUGG, ROBERT
Government official. **Personal:** Born Jun 3, 1941, Topeka, KS; son of Mattie Bugg and Walter Bugg; married Jacqueline Shope Bugg, May 28, 1970; children: Glen, Chris, Anton. **Educ:** Washburn University, Topeka, KS, BA, corrections, 1974; Kansas University, Lawrence, KS, MPA, 1976. **Career:** State of Kansas, Topeka, KS, correctional officer, 1962-66; City of Topeka, Topeka, KS, police officer, 1966-68, field rep human relations, 1968-69; East Topeka Methodist Church, Topeka, KS, director of counselling, 1969-70; Big Brothers/Big Sisters, Topeka, KS, director of vehicles, 1982-87; State of Kansas, Topeka, director of vehicles, 1982-87; City of Topeka, Topeka, KS, personnel director/labor relations, 1987-. **Orgs:** Chairman, Black Democrats Caucus of Kansas, 1982-89; chair, founder, Martin Luther King Birthday Celebration, 1986-. **Military Serv:** US Army, SP 4, 1959-62; Good Conduct, Marksman. **Home Addr:** 3721 Evans Dr, Topeka, KS 66609.

BUGGAGE, CYNTHIA MARIE
City official. **Personal:** Born Oct 26, 1958, Donaldsonville, LA; daughter of Yvonne Stewart Buggage and Wilfred Joseph Buggage Sr. **Educ:** Grambling State Univ, Grambling, LA, BS, 1979; TX Southern Univ, Houston, TX, MPA, 1988. **Career:** Univ of Houston, Houston, TX, adjunct prof, 1986-89; City of Houston Parks & Rec, Houston, TX, grants administrator, 1980-. **Orgs:** Mem, Natl Assn for Female Exec, 1991; mem, Grambling Univ Natl Alumni, 1980-; mem, Natl Forum for Black Public Administrators, 1987-89; bd of dir, Political Activities League, 1986-87; Alpha Kappa Alpha Sorority, Inc. **Honors/Awds:** Human Enrichment of Life Program, Black Achiever of Houston, TX Award, 1994. **Home Addr:** 745 International Blvd, #745, Houston, TX 77024. **Business Phone:** (713)845-1118.

BUGGS, JAMES
Insurance executive. **Personal:** Born Apr 27, 1925, Summerfield, LA; son of Lucille Franklin Buggs and Clifton Buggs; married Johnye; children: James F, Bruce J. **Educ:** Spauling Business Coll. **Career:** Independent, Insurance Exec, field mgr/mgr; real estate salesman 1973-; Caddo Parish Shreveport, LA, deputy tax assessor 1982-85; Primerica Financial Services, life insurance executive. **Orgs:** Past pres Shreveport Negro Chamber of Commerce 1972-73; deacon Galilee Baptist Church; chairman of trustees; mem Amer Legion 525, 1973-78; past Worshipful Master Fred D Lee Lodge Prince Hall affiliation. **Honors/Awds:** Prince Hall Masonic Lodge, Certificate for 50 yrs membership, 1996. **Military Serv:** AUS Corpl 1943-46. **Home Addr:** 2839 Round Grove Ln, Shreveport, LA 71107.

BUIE, SAMPSON, JR.
Educational administrator. **Personal:** Born Sep 18, 1929, Fairmont, NC; married Catherine O; children: Debra, Janice, Velma. **Educ:** NC A&T State Univ, BS 1952; Univ of NC Greensboro, MEd 1973, Doctorate EdD 1982. **Career:** Boy Scouts of Amer, asst scout exec 1954-70; NC A&T State Univ, dir comm relations 1970-82, dir office of alumni affairs 1982-93; State of North Carolina, Dept of Administration, deputy sec for programs, 1993-. **Orgs:** Bd of dir Greensboro Rotary Club 1969-; mem bd of visitors Shaw Univ Div School 1981-; mem NC Comm Devel Commiss 1982-; trustee Gen Baptist State Conv of NC 1982-; mem Coll & Grad Comm, Chamber of Commerce, Greensboro United Fund, Piedmont Triad Criminal Justice/Planning Unit; vice pres Gen Greene Council BSA; mem NC A&T State Univ Natl Alumni Assoc Inc, Phi Beta Sigma, Greensboro Citizens Assoc, Natl Univ Extension Assoc, Guilford Cty Recreation Commiss, Greensboro-Guilford Cty Pulpit Forum, Drug Action Council Personnel Search Comm, NC State Adv Comm on Recruitment of Minorities for State Criminal Justice System; mem at large Natl Council BSA; consult for Monitoring & Tech Asst Training Prof HUD, USHUD; project dir Univ Year for Action Prog; numerousprofessional paper incl "Andragogy Pedagogy, Characteristics of Adults That Impact on Adult Learning & Dev" 1983; "Lifelong Learning, A Necessity & Not a Luxury" 1983. **Honors/Awds:** Nathaniel Greene Awd City of Greensboro 1969; Achievement Awd NC A&T State Univ Alumni Assoc 1969; United Negro Coll Fund Awd Bennett Coll 1972; Silver Beaver Awd BSA 1978; Minister of the Year Deep River Baptist Assoc 1983. **Military Serv:** Infantry 1st lt 1952-54.

BULGER, LUCILLE O.
Business executive. **Personal:** Born Sep 26, 1912; married Robert; children: Neil, Kent. **Educ:** New Sch of Social Research New York City Cornell Univ Extension, 1967-68. **Career:** Comm League of W 159th St Inc, exec dir 1966-. **Orgs:** Pres Comm League of W 159th St 1952-66; founder Comm League of W 159th St Inc 1952; pres Council Dist 6 1954-56; vice pres United Parents Assoc of NY 1957-61; mem Neighborhood Clean-Up Campaign Comm 1966-; bd mem Washington Heights W Harlem Inwood Mental Health Cncl 1969-; bd mem Central Harlem Meals on Wheels 1972; various comm com at Columbia Univ NYC; chmn Health Com of Ofc of Neighborhood Govt; mem Fed Grants Com of Addiction Serv Agy; Dist 6 Health Council 1973-75. **Honors/Awds:** Recipient Certificate of Pub Serv State of NY 1959; New York City Dept of Health Certificate of Merit 1967; Nat Assn of Media Women Inc Awd 1967; New York City Dept of Health Certificate of Merit 1975. **Business Addr:** Executive Dir, Comm League of W 159th St Inc, 508 W 159 St, New York, NY 10032.

BULLARD, EDWARD A., JR.
Educator, accountant, systems analyst. **Personal:** Born Apr 2, 1947, Syracuse, NY; married Terrlyon D; children: Lan R, Edward III, Terron D. **Educ:** Southern Univ, BS 1969; Syracuse Univ, MBA 1972; Univ of Detroit Law School, JD 1978. **Career:** Carrier Corp, analyst 1969; Ernst & Young, accountant 1969-72; Univ of MI Flint, prof, 1972-93; GMI, assoc prof acctg 1972-1993; Detroit College of Business-Flint, prof, currently. **Orgs:** Bd mem Urban League Flint 1984, Flint Comm Devel Corp 1984; mem AICPA, Amer Acctg Assoc; adv Flint City Schools Bus Prog 1985; mem City of Flint Cable TV Advisory Panel; Small business consultant and urban analyst; mem Amer Business Law Assoc; board of directors, Urban League of Flint; board of directors, Flint Community Development Coordination; legal regress committee, executive committee, NAACP of Flint; advisory panel, Flint Cable TV; consultant, Junior Achievement, Beecher High School; mem, Congressional Black Caucus-Flint; numerous others. **Honors/Awds:** CPA NY 1977-; Outstanding Prof Univ of MI Flint 1979; mem Univ of Detroit Law Schl Moot Court Tax Team 1977. **Home Addr:** 3026 Concord, Flint, MI 48504. **Business Addr:** Professor, Detroit College of Business-Flint, 3488 N Jennings Rd, Flint, MI 48504, (810)789-2200.

BULLARD, KEITH
Automobile dealership executive. **Career:** Airport Lincoln Mercury, owner, currently. **Special Achievements:** Company ranked #96 on BE's Top 100 Auto Dealers list, 1992. **Business Addr:** Owner, Airport Lincoln Mercury, 106 Stillwood Dr, Moon Twp, PA 15108, (412)262-3334.

BULLETT, AUDREY KATHRYN
Cleric. **Personal:** Born Feb 12, 1937, Chicago, IL; daughter of Eva Reed Hill and Louis Hill; married Clark Ricardo Bullett Jr, Sep 18, 1965 (deceased); children: Iris J, Stanley A. **Educ:** Ferris State University, AA, 1983, BS, public admin, 1984; University of Metaphysics, Los Angeles CA, MMs, 1986. **Career:** Lake County MI Veterans Trust Fund, authorized agent, 1969-80; Lake County, MI, deputy county clerk and deputy register of deeds, 1970-73, building and grounds manager, courthouse, 1970-80, public service employment program administrator, 1971-80, vice chair, county planning commission, 1975-76, chair 1976-80; TV 9/10, Cadillac MI, news correspondent, 1973-80; 78th District Court, Baldwin MI, court clerk and deputy magistrate, 1974-81; Yates Township, volunteer firefighter, 1968-96, treasurer, Economic Development Corp, 1979-94, Yates Township supervisor/mayor, 1984-92; Dawn's Light Centre, Inc, founder/president, 1985-; Yates Township Building Department, building official, inspector, 1988-92; Yates Township Fire Department, training officer, 1988-93; reiki master, 1995-; aromatherapy practitioner, 1994-; Uriel Temple of Spiritual Understanding Inc, founder, 1994-; Ordained Minister, 1995-. **Orgs:** Chairperson, MI Chapter Natl Conference of Black Mayors, 1988-92; advisory board member, Rural Business Partnership Board, 1989-90; secretary, West Central MI Community Growth Alliance, 1988-90; chairperson, Lake County Democratic Party, 1975-78, 1985-86, 1991-92; Idlewild Lot Owners Assn, natl financial scy, 1997-; NAACP, Lake-Newaygo branch, 1969-; NAACP, life member, 1994; First Baptist Church of Idlewild, deaconess, 1997-. **Honors/Awds:** Robert F Williams Memorial Scholarship, 1983; Victor F Spathelf Award for leadership, 1984; Twenty Year Fire Service Award, Yates Township Fire Department, 1989; Service Award, Yates Township Police Department, 1992; Woman of the Year, First Baptist Church of Idlewild, 1996. **Special Achievements:** Author: Come Colour My Rainbow, copyright 1996; You, Me and God, unpublished book, copyright, 1996; Sweet Marjoram, Life's Reflections As Seen and Expressed, unpublished book, copyright, 1996; Poetry and Rhythmic Prose. **Business Addr:** Minister, Uriel Temple of Spiritual Understanding Inc, 6489 South Broadway, PO Box 144, Idlewild, MI 49642-0144, (616)745-7608.

BULLETT, VICKY
Professional basketball player. **Personal:** Born Oct 4, 1967. **Educ:** Maryland, bachelor's degree in general studies. **Career:** Charlotte Sting, center, 1997-. **Honors/Awds:** US Olympic Basketball Team, Gold Medal, 1988, Bronze Medal, 1992. **Business Addr:** Professional Basketball Player, Charlotte Sting, 2709 Water Ridge Pkwy, Ste 400, Charlotte, NC 28217, (704)424-9622.

BULLINS, ED
Playwright, producer, educator. **Personal:** Born Jul 2, 1935, Philadelphia, PA; son of Bertha Marie Queen Bullins. **Educ:** Los Angeles City College, attended, 1961-63; San Francisco State College; New York School of Visual Arts; New School

Extension; Vista College; University of California Berkeley; William Penn Business Institute, gen business certificate; Antioch University, BA, 1989; San Francisco State University, MFA, 1994. **Career:** Black Arts West, founder, producer, 1965-67; New Lafayette Theatre of Harlem, playwright, assoc director, 1967-73; Black Theatre Magazine, editor, 1968-73; New York Shakespeare Festival, writers unit coordinator/press assistant, 1975-82; New York University, School of Continuing Education, instructor, 1979, dramatic writing, instructor, 1981; Berkeley Black Repertory, public relations director, 1982; The Magic Theatre, promotion director pro tem, 1982-83; Julian Theatre, group sales coordinator, 1983; City College of San Francisco, drama instructor, 1984-88; Antioch University, playwriting instructor, admin asst, public info & recruitment, 1986-87; Bullins Memorial Theatre, producer/playwright, 1988; lecturer, instructor, various universities and colleges throughout the US; Northeastern University, professor of theater, 1995-. **Orgs:** Dramatists Guild. **Honors/Awds:** Vernon Rice Award, The Electronic Nigger and Others, 1968; Village Voice, Obie Award, Distinguished Playwriting, In New England Winter, and The Fabulous Miss Marie, 1971, also won Black Arts Alliance Award both in same year; New York Drama Critics Circle Award, Obie Award for Distinguished Playwriting, The Taking of Miss Janie, 1975; American Place Theatre grant, 1967; Rockefeller Foundation, grants for playwriting, 1968, 1970, 1973; Guggenheim Fellowship grants, 1971, 1976; Creative Artists Program Service grant, 1973; Natl Endowment for the Arts, grant. **Special Achievements:** The Duplex, 1970; A Ritual to Raise the Dead and Foretell the Future, 1970; The Devil Catchers, 1970; In New England Winter, 1971; The Fabulous Miss Marie, 1971; Ya Gonna Let Me Take You Out Tonight, Baby?, 1972; House Party, A Soul Happening, book/lyrics, 1973; The Taking of Miss Janie, 1975; The Mystery of Phyllis Wheatley, 1976; Storyville, 1977; Michael, 1978; Leavings, 1980; Steve & Velma, 1980; The Hungered One, short stories, 1971; The Reluctant Rapist, novel, 1973; wrote play, ''Boy X Man,'' 1994. **Home Addr:** 801 Tremont St, No 412, Boston, MA 02118.

BULLOCK, ELBERT L.
Correctional officer. **Personal:** Born Jan 19, 1934, Houston; married Yvonne M; children: Paula, Jo Anna, Lauren. **Educ:** Fresno State Coll, BA 1957. **Career:** CA Community Realese Bd, hearing rep; CA Med Facility CA Dept Corrections chief human relations section CA Dept Corrections, assoc supt 1972-74; Richmond Serv Center CA, mgr 1970-72; Richmond Serv Center, CA asst Mgr 1969-70; CA Dept Corrections, correctional consultant 1967-69; Cdc, parole agt 1965-67; tchr pub & state 1959-65. **Orgs:** Mem Counseliers W; CA Black Correctional Coalition; past mem Allied Peace Officers Assn Mem; Alpha Phi Alpha Frat; past mem City Richmond Model Cities Com 1968-71; chmn Mayors Cit Com Study Comm Relations Richmond CA 1969; All Conf team Fresno State Coll 1956; All Star Football team USMC 1958; devel first pre-serv ttng acad hiring & training staff CA dept corrections; Affirmative Action plan Cdc. **Military Serv:** USMC lance corpl 1957-59.

BULLOCK, J. JEROME
Business executive. **Personal:** Born Jan 3, 1948, Hogansville, GA; son of Vivian Baker Bullock and Jerry L Bullock; married Alice Gresham; children: Brian Jerome, Alison Whitney. **Educ:** Tuskegee University, BS Political Science 1969; Howard Univ School of Law, JD 1975. **Career:** US Marshals Serv, assoc legal counsel 1975-77, 1982-84, US Marshal 1977-82, chief congressional & public affairs 1984-85; Air Security Corp, vp, 1983-85; Office of Internal Security, chief 1985-89; US Dept of Justice, asst inspector general for Investigations, 1989-94; Decision Strategies International, managing director, 1994-97; Price Waterhouse, LLP, managing dir, 1997-. **Orgs:** Natl Assoc of Flight Instructors 1984-; IA State Bar Assn; Phi Alpha Delta Law Fraternity; Intl Assoc of Chiefs of Police; Kappa Alpha Psi. **Honors/Awds:** Meritorious Serv Award US Marshals Serv 1978; Tuskegee Alumni Award Tuskegee Inst 1979; Distinguished Military Grad Army ROTC Tuskegee Inst 1969; Special Achievement Award US Marshals Serv 1976; appt by Pres Carter US Marshal for DC 1977; Distinguished Service Award, US Marshals Service, 1987; Commercial Pilot, FAA Certified Flight Instructor. **Military Serv:** AUS capt 1969-72. **Home Addr:** 6127 Utah Avenue NW, Washington, DC 20015. **Business Phone:** (202)414-1765.

BULLOCK, JAMES
Educator, attorney. **Personal:** Born Aug 22, 1926, Charleston, MS; married Lois; children: Joseph. **Educ:** Texas Southern Univ, BA, JD, 1970. **Career:** US Postal Service, supvr; TX Southern Univ, assoc dean law, assoc prof law, currently. **Orgs:** Justice Greener Chap Phi Alpha Delta Legal Frat; TX Black Caucus; mem Am Bar Assn; Nat Bar Assn; State Bar TX; Houston Bar Assn; Houston Lawyers Assn; Phi Alpha Delta Legal Frat; mem S & Central YMCA; NAACP; Harris Co Cncl Orgn; TX Assn Coll Tchrs. **Honors/Awds:** Phi Alpha Delta Outstanding Alumnus. **Military Serv:** USAF s/sgt 1947-56. **Business Addr:** Associate Professor, Texas Southern University, School of Law, 3100 Cleburne Avenue, Houston, TX 77004.

BULLOCK, THURMAN RUTHE
Municipal government official. **Personal:** Born Oct 6, 1947, Richmond, VA; son of Dorothy Hargrove Bullock and Warren Bullock; married Anne Leshner, Aug 31, 1976; children: Thurman Martin. **Educ:** Franklin & Marshall Coll, Lancaster, PA, BA, 1970; Temple Univ, Philadelphia, PA, MS, 1979. **Career:** Comptroller of the Currency, Philadelphia, PA, asst natl bank examiner, 1970-75; Deloitte Haskins & Sells, Philadelphia, PA, auditor, 1977-80; Bell of Pennsylvania, Philadelphia, PA, internal auditor, 1980-82; City of Philadelphia Office of the Controller, PA, deputy city controller, 1982-. **Orgs:** Bd mem, Council of Intl Programs, 1981-, Intl Professional Exchange, 1981-, Opportunities Acad of Mgmt Training Inc, 1981-, Philadelphia Clearinghouse, 1989; business advisory bd, House of Umoja, 1986-; past sec, treasurer, 1980-89, pres elect, 1989-, Pennsylvania Inst of Certified Public Accountants; past pres, mem, Philadelphia Federation of Black Business & Professional Org, 1981-; past vice pres, former advisory bd mem, Community Accountants; mem, Natl Assn of Black Accountants, 1979, Amer Inst of Certified Public Accountants, 1980-, Govt Finance Officers Assn, 1981, Accounting Research Assn, 1989, Amer Soc for Public Admin, 1989, Assn of Local Govt Auditors, 1989; Lesbian & Gay Task Force, financial adviser, currently; Natl Jr Tennis League; Zion Nonprofit Trust; NGA, Inc; East Mt Airy Neighbors; Fund the the FUTURE of Philadelphia. **Honors/Awds:** CPA Certificate, 1979; Distinguished Public Serv Award, Pennsylvania Inst of Certified Public Accountants, 1986; appeared in Pennsylvania Inst of Certified Public Accountants career video, ''Is an Accounting Career in Your Future?'', 1987. **Business Addr:** Deputy City Controller, Philadelphia, Office of the Controller, 1230 Municipal Serv Bldg, 1401 John F Kennedy Blvd, Philadelphia, PA 19102-1679.

BUMPHUS, WALTER GAYLE
Educator. **Personal:** Born Mar 19, 1948, Princeton, KY; married Aileen Thompson; children: Michael, Brian, Fran. **Educ:** Murray State Univ, BS 1971, MEd 1974; Univ of TX at Austin, PhD 1985. **Career:** Murray State Univ, counselor & dorm asst, 1970-72, dir, minority affairs, 1972-74; East AR Comm Coll, dean, 1974-78; Howard Comm Coll, dean of students, 1978-86, vp/dean of students, beginning 1986; Brookhaven College, pres, currently. **Orgs:** Consultant for Office of Educ Title IV 1986; chairperson Middle Stated Accred Assoc Team 1986; Pres Natl Assoc of Student Develop; Amer Assn of Community Colleges, chmn, 1996-. **Honors/Awds:** Richardson Fellowship Univ of TX at Austin 1983; Key to City Awd Princeton KY 1984. **Business Addr:** President, Brookhaven College, 3939 Valley View Lane, Farmers Branch, TX 75244-4997.

BUNCHE, CURTIS J.
Automobile dealer. **Personal:** Born Aug 4, 1955, Crystal River, FL; son of Ruth Bunche; married Melinda Bunche, Jan 1, 1982; children: Mykisha, Cetera, Malcolm. **Educ:** Albany State College, 1979. **Career:** Philadelphia Eagles, defensive end, 1979-80; Tampa Bay Bandits, defensive end, 1983-84; C&C Associates, president, 1981-87; Mon-Valley Lincoln-Mercury, president, 1987-93; Riverview Ford Lincoln-Mercury, president, 1994-. **Orgs:** Rotary, 1988-.

BUNDLES, A'LELIA PERRY
Broadcast deputy bureau chief. **Personal:** Born Jun 7, 1952, Chicago, IL; daughter of A'Lelia Mae Perry Bundles (deceased) and S Henry Bundles Jr. **Educ:** Harvard-Radcliffe Coll, AB (magna cum laude) 1974; Columbia Univ Grad Sch of Journalism, MSJ 1976. **Career:** Newsweek Chicago Bureau, intern 1973; WTLC-FM Indpls, anchor/reporter 1974; Du Pont Co, Wilmington, DE, staff asst 1974-75; NBC News NY, Houston & Atlanta bureaus, field producer 1976-85; NBC News Washington, DC, producer 1985-89; ABC News Washington DC, World News Tonight, producer 1989-96; ABC News Washington DC, deputy bureau chief, 1996-. **Orgs:** Schlesiger Library on the History of Women, advisory board, 1986-94; sec Radcliffe Class of '74, 1979-, Nat'l Assoc of Black Jrnlsts 1980-; trustee of Radcliffe Coll, bd of management 1985-89; dir, Harvard Alumni Assn 1989-91; The Links Inc; Alpha Kappa Alpha; Harvard Club of Washington, DC, bd, 1995-; Madam Walker Theatre Center, bd, 1997-; Radcliffe Quarterly Advisory Board, 1996-; Radcliffe College Alumnae Association, first vp, 1997-. **Honors/Awds:** NBC/RCA Fellow at Columbia Schl of Jrnlsm 1975-76; summer resch Fellow Kennedy Inst of Politics Harvard 1973; freelance writer, published in American History, Parade, Ms, Sage, Ebony, Jr, Essence, Radcliffe Quarterly, Seventeen, Indpls, Star, Indpls News; National Assn of Black Journalists 1st Place Features Award 1987; author, Madam CJ Walker: Entrepreneur, Chelsea House Publishers, 1991; National Academy of Television Arts and Sciences, Emmy, 1990; American Book Award, 1992; American Women in Radio & TV, 1st Place Feature Award, 1992; Black Memorabilia Hall of Fame, 1991; North Central High School Hall of Fame, 1992; duPont Gold Baton, 1995. 1992. **Business Addr:** Deputy Bureau Chief, ABC News, 1717 DeSales St NW, Washington, DC 20036.

BUNDY, JAMES LOMAX
Judge (retired). **Personal:** Born Mar 6, 1920, Bluefield, WV; married Sarah J; children: 4. **Educ:** Bluefield State Coll, BS 1942; Univ MD Sch Law, LLB 1949, JD 1969. **Career:** City of Baltimore, asst city solicitor 1962-68; State of MD, asst atty gen 1968-74; District 1, judge. **Orgs:** Mem Natl, MD State Bar Assns; mem Bar Assn Baltimore City; mem Monumental City Bar Assn; mem Bluefield State Coll Baltimore Alumni Chap pres 1970-73; lectr Business Law Morgan State Coll Grad Sch 1970. **Honors/Awds:** Afro-Amer Superior Comm Serv Awd 1958. **Military Serv:** USAF sgt maj 1942-45. **Business Addr:** Judge, District 1, 221 E Madison St, Baltimore, MD 21202.

BUNKLEY, LONNIE R.
Business executive. **Personal:** Born Aug 12, 1932, Denison, TX; son of Ruth Smith Bunkley and C B Bunkley; married Charlene Marie Simpson, Jan 12, 1973; children: Karen Annette, Natalie Anitra. **Educ:** Prairie View Univ, BA 1952; CA State Univ LA, MS 1964; Univ of So CA, grad studies 1965. **Career:** LA Neighborhood Youth Corps Econ & Youth Oppor Agency, dir 1968; East LA Coll & Compton Coll, coll instr 1970-78; LA Co Probation Dept, div chief 1982; Pacific Properties, broker & Developer/pres; Commercial Devel Corp, president; commercial developer of Compton Plaza; Compton Renaissance Plaza. **Orgs:** Mem exec comm Southside LA Jr C of C 1966; mem SE Welfare Planning Council 1973; bd of dir Compton Sickle Cell Anemia Educ & Detection Ctr; mem CA Probation & Parole Assn; mem Black Probation Officers Assn; bd of dir Natl Black United Fund; chmn, bd of trustees Los Angeles Brotherhood Crusade; mem Omega Psi Phi Frat; ruling elder St Paul's Presbyterian Church; chmn, bd of directors, Black Support Group, California State University; Prairie View University, pres, Los Angeles Alumni, 1960. **Honors/Awds:** Outstanding Serv Awd Brotherhood Crusade 1972; Certificate, Ctr for Health Urban Educ & Rsch 1982; Cert of Appreciation US Congress 1983; Awd LA Co Bd ofSupervisors 1984; Certificate Compton Sickle Cell Educ & Detection Ctr 1982; Prairie View Univ Alumni Awd 1970; Commendation Southside Jr Chamber of Commerce 1962; LA Co Bd of Supervisors Awd 1984; Commendatory Resolution City of Compton 1982; Commendation, State of California, 1990; Omega Psi Phi, Lambda Omicrom Chap, Citizen of the Year. **Military Serv:** AUS educ specl 1953-55. **Home Addr:** 6711 Bedford Avenue, Los Angeles, CA 90056.

BUNTE, DORIS
Administrator. **Personal:** Born Jul 2, 1933, New York, NY; divorced; children: Yvette, Harold, Allen. **Educ:** Boston U, Metro Coll, Univ MA Amhurst/Suffolk Univ 1969-73. **Career:** 7th Suffolk Dist, state rep 1972; Boston Housing Authority, comm 1969-75; So End Nghbrhd Action Program Boston, dir pers 1970-72; So End Nghbrhd ActionProgram & Boston, dir housing 1969-70. **Orgs:** Mem Dem Nat Conventions, 1972-76; mem, Electoral Coll Pres Election 1976; mem MALEG Black Caucaus; mem Third World Jobs Clearing Hse; mem MA Assn Paraplegics; mem Combined Black Phi-lanthropies; mem MA Leg Women's Caucus; mem NAACP; mem Nat Order Of Women Legltr; mem Black Polit Task Force; mem MA Conf Human Rights; mem Citizen's Housing & Planning Assn; mem Solomon Carter Fuller Mental Health Ctr; mem Rosbury Multi-Serv Ctr Declaratoion & ''Doris Bunte Day'' 1975; Loeb Fellow, Harvard Grad Sch of Design 1975-76. **Honors/Awds:** Citizen Of Y R Omega Psi Frat Inc Iota Chi Chap 1978; Citizen Of Yr Award Nat Assn Social Wkrs 1980; Notary Public, Commonwealth MA; Appointee Nat RentAdv Bd Phase II Econ Stabilization Act; Award Black Housing Task Force; Award Roxbury Action Prog; Published, Address To City Missionary, 1973; Publ Child Force; Award, Roxbury Action Prog; Published, Address to City Missionary 1973; Publ ''Child Advocacy'' a dependency cycle is not a goal 1977; publ ''our & Third World Comm Revitalization Through Access By Mandte Example & Monitoring''; Guest Lectr Boston Coll, Boston U, John F Kennedy Sch govt, Simmons Coll Suffolk U; So U; Univ of Ma. **Business Addr:** Administrator, Boston Housing Authority, 52 Chauncy St, Boston, MA 02111.

BUNTON, HENRY CLAY
Clergyman. **Personal:** Born Oct 19, 1903, Tuscaloosa, AL; married Alfreda; children: Mattye, Marjorie, Henry, Joseph. **Educ:** A&M U, AB; Denver U, Sch of Theology MTh; Northwestern U, Garret Theol Sem; Meth U, Perkins Sch of Theology of So. **Career:** Christian Meth Episcopal Ch Seventh Episcopal Dist, bishop; Churchs in AL FL AR TX CO TN, former pastor; Miles Coll, Paine Coll KS-MO Annual Conf Trustee, former pres elder. **Orgs:** Mem NAACP; Phi Beta Sigma; mason; contrib editor Christian Index Christimeth Epis Ch1948-60; charter mem SCLC. **Business Addr:** CME Ch, 557 Randolph St NW, Washington, DC 20011.

BUNYON, RONALD S.
Business executive. **Personal:** Born Mar 13, 1935, Philadelphia, PA; son of Mamie Bunyon and Ulysses Bunyon; married Josephine; children: Ronald Jr, Judith, Joann, Joyce, Jodetta. **Educ:** Mitchell Coll, ASE, 1965; Univ of New Haven, CT, BSBus (cum laude), first in class, 1969; Southern Connecticut State University, MS, urban studies; RPI, MS, urban environment, 1992. **Career:** Business Ventures Intl Inc, pres 1979-; Drexel Univ Philadelphia, asst vice pres 1979; Opportunities Ind Ctr Intl, mgmt spec 1976; Zion Investments Philadelphia, business mgr 1973; Natl Prog Asst for Econ Devel, reg dir 1972; Gen Dynamics Nuclear Ship Bldg, sr designer 1958.

Orgs: US Dept of Commerce, Export Council, 1979; World Trade Assn, Philadelphia, 1979; Alpha Ki Alpha Honor Society, 1967; Bd of Education, leadership committee, Philadelphia, 1978; National Teachers Assn, 1986. **Special Achievements:** Author: Black Life Poetic Thinking, Vantage Inc, 1992; Family, short stories for children, 1993; South Philly, novel, 1993; Black Business, from experiences, 1993. **Business Addr:** President, Business Ventures Intl, Inc, PO Box 1324, Philadelphia, PA 19105.

BURCH, REYNOLD EDWARD
Physician. **Personal:** Born Oct 3, 1910, August, ME; married Mary. **Educ:** Bates Coll, BS 1933; Howard U, MD 1942. **Career:** Pvt practice 1946-72, 1976; MJ Med Schl, asso clinical prof 1972-76; Gardiner HS, sci tchr 1934; Booker Washington HS, chem tchr 1935; Bordentown Manual Training Schl, sci tchr; Maternal & Infant Care, NJ Med & Sch, dir. **Orgs:** Bd dir, Pub Serv Electric & Gas; bd trustee, Coll Med & Dent NJ 1972-74; AMA; NMA; United Hosps of Newark; Bethany Lodge 31; Prince Hall Foam Masons; bd dir, Essex Co Youth House 1949-54; adv bd Planned Parenthood Essex Co; chmn bd trustees, Leaguers Ind; 200 Club; NAACP; YMCA. **Honors/Awds:** Diplomat, Am Bd of Obstetrics, 1963; Fellow, Am Coll of Surgeons; fellow Am Coll Obs-gyn; Alpha Phi Alpha; Sigma Pi Phi; Co-author "Heroin Addiction Among Pregant Women & Their Babies" author "A Plan For Family Planning"; 3 Meritious Serv awds, Essex Co Med Soc. **Military Serv:** AUS Air Corps, cpt 1943-46.

BURCHELL, CHARLES R.
Educator. **Personal:** Born Nov 24, 1946, New Orleans; married Paulette Martinez. **Educ:** Tulane U, 1964-66; Southern U, 1966-68; LA State U, BA 1968, MA 1971, PhD 1977. **Career:** LA State Univ, instructor dept of Psychology 1971-; WRBT-TV,TV news & reporter 1972-74, 76; WXOK Radio Baton Rouge, radio announcer 1966-72. **Orgs:** Southern Psychol Assn, 1974-75; Psi Chi, 1968; AFTRA, 1970. **Honors/Awds:** Recipient Welfare Rights Orgn Serv Award 1973. **Business Addr:** LA State Univ, Dept of Psychol, Baton Rouge, LA 70803.

BURDEN, PENNIE L.
Community activist. **Personal:** Born Nov 26, 1910, Waynesboro, GA; daughter of Sarah L Bell and John W Bell; married Sherman J Burden, Nov 4, 1959. **Educ:** Wayne State Univ; Detroit Inst Musical Art; Lewis Business Coll. **Career:** Detroit Gen Hospital, desk clerk registration of patients for clinic, sec in oral surgery l969-70, technician in radiology clinic patients, sr clerk business office. **Orgs:** Natl pres, Eta Phi Beta Sorority, Inc, l962-66; Campfire Girl Leader, l970-80; Campfire Girl Leader l97-80; Historic Sites Committee, l980-; UNCF MI Con Sr Program, l989; St Stephen AME Church Bd of Trustees asst sec; DABO bd of dir; Natl Council Negro Women; St Stephen Dir Sr Citizen; St Stephen pres Goodwill Club, l989; Dir Sr Citizen Program St Stephen AME Church, l980-89. **Honors/Awds:** Life Membership, NAACP; sec Mortgage Fund, St Stephen AME Church, l975; Golden Heritage, NAACP, l988; Town Hall Forum, St Stephen AME Church; Out Reach Program, City Detroit Retirees, l989. **Home Addr:** l3233 Vassar Dr, Detroit, MI 48235.

BURDEN, WILLIE JAMES
Athletics administrator. **Personal:** Born Jul 21, 1951, Longwood, NC; son of Emily H Burden and John Burden; married Velma Stokes; children: Courtney, Willie James Jr, Freddie Hamilton. **Educ:** Ohio Univ, Masters 1983; NC State U, BA 1974; Tennessee State University, EdD, 1990. **Career:** OH Univ, asst football coach 1982-84; Calgary Stampeders of CFL, prof athlete 1974-81; NC State Univ, asst to athletics dir 1976-82, asst Football Coach 1974-76; Tennessee Tech Univ, asst athletic dir 1984-88; Ohio Univ, asst athletic dir 1988-90; North Carolina A&T University, athletics dir, currently. **Orgs:** Sr cnslr Amer Legion Boys State TN 1984 & 1986; pres Friends of Distinction NC 1969-; big bro cnslr PHD Prevent High Sch Drop Outs Prog Raleigh, NC 1973-74; mem, Phi Delta Kappa 1987-; mem, Civitan Civic Organization 1988-90; Nat Greene Kiwanis, 1993-. **Honors/Awds:** Athletic endwmnt schlrshp honoree Univ of Calgary, Alberta, CN 1983-; all-star Canadian Football League 1975-79; mvp Canadian Football League 1975; mvp player of the year, Atlantic Coast Conf Football 1973; Calgary Stampeders, "Wall of Fame," 1992. **Business Addr:** Athletic Department, North Carolina A&T University, Corbett Center, Greensboro, NC 27411.

BURDETTE, LAVERE ELAINE
Clinical psychologist, business executive. **Personal:** Born Dec 30, Chicago, IL; daughter of Dorothy Earl Dixon and Leonard Charles Dixon. **Educ:** Kentucky State University, BA, 1969; Wayne State University, MSW, 1972; Union Graduate School, MPsych, 1982, PhD, 1985. **Career:** Cigna Insurance Co, employee assistance specialist; Blue Cross and Blue Shield of Michigan, advisory board, 1990-; Burdette & Doss Training Inc, president, currently; Burdette & Doss Psychological Services, executive director, currently; clinical practice of psychology, currently. **Orgs:** American Association of Black Psychologists; Michigan Psychological Association; American Psychological Association. **Special Achievements:** Author of: The Self in Search of Unity Through Confrontation, 1985, Stress Management Workbook, 1987, Handling Conflict: Fighting for Happiness, 1991. **Business Addr:** President, Burdette & Doss Associates Inc, 17336 W 12 Mile Rd, Ste 100, Southfield, MI 48076, (313)569-0344.

BURFORD, EFFIE LOIS
Educator. **Personal:** Born Feb 16, 1927, Learned, MS; married; children: Cecelia Adela Boler, Suzette Elaine, Maurice M. **Educ:** Butler U, AB 1950; Christian Theol Sem, MA 1952 1955. **Career:** Indianapolis, teacher 1957-65; Language Arts & Spanish, teacher 1966; Language, Traveling Foreign teacher 1970; Zeta Phi Beta Sor Inc, state dir 1966, reg dir 1968-74. **Orgs:** Bd mem editor Mem Am Tchrs Spanish & Portguese 1974; IFT; bd mem 2nd Christian Ch; comm on ch devel in IN; life mem NAACP; natl chmn Reconciliation Christian Ch; mem Publicity Com. **Honors/Awds:** Black women's intl conf award in journalism Columbia Scholastic Press Assn 1971; regional award Zeta Phi Beta Sor 1972; natl reg dir's award 1974. **Business Addr:** 150 W 40th St, Indianapolis, IN.

BURGER, MARY WILLIAMS
Educational administrator. **Personal:** Born in North Little Rock, AR; children: Nathaniel R III, Henry W. **Educ:** University of Arkansas, BA (magna cum laude), 1959; Colorado State University, MA, English lit, 1961; Washington University, PhD, modern literature, 1973; Harvard University, certified in education management, 1978. **Career:** Lincoln University, instructor, English, 1961-66; University of Missouri, instructor, asst professor, English, 1966-69, 1973-75; University of Maryland, asst provost/asst vice pres, 1975-84; Tennessee State University, vice pres for academic affairs, professor, English, starting 1984; California State University Sacramento, vice pres for academic affairs, currently. **Orgs:** Consultant, Natl Education Assn, 1973; reviewer, Middle States Assn of Colleges & Schools, 1974-75; consultant, Urban Behavioral Research Assn, 1974-79; consultant, Midwest Center for EEO, 1974-75; Alpha Kappa Mu; Alpha Kappa Alpha; Phi Kappa Phi; Sister Cities of Baltimore-Garnga Liberia; College Language Assn; State Planning Committee ACE/NIP. **Honors/Awds:** Black Viewpoint, New American Library, 1971; Ford Foundation Fellow, Washington University, 1972-73; Images of Black Women Sturdy, Black Bridges, Doubleday, 1979; Improving Opportunity for Black Students, NAFEO Proceedings, 1983; Sister Cities, Intl TAP Grant, Gbarnga Liberia, 1983.

BURGES, MELVIN E.
Construction company executive. **Personal:** Born Oct 15, 1951, Chicago, IL; son of Ruth N Burges and Malcolm M Burges, Sr; children: Necco L McKinley. **Educ:** Loyola University, BA, accounting, 1982; DePaul University, MBA (with distinction), 1984. **Career:** Ceco Corporation, regional controller, 1972-90; Winter Construction Co, corporate controller, 1990-92; Sanderson Industries, Inc, vp of finance & administration, 1992-93; System Software Associates, finance application consultant, 1994; Thomas Howell/McLarens Toplis Inc, national finance manager, 1995-97; Harcon, Inc, controller, 1997-. **Orgs:** National Black MBA Association, director of corporate affairs, 1990-; National Association of Black Accountants, 1990-; Ebenezer Baptist Church, trustee, 1992-; Construction Financial Management Association, 1989-; IBT Capital Group Investment Club, 1991-; American Institute of Certified Public Accountants, 1990-; Being Single Magazine Pinnacle Club, 1992. **Honors/Awds:** Being Single Magazine, The Pinnacle Award, 1991; YMCA, Motivator of Youth Award, 1980. **Business Addr:** Controller, Harcon, Inc, 905 Union Hill Rd, Alpharetta, GA 30201, (770)343-9998.

BURGESS, DWIGHT A.
Association executive. **Personal:** Born Dec 16, 1927, Bailey's Bay; married Delores L Caldwell; children: Daphne, Danita. **Educ:** Tuskegee Inst, BS 1952, MEd 1953. **Career:** Birmingham Urban League, aptd exec dir 1972-; Daniel Payne Coll, interim pres 2 months 1969, dean Acad affairs 1968; New Castle HS, head soc & sci dept, oratorical coach, athletic bus mgr 1966; Summer Basic Skills Workshop For Am Ethical Un, dir 1964-66; Hooper City HS, soc studies Tchr, Jeff co bd educ 1955; Francis Patton Sch Bermuda, tchr English Tchr athletic Coach 1953-55. **Orgs:** Aptd to professional rights & responsibilities comm AL State Tchrs Assn 1963; pres Jeff Co Educ Assn 1963-65, exec comm mem 1966; aptd gr ldr soc studies tchrs Jeff Co AL 1968; mem Adv Com AL Cntr for Higher Edn; chmn Faculty Sharing Emp Com AL Cntr for Higher Educ 1968; aptd inst dep AL, Cntr for Higher Educ 1968; aptd Adv Bd Curbar Asso for Higher & Educ 1968; elected sec St John Fed Com 1969; aptd consult in educ Group Research 1969; aptd chmn Health Manpower Adv Com, Comm Health Planning Commn, Comm Serv Cncl of Jeff Co 1969; aptd outreach supvr Health Planner, Comm Serv Council 1970; aptd Comm Liaison Adv, Family Planning, Dept of OB-GYN of Univ of AL Med Sch 1971; cits adv com Birmingham Police Dept 1972; bd dirs Crisis Cntr 1972; coord Jeff Co Drug AbuseCom 1973; AL Com for PublProgs in Humanities 1973; Birmingham Manpower Area Planning Council 1973; C of C Manpower Voc Educ Com 1974; Birmingham Art Club 1974; Birmingham Youth 1974. **Honors/Awds:** Recip Delta Sigma Theta Sor Comm Serv Award 1973; cert outstanding serv OIC 1974; selected Alpha Phi & Alpha Man of Yr 1974. **Business Addr:** 505 N 17 St, Birmingham, AL 35203.

BURGESS, JAMES R., JR. See Obituaries section.

BURGESS, LINDA
Professional basketball player. **Personal:** Born Jul 27, 1969. **Educ:** Univ of Alabama, attended. **Career:** Belinzona (Switzerland), forward, 1992-93; Ramat HaSharon (Israel), 1993-94, 1996-97; Beni-Yeuda (Israel), 1994-95; SPO Rouen (France), 1995-96; Los Angeles Sparks, 1997; Sacramento Monarchs, 1998-. **Business Addr:** Professional Basketball Player, Sacramento Monarchs, One Sports Parkway, Sacramento, CA 95834, (916)928-3650.

BURGESS, LORD. See BURGIE, IRVING LOUIS.

BURGESS, MELVIN THOMAS, SR.
City official (retired). **Personal:** Born May 23, 1938, Memphis, TN; son of Katherine S Burgess and Eddie Burgess; married Johanna Sandridge, Feb 24, 1975; children: Melvin Thomas II, Pamela Camille. **Educ:** Grambling Coll; Memphis State Univ, BA, police admin, 1981. **Career:** City of Memphis, patrol officer, 1962-66, detective sergeant, 1966-79, lt, 1979-81, captain, 1981-85, inspector, 1985-86, chief inspector, 1986-88, dir of police services, 1991-94; Lin-Cris Inc, currently. **Orgs:** Kappa Alpha Psi, vice pres; NAACP, life member; NEI Major Cities Chief of Police, 1992; Intl Assn of Chiefs of Police. **Honors/Awds:** Kappa Alpha Psi, Man of the Year Award, 1992. **Military Serv:** US Air Force, corporal, 1957-61; Overseas Good Conduct Medal. **Business Addr:** Director of Police Services, Memphis Police Department, 201 Poplar Ave, Ste 1201, Memphis, TN 38103, (901)576-5700.

BURGESS, ROBERT E., SR.
Business executive. **Personal:** Born Oct 13, 1937, Lake City, SC; married Mary Elizabeth, Nov 23, 1969; children: W Michael Tiagwad, Tamara Tiagwad Wagner, Robert E Jr. **Educ:** J M Wright Tech School, Electrical 1954-57; Norwalk Comm Coll Cert City Housing Planning & Devel 1973; IBM Mgmt Devel Prog for Community Execs 1983. **Career:** Self-employed, band leader 1958-63; Norden Aircraft, inspector 1963-66; self-employed, restaurant owner 1966-69; Committee on Training & Employment, administrative asst 1966-71; Norwalk Econ Opportunity Now Inc, administrative asst 1970-72, executive director 1972-; Employment & Training Council, 1995; Norwanc Hospital Institutional Review Board, 1994. **Orgs:** Chmn/organizer Fairfield Cty Black Businessmens Assoc 1969; organizer Norwalk Conn Fed Credit Union 1970; mem South Norwalk Comm Ctr Bd 1970, State Manpower Training Council Gov Meskill 1972; bd of dir Springwood Health Unit 1973; mem New England Comm Action Program Dir Assoc 1973, Natl Comm Action Agchmn/org dir Assoc 1973; chmn Norwalk Comm Devel Citizens Partic Comm Mayor Irwin 1974-; mem State Employment Training Council Gov Grasso 1978; pres CT Assoc for Community Action 1978-84; mem State Energy Adv Comm Gov Grasso 1979; State Negotiated Invest Strategy Team Gov O'Neill 1983; mem NAACP Exec Comm 1983-; legislative chmn CT Assoc for Comm Action 1984-; District Heating Comm 1984; mem Review Team ACVS Headstart 1984; mem Exec Comm, Action Housing 1989(Vice Pres); mem Advisory Comm tT Housing Finance Authority by Gov O'Neill 1989; CT Employment & Training Commission by Gov O'Neill 1989; member CT Commission to Study Management of State Government by Gov O'Neill 1989; United Way Commnity Problem Solving Task Force; General Assistance Task Force; UCONN Downstate Initiative Advisory Committee; South West Region CT Housing Coalition by Governor Weicker, co-chair, 1991; Mayor's Blue Ribbon Committee on Race Relations by Mayor Esposito, 1993; Negotiating Team for Police Community Relations by Mayor Esposito, 1993; Norwalk Community Health Center, bd of dirs, 1995. **Honors/Awds:** Roy Wilkins Civil Rights Awd CT State NAACP 1984; Awd for Outstanding Serv to Norwalk Corinthian Lodge 16 F&AM PHA 1982; Citizen of the Year Alpha Nu Chap Omega Psi Phi 1981; Dedicated Serv to Fairfield Cty Kappa Alpha Psi 1985. **Military Serv:** US Army Reserve, pfc, 4 yrs. **Home Addr:** 37 Brooklawn Ave, South Norwalk, CT 06854. **Business Addr:** Executive Dir, Norwalk Economic Opportunity Now, Inc, 98 S Main St, South Norwalk, CT 06854.

BURGEST, DAVID RAYMOND
Educator. **Personal:** Born Dec 10, 1943, Sylvania, GA; married Loretta Jean Black; children: Juanita Marie, Angela Lynore, David Raymond II, Paul Reginald. **Educ:** Paine Coll, BA 1965; Wayne State Univ, MSW 1968; Syracuse Univ, PhD 1974; Univ of Chicago School of Divinity, Postdoctoral studies 1984-85. **Career:** Central State Hosp Milledgeville GA, social work aide 1965-66; chief social worker 1968-69; Syracuse Univ, asst prof 1969-72; SUNY Upstate Med Coll Syracuse, assoc prof of psychology 1971-72; Univ of Nairobi Kenya, vstg prof of sociology 1980-81; Atlanta Univ Sch of Social Work, social work consultant 1986-87; Governors State Univ, prof 1972-80, prof of social work 1981-; Roosevelt Univ, Chicago, IL, part-time prof, African-Amer studies, 1989-90. **Orgs:** Consultant to various local natl & intl social serv orgs in America, Europe, Canada & Africa such as Dept of Family Svcs, Alcoholism Couns, United Charities, & vocational Rehab; founder/pres Circle of Human Learning & Development Specialists Inc 1975-; licensed gospel minister 1976; editorial bd Black Caucus Journal

of Natl Assn of Black Social Workers 1979-80; prison ministry at Stateville Prison Joliet IL & other facilities in IL 1982-; consultant Suburban NAACP 1984-; editorial bd Journal of Pan-Africans Studies 1986-; Univ Park Library Bd 1987-91; pres, Lower North Youth Centers/Chicago, 1989-91; WGCI-AM, mental health youth svcs adviser, 1988-90; pres, Abyssinia Repetory Theatre, 1990-; pres, Self Taught Publishers, 1989-. **Honors/Awds:** Presented various papers, workshops, & Institutes locally, nationally & internationally in Africa, America, Canada & Europe; published in such journals as Black Scholar, Social Work, Black Male/Female Relationships, Black Books Bulletin, Intl Social Work, Journal of Black Studies; author of Ebonics, Black Talk word game; Social Worker of the Year Awd 1968; Everyday People Awd 1975; author, "Social Work Practice with Minorities," Scarecrow 1982, Proverbs for the Young and Not So Young, Self Taught Publishers; Appreciation Awd Far South Suburban NAACP 1983; "Social Casework Intervention with People of Color," Univ Press of Am 1985; Village of Univ Park proclaimed December "Dr David R Burgest Month" 1985;Man of the Year Awd for Excellence 1985; play, Harriet Tubman: One More River to Cros. **Home Addr:** 2692 Lafeville Cir, Apt 1, Cincinnati, OH 45211.

BURGETT, PAUL JOSEPH
Educational administrator. **Personal:** son Of Ruth Garizio Burgett and Arthur C Burgett; married Catherine G Valentine, Jan 1, 1982. **Educ:** Eastman School of Music, University of Rochester, Rochester NY, BM, 1968, MA, 1972, PhD, 1976. **Career:** Hochstein Memorial Music School, executive dir, 1970-72; Nazareth Coll of Rochester NY, lecturer, 1976-77, asst prof of music, 1977-81; Eastman School of Music, Univ of Rochester, dean of students, 1981-88, vice pres & dean of students, 1988-. **Orgs:** Mem, chair, vice chair, Zoning Board of Appeals, 1981-86; dir, Governing Board Hochstein Memorial Music School, 1982-; dir, Corporate Board YMCA of Rochester and Monroe County, 1983-; mem, Natl Advisory Board, Center for Black Music Research, 1985-; dir, bd of trustees, Margaret Woodbury Strong Museum, 1987-; dir bd of dir, Urban League of Rochester, 1987-. **Special Achievements:** Author: Vindication as a Thematic Principle in Alain Locke's Writings on the Music of Black Americans, 1989; Artistry in Student Affairs or Virtuosity in Practicing the Craft of Being Human, 1987; On the Tyranny of Talent: An Analysis of the Myth of Talent in the Art Music World, 1987; From Bach to Beethoven to Boulez and Very Few Women in Sight, 1987; .. On Creativity, 1982. **Military Serv:** US Army, sgt, 1969-75. **Business Addr:** Vice President, University Dean of Students, University of Rochester, 500 Wilson Commons, Rochester, NY 14627.

BURGETTE, JAMES M.
Dentist. **Personal:** Born Aug 18, 1937, Toledo, OH; married Carolyn Harris; children: Stephanie, James, Ngina. **Educ:** Lincoln University, Pennsylvania AB 1959; Howard Univ, DDS 1964. **Career:** YMCA Pittsburgh, counselor 1958; Allegheny Co Health Dept Pittsburgh, 1960; US Post Office Washington DC, 1962; private practice, dentist 1968-. **Orgs:** Pres Wolverine Dental Soc 1975; bd Natl Dental Assn 1975; Omega Psi Phi Chi Delta Mu; BSA. **Military Serv:** USNR ensign 1960; USN lt 1964. **Business Addr:** 23077 Greenfield Road, Southfield, MI 48075.

BURGIE, IRVING LOUIS (LORD BURGESS)
Composer, publisher. **Personal:** Born Jul 28, 1924, Brooklyn, NY; married Page Turner; children: Irving Jr, Andrew. **Educ:** Juilliard Schl of Music, 1946-48; Univ of AR 1948-49; Univ of So CA, 1949-50. **Career:** Self-employed composer, lyricist; composed 37 songs for Harry Belafonte including Jamaica Farewell, Island In the Sun, Day O; composed Belafonte's Calypso Album, 1st album to sell 1 million copies; wrote Ballad for Bimshire, 1963. **Orgs:** Mem ASCAP 1956; Am Guild of Authors & Composers 1956; Local #802 Am Fed of Musicians; pres & publr Caribe Music Corp; life mem NAACP; mem Harlem Writers Guild; United Blk Men of Queens; hon chmn Camp Minisink; hd of Lord Burgess Caribbean Day Assembly Pgrms Publr; The W Indian Song Book 1972; writer of lyrics Barbados Nat Anthem 1966. **Honors/Awds:** Numerous awards & citations; Silver Crown of Merit (Honorary), Barbados Government 1987; Honorary Doctor of Letters, Univ of the West Indies 1989. **Business Addr:** 199-02 111th Ave, Jamaica, NY 11412.

BURGIN, BRUCE L.
Banking executive. **Personal:** Born Oct 22, 1947, Cincinnati, OH; married Ollie Keeton, Sep 20, 1980. **Educ:** North Carolina Central University, BS, commerce, 1970. **Career:** Freedom Savings Bank, branch manager, 1973-85; Empire of America Federal Savings Bank, branch manager, 1986-88; Life Savings Bank, branch manager, 1988-89; Fortune Bank, branch manager, 1989-. **Orgs:** Tampa Alumni Chapter, Kappa Alpha Psi, 1986-; Tampa Bay Urban Bankers, 1986-89. **Honors/Awds:** Tampa Alumni Chapter, Kappa Alpha Psi, Polemarch Award, 1991. **Military Serv:** US Army, sgt, 1970-73. **Business Addr:** Assistant Vice President, Fortune Bank, 13944 N Dale Mabry, Tampa, FL 33618-2463, (813)962-2705.

BURKE, BRIAN
Government official. **Career:** Domestic Policy Council, senior policy analyst, currently. **Business Addr:** Senior Policy Analyst, Domestic Policy Council, The White House, 1600 Pennsylvania Ave, NW, Washington, DC 20500, (202)456-5573.

BURKE, GARY LAMONT
Company executive. **Personal:** Born Oct 4, 1955, Baltimore, MD; son of Gwendolyn I Burke and William A Burke (deceased); married Nina J Abbott Burke, Aug 30, 1987; children: Brandon L, Christopher J, Jonathan D, Amanda J, Rachel N. **Educ:** Babson College, BS, accounting, 1977. **Career:** Coopers & Lybrand, staff accountant, 1977-79, sr accountant, 1979-81; The Rouse Co., internal auditor, 1981-82, sr auditor, 1982-83, acquisitions management, manager, 1983-87; USF&G Realty Inc, investment officer, 1987-89, assistant vice pres, 1989-90, USF&G Corp, chief of staff, 1990-91, USF&G Financial Services Corp, vice pres, 1991, USF&G Corp, vice pres, administration, 1991-93; Fidelity and Guaranty Life Insurance Company, vice president business development, 1994-95, vice president special markets, 1995-97. **Orgs:** Archdiocese of Baltimore, budget committee, 1992-; National Association of Black Accountants, past prs, 1982-; Development Credit Fund, advisory bd; Cardinal Gibbons High School, financial control bd. **Honors/Awds:** Maryland State Board of Public Accounting, Certified Public Accountant, 1983; USF&G, Leadership Award for Confidence, 1992. **Business Addr:** Vice President, Fidelity and Guaranty Life Insurance Company, PO Box 1137, Baltimore, MD 21203, (410)895-0154.

BURKE, KIRKLAND R.
Promotion manager. **Personal:** Born Jan 4, 1948, Chicago, IL; son of Johnnie Irene Burke and Alonzo Waymond Burke. **Educ:** Chicago Tech Coll, 1966; Chicago St U, BA 1986. **Career:** Holy Angels Roman Cath Sch, tchr 1973-74; Reliable Promotions, promotion mgr 1974-75; Warner, Elektra, Atlantic Corp, promotion mgr 1975-78; Warner Bros Records, midwest promotion mgr 1978-; Whitney Young Magnet High School, Girl's Basketball, asst coach 1987-; American Coaching Effectiveness Program, certified coach, 1991-. **Orgs:** Speaker Chicago Pub Sch Youth Motivation Prog 1972-; mem Natl Assoc of TV & Radio Announcers 1972-77; youth div asst to chm Operation PUSH 1972-75, Natl Choir 1972-75; mem Black Music Assoc 1978-; asst coach Near North High Sch Chicago IL Girls Basketball 1986-87. **Honors/Awds:** 54 gold & platinum records, Warner Bros Records, 1975-; Am Legion Natl Chmpnshp Chicago Cavaliers D & B Corps 1969; VFW & Am Legion IL St Championship Chi Cavaliers 1969; Chicago Board of Education Special Arts Festival, Certificate of Merit, 1980; Mesetrey School, Certificate of Merit, 1982; James Madison School, Certificate of Merit, 1985; Executive Producer, The Barrett Sisters Album "I Got a Feeling" 1986; Chicago Public League Girls Basketball City Championship Runner-Up, Whitney Young Magnet High School Assistant Coach, 1988-89, 1992. **Military Serv:** USN 3rd class petty officer E-4 1965-68; Natl Defense Serv Medal 1965-68; Ancient Order of Shellbacks, 1968. **Business Addr:** Promotion Manager, Midwest Region, 500 Wall St, Glendale Heights, IL 60139.

BURKE, LILLIAN W.
Judge. **Personal:** Born Aug 2, 1917, Thomaston, GA; married Ralph Burke; children: Bruce. **Educ:** OH State Univ, BS 1947; Cleveland State Univ, LLB 1951; Cleveland Marshall Law Sch Cleveland State Univ, postgrad work 1963-64; Natl Coll State Judiciary Univ, grad 1974. **Career:** Cleveland, genl practice law 1952-62; sch teacher bus educ & social sciences; State of OH, asst atty gen 1962-66; OH Indus Commn, vice chmn mem 1966-69; Cleveland Community Coll Western Campus, teacher constitutional law; Cleveland Municipal Ct, aptd judge 1969, elected to full term judge 1969-. **Orgs:** Pres Cleveland Chap Natl Council of Negro Women 1955-57; past pres/former woman ward ldr 24th Ward Rep Club 1957-67; Cuyahoga Co Central Com 1958-68;secty E Dist Faily Serv Assn 1959-60; mem Council Human Rel Cleve Citizens League 1959-; pres Cleve Chap Jack & Jill of Amer Inc 1960-61; alternate delegate Natl Rep Conv in Chicago 1960; sec Cuyahoga Co Exec Comm 1962-63; Gov's Comm on the Status of Women 1966-67; bd, dirs chmn minority div Natl Fed Rep Women 1966-68; vice pres at large Greater Cleveland Safety Council 1969-; aptd to serve four yr term Adv Comm of Accreditation & Institutional Eligibility of Bur of Higher Educ 1972; mem Comm on accreditation 1980-; exec bd mem Amer Assn of Univ Women; past Grammateus Alpha Omega Chap Alpha KappaAlpha Sor; Hon Adv mem Women Lawyers Assn; mCuyahoga Co, Cleveland Bar Assns; life mem past bd mem NAACP Cleve Chapt; mem Phyllis Wheatley Assn; bd trustees Consumer's League of OH; mem OH State, Amer Bar Assns; mem Am Judicature Soc, Natl Bar Assn Inc; trustee OH Comm on Status of Women. **Honors/Awds:** Achievement Awd Parkwood CME Church Cleveland 1968; Career Woman of Yr Cleveland Women's Career Clubs Inc 1969; Martin Luther King Citizen Awd of RecogMusic & Arts Com Pgh 1969; Awd in Recog of Outstanding Ach in Field of Law Natl Sor of Phi Delta Kappa 1969; Awd Natl Council of Negro Women 1969; Outstanding Achieve Awd Te-Wa-Si Scholarship Club Cleve 1969; Outstanding Serv Awd Morning Star Grand Chap Cleve 1970; Lectr Heidelburg Coll Tiffin OH 1971; Salute from Amer Woodmen for First Elected Negro Female Judge Cleve 1970; Golden Jubilee Awd Zeta Phi Beta Sor 1970; Outstanding Serv Awd Morning StarGrand Chap 1970; Awd of Honor Cleveland Bus League 1970; Serv Awd St Paul AMe Ch Lima OH 1972; Woman of Achievement Awd 1973; Inter-Club Council 1973. **Business Addr:** Judge, Cleveland Municipal Court, Room 13B Justice Center, 1200 Ontario St, Cleveland, OH 44113.

BURKE, OLGA PICKERING
Business executive. **Personal:** Born Jan 6, 1946, Charleston, SC; daughter of Esther Robinson Pickering and Dr L Irving Pickering; married Philip C Burke Sr; children: Philip C Jr, Brian. **Educ:** Johnson C Smith Univ, AB Economics/Accounting 1968; Natl Rural Development Leaders School, certificate 1976; Life Investors Inc Co, insurance license 1981. **Career:** HA Decosta Co, accountant 1969-70; Allied Chemical Corp, lost accountant 1970-72; Charleston Area Minority Assoc, fiscal officer 1972-75; Minority Development & Mgt Assoc, exec directory 1975-79; Affiliated Management Services Inc, pres 1979-. **Orgs:** Martin Luther King Comm YWCA Charleston 1977-79; organizer SC Rural America 1979; economic adv council Clemson Univ 1978-81; first vice pres Regional Minority Purchasing Coun 1981; policy comm YWCA Charleston 1981; MBE Governor's Comm State of SC 1982; Business Development Sub-Committee City of Charleston 1982; mem Amer Soc of Professional Consultants 1983; mem Natl Assoc of Minority Contr 1983-; mem Charleston Business & Professional Assn 1980-83; bd of dirs/treas SC Sea Island Small Farmers Co-op 1981-83; Columbia Adv Council US Small Business Admin 1981-83; chairperson business comm Charleston Trident Chamber of Comm 1984. **Honors/Awds:** Outstanding Overall Phi Beta Sigma Frat Beta Mu Sigma Chap Charleston 1977. **Business Addr:** President, Affiliated Mgmt Services, 90 Cannon St, Charleston, SC 29403.

BURKE, ROSETTA
Military official. **Personal:** divoRced; children: Tirlon. **Educ:** Long Island Univ, CW Post Center, master's degree. **Career:** New York Army National Guard, asst adjutant general, currently. **Special Achievements:** First female general in the New York Army National Guard. **Business Addr:** Brig General/Asst Adjutant General, NY Army National Guard, 330 Old Niskayuna Rd, Latham, NY 12110-2224.

BURKE, VIVIAN H.
Government official. **Personal:** Born in Charlotte, NC; married Logan Burke; children: Logan Todd. **Educ:** Elizabeth City State Univ, BS; A&T State Univ, MS; certification Guidance Counseling Administration Curriculum Instructional Specialist. **Career:** City of Winston-Salem, alderman. **Orgs:** Bd of dirs Piedmont Health System Agency; minority interest grp for the NC Sch of Science/math; mem Trans Adv Council; chmn America's Four Hundredth Anniversary Comm; mem bd of trustees Elizabeth City State Univ; organized the Flora Buffs Garden Club; past pres PTA East Forsyth Sr HS; mem PTA Adv Council; experiment in Self-Reliance Bd; mem Forsyth Health Council; admin council Patterson Avenue YWCA; mem Recreation & Parks Comm; basileus Alpha Kappa Alpha Sor; natl membership chmn Alpha Kappa Alpha Sor; former chmn Carver Precinct; co-chair 5th Dist Council to elect Jimmy Carter; delegate to local StateDem Conv; NAACP; Alpha Kappa Alpha Sor; Forsyth Assn of Classroom Teachers; NC Assn of Educators; Top Ladies of Distinction Inc; 5th Dist Blk Ldrshp-Caucus; Leagueof Women Voters; Flora Bs; first woman and first black apptd public safety chmn City of Winson-Salem; one of first two women apptd to Public Wks Com; appt to St Dem Affirm Actn Comm 1983; Chmn Mondale for Pres Forsyth Co 1983; bd of dir 1983, mem-at-large 1984 League of Municipalities. **Honors/Awds:** Recipient of a 4 yr academic scholarship Elizabeth City State Univ; RJR Scholarship Univ of VA; NAACP Outstanding Political & Comm Serv; AKA Sor Outstanding Woman of the Year, Pres of the Year, Grad Leadership Awd, Most Distinguished Political Awd; Outstanding Volunteer ESR; Outstanding Volunteer Heart Fund;Genl Alumni Outstanding Political Awd Elizabeth City State Univ; Gov's Order of Long Leaf Pine; Outstanding Political & Comm Serv Awd Black Political Action League; Outstanding Serv in Politics & Comm Northeast Ward; Dedicated Serv Awd 5th Dist Black Leadership Caucus Banquet Chmn; Serv Awd Forsyth Co Health Council; Distinguished Citizen Awd Sophisticated Gents; Outstanding Women's Achievers Awd Prof Business League. **Home Addr:** 3410 Cumberland Rd, Winston-Salem, NC 27105.

BURKE, WILLIAM ARTHUR
Organization executive. **Personal:** Born May 13, 1939, Zanesville, OH; son of Hazel Norris and Leonard Burke; married Yvonne Brathwaite Burke, Jun 14, 1972; children: Christine Burke, Autumn Burke. **Educ:** Miami Univ, BS, 1961, BS; Boston Univ, 1963-64; Harvard Univ, 1963-64; Univ of MA, 1977, EdD; Lane College, DCL, 1991. **Career:** The City of Los Angeles Marathon, pres; South Coast Air Quality Management District, chair; Tennis Commr XXIII Olympiad; pres, Fish and Game Commr, State of CA; pres, Wildlife Conservation Bd, State of CA; chmn of the bd, Genesis Intl; pres of World Mining Devel Co Inc; deputy Los Angeles City Councilman 1966-69; pres, Amer Health Care Delivery Corp; pres, Batik Wine and Spirits Honorary Consul Gen for the Republic of Mali. **Honors/Awds:** Dir of Legislative Radio & TV for CA State Legislature; Meritorious Service Award, City of Los Angeles; Certificate of AUS Citation of Honor, CA State Senate; Alpha Epsilon Rho, Natl Radio and Television Honorary. **Military Serv:** US Air Force, major, 1961-65. **Business Addr:** President, Los Angeles Marathon Inc, 11110 W Ohio Ave, Suite 100, Los Angeles, CA 90025.

BURKE, YVONNE WATSON BRATHWAITE
County official. **Personal:** Born Oct 5, 1932, Los Angeles, CA; daughter of Lola Moore Watson and James A Watson; married Dr William A Burke, Jun 14, 1972; children: Autumn, Roxanne, Christine. **Educ:** Univ of California, AA, 1951; University of California, Los Angeles CA, BA, 1953; Univ of Southern California, JD 1956. **Career:** CA State Assembly, mem, 1966-72; US House of Representatives, mem, 1972-79; Los Angeles County, supervisor, 1979-81; Kutak Rock & Huie, partner, 1981-83; MGM/UA Home Entertainment, mem bd dir; Burke Robinson & Pearman, partner 1984-87; Jones, Day, Reavis & Pogue, Los Angeles CA and Cleveland OH, partner; Los Angeles County Bd of Supvrs, chairperson, currently. **Orgs:** Mem The Trusteeship, Urban League, Women's Lawyer's Assn; pres Coalition of 100 Black Women LA; vice chmn Univ of CA Bd of Regents; bd mem Educ Testing Svc; dir Los Angeles Branch Federal Reserve Bank of San Francisco; mem Bd of Educ Testing Svc; chair Los Angeles Branch Federal Reserve Bank of San Francisco; mem Ford Foundation Board of Trustee; chm Congressional Black Caucus 1976; vice chm 1984 US Olympics Organizing Comm; chm, Founders Savings and Loan. **Honors/Awds:** Loren Miller Award NAACP; fellow Inst Politics J F Kennedy School of Gvt, Harvard 1971-71; Chubb Fellow Yale Univ 1972; Professional Achievement Award UCLA 1974, 1984; Future Leader of America Time Magazine 1974; first black woman from California to be elected to US House of Rep 1972; Outstanding Alumni Award, Univ of Southern California, 1994; Alumni of the Year, Univ of California, Los Angeles, 1996. **Business Addr:** Supervisor, Second District, Los Angeles County Bd of Supvrs Hall of Administration, 500 W Temple St, Los Angeles, CA 90012.

BURKEEN, ERNEST WISDOM, JR.
City official. **Personal:** Born Aug 28, 1948, Chatanooga, TN; son of Mildred J Burkeen and Ernest W Burkeen; divorced 1977; children (previous marriage): Jeannee M, Ernest W III; married Margaret, May 20, 1993. **Educ:** Michigan State University, BS, 1975, MA, 1976. **Career:** Michigan State University, graduate assistant, 1975-76; University of Michigan, assistant director, 1976-77; City of Detroit, recreation instructor, 1977-80; Huron-Clinton Metro Parks, assistant superintendent, 1980-85, superintendent, 1985-94; Detroit Parks and Recreation, director, 1994-. **Orgs:** National Recreation Parks Association, program committee; Kiwanis Club, president; Ethnic Minority Society, board member; Spectrum Human Services, youth services board; Eastern Michigan University, recreation advisory committee; Michigan Recreation & Parks Association, president; National Recreation Ethnic Minority Society, president. **Honors/Awds:** MRPA, Fellowship Award, 1988, Innovated Program Award, 1988; Detroit Metro Youth Fitness, Appreciation Award, 1993; NRPEMS, Service Award, 1994. **Special Achievements:** "Crossroads for Recreation," "Selective Law Enforcement," "Watt Now," Michigan Leisure; "Handicapped Usage of Recreational Facilities," NIRSA Journal; "Affirmative Action as Charades," NIRSA Newsletter. **Military Serv:** US Navy, e-4, 1969-73; Sailor of the Month, Navcomsta Morocco, 1971. **Business Addr:** Director, Parks & Recreation, City of Detroit, 65 Cadillac Sq, Ste 4000, Detroit, MI 48226, (313)224-1123.

BURKETT, GALE E.
Information systems executive. **Career:** GB Tech Inc, CEO, currently. **Special Achievements:** Company is ranked #98 on Black Enterprise magazine's 1997 list of Top 100 Black businesses. **Business Phone:** (281)333-3703.

BURKETTE, TYRONE
College president. **Career:** Barber-Scotia College, Concord, NH, president, currently. **Business Addr:** President, Barber-Scotia College, Concord, NH 28025.

BURKS, DARRELL
Financial co. executive. **Personal:** Born Sep 3, 1956, Indianapolis, IN; married Suzanne F Shank, Sep 5, 1992. **Educ:** Indiana University, BS, 1978. **Career:** Coopers & Lybrand, Indiana, staff, 1978-86, Detroit, manager, 1986-89; Detroit Public Schools, deputy superintendent, 1989-91; Coopers & Lybrand, Detroit, director, 1991-92, partner, 1992-. **Orgs:** New Detroit's Community Funding & Technical Assistance Team; Kappa Alpha Psi, housing chairman, treasurer; Urban Education Alliance, board of directors, treasurer; Health Education Advocacy League, board of directors, treasurer; Homes for Black Children, board of directors; Easter Seals, board of directors, treasurer, personnel & fin committee chairman; Michigan Metro Girl Scouts, board of directors, treasurer; Police Athletic League, board of directors, treasurer. **Honors/Awds:** Indianapolis Leadership Dev Business Committee, Outstanding Achievers Award, 1984, 1985; YMCA, Minority Achievers Award, 1992; Detroit Board of Education, Honorary Educator, 1991; City of Detroit, Detroit City Council & Wayne County, citations for outstanding service. **Special Achievements:** Crain's Detroit Business, "Top Forty Under Forty" executives in Southeastern Michigan, 1991; featured in "Executive Style" supplement to Detroit Monthly & Crain's Detroit Business, p 8, Sept 1992. **Business Addr:** Partner, Coopers & Lybrand, 400 Renaissance Center, Ste 3200, Detroit, MI 48243, (313)446-7271.

BURKS, ELLIS RENA
Professional baseball player. **Personal:** Born Sep 11, 1964, Vicksburg, MS. **Educ:** Ranger Junior College, Ranger, TX, attended. **Career:** Boston Red Sox, outfielder, 1987-92; Chicago White Sox, 1993-94; Colorado Rockies, 1994-. **Honors/Awds:** Named to American League All-Star Team, 1990. **Business Addr:** Professional Baseball Player, Colorado Rockies, 1700 Broadway, Ste 2100, Denver, CO 80290, (303)292-0200.

BURKS, JAMES WILLIAM, JR.
Business executive. **Personal:** Born Feb 4, 1938, Roanoke, VA; married Janice A Kasey. **Educ:** Lincoln U, AB 1959; Univ of VA; NW U; Roanoke Coll; Lynchburg Coll. **Career:** Norfolk Southern Corp, marketing mgr, currently; Addison HS, Tchr. **Orgs:** V chmn Roanoke City Sch; bd, pres, bd of dir Gainsboro Elec Co 1970-; mem Omega Psi Phi Frat; bd dir Magic City Bldg & Loan Assn; City Plng Commn 1973-76; Human Relat Com; bd dir Roanoke Nghbrhd Devel Proj; past dir Roanoke Jaycees; Roanoke Valley Counc of Comm Serv 1974-77; Commn to Study Relatshp between Govtl Entities & Elec Utilities; bd of vis Norfolk Outst Serv Award, board of commissioners Roanoke Redevelopment & Housing Authority; board of commissioners, Roanoke Civic Center; board member Mill Mountain Theatre; board member Roanoke Valley Arts Council; Sigma Pi Phi; co-chair Norfolk State University Cluster Program; Sigma Pi Phi Fraternity. **Honors/Awds:** Outst serv award City Plng Commn; outst serv award Roanoke Jaycees; 1st black on city plng commn. **Military Serv:** AUS spec-4 1960-63. **Business Addr:** 110 Franklin Rd SE, Box 26, Roanoke, VA 24042.

BURKS, JUANITA PAULINE
Business executive. **Personal:** Born Jul 2, 1920, Marion, KY; daughter of Donna Farley and Allen Farley (deceased); married Ishmon C; children: Lt Col Ishmon F, Donna S, Rev Robert C. **Educ:** KY State Univ, 1940-42; Univ of Louisville, 1969-71. **Career:** Park Duvalle Welfare, social worker 1968-71; Metro United Way, suprv 1971-74; Burks Enterprises Inc, owner/pres, CEO 1974-. **Orgs:** Mem Louisville Urban League 1975-, Natl Assn of Christians & Jews 1982-, Professional Bus Women's Assn 1983-, Governor's Scholar Prog 1983-; bd dir Spaulding Univ 1984-. **Honors/Awds:** Women in Business Game 1980; Woman of Achievement Pro Bus Women 1983; Mayor's Citation City of Louisville 1983; Black Enterprise Mag 1983; Comm Serv Eta Zeta 1984; Equality Awd Louisville Urban League 1984; Money Mag 1984. **Business Addr:** Chief Executive Officer, Burks Enterprises Inc, 1602 Heyburn Bldg, Louisville, KY 40202.

BURLESON, HELEN L.
Writer, poet, consultant, realtor. **Personal:** Born Dec 8, 1929, Chicago, IL; daughter of Beatrice Hurley Burleson (deceased) and Blaine Major Burleson (deceased); divorced; children: Earl Fredrick MD III, Erica Elyce Fredrick. **Educ:** Central State Univ, BS 1950; Northwestern Univ, MA 1954; Nova Univ, Dr of Public Adminstration 1984. **Career:** Lover's Lane Sweet Shop, part owner & mgr 1947-56; HS English, tchr 1951-56, 1958-61; HS Eng sponsor Yrbk & Newspaper Washington, tchr 1956-57; WBBM Radio Matters of Opinion, commntr; Bd of Educ Flossmoor IL, 1972-75, 1975-78, re-elected 1978-81; Nurturing Experiences Enterprises, pres/founder 1987-; Century 21, Dabbs & Associates, mega-broker, Homewood Office, currently. **Orgs:** Past pres Women's Aux of Cook County Physicians Assn 1956; mem AKA 1948; NAACP 1950-; Alpha Gamma Pi 1978; apptd IL State Bd of Educ 1981; apptd Gov's Task Force to Study Medical Malpractice 1985; founder, Enhancement Organization of Olympia Fields, 1994. **Honors/Awds:** 1973 Alumni of Yr; Chicago Chap Central State 1974 Humanitarian Awd; St Matthews AME Ch; One of 100 Women Honored by PUSH Found 1975; Literary Achievement Awd Central State Univ 1976; Humanitarian Awd Dr Gavin Found 1977; Outstanding Civic & Freedom of the Arts Awd Links 1978; Outstanding Contrib to the Black Comm UNCF 1979; founded Women's Bd Wash Park YMCA 1979; 1974 pub verse "No Place Is Big Enough to House My Soul" 1975; pub Where Did You Find Me? Anthology of Prose Poetry & Songs; Centurion Award, for real estate sales in excess of $10,000,000.00, Northern Illinois Region of Century 21, 1992. **Home Phone:** (708)747-0919. **Business Phone:** (708)206-6068.

BURLESON, JANE GENEVA
Councilwoman. **Personal:** Born May 22, 1928, Fort Dodge, IA; daughter of Octavia Bivens Jones Dukes and William Kelly Jones; married Walter Burleson, Oct 22, 1954. **Career:** George A Hormel & Co, 1948-81; Ft Dodge School Syst, para professional 1982-; Ft Dodge City Council, council mem 1984-. **Orgs:** Rec sec P-31 United Food & Comm Workers 1974-75; mem League of Women Voters, Mayors Adv Comm 1980; pres A Philip Randolph Inst Ft Dodge Chapt; mem Superintendents Adv Comm 1984; bd mem Jazz Festival 1984-85, Natl Camp Fire 1985-86; mem IA of Tomorrow Comm 1985-; nominating board member, Girl Scouts, 1990; board member, ICCC Illiteracy, 1989-; board member, County Magistrate, 1990-; member, City Finance Committee, Governor Brandstad, 1986-94. **Honors/Awds:** Comm on Status of Women Cert State of IA 1979; Cert of Apprec IA Devel Comm 1983, 1984; First Black Woman Elected to Ft Dodge City Council. **Business Addr:** Councilwoman, Fort Dodge City Council, City Hall, 819 1st Ave So, Fort Dodge, IA 50501.

BURLEW, ANN KATHLEEN
Psychologist, educator. **Personal:** Born Dec 10, 1948, Cincinnati, OH; married John Howard. **Educ:** University of Michigan, BA, 1970, MA, 1972, PhD, 1974. **Career:** Social Tech Systems, senior partner, 1974-80; University of Cincinnati, Dept of Criminal Justice, Dept of Psychology, asst professor, 1972-78, Dept of Psychology, associate professor, 1978-. **Orgs:** Chair, Evaluation Committee & YWCA Shelter for Battered Women, 1977-79; Community Development Advisory Committee, 1980; vice pres, Cincinnati Assn of Black Psychologists, 1979-80; CETA Advisory Committee of United Appeal, 1979-80; board member, United Appeal/Community Chest Planning Board, 1980; vice pres, United Black Assn of Faculty & Staff, 1980. **Honors/Awds:** Summer faculty research grant, University of Cincinnati, 1977, 1980; co-author, Minority Issues in Mental Health; co-author, Reflections on Black Psychology; published numerous articles. **Business Addr:** Professor, Dept of Psychology, ML 376, University of Cincinnati, Cincinnati, OH 45221-0002.

BURLEY, DALE S.
Engineer, producer. **Personal:** Born Aug 6, 1961, New York, NY; son of Anne L. Thompson Burley and Lloyd C. Burley. **Educ:** Morgan State University, Baltimore, MD, BS, 1984. **Career:** WEAA-FM, Baltimore, MD, newswriter/reporter, 1982-84; WLIB-AM, New York, NY, newswriter/assistant editor, 1983, 1984; WINS-AM, New York, NY, production engineer, 1984-86; WNYE-FM, Brooklyn, NY, production engineer, assistant producer, 1986-; The Daily Challenge, Brooklyn, NY, reporter, 1993-. **Orgs:** Member, National Association of Black Journalists, 1988-; member, Omega Psi Phi Fraternity, 1985-; member, NAACP, 1980-; member, Abyssinian Baptist Church, 1988-. **Home Addr:** 100 LaSalle St, New York, NY 10027.

BURLEY, JACK L., SR.
Food company executive. **Personal:** Born Apr 26, 1942, Pittsburgh, PA; son of Andrew C & Lynda Burley; married JoAnne E Burley, May 29, 1965; children: Diana Burley Gant, Jack L Jr. **Educ:** Pennsylvania State Univ, BS, 1965; Univ of Pittsburgh, MBA, 1974. **Career:** Federal Power Commission, accountant, 1965-66; General Foods, financial analyst, 1968-70; HJ Heinz, mgr, financial planning, 1970-80, controller, Heinz USA, 1983-85, vp finance & administration, Heinz USA, 1985-89, vp logistics & administration, Heinz USA, 1989-91, vp operations & logistics, Heinz USA, 1991-93, pres, Heinz Service Co, 1993-. **Orgs:** Exec Leadership Council, bd of dirs; Urban League of Pittsburgh, bd of dirs; Forbes Health System, bd of dirs; Omega Psi Phi Fraternity; Sigma Pi Phi Fraternity; Bethesda Presbyterian Church. **Military Serv:** US Army, spec-4, 1966-68. **Business Addr:** President, Heinz Service Co, An Affiliate of HJ Heinz Co, 2600 Liberty Ave, Pittsburgh, PA 15222.

BURNETT, ARTHUR LOUIS, SR.
Judge. **Personal:** Born Mar 15, 1935, Spotsylvania County, VA; son of Lena Bumbry Burnett and Robert Louis Burnett; married Frisbieann Lloyd, May 14, 1960; children: Darnellena Christalyn, Arthur Louis II, Darryl Lawford, Darlisa Ann, Dionne. **Educ:** Howard Univ, BA (Summa Cum Laude) 1957; NY Univ Sch of Law, LLB 1958 (Law Review & honors). **Career:** Dept of Justice, attorney adviser criminal div, 1958-65; Asst US Atty DC, 1965-68; MPDC (Met Police), legal advisor 1968-69; US Magistrate judge 1969-75; Legal Div US Civil Serv Comm, asst gen counsel 1975-78; Office of Personnel Mgmt, assoc gen counsel 1979-80; US Magistrate, judge, 1980-87; Superior Court of the District of Columbia, judge, 1987-; Catholic Univ Columbus School of Law, adjunct prof, 1997-. **Orgs:** ABA; Natl Bar Assn; Fed Bar Assn; DC Bar Assn; Washington Bar Assn; Amer Judges Assn; Amer Judicature Soc; chmn Conf of Spl Court Judges ABA 1974-75; pres Natl Council of US Magistrates 1983-84; pres DC Chapter FBA 1984-85; chmn Federal Litigation Sect Admin of Justice FBA 1983-85; chmn Criminal Law & Juvenile Justice Comm, Admin Law & Regulatory Practice Sect ABA 1983-85; Council Admin Law & Regulatory Practice Section ABA, 1987-90; assistant secretary Administrative Law & Regulatory Practice Section ABA, 1990-93, secretary, 1993-95; administrative conference of the United States, 1990-94; vice chair, Criminal Rules and Evidence Committee, Criminal Justice Section, ABA, 1985-92, chair, 1992-97; Juvenile Justice Committee, 1987-; Criminal Justice Magazine Editorial Board, Criminal Justice Section, ABA, 1990-, Books Publication Committee, Criminal Justice Section, ABA, 1992-. **Honors/Awds:** Fed Bar Assn Distinguished Serv Award as Chmn of Nat Criminal Law Com; Attorney General's Sustained Superior Performance Award, 1963; US Civil Serv Commn Distinguished Serv Award 1978; Office of Personnel Mgmt Dir Meritorious Serv Award 1980; chmn FBA Natl Com on Utilization of US Magistrates in Fed Cts 1980-; Editor-in-Chief/Author FBA-BNA publ "Labor-Mgmt Relations Civil Serv Reform & EEO in the Fed Serv" 1980; author of numerous articles in law journals & reviews on role of US Magistrates in Fed Judiciary, on Federal Civil Practice, bail and search & seizure; Flaschner Awd Outstanding Special Court Judge in the United States Natl Conf of Special Court Judges Amer Bar Assoc 1985; Fed Bar Assn, President's Award, 1994; Natl Bar Assn, President's Award, 1996; Washington Bar Assn, Ollie Mae Cooper Award, 1997. **Military Serv:** US Army, spec-4, 1958-60; US Army Reserves, 1960-63, 1st lt, Commendation Medal, 1960; E1-E4-drafted, 1958-60,

second lt to 1st lt, 1960-63. **Business Addr:** Judge, Superior Court of the District of Columbia, 500 Indiana Avenue, NW, Room 1020, Washington, DC 20001.

BURNETT, BESCYE P.
Librarian, educator. **Personal:** Born Apr 29, 1950, Roseboro, NC; daughter of Selena Boone Powell and Casey Powell; married Charles Burnett, Feb 24, 1983; children: Denise, Shawn. **Educ:** Winston-Salem State University, Winston-Salem, NC, bachelor's degree, 1972; University of North Carolina, Greensboro, NC, MLS, 1977; Miami University, Oxford, OH, certificate in management, 1990. **Career:** Startown Elementary School, Newton, NC, teacher, 1972-73; Winston-Salem/Forsyth School, Winston-Salem, NC, teacher/librarian, 1973-79; State of North Carolina, Raleigh, NC, media consultant, 1979-80; University of Illinois-Champ/Urbana, Urbana, IL, visiting prof, 1980-81; Fashion Institute, Los Angeles, CA, librarian, 1981-82; County of Los Angeles Public Library, Downey, CA, librarian, literacy librarian, 1982-87; Johnson County Library, Shawnee, KS, volunteer coor adult services, 1988-89; Cleveland Heights-University Heights, deputy dir, 1989-. **Orgs:** Board member, Project Learn, 1989-96; member, ALA, 1987-; member, PLA, 1987-; member, NAACP, 1980-. **Honors/Awds:** Veterans Four Year Scholarship, US Veterans Admin, 1968-72; RJ Reynolds Scholarship, RJ Reynolds/Winston-Salem, Forsyth County, 1976; CH-UH Friends Scholarship, Friends of Lib, 1990. **Business Addr:** Deputy Director, Cleveland Hgts-University Hgts Public Library, 2345 Lee Rd, Cleveland, OH 44118, (216)932-3600.

BURNETT, CALVIN
Educator (retired), painter. **Personal:** Born Jul 18, 1921, Cambridge, MA; son of Dr Nathan Lowe & Adelaide Waller Burnett; married Torrey Milligan, Aug 20, 1960; children: Tobey Burnett Sparks. **Educ:** Massachusetts College of Art, 1938-42, BS Ed, 1951; Boston Univ, MFA, 1960, doctoral candidate, 1962-71. **Career:** Elma Lewis School, instructor, 1951-53; Decordova Museum, instructor, 1952-56; freelance designer, illustrator, 1943-83; Massachusetts College of Art, professor, 1956-87, prof emeritus, 1987. **Orgs:** Boston African-American Artists, co-founder/bd of dirs, 1961-; Northeastern Univ, African-American Master, Artists in Residency Program, 1977-; The Museum of The National Center of African-American Art, juror, 1981-91. **Honors/Awds:** Massachusetts College of Art, Distinguished Service Award, 1979; New York, Associated American Artists, Printmaking Award, 1959; Massachusetts Artists Foundation, Drawing Award Finalist, 1988; New England Print Award, 1960; Liepzig, Germany, Book Award, 1965; Atlanta Univ, numerous prizes & awards, 1959-68; Massachusetts School of Art, Honorary BFA, 1993. **Special Achievements:** Author, Designer, Illustrator, Objective Drawing Techniques, Reinhold Publisher NY, NY, 1966; Maidenhood, Print Portfolio, Woodcuts, Impressions Graphic Workshop, 1962; Portents & Omens, Serigraphs, Impressions Graphic Workshop, 1966. **Home Phone:** (508)533-2153.

BURNETT, CALVIN W.
Educational administrator. **Personal:** Born Mar 16, 1932, Brinkley, AR; son of Vera Rayford Payne and Elmer Clay Burnett; married Martha Alma Ware, Jul 21, 1956 (divorced 1976); children: Vera, Susan, David; children: Tywana. **Educ:** St Louis U, BS 1959, PhD 1963. **Career:** St Louis State Hospital, research social psychologist 1961-63; Health & Welfare Council of Metro St Louis, research dir of special project 1963-66; Catholic Univ of Amer, assoc prof 1966-69; Upward Bound Program, US Office of Educ, consultant 1966-70; Natl Planning Org Washington, consultant 1967-68; Urban Sys Corp Washington, consultant 1967-69; Southern IL Univ, assoc prof 1969-70; Coppin State Coll MD, pres 1970-. **Orgs:** State rep, 1970-74, mem, board of directors, 1984-86, Amer Assn of State Coll & Univ 1970-74; mem bd of dirs Natl Assn for Equal Oppor in Higher Educ 1985-; chm, bd YMCA of Greater Baltimore 1984-86. **Honors/Awds:** St Louis University Alumni Merit Award 1973; Silver Beaver Award Boy Scouts of America 1983; Community Service Award Alpha Phi Alpha 1987. **Military Serv:** US Army, 1953-55. **Business Addr:** President, Coppin State College, 2500 W North Ave, Baltimore, MD 21216.

BURNETT, COLLIE, JR.
Cable television manager. **Personal:** Born Feb 7, 1950, Tucson, AZ; son of Lee Audrey Ransfer and Collie Burnett; married Sondra E Rhoades, Jun 21, 1982; children: Courtney, Colin Taylor. **Educ:** Morehouse College, BS, 1972; Atlanta University, 1974-75. **Career:** Cox Broadcasting, announcer, newsperson, 1972-78; Atlanta Regional Commission, director of communications, 1978-82; Cable America, director of marketing and sales, 1982-86; Prime Cable, vp of marketing, 1986-90; Georgia Cable Television and Communications, vp, system general manager, currently. **Orgs:** Morehouse College National Alumni Association, vp, board of directors, 1979-; Friends of the Atlanta-Fulton Library, chairman of the board, 1990-92; 100 Black Men of Atlanta, 1979-; Heritage Row Historical Society, 1990-; Alpha Phi Alpha Fraternity, 1988-; Cable Television Administration Society, 1982; National Association of Minorities in Cable, local vp, 1992; Boy Scouts of America, fund raising chair, 1992-. **Honors/Awds:** Numerous Community Civic & Professional Awards. **Business Phone:** (404)874-8000.

BURNETT, DAVID LAWRENCE
News reporter, anchor. **Personal:** Born Apr 6, 1956, Indianapolis, IN; son of Mary Ogburn Burnett and Boyd Burnett Jr; married Lauren Jefferson Burnett, Mar 6, 1987; children: David Jr, Janet Elaine. **Educ:** Ball State Univ, Muncie, IN, BS, communications, 1978. **Career:** WTLC-FM, Indianapolis, IN, reporter/anchor, 1979; WTVW-TV, Evansville, IN, reporter, anchor, 1979-81; WFIE-TV, Evansville, IN, reporter, 1981-82; WHIO-TV, Dayton, OH, reporter/anchor, 1982-86; WTTG-TV, Washington, DC, reporter/anchor, 1986-. **Orgs:** President, Washington Assn of Black Journalists, 1989-90; vice president, Dayton Assn of Black Journalists, 1984-85; member, Alpha Phi Alpha Fraternity, 1975-. **Honors/Awds:** Journalism Award, sports 1st place, ''Doug Williams Reflections'' Nat Assoc of Black Journalists, 1988; Journalism Award, series 1st place, ''Collision Course'', National Association of Black Journalists, 1987; Best Series, 1st place, ''Evansville Housing Authority'', Sigma Delta Chi, 1982; Best Spot News, 1st place, ''WIKY Fire'', Sigma Delta Chi, 1982; Best General News Story, ''County Council Fight'', Sigma Delta Chi, 1982; Spot News Reporting, 1st place, ''Washington Strike'', Assoc Press, 1981; Spot Sports Radio, 1st place, ''US Clay Courts Tourney'', Assoc Press, 1980. **Business Addr:** Reporter/Anchor, News Dept, WTTG-TV Fox Television, 5151 Wisconsin Ave, NW, Washington, DC 20016.

BURNETT, LUTHER C.
Urban planner. **Personal:** Born Aug 12, 1925, Detroit, MI; son of Caroline E Burnett and Jesse H Burnett; married Lucille Walston; children: L Carl. **Educ:** MI State U, BS, MS 1952. **Career:** CEHP Inc, sr associate, urban planner, 1991-; Landcore Assoc, president, 1986-; retired from Civil Service 1986; US Department of Interior/Natl Park Service, Program Manager 1975-86; Natl Capital Parks-West, supt 1972-75; Conservation & Cultural Affairs US Virgin Islands, commr 1971-72; Natl Park Service Washington Office, urban planner 1969-70; Bur of Outdoor Recreation, & Interior Dept, urban planner 1960-69; Nat Capital Planning Commn Washington, urban planner 1957-60; Inkster, MI, dir of planning 1955-57; Detroit Regional Planning Commn, urban planner 1954-55; Detroit Met Area Traffic Study, urban planner 1953-54; Detroit Dept of Pub Works, land surveyor 1948-53. **Orgs:** Mem Amer Inst of Planners; Amer Soc of Planning Officials; mem Alpha Phi Alpha Frat; mem Pigskin Club of Washington, DC; pres Blair-Shepard Neighbors 1961-63; 32 degree Mason, Prince Hall; Urban League Housing Comm 1957-61; bd dir March of Dimes 1972-73; Sigma Phi Phi (Epsilon Boule); bd mem American Red Cross, Brookland Chapter, Washington DC. **Honors/Awds:** Outstanding contrib award March of Dimes 1972; Washington Area Walk-A-Thon; gov outstanding service US Virgin Islands. **Military Serv:** AUS 1943-46. **Business Addr:** Senior Associate, Urban Planner, CEHP, Inc, 1133 20th St NW, Ste 200, Washington, DC 20036.

BURNETT, ROBERT BARRY
Professional football player. **Personal:** Born Aug 27, 1967, Livingston, NJ. **Educ:** Syracuse, bachelor's degree in economics. **Career:** Cleveland Browns, defensive end, 1990-95; Baltimore Ravens, 1996-. **Honors/Awds:** Pro Bowl, 1994. **Business Addr:** Professional Football Player, Baltimore Ravens, 11001 Owings Mills Blvd, Owings Mills, MD 21117, (410)654-6200.

BURNETT, SIDNEY OBED
Dentist. **Personal:** Born Dec 4, 1924, Apex, NC; married Faye Valeria Mc Daniel; children: Stephanie Gantt, Sydney Lee, Sharon, Aaron, Angela, Cassandra. **Educ:** Morgan State Univ, 1942-45; Howard Univ Coll of Dentistry, 1945-49. **Career:** Freedmen's Hosp, surgical 1949-50; Dental Coll Howard Univ, instr 1950-51; Barrett School for Girls, dentist 1950-60; Private practice, dentist 1951-; Balt City Health Dept, dentist 1952-65; MD State Bd Dental Examiners, dentist, sec, treas. **Orgs:** Maryland Dental Assn, pres; Baltimore City, State & Amer Dental Associations; Amer Assn of Dental Examiners; Integrated Housing Baltimore; NAACP, Baltimore Alumi Chapter, Kappa Alpha Psi; Apha Psi; fellow, Acad Dentistry Intl, Amer Coll of Dentists; consult examiner NE Reg Bd Dental Examiners 15 states. **Honors/Awds:** Guardsmen Achievement Award, Baltimore Alumni, Kappa Alpha Psi. **Business Addr:** MD State Bd Dental Examiners, 1318 N Caroline St, Baltimore, MD 21213.

BURNETT, ZARON WALTER, JR.
Writer, performance artist. **Personal:** Born Dec 16, 1950, Danville, VA; son of Zaron W Burnett Sr & Johnsie Broadway Burnett; married Pearl Cleage, Mar 23, 1994; children: Zaron W Burnett III, Deignan Cleage-Lomax, Meghan V Burnett. **Educ:** Hampton Institute, 1968-69; Penn State University, 1973-74; Georgia State University, Atlanta GA, BS, 1977. **Career:** Harrisburg Free Clinic, director of public outreach, 1972-74; CDC-VD Contr Prog, health prog rep, 1978; North Cent GA Health Systems Agency, proj review analyst, 1979-80; Atlanta Southside Community Health Ctr, director of research, 1980; Fulton County Government, executive aide chairman, board of commissioners, 1980-83; Just Us Theater Co, executive producer, 1989-. **Honors/Awds:** Rockefeller Foundation, JAGE Grant, 1988; Atlanta Mayor's Office, Mayor's Fellow in Arts, 1990. **Special Achievements:** Performances at the National Black Arts Festival, National Black Theater Festivals, and the National Performance Festival. **Business Addr:** Executive Producer, Just Us Theater Press, PO Box 42271, Atlanta, GA 30311-0271, (404)753-2399.

BURNETTE, ADA PURYEAR
Educator. **Personal:** Born Oct 24, Darlington, SC; married Thomas Carlos Burnette Sr; children: Paul Puryear Jr, Paula Puryear, Anita B Houser, T Carlos Burnette Jr, Diane B Day. **Educ:** Talladega Coll, BA 1953; Univ of Chicago, MA 1958; FL State Univ, PhD 1986; attended Texas Southern University, Chicago State Univ, FL A&M Univ; FL State Univ, certified public mgr 1989. **Career:** Winston Salem NC Public Schools, high school math teacher 1953-54; Chicago Public Schools, elem school teacher 1954-58; Norfolk State, admin & teacher 1958-61; Univ of Chicago Reading Clinic, teacher 1958 summer; Tuskegee Inst, admin, teacher 1961-66; Fisk Univ, admin, teacher 1966-70; FL DOE, admin 1973-88; Bethune-Cookman Coll, admin, teacher, 1988-90; Florida A&M University, Developmental Research School District superintendent and director, 1990-93; Florida A&M University, dept chair, professor, PhD director, currently. **Orgs:** Pres Intl Read Assn Affiliate Concerned Educ of Black Students 1984-86; sec, treas Afro-Amer Research Assn 1968-73; bd dir Christian School Performing Arts; deacon Trinity Presbyterian Church; mem Leon Dem Exec Bd 1982-; pres teen sponsor Jack & Jill of Amer Tallahassee 1984-85; parliamentarian undergrad advisor, treas, sec, Alpha Kappa Alpha; pres, historian, reporter, vice pres Drifters Tallahassee; pres, publicity chmn, initiation chmn Phi Kappa Phi, FSU; mem Phi Delta Kappa, Pi Lambda Theta; National membership chmn, Drifters, Inc; FL Elem and Middle Schools commr, Southern Association of College and Schools, 1978-88; FL Council on Elem Educ; DOE liaison; sec, co-organizer, Societas Docta Inc, 1987-; FL Assn for Supervision and Curriculum Devel Bd, 1988-; pres, Les Beau Monde, 1989-90; FL Assn of Sch-Adm; Amer Assn of Sch-Adm; FL Elem & Middle Sch Principals; Natl Assn of Elem Sch Principals; Natl Assn of Sec Sch Prin; Links; pres, Ladies Art & Social Club; Natl Assn of Female Execs; Friends of the Black Archives; SE Assn of Prof of Ed Lead. **Honors/Awds:** National Now Black Woman of the Year, Drifters Inc 1984; Head Start Honoree of the Year for Florida 1985; Humanitarian of the Year 1987; NAACP Black Achiever, 1991; Key to Cocoa, FL, 1989; First Black Admin in FL Dept of Educ; Serv to Children and Educ Plaque, FL Council on Elementary Educ 1988; co-author, member of early childhood panel, Four and Five Year Old Programs in Public Schools; delivered hundreds of speeches; wrote many articles and books. **Home Addr:** PO Box 7432, Tallahassee, FL 32314-7432, (850)894-4125. **Business Addr:** Chair Professor, Florida A&M University, Dept of Ed Leadership & Human Services, PO Box 7432, Tallahassee, FL 32314-7432, (850)894-4125.

BURNEY, HARRY L., JR.
Educator. **Personal:** Born Sep 29, 1913, Lakeland, FL; married Iona Mack; children: Harry L III, Sandra Burney. **Educ:** Bethune-Cookman Coll, BS 1946; Univ of PA, MS 1954; Univ of PA; FL A&M U; OK U. **Career:** Tivoli High School, Defuniak Springs FL, prin 1946-47; Middleton High School FL, prin 1952-68; Bethune-Cookman Coll, admin asst to pres 1968-76; United Negro Coll Fund, FL St dir 1976-. **Orgs:** Mem Nat Educ Assn; FL Educ Assn; Nat Alumni Assn of Bethune-Cookman Coll; Alumni Assn of Univ Qof PA; Alpha Phi Alpha Frat; chmn Scholarship & Loans Com Daytona Beach Rotary Club; mem Daytona Beach Area C of C; Selective Service Sys Local Bd No 24; Guidance Cntr Bd; Mental Health Bd of Volusia District, Inc; Bethune-Cookman Coll; Edward Waters Coll; State Dept of Edn; Putnam Co Tchr Assn; Central Acad; Middleton High Sch; Alpha Phi Alpha Frat. **Honors/Awds:** United way bd dir awards FL State Tchr Assn; Chapter of Eastern Star named for him. **Military Serv:** AUS. **Business Addr:** 444 Seabreeze Blvd, Ste 925, Daytona Beach, FL 32118.

BURNEY, WILLIAM D., JR.
Government official. **Personal:** Born Apr 23, 1951, Augusta, ME; son of Helen Nicholas Burney and William D. Burney Sr.; married Lynne Godfrey Burney, Jun 16, 1990. **Educ:** Boston University, Boston, MA, BS, public communication, 1969-73; University of Maine School of Law, Portland, ME, JD, 1973-77. **Career:** Maine State Housing Authority, Augusta, ME, assistant development director, 1981-. **Orgs:** Member, Transportation/Communication Steering Committee, National League of Cities, 1990; board of directors, Holocaust Human Rights Center of Maine; board of directors, American Baptist Churches of Maine; nominating committee, Kennebec Girl Scout Council of Maine; board of directors, Yankee Healthcare, Augusta, ME. **Honors/Awds:** Augusta City Council, 1982-88; Mayor, City of Augusta, Maine, 1988-. **Business Addr:** Mayor, City of Augusta, 16 Cony St, Augusta, ME 04330.

BURNHAM, MARGARET ANN
Judge, attorney. **Personal:** Born Dec 28, 1944, Birmingham, AL. **Educ:** Tougaloo Coll, BA 1966; Univ of PA Law Sch, LLB 1969. **Career:** Burnham & Hines, partner; lecturer in political science, MIT; Boston Municipal Court, justice, Boston. **Orgs:** National Director, National Conference of Black Lawyers; fellow, WEB DuBois Institute. **Honors/Awds:** Honorary Degree from Lesley College. **Business Addr:** 25 Kingston St, Boston, MA 02111.

BURNIM, MELLONEE VICTORIA
Educator. **Personal:** Born Sep 27, 1950, Teague, TX; married C Jason Dotson; children: Jamel Arzo. **Educ:** Northern Texas State University, BM (cum laude), music education, 1971; University of Wisconsin Madison, MM, African music ethnomusicology, 1976; Indiana University, PhD, ethnomusicology, 1980. **Career:** Delay Middle School, director of choral music, 1971-73; University of Wisconsin, research asst, 1973, academic advisor, 1973; Indiana University Bloomington, Afro-American Choral Ensemble, director, 1976-82, Opera Theater, choral director, 1976, 1980, Dept of Afro-American Studies, professor, currently. **Orgs:** Musical director, video tapes 2-30 minutes, ''The Life & Works of Undine S Moore,'' Afro-American Arts Institute, Indiana University, 1979; musical director, WTUI Bloomington, ''Contemporary Black Gospel Music,'' 1979; Alpha Lambda Delta, 1968; Sigma Alpha Iota, NTSU, 1969; chapter vice pres, Mortar Board, NTSU, 1970-71; Pi Kappa Lambda, 1971. **Honors/Awds:** Full Music Scholarship, NTSU, 1969-71; Natl Defense Foreign Language Fellow in Arabic, University of Wisconsin, 1973-74; fellow, Natl Fellowships Fund, Univerisity of Wisconsin & Indiana Unviersity, 1973-78; Eli Lilly Postdoctoral Teaching Fellow, 1984; alternate, Natl Research Council Postdoctoral Fellowship, Washington DC, 1984. **Business Addr:** Professor, Dept of Afro-American Studies, Indiana University Bloomington, Bloomington, IN 47405-1101.

BURNIM, MICKEY L.
Educator. **Personal:** Born Jan 19, 1949, Teague, TX; son of Ruby Burnim and A S Burnim; married LaVera Levels; children: Cinnamon, Adrian. **Educ:** North TX State Univ, BA Economics 1970, MA Economics 1972; Univ of WI-Madison, PhD Economics 1977; The Brookings Inst Washington DC, postgraduate work 1980-81. **Career:** FL State Univ, asst prof/ economics 1976-82; The Univ of NC/GA, asst vice pres for academic affairs 1982-86; UNC-Chapel Hill, adj asst prof/ economics 1983-85, adj assoc prof/economics 1985-86; NC Central Univ, vice chancellor academic affairs 1986-, provost and vice chancello, 1990-. **Orgs:** Chmn educ comm NAACP 1979-80; mem bd dirs Tallahassee Urban League 1979-80; consultant Transcentury Corp 1986; American Economic Assn; National Economic Assn; Durham Chamber of Commerce. **Honors/Awds:** Brookings Economic Policy Fellow The Brookings Inst 1980-81. **Business Addr:** Chancellor, Elizabeth City State Univ, 1704 Weeksville Rd, Elizabeth City, NC 27909.

BURNLEY, KENNETH
Educational administrator. **Personal:** marrIed Eileen Burnley; children: Traci, Trevor, Tyler, Jonathan. **Educ:** Univ of Michigan, BS, MA, PhD. **Career:** Numerous positions in education including: Waverly Bd of Educ, asst superintendent of instruction; Eastern Michigan Univ, instructor; Ypsilanti Bd of Educ, dir, principal, asst principal, coordinator, teacher; Univ of Michigan, asst track coach; teacher for various Michigan school districts; Fairbanks North Star Borough School Dist, superintendent/CEO; Colorado Springs School District Eleven, superintendent of schools, 1987-. **Honors/Awds:** American Assn of School Administrators and the Servicemaster Co, Natl Superintendent of the Year, 1993. **Special Achievements:** First African American superintendent of the Fairbanks, Alaska school system. **Business Addr:** Superintendent, Colorado Springs School District, 1115 N El Paso, Colorado Springs, CO 80903, (719)520-2000.

BURNS, CALVIN LOUIS
Journalist, minister. **Personal:** Born Mar 16, 1952, Memphis, TN; son of Freddie McClinton Burns and Andrew Burns; married Regina Whiting Burns, Nov 18, 1989. **Educ:** Memphis State University, Memphis, TN, BA, 1974; Charles Harrison Mason Bible College, associates, 1979; Memphis State University, Memphis, TN, graduate school, 1981-83. **Career:** Memphis Press Scimitar, journalist, 1974-83; Interstate Transportation, mamager, comm, 1985-88; Church of God In Christ, Memphis, TN, associate news director, Host of Convocation, 1979-85; Tri-State Defender, Memphis, TN, managing editor, 1988-. **Orgs:** Executve director, Bethesda Outreach, 1984-; Memphis region communication director, National Association of Black Journalists, 1990-; board member, Memphis State Univ Journalist Alumni, 1991. **Honors/Awds:** Tennessee Outstanding Achievement Award, Governor of Tennessee, 1990; Outstanding citizen Award, Congressman Harold Ford, 1983; Citizen Achievement Award, Shelby County Sheriff's Dept, 1989; Professional Achievement Award, Gospel Academy, Memphis, 1991. **Business Addr:** Managing Editor, News/ Editorial, Tri-State Defender Newspaper, 124 E Calhoun Ave, Memphis, TN 38101.

BURNS, CLARENCE DU
Government official. **Personal:** Born Sep 13, 1918, Baltimore, MD; married Edith Phillips; children: Cheryl Turner. **Career:** City of Baltimore, mem city council 1971-82, vice pres city council 1977-82, pres of city council 1982-87, mayor 1987-. **Orgs:** Chmn exec bd Eastside Democratic Org 1967-87; chmn East Baltimore Comm Corp 1971-82; chmn East Baltimore Medical Plan 1973-82; delegate Democratic Natl Convention 1980,84; mem Regional Planning Council 1982-. **Honors/ Awds:** Service Awd MD Assoc of Equal Oppor Personnel 1983; Disting Serv Awd Central MD Comm Sickle Cell Anemia 1984; Awd for Contributions to Black Economic Develop The Hub Org 1985; Harry Bard Disting Citizenship Awd Comm Coll of Baltimore 1987; Andrew White Medal Loyola Coll in MD 1987. **Military Serv:** AUS Air Corps sgt 1943-46. **Business Addr:** Mayor, City of Baltimore MD, City Hall Room 250, 100 Holliday St, Baltimore, MD 21202.

BURNS, DARGAN J.
Business executive. **Personal:** Born Feb 26, 1925, Sumter, SC; son of Julia Burns and Dargan J Burns Sr; married Joyce Price; children: Dargan III, Cedric Charles. **Educ:** Hampton Inst, 1949; Boston Univ, MS 1952. **Career:** Burns Public Relations Serv, pres, currently; AL State Coll, teacher & public relations; Advertising, Couyahoga Comm Coll; Karamu House, Cleveland, OH, dir of public relations. **Orgs:** Bd mem, Public Relations Soc of Amer; Lutheran Housing Corp; Cleveland Business League; pres, Urban Counselors; bd mem BSA; Omega Psi Phi. **Military Serv:** US Army 1942-46. **Business Addr:** President, Burns Public Relations Service, 668 Euclid Ave, Ste 516, Cleveland, OH 44114.

BURNS, DIANN
Journalist. **Career:** WLS-TV, co-anchor, currently. **Business Addr:** Co-Anchor, Nighttime Newscast, WLS-TV, 190 N. State St., Chicago, IL 60601, (312)750-7777.

BURNS, FELTON
Psychologist, educator. **Personal:** Born Mar 12, 1936, Tillar, AR; married Verlene Dean; children: Gregory L, Pamele E. **Educ:** Fresno St, BA 1962; CA St Univ, Fresno, MA 1972; Univ So CA, EdD 1977; Natl Bd Cert Cnslr, Inc, NCC 1983-. **Career:** County of Fresno, social worker 1962-65; Economic Opportunities Comm, asst dir 1965-68; CA State Univ Fresno, asst to dean of students 1968-71, staff counselor 1971-. **Orgs:** Dir Advncd Rsrch Tech 1978-83; pres Spectrum Asso 1977-85; mem Am Asso Cnslng & Dev 1985, CA Blck Fclty & Stf Asso. **Honors/Awds:** Albright Endwd Chair for Exclnc 1st Rcpnt CA St Univ Fresno Stdnt Afrs Div 1984-85; Troy Awrd Educ Fresno Comm Srvc 1975. **Home Addr:** 6378 N 8th, Fresno, CA 93710. **Business Addr:** Staff Counselor/Prof Rehab, CA State Univ, Fresno, 6378 N 8th, Fresno, CA 93710.

BURNS, GERALDINE HAMILTON
Social worker. **Personal:** Born Feb 20, Cleveland, OH; daughter of Geraldine Johnson Hamilton and James Hamilton; children: William David Burns, James Thomas Burns. **Educ:** Cuyahoga Community College, Cleveland, OH, AA, 1965; Monmouth College, Monmouth, IL, BA, 1967; School of Applied Social Sciences, Case Western Reserve University, Cleveland, OH, MSSA, 1971. **Career:** Cuyahoga Co Dept of Human Services, social worker, 1967-69; Cleveland YWCA, Cleveland, OH, branch exec dir, 1971-73; Neighborhood Centers Assn, Cleveland, OH, sup, youth outreach, 1974-75, dir, early childhood prog, 1976-78; Friendly Inn Settlement, Cleveland, OH, exec dir, 1978-. **Orgs:** Chair, Housing Resource Center, 1990-; member, Association of Black Social Workers, 1986-; member, National Black Child Dev. Inst., 1983-; member, Commission on Poverty, 1990-; member, Neighborhood Progress Inc., 1990-.

BURNS, JEFF, JR.
Business executive. **Personal:** Born Dec 4, Varnesville, SC; son of Genevieve Burns and Jeff Burns Sr (deceased). **Educ:** Howard Univ, BBA 1972. **Career:** Ebony Magazine, advertising director; Howard Univ, MPA Magazine publishing procedures seminar, lecturer; Johnson Publishing Co, sr vice pres, currently. **Orgs:** Mem PUSH Intl; bd of dirs Trade Bureau; mem Caribbean Tourism Organization; judge CEBA Awds; Howard University Alumni Assn of NY; Board of Directors, New York Urban League, member African American Marketing Association; bd of advisors, Arthur Ashe Athletic Assn. **Honors/Awds:** Business Person of the Year, Natl Assn of Negro Business & Professional Women's Clubs 1989; Sylvia Lord Pioneer of Excellence Award, Five Towns Community Center 1991; Howard University Alumni Club of New York, Award of Recognition, 1992; Natl Council of Negro Women, Nassau County Section, Award of Recognition, 1993; NAFEO Award, 1994. **Business Addr:** Senior Vice President, Johnson Publishing Co, 1270 Avenue of the Americas, New York, NY 10020.

BURNS, JESSE L.
Educational administrator. **Educ:** University of South Florida, doctorate in business administration. **Career:** Edward Waters College, interim president, president, currently. **Business Addr:** President, Edward Waters College, 1658 Kings Rd., Jacksonville, FL 32209-6167, (904)355-3030.

BURNS, KEITH BERNARD
Professional football player. **Personal:** Born May 16, 1972, Greelyville, SC; married Michelle; children: Danielle, Rachel. **Educ:** Oaklahoma State. **Career:** Denver Broncos, linebacker, 1994-. **Business Addr:** Professional Football Player, Denver Broncos, 13655 Broncos Pkwy, Englewood, CO 80112, (303)649-9000.

BURNS, KHEPHRA
Writer, editor. **Personal:** Born Oct 2, 1950, Los Angeles, CA; son of Isham A ''Rusty'' and Treneta C Burns; married Susan L Taylor, Aug 19, 1989; children: Shana-Nequai Taylor. **Educ:** MoorPark Community College, AA, liberal arts, 1970; Univ of California at Santa Barbara, BA, English, 1972. **Career:** Golden State Mutual Life Insurance, salesman, 1974-76; Various Bands, musician, 1976-78; WNET-13, writer, associate producer, 1978-80; RTP,Inc, speech writer, publicist, 1980-81; Self-Employed, freelance Writer, editor, 1981-. **Orgs:** Writers Guild of America, East, Inc, 1993-; The Authors Guild of America, 1995-; Sigma Pi Phi Fraternity, Alpha Sigma Boule, 1995-. **Honors/Awds:** Award of Excellence, Communications Excellence to Black Audiences. **Special Achievements:** Black Stars in Orbit, (Harcourt Brace), 1995; ''The Essence Awards'' (CBS, Fox), 1993-95; ''Images and Realities: African Americans'' (NBC), 1992-94; ''Black Stars in Orbit'' (WNET-13), 1989; '' Black Champions'' (WNET-13), 1986; Confirmation: The Spiritual Wisdom That Has Shaped Our Lives, Anchor Books, 1997. **Business Addr:** Faith Childs Literary Agency, 132 W 22nd St, New York, NY 10011.

BURNS, LAMONT
Professional football player. **Personal:** Born Mar 16, 1974; children: Dyion. **Educ:** East Carolina, BA in communications. **Career:** New York Jets, guard, 1997-. **Business Addr:** Professional Football Player, New York Jets, 1000 Fulton Ave, Hempstead, NY 11550, (516)560-8100.

BURNS, LEONARD L.
Podiatrist, travel agent. **Personal:** Born Jan 10, 1922, New Orleans, LA; son of Leona Galle Burns Gauff and George Burton Burns; married Phyllis Charbonnet Burns; children: Debra E Barnes, Gary M Burns, Lenette P Plummer. **Educ:** Xavier Prep, Xavier Univ, New Orleans, LA, pre-med, 1947; Temple Univ, Philadelphia, PA, DPM 1951; Tulane Univ, New Orleans, LA, Leadership MPC, 1966. **Career:** Private medical practice, New Orleans, LA, 1951-; Four Corners Travel Agency, LA, pres, 1963-. **Orgs:** Bd of dir, NAACP, 1963-66; bd of dir, trustee, NAACP Special Contribution Fund, 1966-; pres, InterAmerican Travel Agents Soc, 1974-78; bd mem InterAmerican Travel Agents Society, 1986-; LA Tourist Devel Commn, pres, 1969. **Honors/Awds:** Man of the Year, Psi Chapter Alpha Phi Alpha Philadelphia, PA, 1950; Honorary Award, civic activities, New Orleans United Clubs, 1962; Small Business Council Champion, New Orleans Chamber of Commerce, 1985; Award of Merit, LA/New Orleans Host Comm, 1988. **Military Serv:** US Marine Corp, OCS/S-SGT,1941-46; Bronz Star/First Black Volunteer Eighth District. **Business Addr:** 1813 N Rocheblave St, New Orleans, LA 70119-1403.

BURNS, OLLIE HAMILTON
Educator (RETIRED). **Personal:** Born Jun 13, 1911, Monroe, LA; daughter of Charlotte Davis Hamilton and Ernest Hamilton; married Alex A Burns Jr, Nov 17, 1937; children: Alice, Alex III, Sylvia, Lawrence, Benjamin. **Educ:** Grambling Univ, BS 1947; LA State Univ, MS 1957. **Career:** Jackson Parish Elementary School, teacher 1932-34; Quachita Parish Elementary School, teacher 1934-39; Quachita Parish HS, teacher 1947-60; Quachita Parish School, librarian 1960-76. **Orgs:** Mem Amer Library Assn; mem, Natl Educ Assn; Elec Comm NEA 1972; pres, Library Dept, LEA 1965; pres Quachita Educ Assn 1967-69; dir Quachita Parish Conf; past pres Quachita Human Relations Cncl; past vice pres Women in Politics; mem Quachita Multi-Purpose Comm Action Program, 1965-72; mem, Monroe Branch, Natl Assn of Univ Women; past pres, Quachita League of Women Voter; Organizer & dir, New Way Center; mem, Parish Library Bd; Gov State Drug Abuse Advisory Council; Mayor's Ind Dev Comm; NAACP; consultant, NDEA Inst. **Honors/Awds:** Articles publ ''Library Services in Quachita Parish''; ''Economic Contrib of Blacks in Quachita Parish 1803-1976''; Woman of the Year, NAACP, 1985; Natl Assn of Univ Women, Award, 1989; Modisette Award for Outstanding State Library Trustee, 1991; Inducted into Local Hall of Fame, Named A Trailblazer; Outstanding Citizen Award, The State Assn of Black Mayors.

BURNS, REGINA LYNN
Public affairs director. **Personal:** Born Feb 19, 1961, Memphis, TN; daughter of Rowena Hooks Whiting and Prince Whiting Jr.; married Calvin L. Burns, Nov 18, 1989. **Educ:** Abilene Christian University, Abilene, TX, BA, 1983; State Technical Institute, Memphis, TN, summer and fall, 1989; Memphis State University, Memphis, TN, magazine writing, fall 1990. **Career:** KRBC-TV, Abilene, TX, reporter/photographer, 1982-83; WSLI Radio, Jackson, MS, anchor/reporter, 1984; WMKW, Memphis, TN, anchor, 1984; WLOK-AM, Memphis, TN, news director, 1984-85; WGKX-KIX 106, Memphis, TN, news and public affairs director, 1985-; Tri-State Defender, Memphis, TN, freelance writer, 1986-. **Orgs:** President, Tennessee Associated Broadcasters Association, 1990-91; former president, Memphis Association of Black Journalists, 1990-; member, Radio-Television News Directors Association; member, National Association of Black Journalists. **Honors/Awds:** American Women in Radio and Television Award for ''A Way Out,'' a documentary on family violence, 1991; National Association of Black Journalists Award and International Radio Festival of

New York Award for "Dr Martin Luther King Jr.: The Man, The Movement, The Momentum," 1990; Journalist of the Year, Tennessee Associated Press Broadcasters Association, 1989; Ten Outstanding Young Americans, United States Junior Chamber of Commerce, 1993; Radio-Television News Directors Assn, Award, "Faces of Memphis" documentary, 1992.

BURNS, RONALD MELVIN
Artist. **Personal:** Born Feb 2, 1942, New York, NY; married Edith Bergmann; children: Elizabeth Bergmann, Alexi Bergmann. **Educ:** School of Visual Arts. **Career:** Collections: Museum of Modern Art, Stockholm, Sweden; Lincoln Center; Art for the Working Place, Copenhaggen, Denmark; Kaptensgarden-Borstahusen-Landskrona-Sweden; Exhibitions, Provinceton Gallery-Paul Kessler-USA 1962; Gallery Sari Robinson, PA 1964; Passepartout-Charlotteborg 1966; Passepartout-Bergen 1969; Landskrona Konsthall 1969-70 & 1980; Galleri Heland-Stockholm 1970; Galerie Migros-Lausanne 1970; Teatergalleriet-Malmo 1970; Graphikbienale-Wien 1972; Corcoran Gallery of Art Washington, DC 1975; Gallerie Unicorn 1975; Fundacion Rodriquez-Acosta-Granada 1977; Galleria II Traghetto-Venice 1977-80; Galerie Schindler Bern 1978; Hvidovre Bibliotek 1980; numerous others in the USA, Denmark, Sweden, and Switzerland; Spelman Coll, retrospective exhibition, 1994. **Orgs:** Mem Artist's Exhibition Group AZ-Venice Italy; mem Artist's Exhibition Group-Gallery 2016 Switzerland; mem Artist's Exhibition Group, Gronningen-Denmark-Gallery, Terry Dintenfass, NY. **Honors/Awds:** Honorary Mem of Danish Acad of Art; 2nd Intl Biennale, Malta, First Prize Drawing, Fourth Prize Painting, 1997. **Home Addr:** HC Orsteds Vej 71, 1879-V Copenhagen, Denmark.

BURNS, SARAH ANN
Administrative officer. **Personal:** Born Sep 20, 1938, Tupelo, MS; married Floyd Burns. **Educ:** Univ of Akron, BS 1960. **Career:** Macomb County NAACP, pres 1978-84; US Senator Carl Levin Screening Committee for Military Academies, member 1980-; Natl Council of Negro Women-McLeod Sect, pres 1986-. **Orgs:** Bd of directors Turning Point 1982-; bd of directors League of Women Voters 1983-; member Natl Assn for Female Executives 1983-; pres Natl Council of Negro Women 1984-; member Amer Soc of Military Comptrollers 1984-. **Honors/Awds:** Woman of the Year Natl Council of Negro Women 1981 & 1984; EEO contribution Detroit Federal Executive Bd 1981 & 1984; EEO contribution Army & Air Force Natl Guard Bureau 1984; Community Service Macomb County Branch NAACP 1984; Brotherhood/Sisterhood Awd 1986; Naval Air Facility Detroit Employee of the Year Awd 1986. **Business Addr:** Personnel Administrator, Naval Air Facility US Navy, Naval Air Facility Detroit, Mount Clemens, MI 48043.

BURNS, TOMMIE, JR.
Service company executive. **Personal:** Born Jul 5, 1933. **Career:** Burns Enterprises, Inc, Louisville, KY, chief executive. **Business Addr:** Chief Executive, Burns Enterprises, 822 S 15th St, Box 11395, Louisville, KY 40210.

BURNS, WILLIE MILES
Publishing executive. **Personal:** Born in Lake Village, AR. **Educ:** AM&N Coll, BS. **Career:** Johnson Pub Co Chicago, vice pres, agency mgr 1946-. **Orgs:** Mem State St Bus & Professional Women's Club; bd mem Sears YMCA; mem Cook Co Hosp Governing Commn. **Business Addr:** 820 S Michigan Ave, Chicago, IL 60605.

BURNS-COOPER, ANN
Editor. **Personal:** Born Feb 7, Charleston, SC; daughter of Janie Williams Burns and Walter Burns. **Educ:** SC State Coll, BA 1969; New York Univ, Certificate 1978. **Career:** RR Bowker Co, booklister 1970-73, editorial asst 1974-78, asst editor 1979-81, editorial coord 1982-87; Cahners Publishing Co, staff editor, 1987-. **Honors/Awds:** Frederick Douglass Fellowship in Journalism; Cahners Editorial Medal of Excellence, 1994. **Home Addr:** 1725 Purdy St #6C, Bronx, NY 10462.

BUROSE, RENEE
Broadcast journalist. **Personal:** Born May 17, 1962, Memphis, TN; daughter of Beatrice Lewis Burose and Aron Burose. **Educ:** Memphis State Univ, Memphis, TN, BA, 1984. **Career:** WLOK-AM, Memphis, TN, anchor, producer, 1984-86; WHBQ-TV, Memphis, TN, prod asst, admin asst, 1986-88; WJTV-TV, Jackson, MS, associate prod, 1988-89; WJW-TV 8, Cleveland, OH, producer, 1989-. **Orgs:** Member, Natl Assn Black Journalists, 1989-. **Honors/Awds:** Best Newscast, Associated Press, 1989. **Business Addr:** Producer, WJW-TV Channel 8, 5800 S Marginal Rd, Cleveland, OH 44103.

BURRAS, ALISA
Professional basketball player. **Personal:** Born Jun 23, 1975. **Educ:** Louisiana Tech. **Career:** Colorado Xplosion, center, 1998-. **Business Addr:** Professional Basketball Player, Colorado Xplosion, 800 Grant St, Ste 410, Denver, CO 80203, (303)832-2225.

BURRELL, BARBARA
Advertising company executive. **Personal:** Born Mar 19, 1941, Chicago, IL; daughter of Wiley Jones; children: Bonita, Aldridge, Alexandra, Jason. **Educ:** No IL Univ, BS, 1963. **Career:** Chicago Bd of Educ, teacher, 1963-65, 1966-67; Needham, Harper, Steers, Chicago, media estimator, 1965-66; Continental Bank, Chicago, personnel counselor, 1973-74; Burrell Advertising, Chicago, sr vp, sec-treas, beginning 1974, vchm, currently; Hyde Park Fed Savings, Chicago, dir, 1979-82; South Shore Bank, Chicago, dir, 1982-. **Orgs:** Aux bd, Hyde Park Art Center, Chicago; Hyde Park-Kenwood Dev Corp, Chicago; SE Chicago Commission; adv comm, DuSable Museum of African Amer History, 1983-; educ fund, Inst Psychoanalysis, 1983-; Alpha Gamma Pi; general chairperson, Blackbook's Natl Business & Professional Awards, 1989. **Business Addr:** Vice Chairman, Burrell Communications Group, 20 N Michigan Ave, Chicago, IL 60602-4811.

BURRELL, EMMA P.
Clergywoman. **Personal:** Born Aug 9, Maryland; widowed; children: 1 son (deceased). **Educ:** Howard U, AB, BD, MDiv 1959, DD 1965. **Career:** Tchr; Irwin, VA, prin; DC Census Bureau Engraving, govt employee; Good Hope United Meth Ch, pastor. **Orgs:** Mem C4 Colesville Comm Council Ch 1972-74; 1st woman receive full clerical rights & membership Annual Conf; Those Incredible & Meth; vp, trustee, Intl Assn of Women Ministers 1973-74; dist dir Rel & Race. **Business Addr:** 14655 Good Hope Rd, Silver Spring, MD 20904.

BURRELL, GARLAND
Judge. **Career:** US District Court, Sacramento CA, judge, currently. **Special Achievements:** Presided at the "Unabomber" trial, the first African American judge to hear a high-profile murder case. **Business Addr:** US District Judge, US District Court, US Courthouse, 650 Capital Mall, Rm 4014, Sacramento, CA 95814, (916)498-5765.

BURRELL, GEORGE REED, JR.
Attorney. **Personal:** Born Jan 4, 1948, Camden, NJ; married Doris; children: Stephen, Leslie. **Educ:** Univ PA, LLD 1974; Wharton Sch, BS 1969. **Career:** Mayor Of Philadelphia, dep 1980-; Colonial Penn Ins Co, asst gen counsel 1978-80; Wolf Block Schorr & Solis-Cohen, atty 1977-; Goodis Greenfield, Henry & Edelstein 1974-77. **Orgs:** Mem Empire Sports Inc (Denver Broncos) 1969; mem Nat Bar Assn; reg dir bd dir Phil Baristers Assn; mem Am Judictre Soc; Am Bar Assn; Philadelphia Bar Assn; bd tsts Univ PA; bd dir World Affairs Cncl; bd mgrs Friends Hosp. **Business Addr:** 10th Floor Packard Bldg, Philadelphia, PA 19102.

BURRELL, KENNETH EARL
Musician. **Personal:** Born Jul 31, 1931, Detroit, MI. **Educ:** Wayne State U, MusB 1955. **Career:** Oscar Peterson Trio, guitarist 1955-57; Benny Goodman Orch, 1957-59; Jimmy Smith Trio, 1959; Kenny Burrell Trio, Formed 1960; Kenny Burrell Quartet, 1963; Guitar Player Productions, exec dir; Jazz Heritage Found, pres 1975-78; UCLA, faculty 1978-79; 50 Records, recording artist. **Orgs:** Mem Kappa Alpha Psi; mem Phi Mu Alpha. **Honors/Awds:** Recip Intl Jazz Critics Awards 1957, 60, 65, 69-73; winner Downbeat Reader's Poll 1968-71; Downbeat Critics Poll 1968-73; Swing Journal Poll 1970-72.

BURRELL, LEROY
Athlete, entrepreneur. **Personal:** son Of Delores and Leroy Brown; married Michelle F. Burrell; children: Cameron, Joshua. **Educ:** University of Houston, BA, Communications. **Career:** Olympic athlete, 1992; Modern Men, Inc, partner, currently. **Honors/Awds:** Grand Prix final and Goodwill games, 100 meters, winner, 1990; two world records, 60 meters, 1991; USA/Mobile Outdoor Track and Field Championships, world record, 100 meters, 1991, 1994; Penn Relays, 4x200 meter relay team, world record, 1992; Olympic Games, gold medalist, 4x100 relay, 1992. **Business Addr:** Gold Medalist, 1992 Games, c/o US Olympic Training Center, 1 Olympic Plaza, Colorado Springs, CO 80909, (719)578-4500.

BURRELL, MORRIS
Clergyman. **Personal:** Born Aug 4, 1908, New Orleans, LA; married Desmonia M; children: Morris, Alvin Peter, Joseph Leroy. **Educ:** Dillard U, 1939-45; Leland Coll, AB 1947, DD 1953. **Career:** Union Bapt Theol Seminary, instr 1943; Bath House Commn Hot Spgs AR, mgr. **Orgs:** Mem Nat Bapt Conv; chmn Interracial Com LA Bapt State Conv & So Bapt Conv; sec-treas Dept Christian Edn; mem Finance Com LA MS Bapt State Conv; exec council Negro Div BSA; mem Big Bro Club Milne Municipal Boys Home;parole adv State LA Penal Inst; adv com Safety City New Orleans 1953; trustee Am Bapt Theol Seminary; mem NAACP; mem Interdenom Am Bapt Theol Seminary; mem Interdenominatl Ministerial Alliance; dir Federation Civic Leagues 1936; vice pres Ideal Missionary Bapt & Educ Assn; mem Orleans Parish Progressive Voters League; mem Urban League. **Honors/Awds:** Dem hon deputy criminal sheriff Orleans Parish 1969. **Business Addr:** 2200 2210 Dumaine St, New Orleans, LA 70119.

BURRELL, SCOTT DAVID
Professional basketball player. **Personal:** Born Jan 12, 1971, New Haven, CT. **Educ:** Univ of Connecticut. **Career:** Charlotte Hornets, forward-guard, 1993-96; Golden State Warriors, 1996-97; Chicago Bulls, 1997-. **Special Achievements:** NBA Draft, First round pick, #20, 1993. **Business Addr:** Professional Basketball Player, Chicago Bulls, 1901 W Madison St, Chicago, IL 60612, (312)455-4000.

BURRELL, THOMAS J.
Business executive. **Personal:** Born Mar 18, 1939, Chicago, IL; son of Evelyn Burrell and Thomas Burrell; married Joli; children: 3. **Educ:** Roosevelt Univ Chgo, BA English 1961. **Career:** Wade Advertising Agency, mail room clerk, copy trainee, copywriter 1960-64; Leo Burnett Co Chgo, copywriter 1964-67; Foote Cone & Belding London, 1967-68; Needham Harper & Steers, copy suprv 1968-71; Burrell McBain Advertising, co-owner 1971-74; Burrell Communications Group, owner, chairman, 1974-. **Orgs:** Chicago United, executive committee; Chicago Urban League, board of directors; Chicago Lighthouse for the Blind, board of governors; President's Advisory Council of Roosevelt University; Advisory Council of Howard University School of Communications; Executive's Club of Chicago, Economic Club. **Honors/Awds:** Has worked on accounts for Pillsbury, Swanson Frozen Foods, Vick Chem, Alka-Seltzer, One-a-Day Vitamins, Falstaff, Coca-Cola, Johnson Products Co, Joseph Schlitz Brewing Co, Proctor & Gamble, Jack Daniel Distillers, Stroh Brewing Co, McDonalds, Ford Motor Co, K-Mart; 2 Clio Awds "Street Song" Coca Cola 1978, McDonalds; other prestigious awds for TV & radio commercials & print advertising; 1985 Person of the Year Awd Chicago Advertising Club. **Special Achievements:** Profiled on the PBS show "Bridgebuilders," 1998. **Business Addr:** Chairman, Burrell Communications Group, 20 N Michigan Ave, Chicago, IL 60602.

BURRIS, BERTRAM RAY (RAY BONE)
Entrepreneur, sports administrator, coach, instructor. **Personal:** Born Aug 22, 1950, Idabel, OK; son of Clara Mae Burris and Cornelius Burris; married Debra Marie Foots, Jan 24, 1986; children: Djemal Jermaine, Ramon Jerome, Damon Jevon, Deneen Janice, Bobby J. **Educ:** Southwestern OK St Coll, BA, 1972. **Career:** Professional baseball player, 1972-87; Burris-Neiman & Asso Inc, Canada, pres, 1983-; Neiman & Asso Inc Canada, pres 1983-; Burris-Neiman & Asso Inc US, pres 1985-; Burbrook investments, founder, 1988; Baseball Network, exec vice pres, 1987-; Milwaukee Brewers, admin asst, instructor, 1987-; Circle of Life Sports Agency, vice pres, 1988. **Orgs:** Bd dir, Friendship Pentacostal Holiness Church,; bd of dir, Burris-Neiman & Assocs Inc, US, 1985; Citizen Advisory Bd, United Cancer Council; chmn, athletic Advisory Council; bd of dir, The Baseball Network, BNA- Canada; chmn, Fund Raising Comm, The Baseball Network; bd of dir, Mt Olive Baptist Church; advisory board, Child Abuse Prevention Fund, 1990-. **Honors/Awds:** Player of the Month, Natl League, 1976; MVP, Oakland A'S, 1984; All-Amer, NAIA, Southwestern OK St Coll, 1971; Southwestern OK State Univ, Athletic Hall of Fame, 1985.

BURRIS, CHUCK
City official. **Personal:** marrIed Marcia Baird Burris. **Educ:** Morehouse College, graduated; Marshall Law School, JD. **Career:** City of Atlanta, mayor's administration office; Mountainware, owner, currently; City of Stone Mountain, Mayor, currently. **Special Achievements:** First African American mayor of Stone Mountain, GA.

BURRIS, JEFFREY LAMAR
Professional football player. **Personal:** Born Jun 7, 1972, York, SC. **Educ:** University of Notre Dame. **Career:** Buffalo Bills, defensive back, 1994-. **Honors/Awds:** Football News, All-Rookie Team, 1994; Pro Football Weekly/Pro Football Writers of America, All-Rookie Team, 1994. **Business Addr:** Professional Football Player, Buffalo Bills, One Bills Dr, Orchard Park, NY 14127, (716)648-1800.

BURRIS, JOHN L.
Attorney. **Personal:** Born May 5, 1945, Vallejo, CA; son of Imogene Terrell Burris and DeWitt C Burris; married Ramona Tascoe; children: Damon, Justin, Monique, Courtney, Jonathan. **Educ:** Vallejo Jr Coll, AA 1965; Golden Gate Coll San Francisco, BS 1967; Univ of CA Grad Sch of Bus Berkeley, MBA 1970; Univ of CA Sch of Law, JD 1973. **Career:** Haskins & Sells San Francisco, acct/auditor 1967-69; Jenner & Block Chicago, assoc atty 1973-74; State Atty Office Cook Co Chicago, asst state atty 1975-76; Alameda Co DA Office Oakland, dep dist atty 1976-79; Harris, Alexander & Burris, atty; Law Office of John L Burris, atty, currently. **Orgs:** Past pres CA Assn of Black Lawyers; past president Charles Houston Bar Assn; spl consultant to president Natl Bar Assn; American Trial Lawyers Association; Alameda Co Bar Association; Kappa Alpha Psi Fraternity; Lawyers Committee for Urban Affairs - (SF); African-American Lawyers Against Aparthied; 100 Black Men, San Francisco Bay Chapter; Lawyer Delegate to Ninth Circuit, 1992. **Honors/Awds:** Outstanding Leadership Awd CA Assn of Black Lawyers 1980; Omegas Continental Boys Club, Outstanding Leadership Award, 1986; Second Baptist Church,

Martin Luther King Leadership Award Vallejo, 1985; Clinton White, Outstanding Trial Lawyers, Charles Houston Bar Association, 1987; Loren Miller, Outstanding Civil Rights Lawyer, 1989; Alameda County's Peace Officer for Better Committee Relationship, Outstanding Merit Award, 1991; NAACP Legal Defense Fund, Bay Area Chapter, Pro Bono Award, 1992; Special investigation into fatal shooting of 15-year-old youth, & entry into NAACP offices by Oakland police officers. **Special Achievements:** Presentations: ''Cocaine Mom/Cocaine Babies, Exposing the Crime and Identifying the Victim,'' National Association of Black Prosecutors Annual Convention, June 1989; ''Police Abuse, City of Oakland,'' public hearing sponsored by East Bay Coalition Against Police Harassment, Oakland, August 1991; ''Police Abuse, Ethicial Issues,'' National Black Prosecutors Association, annual meeting, August 1991; ''Police Abuse Litigation,'' California Association of Black Lawyers, for MLE credits, California State Bar, annual conference, 1991; Voir Dire, litigation section, State bar, trial practice symposium, 1992; ''Police Abuse and Mock Trial,'' National Black Prosecutor's Conference, 1992. **Business Addr:** Attorney, Law Office of John L Burris, 1212 Broadway, 12th Floor, Oakland, CA 94612.

BURRIS, ROLAND W.
State attorney general. **Personal:** Born Aug 3, 1937, Centralia, IL; married Berlean Miller; children: Rolanda Sue, Roland Wallace II. **Educ:** So IL Univ, BA 1959; Univ Hamburg Germany, post grad 1959-60; Howard Univ, JD 1963. **Career:** US Treasury Dept, comptroller/natl bank examiner 1963-64; Continental IL Natl Bank & Trust, various positions from tax accountant to 2nd vice pres 1964-71; State of IL Dept Gen Svcs, cabinet appointee/dir 1973-76; Operation PUSH, natl exec dir 1977; State of IL, comptroller 1978-91, attorney general, 1991-. **Orgs:** ABA; IL, Chicago, Cook Co Bar Assns; Amer Inst of Banking; Independent Voters of IL; NAACP; Cosmopolitan Chamber of Commerce; Natl Business League; Chicago SoEnd Jaycees; Assembly of Black State Execs; Alpha Phi Alpha; vice chair Democratic Natl Comm; Natl Assn of State Auditors Comptrollers & Treasurers; immediate past pres & chmn Intergovtl Relations Comm; National Assoication of Attorneys General. **Honors/Awds:** Distinguished Serv Award, Chicago South End Jaycees 1968; Jr Chamber Intl Scholarship 1971; Cook County Bar Public Serv Award 1974-75; 1 of 10 Outstanding Black Business People Black Book Dir 1974; Outstanding Alumnus Award Howard Univ Law School Alumni Assn 1980; Awd of Financial Reporting Achievement Govt Finance Officers Assn of the US & Canada 1985; President's Award, National Association of State Auditors, Comptrollers, and Treasurers Service Award, Government Finanace Officers Association, 1990; One of Top Three Governmant Financial Officers in the Nation, City & State Magazine, 1989; Alumnus of the Year Award, Howard University Alumni Association, 1989; DistinguishedPublic Service Award, Anti-Defamation League of B'nai B'rith, 1988; Award of Financial Reporting Achievement, Goveent Fianace Officers Association of the US & Canada, 1985; One of the 100 Most Influential Black Americans, Ebony Magazine, 1979-90; 1 of 10 Outstanding Black Business People, Black Book Directory, 1974; Cook County Bar Public Service Award, 1974-75; 1 of 1,000 Successful Blacks in America, 1973; Jr Chamber Intl Scholarship, 1971; 1 of 10 Outstanding Young Men of Chicago, 1970, 1972; Distinguished Service Award, Chicago South End Jaycees, 1968; Kappa Alpha Psi, Peace and Justice Award, 1991. **Business Addr:** Attorney General, State of Illinois, Office of the Attorney General, 500 S Second St, Springfield, IL 62706.

BURROUGHS, BALDWIN WESLEY
Educator. **Personal:** Born Feb 22, 1915, Houston, TX; children: Max Anton. **Educ:** Wiley Coll, AB 1936; N Western U, AM 1938; Yale U, MFA 1950; Western Reserve U, PhD 1960. **Career:** Spelman Coll, retired 1979; Spelman Coll, prof 1950-77, prof lang & drama 1942-43; Tillitson Coll, prof 1939-42; Inst of African Studies, Univ Ghana, prof 1971-72. **Orgs:** Alpha-Phi Alpha; African Theatre; drama critic 1964-71; study grant Africa. **Honors/Awds:** Governor's Award for Contribution to Drama 1979; Bronze Jubilee Award for Cotnribution to Drama 1980. **Military Serv:** USN corpsman 3rd class 1943-45. **Business Addr:** 350 Spelman Ln, Atlanta, GA 30314.

BURROUGHS, HUGH CHARLES
Business executive. **Personal:** Born Feb 6, 1940, Trinidad; son of Mr & Mrs Vernon Burroughs; married Linda D Kendrix; children: Kwame, Dawn; married Henrietta E Johnson (divorced). **Educ:** Columbia Univ, BA, 1966, MA, 1969; Nonprofit Mgmt, Harvard Univ, 1973. **Career:** Packard Foundation, prog director, 1993-; Henry Kaiser Family Found, vice pres, 1987-93; Hewlett Foundation, program officer, 1977-87; John Hay Whitney Found, exec dir, 1971-77. **Orgs:** Prgm dir, Woodrow Wilson Natl Fellowshp Found, 1969-71; asst dean, Columbia Univ, 1966-69; chmn, bd of vis, Clark Coll; bd of overseers, Morehouse School of Med; chmn, bd of dir, Assn of Black Found Exec, 1973-77; bd of dir, Women Philanthropy, 1977-80; bd of dirs, Council on Foundations, Northern California Grantmakers, Natl Charities Information Bureau Peninsula Community Foundation; Hispanics in Philanthropy and Civics. **Business Addr:** Packard Foundation, 300 Second St, Los Altos, CA 94022.

BURROUGHS, JOHN ANDREW, JR.
Government official. **Personal:** Born Jul 31, 1936, Washington, DC; son of Mary Virginia Burroughs and John A Burroughs; married Audrey C Shields, Feb 25, 1966. **Educ:** Univ of Iowa, BA, political science, 1959; George Washington Univ, postgrad 1962; Stanford University, postgrad, 1974. **Career:** Dept of State Washington, passport examiner 1960-63; Dept of State Bur of Econ Affairs, admin asst 1963-66; Dept of Navy Washington, employ relations spec 1970-77; Dept of Navy Washington, spl asst for equal employ 1970-77; Dept of State Washington, asst sec for equal employ oppor 1977-81; Republic of Malawi, US ambassador 1981-84; Joint Ctr for Polit Studies, sr rsch fellow 1985-; US State Dept, Cape Town, South Africa, American consul gen 1985-88; Republic of Uganda, U.S. ambassador 1988-. **Orgs:** Pres bd of dir Ridgecrest Condominium 1964-70; mem Kappa Alpha Psi. **Honors/Awds:** Civilian Superior Serv Awd Dept of Navy Washington DC 1977; Superior Honor Awd Dept of State Washington DC 1980. **Military Serv:** US Army, PFC, 1961. **Business Addr:** American Ambassador, Kampala, Uganada (DOS), Washington, DC 20520-2190.

BURROUGHS, LEONARD
Podiatric physician. **Personal:** Born May 31, 1921, Evanston, IL; married Jeweline; children: Dorothy Carroll, Ellen D, Neal D, Nancy E. **Educ:** Central YMCA Coll & Northwestern U1941-42; Univ of IL Urbana, predental 1946-47; IL Coll of Podiatric Medicine Chicago, Dr of Podiatric Medicine 1948-52. **Career:** US Treasury Dept, clk Fraud & Forgery Dept 1945-46; City Of Chicago Welfare Dept, podiatrist Div of Phys & Medicine of Rehab 1952-54; Foster G McGaw Hosp Loyola Univ of Chicago, clinical instructor in podiatric medicine; Schell Coll of Podiatric Medicine Chicago, adj prof podiatric medicine; Private Practice, podiatrist 1954-. **Orgs:** Mem & past pres IL Podiatry Soc; mem/alternate del Am Podiatry Assn; past mem bd of trustees IL Coll of Podiatric Medicine Chicago; past-pres AlumniEduc Found IL Coll of Podiatric Medicine; mem Kappa Alpha Psi Frat Inc 1942; 32nd Degree Mason Prince-Hall 1967; mem Title XIX Spl Proj Cook Co Dept of Pub Aid 1968-69; bd mem Chicago Assembly; mem Duffer's dozen Golf Club; mem St Edmund's Epis Ch Chicago; mem Amer Podiatric Medical Assoc; mem ILPodiatric Medical Soc; mem Acad of Ambulatory Foot Surgery; mem Natl Podiatric Medical Assoc. **Business Addr:** 1525 Hyde Park Blvd, Chicago, IL 60615.

BURROUGHS, MARGARET TAYLOR (MARGARET TAYLOR)
Educator, museum director, artist, author. **Personal:** Born Nov 1, 1917, St Rose, LA; daughter of Octavia Pierre Taylor and Alexander Taylor; married Bernard Goss, 1939 (divorced 1947); children: Paul Nexo, Gayle Goss Hutchinson; children: Paul Nexo (adopted). **Educ:** Chicago Normal College, Elementary Teacher's Certificate, 1935-37; Chicago Teachers College (now Chicago State Univ), 1939; Art Inst of Chicago, BA, art education, 1946, MA, art education, 1948; Esmerelda Art School, Mexico City, 1952-53; Teachers Coll, Columbia Univ, summers, 1958-60; Field Museum of Chicago, Intern under a grant from the Natl Endowment for the Humanities, 1968; Northwestern Univ, Courses in Institute of African Studies, 1968; Illinois State Univ, Grad School, 1970; Art Institute of Chicago, Courses in Printmaking, 1985-87. **Career:** Chicago Bd of Education, sustitute teacher, 1940-45, elementary teacher, 1945-46; DuSable High School, teacher of art, 1946-69; Elmhurst College, African American Art and Culture, prof, 1968; Barat College, African American Art, prof, 1969; Kennedy-King Community Coll, prof of humanities, 1969-79; instructor, African and African-American art history, Chicago Inst of Art, 1968; co-founder, officer, board of directors, South Side Art Community Center, 1939-; co-founder, 1961, dir, 1961-85, dir emeritus, 1985-, DuSable Museum of African-American History; commissioner, Chicago PK District, 1986-93. **Orgs:** Natl Conference of Negro Artists, founder, 1959-63; Phi Delta Kappa; Staff: American Forum for Africa Study for Travel in Africa, 1972-79; Staff of African-American Heritage Studies Program for travel and study in Africa, director, 1980-; Chicago Council on Foreign Relations, bd; Hull House Assn, bd; Urban Getaways Advisory, bd; Art Inst Alumni Assn, bd; South Side Comm Art Center, bd; Am Forum for Intl Study, bd; African-American Heritage Prog, bd. **Honors/Awds:** Better Boys Fdn, Strategy for the New City Award, 1969; Englewood Businessmen's Assn, Distinguished Service Award, 1972; Commended in Resolution #183 in the 78th General Assembly of the Senate, offered by Senator Richard Newhouse/State of Illinois, 1973; Natl Assn of College Women's Award, 1973; Urban Gateways Award for Cultural Contribution to the Arts, 1973; Catalysts for Change, Intl Year of the Woman Award, 1975; American Federation of Teachers, Citation for Service, 1976; Chicago Defender Survey, One of Chicago's ten most influential women (Bettie Pullen Walker), 1977; Top Ladies of Distinction, Inc, President's Humanitarian Award, 1985; Proclaimed ''Dr Margaret Burroughs Day'' in Chicago on February 1, by Mayor Harold Washington, 1986; Chicago/DuSable/Fort Dearborn Historical Commission, Inc, cited for Outstanding Service in the Arts and Humanities, 1986; Selected by Reverend Jesse Jackson to accompany him to President Samora Mached of Mozambique's Funeral, 1986; Univ of Dubuque, Iowa/Black Presidium, Lifetime Service Award, 1989; Phi Delta Kappa Sorority Mu Chapter, Recognition Award, 1989; Frank Bennett School/Chicago, Harold Washington Leadership Award, 1989; Friends of Law Enforcement Humanitarian Award, 1989; Stateville New Era Jaycees, Outstanding Religious Leader Award, 1989; Chicago Woman of the Year, 1989; and numerous other awards. **Special Achievements:** Author, works include: Jaspar, the Drummin' Boy, 1947; Whip Me Whop Me Pudding and Other Stories of Riley Rabbit and His Fabulous Friends, Praga Press, 1966; What Shall I Tell My Children Who Are Black?, MAAH Press, 1968; Sketchbook, 1976; Editor, HOME, Broadside by Charles Burroughs, ''I, Child of the Promise,'' by Gayle Goss Hutchinson, 1984; Editor, Home, poems by Charles Burroughs, 1985; Editor, Jazz Interlude, (12 poems) by Frank Marshall, 1987; Editor, Poems by Gayle Goss Hutchinson, 1987; selected 1 of 16 women to tour China, 1977; 1 of 10 African-American artists honored by President & Mrs Carter at White House, 1980; exhibitions include: Two Centuries of African-American Art, Los Angeles Art Co Museum, 1976; Ten African-American Artists, Corcoran Art Galleries, Washington, 1980; Nicole Gallery, Chicago, 1992; High Museum, Atlanta; Studio Museum, New York; numerous others.

BURROUGHS, ROBERT A.
Attorney. **Personal:** Born Mar 30, 1948, Durham, NC; son of Lottie Edwards Burroughs and Leslie Burroughs; married Laverne Davis; children: James, Christina, Whitney. **Educ:** NC Central U, BA 1971; Emory University, Atlanta, GA, JD 1978. **Career:** State of NC, magistrate 1970-71; USMC, defense counsel; McCalla, Raymer, Padrick, Cobb, Nichols & Clark, partner, 1990-. **Orgs:** Pres De Kalb Lawyers Assn 1985; Gate City Bar Assn; general counsel Natl Assn Real Estate Brokers 1985-. **Military Serv:** USMC captain, 1971-75. **Home Addr:** 4211 Hapsburg Ct, Decatur, GA 30034. **Business Addr:** Attorney, McCalla, Raymer, Padrick, 56 Perimeter Center E, 5th Fl, Atlanta, GA 30346.

BURROUGHS, SAMMIE LEE
Professional football player. **Personal:** Born Jun 21, 1973. **Educ:** Portland State. **Career:** Indianapolis Colts, defensive back, 1996-. **Business Addr:** Professional Football Player, Indianapolis Colts, PO Box 535000, Indianapolis, IN 46253, (317)297-2658.

BURROUGHS, SARAH G.
Advertising agency executive. **Personal:** Born Oct 19, 1943, Nashville, TN; daughter of Celestine Long Wilson and Herman Griffith; divorced; children: Rachael Ann. **Educ:** Lincoln Univ, Jefferson City, MO, BA, 1964; Northwestern Univ, Chicago, Il, 1966-67. **Career:** Foote, Cone & Belding, Chicago, IL, assoc research dir, vice pres, 1964-1974; Burrell Communications Group, Chicago, IL, Atlanta, GA, general manager, senior vice pres, 1974-94; Burrell Communications Group, Chicago, IL, vice chmn, pres/COO, 1994-. **Orgs:** NAACP; Urban League; Bryn Mawr Community Church. **Honors/Awds:** Outstanding Women in Business, Dollars & Sense Magazine, Kizzy Award, Kizzy Foundation. **Business Addr:** Pres/COO, Burrell Communications Group, 20 N Michigan Ave, Chicago, IL 60637.

BURROUGHS, TIM
Professional basketball player. **Career:** Minnesota Timberwolves, 1992-. **Business Addr:** Professional Basketball Player, Minnesota Timberwolves, 600 First Avenue N, Minneapolis, MN 55403, (612)337-3865.

BURROUGHS, TODD STEVEN
Journalist. **Personal:** Born Feb 17, 1968, Newark, NJ; son of Doris Burroughs. **Educ:** Seton Hall University, South Orange, NJ, BA, 1989. **Career:** The Star-Ledger, Star-Ledger Plaza, Newark, NJ, general assignment reporter, 1989-93; Seton Hall University, South Orange, NJ, adjunct professor, 1990-93. **Orgs:** National Association of Black Journalists, 1987-; Garden State Assn of Black Journalists, 1989-93. **Honors/Awds:** Internship Recipient, 1988, Scholarship Recipient, 1987, National Assn of Black Journalists.

BURROW, MARIE BRABHAM
Educator. **Personal:** Born Dec 14, 1915, St Louis, MO; daughter of Ira Mae Haskell Brabham and William S Brabham; married Artis Nathaniel Burrow, Jun 26, 1940; children: Louvon B Brown, Carolyn Burrow (Adjoa Ayetoro). **Educ:** Stowe Tchrs Coll, BS-edn 1937; So IL U, MS-guidance & coun 1965; MO U, cert-adminstr 1969. **Career:** St Louis Bd of Educ, teacher 1937-64, counselor 1964-71, dir career educ 1971-80; Harris Stowe Tchr's Coll, cons-career educ 1975-79; St Louis Pub Schs dir-career educ 1973-78, coord career educ 1978-79, personnel spec Area IV 1979-. **Orgs:** Consult Building Self-Concepts Work Study Hich Sch 1973; cons-mem-presenter Gov's Conf on Educ 1977; consult career educ Webster Coll St Louis 1978; life mem: Delta Sigma Theta Sor 1936-, NAACP; life mem sec St Louis Met Urban League, Board of Dir 1973-81; commr MO Commnon Human Rights 1975, 1978-81; life mem NAACP 1977-; mem Church Counc Pilgrim Congregational Ch 1978-80; pres St Louis State Hospital Auxiliary 1988-91;. **Honors/Awds:** Outstanding Educ Award Clark Sch Comm Assn 1976; Outstanding Workshop Award Nat Career Educ Conf 1977; Achievement Award in Educ Zeta Phi Beta Sor St Louis 1978; Woman of Achievement St Louis Globe Democrat 1981; Achievement Award in Community & Ed Service Sigma Gamma Rho Sor 1981. **Home Addr:** 5126 Labadie, St Louis, MO 63115.

BURROWS, CLARE
Public health administrator. **Personal:** Born Sep 29, 1938, Kansas City, MO; married William L Burrows; children: James Michael Pickens, Joye Nunn Hill, Carla Nunn, Anita Nunn Orme, Maurice Nunn. **Educ:** College St Mary Omaha, BS 1962; UCLA, MPH 1972. **Career:** Stanford Univ Palo Alto, compliance auditor 1975-78; Community Hosp Santa Rosa CA, dir medical records 1978-80; Univ SF UCSF, dir patient service 1980-82; CA Medical Review San Francisco, monitor 1982-86; Beverly Enterprises Inc, dir business admin. **Orgs:** Tutor Urban League 1980-82; consultant Medical Records Assoc 1980-84. **Honors/Awds:** Outstanding Church Work Mt Hermon AME Church 1984. **Military Serv:** USAR capt 6 yrs.

BURROWS DOST, JANICE H.
Human resource director, consultant. **Personal:** Born Oct 24, 1944, Boston, MA; daughter of Bernice E Cross Howard (deceased) and Lloyd F Howard (deceased); married Quentin C Burrows (divorced 1986); children: Matthew Howard, Christopher Lynch; married William A. Dost, 1995. **Educ:** Harvard University, Cambridge, MA, BA, 1966; University of California, Berkeley, CA, MBA, 1987. **Career:** US Civil Service Commission, Boston, MA, Washington, DC, personnel specialist, 1966-68; US General Services Admin, New York, NY, regional training officer, 1971-72; City of Berkeley, Berkeley, CA, personnel specialist, 1974-76; Alta Bates Hospital, Berkeley, CA, personnel director, 1976-85; self-employed consultant, human resource management, Berkeley, CA, 1985-; University of California, Berkeley, CA, dir of library human resources, 1988-. **Orgs:** Humanities West, director. **Honors/Awds:** President, Healthcare Human Resources Management Assn of California, 1984-85; chair, Berkeley Unified School District Personnel Commission, 1978-79, 1987-91; vice president, California School Personnel Commissioners Assn, 1991-92; president, SF Chapter, California Hospital Personnel Managers Assn, 1980-81; member, American Library Assn; Industrial Relations Research Association, member. **Special Achievements:** Author, Minority Recruitment and Retention in ARL Libraries, Association of Research Libraries, Office of Management Services, 1990; ''Onward or Upward? Getting Ahead in an Unfair World,'' Proceedings of the Second National Conference of the Black Caucus of the American Library Association, 1994; ''Training Student Workers in Academic Libraries, How and Why?,'' Journal of Library Administration, Volume 212, #3/4, 1994;'' Minority Recruitment and Retention in ARL Libraries,'' Office of Management Services, Association of Research Libraries, 1990. **Business Addr:** Director, Library Human Resources, University of California, 447 The Library, Berkeley, CA 94720.

BURRUS, CLARK
Banking executive. **Personal:** Born Nov 5, 1928, Chicago, IL; son of Mattie Hall and Lemuel Burrus; married Lucille Thomas; children: James. **Educ:** Roosevelt University, BSC, 1954, MPA, 1972. **Career:** City of Chicago, Dept of Finance, first deputy city comptroller, assistant & comptroller, director of accounting & assistant director of finance, 1954-73, chief fiscal officer/city comptroller, 1973-79; First National Bank of Chicago, senior vice president, Public Banking Dept, co-head, 1979-. **Orgs:** Government Finance Officers Assn of the United States and Canada; board of trustees, Cosmopolitan Chamber of Commerce; member, Chicago Planning Commission; member, National Assn of Securities Professionals; board of directors, Evangelical Health Systems Foundation; board of directors, National Urban Coalition; board of directors, Chicago Council on Urban Affairs; board of directors, Financial Research and Advisory Committee; bd of director, Economic Development Council; bd of director, National Association of Securities Professionals; Chicago Transit Authority, chairman of the board, currently. **Honors/Awds:** Sertoma Intl, Man of the Year, 1975; Blackbook Business & Ref Guide, one of 10 Outstanding Business & Professional People, 1979; Executive Development Alumni, Executive of the Year, 1974. **Special Achievements:** Author: ''Minorities in Public Finance,'' Government Magazine, 1972; ''Issues Concerning the Financing of Mortgages with Tax-exempt Bonds,'' City of Chicago. **Business Addr:** Senior VP, First National Bank of Chicago, One First National Plaza, Ste 0090, Chicago, IL 60670.

BURRUS, WILLIAM HENRY
Business executive. **Personal:** Born Dec 13, 1936, Wheeling, WV; son of Gertude Burrus and William Burrus; married Ethelda I; children: Valerie, Doni, Kimberly, Kristy. **Educ:** WV State, 1957. **Career:** OH Postal Union, dir rsch & educ 1971, pres 1974-80; Amer Postal Workers Union, bus agent 1978-80, exec vice pres 1980-. **Orgs:** Labor del Cleveland Fed AFL-CIO 1977; vice pres Black Trade Labor Union 1977; mem OH Advisory Bd Civil Rights Comm 1979-81; vice pres A Philip Randolph Inst 1982-. **Honors/Awds:** OH House of Rep 1981; Frederick O'Neal Award 1981; A Philip Randolph Achievement Award 1982; num union awds & recognition; Distinguished Service Award, Martin Luther King Center, 1989; National Coalition of Black Voter Participation. **Military Serv:** AUS sgt 3 years. **Business Addr:** Executive Vice President, American Postal Workers Union, AFL-CIO, 1300 L St NW, Washington, DC 20005.

BURSE, LUTHER
Forestry service official. **Personal:** Born Jan 3, 1937, Hopkinsville, KY; son of Ernestine Perry and Monroe Perry (stepfather); married Mamie Joyce Malbon; children: Luther Jr, Elizabeth N. **Educ:** KY State Univ, BS 1958; Univ of IN, MEd 1960; Univ of MD, EdD 1969. **Career:** Chicago Pub Sch, tchr 1958-59; Elizabeth City State Univ, instruct 1960-66; Univ of MD, research asst 1966-69; Cheyney St Coll, prof, 1969-81, acting pres, 1981-82; Chester Pub Sch, consultant, Philadelphia Bd of Exam; Fort Valley State Coll, pres 1983-89; US Forest Service, special asst to chief, 1989-; director of civil rights, currently. **Orgs:** Amer Council on Industrial Tchr Educ; PA State Educ Assn; Amer Assn of State Colls & Univs; past pres Indus Arts Assn of PA; past pres PA Assn for Voc & Practical Arts Educ; NEA, mem Higher Educ Caucus, Black Caucus, Women's Caucus, Vocational Caucus; Alpha Kappa Mu Honor Soc; Omega Psi Phi Frat; Iota Lamda Sigma Frat; life mem NAACP; Amer Council on Educ Leadership Comm; Council of 1890 College Presidents; bd of directors, Georgia Assn of Minority Entrepreneurs; Sigma Pi Phi Fraternity; Georgia Assn of Colleges; Natl Assn of State Univs & Land Grant Colls. **Honors/Awds:** Omega Man of the Yr Nu Upsilon Chap; leadership award in arts assoc; PA State Educ Assn Serv Award; Honorable KY Col Commonwealth of KY; Centennial Alumni Award, Kentucky State Univ; Leadership Award, Natl Educ Assn. **Business Addr:** Director, Civil Rights, US Forestry Service, PO Box 96090, Washington, DC 20090-6090.

BURSE, RAYMOND MALCOLM
Sr counsel. **Personal:** Born Jun 8, 1951, Hopkinsville, KY; son of Lena Belle Burse (deceased) and Joe Burse (deceased); married Kim M; children: Raymond M Jr, Justin Malcolm, Eric M. **Educ:** Centre College of Kentucky, AB Chem & Math 1973; Oxford Univ, Grad work 1973-75; Harvard Law School, JD 1978. **Career:** Kentucky State Univ, pres, 1982-89; Wyatt, Tarrant & Combs, associate, 1978-82, partner, 1989-95; GE Appliances, sr counsel, 1995-. **Orgs:** Amer Bar Assn; KY Bar Assn; Natl Bar Assn; bd chmn Louisville Fed Reserve 1987, 1990; bd mem State YMCA. **Honors/Awds:** Rhodes Scholar; Fred M Vinson Honor Graduate, Centre College; John W Davis Award NAACP Legal Defense and Educational Fund. **Home Addr:** 7010 New Bern Court, Prospect, KY 40059. **Business Addr:** Sr Counsel - Commercial Law, GE Appliances, Appliance Park, AP2-225, Louisville, KY 40225.

BURTON, BARBARA ANN
Company executive. **Personal:** Born Dec 27, 1941, Houston, TX; daughter of Alice Burton and Isiah Burton; married James Henderson, Nov 4, 1980 (divorced). **Educ:** Texas Southern University, BS, 1966, MS, 1972, MEd, 1974. **Career:** City of Houston, community development manager, 1966-70, City Council, exec assistant, 1980-83; Model Cities, program manager, Texas Southern University, Community Development, Soc Ins, director, 1975-80; State of Texas, program manager, community development, 1983-87; Austin Metropolitan Business Resource Center, president, chief executive officer, 1987-. **Orgs:** Capital Metro, chairman of the board, 1987-; Texas Assn of Minority Business Enterprises, president, 1991-; Capital Area Workforce Alliance, committee chair, 1990-; Natl Council of Negro Women, president, 1986-; Conference on Minority Transportation Officials, president, 1991-; Women's Chamber of Commerce, 1990-; Precinct #141, chair, 1991-. **Honors/Awds:** Minority Business News/USA, Women Who Mean Business Award, 1993; Minorities and Women in Business, Women Who Make a Difference Award, 1992; Black Women Achievers, Black Woman's Hall of Fame Inductee, 1992. **Special Achievements:** First African-American & first woman to be elected chair, Capital Metro Transit; responsible for first African-American McDonald's Franchise in Austin; televeision hostess: ''Minority Business Review,'' 1992-. **Home Addr:** 1833 Coronado Hills Dr, Austin, TX 78752, (512)453-2896. **Business Addr:** President, CEO, Austin Metropolitan Business Resource Center, 2028 E Ben White Blvd, PO Box 6206, Austin, TX 78762, (512)322-0177.

BURTON, CALVIN E.
Business executive. **Personal:** chilDren: 1. **Educ:** Morgan St Coll, BA 1964; Rutgers U, MBA. **Career:** NBC Stations, staff producer 1972-; KNBC, adminstr programs 1970-72; Eual Empl Prog, adminstr 1968-70; Direct Hire Prog, adminstr 1967-68; Prog RotatingAssign, corp training 1966-67; RCA Electr Comp Div, interviewer recruiter 1965-66; US Dept Health Educ & Welfare 1964. **Orgs:** Mem Morgan St NJ Alumni Assn; Nat Caht Ofc for Radio & TV; Hollywood Chap Nat Acad of TV Arts & Sci; Oper Breadbasket PUSH; Nat Urban League; pub affairs com LA Urban League; Am Mgnt Assn; chmn radio &TV com United Negro Coll Fund; exec bd mem NAACP; People United to Save Humanity; SCLC W Spl. **Honors/Awds:** Spl consult Inst of Black Am Music; football schlrsp 4 yrs Morgan St Coll; first internal employe to be selected for 6 mo corp personnel training prog RCA Corp Staff; five day AMA Seminar; nominated for Emmy Award; awared resolution CA St Assembly; awared resolution for outstanding prod City Coun of Los Angeles; award for excellence Nat Assn of TV Program Exec 1973; outstanding contrib to Los Angeles Black Comm Los Angeles Urban League 1973; Salute dto Red FoxxABC; 2 spec in conjuction with Rev Jessee Jackson's Oper PUSH NBC; best local TV pub affairs prgm award 10th Annual NAACP Images Award Dinner. **Business Addr:** 3000 W Alameda Ave, Burbank, CA 91523.

BURTON, CHARLES HOWARD, JR.
Army officer. **Personal:** Born Sep 21, 1945, Richmond, VA; married Adline Mildred Johnson; children: Stuart Howard, Stacee Michelle, Stephanie Brouke. **Educ:** VA State Coll, BS 1968; Meharry Medical Coll, MD 1975. **Career:** US Army, chief ob/gyn. **Orgs:** Fellow Amer College Ob/Gyn 1983, Amer College of Surgeons 1984; mem Omega Psi Phi Frat; 32 Degree Mason, Shriner. **Military Serv:** AUS col 18 yrs; Army Commendation Medal 1978. **Home Addr:** 3852 Highgreen Dr, Marietta, GA 30068. **Business Addr:** Chief Ob/Gyn, US Army, Martin Army Hospital, Fort Benning, GA 31905.

BURTON, DAVID LLOYD
Accountant. **Personal:** Born Aug 1, 1956, Detroit, MI; son of C Lutressie Johnson Burton and Freddie George Burton Sr (deceased); married Michele Lisa Simms-Burton, Dec 26, 1987; children: David Malik. **Educ:** Wayne State Univ, BS 1977, MBA 1980. **Career:** Arthur Young & Co CPA, auditor 1980-81; Barrow Aldridge & Co CPA, semi-sr auditor 1981-84; Ford Motor Co, internal auditor/operations rep 1985-88; Reeves & Associates, Griffin, GA, controller, 1988-90; US Securities & Exchange Commission, Washington, DC, staff accountant, 1991-. **Orgs:** Mem Natl Assoc of Black Accountants 1979; Natl Black MBA Assoc 1981; Cascade United Methodist Church 1986. **Honors/Awds:** Certified Public Accountant State of MI 1983. **Home Addr:** 6197 Old Brentford Court, Alexandria, VA 22310, (703)719-9312.

BURTON, DONALD C.
Law enforcement official, consultant. **Personal:** Born Apr 21, 1938, Lawnside, NJ; son of Josephine B Burton and William E Burton Sr; married Marcia E Campbell; children: Donald Jr, Barry D, Jay S, Robert T, Christopher, Matthew. **Educ:** Camden Co Coll, AS 1969-74; Rutger State Univ, BA 1975-77. **Career:** Correction consultant-private business 1973-; Cherry Hill Police Dept, det sgt, polygraph oper 1973-, lieutenant; Camden Co Sheriff's Dept, undersheriff 1984-88; Bergen County Sheriff's Dept, undersheriff 1988-89; Mark Correctional Systems Inc, correctional consultant, 1989-93; D B Assoc, consultant; City of Lawnside, dir of public safety, 1992-96. **Orgs:** Pres Cherry Hill #176 PBA 1969-71; delegate NJ State PBA 1970-72; pres NJ Chap of NOBLE 1983-88; regional vice pres NOBLE 1987-88; trustee HOPE for Ex-Offenders. **Honors/Awds:** Valor Awd Cherry Hill Township 1970; Commissioner Citation US Customs 1973; Alcohol Tobacco & Firearms Citation polygraph expert 1974; numerous awds from law enforcement organizations municipal and from county, state, and national groups. **Military Serv:** AUS reserves 1957-67. **Home Addr:** 22 Ashland Ave, Sicklerville, NJ 08081.

BURTON, IOLA BRANTLEY
Educator. **Personal:** Born Oct 20, Ensley, AL; daughter of Cremonia D Watkins Brantley and Willie Douglas Brantley; married Herman L Burton, Apr 1, 1945; children: Constance Parma Pulliam, Laura J Odem. **Educ:** Miles Coll, Birmingham, AL, AB, 1941; Columbia Univ, New York, NY, 1953; Univ of Denver, Denver, CO 1954-55; Univ of S CA, Los Angeles, CA, 1964. **Career:** Limestone County Bd of Educ, Athens, AL, teacher, 1941-43; Jefferson County Bd of Educ, Birmingham, AL, teacher, 1943-45, 1948-56; Los Angeles County Dept of Social Service, case worker, 1957-60; Centinela Valley Unified School Dist, teacher, 1963-83; Los Angeles City DPT Recreation & Parks, Los Angeles, CA, outreach consultant, 1983-85; Centinela Valley U.S.D., Hawthorne, CA, substitute teacher, 1985-. **Orgs:** Supreme Epistoleus, The Natl Sorority of Phi Delta Kappa Inc 1987-; Supreme Grammateus The Natl Sorority of Phi Delta Kappa, Inc. 1967-71; Clerk of Session , Westminster Presbyterian Church, 1984-; corres sec bd of dir, Natl Alumni Assoc Miles Coll, 1988-. **Honors/Awds:** Service, Los Angeles City, 1974; Natl Sojourner Truth Meritorious Serv, Natl Assn of Negro Business & Professional Women, 1977; Service & Leadership, Natl Sorority Phi Delta Kappa Inc, 1980; Service, Los Angeles City Dept of Rec & Parks, 1985; Service 10 years, Our Authors Study Club/African Festival, 1989; author, The Way It Strikes Me, 1988, Yawl Come on Back Home Again, 1978. **Home Addr:** 3039 Wellington Rd, Los Angeles, CA 90016.

BURTON, JOHN H.
Union negotiator. **Personal:** Born Jul 18, 1910, St Louis, MO; married Willie. **Career:** Intl United Auto Workers Union UAW, rep internat; Ypsilanti, mayor, former city councilman 18 yrs. **Orgs:** Mem bd of Controls Med Center of Univ of MI; bd trustees Chelsea Med Center; exec bd dir Comprehensive Planning Council. **Honors/Awds:** Recipient man of yr award Ford Motor Car Co Ypsilanti & Rawsonville plants; law day award Washtenaw Bar Assn distinguished serv awards MI Assn of Black Women's Clubs & NAACP Office.

BURTON, JUANITA SHARON
Physician. **Personal:** Born Sep 28, 1946, Philadelphia, PA; daughter of Elizabeth T Jessup and David N Jessup; married Ronald A Burton, Jun 19, 1982; children: Ronald William Os-

borne Burton. **Educ:** Cabrini Coll Radnor PA, BS Biology 1973; Jefferson Medical Coll, MD 1977. **Career:** Presbyterian Univ of PA Med Ctr, internship 1977-78; Union Memorial Hosp Baltimore, resident ob/gyn 1978-80; Walter Reed Army Med Ctr DC, resident ob/gyn 1980-82; US Army MEDDAC Shape Belgium, staff physician 1982-85; US Army MEDDAC Ft Jackson SC, staff physician 1985-87, chief ob/gyn serv 1987-88; private practice, 1988-. **Orgs:** Mem Jr Fellow Amer Coll of Ob/Gyn 1980-; mem Assoc of Military Surgeons of US 1982-; mem Amer Med Women's Assoc 1986-. **Honors/Awds:** US Army Commission Capt 1980; US Army Promotion Major 1983; Diplomate Amer Bd of Ob/Gyn 1985. **Military Serv:** AUS major, 1980-88; received Meritorious Service Medal, 1988.

BURTON, KENDRICK
Professional football player. **Personal:** Born Sep 7, 1974, Decatur, AL. **Educ:** Univ of Alabama. **Career:** Tennessee Oilers, defensive end, currently. **Business Addr:** Professional Football Player, Tennessee Oilers, c/o Baptist Sports Park, 7640 H 70-5, Nashville, TN 37221.

BURTON, LANA DOREEN
Educator. **Personal:** Born Mar 25, 1953, Evansville, IN; daughter of Gloria Wickware Beckner and William Dulin; married Rickey Burton, Feb 8, 1977; children: Alexander Richard. **Educ:** Indiana State University, Terre Haute, IN, BS, 1975; University of Evansville, Evansville, IN, MA, elementary education, 1979, administrative certification, 1990. **Career:** Breckinridge Job Corp Center, Morganfield, KY, teacher, 1975-76; Evansville-Vanderburgh School Corp, Evansville, IN, educator, 1976-92, administrator, 1992-. **Orgs:** Vice president, Coalition of African-American Women, 1990-, president, Evansville Chapter, 1985-90; board member, president, YWCA, 1990-; member, Evansville Youth Coalition, 1989-; superintendent, Sunday School, Zion Baptist Church, 1991-94; Junior League of Evansville, 1986-. **Honors/Awds:** Black Women of the Year, Black Women's Task Force, 1985; Outstanding Young American, 1987. **Home Addr:** 1424 Brookside Dr, Evansville, IN 47714.

BURTON, LEROY MELVIN, JR.
Physician. **Personal:** Born Sep 12, 1940, Statesville, NC; son of Mr & Mrs Leroy M Burton Sr; married Barbara Stokes Pannell; children: Randi Pannell, Lori, Albert Pannell II, Leslie. **Educ:** Lincoln Univ PA, BA 1962; NC Coll, MS 1965; Meharry Med Coll, MD 1969. **Career:** Sunny Brook Med Center Raleigh NC, private practice internal med 1977; Meharry Med Coll, student health dir 1973-74; Meharry Med Coll, asst prof 1973-74. **Orgs:** Mem Nat Med Assn 1975; mem Old N State Med Soc 1975; mem LA Scruggs Med Soc 1975; mem Alpha Phi Alpha Frat 1959; mem Prince Hall Mason 1962. **Honors/Awds:** Mem 32nd Degree Prince Hall Mason & Shriner 1976. **Business Addr:** 100 Sunnybrook Rd, Ste 101, Raleigh, NC 27610.

BURTON, LEVAR (LEVARDIS ROBERT MARTYN JR.)
Actor. **Personal:** Born Feb 16, 1957, Landstuhl; son of Erma Christian Burton and Levardis Robert Burton; married Stephanie; children: Michaela. **Educ:** University of Southern California, attended. **Career:** Film appearances include: Looking for Mr Goodbar, 1977; The Hunter, 1980; The Supernaturals, 1987; television appearances include: Roots, 1977; Reading Rainbow, series host, 1983-; Star Trek: The Next Generation, 1987-88; Murder, She Wrote, 1987; Houston Knights, 1987; numerous biographical tv movies; A Special Friendship, 1987; A Roots Christmas: Kunte Kinte's Gift, 1988; various tv specials. **Honors/Awds:** Emmy Award, nomination, Best Actor, Roots, 1977. **Business Addr:** Actor, c/o Paramount Pictures, 555 Melrose Ave., Gower Mills Bldg., RM 117, Los Angeles, CA 90030.

BURTON, RONALD E.
Business executive. **Personal:** Born Jul 25, 1936, Springfield, OH; married JoAnn Jourdain; children: Steven, Elizabeth, Ronald, Jr, Phillip, Paul. **Educ:** NW U,bS Bus & Mktg 1960. **Career:** John Hancock Mutual Life Ins Co, pub rel exec 1966-; Wall St, stockbroker 3 yrs; Boston Patriots, running back 6 yrs; ABC-TV, sports commentators collgame of week 1969; ABC, commentator for Mon night game of week 1972; Pop Warner football league Charlestown, founder 1971. **Orgs:** Mem Republ St Fin Com; Framingham Pk Commn; mem Copr of Framingham Savings Bank; mem Hood Milk Phys Fit Prgm; Boy Scout Coun; Framingham YMCA; bddir Boston Evening Clinic; vice pres Northwestern Univ Club of Boston; advisory bd Salvation Army. **Honors/Awds:** One of ten outs men in Boston 1967; various records & achvmts in football. **Military Serv:** USNG & reserves 1960-65. **Business Addr:** 200 Berkeley St, Boston, MA 02117.

BURTON, RONALD J.
Information services executive. **Personal:** Born Jun 12, 1947, Montclair, NJ; son of Ruth Jackson Burton and Joseph Burton; married Carolyn Ievers, Oct 1975; children: Christopher, Alison. **Educ:** Colgate Univ, Hamilton, NY, BA, History, Economics, 1969; Wharton School, Philadelphia, PA, graduate courses. **Career:** Dallas Cowboys, Dallas, TX, professional athlete, 1969; EI Dupont, Wilmington, DE, mktg mgr, 1969-74; RH Donnelley, New York, NY, mgr, 1975-87, vice pres, 1987-. **Orgs:** Bd mem, vice pres, Colgate Alumni Club, 1975-80, Montclair Public Schools, 1985-87; bd mem, George Jr Republic Assn, Ithaca, NY, 1979-85, Mountainside Hospital, Montclair, NJ, 1987-. **Honors/Awds:** All-Amer Quarterback, Colgate, 1966-68; Maroon Citation, Colgate. **Business Addr:** RH Donnelley, Dun & Bradstreet Co, 287 Bowman Ave, Purchase, NY 10577.

BURTON-JUNIOR, EVA WESTBROOK
Educator. **Personal:** Born Jul 10, 1944, Yazoo City, MS; daughter of Exia M Shortridge Westbrook and Cue Westbrook; married E J Junior Jr; children: Lori M Burton, Lesli M Burton. **Educ:** TN State Univ Nashville, BS 1966, MA Ed 1972. **Career:** Catholic Schools Washington DC, lang arts teacher 1966-67, 1969-70; DC Public Schools, lang arts teacher 1967-69; Fed City Coll Wash DC, English instr 1968-69; Fisk Univ Nashville, reading instr 1974-75; Atlanta Public Schools Atlanta GA, English, reading teacher 1977-80; Spelman Coll Atlanta GA, English instr 1980-81; Fulton County Schools Atlanta GA, English teacher 1981-82; Morris Brown Coll Atlanta GA, English instr 1983-85; Ft Valley State Coll Ft Valley GA, English instr 1986-. **Orgs:** Mem Modern Lang Assn 1968-70, Natl Educ Assn 1968-76, Delta Sigma Theta 1970-, Intl Reading Assn 1974-76, PTA of GA 1977-85 GA Assoc of Educators 1978-82; notary public-at-large State of GA 1978-; mem Girl Scouts of Amer 1979-84, Mayors' Task Force on Educ Atlanta GA 1982-84; Trinity Bapt Church 1986-. **Honors/Awds:** Dean's List TN State Univ 1963-66; Excellence in Teaching Awd Atlanta Public Schools 1977-78; Cert of Outstanding Performance Morris Brown Coll Special Progs 1983-84-85; Cert of Outstanding Achievements and Appreciation for Dedicated Serv Alpha Phi Alpha, Iota Chapter, 1984 Morris Brown Coll. **Home Addr:** 103 Cochran Ct, Byron, GA 31008.

BURTON-LYLES, BLANCHE
Musician, educator. **Personal:** Born Mar 2, 1933, Philadelphia, PA; daughter of Ida Blanche Taylor-Burton (deceased) and Anthony H Burton (deceased); children: Thedric (deceased). **Educ:** Curtis Inst of Music, MusB 1954; Temple U, Phila, BMusEd 1971, MusM 1975. **Career:** Soc Orch of LeRoy Bostic's Mellowaires, pianist; Concert Pianist, US, 1939-; Bd of Education, Philadelphia, PA, teacher, 1960-93. **Orgs:** Mem Delta Sigma Theta Sor 1954; Pro Arts Society; mem, Music Ed Natl Conf, 1970-; Russell Johnson-Negro Assn Musicians, 1990-; Founder of Marian Anderson Historical Society. **Honors/Awds:** 1st and youngest black piano soloist, NY Philharmonic Symphony Orch Carnegie Hall 1947; 1st black woman pianist to graduate, Curtis Inst of Music Philadelphia 1953; 1st black woman pianist to receive degree, Curtis Inst, 1954; Music Specialist, 25 Years, Women in Ed, 1991; Phila Political Congress of Black Women, Award for Achievement in Music Industry, 1994; Natl Black Music Caucus Award, Outstanding Woman in Music, 1995; Coalition Award of 100 Black Women. **Home Addr:** 1118 S 19th St, Philadelphia, PA 19146-2937.

BURTON-SHANNON, CLARINDA
Obstetrician/gynecologist. **Personal:** Born Jan 16, 1959, Philadelphia, PA; daughter of Gracie Burton and James Burton; married Charles Langford Shannon Sr, Jul 9, 1988; children: Michael Joshua Shannon. **Educ:** Cheyney State Coll, BA (Summa Cum Laude) 1980; Meharry Medical Coll, MD 1984. **Career:** Private practice, obstetrician/gynecologist, currently. **Business Addr:** Obstetrician/Gynecologist, Lebanon Women's Clinic, 437 Park Ave, Suite A, Lebanon, TN 37087.

BURTS, EZUNIAL
City official. **Career:** Port of Los Angeles, executive director, currently. **Business Addr:** Executive Director, Port of Los Angeles, 425 S Palos Verdes St, San Pedro, CA 90731, (310)732-3245.

BURWELL, BRYAN ELLIS
Sports journalist/television broadcaster. **Personal:** Born Aug 4, 1955, Washington, DC; son of Ursula Tomas Burwell and Harold H Burwell; married Dawnn Turner Burwell, Jun 23, 1984; children: Victoria Renee. **Educ:** Virginia State University, Petersburg, VA, BA, English Lit, 1977. **Career:** Baltimore Sun, Baltimore, MD, sports reporter, 1977-79; Washington Star, Washing, DC, sports reporter, 1979-80; New York Newsday, New York, NY, NBA writer, 1980-83; New York Daily News, New York, NY, NFL columnist, 1983-89; Detroit News, Detroit, MI, sports columnist, 1989-; HBD Sports, New York, NY, Inside the NFL reporter, 1990-. **Orgs:** Member, Kappa Alpha Psi, 1975-; member, Pro Football Writers of America; member, National Association of Black Journalists. **Honors/Awds:** Number 5 Feature Writer in Country, APSE, 1988; Number 4 Columnist in Country, 1989, Associated Press Sports Editions; Michigan's Top Sports Columnist, UPI, 1989. **Business Addr:** General Sports Columnist, USA Today, 99 W Hawthorne Ave, Valley Stream, NY 11580-6101.

BURWELL, WILLIAM DAVID, JR.
Educator. **Personal:** Born Jan 9, 1942, Birmingham, AL; married Leslie; children: Edith, Anthony, Miata, Mandela, Shabazz. **Educ:** San Fernando Valley State Coll, MA 1974, BA, 1970; Los Angeles Valley Coll, AA, 1967. **Career:** CA State Univ, chmn 1975-, asst prof 1969-75; San Fernando Valley State Coll, teacher operation & headstart, 1964-69, asst dir 1960. **Orgs:** Consult Southern CA Schl Dist; mem Southern CA Black Stud Alliance; consult Kent State Univ 1970; mem United Prof of CA 1969-; mem CA Assn of Black Faculty &Staff, 1976-; cofndr CA State Univ Black Stud Union, 1967; chrm Afro Am of Pacoima, 1966; chrm La Valley Stud. **Honors/Awds:** Recpt Civil Rights Org 1964 San Fernando Valley Youth Serv 1959; publ Right-on-Learning, 1975. **Military Serv:** AUS sp4 1960-63. **Business Addr:** 18111 Nordhoff St, Northridge, CA 91330.

BUSBY, EVERETT C.
Educator. **Personal:** Born in Muskogee, OK. **Educ:** Langston Univ Langston OK, BA Sociology, 1950; Univ of Norman, Cert in Social Work 1951; Univ of TX Austin, MSW 1953. **Career:** Fordham Univ Grad Sch of Social Svc, asso prof 1961-; Private Practice, supervising psychotherapist, triana & asso 1971-80; NIAAA HEW Wash DC, consult 1970-72; Seton Hall Coll of Medicine & Dentistry Jersey City NJ, instr & dept of psychiatry 1959-61; Kings Co Psychiatric Hosp NYC, psychiatric social worker 1956-59; US Army Med Serv Corps, psychiatric social worker 1953-55. **Orgs:** Consult training ed Bedford-Stuyvesant Youth in Act Brooklyn; consult training ed HARYOU-ACT NYC; mem bd Educ & training Nat Council on Alcohol New York City Affl; mem Nat Assn of Black Soc Wrkrs 1985; mem Council on Soc Wrk Educ 1985; mem Am Assn of Univ Prof 1985; mem Nat Conf on Soc Welfare 1985; mem Nat Conf on SocWelfare 1985; mem Am Civil Liberties Union; mem Alpha Phi Alpha Frat. **Military Serv:** AUS spec II 1951-53. **Business Addr:** Fordham Univ Grad & Sch of Soc Sv, Lincoln Center Campus, New York, NY 10023.

BUSBY, JHERYL
Recording company executive. **Personal:** Born in Los Angeles, CA; married; children: three. **Educ:** Long Beach State College, attended. **Career:** Mattel Toys, from inventory clerk to purchasing agent (production supplies) to new-toy coordinator; Stax Records, from regional promotional representative to head, West Coast promotion and marketing; independent album promoter; promotional work for Casablanca, Atlantic Records, CBS Records; A & M Records, 1980-83; MCA Records, from vp to pres, black music dept, 1984-88; Motown Records, CEO, 1988-. **Honors/Awds:** Helped promote Isaac Hayes's album Shaft; with Apollo Theatre (NY), assisted in developing a new label for Motown (a subsidiary of MCA) distribution: Apollo Theatre Records, 1989. **Business Addr:** Motown Record Co., 5750 Wilshire Blvd. Ste. 300, Los Angeles, CA 90036-3697.

BUSBY, V. EUGENE
City official. **Personal:** Born Jun 20, 1937, Martin, TN; son of Louise Holt Busby and V E Busby; married Bonita Watson Busby, Jun 20, 1981. **Educ:** University of Detroit, MI, BBA, 1969. **Career:** Ford Motor Company, various personnel, labor positions, 1969-74; Babcock & Wilcox, mgr, industrial rel, 1974-76; Mobil Oil Company, mgr, management dev & mgr compensation, 1976-81; Riley Stoker Corp (subsidiary of Ashland Oil), vice president, 1981-85; City of Memphis, director, personnel services, 1986-. **Orgs:** Member, Board of Directors, Southern Health Plan, 1988-; member, Board of Directors, Memphis Blues Foundation, 1990-; member, General Advisory Council, State Technical Institute of Memphis, 1989-; member, Board of Advisors for Program Development, United Cerebral Palsy of Mid-South, 1990-. **Military Serv:** US Air Force, Sgt, 1956-69. **Business Addr:** Director, Personnel Services, City of Memphis, 125 Mid-America Mall, Room 406, Memphis, TN 38103.

BUSH, CHARLES VERNON
Electronics company executive. **Personal:** Born Dec 17, 1939, Tallahassee, FL; son of Marie Bush and Charles Bush; married Bettina; children: 3. **Educ:** USAF Acad, BS Engrg 1963; Georgetown Univ, MA Intl Relations 1964; Harvard Univ Grad School of Business Admin, MBA Finance 1972. **Career:** USAF, intelligence officer 1963-70; White Weld & Co Inc, assoc corp finance 1972-74; Celanese Corp, asst treas 1974-78; Max Factor & Co, vp, treas 1978-80, vp, corp controller 1980-83; ICN Pharmaceuticals Inc, vice pres fin, CFO 1983-85; Greenberg, Glusker, Fields, Claman & Machtinger, exec dir 1985-87; Unicel Inc, vice president, 1987-89; Marnel Investment Corp, pres, 1989-91; The Nostalgia Television Network, president, 1991-92; GM Hughes Electronics Corp, vice president, currently. **Orgs:** Bd of dir United Mutual Ins Co 1976-78; mem Financial Exec Inst 1978-; exec council Harvard Bus School Alumni Assn 1978-83; bd of dir Harvard Business School Southern CA Alumni Assoc 1981-84, Harvard Business School Black Alumni Assoc. **Military Serv:** USAF capt; Bronze Star Medal, Joint Serv Commendation Medal, Air Force Commendation Medal with Oak Leaf Cluster. **Home Addr:** 3809 North Paseo Primario, Calabasas, CA 91302.

BUSH, DEVIN
Professional football player. **Personal:** Born Jul 3, 1973, Miami, FL. **Educ:** Florida State University. **Career:** Atlanta Falcons, defensive back, 1995-. **Special Achievements:** Selected in the 1st round/26th overall pick in the 1995 NFL Draft. **Business Addr:** Professional Football Player, Atlanta Falcons, Two Falcon Place, Suwanee, GA 30174, (404)945-1111.

BUSH, EVELYN
Corrections official. **Personal:** Born Jan 8, 1953, Danbury, CT; daughter of Annette Bush and Ruben Bush; children: Maghan Kadijah. **Educ:** Univ of CT Storrs, BA 1975; MS. **Career:** CT State Dept of Corrections, affirmative action officer 1976-77, personnel officer 1977-79, deputy warden 1979-84, warden 1984-92, 1995-; Correctional Services Director, deputy commissioner, 1992-94. **Orgs:** Bd mem House of Bread 1982-83; vice pres bd Families in Crisis 1982-; volunteer counselor YWCA Sexual Assault Crisis 1982-90; commnr City of Hartford Drug/Alcohol 1986-90; mem CT Criminal Justice Assoc, Amer Correctional Assoc, Middle Atlantic States Correctional Assoc; Manch Bd of Educ, 1995-98; Tenn Mentor, 1996-. **Honors/Awds:** CT Zeta of the Year Zeta Phi Beta Sor 1978; Comm Serv Awd Phoenix Soc Firefighters 1985; Comm Serv Awd Hope SDA Church & Metro AME 1985; Govt Service Recognition YWCA 1985; Outstanding Working Women Glamour Magazine 1985; Outstanding Connecticut Women, Connecticut United Nations Assn, 1987. **Business Addr:** Department of Correction, Manson Youth Institute, 42 Jarvis St, Cheshire, CT 06410.

BUSH, GORDON
Mayor. **Career:** Mayor of East St. Louis, currently. **Business Addr:** Mayor, City Hall, City of East St. Louis, 301 River Pk Dr, East St Louis, IL 62201, (618)482-6601.

BUSH, LENORIS
Executive director. **Personal:** Born Jul 18, 1949, Colquitt, GA; married Helen. **Educ:** Para-Prof Inst, Social Serv Aide 1969; Univ of UT, sociology 1975; Westminster Coll, BS Behavioral Science 1977; Univ of Phoenix, MBA 1984. **Career:** Probation Dept Juvenile Court, caseworker 1968-69; Granite Comm Mental Health Center, mental health aide 1969-70; Second Dist Juvenile Court, probation officer 1970-74; UT Opportunity Industrial Center, job developer/indust relations dir 1976, dir program operation 1977, deputy dir 1977-78, exec dir 1978-. **Orgs:** C of C Indust Dev Comm; UTA Adv Bd 1978-; Apprenticeship Outreach Bd 1977-; Co-Op Exoffender Pgm Bd 1977-80; Blacks Unlimited Bd Dir 1977-; CentralCity and Summer Sch Bd 1974; youth rep Salt Lake Cnty ETD Instit Task Force 1978; asst chairpers Support Serv Task Force for ETD 1978; asst chair Salt Lake Cnty Manpower Planning Cncl 1978; mem Exec Dir Assn of OIC's of Amer 1978; mem Reg Plann comm for OIC's of Amer 1978; mem PIC; bd mem Black Adv Cncl; Governor's Vocational Educ Adv Cncl; Natl Alliance of Businessmen 1980; NAACP 1980-; Black Adv Cncl State Bd of Edn; C of C 1979-; NAACP Scholarship Found 1981; mem Minority Coalition 1981; reg adv bd SBA 1983; Vocational Adv Bd Salt Lake Sch Dist 1985; 1st vice pres Salt Lake NAACP 1985; chmn Black Educ ScholarshipFound 1982. **Home Addr:** 2528 Imperial St, Salt Lake City, UT 84109.

BUSH, LEWIS FITZGERALD
Professional football player. **Personal:** Born Dec 2, 1969, Atlanta, GA. **Educ:** Washington State. **Career:** San Diego Chargers, linebacker, 1993-. **Business Addr:** Professional Football Player, San Diego Chargers, Qualcomm Stadium, 9449 Friars Rd, San Diego, CA 92108, (619)280-2111.

BUSH, MARY K.
Banker. **Personal:** Born Apr 9, 1948, Birmingham, AL. **Educ:** Columbia Univ, summer internship 1967; Yale Univ, summer internship 1968; Fisk Univ, BA econ 1969; Univ of Chicago, MBA fin 1971. **Career:** Chase Manhattan Bank NA, credit analyst 1971-73; Citibank NA, account officer 1973-76; Bankers Trust Co, vp, world corp dept 1976-82; US Treasury Dept, exec asst to dep secy 1982-85; Intl Monetary Fund, us alternate ed 1984-. **Orgs:** Vchair, treas Women's World Banking NY 1983-, Exec Women in Gov 1984-, Univ of Chicago Bus School 1979-; bd of trustees YMCA Washington DC 1985-. **Honors/Awds:** Scott Paper Co Leadership Awd; Who's Who in Finance and Industry; Outstanding Young Women of Amer; Who's Who in Amer Coll & Univ. **Home Addr:** 4201 Cathedral Ave NW, Washington, DC 20016. **Business Addr:** US Alternate Exec Dir, Intl Monetary Fund, 700 19th St NW Rm 13-320, Washington, DC 20431.

BUSH, NATHANIEL
Attorney. **Personal:** Born Jan 19, 1949, Washington, DC; son of Elouise Graves Bush and Thelmen Bush; married Marsha Diane Jackson; children: Traci, Nathan, Matthew. **Educ:** Ripon Coll, BA 1973; Cleveland Marshall Coll of Law, JD 1977; Wharton Sch of Business, certificate 1984. **Career:** Distinguished visiting Prof of Law Cambridge Univ, grad asst 1976-77; Bureau of ATF Dept of Treas, attorney 1979-81; Univ of the District of Columbia, adjunct prof criminology 1982-84; DC State Campaign Jesse Jackson for Pres, general counsel 1983-84; DC Bd of Educ, vice pres; Ward VII rep. **Orgs:** Bd of dir Southeast Neighbors Citizens Assoc; bd of dirs Far East Comm Serv Inc; chmn bd of dirs Concerned Citizens on Alcohol & Drug Abuse; mem Bar of the State of OH 1977; mem Bar of the District of Columbia 1979. **Honors/Awds:** Moot Court Bd of Govs Cleveland Marshall Coll of Law; 1st place Third Annual Douglas Moot Court Competition 1975; Jessup Intl Moot Court Competition 1976; Outstanding Young Men of America, 1984. **Home Addr:** 1119 44th Place SE, Washington, DC 20019.

BUSH, PATRICIA
Company executive. **Personal:** Born in Cambridge, MA. **Educ:** Mt Holyoke Coll. **Career:** Polaroid Corp, Channel Operations and Development, dir, currently. **Orgs:** Polaroid, Senior Black Managers, co-chairperson; Natl Coalition of 100 Black Women, Boston Chapter, founder; Urban League of Eastern MA, bd of dirs. **Business Addr:** Director, Channel Operations & Devt, Polarid Corp, 549 Technology Sq, Cambridge, MA 02139, (617)577-2000.

BUSH, T. W.
Law enforcement official. **Personal:** son Of Wanda L Bush and Thomas J Bush. **Educ:** Morehouse Coll Atlanta GA, 1963-64; Univ of GA, Mgmt Devel 1982-; US Dept of Justice, Human Relations 1982; Southern Police Inst GA Police Acad, Admin Officers Training, 1984. **Career:** Dekalb Cty Dept Public Safety, patrolman 1974-79, master patrolman 1979-80, sgt 1980-82, lt 1982-90, capt 1990-. **Honors/Awds:** Numerous Commendations Intradepartmental; Police Officer of the Month DEK Civic Org 1980. **Business Addr:** Captain, Dekalb Cty Public Safety, 4400 Memorial Dr Complex, Decatur, GA 30032.

BUSKEY, JAMES E.
State official. **Personal:** marrIed Virginia. **Educ:** Alabama State Univ, BS; Univ of North Carolina, Chapel Hill, MAT; Univ of Colorado, Boulder, EdS. **Career:** Commonwealth Natl Bank, dir, Franklin Mem Clinic, dir, currently; CETA, coun and job developer; State of Alabama, representative, 99th dist, currently; E S Chastang Middle School, ret administrator. **Orgs:** NEA and Alabama Educ Assn; Alabama New South Coalition; Nonpartisan Voters League; Al State Democratic Exec Comm. **Honors/Awds:** Omega Psi Phi Fraternity, Outstanding legislator, 1987, Citizen of the Year, 1979. **Business Addr:** State Representative, District 99, 104 S Lawerence St, Mobile, AL 36602, (334)432-0482.

BUSKEY, JOHN
State legislator. **Career:** Alabama House of Representatives, Montgomery AL, state representative, district 77, currently. **Business Addr:** House of Representatives, State Capitol, Montgomery, AL 36130.

BUSSEY, CHARLES DAVID
Professional service co. manager. **Personal:** Born Dec 8, 1933, Edgefield, SC; son of Mattie Lou Phillips (deceased) and Alex William Bussey, Sr (deceased); married Eva Lois Gray, Jul 1, 1967 (divorced 1994); children: Terri Lyn, Tonia Marie, Charles F; married Commie Lena Brown, Jun 11, 1994; children: David James. **Educ:** A&T Coll of North Carolina, Greensboro, BS, English 1955; Indiana Univ, MA, Journalism 1970; Shippensburg State, MS, Communications 1974. **Career:** Chief Legislative Liaison HQ, Exec to the Chief, 1975-76; 2nd Infantry Div, Korea, Commander, 2nd Brigade, 1976-77; OFC Chief of Public Affairs HQ, Chief of Policy & Plans, 1977-80; 172D Inf Bde, Deputy Commander, Chief of Staff, 1980-82; HQ Dept of the Army, Dep Chief of Public Affairs, 1982-84, Chief of Public Affairs, 1984-87; HQ AMC, Dep Chief of Staff for Personnel, 1987-89; Manning, Selvage & Lee Public Relations, Senior Counsel, 1990-91; Univ of Maryland, adjunct professor, 1989-; Resource Consultants, Inc, project director, 1991-. **Orgs:** Alpha Phi Alpha, 1953-; Assn of US Army, 1955-; NC A&T State Univ Alumni Assn, 1960-; Indiana Univ Alumni Assn, 1970-; Rocks Inc, 1975-; PRSA, 1986-; American Legion, 1990-; Council for Excellence in Government, 1990-95; chairman, Leadership Task Force, PRSA 1991; president-elect, National Capital Chapter, PRSA 1991. **Honors/Awds:** ROTC Hall of Fame, NC, A&TSU, 1969; Outstanding Alumnus, NC, A&TSU, 1970; Distinguished Alumnus, Indiana Univ, 1983; Articles on Leadership, Management, Discipline & Training published in Army, Armor, Infantry, Military Review, & Buffalo Magazines; Order of the Palmetto, State of South Carolina, 1987; Accredited in Public Relations, PRSA, 1989; chairman, Board of Trustees, North Carolina A & T State Univ, 1989-94; Honorary Doctor of Humanities; NCA and TSU, 1993. **Military Serv:** AUS, Major General, 1955-89; Distinguished Service Medal, With Oak Leaf Cluster, Legion of Merit; Bronze Star, With 2 Oak Leaf Clusters; Meritorious Service Medal, With Oak Leaf Cluster; Air Medal; Army Commendation Medal, With Oak Leaf Cluster; Combat Infantry Badge; Expert Infantry Badge; Parachutist Badge; ROK Order of Natl Security Merit. **Home Addr:** 6368 Brampton Ct, Alexandria, VA 22304-3509.

BUSSEY, REUBEN T.
Attorney. **Personal:** Born Mar 7, 1943, Atlanta, GA. **Educ:** Morris Brown Coll, BA 1965; TX So Univ Law Sch, JD 1969. **Career:** Kennedy, Bussey & Sampson, ptnr 1971-76; Fed Trade Commn, Boston, atty 1969-71; Legal Aid Soc, Inc, Atlanta, staff mem 1969; St Bar of TX, admtd 1969; GA Bar, 1971. **Orgs:** Mem Hsg Task Force; Atlanta C of C; Gate City Bar Assn, & Atlanta; Nat Bar Assn. **Business Addr:** 171 Ashby St SW, Atlanta, GA 30314.

BUSTAMANTE, J. W. ANDRE
Publisher. **Personal:** Born Jun 18, 1961, Cleveland, OH; son of Frances Joy Simmons Bustamante and John Henry Bustamante; children: Auschayla Quinae Brown. **Educ:** Boston University, Boston, BS, 1983. **Career:** Wang Laboratories Inc, Lowell, MA, auditor, 1982; Trustees of Health and Hospitals of the City of Boston, Inc, accountant, budget controller, 1983; Commonwealth of Massachusetts Dept of Revenue, Boston, MA, tax examiner, 1983-84; Harvard Street Health Center, Boston, MA, business manager, 1985; Commonwealth of Massachusetts Dept of Revenue, Boston, MA, tax examiner, 1985-87; First Bank National Association, Cleveland, OH, executive assistant to chairman, 1987-88; Call and Post Newspapers, Cleveland, OH, president/general manager, 1988-95; Bottom Line Productions Inc, vice pres, 1987-; PW Publishing Co Inc, president & general manager, 1988-89; Augrid Corp, vice pres, 1995-. **Orgs:** Urban League, Cleveland Chapter; National Association of Black Accountants, Cleveland Chapter; American Entrepreneurs Association; board of directors, Job Corps Community Relations Committee; Cleveland Schools Summit Council; University Circle Inc, Board of Directors and Nominating Committee; Ohio Citizes Advisory Council; National Minority Golf Association, Board of Directors; Co-Chairman Ohio Bush-Quayle 92; Repubican National Committee; National Rifle Association; NAACP, Cleveland Chapter. **Honors/Awds:** Certificate of Appreciation, CARE, 1987; Certificate of Appreciation, Republican National Committee, 1988, 1989; Certificate of Appreciation, United Negro College Fund, 1990; Certificate of Recognition, Republican Senatorial Inner Circle, 1990; Presidential Commission, 1992; Presidential Advisory Committee Commission, 1992; Senatorial Commission, 1991; Presidential Task Force Honor Roll, 1991; Order of Merit, 1991. **Home Addr:** PO Box 1892, Cleveland, OH 44106. **Business Phone:** (216)521-7017.

BUSTAMANTE, Z. SONALI. See WILSON, SONALI BUSTAMANTE.

BUSTA RHYMES (TREVOR SMITH, JR.)
Rapper. **Personal:** chilDren: Tahiem II (deceased), T'Ziah. **Career:** Rapper, currently. **Special Achievements:** Part of rap group, The Leaders of The New School; Albums include: Future Without A Past, 1991; T.I.M.E The Inner Mind's Eye: The Endless Dispute With Reality, 1993; solo albums include: The Coming, 1996; When Disaster Strikes, 1997; rapped on "Scenario" with Tribe Called Quest, 1991; "Chim Chim Badass Revenge," with Fishbone, 1996; "Hit 'Em High," with Method Man, Coolio, LL Cool J, and B-Real, 1996; "Rumble In The Jumble," with Tribe Called Quest and the Refugee All-Stars, 1997; appeared on Cosby, 1997; appeared in Higher Learning, 1994. **Business Addr:** Rapper, c/o Elektra Entertainemnt, 75 Rockefeller Plaza, New York, NY 10019-6907, (212)275-4000.

BUTCHER, GOLER TEAL
Attorney. **Personal:** Born Jul 13, 1925, Phila; married George T; children: Lily, Georgette, George, Caryl. **Educ:** Univ PA, AB 1946; Howard U, LLB 1957; Univ PA, LLM 1958. **Career:** Judge Hastie 3rd Circuit, law clerk 1958-59; Legal Aid, atty 1960-62; Library of Congress, legal analyst 1962-63; Dept of St, atty 1963-71; Ho Subcom on Africa, cons, Counsel 1971-74; Private Law Practice, 1974-. **Orgs:** Mem Dem Fgn-Affairs Task Force; co-chmn Dem Study Group on Africa; mem bd trustees Lawyers Com on Civil Rights Under Law; mem Com on Soc Respnsblty;exec council Episcopal Ch; mem exec council Am Soc of Interntl Law; mem Disciplinary Bd; DC Bar; mem Nat Conf Black Lawyers; Nat Assn Black Women Attys; Interntl Adv Cncl; African-Am Inst; African Legal Asst Proj Subcom, Lawyers' Com. **Honors/Awds:** Phi Beta Kappa 1945. **Business Addr:** 1156 15 St NW, Ste 302, Washington, DC 20005.

BUTCHER, PHILIP
Educator, author. **Personal:** Born Sep 28, 1918, Washington, DC; son of Jennie Jones Butcher and James W Butcher; married Ruth B; children: 2. **Educ:** Howard Univ, AB, MA; Columbia Univ, PhD. **Career:** Opportunity, Journal of Negro Life 1947-48; Morgan State Coll, English tchr 1947-49, asst prof 1949-56, assoc prof 1956-59; SC State Coll, visiting prof 1958; Morgan State Univ, prof 1959-79, dean grad sch 1972-75, prof emeritus 1979-. **Orgs:** Mem Coll Language Assn; Modern Language Assn; Soc Study So Literature; lectr many coll & univ. **Honors/Awds:** Gen Educ Bd & John Hay Whitney Fellowship; Creative Scholarship Award Coll Language Assn 1964; many research grants; many citations, reference works; many books & articles pub. **Military Serv:** AUS T/Sgt 1943-46.

BUTLER, ANNETTE GARNER
Attorney. **Personal:** Born Jun 23, 1944, Cleveland, OH; daughter of Minnie Garner and Rudolph Garner; divorced; children: Christopher, Kimberley. **Educ:** Case Western Reserve Univ, BA 1966; Cleveland State/Cleveland Marshall Law, JD 1970. **Career:** Civil rights specialist, D/HEW Office of Civil Rights, 1970-74; assoc atty, Guren, Merritt, Sogg & Cohen, 1974-81; dir legal affairs, Office of School Monitoring, 1981-82; asst US Atty, Atty Office ND OH, 1982-. **Orgs:** Trustee, vice pres grievance comm Cleveland Bar Assn; founder, past pres Black Women Lawyers Assn; bar admissions OH 6th Circuit Court of Appeals; Supreme Court of US; trustee, treas, vice-chmn, Cleveland State Univ; past pres Cleveland City Club; past pres Cleveland Heights Univ Library Bd; bd of trustees Shaker Heights Recreation Bd; pres, bd of trustees, Shaker Heights Library Board; vice president, trustee, Citizens League Research Institute. **Honors/Awds:** Distinguished Serv Cleveland Jaycees; Outstanding Achievment Narrator Cleveland Chapter Natl Acad Arts & Sciences; Woman of Year Negro Business & Professional Club; Outstanding Achievement Cuyahoga County Bar Assn; Distinguished Alumnus Award, Cleveland State Univ; member, Golden Key Natl Honor Soc. **Home Addr:** 13901 Larchmere Blvd, Shaker Heights, OH 44120. **Business Addr:** Attorney, US Dept Justice Atty Ofc, 1800 Bank One Center, Cleveland, OH 44114-2600.

BUTLER, BENJAMIN WILLARD. See Obituaries section.

BUTLER, CHARLES H.
Physician. **Personal:** Born Feb 12, 1925, Wilmington, DE; children: Yvonne, Kathy, Charla, Leslie. **Educ:** IN Univ; Univ PA; Meharry Med Coll, MD 1953. **Career:** Private Practice, physician. **Orgs:** Mem Nat Med Assn; Am Acad Faminly Physicians; PA E PA Med Soc; staff Coatesville Hosp; former health officer & Borough S Coatesville; med adv Loacl Draft Bd Pres PA State Conf NAACP; pres Coatesville Br NAACP; vice pres Unite Political Actin Com; Chester County; past pres Chester County Rep Club former exec com 32 deg Mason; mem Charles E Gordon Consistory #65; IBPOE Wilmington; treas past pres Pan-hellenic Assembly Chester County; past v polemarch Wilmington Alumni Chap Kappa Alpha Psi; mem Natl Bd NAACP. **Honors/Awds:** Life mem Humanitarian Award SE; Chester Cou Bus and Prof Women's Culb Inc 1973; Mason & of Yr 1967; Citation Optimist Club of Coatesville 1972; Community Achievement Award Lily of the Valley Lodge #59 1973. **Military Serv:** USN discharged as lt sr grade.

BUTLER, CHARLES W.
Clergyman. **Personal:** Born May 4, 1922, Dermott, AR; married Helen Odean Scoggins; children: Charles Jr, Beverly, Keith, Kevin. **Educ:** Philander Smith Coll, BA 1939; Union Theol Sem, BD 1949, MDiv 1971; Columbia Univ, residence for PhD 1951; Interdenom Theol Ctr Morehouse School of Religion, DD 1980; Birmingham Bapt Bible School, 1980. **Career:** St James Presb Church NYC, asst to the pastor 1947-50; New York City Mission Soc, released time teacher 1950-51; Bapt Ctr NYC, teacher 1950-51; Morehouse Coll Atlanta, teacher Bible lit & religion 1951-54; Met Bapt Church Detroit, pastor 1954-63; New Calvary Bapt Church, pastor 1963-. **Orgs:** Pres MI Progressive Bapt Conv Detroit 1962-64; bd dir Interdenom Theol Ctr Detroit 1978-; mem Morehouse School Religion Atlanta; dir org 1st Ind Natl Bank Detroit 1970; chmn bd Police Comm City Detroit 1976; mem adv bd MI Consol Gas Co Detroit 1980-86; pres Progressive Natl Bapt Conv Washington 1982-84; pres Bapt Pastors Council Detroit 1987-; mem Alpha Phi Alpha; chmn bd, Congress of National Black Churches, 1988. **Honors/Awds:** Man of the Year MI Chronicle 1962. **Military Serv:** AUS 1943-46. **Business Addr:** Pastor, New Calvary Baptist Church, 3975 Concord St, Detroit, MI 48207.

BUTLER, CLARY KENT
Minister, broadcaster. **Personal:** Born Jul 5, 1948, Charleston, SC; son of Mary Capers Butler and Carl Dallas Butler; married Patsy Swint Butler, Sep 20, 1970; children: Tammy R, Clary K Jr, Cora L. **Educ:** South Carolina State Coll, Orangeburg SC, BA, l970; Webster Univ, Charleston (AFB) Branch, l986-87. **Career:** Berkeley Broadcasting Corp. WMCJ Radio, Monicks Corner SC, 1984. **Orgs:** Mem, Omega Psi Phi, l968—; mem/pastor, House of God Church, l980-89; bd mem, Charleston County Branch (Amer Cancer Soc) l985; mem, Berkeley County Chamber of Commerce, l989; dir at large, SC Broadcasters Assn, l989. **Business Addr:** Pres, Berkeley Broadcasting Corp, WMCJ-AM, 314 Rembert Dennis Blvd, P O Box 67, Moncks Corner, SC 29461, (803)761-9625.

BUTLER, DARRAUGH CLAY
Minority business development manager. **Personal:** Born Dec 26, 1955, Paducah, KY; daughter of Mary Elizabeth Glore and Theodore Malcolm Glore Jr; divorced; children: Charles, John, Brandon. **Educ:** Franklin University; Ohio State University. **Career:** The Ohio State University, personnel director, University Health Svc, 1983-90; The Ohio State University, mgr, Minority Business Dev, 1990-. **Orgs:** Columbus Regional Minority Purchasing Council, treasurer, 1992-; OSU Advisory Board, chairman, 1992-; CRMSDC, board of directors, executive committee, 1991-; Minority Business Opportunity Center , 1990-; Ohio Trade Fair Steering Committee, 1991, 1992; Sojourner Truth Frederick Douglass Society, 1992-. **Honors/Awds:** Ohio Assembly of Councils, Corporate Hall of Fame, 1992; Project Unity, Woman of the Year, 1992; OSU Council of Black Students in Administration, Professional Award, 1992. **Special Achievements:** The Ohio State University, MBE Directory, 1991. **Business Addr:** Manager, Minority Business Development, Ohio State University, 1800 Cannon Dr, Rm 850, Lincoln Tower, Columbus, OH 43210, (614)292-2551.

BUTLER, DOUTHARD ROOSEVELT
Educator. **Personal:** Born Oct 7, 1934, Waxahachie, TX; son of Corine McKinney Butler and Lonnie Butler; married Jo Jewell Ray Butler, Dec 11, 1954; children: Douthard Jr, Carolyn, Barbara, Katherine. **Educ:** Prairie View A&M University, Prairie View, TX, BS, 1955; Central Michigan University, Mt Pleasant, MI, MA, 1976; George Mason University, Fairfax, Virginia, DPA, 1992. **Career:** George Mason University, Fairfax, VA, graduate teacher's asst, 1986-88, academic coordinator, 1990-95, assoc athletic dir for academic resources, 1995-; Fairfax County Public School System, VA, math teacher, 1989-90. **Orgs:** President, Mount Vernon, VA Rotary Club, 1987-88; president, Prairie View A&M University National Alumni Assn, 1981-83; president, Northern VA Chapter, National Pan Hellenic Council, 1989-91; president, Washington, DC metro chapter, Prairie View A&M University Alumni Assn, 1978-81; governor, Rotary District 7610, 1993-94. **Honors/Awds:** Meritorious Service Award, Military, NAACP, 1982; Scholar in Residence, Penn State University, 1989. **Military Serv:** US Army, Colonel, 1955-85; Legion of Merit, 1981, 1985; Bronze Star, 1966; Meritorious Service Medal, 1969, 1975; Army Commendation Medal, 1964; Air Medal 1965-66; Master Aviator Badge, 1971. **Business Addr:** Assoc Athletic Director for Academic Resources, Intercollegiate Athletic Dept, George Mason University, Fairfax, VA 22030.

BUTLER, ERNEST DANIEL
Cleric. **Personal:** Born Oct 11, 1913, Connersville, IN; married Mary L Jones; children: Ernest E, Robert J, William D, Grayce L, Albert R, Florence M, Marye Anne, James L. **Educ:** Simmons Univ, BS 1937; Franklin Coll; Simmons Univ; Moody Bible Sch; Central Theological Seminary Indianapolis, IN, DD 1981. **Career:** Mt Zion Bapt Ch, pastor 1934-49; 1st Baptist Ch, pastor 1949-59; 2nd Baptist Church, pastor. **Orgs:** Mem Natl Bapt Conv of Amer 1945-75; dir youth activ IN Shepherd Boy's League 1962-72; vice-moderator/moderator SE Dist IN Missionary Bapt 1964-73; moderator So Eastern Dist 1982-85; chmn IN Missionary Bapt State Educ Bd 1971-75; guest lectr Dept Guidance & Soc Serv IN Univ; Charter mem MU Sigma Chi 1934-73; dir Noblesville Boy's Club 1949-59; NAACP 1958-73; adv bd YMCA 1962-69; v chmn IN Citizens Fair Housing Com 1962-66 (chmn 1966-71); chrmn Mayor's Commn on Human Relations 1964-67; mem bd dir Comm Action Prog 1965-71; bd mem/chmn Family Serv Agency 1965-72; mem IN State Libr Adv Cncl Bloomington Traffic Commn 1973-75; chmn, Martin Luther King Jr Essay Contest, State of Indiana; Indiana Interreligious Comm on Human Equality, IICHE, vp. **Honors/Awds:** Recip Minister of Year Award Hamilton Co IN 1956; Man of the Year Monroe Co Serv Council 1962; Disting Serv Award Omega Psi Phi 1971; Disting Serv Award Joint Action for Comm Serv 1972; Chmn Monroe Cnty Comm Serv Cncl 1983-85; 14 years Disting Serv to Church 1973; Humanitarian Awd Indiana Governor's Volunteer Program 1987; Author poems Sat Evening Post; weekly & monthly sermons & lectures published in city & state publs; Honorary Mayor of Bloomington, In, 1993; International Exchange Club Book of Golden Deeds Award, 1994; National Missionary Baptist Convention Education Board Chairman, 1994; NAACP 15 Year Service Award; Bloomington Housing Authority 20 Year Service Award; SCLC Meritous Award. **Special Achievements:** A full degree scholarship has been established in the name of Rev Dr E D Butler, for Indiana University students. **Business Addr:** Pastor, Second Baptist Church, 321 N Rogers St, Bloomington, IN 47401.

BUTLER, EUGENE THADDEUS, JR.
Educator. **Personal:** Born Dec 3, 1922, Washington, DC; married Dorothy Mary Dickson; children: Eugene T. **Educ:** Modesto Jr Coll, AA 1960; Stanislaus State Coll CA, BA 1965; SD State U, MEd 1969; SD State U, PhD 1980. **Career:** SD State Univ Brookings, EEO compliance officer/Title IX 1975-, Handicapped, coordinator; SD State Univ Brookings, grad research/ Teaching asst 1970-73. **Orgs:** Vp & past sec Pi Gamma Mu Local Nat Social Sci Honor Soc 1973; Alpha Kappa Delta Nat Sociology Honor Soc Gamma Sigma Delta #Pres; Nat Agricultural Honor Soc Phi Kappa Phi. **Honors/Awds:** Co-author of various publ; recipient USAF Commendation Medal; recipient Air Medal with Oak Leaf Cluster/Ggod Conduct Medal/10 Year Combat Crew Duty Cert USAF1943-70. **Military Serv:** USAF lt col 1943-70. **Business Addr:** University Station, Brookings, SD 57007.

BUTLER, EULA M.
Educator. **Personal:** Born Oct 15, 1927, Houston; married Henry C (deceased). **Educ:** TX So Univ, BS 1954, MED 1958; Univ of TX, Grad Study; Prairie View Univ, Educ & Psy, Counseling & Guidance; TX So Univ, Spec Educ, Vstg Teaching, Counselor; Mount Hope Bihle Coll, DM 1984. **Career:** Region IV Educ Serv Center, TX Educ Agency; classroom teacher; visiting teacher, counselor, first teacher certified with Head Start Prog; writing demonstrator; workshop presenter; TX Southern Univ, public relations, community 1985-87; After School Tutorial Prog Inc, founder, dir, educ cons, mgr. **Orgs:** First State Coord Rehab & Prog for Fed Female Offenders; mem Delta Sigma Theta Sor; comm-counselor Parents & Students; mem YWCA Nat Cncl Negro Women Top Ladies of Distin; mem Am Judicature Soc; bd dirs ARC mem Harris Co Grand Jury 1974-; Harris Co bd dirs; Girl Scout bd dirs; mem Task Force Quality Integrate Educ Houston Independent Sch Dist; dir SW Region Delta Sigma Theta; past pres Houston Chap Delta Sigma Theta; Am PGA NEA TSTA Guid & Gounseling Assn; bd mem Natl Delta Rsch & Educ Found Inc, 1985-88, Vstg Nurses Assoc, The Light House of Houston, Natl Housing & Properties, DeltaSigma Theta, Houston Network For Family Life Education; mem of bd Houston Enrichment of Life Prog Inc; bd mem Metro Teacher Educ Ctr, Volunteers In Public School, Houston Independent SchoolDist. **Honors/Awds:** Teacher of the Year Awd 1969; Comm Leadership Awd; Delta Sigma Theta Cert of Appreciation; United Negro Coll Fund Leadership Awd; Golden Life Mem Delta Sigma Theta Sor; Black History in the Making Awd 1986; Christian Serv Awd Beth Baptist Church 1985; Community Serv Awd Mt Corinth Baptist Church 1985; School After School Awd presented by School After School Faculty & Staff 1985; Recognition of Excellence Achievement Awd Phillis Wheatley High School 1985. **Business Addr:** Dir & Founder, Schl After Schl Basic Skills, Tutorial Program Inc, PO Box 15757, Houston, TX 77020.

BUTLER, FREDERICK DOUGLAS
Attorney. **Personal:** Born Nov 5, 1942, Philadelphia, PA; married Sara Vitori; children: Frederick Douglas II. **Educ:** Rutgers Univ, BA 1974; New York Univ, MA 1977; Univ of CA Hastings Coll of Law, JD 1986. **Career:** Newark Housing Authority, dir of family & comm serv 1973-80; White Plains Housing Auth, exec dir 1980-81; Govt of Trinidad & Tobago Natl Housing Auth,consultant 1984-85; Carroll Burdick & McDonough, attorney. **Orgs:** Mem World Affairs Counsel, Amer Soc of Public Administration, Inst of Real Estate Mgmt, Natl Assoc of Housing Officials, Afro-Amer Historical Soc; former pres United Comm Corp Newark NJ, Newark Citizen's Adv Bd, Soul-House Drug Abuse Prog, NJ Coll of Medicine & Dentistry. **Honors/Awds:** Community Service Awds Newark TEnants Council, Service Employees Intl Union, Newark Central Ward Little League, Frontiers Intl; Amer Jurisprudence Awd. **Military Serv:** USAF A2C 4 yrs; Good Conduct Medal. **Business Addr:** Attorney, California Department of Insurance, 45 Fremont St, San Francisco, CA 94105.

BUTLER, HOMER L. See Obituaries section.

BUTLER, J. RAY
Clergyman. **Personal:** Born Aug 5, 1923, Roseboro, NC; son of Mary Francis Cooper Butler and Amos Delonzo Butler; married Marion Lucas Butler, Dec 1943; children: Charles Ervin, Ellis Ray, Larry Davis, Vincent Recardo. **Educ:** Shaw U, BA, BD, MDiv, 1974, DD, 1973; Friendship Coll, DD, 1966; Southeastern Theol Sem 1966-67; McKinley Theol Sem LLD 1976; Southeastern Theol Seminary DTh 1969. **Career:** Ebenezer Bapt Ch Wilmington, pastor 1954-70; First Bapt Ch Creedd-moor, pastor; Mt Olive Bapt Ch Fayeteville, pastor; New Christian Chapel Bapt Ch RoseHill, pastor; Shiloh Bapt Church Winston-Salem, pastor 1970-90; United Cornerstone Baptist Church, Winston-Salem, NC, founder, pastor, 1990-. **Orgs:** Past pres Interdenom Ministerial All; past pres Interracial Minist Assn; past pres Wilmington Civic League; past pres PTA; 1st vice pres NAACP; bd of dirARC; mem Man Power Delvel; mem Citizens Coalition Bd; pres-at-large Gen Bapt State Conv; pres Bapt Ministers Conf & Asso; mem Forsyth Clergy Assn Chmn of Gen Bapt St Conv of NC Inc; mem extension tchg staff of Shaw U; exec bd of Lott Carey Bapt Foreign Missions & Conv; appointed bd of licensed gen contractors Gov Jim Hunt of NC; founder, Shilohian/St Peters Day Care; moderator, Rowan Baptist Missionary Association, 1989-. **Honors/Awds:** Various tours in foreign countries; Pastor of Yr Award Midwestern Bapt Laymen's Fellowship Chicago 1975, 1976; elected Contbng Writer Nat Bapt Sunday Sch Publ Bd; author, The Christian Communion as Related to the Jewish Passover and Monetary Commitment, 1985; From Playtime to Pulpit Svc. **Home Addr:** 2743 Patria St, Winston-Salem, NC 27127.

BUTLER, JEROME M.
Attorney. **Personal:** Born Jul 15, 1944, Chicago, IL; married Jean Brothers. **Educ:** Fisk U, BA 1966; Columbia U, JD 1969. **Career:** Tucker Watson Butler & Todd, Atty. **Orgs:** Mem Cook County Chicago Bar Assns. **Business Addr:** 120 S Riverside Plaza, Chicago, IL 60606.

BUTLER, JERRY
Entertainer, county commissioner. **Personal:** Born Dec 8, 1939, Sunflower Co, MS; son of Arvelia Agnew Butler and Jerry Butler Sr (deceased); married Annette Smith Butler, Jun 21, 1959; children: Randall Allen, Anthony Ali. **Career:** Jerry Butler Productions, Chicago, IL, owner, 1960-; Iceman Beverage Co, Chi-

cago, IL, CEO, 1984-89; Cook County, IL, commissioner, 1985-. **Orgs:** Life member, Chicago Chapter, NAACP; member, North Star Lodge No 1 FAM PHA 33 degree; member, Groove Phi Groove Fellowship; president, board of directors, Firman Comm Services; vice president, Northern Illinois Planning Commission, 1990-; mem, Alpha Phi Alpha; chair, Rhythm & Blues Foundation; grand lecturer, MWPHGL, State of Illinois & Jurisdiction, 1997; pres, Northeastern Illinois Planning Commission, 1997. **Honors/Awds:** Musical Composition Citation of Achievement Broadcast Music, 1960, 1970; 1972 He Will Break Your Heart, Only the Strong Survive, Brand New Me Res; Ceba Award Advertising, 1983; Clio Award Adv, 1972; Mason of the Year Award, Prince Hall Grand Lodge Illinois, 1989; Valuable Resource Award, Chicago Public Schools; 3 Grammy Nominations, Album, Male Vocalist, Song of the Year, 1969; Elected to Rock Hall of Fame, 1991. **Business Addr:** Commissioner, Cook County Board of Commissioners, 118 N Clark St, Suite 567, Chicago, IL 60602.

BUTLER, JOHN DONALD
Physician (retired). **Personal:** Born Feb 2, 1910, Sewickley, PA; son of Harriet G and James E; married Charlita Elizabeth Whitby; children: Beverly Lavergneau, John G, Richard S, Diane, David, Michelle. **Educ:** Lincoln U, PA, AB 1931; Meharry Med Coll, MD 1937; Univ of Pittsburgh Sch Med, Res & Teaching Fellow Dermatology 1947-50. **Career:** Gen Prac Med, Montgomery, WV, 1939-41; Gen Prac Med, Pittsbrgh, PA, 1941-47, Detroit 1951; Wayne State Univ Med Sch, asst clin prof. **Orgs:** Adjunct clinical prof dermatology, Wayne St Univ Med Sch; life mem Am Acad Dermatology; AMA, Natl Med Assn, MI Dermatology Soc; heritage mem NAACP; Alpha Phi Alpha Frat. **Home Addr:** 301 Orange Lake Dr, Bloomfield Hills, MI 48302.

BUTLER, JOHN GORDON
Management consultant. **Personal:** Born Apr 23, 1942, Pittsburgh, PA; son of Marjorie Johnson Butler and John Donald Butler; children: John Mason. **Educ:** Harvard Coll, Cambridge MA, BA Economics, 1963; Harvard Graduate School of Business Admin, Boston MA, MBA, 1966; Graduate Management Inst, Union Coll, Schenectady NY, 1985-87. **Career:** Carver Federal Savings, New York City, admin asst, 1963-64; Mobil Intl Oil Co, New York City, financial analyst, 1966-68; Kaiser-Aetna Partnership, Oakland CA, dir of investment analysis 1970-71; Kiambere Ltd, Nairobi, Kenya, mng dir, 1971-83; State Univ Coll, New Paltz NY, visiting prof, 1983-85; John Butler Assoc, New Paltz NY, consultant, 1985-. **Orgs:** Mem, Alpha Phi Alpha Fraternity, 1963-; lecturer, Univ of Nairobi, Kenya, 1968-69; consultant, Bomas of Kenya Cultural Village, 1972-73; dir, Kiambere Bldg Soc, 1975-83; assoc, African Development Group, 1979-82; mem, Village of New Paltz Planning Bd, 1984-88; fellow, New York African Amer Inst, 1986-88; mem, New Paltz Democratic Comm, 1987-88; treasurer, Harvard Business School African-American Alumni Assn, 1987-97; director, Harvard Business School African American Alumni Association, 1997-.

BUTLER, JOHN O.
Business executive. **Personal:** Born Nov 28, 1926, Bristol, TN; son of Olivia J Butler and Pinkney E Butler; married Marjorie M Jackson; children: Deborah, David, Brian, Bruce. **Educ:** Howard Univ, BS Mech Engrg (magna cum laude) 1950. **Career:** GE Co, design engr 1950-57; Raytheon Co, mgr indus engrg 1958-64; GTE Sylvania Inc, dir value engrg 1965-68; Deerfield Corp, founder/president, currently. **Orgs:** Registered professional engr MA; mem MA Businessmen's Assn; Natl Soc of Professional Engrs; commr MA Gov's Exec Council for Value Analysis 1966-72; commr Framingham Housing Auth; dir Framingham Regional YMCA 1971-75; cooperator Framingham Union Hosp 1968-; mem Rotary Intl; mem Twn Repub Com 1972-; mem Tau Beta Pi Engrg Hon Soc 1952. **Military Serv:** AUS tech fifth grade 1944-46. **Home Addr:** 6 Doyle Circle, Framingham, MA 01701.

BUTLER, JOHN SIBLEY
Educator. **Personal:** Born Jul 19, 1947, New Orleans, LA; son of Johnnie Mae Sibley Butler and Thojest Jefferson Butler; married Rosemary Griffey Butler, Oct 20, 1972; children: John Sibley Butler. **Educ:** Louisiana State University, Baton Rouge, LA, BA, 1969; Northwestern University, Evanston, IL, MA, 1971, PhD, 1974. **Career:** University of Texas, Austin, professor of sociology and management, 1974-; Butler Enterprises, president/CEO. **Orgs:** President, Louisiana State Univ. Alumni Association, Austin, 1988-91; president, American Association of Black Sociologists, 1980-81; member, Sigma Pi Phi (Boule); member, Kappa Alpha Psi; member, Omicron Nu; member, Phi Delta Kappa. **Honors/Awds:** The Dallas TACA Centennial Professorship, Univ. of Texas, 1990; Teaching Excellence Award, A.K.D., Univ. of Texas Chapter, 1978; management consultant, State Farm Insurance, Southwest, 1990; The Arthur James Douglass Centennial Professor, College of Business, the University of Texas, Austin; The Sam Barshop Centennial Fellow, IO, the University of Texas, Austin. **Military Serv:** US Army, Enlisted Five, 1969-71; received: Bronze Star for Combat Valor, Vietnam, 1970. **Business Addr:** Professor, University of Texas at Austin, Department of Sociology, Austin, TX 78712.

BUTLER, JOHNNELLA E.
Educator. **Personal:** Born Feb 28, 1947, Roanoke, VA. **Educ:** College of Our Lady of the Elms, AB, 1968; Johns Hopkins University, MAT, 1969; University of Massachusetts Amherst, EdD, 1979. **Career:** Towson State University, instructor, 1970-84; Smith College, instructor, 1974-79, asst professor, 1979-81, assoc professor with tenure, starting 1981, Dept Afro-American Studies, instructor, 1974-76, asst to dean, 1976-77, dept chair, 1977-79, chairperson of 5 College Black Studies Executive Committee, 1978-79; Womens Studies Dept, Mt Holyoke College, visiting lecturer, 1984; University of Washington Seattle, Dept of Afro-American Studies, professor, currently. **Orgs:** Board of trustees, College of Our Lady of the Elms, 1984-89; consultant, various universities & colleges, 1983-; consultant, Womens Studies Program, University of Illinois Champagne-Urbana, 1984, Racism & Sexism, Patterson College, 1984, Black Women in American Literature, University of Illinois DeKalb, 1984, Black Studies & Womens Studies, Carleton College, 1984, Wellesley Center for Research on Women, 1984, Womens Studies, Faculty Development Project, College of St Mary, 1984; Drew University, Faculty Development Workshop, 1984. **Honors/Awds:** FIPSE Grant, Black Studies/Womens Studies, 1981-83; $1/4 Million Frsty Development Project Coord; author, "Studies & the Liberal Arts Tradition Through the Ddiscipline of Afro-Amer Literature" University Press of America, 1981, "Toward a Pedagogy of Everywoman's Studies", Minority Womens Studies, "Do We Want To Kill a Dream" Intl Women Studies Quarterly, 1984; Ford Foundation Fellowship, Johns Hopkins University, 1968-69, Cazenovia Institute, 1971; Smithsonian Conference Scholarship, Black Scholars & Black Studies, 1983. **Business Addr:** Professor, Dept of Afro-American Studies G N-80, University of Washington, Seattle, WA 98195-0001.

BUTLER, JOYCE M.
Marketing company executive. **Personal:** Born Jun 12, 1941, Gary, IN; daughter of Dorothy Paige Porter and Robert W Porter; married Mitchell Butler, Jun 13, 1965; children: Stephanie Lynn, Adam Mitchell. **Educ:** Wright Coll, Chicago, IL, AA, 1963; DePaul Univ, Chicago, IL, BA, 1976, MS, 1980. **Career:** Loop Coll, Chicago, IL, admin asst, 1963-78; City of Chicago Dept of Planning, Chicago, IL, city planner, 1978-83; City of Chicago, Mayor's Office of Inquiry & Information, Chicago, IL, program mgr, 1983-88, dir of program serv, 1988-89; Michel Marketing, vice pres, 1989-. **Orgs:** Operation PUSH, 1972-; Natl Forum of Black Public Administrators, 1985-; Natl Assn of Female Exec, 1989; Soc of Govt Meeting Planners, 1988-; Publicity Club of Chicago, 1989. **Honors/Awds:** Paul Cornell Award, Hyde Park Historical Soc, 1986; developer, initiator, annual Black History Fair, Murray Language Acad, Chicago, IL, 1985-.

BUTLER, KEITH ANDRE
Clergyman, city official. **Personal:** Born Nov 22, 1955, Detroit, MI; son of Ida L Jackson Butler and Robert L Butler; married Deborah Lorraine Bell Butler, May 31, 1975; children: Keith Andre II, Michelle Andrea, Kristina Maria. **Educ:** Oakland Community College, 1973-74; Eastern Michigan University, Ypsilanti, MI, 1984-85; University of Michigan, Dearborn, MI, Bachelors, 1987. **Career:** Word of Faith, Detroit, MI, CEO, 1979-; City of Detroit, Detroit, MI, city council member, currently. **Orgs:** Detroit Economic Development Plan; advisory board, Henry Ford Hospital Care Program, 1987; corporate board, Holy Cross Hospital; board of trustees, Metropolitan Youth Foundation; Alliance Against Casino Gambling in Detroit; Michigan Cancer Foundation, board of directors, 1992; Teach Michigan, board of directors, 1992. **Honors/Awds:** Five Outstanding Young People of Michigan, 1988; Ten Outstanding Americans, 1989; Honorary Doctorate of Divinity, NW University of London, 1988. **Business Addr:** Pastor, Word of Faith Christian Center, 23800 W Chicago, Redford, MI 48239.

BUTLER, LEROY
Professional football player. **Personal:** Born Jul 19, 1968, Jacksonville, FL; children: Sharon, L'Oreal, Gabrielle. **Educ:** Florida State, attended. **Career:** Green Bay Packers, defensive back, 1990-. **Honors/Awds:** Pro Bowl, 1993, 1996. **Business Addr:** Professional Football Player, Green Bay Packers, 1265 Lombardi Ave, Green Bay, WI 54304, (414)494-2351.

BUTLER, LORETTA M.
Educator (retired). **Personal:** Born in Forest Glen, MD. **Educ:** Miner Tchrs Coll, BS 1937; Catholic Univ of Amer, MA 1946, PhD 1963. **Career:** Roosevelt U Chicago, assoc prof of educ 1971-80, emeritus, 1980; Archdiocese of Washington, DC, Office of Black Catholics, researcher, 1980-; Xavier Univ of LA, prof of educ 1963-71; Educ Res Ctr on Sch Deseg, assoc dir 1970-71; Univ of NE, visiting prof 1968-69; Paine Coll, visiting lectr 1968-71; Cath Univ of Amer, instr 1962; St Philip Elem Sch, tchr 1955-60; Friendship House, supvr 1953-55; Garrison Elem Sch, 1937-53. **Orgs:** Consultant Training prog for staffs of Model Cities Daycare Cntrs 1973; EDPA In-Service Workshop 1971; NCTE Ele Sch Language Conf 1971; EPDA Inst in Eng 1971; Inter-Instl Inst on Deseg 1967; Proj Headstart Madison WI 1966; NDEA Inst on Reading 1965; mem Natl Assn of Tchr Educ; Natl Council of Tchrs of English; Chicago Reading Assn; Assn of Afro-Amer Life & History. **Honors/Awds:** Author of numerous articles, book reviews, essays commenting on educational, racial, social issues, especially in Comm Mag; named Danforth Asso 1974. **Special Achievements:** Contributor, Encyclopedia of African-American Education, Greewood Press, 1996; contributor, Black Women in America, Carlson Pub Co, 1993; contributor, "Rise 'N' Shine Catholic Education in the African-American Community," National Catholic Educational Association, Washington, DC, 1996; contributor, "Black and Catholic - Strangers at a Turning Point in History," Catholic Herald, London England, June 13, 1997. **Home Addr:** 1806 Metzerolt Rd, Adelphi, MD 20783.

BUTLER, MARJORIE JOHNSON
Educator (retired). **Personal:** Born May 18, 1911, Oberlin, OH; daughter of Mary Jane Jones and Frank Johnson; divorced; children: Beverly Lavergneau, John G, Richard. **Educ:** Oberlin Coll, AB 1930; OH State Univ; MA 1934; Univ Pittsburgh, PhD 1965. **Career:** WV State Coll, instructor 1930-31; Prairie View State Coll, 1931-37; Sumner High School, teacher 1937-40; 5th Ave High School 1955-58; Pittsburgh Public Schools, psychologist 1959-62; Univ of Pittsburgh, instructor 1961-65; State Univ of NY, asst prof 1965-67, assoc prof 1967-70, prof 1970-85; Vasser Coll, part-time prof 1971. **Orgs:** Mem Amer Psychology Assn; NY State Psychology Assn; Assn for Study of Afro-Amer Life & Hist; African Heritage Study Assn. **Honors/Awds:** Mem, Alpha Kappa Alpha Sorority; Psi Chi; Pi Lambda Theta; Delta Kappa Gamma Hon Sorority. **Home Addr:** 3 Field Sparrow Court, Hilton Head Island, SC 29926.

BUTLER, MAX R.
Clergyman. **Personal:** Born Jul 10, 1912, St Francisville, LA; married Leona Hickman; children: Angele B (evans). **Educ:** New Orleans U, AB & BD 1935; Inter-Bapt Theological Sem, DD 1972. **Career:** Adult Edn, tchr, supv & parish dir 1937-41; US, letter carrier 1941-70; chemical mgf 1946-74; 10 Meth Ch, pastor 1933-74; Philips & Memi United Meth Ch, pastor. **Orgs:** Asst sec LA Annual Conf of United Meth Ch 1968-71; vice pres Dillard Univ Alumni Assn 1956; mem NAACP; Nat Urban League; 32 degrees Prince Hall Mason of New Orleans LA. **Honors/Awds:** Honorary Atty Gen of LA 1973; New Orleans second most popular cit 1937; Boy Scout leadership award 1973; DD 1972; appntd by Gov Eswards mem adv council to Historical & Cultural Preservation Bd 1973. **Business Addr:** 3236 Burdette Ave, New Orleans, LA.

BUTLER, MELBA
Association executive. **Personal:** Born Apr 18, 1954, New York, NY; daughter of Juanita Jones Butler and Martin Butler; children: Thomas Martin, Sean David Hamilton. **Educ:** Northeastern University, Boston, MA, 1971-73; Long Island University, New York, NY, BA, psychology, 1975; Columbia University, New York, NY, MS, social work, 1979; University of the State of New York, certified social worker. **Career:** St Joseph Children's Services, caseworker, 1975; Queens Family Court, Jamaica, NY, probation intern, 1977-78; Woodside Senior Assistance Center, Woodside, NY, assistant to the director, 1978-79; Madison Square Boys Club, New York, NY, assistant to the director, 1978-79; Senior Counselor State Communities/Aid, project director, 1979-82; New York City Board of Education, New York, NY, school social worker, 1983-84; Brooklyn College Women's Center, Brooklyn, NY, volunteer supervisor, 1983-84; Public Management Systems Inc, New York, NY, consultant/trainer, 1984-86; Harlem Dowling-Westside Center for Children and Family Services, New York, NY, deputy director, 1984-90, executive director, 1990-; Enter, Inc, consultant/supervisor, 1989-90. **Orgs:** Vice chairman, Advisory Committee, Urban Women's Shelter, 1986-88; National Association of Social Workers; National Black Child Development Institute, 1986-; Black Agency Executives, bd of dirs, Council on Family & Child Caring Agencies; bd pres, Harlem Community, Inc. **Business Addr:** Executive Director, Harlem-Dowling Westside Ctr for Children & Family Svcs, 2090 Adam Clayton Powell Jr Blvd, New York, NY 10027.

BUTLER, MICHAEL E.
Editorial services manager. **Personal:** Born Jul 14, 1950, New York City, NY; son of Myrtle Martin & Bernard E Butler Jr; married Eileen Payne, Oct 10, 1982. **Educ:** Pace U, NYC, BBA 1972; Univ of CA, Berkeley, MPH 1974. **Career:** New York City Hlth & Hosps Corp, asso exec dir 1975-80; NYS Comm Hlth Educ & Illness Prvntn, exec dir 1980-81; Comm Fmly Plng Cncl, exec dir 1981-82; NY St Div Yth, rgnl dir NYC; Executive Health Group, vice pres; Lowe McAdams Healthcare, editor, 1991-97; Harrison and Star, editorial services manager, 1997-. **Orgs:** Mem 100 Black Men 1977-85; bd dir Pace Univ, Alumni Assoc 1983-86; mem Pace Univ Bd Educ Plcs Commn 1984-86. **Honors/Awds:** Outstndng Yng Men of Am; US Jaycees 1978; Trustees Awrd Pace Univ 1972. **Home Addr:** 624 E 20th, Apt 4C, New York, NY 10009.

BUTLER, MICHAEL KEITH
Surgeon, hospital administrator. **Personal:** Born Aug 29, 1955, Baton Rouge, LA; son of Felton Earl & Mildred Alexander Butler; married Marian Thompson Butler, Feb 10, 1990; children: Ebony Bolden, Yashica Bolden. **Educ:** Amherst College, BA, 1976; Tulane University, School of Medicine, MD, 1980, School of Public Health, MHA, 1990. **Career:** South LA Medi-

cal Associates, general surgeon, 1986-95; LSU School of Medicine, chief administrative officer, 1995-96; LA Health Care Authority, COO, med director, 1996-. **Orgs:** American College of Surgeons, fellow, 1989; American College of Physician Executives, 1990; American Board of Quality Assurance Utilization Review Physicians, 1994; American Board of Medical Management; American Society of General Surgeons; LA Surgical Association; National Medical Association; National Association of Health Svcs Executives. **Home Addr:** 205 San Antonio Blvd, Houma, LA 70360, (504)851-0392. **Business Addr:** COO/Medical Director, Medical Ctr of Louisiana, 2021 Perdido St, University Campus, 4th Fl, New Orleans, LA 70112, (504)588-3493.

BUTLER, MITCHELL LEON
Professional basketball player. **Personal:** Born Dec 15, 1970, Los Angeles, CA. **Educ:** Univ of California, Los Angeles, 1993. **Career:** Washington Bullets, guard, 1993-96; Portland TrailBlazers, 1996-97; Cleveland Cavaliers, 1997-. **Business Addr:** Professional Basketball Player, Cleveland Cavaliers, One Center Ct, Cleveland, OH 44115-4001, (216)659-9100.

BUTLER, OCTAVIA E.
Author. **Personal:** Born Jun 22, 1947, Pasadena, CA; daughter of Octavia Margaret Butler and Laurice Butler. **Educ:** Pasadena City Coll, AA, 1968; CA State Coll; UCLA. **Career:** Author, Novels include: Patternmaster, 1976, Mind of My Mind, 1977, Survivor, 1978, Kindred, 1979, Wild Seed, 1980, Clay's Ark, 1984, Dawn, 1987, Adulthood Rites, 1988, Imago, 1989; Parable of the Sower, 1993; Parable of the Talents, forthcoming; short fiction includes, Crossover, 1971, Near of Kin, 1979, Speech Sounds, 1983, Bloodchild, 1984, The Evening and the Morning and the Night, 1987; articles include, Lost Races of Science Fiction, Transmission, Summer, 1980, "Writer," Women and Work—Photographs and Personal Writings, 1986, "Birth of a Writer," Essence, May, 1989; "Future Forum," Future Life, March, 1990; Parable of the Sower, 1995. **Orgs:** Science Fiction and Fantasy Writers of America. **Honors/Awds:** YWCA Achievement Awd for Creative Arts 1980; Hugo Award, Best Short Story, 42nd World Science Fiction Convention, 1984; Nebula Award, Best Novelette, Science Fiction Writers of America, 1984; Hugo Award, Best Novelette, 43rd World Science Fiction Convention, 1985; MacArthur Foundation Fellowship Award, $295,000, 1995.

BUTLER, OLIVER RICHARD
Business executive. **Personal:** Born Jul 3, 1941, New Orleans, LA; son of Rose M Desvignes Butler and Richard M Butler; married Naurine M Jackson; children: Janee, Eric, Shann. **Educ:** Xavier Univ of LA, BS Pharmacy 1958-62; Univ of IL Polk St Campus, Graduate Course in Organic Chem 1968; Univ of New Orleans, Graduate Business Courses 1975-77. **Career:** Walgreen Co Chicago, store mgr/pharmacist 1962-69; Bruxelles Pharmacy, store owner 1970-73; Ayerst Labs, sales positions 1974-78, dist mgr 1978-83, asst field sales mgr 1983-84, dir of sales opers 1984-88; Wyeth-Ayerst Labs (all divisions), Sales Administration, exec dir 1988-91, asst vp, 1991-. **Orgs:** Mem New Orleans Comm/Human Relations 1970; mem exec comm LA High Blood Pressure Prog 1978; guest lecturer Xavier Univ Med Tech Dept 1978-81; adv bd Food/Drug Admin 1979; vice pres Ursuline Academy 1979-80; treas Acro I Gymnastic Club 1981-82; pharmacy dean search comm Xavier Univ Coll/Pharmacy 1981-82 adv comm Xavier Univ Coll of Pharmacy 1982-; Apothecary Board of Visitors, Florida A&M College of Pharmacy 1990-93; Ad Hoc Committee on Sampling, Pharmaceutical Manufacturers Assn, 1990-93; Philadelphia Corporate Alliance for Drug Education, 1992. **Honors/Awds:** Achievement Awd Rexall Drug Co 1962; Man of the Year Chi Delta Mu Frat 1969. **Business Addr:** Asst VP, Sales Administration, Wyeth-Ayerst Laboratories, 555 E Lancaster Ave, St Davids, PA 19087.

BUTLER, PATRICK HAMPTON
Business executive, attorney. **Personal:** Born Jul 24, 1933, Gonzales, TX; married Barbara; children: Daphne, Ann Marie. **Educ:** Univ CO Sch of Law, JD 1961; CO Coll, BA 1956. **Career:** Eli Lilly & Co, asst counsel; IN Univ asst pro of law 1966-68; US Dept of Labor, spec asst 1965-66; US Dept of Justice, trial atty 1962-65; Fed Trade & Comn 1961-62. **Orgs:** Bd govs Indianapolis Bar Assn 1972-74. **Military Serv:** AUS 1st lt 1958. **Business Addr:** 307 E Mc Carty St, Indianapolis, IN 46208.

BUTLER, PINKNEY L.
City official. **Personal:** Born May 3, 1948, Greensboro, NC; son of Louise Alexander Thompson and James Butler; married Mary Green Butler, Nov 4, 1972; children: Monecia, Patrick, Prentice. **Educ:** Southwestern Christian, Terrell, TX, AA, 1969; Pepperdine University, Los Angeles, CA, BA, 1971; Corpus Christi State Univ, Corpus Christi, TX, MA, 1980. **Career:** City of Victoria, TX executive director/dep of community affairs, 1974-77; Nueces County Adult Probation, Corpus Christi, TX, adult probation officer, 1977-78; City of Corpus Christi, TX, administrative asst, 1978-83; City of Tyler, TX, assistant city manager, 1983-. **Orgs:** Member/officer, East Texas City Managers Assn, 1983-; member, committee person, Texas City Managers Assn, 1987-; member, International City Managers Assn, 1983-; National Forum for Black Public Administrators, 1986. **Business Addr:** Assistant City Manager, City of Tyler, PO Box 2039, Tyler, TX 75710, (903)531-1250.

BUTLER, REBECCA BATTS
Educator. **Personal:** Born in Norfolk, VA. **Educ:** Temple U, DEd 1965; Temple U, MEd 1958; Glassboro State Coll, BS 1942. **Career:** Camden Public Schools, elementary teacher 1937-51, supvr of guidance 1966-68, dir adult comm prog 1969-74; Camden Secondary School, teacher 1951-59; NJ State Dept of Educ, 1968-69; Glassboro State Coll, adj prof; Organized Lincoln School for Unwed Mothers Camden City, director. **Orgs:** Chrm of Comm Tchr Educ and Prof Stand; natl editor-in-chief KRINON Natl Sor Phi Delta Kappa 1972-76; mem Natl Asso of Negro Bus & Prof Women 1974; dir Adult Cont Educ for NANPW; Girl Sct Leader 1941-60; mem Philadelphia Fellowshp House; organzr & 1st chrmn Comm on educ Chestnut St UAME ch; mem Civil Def Counc Camden City; mem exec bd Camden County Red Cross; mem of exec bd Vstng Nurses assoc; pres Assoc of Negro Bus and Prof Women of Camden and Vicinity; appt one of 1st mem bd of trustees & Thomas A Edison Coll 1973-75; panel men Unites Fund; past mem bd of dir Mary H Thomas Nursery; chmn Nat Adv Com on Comm Servs for Am Asso Ret Persons 1978-80; natl bd dirs AARP 1980; particant White House Briefing for Women 1980; initiative spokesperson for Amer Assoc ofRetired Persons until 1993. **Honors/Awds:** Over 100 Citations and Awards, including: Woman of the Yr Awd Zeta Phi Beta 1977; Outstanding Citizen Afro-Amer Life & History of Camden County 1977; Volunteer of the Year Elks of Camden 1976; Citedfor Volunter Serv Camden County Red Cross 1976; Citation Spanish Spkg Commun of Camden 1974; Citation Camden Bd of Educ 1974; Cited for Commun Serv UnitedFund of Camden Cty 1974; Cited as Adult Educ of Yr Adult Educ of NJ 1973; Educ of Year Oppty Indn Cent 1972, Natl Achievement Awd & Natl Prog Awd Adult Cont Educ NABPW Clubs Inc 1977; Sojourner Truth Awd Camden B&P Club 1977; Outstanding Citizen of the Year Goodwill Ind 1972; Outstanding Citizen AwdAwds Comm of Ninth Annual Observ of Tenth St Baptist Church 1966; Cited for Community Serv Camden Commun Club 1965; Mae S Moore Awd natl Assoc of Bus&Professional Women of Camden & Vicin 1964; Cited for Commun Serv Chapel of the Four Chaplains 1964; Bishop Awd 1954;v Chapel of the Four Chaplns 1964; Bishop Awd 1954; publ "Protraits of Black Role Models In The History of Southern NJ"; "My Thoughts I Write," A Book of Poems, 1990. **Business Addr:** Educational Consultant, 15 Eddy Ln, Cherry Hill, NJ 08002.

BUTLER, ROY (GENE)
Manager. **Personal:** Born Jun 24, 1949, Tyler, TX; son of Gertha McClendon Butler and Roy Butler; married May 15, 1976 (divorced 1989); children: Stephen, Shannon. **Educ:** Univ of Colorado, Boulder, CO, BSCE, 1975. **Career:** Western Slope Gas Co, Denver, CO, engineering tech, 1970-74, special project engineer, 1974-76; Sun Pipe Line Company, Tulsa, OK, senior pipeline engineer, 1976-78; Sun Pipe Line Company, Seminole, OK, manager of field engineering, 1978-80, general foreman of maintenance & operations, 1980-83; Sun Pipe Line Company, Drumright, OK, general foreman of maintenance & operations, 1980-83; Sun Pipe Line Company, Tulsa, OK, manager business operations, 1987-. **Business Addr:** Manager, Business Operations, Sun Pipe Line Company, 907 S Detroit, Room 1119, Tulsa, OK 74120.

BUTLER, VELMA SYDNEY
Educator (retired). **Personal:** Born Feb 6, 1902, Oakland, TX; daughter of Henrietta Eason Sydney and P W Sydney; married Payton Butler (deceased); children: Shirley Vel Butler Green. **Educ:** Houston-Tillotson Coll Austin TX, BA; Univ of Denver Denver CO, MA 1953. **Career:** San Antonio Independent Sch Dist, elem dept; San Antonio Independent Sch Dist, dept spl educ 1930-69; Incarnate Word Coll San Antonio & TX, dept of spl educ 1969-70. **Orgs:** Exec bd Olive St Welfare Assn 1946-75; exec bd Welcome Home Blind & Aged 1946-75; exec bd Mt Zion First Bapt Day Care Center 1950-56; Alpha Phi Zeta Chap Basileus; life mem exec bd Zeta Phi Beta Sor Inc; exec Young Matrons Guild; dir So Reg Amicae; exec bd San Antonio Tchrs Council 1956-59; secYWCA; Interdenominational Courtesy Council; Woman's Pavilion for HemisFair 68, vp; exec bd Project FREE; first woman appointed on selective service bd in Bexar Co 1971-73; Eastside Neighborhood Devel Project; pres & vice pres Co Fed Credit Unoin 1950-77; bd mem Bexar Co Opportunities Industrialization Center Inc 1974-75; San Antonio & Bicentennial Com; region & natl bds & so region exec bd Zeta Phi Beta Sor Inc; natl exec bd Zeta Phi Beta Sor Ch Affiliations; mem MtZion First Bapt Ch; dir Mt Zionrst Bapt Wednesday Morning Fellowship Hour; Ministers, Deacons, & Trustees Wives Aux; pres Mt Zion First Bapt Courtesy Comm; Retired San Antonio Tchrs Council; TX State Tchrs Assn; NEA. **Honors/Awds:** Certificate of appreciation Pres of US; outstanding contrib in comm serv The Western Ares Links Inc; outstanding serv rendered award from Local Regional & Nat Zeta Phi Beta Sor Inc; outstanding tchr of yr Alamo Dist C Of C; distinguished serv award Mt Zion First Bapt Ch; outstanding serv for city improvements City of San Antonio; comm serv Interdenominational Courtesy Council; outstanding leadership & contbns in educ polit comm civic ch life & toward struggle for women's rights State of TX House of Rep; appointed mem of Bicentennial Com by City Council 1974-76.

BUTLER, WASHINGTON ROOSEVELT, JR.
Operations representative. **Personal:** Born Jan 5, 1933, New Orleans, LA; son of Althea Landry Butler and Washington R Butler Sr; divorced; children: Landry, Luthuli, Leiah. **Educ:** Clark Coll, BS 1953; Univ of TN Knoxville, MA 1964; ABD, 1965. **Career:** Urban & Fed Affairs State of TN, commr 1975-79; Riverside Hosp Nashville, TN, vice pres 1981-83; self-empl Madison, TN, devel consult; Advanced Innovative Technology, Inc, former president, 1987-94; adjunct instructor, Vol State Community College 1990-91; Hunan College of Finance & Economics, Changsha, Hunan, People's Republic of China, english instructor, 1993-94; Olsten Staffing Services, temporary data processor, 1994; Participant Services Representative, BT Services Tennessee, Inc, 1994-96; Technical Writer, Bankers Trust Co, 1996-97; MetLife Co, operations rep, 1998-. **Orgs:** Bd dir Oakwood Coll Huntsville, AL 1977-82; bd dir Riverside Hosp Nashville, TN 1975-81; former sec-treas/bd mem Natl Assn for Comm Dev; former bd mem Southeastern Reg Assn of Comm Action Agencies; elect to two four-yr terms on City Cncl Oak Ridge, TN; served on Oak Ridge Reg Planning Commn; Oak Ridge Beer Board; Anderson Co Citizens Welfare Adv Bd; former mem Agricultural Ext Comm ; bd dir Memphis Opport Indust Center; Natl Busn League Memphis Chpt; former pres Memphis Inter-Alumni Cncl of the United Negro Coll Fund; candidate for nom as Gov in Dem Primary of 1974; Former First Elder in Riverside Chapel Seventh-day Adventist Ch Nashville, TN; Former chrmn Building Comm FH Jenkins Elem Sch; former mem bd trustees Oakwood Coll Huntsville, AL andRiverside Adventist Hosp Nashville, TN; candidate Tenn. Public Service Commission, 1985; candidate for Metro Council At Large, 1986. **Honors/Awds:** Beta Kappa Chi Natl Honorary Sci Soc. **Military Serv:** AUS, USAREUR Command spec e-4 1953-56; USAR 5 years.

BUTLER-BUSH, TONIA
Government official. **Career:** White House Office of Communication, Student Correspondence, deputy dir, currently. **Business Phone:** (202)456-1414.

BUTTERFIELD, DON
Musician. **Personal:** Born Apr 1, 1923, Centralia, WA. **Career:** Teddy Charles Charles Mingus, instrumentalist on tuba jazz tuba player 1950's; Radio City Mus Hall Orch NYC, prin tuba player for 18yrs; Am Symphony Orch, tuba player; free-lance rec artist with leading jazz musicians; spl perfmances including & nightclubs film performances with Dizzier Gillispie Orch 1962; Town-Hall concert with Charles Mingus 1962; Newport RI Jazz Festival 1963. **Orgs:** Mem faculty NY U; composer of study materials for low frequency mus instruments; pub through his own co DB Pub Co Office. **Business Addr:** Nydam Lane, Wyckoff, NJ 07481.

BUTTS, CALVIN OTIS, III
Cleric. **Educ:** Morehouse College, bachelors, 1972; Union Theological Seminary, MDiv, 1975; Drew Theological School, DMin, 1982. **Career:** Abyssinian Baptist Church, asst minister, 1972-77, exec minister, 1977-89, pastor, 1989-. **Orgs:** United Way of NYC, vice chair; Black Leadership Commission on AIDS, Replication Project, chair; CT Walker Housing, chmn; Central Park Conservancy, bd mem; Harlem YMCA, bd mem; The New School of Social Research, advisory bd mem; Graham Services to Family & Children, advisory bd; Kappa Alpha Psi Fraternity; Prince Hall Masons, grand chaplin 33 degree. **Honors/Awds:** NY Chamber of Commerce, Living Treasure (Twice); Morehouse College, Man of the Year; Manhattan Magazine, New York Power Broker; Utility Club of NYC, Louise Fisher Morris Humanitarian Award; I AM Corporation, Communications Against Social Injustice Award. **Special Achievements:** Led fight against police brutality, 1983; Spearheaded boycotts against NY institutions for racist policies & led campaign to eliminate negative billboard advertising, discrimination; Led campaign to eliminate negative lyrics in rap music; Spoken at universities, military bases, prisons, government functions, conventions, summits, etc across America and internationally. **Business Addr:** Pastor, Abyssinian Baptist Church, 132 Odell Clark Place, New York, NY 10030, (212)862-7474.

BUTTS, CARLYLE A.
Business executive (retired). **Personal:** Born Nov 10, 1935, Richmond, VA; son of Coral P Butts and Thomas A Butts Sr; married Omeria A Roberts, Jun 11, 1966; children: Brian, Gregory. **Educ:** Howard Univ, BSEE 1963; USC, MBA 1969; UCLA, Executive Mgmt Program 1988. **Career:** Hughes Aircraft Co, staff vp quality, 1994-96, quality director, aerospace and defense sector, 1992-94, quality director, electro-optical & data systems group, 1990-92, assistant division manager, ground systems group 1988-90, product operations manager 1987, dept mgr radar systems group 1978, proj mgr 1977, head facilities planning 1972-76, proj mgr 1970-72, head prod control 1969-70, various positions in material dept 1964-69, electronics test engr 1963-64; Howard Univ, electronic lab instr asst 1958-63; Ladera Career Paths, chairman, bd of dir, 1993-. **Orgs:** Past mem Amer Marketing Assn; Natl Contracts Mgmt Assn; Intercollegiate Council of Black Colleges; Business Mgmt Consultant; mem Hughes Mgmt Club; past pres bd trustees Crenshaw Ch of Religious Sci 1974-77; den leader Webelos Pack 162c Holman Meth Chl 1978; pres Howard Univ Alumni

Club of So CA 1971-73; pres Howard Univ Alumni Club of So CA 1980; Basileus Omega Psi Phi Fraternity, LA chapter, 1994, 1997-98. **Honors/Awds:** Howard Hughes Fellowship 1967; Los Angeles City Resolution for Service to Youth & Community 1983; Lambda Omicron, Omega Man of the Year, 1994, 1992, Omega Psi Phi Fraternity. **Military Serv:** USAF a1/c 1954-57. **Home Addr:** 4906 Maymont Dr, Los Angeles, CA 90043-2032.

BUTTS, CRAIG E.
Business owner. **Personal:** Born Sep 9, 1958, Des Moines, IA; son of Kathryn Butts and Louis Butts; married Maureen, Sep 1980; children: Crystal, Joelle, Daniel. **Educ:** US Air Force Technical School, dipolma, 1977; Des Moines Area Community College, associate's degree, 1980; Nebraska College of Business, currently. **Career:** Des Moines General Hospital, audio/video biomed tech, 1981-83; Video Images, service manager, 1983-84; Dictaphone Corp, customer service rep, 1985-89; US West/Northwestern, customer service technician, 1989-91; Audio Video Works, owner, currently. **Orgs:** Love Inc, board mem, 1992; The Network, founder/president, 1992. **Honors/Awds:** Des Moines Area Community College, certificate of volunteer engineering, 1979; US West, ''It's Up to You,'' 1991. **Military Serv:** US Air Force, airman, 1977. **Business Addr:** Owner, Audio Video Works, 2013 Calhoun St, Bellevue, NE 68005.

BUTTS, HUGH F.
Physician, psychiatrist, psychoanalyst. **Personal:** Born Dec 2, 1926, New York, NY; son of Edith Eliza Higgins Butts and Lucius C. Butts; married Clementine; children: Lucia, Florence, Eric, by previous marriage; Sydney, Samantha, Heather. **Educ:** City Coll NY, BS 1949; Meharry Med Coll, MD 1953; Morrisania City Hosp, intern cert 1955; Bronx VA Hosp, resd 1958; Columbia Univ Psychoanalytic Clinic, Cert Psychoanalytic Med 1962. **Career:** St Lukes Hospital, staff physician, 1958-74; Hillcrest Ctr for Children, staff psych 1959-61; Private practice, psych 1959-74; Wiltwyck School for Boys, clinical dir 1961-63, chief, in-patient psych serv 1962-69; Gracie Square Hospital, staff physician, 1961-66; Montefiore Hospital, staff physician, 1961-65; Beth-Israel Hospital, staff physician, 1962-63; Harlem Hosptial Center, associate professor of psych, 1962-69; Vanderbilt Clinic Presbyterian Hospital, staff physician, 1963-65; New York Department of Vocational Rehabilitation, staff physician, 1963-69; private practice, psychoanalyist, 1962-74; Columbia Univ Coll Phys & Surgeons, asst clin prof psych 1967-74; Albert Einstein College of Medicine, prof of Psychiatry 1974-81; Bronx State Hospital, staff physician, 1974-79;New York St Department of Mental Hygiene, staff physician, 1974-76; Literary Mind Associates, pres 1986-; Clementine Publishing Company, Leeds NY, pres and founder 1989-; The New Hope Guild, Brooklyn NY, psychiatric consultant 1980-; Columbia Law School-Fair Housing Clinic, psychiatric consultant, 1993; The Open Housing Center, psychiatric consultant, 1996-; St. Vincent's Mental Health Services, psychiatrist, 1996-; The New York College of Podiatric Medicine, adjunct professor, 1995-; The Episcopal Diocese of New York, psychiatric consultant, 1989-. **Orgs:** Consult The Neuropsychiatric Ctr NY 1957; psych consult Jewish Bd Guardians 1962; suprv training analyst Columbia Univ Psychoanalytic Clinic for Training & Rsch 1968-; psych consult Fieldston-Ethical Culture School 1970-74; staff psych Manida Juv Detention Ctr 1972-74; suprv psych Bronx State Hosp 1973-79; training analy, suprv analyst Post-Grad Ctr for Mental Health 1975-; act dir resd training Bronx State Hosp 1977-79; psych consult NY City Police Dept Psychol Clinic 1974-76; mem US Fed Ct 1970-75, Allegheny Cty Mental Health & Mental Retardation Assoc 1974-75; mem, NY Psych Inst 1962-74;Natl Med Assoc, AMA, NY Cty Med Soc, Amer Psych Assoc 1970, Assoc for Psychoanalytic Med 1968-71, Amer Orthopsychiatric Assoc 1970-73, Alumni Assoc Psychoan Clinic for Training & Rsch; fellow NY Acadd; Medical Advisory Board, The Medical Herald, Chairman, 1990-. **Honors/Awds:** Numerous awards, citations, and publications. **Special Achievements:** New York State Department of Mental Hygiene, first deputy commissioner, 1975. **Military Serv:** USAF, private 1st class 1944-45, Good Conduct Medal. **Business Addr:** 350 Central Park West, New York, NY 10025.

BUTTS, JANIE PRESSLEY
Educator. **Personal:** Born Aug 25, 1936, Nesmith, SC; daughter of Lillie D Pressley and Ollie Epps Pressley; married Thomas A Butts Jr, Oct 1, 1960; children: Derrick, Steven, Karlton. **Educ:** South Carolina State College, BBA, 1958; Eastern Connecticut State College, elementary certification, 1973. **Career:** Groton Bd of Education, sixth grade teacher, 1968-69; East Lyme Bd of Education, fifth grade teacher, 1969-. **Orgs:** National Education Association; Natl Council of Negro Women Inc; NAACP; Shiloh Baptist Church; Connecticut Cooperating/Mentor Teaching Program. **Honors/Awds:** National Association for Equal Opportunity in Higher Education, Distinguished Alumni Citation of the Year Award, 1992; National Educator Award, 1990; Exemplary Teacher Citation, 1987; Connecticut Celebration of Excellence Award, 1986; Natl Council of Negro Women Inc, Woman of the Year, 1985. **Business Addr:** Fifth Grade Teacher, Flanders Elementary School, Boston Post Rd, East Lyme, CT 06333, (203)739-8475.

BUTTS, MARION STEVENSON, JR.
Professional football player. **Personal:** Born Aug 1, 1966, Sylvester, GA. **Educ:** Northeastern Oklahoma A & M, attended; Florida State Univ, attended. **Career:** San Diego Chargers, running back, beginning 1989; New England Patriots, 199 4-. **Business Addr:** Professional Football Player, New England Patriots, Sullivan Stadium, Rt 1, Foxboro, MA 02035.

BUTTS, WILSON HENRY
Scientist. **Personal:** Born May 18, 1932, Elizabeth City, NC; married Geraldine High; children: Kevin Eric. **Educ:** Fisk Univ, BA 1959. **Career:** Vanderbilt Univ Med Sch, instr surg research 1960-; Fisk Univ Chem Dept, organic research chemist 1959-60. **Orgs:** Mem Am Assn of Clinical Chem; mem AAAS; mem Omega Pso Phi Frat; officer Knights of Peter Claver & Council 5, 1978-. **Honors/Awds:** Registered Clinical Chemistry Tech #690, Nat Registry in Clinical Chemistry; cert Instrumentation Labs 1965; cert Hewlett Packard 1967; cert Technicon 1967; cert Autoanalyzer 1969; cert AACC 1972; licensure Gen Lab Supr State of TN; numerous pub med jours 1969-78; recipent Good Conduct Medal USAF; sharp-shooter medal USAF. **Military Serv:** USAF sgt 1951-55.

BYAM, MILTON S.
Consultant. **Personal:** Born Mar 15, 1922, New York, NY; son of Sybil Williams and Charles Byam; married Yolanda Shervington, Jan 18, 1947; children: Roger. **Educ:** City Coll NY, BSS 1947; Columbia Univ, MS 1949; NYU, grad sch 1950-51; Columbia Univ Sch Library Sci, 1968. **Career:** Brooklyn Pub Libr, librarian trainee 1947-49, librarian 1949-50, asst br librarian 1950-51, br librarian 1951-56, supt br 1956-61; Pratt Inst, teacher 1956-67; Brooklyn Pub Libr, chief pub serv 1961-65, deputy dir 1965-68; chmn St Johns Univ Dept Library Sci 1968-72; dir DC Public Library 1972-74; dir Queens Borough Public Library 1974-79; Byam et al Inc, consultant 1979-. **Honors/Awds:** Many publications; Friends Library Award Brooklyn Pub Library; Commendation Library Serv & Constrn Act DC Adv Council; Cert of Appreciation City of Philadelphia;Library Award Savannah State Coll; Bd of Regents NY State Univ. **Military Serv:** US Army, T/5, 1943-45; Bronze Star. **Business Addr:** Consultant, Byam et al Consultants, 162-04 75 Rd, Flushing, NY 11366.

BYARD, JOHN ARTHUR, JR.
Educator. **Personal:** Born Jun 15, 1922, Worcester, MA; married Louise M Caruso; children: Denise, Diane, Gerald. **Educ:** Comm Sch of Music Schillinger Sch of Music. **Career:** New England Conservatory of Music, music instr 1969-77; Hart Sch of Music, 1974-77; CCNX, 1974-76; SE of MA, 1974-76; Elma Lewis Sch, conductor 1972-76. **Orgs:** Instr Rotary Club & 1974-77; lectr Harvard Univ 1974-77; Univ of Pitts 197375; Univ of MD 1968-70; Bismark Jr Coll 1976-77; rec artist Prestige New Jazz 1959-67; Futura 1967-70; Victor 1971; Lechange; permc around world. **Honors/Awds:** Hon mem Hartford Jazz Sox; Hot Club of France; Jazz Mus of NY; Vibration Soc; Roland Kirk; hon citz New Orleans 1969; cert of merit Black Stud Union of SE MA Univ 1975; act chmn AAS NE Conservatory 1972; tchr pvt Duke Ellington Flwsp Award 1977; talent recog Down Beat 1966. **Military Serv:** AUS 1/sgt 1942-45.

BYARS, KEITH ALLAN
Professional football player. **Personal:** Born Oct 14, 1963, Dayton, OH; married Margaret; children: Taylor Renae, Keith Allan II. **Educ:** Ohio State Univ, attended. **Career:** Philadelphia Eagles, running back, 1986-93; Miami Dolphins, 1993-96; New England Patriots, 1996-. **Honors/Awds:** Philadelphia Sports Writers Assn, Humanitarian of the Year, 1991; Big Brothers/Big Sisters of Philadelphia, Community Service Award, 1991; Pro Bowl, 1993. **Business Addr:** Professional Football Player, New England Patriots, 60 Washington St, Foxboro Stadium, Foxboro, MA 02035, (508)543-7911.

BYAS, THOMAS HAYWOOD
Dentist. **Personal:** Born Mar 10, 1922, St Louis, MO; son of Rosetta Woolfolk Byas and Thomas Haywood Byas; married Ermine Casey Bush, Mar 25, 1950; children: Diane, Timothy. **Educ:** Lemoyne Coll, BS 1943; Howard U, DDS 1951. **Career:** Univ of Rochester Sch of Med & Dent, asst prof 1978; St Mary's Hosp, 1978; Baden St Settlement, dentist 1954. **Orgs:** Mem Intl Coll of Dentist ADA 1979; mem Rochester & Acad of Med 1965; pres Chi-Psi Chap Omega Psi Phi 1942; pres Chi Delta Mu 1950; mem bd dir Montgomery Comm Ctr 1968; Dental Smilemobile Rochester 1970; dental dir Albion Ny Health Ctr 1972; mem bd dir Monroe Co Dntl Soc 1973; pres 1977-1978; Green Hills Golf Club 1970-73; Thunder Ridge Co Club 1976; co-chmn United Negro Coll Fund 1955; Rochester C of C 1966; pres Howard Univ Alumni Assn 1966; volunteer consult Operation Outreach 1976-; Dental Soc of NY; Amer Dental Assn 1953-; founder exec sec Seoul, Korea Dental Soc 1952; pres Seventh Dist Dental Society 1987; Sigma Pi Phi Frat, Gamma Iota chapter, 1985-. **Honors/Awds:** 32nd & 33rd degree mason 1963; award Alpha Phi Alpha 1977; Focal Infections in Periodontal Disease Howard Univ 1950; Fellowship, American College of Dentists, 1989; George D Greenwood Honorary Awd, Seventh District Dental Soc, 1995. **Military Serv:** AUS 1st lt 1943-1948; AUS 1st lt 1951-1953. **Home Addr:** 140 Gate House Trail, Henrietta, NY 14467. **Business Addr:** 316 Chili Ave, Rochester, NY 14611.

BYAS, ULYSSES
Educator (retired). **Personal:** Born Jun 23, 1924, Macon, GA; son of Marie Byas Sharpe; married Annamozel Boyd, Jul 5, 1953; children: 4. **Educ:** Fort Valley State Coll, BS 1950; Columbia Univ, MA 1952; further study, Atlanta Univ, NC Coll, Bennington Coll, Colorado Coll; Univ of MA, EdD 1976. **Career:** Elberton, tchr 1951-53; Hutchison Elem & HS, supr prin; Butler HS, EE 1957-68; GA Tchrs & Educ Assn, asst exec sec 1968; GA Assn Educ, dir 1970; Macon Co Bd of Educ, supt schs 1970-77; Roosevelt Union Free Sch Dist, New York, supt schs 1977-87; Hempstead Union Free School District, New York, superintendent of schools, 1990-91; education consultant, currently. **Orgs:** Mem, Amer Assn Sch Adminstrs, Natl Alliance Black Sch Educ, Nassau Co Chief Sch Assn, NY Assn Sch Adminstrs, Natl Assn Secondary Sch Prins, Phi Delta Kappa; exec comm hon chmn United Negro Scholarship; life mem Kappa Alpha Psi Frat; vice pres Long Island Cancer Council; participant 23rd Annual Air War Coll Natl Security Forum; life mem, Fort Valley State College Alumni Association; mem former chmn CME; past pres GA Cncl Secondary Sch Principals; past pres GA Tchrs & Educators Assn; past pres Natl Alliance of Black Sch Superintendents; National Alliance of Black School Educators, past president; past mem, NY State Examinations Bd, NAACP, Comm Bd; consultant Univ of MA; adjunct prof Long Island Univ; past pres-elect, Nassau County NY Supt; Macon, Georgia Area Habitat for Humanity, Central Georgia AlzheimersAssation. **Honors/Awds:** Ulysses Byas Elementary School, named by Roosevelt, NY Bd of Educ, 1987; Education Hall of Fame, Fort Valley State Coll, Georgia, 1988. **Military Serv:** USNR 1943-46. **Home Addr:** 5675 Kesteven Lane, Macon, GA 31210.

BYAS, WILLIAM HERBERT
Educational administrator. **Personal:** Born Nov 26, 1932, Macon; married Carolyn Kelsey; children: Yolanda E, William H. **Educ:** TN State U, BS 1957; The Ft Valley State Coll, MS 1957; The Univ of TN, EdD 1971. **Career:** Univ of TN, dean of student servs 1979; Memphis State Univ, assoc prof/res 1978-79; Saginaw Valley State Coll, dir acad & support serv & assoc prof educ psychology 1973-78, dir student pers servs 1971-73; New Careers Inst Knoxville Coll, dir 1970; The Ft Valley State Coll, dir coll educ achievement proj 1966-70. **Orgs:** Mem Am Psychological Assn 1972; mem Nat Assn Student Pers Admin 1978; committeeman BSA 1966-69 bd of dirs big bros of am 1971; rotarian Rotary Intl 1971; mem Phi Delta Kappa 1971. **Honors/Awds:** Recipient natl defense award Usn; doctoral fellowship Univ of TN 1970-71;cert for outstanding serv So Assn of Colls & Schs 1973; couns students with splneeds Saginaw Valley State Coll 1974; consult US Officeof Educ 1975. **Military Serv:** USN seaman 1950-52. **Business Addr:** U of Tennessee, 3113 Circle Park Dr, Knoxville, TN 37916.

BYEARS, LATASHA
Professional basketball player. **Personal:** Born Aug 12, 1973. **Educ:** DePaul, attended. **Career:** Sacramento Monarchs, guard, 1997-. **Orgs:** Meals on Wheels. **Business Addr:** Professional Basketball Player, Sacramento Monarchs, One Sports Parkway, Sacramento, CA 95834, (916)928-3650.

BYNAM, SAWYER LEE, III
Building contractor. **Personal:** Born Sep 15, 1933, Houston, TX; married Betty Ann; children: Keith Wayne. **Educ:** Tx So U, BS Certificate In Construction Planning & Estimating. **Career:** Gen & Sub-contractors Assn, contract dev, Est. **Business Addr:** Gen & Sub-Contractors Assn, 2211 Wheeler St, Houston, TX 77004.

BYNER, EARNEST ALEXANDER
Professional football player. **Personal:** Born Sep 15, 1962, Milledgeville, GA; married Tina; children: Semeria, Adrian Monique, Brandi, Kyara. **Educ:** East Carolina Univ, majored in physical education. **Career:** Cleveland Browns, running back, 1984-88, 1994-95; Washington Redskins, running back, 1989-93; Baltimore Ravens, running back, 1996-. **Orgs:** House of Ruth, spokesman. **Honors/Awds:** Post-season play: AFC Championship Game, 1986, 1987; Pro Bowl appearances, 1990, 1991. **Business Addr:** Professional Football Player, Baltimore Ravens, 11001 Owings Mills Blvd, Owings Mills, MD 21117, (410)654-6200.

BYNES, FRANK HOWARD, JR.
Physician. **Personal:** Born Dec 3, 1950, Savannah, GA; son of Frenchye Mason Bynes and Frank H Bynes; married Janice Ann Ratta, Jul 24, 1987; children: Patricia F Bynes, Frenchye D Bynes. **Educ:** Savanna State Coll, BS 1972; Meharry Medical Coll, MD 1977. **Career:** US Air Force, internist, 1986-87; self-employed, internist, 1987-. **Orgs:** Mem Alpha Phi Alpha Frat 1969-, Amer Medical Assoc 1973-, New York Acad of Scis 1983-, AAAS 1984-, Amer Coll of Physicians 1985-, Air Force Assoc 1987-, Assoc of Military Surgeons of the US 1987-. **Military Serv:** USAF major, 1986-87. **Business Addr:** 703 Noble Oaks Dr, Savannah, GA 31406, (912)354-0899.

BYNES, GLENN KENNETH
Audit manager. **Personal:** Born Jan 17, 1946, Orlando, FL; son of Mr & Mrs Arthur Bynes; married Norma Bynes, Jul 31, 1971; children: Glenn K III, Ingrid N. **Educ:** Hampton Jr Coll, AS, 1966; Tennessee State Univ, BS, 1971. **Career:** McDonnell Douglas, aircraft maintenance engineer, 1971-73; EI DuPont deNemours, production supervisor, 1973-74; Martin Marietta, mgr, audit operations, 1974-. **Orgs:** Registrar Accreditation Board, registered lead auditor, 1993-. **Special Achievements:** Plan, develop, implement & manage group audit activities. **Home Addr:** PO Box 770502, Orlando, FL 32877. **Business Addr:** Mgr, Audit Operations, Martin Marietta Info Group, 12506 Lake Underhill Road, Orlando, FL 32825, (407)826-1707.

BYNOE, JOHN GARVEY
Federal executive (retired), attorney. **Personal:** Born Oct 25, 1926, Boston, MA; married Louise V Granville; children: Sandra M, John L, James G, Jonathan K. **Educ:** Boston Univ New England School of Law, JD 1957. **Career:** Roxbury Comm Council, pres 1964-69; Unity Bank & Trust Co, dir 1968-76; Office Civil Rights Dept Health Ed & Welfare Reg I Boston, dir 1982 retired; attny, real estate broker 1982-; Real Estate Developer, 1987. **Orgs:** Former chmn of bd Urban League of Eastern MA 1979-80; former bd mem Freedom House Inc, Boston; past bd dir Legal Asst, Boston Legal Aid Soc; mem Alpha Phi Alpha; pres adv comm Museum of the Natl Ctr of Afro-Amer Artists Inc; bd mem MA Pre-Engrg Prog for Minority Students; legal counsel Natl Bus League Boston Chapt, 1974-80; chmn of the bd, Professional & Bus Club Boston MA; bd mem Natl Ctr of Afro-Amer Artists Inc; bd of dirs Resthaven Inc; mem Big Brother Assoc of Boston, 1963-86, Boy Scouts of Amer Boston Metro Chapt, 1983, Boston Branch NAACP 1987-88; past worshipful master, Widow Son Lodge #28, 1990-; legal adviser to most worshipful grand master, Most Worshipful Prince Hall Grand Lodge of Massachusetts; deputy grand master, 1997-98, sr grand warden, Prince Hall Grand Lodge, jurisdiction of MA, 1995-96; bd mem, clerk, Exec Services Corps of New England 1994-96 Chairman, advisory comm, Roxbury Heritage State Park; bd men, Roxbury Historical Society. **Honors/Awds:** Honorary Doctor of Laws, New England School of Law, 1987; 33 Degree, United Supreme Council, Prince Hall Masons, 1989. **Military Serv:** AUS sgt 1945-46. **Home Addr:** 82 Harold St, Roxbury, MA 02119.

BYNOE, PETER C. B.
Professional sports executive. **Personal:** Born Mar 20, 1951, Boston, MA; son of Ethel M Stewart Bynoe (deceased) and Victor C Bynoe (deceased); married Linda Walker Bynoe, Nov 1987. **Educ:** Harvard College, Cambridge, MA, BA, cum laude, 1972; Harvard Business School, Boston, MA, master of business, 1976; Harvard Law School, Cambridge, MA, JD, 1976. **Career:** Citibank, exec intern, 1976-77; James H Lowry & Assocs, exec vice pres, 1977-82; Telemat Ltd, chmn, 1982-; Illinois Sports Facilities Authority, exec dir, 1988-92; Denver Nuggets, co-owner, 1989-92; Rudnick & Wolfe, partner, 1995-. **Orgs:** Chairman, Chicago Landmarks Commission, 1986-97; director, JACOR Communications, Inc.; vice chairman, Goodman Theatre, 1987-; director, Chicago Economic Club; trustee, Rush-Presbytarian St Luke Hospital; director, UniRoyal Technology Corporation; director, Chicago Council on Foreign Relations; director Illinois Sports Facilities Authority; overseer, Harvard University; chair, Chicago Plan Commission, 1997-; pres, United Center Community Economic Development Fund. **Business Addr:** Rudnick & Wolfe, 203 N. LaSalle, Suite 1800, Chicago, IL 60601, (312)368-4090.

BYNUM, HORACE CHARLES, SR.
Pharmacist. **Personal:** Born Nov 2, 1916, New Orleans, LA; son of Amanda Medlock Bynum and Henry Bynum Jr; married Ethel Frinkle, Feb 14, 1975; children: Adolph F, Horace C Jr. **Educ:** Xavier Univ, New Orleans, LA, BS Pharmacy, 1936. **Career:** US Post Office, New Orleans, LA, carrier 1936-46; Bynum's Pharmacy, New Orleans, LA, pharmacist. **Orgs:** mem, Alpha Phi Alpha Fraternity; pres, NAACP, New Orleans Branch, 1966-69; sec, New Orleans Branch NAACP 1955-66; treasurer, NAACP, State Branch, 1969-75; pres, Natl Pharmaceutical Assn, 1970-71, treasurer, Lafon Home Bd of Dir, 1969-89. **Honors/Awds:** Pharmacist of Year, New Orleans, Progressive Assn; Man of the Year, Chi Delta Mu Fraternity. **Business Addr:** Pharmacist, Owner, Bynum's Pharmacy/DBA Bynum & Son, Inc, 3840 St Bernard Ave, New Orleans, LA 70122.

BYNUM, RALEIGH WESLEY
Optometrist. **Personal:** Born May 27, 1936, Jacksonville, FL; son of Corene Brown Bynum and John T Bynum; married Thelmetia Argrett; children: Raleigh, Monjya, Zerrick. **Educ:** FL A&M Univ, 1954-56; IL Coll of Optometry, BS OD 1956-60; Univ of SC, MPH 1975; Command & General Staff Coll AUS, certificate 1976. **Career:** Natl Optometric Assn, past pres/bd chmn 1979; Amer Acad of Optometry, vice pres NC chap 1980-85; Amer Opt Assn, trustee 1978-; Natl Optometric Foundation, chmn of the bd 1980-88; RMZ Associates, president, currently. **Orgs:** Past pres bd of dirs Charlotte Bethlehem Ctr 1973; regional dir NOA Minority Recruitment Proj 1971-77; mem Natl HBP Coordinating Comm 1976-84; gen partner Westside Prof Assoc 1972-; vice chmn bd of dirs McCrorey Branch YMCA 1983-91; vice chmn bd of dirs Charlotte Mint Museum 1983-87. **Honors/Awds:** Optometrist of the Year Natl Opt Assn 1980; deacon Friendship Baptist Church 1978-; pilot-instr rated single engine land airplane 1975-. **Military Serv:** US Army Col (retired) 32 yrs service-Reserves, Active & National Guard. **Home Addr:** 6426 Heatherbrook Ave, Charlotte, NC 28213. **Business Addr:** President, RMZ Associates, 401 S Independence Blvd, Charlotte, NC 28204.

BYNUM, VALERIE CALLYMORE
Musician. **Personal:** Born Mar 9, 1942, Bronx, NY; married Louis Jr; children: Adam, Tanisha. **Educ:** Itaca Coll Sch of Music, BS 1963. **Career:** Freelance Musician, 1965. **Orgs:** Mem Sym New World 1965-72; tchr Jr HS 1965-67; mem Radio City Music Hall Sym 1963-66; Recording with leading artist, concerts, broadway shows.

BYRD, ALBERT ALEXANDER
Educator (retired). **Personal:** Born Nov 6, 1927, Baltimore, MD; married Alice Muriel Poe; children: Karen Leslie Forgy-Hicks. **Educ:** Howard University, BA, 1949; Temple University, MFA, 1959; Universidad Nacional Autonoma de Mexico, 1959; Instituto Statele D'Arte Per La Porcellana Sesto Florentino, Italy, 1962; Instituto Statale D'Arte Porto Romano Florence, Italy, 1962. **Career:** Baltimore Public School District, art teacher, 1949-63; Sacramento City College, Humanitites and Fine Arts, professor, 1963-91. **Orgs:** American Federation of Teachers; Faculty Assn of California Community Colleges; Kappa Alpha Psi; Howard University Alumni Assn. **Honors/Awds:** United Nations Service Medal, Natl Defense Service; Natl Endowment for the Humanitites, Washington DC, 1972-73; Grant, American Forum for Intl Study, Cleveland OH, 1975. **Military Serv:** US Army, private first class, 1951-53; Korean Service Meadl with 2 Battle Stars. **Business Addr:** Professor, Dept of Humanities & Fine Arts, Retired, Sacramento City College, 3835 Freeport Blvd, Sacramento, CA 95822-1386.

BYRD, ARTHUR W.
Social worker. **Personal:** Born Dec 24, 1943, Washington, DC; son of Doris Littlejohn Byrd and Arthur W Byrd Sr; married Inez Marie Coleman Byrd, Nov 26, 1967; children: Arthur III William, Ashley Wendall, Allyn Winthrop. **Educ:** Livingstone Coll, BS 1965; Univ NC, MSW 1972; Univ of KY, postgraduate; Univ of Chicago. **Career:** Clinch Valey Coll Univ of VA, faculty 1972; Longwood Coll Farmville VA, faculty 1972; Livingstone Coll Salisbyr 1974. **Orgs:** mem, Rowan Co Civic League, 1973; NC Neighborhood Workers Assn 1969; NASW 1970; CSWE 1970; So Assn of Undergrad SW Educ 1973; NAACP 1964; dir Neighborhood Corps 1965-68; Salisbury & Statesville NC; dir, Neighborhood Youth in School & out of School Programs Salisbury NC 1968-70; dir Outreach to Teenage Fathers Durham NC 1970; comm contact Rep Youth Serv Bureau, Winston Salem, NC 1971; state dir of Rsch Facility for Mentally Retarded; Adjunct J Sargent Reynolds Comm Coll, 1975. **Honors/Awds:** Recipient, Babcock Fellow, 1970-72; Distinguished Serv Award, Salisbury Rowan Com Serv Coun; POP Award Coop School for Girls Durham NC; established 1st Afro-Amer Student Org Longwood Coll, 1972-73; established Social Work Action Group SWAG Livingstone Coll 1973-74. **Home Addr:** 6801 West Rd, Chesterfield, VA 23832.

BYRD, CAMOLIA ALCORN
Educator. **Personal:** Born May 16, Baton Rouge, LA; married Lionel Patrick Byrd; children: Cheryl P, Lionel P Jr, Judith I, Roderick J, Janell M. **Educ:** Southern Univ Baton Rouge, BA 1944; Central State Univ, MA 1964. **Career:** Oklahoma City Public Schools, teacher 1959-70, consultant 1970-76, asst coord 1976-80, coord 1980-86; "I Can" Reading/Math Center, dir 1987-. **Orgs:** Mem Assoc for Supervision and Curriculum Develop, Intl Reading Assoc and OK Reading Assoc, Teachers of English to Speaker of Other Languages & OK TESOL, Natl and Local Black Educators Assoc; mem Natl Council of Negro Women, Fed of Col Womens Club, Phi Delta Kappa Inc, Jack & Jill Inc, OK Eastside Culture Club, Alpha Kappa Alpha Sor, Assault on Illiteracy 1986, NTU Art Assoc, African Art Museum; campaign mgr Senator Vicki Lynn Miles LaGrange Oklahoma City OK 1986. **Honors/Awds:** Eminent Women Phi Delta Kappa Inc Gamma Epsilon Chapter 1985. **Home Addr:** 6600 N Carol Dr, Oklahoma City, OK 73141.

BYRD, CORINE WILLIAMS
Educational administrator. **Personal:** Born May 9, 1946, Tunica County, MS; daughter of Carrie Monday Williams and James Cleveland Williams; married Thomas DuBose (divorced 1987); children: Terryl Lynn, Tee Tamu. **Educ:** Boston State College, Boston, MA, BS, 1971; College Board of Financial Aid Inst, certificate, 1973; Massachusetts Association of Financial Aid Admin, certificate, 1982; Institute for Educational Leadership, certificate, 1990. **Career:** University of Massachusetts at Boston, Boston, MA, assistant director of special admissions, 1971-72, assistant director of student financial aid service, 1973-77, associate director, 1977-79, asst to vc academic affairs, currently; Salem State College, Salem, MA, director of financial aid, 1980-83. **Orgs:** Member, past chair, Massachusetts Board of Regents of Higher Education Financial Advisory Committee; member, College Scholarship Service, New England Regional Council, vice president of Financial Aid Division, Executive Council, 1986-89; member, National Association of Student Financial Aid Administrators; member, chair, Minority Concerns Committee, Massachusetts Association of Financial Aid Administrators; member, Public Assistance/Financial Aid Advisory Group. **Honors/Awds:** Certificate of Appreciation, Salem State College, 1983; Certificate of Appreciation, Office of Student Financial Management, University of Massachusetts at Boston, 1986, OES MVP Award, 1990; Certificate of Appreciation, Massachusetts Association of Student Financial Aid Administrators, 1988, 1989; Bernard Sneed Award for Distinguished Professional Service and Leadership, University of Massachusetts at Boston Alumni Association, 1987; hostess of cable televsion show, College Bound: Funds to Go!. **Home Addr:** 215 Callender St, Dorchester, MA 02124, (617)288-7812.

BYRD, EDWIN R.
Educator. **Personal:** Born Feb 23, 1920, Kansas City, KS; married Dorothy Wordlow; children: Terri E. **Educ:** KS State Teachers Coll, BS; Univ of KS, ME 1950. **Career:** MO School Dist, 1946-81 retired, elementary school teacher 1946-55, jr high school teacher 1955-56, counselor jr & sr high schools 1956-60; Yates Elementary School, principal 1960-61; Dunbar School, principal 1961-63; Richardson School, principal 1963-68; Martin Luther King Jr High School, principal 1968-75; Nowlin Jr High School, principal 1975-. **Orgs:** Mem KC School Admin Assoc, NEA, MO State Teachers Assoc, MO Assoc of School Principals, Natl Assoc School Principals, Phi Delta Kappa, PTA, Amer Legion 149, NAACP, YMCA, Kiwanis Club; institutional rep Boy Scouts; elder Swope Pkwy United Christian Church; mem Alpha Phi Alpha, Rsch Acad of KC, Selective Serv Bd 49; mem adv comm Jr Red Cross; pres Inter-City Kiwanis Club 1983-84; mem Amer Assoc of Retired Persons. **Honors/Awds:** Sigma Pi Phi Outstanding Secondary Educator of Amer 1974; Athletic Serv Awd 1973; PTA Serv Awd 1968; YMCA Serv Awd 1962; Kin Comm Serv Awd 1975; Outstanding Mem Awd Beta Lambda Chap of Alpha Phi Alpha 1979; YMCA Super Quota Buster Awd 1984. **Military Serv:** USAF sgt 1942-46. **Business Addr:** Principal, Kansas City School District, Nowlin Jr HS, 2800 S Hardy, Independence, MO 64052.

BYRD, FREDERICK E.
Attorney, judge (retired). **Personal:** Born Mar 6, 1918, Marvell, AR; married Theresa Dooley; children: 4. **Educ:** Northwestern Univ, BS, BA 1942; Wilson Jr Coll, 1938; Univ of Detroit Law School, JD 1948. **Career:** Traffic Ct, traffic ct 1961-73; Common Pleas Ct Detroit, judge, beginning 1973; attorney, currently. **Orgs:** Mem Michigan Bar Assn, Wolverine Bar Assn, mem NBA; mem NAACP; mem Wayne County & Catholic Social Serv; adv bd Providence Hospital; bd mem Wayne County Mental Health Soc; Detroit Libr Comm. **Home Addr:** 3235 Carter St, Detroit, MI 48206.

BYRD, GEORGE EDWARD
General manager. **Personal:** Born Sep 20, 1941, Troy, NY; son of Louise Collins-Byrd and George Byrd, Sr; married Alice Hill-Byrd, Jul 8, 1967; children: Sharon Collins, George Byrd III, Michael Byrd, Christopher Byrd. **Educ:** Boston Univ, Boston MA, BS 1964; Univ of Michigan, Ann Arbor MI, Exec Mgmt Program, 1980. **Career:** Natl Football League (NFL) Buffalo Bills (NY) 1964-70, Denver Broncos (CO), 1970-72; Chrysler/Plymouth Corp, Atlanta GA sales mgr, New Haven CT, operations mgr, 1973-81; Polariod Corp, Oakbrook IL, regional marketing mgr/regional operations mgr, 1981-86, marketing mgr, 1986-87, gen mgr, 1987-. **Orgs:** Mem, The Partnership. **Honors/Awds:** All-Pro, NFL, Buffalo Bills, 1965, 1966, 1968, 1969; man of the year, African Meeting Houses, 1989. **Business Addr:** Gen Mgr, Polaroid/Inner City, Inc, 716 Columbus Ave, 5th Fl, Boston, MA 02120.

BYRD, HARRIETT ELIZABETH
Former state senator. **Personal:** Born Apr 20, 1926, Cheyenne, WY; daughter of Sudie E Smith and Robert C Rhone; married James W Byrd, 1947; children: Robert C, James W II, Linda C. **Educ:** WV State Coll, BS Educ 1949; Univ of WY, MA Elem Educ 1976. **Career:** Wyoming Educ Assn, Wyoming TEPS Comm 1970-73; Marshall Scholarship Comm, comm mem 1972-79; Wyoming State Adv Council, comm mem 1973-80; NEA Albuquerque, inserv training ctrs 1979; Wyoming State Legislature, House of Representatives, state representative, 1981-89; Wyoming State Senate, senator, 1989-93. **Orgs:** Life mem Kappa Delta Pi; Delta Kappa Gamma; Kappa Kappa Iota; mem Laramie Co Coll Booster Club; adv bd Laramie Co Senior Citizens; past vice pres Laramie Co Democratic Women's Club, pres, 1992-95; mem United Medical Center, Cheynne; Univ of Wyoming Alumni; St Mary's Catholic Church; League of Women Voters; Wyoming State Museum, volunteer; State contact for the State of Wyoming for the Dr Martin Luther King Jr, State and City King Holiday Federal Commission; Love and Charity Club. **Honors/Awds:** Instructor Excellence in Teaching Award Instructor magazine 1968.

BYRD, HELEN P.
Educator. **Personal:** Born Feb 27, 1943, Waynesboro, GA; daughter of Josie C Bessent and Oscar S Bessent (deceased);

married Shedrick; children: Shedrick Tyrone. **Educ:** Warren Wilson Coll, AA 1961; Berea Coll, BA 1963; Temple Univ, MEd 1965; Univ of CT, PhD 1972; Columbia Univ Teachers Coll, Postdoctoral Study 1973, 1976; Long Island Post Campus, 1987. **Career:** School Dist of Philadelphia, teacher 1963-65; Atlanta Public School System, teacher 1966-68; Atlanta State Univ, visiting prof 1968; Savannah GA State Coll, visiting prof 1971; Norfolk State Univ, special educ dept, prof 1968-, head 1977-80. **Orgs:** Governor at large, exec committee, sec, membership chmn MR Div; Comm on Minority Groups, Governor at Large Council for Exceptional Children 1972-78; bd of trustees Boggs Acad 1976-83; mem prog agency board United Presbyterian Church USA 1977-83; bd mem 1976-79, vchmn 1979-80 Norfolk Comm for Improvement of Ed; bd mem Hope House Found 1977-; mem Presbyterian Comm on Minority Educ 1982-; sec 1985, mem 1983-88, vice chmn 1988, Norfolk Comm Serv Bd; bd mem Cultural Experiences Unlimited; Norflolk Public Libraries, board, 1992-. **Honors/Awds:** Scholr Wm H Hess Meml Scholarship Fund 1961; Fellow BEH-USOE Mental Retardation 1965-66; Fellow So Fellowship Fund 1970-72; Grant Recipient BEPD USOE Proj 1972-76; Grant Recipient BEH USOE Proj 1977-80; Education Awd Aurora 60 Order of Eastern Star 1983; Delta Beta Sigma Chapter, Sigma Woman of the Year, 1988; Distinguished Scholar, 1988; Special Olympics Award, 1986. **Business Addr:** Professor, Special Education Dept, Norfolk State University, Norfolk, VA 23504.

BYRD, HERBERT LAWRENCE, JR.
Electrical engineer. **Personal:** Born Oct 21, 1943, Hampton, VA; son of Pearline Singleton and Henry Singleton; married Beverly Ann Ramsuer Byrd, Jan 5, 1966; children: David H II. **Educ:** American Institute of Engineering & Technology, BSEE, 1966; Syracuse University, MSEE, 1975. **Career:** IBM Corp, project manager, 1966-78; Sycom, Inc, president, chief executive officer, 1978-. **Military Serv:** US Air Force, a3c, 1962-65. **Business Phone:** (703)378-6200.

BYRD, ISAAC
Professional football player. **Personal:** Born Nov 11, 1974. **Educ:** Kansas. **Career:** Tennessee Oilers, wide receiver, 1997-. **Business Addr:** Professional Football Player, Tennessee Oilers, c/o Baptist Sports Park, 7640 H 70-5, Nashville, TN 37221.

BYRD, ISAAC, JR.
Judge. **Personal:** Born 1952. **Career:** Mississippi Board of Corrections, former vice chairman; former chancery judge for state of Mississippi, 1989. **Business Addr:** 427 E Fortification, Jackson, MS 39202.

BYRD, JAMES W.
Marshal. **Personal:** Born Oct 22, 1925, Newark, NJ; married Harriett Elizabeth Rhone; children: Robert, James, Linda. **Educ:** Laramie Co Comm Coll. **Career:** Cheyenne Police Dept, 25 Yrs; Hwy Safety State of WY, dir 1975-77; US Marshal KC, 1977. **Orgs:** Life mem VFW Am Legion; Internatl Assn Chfs of Police; WY Peace Officers; IBPO Elks of WY Lawman of Year; Kiwanis Internatl 1968; Served In European Thtr; WW II veteran; Korean War. **Business Addr:** PO Box 768, Cheyenne, WY 82001.

BYRD, JERRY STEWART
Attorney. **Personal:** Born Dec 11, 1935, Greenville, SC; son of Ethel Byrd and Elliott Byrd; married Paula Deborah Aughtry; children: Jerry Stewart Jr. **Educ:** Fisk Univ, BA 1961; Howard Univ, JD 1964; Southeastern Univ, ASBA 1975. **Career:** Natl Labor Relations Bd Regional Adv Branch, atty 1964-65; Neighborhood Legal Serv, managing atty 1965-69 and 1974-81, dep dir 1970-71; Howard Univ, polit sci instructor 1971-72; Superior Ct of DC, hearing commissioner 1981-. **Orgs:** Mem Hearing Comm Bd of Professional Responsibility 1982-85; Special Judges Division of the American Bar Association; Washington and National Bar Association; general secretary, Washington Buddhist Vihara Society, Inc; mem bd dir, Hospitality Comm Fed Credit Union; mem DC Consumer Goods Repair Bd 1974-77. **Honors/Awds:** Publication Parental Immunity in Negligence Actions Abolished, 9 How L J 183 (1963); Courts, Slums and Feasibility of Adopting the Warranty of Fitness The DC Housing Research Comm Report 1967; Important Cases, Thompson v Mazo 421 F 2d 1156, 137 US App DC 221 (1970) rev 245 A2d 122 (DC App 1968); Durmu v Gill 227 A2d 104 (DC App 1970); Coleman v District of Columbia 250 A2d 555 (DC App 1968). **Special Achievements:** Nix vs Watson, RS-650-80R; 18 Family Law Reporter (Nov 12, 1991). **Military Serv:** AUS Sp-4 served 3 years. **Home Addr:** 2110 T St SE, Washington, DC 20020. **Business Addr:** Hearing Commissioner, Superior Court of DC, Chambers 4450, 500 Indiana Ave. NW, Washington, DC 20001.

BYRD, JOAN EDA (JOAN EDA)
Media librarian. **Personal:** Born May 12, 1942, Washington, DC; daughter of Edna Carter (deceased) and Robert Carter (deceased); married Leonard Byrd, Oct 5, 1986; children: Kai-Mariama Byrd (step-daughter). **Educ:** Howard University, BFA, 1965; The Catholic University of America, MLS, 1976; The New School for Social Research, Media Studies Department, MA, 1978. **Career:** DC Public Library, librarian, reference, 1965-76; John Jay College-PPM, mgr, library, 1979-81; Brooklyn Public Library, librarian, reference, 1983-86, asst division chief, a/v division, 1986-88; Donnell Media Center, New York Public Library, acting prin, librarian, film/audio, 1996-. **Orgs:** New York Film/Video Council, 1988-; Black Maria Film/Video Festival, pres, bd of trustees. **Honors/Awds:** NJ State Council on the Arts, Fellowship Award, Photography, 1986; Perkins Center for the Arts, Purchase Award, Photography, 1988. **Special Achievements:** Cover art for 10th anniversary publication of The Color Purple (Alice Walker), 1992; photography-in-performance piece: Friends and Friends II, by Blondell Cummings, 1980; numerous photography exhibitions. **Business Addr:** Supervising Librarian, Donnell Media Center, 20 W 53rd St, New York, NY 10019, (212)621-0675.

BYRD, JOSEPH KEYS
Educational administrator. **Personal:** Born Oct 3, 1953, Meadville, MS. **Educ:** William Carey Coll, BS 1975, MEd 1980. **Career:** William Carey Coll, cnslr/instr 1980-82; Univ of New Orleans, devel specialist cnslr 1981-82; Xavier Univ of LA, gen cnslr 1982-83; Univ of New Orleans, asst dir dev ed 1983-86; Xavier Univ, asst dean student serv 1986-. **Orgs:** Cnslr/tutor coord William Carey Coll 1975-80; exec sec Sigma Lambda Chap Alpha Phi Alpha Frat 1982-; adv Omicron Delta Kappa 1978, Chi Beta Phi 1980; mem NAACP New Orleans LA 1984; president, Greater New Orleans Chapter National Pan-Hellenic Council Inc 1989; president, Louisiana Conference - Alpha Phi Alpha Fraternity Inc; steering committee, Greater New Orleans Foundation; bd of directors, Human Services on Cable. **Honors/Awds:** Outstanding Young Educator William Carey Coll 1981; Distinguished Service Award, Alpha Phi Alpha Fraternity Inc 1989; Advisor of the Year - Student Government, Xavier Univ. **Business Addr:** Asst Dean Student Services, Xavier University, Box 101-C, New Orleans, LA 70125.

BYRD, KATIE W.
Supervisory management analyst. **Personal:** Born Jun 26, Mobile, AL; children: Marcus Dalton, Taynetta Joi. **Educ:** Alabama A&M Univ, BS, MS; Pennsylvania State Univ, PhD. **Career:** Previous positions include tchr educ specialist, counselor, equal oppty officer; US Army Missile Command, supervisory management analyst; University Professor. **Orgs:** Mem Women's Equity Action League; Natl Assn Black Psychologists; Natl Assn Adminstr Counselors & Deans; Pi Lambda Theta; past president Huntsville Br NAACP; Phi Beta Kappa; Maryland Association of University Women; chairperson Social Action-Delta Sigma Theta Sor; mem Women's Political Caucus; state recorder, vice pres Huntsville Chap AL New South Coalition; chair, bod, Harris Home for Children & Community Action Agency. **Honors/Awds:** Equal Employment Opportunity Awd; Outstanding Young Women of Amer; Outstanding Black in Human Services; Good Govt Awd Huntsville Jaycees; Outstanding Leadership Awd; Outstanding Comm Serv Awd; Class Achievement Awd.

BYRD, LUMUS, JR.
Iron company president. **Personal:** Born Apr 25, 1942, Clinton, SC; son of Mary J Byrd and Lumus Byrd Sr. **Educ:** SC State Coll, BS Bio 1965, MS Bio 1969. **Career:** Charleston, SC Sch Dist #20, edctr 1965-70; Jos Schlitz Brewing Co, dist mgr 1970-74; Greyhound Lines, Inc, dir Sls 1974-78; The Greyhound Corp, mgr mkt dev 1978-82; T & T Iron Works, pres, beginning 1989; Byrd Enterprises Inc, pres, chmn, CEO, currently. **Orgs:** Vice pres Natl Asso Mkt Dev 1980; treas Am Mktng Asso 1982; vice pres Phoenix Advertising Club 1984; dir bd Valley Ldrshp Inc 1984; vice pres Alpha Hi Alpha Frat 1985; adv bd YMCA 1985. **Honors/Awds:** Distinguished Alumni SC State Coll 1984; Man of the Yr Alpha Phi Alpha Frat 1983; Outstanding Mtr Toastmasters 1984. **Business Addr:** President, T & T Iron Works, 23108 S Normandie Ave, Torrance, CA 90502.

BYRD, MANFORD, JR.
Educational administrator (retired). **Personal:** Born May 29, 1928, Brewton, AL; son of Evelyn Patton Byrd and Manford Byrd; married Cheri; children: Carl, Bradley, Donald. **Educ:** Central Coll, BA 1949; Atlanta University, MA 1954; Northwestern Univ, PhD, 1978. **Career:** Chicago Public Schools, teacher/principal, asst general supt, deputy supt, general supt, 1985-90; consultant, currently. **Orgs:** Bd of dir, Chicago State Univ Joint Negro Appeal, Chicago State Univ Found, Mid-America Chapter, Amer Red Cross; Sigma Pi Phi (Beta Boule) (Natl Treasurer of Sigma Pi Phi Fraternity, 1980); mem, Natl Alliance of Black School Educators; chmn, Christian Educ, Trinity United Church; mem, Large Unit Dist Assn (LUDA); mem, bd of dir, Council of the Great City Schools; mem, Found for Excellence in Teaching.

BYRD, MELVIN L.
Military officer. **Personal:** Born Nov 1, 1935, Suffolk, VA; son of Lenora Pergram Byrd and Harry A Byrd; married Diane Diggs Byrd, Dec 27, 1968; children: Donna, Melanie, Rosslyn, Melvin Jr. **Educ:** Howard University, BA, 1958; Babson Institute, MBA, 1974; Army War College, 1979-80; Harvard University, 1989. **Career:** US Army, Headquarters Department of Army, Washington, DC, inspector general, 1977-79, deputy director for joint actions, DCSLOG, 1980-81, 82nd Airborne Division, Ft Bragg, NC, division support command, commander, 1981-83, Vint Hill Farms Stations, Warrenton, VA, electronics materiel readiness activity, commander, 1983-86, Heidelberg, Germany, army materiel command, commander, 1986-88, Ft Monmouth, NJ, communications electronics command, deputy commanding general, 1988-. **Orgs:** Armed Forces Communications and Electronics Assn; American Society of Military Comptrollers; Assn of US Army, Ft Monmouth Chapter, board of directors; Society of Logistics Engineers. **Military Serv:** US Army, Brigadier General, 1959-; 2 Legion of Merit awards, 3 Bronze Stars, Air Medal, Army Commendation Medal, 3 Meritorious Service Medals, Distinguished Service Medal. **Home Addr:** PO Box 9068, Alexandria, VA 22304-0068.

BYRD, NELLIE J.
Former alderman. **Personal:** Born Jan 28, 1924, Rayvill, LA; married Leandreu Byrd; children: Bobbie Phillips, Marva Martin, Patricia Jackson, Larry Martin, Willie Martin, Travis Martin, Gerald Martin, Reginald Martin. **Educ:** Chicoh Cty Training School, 1942. **Career:** City of Wrightsville, former alderman 1983-85, planning comm 1985-87. **Orgs:** Treas Esther Chap 384 OES; mem NAACP 1972-85, Natl Assoc of Colored Women Club 1982-85, Privident Relief Club Little Rock AR 1980-85. **Honors/Awds:** 1st fin sec for 1st Bapt Church Wrightsville 1966-74. **Home Addr:** PO Box 2043, Wrightsville, AR 72183.

BYRD, PERCY L.
Company manager. **Personal:** Born Jun 14, 1937, Hogansville, GA; son of Ettarean Philpot Byrd (deceased) and Garland Byrd (deceased); married Irene Stahler, Sep 21, 1977. **Educ:** Morehouse Coll, Atlanta, GA, 1956-59; Savannah State Coll, Savannah, GA, BS (cum laude), 1961. **Career:** US Govt, St Louis, MO, Washington, DC, cartographer, geologist, mathematician, 1965-67; Planning Research Corp, St Louis, MO, San Antonio, TX, Washington, DC, sr tech staff mem, 1967-79, 1984; Sperry Univac, Washington, DC, computer salesperson, 1979-80; Magnavox Data Systems, Washington, DC, sr engineer, 1980-81; District of Columbia Govt, Washington, DC, branch mgr, 1981-83; SAIC, Washington, DC, dir, 1983-84; MAXIMA Corp, Washington, DC, Dayton, OH, Los Angeles, CA, sr vice pres, 1984-. **Orgs:** Bd of dir, treasurer, Black Business Assn of Los Angeles, 1989-90; mem, Los Angeles Urban League, 1987-89. **Military Serv:** AUS, E-4, 1961-64.

BYRD, SHERMAN CLIFTON
Clergyman, former criminal investigator. **Personal:** Born Dec 6, 1928, Mesquite, TX; married Dorothy Barksdale; children: Duane Edward, Dorothy Eleanor, James, Henry, Thomas, Nancy Ellen, Sandra Kay, Johnathan Earl, Joyce Jean. **Educ:** St Philip's Coll, attended 1955-56 & 1966; Guadalupe Coll, B Div, DD 1962; Bible World Christian Univ, ATh. **Career:** San Antonio Police Dept, various positions 1953-62; Bexar County DA's Office, criminal invest 1963-78; cert law enforcement instr; 1st Providence Baptist Church, pastor; Holy Land Museum of the Americas, bd chmn, CEO, founder & president; Guadalupe Baptist Theological Seminary. **Orgs:** Providence Bapt Ch; pres founder United Counc of Civic Action; Christian Action for Prog; TX Bapt Min Union; founder Emancipation Day Commn, 1980; Comm Workers Council 1955; Bexar County Fed Credit Union 1964; coord San Antonio Child Care Assn, vice pres 1963; Non Profit 501C3 Corp, Holy Land of the Americas Inc, founder, 1987. **Honors/Awds:** Author "The Transplant," "God's Plan To Heal Our Land;" est min wage law first city in TX. **Military Serv:** USN 1948-50. **Business Addr:** Organizer & Pastor, 1st Providence Baptist Church, 1014 Clark Ave, San Antonio, TX 78203.

BYRD, TAYLOR
Educator. **Personal:** Born Nov 2, 1940, Greene County, AL; married Katie W; children: Marcus Dalton, Taynetta Joy. **Educ:** Al A&M U, BS 1963; Tuskegee Inst, MEd 1969; PA State U, PhD 1972. **Career:** Agribusiness Educ Dept, AL A&M Univ, Normal AL, chmn 1972-; PA State Univ, grad res asst 1970-72; TN Valley High School, instructor, asst prin 1966-70; Woodson High School, Andalusia AL, instructor, asst coach 1964-66; TN Valley High School, instructor, coach 1963-64; AL A&M Univ, NASA tech. **Orgs:** Evaluator of So Reg Agr Educ Conf Mobile, AL 1973; proj dir Cross-Cultural Skills & 2nterpresonal Effect in Urban Enviroment 1972; mem AVA, AVATA, NVATA, AATE, AEA, NEA, ALEA; mem Consistory #150 32 Mason IBPOE of W. **Honors/Awds:** Student Council Avd Award TN Valley HS 1968; Tchr of Yr TN Valley HS1969; grad research assistantship 1970; Outstanding Achievement in Ed Phi Beta Sigma 1973; Nat Alumni-normalite Assn Class Achievement Award 1973; Citation for Outstanding Contributions to Research Devel, Reg Adaptive Tech Cntr, Honolulu, 1975; appted chmn of Search Co for Dean of Sch of Bus AL A&M Univ 1975. **Business Addr:** Dept of Agr Bus Educ, PO Box AL A&M Univ, Normal, AL.

BYRDSONG, RICKY
College basketball coach. **Career:** Iowa State University, asst basketball coach; Western Michigan University, asst basketball coach; Eastern Illinois University, asst basketball coach; Arizona University, asst basketball coach, six seasons; University of Detroit-Mercy, head coach, 1988-93; Northwestern University, head coach, 1993-. **Business Addr:** Head Basketball Coach, Athletic Dept, Northwestern University, 2129 Sheridan Rd, Evanston, IL 60208-0001, (708)491-3682.

C

CABBELL, EDWARD JOSEPH
Educator. **Personal:** Born Jun 26, 1946, Eckman, WV; son of Cassie Haley King and John Marshall Cabbell; married Madeline Harrell (divorced); children: Melissa Yvette, Winnia Denise. **Educ:** Concord Coll, BS Ed 1970; Appalachian State Univ, MA 1983. **Career:** Upward Bound & Spec Serv for Disadvantaged Students, dir 1969-75; John Henry Folk Fest, dir 1975-; John Henry Records, producer 1978-; Black Diamonds Mag, editor 1978-; Appalachian Studies Concord Coll, adj prof 1984-; John Henry Mem Found Inc, founder, dir; Fairmont State Coll, Fairmont, WV, part-time instructor, history, 1989-. **Orgs:** Advisory comm "We Shall Overcome" Fund Admin Royalties for "We Shall Overcome" Civil Rights Theme 1977; chmn City of Princeton Human Relations Commiss 1977-; pres Neighborhood Improvement Assoc Inc 1982-; advisory comm Folklife Festival 1982 Worlds Fair 1982; bd Council of the Southern Mountains 1984; bd mem Highland Rsch & Educ Center; gov appointee bd mem WV Martin Luther King Jr State Holiday Commiss 1986-; bd mem, Comm on Religion in Appalachia, 1988-. **Honors/Awds:** Writer's Scholarship Breadloaf Writers Conf 1970; Black Studies Fellowship Univ of Louisville 1971; Appalachian Studies Fellowship Berea Coll 1980-81; James Still Fellow in Appalachian Studies Univ of KY 1981; co-editor Black in Appalachia Univ Press of Kentucky 1985; Comtemporary Authors 1987; WEB DuBois Fellow, WV Univ, 1987-89. **Home Addr:** PO Box 1172, Morgantown, WV 26507.

CABELL, ENOS M., JR.
Automobile dealer. **Career:** Cabell Motors, Inc, CEO, currently. **Special Achievements:** Company is ranked number 27 on Black Enterprise's list of Top 100 Auto Dealers, 1994. **Business Addr:** CEO, Cabell Motors Inc, 66730 Gulf Fwy, Houston, TX 77087.

CABRERA, ELOISE J.
Educator. **Personal:** Born Dec 9, 1932, Evinston, FL; daughter of Zebbie & Maude S Johnson (both deceased); married Dr Marion C Cabrera (deceased); children: Yolanda Alicia Cabrera-Liggins. **Educ:** Nova Univ, Educational Leadership, EdD, 1985; Michigan State Univ, Comm Educ; Univ of South FL, Adult Educ; Indiana Univ, Guidance, MS, Educ, 1963; FL A&M Univ, BS, educ, 1954. **Career:** Broward County Sch Syst, elementary teacher, 1954-56; Elem Dept School, US Dependent School Baumholder, Germany, 1956-57; Howard W Black High School, teacher, 1958-63, counselor, 1963-66; Neighborhood Youth Corp, Federal Prog, counselor, 1966-77, asst proj dir, 1966-69; Hills Cty Public Schools, supervisor comm educ prog, 1969-77, principal, Williams Elem, 1977-. **Orgs:** Natl Comm Educ Assn; Am Assn of Univ Women; FL Assn for Comm Edn; bd of dirs; Tampa Urban Leag; FL Adult Educ Assn; NAACP Natl Council of Negro Women; Tampa Alumnae Chap Delta Sigma Theta Sor, May Week and Awards Day, Golden Life Mem, chair, Corr Sec; Orgn for Concerned Parents; Eastern Seal Advisory Bd; Girl Scouts, bd of dirs; Hillsborough Comm Coll Foundation, bd of dirs; St Peter Claver Catholic Church, Parish Council for Sunday Masses, chair as Prayer Team Commentator, recording secy. **Honors/Awds:** Plaque for distn serv to FACE; Boy Scouts Award for Merit Svc; Cert for Outstanding Contribution to Hillsborough Comm Coll Adv Comm; Recognized by Former Gov Bob Graham, Outstanding Educator of Fl; The Golden SABLE Inc, Outstanding Education Award, treasurer; ABWA, Boss of the Year; Rising to the Top Award, Amer Univ Women Assn, Principals, 1990; All Star Education Gala, Outstanding Principal, 1991; Recognition by Williams School, numerous awards; Delta Sigma Theta, Outstanding Leadership Award; FL Atlantic Univ, Outstanding Leadership Award, Community Educ; Featured on the Comm Educ Journal Cover, 1974; Honored by Gov Bob Graham, Outstanding Leadership Award Among Minority Educ; Honored as Parishioner of the month of July, St Peter Claver Church, 1992; Honored as 2nd place winner, Ada S Baker, Distinguished Educ Award, 1993; Honored as Hillsborough Cty Outstanding Elem Principal nominee, The Natl District Principal; numerous other honors. **Business Addr:** Instructional Serv Cntr, 707 E Columbus Dr, Tampa, FL 33602.

CADE, ALFRED JACKAL
Brigadier general. **Personal:** Born Feb 4, 1931, Fayetteville, NC. **Educ:** VA State Coll, BS Gen Psych; Syracuse Univ, MBA Comptrollership; Arty Sch; Quartermaster Sch; AUS Field Arty Sch; AUS Command & Gen Staff Coll;Indsl Coll of Armed Forces. **Career:** Over 25 years active commr svc; asst sector adv 1966-67; Phu Yen Province Vietnam, sector adv 1967; US Milit Command Vietnam, dep sr province adv 1967; Pacific-Vietnam, comdr 1st Battalion 92nd Arty 1967-68; budget operations ofcr 1968-69; Dir of Army Budget Wash, exec ofcr 1970-72; Material Command Wash, DC, asst comptroller for budget 1972; 210th Field Arty Group Europe, comdr 1973-74. **Honors/Awds:** Promoted from 2nd Lt to Brigadier Gen Jan, 1954. **Military Serv:** AUS Brig Gen; Recip Legion of Merit (with 2 Oak Leaf Clusters); Bronze Star Medal (with 3 Oak Leaf Clusters); Meritorious Serv Medal; Air Medal; Army Commend Medal; Combat Infantryman Badge; Parachutist Badge.

CADE, HAROLD EDWARD
Educational administrator. **Personal:** Born Aug 25, 1929, Bonami, LA; married Josephine Lockhart; children: Deryl Vernon. **Educ:** Prairie View A&M Univ, BA 1955, BS 1958; Univ of CO, MA 1960; North TX State Univ, MEd 1967. **Career:** VISD Gross HS, football coach 1960; VISD Victoria/Stroman HS, counselor 1965-; TSTA Dist 3, pres 1975; VISD Patti Welder Jr High, principal 1975-85. **Orgs:** Football coach Lockhart Public Schools 1953; football coach FW Gross 1955-66; counselor Victoria HS 1965-67; asst principal Stroman HS 1967; pres Victoria Kiwanis Club 1975; lt governor Div 25 TX/OK Dist 1977; pres Victoria TSTA 1978. **Honors/Awds:** Pres TX State Teacher Assoc 1967; bd of dir Victoria Chamber of Com 1978; superintendent Palestine Baptist Church SS 1979-85; bd of dir YMCA Victoria 1980-85. **Military Serv:** USMC lt 1954-57. **Business Addr:** Principal, Victoria Public Schools, Patti Welder Jr High, 1500 E North St, Victoria, TX 77901.

CADE, VALARIE SWAIN
Educational administrator. **Personal:** Born Sep 16, 1952, Philadelphia, PA; daughter of Ena Lindner Swain and William Arch Swain; children: Ena Marietta, David Lloyd. **Educ:** Penn State Univ, BA 1973; Temple Univ, MEd 1977, DEd 1978; Univ of PA, Philadelphia Child Guidance Clinic Post-Doctoral Family Therapy 1981; Wharton School Exec Educ Mngmt Prog 1987; Harvard University, IEM 1988. **Career:** PA State Univ, tutor 1971-72, peer counselor 1971-73; School Dist of Philadelphia, teacher language arts 1972-74; Camden Schools, language arts & reading teacher 1974-76; Camden County Comm Coll Learning Skills Ctr, administrator and study skills specialist 1976-77, counselor 1976-77; Dept of Educ, field reader & curriculum consultant 1976-; Rutgers Univ, asst prof of English 1976-78; Univ of PA, psychoeducational specialist 1978-80, asst prof/lecturer 1978-82, faculty master WEB DuBois Coll House 1978-80, asst to vice provost for undergrad studies, dir commonwealth prog 1978-83, asst assoc provost 1983-85, exec asst provost 1985-86, asst provost 1986-88; assistant provost and assistant to the president 1989-91; Cheyney Univ, acting pres, 1991-. **Orgs:** PA coord Tri-State Council on Equal Educ Oppor 1978-81; eastern regional rep ACT-101 Adv Comm 1979-81; pres Mid-Eastern Assoc of Educ Oppor 1983; pres PA Assoc of Educ Oppor 1981-83; bd mem and Mid-Atlantic Regional Pres Emeritus Natl Council of Educ Oppor; exec bd mem Mid-Eastern Assoc of Educ Oppor; mem League of United Latin Amer Citizens Adv Bd; mem Amer Foundation for Negro Affairs Medical Steering Comm; mem National Assn for Educ Opportunity 1988; member, Cornell University Visiting Committee, 1990. **Honors/Awds:** Natl Merit Scholar 1969-73; NAACP Achievement Awd 1969; Dean's List Penn State and Temple Univ 1970-78; Temple Univ Doctoral Fellow 1976-77; Onyx Senior Honor Soc Univ of PA 1979; PA Assoc of Educ Oppor Outstanding Achievement Awd 1983; Temple Univ Russell Conwell Ctr Awd 1983; PA State Univ Achievement Awd 1983; IEM Fellowship, Harvard University 1988; Woman of Color Distinguished Service Award, University of Pennsylvania, 1991. **Business Addr:** Acting President, Cheyney University, Cheyney, PA 19319.

CADE, WALTER, III (ZENBOPWE)
Artist, actor, singer, musician. **Personal:** Born in New York, NY; son of Helen Henderson Brehon and Walter Cade; married. **Educ:** Inst of Modern Art NY; private tchrs Lee Strasberg Sch of Dramatic Arts; Muse Drama Workshop. **Career:** Theatre, "Amen Corner" E River Players Repertory Co; "Hatful of Rain" Muse Drama Workshop; "Mateus" "Harle Quinade" others City Ctr Young Peoples Repertory Theatre; "Mary, Mary" Lexiton & London Barn Dinner Theatre; "Don't Bother Me I Can't Cope" Theatre for the Forgotten; movies, Cotton Comes to Harlem, Education of Sonny Carson, The Wiz, Claudine; TV, Joe Franklin Show, Positively Black, Soul, Sammy Davis Telethon, Musical Chairs, Big Blue Marble; Artist in NY WNYC; Controversy WLIB; singing in various inns in NY, Queens, Long Island, MA, WA; Films: F/X, Angel Heart. **Orgs:** Some exhibitions, CW Post Coll LIU Group Show 1968; Whitney Museum Annual Show 1969; Heckscher Mus Group 1969; Whitney Mus Contemporary Black Artist 1971; Fairleigh Dickinson Coll Group 1971; Corcoran Gallery Group 1972; Automation House Ten Black Artists 1973; Bedford Stuyvesant Restoration Ctr African Art & Afro-Amer Artist 1973; Black Expo 1973; Queens Cultural Ctr for the Arts Queens Talent 1973; Ocean Co Coll One Man Show 1977; Jackson State Univ One Man Show 1980; MS Mus of Art Group Show 1981; Tampa Museum Group Show 1982; Tucson Museum of Art Group Show 1983; three man show, Suffolk Community College, 1987; Lewiston Auburn College, ME: Groupe Show, 1994, Two Person Show, 1993; Olin Museum of Art, Bates College, ME: One Man Show, 1993; The New England Fine Arts Institute, MA: Group Show, 1993; permanent collections, Southeast Banking Corp; Rockefeller Found; Fine Arts Museum of the South; VA Beach Art Museum; Bruce Mus; City of Miami Beach; Peter A Juley & Son Collection, National Museum of Art, Smithsonian Institution. **Honors/Awds:** Best in Show, Bruce Museum, CT, 1994; Award of Merit, Linda Balding Shearer, Curator, Museum of Modern Art, NY, 1986; Award of Distinction, Linda Scheaver, Curator, Guggenbeim Museum, NY, 1981; Best In Show, Lloyd Herman, Curator, Renwich Gallery, Smithsonian Institute, Washington DC, 1981; Best in Show, Willaim S Lieberman, Director, 20th Century Art, Metro Museum of Art, NY, 1980; Best in Show, Dr Douglas Lewis, Curator, National Gallery of Art, Washington DC, 1980; Award of Distinction, Thomas W Leavitt, Former Director, National Endowment for the Arts Museum Prog, 1979; Best In Show, Dorothy C Miller, Former Curator, Museum of Modern Art, NY, 1979; Best In Show, Barbara Haskell, Curator Whitney Museum, NY 1978.

CADOGAN, MARJORIE A.
Attorney. **Personal:** Born Dec 11, 1960, New York, NY; daughter of Doreen Leacock Cadogan and George Cadogan. **Educ:** Fordham University, BA, 1982, JD, 1985. **Career:** New York City Law Department, assistant corp counsel, 1985-90; New York City Loft Board, counsel, 1990-91; New York City Department of Parks & Recreation, general counsel, 1991-95; Primary Care Dev Corp, dir of external affairs, currently. **Orgs:** Association of Black Women Attorneys, treasurer, 1991-93, vp, 1993-; American Bar Association, 1985-. **Honors/Awds:** New York City Bar Association, Outstanding Assistant Corp Counsel, 1990; Fordham University School of Law, Robert B McKay Advocacy Award, 1985. **Business Addr:** Director of External Affairs, Primary Care Development Corp, 291 Broadway, 17th Fl, New York, NY 10007, (212)693-1850.

CADORIA, SHERIAN GRACE
Military officer (retired). **Personal:** Born Jan 26, 1940, Marksville, LA; daughter of Bernice McGlory Cadoria and Joseph Cadoria. **Educ:** Southern Univ, BS, Business Educ, 1961; AUS Command & General Staff Coll, Diploma, 1971; Univ of Oklahoma, MA, Human Relations, 1974; AUS War Coll, Diploma, 1979; Natl Defense Univ, Inst of Higher Defense Studies, 1985. **Career:** Women's Army Corps Sch & Ctr, instructor/human relations ofcr 1971-73; Women's Army Corps Branch, US Army Military Personnel Ctr, exec officer/personnel officer 1973-75; Law Enforcement Div Officer of the Deputy Chief of Staff for Personnel Headquarters Dept of the Army, personnel staff officer 1975-76; Military Police Student Battalion, battalion commander 1977-78; Physical Security Div US Army Europe & 7th Army, division chief 1979-82; 1st Region Criminal Invest Command, brigade commander 1982-84; Dept of the Army, chief, Office of Army Law Enforcement 1984-85; Pentagon Organization of the Joint Chiefs of Staff, dir of manpower & personnel (Brigadier General) 1985-; US Total Army Personnel Command, deputy commander/dir for mobilization & operations 1987-90. **Orgs:** LA Association for Developmental Education, honorary member; WAC Veterans Assn 1980-. **Honors/Awds:** Social Aide to the President of the United States 1975-76; Distinguished Alumni Award Southern University 1984; One of Amers Top 100 Black Bus & Professional Women 1985; Distinguished Serv Medal, Hoffstra Univ 1986; Intl Black Woman of the Year, Los Angeles Sentinel 1987; one of 75 Black Women who helped change history in the I Dream A World photo exhibit in Corcoran Gallery, USA West/Life Magazine 1989; Roy Wilkens Meritorious Service Award, NAACP 1989; LA Black History Hall of Fame 1992; Honorary Doctors of Humane Letters, Ohio Dominican College 1992, Illinois Benedictine College, 1993. **Military Serv:** AUS Brigadier General (served 29 yrs); Legion of Merit, 3 Bronze Stars, 2 Meritorious Serv Medals, Air Medal, 4 Army Commendation Medals; Distinguished Service Medal; Defense Superior Serv Medal. **Business Addr:** Cadoria Speaker Service, 322 Azalea Ln, Pineville, LA 71360-4780.

CAESAR, LOIS
Musician, educator. **Personal:** Born Apr 4, 1922, Texarkana, AR; married Richard C. **Educ:** Wiley Coll, AB; State Univ IA, MA; State Univ of IA, MFA. **Career:** Europe & Am, concert pianist 1949-66; Paris, France debut Salle Gaveau 1950; Town Hall, NY Debut 1950; Fisk U, asst prof 1943-49; TN State U, artist in residence 1955-56; Monsieru & Ciampi, Paris repetitrice 1951-53. **Orgs:** Bd dir SF Symphony Found 1st black 1965-75; SF Symphony Assn 1st Black bd govs 1969-; SF Spring Opera 1st Black exec bd 1969-; SF Grand Jurists1972; 10 Outstanding Citizens judge 1972; Mayor's Crim Just Council 1st Black Woman exec bd 1974-; Juvenile Justice Commn 1st black 1st Woman 1st Minoritychmn 1976-78; SF WATF pres; SF Women's Aux Dental Soc 1st Black pres 1977; No State Dental Wives 1st Black pres-elect 1977; SF Links; NAACP life mem; Nat Newsletter of the Auxiliary Am Dental Assn chmn & Editory 1979; SF Bay Area United Way 1st Black exec bd. **Honors/Awds:** First Black Recipient Thomas Jefferson Award for Public Serv Am Inst 1978; 6 Best Dressed Awards; 4 Outst Comm Svc, Incl 1 From City & Co of SF.

CAESAR, SHIRLEY
Singer, evangelist. **Personal:** Born in Durham, NC; married Bishop Harold I Williams. **Educ:** Shaw Univ, Business Mgmt 1984. **Career:** Joined Caravan Singers 1958; Shirley Caesar Outreach Ministries, opened to aid needy families in Durham NC 1969; recorded 30 albums; travels throughout the US singing to crowds of 8,000 to 35,000 people; Mt Calvary Holy Church Winston-Salem, co-pastor, pastor; The Shirley Caesar Outreach Ministries Inc, pres, currently; album: A Miracle in Harlem, 1997. **Orgs:** Active in various community & civic affairs; visits hosps regularly, sr citizen homes & schools; each yr she spends thousands of dollars buying food to feed the

needy; host for the Gospel music indust; hon mem bd of dirs Divinity Sch Shaw Univ 1984; spokeswoman McDonald's Salute to Gospel Music 1987. **Honors/Awds:** Grammy Awd for "Put Your Hand in the Hand of the Man From Galilee" 1972; several songs that sold over a million copies incl "No Charge", "Don't Drive Your Mother Away"; named Best Female Gospel Singer Ebony Magazine 1975; proclamation Oct and Nov as Shirley Caesar's Months in Durham NC 1978; performed at the WhiteHouse for Jimmy Carter 1979; Dr Martin Luther King Jr Drum Major Awd; Top Female Gospel Singer in the Country Ebony Mag Music Poll 1977; Stellar Awd by Peers in Gospel Music Industry 1987; 5 Grammy Awds; 3 Gold Albums. **Business Addr:** President, The Shirley Caesar Outreach Ministries Inc, P O Box 3336, Durham, NC 27702.

CAFFEY, JASON ANDRE
Professional basketball player. **Personal:** Born Jun 12, 1973, Mobile, AL. **Educ:** Alabama. **Career:** Chicago Bulls, forward, 1995-98; Golden State Warriors, 1998-. **Special Achievements:** NBA Draft, First round pick, #20, 1995. **Business Addr:** Professional Basketball Player, Golden State Warriors, 1001 Broadway, Oakland, CA 94607, (510)986-2200.

CAFRITZ, PEGGY COOPER
Television executive. **Personal:** Born Apr 7, 1947, Mobile, AL; daughter of Gladys Mouton Cooper and Algernon Johnson Cooper; married Conrad Cafritz, Dec 21, 1981; children: Zachary Cooper. **Educ:** George Washington U, BA 1968; Nat Law Center George Washington U, JD 1971; Woodrow Wilson Intl Center for Scholars, fellow 1972. **Career:** Post-Newsweek Stations Inc, special asst to pres; The Ellington HS of Fine & Performing Arts Washington DC, founder & developer 1968-; St for People Study to Plan Redevel of Pub Spaces in Downtown Washington, Washington project dir; Trustee Amer Film Inst, independent consult 1970-73; DC Arts Commn, exec comm chmn 1969-74; WETA, Channel 26, Washington, DC, arts critic, 1986-. **Orgs:** Mem DC Bar 1972; mem exec com DC Bd of Higher Educ 1973; Arts Educ & Amer Natl Panel 1975-; exec bd 1980-86, planning comm 1986-, mem Natl Assembly of State Art Agencies 1979-; mem bd of trustees Atlanta Univ 1983-86; mem Washington Performing Arts Soc 1983-; bd of dirs PEN/Faulkner Foundation 1985-88; mem Natl Jazz Serv Org 1985-; bd of trustees Kennedy Ctr for the Performing Arts 1987; bd mem Women's Campaign Fund 1987; chair, Smithsonian Cultural Education Committee, 1989-; co-chair, Smithsonian Cultural Equity Subcommittee, 1988-. **Honors/Awds:** Woodrow Wilson Intl Ctr for Scholars 1971; Presidents Medal Catholic Univ for Outstanding Comm Serv 1974; New York Black Film Festival Awd 1976; 27th Annual Broadcast Media Awd Aspen Inst Alvin Brown Fellow 1977; George Foster Peabody Award for Excellence in TV public affairs prod 1976; finalist Natl Emmy Award 1977; John D Rockefeller Intl Youth Award; Washingtonian of the Yr; Woman of the Yr Mademoiselle Magazine; named to President Clinton's Committee on the Arts and Humanities, 1994. **Home Addr:** 3030 Chain Bridge Rd NW, Washington, DC 20016.

CAGE, MICHAEL JEROME
Professional basketball player. **Personal:** Born Jan 28, 1962, West Memphis, AR; married Jodi; children: Alexis, Michael Jerome Jr. **Educ:** San Diego State Univ, 1980-84. **Career:** Los Angeles Clippers, 1984-88; Seattle SuperSonics, 1988-94; Cleveland Cavaliers, 1994-96; Philadelphia 76ers, 1996-97; New Jersey Nets, 1997-. **Orgs:** Pres, Fellowship of Christian Athletes. **Honors/Awds:** Named Western Athl Conf Player of the Year; second team All-Amer as voted by AP, UPI and Baksetball Weekly; UPI West Coast Player of the Year; Dist Eight selection by US Baksetball Writers; Sports Illustrated's collegiate Player of the Week for period ending Feb 13, 1984; was invited to a US Olympic Team tryouts; led NBA, rebounding, 1988. **Special Achievements:** NBA Draft, First round pick, #14, 1984. **Business Addr:** Professional Basketball Player, New Jersey Nets, Brendan Byrne Arena, 405 Murray Hill Pkwy, East Rutherford, NJ 07073, (201)935-8888.

CAGE, PATRICK B.
Attorney. **Personal:** Born Aug 11, 1958, Chicago, IL; son of Gwendolyn Monroe and Thomas Cage. **Educ:** Illinois State University, BS; Ohio Northern University, JD, 1984. **Career:** City of Chicago, sr attorney, corp counsel, 1985-88; French, Kezelis & Kominiarek, sr associate, 1988-. **Orgs:** Cook County Bar Association, 1984-; American Bar Association, 1984-; Illinois State Bar Association, 1984-; Chicago Bar Association, 1984-; Alpha Phi Alpha, 1978-. **Honors/Awds:** Alpha Phi Alpha, Broker of Year Award, 1979. **Home Addr:** 345 W Fullerton Pkwy, Chicago, IL 60614.

CAGGINS, RUTH PORTER
Educator. **Personal:** Born Jul 11, 1945, Natchez, MS; daughter of Corinne Baines Porter and Henry Chapelle Porter; married Don Randolph Caggins, Jul 1, 1978; children: Elva Rene, Don Randolph Jr, Myles Chapelle. **Educ:** Dillard University, BSN, 1967; New York University, MA, 1973; Texas Woman's University, PhD, 1992. **Career:** Montefiore Hospital & Medical Center, staff & head nurse, 1968-71; Lincoln Comm Mental Health Center, staff nurse & therapist, 1972-73; Metropolitan Hospital & Med Center, nurse clin & clin adm sup, 1973-76; University of Southwestern Louisiana, assistant professor, 1976-78; Prairie View A&M University, associate professor, tenured, 1978-. **Orgs:** Prairie View A&M Univ College of Nursing, LIFT Center project dir, 1994; A K Rice Institute, associate member, Central States Center, 1992-93, general member, Texas Center, 1992-93; Association of Black Nursing Faculty, program chair, 1993 Spring Regional; National Black Nurses Association; Sigma Theta Tau, 1973-93; American Nurses Association; National League for Nursing; Houston Association of Psychiatric Nurses. **Honors/Awds:** Prairie View A&M University, New Achievers Award, 1992; Association of Black Nursing Faculty, Dissertation Award, 1990; Prairie View A&M College of Nursing, Distinguished Faculty Award, 1990; American Nurses Association, Minority Fellowship, 1989-92. **Special Achievements:** Author of: The Caggins Synergy Nursing Model, ABNF Journal, 2(1), pp 15-18, 1991, Professional Cohesiveness Among Registered Nurses (dissertation sent to Dissertations Abstracts Intern), 1992; Violence prevention Grant, US Dept of Health & Human Services, Office of Minority Health, 1997-2000; Urban Family Life Ctr, Prairie View A&M University, College of Nursing, director of clinical research, 1997-2000. **Home Addr:** 5602 Goettee Circle, Houston, TX 77091, (713)956-1885. **Business Addr:** Associate Professor, Prairie View A&M University, College of Nursing, 6436 Fannin St, 9th Fl, Houston, TX 77091, (713)797-7000.

CAHILL, CLYDE S., JR.
Judge. **Personal:** Born Apr 9, 1923, St Louis, MO; married Thelma Newsom; children: Linda Diggs, Marina, Valerian, Randall, Kevin, Myron. **Educ:** Sch of Arts & Sci St Louis U, BS1949; Law Sch St Louis U, JD 1951. **Career:** City of St Louis, asst cir atty 1954-66; Office of Econ Oppor, reg atty 1966-68; Human Devel Corp, genl mgr 1968-72; Legal Aid Soc, genl counsel & dir 1972-75; St Louis Univ Law Sch, lecturer 1974-79; State of MO, circuit judge 1975-80; US District Court for the Eastern District of MO, dist judge 1980-. **Orgs:** Dir St Louis Urban League 1974; dir Met Y 1975-; dir Comprehensive Health Cntr 1975; dir Cardinal Ritter HS 1978; mem Met St Louis Bar Assn; St Louis Lawyers Assn; Mound City Bar; Am Bar Assn; Nat Bar Assn; Am Judicature Soc. **Honors/Awds:** NAACP Disting Serv Awd; St Louis Argus Awd. **Military Serv:** USAF. **Business Addr:** District Judge, Eastern District of MO, 1114 Market St, St Louis, MO 63101.

CAILLIER, JAMES ALLEN
Educational Administrator. **Personal:** Born Sep 24, 1940, Lafayette, LA; married Geraldine Elizabeth Raphael; children: Jennifer, Gerard, Sylvia. **Educ:** Univ of Southwestern LA, BS 1964; So U, MS 1968; LA State U, EdD 1978. **Career:** Univ of Southwestern LA, dean/prof jr div 1975-, dir/prof 1970-; Public Schools, Lafayette LA, supvr 1967-69, teacher 1964-67; US Office of Educ, natl field reader 1972-77, natl consultant 1974; Commr Lafayette Harbor Term & Indsl 1975-. **Orgs:** Bd of dirs Lafayette Chamber of Commerce 1975-; Nat Sci Found Grant 1966-68. **Honors/Awds:** Outstanding Young Businessmen of America; American Legion Honor Award; Pacesetter Award for Exemplary Presidential/CEO Leadership. **Business Addr:** System President, State Office Bldg, 150 Third St, 3rd fl, Baton Rouge, LA 70801.

CAIN, FRANK
Government official (retired). **Personal:** Born Sep 30, 1930, Mocksville, NC; son of Ella Florence Eaton Cain and Arthur Reece Cain; divorced; children: DiShon Franklin. **Educ:** A&T State Univ, BS 1956, MS 1967; Attended, NC State Univ, Univ of OK. **Career:** NC Agr Ext Svc, asst co agent 1957-62; USDA-FmHA, asst co sup 1962-66, co sup 1966-85. **Orgs:** Mem Black & Minority Employee Organization, NC Assoc of County Supervisors; chmn trustee bd, bldg fund Chinquepin Grove Baptist Church; mem Prince Hall Grand Lodge F&A Masons of NC; past pres of Alamance Co Chap A&T State Univ Alumni. **Honors/Awds:** Certificate of Appreciation Human Rights Comm 1981; Certificate of Merit USDA-FmHA 1977,82; first black FmHA supvr in State of NC. **Military Serv:** AUS spec E-4 1953-55; Natl Defense Service Medal, Good Conduct Medal, Letter of Commendation. **Home Addr:** 857 Dewitt Dr, Mebane, NC 27302.

CAIN, FRANK EDWARD, JR.
Attorney. **Personal:** Born Feb 1, 1924, Blenheim, SC; married Dollie M Covington; children: Cherryetta, Anthony. **Educ:** SC State Coll, BA; SC State Coll, LlB 1951. **Career:** Bennettsville, SC, atty priv prac; Kollock Elem Sch Wallace SC, tchr 1653-55. **Orgs:** Mem SC Bar Assn; SC State Bar; SC Black Lawyers Caucus; Marlboro Co Bar; past & Polemarch Cheraw Alumni Chapt; Kappa Alpha Psi Frat; Sr Warden Sawmill Masonic Lodge #375; vice pres Marlboro Co Br NAACP; past comm Am Legion Post 213; admitted to prac US Dist Ct for Dist of SC; US Ct of Appeals. **Honors/Awds:** Pres W Bennettsvl Precinct Dem Party, Marlboro Co; Legal Adv to Reg of Local Bd No 34 Selec Serv Sys 1972; Recip Cert in Dist Educ SC Dept of Educ 1966; cert of Achievement Kappa Alpha Psi Frat 1966; Listed in SC Lives 1962; comm ldrs of Am 1969. **Military Serv:** AUS Signal Corps corpl 1943-46. **Business Addr:** 203 W Market St, Bennettsville, SC 29512.

CAIN, GERRY RONALD
Market research company executive. **Personal:** Born Dec 12, 1961, Ft Bragg, NC; son of Katherine Edmonds Cain and Moses Cain. **Educ:** Bowie State Coll, attended 1980; Prince George's Comm Coll, AA 1981-82; Univ of KS, BS Journalism 1983-85. **Career:** Freelance Researcher Consultant 1985-86; Mellwood Medical Labs, marketing rep 1985-86; Bernstien-Rein Advertising, analyst, marketing research dept 1985-89; TIP Market Research, Kansas City, MO, owner 1989-. **Orgs:** Mem KUAD Club /Advertising Federation of America 1984-85; mem Natl Assoc of Black Journalists 1985-86; mem Univ of KS Alumni Assoc 1985-; mem, American Marketing Assn (Kansas City Chapter) 1988-; group leader, Sickle Cellers Always Networking, KC 1989-; committee member, Communications Committee, AMA, KCMO. **Honors/Awds:** Urban Journalism Workshop Recipient Univ of KS 1977; Clyde & Betty Read Scholarship Recipient Univ of KS 1983-84; Lucile Bluford Scholarship Recipient 1984-85.

CAIN, HERMAN
Restaurant executive. **Personal:** Born Dec 13, 1945, Memphis, TN; son of Lenora Cain and Luther Cain; married Gloria Cain; children: Melanie, Vincent. **Educ:** Morehouse College, Atlanta, GA, BS, 1967; Purdue University, Lafayette, IN, MS, computer science, 1971. **Career:** The Pillsbury Company, Minneapolis, MN, vice pres/corporate systems & services, 1977-82; Burger King Corporation, Philadelphia, PA, regional vice president, 1982-86; Godfather's Pizza Inc, Omaha, NE, president, 1986-88, president/CEO, 1988-96, chairman of the bd, 1996-. **Orgs:** Bd mem, Federal Reserve Bank of Kansas City, 1992-96; pres/chmn of the bd, National Restaurant Association, 1994-95; bd mem, Creighton University, 1989-95; board member, Super Value Inc, 1990-; board member, Utilicorp United Inc, 1992-; board member, Whirlpool Corp., 1992-; bd mem, Nabisco Inc, 1995. **Honors/Awds:** Honorary Doctorate, Morehouse College, 1988; Honorary Doctorate, Tougaloo College, 1989; Honorary Doctorate, University of Nebraska, 1990; Top 25 Black Executives, Black Enterprise, 1988; Entrepreneur of the Year, University of Nebraska, 1990; Operator of the Year/Gold Plate Award, International Foodservice Manufacturers Association, 1991; Hon Doctorate, NY Technical Coll, 1995; Hon Doctorate, Johnson & Wales Univ, 1996; Hon Doctorate, Creighton Univ, 1997. **Business Addr:** Chairman of the Board, Godfather's Pizza Inc, 9140 W Dodge Rd, Omaha, NE 68114.

CAIN, JOHNNIE M.
Educator. **Personal:** Born Jul 27, 1940, Shreveport, LA; married James O; children: Merion Edward, Nicole Rowlett, Phyllis Yevette. **Educ:** Univ Maryland, BA 1964; Northern CO, MA 1964; Univ AZ & Univ NC, grad work. **Career:** Douglas Pur System, English teacher 1968-; ITT Hamiliton Corp, sales 1972; Cochise Co Hosp, nurse asst 1970-71; NC, home sch & social worker 1966; Am Dept Sch, kindergarten teacher 1964-65; AZ Informant, newswriter-rep; working toward PhD Child Care & Clinical Psychology; freelance poet writer poems appeard in 13 anthologies Harlo Young Poets, Man When Born of Fire, Clover Book of Verse, Insearch of the Museum & others. **Orgs:** Only black woman mem Douglas Phi Delta Kappa; mem Poets's Study Club; Poetry Symposium Black Intl Writers Org Chicago; Natl Educ Assn; Douglas EdnAssn; Upward Bound coordinator Cochise Coll Advisory Bd of Upward Bound; mem Youth City Cncl Douglas Lecturd Black Writers Conf 1973; conducted Black Writers Workshop Urban League Phoenix Oct 1974. **Honors/Awds:** Two poetry awards Clover Poetry Assn 1972-74; published two books "Poetrydo You Remember", "White Bastards", presently Celesterial Arts considering vol Poetry for publication; Northwoods Publication, Accepted vol poetry, publication Feb 1975. **Business Addr:** Douglas High School, 1500 15 St, Douglas, AZ 85607.

CAIN, JOSEPH HARRISON, JR.
Professional football player. **Personal:** Born Jun 11, 1965, Los Angeles, CA; children: Ayana, Joseph III. **Educ:** Oregon Tech. **Career:** Seattle Seahawks, linebacker, 1989-92, 1997-; Chicago Bears, 1993-96. **Business Addr:** Professional Football Player, Seattle Seahawks, 11220 NE 53rd St, Kirkland, WA 98033, (206)827-9777.

CAIN, LESTER JAMES, JR.
Educator. **Personal:** Born Mar 24, 1937, Pittsburgh, PA; son of LeGertha Prince Cain and Lester James Cain Sr; children: Stephanie Lynn. **Educ:** US Armed Forces Inst, Certificate 1962; Connelly Skill Learning Ctr, GED 1977. **Career:** Operation Dig Pittsburgh Plan, field supervisor 1971-72, dir field super 1972-74; Univ of Pittsburgh, admin specialist 1977-. **Orgs:** Mem Pittsburgh Branch NAACP 1971-; bd mem Homewood-Brushton Revitalization & Devel 1983-; bd mem Homewood-Brushton Comm Improvement Assoc Inc 1984-. **Honors/Awds:** Airco Tech Inst of Pittsburgh Certificate of Achievement 1978; Community Serv Awd East Hills Park 1983; Contributions to Educ Pittsburgh Public Schools 1984; Recruitment Awd Pittsburgh Branch NAACP 1985; United Negro College Fund Certificate of Appreciation 1985; Distinguished Leadership Awd UNCF Pittsburgh 1986; Univ of Louisville Certificate of Training 1986; Univ of Louisville Black Family in Amer Conference Continuing Studies Certificate 1986; Associates Program Joint Center for Political Studies 1986. **Military**

Serv: AUS E3 1960-66; Honorable Discharge. **Business Addr:** Administrative Specialist, University of Pittsburgh, 3814 Forbes Ave, Pittsburgh, PA 15260.

CAIN, NATHANIEL Z., JR.
Automobile dealer. **Personal:** Born Feb 1, 1946, Gary, IN; son of Evelyn Carr (deceased) and Nathaniel Z Cain Sr; married Jacqueline Weaver Cain, May 26, 1970; children: Fredrick, Jeffrey, Natalie. **Educ:** Purdue Northwest, attended, 1969-70. **Career:** Mad Hatter Rest & Show Lounge, owner, 1976-81; Bart Allen Buick, gen manager, 1982-85; Chuck White Buick, gen manager, 1985-86; Tyson Motor Corp, vice pres, 1986-; Tyson Lincoln Mercury, president & gen manager, 1989-; Tyson Ford, president/CEO, 1996-; Melrose Lincoln Mercury Inc, co-owner/VP, 1997-. **Orgs:** Ford Lincoln Mercury Minority Dealers Association, 1989; Chrysler Minority Dealers Association, 1986; NAMAD, 1990; NADA, 1986; Indiana Chamber of Commerce, 1989; Highland Chamber of Commerce, 1989; Northwest Indiana Auto Dealers Association, 1989; Boys & Girls Clubs of America, bd of dirs; Gary YWCA, bd of trustees; NW Ind Urban League, bd of dirs; Gary Mental Hth Assn, bd of dirs. **Honors/Awds:** 100 Champions Club (top 100 Lincoln Mercury Dealers), 1996. **Special Achievements:** Company is ranked #77 on Black Enterprise magazine's 1997 list of Top 100 Black businesses. **Military Serv:** US Marine Corps, cpl, 1963-67, 2 Vietnam campaign ribbons, good conduct medal. **Home Phone:** (219)985-9621. **Business Addr:** President & CEO, Tyson Lincoln Mercury Inc, 2440 45th St, Highland, IN 46322.

CAIN, ROBERT R., JR.
Attorney. **Personal:** Born Mar 2, 1944, Chicago, IL; married Azucena Becerril; children: Azucena II, Lisa, Carla, Paula. **Educ:** Univ of Nebraska, BS, 1977; Northern Colorado, MA, 1978; Natl Univ, MBA, 1986, JD, 1995. **Career:** US Government Services, 1962-82; Superior Care Inc, clinic dir, 1982-86; Northeast Clinical Care Services, chief exec officer. 1986-88; Cain Enterprises, CEO, currently. **Orgs:** Scottish Rite Mason Shriner 32 degree Mason, 1976-86; Alpha Phi Alpha, 1982. **Military Serv:** US Navy, W-3, 20 yrs; Vietnam Service Medal. **Business Addr:** Chief Executive Officer, Cain Enterprises, PO Box 1486, Bonita, CA 91908.

CAIN, SIMON LAWRENCE
Attorney. **Personal:** Born Dec 19, 1927, Augusta, GA; married Ada Spence. **Educ:** Howard U, BA 1949, LlB 1956. **Career:** Attorney. **Orgs:** Mem Wash Bar Assn, Am Bar Assn, Nat Bar Assn, DC Bar Assn; pres Lamond-Riggs Citizen Assn 1968-70; pres DC Fedn of Civic Assn 1969-71; chmn highways & transp Palisades Citizens Assn 1974. **Honors/Awds:** Recipient Korean/United Nations 3 Battle Stars USAF 1950. **Military Serv:** USAF lt col 26 Yrs Served. **Business Addr:** 1621 New Hampshire Ave NW, Washington, DC 20009.

CAIN, WALDO
Surgeon. **Personal:** Born Sep 29, 1921, Gadsden, AL; son of Evelyn Croft and James L Cain; married Natalia; children: Sheila, Anita. **Educ:** Meharry Med Coll, MD 1945. **Career:** Cain-Tanner Asso, pres, SW Detroit Hosp, chf surg; Wayne State U, associate prof of surgery; Meharry Med Coll, clinical assistant prof of surg 1946-52; Cain-Wood Surgical Assoc, pres. **Orgs:** Fndr First Independence Nat Bank Detroit; life mem NAACP; mem Am Coll Surgeons; Soc Military Surgeons; State MI Judicial Tenure Commn Physician Yr Detroit Med Soc 1969; Detroit Academy of Surgery. **Military Serv:** AUS MC capt 1953-55. **Business Addr:** President, Cain-Wood Surgical Assoc, 4160 John R Road, Detroit, MI 48201.

CAINES, BRUCE STUART
Photographer. **Personal:** Born Jan 7, 1959, Jamaica, NY; son of Inez & David Caines; married Lisa Bernad-Caines, May 1994. **Educ:** School of Visual Arts, BFA, photography, 1981. **Career:** Photographer, currently. **Orgs:** Black Women in Publishing, 1994-; New York Cares, volunteer, 1990-. **Special Achievements:** Our Common Ground, Portraits of Blacks Changing the Face of America, Crown Publishers, 1994; Our Common Ground, Natl Photography Exhibit, Art Institute of Chicago, 1994-95; Contributing Photographer For Jazziz Magazine, LA Style, Essence, Emerge, Newsweek, Philadelphia Inquirer, Sunday Magazine.

CAINES, KEN
Management consultant. **Personal:** Born Sep 22, 1926, New York, NY; son of Monica Caines and Clarence Caines; married Jo Caines, Jun 17, 1950; children: K Christopher, Clarke A, Leslie Jo. **Educ:** New York University, BS, psychology & sociology, 1954; California State College, Los Angeles, experimental psychology, 1964-66; University of California, Los Angeles, management, 1967-68, Irvine, urban planning, 1969. **Career:** TRW Systems, human factors specialist, data systems lab, 1959-60; ITT-Kellogg, supervisor, human factors, communication system, 1960-61; McDonnell Douglas Corp., program manager, skybolt division, 1961-62; Thioko 1-Humetrics, staff scientist, engineering psychology department, 1962-63; Planning Research Corp., human factors specialist, 1963-67; Serendipity, Inc, marketing manager, western division, 1967-68; JOKEN-Human Factors Consultants, director, 1967-74; POS Associates, director, 1969-; University of California, Irvine, lecturer, systems methodology, 1971-72; City of Orange, planning commissioner, 1973-76; American Telecommunications Corp., manager, human resources, 1977-79. **Orgs:** Institute of Electrical & Electronic Engineers, 1967-; Association of Professional Consultants, board of directors, 1984-; American Management Association, 1985-; Human Factors Society, board of directors, 1985-90. **Military Serv:** US Air Force, aviation cadet, 1944-46. **Home Addr:** 1792 N Winlock St, Orange, CA 92665.

CAISON, THELMA JANN
Physician. **Personal:** Born Apr 26, 1950, Brooklyn, NY. **Educ:** Winston-Salem State Univ, BS 1972; State Univ of NY at Buffalo Sch of Med, MD 1977. **Career:** Bd of Educ NYC, biol tchr 1972-73; Harlem Hosp Med Ctr NY, med externship trauma surgery & surgical ICU 1974, med externship obstet & gyn 1975; Downstate Med Ctr Kings Co Hosp Ctr NY, summer med externship in internal med 1976; Montefiore Hosp Med Ctr & N Central Bronx Hosp, physician 1977-83; Henry Ford Hosp Dept of Pediatrics/Div of Adolescent Medicine, division head 1983-. **Orgs:** Mem AMA 1970-80; mem Natl Med Assn 1979-80; mem Com for Residents & Interns 1979-80; mem State Univ of NY at Buffalo/Sch of Med Alumni Assn; mem Delta Sigma Theta Natl Sor; mem Winston-Salem Univ Alumni Assn. **Honors/Awds:** Med Scholastic Hon State Univ of NY at Buffalo Sch of Med 1973-77; Pride in Heritage Awd in field of med Phi Delta Kappa Natl Sor 1978; guest speaker seminar in hypertension & nutrition Phi Delta Kappa Sor 1979; accomplished pianist. **Business Addr:** Henry Ford Hosp, 2799 W Grand Blvd, Dept of Pediatrics, Detroit, MI 48202.

CALBERT, ROOSEVELT
Government official. **Personal:** Born Nov 13, 1931, Philadelphia, MS; son of Ann Calbert and Jim Calbert; married Thelma Nichols; children: Debra C Brown, Jacquelyn C Smith, Rosalyn C Groce, Lori A. **Educ:** Jackson State Univ, BS (Summa Cum Laude) 1954; Univ of Michigan, MA 1960; Univ of Kansas, PhD 1971. **Career:** Alcorn State Univ, physics prof 1960-63; AL State Univ, math & physics coord 1963-68; Univ of KS, rsch asst 1969-71; Inst for Services to Educ, dir coop academic planning 1971-75; Natl Sci Foundation, program dir. **Orgs:** Mem Phi Beta Sigma Frat 1951-; mem Alpha Kappa Mu Natl Honorary Soc 1952-; founder Heritage Fellowship Church 1978; bd chmn Community Investors Corp 1982-; mem AAAS 1984-. **Honors/Awds:** Distinguished Alumnus Awd Jackson State Univ 1986. **Home Addr:** 11331 French Horn Lane, Reston, VA 22091.

CALBERT, WILLIAM EDWARD, SR.
Clergyman. **Personal:** Born Jun 11, 1918, Lemoore, CA; son of Sadie Emma Hackett Calbert (deceased) and William Riley Calbert (deceased); married Katie Rose Baker, Sep 11, 1942 (deceased); children: William (deceased), Rose M Findley, Muriel L, Katherine E Jackson, Yvonne A; married Madlyn G. Williams, Jun 15, 1963; children: William E, Jr. **Educ:** SF State Coll CA, AB 1949; American Baptist Seminary of the West, Berkeley, MDiv 1952; Tchrs Coll Columbia U, MA 1963; Amer Univ, Washington DC, Post Grad Stdy 1970-71. **Career:** US Army, enlisted and warrant officer service, 1942-46, US, Far East, Germany, unit & org chpln 1952-62; Concord Baptist Church Brooklyn, NY, dir chrstn educ part-time 1964-67; US Army Chpln Sch, Brklyn NY, staff & fclty 1963-67; US Army Cmds, Vietnam, stf chpln/dep Stf 1967-68; Hq 1st US Army, Ft Meade MD, asst Army chpln 1968-69; Far East Comm Srvs Anti-Pvrty Agncy, DC, asst dir/exec dir 1970-73; St Elizabeths Hosp, DC, stf chpln 1973-81; Shiloh Bptst Church, mnstr educ Washington, DC, 1981-85; Interim Dir, Chaplaincy & Pastorial Counselling Serv, Amer Baptist Churches, USA, Valley Forge, PA 1986-1987; Shiloh Baptist Church, Washington, DC, pulpit assistant, 1987-. **Orgs:** Membership committee, Association of Mental Health Clergy, 1988-90; member, State Advisory Council on Adult Education, Washington, DC, 1990-93; board member, Housing Devlopment Corp., DC, 1972-76; mem, DC Mayor's Health Planning Advisory Committee, 1972-77; pres, Amer Baptist Seminary of the West, Alumni Assn, Eastern Region, 1989-93, international pres, 1990-92, seminary trustee, 1990-92; past trustee & exec comm mem, Natl Military Chaplains Assn, past pres of Washington DC Chapter; Natl Trustee Board, 1996-99; Comm Mental Health Center, No 2, advisory bd. **Honors/Awds:** Certificate of Appreciation, DC Government, 1973; Superior Performance Award, St Elizabeth's Hospital, Wash, DC, 1981; Certificate of Commendation, American Baptist Churches, 1987; American Baptist Seminary of the West, Alumnus of the Year, 1996. **Military Serv:** US Army, Lt Col, 1942-46, 1952-69; 15 military awards & decorations including the Meritorious Service Medal 1969, Letter of Appreciation, US Army Chief of Chaplains, 1969. **Home Addr:** 1261 Kearney St NE, Washington, DC 20017-4022.

CALDWELL, ADRIAN BERNARD
Professional basketball player. **Personal:** Born Jul 4, 1966, Falls County, TX. **Educ:** Navarro College, Corsicana, TX, 1984-86; Southern Methodist Univ, Dallas, TX, 1986-87; Lamar Univ, Beaumont, TX, 1987-89. **Career:** Houston Rockets, 1989-91; Shamp Clear Cantu (Italy), 1991-93; Sioux Falls Skyforce (CBA), 1993-95; Houston Rockets, 1994; Indiana Pacers, 1995-96; Philadelphia 76ers, 1996-. **Business Addr:** Professional Basketball Player, Philadelphia 76ers, Broad St & Pattison Ave, Veterans Stadium, Philadelphia, PA 19148, (215)339-7600.

CALDWELL, BENJAMIN
Playwright. **Personal:** Born Sep 24, 1937, New York, NY. **Career:** Free-lance writer. **Honors/Awds:** Guggenheim fellowship for playwriting, 1970; author of Prayer Meeting; or, The First Militant Minister, New American Library, 1970; author of "What Is Going On," produced in New York City, 1973; author of "The World of Ben Caldwell," produced in New York City, 1982. **Business Addr:** P O Box 656, Morningside Station, New York, NY 10026.

CALDWELL, EDWIN L., JR.
Agency executive (retired). **Personal:** Born Mar 6, 1935, Durham, NC; son of Pearl Meritt Caldwell and Edwin Caldwell, Sr; married Eva Holmes, Dec 11, 1960 (divorced); children: Stacey Caldwell Thompson, Edwin Caldwell, III. **Educ:** Hampton Inst, Hampton, VA, BS, 1952-57; Univ of NC, Chapel Hill, govt exec, 1980-96, completion of requirements. **Career:** Orange-Chatham Comprehensive Health Serv Inc, asst dir 1972-78; Beaunit Fibers Research, chemist, 1968-72; Monsanto, Research Tri Park NC, Chemist, 1963-68; Delafield Hospital, Columbia Univ, asst supr, biochemist, 1957-63; North Carolina Housing Finance Agency, deputy executive director, 1978-. **Orgs:** Bd organizer Citizens Triangle United Bank; bd dir Chapel Hill Tennis Club; State Adv Council Title IV Programs; bd dir NC School Board Assn; chmn, school bd, Chapel Hill Carrboro School Bd, 1981-83; chmn, Chapel Hill Housing Advisory Bd, 1987-89. **Honors/Awds:** Citizens of the year, Masonic Lodge, Kappa Frat, 1982-87; WTVD-TV, Citizen of the Year, 1989. **Military Serv:** US Army, Sp4, 1958-60.

CALDWELL, ESLY SAMUEL, II
Physician. **Personal:** Born Sep 25, 1938, Lancaster, SC; married Judith Mary Slining; children: Esly II, Christina C, Robert S. **Educ:** Howard Univ, Coll of Liberal Arts BS 1960, Coll of Medicine MD 1964; University of MI Sch of Public Health, MPH 1979. **Career:** Daugherty Medical Group, physician, currently. **Honors/Awds:** Fellow Royal College Physician of Canada; Fellow, American Academy of Family Physicians; Fellow American College of Physicians. **Military Serv:** AUS Medical Group capt 2 yrs. **Business Addr:** Daugherty Medical Group, 629 Oak St, Ste 503, Cincinnati, OH 45206.

CALDWELL, GEORGE THERON, SR.
City official. **Personal:** Born Jun 5, 1939, Mississippi County, AR; son of Mary Alice Warren and Harry Larnell Caldwell; married Jacqueline Romaine Hinch; children: Darri Alice, Jacqueline Michelle, George T II, Robert L, Richard D, Marilynn Kitt, Felecia, Terry, Delores S, Pammela, Shelly Murphy. **Educ:** Gen Coll, Univ of MN, AA 1972; Coll of Liberal Arts, Honors Div, Univ of MN, BA (magna cum laude) 1976. **Career:** Affirmative Action Dept, County of Hennepin, rsch analyst 1973-76, asst dir 1976-80; Dept of Civil Rights, City of Minneapolis, exec dir 1980-84; Minnesota Valley Transportation Co Inc SW, owner 1984-86; Univ of Minnesota, asst dir EO/AA 1986-91, human resources administrator, 1991-97; deputy dir, Department of Civil Rights, City of Minneapolis, Minneapolis Public Schools, 1997-. **Orgs:** Bd of dirs Minneapolis Branch NAACP 1976-77; bd of dirs Benjamin E Mays Fundamental School 1977-81; trustee Mt Olivet Baptist Church 1978-80; chmn Intergovtl Compliance Inst 1978-81; pres MN State Affirmative Action Assoc 1979-80; founder/directorate MN Soc for Open Comm 1983. **Honors/Awds:** NACo New Co Achievement Award, Natl Assn of Counties, 1977; Outstanding Leadership Award, MN Affirmative Action Assn, 1982; Proclamation GTC Day, City of Minneapolis, 1984; Citation of Honor, Hennepin County Bd of Commissioners. 1984; co-owner of one of the first black-owned railroads in US history, Minnesota Valley Transportation Co Inc, Southwest; featured in Ebony magazine, July 1984, and in Black Enterprise, June 1984, The Top 100 Black Businesses. **Military Serv:** AUS spec 5/E-5 1958-64; Good Conduct Medal (1st & 2nd award); Seventh Army Citation Outstanding Soldier 1962. **Home Addr:** 2421 Germain St, St Paul, MN 55109.

CALDWELL, JAMES E.
Attorney. **Personal:** Born May 22, 1930, Louisville, KY; son of Emmie Lou Caldwell and George Caldwell; married Dolores Robinson; children: Janelle, James, Randall. **Educ:** Univ Of Pittsburgh, AB 1952; ROTC Univ of Pittsburgh, grad 1952; Howard Univ Sch of Law, JD 1958; Univ of Chicago, MBA 1973. **Career:** Standard Oil Co, tax counsel 1971-84; Amoco Oil Co, tax atty 1970-71; Chief Counsel's Office & IRS, sr trial atty 1959-70; Gen Counsel US Treasury Dept, Honor Law Graduate Program 1959; Caldwell & Black, 1984-; Chicago Board of Appeals, vice chairman. **Orgs:** Mem, joint bd of trustees St Anne's & St Elizabeth Hospital; pres, Roseland Economic Devel Corp; mem bd of mgrs Chicago Bar Assn 1973-75; Chicago Bar Assn 1975-77; mem Cook Co Bar Assn; Nat Bar Assn; mem IL Bar, Supreme Ct, US Bar; mem bd dirs, Univ of Chicago Club XP Program MBA; alumni Grad Sch of Business, Univ of Chicago; mem bd trustees CBA Pension Fund; mem bd

dirs CAM Health Trust; Commr Supreme Ct of IL; CLEO, pres. **Military Serv:** US Army, Colonel, 1952-81; Commendation Medal, UN Medal. **Business Addr:** 180 W Washington, Suite 300, Chicago, IL 60602.

CALDWELL, JAMES L.
Collegiate football coach. **Personal:** Born Jan 16, 1955, Beloit, WI; son of Mary Evelyn Caldwell and Willie Caldwell; married Cheryl Lynn Johnson Caldwell, Mar 19, 1977; children: Jimmy, Jermaine, Jared, Natalie. **Educ:** University of Iowa, BA, English, 1977. **Career:** University of Iowa, graduate assistant; Southern Illinois University, football coach, defensive backs, defensive coordinator, 1978-81; Northwestern University, football coach, defensive backs, 1981-82; University of Colorado, football coach, outside linebackers, quarterbacks, 1982-85; University of Louisville, football coach, defensive backs, 1985; Pennsylvania State, football coach, quarterbacks, passing game, 1986-92; Wake Forest University, head football coach, currently. **Orgs:** Kappa Alpha Psi Fraternity Inc; Omicron Delta Kappa. **Business Addr:** Head Football Coach, Wake Forest University, Athletic Center, Pruitt Football Complex, Wingate Dr, PO Box 7268, Winston-Salem, NC 27109, (919)759-5796.

CALDWELL, JOHN EDWARD
Life underwriter. **Personal:** Born Feb 10, 1937, Newberry, SC; married Patricia Henderson; children: Sean Edward. **Educ:** Benedict Coll, BS 1965. **Career:** Newberry Co Memorial Hosp, trustee 1970-80, chmn of trustee bd 1980-82; Newberry Co Council, councilman 1982-86, councilman 1987-91; Independent Life and Accident Ins Co, staff sales mgr. **Orgs:** Bd mem Newberry Co Task Force for Educ 1982-87; bd mem United Way of the Midlands 1983-86; bd mem Central Midlands Human Resources 1983-87; Newberry Co Coord for the United Negro Coll Fund 1983-87; bd mem Newberry Co Vocational Educ 1984-87; bd mem Piedmont Area Occupational Training 1986-. **Honors/Awds:** First Black elected to Newberry County Council 1983; Outstanding Alumni Newberry County Alumni Club 1985; Natl Sales Awd Independent Life & Accident Co Inc7 yrs; President's Club Independent Life & Accident Ins Co 8 yrs; First and only black staff mgr for Independent Life and Accident Ins Co. **Military Serv:** AUS sp/4 1960-62; Outstanding Trainee. **Home Addr:** 711 McSwain St, Newberry, SC 29108. **Business Addr:** Staff Sales Mgr, Independent Life/Accident Ins, 211 Montague, Greenwood, SC 29646.

CALDWELL, LISA JEFFRIES
Attorney. **Personal:** Born Jan 14, 1961, Burlington, NC; daughter of Pauline Jeffries and Roy Jeffries; married Alan Lorenzo Caldwell, Jun 23, 1984; children: Tyler Alan, Lauren Brianna. **Educ:** University of North Carolina, Chapel Hill, BS, business administration, 1983; Wake Forest University, School of Law, JD, 1986. **Career:** Womble Carlyle Sandridge & Rice, attorney, 1986-90; West & Banks, attorney, 1990-91; RJ Reynolds Tobacco Co, mgr, employment practices, 1991-93, personnel mgr, Manufacturing Operations, 1993-94; personnel mgr, Eng Environmental/Support, Distribution/Logistics, 1994-96, director of engineering, distribution & logistics & leaf operations, 1996-. **Orgs:** Delta Sigma Theta Sorority, 1988-; The Moles, Inc, constitution committee co-chair, corresponding secretary, 1991-93, recording secretary, 1996-; UNC General Alumni Association, board of directors, 1990-93; Forsyth Co Morehead Scholarship Selection Committee, 1988-93; Goodwill Inc, board of directors, 1995-; Reynolds Federation Credit Union, board of directors, 1995-; West Central Region, Morehead selection comm, 1994-; The Safe Passage group, bd of dirs, 1997-; Hospice, bd of dirs, 1998-; CERTL, bd of dirs, 1997-. **Honors/Awds:** Morehead Foundation, Morehead Scholarship, 1979-83; National Achievement Scholarship, 1979-83; Wake Forest University, Wake Forest Law Scholar, 1983-86. **Business Addr:** Director, Engineering, Distribution & Logistics, Leaf Operations, RJ Reynolds Tobacco Co, 401 N Main St, Bldg 611-16, 1st Fl, PO Box 2959, Winston-Salem, NC 27102, (910)741-7041.

CALDWELL, M. MILFORD
Educator. **Personal:** Born Feb 20, 1928, South Carolina; married Mazie Hammond. **Educ:** SC State Coll, BS 1949; SC State Coll, MS 1950; OH State U, PhD 1959; OH State U, Post Doctoral Fellow. **Career:** DE State Coll, prof of educ; Elizabeth City State Univ, prof of educ 1961-62; OH State Univ, asst prof of educ 1959-61. **Orgs:** Pres Assn of Coll & Sch of Educ in State Univ & Land-Grant Colls; past pres DE Acad of Sci; mem Am Assn of Higher Edn; gov comm of Vocational Edn; mem Century Club YMCA; NAACP; Notary Public; Phi Alpha Theta; Gamma Sigma Delta; Phi Delta Kappa. **Military Serv:** USAF. **Business Addr:** Delaware State College, 1200 N Dupont Hwy, Dover, DE 19901.

CALDWELL, MARION MILFORD, JR.
Educator. **Personal:** Born Mar 11, 1952, San Antonio, TX; son of Mazie Hammond Caldwell (deceased) and Marion Milford Caldwell (deceased); married Priscilla Robertson; children: Priscilla Marina. **Educ:** Delaware State Coll, BS 1978; Univ of the District of Columbia, MBA 1983; Howard University, Doctoral Student, 1995-. **Career:** Delaware Tech Comm Coll, instructor of Business 1984; Delaware State Coll, prof of mktg 1984-91. **Orgs:** Mem Omega Psi Phi Inc 1971-, Prince Hall Mason Prudence Lodge #6 1980-, Amer Mktg Assoc 1981-, Natl Black MBA Assoc Inc 1986-, MBA Exec Inc 1986-; mem NAACP; rep Faculty Senate; Intl Platform Assn; Prudence Lodge #6F&AM, PHA; Speech Communication Association, 1995. **Honors/Awds:** DE State Coll State Scholarship Award 1971; Omega Psi Phi Inc Psi Epsilon Chapter Service Award 1980; Certificate of Recognition for Service, Delaware State College, 1989, 1990; Certificate of Appreciation, 18th Annual Office Education Leadership Conference, Delaware State College, 1986. **Business Addr:** Doctoral Student, Howard University, School of Communications, C P Powell Bldg, Washington, DC 20059.

CALDWELL, MIKE ISIAH
Professional football player. **Personal:** Born Aug 31, 1971, Oak Ridge, TN. **Educ:** Middle Tennessee State, bachelor's degree in business administration, 1996. **Career:** Cleveland Browns, linebacker, 1993-95; Baltimore Ravens, 1996; Arizona Cardinals, 1997-. **Business Addr:** Professional Football Player, Arizona Cardinals, 8701 S Hardy, Tempe, AZ 85284, (602)379-0101.

CALDWELL, ROSSIE JUANITA BROWER
Educator, librarian (retired). **Personal:** Born Nov 4, 1917, Columbia, SC; daughter of Henrietta Irby Brower and Reverend Rossie Lee Brower; married Dr. Harlowe Evans Caldwell, Aug 6, 1943 (deceased); children: Rossie Laverne Caldwell-Jenkins. **Educ:** Claflin College, Orangeburg, SC, AB, 1937; South Carolina State, Orangeburg, SC, MSEd, 1952; University of Illinois, Urbana, IL, MSLS, 1959; Columbia University, New York, NY, 1961; Duquesne University, Pittsburgh, PA, 1965. **Career:** Reed St High School, teacher/librarian, 1937-39; Emmett Scott High School, teacher/librarian, 1939-1942; Wilkinson High School, teacher/librarian, 1942-43; Tuskegee Army Air Field, clerk, stenographer, 1943-45; Wilkinson High School, librarian, 1945-57; South Carolina State College, library science educator, 1957-83. **Orgs:** Sunlight Community Club; As You Like It Bridge Club; life member, NAACP; life member, Veterans of Foreign Wars Aux; Links Inc; Daughters of Isis; Palmetto Education Assn, 1937-62; South Carolina Education Assn, 1962-83; continuing mem, American Library Assn, 1948-; Alpha Beta Alpha; American Assn of University Professors; American Assn of University Women Editors; Phi Delta Kappa; former state pres, Palmetto Medical Dental Pharmaceutical Auxiliary (PMDPA); former Basileus Alpha Kappa Alpha Sorority Inc; life member, undergraduate library science adviser, South Carolina Library Assn, honorary life mem; Archousa, Sigma Pi Phi; communications coord, Trinity United Methodist; found, Forerunners club; co-found, Golden Scholarship Club. **Honors/Awds:** Beta Phi Mu International Library Science Honorary Fraternity, 1959-; Magna Cum Laude, Claflin College, 1937; University of Illinois Founder Forerunners and Co-Founder Golden Scholarship Club; Black College Hall of Fame, 1991; Claflin Coll Alumni, Honoree of the Year, 1994, Hall of Fame, 1997; Heritage Club Honoree, 1997. **Home Addr:** 1320 Ward Lane, Orangeburg, SC 29118.

CALDWELL, SANDRA ISHMAEL
Dentist. **Personal:** Born Aug 23, 1948, Fort Knox, KY; children: Rhonda. **Educ:** Howard Univ, BS 1971; Howard Univ Coll of Dentistry, DDS 1981. **Career:** Food & Drug Admin, microbiologist 1971-77; Ton Ron Productions, vice pres 1985-; Private practice, dentist 1991-. **Orgs:** Mem Natl Dental Assoc, Acad General Dentistry, Beta Kappa Chi Honor Soc, Prince George's Soc of Health Profls, Sigma Xi Scientific Rsch Soc; co-chair,secty Robert T Freeman Dental Soc; mem co-chair Delta Sigma Theta Sor Inc; dental alumni recruiter Howard Univ; mem Minority Women in Science. **Honors/Awds:** Natl Health Serv Corp Scholarship 1978; Delta Sigma Theta Scholarship 1978; Outstanding Young Women of Amer 1980; Who's Who Among Students in Amer Univs & Colls 1981. **Home Addr:** 101 Prospect Dr, Upper Marlboro, MD 20772.

CALHOUN, CALVIN LEE
Educator. **Personal:** Born Jan 7, 1927, Atlanta, GA; married Evelyn; children: Calvin Jr. **Educ:** Morehouse Coll, BS 1948; Atlanta U, MS 1950; Meharry Med Coll, MD 1960; GW Hubbard Hosp, internship 1960-61; GW Hubbard Hosp, residency 1961-62; Univ MN, neurology residency 1962-65; Univ MN, NIH rsrch fellow 1965-66. **Career:** Hubbard Hosp, prof, anatomy, neurology emeritus, 1991-; Meharry Med Coll, prof of medicine, 1973-91, prof of anatomy, 1972-91, prof 1966-72; Meharry, assc prof 1968-71; prof chmn 1971; Meharry Med Coll, chief 1966; Hubbard Hosp, dir 1966; Meharry, asst prof 1961-62; Meharry, instr 1951-57; Morehouse Coll, instr 1950-51. **Orgs:** Mem Am Acad of Neurology; Nat Med Assn; AAAS; Am Assn of Anatomists; TN Med Assn; volunteer State Med Assn; Am Assn of Univ Profs Am Assn of Dental Schs; Assn of Univ Profs of Neurology; Assn of Anatomy Dept; NY Acad of Scis; fellow Stroke Council Am Heart Assn; mem TN Anatomical Bd; bddir Nashville-Davidson Co Chap Am Nat Red Cross; So Soc of Anatomists Alpha Omega Alpha; Beta Kappa Chi; vis prof Univ W Indies Med Sch 1975; resource Consult Elem Curriculum MN City Schs 1965-66;team Physician MN HS 1965; mem professional adv bd Epilepsy Found of Am; deacon 1st Bapt Ch; Am Men Of Sci 1967. **Military Serv:** AUS pvt 1945. **Business Addr:** 1005 18th Ave N, Nashville, TN 37200.

CALHOUN, CECELIA C.
Educator, nurse. **Personal:** Born Sep 22, 1922, New Roads, LA; daughter of Celesea Christopher and Elie Christopher; married Noah R Calhoun; children: Stephen, Marc, Cecelia Noel Calhoun Wells. **Educ:** Southern Univ, BS 1944; Catholic Univ, BS NEd 1950; Univ of Chicago, MS 1953; The Catholic Univ of Amer Washington DC, grad work in psychiatric nursing 1962. **Career:** VA Med Ctr, staff nurse, head nurse, supr, rsch nurse, skin integrity, nursing instr 1950-. **Orgs:** Consultant Life Styles for Wellness; participant Catholic Renewal Prog. President, Alpha Wives District of Columbia. **Honors/Awds:** Pi Lambda Theta Univ Women of Higher Ed Univ of Chicago 1950; Incentive Awds for Work Improvement with VA 1960; board JB Nursing Home; Recognition as Woman of Culture 1974; Friend & Volunteer of the Kennedy Ctr 1974; AKA Sorority; Alpha Wives of Washington; Sigma Theta Tau Nurses Hon Soc. **Business Addr:** Nursing Instructor, Veterans Admin Medical Center, 50 Irving St NW, Washington, DC 20422.

CALHOUN, DOROTHY EUNICE
Administrator (retired). **Personal:** Born Jul 16, 1936, Salitpa, AL; daughter of Maggie Cunningham Jackson and Joshua Jackson; married Roosevelt Calhoun, Apr 11, 1969; children: Michael W Moore, Daryl T Moore. **Educ:** AL State U, BS 1957; Atlanta U, MLS 1972; Auburn U, 1973. **Career:** Clarke Co Bd of Educ, tchr 1957-59; Mntgmry Co Bd of Educ, tchr-Lbrn 1959-70; Maxwell AFB, AL, lbrn 1970-94, chief, cataloging section, currently. **Orgs:** Mem Amer Library Assn 1970-85, AL Lbry Assn 1979-83, NEA 1959-70, Delta Sigma Theta Sor; Special Libraries Assn 1986-. **Honors/Awds:** 2 Sustained Superior Awrds USAF 1971-84; Lbrn of Yr ATC Cmd 1980; Tchr of Yr Clarke Co Bd of Educ 1958; Ten Year Cert of Serv USAF 1980; Theses, A Study of the Jr High Sch Lbry Fclts & Svcs, Atlanta Univ 1972; Twenty Years Certificate of Service 1970-90, Outstanding Award 1989, United States Air Force. **Home Addr:** 2937 Alta Rd, Montgomery, AL 36110. **Business Addr:** Chief Cataloging Section, Air University Library, AUL/LSF, Bldg 1405, Maxwell AFB, AL 36112-6424.

CALHOUN, ERIC A.
Government official. **Personal:** Born Nov 20, 1950, Gary, IN; son of Lillian B Calhoun and William Calhoun; married Delores Brown Calhoun, Apr 22, 1983; children: Asha D Calhoun. **Educ:** Wilberforce Univ, Wilberforce, OH, BS, Accounting, 1974; Kentucky State Univ, Frankfor, KY, MPA, 1982; Miles Law School, Fairfield, AL, Juris Doctorate (cum laude), 1989. **Career:** Central State Univ, Wilberforce, OH, admin, 1972-78; Wendy's Intl, Dayton, OH, store co-mgr, 1978-79; Kentucky State Univ, Frankfort, KY, admin, 1979-83; Miles Coll, Fairfield, AL, admin, 1983-85; City of Birmingham, Birmingham, AL, admin analyst, 1985-87; Mayor's Office, Birmingham, AL, admin asst, 1987-90, admin analyst 1990-. **Orgs:** Mem, Drug Abuse Task Force, Bethel Baptist Church, 1989-; UAB Special Studies Advisory Committee of Black Professionals, 1989-. **Honors/Awds:** Deans List, 1987. **Business Addr:** Admin Analyst to the Mayor, City of Birmingham, 710 N 20th Street, Birmingham, AL 35203.

CALHOUN, FRED STEVERSON
Educator. **Personal:** Born Mar 20, 1947, McDonough, GA; son of Mattie W Calhoun and Willie M Calhoun (deceased); married M Janice Wright. **Educ:** Fullerton College, 1965-66; Cypress College, AA, 1971; University of California, Irvi ne, BA, social ecology, 1973; California State University, Long Beach, MA, psychology, 1977; Nova University, EdD, 1989. **Career:** Cypress Coll, Student Educational Development Center, work study jobs and recruitment coordinator 1968-71; UC Irvine/Social Ecology Dept, research asst 1971-73; Corbin Center, asst coordinator 1973; Cypress Coll, Student Educational Development Center, asst dir 1973-79, dir 1979-. **Orgs:** North Orange County Community Coll Affirmative Action Task Force; Cypress Coll Affirmative Action Comm, North Orange County Comm Coll District; Mgmt Group, North Orange County Comm Coll District; EOPS Advisory Comm, Cypress Coll; Extended Opportunities Programs and Services Assn. **Honors/Awds:** Ford Foundation Upper Division Scholarship for Outstanding Minority Students, 1971; United States Army "Old Guard"; voted co-captain, Cypress College football team, 1968; Certificate of Merit, Mentoring Program, 1991; developed and implemented a Cooperative Agencies Resources for Education, CARE, Program, designed for single parent college students, 1992; North Orange County Comm Coll Bd of Trustees 1988; Devel Summer Readiness Program for pre-college students, 1980, scholarship program 1980, English as a second language conversational groups, 1981, Adult Literacy Program, 1987, and implemented classes in self-concept, 1987, developed the Mentoring Program, 1991. **Military Serv:** US Army, sergeant, 1966-68; Good Conduct Medal. **Business Addr:** Dir, Student Educ Devt Ctr, Cypress College, 9200 Valley View St, Cypress, CA 90630.

CALHOUN, GREGORY BERNARD
Entrepreneur. **Personal:** Born Sep 10, 1952, Detroit, MI; son of Coretta Calhoun and Thomas Calhoun; married Verlyn Pressley; children: Malcolm, Shakenya, Gregory. **Educ:** Trenholm Junior College, 1973; Cornell University, 1979. **Career:** Hudson & Thompson Supermarkets, package clerk, 1970-71, stock

clerk, 1972-73, assistant manager, 1973-75, co-manager, 1975-79, manager, 1979-82, public relations director, 1982-84; Calhoun Enterprises Inc, president, chief executive officer, currently. **Orgs:** Food Marketing Inst, bd mem, 1994-; Sterling Bank, board member, 1990-; Montgomery Area Chamber of Commerce, board member; Tuskegee Savings and Loan, board member; Montgomery Area Lions Club; Hot 105 Radio, board member; IGA Inc, executive roundtable; Sickle Cell Anemia Foundation, president, board of directors; Montgomery Area Committee of 100, board member. **Honors/Awds:** US Department of Commerce, National Minority Retailer of the Year, 1990, Regional Minority Retailer of the Year, 1990; SCLC, Progressive Junior Collegian, 1989, Annual Leadership Award, 1987; MLK Foundation, Entrepreneur Dreamer Award, 1988; Governor of Alabama, Mar 24, "Greg Calhoun Day", Honoree, 1992. **Military Serv:** US Army, sgt, 1971-72. **Business Addr:** President, Chief Executive Officer, Calhoun Enterprises, Inc, 810 W South Blvd, #B, Montgomery, AL 36105-3019, (205)272-4400.

CALHOUN, JACK JOHNSON, JR.

Jail administrator. **Personal:** Born Sep 5, 1938, Canton, OH; son of Jessie Mae Calhoun and Jack Johnson Calhoun Sr; married Constance Butler, Jun 2, 1979; children: Jack III, Leslie A, Lisa J, Rayetta J. **Educ:** Central State, Wilberforce, OH, 1956-58; Kent State, Kent, OH, 1988-89. **Career:** Republic Steel, Canton, OH, security guard, 1966-69; Canton Police Dept, Canton, OH, patrolman, 1969-79; Stark County Sheriff, Canton, OH, deputy sheriff, 1979-81; sergeant, 1981-85; lieutenant, 1985-90, captain, 1990-. **Orgs:** Mem Buckeye Sheriff, 1979-; mem Amer Jail Assn, 1986-; mem Ohio Correctional Court Serv Assn (OCCSA) 1986-; consultant, TANO, State of Ohio, 1987-; pres Ebony Police Assn of Stark County, 1983-89; Natl Black Police Assn, 1983-; Fraternal Order of Police, 1969-; National Organization of Black Law Enforcement Executives, 1990-; Central Mental Health, board of trustees, Canton Chamber of Commerce; American Corrections Association. **Honors/Awds:** Stark County Amateur Baseball Hall of Fame, 1989. **Military Serv:** AUS SP 4 1961-1965. **Business Addr:** Jail Administrator, Stark County Sheriff Department, 4500 Atlantic Blvd NE, Canton, OH 44705.

CALHOUN, JOSHUA WESLEY

Psychiatrist. **Personal:** Born Mar 21, 1956, Macon, GA; son of Harriett Hixon Williams and E M Calhoun (deceased); married Deloris Davis, Dec 21, 1981; children: Joshua W II, Amanda Joy. **Educ:** Yale Univ, BA 1978; Univ of Cincinnati, MD 1982. **Career:** Cincinnati General Hosp, medical internship 1982-83; MA Mental Health Ctr, resident in psychiatry 1983-87, chief resident in child psychiatry 1986-87; Harvard Medical School, clinical fellow in psychiatry; St Louis University Medical School, clinical instructor, 1987-; Private Practice, 1990-. **Orgs:** Adolescent Task Force 1986-87; consultant, Annie Malone Children's Home 1988-90; consultant, Children's Center for Behavioral Development, 1987-90; American Psychiatric Association; American Academy of Child Psychiatry; Black Psychiatrists of America; American Medical Association. **Honors/Awds:** Fellow Amer Psychiatric Assoc, Natl Institute of Mental Health 1983-86; editorial bd Jefferson Journal of Psychiatry 1985-87. **Home Addr:** 239 Westgate Ave, St Louis, MO 63130-4709. **Business Addr:** Director of Child/Adolescent Psychiatry, St John's Mercy Medical Ctr, 615 S New Ballas Rd, St Louis, MO 63141.

CALHOUN, LILLIAN SCOTT

Business executive. **Personal:** Born in Savannah, GA; daughter of Laura McDowell Scott and Walter S Scott; married Harold; children: Laura, Harold Jr, Walter, Karen. **Educ:** Ohio St U, BA. **Career:** Ebony-Jet Mag, assoc editor 1961-63; Chicago Daily Defender, feature editor, columnist 1963-65; Chicago Sun-Times, reporter 1965-68; Integrated Educ: Race & Schools, managing editor 1968-71; Chicago Journalism Rev, columnist 1969-74; Black Forum WLS-AM Radio, consultant, program moderator 1969-74; US Dept of Labor, information officer, dir Chicago regional information office 1971-73; The Chicago Reporter, co-editor 1973-76; WGN-TV "Issues Unlimited", semi-regular participant 1974-76; US Dept of Labor, writer-editor 1976-77; "The Business of Rights," Crain's Chicago Business, columnist 1978-80; "Matter of Opinion" WBBM-AM Radio, commentator 1979-80; Calmar Communications Inc, founder, pres 1978-. **Orgs:** Member Governor's Commn on Status of Women 1965-67; Governor's Advisory Council on Manpower 1973-75; past bd member Oppor Cntrs; Woman's Bd, Chicago Urban League; Hyde Park Coop Society; Amer Civil Liberties Union; Erikson Inst For Early Educ; mem Alpha Kappa Alpha; Alpha Gamma Pi; Society of Midland Authors; Chicago Press Club; Publicity Club of Chicago; Arts Club of Chicago; life member NAACP; member, bd of trustees, Chicago Educ TV Assn (WTTW-TV). **Honors/Awds:** Second Prize Natl Negro Publisher's Assn Feature Competition 1963; second prize IL Associated Press Feature Competition 1966, 1967; Journalistic Excellence North Shore Chapter LINKS; Operation PUSH Communicator of Year 1975; YWCA Leader Award Communications 1984.

CALHOUN, NOAH ROBERT

Oral/maxillofacial surgeon. **Personal:** Born Mar 23, 1921, Clarendon, AR; married Cecelia C; children: Stephen M, Cecelia N. **Educ:** Dental Sch Howard U, DDS 1948; Tufts Med & Dent Coll, MSD 1955. **Career:** Med Ctr VA, asst oral surgeon 1964-72, asst chief dentist 1972-75, chief dental surgeon 1975-82, coord, Dental Rsch, Dental School Howard Univ; prof oral maxillofacial Surgery 1982. **Orgs:** Oral surgeon Med Ctr Tuskegee AL VA 1950-64; prof lecturer Georgetown Dental 1970-; consultant VA & Atena Ins Co 1982-; dir Red Cross Tuskegee Inst 1962-64; dir vice pres Credit Union VA 1982; adv comm Amer Bd Oral Surgery 8 yrs. Institute of Medicine, selection editor & editoral board, Intl Oral & Maxillofacial Surgery. **Honors/Awds:** Fellow Amer Coll Dentistry; Fellow Intl Coll Dentistry; mem Inst of Med 1982; Dental Alumni Awrd Howard Univ 1972. **Military Serv:** USAF cptn 2 yrs. **Home Addr:** 1413 Leegate Rd NW, Washington, DC 20012. **Business Addr:** Prof Oral & Maxillofacial Surgery, Dental Sch Howard Univ, Washington, DC 20059.

CALHOUN, THOMAS

Educator. **Personal:** Born Oct 6, 1932, Marianna, FL; son of Sylvia Barnes Thompson and Thomas Pittman; married Shirley Kathryn Jones; children: Thomas Jr, Christine, Kathy, Maria. **Educ:** Florida A&M Univ, BS 1954; Fisk Univ, grad school; Meharry Med Coll, MD 1963. **Career:** Fisk Univ, instr 1957-58; Tennis Circuit, amateur traveller 1958; US Postal WA, employee 1958-59; Howard Univ, clinical assoc prof of surgery. **Orgs:** Mem Amer Tennis Assn; Amer Medical Tennis Assn; US Tennis Assn; District of Columbia Medical Soc; Bd of Surgeons Police Fire Dept; St Thomas Apostle Catholic Church; Diplomate Amer Bd of Surgery 1971; fellow Amer Coll of Surgery 1972; fellow Amer Assn of Abdominal Surgeons 1977; med adviser Care-Plus, Delmarva regional medical director; fellow Amer Coll of Nutrition; president elect, Med-Dental Staff, Providence Hosp, Washington DC. **Honors/Awds:** Certified by American Board of Quality Assurance and Utilization Review Physicians Inc, 1991. **Military Serv:** AUS 2nd lt 1954-56. **Business Addr:** Clinical Assoc Prof of Surgery, 1160 Varnum St NE, Washington, DC 20017.

CALLAHAN, SAMUEL P.

Dentist, clergyman. **Personal:** Born Apr 15, 1924, Galax, VA; son of Nannie C Callahan and William Thomas Callahan; married Maude R Harris; children: Samuel, Maria, William, Angela. **Educ:** Fisk U, BA; Meharry Med Coll, DDS; Wesley Theol Sem, MDiv. **Career:** Self employed dentist; Christ Is The Answer Deliverance Center, pastor; NAACP, chmn legal redress com. **Orgs:** Mem Anne Arundel Co Human Relation & Com; 32 Deg Mason; shriner; Alpha Phi Alpha. **Honors/Awds:** Recipient Certificate for Creative Achievement in Dentistry. **Military Serv:** USN 1944-46.

CALLAWAY, DWIGHT W.

Automotive component manufacturing executive (retired). **Personal:** Born May 22, 1932, Cincinnati, OH; son of Virginia Moody Gordon (deceased) and H C Callaway (deceased); married Roberta F Leahr, Aug 6, 1955; children: Denise Callaway-Reistad, Gordon C Callaway, Dwight W Callaway II. **Educ:** Morehouse Coll, Atlanta, GA, BS, 1953; Univ of Cincinnati, Cincinnati, OH, MS, 1956; Pennsylvania State Univ, eight week Exec Mgmt, 1979. **Career:** D H Baldwin Co, Cincinnati, OH, sr engineer, 1955-62; Electra Mfg Co, Independence, KS, mgr research & devel, 1962-64; Delco Electronic Div, GMC, Kokomo, IN, chief engineer, 1964-81; Youngwood Electronic Metals, Murraysville, PA, CEO, exec vice pres, 1981-82; A C Rochester Div, GMC, Flint, MI, dir intl operations, beginning 1982; board of directors, Bumex Corp, Mexico City, Mexico, 1986; board of directors, GM Luexenbourg, 1987; bd of dir, AG Australia, Melbourne, beginning 1986. **Orgs:** Pres, 1970-72, bd of dir, 1972-, Intl Soc for Hybrid Microelectronics; mem Alpha Phi Alpha Fraternity, 1952-; mem Sigma Pi Phi Fraternity, 1984-; mem Air Port Authority, Flint, MI, 1986-; bd of dir, Flint School System Pre Engineering Program; bd of dir, Howard Community Hospital, Kokomo, IN, United Way, Kokomo, IN, YMCA, Carver Community Center, Kokomo, IN; pres of bd, Kokomo OIC. **Honors/Awds:** Engineer of the Year, Natl Electronic Production Conf, 1970; Daniel M Hughes Award, Intl Society for Hybrid Microelectronics, 1972; patent issued, Plat/gold W B Semi conductors, 1969. **Home Addr:** 2620 Indian Bow Trail, Flint, MI 48507.

CALLAWAY, LOUIS MARSHALL, JR.

Plant manager. **Personal:** Born Jan 22, 1939, Chicago, IL; married Duryea Dickson. **Educ:** Drake U, BA 1961. **Career:** Ford Motor Co, plant mgr; Ford, asst plant mgr; Ford Truck plant, asst plant mgr; Ford, quality control mgr; Ford, pre-delivery mgr; Ford, supt; AAD Div, indsl rep. **Orgs:** Mem Chicago S C of C; dir Chicago Assn Commerce & Indus; coporate mem Blue Cross Blue Shield. **Business Addr:** 12600 S Torrence Ave, Chicago, IL 60633.

CALLENDER, CARL O.

Commissioner, attorney. **Personal:** Born Nov 16, 1936, New York, NY; married Leola Rhames. **Educ:** Brooklyn Comm Coll Brooklyn NY, 1960-61; Hunter Coll Bronx NY, AB 1961-64; Howard Univ Sch Law Washington DC, JD. **Career:** Housing Litigation Bur NYC, dir 1975-76; Comm Law Ofcs Prgm, dir 1972-75; Comm Law Ofcs, deputy dir 1971-72; Comm Law & Ofcs, asso dir 1971; CALS Reginald Heber Smith Fellow Prgm NYC, COORD 1970-71; Regin Ald Heber Smith fellow Harlem Assertion of Rights Inc, 1969-70; Harlem Assertion of Rights Inc, staff atty 1968-69; Prentice-Hall's Federal Tax Service Bulletins NJ, legal edit 1968; Palystreet NYC, dir 1967; Hunter Coll NYC, asst libr aide 1966; Ebenezer Gospel Tabernacle, ordained minister 1972. **Orgs:** Chmn & pres Natl Young People's Christian Assn Inc; chmn & pres Christian Leaders United Inc; mem elec com of Student Bar Assnadministrv asst; Housing Research Com; Phi Alpha Delta Legal Fraternity. **Honors/Awds:** "Student who made most & significant progress in senior year" 1967; Am Jurisprudence Award for Insurance 1967; half hour film on channel 2 "Eye On New York"; brief Biog; Sketch Life Entitled "Attorney For The Defenseless" 1970. **Military Serv:** USAF airman 1st class 1951-55. **Business Addr:** 415 Louis Ave, Floral Park, NY 11001.

CALLENDER, CLIVE ORVILLE

Educator, physician. **Personal:** Born Nov 16, 1936, New York, NY; son of Ida Burke and Joseph Burke; married Fern Irene Marshall; children: Joseph, Ealena, Arianne. **Educ:** Hunter Coll, AB 1959; Meharry Med Coll, MD 1963. **Career:** Univ of Cincinnati, internship 1963-64; Harlem Hosp, asst resident 1964-65; Howard Univ & Freedmen's Hosp, asst resident 1965-66; Memorial Hosp for Cancer & Allied Diseases, asst resident 1966-67; Howard Univ & Freedmen's Hosp, chief resident 1967-69, instr 1969-70; DC Gen Hosp, med ofcr 1970-71; Port Harcourt Gen Hosp Nigeria, consult 1970-71; Howard Univ Med Coll, asst prof, 1973-76, assoc prof, 1976-80, prof, 1980-; Howard Univ, prof vice chmn dept of surgery 1982-95, dir transplant center 1973-, chair department of surgery and LaSalle D Leffall Jr, prof of surgery, 1996-. **Orgs:** Mem DC Med Soc; Soc of Acad Surg; Transplant Soc; Amer Soc of Transplant Surg; edtrl adv bd New Directions; bd dir Kidney Found Natl Capital Area; Fellow of Amer Coll of Surg 1975; pres Natl Kidney Found of Natl Capital Area 1979-; chmn membership com Amer Soc of Transplant Surgeons; pres Med Dental Staff of Howard Univ Hosp 1980; pres Alpha Phi Omega Frat 1959; pres Alpha Omega Alpha; Alpha Phi Alpha; dip Amer Bd of Surgery 1970; End Stage Renal Disease Data, advisory committee to the secretary of health, 1990-; founder and principal investigator of MOTTEP-the Natl Minority Organ/tissue transplant education program. **Honors/Awds:** Hoffman LaRoche Awrd 1961; Natl Med Assn Aux Scholarship 1961; Joseph Collins Scholarship Award 1961-63; Charles Nelson Gold Medal Meharry Med Coll 1963; Hudson Meadows Award Meharry Med Coll 1963; Natl Med Assn Scholarship Award 1963; Fellow Amer Cancer Soc 1965-66; Charles R Drew Rsch Award Howard Univ & Freedmen's Hosp 1968; Daniel Hale Williams Award Howard Univ & Freedmen's Hosp 1969; Spec Postdoctoral NIH Rsch Fellow 1971-73; Clin Transp Fellow Univ of MN 1971-72; Univ Pittsburgh, visiting transplant fellowship, liver, 1987-88; numerous presentations, publications & abstracts; Hall of Fame, Hunter College Alumni 1989; Physician of the Year Award, National Med Association 1989; Distinguished Surgeon Award, Howard University, Department of Surgery 1989; Distinguished Service Award, National Med Association, Surgical Section 1990; elected to the American Surgical Assn, 1991; AAKP, Amer Assn of Kidney Patients, Medal of Excellence, 1997; Elected to the Southern Surgical Assn, 1996. **Business Addr:** Professor/Chair, Department of Surgery, Howard University Medical College, 2041 Georgia Ave, Washington, DC 20060, (202)865-1441.

CALLENDER, LEROY R.

Structural engineer. **Personal:** Born Feb 29, 1932, New York City, NY; divorced; children: Eric. **Educ:** City Coll City Of NY, BCE 1958. **Career:** LeRoy Callender PC Consulting Engineers, founder, 1969-. **Honors/Awds:** Black Engineer of the Year Award, 1992. **Business Addr:** Founder, LeRoy Callender/PC Consulting Engineers, 236 W 26th St, New York, NY 10001.

CALLENDER, LUCINDA R.

Educator. **Personal:** Born Oct 26, 1957, Xenia, OH; daughter of Isabel Long Callender and Richard E Callender Sr. **Educ:** The Ohio State University, Columbus, OH, BA, 1979, MA, 1980, PhD, 1985. **Career:** Ohio Wesleyan University Upward Bound Project, Delaware, OH, teacher & acting associate director, 1977-84; The Ohio State University, Columbus, OH, graduate teaching associate, 1980-85; University of Missouri-Columbia, Columbia, MO, assistant profesor, 1985-88; San Diego State University, San Diego, CA, assistant professor, 1988-. **Orgs:** Member, Western Political Science Association, 1990-; member, Midwest Political Science Association, 1983-89; member, Southern Political Science Association, 1989-90; member, American Political Science Association, 1985-90; Natl Conference for Black Political Scientists. **Honors/Awds:** Outstanding Faculty Award, San Diego State Univ, 1990; Honorary Coach of University of Missouri-Columbia Male Basketball Team, Univ of Missouri-Columbia, 1987-88; Summer Research Fellowship, University of Missouri-Columbia, 1986; Commendation for excellence in many pursuits, Ohio House of Representatives, 1985; William Jennings Bryan Prize, which is a dissertation award given to a manuscript judged outstanding, The Ohio State University, 1984; Summer Research Fellowship, San Diego State University, 1991, Research, Scholarship and Creative Activity Award, 1991, Outstanding Faculty Award, 1993. **Business Addr:** Assistant Professor, San Diego State University, Dept of Political Science, San Diego, CA 92182.

CALLENDER, VALERIE DAWN
Physician, dermatologist. **Personal:** Born Oct 1, 1960, Port Chester, NY; daughter of Nancy S Callender and Joseph H Callender. **Educ:** Bennett Coll, BS 1982; Howard Univ Coll of Medicine, MD 1986. **Career:** Health Science Acad Howard Univ Coll of Medicine, program asst coord 1983; Howard Univ Hospital, postgraduate physician, 1986-87, internal medicine, 1987-90, dermatology, 1990. **Orgs:** Mem NAACP 1978-, Amer & Natl Medical Assocs 1982-, District of Columbia Medical Soc 1983-, Amer Medical Women's Assoc 1984-; mem Amer Academy of Dermatology 1990-; mem, District of Columbia Dermatologic Society, 1991-. **Honors/Awds:** First prize Syntex Lab Outstanding Student Rsch Howard Univ Coll Medicine 1984; 2nd prize Student Natl Medical Assoc Rsch Forum, 1985; 2nd prize Howard Univ Residents Research Forum, 1988. **Business Addr:** Dermatologist, 2100 Brightseat Rd W, Ste 201, Landover, MD 20785.

CALLENDER, WILFRED A.
Educator, attorney. **Personal:** Born Mar 23, 1929, Colon, Panama; son of Isaline Brathwaite (deceased) and Newton N Callender (deceased); married Beth Robinson; children: Neil, Melissa. **Educ:** Brooklyn Coll, BA 1954; Brooklyn Coll, MA 1963; Brooklyn Law Sch, JD 1969. **Career:** Boys High School Brooklyn, educator 1957-69; Dept Real Estate Commerce Labor Industry Corp Kings, asst dir 1969-70; Wade & Callender, atty 1972-; Hostos Community College, prof 1970-91; Wade & Callender ESQS Practice of Law. **Orgs:** Mem Brooklyn Bar Assn; Bedford Stuyvesant Lawyers Assn; Natl Conf Black Lawyers; bd Trustees Encampment for Citizenship 1971-; pres Black Caucus Hostos 1972-; mem bd trustees Social Serv; bd NY Soc Ethical Culture. **Military Serv:** AUS pvt 2 1954-56. **Business Addr:** 1501 No Strand Ave, Brooklyn, NY 11226.

CALLOWAY, CHRISTOPHER FITZPATRICK
Professional football player. **Personal:** Born Mar 29, 1968, Chicago, IL. **Educ:** Univ of Michigan, bachelor's degree in communications and film. **Career:** Pittsburgh Steelers, wide receiver, 1990-91; New York Giants, 1992-. **Business Addr:** Professional Football Player, New York Giants, Giants Stadium, East Rutherford, NJ 07073, (201)935-8111.

CALLOWAY, DEVERNE LEE
Legislator. **Personal:** Born Jun 17, 1916, Memphis, TN; daughter of Sadie Lee and Charles Lee; married Ernest Calloway. **Educ:** LeMoyne-Owen Coll, AB 1938; Atlanta Univ & Northwestern U, grad studies in English. **Career:** 81st Dist St Louis, state rep for nine consecutive terms. **Orgs:** Mem of numerous city & state coms. **Honors/Awds:** First black woman to be elected in MO; commendation by St Louis Comm for efforts to educate average citizens in the effectiveness & need for polit participation on local, state & fed lLevels. **Home Addr:** 4309 Enright, St Louis, MO 63108.

CALLOWAY, VANESSA BELL
Actress. **Personal:** marrIed Anthony Calloway, Sep 1988; children: Ashley, Alexandra. **Career:** Actress; television appearances include: Polly, 1989; Piece of Cake, 1990; Memphis, 1992; Stompin' at the Savoy, 1990; Rhythm and Blues, 1992; All My Children; Under One Roof, Orleans; films: Coming to America; Bebe's Kids; What's Love Got to Do With It; Crimson Tide; The Inkwell. **Business Addr:** Actress, c/o Fred Amsel & Associates, 6310 San Vicente Blvd, Ste 407, Los Angeles, CA 90048, (213)939-1188.

CALLUM, AGNES KANE
Genealogist, historian. **Personal:** Born Feb 24, 1925, Baltimore, MD; daughter of Mary Priscilla Gough Kane and Philip Moten Kane; married Solomon Melvin Callum, Jul 7, 1944 (deceased); children: Paul A Foster, Agnes H Lightfoot, Arthur M Callum, Martin J Callum, Martina P Callum. **Educ:** Morgan State Univ, BA, 1973; Univ of Ghana, West Africa, 1973; Morgan State Univ, MS, 1975. **Career:** Beauty Queen Co, Baltimore MD, sales manager 1954-58; North Carolina Mutual Life Insurance Co, Baltimore MD, 1958-62; Rosewood State Hospital, Ownings MD, practical nurse, 1962-66; US Postal Serv, Baltimore MD, review clk, 1966-86; Douglass High Evening School, Baltimore MD, teacher 1977-80; Coppin State Coll, Baltimore MD, teacher 1978. **Orgs:** Mem NAACP 1950-89; mem Assn for Study of Afro-Amer Life and History 1966-89; commn mem Baltimore City Hospital 1976-78; mem Maryland Genealogical Society 1978-89; corresponding sec Afro-Amer Historical & Genealogical Society 1986-89; historian Natl Alliance Postal & Federal Employees Local #202 1986-; historian St Francis Xavier Catholic Church 1988-; Advisory Committee Maryland State Archives 1989; mem Archive Committee Maryland Comm Afro-Amer Life & Culture; trustee, Satterly Plantation Mansion, Hollywood, MD, 1991-; commissioner, Maryland Civil War Heritage Commission, 1993-95. **Honors/Awds:** City of Baltimore Mayor's Citation, Citizenship 1967; Author, Kane-Butler Family Genealogical History of a Black Family 1978; founder, editor Kane Family News Notes 1979; founder, editor, publisher, Flower of the Forest Black Genealogical Journal 1982-; author, Inscriptions From The Tomb Stones at Mt Calvary Cemetery 1926-1982, 1985; Senate of Maryland Award Outstanding Community Worker 1986; City Council of Baltimore Retirement 1986; Citizen Citation of Baltimore Leadership 1986; US Postal Service 20 year Service Award 1986; Natl Council of Negro Women Historian Award 1988. **Special Achievements:** Author: Black Marriages of St Mary's County, Maryland; 19 Colored Volunteers of Maryland, 7th Regiment United States Colored Troops, 1863-66; Black Marriages of Anne Arundel County, Maryland 1850-86, 1993.

CALOMEE, ANNIE E.
Educator (retired). **Personal:** Born Feb 2, 1910, Beaumont, MS; married Andrew; children: Doris, Gloria, Andrea. **Educ:** Univ of So CA, BS MS; UCLA Pepperdine U, spl Study. **Career:** Multicultural Educ, teacher, consultant, lecturer; LA City School Dist Coord, teacher reading, splst coord; 1st workshop in Tech & Materials for Teaching Black History to classroom teachers LA City Schools, leadrr, consult 1967; inserv classes for teachers; Afro-Am History, consultant lecturer. **Orgs:** Life mem NAACP; Nat Counc of Negro Women; Assn for Study of Afro-Am Life & Hist; Nat Sor of Phi Delta Kappa; Women in Educ Ldrshp; CTA; NEA; United Tchrs of LA. **Honors/Awds:** Woman of yr Ward African Meth Epis Ch Phi Delta Kappa 1965; City Counc Resolution for contrib to Am Hist; fdr chmn Negro Hist Workshop for Youth Pepsi Cola Bottling Co 1965; United Tchrs; plaque contrib to students & tchrs in Multicultural Edn. **Home Addr:** 3856 Roxton Ave, Los Angeles, CA 90008.

CALVERT, WILMA JEAN
Nursing educator. **Personal:** Born Nov 25, 1958, St Louis, MO; daughter of Amanda Bond Calvert and John Phillip Calvert. **Educ:** Oral Roberts University, BSN, 1981; University of Oklahoma, MS, 1986. **Career:** Deaconess Hospital, staff nurse, 1981-82; St John Medical Center, staff nurse, 1982-84; City of Faith, Tulsa, OK, staff nurse, 1984-87; Oral Roberts University, instructor, 1987-82; Hillcrest Medical Center, staff nurse, 1989-91; St John Medical Center, staff nurse, 1991-92; Barnes College, asst professor, 1992-. **Orgs:** National Black Nurses Association, scholarship & awards committee, 1991-; Association of Black Nursing Faculty, research committee, 1990-; Mu Iota Chapter, Sigma Theta Tau, faculty counselor, 1990-; NAACOG, 1989-; American Nurses Association, 1987-; National League for Nursing, 1987-. **Honors/Awds:** Oral Roberts University, Service Award, 1992; Sigma Theta Tau, Mu Iota Chapter, 1990; State of Oklahoma, Scholar-Leadership Enrichment Program, 1986. **Special Achievements:** Medical mission trip to Guatemala, 1992; completing research related to the relinquishing mother, 1992; completing research on black adolescent fFathers. **Home Addr:** 4875 Cote Brilliante Ave, St Louis, MO 63113-1816, (314)531-3713. **Business Addr:** Clinical Asst Professor, Barnes College, 416 S Kingshighway, St Louis, MO 63110, (314)362-5656.

CALVIN, MICHAEL BYRON
Judge, attorney. **Personal:** Born Feb 16, Nashville, TN; divorced; children: Michael Langston, Justin Kinnard. **Educ:** Hist/Govt Monmouth Coll, BA 1972; St Louis Univ Sch of Law, JD 1975. **Career:** City of St Louis, circuit judge; Black Am Law Students Assn BALSA Reports, former editor . **Orgs:** Mem Mound City Bar Association. **Honors/Awds:** Outstanding Young Alumnus Monmouth Coll IL 1979; BALSA Alumnus Award Black Am Law Students St Louis Univ 1979. **Business Addr:** Circuit Court Judge, State of MO, 12th & Market Sts, St Louis, MO 63101.

CALVIN, VIRGINIA BROWN
Educational administrator. **Personal:** Born Jun 16, 1945, Lake Providence, LA; daughter of Vera Brown and Arthur Brown; married Richmond E Calvin; children: Brent Tremayne, Shannon D'Ann. **Educ:** Alcorn State U, BS 1966; NM Highlands U, MA 1970; TX Wmns U, EdD 1973; North TX State U, 1970; IN Univ South Bend, 1979. **Career:** LA, NM & TX, teacher 1967-71; South Bend Community School Corp, counselor 1972-76, admin 1977-, Muessel Elem School, principal, acting executive director, division of instruction and curriculum, 1991-92; superintendent of schools, 1992-. **Orgs:** State cnsltnt IN Head Start Training 1980; chprsn Validation-Head Start 1979; sec Delta Kappa Gamma Hnr Scty 1984; bd dir Jr League of So Bend 1984, Art Ctr 1985; board member, St Joseph County Parks Board, 1990-; board member, Broadway Theatre League 1986-; president, Alpha Kappa Alpha Sorority, 1991-93; bd mem, United Way of St Joseph County, 1991-92; bd mem, Leadership Chamber of Commerce, 1985-93; bd mem, Chamber of Commerce, 1992-; bd mem, St Joseph County Children's Ctr, 1992-; bd mem, Firefly Festival, 1992-; bd mem, Healthy Comm Initiative, 1992-; bd mem, Jr Achievement. **Honors/Awds:** Wmn of Yr Plano, TX 1971; Monograph "Supt Intern" SBCSC 1979; Wmn of Yr SBCSC YWCA 1984; Educator of the Year, Executive Journal, 1991; Bond Award, AKA, 1976, 1991; Natl Blue Ribbon School Award, Muessel Elem School, 1992; Redbook Magazine's America's Best Elem School Award, Muessel Elem School, 1993; Educ of the Year, Comm Educ Roundtable, 1991; Indiana State Superintendent of the Year, 1996. **Home Addr:** 17530 Bending Oaks, Granger, IN 46530. **Business Addr:** Superintendent of Schools, South Bend Community School Corp, 635 S Main St, South Bend, IN 46601.

CAMBOSOS, BRUCE MICHAEL
Educator. **Personal:** Born Jul 20, 1941, New Haven, CT; married Syleatha Hughes; children: Shanay. **Educ:** George Washington U, 1961; Howard U, BS 1964; Howard U, MD 1969. **Career:** Ugast Treatment Center WA, staff psychiatrist 1976-; VA Hospital, staff pyschiatrist 1973-75. **Orgs:** Am Psy Assn; WA Psy Assn; St George Soc; Capital Med Soc Trustee. **Honors/Awds:** Scholarship GWU 1959; tutorial scholarship Howard Univ 1965; ey Williams Award Howard Univ 1969. **Business Addr:** 2041 Georgia Ave, Washington, DC 20060.

CAMBRIDGE, DEXTER
Professional basketball player. **Career:** Dallas Mavericks, currently. **Business Addr:** Professional Basketball Player, Dallas Mavericks, ReUnion Arena, 777 Sports St, Dallas, TX 75207, (214)988-0117.

CAMBY, MARCUS D.
Professional basketball player. **Personal:** Born Mar 22, 1974, Hartford, CT. **Educ:** Massachusetts. **Career:** Toronto Raptors, forward-center, 1996-. **Honors/Awds:** James A Naismith award, 1996; John Wooden award, 1996; NBA, All Rookie Team, 1997. **Special Achievements:** NBA Draft, First round pick, #2, 1996. **Business Addr:** Professional Basketball Player, Toronto Raptors, 150 York St, Ste 110, Toronto, ON, Canada M5H 3S5, (416)214-2255.

CAMERON, JAMES
Museum curator, educator. **Personal:** Born Feb 25, 1914, LaCrosse, WI; son of James Herbert & Vera Carter-Cameron; married Virginia, May 15, 1938; children: James Herbert, Walter, Virgil, David, Dolores Donzetta. **Educ:** Wayne State Univ; Milwaukee Area Technical College. **Career:** Hoods Laundry, 1935-37; Detroit Creamery, delivery boy, 1935-36; Lehigh Coal Yard, 1937-43; Delco Remy-Anderson, 1943-46; self-employed, 1946-53; Inland Container Corp, 1953-64; Mayfair Shopping Mall, 1964-82; America's Black Holocaust Museum, president/CEO, currently. **Orgs:** NAACP; National Urban League; Improved Benevolent Protective Order of Elks of the World; CIO-UAW; Brainstorming Conference of Milwaukee; All Saints Catholic Church, Milwaukee; For My Brothers, Inc, Assn for the Study of African Amer History (Woodson). **Honors/Awds:** Numerous honors. **Special Achievements:** Author, A Time of Terror; Lecturer at colleges and universities; world traveler. **Business Addr:** President/CEO, America's Black Holocaust Museum, Inc, 2233 N Fourth St, Single Building, Milwaukee, WI 53212, (414)264-2500.

CAMERON, JOHN E.
Clergyman. **Personal:** Born Jun 11, 1932, Hattiesburg, MS; married Lenora Woods; children: Jonetta, John Earl Jr. **Educ:** Alcorn A&M Coll; Am Bapt Theo Sem, BTh 1956; Rust Coll, BS 1957. **Career:** Mt Calvary Bapt Ch, Minister; Mt Calvary Comm Devel Agency Inc, coord 1974-; Div of Youth Affairs at Gov's Ofc Jackson, coord 1972; Star Inc Jackson, job coach 1968-71; Star Inc Natchez, cntr dir 1966-68; Minister's Proj under auspices of Presb Commn on Religion & Race Hattiesburg , dir 1954-65. **Orgs:** Candidate US Congress 5th Congressional Dist of MS 1964; ambassador Cntrl Am 1954; pres Nat Bapt Student Union 1954; job Devel Specialist Star Inc 1969-71; sponsor Boy Scouts; Mason; historian for Progressive Nat Bapt Conv; commr Criminal Justice Sys for State Of MS Commr LEAA. **Business Addr:** 901 Lynch St, Jackson, MS.

CAMERON, JOSEPH A.
Educator. **Personal:** Born Apr 25, 1942, Fairfield, AL; son of Searcie Cameron and Arthur Cameron; married Mary E Stiles; children: Joseph Jr, Jozetta, Cecelia, Juanita. **Educ:** TN State U, BS 1963; TX So U, MS 1965; MI State U, PhD 1973. **Career:** TX Southern Univ, graduate teaching asst 1965; Dept of Biological Science, Grambling State Univ, instructor 1965-66, asst prof 1967-69; Dept Natural Science, MI State Univ, instructor 1969-73; Dept of Nat Science, MI State Univ, asst prof 1973-74; Dept of Biology, Jackson State Univ, asst prof 1974-78, coordinator, graduate programs, 1976-85, prof, 1978-, director, biomedical sciences program, 1980-84, acting dean, School of Science and Technology, 1984, director of minority institutional research training program, 1986-; Bridges to the Baccalaureate Degree Program, dir, 1993-95; Univ of Mississippi Med Ctr/Jackson State Univ, health careers opportunity program, faculty, 1985-; National Science Foundation, consultant and reviewer, 1978-91; Natl Inst of Health, consultant and proposal reviewer, 1978-95; Equal Opportunity Program, MI StateUniv, ulty tutor 1969-71; high school sci teacher, consultant 1967-69; Natural Science Lab Manual, MI State Univ, contributing author 1971; published professional journals. **Orgs:** Mem Tri Beta Biol Honor Soc; Am Soc Zool; Am Assn Univ Prof; Tissue Culture Assn; Soc Sigma XI; AAAS; Miss Acad Sci, Alpha Phi Alpha Frat Inc; mem, American Heart Associa-

tion, Endocrine Soc, Phi Delta Kappa; pres, Phi Kappa Phi, 1990. **Honors/Awds:** Academic Tuition Scholarship Univ IA 1966-67; Soc Sigma XI Award Meritorious Research MSU 1973; apptd Fairfield Ind HS Hall Fame 1973; King/Chavez/Parks Visiting Prof, MI State Univ, 1992. **Business Addr:** Professor, Dept of Biology, Jackson State University, 1400 Lynch St, Jackson, MS 39217.

CAMERON, KRYSTOL
Business executive. **Personal:** Born Mar 14, 1967, Brooklyn, NY; son of Jean Clark and John Cameron; married Deidre DeRiggs, Aug 15, 1987. **Educ:** MIT, computer engineering, 1980. **Career:** IBM, sr design engineer, 1984-85; Cameron Systems Inc, president, 1987-. **Orgs:** Black Filmmaker Foundation, patron, 1988-; Chase Records, Inc, vice pres, production, 1990-; Facile Management, vice pres, communications, 1990-; ATC Music, president, publishing, 1992-; Ashton Film, Inc, president, 1992-. **Honors/Awds:** Ernst & Young, Entrepreneur of the Year, 1987; Computer Land, Local Area Network Degree, 1986; IBM, Authorized Dealer, 1990. **Special Achievements:** Developed two ROM Chips for the IBM XT-286, 1985; revamped, Billboard, Essence, Class, and Carib News through computers, 1988-; automated the Black Filmmaker Foundation business in New York and California. **Business Phone:** (718)322-9510.

CAMERON, MARY EVELYN
Educator. **Personal:** Born Sep 8, 1944, Memphis, TN; married Dr Joseph Alexander; children: Jozetta Louise, Joseph Alexander Jr, Cecelia Denise, Juanita Evette. **Educ:** Marian Coll Indianapolis IN, BA 1962-66; Univ of IA Med Ctr, ADA Cert 1966-67; Jackson State Univ, MS 1979. **Career:** State of MS, nutritionist, mem of survey team 1967-68; Grambling State Univ; admin dietitian 1968-69; Sparrow Hosp, clinical dietitian 1969-74; Hinds Gen Hosp, clinical dietitian 1974-79; VA Med Ctr, clinical dietitian 1979; Univ of MS Med Ctr, asst prof 1979-. **Orgs:** Pre Central Dist Dietetic Assn 1978-79; rsch nutritionist Univ Med Ctr 1980-84; pres Nutritionists in Nursing Ed 1981-82; mem MS Heart Assn Professional Ed Comm 1982-84; chmn Nutrition Subcomm Professional Ed Comm 1982-85; nutrition consult Oper Headstart Prog 1982-; mem MS Heart Ass Nutrition Comm 1983-; pres MS Dietetic Assoc 1983-84; Pres, Health Advisory Comm of Hinds County Project Headstart, 1987; mem, board of dirs, MS Dietetic Assn, 1985-; The Amer Cancer Society (MS Division), 1987-; American Heart Assn (MS Division), 1991-; PTSA Pres, Forest Hill HS, 1991-. **Honors/Awds:** Appt mem of Diocesan School Bd 1982-86; Reviewed several articles for professional jrnl 1982-84; Presented res abstract at Reg Hypertension Mtg 1983; Reviewed a major nutrition text Mosby Publ 1984; Publ article in professional refereed jrnl 1985; appt mem bd of CUP Univ S MS; mem Tri Beta Biological Hon Soc 1979-; mem Phi Delta Kappa Hon Soc. **Business Addr:** Asst Prof of SHRP/Clinical-Research Dietician, Dept of Medicine, 2500 N State St, Jackson, MS 39216-4505.

CAMERON, MICHAEL TERRANCE
Professional baseball player. **Personal:** Born Jan 8, 1973, La Grange, GA. **Career:** Chicago White Sox, outfielder, 1995-. **Business Addr:** Professional Baseball Player, Chicago White Sox, 333 W 35th St, Chicago, IL 60616, (312)924-1000.

CAMERON, RANDOLPH W.
Marketing/public relations consultant. **Personal:** Born in Jersey City, NJ; son of Randolph W Cameron; married Martha; children: Randolph Jr, Michele. **Educ:** Delaware State Coll, BS Business Admin 1958; New School for Social Rsch, MA Communications 1985. **Career:** D Parke Gibson Assocs Inc, vice pres 1962-72; Avon Products Inc, div sales mgr 1972-73, dir field sales support, dir of corp communications 1978-85; Cameron Enterprises, pres. **Orgs:** Former bd mem Amer Cancer Soc; Economic Advisory Comm; New York City Business Society; advisory committee, New York Jobs for Youth. **Honors/Awds:** Black Achievers in Industry; Author of "The Minority Executives' Handbook," Warner Books, 1989; Athletic Hall of Fame, Delaware State College, 1989. **Military Serv:** US Army, PFC. **Business Addr:** President, Cameron Enterprises, 100 West 94th St, New York, NY 10025.

CAMERON, ULYSSES
Librarian (retired). **Personal:** Born Dec 4, 1930, Sanford Hts, NC; son of Pearlie Judd (deceased) and Archie Cameron (deceased); married Ida R Womack; children: Sylvia Mortensen, Byron, Cynthia Moorman, Myrna Maunuksela. **Educ:** Howard Univ, BMusEd (cum laude) 1952; Atlanta Univ, MSLS 1965; Federal City Coll, MA 1974; VA Polytech Inst & State Univ, CAGS 1977, EdD 1984. **Career:** Enoch Pratt Free Library, librarian 1965-68; Federal City Coll Media Ctr, assoc dir 1968-74, deputy dir 1974-77; Univ of DC, assoc dir univ libraries 1977-82, head librarian, bus library 1982-84, head librarian educ library 1984-86, librarian & special proj dir serials librarian, 1986-94. **Orgs:** Mem Phi Delta Kappa. **Honors/Awds:** "What's Wrong with our Library Schools," Cameron et al 1966. **Military Serv:** USAF captain 1953-62. **Home Addr:** 4117 Raleigh Rd, Baltimore, MD 21208.

CAMERON, WILBURN MACIO, JR.
Dentist. **Personal:** Born in Richmond, VA; married Jacqueline Amelia; children: Wilburn Macin III, Charles Anderson. **Educ:** Virginia State, BS 1950; Howard Univ Grad Sch; Meharry Med Coll, 1956. **Career:** Richmond VA, private practice in dentistry, 1958-. **Orgs:** Past pres Peter B Ramsey Dental Soc 1967-75; Dr Wilburn M Cameron & Jr Professional Corp 1975-77; pres Old Dominion Dental Soc 1977-79; sec tres VA Acad Gen Dentistry 1977-79, vice pres 1979-; grand organizer Chi Delta Mu Frat 1967-73; bd of dir YMCA 1970-75; mem Richmond C of C Kappa Alpha Psi Frat; pres VA Academy of General Dentistry, 1980-81. **Honors/Awds:** Fellowship VA, Acad of Gen Dentistry 1976; pres award Old Dominion Dentist Soc 1977, 1978; Fellowship Intl Academy of General Dentistry, 1982; Meharry's Presidents Award, Service to Mankind 25 years, 1956-81. **Military Serv:** AUS capt 1946-48, 1956-58. **Business Addr:** 10 & 12 W Marshall St, Richmond, VA 23220.

CAMMACK, CHARLES LEE, JR.
Human resources manager. **Personal:** Born Oct 8, 1954, Fort Wayne, IN; son of Sarah Elizabeth Jackson Cammack and Charles Lee Cammack Sr; married Michelle Lynn Duncan Cammack, Aug 10, 1986. **Educ:** Purdue University, West Lafayette, IN, BA, 1977; University of Wisconsin, Madison, WI, MA, 1978. **Career:** WKJG-TV, Fort Wayne, IN, broadcast journalist, 1978-89; Fort Wayne Newspapers, Fort Wayne, IN, management trainee, 1987-89, benefits/systems manager, 1989-, manager, employment, safety, security, 1992-. **Orgs:** Bd Diversity Committee, Newspaper Assn of America; chairman, Workplace Issues Committee of Newspaper Assn of America; co-chairman Youth Leadership, Ft Wayne; bd member, Leadership Fort Wayne; Youth as Resources, 1988-. **Honors/Awds:** Community Service Award, Union Baptist Church, 1982; 2nd Place News Documentary, "Excellence in Education," Indiana Press Photographers Association, 1982; 1st Place News Feature, "Singing Hands," Indiana Associated Press, 1981; 1st Place News Documentary, "Success by a Different Yardstick," Indiana Associated Press, 1980.

CAMP, KIMBERLY
Artist, arts administrator. **Personal:** Born Sep 11, 1956, Camden, NJ; daughter of Marie Dimery Camp and Hubert E Camp; married Seydou Coulibaly. **Educ:** American University, Washington, DC, 1973-74; University of Pittsburgh, Pittsburgh, PA, BA, 1978; Drexel University, Philadelphia, PA, MS, 1986. **Career:** City of Camden, New Jersey, visual arts director, 1983-86; Commonwealth of Pennsylvania/Council on the Arts Harrisburg, PA, director, artist in education & minority arts services, 1986-89; Smithsonian Institution, Washington, DC, director, The Experimental Gallery, 1989-94; Museum of African-American History, exec dir, pres, currently. **Orgs:** Member, Links Inc, Detroit Chapter; Member, Links, Inc, Arlington VA Chapter, 1990-94; vice chair, Association of American Cultures, 1984-89; board member, Intercultural Advancement Inst Gettysburg College, 1988-; board member, Arlington Art Center, 1990-; natl advisory committee member, National Assoc of Artists Organizations, 1989-; board member, Business Volunteers for the Arts, 1994-; advisory board, Junior League, 1994-; board member, Empowerment Zone Development Corp, 1996-; board member, American Assn of Museums, 1995-. **Honors/Awds:** Arts Mgt Fellowship, National Endowment F/T Arts, 1986; New Jersey Senate Citation, 1986; City of Camden Arts Achievement Award, 1986; Purchase award, JB Speed Museum, KY, 1988; Exhibitions at over 50 museums, galleries and organizations in the USA, 1988-. **Business Addr:** President, Museum of African-American History, 315 E Warren, Detroit, MI 48201.

CAMP, MARVA JO
Attorney, businesswoman. **Personal:** Born Sep 17, 1961, Washington, DC; daughter of Ernestine Alford Camp and Fab Camp Jr. **Educ:** Univ of Virginia, Charlottesville, VA, BA, 1983; Univ of Virginia, School of Law, Charlottesville, VA, JD, 1986. **Career:** Gartrell and Alexander Law Firm, Silver Spring, MD, atty, assoc, 1986-87; Congressman Harold E Ford, Washington, DC, legislative dir, tax counsel, 1987-88; Congressman Mervyn M Dymally, Washington, DC, advisor, 1988-; Congressional Task Force on Minority Business, Washington, DC, dir, legal counsel, 1987-; Crenshaw Intl Corp, Washington, DC, pres, CEO, 1988-. **Orgs:** Legal counsel, Inst on Science, Space, and Technology, 1987-; consultant, Minority and Small Business, 1987; advisor, Democratic Natl Comm, 1988; legal counsel, Carribean Amer Research Inst, 1988; pres, bd of dir, Young Black Professionals, 1988-; co-chair, treasurer, African-Amer Political Fund, 1988; vice pres, bd of dir, Edward C Mazique Parent Child Center, 1986; bd of dir, 14th & U Coalition, 1988; advisor to pres, Congressional Black Assoc, 1988. **Honors/Awds:** Soc of Outstanding Young Amer; Congressional Certificate of Recognition; author, Federal Compliance with Minority Set-Asides, 1988, Future of African-Amer, 1988.

CAMPBELL, ALMA PORTER
Educator. **Personal:** Born Jan 5, 1948, Savannah, GA; daughter of Gladys B Porter and William Porter; divorced 1978. **Educ:** Savannah State, BS, 1969; State Univ of New York College at Brockport, NY, MS, 1971, CAS, 1988. **Career:** Rochester City School, Rochester, NY, 3rd grade teacher, 1974-87, chp. 1 reading teacher, 1987, basic skills cadre, 1988-90, lead teacher mentor, 1991-92, principal school #43, 1992-. **Orgs:** Chairman, Nominating Comm, Alpha Kappa Alpha, 1988-90; member, Phi Delta Kappa Honorary Fraternity in Educ, 1989-; member, Bd of Directors, Hamm House, 1990-91; member, Bd of Directors, Jefferson Ave Early Childhood Center, 1990-91; member, Bd of Christian Ed, Memorial AME Zion Church, 1986-; Alpha Kappa Alpha, Ivy Leaf reporter; African-American Leadership Development Program, steering-committee; chairperson, Climate Committee, No 43 School, Introduced 24 staff mems to Peer-Mediation Training Module; chairperson, Artist in Residence Programs; Cooperative Learning, teacher trainer; Leadership Group, Local Statewide Systemic Initiative, R&D Schools; LARC-Lyell Ave Revitalization Comm; RCEL, Rochester Council of Elem Adm; Internal Reading Leadership Assn; Rochester Teaching Center and the Steering Comm; Phi Delta Kappa Honorary Education Fraternity, treasurer. **Honors/Awds:** Phi Delta Kappa Honorary Education Fraternity; Professional Development Academy, appointed to focus group. **Special Achievements:** Co-author: Quick Reference Manual for Teachers, RCSD, 1990-; Super Teaching Tips, 1992; Submitted two curriculum guides to the New York State Education Department to be included in the New York Academy for Excellence in Teaching and Learning. **Business Addr:** Principal, Theodore Roosevelt School #43, Rochester, NY 14606.

CAMPBELL, ARTHUR REE
Nurse, educator. **Personal:** Born Feb 20, 1943, Bessemer, AL; daughter of Menyarn Miller Williams and Levi Williams Sr; married Shadrach Campbell, Jun 25, 1966; children: Korey Lanier, Kareem Damohn, Kheela Delores. **Educ:** Tuskegee University, Tuskegee, AL, BS, 1965; University of Maryland, Baltimore, MD, MS, 1967; University of Alabama, Tuscaloosa, Al, EdD, 1984. **Career:** University of Alabama Hospital, Birmingham, AL, charge nurse, 1965; Jefferson County Department of Health, Birmingham, Al, psyciatric nurse, 1967-75; University of Alabama, Birmingham, Birmingham, AL, associate professor, 1975-. **Orgs:** President, Mental Health Assn of Central Alabama, treasurer/vice president, Family and Child Service, member, YWCA, member, American Red Cross. **Honors/Awds:** Volunteer of the Year Award, Mental Health Assn of Central Alabama, 1987; Craig Award, Volunteer of the Year, Family Court of Jefferson County, 1984; Outstanding Volunteer, American Red Cross, 1980; Distinguished Service Award, Alabama State Nurses Assn, 1981. **Business Addr:** Associate Professor, School of Nursing, University of Alabama at Birmingham, UBA Station, 50N, Room, 117, Birmingham, AL 35294.

CAMPBELL, BEBE MOORE
Author. **Personal:** marrIed Ellis Gordon, Jr; children: Maia Campbell, Ellis Gordon III. **Career:** Author, works include: Successful Women, Angry Men, nonfiction, 1986; Sweet Summer: Growing Up With and Without My Dad, nonfiction, 1989; Your Blues Ain't Like Mine, fiction, 1992; Brothers and Sisters, 1994. **Orgs:** Alpha Kappa Alpha Sorority. **Honors/Awds:** Natl Endowment for the Arts, literary grant, 1980; Midwestern Radio Theatre Workshop Competition, winner; Natl Assn of Negro Business and Professional Women, Body of Work Award, 1978; NAACP Image Award for Literature, 1995; NY Times Notable Book of the Year. **Special Achievements:** Guest appearances on Oprah and Donahue. **Business Addr:** Author, Brothers and Sisters, c/o Editor Faith Sale, Putnam Berkley Group Inc, 200 Madison Ave, New York, NY 10016, (212)951-8400.

CAMPBELL, BLANCH
Telephone company administrator (retired). **Personal:** Born Jan 24, 1941, Biscoe, AR; daughter of Louella Calbert Louderdale and Oscar Louderdale; divorced; children: Tanja Marie Smith. **Educ:** Webster Coll, St Louis, MO, BA, 1981. **Career:** Southwestern Bell Telephone, St Louis, MO, serv asst, 1966-68, group chief operator, 1968-72, supvr business serv, 1972-74, supvr course devel, 1974-75, staff mgr training, 1975-78, district mgr, 1978-91; Trip With Me Travelers Inc, founder, chief executive officer, currently. **Orgs:** Pres, Junior Kindergarten Bd, 1981-87; pres, Project Energy Care Bd, 1984; loan exec, United Way, 1984-85; pres elect 1985-86, pres 1986-88, City North Y's Men Club; mem, Monsanto YMCA Bd of Dir, 1989; chairperson, mem placement and education information comm, Greater Mount Carmel Baptist Church; mem, Women in Leadership, 1984-; consultant, Emprise Designs, 1988-89; regional dir elect, 1990-91, regional dir, 1991-92, Y's Men International; pres Continental Societies Inc, St Louis Chap, 1989-; mem, admin council, 1993-97; Phyllis Wheatley YWCA, 1991; regional dir Continental Societies Inc Midwest-Western Region, 1997-. **Honors/Awds:** Volunteer Serv Award, United Way of Greater St Louis, 1984; Outstanding Leadership, The Junior Kindergarten, 1984, 1985; Continental Soc Volunteer Award Educ Div, 1986; Y's Men of the Year, City North Y's Men, 1987-90; Youth Serv Award, Monsanto YMCA, 1989; Finalist, Missouri Mother/Daughter Pageant, 1989; Outstanding New Mem, Continental Societies Inc, 1993-; Volunteer Award, Top Ladies of Distinction, 1991; Division Leader, Monsanto YMCA Partner with Youth Campaign, 1992; Y's Men International, Golden Book Endowment Award, 1996. **Business Addr:** CEO, Trip With Me Travelers Inc, 7242 Natural Bridge, Normandy, MO 63121.

CAMPBELL, BOBBY LAMAR
City official & business executive. **Personal:** Born Sep 30, 1949, Fairmont, NC. **Educ:** Brooklyn Coll, BA 1975-79; Howard Univ, MCP 1980-82; Natl Inst Power Engrs, 3rd class engr 1984. **Career:** US HUD, prog analyst 1980-81; Howard Univ, researcher 1981-82; Polinger Mgt Co, resident mgr 1983-85; DC Mutual Housing Assn Inc, prop mgr 1985-. **Orgs:** Vet counselor Brooklyn Coll 1975-79; student rep Amer Planning Assn 1981-82; site coord Natl Capitol Health Fair Project 1982; steering comm mem DC office of planning 1983-84; pres Upper Northwest Civic Group 1984; ANC comm 4D Advisory Neighborhood Comm 1980-84. **Honors/Awds:** Outstanding comm svs DC Recreation Dept 1983; contrib author Washington on Foot NCAC APA/Smithsonian Press 1983; outstanding comm svs 4D Advisory Neighborhood Comm 1984. **Military Serv:** USAF SS6T 4 yrs; Air Force Accomendation Awd 1970-71. **Business Addr:** Property Manager, DC Mutual Housing Assoc, Inc, 1436 Independence Ave, SE, Washington, DC 20003.

CAMPBELL, CALVIN C.
Judge. **Personal:** Born Aug 20, 1924, Roanoke, VA; children: Cathleen. **Educ:** Howard U, BA Econ 1948; Univ Of Chicago Law Sch, JD 1951. **Career:** Appellate Ct Of IL, justice 1978-; Circuit Ct, judge 1977-78; IL, asst atty gen 1957-77; Revenue Litigation, chief. **Orgs:** Mem Cook Co Bar Assn present; mem IL State Bar Assn; mem Forty Club of Chicago. **Honors/Awds:** Recipient bronze Star; AUS 1945; outstanding alumni Chicago Howard Univ Alumni 1965; outstanding State of IL Employee Office of Atty Gen State Of IL 1976. **Military Serv:** AUS pfc 1943-45. **Business Addr:** Presiding Judge, First Division, First Appellate District, Chicago, IL 60601.

CAMPBELL, CARLOS, SR.
Production control manager. **Personal:** Born Dec 23, 1946, Warrenton, VA; son of Martha Campbell and Albert Campbell; married Ethel Douglas; children: Carlos II. **Educ:** US Army Air Defense School, Certificate of Completion Opers and Intelligence Specialist 1967; North AL Coll of Commerce, Certificate of Completion Business Admin and Accounting 1972; Alabama A&M Univ, BS 1975; Alabama A&M Univ, MBA graduate studies. **Career:** AL A&M Univ, univ recruiter 1975-76, dir of veterans affairs 1975-76; Chesebrough Ponds Inc Prince Matchabelli Div, production scheduler 1976-78, sr production planner 1978-80, supervisor of warehousing and inventory control 1980-86, senior production supervisor 1986-87; Consolidated Industries, production control manager 1989-. **Orgs:** Mem Madison Co Democratic Exec Comm, Exec Bd Madison Co NAACP; vice chmn AL Democratic Conf Exec Bd; chmn Univ and Industry Cluster AL A&M Univ; chmn bd of managers North West YMCA; chmn athletic exec bd AL A&M Univ; prof Black Exec Exchange Prog Natl Urban League; mem Youth Motivation Task Force Natl Alliance of Business; mem Alpha Phi Alpha Frat, Govtl Relations Comm AL A&M Univ; North Alabama Regional Hospital Board of Directors; exec bd Police Athletic Association; president JD Johnson High School PTA, president, School Band Parents Association. **Honors/Awds:** Presidential Citation The Natl Assn for Equal Oppor in Higher Educ; Outstanding Leadership Awd Natl Alliance of Business Washington DC; Alumni of the Year Sch of Business AL A&M Univ; Distinguished Serv Awd, Outstanding Serv Awd AL A&M Univ; Citation the Natl Urban League, Natl Alliance of Business, AL Veteran Affairs Assoc of AL; Distinguished Serv Awd Phi Beta Lambda Professional Business Frat; life mem 1814 Color Guard US Army Air Defense Command; Outstanding Young Man of America, US Jaycees. **Military Serv:** AUS Air Defense Command 1966-72; Vietnam Vet 1970. **Home Addr:** 6726 Hollow Rd NW, Huntsville, AL 35810.

CAMPBELL, CARLOS CARDOZO
Banking executive, writer, actor. **Personal:** Born Jul 19, 1937, New York, NY; married Sammie Marye Day (divorced 1988); children: Kimberly, Scott. **Educ:** MI State Univ, BS 1959; US Naval Post Grad School, Diploma Engrg Sci 1965; Catholic Univ of Amer, MA City & Reg Plnng 1968. **Career:** VA Polytech Inst & State Univ, adj prof summer 1974; Amer Revolution Bicentennial Admin, dep asst admin 1974-76; Carlos C Campbell & Assoc, principal & owner 1976-81; US Dept of Comm, asst sec for economic devel 1981-84; Inter-Amer Devel Bank, alternate exec dir designee; CC Campbell and Co, management, consultant, 1985-; Cataray, Inc, bd of dirs, 1985-89; Graphic Scanning Inc, 1987-89; Dominion Bank, Tysons, 1988-92; Computer Dynamics Inc, 1992-96; Resource America Inc, 1992-; Fidelity Leasing Inc, 1996-. **Orgs:** Sr systems analyst Control Data Corp 1968-69; spec asst US Dept of Housing & Urban Dev 1969-72; vice pres Corp for Comm Devel 1973-74; bd of dir Amer Soc of Plnng Officials 1973-74; bd of dir McLean Savings & Loan Assoc 1975-77; vice pres Amer Council on Intl Sports 1978-81; commiss Northern VA Reg Plnng Dist Comm 1980-82; Screen Actors Guild, 1972-. **Honors/Awds:** Grant Natl Endowment for the Arts 1972, Ford Found 1973; Author New Towns, Another Way to Live 1976; Book of the Month Club Alternate Selection 1976. **Military Serv:** USN lt comm 1959-68; Naval Flight Officer, Navy Achievement Medal, Natl Defense Medal. **Home Addr:** 11530 Links Dr, Reston, VA 22090.

CAMPBELL, CHARLES EVERETT
Dentist (retired). **Personal:** Born Aug 13, 1933, Statesboro, GA; son of Earnestine Campbell and Fred Campbell; married Phyllis; children: Charles, Jacqueline, Andrea. **Educ:** Oakwood Coll, 1959; Meharry Med Coll, 1968; Univ NC, School of PH, 1974. **Career:** Nghbrhd Hlth Ctr, staff dentist 1969-73; Hubbard Hosp & VA Hosp, dental intern 1968-69; VA Hosp, med tech 1960-64; Mt Sinai Hosp, 1959-60; Orange Chatham Comprehensive Health Services, Inc, Carrboro, NC, dental director, 1974-94. **Orgs:** Mem Old N State Dental Soc; Durham Acad Med; Nat Dental Assn; Black Adventist Med Dental Assn; S Atlantic Conf SDA Dental Hlth Sec; mem Oakwood Coll Natl Alumni Assn; Meharry Med Coll Alumni Assn; Immanuel Temple SDA Church, Durham, NC. **Honors/Awds:** Recpt Nashville Dental Prize; John Bluford Award; Sch Dentistry Meharry Med Coll 1968; Cumberland Chap Oakwood Coll Alumni Assn Award 1973. **Military Serv:** AUS mc 1956-58. **Home Addr:** 343 Warren Court, Chapel Hill, NC 27516.

CAMPBELL, CHRISTOPHER LUNDY
Attorney, athlete. **Personal:** Born Sep 21, 1954, Westfield, NJ; son of Marjorie Lee and Howard Thomas; married Laura Sue Beving, Mar 11, 1979; children: Christopher Lundy, Auasa Ebony, Jonathan Edward. **Educ:** University of Iowa, BS, sociology, 1979; Iowa State University, 1980-83; Cornell Law School, JD, 1987. **Career:** Iowa State University, assistant wrestling coach, 1979-83; Iowa University, assistant wrestling coach, 1983-84; Cornell University, assistant wrestling coach, 1985-87; United Technologies Corp., staff attorney, 1987-88; Carrier Corp., attorney, 1988-. **Orgs:** USA Wrestling, board of directors, member of executive committee, 1992; Black Law Student Association, chairman education committee, 1986; US Olympic Committee Athletes Advisory Board, 1992; US Olympic Committee, bd of dirs, 1993; Vegetarian Times, bd of dirs, 1993. **Honors/Awds:** US Olympic Team, bronze medal winner, Barcelona, 1992; Olympic Trials Champion, 1980, 1992; world champion, selected as the ''world's most technically prepared wrestler,'' first American to receive that award, 1981; world silver medalist, 1990; World Cup champion, 1981, 1983, 1984, 1991; Tbilisi champion, 1991; Sullivan Award, 1981; National Freestyle Champion, 1980, 1983, 1990, 1991. **Business Addr:** Executive Director, US Amateur Boxing (USA Boxing), One Olympic Plaza, Colorado Springs, CO 80909, (719)578-4506.

CAMPBELL, E. ALEXANDER
Minister. **Personal:** Born Jan 31, 1927, Montego Bay, Jamaica; married Estelle Jones; children: Alexis, Paula, Edwin, Susan. **Educ:** Cornwall Coll Jamaica, 1944; VA Union Univ, BA 1952; VA Union Theol Sem, MDiv 1955; Hartford Seminary Found, MA 1957; McCormick Theological Sem, DMin 1975. **Career:** Churches-in-Transition Proj, dir, prog devel; Urban Ch Strategy IN-KY Conf UCC, cons. **Orgs:** Dorm dir, counselor for men VA Union Univ 1954-55; assoc conf minister RI Conf United Ch of Christ 1962-72; area chmn NE Comm of Church Leaders 1971-72; dir, host Church & Comm TV Prog RI; chairperson Oak River Forest HS Human Relations Comm; past pres Christian Ed Council United Church of Christ; past vice pres Greater Hartford Council of Church; past vice pres NE Comm of United Ministry in Highr Ed; bd dir United Church Bd for World Ministries; dir Black Church Empowerment Prog; past vice pres Barrington Prog for Action; past bd mem RI People Against Poverty; bd mem Ed Comm RI Childrens Ctr; bd dir Oak Park Housing Ctr; lecturer Negro Hist & Culture; mem Alpha Phi Alpha, Urban League; pres Louisville Interdenominational Ministerial Alliance; bd mem NAACP. **Honors/Awds:** Citation UCC Churches in Chicago; Citation for Outstanding Leadership RI United Church of Christ Conf; Citation for Achievement in Bringing Understanding of Church & Comm through TV RI Council of Church.

CAMPBELL, EDNA
Professional basketball player. **Personal:** Born Nov 26, 1968. **Educ:** Univ of Texas. **Career:** Colorado Xplosion, guard, 1996-. **Business Addr:** Professional Basketball Player, Colorado Xplosion, 800 Grant St, Ste 410, Denver, CO 80203, (303)832-2225.

CAMPBELL, ELDEN
Professional basketball player. **Personal:** Born Jul 23, 1968, Los Angeles, CA. **Educ:** Clemson. **Career:** Los Angeles Lakers, forward-center, 1990-. **Business Addr:** Professional Basketball Player, Los Angeles Lakers, PO Box 10, Inglewood, CA 90306, (310)419-3100.

CAMPBELL, EMMETT EARLE
Educator, physician. **Personal:** Born Dec 22, 1927, Dayton, OH; married Geneva Sydney; children: Michael, Heather, Kimberly, Laura. **Educ:** Univ Dayton, Pre-med 1948; Univ Cinn, MD 1953. **Career:** Am Coll Of Surgeons, fellow 1969; Am Acad Opthalmology & Otolaryngology, fellow 1966; Am Bd Of Otolaryngology, diplmt 1966; Temporal Bone & Lab NY Eye & Ear Infirmary, asst dir; Cleft Palate Clinic N Shore Univ Hosp, cons. **Orgs:** Mem Nassau Co Med Soc; Nassau Surgical Soc; AMA; Nassau Otolaryngol Soc; NY St Soc Of Surgeons; Empire Med Polit Action Com; Nassau Physicians Guild; Am Council Of Otolaryngology; Nat Med. **Honors/Awds:** Assn phy recognition award 1977; paper ''Tympanoplasty Using Homograft Tympanic Membranes & Ossicles'' Nat Med Assn 1976. **Military Serv:** USAF base flight surgeon 1954-57. **Business Addr:** 520 Franklin Ave, Garden City, NY 11530.

CAMPBELL, EMORY SHAW
Community service director. **Personal:** Born Oct 11, 1941, Hilton Head Is, SC; married Emma Joffrion; children: Ochieng, Ayaka. **Educ:** Savannah State Coll, BS Bio 1965; Tufts Univ, MS Env Eng 1971. **Career:** Harvard School of Public Health, Boston MA, rsrch asst 1965-68; Process Rsrch Cambridge, Boston MA, biologist 1968-70; Bramley Health Comm Center, Boston MA, asst dir1971; Beaufort Jasper Comprehensive Health, dir comm serv 1971-80; Penn Center, exec dir. **Orgs:** Plng comm Beaufort Co Plng Comm 1982-; bd dir Beaufort Jasper Water Admin 1978-82, Hilton Head Rural Water 1980-. **Home Addr:** 208 Spanish Wells Rd, Hilton Head Island, SC 29928.

CAMPBELL, EVERETT O.
Physician. **Personal:** Born Nov 15, 1934, Chicago, IL; married Anne Big Ford. **Educ:** Univ Of MI, MD 1958; Ucla, Chas Drew Post, Grad Med Schl. **Career:** Physician; Ucla, asst clinical prof; Chas Drew Post Grad Med Schl, asst prof; Martin Luther King Hosp. **Orgs:** Mem AMA; CA Med Assn; Los Angeles Co Med Assn; mem Applied Health Research. **Honors/Awds:** Author of paper on cancer; organizing dept of Sexual studies at Martin Luther King Hosp. **Military Serv:** AUS chf dept obgyn, 1962-64. **Business Addr:** 1141 W Rodondo Beach Blvd, Gardena, CA 90247.

CAMPBELL, FRANKLYN D.
Airline pilot. **Personal:** Born Feb 11, 1947, Washington, DC. **Educ:** BS 1971. **Career:** The Flying Tiger Line, Inc, Airline Pilot 1974; Garrett Airesearch Aviation Co, test pilot 1974; Saturn Airways, Inc, aircraft planner 1971-72; Embry RiddleAero U, student flight dispatcher, tchr 1970-71; Page Airways, Inc, lineman 1970; Dept of Recreation, neighborhood yth corps coord 1969. **Orgs:** Mem, Nat Coll Flight Safety Council; mem NAACP; Brotherhood Crusade; Airline Pilot Assn; Negro Airman Internat, Inc. **Honors/Awds:** Outstanding Flight Student 1970. **Business Addr:** Flying Tigers, 7401 World Way West, Los Angeles, CA 90009.

CAMPBELL, GARY LLOYD
Educator. **Personal:** Born Feb 15, 1951, Ennis, TX; married Alola McKinney; children: Phyllis, Traci, Bryan. **Educ:** UCLA, BA Sociology 1973. **Career:** UCLA, asst coach 1976-78; Southern Univ, asst coach 1978-80; Howard Univ, asst coach 1981; Pacific Univ, asst coach 1982; Univ of OR, asst coach 1983-. **Orgs:** Mem Amer Football Coaches Assoc 1978-, Amer Congress on Real Estate 1984-. **Business Addr:** Asst Football Coach, Univ of Oregon, McArthur Court, Eugene, OR 97403.

CAMPBELL, GEORGE, JR.
Organization executive. **Personal:** Born Dec 2, 1945, Richmond, VA; son of Lillian Britt Campbell (deceased) and George Campbell; married Mary Schmidt Campbell, Aug 24, 1968; children: Garikai, Sekou, Britt. **Educ:** Drexel University, Philadelphia, PA, BS, 1968; Syracuse University, Syracuse, NY, PhD, 1977; Yale University, New Haven, CT, Executive Management Program, 1988. **Career:** Nkumbi College, Kabwe, Zambia, senior faculty, 1969-71; AT&T Bell Laboratories,Holmdel, NJ, technical staff member, 1977-83, third level manager, 1983-88; NACME, Inc, New York, NY, president, 1989-. **Orgs:** Emeritus member, Secretary of Energy Advisory Board, 1989-; AAAS Committee on Science Engineering & Public Policy, 1990-; American Physical Society, 1968-; President Council of the New York Academy of Sciences, 1984-; National Society of Black Physicists, 1977-; chairman, National Advisory Committee, NSF Comprehensive Regional Center for Minorities, 1989-91; board of trustees, Rensselaer Polytechnic Institute, 1992-; board of trustees, Crossroads Theater Company, 1991-. **Honors/Awds:** Simon Guggenheim Scholar, Drexel University, 1963-67; Sigma Pi Sigma, 1967; AT&T Bell Laboratories Exceptional Contribution Award, AT&T, 1985, 1986, 1987; Black Achiever in Industry, Harlem YMCA, 1988; Outstanding Black American Scientist, Brooklyn Science Skills Center, 1990; Synthesis Medallion, National Engineering Education Coalition, 1992; Centennial Medal, Drexel University, 1992; Arents Pioneer Medal in Science, 1993. **Business Addr:** President, National Action Council for Minorities in Engineering, Inc, 350 5th Ave, Ste 2212, New York, NY 10118-2299.

CAMPBELL, GERTRUDE M.
Association executive. **Personal:** Born Aug 3, 1923, Dallas; married Quintell O; children: Patricia. **Educ:** Prairie View Coll, BS 1943; USC, 1968. **Career:** US Energy Res & Dev Adminstrn, dir ofc mgmt Serv 1st Female 1975;Oakland Adult Minor Proj, one of 1st Demon Projs US employ disadv Adults; brmgr; Berkeley Human Res Dev Cntr, 1st & female cntr mgr. **Orgs:** 1st Pres, Past Western Dist Gov & Life mem; E Bay Area Nat Assn Negro Bus & Prof Women's Clubs; Life mem Nat Coun Negro Wmn; Zeta Phi Beta; past matron Order Eastern Star; sec El Cerrito Br NAACP; mem Golden State Bus League; Prairie View Alumnae Assn; Bay Area Personnel Women; N CA Ind rel coun Who's Who Am Women 1971; com mem Gov's

Commn Status Women. **Honors/Awds:** 3 serv awards Zeta Phi Beta; commun serv award Order Eastern Star; empl awards Nat Assn Negro Bus & Prof Women. **Business Addr:** 1333 Broadway, Oakland, CA.

CAMPBELL, GERTRUDE SIMS
Postal administrator. **Personal:** Born May 13, 1942, Greenville, MS; daughter of Eugene Sims & Beatrice Parker Smith; married Willie James Campbell, Jul 1, 1960 (deceased); children: Kimberly Jamille. **Educ:** Wm F Bolger Academy, Supervisor Skills Training, Memphis, TN, 1990. **Career:** US Postal Service, clerk positions, 1966-1990, supervisor customer svc, 1990, postmaster, 1997-. **Orgs:** National Association Postal Supervisors, 1993; National Association Postmasters United States, 1997; League of Postmasters, 1992; Afro Americans United for the Success of the Postal Svc, 1990-93. **Honors/Awds:** US Postal Service, Special Achievement Awd, 1973, 1987, Diversity Peacesetters Awd, 1996.

CAMPBELL, GILBERT GODFREY
Cleric (retired). **Personal:** Born Jan 16, 1920, Plainfield, NJ; son of Lulu Conover Campbell (deceased) and Daniel Young Campbell (deceased); married Bertha Vernice Morgan; children: Gilbert G Jr, Rosalind V Taylor. **Educ:** Union Univ Richmond VA, AB 1941; Union Univ VA, MDiv 1944; Union Univ Va, DD 1967. **Career:** Moore St Bapt Ch, pastor, until 1994; VA Union U, pastor 1971-88; 1st Gravel Hill Bapt Ch Rushmore & VA, pastor 1953-64; Chesapeake Pub Sch, prin/tchr 1950-64; Gethsemane Bapt Ch Suffolk, VA, pastor 1950-64; Grove Bapt Ch Portsmouth VA, pastor 1949-64; Theol Dept VA Sem & Coll, dean 1947-50; 1st Bapt Ch Cape Charles VA, pastor 1946-49. **Orgs:** Dir of Christian Educ Bapt Gen Convention of VA 1944-46; bd mem Richmond OIC 1965; pres Bapt Gen Convention of VA 1970-73; bd mem Richmond NAACP/Sickle Cell Anemia 1977-. **Honors/Awds:** Outstndng leadership Award VA Union Univ 1977; past pres Award Bapt Gen Convention Of VA 1979; Gold Key Award OIC 1980.

CAMPBELL, GRAHAM F.
Personnel executive. **Personal:** Born Oct 20, 1939, Winston-Salem, NC; married Gloria Watson; children: Gregory, Gigi, Garry. **Educ:** Johnson C Smith U, 1958-59; Winston-Salem State U, 1972-74; Dominican Coll, BS Mgmt 1982. **Career:** Joyce-Munden Co, Winston-Salem NC, warehouse mgr 1957-62, 1965-69; Hanes Knitwear, Winston-Salem NC, mgr-personnel admin 169-74; L & M Tobacco Co, Durham NC, asst dir personnel 1975-76; Grand Met USA, Inc, Montvale NJ, mgr compensation 1976-87; Guilford County School System, sr dir of personnel 1987-. **Orgs:** Am Mgmt Assn 1976-; Am Cmpstn Assn 1976-; dir & treas Am Scty Persnl Admin 1972-; Admin Mgmt Scty 1977-; chmn hsng task force Winston-Salem Model Cities Pgm 1967-71; Natl Urban League 1980-; Chmbr Comm Durham, NC 1975-79, Winston-Salem NC 1967-74. **Military Serv:** AUS sgt E-5 1962-65. **Home Addr:** 6110 Westwind Dr, Greensboro, NC 27410.

CAMPBELL, JAMES W.
Clergyman. **Personal:** Born Mar 17, 1945, Chicago, IL; married Anne; children: James, Jesse, Jared, Bridgett. **Educ:** Wilson Jr Coll; Moody Bible Inst. **Career:** St James Ch God in Christ, supt State 1977; 5th Jurisdiction IL, sec 1973; dist supt 1972; pastorate 1970; ministry 1966. **Orgs:** Mem Resolution Com for Nat & Elders Cncl 1975-77; mem Westside br NAACP; Nat Petrolmans Assn; NACD; Intl bd Minister's; Intl Assn Pastor's; Nat Elder's Cncl. **Honors/Awds:** COGIC spl citation City Chicago; pastor of the year Award Christian Guild Society 1979; Award for Dedicated & Faithful Servs as State Sunday Sch supt Sunday Sch Dept of IL 1980. **Business Addr:** 4147 W Roosevelt Rd, Chicago, IL 60623.

CAMPBELL, JESSE
Professional football player. **Personal:** Born Apr 11, 1969, Washington, NC; married Belinda. **Educ:** North Carolina State, attended. **Career:** New York Giants, defensive back, 1992-96; Washington Redskins, 1997-. **Business Addr:** Professional Football Player, Washington Redskins, 13832 Redskin Dr, Herndon, VA 22071, (703)471-9100.

CAMPBELL, MAIA
Actress. **Personal:** daugHter of Bebe Moore Campbell. **Career:** Actress, UPN's In The House, currently. **Business Addr:** Actress, Gold/Marshak/Liedtke, 3500 W Olive Ave, Ste 1400, Burbank, CA 91505, (818)972-4300.

CAMPBELL, MARGIE
Educator. **Personal:** Born Jun 17, 1954, Musella, GA; daughter of Margret Smith; children: MeQuanta. **Educ:** Gordon College, AS, 1991, Mercer University, BS, 1995. **Career:** Monroe County Bd of Education, school secretary, 1978-; Hospital/Homebound teacher, currently. **Orgs:** Parker Chapel AME Church; GA Municipal Assn 1984; Gov's Project Steering Comm 1984; Volunteer Fire Fighter, 1977-; Band Booster, vice pres, 1990-; Basketball Tip-Off Club, vice pres, 1991. **Honors/Awds:** Comm Leader Awd Gov's Project Competition Atlanta 1982; selected as one of the 50 most influential Black women in GA-GA Informer 1983. **Home Addr:** PO Box 13, Culloden, GA 31016.

CAMPBELL, MARK
Professional football player. **Personal:** Born Sep 12, 1972, Jamaica. **Educ:** Univ of Florida, attended. **Career:** Arizona Cardinals, defensive tackle, 1997-. **Business Addr:** Professional Football Player, Arizona Cardinals, 8701 S Hardy, Tempe, AZ 85284, (602)379-0101.

CAMPBELL, MARY ALLISON
Educator. **Personal:** Born Feb 18, 1937, Shelby, NC; daughter of Mr & Mrs A C Allison; married Fred N Campbell Sr; children: Alison Winifred, Fred N Jr. **Educ:** Benedict Coll, BS 1960; Winthrop Coll, Early Childhood 1973. **Career:** Harold Fagges Assoc NYC, clerk 1963-68; Clover Town Council, councilmember; Clover Sch Dist, teacher 1968-. **Orgs:** Pres The Progressive Women's Club Inc 1970-75; assoc matron Magnolia Chap OES #144 1982-84; YCEA Pres, 1988-89. **Honors/Awds:** School Yearbook Dedication Roosevelt Sch 1970; Appreciation Awd United Men's Club 1980; Outstanding Black Citizen of Clover Community, 1989. **Home Addr:** 104 Wilson St, Clover, SC 29710. **Business Addr:** Teacher, Clover School District, 201 Pressly St, Clover, SC 29710.

CAMPBELL, MARY DELOIS
Administrator. **Personal:** Born Jul 21, 1940, Greenville, TX; married David; children: Keith Devlin. **Educ:** Jarvis Christian Coll Hawkins, Tx, BS Bus Admin 1957-62; Bishop Coll Dallas, 1962-63. **Career:** Housing Auth of City of Dallas, asst dir res selection 1980; Housing Auth of City of Dallas, asst dir of Soc Serv 1979-80; N Central TX Council of Govt, human serv & planner 1976-77; N Central TX Council of T, manpower planner 1971-76; City Of Dallas, asst youth coord 1969-71; Dallas Co Comm Action Inc, Neighborhood Center coord 1968-69; Bishop Coll Dallas Co Comm Action, clerical 1962-68. **Orgs:** Bd of dir Dallas Urban League 1974-77; mem Dallas Commn on Children & Youth 1975; pres bd of dir Dallas Urban League 1977-78; bd of dir Goals for Dallas 1977-79. **Business Addr:** Housing Auth City of Dallas, 2525 Lucas Dr, Dallas, TX 75219.

CAMPBELL, MARY SCHMIDT
Dean. **Personal:** Born Oct 21, 1947, Philadelphia, PA; daughter of Elaine Harris Schmidt (deceased) and Harvey N. Schmidt; married George Campbell Jr, Aug 24, 1968; children: Garikai, Sekou, Britt Jackson. **Educ:** Swarthmore Coll, BA English Lit 1969; Syracuse Univ, MA art history 1973, PhD, 1982. **Career:** Syracuse University, Syracuse, NY, lecturer; Nkumbi Intl Coll, Kabwe, Zambia, instr, 1969-71; Syracuse New Times, writer, art editor, 1973-77; Everson Museum, curator, guest curator, 1974-76; The Studio Museum in Harlem, exec dir, 1977-87; New York City Department of Cultural Affairs, New York, commissioner, 1987-91; Tisch School, dean, 1991-. **Orgs:** Chair, Student Life Committee, Swarthmore College Board of Managers, 1991-; member, Visiting Committee on Fine Arts, Harvard College Board of Overseers, 1991-93; chair, Advisory Committee for African American Institutional Study, Smithsonian Institute, 1989-91; advisory board member , Barnes Foundation, 1991-; fellow, Institute for Humanities, New York University, 1989-. **Honors/Awds:** Ford Fellow, 1973-77; Rockefeller Fellowship in the Humanities, 1985; Municipal Art Society Certificate, 1985; Candace Award, 100 Black Women, 1986; author, Black American Art & Harlem Renaissance, 1987; author of numerous articles on Black American art; consultant to the Ford Foundation as part of their mid-decade review; lectures on American & African-American Art, The Studio Museum in Harlem and the issues involved in the Institutionalization of Diverse Cultures and Public Policy and the Arts; City College, NY, Honorary Doctorate, 1992. **Business Addr:** Dean, Tisch School of the Arts, New York University, 721 Broadway, New York, NY 10003.

CAMPBELL, MICHELE
Professional basketball player. **Personal:** Born Feb 20, 1974. **Educ:** Univ of Southern California. **Career:** Philadelphia Rage, center, 1997-. **Business Addr:** Professional Basketball Player, Philadelphia Rage, 123 Chestnut St, Fourth Flr, Philadelphia, PA 19106, (215)629-1976.

CAMPBELL, MILTON GRAY
Athlete, lecturer. **Personal:** Born Dec 9, 1933, Plainfield, NJ. **Educ:** Indiana University, 1957. **Career:** US Olympic Team, decathlete, 1952, 1956; community service, work with underpriviledged children, lecturer, currently. **Orgs:** NFL Cleveland Browns; CFL Hamilton Tiger Cats & Toronto Argunauts. **Honors/Awds:** AAU Decathlon, winner, 1953; AAU and NCAA high hurdles, first place, 1955; World Record, 120 yard hurdles; Silver Medal, decathlon, 1952; Gold Medal/Olympic Record, decathlon, 1956; Intl Swimming Hall of Fame, 1995; NJ Sports Hall of Fame; Natl Track and Field, Hall of Fame; Indiana Univ, Hall Of Fame; NJ Interscholastic Hall of Fame; US Olympic Hall of Fame; NFL Cleveland Browns. **Military Serv:** US Navy, 1955-56.

CAMPBELL, OTIS, JR.
Physician. **Personal:** Born Sep 9, 1953, Tampa, FL; son of Georgia Mae Anthony Campbell and Otis Campbell; married Carol Y Clarke; children: Davin, Desmond, Donovon, Danyel. **Educ:** FL A&M Univ, BS Biology 1973; Meharry Medical Coll, PhD Pharmacology 1982; Meharry Medical Coll, MD 1986; Hubbard Hospital, Nashville, TN, internal medicine residency 1986-89. **Career:** Special Medical Prog Meharry Medical Coll, instructor 1982-84; Biomedical Science Prog Meharry Medical Coll, instructor 1982-84; UNCF Fisk Univ Pre-Med Inst, 1982-84; TN State Univ Weekend Coll, prof 1982-86; Meharry Medical College, Dept of Pharmacology, Nashville, TN, professor, 1986-; private practice, internal medicine, McMinnville, TN, 1990-. **Orgs:** Mem Middle TN Neuroscience Soc; mem Amer Medical Assoc. **Honors/Awds:** Post Doctoral Rsch Fellow in hypertension Vanderbilt Univ 1982-85 summers; Alpha Omega Alpha Medical Honor Soc 1986; Hall of Natural Scientists Florida A&M Univ 1987; Diplomate of the American Board of International Medicine. **Home Addr:** 3723 Stevens Lane, Nashville, TN 37218. **Business Addr:** Physician, 140 Vo-Tech Dr, Ste 5, Mc Minnville, TN 37110, (615)473-9529.

CAMPBELL, OTIS LEVY
Owner/manager. **Personal:** Born Jan 9, 1935, Slidell, LA; married Lois Ziegler; children: Cherry Ann, Barry, Maynard, Lajuana. **Educ:** Worsham Coll of Mortuary Sci, 1962; Christian Bible Coll Kenner La, BA/Theology 1980. **Career:** Campbell's Funeral Hm, mgr ownr 1952; O L Campbell Agy, broker/mgr 1952; St Tammany & Progressive Civic League, 1952-62. **Orgs:** Sec NAACP Local Chap 1952-62; Vice Pres CBC Citizens for a Better Comm 1974; Elected 1st Black Mem to Sch bd Saint Tammany Parish La 1978. **Business Addr:** Campbells Funeral Home, 2522 4th St, Slidell, LA 70458.

CAMPBELL, ROGERS EDWARD, III
Pharmaceutical company executive. **Personal:** Born Jul 14, 1951, Jersey City, NJ; son of Anne Mae Powell and Rogers E Campbell, Jr. **Educ:** Saint Peter's Coll, BS 1973; Rutgers Univ, MBA 1974. **Career:** General Mills Inc, asst product mgr 1978-81; Mattel Electronics, product mgr 1982-83; Schering-Plough Corp, dir of marketing, 1983-88; Marketcare Consumer Health, vice pres, managing director, 1988-. **Orgs:** Admissions liaison officer US Military Acad; chmn public relations comm Rutgers Grad Sch of Business; IOTA Phi Theta Fraternity; Clinton Hill Development Corp. **Honors/Awds:** Distinguished Military Graduate. **Military Serv:** US Army, 1st lt, 1974-77; Army Commendation Medal for Meritorious Svcs. **Home Addr:** 66 Highland Ave, Maplewood, NJ 07040.

CAMPBELL, SYLVAN LLOYD
Physician. **Personal:** Born Oct 8, 1931, Boston, MA; son of Vera Campbell and Silvanis Campbell; children: Steven. **Educ:** Boston Coll, AB 1953; Howard U, MD 1961. **Career:** Philadelphia Gen Hosp, intern 1961-62, res 1962-65; Boston, Pvt Practice med, specializing in ob & gynecology 1965; Beth Israel Hospital, Boston, MA, obstetrician-gynecologist, 1965-; Harvard U, Obstetrics Gynecology Obstetrics asst cl prof 1975. **Orgs:** Mem Attending Staff Beth Israel Hosp & Univ Hosp Boston; mem Am Bd Obstetrics-Gynecology Boston Obstetrical Soc; mem American College of Obstetricians-Gynecologists, 1969-; mem Massachusetts Medical Society, 1966-. **Military Serv:** USNR, lt jg, 1953-57.

CAMPBELL, TEVIN
Vocalist. **Personal:** Born Nov 19, 1978, Dallas, TX; son of Rhonda Byrd. **Career:** Vocalist; albums: TEVIN, 1991; I'm Ready, 1993. **Special Achievements:** Single, "Round and Round," featured on Prince's album Graffiti Bridge; Grammy nomination for Best Male R&B Vocalist; television appearances include: Saturday Night Live, Arsenio Hall, Fresh Prince of Bel Air, and Oprah; single, "Tell Me What You Want Me to Do," reached top ten charts.

CAMPBELL, THOMAS W.
Musician. **Personal:** Born Feb 14, 1957, Norristown, PA. **Educ:** Berklee Coll of Music, Attended. **Career:** Dizzy Gillespie Band, professional jazz drummer 1985; Baird Hersey & Yr of the Ear, drummer; Own Group "TCB" Boston, drummer; MarLena Shaw/Gap Mangione, drummer 1979; Webster Lewis, drummer 1978. **Orgs:** Big Brother Activities; org First Music Group & "The Mandells" 15 yrs; conducted music clinics Berklee Coll. **Honors/Awds:** Recorded Album with Baird Hersey 1978; concert Berklee Performance Ctr 1979; toured US/Can/S Am/E Europe/Scandinavian Counties/Asia & Africa 1979-80. **Business Addr:** Sutton Artists Corp, 119 W 57 Ste 818, New York, NY 10019.

CAMPBELL, TISHA
Actress. **Personal:** daugHter of Mona Campbell; married. **Career:** Actress, movies include: Little Shop of Horror, House Party, Boomerang; Sprung; television, plays Gina on Martin, 1992-97; Singer, currently. **Business Addr:** Actress, c/o Michelle Marx Inc., 6308 W 89th St #338, Los Angeles, CA 90045-3602.

CAMPBELL, TONY
Professional basketball player. **Personal:** Born May 7, 1962, Teaneck, NJ. **Educ:** Ohio State Univ, Columbus, OH, 1980-84. **Career:** Albany Patroons, 1987-88; Detroit Pistons, 1984-87; Los Angeles Lakers, 1987-89; Minnesota Timberwolves, 1989-

92; New York Knicks, 1992-94; Dallas Mavericks, 1994-. **Honors/Awds:** NBA championship team, 1988; CBA All-Star First Team, 1988; CBA Newcomer of the Year, 1988. **Business Addr:** Professional Basketball Player, Dallas Mavericks, Reunion Arena, 777 Sports St, Dallas, TX 75207.

CAMPBELL, WENDELL J.
Business executive. **Personal:** Born Apr 27, 1927, East Chicago, IN; son of Selma Campbell and Herman Campbell; married June Crusor Campbell, Nov 6, 1955; children: Susan, Leslie. **Educ:** IL Inst Tech, BA 1956. **Career:** Purdue Calumet Devel Foundation, staff architect & dir rehab; Wendell Campbell Assoc, Inc, owner; Campbell & Macsai Architects Inc, owner. **Orgs:** Pres lecturer Yale Univ MA Inst Tech, Univ IL; mem Urban Planning & Design Comm Amer Inst Architects; bd dir Chicago Amer Inst-Architects; mem Natl Organization Minority Architects; mem Chicago C of C; Chicago Assn Commerce & Ind; NAACP; Natl Urban League Devel Foundation. **Honors/Awds:** Distinguished Bldg Award 1973; Construction Man Yr 1973; Engineering News Record 1973; AIA Whitney M Young Jr Medal 1976; Fellow Amer Inst of Arch 1979. **Military Serv:** AUS sgt major. **Business Addr:** President, Wendell Campbell Assocs Inc, 1326 S Michigan Ave, Chicago, IL 60605.

CAMPBELL, WILLIAM
City official. **Personal:** Born 1953, Raleigh, NC; married Sharon; children: Billy, Christina. **Educ:** Vanderbilt Univ; Duke Univ, law degree. **Career:** Atlanta City Council, 12 yrs; City of Atlanta, mayor, currently. **Business Addr:** Mayor, City of Atlanta, 68 Mitchell St, SW, Ste 2400, Atlanta, GA 30335, (404)330-6100.

CAMPBELL, WILLIAM EARL
City official. **Personal:** Born Aug 26, 1965, Dermott, AR; son of Alice Allen Campbell and Eddie Campbell Sr (deceased). **Educ:** University of Arkansas-Monticello, Monticello, AR. **Career:** Dixie Dandy, night mgr, 1983-86; Piggly Wiggly, night mgr, 1986-91; Desha-Drew School System, substitute teacher, 1983-86; City of Reed, AR, mayor, currently; McGehee Auto Plaza, sales consultant, currently. **Orgs:** General secretary, board of directors, New Hope Baptist Church, 1985-91; Desha County Quorum Court, 1991-; Reed Neighborhood Crimewatch Program, president; United Negros Interacting Todays Youth, historian; Southeast Arkansas Literacy Council; Arkansas Municipal League. **Honors/Awds:** Valedictorian, Tillar High School, 1983; Mr Boss, Black Organization for Special Services, University of Arkansas-Monticello, 1990; Southeastern Arkansas Charity Organization, Andrew Gregory Man of the Year Award, 1991. **Business Addr:** Mayor, City of Reed, PO Box 233, Reed, AR 71670.

CAMPBELL, ZERRIE D.
Educator, educational administrator. **Personal:** Born Feb 9, 1951, Chicago, IL; daughter of Lorraince Rice and Robert Rice; children: Sydney Adams. **Educ:** Northern Illinois University, BA, 1972, MS, 1974; Chicago State University, MA, 1978. **Career:** Northern Illinois University, graduate assistant, 1972-73, assistant dormitory director, 1973-74; Malcolm X College, director, student supportive services, 1974-77, instructor, English and communications, 1977-82; Harold Washington College, assistant professor, English grammar, 1983-87; City Colleges of Chicago, acting associate, vice chancellor, liberal arts and sciences, 1987-89; Malcolm X College, vice pres, academic affairs, 1989-92, president, 1992-. **Orgs:** Alpha Kappa Alpha, Xi Nu Omega Chapter, past president; Monarch Awards Foundation, past president; Langston Hughes Literary Association; NIU Black Alumni Council; Modern Language Association; Illinois Committee on Black Concerns in Higher Education; National Council of Instructional Administrators; American Council on Educational/National ID Program for the AWHE; American Association of Women in Community Colleges; American Association of University Women, National Association of Female Executives. **Honors/Awds:** Kathy Osterman Award for Outstanding Executive Employee (finalist) 1994, Eta Phi Beta Sorority, Inc, Woman of the year, 1994, Proviso Leyden Council for Community Action Inc, Woman of the Year, 1993, National Association of University Women, Chicago Branch, Distinctive Imprint Award, 1993; Midwest Community College, Distinguished Service in Education Award, 1992; Malcolm X College, Spirit Award, 1991; Work Force 2000: Women's Day, Chancellor's Award, 1991; Fred Hampton Image Award, 1990; 2,000 Notable American Award, 1990; Malcolm X College, Administrator Appreciation Award, 1990. **Business Addr:** President, Malcolm X College, 1900 W Van Buren, Rm 1100, Chicago, IL 60612-3197.

CAMPER, DIANE G.
Journalist. **Personal:** Born Feb 27, 1948, New York, NY; daughter of Clinice Coleman Camper and Roosevelt P. Camper (deceased). **Educ:** Syracuse University, Syracuse, NY, BA, 1968; Yale University, New Haven, CT, master of studies in law, 1977. **Career:** Newsweek, editorial assistant, 1968-72, Washington Bureau correspondent, 1972-83; The New York Times, New York, NY, editorial writer, 1983-. **Orgs:** Member, Women in Communications, Inc, 1968-; member, National Association of Black Journalists, 1985-; member, Delta Sigma Theta Sorority, 1974-. **Honors/Awds:** George Arents Pioneer Medal, 1990, Chancellor's Citation, 1986, Syracuse University; Page One Award, New York Newspaper Guild, 1977; New York Times, Publisher's Awards, 1988, 1990. **Business Addr:** Editorial Writer, New York Times Co, 229 W 43rd St, 10th Fl, New York, NY 10036.

CAMPHOR, MICHAEL GERARD
Health services administrator. **Personal:** son Of Lillie Camphor and James Camphor. **Educ:** Morgan State Univ, BA 1978; Univ of Baltimore, MPA Health Serv Admin 1984; Naval Health Sciences Education and Training Command, Certificate Financial/Supply Management 1986. **Career:** Columbia Rsch Syst, rsch asst 1976-77; N Central Baltimore Health Corp, center admin 1980-84; Dept Housing & Community Devel, project mgr 1983-84; Central MD Health Systems Agency, health implementor/liaison 1984-85; US Naval Hospital Philadelphia PA, comptroller/hosp administrator 1985-; US Naval Hospital, Yokosuku Japan, Materials Management/Contracting, head officer. **Orgs:** Mem E Baltimore Comm Org 198-83, Waverly Human Serv Coord Council 1980-83; site coord Natl Health Screening Council for Volunteer Org 1980-83; mem Dallas F Nicholas Elem School Advisory Bd 1981-84; mem Johns Hopkins Hosp Comm Devel Advisory Bd 1983-84; National Naval Officers Association, life mem. **Honors/Awds:** Senatorial Scholarship Sen Clarence Blount 1973-77; MJ Naylor Awd Highest Dept Average Morgan State Univ 1978; Admin of the Year N Central Baltimore Health Corp 1981; Outstanding Young Men of Amer Jaycees 1983; Recipient of Grad Studies Fellowship from Dept Housing & Urban Devel. **Military Serv:** US Navy, Medical Officers Corp, lcdr, 1992; Navy Achievement Medal, 1988, 1990; Overseas Service Ribbon; Armed Forces Service Medal, 1991.

CANADA, BENJAMIN OLEANDER
Educational administrator. **Personal:** Born Nov 22, 1944, Tallulah, LA; son of Thelma Victoria Harrison Canada and Archie Canada; married Doris Malinda Colbert Canada, Aug 17, 1968; children: Julie Malinda, Christina Malinda. **Educ:** Southern University, BA, 1967; University of Washington, MEd, 1971; University of Texas at Austin, PhD, 1989. **Career:** Las Vegas School District, elementary teacher, 1967-68; Seattle School District, secondary teacher, middle school asst principal, elementary school principal, junior high school principal, senior high school principal, 1968-83; Tucson Unified School Dist, regional asst supt, 1983-86, assistant supt, 1987-88, deputy supt, 1988-90; Texas Assn of School Boards, consultant and trainer, 1986-87; Jackson Public Schools, superintendent, 1990-94; Atlanta Public Schools, superintendent, currently. **Orgs:** Alliance Theater Co, bd of dirs; American Red Cross, advisory bd; 100 Black Men of Atlanta; Chamber of Commerce Education Comm; Rotary Club of Atlanta, Governor's Georgia P-16 Council; Center for Research on Evaluation, Standards & Students Testing, natl advisory bd, 1996; The Horace Mann League; American Assn of Colleges and Schools, commission on colleges, 1992-; Natl Commission on Chap 1, 1991-; Southern Assn of Colleges and Schools, commission on colleges, 1992-; Natl Urban Reform Network, bd mem, 1992-; Active Citizenship Today, natl advisory bd, 1992; Natl Federation of Urban-Suburban School Districts, executive comm, 1991-; Southern Regional Education Board Commission for Educational Quality, 1992-; Learning Matters, natl advisory bd, 1992-. **Honors/Awds:** University of Washington, fellowship, 1970-71; University of Texas at Austin, Superintendent's Program, 1986-87; Phi Kappa Phi; Kappa Delta Phi; Rotary International, Urban Superintendents; Large City School Superintendents; Tucson/Pima County Arts Council, various awards for participation; Harvard University, Graduate Seminar for Superintendents, 1991; Jackson Urban League Guild, Outstanding Service and Achievement Award. **Special Achievements:** Sang theme song, "CBS This Morning," CBS-TV. **Business Addr:** Superintendent of Schools, Atlanta Public Schools, 210 Pryor St SW, Atlanta, GA 30335.

CANADY, ALEXA I. (ALEXA CANADY-DAVIS)
Physician. **Personal:** Born Nov 7, 1950, Lansing, MI; daughter of Hortense Golden Canady and Clinton Canady Jr.; married George Davis, Jun 18, 1988. **Educ:** Univ of Michigan, Ann Arbor MI, BS, 1971, MD, (cum laude) 1975. **Career:** Univ of Pennsylvania, instructor in neurosurgery, 1981-82; Henry Ford Hosp, Detroit MI, instructor in neurosurgery, 1982-83; Wayne State Univ, School of Medicine, Detroit, MI, clinical instructor, 1985, clinical assoc prof, 1987-90, associate prof of neurosurgery, 1990-; vice chairman, department of neurosurgery, 1991-; Children's Hosp of Michigan, Detroit MI, asst dir of neurosurgery, 1986-87, chief of neurosurgery, 1987—. **Orgs:** American College of Surgeons, American Association of Neurological Surgeons, Congress of Neurological Surgeons, American Medical Association, National Medical Association, American Society of Pediatric Neurosurgery, Michigan State Medical Society. **Honors/Awds:** Womens Medical Association citation, 1975; Teacher of the Year, Children's Hospital of Michigan, 1984; Woman of the Year Award, Detroit Club of National Association of Negro Business & Professional Women's Club, 1986; Candace Award, National Coalition of 100 Black Women, 1986; Michigan Womans Hall of Fame; American Women's Medical Assn, Woman of the Year, 1993.

CANADY, BLANTON THANDREUS
Company executive. **Personal:** Born Nov 25, 1948, West Point, GA; son of Grace Warrick Canady and William Canady Jr; married Mae Newbern Canady; children: Andre Reynolds, Blanton T Canady II. **Educ:** University of Illinois, BA, 1970; University of Chicago, MBA, 1975. **Career:** IL Bell Telephone, Chicago, IL, communications consultant, 1970-73; Xerox Corp, Des Plaines, IL, telecomm mgr, 1973-76; Amer Hosp Supply, Waukegan, IL, fin mgr, 1976-80; BT II, Inc, Chicago, IL, pres, 1981-. **Orgs:** Pres, McDonald's Owners of Chicagoland & NW IN, 1990-92, vice pres, 1988-90; pres, Black McDonald's Owners Assn of Chicago, 1986-88; exec comm, South Side Planning Bd, 1990-; bd mem, Midwest Assn of Sickle Cell Anemia, 1990-. **Honors/Awds:** Dollars & Sense Magazine, 1991; Business & Professional Awards, Donald C Walker Publisher; The Empire Salute Award, Black McDonald's Owners Assn, 1990; The Monarch Award, Alpha Kappa Alpha, 1990. **Military Serv:** IL Natl Guard, E4, 1970-76. **Business Addr:** President, BT II, Inc, DBA McDonald's, 2525 Martin L King Dr, Chicago, IL 60616.

CANADY, HERMAN G., JR.
Judge. **Career:** Circuit Court, Charleston, WV, judge. **Business Addr:** Judge of the Circuit Court, Kanawha County Courthouse, 4th Floor, Judicial Annex, 409 Virginia St E, Charleston, WV 25301.

CANADY, HORTENSE GOLDEN
Educational administrator (retired). **Personal:** Born Aug 18, 1927, Chicago, IL; daughter of Essie Atwater Golden (deceased) and Alexander H Golden (deceased); married Clinton Canady Jr; children: Clinton III, Alexa I, Alan L, Mark H. **Educ:** Fisk Univ, BA 1947; Michigan State Univ, MA 1977. **Career:** Community Nursery School, dir 1947-48; Lansing Bd of Educ, elected bd mem 1969-72; Women's Commission State of MI, establishing comm 1967-71; Auxiliary to the NDA, natl pres 1976-77; Lansing Comm Coll, Lansing Community College Foundation, director. **Orgs:** President, Delta Research & Educational Foundation, currently; natl pres Delta Sigma Theta Sor Inc 1983-88; natl bd YWCA 1976-82; bd dirs First of Amer Central Bank, 1977-92; First of Amer Corp Bd, 1985-92; charter mem Lansing-East Lansing Chapter Links, AAUW, NAACP, League of Women Voters; advisory bd, Wheaton Center Performing Arts. **Honors/Awds:** DIANA Awd YWCA 1977; Sojourner Truth Awd Negro Bus & Professional Women; Black Book Awd 1984; 100 Top Black Business & Professional Women 1985; Hugo Lundberg Awd Lansing Human Relations Comm; Athena Award, Lansing Regional Chamber of Commerce. **Home Addr:** 3808 W Holmes Rd, Lansing, MI 48911.

CANADY-DAVIS, ALEXA. See CANADY, ALEXA I.

CANNADY, ALONZO JAMES. See MUWAKKIL, SALIM.

CANNON, ALETA
City official. **Personal:** Born Jan 19, 1942, Greenville, MS; daughter of Leatha D Cannon and Daniel Cannon; married Robert Lewis Dowell; children: Gerald, Marian, William, Gregory. **Educ:** Garland Coll, AA 1968; Laney Coll, AA 1977; Univ of San Francisco, BS 1979. **Career:** Tufts Univ, sec 1968-72; CA Legislature, sec 1972-78, admin asst 1978-; City of Oakland, city councilmember, currently. **Orgs:** Mem NAACP, CA Elected Women for Ed & Rsch, League of Women Voters, Natl Council of Negro Women. **Honors/Awds:** Medal of Merit CA Natl Guard. **Business Addr:** City Councilmember, City of Oakland, 1 City Hall Plz, Oakland, CA 94612.

CANNON, BARBARA E. M.
Educational administrator (retired). **Personal:** Born Jan 17, 1936, Big Sandy, TX; daughter of Jimmie Jones Cannon and Archie Cannon; married Rev Dr Booker T Anderson Jr (deceased). **Educ:** San Francisco State Univ, BA, 1957, MA 1965; Sorbonne Univ of Paris, Cert Pedagogiques, 1967; Alliance Francaise, Paris, Cert Pedagogiques, 1967; Univ of California, Berkeley, Admin Credit, 1973; Stanford Univ, MA, 1975, EdD, 1977. **Career:** Berkeley Public Schools, teacher, staff devel, assoc admin, 1958-74; Stanford Univ, teaching fellow, rsch assoc, 1974-75; Natl Teacher Corp, US Office of Educ, Washington, DC, educ policy fellow, 1975-76; Coll of Alameda, asst dean, 1978-85; Merritt Coll, asst dean, 1985-95, Math & science Div, dean, 1995-96, dean emeritus, 1996-. **Orgs:** Urban Educ Inst, 1982-83; exec bd mem, East Bay Consortium of Educ Inst, 1982-84; mem, Soroptimist Intl Alameda, 1984-86; Business & Professional Women of Alameda, 1984-; Black Women Org Political Action 1981-; Women's Day Speaker, St Mark's United Methodist Church, 1983; Black History Speaker, Easter Hill United Methodist Church, 1984; Women's Day Speaker, 1984, Women's Day co-chair, 1985, Women's Day Chair, 1986, Jones United Methodist Church; Assn of California Community College Administration; Pi Lambda Theta; Phi Delta Kappa; Today's Women Inc, advisory bd; Mayor's Literacy, steering committee; Mayor's Church City Coalition; Oakland Sharing The Vision: Education & Lifelong Learning Task Force; New Oakland Comm Race Relations Roundtable; Black Women's Roundtable; Black Women Organized for Political

Action. **Honors/Awds:** Theodore Presser Found Music Scholarship Recipient, San Francisco State Univ, 1956; Outstanding Sr of Yr, Mu Phi Epsilon, San Francisco State Univ, 1957; Sabbatical Berkeley Public School, 1966-67, 1974-75; govt fellow, Univ of CA, Univ of Ghana, 1968; educ policy fellow, Inst for Educ Leadership, Washington, DC, 1975-76; Status & Role of Women Shattuck Ave, United Methodist Church, 1987; Dissertation, School Community Councils: Parity in Decision Making, 1977; US Office of Education Monograph: Involvement: Parity in Decision Making, 1977; trustee, The Foundation, San Francisco Community College District; board of directors, Children's Advocate Newspaper; chair, advisory council, Jones Memorial United Methodist Church Preparatory School; board of directors, Successful Black/Minority Scl Project; Consortium of Doctors, Ltd, 1993; Honoree: Outstanding Bay Area Educator, Iota Phi Lambda, 1994; Outstanding Educator Award, Black Business/Professional Women, 1996; Educ Editor Prestige Mag, 1997; Host: ''Oakland Is'' TV Show, 1990-; Co-Host/Producer: ''Just A Look'' Intergenerational Family Comm Based Educational TV Show, 1997. **Business Addr:** Asst Dean, Instruction, Merritt College, Outreach & Library/Learning Resources Center, 12500 Campus Dr, Oakland, CA 94619.

CANNON, CALVIN CURTIS
Manager information systems. **Personal:** Born Mar 2, 1952, Lenoir, NC; married Anna Laura Copney; children: Calvin IV. **Educ:** Univ of MI Grad School of Business, BBA 1974; Attended, Wayne State Univ Sch of Engrg, Howard Univ Sch of Divinity. **Career:** Proctor and Gamble Co, client rep 1974-76; Vitro Laboratories, section leader 1977-79; Planning Rsch Corp, unit manager 1979-81; General Elec Information Serv Co, project coord 1981-83; Comp-U-Staff, staff mgr 1983-84; Executive Office of the President Washington DC, manager information serv 1984-. **Orgs:** Mem African Methodist Episcopal Zion Church. **Home Addr:** 10606 Wheatley St, Kensington, MD 20895.

CANNON, CHAPMAN ROOSEVELT, JR.
Business executive. **Personal:** Born Nov 14, 1934, St Louis, MO; son of Geneva Gaines Cannon and Chapman Roosevelt Cannon Sr; married Donnie Easter Cannon, Oct 10, 1954; children: Donald Chatman, Emily Easter. **Educ:** Michigan State University, BS, business administration, 1964. **Career:** American Beauty Products Co Inc, chief executive officer, currently. **Orgs:** NAACP, 1965-; Metropolitan Baptist Church; United Church-Science of Living Institute; Metropolitan Tulsa Chamber of Commerce, 1975-; Greenwood Chamber of Commerce, 1980-; American Health & Beauty Aids Institute, board of directors, 1981-. **Honors/Awds:** Black Hair Olympics, Outstanding Achievement Award, 1982, Manufacturer of the Year Award, 1983; Top Businessman of the Year, 1984; Tulsa Urban League, Outstanding Achievement Award, 1984; Tulsa Metro Chamber Commerce, Small Businessman of the Year, 1985; Black Enterprise 100 listing of America's Most Successful Black Owned Companies; 1985, 1986, 1987. **Special Achievements:** Co-author, autobiography, How We Made Millions & Never Left the Ghetto, 1983; co-publisher, Beauty Classic Magazine, 1984-87; co-founder, NY Beauty Classic Rolls Royce Competition; composer/singer, Rejuvenation, record, 1984; artist, painting, New York skyline, 1961. **Military Serv:** US Air Force, captain, 1952-68; served in USA, SE Asia, Japan, Vietnam, Republic of China, Dominican Republic. **Business Addr:** Chairman of the Board/Chief Executive Officer, American Beauty Products Co., Inc, 1623 E Apache, Tulsa, OK 74106, (918)428-2577.

CANNON, CHARLES EARL
Educator. **Personal:** Born Jan 30, 1946, Sylacauga, AL; son of Carrie Cannon and Eugene Cannon (deceased). **Educ:** AL A&M Univ, BS (w/Great Honors) 1968; Univ of WI-Milwaukee, PhD 1975. **Career:** Amoco Corp, rsch scientist 1974-85; West Aurora Sch Dist, educator 1985-86; Elmhurst Coll, adjunct faculty 1984-87; IL Math & Sci Acad, prof of chemistry 1986-92; Columbia College, chair, science and math department, 1992-. **Orgs:** American Chem Soc Chicago, 1974-; National Association of Negro Musicians, director, 1975-; The Amer Inst of Chemists, fellow, 1979-92; Executives Interested in Politics, 1982-88; Natl Alumni Assoc AL A&M Univ, past president, 1984-86; Apostolic Church of God, Chicago; Great Lakes Regional ACS Meeting Planning Comm, 1986-87, at-large, 1987-88; National Association for the Advancement of Black Chemists and Chemical Engineers. **Honors/Awds:** Merit Awd Public Service Cultural Citizen Foundation; J Org Chem 41,1191 1976; Grignard Reagents Rearrangements ACS Natl Mtg Fall 1985; paper Semi-Automated Sep of Oils Resins Asphalcenes; ''Greenhouse Effect and Other Environmental Issues.'' ISTA, Fall 1990; Alabama A&M Univ, Alumnus of the Year, 1992; Natl Assn of Negro Musicians, Inc, Distinguished Service Award, 1992; Lilly Multicultural Award, Columbia Coll, 1994; Spectroscopy Society of Pittsburgh, Host College Grant, 1996. **Home Addr:** 8120-B Prairie Park Pl, Chicago, IL 60619, (773)651-4588. **Business Addr:** Chair, Science & Math Department, Columbia College, 600 S Michigan Ave, Chicago, IL 60605, (312)344-7396.

CANNON, DAVITA LOUISE BURGESS
Editor. **Personal:** Born Mar 17, 1949, Jersey City, NJ; daughter of Bernice Cannon and James Cannon (deceased). **Educ:** St Peters College, BS Marketing Management 1967-73; NYU Graduate School of Business, Advanced Mgmt Program 1979-83; America Computa, 1988. **Career:** JM Fields, dicta sec 1978-79; NJ Afro Amer, columnist 1980; Office Force Inc, exec sec/admin asst 1979-83; Cannon Clues, publisher, chairman, 1981-, owner 1988-; public relations consultant/mktg specialist 1981-. **Orgs:** Pr chair NY metro Area Chapter Amer assn of Blacks in Energy 1983-84; chairman, US Rep Parren J Mitchell Brain Trust 1984; Natl Bd of Advisors Amer Biographical Inst 1985; Bayonne Youth Cntr, bd of dir 1974-92; Governors Advisory Council on Minority Business Devel, reappointed councilmember 1987-92; NJ Coalition of 100 Black Women, pr officer 1986-91; Concerned Comm Women of JC, Inc, pr chair 1986-92; Governor's Planning Comm; 1986-87; NJ Devel Authority for Small Minority & Women's Business, commissioner 1987-92; vice chair, charter mem, Republican Presidential Task Force, 1989-; The Council on HOS, vice chairman; Chandeliers of the United Nations, 1992-; Presidential Commission on the American Agenda, commissioner. **Honors/Awds:** Distinguished Serv Award Pavonia Girl Scout Council 1981; Mary McLeod Bethune Award Com-Bin-Nations Jersey City 1984; VIP Award Concerned Comm Women of Jersey City Inc 1984; Small Business Award Roselle Branch NAACP 1984; Jersey Journal, Woman of Achievement 1986; Governor's Conf on Minority Business Devel, keynote speaker 1986; Govs Conf on Small Business, panelist 1986; moderator; Concerned Comm Women of JC, Inc, women advancing through adversity 1986; Black Leadership Reception 100 Black Men of New Jersey, 1988. **Home Addr:** 528 Avenue A-5, Bayonne, NJ 07002.

CANNON, DONNIE E.
Business executive. **Personal:** Born in Magnolia, AR; married Chapman R Jr; children: Donald Chatman. **Educ:** MME C J Walker Beauty Coll, Grad; Eugene Hairstyling Acad, Paris France; Myriam Carriages Inst De Beaute Paris France; The Ophelia De Voores Modeling & Charm Sch, Grad. **Career:** Am Beauty Prod Co, Inc, co-owner & treas 1966; Johnson Prods, natl rep; La Roberts & Gray's Beauty Sch, NY. **Orgs:** Mem Alpha-Chi Pi Omega organized 1st chap in Hempstead; Tulsa Urban League Guild; Greenwood C of C; mem Tulsa Comm Devel Cntr; mem OK Beauty Culturist League; Tulsa Urban League, Inc; hon mem YWCA; mem Natl Beauty Culturist League; board of trustees Bethune-Cookman Coll; mem Tulsa C of C; mem NAACP. **Honors/Awds:** Bus & Ind Award, 1973; Service Awd Greenwood C of C, 1974; Basilleus Tulsa Chap Alpha Chi Pi Omega; noted as Black Woman Mnf Black Bus Women of OK; Top 100 Black Bus and Prof Women in America, 1985; Hon Deg Doctor of Law, 1984; Outstanding Women in Industry YWCA, 1977; Outstanding Achievement Award Natl Beauty Culturists League, 1982; Outstanding Achievement Award Black Hair Olympics, 1982; Mfr of the Year Award Black Hair Olympics, 1983; Hon Alumnus Award Langston Univ. **Special Achievements:** Co-author, autobiography, How We MAde Millions and Never Left the Ghetto, 1983; co-publisher, Beauty Classic Magazine, 1984-87; co-founder NY Beauty Classic Rolls Royce Competition. **Business Addr:** Co-Owner/Treasurer, American Beauty Products Co Inc, 1623 E Apache, Tulsa, OK 74106, (918)428-2577.

CANNON, EDITH H.
Educator. **Personal:** Born Aug 8, 1940, Tougaloo, MS; married Dan Cannon Jr; children: Audra Charmaine, Portia Camille. **Educ:** Tougaloo Coll, BS 1961; Boston State Coll, Grad Studies 1975-76; Bridgewater State Coll, Grad Studies 1982-83; Eastern nazarene Coll, MEd 1984. **Career:** Greenville MS Public Schools, elem teach 1961-65; Boston Head Start, educ dir 1969-73; Randolph Public Schools, elem teach 1973-81; North Jr HS, diagnostic prescriptive teach of reading 1981-. **Orgs:** Past vice chmn Randolph Fair Practices 1980-81; conference presenter MA Teachers Assn 1982-84; mem The Governor's Task Force on Educ Reform 1983-84; bd mem South Shore Council for Children 1983-85; mem Randolph Fair Practices 1973-; chair minority affairs comm MA Teachers Assn 1982-; bd dir Norfolk Co Teachers Assn 1983-; communication comm MA Teachers Assn 1984-. **Honors/Awds:** Outstanding Serv Randolph Teachers assn 1980, 1981, 1982; Citation for Serv Gov Michael Dukakis 1983; mem Delta Kappa Gamma Soc Intl Honor Soc for Women Educators 1985. **Home Addr:** 38 Sunset Drive, Randolph, MA 02368. **Business Addr:** Diag Prescr Teacher of Reading, North Jr HS, High St, Randolph, MA 02368.

CANNON, EUGENE NATHANIEL
Educational administrator (retired). **Personal:** Born Sep 13, 1944, Wilmington, DE; son of Alice Henry; married Lillian; children: Eugene. **Educ:** Delaware State Coll, BS 1972; Southern Illinois Univ, MBA 1976. **Career:** Bankers Trust, investment banking 1969-70; A Kelley Jr Construction Co, business mgr 1971-72; DE Opportunities Industrialization Ctr, dir of higher educ programs 1972-75; Penn State Univ, dir of business services 1976-84. **Orgs:** Mem Amer Mgmt Assn 1979-80; pres Int Rotary Club 1980-81; mem Assn of MBA Executives 1980-84; mem Natl Assn of College Bus Offices 1980-84. **Military Serv:** USN Petty Officer 4 yrs. **Home Addr:** 2510 Pennington Way, Wilmington, DE 19810.

CANNON, H. LEROY
Attorney. **Personal:** Born Jan 22, 1916, Georgetown, DE; married Eddie M; children: Muriel. **Educ:** DE State Coll, BS 1933-37; Atlanta U, 1941-42; Hastings Coll of Law, JD 1949-52. **Career:** San Francisco Unified School Dist, legal advisor 1974-; City & County of San Francisco, deputy city atty 1963-74; Private Practice, atty 1952-63; United Methodist Church, supply pastor 1956-58. **Orgs:** Mem CA & State Bar; SF Bar Assn; bd of gov SF Lawyers Club; Nat Bar Assn; Am Bar Assn; Am Bar Assn; Charles Houston Bar Assn; CA Assn of Black Lawyers; Am Judicature Soc; past pres SW Conf on Intergp Relations 1968-72; past pres bd of gov SF Br NAACP; past pres Com on Religion & Race; CA-NV Annual Conf United Meth Ch; dist dir CA Dem Cncl 1961-63; bd of gov No CA Ecumenical Cncl JSAC; exec com Cncl on Ministries; past pres Civil Liberties Com; past chaplain LJ Williams Lodge. **Honors/Awds:** First black legal advr SFUSD. **Military Serv:** AUS CWO 1942-46. **Business Addr:** 135 Van Ness Ave, San Francisco, CA 94102.

CANNON, JOSEPH NEVEL
Educator, chemical engineer. **Personal:** Born May 2, 1942, Weldon, AR; son of Elmer Lewis Cannon and Joseph Henry Cannon; married Carmen Bianchi Cannon, Jan 1, 1978; children: Devi, Arville, Bianca, Changa, Erin. **Educ:** University of Wisconsin, Madison, WI, BSChE, 1964; University of Colorado, Boulder, CO, MSChE, 1966, PhD, 1971. **Career:** Dow Chemical Co, Midland, MI, process engr, 1964; Procter & Gamble, Cincinnati, OH, res. chemical engr, 1965-68; National Institutes of Health, Bethesda, MD, research chem engr, 1972-78; Howard University, Washington, DC, professor, 1971-. **Orgs:** Charter member, Natl Org of Black Chemists & Chem Engineers; member, Amer Inst of Chem Engineers, 1970-; member, Tau Beta Pi Natl Honor Society, 1980-; member, Sigma Xi Scientific Research Society, 1980-; member, Amer Assn for Advancement of Science, 1978-. **Honors/Awds:** Univ of CO, Coll of Engineering and Appl Sci, Centennial Medal, 1994; Distinguished Engr Alumnus, Univ of CO, School of Engineering, 1989; Outstanding Professor, Natl Org of Black Chemists & Chem Engrs, 1983; Outstanding Faculty, Chem Engr Student Societies, 1977, 1979, 1981, 1986. **Business Addr:** Professor, Chemical Engineering, Howard University, School of Engineering, 2300 6th St, NW, Washington, DC 20059, (202)806-6626.

CANNON, KATIE GENEVA
Educator, theological ethicist. **Personal:** Born Jan 3, 1950, Concord, NC; daughter of Corine Lytle Cannon and Esau Cannon. **Educ:** Barber-Scotia Coll, BS, Elementary Education (magna cum laude), 1971; Johnson C Smith Seminary, Atlanta, MDiv, 1974; Union Theological Seminary, New York, NY, MPhil, 1983, PhD, Christian Ethics, 1983. **Career:** Episcopal Divinity School, asst prof; New York Theological Seminary, admin faculty, 1977-80; Ascension Presbyterian Church, first African-American female pastor, 1975-77; Yale Divinity School, visiting lecturer, 1987; Harvard Divinity School, visiting scholar, 1983-84; Wellesley College, visiting professor, 1991; Temple University, Department of Religion, associate professor of Christian ethics, currently. **Orgs:** Ecumenical dialogue, Third World theologians, 1976-80; Middle East travel guide, NY Theological Seminary, 1978-80; editor, Que Pasa, 1982-; member, Amer Acad of Religion, 1983-, Assn of Black Women in Higher Educ, 1984-; bd of dir, Women's Theological Center 1984-; member bd dir, Soc of Christian Ethics, 1986-90; member, Soc for the Study of Black Religion 1986-; World Alliance of Reformed Churches Presbyterian & Congregational, 1986-91. **Honors/Awds:** Isaac R Clark Preaching Award, Interdenominational Theological Center, 1973; Rockfeller Protestant Fellow Fund for Theological Educ, 1972-74; Rockefeller Doctoral Fellow Fund for Theological Educ, 1974-76; Ford Found Fellow Natl Fellowships Fund, 1976-77; Roothbert Fellow, 1981-83; Harvard Divinity School, woman research assoc, Ethics, 1983-84; Radcliffe Coll Bunting Inst, 1987-88; Episcopal Church's Conant Grant, 1987-88; Assn of Theological School Young Scholar Award, 1987-88; author, Black Womanist Ethics, Scholars Press, 1988; co-editor, Inheriting Our Mothers' Garden, Westminster Press, 1988; Katie's Canon: Womanism and the Soul of the Black Community, 1995. **Business Addr:** Associate Professor of Christian Ethics, Department of Religion, Temple University, 646 Anderson Hall, Philadelphia, PA 19122-2228.

CANNON, PAUL L., JR.
Research chemist. **Personal:** Born Nov 21, 1934, Harrisburg, PA; son of Mildred A Mercer Cannon and Paul L Cannon. **Educ:** Lincoln University, AB 1956. **Career:** Harrisbrg Hospital, clinical chem 1956-58; PA Dept of Highways, chem 1958; Dept of the Army, rsrch chem beginning 1958, US Army Edgewood Res Dev Eng Ctr, research chemist, currently. **Orgs:** Omega Psi Phi; Sigma Xi. **Honors/Awds:** Electrochemistry Patents US; published articles on electrochemistry and analytical chemistry. **Military Serv:** US Army, PFC, 1958-60. **Home Addr:** 21 N 15th St, Harrisburg, PA 17103-2302, (717)238-7639. **Business Addr:** Research Chemist, US Army, Edgewood Res Dev Eng Ctr, SCBRD-RTC, Aberdeen Proving Ground, MD 21010-5423, (410)612-7639.

CANNON, REUBEN
Business executive, television producer. **Personal:** Born Feb 11, 1946, Chicago, IL; married Linda Elsenhout; children: Tonya, Reuben Jr, Christopher, Sydney. **Educ:** SE City Coll. **Career:** Univ Studios, mail room clerk, sec casting dept, casting dir 1970-77; Warner Bros, head of TV casting 1977-78; casted roles for The Rockford Files, Roots II, The Next Generation, A Soldier's Story, The Color Purple, The A-Team, Hunter, Riptide, Moonlighting, Amen, Amerika, Ironside; Under One Roof, Touched By An Angel; Eddie What's Love Got to Do With It, American Heart, Who Framed Roger Rabbitt; Producer "The Women of Brewster Place"; Reuben Cannon & Assoc, owner 1979-; Spike Lee's Film "Get On The Bus," producer, 1996. **Orgs:** Los Angeles Urban League, board of dir. **Honors/Awds:** Emmy Roots II TV Academy 1979. **Business Addr:** President, Reuben Cannon & Assoc, 5225 Wilshire Blvd, Ste 526, Los Angeles, CA 90036.

CANNON, TYRONE HEATH
Library administrator. **Personal:** Born Jan 16, 1949, Hartford, CT; son of Laura R Cohens and Jesse Heath Cannon. **Educ:** University of Connecticut, BS, 1973, MSW, 1975; University of Pittsburgh, MLS, 1981. **Career:** Hartford Public Schools, school social worker, 1975-77; Child and Family Services Inc, clinical social worker, 1977-80; University of Texas at Arlington, social sciences librarian, 1981-83; Columbia University, social work librarian, 1984-88; Oklahoma State University, Social Sciences Division, head, 1988-89; Boston College, head of reference, 1989-91, senior associate university librarian, 1991-. **Orgs:** American Library Assn; Assn of College and Reference Libraries; Black Caucus of the American Library Assn. **Honors/Awds:** University of Pittsburgh, Title IIB Fellowship, 1980. **Business Addr:** Senior Associate University Librarian, Boston College Libraries, Thomas P O'Neill Jr Library, Rm 410B, Chestnut Hill, MA 02167, (617)552-4470.

CANSON, FANNIE JOANNA
Educator. **Personal:** Born Apr 26, 1926, Bainbridge, GA; married Robert L. **Educ:** Spelman Coll Tuskegee Inst, BS 1945; Univ of OR, MS 1967, PhD 1967. **Career:** CA State Univ Sacramento, assoc prof; former high school teacher; univ admin dir; teacher corps Corrections Project; Natl Council of Chs, teacher; licensed marriage & family counselor. **Orgs:** Conducted numerous workshops self concept theories, curriculum in correctional instns & Personnel Panels for State of CA; mem Numerous professional & Civic Orgn teaching fellow Univ of OR. **Business Addr:** CA State Univ, 6000 Jay St, Sacramento, CA.

CANSON, VIRNA M.
Association executive. **Personal:** Born Jun 10, 1921, Bridgeport, OK; married Clarence B Canson; children: Clarence B Jr, Faythe. **Educ:** Tuskegee Inst; Univ of WI; Credit Union Nat Assn Sch for Credit, Grad. **Career:** NAACP Credit Union Sacramento Br, treas/mgr 1953-; CA State Office of Econ Oppor, credit union & consumer educ & spec 1965-67; West Coast Region I NAACP, field dir & legislative advocate 1967-74, reg dir 1974-. **Orgs:** mem, People to People Sacramento Chapter, Oak Park United Church of Christ; Subscribing Golden Heritage life mem NAACP; mem Founders Club, Credit Union Natl Assoc; life mem Natl Council of Negro Women; mem Women's Civic Improvement Club Sacramento; mem comm adv panel, CA State Univ Syst. **Honors/Awds:** 1st winner D D Mattocks Award for Serv to Comm Sacramento Branch NAACP; Bus Week Award Iota Phi Lamba 1957 & 1962; Outstanding Serv Award So Area Conf NAACP; Outstanding Serv Awd Natl Council of Negro Women; Service Awd Black Police Officers Assoc Los Angeles; El Cerrito Branch NAACP; CA Credit Union League; City of Long Beach; Operation Second Chance San Bernardino CA. **Business Addr:** Dir West Coast Region, NAACP, 1975 Sutter St Ste #1, San Francisco, CA 94115.

CANTARELLA, MARCIA Y.
Consultant. **Personal:** Born Oct 31, 1946, Minneapolis, MN; daughter of Margaret Buckner Young and Whitney M Young Jr; married Francesco Cantarella, May 24, 1980; children: Mark Boles, Michele Cantarella, Maratea Cantarella. **Educ:** Bryn Mawr Coll, Bryn Mawr PA, BA (with honors), 1968; Univ of Iowa Law School, 1968; Simmons Coll, Boston MA, middle mgmt program, NYU, 1991-; NY Univ, MA, American Studies, 1992, PhD, 1996. **Career:** Sen Robert F Kennedy's Washington Office, summer intern 1967; Rabat Amer School, Rabat Morocco, social studies teacher grades 6-8, 1970-71; Zebra Assoc, New York City, advertising, 1971-72; Avon Products Inc, New York City, dir sales devel, dir 1972-85; Mom's Amazing, New York City, pres, 1985-88; Natl Coalition for Women's Enterprise, New York City, exec dir; NYU Stern School of Business, management consultant, 1988-90; Academic Enhancement, NYU, Coll of Arts & Science, dir, 1991-; NYU Gallatin School of Individualized Study, faculty, 1995-. **Orgs:** Bd of dir New York City Police Foundation, 1988-91; mem Vaseline Baby Care Council, 1987-88; dir Children's Museum of Manhattan, 1986-91; Equity Institute, 1990-92; planning comm, Support Center of NY, 1992-. **Honors/Awds:** Woman of the Year, NCNW, 1976; published articles in Working Mother, McCalls, Essence, Working Parent, Boardroom Reports, Lears. **Business Addr:** 905 Main Bldg, 100 Washington SE, NY University, New York, NY 10003.

CANTON, DOUGLAS E.
Senator. **Personal:** Born Jan 6, 1931, St Croix, Virgin Islands of the United States; married Pauline Edith; children: Denise, David, Douglas Jr, Danny, Leone, Dinah, Robert, Devin. **Educ:** Central CT State Coll VI, Certificate. **Career:** Self-employed, carpenter 1953-60; Canton's Construction, contractor 1973; St Croix Central HS, vocational educ instructor 1973-86; Legislature of the Virgin Islands, senator, currently. **Orgs:** Mem, bd of dirs Amer Red Cross STX; mem, St Croix Central HS Parent/_ Teacher Assn; mem, Frederiksted Citizen Assn, 1987-88; mem, Majority Coalition 17th Legislature; vice chmn, Housing & Planning; mem Educ & Youth Rules & Nominations. **Military Serv:** USMC 3 yrs.

CANTRELL, FORREST DANIEL
Business executive. **Personal:** Born Dec 30, 1938, Atlanta, GA; married Cheryl Francis; children: John Daniel. **Educ:** San Francisco State U, BA 1968; Univ of CA, MBA 1970; Harvard Bus Sch, AMP 1977. **Career:** Mile Sq Health Center Inc, pres, former proj dir, former admnstr; San Francisco Police Dept, former police & Officer; Vallejo Police Dept, patrolman; Dept of Corrections, corr ofcr. **Orgs:** Past pres Nat Asn of Neighborhood Health Cntrs Inc; pres bd dir Miles Sq Serv Corp; commr Chicago Hlth Planning & Resources Devel Commin; bd dir Chica United Black Appeal Fund. **Military Serv:** USN airman 1955-58. **Business Addr:** 1508 W Jackson Blvd, Chicago, IL 60607.

CANTWELL, KATHLEEN GORDON
Physician/radiologist. **Personal:** Born May 17, 1945, Beaumont, TX; daughter of Mildred Portis Gordon; children: Jennifer, John. **Educ:** Univ of TX at Austin, BA 1967; Howard Univ Coll of Medicine, MD 1975. **Career:** Howard Univ Coll of Medicine, faculty 1979-80; Hadley Hospital, radiologist 1979-; Doctor's Hospital Lanham MD, radiologist 1980-83; Drs Press & Cantwell PC, radiologist/partner 1981-. **Orgs:** Sec 1983-85, pres 1985-86 DC Chap Amer College of Radiology; chmn Radiology Section Medical Soc of DC 1985-86; mem bd dirs Southeast House 1985-87; assoc clinical prof radiology George Washington Univ 1986-87; Chairman, Women Physicians Section, Medical Society of DC 1988-1989; member-at-large, Executive Board, Medical Society of DC 1989-1991; Alternate Councilor, D.C. Metropolitan Chapter, Amer College of Radiology 1989-. **Honors/Awds:** Most Outstanding Resident Howard Univ Hospital 1979; 13 journal articles in radiology.

CANTY, CHRIS
Professional football player. **Educ:** Kansas State. **Career:** New England Patriots, 1997-. **Special Achievements:** NFL Draft, First round pick, #29, 1997. **Business Addr:** Professional Football Player, New England Patriots, Rt 1, Sullivan Stadium, Foxboro, MA 02035, (508)543-7911.

CANTY, GEORGE
Chemical company supervisor. **Personal:** Born Dec 7, 1931, Manning, SC; married Mabel Lucille Scott; children: Andria G, Alison D. **Educ:** Univ of Pittsburgh, BS Chemistry 1954; Am U, MS Physics & Chemistry 1966. **Career:** 3m Co St Paul MN, supr prod devel 1973-; Celanese Research Co Summit NJ, sr research chemist 1967-73; Gillete & Research Inst Wash DC, rsrch/develchemist 1965-67; Nat Bur of Standards Wash DC, chemist 1961-63; NIH Bethesda MD, chemist 1958-63. **Orgs:** Mem Am Chem Soc 1960-; mem MN Chem Soc 1973-; mem & past basileus NJ Chap Omega Psi Phi Frat 1953-; guest lectr Black Exec Exchange Prog Nat Urban League 1974-; pub "The Melting & Crystallization of Fibrous Protein in Non-Aqueous Media" J Physics Chemistry 67 1963; pub "Stereoregularity in Ionic Polyumerization of Acenaph-Thalene" J Nat Bur of Standards 68a 1964. **Honors/Awds:** Catalyst Club Award 3m Co Film & Allied Prod Div 1977; patented Photosensitive Composite Sheet Material 1979. **Military Serv:** USN seaman recruit 1952. **Business Addr:** Chemical Supervisor, 3M Center, Building 236-1A, St Paul, MN 55101.

CANTY, MIRIAM MONROE
Educator, lecturer. **Personal:** Born May 6, 1916, Savannah, GA; married E J. **Educ:** CA State U, BA 1959; Mt St Mary's Coll, MS 1971. **Career:** Promotional Personnel, Los Angeles City Unified School Dist, consultant 1972-; Mt St Mary's Coll, instructor; Educ Professional Develop Act Internship Program, teacher, training coord 1969-72, special educ consultant 1968-69, special educ teacher 1963-68, first grade teacher 1960-63; Child Devel Center, dir 1948-60. **Orgs:** Charter mem CA Council for Exceptional Children; mem Nat Council for Exception Children; prof educ of Los Angeles; past mem Exec Bd Assn Tchrs of LosAngeles; co-chmn Delta Sigma Theta Golden Life Mem Com 1971-75; Ch of Christian Fellowship Achieve Funds 1975-77; chmn Ad Hoc Com Delta Reading Prog 1975-76; life mem Delta Sigma Theta; Nat Council of Negro Women Inc; CA State Univ Alumni Assn; mem Phi Delta Kappa; Alpha Chi Pi Omega; Magellan C Mars Am Leg Aux; CA Music Tchrs Assn. **Honors/Awds:** Certificate of Serv Delta Sigma Theat 1971 & 1975; Los Angeles & Alumni Chap Delta Sigma Theta Leadership Award 1971-76; Certificates of Appreciation Ch of Christian Fellowship 1970-74; holder of six CA Credentials. **Business Addr:** 8817 Langdon Ave, Sepulveda, CA 91343.

CANTY, OTIS ANDREW
Professional sports team administrator. **Personal:** Born May 12, 1934, Troy, AL; son of Candus McGhee Canty and Roscoe Canty; married Flora (divorced 1990); children: Virginia, Elezibeth, Barbara, Sandra, Marian, Sheila. **Career:** The Detroit Lions, Inc, Pontiac, MI, director of player relations, beginning 1966. **Honors/Awds:** First African American to serve on a National Football League team video crew. **Business Addr:** Director of Player Relations, Detroit Lions, 1200 Featherstone Rd, Pontiac, MI 48342.

CANTY, RALPH WALDO
Clergyman. **Personal:** Born Oct 9, 1945, Sumter, SC; married Jacqueline Wright; children: Ralph Jr, Serena. **Educ:** Morris Coll, AB 1967, BD 1970, DD 1978. **Career:** Morris Coll, pub rel dir 1970-75; BF Goodrich (Elgin Plant), asst personnel dir 1975-78; Savannah Grove Bapt Ch, pastor. **Orgs:** Pres/chrm bd Job's Mortuary 1970-; pres Brenca 1976-; bd mem Natl Cncl of Churches 1980; bd mem Bapt World Alliance 1980; bd mem Morris Coll 1982. **Honors/Awds:** Omega Man of the Yr Gamma Iota Chap 1985; Citizen of the Yr Key Publns 1980; Citizen of the Yr Gamma Iota Chptr 1979. **Business Addr:** Pastor, Savannah Grove Baptist Church, Route 3 Box 475, Effingham, SC 29541.

CAPEHART, JOHNNIE LAWRENCE
Law enforcement. **Personal:** Born Apr 2, 1947, Windsor, NC; son of Florence Slade Jordan and Willie Cecil Capehart; married Geneva Kendall; children: Gregory, Deloris, Willie. **Educ:** Newport News Police Academy, Certificate Award 1971; Saint Leo College, AA 1978, BA 1979; FBI Academy Executive Development School, Quantico VA 1985. **Career:** Newport News Police Dept, police officer 1971-73; Christopher Newport College, campus police officer 1973-76; Williamsburg Police Dept, police detective 1976-78; Christopher Newport College, campus police chief. **Orgs:** Member Fraternal Order of Police 1971-; member Masonic Lodge 1973-; member Virginia Campus Police Chief Assn 1978-; member Virginia Crime Prevention Assn 1979-; member NAACP 1982-; member Intl Chief of Police Assn 1983-; member Conference of Minority Public Administrators 1983-. **Honors/Awds:** Staff Member of Year Christopher Newport College 1975; 100 Club Award Sewart AFB, TN 1967; Airman of the Month USAF 1967; Candidate for Sheriff Bertie County, NC 1982. **Military Serv:** USAF Staff Sgt (Admin Specialist), 1966-70; VA ANG Munition Specialist 1978-; USAF Accom Medal, Good Conduct Medal, Pres Citation, Airman of Month Awd, 100 Club Awd; Virginia Air National Guard, technical sergeant 1985-; Drug and Alcohol NCO.

CAPEL, FELTON
College basketball coach. **Personal:** son Of Jean and Felton Jeffrey. **Career:** Wake Forest Univ, asst coach; Fayetteville State Univ, coach; North Carolina A & T State Univ, head coach, 1993-. **Business Addr:** Head Basketball Coach, North Carolina A & T State University, 1601 E Market St, Greensboro, NC 27411, (919)334-7500.

CAPEL, FELTON JEFFREY
Business executive. **Personal:** Born Feb 26, 1927, Ellerbe, NC; son of Elnora Leak Capel and Acie Capel; married Jean Walden, Jul 12, 1951; children: Jeff, Mitch, Ken. **Educ:** Hampton Univ, BS 1951. **Career:** Century Metal Craft Corp, salesman 1958-61, sales mgr 1958-61, reg sales mgr 1965-77; Century Assn of NC, pres, CEO, 1977-. **Orgs:** City councilman, Southern Pines 1959-68; dir, Carolina P & L Co 1972-, Southern Natl Bank 1974-85, First Federal Savings & Loan 1978-85, North Carolina Assn of Minority Businesses Durham NC 1986, Durham Corp 1988-, Durham Life Insurance 1988-, North Carolina Citizens for Business and Industry Raleigh NC 1988-, Wachovia Corp Winston-Salem NC 1989, Wachovia Bank and Trust Co NA Winston-Salem NC 1989; city treasurer and chmn of Moore County Bd of Elections 1980-86; dist governor, Rotary Intl 1981-82; chmn, Moore Co United Way 1983; chairman, Moore County Chapter Amer Red Cross 1983-85; member, North Carolina Comm for Educ, 1989; chairman, board of trustees, Fayetteville State University, 1980-89. **Honors/Awds:** Intl Mgr Sales Award Century Metalcrft 1962; Bd Mem of Year North Carolina Dept of Conservation & Devel 1971; chmn of the year, Sandhills Area Chamber of Commerce 1977; Delta Mu Delta Natl Honor in Business FSU 1983; Fayetteville State University, Basketball Arena Named Felton J Capel Arena, 1995; Rotary International, International Service Award, 1995, 1996. **Military Serv:** US Army, staff sergeant, two years. **Business Addr:** PO Drawer 37, 1800 S Walnut St, Pinebluff, NC 28373-0037.

CAPEL, WALLACE
Physician (retired). **Personal:** Born Nov 12, 1915, Andalusia, AL; son of Callie Capel and Henry Capel; married Carrie Ford; children: Carolyn Capel Harrison, Jacqueline D, Denise L, Wallace Capel Jr. **Educ:** Howard Univ, BS 1940, MD 1944; Baylor Univ, MHA 1970. **Career:** VA Medical Ctr, chief of staff. **Orgs:** Mem Amer and Natl Medical Assoc, 1970, Macon Co Medical Soc 1973. **Honors/Awds:** Exec of Year Professional Secretaries Intl 1979. **Military Serv:** AUS col 20 yrs; Legion of Merit w/Oak Leaf Cluster.

CAPERS, ELIZA VIRGINIA
Actress, singer. **Personal:** Born Sep 22, 1925, Sumter, SC; children: Glenn S. **Educ:** Howard U, 1943-45; Juilliard Sch Music, 1946-50. **Career:** Actress in motion pictures, on stage, and on TV; singer; licensed agent. **Orgs:** Mem San Fernando Fair Housing Council; bd mem Muscular Dystrophy Assn; life mem NAACP; chmn CARE Intl Children's Party; World's Poet & Resources Ctr Inc; Meth Women; Women's Ort Lane Bryant for Operation Reach Out; mem Nat Acad TV Arts. **Honors/ Awds:** Lorraine Hansberry Fine Arts Award 1975; drama award Satellite Academy; Tony Award 1974. **Business Addr:** C/O Lunt Fontanne Theater, 205 W 46 St, New York, NY 10036.

CAPERS, JAMES
Professional basketball referee. **Career:** NBA official, currently. **Business Addr:** NBA Official, c/o National Basketball Association (NBA), 645 5th Ave, 15th Fl, New York, NY 10022-5986.

CARAWAY, YOLANDA H.
Public relations, event management. **Personal:** Born Sep 1, 1950, Rochester, NY; daughter of Cecile Carr Harris and Earl Harris; divorced; children: Theron Tucker Jr. **Career:** State Representative Wendell Phillips, administrative assistant, 1976-80; Congresswoman Barbara Mikulski, legislative aide, 1980-81; Democratic National Committee, director of education and training, 1981-85; Mondale/Ferraro General Election Campaign, deputy assistant political director, 1984; Democratic National Committee, special assistant to the chairman and staff director for the Fairness Commission, 1985; National Rainbow Coalition, chief of staff, 1985-86; Citizenship Education Fund, executive director, 1986-87; Jesse Jackson for President, chief of staff, 1987-88; Democratic National Committee Chairman Paul G. Kirk, Jr., deputy chair, 1988-89; Presidential Inaugural Committee, Office of the Chairman, director, 1992-93; The Caraway Group Inc, pres & CEO, currently. **Orgs:** At-large member, Democratic National Committee; member, board of directors, American University's Campaign Management Institute; member, board of directors, Americans for Democratic Action Education Fund; member, American Council of Young Political Leaders; steering committee, Ronald H Brown Foundation. **Business Addr:** 1010 Wisconsin Ave NW, Ste 440, Washington, DC 20007.

CARBY, HAZEL V.
Educator. **Personal:** Born Jan 15, 1948, Oakhampton, Devon, England; daughter of Iris Muriel Carby and Carl Colin Carby; married Michael Denning, May 29, 1982; children: Nicholas Carby-Denning. **Educ:** Birmingham University, Center for Contemporary Cultural Studies, PhD, 1984. **Career:** Wesleyan University, associate professor, 1982-89; Yale University, professor, 1989-. **Business Addr:** Chair, African & African-American Studies, Yale University, PO Box 3388, Yale Station, New Haven, CT 06520, (203)432-1170.

CARD, LARRY D.
Judge. **Personal:** Born in Kansas. **Career:** State of AK, Superior Court, judge, currently. **Orgs:** Inns of Court; Alaska Bar Assn; Anchorage Bar Assn. **Special Achievements:** First African American judge in Alaska, 1993. **Military Serv:** US Air Force, captain, attorney. **Business Addr:** Judge, Alaska Superior Court, 305 K St, Anchorage, AK 99501, (907)264-0414.

CAREW, RODNEY CLINE
Professional athlete (retired). **Personal:** Born Oct 1, 1945, Gatun, Panama; son of Olga and Eric; married Marilynn Levy; children: Charryse, Stephanie, Michelle (deceased). **Career:** MN Twins, second baseman 1967-78; CA Angels, 1st baseman, 2nd baseman 1979-86, batting coach. **Orgs:** Works with underprivileged youth Atwood Rec Ctr Placentia CA; gives talks to schools in Orange Cty area regarding child abuse; private charity work at local high schools and Little League. **Honors/Awds:** Rookie of the Year, BBWAA 1967; batting champ 1969, 1972-75, 1978; Rookie of the Year, Amer League 1967; Most Valuable Player Amer League 1977; Selected Top Hitter of Decade, 1969-79, for compiling a .343 average; selected to All-Star team for 18th consecutive seasons; winner of seven batting titles; named AL's MVP Major League Player of the Year, MN Sports Personality of the Year, Roberto Clemente Awd, Calvin Griffith Awd; 1st player to win AL Player of the Month twice in a season; 3 time winner AL Player of the Week; 4 time winner AL Player of the Month; all-time top vote-getter in All-Star balloting with total vote count approaching 32 million; set club record 339average 1983; 16th player in major league history to get 3,000 hits Aug 4 1986; mem, Baseball Hall of Fame, 1990.

CAREY, ADDISON, JR.
Educator. **Personal:** Born Mar 10, 1933, Crescent City, FL; son of Laura Dowdell Carey and Addison Carey Sr; married Clara Lee Parker; children: Leon, Alphonso, Pamela, Katrenia, Addison III, Michael, Douglas. **Educ:** FL A&M Univ, BS 1958; The OH State Univ, MA 1960; Tulane Univ, PhD 1971. **Career:** Southern Univ at New Orleans, dir visiting scholars lecture series 1972-78, admin asst to the chancellor 1983-85, prof of political sci 1960-. **Orgs:** Bd mem YMCA 1978-; pres, Retired Military Assoc of New Orleans 1980-; pres Economic Develop Unit 1984-; mem Civil Service Commn City of New Orleans LA 1987-; past pres LA Political Science Assoc; mem Natl Conf of Black Political Scientists; mem, Pi Sigma Alpha Honorary Society; mem, African American Heritage Assn. **Honors/ Awds:** Ford Foundation Fellow; Southern Fellowships Foundation Fellow; Outstanding Professor Southern Univ at New Orleans 1965,74; Citations for work in voter registration drives YMCA and student organizations. **Military Serv:** AUS pfc 3 yrs; Purple Heart, Korean Serv Medal, Sigman Rhee Citation, National Defense Medal 1950-53. **Home Addr:** 4844 Mendez St, New Orleans, LA 70126, (504)288-5400. **Business Addr:** Professor of Political Science, Southern Univ at New Orleans, 6400 Press Dr, New Orleans, LA 70126, (504)286-5368.

CAREY, AUDREY L.
Elected official. **Personal:** Born Nov 28, 1937, Newburgh, NY; widowed; children: Davina Henry, Dana, David C Jr. **Educ:** St Luke's Hosp Sch of Nursing, Registered Prof Nurse (honors) 1961; NY State Dept of Educ, permanent certification sch nurse teacher 1971; NY Univ Graduate Sch of Educ, advanced degree admin & super 1971-76; UpState medical Coll SUNY, pediatric nurse practitioner certification 1980; State Univ Coll at Oneonta, BS Education/Nursing. **Career:** St Luke's Hosp, asst head nurse 1963-69; Headstart & N Jr HS, school nurse teacher 1966-69; Newburgh Sch Dist, drug educ coord 1969-74; Newburgh Free Academy, school nurse teacher 1975-80; Newburgh Free Academy HS, pediatric nurse practitioner 1980-; City of Newburgh, councilwoman. **Orgs:** Bd of dirs, Orange Co Dept of Mental Health, 1971-73; Inst of Black Studies Mt St Mary's Coll, 1973-74; assoc coord Non-Credit Progs St Mary's Coll, 1973-74; panelist NYS Bd of Regents Conf, 1973-74; bd of dirs YWCA, 1975-76; bd of trustees Orange Co Comm Coll, 1973-82; panelist Robert Wood Johnson Found Sch Health Conf, 1980-81; chmn, Newburgh Comm Action Head Start Policy Advisory Council, 1983-84; Newburgh City Councilwoman, 1977-. **Honors/Awds:** Professional Achievement Awd Omega Psi Phi Frat Upsilon Tau Chap 1961; Disting Serv Awd Jaycees 1973; Outstanding Comm Serv Awd Nimrod Lodge #82 AF&AM 1977; Continuous Serv Awd Black Commonwealth of Newburgh 1979; Disting Serv Awd NAACP 1981; Outstanding Comm Serv HVOIC Mary C Christian Awd 1982; Achievement Awd Newburgh Comm Action Head Start 1984; Comm Achievement Awd Black History Month 1985; Recognition Awd Newburgh Optimist Club 1985; publication"Adolescence, Feeling Good, Looking Fine, Acting Fit" Natl Sch Health Digest 1981. **Business Addr:** Councilwoman, City of Newburgh, PO Box 4, Newburgh, NY 12550.

CAREY, CARNICE
Government contract compliance coordinator. **Personal:** Born Dec 17, 1945, Chicago, IL; daughter of Ora Gardner Stephen and Joe Stephen; married Lloyd L Carey, Oct 29, 1966; children: Patrice Carey, Leslie Carey. **Educ:** Loop Jr Coll, Chicago, IL; Northeastern Illinois Univ, Chicago, IL. **Career:** City of Chicago, Chicago, IL, contract compliance coord, 1972-75; Regional Transportation Authority, Chicago, IL, eeo officer, 1975-84; City of Chicago, Chicago, IL, contract compliance coord, 1985-. **Orgs:** Administrative bd, Redeemer Methodist Church, 1970; mem, Wesley Methodist Church, 1980-; consultant, Seventh Ward Democratic Org, 1988-.

CAREY, CLAIRE LAMAR
Manager. **Personal:** Born Aug 11, 1943, Augusta, GA; daughter of Serena James Lamar and Peter W Lamar; married Harmon Roderick; children: Roderick Lamar. **Educ:** Fisk Univ, BS Chemistry 1964; OH Univ, graduate study, Chemistry, 1965; Univ of DE, mgmt certificate, 1975. **Career:** Hercules Inc, since 1965, mgr of professional staffing & devel, dir workforce diversity, college relations and regulatory compliance, currently. **Orgs:** Pres, Alpha Kappa Alpha Sorority Inc Zeta Omega 1962-; mem Sigma Xi Sci Honor Soc 1969-; mem Amer Chem Soc Educ Comm 1974-; mem DE Tech Comm Coll Advisory Bd 1974-76; consult personnel affairs Human Resources Consultant; sec Gov's Commn Magistrates Screening; vice pres YWCA bd of dirs; mem NCCJ board of directors; president, YWCA board of directors, 1987-89; mem, Boy Scouts board of directors; board of directors, National YWCA, 1990. **Honors/ Awds:** Comm Serv Award United Way of DE 1975; Mem, Acquisition Award Wilmington DE Chapter NAACP 1976; Minority Achiever in Industry Award Wilmington Branch YMCA 1976; Leadership Award Alpha Kappa Alpha N Atlantic Region 1979; Outstanding Achiever in Industry-Brandywine Professional Assn 1985; inducted into Delaware's Womens Hall of Fame, 1992. **Business Addr:** Director, Workforce Diversity, Hercules Inc, Hercules Plaza, 1313 N Market St, Wilmington, DE 19894-0001.

CAREY, HARMON RODERICK
Social services agency executive, businessman. **Personal:** Born Jul 7, 1936, Wilmington, DE; married Claire D Lamar; children: Roderick. **Educ:** Central State Univ, AB 1957; Univ of PA, MSW 1962, post grad; Temple Univ Law Sch, post grad 1963-65; Univ of DE, MA 1977; Univ of DE, doc candidate 1996. **Career:** Dept Public Welfare Wilmington, caseworker 1958-60; YMCA, dir youth lounge 1959-64; Family Ct, supr 1960-65; Peoples Settlement Assn, prog dir exec dir 1965-70; Assn Greater Wilmington Neighborhood Ctrs, exec dir 1970-74; Pine Beverage Inc, pres; Bar-B-Que Pit Windsor Market & Deli, owner/operator; HaralRealty, pres; Human Resources Consultants, founder/pres; Afro-Amer Historical Soc of DE, founder/pres/executive director. **Orgs:** Mem bd dir Equity Farm Trust; instr Univ of DE Extension Div; founder King Collection; vice pres Communigraphics Inc; conf coord Natl Fed Settlements 1971; mem Natl Assn Social Workers, Acad Certified Soc Workers; mem NAACP, Black Alliance, Kappa Alpha Psi, Alpha Kappa Mu, Equity of DE Monday Club; numerous publications; founder Minority Business Assn of DE; pres Carey Enterprises Unlimited; founder/pres, African-American Heritage Coalition; founder, African-American Family Reunion Festival; founder, African-American Heritage Day in DE; co-founder, Slave Ship Replica Project; pres, African-American Heritage Tours of DE; exec asst, African-American Heritage, Department of Historical & Cultural Affairs, State of DE. **Honors/Awds:** Numerous honors & awds. **Military Serv:** 2nd lt AUS 1957-58. **Business Addr:** Executive Director, Afro-Amer Hist Soc of DE, 512 E 4th St, Wilmington, DE 19801, (302)571-9300.

CAREY, HOWARD H.
Association executive. **Personal:** Born Jan 6, 1937, Lexington, MS; married Yvonne A Arnold; children: Melba, Rodney. **Educ:** Morehouse Coll, AB 1957; Atlanta Univ, MSW 1963; US International Univ, PhD 1977. **Career:** San Diego Urban League, assoc dir 1963-66; Economic Oppor Commn, prog dev specialist 1966-69; Neighborhood House Assn, prog dir 1969-72. **Orgs:** Charter mem/treas LEAD; certification comm Natl Assn of Social Workers; Natl Assn of Black Social Workers; Alpha Phi Alpha Frat; Sigma Pi Phi Frat, Alpha Pi Boule; Alpha Kappa Delta; Morehouse Coll Alumni Assn San Diego Chap; Natl Conf of Social Welfare; adv comm San Diego City Coll Adv Comm; US Intl Univ Alumni Assn; integration task force, human relations comm San Diego Unified Sch Dist; bd dir United Way Comm Serv Div; United Way Agency Executives Assn; held various offices United Neighborhood Centers of Amer; fndg mem Black Leadership Cncl; Congressman Jim Bates Adv Comm; Congressman Duncan Hunter's Black Affairs Sub-Comm; Black-Jewish Dialogue; Catfish Club; Bethel Baptist Ch; mem governingbd Physicians & Surgeons Hosp; sec Natl Head Start Friends Assn; Co of San Diego Child Care k Force; bd of dir Natl Head Start Assn; Mayor O'Connor's Black Adv Comm; bd of visitors The Bishop's School. **Honors/ Awds:** Cert of Appreciation as Educ Consul San Diego State Univ 1973-74; Special Thanks for Outstanding Contribs in Black Comm Black Federation of San Diego 1973; Significant Contrib to the Comm Educ Comm San Diego Urban League 1974; Citation for Dedication United Way of San Diego 1977; Thanks Coach Allied Gardens Little League 1977; Outstanding Achievement Awd Action Intrprises Develop 1980; Comm Serv San Diego Bd of Realists 1980-81; Dedicated & Outstanding Serv Neighborhood Home Loan Counseling Serv 1981; Cert of Honor Morehouse Coll 1957-82; Providing Competent Child Care Child Develop Assn 1983; Outstanding Leadership Neighborhood House Assn Bd dirs 1983; Concern for & Contributions Toward Well-being of Humanity Christ Church 1984. **Military Serv:** USN e-5 4 yrs. **Business Addr:** Executive Dir, Neighborhood House Assoc, 841 S 41st St, San Diego, CA 92113.

CAREY, JENNIFER DAVIS
Educator. **Personal:** Born Oct 2, 1956, Brooklyn, NY; daughter of Phillippa Stoute Davis and Reuben K Davis; married Robert J Carey Jr; children: Michael, Christopher, Helena. **Educ:** Harvard & Radcliffe Coll, AB 1978; Harvard Graduate School of Educ, EdM, 1979. **Career:** Ohio Univ, asst dir student prog 1979-81; Harvard & Radcliffe Coll, dir of minority recruitment program, 1982-. **Orgs:** Albert Oliver Prog, mem, bd of dir 1983-; The Vista Group, partner 1986; NAACP, mem; Assoc of Afro-American Museums, mem 1986; Visions Foundation, mem 1986. **Business Addr:** Dir, Minority Recruitment, Harvard and Radcliff College, Byerly Hall, 8 Garden St, Cambridge, MA 02138.

CAREY, MARIAH
Vocalist, songwriter. **Personal:** Born 1970, New York, NY; daughter of Patricia Carey and Alfred Roy Carey; married Tommy Mottola, Jun 1993. **Career:** Various jobs including: waitress, hat checker, hostess, until 1987; vocalist, songwriter, record producer, 1987-; albums include: Mariah Carey, 1990; Emotions, 1991; Daydream, 1995. **Honors/Awds:** Grammy nominations for Best Album, Song of the Year, Record of the Year, 1990, won Grammy Awards for Best New Artist, Best Pop Vocal Performance by Female, 1990; People magazine, named one of Twenty-Five Most Most Intriguing People, 1991. **Special Achievements:** Song included on MTV Unplugged EP, 1992; Natl Assn of Recording Merchandisers convention, live performance, 1990; The Arsenio Hall Show, guest appearance, 1990. **Business Addr:** ATTN: Tommy Mottola, Sony Music Entertainment Inc, 550 Madison Ave, 32nd Fl, New York, NY 10022, (212)833-8000.

CAREY, PATRICIA M.
Educational administrator. **Personal:** Born in Chicago, IL; daughter of Mildred Fowler Morris and Ezekiel J Morris, Jr;

married Robert B Carey, Aug 28, 1965; children: Meredith Brooke, Jason Morris. **Educ:** Michigan State Univ, East Lansing MI, BA, 1962, MA, 1963; New York Univ, New York NY, PhD, 1982. **Career:** Marketing Research, New York NY, psychologist, 1968-69; New York Univ, New York NY, counselor, 1970-76, dir of counseling services, 1976-79, dean for student affairs, 1979-; asst chancellor, currently. **Orgs:** American Assn of University Women, American Psychological Assn, Assn of Black Women in Higher Education, Inc; Trustee, Bennett College 1987-; member, NY City Commission on Status of Women 1986-; National Association of Women in Higher Education; Arts Connection Board, 1989-; Manhattan Country School Board, 1991-. **Honors/Awds:** Distinguished Service Award, Graduate School Organization, New York University, 1987; Distinguished Alumnus Award, New York University Black Alumni Association; Outstanding Leadership Award, Higher Education Opportunities Program, New York University, 1987; Named One of America's top 100 Black Business and Professional Women by Dollar & Sense Magazine, 1988; NYU, Faculty Resource Network Achievement Award, 1991; Martin Luther King Jr, Scholars Program Leadership Award, 1992. **Business Addr:** Dean for Student Affairs, Asst Chancellor, New York University, 32 Washington Place, #31, New York, NY 10003.

CAREY, PEARL M.

Beauty consultant. **Personal:** Born May 13; married. **Educ:** Chatman Coll, AA. **Career:** Monterey Peninsula Unified School Dist, CETA coord; EDD, man-power specialist; Child Care Center, owner; Naval Post Graduate Cafeteria, supr; Youth Corps/Job Corps, employ interviewer; NYC, employ clerk. **Orgs:** Mem Comn on Status of Women; life mem & registrar PTA; pres Western States Golf Assn; past pres Dem Womens Club 1976; past pres life mem NAACP 1976; past pres Business & Professional Womens Club 1973; past exec bd mem YMCA; United Fund; Welfare Rights; Natl Council of Negro Women; CA Elected Womens Assn; Eskaton Aux Vol; past council woman Heart Fund & Infant Care Center 1970; Natl Dem Com Woman; Monterey Area Director, Pacific Women's Golf Assn, 1989-; Golf Course Rating Director, Pacific Womens Golf Assn, 1989-. **Honors/Awds:** CA Woman of Achievement BPWC; valedictorian class 1974, MPC; 5 most activist women Monterey Peninsula Herald 1977; Outstanding Woman Monterey County, Monterey County Commission on Status of Women, 1988; Secretary, CA AARP State Legislative Committee, 1989; Monterey County Juvenile Justice Commissioner, 1989-.

CAREY, PHILLIP

Educational administrator. **Personal:** Born Mar 3, 1942, Andros, Bahamas; son of Edna Smith Lewis and Gerald Carey; married Jean Harvey Carey, May 27, 1973; children: Phillipa, Phillip Jr, Peter. **Educ:** Oklahoma State University, Stillwater, OK, BS, 1969, MS, 1970, PhD, 1975. **Career:** American Sociological Assn, Washington, DC, director, fellowship program, 1975-76; Arkansas State, Jonesboro, AR, chair, arts & sciences, 1976-77; Univ of Minnesota, Minneapolis, MN, director, minority affairs, 1977-79; Morgan State Univ, Baltimore, MD, director, urban research, 1979-81; Bahamas Govt, Nassau, director, national ins board, 1981-84; Austin Peay State, Clarksville, MD, assistant to the president, 1989-90; Langston Univ, Langston, OK, associate vice president, academic affairs, 1990-91. **Orgs:** Chair, Academic Policies & Cirriculum Committee, Langston Univ, 1990-; chair, Academic Retention Task Force Committee, Langston, Univ, 1990; chair, Presidential Special Committee, Langston Univ, 1990-; member, Oklahoma Academy for State Goals, State of Oklahoma, 1990-; member, Association of Higher Education, 1990-; member, American Sociological Association, Washington, DC, 1975-. **Honors/Awds:** Community Service Award, Oklahoma Community Services, 1991; Recognition in Profiles of Service, Caucus of Black SDA Administration, 1990; Outstanding Counseling Award, Alpha Phi Alpha, Oklahoma State University, 1974; Graduate Excellence Award, Oklahoma State University, 1973; Fellow, US Department of Labor Manpower, Oklahoma State Univ, 1969-70. **Business Addr:** Associate Vice President for Academic Affairs, Langston University, University Women Building, Langston, OK 73050.

CAREY, WAYNE E.

Human resources executive. **Personal:** Born Feb 8, 1945, Norwalk, CT; son of Etta J Carey and Edward E Carey; married Olivia Thompson, Jun 19, 1986. **Educ:** Howard University, College of Liberal Arts, BA, 1968, School of Law, JD, 1971. **Career:** Bendix Corp, numerous positions including: contracts manager, program development manager, Affirmative Action Affairs, corporate director, Social Responsibility, corporate director; Michigan National Corp, corporate director, staffing-staff relations; Abbott Laboratories, director, Corporate Staffing, currently. **Orgs:** Society For Human Resources Management; Employment Management Association; Sigma Pi Phi Fraternity. **Honors/Awds:** Key Women's Club of America, Man of the Year, 1981. **Business Addr:** Director, Workforce Diversity, Abbott Laboratories, 200 Abbott Park Rd, D39F, AP51, Abbott Park, IL 60064, (847)938-1183.

CARGILE, C. B., JR.

Personnel administrator (retired). **Personal:** Born May 17, 1926, Bastrop, LA. **Educ:** Rutgers State Univ NJ, BA Pol Sci 1973; Rider Coll, MA Mgmt 1980. **Career:** NJ State Govt, admin 1966-70; Ocean Cty Coll, asst dean of bus 1973-. **Orgs:** Exec dir Black Amer 1970-, Black Political Org; life mem NAACP, Alpha Phi Alpha; 1st black elected dem municipal chmn Lakewood NJ; 1st black cand for cty freeholder Monmouth Cty NJ; mem Ocean Cty Coll Speakers Bur; compliance chmn Toms River NJ Br of NAACP. **Honors/Awds:** Disting Comm Serv Awd Concerned Citizens 1970; Pol Awareness Awd Camden NJ Action Council 1979; Disting Serv Awd for Five Yrs Serv as Chmn Ocean Cty CETA Adv Council. **Military Serv:** AUS cwo3 1942-65; AUS Commendation Medal 1959; Oak Leaf Clusters 1963-64.

CARGILE, WILLIAM, III

Construction company executive. **Career:** William Cargile Contractor Inc, Cincinnati, OH, chief executive. **Business Addr:** Chief Executive, William Cargile Contractor Inc, 2008 Freeman Ave, Cincinnati, OH 45214.

CARGILL, GILBERT ALLEN

Government official. **Personal:** Born Jun 4, 1916, Oberlin, OH; son of Mayora Louise Mosby Cargill and Edward James Cargill; divorced; children: Thomas Gilbert. **Educ:** Oberlin Coll, AB, 1937; Case School of Science, 1959-60; Wayne State Univ, 1970-72. **Career:** US Army, flight instructor, 1945-46; Bd of Educ, teacher, 1946-66; Berz Aviation, charter pilot/flight instr, 1967-85; Detroit Board of Education, Detroit, MI, teacher 1967-85. **Orgs:** Organizer, Airway Intruders Flying Club, 1945-67; Flight Instructor, Independent, 1967-85; FAA Designated Pilot Examiner, 1972-89; FAA Safety Counselor, 1972-89; natl pre, Negro Airmen Intl, 1976-78; pres, Detroit Chapter NIA, 1976-; mem, Tuskegee Airmen, 1976-; pres, Trojan-Hessel Block Club, 1981-82; production test pilot, Adams Industries, 1982; mem, British Methodist Episcopal Church, 1982-; sec of trustees of BME Church, 1984-; sec of stewards of BME, 1984-; treasurer of stewards of BME Church, 1984-; mem, Detroit Airport Advisory Commission, 1984-86; mem/chairman, Michigan Aeronautics Commission, 1985-; mem, Michigan Aviation Assn, 1987-88. **Honors/Awds:** Great Lakes Region FAA Award for Outstanding Support of Safety Counselor Program, 1979; Aviation Radio Station "CARGL" named after him by the Federal Aviation Admin, 1981; Chapter Award given by the Detroit Chapter of NAI, 1982; Troy Citizenship Award given by City of Troy, MI, 1982; Detroit City Council Resolution, 1982; Mayoral Proclamation given by Mayor Coleman Young, 1982; C Alfred Anderson Award given by NBCFAE (Natl Black Coalition of Federal Aviation Employees), 1983; Honorary Commission in the AL State Militia given by Governor George Wallace, 1983; City of Holland Certificate given by the City of Holland, MI, 1986; Sesquicentennial Aviation Certificate given by MI Sesquicentennial Committee, 1987; MI Aeronautics Commission Leadership Award given by MI Aeronautics Commission, 1992; elected to the MI Aviation Hall of Fame in November 1988, first African-American person to become enshrined in this organization, 1989. **Military Serv:** Army Air Corps, f/o, 1945; State of MI special tribute. **Home Addr:** 20213 Faust Road, Detroit, MI 48219.

CARGILL, SANDRA MORRIS

Management consulting company executive. **Personal:** Born May 8, 1953, Boston, MA; daughter of Ida R Morris and Richard B Morris; married Ronald Glanville Cargill. **Educ:** Univ of Redlands, BS, business administration, 1984. **Career:** Amer Acquisitions Inc, admin asst 1976-77; Mode O' Day Co, asst buyer, sec 1977-78; Loral (Xerox) Electro Optical Systems, sr contract admin 1978-85; CA Inst of Tech Jet Propulsion Lab, contract specialist 1985-91; Cargill Assocs, pres, 1990-. **Orgs:** Pres, principal developer Xerox Electro Optical Systems Tutorial Prog 1980-83; mem Black Women's Forum 1980-83; lecturer Youth Motivation Task Force 1981-83; mem Loral EOS Mgmt Club 1983-85; gen mem 1983-85, bd dir logistics 1986-87, exec adv Jr Achievement Prog 1984-85; member, National Contract Management Association, San Gabriel Valley, 1983-; member, Caltech Management Club, California Institute of Technology, 1985-. **Honors/Awds:** Outstanding Achievement in Contract Admin Xerox Electro Optical Systems 1981; Recognition for Leadership in Developing & Coord the XEOS Tutorial Prog Xerox Electro Optical Systs 1981; Rec for Volunteer Serv to Students Pasadena Unified School Dist 1981; Recognition for Volunteer Serv to Students Youth Motivation Task Force 1981-83; Recognition for Outstanding Contribs in Community Serv So CA Volunteers Assoc 1981; Recognition of Volunteer Serv Jr Achievement Assoc 1985; Recognition of Extraordinary Serv & Leadership Mgmt Devel Comm Loral EOS Mgmt Club 1985; Recognition of Volunteer Support to Students Jr Achievement Loral EOS Mgmt Club 1985; Outstanding Achievement Award, General W Harmon, 1990; Outstanding Achievement Award, NCMA, 1990; Group Achievement Award, NASA, 1989; Clinton's Natl Svc Prog Award, Los Angeles Pilot, 1993. **Business Addr:** President, Cargill Associates Management Consultation, 6442 Coldwater Canyon, Ste 209, North Hollywood, CA 91606, (818)760-0289.

CARL, EARL LAWRENCE. See Obituaries section.

CARLINE, WILLIAM RALPH

Dentist. **Personal:** Born Oct 21, 1910, Lake Charles, LA; married Gen. **Educ:** Wiley Coll, BA; Meharry Dental Coll, DDS honors. **Career:** Carline Dental Clinic, Corpus Christi, TX, practioner in dentistry. **Orgs:** Past pres Gulf State Dental Assn 1955; Phi Beta Sigma 1932; apptd citizens Com for revision of TX Constitution 1973; mem United & Methodist Ch; mem Nat-Dental Assn; life mem NAACP; mem various other Local, State, Nat Orgns. **Honors/Awds:** 1 of 5 chosen in nation Research Randolph Air Force 1956. **Military Serv:** USAF group dental surgeon 1943-43. **Business Addr:** 1211 Sam Rankin St, Corpus Christi, TX 78401.

CARLISLE, JAMES EDWARD, JR.

Educator, lawyer. **Personal:** Born May 30, 1944, Acmar, AL; son of Juanita Carlisle and James E Carlisle Sr; married Deborah Ann Carter, Jun 19, 1976; children: Constance Isabelle, Phillip Joseph. **Educ:** Youngstown State University, BA, 1967; Bowling Green State University, MEd, 1978; University of Toledo College of Law, JD, 1985. **Career:** Perkins Board of Education, 1967-69; Toledo Board of Education, 1969-; Waite High School, educator, currently. **Orgs:** Youngstown University Chapter of NAACP, president, 1966-67; Big Brothers of America, 1970-73; American Federation of Teachers, 1969-; Homeless Awareness Project, 1988-; National Bar Association, Ren Daniels for President, campaign organizer, 1992; Nubia, reading coordinator; Toledo Alliance of Black Educators. **Honors/Awds:** American Jurisprudence Award, 1985. **Home Addr:** 110 Harmony Ln, Toledo, OH 43615. **Business Addr:** Educator, Waite High School, 301 Morrison Dr, Toledo, OH 43605.

CARLO, NELSON

Corporate executive. **Career:** Abbott Products Inc, Chicago, IL, chief executive.

CARLTON, PAMELA GEAN

Banker. **Personal:** Born Oct 17, 1954, Cleveland, OH; daughter of Mildred Myers Carlton and Alphonso A Carlton; married Charles Jordan Hamilton Jr; children: Charles III, Samuel Aaron Hamilton. **Educ:** Williams Coll, BA Pol Econ 1976; Yale Sch of Management, MPPM Business 1980; Yale Law School, JD 1980. **Career:** Cleary Gottlieb Stein & Hamilton, assoc counsel 1980-82; Morgan Stanley Co Inc, assoc investment banking 1982-85, vice pres investment banking, beginning 1985, principal, finance department currently. **Orgs:** Mem NY State Bar 1981-; bd mem Studio Museum in Harlem 1982-87; mem Westchester Bd Planned Parenthood 1987-89; bd mem, Graduate School of City University of New York; executive comm 1988-91; bd mem, World Resources Institute 1991-94. **Business Addr:** Principal, Finance Department, Morgan Stanley & Co Inc, 1251 Avenue of the Americas, New York, NY 10020.

CARMAN, EDWIN G.

Elected official. **Personal:** Born Feb 13, 1951, New Brunswick, NJ; married Pamela M Vaughan. **Educ:** Rutgers Univ, BA 1974. **Career:** Middlesex Cty Coll Found, bd mem 1980-; Middlesex Cty Econ Oppty Corp, bd mem 1975-, chmn 1981-84; City of New Brunswick, councilman 1975, council pres 1987. **Orgs:** Aide to the speaker of the house NJ Gen Assembly 1979-81; mem American Council of Young Political Leaders; bd mem NJ Foster Grandparents 1986. **Honors/Awds:** Political Action Awd New Brunswick Area NAACP 1983. **Business Addr:** Councilmember, City of New Brunswick, 78 Bayard St, New Brunswick, NJ 08901.

CARMICHAEL, BENJAMIN G.

Educator. **Personal:** Born Jul 7, 1938, Atlanta, GA; married Dorothy; children: Christopher, Jennifer. **Educ:** San Francisco St Coll, BA 1963; Univ of CA, MA 1972. **Career:** CA State Univ, prof 1969-; US Comm on Porno, princ invest; Transit Robby Study, Univ of CA, asst proj dir 1968-70; Univ of San Francisco, lecturer 1968-69; Hunters Pt Comm Devel Proj, proj dir 1966-68. **Orgs:** Dir Crim Just Admin Prgm CA St U; consul Law Enforce Assis Admin; advis bd me Admin of Just Prgm Ohlone Jr Coll Alpha Phi Alpha; Natl UrbanLeague; Natl Coun on Cr & Delinq Youth Cr in Urban Comm, St Hustlers & Their Crimes, Crime & Delinq Vol 21, 1975; The Hunters Pt Riot, Pol of theFrust, Issues in Crime, Vol 4 1969. **Honors/Awds:** Fellow Natl Inst of Mental Hlth Univ of CA 1966-68. **Military Serv:** AUS 1957. **Business Addr:** 25800 Hillary St, Hayward, CA 94542.

CARMICHAEL, CAROLE A.

Journalist. **Personal:** Born Jul 9, 1950, Brooklyn, NY. **Educ:** NY U, BA 1972. **Career:** Seattle Times, asst news managing editor, currently; Chicago Tribune, former careers editor; Clmb Coll Chicago, instr journalism 1978-79; Fairchild Publ Inc NY, news reporter 1976; UPI Omaha & NY, news reporter 1973-76; Stephen Decatur Jr High School, English tchr 1972-73; Philadelphia Daily News, news reporter. **Orgs:** Contrib wrtr Working Wmn Mag 1977-; contrib wrtr Essence Mag 1979; pres Chicago Assn of Blk Jrnlsts 1978-80; mem bd of dir YWCA Metro Chicago 1978-79. **Honors/Awds:** Adv Study Fellow Econ for Jrnlsts Brkngs Instn Wash 1978; slctd as 1 of 50 ftr ldrs of Am Ebony Mag 1978; Sojrnr Truth Awd Nat Assn of Negro Bus &

Professional Wmn NY 1980; Comm Serv Awd Nat Assn of Negro Bus & Professional Wmn Chicago 1980. **Business Addr:** Asst News Managing Editor, Seattle Times, 1120 John St, Seattle, WA 98109.

CARMICHAEL, STOKELY (KWAME TOURE)
Political activist. **Personal:** Born Jun 29, 1941, Port-of-Spain, Trinidad and Tobago; son of Mabel F and Adolphus; married Miriam Makeba, Apr 1968 (divorced); children: Miriam Makeba. **Educ:** Howard University, BA, 1964. **Career:** Student Nonviolent Coordinating Committee (SNCC), Atlanta, GA, organizer, 1964-66, chairman, 1966-67; Black Panthers, Oakland, CA, prime minister, 1967-69; All Afrikan People's Revolutionary Party, organizer. **Honors/Awds:** Coauthor, Black Power: The Politics of Liberation in America, Random House, 1967; author, Stokely Speaks: Black Power Back to Pan-Africanism, Random House, 1971; LLD, Shaw University. **Business Addr:** Stokely Carmichael, c/o Random House, 201 East 50th Street, New York, NY 10022.

CARNEGIE, RANDOLPH DAVID
Business executive. **Personal:** Born Jan 23, 1952, Kingston, Jamaica; son of Nola E Lindo and Anthony C Carnegie. **Educ:** Franklin and Marshall Coll, BA 1974; Pace Univ, MBA 1981. **Career:** Dow Jones & Co, account rep, 1974-75; Time Inc, account rep, 1975-81; Conoco Inc, sr analyst, 1981-86; dir, TAG Productions, 1986. **Orgs:** NBMBAA, Houston Chapter, pres, 1985-86; Natl Conf Co-Chair, NBMBAA 1988.

CARNELL, LOUGENIA LITTLEJOHN
Program analyst. **Personal:** Born Mar 12, 1947, Memphis, TN; children: Gizele Montrece. **Educ:** Dept of Agr Grad Sch; Catholic U; Univ of DC Chester. **Career:** Dept of Energy, prog analyst; Dept of Energy, personal asst to dep asst adminstr 1977-78; Interagency Council for Minority Business Enterprise Dept of Commerce, prsnl asst to exec dir 1975-76; Staff Chaplain Mil Dist Wash DC, admin sec steno 1973-75; MEECN Systems Engineering Office Def Communications Agency Wash DC, div sec steno 1971-73. **Orgs:** Mem Fed Women's Prof 1978-; 1st chmn Dept of Energy Task Force On Concerns of Minority Women 1979-80; mem Nat Council of Career Women 1979-; Nat mem Smithsonian Assos 1979-; med asst vol ARC Alexandria Chap 1973-76. **Honors/Awds:** Key to City New Orleans 1975; recital WTOP-TV Wash DC 1975; cert & 3-yr serv pin ARC Alexandria Chap 1976; pub poetry & prose; 1st female in 108 yrs to be mem of bd of & trustees Mt Olive Bapt Ch Arlington 1977; first chmn Dept of Energy Task Force on Concerns of Minority Women Wash DC 1979; Peopleon the Move Black Enterprise Mag 1979; designated to address DOE-FWPMs Nat FEW Conf Seattle 1979; Women in Energy Newsletter 1979; cert of participation IL Ofc of Minority Bus Enterprise Statewide Annual Conf 1979; observance of black history month Prog Adv Dept of Energy. **Business Addr:** 2000 M St NW, Washington, DC 20416.

CARNEY, ALFONSO LINWOOD, JR.
Attorney. **Personal:** Born Aug 7, 1949, Norfolk, VA; married Cassandra E Henderson MD; children: Alison Lynette. **Educ:** Trinity Coll Hartford CT, BA 1971; Univ of VA Sch of Law, JD 1974. **Career:** General Foods Corp, asst div counsel 1974-78, Washington counsel 1978-81, intl counsel 1981-86, sr intl counsel 1987-. **Orgs:** Mem Natl Bar Assoc 1976-, Amer Bar Assoc 1980-; chmn Law Dept Recruiting Comm 1983-85; mem Law Dept Mgmt Comm 1985; bd of dirs Volunteer Serv Bureau of Westchester 1985-. **Honors/Awds:** Earl Warren Fellow Legal Defense & Educ Fund; Black Achiever Awd Harlem YMCA 1985; Financial Achievement Awd General Foods Corp 1986. **Business Addr:** Sr International Counsel, General Foods Corp, 250 North St, White Plains, NY 10625.

CARNEY, ROBERT MATTHEW
Physician (retired). **Personal:** Born Feb 28, 1928, Steubenville, OH; divorced; children: Ruby, Darla, Wendi. **Educ:** Univ of HI, attended; Fisk Univ, BA 1952; Meharry Med Coll, grad degree program, 1952-54, MD 1958; Mercy Hosp, intern 1958-59. **Career:** Private practice, physician. **Orgs:** Bd dir Brookhaven Nursing Home; staff sec Grinnel Gen Hosp; professional chmn Cty Chap Amer Cancer Soc, Poweshiek Cty Med Examiner; clinical tutorial staff Grinnel-Rush Med Students; assoc prof Alcohol/Drug Abuse Counselors; mem Poweshiek Cty Mental Health Assoc; lecturer HS Sex Ed; preceptor Univ IA Med Students; mem Amer Acad Family Physicians 1963-, Poweshiek Cty Med Soc 1959-, IA Family Practice Club, Amer Legion, United Presbyterian Church, Amer Bowling Assoc, Oakland Acres Golf Club; team physician HS Football 1960-, Army Tennis Team 1948-49. **Honors/Awds:** Dr of the Day IA House & Senate 1976-77; Citizen Awd Prog 1969. **Military Serv:** AUS 1946-49.

CAROLINE, J. C.
Football coach. **Personal:** Born Jan 17, 1933, Warrenton, GA; married Laverne Dillon; children: Jayna. **Educ:** BS 1967. **Career:** Univ of IL Athletics Assn, asst ftball coach 1966-; Chicago Bears, 1956-; Montreal Allouetts, 1955-56. **Orgs:** Bd of dir Don Moyers Boys Club. **Honors/Awds:** All-am Football 1653; All Professional 1956. **Business Addr:** 123 Assembly Hall, Champaign, IL 61820.

CARPENTER, ANN M.
Chiropractor, educator. **Personal:** Born Jul 1, 1934, New York, NY; daughter of Charity Gowdy and James Gowdy; divorced; children: Karen, Marie. **Educ:** City Coll of New York, MA/BS Educ 1956-60; NY Chiropractic Coll, DC 1978; Univ of Bridgeport CT, MS Nutrition 1980. **Career:** Harlem Prep Sch prin 1975; Harlem Prep Sch, asst prin tchr educ & curriculum 1968-75; Haaren Hs NY, chmn Eng dept 1967-68; Haaren HS NY, tchr Eng 1957-67; Beacon NY, chiropractor 1980. **Orgs:** Mem Natl Assn of Secondary Sch Admin 1979; mem NY Assn Mem Black Educators II 1978-; mem Amer Chiropractic Assn 1975-; Bergen Co NJ Urban League of Bergen Co 1978; NY State Chiropractic Assoc 1979-; Amer Black Chiropractors Assoc 1985-; mem NY State Bd for Chiropractic 1985; pres NYSCA Dist Nine 1985-86, 1986-87; Chair NY State Bd for Chiropractic, 1988-89 . **Honors/Awds:** Community service award Harlem Prep Sch 1976; youth guidance award Bergen Co Negro Bus & Professional Women 1974; Citizen of the Year Awards in Black; Service to profession, NY State Chiropractic Association, 1988; Fellow, American College of Chiropractors, 1992. **Business Addr:** Chiropractor, Beacon Chiropractic Office, 125 South Chestnut St, Beacon, NY 12508.

CARPENTER, BARBARA WEST
Organization executive, educator. **Educ:** Southern Univ, BS, vocational education and general science, master's degree in secondary education and administration. **Career:** Southern Univ, professor and administrator, currently. **Orgs:** Zeta Phi Beta Sorority Inc, director of education, director of illiteracy eradication, international pres, currently. **Business Addr:** President, Zeta Phi Beta Sorority Inc, 1734 New Hampshire Ave NW, Washington, DC 20009, (202)387-3103.

CARPENTER, CARL ANTHONY
Educational administrator. **Personal:** Born Feb 29, 1944, Gaffney, SC; son of Teacora Carpenter and John H Carpenter; married Parthelia Davis Carpenter, Aug 6, 1967; children: Carla P Adams, Carl A II. **Educ:** South Carolina State University, BS, 1966, MEd, 1970; University of South Carolina, PhD, 1973. **Career:** Sumter, South Carolina School District #17, teacher, 1966-70; South Carolina State Department of Education, 1972; South Carolina State University, assistant-associate professor, 1972-75, assistant vice president academic affairs, 1975-80, vice president academic affairs, 1980-86, professor, 1986-92, interim president, 1992-93, professor of education, 1993-94; Consolidated Consultative Services, pres, 1994-96; Voohees College, executive vp/academic dean, 1996-. **Orgs:** NAFEO; MEAC Council of Presidents; NAACP; Omega Psi Phi Fraternity Inc; Phi Delta Kappa Educational Fraternity; Alpha Kappa Mu; board of trustees, Presbyterian College and Rabun Gap Nacoochee School; Presbyterian Church (USA) Foundation board of directors; Heritage Corridor Partnership board of directors. **Honors/Awds:** Omega Psi Phi Fraternity Inc, Epsilon Omega Chapter, Man of the Year, 1992; Omega Psi Phi Fraternity Inc, Citizen of the Year, 1981; Outstanding Educators of America, 1974. **Special Achievements:** Institutional Effectiveness Measures for Adult and Continuing Education, 1992; Factors Influencing Access & Equality in Higher Education, 1991; Review, Analysis & Projections of Academic Programs, 1978; Performance Based Teacher Education Specifications, 1973. **Home Phone:** (803)536-1793. **Business Addr:** Exec. VP/Academic Dean, Voorhees College, 1411 Voorhees Rd., Denmark, SC 29042, (803)793-3351.

CARPENTER, CLARENCE E., JR.
Company executive. **Personal:** Born Feb 5, 1941, Nashville, TN; son of Mary Carney Carpenter and Clarence E Carpenter Sr (deceased); married Faye Powell Carpenter, Apr 7, 1990; children: Brenda Thomas, Yvonne Campbell, Gail, Clarence E III, Tiffany. **Educ:** Southwestern Christian College, Terrell, TX, AA, 1961; Northeastern Illinois University, Chicago, IL, BA, 1988. **Career:** Mother of Savior Seminar, Blackwood, NJ, mgr, administration, 1962-65; Chemical Co, Davisboro, NJ, shipping mgr, 1965-68; Kraft, Philadelphia, PA, account exec, 1968-71; Kraft, New York, NY, Washington, DC, supervisor, zone mgr, 1971-76; Kraft, Albany, NY, Rochester, NY, district mgr, area mgr, 1976-82; Kraft, Chicago, IL, region grocery mgr, region vice president, 1982-89; Kraft General Foods, Glenview, IL, vice president retail operations, 1989-. **Orgs:** Visiting professor, executive, Urban League, 1988-. **Honors/Awds:** Chicago YMCA Black Achievers Award, YMCA Metropolitan Chicago, 1988; Food Marketing Institute Award, Food Market Institute, 1990; Martin Luther King Award, Minority Economic Council, 1989. **Home Addr:** PO Box 3487, Barrington, IL 60010.

CARPENTER, JOSEPH, II
Educator. **Personal:** Born Jul 21, 1937, Aliceville, AL; married; children: Martin, Brenda, Richard. **Educ:** MATC, AA 1965; Marquette U, BA 1967; Fisk U, 1968-69; Marquette U, PhD 1970; Univ of IA, Post Doctorate 1972. **Career:** Univ of WI, prof Afro-Educ, soc research 1972-. **Orgs:** Dir Carthage Coll 1970-72; asst prof Lehman Coll Bronx Summer 1971; NEA Fellow Marquette Univ 1968-70; chmn City of Milwaukee Bd of Election Commr; chmn bd dir Northcott Youth Serv Bur for Prevention of Juvenile Delinq; chmn Univ of WI Afro-am Stud Comm Rel Comm; exec bd mem Social Studies Council of WI; consult State of NJ Dept of Ed; mem Phi Delta Kappa; alpha Psi Alpha; Milwaukee Frontiers Internat; bd dir Nat Council for Black Child Develop Inc. **Honors/Awds:** Author of numerous articles; Distinguished Christian Fellowship Award for Comm Serv 1973; distinguished political serv Award 1974. **Military Serv:** USAF comm spl 1955-60. **Business Addr:** Dept of Afro Am Studies, U of WI, Milwaukee, WI 53201.

CARPENTER, LEWIS
City government official, banker (retired). **Personal:** Born Feb 1, 1928, Brantley, AL; son of Bessie Carpenter and H D Carpenter; married Myrtice Bryant Carpenter, Nov 18, 1950. **Educ:** Covington Cty Training School, AA 1956; LBW Jr Coll, Acct 1982. **Career:** Covington Cty Bank, custodian 1959; City of Andalusia, councilman, 1984-; Covington County Bank, banker, retired. **Orgs:** Mem Masonic Rose of Sharon Lodge 1965-, Advisory Comm LBW Jr Coll 1970-, Covington Cty Sheriff Reserve 1970-; mem advisory Local Draft Bd 1980-; advisory OCAP Comm 1982-. **Honors/Awds:** 1st black City Councilman Andalusia City Council 1984. **Military Serv:** US Army, corporal, 1952-54, 18 mos in Korea. **Home Addr:** 210 Lowe Ave, Andalusia, AL 36420.

CARPENTER, RAYMOND PRINCE
Attorney. **Personal:** Born Apr 2, 1944, Little Rock, AR; son of Reuben & Ellen Carpenter; married Barbara Pearson, Sep 2, 1971; children: Raymond Prince Jr. **Educ:** Philander Smith College, 1962-63; University of AR, BA, 1966; Emory University School of Law, JD, 1975. **Career:** Lockheed Georgia Co, associate attorney, 1975-76; City of Atlanta-Solicitor's Office, assistant solicitor, 1976-78; Sears Roebuck & Co., sr attorney, 1978-86; Price Waterhouse LLP, managing director, 1986-92; Huey, Guilday & Tucker, managing partner, 1992-94; Holland & Knight, partner, 1994-. **Orgs:** State Bar of Georgia, chair-elect taxation section, 1995-97; Atlanta Bar Association, secretary-treasurer, 1996-; National Institute on State Taxation, board member, 1990-; American Bar Association, state tax section bd, 1990-. **Honors/Awds:** Fulton County Georgia, Outstanding Public Achievement, 1990. **Special Achievements:** Keynote Speaker, ML King Holiday Celebration, 1992; Keynote Speaker, Tax Executive Institute, National Mtg, 1989; Journal of State Taxation, Florida Svc Taxes, 1986; Georgia Bar Journal, State Tax Issues, 1989. **Military Serv:** US Marine Corps, cpl, 1969-70. **Business Addr:** Attorney, Holland & Knight, 1207 W Peachtree St, Ste 2000, 1 Atlantic Ctr, Atlanta, GA 30309.

CARPENTER, THELMA. See Obituaries section.

CARPENTER, VIVIAN L. (VIVIAN CARPENTER STRATHER)
Educator. **Personal:** Born Nov 3, 1952, Detroit, MI; daughter of Jennie Pettway Thomas and Doyal Wilson Thomas (deceased); married Herbert J Strather (died 1978); children: Andrea Nicole Strather, Carmen Laverne Strather. **Educ:** University of Michigan, Ann Arbor, MI, BSE, 1973, MBA, 1975, PhD, 1985. **Career:** Ford Motor Co, Dearborn, MI, research engineer, 1972-73; Arthur Andersen & Co, Detroit, MI, sr consultant, 1975-77; Michigan Dept of Treasury, Lansing, MI, deputy state treasurer, 1979-81; University of Michigan, Ann Arbor, MI, visiting prof of industrial & operations engineering, 1990-91; Wayne State University, Detroit, MI, asst prof of accounting, 1984-92; Florida A&M University, associate professor, director of academic programs, 1992-95; School of Business and Industry, assistant dean, 1995-. **Orgs:** American Accounting Assn, 1984-; American Institute of CPA's, 1979-; Michigan Assn of CPA's, 1979-; Government Finance Officers Assn, 1978-84, 1990-; National Assn of Black Accountants, 1979-90, 1994-95; Atwater Entertainment Associates, director. **Honors/Awds:** National Assn of Black Accountants National Award, 1991; National Science Foundation, 1987, 1990; Ford Foundation Fellow, 1985; Association of Government Accountants Author's Award, 1991; Decision Sciences Institute, Best Interdisciplinary Paper Award, 1991; Nissan International Fellow, 1993. **Business Addr:** Assistant Dean, Florida A&M University, School of Business & Industry, 1 SBI Plaza, Tallahassee, FL 32307.

CARPENTER, WILLIAM ARTHUR, II (BILL)
Writer. **Personal:** Born Oct 14, 1965, Fayettesville, NC; son of Via Maria Randall-Carpenter and William A Carpenter, Sr. **Educ:** Univ of Dijon France, Certificate 1985; The Amer Univ, BA, 1990. **Career:** Smithsonian-Natl Museum of Amer History, exhibit writer 1987; Bush/Quayle Campaign, Washington DC, campaign worker 1988-89, 1992; Vietnam Veterans of Amer, Washington DC, press asst 1987; Gospel Highlights Newsletter, editor, 1987-89; Journal of Gospel Music, Mitchellville, MD, editor, 1990-92; The Washington New Observer, staff writer, 1990-93; Carp Shank Entertainment, sr publicist, 1992-95; Capital Entertainment, co-founder, 1996-. **Orgs:** National Association of Black Journalists; Gospel Music Professional Network. **Special Achievements:** Freelance articles published in: American Gospel, Destiny, Goldmine, Living Blues, YSB, Players, People Magazine, Rejoice, The Washington Post; gospel editor, All-Music Guide, Miller-Freeman, 1992. **Business Addr:** Co-Founder, Capital Entertainment, PO Box 66661, Washington Sq Station, Washington, DC 20035, (202)986-0693.

CARPER, GLORIA G.
Educator. **Personal:** Born Aug 10, 1930, Montclair, NJ; widowed; children: Gladyce, Terri. **Educ:** Morgan State Coll, BS 1950; WV Univ, MA 1971. **Career:** WV Dept of Welfare, social worker 1961-64; WV Dept of Mental Health, welfare supvr 1964-67, admin asst med div 1967-72; Day Care Center, Mentally Retarded Children, Dept of Mental Health, dir 1972-73; WV State Coll, acting dir of guidance & placement, foreign student advisory, counselor for devel serv 1982-. **Orgs:** Mem natl Assoc for Retarded Children Inc, Kanawha Assoc for Retarded Children Inc; past pres Charleston Inst; mem Delta Sigma Theta, Charleston Inst Chapt, The Links Inc; bd mem Charleston Oppty Indust Ctr Inc; organist 1st Bapt Church. **Honors/Awds:** Mother of the Year 1st Bapt Church 1972. **Business Addr:** Foreign Student Adv, Couns, West Virginia State Coll, Developmental Serv, Institute, WV 25112.

CARR, ANTOINE LABOTTE
Professional basketball player. **Personal:** Born Jul 23, 1961, Oklahoma City, OK. **Educ:** Wichita State Univ, Wichita, KS, 1979-83. **Career:** Played in the Italian league, forward, 1983-84; Atlanta Hawks, 1984-90; Sacramento Kings, 1990-91; San Antonio Spurs, 1991-94; Utah Jazz, 1994-. **Special Achievements:** NBA Draft, First round pick, #8, 1983. **Business Addr:** Professional Basketball Player, Utah Jazz, 301 W South Temple, Salt Lake City, UT 84101-1216, (801)575-7800.

CARR, CHRIS DEAN
Professional basketball player. **Personal:** Born Mar 12, 1974, Ironton, MO. **Educ:** Southern Illinois. **Career:** Phoenix Suns, guard, 1995-96; Minnesota Timberwolves, 1996-. **Business Addr:** Professional Basketball Player, Minnesota Timberwolves, 600 1st Ave N, Minneapolis, MN 55403, (612)337-3865.

CARR, CLARA B.
Data entry inspector. **Personal:** Born Aug 31, 1948, Opelika, AL; daughter of Princella Ingram and Ben Baker; married Lonnie Carr Jr, Jan 20, 1968 (divorced); children: Amy Arletha Carr, Amaris Artreja Carr. **Educ:** Opelika State Technical Jr Coll, Business, 1966-67. **Career:** Ampex Corp, Opelika, AL, record insp II. **Orgs:** Past grand matron, Silver Queen Grand Chapter, Order of the Eastern Star, 1986-89; worthy matron, Queen Esther Chapter, Order of the Eastern Star, 1980-; food share unit clerk, Food Share, 1989; financial sec, Nazareth Baptist Church, 1988; sec, Mitchell Quarter Water System, 1983-88.

CARR, KENNY
Professional basketball player. **Personal:** Born Aug 15, 1955, Washington, DC; married Adrianna; children: Cameron, Devon Roberts. **Educ:** NC State Univ, 1978. **Career:** Los Angeles Lakers, forward 1977-79; Cleveland Cavaliers, forward 1980-81; Detroit Pistons, forward 1981-82; Portland Trail Blazers, forward 1982-87. **Honors/Awds:** 5th highest scorer in the nation 266 points a game sr yr NC State; Scored 798 point second only to David Thompson in NC State history; ACC's leading scorer & rebounder as a jr; Selected to the Sporting News 1st team All Amer squad; Gold Medal in Montreal with the US Olympic team 1976.

CARR, KIPLEY DEANE
Civil rights activist, political consultant. **Personal:** Born Mar 28, 1967, Bowling Green, KY; son of Georgianna Smith Carr Hendrix and Billy Zack Carr (deceased). **Educ:** Shepherd College, 1987-88, 1990-91; Georgia State University, 1989. **Career:** United States Senate, Minority Secretary, aide, 1985; Martinsburg Journal, interim office manager, 1986; Democratic National Convention, deputy delegate liasion, 1988; Michael Lomax for Atlanta Mayor, issues advisor, 1988-89; Joint Action in Community Service, counselor, 1989-91; free-lance political consultant, 1989-; Atlanta NAACP Branch, volunteer staff mem, 1988-89; NAACP Southeast Regional Office, volunteer staff mem, 1988-89; Atlanta Public Schools, aide, 1988-89; Shepherd Coll, asst to the dir, Media Services, 1993-94. **Orgs:** Bowling Green Board of Education, student representative, 1984; Jefferson County Young Democrats, parliamentarian, 1986-87; Atlanta NAACP Youth, chair, executive committee, 1988-89; Eastern Panhandle Association of Student Councils, founder, 1988; West Virginia State Dem Executive Committee, 1991-; NAACP, West Virginia State Branch, assistant state advisor, 1992-; Bowling Green NAACP Youth Council, charter mem, 1978, Program & Research Committee, chairman, 1981-83, acting vp, 1982-83, pres, 1983-84; KY State NAACP Youth Conference, pres, 1984-85; Jefferson County (WV) NAACP, exec committee mem, 1985-87; SCLC Natl Office, office volunteer, 1988; NAACP Natl Bd of Dirs, regional youth nominee, 1989; West VA Delegate Selection Plan Committee, 2nd cong dist rep, 1992, Democratic Natl Convention, 1991-92; WV Young Democrats, acting natl committeeman, 1991; Berkeley Co, Chamber of Commerce, participant, Leadership Berkeley, 1993-94; Carter G Woodson Historical Assn, chairman, Bylaws Committee, 1992-94; WV NAACP, asst state youth advisor, 1992-94; Martinsburg (WV), Dem Exec Comm, acting ward 1 committeeman, 1993-94, at large committeeman/secretary, 1994; Political Empowerment Project, founder & chairman, 1994-; Bowling Green/Warren County Young Democrats, acting pres, 1994-; KY State NAACP Conf, chairman, Legislative Affairs Committee, 1995-, chairman, Youth Work Committee, 1995-; NAACP Youth & College Division, special advisor to the dir, 1995-. **Honors/Awds:** Kentucky State NAACP, Honor Roll of Civil Rights Veterans, 1984; Jefferson County Board of Education, Academic Excellence, 1986; Bowling Green/Warren County NAACP, Distinguished Service, 1983; KY NAACP, Honor Roll of Civil Rights Veterans, 1984; Jefferson County (WV), Bd of Ed, Academic Excellence Award, 1985; Gloster B Current Youth Leadership Award, Nominee, 1989. **Special Achievements:** Publisher, State Street Baptist Church Youth Times, 1984; youngest African-American ever to serve in a state party office in West Virginia, 1991; First person to serve as a junior deacon in the 145 year history of State Street Baptist Church, 1983; First African-American to serve as student representative to the BG Bd of Educ, 1983; First person from Southern KY ever elected as Pres of the State Youth Conference, 1984; Youngest person ever in the history of the WV NAACP to be elected to a branch exec comm seat, 1985; First African-American ever to run for political party office in Eastern WV, 1990; First African-American to successfully manage a political campaign in Eastern WV, 1990; First African American to successfully manage a presidential campaign in WV, 1992; First African American to serve as a political commentator in Eastern WV, 1990; First African American to win a city-wide election in Eastern WV, 1994; First African American ever to represent West VA at a Natl Young Dem Meeting, 1991; First African American ever to represent WV at the President's State of the Union Address, 1991. **Home Addr:** 1036 Kenton Street, Bowling Green, KY 42101-2502.

CARR, LENFORD
City official. **Personal:** Born Sep 21, 1938, Haywood Co Bural, TN; married Ella R Porter; children: Vincent Louis, Bridgett Genese. **Educ:** Knoxville Coll, 1957-58. **Career:** Humboldt City Park Comm, mem 1977-85; Humboldt City School Board, mem/secretary 1979-88. **Orgs:** Mem City Schools-Transportation-Building and Calendar Comm; mem Morning Star Baptist Church; mem NAACP Humboldt Chapt; pres Humboldt Demo Concerned Citizens Club; mem Gibson Co Demo Exec. **Honors/Awds:** Plant Mgrs Awd Martin Marietta Aluminum Sales 1970; culinary serv Morning Star Baptist Church 1977; community serv NAACP-, IBPOWELK 1980-83; ed boardsmanship Humboldt City Schools Board 1983; Outstanding Citizen Political Involvement AKA Sorority 1983. **Military Serv:** AUS Sp4 1961-64. **Home Addr:** 94 Maple St, Humboldt, TN 38343.

CARR, LEONARD G.
Clergyman. **Personal:** Born Oct 25, 1902, Bridgewater, VA; married Juanita; children: Leonita. **Educ:** Lincoln U, STB 1933; VA Theol Sem, DD 1949; Lincoln Univ PA, 1950. **Career:** Vine Meml Bapt Ch, founder pastor. **Orgs:** Treas, Nat Bapt Conv USA 20 Yrs; pres PA Bapt State Conv 1945; mem Eastern Keystone Assn; Home Mission Bd; YMCA; Lincoln Alumni Assn; Berean Inst; bd dirs Better Family Planning; Mason; mem Phi Beta Sigma. **Honors/Awds:** Numerous honors & awards. **Business Addr:** Vine Meml Bapt Ch, 5600 Girard Ave, Philadelphia, PA.

CARR, M. L. (MICHAEL LEON)
Basketball coach (retired), sports executive. **Personal:** Born Jan 9, 1951, Wallace, NC. **Career:** Detroit Pistons, 1976-79; Boston Celtics, forward, 1979-85, scout, 1985-91, director of community relations, 1991-94, senior executive vice president and director of basketball group, 1994-, head coach, 1995-97. **Business Addr:** Dir, Basketball Operations, Boston Celtics, 151 Merrimac St, 5th Fl, Boston, MA 02114, (617)523-6050.

CARR, PERCY L.
Basketball coach. **Personal:** Born Nov 19, 1941, Longview, TX; married Fredella Scott; children: Kacy. **Educ:** CA State Univ, BS, Phys Educ 1968, MA, Phys Educ 1972. **Career:** San Jose City Coll, head basketball coach; Stanford Univ, asst basketball coach 1974-75; Edison HS, coach 1970-74; Tulare Union HS, 1968-70; Edison HS, teacher, asst vice principal & dean of boys 1970-74; Tulare Union HS, teacher & coach 1968-70; has worked in various basketball camps & clinics 1971-74. **Orgs:** Mem Masonic Lodge; Alpha Phi Alpha. **Honors/Awds:** All metro coach of the Year, 1971; Coach of the Year, Central CA Basketball Coaches Assn, 1974; All metro coach of the year Fresno Bee 1974; Coach of the Year, 1976; Outstanding Teacher-Coach Award, 1988. **Business Addr:** Basletball Coach, Athletic Dept, San Jose City College, 2800 Moorpark Ave, San Jose, CA 95128.

CARR, RODERICH MARION
Investment banker. **Personal:** Born Nov 5, 1956, Birmingham, AL; son of Edgar A Carr; married Charlotte Bland; children: Hamilton Taylor, Chesleigh Marie. **Educ:** Johns Hopkins Univ, BSEE 1978; Univ of Chicago Grad Sch of Business, MBA Finance & Marketing 1980. **Career:** Salomon Brothers Inc, vice pres 1980-. **Orgs:** Vice pres 1978-80, mem Natl Black MBA Assoc 1978-; bd of dirs Jobs for Youth 1986-. **Home Addr:** 2437 N Janssen Ave, Chicago, IL 60614.

CARR, SANDRA JEAN IRONS
Union president. **Personal:** Born Jul 17, 1940, Middlesboro, KY; divorced. **Educ:** Kentucky State Univ, Frankfort KY, BS 1960; Purdue Univ, West Lafayette IN, MAT 1965; Indiana Univ, Gary IN, MA plus 30 1980. **Career:** Gary Teachers Union Gary, IN, div pres 1971-; Gary Sch System Gary, IN, tchr 1961-71; State of OH Div Aid for Aged, social caseworker 1960-61. **Orgs:** Vp IN Fedn of Tchers 1971-; vice pres Am Fedn of Tchrs 1974-; trustee 1976-79, treas 1986 Lake Area United Way bd of trustees; co-chairperson/mem com NAACP 1977; Gamma Psi Omega Chap AKA; mem mayoral appt Gary Commn on the Status of Women; co-dir Christian Educ New Revelation Baptist Church Gary 1980-; mem Citizens Task Force on St Gangs & School Discipline 1983-; sec Gary Educ Devel Found 1984-; pres Mental Health Assoc in Lake County 1985-. **Business Addr:** President, Gary Teachers Union, 1301 Virginia St, Gary, IN 46407.

CARR, VIRGIL H.
Association executive. **Personal:** marrIed Mygene. **Educ:** Iowa State Univ, BA education-speech 1958-62; George Warren Brown School of Social Work-Washington University, MSW community development and administration. **Career:** Neighborhood Centers OEO Program, dir 1961-68, comm organizer 1961-68; Pruitt Igoe Housing, comm organizer 1961-68; Family Service of Omaha, director, multi-service program 1968-71; United Charities of Chicago, dir of inner city operations 1970-75, dir of personnel 1975-76, assoc exec dir 1976-79; Family Service of Detroit and Wayne County, president 1979-85; United Way of Chicago, pres, CEO, 1985-93; United Way for Southeastern Michigan, pres, 1993-. **Orgs:** Appointed to Mayor Washington's Committee on Infant Mortality 1986; appointed to state advisory committee for the Illinois Dept of Public Aid 1986; HEW, nat'l consultant parent-child centers, nat'l task force to develope parent-child center standards; NIMH, nat'l consultant; MI Voluntary Agency Group Plan for Unemployment Compensation, Inc, board mem; Agape House, board mem; Family Financial Counseling Services, board mem; Black Human Service Administrators, co-founder and chairman; White House Conference on Families, governor's appointee; Select Committee of Childern, Youth, Families, appointed by Congressman Sandor Levin to chair committee to plan for site hearings. **Honors/Awds:** Family Service America, Grady B Murdock Humanitarian award 1979; Metropolitan Detroit Area, executive of the year 1983; George Warren Brown School of Social Work, Washington Univ, distinguished alumni award 1984; Chicago Committee for Excellence award 1985. **Business Addr:** President/CEO, United Way Community Svcs, 1212 Griswold, Detroit, MI 48226, (313)226-9200.

CARR, WILLIAM
Professional football player. **Personal:** Born Jan 13, 1975. **Educ:** Univ of Michigan. **Career:** Carolina Panthers, defensive tackle, 1997-. **Business Addr:** Professional Football Player, Carolina Panthers, 800 Mint St, Ericsson Stadium, Charlotte, NC 28202, (704)358-7000.

CARREATHERS, KEVIN R.
Educator. **Personal:** Born Feb 26, 1957, Denison, TX; son of Ernestine Thurston-Carreathers and Raymond E Carreathers. **Educ:** North Texas State Univ, BS 1979; Prairie View A&M Univ, MEd 1980. **Career:** Depauw Univ, asst to the dean of students 1980-82; East Texas State Univ, head resident advisor 1982-83; Texas A&M Univ, student dev specialist 1983-88; Texas A&M University, Multicultural Services Coordinator 1988-, Department of Multicultural Services, director 1989-, asst to the pres, 1994. **Orgs:** Life mem Alpha Phi Alpha 1976-; personnel admin TX Assoc of Univ and Coll Student 1982-; mem TX Assoc of Black Personnel in Higher Education 1982-; mem minority recruitment and retention comm coord bd Texas Coll and Univ System 1985-88; T.A.M.U. National Youth Sports Program advisory bd, Minority Leadership Development advisory bd; mem Statewide Retention Comm. **Honors/Awds:** Certificate of Appreciation TX Assoc of Coll and Univ Personnel Administrators 1985; Certificate of Appreciation Prairie View A&M Univ 1985; Certificate ofRecognition Delta Sigma Pi 1986; Certificate of Appreciation Delta Sigma Theta Sor Inc 1987; Houston Young Black Achiever Human Enrichment Program 1988; John J. Koldus Faculty/Staff Award, Texas A&M University 1989; Faculty Distinguished Service Award. **Business Addr:** Director, Multicultural Services, Texas A&M University, 137 MSC, College Station, TX 77843-1121.

CARREKER, WILLIAM, JR.
Educator. **Personal:** Born Oct 17, 1936, Detroit, MI. **Educ:** City Coll of San Francisco, AA 1964; Univ of CA, AB 1966, MSW 1968, MPH 1971; Univ of CA at Berkeley. **Career:** Columbia Univ School of Social Work, asst dir of admissions, financial aid officer; Golden State Medical Assn, proj dir 1972-73; Univ of CA Medical Center, staff asso 1971-72; Tufts-Delta Health Center, intern 1971; Alameda County Welfare Dept, child welfare worker 1968-70. **Orgs:** Vol couns Jr Ldrshp Prgm 1968; CA State Sch for Deaf & Blind 1971; Offenders Aid & Restoration 1974-75; Nat Assn of Black Soc Wrkrs 1974-77; publ article Comm Hlth Agency Partic in Plng; a Univ Ambulatory Care Prgm; contbd papers Am Pub Hlth Assn 1972. **Military Serv:** 1955-59. **Business Addr:** 622 W 113th St, New York, NY 10025.

CARRIER, CLARA L. DEGAY
Educator. **Personal:** Born Jan 15, 1939, Weeks Island, LA; daughter of Georgianne Henry DeRoven and Clarence DeGay; divorced; children: Glenda, Melvin T, Marcus W, Robby Bethel, Clarence (dec), Patrick R, Dawn Nicole. **Educ:** Dillard Univ, 1956-57; Univ of Southwestern, 1976-80. **Career:** JHH School Student Body, pres 1955-56; JB Livingston Elem PTC, sec 1961-67; Les Aimu Civic & Social Club, sec 1974-; Iberia Parish School Bd, exec mem at large 1979-82; Iberia Parish School Bd, vice pres 1985-; Smile, CAA, teacher; Iberia Parish School Board, school board vice member, pres; City of New Iberia Parks and Recreations, supervisor. **Orgs:** Mem NAACP 1963-65; teacher's aide Acadiana Nursery Head Start 1965; teacher's aide SMILE CAA Head Start 1970-76; social worker SMILE CAA 1976-79; mem LA Caucus of Black School Bd Mems 1980-85; bd of dir Bayou Girls Scout Council 1983-84; mem LA School Bd Assoc, Natl School Bd Assoc (LSBA); Louisiana School Bd Assn, bd of dirs, 1993. **Honors/Awds:** USL Honor Soc Psi Beta Honr Soc 1978; Service to Youth Awd Park Elem 1982-84; The President's Awd Park Elem 1982-84; Cert of Recognition for Contrib to the Comm Zeta Phi Beta Sor 1983; Omega's Citizen of the Year Omega Rho Omicron Chap 1983; Martin Luther King Jr Award, 1995. **Special Achievements:** First African-American and woman to be elected president in the Iberia Parish School System, 1992. **Home Addr:** 717 Elizabeth St, New Iberia, LA 70560. **Business Addr:** President, Iberia Parish School Board, 1500 Jane St, New Iberia, LA 70560.

CARRIER, MARK
Professional football player. **Personal:** Born Oct 28, 1965, Lafayette, LA. **Educ:** Nicholls State Univ. **Career:** Tampa Bay Buccaneers, wide receiver, 1987-93; Cleveland Browns, 1993-95; Carolina Panthers, 1995-. **Honors/Awds:** Post-season play: Pro Bowl, 1989. **Business Addr:** Professional Football Player, Carolina Panthers, 800 Mint St, Ericsson Statdium, Charlotte, NC 28202.

CARRIER, MARK ANTHONY
Professional football player. **Personal:** Born Apr 28, 1968, Lake Charles, LA; married Andrea; children: Mark Anthony III. **Educ:** USC, BA in communications, 1991. **Career:** Chicago Bears, defensive back, 1990-97; Detroit Lions, 1997-. **Honors/Awds:** Pro Bowl, 1990, 1991, 1993; Associated Press, Defensive Rookie of the Year, 1990; Football News, Defensive Rookie of the Year, 1990. **Business Addr:** Professional Football Player, Detroit Lions, 1200 Featherstone Rd, Pontiac, MI 48342, (248)335-4131.

CARRINGTON, CHRISTINE H.
Psychologist. **Personal:** Born Jun 7, 1941, Palatka, FL; divorced; children: Michael, David, Lisa. **Educ:** Howard Univ, BS 1962, MS 1965; Univ of MD, PhD Psychology 1979. **Career:** DC Public Schs, sch psychologist 1966-70, consult sch psychol 1971-72; Bowie State Coll, instr 1970-74; Fed City Coll, asst prof 1972; Bowie State Coll, rsch consult 1974-75; Howard Univ Hosp, Psychiatric Inst of Wash, Psychiatric Inst of Mont Co, consult psychologist privileges; Dept of Human Resources Washington DC, consulting psychologist; Howard Univ Couns Serv, couns psychologist. **Orgs:** Couns therapist Family Life Ctr Columbia MD; psychologist Rsch Team Howard Univ Med Sch; mem Amer Psychol Assn; Amer Assn for Psychologists in Private Practice; Assn of Counseling Ctr Training Dirs 1981-; Natl Assn Sch Psychol 1970-79; Amer Assn Univ Profs 1972-; Natl Assn Black Psychol 1970-; DC Psychol Assn 1969; bd of dirs Assn of Psychology Internship Ctrs; liaison to bd of APA; mem DC Assn of Black Psychol 1972-. **Business Addr:** Cons Psychologist, Howard Univ, Counseling Center, Washington, DC 20059.

CARRINGTON, TERRI LYNE
Musician, recording artist, singer, songwriter. **Personal:** Born Aug 4, 1965, Medford, MA; daughter of Judith Ann Sherwood Carrington and Solomon Mathew Carrington. **Educ:** Berklee College of Music, Boston, MA, 1982-83. **Career:** Clark Terry, New York, NY, drummer, 1984; David Sanborn, New York, NY, drummer, 1986-; Stan Getz, Los Angeles, CA, drummer, 1988, 1990; Arsenio Hall Show, Los Angeles, CA, drummer, 1989; Wayne Shorter, Los Angeles, CA, drummer, 1986-; Polygram Records, New York, NY, recording artist, singer, songwriter, drummer, 1988-; Herbie Hancock, LA, drummer, 1994; house drummer for Vibe TV show, 1997; Al Jarreau, Los Angeles, CA, drummer, 1991-94; Dianne Reeves, Los Angeles, CA, drummer, 1996-97, producer, 1997. **Orgs:** NARAS. **Honors/Awds:** Youth Achiever Award, & Music, NAJE, 1981; Boston Music Awards, 1988, 1989; Nominated for Grammy, NARAS, 1990; Nominated for NAACP Image Award, NAACP, 1990; Dr Martin Luther King Music Achiever Award, City of Boston, 1991. **Business Addr:** 366 W California Ave, #1, Glendale, CA 91203, (818)569-5479.

CARROLL, ANNIE HAYWOOD
Social service executive. **Personal:** Born Sep 14, 1904, Raleigh, NC; married Richard Alexander Carroll Jr; children: Howard Livingston. **Educ:** Fisk Univ; Shaw Univ, BA 1928. **Career:** Wake Cty Sch NC, teacher 1928-41; Acct Div Bureau of Empl Sec Dept Labor and Ind Harrisburg PA, clerk, supr 1943-69. **Orgs:** Exec com RSVP 1972-75; vol Radio Announcer Station WMSP Harrisburg PA 1973-74; mgr Capital Presby Sr Ctr 1984-. **Honors/Awds:** Elder First Presbyterian Church of Honolulu 1987. **Home Addr:** 2333 Kapiolani Blvd #304, Honolulu, HI 96826.

CARROLL, BEVERLY A.
Catholic church official. **Personal:** Born Oct 23, 1946, Baltimore, MD; daughter of Lillian N Mercer Carroll and James E Carroll; children: Rudolph Weeks II. **Educ:** University of Maryland, College Park, MD, BA, 1981; Towson State University, Towson, MD, MA, 1987. **Career:** Archdiocese of Baltimore, Baltimore, MD, exec director, assoc director, clerk typist, 1967-87; National Conference of Catholic Bishops, Secretariat for African-American Catholics, Washington, DC, exec director, 1988-. **Orgs:** President, Fr Charles A Hall School Board, 1970-75; secretary, National Assoc of Black Catholic Administrators, 1985-87; member, Mayor's Committee on Alt Use of Firehouses, 1988-. **Honors/Awds:** Ambassador to Eucharistic Congress in Nairobi, Kenya, Archdiocese of Baltimore, 1985; Alpha Phi Beta Sorority, Woman of the Year Award, 1988; Martin Luther King Award for Community Service, Archdiocese of Baltimore, 1988; Women of Excellence Award, Emmanuel C C Church, 1988. **Business Addr:** Executive Director, Secretariat for African-American Catholics, 3211 4th St, NE, National Conference of Catholic Bishops, Washington, DC 20017-1194.

CARROLL, CHARLENE O.
Business executive. **Personal:** Born Apr 17, 1950, Boston, MA; married Ronald Carroll; children: Kiet, Robyn, Ronald. **Educ:** La Newton Beauty Rama, Diploma 1971; John Delloria, certificate 1973; Chadwicks Masterclass NY, certificate 1979; Bruno's School of Hair Design, diploma 1980; Vidal Sassoon Hair Design, dipl 1980-82; Pivot Point, certificate 1981; Floyd Kenyetta/Fingertips Intl Workshop, certificate 1982; Jingles Intl, diploma 1978/83-84. **Career:** Black Hair Olympics Inc, pres 1985; Charlene's Hair Salon Inc, pres, currently. **Orgs:** Platform artist & stylist Revlon Co 1978-79; mem Natl Hairdresser & Cosmotology Assoc 1980-85; traveling consultant Soft Sheen Co 1984; consultant Amer Beauty Products Co 1985. **Honors/Awds:** Honorable recognition Greater Boston Cosmetologist Assoc 1975; honorable recognition Black Hair Olympics Silver Spring MD 1982; stylist of the year Black Hair Olympics Inc Washington 1984. **Business Addr:** President, Charlenes Hair Salon, Inc, 634 Warren St, Roxbury, MA 02119.

CARROLL, CHARLES H.
Personnel officer. **Personal:** Born May 31, 1910, Washington, DC; married Julia E Mack. **Educ:** Howard U, BS 1943. **Career:** Univ of MD, personnel officer; Public Empolyees Safety Assn of MD, 3rd vp; City of Coll Park, MD, Councilman. **Orgs:** Mem Elks, Mason, Am Legion, Shriner; mem of Counicl of Gov't; Municpal League of MD; Transp Com of Met of Washington; pres Plutocrats Inc; pres Pub Employees Safety Assn of MD; mem 25 Club Inc. **Military Serv:** Usn 1st class spl 1944-45. **Business Addr:** Personnel Office, Univ of Maryland, College Park, MD 20742.

CARROLL, CONSTANCE MARIE
Educational administrator. **Personal:** Born Sep 12, 1945, Baltimore, MD. **Educ:** Duquesne U, BA 1966; Knubly Univ Athens Greece, cert 1967; Univ of Pittsburg, MA 1969; University of Pgh, PhD candidate. **Career:** Univ of Pittsburgh, teaching asst dept of classics 1968-69, academic advisor College of Arts and Scis 1969-70, College of Arts and Scis Adv Ctr 1970-71, dir of freshman adv and pre-profl programs College of Arts and Scis 1971-72; Univ of Maine Coll of Arts & Scis, asst dean 1972-73, asst prof of classics 1973-77; Marin Comm College District, interim chancellor 1979-80; Indian Valley Colleges Marin Comm Coll District, president 1977-83. **Orgs:** Mem CA Council for the Humanities; mem adv bd Inst for Leadership Develop; mem adv bd Policy Analysis of CA Education; mem Natl Humanities Faculty; mem CA Postsecondary Educ Comm Task Force on Women and Minorities; evaluator Western Assn of Schools and Colleges; mem Amer Philological Assn, Classical Assn of New England, Vergilian Soc of Amer, Natl Assn of Black Professional Women in Higher Educ, Council of Colleges of Arts & Scis, Comm for the Concerns ofWomen in New England Colls and Univs; bd mem Film Study Ctr of Portland; mem Commonwealth Club of CA, Comm for the Concerns of Women in CA Colls and Univs; mem Council on Black American Affairs Western Region, Assn of CA Comm Coll Administrators. **Honors/Awds:** John Hay Whitney Scholarship Marshall Fellowship in Classics 1968; College of Arts & Scis Distinguished Teaching Awd University of Pgh 1971; Outstanding Educators of America 1975; Excellence in Education Awd YWCA South Orange County 1984; numerous publications. **Business Addr:** President, Saddleback College, 28000 Marguerite Parkway, Mission Viejo, CA 92692.

CARROLL, DIAHANN (CAROL DIAHANN JOHNSON)
Actress, singer. **Personal:** Born Jul 17, 1935, Bronx, NY; daughter of Mabel Faulk and John Johnson; married Monte Kay (divorced); children: Suzanne Ottilie; married Robert DeLeon, 1975 (died 1977); married Vic Damone, Jan 1987 (divorced). **Educ:** Attended NYU. **Career:** Actress and singer. Starred in motion pictures Carmen Jones; Porgy & Bess; Paris Blues; Hurry Sundown; Claudine; Sister, Sister, 1982; The Five Heartbeats, 1991; TV series: Julia, co-starred in Dynasty, 1984-87; Lonesome Dove, 1994; Eve's Bayou, 1997; starred in "Sunset Blvd," 1996-97. **Orgs:** Mem AEA, AFTRA, SAG. **Honors/Awds:** Tony Award for Broadway role in "No Strings" 1962; 2 Emmy nominations; Entertainer of the Year Cue Mag; Oscar nomination for "Claudine" 1974; recip NAACP 8th Image Award (Best Actress) Black Filmmaker's Hall of Fame 1976; Crystal Award, Women in Film, 1993; Ten Intl Best Dressed List; Patron Performer John F Kennedy Center; author, Diahann: An Autobiography, 1986. **Special Achievements:** Own Designer Label of clothes, 1998. **Business Addr:** Jeffrey Lane Assoc, 8380 Melrose Ave, Ste 200, Los Angeles, CA 90069.

CARROLL, EDWARD GONZALEZ
Cleric. **Personal:** Born Jan 7, 1910, Wheeling, WV; son of Florence Dungee Carroll and Julius Carroll Sr; married Phenola Valentine Carroll, Jul 3, 1934; children: Edward G Carroll Jr, Nansi Ethelene Carroll. **Educ:** Morgan State Univ, AB 1930; Yale Univ, BD 1933; Columbia Univ, MA 1941. **Career:** Nat'l Student YMCA, assoc sec 1945-49; St Marks United Methodist Church, dir of christian ed 1949-53; Epworth United Methodist Church, pastor 1953-55; Sharp St Mem United Methodist Church, pastor 1955-62; Washington Conf Washington Dist, dist superintendent 1962-64; Baltimore Conf Washington W Dist, dist superintendent 1964-68; Marvin Mem United Methodist Church, pastor 1968-72; Boston Area United Methodist church, bishop 1972-80; Morgan Christian Ctr, retired interim dir. **Orgs:** Dir Black Methodists for Church 1972-; trustee Boston Univ 1972-80; hon Boston Univ 1980-; visiting prof and bishop in residence Boston Univ Sch of Theology 1980-81; interim dir Black Methodist for Church Renwal 1981-82; interim dir Morgan Christian Center Morgan St Univ 1983-84; life mem NAACP, Black Methodist for Church Renewal, Common Cuase, Torch Club. **Honors/Awds:** LLD Morgan State Univ 1967; Alumnus of the Year Morgan St Coll Alumni Assoc 1973; DD Barrington Coll 1979; DLitt Univ of MA 1980; Children's Center; honorary trustee The New England Deaconess Hosp 1981. **Military Serv:** AUS chaplain maj 1941-45.

CARROLL, EDWARD MAJOR
Educator. **Personal:** Born Dec 30, 1916, Corsicana, TX; son of Estella Steward Carroll and Ezra Carroll; married Arnell Lewis Carroll, Jul 13, 1941; children: Maria Voncielle Carroll Green, Ed Nelvyn Lezette Carroll Evans. **Educ:** Bishop Coll, BS 1939; Columbia U, MA 1952, EdD 1964. **Career:** Educ NYU, prof math 1965-; Dwight Morrow HS NJ, math teacher 1958-65; Bishop Coll TX, asst to pres, dir of pub relations, prof of math 1946-57. **Orgs:** Mem Mathematical Assn of Amer; Amer Educ Research Assn; Natl Council of Teachers of Math; Amer Math Soc; mem NY Acad of Sci; trustee Social Serv Found, Englewood, NJ 1966-74; trustee & treas Greater Englewood Housing Corp 1969-; alumni of yr Bishop Coll 1965. **Military Serv:** AUS 1st Sgt 1944-46. **Business Addr:** Emeritus Professor of Mathematics Education, New York University, 933 Shimkin Hall, New York, NY 10003.

CARROLL, GEORGE D.
Judge (retired). **Personal:** Born Jan 6, 1923, Brooklyn, NY; married Janie. **Educ:** Brooklyn Coll, BA (Cum Laude) 1943; Brooklyn Law School, JD (Cum Laude) 1950. **Career:** Richmond City Council, councilmember 1961; City of Ricmond, mayor 1964; Gov Edmund E Brown, appt judge 1965; Bay Municipal Ct, judge 1970, 1976,1982, retired 1985. **Orgs:** Mem CA Bar 1953, NY Bar 1950, Jud Council of Natl Bar Assoc, CA Judge Assoc, Amer Bar Assoc, Jud Admin Sect; past pres Richmond Bar Assoc; life mem NAACP. **Honors/Awds:** John Russwurm Awd 1965; Man of the Year San Francisco Sun Reporter 1964. **Military Serv:** AUS s/sgt 1943-45.

CARROLL, JAMES S.
Attorney. **Personal:** Born Sep 17, 1945, Brooklyn, NY; son of Mabel G Duncan Carroll and James S Carroll Jr; married Celia Antonia; children: Jason Sean, Jamaal Samuel. **Educ:** NY Univ, BA 1966; Howard Law Sch, JD 1970. **Career:** Natl Conf of Black Lawyers, attorney 1970-72; Comm Devel Harlem Assertion of Rights, dir 1972-73; Private Practice, attorney 1973-79; Virgin Islands, asst US attorney 1979-92, sr litigation counsel, 1992-95, civil chief, 1995-. **Orgs:** Nat Bar Assn; American Bar Association; Natl Assn of Assistant US Attorneys; Natl Black Prosecutors Assn. **Honors/Awds:** Recipient Root-Tilden Scholarship to NY Univ Law Sch; Reginald Heber Smith Fellowship 1970-72; Directors Award, Attorney General of the US, 1990; US Dept of Justice, Special Achievement Award, 1992, Special Commendation, 1995. **Business Addr:** Civil chief, Office of US Attorney, District of VI, 5500 Veterans Dr, Ste 260, St Thomas, Virgin Islands of the United States 00802, (809)774-5757.

CARROLL, JOE BARRY
Professional basketball player. **Personal:** Born Jul 24, 1958, Pine Bluff, AK. **Educ:** Purdue, BA, 1980. **Career:** Golden State Warriors, center, 1980-87; Houston Rockets, 1987-88; New Jersey Nets, 1988-90; Denver Nuggets, 1990-91; Phoenix Suns, 1991-. **Orgs:** Bay Area Special Olympics Program. **Hon-**

ors/Awds: Joined Julius Erving & Bobby Jones as only members of the Century Club; All-Amer his senior year at Purdue; first Team All-Big Ten his junior & senior years; captured the Big Ten scoring crown his junior season; Basketball Digest's Rookie-of-the-Year 1980-81; unanimous selection to NBA's All-Rookie Team 1980-81; Warrior's all-time career leader in blocked shots,with 690; ranks in the top ten in six categories; played for SIMAC in Milan Italy, and led team to both the Italian Natl Championship and the 1985 European Kirac Cup Championship.

CARROLL, LAWRENCE W.
Judge. **Personal:** Born Mar 7, 1923, Chicago, IL; son of Lucille Blackwell Carroll and Lawrence W Carroll; married Annie Lee Goode; children: Lawrence W III. **Educ:** Herzl Jr Coll, AA 1942; Univ of IL, 1942-44; Loyola Univ, JD 1950. **Career:** USAF, multi-engine pilot 1944-46; Chicago Title and Trust Comp, lawyer & title examiner asst chief title Officer, Office Counsel 1950-82; Atty Reg Comm of the Supreme Court of IL, counsel to admin 1982-84; Circuit Court of Cook Cty IL, assoc judge 1984-. **Orgs:** Exec VP The Woodlawn Organization, 2 terms; Chmn of bd Woodlawn Mental Health Ctr 1973-78; pres CEO TWO Hillmans Company 1970-84; mental health corp State of IL 1973-80; bd mem Woodlawn Comm Develpment Corp 1976-85. **Honors/Awds:** Edward H Wright Award Cook Cty Bar Assn 1981. **Military Serv:** USAF, pilot, 2nd lt 1944-46. **Business Addr:** Associate Judge, Circuit Court Cook Cty IL, 16501 S Kedzie Parkway, Markham, IL 60426.

CARROLL, LAWRENCE WILLIAM, III
Broadcast journalist. **Personal:** Born Dec 11, 1950, Chicago, IL; son of Annie Lee Goode Carroll and Lawrence William Carroll Jr; married Roman Abebe Wolder-Selassie Carroll, Apr 19, 1986; children: Yenea Lucille, Lawrence William IV. **Educ:** Pomona College, Claremont, CA, BA, 1973. **Career:** KABC-TV, Los Angeles, CA, reporter/anchor, 1973-89; KCAL-TV, Los Angeles, CA, news anchor, 1989-. **Orgs:** Member, Academy of Television Arts & Sciences, 1989-; member, Radio Television News Assn, 1989-. **Honors/Awds:** 20th Anniversary Award for Television Programming, Congressional Black Caucus, 1990; Nominations (5), Academy of Television Arts & Sciences, 1976-77, 1984, 1990; Nomination, NAACP Image Award, 1984; Winner of 2 Golden Mile Awards, 1992. **Business Addr:** News Anchor, KCAL-TV, 5515 Melrose Ave, Los Angeles, CA 90038.

CARROLL, RAOUL LORD
Attorney. **Personal:** Born Mar 16, 1950, Washington, DC; son of Gertrude B Jenkins Carroll (deceased) and John Thomas Carroll; married Elizabeth Jane Coleman, Mar 22, 1979; children: Alexandria Nicole, Christina Elizabeth. **Educ:** Morgan State Coll, BS 1972; St John's Univ Sch of Law, JD 1975; Georgetown Univ Law Center, 1980-81. **Career:** Dept of Justice, asst US atty 1979-80; US Bd of Veterans Appeals, assoc mem 1980-81; Hart Carroll & Chavers, partner 1981-86; Bishop Cook Purcell & Reynolds, partner 1986-89; US Dept of Veterans Affairs, Washington, DC, general counsel 1989-91; US Dept of Housing and Urban Development, pres, Government National Mortgage Assn 1991-92; chief operating officer, M.R. Beal & Company, New York, NY, 1992-95; Wincom Corp, Los Angeles, CA, chmn, currently. **Orgs:** Washington Bar Assn, 1976-, District of Columbia Bar, 1979-; New York Bar, 1976-; Natl Bar Assn, 1977-; pres Black Asst US Attorney Assoc 1981-83; trustee, Christian Brothers Investment Services, Inc; chmn Amer Ctr for Intl Leadership 1985; trustee, The Enterprise Foundation. **Honors/Awds:** "After the Dust Settles, Other Modes of Relief," The Advocate Vol 10 No 6 1978. **Military Serv:** AUS capt 1975-79; Joint Serv Commendation Medal, Army Commendation Medal. **Business Addr:** 1420 Sixteenth Street, NW, US Dept of Housing and Urban Development, Washington, DC 20036.

CARROLL, ROBERT F.
Business executive. **Personal:** Born Jun 18, 1931, Bartow, FL; son of Emma Harris Carroll (deceased) and Robert Carroll Sr (deceased); married Gwendolyn Jackson; children: Tosca, Denise, Robert III. **Educ:** FL A&M Univ, BA 1960; Univ of CT, further study 1961; Columbia Univ, MA 1963; Yale Univ, further study 1964-. **Career:** NY City Dept of Soc Services, deputy comm 1967-71; NY City Human Resources Admin, deputy admin 1971-74; City Coll of NY, vice pres 1974-78; Cong Chas B Rangel, chief of staff 1978-81; R F Carroll and Comp, chmn CEO. **Orgs:** Bd mem WNET TV 1982-85; chmn bd R F Carroll and Comp Inc 1981-; mem Public Rel Soc of Amer, Amer Assn of Political Science, American Association of Public Administration, 1973-; Alpha Phi Alpha Frat; pres, The Fellas 1970-73; board of governors, Mill River Country Club; Metropolitan Golf Assn, Exec Committee, bd mem. **Honors/Awds:** Educ of year Assc of Black Educ 1975; distinguished srv award Univ of Taiwan 1979; public srv award US Dept HEW 1970. **Military Serv:** USAF t/sgt; srv medal 1955. **Home Addr:** 37 Reynolds Rd, Glen Cove, NY 11542. **Business Addr:** Chairman/CEO, R F Carroll & Co, Inc, One World Trade Ctr, Ste 2143, New York, NY 10048.

CARROLL, SALLY G.
Association executive. **Personal:** Born in Roanoke, VA. **Educ:** Essex Jr Coll. **Career:** Newark Police Dept, 1949-51; Essex Co Sheriff's Office, court attendant 1951-. **Orgs:** Life mem 1970-, former sec treas pres Newark Br NAACP; trustee Bd of Gr Newark Urban Coalition; Newark Museum; Milt Campbell Youth Center; chmn Newark NAACP Day Care Bd; pres Batons Inc; mem Nat Assn of Negro Bus & Professional Women's Club; adv bd Profect COED; Hich Impact Anti-Crime Bd; Affirmative ActionReview Council; mem Citizens Adv Bd Mayor's Policy & Devel Office. **Honors/Awds:** Recipient Woman of the Year Award Frontiers Internat; Sojourner Truth Award Bus & Professional Women; Outstanding Negro Woman Imperial Court Of Isis PHA; 1st woman in hist of NJ apptd to NJ St Parole Bd by Gov Brendan T Bryne confirmed by NJ St Senate for 6-yr Term.

CARROLL, VINNETTE JUSTINE
Director, actress. **Personal:** Born in New York, NY; daughter of Florence Morris Carroll and Edgar Edgerton Carroll. **Educ:** Long Island University, BA, 1944; Columbia University, grad work, 1945-46; New York University, MA 1946; New School for Social Research, postgrad 1948-50; trained for stage with Erwin Piscator, Lee Strasberg, Stella Adler. **Career:** Theater work includes: Deep Are the Roots, actress, 1949; A Streetcar Named Desire, actress, 1956; A Grass Harp, actress, 1956; The Crucible, actress, 1958; The Octoroon, actress, 1961; Dark of the Moon, director, 1960; The Disenchanted, director, 1962; The Prodigal Son, director, 1965; Bury the Dead, director, 1971; Don't Bother Me, I Can't Cope, director/playwright, 1971; When Hell Freezes Over, I'll Skate, director/playwright, 1979; Lost in the Stars, director, 1980; Your Arms Too Short to Box with God, director/playwright, 1980; The Flies, director, 1966; variety show, toured in US and West Indies, 1952-57; film work includes: A Morning for Jimmy, actress, 1960; One Potato, Two Potato, 1964; Up the Down Staircase, actress, 1967; Alice's Restaurant, actress, 1969; Ghetto Arts Project Director; Urban Arts Corps Theatre, founder/artistic director; Vinnette Carrol Repertory Company, founder/director, 1986-; School for the Performing Arts, teacher of drama; also appeared in various television shows, 1962-79. **Orgs:** Actors' Equity Assn; Screen Actors Guild; American Federation of Television & Radio Artists. **Honors/Awds:** Obie Award, Distinguished Performance, Moon on a Rainbow Shawl, 1961; Emmy Award, conception/supervision, Beyond the Blues, 1964; New York Outer Critics Circle Award, Best Director, Don't Bother Me, I Can't Cope, 1972; Los Angeles Drama Critics Award, Don't Bother Me, I Can't Cope, 1972; NAACP Image Award; Golden Circle Award, 1979; Black Filmmakers Hall of Fame Award, 1979; Tony nominee, Don't Bother Me, I Can't Cope, 1975. **Business Addr:** Founder/Artistic Director, Vinnette Carroll Theater, PO Box 030473, Fort Lauderdale, FL 33303.

CARROLL, WILLIAM
Educator. **Personal:** Born Jan 4, 1936, Brooklyn, NY; son of Willie Ann Carroll and Grover Cleveland Chatman; married Thelma Ellen Young, Nov 26, 1966; children: William Stewart Carroll, Valinda Sue Carroll. **Educ:** Harvard Univ, Cambridge MA, 1964; Norfolk State Coll, Norfolk VA, BA 1965; Temple Univ, Philadelphia PA, MA 1967; Univ of North Carolina, Chapel Hill NC, PhD 1978. **Career:** Norfolk State Univ, Norfolk VA, instructor 1967-73, asst prof 1974-77, assoc prof 1978-95, prof, 1995-. **Orgs:** Mem Alpha Kappa Mu Natl Honor Society 1963-; mem Norfolk State Univ Alumni Assn 1965-; mem Coll Language Assn 1967-70, 1984-; mem Amer Assn of Univ Prof 1969-; vice pres Tidewater Fair Housing Inc 1969-70; mem Natl Council of Teachers of English 1975-86, 1988-; mem Sigma Tau Delta Intl Honor Society 1979-; mem NAACP 1982-; publicity dir Voter Registration 1982-84; mem United Council of Citizens & Civic Leagues 1982-; advisory board, Planned Parenthood of Southeastern Virginia, 1993; bd mem George Moses Horton Society; Middle Atlantic Writer's Assn, life mem, 1987-, vp, 1992-94. **Honors/Awds:** Summer School Cooperative Scholarship, Harvard Univ, 1964; Teaching Fellowship, Univ of North Carolina, 1971; co-author Rhetoric and Readings for Writing, 1981, Variations on Humankind: An Introduction to World Literature, 1990; author, "George Moses Horton," Dictionary of Literary Biography, 1986; contributor, Fifty More Southern Writers. **Military Serv:** AUS specialist E4, 1959-62. **Business Addr:** Professor, Norfolk State University, 2401 Corprew Ave, 205 Madison Communication Building, Norfolk, VA 23504.

CARRUTH, RAE
Professional football player. **Personal:** Born Jan 20, 1974. **Educ:** Colorado. **Career:** Carolina Panthers, 1997-. **Special Achievements:** NFL Draft, First round pick, #27, 1997. **Business Addr:** Professional Football Player, Carolina Panthers, 800 Mint St, Ericsson Stadium, Charlotte, NC 28202, (704)358-7000.

CARRUTHERS, GEORGE ROBERT
Physicist. **Personal:** Born Oct 1, 1939, Cincinnati, OH. **Educ:** Univ of IL, BS 1961, MS 1962, PhD 1964. **Career:** Space Sci Div NRL, research physicist 1964-82, head ultraviolet measurements brnch 1980-82, sr astrophysicist 1982-. **Orgs:** Mem Amer Astronomical Soc, Amer Geophysical Union, Amer Inst of Aeronautics and Astronautics, Amer Assc for the Advancement of Science, Natl Tech Assc, chrmn edit review comm and edit of journal Natl Tech Assc 1983-; Science, Mathematics, Aerospace, Research, and Technology (SMART), Inc, 1990-, vp 1995-; Council of the Smithsonian Institute, 1995-. **Honors/Awds:** Arthur S Flemming Awd Washington Jaycees 1971; Apollo 16 excep sci achvmnt medal Natl Aeronautics & Space Admin 1972; Warner Prize Amer Astronomical Soc 1973; excep achievement awd Natl Civil Srv League 1973; honorary degree doctor of engr MI Tech Univ 1973; Samuel Cheevers Award Natl Tech Assc 1977. **Business Addr:** Senior Astrophysicist, Space Sci Div Naval Res Lab, Code 7609 Naval Research Lab, Washington, DC 20375-5320.

CARRY, HELEN WARD
Educational administrator. **Personal:** Born Mar 22, Chicago, IL; daughter of Minnie Ward and Anderson Ward; widowed; children: Ronald, Julius J III. **Educ:** Xavier Univ New Orleans, LA, BA 1946; Loyola Univ Chicago, MEd 1963. **Career:** Chicago Public Schools, teacher 1952, adjustment counselor 1962; Chicago Public Schools Head Start, coord 1965-69; Webster School, Chicago Public Schools, asst prin 1965, prin 1970; Christ Univ Temple, asst to minister 1976-; Johnnie Colemon Institute, dir 1976-; Christ Universal Temple, Chicago, IL, assistant minister, 1990-. **Orgs:** Consult David Cook Publishing; mem Delta Sigma Theta Sor. **Honors/Awds:** Alpha Kappa Mu Hon Soc New Orleans, LA 1945; Outstanding Principal Dist 8 Chicago Publ Schools; Black Rose Award, League of Black Women, 1987; America's Top 100 Business & Professional Women, Dollars and Sense Magazine, 1986; Lifetime Career Achievement Award, National Publications, 1990; Positive Image Award, Westside Center of Truth, 1990; Tubman/Truth Woman of the Year Award, 1992. **Business Addr:** Dir, Johnnie Colemon Institute, 11901 S Ashland Ave, Chicago, IL 60643, (312)568-2282.

CARRY, JULIUS J., III
Actor. **Personal:** Born Mar 12, 1952, Chicago, IL; son of Helen W Carry and Julius J Carry Jr. **Educ:** Quincy College, 1970-72; Loyola-Marymount University, BA, 1977, MA, 1978. **Career:** Actor, television appearances: "Dribble," 1980; "Goldie and the Bears," 1985; "Independence," 1987; "Why on Earth," 1988; "Perry Mason: The Case of the All-Star Assassin," 1989; "Jake Spanner, Private Eye," 1989; "Doctor, Doctor," 1989; "Misery Loves Co.," 1995; "Cosby, 1997," "Murphy Brown;" movie apperances: The Fish That Saved Pittsburgh, 1979; The Last Dragon, 1985; The Man With One Red Shoe, 1985; World Gone Wild, 1988; The Adventures of Brisco County Jr, cast member, 1993; guest starred in several sitcoms. **Business Addr:** Innovative Artists, 1999 Avenue of the Stars, Ste 2850, Los Angeles, CA 90067.

CARSON, BENJAMIN SOLOMON, SR.
Physician, neurosurgeon. **Personal:** Born Sep 18, 1951, Detroit, MI; son of Sonya Copeland Carson and Robert Solomon Carson; married Lacena (Candy) Rustin Carson, Jul 6, 1975; children: Murray Nedlands, Benjamin Jr, Rhoeyce Harrington. **Educ:** Yale Univ, New Haven CT, BA 1973; Univ of Michigan, Ann Arbor MI, MD 1977. **Career:** Johns Hopkins Univ, Baltimore MD, chief resident neurosurgery, 1982-83; asst prof neurosurgery 1984-, asst prof oncology 1984-, asst prof pediatrics 1987-, dir pediatric neurosurgery 1985-91, assoc prof, 1991-; Queen Elizabeth II Medical Center, Perth, Australia, senior registrar neurosurgery, 1983-84. **Orgs:** Amer Assn for the Advancement of Science, 1982-; Natl Pediatric Oncology Group, 1985-; Natl Medical Assn, 1986-; honorary chmn Regional Red Cross Cabinet, 1987-; medical advisory bd, Children's Cancer Foundation, 1987-; life mem, Maryland Congress of Parents and Teachers, 1988-; Amer Assn of Neurological Surgeons, 1989-; Congress of Neurological Surgeons, 1989-. **Honors/Awds:** Citations for Excellence, Detroit City Council, 1987, Philadelphia City Council, 1987, Michigan State Senate, 1987, PA House of Reps, 1989, Detroit Medical Soc, 1987; American Black Achievement Award, Business & Professional, Ebony & Johnson Publications, 1988; Clinical Practitioner of the Year, Natl Medical Assn Region II, 1988; Certificate of Honor for Outstanding Achievement in the Field of Med, Natl Med Fellowship Inc, 1988; Honorary Doctor of Science Degrees, Gettysburg Coll, 1988, Andrews Univ, 1989, North Carolina A&T, 1989, Sojourner-Douglass Coll, 1989; Candle Award for Science and Technology, Morehouse Coll, 1989; numerous scientific publications (books and journals 1982-); numerous natl network television appearances (med & social issues), 1985-; performed first intrauterine shunting procedure for a hydrocephalic twin, 1986, first successful separation of occipital craniopagus Siamese twins, 1987; author of Gifted Hands (autobiographic sketch), scheduled for publication, 1990; Honorary Doctor of Science, Jersey City State Coll, 1990; Honorary Doctor of Science, Shippensburg Univ, 1990; Blackbook Humanitarian Award, Blackbook Publishing, 1991. **Business Addr:** Associate Professor, Johns Hopkins Medical Institutions, Meyer 5-109, 600 N Wolfe, Baltimore, MD 21205.

CARSON, CURTIS C., JR.
Judge (retired). **Personal:** Born Feb 5, 1920, Cowpens, SC; married Vida Timbers; children: Curtis III, Gregory, Carol. **Educ:** VA State Coll, AB; Univ of PA Law Sch, LLB; National

Judicial College in Reno Nevada, 1975. **Career:** Law Office of Raymond Alexander, private practice, 1946-49, sole practitioner, 1946-52; Trial Asst District Atty, 1952-57; private practice, 1957-71; Phila Common Pleas Court, 1972-90, senior judge, 1993. **Orgs:** Philadelphia Bar Assn, 1946-; Barristers Assn, charter mem, author of its Original Constitution & By-Laws, 1950-; Judicial Section of National Bar Assn; Phila Anti-Poverty Commission; Phila Bar Rep, Bd of Community Legal Services; Phila Law Examiners, 1966-69; American Arbitration Assn, 1966-71; Parkside YMCA, bd & chairman, 1950-71; Phila NAACP, 1946-80, chairman of its Legal Redress Committee, 1962-69; John M Langston Law Assn, 1945-50; Constitution of Phila Barrister Assn, pres & author, 1949-; PA Sentencing Commission, 1980-86; Germantown Community Presbyterian Church, elder. **Special Achievements:** Appointed by the Judicial College as Faculty Advisor, 1979, 1983; Appointed by the Judicial College to serve on its Committee to critique a proposed course to be inserted in the College Curriculum.

CARSON, DWIGHT KEITH
Physician. **Personal:** Born Jul 27, 1951, Franklin, VA; son of Olga C Walden Chambers and John D Carson; married Maria Margaret Fisher, Dec 21, 1979; children: Shayla-Marie, Ilea Janelle. **Educ:** Howard Univ, BS Zoology 1973; Meharry Medical Coll, MD 1977. **Career:** US Public Health Serv Hospital, internship 1977-78; West Baltimore Comm Health Care Corp, primary care physician 1978-80; Hahnemann Hospital, 2nd yr resident 1980-81; Norfolk General Hosp, 3rd yr resident 1982-83; Allen Memoiral Hospital, chairman infectious control comm 1986-; The Oberlin Clinic Inc, staff physician, chairman of family medicine department, 1988-89. **Orgs:** Guest lecturer local schools, churches etc 1983-; mem Lorain Co Medical Soc 1983-, Amer Medical Assoc 1983-; diplomate Amer Acad of Family Physicians 1984-91; appointee to public/profl relations comm OH Acad of Family Physicians 1984-; guest interviewee WBEA Radio subject-family health month 1985; member, National Medical Assn, 1990-. **Honors/Awds:** Honorarium, West Baltimore Community Health Care Corp, 1980.

CARSON, EMMETT D.
Association executive. **Personal:** Born Oct 6, 1959, Chicago, IL; son of Emmett & Mary. **Educ:** Morehouse Coll, BA (magna cum laude), economics, 1980; Princeton Univ, MPA, public & international affairs, 1983, PhD, public & international affairs, 1985. **Career:** Library of Congress, social legislation analyst, 1985-86; Univ of Maryland, Coll Park, adjuct lecturer, 1987-89; Joint Ctr for Political & Economic Studies, proj dir, 1986-89; Ford Foundation, Rights & Social Justice Program, prog officer, 1989-92, Governance & Public Policy Program, prog officer, 1989-92; Minneapolis Foundation, pres & CEO, 1994. **Orgs:** Assn of Black Foundation Executives, chair, bd of dirs, 1994-; National Economics Assn, bd of dirs, 1993-. **Honors/Awds:** Joint Ctr for Political & Economic Studies, Superior Performance Award, 1988; Natl Economic Assn, Dissertation Award, 1985; Princeton Univ Graduate Fellowship, 1981-85; Phi Beta Kappa, 1981; Morehouse College, E B Williams Economics & Business Award, 1981. **Special Achievements:** Designed and directed the first national comparative study of the charitable giving and volunteer behavior of Black and White Americans. **Business Addr:** Pres/CEO, The Minneapolis Foundation, 821 Marquette Ave South, A200 Foshay Tower, Minneapolis, MN 55402, (612)672-3838.

CARSON, IRMA
Counselor. **Personal:** Born Jun 24, 1935, Monroe, LA; children: Sharon, Karen, Camille. **Educ:** Bakersfield Coll, AA; CA State Coll, BA; Kern Co Law Enforcement Acad, Graduate; Univ of Santa Barbara, Certificate in Criminal Justice; Univ of CA, Cert of Instruction; CA Teaching Credential. **Career:** Bakersfield City Sch Dist; bd mem; Bakersfield City Police, police sgt; Bakersfield City Schools, president of bd of education, currently; Ebony Counseling Center, director, currently. **Orgs:** Mem Amer Business Women's Assn; mem Kern Co Child Sex Abuse Treatment Comm; mem Black History Comm; mem BAPAC; mem NAACP; mem CFBL; mem Cain Memorial AME Church; co-author The Handbook for Battered Women; Rape Prevention Workshop; Parent's Rights & Responsibilities Workshop; Natl Political Inst Workshop 1984; NSBA Urban Board of Education Council; State Supt, Ethic Advisory Council; Democratic Nominee State Assembly, 1992. **Honors/Awds:** Officer of the Yr 1974; NAACP Comm Serv Awd 1979; People's Baptist Church Comm Serv Awd 1980; Black History Parade Grant Marshal 1980; The Golden West Leadership Awd 1981; Elks Lodge Comm Serv Awd 1981; CA Alliance of Black Educators Disting Serv Awd 1982; Comm Appreciation Reception 1982; Black History Parade Grand Marshal 1983. **Business Addr:** Director, Ebony Counseling Center, 1313 California Ave, Bakersfield, CA 93304.

CARSON, JULIA M.
Federal official. **Personal:** Born Jul 8, 1938, Louisville, KY; daughter of Velma Porter Carson; divorced; children: 2. **Educ:** Indiana Univ, 1970-72; St Mary of the Woods, 1976-78. **Career:** Congressman Andrew Jacobs (IN), area office dir, 1965-72; State of IN, state rep, 1972-76, state senator, 1976-90; Center Township Trustee, 1991-96; Cummins Engine Co, 1973-; J Carson's, owner; US House of Representatives, congresswoman, 1996-. **Orgs:** Mem NAACP; Urban League; trustee YMCA; bd of dir Pub Serv Acad; Georgetown U; Nat Council Negro Women; Tabernacle Bapt Ch; committeewoman Nat Dem Party; vice pres Gtr Indianapolis Prog Com. **Honors/Awds:** Woman of Yr IN 1974; Outstanding Leadership AKA; Humanitarian Award Christian Theol Sem. **Business Addr:** Congresswoman, US House of Representatives, 1541 Longworth, House Office Bldg, Washington, DC 20515-1410.

CARSON, LOIS MONTGOMERY
Public administrator. **Personal:** Born Jul 3, 1931, Memphis, TN; married Harry L Carson; children: Harry, Jr, William, Patricia, John, Brian, Felicia. **Educ:** Wilberforce Univ; CA State Coll, BA 1967; Univ of CA, MA 1974; CA State, Secondary Teaching Credential 1970. **Career:** Freewalk Gazette, 1963-64; San Bernardino County Probation Dept, counselor 1964-68; precinct reporter 1964-69; San Bernardino County Schools, teacher 1968-72; Am News, 1969; Univ of CA, dir proj Upward Bound 1973-76; CA State Univ, prof English & Educ 1977-78; Comm Serv Dept, deputy dir 1978-80; Community Action Dept Riverside County, exec dir. **Orgs:** Mem CA Tchrs Assn 1968-73; CA Conf Black Elected Officials 1973-74; mem Military Acad Bd 38th Cong Dist 1973-74; past pres bd San Bernardino Comm Coll Dist 1973; state v chairperson CA Adv Health Council 1976-; Nat Bd Assn of Comm Coll Trustees 1978; mem Delta Kappa Gamma Intl Soc; Alpha KappaAlpha Sor; mem CA OEO Advisory Bd; sec Nat Bd Nat Council Negro Women. **Honors/Awds:** Disting Achievement Award 1969; CA State Assembly Pub Serv Award 1973; Woman of Yr Inland Empire Sect NCNW 1973; Black Woman of Yr San Bernardino 1974; Women of Achievement of San Bernardino 1975; good citizenship award Alpha Kappa Alpha 1976; Outstanding Achievement Award Far Western Region 1979 & 84; Public Administrator of the Year 1980; CA State Distinguished Alumnus 1980. **Business Addr:** Executive Dir, County of Riverside, Community Action Dept, 3556 Tenth St, Riverside, CA 92501.

CARSON, REGINA E. EDWARDS
Educator. **Personal:** Born in Washington, DC; daughter of Arcola M Gold Edwards and Reginald Edwards; married Marcus T Carson, Jan 12, 1967; children: Marcus Reginald, Ellis Khari, Imani Regina. **Educ:** Howard Univ Coll of Pharmacy, BS, 1973; Loyola Coll, Baltimore, MD, MBA, marketing, 1987, health services admini, 1987. **Career:** Provident Hospital, Baltimore, MD, dir, pharmacy services, 1979-86; Ridgeway Manor, Catonsville, MD, mgr, pharmacy services, 1986-87; Univ of MD, School of Pharmacy, asst prof, 1986-88; Howard Univ, Coll of Pharmacy and Pharmacal Sciences, coordinator professional practice prog, asst prof, 1988-; Office of Education, consultant, 1990-; Marrell Consulting, consultant. **Orgs:** Chair, Business & Economic Devt Comm, 1991-92; Natl Black MBAs, DC Chapter; bd mem, Auxiliary, Northwest Hospital Center; steering comm, Home Health Care Comm, 1990-92; NARD; National Pharmacist Association, life member; National Association of Health Service Executives; American Society of Consultant Pharmacists, fellow; American Association of Colleges of Pharmacy. **Honors/Awds:** Women Pharmacists of the Year, MD Pharm Society, 1984; Outstanding Women in Pharmacy, Student Natl Pharmacist Assn, 1984; Outstanding Alumni, HU Copps, 1992. **Business Addr:** Coordinator, Professional Practice Program, Howard University, College of Pharmacy and Pharmacal Sciences, 2300 4th St NW, Washington, DC 20059.

CARSON, WARREN JASON, JR.
Educator. **Personal:** Born Feb 12, 1953, Tryon, NC; son of Esther Maybrey Carson and Warren J Carson (deceased). **Educ:** Univ of NC, AB 1974; Atlanta Univ, MA 1975; Univ of SC, Columbia, SC, PhD, 1990. **Career:** Isothermal Community Coll, instructor 1975-76; Piedmont OIC, head of career prep div 1975-80; Rutledge Coll, dean for acad affairs 1980-84; Univ of SC at Spartanburg, prog dir, prof dept of English, 1984-. **Orgs:** Pres Polk Cty NAACP 1976-; chrmn Mayor's Adv Task Force 1980-83; pres Tryon Schls PTA 1980-81; member, Polk Co (NC) Board of County Commissioners, 1986-88; member, City Council, Tryon, NC, 1989-; member, Polk Co Dept of Social Services, 1986-94; mem, Polk County Child Protection Team, 1993-. **Honors/Awds:** Church And Comm Award 1984; Outstanding Teacher Award Piedmont OIC 1980; Outstanding Teacher Award Rutledge Clge 1982-83; Teacher of the Year, USC-Spartanburg, 1989; Amoco Outstanding Teacher Award, Univ of SC, 1989; Governor's Distinguished Professor, SC Commission on Higher Education, Governor's Office, 1989. **Home Addr:** PO Box 595, Tryon, NC 28782. **Business Addr:** Professor, English, University of South Carolina at Spartanburg, 800 University Way, Spartanburg, SC 29303.

CARSWELL, DWAYNE
Professional football player. **Personal:** Born Jan 18, 1972, Jacksonville, FL; married Tamara. **Educ:** Liberty Univ. **Career:** Denver Broncos, tight end, 1994-. **Business Addr:** Professional Football Player, Denver Broncos, 13655 Broncos Pkwy, Englewood, CO 80112, (303)649-9000.

CARSWELL, GLORIA NADINE SHERMAN
Certified public accountant. **Personal:** Born Dec 27, 1951, Cairo, GA; daughter of Mary Martin Sherman and Eugene Martin Sherman; married Willie F Carswell Jr; children: Mercedes Elaine, John Garfield. **Educ:** Mercer Univ Macon GA, BS (magna cum laude) 1972; FL State Univ, MA 1976. **Career:** Grady Cty Bd of Ed, math instr 1972-74; Deloitte Haskins & Sells, sr accountant 1976-81; Charter Oil Co, plng analyst 1981-82; The Charter Co, sr internal auditor 1982-83, mgr internal finance reporting 1983-86; AT&T American Transtech, mgr ESOP recordkeeping, 1986-94; Jackson Electric Authority, manager, employee benefits, 1994-. **Orgs:** Mem FL Inst of CPA's, Amer Inst of CPA's; Natl Assn of Black Accountants, Jacksonville Women Network; Volunteer Jacksonville Inc; bd dir Jr League of Jacksonville; treasurer, Jacksonville Community Council Inc; State Public Affairs Committee, Junior Leagues of Florida; YWCA of Northeast FL. **Honors/Awds:** Outstanding Leadership Award, Jacksonville Chapter, National Assn of Black Accountants 1981. **Home Addr:** 1634 Dunsford Rd, Jacksonville, FL 32207. **Business Addr:** Manager, Employee Benefits, Jacksonville Electric Authority, 21 W Church Street, Jacksonville, FL 32202, (904)632-6257.

CARTER, ALLEN D. (BIG AL)
Educator, artist. **Personal:** Born Jun 29, 1947, Arlington, VA; married Mae Ira; children: Flora Ophelia, Cecilia. **Educ:** Columbus Coll Art & Design, BFA 1972; Northern Virginia Community College, Arlington, VA; University of Virginia Consortium, Arlington, Virginia; Amer Univ, Grad Study. **Career:** Adult Educ Program, art instructor; artist. **Orgs:** Arlington Independence Day Celebration Comm 1974; Childrens Day Smithsonian Inst 1974; Natl Portrait Gallery 1975. **Honors/Awds:** 1st prize N VA Art League 1973; Disting Merit Awd 5th Annual Juried Athenaeum Show 1974; Kansas City key to the city 1986; Virginia Museum of Fine Arts fellowship award 1987; solo exhibitions: Anton Gallery Shows, Washington, DC 1982, 1986; group exhibitions: Next Generations, Southeastern Center for Contemporary Art, Winston-Salem, NC 1990-92; Contemporary Modes of Expression, Marsh Gallery, Richnmond, VA 1987; Artist for Univ of North Carolina; Bicentennial Observance, 1993-94; Big Al Carter, painting, drawing & murals, Knight Gallery/Spirit Square Charlotte, North Carolina, 1992; Virginia Museum of Fine Arts, One Man Show, 1993; The Arts Center, Portsmouth Museums, 1993; New York Times, painting, I Made a Step, cover & review by Michael Brenson, 1990; 23 works at Madeira School/Big Al Carter Drawing & Prints.

CARTER, ALPHONSE H.
Educational Administrator, management consultant (retired). **Personal:** Born Oct 3, 1928, Baton Rouge, LA; son of Elvinna Pritchard Yarborough (deceased) and Haley Carter (deceased); married Carolyn McCraw; children: Cynthia Susan. **Educ:** Albany State Coll, 1956-57; Duquesne U, BS 1961; Univ of Cincinnati, PhD 1975. **Career:** Housing Authority City of Pittsburgh, interviewer 1961-62, asst mgr 1962; Kroger Co, mgmt trainee 1962-63, store mgmt 1963-65, div industrial engineering 1965-66, div personnel mgmt 1966-68, corp personnel coord 1968-72; Carter Carter & Assoc Inc, mgmt consult pres; 1972-76, director, human resources, 1976-81; Westinghouse Electric Corp, Pittsburgh, PA, mgr, Corp Quality training, 1981-86; Grambling State Univ, Grambling, LA, assoc prof, mgmt, 1986-88; Hampton Univ, Hampton, VA, dean, school of business, 1988-94. **Orgs:** Mem Nat Alliance of Businessmen Coll Cluster 1969-72; bd mem Opportunities Industrialization Center 1969-72; block club pres Homewood-Brushton Improvement Assn 1958-61; bd mem Victory Neighborhood Serv Agency 1969-72; Community Chest 1970-72; Nat Urban League 1970-71; met dir Nat Alliance of Businessmen 1971; trustee Funds for Self Enterprise 1972-; mem Task Force Com Univ of Cincinnati Sch of Educ 1972; life mem NAACP 1946-; Soc for Advancement of Mgmt 1958-; Urban League 1958-; BOAZF & AM 1960-; Personnel Assn 1966-; bd mem Cit Com on Youth 1969; mem adv com Retired Sr Volunteer Program 1972-73; Alpha Mu Sigma Professional Fraternity in Mgmt Devel 1974; pres Churchill Area Kiwanis 1978-79; lt gov Kiwanis Div 6-A 1980-81; bd mem Allegheny Trails Boy ScoutCouncil 1979; board mem, HamptParking Authority, 1990-; board mem, Virginia Peninsula Chamber of Commerce 1991-; board mem, Penninsula Chapter, Natl Conf of Christians & Jews, 1990; mem, Delta Beta Lambda Chapter, Alpha Phi Alpha Fraternity, 1991. **Honors/Awds:** Alpha Mu Sigma Award for Excellence in Scholarship Achievement in Mgmt 1975. **Home Addr:** 13 Estate Dr, Hampton, VA 23666-1870.

CARTER, ANTHONY
Professional football player. **Personal:** Born Sep 17, 1960, Riviera Beach, FL; married Ortancis; children: Tara, Nikki. **Educ:** Univ of Michigan. **Career:** Michigan; Oakland Invaders, wide receiver 1984-90; Minnesota Vikings, 1990-94; Detroit Lions, 1994-. **Honors/Awds:** Clinched USFL title with 48-yd touchdown catch ending game with 9 catches for 179 yds & a touchdown; named All-USFL by Pro Football Weekly & also selected second team All-League; also named All-USFL as punt returner by Sporting News; became 1st USFL player to return a punt for a touchdown, a 57 ydr in 43-7 win vs Tampa Bay. **Business Addr:** Professional Football Player, Detroit Lions, 1200 Featherstone Rd, Pontiac, MI 48342.

CARTER, ANTHONY JEROME
Programmer analyst. **Personal:** Born Jun 28, 1956, Tuscaloosa, AL; son of Hazel Carter and George Carter Jr; married Anna Carter, Aug 7, 1977; children: Anthony Jerrard. **Educ:** Barry University, BS (cum laude), computer science, 1988. **Career:** SystemOne, sr system analyst/team leader, 1978-89; Burger King Corp., sr programmer analyst, 1989-. **Orgs:** Boy Scouts of America, cub master, 1991-; Leadership Miami, 1992-; Burger King REACH Advisory Committee; Corporate Academy's Cities in Schools/Burger King Academy Program; Kids and the Power of Work Program; Junior Achievement, advisor. **Honors/Awds:** Dollars and Sense Magazine, American's Best and Brightest, Sept 1992. **Business Addr:** Senior Programmer Analyst, Burger King Corp, 17777 Old Cutler Road, Miami, FL 33157, (305)378-3112.

CARTER, ARLINGTON W., JR.
Boeing company executive. **Personal:** Born Mar 13, 1933, Chicago, IL; son of Martha Carter and Arlington Carter Sr; married Constance E Hardiman. **Educ:** IL Inst of Tech, BSEE 1961. **Career:** Seattle Housing Development, exec dir, 1971-73; The Boeing Co, program mgr, 1973-77, general mgr, 1977-81, prog mgr, 1981-85, general mgr space systems, 1985-88, Defense Systems Division, vice pres, 1988-89, Missile Systems Division, vice pres & general mgr 1989-90, CQ 1, vp, 1990-93, Facilities & CQ 1, vp, 1993-. **Orgs:** Pres Boeing Mgmt Assn 1982-84; mem Natl Space Club 1981-85; exec bd mem Seattle Comm Coll Foundation 1982-85; chmn King County Personnel Bd 1970-77; chmn Western Region of NAACP 1966; exec bd mem United Way 1978-82; mem Amer Defense Prepared Assoc; exec bd mem Metropolitan YMCA; mem Seattle Urban League; exec bd mem Seattle Hearing & Speech Center; sec/treasurer Northwest Chapter of Ill Inst Alumni Assn; North Carolina A&T Board of Visitors; Amer Inst of Aeronautics and Astronautics; Ill Inst of Technology President's Council; Nat Advisory Committee for the Natl Engineering Education Coaltion; bd of dir, Seattle Alliance for Educ; bd of dir, Seattle Public Library Foundation; bd of dirs, Sand Point Country Club; co-chairman, exec advisory committee, Advancing Minority Interest in Engineering, (AMIE). **Honors/Awds:** Black Engineer of the Year, 1990; Illinois Institute of Technology, Professional Achievement Award, 1991. **Military Serv:** US Air Force, SSgt. **Business Addr:** Vice President & General Manager, The Boeing Co, PO Box 3999, Seattle, WA 98124.

CARTER, ARTHUR MICHAEL
Government official. **Personal:** Born Apr 27, 1940, Detroit, MI; son of Alberta Carter and Arthur Carter. **Educ:** Wayne State Univ, Detroit, MI, BA, 1962, MA, 1964, ED, 1971. **Career:** Detroit Public Schools, Detroit, MI, teacher; Wayne County Community Coll, Detroit, MI, dean; Wayne County Gov chairman; Governmental Relations & Community Service, deputy superintendent, currently. **Orgs:** Executive producer, host, Showcase Detroit, Barden Channel 6, Cable TV Program; mem, Detroit Science Center. **Honors/Awds:** Film, I Am Somebody, 1969; contributor, Career and Vocational Devel, 1972; author, Black Family Role in Political Educ, 1987. **Business Addr:** Deputy Spt of Government & Community Relations, 5057 Woodward Ave Rm 270, Detroit, MI 48202.

CARTER, BARBARA LILLIAN
Educator. **Personal:** Born Jun 20, 1942, Mexia, TX. **Educ:** Fisk Univ, AB 1963; Brandeis Univ, MA 1967, PhD 1972; Harvard Univ Inst of Educ Mgmt, attended 1984. **Career:** Federal City College, asst prof 1969-72, assoc provost and assoc prof 1972-77; Univ of District of Columbia, assoc vice pres and prof 1977-80, vice pres for academic affairs 1980-81; Spelman Coll, vice pres for academic affairs and dean 1981-, acting dean 1986-87. **Orgs:** Mem Amer Sociological Assoc 1969-; bd dirs YWCA of Atlanta 1982-; bd dirs United Way of Atlanta 1985-, Public Broadcast Assoc 1985-; bd trustees Atlanta Coll of Art 1986-; bd of trustees Chatham Coll. **Honors/Awds:** Woodrow Wilson Fellow 1963; Phi Beta Kappa 1963; Fellow Natl Inst of Mental Health 1964-67; Aspen Institute for Humanistic Studies Fellowship 1981; co-author "Protest, Politics and Prosperity" 1978. **Business Addr:** Vice Pres for Academic Afrs, Spelman College, 350 Spelman Ln SW, Atlanta, GA 30314.

CARTER, BETTY
Jazz singer, songwriter. **Personal:** Born May 16, 1930, Flint, MI; children: Myles, Kagle. **Educ:** Detroit Conservatory of Music, studied piano. **Career:** Lionel Hampton Band, singer 1948-51; conducted workshops at Harvard Univ, Goddard Coll and Dartmouth Univ; founded BeCar Productions, 1969; performer at various nightclubs with Theolonius Monk, Muddy Waters, Miles Davis, Moms Mably, Ray Charles and T-Bone Walker; appeared in play "Don't Call Me Man," Billie Holiday Theatre, 1975; Carnegie Hall, singer, 1977; Newport Jazz Festival, 1977-78; Shubert Theatre on Broadway; writer of compositions including: "I Can't Help It," "Who, What, Why, Where, When," "With No Words," "Happy," "Someone Else Will Soon Grow Old Too," "What Is It?," "New Blues," "Tight," "Sounds," "Open the Door," "We Tried". **Honors/Awds:** Grammy Nominee, 1981; TV Appearances incuding, Saturday Night Live, 1976; "But Then She's Betty Carter" PBS, 1980; Over Easy PBS, 1981; The Tomorrow Show NBC, 1981; Live At Resorts Intl Cable, 1981; "Call Me Betty Carter" CBS Cable, 1981; "A Tribute to Lionel Hampton" Kennedy Center, White House, CBS, 1981; radio programs include, "All Things Considered," Natl Public Radio, "Jazz Alive," Natl Public Radio; participant in festivals in Europe, US, Brazil, and Japan; Recipient of Special Award, Natl Assn of Independent Record Distributors, 1981; Grammy Award for best female jazz vocal performance for album, "Look What I Got!," 1989. **Business Addr:** Bet-Car Productions, 117 St Felix St, Brooklyn, NY 11217.

CARTER, BILLY L.
Associate attorney. **Personal:** Born in Montgomery, AL; married Brenda T. **Educ:** Tuskegee Inst, BS 1967; Howard Univ Law School, JD 1970; Univ of VA, 1971. **Career:** Gray Seay & Langford, atty 1970-71; AUS Ft Meade, MD, chief defence counsel; Gray Seay & Langford, assoc atty 1974-; Recorder's Court City of Tuskegee, pros atty 1974-. **Orgs:** Mem ABA; NBA; Am Trial Lawyers Assn; AL Bar Assn; AL Black Lawyers Assn; DC Bar Assn; Kappa Alpha Psi. **Honors/Awds:** Recipient Army Commendation Medal for Meritorious Serv 1974; Distinguished Military Graduate 1967. **Military Serv:** AUS capt 1971-74. **Business Addr:** PO Box 539, Tuskegee, AL 36083.

CARTER, CAROLYN MCCRAW
Nursing consultant. **Personal:** Born Nov 25, 1932, Monessen, PA; daughter of Ruby E Draper McCraw and Harry K McCraw; married Alphonse H Carter; children: Cynthia S. **Educ:** St Francis Hosp Sch of Nursing, dip 1953; Univ of Pittsburgh Sch of Nursing, BSN 1958, MSN 1966; Univ of Pittsburgh Sch of Edn, Ph D. **Career:** Univ of Cincinnati College of Nursing & Health, assoc prof of nursing & dir of Minority Affairs; Univ of Pittsburgh School of Nursing, asst prof & dir of Minority Affairs 1976, asst prof & dir of Minority Nursing Prgm 1969-76; Hill Team Comm Mental Health Center, Western Psychiatric Inst & Clinic, nurs consult num inst coord 1967-68, asst dir of nurs 1964-67; VA Hospital, staff head nurse & relief supvr 1954-62; St Francis Hospital, staff nurse 1953-54; Carter Carter & Assoc Inc, vice pres. **Orgs:** Mem Academy of Nursing; mem, American Nurses Assn; bd dirs PA Nurses Assn; Human Rights Com Dist #6 Nurses Assn; Nat League for Nursing; PA League for Nursing; Mercy Hosp Adv Com on Hlth Care; Chi Eta Phi Sor Inc; Alpha Kappa Alpha Sor Inc; Jack & Jill Inc; mem, Pittsburgh Chap Girl Friends Inc; mem Club 21; Churchill Woman's Club; St Francis Alumni Univ of Pittsburgh Alumni; Sigma Theta Tau; consult Spec Action Ofc of Drug Abuse Prevention Exec Ofc of White House 1973. **Honors/Awds:** Outst Girl Grad Award Monessen Woman's Club 1950; Black Achievers Award Mon Valley 1974; commendation OH Senate 1976; WCIN Citz of Day 1976; Cincinnati Mental Hlth Assn Reach Out Award 1976; picture hung un Univ of Cincinnati Coll of Nursing Library 1976; Mary Mahoney Award Am Nurses Assn 1976. **Home Addr:** 13 Estate Dr, Hampton, VA 23666-1870.

CARTER, CHARLES EDWARD
Attorney. **Personal:** Born Jun 20, 1925, Springfield, OH; son of Mary B Carter and Brindley Carter; divorced; children: Bette Brown, Norman. **Educ:** Miami Univ OH, AB 1950; OH State Univ, LLB 1957, JD 1967. **Career:** City of Springfield, OH, law dir 1960-69; Mahoming Co Legal Serv Youngstown, OH, 1969-71; NAACP, assoc gen counsel 1971-86; Corporate Counsel 1986-. **Honors/Awds:** Published "Civil Rights Handbook" NAACP 1979. **Military Serv:** USN Yeoman 2nd Class 1943-46. **Business Addr:** Corporate Counsel, NAACP, 4805 Mt Hope Drive, Baltimore, MD 21215.

CARTER, CHARLES MICHAEL
Attorney, company executive. **Personal:** Born Apr 18, 1943, Boston, MA; son of Florence Carter and Charles Carter; children: Brandon H, Chad F, Courtney C, Candice A. **Educ:** Univ of CA Berkley, BS 1967; George Washington Univ Schl of Law, JD 1973. **Career:** Winthrop, Stimson, Putnam, and Roberts, assc 1973-81; The Singer Comp, div counsel & finance staff and investment counsel 1981-83; RJR Nabisco Inc, sr corporate counsel 1983-87; Concurrent Computer Corporation, vice pres, general counsel & secretary of Corporate Development 1987-. **Orgs:** Mem Amer Bar Assn, Natl Bar Assn. **Business Addr:** Vice Pres, General Counsel, and Secretary, Corporate Development, Concurrent Computer Corp., 2 Crescent Place, Oceanport, NJ 07757.

CARTER, CHESTER C.
Business executive. **Personal:** Born Feb 14, 1921, Emporia, KS; married Claudia; children: Chester Jr, Marise, Carol. **Educ:** USC, AB 1944, MA 1952; Loyola Law Sch, JD 1958. **Career:** Capitol City Liquor Co Wholesale, pres chmn of bd; US State Dept, ambassador Peace Corps 1962-68; Sup Ct of LA Co, juvenile traffic hearing ofcr 1956-62. **Military Serv:** AUS 1st lt 1942-46, major 1950-52. **Business Addr:** 645 Taylor St NE, Washington, DC.

CARTER, CHRISTOPHER ANTHONY
Police officer. **Personal:** Born Jul 23, 1963, Columbus, GA; son of Artha Dean Carter and Jeff Fred Carter; married Gwendolyn Denise Martin Carter, Dec 27, 1987; children: Precious Gwendolyn. **Educ:** Columbus College, 1981-83; Columbus Area Vocational School, 1983-84. **Career:** Blue Cross/Blue Shield, electronic data processor, 1980-81; Manpower Temp Service, data entry operator, 1983-84; Columbus Police Department, patrolman, beginning 1984; Georgia State Patrol, trooper, currently. **Orgs:** YMCA, 1984; FLBA, 1981; VOT, 1981; PBA, currently; FOP, currently; Pathfinders, master guide, 1990. **Honors/Awds:** Columbus Exchange Club, Officer of the Year, 1992; Optimist Club, Officer of the Year, 1992; American Legion #35, Officer of the Year, 1992; Columbus Police Department, Officer of the Year, 1992; American Legion 40/8, Georgia's Officer of the Year, 1992. **Special Achievements:** Most commendated officer in the history of the Columbus Police Department, 1992; third place winner for Officer of the Year for the United States, 1992; poems published by the Columbus Times, Columbus Ledger/Enquirer, and various other sources, 1987-; first black officer to be Officer of the Year for Columbus, 1992; Published: From My Heart To You. **Home Addr:** Rte 1, Box 87-A, Junction City, GA 31812. **Business Phone:** (706)846-3106.

CARTER, CRIS
Professional football player. **Personal:** Born Nov 25, 1965, Middletown, OH; married Melanie; children: Duron Christopher, Monteray. **Educ:** Ohio State Univ. **Career:** Philadelphia Eagles, 1987-90; Minnesota Vikings, 1990-. **Honors/Awds:** Pro Bowl, 1993, 1994, 1995, 1996; NFL Extra Effort Award, 1994; Athletes in Action, Bart Starr Award, 1995; Midwest Sports Channel, Citizen Athlete Award, 1995. **Business Addr:** Professional Football Player, Minnesota Vikings, 9520 Viking Dr, Eden Prairie, MN 55344, (612)828-6500.

CARTER, DAISY
City official. **Personal:** Born Oct 17, 1931, Stuart, FL; daughter of Lottie Thompson Simmons and Robert C. Carter (deceased); children: Marilyn D Jewett. **Educ:** St Joseph's Coll, Social Work, 1972; Temple Univ, BS, Recreation Admin, 1980. **Career:** Philadelphia Dept of Recreation, center recreation leader, asst day camp dir, drama specialist, dist coordinator for retarded program, 1968-71; Zion Church, ctr supvr, 1969-70, sr citizen's community worker, 1971-72; East Germantown Recreation Center, day camp dir, 1972-78; sr citizen's program supvr, sr citizen's program supvr, 1972-81; Penrose Playground, ctr supvr, 1981-88; Juniata Park Older Adult Center, program dir, 1989-91, therapeutic recreation program dir, 1989-91; City of Philadelphia, Dept of Recreation, center supervisor, 1991-. **Orgs:** Mem, PA Park & Recreation Soc, PA Therapeutic Recreation Soc, Black Social Workers Assn, Natl Park & Recreation Assn, Natl Therapeutic Recreation Assn, Natl Recreation & Parks Assn Ethnic Minority Soc, Philadelphia YWCA, NAACP, Philadelphia People Fund, West Mt Airy Neighbors; chairperson, PA Park & Recreation Soc Minority & Women Comm; comm chairperson for State Rep David P Richardson Jr, Sr Citizens & Recreation Programs; bd dir, Ile Ife Museum; bd dir, Temple Univ Health, Physical Educ, Recreation, & Dance Alumni Comm Chmn; bd dir, HPERD Alumni to the Temple's General Alumni Bd; vice pres, Temple Alumni Bd of Dir; board member, Pennsylvania Chapter, National Coalition of 100 Black Women, 1986; member, National Council of Negro Women Inc, 1986-; board member, Quantum Leap Publisher I 1990-; member, Temple University Alumni Athletic Committee, 1987-; president, Temple University College of HPERd Alumni Association; board member, historian, Ethnic Minority Society, National Recreation & Parks; advisory comm, Intercollegiate Athletics, Temple Univ, 1998, steering comm. **Honors/Awds:** East Germantown Sr Citizens Service Award, 1976; Commonwealth of PA House of Rep Citation, Sr Citizens & Comm Programs, 1976; finalist, NRPA West Francis Audio Visual Contest, 1976; Citation Award, Natl Recreation & Park Ethnic Minority Soc, 1977, 1979; Appreciation Award, Lincoln Univ, 1981; Admiration & Appreciation Award, East Germantown Sr Citizens, 1981; Certificate of Appreciation, Recreation Dept, Lincoln Univ, 1982; NRPA Ethnic Minority Soc Recognition Award, 1982; President's Certificate, EMS, 1983; North Philadelphia Branch, NAACP, Youth Award, 1986; Philadelphia Child-Parent Assn, Serv Award, 1988; Ernest T Atwell Award, 1993; Woman of Distinction Awd, Philadelphia Soroptimist International of 5 Points Magenta, 1995. **Business Phone:** (215)686-6118.

CARTER, DALE LAVELLE
Professional football player. **Personal:** Born Nov 28, 1969, Covington, GA. **Educ:** Univ of Tennessee. **Career:** Kansas City Chiefs, defensive back, 1992-. **Special Achievements:** Pro Football Writers, NFL Rookie of the Year, 1992; Bert Bell Trophy, 1992; Pro Bowl, 1994, 1995, 1996. **Business Addr:** Professional Football Player, Kansas City Chiefs, One Arrowhead Dr, Kansas City, MO 64129, (816)924-9300.

CARTER, DARLINE LOURETHA
Library administrator. **Personal:** Born Dec 7, 1933, Pinola, MS; daughter of Cora Lee Carter and Gennie Carter. **Educ:** Tougaloo Coll MS, BS Elementary Educ 1955; Syracuse Univ NY, MLS 1960. **Career:** Cleveland MS, school librarian 1955-59; Syracuse Univ, asst librarian 1959-60; Tougaloo Coll MS, circulation librarian 1960-62; West Islip Public Library NY, children's librarian 1962-66, asst dir 1966-69, library dir 1969-. **Orgs:** Member, Amer Library Week Comm, HW Wilson

Awards Jury, Membership Comm Amer Libr Assn 1969-85, Exhibits Comm, Membership Comm NY Library Assn 1962-85; vice pres, recording sec, chmn Public Library Dir Assn 1969-85; pres, Spring Inst; exec bd Suffolk County Library Assn 1973-85, Univ of MD 6th Annual Library Admin Devel Program 1972; honorary life membership West Islip PTA 1971; reaccreditation comm Palmer School of Library and Information Science, Long Island Univ, CW Post Center 1983; pres, Suffolk Library Consortium Inc 1986-92. **Business Addr:** Dir, West Islip Public Library, Three Higbie Ln, West Islip, NY 11795.

CARTER, DAVID G., SR.
Educator, educational administrator. **Personal:** Born Oct 25, 1942, Dayton, OH; son of Esther Dunn Carter and Richard Carter; children: Ehrika Aileen, Jessica Faye, David George Jr. **Educ:** Central State Univ, BS 1962-65; Miami Univ, MEd 1967-68; The OH State Univ, PhD 1969-71. **Career:** Dayton City Schools, 6th grade tchr 1965-68, asst prin 1968-69, elem prin 1969-70, unit facilitator 1970-71; Dayton Publ Schools, serv unit dir (dist supt) 1971-73; Wright State Univ, adj prof 1972; Penn State Univ, asst prof dept of educ admn 1973-75, assoc prof dept educ admn 1975-77; Univ of CT, assoc prof dept educ admin 1977-79, prof dept educ admn 1980-, assoc dean/sch educ 1977-82, assoc vice pres acad affairs 1982-; Univ of CT, Storrs, CT, assoc vice pres academicaffairs, 1982-88; Eastern CT State Univ, Willimantic, CT, president 1988-. **Orgs:** Commission's Division III NCAA, chair, 1994-97; Urban League of Greater Hartford, bd of dirs, 1994-97; Consult Professional Devel Assoc 1979-80; consult Milwaukee Pub Schools 1980; consult Syracuse Univ Research Corp 1976; consult PA Dept of Educ 1973-77; consult So Ea Delco Sch Dist 1973-83; consult Booz-Allen and Hamilton Inc 1972-73; bd trustees Dayton Museum of Natl Hist 1973; mem Centre Cnty Mental Hlth and Mental Retardation Adv Bd 1974-76; mem Adv Cncl to the Bd of Mental Health for Program Dev 1977-80; mem Governor's Task Force on Jail and Prison Overcrowding 1980; bd dir New Engl Reg Exch 1981-; corporator Windham Meml Comm Hosp 1982; trustee Windham Meml Comm Hosp 1984; dir Windham Healthcare Sys Inc 1984; mem Phi Delta Kappa; mem Amer Educ Rsch Assn; mem NAACP; mem Pi Lambda Theta; mem Phi Kappa Phi; bd dir Natl Organiz on LegalProbl in Education 1980-83; ed bd Journal of Eduquity and Leadership 1980; mem Good Samaritan Mental Health Adv 1968-73. **Honors/Awds:** NAACP, Roy Wilkins Civil Rights Award, 1994; Connecticut American Legion Dept, 39th Americanism Award, 1994; Inducted into the Donald K Anthony Achievement Hall of Fame, 1993; Central State University, Wilberforce, OH, 1993; Selected Young Man of the Year Dayton Jr C of C 1973; published over 70 articles and chapters incl, "Students Rights and Responsibilities, Challenge or Revolt" The Penna School Master Journal for Secondary Principals 1974; "Implications of Teacher Performance Appraisal" The Penna School Master 1975; "Minority Students, Ability Grouping and Career Development" Journal of Black Studies with Frank Brown and J John Harris 1978; "Race, Language and Sex Discrimination" in A Digest of Supreme Court Decisions Affecting Education 1978. **Business Addr:** President, Eastern Connecticut State University, 83 Windham St, Willimantic, CT 06226-2295.

CARTER, DEBORAH
Professional basketball player. **Personal:** Born Jan 3, 1972; children: Jeremica. **Educ:** Georgia, attended. **Career:** Utah Starzz, forward, 1997; Washington Mystics, 1998-. **Business Addr:** Professional Basketball Player, Washington Mystics, MCI Center, 601 F St NW, Washington, DC 20071, (301)622-3865.

CARTER, DORVAL RONALD
Obstetrician, gynecologist. **Personal:** Born Feb 13, 1935, Donora, PA; married Vivian Ann Johnson; children: Dorval Jr, Melanie. **Educ:** Howard U, BS 1956; Howard Univ Coll of Med, MD 1962. **Career:** Self-employed ob/gyn; Freedmen's Hosp, medical intern; Cook Co Hosp, pathology resident, ob/gyn resident, sr attending physician 1970-73; Bethany MedCtr, dept chrmn Cons; St Francis Cabrini Hosp, dept chrmn; Columbus-Cabrini Med Center, cons; NW Univ Med Sch, clinical instr; Johnson Rehab Nursing Center, med dir & cons. **Orgs:** Mem AMA; Chicago Med Soc; Nat Med Assn. **Honors/Awds:** Recipient Outstanding Black Achievement Award 1975; Fellow Am Coll of Ob/Gyn; Fellow Am Coll of Surgeons; Fellow Internatl Coll o Surgeons. **Military Serv:** US Army Med Corp 1st lt 1956-58. **Business Addr:** 815 W Van Buren St, Ste 314, Chicago, IL 60607.

CARTER, EDWARD EARL
Company Executive (retired). **Personal:** Born Oct 9, 1939, Havelock, NC; son of Nettie Morris Carter and Leander Carter; married Evelyn Jean Carter, Jan 17, 1966; children: Regina Yvette, Tonya Denise, Jacquelyn. **Educ:** Virginia State Univ, Petersburg, VA, BS, 1963; Pitt Community Coll, Greenville, NC, AAS, 1979. **Career:** Hudson Labs, Columbia University, Dobbs Ferry, NY, research asst, 1962-63; Burroughs Wellcome Co, Greenville, NC, Administrative Services, dept head, 1971-95. **Orgs:** Life mem, Alpha Phi Alpha Fraternity, 1960-; master mason, Mt Calvary Masonic Lodge 669, 1973-; transportation policy communication safety comm, North Carolina League of Cities, 1988-89; transportation policy communication safety comm, Natl League of Cities, 1988-89; mem, Pitt County Mayors Assn, 1987-89; Black Natl Conf of Mayors, 1987-89, Black Mayors Conf, 1987-89; bd of dir, Governors Crime Commn of North Carolina, 1988-; bd of dir, Pitt-Greenville Chamber of Commerce, 1988-; bd of dir, Project Parenting, 1988-. **Honors/Awds:** Appeared in army air defense movie, Nike-In-the-Attack, 1965; appeared in New York Times and New York Times Magazine army promotional, 1965; TAR-Heel-of-the-Week, Raleigh News & Observer, 1979; Gus Witherspoon Leadership Award, North Carolina Assn of Alpha men, 1975; Omega Psi Pi, Community Serv Award, 1975; Citizen of the Year, Mid Atlantic Region of Alpha Kappa Alpha Sorority, 1989. **Military Serv:** AUS captain, 1963-71; two Bronze Stars, 1971, three Army Commendation medals, 1964, 1966, 1971; Vietnam Cross of Gallantry. **Home Addr:** 104 Fireside, Greenville, NC 27834.

CARTER, ESTHER YOUNG
Educator (retired). **Personal:** Born Feb 8, 1930, North Carolina; daughter of Bertha Perry Young and Johnny Argro Young; married Robert Carter, Jun 25, 1950; children: Gwendolyn C Adamson, Johnny Jerome, Robert Gilbert. **Educ:** North Carolina Central University, BS, 1953; Johnson C Smith University, elem education certification; North Carolina A&T State University, MS, 1975. **Career:** Carver College, secretary & teacher, 1954-59; Douglas Aircraft Company, secretary, 1959-66; Greensboro Public Schools, teacher, 1966-92. **Orgs:** NEA-R 1993-; NEA, 1966-92; Greensboro Alumnae Chapter, 1976; Delta Sigma Theta Sorority Inc, corresponding secretary, 1986-90, president, 1990-94; Greensboro Chapter, Pinochle Bugs Social & Civic Club, Inc, president, 1991-; North Carolina Central Alumni Association, life member, currently; Metropolitan Council of Negro Women, 1989-; Black Child Development Institute, 1988-. **Honors/Awds:** W M Hampton Elementary School, Teacher of the Year, 1988.

CARTER, FRED
Professional basketball player (retired), professional basketball coach. **Personal:** Born Feb 14, 1945; married Jacqueline Carter; children: Stephanie, Mia, Christopher, Amee, Jason, Aaron. **Educ:** Mount St Mary's College Emmitsburg MD, grad 1969. **Career:** Player, Baltimore Bullets (Washington Bullets from 1974-), 1970-72, Philadelphia 76ers, 1972-76, Milwaukee Bucks, 1977; assistant coach, Washington Bullets, Chicago Bulls, Atlanta Hawks (1987-). **Orgs:** Instrumental in the devt & instruction of Mayor Washington's inner-city basketball clinics; involved with Little City Foundation. **Honors/Awds:** Played 8 seasons in The NBA scoring 9,271 from 1969-77; ended career after 611 games with a 15.2 points-per-game average; captained the 76er's for 3 seasons; player rep, 4 years. **Business Addr:** Assistant Coach, Philadelphia 76ers, Broad St & Pattison Ave, Spectrum, Philadelphia, PA 19147.

CARTER, GENE RAYMOND
Educational administrator. **Personal:** Born Apr 10, 1939, Staunton, VA; married Lillian Young; children: Gene Raymond Jr, Scott Robert. **Educ:** VA State Univ Petersburg, BA 1960; Boston Univ, ME 1967; Teachers Coll Columbia Univ NY, EdD 1973. **Career:** St Emma Mil Acad & Norfolk Public Schools, teacher 1960-69; Campostella Jr High School, educ devel spec, intern principal 1969-70; Maury High School, Norfolk VA, asst principal for instr 1970-71; Englewood Public Schools NJ, admin asst for rsch & planning 1972-73; Norfolk Public Schools, supvr of curriculum resources 1973-74; School of Educ Old Dominion Univ, Norfolk VA, adj assoc prof 1974-; Norfolk Public Schools, reg asst supt 1979-83, supt of schools 1983-. **Orgs:** Bd mem, Tidewater Juvenile Detention Home Adv Bd, 1978-80; bd mem, Comm of Mgmt Serv YMCA Norfolk, 1978-80; pres, exec bd mem Sunrise Optimist Club of Norfolk, VA, 1979-80; pres Gene R Carter & Assoc, Chesapeake VA, 1979-; bd mem, St Marys Infant Home Norfolk, 1980-. **Honors/Awds:** Natl Grad Fellow Training, Teachers of Teachers, Teachers Coll, Columbia Univ, 1971-72; Minority Student Scholarship, Teachers Coll, Columbia Univ NY 1972; selected by Minority Affairs Adv Comm to serve as a resource in its Talent Bank of Consult Amer Assn of School Admin 1979-; Optimist of the Year Sunrise Optimist Club Norfolk VA 1979-80. **Business Addr:** Superintendent, Norfolk Pub Sch Admin Bldg, 800 E City Hall Ave, Norfolk, VA 23510.

CARTER, GEOFFREY NORTON
Commissioner. **Personal:** Born Jan 28, 1944, St Louis, MO; son of Daphne Louise Tyus Carter and Robert Carter. **Educ:** St Louis Univ School of Arts & Science, AB cum laude 1966; St Louis Univ Law School, JD 1969. **Career:** Atty private practice 1975-88; USAF, judge advocate 1970-74; Legal Aid Soc of St Louis, staff atty 1969-70; Oakland Municipal Ct, Oakland, CA, commr, 1988-. **Orgs:** Treasurer CA Assn of Black Lawyers 1978 & 1979; vice pres Charles Houston Bar Assn 1980; cmmr City of Oakland Citizens' Complaint Bd 1980; mem, board of directors, Heritage Trails Fund, 1987-97. **Honors/Awds:** Full tuition scholarship St Louis Univ School of Law 1966; USAF Commendation Medal 1974. **Military Serv:** USAF captain 1970-74. **Business Addr:** Commissioner, Oakland-Piedmont-Emeryville Municipal Court, 661 Washington St, Oakland, CA 94607, (510)268-7606.

CARTER, GEORGE E.
Association executive. **Personal:** Born Jul 3, 1925, Philadelphia, PA; son of Amita Mitchel Carter and George Carter; married Margaret Scully, Apr 4, 1981; children: Stephan George, Laurent George. **Educ:** Lincoln University, AB, 1949; Harvard University, 1949-52. **Career:** Peace Corps, Ghana, director, 1961-64; United States Peace Corps, assistant director, 1964-66; IBM, director of budgets, 1966-88; Crossroads Africa, president, CEO, 1988-90; NAACP, dep executive director, beginning 1990. **Orgs:** Council on Foreign Relations, 1966-; Woodrow Wilson Fellow, 1968-78; Transcentory Foundation, chairman of board, 1975-85; OXFAM America, board member, 1983-88. **Special Achievements:** Pan Africanism Reconsidered, 1959. **Home Addr:** Valeria 78, Cortlandt Manor, NY 10566.

CARTER, GILBERT LINO
Appointed official. **Personal:** Born Jul 6, 1945, Richmond, VA; married Joyce Jones; children: Jana, Gilbert Jr, Ridgely. **Educ:** Morgan State Univ, AB 1967; Howard Univ, JD 1970. **Career:** VA Commonwealth Univ, asst dean of student life 1971-73; Commonwealth of VA, asst dir 1973-75. **Orgs:** Exec dir Model Cities/City of Richmond 1975-77; vice-chair assts Intl City Management Assoc 1983-. **Business Addr:** Exec Staff Asst City Mgr, City of Richmond, 900 E Broad St Room 104, Richmond, VA 23219.

CARTER, GWENDOLYN BURNS
Educator. **Personal:** Born Nov 21, 1932, Lufkin, TX; daughter of Tressie Stokes Burns and Robert Burns; married Purvis Melvin Carter, Jun 2, 1957; children: Purvis Melvin III, Frederick Earl, Burnest Denise. **Educ:** Attended, Univ of Denver, Univ of CO, Univ of So IL, Univ of TX; Huston Tilloston Coll, BS 1954; Prairie View A&M Univ, MEd 1960. **Career:** Hempstead Elementary Sch, resource teacher. **Orgs:** Pres Jack and Jill of Amer Inc 1980-82; pres Waller Co Teachers Assoc 1983-84; mem Delta Sigma Theta Sor; career treas Top Ladies of Distinction Inc 1985-87; mem The Council for Exceptional Children, Natl Educ Assoc; mem adv council for Exceptional Children 1986-; mem youth develop comm Mount Corinth Baptist Church 1986-; president Top Ladies of Distinction, 1988-; vice president, Delta Sigma Theta Sorority, 1988-. **Honors/Awds:** Outstanding Leadership Awd Girl Scouts 1984; San Jacinto Council Appreciation Awd 1984; Disting Serv Prairie View Local Alumni Assoc 1984; Certificate of Recognition Mt Corinth Baptist Church 1985; Human Relations Awd Waller Co Teachers Assoc 1986; Outstanding Serv Awd Top Teens of Amer Inc 1986; Certificate of Recognition Prairie View Local Alumni Assoc 1986; Top Lady of The Year, Top Ladies of Distinction 1989. **Home Addr:** 319 Pine St, PO Box 2243, Prairie View, TX 77446. **Business Addr:** Resource Teacher, Hempstead Elementary School, Hempstead, TX 77445.

CARTER, HARRIET LASHUN
Account executive. **Personal:** Born Feb 16, 1963, Muskegon, MI; daughter of LuLa Fae Williams Carter and John Edward Carter. **Educ:** Michigan State University, East Lansing, MI, BA, 1985. **Career:** Muskegon Harbour Hilton, Muskegon, MI, supervisor, night auditor, 1986-88; Radisson Resort Hotel, Ypsilanti, MI, sales manager, 1988-89; Metropolitan Detroit Convention & Visitors Bureau, Detroit, MI, account executive, 1989-. **Orgs:** Alpha Kappa Alpha Sorority Inc; National Coalition of Black Meeting Planners. **Home Addr:** 200 Riverfront Dr, # 20F, Detroit, MI 48226.

CARTER, HAZO WILLIAM, JR.
Educational administrator. **Personal:** Born in Nashville, TN; son of Elizabeth Forbes Carter and Hazo William Carter Sr; married Phyllis Harden; children: Angela Mable Elizabeth. **Educ:** Tennessee State Univ, BS, 1968; Univ of Illinois, MS, 1969; Vanderbilt Univ, EdD, 1975. **Career:** Southwestern Bell, Chicago, IL, supr services, 1969-71; Norfolk State Univ, asst to pres, 1975-76, asst vice pres of student affairs, 1976-77, vice pres of student affairs, 1977-83; Philander Smith College, Little Rock, AR, pres, 1983-87; West Virginia State College, Institute, WV, pres, 1987-. **Orgs:** National Assn of Personnel Workers; NAACP; Civic League; memPhi Delta Kappa; Alpha Kappa Mu; Psi Chi; Peabody Alumni Board of Vanderbilt University, 1993-; American Council on Education, Commission on Educational Credit and Credentials; American Association of State Colleges and Universities Committee on Accreditation; National Association for Equal Opportunity in Higher Education; chairman, Advsory Council of Presidents for the State College System of WV; board of directors, WV Quality Council Inc; National Institute for Chemical Studies; Association of College an University Presidents. **Honors/Awds:** Outstanding Service Award, KWTD-FM, 1985. **Business Addr:** President, West Virginia State College, PO Box 399, Institute, WV 25112-0399.

CARTER, HERBERT E.
Educator (retired). **Personal:** Born Sep 27, 1919, Amory, MS; son of Willie Sykes Carter and George Carter; married Mildred L Hemmons; children: Herbert E Jr, Gene Kay, Kurt Vincent. **Educ:** Tuskegee Univ, BSc 1955, MEd 1969. **Career:** United States Air Force, fighter pilot 1943-44, group maintenance officer 1945-48, flight test maintenance officer 1948-50, prof air

science 1950-55, deputy dir military adv group to German Air Force 1955-59, chief of maintenance 1959-63, 1963-65; Tuskegee Inst, prof aerospace studies 1965-69, assoc dean student services 1970-75, assoc dean admissions and recruiting 1975-84 (retired). **Orgs:** Mem Presidential Scholars Review Comm; mem Coll Bd Educ Testing Serv; mem Amer Assn Collegiate Registrars and Admissions Officers; mem Sigma Pi Phi, Kappa Delta Pi; mem Natl Assn Coll Admissions Counselors; pres Tuskegee Chap Tuskegee Airmen Inc; numerous speaking engagements over the past five years on ''Professionalism, Commitment and Performance of Blacks in Aerospace Careers.''. **Honors/Awds:** Air Medal w/4 Clusters; Air Force Commendation Medal; Distingushed Unit Citation; European Theater Medal w/5 Bronze Stars; Natl Defense Medal w/1 Bronze Star; Air Force Longevity Awd w/5 Oak Leaf Clusters; Tuskegee University, Alumni Merit Award, 1994; Tuskegee Airmen BG Noel F Parris Gold Medallion Medal, 1993. **Military Serv:** USAF lt col (retired). **Home Addr:** 2704 Bulls Ave, Tuskegee Institute, AL 36088.

CARTER, HOWARD PAYNE
Educator. **Personal:** Born Sep 9, 1921, Houston, TX; married Lolla Patterson; children: Vicki, Howard. **Educ:** Tuskegee Inst, BS, 1966; Columbia Univ, MA, 1950; U of CA, MA, 1956; U of WI, PhD, 1964; U of CA, post doctoral training, 1966. **Career:** Tuskegee Inst, dean 1968-, prof Biology 1974, assoc prof Biology 1964-74, asst prof Biology 1957-64, instructor Biology 1957. **Orgs:** Mem Soc of Protozoologists; Am Soc of Parasitologists; Am Assn for Higher Edn; Am Inst of Biological Sci; Soc of Sigma Xi; Beta Kappa Chi Phi Boule; Alpha Phi Alpha; Scabbard & Blade; Tuskegee Civic Assn; NAACP numerous papers. **Military Serv:** AUS 1st lt 1942-46. **Business Addr:** Professor of Biology, Tuskegee University, Tuskegee Institute, AL 36088.

CARTER, J. B., JR.
Manager. **Personal:** Born Oct 5, 1937, Pascagoula, MS; married Mary Mallard; children: J B III, Joy Bonita, Janelle Betrice. **Educ:** Tougaloo Coll, BA 1960. **Career:** Pub Schs MS, tchr coord; Litton Industries, labr Rltns, rep EEO coor mgr; Keesler AFB, mgmt specialist; MS St Employment Security Com, employment interviewer; Jackson County Neighborhood Youth Corps, dir; Gulf Coast Safety Soc, sec 1975. **Orgs:** Adv bd Jackson County Salvation Army's Bldg Fund Drive 1975; mem Jackson County Civic Action Com 1969; decon, 1st Christian Ch; mem Omega Psi Phi Frat;chmn Pas-point Handicap Com 1972; co-chmn Bi-racial Com, Moss Point Sch System 1972; mem Jackson County Pres Task Force; sec bd trustees, Moss Point Municipal Separate Sch Dist 1975. **Honors/Awds:** Outstanding Citizen, Jackson County Non-partisan Voters Leg 1974; Distinguished Serv Awd, Pas Point Jaycees 1972; Omega Man of Yr 1967.

CARTER, JAMES
Educator, mayor, businessman. **Personal:** Born Jul 6, 1944, Woodland, GA; son of Mae Bell Carter and Jimmie L Carter. **Educ:** Albany State Coll, Albany, GA, BS, Business, minor Math, PE; Georgia State Univ, Atlanta, GA; Univ of Georgia, Athens, GA, Finance. **Career:** City of Woodland, Woodland, GA, mayor, 1982-; Self-employed, small business manager; Homes of the South, Greenville, GA, contract writer, 1988. **Orgs:** Baptist Student Union; National Conf of Black Mayors; Joint Center for Political Studies-SBCC; Natl Towns and Townships-GRWA; Small Towns; Georgia Conference of Black Mayors; Master Mason. **Honors/Awds:** Teacher of the Year, Central High School, 1979; Man of the Century Award, Concerned Citizens, 1988; Special Alumni Award, Albany State Coll, Albany, GA, 1989; appeared in Albany State Coll Magazine, Albany, GA, 1989; GMA Community Leadership Award, 1993; NAACP Community Leader Award, 1993; NAACP Man of the Year Award, 1994; Montel Williams Award, 1994; Outstanding Service awd, Rural Develpmnt Ctr, 1997; Outstanding Citizen Award, Farm City, 1997. **Special Achievements:** First African American mayor and judge of Woodland, GA.

CARTER, JAMES EARL, JR.
Physician. **Personal:** Born Oct 13, 1943, Kansas City, KS; son of Anna Sneed Carter and James E Carter Sr; married Nina Sharon Escoe; children: Chisty, Kimberly. **Educ:** UMKC, BS 1965; Univ MO, MD 1969; Walter Reed Hosp, intern 1969-70; residency, Ventura County Hospital 1972-73. **Career:** Family practitioner 1975; Wayne Miner Health Ctr, family physician 1973-75; James E Carter, M.D., P.C. Kansas City MO, family physician & president 1975-. **Orgs:** Amer Heart Assn Kansas City Chap; life mem NAACP; life mem Africare; Sunday School Teacher, Baptist Church; Metropolitan Medical Society; deacon, Paseo Baptist Church. **Honors/Awds:** Fellowship Award Amer Acad of Family Practice 1975. **Military Serv:** AUS med corp cpt 1969-72. **Business Addr:** 7800 Paseo, Kansas City, MO 64131.

CARTER, JAMES EDWARD, III
Educational administrator (retired). **Personal:** Born Sep 3, 1938, Columbia, SC; son of Dr & Mrs James E Carter Jr; married Judy Luchey; children: James E IV, Mason Johnson III. **Educ:** Howard Univ, 1958; Paine Coll, BS, 1958-60; South Carolina State Coll, MEd, 1971-73; Faith Coll, LHD, 1978. **Career:** Richmond County Bd of Educ, teacher, counselor, principal, 1960-73; AUS, AUSR, instructor of med corps, 1963-67; Franklin Life Insurance Co, agent, financial consultant, 1969-72; Med Coll of GA, recruiter, counselor, asst dean, Student Affairs, 1973-97. **Orgs:** pres, Belair Hills Assn, 1973-75; vice dist rep, 7th Dist, Omega Psi Phi, 1974-77; Black Heritage Comm, 1975-; pres, Alpha Mu Boule; Sigma Pi Phi, 1979-81; appointee Govenor's Advisory Council on Energy, 1980-82; pres, National Assn of Med Minority Education, 1983-85; pres, Natl Assn of Student Personnel Workers, 1987-88; appointee, Govenor's Intercultural Speakers Bureau, Human Relations Commission, State of Georgia, 1990; appointee, Richmond County Commission on Historic Preservation, 1990; board of directors, Health Central, 1988-91. **Honors/Awds:** United Negro Coll Found Distinguished Achievement Awards, 1977-83; Paine Coll, Pres Alumni Award, 1979, 1997; Lucy C Laney High School Distinguished Alumni Award, 1983; Arkansas Governor's Award, 1984; Presidential Award, Natl Assn of Personnel Workers, 1985, 1989, 1991, 1996; Presidential Citation, Natl Assn of Med Minority Educators, 1982, 1984, 1985, 1987, 1990, 1996; Article, ''The Need for Minorities in the Health Professions in the 80's: The National Crisis and the Plan for Action,'' 1986. **Military Serv:** AUS, Good Conduct Medal, 1963; Honorable Discharge, 1969. **Home Addr:** 1528 Flagler Rd, Augusta, GA 30909.

CARTER, JAMES HARVEY
Psychiatrist, educator. **Personal:** Born May 11, 1934, Maysville, NC; son of Irene Barber Carter and Thomas Carter (deceased); married Elsie Richardson-McDonald Carter, Aug 26, 1988; children: James Harvey Jr, Saunja McDonald-Wilson. **Educ:** NC Central Univ, BS 1956; Howard Univ Med College, MD 1966. **Career:** Walter Reed Army Hosp, internship 1966-67; Duke Univ Med Ctr, assoc prof 1967-83, prof of psychiatry 1983-; Dept of Corr Raleigh NC, sr psychiatrist 1984-. **Orgs:** Consulting psychiatrist Lincoln Community Health Ctr 1972-; consultant on minority mental health NIMH 1974-78; consultant on drug abuse NC State Univ 1970-71; commander 3274th USAR Hosp 1984-89; chairperson Achievement Awards Bd Amer Psychiatric Assn 1984; mem US Senate on Aging and USAR Aged Blacks 1972-74; mem Committee of Black Psychiatrists 1984-86. **Honors/Awds:** Macy Faculty Fellow Duke Univ Med School 1970-74; Faulk Fellow Amer Psychiatric Assn 1968-70; Fellow Orthopsychiatric Assn 1986; awarded the ''A'' Prof Designation by the Army Surgeon General Excellence in Psychiatry; Beta Kappa Chi Honorary Scientific Society NC Central Univ 1956; Fellow of the Amer Psychiatric Assn 1980; Assn of Military Surgeons of the US; Physicians for Human Rights; Amer Society of Addicted Diseases; author, 56 articles in refereed journals, 3 chapters in textbooks. **Military Serv:** AUSR col 1956-; Army Achievement Medal 1971; Army Comm 1980; Army Meritorious Serv 1986; Order of Military Merit 1988. **Home Addr:** 3310 Pine Grove Rd, Raleigh, NC 27610. **Business Addr:** Professor of Psychiatry, Duke Univ Med School, Dept of Psychiatry, Box 3106, Durham, NC 27710, (919)684-6102.

CARTER, JAMES L.
Social worker. **Personal:** Born May 20, 1933, Camden, NJ. **Educ:** Howard U, BA; NY U, MSW. **Career:** Univ FL, clin soc worker 1975; Inst Black Culture Univ FL, fndr acting dir 1971-72; Student Devel Univ FL, asst dean 1971-72; Black Cultural Cntr Penn State U, dir 1972-73. **Orgs:** Mem Nat Assn Soc Workers; Assn Black Soc Workers; Acad & Cert Soc Workers; citizen adv com Alachua Co Div Corrections. **Honors/Awds:** Radio sta WRUF Salute dist comm serv 1972. **Business Addr:** Univ FL, Gainesville, FL.

CARTER, JAMES P.
Educator. **Personal:** Born in Chicago, IL. **Educ:** Northwestern U, BS; Columbia Univ Sch Pub Hlth, MS, PhD. **Career:** Dept of Nutrition & Nursing, Tulane Univ School of Public Health, chmn; Ibadan Univ, chmn; Egypt, staff pediatrician. **Honors/Awds:** Numerous publ. **Business Addr:** Tulane Univ, Dept of Nutrition, Sch of Pub Hlth & Trop Med, 1430 Tulane Avenue, New Orleans, LA 70112.

CARTER, JANDRA D.
Government official. **Personal:** Born May 11, 1948, St Louis, MO; daughter of Mamie France Spinks and Larry Spinks; married Alvin Carter, Jul 24, 1971; children: Brian, Traci Carter-Evans, Chaun. **Educ:** Univ of Missouri, Columbia, MO, BS, 1979; Central Missouri State Univ, Warrensburg, MO, MS, 1984. **Career:** Missouri Division of Youth Services, Jefferson City, MO, training officer, delinquency prev spec, facility mamanger, group leader, youth spec, 1971-81; Missouri Department of Mental Health, Jefferson City, staff development, 1981-84; Missouri Department of Corrections, Jefferson City, director of training, 1984-; Missouri Department of Mental Health, Jefferson City, director of investigation, 1989-92, program coordinator, 1992-95, dir caring communities, 1995-. **Orgs:** Chair, advisory board, William Woods College School of Social Work, 1991-92; member, Natl Assn of Blacks in Criminal Justice, 1979-; president, Missouri Chapter NABCJ, 1985-87; member, Self Eval Task Force Girl Scouts, 1990-; member, State Training Advisory Board State of Missouri, 1984-89. **Honors/Awds:** Phi Kappa Phi Honor Society; Governor's Diversity Award, 1995. **Business Addr:** Director, Caring Communities, Missouri Dept of Mental Health, PO Box 687, 1706 E Elm, Jefferson City, MO 65102, (314)751-8575.

CARTER, JESSE LEE, SR.
Business executive. **Personal:** Born Aug 1, 1926, Indianapolis; married; children: 3. **Educ:** Butler U; IN U; Howard U. **Career:** Owner dry cleaners & household maintenance svc9 1950-65. **Orgs:** Indianapolis C of C 1965-69; dir Indianapolis Urban League 1969-72; Manpower Commn1972-74; presently pres Devel Plus Mem; mem Indianapolis Alumni Chpt; Kappa Alpha Psi; Frat; Urban League; C of C; life mem NAACP. **Military Serv:** AUS 1946; 1st lt IN Guard Reserve.

CARTER, JOANNE WILLIAMS
Educator, artist, community activist. **Personal:** Born Mar 19, 1935, Brooklyn, NY; daughter of Elnora Bing Williams Morris and Edgar T. Williams; married Robert L. Carter, Sep 17, 1960; children: Anthony Tyrone, Tiffany Lucille, Janine Lynn Carter-Chevalier. **Educ:** Brooklyn College, City University of New York, Brooklyn, NY, BA (cum laude), 1976, MA, 1986. **Career:** NYC, bd of educ, 1974-94; professional artist, 1980-. **Orgs:** Patron, The Studio Museum of Harlem; trustee, The Brooklyn Museum; former pres, Society for the Preservation of Weeksville and Bedford/Stuyvesant History (an African American Museum); charter member, The Schomberg Society of the Schomberg Library of New York; charter member, The National Museum of Women in the Arts; member/patron, Prospect-Lefferts Gardens Neighborhood Association; member, Delta Rho Chapter, Alpha Kappa Alpha Sorority; member, Church Women United; member, Brooklyn Chapter, LINKS, Inc; member, African and Caribbean American Artists; founding member, Emily Pickens Club; member, Historic Preservation and Architectural Review Board, Sag Harbor, NY; pres, Eastville Historical Society of Sag Harbor; mem, Artists Alliance of East Hampton, NY. **Honors/Awds:** Prize winning painting, Kingsboro Community Art Gallery, 1988; participant, Sag Harbor Initiative, an annual gathering of artists, philosophers, and writers, 1987-89. **Home Addr:** 153 Hampton St, Sag Harbor, NY 11963.

CARTER, JOHN H.
Telecommunications company executive. **Personal:** Born Sep 26, 1948, Thomaston, GA; son of Rosa Matthews Carter and Augustus Carter Jr; married Susan Gibson Carter, Aug 20, 1970; children: Gregory L, Candace M. **Educ:** Robt E Lee Inst, attended 1965-66; Morris Brown Coll, BA 1970; Univ of UT, MS 1977; Univ of Southern CA, MS 1989. **Career:** Cambridge Sch System, instr 1970; So Bell Tele & Teleg Co Atlanta, mgmt asst 1972-73, bus office mgr 1973-74, personnel supr 1974-76, bus office mgr 1976-77; Amer Tele & Teleg Co Basking Ridge NJ, dist mgr eeo goals/analysis 1977-79; So Bell Tele & Teleg Co Atlanta, dist mgr personnel admin 1979-80; dist mgr assessment American Tel & Tel Co Atlanta GA 1980-81; Southern Bell dist mgr copr plg 1982-87 Operations mgr supplier relations; dir of purchasing 1987-88; BellSouth Fellow Univ of Southern CA 1988-89; general manager, property and service Southern Bell 1989-91, assistant vice pres, procurement, property and services management, 1991-92; City of Atlanta, Mayor's Office, loan executive, 1992; asst vice president, Fleet and Services, 1992-93; pres, Operator Services, 1993-. **Orgs:** President Alpha Phi Alpha Frat 1969-70; pres Mt Olive Jaycees NJ 1977-78; chairman of administrative bd SuccaSunna United Meth Ch 1978-79; board of directors Atlanta Met Fair Housing 1983-84; loan exec Fulton Co Comm GA 1981-82; pres Huntington Comm Assn Atlanta 1981-82; vice pres, Seaborn Lee Sch PTA Atlanta 1983-84; Clark Coll Allied Health Comm Atlanta 1981-, vice pres; Fulton Co Zoning Orgin Review Comm, vice president, 1982-; Econom Devel Advisory Bd 1985-; chairman Douglas HS Bus Advis Cncl 1985-92; Adult Schl Super Ben Hill United Meth Church 1986-87; board of directors Renaisssance Capital Corp. 1987; American Lung Association, board of directors, 1990-94; American Red Cross, board of directors, 1992-; Opportunities Industrialization Center, board of directors, 1989-92; Bobby Dodd Center, board of directors, 1989-92; Alpha Phi Alpha Fraternity, Georgia District, director of education, 1991-94. **Honors/Awds:** Natl Chap of Yr Natl Alpha Phi Alpha Frat 1970; Jaycee of Yr Coll Park Jaycees GA 1977; Jaycee of Yr Mt Olive Jaycees NJ 1979; Outstanding Pres in Region NJ Jaycees 1978; Bell South ServicesPresident's Award 1987; Man of the Year, Alpha Phi Alpha, 1990; National Alpha Phi Alpha, Alumni Brother of the Year, 1992; Douglass High School, Businessman of the Year, 1989. **Military Serv:** US Army sp/5 1970-72; Good Conduct Medal. **Home Addr:** 3465 Somerset Trail, Atlanta, GA 30331. **Business Addr:** President, Operative Services, Southern Bell Center, Rm 4406, Atlanta, GA 30375.

CARTER, JOHN R.
Mayor. **Personal:** Born Sep 2, 1941, Laurens County, SC; married Carrie; children: Anthony, Wadis, Kris. **Career:** Mayor Town of Gray Court, currently; Laurens County Dept Soc Ser, human services specialist; laborer 1960-69. **Orgs:** President SC Conference of Black Mayors; President, Laurens Chapter, State Employees Assn; Deacon Pleasant View Baptist Church; Opport Off & Assoc; past-pres Laurens Cty Chptr NAACP; worsh-

pfl mstr Red Cross Masonic Ldg FMPHA; pres SC Equal Opport Assoc; former mem Laurens Cty Select Serv Bd Town Coun of Gray Court SC (2 yrs). **Honors/Awds:** First African-American to serve on Gray Ct Council; numerous others. **Business Addr:** PO Box 2001, Laurens, SC 29360.

CARTER, JOSEPH, JR.
Realtor. **Personal:** Born May 12, 1927, Newark, NJ; married Ann; children: 5. **Educ:** Grant Tech Coll, 1952-54; Am River Coll, 1955-56; Sacramento State Coll, 1957-59; Realtors Inst, grad 1972; Sacramento State U, housing mgmt 1972-73; Sacramento Jr Coll, ghetto econ 1973. **Career:** Realtor, currently. **Orgs:** Mem NAACP; Urban League; Sacramento Bd of Realtors; CA Bd of Realtors; Sacramento Valley Chap of Inst of Real Estate Mgmt; Building Consultant Showcase Homes; Co-founder Minority Broker Assn; Co-founder New Start Inc; chmn Marketing Com; Operation Breakthrough; chmn Oak Park Redevel; Project Area Com; Sacramento City Housing Code Adv & Appeals Bd. **Honors/Awds:** Sacramento Bd of Realtors Victory Medal. **Military Serv:** USAF s/sgt 1945. **Business Addr:** 400 21 St, Sacramento, CA 95818.

CARTER, JOSEPH CHRIS
Professional baseball player. **Personal:** Born Mar 7, 1960, Oklahoma City, OK. **Educ:** Wichita State. **Career:** Chicago Cubs, outfielder, 1983; Cleveland Indians, outfielder/infielder, 1984-89; San Diego Padres, outfielder/infielder, 1990; Toronto Blue Jays, outfielder/infielder, 1991-97; Baltimore Orioles, 1998-. **Business Addr:** Professional Baseball Player, Baltimore Orioles, 333 W Camden St, Baltimore, MD 21201, (410)685-9800.

CARTER, JOYE
City official. **Educ:** Howard Univ, medicine. **Career:** Howard Univ, pathology, chief resident; Dade County, forensic pathology, fellow; US Air Force Medical Corps, chief physician, forensic pathologist; Washington, DC, chief medical officer; Harris County, Texas, chief medical officer, currently; Howard University, instructor, currently; Baylor College of Medicine, currently. **Special Achievements:** First African American chief medical examiner in Houston (Harris County); first woman chief medical examiner in Houston. **Business Addr:** Chief Medical Examiner, c/o Harris County Medical Examiner's Office, 1885 Old Spanish Trail, Houston, TX 77054, (713)796-9292.

CARTER, JUDY L.
Educator. **Personal:** Born Jun 7, 1942, McCormick, SC; daughter of Willie Moton Luchey; married James Carter III, Feb 10, 1968; children: James IV, Mason III. **Educ:** Paine College, Augusta, GA, BA, 1967; Augusta College, Augusta, GA, MEd, 1976; University of South Carolina, Columbia, SC, EdD, 1981. **Career:** Richmond County Bd of Ed, Augusta, GA, teacher, 1967-76; Paine College, Augusta, GA, instructor, 1976-80; University of South Carolina, Aiken, SC, dir of student teaching, 1980-84; Paine College, Augusta, GA, chair, div of education, 1984-. **Orgs:** Vice-president, Alpha Kappa Alpha Sorority Inc, 1985-87; president, The Augusta Chapter of Links Inc, 1986-89; chairperson, Georgia Advisory Council, 1988-89; director, Bush Faculty Development Program, 1988-; site coordinator, Ford Teacher-Scholar Program, 1990-; member, Georgia Assn of Colleges for Teacher Education, 1985-. **Honors/Awds:** Teacher of the Year, Paine College, 1979-80; Graduate Advisor of the Year, Alpha Kappa Alpha Sorority Inc, 1988; Minority Teacher Recruitment Project, Consortium for the Advancement of Private Higher Education, 1988-90; Outstanding Community Leader, Wrights Enterprise, 1990. **Home Addr:** 1528 Flagler Rd, Augusta, GA 30909.

CARTER, JUDY SHARON
Personnel administrator. **Personal:** Born Dec 22, 1951, Miami, FL; daughter of Ola Carter and James Carter. **Educ:** Fisk Univ, BS (Magna Cum Laude, Dept Honors) 1969-73; Univ of MI, MA 1973-74, Coll of Financial Planning, AFP (CFP designation pending). **Career:** Dade Cty School Miami FL, teacher 1974-75; City of Miami FL, admin asst 1975-77, personnel officer 1977-78, sr personnel officer 1978-79, exec dir civil serv bd (1st Black & 1st Black woman exec dir) 1979-; Assoc Financial Planing (1st Black Woman in Dade County). **Orgs:** 1st black trustee Bd of Trustees City of Miami Pension Bd 1980; pres Natl Assoc of Civil Serv Commiss 1983; mem Leadership Miami Alumni Assoc; mem Natl Forum for Black Public Admin, Intl Personnel Mgmt Assoc, FL Public Personnel Assoc, Federal Selective Serv Syst Be, Natl Assoc of Female Exec; mem, Delta Sigma Theta Inc; sec Miami-Fisk Alumni Club; mem Young Adult Choir/New Way Fellowship Baptist; mem Natl Assoc of Negro & Professional Womens Club, Credit Union Loan Committee, Carver Young Mens Christian Assoc, Greater Miami Urban League, Amer Assoc of Individual Investors, Intl Assoc of Financial Planners; YWCA; Coordinator, Women's Growth Inst, New Way Fellowship Baptist; NAACP; Inst of Certified Financial Planners. **Honors/Awds:** Grad Class Leadership in Miami Greater Miami Chamber of Commerce 1980; article & publications, Carter, Judy S & Timmons, Wm M ''Conflicting Roles in PersonalBds, Adjudications vs Policy Making ''Public Personnel Mgmt, Vol 14, #2, 1985. **Business Addr:** Executive Dir Civil Serv Bd, City of Miami, 1145 NW 11th St, Miami, FL 33136.

CARTER, KELLY ELIZABETH
Sportswriter. **Personal:** Born Nov 27, 1962, Los Angeles, CA; daughter of Lucille Turner Carter and Ernest Carter. **Educ:** Univ of Southern California, Los Angeles, CA, AB, Journalism, 1985. **Career:** Iowa City Press-Citizen, Iowa City, IA, sportswriter, 1986-87; Pittsburgh Press, Pittsburgh, PA, sportswriter, 1987-89; Dallas Morning News, Dallas, TX, sportswriter, 1990-. **Orgs:** Member, Delta Sigma Theta Sorority, Inc, 1982-; regional coordinator, Association for Women in Sports Media, 1986-; member, National Assn of Black Journalists, 1986-; member, Dallas-Fort Worth Assn of Black Communicators, Currently. **Honors/Awds:** Golden Quill Award, Pittsburgh Press Club, 1989. **Business Addr:** Sportswriter, Sports Dept, Dallas Morning News, Communications Center, Dallas, TX 75265.

CARTER, KENNETH GREGORY
Business executive. **Personal:** Born Aug 12, 1959, Louisville, KY; son of Laura L Grant Offutt and Garland K Offutt; married Ellen Melissa Pullen Carter, Feb 14, 1987; children: Kenneth Jr, Brandon G. **Educ:** University of Louisville, Louisville, KY, BSC, 1981; Ohio State University, Columbus, OH, MBA, 1983. **Career:** International Business Machines, Louisville, KY, sales, 1980-90; Brown-Forman, Louisville, KY, national senior brand manager, 1990-. **Orgs:** Board of directors, Urban League, 1990; member, NAACP. **Honors/Awds:** Black Achiever, YMCA, 1987; America's Best and Brightest, Dollars and Sense Magazine, 1988; Kentucky Colonel, Jaycees, 1989; Key to the City, New Orleans City Government, 1990. **Business Addr:** National Senior Brand Manager, Early Times-Marketing, Brown-Forman Beverage Company, 850 Dixie Hwy, Louisville, KY 40201.

CARTER, KENNETH WAYNE
Advertising executive. **Personal:** Born Sep 8, 1954, Muskogee, OK; son of Doris and Ira Carter McCoy; married Constance Burch, Sep 3, 1988. **Educ:** Southern University, BA, 1976. **Career:** KALO Radio, sports director, 1976-77; American Heart Association, director of public relations, 1977-81; Focus Communications, exec vp, 1981-87, president/CEO, 1988-. **Orgs:** PRSA, Multicultural Affairs Committee, 1982-; Dallas/Ft Worth Minority Business Development Division Council, board member, 1983-86; City of Dallas, Public Information Task Force, 1990; Dallas Citizens Council, mem, 1994-95; Dallas Urban League, bd mem, 1994-98; Dallas Convention & Visitors Bureau, bd mem, 1996-. **Honors/Awds:** Dallas Black Chamber of Commerce, Quest for Success, 1987; National Association of Negro Business & Professional Women, Man of the Year, 1986. **Special Achievements:** First Black member, Board of Directors, Public Relations Society of America, North Texas Chapter, serving two terms, one as secretary; only Black member, Public Information Task Force, City of Dallas, also serving on Steering Committee. **Business Addr:** President/CEO, Focus Communications Inc, 1401 Elm St, Ste 1900, Dallas, TX 75202, (214)744-1428.

CARTER, KEVIN ANTONY
Investment executive. **Personal:** Born May 23, 1960, Cleveland, OH; son of John & Lavenia Carter; divorced. **Educ:** Vanderbilt University, BA, philosophy, 1982; Weatherhead School of Management, Case Western Reserve University, MBA, finance, 1987. **Career:** Ernst & Young, senior consultant, strategic planning, 1986-89; LTV Corporation, senior analyst, strategic planning, 1989-93; McDonald & Company Investment, vp & director of diversity & business development, 1993-. **Orgs:** United Negro College Fund, Cleveland/Canton/Akron, telethon chairperson, 1993-; Kaleidoscope Magazine, advisory bd chairperson, 1994-; City of Cleveland Community Relations Board Chair, youth subcommittee, 1994-; City of Cleveland Investment Oversight Committee, 1994-; NAACP, Cleveland Branch, executive committee member, 1992-94; National Black MBA Assn, national bd member, 1994-; African American Business Consortium, chairperson, 1992-. **Honors/Awds:** Kaleidoscope Magazine, Man of the Year, 1994; National Black MBA Assn, H Naylor Fitzhugh Award of Excellence, 1993; Cleveland Crains' Business, 40 under 40 Club, 1993; Kaleidoscope Magazine, Forty-Forty Club, 1994; Cleveland SuccessGuide, Top Ten to Watch, 1991. **Special Achievements:** Columnist, Call & Post Newspaper, Minority Investor Forum, weekly column, Feb 1993-; Serie 7 & 63, Investment Securities Licenses; Leadership Cleveland, Class of 1993-94. **Business Addr:** Director, Diversity Business Development, McDonald & Company Investments, 800 Superior Ave, Ste 2100, Cleveland, OH 44114-2603, (216)443-3843.

CARTER, KEVIN LOUIS
Professional football player. **Personal:** Born Sep 21, 1973, Miami, FL; married Shima. **Educ:** Florida. **Career:** St Louis Rams, defensive end, 1995-. **Special Achievements:** 1st round/6th overall NFL draft pick, 1995; Carroll Rosenbloom Award, 1995. **Business Addr:** Professional Football Player, St Louis Rams, One Rams Way, St Louis, MO 63045, (314)982-7267.

CARTER, KI-JANA (KENNETH LEONARD)
Professional football player. **Personal:** Born Sep 12, 1973, Westerville, OH. **Educ:** Penn State University. **Career:** Cincinnati Bengals, running back, 1995-. **Special Achievements:** Selected in the 1st round/1st overall pick in the 1995 NFL Draft. **Business Addr:** Professional Football Player, Cincinnati Bengals, One Bengals Dr, Cincinnati, OH 45202, (513)621-3550.

CARTER, LAMORE JOSEPH
Educational administrator, psychologist. **Personal:** Born Apr 18, 1925, Carthage, TX; married Lena Mae Jones; children: Greta Lisa, Kris-Lana. **Educ:** Wiley Coll, 1946-47; Fisk U, AB 1950; Univ of WI, MS 1952; State Univ of IA, PhD 1958; Univ of Chicago, postgrad 1954; Univ of TX, 1966; Columbia, 1967; Emory U, 1970; Harvard U, 1976. **Career:** Grambling Coll LA, instructor 1952-54; asst 1961-66; State Univ of IA, rsch asst 1956-58; Institutional Research, admin 1966-68; Southern Assn of Colls & Schools, research fellow postdoctoral 1969-70; Morehouse Coll, visiting distinguished prof Psychology 1970; TX Southern Univ Houston, dean of faculties 1970-71; Grambling State Univ, assoc dean for admin 1971-76; consultant Peace Corps West Africa 1971-76; Southern Assoc of Colls & Schools, consultant 1971-82; Amer Council on Educ, fellow in academic admin 1976-77; Grambling State Univ, provost and vice pres academic affairs, beginning 1977; Wiley College, pres, 1993-. **Orgs:** Am Educ Research Assn; diplomate Am Bd Professional Psychology; chap pres Am Assn Univ Prof 1960-63; consultant Headstart Program 1968-76; Am Southwestern; LA Psychol Assn; Am Assn for Higher Edn; Am Assn on Mental Deficiency; Natl Soc for Study Edn; LA Assn Mental Health; Nat Educ Assn; Phi Delta Kappa; Phi Beta Sigma; Dem; Meth; Amer Psychological Assn; founder & pres Lions Club Intl 1981-84; bd of dirs, United Campus Ministry. **Honors/Awds:** Mason 33rd degree; Fellow Amer Assoc on Mental Deficiency; Diplomate Amer Bd of Professional Psychology; Licensed School Psychologist by LA Bd of Examiners of Psychologists; contrib articles to professional jours books monographs. **Military Serv:** AUS; Bronze Star. **Business Addr:** President, Wiley College, 711 Wiley Ave, Marshall, TX 75670, (903)927-3200.

CARTER, LAWRENCE
University administrator. **Personal:** Born Oct 4, 1942, Valdosta, GA; son of Mrs Isabell Beady Carter; married Mrs Marva L Moore, Jan 28, 1968; children: Mauri D Carter, Laurent L Carter. **Educ:** Fort Valley State College, Ft Valley GA, BS, 1968; Tuskegee Institute, Tuskegee AL, MS, 1969; Florida State Univ, Tallahassee FL, EdS, 1973, PhD, 1976. **Career:** Goldkist Industries, Atlanta GA, mgr trainee, 1969-71; Tuskegee Inst, Tuskegee AL, asst prof of Adult Educ, 1973-74; Florida A&M Univ, Tallahassee FL, ext rural devel specialist, 1974-80, acting dir agricultural research, 1980-87, dir cooperative extension, 1980-. **Orgs:** Mem, Fort Valley State Coll Alumni Assn, 1968, Tuskegee Alumni Assn, 1969, Adult Education Assn of America, 1973, Florida A&M Univ Alumni Assn, 1974; consultant, Univ of Florida Int Program, 1980; dir, Steering Comm, Bethel Baptist Church, 1982-84; mem, bd of dir, Southern Rural Devel Center, 1987; pres, Phi Beta Sigma, Local Chapter, 1987; consultant, Kellog Project, North Carolina A&T Univ, 1988; mem, Policy Comm, Extension Serv, USDA. 1989. **Honors/Awds:** Author, Thesis, ''Adult Educ,'' 1969 The Effect of Readability on Comprehensive of Consumer Laws, 1976 A Package Approach for Rural Clientele, 1979 Small Farm Development in Florida's Vegetable Industry, 1979; Certificate of Appreciation, Governor's Office, State of Florida, 1981; Certificate of Appreciation, Florida A&M Univ, 1984; Strategic Planning for Cooperative Extension Involvement in International Programs, 1985; Meritorious Achievement Award, Univ of Florida, 1986; Certificate of Appreciation, Florida A&M Univ, 1987; Service Award, Florida A&M Univ, 1988. **Military Serv:** AUS, Spec 4, 1961-65; Good Conduct Medal, 1964.

CARTER, LAWRENCE E., SR.
Clergyman, educational administrator, counselor. **Personal:** Born Sep 23, 1941, Dawson, GA; son of Mr and Mrs John Henry Carter III; married Marva Lois Griffin; children: Lawrence Edward Jr. **Educ:** VA Univ of Lynchburg, BA Soc Studies 1964; Boston Univ, MDiv Theol 1968, STM Pastoral Care 1970, PhD Pastoral Care & Counseling 1978; Andover Newton Theol School, OH State Univ, New York University, Harvard University, Georgia State University, attended; Univ of Wisconsin, George Washington Univ, attended. **Career:** Roxbury United Presbyterian Church, minister to youth 1965-67; Boston Public Schools, sub teacher 1966-77; Twelfth Baptists Church, minister of counseling 1968-71; Boston Univ Warren Residence Hall, resident counselor & asst dir 1968-71; Boston University MLK Jr African-American Cultural Center, director, 1971-73; People's Baptist Church, assoc minister 1971-78; Harvard Univ Divinity School, clergy teaching advisor 1976-77; Marsh Chapel Boston Univ, assoc dean 1978-79; Morehouse Coll, prof, dept of philosophy & religion 1979-; Martin Luther King Jr Intl Chapel Morehouse Coll, dean 1979-, archivist/curator, 1982-97. **Orgs:** Mem Atlanta United Nations Assoc; board of directors Natl Council of Chuches of Christ 1983-90; mem Natl Assoc of Coll & Univ Chaplains, ACLU, Amer Acad of Religion, Assoc of Black Prof of Religion, Ministries to Blacks in Higher Ed, NAACP; coord Afro-Amer Studies Prog Simmons Coll, coord 1977-78; mem Soc for the Study of Black Religion, Class of Leadership Atlanta 1986; American Academy of Religion, 1979-. **Honors/Awds:** Fulbright Scholar, Brazil, 1994; Citizenship Medal of the Year VA

Coll 1964; Recognition of Outstanding Achievement in the field of Religion & Humanitarianism Omega Scroll of Honor Morehouse Coll 1979; Natl Black Christian Student Leadership Consultation Awd in Appreciation for Support & Commitment to Devel of Black Christian Leadership 1980; Delegate to United Nations Spec Committee Against Apartheid 1984; numerous radio & TV appearances including Ebenezer Church Serv WAGA Channel 5 Atlanta GA, "The Role of the Black Church" WAOK Interview Atlanta GA, WCNN Radio Anthony Johnson Commentary 1984, CNN Roy Patterson Interview 1984; Voted Faculty Mem of the Year Morehouse Coll Student Newspaper; Del to the 6th Assembly of the World Council of Churches 1983; Del to the World Baptist Youth Conf in Argentina, 1984; Del to 4thtl Council of Churches Dialogue between the Soviety Union Clergy & Amer Clergy in Moscow; Senate Concurrent Resolution by the State of MI in Honor of Dr Carter, 32nd Degree Mason Prince Hall Lodge, 1985. **Business Addr:** Dean of Chapel, Professor of Philosopy and Religion, Morehouse College, Martin Luther King Jr Intl Chapel, 830 Westview Dr, PO Box 24, Atlanta, GA 30314.

CARTER, LAWRENCE ROBERT

Educator. **Personal:** Born Nov 24, 1936, Washington, DC; son of Mary Magdalene King Carter (deceased) and John Harold Carter, Sr (deceased); married Maile Louise Crooker Carter; children: Elizabeth Miriam Carter, Christopher Lawrence Carter. **Educ:** Howard University, Washington, DC, BS, 1958; University of Oregon, Eugene, OR, MA, 1970, PhD, 1973. **Career:** Lane County Youth Project, community organizer, 1965-67; Univ of Oregon, research asst, instructor, 1967-71; Univ of the Pacific, asst prof, 1971-73; Univ of Oregon, asst prof, 1973-75; Social Science Research Council, staff associate, 1975-76; Univ of Oregon, asst professor, associate professor, 1976-;. **Orgs:** Eugene Human Rights Commission, commissioner, 1967-71; Oregon Health Council, vice chair, 1988-91, commissioner, 1988-; City Club of Eugene, 1990-; Population Assn of America, 1970-; American Statistical Assn, 1989-. **Honors/Awds:** Pre-doctoral Fellowship, US Office of Education, 1969, NSF Fellowship, National Science Foundation, 1971; Citation for Service, City of Eugene, 1970-71; Danforth Associate, The Danforth Foundation, 1973. **Military Serv:** USAF, captain, 1959-65. **Home Addr:** 2112 Agate Street, Eugene, OR 97403. **Business Addr:** Associate Professor and Graduate Program Coordinator, University of Oregon, Department of Sociology, Eugene, OR 97403, (503)346-5169.

CARTER, LEMORIE, JR.

Franchise owner. **Personal:** Born Dec 9, 1944, Birmingham, AL; son of Gloria Carter and Lemorie Carter; children: Kristie, Ronnie, Lemorie III. **Educ:** Morehouse Coll, 1963-65; Miles Coll, BA Soc Sci 1967; Life Underwriter Training Council, 1972. **Career:** Firestone Tire & Rubber Co, sales mgr 1968-70; Met Life Ins Co, sales rep 197-77; Lemorie Carter Ins Agency, Midland Natl Life Ins Co, ins broker, gen agent 1977-; AL Williams Fin Serv Org, sr vice pres 1983-; Carter-Carter Ins Agency, owner; Mayor Richard Arrington Jr Birmingham AL, admin asst 1977-; sr vice pres First Amer Natl Securities & The A L Williams Corp; Primerica Financial Services, national sales director, 1989-. **Orgs:** Adv bd Sickle Cell Anemia Screening Found 1979, Birmingham Creative Dance Co 1980; instr ins seminars Miles Coll, Daniel Payne Coll, Lawson State Comm-Coll; treas Birmingham Urban League 1973-; initiated voter reg Birmingham 1973; publ rel dir Alpha Phi Alpha Omicron Lambda Chapt; budget comm Six Ave Bapt Church; board of directors Positive Maturity, United Way Agency. **Honors/Awds:** Num ins org awds, frat awd; Outstanding Young Men in Amer 1972-77; Outstanding Bd Mem Awd, Outstanding Serv Pin Birmingham Urban League 1975,78; several Financial Services Industry Awards. **Business Addr:** 2090 Columbiana Rd, Vestavia Commerce Center, Ste 1200, Birmingham, AL 35216.

CARTER, LENORA

Publisher. **Personal:** Born Mar 12, 1941, Corrigan, TX; widowed; children: Constance, Karen. **Career:** Forward Times Newspaper, chmn of bd, publisher. **Orgs:** Mem Riverside Hosp, Eliza Johnson Home for Aged, 20th Century Fund, Natl Assn Market Developers; member, secretary, Natl Newspaper Publishers Assn; mem American Red Cross, United Fund, United Negro College Fund, Eta Phi Beta, Gamma Phi Delta. **Honors/Awds:** Recipient Natl Emphasis Award NAMD; Fred D Patterson Leadership Award; Natl Assn of Media Women; Houston Med Forum Recognition Award; Outstanding Citizen, State of Michigan. **Business Addr:** Publisher, Chairman of the Bd, Forward Times, P O Box 2962, Houston, TX 77004.

CARTER, LEWIS WINSTON

Real estate broker. **Personal:** Born Jul 16, 1920, Middletown, OH; children: 4. **Educ:** Hampton Inst, grad 1944; Detroit Inst Tech, 1961; Univ Detroit, 1963. **Career:** Self-employed, real estate broker. **Orgs:** Sec Demo Dist #16; bd educ Region #2; mem United Citizens of SW Detroit; pres St Andrew & Benedict Dads Club; life mem NAACP; mem & Sts Andrew& Benedict Ch; mem Nat Lawyers Guild. **Honors/Awds:** Police award 1960; Sch Achievement Award; State Legislature Common Council Detroit 1963. **Military Serv:** USN 1943-46. **Business Addr:** 2311 S Fort St, Detroit, MI.

CARTER, MARGARET LOUISE

Elected official, educator. **Personal:** Born Dec 29, 1935, Shreveport, LA. **Educ:** Portland State Univ, BA; Washington State Univ, Post-Grad Studies, OR State Univ, MEd. **Career:** Albina Youth Opportunity School, instr 1971-73; Portland Comm Coll, counselor 1973-; business woman 1975-; House Educ Comm, mem 1985-; Conf Comm on Martin Luther King Jr State Holiday, co-chair 1985; Joint House-Senate Comm on Trade & Economic Development 1985-; Special Joint Comm on Health Care, mem 1986; OR House Human Resources Comm, vchair 1987-; OR State, state rep, currently. **Orgs:** Mem OR Alliance for Black School Ed, Portland Teachers' Assoc, OR Assembly for Black Affairs, Amer Fed of Teachers, Spec Commiss for the Parole Bd on the Matrix Syst, NAACP, OR Political Women's Caucus, Alpha Kappa Sor; co-founder Black Leadership Conf 1986; gov appointee OR Task Force on Drug Abuse 1986-; gen adv comm Victims Rights 1986-. **Honors/Awds:** Zeta Phi Beta Sor Awd; Musical Dir of the Joyful Sound Piedmont Church of Christ Portland; Appointed to OR State Commiss on Post-Secondary Ed; First black woman in history to be elected to OR Leg Assembly; Jeanette Rankin First Woman Awd OR Women's Political Caucus 1985; Jefferson Image Awd 1985. **Business Addr:** State Representative, State of Oregon, District 18, 364 State Capitol, Salem, OR 97310.

CARTER, MARION ELIZABETH

Educator. **Personal:** Born Jan 25, Washington, DC; daughter of Marion Jackson Carter and James Martin Carter. **Educ:** Wellesley College; Howard University, MA; Middlebury College, MA; Georgetown University, MS; Catholic University, PhD; Georgetown University, PhD. **Career:** Wellesley College, visiting prof; Gordon College, prof; Teachers College, prof; Howard University, instructor; Barber Scotia College, instructor; Wiley College, assoc prof; University of La Gaguna, lecturer; American Language Institute of Georgetown University, teacher; St Mary University Nova Scotia, lecturer. **Orgs:** Natl Assn of Foreign Student Affairs; mem Le Droit Park Civic Assn; mem Smithsonian Inst; past sec, Amer Assn of Teachers of Spanish & Portuguese; mem AAUP, AAUW, IBC, ABI; trustee, World University; elected mem, Order of International Fellowship. **Honors/Awds:** Intl Biog Ctrt; Buena Aires Conv Award; Agnes Meyer Award; AATSP Award, Spain; Directory of Amer Scholars; Fulbright Award Spain; placque, Lifetime Bd of Governors, American Biographical Inst, Intl Hall of Leaders, IBC Book of Dedications.

CARTER, MARTIN JOSEPH

Clergyman. **Personal:** Born Jul 31, 1930, High Point, NC. **Educ:** Cornell Univ, MEd 1960, BA 1956; Emersin Coll, BA 1956. **Career:** Archdiocese Kingston, Jamaica, pastor 1976-; St Francis De Sales Church, 1975-76; St Joseph Comm Parochial School, tchr coord facilitator 1970-75; Harvard Univ, consult 1970-74; Dissemination Prog, participant 1971-72; Univ of Illinois Curriculum Studies in Math, model tchr. **Orgs:** Mem Natl Black Catholic Clergy Caucus 1968-77; Caribbean Ecumenical Const for Devel 1976-77; exec for Jamaica Council of Churches 1976-77. **Honors/Awds:** Published "Teen-Age Marriage" 1974; "Homiletic & Pastoral Rev - Diocesan Policy on Teenage Marriages" 1975; "Dignitatis Humanae Declaration on Religious Freedom"; The New Catholic Encyclopedia 1979. **Business Addr:** Church of Reconciliation, Kenton Ave, Bridge Port, Jamaica.

CARTER, MARTY LAVINCENT

Professional football player. **Personal:** Born Dec 17, 1969, LaGrange, GA. **Educ:** Middle Tennessee State, attended. **Career:** Tampa Bay Buccaneers, defensive back, 1991-94; Chicago Bears, 1995-. **Business Addr:** Professional Football Player, Chicago Bears, 1000 Football Dr, Halas Hall at Conway Park, Lake Forest, IL 60045-4829, (847)295-6600.

CARTER, MARVA GRIFFIN

Educator. **Personal:** Born Jun 4, 1947, Cleveland, OH; daughter of Dr and Mrs Marvin C Griffin; married Dr Lawrence E Carter Sr, Jun 22, 1969; children: Lawrence E Jr. **Educ:** Boston Conservatory of Music, BM, 1968; New England Conservatory of Music, MM, 1970; Boston Univ, MA, 1975; Univ of Illinois, PhD, 1988. **Career:** Boston Univ, administrative assistant, Afro-American Studies Program, 1970-71, coordinator of freshman/sophomore seminars, 1972-73; Simmons College, coordinator of Afro-Am studies program, 1973-77; Clark Atlanta Univ, adjunct assoc prof of music, 1988-89; Ebenezer Baptist Church, organist and music coord, 1982-92; Morris Brown Coll, coordinator of music, 1988-93; Georgia State Univ, asst director, School of Music, 1993-95, asst prof of music hist & lit, currently. **Orgs:** American Musicological Society, cultural diversity and the committee on the publication of American music, 1973-77, 1993-; Sonneck Society for American Music, nominating committee, education committee and cultural diversity committee, 1973-77, 1993-; Center for Black Music Research, associate mem, 1993-; Society for Ethnomusicology, 1973-77, 1993-; Young Audiences of Atlanta, board member, ed comm, 1992-94; Atlanta Symphony Action Committee for Black Audience Development, 1992-94. **Honors/Awds:** Miss Texas High, poise, 1964; Winner of piano award, 1964; Smithsonian Institution Research Fellow, 1983. **Special Achievements:** First African American to receive the PhD in musicology from the Univ of Illinois, 1988; Roland Hayes, Expresser of the Soul in Song, Black Perspective in Music, pp 189-220, Fall, 1977; Articles published in Black Women in the US and Notable Black American Women; musical biography on Will Marion Cook, forthcoming. **Business Addr:** Asst Director of the School of Music, Georgia State Univ., Unversity Plaza, Room 117, Atlanta, GA 30303, (404)651-3513.

CARTER, MARY LOUISE

City official. **Personal:** Born Jun 27, 1937, Clarksdale, MS; daughter of Mrs Julia M Turner; married Everett L Carter; children: Danny C, Eric L. **Educ:** Coahoma Jr Coll, AA 1959; Alcorn Coll, 1959-60; Fontbonne Coll, 1977. **Career:** Sears Credit Central, credit analyst 1969-; City of Pagedale, alderperson, 1981-92, acting mayor, 1984-85, mayor, 1992-; MO Division of Families Svcs, caseworker, 1995-. **Orgs:** Bd mem Normandy Mun Council 1981-88; bd mem Adult Basic Educ 1981-86; acting pres of bd City of Pagedale 1984-86; chairperson Public Awareness Adult Basic Educ 1984-85; Black Elected Officals of St Louis County 1990-; Natl Conference of Black Mayors, mem. **Honors/Awds:** Positive Imate; Outstanding Contribution in Adult Literarcy, 1994; Award for Services to Scout Troop #606, 1995. **Home Addr:** 1284 Kingsland, Pagedale, MO 63133. **Business Addr:** Mayor, City of Pagedale, 1404 Ferguson Ave, Pagedale, MO 63133.

CARTER, MILTON O., SR.

Business executive. **Personal:** Born Mar 17, 1912, St Louis, MO; married Ida M; children: Catherine E Lindsey, Milton, Jr. **Educ:** Wilson Jr Coll, attended 2 years; Central YMCA Coll, attended 2 years; George William Coll, attended 1 year. **Career:** St Charles School for Boys, rec dir 1983-41; Pine St YMCA St Louis, boys work sec 1941-45; N Webster YMCA St Louis, exec dir 1945-48; Wabash Ave YMCA Chicago, dir comm serv for outpost work 1948-50; Southtown YMCA Chicago, 1st Black staff mem 1951-53; Maxwell St YMCA Chicago, exec dir 1953-66; Wabash Ave YMCA, exec dir 1967-69; Univ of IL Chicago, spec asst to vice chancellor 1970-78; retired. **Orgs:** Mem adv bds, Near Westside Council, City wide Mental Health Bureau; chmn of Univ of IL Chicago Campus of Natl Youth Sports Program; Eisenberg Boy's Club Chicago. **Honors/Awds:** Outstanding Work Award YMCA of Chicago 1958; Man of the Year Old Town Chicago Boy's Club 1975; Recognition Award Board of Trust Univ of IL Chicago 1977; Model Cities Chicago Comm on Urban Oppty Serv 1975; Humanitarian of the Year Near West Side Council 1977; Continuous Leadership Halsted-South Lawndale Citizens Adv Cncl to the City of Chicago 1978; Cert of Appreciation Dist 9 Chicago Bd of Educ 1978; Achievement Award for Vol Serv Chicago Police Dept 1978; Mayor Bilandic's Proclamation Day 1978; YMCA Olde Tymer Inc St Louis for Man of Compassion 1982; Apprec of Serv as Chmn of Adv Bd Salvation Army Chicago 1983.

CARTER, NANETTE CAROLYN

Professional artist. **Personal:** Born Jan 30, 1954, Columbus, OH; daughter of Frances Hill Carter and Matthew G Carter. **Educ:** L'Accademia di Belle Arti, Perugia Italy, 1974-75; Oberlin Coll, Oberlin OH, BA, 1976; Pratt Inst of Art, Brooklyn NY, MFA, 1978. **Career:** Dwight-Englewood School, Englewood NJ, teacher of printmaking and drawing, 1978-87; self-employed artist and painter, 1987-; City College of New York, adj prof, 1992-93. **Orgs:** NARAL, 1988-; Amnesty Int, 1988-; College Art Association. **Honors/Awds:** Jerome Found Grant, 1981; Natl Endowment for the Arts Grant, 1981; Artist in Residence Grant, New York State Council on the Arts, 1984; New Jersey State Council Grant, New Jersey State Council on the Arts, 1985; Exhibition, Newark Museum, "Twentieth Century Afro-American Artist," Newark NJ, 1985; featured in The Christian Science Monitor, "Artist at Work-Nanette Carter," 1986; Exhibition, Studio Museum in Harlem, New York, NY, 1988; Solo Exhibition, Montclair Art Museum, Montclair NJ, 1988; Fellowship, Bob Blackburn's Printmaking Workshop, 1989; New York Foundation for the Arts Grant, 1990; Solo: June Kelly Gallery, New York, 1990, Jersey City Museum, New Jersey, 1990; N'Namdi Gallery, Birmingham, MI, 1989; Sande Webster Gallery, Philadelphia, PA, Solo, 1993; June Kelly Gallery, NY, NY, Solo, 1994; Pollock-Krasner Foundation, Inc, Grant, 1994-; The Wheeler Foundation, Grant, 1996; solo shows of 1997; Hodges-Taylor Gallery, Charlotte, NC; Sante Webster Gallery, Phila, PA; June Kelly Gallery, NYC, NY. **Special Achievements:** Yale Gallery of Art, New Haven CT; Museum of Art, Rhode Island School of Design, RI; ARCO, Philadelphia, PA; Studio Museum in Harlem, NY; Merck Pharmaceutical Co, PA; Motown Corp., CA; MCI Telecommunication IL; IBM, CT; Pepsi-Cola, NY. **Business Addr:** 788 Riverside Drive, Apt #3C, New York, NY 10032, (212)690-7512.

CARTER, NELL

Actress, singer. **Personal:** Born Sep 13, 1948, Birmingham, AL; married George Krynick, 1982. **Educ:** Bill Russell's School of Drama, attended. **Career:** Num radio & TV appearances in AL; num club appearances & concerts incl Los Angeles Philharmonic; Hair, Modern Problems 1981, Back Roads 1981, Baryshnikov on Broadway, The Big Show, Dude, Don't Bother Me, I Can't Cope, Jesus Christ Superstar, Bury the

Dead, Rhapsody in Gershwin, Blues is a Woman, Black Broadway, Ain't Misbehavin', actress; Gimme a Break, star. **Orgs:** Mem AFTRA, Screen Actors Guild, Equity; life mem NAACP. **Honors/Awds:** Tony Awd; OBIE Awd; Drama Desk Awd; Soho News Awd for Ain't Misbehavin'; performed at George Bush's Inaugural Gala, 1989.

CARTER, NIGEA
Professional football player. **Personal:** Born Sep 1, 1974. **Educ:** Michigan State, attended. **Career:** Tampa Bay Buccaneers, wide receiver, 1997-. **Business Addr:** Professional Football Player, Tampa Bay Buccaneers, One Buccaneer Place, Tampa, FL 33607, (813)870-2700.

CARTER, NORMAN L.
Electric company executive. **Personal:** Born Jun 16, 1949, Pittsburgh, PA; married Zelia, Jul 19, 1986; children: Norman IV. **Educ:** Indiana Univ of PA, BA, 1971; Johns Hopkins Univ, MS, 1997. **Career:** Brown and Root, Inc, Houston, TX, sr auditor; Ernst & Young, sr accountant; Westinghouse Electric Corp, internal auditor; PEPCo, mgr of minority business devel, sr auditor, division mgr, 1981-. **Orgs:** American Institute of Certified Public Accountants; Pittsburgh PA, Natl Assn of Black Accountants, founder, past pres; Prince Georges Chamber of Commerce, treas, bd of dirs; Utility Network for Community Based Devel, chair; Washington Cathedral Choral Society, bd of dirs; Prince Georges Economic Devel Corp, bd of dirs; Maryland/District of Columbia Minority Supplier Devel Council, vp. **Business Addr:** Manager, Economic Development, Potomac Electric Power Co, 1900 Pennsylvania Ave NW, Ste K420, Washington, DC 20068, (202)872-3357.

CARTER, ORA WILLIAMS
Educator, artist. **Personal:** Born Aug 25, 1925, Ferndale, MI; daughter of Emma Kinney Williams and Samuel Williams; married Walter H Carter (deceased). **Educ:** Black Mountain Coll, Rosenwald Fellowship to attend summer art inst 1946; Clark Coll, AB 1947; Wayne State Univ, MEd 1963; Harvard Univ, Rosenwald Fellowship to attend summer inst in urban educ 1965. **Career:** Detroit Bd of Educ, teacher 1953-67; Communication Skills Center, instructor/diagnostician 1967-72; Bow Elementary School, instructor 1972-76; Roosevelt Elementary School, precision teacher 1976-81; Ora's Studio, artist 1978-. **Orgs:** Mem MI Assn of Calligraphers, Natl Conf of Artists, Met Detroit Reading Council 1965-81, Detroit Federation of Teachers; pres Detroit Alumnae Chapter Delta Sigma Theta Sorority 1973-75; charter mem Fred Hart Williams Genealogical Soc, Founders Soc & Friends of African Art; life mem NAACP; mem Museum of African Amer History, Bd of Mgmt YWCA 1972-79 1980-84; chairperson Bd of Mission Educ & Social Action 1976-80, vice moderator, church council 1991-, chp, diaconate 1991, Mayflower Congregational United Church of Christ; mem Div of Mission Detroit Metro Assn United Church of Christ; chairperson Women's Day Comm Mayflower cong UCC 1984; mem bd dirs Delta Home for Girls 1968-78; mem bd of dirs Federation of Girls homes 1975-78; recording sec March of Dimes Fashion Extravaganza 1970-75; memN-Detroit Arts Comm 1982-89; exhibited in juried calligraphy shows; 1st vice pres, Top Ladies of Distinction, 1987-88. Clark Atlanta University Alumni Association. **Honors/Awds:** Artist of the Month, Afro-Amer Museum of Detroit 1975; Community Service Award, 1993. **Home Addr:** 19501 Hubbell, Detroit, MI 48235.

CARTER, OSCAR EARL, JR.
Physician. **Personal:** Born Aug 2, 1922, Chesterbrook, VA; married Edna; children: Oscar III, Don, Donna, Kim. **Educ:** Meharry Med Coll, MD 1952; Dillard U, BA 1948. **Career:** Lower 9 Methadone Clinic Inc, med dir sponsor; physician family prac 1959-76; Well Baby Clinics Eastside Hlth Dist, dir 1954-59; gen prac 1953-59; Lower 9 Methadone Clinic Inc, dir 1970-76; Desire Narcotics Rehab Ctr, med dir 1971-72; Com Alcoholism & Drug Abuse, med coord 1971-72. **Orgs:** Mem Sanity Commn Sect I Criminal Dist Ct 1971-72; Drug Abuse Rehab Team; consult SUNO'S Dept Drug Abuse; Dist I Adv Bd La; adv bd bur Drug Affairs New Orleans; New Orleans Med Soc; Nat Med Assn Cert Drug Abuse; Univ Miami Dept Urban Studies 1972; LSU Med Sch Dept Continuing Med Educ 1975. **Business Addr:** 2017 Caffin, New Orleans, LA 70117.

CARTER, PAMELA LYNN
State government official. **Personal:** Born Aug 20, 1949, South Haven, MI; daughter of Dorothy Elizabeth Hadley Fanning and Roscoe Hollis Fanning; married Michael Anthony Carter, Aug 21, 1971; children: Michael Anthony Jr, Marcya Alicia. **Educ:** University of Detroit, BA (cum laude), 1971; University of Michigan, MSW, 1973; Indiana University, JD, 1984. **Career:** University of Michigan, School of Public Health, research analyst, treatment director, UAW, Detroit, 1973-75; Mental Health Center for Women and Children, executive director, 1975-77; UAW-General Motors Legal Services, Indianapolis, consumer litigation attorney, 1983-87; Secretary of State, Indiana, securities attorney, 1987-89; Governor of Indiana, executive assistant for health and human services, starting 1989; State of Indiana, attorney general, 1992-. **Orgs:** Indiana Bar Assn, 1984-; Catholic Social Services; Junior League; Natl Bar Assn; Coalition of 100 Black Women. **Special Achievements:** First African American female to become a State's Attorney General. **Business Addr:** Attorney General, State of Indiana, 219 State House, 200 Washington, Indianapolis, IN 46209, (317)232-6201.

CARTER, PAT
Professional football player. **Personal:** Born Aug 1, 1966, Sarasota, FL; married Charlene; children: Jamelle, Alec. **Educ:** Florida State, attended. **Career:** Detroit Lions, tight end, 1988; Los Angeles Rams, 1989-93; Houston Oilers, 1994; St Louis Rams, 1995; Arizona Cardinals, 1996-. **Business Addr:** Professional Football Player, Arizona Cardinals, 8701 S Hardy, Tempe, AZ 85284, (602)379-0101.

CARTER, PATRICK HENRY, JR.
Sports team executive. **Personal:** Born Jan 8, 1939, Memphis, TN; son of Annie Carter and Patrick Carter; married Mattie Pearl Bland; children: Kimberly, Patrick H III. **Educ:** Attended, Mississippi Valley State Univ, LeMoyne Coll, General Motors Inst. **Career:** Exxon USA, instructor 1972; Pat Carter Pontiac Inc, president; Superior Services, partner 1990-; Memphis Rockets Basketball Team, owner; Olympic Staffing Inc, owner, 1993-. **Orgs:** Exec bd Liberty Bowl 1982-; bd mem Boy Scouts of America 1986; bd mem Memphis in May 1990; bd mem Memphis Urban League 1990-95; bd mem Public Bldg Authority 1988-94; bd mem Senior Citizens 1990-95; Chamber of Commerce, 1992-94; pres, Whitehaven Community Development Corporation, 1994-; deacon, Middle Baptist Church, 1970-. **Honors/Awds:** Achiever Pontiac Motor Div 1984-86; Top 100 Black Businesses, Black Enterprise Magazine, 1984, 1985, 1986, 1987; Small Business of the Year (25-75 employees), Memphis Business Journal 1988. **Military Serv:** USN petty officer second class, 4 yrs. **Business Addr:** Owner, Olympic Staffing Inc, 2050 Elvis Presley Blvd, Memphis, TN 38106.

CARTER, PERCY A., JR.
Clergyman. **Personal:** Born Jul 4, 1929, Hampton, VA; married Evelyn; children: Allen, Audrey, Mildred, Mark, Daniel. **Educ:** VA Union U, AB 1949; Harvard Sch of Bus Adminstrn, 1951-52; M Div Andover-Newton, 1953; Boston Univ Sch of Theology, MST 1953; Harvard Divinity Sch, 1953-55; Brown U, 1958-59. **Career:** Olney St Bapt Ch Providence RI, formerly pastored; Mt Calvary Bapt Ch Mansfield OH; Hosack St Bapt Ch Columbus OH, pastor, currently; Eastern Union Bible College of Columbus, OH, instructor, currently. **Orgs:** Mem Bapt Pastor's Conf; mem Ministerial Alliance; mem Interdenom of Ministerial Alliance of Columbus OH; Met Area Church Bd Affiliate; broadcasts on radio weekly; previously served as substitute tchr on secondary level in pub sch; past chmn Mansfield Alliance for Progress; past chmn & founder Opport Indusl Cntr of Mansfield OH. **Honors/Awds:** Contrib "What Jesus Means to Me", "Seven Black Preachers" 1971. **Military Serv:** USAF 1963-68. **Business Addr:** Pastor, Hosack Street Baptist Church, 1160 Watkins Rd, Columbus, OH 43207.

CARTER, PERRY LYNN
Professional football player. **Personal:** Born Aug 15, 1971, McComb, MS; married; children: one. **Educ:** Southern Mississippi. **Career:** Kansas City Chiefs, defensive back, 1995; Oakland Raiders, 1996-. **Business Addr:** Professional Football Player, Oakland Raiders, 1220 Harbor Bay Pkwy, Alameda, CA 94502, (510)615-1875.

CARTER, PERRY W.
Data systems officer. **Personal:** Born May 24, 1960, Washington, DC; son of Viola Green Carter and Charles P Carter. **Educ:** US Air Force Acad Prep School, Colorado Springs CO, 1978-79; US Air Force Acad, Colorado Springs CO, 1979-81; Temple Univ, Philadelphia PA, BA, 1985; Golden Gate Univ, Ft Myer VA, 1988-. **Career:** US Marine Corps, Washington DC, data systems officer, 1985-; Joint Education Facilities Inc, Washington DC, instructor, 1989-; Meridian Publishing, Washington DC, CEO, 1989-, chmn of the bd, 1989-. **Orgs:** Public affairs dir, Natl Naval Officers Assn, 1987-; asst editor, Journal of Black Data Processing Assoc, 1988-; editor, Articles of the Coalition, Washington DC Coalition of Black Professional Org, 1989-. **Honors/Awds:** Co-founder, Temple Univ Student Chapter, BDPA, 1984; Outstanding Young Men of America, 1986, 1988; founding editor, NNOA Meridian, 1987, Articles of the Coalition, 1989; founder, chairman, CEO, Meridian Publishing Inc, 1989. **Military Serv:** USAF, USMC, First Lt, 1978-; Certificate of Commendation, 1987.

CARTER, PHILIP W., JR.
Educational administration. **Personal:** Born Feb 1, 1941, Widen, WV; married Beverly Thomas; children: Philippa, Stacey, Frederick. **Educ:** Marshall Univ, BA Pol Sci 1964; Univ of Pittsburgh, MSW 1970. **Career:** Congress of Racial Equality, dir Cleveland 1967-68; Univ of Pittsburgh Graduate School of Public Intl Affairs, instr 1970-78; Comm Action Reg Training, dir 1972-73; Univ of Pittsburgh, asst to the provost 1979; DIGIT Inc, pres 1967-; Marshall Univ, dir soc work prog. **Orgs:** Consult Intercultural House Univ of Pittsburgh 1969-70; consult Clarion Univ of PA 1973,76,80,81,83,84,85; campaign mgr Mel King for Mayor in Boston 1979; bd mem Schuman Juvenile Ctr 1979-81; bd mem Human Relations Commiss 1982-; bd mem Barnett Day Care Ctr Huntington WV 1982-84; chairman Western PA Black Polit Assembly 1974-; campaign mgr Doris Smith for Judge Spring 1985. **Honors/Awds:** Recipient Ford Found Fellowshp 1968; Outstanding Man of the Year Talk Mag 1974; Outstanding Contrib in Politics Black Republicans 1978; Outstanding Black Alumni Marshall Univ 1978; recognized by Herald Dispatch Newspaper as Major Architect of 1960's Student Movement 1983; Summa Cum Lauda in Tchng Excellence Marshall Univ Minority Affairs 1985. **Business Addr:** Director, Social Work Program, Marshall Univ, 749 Smith Hall, Huntington, WV 25701.

CARTER, PHYLLIS HARDEN
State government official. **Personal:** Born Oct 28, 1948, Norfolk, VA; daughter of Mable Harden and Wilbur Harden; married Hazo W Carter Jr, Aug 8, 1981; children: Angela Mable Elizabeth. **Educ:** Institute of European Studies, Paris, France, 1969-70; L'Alliance Francaise, Paris, France, 1970; St Augustine's College, BA, history and French, 1971; College of William and Mary, Marshall-Wythe School of Law, JD, 1975. **Career:** Little Rock, Arkansas, assistant city attorney; Charleston, West Virginia, assistant attorney general; West Virginia Human Rights Commission, director; Department of Human Services, commissioner; State-Federal Relations, Office of the Governor, Charleston, West Virginia, director, currently. **Orgs:** Delta Sigma Theta Sorority, Inc, president, Charleston-Institute Alumnae Chapter, 1990-92, Social Action Commission, 1992-94; American Red Cross, Central West Virginia, 1992-95; Black Diamond Girl Scouts, 1989-93; Appalachian Education Laboratory, 1991-93; Methodist Charities of West Virginia, 1989-93; West Virginia Literacy Council, 1991-94. **Honors/Awds:** Outstanding Personalities of the South, 1984; City Council of Little Rock, Arkansas, Commendation, 1987; Governor Bill Clinton, Merit Award, 1987; National Organization of Women, West Virginia Chapter, Outstanding African American Women in the Kanawna Valley, 1991. **Special Achievements:** Author: "Judge George Howard," Arkansas Lawyer, 1987; "Scholars, Balancing Out the Under Representation," Arkansas Lawyer, 1987; "Has the Color Barrier Fallen," Arkansas Lawyer, 1988. **Home Addr:** PO Box 622, Institute, WV 25112. **Business Addr:** Director of State and Federal Relations, State of West Virginia, Officer of the Governor, 1900 Kanawha Blvd E, Bldg 1, Charleston, WV 25305-0370, (304)558-3829.

CARTER, RAYMOND GENE, SR.
Educator. **Personal:** Born Nov 12, 1936, Youngstown, OH; married Virginia Averhart; children: Raymond Gene, John Amos, Dewayne Dwight. **Educ:** Youngstown State U, BA 1959, MEd 1975; Univ of Pittsburgh, PhD candidate. **Career:** McGuffey Ctr Inc, admin dir, 1976-86; Youngstown State Univ, ltd serv faculty 1976-; Model City, dep dir; Curbstone Coaches, bd dir; Youngstown State Univ, limited serv faculty political & social dept; Parkview Counseling Ctr, currently. **Orgs:** Minority rep Stub Canal Private Sector; chmn Welf Adv Bd; Social Serv; bd dir Asso Neighborhood Ctr; vice pres bd dir Meth Comm Ctr; Eval Com - Area Health; bd dir C of C; mem Kiwanis Club; Big Brothers; bd dir Eastern Mental Health High Sch; mem Selective Svc; foreman Mahoning County Jury 1981. **Honors/Awds:** Leadership & Citizenship Award; Coll Most Valuable Athlete; Curbstone Coaches Hall of Fame Youngstown; Athletic Achievement Awd Serv Awd Youngstown City Mayor; Community Serv Awd Black Knight Police Assoc; Choffin Career Ctr Award, 1988; Youngstown State Univ Football Hall of Fame, 1997. **Military Serv:** AUS 1960-62. **Business Addr:** Parkview Counsleing Center, 611 Belmont Avenue, Youngstown, OH 44502.

CARTER, ROBERT HENRY, III
Insurance company executive. **Personal:** Born Aug 2, 1941, Chicago, IL; married Marlene Y Hunt; children: Robert H IV, Kimberly, Brandon Robert. **Educ:** Chicago City Colleges, attended 1962; Worshams Coll of Mortuary Science, attended 1963; IL Inst of Technology, attended 1964. **Career:** Lawndale Packaging Corp, sales mgr 1971-72; Chicago Minority Purchasing Council, purchasing specialist 1972-75; Robert H Carter, III & Assocs, Inc, pres 1975-; Group Insurance Administration Inc, pres 1982-. **Orgs:** Mem Cosmopolitan Chamber of Commerce 1972-, Chicago Urban League 1975-, Chicago Assoc of Commerce & Industry 1979-, Self Insurance Inst of Amer 1983, Soc of Professional Benefit Administrators 1984-, Professional Ins Marketing Assn 1986-. **Honors/Awds:** Ten Outstanding Young Men of Chicago Jaycees, 1974. **Business Addr:** President, Group Insuance Admn Inc, 850 W Jackson, Chicago, IL 60607.

CARTER, ROBERT LEE
Judge. **Personal:** Born Mar 11, 1917, Caryville, FL; widowed; children: John, David. **Educ:** Lincoln Univ, AB 1937; Howard Univ, LLB (Magna Cum Laude) 1940; Columbia Univ, LLM 1941; Lincoln Univ, DCL 1964. **Career:** NAACP Legal Defense and Education Fund, asst counsel, 1945-56; NAACP, gener al counsel, 1956-68; Poletti, Freiden, Prashker, Feldman & Gartner, member of f irm, 1969-72; US District Ct, So District, judge, 1972-. **Orgs:** Mem NY Bar Assn 1941-; mem New York City Mayor's Jucic Comm 1968-72; educ bd NY Law Journ 1969-72; pres Natl Comm Against Descrim in Housing 1966-72; mem NY State Spl Comm on Attica, NY Ct Reform

1970-72; mem Natl Conf Black Lawyers. **Honors/Awds:** Recipient Howard Univ Disting Alumni Award 1980; Fellow Columbia Urban Center 1968-69; Resenwald Fellow 1940-41; Lincoln Univ, Honorary Doctor o f Laws, 1965; NorthEastern Univ, Honorary Doctor of Laws, 1985; Holy Cross, Hon orary Doctor of Laws, 1990; Howard Univ, Honorary Doctor of Laws, 1994. **Military Serv:** USAF 2nd Lt 1941-44. **Business Addr:** Judge, U S Dist Ct So District, U S Courthouse, Foley Square, New York, NY 10007.

CARTER, ROBERT LOUIS, JR.
Educator, educational administrator. **Personal:** Born Nov 11, 1937, Loganville, GA; son of Elizabeth Carter and Robert Louis Carter; married Cathleen Jane Cole, Jun 4, 1974; children: Robert Louis, William Stephen, Joyce Elizabeth, Valerie Denise. **Educ:** Beloit College, classics, 1962; Northwestern University, classics, 1964, 1980. **Career:** University of Illinois, classics instructor; Beloit College, classics instructor, director of High Potential Program, executive director of the Beloit Improvement Coalition, 1971-73, special assistant to the provost, 1969-73; Associated Colleges of the Midwest, director, Educational Development Program, 1973-83; Wayne State University, director, University Studies, Weekend College Program, 1984-86, associate dean for Adult Degree Programs, 1986-87, dean, College of Lifelong Learning, 1988-. **Orgs:** Coordinating Council for Continuing Higher Education, chair, 1991-; Mid-America Association of Educational Opportunity Program Personnel, president, 1981, president-elect, 1980, past president 1983, executive secretary, 1984; National Council of Educational Opportunity Associations, board of directors, 1980-82; National University Continuing Education Association, 1987-; Association of Continuing Higher Education. **Honors/Awds:** MAEOPP, Outstanding Service & Leadership, 1981; Northwestern University Fellowship, 1962-65; Wisconsin Higher Educational Aids Board, executive board, 1982-84. **Special Achievements:** Systematic Thinking Curriculum, Kendall/Hunt Publishing Co, 1980; ''The Role of Formal Syntax in Critical Thinking,'' MAEOPP Journal of Educational Opportunity, 1986; ''Uncle Tom and the Pedestal,'' Chicago Defender, 1968. **Business Addr:** Dean, College of Lifelong Learning, Wayne State University, 6001 Cass, Rm 200, Detroit, MI 48202, (313)577-4675.

CARTER, ROBERT T.
Business executive. **Personal:** Born Mar 21, 1938, Cleveland, OH; married Virginia; children: Robert John. **Educ:** Baldwin Wallace Coll, BA 1959; Pepperdine Grad Sch of Business. **Career:** KFI Radio Inc, accnt exec 1968-; Hoffman LaRoche, sales & hosp rep 1966-68; Shell Oil Co Long Beach, sales rep 1964-66; Cleveland, tchr 1959-64. **Orgs:** Mem Natl Assn Market Developers; Radio Salesman of LA; mem Southern California Broadcasters; mem LA Brotherhood Crusade; New Frontier Dem Club; United Crusade Fund Raising Comm 1974-75; Leukemia Soc of Amer; Southern California Striders Track Club. **Honors/Awds:** Martha Jennings Teaching Award 1963; Pharmaceuticals Sales Award LaRoche 1968; California delegate to Democratic Convention 1968; California Democratic Council 1968; Democratic State Central Comm 1968. **Business Addr:** 610 S Ardmore, Los Angeles, CA 90005.

CARTER, ROBERT THOMPSON
Education program executive. **Personal:** Born Mar 16, 1937, Cleveland, OH; son of Evelyn Carter (deceased) and Robert Carter (deceased); married Tessa Rosemary Felton; children: Robert, Jacqueline. **Educ:** Dartmouth Coll, BA 1959. **Career:** Joseph T Ryerson & Son Inc, supervisor personnel admin 1967-68, mgr comm relations 1968-70; North Lawndale Econ Devel Corp, asst genl mgr 1970-72; Inland Steel Develop Corp, asst regional mgr & project mgr 1972-77; Inland Steel-Ryerson Foundation, exec dir, sec 1981-86; Dearborn Park Corp, vice pres corp communications and corp sec 1977-81; Natl Merit Scholarship Corp, exec dir, 1987-88, vice pres, 1988-. **Orgs:** Co-fndr Black Contractors United 1979; bd chairperson Just Jobs Inc 1982-86; dir Performance Comm 1982-86; vice pres Assoc of Black Foundation Execs 1984-86; founding mem/dir Indiana Donors Alliance 1984-86; corp adv bd Independent Coll Funds of Amer 1984-86; vice pres Music/Theatre Workshop 1986-; dir Brass Foundation Inc 1987; dir Blacks in Development 1987-; trustee, Gaylord & Dorothy Donnelley Foundation 1988-; Horizon Hospice, director, 1992-. **Honors/Awds:** Leadership Awd Black Contractors United 1979; Beautiful People Awd Chicago Urban League 1980. **Military Serv:** USAF capt 1959-66; Air Force Commendation Medal 1964. **Business Addr:** VP, Achievement Program, National Merit Scholarship Corp, 1560 Sherman Ave, Suite 200, Evanston, IL 60201-4897.

CARTER, ROMELIA MAE
Chief executive officer. **Personal:** Born Jan 1, 1934, Youngstown, OH; divorced. **Educ:** Youngstown State Univ, BA 1974; WV Univ, MSW 1976. **Career:** Youngstown Comm Action Council, comm org 1967-70; Youth Devel Agency, proj dir children & family serv 1976-79; Assoc Neighborhood Ctrs, exec dir. **Orgs:** Mem Natl Assoc Black Soc Workers, Mattoning Cty Assoc of Counselors, Delta Sigma Theta Sor, Youngstown Urban League; issues chmn Youngstown Chap of OH Black Womens Leadership Caucus; mem Natl Council of Negro Women. **Honors/Awds:** N Side Youth Serv Awd N Side Youth Council 1970; Serv Awd N Side Oldtimers 1972; Warren Black Youth Serv Awd Warren Black Youth 1974; Civic Soc Awd OH Black Womens Leadership Caucus 1976; Comm Serv Awd Child & Adult Mental Health Ctr 1977. **Business Addr:** Community Organizer, Assoc Neighborhood Centers, 755 Lexington Ave, Youngstown, OH 44510.

CARTER, RUTH DURLEY
Orthodonist. **Personal:** Born Apr 1, 1922, LaFollette, TN; children: Ann, Bekka. **Educ:** Meharry Med Coll Sch of Dentistry, DDS 1948; Orthodontic Sch St Louis U, post grad 1958. **Career:** Self-employed orthodontist; Mound City Dental Soc. **Orgs:** Past pres Mound City Dental Soc; past pres Mid-Western St Dental assn; past mem Assoc Amer Women Dentists; Delta Sigma; Theta Sor; vice pres Comm Rel Educ Found 1966. **Honors/Awds:** 1st female honored Mid-Western St Dental Assn; 1st black St Louis Dental Soc. **Business Addr:** 1326 Avalon Blvd, Wilmington, CA 90744.

CARTER, THEODORE ULYSSES
Attorney. **Personal:** Born Oct 16, 1931, Birmingham; married Joyce A; children: Theodore N, Julia W. **Educ:** Howard U, BA 1955; JD 1958; NY U, postgrad 1962-63. **Career:** PA NJ bars, atty; IRS Phila, atty 1961-; Glassboro NJ State Coll, adj prof justice. **Orgs:** Vol counsel Camden Legal Servs 1970-; mem Am Jud & Soc; Am Nat PA NJ Bar Assns; Howard Univ Alumni Assn.

CARTER, THOMAS
Professional football player. **Personal:** Born Sep 5, 1972, St Petersburg, FL; married Renee; children: Alexander, Madison. **Educ:** Notre Dame, attended. **Career:** Washington Redskins, defensive back, 1993-96; Chicago Bears, 1997-. **Business Addr:** Professional Football Player, Chicago Bears, 1000 Football Dr, Halas Hall at Conway Park, Lake Forest, IL 60045-4829, (847)295-6600.

CARTER, THOMAS, II (T. C)
Attorney at Law. **Personal:** Born Feb 27, 1953, St Louis, MO; son of Thomas & Everline Carter; married Dorothy L Carter, Sep 25, 1972; children: LaDon D Carter. **Educ:** Univ of Maryland, BS, 1980; St Louis Univ School of Law, JD, 1983. **Career:** Law Officers of Bussey & Jordan, law clerk, 1981-93, assoc, 1993-94; Office of the Attorney General, asst attorney general, 1984-85; Moser & Marsalek, PC associate, 1985-92, shareholder, 1992-95; Collier, Dorsey, Carter, Williams, partner, 1995-. **Orgs:** American Bar Assn, 1980-; MO Bar Assn, 1984-; Bar Assn of Metropolitan St Louis, 1985-; Mound City Bar Assn, 1985-, president, 1991-92; MO Organization of Defense Lawyers, 1985-; Assn of Defense Counsel of St Louis, 1985-; The Natl Bar Assn, 1986-; IL State Bar Assn, 1986-. **Honors/Awds:** State of MO, License, 1984; US District Court of Eastern MO, Admission, 1985; US District Court of Western MO, Admission, 1985; State of IL, License, 1986; US Court of Appeals, 8th Circuit, Admission, 1987. **Special Achievements:** Lawyers Role - Political Empowerment: the Struggle Continues Minorities & Women, St Louis Daily Records, May 1, 1990. **Military Serv:** US Air Force, ssgt, 1972-80; Two Air Force Commendation Medals. **Business Addr:** Attorney at Law, Collier, Dorsey, Carter & Williams, 625 N Euclid, Ste 402, St Louis, MO 63108-1660, (314)367-6888.

CARTER, THOMAS ALLEN
Consultant. **Personal:** Born Jul 12, 1935, Cincinnati, OH; son of Mary Gladys Gover Carter and Fernando Albert Carter; married Janet Tucker, Oct 14, 1956; children: Barry E, Duane A, Sarita A. **Educ:** Jones Coll, AB (cum laude) 1980, BBA (cum laude) 1982. **Career:** Red Lobster Restaurant Const Dept, contract administrator 1976-78; Harcar, Inc, pres 1978-80; Blacando Develop Corp, exec sec 1980-84; Solomon A Williams Inc, project engr 1984-, chief engineer, currently. **Orgs:** Consult cost estimating JH Dunlap Roofing Co 1978-84, Robinson's Custom Homes 1980-84; mem Bluejackets Choir USN, Bluejackets Octet USN, Fleet Reserve Association; Rafman Club, Inc. **Honors/Awds:** Sailor of the Year 9th Naval Dist 1960; SeaBee of the Month Argentia Newfoundland Canada 1965; Certified Construction Inspector. **Military Serv:** USN master chief constructionman, 22yrs; Navy Commendation, Naval Unit Citation, Vietnam Expo, Good Conduct Medals (5), Presidential Unit Citation, Expert Rifleman. **Home Addr:** 4128 Arajo Ct, Orlando, FL 32812. **Business Addr:** Chief Engineer, Soloman A Williams Inc, 7041 Grand National Drive, Orlando, FL 32819.

CARTER, TONY
Professional football player. **Personal:** Born Aug 23, 1972, Columbus, OH. **Educ:** Univ of Minnesota. **Career:** Chicago Bears, running back, 1994-. **Business Addr:** Professional Football Player, Chicago Bears, 1000 Football Dr, Halas Hall at Conway Park, Lake Forest, IL 60045-4829, (847)295-6600.

CARTER, TROY A.
Government representative, engineering executive. **Personal:** Born Oct 26, 1963, New Orleans, LA; son of Eartha F Carter and Theodore R Carter. **Educ:** BA, political science/business administration, 1986; Carnegie-Mellon School of Urban and Public Affairs, MPA. **Career:** Executive assistant to mayor of New Orleans; Louisiana state representative, currently; WD Scott Group Inc Environmental Engineering Consultants, vice pres, currently. **Orgs:** Big Brothers/Big Sisters, board of directors; National Youth Sport Foundation, board of directors; Orleans Parish Democratic Executive Committee, chairman district C; 100 Black Men of New Orleans, charter member; NAACP; National Organization of Black Public Administration; Kappa Alpha Psi Fraternity, Inc. **Special Achievements:** Featured in Ebony Magazine as 1 of 30 leaders of America; featured in Jet Magazine for being first African-American elected Dist. 102; sponsored and passed legislation banning guns around schools (within 1,000 yards), creating a gun-free zone around all schools in LA. **Home Addr:** 2319 Easter Lane, New Orleans, LA 70114, (504)392-6213.

CARTER, VINCENT G.
Company executive, educator, interior designer. **Personal:** Born Feb 22, 1956, Milwaukee, WI; son of Lessie M & Walter A Carter Sr; divorced. **Educ:** Univ of Wisconsin-Milwaukee, BA, 1977; Univ of Wisconsin-Madison, MS, 1983. **Career:** Visual Graphics Created, designer, 1980-; The World Bank, client rep, 1983-95; Howard Univ, asst prof, 1984-; Vincent G. Carter Associates, Inc, principal, 1994-; senior interior designer, Karn Charuhas Chapman Twohey Architects, 1997. **Orgs:** Amer Soc of Interior Designers, 1980-; Natl Council for Interior Design Qualifications, 1991-; Natl Legislative Coalition for Interior Design, 1992-; Interior Design Educator's Council, 1990-; Intl Facilities Mgmt Assn, 1988-; Intl Interior Design Assn, 1991-; Washington, DC Bd of Interior Designers, Chair, 1993-97; mem, Woodlawn Plantation/Pope-Leighey House Council, 1997-. **Honors/Awds:** Omicron Nu National Honor Society Scholarship, 1980; Phi Upsilon Omicron National Honor Society, Scholarship, 1981; America's Best & Brightest Young Business Professionals, 1990; Howard Univ Teaching Award, 1994. **Home Phone:** (202)265-7916. **Business Addr:** 2208 First St NW, Washington, DC 20001-1016.

CARTER, WARRICK L.
Educator, composer. **Personal:** Born May 6, 1942, Charlottesville, VA; son of Evelyn Carter and Charles M Carter; married Laurel (Latta) Carter, Apr 17, 1993; children: Keisha. **Educ:** TN State Univ, BS; Blair Acad of Music, Advanced Percussion 1964-65; MI State Univ, MM 1966, PhD 1970; Univ of Chicago, Certificate in Fund Raising 1978. **Career:** Univ of MD, asst prof dept of music 1966, 1967, 1971; MI State Univ, dir dept of music 1970, 1971; Governors State Univ, coordinator in fine & performing 1971-76, coord music program 1976-79; Northwestern Univ, guest prof Afro-Amer Studies 1977-84; Governors State Univ, chmn div Fine & Performing Arts 1979-84; Univ of Santa Cantarina Florianopolis Brazil, guest lecturer dept music 1980; Berklee Coll of Music, dean of faculty 1984-95; CA State Univ LA, visiting prof, Music Dept; School of Music Univ of Sao Paulo Brazil, guest lecturer, 1976; Berklee School of Music, provost/vice pres of academic affairs, 1995-96; Walt Disney Attractions, dir of academic arts, 1996-. **Orgs:** past pres NAJE 1982-84; chmn Jazz Panel Natl Endow for the Arts 1982-85; co-chair Music Policy Panel Natl Endowment for the Arts 1983-84; natl sec Black Music Caucus 1974-78; ASCAP; bd mem Natl Jazz Cable Network 1982-84; bd mem Found for the Advancement of Music 1982; on adv bds of MusicFest USA and EPCOT Inst of Entertainment Arts; bd of directors, International House of Blues Foundation, 1993-; IAJE, 1982-. **Honors/Awds:** Distinguished Teacher Award Gov's State Univ 1974; Best Drummer Award Collegiante Jazz Festival Notre Dame Univ 1970; Faculty Mem of the Yr Univ of MD 1967-68; Graduate Fellow Center of Urban Affairs MI State Univ 1969-70; named as one of ten Outstanding Music Educators by School Musician 1983; ''The Whistle'' commissioned by the Natl Endowment for the Arts, 1982-83; IAJE, Hall of Fame, 1997. **Business Addr:** Director of Entertainment Arts, Walt Disney Attractions, PO Box 10000, Lake Buena Vista, FL 32830-1000.

CARTER, WEPTANOMAH WASHINGTON
Educator, author, executive. **Personal:** Born Feb 15, 1937, Ossining; married Harold A; children: Weptanomah, Harold A, Jr. **Educ:** Millersville State Tchr Coll, BS 1959; VA Sem Lynchburg, M of Divinity 1975; VA Sem Lynchburg, D of Lit 1977. **Career:** MD Bapt Sch of Rel, dean of church admin 1976-; MD Bapt Sch of Rel, instructor 1971-76; The Carter Foundation, pres. **Orgs:** Mem Bd of Trustees Community Coll of Baltimore 1977-83; co-ordinator of Christian Outreach New Shilow Bapt Ch1975-; announeer for radio ministry New Shiloh Bapt Ch; pres The Carter Found Inc. **Honors/Awds:** Afro Honor Roll for Superior Service; Baltimore Afro-Am Newspapers 1971; author ''The Black Ministers Wife''; Progressive Nat Pub Co 1976; Woman of the Year-Hon Mention Greyhound Corp 1976; Distinguished Serv Award Millersville Alumni Assn 1978; author ''For Such A Time As Time'' Gateway Press 1980.

CARTER, WESLEY BYRD
Child psychiatrist. **Personal:** Born Apr 22, 1942, Richmond, VA; son of Mr and Mrs Wesley T Carter; married Norma Archer. **Educ:** VA Union U, BS 1964; Med Coll of VA, 1968; Med Coll of VA, pediatric internship 1969; Gen Psychiatry

Residency, MCV 1971; VA Treatment Ctr for Children, child psychiatry fellowship 1973. **Career:** Richmond Pub Schools, psych cons; Caroline County Public Schools, psych cons; Friends Assn of Richmond, psych cons; Psych Med Coll of VA, asst clinical prof; Real School Richmond Pub Schools, spec cons; St Mary's Hosp, Stuart Circle, Richmond Meml, Richmond Comm Hosp, Richmond Metro Hosp, Westbrook Hosp, Psych Inst of Richmond, Med Coll of VA, Chippenham Hosp, hosp appts; Psych Inst of Richmond Childrens Unit, med chief, 1983-87; Child Psych Ltd, child psych 1975-83; Horizons Inc, pres, 1986-93; Psychiatric Inst of Richmond, acting med dir, 1986; Charter Westbrook Hosp, clinical dir of adult services, 1987, clinical dir of RTP, 1989-92, acting medical dir, 1990; Host Radio Show Whats on Your Mind, WANI Richmond. **Orgs:** Mem Yth Serv Commin Richmond; Spcl Educ Adv Com; Richmond Public Schools; Med Coll of VA Soph Med Curr Com; Richmond Acad of Med; past pres Richmond Med Soc; past pres VA Coun of Child Psychiatry; past pres-psychiatric Soc of VA; VA Soc for Adolescent Psychiatry; Med Soc of VA; Am Psychiat Assn; Am Acad of Child Psy; Black Psychiat of Am; Assn of Air Force Psychiat; Chi Delta Mu; Alpha Phi Alpha; Mental Health Assn of VA, bd of directors, 1991; mem Thebans of Richmond; mem Old Dominion Medical Soc; mem National Medical Assn; mem American Medical Assn; State Human Rights Committee of Virginia Dept of Mental Health, Mental Retardation & Substance Abuse Services; American Academy of Child and Adolescent Psychiatry. **Honors/Awds:** Fellow, Amer Psych Assn, Alpha Kappa Mu, Beta Kappa Chi. **Military Serv:** USAF 1973-75; Commendation Medal. **Home Phone:** (804)353-8006. **Business Addr:** Child Psychiatrist, Memorial Child Guidance Clinic, 2319 E Broad Street, Richmond, VA 23223, (804)649-1605.

CARTER, WILL J.
Transportation company executive. **Career:** Carter Industrial Services Inc and Carter Express Inc, Anderson, IN, chief executive.

CARTER, WILLIAM BEVERLY, III
International education specialist. **Personal:** Born Feb 22, 1947, Philadelphia, PA; son of Rosalie A Terry Carter and W Beverly Carter Jr; married Kay Sebekos; children: Terence. **Educ:** Univ Clge Nairobi Kenya 1965-66; Univ de Paris Sorbonne 1966; Howard Univ BA 1971; Johns Hopkins Univ Schl of Adv Intl Studies MA 1971-73. **Career:** US Comm on the Organization of Govt for Conduct of Foreign Policy, staff mem 1972-75; US Dept of State, escort interpreter 1972-75; Brookings Inst, res asst 1974-75; US Dept of Energy, foreign affairs officer 1976-81; Inst of Intl Educ, Professional Exchange Programs, senior program officer, currently. **Orgs:** Bd dir, Lupus Fnd of Greater Wash DC 1984-93; Natl Genealogical Soc 1974-; advisory board, Lupus Fnd of Greater Wash, 1993-; bd dir, National Council of International Visitors, NCIV, 1994-; chairman, National Advisory Committee on Diversity, NCIV, 1993-96. **Honors/Awds:** William C Foster Award JH Univ Schl of Advanced Intl Studies 1972-73, Rockefeller-Luce Fellowship 1971-73. **Military Serv:** AUS sgt; Bronze Star Ach 1967-70. **Home Addr:** 3117 Brooklawn Terrace, Chevy Chase, MD 20815. **Business Addr:** Program Officer, Professional Exchange Program, Institute of International Education, 1400 K St NW, Suite 650, Washington, DC 20005.

CARTER, WILLIAM THOMAS, JR.
Physician. **Personal:** Born Apr 27, 1944, Norfolk, VA; married Juatina M Redd; children: William III, Dominique Michelle, Tiasha Malitha. **Educ:** Fisk Univ, AB 1967; TN A&I State Univ, MS 1969; Meharry Medical Coll, MD 1973. **Career:** United States Navy, dir of emergency medicine. **Orgs:** Mem Kappa Alpha Psi Frat 1963-; dir of emergency medicine Natl Naval Medical Ctr 1980-82; mem Assoc of Military Surgeons of United States 1981-; ATLS instructor Amer Coll of Surgeons 1982-; mem Pigskin Club Inc 1984-, NAACP 1987-, Natl Medical Assoc 1987-, Amer Coll of Emergency Physicians 1987-. **Honors/Awds:** Publication "Gunshot Wounds to the Penis," NY Acad of Urology 1979. **Military Serv:** USN commander 9 yrs; Navy Commendation Medal, Meritorious Achievement 1984. **Home Addr:** 4411 Marquis Pl, Woodbridge, VA 22192. **Business Addr:** Dir of Emergency Medicine, United States Navy, Naval Medical Clinic, Quantico, VA 22134.

CARTER, WILLIE A.
Carpenter, associate president. **Personal:** Born Sep 5, 1909, Buckingham, CO; married Amanda Carey; children: Fannie, Ernest, James. **Career:** Prince Edward Co Br, pres. **Orgs:** NAACP; Mason; mem Human Relations; Prince Edward Co Voters League; Deacon Oak Grove Bapt Ch. **Honors/Awds:** VFW award; NAACP; past Worshipful Master Mason.

CARTER, WILMOTH ANNETTE
Educational administrator (retired). **Personal:** Born in Reidsville, NC; daughter of Margaret Lee Milner Carter (deceased) and William Percy Carter (deceased). **Educ:** Shaw Univ, BA 1937; Atlanta Univ, MA 1941; Univ of Chicago, PhD 1959; Shaw Univ, LHD 1986. **Career:** Atlanta Univ, grad asst, dept of soc, 1943-47; Shaw Univ, Raleigh, chmn, soc dept, 1959-63, chmn, soc sci div, 1966-69, educ devel officer, 1972-73, dir of research, 1969-72, vice pres inst research, 1973-76, vice pres acad app acad affairs & res, 1978-86; Univ of MI, res assoc, 1964-65; Tuskegee Inst, res assoc, 1965-66. **Orgs:** Mem Delta Kappa Gamma 1974-, Delta Sigma Theta Sor 1935-; Natl Council of Alpha Chi Scholarship Soc 1977-89. **Honors/Awds:** Honor soc Alpha Omicron Shaw Univ 1936-37; Alpha Kappa Delta Atlanta Univ 1941-42; Rosenwald Fellow Study at Univ of Chicago 1947-49, Danforth Fellow 1957-59; Delta Kappa Gamma 1973-; Alpha Chi Honor Society 1979-; author of The Urban Negro in the South, published 1961; author of The New Negro of the South, published 1967; author of Shaw's Universe, published 1973. **Home Addr:** 1400 E Davie St, Raleigh, NC 27610.

CARTER, YVONNE P.
Educator, artist. **Personal:** Born Feb 6, 1939, Washington, DC; daughter of Esther Robinson Pickering and Lorenzo Irving Pickering; married Joseph Payne (divorced); children: Cornelia Malisia. **Educ:** Howard Univ, BA 1962, MFA 1968; Traphagen School Design, NY, certificate Interior Design 1959. **Career:** Dist Display Washington, DC, display coordinator, 1962-63; Howard University, library assistant, 1963-68, assistant librarian, 1968-71; Fed City College, assistant professor of art; University of District of Columbia, Art Department, professor of art, currently; chairperson of the Dept of (MMUPA) Mass Media Visual & Performing Arts, 1995. **Orgs:** Mem Coll Art Assn 1971-; Am Assn Univ Prof 1974-; DC Registery 1973-74; Am Soc African Culture 1966; Natl Assn Study Negro Life & History 1971-72; Artists Equity, 1987-89; Women's Caucus for Art, 1976-; College Art Assoc, 1976-; WOCA, 1996-97; MOCA, 1996-97. **Honors/Awds:** Visual Artist Grant, DC Commission of the Arts & Humanities, 1981, 1982, 1995. Corrine Matchell Award (WCA/DC); Commonwealth Rev. George Mason U. 1990-92. Mobile Oil Grant, Artisisin Kazakstan. **Special Achievements:** Exhibitor, Howard Univ JA Porter Gallery, one-woman show 1973; Paintings WA Gallery Wash DC, two-woman show; Smith-Mason Gallery Nat Exhbn Black Artist Wash DC; selected group shows & performances: NJ State Museum black artist show; Howard Univ Art Gallery; Franz Bader Gallery Wash DC; Corcoran Gallery of Art; Miami-Dade Public Library; Los Angeles African-Amer Museum; Kenkelaba House, New York, NY; Baltimore Museum; Fendrick Gallery; Walters Art Gallery, MD; CA Afro-American Museum; Anacostia Museum Kenkeleba Gallery; NY, Bronx Museum of Arts; Natl Museum of Women in the Arts; Publ imprints by American Negro artists, 1962, 1965; Gumbo Yayya: Anthology of Contemporary African American Women Artists, 1989; Gathered Visions: Selected Works by African American Women Artists by Robert Hall 1990; "..My Magic Pours Secret Libations," by Monifa Love, 1996; "Environments of Spirit, Mind, and Space: The World We Create," Nathan Cummings Foundation, 1996. **Business Addr:** Professor, University of the District of Columbia, Art Dept, MB10-01, 4200 Connecticut Ave NW, Washington, DC 20008.

CARTER, ZACHARY WARREN
US attorney. **Personal:** Born Mar 19, 1950, Washington, DC; son of Joseph W & Margaret G Carter; married Rosalind Clay, Apr 4, 1992; children: Chandler Clay Carter. **Educ:** Cornell Univ, BA, 1972; NY Univ School of Law, JD, 1975. **Career:** EDNY Deputy Chief, Crim Div, asst US attorney, 1975-80; Patterson, Belknap, Webb & Tyler, gen litigation, 1980-81; DA Kings County DA's Office, exec asst, 1982-87; NYC Courts, exec asst to the deputy chief admin, 1987; Criminal Court, city of NY-Queens, County, judge, 1987-91; EDNY, US magistrate judge, 1991-93; US Dept of Justice, US attorney - EDNY, 1993-. **Orgs:** NY State Bar Assn, exec committee mem, crim law section; Assoc of the Bar, comm to encourage judicial service; Federal Bar Council, bd of trustees; NYU Law Foundation, bd of trustrees; Community Action for Legal Services, past vice chair, bd of dirs; Natl Black Prosecutors Assn, past vice pres. **Business Addr:** US Attorney, EDNY, US Attorney's Office - EDNY, 147 Pierrepont St, Brooklyn, NY 11201.

CARTHAN, EDDIE JAMES
Government official. **Personal:** Born Oct 18, 1949, Tchula, MS; married Shirley; children: Cissye, Neketa. **Educ:** MS Valley State U, BS 1971; Jackson State U, MS 1977; Univ MS. **Career:** Carthan's Convenience Store, owner mgr; Carthan's Pkg Store; Crystal Rest; Lexington Bus Serv Inc, bus specl 1973; Holmes Co Bd & Edn, pres 1973; St Coll, instr 1972. **Orgs:** Bd dir Delta Found; mem Gov Midas Com; King David Mason Lodge #112; Holmes Co Bd Edn; Holmes Co Elks. **Honors/Awds:** Pulbl "The Last Hired & First Fired"; "Success & Hard Work"; editor "If Things Could Talk"; "We've Come A Long Way, Baby"; "Bus Ruralite". **Business Addr:** PO Box 356, Tchula, MS 39169.

CARTHEN, JOHN, JR.
Automobile dealership owner. **Career:** River View Ford-Mercury Inc, owner, currently; Lakeland Ford-Lincoln-Mercury Inc, owner, currently. **Special Achievements:** Listed 42 of 100 top auto dealers, Black Enterprise, 1992. **Business Addr:** Owner, Lakeland Ford-Lincoln-Mercury, 901 North Park Ave, Herrin, IL 62948, (618)942-2102.

CARTLIDGE, ARTHUR J.
Educator. **Personal:** Born Jun 28, 1942, Rolling Fork, MS; married Helen Rose King; children: Byron Darnell, Arthur J, Jr, Kirsten Jamille. **Educ:** MS Valley State Univ, BS 1965; Delta State Univ, MS 1972; Spec Degree in Adm 1977. **Career:** T L Weston High School, teacher 1965-70; H W Solomon Jr High School, 1970-72, asst prin 1973-. **Orgs:** Mem Math Tchr Assn; Greenville Tchr Assn; Dist Tchr Assn; MS Tchr Assn; Nat Ed Assn; Nat Council of Secondary Prin; mem Uniserve Bd; #Jr warden Lake Vista Masonic Lodge; deacon; Mt Horeb Bapt Ch; mem Presidenths Comm; MVSU 1964-65. **Honors/Awds:** Outs Tchr of Year Weston HS 1969-70; Outs Tchr of Year Solomon Jr Hi 1970-71. **Business Addr:** 556 Bowman, Greenville, MS.

CARTWRIGHT, BILL (JAMES WILLIAM)
Professional basketball player (retired). **Personal:** Born Jul 30, 1957, Lodi, CA; married Sheri Johnson; children: Justin William, Jason James Allen, Kristen. **Educ:** University of San Francisco, BA. **Career:** New York Knicks, 1980-84, 1986-88, Chicago Bulls, 1989-94; Seattle Supersonics, beginning 1994; West Coast consultant, currently. **Orgs:** Charity work Easter Seals; Boys Hope, Chicago. **Honors/Awds:** Ranks 5th among NBA's all-time field goal perc shooters with his 557 Norm; matched the league record for most free throws without a miss going 19 for 19 vs KC at the Garden; first Knickerbocker ctr to start in every game; shattered USF single seas shooting perc mark with 667 pace as a junior; playing 14th year in the NBA; starting center, World Champion Chicago Bulls, 1991, 1992. **Business Addr:** West Coast Consultant, c/o Seattle Supersonics, PO Box 900911, Seattle, WA 98109.

CARTWRIGHT, CAROLE B.
Producer. **Personal:** Born Aug 3, 1940, Chicago, IL; daughter of Margaret Beard and Donald Beard; married Eugene; children: Karen, Shari. **Educ:** DePaul Univ, BS 1962. **Career:** KNBC-TV, dir of programing; WMAO-TV, mgr comm programs; "On Q" TV Program, WMAO-TV, exec producer/on air hostess, "As We See It-2" US Dept of Health Educ & Welfare, project dir, exec producer, 1977-79; WMAQ-TV, producer, 1970-77; Public Affairs Channel 5, Sec, 1962. **Orgs:** Bd dir, Ada McKinley Org; mem, Amer Women in Radio & TV; mem, Natl Assn of Media Women; Natl Broadcast Assn of Fomm Affairs; bd dir, The Bedside Network; Bd of Governors, Academy of TV, Arts & Sciences. **Honors/Awds:** Alpha Kappa Alpha Sorority Serv Award, Chicago School & workshop for Retarded, 1977; Outstanding Program Award, Natl Assn of TV Program Execs, 1976; Producer, Outstanding Children's Program Award, Medinah Shrine Temple, 1971.

CARTWRIGHT, CHARLES (CHIP)
Government official. **Personal:** Born Aug 4, 1948, Petersburg, VA; son of Charles W Sr and Dorothy S Cartwright; married Valorie, Jan 25, 1974; children: Shannon, Michael. **Educ:** Virginia Polytechnic Institute & State University, BS, forestry & wildlife management, 1970; US War College, Diploma, 1988. **Career:** US Department of Agrigculture, Forest Service, various positions, beginning 1967, regional forester, southwest region, 1994-. **Orgs:** Society of American Foresters; Boy Scouts of America; Virginia Polytechnic Institute & State University, School of Forestry & Wildlife Resources, advisory bd member; Pennsylvania State University; School of Forestry Resources, advisory bd member; Society of Range Management. **Honors/Awds:** Various Awards in achievement for the management of natural resources on public lands; The Boy Scouts of America Award for leadership and involvement in the community. **Special Achievements:** First African American District Forester, 1979; First African-American Forest Supervisor, 1988; First African-American Regional Forester, 1994. **Military Serv:** US Air Force, first lieutenant, 1971-73. **Business Addr:** Regional Forester, SW Region, US Dept of Agriculture, Forest Service, 517 Gold Ave, SW, Executive Suite, Albuquerque, NM 87102.

CARTWRIGHT, JAMES ELGIN
Securities company executive, banker. **Personal:** Born Jul 17, 1943, Memphis, TN; son of Rachel Richards Cartwright and James A Cartwright; children: Jennea. **Educ:** San Diego State Coll, BA 1963; Stanford Univ of Law, 2 yrs 1963-66; Oxford Univ-Trinity Coll, M Intl Law 1968. **Career:** SEC, legal 1968-69; Shearson Hammil & Co, compliance examiner-legal 1969-71; 1st Harlem Securities Inc, investment exec 1971-75; Daniels & Cartwright Inc, exec vice pres 1976-84; Cartwright & Daniels Inc, pres, 1984-; Pres, Cartwright Securities Inc, 1985-. **Orgs:** Consultant, Org of African Unity 1968-; consultant, Social & Econ Council UN, 1969; guest lecturer various high schools & colls in US, 1970-; mem, NAACP 1959-, Omega Psi Phi, 1970-, Council of Concerned Black Execs 1978-; mem NAACP 1959; mem 100 Black Men, Los Angeles Chapter 1988-; member, board of directors, National Association of Securities Professionals, 1990-. **Honors/Awds:** Oxford Fellowship Trinity Coll Oxford Eng 1966-68.

CARTWRIGHT, JOAN S.
Judge. **Personal:** married Lawrence R Neblett. **Educ:** Michigan State University, BA, 1965; University of Iowa College of Law, JD, 1976. **Career:** Alameda County Superior Court, judge, currently. **Business Addr:** Judge, Alameda County Superior Court, 1225 Fallon St, Oakland, CA 94612.

CARTWRIGHT, MARGUERITE DORSEY
Educator research. **Personal:** Born May 17, Boston, MA; married Leonard Carl Cartwright (deceased). **Educ:** Boston Univ, BS, MS; NY Univ, PhD 1948. **Career:** Hunter Coll of the City Univ of NY, teacher, lecturer; communications, journalism other media; adv educ in foregin countries; Phelps Stokes Inst, rsch. **Orgs:** Mem Provisional Council of Univ of Nigeria; served on various delegations & com; covered intl conf including Bandung Middle East African States African Peoples; state guest several Independence Celeb in Africa; mem Govs & Vice Pres Overseas Press Club of Amer bd mem Intl League for Human Rights & various civic orgns; mem UN Corres Assn; Women in Communications Inc; World Assn of Women Journalists & Writers other organs. **Honors/Awds:** Phi Beta Kappa other scholarly hons & awds; Headliners Awd 1975; Highest Natl Awd of Women in Communications Inc; Awds from Ford Found, Links, various civic & professional groups; Amoris Alumna Pax Pope Paul VI; Knight Commander Order of African Redemption Rep of Liberia; Keys to Cities Wilmington Xenia Zurich; street name in Nigeria for serv to Univ of Nigeria; subj of various feature articles. **Business Addr:** Phelps Stokes Inst, 10 East 87th St, New York, NY 10028.

CARTY-BENNIA, DENISE S.
Educator. **Personal:** Born Jun 28, 1947, Reed City, MI. **Educ:** Barnard Coll Columbia U, BA 1969; Sch of Law Columbia U, JD 1973. **Career:** Northeastern Univ School of Law, prof of law; Wayne State Univ Law School, pres, assoc prof of law 1975-77; Kaye/Scholer/Fierman/Hays & Handler, assoc atty 1973-75. **Orgs:** Mem Am Bar Assn, NY State Bar Assn, mem Nat Bar & Assn 1974; mem bd of dir Affirmative Action Coordinating Center, 1978-; co-chmn bd of dir NCBL 1979-; Minority Group Sec Assn of Am Law Sch 1975-; Faculty & Legal Advisor Nat Black Am Law Students Assn 1977-; Cooperating Atty Cntr For Constitutional Rights Research Fellow Inst for the Stury of Educ Policy Howard Univ 1978. **Honors/Awds:** Outstandint serv award Nat Black Am Law Students Assn 1979; presidents award, Nat Bar Assn 1979; revson fellow, Greenburg Center for Law & Soc Policy City Coll NY 1979-80; appreciation award, NE Region Black Am Law Students As, 1980; summer humanities seminar award, Nat Endowment for the Humanities, 1980.

CARUTHERS, PATRICIA WAYNE
Educational administrator (retired). **Personal:** Born Aug 28, 1939, Kansas City, KS; daughter of Mrs Evelyn W Caruthers and Dr Bertram Caruthers Sr. **Educ:** Emporia State Univ, BS 1962; Univ of MO Kansas City, MA 1965, PhD 1975. **Career:** US Dist #500, teacher 1962-69; Kansas City KS Comm Coll, teacher 1969-72, asst dean of cont educ 1972-76, asst to the pres 1978-92, vp, 1992-94; Donnelly Coll, pt-time instructor, 1997; Penn Valley Comm Coll, pt-time instructor, 1997. **Orgs:** Comm KCK Planning & Zoning Bd 1975-; govt intern Office of Educ HEW 1976-78; past pres Alpha Kappa Alpha Sorority, 1981-83; chmn KC KS Economic Devel Comm 1980-; regent KS Bd of Regents 1982-86; treas, Links Inc 1984-86; mem Kanas City Zoning Appeals Bd; mem, Youth Empowerment Task Force, 1994; mem, Kansas City Consensus, 1990-94; mem, Empowerment Zone Comm, 1994; commissioner, Kansas City Area Transportation Authority, 1994-; bd of dirs, Friends of the Union Station, 1994. **Honors/Awds:** Top Girl Winner Gr KC Science Fair 4th Place Tokyo 1957; Most Outstanding Young Woman in Amer 1976; Mary McLeod Bethune Alpha Phi Alpha Fraternity, 1982; Alumni Achievement Award, Univ of Missouri/Kansas City, 1994; School of Ed, Alumni Achievement Award, Univ of Missouri/Kansas City, 1994; AME Missionaries Higher Ed Award, 1995.

CARVER, PATRICIA ANNE
Consultant. **Personal:** Born Aug 29, 1950, Atlantic City, NJ; daughter of Gloria C Livingston Graham and Williard Bernard Hall Sr; children: Thomas H Miller III, Dion B Miller. **Educ:** Atlantic Community Coll, Mays Landing, NJ, AA, 1970; New York Univ, New York, NY, BS, 1972; Yeshiva Univ, New York, NY, 1973-75; Rutgers Univ, Newark, NJ, MPA, 1988. **Career:** Atlantic Community Coll, Mays Landing, NJ, counselor, 1972-73, dir, 1973-78; Atlanta Univ, Atlanta, GA, consultant, 1978-79, assoc dir, NCLD, 1979-81; Stockton State Coll, Pomona, NJ, admin rep, 1981-82, dir of admissions, 1982-88; Honeywell, Inc, Minneapolis, MN, mgr org devt, 1988-89, dir exec devt, 1989-91; Pecos River Learning Ctr, Santa Fe, NM, consultant, 1991-92; Carver and Associates, management consulting firm, president, 1992-. **Orgs:** Sec, Atlanta County Transportation Authority, 1983-86; pres, Stockton State Coll-Black Faculty & Staff, 1987-88; Galloway Township Bd of Education, 1985-88. **Honors/Awds:** 100 Top Black Women in Corporate Amer, Ebony Magazine, 1991; 84 People to Watch in 84, Atlantic City Magazine, 1984.

CARVER, SHANTE
Professional football player. **Personal:** Born Feb 12, 1971, Stockton, CA. **Educ:** Arizona State, attended. **Career:** Dallas Cowboys, defensive end, 1994-. **Business Addr:** Professional Football Player, Dallas Cowboys, One Cowboys Pkwy, Irving, TX 75063, (214)556-9900.

CARY, LORENE
Writer. **Personal:** Born Nov 29, 1956, Philadelphia, PA; daughter of Carole J Cary and John W Cary; married R C Smith, Aug 27, 1983; children: Geoffrey Smith (stepson), Laura & Zoe Smith. **Educ:** University of Pennsylvania, BA, MA, 1978; Sussex University, MA, 1980. **Career:** Time, intern writer, 1980; TV Guide, associate editor, 1980-82; St Paul's School, teacher, 1982-83; Antioch University, Phila campus, lecturer, 1983-84; Phila University of the Arts, lecturer, 1984-86; Essence, American Visions, The Philadelphia Inquirer Sunday Magazine, Philadelphia TV Guide, freelance writer, 1985-88; Newsweek, contributing editor, 1991-93; University of Pennsylvania, lecturer, 1995-; author, Black Ice, 1991; author, The Price of A Child, 1995, Pride, 1988. **Orgs:** Author's Guild, 1991-. **Honors/Awds:** Colby College, Honorary Doctorate, Letters, 1992; American Library Association, Notable Books Citation, Black Ice, 1992; National Hook-up of Black Women, Bronze Star Award, 1992; Keene State Coll, Honorary Doctorate, 1997; Chestnut Hill Coll, Honorary Doctorate, 1997. **Business Addr:** Writer, c/o Alfred A Knopf Inc, 201 East 50th Street, New York, NY 10022.

CARY, REBY
Educator. **Personal:** Born Sep 9, 1920, Ft Worth, TX; married Nadine S; children: Faith Annette. **Educ:** Prairie View A & M, BA, MS 1948; TX Christian U, 1951-53; N TX State U, 1961-71. **Career:** McDonald Coll Industrial Arts, dir, teacher 1946-49; Tarrant County/Johnson County Vocational School, lead teacher 1954-64; Dunbar High School, counselor 1953-64, asst prof 1964-67; Tarrant County Jr Coll, asst prof 1966-69; Univ of TX Arlington, assoc dean student life, asst prof history 1969-78; TX House of Representatives, Dist 32-B State Legislature, state representative 1978-82; Real Estate Broker, Cary's Real Estate, 1980-. **Orgs:** Mem Nat Educ Found Bd; Alpha Phi Frat 1974-75; reg educ dir 1972-75; sec Ft Worth Independent Sch Bd 1974-75; trustee, choir dir New Rising Star Bapt Ch; bd dirs Boy Scouts Am; bd mem Tarrant County United Way; community dev bd city Ft Worth. **Honors/Awds:** Man of yr Omega Psi Phi 1974; outstanding citizen award, St James AME Ch 1975. **Military Serv:** USCG 1942-45. **Business Addr:** 1804 Bunche Dr, Fort Worth, TX 76112.

CARY, WILLIAM STERLING
Minister (retired). **Personal:** Born Aug 10, 1927, Plainfield, NJ; son of Sadie Cary and Andrew Cary; married Marie B Phillips; children: Yvonne, Denise, Sterling, Patricia. **Educ:** Morehouse Coll, BA 1949; Union Theolog Seminary, MDiv 1952; Morehouse Coll, DD 1973; Bishop Coll Dallas, TX, hon LLD 1973; Elmhurst Coll Elmhurst, IL, hon DD 1973; Allen Univ Columbia, SC, hon HD 1975; IL Coll, doctor of human letters, 1988. **Career:** Butler Meml Presbyterian Ch, pastor 1953-55; Intl Ch of the Open Door Brooklyn, NY, pastor 1955-58; Grace Congr Ch NYC, pastor 1958-68; Metro & Suffolk Assns NY Conf United Ch of Christ, area minister 1968-75; IL Conf of United Ch of Christ, conf minister 1975-94. **Orgs:** Chr Comm for Racial Justice; mem gov bodies Cncl for Christian Soc Action and Off Communication; appointed by Pres Ford to 17 mem Task Force on Vietnamese Refugee Relocation; mem of 1977 UCC Cncl on Ecumenism; UCC rep to consult on Church Union; Natl Ministerial Adv Cncl; Chicago Theol Seminary Bd; Committee of Denominational Exec IL Conf of Churches; Exec Cncl United Ch of Christ; Church World Serv Comm; pres & vice pres Natl Cncl of Churches in Amer 1972-79; chr Council of Religious Leaders of Metropolitan Chicago; chmn Council of Religious Leaders, Chicago, 1987-88; mem Council of Religious Leaders, Chicago. **Business Addr:** Conf Minister (Retired), IL Conf of United Church of Christ, 1840 Westchester Blvd Ste 200, Westchester, IL 60154.

CASE, ARTHUR M.
Dentist. **Personal:** Born May 18, 1950, Philadelphia, PA. **Educ:** Temple Univ, DDS 1979. **Career:** Private Practice, dentist; JFK Memorial Hosp, staff. **Orgs:** Mem Alpha Omega Frat, New Era Dental Soc. **Honors/Awds:** Mem Oral Surgery Honor Soc, Peridontal Honor Soc. **Business Addr:** 5555 Wissahickon Ave, Philadelphia, PA 19144.

CASEY, CAREY WALDEN, SR.
Minister. **Personal:** Born Oct 12, 1955, Radford, VA; son of Sarah Adline Coles Casey and Ralph Waldo Casey Jr; married Melanie Little, May 15, 1977; children: Christie, Patrice, Marcellus. **Educ:** Northeastern Oklahoma, Miami, OK, Physical Ed, 1974-76; Univ of North Carolina at Chapel Hill, BA Religion, 1979; Gordon-Conwell Theological Seminary, S Hamilton MA, MDiv, 1981; School of Theology Virginia Union Univ, Richmond VA, MDiv, 1984. **Career:** Northeastern Univ, Boston, MA, counselor for student athletes, 1980-81; Total Action Against Poverty, Roanoke, VA, youth employment coord, 1981; First Baptist Church, Petersburg, VA, minister in residence, 1982-83; Fellowship of Christian Athletes, Dallas, TX, urban dir, 1983-88; Mount Hebron Baptist Church, Garland, TX, interim pastor, 1984-85; Dallas Cowboys Football Club Training Camp, counselor, 1986-87; Fellowship of Christian Athletes, Kansas City, MO, natl urban dir, 1988-92; Olympic Protestant Chaplain, Seoul, Korea, 1988; Lawndale Community Church, Chicago, IL, pastor, 1992-. **Orgs:** Comm, Martin Luther King Center, Dallas, TX, 1984-88; speaker, Athletes in Action, 1984-, Boys & Girls Clubs of Amer, 1986-, mem, NAACP, 1986-; natl consultant, Salvation Army, 1988-; consultant to bd, International Sports Coalition, 1988-; steering comm, Kansas City Star-Times, 1989-; board member, sports Outreach USA, 1990-; board member, Michigan Assn for Leadership Development Inc, 1989-; board member, Urban Life Outreach, Kansas City, MO, 1990-. **Honors/Awds:** Football Scholarship, Univ of North Carolina, 1976-79; Theological Scholarship, Billy Graham Evangelistic Assn, 1979; Outstanding Young Men of America, US Jaycees, 1980; NFL, Major League Baseball Chapel Speaker USA, 1980-; Juanita Craft Contribution to Sports in Comm, NAACP, 1984; L K Williams Inst Bishop Coll, Speaker, 1985; Proclamation Carey Casey Day, City of Louisville, KY, December 5, 1988; World Congress on Sports, Seoul, Korea, Speaker, 1988; Guest lecturer, University of Missouri, Kansas City, MO, Understanding 1990 Cultural Diversity. **Business Addr:** Pastor, Lawndale Community Church, 3828 W Ogden Ave, Chicago, IL 60623.

CASEY, CLIFTON G.
Police commander (retired). **Personal:** Born Oct 22, 1924, Yolande, AL; son of Irene Casey and Simpson Casey; divorced. **Educ:** FBI National Academy, 1972; Wayne State Univ, BS 1974; Tuskegee Inst. **Career:** Detroit Police Dept, promoted through the ranks to police commander 25 yrs, retired; State of Michigan Liquor Control Commission, deputy dir retired 1989. **Orgs:** Mem Intl Assoc Chiefs of Police, MI Assoc Chiefs of Police, Natl Acad Assoc, FBI; life mem NAACP; mem Amer Legion, Tuskegee Airman. **Military Serv:** USAF fighter pilot 1943-46.

CASEY, EDMUND C. See Obituaries section.

CASEY, FRANK LESLIE
Television reporter, journalist. **Personal:** Born Jan 29, 1935, Stotesbury, WV; son of Mary and Conston Casey; married Lenore Thompson, Apr 16, 1988; children: Zauditu, Tamarat, Bakaffa, Charles Arnold. **Educ:** WV State Coll, BS 1962. **Career:** WPIX-TV New York City, TV reporter; New York City Dept of Welfare, social worker 1969; Repub Aviation, tech illustrator 1963. **Orgs:** NAACP. **Honors/Awds:** Good Conduct Medal; New York Area Television Academy Award, The National Academy of Tevelision Arts & Scienced 1976-77; Uniformed Firefighters Association Award for excellence in T.V. coverage for fire fighting 1971; Humorous Writing Award, Society of the Silurians, New York 1986; Honorary Membership for Fair & Impartial Reporting for Police Stories, Retired Dectectives of the Police Dept of the city of New York Inc 1984. **Military Serv:** AUS sp2 1954-57. **Business Addr:** News Reporter, WPIX TV, 200 E 42nd St, New York, NY 10017.

CASEY, JOSEPH F.
Physician. **Personal:** Born Mar 14, 1914, Weaver, IN; married Amye; children: 1. **Educ:** IL Coll, Podiatric Med 1937. **Career:** Private Practice Podiatric Med, dr. **Orgs:** Mem IN State Parole Bd 1953-58; mem IN State Podiatry Assn pres 1972; staff consult Podiatry for VA Hosp; past pres Marion Urban League 1955, 1965; mem Exchange Club Metro Marion; Marion C of C; bd trustees & past pres Bd of Educ 1966-75. **Honors/Awds:** 33 deg Mason No Jurisdiction Mason of Yr 1960; Podiatrist of Yr 1970. **Military Serv:** USN 1943-46.

CASH, BETTYE JOYCE
Business executive. **Personal:** Born Feb 19, 1936, Fort Worth, TX; divorced; children: Ardranae, James Jr, Anthony, Lisa, Janine. **Educ:** Contra Costa Coll, 1963, AA 1975. **Career:** W Contra Costa Co, dist hosp dir. **Orgs:** Mem 2nd yr of 2nd 4 yrs term Natl Womens Pol Caucus, Black Bus & Professional Assoc, Church Missionary, CA Hosp Assoc, Med Staff, Assoc of W Hosp, AmerHosp Assoc, Assoc of Dist Hosps Dist Hosp; dir W Contra Costa Hosp. **Honors/Awds:** 1st & only black elected female W Contra Costa Cty 1974; Woman of the Year Honor Soc 1976-77; num other honors. **Business Addr:** District Hospital Dir, W Contra Costa Hospital Dist, 2000 Vate Rd, San Pablo, CA 94806.

CASH, JAMES IRELAND, JR.
Educator. **Personal:** Born Oct 25, 1947, Fort Worth, TX; married Clemmie; children: Tari, Derek. **Educ:** TX Christian Univ, BS mathematics and computer science 1969; Purdue Univ, MS computer science 1974, PhD management information systems & accounting 1976. **Career:** TX Christian Univ Computer Ctr, systems programmer 1969; Langston Univ, dir of computer ctr 1969-72, instructor/asst professor in vo-tech program 1969-72; Arth Drug Stores, Inc, systems analyst & programmer consultant 1973-76; Inst of Educational Management, exec educ course MIS instructor 1977-79; Harvard Grad School of Bus Admin, asst prof 1976-81, instructor in exec educ course 1978-; IBM Systems Research Inst, adjunct prof 1980; Harvard Grad School of Bus Admin, assoc prof of bus admin 1981-85, prof of bus admin 1985-. **Orgs:** Bd of advisors Amer Accounting Assoc; Assoc for Computing Machinery; Quality Assurance Inst; adv bd Society for Information Management; Strategic Management Society; US Dept of State Advisory Comm on Transnational Enterprises 1976-83; Index Systems, Inc 1978-; bd of trustees The Park School 1983-; adv bd BOSCOM 1983-;

editorial bd Harvard Business Review 1983-; MA Governor's Advisory Comm on Information Processing 1983-88. **Honors/Awds:** 3 books and 13 papers published; All American Academic Basketball team 1968; Outstanding Instructor Awd Vo-Tech Dept of Langston Univ 1971; Purdue Univ fellowship 1972; Phi Kappa Phi 1974; Hall of Fame TX Christian Univ 1982; 1st Century Disting Alumni Ft Worth Independent School Dist 1983. **Business Addr:** James E Robison Professor of Business Administration, Harvard Grad Sch Bus Admin, Loeb #14, Soldiers Field, Boston, MA 02163.

CASH, PAMELA J.
Librarian. **Personal:** Born Oct 26, 1948, Cleburne, TX; daughter of Juanita Beatty Cash and James Cash; married Gervis A Menzies Sr, Sep 17, 1983; children: Gervis A Menzies Jr. **Educ:** Univ of OK, BA 1970; Univ of IL, MLS, 1972. **Career:** Univ of IL, asst Afro-Amer bibliographer 1970-71, librarian of Afro-Amer studies 1971-72; Univ of TX, humanities librarian 1972-73; Johnson Publishing Co, librarian. **Orgs:** Mem Black Caucus of Amer Library Assn, Special Library Assn, Assn of Black Librarians of Chicago. **Business Addr:** Librarian, Johnson Pub Co, 820 S Michigan Ave, Chicago, IL 60605.

CASHIN, SHERYLL
Government official. **Career:** Office of the Vice Pres, Community Empowerment Bd, staff dir, currently. **Business Addr:** Staff Dir, Office of the Vice Pres, Community Empowerment Bd, 1600 Pennsylvania Ave, NW, Washington, DC 20500, (202)456-1414.

CASH-RHODES, WINIFRED E.
Educator (retired). **Personal:** Born in Savannah, GA; daughter of Mrs Clifford Brown Cash and Rev William L Cash Sr; married Augustus H Rhodes; children: Eva Carol, Lydia Ann, Victoria Elizabeth. **Educ:** Fisk Univ, AB 1934; Univ of S California, MS 1959; New York Univ, Fellowship 1970; Univ of California-Berkley, fellowship 1960. **Career:** Tchr of Secondary Math, 1935-40, 1945-52; Dept Chairperson Math, 1957-65; Los Angeles Unified Sch, supr of secondary Math tchrs 1966-68, Spclst in Resch & Dvlpmnt 1968-78. **Orgs:** Sec Baldwin Hills Homeowners Assoc 1976-82; dir Far Western Rgnl Dir Alpha Kappa Alpha Sor Inc 1970-74; mem Exec Council of United Church of Christ representing So, CA and NV (first black) 1981-87; chmn Nominating Comm, Southern California Ecumenical Council 1987-; mem Southern California Interfaith Coalition on Aging Board 1989-. **Honors/Awds:** Natl Sci Fdn US Gov't 1957-59; research fellowship New York Univ 1970; Article "What Jesus Means to Me" United Church of Christ New York 1982. **Home Addr:** 4554 Don Felipe Dr, Los Angeles, CA 90008.

CASON, DAVID, JR.
Urban planner. **Personal:** Born Jun 20, 1923, Selma, AL; son of Mattie Clark and David Cason Sr; married Armene B. **Educ:** BA 1950; MA 1959; Wayne State U, MUP 1966; Univ of Manchester Eng, 1972; Univ of MI, PhD 1976. **Career:** Univ of MI, adj prof 1977-; CRW Assoc Consult in Planning Detroit, pres 1977; Univ of MI, lectr in urban planning; Research Assoc Environmental Research Inst of MI, 1972-73; Univ of MI Dept of Urban Planning, instr 1970-; MI Dept of Corrections Program Bureau, asst bureau chief 1985-89, director of programs 1989-. **Orgs:** Dir Model Neighborhood Agency Detroit 1967-70; tchr Merrill-Palmer Inst 1975; proj mgr Neighborhood Conservation Housing Commn 1962-65; dir Urban Renewal Ypsilanti 1961-62; pub aide worker Receiving Hosp Detroit 1956-61; part-time work in studies field Wayne State Univ 1966-67; past mem Natl Assn of Redevel & Housing Officials; MI Soc of Planning Officials, Amer Inst of Planners; has written several articles; past trustee Met Fund Detroit; co-vice chairperson Southeastern MI Regional Citizens; bd mem, vice president, 1987. MI Council of Girl Scouts, Detroit Area Agency on Aging, Center for Humanistic Studies; mem Alpha Phi Alpha; vice pres, The Prometheas 1988-. **Military Serv:** US Army, infantry, 92nd div, PFC, 1944-45. **Business Addr:** Director of Programs, MI Dept of Corrections, Stevens T Mason Bldg, PO Box 30003, Lansing, MI 48909.

CASON, JOSEPH L.
Educational administrator. **Personal:** Born Mar 24, 1939, Anderson County, SC; son of Conyers Williams Cason and William Cason; married Margaret Johnson; children: Ajena Lynette, Kenneth Todd, Shawn Douglas, Valerie Kay. **Educ:** Hampton Inst, BS. **Career:** Roanoke Valley Bus League, exec dir 1973-81; Cason Enterprises, owner 1970-;Eli Lily Corp, indsl engr tech 1968-70; City of Roanoke, proj engr 1967-68; Better Housing Inc, mgr 1965-67; Roanke City School Bd, Roanke, VA, coordinator for maintenance & construction systems, 1988-. **Orgs:** Charter mem pres Roanoke Vly Contractors Assn 1970; dir Roanoke Valley Bus League; charter mem vice pres Afro-Am Builders of VA 1973; bd mem SW VA Comm Devel Fund 1971-75; mem Roanoke C of C; mem Hunton YMCA; group chmn United Fund 1977; mem Minority Bus Oppty Com Mem Kappa Alpha Psi; mem Comm Orgn for Rsrch & Devel; mem Nat Bus League; mem dir Nethel AME Ch; mem Hampton Inst Alumni Assn; mem US Army Res; 1st black professional hired by City of Roanoke 1967; instrumental in orgnizing 3 minority contractros assns in VA; 1st State Registerd Gen Contractor in SW VA; originated & administrated 9 yrs Office of Minority Bus Enterprise Prgr for SW VA. **Military Serv:** AUS capt 1963-65. **Home Addr:** 1449 Leon St NW, Roanoke, VA 24017. **Business Addr:** Coordinator of Maintenance & Construction Systems, Roanoke City Schools, Maintenance & Operations Dept, 250 Reserve Ave SW, Roanoke, VA 24016.

CASON, MARILYNN JEAN
Corporate officer. **Personal:** Born May 18, 1943, Denver, CO; daughter of Evelyn L Clark Cason and Eugene M Cason; married P Wesley Kriebel, Dec 12, 1987. **Educ:** Stanford Univ, BA Polit Sci 1965; Univ of MI Law Sch, JD 1969; Roosevelt Univ, MBA 1977. **Career:** Dawson Nagel Sherman & Howard, assoc atty 1969-73; Kraft Inc, attorney 1973-76; Johnson Prods Co Inc, vp, managing dir 1980-83, vp & corp counsel 1976-86, vp-intl 1986-88; DeVry Inc, vice pres & gen counsel, 1989-96, senior vp & gen counsel, currently. **Orgs:** Dir Arthritis Found IL Chap 1979-; Il Humanities Council 1987-96. **Business Addr:** Senior VP & General Counsel, DeVry Inc, 1 Tower Ln, Oakbrook Terrace, IL 60181.

CASON, UDELL, JR.
Educational administrator. **Personal:** Born Jul 30, 1940, Glasgow, MO; married Emma R Bothwell; children: Carmen Q, Udell Q. **Educ:** Drake U, BS 1965; Drake U, MS 1970. **Career:** Des Moines Pub Sch, prin 1972-, coord 1970-72, tchr 1968-70; City of Des Moines, admin asst 1965-68. **Orgs:** Chmn & v chmn & trustee bd Union Bapt Ch 1965-; pres United Black Fedn 1967-69; sec chmn prin DMPS; pres Kappa Alpha Psi Frat 1980-81; chmn board of directors, Iowa Children and Family Services 1984-89; board of directors, Des Moines YMCA 1982-89. **Honors/Awds:** Task force award State of Iowa 1968; mayor task force award City of Des Moines 1968; outstanding achievement Kappa Alpha Psi 1975; Double D Award Drake Univ 1979; Service to Youth Award YMCA 1988; Tae Kwon Do Instructor YMCA 1979-. **Business Addr:** Moore Elem School, 3725 52nd St, Des Moines, IA 50310.

CASPER, BANJO
Artist. **Personal:** Born Feb 13, 1937, Memphis, TN. **Educ:** Laney Coll AA 1970; SF Art Inst, BFA 1973, MFA 1975. **Career:** Booth Memorial Home for Adults, 1970; Laney College Art Dept, teacher asst, 1971-72; Oakland Public School District, asst teacher, 1972-73; San Francisco Art Institute, asst teacher, 1974-75; San Francisco State Univ Art Dept, lectures series, 1979-81; selected exhibitions: Aesthetic of Graffiti: Catalog, San Francisco Museum of Modern Art, 1979; On Our Own Terms, Berkeley Plaza Gallery, 1989; Continuing Traditions-The National Black Art Festival, 1990; Juneteenth Festival, The Black Repertory Theater Gallery, 1990; Sister Kenny Institute Inte rnational Artists Exhibition, 1991; 13th Southwest Black Art Exhibition, Museum of African American Life & Culture, 1991; Self Portrait Show, Center of the Visual Arts, 1993; Diversity and Vision of Print Image, California Society of Print Makers, 1994; Small Works, Center for the Visual Arts, 1994; Love is Love, Center for the Visual Arts, 1995; The Seeing Soul: 13 Bay Area African American Artists, The Oakland Museum Collectors Gallery, 1995; Artistic License Part II, Center for the Visual Arts, 1996; Sister Kenny International Artists Exhibition, 33rd Annual Disabilities Art Show, 1996. **Honors/Awds:** Black Filmmakers Hall of Fame, 1991; Oakland Chamber of Commerce, Oakland B usiness Art Award, 1994.

CASSELL, SAMUEL JAMES (SAMUEL JAMES)
Professional basketball player. **Personal:** Born Nov 18, 1969, Baltimore, MD. **Educ:** San Jacinto College; Florida State. **Career:** Houston Rockets, guard, 1993-96; Phoenix Suns, 1996; New Jersey Nets, 1996-. **Special Achievements:** NBA, Championship, 1994, 1995. **Business Addr:** Professional Basketball Player, New Jersey Nets, Brendan Byrne Arena, East Rutherford, NJ 07073, (201)935-8888.

CASSIS, GLENN ALBERT
Educational administrator. **Personal:** Born Nov 11, 1951, Jamaica, NY; married Glynis R; children: Glenn Jr. **Educ:** Univ of Ct, BA pol sci 1973; Univ of CT, MFA arts adminstrn 1974. **Career:** N Adams State Coll, dir of campus center 1978; Oakland Center, Oakland Univ, Rochester MI, asst dir 1976-78, asst dir student act 1974-76; Jorgensen Auditorium, Univ of CT, Storrs CT, admin asst 1973-74; Assoc of Coll Union-Intl, region I comp coord 1979-. **Orgs:** Bd of dir Nat Entertainment and Campus Act Assoc 1972-74; co-founder minority affairs comm Nat Entertainment and Campus Act Asso 1973; advisory bd Salvation Army 1980-; mem Min Counc on Comm Concerns 1980-. **Honors/Awds:** Founders award Nat Entertainment & Campus Act Assoc 1974; black faculty & admin service award Oakland Univ Rochester MI 1977. **Business Addr:** 8 Puritan Dr, Bloomfield, CT 06002.

CASTENELL, LOUIS ANTHONY, JR.
Educational administrator. **Personal:** Born Oct 20, 1947, New York, NY; son of Louis and Marguerite; married Mae E Beckett; children: Louis C, Elizabeth M. **Educ:** Xavier Univ of LA, BA Educ 1968; Univ of WI Milwaukee, MS Educ Psych 1973; Univ of IL, PhD Educ Psych 1980. **Career:** Univ of WI-Milwaukee, academic adv 1971-74; Xavier Univ, dir alumni affairs 1974-77, asst prof 1980-81, dean grad sch; University of Cincinnati, dean, college of education, currently. **Orgs:** Editorial Boards, Journal of Curriculum Theorizing 1990-95; reviewer, Journal of Teacher Education; reviewer, Journal of Educational Foundations, Educ Task Force Urban League 1984; chair Human Rights and Academic Freedom AERA 1985-86; consultant Sch of Educ 1980-; bd mem Ronald McDonald House of Louisiana, 1987; board member, NAACP; Children Museum of Cincinnati, board member. **Honors/Awds:** Craig Rice Scholarship Xavier Univ 1968; Fellowship Univ of IL 1977-78; Fellowship Natl Inst of Mental Health 1978-80; over 15 published works on aspects of educ; American Educational Studies Association, Critic's Choice Awards, 1993; Presidential Award, Networking Together Inc, 1996. **Military Serv:** AUS sgt 2yrs. **Business Addr:** Dean and Professor, College of Education, University of Cincinnati, ML002, Cincinnati, OH 45215.

CASTER, CAROLEIGH TUITT
Federal official. **Personal:** Born Jan 25, 1947, Bronx, NY; daughter of Carmen L Charles Tuitt and James M Tuitt; married Dwight O Caster, Mar 30, 1985. **Educ:** Howard Univ, BA 1968, JD 1972. **Career:** IRS, tax law specialist 1972-; OEO, law clerk 1971; Harlem Assertion of Rights, law asst 1970; DC Public Schools, substitute teacher, 1970-72; Library of Congress, library tech 1968-69; WA Saturday Coll, Washington, DC, coordinator/teacher, 1989-. **Orgs:** Mem Howard Univ Law School Alumni Assn; Natl Bar Assn; Kappa Beta Pi Intl Legal Sorority 1971-72; mem, Greater Washington Area Chapter, Women's Division National Bar Assn, 1972-; mem DC Law Students in Ct Comm Income Tax Clinic 1971-72; pres Howard Law Alumni Assn, Greater Washington Area, 1988-90.

CASTERLOW, CAROLYN B.
Computer consultant. **Personal:** Born Jul 16, 1948, Rich Square, NC; daughter of Zeophia Casterlow and Jesse Casterlow. **Educ:** Fayetteville State Univ, BS Business 1970; State Univ of NY at Albany, MS Business 1972; Georgia State Univ, advanced grad business courses 1976-78; GA Institute of Technology, Atlanta, GA, MS Information and Computer Sc. 1989-91. **Career:** Georgia Real Estate License, salesperson 1974-77, broker 1977-83; Atlanta EREB Chap of Women's Council, treasurer 1980-82; Atlanta Empire Real Estate Bd, sec 1981-83; City of Atlanta, Atlanta, GA, Consultant 1988-. **Orgs:** Owner/broker VIP Realty Co Atlanta 1977-83; mem Atlanta Bd of Realtors 1978-82; mem GA Assoc of Realtors 1978-82; treasurer Natl Women's Council of NAREB 1981-83; mem Assoc of MBA Execs 1985-86, Amer Assoc of Univ Women 1985-86; mem National Political Congress of Black Women 1988-; Owner/Senior Consultant, Consultants Unlimited, Atlanta, GA 1988-. **Honors/Awds:** Mem Phi Theta Kappa Honor Soc 1986-; mem Who's Who In Professional and Executive Women 1989. **Business Addr:** Senior Consultant, Consultants Unlimited, PO Box 311217, Atlanta, GA 30331.

CASTLE, KEITH L.
Corporate executive. **Career:** Phase One Office Products Inc, Cambridge, MA, president, currently. **Orgs:** New England Minority Purchasing Council; Cambridge Chamber of Commerce. **Honors/Awds:** New England Minority Purchasing Council, Vendor of the Year, 1981, 1991; SBA, Award for Excellence; Black Enterprise Top 100, 1989, 1991; Gillette Co., Outstanding Service and Quality Award, 1991. **Business Addr:** President, Phase One Office Products Inc, 89 Fulkerson Cam, Cambridge, MA 02141.

CASTLEBERRY, EDWARD J.
Newscaster. **Personal:** Born Jul 28, 1928, Birmingham, AL; son of Lillian Castleberry and Edward Castleberry; married Frances Bassett (deceased); children: Terrie Wade, Sharon Bryant, Susan, Bradley. **Educ:** Miles Coll Birmingham, AL, 1950-51. **Career:** WEDR, WJLD Birmingham, AL, disc jockey, 1950-55; WMBM, Miami, FL, prog dir, disc jockey, 1955-58; WCIN, Cincinnati, OH, disc jockey, newsman, 1958-61; WABQ, Cleveland, OH, disc jockey, newsman, 1961-64; WVKO, Columbus, OH, program dir, disc jockey, 1964-67; WHAT, Philadelphia, PA, disc jockey, 1967-68; WEBB, Baltimore, MD, disc jockey, newsman; Mutual & Natl Black Networks, anchorman, entertainment editor. **Honors/Awds:** Newsman of the Year, Coalition of Black Media Womn, NY, 1980; Newsman of the Year, Jack the Rapper Family Affair, Atlanta, 1980; Outstanding Citizen Award, AL House of Representatives, Montgomery, 1983; Honored, Smithsonian Institute, Washington, 1985; Part of the first black newsteam to broadcast a presidential election, 1972. **Military Serv:** USN Yeoman 3rd Class, served three years; WWII Victory Medal, 1945-47. **Business Addr:** Anchorman/Entertainment Editor, Natl Black Network, 41-30 58th St, Woodside, NY 11377.

CASTLEBERRY, RHEBENA TAYLOR
Educational administrator. **Personal:** Born Nov 17, 1917, Wilson, NC; daughter of Alice Taylor and Armstrong Taylor; married Henry A Castleberry; children: Dr Curtis A Leonard. **Educ:** Cheyney State Coll, BS 1941; Temple Univ, MEd 1948-49, Doctoral Studies 1949-51; Univ of HI, Cert in Asian Studies 1968. **Career:** Ft Valley Coll Lab School, elem teacher 1941-42; Martha Washington School, elem teacher 1949-65, grad

chmn & supr 1965-75; Natl Assn of Univ Women, natl pres; commr Philadelphia Fellowship Commn; mem bd dir Natl Conf of Christians and Jews; mem PA Coalition of 100 Black Women; mem bd dir, exec comm of Natl Polit Congress of Black Women; mem Mayor's Commn for Women. **Orgs:** Consultant to Dept of Christian Educ African Methodist Episcopal Church 1964-72; natl pres Natl Assn of Univ Women 1982-; mem of bd of dir Natl Conf of Women Christians & Jew 1983-; vice pres PA Council of Churches 1984-; bd dir Philadelphia Fellowship Commn. **Honors/Awds:** Outstanding Serv Award Chapel of Four Chaplains 1980; Dedicated Serv in Secular & Christian Ed Awd AME Church 1981; Woman of Year Award Natl Assn of Univ Women 1982; Churchwoman of the Year African Methodist Episcopal Church 1984; Woman of the Year Award, Jones Tabernacle AME Church.

CASTLEMAN, ELISE MARIE
Social worker. **Personal:** Born May 30, 1925, Duquesne, PA; daughter of Fannie M Ridley (deceased) and Guy L Tucker (deceased); divorced; children: John II. **Educ:** Howard Univ, BA 1947; Univ of Pittsburgh, M 1949. **Career:** Family & Childrens Agency, social worker 1949-53; DC General Hospital, social worker 1953-58; Wayne County General Hospital & Consulting Center, social worker 1958-59; United Cerebral Palsy, social worker 1960-66; Mental Hygiene Clinic Veterans Admin, social worker 1967-; Defense Construction Supply Center, mgmt analyst 1982-85. **Orgs:** Mem Columbus Bd of Ed 1971-79; exec adv comm Office of Minority Affairs OH State Univ 1972-73; adv bd Martin Luther King Serv Ctr 1963-67; Howard Univ Womens Club 1953-58; exec comm OH School Bds Assn; bd mem YWCA 1974-76; bd mem Columbus Civil Rights Council 1973-, OH School Bd Assn 1972-, NAACP, Black Womens Leadership 1973-76; fellowship for graduate study in social work Family Serv Assn 1947-49. **Honors/Awds:** Public Serv Award 1979; Public Serv Award Inner City Sertoma Club 1978; Public Serv Award NAACP Columbus Chapter 1980; Cert of Appreciation for Serv & Leadership in the Field of Public Educ KEDs Kent State Univ 1980; Award for Distinguished Community Serv OH House of Rep 1981.

CASTRO, GEORGE A.
State representative, association executive. **Personal:** Born Dec 27, 1936, Providence, RI; married Avis L; children: Regina, Terri, Brian Dave. **Educ:** Providence College. **Career:** Blacks Interested in Communications, director, currently; Rhode Island General Assembly, state representative, district 20, currently. **Orgs:** Martin Luther King, Jr. State Holiday Commission, chairman; Rhode Island Black Heritage Society, board; International Institute; Cranston General Hospital Corp, board; NAACP, Newport Chapter; Commission on Boxing and Wrestling in Rhode Island, chairman; Governor's Advisory Commission on Senior Citizens; Urban Education Center; Radio & Tv, advisory committee; Minority Advisory Committee; Pep Mgmt Advisory Committee, boxing, wrestling, kickboxing. **Home Addr:** 57 Carolina Ave, Providence, RI 02905.

CASWELL, CATHERYNE WILLIS
Councilwoman, teacher. **Personal:** Born Aug 27, 1917, Troy, AL; divorced; children: James, Leon, Bettye. **Educ:** AL A&M U, BS 1946, M 1962. **Career:** Geneva Cty Pub Sch Sys & Montgomery Cty, teacher; Catheryne's Rec Ctr, owner & dir; G & W Grocery & Market, owner; Toliver's Place, owner; G & W Rec Ctr, owner. **Orgs:** Pres Geneva Cty Teachers Assoc; advisory coun mem ACT-NEA; mem AL St Teachers' Assn; 8 6 mem Natl Democ Party AL; mem dir United Mem Natl Bank; dirc West Side Improve Assn; rep Minority Prob on Democ Comm; capt Tuberculosis Heart and March of Dimes Drives. **Honors/Awds:** Teacher of yr award Geneva Teachers Assoc; only Negro to serve actively with Democ 30 yrs ago.

CATCHINGS, HOWARD DOUGLAS
Insurance salesman. **Personal:** Born Jun 19, 1939, Copiah County, MS; son of Corean Catchings and H D Catchings; married Danella Brownridge; children: Sebrena, Douglas, James, Daniel. **Educ:** Jackson State Univ, BEd 1963, MEd 1973. **Career:** Jackson Public Schools, teacher 1963-80; United Founders Ins Co, rep 1967-68; PFL Life/NOL Division, Natl Old Line Ins Co, rep 1968-. **Orgs:** Pres Jackson State Univ 1984-88; regional vice pres, president, 1993-94; MS Assn of Life 1985-89 pres 1993-94; comm mem Million Dollar Round Table; pres Jackson GAMA 1986-87; BD dirs Junior Achievement; State Job Training Coordinating Council; council member Business/Industry/Edu Regional Council; past chmn of bd, Jackson Chamber of Commerce; regional officer, GAMC; national board mem, Public Education Forum; past pres, Mississippi Association of Association of Life Underwriters; chmn, Junior Achievement of Mississippi. **Honors/Awds:** Outstanding Teacher in Human Relations Jackson Public Schools 1972; Outstanding Achievement Awd Jackson State Univ Natl Alumni Assn; Natl Sales Rep 1993-97; No 1 Salesman (Nationally) 1986, 1993-95; Natl Old Line Ins Co; one of top ten agents 1971-. **Business Addr:** General Agent, PFL Life/Catching Insurance Agency, PO Box 2509, Jackson, MS 39207.

CATCHINGS, WALTER J.
Automobile dealer. **Personal:** Born Nov 8, 1933, Drew, MS; son of Mable Deshazer-Trotter and Walter Catchings Sr.; married Bobby Catchings, Jan 3, 1987. **Career:** Kessler Buick, Detroit MI, salesman, 1960; Shore Severs Cadillac, Detroit MI, salesman, 1972; Dick Harris Cadillac, Detroit MI, salesman, 1978, general sales manager, 1979-86; Eldorado Ford/Lincoln-Mercury Inc, president, 1986-. **Orgs:** Mem, Boys Club, Eldorado AR, Kiwanis Club, Eldorado AR.

CATCHINGS, YVONNE PARKS
Educator. **Personal:** Born in Atlanta, GA; daughter of Hattie Marie Brookins Parks and Andrew Walter Parks; married James Albert A Catchings; children: Andrea Hunt Warner, Wanda Hunt McLean, James A A Jr. **Educ:** Spelman Coll, AB 1955; Tchrs Coll Columbia, MA 1958; Univ of Michigan, MMP 1971, PhD 1981. **Career:** Spelman Coll, instr 1956-57; Marygrove Coll, instr 1970-72; Specialist; Detroit Bd of Educ, instr 1959-; Valdosta State Coll, assistant professor of art 1987-88; Detroit Board of Education, specialist 1988-. **Orgs:** Presenter Natl Art Educ Assn 1956-; natl treasurer, The Smart Set 1976-78; archivist pub rel MI Art Therapy Assn 1981-; reg art therapist Amer Art Therapy 1981-; prog chr bd mem Detroit Soc Genelogical Research 1965-; chmn Heritage Archives Delta Sigma Theta Sor 1983-; bd chr peace Amer Assn Univ Women 1981-; art chr The Links 1981-. **Honors/Awds:** James D Parks Award Natl Conf of Artist 1979; Pres Spec Award Natl Dental Assoc 1973; 1st Award Art & Letters Delta Sigma Theta Sorority 1978; Mayor's Award of Merit Mayor Coleman Young 1978; Fulbright Hayes Award Study in Zimbabwe 1982; Outstanding Black Woman in Michigan 1785-1985, Detroit Historical Museum 1985; Service Award, Afro American Museum, 1983; Exhibited Atlanta University Negro Art Show, 1953-63; Won Honorable Mention 4 times, Clark Atlanta Univ; 3 One-Woman Shows; Exhibited in many Museums and Galleries in America; Exhibited Forever Fun Art, African-American Women 1862-80, show traveled throughout America; Black Artist South, Hunterville Museum, 1978; One Woman Art Show, Through the Year, National Dental Assn, 1973; Included in many art books and periodicals. **Home Addr:** 1306 Joliet Pl, Detroit, MI 48207.

CATES, SIDNEY HAYWARD, III
Government official. **Personal:** Born Mar 10, 1931, New Orleans, LA; married Betty; children: Sidney IV, Kim. **Educ:** Loyola U, BA 1968. **Career:** Housing Authority of New Orleans, exec dir; LA Dept of Justice, atty gen gss inc, vice pres-gen mgr; Hibernia natl bank, mrktng off; City of New Orleans, asst chief admin off; New Orleans Police Dept, deputy chief for admin. **Orgs:** Bd of dir Loyola U; Red Cross; Boy Scouts of Amer; United Way; Goodwill; St Claude Gen Hosp; mem Mid Winter Sports Assoc (Sugar Bowl); 4th degree Knights of St Peter Claver; Equestrian Knights of the Holy Sepulchre; pres Studs Club; mem Chamber of Comm; vice-chrm Bicentennial Comm City of New Orleans; consul Law Enforce Ass Admin Alfred E Clay award; Children's Bureau City of New Orleans. **Honors/Awds:** Charles E Dunbar, hon mention; St of LA, Career Civil Service Award. **Military Serv:** Sgt 1951-53.

CATLETT, ELIZABETH
Sculptor/printmaker. **Personal:** Born Apr 15, 1915, Washington, DC; daughter of Mary Carson Catlett and John H. Catlett; married Francisco Mora, Oct 31, 1946; children: Francisco, Juan, David. **Educ:** Howard University, Washington DC, BS, 1935; State University of Iowa, Iowa City IA, MFA, 1940; Art Institute of Chicago, Chicago IL, 1941, Art Students' League, New York NY, 1943; privately with Ossip Zadkine, New York, NY, 1943; Esmeralda, Escuela de Pintura y Escultura, Mexico City, 1948. **Career:** Teacher in Texas, Louisiana, Virginia, and New York City; National School of Fine Arts, National Autonomous University of Mexico, professor of sculpture, department head, 1959-73; free-lance sculptor/printmaker. **Orgs:** Member, Delta Sigma Theta, 1932-. **Honors/Awds:** First prize in sculpture, Golden Jubilee Nation Exposition (Chicago IL), 1941; Tlatilco Prize, First Sculpture Biannual (Mexico), 1962; Xipe Totec Prize, Second Sculpture Biannual (Mexico), 1964; first prize in sculpture, Atlanta University Annual, 1965; first purchase prize, National Print Salon (Mexico), 1969; prize to study and travel in West Germany, Intergrafic Exhibition (Berlin), 1970; Alumni Award, Howard University, 1979; award from Women's Caucus for Art, National Congress (San Francisco), 1981; Brandywine Workshop Award, Philadelphia Museum of Art, 1982; purchase prize, Salon de la Plastica Mexicana, Drawing Salon (Mexico), 1985; honoree, National Sculpture Conference: Works by Women (Cincinnati OH), 1987; numerous individual exhibitions throughout US and Mexico; Art Award, AMISTAD Research Center, 1990; Morgan State Univ, Honorary Doctorate of Human Letters, 1993; New School for Social Research, Parsons, Honorary Doctorate of Fine Arts, 1995; Tulane University, Honorary Doctorate of Humane Letters, 1995; Spelman College, Honorary Doctorate in Fine Arts, 1995; Howard University, Honorary Doctorate in Humane Letters, 1996; Cornell College, Honorary Doctorate in Fine Arts, 1996. **Home Addr:** PO Box AP694, 62000 Cuernavaca, Mexico.

CATLIN, ROBERT A.
Educator, educational administrator. **Personal:** Born Jun 14, 1940, Chicago, IL; son of Julia Jackson Catlin and Robert T. Catlin; married Ethel Long Catlin, Dec 1977; children: Janell, Michelle. **Educ:** Illinois Institute of Technology, Chicago, IL, BS, 1961; Columbia University, New York, NY, MSURP, 1972; Claremont Graduate School, Claremont, CA, PhD, 1976. **Career:** Professional urban planner, 1961-72; California State Polytechnic University, Pomona, CA, assistant professor, 1972-76; University of South Florida, Tampa, FL, chair, Department of Political Science, 1977-82; Indiana University, Gary, IN, chair, Department of Minority Studies, 1982-87; Florida Atlantic University, Boca Raton, FL, dean, College of Social Science, 1987-89; University of Florida, Gainesville, FL, professor, 1989-92; Rutgers University, Camden College of Arts and Sciences, dean, 1992-. **Orgs:** Chairman, Gary Airport Promotion and Development Commission, 1986-87; member, Hillsborough Area Transit Authority, 1981-83; member, Hillsborough County-Tampa Planning Commission, 1978-81; charter member, American Institute of Certified Planners, 1978. **Honors/Awds:** Administrator of the Year, Florida Atlantic University Faculty, 1988; Resolution of Appreciation for Comprehensive Urban Planning, Gary City Council, 1987; Leadership Award, Tampa Urban League, 1982. **Business Addr:** Dean, Camden College of Arts and Sciences and University College, Rutgers University, 311 N 5th St, Camden, NJ 08102.

CATO, KELVIN
Professional basketball player. **Personal:** Born Aug 26, 1974. **Educ:** Iowa State. **Career:** Portland TrailBlazers, center, 1997-. **Business Addr:** Professional Basketball Player, Portland TrailBlazers, 1 Center Court, Ste 200, Portland, OR 97227, (503)234-9291.

CAUSWELL, DUANE
Professional basketball player. **Personal:** Born May 31, 1968, Queens Village, NY; married Leslie; children: Kaelyn Alana. **Educ:** Temple Univ, 1987-90. **Career:** Sacramento Kings, center, 1990-97; Miami Heat, 1997-. **Business Addr:** Professional Basketball Player, Miami Heat, 721 NW 1st Ave, Miami Arena, Miami, FL 33136, (305)577-4328.

CAUTHEN, CHERYL G.
Ophthalmologist. **Personal:** Born Nov 13, 1957, Flint, MI; daughter of Dr and Mrs Joseph Cauthen Jr. **Educ:** Attended, Howard Univ 1974-77; Howard Univ Coll of Medicine, MD 1981. **Career:** DC General Hosp, intern-medicine 1981-82; Howard Univ Hosp, resident ophthalmology 1982-85; Howard Univ Coll of Medicine, instructor dept of surgery ophthalmology div 1985-86; Norfolk Eye Physicians & Surgeons, physician 1986-. **Orgs:** Mem Amer Acad of Ophthalmology, Natl Medical Assoc, Amer Medical Assoc, Norfolk Medical Soc, Norfolk Acad of Medicine, Old Dominion Medical Soc, The Medical Soc of VA. **Business Addr:** Ophthalmologist, Norfolk Eye Physicians & Surg, 1005 May Ave, Norfolk, VA 23504.

CAUTHEN, RICHARD L.
Attorney, educator. **Personal:** Born Dec 4, 1944, Canonsburg, PA; son of Mazella Bester Cauthen and John Cauthen Sr; divorced. **Educ:** Wabash Coll, BA 1966; Wayne State Univ Law Sch, JD 1975. **Career:** Gary Froebel HS, Spanish tchr/dept head/head wrestling coach 1966-68; Detroit Public Schs, English history Spanish instr 1968-80; AIM Enterprises Assoc, curriculum coord 1971; Project CHILD, asst supvr Latch Key Prog 1972; CETA Summer Youth Prog, asst coord 1973-75; Comm Educ & Training Prog Coord, clients council policy bd 1976-77; Detroit Non-Profit Housing Corp, prog coord & office adminstr 1977-80, deputy dir 1979-84; Jordan Coll, instr acctg & bus law 1982-83; DMCC, financial consul 1989-; Renaissance HS Detroit, bilingual instr. **Orgs:** Tech adv Brush Park Subdiv Property Owners Assn 1980-84; sec bd dirs Wayne Co Neighborhood Legal Serv Inc 1977-80; mem citizens adv comm Mayors Comm for Human Resources Develop 1971-76; chmn Citizens Adv Cncl MCHRD 1970-71; mem Amer Assn of Tchrs of Spanish & Portuguese; Amer Bar Assn; Detroit Energy Corp Consortium; MI Federation of Housing Counselors; MI State Clients Cncl; Natl Black Caucus; Natl Caucus & Ctr on Black Aged; Natl Fed of Housing Counselors; Phi Alpha Delta Legal Frat; State Bar of MI; Tau Kappa Epsilon Frat; Wayne Co Clients Cncl Policy Bd; Wayne State Univ Alumni Assn; Wolverine Bar Assn; deacon, Agape Fellowship of the Savior; mem Citizens for Better Govt. **Honors/Awds:** Mem Student Bd of Govs Wayne State Univ Law Sch 1971-72; finalist, Michigan Teacher of the Year, 1990; inducted in Wabash College Sports Hall of Fame, 1990; Achievement Award for Education & Law, Detroit Non-Profit Housing Corp, 1990. **Home Addr:** 18934 Ohio, Detroit, MI 48221-2060. **Business Addr:** Bilingual Instructor, Renaissance High School, 6565 W Outer Dr, Detroit, MI 48235.

CAVE, ALFRED EARL
Physician. **Personal:** Born Jan 23, 1940, Brooklyn, NY; son of Theodora Cave and Alfred Cave Sr; married Jeanne Byrnes; children: Christine. **Educ:** Columbia Coll, BA 1961; Downstate Medical Ctr, MD 1965. **Career:** Downstate Medical Ctr, instructor 1971, asst prof surgery 1971-77; Kings County Hosp Brooklyn, attending physician 1971-77; Long Beach Memorial Hosp, attending surgeon 1976-79; Lydia Hall Hosp, attending surgeon 1977-78; Nassau Co Med Ctr, attending surgeon 1978-; Syosset Comm Hosp, attending surgeon 1978-. **Orgs:** Mem Sigma Pi Phi Frat. **Honors/Awds:** Natl Medical Fellowship Awd 1961; New York State Medical Scholarship 1961. **Military Serv:** US Army Reserve capt 6 yrs; Honorable Discharge 1972. **Home Addr:** 1 Hutch Ct, Dix Hills, NY 11746.

CAVE, CLAUDE BERTRAND
Physician. **Personal:** Born Jan 29, 1910, Brooklyn, NY; married Nora Elizabeth Wallace; children: Claude Bertrand II, Carol Ann, Curtis Bryan. **Educ:** Coll of the City of NY, BS 1932; Loma Linda U, MD 1938. **Career:** Prt Practice, family physician 1965-75; Kingsbrook Flatbush Gen Lefferts Gen Hosp, asst surg 1956-74; Brookdale Hosp Unity Flatbush Lefferts Empire MedGroup, staff physician 1950-74; Harlem Hosp, staff member 1939-44. **Orgs:** Mem Kings Co Med Soc; NY State Med Soc 1944-; pres Provident Clinical Soc 1945-46; mem AMA; AAFP; NMA 1949; Charter Fellowship, AAFP Nat Group NY Chap 1974; life mem Kappa Alpha Psi Brooklyn LI Chap 1974. **Honors/Awds:** Award of Excellence; Woodrow Lewis Assemblyman. **Business Addr:** 1349 Dean St, Brooklyn, NY 11216.

CAVE, HERBERT G.
Physician, educator. **Personal:** Born Jul 16, 1922, Colon, Panama; married Francis; children: Herbert Jr, LaVerne. **Educ:** Coll of NYC, 1940-42; Howard Univ Washington Dc, 1942-44; Howard Univ Coll of Med, MDD 1947; Harlem Hosp Ctr, internship 1947-48. **Career:** Col U, assoc prof anestesolgy 1973-; Harlem Hosp, dir anestesolgy dept 1961-; Mitchell AFB Hosp, conslt 1959-61; Italian Hosp, attndg anesthesolgst 1957-61; Manhattan State Hosp, attndg anesthesolgst 1956. **Orgs:** Past mem House of Del NMA 1960; past mem Anesthsia Study Commn NY Co Med Soc 1633-64; past chmn Adv Coun of Med Bds Dept of Hosp 1969-70; mem Blk Caucus of Harlem Hlth Wrks NY 1969-; mem 369th VA Westchester Dist; chmn Educ Com 369th VA; mem Mt Vernon Narc Gdnc Coun 1969-; past mem Mayor's Com for Recptn of New Res Mt Vern 1970-71; past mem Sel Serv Be #10 1968-76; past participation Med Presence MS 1964; commr Mt Vern Plng Bd 1967-68; chmn Mt Vern Com Actn Grp 1976-; past host WLIB Radio Stn NY wkly show Hlth Your Grtst Invst 1972; past mem Com for Hlth Careers forDisadvantaged Manhattan 1968; mem Econ Devel Coun of Mt Vern 1976-; mem NAACP Articles a comprsn of Thiopental Sodium & Methohexital Sodium in Shrt Surgl Prcks SAA NA 1962; Anesthesia Prblms inEmerg Srgy JAANA 1964; AnesthetMgmt of Drug Addict Med Aspts of Drug Abuse 1975. **Honors/Awds:** Dist serv aw Caucus of Blk Legltrs St of NY 1971; natl com aw Nat Assn of Bus and Prfsnl Wmns Clubs Inc 1972; humanitarian aw Key Wmn of Am Mt Vern Br. **Military Serv:** AUS Med Corps capt 1952-54. **Business Addr:** Harlem Hosp Ctr, Anesthesia Dept, 506 Lenox Ave, New York, NY 10037.

CAVE, PERSTEIN RONALD
Educational administrator. **Personal:** Born Sep 24, 1947, Brooklyn, NY; son of Dorothy Cave and Perstein Cave; married Jeanette; children: Christopher, Joscelyn, Jerilynn. **Educ:** Kingsborough Comm Coll, AA 1967; The City Coll of NY, BA 1970; The Univ of Hartford, MBA 1981. **Career:** The Aetna Life & Casualty Ins Co, expense coord 1977-80; ESPN/ABC Television, special Projects consultant 1980-85; Asnuntuck Comm Coll, business mgr/assoc dean 1985-; Twins Community Coll, business mgr 1988-89; State of Connecticut, asst financial dir, 1989-. **Orgs:** Ministerial servant Windsor CT Congregation of Jehovah's Witnesses 1980-; mem Natl Assoc of Accountants 1980-, Natl Black MBA Assoc 1982-; comm mem Asnuntuck Comm Coll Affirmative Action Comm 1985-. **Honors/Awds:** Citation for Outstanding Community Service. **Home Addr:** 20 Maythorpe Dr, Windsor, CT 06095.

CAVER, CARMEN C. MURPHY
Business executive (retired). **Personal:** Born Oct 20, 1915, Auvergne, AR; daughter of Sarah Crofford and Henry Lutenant Caver; married Scipio G Murphy, Sep 12, 1935; children: Robert Caver, Scipio G. **Educ:** Wayne Univ, attd; Mary Hall Acad; School of Cosmetology. **Career:** House of Beauty, ret fnd & head 1948-74; Carmen Cosmetics, beauty/travel consult 1955; House of Beauty Record Co beginning 1957. **Orgs:** Consult Amalgamated Press; beauty consult Detroit Bd Educ resource adv 1960-; mem Com of 1000 Women; Serv Guild Blvd Gen Hosp Detroit; bd dir Detroit YMCA; Detroit Urban League Guild. **Honors/Awds:** Recipt Bus Award Wilberforce Univ 1967; 7-Up Co 1968; Booker T Washington Bus Assn & Cham of Comm Top Ten Working Women Award 1970; mem Wilberforce Univ Alumni; Natl Assn Negro Bus & Prof Women's Clubs; NAACP; Women's Aux to Natl Med Assn; pres Detroit Med Soc Aux 1978-80; bd dir Sickle Cell Detection & Info Prog Inc; vol ARC Southeastern MI Chpt; chmn Women's Com United Negro Clge Fund 1979; chrt mem; Natl Assc Market Developers; Natl Assn Fashion & Accessory Designers; Natl Assc Media Women; Women's Econ Club; others.

CAVIN, ALONZO C.
Educational administrator. **Personal:** Born Jul 17, 1939, Savannah, GA; son of Willie Cavin Dale; married Gwendolyn Mary Wells; children: Alonzo, William. **Educ:** Cheyney State College PA, BS 1961; West Chester State College PA, MA 1969; Temple Univ, EdD 1979. **Career:** Bayard Middle Schl, eng tchr 1965-69; PMC Clge, dir proj prepare 1972-; Widener Univ, assoc prof/dir state and fed prog 1979-. **Orgs:** Mem Assn for Supv and Curriculum Dev 1972-, PA Assn for Supv and Curriculum Dev 1972-, Mid-Eastern Assn of Educ Opportunity Prog Personnel 1972-; pres Chester PA Rotary Inc 1985; bd mem DE Governor's Council Exceptional Citizens 1979-, Wallingford Chester Amer Red Cross 1985. **Honors/Awds:** Legion of Honor Chapel of Four Chaplains 1980; publ Cognitive Dissonance affective Domain ERIC 1979, Affective Variable Indicating Acad Success ERIC 1978, Pre College Exper, An Oppor Assessment PA Dept Educ 1974; Chairman Chester-Wallingford American Red Cross 1989-90; Service Award Omega Psi Phi Fraternity, Inc Epsilon Pi Chapter 1987; Outstanding Service Award, Act 101 Directors' Association 1990; Lucy G Hathaway Memorial Award, American Red Cross, Chester-Wallingford Chapter 1992; Rotarian of the Year Award, Chester Rotary Club 1991; Award of Advocate, National Council of Educational Opportunity Association 1990. **Special Achievements:** Discussions/interviews: ''Legislation and Higher Education,'' Edie Huggins, WCAU-TV, Philadelphia, 1992; ''Higher Education and Black America,'' Rica Duffus, WPHL-TV, Philadelphia, 1992; testimony: ''The Philadelphia Higher Education Equal Opportunity Act (Act 101),'' Pennsylvania Legislative Black Caucus Public Hearing, Pittsburgh, 1991. **Military Serv:** USN lt jg 1961-65. **Business Addr:** Assoc Prof/Dir, State/Federal Program, Widener Univ, Sparrow Hall, Chester, PA 19013.

CAVINESS, E. THEOPHILUS
Clergyman. **Personal:** Born May 23, 1928, Marshall, TX; married Jimmie; children: Theophilus James, Theodosia Jacqueline. **Educ:** Bishop Coll, BA; Eden Theol Sem, BD; VA Seminary & Coll, DD. **Career:** Greater Abyssinia Bapt Ch, pastor; 1961; Greater Abyssinia Bapt Ch Fed Credit Union, pres. **Orgs:** Historian & mem bd dir Nat Bapt Conv USA Inc; pres OH Bapt State Conv; pres Bapt Min Conf; exec asst Mayor of Cleveland Office. **Business Addr:** Greater Abyssinia Baptist Church, 1161 E 105 St, Cleveland, OH 44108.

CAVINESS, LORRAINE F.
Educator. **Personal:** Born Apr 8, 1914, Atlanta; married Clyde E; children: Muriel E. **Educ:** Spelman Coll, BA 1936; Atlanta U, postgrad study 1947-48; Am U, 1951-52; DC Tchrs Coll, 1959-60. **Career:** Winston-Salem Teachers Coll, asst teacher 1936-37; Vocational High School, teacher 1937-38; US Govt Dept of Labor, research asst 1942-44; Dept of Army, 1947-51; Washington DC Public Schools, 1946, 1963-64. **Orgs:** Mem Spelman Coll Alumnae Assn; mem Century Club Spelman Coll 1977; DC Nat Retired Tchrs Assns; Washington Urban League; mem Brightwood Community Assntreas 1968-70; del Beautification Com; Educ Com precinct chmn 1969; Federaton Civic Assns; mem Adv Neighborhood Council; Task Force which defined areaboundaries Summer 1975. **Honors/Awds:** Honorable serv award US Dept Labor 1958; Wash Real Estate Brokers Award 1970; Grass Roots Honoree Award DC Federation Civic Assns 1969.

CAYOU, NONTSIZI KIRTON
Educator. **Personal:** Born May 19, 1937, New Orleans; married William. **Educ:** SF State U, AB 1962; SF State U, 1963; Univ Ca; SF State U, MA 1970;-73; tchr guest artist 1969-70; SF State U, tchr dance prgm 1963 , 65, 67; SF Unifed Sch Dist & Woodrow Wilson HS, dancer choreographer revues supper clubs dance theatres mus 1955. **Career:** San Francisco State Univ, coord dance program Presently; Stanford Univ, 1976-77; Univ of San Francisco 1972-73; teacher guest artist 1969-70; San Francisco State Univ, teacher dance program 1963, 1965, 1967; San Francisco Unified School Dist & Woodrow Wilson High School 1963; dancer choreograper revues supper clubs dance theatres museums 1955. **Orgs:** Dir founder Wajumbe Cultural Ensemble 1969; chmn Oakland Dance Assn 1966-68; chmn Comm of Black Dance 1969; CA Dance Educators Assn; Nat Dance Assn; Griot Soc Publ ''The Dance is People'' New African article 1965; article ''Origins of Jazz Dance'' Black Scholar 1970; book ''Modern Jazz Dance'' 1973. **Business Addr:** 1600 Holloway Ave, San Francisco, CA 94132.

CAZENAVE, NOEL ANTHONY
Educator. **Personal:** Born Oct 25, 1948, Washington, DC; son of Mildred Depland Cazenave and Herman Joseph Cazenave; married Anita Washington, Jun 20, 1971; children: Anika Tene. **Educ:** Dillard Univ, BA Psychology (Magna Cum Laude) 1970; Univ of MI, MA Psychology 1971; Tulane Univ, PhD Sociology 1977; Univ of New Hampshire, Post-Doctoral Study 1977-78; Univ of Pennsylvania, Fall 1989. **Career:** Temple Univ, assistant and assoc prof dept of sociology; Univ of Connecticut, associate professor of sociology, currently. **Orgs:** Mem Amer Sociological Assoc, Soc for the Study of Social Problems. **Honors/Awds:** Numerous articles published; National Science Foundation Grants, 1988-89, 1991-93. **Business Addr:** Associate Professor of Sociology, The University of Connecticut, 344 Manfield Rd, Box U-68, Rm 123, Storrs Mansfield, CT 06269-2068.

CEASAR, SHERITA THERESE
Company executive. **Personal:** Born Apr 21, 1959, Chicago, IL; daughter of Christine E Miller and Johnathan A Brown; married Cedric Ceasar, Apr 10, 1987. **Educ:** Illinois Institute of Technology, BSME, 1981, MSME, 1984. **Career:** Northrop DSD, engineer, 1984-85, senior engineer, 1985-87, engineering specialist, 1987-88; Motorola CPD, staff engineer, 1988-90, engineering group leader, 1990, manufacturing manager, 1990-92; Motorola PPG, manufacturing director, 1992-. **Orgs:** Society of Women Engineers, national vice pres of student services, 1992-; IIT Alumni Board, board of directors, 1992-; American Society of Quality Control, 1992-; American Society of Mechanical Engineers, associate member, 1982-; Chicago Technical Exchange, founding member, 1989-92; Illinois Engineering Council, director, 1985-88. **Honors/Awds:** Society of Women Engineers, Distinguished New Engineer of the Year, 1991; US Black Engineer Magazine, Special Recognition, 1991; IIT Alumni Association, Certificate of Appreciation, 1994; YMCA of Metropolitan Chicago, Black & Hispanic Achievers of Industry, 1986; Association of Old Crows, Award of Excellence, 1984. **Special Achievements:** University of Washington, Role Model of the Year, 1993; Motorola coordinator for ''I Dream a World'' Sojourner Program, 1991; founder, Chicago Technical Exchange, 1989; videotape panelist, Trinton Community College, 1987; panelist, ''Objective Jobs: Women in Engineering Series,'' WBBM TV, 1986. **Business Addr:** Director of Manufacturing, Motorola, 1500 NW Gateway Blvd, FL19-MS37, Boynton Beach, FL 33426, (407)739-2021.

CEBALLOS, CEDRIC Z.
Professional basketball player. **Personal:** Born Aug 2, 1969, Maui, HI. **Educ:** Ventura College, Ventura, CA, 1986-88; California State Univ at Fullerton, Fullerton, CA, 1988-90. **Career:** Phoenix Suns, forward, 1990-94, 1997-98; Los Angeles Lakers, 1994-97; Dallas Mavericks, 1998-. **Honors/Awds:** NBA All-Star, 1995. **Business Addr:** Professional Basketball Player, Dallas Mavericks, 777 Sports St, Reunion Arena, Dallas, TX 75207, (214)748-1808.

CEDENO, CESAR
Professional baseball player (retired). **Personal:** Born Feb 25, 1957, Santo Domingo; married Cora Lefevre; children: Cesar Jr, Cesar Roberto, Cesar Richard. **Career:** Houston Astros, outfielder 1970-81; Cincinnati Reds, outfielder 1982-85; St Louis Cardinals, outfielder, 1985; Los Angeles Dodgers, outfielder, 1986. **Honors/Awds:** Only player in major league history to hit 20 or more homers and steal 50 or more bases in the same season three years in a row; had 50 or more steals six years in a row; named to the NL All-Star team four times; Gold Glove winner for defensive excellence in the outfield five years in a row 1972-76; named to the post-season NL All-Star team by Sporting News three times.

CELESTIN, TOUSSAINT A.
Physician. **Personal:** Born Nov 17, 1930, Cap Haitien, Haiti; married Jessie, Dec 15, 1956; children: Nadhia, Ramses, Marthe, Marie, Toussaint, Victoria. **Educ:** Lycee Nat Philippe Guerrier, BA 1950; Faculte de Med Univ Haiti, MD 1956. **Career:** Howard Univ Coll Med, asst prof psychiatry 1974-; Albany M Ed Coll Union U, 1971-74; Columbia Univ Coll & Physicians & Surgeons, staff psychiat 1964-71; Columbia Univ Coll Physicians & Surgeons Harlem Hosp, resd psychiat inst 1964-67; post grad 1961-63; Univ Haiti, physician 1956-68; Area C Mental Hlth Ctr Dept Human Resources DC, dir in-patient serv; Clinical Hypnosis Inst Howard U, dir; Intl Soc Papplied Studies Transcultural Adaptation Inc pres; St Thomas RC Ch, consult 1971. **Orgs:** Mem Shiloh Bapt Ch 1973; All Angels Episcopal Ch 1973; Christ Ch Meth; publ ''Adaptation of the Haitian Physician & His Family to the Am Soc''.

CENTERS, LARRY
Professional football player. **Personal:** Born Jun 1, 1968, Tatum, TX. **Educ:** Stephen F. Austin State, attended. **Career:** Phoenix Cardinals, running back, 1990-93; Arizona Cardinals, 1994-. **Honors/Awds:** Pro Bowl, 1995, 1996. **Business Addr:** Professional Football Player, Arizona Cardinals, 8701 S Hardy, Tempe, AZ 85284, (602)379-0101.

CHAFFERS, JAMES A.
Educator. **Personal:** Born Nov 30, 1941, Ruston, LA; married Geraldine; children: Pedra, Michael. **Educ:** So Univ Baton Rouge, BArch (cum laude) 1964; Univ of MI, MArch 1969, DArch 1971. **Career:** Coll of Arch & Urban Plng, prof; Wastenaw Co, commnr 1970-71; Nathan Johnson & Asso, arch; So U, tchr 2 yrs; Univ of MI, 2 yrs. **Orgs:** Chmn So Univ Dept of Arch; dir Comm based Design Wrkshps N Cntrl Ann Arbor & SW Detroit; cntrbn author to ''The Blk 70'S''. **Honors/Awds:** Recip Woodrow Wilson Fellow; outst tchr award So Univ 1971-72. **Military Serv:** AUS Corps of Engr capt 5 yrs. **Business Addr:** University of Michigan, College of Architecture, Ann Arbor, MI 48103.

CHALLENOR, HERSCHELLE
Educational administrator. **Personal:** Born Oct 5, 1938, Atlanta, GA; divorced. **Educ:** Spelman Coll, BA; Univ Grenoble, attended; Sorbonne Univ, attended; Johns Hopkins, MA; Columbia Univ, PhD. **Career:** Political Sci Dept Brooklyn Coll, asst prof 1969-72; Amer Pol Sci Assoc, cong fellow 1972-73; Div Ed & Rsch Ford Found, prog officer 1973-75; UN Ed Sci & Cultural Org Wash Liaison Office, dir 1978-93; Clark Atlanta Univ, School of Pub & Intl Affairs, dean, 1993-. **Orgs:** Consult Sub-com on Africa; mem UN Assoc Council on Foreign Rel, Amer Pol Sci Assoc, Natl Conf Black Pol Sci, Bd of Oper Crossroads Africa; bd mem Intl Block United Fund; mem Spel-

man Coll Scholarship. **Honors/Awds:** Charles Merill Study Travel Awd; Woodrow Wilson Fellowship; John Hay Whitney Fellowship; NY State Merit Fellowship; Amer Assoc Univ Women Fields Rsch Grant; Fellow Adlai Stevenson Inst Intl Affairs Chgo; Ford Found Travel & Study Awd. **Business Addr:** Dean, Clark Atlanta Univ, James P Brawley Dr & Fair St SW, Atlanta, GA 30314.

CHALMERS, THELMA FAYE
Executive director. **Personal:** Born Feb 21, 1947, Shreveport, LA; daughter of Ivy Williams Hampton and Leonard Hampton; married Jimmy Chalmers; children: Troy, Douglas, Celeste. **Educ:** Chandler College, Associates Degree 1966. **Career:** St Clair County Intergovernmental Grants Dept, program monitor 1979-81, program planner 1981-83, special assignment supvr 1983-86, div mgr 1988-90, executive director 1990-. **Orgs:** Equal employment opportunity officer St Clair County Grants Dept 1982-; staff liaison Service Delivery Area 24 Private Industry Council 1984-; mem Illinois Employment & Training Assn 1985; board member Illinois employment & Training Association 1989-90; member, Illinois Employment & Training Partnership, 1988-91; member, IETP Professional Development Committee 1989-90; vice chair, Advisory Council Program Services for Older Persons, currently. **Honors/Awds:** Assertive Mgmt Certificate, Southern Illinois Univ Edwardsville School of Business 1985; Image and Communication Skills Certificate, The Business Women's Training Institute 1986; Staff Award, Annual Job Training Partnership Act, 1989. **Home Addr:** 1517 Oak Meadow Dr, O Fallon, IL 62269. **Business Addr:** Executive Director, St Clair County Intergovernmental Grants Dept, 1220 Centreville Ave, Belleville, IL 62220.

CHAMBERLAIN, BYRON
Professional football player. **Personal:** Born Oct 17, 1971, Honolulu, HI. **Educ:** Wayne State (Neb.). **Career:** Denver Broncos, tight end, 1995-. **Business Addr:** Professional Football Player, Denver Broncos, 13655 Broncos Pkwy, Englewood, CO 80112, (303)649-9000.

CHAMBERLAIN, WESLEY POLK
Professional baseball player. **Personal:** Born Apr 13, 1966, Chicago, IL; son of Bettie L Chamberlain; children: Wesley Polk II. **Educ:** Simeon Vocational; Jackson State University. **Career:** Pittsburgh Pirates, 1987-90; Philadelphia Phillies, outfielder, 1990-. **Orgs:** SAA. **Honors/Awds:** Pittsburgh Pirates: 4th-round pick, 1987; MVP, Eastern League, 1989; Minor League Player of the Year, 1989; NL Player of the Week, Jul 27-Aug 2, 1991; Topps All-Star, 1989; Eastern League All-Star, 1989; Player of the Month, May-Jul, 1989; Topps Player of the Month, Aug 1989; High School All-American; All-Southwestern Conference, 1985, 1986, 1987. **Business Addr:** Professional Baseball Player, Philadelphia Phillies, PO Box 7575, Philadelphia, PA 19101, (215)463-6000.

CHAMBERLAIN, WILT NORMAN (WILT THE STILT)
Professional basketball player (retired), business executive. **Personal:** Born Aug 21, 1936, Philadelphia, PA. **Educ:** KS Univ, 1954-58. **Career:** Harlem Globetrotters, player 1958-59; Philadelphia Warriors, player 1959-65; Philadelphia 76ers, player 1965-68; LA Lakers, center 1968-73; San Diego Conquistadors (ABA), coach 1973-74; Wilt's Athletic Club, owner; Big Wilt's Smalls Paradise Niteclub, owner; actor in various movies (Conan the Destroyer, 1982) and adv endorsements; USTA League Tennis; Wilt Chamberlain's Restaurants Inc, owner, 1992-. **Honors/Awds:** NBA Rookie of the Year 1960; led NBA League in total points scored per season 7 years straight; holds following records: all-time professional lead in points scored (more than 30,000), most points scored by individual in one game (100 Points) 1962; named NBA MVP 4 times; averaged 30.1 points per game and led League in rebounds 11 times; inducted Basketball Hall of Fame 1978; Philadelphia Sports Writers Assn, Living Legend Award, 1991.

CHAMBERS, ALEX A.
Educational administrator, minister. **Personal:** Born Dec 10, 1934, Lorman, MS; son of Henrietta Hooks Chambers and McKinley Chambers; married Rilla George Morrison, 1960; children: Twan-Alexis Chambers. **Educ:** Stillman College, AB, 1960; Duke Univ, MDiv, 1968; Southeastern Univ, STD, 1971. **Career:** Hayes Tabernacle Christian Methodist Church, minister; Vermont Avenue Presbyternian Church, minister to youth; St Joseph Christian Methodist Episcopal Church, minister; JC Penny, auditor; Kittrel College, visiting professor, 1966-67; Furman Univ, professor of religion, 1972-; Williams CME Church, Memphis, TN, minister; Mount Olive CME Church, Memphis, TN, minister, 1982-86; Lane College, Jackson, TN, president, 1986-. **Orgs:** United Fund; editor, Eastern Index; exec vice pres/general, Van Hoose Mortuary. **Honors/Awds:** Author, "The Negro in the United States," Journal of Negro History, 1961; Honorary Degrees: Kittrell Coll, DD; Natl Theological Seminary, LittD; Stillman Coll, LHD; Alumni of the Year, 1968, Distinguished Alumni Award, Stillman Coll, 1970. **Military Serv:** US Army, SP-4, 1956-58; Good Conduct Medal. **Home Addr:** 1224 Highland Ave, Jackson, TN 38301. **Business Addr:** President, Lane College, 545 Lane Avenue, Jackson, TN 38301-4598.

CHAMBERS, CLARICE LORRAINE
Elected official, clergyman. **Personal:** Born Oct 7, 1938, Ossining, NY; daughter of Louise McDonald Cross (deceased) and Willie Cross (deceased); married Albert W, Jun 9, 1962; children: Albert W Jr, Cheryl L Fultz. **Educ:** Manna Bible Inst, Teachers Cert 1965; Trinity Coll of Bible, B Biblical Studies 1983; International Bible College & Seminary, Orlando FL, Masters Biblical Theology 1986. **Career:** Naval Supply Depot, master data spec 1957-65; dir of training Tri-Cty OIC 1970-72; PA State Dept of Revenue, asst public info dir 1972-79; Antioch Tabernacle UHC of A, pastor 1979-; Harrisburg School Bd, member. **Orgs:** Sec Tri-Cty OIC Bd 1980-; mem Tri-Cty United Way Bd 1983-89, South Central PA Food Bank Bd 1983-89; bd mem, YMCA 1989-; bd mem, Delta Dental 1989-95; council of trustees, Shippenburg University 1989-96; board of directors, PA 2000 1992-96; PA Standards and Practices Commission 1992-96; president, PA School Boards Association 1992; Natl School Bds Assn, 1993-. **Honors/Awds:** Volunteer Comm Serv Tri-Cty OIC 1977; Community Serv Awd Natl Assoc Black Accountants 1984; Cert of Recognition Christian Churches United 1984; African-American Comm Service Award, Harrisburg Chapter Black United Fund of Pennsylvania 1989. **Home Addr:** 147 Sylvan Terr, Harrisburg, PA 17104. **Business Addr:** Member, Harrisburg School Board, 1201 N 6th St, Harrisburg, PA 17101.

CHAMBERS, DONALD C.
Physician. **Personal:** Born May 17, 1936; married Jacqueline; children: Christopher, Kimberly, Bradley. **Educ:** NY U, BA 1957; Howard U, MS 1961. **Career:** Ings Co Hosp Ctr, res training 1961-66; St Univ NY, asst prof 1964-66; Baltimore Pvt Prac, 1968-; Sinai Hosp, physician; Provident Hosp, physician; Lutheran Hosp, physician. **Orgs:** Mem Pan Am Med Soc; Am Soc Abdominal Surgeons; mem NAACP; Monumental City Med Soc; Hlth Care Standards Com; MD Found Hlth Care. **Honors/Awds:** Contrib author Urban Hlth Mag; fellow Am Coll Abstericians Gynecologists 1969; fellow Am Coll Surgeons 1973; fellow Royal Soc Hlth. **Military Serv:** USAF cpat 1966-68. **Business Addr:** 2300 Garrison Blvd, Ste 200, Baltimore, MD 21216.

CHAMBERS, FREDRICK
Educator (retired). **Personal:** Born Mar 28, 1928, Waterloo, IA; married Doris Foster (deceased); children: Ivie Cecilia, Fredrick Foster. **Educ:** Univ of AR at Pine Bluff, BA 1955; Univ of AR, MEd 1959; Ball State U, EdD 1970. **Career:** Kent State Univ, assoc prof, assoc prof emeritus; Univ of AR at Pine Bluff, assoc prof 1959-71; Ball State Univ, teaching fellow History 1967-70; Phelix High School, social science teacher 1957-59; Mound Bayou High School, social science teacher 1955-57; AR Boy's Ind School, counselor 1955; Natl Teachers Ex Educ Testing Service, supr 1960-63. **Orgs:** Commr AR on Higher Educ 1970; exec com AR Conf of AAUP 1965-67; state sec & bd mem OH Am Civil Liberties 1976-. **Honors/Awds:** Author "Histories of Black Coll" Journal of Negro History 1972; Black Higher Educ in the US Greenwood Press Inc 1978. **Military Serv:** AUS pfc 1952-54. **Home Addr:** 2010 Carlton Dr, Kent, OH 44240.

CHAMBERS, HARRY, JR.
Consultant, educator. **Personal:** Born Jul 4, 1956, Birmingham, AL; son of Bessie Chambers and Harry Chambers Sr; married Linda Giles; children: Hali Alexandria, Harry Alonso III, Kayla Melissa. **Educ:** Alabama State Univ, BS 1979; Samford Univ, MBA 1985; Dale Carnegie, Human Relations & Leadership Training. **Career:** US General Accounting Office, co-op student 1976-77; Bank of Amer NT & SA, intl auditor Europe 1979-80; Amsouth Bank NA, div accounting officer opers 1980-86; US Treasury, IRS agent 1987-88; Chambers Consulting Ltd, financial partner, 1985-; Birmingham Southern College, adjunct prof, 1988-; Star Net Inc, vice pres, comptroller; Drake Beam Morin, consultant, 1996-. **Orgs:** Life mem Kappa Alpha Psi 1980-; life member Natl Black MBA Association Birmingham Chap 1985-; Sunday school teacher Sixth Ave Baptist Church 1985-; managing partner Chambers Consulting Ltd 1986-; deacon Sixth Ave Bapt Church 1986-; treasurer, bd mem, Academy of Fine Arts Inc, Birmingham AL, 1988-. **Honors/Awds:** Woodrow Wilson designee Woodrow Wilson Fellowship Found 1985; Birmingham Jefferson Metro Chamber of Commerce, charter member, 1992; City of Birmingham Cable Television Commission, 1995; Library Pension Board, bd member, 1995. **Home Addr:** 1040 50th St, Birmingham, AL 35208.

CHAMBERS, JOHN CURRY, JR.
Attorney. **Personal:** Born May 22, 1956, Newark, NJ; son of Naomi McGriff & John Chambers; married Georgette Sims-Chambers, Nov 28, 1981; children: John Curry III, Candace Dane. **Educ:** Univ of Pennsylvania, BA; The Washington College of Law, American Univ, JD. **Career:** American Petroleum Institute, principal RCRA attorney, 1981-84; CONOCO, in-house counsel, 1985; McKenna & Cuneo, partner, currently. **Orgs:** DC Bar; ABA, National Bar Assn; Environmental Law Editorial Institute, advisory bd, Journal of Environmental Permitting; advisory committee, ABA Conference on Minority Partners; committee, National Institute for the Environment; vice chair, ABA Teleconference & Video Programs Sonreel; vice chair, ABA Sonreel Diversity Committee; guest commentator, Natl Public Radio; founder, Brownfields Business Information Network; co-chair, ABA Video Teleconferences Committee. **Special Achievements:** McKenna & Cuneo, first African American equity partner in its history; Panelist for ABA Satellite Seminars; Lecturer; numerous publications. **Business Addr:** Partner, McKenna & Cuneo, 1900 K St, NW, Washington, DC 20006, (202)496-7698.

CHAMBERS, JULIUS LEVONNE
Attorney. **Personal:** Born Oct 6, 1936, Montgomery Co, NC; son of Matilda Chambers and William Chambers; married Vivian Verdell Giles; children: Derrick, Judy. **Educ:** NC Central Univ Durham, BA History (summa cum laude) 1958; Univ of MI, MA 1959; Univ of NC Sch of Law, JD 1962; Columbia Univ Sch of Law ML 1963. **Career:** Columbia Univ Sch of Law, assoc in law 1962-63; NAACP Legal Def & Educ Fund Inc, legal intern 1963-64; Chambers Stein Ferguson & Becton PA, pres 1964-84; Harvard Univ Law Sch, lecturer 1965; Univ of VA Law Sch, guest lecturer 1971-72; Univ of PA Sch of Law, lecturer 1972-90; Columbia University School of Law, adjunct 1978-91; NAACP Legal & Educ Fund Inc, dir counsel 1984-92; University of Michigan Law School, adjunct 1989-92; North Carolina Central University, chancellor 1993-. **Orgs:** Mem numerous cts of practice 1962-; mem Amer, Natl, 26th Judicial Dist NC Bar Assns; NC Assn of Black Lawyers; mem Amer Bar Assn Section on Indiv Rights & Responsibilities; adv com Natl Bar Assn Equal Employment Oppor; mem NC Bar Assn Com on Rules of Appellate Procedure; mem NC State Bar Assn Const Study Com; mem various NAACP brs; mem various legal assns; bd of dirs Epilepsy Assn of NC; mem various Univ bds; mem various alumni assns; mem various frats; mem Friendship Baptist Church Charlotte. **Honors/Awds:** WEB DuBois Awd Scotland Co 1973; Hall of Fame Awd NAACP 1975; numerous hon LLD degrees; various distinguished serv awds, frats & Assns. **Military Serv:** USNR 1960-63; AUSR 1963-66. **Business Addr:** Chancellor, North Carolina Central University, Durham, NC 27707.

CHAMBERS, MADRITH BENNETT
Appointed official. **Personal:** Born Oct 23, 1935, Beckley, WV; married Robert E Chambers; children: Stephanie M Rosario, Gregory B, Patrick M, Jennifer E, Sharri L. **Educ:** Bluefield State College, AS Law Enforcement, BS Criminal Justice Adm 1985. **Career:** Social Security Admin, contact representative. **Orgs:** Councilwoman City of Pax 1972-74; vice-pres Amer Legion Women's Aux 1982-84; chairperson City of Beckley Human Rights Comm 1978-; pres Beckley Chap Bluefield St Coll Alumni Assn 1983-; mem Alpha Kappa Alpha. **Honors/Awds:** DHHS Special Award Social Sec Admn 1980; Outstanding Service Awd Bluefield St Coll Alumni Assn 1984; Mountain State Bar Assn Citation Mt State Bar Assn 1984. **Business Addr:** Contact Representative, Social Security Adm, 214 N Kanawna St, Beckley, WV 25801.

CHAMBERS, OLIVIA MARIE
Government service. **Personal:** Born Sep 27, 1942, Denver, CO; married Bill D Chambers; children: Maria. **Educ:** Dale Carnegie Crs Human Rel, Cert 1977; Univ of Denver, Mgmt Cert Prog 1983; CO Univ Ext Cntr and Comm Clge. **Career:** State of CO Interstate Dept of Employ and Training Unit, mgr 1976-77; State of CO Dept of Employ and Trng, chief of benefits 1977-84; chief of tax department, 1984-. **Orgs:** Mem IAPES; bd mem Comm Homemaker Suc 1981-83. **Honors/Awds:** Citation hnrbl mntn Distgnshd State Serv Award Denver Federal Exec Bd 1981; rec Ebony Mag Speaking of People 1979. **Business Addr:** Dept of Employment & Training, 251 E 12th Ave, Denver, CO 80203.

CHAMBERS, PAMELA S.
Police sergeant. **Personal:** Born Nov 5, 1961, Gasden, AL; daughter of Mildred L Douglas Chambers and Hurley S Chambers. **Educ:** Ferris State College, Big Rapids MI, AA pre-law, 1982. **Career:** City of Pontiac MI, police cadet, 1982, police officer, 1982, police sergeant, 1988; owner, president, Not Just Nails, a nail salon, 1989. **Orgs:** Sec, Soc of Afro-American Police; bd mem, The Natl Black Police Assn; assoc mem, Natl Org of Black Law Exec (NOBLE). **Honors/Awds:** Distinction of being the first black woman promoted to police sergeant in the history of the city of Pontiac; also the youngest person ever to be promoted to sergeant in the city of Pontiac. **Business Addr:** Sergeant, Pontiac Police Department, 110 E Pike St, Pontiac, MI 48341.

CHAMBERS, VAN B.
Educator, artist. **Personal:** Born Mar 23, 1940, Lyon, MS; children: three. **Educ:** Xavier Univ, BA in fine arts, 1961; Notre Dame Univ, MFA, 1963. **Career:** Practicing artist, 1963-; Southern University, instructor of fine arts, 1963-69, asst professor, 1969-74, associate professor, 1974-. **Orgs:** Baton Rouge Gallery, 1971-.

CHAMBERS, YJEAN S.
Educator. **Personal:** Born Dec 9, 1921, Bluediamond, KY; daughter of Hester A Hutcherson Staples and Thomas H Staples; married Herman; children: Lanel R. **Educ:** Illinois State

Univ, BEd, 1943; Purdue Univ, MA, 1973; Purdue Univ, Litt, H D, 1993. **Career:** School Madison Illinois, 1943-45; Roosevelt HS Gary Indiana, 1945-71; Purdue Univ, Calumet, guest lecturer, 1969-71; grad instructor, 1971-73; Purdue Univ, Calumet, asst prof, 1973-79, assoc prof 1979-90, professor emerita, 1990-. **Orgs:** Pres, Gamma Psi Omega Chapter (Alpha Kappa Alpha Sor Inc), 1960-64; Gen Chmn, 29th & 39th Central Region Conf of AKA; Program Com Co-Chairperson; Gary Br, NAACP life mem com, 1963-88; bd mem, Gary School Trustees, 1973-77, pres, 1974; bd mem, Indiana School Bd Assn, 1974-77; chair, Northwest Indiana Regional School Bd Assn, 1974-77; mem, Central States Communication Assn; mem, Van Buren Baptist Church; chair, African American History Com, 1993-; dir, Miss Gary Scholarship Pageant, 1969-73; adv bd, Bank One; bd of dirs, pres, vp, Gary Educ Devel Found, 1977-; apptd by Gov Robt Orr Calumet Township Control Bd; dir, Miss Black Indiana Pageant, 1980-85; acting head, communication & creative arts dept, Purdue University, Calumet, 1981-83; vice pres, bd of dirs, Steel City Hall of Fame 1988-96, pres, 1996-; chmn, Quality Assurance Comm & Asst Secretary, bd of dirs, Methodist Hospital,Inc, 1981-; mem, Speech Communication Assn, 1971-; mem, Popular Culturel/Amer Culture Assns, 1987-; mem, bd of dirs, Visiting Nurses Assn of Northwest Indiana, 1990-96; mem, Academy Selection Board of Congressman Peter Visclosky, 1990-; steering committee mem, Jewish Federation Cultural Outreach Project, 1990-91; Northwest Indiana Visiting Nurse Assn Foundation, bd, 1997-. **Honors/Awds:** Amoco Foundation, Outstanding Teacher Award, Purdur Univ, Calumet, 1974, 1981; Outstanding Educator Awd Natl Sor of Phi Kappa Delta, Beta Nu Chap 1985; Gary City Council Resolution A Tribute for Academic Contributions to IN Youth & Adults 1986; Bethune Achievement Awd in Communication Miller Sect Natl Council of Negro Women 1986; named by IN Speech Assoc as one of Three Top Communication Educators in the State 1987; distinguished service award, Purdue University Alumni Assoc Calumet, 1987; Edgar L Mills Communication Award, The Communicators of Northwest Ind 1988; The Golden Apple Award, Gary Ambassadors of Education 1988; Educational Vision Award, IU Dons & Donnetts, 1988; ''Pronunciation Needs Attention'', The Times, 1986; ''Good Speech and the Job Interview'' The Times 1988; ''Gary Ind, remembered in the Diamond Time'' (a narrative poem with musical interpolations) excerpted in The Skylark, public performance, 1983; ''Reverent Resonances: M L King Remembered'' public performance 1986; Indianian African-American Heritage Award, Gary Community School Corp, Beckman School, 1991; Outstanding Service Award, Illinois State Univ, Alumni Assn, 1994; Inductee, Steel City Hall of Fame, 1994; Purdue Univ, Hall of Fame, 1997; Indiana Northwest Women's History Museum, inductee, 1997. **Home Addr:** 2969 W 20 Pl, Gary, IN 46404, (219)944-9242. **Business Addr:** Professor Emerita, Purdue University-Calumet, Porter Bldg, Hammond, IN 46323, (219)989-2393.

CHAMBLISS, ALVIN ODELL, JR. (IKE-MO)
Lawyer. **Personal:** Born Jan 22, 1944, Vicksburg, MS; son of Ledorsha A Chambliss and Alvin O Chambliss Sr; married Josephine Johnson Chambliss, Dec 31, 1973; children: Sadarie, Alvin O III, Alvenia. **Educ:** Jackson State Univ, BA, 1967; Howard Univ, JD, 1970; Univ of Calif, Masters of Law, 1972. **Career:** Natl Conf of Black Mayors; Operation PUSH; Legal Aid Society of Alameda County; New Orleans Legal Assistance; Cohon, Jones & Fazande Law Firm, 1972-74; North Mississippi Rural Legal Services, lawyer, 1974-. **Orgs:** Natl Black Media Coalition, vice chair; Black Mississippian Council for Higher Educ, gen counsel; Oxford-Lafayette County Branch NAACP, pres; Natl Conf of Black Mayors, chairman; Magnolia Bar Assn, court watch chair; Mississippi Assn of Educators, affiliate advisor; Methodist Men of Burns, community liaison. **Honors/Awds:** NAACP, Ming Award Lawyer of the Year, 1992; SCLC Chauncy Estridge Distinguished Barrister of Law, 1992; Mississippi Education Assn, Lawyer of the Year, 1993; Mississippi Legislative Black Caucus, Lawyer of the Year, 1993; Masonic Orders, PHA North Mississippi, Man of the Year, 1993. **Special Achievements:** Natl NAACP 8th Lawyers CLE Seminar: Honoring Our Past, Fulfilling Our Present, Preparing for Our Future; Voting Rights & Citizen Participation Manual, 1986; Ayers Brown III The New Frontier in Higher Education, 1989; Trends in the Eighties, Mississippi State Practice, 1989; Natl NAACP Summit on Higher Education, Higher Education Desegregation Advancing African-Americans Towards Equality, 1992; Ayers v Fordice, ''Where Do We Go From Here in Higher Education Desegration,'' 1993; Ayers v Fordice, Reversing the Trend in Higher Education Desegration From Closure to Parity for HBCUs, 1993; ''Black Colleges Under Fire,'' Emerge, 1993. **Business Addr:** Attorney, North Mississippi Rural Legal Services, Inc, PO Box 928, 2136 W Jackson Ave, Oxford, MS 38655, (601)234-2918.

CHAMBLISS, CHRIS (CARROLL CHRISTOPHER)
Professional baseball coach, professional baseball player (retired). **Personal:** Born Dec 26, 1948, Dayton, OH; son of Christene H Knew Chambliss and Carroll R Chambliss; married Audry C Garvin Chambliss, Sep 30, 1973; children: Russell J. **Educ:** Miracosta Junior College, Oceanside, CA, AA, 1968; UCLA, 1969; Monclair State University, Upper Monclair, NJ, BS, 1980. **Career:** Cleveland Indians, first baseman, 1971-73; New York Yankees, first baseman, designated hitter, 1974-79; Atlanta Braves, first baseman, 1980-86; New York Yankees, 1988; London Tigers, manager, 1990; Greenville Braves, manager; St Louis Cardinals, hitting instructor, 1992-. **Honors/Awds:** 37 doubles in 1980; tied the Atlanta record set by Hank Aaron; Indian's No 1 pick, Jan 1970 free agent draft; World Series Champion, New York Yankees 1977, 1978; Golden Glove, 1st Base, Yankees 1978; Rookie of the Year, Cleveland Indians 1971; American League All Star, New York Yankees, 1976. **Military Serv:** Air National Guard, airman, 1970-76. **Business Addr:** Hitting Instructor, St Louis Cardinals, Busch Memorial Stadium, 250 Stadium Plaza, St Louis, MO 63102.

CHAMBLISS, PRINCE C., JR.
Attorney. **Personal:** Born Oct 3, 1948, Birmingham, AL; son of Rev & Mrs Prince C Chambliss Sr; married Patricia Toney Chambliss, Dec 26, 1971; children: Patience Bradyn. **Educ:** Wesleyan Univ, 1966-68; Univ of Alabama, Birmingham, BA, 1971; Harvard Univ School of Law, JD, 1974. **Career:** Univ of Alabama-Birmingham, special asst to pres, 1974-75; Judge Sam C Pointer Jr, law clerk, 1975-76; Armstrong Allen, et al, attorney, 1976-. **Orgs:** Tennessee Bd of Law Examiners, vp, 1988-; Tennessee Bar Assn, scy, 1994-97; Memphis Bar Assn, bd of dirs, 1994-, president, 1997-98; Ben F Jones Chapter of the National Bar Assn, chairman, judicial recommendations committee, 1978-; Grant Information Ctr Inc, chairman-elect, 1994-; Memphis Mid-South Chapter, bd of dirs American Red Cross, bd of dirs, 1987-. **Honors/Awds:** National Bar Assn, Judicial Conference Community Service Award, 1986; Memphis Legal Secretaries Assn, Boss of the Year, 1983. **Special Achievements:** ''Legal Ethics for Trial Lawyers,'' The Litigator; ''Inconsistent Verdicts: How to Recognize & Cope With,'' The Litigator. **Business Addr:** Attorney, Armstrong, Allen, Prewitt, Gentry, Johnston & Holmes, 80 Monroe Avenue, Ste 700, Brinkley Plaza, Memphis, TN 38103, (901)524-4951.

CHAMPION, JAMES A.
Human resources executive. **Personal:** Born May 9, 1947, Bronx, NY; son of Jean Simmons Champion and James William Champion; married Victoria Lindsey Champion, May 25, 1985; children: Nicole, Jayson, Christopher, Lindsey. **Educ:** Alabama A & M University, Huntsville, AL, BS, 1970; Rutgers University, New Brunswick, NJ, graduate school of education, 1975-76. **Career:** Chase Manhattan Bank, New York , NY, asst educational coordinator, 1970-72; US Dept of Labor Recruitment & Training Program, New York, NY, director, 1972-79; Merrill Lynch & Co, New York, NY, asst vice president, human resources, 1979-85; Ryder Truck Rental Inc, Miami, FL, director, employee relations, 1985-87; Ryder System Inc, Miami, FL, corporate director, human resources, 1987-92, director, corporate diversity/employee affairs, 1992-. **Orgs:** Board member, Miami/Dade Chamber of Commerce, 1992-; president, Assn of Affirmative Action Professionals, Miami, 1989-; board member, Jobs for Progress, Miami, 1992-; chairman of advisory group, The Focal Point for the Elderly, 1991-; board member, The Epilepsy Foundation of Miami, 1992-; member, Kappa Alpha Psi Fraternity, 1968-. **Honors/Awds:** Black Achiever, Harlem YMCA, 1982; Black Achiever, Family Christian Association of America, 1987; Humanitarian Award, 1990; Service Award, 1990. **Business Addr:** Director, Corporate Diversity/ Employee Affairs, Ryder System, 3600 NW 82nd Ave, Miami, FL 33166.

CHAMPION, JESSE
Journalist (retired). **Personal:** Born Aug 27, 1927, Dolomite, AL; divorced; children: Hermenia Gwynette, Sharmayn Lil Margo, Jesse II. **Educ:** AL A&M U, grad 1951. **Career:** WERC Radio, dir; news report; Southwestern HS, instr 1963-71; Council Elem Sch, tchr 1954-63; Carver HS, tchr 1950-54. **Orgs:** Mem AL Educ Assoc; mem Nat Educ Assn 1950-63; mem Amer Fed of Tchrs; Flint Tchrs Assn 1963-71; mem Amer Fed of Musicians; mem Prof Journalism Soc; NAACCP; B'ham Urban Leag; B'ham Press Club; Knights of Columbus; Alpha Phi Chap; ed past chrm Omega Psi Phi Frat; Sigma Delta Chi. **Honors/Awds:** Outstanding Clarinetist, Morehouse Coll Award 1946; Acad Award, AL A&M Univ dram club; Fellowship Grant; Univ of Notre Dame 1951; Outst Newsman Award, B'hamFirefighters 1973; Best Public Affairs Dir, State Assn Press 1975; hon mention Active Partic during Civil rights struggle 1962-63. **Business Addr:** 800 14th St, SW, Birmingham, AL 35211.

CHAMPION, TEMPII BRIDGENE
Speech/language pathologist. **Personal:** Born Sep 2, 1961, Brooklyn, NY. **Educ:** Northeastern Univ, BS 1983; Hampton Univ, MA 1986. **Career:** Bd of Educ New York, speech therapist 1983-84; Northern Westchester Ctr for Speech Disorders, speech therapist 1986-87; Federation Employment & Guidance Svcs, speech therapist 1987-. **Orgs:** Mem Amer Speech & Hearing Assoc, New York City Speech & Hearing Assoc, Natl Assoc of the Deaf, NAACP; mem Black Speech Language Hearing Assoc. **Honors/Awds:** Graduate Fellowship 1984-86; Who's Who Among Outstanding Young Women of Amer 1985; Cert Speech Lang Pathologist (ASHA); NYS Lic Speech Language Pathologist. **Home Addr:** 334 Eastern Parkway, Brooklyn, NY 11225. **Business Addr:** Speech/Language Pathologist, Federation Employ & Guid Serv, 510 6th Ave, New York, NY 10011.

CHANCE, KENNETH BERNARD
Endodontist, educator, consultant. **Personal:** Born Dec 8, 1953, New York, NY; son of Janie Bolles Chance and George E Chance; married Sharon L Lewis; children: Kenneth B II, Dana Marie, Christopher Weldon, Jacquelyne Lee. **Educ:** Fordham Univ, BS 1975; Case Western Reserve Univ Dental Sch, DDS 1979; Jamaica Hospital GP Residency Prog, Certificate 1980; NJ Dental School, Certificate in Endodontics 1982; PEW Natl Dental Educ Prog, Certificate 1986. **Career:** Harlem Hosp, attending 1981-90; North Central Bronx Medical Ctr, asst attending 1982-; Jamaica Hosp, asst attending 1982-86; Kings Co Medical Ctr, chief of endodontics 1983-91; Kingsbrook Jewish Medical Ctr, asst attending 1985-89; NJ Dental Sch, dir of external affairs 1985-89, assoc prof of endodontics 1987-97; Univ of Medicine & Dentistry of New Jersey, asst dean for external affairs & urban resource devel, 1989-97; Commissioner of Health, Department of Health of New Jersey, consultant, 1991-97; Health Policy Program, The Joint Center for Political and Economics Studies, director, 1992-93; United States Senator Frank Lautenberg (D-NJ), health policy advisor, 1992-; Meharry Med Coll, School of Dentistry, dean, prof, 1997-. **Orgs:** Mem Amer Assn of Endodontists 1980-86, Natl Dental Assn 1980-; minister of music and sr organist Sharon Bapt Ch 1983-94; mem Intl Assn of Dental Rsch 1984-; pres elect Greater Metro Dental Soc of NY 1985-86; consultant Commonwealth Dental Soc of NJ 1985-97; member American Association of Dental Schools 1990-. **Honors/Awds:** Dr Paul P Sherwood Awd Case Western Reserve Dental Sch 1979; Awd for Excellent Serv Jamaica Hosp 1981; Rsch Awd The Foundation of the UMDNJ 1985; Exceptional Merit Awd NJ Dental Sch 1986; Nom for Excellence in Teaching Awd NJ Dental School 1985; University of Medicine and Denistry of New Jersey Award in Education 1990; Robert Wood Johnson Health Policy Fellowship Award 1991; Pew National Dental Leadership Development Fellowship Award, 1991; Fellow, Omicron Kappa Upsilon Honor Dental Society, Omega Omega Chapter, 1992; Intl College of Dentists, American College of Dentists, 1993; Pierre Fauchard Academy Intl Honor Organization, 1994. **Home Addr:** 570 Church St E, Apt 304, Brentwood, TN 37027. **Business Addr:** Dean, School of Dentistry, Meharry Medical College, 1005 Dr D B Todd Jr, Blvd, Nashville, TN 37208-3599.

CHANCELLOR, CARL EUGENE
Retired attorney. **Personal:** Born Mar 1, 1929, Cleveland, OH; son of Helen L Leonard Summons and James H Summons (stepfather); married Joyce Marshall; children: Carl C, Bruce E, Steven E, Yvette. **Educ:** OH State Univ, BA 1951; Case Western Res Law School, JD 1954; Univ of MI Grad School of Bus Admin, Publ Utility Exec Prog Cert 1973. **Career:** Cleveland Electric Illuminating Co, assoc attny, attny, sr attny, gen suprv attny claims 1954-72, mgr legal serv dept 1972-82, asst gen counsel 1982-, sec and general counsel 1986-90 (retired). **Orgs:** Spec counsel Attny Gen of OH 1953-69; sec, bd of dir Raymilton Land Co Coal Mining 1956-64; labor adv comm OH C of C 1977-; pres Self Insurers Group of OH 1965-70; chmn Edison Elec Inst Claims Comm 1985-86, Frankfort Pol Action Comm 1977-84; exec bd, life mem Cleveland Br NAACP; mem Alpha Phi Alpha. **Honors/Awds:** Cert of Appreciation Vice Pres Humphreys Plans for Prog Comm 1969; Meritorious Serv Awd Cleveland Bar Assn 1972; Legal Study Scholarship Rainey Found 1951-54.

CHANDLER, ALLEN EUGENE
Physician, military officer. **Personal:** Born Sep 16, 1935, Hagerstown, MD; married Barbara Hardiman Chandler; children: Allen (deceased), Rodney, Roderick. **Educ:** Morgan State College, Baltimore, MD, BS, (summa cum laude), chemistry, 1957; Jefferson Medical College, Philadelphia, PA, MD, 1961. **Career:** General Leonard Wood Army Hospital, Fort Leonard Wood, MS, chief of pediatric department, 1964-66; Pennsylvania Army National Guard, 108th Combat Support Hospital, chief of medical services, 1976-83, state surgeon, Headquarters State Area Command, 1983, advisor to the National Guard Bureau Surgeon, 1984, assistant adjutant general, State Area Command, 1987-; private medical practice, Philadelphia, PA, currently; Philadelphia Health Department, senior pediatrician, currently. **Orgs:** Member, Natl Medical Assn; member, American Academy of Pediatrics; member, US Military Academies Selection Committee for Congressman and House Majority Whip William H Gray; member, National Guard Assn of Pennsylvania; member, Natl Guard Assn of the US; member, Assn of Military Surgeons. **Military Serv:** Pennsylvania Army National Guard, Brigadier General, 1976-; Meritorious Service Medal, Army Commendation Medal, Army Reserve Components Achievement Medal with one Oak Leaf Cluster, Armed Forces Reserve Medal, National Defense Service Medal, Army Service Ribbon, Pennsylvania Twenty-year Service Medal, General Thomas R White Ribbon, General Thomas J Stewart Medal, Adjutant General's Staff Identification Badge. **Business Addr:** Dir, Pediatrics, City of Philadelphia, Dept of Health, 1720 S Broad, Philadelphia, PA 19145.

CHANDLER, ALTON H.
Publisher. **Personal:** Born Oct 4, 1942, Philadelphia, PA; son of Frances Houston-Chandler Leysath and Herman A. Chandler. **Educ:** Penn State University, University Park, PA, advertising art, 1960-64; Cooper School of Art, Cleveland, OH, design, 1964-65; Philadelphia College of Textiles & Sciences,

Philadelphia, PA, textile design, 1966-67; Philadelphia College of Art, Philadelphia, PA, ad market, 1967-69. **Career:** AT&T, Wayne, PA/Newark, NJ, art director, 1964-70; American Baptist Churches, Valley Forge, PA, art director, 1975-76; Perkasie Industries Corporation, Perkasie, PA, advertising & marketing director, 1976-80; Magnatite Inc, Boston, MA, advertising & marketing director, 1980-84; Black Family Magazine, Chicago, IL, creative director, 1984-85; Chandler/White Publishing Co., Chicago, IL, president, 1985-. **Business Addr:** President, Chandler/White Publishing Co Inc, 30 E Huron, Suite 4403, Chicago, IL 60611.

CHANDLER, EFFIE L.
Business executive. **Personal:** Born Aug 13, 1927, Houston, TX; divorced; children: Donald C. **Educ:** Massey Bus Coll, 1967-68; TX So U, BA 1966; TX So U, MEd 1975; Franklin Beauty Coll, Cosmetology TX License 1945. **Career:** US Postal Svc, dist EEO splst 1973-; asso employee devel advisor 1973; asst learning counselor 1971-73; acting & employment asst 1968-74; Personnel Section, clk steno 1965-68; scheme instr 1963-65; job instr 1963-65; distribution clk 1959-63. **Orgs:** Mem Nat Council of Negro Women; YWCA; Nat Assn of Postal Supr Br 122; Fed Minority Bus Opportunity Com; instr EEO Div, So Region Headquarters chrtr mem Cit Against Drug Abuse Com; past society editor for Houston's Oldest Black Weekly Newspaper, Effie's Excerpts 1973-74; sec Cambridge Civic Club 1967; sec treas 1968-69; pres Cambridge Village Civic Club 1973-74; chmn exec adv bd Anti-Basileus for Gamma Phi Sigma Chpt; Sigma Gamma Rho Sorority; campus advisor Alpha Lambda Chpt; Sigma Gama Rho Sorority TX So Univ 1974-. **Honors/Awds:** Outstdng Serv to Comm, Cambridge Village Civic Club 1977; The Lt Col Cleveland Roy Petit Merit Award; Cert of Appreciation in recognition of performance in interest of improved Postal Svc, US Postal Svc, So Region; recipient Certificate & cash award for adopted suggestion, US PO 1967; Superior Accomplishment Award with cash award, US PO 1968; Quality Step Increase 1968; nominated for Fedl Women's Award 1975. **Business Addr:** 401 Franklin Ave, Houston, TX 77201.

CHANDLER, EVERETT A.
Attorney. **Personal:** Born Sep 21, 1926, Columbus, OH; son of Mary Turner Chandler and Everett P Chandler; divorced; children: Wayne B, Brian E, V Rhette, Mae Evette. **Educ:** Ohio State Univ, BSc in Educ 1955; Howard Univ Law School, JD 1958. **Career:** Juvenile Ct Cuyahoga County, referee, support dept 1959; City of Cleveland OH, hous insp 1960; Cuyahoga County Welfare Dept, legal inv 1960-64; Cuyahoga County OH, asst cty pros 1968-71; City of Cleveland OH, chief police prosecutor 1971-75; private practice, attorney 1975-. **Orgs:** Bd mem, Cedar Branch YMCA, 1965; Comm Action Against Addiction, 1975-80, bd chrmn, 1980-87; bd mem, Legal Aid Soc of Cleveland, 1980; polemarch and bd chmn, Kappa Alpha Psi Inc, Cleveland Alumni Chapter, 1976, 1980-83; NAACP; Urban League; bd mem, past bd pres, CIT Mental Health; Excelsior Lodge #11 F&AM; Mt Olive Missionary Baptist Church, 1958-. **Honors/Awds:** Book review vol 21 #2 Cleveland State Law School Law Review 1972; main speaker banquet Frontiers Intl Columbus OH 1972; Cleveland Bar Association, Meritorious Service Award, 1972. **Military Serv:** USN qmq2. **Home Addr:** 16010 Talford Ave, Cleveland, OH 44128. **Business Addr:** Attorney, PO Box 28459, Cleveland, OH 44128-0459.

CHANDLER, HAROLD R.
Librarian. **Personal:** Born Sep 8, 1941, Louisville, KY; son of Nellie M. Chandler and Joseph F. Chandler. **Educ:** Morehouse Coll, BS, Biology 1965; Atlanta Univ, MSLS 1965; Univ of TN Med School, Certified Med Librarian 1972; Memphis Theological Sem, MDiv 1978, MAR 1987. **Career:** Memphis Theological Seminary, librarian-acquisitions/minister; Univ of TN Center for Health Science, rsch bibliographer 1972-76; Watkins Chapel CME Church Memphis, minister of music; Regional Med Center, Memphis, med librarian 1984-; Teaches class on ministry to the terminally ill. **Orgs:** HEW Fellowship for Science Librarians 1971-72; mem Memphis Ministerial Assn 2 yrs; steering com 1st Annual Lecture Series LeMoyne-Owen Coll 1980; post grad librarian fellowship Univ TN Med School; delegate to the World Methodist Conference Nairobi Kenya 1986; mem, Memphi, 1989. **Honors/Awds:** Outstanding young man of year 1978; Commendation medal USAF; Honored for teaching class on death & dying, Mt Vernon Baptist Church Westwood; Organized the Black History Program at the MED, 1985-present. **Military Serv:** USAF staff sgt 4 years served.

CHANDLER, JAMES P.
Attorney, educator. **Personal:** Born Aug 15, 1938, Bakersfield, CA; married Elizabeth Thompson; children: Elizabeth Lynne, James Jr, Isaac, Dennis Augustine, Ruth Rebekah, Aaron Daniel Pushkin, David Martin Thompson. **Educ:** Univ CA, AB, JD; Havard U, LLM. **Career:** The Natl Law Center, George Washington Univ, prof of law 1977-; Univ CA, research asst; Boston Univ Law School, instructor 1970-71; Univ of MD Law School, asst assoc prof 1971-75; Univ of MS Law Center, distinguished visiting prof of law 1976; Univ CO Law School, visiting prof of law 1977. **Orgs:** DC Bar; Am Soc Intl Law 1969-; Am Assn Univ Profs 1971-; Am Soc Law Profs 1974-; Alpha Phi Alpha Frat 1961-; bd dirs Ch God Evening Light Saints 1972-; Computer Law Assn 1974-; Woodbourne Ctr Inc 1974-76; sect council mem Am Bar Assn; consult Adminstrn Officer Cts St MD 1974-76; US Gen Acctng Office 1973-81.

CHANDLER, MITTIE OLION
Educator, researcher, consultant. **Personal:** Born Jul 25, 1949, Detroit, MI; daughter of Lurie Mae Johnson Davis; children: Mae Evette Chandler. **Educ:** Michigan State University, Lansing, MI, BA, 1971; Wayne State University, Detroit, MI, MUP, 1979, PhD, 1985. **Career:** Detroit Housing Department, public housing manager, 1972-77; Detroit Community and Economic Development Dept, city planner, 1977-81; New Detroit Inc, Detroit, MI, director, neighborhood stabilization & housing division, 1981-85; Cleveland State University, Cleveland, OH, assistant professor, 1985-91; associate professor, 1991-; Master of Urban Planning, Design & Dev Prog, dir, 1993-; Master of Science in Urban Studies Program, director, 1995-. **Orgs:** Board of trustees, North Coast Community Homes, 1997-; bd of trustees, The Empowerment Ctr of Greater Cleveland, 1997-; board of trustees, Living in Cleveland Center, 1987-94; president, board of trustees, Living In Cleveland Center, 1990-92; board of trustees, Garden Valley Neighborhood House, 1987-93; president, board of trustees, Garden Valley Neighborhood House, 1991-93; board of trustees, Professional Housing Services, 1990-92; Alpha Kappa Alpha Sorority, 1969-; Urban League of Greater Cleveland, 1989-; National Conference of Black Political Scientists, 1990-; Natl Assn for the Advancement of Colored People, life mem. **Honors/Awds:** Urban Homesteading: Programs and Policies, Greenwood Press Inc, 1988; Clifford Kaufman Memorial Award in Urban Politics, Wayne State University, 1986; Pi Alpha Alpha, National Honor Society for Public Affairs and Administration, 1982; Minority Fellowship Award, Urban Institute, 1984; Outstanding Young Woman of Amer, 1979. **Home Addr:** 3491 W 159th St, Cleveland, OH 44111, (216)671-2109. **Business Addr:** Director, Master of Science in Urban Studies Program, Cleveland State University, College of Urban Affairs, Cleveland, OH 44115, (216)687-3861.

CHANDLER, THEODORE ALAN
Educator. **Personal:** Born Sep 19, 1949, St Louis, MO. **Educ:** Northwest MO State Univ, BS 1973; Southern IL Univ Edwardsville, MA 1980; Univ of FL, PhD 1986. **Career:** Cleveland HS, secondary teacher 1976-79; New Student Life-SIU Edwardsville, consul 1980; SIU Edwardsville, grad teaching asst 1979-80; Univ of FL, grad teaching asst 1980-83; Sex Equity in Voc Ed, project asst 1983; FL Keys Comm Coll, prof & ea/eo coord 1983-90, Arts & Sciences Division, chairman, 1990-. **Orgs:** Mem FL Speech Comm Assn 1981-; mem Speech Comm Assn 1980-; mem Southern Speech Comm Assn 1981-; mem FL Assn of Equal Oppor Profs 1983-; mem Tennessee Williams Fine Arts Ctr Founders Soc, Key West, 1985-; board of directors Helpline Inc, secretary 1992-93, president 1993-94; AIDS Help Inc, volunteer, 1988-93. **Honors/Awds:** Top Ranked Paper Competitive FL Speech Comm Assn 1982; Outstanding Young Men of Amer Jaycees 1984; Teaching Excellence Awds SIU-E, 1980, Univ of FL, 1983; Outstanding Faculty Member Phi Theta Kappa 1989-90. **Business Addr:** Professor & Chairman, Arts & Science Division, Florida Keys Comm College, 5901 W College Rd, Key West, FL 33040.

CHANEY, ALPHONSE
Insurance agency manager. **Personal:** Born Jul 24, 1944, Detroit, MI; son of Gussie Chaney and Norman Chaney; married Clara Hinton, Feb 14, 1981; children: Kristina, Stacy Sanders, Jason. **Educ:** Western Michigan University, BS, 1967; University of Michigan, 1969-70. **Career:** DC Heath and Co, sales representative, 1973-87; State Farm Insurance Companies, agent, 1987-92, agency manager, 1992-. **Orgs:** National Association of Life Underwriters. **Honors/Awds:** DC Heath and Co, National Sales Acheievement Award, 1985; State Farm Insurance, Michigan Life Hall of Fame, Charter Member Health Hall of Fame, 1987, Michigan Life Hall of Fame, 1988, 1989, 1990, 1991; Michigan Life Hall of Fame, 1987, 1993. **Business Phone:** (313)228-2858.

CHANEY, DON
Former professional basketball coach. **Personal:** Born Mar 22, 1946, Baton Rouge, LA; married Jackie; children: Michael, Donna, Kara. **Educ:** Univ of Houston, graduated, 1968. **Career:** Boston Celtics, 1968-75, 1978-80; St Louis Spirits, 1975-76; Los Angeles Lakers, 1976-78; San Diego Clippers, asst coach, 1983-85; LA Clippers, head coach, 1985-87; Atlanta Hawks, asst coach, 1987-88; Houston Rockets, head coach, 1988-92; Detroit Pistons, asst coach, 1980-83, 1992-93, head coach, 1993-95. **Business Addr:** Former Head Coach, Detroit Pistons, 2 Championship Dr, Auburn Hills, MI 48326, (810)377-0100.

CHANEY, JOHN
Head coach. **Educ:** Bethune-Cookman, BS, education; Antioch, Master's Degree. **Career:** Cheyney State Coll, basketball coach; Temple Univ, basketball coach, currently. **Honors/Awds:** Philadelphia Public League's MVP Player 1951; NAIA All-Amer at Bethune-Cookman.

CHANNELL, EULA L.
Business assistant. **Personal:** Born Jan 29, 1928, Greenville, SC; daughter of Ruby Davenport Channell (deceased) and Caesar Channell. **Educ:** Benedict Coll; Greenville Tech Coll, AA 1974. **Career:** Allen Music Co, mgr sheet music dept; SC Commn on Aging Greenville, office worker 1972; Phillis Wheatley Assn Greenville, girls worker 1965-69; Recreation Dept City of Greenville, supvr 1955-65. **Orgs:** Mem Greenville Urban League; mem NAACP; mem ARC; mem Bethel Church of God; Blu Triangle Garden Club; Lend-A-Hand Federated Club; Greenville Dem Women; SC Literacy Assn; YWCA; Adv Housing Com; Girl Scout Leader; Greenville Chapter of Human Services; mem SC Fed of Women and Girls' Club; pres Lend-A-Hand Fed Club; mem PTA; delegate to state convention Guille County Dems; charter mem, sec Greenville Chap Top Ladies of Distinction. **Honors/Awds:** Honored for serv rendered Family Planning Assn; Citizen of week Focus Newspaper; received letter of congratulations US Senator James R Mann; Camp for Pregnant Girls; Girl Scouts; Boy Scouts; Cancer Soc; 1st runner up Woman of Yr Greenville Chap NAACP; hon Mayor of City vol Serv in recreation; rec'd of award vol serv by exec dir of Phyllis Wheatley Assn; part in City wide voter registration proj Political Action Com; Heart Fund; Arthritis Found; March of Dimes; United Fund. **Home Addr:** 144 Catlin Circle, Hyde Park, Greenville, SC 29607.

CHAPMAN, ALICE MARIAH
Deputy Director, Human Resources. **Personal:** Born Dec 31, 1947, New York, NY; daughter of Elizabeth Brooks Chapman and Elijah Chapman Sr (deceased); divorced. **Educ:** City Univ of NY, Liberal Arts 1969; New York Univ, Business Admin 1974. **Career:** WOR Radio, dir public serv & comm affairs 1978-80; Waxy Radio, dir public affairs & comm relations 1980-83; RKO General Inc, corp equal employment compliance mgr 1976-78, corp dir equal employment oppor 1983-87; City of NY, deputy city personnel dir-equal employment opportunity 1987-89; New York City Health and Hospitals Corporation, acting vice president, Affirmative Action, 1989-92; Darryl E Greene & Associates, chief executive officer, 1992-94; New York State Unified Court System, deputy director, Human Resources, Equal Employment Opportunity Division, 1994-. **Orgs:** Raritan Valley Chapter, The Links Inc. **Honors/Awds:** Black Achievers in Industry Awd Harlem YMCA 1979; Cecelia Cabiness Saunders Awd New Harlem YWCA 1985; Corporate Recognition Awd Metropolitan Council of NAACP Br 1987. **Home Addr:** 21 E Lincoln Place, North Brunswick, NJ 08902. **Business Addr:** Dep Dir, Human Resources, Equal Emp Opportunity Div, New York State Unified Court System, 25 Beaver St, Rm 1009, New York, NY 10004.

CHAPMAN, AUDREY BRIDGEFORTH
Family therapist, author, trainer. **Personal:** Born Aug 30, 1941, Yonkers, NY; daughter of Alice Lee Bridgeforth Chapman and Leon Charles Chapman. **Educ:** Goddard College, Plainfield, VT, BA, 1974; University of Bridgeport, Bridgeport, CT, MA, 1976; The Fielding Institute, Santa Barbara, CA, pre-doctorate psychology candidate, currently. **Career:** Hamden Mental Health Service, mental health therapist, 1976-78; Center for Systems and Program Development, staff development, trainer, 1979-80; Howard University, Inst of Urban Affairs & Dev, director of community action program, 1980-81, Counseling Service, family marriage counselor and trainer, 1981-; A B Chapman Associates, president of human relations training and staff management, 1988-. **Orgs:** National Board of Certified Counselors, 1983-; Counselors Assn, 1983-. **Honors/Awds:** APA Minority Fellowship for Social Research, 1983; Certification of Appreciation, Howard University, Division of Student Affairs, 1988. **Special Achievements:** Author: Mansharing: Black Men and Women: Battle For Love and Power; ''Black Men Do Feel About Love,'' article; WHUR-FM, ''All About Love,'' hostess, 1981-; Entitled to Good Loving: Black Men and Women and the Battle for Love and Power, Henry Holt, 1994. **Business Addr:** Family Therapist, 1800 Diagianal Road, Ste 600, Alexandria, VA 22314.

CHAPMAN, CHARLES F.
Human resources executive. **Personal:** Born Jul 11, 1947, Charlottesville, VA; son of Catherine Banks Chapman and Charles Chapman; married Kathy Williams; children: Weusi, Kia. **Educ:** Rutgers Univ, BA 1971. **Career:** Ramapo Coll of NJ, dir community affairs 1972-75; NJ Dept Comm Affairs, EEO officer 1975-78; Legal Serv Corp, dir civil rights 1978-83; CNT, partner, consultant 1982-; Durham Co Hospital Corp, vp, Human Resources, 1984-94; CFC & Associates, CEO/president, 1994-. **Orgs:** Bd dirs NJ Public Policy Rsch Inst 1976-; commissioner NJ Commission EEO & Affirmative Action 1976-80; advisory bd Willingboro, NJ Township 1977-78; vice pres Natl Congress of Affirmative Action Assocs 1978; Amer Bar Assn Task Force on Minorities in the Profession 1982-84; consultant, Natl Legal Aid & Defenders Assoc 1983; consultant Puerto Rico Legal Services Inc 1983-84; president NC Chapter Amer Assn for Affirmative Action 1985-88; mem NC Health Manpower Advisory Council 1985-; mem Triangle Area Business Advisory Council 1986-; admin NC Girls Olympic Devel Soccer Program 1986-90; vice pres Durham County Hospital Corp, 1984; pres Durham Day Care Council, 1990-95; Durham County Board of Health, 1992-; Governors Health District Board. **Business Addr:** CEO/President, CFC & Associates Inc, 3516 Manford Drive, Durham, NC 27707.

CHAPMAN, CLEVELAND M.
Construction company executive. **Career:** Englewood Construction Co, Chicago, IL, chief executive.

CHAPMAN, DAVID ANTHONY
Attorney. **Personal:** Born Nov 6, 1949, Akron, OH; married Sharon Gail McGee; children: Brandon. **Educ:** Univ of Akron, BA 1972; Univ of Cincinnati Coll of Law, JD 1975. **Career:** City of Cincinnati Law Dept, asst city solicitor 1975-; Civil Practice Cincinnati, atty gen 1975. **Orgs:** Mem Mayor's Tack Force on Minority Bus Enterprise 1978; mem OH State Bar Assn 1975; mem Cincinnati Bar Assn 1975; mem Black Lawyers Assn of Cincinnati1975. **Business Addr:** City of Cincinnati Law Dept, Room 214 City Hall, Cincinnati, OH 45202.

CHAPMAN, DIANA CECELIA
Detective. **Personal:** Born Sep 3, 1954, Mobile, AL; daughter of Cleo Miller Williams and John Williams; married Nathan Chapman (divorced 1985); children: Miquel. **Educ:** Jarvis Christian College, Hawkins, TX, BS, 1977. **Career:** Mobile County Youth Center, Mobile, AL, house-parent, 1982-83; Mobile Police Dept, Mobile, AL, detective, 1983-. **Orgs:** Vice pres, Mobile Police Benevolent Assn, 1990-; secretary, South Region of National Black Police Assn, 1990-94; member, Semper Fidelis Federated Club, 1990-; member, Zeta Phi Beta Sorority, 1973-; Mobile Police Benevelent Assn, treasurer, 1993-; Azalza City Elks, organist, 1992-93; Mobile Police Benevolent assn, vp, 1990-93; board of directors, National Black Police Association, 1996-. **Honors/Awds:** Wille "WD" Camron Leadership Award, 1991. **Business Addr:** Detective, Youth Services, Mobile Police Department, 350 St Joseph St, Mobile, AL 36603.

CHAPMAN, DOROTHY HILTON
Librarian. **Personal:** Born Sep 4, 1934, Victoria, TX; divorced; children: Dessalyn, Karen. **Educ:** Tuskegee Inst, BS 1958; Carnegie Inst, MLS 1960. **Career:** Richard B Harrison Pub Lib, cataloger 1960-61; St Augustines Coll Benson Lib; TX So Univ Lib, curator spl collections 1969-. **Orgs:** Mem Am & TX Lib Assns; TX Assn Coll Tchrs; mem Wheeler Bapt Ch Index Black Poetry GK Hall & Co 1974. **Honors/Awds:** Index to Poetry by Black Amer Women Greenwood Press 1986. **Business Addr:** Curator Special Collections, Texas Southern Univ Library, 3201 Wheeler Ave, Houston, TX 77004.

CHAPMAN, GEORGE WALLACE, JR.
Educator. **Personal:** Born May 14, 1940, Somerville, TX; son of Angelona Goin Chapman and George W Chapman; divorced; children: Craig, Kevin, Jennifer. **Educ:** Prairie View A&M Univ, BS 1957; Howard Univ, MD 1966. **Career:** Univ of Iowa, asst prof 1981-83; Boston Univ, asst prof 1983-85; Louisiana State Univ, asst prof 1985-89; asst prof Univ of CA-Irvine 1988-; New Jersey Medical School, associate professor, 1989-92; Howard University Hopital, associate professor, currently. **Military Serv:** US Army Medical Corp capt 1966-67. **Business Addr:** Associate Professor, Howard Univ Hospital, 2401 Georgia Ave, NW, Washington, DC 20060.

CHAPMAN, GILBERT BRYANT, II
Automobile company executive. **Personal:** Born Jul 8, 1935, Uniontown, AL; son of Annie Lillie Stallworth Chapman-Bickley and Gilbert Bryant Chapman; married Loretta Woodard Chapman, Jun 5, 1960 (deceased); children: Annie L, Bernice M, Gilbert B III, Cedric N, David O, Ernest P, Frances Q H. **Educ:** Baldwin Wallace Coll, BS 1968; Cleveland State Univ, MS 1973; Michigan State Univ, MBA, 1990. **Career:** NACA Lewis Rsch Ctr, propulsion test tech 1953-58; NASA Lewis Rsch Ctr, matls characterization engr 1961-77; Ford Motor Co Rsch, project engr leader 1977-86; Chrysler Corp Engrg, advanced material testing specialist, 1986-89, advanced materials specialist, 1989-91, advanced product specialist, 1991-94, advanced materials consultant, currently. **Orgs:** Vice chair & prog chair Cleveland Sect SAS 1977; lay leader SDA Church of Southfield 1983-95; chairman Detroit Sect ASNT 1985-86; bd mem Mt Vernon Acad; advisory bd, chair, SME/CMA, 1996; Intl Symposium on Automotive Technology and Automation (ISATA), materials conference, 1996; Automotive Composites Consortium (ACC), 1996; mem AAAS, ACS, APS, ASC, ASM ASNT, ASTM, ESD, NTA, SAE, SAS, SME, Sigma Pi Sigma; member, National Physics Honor Society; member, American Society for Nondestructive Testing; industrial advisory board member, Iowa State Univ, 1990; Univ of TX Pan American, Wayne State Univ. **Honors/Awds:** Apollo Achievement Awd NASA 1969; Group Achievement Awd to Outstanding Employees Actively Participating in the EEO Prog NASA-Lewis 1970; Kent State Univ Chap Natl Physics Honor Soc; mem Sigma Pi Sigma 1975; Excellence in Oral Presentation Awd SAE 1982; Henry Ford Tech Awd nom Ford Motor Co 1981, 1982; Fellow Amer Soc for Nondestructive Testing 1987; "Speaking of People," Ebony Magazine; Spirit of Detroit Award, Science and Service to Youth; holds US Patents. **Military Serv:** US Air Force, aviation cadet, 1959-61. **Home Addr:** 17860 Bonstelle, Southfield, MI 48075, (810)557-8067. **Business Addr:** Advanced Products Consultant, Chrysler Corporation, Liberty Concept Vehicle Development and Technical Affairs, 30900 Stephenson Hwy, Madison Heights, MI 48071, (810)583-5214.

CHAPMAN, JOSEPH CONRAD, JR.
Physician. **Personal:** Born Nov 18, 1937, Poplar Bluff, MO; son of Louise Chapman and Joseph Chapman; married Myrna Loy; children: Joseph, Christopher. **Educ:** Howard Univ, BS 1959, MD 1953; Georgetown Univ Hosp, residency 1968. **Career:** Private practice, otolaryngologist. **Orgs:** Mem Medico-Chururgical Soc of DC, Med Soc of DC, Natl Med Assn, Amer Acad of Otolaryngology, Amer Council of Otolaryngology; asst clinical prof Howard Univ; mem Alpha Phi Alpha; fellow Amer Bd of Otolaryngology 1970. **Military Serv:** USN lt cmdr 1968-70.

CHAPMAN, JULIUS
Educator. **Personal:** Born Apr 1, Kellyton, AL. **Educ:** Tuskegee Inst, BS 1961, MEd 1967; Loyola Coll, EdS 1974. **Career:** Towson State Univ Baltimore, assoc dean 1969; Wilberforce Univ, assoc dir of admissions 1968-69; Residence Life Tuskegee Inst, counselor, dir 1966-68; Case-western Reserve Univ, research tech 1962-64; Assn for African-Amer Studies, dir cofounder 1972-; Amer Assn of Higher Educ; MD Black Coalition for Higher Educ. **Orgs:** Mem Baltimore-tuskegee Alumni Assn; Am Coll Personnel Assn; Omega Psi Phi Frat. **Business Addr:** Voorhees College, Denmark, SC 29042.

CHAPMAN, LEE MANUEL
Insurance company executive. **Personal:** Born Aug 4, 1932, Chesterfield, SC; son of Marie M Chapman Merriman and Jesse Chapman; married Emily Bernice Chapman, Jun 16, 1957; children: Victoria Lenice, Leander M. **Educ:** SC State College, Orangeburg, SC, BA, 1954; Biblical Sch of Theology, Hatfield, PA, 1957-58; Temple Univ, Philadelphia, PA, 1958. **Career:** NC Mutual, special ordinary agent, 1957-60; Equitable Life Assur Soc, agency manager, 1960-81; Lee M Chapman & Assoc, financial planner, 1981-. **Orgs:** Gideon Intl, camp pres & regional dir, 1986-; Christian Business Men Intl, 1982-; Intl Assn for Stewardship, pres, 1990-. **Honors/Awds:** Natl Assn Amer Fellow Award Chaplain of 4 Chaplains; Young Man of Year Jaycees Awards 1967; Natl Assn of Marketing Developers Award, 1967; Natl Citation Award, Equitable Life Assur Soc, 1967, 1968, 1980. **Military Serv:** US Army, 1st Lt, 1954-56; received platoon leader awards. **Business Addr:** Financial Planner, Lee M Chapman & Associates, 6850 Anderson St, Philadelphia, PA 19119.

CHAPMAN, MELVIN
Association executive. **Personal:** Born Mar 16, 1928, Detroit, MI; married Elizabeth Patton; children: Carolyn, Melvin. **Educ:** Wayne State U, BA 1949, MEd 1953, EdSpec 1965, EdD 1973. **Career:** Detroit, teacher 1949; Northwestern High School, counselor 1962; Wayne State Univ, dir high educ opportunity com 1964; Central High School, asst prin 1966; Northwestern High School, prin 1967; Detroit Public Schools, asst supt 1970-. **Orgs:** Mem Corporate Body MI Blue Shield; Trio Adv Com; Nat Alliance Black Sch Edn; MI Assn Children with Learning Disabilities; Met Detroit Soc Black Educ Adminstrs; Am Assn Sch Adminstr; mem NAACP; Kappa Alpha Psi USC of C. **Honors/Awds:** Leadership award Chrysler Corp & NW HS 1968. **Business Addr:** Region 4 Office, 14111 Puritan, Detroit, MI 48227.

CHAPMAN, NATHAN A.
Banker. **Career:** The Chapman Co, chief executive officer, 1986-. **Special Achievements:** Company is ranked #5 on Black Enterprise's list of top investment banks, 1994. **Business Addr:** CEO, The Chapman Co., World Trade Center-Baltimore, 401 E. Pratt St., 28th Fl., Baltimore, MD 21202, (410)625-9656.

CHAPMAN, ROBERT L., SR.
Clergyman. **Personal:** Born Apr 13, 1923, Saluda, SC; son of Florence Chapman and Furman Chapman; married Geraldine Chisholm; children: Robert L Jr, Jacques, Harold, Irwin. **Educ:** Erma Lee's Barber Coll 1951; attended Cleveland Coll 1949-51, Cleveland Bible Coll 1956, Mary Beach Sch of the Bible, Cleveland State Univ 1974. **Career:** Church of God in Christ, supt of Sunday sch 1947, pres Young People Willing Workers 1953, licensed minister 1953, dir religious educ 1954-58; Church of God in Christ Kent OH, pastorate appt 1957; Church of God in Christ Ashtabula, pastorate appt 1959; No OH Church of God in Christ, state pres Young People Willing Workers 1960-66; founded E 116th St Church of God in Christ Cleveland 1966; No OH Ch of God in Christ, prog chmn 1967; R Chapman Realty Cleveland 1953-74. **Orgs:** Institutional rep for Boy Scouts of Amer 1952-55; vice chmn Intl Youth Congress Steering Comm 1966-68; admin asst to bishop NW OH 1967-72; dist supt OH NW Buckeye Dist 1968; asst pastor to bishop Jonas Temple Church of God in Christ Cleveland 1972-73; hon mem Fraternal Order of Police 1972-74; mem Urban League1974; mem YMCA Bus Men Club 1974; mem NAACP 1974; bd dir for the C H Mason Bible Coll 1974; consecrated bishop NW OH Juridsiction 1974; personal admin asst to the natl chmn of the Genl Assembly of the Church of God in Christ Inc 1982-. **Honors/Awds:** Letter of Commendation for Outstanding Comm Serv City of Ashtabula OH 1967; nominated for Honorary Dr of Divinity Degree Trinity Hall Coll 1973-74; Proclamation of May 4, 1974 as "Robert L Chapman Day" by Mayor Ralph J Perk City of Cleveland; resolution of congratulations Cleveland City Council 1974; commendations Howard M Metzenbaum US Senate 1974; commendations Louis Stokes US House of Rep 1974; commendations Intl presiding Bishop J O Patterson & Gen Bd of Bishops of Ch of God in Christ Inc 1974; Awd of Merit Emanuel Ch of God in Christ Harrisburg PA 1974; Letter of Congratulations US Dept of Labor 1974. **Military Serv:** US Army, 1943-46. **Business Addr:** 11814 Buckeye Road, Ste 200, Cleveland, OH 44120.

CHAPMAN, ROSYLN C.
Sales executive. **Personal:** Born Mar 10, 1956, Richmond, VA; daughter of Howard Chapman (deceased) and Bertha Chapman. **Educ:** Hampton Inst, BA 1978. **Career:** Johnson Products Co, sales rep 1979-80, key acct mgr 1980-81, dist mgr 1981-83, regional mgr 1983-84, natl accts mgr 1984-85; Alberto Culver Co, natl accts mgr 1985-90; Alberto Culver Co, national sales manager, 1990-94, dir of retail sales, 1994-. **Orgs:** Cabrini Green Tutorial Bd; Midwest Women's Center Bd; Delta Sigma Theta Sor, Natl Black MBA. **Home Addr:** 4170 N Marine Dr #21K, Chicago, IL 60613.

CHAPMAN, SAMUEL MILTON
Dentist. **Personal:** Born Sep 10, 1920, Mangham, LA; son of Idella Ross Chapman and Frank J Chapman; married Pauline Earl; children: Gregory Milton, Greta Michaele, Frances Delano, Pamela Chapman Wallace. **Educ:** Morehouse Coll, BS 1947; Meharry Medical Coll, DDS 1951. **Career:** Private Practice, dentist. **Orgs:** Mem Sigma Frat 30 yrs; life mem NAACP. **Honors/Awds:** 25 Year Awd Meharry Medical Coll 1976. **Military Serv:** Infantry Medical Corps m/sgt 1943-45. **Home Addr:** 3917 W Bethany Home Rd, Phoenix, AZ 85019.

CHAPMAN, SHARON JEANETTE
Marketing executive. **Personal:** Born Oct 25, 1949, St Louis, MO; children: Leslie Michelle Lee. **Educ:** Southern IL Univ, BS 1970; College of St Thomas, MBA 1981. **Career:** Famous Barr Dept Store, asst buyer 1971-72; Donaldson's Dept Store, dept mgr 1972-75; IBM, systems engr 1976-83, mktg rep 1983-86; Job Trak Systems Inc, dir of mktg & sales 1986-. **Orgs:** 2nd vice pres 1983-85, pres, bd mem 1985-87 Twin Cities Chap Black MBA's; trustee Pilgrim Bapt Church 1984-87; bd of dirs Survival Skills Inst 1985-;chapter pres Delta Sigma Theta 1987-; mem Minneapolis Urban League, St Paul NAACP. **Home Addr:** 4745 Zenith Ave South, Minneapolis, MN 55410. **Business Addr:** Dir of Mktg & Opers, Jobtrack Systems Inc, 7269 Flying Cloud Dr, Eden Prairie, MN 55344.

CHAPMAN, TRACY
Singer, songwriter. **Personal:** Born Mar 30, 1964, Cleveland, OH; daughter of Hazel Winters Chapman and George Chapman. **Educ:** Tufts University, BA (cum laude), anthropology, 1986. **Career:** Album, "Tracy Chapman," Elektra Records, includes "Fast Car," "Baby Can I Hold You," "Talkin' bout a Revolution," 1988; Albums: "Crossroads," 1989; "Matters of the Heart," 1992. **Honors/Awds:** Numerous Grammy Awards including, Best New Artist, Best Contemporary Folk Recording, Best Female Pop Vocal Performance, 1988; Best Selling Album by a New Artist, Best Selling Album by a Female Artist, Natl Assn of Recording Merchandisers, 1988; Best Intl Newcomer, Best Intl Female Artist, The Brits, 1989; Favorite New Artist Pop/Rock, American Music Awards, 1989. **Special Achievements:** Plays the ukelele, organ, clarinet, and guitar; played at Wembley Stadium, England, for the Nelson Mandela Birthday Tribute.

CHAPMAN, WILLIAM TALBERT
Neurologist. **Personal:** Born Oct 15, 1944, Camden, NJ; married Ingrid; children: William Jr, Marcus, Blaire, Leigh. **Educ:** Rutgers Univ, BA 1966; Howard Univ Coll of Medicine, MD 1971. **Career:** 97th General Hospital, asst chief neurology 1976-78; Silas B Hayes Hosp, chief of neurology 1978-79; Private Practice, neurologist 1979-. **Orgs:** Mem Natl Medical Assoc 1971, Amer Bd of Neurology 1977, Amer Bd of Electroencephalography 1985, Amer Medical Assoc 1987. **Honors/Awds:** Alpha Omega Alpha Med Hon Soc. **Military Serv:** AUS major 1976-79; Army Commendation Medal 1979. **Home Addr:** 3951 The Hill Rd, Bonita, CA 91902. **Business Addr:** Neurologist, 2340 East 8th St, Ste G, National City, CA 91950.

CHAPMAN, WILLIE R.
Research scientist. **Personal:** Born Sep 2, 1942, Memphis, TN; married Marion N Evans; children: William Eric, Lamont Everett. **Educ:** LeMoyne Owen Coll, BS Chemistry (Cum Laude) 1964; Memphis State Univ, MAT Chemistry 1975. **Career:** Schering/Plough Inc, sr rsch chemist 1965-77; Chattem Inc, mgr/rsch and devel 1977-87; Chattanooga State Technical Comm Coll, instructor of Chemistry; currently. **Orgs:** Soc of Cosmetic Chemists mem conduct & ethics comm, chapter affairs comm 1982, chmn professional relations and status 1983, area dir 1984-86, chmn educ comm 1986-; Alpha Phi Alpha founder/minority leadership conf 1985-87, social chmn 1985-86, chair educ comm 1986-87; mem Sigma Phi Fraternity; NAACP; Explorer Program/BSA; Alpha Phi Alpha Fraternity; Urban League. **Honors/Awds:** Golden Parade Gallery LeMoyne Coll 1982; guest lecturer Summer enrichment workshops Univ TN Chattanooga 1984-; Role Models for Chattanooga Afro-Amer Museum 1986-87; author "Cosmetic Creams

and Lotions for Dark Tone Skins,'' March 1980, Cosmetics and Toiletries; ''The Development of Skin Lighteners'' May 1983 Cosmetics and Toiletries; Phi Delta Kappa 1987; Leadership Chattanooga 1987.

CHAPPELL, EMMA CAROLYN
Banker. **Personal:** Born Feb 18, 1941, Philadelphia, PA; daughter of Emma Lewis Bayton (deceased) and George Bayton, Sr.; married Verdayne (deceased); children: Tracey, Verdaynea. **Educ:** Berean Business Inst, Temple Univ, Amer Inst of Banking, Stonier Graduate School of Banking, Rutgers Univ. **Career:** Continental Bank Philadelphia, beginning 1959; United Bank of Philadelphia, chair, CEO/Pres, currently. **Orgs:** Mem, Amer Bankers Assn; Natl Bankers Assn; Robert Morris Assn; Natl bd mem, PUSH; advisory bd dir, Girl Scouts of Greater Philadelphia Inc; mem, vice pres, admin & treasurer, Natl Rainbow Coalition; Founded/chair, Women's Network for Good Govt; Bd mem, Temple Univ, Coll of Arts & Sciences, Chestnut Hill Coll Pres' Council, Cheyney Univ Found, United Way of Southeastern Pennsylvania, United Negro Coll Fund, Philadelphia Chapter, PA Economic Devel Partnership Bd, March of Dimes, Delaware Valley Chapter; Vice Chmn, African Devel Found. **Honors/Awds:** Motivational Speaking Exec Leadership & Professional Salesmanship Achievement Award, Dale Carnegie Inst; Achievement Award, Philadelphia Police Dept; Certificate of Appreciation, Soc for Advancement of Mgmt; Couns Selling Achievement Award, Larry & Willson; Achievement Award, N Philadelphia Action Branch of NAACP; Pres Award, Natl Assn of Colored Women's Clubs Inc; Recognition Award, PA Contractors Coalition Inc; Achievement Awd, Club VIP; Honored as One of America's Top 100 Black Business & Professional Women by Dollars and Sense Magazine, 1986; Business & Professional Award, Blackbook Magazine, 1987; Bishop R R Wright Humanitarian Award, Ward AME Church, 1987; Achievement Award, West Philadelphia Economic Devel Corp, 1988; Texas Assn of Minority Enterprises, Outstanding Businesswoman the Year, 1993. **Business Addr:** CEO, Chair, United Bank of Philadelphia, 714 Market St, Philadelphia, PA 19106, (215)829-2265.

CHAPPELL, MICHAEL JAMES
Government manager. **Personal:** Born Dec 27, 1946, Ann Arbor, MI; son of Dorothy Freemen Chappell and Willie Chappell; married Betty Brown-Chappell, Oct 1, 1975; children: Michael Jahi, Aisha Ebony. **Educ:** Eastern Michigan University, BS, 1970; Keller Graduate School of Management, MBA, 1982. **Career:** Northeastern Illinois University, part-time instructor, 1983; Social Security Adm, district mgr, 1971-; Detroit College of Business, part-time instructor, 1995-. **Orgs:** Black Affairs Advisory Council, advisor/mentor; Chicago Social Security Management Assn, pres; The Sr Alliance (Western Wayne County), Area Agency on Aging, chair, advisory council mem/alternate board member; African-American Gerontology Network, treasurer. **Honors/Awds:** Regional Director's Citation, Dept of Health and Human Service, 1988; Vice President, Chicago Region Social Security Management Assn, 1988-90; Social Security Administration Black Caucus, Charles E Lawrence Award, 1992; The Government College Relations Council, Honor Award, 1992; The Senior Alliance Meritorious Svc Awd, 1996; Detroit Federal Executive Bd, Certificate of Appreciation, 1997. **Business Addr:** District Manager, Social Security Administration, 3101 S Gulley Rd, Dearborn, MI 48124.

CHAPPELL, RUTH RAX
Management consultant. **Personal:** Born Apr 20, 1932, Los Angeles, CA; daughter of Helen Finley Rax and George Rax; married Joseph Chappell; children: Valinda, Patricia, Jerome, Kevin, Michael, Michelle, Sakeenah. **Educ:** CA State Univ, BS 1977, MA 1986. **Career:** State Personnel Bd, training officer 1976-79, mgr admin serv 1979-81, asst mgr statewide women's program 1981-82, mgr appeals div 1982-83; Private Consultant, 1983-87. **Orgs:** Mem Natl League Women Political Caucus; chairperson Human Right Comm CA State Employees Assoc 1987-; mem NAACP. **Honors/Awds:** Certificate of Merit CA State Govt. **Business Addr:** Communications Consultant, CA State Personnel Bd, 2551 5th Avenue, Sacramento, CA 95818.

CHAPPELLE, THOMAS OSCAR, SR.
Clergyman. **Personal:** married Elizabeth; children: 2. **Educ:** Bishop Coll, attended; Amer Baptist Theol Sem, Grad; Honorary Degrees, Wright School of Religion Memphis, DD 1953, Morris Booker Coll Dermott AR, DD 1955, Birmingham Baptist Coll Birmingham, DD 1962, OK School of Religion Langston, DD 1964, Bishop Coll Dallas TX, LLD 1972, TN School of Religion, LLD 1981, Univ of Central Amer 1983. **Career:** OK Baptist State Convention, pres; Natl Baptist Congress of Christian Ed, pres. **Orgs:** Mem bd of regents Tulsa Jr Coll; mem bd of dir OK State Nursing Home Assoc, Northside State Bank; mem bd of trustees N Tulsa Hosp Assoc, Bishop Coll; mem adv bd St John Hosp; mem bd of dir Moton Comprehensive Health Assoc; natl chmn Church Rel Bd Bishop Coll; chmn of bd of trustees OK School of Religion; life mem NAACP, Hutcherson Br YMCA, Greenwood C of C, Tulsa Urban League; mem Omega Psi Phi. **Honors/Awds:** Traveled in all 50 states & made 6 trips abroad visiting Europe, Asia, Africa, Holy Land, Australia, Japan, Philippines; Disting Serv Awd Bishop Coll 1970; Disting Serv Awd OK State Nursing Home Assoc 1970; Disting Serv Awd Youth Rally of Natl Sunday School & BT Univ Congress 1975; Omega Psi Phi Frat Awd 1977; Disting Serv Awd Carrie B Neely Art Guild 1978; MN Taylor Awd Tulsa Urban League 1978; Good Shepherd Awd Boy Scouts of Amer 1980. **Business Addr:** Pastor, Morningside Baptist Church, 1014 E Pine St, Tulsa, OK 74106.

CHARBONNET, LOUIS, III
Funeral director. **Personal:** Born Mar 12, 1939, New Orleans, LA; son of Myrtle Labat Charbonnet and Louis Charbonnet Jr.; married Simone Monette; children: Kim Marie. **Educ:** Commonwealth Coll of Sci, BS 1957. **Career:** State of Louisiana, state representative; Total Community Action Agency, president, 1973-; Cresent City Funeral Home, director, currently. **Orgs:** Mem Cresent City Funeral Dir Assn; bd dir Treme Child & Enrichment Ctr; bd mem Criminal Justice for State of LA; vice chmn Bd of Appropriations State of LA; bd dir LA State Museum Bd. **Military Serv:** US Army, SP-4. **Business Addr:** Funeral Director, 1615 St Phillip St, New Orleans, LA 70116.

CHARGOIS, JAMES M.
Automobile dealership executive. **Career:** Pavillion Lincoln-Mercury, Inc, CEO, currently. **Honors/Awds:** Co. is ranked #2 on Black Enterprise magazine's list of top 100 auto dealers, 1992. **Business Addr:** Chief Executive Officer, Pavillion Lincoln-Mercury Inc, PO Box 201930, Austin, TX 78720-1930, (512)258-7711.

CHARGOIS, JENELLE M.
Foundation director. **Personal:** Born Nov 19, 1949, Lafayette, LA; daughter of Effie Jeanlouis Alfred and Alton J Alfred; married Paul R Chargois, Dec 7, 1973; children: Jared Kiburi, Maisha Z. **Educ:** Xavier U, 1 yr; Univ of Southwestern, 3 yrs; Spencer's Bus Coll, Accounting Cert. **Career:** So Coop Devel Fund, dir of pub relations; People's Enterprise, mgr 1972; So Consumers Educ Found, dir 1971; Supply Group, Lafayette, LA, pres, 1986-. **Orgs:** Mem St Paul's Credit Union; So Consumer Coop; People's Enterprise; So Consumer Educ Found; volunteer; counselor Scholarship Bd; mem Lafayette Juvenile; League of Women Voters; Black LA Action Comm; NAACP; Women Involved in Comm; Lafayette Comm Devel Program; adv council Lafayette Bi-Racial Comm; chmn Labor & Industry Comm; vice pres Black Alliance for Progress; sec So Coop Council; counselor Young Gifted Black Youth; pres, Northside Organization for Nurturing Arts, 1990-91; pres, Pat Taylor Kids Truman Elem, 1990-91. **Honors/Awds:** Key To City Lafayette 1972; 1st place honors Dist & State Competitions (Spanish) 1966-67; outstanding youth 1966; outstanding black citizen award 1972; comm orgn award 1972; Outstanding Black Citizen, Southern Education Foundation, 1986; PBS Pinchback Award, LA Republican Party, 1988. **Business Addr:** President, The Supply Group, 729 John LeBlanc Rd, Duson, LA 70529.

CHARIS, SISTER (SHARON DIANA JONES)
Cleric. **Personal:** Born Nov 14, 1948, Fort Riley, KS; daughter of Agnes D Burrus Jones and Theodore D Jones. **Educ:** Missouri Valley College, Marshall, MO, BA, magna cum laude, 1970; Georgia State University, Atlanta, GA, MA, cum laude, 1974; University of California, Santa Barbara, Santa Barbara, CA, 1988. **Career:** Muscogee County School District, Columbus, GA, math teacher, 1970-78; Sisterhood of the Holy Nativity, Fond Du Lac, WI, religious sister, 1978-. **Orgs:** Member, Gamma Sigma Sigma Sorority, 1968-70; member, Union of Black Episcopalians, 1988-. **Honors/Awds:** Numerous religious awards, 1979-. **Home Addr:** 338 Academy St, Madison, GA 30650.

CHARITY, LAWRENCE EVERETT
Business executive. **Personal:** Born Jun 21, 1935, Washington, DC; married Suzanne G Leach; children: Alexander PL, Danika EN. **Educ:** Rhode Island School of Design, BFA/Int Arch Des 1953-57; Cranbrook Academy of Art, MFA/Design 1957-58. **Career:** Skidmore, Owings & Merrill, designer 1958-68; Sewell & Charity Ltd Designers, principal 1968-74; Interior Concepts, Inc, principal 1974-86; Lawrence Charity Design, 1986-. **Orgs:** Adjunct asst prof/design Rhode Island School of Design 1972-73; Industrial Designers Society of America 1974-. **Honors/Awds:** Canopy design US Patent 214,226 issued 1969; chair design US Patent 224,856 issued 1972; door pull design US Patent 3,894,760 issued 1975; Institute of Business Designers, Best of Competition Award for design of ''Davidoff of Geneva,'' 1992; American Society of Interior Designers, 1st Place Retail Design Award for design of ''Davidoff of Geneva,'' 1992. **Military Serv:** AUS sp4 1959-62. **Home Addr:** 8 Gracie Sq, New York, NY 10028. **Business Addr:** Principal/Designer, Lawrence Charity Design, Eight Gracie Sq, New York, NY 10028.

CHARITY, RUTH HARVEY
Consultant, attorney. **Personal:** Born in Pittsylvania Count, VA; married Ronald K Charity; children: Khris Wayne. **Educ:** Howard Univ, BA, JD. **Career:** Formerly asst to dir President's Cncl on Consumer Affairs; Indust Rel Analyst Wage Stabil Bd; law prof formerly pract law under name of Ruth L Harvey; former Dem Natl Committeewoman; 1st Black woman South of Mason Dixon line to serve this capacity and as mem of Natl Dem Exec Comm. **Orgs:** Mem Pres's Comm on Civil Rights under the Law; past pres Old Dominion Bar Assn (1st woman to serve this capacity); mem Natl Bar Assn; formerly vice pres of Natl Bar Assn(1st woman to serve as vice pres of NBA at time of election); organiz Women's Sect Natl Bar Assn (1st natl orgn of Black women lawyers); mem Intl Fedn of Women Lawyers; past pres of Natl Assn of Black Women Lawyers; founder/pres VA Assn of Black Women Lawyers; past mem trustee bd Howard Univ;past mem trustee bd Palmer Meml Inst; mem bd of VA Seminary; past chrpsn VA State Adv Com US Civil Rights Comm (1st woman in VA to serve as chrpsn); mem Amer Assn of Univ Women; League of Women Voters; NOW; past mem Legal Staff State Conf NAACP; past natl parliamentarian Natl Cncl of Negro Women; pastgrand legal advisor Grand Templeughters IBPOE of W; past pres Chums Inc. **Honors/Awds:** To date 1st and only Black woman elected to Danville, VA City Council 1970-74; Founder/President Black Women for Political Action; Charter Mem natl Women's Chamber of Commerce; numerous awards received from various organizations and groups including, Natl Fedn of Dem Women Mid-Atlantic Region; Alpha Kappa Alpha Sor; NAACP; listed in Biography of Charlotte Hawkins Brown, Rights on Trial; Lecturer & consultant to political & civil rights & educational groups.

CHARLES, BERNARD L.
Educator. **Personal:** Born Feb 27, 1927, New York, NY; married Eleanor; children: Bernard II, Dominique, Bridgette. **Educ:** Fisk U, BA 1952; Yeshiua U, MS 1965; Rutgers Univ Grad Sch of Edn. **Career:** Livingston Coll Rutgers Univ, prof of educ, chmn dept urban educ 1970-; Town of Ramapo, councilman & deputy supvr 1966-74; Rockland Co Legis, vice chmn 1975-77; Dem Natl Comm NY State Voter Reg Drive, dir 1976; NY State Council of Black Elected Democrats, treas 1965-77; Office of Master Plan Bd of Higher Educ City Univ of NY, coordinator 1968-70. **Orgs:** Dir of spl projects Human Resources Admin 1968; dep dir Office of Civil Rights Region II NY 1966-68; dir of Life Skills Educ Training Resources for Youth 1965-66; asst to dir Jr Guidance Classed Program New York City Bd of Educ 1962-66; tchr Pub Sch 613 Brooklin Pub Sch 614 Bronx 1955-62; street club worker New York City Youth Bd 1954-55; co-dir Univ of Summer workshop for tchrs of Emotionally & socially maladjusted childred; guest lecturer; mem Assn of Tchr Edn; Am Assn of Higher Edn; Am Assn of Univ Prof; Am Assn of Sch Administr; Nat Advisory Council; Nat Advisory Health Council; treas Inst for Mediation & Conflict Resolution; pres Broadjump Inc; dir Action Priorities Inc; Rockland Comm Action Council; bd of dir World Rehabilitation Fund; BulovaWatchmaking SchState Cord Gov Samuels paign 1974; chairman New York State Governor's Advisory Comm for Black Affairs. **Business Addr:** Livingston College, New Brunswick, NJ 08903.

CHARLES, DAEDRA
Professional basketball player. **Personal:** Born Nov 22, 1968; daughter of Helen Charles. **Educ:** Tennessee State Univ, bachelor's degree, early childhood education, 1991. **Career:** Como (Italy), center, 1991-92; DKB (Japan), 1992-93; Sireg (Italy), 1993-94; Tarbes (France), 1994-95; Galatasaray (Turkey), 1995-96; Sopron (Hungary), 1996-97; Los Angeles Sparks, 1997-. **Honors/Awds:** Natl Assn for Girls and Women in Sports, Wade Trophy, 1991; Sports Illustrated, Player of the Week, March 4, 1991; NCAA Women's Div I, one of the best rebound averages in basketball tournaments held between 1983 and 1992; Olympic Games, Bronze Medal, 1992, Gold Medal, 1996; World Championship Team, Bronze Medal, 1994. **Business Addr:** Professional Basketball Player, Los Angeles Sparks, 3900 W Manchester Blvd, Inglewood, CA 90306, 800-978-9622.

CHARLES, DOREEN ALICIA. **See LATIF, NAIMAH.**

CHARLES, JOSEPH C.
Probation officer. **Personal:** Born Jan 12, 1941, Lake Charles, LA; married Doris J Charles; children: Caron Scott. **Educ:** BA AA 1969. **Career:** Mitchell Pacific Devel Corp, pres; San Diego Co Probation Dept, dep probation officer II; Webchar Construction Corp, pres. **Orgs:** Mem Black Businessmen Assn; Black Investors Inc; sec Reserve Officers Assn; charter mem Black Student Union San Diego State Coll; mem San Diego Co Emp Assn; mem CA State Corrections Assn. **Honors/Awds:** Recipient Fed & State Commissions as Nat Guard Lt 1966. **Military Serv:** USAR capt.

CHARLES, LEWIS
Welder. **Personal:** Born Aug 24, 1945, Jackins Co, GA; married Rosetta W; children: Tracy C. **Educ:** Atlana U, 1 yr. **Career:** Fulghum Industrial Mgt Co, demonstrator; Hudson Mortuary Wadley, GA, asst mgr. **Orgs:** Mem GA State Fireman of Wadley, GA No 2217; mem Dem Party of GA 1972; mem Free & Accepted Mason; mem Brinson Hill Bapt C; life mem GA Municipal Assn; mem Wadley & Borlow Cit League; mem Nat Pilots Assn; ciy-councilman 1970-. **Honors/Awds:** Award Wadley & Borlow Cit League 1972; spl award Brinson Hill Bapt Ch 1973. **Business Addr:** Fulghum Industrial Mfg Co, Wadley, GA.

CHARLES, RAY (RAY CHARLES ROBINSON)
Singer, arranger, composer, band leader. **Personal:** Born Sep 23, 1930, Albany, GA; son of Aretha Robinson and Bailey Robinson; married Della Charles; children: Ray Jr, David, Robert. **Career:** At age 7 began playing piano while attending St Augustine School for the Blind; joined Lowell Fulsom's Blues Band; began touring with dance bands at age 15; Atlantic Records, 1954-59; signed on with Florida Playboys 1954, recorded 1st major hit ''I Got A Woman 1954''; ABC Records, 1959-62; wrote ''What I Say'' 1959; formed Maxim Trio in Seattle; RPM Intl, owner; recorded country album featuring Willie Nelson ''Friendship'' 1984; Ray Charles Enterprises, owner; Tangerine Records, 1962-73; Crossover Records, 1973-82; Columbia Records, 1982-; appeared in Commercials for Diet Pepsi; Genius & Soul: The Fiftieth Anniversary Collection, Rhino Records, 1997. **Honors/Awds:** Bronze Medallion presented by French Republic; 10 Grammy Awds; New Star Awd Down Beat Critic's Poll 1958, 1961-64; No 1 Male Singer Int Jazz Critics' Poll 1968; Playboy Jazz & Pop Hall of Fame; Songwriters' Hall of Fame; Hon Life Chmn Rhythm & Blues Hall of Fame; Ebony Black Music Hall of Fame; Gold records include, ''Ray Charles Greatest Hits'', ''Modern Sounds in Country & Western Music'', ''Ray Charles A Man and His Soul''; B'nai B'rith Man of the Year; Kennedy Center Honors Medal 1986; Rock and Roll Hall of Fame 1986; Hall of Fame Award, NAACP Image Awards 1983; Man of Distinction Award, National Assn for Sickle-Cell Disease 1975; movie, The Blues Brothers, 1980; The Ebony Magazine Lifetime Achievement Award, 1993. **Business Addr:** Singer, Ray Charles Enterprises, 2107 W Washington Blvd, Los Angeles, CA 90018.

CHARLES, RODERICK EDWARD
Psychiatrist. **Personal:** Born Sep 4, 1927, Baltimore, MD; married Mamie Rose Debnam; children: Kimberly Anne, Roderick Todd. **Educ:** Howard Univ, BS 1951; Univ of MD, MD 1955. **Career:** Mil City Gen Hosp, internship 1955-56; Meyer Meml Hosp, psych resident 1956-59; NYS Fellow, 1959-60; Erie County Med Center (formerly Meyer Hosp), att psychiatry 1960-66; SUNY Brooklyn Sch of Medicine, asst clinical prof 1966-96; private practice, psychiatry 1966-. **Orgs:** Asst psych Buff Gen Hosp; dir Migrant H Clinic 1968-71; BUILD Acad H Progm 1971-75; mem state council Met H Plan 1977-81; pres WNY Psych Assn 1967-68; Fedr Citizens Council Human Rel 1964; Fellow Amer Psych Assn; mem Black Psychiatrists of Amer; Natl Med Assn; advisor SMNA Univ of Buffalo 1975; consultant Gowando State Hosp 1982-87. **Military Serv:** USN 1944-46. **Business Addr:** 142 N Pearl, Buffalo, NY 14202.

CHARLESTON, GOMEZ, JR.
Physician/cardiologist. **Personal:** Born Mar 19, 1950, Chicago, IL; son of Margie Williams Charleston and Gomez Charleston; married Robin Prince, Jun 21, 1975. **Educ:** Univ of Chicago, BA, 1971, MD, 1975. **Career:** Stony Island Medical Associates, Chicago IL, partner, 1980—; Michael Reese Hosp, Chicago, attending physician cardiology, 1980—, dir of cardiac catheterization lab, 1987-88, Pritzker School of Medicine, Univ of Chicago, asst clinical prof of medicine, 1980—. **Orgs:** American Medical Association, Illinois Medical Society, Chicago Cardiology Group. **Honors/Awds:** Sigmund E. Edelstone fellow in cardiology, Michael Reese Hospital & Medical Center, 1980; fellow of American College of Cardiology, 1982. **Business Addr:** Stony Island Medical Assn, 9000 South Stony Island, Chicago, IL 60617.

CHARLTON, CHARLES HAYES
Pastor. **Personal:** Born Dec 22, 1940, Radford, VA; son of Ollie and Lawrence; married Janet Lee Lewis; children: Charles. **Educ:** Christiansburg Inst, 1959; VA Seminary, attended; E TN State Univ, attended; ETSU, BS 1982, M Ed 1984; Emmaus Bible Institute of Seminary, Elizabeth, TN, ThD, 1986; Cornerstone Univ, PhD Temperament Therapy. **Career:** Radford City School Bd, 1972-74; City of Radford VA, mayor 1974-76; Friendship Bapt Church, pastor; CASA Northeast, Johnson City, TN, coordinator, 1987-; CASA, 1987-92; ETSU, Johnson City, TN, career counselor, 1991-92; City of Johnson City, planning commission, 1990-; Northeast State Tech Comm Coll, instructor, 1992-, counselor & advisor, 1994-; Emmaus Bible Inst & Seminary, Elizabethton, TN, dean of educ, 1984-89. **Orgs:** Moderator Schaetter Meml Assoc of SW VA 1974-77; treas Bethel Dist Assoc; vice pres Radford Jaycees; moderator Bethel Dist Assoc of TN 1982-; dean ed Emmaus Bible Inst & Seminary Elizabethton TN 1984-; dir Pastors Conf of the TN BM&E Convention 1984-; pres, Black Ministers Alliance, 1990-91; zone chairman, Washington County Democratic Party, 1994-; City of Johnson City, TN, Board of Education, 1996-. **Honors/Awds:** Radfords Outstanding Young Men Radford Jaycees 1973; publ 2 weekly religious-columns Radford News Jrnl. **Special Achievements:** Published Agony & Ecstasy of the Ministry, Making The Fundamentals Fun, 1993; Love is the Key, To Love And Be Loved, How To Really Love Your Pastor, This We Believe, Meditations on Love, 1994.

CHARLTON, GEORGE N., JR.
Executive director (retired). **Personal:** Born Apr 12, 1923, Pittsburgh, PA; son of Mildred F Woods Charlton and George N Charlton Sr; married H Nadine Branch, Jun 1964; children: George N III, Diana C Jones, Susan C Harrison, Ronald, Lena Coleman. **Educ:** Univ of Pittsburgh, BBA 1955. **Career:** AUS, clerk-typist 1943-45, transfer unit asst suprv, analyst admin div 1945-48; VA Pittsburgh, regis clerk 1948, collec officer, collec div 1948-51; US Treas Dept IRS Intell Div Pittsburgh, spec agent 1953-63; Pittsburgh Private practice, spec investigator 1964-65; Commonwealth of PA Dept of Revenue Bur of Sales & Use Tax Harrisburg, spec audit staff 1965-67; Opps Indus Ctr Inc Pittsburgh, dir admin serv 1967-68; Homewood-Brushton Neighborhood HealthCtr Inc Pittsburgh, bus mgr 1968-71; Pittsburgh Model Cities, asst exec dir 1971-73, exec dir 1973-76; Public Parking Authority of Pittsburgh, exec dir 1976-88, retired; self-employed real estate property mgr, 1988-. **Orgs:** Mem, treas, bd dir Housing Auth Pittsburgh, 1973-78; mem Mayors Econ Manpower Adv Comm, 1974-83; mem, treas Comm Action Pittsburgh Bd, 1975-78; mem Reg Personnel Serv Ctr of SW PA, 1974-78; life mem Kappa Alpha Psi, 1969-; life mem Reserve Officers Assn; mem, 1st vchmn Bd Mgmt of Homewood-Brushton YMCA Prog Ctr, 1970-77; Province Polemarch, East Central Province, Kappa Alpha Psi Frat Inc 1971-84; Grand Bd of Dirs Kappa Alpha Psi Frat Inc 1985-88; bd of governors, mem, co-vice chmn, National Parking Assn 1983-88; United Way of Pittsburgh 1986-89; exec mem, Urban League of Pittsburgh Inc 1986-89; St Cyprian-Alpha Lodge #13 F & A M 1970-; life mem, NAACP 1981; life mem, sr vice commander 1965, Angell-Bolen VFW Post #4040; mem, chm, trustee bd, Grace Memorial PresbyterianChurch; member, Chadwick Civic League, 1975-; pres, Chap 4542 American Association of Retired Persons, Inc, 1996-. **Honors/Awds:** Man of the Year Achievement Awd Pittsburgh Alumni Chap 1971; Meritorious Serv Opp Indus Ctr Inc Pittsburgh 1972; Achievement Delta & Delta Zeta 1973; Serv to Youth Black Achievers Awd YMCA of Pittsburgh 1973; Outstanding Achievement E Cntrl Province 1974; Leadership Dayton Kappa League 1974; Meritorious Serv Medal 1976; Honor Black Cath Ministers & Laymen's Council 1976; Comm Leader Awd 1977; Citation 26 yrs of serv AUS 1976; selected as 1 of 25 most influential blacks in Metro Pittsburgh Talk Mag 1975; Elder Watson Diggs Achievement Award, Kappa Alpha Psi Frat Inc 1986; Certificate of Achievement, Natl Parking Assn 1987. **Military Serv:** AUS lt col retired WWII Vet 23 yrs; received Army Meritorious Service Medal, 1976; Society for the Preservation & Encouragement of Barber Shop Quartet Singing in America, (SPEBQSA), 1991. **Home Addr:** 1714 Lincoln Ave, Pittsburgh, PA 15206.

CHARLTON, JACK FIELDS
Engineer. **Personal:** Born Apr 30, 1928, Bellaire, OH; son of Grace Stone Charlton and Harold L Charlton; married Audrey Perry; children: Michael, James Eric. **Educ:** Fenn Coll, BMechEng 1957; Tufts Univ, BMetEng 1963; Case Inst of Tech, MS 1965. **Career:** Euclid, div of GMC superintendent 1966-70, sub of White Motor dir 1970-77, sub of Mercedes-Benz vice pres 1977-84; Mercedes-Benz Truck Co, dir quality assurance 1984-87; Freightliner Corp Dir Gov't Proj 1987-; Private Practice, prof consulting eng, 1992; US Dept of Defense, consultant, 1993. **Orgs:** Special Task Force on Youth Motivation, vice pres of US; McGill Univ, lecturer 1968; Nat'l Professional Engrs, mem 1973, treasurer 1975/79; Cleveland Public Sch, advisor in economic education 1980; Ohio State Board of Education, advisor in economic education 1981; pres Williamsburg Mens Club 1988; engineer consultant NATO 1988. **Honors/Awds:** Royal Canadian Soc of Engrs, fellow 1978; Soc of Military Engrs, fellow 1979. **Military Serv:** AUS, col, corp of engrs 25 yrs (retired). **Home Addr:** 42 Whittakers Mill, Williamsburg, VA 23185.

CHASE, ARNETT C.
Business executive. **Personal:** Born Apr 5, 1940, Green Cove Spgs, FL; married Dianne J Thomas; children: Avis Chiquita, Arnett Cameron. **Educ:** Am Acad Funeral Serv, 1963; Univ FL, Certified Ophthalmology 1972. **Career:** Apprentice embalmer & funeral dir 1965, mgr 1970. **Orgs:** Mem Nat Funeral Dir & Morticians Assn; mem State Auditor FL Morticians Asn; chmn 4th Regional & Dist Morticians Assn; sec SDW Smith Lodge 481 F &AM; mem Jaycees; mem USO Council; mem Council Aged; mem Ancient City Charity Club; lifetime mem, NAACP. **Honors/Awds:** Award FL Morticians Serv 1974; certificate appreciation St Paul AME Ch 1973. **Military Serv:** AUS sp/5 1963-65. **Business Addr:** Funeral Dir, Leo C Chase Funeral Home, 262 W King St, St Augustine, FL 32095.

CHASE, JOHN S.
Architect. **Personal:** Born Jan 23, 1925, Annapolis, MD; married Drucie Rucker; children: John Jr, Anthony, Saundria. **Educ:** Hampton Inst, BS 1948; Univ of TX, MArch 1952. **Career:** TX Southern Univ, asst prof; John S Chase FAIA Architect Inc, pres/chmn of the bd. **Orgs:** Mem AIA; mem TX Soc of Architects; notable contr to the advcmt of archt Coll of Fellows AIA 1977; pres Nat Orgn of & Minority Architects; consult architect to TX So Univ Bd of Regents; mem bd Huston-Tillotson Coll; mem bd Standard Savings & Loan Assn; mem Houston Engineering & Sci Soc; mem Univ of TX Adv Council; sec Greater Houston Convention & Visitors Council; mem bd Houston Visitors & Convention Council; mem bd of trustees Herman Hospital, Hampton Univ; served on the US Commn of Fine Arts; mem bd of trustees Antioch Bapt Ch; mem bd of trustees Univ of Houston Foundation; mem TX Southern Univ; served on Univ of TX Presidential Search Comm; mem bd of dirs Golden State Mutual Life Ins Co; bd of dir TX Southern Univ Foundation. **Honors/Awds:** Nu Phi Chap of Omega Si; trustee Antioch Bapt Ch; Whitney M Young Citation; NOMA Design Excellence Awd; John S Chase Scholarship in Architecture; McGraw Hill Publishing Co Golden 100 Fleet Awd. **Military Serv:** AUS. **Business Addr:** President/Chmn of the Board, John S Chase FAIA Arch Inc, 1201 Southmore, Houston, TX 77004.

CHASE-RIBOUD, BARBARA DEWAYNE
Author, sculptor. **Personal:** Born Jun 26, 1939, Philadelphia, PA; daughter of Vivian May Braithwaite West Chase and Charles Edward Chase; married Marc Eugene Riboud, Dec 25, 1961 (divorced); children: David, Alexis; married Sergio G Tosi, Jul 4, 1981. **Educ:** Temple Univ, BFA, 1957; Yale Univ, MFA, 1960. **Career:** One-woman shows include those at The University Museum, Berkeley, CA, The Museum of Modern Art, Paris, France, The Kunstmuseum, Dusseldorf, Germany, The Detroit Art Institute, Detroit, MI, The Indianapolis Art Museum, Indianapolis, IN, The Museum of Modern Art, New York, NY, The Kunstmuseum, Freilburg, West Germany, 1976, The Musee Reattu, Arles, France, 1976, European Drawings, Berlin, West Germany, 1980, five-museum tour in Australia, 1980-81, Studio Museum, 1996; Milwaukee Art Museum, 1997, Chicago Cultural Center, 1997, Museum of South Carolina, 1997, Mint Museum, 1997, Los Angeles Museum of Contemporary Art, 1997, Smithsonian, 1998 and many more; selected group exhibitions include ''Documenta 77'' Kessel, West Germany, 1977, Museum of Contemporary Crafts, New York, 1977, Smithsonian Inst Renwick Gallery, 1977, Noeuds et Ligatures Fondation Nationale des Arts, 1983, California Museum of Afro-Amer Art, 1985; selected public collections at The Philadelphia Art Alliance, The Scnburg Collection New York, New York State Council on the Arts, St John's Univ, Harlem State Office Bldg, The Metropolitan Museum of Art, New York, The Natl Collections, France, Museum of Modern Art, Berkley Museum Los Angeles; Foley Square African Burial Ground. **Orgs:** PEN; PEN American Center; The Century Association; Yale Alumni Association; Alpha Kappa Alpha. **Honors/Awds:** John Hay Whitney Foundation Fellowship, 1957-58; National Fellowship for the Arts; Carl Sandburg Poetry Award as Best American Poet, 1988; Janet Kafka Award for Best Novel by an American Woman, 1979; Honorary Doctorate of Arts & Humanities, Temple Univ, 1981. Muhlenberg College, Honorary LHD, 1993; Van der Zee Achievement Award, 1995; Connecticut State University, Honorary Doctorate, 1996; Government of France, Knighthood for Contributions to Arts and Letters, 1996. **Special Achievements:** Author: From Memphis to Peking, poems, Random House, 1974; Sally Hemings, Viking, 1979; Albin Michel, 1981; Valide, Morrow Publishing, 1986; Portrait of a Nude Woman as Cleopatra, Morrow Publishing, 1987; Echo of Lions, Morrow Publishing, 1989; The President's Daughter, 1994; Egypt's Nights, 1994; numerous others.

CHASTANG, MARK J.
Hospital administrator. **Educ:** Univ of Kansas, MPA; Georgia Stae Univ, MBA. **Career:** DC General Hospital, executive dir, chief executive, 1989-95; East Orange General Hospital, pres/CEO, 1995-. **Business Addr:** President/Chief Executive Officer, East Orange General Hospital, 300 Central Ave, East Orange, NJ 07018-2897, (201)678-8300.

CHATMAN, ALEX
Educator, magistrate. **Personal:** Born Oct 6, 1943, Greeleyville, SC; son of Alma Montgomery Chatman and Alex Oscar Chatman; married Mariah Williams Chatman, Sep 26, 1986. **Educ:** Williamsburg County Training Sch 1962; Benedict Coll, diploma 1965; SC State Coll, BS 1973; Univ RI, ME 1966; Univ SC, Certificate 1970. **Career:** Tchr 1965-; Greeleyville, magistrate 1973-81; Williamsburg County Council, supervisor, chmn 1982-. **Orgs:** Pres Williamsburg County Educ Assn 1974-75; mem Credential Com State Dem Conv 1971 & 1974; pres Greeleyville Br Nat Bus Leauge 1970-; mem NAACP; mem United Teaching Professional; mem Nat Bus League; mem Official Black Caucus Nat Educ Assn; mem SC Magistrate's Assn; chmn 6th Congressional Dist Polit Action Com for Educ 1974; SC Assn of Counties 1982-; Governor's Council on Rural Devel 1982-86; SC Private Industry Council 1984-87. **Honors/Awds:** Award Phi Beta Sigma Frat 1973; award SC Educ Assn 1975; Presidential Citation, Natl Assn for Equal Opportunity in Higher Education 1985; Citizen of the Year for Outstanding Public Service, Delta Rho Chapter Omega Psi Phi Frat 1982; Distinguished Service Award, Williamsburg Branch NAACP 1985; Certificate of Appreciation, Kingstree Kiwanis Club 1988.

CHATMAN, ANNA LEE
Administrator. **Personal:** Born Aug 21, 1919, Monroe, GA; married Rev Marcellus; children: Marcella Ann McElroy, Ruby Marie Alexander. **Educ:** Cuy Comm Coll, Cert Comm Org 1969, Bus Admin 1969. **Career:** 21st Cong Dist Caucus, exec dir 1969-; Congressman Louis Stokes, cong aide 1976-; Harvest Day Care Ctr, admin 1969-. **Orgs:** Dir MC Chatman Meml Found 1978-; mem Zoning Bd of Appeals Cleveland 1977-; pres Bapt Ministers Wives & Widows 1972-; mother of the church Harvest Missionary Bapt Church 1978-; co-sponsor

Womens Com Leadership Defense Fund 1979. **Honors/Awds:** Leadership Awd Cleveland Br NAACP; Congressional Awd Cong Louis Stokes; Recipient of numerous awds. **Business Addr:** Administrator, Harvest Day Care Center, 1240 E 9th St, Cleveland, OH 44199.

CHATMAN, DONALD LEVERITT
Physician. **Personal:** Born Dec 27, 1934, New Orleans, LA; married Eleanor; children: Lynn Ann, Eleanor Louise, Eric Leveritt. **Educ:** Harvard U, AB 1956; Meharry Med Coll, MD 1960; Cooper Hosp NJ, rotating intrnshp 1960-61; Michael Reese Hosp, resident 1965-69. **Career:** Chicago, ob gyn 1969-; Lake Charles LA, gen Prac 1961-63; Dept of Ob Gyn Michael Reese Hosp & Med Cntr, asst Attndng 1969-74; Dept Ob Gyn Univ of Chicago-Pritzker Sch Diamine Oxidase in Prgncy, clncl instr; USAF, cpt 1963-65. **Orgs:** Mem Chicago Med Soc; pres Chicago Med Soc S Chicago Br 1969-70; mem Am Assn of Gynecologic Laparoscopists 1974-; mem IL State Med Soc; mem Am Med Soc; mem NMA; mem Am Coll of Ob & Gyn Diplomate Am Bd of Ob & Gyn 1972; rsrchr of, "Endometriosis & the Black Female" Am Jour of Ob & Gyn 1976, "Endometriosis & the Black Woman" Jour of Reproductive Med 1976, "Endometriosis & the Black Female" Adio-Digest 1976, "Laparoscopy-Falope Ring Sterilization" Am Jour of Ob & Gyn 1978, "Commentary on Inaugural Thesis-Laparscopic Cautery of Endometriotic Implants" Am Jour of Ob & Gyn 1979, "Pelvic Peritoneal Defects & Endometriosis-Allen-Masters Syndrome Revisited" in press, Direct Trochar Falope Ring Sterilization in press; presently resrchng, Laparoscopic Evaluation &Functional Classification of Endomiosis, The Concept of Pre-Clinical or "Emerging" Endometriosis, The Long Term Effectiveness & Complications of Falope Ring Sterilization, The Efficacy of Direct Trochar Laparoscopic Falope Ring Sterlization. **Military Serv:** USAF capt 1963-65. **Business Addr:** 8811 S Stony Island, Chicago, IL 60617.

CHATMAN, JACOB L.
Pastor. **Personal:** Born Aug 5, 1938, Patterson, GA; married Etty; children: Mario. **Educ:** FL Meml, BS 1963; Eastern Theol Sem, MDiv 1968; Univ of Ma, DEd 1974. **Career:** Scnd Bapt Ch Coatesville PA, pastor; organized coordinated tutorial progs for socially deprived children; written training curr for employable disadvantaged of Chester; counseling drop-outs, drugs, planned parenthood, family counseling, organizer Day Care, chmn comm support. **Orgs:** Dir Pinn; mem Center PA Chmn Title I Coatesville Sch Dist; mem Am Assn of Univ Profs; Coatesville Area Clergy; Kappa Alpha Psi Frat; trustee Cheyney State Tchrs Coll; pres Commn to Disadvantaged Eastern Sem; bd mgrs, exec bd PA DE Chs of Am Bapt Conv; Task Force on Foreign Mission; Black Churchmen of Am Bapt Conv; vice pres Coatesville Opp Council; chmn Non-profit Hsng Corp Scnd Bapt Ch; past chmn Comm Support Day Care; Coatesville vice-chmn Task Force on World Hunger; Am Bapt Conv; rotary mem. **Honors/Awds:** Recip citizenship YMCA 1955; Eagle Scout 1955; Chapel of Four Chaplains Award 1969; cit award Mt Labanon HRAM of PA 1972; FL mem coll outsanding serv award 1972; Humanitarian Award 1973; outstanding youth man of Am 1972; cited by Coatesville Record for Outstanding Serv 1970-74. **Business Addr:** St John Missionary Church, 34 W Pleasant St, Springfield, OH 45506.

CHATMAN, MELVIN E.
Educator (retired). **Personal:** Born Feb 9, 1933, Springfield, TN; married Velma R; children: Vera, Melvin Jr, Carol, Bobby, Jeff, Karl. **Educ:** Lane Coll, BS 1955; Fisk Univ, MA 1963; Univ of TN, EdS 1975; American Baptist College, ThB 1996. **Career:** Bransford High School, teacher, coach 1957-68; Springfield High School, teacher 1968-70, asst principal 1970-73, supvr special educ 1973-95. **Orgs:** Mem NEA, TEA, Robertson Cty Teacher Assoc, Council for Excpetional Children, TN Assoc for Suprv & Curriculum Devel; former mem Mid-Cumberland Council Gov, Mental Health Harriett Cty; mem num offices, coms Dem Party Selected Serv Bd; mem TN Voter Council, Cty Ct 1972-74, 33 Deg Mason, Shriner, Alpha Phi Alpha, Beard Chapel Baptist Church. **Military Serv:** US Army, 1955-57.

CHATMAN-DRIVER, PATRICIA ANN (PAT DRIVER)
Senior software engineer. **Personal:** Born Jul 19, 1956; daughter of Mamie Chatman; married Allen Jerome Driver, Aug 9, 1985; children: Khaalid, Allen Jr, Amanda. **Educ:** SC State College, BS mathematics, 1979. **Career:** Vitro Laboratories, mathematician, 1979-82; Sperry/UNISYS, mem of engineering staff, 1982-87; self-employed, 1987-88; Mystech Associates, Inc, sr software engineer, 1988-. **Business Addr:** Senior Software Engineer, Mystech Associates, Inc, 5205 Leesburg Pike, Ste 1200, Falls Church, VA 22041, (703)671-8680.

CHATMON, LINDA CAROL
Educator. **Personal:** Born Nov 13, 1951, Louisville, KY; daughter of Betty A Savage and L C Fox; children: Dana Marie. **Educ:** Univ of Louisville, BA 1980, MSSW 1982; currently pursuing EdD in Educational Administration, Univ of Louisville. **Career:** Creative Employment Project; counselor 1982-84; Univ of Louisville, coord of cooperative educ 1984, instructor/counselor 1984-89; Univ of Louisville, Kent School of Social Work, dir of admissions and student services, adjunt assistant professor, 1989-;. **Orgs:** Mem comm chair Urban League 1982-88, Youth Performing Arts School 1983-87; consultant GYSG Corp 1986-88. **Honors/Awds:** Association of Black Psychologists Kentucky Chapter, Martha Davis Scholarship for Grad Study Univ of Louisville 1980-82; Outstanding Young Women of America 1984. **Home Addr:** 1946 Goldsmith Ln, Bldg #7, Louisville, KY 40218. **Business Addr:** Director of Admissions & Student Svcs, Kent School of Social Work, University of Louisville, Belknap Campus, Louisville, KY 40292.

CHATTERJEE, LOIS JORDAN
Bank officer. **Personal:** Born Aug 4, 1940, Nashville; married Dr Suchindran S Chatterjee. **Educ:** TN State U, BS 1962; Univ TN, 1963. **Career:** Commerce Union Bank, bank officer bus devel 1972-; Model Cities Prog, evaluator 1971; St Dept Corrections, couns youthful offenders 1966-70; Juvenile CtDavidson Co, legal sec 1962-66. **Orgs:** 1st black female mem Met Council 1971-; mem Negro Bus & Professional Womens League; Middle TN Bus Assn; Nat Bus League; sec SE Nashville Civic League; charter mem Dudley Park Day Care Cntr; bd dirs Goodwill Indus; The House Between; mem Nashville C of C; League Women Voters; YWCA; Nat Council Crime & Delinquency; Nat League Citizens. **Honors/Awds:** Pub Essence mag 1974. **Business Addr:** Educator, Metropolitan School System, 2601 Bradford Ave, Nashville, TN 37204.

CHAUNCEY, MINION KENNETH. See MORRISON, K. C.

CHAVIS, OMEGA ROCHELLE (WENDI)
Banker. **Personal:** Born Dec 31, Tennessee; daughter of Eddie H and Estella M Chavis. **Educ:** Wayne State Univ, bachelors degree, 1970. **Career:** Security Pacific Natl Bank, asst vp, 1973-86; Fox Film Corp, assoc dir, 1986-87; Glendale Federal Bank, sr vp, 1987-. **Orgs:** Savings Assn Mortgage Co Inc, bd of dirs; Los Angeles Home Loan Counseling Ctr, exec bd; United Negro College Fund; Natl Assn of Female Executives; Los Angeles Urban Bankers; Children's Defense Fund; Alpha Kappa Alpha Sorority, Inc; First AME Church. **Honors/Awds:** State of California Health & Welfare Agency Public Service Award; LDF Black Woman of Achievement. **Special Achievements:** Co-founder, California State EDD Advisory Council. **Business Addr:** Senior VP, Glendale Federal Bank, 401 N Brand Blvd, Ste 200, Glendale, CA 91203.

CHAVIS, THEODORE R.
Educator. **Personal:** Born Jun 14, 1922, Asheville, NC; son of Anna Chavis and Theodore Chavis; married Montios; children: Carolyn, Lisa. **Educ:** Talladega Coll, AB 1942; Atlanta Univ, MSW 1951; Smith Coll School of Soc Work, Grad Studies; Univ of MI School of Soc Work, attended. **Career:** NC Employment Security Comm, interviewer 1947-49; VA Guidance Ctr Atlanta GA, trainee 1949; Bur of Mental Hygiene Wash DC, 1950-51; Percy Jones Army Hosp, soc worker 1951-53; VA Hosp Battle Creek MI, asst chief soc work serv 1953-65; MI State Univ, School of Soc Work, professor and past coord practicum instructim 1965-88, professor emeritus, 1988-. **Orgs:** Past Mem MI Chap Professional Standards Comm, ACSW, Natl Assn of Social Workers; past mem Council on Social Work Ed, past mem Budget Panel United Way; past bd mem, chmn serv comm Big Brothers/Big Sisters; past bd mem Capitol Area Child & Family Svc; mem, past chap chmn, treas, Natl Assembly Delegate NASW; past mem Legislative Task Force, MI Chap AARP; past coordinator Capitol City Task Force, past MI State Legislative comm, AARP 1987-; past bd mem, Capital Area Interfaith Respite; State of Michigan Advisory Council on Aging, 1994-. **Honors/Awds:** Outstanding Performance Awd, VA Hosp Battle Creek MI, 1957. **Military Serv:** AUS 1942-46. **Home Phone:** (517)351-6687.

CHAVOUS, BARNEY LEWIS
Executive. **Personal:** Born Mar 22, 1951, Aiken, SC; married Odessa; children: Shedric, Jasmine, Nikeya Monique. **Educ:** SC State U, Phys Ed. **Career:** Denver Broncos, defensive end 1973-1986; Minority Arts & Education Foundation, chairman 1986. **Honors/Awds:** Pittsburgh Courier's NFL Defensive Lineman of the Yr 1978; NFLPA Defensive Rookie of the Yr Hon 1973; All-Conf & defensive MVP at SC State; All-Am by AP;collegiate Defensive Lineman of the Yr; North-South Game; The Senior Bowl; Coaches' All-Am Game. **Business Addr:** Chairman, Minority Arts & Ed Foundation, 6670 S Billings Way, Englewood, CO 80111.

CHAVOUS, MILDRED L.
Educational Administrator, author, journalist. **Personal:** Born Nov 12, Columbia, AL; daughter of Juanita Jackson Lynn and William H Lynn; married Jarret C Chavous, Oct 2, 1951. **Educ:** Franklin University, BS, 1946. **Career:** Ohio State University Graduate School, counselor, 1964-1977, academic counselor, 1977-84, academic counselor & staff asst, 1984-86, administrative associate, 1986-90, director of graduation services, 1990-. **Orgs:** Commission on Public School Personnel Policies in Ohio, 1971-73; Ohio Humanities Council, 1st African American woman, executive committee, 1974-1980; Metropolitan Human Services Commission, founding mem, 1977-90; State Library of Ohio, Advisory Committee Federal Library Program, 1984-1987; League of Women Voters, board of directors, chairperson of the education committee, 1965-; Thurber House, trustee, Thurber National Award for American Humor Comm, 1995-; European Womens Management Network, 1992-; Players Theatre Columbus, trustee and chairperson Outreach Committee, 1989-95; Council on Academic Excellence for Women, 1994-; The Links, Inc; Assn of Faculty and Professional Women; The Crichton Club, past treasurer; Scioto Valley Health Systems Agency, trustee, 1996-; Ohio State Univ Critical Difference for Women, Intl Council; Circle-Lets, Inc, natl vp, 1997-; Ohio State Univ Critical Difference for Women, Intl Council, bd of governors, 1996-. **Honors/Awds:** Ohio House of Representatives 110th General Assembly, Commendation, 1971; United Negro College Fund, Distinguished Service Award, 1981; City of Columbus, Mayors Certificate of Recognition, 1982; Ohio House of Representatives 116th General Assembly, Commendation, 1983; Ohio Senate 116th General Assembly, Commendation, 1983; The Ohio State University, Distinguished Staff Award, 1986; Coalition of 100 Black Women Honoree, 1992; Black Women of Courage Honoree, 1995; Health Plan Review, Cert of Appreciation for Distinguished Svc, 1988-95; Council of the City of Columbus, Commendation, 1996; Ohio House of Representatives, 121 General Assembly, Commendation, Recognition of Accomplishments, 1995. **Special Achievements:** 1st African American and woman co-chair, Ohio State University, United Way Annual Campaign, 1981; 1st woman general chair, United Negro College Fund Annual Telethon, Central Ohio, 1982; chair, Ohio State University Graduate School, 75th Anniversity Celebration, 1987; co-editor, "Graduate School News," The Ohio State University, 1990-; women's editor, Columbus Call and Post, 1970-1985; 1st African American President, board of directors, Columbus Cancer Clinic, 1993-.

CHEADLE, DON
Actor. **Career:** Actor, currently. **Special Achievements:** Appeared on "Picket Fences"; Films include: Devil In A Blue Dress; Rosewood; Boogie Nights, 1997.

CHEANEY, CALBERT N.
Professional basketball player. **Personal:** Born Jul 17, 1971, Evansville, IN. **Educ:** Indiana. **Career:** Washington Wizards, guard-forward, 1993-. **Special Achievements:** NBA Draft, first round, sixth pick, 1993. **Business Addr:** Professional Basketball Player, Washington Wizards, MCI Center, 601 F St NW, Washington, DC 20071, (301)622-3865.

CHEATHAM, BETTY L.
Appointed official. **Personal:** Born Dec 5, 1940, South Carolina. **Educ:** Benedict Coll, BS Bus Admin 1962. **Career:** Intl City Mgmt Assn, prog mgr 1974-80, minority prog dir 1980-83; DC Dept of Public Works, chief office of contract admin. **Orgs:** Mem Coalition of Black Public Admins 1982-85; mem Black Public Admins Forum 1984-85; mem Intl City Mgmt Assn 1983-85. **Honors/Awds:** Awd Coalition of Black Public Admins 1982. **Home Addr:** 859 Venable Place, Washington, DC 20012. **Business Addr:** Chief Office of Contract Admin, DC Public Works Department, 2000 14th St NW 5th Fl, Washington, DC 20009.

CHEATHAM, DOC. See Obituaries section.

CHEATHAM, HENRY BOLES
Television camera operator/director. **Personal:** Born Oct 5, 1943, Bentonia, MS; son of Maude Boles and Thomas Cheatham; married Helen M Hughes, Nov 23, 1966; children: Tonita R, Jomo K. **Educ:** Columbia Coll, BA 1973; Univ of IL at Chicago, MA 1980. **Career:** Ford Motor Co, utility man 1965-73; WISH-TV Indianapolis, tv-production 1973; WSNS-TV Chicago, prod dir camer oper 1973-; Yoton Communications, Inc, president, founder/owner, 1980-. **Orgs:** Union steward ex bd NABET 1980-; mem Chicago Area Broadcast Public Affairs Assoc 1980-83; mem Natl Black United Front 1983-, Operation PUSH 1983-. **Honors/Awds:** Image Awd Fred Hampton Foundation 1983; article published in following publications, NABET-NEWS, Beverly Review, Chicago Defender. **Military Serv:** AUS E-4 2 yrs; Honorable Discharge 1965. **Business Addr:** Producer/Director/Camera Oper, WSNS TV, 430 W Grant Place, Chicago, IL 60614.

CHEATHAM, LINDA MOYE
City official. **Personal:** Born Nov 2, 1948, Richmond, VA; married Harold D Cheatham Jr; children: Michelle, Maxanne, Harold,III. **Educ:** Wheaton Coll, BA, 1970; Virginia Commonwealth Univ. **Career:** City of Norfolk, planner 1970-72; City of Richmond, planner 1972-75, operations mgr 1975-79, senior budget analyst 1979-84, dir of general serv 1984-87, budget dir 1987-. **Orgs:** Mem, Intl City Mgmt Assn, 1980-; bd of governors, William Byrd Community House, 1983-; mem, Conf of Minority Public Admin 1983-; bd of dirs, City of Richmond, Fed Credit Union, 1984; chapter council VA Chapter Amer Soc of Public Admin, 1984-; treasurer, John B Cary PTA 1985-88. **Honors/Awds:** Outstanding Woman of 1984; North Richmond YMCA Black Achiever 1985. **Home Addr:** 3112 Rendale Ave, Richmond, VA 23221. **Business Addr:** Budget Dir, City of Richmond, 900 East Broad St, Richmond, VA 23230.

CHEATHAM, ROY E.
Educator. **Personal:** Born Sep 14, 1941, Memphis; married Gertie Brenell Wilson; children: Roy III, Gina Rochele. **Educ:** Lincoln U, BA 1965; St Louis U, MA 1969; St Louis U, PhD 1975. **Career:** Metropolitan College, dean; St Louis Univ, dir special acad prog, dir coll assistance prog & upward bound 1970-73; Coll of Arts & Science, St Louis Univ, asst to dean 1969-70; Human Dev Corp, adult & educ coord 1966-67; adult educ curriculum specialist 1969. **Orgs:** Mem Am Coll Pesonnel Assn's Commn XIV 1973-76; mem Basic Educ Oppor Grant Planning Com 1972; Reg VII Office of Higher Edn; pres Roy Cheatham & Asso; mem Financial Aid Panel 1973; pres 1976-77; bd educ Univ City Pub Sch Dist 1974-77; v-chmn bd dir Inroads Inc 1973-76; commr Mark Twain Boy ScoutDist; mem bd dir Comm Learning Ctr; mem bd dir Sophia House; Educ Enrichment Prog 1972-75. **Honors/Awds:** Comm serv award Orgn of Black Entrepreneurs 1972; meritorious serv award Lincoln Univ Alumni Assn 1973; outstanding serv award Black Students of St Louis U1973; NDEA Fellow St Louis & Univ 1967-69. **Business Addr:** St Louis University, 221 N Grand Blvd, St Louis, MO 63103.

CHECKER, CHUBBY (ERNEST EVANS)
Recording artist. **Personal:** Born Oct 3, 1941, Spring Gulley, SC; married Rina Lodder, 1964; children: three. **Career:** Appeared in night clubs, movies, theatres; popularized "The Twist" dance; TV appearances: Midnight Special, American Bandstand, Mike Douglas, Discomania; recordings include: The Class, 1959; Dancing Dinosaur, 1959; The Twist, 1960; Let's Twist Again, 1962; Pony Time, 1961; Slow Twistin (w/ Dee Dee Sharp), 1962; Limbo Rock. 1963; others. **Orgs:** ASCAP. **Honors/Awds:** Grammy Award 1961.

CHECOLE, KASSAHUN
Publisher. **Personal:** Born Jan 22, 1947, Asmara, Ethiopia; married Nevolia E Ogletree; children: MuluBirhan, Senait. **Educ:** SUNY Binghamton, BA Hnrs 1974, MA 1976. **Career:** Rutgers Univ, instructor 1979-85; Africa Research and Publishing Proj, dir 1979-; El Colegio De Mexico, research prof 1982-; The Red Sea Press, publisher 1982-; Washington School Inst for Policy Studies, lecturer; Africa World Press, publisher. **Orgs:** Vice chrmn Eritrean Relief Comm Inc 1983-85; editorial bd Saga Race Relations Abstracts, Horn of Africa; editor RSP current issues series. **Business Addr:** Publisher, Africa World Press, PO Box 1892, Trenton, NJ 08607.

CHEEK, DONALD KATO
Educator. **Personal:** Born Mar 24, 1930, New York, NY; married Calista Patricia Duff (deceased); children: Don Jr, Gary, Alan, Stephan, Donna; married Patti Dorothy Walker. **Educ:** Seton Hall Univ, BS 1953; Fordham Schl of Soc Srv, MSW 1955; Temple Univ, PhD 1971. **Career:** Lincoln Univ PA, vice pres student affairs, dean, lecturer 1967-69; Claremont Coll CA, dir of black studies 1969-73; CA Polytechnic State Univ, prof 1973-; rehabilitation counselor 1984-; ordained minister 1987-. **Orgs:** Consult spkr wrkshp facilitator Milwaukee WI Mental Health Ctr, Orangeburg SC Annual Guidance Conf NY Salomon Brothers, Las Vegas NV Amer Personnel & Guidance Assc Conv, New Orleans LA Assc of Blk Soc Wrks, Dallas TX Drug Educ Prev and Treatment, Daytona Bch FL, Bethune Cookman Clge, Emporia KS State Univ, Omaha NE Crighton Univ, Sanford FL Seminole Comm Clge, Xenia OH Cty Mental Health, Evansville IN Human Rel Comm, Univ of Cincinnati Clge of Nursing, Cleveland OH Urban Minority Alcoholism Outreach Proj, SC Schl of Alcohol and Drug Studies, City of Portland OR, Univ of ND, LA Black Prof Engrs. **Honors/Awds:** Invited pres sci paper Intl Congress of Behavior Therapy Uppsala Sweden 1977; recipient of Natl Inst Mental Health Grad Flwshp 1967; presenter Intl Consult Counslng and Ethnic Minorities Univ of Utrecht Netherlands 1985; publ Assertive Black Puzzled White. **Home Addr:** PO Box 1476, Atascadero, CA 93423. **Business Addr:** Professor, CA Polytechnic State Univ, San Luis Obispo, CA 93407.

CHEEK, DONNA MARIE
Equestrian. **Personal:** Born Dec 5, 1963, Philadelphia, PA. **Educ:** CA Polytech State Univ. **Career:** "One More Hurdle" Autobiography NBC TV, starred in one hour drama 1984; "Profiles in Pride" NBC TV, starred 1985; equestrian; Exhibition Equestrian, Coors; Seven Star Farms, Hunter/Jumper Training Facility for Horses and Riders, owner/operator. **Orgs:** Corp sponsorship Univox CA Inc, Pro-Line Corp, Quincy Jones Prod, Ed Lara's Westside Distr; spokesperson Involvement for Young Achievers Inc 1982-. **Honors/Awds:** Financial Grant Black Equestrian Sports Talent 1980-, Avon Found NY 1983; Publ "Going for the Gold-The Story of Black Women in Sports," 1983; NAACP Image Awd for "One More Hurdle-The Donna Cheek Story," 1984; first equestrienne inductee, Women's Sports Hall of Fame, 1990; first black on US Equestrian Team. **Home Addr:** PO Box 1476, Atascadero, CA 93423.

CHEEK, JAMES EDWARD
Educational administrator (retired). **Personal:** Born Dec 4, 1932, Roanoke Rapids, NC; son of Lee Ella Williams Cheek and King Virgil Cheek; married Celestine Juanita Williams, Jun 14, 1953; children: James Edward, Janet Elizabeth. **Educ:** Shaw Univ, BA 1955; Colgate-Rochester Div Sch, M Div 1958; Drew Univ, PhD 1962. **Career:** Drew Theology School, teaching asst 1959-60; Union Jr Coll, instructor Western History 1959-61; VA Union Univ, asst prof NT hist theology 1961-63; Shaw Univ, pres 1963-69; Howard Univ, pres 1969-89, pres emeritus; Tennessee Wesleyan College, pres, currently. **Orgs:** Bd mem, trustee, and advisory bd mem of numerous professional and civic associations and committees; mem Alpha Theta Nu, Alpha Phi Alpha, Sigma Pi Sigma, American Society of Church History, American Assn of Univ Profs, American Academy of Religion. **Honors/Awds:** Presidential Medal of Freedom, February 23, 1983; honorary degrees: Shaw Univ, 1970, Drew Univ, 1971, Trinity College, 1970, A&T State Univ, 1971; L'Universite d'Etat d'Haiti, 1972, Deleware State College, 1972, Univ of Maryland, 1975, Bucknell Univ, 1975, New York Institute of Technology, 1980, Univ of North Carolina, 1980, Duke Univ, 1982, Fisk Univ, 1984, Central State Univ, 1988, Tuskegee Univ, 1989, Adelphi Univ, 1989, Rider College, 1989. **Military Serv:** USAF 1950-51. **Business Addr:** President, Tennessee Wesleyan College, PO Box 40, Athens, TN 37303.

CHEEK, KING VIRGIL, JR.
Educator, attorney (retired). **Personal:** Born May 26, 1937, Weldon, NC; married Annette Walker; children: King Virgil III, Kahlil, Antoinette, Antoine. **Educ:** Bates Coll ME, BA 1959; Univ of Chicago, MA 1960; Univ of Chicago Law School, JD 1964. **Career:** Shaw Univ Raleigh, NC, asst econs prof 1964-65, acting dean 1956-66, dean 1966-67; private practice law Raleigh 1965-69; Shaw Univ, vice pres acad affairs 1965-69; Citizinship Lab, lectr 1968-69; Shaw Univ, pres 1969-71; Morgan State Coll, pres 1971-74; Union for Experimenting Colls & Univs, vice pres for planning & devel 1974-76, pres, 1976-78; New York Inst of Tech, exec dir ctr for leadership and career develop 1978-85; New York Inst of Tech, Ctr for Leadership and Career Develop, vice pres, dean of grad studies, exec dir 1985-89, vice pres institutional advancement, 1989-91, vice pres academic affairs, 1991-96. **Orgs:** Bd of dir Baltimore Contractors 1974-; bd of dir Inst for Econ Devel 1978-; bd of trustees Martin Center Coll; bd of trustees Shaw Coll Detroit; bd of visitors Univ of Chicago Law Sch; bd of trustees Warnborough Coll Oxford England. **Honors/Awds:** Grand Commdr of Order of Star Africa 1971; Top Young Leaders in Amer Acad Change Magazine 1978; Disting Civilian Award AUS 1973; LLD DE State Coll 1970,Bates Coll, Univ of MD 1972; LHD Shaw Coll at Detroit 1983.

CHEEK, ROBERT BENJAMIN, III
Dentist. **Personal:** Born Sep 12, 1931, New York, NY; married Geraldine M Manley; children: Albert, Sonseeahray. **Educ:** NC Coll, BS 1954; Howard Univ, DDS 1962. **Career:** Robert B Cheek DDS PC, pres 1956-; Am Airlines, sales rep 1956; Underwood Corp, sales rep 1954. **Orgs:** Mem Nat Dental Assn; mem Acad of Gen Dentistry; mem Bridgeport Dental Assn; mem Guardsmen; life mem NAACP. **Honors/Awds:** Fighter Wings USAF 1956. **Military Serv:** USAF 2nd lt 2 yrs. **Business Addr:** President, 1211 Reservoir Ave, Bridgeport, CT 06606.

CHEEKS, CARL L.
Dentist. **Personal:** Born Jul 7, 1937, Poplar Bluff, MO; married Shirley K Magness; children: Darryl, Shalonda. **Educ:** Fisk Univ Nashville, BA 1960; Meharry Med Sch, DDS 1965. **Career:** Self-Employed Evanston IL, dr dntl surgery 1967-. **Orgs:** Am Dental Assn; Nat Dental Assn; Northshore Dental Assn; Lincoln Dental Soc; Am Acad Gen Dentistry; mem Relative Analgesia Seminars; Chicago Dental Soc; life mem NAACP; life mem Kappa Alpha Psi Frat; mem, trustee, teacher song leader Monroe Street Ch Christ; bd dir United Community Services Evanston 1969-71; chmn nominating com Martin Luther King Lab Sch PTA 1975; mem Black Bus & Professional Assn; exec com Evanston Sch Bd 1969-71; former mem Fisk Jubilee Singers; served spl bd recruitment black hs male students Naval Acad; served com human relations Great Lakes, IL. **Honors/Awds:** Certificate merit Minority Youth Motivation 1968-74; Chessman Club Award for aiding civic program; certificate Council Nat Bd Dental Examiners. **Military Serv:** USN dental & lt 1965-67. **Business Addr:** 1626 Darrow Ave, Evanston, IL 60201.

CHEEKS, DARRYL LAMONT
Auditor. **Personal:** Born Apr 7, 1968, Evanston, IL; son of Beaulah Brittain Cheeks and Carl Cheeks. **Educ:** University of Illinois, Champaign, IL, BS, accounting, 1990. **Career:** Dr Carl L Cheeks, Evanston, IL, dental assistant, 1978-86; Golden Touch Cleaners, Evanson, IL, owner/manager, 1987-88; Krispy Kits Karmel Korn, Evanston,IL, owner/manager, 1988; Arthur Andersen, Chicago, IL, auditor, 1989-93; Abbott Laboratories, North Chicago IL, financial & operational consultant, 1993-95; Hoyt Fastener Co, Niles, IL, controller, 1995-. **Orgs:** Dir of education, assist minister, jail ministry dir, trustee, Monroe St Church of Christ, 1989-; bd of dirs, treasurer, Reba Place Day Nursery, 1992-; bd of dirs, treasurer, Jan Erkert & Dancers, 1994-; Natl Assoc of Black Accountants, 1991-; IL CPA Society, 1992-. **Honors/Awds:** Outstanding College Students of America, Outstanding College Students Of America, 1987-90; Mom's Day Scholastic Award, University of Illinois, 1987, 1988, 1990; High Honor Roll, Dean's List, University of IL, 1987; Fred G Carpenter Award, Business, Evanston Township, MS, 1986; President's Scholarship Award, University of IL, 1986-90; Certified Public Accountant, 1992; Ebony Magazine, August 1990. **Business Addr:** Controller, Hoyt Fastener Corp, 7300 N Oak Park Ave, Niles, IL 60714, (708)647-5402.

CHEEKS, MAURICE EDWARD
Professional basketball player. **Personal:** Born Sep 8, 1956, Chicago, IL. **Educ:** West Texas State. **Career:** Guard: Philadelphia 76er's, 1978-89, San Antonio Spurs, 1990, New York Knicks, 1990-91, Atlanta Hawks, 1991-93, New Jersey Nets, 1993-. **Business Addr:** Professional Basketball Player, New Jersey Nets, Brendan Byrne Arena, East Rutherford, NJ 07073.

CHENAULT, KENNETH
Business executive. **Educ:** Bowdoin Coll, graduate; Harvard Law School, graduate. **Career:** Attorney, firm of Rogers & Wells; management Consultant, Bain & Company; American Express, div head of green cards, 1981-89, pres, Consumer Card Group U S, 1989-, pres of Travel Related Services, US Division, 1993-95, vice chairman, 1995-. **Business Addr:** Vice Chairman, American Express Co, American Express Tower C, New York, NY 10285-5000.

CHENAULT, MYRON MAURICE
Vice chancellor. **Personal:** Born Mar 3, 1949, Richmond, IN; married Vivian Michelle Chiles; children: Myron. **Educ:** Manchester Coll, BA 1971; Valparaiso Univ Sch of Law, JD 1974. **Career:** Bowling Green Univ, asst vice pres 1978-80, assoc vice pres legal staff cont rel 1980-82; Winston-Salem State Univ, vice chancellor 1982-. **Orgs:** Bd mem Winston-Salem Housing Foundation 1984-, Greater Winston-Salem Chamber of Commerce 1984-; bd mem Southeastern Ctr for Contemporary Art 1985-, NatureScience Ctr 1985-; mem Phi Alpha Delta, Omicron Delta Kappa, Phi Beta Sigma, Leadership Winston-Salem; mem Ohio, America Bar Assocs; mem Council for Advancement and Support Educ; mem Ohio US Dist Court Northern Div. **Business Addr:** Vice Chancellor, Winston-Salem State Univ, PO Box 13325, Winston-Salem, NC 27102.

CHENAULT, WILLIAM J.
Business executive. **Personal:** Born Sep 20, 1928, Cincinnati, OH; son of Dora E Hill Chenault and James Chenault (deceased); married Betty R; children: Lisa Ann, Constance Louise, Karla Ann, Kenneth Luther, Edward Alan. **Educ:** Univ of Cincinnati, BBA 1959. **Career:** City of Cincinnati, city council mem 1968-75, vice mayor 1971, 1973, 1975; Chenault and Assoc Real Estate Appraisal and Consulting, owner & CEO 1971-; State of Ohio Dept of Tax Equal, appraisal supr 1977-84; J Ruth Corp Holding Company, pres & CEO 1982-89. **Orgs:** Pres & founding mem, Appraiser's Network, 1994-; instr, Univ of Cincinnati Evening Coll, 1978-81; chmn of admissions comm, Natl Assn of Independent Fee Appraisers, Cincinnati Chap, 1973; mem, Ohio, Kentucky, Indiana Regional Planning Commn, 1971-75; pres & treas, Cincinnati-Hamilton County Criminal Justice Regional Planning Unit, 1969-75; pres & founding mem, Political Action Programming Assembly, 1963-65; vice pres & bd dir, Jaycees Greater Cincinnati, 1960-62; vice pres, Hamilton County Democratic Party, 1969-75; first vice pres 1985-87, pres 1987-88, public relations comm chmn 1988-89, Columbus Chap, Amer Soc of Appraisers, 1985-87, 1990-91. **Honors/Awds:** Public Serv Award, Prudential Insurance Co of Amer, 1967; Recognition of Serv, Ohio, Kentucky, Indiana Regional Planning Commn, 1975; Honorary Citizen of State of Tennessee, 1975; Honorary Sergeant-at-Arms, Tennessee State Legislature, 1975. **Military Serv:** AUS Med Corps pfc; Good Conduct Medal; honorable discharge. **Business Addr:** CEO and Owner, Chenault & Associates, 7761 Wayfaring Ct, Reynoldsburg, OH 43068, (614)861-0237.

CHENEVERT, PHILLIP JOSEPH
Physician. **Personal:** Born Feb 15, 1948, Detroit, MI; son of Mary Chenenert Pembroke and Wendell Sr (deceased); married Judith Grandy; children: Belen, Amber. **Educ:** Highland Park Comm Coll, AA 1970; North Carolina Central Univ, BS (Cum Laude) 1974; Meharry Medical Coll, MD 1978; Children's Hospital of Michigan, Residency 1978-81. **Career:** Private Practice, physician 1981-86; Cigna Health Plan of TX, pediatrics 1986-; Univ of Texas Southwestern Medical Center, Dallas Fellow Developmental and Ambulatory Pediatrics 1988-91. **Orgs:** Bd of dirs AYD Youth Job 1982-83; chief of pediatrics L Richardson Memorial Hosp 1982-86; med dir United Way Greensboro NC 1983-84; bd of dirs Amer Diabetes Assoc Greensboro NC 1985-86; volunteer Medical Instructor PA Prog Bowman Gray Sch of Medicine 1985-86; bd of dirs Arlington Charities 1986-. **Honors/Awds:** Fellowship Natl Inst of Health; Outstanding Young Men of Amer 1986.

CHENEVERT-BRAGG, IRMA J.
Judge. **Personal:** Born Nov 17, 1951, Detroit, MI; daughter of Arthur & Ruth Green; married Sidney Bragg, Sr, Mar 7, 1992; children: Arica Chenevert, Arianna Powers. **Educ:** Eastern Michigan University, BS, 1973; Detroit College of Law, JD, 1982. **Career:** Wayne County Prosecutor's Office, assistant prosecuting attorney, 1984-85; Joselyn Rowe Etal, attorney,

1985-86; Detroit Board of Police Commissioner, special proj assistant, 1986-87; self-employed, attorney, 1986-89; State of Michigan, administrative, law judge, 1986-89; 36th District Court, magistrate, 1989-. **Orgs:** State Bar of Michigan, 1985-. **Honors/Awds:** Handgun Intervention Prog, HIP Awd, 1996; American Business Women's Association, Business Association of the Year, 1992-93; Wolverine Student Bar Association, Special Alumni Awd, 1985. **Business Addr:** Magistrate, 36th District Court, 421 Madison Ave, Ste 1063, Detroit, MI 48226, (313)965-5220.

CHENNAULT, MADELYN
Educator. **Personal:** Born Jul 15, 1934, Atlanta, GA; daughter of Othello Ann Jones and Benjamin Q Chennault; married Thomas Mark, Jul 14, 1982 (deceased). **Educ:** Morris Brown Coll, BS 1957; Univ of MI, MA 1961; IN Univ, PhD; Univ of GA, Post Doctoral Study in Clinical Psychology; Univ of MS Med Ctr, Post Doctoral Internship. **Career:** Public Schls GA, CA, MI, educator 1957-62; Albany State Coll, asst prof of Psychology 1962-64; IN Univ, rsch asst 1964-66; Atlanta Univ, asst prof educ 1966-67; Ft Valley State Coll, assoc prof educ 1967-70, prof educ 1970-72, prof educ & clinical dir of Community Hypertension Intervention Program, 1972-89; Chennault Enterprise, pres 1974-. **Orgs:** Counsel Exceptional Children's Regional Meeting; consul Atlanta GA 1967; spl educ consult Grambling Coll 1968; educ psych consult Univ of CT 1969; elementary educ consult AL A&M Univ 1969; mental retardation consul GA State Dept Educ 1969-71; sch integration consul Americus GA Pub Schs 1970; spec educ vis scholar NC Central Univ 1971; Natl Sci Found Visit Scientist AL State Univ 1971; Head Start consul for Heart of GA Project 1970-71; spec serv proj consult Ft Valley State Coll 1971-72; Natl Sci Found Vis Scientist Talledega Coll 1972; main speaker Alpha Kappa Alpha Sor Founders Day Prog 1972; spec educ consult & psychometrist Peach Co Pub Sch 1972; So Regional Rep Assn Black Psychologists 1972-74; served on exec adv com of Comm-Clinical Psych Project So Reg Educ BdAtlanta 1972-75; cont psych Jackson Hinds Comm Mental Health Ctr 1973; psych consul MS State Univ 1973; mem Assn Adv of Behav Therapy, Am Assn on Mental Def, Am Assn of Univ Profs, Amer Psych Assn, Am Rsch Assn, GA Psych Assn, Nat Educ Assn, Alpha Kappa Alpha Sor, Links, Inc. **Honors/Awds:** Pub Law Fellowship 88-164, 1964-66 IN Univ Bloomington; Post Doc Fellowship in Clinical Psych Univ of GA; published numerous articles. **Home Addr:** 215 Piedmont Ave NE, #1006, Atlanta, GA 30308.

CHEROT, NICHOLAS MAURICE
Attorney. **Personal:** Born Jun 30, 1947, Ann Arbor, MI. **Educ:** Univ of MI, BA 1969; NYU Sch of Law, JD 1972. **Career:** Autumn Industries Inc, sec-treas 1977-; Autumn-Everseal Mfg Co Inc, sec-treas 1979-. **Orgs:** Dir-partner Powell Blvd Holdin Co Inc & Powell Blvd Assoc 1979-; mem Harlem Lawyers & Assn NYC; mem NY Co Lawyers Assn; Natl Bar Assn; mem Black Allied Law Students Assn Invitations, law jours. **Business Addr:** Cherot & Michael, PC, 305 Broadway, Room 600, New York, NY 10007.

CHERRELLE (CHERYL NORTON)
Singer, songwriter, producer. **Career:** Albums and singles include: Fragile, High Priority, Affair, "I Didn't Mean to Turn You On," "Artificial Heart," numerous others; duet with Alexander O'Neal, "Saturday Love"; Tabu Records; CBS Records Inc, currently. **Business Phone:** (212)975-4321.

CHERRY, ANDREW JACKSON
Clergyman. **Personal:** Born Feb 8, 1927, Harrellsville, NC; married Bernice Britt; children: Vivian L Carter, Andrew J Jr, Ada E. **Educ:** Shaw University, AB 1950; Shaw Divinity School, BD 1950, DD, 1984. **Career:** Minister, currently. **Orgs:** President, Bertie United Concerned Citizens 1953; president, Bertie NAACP Branch 1954-56; West Roanoke Missionary Baptist Assn 1944-85; Roanoke Missionary Baptist Assn 1952-85; Bertie Board of Education 1976-84. **Home Addr:** 226 Republican Rd, Windsor, NC 27983.

CHERRY, CASSANDRA BRABBLE
Education specialist. **Personal:** Born May 29, 1947, Norfolk, VA; married Capt Maurice L Cherry (deceased). **Educ:** Bennett Coll, BA 1969; VA State Univ, MEd 1974; Richard Bland Coll of the Coll of Wm and Mary, Management diploma 1975; Nova Univ, EdD 1980. **Career:** US Army Quartermaster School, educ specialist 1974; US Army Logistics Ctr, educ specialist 1974-78; US Army Training Support Ctr, educ specialist 1978-79;Naval Supply Ctr, employee develop specialist 1979; Defense Activity for Non-Traditional Educ Support, mgr instructional delivery programs 1980-. **Orgs:** Mem Phi Delta Kappa 1980-; bd dirs Minorities in Media 1982-83; mem Federally Employed Women 1985-; publicity chmn Equal Employment Oppor Council Pensacola Naval Complex 1985, 86; mem Amer Inst of Mortgage Brokers 1986-; mem NAACP 1986-. **Honors/Awds:** One Woman Art Exhibit at Bennett College 1969. **Home Addr:** 7811 Bay Meadows Court, Pensacola, FL 32507.

CHERRY, CHARLES WILLIAM
Publisher. **Personal:** Born Oct 13, 1928, Americus, GA; son of Janie Cherry and Grady Cherry; married Julia Troutman; children: Charles II, Glenn, Cassandra. **Educ:** Morehouse Coll, BA 1949; AL State U, MA 1953. **Career:** Bethune Cookman Coll, acct 1953-56; Claflin Coll, mgr 1956-58; Volusia Co Com Coll, mgr 1958-61; Bethune Cookman Coll, dir & asst prof 1961-79; Daytona Times & Florida Courier, pub, 1977-; WPVL, gen mgr, 1988-; City of Daytona Beach, city commissioner, 1995-. **Orgs:** Mem Nat & Campgn Staff of Sen McGovern Pres 1971-72; pres Volusia Cnty NAACP 1972-76; pres FL State Conf NAACP 1974-84; mem Nat Bd of Dir NAACP, 1975-87; chrm of bd RV Moore Comm Ctr Inc; mem SHCC. **Military Serv:** AUS 1950-52.

CHERRY, DERON
Sports administrator, former professional football player. **Personal:** Born Sep 12, 1959, Riverside, NJ. **Career:** Kansas City Chiefs, safety, 1981-91; Anheuser-Busch, beverage distributor; Jacksonville Jaguars, co-owner, currently. **Honors/Awds:** Tied NFL record for most interceptions in a game (4) against Seattle Seahawks, 1985; played in Pro-Bowl, 1983-88 seasons. **Special Achievements:** Second African American to attain part ownership in an NFL franchise, 1993. **Business Addr:** Co-owner, Jacksonville Jaguars, 1 Stadium Place, Jacksonville, FL 32202, (904)633-6000.

CHERRY, EDWARD EARL, SR.
Business executive. **Personal:** Born Dec 4, 1926, Greenville, NC; son of Velma Smith Cherry and Jasper Cherry; married Mary Jean Jordan (deceased); children: Edward Jr, Todd J (deceased). **Educ:** Howard Univ, BArch 1953. **Career:** Edward Cherry Architect, pres 1963-; Yale Univ School of Architecture, asst prof 1971, visiting critic 1972-81. **Orgs:** Founder, bd dir, past pres, Greater New Haven Business Prof Assn 1964-; pres, Heritage Hall Devel Corp 1980; corporate mem, Connecticut Soc of Architects, AIA 1960-; worshipful master, Oriental Lodge No 6, F&AM PHA 1966-68; New Haven Consistory No 7, AASR PHA 1968-; mem, past basileus, Chi Omicran Chapter, Omega Psi Phi Frat 1957-; mem, State Historic Preservation Review Bd, Connecticut Historical Comm 1980-; grand inspector general, AASR, PHA, Northern Jurisdiction 1986; archon, Beta Tau Boule, Sigma Pi Phi 1986; bd dir, Foundation for the New Haven Green 1986-89. **Honors/Awds:** AIA Design Award, Connecticut Soc Arch, AIA; Man of the Year, New England States, 1st Dist, Omega Psi Phi Frat, 1979; Grand Basileus Service Award, Omega Psi Phi, 1979; College of Fellows, AIA, 1996. **Military Serv:** AUS pvt 1945-46; Victory Medal, Occup Medal 1946. **Home Addr:** 22 Pine Ridge Rd, Woodbridge, CT 06525. **Business Addr:** President, Edward E Cherry FAIA Arch, 60 Connolly Pkwy, Hamden, CT 06514, (203)281-1300.

CHERRY, JE'ROD
Professional football player. **Personal:** Born May 30, 1973, Charlotte, NC; married Lisa. **Educ:** University of California, bachelor's degree in political science, 1995. **Career:** New Orleans Saints, defensive back, 1996-. **Business Addr:** Professional Football Player, New Orleans Saints, 5800 Airline Hwy, Metairie, LA 70003, (504)733-0255.

CHERRY, LEE OTIS
Researcher. **Personal:** Born Nov 20, 1944, Oakland, CA; married Lauran Michelle Waters; children: Aminah Louise. **Educ:** Merritt Comm Coll, AA 1965; San Jose State Univ, BSEE 1968; Hazardous Material Management, Univ of CA, certificate, 1995; Site Assessment & Remediation, registered environ assessor, CA, 1997. **Career:** Intl Business Machines, systems analyst 1968-69; Pacific Gas & Electric Co, electrical engineer 1969-79; Dept of Defense, project mgr 1979-; African Scientific Inst, exec dir 1967-. **Orgs:** Sr consultant Develop Consultants and Assocs 1972-; proprietor L & L and Assocs Network Marketing 1980-; co-founder, African Science Inst, International, 1967-. **Honors/Awds:** Published "Technology Transfer," a monthly magazine 1979-83; Co-Founder/Vice Pres of the Ghanaian-American Chamber of Commerce; Developer of "Blacks in Science Calendar" annually 1986-; produced general and technical conferences; performed public speaking; made numerous TV appearances and radio shows; written articles for various newspapers and magazines; Publisher, "Sci Tech," nationally distributed newspaper about developments in science and technology. **Business Addr:** Exec Dir, African Scientific Institute, PO Box 12161, Oakland, CA 94604.

CHERRY, ROBERT LEE
Educational administrator. **Personal:** Born Feb 17, 1941, Barrackville, WV; married Anna Luckett; children: Mary Elizabeth, Robert Lee, Ebon Michael. **Educ:** Wittenberg U, EdB 1964; Wright State U, EdM 1973. **Career:** Clark Tech Coll, dir student serv 1975; DMVC-EDNL Opportunity Center, exec dir 1975; Clark Tech Coll, admissions officer 1973; Upward Bound Program Wittenberg Univ, program dir 1968; Intl Harvester Co, supr 1964. **Orgs:** Past mem & pres OH Assn of Upward Bound Dir 1970; certification com mem OH Assn of Student Financial Aid Adminstr 1974; mem OH Assn of Student Serv Dir 1977; bd mem Opportunities Industrialization Center 1974; city commnr Springfield OH, 1974; chmn Clark Co 648 Mental Health & Retardation Bd 1975. **Honors/Awds:** Comm merit award Springfield Frontiers Intl 1962; Outstanding Young Men of Am OYMA Bd of Advisors 1970; comm Serv award St John Bapt Ch 1980. **Business Addr:** Educational administrator, PO Box 570, Springfield, OH 45505.

CHERRY, THEODORE W.
Elected government official. **Personal:** Born Dec 5, 1932, Woodland, NC; son of Laura Cherry (deceased) and Noah Cherry (deceased); married Evelyn Maggett; children: Theodore Jr. **Educ:** NC Central Univ, BS 1952-56; Hampton Inst, MS 1965-66. **Career:** Ralph J Bunche School, Weldon NC, chmn sci & math 1958-59; James Weldon Johnson School, Yorktown VA, chmn sci & math 1959-67; Hampton Inst VA, teacher 1966-67; Crossroads School, Monmouth Jct NJ, chmn sci dept 1967-87; Horizon for Youth PA, NY, UT, dir 1969-72; US Dept of Intl Youth Conservation Corp 1973; S Brunswick Township, mayor 1979-81, commissioner of police, 1989-, committeeman until 1990; MCEOC, dir 1981-; South Brunswick Board of Education, Monmouth Junction, NJ, chairman of the science dept, 1986-. **Orgs:** Mem NAACP 1967-, NEA, NJEA, MEA, SBEA 1967-, Sci Club of Amer 1968; mem South Brunswick Township Lions Club 1986-; member, Concerned Black Parents & Citizens of South Brunswick, 1969-. **Honors/Awds:** Meritorious Teacher of the Year Awd VA Teacher Assn 1965; Outstanding Educator Awd Jaycees of S Brunswick 1975; Mayors Apprec Awd S Brunswick Twp Com 1976; Outstanding Citizens Awd NAACP 1979; Concerned Black Parents & Citizens of South Brunswick Service Award, 1989. **Military Serv:** US Army, spec5, 1956-58. **Business Addr:** Dir, MCEOC, Municipal Bldg, Monmouth Junction, NJ 08852.

CHESLEY, ROGER T., SR.
Journalist. **Personal:** Born Oct 31, 1959, Washington, DC; son of Virginia C Hamilton Chesley (deceased) and Joseph W Chesley Sr (deceased); married Michele Vernon-Chesley, Sep 19, 1987; children: Roger T Jr, Christine J. and Maya A. **Educ:** Howard University, Washington, DC, BA(magna cum laude), 1981. **Career:** Washington Star, Washington, DC, reporter intern, 1981; Courier-Post, Camden, NJ, copy editor, 1981-83; Detroit Free Press, Detroit, MI, editor, 1983-88, reporter, 1988-. **Orgs:** President, vice pres, treasurer, Detroit Chapter, National Assn of Black Journalists, member, Newspaper Guild of Detroit, 1983-; lector, St Aloysius Catholic Church, 1988-92; member, East English Village Assn, 1990-; member, Phi Alpha Theta Society, 1981. **Honors/Awds:** Olive Branch Award, New York University's Center for War, Peace and the News Media, 1990.

CHESS, EVA
Company executive. **Personal:** Born Feb 6, 1960, High Point, NC; daughter of Hon & Mrs Sammie Chess Jr. **Educ:** Univ of NC, Chapel Hill, BA, 1982; Univ of VA, JD, 1985. **Career:** JP Morgan & Co, Inc, private banker, 1985-91; Sara Lee Corp, sr mgr, public responsibility, 1991-. **Orgs:** United Way of Stamford, CT, bd of dirs; Coalition of 100 Black Women of Lower Fairfield County, CT, officer, bd of dires; Business Policy Review Council; Urban Bankers Coalition, American & VA Bar Assns; Chicago Cosmopolitan Chamber of Commerce, bd of dirs; Chicago United, deacon; Center for Women Policy Studies, corp advisory comm; League of Women Voters, corp advisory council; American Assn of Univ Women Educ Foundation, bd of dirs; Midwest Women's Center, bd of dirs. **Honors/Awds:** Dollars & Sense Magazine, America's Best & Brightest, 1993.

CHESS, SAMMIE, JR.
Attorney. **Personal:** Born Mar 28, 1934, Allendale, SC; married Marlene Enoch; children: Eva, Janet. **Educ:** NC Central U, LLB 1958. **Career:** Pvt Practice, atty 1960-71; spl superior ct judge 1971-75. **Orgs:** Mem NC Bd Higher Educ 1968-71; mem High Point Parks & Recreation Commn 1962-65; High Point Bar Assn; Am Assn; trustee Winston-Salem State U. **Honors/Awds:** Outstanding & serv award High Point Bus & Professional Members Club; award of merit NC Central Univ 1973; citizen of yr award Alpha Phi Alpha Frat. **Military Serv:** AUS 1958-60. **Business Addr:** 1222 Montlieu Ave, High Point, NC 27260.

CHESTANG, LEON WILBERT
Educator. **Personal:** Born May 16, 1937, Mobile, AL; married Aurelia C Taylor; children: Nicole, Yvette. **Educ:** Blackburn College, AB 1959; Washington Univ, MSW 1961; The Univ of Chicago, PhD 1977. **Career:** IL Dept of Children and Family Serv, supervisor 1961-65; IL Dept of Public Aid, social casework instr 1967-68; Family Care of Chicago, dir of casework services 1968-71; Univ of Chicago, asst prof 1971-78; Univ of Alabama, prof 1978-81; Wayne State Univ, dean and prof 1981-. **Orgs:** Bd mem Childrens Aid Soc of Detroit 1984-; bd mem Detroit Urban League 1985-; bd mem Natl Assn of Social Workers 1985-88. **Honors/Awds:** ACE Fellow 1979; Distinguished Commonwealth Prof VA Univ Commonwealth 1984-86; Disting Lydia Rapaport Prof Smith Coll 1985; Disting Service Awd MI Assn of School Social Workers 1986; Howard Univ, visiting Cosby Scholar, 1992. **Home Addr:** 682 Pallister Ave, Detroit, MI 48202. **Business Addr:** Dean, Professor, Wayne State Univ, School of Social Work, Detroit, MI 48202.

CHESTNUT, DENNIS EARL

Educator, psychologist. **Personal:** Born May 17, 1947, Green Sea, SC. **Educ:** East Carolina Univ, BA Psych & Soc 1965-69, MA Clinical Psych 1971; Univ of utah, Doc Prog Clin Psy 1971-74; NY Univ, PhD Comm Psych 1982. **Career:** Camden Co MH Ctr, psychological consul 1974-75; Neuse Mental Health Ctr, qual assurance consult 1975-77; Medgar Evers Coll CUNY, instr psychology 1979-81; East Carolina Univ, asst prof psychol 1974-, prof of psychol. **Orgs:** Pres Young People's Holiness Assoc United Pentecostal Holiness Churches of Amer Inc; Alpha Phi Alpha Frat; natl treas Assoc of Black Psychologists 1983-84; organizational liaison Assoc for Humanistic Psychology 1983-84; s regional rep Assoc of Black Psychologists 1984-85; mem at large bd of dirs Assn for Humanistic Psychology 1984-85; reg rep NC Group Behavior Soc 1981-; vice bishop United Pentecostal Holiness Churches of Amer 1981-; pastor Mt Olive Holiness Church Tabor City NC 1984-; treas NC Assoc Black Psychologists; mem Pitt Cty Mental Health Assoc; pres NC Chap Assoc Black Psychologists 1986-87; dir Minority Affairs Assoc for Humanistic Psychology 1986-; co-chmn Natl Black Family Task Force of the Assoc of Black Psychologists. **Honors/Awds:** Outstanding Sr Dept of Sociology E Carolina Univ 1969; NIMH Fellow Univ Utah 1971-74; NIMH Fellow NY Univ 1978; NEH Summer Stipend for study of Southern Black Culture 1982. **Home Addr:** 1801 East Fifth St, Greenville, NC 27834. **Business Addr:** Prof of Psychology, East Carolina Univ, Dept Psychol, Greenville, NC 27834.

CHESTNUT, EDWIN, SR.

Insurance company executive. **Personal:** Born Jan 14, 1924, Louisville; married Jacqueline Eades Chestnut, Nov 17, 1979. **Educ:** Univ Louisville, BS 1952. **Career:** Mammoth Life & Accident Ins Co Louisville, vice pres cont 1975-, various pos. **Orgs:** 23 yrs mem Ins Acct & Stat Assn; Nat Accountants Assn; pres USO 1975; former sec Musicians Local #637. **Military Serv:** USN petty officer 1st class 1942-45. **Home Addr:** 629 S 41st Street, Louisville, KY 40211.

CHESTNUT, MORRIS

Actor. **Personal:** Born in Los Angeles, CA. **Educ:** University of California at Northridge, finance, acting. **Career:** Bank teller; actor; movies include: Boyz 'N the Hood, 1991; Under Seige 2, 1995; TV credits include: "In the Line of Duty: Street War," 1992, "The Ernest Green Story," 1992; "Out All Night," 1992. **Business Phone:** (310)551-3000.

CHEW, BETTYE L.

Secretary. **Personal:** Born Dec 10, 1940; children: Gordon W, Cheryl L, Donna V. **Educ:** Rosenwald Comm Jr Coll, 1959; Cortez W Peters Bus Sch, Grad 1964; Bowie State Coll, Spec Student. **Career:** Bowie State Coll, Bowie MD, Office of Dean, sec 1972-; Univ of MD Cooperative Extension Serv, Annapolis MD, sec 1969-72; Annapolis Urban Renewal & Program, sec 1967-69. **Orgs:** Corr sec 1966-70; rec sec 1974-; NAACP; reg rep of Annapolis Sr HS Citizens Adv Com 1974-; sudnay sch tchr First Bapt Ch 1964-; Offender Aid & Restoration Counselor at Anne Arundel Co Detention Cntr; chmn Citizen Adv Com Annapolis Sr HS 1976-77; mem Human Rel Com Annapolis Sr HS 1977; proj coord Am Issues Forum Prgm Bowie St Coll 1976; ldr Girl Scout Troop 43 1974-. **Honors/Awds:** Certificate for serv NAACP 1974; employee of month award Bowie State Coll 1974; 5 yr serv award Bowie State Coll 1975. **Business Addr:** Bowie State Coll, Office of Dean, Bowie, MD 20715.

CHICOYE, ETZER

Research administrator (retired). **Personal:** Born Nov 4, 1926, Jacmel, Haiti; son of Appoline Briffault Chicoye and Rigaud Chicoye; married Dolores Bruce; children: Lorena, Rigaud. **Educ:** Univ of Haiti Port Au Prince, BS 1948; Univ of WI Madison, MS 1954; Univ of WI, PhD 1968. **Career:** Chicago Pharmacal, chemist quality control 1955-57; Julian Labs, prod chemist 1957-62; Julian Labs Chgo, chemist r&d 1962-64; Miller Brewing Co, chem rsch suprv 1968-72, mgr rsch 1972-77, dir of rsch 1977-92. **Honors/Awds:** Black Achiever Harlem YMCA 1979. **Special Achievements:** Several technical publications and 18 patents dealing with steroid chemistry, food and brewing technology.

CHIDEYA, FARAI NDUU

Author/reporter. **Personal:** Born Jul 26, 1969, Baltimore, MD; daughter of Cynthia & Lucas Chideya. **Educ:** Harvard University, BA, Magna Cum Laude, 1990. **Career:** Newsweek, researcher, reporter, NY, 1990-93, reporter, Washington bureau, 1993-94; MTV News, assignment editor, 1994-96; CNN, political analyst, 1996-97; ABC News, correspondent, 1997-. **Orgs:** Natl Assn of Black Journalists, 1992-. **Honors/Awds:** NABJ Unity Award, 1994; GLAAD, Glaad Media Award, 1994; Natl Education Reporting Award, 1992; Ed Press Award, 1992. **Business Addr:** Correspondent ABC News, 200 E 10th St, Ste 712, New York, NY 10003.

CHIGBU, GIBSON CHUKS

Construction company president. **Personal:** Born Sep 21, 1956, Aba, Imo State, Nigeria; son of Rhoda N Amadi Chigbu and Jason N Chigbu; married Florence Ihekwoaba Chigbu, Sep 13, 1986; children: Gibson Jr, Krystal, Jasmine. **Educ:** Southern

University, Baton Rouge, LA, Bachelors, Architecture, 1981, Masters, Arts, 1982. **Career:** Hunt-Thurman & Associates, Baton Rouge, LA, draftman, 1979-81; Barber & Johnson Engineers, Baton Rouge, LA, designer, 1981-82; Hewitt-Washington Architects, New Orleans, LA, project architect, 1982-85; Gee Cee Group, Inc, New Orleans, LA, owner, pres, 1985-. **Orgs:** Chmn, construction committee, Black Economic Dev Council, 1991; Natl Public Relation Officer, Organization of Nigerian Professionals-USA, 1984-86; pres, Assn of Nigerians in New Orleans, 1985, 1986; provost, Organization of Nigerian Professionals-USA, 1986-87; Natl Pres, Org of Nigerian Profs, USA Inc, 1992-; bd mem, Urban League of Greater New Orleans; pres, Louisiana Contractors Assn; bd mem, Specialty Bus & Industrial Development Corp; national bd of dirs, National Business League, 1996-; national president, Nkwerre Aborigine's Union, USA, elected in Dallas, TX, 1996. **Honors/Awds:** Certificate of Recognition, US Dept of Commerce, 1989-90; In Construction, Dallas Region Office. **Special Achievements:** Louisiana State Licensing Bd for contractors, appointed by Gov Mike Foster, for six year term, 1996. **Business Addr:** President, Gee Cee Group, Inc, 13020 Carrere Court, New Orleans, LA 70129, (504)254-1212.

CHILDRESS, RANDOLPH

Professional basketball player. **Educ:** Wake Forest. **Career:** Detroit Pistons, professional basketball player, 1995-. **Special Achievements:** NBA, First Round Draft Pick, #19 Pick, 1995. **Business Addr:** Professional Basketball Player, Detroit Pistons, 2 Championship Dr, Auburn Hills, MI 48326, (313)377-0100.

CHILDS, CHRIS

Professional basketball player. **Personal:** Born Nov 20, 1967, Bakersfield, CA; son of James Childs; married Karla; children: Jesse, Jenne, Jade. **Educ:** Boise State. **Career:** CBA: Columbus Horizon, 1989-90, 1990-91; Rapid City Thrillers, 1989-90; La Crosse Catbirds, 1990-91; Rockford Lightning, 1990-91, 1991-92; Bakersfield Jammers, 1991-92; Quad City Thunder, 1992-93, 1993-94; US Basketball League: Miami Tropics, 1993, 1994; NBA: New Jersey Nets, guard, 1994-96; New York Knicks, 1996-. **Honors/Awds:** CBA, MVP, 1994. **Special Achievements:** CBA, Championship, 1994. **Business Addr:** Professional Basketball Player, New York Knicks, 2 Pennsylvania Plaza, New York, NY 10121, (212)465-5867.

CHILDS, FRANCINE C.

Educator. **Personal:** Born Feb 8, Wellington, TX; children: Jimmy Fenley. **Educ:** Paul Quinn Coll, BS 1962; East TX State Univ, MEd 1970, EdD 1975. **Career:** Wiley Coll, dean of students 1970-72; East TX State Univ, part-time project dir special svcs/full time doctorial student 1972-74; Ohio Univ, prof afro-amer studies 1974-85, chair/prof afro-amer studies 1985-. **Orgs:** Local pres & advisor OH Univ Chap NAACP 1971-; mem League of Women Voters 1977-; educ chair OH Conf of Branches NAACP 1978-; natl coord Booker T Washington Alumni Assoc 1982-; prayer coord Athens Christian Women Club 1984-86; workshop leader Ohio Bapt Women Aux Convention 1985-; local conf host and progcomm Natl Cncl on Black Studies 1987; National Alliance of Blk School Education; Mt Zion Baptist Ch, assoc pastor, currently. **Honors/Awds:** Paul Quin Coll Outstanding Alumni 1982; Individual Witness for Peace & Justice Awd 1985; OU Higher Educ Mgmt Develop Prog 1985-86; Outstanding Black Alumni Awd 1986; Fulbright Hays Scholarship 1986; Peace Corp Black Educator of Year, 1988-89; Anna Cooper Presidential Award, 1992; Phenomenal Woman Award, 1996; Marcus Foster Distinguished Educators Award, 1996; Ohio University Honorary Alumni Award, 1997. **Business Addr:** Prof African Amer Studies, Ohio University, 302 Lindley, Athens, OH 45701.

CHILDS, JOSIE L.

City official. **Personal:** Born Oct 13, Clarksdale, MS; married James M Childs Sr, May 24, 1969. **Career:** City of Chicago, director of planning, 1989-. **Orgs:** Board member, Friend of Chicago Public Library; board member, Know Your Chicago. **Home Addr:** 6935 S Crandon Ave, Chicago, IL 60649.

CHILDS, JOY

Attorney. **Personal:** Born Apr 10, 1951, Wilmington, NC; daughter of Mable Childs and Joseph Childs. **Educ:** UCLA, BA 1973, MA 1975; Georgetown Univ Law Ctr, JD 1981. **Career:** Screen Actors Guild, contract admin 1981-83; Atlantic Richfield Co Legal Dept, paralegal 1983-84; Peace Officers Rsch Assoc of CA, labor relations rep 1984-86; CA State Univ, employee relations admin, 1986-90; Hughes Aircraft Company, senior labor relations consultant, 1990-94; Warner Bros, Employee Relations, mgr, currently. **Orgs:** Mem KCET Comm Adv Bd 1984-, UCLA Black Alumni Assn 1985-, Black Labor Attorneys of LA 1985-, Black Entertainment & Sports Lawyers Assn 1986-; Women of Color, 1987-. **Business Addr:** Manager, Employee Relations, Warner Bros, 4000 Warner Blvd, Burbank, CA 91522.

CHILDS, OLIVER BERNARD, SR.

Non-profit organization executive. **Personal:** Born Jan 15, 1933, Philadelphia, PA; son of Ogetta Faust Childs and Ed-

mond A Childs Sr; married Dorothy Collins, Feb 7, 1953; children: Renee Olivia, Oliver Jr, Sean Vincent. **Educ:** Cheyney State Teachers Coll, Cheyney PA, BS, El Educ, 1958; Univ of Utah, Salt Lake City UT, MS, Human Resource Mgmt, Economics, 1980. **Career:** Philadelphia Board of Educ, Philadelphia PA, teacher, 1958-65; Opportunities Industrialization Centers, Philadelphia PA, dir training, 1965-66, Los Angeles CA, exec dir, 1966-68; OIC Inst, Philadelphia PA, asst dir Ext Serv, 1968-71; OIC America, Dallas TX, regional dir, 1971-74, Philadelphia PA, dir Fund Devel, 1974-83; OIC Intl, Philadelphia PA, dir Resource Devel, 1984-; Univ of Maryland, Eastern Shore, asst prof, 1990-94; Richard A Henson Conference Ctr, dir, currently. **Orgs:** Mem, Kappa Alpha Psi Fraternity, 1956-, Natl Soc Fund Raising Exec, 1976-, NAACP, Philadelphia PA, 1978-; chmn, Troop Comm, Boy Scouts of Amer, Philadelphia PA, 1980-; bd mem, Independent Charities of America, 1989-; Minority Advisory Comm, Philadelphia Visitors & Convention Bureau, 1989-; president, bd of directors, National Coalition Black Mtg Planners, 1989. **Honors/Awds:** Mayoralty Awards, Los Angeles CA, 1968, New Orleans LA, 1972, Lubbock TX, 1972; Honorary State Senator, State of Louisiana, 1973. **Military Serv:** AUS, corporal, 1952-54. **Business Addr:** Director, Richard A Henson Conference Ctr, University of Maryland, Eastern Shore, Princess Anne, MD 21853.

CHILDS, THEODORE FRANCIS

Educator (retired). **Personal:** Born Feb 17, 1921, Jamaica, NY; son of Maude Childs and Andrew Childs; married Marie J; children: Sheila Childs-Berg, Theodore W. **Educ:** Shaw Univ, BS 1944; State Univ IA, RPT 1948; Columbia Univ, MA 1958; Masonic Congress, Honorary Doctorate 1972; Columbia Univ, EdD 1976. **Career:** Brooklyn VA Hospital, chief pt 1955-65; US Comm Rehab Africa, vol exec dir 1962-75; NY Univ Medical Center, dir pt servs 1965-68; Long Island Univ, dir spec educ 1968-75; Nassau Coop Educ, school bd mem 1970-76; Tuskegee Inst, dir health science 1975-83; United Cerebral Palsy Assn, civil vice pres 1982-; AL State Univ, assoc prof, dir interdisciplinary studies program, retired; Columbia Univ-Harlem Hospital, New York, NY, director of pediatric rehabilitation & clinical professor physical therapy, retired. **Orgs:** Vice president of board, United Cerebral Palsy, 1982-89. **Honors/Awds:** Man of the Year Westbury NY 1971; Brooklyn Hall of Fame Brooklyn NY 1973; Travel Flwshp Natl Fnd Europe and Africa 1957; Distinguished Alumni, Shaw Univ, Raleigh, NC, 1991; mem US Medical Team, 1992 Olympic Games Barcelona Spain; Shaw University, Football Hall of Fame, 1995; Alabama Athletic Trainers, Hall of Fame, 1996. **Military Serv:** AUS lt col 1944-46; Assc Pacific Theatre of War WWII 1944-76; Army Reserves, retired, 1982. **Home Addr:** PO Box 86, Tuskegee Institute, AL 36088.

CHILDS, WINSTON

Attorney, board chairman, chief executive officer. **Personal:** Born Feb 14, 1931, Savannah, GA; son of Inez Childs Scoggins; children: Evan, Julie, Stephanie. **Educ:** Amer Univ, AB 1957, JD 1959. **Career:** Booker T Washington Found, special counsel; Minority Consult & Urbanologists, natl assn; GEOC, CIO Labor Union, pres; stock broker; private law pratice; DC Republican Central Committee, gen counsel; Natl Business League, gen counsel; Graham Building Associates Real Estate Development Company, pres; Amer Univ Law School, adjunct prof; MSI Services Inc, a systems engineering and mgmt consulting firm, Washington DC, founder, chairman, CEO, 1976-. **Orgs:** DC Bar Assn; Amer Management Assn; Armed Forces Communication and Electronics Assn; Republican Senatorial Inner Circle; DC Metropolitan Boys/Girls Club; bd mem, Georgetown Symphony Orchestra; John Sherman Myers Society. **Business Addr:** Board Chairman & CEO, MSI Services, Inc, One Farragut Square South, Suite 610, Washington, DC 20006.

CHINN, JOHN CLARENCE

Writer, audio programmer. **Personal:** Born Dec 15, 1938, Meadville, PA; son of Marquerite Lucas Chinn and Horace P Chinn. **Educ:** Bowling Green Univ, BA 1960; Syracuse Univ, MS 1962. **Career:** J Walter Thompson NYC, advertising copywriter 1963-67; First Edition radio book discussion prog, assoc prod creative dir 1973; freelance writer for feature film, TV & radio drama, scripts, short stories & poetry; Inflight Serv Inc NYC, dir audio prog; freelance writer/radio producer, currently. **Orgs:** Joined bd of editors of Literary Guild of Amer Book Club; created music entertainment channels; mem Writers Guild of Amer; Natl Acad of Rec Arts & Sci; Airline Entertainment Assn; poetry published in NY Quarterly. **Honors/Awds:** Author "Jelly Roll" musical on Jelly Roll Morton; produced series of multiple record albums entitled, Body & Soul-Five Decades of Jazz Era Song Satchmo-Louis Armstrong 1900-1971, A Silver Screen Symphony, Broadway Babies, others in coop with Columbia Spec Prod Div & Literary Guild 1970.

CHISHOLM, JOSEPH CARREL, JR.

Physician. **Personal:** Born May 16, 1935, Detroit, MI; son of Maizie Jones Chisholm and Joseph Chisholm; married Maurita, Nov 6, 1965; children: John, Lynn, Kim, Kelly. **Educ:** Univ Chicago, BS 1958, MS 1960; Meharry Med College, MD 1962. **Career:** VA Hosp Wash DC, consultant 1968-77; US Dept of State, consultant 1970-; DC Soc Internal Med, mem exec bd

1972-80; DC VNA, mem exec bd 1982-; Amer College of Physicians Washington DC, governor's bd 1984-; physician. **Orgs:** Mem DC Soc Internal Med 1970, Southern Med Soc 1980-, NY Acad Sci 1975-, Alpha Phi Alpha Inc 1957, Alpha Omega Alpha Honor Soc 1960-, NAACP 1978-, NMA, DC Thoracic Soc, Amer Lung Assn 1970-, DC Heart Assn, DC Med Soc, Amer Heart Assn 1970; mem Sigma Pi Phi Frat, 1986-; mem Viceroys, 1990-. **Honors/Awds:** Rockefeller Research School Allergy Immunology 1959-61; Pulmonary Research School NIH 1965-66; Fellow Amer College of Physicians 1970-; Order of the C Univ Chicago 1954-; mem Pigskinners of Washington DC 1980-. **Military Serv:** USN comdr 1962-68; Korean Serv Medal; Vietnam Serv Medal 1966-68. **Business Addr:** Physician, 106 Irving St NW, Ste 206, Washington, DC 20010.

CHISHOLM, JUNE FAYE
Clinical psychologist, educator. **Personal:** Born Apr 29, 1949, New York, NY; daughter of Luretta Brawley Chisholm and Wallace Chisholm. **Educ:** Syracuse U, BA Psych 1971; Univ of MA Amherst, MS Psych 1974; Univ of MA, PhD Psych 1978. **Career:** NY Univ Med Centr Bellevue, intern psych 1975-77; Harlem Hospital NY senior psychologist 1982-; Pace Univ NY asst prof 1986-; private practice, 1980-; adjunct prof NYU Medical Center 1984-. **Orgs:** Mem NY Assn of & Black Psychol 1977-; mem Am Psychol Assn 1979-; mem NY Society of Clinical Psychologists 1980-; mem NYSPA 1980; mem EPA 1988-. **Honors/Awds:** Teaching flwshp NY Univ Med Cntr 1976-77. **Business Addr:** 260 W 72 St, Ste 1-B, New York, NY 10023.

CHISHOLM, REGINALD CONSTANTINE
Educator. **Personal:** Born Oct 13, 1934, Jamaica, WI; married Cecilin Coy. **Educ:** Howard U, BS 1962, MD 1966. **Career:** Howard U, chief med oncology; NCI-VA Oncology Serv WA, fellow clinical assoc 1971-73; Freedmens Hosp, residency internal med 1967-70, intern 1966-67; Shaw Comm Health Clinic, internist 1970-71; Cancer Screening & Detection Clinic, chf 1977; Howard U, assoc dir 1977. **Orgs:** Mem DC Med Soc; WA Soc of Oncology; Nat Med Assn Publ ''Hypercalcitonemig in Cancer of the Breast'' 1975. **Honors/Awds:** Post-grad fellowship 1971-73. **Business Addr:** Howard Univ Hosp, 2041 Georgia Ave NW, Washington, DC 20060.

CHISHOLM, SAMUEL JACKSON
Advertising executive. **Personal:** Born May 15, 1942, Philadelphia, PA; son of May L Jackson Chisholm and Thomas J Chisholm; married Thelester McGinns Chisholm, May 13, 1979; children: Heather, Jason. **Educ:** Virginia State University, Petersburg, VA, BS, Business Admin & accounting, 1965, Graduate Studies, NYU. **Career:** Corn Products Corp, New York, NY, claims adjuster, 1965-66; Phelps Dodge, New York, NY, jr accountant, 1967; Benton & Bowles, New York, NY, media planner, 1967-69; Jack Tinker & Partner, New York, NY, asst media dir, 1969; Continental Can Company, New York, NY, adv dir, 1969-74; The Malk Company & Uniworld Group Inc, New York, NY, Account Sup 1974-80, The Chisholm- Mingo Group, New York, NY, vp, & Management Sup, 1980-84; sr vp & dir of clients, 1984-86, ex vp & gen manager, 1986-88, president 1988-90, CEO, 1990. **Orgs:** Kappa Alpha Psi Fraternity, member, Advertising Council; Connecticut Comm Regional Planning Assoc, bd; Traffic Audit Bureau; NY Bd Governors of the 4/a's; Worldwide Partners; Ad Hall of Fame Council of Judges; Urban League of 4/a's SW Conn. **Honors/Awds:** National Business & Professional Men & Women, Dollars & Sense, 1990; Kappa Alpha Psi Community Award, 1990. **Military Serv:** US Army, Spc 4, 1966-75; National Guard. **Business Addr:** President, The Mingo Group Inc, 228 E 45th St, New York, NY 10017.

CHISHOLM, SHIRLEY
US ambassador. **Personal:** Born Nov 30, 1924, New York, NY; daughter of Ruby St Hill and Charles St Hill; married Arthur Hardwick Jr. **Educ:** Brooklyn Coll, BA (cum laude); Columbia U, MA. **Career:** New York State Legislature, assemblywoman; 12th Cong Dist NY, US rep, 1969-83; Veterans Affairs Com House Education & Labor Com Select Education; Mt Holyoke Coll, MA, Purington chair 1983-87; US ambassador to Jamaica, 1993-. **Orgs:** General Education & Agricultural Labor Subcommittees; mem comm on rules Sec of Dem Caucus; mem of Congressional Black Caucus Candidate for President of US 1972; first woman to ever actively ever run for president; member of numerous civic & professional organizations including League of Women Voters, Brooklyn Br NAACP, Delta Sigma Theta, Nat Bd of Americans for Dem Action, Adv Council, NOW, Hon Com Mem United Negro College Fund, Natl Assoc Coll Women, Brooklyn Coll Alumni, Key Women; pres National Congress of Black Women. **Honors/Awds:** Recipient Clairol's ''Woman of Year'' award for outstanding achievement in pub affairs 1973; Gallup poll's list of ten most admired women in the world 3 yrs; recipient of numerous honorary degrees; author ''Unbought & Unbossed,'' 1970; ''The Good Fight''; First black women to be elected to the US Congress, 1968-82.

CHISM, HAROLYN B.
Financial administrator. **Personal:** Born Jan 4, 1941, Columbia, SC; divorced; children: John Patrick, Sharon Elizabeth. **Educ:** Benedict Coll, BS 1967. **Career:** US Dept of Commerce Minority Bus Devel Agency, budget ofcr 1978; USDA-animal & Plant Health Insptn Serv & Food Safety And Quality Serv, supr bdgt analyst 1972-78; USDA-Office Of Mgmt Serv, budget analyst 1967-72; IRS, sec 1964-65; Fed Power Commn, clk typist 1963-64; Gen Accounting Office, clk typist 1962-63. **Orgs:** Mem Am Assn of Budget and Program Analyst 1980; sec Boy Scouts of Am T351 1973-75; EEO counsellor USDA APHIS and FSQS 1974-78; bd mem USDA Credit Union 1977-78. **Honors/Awds:** Incentive award Fed Power Commn 1964; cert of merit USDA/APHIS 1975; cert of merit USDA/FSQS 1978. **Business Addr:** 14th & Constitution Ave NW, Washington, DC.

CHISSELL, JOHN T.
Physician, optimal health educator. **Personal:** Born May 31, 1926, Charlottesville, VA; son of Herbert G Chissell, Sr & Connie B Sitgraves; divorced; children: Carla, Crystal. **Educ:** Virginia State University, BS, 1950; Meharry Medical College, MD, 1954. **Career:** Self Employed, board certified family practice, physician, 1955-87; Self Employed, the Positive Perceptions Group, chief executive officer, 1987-. **Orgs:** National Medical Association, founder region II, past chairman-family practice section, 1955-; American Academy of Family Physicians, 1960-; Maryland Academy of Family Physicians, president, 1970-71; NAACP, life member; Kappa Alpha Psi Fraternity, life member; Physicians Committee for Responsible Medicine; American Public Health Association. **Special Achievements:** Author: Pyramids of Power!, An Ancient African Centered Approach to Optimal Health, 1993. **Military Serv:** US Army, cpl/tech 4, 1945-46. **Business Addr:** Chief Executive Officer, The Positive Perceptions Group, PO Box 31509, Baltimore, MD 21207-8509, (410)448-0116.

CHISUM, GLORIA TWINE
Psychologist. **Personal:** Born May 17, 1930, Muskogee, OK; daughter of Nadine Davis Twine (deceased) and Chauncey Depew Twine (deceased); married Melvin Jackson Chisum. **Educ:** Howard Univ, BS 1951, MS 1953; Univ of PA, PhD 1960. **Career:** Univ of PA, lecturer in psych 1958-68; Naval Air Devel Ctr, rsch psych 1960-65, head vision lab 1965-80, head environ physiol rsch team 1980-90, retired. **Orgs:** Trustee Philadelphia Saving Fund Soc 1977-85; dir Fischer & Porter Co 1978-1994; bd mem Arthritis Found of E PA 1972-80; trustee 1974-, vice chair 1990-, University of PA; bd mem World Affairs Council of Philadelphia 1977-80, Philadelphia Orch Assn 1979-85; dir Meritor Financial Group 1985-92; bd mem, 1979-1993, chm, bd of trustees, 1990-1993, Free Library of Philadelphia. **Honors/Awds:** Raymond F Longacre Award Aerospace Med Assn, 1979; Distinguished Daughter of Pennsylvania 1983; Oklahoma Hall of Fame 1984; first black chm, bd of trustees, Free Library of Philadelphia.

CHITTY, MURELA ELIZABETH (M. ELIZABETH CHITTY)
Librarian. **Personal:** Born May 28, 1928, Pittsburgh, PA; daughter of Joliver Jackson Williams and Earl Sandidge; married Vernon, Jan 17, 1956 (deceased); children: Treka Spragine, David Francis. **Educ:** Columbia, 1961; MLS. **Career:** VA Somerville Supply Depot, admin lib & chief books & periodicals 1973-83; Lyons VA Hosp, acting chief med lib 1969-73; retired, 1983; Fairchilde International Library Inst, founder and director, currently. **Orgs:** Mem Pres, NJ Black Librarians Network; African Women's Conf; bibliothrpst-founder Plainfield & Reading Prog; Model Cities Educ Task Force; Plainfield Bd Educ, mem 1969, pres 1974; NJ School Bds; ALA; Catholic Library Assn; Hosp & Inst Lib Assn; Amer Benedictine Acad Fellow; Plainfield Cit Adv Comm; vice pres finance NJSBA; bd dir NJ School Bd Assn 1973-77; Natl Commn Child Abuse & Neglect (Educ Commn of States); Union County Legislative Comm Lisle Fellowship student, Univ of Colorado; Delta Sigma Theta Sor. **Honors/Awds:** Plainfield Public High School Library named M Elizabeth Chitty Library, 1977; Margaret C Scroggins Award, young adult lib; NY Public Library Merit Award; Pro Ecclesia et Pontifice, Vatican City; Mem, Union County Status of Libraries, Honorary Member, NJ Library Trustee Executive Bd.

CHIVERS, GWENDOLYN ANN
Chief pharmacist, clinical instructor. **Personal:** Born Jun 30, 1946, Sturgis, KY; daughter of Herman & Lillian McGee; married Richard, Oct 10, 1972. **Educ:** Kellogg Comm College, associate degree, 1968; Univ of MI, BS, 1972; Century Univ, MBA, health care management, 1993. **Career:** Catherine McAuley Hosp, pharmacist, 1983-85; Perry Drugs, pharmacist, 1988-89; Univ of MI, pharmacist, 1972-76, asst chief pharmacist, 1976-83, chief pharmacist/clinical instructor, 1983-. **Orgs:** Univ of MI Health Service, member of administration comm, 1994-; Amer Society for Pharmacy Law, bd of dirs, 1994-96; State of MI Health Occupations Council, 1991-93; Univ of MI Pharmacy Alumni Bd of Governors, 1992-94; Amer Pharmaceutical Assn, 1985-; MI Pharmacists Assn, 1993-; Amer College Health Assn. **Special Achievements:** Appointed by Governor of MI to State Health Occupations Council; Selected to represent US Pharmacists at a Women in Pharmacy Leadership Symposium in Europe. **Business Addr:** Chief Pharmacist, University of Michigan Health Service, 207 Fletcher Avenue, Ann Arbor, MI 48109-1050, (313)764-7387.

CHIVIS, MARTIN LEWIS
Banker. **Personal:** Born Oct 5, 1952, Washington, DC; son of Odesa Penn Chivis and Samuel Lewis Chivis. **Educ:** Drexel Univ, BS 1976; American Inst of Banking, graduated, 1983; Stonier Graduate School of Banking, 1988. **Career:** NASA, aide 1969-70; Comptroller of the Currency, fellowship 1971-72; Peat Marwick Mitchell, pre pro intern 1973-74; Covington & Burling, coll co-op 1975-76; Continental Bank, exec trainee 1976-89; Industrial Bank, funds mgr. **Orgs:** Mem NABA, NBMBA, BDPA; bd mem Urban Bankers; mem Concerned Black Men, 21st Century PAC; jr deacon, 12th St Christian Church. **Honors/Awds:** Most Outstanding Employee OCC 1971; Outstanding Professional Business Exchange Network Inc 1987. **Business Addr:** Funds Manager, Industrial Bank, 4812 Georgia Ave NW, Washington, DC 20011.

CHONG, RAE DAWN
Actress. **Personal:** Born 1962, British Columbia;daughter of Tommy Chong; married Owen Baylis; children: Morgan. **Career:** Film credits include: Stony Island, 1978; Quest for Fire, 1982; Beat Street, 1984; The Corsican Brothers, 1984; Choose Me, 1984; Fear City, 1984; American Flyers, 1985; City Limits, 1985; The Color Purple, 1985; Commando, 1985; Running Out of Luck, 1986; Soul Man, 1986; The Squeeze, 1987; The Principal, 1987; Walking After Midnight, 1988; Far Out, Man!, 1990; Tales from the Darkside: the Movie, 1990; Denial: the Dark Side of Passion, 1991; Loon; Chaindance; In Exile; The Borrower, 1991; Amazon, 1992; When the Party's Over, 1992; television appearances include: ''Whiz Kid of Riverton''; ''Friends,'' 1978; television movies include: Top of the Hill, 1980; Badge of the Assassian, 1985; Curiosity Kills, 1990; Prison Stories: Women on the Inside, 1991; Broadway credits: Oh Kay!, 1991. **Orgs:** Screen Actors Guild; American Federation of Television Recording Arts and Radio Artists. **Honors/Awds:** Black Filmmakers Hall of Fame, Clarence Muse Award, 1986. **Special Achievements:** Sex, Drugs, and AIDS, educational documentary, narrator; Sex, Drugs, and AIDS, book, contributor, 1987. **Business Phone:** (310)855-1700.

CHOWNING, FRANK EDMOND
Dentist. **Personal:** married Edith Mae Jenkins. **Career:** Morgan Health Ctr, dentist. **Orgs:** Mem Kappa Alpha Psi Frat; mem Sigma Pi Phi Frat; past pres Ethical Culture Soc; past pres Nat Dntl Assn; past trustee Natl Dntl Assn; trustee & past asst supr Allen Chapel AME Ch; bd of dir Alpha Home; bd of Dir Citizens Forum; past bd mem YMCA Exec Bd; mem Clncn Nat Dntl Assn; mem Clncn IN State Dntl Assn; past Polemarch Kappa Alpha Psi; mem Sigma Pi Phi; life mem NAACP; past pres IN State Med Dntl & Pharm Assn; past pres Indianapolis Frntrs Serv Clb; past mem Peer Review Com. **Honors/Awds:** Dentist of the Yr Nat Dental Assn; fellow Am Coll Dentists; fellow Intenat Coll of Dentists; mem Am Dental Assn; mem Am Prosthodontic Soc.

CHRETIEN, GLADYS M.
Business executive. **Personal:** Born Dec 16, Texas; divorced; children: Joseph P, III, Perry Duncan. **Educ:** Prairie View Coll; Wiley Coll. **Career:** Salesman 1961; broker 1962; Gladys M Chretien Realty Co, real estate broker, realtor & realtist; Consolidated Realty Bd, 2nd women to serve as pres in 27 yrs of existence 1976; Multiple Listing, one women chmn; Wash Escrow Co, pres elect, part owner & vp; Wall St Enterprises & Wash Reconveyance Corp,part owner & stockholder; Century 21 Chretien Realty, owner. **Orgs:** Mem Ch Christ; LA Co Tax Appeals Bd Fndrs 3 yr term. **Honors/Awds:** LA Co Tax Appeals Bd Fndrs Achvmnt Awrd Consolidated Rlty Bd 1969-70; Top Ten Cntrbtrs Consolidated Rlty; many sales awards. **Business Addr:** 3754 W 54 St, Los Angeles, CA.

CHRICHLOW, LIVINGSTON L.
Church administrator (retired). **Personal:** Born May 13, 1925, Brooklyn, NY; son of Viola Chrichlow and Alfred Chrichlow; married Mary Atkinson; children: Gordon H. **Educ:** Queens Clge City Univ NY, BA 1975; Baruch Clge City Univ NY, MPA 1979. **Career:** Dept of Defense, contract admin 1951-80; Lutheran Immigration and Refugee Srv, coordinator 1980-82; Lutheran Church in Amer, dir urban ministry 1982-1987. **Orgs:** Sec Assn of Black Lutherans 1979-88; chmn Finance Comm New Hope Church 1975-89; dir Proj Equality NY 1980-1987; mem chmn Minority Concerns Comm NY Synod 1979-1987; pres Parkhurst Civic Assn 1984-96; past pres Better Comm Civil Assn 1955-57; mem vice pres Comm Schl Bd 27 Queens 1965-70; sec Boy Scouts of Amer Alumni 1980-; treasurer New Hope Church 1990-93; stewardship committee, Metro NY Synod, Lutheran Church in America, 1990-93; vp, New Hope Church, 1994-. **Honors/Awds:** Distinguished discipleship Metro NY Synod Lutheran Church in Amer 1970; Distinguished Citizen Springfield Gardens Sr Citizens 1980; Community Service Award, Elmont Youth Outreach, 1994. **Military Serv:** USN elec mate 2nd class; Good Conduct Amer Theatre USN 1944. **Home Addr:** 2232 Leighton Rd, Elmont, NY 11003.

CHRISS, HENRY THOMAS
Sports and fitness company manager. **Personal:** Born Nov 24, 1964, Cleveland, OH; son of Frank James and Mary Glynn; married Sandra Renee, Aug 10, 1985; children: Henry II, Jas-

mine, Tiffany. **Educ:** Bowling Green State, business administration, 1984-86; Akron University, polymer science, 1985-86; Kent State University, business manangement, 1990. **Career:** Polychem Dispersions, production/laboratory manager, 1985-87; Duramax Johnson Rubber, production supervisor, 1987-88, product technician, 1988-89, q/c chemistry lab supervisor, 1989-91; NIKE Inc, chemistry lab manager, 1991-93, environmental affairs dir, 1993-94, director account logistics, 1995-. **Orgs:** American Black Sporting Goods Professionals, 1992-; American Chemical Society (Akron Rubber Group), 1991-. **Honors/Awds:** Congressional nomination to West Point, 1982; Ohio High School Athletic Association, State qualifier, wrestling, 1983; US Semi-Pro Football Leauge, 2nd Team All Nation, 1987. **Special Achievements:** US Patent, Recycling Polymer Technology, 1994. **Business Addr:** Director, JCP Account Logistics, NIKE Inc, 1 Bowerman Dr, #AS-1, Beaverton, OR 97005-6453, (503)671-6453.

CHRISTIAN, ALMERIC L.
Retired chief judge. **Personal:** Born Nov 23, 1919, St Croix, Virgin Islands of the United States; son of Elena L Davis Christian and Adam E Christian (deceased); married Shirley C Frorup; children: Donna Marie, Adam Gregory, Rebecca Therese. **Educ:** Columbia U, AB 1942, LLB 1947. **Career:** Chief judge 1970; Dist Ct VI, judge 1969; VI, US atty 1962-69; US Ct of Appeals 3 circuit; Supreme Ct; Pvt Pract, 1947-62. **Orgs:** Mem bd of visitors of Columbia Univ Sch of Law; mem VI Bar Assn; mem Jr & Sr Warden All Saints Episcopal Ch 1966-67; Missionary Diocese VI; Commn propose Amendments 1936 Organic Act Testimonial St Lukes Anglican Ch 1974; hon VI Bar Assn 1968. **Military Serv:** 1st lt 1942-54. **Home Addr:** 19-0 Solberg Box 7157, St Thomas, Virgin Islands of the United States 00801.

CHRISTIAN, CORA LEETHEL
Physician. **Personal:** Born Sep 11, 1947, St Thomas, Virgin Islands of the United States; daughter of Ruth Christian and Alphonso Christian; married Simon B Jones-Hendrikson; children: Marcus Benjamin, Nesha Rosita. **Educ:** Marquette Univ Milwaukee WICS, BS 1967; Jefferson Med Coll Phila, PA, Medical Dr 1971; Johns Hopkins Univ Baltimore, MD, MPH 1975. **Career:** Howard Univ Family Practice, admin chief resident 1973-74, instr 1974-75; Ingeborg Nesbitt Clinic Dept of Hlth, physician in charge 1975-77; VI Med Inst, exec dir/med dir 1977-94; VI Dept of Hlth, asst commr 1977-81, asst commr for ambulatory care serv 1981-87; asst commr prevention, health promotion & protection 1987-92; Hess Oil Virgin Islands Corp., med director, 1992-; Thomas Jeffer University, lecturer, 1990-; Meddar/PCC, VI med inst, 1994-. **Orgs:** Dir of family planning VI Dept of Hlth 1979-, proj dir Frederiksted Hlth Ctr 1978-80, act dir MCH 1982-, chief staff 1983; delegate Am Pub Hlth Assn; mem League of Women Voters VI 1979; pres Charles Harwood Mem Hosp Med Staff 1978-79, vice pres 1977-78; sec VI Med Soc 1976-77, treas 1980-81 & 1983-84, pres 1985-; pres Am Acad Family Pract 1978-; vice territory chief, Caribbean Terrtory Soka Gakkau Intl; exec scy/treas, Virgin Islands Medical Society 1997-2002. **Honors/Awds:** Wilmont Blyden Scholarship VI 1963; John Hay Whitney Fellowship John Hay Whitney Found 1969; Nat Urban Coalition Fellowship National Urban Coalition Found 1974; Outstanding Woman, AKA, 1997; Paul Harris Fellow, 1997. **Home Addr:** PO Box 1338, Frederiksted, St Croix, Virgin Islands of the United States 00841. **Business Addr:** Med Director, Hess Oil Virgin Island Corp., 40 E G La Grange, Frederiksted, Virgin Islands of the United States 00841.

CHRISTIAN, DOLLY LEWIS
Business executive. **Personal:** Born in New York, NY; daughter of Adeline Walton Lewis and Daniel Lewis; divorced. **Educ:** Manhattan Comm Coll. **Career:** The Sperry & Hutchison Co, dir civic affairs, personnel mgr, supvr, special project & records, employment specialist; IBM Corp, program mgr affirmative action program. **Orgs:** Chmn bd NY Urban League 1977-85; Panel of Arbitrators Amer Arbitration Assn 1978; bd mem Coalition Of 100 Black Women 1979; past vice pres The Edges Group Inc; mem Council of Concerned Black Exec; Natl Urban Affairs Council Office; mem Mngmt Assistance Comm Greater NY Fund; commissioner, New York City, Commission on Human Rights, 1987-90. **Honors/Awds:** Scroll of Honor Natl Council of Negro Business & Professional Women's Clubs; Community Serv Award; Ambudswoman Award; Youth Salute to Black Corp Exec Awd, Natl Youth Movement; Corp Recp of Mary McCleod Bethune Awd; Natl Council of Negro Women; Spec Corp Recognition Award; Metro Council of Brances; NAACP; Woman Achiever, YWCA of NY; Black Achiever, Harlem YMCA.

CHRISTIAN, ERIC OLIVER, JR.
Government consultant. **Personal:** Born Jan 1, 1951, Tortola, Virgin Islands of the United States; son of Ethel Trotman Thomas and Eric O Christian Sr; married Shelia Christian, Dec 23, 1973; children: Eric O III, Cosine. **Educ:** Tennessee State University, BSEd, 1973. **Career:** Government of the Virgin Islands, teacher, 1973-85; American Bankers Life, manager, 1975-89; Black Business Chamber of Commerce, president, 1988-; Government of St Kitts, West Indies, consultant, 1989-90; Caribbean Small Business Association, consultant, 1989-; Government of Virgin Islands, consultant, 1990-. **Orgs:** American Federation of Teachers, executive council, 1973-85; Tony Brown's Buy Freedom Movement, executive member, 1989-; National Association of Black Chambers; Status Commission, Virgin Islands, 1989-; Black Meeting Planners, 1990-. **Honors/Awds:** AT&T, Musician and Choral Director of the Year, 1991; American Bankers Life, Manager of the Year, 1990. **Home Addr:** 39 L Lindberg Bay, St Thomas, Virgin Islands of the United States 00801, (809)776-4433. **Business Phone:** (809)774-8784.

CHRISTIAN, GERALDINE ASHLEY MCCONNELL
Pharmacist. **Personal:** Born May 1, 1929, Denver, CO; daughter of Mary Owens Ashley and Frederick Douglas Ashley; widowed; children: Conrad P McConnell. **Educ:** Univ of Denver, 1946-47; Univ of CO, BS 1950. **Career:** Rocky Mountain Arsenal Dept Army Chem Corps, phrmst 1951-55; VA Outpatient Clinic, Portland OR, pharmacist 1957-68, 1973-78; Crestview Hospital, pharmacist manager, 1968-73; retired 1978. **Orgs:** Mem, bd of dir, Urban League of Portland, 1974-78; first female pres, bd of State of Oregon; Portland Chapter, The Links Inc, 1965; Jacks & Jill of Amer, 1957-67; Alpha Kappa Alpha Sorority, 1947-; School Board Advisory Committee, 1973-75; Young Audiences Board, 1966-68; appointed by Governor to Amer Revolution Bicentennial Commission, 1974-77; appointed by Governor to Oregon Commission on Black Affairs, 1980-83. **Honors/Awds:** Recipient Alpha Kappa Alpha Award 1966; named woman of year, Portland Fedn Women's Orgns; Superior Performance Award; Superior Performances Awards VA, 1963, 1973; numerous awards, certificates. **Business Addr:** 426 SW Stark St, Portland, OR 97204.

CHRISTIAN, JOHN L.
Corporate executive. **Personal:** Born Jan 27, 1940, Winton, NC; son of Addie Beatrice Weaver and John Albert Christian; married Lesley Evans Christian; children: Andrea Lenore, John A II. **Educ:** Hampton University, Hampton, VA, BS, 1961; Wharton School, Philadelphia, PA, certificate, 1978; Harvard School of Public Health, Boston, MA, certificate, 1988. **Career:** Lesasco Systems & Research Corp, Bethesda, MD, div manager, 1964-69; Polaroid Corp, Cambridge, MA, div manager, 1969-74; Trustees of Health & Hospitals, Boston, MA, VP, 1974-92; The Enterprise Group Ltd, exec vp/treasurer, currently. **Orgs:** President, International Society of Research Administrators, 1988-89; President, National Guardsmen Inc, 1978-79; board chairman, Crispus Attucks Children's Center, 1972-; President, Sigma Pi Phi-Beta Beta, 1981-82; board, Brookline Community Fund, 1988-; allocations review committee, United Way of Massachusetts Bay, 1980-91. **Honors/Awds:** Outstanding Citizen, NAACP, 1982; Hartford-Nicholson Service Award, Society of Research Administrators, 1985. **Business Addr:** Exec VP & Treasurer, The Enterprise Group, Ltd, PO Box 925, Brookline, MA 02146-0007, (617)232-9790.

CHRISTIAN, MARY T.
State Representative. **Personal:** Born Jul 9, 1924, Hampton, VA; married Wilbur B Christian; children: Benita D Toler, Carolyn D, James M. **Educ:** Hampton Inst, BS; Columbia Univ, MA; Michigan State Univ, PhD. **Career:** Hampton Univ, School of Educ, prof, dean; VA House of Reps, state rep, currently. **Orgs:** First Baptist Church Auxiliary; Peninsula Assn Sickle Cell Anemia, bd mem; American Assn Univ Women; NAACP; Groups Representing Orgn United for Progress, chairman; Hampton Crusade for Voters; Coalition of 100 Black Women; American Lung Assn; Jr League Hampton Roads; VA Advisory Bd on Gifted Education. **Business Addr:** State Representative, Virginia House of Reps, House of Delegates, POB 406, Richmond, VA 23203, (804)786-8826.

CHRISTIAN, SPENCER
Weatherman, television host. **Personal:** Born Jul 23, 1947, Newport News, VA; son of Lucy Greene Christian (deceased) and Spencer Christian; married Diane Chambers Christian, Jun 20, 1970; children: Jason, Jessica. **Educ:** Hampton Univ, Hampton, VA, BA, English, 1970. **Career:** Stony Brook Prep School, Long Island, NY, teacher, 1970; WWBT-TV, Richmond, VA, news reporter, 1971, weatherman, 1972-75; WBAL-TV, Baltimore, MD, weatherman, 1975-77; WABC-TV, New York, NY, weatherman, 1977-86; Good Morning America, weatherman, co-host, interviewer, 1986-; BET, ''Triple Threat'' game show, host, 1993-. **Orgs:** Has worked with numerous charities including: March of Dimes, Special Olympics, Cystic Fibrosis Foundation, American Cancer Society, Big Brothers, Girl Scouts of America, Tomorrow's Children, United Negro College Fund; Up With People; Daytop Village. **Honors/Awds:** Better Life Award; Whitney M Young Jr Service Award, Greater New York Councils of the Boy Scouts of America, 1990; Honorary Chairman, North Jersey Chapter, March of Dimes, 1979; Virginia Communication's Hall of Fame, 1993. **Military Serv:** US Army Reserves. **Business Addr:** Weatherman/Host, Good Morning America, ABC, Inc, 147 Columbus Ave, New York, NY 10023.

CHRISTIAN, THERESA
Educator (retired). **Personal:** Born in Philadelphia, PA; daughter of Mary Christian and Charles Christian. **Educ:** Freedmen's Hospital School of Nursing; Howard University, diploma; Loyola U, BSN; Univ of Toronto, certificate; Univ of Chicago, MSN. **Career:** Provident Hospital School of Nursing, supvr instructor; Univ of Chicago Clinics; Univ of KS, supvr asst & prof; Cornell Univ, instructor, supvr; Villanova Univ, associate professor, associate professor emeritus, 1988. **Orgs:** Acad policy com, admissions, promotions com, Villanova U; treas Am Assn of Univ Profs; Am Council of Churches; Am Nurses Assn; Black Conf on Higher Education; pres Beta Chap Chi Eta Phi; bd mgrs Ellen Cushing Jr Coll; Freedmans Hosp Alumni Assn; PA Nurses' Assn; Sigma Theta Tau; University of Toronto Alumni Assn; Loyola Univ of Chicago Alumni Assn; Women's League of Voters; Womens Missionary Soc; board of directors Philadelphia Nat League of Nursing; rep Am Bapt Women; board member, Community Health Affiliates; American Medical Association; American Nurses Federation. **Honors/Awds:** Three Chaplains Philadelphia, Citation for Citizenship; American Institute of Pakistan Studies, grant; Rockefeller Foundation, grant. **Special Achievements:** Author: articles for various professional publications. **Business Addr:** Associate Professor Emerita, Villanova University, College of Nursing, Villanova, PA 19085.

CHRISTIAN, WILLIAM LEONARD
Actor. **Personal:** Born Sep 30, 1955, Washington, DC; son of William L Christian and Evelyn M Shaw. **Educ:** The Catholic University of America, BA, 1976; The American University, MA, 1980. **Career:** Capital Cities/ABC, Inc, disney actor, All My Children, 1990-; Appeared in off broadway play The Boy in the Band: appearances on The Cosby Show, Matlock, and Tattingers. **Honors/Awds:** Daytime Emmy Award Nominee, Outstanding Supporting Actor, 1991.

CHRISTIAN-GREEN, DONNA-MARIE
Congresswoman. **Personal:** Born Sep 19, 1945, Teaneck, NJ; daughter of Virginia Sterling Christian and Almeric Leander Christian; married Carl L Green, Sep 21, 1974 (divorced 1980); children: Rabiah Layla, Karida Yasmeen. **Educ:** St Mary's College, South Bend, IN, BA, 1966; George Washington Univ, Washington, DC, MD, 1970. **Career:** Virgin Islands Department of Health, St Croix, Virgin Islands, various positions, 1975-80; F'sted Health Center, St Croix, Virgin Islands, medical director, 1980-85; Dir Mch and Family Planning, St Croix, Virgin Islands, medical director, 1985-87; St Croix Hospital, St Croix, Virgin Islands, medical director, 1987-88; Virgin Islands Department of Health, St Croix, Virgin Islands, assistant commissioner, 1988-92; US House of Representatives, congresswoman, 1997-. **Orgs:** Member, Democratic National Women Committee, 1984-; member, Democratic Territorial Committee, 1980-; member, Virgin Islands Board of Education, 1984-86; president, Virgin Islands Medical Society, 1990-91; Christian ed chair, Friedenstal Moravian Church, 1988-. **Business Addr:** Congresswoman, US House of Representatives, 1711 Longworth House Office Bldg, Washington, DC 20515-5501.

CHRISTIE, DOUGLAS DALE
Professional basketball player. **Personal:** Born May 9, 1970, Seattle, WA; children: Chantell. **Educ:** Pepperdine Univ. **Career:** Seattle Supersonics, guard-forward, 1992-93; Los Angeles Lakers, 1993-94; New York Knicks, 1994-96; Toronto Raptors, 1996-. **Special Achievements:** NBA Draft, First round pick, #17, 1992. **Business Addr:** Professional Basketball Player, Toronto Raptors, 150 York St, Ste 110, Toronto, ON, Canada M5H 3S5, (416)214-2255.

CHRISTOPHE, CLEVELAND A.
Private equity investor. **Personal:** Born Jan 1, 1946, Savannah, GA; son of Cleveland & Lucy Christophe; married Cheryl S Chistophe, Dec 28, 1966; children: Jon Scott (deceased), Jean-Paul, Kimberly D. **Educ:** Howard Univ, BA, 1966; Univ of MI, Graduate School of Business, MBA, 1967. **Career:** Citibank, NA, country head for Colombia, pres of Banco International de Colombia, 1967-87; TLC Group, LP, sr vice pres, 1987-88; The Christophe Corp, pres, 1988-90; Equico Capital Corp, vice pres, 1990-92; TSG Ventures Inc, principal, 1992-; TSG Capital Group, LLC, managing partner, 1995-. **Orgs:** Hayes Lemmerz Intl, Inc, dir, 1996-; Envirotest Systems Corp, bd of dirs, 1990-; Midwest Stamping & Manufacturing, Inc, dir, 1993-; Natl Assn of Investment Companies, dir, 1992-. **Honors/Awds:** Institute of Chartered Financial Analysts, Chartered Financial Analyst, 1975. **Special Achievements:** Competition in Financial Services, Citicorp, 1974. **Business Addr:** Managing Partner, TSG Capital Group, LLC, 177 Broad St, #12 Fl, Stamford, CT 06901-2048, (203)406-1500.

CHRISTOPHER, JOHN A.
Microbiologist, immunologist. **Personal:** Born Aug 19, 1941, Shreveport, LA. **Educ:** Bishop Coll, BS 1964; Baylor U, MS 1967; IA State U, PhD 1971; TX S U, NIH Undergrad Research Fellow 1963. **Career:** Univ TX SW Med Sch, research tech 1964-65; Inst Of Baylor Univ, grad research fellow 1965-67; IA State U, grad research/tchr asst 1967-71; Univ MN Med Sch, postdoctoral research fellow 1971-73; So Univ Mem Soc for Microbiology, prof dept chm. **Orgs:** Am Assn For The Advancement of Sci; Soc of Sigma Xi; So Cntrl Br Am Soc for Microbiology; mem YWCA; NAACP; Community Cncl Inc; Natl Fnd March of Dimes. **Business Addr:** So Univ, 3050 Cooper Rd, Shreveport, LA 71107.

CHUBB, LOUISE B.
Business executive. **Personal:** Born Jun 15, 1927, Bronwood, GA; married Edward; children: Mrs Charles L McCoy. **Educ:** Ft Vly State Coll, BS 1957; Ga State Univ, MS 1975; Smith Coll Grad Sc Hl Univ TN; GA State Univ. **Career:** GA School for the Deaf, retired English dept chairperson; Success, Inc, sales dir. **Orgs:** Community Youth Worker; mem NEA; CAID; GA Assn Edn; GA Educ Hearing Impaired; United Meth Ch; Minority Bus Assn; Delta Sigma Theta; Natl Council Negro Women. **Honors/Awds:** Sr class pres & Miss summer sch Ft Vly State Coll 1957; tchr yr GSD 1963; Outstanding state serv 1960, 65, 70, 75. **Business Addr:** Sales Dir, Success, Inc, 1185 Chubb Rd, SW, Cave Spring, GA 30124.

CHUCK D (CARLTON RIDENHOUR)
Rapper, activist, author, journalist. **Personal:** Born 1960, Long Island, NY. **Educ:** Adelphi Coll, NY, attended. **Career:** Rapper, with group Public Enemy, 1987-; lecturer; activist; author; Fox News Channel, commentator/correspondent, 1998-. **Special Achievements:** Albums include: Yo! Bum Rush The Show, 1987; It Takes A Nation of Millions to Hold Us Back, 1988; Fear Of A Black Planet, 1990; Apocalypse '91: The Enemy Strikes Black, 1991; Greatest Misses, 1992; Muse Sick n Hour Mess Age, 1994; Singles include: "Fight The Power," 1989; "911 Is A Joke;" "Don't Believe The Hype," 1988; collaborated with rock group Anthrax on remake of "Bring The Noise," 1991; "Hip Hop: Talk Back," Lecture series, participant, 1993; MTV "Enough Is Enough" antidrugs/antiviolence program, spokesperson, 1993; MTV News, reporter for Republican Convention; co-author, Fight The Power: Rap, Race, Reality, 1997. **Business Addr:** Rapper, Public Enemy, Def Jam Recordings Group Inc, 160 Varick St, 12th Fl, New York, NY 10013, (212)229-5200.

CHUCKS, JERRY. See **CHUKWUEKE, GERALD NDUDI.**

CHUKS-ORJI, AUSTIN
Automobile dealership executive. **Career:** Mission Boulevard Lincoln-Mercury Inc, chief executive officer, currently. **Special Achievements:** Listed 69 of 100 top auto dealers, Black Enterprise, 1992. **Business Addr:** Chief Executive Officer, Mission Blvd Lincoln-Mercury Inc, 24644 Mission Blvd, Hayward, CA 94544, (415)886-5052.

CHUKWUEKE, GERALD NDUDI (JERRY CHUCKS)
Automobile dealer. **Personal:** Born Jan 28, 1957, Port-Harcourt, Rivers State, Nigeria; son of Martha Ego Chukwueke and Thedeous Uba Chukwueke; married Chinelo Catherine Chukwueke, Mar 16, 1987; children: Nicole, Megan. **Educ:** Morgan State Univ, Baltimore, MD, BA, political science, 1984, MBA, marketing, 1987. **Career:** Sherwood Ford, Baltimore, MD, asst sales manager, 1981-84, sales manager, 1984-87; Dominion Lincoln/Mercury, Culpeper, VA, chairman & CEO, 1987-; Dominion Lincoln/Mercury, Waynesboro, VA, chairman & CEO, 1988-. **Orgs:** Member, Rotary International, 1990-. **Honors/Awds:** America's Top 100 Businesses, Black Enterprise Magazine, 1989, 1990.

CHUNN, JAY CARRINGTON, II
Educator, researcher. **Personal:** Born Dec 26, 1938, Atlanta, GA; son of Carrie Reid Morgan and Jay Carrington Chunn Sr; married Brenda, Oct 18, 1987; children: Tracy, Jay III, Lauren Ruth. **Educ:** Ohio Univ, BS 1957, BA 1961; Case Western Reserve Univ, MS 1965; Univ of MD, PhD 1978. **Career:** Community Coordinated Child Care, staff coordinator 1970; Council for Economic Opportunity in Greater Cleveland, child devel coordinator 1970; Natl Child Devel Day Care and Child Develop of Amer, pres 1970-71; Natl Child Devel and Day Care Consultants, president 1971-73; Howard Univ, prof 1972-74, dean of social work 1974-84; Medgar Evers Coll, president 1984-. **Orgs:** Natl pres Natl Assoc of Black Social Workers CA 1974-76, re-elected in Baltimore, MD for term ending in 1978; chairman 100 Black Men Intl Affairs Comm 1985-; mem 100 Black Men, Inc 1986-; mem Governor's Adv Comm for Black Affairs 1986. **Honors/Awds:** Author "The Black Aged and Social Policy" in Aging 1978, "Mental Health & People of Color, Curriculum Development and Change," Univ Press 1983; "Stress Management and the Black Female in Corporate Environment," 1983. **Military Serv:** Marine Reserves 6 months. **Business Addr:** Director/Professor of Research & Development, Hunter College, 425 E 25th St, New York, NY 10010.

CHURCH, ROBERT T., SR.
City councilman (retired), county agricultural agent. **Personal:** Born Sep 26, 1909, Athens, GA; son of Pearl Billups Church and Arthur Church; married Ruby Summers, Jun 26, 1938; children: Robert T Jr, Ruby A. **Educ:** Hampton Inst, BS Agr 1934; Tuskegee Inst, MS Agr Educ 1958. **Career:** Washington GA Bd of Educ, asst principal & vocational agricultural teacher, 1934-36; Millen GA Bd of Educ, principal & voc agr teacher, 1936-38; Jenkins Co, co agent, 1938-46; Clarke Co, co agt 1946-48; Peach Co Ft Valley, co agt 1948-69; Ft Valley, GA, city councilman 1974-82 (retired); farmer, 1969-86; Church's Enterprises, Mgr, 1969-89. **Orgs:** Sponsored 4H winner of local/state & natl contest; keeper of fin Lambda Phi Chap Omega Psi Phi; mem Ft Valley City Council; chmn bd dir Div of Peach Co Family & Child Svcs; mem Deacon Bd Trinity Bapt Ch; Epsilon Sigma Phi 1968; Grammatues Beta Chi Boule 1984; appointed to Peach Cty Jurors Commission, 1986; Pres, Central GA Chapter of Hampton Univ Alumni Assn, 1985-; President, Tabor Hts Community Club, 1986-; chairman of board, Peach County Family & Children Services, 1991-. **Honors/Awds:** Omega Man of the Year Awd 1968; Plaques for Distinguished Serv GA Agr Ext Serv 1969; Peach Co Bd of Commrs 1969; Silver Serv Farmers of Peach Co 1970; Omega Citizen of the Year Award 1975; Man of the Year Award Trinity Bapt Ch 1975; Public Serv Awd 1980; Houston Stallworth Awd for Outstanding Leadership from Citizens Ed Commiss 1982; Southeastern Region Natl Hampton Alumni Assn Inc Awd for Outstanding Unselfish & Dedicated Serv 1986; Certificate of Appreciation for Outstanding & Dedicated Serv, Peach Co Div of Family & Children Serv, 1988; Fifty Year Award, Omega Psi Phi Fraternity, 1988; Board Member of the Year, GA Welfare Assn, 1989; Man of the Year for Community Service, Trinity Baptist Church, 1990; Outstanding Service Award, Jenkins County Alumni Assn, 1996; Distinguished Service Award, Peach County Dept of Family and Children Service Board, 1996. **Special Achievements:** Selected to serve on the advisory council of President of Ft Valley State Univ, 1996. **Home Addr:** 901 S Carver Dr, Fort Valley, GA 31030.

CHURCHWELL, CAESAR ALFRED
Dentist. **Personal:** Born Nov 26, 1932, Newton, GA; married Ruth; children: Caesar Jr, Gabrielle, Eric. **Educ:** Mt Union Coll, BS 1956; Howard Univ Coll Dentistry, DDS 1967. **Career:** Self-Employed, dntst. **Orgs:** Mem ADA; SFDS; CDS; Western Peridontal Soc; SF Dental Fnd 1975; SF Dental Forum; Acad Gen Dentistry; No Chap Med; Dental & Pharm Assn; past pres NCNDA 1974; mem Bicentennial Com So SF 1975-76; Co San Mateo 1975-76; mem NAACP; personnel com mem NAACP Urban League Bd Dir 1971-72; adv bd Fulcrum Saving & Loan 1973; mem Black Ldrsp Forum; Men of Tomorrow; Black Unity Cnsl; past pres W Twin Peaks Lions Club 1973; actvty chm BSA 1974. **Military Serv:** AUS pvt 1955-56. **Business Addr:** 933 Geneva Ave, San Francisco, CA 94112.

CHURCHWELL, CHARLES DARRETT
Educational administrator. **Personal:** Born Nov 7, 1926, Dunnellon, FL; married Yvonne; children: Linda, Cynthia. **Educ:** Morehouse College, BS, 1952; Atlanta University, MLS, 1953; University of Illinois, PhD, library science, 1966; additional courses: City College, Hunter College, New York University, 1959-61. **Career:** Numerous teaching experiences, 1953-68; Miami University, professor, director of libraries, 1969-72, professor, associate provost for academic services, 1972-74; University of Michigan, visiting lecturer, 1972, 1976; Brown University, librarian, 1974-78; Washington University, dean of library services, 1978-87; Wayne State University, visiting professor, library science, 1987, professor, 1988-90; Clark Atlanta University, School of Library and Information Studies, dean, 1990-, interim provost, vice president academic affairs, 1990-91; Atlanta University Center, Robert W Woodruff Library, director, 1991-. **Orgs:** American Library Association, life member, 1968-; NAACP, life member; Georgia Library Association; Council of Library Resources, vice chairman, board of directors. **Honors/Awds:** American Council on Education, Academic Administration Fellow, 1971-72; Atlanta University, School of Library and Information Studies, Outstanding Alumni Award, 1986. **Business Addr:** Dean, School of Library and Information Studies, Clark Atlanta University, James P Brawley Drive at Fair St SW, Atlanta, GA 30314.

CISSOKO, ALIOUNE BADARA
Educational administrator, psychotherapist, artist. **Personal:** Born Jun 15, 1952, Kolda Casamance, Senegal; son of Fatoumata Mara and Moussa Balla; married Sonia H; children: Moussa Balla, Fatoumata, Djibril Kalif. **Educ:** Univ Dakar Inst Arts, BA 1975; RI Schl Design, MFA 1979; Univ RI, Arts Mgmt Cert 1982; Northeastern Univ, MA 1984, PhD; certified case manager. **Career:** Intl House RI, prog asst 1978-80; Soc Cons, arts consult 1979-; Amer Sociological Assc, mem 1983-; Amer Anthropological Assc, mem 1983-; Northern RI Community Mental Health Center Psychiatric Counselor Crisis Beds, psycho-social counselor & therapist; Southeastern MA Univ, publ rel prof of arts 1985-; Brown Univ, Dept Police & Security, mgr special services, 1993-. **Orgs:** Fine artist Performing Arts RI 1977-; folk artist artist in educ RI State Council on Arts 1980-; listed Talent Bank NEA Wash DC 1983-; mem RI Black Heritage Soc 1979-, Intl House of RI 1979-; mem Natl Council on Creative Educ Therapy; mem & co-founder Black Artists of RI. **Honors/Awds:** Citation State of RI and Providence Plantations 1984; fndr of Dougouto Ngnagnya African Drums and Dance Ensemble 1982-; RI State Council Awd on Creative Educ Therapy. **Home Addr:** PO Box 603227, Providence, RI 02906-0227. **Business Addr:** PO Box 603227, Providence, RI 02906-0227.

CLACK, DORIS H.
Educator. **Personal:** Born Mar 24, 1928, Wakulla, FL; daughter of Delia Green Hargrett and Andrew Joshua Hargrett; married Harold Lee Clack; children: Harold Levi, Herek Lerron. **Educ:** FL A&M Univ, AB 1949; attended Univ of MI 1956; Univ of Pittsburgh, PhD 1973; Univ of Toronto, certificate 1981. **Career:** Shadesville HS, teacher 1952-54; FL A&M Univ, librarian 1955-68; Univ of Pgh, lecturer 1969-70; Univ of IA, vstg prof 1978-80 summers; Library of Congress, cataloger 1984; Univ of Maiduquri Nigeria, vstg prof 1987-88; FL State Univ Sch of Lib & Info Studies, prof 1973-. **Orgs:** Mem Amer Lib Assn; chairperson ALA/RTSD Council of Regional Groups; mem ALA Rsch Comm RTSD/CCS CC,DA; Frontiers Intl Aux; NAACP; mem Bethel Baptist Ch; chair ALA/RTSD Cataloging & Classification Section; councillor SELA. **Honors/Awds:** Title II Fellowship Univ of Pgh 1970-73; Disting Alumni Awd Univ of MI 1979; Beta Phi Mu Hon Frat; Distinguished Teaching Award Florida State University, 1988; University Leadership Award, Florida State University, 1991. **Business Addr:** Professor, Florida State Univ, Sch of Library & Info Studies, Tallahassee, FL 32306.

CLACK, FLOYD
State representative. **Personal:** Born Dec 21, 1940, Houston, TX; married Brenda J Jones; children: Michael, Mia. **Educ:** TX So Univ, BS 1965; TX So Univ School of Law, 1966; Eastern MI Univ, MA 1972, studies in educational leadership, 1985. **Career:** Old Fisher Body Plant, factory worker; Houston Public Schools, teacher; Federal Government Job Corps Center, teacher, 1967-68; Flint Community School System, teacher, 1968-82; Michigan House of Representatives, state representative, 1980-96; Genesee County Board of Commissioners, commissioner, 1997-. **Orgs:** Kappa Alpha Psi Fraternity; National Conference of State Legislators; National Conference of Black Legislators; Michigan Alternative Education Assn; National Alternative Education Assn; Urban League of Flint; Genesee County Boy Scouts of America, board of directors; Council of State Governments; The Academy of Criminal Justice; American Corrections Association; Michigan Corrections Association; Flint Inner City Lions Club; Kentucky Colonels; Genesee County Community Action Agency; Metropolitan Chamber of Commerce; Michigan Political History Society; National Democratic Party; Democratic Leadership Conference; Democratic Black Caucus; Michigan State Alumni Assn; Eastern Michigan Alumni Assn; Buckham Alley Theater; National Civic League; American Legislative Exchange Council; CARE Advisory Board. **Honors/Awds:** Michigan Education Assn, David McMahon Award, 1988; City of Flint, Boy Scouts of America Appreciation, 1989; Metropolitan Chamber of Commerce, Supportive Services Award, 1989, Harry L Redds Award, 1991; Urban League, Equal Opportunity Award, 1990; Genesee County Community Action Agency, Appreciation Award, 1990; Flint NAACP, Leadership Award, 1990, Service Award, 1990; Alpha Kappa Alpha Sorority, Outstanding Service to Mankind Award, 1990; Concerned Pastors for Social Action, Outstanding Service Award, 1990; Genesee County Tribute Committee, Martin Luther King Memorial Award, 1990; The Forum Magazine, Appreciation Award, 1991; Kappa Alpha Psi, Good Old Kappa Spirit Award, 1991; Greater Flint Jaycees, Outstanding Service Award, 1991; Panhellic Council, Floyd J McCree Leadership, 1991; Flint Inner City Lions Club, Man of the Year, 1991; Genesee Federation of the Blind Inc, Certificate of Appreciation, 1992; American Red Cross, Gift of Life Award, 1994; Foss Avenue Baptist Church Award, 1994; WJRT TV Channel 12, Person of the Week Award, 1994; University of Michigan-Flint, Black History Month Award, 1996. **Special Achievements:** Youth Leadership Inst in Flint, founder; Floyd Clack Thanksgiving Dinner for Sr Citizens, founder, 1983; Floyd Clack Comm Projects; Flint Inner City Lions Club, charter mem.

CLACK, R. C.
Human resources executive. **Personal:** Born Dec 16, 1938, Houston, TX; son of Thelma Hollingsworth Dightman and R C Clack; married Donna Wise, Jul 1964; children: Kim, Carla, Dana, Chris, Ben. **Educ:** Prairie View A&M Univ., Prairie View, TX, BS, 1961; Southern Methodist Univ., Dallas, TX, MS, 1975. **Career:** FBI, Washington, DC, special agent, 1965-70; Shoprite Foods, Dallas, TX, dir of personnel, 1970-72; Campbell Toggart, Inc., Dallas, TX, vice pres human resources, 1972-. **Orgs:** Chairman, ABA Industrial Relations Committee, 1991-; board of directors, Campbell Toggart, 1990-; secretary, BCT Fund, 1986-. **Military Serv:** US Army, Capt, 1961-65.

CLAIBORNE, LLOYD R.
Government official (retired). **Personal:** Born Feb 15, 1936, Newport News, VA; son of Alma E Dennis and John Claiborne; married Dorma J Robinson; children: Renee, Cheryl, Denise, Lloyd II. **Educ:** City Coll of NY, BS 1958. **Career:** FDA NY, food & drug insp 1958-67, suprv food & drug insp 1967; DHEW/PHS/FDA Bureau of Compliance Washington, prog analyst FDA exec devel prog 1968-71; DHEW/PHS/FDA Kansas City, dep & reg food & drug dir 1971-77; US Food & Drug Admin: Chicago, IL, regional food & drug dir 1977-81, San Francisco, CA, regional food & drug dir 1981-90, Kansas City, MO, asst to assoc commissioner for regulatory affairs 1990-91; Retired 1991. **Orgs:** Mem NAACP 1971-72; mem Assoc of Food & Drug Ofcls 1971-90; chmn DHEW, PHS, FDA Field Med Device Adv Comm 1978-83; chmn DHEW, PHS, FDA Mid-Level Career Dev Prog Comm 1978-84. **Honors/Awds:** Commendable Service Award, US Food & Drug Admin 1985; Commissioner's Special Citation, US Food & Drug Admin

1985. **Home Addr:** 12900 Mastin St, Overland Park, KS 66213.

CLAIR, AREATHA G.

Educator (retired). **Personal:** Born Sep 5, 1931, Jacksonville, FL; daughter of Mary Lee Anderson (deceased) and John Anderson; married Alford; children: Andre, Armand. **Educ:** FL A&M Univ, BS 1953; Chicago Teachers Coll; CO Coll, Univ of CO Springs, Grad Studies; Western State Coll, Type D Admin Cert, MA. **Career:** Chicago Public School, teacher 1962-65; CO Springs Teacher Assoc, prof negotiator 1970-72; Zebulon Pike Elementary School, principal 1977-78; Garfield Elementary School, principal 1978-80; Mark Twain & US Grant Schools, elem asst principal; CO Springs School Dist 11, teacher; Taylor Elementary School, principal 1980-91. **Orgs:** Pres CO Springs Alumnae Delta Sigma Theta, 1989-91; past comm Woman Dem Party CO Springs; del Delta's Natl Conv Atlanta 1972, CO Dem State Conv Denver 1974; writer for Drug Curr 1970; team leader CO Springs School Dist 11, Univ of So CO Teacher Corps Proj 1975; bd mem UCCS Alumni Assoc; University of Southern Colorado, part-time supervisor of student teachers, currently. **Honors/Awds:** Outstanding Delta Award, Colorado Springs Alumnae Chapter, Delta Sigma Theta Sorority, 1988-89; Outstanding Volunteer Service Plaque, Alumni Board UCCS, Colorado Springs, CO, 1989.

CLANAGAN, MAZZETTA PRICE

Company marketing executive. **Personal:** Born Oct 14, 1920, Rankin, PA; daughter of Gyrlie Geane Miller (deceased) and William Heintzelman Price Sr (deceased); married Robert A Clanagan (deceased); children: Robin Clanagan Moore. **Educ:** Keller Schl Dressmaking & Design, Certf Grad 1943; Grad Schl of Pblc & Intrntl Affairs Univ of Pgh, Master Pblc Admn 1971, Doctoral Candidate Deferred 1975; Regional Prsnl Serv Cntr of Southwestern PA, Cert Prsnl Law 1977. **Career:** Bureau of Emplymnt Security PA, manpower speclst emplymnt intrviewer emplyr reltns rep 1960-70; Univ of Pittsburgh, admsns ofcr 1971-74; Allegheny Cnty Gov't Pittsburgh PA, EEO speclst & contract compliance ofcr 1974-78; Claybar Intrntl, Inc Pittsburgh, PA Claybar Constrctn & Contrctrs Equip Corp, vice pres 1978-80; Allegheny Cnty Govt, soc serv cordinator, 1983-89; Allegheny Fabricating & Supplies, Inc, vice pres/dir of marketing, 1989-. **Orgs:** Mgmt cnsltnt self-emplyd penal reforn consltnt & coal broker Mazzetta Price Clanagan Co Pittsburgh, PA 1971-; co-owner-partnrshp P&M Assc Pgh PA 1978-80; cnsltnt-filming of documentary KDKA TV Channel 2 1973; Councilwoman Borough of Rankin, Rankin, PA 1976-84; mem Natl Black Caucus of Local Elected Pblc Offcls 1976-84; oral examiner PA State Civil Serv Comm 1972-; guest lecturer, Univ of Pittsburgh; pblc spkr Churches Univ Etc. **Honors/Awds:** Jessie Smith Noyes Foundation & Carnegie Foundation flwship Grad Schl of Intrntl Affairs Univ of Pittsburgh 1969-71; author Article ''Forgotten Inmates-Women'' Commission for Racial Justice Reprtr.

CLANCY, MAGALENE ALDOSHIA

Elected official (retired). **Personal:** Born Jan 2, 1938, Midway, GA; children: Eric G, Delia A, Lorenzo K. **Educ:** Johnson C Smith Univ, 1957-59. **Career:** Liberty Elem School, sub teacher 1962-65; Liberty Co, oeo worker 1966-68; Ft Stewart GA, nurses asst 1968-92. **Orgs:** Usher bd, chmn youth group, Midway 1st Presbyterian Church; re-elected for fifth term, councilperson for City of Midway, 1992; eigth years as mayor-protem, City of Midway. **Honors/Awds:** Outstanding Awd Ft Stewart USAH 1978; 15 Yrs Cert Ft Stewart USAH 1983. **Home Addr:** PO Box 166, Midway, GA 31320.

CLANTON, LEMUEL JACQUE

Physician. **Personal:** Born Mar 11, 1931, New Orleans, LA; married Barbara Guy; children: Mark, Lynn, Justine, Lemuel J, Leslie. **Educ:** Howard U, BS 1952; Meharry Med Coll, MD 1956. **Career:** Med Asso, physician. **Orgs:** Bd Certified Surgeon; Am Bd Of Surgery; mem AMA; mem Nat Med Assn; bd mem Lafon Home for Aged 1975. **Business Addr:** 517 Newton, New Orleans, LA 70126.

CLARDY, WILLIAM J.

Manager. **Personal:** Born May 1, 1935, Newalla, OK; married Patricia Ann Lomax; children: D Vincent, Terri Lynette, William Gerald. **Educ:** OK St U, ass eng degree 1960; USN Comm Tech Class A Sch; Iowa St U, 1971-72. **Career:** Lennox Ind Inc Pacific Div, terr mgr htg & air cond equip, instr; LA Unified Sch Dist, instr; Lincoln Job Corp Ctr Northern Sys Co, sr instr htg & air cond; Cal-Poly Workshop, made presentation 1972; Annual Ed Con CARSES, made presentation May 1974; Utah Sheet Metal Con Assn, conducted workshop Aug 1971. **Orgs:** Bd dir Marshalltown Chap Jaycees; bd dir Marshalltown Chap Am Field Ser; bd dir YMCA Omaha; mem Marshalltown, IA Optimist Club Intl. **Military Serv:** USN tech 3 class 1952-56. **Business Addr:** 2041 S Saybrook Ave, Los Angeles, CA 90022.

CLARK, AUGUSTA ALEXANDER

Attorney, city offical. **Personal:** Born Mar 5, 1932, Uniontown, AL; married Leroy W Clark; children: Mark, Adrienne. **Educ:** WV State Coll, BSBA (cum laude) 1954; Drexel Univ, MLS 1958; Temple Univ, JD 1976. **Career:** Fed Defense Installations & Free Library of Phila, librarian 1958-66; Gen Elect Co RESD, market rsch analyst 1967-69; Auerbach Corp, consult 1970-71; Philadelphia Model Cities Prog, admin 1971-73; Gen Elect Co, affirm action requirement mgr 1973-75; Majority Whip of The City Council of Philadelphia, councilwoman-at-large, attorney. **Orgs:** Bd of dir Friends of Free Library of Philadelphia, New Horizons Rsch Inst, Horizon House, Shalom Inc, North Central Branch YWCA, Organization for Women & Girls Offenders, PILCPO; bd of trustees Philadelphia Coll of Arts; advisory bd PA Women's Campaign Fund; law comm Amer Baptist Churches USA Inc; founder &co-chair Bright Hope Survival Prog; sponsor The Month of the Woman 1983; delegate Natl Women's Conf Houston; co-chair PA Intl Women's Year Coord Comm; mem Barristers, PA Bar Assoc, Alpha Kappa Alpha Sor, West of Broad St Coalition, WV State Alumni, Steering Comm for Chessfest, Black Women's Network; organizer Jefferson Manor Tenant Assoc; counsel Minority Contractors Advisory Comm. **Honors/Awds:** Oustanding Serv in the Community Nu Sigma Natl Sor 1980; Alumnus of the Year & Outstanding Citizen & Humanitarian WV State Coll Theta Chap of Theta 1981; Support to Delta Iota Chap Alpha Kappa Alpha Sor Inc 1983; Sponsored a number of Bills & Resolutions to assist in improving the quality of life; Honorary Doctorates Degree Drexel University 1985. **Business Addr:** Councilwoman-at-Large, City Council of Philadelphia, City Hall Room 580, Philadelphia, PA 19107.

CLARK, BENJAMIN F.

Dentist. **Personal:** Born Sep 19, 1910, Charleston, WV; son of Mary Brown Clark and Benjamin F Clark Sr; married Alice Robinson. **Educ:** WV State Coll, BS 1933; Howard Univ Sch of Dentistry, DDS 1944; Univ of MI Sch of Dentistry, Grad Work 1948. **Career:** WV gen practice, dentistry; Lakin State Hosp, dir dental serv (retired). **Orgs:** Past pres Capital City Med Soc Bachelor Benedict Club; past post commander & exec bd mem Col Charles Young Post 57 of Amer Legion; mem exec, past state dept vice commander WV Dept of Amer Legion; past state vice pres Natl Dental Assn; mem Amer Assn of Hosp Dentists; dir Dental Prog of State Assn of IBPOE of World; mem NAACP; Omega Psi Phi Frat; Chi Delta Mu Med Frat; assoc mem Chicago Dental Soc; sec-treas WV Med Soc; vice pres Economic Comm Housing Opportunity; past treas and mem of trustee bd, First Baptist Church; advisory bd mem, Martin Luther King Recreation Center. **Honors/Awds:** Recip Doctor of Yr Award WV Med Soc 1973; Sports Hall of Fame inductee, West Virginia State College, 1983; Omega Psi Phi Fraternity, 50 Year Award, 1992. **Military Serv:** AUS capt Dental Corps 1944-47.

CLARK, BERTHA SMITH

Educator. **Personal:** Born Sep 26, 1943, Nashville, TN; daughter of Louise Smith and James Robert Smith; married Phillip Hickman Clark, Apr 21, 1973; children: Phillipa Jayne, Margaret Ann, Sheryll Clark Nelson. **Educ:** TN State Univ, BS (high distinction) 1964; George Peabody Clg for Tchrs, MA 1965; Natl Inst of Mental Hlth, Pre Doctoral Fellow 1978-80; Vanderbilt Univ, PhD 1982. **Career:** Bill Wilkerson Hearing & Speech Center (BWHSC), head tchr OE #1 project 1965-70, speech pathologist 1965-78, 1980-87; TN State Univ, supvr of clinical practicum 1969-78, 1980-87; Mama Lere Parent Infant Home, Bill Wilkerson Hearing & Speech Center, parent-infant trainer 1982-86; Vanderbilt Univ, div of hearing and speech sciences, 1970-87, adjunct assistant professor, 1987-98; Middle TN State Univ, prof, currently. **Orgs:** Board of dir League for the Hearing Impaired 1973-87, The Childrens House (A Montessori Preschool) 1984-86; advsry Cmt Early Devel & Assistance Project Kennedy Cntr 1984-88; co-chrprsn mem YWCA 1985; mem Delta Sigma Theta Sorority, Inc 1962-; admin comm, vice pres for educ TN Speech and Hearing Assn 1985-87; chairperson Cochlear Implant Scholarship Comm, 1985-86; mem Compton Scholarship Comm Vanderbilt Univ 1985-86; bd of dirs Peabody Alumni 1986-89; board of directors Bill Wilkerson Center 1990-95; board of directors Effective Advocacy for Citizens with Handicaps 1991-92; board of directors CFAW, MTSU 1991-. **Honors/Awds:** Honors grad Haynes HS 1960, TN State Univ 1964; predoctoral flwshp Natl Inst of Mental Hlth 1978-80; Honors of TSHA, In Speech, Language Hearing Assn 1988; Office of Education Trainee, Office of Education 1964-65; Fellow, Southern Education Foundation 1964. **Business Addr:** Professor, Middle Tennessee State University, Dept of Speech & Theatre, Communication Disorders, Murfreesboro, TN 37132.

CLARK, BETTIE I.

Physician (retired). **Personal:** Born Feb 12, 1927, Mt Holly, NJ; daughter of Viola Edna Stanley Graves and Norman Norwood Graves; married Dr Ross J Clark, Sep 4, 1953 (deceased); children: Ross James Jr, Patricia Leigh, Robyn Marie. **Educ:** Morgan State Coll Baltimore, BS 1949; Howard Univ Coll of Med, MD 1954; Johns Hopkins Univ, School of Hygiene & Publ Health, MPH 1973. **Career:** Howard Univ Coll of Med, clinical instr dept of ped 1957-60; DC Govt Ambulatory Health Care Admin, pediatric med officer 1960-80; Coll of Med Howard Univ, asst clinical prof of ped 1966-80, retired. **Orgs:** Mem Amer Acad of Ped, DC Med Soc, Pan Amer Med Assn, Amer Publ Health Assn, Howard Univ Med Alumni Assn; pres bd of dir Metro Lab Inc Wash DC 1974-78; sec, treas DC Chap Amer Acad of Ped 1976-79; bd of dir Columbia Hosp for Women Wash DC 1979-91; trustee emeritus, 1991-; cert in ped Amer Bd of Ped 1961; fellow Amer Acad of Ped 1962; apptd trustee The Holton-Arms School Bethesda MD 1982-88.

CLARK, BEVERLY GAIL

Writer. **Personal:** Born Jul 23, 1947, Oklahoma City, OK; daughter of James & Isabella; married Alvin Clark, Oct 1, 1966; children: Catana Clark-Hughes, Alvin Jr, Dayna, Ericca, Gloria. **Educ:** LTU, Genre Fiction Writing. **Career:** Book Nook, bookseller, 1992-; Walden Books, bookseller, 1996-98, Book Stop, bookseller, 1998-. **Orgs:** Friends of the Library, 1991-; Romance Writer of America (RWA), 1990-. **Honors/Awds:** RWA, Published Writer-Fiction, 1996. **Special Achievements:** Published 120 short stories, 1989-94; Yesterday is Gone, 1997; A Love to Cherish, 1998. **Home Addr:** 1814 W Ave J-15, No 3, Lancaster, CA 93534, (805)948-9522.

CLARK, CAESAR A. W.

Clergyman. **Personal:** Born Dec 13, 1914, Shreveport, LA; married Carolyn Elaine Bunche, Apr 16, 1987; children: Caesar Jr. **Educ:** Bishop Coll, BA, BTh, LLD, DD. **Career:** Good St Baptist Church Dallas, pastor; nationally known evangelist; National Baptist Convention USA Inc, vice pres at large; Baptist Missionary and Education Convention of Texas, pres. **Orgs:** Mem bd dir Nat Baptist Conventionnv; numerous other church & civic groups. **Honors/Awds:** Recipient of numerous citations & awards. **Business Addr:** 3110 Bonnie View Rd, Dallas, TX 75216.

CLARK, CHARLES WARFIELD

Physician, educator (retired). **Personal:** Born Dec 6, 1917, Washington, DC; married Savanna Marie Vaughn. **Educ:** Univ of MI, BS 1939; Howard Univ, MD 1944; internship Freedmen's Hospital 1944. **Career:** Sr attending urologist Howard Univ Hospital, Washington Hospital Center, Children's Natl Med Center Washington; Trinity Hospital, house physician 1944-46; Freedman's Hospital, chief resident urology 1952-53; Howard Univ School of Medicine, clinical instructor in Urology 1946-52, 1955-59, clinical asst prof of Urology. **Orgs:** Mid-Atlantic Section of Amer Urologic Assn; Amer Assn of Clinical Urologists; Amer Urologic Assn; National Med Assn; Medico-Chirurgical Soc of DC; Med Soc of DC; Amer Med Assn; Washington Urologic Soc; Soc Internationale d'Urologie; fellow Amer Coll of Surgeons; mem Sigma Pi Phi Fraternity Epsilon Boule; Amer Fertility Soc; Chi Delta Mu Fraternity; Friends of Kennedy Center; Mus of African Art; Pigskin Club of Washington; Smithsonian Assoc; Urban League; NAACP; YMCA; natl social dir Omega Psi Phi Frat; Plymouth Congregational Church; Washington Urology Association, president, 1984-85; life mem, 50 Year Club of American Medicine. **Honors/Awds:** Washington Hospital Center, W Dabney Jarman Teaching Award. **Special Achievements:** Author of three publications; National Museum of Women in the Arts, donor. **Military Serv:** AUS med corps capt 1953-55.

CLARK, CLARENCE BENDENSON, JR.

Dentist. **Personal:** Born Jun 15, 1943, Nashville, TN; son of Dr & Mrs C B Clark Sr; married Jeana; children: Clarence III, Dominick, Jessica. **Educ:** Loyola Univ, BS 1965; Meharry Med Coll, DDS 1974. **Career:** Private practice, dentist. **Orgs:** Mem MS Dental Soc, N MS Med, Dental, Pharm Soc. **Business Addr:** Harris County Dental Center, 1612 Fannin, Houston, TX 77004.

CLARK, CLAUDE LOCKHART

Artist, educator, businessman. **Personal:** Born Mar 28, 1945, Philadelphia, PA; son of Daima Mary Lockhart Clark and Claude Clark. **Educ:** CA Coll of Arts & Crafts, BA 1968; Univ of CA Berkeley, MA 1972. **Career:** House of Vai African Imports, owner 1977-; San Jose St Univ Afro-Am Studies Dept, instr crafts course 1974-; UC Berkeley Afro-Am Studies Dept, ''Black Art in the New World'' 1974, 1977; CA Coll of Arts & Crafts, instr 1970-; Coll of Alameda, instr 1971-72; Oakland HS, instr 1969-70; Univ of CA Berkeley, SOS upward bound prog; Craftsman, photography, painting, lithography, ceramics, jewelry, wood carving, murals; numerous one man & group shows since 1962; University of California, Berkeley, Berkeley, CA, 1974-80; San Jose University, 1974-80; California College of Arts & Crafts, 1970-80. **Orgs:** Mem, Smithsonian Inst 1980, World Print Council 1979; participant, 1st Natl African-Amer Crafts Conf & Jubilee Memphis 1979; mem, Music Publications of Amer 1947; Acts of art gallery NYC 1973; mem, Amer Federation of Arts 1976; catalogue exhibits Emanuel Walter & Atholl Mcbean Galleries San Francisco Art Inst 1976; Amistad II Afro-Amer art, Dept of Art, Fisk Univ, 1975-76; West Coast 1974 the Black Image, Eb Crocker Art Gallery 1974-75; A third world painting/sculpture exhibition San Francisco Museum of Art 1974; Tuesday Club Picture Rental Serv Sacramento 1972; catalogue exhibits Black Artist Huntsville AL 1979; Contemporary African-Am Crafts Exhibition Brooks Memorial Art Gallery Memphis 1979; mosaic exhibit Meml Union-Art Gallery UC Davis CA; freein' thespirit-the chin the black comxhibit. **Honors/Awds:** ''The Complete Annotated Resource Guide to Black Am Art'' 1978; included Numerous Private Collections 1971-; recipient 3rd prize Nat Ford Indus Arts Contest; 1st prize Oakland Art Museum's Exhibit for Public Schools; elected citizen of the day KABL Radio San Francisco; scholarship CA Coll of Arts & Crafts 1963. **Business Addr:** Owner, House of Vai, PO Box 8172, Oakland, CA 94662.

CLARK, DAVID EARL
Professional baseball player. **Personal:** Born Sep 3, 1962, Tupelo, MS. **Educ:** Jackson State. **Career:** Cleveland Indians, outfielder, 1986-89; Chicago Cubs, 1990; Kansas City Royals, 1991; Pittsburgh Pirates, 1992-96; Los Angeles Dodgers, 1996; Chicago Cubs, 1997; Houston Astros, 1998-. **Business Addr:** Professional Baseball Player, Houston Astros, PO Box 288, Houston, TX 77001-0288, (713)799-9500.

CLARK, DOUGLAS L.
Educator. **Personal:** Born May 2, 1935, Swedesboro, NJ; married Ellen; children: Douglas Jr, Dana Lynn. **Educ:** Glassboro State Tchrs Coll, BS 1956, MA 1970; Laurence U, PhD 1975. **Career:** Glassboro State Coll, dir educ opportunity program 1970-, asst dir 1968-70; NJ Rural Manpower Prog, educ specialist 1967-68; jr high school NJ, instructor 1956-67; Real Estate, licensed salesman 1963-. **Orgs:** Mem Mt Calvary Bapt Ch; Businessman Assn 1975-; NJ Dirs Assn EOF; mem NAACP; bd dirs UYA. **Business Addr:** La Spata House, Glassboro State Coll, Glassboro, NJ 08028.

CLARK, EDWARD
Artist. **Personal:** Born May 6, 1926, New Orleans, LA; son of Merion Clark and Edward Clark. **Educ:** Art Inst Chgo, 1947-51; L'Academie de la Grande Paris, 1947-52. **Career:** Univ of DE, Univ of OR, Art Inst Chgo, Showkegan School of Painting & Sculpture, OH State Univ, LA State Univ, vstg artist 1969-78; Syracuse Univesity, 1985; artist, currently. **Orgs:** Bd of dir Org of Independent Artist NY; bd of adv Cinque Gallery NY. **Honors/Awds:** Numerous exhibits & one-man shows Cont Arts Ctr New Orleans, NC A&T Univ, Randall Gallery NYC, Mus of Solidarity Titograd Yugoslavia, Art Salon NYC, LA State Univ, "Contemp Black Art" FL Intl Univ, Sullivant Gallery OH State Univ, James Yu Gallery NYC, Acad of Arts & Letters NYC, Whitney Mus NYC, Lehman Coll NYC, Afro-Amer Exhib Mus of Fine Arts Boston, Morgan State Coll, Mod Mus Tokyo, Stockholm, Nova Gall Boston, Amer Ctr Artists, Amer Embassy Paris, Gall Creuze Paris, Salon d'Automne Paris, num others 1952-; Adolph Grant 1981, Natl Endowment Grant 1982.

CLARK, EDWARD DEPRIEST, SR.
Educator. **Personal:** Born May 24, 1930, Wilmington, NC; son of Ethel Exum Clay and Junius Clark; married Evangeline Merritt (divorced 1961); children: Edward D Jr. **Educ:** North Carolina A&T State University, Greensboro, NC, BS, 1948; New York University, New York, NY, MA, 1955; Syracuse University, Syracuse, NY, PhD, 1971. **Career:** Union Point High School, Union Point, GA, English dept head, 1948-51; Greensboro High School, Greensboro, GA, English dept head, 1953-54; Emanuel County High School, Swainsboro, GA, English dept head, 1954-57; Albany State College, Albany, GA, asst prof, English, 1957-59; Southern University, Baton Rouge, LA, asst prof, English, 1960-61; Fayetteville State University, Fayetteville, NC, assoc prof, chairman, 1961-66, chairman, prof, English, 1971-75; North Carolina State University, Raleigh, NC, assoc prof, English, 1975-. **Orgs:** Member, College Language Assn, 1961-; member, Modern Language Assn, 1961-; member, South Atlanta Modeern Language Assn, 1975-. **Honors/Awds:** Outstanding Teacher Award, 1989, elected to Academy of Outstanding Teachers, 1989, North Carolina State University; Alumni Outstanding Teacher Award, North Carolina State University, 1989. **Military Serv:** US Army, Sgt, 1951-53; Outstanding Teaching Award, 1952, 1953. **Business Addr:** Professor, English, North Carolina State Univ, Raleigh, NC 27602.

CLARK, FRED ALLEN
Psychologist. **Personal:** Born Jul 8, 1929, Toledo, OH; son of Rose Clark and Idus Clark; divorced; children: Kevin, Kim. **Educ:** San Francisco State College, BA, 1967, MA, 1968; Wright Institute, PhD, psychology, 1971. **Career:** Counseling Clinics Inc, executive director, 1972-81; California Youth Authority, staff psychologist, 1982-89; private practice, psychologist, 1989-; National University, instructor; Clarico Enterprises, owner/ceo, currently. **Orgs:** American Psychological Association; California Association of Marriage Counselors. **Special Achievements:** Author: Teenage Gangs, 1993; All for Nothing, 1989; articles: Series on Teenage Gangs; Ebony Magazine, Sep 1992; Observer Newspaper, 1992; lecturer, "Teenage Gangs," Sierra Vista Hospital, 1991-92; Author, Teenage Street Gangs, 1996. **Business Addr:** Psychologist, PO Box 162550, Sacramento, CA 95816, (916)488-8068.

CLARK, GARY C.
Professional football player. **Personal:** Born May 1, 1962, Radford, VA. **Educ:** Attended, James Madison Univ. **Career:** Washington Redskins, wide receiver 1985-93; Phoenix Cardinals, 1993-. **Honors/Awds:** Team MVP sr yr coll; Coll Offensive Player of the Year in VA, James Madison Univ, 1983; Redskins Offensive Player of the Game against Cleveland, 1985; Redskins leading receiver four times with three 100 yd games; played in Pro Bowl, 1986, 1987.

CLARK, GRANVILLE E., SR.
Physician. **Personal:** Born Jun 14, 1927, Santiago, Cuba; married Mary; children: Granville Jr, Robert, Joseph, James. **Educ:** Institute DeSegunda Ensenanta De Santiago, BS 1947; Univ Havana, MD 1954. **Career:** Pvt Prac, physician 1959; Resd Gen Hosp, physician 1957-59; Norfolk Comm Hosp, physician 1955-57; Provident Hosp, intern 1954-55. **Orgs:** Mem SW Pediatric & Soc; KC Me Soc; Pan-MO State Med Soc; NMA; Jackson Co Med Soc; MO Med Assn; Cncl Selection Med Sch; bd mem Lead Poison Prgm; KC Sickle Cell Anemia; past mem Mid-Am Comprehensive Hlth Planning Agy; chmn Med Exec Com Martin Luther King Hosp; pediatrician consult KCMC DayCare Ctr; adv bd Douglas State Bank; pres Metro-Metic Clinic; life mem NAACP; mem YMCA; Grtr KC Boys Club. **Honors/Awds:** Num awards & recognitions. **Business Addr:** 3718 Prospect, Kansas City, MO 64128.

CLARK, HARRY W.
Physician, educator. **Personal:** Born Sep 6, 1946, Detroit, MI. **Educ:** Wayne State U, BA 1969; Univ of MI Med Sch, MD 1973; Univ of MI Sch of Public Hlth, MPH 1974. **Career:** Exec asst Div of Mental Hlth Serv Prgms, Comm Mental Hlth Serv, Nat Inst of Mental Hlth; Psychiatrist. **Business Addr:** Room 11 C 23 Parklawn Bldg, 5600 Fisher's Ln, Rockville, MD 20852.

CLARK, IRMA
Educational administrator. **Career:** Wayne County, MI, Wayne County Human Relations Division, director; Detroit School Board, pres, currently. **Orgs:** NAACP, life member; God Land Unity Church, vice president of the board of directors; Michigan Democratic Party; Travelers Aid Society; March of Dimes; Detroit Goodfellows; Civic Center Optimist Club; TULC; United Way Community Services, vice co-chair Detroit Public Schools. **Honors/Awds:** Adelita Award, MANA de Michigan; the Spirit of Detroit Award, City of Detroit; Distinguished Service Award, Wayne County Clerk; State of Michigan Executive Declaration Award. **Business Addr:** President, Detroit School Board, 5057 Woodward, Detroit, MI 48202, (313)494-1000.

CLARK, JAMES IRVING, JR.
Manager, clergyman. **Personal:** Born Apr 18, 1936, Paterson, NJ; married Shirley Lorraine Matthews; children: James I III, Renee Therese, Rhonda Ellise. **Educ:** Am Divinity Sch, BTH 1966; Baruch Coll, 1966-68; Columbia U, MBA 1973. **Career:** Pfizer Diagnostics, mgr training & devel 1978, mgr professional placement 1975-78, personnel rela mgr 1973-75; New Era Learning Corp, exec vice pres 1969 -71; Slant/Fin Corp, asst ind rela mgr 1962-69; Christ Temple Ch, pastor 1969; Ch of Christ Bible Inst, acting dean 1971. **Orgs:** Pres vice pres 1st black pres pro tem Grad Bus Assn Columbia Univ Grad Sch of Bus 1971-73; COGME Fellowship Columbia Univ 1971. **Honors/Awds:** Serv award Columbia Univ Grad Sch of Bus 1973; black achiever award Pfizer In & YMCA NY 1974. **Military Serv:** USAF a/2c served 3 1/2 years. **Business Addr:** Pfizer Diagnostics, 235 E 42nd St, New York, NY 10017.

CLARK, JAMES N.
Dentist, consultant. **Personal:** Born Sep 16, 1934, Brooklyn, NY; son of Augusta Neale Clark and Luther Clark; married Patricia; children: Melissa, Holly, James II. **Educ:** CCNY, BS 1956; Columbia Univ, DDS 1964; Acad of Gen Dentistry, FAGD (Hon) 1974; AM Coll of Dentists, FACD (Hon) 1980-. **Career:** ITT, dental dir 1965-69; Private practice, dentist; World Wide ITT, dental consult 1969-90. **Orgs:** Mem NAACP, Omega Psi Phi 1955-; sec Commonwelath Dental Assoc 1969; Newark Beth Israel Hosp Attendant 1969; Civil Defense 1972-79; pres Amer Assoc of Indust Dentists 1973; co-chmn United Way 1973; sec Central Pkwy Assoc 1974; mem 100 Black Men 1975; Life mem Omega Psi Phi 1976; pres Ad Hoc Comm Orange Central YMCA 1976-80; sec 100 Black Men 1980; fellow Amer Coll of Dentists 1980-; bd of trustees Rampo Coll 1982-93; pres, UMDNJ Dental Assting Advisory Bd 1986-90; chairman, board of trustees, Ramapo College 1988-; vice pres, external affair, 100 Black Men, Inc. 1988-94; treasurer, Columbia Univ Alumni Assn, 1986-92; Ramapo Coll, bd of governors, 1993-; Essex County Vincinage Committee, Minority Concerns Judicial, 1994-; NJ Corrections Dept, advisory council, 1994; Hosp Ctr of Orange, Dental assoc attendant, 1988-. **Honors/Awds:** John Hay Whitney Fellowship 1963; Smith & Noyes Scholarship 1960, 1964; Gold Foil Awd 1st Prize Dental Student Exhibit; Superstar Awd YMCA 1979; Centennial Comm of Orange Award, 1989; Minority Achievement Award, Ramapo College, 1990. **Military Serv:** US Army, private. **Business Addr:** Dentist, 185 Central Ave Suite 301, East Orange, NJ 07018, (201)672-1717.

CLARK, JERALD DWAYNE
Professional baseball player. **Personal:** Born Aug 10, 1963, Crockett, TX. **Educ:** Lamar Univ, 1981-85. **Career:** Colorado Rockies, 1992-. **Orgs:** Microsoft Certified Professionals.

CLARK, JESSE B., III
Director. **Personal:** Born Feb 12, 1925, Philadelphia, PA; married Lucille Field; children: Bruce, Kevin, Blair, Cynthia. **Educ:** PA State Univ, BA 1950; Grad Work Univ of PA, 1951-52. **Career:** Urban League, dir vocaliors 1954-59; Campbell Soct Co, persnl speclst 1959-62; Abbotts Dairies, dir pblc rltns 1962-1964. **Orgs:** Pres & board chrmn St Edmonds Home for Children 1983-; trustee St Charles Seminary Archdiocece of Philadelphia 1984, Mercy Catholic Medical Cntr 1974-; past pres Serra Club of Philadelphia 1972; tres Catholic Soc Serv Board 1974-; trustee Villanora Univ Villanora PA 1974-84; commissioner Charter Revision Commn Philadelphia 1976; board mem Natl Catholic Stwrdshp Cncl 1983-; bd mem Institutions for Mentally Retarded 1985-; sec Natl Adv Comm US Conference of Bishops 1987. **Honors/Awds:** Knight of the Order Saint Gregory the Great 1977; Commandor Knight of the Order Saint Gregory the Great 1986. **Military Serv:** USNA s/sgt. **Business Addr:** Dir of Development, Archdiocese of Philadelphia, Rm 1100 222 N 17th St, Philadelphia, PA 19103.

CLARK, JOE LOUIS
Educator, educational administrator. **Personal:** Born May 7, 1939, Rochelle, GA; son of Maggie Majors Clark and Rhomie Clark; married; children: Joetta, Joe Jr, Hazel. **Educ:** William Paterson College, BA, 1960; Seton Hall University, MA, 1974. **Career:** Board of Education, Paterson NJ, teacher, 1960-74, coordinator of language arts, 1976-79, elementary school principal, 1979-82, secondary school principal, 1983-90; Essex County Juvenile Detention Ctr, Newark, NJ, director, division of youth svcs, currently; Keppler Associates, lecturer, currently. **Orgs:** Natl Assn of Secondary School Principals; NAACP; New Jersey Principals & Administrators Assn; Paterson Principals Assn. **Honors/Awds:** NAACP Paterson Chapter, Community Service Award, 1983; New Jerseyan of the Year, Newark Star Ledger, 1983; New Jersey Monthly magazine, Outstanding Educator, 1984; Seton Hall University, Distinguished Alumnus Award, 1985; Fairleigh Dickinson University, Distinguished Service Award, 1985; honored at presidential conference on academic and displinary excllence at White House, 1985; Natl School Safety Center, Principal of Leadership Award, 1986; Natl Black Policemen's Assn, Humanitarian Award, 1988; 60 Minute Profile; Presidential Citations. **Special Achievements:** Dramatized version of his struggle in ridding Eastside High School of violence and drugs depicted in major motion picture, Lean On Me, 1989; Book: Laying Down The Law; Time Cover, Feb 1988; 60 Minute Profile; Presidential Citations. **Military Serv:** US Army Reserves, e5, 1958-66. **Business Addr:** Director, Division of Youth Svcs, Essex County Juvenile Detention Ctr, 208 Sussex Ave, Newark, NJ 07103.

CLARK, JOHN JOSEPH
Business manager. **Personal:** Born Jun 26, 1954, Pittsburgh, PA; son of Anna Bluett Clark and John L Clark; married C Lynne Clark, Jun 24, 1989. **Educ:** Northeastern Univ Boston, BS, BA 1977; Univ of Chicago, MBA 1985. **Career:** Arthur Andersen & Co, auditor 1977-80; Bell & Howell, sr auditor 1980-81; Baxter Travenol Labs, mktg mgr 1981-86; Clark & Associates, pres 1986-, professor, Community College of Allegheny County 1992-97. **Orgs:** School coord Chicago Assoc of Commerce & Industry Youth Motivation Program 1977-; mem 1978-86, treas 1980 Natl Assoc of Black Accountants; mem Natl Black MBA Assoc 1985-96; bd mem Hollywood Tower Condo Assoc 1986-88; mem Greater Pittsburgh Chamber of Commerce 1987, Pittsburgh Regional Minority Purchasing Cncl 1996; mem Alumni Assocs, Chicago Council Foreign Relations; commission mem PACE 1990-93; co-chair Allegheny County MBE Advisory Committee 1990-92, board of directors, Garfield Jubilee Association 1991-95, board of directors, East Liberty Development, Inc., 1993-95; American Mktg Association, Pittsburgh Chap, vice pres of communications. **Honors/Awds:** Beta Alpha Psi 1975-77; drafted by Boston Celtics in Natl Basketball Assoc 1976; Outstanding Young Men of Amer 1985; Certificate of Appreciation Chicago Assoc of Commerce 1986; inducted into Northeastern University Athletic Hall of Fame 1987. **Business Addr:** President, Clark Market Research, 5933 Baum Blvd, Pittsburgh, PA 15206.

CLARK, KENNETH BANCROFT
Business executive. **Personal:** Born Jul 24, 1914; son of Kate Florence and Harold Hilton; widowed; children: Kate Miriam Harris, Hilton Bancroft. **Educ:** Howard Univ, AB 1935; Howard Univ, MS 1936; Columbia Univ, PhD Psychology 1940. **Career:** Pyschology Emeritus City Clg, distinguished prof 1942-75; Columbia Univ, visiting prof; Univ Of CA, Berkeley, visiting prof; Harvard Univ, Cambridge, visiting prof; Kenneth B Clark & Associates, president, currently. **Orgs:** Fndr/dir Northside Center for Child Devel 1946-; fndr/pres Metropolitan Applied Research Ctr 1967-75; mem NY State Board of Regents 1966-86; trustee Chicago Univ; mem Phi Beta Kappa, Sigma Xi; past pres Amer Psychological Assn, 1970-71; Soc for Psychological Studies of Social Issues, 1959-60; Metro Applied Rsch Ctr, 1967-75; trustee Woodrow Wilson Intl Ctr for Scholars; fndr Harlem Youth Oppor Unlimited, 1964-66. **Honors/Awds:** Spingarn Medal 1961; Kurt Lewin Memorial Award 1965; Disting Professor of Psychology City College 1971; honorary degrees several colleges & univ 1980; Sidney Hilman Award Dark Getto 1965. **Special Achievements:** Author, "Prejudice and Your Child," 1963; "Dark Getto," 1965; "A Possible Reality," 1972; "Pathos of Power," 1974. **Business Phone:** (914)478-1010.

CLARK, LARON JEFFERSON, JR.
Educational administrator. **Personal:** Born Dec 6, 1938, Atlanta, GA; son of Doshia Mary Alice Blasingame Clark and Laron Jefferson Clark, Sr; married Mary Ellen Smith; children: Laron III, Jeremy, Allison. **Educ:** Morehouse Coll, AB 1961; Atlanta Univ, MS 1965; Univ of Tulsa, 1968. **Career:** Langton Univ, dir of devel 1968-71; Atlanta Univ, exec dir, univ relations & devel 1971-75; Hampton Univ, vice pres for devel 1975-. **Orgs:** Adult serv librarian Brooklyn Public Library 1961-63; suprv branch librarian Queensborough Public Library 1963-66; chief librarian, Library Sci Dept chm, and assoc prof Langston Univ 1966-68; trustees Hampton Rd Acad 1978-; mem Kiwanis Club 1979-, Tidewater Longshoremen Scholarship Cmte 1982-, Soc of Fund Raisers 1980-; mem bd of dirs Cultural Alliance of Greater Hampton Roads 1985-; secretary/board of directors, Cultural Alliance of Greater Hampton Roads; member, Fund Raising Committee, Virginia Air and Space Center Museum; treasurer, Cultural Alliance of Greater Hampton Roads, 1990-. **Honors/Awds:** Acad Scholarship Morehouse Coll 1956; Fellowship Univ of Tulsa 1968. **Home Addr:** 94 E College Place, Hampton, VA 23669.

CLARK, LAWANNA GIBBS
Government official. **Personal:** Born Feb 5, 1941, Calvert, TX; daughter of Mildred Bunns and Wilbert Gibbs; divorced. **Educ:** Attended, Texas Southern Univ 1958-59, Univ of NV 1959-60 1972, Nevada College of Commerce 1961; ofc of Personnel Management Executive Semninar Center. **Career:** Energy Rsch & Devel Admin, exec asst to mgr 1975-77; Dept of Energy, exec asst to asst sec 1977-79, exec asst to under sec 1979-81, staff asst to sec 1981-85, special asst to mgr and eeo program mgr 1985-88; Equal Employment Specialist 1988-. **Orgs:** Leadership Las Vegas Chamber of Commerce 1986-87; life mem NAACP, Natl Council of Negro Women; mem Metropolitan Baptist Church, Washington, DC. **Honors/Awds:** Special Citation for Outstanding Performance Dept of Energy 1981; Monetary Awd for Spec Act or Service Dept of Energy 1981; Certificate of Appreciation Dept of Energy 1985; Monetary Awd for Superior Performance Dept of Energy 1986; Good Service Awd Second Baptist Church 1986; Monetary Award for Superior Service, 1987, Dept of Energy; Quality Step Increase, Dept of Energy, 1988. **Business Addr:** Equal Opportunity Specialist, US Dept of Energy, 1000 Independence Ave SW, Rm 4B-112, Washington, DC 20585.

CLARK, LAWRENCE M., SR.
Educator, educational administrator. **Personal:** Born Apr 4, 1934, Danville, VA; son of Ida Bell Clark and Lawrence U Clark; married Irene Reynolds Clark, Aug 20, 1960; children: Deborah, Linda, Lawrence Jr, Shelia. **Educ:** Virginia State University, Petersburg, VA, BS, 1960; University of Virginia, Charlottesville, VA, MS, 1964, EdD, 1967. **Career:** Norfolk State Univ, Norfolk, VA, assoc professor of mathematics, 1969-70; Florida State Univ, Tallahassee, Fl, associate professor of mathematics, 1970-74; North Carolina State Univ, Raleigh, NC, associate provost/prof, math ed, 1974-. **Honors/Awds:** Kappa Mu Epsilon, Mathematics Honorary Soc, 1959; Phi Delta Kappa, 1965; American Council on Ed, Administrative Fellow, 1976-77; Phi Kappa Phi, North Carolina State Univ, 1977; Alpha Phi Alpha Fraternity. **Military Serv:** Army, Corporal, 1954-56. **Business Addr:** Associate Provost, Provost's Office, North Carolina State University, 208 Holladay Hall, Box 7101, Raleigh, NC 27606.

CLARK, LEON HENRY
Airline pilot. **Personal:** Born Aug 8, 1941, Hallandale, FL; married Pearlie; children: Tangela, Robbie. **Educ:** TN State A&I U, BS 1965. **Career:** Substitute school teacher, 1970-71; Delta Airlines, flight engr, co-pilot, captain, currently. **Orgs:** FL State, dir; Negro Airmens International; Black Airline Pilots Assn; Broward Co Affirmitive Action Coalition. **Military Serv:** US Navy, lt jg, 1966-69; US Army, instructor, 1971-72; Vietnam Service Medal. **Business Addr:** Co-Pilot, Delta Airlines, Miami International Airport, Miami, FL 33055.

CLARK, LEON STANLEY
Educator, government official. **Personal:** Born Mar 31, 1930, Bunkie, LA; son of Leola Dodson and Daniel Clark; married Ernestine Mack, Nov 11, 1913; children: Mary D, Leon S Clark Jr. **Educ:** Southern University, Baton Rouge, LA, BS, 1959, MEd 1966, Certificate in Supervision and Administration, 1970. **Career:** Avoyelles Parish School, Marksville, LA, teacher, 1959-69; Avoyelles Parish School, Alexendria, LA, teacher, 1969-70; Saginaw Schools, Saginaw, MI, teacher, 1970-83; Saginaw County Juven, Sagniaw, MI, unit supvr, 1970-74; Buena Vista Charter Township, supervisor, Currently. **Honors/Awds:** Outstanding Award for services rendered in community as Cub Scout master, 1976; Booker T Washington Certificate for Outstanding Service, 1987; Outstanding Services Award, Buena Vista Men's Club, 1984; Appreciation for Continued Service, Buena Vista Parks & Rec, 1990. **Military Serv:** Army, Pfc, 1950-54; Received: KSM, UN, SM, NDSM, GCM Awards. **Business Addr:** Supervisor, Buena Vista Charter Township, 1160 S Outer Dr, Saginaw, MI 48601.

CLARK, LEONARD WESLORN, JR.
Attorney. **Personal:** Born Oct 8, 1942, Lawrence, KS; son of Letha Posten Clark (deceased) and Leonard Weslorn Clark, Sr (deceased); married Leatha Johnson Clark, Jan 21, 1967; children: Teresa Lynne, Mary Elizabeth, John Weslorn, Laura Anne. **Educ:** Wichita State University, Wichita, KS, BA, education, 1960-65; The University of Kansas, Lawrence, KS, JD, 1969-73. **Career:** National Labor Relations Board, Kansas City, KS, field attorney, 1973-78; Catt & Prater, Lawrence, KS, attorney, 1978-80; District Attorney, 7th Judicial District, Lawrence, KS, deputy district attorney, 1979-80; Commerce Bank of Kansas City, Kansas City, MO, corporate trust administrator, 1980; US Dept of Housing and Urban Development, Kansas City, MO, systemic branch chief/legal analyst, 1980-82; Hall & Evans, Denver, CO, attorney, 1982-84; State of Colorado, State Personnel Board, Denver, CO, hearing officer, 1984; self-employed attorney, 1985; US Dept of Energy, Western Area Power Authority, Golden, CO, equal employment specialist, 1985; US EEOC, Denver, CO, supervisory equal opportunity specialist, 1985; State of Kansas, Topeka, KS, director, state office of EEO, 1985-88; Hillsborh County, Tampa, FL, director of equal opportunity and human relations dept, 1988-89; Kentucky Commission on Human Rights, Louisville, KY, executive director, 1989-. **Orgs:** African-American Arts Consortium of Kentucky; secretary-treasurer and member, Lawrence Human Relations Commission, 1966-69; board of directors, Lawrence United Fund, 1968-69; board of directors, 1968-78, president, 1976-77, Achievement Place; member and board of governors, Lawrence Memorial Hospital Endowment Assn, 1971-73; board of directors/member, Kansas University Memorial Union Corporation, 1979-82. **Honors/Awds:** Kentucky Colonel; Martin Luther King Jr. Equality Award, 1991.

CLARK, LEROY D.
Union executive. **Personal:** Born Nov 19, 1917, Canal Zone, Panama; married Alzada Bradley; children: Leroy Jr. **Career:** So Region United Furn Workers of Am, AFL-CIO, vice pres 1970-; Intl Rep Chicago & Southern Reg 1957-70; Local Union Organizer NY, 1940-41; Factory Worker NY, 1937-40. **Orgs:** Mem Am Negro Labor Council; mem Memphis Chap A Philip Randolph Inst; mem Coalition of Black Trade Unionists; vice pres TN State Labor Council AFL-CIO; presMemphis Br NAACP 1969-72; Shelby County Dem Club 1964-73; Shelby Co Dem Voters Council 1973; Shelby United Neighbors 1970. **Military Serv:** AUS sgt 1941-45. **Business Addr:** Ste 132, 2881 Lamar, Memphis, TN 38114.

CLARK, LOUIS JAMES
Manager. **Personal:** Born Apr 28, 1940, Camden, SC; married Beverly Jean Smith; children: Marcia, Louis, Christopher. **Educ:** Wayne State U, BS 1973; IA State Univ Engring, 1973; Univ of MI Bus Admin 1979-. **Career:** MI Bell, dist eng mgr 1978-, design engr 1977-78, methods engr 1975-77, supervising engr 1973-, area engr 1973-74. **Orgs:** Mem Engineering Soc of Detroit 1975; contributor of articles Nat Electric Inst 1975; mem bd of dir Detroit Alumni & No Province of Kappa Alpha Psi 1975-; pres sch bd Presentation Sch 1975-. **Honors/Awds:** Service award No Providence Kappa Alpha Psi 1979; Vietnam Service & Combat Award 1966. **Military Serv:** AUS e-4 1964-66. **Business Addr:** Michigan Bell Telephone Co, 100 S Gratiot, Mount Clemens, MI 48043.

CLARK, MAJOR
Military officer (retired), historian. **Personal:** Born Dec 7, 1917, Headland, AL; son of Marcus Elijah Clark and Elizabeth Bailey; widowed; children: William Marcus, Vivian Noreen, Gregory Lewis. **Educ:** Ft Sill OK, Field Artillery School, Officer Candidate Course 1942, Artillery Officer Adv Course 1953-54; Ft Leavenworth KS, Command & Gen Staff Coll, Assoc Command & Gen Staff Officer Course 1955, Spec Weapons Course 1956, Sr Officers Nuclear Weapons Employment Course 1958. **Career:** Battery commander, batallion intelligence officer, unit historian, 597 FABN, 1942-45; asst PMS&T, Hampton Inst VA, 1947-51; Korea, sr artillery advisor 3d ROK div, Korea, 1951-52; army gen staff officer, Dept Chief of Staff Military Oper Pentagon, 1956-60; McDonnell Douglas Tulsa, 1962-79. **Orgs:** Mem, Retired Officers Assn, 92nd Infantry World War II Assn, 1982-91, Oklahoma Historical Society. **Honors/Awds:** Inducted into Field Artillery OCS Hall of Fame Ft Sill OK 1980; Spurgeon H Burris Award, 92nd Infantry Div World War II Assn 1987; Special Veteran's Recognition Award, Oklahoma Historical Society 1988; author Black Military History Material. **Special Achievements:** Researcher and consultant, video documentary, "African Americans in World War II: A Legacy of Patriotism and Valor.". **Military Serv:** AUS pvt to lt col 1940-60; Bronze Star Medal & Cross for Merit of War Italy 1945; Oak Leaf Cluster-Bronze Star 1952; Chungmu Medal with Gold Star & ROK Presidential Unit Citation Korea 1952; Army Commendation Medal 1960. **Home Addr:** 503 E 27 Pl N, Tulsa, OK 74106.

CLARK, MARIO SEAN
Business executive. **Personal:** Born Mar 29, 1954, Pasadena, CA; son of Lois Prince Clark and Oscar Clark; married Lisa Clark Adkins; children: Taylor Alexander Clark. **Educ:** Univ of Oregon, interior design, 1972-76. **Career:** Buffalo Bills, San Francisco 49ers, Defensive Back; owner Elegant Pillow Upholstery; Community Outreach Coord, currently. **Orgs:** Bd mem, George Steuart Memory Football Camp, 1985; consultant, Boys Club of Pasadena 1985; counselor of disadvantaged youth, Pride; community outreach coordinator for the Rose Bowl. **Honors/Awds:** All-rookie team Buffalo Bills 1976; super bowl winner San Francisco 49ers 1985; Certificate of Appreciation, Pasadena Police Department; Pasadena High School Hall of Fame, 1996. **Business Addr:** Community Outreach Coordinator, 1001 Rosebowl Dr, Pasadena, CA 91103, (818)577-3176.

CLARK, MILDRED E.
Educator. **Personal:** Born Dec 16, 1936, Columbus, GA; married Henry L; children: Henry L, Kenneth. **Educ:** Univ of Toledo, Master of Educ, 1982, BA, 1963; Davis Business Coll, Computer Programming, 1981; Elsa Cooper School, Detroit, MI, Court Reporting, 1960; Wayne State Univ, Detroit, MI, Adult Educ Training, 1958; Lane Coll, Jackson, TN, Liberal Arts, 1957; Jesup W Scott High School, 1954. **Career:** Toledo, legal sec 1958-59; Realty Co, sec 1960-61; Rossford Ordinance, clerk typist 1961-63; Eli B Williams Sch, educator 1963-65; Anna Pickett Elementary Sch, educator 1963-; Toledo Public School System, 1963-93, adult educ classes, 1982, grad assist, 1965-67, adult night classes, instructor; Martin Luther King Jr Elementary School, 1983; WNGT-TV, channel 48, co-owner, 1996-; Ghana's Academies & Cul Arts Academy, Founder & Admin, 1997. **Orgs:** Founder Ghanited Neighborhood Org 1970-; Toledo Fed of Teachers 1973; The Black Caucus of Toledo Teachers; Frederick Douglass Comm Assn NAACP; mem Toledo Educ Assn 1965-72; Black African Peoples Assn; Black Historical Soc; Sec PTA; chmn Human Relations Bd Toledo Educ Assn, 1966-67, 1973; building rep, Toledo Federation of Teachers, 1983. **Honors/Awds:** Outstanding serv Doer's Awd Toledo Educ Assoc. **Special Achievements:** Developed career unit for students' enrichment; produced and directed TV program for elem students, "The Beat Goes On," channel 30, WGTE-TV, 1970; initiated, produced First Annual Black History Quiz Bowl for elem students, Toledo, channel 13, WTVG-TV, 1977; Office of Minority Affairs, organized, prepared job opportunity announcements in the Collegiate newspaper, Univ of Toledo, 1982; founder, Honor Society to honor Dr Martin Luther King Jr, (Martin Luther King, Jr School - "King's Honor Society"), 1983-; organized city-wide "King's Oratorical" contest: a celebration of Dr King's birthday and holiday, 1984-; organized and developed NUBIA's, (New Union of Blacks to Improve America), after school tutorial program, 1978; founded and organized The "Ghanaian" Foundation, 1993-; programming and the perfecting of talent abilities, exposure for young talent in the Arts and Academics, 1982; Ex Producer & Dir of "Step Up Toledo", tv program, 1996. **Business Addr:** Ghanashia, 11 South Centennial, Holland, OH 43528.

CLARK, MORRIS SHANDELL
Surgeon. **Personal:** Born Nov 27, 1945, Princeton, WV; son of Clarie Clark and Willie R Clark Sr; married Maureen Pamela Mercier; children: Gregory Morris, Angela Maureen. **Educ:** WV State Coll, BS 1967; Univ of CA, San Francisco, BDS 1973, DDS 1973. **Career:** Oral and maxillo, facial prog, Columbia Univ, 1976, internship & residency 1976; asst prof, Univ of Medicine & Dentistry, asst prof oral & maxillofacial surgery 1976-81; Univ of CO School of Dentistry, assoc prof of otolaryngology, assoc prof oral & maxillofacial; Univ of CO School of Medicine, dir of anesthesia 1982-. **Orgs:** Fellow Amer Soc of Oral and Maxillofacial Surgery, Amer Soc of Dental Anesthesiology, Intl Soc of Oral and Maxillofacial Surgery; pres, Amer Assn for the Advancement of Anesthesia in Dentistry 1991-93; bd of dirs, National Foundation for Child Abuse and Neglect; bd of dirs, Make-A-Wish-Foundation. **Honors/Awds:** Excellence in Teaching Awd 1981; Fellow Amer Coll of Dentists 1986; over 50 publications in medical & dental literature; 2 books; 15 major research projects; spoken and lectured throughout the world. **Home Addr:** 17 Cherry Hills Farm Drive, Englewood, CO 80110, (303)761-3779. **Business Addr:** Assoc Prof/Dir of Anesthesia, Univ of Colorado Health Sciences Ctr, 4200 E 9th Ave, Box C-284, Denver, CO 80262.

CLARK, PATRICIA ANN
Research librarian. **Personal:** Born May 12, 1951, Philadelphia, PA; daughter of Rosalie Maynor Clark and George Clark. **Educ:** Barnard College, BA, 1972; Columbia University, School of Library Services, MLS, 1974. **Career:** Columbia University, reference librarian, 1974-76; Time Warner Inc, research librarian, 1976-92, The Research Center, Time Inc, mgr central research group, 1992-. **Orgs:** Special Libraries Association, 1990-. **Business Addr:** Head Research Librarian, Time Warner Inc, 1271 Ave of the Americas, Time-life Bldg, Rm 2613-B, New York, NY 10020-1393.

CLARK, PATRICK. See Obituaries section.

CLARK, RANDOLPH A.
Architect. **Personal:** Born Nov 25, 1939, Marshall, TX; married Mae A Wesley; children: Dawn, Randalyn. **Educ:** Prairie View A&M U, BS 1961. **Career:** Randolph A Clark & Asso Architects, owner 1973-; Hex Learning Ctr Urban Six Prtnship, owner; Gen Serv Adminstrn, architect 1963-73. **Orgs:** Mem AIA Nat Orgn of Minority Architects Rotary Intl Ft & Worth C of C; mem Alpha Phi Alpha Inc; bd dir Hex Learning Center. **Military Serv:** AUS capt 1963. **Business Addr:** 3113 S Univ Dr, Fort Worth, TX.

CLARK, RICO
Professional football player. **Personal:** Born Jun 6, 1974. **Educ:** Louisville. **Career:** Indianapolis Colts, defensive back, 1997-. **Business Addr:** Professional Football Player, Indianapolis Colts, PO Box 535000, Indianapolis, IN 46253, (317)297-2653.

CLARK, ROBERT G.
State representative. **Personal:** Born Oct 3, 1929, Ebenezer, MS; son of Julian Williams Clark and Robert Fletcher Clark; married Essie B Austin, 1970 (deceased); children: Robert George III, Bryant Wandrick. **Educ:** Jackson State Coll, BS, 1953; Mississippi Valley State; Michigan State Univ, MA, 1959; Florida A&M Univ, 1960; Western Michigan Univ, 1965. **Career:** State of Mississippi, Holmes & Vazoo Counties, Dist 49, representative 1968-; House of Clark Furniture Store, currently. **Orgs:** Founder & bd mem Central MS Inc of Comm Action Progs; mem Intl Bd of Basketball Officials; past pres Central MS Bd of Athletic Officials; fellow Inst of Politics John F Kennedy School of Govt Harvard Univ 1979; dem party nominee Congressional Seat 1982, 1984; past pres Fine Housing Enterprises; chmn ed comm House of Reps; mem appropriations comm House of Reps; sec rules comm House of Reps; pres bd of trustees Childrens Ctr of Lexington; mem Natl Coalition of Advocates for Students; mem Dem Natl Comm Voter Participation Task Force; co-chmn MS Del So Reg Council; pres, Holmes Co Teachers Assn, 1969-. **Honors/Awds:** Alumnus of the Year, Jackson State College, 1968; Outstanding Service & Inspiration to Humanity Award; Distinguished Alumni, National Assn Equal Opportunity in Higher Education, 1982. **Business Addr:** Representative, State of Mississippi Dist 47, Box 179, Lexington, MS 39095.

CLARK, ROSALIND K.
Singer, actress. **Personal:** Born Nov 16, 1943, Dallas, TX. **Educ:** TX So U, BMus 1965. **Career:** Las Vegas Hilton, nightclub performer; Playboy Club, nightclub performer; Jackson's Penthouse, nightclub performer; After Dark, nightclub performer; Studio One, nightclub Performer; The Tonight Show, Guest; Merv Griffin, Guest; Dinah, Guest; Paul Lynde, Toured. **Orgs:** Vp Celebration Soc Inc 1970-74; Alpha Kappa Alpha Sor. **Honors/Awds:** Entertainment hall of fame awards The Wiz, Hair, Two Worlds & It's About Time. **Business Addr:** c/o Actors Equity, 165 West 46th St, Attn: Jackie Veglie, New York, NY 10036.

CLARK, ROSLYN M.
Law enforcement. **Personal:** Born Dec 4, 1950, Miami, FL; daughter of Augusta Glass & Robert McGruder; married Edgar E Clark, Jul 30, 1989; children: Keenan Xavier Clark. **Educ:** Miami-Dade Junior College, AA, 1970; Florida Atlantic University, BA, 1972, MA, 1972-74; Biscayne College, MS, 1980. **Career:** Boca Raton Police Dept, police off, 1971-73; Dade Cty Public Safety Dept, police off, 1973-81; Florida Dept of Law Enforcement, proj dir/special agent, 1981-82; Metro-Dade Police Dept, police off, sergeant, police commander, lieutenant, captain, police bureau commander, 1982-. **Orgs:** Intl Assn of Women Police, mem, 1991-; Natl Organization of Black Law Enforcement Executives, local, 1991-, national, 1997-; Police Benevolent Assn, mem, 1982-; Progressive Officers Club, mem, 1983-; Florida Sex Crimes Investigators Assn, Inc, mem, 1996; S Florida Police Inst Alumni Assn, 1996-. **Honors/Awds:** Dade Cty Manager's Off, Special Recognition Merit, 1984; Dade Cty HUD, Arthur Mays Villas-Ladies of Distinction, 1992; African-American Women Leadership Certificate, N Miami Elementary, 1996; The Progressive Officers Club, Historic Achievement Award, 1997. **Special Achievements:** First Female Officer, City of Boca Raton, FL, 1971; Highest Ranking African-American Women, Metro-Dade Police, 1995; While still holding the appointed rank of Police Bureau Commander, became the first African-American Female Police Captain in the history of the Metro-Dade Police Department. **Business Addr:** Police Bureau Commander, Metro-Dade Police Department-Sexual Crimes Bureau, 7955 NW 12 St, ITT Bldg, Ste 321, Miami, FL 33126, (305)477-1112.

CLARK, SANZA BARBARA
Educator. **Personal:** Born Jul 3, 1940, Cleveland, OH; daughter of Gladys Sanders Davis and Dewell Davis; divorced; children: Msia. **Educ:** Kent State Univ, BA 1967; Duquesne Univ, MA 1970; Howard Univ, CAS 1980; Univ of IL, PhD 1985. **Career:** Univ of Pittsburgh, Swahili instructor 1969-72; Tanzanian Min of Natl Educ, educ officer IIA 1972-78; University of Illinois, statistical consultant, 1980-83; OH State Univ, Swahili instructor 1983-84; Cleveland State Univ, assoc prof educ/rsch 1985-. **Orgs:** Pres Orchard Family Housing Council 1981-83; pres Parents for Quality Educ 1986-87; chmn, Mali Yetu Alternative Educ School 1988-; trustee, Center for Human Services, 1989-91. **Honors/Awds:** Mem Phi Delta Kappa Professional Soc; mem Phi Kappa Phi Honor Soc; Guide-Formulas-Hypothesis Testing Univ of IL 1982; Effects-Parental Educ & Sch on Ach Univ of IL 1985; Ed Refugees in Tanzania Comp & Intl Educ Soc 1986; Honoree, Outstanding African-American Women, 1996; Queen Mother Award, Excellence in Service & Community, 1996. **Special Achievements:** "African-American Research," The State of Black Cleveland, 1989; "Persistence Patterns of African-American College Students," Readings on the State of Education in Urban America, 1991; "An Analysis of African-American First Year College Student Attitudes & Attrition Rates," Journal of Urban Education, 1992; "The Great Migration," Mali Yetu, 1993; "The Schooling of Cultural and Ethnic Subordinate Groups," Comparative Education Review, 1993; "Rediscovering Our Roots in Ghana, Africa," Mali Yetu, 1995. **Business Addr:** Assoc Prof of Education/Research, Cleveland State Univ, Dept Curr & Fds, 1451 Rhodes Tower, Cleveland, OH 44115.

CLARK, SAVANNA M. VAUGHN
Educator. **Personal:** Born Mar 10, Hutchinson, KS; daughter of Helen Vermal Grice Vaughn and Charles Theola Vaughn; married Charles Warfield Clark. **Educ:** Prairie View A&M Univ, Prairie View TX, BS, 1949; Univ of Oklahoma, Norman OK, MEd; Oklahoma State Univ, Stillwater OK, postgraduate and doctoral studies. **Career:** Southern Univ, Baton Rouge LA, instructor, 1954-60; Ponca City Public Schools, Ponca City OK, instructor, 1960-65; North Carolina Central Univ, Durham NC, instructor, 1965-67; Langston Univ, Langston OK, asst prof, 1967-69; Univ of the District of Columbia, asst prof, 1974-. **Orgs:** Amer Public Health Assn; Amer Alliance for Health, Physical Educ, Recreation and Dance; Natl Educ Assn; Amer Medical Auxiliary Assn Inc; founding mem, Phi Delta Kappa, Univ of the District of Columbia Chapter; Delta Sigma Theta Sorority; founding mem, Friends of the Kennedy Center; vice pres, Women's Comm, Washington Ballet; patron, Museum of African Art; donor, Museum of Women in the Arts, Washington DC; exec bd mem, YWCA, Washington DC area, 1974; founder 1979, pres 1981, Capital City Links Inc, Washington DC; chairperson, Northwest Quadrant, Amer Cancer Soc, 1984; chairperson, Fund-Raiser for the Arts, Children's Museum, 1988. **Honors/Awds:** Award of Appreciation, Prairie View Univ Student Body; alumnus of Prairie View A&M University, Nafes Award; Award of Contribution and Presidents Club, Prairie View Univ; fund-raiser chairperson, raised $100,000 for Gems Program for Minority Medical Students, Georgetown Univ Medical School; honoree, Georgetown Univ Medical School, 1988, 1989; Texas Hall of Fame; James Wells $30,000 Art donated to Prairie View Univ of Texas of Black Americans; Richard Dempey-Samuel Gilliam and Africa sculpture from Kenya, West Africa; 3 Citations, Best Dressed Woman, 1967, 1975, 1983; Exhibition of my Couture wardrobe at Neiman Marcus, 1996, a selection from 1960-80; Women's Inner Circle of Achievements, 1997. **Home Addr:** 2922 Ellicott Terrace, NW, Washington, DC 20008.

CLARK, SHEILA WHEATLEY
Account executive. **Personal:** Born Sep 4, 1948, Houston, TX; daughter of Helen Wheatley and Reuben Wheatley; divorced. **Educ:** University of North Texas BBA Acctg 1969, MBA Acctg 1972. **Career:** Shell Oil Co, gas accountant 1969-70; Peat Marwick Main & Co, audit partner 1972-. **Orgs:** Memberships Amer Inst of Certified Public Accountants; Natl Assn of Black Accountants; Amer Women's Soc of CPA's; Comm on Tech Standards TX State Bd of Public Accountancy; TX Soc of CPA;s; TASBO; N TX State Univ Dept of Acctg; held various offices in Delta Sigma Theta Sor Inc; Houston Bus Forum; BOLD the Black Organ for Leadership Develop; NAACP; Houston Chamber of Comm; United Way of Houston; YWCA; Prof Christian Women Assn; Natl Coalition of 100 Black Women; INROADS; acctg instructor TX Southern Univ 1977-78; teaching fellow N TX State Univ; instructor TX Soc of CPA's Continuing Prof Educ seminars 1976-; auditing instructor Miller CPA Review Courses 1980-82; guest lecturer AICPA summer seminar 1978 & 1983; bd of regents TX State Univ System 1986-; Chairman ofBoard, Inroads Houston, I1987-. **Honors/Awds:** Natl Acctg Achievement Awd NABA; Acctg Achievement Awd NABA Houston Chapt; Cert of Appreciation NABA 8th Annual Convention 1981; Alumni of the Yr Phillis Wheatley Sr HS 1982; NABA Achievement Awd NY Chap 1982; Outstanding Alumni Awd North TX State Univ 1987; Women on the Move Houston Post, Texas Executive Women 1986; Eagle within Award, Inroads 1986.

CLARK, SHIRLEY LORRAINE
Business executive. **Personal:** Born Oct 26, 1936, Boston, MA; married James I Jr; children: James I III, Renee T, Rhonda E. **Educ:** Am Bible Coll, BRE 1961; CPCU Coll of Insurance, 1978; Am Inst for Prop & Liability Underwriters, 1978. **Career:** E G Bowman Co Inc, vp, 1980, asst vice pres 1978, mgr 1975, supr 1974. **Orgs:** Mem NY Chap Soc of Chartered Pro and Casualty Underwriters 1979-80; dir Christian educ Christ Temple Inc of the Apostolic Faith 1975-80. **Honors/Awds:** 1st black woman in US to receive CPCU Designation Chartered Prop/Casualty Underwriter 1978. **Special Achievements:** Notary Public, 1980. **Business Addr:** 97 Wall St, New York, NY 10005.

CLARK, TAMA MYERS
Judge. **Educ:** Univ of PA Law School, JD 1972; Univ of PA Grad School, MA City Planning 1972; Morgan State Univ, BS 1968. **Career:** Office of the Dist Attny for the City & Cty of Philadelphia, asst dist attny 1973-80; Human Serv Div City of Philadelphia Law Dept, dep city solicitor 1980-83; Court of Common Please Criminal Trial Div, judge 1984-. **Orgs:** Mem PA State Conf of Trial Judges; bd of dir Comm Serv Planning Council, Prisoners; Family Welfare Assoc; mem The Links Inc, Coalition of 100 Black Women, Women & Girl Offenders Task Force, Mayor's Comm for Women. **Honors/Awds:** Woman of the Year Natl Sports Found 1984; Morgan State Univ Disting Alumni of the Year Natl Assn for Equal Opport in Higher Ed 1984; Outstanding Woman of the Community Bright Hope Baptist Church Women's Comm 1984; Disting Alumnus Philadelphia Chap Morgan State Univ Alumni Assoc 1984.

CLARK, THEODORE LEE
Mayor. **Personal:** Born Aug 29, 1907, Osceola, AR; married Bernice Walker; children: Theoplis, LeEvertt, James, Lorene Mc Cullough, Theodore Jr, Margarie McGee, Ardeen, Charles, Gloria Adams, David, Linda Rosten. **Career:** Village of N Lilbourn, mayor; AME Ch, minister 38 yrs; PTA, pres 14 yrs; Master Masons, sr warden 28 yrs. **Orgs:** Treas Bootheel Mayors Assn 2 yrs. **Honors/Awds:** Ebony Mag 1975. **Business Addr:** PO Box 139, Lilbourn, MO 63862.

CLARK, TONY (ANTHONY CHRISTOPHER)
Professional baseball player. **Personal:** Born Jun 15, 1972, El Cajon, CA. **Educ:** Arizona; San Diego State. **Career:** Detroit Tigers, infielder, 1995-. **Honors/Awds:** Honey Baked Ham, Iron Man Award, 1997. **Business Addr:** Professional Baseball Player, Detroit Tigers, 2121 Trumbull St, Detroit, MI 48216, (313)962-4000.

CLARK, VERNON L.
Educational administrator. **Career:** Texas Southern Univ, provost, sr vp; Bowie State Univ, provost, sr vp, 1995-. **Business Addr:** Provost/Senior VP Acad Affairs, Bowie State University, 14000 Jericho Park Rd, Bowie, MD 20715, (301)464-3000.

CLARK, VEVE A.
Educator. **Personal:** Born Dec 14, 1944, Jamaica, NY; daughter of Pauline Kirton and Alonzo Clark. **Educ:** Univ of CA Berkeley, PhD; Queens Coll NY, MA; Univ de Nancy France, Cert d'Etudes Superieures; Queens Coll NY, BA. **Career:** Univ of CA Berkeley, lecturer 1974-79; Tufts Univ, assoc prof 1980-90; Univ of California, Berkeley, associate professor, 1991-. **Orgs:** Archivist The Katherine Dunham Fund 1977-; coord Africa & The New World Program at Tufts Univ 1981-; bd mem Fenway Comm Devel Corp 1981-83. **Honors/Awds:** Natl Endowment for the Arts Grants for Maya Deren Proj & Katherine Dunham Proj 1980-81; Merrill Ingram Found Writing Grant for Deren Proj 1982; Mellon Faculty Rsch Awd Tufts Univ 1983-84; co-editor The Legend of Maya Deren, Film Culture NY 1985; Gussenheim Fellow, 1987; Brown University Fellow, Rites and Reason and Univ Massachusetts, Boston, MA, 1988. **Business Addr:** Associate Professor, University of California Berkeley, 660 Barrows Hall, Berkeley, CA 94720-2572.

CLARK, VINCENT W.
City official. **Personal:** Born Apr 11, 1950, Bronx, NY; son of Gladys Young Clark and Vincent Clark; married LaVerne McBride; children: Derrick, Noelle. **Educ:** LaGuardia Comm Coll, AS 1979; York Coll, BA 1983; New York Univ, MPA 1987. **Career:** New York City Bd of Education, asst director, management analyst, business manager, budget director; NYC Bd of Education, Various positions 1980-90; NYC Emergency Medical Service, assoc executive director 1990-; NYC Health and Hospitals Corp, senior asst vp. **Orgs:** Mem Amer Soc of Public Administrators 1982-, Assn for School Bus Officials. **Honors/Awds:** Mayor's Scholarship New York Univ 1985-86; Top 40 Program New York City 1986-87. **Home Addr:** 120 Maryton Road, White Plains, NY 10603. **Business Addr:** Senior Asst Vice President, NYC Health and Hospitals Corporation, 125 Worth Street, New York, NY 10013.

CLARK, WALTER H.
Financial consultant. **Personal:** Born Jun 5, 1928, Athens, GA; son of Beulah Clark and John Clark; married Juanita E Dillard; children: Hilton P, Jaunine C. **Educ:** So IL Univ, BBA 1951; DePaul Univ, MBA 1958; Harvard Univ, Postgrad 1971. **Career:** IL Fed Savings & Loan Assn, 1952, 1954-55; 1st Fed Savings & Loan Assoc Chgo, exec vp, mem bd of dir 1955-; Citicorp, 1983-86; Chicago Transit Authority, chairman, 1986-88; Bear Stearns Co Inc, vice president, 1986-91; financial consultant, beginning 1991; Wheat First Securities Inc, sr financial analyst & broker, currently. **Orgs:** Invest Comm, YMCA Metro Chicago; bd of dirs, Better Govt Assn; adv council, Coll Bus Admin; Univ of IL, Urbana, Natl Soc Controllers & Financial Officers, Financial Exec Inst Econ Club Mem, Travelers Aid Soc Serv League, 1967, Alpha Phi Alpha, Union League Club; bd of dirs, Harvard Bus School, Snakes Soc Club; trustee, Park Manor Congregational Church. **Honors/Awds:** Black Achievers of Indust Recog Awd YMCA 1974; Business School Hall of Fame, Southern Illinois University, 1986. **Military Serv:** US Army, sgt, 1952-54. **Business Addr:** Senior Financial Analyst, Wheat First Securities Inc, 901 E Byrd St, Richmond, VA 23219.

CLARK, WALTER L.
Financial executive. **Personal:** Born Dec 5, 1963, Baltimore, MD; married Mikki Clark; children: Aaron. **Educ:** RETS Elec-

tronic Engineering, AA, 1985; Howard County Community College, AA, 1995; Johns Hopkins University, BS, finance, 1996. **Career:** Gruntal & Co, LLC, vp of investment; Wheat First Securities, vp of investment.

CLARK, WILLIAM
State representative. **Personal:** Born May 16, 1937, Meridian, MS; married Hattie Giles; children: William H, Reginald A. **Educ:** Dillard Univ, BA 1961; Tuskegee Inst, MEd 1967; AL State Univ, EdS 1978. **Career:** Mobile Co Training Sch, teacher/coach 1961-70; Vigor HS, asst principal 1972-73; Property Realty Inc, pres 1974-; Citronelle HS, asst principal, 1977-86, principal, 1986; State of AL, state rep, currently. **Orgs:** Mem Elks 1980-, Mobile United 1982-85, Phi Delta Kappa 1982-85. **Home Addr:** 711 Atmore Ave, Prichard, AL 36610. **Business Addr:** State Representative, Dist 98, State of Alabama, PO Box 10434, Prichard, AL 36610.

CLARK, WILLIE CALVIN
Professional football player. **Personal:** Born Jan 6, 1972, New Haven, CT. **Educ:** Univ of Notre Dame, attended. **Career:** San Diego Chargers, defensive back, 1994-96; Philadelphia Eagles, 1997-. **Business Addr:** Professional Football Player, Philadelphia Eagles, 3501 S Broad St, Philadelphia, PA 19148, (215)463-2500.

CLARKE, ALYCE GRIFFIN
State legislator. **Personal:** Born Jul 3, 1939, Yazoo, MS; daughter of Fannie Merriweather Griffin and Henry Griffin; married L W Clarke Jr, Jun 24, 1972; children: DeMarquis Clarke. **Educ:** Alcorn State Univ, Lorman MS, BS, 1961; Tuskegee Univ, Tuskegee AL, MS, 1965; Mississippi Coll, Clinton MS, 1977-79; Jackson State, Jackson MS, 1982. **Career:** Washington County Public Schools, Leland MS, teacher, 1961-68; Mississippi Action for Progress, Jackson MS, nutritionist, 1969-71; Jackson Hinds Health Center, Jackson MS, nutritionist, 1971-87; Mississippi State Legislature, Jackson MS, state representative, 1985-. **Orgs:** Mem, Alcorn State Univ Alumni, 1961-89, Mississippi Assoc Community Health Centers, 1971-89, Natl Society of Nutrition, 1980-89, Mayor's Advisory Comm, 1980-89; bd mem, Mississippi Multiple Sclerosis Natl Soc, 1984-89; Mississippi Food Network, 1985-89; mem, Natl Women's Political Caucus, 1985-89; bd mem, United Way, 1986-89, Southeastern Educ Improvement Lab, 1986-89; chmn, Jackson Crime Prevention Comm, 1988. **Honors/Awds:** WIC Coord of the Year, Mississippi Bd of Health, 1984; Employee of the Year, Jackson Hind Health Center, 1984; Outstanding Serv to Educ, Intl Alumni Council, 1984; Mississippi Woman of the Year, Hind County Federation of Democratic Women, 1985; distinction of being the first black woman legislator in Mississippi, 1985; Alcornite of the Year, Alcorn State Alumni, 1987; Leadership & Serv Award, Alpha Kappa Alpha Sorority, 1987.

CLARKE, ANGELA WEBB
Physician. **Personal:** Born Nov 4, 1932, Baltimore, MD; daughter of Cora Mayfield Webb and Luke E Webb; divorced; children: Wuan, Indranee, Tarita. **Educ:** Univ of MD School of Med, MD 1961. **Career:** UCLA Dept Comm Med, assoc prof 1970-76; Univ of NV Medical School, assoc prof, 1978-; Amer Bd of Family Practice, diplomate 1972; Private practice, 1962-87. **Orgs:** Mem, Links, Inc, 1983-92; Phi Beta Kappa; Clark County Med Society, pres, 1985; CI West Chapter of NMA, pres, 1984; NAACP, life mem. **Military Serv:** WAF 1951-53; USAFR Lt col 1985-87. **Home Addr:** 2505 Desert Butte Dr, Las Vegas, NV 89134-8869.

CLARKE, ANNE-MARIE
Attorney. **Personal:** Born in St Louis, MO; daughter of Thomas P & Mary Ann Vincent Clarke; married Richard K Gaines, Apr 3, 1979. **Educ:** Forest Park Comm Coll, 1967-68; Northwest MO State Univ, BA, 1970; St Louis Univ School of Law, JD, 1973. **Career:** Arthur D Little Inc, researcher, 1974-94; Northeast Utilities, asst corp sec, 1974-77; Bi-State Develop Agency, staff counsel, 1977-79; Self Employed, private practice of law, 1980-92; City of St Louis, hearing officer, family court, 1986-. **Orgs:** The MO Bar, bd of governors, 1986-90, 1991-95; Mound City Bar Assn, pris, 1981-83; Confluence St Louis, chair, prevention of juvenile crime task force, 1993; Delta Sigma Theta Sorority, Inc; The Bar Plan Mutual Insurance Co., director, 1986-. **Honors/Awds:** Natl Council of Negro Women Bertha Black Rhoda Section, Achievement Award, 1990; Natl Organization of Blacks in Law Enforcement (NOBLE), Achievement Award, 1993; MO Legislative Black Caucus, Jordan-McNeal Award, 1994. **Special Achievements:** The History of the Black Bar, St Louis bar Journal, Spring 1984. **Business Addr:** President, Bd of Police Commissioners, St Louis Police Dept, 1200 Clark, St Louis, MO 63103, (314)444-5600.

CLARKE, BENJAMIN LOUIS
Personnel supervisor. **Personal:** Born Mar 5, 1944, Springfield, OH; married Janet; children: Bryan, Darryl. **Educ:** Lincoln Univ, BS Social Science 1966; Xavier Univ, MEd Counseling 1972; Univ of Cincinnati, MA Industrial Relations 1984. **Career:** Ford Motor Company, supervisor of personnel. **Orgs:** Just Us Indiv Investment Club 1985-; unit comm Detroit Boy Scout Leader 1985-; Hartford Optimist Club; Lincoln University Alumni Association; Xavier University Alumni Association; University of Cincinnati Alumni Association. **Military Serv:** AUS capt 2 1/2 yrs; Army Commendation Medal 1967. **Business Addr:** Staff Human Relations Associate, Ford Motor Co., 3001 Miller Rd, Dearborn, MI 48121.

CLARKE, DONALD DUDLEY
Educator, scientist. **Personal:** Born Mar 20, 1930, Kingston, Jamaica; son of Ivy Burrowes Clarke and I Dudley Clarke; married Marie B Burrowes; children: Carol, Stephen, Paula, David, Ian, Sylvia, Peter. **Educ:** Fordham Clg, BS (cum laude) 1950; Fordham Univ, MS 1955, PhD 1955; Univ of Toronto, post doctoral res 1955-57. **Career:** NY Psychiatric Inst, research assc 1957-62; Columbia Univ Med Schl, sr res scientist 1960-62; Fordham Univ, assc prof 1962-70, prof 1970-. **Orgs:** Consultant Natl Inst of Mental Hlth 1972-76, Natl Inst of Hlth 1981-85; chmn chem dept Fordham Univ 1978-84; chmn, councillor NY sect Amer Chemical Socy 1976-; co-chmn Kingsbridge Manor Neighborhood Assn 1980-84. **Honors/Awds:** NIH special fellowship Univ of PA, 1971-72; Research Publications in Professional Journals; NIH Marc Faculty Fellowship, Mt Sinai Sch Med, 1993-94. **Business Addr:** Professor of Chemistry, Fordham Univ, Chemistry Dept, Bronx, NY 10458.

CLARKE, EUGENE H., JR.
Judge. **Personal:** Born Jul 26, 1920, Philadelphia, PA; son of Mary Emma Bell Clarke (deceased) and Eugene H Clarke Sr (deceased); married Anne B; children: Shirley Franklin, Ernestine Cheeves, Beverly Williams. **Educ:** Howard Univ, BA 1940; Howard Univ Sch of Law, LLB 1943. **Career:** NAACP, chief legal counsel 1945-47; John M Langston Law Club, pres 1947; US Selective Bd, 1948-49; Criminal Justice Sect Philadelphia Bar Assn, chmn 1979; Court of Common Pleas, judge. **Orgs:** Pres Prisoner Family Welfare Assn 1983; chmn of Bd Women's Christian Alliance 1984; chairman, Pennsylvania Board of Law Examiners, 1995-97. **Honors/Awds:** Distinguished Alumnus Awd Howard Univ 1978; J Austin Norris Barrister's Assn 1979; Philadelphia Bar Assn Criminal Justice Sect 1979 & 81; Award of Merit Olde Philadelphia Club 1980, 1983. **Business Addr:** Judge, 1st Judicial Dist, 1289 Wanamaker Bldg, 1300 Market St, Philadelphia, PA 19107.

CLARKE, EVEREE JIMERSON
Educator. **Personal:** Born Jul 6, 1926, Merritt Island, FL; divorced; children: Frances Yvette. **Educ:** Attended, Lincoln Univ 1945-48, Juilliard Sch of Music 1952-54, Nova Univ 1979-82. **Career:** Everee Clarke Sch of Charm and Dance Inc, pres 1960-; Tri County Chap NBL, pres elegante intl; Natl Business League, natl sec 1972-76, asst regional vice pres 1986-, pres/ceo 1987. **Orgs:** Professional beauty/talent pageant consultant; consultant Frances Bright Women's Club Debutante Cotillion, "The Children's Hour" early childhood development prog, Palm Beach Co Cities in Schools prog 1985-86; mem Broward Co Republican Exec Comm 1985-88; mem City of West Palm Beach HCD Educ Comm 1987; mem BrowardCo Cncl for Black Economic Develop; mem Urban League, NAACP, Voters League. **Honors/Awds:** Service Awd Natl Business League Washington DC 1977; Broward County Historic Preservation Board of Trustees, Governor's Appointee, 1991-93. **Special Achievements:** Founder, Service Tri-County Chapter, National Business League, 1986. **Home Addr:** 4290 NW 19th St, Fort Lauderdale, FL 33313.

CLARKE, GRETA FIELDS
Physician, dermatologist. **Personal:** Born in Detroit, MI; daughter of Willa Fields and George Fields; divorced; children: Richard. **Educ:** Univ of MI, BS 1962; Howard Univ, MD 1967. **Career:** Harlem Hospital New York, internship 1967-68, residency internal medicine 1968-69; NY Univ Medical Ctr, residency dermatology 1969-72; Private Practice NY, dermatologist 1972-77; Arlington Medical Group Oakland CA, dermatologist 1977-79; Private Practice Berkeley CA, dermatologist 1979-. **Orgs:** Mem Amer Acad of Dermatology 1974-, trustee, Natl Medical Assoc 1990-92; CA Medical Assoc 1977-; San Francisco Dermatological Soc 1977-; mem Jack and Jill of Amer 1977-88; founding mem Northern CA Black Women Physicians 1981-; chmn Council on the Concerns of Women Physicians NMA 1983-89; bd of dirs Bay Area Black United Fund 1985-89; mem The Links Inc 1985-92; chmn Region VI Natl Medical Assoc 1986-90; mem Comm on Women in Med CA Med Assoc 1986-90; Oakland Chapter Carrousels, Inc, 1990-. **Honors/Awds:** Certificate of Merit Natl Medical Assoc, 1985; Professional Achievement Awd Sinkler Miller Med Assoc 1986; Founders Awd No CA Black Women Physicians 1986; Amer Spirit Awd 1987. **Special Achievements:** Established the Fields Dermatologic Group, Inc, Parent company of The Clarke Collection, 1992. **Business Addr:** Dermatologist, 2500 Milvia St Ste 124, Berkeley, CA 94704, (510)843-2384.

CLARKE, HENRY LOUIS
Educational administrator. **Personal:** Born May 28, 1908, Pickens, MS; married Dorethea Doris Falconer; children: 9. **Educ:** Alcorn State Univ, BSA 1953; Tuskegee Inst, ME 1963; MS State Univ Further Study. **Career:** Holy City MB Church, sec 12 yrs; Cty ECM, sec 1980-85; Sec State Task Force Comm, mem 1984-85; State Election Commiss, adv bd election commissioner 1984-85. **Orgs:** Mem Democratic Party 1985, State Cty Retired Teachers Assn 1985, NEA Assn. **Honors/Awds:** Elected Vice Pres of the State Election Comm March, 1985; 32nd Degree Mason. **Home Addr:** 384 Clark Rd, Pickens, MS 39146.

CLARKE, JAMES ALEXANDER
Educator (retired). **Personal:** Born Jul 4, 1925, Jacksonville, FL; son of Josephine Jones Clarke and Rev Henry J Clarke (deceased); married Mary Ada Zeigler, Jan 26, 1946; children: James Alexander Clarke II, grand: Jevon, Jarrett. **Educ:** Morehouse Coll, attended 1946-47; Johnson C Smith Univ, BS 1949; NC A&T State Univ, MS 1954; Columbia Univ, MA 1963; Univ of NC-Chapel Hill, EdD 1976. **Career:** Kannapolis City Schools, teacher 1949-51; Rowan Co Schools, principal 1951-56; Charlotte-Mecklenburg Schools, principal & program dir 1956-72; Asheville City Schools, assoc supt 1972-77; NC Dept of Public Instruction, state dir 1977-82; Halifax County Schools, superintendent 1982-86 (retired); part-time, coll professor. **Orgs:** Pres Div of Superintendents NC Dist VIII 1975-76; dir exec bd Natl Alliance of Black School Educators 1976-82; mem bd dirs Natl Community Educ Assoc 1980-82; deacon Martin St Baptist Church Raleigh 1980-; regional dir SE Region of Phi Beta Sigma Frat Inc 1981-84; mem AASA, NCASA, NCAE, NSBA, Sigma Pi Phi Frat, NASSP, NAACP; NC state & area 3 housing coord, AARP, 1988-94; AARP Association, state director NC: deacon Martin Street Baptist Church, Raleigh, NC, 1982-; natl dir of educ, Phi Beta Sigma 1987-91. **Honors/Awds:** First black associate superintendent in NC; first black superintendent of Halifax County Schools; The Order of the Long Leaf Pine presented by Gov James Hunt of NC 1982; Educ Service Awd Phi Beta Sigma Frat 1984; Distinguished Alumni Awd Natl Assn of Equal Oppor in Higher Educ 1985; Outstanding Educ Leadership Award, Phi Beta Sigma, 1989; Distinguished Service Chapter of Phi Beta Sigma Fraternity, 1990; Hall of Fame, National Alliance of Black School Educators, 1996. **Military Serv:** AUS tech sgt 3 yrs. **Home Addr:** Box 37067, Raleigh, NC 27627.

CLARKE, JOHN HENRIK
Author, educator, historian. **Personal:** Born Jan 1, 1915, Union Springs, AL; son of Willella Mays Clarke and John Clarke; married Sybil Williams Clarke, Dec 24, 1961; children: Nzingha Marie, Sonni Kojo. **Educ:** New York University, 1948-52; New School for Social Research, 1956-58; Pacific Western University, BA 1992, PhD 1994. **Career:** Co-founder and associate editor of Harlem Quarterly, 1949-51; New School for Social Research, New York NY, teacher of African and Afro-American history, 1956-58, developer of African Study Center, 1957-59, assistant to director, 1958-60; feature writer for Pittsburgh Courier, 1957-58, Ghana Evening News, 1958; editor of African Heritage, 1959; assistant editor of Freedomways magazine, 1962-82; director of HARYOU-ACT Heritage Teaching Program, 1964-69; Hunter College of the City University of New York, New York NY, associate professor of Black and Puerto Rican studies, 1970-86. **Orgs:** International Society of African Culture, African Studies Association, American Society of African Culture, founding member of Black Academy of Arts and Letters, Association for Study of Negro Life and History, American Historical Society, American Academy of Political and Social Science, African Heritage Studies Association, African Scholars Council, founding member of Harlem Writers Guild. **Honors/Awds:** Carter G. Woodson Award, 1968, for creative contribution in editing, and 1971, for excellence in teaching; National Association for Television and Radio Announcers citation for meritorious achievement in educational television, 1969; LHD from University of Denver, 1970. **Special Achievements:** Author and/or editor of 23 books. **Military Serv:** US Army Air Forces, master sergeant, 1941-45. **Home Addr:** 223 West 137 St, New York, NY 10030.

CLARKE, JOSEPH LANCE
Business executive. **Personal:** Born Apr 6, 1941, New York, NY; married Marion Joyce Herron; children: Bernadette, Leslie, Lancelot. **Educ:** So IL Univ Carbondale IL, 1960-63; City Coll of NY, BA 1967; NYU, 1967-68. **Career:** Fashion Fair Cosmetics, exec vice pres 1974-, dir of sales 1973-74; Supreme Beauty Products, dir of sales 1971-73; Livingston Inst, mgr 1966-67. **Orgs:** VP Alpha Phi Alpha Frat Beta Eta Chap 1962-63; vice pres Young Dem of Mt Vernon NY 1966-68. **Honors/Awds:** Plaque for Exemplary Serv AUS 1963-66; Letter of Accommodation AUS 1963-66; bus award Supreme Beauty Products 1970. **Military Serv:** AUS spec/e5 1963-66. **Business Addr:** 820 S Michigan Ave, Chicago, IL 60605.

CLARKE, JOY ADELE LONG
Library media specialist. **Personal:** Born Sep 27, 1937, Springfield, OH; daughter of Joy Christobel White Long and Albert Edward Long; married Ronald Eugene Clarke, Nov 19, 1960; children: Dylan Terence, Kelcey Lamar, Darcy Marie. **Educ:** Central State University, Wilberforce, OH, BS, elementary education, 1960; University of Northern Colorado, Greeley, CO, MA, 1978. **Career:** Springfield Public Schools, Springfield, OH, teacher, 1960-62; Pershing Elementary School, Fort Leonard Wood, MO, 1962-63; Boulder Valley Schools, Boulder, CO, teacher, 1972-83; Tucson Public Schools, Tucson, AZ, library media specialist, 1978-81; Denver Public Schools, Den-

ver, CO, library media specialist; Aims Community College, Greeley CO, teacher of multicultural diversity, currently. **Orgs:** Alpha Delta Kappa Teacher's Sorority; NAACP; American Library Association; American School Librarians; Assn Black Caucus of the American Library Association; Alpha Kappa Alpha Sorority. **Honors/Awds:** Miss Ohio Campus Queen, Central State University, Wilberforce, OH; Oratorical contest winner, National Sunday School, BTU Congress; published a devotional book entitled Spiritual Nourishment; author of Multicultural Social Studies Unit Who Am I?; Black History Activities Book for K-12. **Home Addr:** 6919 Roaring Fork Trail, Boulder, CO 80301.

CLARKE, KENTON
Company executive. **Personal:** Born Nov 17, 1951, Bridgeport, CT; son of Ruth and Haywood. **Educ:** Norwalk State Technical College, AS, 1972; University of New Haven, BS, 1979. **Career:** Computer Consulting Associates, president, 1980-. **Orgs:** Nortech Foundation, director, 1989-; Connecticut Minority Purchasing Council, bd of dirs; Norwalk Community Technical College, bd of dirs. **Honors/Awds:** Connecticut Minority Purchasing Council, Supplier of the Year, 1990; United Negro College Fund, 1991; CMPC Shining Star, 1996. **Business Addr:** President, Computer Consulting Associates, 578 Post Rd, Ste 503, Westport, CT 06880, (203)255-8966.

CLARKE, LEON EDISON
Hospital administator. **Personal:** Born Nov 17, 1949, Monrovia; married Fatu; children: Tanya, Nina, Lee Ann. **Educ:** George Washington Univ, MD, 1975; Hospital of the Univ of PA, Surgical Residency, 1975-77; Medical College of PA, 1977-80; Surgical Oncology, Medical College of PA, 1980. **Career:** Veterans Administration Hospital, Philadelphia PA, consultant, 1981-; Medical College of PA, attending surgeon, beginning 1981-, instructor of surgery, 1982-, medical director of surgical procedure unit, 1985-; Mercy Catholic Medical Center, director of surgery, 1988-; Thomas Jefferson University Hospital, clinical associate professor of surgery, currently; Misericordia Hospital, director of surgery, currently. **Orgs:** American Cancer Society; Amer Coll of Physician Executives; Society of Black Academic Surgeons. **Honors/Awds:** Valedictoria (Dux) High School; Phi Sigma Biology Honorary Society Washington & Jefferson Coll Graduatation Cum Laude; Student Representative on the Committee for New Chairman, Dept of Anatomy, George Washington Univ School of Medicine; Golden Apple Award 1978-79, two consective academic yars Senior Medical Students Selection of the Best Teacher The Medical College of PA; Summer Research 1973; Histamine Release from Mast Cells: The Possible Effect of Papain on Bee Venom George Washington Univ School of Medicine. **Business Addr:** Director of Surgery, Misericordia Hospital, 53rd & Cedar Avenue, 5th Floor, Philadelphia, PA 19143.

CLARKE, LEROY P.
Artist, poet. **Personal:** Born Nov 7, 1938, Port-of-Spain, Trinidad and Tobago; divorced; children: Kappel, Ra-nkosane. **Career:** Artist; poet; tchr 1959-67. **Orgs:** Numerous exhibits 1969-; one-man exhibition, Studio Mus 1972; artist-in-residence, Studio Mus 1973-76. **Honors/Awds:** Published portfolios of drawings, Fragments of a Spiritual 1972; Douens 1976; poems & drawings, Taste of Endless Fruit 1974; drawings, In a Quiet Way 1971; one-man exhibition, Douens at Howard Univ 1976; complete Douens' series exhibition, Port-of-Spain, Trinidad 1979.

CLARKE, PRISCILLA
Accountant, business owner, publicist, photographer, producer, martial arts instructor. **Personal:** Born Aug 3, 1960; daughter of Dorothy Sharples Clarke and Gilbert Lee Clarke; children: Huda, Ilyas, Qasim. **Educ:** Columbia Union, BA, business administration; North American School of Firearms, PA, gun professional; WNEC, BA, accounting; Rouse School of Special Detective Training, private investigator. **Career:** Channel 10 Fairfax County Television, producer; Eat To Live Health food Store, owner, 1988-; NEB Security, president & owner, 1992-; N.E.B. Entertainment, president, 1995-. **Orgs:** Maryland State Director for United States Karate Association, 1990; member, National Association of Female Executives, 1986-; volunteer, Connecticut State Black Caucus; officer, National Association of Executive Bodyguards, Inc, 1990-; Maryland state representative for United States Karate Association, 1990-93; Rouse Detective Assn; National Council of Negro Women; Parent Teachers Assn. **Honors/Awds:** Black Enterprise Magazine Articles, 1990, 1991; Featured on Channel 13, WJZ Baltimore, MD, 1991; Black Belt Chinese Kenpo Karate, Martial Arts Instructor; Held Top Female Black Belt titles: Number 1 female champion on the east coast for serveral years, ranked #2 in the United States, also held AAU Female Black Belt Championship title; Presidential Sports Award for Karate; held #1 Canadian Championship in Karate for 3 years. **Special Achievements:** Worked security/bodyguard positions for Alan Haymon Concert Productions, other celebrities; conducted rape prevention/self defense seminars on television, colleges; Production and PR contracts include: Johnnie Cochran, Russell Simmons DEF Comedy Jam, 1996 Essence Awards, "The First Kid," movie with Sinbad, Telly Awards, the "Comedy Tonight" Show, etc., mem of International Who's Who of Professionals. **Business Addr:** President, Publicist, Photographer, Producer, N.E.B. Entertainment & Production, 2020 Pennsylvania Ave NW, Suite 271, Washington, DC 20006.

CLARKE, RAYMOND
Organization executive. **Personal:** Born Aug 2, 1950, Cincinnati, OH; son of Genie Johnson Clarke (deceased) and William Clarke (deceased); married Debra, Dec 29, 1984; children: Terri, Paul. **Educ:** Univ of Arizona, Tucson AZ, BS 1973, MS, 1978. **Career:** Univ of AZ, counselor, youth, 1971, 1972; Pima County Juvenile Court Center, deputy dir, probation, 1973-84; University of Arizona, consultants, student athletes 1980-81; Governor Bruce Babbitt, exec dir, health council 1984-86; Tucson Urban League Inc, pres/ceo Agency 1986-. **Orgs:** Mem, Pi Lambda Theta, 1977-; pres, Tucson Chapter Natl Assn of Black Social Workers, 1978-79; mem, AZ Small Businessmen Assn, 1979; mem, Mayor's Task Force, Economic Development, 1988-89; mem, Governor's Task Force on Welfare Reform, 1988-89; mem, Regents Ad-Hoc Committee, Minority Access and Retention, 1988-; mem, State Supreme Court Taskforce, 1989; mem, Tucson Community Foundation Grants Committee, 1988-; member, US Selective Service System, 1981-; Citizens-Police Advisory Committee, City of Tucson, 1984; vice pres, western regional council of executives, National Urban League, 1991; Tucson Local Development Corp, City of Tucson, 1987; Tucson Civil Rights Coalition, Tucson Community, 1990. **Honors/Awds:** One of the Youngest Administrator in the Juvenile Justice System, 1975; Co-Founder of the Tucson Chapter of the Natl Assn of Black Soc, 1978; Development and Implemection of an Educational and Career Development Project for Student Athletes, 1979; Meritorious Recognition/Natl for Juvenile Delinquency Prevention, 1980; State Image Award, NAACP, 1980; Outstanding Young Men, OYM of America, 1980, 1982; Service to Youth, Foundation, Pima County, 1983; Service to Community, Optimist Club, Tucson, 1983; UA Black Alumni Award, 1988; Panelist, Documented Forum on Civil Rights in AZ, 1989; Certificate of Dedication, Southern Arizona Chapter, A Philip Randolph Institute, 1990; Mayor's Copper Letter of Appreciation, Mayor of Tucson, 1984, 1989; Corporate Solicitor-Professional, United Way, 1987;Cificate of Appreciation, Tucson Human Relations Commission, 1990; Community Service Award, NAACP-Tucson, 1990. **Business Addr:** President and Chief Executive Officer, Tucson Urban League, Inc, 2305 S Park Avenue, Tucson, AZ 85713.

CLARKE, RICHARD V.
Business executive. **Personal:** Born Jun 11, 1927, New York, NY; divorced; children: Tracy, Chip. **Educ:** City Coll of NY City. **Career:** Richard Clarke Assos Inc, pres 1964-; Hallmark Employment Agy, fdr 1957; consult to fed, state & pvt agencies. **Orgs:** Mem NY State Econ Devel Bd; mem NY State Bd of Tourism; bd dirs NY State Council of the Arts. **Business Addr:** President, Richard Clarke Associates, Inc, 9 West 95th St, Suite C, New York, NY 10025.

CLARKE, STANLEY MARVIN
Composer, musician. **Personal:** Born Jun 31, 1951, Philadelphia, PA; son of Blanche Bundy Clarke and Marvin Clarke; married Carolyn Helene Reese, Nov 29, 1974; children: Christopher Ivanhoe. **Educ:** Philadelphia Music Academy, 1968-71. **Career:** Member, Horace Silver Band, 1970, Joe Henderson Band, 1971, Stan Getz Band, 1971-72, Return to Forever, 1972-76, New Barbarians tour group (with Rolling Stones members Keith Richard, Ron Wood), 1979, Clarke/Duke Project, 1980-; Stanley Clarke Group, leader, 1976-. **Orgs:** Musicians Local 802 Union; Ntl Academy of Recording Arts & Sciences; AFTRA; Screen Actors Guild; Hubbard Assn Scientologists Intl. **Honors/Awds:** Composer, Life is Just a Game, Stanley Clarke Songbook (1977), I Wanna Play for You Songbook (1979); albums recorded include Find Out (1985), Modern Man (1985), If This Bass Could Only Talk (1988), Midnight Magic (with Chick Corea and Return to Forever group), Hideaway (1986, with George Howard, Herbie Hancock, others), The Clarke/Duke Project (1981, with George Duke), The Clarke Duke Project II (1983, with George Duke), others; produced albums for himself and artists such as Roy Buchanan, Dee Dee Bridgewater, Flora Purim; recorded hit song Sweet Baby (1981, with George Duke); featured on albums by numerous artists, including Aretha Franklin, Carlos Santana, Quincy Jones, and Dianne Reeves; Grammy award nominee, 1976, 1978, 1981; Bassist of the Year, 1973, Electric Bassist of the Year,4; Bassist of the Year, Playboy Readers' Poll, 1976, 1977, 1978, 1979, 1980; Jazz Artist of the Year, Rolling Stone Music Critics' Poll, 1977; named to Guitar Gallery of Greats, 1980.

CLARKE, THEODORE HENSON
Podiatric physician & surgeon. **Personal:** Born Feb 18, 1923, Martins Ferry, OH; married Ada Miller; children: Jeffrey Allen, Wendell Howard. **Educ:** Sumner Coll KS City MO, Prepodiatry 1943; IL Coll of Podriatric Med, DPM 1950. **Career:** Podiatry Clinic Ltd, doctor of podiatric med 1950-; Meridian & Foot Clinic Indianapolis, part owner 1972-. **Orgs:** Past pres, mem, Am Podiatry Assn 1950-; past pres, mem IN State Podiatry Assn 1950-; past pres, fellow, mem Am Acad of Podiatric Adminstrn 1956-; fellow, mem, Am Coll of Foot Surgeons 1970; past liaison, present mem, bd of trustees, Nat Podiatry Assn 1972; fellow, mem, Acad of Ambulatory Foot Surgery 1975; past pres, mem, Alumni Edn Found ICPM 1967-; mem, bd of trustees, ICPM; past mem, action bd, present mem governing council, Am Pub Health Assn; mem, IN Pub Health Assn; mem, bd trustees, Howard Co Diabetes Assn; mem, Am Acad of Human Serv; mem, Intl Physician's Fellowship; mem, Am Acad of Podiatric & Sports Medicine; mem, Am Assn of Hosp Podiatrists; fellow, mem, Am Soc of Podiatric Medicine; other present & past professional ofcs. **Honors/Awds:** Numerous honors; author of many pub lectures books & papers; editor Yearbook of Podiatric Medicine & Surgery Futura Publs. **Home Addr:** 4175 E Co Rd 50 S, Kokomo, IN 46901.

CLARKE, VELMA GREENE
Educator/administrator. **Personal:** Born Sep 20, 1930, Chicago, IL; daughter of Zadie Morgan Greene and Sherman L Greene Jr.; divorced; children: Gwendolyn Clarke-Sills. **Educ:** Fisk Univ Nashville, AB 1957, MA 1961; The Univ of MI, ABD 1973. **Career:** Talladega Coll, dean of women 1960-62; Edward Waters Coll, dir prof 1962-65; Shaw Univ, dir prof 1965-71; Eastern MI Univ Coll of Arts & Scis, adminis assoc. **Orgs:** Bd dirs Amer Assoc on Higher Educ 1972-74; mem Executive Comm on Higher Educ AME Church 1973-76; Delta Sigma Theta Sorority 1987-. **Honors/Awds:** Ford Foundation Advanced Study Fellowship 1971-74; The Univ of MI Rackham Awd 1972-73. **Business Addr:** Administrative Associate, Eastern MI University, College of Arts & Sciences, Ypsilanti, MI 48197.

CLARK-GATES, BRENDA
Lawyer. **Personal:** Born in Baltimore, MD; daughter of Janice Dorsey Clark and Bernard R Clark; married Bobby G Gates, Nov 24, 1990; children: Graeme Gates. **Educ:** Univ of Maryland, Baltimore, MD, BA, 1974; Univ of MD School of Law, Baltimore, MD, JD, 1977. **Career:** Mann & Clark, PA, Baltimore, MD, partner, 1978-. **Orgs:** Chairperson, Arbitration Comm, Baltimore Co Bar Assn, 1988-89; mem, Legal Aid Bureau Bd of Dir, 1987-90; vice pres, Monumental City Bar Assn, 1988-90; mem, J Dudley Diggs INWS of Court, 1988-90. **Business Addr:** Lawyer, Mann & Clark, PA, 1142 York Rd, Lutherville, MD 21093.

CLARK-HUDSON, VERONICA L.
Educator, administrator. **Personal:** Born Aug 22, 1946, Baltimore, MA; daughter of Flozella R & Harold A Clark; married Arturio M Hudson; children: Kristin Hudson Jordan. **Educ:** Albright College, 1963; Howard University, BA, 1967; University of Pennsylvania School of Law, 1972; Gemological Institute of America, GG, CG, 1985. **Career:** IBM Corp, instructor, analyst, 1967-70; Sperry Rand Corp, Univac Div, instructor, mktg, 1971-72; Hong Kong Intl School, instructor, upper div, 1974-78; ABC TV, 1984 Summer Olympics, microcomputer analyst, 1981-84; Hospitality Lane Flowers, owner, 1984-87; Best Jewelry, asst store mgr, 1987-89; Gemological Institute of America (GIA), instructor, 1989-92, sales mgr, 1992-97, dir of education, 1997-. **Orgs:** Women's Jewelry Association, prog chmn, 1997-; American Gem Society, 1990-; GIA Alumni Association, 1986-. **Honors/Awds:** National Association of Trade & Technical Schools, Personal Achievement, 1990; Staff Member of the Year, 1993. **Special Achievements:** First African American woman director of education at institute. **Business Addr:** Director of Education, Gemological Inst of America, 550 S Hill St, Ste 901, Los Angeles, CA 90013-2407, (213)833-0115.

CLARK-TAYLOR, KRISTIN
Telecommunications company executive. **Personal:** Born 1959; daughter of Elizabeth Clark (deceased) and James Clark; married Lonnie; children: Lonnie Paul, Mary Elizabeth. **Educ:** Michigan State Univ. **Career:** USA Today, editorial board, 1982-87; White House, dir of media relations, 1987-90; BellSouth Corp, dir of communications, 1990-. **Special Achievements:** The First to Speak, Doubleday, 1993. **Business Addr:** Director of Communications, BellSouth Corp, 1155 Peachtree St, SE, Atlanta, GA 30367-6000.

CLARK-THOMAS, ELEANOR M. (ELEANOR M. THOMAS)
Educator. **Personal:** Born Sep 18, 1938, Houston, TX; daughter of Alberta Palmer Henderson and George Clark Jr (deceased); married Bob Thomas; children: Natalie, Brandon, Shannon. **Educ:** Kent St Univ, BS 1960; CA St Univ, MA 1973; ASHA, Certificate Clinical Competence Speech Pathology, Certificate Clinical Competence Audiology; Univ So CA, EdD pending. **Career:** Stockton Unified School Dist, speech & hearing therapist 1960-61; Ella School Dist & Olivehurst, speech & hearing therapist 1961-63; Sacramento City Unified School Dist, speech & hearing specialist 1963-76; St Dept of Educ, consultant, educ of communicable handicapped 1976; CA St Univ Northridge, assoc prof 1985; Folsom Cordova School Dist, speech therapist; Sacramento Co Schools, speech therapist for children, admin asst special educ, compliance unit manager, currently. **Orgs:** Mem Delta Kappa Gamma 1977; mem CA Speech & Hearing Assn 1986-87; selected mem, bd dir Sacramento Hearing Soc 1974-; mem Amer Speech & Hearing Assn; mem, treasurer, coordinator council Sacramento Area Speech & Hearing Assn; mem NAUW, NBLSHA, NASDSE; pres, LA South Bay Alumnae Chapter, Delta Sigma Theta, 1989-91. **Honors/Awds:** Sustained Superior Accomplishment Award State Dept of Educ

1983-85; State Guidelines for Language-Speech Specialists, 1989. **Business Addr:** Compliance Unit Mnanger, Dept of Education, 721 Capitol Mall, Sacramento, CA 95814.

CLASH, KEVIN
Puppeteer. **Personal:** Born 1961, Baltimore, MD; son of George Clash and Gladys Clash; married Genia; children: Shannon Elise. **Career:** Jim Henson Productions, principal muppeteer, currently. **Honors/Awds:** Emmy Award, Outstanding Performer in a Children's Series for "Sesame Street," 1993. **Special Achievements:** Puppeteered on "Captain Kangaroo," 1979-85; "Sesame Street," 1980, 1985-; "The Great Space Coaster;" Created "Elmo" on "Sesame Street," 1985-; puppeteered "Baby Natasha," "Hoots the Owl," on "Sesame Street;" "Baby Sinclair," on "Dinosaurs;" "Splinter" in two of Teenage Mutant Ninja Turtles films; "Bad Polly" in Muppet Treasure Island; puppeteered on tv shows including: "The Jim Henson Hour," 1989; "Muppets Tonight!" 1996-97. **Business Addr:** Principal Muppeteer, Jim Henson Productions, 117 E 69th St, New York, NY 10021, (212)794-2400.

CLAXTON, MELVIN L.
Journalist. **Personal:** Born in Antigua-Barbuda. **Career:** The Daily News, reporter/writer, currently. **Honors/Awds:** Lead reporter and writer for a 10-day series on crime and corruption which won his newspaper a Pulitzer Prize for public service reporting, 1995. **Business Addr:** Reporter/Writer, The Daily News, PO Box 7760, St Thomas, Virgin Islands of the United States 00801, (809)774-8772.

CLAY, CAMILLE ALFREDA
Educational administrator, mental health counselor. **Personal:** Born Aug 21, 1946, Washington, DC; daughter of Doris Coates CLay and James Clay. **Educ:** Hampton Inst, BA 1968; Univ of DC, MA 1974; Psychiatric Inst Ctr for Group Studies, certificate 1972-74; George Washington Univ, EdD 1984. **Career:** DC Comm Mental Health Dept, mental health specialist 1971-72; SW Interagency Training Ctr, manpower develop specialist 1972-74; Private Practice, group therapist 1973-79; City of Bowie MD Youth Serv Bureau, asst dir 1974-76; Private Practice, mental health and career counselor 1983-; Towson State Univ, couns/sr counselor 1977-85, asst vice pres for diversity 1986-. **Orgs:** Mem NAACP, Phi Delta Kappa, Alpha Kappa Alpha; bd dirs Alfred Adler Inst of DC; past pres DC Mental Health Counselors Assn; mem Amer Counseling Assn, DCCA; Assn for Multi-Cultural Counseling and Develop; Amer Mental Health Counselors Assn; Assn of Black Psychologists; past president, DC Mental Health Counselor Assn; chair Bd of Professional Counselors, 1993-; chairperson, Licensure DCACD 1988-; member, AAHE, NAWDAC. **Honors/Awds:** Study in Germany, Experiment in International Living 1966; mem Omicron Delta Kappa Honor Leadership Society 1988; published dissertation, The Psychosocial Development of Middle Class African American Men & Women 1984; certification, Natl Certified Counselor NBCC/AACD, 1983; TSU Outstanding Black Faculty/Staff Award, TSU Black Alumni, 1989; McCully Award, DCCA, 1997. **Business Addr:** Asst Vice Pres for Diversity, Towson University, Towson, MD 21204.

CLAY, CASSIUS MARCELLUS. See ALI, MUHAMMAD.

CLAY, CLIFF
Artist. **Personal:** Born in Greenwood, MS. **Educ:** Cleveland Inst Art; Cooper Art Sch. **Career:** Prof Paul Travis, aprntc; Self Employed, painting tanned animal skins various other forms of painting. **Orgs:** Hon yet offcl deputy sheriff in Kay Co OK; mem The Karamu House; mem NAACP; Urban League Hon Amer Indian PowWow 1969; hon mem 101 Ranch Ponca &City OK; me report on health conditions of Am Indian Am Med Assn 1974; bd mem 101 Ranch Restoration Found Ponca City OK; bd mem Afro Am Hist & Cult Museum, Cleveland OH; guest speaker & instr; has had various exhibits & one man hsows; scout for Red Carpet County; promote Hist Landmarks in 19 Counties in NW OK. **Business Addr:** 10605 Chester Ave, Cleveland, OH 44106.

CLAY, ERIC LEE
Attorney. **Personal:** Born Jan 18, 1948, Durham, NC; son of Betty Allen Clay (deceased) and Austin Burnett Clay. **Educ:** Univ of NC, BA 1969; Yale Univ Law School, JD 1972. **Career:** US Dist Ct for the Eastern Dist of MI, law clerk 1972-73; State of MI, special asst atty general 1974-75; Lewis White & Clay PC, dir, atty, 1973-. **Orgs:** Arbitrator Amer Arbitration Assn 1976-; mem MI Soc of Hospital Atty 1978-; life mem 6th Circuit Jud Conf 1979; mem State Bar of MI 1972-, Wolverine Bar Assn 1973-, Amer Bar Assn 1973-, Detroit Bar Assn 1973-; mem Phi Beta Kappa; life mem Natl Bar Assn; life mem NAACP; mem Natl Assn of Railroad Trial Counsel; mem State Bar of MI Insurance Law Comm 1984-88; trustee Detroit Bar Assn Foundation 1985-88; mem, Merit Selection Panel on Bankruptcy Judgeships, 1986-87; mem, Sixth Circuit Committee on the Bicentennial of the Constitution, 1986-; mem, Executive Committee, Yale Law School Assn, 1989-; mem Merit Selection Panel on US Magistrates 1980-81; mem bd of dires Detroit Bar Assn 1990-; co-chairperson public advisory committee Detroit Bar Assn, 1988-90. **Honors/Awds:** Admitted to practice State of MI 1972, US Dist Ct for the Eastern Dist of MI 1972, US Ct of Appeals for the Sixth Circuit 1978, US Supreme Ct 1977. **Business Addr:** Judge, U.S. Court of Appeals For the Sixth Circuit, 231 W. Lafayette Blvd., Detroit, MI 48226.

CLAY, ERNEST H., III
Architect. **Personal:** Born Feb 17, 1972, Chicago, IL; son of Beatrice and Ernest. **Educ:** University of Illinois at Urbana, BAr, 1969, MAr, 1970; State of Illinois, licensed to practice architecture, by examination, 1973. **Career:** Hardwick & Clay, Architects, partner; Hardwick, Clay, Voelker, & Petterson, Architects, owner/partner; School of Architecture, Urbana IL, associate professor; E H Edric Clay & Associates, CEO, currently. **Orgs:** AIA; NOMA, National Organization of Minority Architects, Illinois Chapter, founding member. **Honors/Awds:** National Aeronautics and Space Administration, Research Fellow, 1978-79; Illinois House of Representatives, Certificate of Recognition in Architecture, 1991; National Council of Architectural Registration Boards, Exam Review Member, 1979; City of Champaign, Illinois Public Service Award, Excellence in Design, 1979-82; Society of the Gargoyle, Execellence in Architecture, 1971. **Special Achievements:** Appointed a NASA Research Fellow in 1978, 1979 to begin preliminary design work on Space Station Freedom. **Business Addr:** President & Chief Executive Officer, E Hedric Clay & Associates, PO Box 362, Champaign, IL 61820, (217)356-6077.

CLAY, HENRY CARROLL, JR.
Clergyman. **Personal:** Born Jun 8, 1928, Yazoo City, MS; married Effie Husbands; children: Henry III. **Educ:** Rust Coll, AB, MS 1952, DD 1969; Gammom Theol Sem, BD 1956. **Career:** Central United Meth Ch Jackson MS, min 1978-; Jackson Dist & United Meth Ch, dist supt 1967-73; Christian Educ MS Conf, exec sec 1959-67; St Paul UMC, pstr 1961-67; St Mark UMC, pastor 1956-61; MS Ann Conf, full connection 1956, on trail 1954; UMC, elder 1956, deacon 1954; Pub Sch, tchr 1952-53. **Orgs:** Staff mem MS Conf Cncl on Ministries United Meth Ch 1973-78; mem MS Conf Bd of Ministry 1968-76; Gen Bd of Discipleship UMC 1972-; staff mem UMC 1973-; pres MS Religious Ldrsp Conf 1975-76; del Gen Conf UMC 1976-80; 13th World Meth Conf; chmn Rust Coll Bd of Tst 1971-77; mem Bethlehem Ctr Bd Dir 1967; bd dir MS Cncl on Human Rels; mem Operation Shoestring Bd Dir; mem NAACP; bd dir Mississippians for Educ TV; MS YMCA Nat Meth Schlrsp 1954-55; Gammon Faculty & Schlrsp9 195. **Honors/Awds:** Citz yr award Omega Psi Phi Frat; outstsdng religious ldr award MS Religious Ldrsp Conf. **Business Addr:** East Jackson Dist United Methodist Church, 6658 Franklin D Roosevelt Dr, Jackson, MS 39213.

CLAY, JULIUS C.
Cleric. **Personal:** marrIed Denise M Cummings-Clay; children: Kimberly. **Educ:** Lane College, BS; Univ of Missouri, MEd; Eden Theological Seminary, MDiv; United Theological Seminary, candidate, ThM. **Career:** Israel Metropolitan Christian Methodist Episcopal Church, paster, currently. **Orgs:** Interfaith Clergy Council, president, 1993-94, vp, 1992; Police Chaplaincy, vp; NAACP, Milwaukee Chapter, third vp; Friends of Phillips School of Theology, national chairman; Gary District Leadership School, CME Church, dean; Omega Psi Phi Faternity. **Honors/Awds:** Distinguished Man of the Milwaukee Top Ladies of Distinction, Inc; Lane College, Student-Christian Assn Award. **Special Achievements:** Delegate, World Methodist Council, Nairobi, Kenya, 1986.

CLAY, REUBEN ANDERSON, JR.
Physician. **Personal:** Born Feb 8, 1938, Richmond, VA; son of Sue Clarke Clay and Rueben R Clay; married Ardelia Brown, Jun 17, 1987; children: Raymond Alan, Adrienne Beth. **Educ:** Amherst Coll, BA 1960; Univ of Rochester, MD 1964. **Career:** San Francisco Gen Hosp, internship 1964-65; Cornell Univ Med Ctr, resd 1967-68; Univ of CA, resd ob-gyn 1968-71; private practice, physician; UCSF, assoc clin prof 1981-; Ralph K Davies Med Ctr, chief of gynecology 1982-86. **Orgs:** Mem San Francisco Cty Med Soc, CMA, NMA, AMA, Amer Fert Soc; diplomate Amer Bd Ob Gyn 1973; fellow Amer Coll of Ob Gyn 1974; asst clin prof UCSF 1974-; mem San Francisco Gyn Soc; pres Parnassus Hts Ob Gyn Med Group Inc 1979-89; sec Dist IX Amer Coll of Ob Gyn 1981-88. **Military Serv:** USAF capt 1965-67. **Business Addr:** Pacific Gynecology and Obstetrics Medical Group, 2100 Webster St #319, San Francisco, CA 94115.

CLAY, ROSS COLLINS
Educator. **Personal:** Born Dec 15, 1908, Conehatta, MS; married Ollie Dolores Billingslea; children: Ross, Jr. **Educ:** Jackson State U, Atnd 1934; Fisk U, MA 1940; Northwestern U, MUSM Educ 1953; IN U, Study 1961-62; MS Southern U, Workshop 1970. **Career:** Jackson State Univ, dir music educ, tutorial teacher 1953-74; Lane Coll, dir music 1948-53; Philander Smith Coll, dir music 1946-48; Friendship Jr Coll, dir music defense worker 1943-46; Geeter High School, music educ 1940-43; AR Baptist Coll, music educ 1936-38; Humphries Co Tr School, music educ 1935-36; Corinth Hihg School, dir music 1934-35; Dir Music Educ Tutorial Teacher, composer ch music, piano, organ, instruments, voices. **Orgs:** Mem Music Educators Nat Con; mem NEA; mem MTA; mem Am Assn of Univ Profs; mem Nat Council of Sr Cits; AARP. **Honors/Awds:** Recip NART Cert Merit JSU1974; plaque in honor of retirement Farish Bapt Ch 1974; trophy Student Chap MENC; guest performer Retired Cits Paterson NJ 1975; 32 deg Mason; McKinley Theological Seminary, Honorary Doctorate of Divinity, 1981; Farish Street Baptist Church, Centennial Plaque, 1993.

CLAY, RUDOLPH
Elected government official. **Personal:** Born Jul 16, 1935, Gary, IN; son of Willie; married Christine Swan Clay; children: Rudolph Jr. **Educ:** IN Univ, 1956. **Career:** State of IN, state senator 1972-76; Lake Co IN, county councilman 1978-85, recorder 1985-, county commissioner 1987-. **Honors/Awds:** 50 Outstanding Service Awards, 1994; 50 awards in last 15 years from various organizations; City Chairman, Gary Democratic Precinct Org, 1993. **Military Serv:** US Army, SP4, 1960; Good Conduct Medal. **Home Addr:** 4201 W 10th, Gary, IN 46404.

CLAY, STANLEY BENNETT
Actor, writer, producer, director. **Personal:** Born Mar 18, 1950, Chicago, IL; son of Bertha Florence Clay Fleming and Raymond Leon Fleming. **Career:** Motion Pictures, TV Shows, Commercials, Stage Plays, 200 starring, co-starring roles 1968-; Argo Reportory Co, artistic dir 1971-74; One Flight Up Theatre Co, resident dir playwright 1974-80; Preceptor Communications, producer/director/playwright; Los Angeles Theatre Review, theatre critic 1989-91, producer/dir/co-writer, 2nd Annual NAACP Theatre Awards 1989, producer/dir, Los Angeles Black Family Reunion Concerts sponsored by Natl Council of Negro Women 1989, dir 7th Annual Ira Aldridge Awards 1989. **Orgs:** Mem exec comm NAACP Beverly Hills Hollywood Branch 1977-80; entertainment editor Sepia magazine 1981; publisher/editor-in-chief SBC Hollywood monthly magazine 1983-86; Amer corres for London's Blues and Soul magazine 1984-87; mem bd of dirs The Intl Friendship Network; producer dir and author of "Ritual" at Theatre of Arts LA; vice pres, bd of dirs The Los Angeles Black Theatre 1989-92; mem Los Angeles Black Playwrights 1988-; vp bd of directors Minority AIDS Project 1990-97; publisher, editor, SBC Magazine, 1992-. **Honors/Awds:** Three Drama Logue Awds for Disting Writing Direction Production of "Ritual" 1982; Drama Logue Awd/Best Actor starring in "Zoomen and the Sign" 1984; NAACP Image Awd/Best Actor for starring in "Anna Lucasta" 1986; 3 NAACP Theatre Awards, NAACP 1987; author of novel, Diva (Holloway House) 1987; author of play, The Night The Queen of Outerspace Played Z, produced at Inner City Cultural Center 1988; producer, director and author of Ritual at Theater of Arts LA; producer of William of Esther, at Theatre of Arts LA, 1990; author/producer/dir, In Search of Pretty Young Black Men, Ebony Showcase Theatre LA, 1991; Outstanding Cultural Achievement Award, African American Gay and Lesbian Cultural Alliance 1990; Drama-Logue Award/Best Director for Jonin, Drama-Logue Magazine, 1989; Genre Magazine, Lifeguard/Role Model Award, 1993; Intl Black Writers & Artists, Edna Crutchfield Founders Literary Achievement Award, 1997. **Business Addr:** Producer/Director/Playwright, SBC Publishers, 1155 4th Ave, Los Angeles, CA 90019.

CLAY, TIMOTHY BYRON
Project director. **Personal:** Born Sep 22, 1955, Louisville, KY; son of Louise Middleton Clay and Bernard H Clay; married Phyllis Wells Clay, May 11, 1978; children: Jacqueline Simone Clay, Arielle Christine Clay. **Educ:** Oakwood Coll, Huntsville AL, BS 1976-78; Univ of AL, Birmingham AL, MBA 1978-82. **Career:** Bell South Svcs, staff analyst 1978-86; Protective Indus Insurance Co, Birmingham AL, comptroller, 1986-87; Porter White Yardley Capitol Inc, Birmingham AL, project dir 1987-. **Orgs:** Instructor Miles Coll; writer Birmingham Times; mem Big Brothers/Big Sisters; mem Birmingham Assn of Urban Bankers, 1988-. **Honors/Awds:** Leadership Award, Birmingham AL, 1989.

CLAY, WILLIAM L.
Congressman. **Personal:** Born Apr 30, 1931, St Louis, MO; son of Luella Hyatt Clay and Irving C Clay; married Carol Ann Johnson, 1953; children: Vicki Flynn, William Jr, Michelle Katherine. **Educ:** St Louis Univ, BS, history & political science, 1953. **Career:** Real estate broker, St Louis, MO, 1955-59; Indust Life Ins Co, manager, 1959-61; Democratic alderman, 26th Ward, St Louis, MO, 1959-1964; St Co & Municipal Employees Union, bus rep, 1961-1964; 26th Ward, dem committeeman 1964-85; US House of Representatives, congressman, 1969-. **Orgs:** Member, NAACP; member, CORE; member, St Louis Junior Chamber of Commerce. **Honors/Awds:** Distinguished Citizens Award, Alpha Kappa Alpha, 1969; Argus Award, St Louis Argus Newspaper, 1969; Honorary LLD, Lincoln Univ. **Military Serv:** US Army, 1953-55. **Business Addr:** Congressman, US House of Representatives, Washington, DC 20515.

CLAY, WILLIAM LACY, JR.
Government official. **Personal:** Born Jul 27, 1956, St Louis, MO; son of Carol A Clay and William L Clay; married Ivie. **Educ:** Univ of MD, BS Political Sci 1983, Cert in Paralegal

Studies 1982. **Career:** US House of Rep, asst doorkeeper 1976-83; paralegal; Missouri General Assembly, senator, currently. **Orgs:** Mem bd of dirs, William L Clay Scholarship and Research Fund 1989-; Missouri Legislative Black Caucus; Democratic National Committee. **Home Addr:** 6136 Washington, St Louis, MO 63112. **Business Addr:** Senator, Missouri General Assembly, State Capitol Bldg, Rm 429, Jefferson City, MO 65101.

CLAY, WILLIAM ROGER
Judge. **Personal:** Born Oct 16, 1919, Phoenix, AZ; married Jacqueline Laura Banks; children: William R III, Benjamin R. **Educ:** Southwestern Univ, LLB 1956. **Career:** LA Police Dept, policeman 1946-66; LA Co Publ Defenders Off, atty 1966; LA Neighborhood Legal Serv Soc, atty 1966-68; LA Superior Ct, referee 1968-70; LA Co, comm 1970-73; Inglewood Municip Ct, judge 1973-76; LA Co Superior Ct, judge 1976-. **Orgs:** Past pres Congr 1971; chrmn Parish Educ Bd; mem trustee bd Men's Club; comm Lutheran Ch & Ascension Luth Ch; mem Crenshaw YMCA & Y's Men's Club; bdmem YMCA; bd mem Boy's Club; mem LA Co Bar Assn; mem Natl Bar Assn; Judicature; mem CA Judges Assn; mem Retired Police Officer's Assn; NAACP mem Urban League. **Honors/Awds:** Citation LA City Council. **Military Serv:** AUS Staff Sgt 1940-44; AUS Reserves 1st Lt 1944-45, Major 1945-56. **Business Addr:** Judge, Kenyon Juvenile Justice Center, 7625 S Central, Los Angeles, CA 90001.

CLAY, WILLIE B.
Minister. **Personal:** Born Feb 16, 1929, Yazoo City, MS; married Ruth Davis; children: Gladys, Willie Jr, Jonathan, Margo, Lara. **Educ:** Rust Coll, Grad; Gammon Theol Sem, Grad; Wiley Coll, DD. **Career:** North IL Conf Unit Meth Ch, council dir 6 yrs; MS, pastorates; IN, pastorates; IL, pastorates; Chic So Dist of North IL, dist supt 6 yrs; Gorham United Methodist Church, minister. **Orgs:** Mem Bd of Trustees N Cent Coll; mem Gammon & Theol Sem; del Gen Conf & Juris Conf of Unit Meth Ch; mem Rotary Club of Chic. **Business Addr:** Minister, Gorham UM Church, 5600 S Indiana Ave, Chicago, IL 60637.

CLAY, WILLIE JAMES
Professional football player. **Personal:** Born Sep 5, 1970, Pittsburgh, PA. **Educ:** Georgia Tech, attended. **Career:** Detroit Lions, defensive back, 1992-95; New England Patriots, 1996-. **Business Addr:** Professional Football Player, New England Patriots, 60 Washington St, Foxboro Stadium, Foxboro, MA 02035, (508)543-7911.

CLAYBORN, RAY DEWAYNE
Professional athlete. **Personal:** Born Jan 2, 1955, Fort Worth, TX; son of Jessie Wilson Clayborn and Adell Clayborn; married Cindy Cavazos Clayborn, Nov 12, 1984; children: Lindsey Marie. **Educ:** University of Texas, Austin, TX; B.S. Communications, 1977. **Career:** New England Patriots, corner back 1977-. **Honors/Awds:** As rookie named to Pro Football Weekly's All-AFC and All-Pro squads as a kickoff returner; set 5 Patriot kickoff return records as a rookie; 2nd team All-AFC by UPI; 2nd team All-Pro by Coll and Pro Football Newsweekly; 2nd team All-NFL by NEA; mem Pro Bowl teams 1984,86,87; mem, Natl Found and Hall of Fame. **Business Addr:** New England Patriots, Sullivan Stadium Route 1, Foxboro, MA 02035.

CLAYBORN, WILMA W.
Business Executive, educator, educational administrator. **Personal:** Born Aug 21, Louisville, KY; daughter of Loreta Kline Westfield and Louis Albert Westfield; widowed; children: Terrence A, Jocelyn L Clayborn Raymore. **Educ:** KY State Univ, BS 1960; Catherine Spalding Univ, MEd 1971; IN Univ SE, grad work; Univ of Louisville, post grad. **Career:** McCracken Co, Independent School System, Sci/Physical Ed teacher, 1960-62; JCPS, Biology, Gen Sci, Anatomy & Physiology, Physical Sci & Physical Ed, 1963-89; Grace Gospel Music Co, entrepreneur/publisher/promoter 1969-; Jefferson Co Public Schools, science tchr 1964-76, instructional coord 1976-78, tchr of biology science 1963-89; Math, Science, Technology Program, sci specialist, 1987-89; Math, Science, Technology Magnet Science Resource Consultant, Jeff Co Public School 1987-89 (retired); Lincoln Foundation, Inc, Math/Science Program, teacher, 1981-90, The Whitney M Young Scholars Program, director, 1990-, assoc prog officer, 1995-. **Orgs:** Mem Natl C of Gospel Choirs & Choruses Inc; NEA, KEA, LEA; chairperson Minority Involv Caucus; LEA 1971-74; coord Human Relations Workshop 1972-74; mem bd dir KY Assn for Progress in Sci 1974; natl reg local directress Youth & Young Adult Choirs Ch of God 1967-; directress various gospel choirs; mem Religious Radio Announcers Guild 1977-90; officer Louisville Gospel Choral Union 1968-88; founder, president Metropolitan Gospel Music Connection 1989-; Kentucky Retired Teachers Assn; Jefferson County Retired Teachers Assn; AARP; NEA-R; KEA-R; Jefferson County Retired Teachers; African Amer Pioneers in Science & Industry, lecturer, facilitator, consultant; mem of several advisory bds. **Honors/Awds:** Outstanding Young Educator Awd Louisville Jaycees 1972; Citation Pioneer in Educ for Innovations in Educ 1970-71; Outstanding Secondary Educators Amer 1973; Words & Music to song: ''Jesus Is The Sunshine of My Life''; Adult Black Achievers, 1991; Torch Bearer & Trail Blazers Award, 1991. **Business Addr:** Owner/Entrepreneur, Grace Music Co, PO Box 2138, Louisville, KY 40201.

CLAYBORNE, ONEAL
Elected official. **Personal:** Born Dec 17, 1940, DeKalb, MS; married Deborah Roberts; children: Michelle, Shaneal. **Educ:** Whisenton High Dekalb MS, diploma. **Career:** Pct #48 E St Louis, pct committeeman 1979-87; Aldermanic Pub Safety Comm, chmn 1981-85; City of E St Louis, alderman 1979-87. **Orgs:** Chmn Project ONEAL Citizen Patrol Neighborhood Watch 1982-85. **Honors/Awds:** Special Achievement Awd Natl Coalition to Ban Handguns 1982. **Home Addr:** 840 N 79th St, East St Louis, IL 62203.

CLAYBOURNE, EDWARD P.
Educator. **Personal:** Born Apr 7, 1927, Chattanooga, TN; married Earnestine Crawford; children: Kimberly, Karen, Kaye, Kenneth. **Educ:** TN State U, BS 1952, MS 1968. **Career:** Harrison HS, asst prin/dean 1980; Harrison HS Evansville, asst 1975-; Central HS Evansville IN, counselor 1966-75; Lincoln HS Evansville, coach & tchr 1957-62; Educator, coach & tchr 1952-57; I & II Regional Tournament, football play-off champs. **Orgs:** Mem NEA; IN Tchr Assn; TN Tchr Assn; Evansville Tchr Assn; Assn Tchr Educators; HPER Assn Counselor Assn 33 deg Mason; mem NAACP Frofl Contract; coll soph LA Rams; 1st Black Coach Predom White Sch. **Business Addr:** 5400 N First Ave, Evansville, IN.

CLAYE, CHARLENE MARETTE
Art historian. **Personal:** Born Apr 6, 1945, Chicago, IL; daughter of Anne Claye and Clifton Claye; divorced. **Educ:** Univ of Bridgeport, BA 1966; Univ of Paris, certificate 1968; Howard Univ, MA 1970. **Career:** Univ of DC, instructor, 1970, 1973; Howard Univ Washington, instructor, 1970 1973; Spelman Coll Atlanta, instructor, 1971-72; Clayton Jr Coll, instructor, 1972-; New Muse, exec dir 1974-78; CA Afro Amer Museum, exec dir 1982-83; The Claye Institute, exec dir, currently. **Orgs:** Pres Natl Conf of Artists 1976-78; assoc dir African Cultural Serv 1970; Amer Soc for Aesthetics; member, National Education Association. **Honors/Awds:** Pubished curator ''The Black Artist in the WPA'' 1933-43; article on symbolism of African Textiles Contemporary Weavers Assn of TX; cover design for Logic for Black Undergrad; Curator permanent exhibit on ''The Black Contrib to Devel of Brooklyn 1660-1960''; grants, Travel for Mus Professional Natl Mus Act 1976; Aid to Special Exhibitions Natl Endowment of the Art 1976, 1977; Planning Grant Natl Endowment for the Humanities 1976. **Home Addr:** 3209 Ewing St, Houston, TX 77004.

CLAYTON, CONSTANCE ELAINE
Educational administrator. **Personal:** Born in Philadelphia, PA; daughter of Willabell Harris Clayton and Levi Clayton. **Educ:** Temple University, BA, elementary education, MA, elementary school administration, 1955; University of Pennsylvania, PhD, 1981. **Career:** Philadelphia Public School System, Harrison Elementary School, fourth grade teacher, 1955-64, social studies curricula designer, 1964-69, African & Afro-American studies program, head, 1969-71, Early Childhood Development Program, director, 1973-83, associate superintendent, superintendent, 1982-; US Dept of Labor, Women's Bureau, director, Middle Atlantic States, 1971-72. **Orgs:** St Paul's Baptist Church; NAACP; Delta Sigma Theta. **Honors/Awds:** Rockefeller Foundation fellowship. **Business Addr:** Superintendent, Philadelphia Public School System, 21st & Parkway, Philadelphia, PA 19103.

CLAYTON, EVA
Congresswoman. **Personal:** Born Sep 16, 1938. **Educ:** North Carolina Central University, MS. **Career:** Warren County Commission, chairperson, 1982-90, commissioner, 1990-92; US House of Representatives, congresswoman, 1992-. **Honors/Awds:** North Carolina Assn of County Commissioners, Outstanding County Commissioner, 1990. **Special Achievements:** One of the first two African Americans voted into Congress from North Carolina in the 20th Century. **Business Addr:** Congresswoman, ATTN: Lenwood Long or Janice Crump, US House of Representatives, 222 Cannon House Office Bldg, Washington, DC 20515-3301, (202)225-3101.

CLAYTON, JAMES HENRY
Educator. **Personal:** Born Jul 10, 1944, Marianna, AR; married Dorothy; children: Kamillah, Keith, Denise. **Educ:** IL State U, BS 1967, MEd 1972. **Career:** CA State, dir educ opportunity program; Special Recruitment & Asmissions Program, dir 1974-75; Special Progress Parkland Community Coll, coord 1972-74; Upward Bound Univ of IL, dir 1970-72; Special Educ Opportunity, co-dir 1969-70. **Orgs:** Dir CA Assn of EOP Dir; pres CA State Dom Hills Black Faculty & Staff Assn; proposal consult Carson Comm Thtr Mem NAACP; Intl Reading Assn; Phi Delta Kappa; chmn Comm Support; adv bd Carson Employment Readiness Support Ctrco-author, musical play Cinderella Brown 1976-77. **Business Addr:** California State University, 1000 E Victoria, Long Beach, CA 90840.

CLAYTON, JANET THERESA
Journalist. **Personal:** Born May 10, 1955, Los Angeles, CA; daughter of Pinkie B Hodges Clayton and Pronzell B Clayton; married Michael D Johnson, Jul 27, 1985; children: Jocelyn Michelle, Aaron Clayton. **Educ:** USC, Los Angeles, CA, BA, 1977. **Career:** Los Angeles Times, staff writer, 1977-87, editorial writer, 1990, asst editor of editorial page, 1990-95, editor of editorial pages, 1995-97, vice president, 1997-. **Orgs:** Member, Black Journalists Assn of Southern California, 1980-; member, National Assn of Black Journalists, reporting team, 1986-; American Society of Newspaper Editors. **Honors/Awds:** Reporting Team Award, National Association of Black Journalists, 1983; Black Woman of Achievement, NAACP Legal Defense Fund. **Business Addr:** Vice President, The Los Angeles Times, Times Mirror Square, Los Angeles, CA 90053.

CLAYTON, KATHLEEN R.
Business executive. **Personal:** Born Jun 4, 1952, New Orleans, LA; married Lawrence Clayton Jr; children: Lisa, Lawrence III, Wesley. **Educ:** Rice Univ, BA Behavioral Sci 1976. **Career:** Prudential Ins Co, cost analyst 1976-79; Bank of New Orleans, asst vice pres & mgr 1980-83; Liberty Bank & Trust Co, vp, human resource dir. **Orgs:** Mem Amer Compensation Assoc 1984-85, Black Heritage Comm New Orleans Museum of Art 1984-.

CLAYTON, LAURA ANCELINA
Attorney. **Personal:** Born Aug 22, 1960, St George's, Bermuda; daughter of Barbara Joan Milton and Sylvester Valentine Clayton Jr; married Henry Hutchins; children: Clayton Enrique Hutchins, Taji Alessandra Hutchins. **Educ:** De Anza College, Cupertino, CA, AA/AS, 1980; San Jose State Univ, San Jose, CA, BS, 1981; University of California Berkeley, Berkeley, CA, MBA, 1985; University of California Berkeley, Berkeley, CA, JD, 1985. **Career:** Lillick & Charles, San Francisco, CA, associate, 1985-86; Pettit & Martin, San Francisco, CA, associate, 1986-89; Apple Computer Inc, Cupertino, CA, sr counsel, 1989-. **Orgs:** President, Natl Black MBA Assn, San Francisco Chapter, 1989-90; director, Youth Entrepreneurial Svcs Intl, 1988-90; director, Natl Economic Development & Law Center, 1988-90; advisory board member, Natl Institute for Managing Diversity, 1990-92; president-elect, Barristers Clubs, Santa Clara County Bar Association, 1993-; Bankers Section Santa Clara County Bar Assn, pres, 1994; Educ Comm, Santa Clara County Bar Assn, chair, 1995, bd of trustees, 1995-; CA Young Lawyers Assn, District #3, bd mem, 1995-. **Business Addr:** Counsel, Legal Department, Apple Computer Inc, 1 Infinite Loup M/S 73-LG, Cupertino, CA 95014.

CLAYTON, LLOYD E.
Association executive. **Personal:** Born Jul 8, 1921, Mobile, AL; son of Ruby Roberts Clayton and William H Clayton; married Lela Maxwell, Aug 4, 1947; children: Kenneth R, Robert L, Carole M. **Educ:** Howard Univ, BS 1955. **Career:** Walter Reed Army Inst Res, res chemist 1951-68; Task Force Health Care Disadvantaged, dep chmn 1968-71; Task Force Health Care Disadvantaged 1968-71; Status Health Black Comm, proj officer 1971; Status Dental Health Black Comm, proj officer 1972; Minority Physician Recruitment Natl Health Serv Corps, proj officer 1973; Sickle Cell Disease Prog, proj officer 1976; Black Congress on Health & Law, proj officer 1980, staff consultant 1980-88. **Orgs:** Vol coord trnsp between Poor People's Campaign HQ & Resurrection City 1968; mem Assoc Sports Intl Track Club 1967; official timer Natl Invitational Track Meet 1967-68. **Honors/Awds:** Appreciation and Gratitude Awd for Outstanding Leadership in the Field of Sickle Cell Anemia San Juan PR 1978; spec presentation for Contrib to the health field Black Congress on Health and Law Dallas TX 1980; Superior Serv Awd Natl Black Health Planners Assn Wintergreen VA 1986; Meeting Planner of the Year, Natio nal Coalition of Black Meeting Planners, 1989. **Military Serv:** US Army, tech sgt, 1944-46. **Home Addr:** 4821 Blagden Ave NW, Washington, DC 20011. **Business Addr:** President, Clayton & Associates, 4821 Blagden Ave, NW, Washington, DC 20011.

CLAYTON, MATTHEW D.
Counsel. **Personal:** Born Mar 5, 1941, Philadelphia, PA; married Ramona Carter; children: Rebecca, Janice, Matthew D III. **Educ:** Univ of MD, 1960-61; Uof MN, 1962-63; PA State U, BA 1966; Howard Univ Sch of Law, JD 1966-69. **Career:** Philadelphia Prisons System, correctional officer 1963; Philadelphia Crime Presention Assoc, staff 1966; Small Business Admin, legal asst 1968; US Dept of Labor, regional trial atty 1969-72; Counsel Corp Law, 1972-74; Smith Kline Corp, corporate employee relations & litigation counsel 1974-. **Orgs:** Mem Natl Bar Assn; Am Bar Assn; Fed Bar Assn; PA Bar Assn; Philadelphia Bar Assn; Indsl Relat Resrch Assn; mem sec of labor study on young professional US Dept of Labor 1970-72; coord US Dept of Labor; mem Nat Urban League; Natl Panel of Arbitrators; Am Arbitration Assn; Am Mgmt Assn; Am Trial Lawyers Assn; mem Barristers Club; fdng mem World Lawyers Assn. **Honors/Awds:** Outstanding Academic Achievement Amer Jurisprudence Awd; Outstanding Legal Service Small Business Admin. **Military Serv:** USAF 1959-63. **Business Addr:** 865 Belmont Ave, Philadelphia, PA 19104.

CLAYTON, MAYME AGNEW
Business executive. **Personal:** Born Aug 4, 1923, Van Buren, AR; daughter of Mary D Agnew and Jerry M; married Andrew Lee Clayton; children: Averyie, Renai, Lloyd, Andy. **Educ:** UWW Berkeley, BA 1974; Goddard Coll, grad prog 1974; AR Baptist Coll, attended 1940-41; Lincoln Univ MO 1944-46;

Univ of So CA, attended 1958-59; Sierra University, PhD 1983. **Career:** UCLA, law library, 1959-72; USC, asst lib for engrg lib 1956-59, dir of circulation & spl serv asst for law lib 1959-71, consult librarian for Afro-Amer Study Ctr 1970-71; UWW Berkeley, natl field rep adjunct faculty 1972-74; Universal Books, co-owner 1971-72; Special Black Achievement, consul & lectr; Third World Ethnic Books, owner/pres (largest black collection on W Coast OP specialist) 1972-. **Orgs:** Founder/executive director, Western States Black Research Center, 1976; founder Black Amer Cinema Soc 1974-; producer Black Talkies on Parade 13th Annual Film Festival 1991; consult Claremont Coll Black Oral History Dept 1973-74; organizer of Intl Black Bookdealers 1973; African Work & Study Proj 1971; KCOP TV Minority Comm Rsch & Historian 1974-; KNBC-TV "What It Is" Rsch & Consult 1973-74; mem Iota Phi Lambda Sor Inc; Gamma Mu Chap LA 1973; Natl News Media Women Hollywood/Beverly Hills Chap 1973; founder Black Amer Cinema Soc 1976; art & cult coord Dist 8 Councilmatie; LA Coin Club 1974; founder Black Cultural Entertainment Network 1982; Producer Black Progs for TV & Cable; founder, exec dir Western States Black Research Center 1975 (non-profit); bd of dir Sierra Univ Santa Monica, C. **Honors/Awds:** Woman of the Yr Awd Iota Phi Lambda 1973; Feature article Third World Book Store Owner Black Profile Sepia Mag June 1974; Black Filmmakers Awd; Image Award, NAACP, 1980; Rosa Parks Award, 1991. **Special Achievements:** Contributed over $50,000 in cash grants for independent and student black filmmakers, Black American Cinema Society Awards, 1993. **Business Addr:** President, Third World Ethnic Books, 3617 1/2 Mont Clair St, Los Angeles, CA 90018.

CLAYTON, MINNIE H.
Librarian. **Personal:** married Robert L; children: Robert J III, Myrna A. **Educ:** Alabama State University, BS, 1954; Atlanta University, MLS, 1970. **Career:** Dev and Book College on Porton, all ages, cons; Black History & Bibliography of Civil Rights, author, 1954; Lectures & Life of Martin Luther King Jr, author; Martin Luther King Center for Social Change, library archivist, 1969-78; Atlanta University Center, Southern Regional Council Archives Project, Dept of Archives and Records Management, project archivist, 1978-80, RW Woodruff Library, Div of Archives and Special Collections, director, 1982-88, processing archivist, 1988-. **Orgs:** American Library Assn; Georgia Library Assn; Metro-Atlanta Library Assn; Natl Hist Society; Society of American Archivists; American Assn of University Professors; African American Family Hist Assn; Georgia Archivists. **Honors/Awds:** Coretta King Award Committee; League of Women Voters; NAACP, Jessie S Noyes Foundation Grant, 1966-68; State Historical Record, Advisory Bd of Georgia; cert, Archival Adm, Emory University, 1973; Danforth Foundation Assn, 1966-67.

CLAYTON, ROBERT L.
Personnel executive. **Personal:** Born Dec 6, 1938, Morris Station, GA; son of Willie Mae Mercer Clayton and Henry Clayton; married Sharon Cage, Mar 25, 1966; children: Robert, Angela. **Educ:** Central State Univ, Wilberforce, OH, BS, business admin, 1962; Akron Univ, Akron, OH, post-graduate studies, 1965-66. **Career:** Co-op Supermarkets, Akron, OH, comptroller, 1965-73; Fiberboard, San Francisco, CA, sr financial analyst, 1973-79; CH2M Hill, Denver, CO, vp Employee Relations and Diversity 1979-. **Orgs:** Mem, Amer Soc Personnel Admin, 1980-, Natl Assn of Minority Engineering Program Admin, 1983-, Natl Forum of Black Public Admin, 1984-, UCLA Advisory Bd, 1986-, Industrial Technical Advisory Bd, Statewide MESA, 1986-, Univ of California Fullerton, Minority Engineering Bd, 1988-; member Kappa Alpha Psi Fraternity; 32nd Degree, Mason Shrine. **Military Serv:** US Army, 1st lt, 1962-65. **Home Phone:** (303)791-8964. **Business Addr:** Vice President Employee Relations, CH2M Hill, 6060 S Willow Dr, Greenwood Village, CO 80111-5142, (303)771-0900.

CLAYTON, THEAOSEUS T.
Attorney. **Personal:** Born Oct 2, 1930, Roxboro, NC; married Eva McPherson; children: Joanne A, Theaoseus T, Jr. **Educ:** Johnson C Smith U, AB 1955; Central Univ Sch of Law, JS, JD 1958. **Career:** Theaoseus T Clayton PA Inc, pres 1979-; Clayton & Ballance, sr partner 1966-78; Theaoseus T Clayton, sole propietorship 1963-66; Gilliland & Clayton, jr partner 1961-66; McKissick & Berry Durham, NC, atty 1961. **Orgs:** Mem Nat Bar Assn; mem Am Bar Assn; mem NC State Bar; mem NC Bar Assn; mem NC Trial Lawyers Assn; mem NC Assn Black Lawyers; mem Nat Conf Black Lawyers; past sec/treas 9th Jud Dist Bar Assn; pres Charles Williamson Bar Assn; chief counsel Floyd B McKissick & Floyd B McKissick Enterprises Inc Life mem/past state vice pres NAACP; mem Warren Co Dem Party; mem Warren Co Polit Action Council; mem 2nd Congressional Dist Black Caucus; past v chmn NC Bd Youth Devel. **Military Serv:** AUS corpl 1952-54.

CLAYTON, WILLIE BURKE, JR.
Law enforcement official. **Personal:** Born May 4, 1922, Sparta, GA; married Peggy Joyce; children: Eric, Craig, Deirdre, John, Kevin, Anthony, Peggy. **Educ:** NJ Coll of Commerce, 1951; Temple U, 1952-59; MI State U, Cert 1968; Trenton State Coll, 1973; Montclair State Coll Grad Sch, 1973; Am Intl Open U, PhD Cand; Stockton State Coll, BA 1973; Atlantic Comm Coll, Resd Study Course 1974; Glassboro State Coll, MA 1974; Univ of DE, Cert Grad 1977. **Career:** Roy E Hager Acctnts, pub acct 1968; You're in Touch WUSS Radio Sta, host 1976; Community Relations Unit, dir; Atlantic City Police Dept, capt; Atlantic City Police Dept, col & comdr of serv bur 1979-80; Atlantic City NJ, elected city commr 1980-84; Atlantic City, commr & dir of publ safety 1980;; Atlantic County Transportation Auth, sec 1987. **Orgs:** Vp bd of dir Atlantic Bus Comm Devel Corp; 1st pres NJ Conf of Police Professional 1976; treas Superior Ofcrs Assn ACPD 1977; past Nat treas Nat Counc of Police Soc Inc; charter mem Nat Orgn of Black Law Enforcement Exec 1977; pres NJ Statewide Assn of Comm Relat Ofcrs 1977; prgm advr Atlantic Comm Coll Bd; dir Boys Club of Am 1977; bd of trustees Nat Multiple Sclerosis Soc; life mem NAACP; mem League of Women Voters of Atlantic Co vp Ring #12 of Nat Vet Boxers Assn 1977; assisted in orgn Atlantic City Jr Police; assisted in establ & comdg ofcr Police Athletic League; mem Intl Assoc of Chiefs of Police IACP; pres Mothers Against Drugs Inc; golden heritage mem NAACP; vice pres Mainland Br NAACP. **Honors/Awds:** Plaque for Serv Rendered to Comm 3 R's Social Club 1975; Outstanding Serv in Human Realt Bus & Professional Women of NJ 1975; Cert of Honor Mainland Br NAACP 1975; Policeman of the Year 1977; Plaque Miss Black Amer Beauty Pagent of NJ for Outstanding Serv 1979; Plaque Natl Multiple Sclerosis Soc Greater Chap Outstanding Volunteer of the Year 1980; Plaque Atlantic City Taxicab Assoc 1980; Plaque K-9 Corps Awd AC Police Dept 1980; Plaque Black Atlantic City Mag Awd 1982; Martin Luther King Awd 1983; Mainland Br NAACP Martin Luther King Awd Plaque 1986; 27 commendations for merit serv Atlantic City Police Dept. **Military Serv:** US Army, tech/5 1944-46. **Business Addr:** Secretary, Atlantic City Police Dept, Tennessee & Arctic Avs, Atlantic City, NJ 08401.

CLAYTON, XERNONA
Television executive. **Personal:** Born Aug 30, 1930, Muskogee, OK; daughter of Rev & Mrs James Brewster; married Paul Brady. **Educ:** TN State U, BS 1952; Ru-Jac Sch of Modeling Chgo. **Career:** "The Xernona Clayton Show" WAGA-TV, hostess; Atlanta Voice, newspaper columnist; Chicago & LA, tchr pub schs; photographic & fashion modeling; Turner Broadcasting Systems, Inc, corporate vice president, retired. **Orgs:** Mem Atlanta Women's C of C; State & Manpower Adv Com for GA Dept of Labor; Nat Assn of Market Developers; Arts Alliance Guild; Am Women in Radio & TV; Nat Assn of Media Women; Nat Assn of Press Women; Atlanta Chap of Sigma Delta Chi; Atlanta Broadcast Exec Club; founder Atlanta Chap Media Women; mem Nat Academy of TV Arts & Sci; mem Ebenezer Bapt Ch; Alpha Kappa Alpha Sorority; bd dir Greater Atlanta Multiple Sclerosis Soc; honorary asso So Ballet. **Honors/Awds:** Outstanding Leadership Award winner Nat Assn of Market Developers 1968; First Negro Woman in TV Award Women's Orgn of Allen Temple AME Ch 1968; Bronze Woman of Yr in Human Relations Award Phi Delta Kappa Sorority 1969; Hadassah Women planted tree in her honor in Freedom Forest in Israel 1969; recipient GA Associated Press Award for Superior TV Programming 1969-71; awarded Excellence in TV Programming Los Angeles Chap of Negro Business & Professional Women 1970; Mother of Yr Future Homemakers of Am of Douglas HS 1969; Flying Orchid Award Delta Airline; included in Leadership Atlanta C of C 1971; named Atlanta's Five Best Dressed Brentwood Models Assn 1971; named Atlanta's Ten Best Dressed Women Women's C of C 1972; appointed by Gov of GA to Motion Picture & TV Commn for4-yr term 1972-76o-starred in major motion picture "House on Skull Mountain". **Business Addr:** Corporate Vice President Urban Affairs, Turner Broadcasting System, One CNN Center, Atlanta, GA 30303.

CLAYTOR, CHARLES E.
Association executive. **Personal:** Born Jun 2, 1936, Hotcoal, WV; son of Fairy Hickman Claytor and Harvey Claytor; married Annette Broadnax; children: Dreama, Charles Jr, Brien. **Educ:** NYCC. **Career:** Local 2947 United Brotherhood Carpenters, pres 1967-. **Business Addr:** 87-80 153 St, Jamaica, NY 11432.

CLEAGE, ALBERT B., JR.
Clergyman. **Personal:** Born Jun 13, 1911, Indpls, IN; divorced; children: Mrs Pearl Lomax, Mrs Kristin Williams. **Educ:** Wayne State U, AB; Oberlin Grad Sch of Theol, BD. **Career:** Shrine of Black Madonna Detroit, minister. **Orgs:** Nat chmn Black Christian Nationalist Ch Inc; mem natl bds of interreligious Foun for Comm Rogn; Nat Com of Black Churchmen; Comm for Racial Justice. **Honors/Awds:** Author "The Black Messiah"; "Black Christian Nationalism". **Business Addr:** Pan African Orthodox Christian, 13535 Livernois, Detroit, MI 48238.

CLEAGE, PEARL MICHELLE
Writer. **Personal:** Born Dec 7, 1948, Springfield, MA; daughter of Doris Graham Cleage & Albert B Cleage, Jr; married Zaron W Burnett, Jr, Mar 23, 1994; children: Deignan Cleage Lomax. **Educ:** Howard Univ, attended, 1966-69; Spelman College, BA, 1971. **Career:** Writer, currently. Just Us Theater Co, playwright-in-residence, 1981-86, artistic dir, 1987-94; CATALYST Magazine, founding editor, 1986-96; Atlanta Tribune, columnist, 1988-; Spelman Coll, playwright-in-residence, instr in drama, 1991-93; Smith Coll, playwright-in-residence, 1994; Agnes Scott Coll, Laney prof-in-residence, 1997; Writer, currently. **Honors/Awds:** Bronze Jubilee Award, Literature, 1983; NEA Grant, Just Us Theater Co, 1983-87; Atlanta Assn of Black Journalists, Outstanding Columnist Award, 1991; AT&T, Onstage Award, Outstanding New Play, 1992; Atlanta Assn of Media Women, Outstanding Columnist Award, 1993; Assn of Southern Writers, Award, 1994; Spelman Coll, Scholar-in-Residence, 1996; Univ of Mass at Amherst, Bateman Scholar-in-Residence, 1996; 2 Audellco Awards, Honoring off Broadway Achievements, Best Play and Best Playwright. **Special Achievements:** Publications: Flyin' West, play, 1992; Blues for An Alabama Sky, play, 1995; Mad at Miles: A Black Woman's Guide to Truth, essays, 1990; What Looks Like Crazy on An Ordinary Day, novel, 1997; author of numerous plays, essays and poems.

CLEAMONS, JAMES MITCHELL (JIM)
Professional basketball coach. **Personal:** Born Sep 13, 1949, Lincolnton, NC. **Educ:** Ohio State. **Career:** Los Angeles Lakers, 1971-72; Cleveland Cavaliers, 1972-77; New York Knicks, 1977-79; Washington Bullets, 1980; Furman Univ, asst coach, 1982-83; Ohio State Univ, asst coach, 1983-87, coach, 1987-89; Chicago Bulls, asst coach, 1989-96; Dallas Mavericks, coach, 1996-98. **Honors/Awds:** NBA, All-Defensive second team, 1976. **Special Achievements:** NBA Draft, First round pick, #13, 1971; NBA, Championship, 1972. **Business Addr:** Head Coach, Dallas Mavericks, Reunion Arena, 777 Sports St, Dallas, TX 75207, (214)988-0117.

CLEAVER, ELDRIDGE. **See Obituaries section.**

CLEAVER, EMANUEL, II
Mayor. **Personal:** Born Oct 26, 1944, Waxahachie, TX; married Dianne; children: Evan Donaldson, Emanuel III, Emiel Davenport, Marissa Dianne. **Educ:** Prairie View A&M Coll, BA; St Paul School of Theology Kansas City, MDiv; St Paul School of Theology, DSE. **Career:** St James-Paseo United Methodist Church, pastor; Kansas City, City Council, councilman; City of Kansas City, mayor, 1991-. **Orgs:** Bd of dir De La Salle Ed Ctr; mid-central reg vice pres Southern Christian Leadership Conf; pres, bd of trustees Leon Jordan Scholarship Fund; bd of trustees St Paul School of Theology; council on finance United Methodist Conf; bd of dir, former Chmn of bd Freedom Inc; mem Alpha Phi Alpha, NAACP. **Honors/Awds:** 41 achievements & honors incl Man of the Year Alpha Phi Alpha 1968; Community Leaders in Amer 1971; Builder of Boys Award Boys Club of Amer 1976; White House Guest of Pres Jimmy Carter 1977; Recognition of Thanks Woodland Elem School 1983; Apprec Award NAACP 1984; Black History Award Univ of MO-Kansas City 1984; Disting Serv Award Exceptional Leadership & Devoted Serv to Civil Rights Alpha Phi Alpha 1984; Award for Outstanding Serv Freedom Inc 1984; Citizen of the Year Omega Psi Phi.

CLEGG, LEGRAND H., II
Attorney. **Personal:** Born Jun 29, 1944, Los Angeles. **Educ:** UCLA, BA 1966; Howard Univ Sch Law, JD 1969. **Career:** City of Compton CA, deputy city atty; Compton Community Coll, instructor; Robert Edelen Law Offices, atty 1975-; LA, legal aid found 1972-74; Compton CA, admin asst 1970-72; Dept Justice Washington, legal intern 1968-69. **Orgs:** Mem LA Bar Assn; CA Lawyers Criminal Justice; Langston Law Club; Nat Conf Black Lawyers; Compton Cultural Commn; Assn Black Psychol; Pilgrim Missionary Bapt Ch. **Honors/Awds:** Pubs LA Times 1974; current bibliography on African Affairs 1969, 1972; guest lecturer Vassar Coll/NY U/UCLA/U of So CA 1978-79. **Business Addr:** Compton City Hall, Compton, CA 90224.

CLEMENDOR, ANTHONY ARNOLD
Physician, educator. **Personal:** Born Nov 8, 1933; son of Beatrice Stewart Thompson and Anthony Clemendor; married Elaine C Browne (died 1991); children: Anthony A, David A; married Janat Jenkins, Sep 23, 1993. **Educ:** NY Univ, BA 1959; Howard Univ Coll Med, MD 1963. **Career:** NY Med College, prof of clinical OB-GYN, dir office minority affairs, assoc dean. **Orgs:** Life mem NAACP; mem 100 Black Men Inc; mem NY Urban League; bd mem Elmcor; fellow Amer Coll OB-Gyn; mem Amer Pub Health Assn; pres Student Amer Med Assn Chapter Howard Univ 1961-62; dir Office of Minority Affairs NY Med Coll 1974-97; pres, New York Gynecological Society Inc 1988; bd of directors, Caribbean American Center 1988; pres, New York County Medical Society 1992; mem, National Urban League. **Honors/Awds:** Publ "Transient Asymptomatic Hydrothorax in Pregnancy" 1976; "Achalasia & Nutritional Deficiency During Pregnancy" 1969; SNMA Award Univ of Buffalo Chap 1984; T & T Alliance Award Trinidad & Tobago Alliance of NA 1984; Trinidad & Tobago Nurses Assn of America Inc Award 1988; National Award, The National Assn of Medical Minority Educators, Inc, 1989; Physician of the Year Award, Manhattan Central Medical Society, 1989. **Business Addr:** Professor of Clinical OB-GYN, 125 East 80 St, New York, NY 10021.

CLEMENT, JOSEPHINE DOBBS
County commissioner (retired). **Personal:** Born Feb 9, 1918, Atlanta, GA; daughter of Irene Thompson Dobbs and John Wesley Dobbs; married William Alexander Clement, Dec 24, 1941; children: Alexine Jackson, William Jr, Wesley, Arthur, Kathleen, Josephine. **Educ:** Spelman Coll, Atlanta GA, BS 1933-37; Columbia Univ, New York, NY, MA 1937-38. **Career:** Durham City Bd of Educ, chmn; GA State Coll, tchr; NC Central Univ; GA State Coll, Savannah GA, instr, 1938-41; Morris Brown Coll, Atlanta GA, instr, 1943-45; North Carolina Central Univ, instr, 1951-57. **Orgs:** Mem Durham Co Libr; NC Symphony; editorial bd Negro Braile Mag; Durham City Co Chrtr Commn 1971-74; Delta Sigma Theta; Links; docent Duke Univ Mus of Art; mem and chmn, Durham City Bd of Educ, 1973-83; bd mem Shaw Univ; bd mem Z Smith Reynolds Found. **Honors/Awds:** Shaw Univ, Doctor of Humane Letters; Durham Chamber of Commerce, Distinguished Award; Women of Achievement, YWCA; NAACP, Citizens Award; NC Cen Univ, Honorary Doctor of Humanities, 1996. **Home Addr:** 3747 Peachtree St NE, Apt 1101, Atlanta, GA 30319.

CLEMENT, WILLIAM A.
Business executive (retired). **Personal:** Born May 6, 1912, Charleston, SC; son of Sadie K Jones Clement and Arthur J Clement; married Josephine Dobbs; children: Alexine C, William A Jr, Wesley, Arthur, John, Kathleen Ophelia, Josephine Millicent. **Educ:** Talladega Coll, BA 1934. **Career:** NC Mutual Life Ins Co, agency dir 1961, vice pres 1962, agency vice pres in charge of field opers 1966, sr vice pres 1969-75, retired exec vice pres 1975-78. **Orgs:** 33 Degree Mason Prince Hall 1945; earned CLU designation 1953; mem bd of dir NC Mutual Life Ins Co 1961-85; pres Durham's United Fund 1970; mem bd dir Wachovia Bank & Trust Co; dep grand master Prince Hall Grand Lodge 1975; chmn trustee bd NC Central Univ 1975; trustee Durham Co Gen Hosp Corp 1976; mem Raleigh-Durham Airport Auth 1979; grand master Prince Hall Grand Lodge of NC 1981; chmn Raleigh-Durham Airport Authority 1985; trustee Amer Coll Bryn Mawr PA; dir NC Mutual Life Ins Co; mem Durham Rotary Club; Durham Bus & Professional Chain; mem exec comm Durham Comm on Negro Affairs; mem bd dir Scarborough Nursery. **Honors/Awds:** Silver Beaver Awd BSA 1966; Durham Chamber of Commerce Civic Awd 1987; Honorary Degree, North Carolina Central University Doctor of Law. **Home Addr:** 3747 Peachtree Rd NE, Apt 1101, Atlanta, GA 30319-1364.

CLEMENT, WILLIAM A., JR.
Computer company executive. **Personal:** Born Jan 22, 1943, Atlanta, GA; married Ressie Guy; children: Anika P, Leanetta Spencer. **Educ:** Morehouse Coll, BA; Wharton Sch of Finance & Commerce Univ of PA, MBA; Amer Coll of Life Underwriters, CLU. **Career:** North Carolina Mutual Life Ins Co, life insurance agent; Robinson Humphrey/American Express Inc, stockbroker; Prudential-Bache Securities Inc, stockbroker; North Carolina Natl Bank, credit analyst/commercial loan officer; Citizens Trust Bank, vice pres & sr loan officer; US Small Business Administration-Carter Administration, assoc administrator; Dobbs Corporation, pres/CEO; Dobbs Ram & Co, chairman/CEO, currently. **Orgs:** The Dobbs Corp., Natl Bank of Washington, Natl Consumer Cooperative Bank; chmn bd dirs USEP Inc; mem bd dirs Business League, Atlanta Urban League, Butler St YMCA, Big Bros of Atlanta, vice pres and sr loan officer Citizens Trust Bank Atlanta; bd chm, chief volunteer officer, Atlanta Business League; board of directors, Atlanta Chamber of Commerce; board of directors, The Metropolitan Atlanta Community Foundation; board of directors, Leadership Atlanta; board of directors, Atlanta Convention & Visitors Bureau; bd mem, Research Atlanta, The Atlanta Exchange, The Alliance Theatre Co; Atlanta Coalition of 100 Black Men; Soc of Intl Business Fellows. **Honors/Awds:** Intl Business Fellow, London Business School; Crim High School, Entrepreneur of the Year, 1992; Atlanta Tribune, Business Owner of the Year, 1992; SuccessGuide, Entrepreneur of the Year, 1992; NABMBA, Entrepreneur of the Year, 1990; Atlanta Chamber of Commerce, Finalist, Small Business Person of the Year, 1990. **Business Addr:** Chairman & CEO, Dobbs, Ram & Co, 615 Peachtree St NE, Ste 1200, Atlanta, GA 30308.

CLEMENTS, GEORGE H.
Priest. **Personal:** Born Jan 26, 1932, Chicago, IL. **Educ:** St Mary of the Lake Sem, BA; St Mary of the Lake Sem, MA philosophy. **Career:** Quigley Sem, 1st black grad ordained in 1957; Holy Angels Roman Catholic Church, pastor, currently. **Orgs:** Oranized Black Clergy Caucus; chaplain Afro-Am Patrolmen's League; Afro-AmFiremen's League; Postal Workers' League; highly active in civic & comm affairs & has organized several neighborhood assns; mem bd SCLC's Operation Breadbasket; NAACP; Urban League; Better Boys Found; Black Panther party Malcolm X Coll; organizer, Black Clergy Caucus. **Honors/Awds:** Trumpet Awards, Family Spirit Award, 1998. **Business Addr:** Founder, One Church, One Addict, 1101 14th St. NW, Ste. 630, Washington, DC 20005.

CLEMENTS, WALTER H.
Attorney. **Personal:** Born Oct 28, 1928, Atlanta, GA; son of Lucile Clements and Emanuel Clements; divorced; children: Kevin M, Alisa C. **Educ:** Morehouse Coll, BA 1949; Univ of MI Law School, JD 1952. **Career:** Private practice, attny 1953-59; Vet Admin, adjudicator 1962-65; Small Bus Admin, asst area counsel 1966-69; State of MI, asst attny gen 1969-73; Southeastern MI Transp Auth, gen counsel 1973-88; Wayne County Community College, gen counsel, 1988-. **Orgs:** Mem State Bar of MI, Wolverine Bar Assoc, Natl Bar Assoc, Amer Arbitration Assoc; referee MI Civil Rights Comm. **Home Addr:** 20070 Lichfield, Detroit, MI 48221.

CLEMMONS, CLIFFORD R.
Probation branch chief (retired). **Personal:** Born in Kansas City, KS; son of Constance Alice Sargent Clemmons and H B Clemmons; married Jimmie E Hill; children: Jennifer M Johnson-Barnett, C Robert Jr. **Educ:** Oakwood Jr Coll, Huntsville, AL, Diploma, 1939; Central State Univ, Wilberforce OH, BS, Social Work, 1948; OH State Univ, Masters of Social Admin, 1950; NYU, Columbia Univ, attended. **Career:** Greenpoint Hospital, Med Social Worker 1950; Probation Dept NY, Probation Officer, 1951-66, Supvr Probation Officer 1966-82; City of NY Dept of Probation, branch chief 1982-87. **Orgs:** Chmn emeritus, bd dir, Sickle Cell Disease Found, Greater NY 1972-87; vice pres bd dir Muncipal Credit Union, 1971-77; chmn bd of dir, Federation of Negro Serv Org Inc, 1968-77; state dir, Alpha Phi Alpha Fraternity Inc 1971-87; pres, Counselors, Probation & Parole Officers, 1964-68; pres, bd of dir, United Veterans Mutual Housing Company, 1967-70; pres, Consumer Groups of Greater New York, 1973-75. **Honors/Awds:** Middleton Spike Harris Award Counseliers Inc NY 1978; Commr of Probation Merit Award, Probation Dept NY, 1980; Alpha Award of Merit, Alpha Phi Alpha Fraternity Inc, Queens Chapter, 1972; Comm Serv Award, Leadership Bell Park Manor Terrace Comm Council Inc, 1964; over 35 awards & citations. **Military Serv:** AUS 1st sgt. **Home Addr:** 4345 Senna Dr, Las Cruces, NM 88011.

CLEMMONS, JACKSON JOSHUA WALTER
Pathologist, educator. **Personal:** Born Mar 24, 1923, Beloit, WI; son of Ora Bell Clemmons and Henry Clemmons; married Lydia Monroe Clemmons, Dec 27, 1952; children: Jackson, Lydia, Laura, Jocelyn, Naomi. **Educ:** Univ of WI, BS Biochem 1947, MS Biochem 1949, PhD Biochem & Exper Pathology 1955; Western Reserve Univ, MD, 1959. **Career:** Univ of WI Madison, rsch asst, Biochem, 1942-43, res assoc in biochemistry/exper pathology 1947-52; Karolinska Inst of Biophysics & Cell Res Stockholm, Sweden, res fellow 1950; Sloan Kettering Inst for Cancer Res NY, special res fellow 1953; Univ of WI Madison, WI, project assoc in exper pathology 1953-55; Amer Cancer Soc Inst of Pathology, Western Reserve Univ, Cleveland OH, postdoctoral fellow 1956-57, fellow of pathology 1957-61, Helen Hay Whitney fellow 1961-64; Univ of VT Coll of Med, Burlington VT, asst prof, Pathology 1962-64. **Orgs:** Amer Bd of Pathology Anatomic Pathology 1964; Am Med Assn; Am Assn of Path & Bacteriologists; VT State Med Soc; Chittenden Co Med Soc; New England Rheumatism Soc; Sigma Xi; Phi Lambda Upsilon; Gamma Alpha; Am Soc for Experimental Pathology; Intl Acad of Pathology; Am Soc for Clinical Chem; NY Acad of Science; Am Soc of Clinical Pathologists; Univ of VT Radioisotope Com 1968-; Exec Com Graduate School Faculty 1969-71; vp Univ of VT Chap of Sigma Xi 1971-72, pres 1971-72; Univ of VT Admin Policy Com 1971-76; admissions com Univ of VT Coll of Med, student affairs com 1974-; admissions com Univ of VT 1977-, exec com 1977-; school dir Champlaign Vlly Union HS 1967-74, vice chmn Gov Advisory Comm to Council onAging 1970-72; deleg VT White House Conf on Children & Youth 1971; pathology trainicomm of Natl Inst General Med Science, 1971-73; natl advisory council Health Professional Educ, 1975-78. **Honors/Awds:** "Influence in Estrogen on Nuclear Volumes & Chemical Composition" 1955; "Thermoluminescence & Fluorescence in Alkai Halide Crystals Induced by Soft X-Ray" 1955; "Occurrence of Multiple Fractures in Suckling Rats Injured with B-Aminopropionitrile" 1957; "Quantitative Historadiography" 1957; "Inhibition of Cytochrome Oxidase by Aminoacetonitrile" 1962; "Proline Metabolism Collagen Formation & Lathyrism" 1966; "Effect of Lathyrogenic Compounds on Oxygen Consumption of Devel Chick Embroys" 1966; Radiorespirometer for the Study of C14-Labeled Substance Administered to Chick Embryos 1971; "Ornithine as a Precursor of Collagen Proline & Hydroxyproline in the Chick Embryo" 1973; "Embryonic Renal Injury-A Possible Factor in Fetal Malnutrition" 1977; "Electrolytic Radiorespirometer for Continuouonitoring of Chick Embryo Devel" 1979; "Fetal-Maternal Hemorrhage, A Spectrum of Disease" 1980. **Home Addr:** Green Bush Rd, Charlotte, VT 05445. **Business Addr:** Professor of Pathology, Univ of Vermont, College of Medicine, Burlington, VT 05405.

CLEMON, U. W.
Federal judge. **Personal:** Born Apr 9, 1943, Fairfield, AL; son of Addie Bush Clemon and Mose Clemon; married Barbara Lang Clemon; children: Herman Isaac, Addine Michelle. **Educ:** Morehouse Coll, Atlanta, GA, 1961; Miles Coll, Birmingham, AL, BS, 1965; Columbia Univ School of Law, New York, NY, JD, 1968. **Career:** NAACP Legal Defense Fund, New York, NY, law clerk, 1966-69; Adams, Burg & Baker, Birmingham, AL, assoc, 1969-70; Adams, Baker & Clemon, Birmingham, AL, partner, 1970-77; Adams & Clemon, Birmingham, AL, partner, 1977-80; State of AL, Montgomery, AL, senator, 1974-80; US Courts, Birmingham, AL, district judge, 1980-. **Orgs:** Pres, AL Black Lawyers Assn, 1976-78; council mem, Section on Individual Rights, 1976-79; legal council, AL Chap, Southern Christian Leadership Conference, 1974-80. **Honors/Awds:** C Francis Stradford Award, Natl Bar Assn, 1986; Drum Major Award, Southern Christian Leadership Conference, 1980; William H Hastie Award, Judicial Council, Natl Bar Assn, 1987. **Business Addr:** Judge, Federal Courthouse, Birmingham, AL 35203.

CLEMONS, ALOIS RICARDO (RICKY)
Public relations director. **Personal:** Born Jan 19, 1956, Durham, NC; son of Mary Alice Clemons and Theodore Quick; married Gail Melinda Shaw, Feb 4, 1983; children: Jason Alois, Perry Ricardo. **Educ:** University of Maryland, BS, journalism, 1977, pursuing MA, journalism. **Career:** Howard University, assistant sports information director, 1980-82, sports information director, 1982-85, assistant athletic director, 1989-91; Miller Brewing Co., marketing communications supervisor, 1985-88; ARC & Associates, president, 1988-91; Major League Baseball, manager, public relations, begin 1991; the National League of Professional Baseball Clubs, executive director of public relations, 1994-. **Orgs:** Kappa Alpha Psi Fraternity, Theta Theta Chapter, president, 1977-78; NABJ, 1989; Institute for Community Development. **Honors/Awds:** The Southwestern Co., Tough-Minded Businessman, 1979, Salesmanship Award, 1979; University of Maryland, Journalism Grant, 1989, Outstanding Alumni Award, 1988. **Special Achievements:** Facilities for Journalists, Vol 1 & 2, Los Angeles Olympic Committee, 1984; The Olympian, United States Olympic Committee, 1985; Howard University Spring Media Guides, 2nd place, College and Sports Information Directors of America, 1985; produced more than 50 media guides for Howard University Athletic Department, 1980-85; venue press chief for Olympics, 1984; press liasion, USOC, 1985; track & field interview room Manager, for Olympics, 1996. **Business Addr:** Executive Director, Public Relations, The National League of Professional Baseball Clubs, 350 Park Ave, New York, NY 10022, (212)339-7700.

CLEMONS, DUANE
Professional football player. **Personal:** Born May 23, 1974, Riverside, CA; married Rana. **Educ:** Univ of California. **Career:** Minnesota Vikings, defensive end, 1996-; Unicept, coowner. **Business Addr:** Professional Basketball Player, Minnesota Vikings, 9520 Viking Dr, Eden Prairie, MN 55344, (612)828-6500.

CLEMONS, EARLIE, JR.
Cleric. **Personal:** Born Oct 9, 1946, Austin, TX; son of Velma Piper Clemons and Earlie Clemons Sr; married Carolyn Hickman, Jul 7, 1967; children: Rodney L, Roland E. **Educ:** Texas Southern University, BS, 1969; Episcopal Theological Seminary, MDiv, 1982. **Career:** Walgreen's Drugs, chief pharmacist, 1971-76; Medi Save Pharmacy, pharmacist/manager, 1976-79; Paul Quinn College, assistant professor, 1983-85; St James Church, vicar, 1987-90; Chaplain Prairie View, chaplain, 1990-; St Francis Church, rector/vicar, 1990-. **Orgs:** Alpha Phi Alpha Fraternity, 1972; Chi Delta Mu Professional Fraternity, 1968; Episcopal Commission for Black Ministry, vice chairman, 1990; Diocesan Commission for Black Ministry, chairman, 1991; Episcopal Society for Ministry in Higher Education, steering committee, 1991; Episcopal Coalition for Human Needs, 1990; Prairie View-Waller Ministerial Alliance, 1990; Waller Closet & Pantry, board member, 1990. **Honors/Awds:** Black Cultural Workshop, Merit Award, 1985. **Business Addr:** Rector, St Francis Episcopal Church, PO Box 246, Prairie View, TX 77446.

CLEMONS, FLENOR
Business executive. **Personal:** Born Aug 30, 1921, Chicago, IL; married Thomasine Crisler; children: Felicia, Dwayne. **Career:** Clemons Cartage, owner; IL St Empl Bur; Ammun Cont Corp, ship clerk. **Orgs:** Bd of auditors Bremen Twnship; bd of ed Posen Robbins Sch Dist; pres Clemons Real Est mem Robbins Ind Comm; mem Robbins Human Rel Res Commn. **Business Addr:** Clemons Cartage, 3707 W 135 St, Robbins, IL 60472.

CLEMONS, JAMES ALBERT, III (J.C)
Journalist. **Personal:** Born Nov 10, 1953, Lake Charles, LA; son of James A Clemons Jr & Rupert Florence Richardson; married Linda E Lewis-Clemons, Nov 24, 1990; children: Anitra Jernell, Jasmine Angelle, James A IV. **Educ:** University of Southwestern LA, 1971-73; McNeese State University, 1980-82; Georgia State University, currently. **Career:** Hughes Tool Co, assembly line worker, 1975-76; LA Department of Corrections, prison guard, 1977; Cities Svc Oil Co, operating engineer, 1977-83; Lake Charles LA, American Press, sports writer, 1979-81; Lake Charles LA, Recorder, owner/publisher, 1980-82; Monroe, LA, News Star World, sports writer, 1983-84; Louisville KY, Courier-Journal, sports writer, 1984-89; Atlanta Journal Consitution, night sports editor, 1989-. **Orgs:** National Association of Black Journalists, 1984-; Atlanta Association of Black Journalists, 1996-; Associated Press Sports Editors, 1996-; Society of Professional Journalists, 1996-; Atlanta Press Club, 1996-; NAACP; Laborers International Union of North America, Local #706. **Honors/Awds:** Gumbeaux Magazine,

Man of the Year, 1996; Georgia Sports Writers Association, First Place Editing, 1991; National Association Women's Basketball Coaches, Salute, 1996; LA Sportswriters Association Contest, Second Place, 1984. **Home Addr:** 2048 Quilt Ct, Lithonia, GA 30058, (770)322-0663. **Business Addr:** Night Sports Editor, Atlanta Journal-Constitution, 72 Marietta St, 8th Fl, Atlanta, GA 30302, (404)526-5334.

CLEMONS, JOHN GREGORY
Public relations executive. **Personal:** Born Mar 24, 1954, Newark, NJ; son of Laura Christine Adams Clemons and John Clemons; married Corine Kendrick Clemons, Aug 31, 1981; children: Diarra Joi. **Educ:** Seton Hall Univ, South Orange, NJ, 1972-73; Syracuse Univ, Syracuse, NY, BS, News Journalism, 1973-76. **Career:** The Star-Ledger, Newark, NJ, reporter, 1976-79; Black Enterprise Magazine, New York, NY, Associate Editor, 1979-81; AT&T, Basking Ridge, NJ, & Atlanta, GA, public rels specialist, 1981-87; Contel Corp, Atlanta, GA, mgr-internal communications, 1987-88; GTE, Tampa, FL, public affairs director, 1989-93; Joint Ctr for Political & Economic Studies, vp of communications, 1992-. **Orgs:** Public Relations Society of America, 1987-; Tampa Chamber of Commerce, 1989-92; Tampa Bay Male Club, 1990-92; dir, exec bd, International Assoc of Business Communicators, 1990-92; PRSA Natl Capital Chapter, bd of dirs, 1994; Capital Press Club; Black Public Relations Society. **Honors/Awds:** Golden Flame, International Assoc of Business Communicators/Atlanta, 1988; Newsletter Award-First Place, IABC/Atlanta, 1987. **Special Achievements:** Hearst Visting Professional, Univ of FL, Coll of Journalism & Communications, 1995. **Business Addr:** VP, Communications, Joint Ctr for Political & Economic Studies, 1090 Vermont Ave NW, Ste 1100, Washington, DC 20005, (202)789-3504.

CLEMONS, LINDA K.
Association executive. **Personal:** Born Dec 26, 1957, Cleveland, OH; divorced. **Educ:** Ball State University, BA, currently. **Career:** Christ In My Life Foundation, founder; Living Legends in Black, founder; Women of the Rainbow, Award of Excelience, national founder; National Association of African American Entrepreneurs, founder, president, currently. **Honors/Awds:** Minorities & Women in Business, Role Model of Year, 1992; listed in the Congressional Record of United States, 1992, proclamation from governor of Indiana, 1992. **Special Achievements:** Artistic director/writer, two plays: When God Calls A Woman, Lord I Wanna Dance. **Business Addr:** President, Founder, National Association of African American Entrepreneurs, PO Box 1191, Indianapolis, IN 46206, (317)466-9556.

CLEMONS, MICHAEL L.
Professor, educational administrator. **Personal:** Born Jul 18, 1955, Worth, WV; son of Delores S. and Lawrence D. Clemons; married Sharon D Brown Clemons, Aug 14, 1982; children: Misha Michelle, Nyasha Denise. **Educ:** University of Maryland, College Park, MD, BA, 1976, MA, 1979; Atlanta University, Atlanta, GA, PhD, 1987. **Career:** Honeywell Information Systems, McLean, VA, associate systems analyst, 1977-79; Gen Electric Information Svc, Atlanta, GA, programmer/analyst, 1979-80; Atlanta Junior College, Atlanta, GA, research associate systems analyst, 1981-84; State University of New York, Oswego, NY, director, institutional research and MIS, 1984-87; Old Dominion University, Norfolk, VA, director, university planning and institutional research, 1987-. **Orgs:** Mem, Association for Institutional Research; mem, Virginia Assn for Management & Planning, 1987-; member, Southern Assn for Institutional Research, 1987-; member, American Political Science Association, 1986-; member, Natl Conf of Black Political Scientist, 1982-; member, Society for College and University Planners, 1986-. **Honors/Awds:** Virginia Management Institute, 1989; National Science Foundation Fellow Dept of Political Science, Atlanta Univ, 1979-82; Graduate Fellowship, Univ of Maryland/Urban Studies, 1977-78; Omicron Delta Kappa Natl Honor and Leadership Society, 1977. **Business Addr:** Assistant Professor, Dept of Political Science, Dominion Univ, 704 Batten Arts & Letters Bldg, Norfolk, VA 23529.

CLEMONS, THOMASINA
University administrator. **Personal:** Born Nov 23, 1938, Charleston, WV; daughter of Fannie Estelle Hairston Coles and Charles Henry Clemons; married Otis William Wade (divorced 1972). **Educ:** Howard University, Washington, DC, 1956-58; University of Hartford, West Hartford, CT, BA (cum laude), 1964; University of Connecticut, Storrs, CT, MBA, 1982. **Career:** CT Commission on Human Rights and Opportunities, New London, CT, investigator, regional mgr, 1967-75; University of Connecticut, Storrs, CT, dir, affirmative action, 1975-. **Orgs:** President, Northeastern Connecticut Chapter, 1990-; member, National Coalition of 100 Black Women, Vernon Democratic Town Committee, 1980-83, 1986-; member, board of directors, Hockanum Valley, 1990-; member, past state coordinator, Community Council, American Assn for Affirmative Action, 1978-. **Honors/Awds:** Chair, Employment Task Force, CT Department of Higher Education, 1983-85; Management Development Program, Harvard University, 1990; Certificate of Appreciation, National Coalition of 100 Black Women, 1990; Search Handbook, University of Connecticut, 1980, 1991.

CLENDENINN, NEIL J.
Physician. **Personal:** Born Apr 7, 1949, New York, NY; married Mary Lavinia Neely. **Educ:** Wesleyan Univ, BA 1971; New York Univ, MA, MD, PhD 1977. **Career:** Univ of WA Affiliated Hosp, residency 1977-81; Natl Inst of Health/Natl Cancer Inst, clinical pharmacology fellow 1981-83, oncology fellow 1983-84, medical staff 1984-85; Burroughs Wellcome, sr clinical research scientist 1985-. **Orgs:** Trustee Wesleyan Univ 1984-. **Honors/Awds:** Numerous scientific articles and book chapts.

CLENDENON, DONN A.
Attorney, counselor. **Personal:** Born Jul 15, 1935, Neosho, MO; son of Helen Moore Clendenon and Claude Clendenon; divorced; children: Eric Val, Donn A Jr, Donna Alexis. **Educ:** Morehouse College, BA, 1956; Duquesne University School of Law, JD, 1978. **Career:** Bostich, Gurren & Clendenon, attorney, 1977-80; Dap Inc, director of personnel, 1978-80; Western International Contractors Inc, president/CEO, 1980-85; Chicago Economic Development, president/CEO, 1985-86; Anderson, Carlson, Carter & Hay, attorney, 1986-88; Keystone Carroll Treatment Center, counselor, 1988-92; Interstate Audit Corp, general counsel, 1992-. **Orgs:** South Dakota Chemical Dependency Counselors Association, 1989-; Ohio Bar Association, 1978-; Dayton Bar Association, 1978-80; National Chemical Dependence Counselors Association, 1990-; Major League Baseball Alumni Associate, 1972-. **Honors/Awds:** Major League Baseball, 1969 World Series MVP, 1969. **Special Achievements:** Duquesne Law School, Honors Law Review, published article, 1976-77. **Military Serv:** Army, SSgt, 1958-64. **Business Phone:** (605)335-7267.

CLERMONT, VOLNA
Medical director, physician. **Personal:** Born Sep 15, 1924, Jeremie, Haiti; married Hazel Baggett; children: Karen, Kimberly, Christopher. **Educ:** Lycee Petion of Port-au-Prince Haiti, BA 1943; Ecole Nationale de Medecine et de Pharmacie Univ d'Haiti Port-au-Prince Haiti, MD 1949. **Career:** Childrens Hosp of MI, pathologist 1960-69; Compr Neighborhood Health Ctr, chief pediatrics 1969-72; SW Detroit Hosp, chief of staff; DMIC-PLRESCAD, med dir 1972-; Private Practice, pediatrician. **Orgs:** Mem Detroit Med Soc; life mem NAACP; Natl Med Assn; Detroit Pediatric Soc; Dip of Bd of Pediatrics Wayne Co Med Soc; MI State Med Soc; mem medical staff Hutzel Hosp, Children's Hosp, Grace Hosp; mem Urban League, Founders Soc of MI; African Art Gallery, Intl African Museum Soc; Alpha Phi Alpha Frat. **Business Addr:** 3800 Woodward, Detroit, MI 48203.

CLEVELAND, CLYDE
Councilman. **Personal:** Born May 22, 1935, Detroit. **Educ:** Wayne State Univ. **Career:** Detroit City councilman, 1974-; Comm Devel Div, New Detroit Inc, proj dir 1971-1973; Comm Org, New Detroit Inc, specialist, 1970-71; Inner City Business Improvement Forum, comm planner 1968-70; Comm of Human Resources Devel, community serv mayor, 1965-68; public aid worker 1958, 1960-64. **Orgs:** mem, MI Democratic Party, various committees in first dist Democratic Party; Nacirema Club; Trade Union Leadership Council; MI Comm on Law & Housing; Assn for Study of Negro Life & History; Assn of Black Soc Workers; Booker T Washington Business Assn; Advisory bd of Black Caucus; NAACP; Operation PUSH; 33 Degree Mason; Past Grand Exalted Ruler (Elks). **Honors/Awds:** Has received numerous service & community awards. **Military Serv:** AUS sp 4th class 1958-60. **Business Addr:** City Councilman, City of Detroit, City County Bldg, Detroit, MI 48226.

CLEVELAND, GRANVILLE E.
Librarian. **Personal:** Born Nov 25, 1937, Springfield, OH; married Juanita; children: Granville, Tivonnia. **Educ:** Tougaloo So CC, attnd 1956-57; Central State Coll, 1957-60; Wittenberg U, 1963. **Career:** Univ Notre Dame Law Sch, asst law lib & faculty mem 1969-; Springfield Bar & Law Lib Assn, lib & exec sec 1963-68. **Orgs:** Mem Am Assn Law Libs 1964-; mem & past pres OH Reg Assn Law Libs 1964-; mem Affirmative Action Com Univ Notre Dame 1973-; past sec Community Wel Council; chmn Housing & Jobs Human Rel Com; adult adv Springfield Youth Club; Legal Aid Soc; United Appeal Fund; vice pres Young Rep; adv & supr City Rec Dept; mem Planned Parenthood; YMCA; basketball referee; acting dir Black Studies Univ Notre Dame 1972-73; chmn Black Student Affairs Com 1973-74; asst dir Civil Rights Center 1973-74. **Honors/Awds:** Black Am Law Studies Assn Awd, Univ Notre Dame Law Sch 1973-74. **Military Serv:** Air Nat Guard sgt 1956-60. **Business Addr:** Asst Law Librarian, Notre Dame Law School, Notre Dame, IN 46556.

CLEVELAND, HATTYE M.
Therapist (retired). **Personal:** Born Sep 22, 1911, Laurens, SC; daughter of RosaLee Fuller Johnson (deceased) and William Guy Johnson (deceased); married John M Cleveland, Aug 29, 1936 (deceased). **Educ:** Shaw Univ, BS, sci/home economics, 1935; NY Univ, post graduate cert, Occup Therapy, 1956; Pace Univ, cert mgmt of vol organizations/issues in committee devel, 1975; Westchester Community College, Fordham Univ, Lincoln Center, business seminars, 1978, women in politics II lobbying sem, 1978; Mary Mt Manhattan College, blissymbolics 1979. **Career:** Willowbrook State Sch, therapist 1956-60; Beth Abraham Home, sr therapist 1960-65; Monte-Mor Affil, asst supr occupational therapy 1965-72, supr occupational therapy 1973-76; Montefiore Hospital N Central Bx Affil, head occupat therapy serv 1976-77 (retired). **Orgs:** Charter mem Delta Sigma Theta, Alpha Rho Chap Shaw Univ 1934; AOTA, WFOT's 1956-93; S Side Res Assn 1966-67; World Federation Occ Therapy 1970-; pres Westchester Co Natl Council of Negro Women, life mem 1970-; Women's Task Force 1974-78; Amer Biog Assn 1977-; IFABI 1979; ABIRA 1980-; researcher no 370 for the Amer Cancer Soc CPSII 1982-86; League of Women Voters 1985-; NY State & NY Dist OTA; Nat'l Alumni Association & Alumni Club Shaw Univ; Grace Baptist Church 1989; exec bd, chair, Scholarship Fund; life mem, Mt Vernon Branch NAACP 1988; committee mem, Home Health Care of Mt Vernon NY Inc 1988-; guild chair, Life Member's Guild of the Natl Council of Negro Women Inc, Westchester County Section, 1985-; Democratic Natl Party, mem, 1988-94; World Jewish Congress, diplomat, 1994; Mt Vernon Home Health Care Quality Assurance Comm, bod, 1993-. **Honors/Awds:** Mary McLeod Bethune Centennial Awd Natl Council of Negro Women Inc 1975; pin 10 yrs Cont Dedicated & Outstanding Serv Montefiore Hosp & Med Ctr 1976; Committee Apprec Awd Morrisania City Hosp Emp Council 1976; Alumni Achievement Awd Administration Committee Ldr & Humanitarian Shaw Univ Natl Alumni Assn 1976; Spec Awd of Loyalty Grace Baptist Ch 1979; Hon Appt to the Natl Adv Bd ABI 1982; Cert of Recog as sustaining mem Democratic Natl Comm 1982-; Appreciation Awd for Serv Church Supt Council of Westchester Co 1984; 5 yr & 10 yr Serv Awd Montefiore Hosp & Med Ctr; 3 yr & 5 yr Serv Awd Beth Abraham Home; United Way of Mt Vernon, NY, citation for community service 1985-; Westchester County Department Mental Health Community Systems, Mental Health Award, 1985; John F Kennedy Library, Honorary Fellow, 1988-; American Biographical Institute, Woman of the Year, 1990; w University, Half A Century Award, 1985; Shaw University, 3 Plaques, Appreciation of Contributions; Shaw Univ Elizah Shaw Club, Honor, 1991-93; Honorary Inductees inducted to the Senior Citizens Hall of Fame, Westchester County, NY by County Exec, 1995; Distinguished Service Awd, Westchester County Clerk, 1995; Certificate of Sponsorship, Andrus Foundation, 1994; Certificate, NY Easter Seals Society. **Special Achievements:** Selected as Charter Member, "Americans for Change," Presidential Task Force; Recipient of: The 52nd Presidential Inaugural, An American Reunion, 1993 Commemorative Invitation. **Home Addr:** 22 Union Ave, Mount Vernon, NY 10550-3511.

CLEVELAND, TESSIE ANITA SMITH
Health services administrator. **Personal:** Born Sep 17, 1939, Loverne, AL; married Lawrence J. **Educ:** AL State Coll, BS 1959; Atlanta U, MSW 1964; Univ of CA at Los Angeles, postgrad 1968-69. **Career:** Tuskegee VA Hosp, asst sec chief med serv 1959-62; Los Angeles Co Gen Hosp, med social worker diabetic serv 1964-66; Home Care Prog, sr med social worker 1966-67; Met State Hosp Norwalk CA, psychiataric social worker 1966-67; Allison Home for Girls Los Angeles, psychiatric social worker, beginning 1966; Shaw's Home for Girls Los Angeles, psychiatric social worker, beginning 1969; King Drew Medical Center, dir of hospital social services, currently. **Orgs:** Dir Med Social Serv 1970-; dir Comm Outreach Prog 1971-; med soc work consult Teen Pregnancy Project 1968-70; mem prog session TB & Heart Assn 1969; mem Assn Black Social Workers; Nat Assn Social Workers; bd dir SE Welfare Planning Council; mem Nat Council Negro Women; Iota Phi. **Business Addr:** Director, Hospital Social Services, King Drew Medical Center, 12012 Compton Ave, Los Angeles, CA 90059.

CLEVERT, CHARLES N., JR.
Judge. **Personal:** Born Oct 11, 1947, Richmond, VA. **Educ:** Davis & Elkins Coll Elkins WV, BA 1969; Georgetown Univ Law Center Washington DC, JD 1972. **Career:** Milwaukee Cty Dist Atty's Office, asst dist atty 1972-75; US Atty's Office Eastern Dist of WI, asst US atty 1975-77; US Bankruptcy, judge 1977-86; US Bankruptcy Court Eastern Dist of WI, chief US bankruptcy judge 1986-96; US District Judge, 1996-. **Orgs:** Mem WI Bar Assn, Milwaukee Bar Assn, WI Association of Minority Attorneys; 7th Circuit Bar Assn, Alpha Phi Alpha, Judicial Council NBA; African Methodist Episcopal Church; vice chair, Natl Conference Federal Trial Judges; bd mem, American Bankruptcy Inst; bd mem, American Judicature Society; immediate past pres, Thomas Fairchild American Inn of Court; bd mem, Men of Tomorrow; bd mem, Anvil Housing Corp; comm on the budget, Judicial Conference of the United States; mem, Sigma Pi Phi. **Honors/Awds:** American Coll of Bankruptcy, Fellow; Milwaukee Times Black Excellence Award; Milwaukee Federal Executives Assn, Federal Employee of the Year, 1991; Natl Conference of Bankruptcy Clerks, Administrative Excellence Award. **Business Addr:** Judge, US District Court, 162 US Courthouse, Milwaukee, WI 53202.

CLIFFORD, CHARLES H.
Human relations consultant. **Personal:** Born Sep 8, 1933, Sacramento, CA; married Claudean Akers; children: Carla, Carolyn, Caren. **Educ:** Sacramento Jr Coll, AA 1958; Sacramento State Coll, BA 1965. **Career:** Dept of Corr State of CA, human rel consult 1964-. **Orgs:** Mem area pres Black Corr Coalition; past pres CA Corr Officers 1969-72; mem Urban League, Black

Caucus, NAACP, CA Young Dems. **Honors/Awds:** Co-author Dept Corrs Affirmative Action Plan; 1st black dep sheriff Sacramento Co 1960; 1st black corr sgt Folsom Prison; 1st black Lt Folsom 1970. **Military Serv:** USN 1951-55. **Business Addr:** 719 P St, Sacramento, CA.

CLIFFORD, MAURICE C.

Educational administrator. **Personal:** Born Aug 9, 1920, Washington, DC; son of Rosa P Linberry Clifford and Maurice C Clifford; married Patricia; children: Maurice C III, Jay PL, Rosemary Clifford McDaniel. **Educ:** Hamilton Coll Clinton NY, BA 1941; Univ of Chicago, MA 1942; Meharry Med Coll, MD 1947. **Career:** Obstetrics & Gynecology, private practice 1951-78; Med Coll of PA, vice pres med affairs 1978-79, acting pres 1979-80, pres 1980-86; Dept of Public Health City of Phila, commissioner; Lomax Health Services, currently. **Orgs:** Trustee Meharry Med Coll 1963-88; mem bd of mgrs Germantown Savings Bank 1968-; trustee Acad of Natural Sci Philadelphia 1974-85, Philadelphia Museum of Art 1982-; mem Bd of Ethics City of Philadelphia 1984-86; trustee, Philadelphia College of Textiles and Science 1982-. **Honors/Awds:** Martin Luther King Jr Awd Operation PUSH Philadelphia 1981; Natl Serv Awd Salem Baptist Church Philadelphia 1982; George Washington Carver Awd G Washington Carver Committee Philadelphia 1982; Disting Serv Awd Frontiers of Amer 1983; Frederick D Patterson Awd Philadelphia Inter Frat Counc UNCF 1985; Doctor of Humane Letters LaSalle University 1981; Honorary Degree Hamilton College 1982; Doctor of Science Honorary Degree Hahnemann Univ 1985; Doctor of Laws Honorary Degree Medical College of Pennsylvania 1986. **Military Serv:** AUS capt 1952-54. **Business Addr:** Lomax Health Services, 200 Highpoint Dr, Ste 215, Chalfont, PA 18914.

CLIFFORD, PAUL INGRAHAM

Psychologist. **Personal:** Born Jan 22, 1914, Martinsburg, WV; son of Mabel Grace Douglass Clifford and J Paul Clifford; married Margaret Earnestine Washington, Nov 26, 1975. **Educ:** Shippensburg Univ, BS 1938; Atlanta Univ, AM 1948; Univ Chicago, PhD 1953. **Career:** Tuskegee Army Air Field, Tuskegee, AL, Admin, 1941-45; Paine Coll, prof 1947-48; Atlanta Univ, instructor 1948-51, asst prof 1952-54, registrar 1954-66, prof dir summer school 1957-68; US Office Educ Washington, consultant 1961-68; Emory Univ, visiting lecturer 1964-66; Univ CA, 1968-69; Amer Mgmt Psychols Inc, staff psychologist 1966-70; Prof Serv Amer Mgmt Psychols Inc, regional dir 1970-71, natl dir 1971-72; SC State Coll, prof dept chmn 1972-76; Career Mgmt of Atlanta Inc, psychologist. **Orgs:** Special lecturer, numerous institutions of higher learning; fellow, AAAS; GA Psychology Assn; mem Alumni Assn of Shippensburg Univ; Amer Acad Political & Social Science; Amer Assn School Admins; Amer Assn Univ Profs; Amer Educ Rsch Assn; Amer Assn for Counseling & Devel; Amer Psychol Assn; Assn for Higher Educ of Natl Educ Assn; GA Branch Assn for Counseling & Devel; IL Psychology Assn; Midwestern Psychology Assn; Natl Alumni Assn; Atlanta Univ; Natl Council on Measurements Used in Educ; communicant Protestant Episcopal Church; life mem Univ Chicago Alumni Assn; mem Natl Soc for Study of Educ; NY Acad Sciences; Omega Psi Phi Fraternity Inc Eta Omega Chapter; PA Psychology Assn; Phi Delta Kappa Zeta Chapter; Soc for Psychol Study of Social Issues;charter mem SE Psychols Assn; contributojournals, papers, author in field; mem numerous bds & comms; independent practice counseling/clinical/consulting psychologist 1962-. **Honors/Awds:** Numerous honors; numerous publications in educational and psychological journals.

CLIFFORD, THOMAS E.

Military official (retired), automobile dealership owner. **Personal:** Born Mar 9, 1929, Washington, DC; married Edith Sanders; children: Maria, Edwin, Larry, Mark. **Educ:** Howard Univ, BA (cum laude) 1949; George Washington Univ, MBA 1963. **Career:** US Air Force, jet fighter pilot and officer 1949-79; General Motors Corp, plant mgr 1979-86; Clifford Motors, owner, 1987-. **Orgs:** VFW; American Legion; BPOE; NAACP; Urban League. **Military Serv:** US Air Force, major gen, 30 yrs; Distinguished Flying Cross; numerous others. **Business Addr:** Owner, Clifford Motors, PO Box 1060, Blythe, CA 92226.

CLIFT, JOSEPH WILLIAM

Physician. **Personal:** Born Apr 24, 1938, Patoka, IN; son of Mary Esther Lucas Clift and Cecil William Clift; married Ulyssine Gibson Clift, Aug 10, 1963; children: Kory Grant Clift, Nathalie Louise Clift. **Educ:** TX So Univ, BS 1959; Univ TX Med Br, MD 1965. **Career:** Physician self employed. **Orgs:** Pres Delta Theta Chap Alpha Phi Alpha Fraternity 1959; pres Alameda Contra Costa Co Diabetes Assn 1975; mem bd dir Samuel Merritt Hosp 1976-79; diplomate Amer Bd of Internal Med 1978; pres of medical staff Highland General Hospital 1983-84; pres East Bay Soc of Internal Med 1984-; mem Nat Med Assn; AMA; CA Med Assn; mem, counselor, president Alameda-Contra-Costa Med Assn, 1992-; California Society of Internal Medicine, 1991-92. **Honors/Awds:** Resident of the Year, Highland General Hospital 1971. **Military Serv:** USAF MC captain 1967-69; Commendation Medal USAF 1969. **Home Addr:** 14030 Broadway Terr, Oakland, CA 94611, (510)547-7352. **Business Addr:** Physician, 3300 Webster, Ste 702, Oakland, CA 94609, (510)832-0147.

CLIFTON, IVERY DWIGHT

Educator. **Personal:** Born Apr 6, 1943, Statesboro, GA; son of B J (deceased) & Rosetta B Clifton; married Patricia A Davis, May 28, 1967; children: Kalisa, Kelli. **Educ:** Tuskegee Inst, BS 1965; Tuskegee Inst, MS 1967; Univ Of IL, PhD 1976. **Career:** Univ of GA, prof and vice pres for Academic Affairs, assoc dean, Coll of Agriculture, 1988-; US Dept of Agriculture, Washington DC, agricultural economist 1970-76; AUS VA and Vietnam, officer advisor 1967-70; TVA AL, agricultural economist 1967. **Orgs:** Special asst to & vice pres for acad affairs Univ of GA 1977-78; consult Resources for the Future 1979; sec Alpha Phi Alpha 1975; pres Steward Bd First AME Church 1979-80. **Honors/Awds:** AUS commendation bronze star Natl Defense 1967-70; achievement award USDA 1971; Chi Gamma Iota Univ of IL Chapter Urbana 1975; Phi Kappa Phi Univ of GA Chapter Athens 1979; gamma sigma delta Univ of GA Chapter Athens 1980. **Military Serv:** AUS qm ltc(p) reserves 20 years served. **Home Addr:** 162 Doubles Bridges Xing, Winterville, GA 30683-9674.

CLIFTON, LUCILLE

Poet, author, educator. **Personal:** Born Jun 27, 1936, Depew, NY; daughter of Thelma Moore Sayles and Samuel Sayles Sr; married Fred J Clifton, May 10, 1958 (deceased); children: Sidney, Fredrica, Channing, Gillian, Graham, Alexia. **Educ:** Howard Univ, Washington DC, 1953-55; Fredonia State Teachers College, Fredonia, NY, 1955. **Career:** New York State Div of Employment, Buffalo, NY, claims clerk, 1958-60; US Office of Educ, Washington, DC, literature asst for Central Atlantic Regional Educ Laboratory, 1969-71; Coppin State College, Baltimore, MD, poet in residence, 1971-74; Columbia University School of the Arts, visiting writer; George Washington University, Jerry Moore visiting writer, 1982-83; Univ of California, Santa Cruz, prof of literature and creative writing, 1985-89; St Mary's College of Maryland, St Mary's City, MD, distinguished professor of humanities, 1989-; Columbia University, professor of writing, 1994-96. **Orgs:** Mem, Intl PEN, Authors Guild, Authors League of Amer. **Honors/Awds:** Discovery Award, New York YW-YMHA Poetry Center, 1969; Natl Endowment for the Arts fellowships, 1970, 1972; honorary degrees from Univ of Maryland and Towson State Univ; Poet Laureate of the State of Maryland, 1979-84; nominated for Pulitzer Prize for poetry, 1980, 1988; Juniper Prize, Univ of Massachusetts, 1980; Coretta Scott King Award, Amer Library Assn, 1984; author, 21 children's books, including The Black BCs, 1970, All Us Come Cross the Water, 1973, Three Wishes, 1976, Everett Anderson's Goodbye, 1983; author, eight books of poetry, including Good Times: Poems, 1969, An Ordinary Woman, 1974, Next: New Poems, 1987; Book of Light, 1993; author, Generations: A Memoir, 1976; The Terrible Stories; contributor to anthologies and periodicals. **Business Addr:** Distinguished Professor of Humanities, St Marys College of Maryland, St Marys City, MD 20686.

CLIFTON, ROSALIND MARIA

Health services administrator. **Personal:** Born Oct 23, 1950, St Louis, MO; son of Lois and Houston Gant. **Career:** Claims Overload System, bus mgr, 1986-89; Blacklog Ltd, owner/pres/ceo, 1989-.

CLIMMONS, WILLIE MATHEW

Educational administrator. **Personal:** Born Mar 18, 1923, Magnolia, MS; married Vera Lois Chachere; children: Gwendoly Faye. **Educ:** Leland Coll Baker LA, BS 1952; TX So Univ Houston, MEd 1960; LSU Baton Rouge LA, reading courses 1968-69. **Career:** Plaquemine Point Elementary School, St Landry Parish School Bd, prin 1958-; St Landry Parish School Bd, teacher Math, Chemistry, Biology & Science 1952-58. **Orgs:** Treas St Landry Parish Educ Assn Fed Credit Union 1962-; treas St Landry Parish Educ Assn 1967-; pres 7th Dist JK Haynes Found & Legal Defense FundInc 1977-; past pres & state dir Frontiers Intl past m & chmn audit com Keystone Lodge No 196 Opelousas LA; 1st lt comdr CF Ladd Consistory No 80. **Honors/Awds:** Recipient good conduct medal & eto ribbon & 5 battle stars AUS 1943-46; natl sci found grant TX So Univ Houston 1958; Frontiersman of the year award Frontiers Intl Opelousas LA 1975; black outstanding educator awards SRRYHO 1975; disting serv award Dist 5 Frontiers Intl 1979; past exalted ruler degree 33rd Degree of Masonary PHA 1979. **Military Serv:** AUS pfc 1943-46. **Business Addr:** PO Box 850, Opelousas, LA 70570.

CLINE, EILEEN TATE

Educational administrator. **Personal:** Born Jun 25, 1935, Chicago, IL; daughter of Inez Duke Tate and Herman Tate; married William P Cline (deceased); children: Jon Christopher, Joy Michele. **Educ:** Geneva C Robinson Chicago Musical Coll, priv piano study 1947-52; Univ of Chicago, liberal arts 1950-52; Helen Curtis Chicago Musical Coll, class piano course 1950; Rudolph Ganz scholarship student, priv piano study 1956-58; Oberlin Conserv of Music, BMus Ed 1956, B Mus piano perf 1956; Univ of CO Boulder, MMus piano perf 1960; independent piano studio, 1960-75; IN Univ Sch of Music, Doctor Mus Educ, 1985; Harvard Institute for Educational Mgt, 1986. **Career:** Univ of CO, coord of cont educ piano 1965-75; Neighborhood Mus Sch New Haven, CT, exec dir 1980-82; Peabody Conserv of Mus The Johns Hopkins Univ, assoc dean 1982-83, dean 1983-95; Institute for Policy Studies, The Johns Hopkins Univ, sr fellow. **Orgs:** Founder/dir Boulder Children's Choir 1972-75; student activities chmn CO State Music Teachers' Assn, student activities chmn, exec bd; prog chmn Boulder Area Music Tchrs' Assn; Music Prog Professional Training Panel Natl Endowment for the Arts 1980-; pres Young Musicians of Boulder; alumni-elected trustee Oberlin Coll 1981-88; bd trustees Hopkins Sch 1981-82; bd mem Natl Guild of Comm Schools of the Arts 1982-88; natl Keyboard Comm Music Educators Natl Conf; adv bd YWCA Univ of CO; Music Comm CO Council for the Arts and Humanities; Coll Bd Theory AP Test Devel Comm ETS 1983-; Eval Team Middle States Accredit Assn 1983-; MTNA, MENC, Coll Music Soc, Natl Guild of Piano Teachers, Society for Values in Higher Education, bd mem, American Symphony Orchestra League, 1989-; Baltimore Symphony Orchestra Community Outreach Committee, Educational Outreach, 1989-95, music comm, 1993-; bd mem National Guild Community Schools of the Arts, 1982-88; Kenan Inst for the Arts, bd mem; Harvard Univ Kennedy School Program for Non-Profit Leadership, advisory bd mem; MD State Dept of Education, arts advisory panel, 1995-; bd mem, Marlboro Music; advisory bd, El Paso Pro Musica; advisory bd, Van Cliburn Intl Piano Competition; advisory bd, Amer Bach Society. **Honors/Awds:** Research grants, IN Univ Found, IN Univ Office of Rsch and Grad Devel; Oberlin Coll Alumni Rsch Grant; academic scholarships and honors Univ of CO 1958-60, Oberlin Coll 1953-56; Danforth Found Fellowship 1975-; "Reflections of Cultural Synthesis and Social Reality as Seen in George Walker's Sonata No 2" Soc for Values in Higher Education Conf Dickinson Coll 1979; "The Competition Explosion, Impact on Higher Education" MTNA Natl Convention 1980; "Education Relationships to Professional Training and Career Entry" NASM Conv Dallas, TX 1981; published, "The Competition Explosion, Impact on Education" The American Music Teacher Parts I-III Jan-March 1982; lectures, performance competitions; Outstanding Woman Awd Natl Exec Club 1984; Outstanding Alumni Awd Univ ofColorado College of Music 19 Peabody Faculty and Administration Award for Outstanding Contribution to the Peabody Community, 1986; Article of the Year Award for "Anyone Can Win . . . ," a two-part article in American Music Teachers, 1990; Keynote speaker ASOL/Unv of Chicago/Chicago Symphony Orchestra 100th Anniversary Symposium: "The Training of Orchestral Musicians"; Torch Bearer Award for distinguished service, Coalition of 100 Black Women, 1991; Panelist: NJ State Arts Council; Massachusetts Cultural Council; Keynote Speaker, Coll Music Society Annual Mtg, 1995; My Father Never Told Me.., or, A View From this Bridge; NASM Task Force Report: Minority Access to Music Study, Nov 1994. **Business Addr:** Sr Fellow, Institute for Policy Studies, Johns Hopkins University, 3400 N Charles St, Baltimore, MD 21218-2696.

CLINGMAN, KEVIN LOREN

Business executive. **Personal:** Born Oct 9, 1961, Detroit, MI; son of Gloria Clingman and Simeon Clingman; married Sherry Bryant, Jul 2, 1988; children: Kameron. **Educ:** Morehouse College, AB, economics, 1985. **Career:** Owens Corning Fiberglass, supervisor, materials and logistics, 1985-86; Union Pacific Railroad, product manager, 1988-92; Omaha Small Business Network, president, 1993-96; North Omaha Business Development Corporation, 1993-96; LCBD Enterprise Group, pres, 1996-. **Orgs:** Omaha Small Business Network, board of directors, 1992-96; North Omaha Business Development Corp., board of directors, 1992-96; Center Stage Theatre, board of directors, 1989-94; Black Employee Network of Union Pacific Railroad, president, 1992; Salem Baptist Church, finance committee, 1989-96; National Business Incubation Association, Board of Directors, 1996-. **Honors/Awds:** Union Pacific Railroad, Special Commendation, 1989. National Business Incu bation Association, Microenterprise Incubator of the Year, 1996. **Business Addr:** LCDB Enterprise Group, 2901 W Broadway, Louisville, KY 40251, (502)778-6000.

CLINKSCALES, JERRY A.

Educator. **Personal:** Born Sep 25, 1933, Abbeville, SC; married Jerrolyn Holtzclaw; children: Mary, Jerry, David, Stephen. **Educ:** SC State Coll, BSA 1956; Tuskegee Inst, DVM 1960; Univ IL, advanced training 1972; Univ TX, advanced training, 1981. **Career:** Tuskegee Inst, instructor 1960; USDA, poultry insp div 1966; Tuskegee Inst, instructor 1967; head small animal clinic 1968; asst prof 1971-; Tuskegee University, director of veterinary admission, 1994-. **Orgs:** Mem Am Vet Me Assn 1960-; Am Assn Vet Clinicans 1961-; Am Animal Hosp Assn 1965-; mem Tuskegee Area C of C; Omega Psi Phi Frat; Phi Zeta Hon Vet Frat; adv City Recreation Detp; City Canine Control Center. **Honors/Awds:** Outstanding tchr of yr award Norden's 1972-73. **Military Serv:** AUSR 1956-90.

CLINKSCALES, JOHN WILLIAM, JR.

Clergyman. **Personal:** Born Mar 5, 1925, Chicago, IL. **Educ:** VA Union U, AB 1946; McCormick Theol Sem, MDiv 1950. **Career:** Beth Eden Bapt Ch, asst min 1946-55; Lebannon Bapt Ch, min 1955-; St Bernard Hosp, chaplain 1974-80; Chicago Baptist Inst, instr 1980-. **Orgs:** Mem Amer Bapt Ministers Assn; vice pres Chicago Chapter VA & Union Univ Alumni Assn; bd mem Morgan Park Coop Credit Union; bd mem Englewood Quality of LifeNetwork; mem Chicago Heights Alumni Chap Kappa Alpha Psi; adv council Harper HS; neighborhood adv council Ogden Park; neighborhood social serv adv council Chicago Urban League; mem Southwestern Ministers Assoc; treas Interdenominational Ministers Alliance. **Military Serv:** USAR retired col chaplain.

CLIPPER, MILTON CLIFTON, JR.
President. **Personal:** Born Feb 3, 1948, Washington, DC; son of Gladys Robertson Clipper and Milton Clipper, Sr; divorced; children: Faith Ann Clipper, Jaime Marie Clipper. **Educ:** Montgomery Coll; Corcoran Sch of Art. **Career:** WA Post, graphic designer 1976-; Corcoran Sch of Art, art tchr 1976-; WJXT-TV, art dir 1974-76; WTOP-TV, artist 1970-73; WDVM TV 9 Washington DC, Asst Promotions Mgr, 1985. **Orgs:** Editorial bd WJXT-TV 1975-76; mem Metro Art Dirs & Club of WA; guest lectr TV & Newspaper Graphics; mem Black Ski; Washington Urban League; mem Amer Film Inst; advisory bd mem Big Brothers of the Natl Capital area. **Honors/Awds:** 2nd place Metro Art Dirs Club 1972; exhibition of abstract art 1973; Gold Award, Broadcast Designers Assn, 1984; Finalist Intl Film Festival, 1984. **Business Addr:** Pres, Design Concepts Inc, 300 I St NE, Suite 212, Washington, DC 20002.

CLOSS, KEITH
Professional basketball player. **Personal:** Born Apr 3, 1976. **Educ:** Central Connecticut State. **Career:** Los Angeles Clippers, 1997-. **Business Addr:** Professional Baskeball Player, Los Angeles Clippers, 3939 S Figueroa St, Los Angeles Sports Arena, Los Angeles, CA 90037, (213)748-8000.

CLOUD, SANFORD, JR.
Insurance company executive. **Personal:** Born Nov 27, 1944, Hartford, CT; son of Inez Morgan Cloud and Sanford Cloud Sr; married Diane Brown; children: Adam, Christopher, Robin. **Educ:** Univ of Az; Howard U, BA 1966; Howard Univ Sch of Law, JD cum laude 1969. **Career:** Cloud & Ibarguen, partner 1977-78; Robinson Robinson & Cole, atty 1970-76; CT General Assembly, couns 1971-72; Aetna Life & Casualty Law Dept, atty 1969; Covington & Burling, law clk 1968-69; US Sen Thomas Dodd, res asst 1964-67; Aetna Life & Casualty, Hartford CT, vice president, corporate public involvement 1986-; Aetna Life & Casualty, Hartford, CT, Law Department 1978-86; State of Connecticut, Hartford, CT, state senator 1977-81. **Orgs:** Bd of dirs, Soc for Savings Bancorp, 1990; bd of trustees, Hartford Seminary, 1991; bd of trustees, Wadsworth Atheneum, 1985-. **Honors/Awds:** United Way Community Service Award, United Way 1990; Distinguished Service Award, Howard University School of Law 1982; Charter Oak Leadership Medal, Greater Hartford Chamber of Commerce 1979.

CLOUD, W. ERIC
Attorney. **Personal:** Born Feb 26, 1946, Cleveland, OH; son of Alfreda Ruth Cloud and William Walter Cloud; married Carole Anne Henderson; children: Andre, Sharrieff. **Educ:** Morris Brown Coll, BA (cum laude) 1973; Dag Hammarskjold Coll, fellowship (highest honors) 1974; Antioch Sch of Law, JD 1977; George Washington Law Sch, LLM Intl & Comparative Law 1980. **Career:** Pvt Practice Intl Law, atty; US Dept of Treasury, consult 1979-80; US Dept of Labor, spl asst to intl tax counsel 1976-78; Cloud, Henderson & Cloud, attorney, 1982-; Washington Afro-American Newspaper, correspondent, 1988-; Morris Brown College, lecturer, 1990-. **Orgs:** Mem, Am Bar Assn 1977; mem, Nat Bar Assn; mem, Morris Brown College Alumni Assn, 1988-. **Honors/Awds:** Good Samaritan of the Year Mayor Carl Stokes 1968; fellowship Dag Hammarskjold Coll Dag Hammarskjold Found 1973; article in George Washington Law Review "Tax Treaties the need for the us to extend its treaty network to developing countries in light of the new Intl Economic and Polit Realities"; Four Walls/Eight Window, 1990; Award for Best Article of 1990. **Business Addr:** Attorney, Cloud and Henderson, 10605 Woodlawn Blvd, Largo, MD 20772.

CLOUDEN, LAVERNE C.
Music director. **Personal:** Born Dec 6, 1933, Cleveland, OH; married Aubrey B Clouden; children: Norman, Karen, Nathan. **Educ:** Case Western Res U, BS (cum laude) 1966; MA 1970. **Career:** Buckeye State Band, dir 1958-; F D Roosevelt Jr High School, instructor, dir 1966-72; Music Dept Nathan Hale Jr High School, chmn 1972-74; John F Kennedy High School, music dir 1974-85; East High School, fine arts dept chmn/instructor, dir/vocal dir 1985-. **Orgs:** Mem Mt Pleasant Symphony Orch Parma Symphony; Cleveland Women's Symphony; Buckeye State Band; Mt Pleasant Musician's Guild; dir Musicians Umion #4; MusicEducators Nat Conf OH Music Educators Assn; Women Band Dirs Nat Assn; mem Nat Band Assn; mem Intl Platform Assn; mem Nat Assn of Music Therapy; mem Mu Phi Epsilon. **Honors/Awds:** Congrats resolution Mayor & City Cleveland 1975; feat newspapers & Mags; apptd Natl Bd of Am Youth Symphony& Chorus; 1st female marching band band dir Cleveland HS. **Business Addr:** Fine Arts Dept Chairman, East High School, 1349 E 79th Stv, Cleveland, OH 44103.

CLOWNEY, AUDREY E.
Brand manager. **Personal:** Born Aug 29, 1961, Pittsburgh, PA; daughter of Helen A Clowney and Gordon W Clowney. **Educ:** Univ of MI, Ann Arbor, MI, BSE, 1983; Columbia Univ, New York, NY, MBA, 1985. **Career:** Quaker Oats Co, Chicago, IL, brand mgr, 1985-. **Orgs:** The Natl Black MBA Assn-Chicago Chapter, 1990-; The Arts Forum, 1990-; Youth Guidance, 1988-89. **Honors/Awds:** One of "The 100 Most Promising Black Women in Corporate America," Ebony Magazine, 1991. **Business Addr:** Brand Manager, Quaker Oats Compnay, 321 N Clark St, 13-10, Chicago, IL 60610.

CLUSE, KENNY JOSEPH
Educator. **Personal:** Born Sep 25, 1945, Houston, TX; son of Elsie Green Cluse and McKinley Cluse. **Educ:** Texas Southern University, BA 1971; Univ of Houston, BA Radio TV 1973. **Career:** KCOH-AM Houston, Texas, newscaster 1973-75; KTSU-FM radio Houston, TX, sportscaster 1977; HISD Houston Texas, teacher 1978-89; KCOH Radio Houston, newsman. **Orgs:** Mem Sigma Delta Chi Journalistic Soc 1972. **Honors/Awds:** Plaque Lynn Eusann Inst 1973; certificate of Appreciation Prairie View A&M Univ 1974.

CLYBURN, JAMES E.
Congressman. **Personal:** Born Jul 21, 1940, Sumter, SC; son of Almeta Clyburn and E L Clyburn; married Emily; children: Mignon, Jennifer, Angela. **Educ:** SC State Coll, BS 1962; USC Law Sch, 1972-74. **Career:** US House of Representatives, congressman, 1993-; South Carolina Human Affairs Commission, commissioner, 1974-92; Gov John C West of SC, spec asst (for human resource devel) 1971-74; SC Commn for Farm Workers Inc, exec dir 1968-71; Neighborhood Youth Corps, dir 1966-68; SC Employee Sec Commn, couns 1965-68; high school history teacher 1962-65. **Orgs:** Mem of numerous political & civic orgns. **Honors/Awds:** 1st black pres SC Young Democrats; recipient of 36 citations & awards. **Business Addr:** Congressman, US House of Representatives, 319 Cannon House Office Bldg, Washington, DC 20515-4006.

CLYBURN, JOHN B.
Business executive. **Personal:** Born Oct 22, 1942, Sumter, SC; married Vivian Hilton; children: Jeffrey, Erica, Kimberly. **Educ:** SC State Coll, BS 1964; Northeastern Univ, MEd 1968; Univ of WI, PhD Urban Ed. **Career:** Wiltwyck School for Boys Inc, sr counselor; New England Home, weekend suprv; Hayden Goodwill Inn School for Boys, exec asst; SC Vocational Rehab Dept, vocational rehab counselor; ESC, natl coord 1969-70, proj dir 1970-71, vice pres 1971-72, exec vice pres 1972-73; Decision Info Systems Corp, chmn; Precise Solutions, Inc, chmn/CEO. **Orgs:** Mem Natl Assoc Market Developers, Amer Mgmt Assoc, Child Care Proj Adv Comm, Natl Rehab Assoc, Day Care & Child Devel Corp Amer, Natl Assoc Ed Young Children, Delta Psi Omega; lecturer Natl Head Start Conf, Natl Assoc Black Social Workers, Natl Conf Inst Svc. **Honors/Awds:** Deviant Youth; "Use Your Aides Effectively" interview, edited & publ Tech Asst Bulletin; "Challenge Pre-School Ed" promo brochure; "New Horizons Migrant & Seasonal Farm Worker Youths" Publ Idea Exchange 1970. **Home Addr:** 2711 Unicorn Ln, NW, Washington, DC 20015.

CLYMER, LEWIS W.
Judge (retired). **Personal:** Born Dec 16, 1910, Neosho, MO; married Janet L Blackwell; children: Willa Lynn. **Educ:** Lincoln Univ, 1928-29; Howard Univ, 1935-36; Howard Univ School of Law, LLB 1939. **Career:** State of MO, asst attny gen 1935-60; War Manpower Comm Region 9 AR, KS, MO, OK, minorities placement spec 1941-45; Kansas City MO, gen practice 1945; Jackson Cty MO, asst pros 1948-52; Municipal Court MO, apptd judge 1960; Municipal Cty Mar, elected judge 1963; Non-partisan Ct Plan, re-elected 1967-71; 16th Judicial Circuit of MO 1970, judge retired 1980. **Orgs:** Former bd mem N Amer Judges Assoc, MO Munic & Magistrate Judges Assoc; mem Amer Bar Assoc, KC Bar Assoc, Jackson Cty Bar Assoc, Natl Bar Assoc, Cts & Judiciary Comm, The MO Bar & Adv Comm on Cit Ed, The MO Bar; mem bd of dirs urban League of KC, Blue Cross of KC; bd curators Lincoln Univ; vice pres Trumon Amer Eye Ctr; bd dir Gr KC Chap ARC; bd dir Acad of Health Prof; mem MO Statewide Prof Standards Review Council; bd mem at large School Dist of Kansas City MO.

CLYNE, JOHN RENNEL
Lawyer, senior foreign service officer. **Personal:** Born Feb 25, 1926, New York, NY; son of Urielle Linard Clyne and Reginald Clyne; married Jessie MacFarlane, Dec 28, 1954; children: Diana, Reginald, Robert. **Educ:** St Johns Univ School of Law, LLB 1958; St Johns Univ School of Law, JD 1968. **Career:** US & W Indies, engr 1958; private practice NY, lawyer 1958-62; New York City Transit Auth, attny 1963-65; US Agency Intl Devel Nigeria, Brazil, Nicaragua, Honduras, regional legal adv 1965-83; US Agency Intl Devel, asst general counsel 1983-85; self-employed, econ devel consultant. **Orgs:** Dir Amer Intl School Managua, Amer Intl School Lagos. **Honors/Awds:** Nominated Fed Exec Sr Sem 1977; Sr Foreign Serv Awd 1984; Secretary of State's Tribute of Appreciation for Distinguished Service in Foreign Disaster Assistance 1985. **Military Serv:** USN 1944-46. **Home Addr:** 2200 Eugenia Ct, Oviedo, FL 32765.

COACHMAN, WINFRED CHARLES
Educator. **Personal:** Born Oct 8, 1927, McDonald, PA; divorced; children: Winfred, Tonya, Sherrie, Sandy. **Educ:** Univ of PA, MEd; Univ of PA, Cert Doctrl Cand. **Career:** Human Serv Neighborhood Centers Assn, dir 1977-; PA Bd of Educ Manchester Floating Classroom, prin; PA Blk Action Drug Abuse Center Inc, durg counselor, co-ord educ therapy 1970-71; Com Sch Partnership Program, co-ord 1970; Black History Bidwell Cultural Training Center, instructor 1968-70. **Orgs:** Chmn Manchester Comprehensive Educ Com; mem St Joseph's Comm Sch Bd Dir; mem Advsry Com Act 101 Allegheny Comm Coll; mem PA Br NAACP; memAdvsry Com and Sec Task Force PA Bd of Edn; mem N Side Com on Humn Resrcs Inc; mem PA Drug Advsry Task Frc Com Aw Manchester Fltng Clsrm 1975; com aw N Side Comm ; testimonial N Side Resdnts Co-wrks and Sch Persnl; achvmnt aw Manchester Fltng Clsrm. **Honors/Awds:** Biol art SCOPE Allis Chalmers publ 1973. **Military Serv:** AUS 1945-47.

COAKLEY, DEXTER
Professional football player. **Personal:** Born Oct 20, 1972. **Educ:** Appalachian State, attended. **Career:** Dallas Cowboys, linebacker, 1997-. **Business Addr:** Professional Football Player, Dallas Cowboys, One Cowboys Pkwy, Irving, TX 75063, (214)556-9900.

COASTON, SHIRLEY ANN DUMAS
Educator. **Personal:** Born Nov 27, 1939, New Orleans, LA; daughter of Pearl Bailey Dumas and Cornelius Dumas; married George Ellis Coaston Sr, Jul 21, 1962; children: Debra Coaston Ford, George E Jr, Angela R. **Educ:** Dillard University, New Orleans, LA, BA, 1962; University of California, Berkeley, CA, MLS, 1970. **Career:** University of California, San Francisco, CA, library asst, 1966-69; Peralta Community College District, Oakland, CA, evening, reference and head librarian, dir, 1970-87; Contra Costa Community College District, Richmond, CA, reference librarian, 1987-88; Peralta Community College District, Oakland, CA, head librarian, 1988-. **Orgs:** Chairperson, Professional Development Comm, Laney College, 1989-91; treasurer, California Librarians Black Caucus, North, 1980-; member, secretary, board of directors, Salem Lutheran Home, 1986-91; secretary, BayNet, 1990-92; member, American Library Assn; member, ALA Black Caucus; member, Delta Sigma Theta Sorority; member, NAACP; lamplighter, Aid Assn for Lutherans, 1989-; vice pres, Peralta Federation of Teachers, 1991-; member, Professional Development Commission, Laney College, 1991-; member, California Library Association, annual convention planing committee, 1993; assistant secretary, San Francisco Bay Area Panhellenic Council, 1992-. **Honors/Awds:** Author, Books by and about Blacks in the Laney College Library, Laney College, 1973. **Business Addr:** Head Librarian, Laney College, 900 Fallon St, Oakland, CA 94607.

COATES, BEN TERRENCE
Professional football player. **Personal:** Born Aug 16, 1969, Greenwood, SC; married Yvette; children: Lauren, Brianna, Destiny. **Educ:** Livingstone, attended. **Career:** New England Patriots, tight end, 1991-. **Honors/Awds:** 1776 Quarterback Club of New England, Offensive Player of the Year, 1993; Pro Bowl, 1994, 1995, 1996. **Business Addr:** Professional Football Player, New England Patriots, 60 Washington St, Foxboro Stadium, Foxboro, MA 02035, (508)543-7911.

COATES, JANICE E.
Optometrist. **Personal:** Born Aug 27, 1942, Zanesville, OH; daughter of Bessie Kennedy Mayle and Urschel Mayle; children: Stephanie, Stephlynn, Melissa, Tischa. **Educ:** Marion Coll, undergrad work 1960-62; Wright State Univ, BS Comprehensive Sciences and BS Secondary Educ 1974; Indiana Univ, Dr of Optometry 1979. **Career:** Dr Frederick Grigsby, urologist asst 1963-65; Sanders Stone Ins Agency, insurance rater 1965-66; Montgomery Co Welfare Dept, welfare worker 1967-69; Dayton Bd of Educ, substitute teacher 1969-74, science teacher 1974-75; Capital Univ, educator 1980-82; optometrist private practice 1980-. **Orgs:** Prog coord 1982-83, treas 1983-84 Amer Bus Womens Assn; mem of minority recuirt Amer Optometric Assn Ohio Optometric Assn 1980-; liasion to state rep Miami Valley Soc of Optometrists 1981-; mem Gem City Med Soc 1982-; trustee Natl Optometric Assn 1983-, secretary, 1985-87, exec bd, 1983-89; mem NAACP 1983-; exec bd Youth Engaged for Success 1985-97. **Home Addr:** 1000 Amherst Pl, Dayton, OH 45406. **Business Addr:** Optometrist, 4387 Parkway Dr, Dayton, OH 45416-1618.

COATES, SHELBY L.
Business executive. **Personal:** Born Mar 25, 1931, Washington, DC; married Lysette D'Amours. **Educ:** Dept of Agr Grad Sch, Cert 1965-66; Inst of Computer Tech, Cert 1965-66; USAF Supply Analysis & Design Sch, Cert 1969. **Career:** MISSO Serv Corp, pres, CEO 1976-; AUSNG, computer specialist 1966-78. **Orgs:** Mem DAV 1970-; mem Republican Natl Finance Comm EAGLE. **Honors/Awds:** Recipient 3 outstanding performance awards AUS 1971, 1974, 1978. **Military Serv:** AUS pfc, 1948-55. **Business Addr:** President & CEO, MISSO Services Corp, 6715 Little River Turnpike, Ste 203, Annandale, VA 22003.

COATIE, ROBERT MASON
Educator. **Personal:** Born May 19, 1945, Mound City, IL; son of Georgia B Mason Coatie (deceased) and Rev Dixon C Coatie; married Birdeen Golden, Jun 29, 1968; children: Dionne, Robert M II. **Educ:** Ball State Univ, BS 1968, MA 1972. **Career:** Muncie Comm Sch Corp, tchr 1967-68; IN Civil Rights Commission, proj dir 1968-69; Ball State Univ, assc dir minority student development 1969-84; Univ Louisville, dir Center for Academic Achievement 1984-92; Florida International Univ, Student Services, director, 1993-. **Orgs:** Bd mem Hooisers for Excellence 1983-85; past chmn, tres Area VI Council on Aging 1974-84; mem Kappa Alpha Psi Frat 1964-, Natl Assn Dev Educ 1985-, Southeastern Assn Educ Prog Personnel 1986-90, Amer Assn Counseling & Devel 1987-90, Natl Assn Student Personnel Admin 1987-90; mem Assoc for Supervision and Curriculum Development 1987-90; mem YMCA Black Achiever's Parent Advisory Committee 1986-89; vice president Central High School Parent Teachers Assoc 1985-89; secretary Brown School Parent Teachers Association 1986-89; American Assn University Administrators 1989-92; American Assn Higher Education. **Honors/Awds:** Observer White House Conf on Aging 1981; Black Achiever, Muncie, Indiana 1988; Athletic Hall of Fame, Delaware County (Indiana) 1988; mem, Kappa Delta Pi 1974-84. **Home Addr:** 8360 NW 166 Terrace, Hialeah, FL 33016. **Business Addr:** Director, Minority Student Services, Florida International University, University Park, GC, 216C, Miami, FL 33199.

COAXUM, CALLIE B.
Educational administrator. **Personal:** Born Jun 7, 1930, Clinton, NC; married Lymon A Coaxum; children: Donald, Ronald, Kelvin. **Educ:** Johnson C Smith Univ, BA (cum laude) 1949; SC State Coll, MS 1960; VA State Coll, post grad 1963; IN Univ, post grad 1964; Univ of SC, post grad 1969; SIU, DPhil in Educ 1976. **Career:** Porter Elementary School, prin 1951-52; St Helena High School, teacher, counselor 1955-69; Coll Counseling & Asst Dean of Students, dir 1970-72; Winston-Salem State Univ, prof of English, asst to vice chancellor for academic affairs 1977-83, vice chancellor for academic affairs 1983-86; Fayetteville State University, associate vice chancellor for academic affairs, 1986-. **Orgs:** Informal consul Ford Found Leadership Dev Prog 1972; pres Lady's Island Dem Precinct 1968; Alpha Kappa Alpha Sor; SC Coll Student Pers Assoc 1970-; Amer Coll Pers Assoc Summer Fellowship French VA State Coll 1963; Top Ladies of Distinction, Winston-Salem Chapter, founder, 1980. **Honors/Awds:** Phi Kappa Alpha. **Special Achievements:** Contributor, numerous articles to education magazines & publishers. **Business Addr:** Associate Vice Chancellor for Academic Affairs, Fayetteville State University, Fayetteville, NC 28301.

COAXUM, HARRY LEE
Restaurant executive. **Personal:** Born Sep 25, 1953, Awendaw, SC; son of Henry Sr (deceased) & Myrtle W Coaxum; married Donna Bunch Coaxum; children: Todriq, Nia. **Educ:** Talladega Coll, BA, economics, 1975. **Career:** McDonald's Corp, multi dept head, Philadelphia region, 1986-89, dir, field training, 1989-90, dir, minority operations, 1990-94, dept dir, western zone, beginning 1994, asst vice pres, franchising, currently. **Orgs:** Omega Psi Phi Fraternity, 1972; Trinity United Church of Christ, 1993; Urban League Leadership Institute Philadelphia charter, mem, 1988; 100 Black Men of America, Chicago. **Honors/Awds:** Natl Black McDonald's Operator Assn, Corp Award, 1991, 1993; Natl Alumni Council UNCF, Presenters Award, 1993; Dollar & Sense Magazine, America's Best & Brightest, 1993; McDonald's Corp, Outstanding Contributor, Business Consultant, 1985, Restaurant Security Award, 1978. **Special Achievements:** Economic Development: Capacity Building for Community Development, 1988. **Business Addr:** Assistant Vice President, Franchising, McDonald's Corp, 711 Jorie Blvd, Oak Brook, IL 60521, (630)623-5836.

COAXUM, HENRY L., JR.
Restauranteur. **Personal:** Born Jan 27, 1951, Charleston, SC. **Educ:** Talladega Coll, BA History, Pol Sci 1969-73; IN Univ, MPA 1973-75. **Career:** City of Chicago, planning analyst 1975-79; DuSable Museum African-Amer History, devel officer 1979-81; Southtown Planning Assoc, exec dir, 1981-83; Amistad Rsch Ctr, dir of devel 1983-84; McDonalds Corp, various mgmt positions, currently. **Orgs:** Pres Chicago Talladega Coll Alumni Club 1977-81; mem Natl Soc of Fund Raising Exec 1980-84, Comm Arts Comm of Chicago Council on Fine Arts 1981-82; dir, United Bank & Trust, New Orleans, 1995-; 100 Black Men of Metro New Orleans, 1995-; certified facilitator, Covey Leadership Center, 1994-. **Honors/Awds:** Cert Chief Planning Analyst City of Chicago Dept of Personnel 1979; Alumni Devel Robert R Moton Inst VA 1981; Commercial Redevel Natl Devel Council Atlanta 1982; Comm Exec Prog IBM Corp NY 1982. **Business Addr:** Field Service Manager, McDonald's Corp, 3850 N Causeway Blvd, Ste 1600, Metairie, LA 70002-7200, (504)837-4111.

COBB, CHARLES E.
Association executive. **Personal:** Born Sep 28, 1916, Durham, NC; married Martha Kendrick. **Educ:** BA 1940; BD 1944; STM1954; DD 1972. **Career:** KY State Coll, chaplain dean men; St Mark Social Center, dir; St John AME Ch, pastor; St Johns Congregational Ch; Charlotte Edition Carolina & Times, mgn editor; Commn for Racial Justice United Ch Christ, exec dir. **Orgs:** Mem Ministers for Racial & Social Justice; Nat Council Chs; Commr Pub Welf Springfield; chmn spl com Black Clergy 1966 Omega Psi Phi Frat; UCC United Black Christian; Black Execs in Denominations Religious Orgns & Communions Orgn Sch Civic Responsibility Springfield 1952; bd dirs Child & Family Serv 1955-66. **Honors/Awds:** Man Of Yr Omega Psi Phi New England Reg Award 1954; NAACP New England Reg Award 1958; Frederick Douglass Citation 1972; City Wide Clergy Award 1971; Nazarene Brotherhood Award 1972; Richard Allen Brotherhood Award 1964. **Business Addr:** Commission for Racial Justice, United Church of Christ, 475 Riverside Dr, New York, NY 10027.

COBB, CYNTHIA JOAN
Staffing manager. **Personal:** Born Sep 22, 1959, Indianapolis, IN; daughter of Marcella Jean Collins Taylor and Henry Marshall Taylor; married Arthur Cobbs Jr, Aug 31, 1985. **Educ:** Purdue University, West Lafayette, IN, BSE, 1981; Indiana University, Bloomington, IN, MBA, 1985. **Career:** Corning Medical, Medfield, MA, process engineer, 1981-83; Eli Lilly, Indianapolis, IN, summer intern, 1984; Baxter Healthcare Corporation, Deerfield, IL, compensation analyst, 1985, senior compensation analyst, 1986, associate, college relations, 1986-88, supervisor, college relations, 1988, staffing manager, 1988-. **Orgs:** Vice president-employer, 1990-91, vice chair, editorial advisory board, 1989-90, member, assembly, 1989-90, chair, pharmaceutical/HC employers, 1987-89, Midwest College Placement Assn. **Honors/Awds:** 100 Most Promising Black Women in Corporate America, Ebony/Johnson Publishing 1991; Consortium for Graduate Study in Management Fellowship, 1983. **Business Addr:** Staffing Manager, IV Systems Division, Baxter Healthcare Corporation, 1425 Lake Cook Rd, LC11-1, Deerfield, IL 60015-4625.

COBB, DELMARIE L.
Media consultant. **Personal:** Born Jul 28, Chicago, IL; daughter of Johnnie Mae Cobb Wells and James A Wells. **Educ:** University of Cincinnati; Northwestern University. **Career:** WSBT-TV (CBS), general assignment reporter, 1981-83; WVEC-TV (ABC), general assignment reporter, 1983-85; WTHR-TV (NBC), general assignment reporter, 1985-87; Jackson For Pres, natl traveling press secy, 1988; WVON-AM, talk show host, 1988-89; Democratic National Convention Committee, press secy, 1996-. **Orgs:** Chicago Association of Black Journalist, at large bd mem, 1996-97; Fairness & Accuracy in Reporting, women & media proj advisory bd, 1995-. **Honors/Awds:** League of Black Women, Black Rose Award, 1992; Lincoln University, Unity Awards in Media, 1993; Delta Sigma Theta, Echoes of Excellence, 1995; Operation Push, Achievement Award, 1996; N'Digo Foundation, N'Voice, 1997. **Special Achievements:** Street Life, TV newsmagazine program (PBS-TV), 1990, 1991; Congressman Bobby Rush Camp, dir of communications, 1992; Congressman Jesse Jackson Jr Camp, dir of communications, 1995. **Business Addr:** Owner/President, The Publicity Works, Deleco Communications, Inc, 28 E Jackson Blvd, Ste 1101, Chicago, IL 60604, (312)939-7740.

COBB, ETHEL WASHINGTON
Elected official. **Personal:** Born Jun 10, 1925, Ravenel, SC; married Shedrick Cobb; children: 7. **Career:** City of Ravenel, bd of execs 1970-. **Orgs:** Mem St John Baptist Church, recording sec & pres The Pulpit Aid Bd, mem Missionary Bd, mem church choir; founder/chmn St John Day Care Ctr; mem Yonges Island Headstart Bd; mem Daycare Ctr Bd; mem Rural Mission Council; mem Biracial Comm Charleston Co Comm Develop Bd; vol firefighter Sea Island Prog; Clemson Univ Ext Comm Develop Progs; mem Democratic Party, exec comm, poll mgr for Primary & Presidential Elections; precinct chmn Pol Action Comm Dist 116; mem Democratic Council 1984; mem Budget Proposal Comm; represented Ravenel in Charleston Berkley & Dorchester Comm; represented Ravenel in Firemen Assn; mem Eastern Star; elected First Black Woman to the Bd of Execs in Ravenel. **Honors/Awds:** Civil Defense Awd; 5 yr Recognition Awd Clemson Univ Ext Prog; Outstanding Assistance Awd, Who's Who Among Southern Americans; Outstanding Assistance Awd for the Baptist Hill HS Athletic Dept; Outstanding Democratic Female; cert from Gov's Rural School.

COBB, HAROLD
Clergyman, elected official. **Personal:** Born Jul 20, 1941, Covington, GA; son of Mary Alice Cobb and Toy Quintella Cobb; married Reta Jean Davis; children: Sheila, Shermekia, Harrell. **Educ:** Atlanta Area Tech School, 1970; Marsh-Drangron Bus Coll, 1971-72; Oxford Coll of Emory Univ 1978; DeKalb Comm Coll 1981; Emory Univ, ministerial course, 1984-89. **Career:** City of Covington, lab analyst, water treatment 1974-78; Ford Motor Co, lab analyst, water treatment 1978-; City of Covington, commission; United Methodist Church, minister. **Orgs:** Masonic Lodge Friendship #20 F&AM 1969-; pres & founder Newton Cty Voter League 1970-77; founder & owner Cobb's Printing 1971-80; pres Cousins Middle School PTO 1973-75; bd of dir Newton Cty Mental Health 1974-76, Washington St Comm Ctr 1980-83; bd mem Newton Cty Public Defenders 1980-; founder-owner C&C Rental 1984-; co-founder Newton County King Scholar Prog Emory Univ of Oxford Coll 1986-. **Honors/Awds:** Outstanding Serv to God & Country 1981; Inkind Contrib Headstart 1977; Outstanding Progress to Newton Cty 1978; Appreciation Awards Recreation Dept Supporter 1981-84; Gaithers Chapel United Methodist Church Appreciation 1983; Support of Industrial Growth Newton Cty Chamber Commerce 1984; "I Have A Dream Award" Martin Luther King Scholarship Fund 1988; Outstanding service, Toney Gardens Civic Assn 1989; Appreciation Award, Union Grove Church 1990. **Military Serv:** USAF E-3 4 yrs. **Home Addr:** 5224 Avery St, Covington, GA 30209.

COBB, HAROLD JAMES, JR.
Cleric. **Personal:** Born Jun 10, 1958, Burlington, NC; son of Armadia Goodson Cobb and Harold James Cobb Sr; married Sheliah Jeffries Cobb, Jun 29, 1991. **Educ:** University of North Carolina at Chapel Hill, BA, 1982; Episcopal Theological Seminary, MDiv, 1990. **Career:** Good Samaritan Church, pastor & founder, 1980-87; Saint Stephen's Church, rector, 1990-. **Orgs:** Episcopal Seminary, alumni executive committee, 1990-91; Diocese of North Carolina, Board of Higher Education, 1990-, Youth Commission, 1990-; North Carolina Episcopal Clergy Association, 1990-; North Carolina Governor's Commission for the Family, commissioner, 1985-88; Alpha Phi Alpha; The Order of the Cross; The Royal Order of the Society of Saint George. **Honors/Awds:** City of Atlantic City, NJ, Harold J Cobb Jr Day, August 1989. **Special Achievements:** Author, The Organization of Black Episcopal Seminarians, Virginia Seminary Journal, 1987. **Business Addr:** Rector, Saint Stephen's Episcopal Church, 810 Highland Ave, Winston-Salem, NC 27101.

COBB, JEWEL PLUMMER
Cancer researcher, university president. **Personal:** Born Jan 17, 1924, Chicago, IL; daughter of Carriebel Cole Plummer and Frank V Plummer; married Roy Cobb, Jul 4, 1954 (divorced); children: Jonathan Cobb. **Educ:** Talladega Coll, Talladega AL, BA, 1944; New York Univ, New York NY, MS, 1947, PhD, 1950. **Career:** New York Univ, New York City, instructor, 1955-56, asst prof, 1956-60; Hunter Coll, visiting lecturer, 1956-57; Sarah Lawrence Coll, Bronxville NY, biology prof, 1960-69; Connecticut Coll, New London CT, zoology prof, dean, 1969-76; Rutgers Univ, Douglass Coll, New Brunswick NJ, biology prof, dean, 1976-81; California State Univ, Fullerton CA, pres, 1981-. **Orgs:** Mem bd trustees, Inst Educ Mgmt, 1973-; developer & dir, Fifth Year Post Bacc Pre-Med Prog; bd dir, Amer Coun Educ, 1973-76; bd dir, Educ Policy Center, New York City; Natl Acad of Sciences, Human Resources Commn, 1974-; Natl Science Found, 1974-; bd dir, Travelers Insurance Co, 1974-; bd dir, 21st Century Found; trustee, Natl Fund for Minority Engineering Students, 1978-; bd dir, Californians Preventing Violence, 1983-; bd dir, First Interstate Bancorp, 1985-; bd dir, Amer Assembly of Barbard Coll, 1986-; bd mem, Newport Harbor Museum. **Honors/Awds:** Research grant, Amer Cancer Soc, 1969-74, 1971-73, 1974-77; honorary doctorates from Wheaton Coll (1971), Lowell Technical Inst (1972), Pennsylvania Medical Coll (1975), City Coll of the City Univ of NY, St Lawrence Univ, Coll of New Rochelle, Tuskegee Univ, Fairleigh Dickinson Univ; author of Filters for Women in Science, 1979, Breaking Down Barriers to Women Entering Science, 1979, Issues and Problems: A Debate, 1979. **Business Addr:** President, California State University, Fullerton, 800 North State College Blvd, Fullerton, CA 92634.

COBB, JOHN HUNTER, JR.
Lawyer. **Personal:** Born May 5, 1953, Rocky Mount, NC; son of Annie Lee Cobb and John H Cobb; married Regina LaVerne Payne. **Educ:** Hampton Univ, BA 1975; Howard Univ, JD 1979. **Career:** Michie Company, senior editor 1979-85; Robinson Buchanan & Johnson, associate 1985-; Virginia Union University, business law prof 1985-86; solo practicioner 1988-. **Orgs:** Mem Old Dominion Bar Assoc 1979-; Young Lawyers Conf VA State Bar 1979-; legal advisor Time Investment Corp 1985-; mem VA Trial Lawyers Assoc 1985-; comm mem Guardian Ad Litem Seminar 1987. **Honors/Awds:** Litigation Section VA State Bar 1985-.

COBB, KEITH HAMILTON
Actor. **Career:** All My Children, 1994-. **Honors/Awds:** Soap Opera Digest, Award for Outstanding Male Newcomer, 1995; Emmy nominee, Award for Outstanding Younger Actor in a Drama Series, 1995. **Business Phone:** (310)289-0909.

COBB, REGINALD JOHN
Professional football player. **Personal:** Born Jul 7, 1968, Knoxville, TN. **Educ:** Univ of Tennessee, attended. **Career:** Tampa Bay Buccaneers, running back, 1990-94; Green Bay Packers, 1994-. **Honors/Awds:** MVP, Peach Bowl, 1987. **Business Addr:** Professional Football Player, Green Bay Packers, 1265 Lombardi Ave, Green Bay, WI 54304.

COBB, THELMA M.
Educator. **Personal:** Born Apr 3, Portsmouth, VA; married Henry E Cobb (deceased). **Educ:** Hampton Inst, BS 1941, MA 1946; Univ of Houston, EdD 1976; Temple Univ; Univ of CT, further study. **Career:** Tuskege Inst, instructor 1948-52; FL A&M, asst prof 1952-55; Southern Univ, prof 1958-89, prof

emeritus, 1989-. **Orgs:** Consultant Black Lit, Multicultural Studies, Women's Lit; reg dir Delta Sigma Theta; CLA; Delta Sigma Theta, YWCA, Phi Delta Kappa, Pi Gamma Mu, NCTE; admin bd Camphor Memorial United Methodist Church; The Links, Inc. **Honors/Awds:** Gen Educ Bd Fellow; Outstanding Woman in Educ Baton Rouge Delta Sigma Theta; Tchr of the Yr Southern Univ and Alumni Fed. **Home Addr:** 2145 78th Ave, Baton Rouge, LA 70807.

COBBIN, GLORIA CONSTANCE
Organization executive. **Personal:** Born Dec 2, 1939, Detroit, MI; daughter of Marissa L Wright Taylor and Arthur Wardell Taylor; married Ward Robert Cobbin, Sep 15, 1962 (deceased); children: Darryl, Lynnette. **Educ:** Labor School, Cert 1972; Wayne State Univ, 1973-76. **Career:** City of Detroit Human Rights Dept, office mgr 1962-82; MI AFSCME Council, political action coord/lobbyist 1982-; Detroit Bd of Educ, vp, 1983-86, pres, 1986-88; mem, until 1994; Collaborative on Offender Training and Employment, dir, 1989; vice pres, Assn for Community Correction in Michigan, 1990-. **Orgs:** Chairperson City-Wide School Board Member Caucus 1978; exec board member SACVE 1979; Newly Structured Detroit Bd of Ed 1982; delegate Natl Dem Convention 1976, 1980, 1984, 1988, 1992; chair Women's Comm; 1st dist adv & org 1st Dist Young Dems Comm; mem MI Dem Party Women's Comm; exec vice pres AFSCME #1329; co-founder Young Individualists for COPE; mem, steering comm Coaliton of Labor Union Women; former spokesperson Women United for Action; mem Policy Adv Comm Catholic Soc Serv Head Start Prog; moderator Bd of Educ Digest WDET FM 909; vice pres Central Region Natl Caucus of Black School Bd Members; secretary-treasurer, Metropolitan Detroit AFL-CIO 1988-; sec, Wayne County Community Corrections Advisory Board, 1989; chair, 15th Congressional District Democratic Party; AFSCME, intl vp; Detroit Public Schools Citizens Bond Monitoring Panel, chair; AFL, COTE, dir. **Honors/Awds:** Conducted study of state boards of educ; received Awd for Outstanding Dem Woman of the Year; Harriet Tubman Awd; Martin Luther King Awd MI AFSCME; first black female elected president Detroit Bd of Educ, 1986-88; elected International Vice Pres AFSME, AFL-CIO, 1992. **Special Achievements:** First African American female to be elected president of the Detroit Board of Education; first female to be named secretary/treasurer of the Metropolitan Detroit AFL-CIO; first female to be elected chair of the 15th Congressional District Democratic Party. **Business Addr:** Director, COTE Program, 2550 W Grand Blvd, Detroit, MI 48208.

COBBIN, W. FRANK, JR.
Business executive. **Personal:** Born Jul 2, 1947, Youngstown, OH; married Deborah Walk; children: Kevin, Kimberly. **Educ:** Cleveland State Univ, BA Psych, English 1971; IN Univ Exec Program, Prof Mgr & Bus Functions 1980-81. **Career:** OH Bell Telephone Co, mgr bus office 1973-77, mgr installation 1977-78, dist mgr installation 1978-79, mktg mgr 1979, dist mgr 1979-82; AT&T AmericanTranstech, dir telephone response ctr 1982-83, exec dir mktg svc, vice pres direct mktg serv 1987-. **Orgs:** Mem Direct Mktg Assoc, Telemarketing Assoc, Mayor's Econ Devel Council, Jax Urban League Bd; Basileus Omega Psi Phi Frat Inc; mem United Way, Univ of North FL Business Adv Cncl, Jacksonville Univ Career Beginnings Prog. **Military Serv:** Reserves staff sgt 6 yrs; #1 in class NCO Acad. **Business Addr:** Vice President, AT&T American Transtech, 8000 Baymeadows Way, Jacksonville, FL 32216.

COBBINS, LYRON
Professional football player. **Personal:** Born Sep 17, 1974. **Educ:** Notre Dame, attended. **Career:** Arizona Cardinals, linebacker, 1997-. **Business Addr:** Professional Football Player, Arizona Cardinals, 8701 S Hardy, Tempe, AZ 85284, (602)379-0101.

COBBS, DAVID E.
Educator. **Personal:** Born May 26, 1940, Nashville, TN; married Margaret; children: Amy Elizabeth. **Educ:** TN State U, BS; MI U, MMus; Univ of MA, MMus; No TX State Univ USC, Grad Study. **Career:** Music Conservatory Compton Community Coll, dir 1970-; Prairie View Coll, 1963-70; Edward Waters Coll, Jacksonville FL, 1962-63; Univ of MA, teaching asst 1967-68; USC, teaching asst 1971-73. **Orgs:** Mem bd dir Compton & Comm Symphony; western rep Black Music Caucus Mu Sic Educ Nat Conf. **Honors/Awds:** Award instrumental music; award asst dir of marching bands. **Business Addr:** 1111 E Artesia Blvd, Compton, CA 90221.

COBBS, HARVEY, JR.
Corrections counselor, supervisor. **Personal:** Born Mar 19, 1952, Twist, AR; son of Paralee Jackson and Harvey Cobbs; married Willie Mae Lewis, Apr 27, 1973; children: Harvey III, Carolyn, Davina, Yvonne. **Educ:** Bakersfield College, AA, 1976; California State University-Bakersfield, BA, 1980. **Career:** US Army, military policeman, sentry dog handler, 1972; California Department of Corrections, correctional officer, 1979-82, Junipero Serra-Work Furlough, inmate supervisor, counselor, 1987-. **Orgs:** NAACP, life & golden heritage member, 1990; California Correctional Officers Association, 1987; American Correctional Officers Association, 1989; life mem, National Association of Black Veterans. **Honors/Awds:** NAACP, Golden Heritage Award, 1990; California Corrections Officers Association, Certificate and Badge (w/ribbon), 1987; American Criminal Justice Association, Recognition Plaque, 1990; International Association of Correctional Officers, Certificate; Nat Assn of Black Veterans, 1971; CA State Senator Jim Coste, Cert of Rec, 1997. **Military Serv:** US Army, spec-4, 1972-73; Good Conduct Medal, 1973, National Defense Medal, 1973. **Business Addr:** Supervisor, Counselor, California Department of Correction, Junipero Serra-Work Furlough, 700 19th St, Bakersfield, CA 93301, (805)324-6125.

COBBS, PRICE MASHAW
Business executive, psychiatrist. **Personal:** Born Nov 2, 1928, Los Angeles, CA; son of Rose Mashaw Cobbs and Peter Price Cobbs; married Evadne Priester, May 30, 1957 (died 1973); children: Price Priester, Marion Renata; married Frederica Maxwell, May 26, 1985. **Educ:** Univ of CA Berkeley, BA 1953; Meharry Med College, MD, 1958. **Career:** San Francisco Gen Hosp, intern 1958-59; Mendocino State Hosp, psychiatric res 1959-61; Langley Porter Neuropsychiatric Inst, psych res 1961-62; Pacific Mgmt Systems, pres 1967-; Cobbs Inc, CEO. **Orgs:** Natl Medical Assn; life mem NAACP; consultant to many Fortune 500 companies, govt agencies and comm groups; charter member, Natl Urban League; chair First National Diversity Conf; co-founder/pres Renaissance Books; advisory board, Black Scholar; bd of dirs, Foundation for National Progress; fellow, American Psychiatric Assn; Natl Academy of the Sciences. **Honors/Awds:** Black Enterprise, Outstanding Psychiatrist, 1988; Assn of Humanistic Psychology, Pathfinder Award, 1993. **Military Serv:** US Army, corporal, 1951-53. **Business Addr:** President, Pacific Mgmt Systems, 3528 Sacramento St, San Francisco, CA 94118-1847.

COBBS, SUSIE ANN
Educator (retired). **Personal:** Born Feb 8, 1924, Toledo, OH; married Dr Therion D Cobbs; children: Therion, Therman, Jonathan. **Educ:** Central State Univ, BS 1948; Univ of MO Kansas City, attended; Univ of KS, MS Ed; George Peabody Coll, attended; Central State Univ, BS; Univ of KS, MS. **Career:** Kansas City MO, physical educ teacher; San Diego School Dist, teacher; Fisk Univ, recreation dir, assoc prof retired. **Orgs:** Mem Alpha Kappa Alpha Sor, AME Ministers Wives Alliance; pres Progressive Matrons Club, Water Safety Instr; 1st aid instr ARC; mem St Peter AME Church, Womens Civic Forum of Nashville, The Assoc of Coll Women of Nashville, The TN Coll Womens Sports Fed, The Natl Assoc of Health Phys Ed & Rec; former staff mem, rec dir Martha O'Brian Comm Ctr; sub teacher Nashville Bd of Ed. **Honors/Awds:** Natl ARC Serv Awd Frist Aid 1973; Adv of the Year Pi Chap of Alpha Kappa Alpha Sor 1974. **Home Addr:** 617 Malta Dr, Nashville, TN 37207.

COBBS, WINSTON H. B., JR.
Physician. **Personal:** Born May 7, 1955, Flushing, NY; married Valerie Crouch; children: Noelle Bianca, Paige Alfreda. **Educ:** Boston Univ, BA biology 1976; Meharry Medical Coll, MD 1980. **Career:** Long Island Jewish Medical Ctr, internship internal medicine 1980-81; Nassau Co Medical Ctr, residence in internal medicine 1983-85; Booth Memorial Medical Ctr, fellow in pulmonary medicine 1986-88; in private practice 1988-. **Orgs:** Mem Amer Soc of Intl Medicine, Amer Thoracic Soc; assoc mem Amer Coll of Physicians, Amer Coll of Chest Physicians; Fellow-American Coll of Chest Physicians. **Honors/Awds:** Martin Luther King Scholarship Awd for Excellence in Education; Publications, "The Effects of Phospho-Diesterase on Insulin Metabolism," A Research Study The Diabetes and Endocrinology Ctr Nashville 1972; "The Spirometric Standards for Healthy Black Adults," A Research Study Meharry Medical Coll Nashville, The Journal of the Natl Medical Assoc 1981; secretary of medical staff, Franklin Hosp and Medical Center. **Business Addr:** 1800 Dutch Broadway, Elmont, NY 11003.

COCHRAN, DONNIE L.
Naval aviator (retired). **Personal:** Born Jul 6, 1954, Pelham, GA; son of Addie B Cochram and I C Cochran; married Donna F Townsell, Mar 18, 1978; children: Donnie L Jr, Destiny L. **Educ:** Savannah State Coll, BS Civ Engr 1976. **Career:** VT-27, VT-23, VT-21 (Training Command), student aviator 1976-78; VFP-63 DET-5 RF-86, detach operation officer 1978-80; VF-124 F-14A, fleet replacement pilot 1980-81; VF-213 F-14A, fleet pilot 1981-85; VF-124 F-14A, instructor pilot 1985; Blue Angels, pilot number three 1986; Blue Angel #3 1987; Blue Angel #4 1988; US Navy NAS MIRAMAR, CDR. **Orgs:** Mem Tail Hook, Natl Naval Officers Assoc 1976. **Honors/Awds:** Black Engineer of the Year, 1989. **Special Achievements:** First African-American pilot to fly with the Blue Angels, 1985-89. **Military Serv:** US Navy, lt comm, 1976-; Meritorius Unit Commendation; Navy Expeditionary Medal; Meritorious Service Medal. **Business Addr:** RM7800 University Inn Bldg, #157, Maxwell AFB, AL 36112.

COCHRAN, EDWARD G.
Telecommunications manager. **Personal:** Born Jun 16, 1953, Chicago, IL; married Barbara Porter; children: Rashida, Marcus. **Educ:** Lake Forest Coll, BA (w/Honors) 1975; DePaul Univ, MBA 1985. **Career:** Continental Bank, operations analyst 1975-77; IBM, systems engr 1977-81; Sears Communications, telecomm mgr 1981-; Consultant Telecommunications, 1984-; Mundelein College, undegrad, adjunct faculty, 1986-; DePaul University, grad, adjunct faculty, 1987-. **Honors/Awds:** Several articles and papers published on Telecommunications. **Business Addr:** Manager, Sears Communications, 231 N Martingale Rd, Schaumburg, IL 60173-2254.

COCHRAN, HAROLD LLOYD, JR.
Company executive. **Personal:** Born Aug 14, 1957, Columbus, OH; son of Harold & Margret Cochran; married Linda, Dec 28, 1983; children: Courtney Elest, Taylor Lloy. **Educ:** Kent State Univ, BA, 1980; Univ of CT, MBA, 1986; Dallas Baptist Univ, Exec MBA Program, 1992. **Career:** JC Penney Co: financial controls supervisor, 1980-84, financial planning mgr, 1984-88, mgr of marketing, Speciality Markets, 1988-92, mgr of strategic planning, 1990-92; Dell Computer, dir of segment marketing, sales, 1992-94; Corporate Software Inc, dir of marketing, Direct Bus Unit, 1994-95, dir of marketing, Global Demand, 1995-. **Orgs:** American Management Assn, NY Chapter, president, 1986-88; Direct Marketing Assn, Dallas TX Chapter, 1st vp, 1988-89; Alpha Phi Alpha Fraternity, Graduate Chapter, treasurer, 1984-86; Institute of Internal Auditors, NY Chapter, secretary, 1987; National Assn of Accountants, chairperson, steering comm, 1988; Black Assn of Accountants, 2nd vp, 1986; Jack & Jill Inc, Dallas, TX Chapter, chairperson, Charity Ball (annual) 1987-88. **Honors/Awds:** DECA, Outstanding Leadership Award, 1989-90; Kent State Univ, Outstanding Black Athlete Award, 1979, Distinguished Alumni Award, 1992; JC Penney Co, Community Service Award, 1986; Dell Computer, President Leadership Gold Pin, 1993. **Special Achievements:** Creation of the country's first major catalog, targeted to African Americans, Fashion Influences, JC Penney, 1992. **Business Addr:** Dir of Marketing, Corp Software Inc, 2 Edge Water Dr, Corp Headquarters, Norwood, MA 02062-4637, (617)440-1623.

COCHRAN, JAMES DAVID, JR.
Pediatrician. **Personal:** Born Oct 24, 1951, Muskegon, MI. **Educ:** Univ of MI, BS 1973; Howard Univ, MD 1977. **Career:** Howard Univ Hosp, pediatric resident 1977-80; Natl Health Serv Corps, medical officer 1980-83; Collier Health Svcs, staff physician 1983-84; Collier Health Serv Inc, medical dir 1984-. **Orgs:** Mem local vice polemarch Kappa Alpha Psi Frat 1980-; mem Amer, Natl Medical Assocs 1981-; mem Collier County Medical Soc 1983-; counselor Collier County Youth Guidance 1985-; mem Big Bros Collier County 1985-. **Honors/Awds:** Publication "Study of Sickle Cell in an Animal Model," Journal of NMA 1980. **Business Addr:** Medical Dir, Collier Health Serv Inc, 419 N First St, Immokalee, FL 33934.

COCHRAN, JOHNNIE L., JR.
Attorney. **Personal:** Born Oct 2, 1937, Shreveport, LA; son of Hattie Bass Cochran and Johnnie L Cochran Sr; married Sylvia Dale Cochran; children: Melodie, Tiffany, Jonathan. **Educ:** University of California, Los Angeles, BS, bus adm, 1959; Loyola University, School of Law, JD, 1962; University of Southern California, Los Angeles, grad work in law. **Career:** City of Los Angeles, deputy city attorney, 1963-65; Cochran, Atkins & Evans, founder, attorney, 1966-78; Los Angeles County, asst district attorney, 1978-80; Johnnie L Cochran Jr Inc, private practice of law, 1981-. **Orgs:** Second Baptist Church; Criminal Courts Bar Assn, bd of dirs; Langston Bar Assn, bd of dirs; Los Angeles Urban League, bd of dirs; Oscar Joel Bryant Foundation, bd of dirs; 28th St YMCA, bd of dirs; Los Angeles Family Housing Corp, bd of dirs; Los Angeles African American Chamber of Commerce, bd of dirs; Bd of Airport Commissioners for City of Los Angeles, 1981-93; Intl Academy of Trial Lawyers, 1982; UCLA Foundation, bd of trustees, 1983; American Civil Liberties Union Foundation of Southern California, bd of dirs, 1984; Democratic Natl Conv, Rules Committee, special council to the chairman, 1984; Greater Los Angeles Visitors and Convention Bureau, bd of dirs, 1985; Dance Gallery of Los Angeles, bd of trustees, 1987; Children's Inst Intl, bd of trustees, 1988; Judicial Council of the State of California, 1989, Executive Committee, 1990; Black Business Assn of Los Angeles, pres, 1989; Chancery Club of Los Angeles, 1990; UCLA Alumni Assn, General Counsel, 1990; Lawyers Mutual Insurance Co, bd of dirs, 1991; Judicial Council of California, Advisory Committee on Racial and Ethnic Bias, 1991; American Bar Foundation, fellow, 1991; Rebuild LA Project, bd of dirs, 1992; American College of Trial Lawyers, 1993; State Bar of California, Bd of the Legal Service Corps, co-chair, 1993; Daniel Freeman Hosp, bd of dirs, 1993; Montgomery Watson Inc, bd of dirs, 1993. **Honors/Awds:** Los Angeles Criminal Courts Bar Assn, Criminal Trial Lawyer of the Year, 1977; Los Angeles Brotherhood Crusade, Pioneer of Black Legal Leadership Award, 1979; California Trial Lawyers Assn, Outstanding Law Enforcement Officer, 1979; John M Langston Bar Assn, Honorable Loren Miller Award as Trial Lawyer of the Year, 1983; California Assn of Black Lawyers, Loren Miller Award as Trial Lawyer of the Year, 1983; Legal Defense Fund of the NAACP, Equal Justice in Law Award, 1984; Los Angeles High School Alumni Hall of Fame, 1987; UCLA Black Alumni Assn, Distinguished Alumni Assn, 1988; UCLA Alumni Assn, Alumni Award for Excellence in Professional Achievement, 1988; Los Angeles Magazine, One of LA's Secret Power Elite, 1988; Los Angeles Times Magazine, one of California's Outstanding

Criminal Defense Attorneys, 1989; Los Angeles Trial Lawyers Assn, Trial Lawyer of the Year, 1990; Westminster Neighborhood Assn, Outstanding Citizen of the Year, 1991; Kappa Alpha Psi Fraternity, 1990 Trial Lawyer of the Year, 1991; NAACP Legal Defense Fund, Los Angeles Chapter, Civil Rights Lawyer of the Year Award, 1991; NAACP, Los Angeles Chapter, Presidential Award, 1991; NAACP, Pasadena Branch, Lifetinme Achievement Award, 1991; Los Angeles Intl Airport Kiwanis Club, Man of the Year, 1991; Vice Chancellor Winston Doby for establishing the Johnnie L Chochran Sr Scholarship for UCLA Afrian American Males, 1991; Natl Law Journal, named One of the 10 Most Successful Litigators in the Country, 1992; Criminal Courts Bar Assn of Los Angeles, Morton Herbert Community Service Award, 1994; PTA of the Frank D Parent School, Positive Image Award, 1994; Women Aware Inc, Renaissance Man of the Year Award, 1994; Kappa Alpha Psi Fraternity, honored in its Annual Scholarship Extravaganza, 1994; Black Enterprise Magazine, named of of Top 50 Powerbrokers in the Entertainment Industry, 1994; Entertainment Weekly Magazine's Feature, "Power 100," named One of Hollywood's Hottest Players, 1994; Brotherhood Crusade, Walter Bremond Pioneer of African American Achievement Award, 1994; Watts Christman Parade, Role Model of the Year/ Grand Marshall, 1994. **Special Achievements:** Obtained the largest jury verdict, at that time, in the history of the City of Los Angeles of $1.3 million in the case of Herbert Avery vs The City of Los Angeles, 1982; negoitated the largest settlement in a case of this type in the history of the State of California in the case of Helen and Donnell Settles vs The City of Signal Hill, 1983; appeared as a guest attorney on NBC TV Program "Headlines on Trial"; his law firm was appointed as Special Counsel to the Committee on Standards of Official Conduct, Ethics Committee, of the House of Representatives, 99th Congress, 1986; according to LA Times, obtained the largest jury verdict ($2,230,000) in the history of the city of Los Angeles in a police abuse case in Murphy and Katie Pierson vs The City of Los Angeles, 1989; obtained an acquittal for actor Todd Bridges on charges of attempted murder and voluntary manslaughter, 1989; according to LA Times, negotiated the largest settlement in the history of the Los Angeles Unified School District in a child abuse case in the amount of $6,015,000 in La Shaunda Acker, et al vs LAUSD, 1990; selected as correspondent for CBS News Show "Whose Side Are You On?" 1991; his firm received the highest jury award in the history of the City of Los Angeles in a police misconduct case, $9.4 million plus attorneys' fees, in the case of Patricia and Alicia Diaz vs The City of Los Angeles, et al; retained as special legal counsel for NBC News regarding the OJ Simpson Preliminary Hearing, 1994; member of OJ Simpson's legal defense team, 1994. **Business Addr:** President, Law Offices of Johnnie L Cochran, Jr, 4929 Wilshire Blvd, Ste 1010, Los Angeles, CA 90010.

COCHRAN, S. THOMAS

Sales manager. **Personal:** Born Jun 8, 1950, Columbus, OH; son of Dorothy Saunders Cochran and Sylvester M Cochran; married Lynne Rankin; children: Clanci Marie, Camille Alexandra, Cameron Thomas. **Educ:** OH U, BSC 1972. **Career:** WOUB-Radio, newscaster 1971-72; Taft Broad WTVN-TV, dir film & Ed floor dir 1972-75; Taft Broad WGR-TV, prod dir 1975-77; Langston Hughes Ctr for Vis & Perform Arts, adv 1976; Astro Adv Agency, consultant 1976; WGR-TV Taft Bdcst, acct exec; Buffalo State Coll, part-time prof of communications 1978-80;SUNY Buffalo, part-time prof of communications 1978-; TV for Black Hist, prod dir independent proj; WGRZ-TV, sales mgr local and Canadian. **Orgs:** Conduct seminars for Buffalo Black Media Coalition; mem Professional Communicators of WNY; minority bd rep WGRZ-TV; mem Buffalo Area Chamber of Commerce; bd of dir William-Emslie YMCA. **Honors/Awds:** Guest speak for comm stud at coll & u wk; Black Acheivers Award in Ind 1976; Sales Achievement Awards Taft Broadcasting Co 1978-80. **Business Addr:** Sales Manager, WGRZ-TV, 259 Delaware Ave, Buffalo, NY 14206.

COCHRAN, TODD S.

Business executive (retired). **Personal:** Born Sep 1, 1920, San Francisco, CA; married Inis; children: Todd, Walter. **Career:** Bethlehem Steel, elect 1944-45; Nichols Dodge, auto salesman & mgr 1963-65, fleet mgr 1965-68; KC Dodge Inc, pres, owner 1968-88. **Orgs:** Mem Natl Auto Dealers Assoc, SF Auto Dealers Assoc, Dodge Dealer Assoc, Driver Training Prog for San Francisco, Kiwanis Club; dir Bay Area Dealer Adversting Assoc, Chrysler Black Dealers Assoc; mem Natl Assoc of Minority Dealers. **Honors/Awds:** Grand Awd for Dodge Sales 1964-67; Oldest Black Dealer for Chrysler Corp. **Business Addr:** President, KC Dodge Inc, 3030 Mission St, San Francisco, CA 94110.

COCKBURN, ALDEN G., JR.

Surgeon. **Personal:** Born Mar 8, 1947, Ancon, Panama; son of Edith E Gittens Cockburn and Alden G Cockburn Sr; divorced; children: Alexis, Justin. **Educ:** Tufts University, Boston, MA, medical degree, 1974; Tufts-New England Medical Center Hospital, Boston, MA, surgical intern, 1974-75, surgical assistant resident, 1975-76; Lahey Clinic Foundation Hospital, Burlington, MA, urological resident, 1976-79; Memorial-Sloan Kettering Cancer Center, New York, NY, urological-oncology fellow, 1980-81. **Career:** Lahey Clinic, Boston, MA, assistant attendant urologist, 1979-80; Harlem Hospital Medical Center, New York, NY, director, division of urology, 1981-85; Columbia University School of Medicine, New York, NY, assistant professor of urology, 1981-85; self-employed surgeon, Tampa, FL, 1985-. **Orgs:** Former president, member, Bay Area Medical Association; member, Sigma Pi Phi. **Business Addr:** Surgeon, 4700 N Habana Ave, Tampa, FL 33614.

COCKERHAM, GLORIA ROSS

Telecommunications company executive. **Personal:** Born Dec 17, 1953, Charlotte, NC; daughter of Calvene Fincher Ross and Emanuel H. Ross; married James Allen Cockerham, Aug 21, 1982. **Educ:** Winston-Salem State Univ, Winston-Salem, NC, BA, English/psychology, 1976; Penn State Univ, University Park, PA, executive program, 1989. **Career:** Southern Bell, Winston Salem, NC, marketing/business sales representative, 1977-82; Southern Bell, Charlotte, NC, management instructor, 1982-87, business sales mgr, 1987-90; BellSouth Services, Birmingham, AL, operations mgr, 1990-. **Orgs:** Board member, Charlotte Chapter, National Conference of Christians and Jews, 1988-89; member/seminar instructor, National Urban League, 1982-; board member, Charlotte Housing Authority Scholarship Fund Committee, 1988-89; member/volunteer, Junior Achievement, 1983-; member, Women in Sales, 1984-; member, Executive Women, 1986-89; counselor, Youth Involvement Council, 1984-; member, The Society for the Advancement of Management, 1980-91; member, Toastmaster's International, 1979-; member, Black Executive Exchange Program, 1978-83; member, National Alliance of Business Youth Motivation Task Force, 1981-82; Birmingham Charter Chapter. **Honors/Awds:** Keynote speaker, Success '91 Small Business Symposium, 1991; President's Club, 1987, Achiever's Club, 1987, 1988, Southern Bell; Pursuit of Excellence, Southern Bell Marketing Dept in North Carolina, 1988; Community Service Award, March of Dimes, 1987; Commitment to Youth Award, Junior Achievement, 1985; Volunteerism Award, National Urban League, 1984; Volunteerism Award, National Alliance of Business, 1982; Carolinas Minority Supplier Development Councils, Inc, 1989, 1993; American Business Women's Assn, Business Assoc of the Year, 1992.

COCKERHAM, HAVEN EARL

Human resources administrator. **Personal:** Born Aug 13, 1947, Winston-Salem, NC; married Terry Ward; children: Haven Earl Jr, Audra. **Educ:** NC A&T, BS Economics 1969; MI State, MBA 1979. **Career:** GMC, personnel admin exec comp 1978-79, admin personnel 1979-80; Fisher Body, genl offices gen admin 1980-82, Pgh plant dir personnel 1982-83; General Motors, world headquarters dir personnel 1983-84, gen dir personnel; McCain & Assocs, pres; Detroit Edison, vice pres of human resources, 1994-. **Orgs:** Pres Detroit Chap Natl Black MBA Assn 1981; bd mem Natl Black MBA Assn 1981; mem Mon-Yough Chamber of Commerce Pgh 1982-83; leadership mem Leadership Detroit Chamber of Comm; bd mem Detroit South Macomb Hosp; chmn east central sec Detroit Area Council Boy Scouts of Amer. **Honors/Awds:** Outstanding Leadership Detroit Chap Natl Black MBA Assoc 1982; Outstanding Serv Detroit Area Bou Scouts. **Business Addr:** VP, Human Resources, Detroit Edison, 2000 Second Ave, Detroit, MI 48226.

COCKERHAM, PEGGY

Automobile dealership owner. **Personal:** marrIed John Ali; children: Pam, Anwar. **Career:** Southlake Buick & Imports, pres, currently. **Special Achievements:** Company is ranked #94 on Black Enterprise magazine's 1997 list of Top 100 Black businesses.

COCKRELL, MECHERA ANN

Insurance agent. **Personal:** Born Jul 8, 1953, Brookshire, TX; married Thomas Cockrell; children: Twanna Nicole Randle. **Educ:** TX Southern Univ, BS 1975, MA 1978; Espanola's Beauty Coll, Licensed Cosmetologist 1978; Leonard's Sch of Insurance, Group II license 1986. **Career:** Cockrell Insurance, general agent. **Orgs:** Mem Teachers Educ Assoc 1975-; advisor Jack & Jill of Amer 1985-; teacher 4H Prairie View Chap 1985-; mem Home Economics Educators of Amer. **Business Addr:** General Agent, Cockrell Insurance, 33405 Reynolds Rd, Simonton, TX 77476.

CODY, HENRY LEROY

Educator. **Personal:** Born May 22, 1922, Tuscaloosa, AL; married Betty Frazier; children: Henry Leroy Jr, Patricia Elaine, Cynthia Jane. **Educ:** NC A&T Univ Greensboro, BS 1957; OH State Univ Columbus, MA radio & TV 1959;Teacher Coll Columbia Univ NY, EdD 1978. **Career:** NC A&T Univ Greensboro, prof, military science & tactics 1954-58; AUS Signal School Ft Monmouth NJ,TV prod off 1959-62; AUS Pictorial Center NYC, motion picture off 1964-65; Amer Forces Network Europe, commanding officer 1966-68; AUS SE Asia Signal School Vietnam, commanding officer 1969-70; Brookdale Comm Coll, affirm action officer. **Orgs:** mem, 32nd Degree Mason Greensboro Consistory 106 NC 1956-85; pres Laymens Movement Seacoast Missionary Baptist Assn, 1977-85; past pres, NJ Assn for Affirm Action in Higher Educ, 1980-81; vice pres at large Natl Laymens Movement Natl Baptist Convention USA Inc 1983-85; pres, Laymens Movement General Baptist State Convention NJ. **Honors/Awds:** Educ Bd Div of News Publications Co 1971; Considerations for Textbook Selection Teacher Coll Columbia Univ 1978; Elected Councilman of Laymens Movement of Men's Dept Bapt World Alliance 1980-85. **Military Serv:** AUS lt col 29 yrs; Natl Serv & Legion of Merit 1971.

CODY, WILLIAM L.

Clergyman. **Personal:** Born Jun 9, 1934, Philadelphia, PA. **Educ:** Univ PA, AB 1951-55; Temple U, STB 1955-58; Monrovia Coll, DD; St Davis Sem, DD. **Career:** St James AME Ch, pstr 1972-; Grant AME Ch, 1966-72; Fisk Chpl AME Ch, 1964-66; Vernon Tmpl AME Ch, 1960-64; Union AME Ch, 1958-60; St Paul AME Ch Malvern, 1956-58; St Paul AME Ch Ben Salem, 1955-56. **Orgs:** Past pres Grtr Boston Inter-Denominational & Inter-Racial Ministers Alliance; past bd dir Boston Br NAACP; Cooper Comm Ctr; Conv Cncl Black Ecumenical Commn; past tst Boston Univ Without Walls; past pres bd dir Grant Manor Apts; past mem Black Studies Com Boston Theol Inst; Steering Com Metro Boston Com Black Chmn Act; presiding elder Atlantic City Dist African Met Epis Ch; 1st vice pres Atlantic City NAACP; pres Atlantic City Chap Frontiers Internat; tst Atlantic Comm Coll; mgr Bright's Villa N & Bright's Villa S; chmn NAACP Atlantic City Housing Corp.

COELHO, PETER J.

Business executive. **Personal:** Born May 10, 1921, E Providence, RI; married Julia; children: Jean, Carol, Julie, Sheila, Susan. **Educ:** Inst of Applied Sci, 1944-45; Univ RI, 1961-62. **Career:** RI Housing Investment Fund, exec dir 1972-77; Homes for Hope Found, 1968-72; PJ Coelho Painting Co, owner 1947-65. **Orgs:** V chmn RI Housing & Mortgage Fin Corp; past dir Blue Corss of RI 1973-76; chmn com on corp RI Ho of Reps; past pres chmn bd Cape verdean ProgCtr; area cat num maj fund drives. **Honors/Awds:** First black elected RI Gen Assembly 1966; re-elected Biennialcy. **Military Serv:** USAAF sgt 1942-46. **Business Addr:** 155 Leonard Ave, East Providence, RI 02914.

COFER, JAMES HENRY

Mortician & city official. **Personal:** Born Mar 24, 1925, New York, NY; married Marion D Willis; children: James H III, Linda S Hawkins. **Educ:** Amer Acad of Mortuary Science, 1961. **Career:** Ft Monmouth NJ, electronic tech 1947-50; Long Branch Police Dept, patrolman 1951-60; Long Branch NJ, vice pres city council. **Orgs:** Mem NJ State Funeral Directors 1964-73; owner-mgr Cofer Memorial Home 1976-; pres Cofer-Willis Corp 1976-; dir Cofer-Hawkins Funeral Home 1981-; bd mem United Way, Red Bank Rotary Club, Cancer Soc, Second Baptist Church of Long Branch, Amer Red Cross, Long Branch Public Health; vice pres Long Branch City Council; former trustee PBA Local #10. **Honors/Awds:** Lewis R Peet Awd NY 1961; NY State Merit Cert NY 1961; Conf FS Examining Bd of US 1961; Natl Conf of Christians & Jews. **Special Achievements:** First Black police officer to qualify for rank of SGT in Long Branch, NJ. **Military Serv:** AUS corpl 3 yrs. **Business Addr:** Vice Pres City Council, Long Branch NJ 07740, 240 Shrewsbury Ave, Red Bank, NJ 07701.

COFER, MICHAEL LYNN

Professional football player. **Personal:** Born Apr 7, 1960, Knoxville, TN. **Educ:** Univ of Tennessee, attended. **Career:** Detroit Lions, linebacker, 1983-. **Honors/Awds:** Played in Pro Bowl, post-1988 season. **Business Addr:** 905 Kitelake Trail, Fairburn, GA 30213.

COFFEE, LAWRENCE WINSTON

Dentist. **Personal:** Born Apr 29, 1929, Detroit, MI; married Drexell R; children: Lawrence Jr, Roderic, LaJuan. **Educ:** Wayne State Univ, BS 1957; Meharry Medical College, DDS 1961. **Career:** Private practice, dental surgeon; Children's Hospital of Michigan, medical tech 1955-57; Detroit First Aid Co, drug shipper 1953-55; Chrysler Corp, machine operator 1949-51. **Orgs:** Mem Michigan Dental Assn; Amer Dental Assn; Natl Dental Assn; Wolverine Dental Soc; Detroit Dist Dental Soc; past trustee St Stephen AME Church; mem BSA; past dist commr Chi Health & Safety 1968-77; bd mgmt Meharry Medical College Alumni Assn; pres Meharry Medical College Alumni Assn. **Honors/Awds:** Dentist of the Year 1972; trophies BSA 1966-67; Dentist of the Year, Meharry Detroit Chap 1972. **Military Serv:** AUS mc corpl 1951-53. **Home Addr:** 7640 Tireman, Detroit, MI 48204.

COFFEY, BARBARA J.

Educator. **Personal:** Born Nov 24, 1931, Omaha, NE; daughter of Eva Williams Waldron-Cooper and Earl L Waldron, Sr; divorced; children: William Jai III. **Educ:** Univ of NE, BA 1951; Fisk Univ, MA 1953; Univ of NE, PhD 1976. **Career:** US Dept of Commerce, Chicago Regional Office, survey statistian 1963-65; United Comm Serv Omaha, planning assoc 1965-67; Greater Omaha Comm Action Inc, dep dir 1967-70; Univ of NE Omaha, assoc dean of students & instrutor of sociology 1970-71; US Dept of HEW, consultant region VII 1971-; Univ of NE Syst, asst to pres, equal opportunity coordinator 1971-78; Northwestern Bell Telephone Co, supvr mgmt training 1978-81; Metro Communtiy Coll, south campus mgr 1981-84, dir of mktg 1984-. **Orgs:** Grad rsch fellowship Fisk Univ, 1951-53, State Univ of IA 1954-55; bd of dir United Comm Serv 1972-

74; past vp, found dir NE Civil Liberties Union; mem Omaha Metro NAACP, Hon Soc; mem Natl Assoc of Women Deans Admin & Couns; chairperson NE Equal Opportunity Comm; mem Alpha Kappa Delta, Alpha Lambda Delta, Phi Delta Kappa; pres Omaha Chapter Links Inc; charter mem Omaha Chapter Jack & Jill Inc; mem Delta Sigma Theta Sorority, United Methodist Comm Center, Urban League of NE, Episcopal Church of Resurrection; mem vestry, layreader; bd dir Omaha Head Start Child Devel Corp; bd dir United Way of the Midlands, 1988-. **Honors/Awds:** One of Outstanding Black Women of Omaha Quinn Chapel AME Church 1975; Omicron Delta Kappa Natl Leaderhip Honor 1986. **Business Addr:** Dir of Marketing, Metropolitan Community College, PO Box 3777, Omaha, NE 68103.

COFFEY, GILBERT HAVEN, JR.
Government official, physician. **Personal:** Born Nov 27, 1926, Lackawanna, NY; married Madelyn Elizabeth Brewer; children: Denise E. **Educ:** Univ of Buffalo, BA 1952; certificate in phys therapy 1955; Meharry Med Coll, MD 1963. **Career:** Wayne Co Gen Hosp Eloise MI, phys therapist 1956-59; intern 1963; VA Hosp Buffalo, resident 1964-67; asst chief phys medicine & Rehab serv 1967-69; chief phys medicine & rehab serv 1969-70; Central Ofc VA Washington, prog devel policy chief phys medicine & rehab 1970; Univ of Buffalo Med Sch, prof 1968-70; Howard Univ Med Sch Washington 1971; George Washington u med sch, asst dir prof 1971-; diplomate am Bd Phys Medicine & Rehab; Nat Med Assn; Am Congress Rehab; Am Acad Phs Medicine & Rehab Commr Parks & Recreation Inster, MI 1958-59. **Orgs:** Mem Alpha Phi Alpha; Rep; Mason 32nd degree; contrib articles professional jours. **Military Serv:** AUS 1946-47. **Business Addr:** Howard University Hospital, Medical School, Dept PMER, 2041 Georgia Ave Nw, Washington, DC 20060.

COFFEY, RICHARD
Professional basketball player. **Career:** Minnesota Timberwolves, currently. **Business Addr:** Professional Basketball Player, Minnesota Timberwolves, 600 1st Ave, Minneapolis, MN 55403-1416.

COFIELD, ELIZABETH BIAS
County official, educator. **Personal:** Born Jan 21, 1920, Raleigh, NC; married James; children: James Edward, Juan Medford. **Educ:** Hampton Inst, BS; Columbia U, MA; diploma in adminstrn & supervision. **Career:** Wade County Bd of Commrs, Juan Medford co commr 1972; Shaw Univ, prof of educ. **Orgs:** Elected to Raleigh Sch Bd 1969-72. **Business Addr:** Professor of Education, Shaw University, 118 E South St, Raleigh, NC 27602.

COFIELD, JAMES E., JR.
Business executive. **Personal:** Born May 16, 1945, Norfolk, VA; son of Elizabeth B Cofield and James E Cofield Sr; divorced; children: Nicole. **Educ:** Univ NC, BS 1967; Stanford Univ Grad Sch of Bus, MBA 1970; Howard Univ Law Sch. **Career:** Cofield Properties, Inc, Brookline, MA. **Orgs:** Chairman, Roxse Homes, Inc.; director, National Center for African-American Artists. **Honors/Awds:** Outstanding Comm Serv Annual Awds Com of Boston 1979; Ten Outstanding Young Leaders Boston Jaycees 1980; Massachusetts Black Legislative Caucus, Minority Business Award, 1991. **Business Addr:** President, Cofield Properties, Inc, PO Box 470827, Brookline Village, MA 02147.

COGDELL, D. PARTHENIA
Educational Administrator. **Personal:** Born Sep 12, 1938, Wayne County, NC; daughter of Geneva Herring Cogdell and Nathaniel Cogdell; divorced; children: Samuel George Sanders III. **Educ:** Fayetteville State NC, BS 1959; Trenton State NJ, MA 1971; Glassboro State NJ, 1973-74; Hunter Coll NY, 1982. **Career:** Burlington Co Special Servs, principal 1974-76, program dir 1976-79; NJ Dept of Educ, admin asst 1979-81, bureau dir 1981-92; Camden City Schools, Office of Personnel Services, currently. **Orgs:** Project dir, Low Incidence Handicap Project, 1979-80; reader, US Dept of Educ & Special Educ Office 1974-79; chairperson, NJ State Advisory Council Handicap, 1974-76; pres, Intl Council for Exceptional Children 1978-79; Phi Delta Kappa; pres, Rancocas Valley, Delta Sigma Theta Sor, 1988-92; pres, Found for Exceptional Children, 1989-91. **Honors/Awds:** Dan Ringeheim Award of Excellence, NJ State Federation; Outstanding Special Educator, Intl Council for Exceptional Children; Woman of the Year, Zeta Phi Beta Sorority. **Business Addr:** Director, Office of Personnel Svcs, Camden City Schools, 201 North Front St, Camden, NJ 08102.

COGGS, GRANVILLE COLERIDGE
Physician. **Personal:** Born Jul 30, 1925, Pine Bluff, AR; son of Nannie and Tandy; married Maud; children: Anita, Carolyn. **Educ:** Univ of Nebraska, BS 1949; Harvard Medical School, MD 1953. **Career:** Univ of Texas Health Science Center, prof radiology dept 1975-89; Univ California School of Medicine, assoc clinical prof 1971-75; asst chief 1969-71; Kaiser Hospital, staff radiologist 1959-71; Univ of California, resident 1955-58; Letterman Gen Hospital, intern 1954; Murphy Army Hospital, 1953-54. **Orgs:** Mem Harvard Medical School Alumni Survey Comm 1973-78; assoc mem Sigma Xi; mem Amer Coll of Radiology 1959-; fellow ACR 1972; Amer Inst Ultrasound Medicine 1972-82; Amer Thermographic Soc 1972-80; mem Phi Beta Kappa 1949. **Military Serv:** USAAC 1943-46; USAF 1953-55; USAFR lieutenant Colnel 1956-85 (retired). **Home Addr:** PO Box 690647, San Antonio, TX 78269-0647, (210)699-6824.

COGSVILLE, DONALD J.
Business executive. **Personal:** Born May 16, 1937, New York, NY; son of Frances Cogsville and Johnny Cogsville; married Carol Atherton Cogsville (deceased); children: Rachel, Donald Paul. **Educ:** Mt Union Coll, BA 1963. **Career:** Harlem Urban Devel Corp, pres & chief exec 1971-; Office of Economic Opportunity deputy dir 1968-71; Econ Devel State of NJ, dir 1968-71; Harlem Urban Devel Corp, general mgr; NY State Urban Devel Corp, Affirmative Action officer. **Orgs:** Mem Natl Task Force on Educ & Training for Minority Business; Affirmative Action advisor Clark-Phipps-Clark & Harris Consultants Firm; pres NY Urban League Trenton, NJ. **Military Serv:** US Army spec 4th class 1958-60. **Business Addr:** Chief Executive Officer, Harlem Urban Development Corporation, 163 W 125th St, 17th Fl, New York, NY 10027.

COHEN, AMAZIAH VANBUREN
Dentist (retired). **Personal:** Born Nov 8, 1916, Miami, FL. **Educ:** FL A&M U, 1943; Meharry Med Coll, DDS 1947. **Career:** Fulton Co Health Dept, dentist 1947-; prv prac. **Orgs:** Life mem GA Dental Assn; Am Dental Assn; Nat Dental Assn; Acad of Gen Dentistry; mem YMCA; NAACP. **Honors/Awds:** Numerous awards for public service. **Military Serv:** Spl assignment 1943-45. **Business Addr:** PO Box 92541, Atlanta, GA 30314.

COHEN, GWEN A.
Investment executive. **Personal:** Born Nov 8, Eufaula, AL; daughter of Johnie & Clementine Morris Gilbert; married Paul M Cohen, Feb 3, 1990. **Educ:** Tuskegee Univ, BS, 1974; Northwestern University's Kellogg Grad School of Mgmt, MBA, 1982. **Career:** IBM, marketing, manufacturing, 1974-80; Quaker Oats, brand management, 1982-84; Dean Witter, account exec, associate vp, vp investments, 1986-. **Orgs:** Leadership IL, pres, 1992-94, exec comm, 1990-; Natl Black MBA, Chicago, exec comm, 1984-89; ETA Cultural Arts, co-chair, Gala, 1994-; Hugh O'Brian Youth Foun, judge, 1993-; America's Jr Miss, IL, judge, 1994-; Miss America, Chicago, judge, 1995-; Children's Hosp, chair, child life, 1976-80. **Honors/Awds:** Who's Who in Amer Colleges & Universities, 1974; Outstanding Young Women of America, 1986; Childrens Memorial Hosp Humanitarian Award, 1979; Leadership IL, Achievement Award, 1993; Urban Potential IA, Achievement Award, 1994. **Special Achievements:** Black Enterprise, "Money Moves for 1995," 1995; Chicago Sun Times Supplement, "Municipal Bonds," Aug 1990; N'Digo Magazine, Charitable Givings, Retirement Planning, etc, 1994; Afrique, "Global Investing," Tax Deferral Strategies, 1994; Keynote speaker for HOBY, General Federations of Women's Clubs, etc, 1992-; Writer of quarterly newsletter; Judge, Miss Illinois Scholarship Competition, 1996; Ebony, "Retirement Nestegg," Sept 1996. **Home Phone:** (312)225-2532. **Business Addr:** Vice President of Investments, Dean Witter, 70 W Madison, Ste 300, Chicago, IL 60602, (312)984-4107.

COHEN, VINCENT H.
Attorney. **Personal:** Born Apr 7, 1936, Brooklyn, NY; son of Marion Cohen and Victor Cohen; married Diane Hasbrouck; children: Robyn, Traci, Vincent Jr. **Educ:** Syracuse Univ, BA 1957, LLB 1960. **Career:** Consol Edison Co NY, 1960-62; US Dept of Justice, 1962-67; EEOC, 1967-69; Hogan & Hartson, partner 1969-. **Orgs:** Admission NY Bar 1960, US Supreme Ct 1966, OH 1967, DC 1968; mem Amer, Natl NY State Bar Assns; Justinian Law Soc; Natl Jud Conf DC Circuit 1972, 1975; sec Commn Med Malpractice; bd visitors Syracuse Univ Coll of Law; bd of gov's DC Bar; bd dirs ACLU; Young Lawyers Sect Bar Assn DC; Neighborhood Legal Serv Prog. **Honors/Awds:** Helms Found All-Amer Basketball Team; AP All Amer; UP All-Amer 1957; Syracuse Law Review; Order of the Coif. **Military Serv:** 1st lt 1957-65. **Business Addr:** Attorney, Hogan & Hartson, 555 13th Street, NW, Suite 13W202, Washington, DC 20004-1109.

COKER, ADENIYI ADETOKUNBO
Educator. **Personal:** Born Sep 27, 1962, Nigeria; son of Adeniyi & Modupe Coker; married Angela Denise Johnson, Jan 2, 1987; children: Kikelomo, Morenike, Modupeola. **Educ:** Univ of Ife, Nigeria, BA, 1983; City Univ of New York, Brooklyn Coll, MFA, 1987; Temple Univ, PhD, 1991. **Career:** William Paterson College NJ, asst prof, 1987-91; Univ of Colorado, assoc prof, 1991-1992; Univ of WY, dir & assoc prof; Eastern Illinois Univ, dir & assoc prof, currently. **Orgs:** Natl Council of Black Studies Inc, exec bd mem, 1994-; Journal of Black Studies, editorial bd, 1993-. **Honors/Awds:** Emmy Award Nomination. **Special Achievements:** Ouray, A Historical Drama on Southern Ute Indians of Colorado, 1992; Sizwe Bansi Is Dead, Fringe Theater Festival Canada, 1990; Woza Albert, Eulipions Theater, Denver, 1991. **Business Addr:** Assoc Prof & Dir, African American Studies, Eastern Illinois University, Charleston, IL 61920, (217)581-5719.

COLBERT, BENJAMIN JAMES
Educator. **Personal:** Born Jun 2, 1942, Savannah, GA; son of Anna Chaplin Colbert and Jack B Colbert; married Deborah Raikes Colbert, Dec 1982; children: Edwin, Kenneth, Jonathan. **Educ:** Savannah State Coll, BS 1963; Univ of GA, MFA 1971. **Career:** Metro Atlanta Talent Search Progrm, dir; Natl Scholarship Serv & Fund for Negro Students; assoc regional dir; Univ of GA, admissions counselor, instructor; Savannah Bd of Educ, teacher, assoc program dir admissions testing program; HHS Fellow 1980-81; Educ Testing Svc, assoc dir sponsored scholaship program, 1981-. **Orgs:** Consultant Coll Entrance Exam Bd & US Office Educ Trio Program; advisory bd, Southern Educ Found, Human Relations Comm, Natl Assn of Coll Admissions Counselors, Natl Scholarship Serv & Fund for Negro Students; mem NAACP, APGA, Alpha Phi Alpha; Elder Witherspoon Presbyterian Church. **Honors/Awds:** Callaway Found Award, Painting, 1970. **Business Addr:** Director of Sponsored Scholarship Programs, Educational Testing Serv, Rosedale Rd, Princeton, NJ 08541.

COLBERT, ERNEST, SR.
Business manager. **Personal:** Born Aug 2, 1916, Lettsworth, LA; married Gloria Kelly; children: Claudette, Barbara, Ernest Jr, Zanda. **Educ:** Loyola Univ, Tulane Univ, attended. **Career:** Union 689, bus mgr constr & gen labor 1934-. **Orgs:** Vice pres LA AFL-CIO; chmn Local 689; bd mem Grtr New Orleans AFL-CIO; state pres LA A Philips Randolph Inst; sec treas SE LA Laborers Dist Cncl; past mem Commerce & Ind Bd; past commr LA Stadium & Exposition Dist; mem IBPOEW, Bon Temps Soc Club. **Honors/Awds:** Awd Human Relations Dept Loyola Univ. **Business Addr:** Bus Mgr, Union 689, 400 Soniat St, New Orleans, LA 70115.

COLBERT, GEORGE CLIFFORD
Educational administrator. **Personal:** Born Mar 22, 1949, Cedar Rapids, IA; married Marion Patricia Clark; children: Bridget Lynette Clark, Donta Kami Colbert. **Educ:** Kirkwood Comm Coll, AA 1972; Mt Mercy Coll, BA 1974; Northern Arizona University, MED, 1993. **Career:** IA State Men's Reformatory, correctional officer II, 1975-76; Rockwell Intl, security guard, 1976-78; Kirkwood Community Coll, outreach worker/ employer, school program 1978-89; Central Arizona College, director, community education/ student services, 1989-. **Orgs:** Chmn, Genl Mills, FMC Minority Scholarship Prog, 1978; vice pres, NAACP, 1978; founder/chmn, Higher Educ Minority Scholarship Prog, 1979; mem, Natl Council of Instructional Administrators; mem, Natl Council for Community Services and Continuing Education; lifetime mem, AMVETS Post 15. **Honors/Awds:** Cert Vol Serv Awd, Jane Boyd Comm House, 1974; Cert Vol Probation Officer, Linn Co Juvenile Ct, State of Iowa, 1974; Humanities Awd, NAACP Freedom Fund Banquet, 1979; Appreciation in Recog of Serv to Student Affairs, Kirkwood Comm Coll, 1979; several awards for service, Apache Junction Community School System. **Military Serv:** USMC E-3 1967-69; Natl Defense Serv Medal; Purple Heart; Pres Citation; Vietnam Campaign; Vietnam Serv Medal. **Business Addr:** Student Service Associate, Central Arizona College, 8740 North Overfield Rd, Coolidge, AZ 85228.

COLBERT, VIRGIS W.
Brewing company executive. **Personal:** Born Oct 13, 1939, Mississippi; son of Eddie Mae Colbert and Quillie Colbert (deceased); married Angela Johnson; children: Jillian, Alyssa, V William II. **Educ:** Central MI Univ, BS; Graduate of Earlham College Executive Institute. **Career:** Chrysler Corp, gen mfg superintendent 1977-79; Miller Brewing Co, asst to plant mgr 1979-80, production mgr 1980-81, plant mgr 1981-87, asst dir can mfg 1987-88, director can mfg 1988-89, vice president materials manufacturing 1989-90, vice president plant operations 1990-93, senior vice president of operations, 1993-95, senior vice president of worldwide operations, 1995-97, executive vice president, 1997-. **Orgs:** Board Member, Urban Day School, Goodwill, OIC, Fisk University; adv comm Business School, Marquette University; Omega Psi Phi; Prince Hall Masons; Shriners; NAACP; NUL Black Exec Exchange Prog; Executive Advisory Council, Sigma Pi Phi. **Honors/Awds:** Scott High School Hall of Fame Toledo OH; Black Achiever Milwaukee YMCA; Harlem YMCA; Role Model Natl Alliance of Business; Silver Ring Merit Awd Philip Morris Co Inc; Role Model Several Black Colleges. **Business Addr:** Executive VP, Miller Brewing Co, 3939 W Highland Blvd, Milwaukee, WI 53201-0482.

COLE, ADOLPH
Cleric. **Personal:** Born Jul 18, 1923, Shreveport; married Elizabeth. **Educ:** Univ So CA. **Career:** "Shadows of the Future" & many religious tracts, author; Cole Brown Ward Coll & Seminary, founder. **Business Addr:** 3635 W Slauson, Los Angeles, CA.

COLE, ARTHUR
Educator. **Personal:** Born Nov 6, 1942, Buffalo, NY; married Alice Bailey; children: Arthur, Brandon. **Educ:** State Univ Coll at Buffalo, BS 1964; State Univ of NY Buffalo, MS 1968, PhD 1974. **Career:** State Univ Coll at Buffalo, counselor 1967-68, rsch asst 1968-70, personnel dir libraries 1973-75; US Office of Educ, educ prog specialist 1975-79; The White House, asst to

deputy asst to pres 1979-80; US Dept of Educ, deputy dir Horace Mann Learning Center. **Orgs:** Vice pres Earmark Inc 1979-; chap sec Omega Psi Phi 1967-69; mem Phi delta Kappa 1967-; mem Amer Lib Assn 1973-. **Honors/Awds:** Fellowship State Univ of NY Buffalo 1968; Fellow Dept of HEW 1975. **Business Addr:** Dep Dir H Mann Learning Ctr, US Dept of Education, 400 Maryland Ave SW, Washington, DC 20202.

COLE, CHARLES ZHIVAGA
Association secretary. **Personal:** Born Oct 7, 1957, Birmingham, AL; son of Mrs Louise Cole and Mr Howard Hover Cole. **Educ:** McNeese State Univ, (law major). **Career:** NAACP Cameron, assoc sec 1978-85; CBC Organ & McNeese, former mr calendar/rep 1978; Student Govt NAACP Christian Educ, natl youth ambassador 1980-84; John G Lewis Consistory, 32nd degree mason natl 1981-85; S Bapt Convention, travels local state and natl ambassador of goodwill, speaks lectures and teaches, natl volunteer consultant. **Orgs:** Musician dir Music Ministry NJ Bapt LC Religious Inst Local State & Natl 1985; North Lake Charles Kiwanis 1977; McNeese State Lions Club 1978; civil rights activist NAACP 1984-; natl ambassador speaker Christian Educ Special Scientific Olympic 1984-; ROTC 1977-78; Sr Reserve Training 1978; minister of music choir & workshop Cheron Chapel, Star of Bethlehem Baptist Center; Macedonia Baptist, Cameron LA. **Honors/Awds:** Foreign Mission Planned Seoul Korea, Zimbabwe Africa; Special Citation, Gov Ann Richards/Ambassador Charles Zhivaga, Distinguished Citizen, War on Drugs, Social Change Movement; Special citation, US Senate & US Congress, cited him along with Madame Pres NAACP/Mrs Louise Cole; Emory Univ, Distinguished Am Citizens, 1993-1994; Law School offers, Tulane Univ & Loyola Law School, New Orleans, LA, Howard Univ, Emory Univ; Nation Speaker, Prison Ministry Reform, Natl Spokesman War on Drugs; Voice of Democracy, Natl Essay Winner, In My Youth I See: What's Your Problem the Struggle Still Continues; Cited for Outstanding Accomplishments Govt Dave C Treen 1981; All Star Drum Major 1973-74; Mr Calendar 1978 McNeese State; Natl Delegate Lobbyist 1980-84; Pres Dr Jack Doland 1985; Governors Award; Outstanding Leadership Award for Serv to Comm; LA State Senatorial Award Hon State Senator Clifford L Newman 1986; Hutt River Province, Royal Proclamation, 1996. **Military Serv:** ROTC 1976-78, A Scholar, Prolific Speaker. **Home Addr:** 2817 1/2 Fitz/M L King, Lake Charles, LA 70601.

COLE, EDYTH BRYANT
Educational administrator. **Personal:** Born in Detroit, MI; children: Charles R, Constance A, Leslie B. **Educ:** Eastern MI U, BA 1945; Eastern MI U, MA 1952; Univ of MI, EdD 1972; Univ of Toledo OH. **Career:** NC State Univ, Elizabeth City, chmn dept of educ & psychology 1972-, dir of summer sessions 1973-80; Highland Park MI Public Schools, admin asst for curriculum 1969-71; Wayne County MI Intermediate School Dist, educ consultant redesegregation 1966-69; Ypsilanti MI Public Schools, teacher 1945-66; Wayne Coutny Intermediate School Dist, shared learning experiences program 1967-69; Natl Resolutions Comm, assn for supervision & curriculum devel 1971-74. **Orgs:** Chmn of tchr educ Elizabeth City State Univ 1972-78; former chap basileus Alpha Kappa Alpha Sorority 1976-78; former pres L'Esprit Club; bd of dir Mus of Albermarle 1977-79; Scholarship Social Studies Ypsilanti MI Pub Sch; NDEA Grant Univ of Toledo 1965; pub article re curriculum changes "Curriculum Trends" Croft Pub Co 1974. **Business Addr:** Elizabeth City State Univ, Campus Box 982, Elizabeth City, NC 27909.

COLE, HARRY A.
Judge. **Personal:** Born Jan 1, 1921, Washington, DC; children: Susan, Harriette, Stephanie. **Educ:** Morgan State U, AB 1943; Univ of MD, LlB 1949. **Career:** Ct of Appeals Annapolis, judge Presently; Baltimore, asso judge 1968; Asst Atty General 1953; Sub Magistrate 1952; Justice of Peace 1951; State Senate of MD, Elected 1954-58. **Orgs:** Mem Exec Com US Nat Commn for UNESCO; chmn MD Adv Com on Civil Rights; mem Adv Bd Dept Parole & Probation; mem Monumental City Bar Assn Baltimore Bar Assn MD Bar Assn; NBA; Am Judicature Soc. **Honors/Awds:** Life member NAACP; man of the year Alpha Phi Alpha; Alpha Kappa Mu Nat Honor Soc. **Military Serv:** AUS 1st lt 1943-46. **Business Addr:** 6th Judicial Circuit, Calvert & Fayette Sts, Baltimore, MD 21202.

COLE, JAMES O.
Attorney. **Personal:** Born Feb 6, 1941, Florence, AL; married Ada; children: Barry. **Educ:** Talladega Coll, BA 1962; Harvard Univ Law Sch, JD 1971. **Career:** Republic Industries, sup, gen. counsel & secretary, currently; The Clorox Co, vp, corp affairs, 1993-97; Kirkland & Ellis Chicago, assoc general counsel, 1985-93, sr counsel, 1973-85, atty 1971-73; Mayor's Office Boston, manpower dir 1968-71; Honeywell Inc Chicago, prod planning mgr 1963-68; Union Carbide Sheffield, chemist 1962-63. **Orgs:** IL Bar Assn; Am Bar Assn; Alpha Phi Alpha; mem Urban League; past pres, Natl Bar Assn; CA Assn of Black Lawyers; Charles Houston Bar Assn; past chair, State Bar's Judicial Nominations Evaluations Comm; bd of dirs, Black Filmmakers Hall of Fame; NAACP, Legal Defense & Educ Fund. **Honors/Awds:** Program Award for Volunteer Legal Service; Charles Houston Bar Assoc, Hall of Fame. **Business Addr:** Sup, Gen Counselor & Secretary, Republic Industries, Inc, 110 SE 6th St, 20th Fl, Fort Lauderdale, FL 33301.

COLE, JOHN L., JR.
Association executive (retired). **Personal:** Born Nov 8, 1928, Johnstown, PA; son of Susie L Cole and John L Cole; children: Keia D. **Educ:** Millard Fillmore Coll Univ of Buffalo, attended 1956-58; attended, Graduate Bryant & Stratton Coll. **Career:** Dept Comm Devel, exec asst; City of Cleveland, contract compliance officer 1966-72; Metro Atlanta Rapid Transit Auth, asst gen mgr. **Orgs:** Bd dir Greater Cleveland Growth Assn 1971-72; bd of dir Cleveland Urban League 1971-72; Amer Public Transit Assn Comm Minority Affairs; comm chmn Urban League Cleveland. **Honors/Awds:** Outstanding Serv Awd 1971; NAACP Cleveland Branch, Meritorious Public Serv Municipal Govt in Pursuit True Dem Ideals 1971. **Military Serv:** AUS pfc 1951-53.

COLE, JOHNNETTA BETSCH
Educator. **Personal:** Born Oct 19, 1936, Jacksonville, FL; married Arthur J Robinson Jr; children: David, Aaron, Ethan. **Educ:** Oberlin Coll, BA 1957; Northwestern Univ, MA 1959, PhD 1967. **Career:** WA State Univ, asst prof & instructor of anthropology, dir of black studies, 1964-70; Univ of MA, faculty in anthropology & Afro-Amer studies, 1970-84; Hunter Coll, Russell Sage visiting prof of anthropology 1983-84, prof of anthropology, beginning 1984; Spelman College, Atlanta, pres, 1987-1997. **Orgs:** Fellow Amer Anthrop Assn 1970-; mem Coalition of 100 Black Women; contrib & adv ed The Black Scholar 1979-; pres Assn of Black Anthropologists 1980. **Honors/Awds:** Outstanding Faculty Mem of the Year, WA State Univ 1969-70; conducted anthrop field work Liberia Cuba & Afro-Amer Comm in US; Emory Univ, Presidential Distinguished Professor of Anthropology Woman's Studies, and African American Studies, 1998-. **Special Achievements:** Profiled on the PBS show "Bridgebuilders," 1998. **Business Addr:** Anthology Dept, Emory University, Atlanta, GA 30327.

COLE, JOSEPH H.
City official. **Personal:** Born Feb 13, 1913, Philadelphia, PA; married Laura; children: Mrs 5Sylvia Ann Mackey, Mrs Kathleen Teresa Hopkins. **Educ:** Howard U, BS 1935; Howard Univ & NY U, addl study toward master's degree; Cath U, studied human rel; Holy Cross Coll, coaching. **Career:** Park & Recreation, retired consult 1975-80; DC Dept of Recreation, dir 1966-75; started with dept in 1938 as playground dir, area dir, dir of city-wide programs; asst supt. **Orgs:** Mem Nat Recreation & Park Assn; mem Brookland Civic Assn; exec bd Police Boy's Club; C & O Canal Commn; Howard Univ Alumni Assn; NAACP; Omega Psi Phi. **Business Addr:** 3149 16 St NW, Washington, DC 20010.

COLE, LYDIA
Cable programming executive. **Personal:** marrIed Dr. Reginald Cole; children: Iman, Maya. **Educ:** Howard University. **Career:** Black Entertainment Television, dir of music and programming management, 1987-96; BET Cable Network and BET on Jazz, vice pres of programming, 1997-. **Special Achievements:** Created cable shows such as "Unreal", "The Hit List".

COLE, MACEOLA LOUISE
Physician (retired). **Personal:** Born Jun 18, 1934, Brentwood, MO; daughter of Anna C Tibbs Cole and Maceo L Cole. **Educ:** St Louis U, BS 1954, MD 1958. **Career:** Sole Practitioner, currently. **Honors/Awds:** Diplomate Am Bd of Pediatrics 1964.

COLE, NATALIE
Vocalist, actress. **Personal:** Born Feb 6, 1950, Los Angeles, CA; daughter of Maria Hawkins Cole and Nathaniel Adam Cole; married Marvin J. Yancy, Jul 30, 1976 (divorced 1979); children: Robert Adam. **Career:** Capitol Records, recording artist 1975-; Big Break, television show, host and performer, 1990-; co-starred in the HBO film "Socrates," 1998. **Honors/Awds:** Gold Record, Inseparable; Grammy awards for This Will Be (single), Inseparable; four gold albums; two platinum albums; albums include Inseparable (1975), Thankful (1978), I'm Ready (1983), Dangerous (1985), Everlasting (1987), Good To Be Back (1989), Unforgettable (1991); Holly and Ivy; Image Awards, 1976, 1977, NAACP; American Music Award, 1978. **Special Achievements:** Television debut, Lily in Winter, USA Pictures Original-Special Presentation, 1994; Abducted; A Father's Love, 1997. **Business Addr:** Singer, c/o Capitol Records, Inc, 1750 N Vine St, Hollywood, CA 90028.

COLE, PATRICIA A.
Consultant, company executive. **Personal:** Born Oct 25, 1940, Detroit, MI; daughter of C Marie Johnson Wilson and Thomas Aaron Allen; married Jun 1, 1965 (divorced); children: B Derek, Jason A. **Educ:** University of Detroit, Detroit, MI, BA, Business Admin, 1980. **Career:** Cole Financial Services, Detroit, MI, president, 1983-. **Orgs:** Member, general chairperson, American Assn of Professional Consultants, SE Conference, 1987-; national advisory board, Black Career Women, Execucircle, 1989-; member, National Association of Woman Consultants, 1990-; counselor, presentor, Score, SBA Chapter 48, 1990-; membership co-chairperson, Metro Atlanta Coalition of 100 Black Women, 1990-. **Honors/Awds:** Outstanding Volunteerism, Optimist Club of NW Detroit, 1987; National Advisory Board, Black Career Women, 1989; Certified Professional Manager, Professional Services Management Institute, 1990; Registered Professional Consultant of American Assn Professional Consultants, currently; Women Who Make a Difference, Minorities and Women in Business, currently.

COLE, RANSEY GUY, JR.
Attorney. **Personal:** Born May 23, 1951, Birmingham, AL; son of Sarah Coker Cole and Ransey G Cole Sr; married Kathleine Kelley, Nov 26, 1983; children: Justin, Jordan, Alexandra. **Educ:** Tufts University, BA, 1972; Yale Law School, JD, 1975. **Career:** US Bankruptcy Court, judge, 1987-93; Varys, Sater, Seymour, & Pease Law Firm, partner, 1975-78, 1980-87, 1993-. **Orgs:** Children's Hospital, trustee, 1990-; American Bankruptcy Board of Certification, director, 1993-; Bankrupty Arbitration & Mediation Services, dir; US Health Corp, Community Health & Wellness, trustee; I Know I Can, trustee; Columbus Bar Association, board of governors, 1990-94; University Club, trustee, 1992-. **Honors/Awds:** Alpha Phi Alpha Fraternity, Founders Day Award. **Business Addr:** Attorney, Vorys Sater Seymour and Pease, 52 East Gay St, PO Box 1008, Columbus, OH 43216, (614)464-5603.

COLE, THOMAS WINSTON, SR.
Educator. **Personal:** Born Oct 24, 1915, Navasota, TX; married Eva M Sharp. **Educ:** Wiley Coll, BS 1934; Univ of WI, MS 1947; Univ of TX, EdD 1955. **Career:** Dean of Acad Affairs for Instr Serv & Univ Ombudsman, Univ of FL, asst dean 1971-72; Wiley Coll, pres 1958-71, prev dean reg & prof 1948-58; Graduate Extension Program Prairie View Coll, dir grad 1950-71; Wash Elementary School, prin 1944-50; Wash High School, prin 1934-44. **Orgs:** Apptd by Pres of US to Advisory Com on Developing Institutions 1965-66; appted by Pres Commn on Presidential Scholars 1969-74; appted by Pres Nat Commn on Equality of Educational Opportunity 1972-76; delegate to World Conf of Meth Ch Oslo, Norway 1961 & London 1966; visited as rep of Bd Educ of Meth Ch all major universities in Europe & British Isles including Univ of Leningrad, Moscow & Kiev; Univ of Rome; the Sorbonne etc 1960; chmn work area on higher educ FL Conf United Meth Ch 1973-75; sec program Commn on Gen & Conf United Meth Ch 1968-76; numerous local state & federal appointments; mem Phi Delta Kappa; pres Alpha Phi Alpha; Sigma Pi Phi; Masonic Lodge; Rotary Internt; Omicron Delta Kappa Phi Kappa Phi; pres council Am Inst of mgmt; Am Assn ofcoll; Various others; author "Duties Acad Deans in Meth Ch Related Coll" 1955; co-author "Quality Edn" 1974. **Business Addr:** 231 Tigert Hall, U of FL, Gainesville, FL 32611.

COLE, THOMAS WINSTON, JR.
Educational administrator. **Personal:** Born Jan 11, 1941, Vernon, TX; son of Eva Sharp Cole and Thomas Cole; married Brenda S Hill, Jun 14, 1964; children: Kelley S, Thomas Winston III. **Educ:** Wiley Coll Marshall TX, BS 1961; Univ of Chgo, PhD 1966. **Career:** Atlanta Univ, mem faculty 1966-82, prof chem, chmn dept 1971-82, Fuller E Callaway prof 1969-80, proj dir resource ctr sci & engrg 1978-82, univ provost, vice pres acad affairs 1979-82; Univ of IL, vstg prof 1972; MIT, vstg prof 1973-74; Miami Valley Lab Procter & Gamble Co, summer chemist 1967; Celanese Corp Charlotte NC, chemist, 1974; UNCF, lecturer 1975-84; WV State Coll Inst, pres 1982-86; WV Bd of Regents, chancellor 1986-88; Clark Atlanta Univ, Atlanta, GA, president, currently. **Orgs:** Mem Leadership Atlanta; mem Amer Chem Soc, AAAS, Natl Inst Sci, Natl Org Professional Advancement Black Chemists & Chem Engrs, Sigma Xi, Sigma Pi Phi, Alpha Phi Alpha, Rotary; member, Oak Ridge Associates, 1988-; board member, Fernbank Museum, 1989-. **Honors/Awds:** So Regional Fellow summer 1961; Woodrow Wilson Fellow 1961-62; Allied Chem Fellow 1963; Honorus Causa DLL, West Virginia State College, 1987; Honorus Causa DHL, University of Charleston, 1988. **Business Addr:** President, Clark Atlanta University, James P Brawley Dr at Fair St, SW, Atlanta, GA 30314.

COLE CAREY, WILHEMINA
Consultant, owner. **Personal:** daugHter of Estell Swinton Nesmith; children: Gilbert Flemin Jr, Tyrone Sr. **Educ:** Univ of Maryland, Western State Univ for Professionals, AA, BS, MBA, PhD; Anna Burdick, Washington, DC, LPN; St Elizabeths Hospital, Washington DC, postgrad course in psychiatry, 1960; executive housekeeper certification, 1967; Cornell Univ, attended; Lewis Hotel/Motel Training School; attended seminars and collegiate studies in historic preservation at Univ of MD, Smithsonian Institute. **Career:** Executive housekeeper, 1951-58; St Elizabeths Hospital, lpn, lpn supervisor, 1960-65, asst hospital housekeeping officer, 1965-78, hosp housekeeping off, 1978-89; federal govt employee, 1960-87; city govt employee, 1987-91; Logistics Mgmt Branch, deputy chief, 1984-91; Carey and Hester, Inc, consultant, owner, 1991-; Arlington Public Schools, teacher, marketing, currently. **Orgs:** St Elizabeths Hospital Museum, founder, curator mgr; Upper Room Baptist Church, Sr Citizens Program, coord, 1991; International Executive Housekeepers Assn, natl bd. **Honors/Awds:** Saint Elizabeths Hospital, DC government, The Wilhemina C. Carey Retirement Resolution, for 30 yrs of Outstanding Public and Dedicated Service, 1992. **Special Achievements:** Designed and established a library which is affiliated with the DC Library; de-

veloped and implemented a nine month Housekeeping Training Program for two Liberian students under the auspices of the Agency for Intl Development, US Dept of State; Wrote, The Housekeeping Manual, 1979; researched, wrote, "Hospital Housekeeping Education and Training, A Case Study," with George P. Garrett, Professional Sanitation Management, spring 1971; first woman to be Supreme Master of the Natl Ideal Benefit Society; developed and implemented programs of lesser training for others under similar housekeeping programs for US Dept of State; published various articles in the Natl Exec Housekeepers Assn, Environmental Mgmt Assn journals; has spoken at various conferences and seminars. **Business Addr:** Consultant/Owner, Carey and Hester, Inc, 33 54th St SE, Washington, DC 20019-6560, (202)584-7010.

COLEMAN, ANDRE CLINTONIAN
Professional football player. **Personal:** Born Sep 19, 1972, Hermitage, PA. **Educ:** Kansas State Univ. **Career:** San Diego Chargers, wide receiver, 1994-96; Seattle Seahawks, 1997; Pittsburgh Steelers, 1997-. **Business Addr:** Professional Football Player, Pittsburgh Steelers, Three Rivers Stadium, 300 Stadium Circle, Pittsburgh, PA 15212, (412)323-1200.

COLEMAN, ANDREW LEE
Corrections officer. **Personal:** Born Jan 30, 1960, Humboldt, TN; son of Mae Doris Scott Lovelady and Lonnie Lee Coleman. **Educ:** Vanderbilt Univ, BS Political Science, Sociology 1982; Dyersburg Comm Coll, principles of real estate, parole officer training, 1990; Jackson State Community Coll, Jackson, TN, parole training, 1987; Memphis State Graduate School, Memphis, TN, 1990-; Jackson State Comm Coll, 1993-. **Career:** Humboldt City Parks, asst supvr summer, 1977; Jones Mfg Co, laborer, 1978-79; Foster & Creighton Const Co, laborer, 1981; Denver Broncos, professional football player, 1982; New Orleans Saints, professional football player 1982; Classic I Kitchenware Inc, sales distr, 1983; Humboldt Schools, sub teacher, 1983; City of Humboldt, alderman, 1983; Gibson Cty Vote Coord, Get Out the Vote, coord for Albert Gore Jr, 1984; Jesse Jackson for Pres, coord 1984; The Drew Enterprise (publ rel/pers svcs), pres, 1985-; Jonah, Inc, organizer/office mgr, 1985; Al Williams, Inc, sales rep, 1986; TN Bd of Paroles, parole officer/counselor, 1986-; Morgan & Assocs Realtors, affiliate broker 1987; co-chairman Humboldt Strawberry Patch, 1988; Jackson State Community Coll, 1993-. **Orgs:** Volunteer/coach, Special Olympics; mem, TN Black Elected Officials, 1984-, TN Voters Council, 1984-, Gibson Cty Voters Council, 1984; lecturing knight, WJO Lee Elks #1290, 1985-; mem, NAACP; vice president, 1988, president, 1991-92, Humboldt NAACP; mem Jonah; financial sec, WJO Lee Elks 1290; past exalted ruler, Council #42, 3 yr trustee; Celestial Lodge #80; mem in dept of health & environment Amer Probation & Paroles 1988; bd mem, Decatur County Community Corrections advisory bd, 1988-; patron Order of Eastern Star 1988; mem Gibson County Fraternal Order of Police, 1988-; mem, Brownstown Alumni Club of Memphis, 1990; mem, Lane College Alumni Assn, 1989; chancellor, T.P. Haroldson Consistory 94, 1989-90; TN State Troopers Assn, #4; TN Correctional Assn; Amer Correctional Assn; JONAH (Just Organized Neighborhood Area Headquarters); Steward, Lane Chapel CME Church; TN Sheriff Assn; NAACP, Golden Heritage life mem; Jonah CHDO (Community Housing Development Organization), president, 1995; Jackson Halfway House, volunteer; 100 Black Men of West Tennessee, Inc; Apha Phi Alpha Fraternity Inc, life mem; past state pres, Past Grand Exalted Ruler, 1997. **Honors/Awds:** Most Valuable Player Vanderbilt Football 1980; voted Most Athletic Class of 1982; All Amer Middle Linebacker Vanderbilt Univ 1982; Amer Outstanding Names & Faces Natl Org 1982; Community Service Award, Humboldt NAACP, 1988; Community Service Award, Phi Delta Kappa, 1992; Lane College, Asst Football Coach, 1992, 1994; Gibson Co Habitat for Humanity, VP, 1994; Outstanding Young Men of America, National Nominating Comm. **Home Addr:** 1610 Osborne, Humboldt, TN 38343.

COLEMAN, APRIL HOWARD
Attorney, educational administrator. **Personal:** marrIed Donald Coleman; children: Rebekah, Donald. **Educ:** Univ of Michigan; Texas Southern Univ, Thurgood Marshall School of Law. **Career:** Univ of Detroit Mercy, adjunct prof; Wayne State Univ, adjunct prof; Swanson, Torgow & Lyons, PC, attorney; Detroit Board of Education, past pres, mem, currently. **Orgs:** Detroit Teen Anti-Violence Program, founder; Detroit City Council's Youth Advisory Commission, charter mem; Wayne County, MI, Youth Task Force Citizens Committee, chair; Detroit Street Law Project, founder; Detroit School Bd, 1989, community confidence committee, chair, 1991, 1992. **Military Serv:** US Army Reserve, first lieutenant. **Business Addr:** Member, Detroit Board of Education, 5057 Woodward, Detroit, MI 48202, (313)494-1010.

COLEMAN, ARTHUR H.
Business executive, physician, attorney. **Personal:** Born Feb 18, 1920, Philadelphia, PA; son of Virgina Hines Coleman and Jessie Coleman; married Renee Dorsey, Nov 21, 1987; children: Ruth Karnell, Patricia, John, Kurt. **Educ:** PA State U, BS 1941; Howard U, MD 1944; Golden Gate Coll, LlB 1956; Golden Gate Coll, JD 1968. **Career:** Medicine, pvt practice 1948-; San Francisco Med Assoc, pres. **Orgs:** Bd dir Sec Drew Inv Corp 1952; pres co-founder Amer Health Care Plan 1973; bd dir Fidelity Savings & Loan Assn 1966; co-founder pres SF Med Assn Inc; exec dir Hunters Point Baypoint Comm Health Serv 1968-72; chmn SF Econ Opportunity Council 1964-67; pres chmn of bd Trans-Bay Fed Savings & Loan Assn 1964-66; guest lectr Golden Gate Coll of Law 1958-60; lectr Univ CA 1968; mem Pathway Comm for Family Med Univ CA Med Ctr 1970; internship Homer G Phillips Hosp 1945; mem AMA 1948; mem CA Med Assn 1948; mem SF Med Soc 1948-; pres Natl Med Assn 1976-77; pres John Hale Med Soc 1970-71; fellow Amer Acad of Forensic Sci 1958; fellow bd of govs Amer Coll of Legal Med 1961; pres Northern California Med Dental Pharm Assn 1964; pres bd Dir Golden State Med Assn 1970-74; memWorld Med Assn 1971-; mem Acad of Med 1971; coord com SF Alliance for Health Care; vice pres Amer Cancer Soc 1969-71; bd of dir SF Hunters Point Boys Club; bd dir adv council SF Planning & Ren Assn 1969-75; pres Amer Coll of Legal Medicine 1983-84; vice pres bd of dir Drew Medical Univ 1987; pres Port of San Francisco 1984-87. **Honors/Awds:** Bay Area Howard Univ Alumni Award 1966; SF Bay Area Council Certificate 1965-67; SF bd of supres Certificate of Award 1968; SF Dept of Health Commendation 1976; Omega Psi Phi Award for Distingushed Serv 1973; numerous articles and other publications; Distinguished Alumnus, Penn State Univ 1977. **Military Serv:** USAF capt 1945-48. **Business Addr:** President, San Francisco Medical Assoc, 6301 Third St, San Francisco, CA 94124.

COLEMAN, AUDREY RACHELLE
Educational administrator. **Personal:** Born Aug 26, 1934, Duquesne, PA; daughter of Ola Dixon Ward and Dave Ward; married William Franklin Coleman Sr; children: William Franklin Jr. **Educ:** Youngstown Univ, BMus 1956; Boston State Coll, MEd 1965, Advanced Admin 1978. **Career:** Youngstown OH Public Schools, teacher 1957-61; Boston Public Schools, teacher 1961-75, asst principal 1975-76, admin, asst director, director of comprehensive school planning, currently. **Orgs:** Natl First Anti-Basileus Lambda Kappa Mu 1976-79; conductor Natl Workshops Lambda Kappa Mu 1976-; conductor Citywide Workshops Boston Public Schools 1977-; mem MA State Review Team Chap I Prog 1978; grand basileus Lambda Kappa Mu 1981-85; bd of dir Natl Coalition-Black Meeting Planners 1984-86; natl bd mem, Lambda Kappa Mu (past natl pres); natl vice pres, American Federation of School Admin; board member, Boston Convention and Visitor's Bureau; president Middlesex County Chapter Links Inc; national nominating committee 1992, national protocol committee, foundation board member-at-large, Links Inc. **Honors/Awds:** Certificate of Achievement & Leadership Urban League 1979; Mary M Bethune Awd Natl Council Negro Women 1982; Distinguished Serv Key Awd Lambda Kappa Mu 1983; featured on front cover of Black Monitor Magazine 1984; Dollars & Sense Magazine Award to Outstanding Afro-American Women 1989; Mayor of Boston Award for Leadership 1988; Humanitarian Award, South Shore United Methodist Church, Chicago, IL, 1987; National Freedom's Foundation Award; Board member, Mass Lodging Assn Educational Foundation. **Business Addr:** Director of Comprehensive School Planning, Boston Public Schools, 396 Northampton St, Springfield, MA 01109.

COLEMAN, AVANT PATRICK
Educator. **Personal:** Born Jun 16, 1936, Rocky Mount, NC; son of Bessie D Phillips Coleman and Edward William Coleman; married Willa Jean Monroe Coleman, Apr 28, 1960; children: Jacqueline, Elliotte, Wanda. **Educ:** Agr & Tech State Univ, BS 1960; NC State Univ, MS 1978. **Career:** Lenoir Cty Bd of Ed, teacher, vocational agr 1960-61; Greene Cty Bd of Ed, teacher, vocational agr 1961-62; NC Agr Extension Svc, extension agent 4-H 1962-. **Orgs:** Sec NC State 4-H Agents Assoc 1972-73; city council 1975-77, 1980-85, mayor pro tem 1982-91 City of Wilson; pres Kiwanis Club of Wilson All Amer 1981-82; pres Men's Civic Club 1982; bd mem United Way of Wilson Cty Inc 1983-85; 1st vice pres Red Cross Wilson County Chapter 1986-87; chapter chairman, Wilson Chapter American Red Cross, 1987-88; bd mem, NC Housing Partnership NC League of Municipalities, 1987-; chairman, Regional L Council of Governments, 1988-90; bd mem, Small Cities Council Natl League of Cities, 1988-89; 3rd vice pres, NC League of Municipalities, 1988-89, 1st vice president NC League of Municipalities, 1990-91. **Honors/Awds:** Distinguished Serv Award State Natl Assoc of 4-H Agents 1975; Certificate of Appreciation Mid-Atlantic Reg MD-NC 4-H Caravan Six Weeks 1977; Distinguished Serv Award Alpha Kappa Alpha Sorority 1982; Distinguished Humanitarian Award Gamma Beta Omega Chap Alpha Kappa Alpha Sorority 1982; Tour of United Kingdom Natl 4-H Council Washington DC; NCNB, bd of dir; NC League of Municipalities, bd of dir 1986-87; appointed to the Natl League Comm & Economic Devel Comm 1986-87; 25 yr Service, Natl Assn of Extension 4H Agents, 1987; Recipient of the Outstanding Leadership Award by th NC Ag Extension Service, 1989. **Home Addr:** 2406 Belair Ave, PO Box 4185, Wilson, NC 27893.

COLEMAN, BARBARA SIMS
Social worker (retired). **Personal:** Born Mar 5, 1932, Wichita, KS; daughter of Rossa Velma Whitehead Sims and Hugh Napoleon Sims; married Julian D Coleman Jr, Aug 8, 1953; children: Julian, Hugh, Mark. **Educ:** Howard Univ, BS 1953; Univ of WI, MSSW 1956. **Career:** Larue Carteer Memrl Hosp, asst dir soc work 1957-73, sprvr 1957-73, psychiatric soc worker 1957-73; Indiana University Medical Center, asst dir soc work/psychiatry Riley Child Psychiatry Clinic 1973-93. **Orgs:** Conslnt sprvsr Christian Theological Smnry Pastoral Cnslng Pgm 1972-; mem of bd Plnd Parenthood Cntrl IN 1980-89; mem bd pres Raines Cnslng Cntr 1968-84; Natl Assn of Social Workers & Academy of Certified Social Workers; board of directors Children's Bureau of Indianpolis Inc, 1993-; advisory council, Buchanan Counseling Center, 1994-; Greater Indianapolis Literary League, 1995-. **Honors/Awds:** Social Worker of the Year, Region 7, Indiana, National Assn of Social Workers, 1989. **Home Addr:** 4370 Knollton Rd, Indianapolis, IN 46208.

COLEMAN, BENJAMIN LEON
Professional football player. **Personal:** Born May 18, 1971, South Hill, VA; married Krista; children: Haley. **Educ:** Wake Forest, attended. **Career:** Arizona Cardinals, guard, 1994-95; Jacksonville Jaguars, 1996-. **Business Addr:** Professional Football Player, Jacksonville Jaguars, One Stadium Place, Jacksonville, FL 32202, (904)633-6000.

COLEMAN, CAESAR DAVID
Cleric. **Personal:** Born Oct 4, 1919, Pickens, MS; son of Eddye Love Coleman (deceased) and Ira Leigh Coleman (deceased); married Elizabeth Luellen Coleman, Nov 11, 1955; children: Rev Daryll H Coleman. **Educ:** Mary Holmes Jr Coll, West Point, MS; Mississippi Industrial Coll, Holly Springs, MS, AB, 1947; Lincoln Univ, Lincoln Univ, PA, BD, 1950. **Career:** Miles Chapel CME Church, Sardis, MS, pastor, 1952-57; Mississippi Industrial, Holly Springs, MS, prof of religion & philosophy, 1952-57; Christian Methodist Epis Church, N Mississippi Conf, presiding elder, 1956-58; General Bd of Christian Educ, CME Church, Chicago, IL, exec sec, 1958-74; Christian Methodist, Dallas, TX, presiding bishop, 1974-; Episcopal Church, Dallas, TX, sr bishop & CEO, 1986-. **Orgs:** Founder & trustee, Interdemonational Theology Center, 1960-76; chmn, bd of trustees, Texas Coll, 1974-; Dallas Area Ministers' Alliance, 1974-; chmn & chief endorser, Comm on Chaplaincy, 1978-86; pres, Gen Bd of Personnel Serv, 1982-86; sec, Coll of Bishops, vice pres, The Natl Congress of Black Churches, 1982-86; treasurer, Texas Conf of Churches, 1982-86; patron bishop, Women's Missionary Council CME Church, 1986-; dir, AMI Securities, 1988-; life mem, Natl Urban League, Consultation on Church Union, Urban Ministries Inc; mem, NAACP, Greater Dallas Community of Churches. **Honors/Awds:** Doctor of Divinity, Lane Coll, 1960; Doctor of Laws, Mississippi Indus Coll, 1967; Doctor of Divinity, Interdenominational Theology Center, 1976; 100 Most Influential Black Amer, Ebony Magazine, 1986-; Trailblazer Award, South Dallas Business & Professional Women's Club, 1987; Outstanding Minister, Dallas Interdenomational Ministers' Alliance, 1988; Honorary Mayor, Kenny Dill, Mayor of West Point, MS, 1989; author, The CME Primer, Beyond Blackness to Destiny, Organizational Manual & Guide for Christian Youth Fellowship, CME Church; editor in chief, Civil Rights. **Military Serv:** US Armed Forces, WW II, commissioned officer.

COLEMAN, CECIL R.
Business executive. **Personal:** Born May 15, 1934, Centralia, IL; married Betti Thomas; children: Karla M, Mark C. **Educ:** Northwestern U, BBA 1970; Northwestern U, Grad Sch of Mgmt. **Career:** Harris Trust & Savs Bank, dir 1980-; Harris Trust & Savs Bank, vice pres 1978-80; Harris Trust & Savings Bank, former asst mp 1965; Mammoth Life Ins Co, sales rep asst & mgr & mrg 1954-65. **Orgs:** Mem Chicago Chap AIB Bd Regents; TAP Cons; Alpha Delta Sigma; Human Resources Com IL State C of C chmn; Chicago Student Symposium ; Sci & Math Conf 1973; bd dir Chatham YMCA; mem Comm Fund Review Panel; mem Old Town Boys Club. **Honors/Awds:** Chicago black achiever 1974; WGRT Radio "Great Guy Award 1973"; jacee of the month Chicago Chap 1969; Chicago merit Employee of week 1967; num Nat Ins Assn awards for sales achievement. **Military Serv:** AUS sp/4 1956-58. **Business Addr:** Harris Trust & Sav Bank, 111 W Monroe St, Chicago, IL 60690.

COLEMAN, CHRISENA ANNE
Journalist. **Personal:** Born Mar 20, 1963, Hackensack, NJ; daughter of Dorothy Coleman and Wilbert Coleman. **Educ:** Emerson College, attended, 1981-82; Northeastern University, BA, 1968. **Career:** Hackensack Board of Education, counselor for family literacy program; The Record, journalist, currently. **Orgs:** Garden State Association of Black Journalists, vice pres; National Association of Black Journalists; Alpha Kappa Alpha Sorority Inc. **Honors/Awds:** NAACP, Passaic Chapter, Black History Honoree; Alpha Kappa Alpha, Bergen Chapter, Black Woman of Inspiration, 1992. **Business Addr:** Journalist, The Record, Bergen Record Corp, 150 River St, Hackensack, NJ 07601, (201)646-4100.

COLEMAN, CLAUDE M.
Law enforcement executive, attorney-at-law. **Personal:** Born Oct 26, 1940, Newberry, SC; son of Roberta Spearman Coleman and Willie Coleman; married Barbara Saunders Coleman, Apr 16, 1983. **Educ:** Rutgers University, Newark, NJ, BS,

1971-74; Rutgers Law School, Newark, NJ, JD, 1974-77; FBI National Academy, VA, 1978; National Fire Academy, MD, 1987. **Career:** City of Newark, NJ, police officer, 1964-80, police legal adviser, 1980-86, fire director, 1986-88; police director, 1988-. **Orgs:** Former president, chairman, Bronze Shields, Inc, 1964-; member, 100 Black Men of New Jersey; member, National Orgn of Black Law Enforcement Executives, member, IACP; chairman, Law Enforcement Executive Forum. **Military Serv:** USAF, Sgt 1st class, 1959-63; Good Conduct. **Business Addr:** Police Director, City of Newark, Police Dept, 31 Green St, 4th Floor, Newark, NJ 07102.

COLEMAN, COLLIE
Educational administrator. **Career:** Allen University, academic dean; Shorter College, Little Rock, AR, academic dean; Allen University, president, chancellor, 1984-. **Business Addr:** President/Chancellor, Allen University, 1530 Harden St, Columbia, SC 29204, (803)254-4165.

COLEMAN, COLUMBUS E., JR.
Corporate officer. **Personal:** Born Jul 13, 1948, Wharton, TX. **Educ:** Univ of TX, BS 1970; Univ of NC, MBA 1973-75; Univ of San Francisco, Law Courses 1978-79. **Career:** Wells Fargo Securities Clearance Corp, exec vice pres & gen mgr 1979-; Wells Fargo Bank, asst vice pres 1977-79; First Nat Bank in Dallas, corporate banking officer 1975-77; Gulf & Oil Co, elec engr 1970-71. **Orgs:** Adv capt Am Cancer Assn Dr 1977; Small Bus Assn 1978-; adv Jr Achievement 1978; pres Alpha Phi Alpha Epsilon Iota Chap 1970-71; mem & participant Big Brothers Assn 1978-; mem NAACP 1979-. **Honors/Awds:** Hon mem Phi Theta Kappa Frat 1967-; Consortium Fellow 1973-75; Soldier of Year AUS 1971. **Military Serv:** AUS spec-5 1971-72. **Business Addr:** 45 Broad St, New York, NY 10004.

COLEMAN, DENNIS
Entrepreneur. **Personal:** Born Dec 31, 1951, North Chicago, IL; son of Eupha Lee Coleman and J C Coleman Sr; married Cheryl Diane Jarnigan, Aug 31, 1974; children: Dennis II, Felicia Marie, Steven Anton. **Educ:** Knoxville College, BS, business, 1974. **Career:** Burger King Corp, crew supervisor, 1970-74, restaurant manager, 1974-77, district manager, 1977-81; Coleman Enterprises, president, 1981-90; Five Star Inc, DBA Rally's Hamburgers, president, 1992-. **Orgs:** Phi Beta Sigma, 1971-; Big Fellas Association; Minority Franchise Association. **Honors/Awds:** Michigan Dept of Commerce, Minority Franchisee of the Year, 1992. **Special Achievements:** First minority to own a Rally's Franchise in the country, 1992; highest award received at Whopper College, 1974; Top Ten Graduates at Burger King University. **Business Addr:** President, Five Star, Inc/DBA Rally's Hamburgers, 19801 W Eight Mile Rd, Detroit, MI 48219, (313)255-5455.

COLEMAN, DERRICK D.
Professional basketball player. **Personal:** Born Jun 21, 1967, Mobile, AL. **Educ:** Syracuse Univ, Syracuse, NY, 1986-90. **Career:** New Jersey Nets, forward, 1990-95; Philadelphia 76ers, 1995-. **Honors/Awds:** NBA Rookie of the Year, 1991; NBA All-Star, 1994. **Business Addr:** Professional Basketball Player, Philadelphia 76ers, One Corestates Complex, Philadelphia, PA 19148, (215)339-7676.

COLEMAN, DON EDWIN
Educator. **Personal:** Born May 4, 1928, Ponca City, OK; son of Nancy Coleman and George Coleman; married Geraldine J Johnson; children: Stephanie Lynn. **Educ:** MI State Univ, BS 1952, MS 1956, MA 1958, PhD 1971. **Career:** Flint MI Schools, teacher 1954-67; Doyle Comm School, prin 1966-68; MI State Univ, teacher, coach 1968-69, asst dean graduate school 1978-, College of Osteopathic Medicine, professor, community health science, currently. **Orgs:** Pres MI Health Council 1980; mem Amer Pub Health Assn; mem Amer Coll Pers Assn; mem Natl Assn Student Pers Admin; past mem Natl Comm Sch Dir Assn 1963-67; past mem MI Elem Principal Assn 1967-68; mem Phi Delta Kappa; mem Alpha Phi Alpha Frat 1949; past pres Epsilon Upsilon Lambda 1965-67; past pres fdr Kappa Delta Lambda 1972; Red Feather United Fund 1964-68; past dir BS of Amer 1965-68; Prince Hall Masonic Order 1954; Elks Genesee Temple 1956-68; NAACP 1954; mem Urban League 1954; exec comm Planned Parenthood 1952-60; mem Flint Jr Chamber of Comm 1960-64; bd mem Listening Ear 1970-73; Air Pollution Bd 1970-74; past mem Tri-Co Plng Comm 1974-76; MI State Univ Athletic Coun 1975; life mem Alpha Phi Alpha Frat 1980; exec dir Black Child & Family Inst 1986; chmn Ingham County Bd of Health 1987; bf trustees, Mich Capital Medical Center, 1988. **Honors/Awds:** 10 Yr Awd Big Brothers of Amer 1955-68; Blue Key Natl Scholastic Honor; Unanimous All-Amer Tackle 1950-51; Outstanding Lineman 1951 1952; Coll All Star game 1952; 1st football jersey (78) retired at MSU 1952; Outstanding Lineman Hula Bowl Silver Anniv 1971; inductee Natl Football Found & Hall of Fame 1975; NCAA Silver Anniv Awd 1976. **Military Serv:** AUS 1st lt 1952-54. **Business Addr:** Professor Emeritus, Michigan State University, College of Osteopathic Medicine, 535 E Fee, East Lansing, MI 48824.

COLEMAN, DONALD
Police officer. **Personal:** Born Aug 18, 1953, Marion, AL; son of Elijah (deceased) & Alma Coleman; married Constance Lin Coleman, Jan 6, 1979; children: Benjamin Ashley, Christopher Andrew. **Educ:** New Hampshire College, BS, bus mgmt, 1976. **Career:** City of Detroit, police officer, 1987-; Flowers by Miss Marion, co-owner, currently. **Orgs:** Kappa Sigma International Fraternity, 1974; Barney McCosky Baseball League, little league coach, 1986-93. **Honors/Awds:** Fraternity Brother of the Year, 1975; 8th Precinct, Police Officer of the Year, 1993; Police Officer of the Month, 3 times; Performance Award, 6 times.

COLEMAN, DONALD ALVIN
Advertising executive. **Personal:** Born Jan 11, 1952, Toledo, OH; son of Dorothy Bowers Coleman and Augustus Coleman; married Jo Moore Coleman, Oct 5, 1976; children: Kelli. **Educ:** University of Michigan, Ann Arbor MI, BA, journalism, 1974; Hofstra University, Hempstead, NY, MBA, 1976. **Career:** Lintas Campbell-Ewald Advertising, Warren, MI, vice president, 1977-85; Burrell Advertising, Chicago, IL, senior vice president, 1985-87; Don Coleman & Assoc, Southfield, MI, president & ceo, 1987-. **Orgs:** Member, American Assoc of Advertising Agencies, 1988; member, National Football League Players Assoc, 1975; advisory committee, Reggie McKenzie Foundation, 1988; member, NAACP, 1972; member, National Assoc of Market Developers, 1989. **Business Addr:** CEO, Don Coleman & Associates, 26555 Evergreen Rd., 18th Floor, Southfield, MI 48076.

COLEMAN, EDWIN LEON, II
Educator. **Personal:** Born Mar 17, 1932, El Dorado, AR; son of Mae Otis and Edwin; married Charmaine Joyce Thompson; children: Edwin III, Callan. **Educ:** City Coll of San Francisco, AA 1955; San Francisco State Univ, BA 1960, MA 1962; Univ of OR, PhD 1971. **Career:** Melodyland Theatre, technician, 1960; Chico State Univ, Speech Dept, asst prof, 1963-66; Univ of OR Dept of English, dir, Folklore 1 Ethnic Program, currently; professional musician, currently. **Orgs:** Bd Campus Interfaith Ministry 1975-; bd Sponsors Inc 1980-; bd Clergy & Laity Concerned 1980-; bd OR Arts Found 1981-84; pres OR Folklore Soc 1983-84; consul Natl Endowment for the Arts 1983-; Natl Humanities, faculty; mem Amer Folklore Soc; NAACP; Kappa Alpha Psi; Oregon Track Club; bd, Western States Arts Foundation. **Honors/Awds:** Ford Fellow Educ Grant 1970; Danforth Assoc 1977-; Distinguished Black Faculty 1978; Outstanding Faculty Natl Mag OR Art Commission 1982; Frederick Douglass Scholarship Awd Natl Council of Black Studies 1986; University of Oregon, Charles S. Johnson Service Award; NAACP Lifetime Achievement Award. **Military Serv:** USAF Staff Sgt 1951-56. **Business Addr:** Professor of English, Univ of Oregon, Dept of English, Eugene, OR 97403.

COLEMAN, ELIZABETH SHEPPARD
Performing arts director. **Personal:** chilDren: Nedra, Andre, Jalinda, Angela, Aretha. **Educ:** Muskegon Comm Clg, Assc 1973; Grand Valley State Clg, BS 1975, Masters Gen & Urban Educ 1979. **Career:** Advisory Cncl Muskegon Hghts Police, mem 1975-77; Muskegon Hghts Bd of Educ, trst sec 1975-81; Muskegon Cnty Cncl of Black Orgn, mem sec 1975-77; Muskegon Cnty Human Resrc Cmt, mem 1977-79; Muskegon Cnty Repertory Cntr, dir 1976-85; NAACP, civic serv mem. **Orgs:** Mem & sec Muskegon Co Black Orgn 1977-79; mem Muskegon Co Human Resource 1979-; mem Muskegon Co NAACP. **Business Addr:** Dir, Muskegon Cnty Repertory, 706 Overbrook Dr, Muskegon, MI 49444.

COLEMAN, ERIC DEAN
Elected official, attorney. **Personal:** Born May 26, 1951, New Haven, CT; son of Rebecca Ann Simmons Coleman and Julius Coleman; married Pamela Lynette Greene, May 19, 1979; children: Trevonn Rakeim, Lamar Ericson, Erica Lynette. **Educ:** Columbia Univ, BA 1973; Univ of CT, JD 1977. **Career:** Hartford Neighborhood Legal Svcs, staff atty 1977-78; CT Div of Pub Def Services, asst public defender 1978-81; Aetna Life & Casualty, consultant 1981-86; CT General Assembly, state rep 1983-95; State senator, 1995-. **Orgs:** Mem Greater Hartford Urban League 1974-, Greater Hartford NAACP 1974-, Amer Bar Assoc 1978-, CT Bar Assoc 1978-, George Crawford Law Assoc 1978-, Action Plan for Infant Health 1984-; mem Oper PUSH 1974-, Charter Oak Lodge of Elks 1982-, Omega Psi Phi, Bloomfield Dem Town Comm 1984-, Greater Hartford Black Dem Club 1978-, Metro AME Zion Church; mem bd of dirs Mutual Housing Assn of Greater Hartford, 1989-. **Honors/Awds:** Citizen of the Year Omega Psi Phi Frat Tau Iota CT, 1982; Citizen of the Year Omega Psi Phi Frat Delta Lambda CT 1983; First Report (Weekly Neighborhood Newspaper Column) 1983-; Marital Deduction Planning under ERTA 1981. **Home Addr:** 77 Wintonbury Ave, Bloomfield, CT 06002.

COLEMAN, EVEROD A.
Consultant. **Personal:** Born Sep 24, 1920, Mounds, LA; son of Florence Blackburn Coleman and Frank Harrison Coleman; married Willie Mae Dixon; children: Everod Coleman Jr, Rene Martin. **Educ:** Lincoln Univ, BS 1947; Attended, Wayne State Univ, Univ of Detroit. **Career:** White & Griffin Arch & Eng, steel designer 1947-49; City of Detroit, coord phys devel comm & econ devel dept (retired 1980); City of Inkster MI, interim chief bldg inspector & consul 1982; Architects Intl, consultant. **Orgs:** 1st black building insp City of Detroit 1949-; housing consul bd dir Phoenix Housing Corp; mem SMED; Natl Assn of Housing Rehab Officials; Natl Tech Assn Omega Psi Phi Frat; NAACP; past elder & trustee Calvary Presby Ch; mem Detroit Housing Corp. **Honors/Awds:** Father of Yr 1955 United Christian Ch; Distinguished Alumni Award, Lincoln University, MD, National Alumni Assn, 1985; Fifty Years Devotion & Service Award, Omega Psi Phi Fraternity Inc, 1983. **Military Serv:** Vet WW II. **Home Addr:** 4058 Clements St, Detroit, MI 48238.

COLEMAN, FRANKIE LYNN
Employment/training executive director. **Personal:** Born Aug 21, 1950, Columbus, OH; daughter of Mary A Young and Franklin L R Young (deceased); married Micheal Bennett Coleman, Aug 31, 1973; children: Kimberly, Justin, John-David. **Educ:** Mount Union College, BA, 1972; Central Michigan University, MA, 1974. **Career:** City of Columbus, lead planner, 1974-83; State of Ohio, Job Training Partnership, director, 1983-88; The Private Industry Council Inc, executive director, 1988-. **Orgs:** Governor's Black Male Commission, employment committee chair, 1990-; Ohio Job Training Partnership, executive bd, 1992-93; Jack & Jill, Columbus Chapter, fundraising co-chair, 1993-94; Links Inc, Columbus Chapter; Natl Assn of Private Industry; councils bd of dirs, 1996-; Communications Committee, chair; Columbus Rotary Club; Columbus One-Step Governace, bd; Magazine Editorial Board, CEO. **Honors/Awds:** YWCA Woman of Achievement, 1994, YMCA, Woman of the Year, 1991; Mayor's Excellence in Business Award, 1991; WCKX, Excellence in Community Service Award, 1990; Columbus Urban League, EEO Award, 1992. **Special Achievements:** Co-Author, The State of Black Males in Ohio, 1991. **Business Addr:** Executive Director, CEO, The Private Industry Council, Inc, 400 E Town St, Suite 220, Columbus, OH 43215, (614)228-3907.

COLEMAN, GARY
Actor. **Personal:** Born Feb 8, 1968, Lima, OH; son of Sue Coleman and W G Coleman. **Career:** TV commercials; guest starred, Good Times, The Jeffersons, The Johnny Carson Show; TV pilot, Little Rascals 1978; co-star Different Strokes, 1978-86; movies include The Kid From Left Field, 1979; Scout's Honor, 1980; On the Right Track, 1981; Jimmy the Kid, 1983; The Fantastic World of DC Comics, 1983; Playing With Fire, 1984. **Orgs:** Honorary Gift of Life Chmn Natl Kidney Foundation. **Honors/Awds:** Biography "Gary Coleman-Medical Miracle".

COLEMAN, GEORGE EDWARD
Saxophonist, bandleader. **Personal:** Born Mar 8, 1935, Memphis, TN; son of Indiana Lyle Coleman and George Coleman; married Gloria Bell (divorced); children: George, Gloria; married Carol Hollister, Sep 7, 1985. **Career:** Tenor alto and soprano saxophonist; mem BB King Band 1952, 1955; mem Max Roach Quintet 1958-59, Miles Davis Quartet 1963-64, Lionel Hampton Orch 1965-66, Lee Morgan Quintet 1969, Elvin Jones Quartet 1970; writer arranger of mus shows; Lenox MA Jazz Sch of Mus, consult 1958; George Coleman Quartet & George Coleman Octet, 1974-; consultant, New York Univ, Long Island Univ, New School for Social Research. **Honors/Awds:** Selected by Intl Jazz Critics Poll 1958; Artist of the Yr Record World Mag 1969; Knight of Mark Twain 1972; Beale St Mus Festival Awd 1977; Tip of the Derby Awd 1978, 1979, 1980; New York Jazz Awd 1979; Grantee National Endowment of the Arts 1975, 1985; Gold Note Jazz Award 1982; Key to the City of Memphis 1992; Life Achievement Award, The Jazz Foundation of America, 1997. **Special Achievements:** Films: Sweet Love Bitter, 1970; Comedie (French), 1985; Freejack, 1991; The Preacher's Wife, 1996. **Home Addr:** 63 East 9th St, New York, NY 10003.

COLEMAN, GILBERT IRVING
Educator. **Personal:** Born Jan 20, 1940, Fredericksburg, VA; married Pearlie Ball; children: Darryl Langston. **Educ:** VA Union Univ, BS 1956-60; Howard Univ, MS 1960-62; Univ of VA, EdD 1980-. **Career:** Microbiological Assoc, rsch assoc 1962-63; Natl Institutions of Health, rsch asst 1963-64; Smithsonian Inst, jr rsch analyst 1964-68; Spotsylvania SrHS, biology teacher 1968-70; Germann Comm Coll, instructor 1970-73, asst prof 1973-76, assoc prof 1976- 92, Prof, 1992; div chmn arts sciences & nursing. **Orgs:** Mem Shiloh Baptist Church 1949-; mem Personnel Bd Mary Washington Hosp 1984-; mem of the bd Rappahannock Serv Corp 1984-. **Honors/Awds:** Man of the Year Veterans of Foreign Wars 1984; Man of the Year Fraternal Order of Police 1984. **Home Addr:** HC 72 Box 355, Locust Grove, VA 22508-9515. **Business Addr:** The National Center for Community College Education, George Mason University, Associate Director, 221 Thompson Hall, MSN 1B3, Fairfax, VA 22030-4444.

COLEMAN, HARRY THEODORE
Dentist. **Personal:** Born Jul 6, 1943, Somerville, TN; married Olivia Jackson; children: Brian, Chandra. **Educ:** Johnson C Smith U, BS1965; Meharry Med Coll, DDS 1970. **Career:** Self, dentist; Hubbard Hosp, intership 1970-71. **Orgs:** Mem Nat Dental Assn; Shelby Co Dental Soc; Pan-TN Dental Assn; Am

Dental Assn; mem Memphis Jr C of C; Kappa Alpha & Psifrat; NAACP YMCA; bd dir Boys Club. **Military Serv:** USN lt 1971-73. **Business Addr:** 3087 Park Ave, Memphis, TN 38111.

COLEMAN, HERMAN W.
Association executive. **Personal:** Born Sep 10, 1939, Brookhaven, MS; married Kay G; children: Hope, Michelle. **Educ:** Alcorn A&M Coll Lorman, MS, BS 1962; Western MI Univ Kalamazoo, MI, 1965 & 1968; Eastern MI Univ Ypsilanti, MI, 1968-69. **Career:** Michigan Ed Assn Assoc, exec sec; Div of Minority Affairs, exec sec; Urban Ed Prog Rochester & Public Sch Rochester, NY, dir. **Orgs:** Critic guest lecturer and/or consultant at Univ of MI MI State Univ and Harvard U; consultative resource to US Off of Ed Nat Ed Assn & St Assn; Fmem State Com on Security & Privacy 1974; Urban League; NAACP; Omega Psi Phi Frat; MASCD; NEA; MEA; Nat Assn of Black Sch Adm; nom for alumni of yr award 1973-74; Mott Foundation Fellowship in Ed Admin 1968-69; 1st black exec sec of a St Ed Assn. **Business Addr:** 1216 Kendale Blvd East, East Lansing, MI 48823.

COLEMAN, HURLEY J., JR.
County parks and recreation director. **Personal:** Born Apr 14, 1953, Saginaw, MI; son of Martha Chatman Coleman and Hurley J Coleman Jr; married Sandra Morris, Jul 18, 1981; children: Natoya Dinise, Hurley J III, Tasha Noel. **Educ:** Eastern Michigan Univ, Ypsilanti, MI, BA, Com Recreation Admin, 1977. **Career:** Washtenaw County Parks & Recreation Com, Ann Arbor, MI, program specialist, 1977-78; Saginaw County Parks & Recreation Com, Saginaw, MI, recreation program coord, 1979-85; City of Saginaw Recreation Div, Saginaw, MI, recreation admin, 1985-89. **Orgs:** Exec mem, Michigan Recreation & Park Assn; mem, Michigan State Univ, Natural Resources/Public Policy, 1986-88; mem exec bd, Saginaw County Leadership Saginaw Program, 1987-88; chmn, Governor's Recreation Advisory Comm, 1988-; pres-elect, Michigan Recreation & Park Assn, 1988; mem, Michigan State Univ, Michigan Outdoor Recreation Task Force, 1988; comm mem, Natl Recreation & Park Assn; mem, Natl Forum for Black Public Admin, United Way of Saginaw County, Kappa Alpha Psi Fraternity; various church affiliations; past mem, Saginaw Human Relations Comm, Optimist Club, Lions Club; Ethnic Minority Society, Natl Rec & Park Assn, bd mem, 1987-96, pres-elect, 1995, pres, 1995-96. **Honors/Awds:** Ten Outstanding Young People in Michigan, Jaycees, 1986; Distinguished Alumni, Eastern Michigan Univ, 1988; Community Service, A Phillip Randolph Inst, 1988; Service Award, Natl Parks & Recreation Assoc, 1991, Presidential Award, 1995; NRPA EMS Young Professional Award, 1993; MRPA Fellowship Award, 1994; Employee of the Year, 1996. **Business Addr:** Wayne County Parks and Recreation Dir, 33175 Ann Arbor Trail, Westland, MI 48185.

COLEMAN, JAMES WILLIAM
Builder. **Personal:** Born Mar 29, 1935, Mound Bayou, MS; son of Harriet B Coleman and Gus C Coleman Sr; married Lois Bradley Coleman, Sep 12, 1964; children: Bradley C. **Educ:** Tougaloo College, BS, 1957; Tuskegee University, MS, 1965; University of Louisville, PhD, 1972. **Career:** Joseph E Seagram & Sons, Inc, senior research scientist, 1969-85; Coleman Builders, builder, currently. **Orgs:** Beta Kappa Chi Scientific Society, 1958-; American Society for Microbiology, 1958-85; NAACP, Louisville Branch, first vice pres, 1972-74, 1990-92. **Military Serv:** US Air Force, a1c, 1958-62. **Home Addr:** 8622 Blackpool Dr, Louisville, KY 40222, (502)426-5815.

COLEMAN, JEAN ELLEN
Librarian. **Personal:** Born in Brooklyn, NY; daughter of Hughie Boyer Coleman and John Milton Coleman. **Educ:** Hunter Coll, AB, MS; Pratt Inst, MLS; Rutgers Univ, PhD candidate. **Career:** San Carlos Indian School, teacher, 1957-58; Jewish Guild for the Blind, teacher, 1958-62; Lexington School for the Deaf, assistant librarian, 1964-65; Brooklyn Public Library, children's librarian, Bedford branch, 1965-66, assistant coordinator, central children's room, 1966-68; Central Brooklyn Model Cities, Brooklyn, NY, librarian administrator, 1968-73; American Library Association, Office for Library Outreach Services, Chicago, IL, director, 1973-86. **Orgs:** Member, American Library Association, 1971-; life member, Beta Phi Mu Theta Chapter, 1964-. **Honors/Awds:** Outstanding Student Award, Beta Phi Mu Theta Chapter, Pratt Institute, 1964; Outstanding Service, American Library Association Black Caucus of Librarians, 1982, 1986.

COLEMAN, JOHN H.
Government employee. **Personal:** Born Jul 29, 1928, Memphis; married Willa Nicholson; children: Patrice, Sylvia, John, Jr, Elissia, Tracey. **Educ:** IN U, BS phys educ 1951; IL U. **Career:** Quad Co IL Dept of Pub Aid, bldg operation supvr 1974-; adminstrv asst 1972; ofc mgr 1969; caseworker 1959; worked steel mills post ofc 1955-59. **Orgs:** Mem planning com IL Welfare Assn; bd mem Strong Cntr; Maple Park United Meth Ch; prog chmn Maple Park Meth Men's Club; vice pres 116 Ada St Block Club; mem Maple Park Homeowners Assn. **Military Serv:** USAF 1951-55. **Business Addr:** 624 S Michigan, Chicago, IL.

COLEMAN, JOSEPH E.
Councilman. **Personal:** Born Oct 8, 1922, West Point, MS; married Jessie L Bryant; children: 3. **Educ:** BS chem 1948; MS 1952; LlB 1963; LlD 1967; LHD 1969; AHC 1972. **Career:** Celanese Corp NY Hdq, patent atty 1962-65; USDA, res chem; City Council Philadelphia city planner 1965-71, councilman 1972, pres of council 1980-. **Orgs:** Mem Philadelphia Bar Assn; PA Bar Assn; mem all comm & civic organ in 8th Councilmanic Dist. **Honors/Awds:** Recip Gold Bond Awdd Am Oil Chem Soc 1957. **Military Serv:** USAF cpl. **Business Addr:** President, Philadelphia City Council, Room 494, City Hall, Philadelphia, PA 19107.

COLEMAN, KENNETH L.
Computer co. executive. **Personal:** Born Dec 1, 1942, Centralia, IL; married Caretha; children: Kennetha, Karen, Kimberly, Kristen, Kenneth. **Educ:** OH State Univ, BS Indus Mgmt 1965, MBA 1972. **Career:** Hewlett-Packard Co, corp staffing mgr division personnel, mgr northern European personnel, mgr 1972-82; Activision Inc, vice pres human resources, vice pres prod develop; Silicon Graphics Computer Systems, vice pres admin, currently. **Orgs:** Mem St of CA MESA Bd 1984-85; bd mem Bay Area Black United Fund 1984-85; mem Univ of Santa Clara Indus Adv Comm 1984-85; mem OH State Bus Adv Bd 1984-85; mem past pres Peninsula Assoc of Black Pers Admin 1975-; industry advisor, Bay Area Black MBA Association; bd mem, San Francisco Exploratorium, Ohio State University College of Business Dean's Advisory Council; bd mem, Children's Health Council; bd mem, The Community Foundation of Santa Clara County; bd mem, University of California San Francisco. **Honors/Awds:** Awd for Excellence in Comm Serv San Jose CA 1981. **Military Serv:** USAF capt 1968-72.

COLEMAN, LEMON, JR.
Educational administrator. **Personal:** Born Jan 14, 1935, Pineville, LA; son of Bessie Coleman and Lemon Coleman Sr; married Dorothy Ruth Wilson; children: Valerie. **Educ:** Grambling State Univ, BS 1957; So Univ, EdM 1968. **Career:** Pinecrest State School for the Mentally Retarded, teacher, recreation worker 1957; CC Raymond High School Lecompte, coach, teacher 1960-69; Lincoln State Hospital, rec sup therapist 1964; Boyce High School, coach, teacher 1969-71; Rapides High School, asst principal 1971-72; Slocum High School, asst principal 1972-73; Pineville High School, asst principal 1973-80, principal 1980; Pineville Jr High, principal, currently. **Orgs:** Mem Natl Ed Assoc 1957, LA Ed Assoc 1957, Rapides Parish Ed Assoc 1957; asst exec dir Rapides Parish Poverty Agency 1965; mem Central LA Hosp Bd 1970-, Goals LA Comm 1970, Priorities for LA Conv 1979; mayor pro-tem 1979,83; del 8th Cong Dist Dem Party Natl Conv 1980; mem NAACP; bd of dir Family Serv Agency; mem Reg VI mental Health Bd, Omega Psi Phi, Bro & Sisters Solidarity, Pineville Neighborhood Council, N Rapides Civic & Polit Org, Natl Black Caucus; bd of dir Boys Club of Alexandria-Pineville. **Honors/Awds:** 1st Negro Mem City Pineville Recreation Bd; 1st Negro City Councilman History Pineville; 1st Negro Mem Central LA Hosp Bd Dir. **Military Serv:** USAR E-3. **Business Addr:** Principal, Pineville Jr High School, 501 Edgewood Drive, Pineville, LA 71360.

COLEMAN, LEONARD
Professional baseball executive. **Career:** Office of the Baseball Commissioner, Market Development, director; Natl League of Pro Baseball, Major League Baseball, president, 1994-. **Orgs:** Major League Baseball, exec council. **Special Achievements:** One of the highest ranking African-American executives in the sports world; Only the second African-American to assume the role of president of the Natl League. **Business Addr:** President, Natl League of Pro Baseball, Major League Baseball, 350 Park Ave, New York, NY 10022, (212)371-7300.

COLEMAN, MARCO DARNELL
Professional football player. **Personal:** Born Dec 18, 1969, Dayton, OH; married Katrina. **Educ:** Georgia Tech, majored in management. **Career:** Miami Dolphins, defensive end, 1992-95; San Diego Chargers, 1996-. **Honors/Awds:** Sports Illustrated, NFL Rookie of the Year, 1992; Football News, Defensive Rookie of the Year, 1992. **Business Addr:** Professional Football Player, San Diego Chargers, Qualcomm Stadium, 9449 Friars Rd, San Diego, CA 92108, (619)280-2111.

COLEMAN, MARCUS
Professional football player. **Personal:** Born May 24, 1974, Dallas, TX. **Educ:** Texas Tech, attended. **Career:** New York Jets, defensive back, 1996-. **Business Addr:** Professional Football Player, New York Jets, 1000 Fulton Ave, Hempstead, NY 11550, (516)560-8100.

COLEMAN, MARIAN M.
Educator. **Personal:** Born Aug 7, 1948, Laurens Co. **Educ:** Friendship Jr Coll, AA 1967; Claflin Coll, BS 1969. **Career:** Gleams Community Action Inc, counselor 1974-; Comprehensive Employment Training Act, couns; Laurens Community Action Inc, social worker 1973-74; Pamplico Middle School, instructor 1970-72; Benning Terrace Recreation Center, recreational specialist 1970; Palmetto High School, instructor 1969-70. **Orgs:** Mem SC Head Start Assn 1975; mem SC Educ Assn 1969-73; advisor Youth Chap NAACP 1974; asst sec April Shower Chap 184 OES 1974-75; asst sec Union Bd White Plain Bapt Ch 1973-75. **Business Addr:** PO Box 1001, Laurens, SC.

COLEMAN, MELVIN D.
Psychologist. **Personal:** Born Oct 9, 1948, Cleveland, OH; son of Neda Coleman and James Coleman. **Educ:** Univ of WI Stout, BS 1969, MS 1974; Univ of MN Extension, certificate, behavioral analysis, 1978. **Career:** Youth Employment Org, youth counselor summers 1967-68; Cuyahoga County Welfare, social worker 1969-70; OH Youth Commn, parole officer 1970; Univ of WI Stout, teaching asst 1970-71; State of MN, med disability adj 1971-72, vocational rehab 1972-79; Harley Clinic of MN, psychologist 1978-92. **Orgs:** MN Behavioral Analysis Assoc 1978-87; consult Pilgrim Baptist Church 1984-90, Bryn Mawr & Queen Nursing Homes 1985-90; consultant Institution on Black Chemical Abuse 1990-91; established Gestalt Family Preservation Consultation Services, 1990. **Honors/Awds:** Basketball All Amer 1st Team Natl Assoc Inter Coll Ath 1969; 3rd Round Draft Choice Carolina Cougars Basketball ABA 1969; 6th Round Draft Choice Cincinnati Royals Basketball NBA 1969; Univ of WI Stout Basketball Hall of Fame 1978; established Gestalt Publications as distribution outlet for positive black literature; The Black Gestalt 1987; Reclaiming The Black Child 1989; Florence Meets Africa: A Jazz Concerto 1988; BC & Phoenicia, 1998. **Home Addr:** 3828 Clinton Ave So, Minneapolis, MN 55409.

COLEMAN, MICHAEL BENNETT
City official, attorney. **Personal:** married Frankie L Coleman; children: Kimberly, Justin, John David. **Educ:** Univ of Cincinnati, bachelor's, political science, 1977; University of Dayton School of Law, JD, 1980. **Career:** City of Columbus, councilman, 1992-; City Council's Finance & Zoning Comm, chair, currently; Council Utilities's Safety & Judiciary, development, rules & reference committees; Schottenstein, Zox & Dunn, partner. **Orgs:** Union Grove Baptist Church; Ohio State Bar Assn, council of delegates, 1990-; American Bar Assn, Minority Counsel Demonstration Program, 1990-; Robert B Elliot Law Club, vice pres, 1989; Natl Conf of Black Lawyers, 1980-; Downtown Devt Corporation's Retailer's Task Force, 1987; Columbus Convention Center Citizens Advisory Group, 1986; Comm Housing Network Inc; CMACAO; Columbus Youth Corps, Inc; Rosemont Ctr; Veterans Memorial Convention Ctr; Black Family Adoption; Central OH Transit Authority, bd mem; numerous others. **Honors/Awds:** Columbus Bar Assn, Community Service Award; Citizen's Leadership Award; WCKX Citizen of the Week. **Special Achievements:** Accomplishments since becoming city councilman: Urban Recovery Fair to repair and rebuild the inner-city; Boys to Men Volunteers Fair (mentor program); Bikeway Advisory Committee, which designed and constructed bikeways, bikepaths, and bike routes; Neighborhood Partnership Fund; Central City Development Corp; Summer Urban Repair & Fix-Up Program; "Constituency Days.". **Business Addr:** Councilman, Columbus City Council, 90 W Broad St, Columbus, OH 43215.

COLEMAN, MICHAEL VICTOR
Government official, attorney. **Personal:** Born Oct 12, 1953, Detroit, MI; son of Mary Elizabeth Coleman (deceased) and Osborn V Coleman (deceased); married Frankie Moorhead, Jun 4, 1977; children: Lauren Coleman, Ashley Coleman, Christopher Smith. **Educ:** University of Evansville, BS, 1976; Vanderbilt University School of Law, JD, 1979. **Career:** Manson, Jackson & Associates, law clerk, 1977-78; Tennessee State Attorney Gen Office, law clerk, 1978-79; Securities Division, Tennessee Department of Insurance, staff attorney, 1979-80; Hon Horace T Ward, law clerk, 1981-82; Wildman, Harrold, Allen, Dixon & Branch, associate, 1982-84; Trotter, Smith & Jacobs, associate, 1984-88, shareholder, 1988-90; City of Atlanta, city attorney, 1990-. **Orgs:** Grady Hospital Board of Visitors, 1983-; Gate City Bar Association, chairman, CLE committee, 1984, executive committee, 1984-88; Butler Street YMCA, board of directors, 1986; American Civil Liberties Union of Georgia, board of directors, 1986-88; National Association of Securities Professionals, 1989-. **Honors/Awds:** Dollars & Sense Magazine, Outstanding Business and Professional Award, 1991. **Special Achievements:** Co-author, "Regulatory Evolution of Limited Offerings Georgia," 1984; author, "A Review of the Business Judgment Rule," 1990; panelist, The Purchase & Sale of a Going Concern, NBA Convention, 1990. **Home Addr:** 720 Delmar Ave SE, Atlanta, GA 30312, (404)627-6732. **Business Addr:** City Attorney, City of Atlanta, 68 Mitchell St SW, Ste 4100, Atlanta, GA 30335-0032, (404)330-6400.

COLEMAN, MONTE
Professional football player (retired); computer co. executive. **Personal:** Born Nov 4, 1957, Pine Bluff, AR. **Educ:** Central Arkansas Univ, attended. **Career:** Washington Redskins, linebacker, 1979-95; Decision Support Systems, vice pres of public relations, currently. **Honors/Awds:** Post-season play: NFC Championship Game, 1982, 1983, 1986, 1987, NFL Championship Game, 1982, 1983, 1987; Redskin Ring of Stars, played more games & years than any other Redskin in history, 216; helped Redskins win four Super Bowls. **Business Addr:** Professional Football Player, Washington Redskins, 21300 Redskin Dr, Ashburn, VA 22011-6100.

COLEMAN, ORNETTE
Composer, musician. **Personal:** Born Mar 19, 1930, Fort Worth, TX; married Jayne Cortez, 1954 (divorced 1964); children: Denardo. **Educ:** School of Jazz, Lenox, MA, 1959. **Career:** Tenor alto saxophone trumpet violin basson; Formed a quartet with Don Cherry, Eddie Blackwell & Charlie Haden; Recording include: "Something Else!," 1958; "Ornette," 1961; "Dancing in Your Head," 1977; "Opening the Caravan of Dreams," 1986; "Tone Dialing," 1995. **Honors/Awds:** Jazz Man of the Year, Jazz & Pop 3rd Annual Readers Poll, 1968; Guggenheim Foundation Fellow, 1967; developed theory concept called "Harmoldic" for composer & players; pioneered use of double quartets; noted for atonal style; over 100 compositions for small jazz groups & larger ensembles; works for string quartet & woodwind quintet recorded for London Symphony Orchestra. **Home Addr:** pOB 12, Canel St, New York, NY 10002.

COLEMAN, RAYMOND CATO
City official. **Personal:** Born Jun 17, 1918, Ennis, TX; married; children: 7. **Career:** So Pacific RR Co, 1943-64; City of Ennis, policeman 1965-72; Ennis, city marshal 1973-. **Orgs:** Mem Ennis Evening Lion's Club; Intl Police Chief's Assn. **Honors/Awds:** 1st Black Elected City Marshal in State of TX. **Business Addr:** 119 W Brown, Ennis, TX 75119.

COLEMAN, ROBERT A.
City official, mailman. **Personal:** Born Feb 8, 1932, Hopkinsville; married; children: Dominic Joseph. **Educ:** Paducah Community Coll. **Career:** US Postal Serv, letter carrier; Paducah, city commissioner 1973-. **Orgs:** Mem Nat Assn Letter Carriers, pres Paducah Br #383 1971, 73; chmn exec bd KY State 1974; mayor protem 1980-81; mem bd of dir Paducah McCracken-County Red Cross Chpt; mem bd of dir Boys Club of Paducah; mem advisory bd Paducah Community Coll; mem bd of dir Opportunity Industrilization Cntr; mem bd of dir Family "Y" of Paducah mem KY Crime Commission. **Honors/Awds:** 32 Degree Mason; past master Stone Sq Lodge #5; former editor Masonic Herald. **Military Serv:** USAF sgt 1950-54. **Business Addr:** US Post Office & City Hall, Paducah, KY 42001.

COLEMAN, ROBERT EARL, JR.
Journalist. **Personal:** Born Jan 27, 1961, St Louis, MO; son of Fredonia West Coleman and Robert E Coleman Sr. **Educ:** St Louis University, St Louis, MO, BA, 1987. **Career:** KMOX-AM, St Louis, MO, writer, editor, 1982-83; Church of God in Christ, St Louis, MO, dir of public relations, 1984-90; KTVI-TV, St Louis, MO, St Louis, MO, video tape editor, 1983-. **Orgs:** Member, National Assoc of Black Journalists, 1987-; member, Greater St Louis Assoc of Black Journalists, 1987-; member, National Academy of TV Arts and Sciences, 1987-; member, NAACP, 1988-. **Honors/Awds:** Delegate Elect to Inter Radio & TV Society Workshop, 1984; Best Business & Professional Speech, St Louis Univ, 1985; Best Video Content Award, United Press International, 1987, 1988; Emmy Nominee, St Louis Chapter (NATAS), 1988, 1992; Double Black Excellence Award Winner, St Louis Assoc of Black Journalists, 1989; Graduate of the Poynter Institute for Media Studies, 1990.

COLEMAN, ROBERT L.
Business executive. **Career:** Composite Holdings LLC, chair, currently. **Business Addr:** Chairman, Composite Holdings LLC, 1537 Knollway Dr, St Louis, MO 63135-1405, (314)522-2337.

COLEMAN, RODNEY ALBERT
Government official. **Personal:** Born Oct 12, 1938, Newburgh, NY; son of Reba Belden Coleman and Samuel C Coleman (deceased); divorced; children: Terri Lynne, Stephen A. **Educ:** Howard Univ, Washington, DC, BArch, 1963; Univ of Michigan, Ann Arbor, MI, Exec Mgmt Program, 1988. **Career:** US Air Force, captain/project architect, 1963-73; The White House, White House Fellow, 1970-71; District of Columbia City Council, exec asst to chmn, 1973-78; Pennsylvania Ave Devel Corp, design consultant, 1978-80; General Motors Corp, dir of government relations, 1980-85, dir of municipal govt affairs, 1985-90, executive dir of urban and municipal affairs, 1990-94; US Air Force, asst secretary, Dept of Air Force, 1994-. **Orgs:** White House Fellows Assn, 1971-; bd of dir, Natl Council for Urban Economic Devel, 1986-93; corporate representative, Natl League of Cities, 1986-94, The US Conference of Mayors, 1986-94; alternate representative to bd, New Detroit Inc, 1986-94, Detroit Economic Growth Corp, 1986-94; Urban Affairs Comm, Greater Detroit, Chamber of Commerce, 1986-94, corporate representative, Natl Forum for Black Public Admin, 1987-94; Executive Leadership Council, 1991-. **Honors/Awds:** Pony Baseball Man of the Year, Pony League, Newburgh, NY, 1960; Distinguished Alumus Award, Newburgh Free Academy, 1994; The Air Force Commendation Medal, 1965; The Air Force Meritorious Service Medal, 1968; Republic of Vietnam Honor Medal, 1972; The Bronze Star Medal, 1972; Distinguished Alumni Award for Postgraduate Achievement in Corporate and Government Service, Howard University, 1996; The Tuskegee Airmen, Distinguished Achievement Award, 1996; The Black Engineer of the Year Dean's Award, 1996; US Air Force, Execptional Civilian Service Award, 1997. **Military Serv:** USAF Captain, project architect, 1963-73. **Business Addr:** Asst Secretary, US Air Force 4E 1020, The Pentagon, Washington, DC 20330.

COLEMAN, RONALD GERALD
Educator, association executive. **Personal:** Born Apr 3, 1944, San Francisco, CA; son of Gertrude Coleman Hughes and Jesse Coleman; children: Danielle D, Joron S, Cori D. **Educ:** Univ of UT, BS Sociology 1966, PhD History 1980; CA State Univ Sacramento, CA teaching certificate secondary 1968, MA Social Science 1973. **Career:** General Mills Inc, grocery sales rep 1966-67; San Francisco Unified Sch Dist, faculty teacher social studies phys ed 1968-70; Sacramento City Coll, faculty instructor social science 1970-73; Univ of UT, dir of Afro-Amer studies 1981-, coord of ethnic studies 1984-; CA State Univ Haywood, visiting prof Afro-Amer studies 1981; Univ of UT, prof of history, Diversity and Faculty Development, associate vice president 1989-. **Orgs:** Consultant UT State Cultural Awareness Training Prog 1974-76; consultant UT State Bd of Educ 1981; consultant UT State Historical Soc 1981; mem UT Endowment for the Humanities 1982-88; commissioner Salt Lake City Civil Service Comm 1983-; chairperson Salt Lake City Branch NAACP Educ Comm 1984-85; mem UT Chapter American Civil Liberties Union 1989-; mem Salt Lake Sports Advisory Board 1990-. **Honors/Awds:** "Blacks in Pioneer Utah 1847-1869" UOMOJA Scholar/Journal of Black Studies 1979; "Blacks in Utah History: An Unknown Legacy" The Peoples of Utah 1976; "The Buffalo Soldiers, Guardians of the Uintah Frontier 1886-1901" Utah Historical Quarterly 1979; Martin Luther King Jr: Apostle of Social Justice, Peace and Love pamphlet printed for Univ of Utah Martin Luther King Jr Comm 1985; Phi Kappa Phi 1979; Merit Society for Distinguished Alumni George Washington High School; University of Utah, Hatch Price Award for Distinguished Teaching, 1990. **Business Addr:** Professor of History, University of Utah, Dept of History, Salt Lake City, UT 84112.

COLEMAN, RONALD K.
Broadcast and print journalist. **Personal:** Born May 11, 1934, Kimberley, WV; son of Emma Vaughn Coleman and Isaiah Edward Coleman; married Charissa Foster Coleman, Feb 11, 1984; children: Nikita L, Diedra M, Akevia M, Regina S, Arisa, Isaiah T. **Educ:** Ohio State University, Columbus, OH, 1953-55, Journalism, 1986; MATA College, Columbus, OH, Computer Programming, 1964; Capital University, Columbus, OH, Appropriate Technology, 1979. **Career:** CMACAO, Columbus, OH, Center Director, 1965-68; WOSU/NPR News, Columbus, OH, Morning Editor/Anchor, 1968-74; Onyx Newspaper, Columbus, OH, Associate Editor, 1974-78; Capital University, Columbus, OH, Research Associate, 1979-80; John Foster and Associates, Technical Writer, 1984-85; Vision Service Plan, Columbus, OH, Programmer/Analyst, 1985-89. **Orgs:** President/founder, Black United Fund of Central Ohio, 1986-; president/founder, Star and Crescent Parapsychology Experimental Research, 1974-81; member/assoc, Smithsonian Institution, 1975-; member, National Audubon Society, 1981; nominee, American Association for the Advancement of Science. **Honors/Awds:** Excellence in Journalism, Associated Press, 1974; poetry has been published in The Journal for the Study of Negro Life and History, and Black Children: Their Culture and Learning Styles; contributor of news articles and poetry to numerous newspapers and magazines, currently. **Military Serv:** US Army, spc-3, 1966-68; Good Conduct Medal. **Home Addr:** 1274 E 21st Ave, Columbus, OH 43211.

COLEMAN, RUDOLPH W.
Counselor, clergyman. **Personal:** Born Aug 19, 1929, Live Oak, FL; son of Dr & Mrs D C Coleman; married Cecile Bryant; children: Princess, Cheryl. **Educ:** Wilberforce U, BS 1954; Payne Seminary, BD 1956; Princeton Seminary, ThM 1968. **Career:** DE State Coll, academic counselor & coll chaplain; Mt Zion AME Ch; Var Chs, pastor 1956-74; Kent, Co, adminstrv coord & counselor for adult basic adn 1968-71. **Orgs:** Chaplain Rotary Intl 1978; Chaplain Tuskegee Airmen Inc 1989. **Honors/Awds:** Outstanding citizenship award DE State Coll 1970; AME Ch Award 1972. **Military Serv:** USAF corpl 1945-48. **Business Addr:** DE State Coll, Dover, DE 19901.

COLEMAN, RUDY B.
Judge. **Career:** Carpenter, Bennett and Morissey law firm, atty; Superior Court of NJ, judge, 1995-. **Business Addr:** Judge, Superior Court of New Jersey, Union County Courthouse, 2 Broad St, Elizabeth, NJ 07207, (908)527-4738.

COLEMAN, SINCLAIR B.
Statistician, economist. **Personal:** Born Feb 17, 1946, Halifax, VA; son of Bessie Bowman Coleman and N Wyatt Coleman. **Educ:** Hampton Inst, BA 1967; Univ of Chicago, MS 1970; Rand Graduate School, PhD, 1975. **Career:** US Congressional Budget Office, analytic staff 1976-78; The Rand Corp, rsch staff/consultant, 1968-76, 1978-. **Honors/Awds:** Woodrow Wilson Fellow, Univ of Chicago, 1967-68; Published numerous articles, reports & reviews; seminars & briefings at univs, rsch institutions, govt agencies, confs, & professional meetings. **Business Addr:** Consultant, PO Box 262, Manhattan Beach, CA 90267.

COLEMAN, TREVOR W.
Journalist. **Personal:** Born Jan 12, 1960, Hudson, NY; son of Mary C Coleman & Leonard Gresham; married Karl Elaine Coleman, Sep 3, 1988; children: Sydnie Lianne, Trevor W II. **Educ:** Ohio State University, BA, 1986. **Career:** Satin Magazine, reporter, 1985-86; The Times, reporter, 1987; The Hartford Courant, reporter, 1987-90; The Detroit News, reporter, 1990-93; The Cincinnati Enquirer, editorial writer, 1993-94; The Hartford Courant, columnist/reporter, 1994-96; The Detroit Free Press, editorial writer, 1996-. **Orgs:** The National Association of Black Journalist, 1987-; The National Conference of Editorial Writers, vice chair, 1994-; The Detroit Press Club, 1992-; Alpha Phi Alpha Fraternity Inc, 1982-; Detroit Chapter of National Association of Black Journalist, 1990-; The Ohio State University Black Alumni Society, 1990-. **Honors/Awds:** Kappa Chapter & Alpha Phi Alpha, Distinguished Alumni Award, 1992; Detroit Press Club Foundation, 1st Place Award for News Reporting, 1992; Lincoln University, Unity Award, 1st Place for Coverage of Minority Affairs & Social Issues, 1992; Best of Gannet Award, Public Service Reporting, 1992; Columbia County NAACP, Award for Distinguished Journalism, 1992; Nominated for 1992 Pulitzer Prize for Public Service Reporting. **Special Achievements:** Fellow, Knight Center for Specialized Journalism at the University of Maryland, 1996; American Press Institute, seminar for Editorial Writers & Editors, graduate, 1996; Cover Story for Emerge Magazine on Clarence Thomas, writer, Nov 1993; Cover Story for Emerge Magazine on Clarence Thomas, co-writer, Dec 1996; Author, Essay a Black Child for NABJ published "Friend of a Friend," 1996; Hudson (NY) High School, Commencement Speaker, 1994. **Business Addr:** Editorial Writer, Detroit Free Press, 321 W Lafayette, Rm 544, Detroit, MI 48226.

COLEMAN, VERONICA F.
Government official. **Personal:** daugHter of Robert and Mary Freeman. **Educ:** Howard Univ; Memphis State Univ, JD. **Career:** Federal Express Corp, senior attorney; Memphis State Univ, legal counsel to the president; district attorney; general public defender; Western District of Tennessee, US attorney, currently. **Orgs:** Tennessee Commission on Criminal Rules Procedures; Board of Law Examiners, assistant. **Special Achievements:** Third African-American female US Attorney in the country. **Business Addr:** US Attorney, Western District of Tennessee, 167 N Main, Jackson, TN 38301, (901)427-6586.

COLEMAN, WANDA
Author. **Career:** "Days of Our Lives," NBC-TV, staff writer, 1975-76; writer, poet, and performer; Loyola Marymount, Dept of English, assoc prof, Fletcher Jones Chair, 1994. **Orgs:** Writers Guild of America, West, 1969-; PEN Center, West, 1983-. **Honors/Awds:** Emmy Award, Academy of Television Arts & Sciences, 1976; Harriette Simpson Arnow Prize for Fiction, The American Voice, 1990; author, Art In The Court of The Blue Fag (chapbook), 1977; author, Mad Dog Black Lady, 1979; Grant, Natl Endowment for the Arts, 1981-82; author, Imagoes, 1983; Guggenheim Fellowship, Poetry, 1984; author, Heavy Daughter Blues: Poems & Stories 1968-86, 1987; author, A War of Eyes and Other Stories, 1988; Vesta Ward, Writing Woman's Building/LA, 1988; author, Dicksboro Hotel and Other Travels, 1989; author, African Sleeping Sickness: Stories and Poems, 1990; spoken performances include: On Voices of the Angels, 1981; On English as a Second Language, 1982; On Neighborhood Rhythms, 1984; Twin Sisters, 1985; Black Angeles,1988; Nation of Poets, 1990; High Priestess Word, 1990; Black and Blue News, 1990; Berserk On Hollywood Blvd, 1992; work has appeared in the anthologies Deep Down Inside; Poetry Loves Poetry; Yellow Silk; The Best American Poetry, 1988, 1996; Breaking Ice—Contemporary African-American Fiction. **Special Achievements:** Author: Hand Dance, 1993; Author: American Sonnets (chapbook), 1994; Author: Native in a Strange Land: Trails & Tremors, 1996. **Home Addr:** PO Box 29154, Los Angeles, CA 90029.

COLEMAN, WARREN B.
Educator. **Personal:** Born Aug 8, 1932, Swarthmore, PA; married Carole Berry; children: Warren, Kim, Fawn, Carole. **Educ:** Hampton Inst, BS 1956; PA State U, MED 1974. **Career:** PA State Univ, asst prof of physical education 1968-; Carver High School, Newport News VA, head football & track coach 1956-68. **Orgs:** Real Estate Asso; mem bd dir PSU Black Christian Fellowship; originator of Black Cultural Center PA State U. **Military Serv:** AUS 2d lt. **Business Addr:** Pennsylvania State University, Room 60 Recreation Bldg, University Park, PA 16802.

COLEMAN, WILLIAM T., JR.
Attorney. **Personal:** Born Jul 7, 1920, Germantown, PA; married Lovida Hardin; children: William T III, Livida Hardin Jr, Hardin L. **Educ:** Univ of PA, AB (summa cum laude) 1941; Attended, Harvard Bus Sch; Harvard Law Sch, LLB (magna cum laude) 1946. **Career:** Judge Herbert F Goodrich US Ct of Appeals for 3rd Circuit, law sec 1947-48; Justice Felix Frankfurter Assoc Judge Supreme Ct, law sec 1948-49; Paul Weiss Rifkind Wharton & Garrison NY, assoc 1949-52; City of Phila, spl counsel transit matters 1952-63; Dilworth Paxson Kalish Levy & Coleman, partner law firm 1956-75; retained by Gov Scranton to represent Atty Gen of PA & Commonwealth of PA in liti-

gation to remove racial restrictions at Girard Coll 1965; US Dept of Trans, sec 1975-77; SE PA Trans Auth, spl counsel 1968-; O'Melveny & Meyer, sr partner 1977-. **Orgs:** Dir Pan Am World Airways Inc; dir IBM; dir Pepsi Co; dir Chase Manhattan Corp; dir Amax Inc; dir CIGNA Corp; dir Philadelphia Elec Co; vice pres Philadelphia Museum of Art; chmn bd NAACP Legal Defense & Educ Fund; trustee The Rand Corp; trustee The Brookings Inst; fellow Amer Coll of Trial Lawyers; mem Trilateral Commn Council on Foreign Relations; officer French Legion of Honor; council Amer Law Inst; Amer Bar Assn; Amer Bar Assn Task Force on Judicial Admin; Philadelphia Bar Assn; DC Bar Assn; mem Amer Arbitration Assn; mem numerous public serv orgns. **Honors/Awds:** Author coauthor contributor numerous legal writings; Presidential Medal of Freedom recipient; NAACP Legal Defense & Educ Fund, Thurgood Marshall Lifetime Achievement Award. **Business Addr:** O'Melveny & Myers LLP, 555 13th St NW, Washington, DC 20004.

COLEMAN, WILLIAM T., III
Attorney, military official. **Career:** Pepper, Hamilton & Scheetz, partner; Department of the Army, chief legal officer, currently. **Business Addr:** General Counsel, Office of the Army, 104 Army Pentagon 2E722, Washington, DC 20310-0104, (202)697-9235.

COLEMAN, WINSON. See Obituaries section.

COLEMAN, WISDOM F.
Dentist. **Personal:** Born Jun 20, 1944, Batesville, MS; married Veronica Freemon; children: Wisdom III, Daivd, Anthony. **Educ:** Howard U, BS 1965, DDS 1969. **Career:** Emory Coll of Dentistry, instructor; VA Hospital, Atlanta GA, dentist 1970-71; VA Hospital St Louis, internship 1969-70. **Orgs:** Dental dir Memphis & Shelby Co Head Start 1974-77; exec sec Pan TN Dental Soc; pres Shelby Co Dental Soc 1974-77. **Honors/Awds:** Dean's hon soc Univ TN 1976. **Business Addr:** 3087 Park Ave, Memphis, TN 38106.

COLEMAN-BURNS, PATRICIA WENDOLYN
Educator. **Personal:** Born Nov 23, 1947, Detroit, MI; daughter of Jessie Mae Ray Coleman and Dandie Coleman; married John Burns II, Jul 29, 1977; children: Robert Burns. **Educ:** Wayne State University, Detroit, MI, BA, 1969, MA, 1978, PhD, 1987. **Career:** Motown Records, Detroit, MI, admin asst, 1969-72; Institute for Labor Studies, Detroit, MI, part time faculty, 1972-87; Wayne State University Detroit, Mi, speech comm, grad asst, 1972-76, Africana studies, grad asst, 1976-78, part-time faculty, 1976-, Africana studies, lecturer, 1978-91; University of Michigan, assistant professor, director, office of multicultural affairs, 1991-. **Orgs:** Member, chairperson, WSU President's Commission on Status of Women, 1985-1989; member, Pres Council of Non-Discrimination, Affirmative Action, 1986-90; member, pres board of directors, Women's Justice Center, 1990-;. **Honors/Awds:** Minority Faculty Research Awards: WSU, 1987-88, U of M, 1992-93; Woman of the Year, Dorcas Society, 1988; Article, African-American Women in Higher Educ Sex Roles, 1989; Participant, Summer Institute for Women in Higher Education, 1990; Fellowship, National Council of Black Studies, 1990. **Business Addr:** Assistant PRO, Director, Multicultural Affairs, School of Nursing, University of Michigan, Ann Arbor, MI 48109-0482.

COLEMAN MORRIS, VALERIE DICKERSON
Journalist. **Personal:** Born Nov 25, 1946, Philadelphia, PA; daughter of Vivien A Dickerson and William O Dickerson; married Robert Lee Morris Jr, Dec 31, 1993; children: Michon Allyce, Ciara Ashley. **Educ:** San Jose State College, BS, 1968; Columbia University Graduate School of Journalism, BA, 1969. **Career:** KRON-TV, production assistant & researcher, 1969-73; KGO-TV, reporter, 1974-79; KRON-TV, news anchor/reporter, 1979-82; KGO-TV, news anchor/reporter, 1982-85; KCBS-Radio, news anchor, 1985-87; KCBS-TV, news anchor/reporter, 1987-89; KCBS-Radio, news anchor, beginning 1989; WPIX-TV, reporter, currently. **Orgs:** Delta Sigma Theta Sorority, 1968-; Oakland Bay Area Links, 1989-; Hearing Society for the Bay Area, vp, 1983-; Chronic Fatigue Foundation, advisory board, 1984-; Children's Hosp, board of directors, 1990-92; Alumnae Resources, vp, 1990-. **Honors/Awds:** Received three Emmy Awards between 1975 and 1988; RTNDA Best Live Coverage News Story, Class A Division, "Earthquake" 1987; Soulbeat Civic Award, 1990; National Organization for Women, Los Angeles Chapter, Award of Courage, 1987. **Special Achievements:** Contributing editor, Northern California Women Magazine, 1992-. **Business Addr:** Reporter, WPIX-TV, 220 E 42nd St, 10th Fl, New York, NY 10017, (212)949-1100.

COLEMON, JOHNNIE (JOHNNIE COLEMON NEDD)
Clergyman. **Personal:** Born in Centerville, AL; daughter of Lula Haley and John Haley; married Don Nedd. **Educ:** Wiley Coll, BA 1943, DD 1977, DHL. **Career:** Chicago Mkt Cntr, price analyst; Chicago Pub Schools, teacher; Christ Univ Temple, fdr; Christ Univ Temple for Better Living, pastor, fdr, 1974-; Johnnie Coleman Institute, fdr, pres, 1974-. **Orgs:** Elect pres (1st Black woman) of exec bd Unity Sch of Christianity; orgn of Univ Found for Better Living (UFBL); guest spkr Festival of Mind & Body in London, Eng; guest spkr & consult seen on radio & TV shows; mem Intl Thought Alliance; dist pres & bd of dir chrprsn 60th anniv INTA Congress; dedication of largest New Thought Church in the World 4,000 seating 1985; guest speaker AKA Boule 1986; guest speaker Prayer Breakfast Atlanta GA. **Honors/Awds:** Tremendous "Ten Years" Unity Chicagoland Assn 1966; Deep Appreciation of Unity Assn of Unity Churches 1969-70; major contributions Assn of Unity Churches 1970; Golden Anniv Awd Alpha Kappa Alpha Sor 1972; Recognition Awd Serv to Humanity 1st CP Church 1972; Serv to Youth YMCA 1973; Outstndg Achvmnt in Gospel Ministry Youth for Christ 1974; Love with Sincere Appreciation Award Hillside Chapel & Truth Ctr 1974; Outstndg Christian Serv Civic Liberty League of IL 1974; Women's Day Annual Black Excell Operation PUSH 1974; "The Year of the Woman" Award PUSH Found 1975; Cert of Apprec Chicago Cncl BSA 1975; Cert of Appreciation Comm Civic & Cultural Affairs 1975; Outstanding & Dedicated Serv as chairperson 60th Anniversary INTA Congress 1975; Blackbook's Humanit AwdBlackbook Bus & Ref Guide 1; Excellence in Religion PUSH Foundation 1977; 100 Outstanding Black Women Dallas 1985; Blackbook's Par Excellence 1986; Dr Martin L King Drum Major Awd 1987; Awds and Key to the Cities Brooklyn NY, Atlanta GA, Detroit MI, Chicago IL; Candace Awd 1987; "A Woman Called Johnnie" TV Channel 2; Appreciation Award for Service Thompson Company Singers 1989; Stellar Award For Inspiration Central City Productions 1991. **Business Addr:** Pastor, Christ Univ Temple Better Liv, 11901 So Ashland Ave, Chicago, IL 60643.

COLES, ANNA BAILEY
Educational administrator (retired). **Personal:** Born Jan 16, 1925, Kansas City, KS; daughter of Lillie Mai Buchanan Thomas and Gordon Alonzo Bailey; married Herbert R Coles, May 19, 1953 (divorced); children: Margot, Michelle, Gina. **Educ:** Avila College, Kansas City, MO, BS, nursing, 1958; Catholic University of America, Washington, DC, MS, nursing, 1960, PhD, 1967. **Career:** VA Hosp, Topeka, KS, supervisor, 1950-58; Freedmen's Hosp, Washington, DC, director of nursing, 1961-68; Howard Univ Coll of Nursing, Washington, DC, dean 1968-86. **Orgs:** Member, Institute of Medicine, 1974-; member, National League for Nursing, 1966-; member, Alpha Kappa Alpha Sorority, 1950-; member-president, Societas Docta, Inc, 1987-. **Honors/Awds:** Sustained superior Performance, Dept of Health, Education, and Welfare, 1965; Avila Medal of Honor, Avila College, 1967; Distinguished Alumni Award, Howard University, 1990; Director of Minority Development University of Kansas School of Nurshing, Kansas City, Kansas, 1991-95. **Home Addr:** 15107 Interlachem Dr, #205, Silver Spring, MD 20906-5627.

COLES, BIMBO (VERNELL EUFAYE)
Professional basketball player. **Personal:** Born Apr 22, 1968, Covington, VA. **Educ:** Virginia Polytechnic Institute and State Univ, Blacksburg, VA, 1986-90. **Career:** Miami Heat, guard, 1990-96; Golden State Warriors, 1996-. **Honors/Awds:** Member of the US Olympic team, 1988. **Business Addr:** Professional Basketball Player, Golden State Warriors, 1001 Broadway, Oakland, CA 94607, (510)986-2200.

COLES, DARNELL
Professional baseball player. **Personal:** Born Jun 2, 1962, San Bernardino, CA; married Shari; children: Deanna. **Educ:** Orange Coast College, Costa Mesa, CA, attended. **Career:** Seattle Mariners, infielder 1983-85; Detroit Tigers, infielder, 1986-87; Pittsburgh Pirates, infielder/outfielder, 1987-88; Seattle Mariners, infielder/outfielder, 1988-90; Detroit Tigers, infielder/outfielder, 1990; Toronto Blue Jays, beginning 1992; St Louis Cardinals, currently. **Business Addr:** Professional Baseball Player, St Louis Cardinals, Busch Memorial Stadium, 250 Stadium Plaza, St Louis, MO 63102, (314)421-3060.

COLES, JOHN EDWARD
Chief executive officer. **Personal:** Born Jul 18, 1951, Roanoke, VA; married Jerelena Perdue; children: Caron N, Jonlyn E, John E Jr, Christin N. **Educ:** TN State Univ, 1969-70; Hampton Univ, BS Bus Mgmt 1973; Golden Gate Univ,. **Career:** Citizens Bdgt Advsry Cmt, mem 1980-81; Consumer Crdt Cnslng of Peninsula, mem 1982 bd of educ City of Hampton, VA, mem 1982-83; A Bldrs of VA, dir1983-; People's Sav & Loan, chief exec ofcr. **Orgs:** Mem VA Peninsula Econ Dev Cncl 1982-; life mem NAACP, Omega Psi Phi Frat, Inc; tres Peninsula Assc for Mental Retrdtn 1982-84; pres Citizen's Boys' Clb of Hampton 1982-84; keeper of fin Omega Psi Phi Frat Zeta Omicron 1977-80. **Honors/Awds:** Otstndg Young Men of Am Awrd 1981; Distngshd Ldrshp Awrd United Negro Clg Fund 1982; Omega Man of Yr Omega Psi Phi Frat Zeta Omicron Chptr Hampton, VA 1982. **Home Addr:** 7 Balmoral Dr, Hampton, VA 23669.

COLES, JOSEPH C.
Association executive. **Personal:** Born Aug 26, 1902, South Boston, VA; married Ruth White; children: Joseph C, Jr. **Educ:** Paine Coll; Howard U. **Career:** Bankruptcy, trustee; MI Civ Serv Comm, hearings offcr & mediat 1969-72. **Orgs:** Asst dir Detroit Comm on Human Rights Fdr; vchmn & mem Bd of Natl Assn of Intergroup Rel Officials; mem Bd of Nat Alumni Coun of Unit Negro Coll Fund for 10 Yrs; official Office of Price Adminstrn in WA, WW II; founder vice chmn MI Chap of Unit Negro Coll Fund; bd mem SW Gen Hosp; memexec bd of Paine Coll Natl Alumni Assn Natl Leader, Dem 30 yrs; mem ex-chmn Freedom Fund Dinner of the NAACP for 20 yrs. **Honors/Awds:** 1st black del to St Dem Conv 1928; cited by NAACP at Natl Conv, Atlantic City for raisiing highest amount to date 1968; cited by Natl Alumni CounUnit Coll Fund at Ann Conv in New Orleans 1967; cited comm leadership Booker T Wash Bus Assn 1964; inv to White House in honor of Prime Min of Australia Pres Johnson 1964; attend Civil Rights Meet at White House Pres Johnson; mem JFK staff Natl Dem Conv 1960; consult Unit Conf of Mayor's Dept of Race Rel for several yrs; guest of Pres Truman on his train from Grand Rapids to Det, 1st black to be so honored 1948; honored at Testimonial Dinner 1974.

COLES, KIM
Actress, writer, producer. **Personal:** Born Jan 11, Brooklyn, NY; divorced. **Career:** Comedian, currently; actress, currently. **Special Achievements:** Starred in "In Living Color;" "Living Single;" Performed "Homework", HERE Theater in NYC; wrote "I'm Free, But It'll Cost You: The Single Life According to Kim Coles," 1997.

COLES, ROBERT TRAYNHAM
Architect. **Personal:** Born Aug 24, 1929, Buffalo, NY; son of Helena Vesta Traynham Coles and George Edward Coles; married Sylvia Rose Meyn; children: Marion B, Darcy E. **Educ:** MIT, MArch 1955; Univ of MN, BArch 1953, BA 1951; Hampton Inst, attended. **Career:** Perry Shaw Hepburn & Dean 1955-57, Shepley Bulfinch Richardson & Abbot 1957-58, Carl Koch & Assoc 1958-59, designer; Boston Architectural Ctr 1957-59, NY State Univ Coll 1967, Hampton Inst 1968-70, Univ of KS 1969, teacher; Adv Planning Assoc, assoc 1959-60; Techbuilt Inc, design mgr 1959-60; Deleuw Cather & Brill Engrs, coord architect 1960-63; Robert Traynham Coles Architect PC, pres 1963-; Amer Inst Architects, dep vice pres minority affairs 1974-75; University of Kansas, professor architecture & urban studies; Carnegie Mellon University, Pittsburgh, PA, assoc prof, 1990-. **Orgs:** Fellow AIA 1981, exec committee, 1990-95, chancellor, 1995; consult Union Carbide Corp 1963; lecturer many coll & univ; treas 1975-77, vice pres 1977-79 Natl Org of Minority Architects; sec bd of dir Preservation League of NY State Inc 1976-; AIA, Comm Planning Assistance Ctr, Assoc Comm Design Devel Ctrs, NY State Assoc Architects; mayors adv com Buffalo Urban Caucus, BANC, Cit Adv Council, Goals Met Buffalo, comm Urban Univ, E Side Comm Org, Ellicott Talbert Study Comm, NY State Sub-Com US Comm Civil Rights, Com Community Improvement, Friendship House Study Comm; vice pres Buffalo Arch Guidebook Corp 1979-82; pres Amer Arch Mus & Resource Ctr 1980-82; trustee Western NY Public Broadcasting Assoc 1981-; NY State Bd for Architecture 1984-; commissioner, Erie County Horizons Waterfront Committee, 1989-94; chairperson, NY State Board for Architecture, 1990-91. **Honors/Awds:** Whitney E Young Awd AIA 1981; Outstanding Prof Achievement Urban League 1961; Langston Hughes Distinguished Professor of Architecture & Urban Design, Univ of Kansas 1989; Sam Gibbons Chair Nominee, University of South Florida, Tampa, FL, 1990; Centennial Medal, Medaille College 1975; Honorary Doctor of Letter, Medaille College 1975. **Business Addr:** President, Robert Traynham Coles Arch PC, 730 Ellicot Square, Buffalo, NY 14203.

COLEY, DONALD LEE
Educator. **Personal:** Born Feb 25, 1953, Baltimore, MD; son of Emma Harrell Sessoms and Letell Sessoms; married Linda Carol McNair, Jun 23, 1979; children: Natasha Shenee Coley. **Educ:** St Augustine's Coll, BS (Cum Laude) 1975; East Carolina Univ, MAEd 1983. **Career:** Wake County Schools, teacher/coach 1975-79; Bertie Co Schools, coach/director alternative adjustment 1980-83; New York Yankees, scout 1978-91; Montreal Expos, scout 1991-; BHS Extended Day School, principal, 1983-89, dropout prevention coord, 1989-92, dir of student services, 1992-95; Windsor Elem Sch, principal, 1995-. **Orgs:** Mem State of NC AAA Championship Basketball Team 1971; head coach of championship teams baseball 1976,78, football 1978, basketball 1980, 1982; chairperson Bertie County Youth Task Force 1981-87; mem Palestine Masonic Lodge 1982-; rep NC Extended Day Assoc 1985-87; mem NCAE, NEA 1986-87, Kiwanis Intl 1986-, NC Employment & Training Assoc 1986-; consultant/dropout prevention Weldon City Schools 1986; commentator of weekly radio program "Extended Day School Highlights"; mem NC Employment and Training Assoc; vice pres, NC Dropout Prevention Assn, 1988-; pastor, St John 2nd Baptist Church, 1987-; asst pastor, Indian Woods Baptist Church, 1988-90; pres, Grace Unlimited Consulting Service; pastor, Elm Grove Baptist Church, 1990. **Honors/Awds:** Phi Beta Signia Scholarship 1973; Drop Prevention Leadership Exchange, NC Dept of Public Instruction, 1988; Exemplary Program in Dropout Prevention, NC State Bd of Educ; Author: Effectively Serving At-Risk Children, 1996; Southeastern US Award Winner, Alcohol/Drug Prevention, 1996. **Home Addr:** PO Box 7, Powellsville, NC 27967. **Business Addr:** 104 Cooper Hill Rd, Windsor, NC 27983.

COLIN, GEORGE H.
Educator, funeral director. **Personal:** Born Apr 15, Cleveland, OH. **Educ:** Coll Conservatory of Music Cincinnati, Mus B; Temple Bible Coll, AB; Miami U, AM; Temple Bible Coll & Sem, SMD. **Career:** Geo H Colin Mortuary, owner; Cincinnati, min music 22 yrs; Cincinnati, tchr music 15 yrs. **Orgs:** Pres Buckeye State Funeral Dirs & Embalmers Assn; bd dirs NAACP & Cincinnati Br; trustee Temple Bible Coll; bd mem Small Business Found Cincinnati; mem Phi Mu Alpha Frat; Hamilton Co Black Caucus; Amer Guild of Organists; Local, State, & Natl Funeral Dirs Assn. **Honors/Awds:** Recip Hon Dr of Music 1962. **Military Serv:** AUS sp4.

COLLETON, KATRINA
Professional basketball player. **Personal:** Born Nov 22, 1968; daughter of Pamela Colleton. **Educ:** Univ of Maryland, bachelor's degree in criminal justice. **Career:** Los Angeles Sparks, guard, 1997-. **Business Addr:** Professional Basketball Player, Los Angeles Sparks, 3900 W Manchester Blvd, Inglewood, CA 90306, 800-978-9622.

COLLEY, NATHANIEL S.
Playwright. **Personal:** Born Jun 8, 1956, Sacramento; son of Jerlean J Colley and Nathaniel S Colley, Sr; married Toni Denise Conner (divorced); children: Jasmine Nicole, Aishah Simone, Mazuri Francis. **Educ:** University of Michigan, BA, 1977, Law School, JD, 1979; UC Davis, graduate study, anthropology. **Career:** Colley-Lindsey & Colley, partner, 1980; Sextus Products (entertainment), partner, 1974-; WCBN-FM Radio Station, general manager, 1979, program director, 1978, talk show host, 1976-78, disc jockey, 1974-76; playwright, currently. **Orgs:** California Bar Assn, 1980; American Legion Boy's State CA, 1973; California Youth Senate, 1973; University of Michigan Assn of Black Communicators, 1974; vice pres, Sacramento NAACP Youth Council, 1973-74; natl bd dirs, NAACP 1972-75; Black Music Assn, 1979-. **Honors/Awds:** Natl Merit Scholarship Finalist, 1974. **Special Achievements:** Playwright: ''The Shoebox,'' Lorraine Hansberry Theatre; ''A Sensitive Man,''; Moving Arts, LA Winner of 5 Dramalogue Awards; film: ''The Abortion of Mary Williams,''; finalist ''Showtime's Black Filmmaker Program,'' premiered on Showtime, 1998. **Business Addr:** PO Box 741825, Los Angeles, CA 90004.

COLLIE, KELSEY E.
Educator, playwright, talent agent. **Personal:** Born Feb 21, 1935, Miami, FL; son of Elizabeth Malinda Moxey Collie and James George Collie; divorced; children: Kim Denyse, Vaughn Hayse. **Educ:** Hampton Inst, AB 1967; George Washington Univ, MFA 1970; Howard Univ, PhD. **Career:** Library of Congress, accessioner & documents librarian 1960-70; Coll of Fine Arts Drama Dept, prof, asst dean 1976-79; Kelsey E Collie Playmakers Repertory Co, artistic dir 1976-; Diva Productions, artistic dir 1986; Howard Univ Children's Theatre, playwright; Kelsey E Collie Talent Assoc, talent mgr; Howard Univ, prof of drama 1973-. **Orgs:** Bd dir Pierce Warwick Adoption Serv 1973-89; mem Amer Community Theatre Assn 1977-; Theatre Arts Productions Inc 1980-87; mem Artist-in-Educ Panel DC Commission on the Arts 1983-85; mem Amer Council on the Arts 1985-; mem Black Theatre Network 1986-; artistic dir, Color Me Human Players, 1986-; pres, OPM Productions, 1991-. **Honors/Awds:** Community Serv Award, Salisbury Cultural Arts Comm, 1978; Distinguished Serv Award, Univ Without Walls, 1980; Coalition of Professional Youth on the Move Award, 1981; appreciation award, Syphax School, Washington DC, 1989; director, Night of the Divas: Tribute to Marian Anderson, J F Kennedy Center, 1985; President's Award for play Black Images/Black Reflections, Dundalk International Maytime Festival, Ireland, 1977; Premiere Award for play Brother, Brother, Brother Mine, Dundalk International Maytime Festival, Ireland, 1979. **Military Serv:** AUS Sp4 1958-60. **Business Addr:** Executive Director, Kelsey E Collie Talent Associates, 473 Florida Ave NW, Washington, DC 20001.

COLLIER, ALBERT, III
Educator (retired). **Personal:** Born Jul 26, 1926, Newark, NJ; son of Adelaide Coleman Collier and Albert Collier II; married Juanita Malia Augustono; children: Albert IV, Byron Joel. **Educ:** Howard Univ, BA, 1951; Seton Hall Univ, MA 1956; Teachers Coll Columbia Univ, Prof's Diploma, 1961. **Career:** Friendly Neighborhood House, NJ, Groupleader, 1951-54; Cleveland Jr HS NJ, teacher, 1954-62; Somerset Public Schools NJ, dir special educ, 1963-66; Orange Public Schools NJ, dir spec serv 1967-70; Piscataway NJ, admn asst pupil personnel, 1970-75, asst supt schools 1975-90. **Orgs:** NJEA; NEA; Amer Personnel & Guidance Assn; NJ Assn Pupil Personnel Admn; Council For Exceptional Children; Intern Assn Pupil Personnel Admin; Phi Delta Kappa; trustee Kean Coll NJ 1973-79; Bd of Educ, Highland Pk NJ 1969-72; pres NJ Assc Pupil Personal Admin 1980-82; mem Salvation Army, Urban League, Mental Health Alpha Phi Alpha Frat. **Honors/Awds:** NDEA Fellow Columbia Univ Teachers Coll, 1960-61. **Military Serv:** USN. **Home Addr:** 222 S 8th Ave, Highland Park, NJ 08904.

COLLIER, CLARENCE MARIE
Educator. **Personal:** Born in St Francisville, LA. **Educ:** Southern Univ, BS; Tuskegee Inst, MS; Louisiana State Univ, MS; Grambling State Univ; New York Univ System. **Career:** Southern Univ, vice pres; Teacher Corps Program, admin; Parish School System, elementary principal, supvr of educ. **Orgs:** Mem Assn of Supr & Curriculum Devel; Phi Delta Kappa; NEA; Louisiana Educ Assn; Natl Alliance of Black School Educators; Amer Council on Educ; Natl Assn of Women Deans, Administrators, & Counselors; SW Assn of Student Personnel; admin co-chmn Louisiana Commn on Observance of Intl Women's Yr; Delta Sigma Theta; State & Natl Women's Political Caucus; Leauge of Women Voters; Women in Politics; Natl Council of Negro Women; Comm Assn for Welfare of Sch Children; bd of dir YWCA. **Honors/Awds:** Operation Upgrade Advancement of Women Award Natl Orgn for Women; Arts & Letters Award Delta Sigma Theta Inc; Certificate of Merit Gov of Louisiana; Certificate of Recognition E Baton Rouge City Parish Council; cit of outstanding contrib to educ Prince Hall Masons. **Business Addr:** Southern Univ, Baton Rouge, LA 70813.

COLLIER, EUGENIA W.
Educator, writer (retired). **Personal:** Born Apr 6, 1928, Baltimore, MD; daughter of Eugenia Jackson Williams and H Maceo Williams; divorced; children: Charles Maceo, Robert Nelson, Philip Gilles. **Educ:** Univ of MD, PhD 1976; Columbia Univ, MA 1950; Howard Univ, BA (magna cum laude) 1948. **Career:** Balt Dept of Public Welfare, case worker 1950-55; Morgan State Univ, asst prof 1955-66; Comm Coll of Baltimore, prof 1966-74; So IL Univ, visiting prof 1970; Atlanta Univ, visiting prof 1974; Univ of MD, assoc prof 1974-77; Howard Univ, assoc prof 1977-87; Coppin State Coll, prof, 1987-92; Morgan State University, professor of English, 1992-96. **Orgs:** National Conference on African-American Theater; National Council of Teachers of English; Middle Alantic Writers Association; College Language Association; African-American Writers' Guild; Arena Players, Baltimore, MD. **Honors/Awds:** Gwendolyn Brooks Award for Fiction 1969; MAW, Creative Writing Award, 1984. **Special Achievements:** Author: Breeder and Other Stories, 1994; co-editor, Afro-American Writing, w/ Richard A Long. **Home Addr:** 2608 Chelsea Terr, Baltimore, MD 21216.

COLLIER, LOUIS KEITH
Professional baseball player. **Personal:** Born Aug 21, 1973, Chicago, IL. **Educ:** Triton Community College. **Career:** Pittsburgh Pirates, infielder, 1997-. **Business Addr:** Professional Baseball Player, Pittsburgh Pirates, PO Box 7000, Pittsburgh, PA 15212, (412)323-5000.

COLLIER, LOUIS MALCOLM
Educator. **Personal:** Born May 19, 1919, Little Rock, AR; son of Ludia Lewis Collier and Albert Collier; married Pearlie B May Collier; children: James Bernard, Irving Orlando, Albert Jerome, Phillip Louis, Eric Wayne. **Educ:** Grambling State Univ, BS 1954; OK State Univ, MS 1960; Cornell Univ, postgraduate 1961; OK State Univ, 1962-64. **Career:** Central HS Calhoun LA, teacher, chmn Science & Math dept 1955-62; So Univ, instructor Physic & Math 1962-65; Grambling Coll, instructor of Phys & Chem 1966-67; Hopewell HS Dubach LA, chmn Sci & Math dept; So Univ, assoc prof phys, chmn of dept 1967-75; So Univ Shreveport, chmn Physics 1975-; Caddo Parish School Bd, Shreveport, LA, pres, l986. **Orgs:** Exec bd mem Amer Inst Physics; pres Ouachita Ed Assoc; dir 8th Dist LA Acad Sci; 2yr coll rep Natl Council Teachers of Math; mem Shreveport Cof C, Shreveport Negro Chamber of Commerce, LA Ed Assoc, Amer Assoc of Univ Prof, AAAS; exec bd mem, sec YMCA 1972; mem Kiwanis Club 1974; chmn advisory bd Caddo Parish School Bd 1974; vice pres Newton Smith PTA 1973; pres Cooper Rd Health Club 1973; bd mem Caddo Parish School Bd 1980-86; deacon, trustee Little Union BC 1973-; AARP, Minority Affairs, spokesperson, l986-; State Leadership Team Forla-AARP, l988-. **Honors/Awds:** Science Educ Leadership Award LA Educ Assoc 1973; Selected by Gov of LA to serve as 1st & only Afro-Amer mem of LA Sci Found Bd; Teacher of the Year Freedom Found 1962; Shell Merit Fellowship Award Stanford Univ 1962; Ed Leadership Award LA Ed Assoc 1973; Outstanding Club Leadership Award N Shreveport Kiwanis Club 1975; Comm Leadership & Serv Award 1975; Comm Serv Awd Phi Beta Sigma Frat 1976; Leadership Awd Caddo Ed Assoc & Caddo Teachers Assoc 1977; Distinguished Serv Award, Gulf Coast Region (LA & TX) IBE, Phi Beta Sigma Fraternity, Inc, l978; Distinguished Educ Award, Gulf Coast Region (LA & TX); Phi Delta Kappa, membership, l987. **Military Serv:** Sgt WWII. **Business Addr:** Chairman, Physics Department, Southern Univ, 3050 Cooper Rd, Shreveport, LA 71107.

COLLIER, MILLARD JAMES, JR.
Physician. **Personal:** Born Nov 8, 1957, Atlanta, GA; son of Catherine Walker & Millard James Collier, Sr; married Michelle B Collier, Aug 2, 1987; children: Millard J Collier, III. **Educ:** Morehouse College, BS; Medical College of Georgia, MD. **Career:** Atlanta West Health Care, PC, medical director, 1990-. **Orgs:** American Medical Association; Atlanta Medical Association; National Medical Association; American Academy of Family Physicians; Georgia Academy of Family Physicians; Georgia State Medical Association; 100 Black Men of America; Alpha Phi Alpha Fraternity Inc. **Honors/Awds:** Atlanta Medical Association, Young Physician of the Year, 1996; 100 Black Men, Member of the Year, 1996; AAFP, Teaching Recognition Awd, 1996. **Special Achievements:** Radio Talk Show Host ''Your Health is Important'', WYZE 1480 AM. **Business Addr:** 939 Thornton Rd, Lithia Springs, GA 30057.

COLLIER, TORRENCE JUNIS
Physician. **Personal:** Born Sep 3, 1932, Texarkana, AR; married Gisele. **Educ:** Morehouse, BS; Meharry, MD; Harvard, MPH. **Career:** Schering Plough Pharm Corp, dir, med liaison; Preventive Med, NY Med Coll, instr 1963. **Orgs:** Mem Drug Info Assn; Mental Hlth Assn; Meaning of Global Econ to Western Econ & Culture; past mem NMA; mem Urban League; Human Rights Commn; Adv Youth Rec Ctr; need for differentiated self-acknowledged & implemented role of black lawyers in pvt prac especially to ''Get Down'' & become accessible; mem Politics of Hlth Care. **Honors/Awds:** Hon grades Morehouse; Harvard; Brook Army Med Ctr 1957; Roosevelt Univ 1948-49; Sorbonne 1960. **Military Serv:** US Army, 1957-61.

COLLIER, TROY
Educator. **Personal:** Born Apr 19, 1941, Nacogdoches, TX; married Claudette Liggns. **Educ:** Phoenix Coll, AA, Bus Adminstrn, 1962; UT State U, BS, social work, 1964; S Meth U, MLA, 1971; Nova U, PhD candidate. **Career:** Univ of Southern FL, asst to vice pres for sudent affairs; Clearfield Job Corps Center, res life counselor 1969-71; Youth Programs Coord & Neighborhood, organizer supvr 1968-69; City of Phoenix AZ, youth programs coord & neighborhood organizer, supvr 1967-68; Harlem Globetrotters Basketball Team, professional basketball player 1964-67. **Orgs:** Bd of dir DACCO; mem Citizens Adv Com, Hillsborough Co Sch Bd; Am Civil Liberties Union, State Bd & Tampa Chpt; bd mem Nat Assn Human Rights Workers; So Assn Black Adminstr; Am Assn Affirmative Action; Tampa Urban League; NAACP; Tampa-Hillsborough Manpower Council. **Business Addr:** 4202 Fowler, Tampa, FL 33620.

COLLIER, WILLYE
Educator. **Personal:** Born Sep 26, 1922, Hattiesburg, MS; married Cisero. **Educ:** Tuskegee Inst, BS 1943; John AAMHosp Tuskegee Inst, intern 1944; Univ of WI, MS 1946. **Career:** Bakersfield Coll, prof Food & Nutrition 1964-; San Luis Obispo City Schools, teacher 1960-64; Los Angeles Paso Robles & San Luis Obispo, consult diet 1956-57; Southern Univ, dir dietetics 1949-56; SC Public Schools, home economics teacher 1946-49. **Orgs:** Chmn Home Econ Dept Benedict Coll; Liasion Rep, Home Con Assn to CA Tchrs Assn/NEA; mem Amer Dietetic Assn; mem Amer Pub Hlth Assn; mem Amer Home Econ Assn; Intnl Fed of Home Econ; chmn bd Kern County Hlth Assn 1976-; chmn Nut Com KC Heart Assn 1970-76; mem of the Bd Kern Co MentHlth Assn 1974-80, organizer, pres 1977-79; chmn of bd Kem Co Mental Hlth Assn 1980-81; Links of Bakersfield 1977; mem NAACP; Basileus, Gamma Alpha Sigma Chap Sigma Gamma Rho Inc, 1976-78. **Honors/Awds:** Who award CA Higher Educ 1976; sigma of the yr Sigma Gamma Rho Sor 1975; outstanding Contrib Kern County Heart Assn 1974. **Business Addr:** 1801 Panorama Dr, Bakersfield, CA 93305.

COLLIER-BRIDGEFORTH, BARBARA (BARBARA COLLIER LONG)
Federal government official. **Personal:** Born Dec 18, 1943, Athens, AL; daughter of Eunice Louise Collier and John Robert Collier; married John Henry Bridgeforth; children: Tracey Dione. **Educ:** Alabama A&M Univ, BS 1965; Atlanta School of Biblical Studies, MA, 1996. **Career:** Dept of Energy, compliance officer 1973-78; Dept of Labor, program analyst 1978-79, supervisor 1979-80, area office dir 1980-84, asst district dir, sr compliance officer, currently. **Orgs:** Black Pilots Association; Flying Doctors; Biblical Counseling; NAACP; Zeta Phi Beta Sor; American Cancer Association, volunteer fundraiser; Atlanta Botanical Gardens; Black Cowboy Assn; Atlanta Preservation Center volunteer; Kiwanas, Atlanta; Toastmasters; Zone III Photography. **Honors/Awds:** BACS 1982, VEVA 1984; Special Achievement Dept of Energy 1976, Dept of Labor 1984; Outstanding Young Women Women's Suffrage Awd 1984; Outstanding Young Women of Amer 1986; Community EEO/AA Action Award, Top Ladies of Distinction, 1989; Distinguished Career Service Award, 1994. **Home Addr:** 5687 Hunters Chase Ct, Lithonia, GA 30038-1646. **Business Addr:** Sr Compliance Officer, US Department of Labor-OFCCP, 61 Forsyth St Suite 7B75, Atlanta, GA 30309.

COLLIER-GRIFFITH, JULIA MARIE
Educational administrator. **Personal:** Born Aug 23, 1949, Athens, AL; daughter of Louise Bluford Collier and John Robert Collier Sr. **Educ:** Berea Coll, BA 1971; Temple Univ, MEd 1973; Eastern KY Univ, MA 1979. **Career:** Ministry of Educ, faculty Nassau, Bahamas 1973-76; Manchester Coll, faculty 1978-79; Franklin Wright Settlement, admin coord 1979-80; Aldine Independent Sch Dist, counselor 1980-83; Kennesaw Assoc, associate dir of admissions, currently; Nat Expansion Leader, Independent Rep, Amer Comm Network, currently. **Orgs:** Comm mem Southern Assoc of Collegiate Registrar & Admission Offices 1985; conference presenter Southern Assoc of Collegiate Registrar & Admission Offices 1986-87; work-

shop presenter ELS Language Ctr 1986; comm mem GA Educ Articulation Comm 1987-89; chmn, Georgia Assn for Foreign Student Affairs, 1989-90; bd mem, ELS Language Center; Georgia Association of Colegiate Registrars & Admissions Officers, executive committee, 1988-95; Natl Advisory Board Committee, ELS, Language Centers. **Honors/Awds:** Fulbright Scholar to Germany, 1987; Outstanding New Professional, Georgia Assn for Collegiate Registrars & Admissions Officers 1988; Omega Psi Phi Fraternity, Humanitarian of the Year, 1990.

COLLIER-THOMAS, BETTYE

Educator. **Personal:** Born in Macon, GA; married Charles John Thomas. **Educ:** Allen U, BA (magna cum laude) 1963; Atlanta U, MA 1966; Geo Wash U, PhD 1974. **Career:** Univ of MD, lecturer, history, beginning 1971; William & Mary Coll, assoc prof 1969-70; Wash Tech Inst, asst prof 1969-71; Howard Univ Coll of Lib Arts, dir honors pgm 1969-71; Howard Univ, instr 1966-69; WA Perry Jr HS Columbia SC, instr 1963-65; Temple Univ, assoc history prof; Center for African-American History and Culture, Temple Univ, director, 1989-. **Orgs:** Mem Am Assn of Univ Profs; Nat Educ Assn; mem Assn for Study of Afro-Am Life & Hist; Alpha Kappa Alpha; Orgn of Am Historians; American Historical Association; founding director, Bethune Museum and Archives National Historic Site, Washington, DC. **Honors/Awds:** Schlrshp Awrd Delta Sigma Theta 1960; Mark Schaefer History Awrd 1963; Nat Assn of Coll Women's Awrd 1963; Presdntl Schlrshp Atlanta Univ 1965-66; Ford Fdn fellowship; Howard Univ Rsrch Grant; author of various articles; Conservation Services Award, Dept of the Interior, 1994. **Business Addr:** Director, Center for African-American History and Culture, Temple University, 13th & Cecil B. Moore Ave, Weiss Hall, Ste B-18, Philadelphia, PA 19122.

COLLINET, GEORGES ANDRE

Television and radio producer. **Personal:** Born Dec 16, 1940, Sangmelima, Cameroon; son of Myriam Nyangono K'Pwan and Raymond Maurice Collinet; married Louise Wilma Lutkefedder, Sep 21, 1980; children: Georges-Alexandre William Zuom. **Educ:** Universite de Caen, France, BA. **Career:** Soul Music Magazine, founder, editor, 1975-79; GC Productions, president, 1979-; USIA TV, talent coordinator, 1976-; Voice of America, producer, 1964-; Afropop Worldwide, host, currently. **Orgs:** Marracas d'Or, founding mem, 1975-78; Prix de la Jeune Chanson Francaise, 1976-78; Sharon Pratt Kelly, art steering committee. **Honors/Awds:** Corp. for Public Broadcasting, Gold Award for Best Series, Silver Award for Best Program. **Business Addr:** Host, Afropop Worldwide, G.C. Productions, National Public Radio, 2025 M St NW, Washington, DC 20036.

COLLINS, ANDRE PIERRE

Professional football player. **Personal:** Born May 4, 1968, Riverside, NJ. **Educ:** Penn State Univ. **Career:** Washington Redskins, linebacker, 1990-94; Cincinnati Bengals, linebacker, 1995-. **Honors/Awds:** First-team All-America selection, Football Writers Assn, 1989. **Business Addr:** Professional Football Player, Cincinnati Bengals, One Bengals Dr, Cincinnati, OH 45202, (513)621-3550.

COLLINS, BARBARA-ROSE

Congresswoman. **Personal:** Born Apr 13, 1939, Detroit, MI; daughter of Versa Richardson; widowed; children: Cynthia, Christopher. **Educ:** Attended Wayne State Univ. **Career:** Wayne State Univ, business mgr, physics dept, 9 yrs, office asst in equal opportunity office, neighborhood relations; Detroit School Region I, bd mem 1970-73; Michigan House of Rep, 21st Dist of Detroit, state representative, 1974-82; City of Detroit, councilwoman 1982-90; U.S. House of Representatives, congresswoman 1991-. **Orgs:** Regional coord Michigan, Ohio Natl Black Caucus of Local Elected Officials 1985; trustee Michigan Municpal League 1985; bd mem Comprehensive Health Planning Council of Southeastern Michigan 1985; trustee Intl Afro-Amer Museum; chairperson Region I Political Action Comm; mem City-Wide Citizens Action Council, Democratic Party, ACLU, League of Women Voters, Amer for Democratic Action, Kenyatta Homeowners & Tenants Assoc, Black Teachers Caucus, Black Parents for Quality Educ, Inner-City Parents Council, Natl Order of Women Legislators; bd mem Detroit Black United Fund; mem Special Comm on Affirmative Action, Shrine of the Black Madonna Church, IWY State Coord Comm Natl Intl Women's Year Comm, Michigan Delegate to IWY Convention; chairperson ConstlRevision & Women's Rights Comm; principal nsor of bills which were later passed, including The Food Dating Bill, The Sex Educ Bill, The Pregnancy Insurance Bill; past mem Detroit Human Rights Comm; regional dir Natl Black Caucus of Local Elected Officials. **Honors/Awds:** Feminist of the Year Awd, 1977; featured in ''How Michigan Women Make It Happen,'' Redbook Mag, 1978; Woman of the Year Awd, Eta Phi Beta Sor Inc, Eta Lambda Zeta Chap, 1979; Invaluable Serv, Pershing High School, Detroit Public Schools, 1985; Devoted Serv, Metro Boy Scouts of Amer, 1984; Valuable Serv, Intl Freedom Festival, 1983; Distinguished Serv, Shrine of the Black Madonna Pan African Orthodox Christian Church, 1981. **Business Addr:** Congresswoman, US House of Representatives, 401 Cannon, House Office Bldg, Washington, DC 20515.

COLLINS, BERNICE ELAINE

Circus administrative assistant. **Personal:** Born Oct 24, 1957, Kansas City, KS; daughter of Wanda J Coby Collins and William H Collins. **Educ:** Ringling Brothers Barnum Bailey Clown Coll, Diploma 1977; Transworld Travel Coll, Kansas City, KS, Diploma 1985. **Career:** Dr's Office, receptionist 1975-77; Ringling Brothers Barnum Bailey Circus, clown 1978-79, dancer/showgirl 1980-84, apprentice tiger trainer 1983; Trans World Airlines, intl flight attendent 1985-86; Kansas City Riverboat, entertainer/asst mgr; Ringling Brothers Barnum & Bailey Circus, dancer/showgirl, 1988-90; horse act, 1992-94, administrative assistant, 1994-. **Honors/Awds:** Gold Key Awards HS Art Award 1974-75; 1st African-American woman clown Ringling Brothers Barnum & Bailey Circus 1978, 1st African-American woman tiger Trainer 1983. **Home Addr:** 3507 Oak Ave, Kansas City, KS 66104.

COLLINS, BERT

Insurance executive. **Personal:** Born Nov 9, 1934, Austin, TX; son of Marie Collins (deceased) and James K Collins (deceased); married Carolyn Porter; children: Suane, Brandy Collins Suggs, Bert E. **Educ:** Hoston-Tillotson Coll, BBA, 1955; Univ of Detroit, MBA 1959; North Carolina Central Univ Law School, JD 1970; Univ of North Carolina-Chapel Hill, Young Exec Prog. **Career:** Sidney A Sumby Meml Hosp, chief accountant 1956-61; Austin Washington & Davenport CPA's, sr staff accountant 1962-67; North Carolina Mutual Life Insurance Co, admin asst 1967, asst vice pres, official staff 1970, vice pres, controller 1974, bd dir, exec comm 1978, finance comm 1979, sr vice pres, controller 1982, sr vice pres, admin 1983, chmn of securities comm 1983, chmn field comm 1986, exec vice pres, COO 1987-90; president/CEO, 1990-. **Orgs:** Board of directors, Durham Rotary Club; Kappa Alpha Psi; Sigma Pi Phi Boule'; First Church of Christ Scientist; mem, Michigan Assn of CPA's; North Carolina Assn of CPA's; Amer Inst of CPA's; Amer Bar Assn; American College; North Carolina State Bar; George White Bar Assn; bd dir, Amer Citizens Life Insurance Co; business advisory council, School of Business, North Carolina Central Univ; board of visitors, North Carolina A&T State University; mem, Durham Comm on the Affairs of Black People; Durham Business & Professional Chain; Durham Chamber of Commerce; bd dir, treas, former pres, State Easter Seal Soc; vice chair, exec comm, board of directors, Mutual Savings & Loan Assn; bd dir, United Durham Inc; advisory bd, North Carolina Central Univ Law School; advisory bd, Duke Univ NC Business; council of management, bd dir, NC Amateur Sports;mem, Africa News; appointed to Bd of Arts and Humanities (NC); chairman of board of trustees, North Carolina Central University, 1992-93; member, National Board of Boys and Girls Clubs of America; member, North Carolina Business Council of Management and Development. **Honors/Awds:** Barber Scotia College, Doctor of Humane Letters; The National Business League, CC Spaulding Award. **Business Addr:** President, North Carolina Mutual Insurance Co, 411 W Chapel Hill St, Durham, NC 27701.

COLLINS, BOBBY L.

Dentist. **Educ:** Univ of Iowa, College of Dentistry, graduated, 1975. **Career:** Dentist, currently. **Orgs:** Tennessee Board of Dentistry, 1988-, pres, 1993-. **Special Achievements:** First African-American president, second African-American appointed mem, Tennessee Board of Dentistry. **Business Phone:** (615)367-6228.

COLLINS, CARDISS

Congresswoman (retired). **Personal:** Born Sep 24, 1931, St Louis, MO; daughter of Rosia Mae Robertson and Finley Robertson; married George Collins (deceased); children: Kevin. **Educ:** Northwestern Univ, grad 1967. **Career:** IL Dept of Revenue, revenue auditor; US House of Representatives, member, 7th Illinois District, beginning 1973. **Orgs:** SComm on Govt Ops, Subcomms on Oversight and Investigations, Energy & Commerce Comm, chair of commerce, consumer protection and competitiveness; House Select Comm Drug Abuse & Control; past chairwoman Mems of Congress for Peace through Law Subcomm on Africa; active secretary, vice chair, chair, Congressional Black Caucus; Democratic committeewoman 24th Ward Chicago, mem NAACP; Chicago Urban League; Northern Virginia Urban League; Natl Council Negro Women, Natl Women's Political Caucus; Alpha Kappa Alpha, Alpha Kappa Psi; Black Women's Agenda; secretary, Congressional Women's Caucus; Links. **Honors/Awds:** Honorary degrees: Spelman College, Winston-Salem State Univ, Barber-Scotia College. **Business Addr:** Congresswoman, House of Representatives, 2308 Rayburn House Office Bldg, Washington, DC 20515.

COLLINS, CARTER H.

Educator. **Personal:** Born Mar 13, 1928, Torresdale, PA. **Educ:** Amer Univ, EdD 1972; Georgetown Univ, doctoral studies 1960; Univ de las Americas, MA 1958; LaSalle Coll, BA 1953. **Career:** Washington DC & Philadelphia PA, tchr 5 yrs; USIA, cultural affairs & educ 3 yrs; State/AID, intl relations officer 2 yrs; CSA, prog mgmt, formulation, evalation, presentation, supervision 7 yrs. **Orgs:** Vice pres Paul Jr HS Adv Council; consult Brightwood Elem Sch Parent Council; proj officer SW Educ Devel Lab; Educ Equity Officer. **Honors/Awds:** Govt Career Serv Award; Rotary Scholarship; produced or contributed numerous govt reports, papers, training manuals, audiovisual packages.

COLLINS, CHARLES MILLER

Real estate executive. **Personal:** Born Nov 22, 1947, San Francisco, CA; son of Dr & Mrs Daniel A Collins; married Paula Robinson; children: Sara, Julia. **Educ:** Williams Coll, BA (w/ honors) 1969; Athens Center of Ekistics, Athens, Greece, Certificate 1971; MIT, MCP 1973; Harvard Law School, JD 1976. **Career:** Private law practice, attorney 1976-79; State of California, Deputy Sec Business, Transportation and Housing 1980-82; WDG Ventures Ltd, managing general partner 1987-; Western Development Group Inc, principal, 1982-87; Chairman/President, WDG Ventures, Inc. 1987-. **Orgs:** Trustee Howard Thurman Educ Trust 1976-97; mem Alpha Phi Alpha, Sigma Pi Phi; trustee, Natl Urban League 1989-; trustee, San Francisco Museum of Modern Art, trustee; chmn, special awards comm, San Francisco Foundation. **Honors/Awds:** Thomas J Watson Foundation Fellowship 1969-71. **Special Achievements:** Editor, ''The African Americans A Celebration of Achievement'', Viking Studio Books, 1993. **Business Addr:** Chairman, WDG Ventures, Inc, 100 First St, Ste 2350, San Francisco, CA 94105.

COLLINS, CLIFFORD JACOB, III

Organization executive. **Personal:** Born Mar 6, 1947, Jamaica, NY; son of Mamie Hale Collins and Clifford Collins Jr; married Electra Bazemore Collins, Jan 13, 1973; children: Makina, Ahmed. **Educ:** Roger Williams College, Bristol, RI, AA, 1970; Shaw University, Raleigh, NC, BA, 1975; Georgia State University, Atlanta, GA, MEd, 1977. **Career:** Goodwill Industries, Atlanta, GA, director, industrial services, 1983-84; Atlanta Regional Comm, Atlanta, GA, chief planner, 1985-86, principal planner, 1986-87; NAACP Baltimore, MD, assistant to the director, back-to-school/stay-in school, 1987-88, promotion director, back-to-school/stay-in school, 1988, 1992-, director, voter education, 1989-. **Orgs:** Board of directors, National Coalition on Black Voter Participation, 1990-; Minority Education Coordinating Council Baltimore County Public Schools, 1990-; Citizens Advisory Committee Gifted and Talented Program, Baltimore Co Public Schools, 1990-; National Commission for Renewal of American Democracy; National Association of Secretaries of State; 2000 Census Advisory Committee, US Census Bureau. **Honors/Awds:** 1990 Award for Outstanding Cooperation in Advancing Public Understanding, Census; US Dept of Commerce Bureau of the Census, 1991; Co-author, NAACP Redistricting Project Handbook, NAACP, 1991; Certificate of Recognition for Outstanding Volunteer Service, Old Court Middle Sch, 1990; Publication: Personal Care Homes: A Local Government Perspective, research study of personal care homes in Atlanta, GA, Atlanta Regional Commission, 1987. **Business Addr:** Director of Voter Education and Back-To-School Programs, Programs Department, NAACP, 4805 Mt Hope Dr, Baltimore, MD 21215.

COLLINS, CONSTANCE RENEE WILSON

Executive director. **Personal:** Born Nov 25, 1932, New York, NY; married Alphonzo S; children: Michael Alan, Tonilyn. **Educ:** Skidmore Univ 1975; Harvard U, MEd 1979. **Career:** CT United Labor Agency of New Britain, exec dir 1982-87; Poor People's Fedn Inc, exec dir 1972-80; Silver Strands System Inc Consult Firm, dir of Adminstrn 1976-80; Arsenal Devel Corp, asso dir 1969- 72; United & Elec Workers of Am Local 207, pres 1965-69. **Orgs:** Alderman City of New Britian 1969-75; bd of advs Burrit Bank of New Britain Ct 1975-80; dir City Plan Commn 1978-80; grand dist dep IBPO of Elks of the World 1961-80; natl bd mem Opportunites Indsl Ctrs of Am 1972-80; organizer bd chmn OIC of New Britain, CT 1976-80; alderman City of New Britain 1985-. **Honors/Awds:** Recipient Dedication Award for Serv Bd & Staff Poor People's Fedn Inc 1974; Torch Bearer Award OIC's of Am 1976; Martin Luther King Comm Serv Award MLK Monument Com 1977; Elk of the Yr Award; New Eng Sts & Eastern Canada Assn IBPOE of W 1979; Outstanding Woman of the Year Awd State of CT Gov Ella Grasso 1979; Leader of the Month of Greater Hartford CT Mutual Ins Co 1979; One of CT Outstanding Woman in Labor CT Historial Cos 1984. **Business Addr:** Executive Dir, CT United Labor Agency, 1 Grove St, Ste 315B, New Britain, CT 06053, (860)225-8864.

COLLINS, CORENE

Government administrator. **Personal:** Born Apr 20, 1948; married Tony Collins; children: Craig, Kisten. **Educ:** FL A&M Univ, BA Sociology/Criminology 1970; Rutgers Univ, MA Criminal Justice Admin (Outstanding Thesis). **Career:** Youth Serv Bureau East Orange NJ, dir 1974-78; United Way Comm Plnng & Devel Newark NJ, dir 1978-80; Div of Comm Serv Tampa FL, dep dir 1981-85; Divof Cultural Serv Hillsborough Cty, dir. **Orgs:** Exec dir volunteer Oper PUSH 1977-79; producer & host volunteer Black Spectrum TV Show 1978-79; public relations coord & newsletter co-editor Tampa Org of Black Affairs 1980-84; pres Tampa Bay Investment Club 1982-85; mem Natl Forum for Black Publ Admin, Tampa Chamber of Commerce Govt Comm; bd mem, Amer Cancer Society. **Honors/Awds:** Natl PUSH Awd for Outstanding Chap Devel 1978; Outstanding Young Woman of Amer 1979; Selected 1 of 33 Women Achievers Tampa Tribune Newspaper 1982; Selected Minority Woman of the Year Zeta Phi Beta Sor 1984; Up and Comers Awd- price waterhouse. **Home Addr:** 4708 Soap Stone Dr, Tampa, FL 33615. **Business Addr:** Dir, Hillsborough County, Division of Cultural Services, P O Box 1110, Tampa, FL 33601.

COLLINS, DAISY G.

Judge (retired), attorney. **Personal:** Born Feb 5, 1937, Butler, AL; daughter of Luevinia Mitchell Collins and Booker T Collins Sr (deceased); divorced. **Educ:** OH State Univ, Acct major, 1955-58, BS Business Admin (cum laude) 1958; Howard Univ Sch of Law, JD (cum laude) 1970. **Career:** Mgt trainee, Commonwealth Edison Co, Chicago, 1958-60; acct, City of Detroit, 1960-64; General Foods Corp, White Plains, cost & budget anal, 1964-66; Student asst to asst legal advisor, US State Dept, African Affairs, 1969; N MS Rural Legal Serv Greenwood, staff atty, 1970-71; OH Turnpike Comm, asst gen cnsl & stflwyr, 1973-74; No Dist of OH, asst us atty, 1975-77; Capital Univ Law School, vis assc prof of law, 1981-82; Equal Opportunity Commn Cleveland Dist Office, administrative judge, 1986-90; administrative law judge, Office of Hearings & Appeals, Social Security Administration, 1990-94; part-time instructor, Business Law & Acct, Cleveland State Univ & Cuy CC. **Orgs:** exec sec Cleveland Branch NAACP 1979-80; Alpha Kappa Alpha Sor, life mem, NAACP. **Honors/Awds:** Hon Mention, Cleveland Federal Exec Bd for Community Service, 1976; Cleveland Bar Assn Meritorious Serv Awards, 1972-73; Six Am Jurisprudence Awds for Exc Achievement; articles published in Howard Law Journal & Crnt Bibliography of African Affairs; HLJ Notes Editor; Appreciation Award Law Journal Notes Editor 1970; Beta Gamma Sigma Natl Comr Hon 1956; Beta Alpha Psi; Phi Chi Theta Scholarship Key Most Outstanding Grad Woman Coll C & Admin. **Home Addr:** 12501 Brooklawn Ave, Cleveland, OH 44111.

COLLINS, DANIEL A.

Business executive, dentist. **Personal:** Born Jan 11, 1916, Darlington, SC; son of Lucy Miller Collins and Andrew Sumner Collins; married DeReath C James; children: Daniel Jr, Edward J, Charles M, Craig S. **Educ:** Paine Coll Augusta, GA, AB 1936; Meharry Med Coll Nashville, TN, DDS 1941; Univ of CA, MS Dentistry 1944; Guggenheim Dental Clinic NYC, Cert in Chldrns Dentistry 1941; Armed Forces Inst of Pathlogy, Cert 1958; Am bd of Oral Pathology, Diplomat 1958. **Career:** Bay Area Dental Prac Coll of Dentistry Univ of CA, research asst/research fellow/instructor/asst prof 1942-60; Comprehensive Dental Hlth Care Project Mt Zion Hosp, co-dir; Div of Urban Educ San Fran Ofc Harcourt Brace Jovanovich New York, NY, president. **Orgs:** Mem Am Dental Assn; Nat Dental Assn; Omicron Kappa Upsillon; Sigma Pi Phi; House of Delegates CA State Dental Assn; Am Acad of Oral Pathology; dental staff Mt Zion Hosp San Fran, CA; Intl Assn of Pathology; La Fed Dentaire Intl; The Royal Soc of Hlth; lecturer/clinician Univ of CA Dental Coll Alumni Assn; CA State Dental Assn; Meharry Med Coll; Howard U; Georgetown U; Stanford Med Coll; Annual Convention of ADA & NDA; bd of dir San Fran Dental Soc; bd of trustees Meharry Med Coll; bd of dir Paine Coll; bd of dir Golden Gate U; World Coll West; fellow Intl Coll of Dentists; Fellow Am Assn for the Advancement of Sci; trustee Am Fund for Dental Edn; founder Oral-Facial Consultative Svc, College of Dentistry, University of California; founder & sec Beneficial Savings & Loan Assn; dir Harcourt Brace Jovanovich Inc; dir Natomas Co; consultmn Harcourt Brace Jovanovich; Western Devel Group Inc; partner San Fran Airport Parking Group. **Honors/Awds:** Citation of Merit Paine Coll; Disting Alumni Award United Negro Coll Fund; Alumnus of the Yr Meharry Med Coll; Cited Am Men of Sci; Disting Serv in Trusteeship Award The Assn of Governing Bds of Univ & Coll; Whitney Young Award, National Urban League; Doctor of Humane Letters, Meharry Medical College 1991; Paine College. **Military Serv:** USAR Armed Forces Inst of Pathology lt col Honorable Discharge 1958.

COLLINS, DOROTHY LEE

Educator. **Personal:** Born Jan 19, 1932, Nacogdoches, TX; married Samuel M Prin. **Educ:** TX So U, 1952; Our Lady of the Lake U, MEd 1973; Trinity U, postgrad 1976-77. **Career:** Las Palmas Elementary School San Antonio; Edgewood Independent School Dist, prin 1973; jr high school, counselor 1971-73; Edgewood Independent School Dist, elementary teacher 1957-71. **Orgs:** Mem TX State Tchrs Assn/Nat Educ Assn 1966-; TX Elem Prins Assn 1973-; vice pres San Antonio Leag of Bus & Professional Women Inc 1971-76; mem State Bd ofExam for Tchr Educ 1975-77; adv bd educ dept Our Lady of Lake Univ 1976-77; Nat Educ Assn Task Force on Testing 1972-75; pres Edgewood Classroom Tchrs Assn 1969-71; pres Edgewood Admin & Servs Personnel Assn 1976-77; exec com TX State Tchrs Assn 1971-77; life mem Nat Council of Negro Women Inc 1979; vice pres San Antonio Chap Our Lady of the Lake Univ Alumni Asn 1979-80; chmn TX Educ Agency Tchr Educ Evaluation Team Visit to Hardin-Simmons Univ Abilene 1979; treas Dist XX TX Elem Prin & Supr Assn 1980-81; mem exec com United Negro Coll Fund Inc 1980-; bd of dir Young & Women Christian Assn 1966-69;Ella Austine Comm Ctr1969-77; adv bd ewood ISD 1970-75; rep proj area com San Antonio Devel Agency 1973-78; bd of dir Bexar Co Opptys Indslzn Ctr 1974-; life mem NAACP spec state mem com TX State Tchrs Assn. **Honors/Awds:** Hon roll cert TX So Univ 1951; 1st black to Integrat Tchng Profn Edgewood ISD 1963; Citation-Historical Achvmt Among Negroes of San Antonio Smart Set Club 1965; citation Woman's Pavilion Hemisfair 68 Vol Guide 1968; hon & life mem TX Congress of Parents & Tchrs 1969; 1st black pres TX State Tchrs AssnAffiliate 1969-71; cit outst work with Youth City of San Antonio 1970; ambassador of Good Will Sstate of TX 1970; past pres award Edgewood Classroom TchrsAssn 1971; disting educ serv award Prince & Princess Soc & Civic Club Inc 1971f cit Ella Austin Comm Ctr 1973,77; outst educ award Zeta Phi Beta Sor1973; TX Classroom Tchrs Assn Serv Award 1973; disting serv award Task Force on Testing Nat Educ Assn 1976; miss black san antonio bd of dir model comm ldrsaward 1976; serv award TX State Thcrssn 1977; cert of apprec TX State Tchrs Assn 1977; 1st black mem TX Classroom Tchrs Asn Bd of Dirs Rep Dist 1973-73; boss of the yr Mission City Chap Am Bus Women's Assn 1978; educ adminstr of the yr Delta Rho Lambda Ch Alpha Phi Alpha Frat 1978; cert of apprec Edgewood Inde Sch Dist 1978.

COLLINS, ELLIOTT

Educator. **Personal:** Born Mar 18, 1943, Eastman, GA; son of Elvin W Collins (deceased) and Johnnie C Collins (deceased); married Carol Jones, Sep 9, 1967; children: Kimberly L. **Educ:** Univ of DE, BA 1966; New York Univ, MPA 1971; Drew Univ, Madison, NJ, MA, political science, 1983; NYU, American Studies, candidate PhD. **Career:** Passaic Cty Community College, president, 1991-96, interim president, 1990-91, dean of academic services, 1986-89, dean of students, 1979-86; Upsala College, East Orange, NJ, coordinator of science enrichment program, 1976-77; Upsala Coll, Drew Univ, lecturer political science 1974-; Upsala Coll, asst dean for acad counseling 1976-77; Upsala Coll, affirmative action officer 1974-77; Educ Opportunity Fund Program Upsala Coll, dir and coordinator 1970-76; City of E Orange NJ, asst city planner 1969; Passaic (NJ) County Community College, Paterson, NJ, Professor, History and Political Science, 1996-. **Orgs:** Vp United Way & Community Serv Council 1971-75; vice pres bd of dir Rotary Club of E Orange NJ 1971-72; bd of trustees Family Servs & Child Guidance Center 1975-76; board of directors, Opportunities Industrialization Center, 1987-95; board of directors, Paterson YMCA, 1983-87; board of trustees, Passaic-Clifton YMCA, 1989-93; United Way of Passaic Valley, board of directors, 1992-95; Inner City Christian Action for Housing Inc, board of trustees, 1992-96; North Jersey Regional Chamber of Commerce, 1991-95; Greater Paterson Chamber of Commerce, 1991-95; Passaic Valley Council Boy Scouts of America, executive board member, 1992-95. **Honors/Awds:** Alpha Phi Alpha Scholarship 1962-64; Young Man of the Year Unity Club Wilmington DE 1965; Martin Luther King Scholarship 1968-70. **Business Addr:** College Blvd, Paterson, NJ 07509.

COLLINS, ELSIE

Educator. **Personal:** Born Apr 25, Durham, NC; divorced; children: Leslie Jean, Kimberly Ruth. **Educ:** DE St Coll, BA 1945; Columbia U, MA 1952; Union Grad Sch, PhD 1977. **Career:** Trenton State Coll, asst prof 1971-; Trenton, NJ, asst dir of COP 1971; Natl Teachers Corp, Trenton NJ, team leader 1968-71; Core Curr Jr High School, Trenton NJ, teacher 1961-62, 1964-68, demonstration teacher 1965-68; Trenton State Coll, supvr summer semester for teachers 1965-75; Dover DE Jr & Sr High Schools, teacher 1945-59; Beth Jacob Jewish High School New York City, teacher 1960-61; Consult Serv & In-serv Workshops Trenton; Teahcer Educ NJ State Dept Higher Educ 1967-72; Afro-Amer Studies 1969-76; Urban Educ Curriculum Spec 1972-. **Orgs:** Mem Community Leaders & Noteworthy Am 1979; mem Doctorate Assn of NY Educators 1980; mem Amer Assn Univ Women 1954-60; current membrshp New Jersey HistSoc Am Assn Negro Mus; NAACP; Urban Leag Couns of Soc Studies NEA NJEA Poverty Law Ctr AKA Assn for Superv & Curriculum Devel. **Honors/Awds:** Valedictorian high sch schlrship high honor DE St Coll; scholarship student of music Tchrs Coll Columbia Univ 1950-57; soloist St Paul United Meth Ch Trenton 1967-; publ "Poverty & the Poor" 1968; contributed to Devl of Urban Educ Series Prob of Amer Soc 1966-68; special award World Who's Who of Women in Educ 1977-78; Internatl Artists & Fellows of Distinction 1980. **Business Addr:** 371 Education Bldg, Trenton St Coll, Trenton, NJ 08625.

COLLINS, GORDON GEOFFREY

Public relations executive, educator. **Personal:** Born Nov 7, 1958, Bronx, NY; son of Nellie Faison Collins and Clyde Rogers Collins Sr; married Dale Jenkins Collins, Jul 28, 1990. **Educ:** The Coll of St Rose, Albany, NY, BA, 1982; Baruch Coll, New York, NY, MPA, 1988. **Career:** Town of Hempstead, Dept of Occupational Resources, Hempstead, NY, educ and training monitor, 1978; New York State Alliance of Comm Action Programs Inc, Albany, NY, public information specialist, 1981-84; Office of the Mayor, Cleveland, OH, exec asst to the Mayor, 1984-85; Springfield Gardens High School, Springfield Gardens, NY, dean of students, 1986-90; Queensborough Comm Coll, Bayside, NY, adjunct lecturer, 1988-90; Collins Associates, Largo, MD, pres, 1985-; Prince George's County Public Schools, Upper Marlboro, MG, teacher, 1990-. **Orgs:** Mem, Amer Political Science Assn, 1985-, Amer Soc for Public Admin, 1985-, New York State United Teachers, 1986-90, New York Alliance of Black School Educators, 1987-90; delegate, United Federation of Teachers Delegate Assembly, New York, NY, 1987-90; mem, New York Urban League, 1988-; conf coord, Second Annual Black Man and Family Conf, New York, NY, 1988-89; mem, Queens Summit on Racial and Religious Harmony, New York, NY, 1988-90; bd mem, Positive Images Found Inc, Queens, NY, 1989-90; mem, Queens Martin Luther King Memorial Commn, New York, NY, 1989-90; pres elect, Council for the Social Studies, 1991-; board member, advisory board, POWERS, Inc, 1990-; area rep, Largo Civic Assn, Inc, 1991-; mem, National Council for the Social Studies, 1991-. **Honors/Awds:** Martin Luther King Scholarship Award, Nassau Community Coll, 1978; editor, New York State Alliance of Comm Action Programs Newsletter, 1981-84; Presidential Award, NAACP, Albany, NY, 1983; Natl Urban Fellow, Natl Urban Fellows Inc, 1984; Sidney Langsam Award, Springfield Gardens High School, New York , NY, 1988.

COLLINS, JAMES

Professional basketball player. **Personal:** Born Nov 5, 1973. **Educ:** Florida State. **Career:** Los Angeles Clippers, guard, 1997-. **Business Addr:** Professional Basketball Player, Los Angeles Clippers, 3939 S Figueroa St, Los Angeles Sports Arena, Los Angeles, CA 90037, (213)748-8000.

COLLINS, JAMES DOUGLAS

Educator, radiologist. **Personal:** Born Dec 11, 1931, Los Angeles, CA; son of Edna Alice O'Bryant Collins and James Douglas Collins; married Cecila Edith Lyons, Feb 7, 1954; children: Keith, Jelana Carnes, Jenine. **Educ:** Univ of CA, BA 1957; Univ of CA, MA 1959; Meharry Med Coll Nashville, MD 1963. **Career:** UCLA, assoc prof in radiology 1976-96, prof 1996-; UCLA, resident in radiology 1964-68; LA City General Hospital intern, 1963-64; Vet Admin (Wadworth/Spelveda), attending radiologist 1972-; Martin Luther King Jr Gen Hosp LA, attending radiologist 1973-; Olive View Mid-Valley Hosp Van Nuys, attending radiologist 1976-; Martin Luther King Jr Hosp, attending physician 1969-. **Orgs:** Mem Search Committee for Chmn of Radiology Dept of Martin Luther King Jr General Hosp 1969-70; vol Venice Community Health Center; Los Angeles County Radiology Society; National Medical Association Radiological Society of North America, 1969-; Radiological Society of North America, 1992-; Los Angeles County Radiological Society, 1968-; Association of University Radiologist, 1971-; American Assn of Clinical Anatomists, 1993-; American Assn of Anatomists, 1996-. **Honors/Awds:** Josiah Macey Fellow, 1959-63; AOA, 1992; Sigma Xi, 1957-; William Allan Jr, MD, Memorial Lecture, 98th NMA, 1993. **Military Serv:** US Army Medic, Corpl, acting first sargent, 1954-56. **Business Addr:** Prof, Radiology, UCLA, Dept of Radiological Sciences, 405 Hilgard, Los Angeles, CA 90024.

COLLINS, JAMES H.

Personnel manager. **Personal:** Born Feb 1, 1946, Moline, IL; son of Mattie Pennington Collins and Alphonso Collins; married Karen J Raebel; children: James Jr, Kimberly, Candace, Anthony, Kevin. **Educ:** St Ambrose Coll, BA Sociology 1969. **Career:** Proj Now Comm Action Agy, exec dir 1968-71; John Deere, industrial relations rep 1971-74, EEO crdtr 1974-75, mgr prsnl 1975-83; Deere & Co, dir affirmative action. **Orgs:** Vice pres Milan, IL C of C 1981; advisor Jr Achvmt 1975; vice pres Quad Cities Merit Employment Council 1975; chmn Dubuque, IA Human Rts Comm 1973; bd Quad Cities United Way 1975-78; pres Quad Cities Council on Crime & Delinquency 1978-79; chmn Human Rights & Employment Practices Comm Iowa Assn of Bus & Ind; chmn PIC/JTPA; chmn, Business Advisory Council, Illinois Dept of Rehabilitation Services 1988-90; commissioner, Iowa Civil Rights Commission 1989-92. **Honors/Awds:** Amer Legion Rock Island, IL 1961, Rotary 1964; Athletic Hall of Fame St Ambrose Coll 1984; Citizen Community Rehabilitation Service Award, Illinois Rehabilitation Assn 1989. **Business Addr:** Dir of Affirmative Action, Deere & Co, John Deere Rd, Moline, IL 61265.

COLLINS, JEFFREY

Judge. **Career:** Detroit Recorder's Court, judge, currently. **Orgs:** Associated Black Judges of Michigan, president-elect; Man to Man, mentor; Plymouth United Church of Christ, deacon; Wayne County Criminal Advocacy Program, chairman. **Business Addr:** Judge, Recorder's Court, 1441 St Antoine, Rm 402, Detroit, MI 48226, (313)224-2276.

COLLINS, JOANN RUTH

Educational administrator. **Personal:** Born Jan 26, Nashville; married John H; children: John K, Guy R. **Educ:** MI State U, BS 1971; MI State U, MA 1973; MI State U, PhD Candidate. **Career:** Dept of Civil Serv, State of MI, women's training officer; MI State Univ, coord college work study program; Breckinridge Job Corps Center KY, dir family servs, dir & nursery & kindergarten. **Orgs:** Pres Nat Assn of Financial Assistance to Minority Students 1974-; mem Nat Task Force on Student Aid Problems; mem Black Faculty & Adminstrn MI State U1973; mem bd dir Lansing Senior Citizens Inc 1974-76; mem women's steering com MI State Univ 1973; mem adv com to bus & office Educ Clubs MI HS 1974-.

COLLINS, JOANNE MARCELLA
Banker, community volunteer. **Personal:** Born Aug 29, 1935, Kansas City, MO; daughter of Mary Frances Porter Mitchell and William Mitchell; married Gerald A Spence (divorced 1961); children: Jerri Ann, Francis Damont; married Robert Lawrence Collins, Jun 10, 1962. **Educ:** Kansas Univ, 1953-55; Stephens Clg, BA, 1988; Baker Univ, MS, 1990; St Louis Univ, certificate; Weaver Schl of Real Estate, sales & property mgmt. **Career:** University of Kansas Medical Center, Clendenning Medical Library, library clerk, 1955-58; Robert Hughes and Company Real Estate, agent, 1958-62; US Post Office, postal clerk, 1960-63; Wheatley Provident Hospital, The Greater Kansas City Baptist and Community Hospital Assn, administrative assistant, 1964-72; US Department of Commerce, Metropolitan Kansas City, supervisor of dicennial census, 1970-71; Kansas City, MO, city cncl woman, 1974-; Halls Crown Center, Retail Sales Division, 1973-75; Connecticut Mutual Life Insurance Co, associate, 1977-79; United Missouri Bank of Kansas City, NA, asst vp, 1983-. **Orgs:** Salvation Army, Greater Kansas City Chapter, Adult Rehabilitation Center, bd of dirs; life member, NAACP; Delta Sigma Theta; Urban League of Greater Kansas City; St Paul AME Zion Church; Women's Public Service Network; numerous others; Emily Taylor's Women Resource, board member; Liberty Memorial Association, board of directors; Missouri Capital Punishment Resource Center, board of directors; United Minority Media Association, advisory board; Urban Youth Corps, advisory group; Women's Leadership Fountain Committee; Women's Public Service Network; Fifth Congressional District Republican Club; Soroptimist International Inc; Financial Women International; Ethnic Enrichment Commission; Avila College School of Nursing, advisory board; Stephens College Alumnae Association, board of directors. **Honors/Awds:** Distinguished Service Award, Eleventh Episcopal District, AME Zion Church; Award of Appreciation for Community Service, Women's Political Caucus; Builder of Boys Award, Boys Club; Honoree, Greater Kansas City Commission on the Status of Women; YWCA Volunteer Award; AT&T Margit Lasker Award; Women's Hall of Fame, University of Kansas; Zonta International Award; Women of Achievement Award, Girl Scouts of America, Kansas City Chapter; Junior Achievement, Recognition Award; Black Economic Union, Hawk Award; Omega Psi Phi, Citizen of the Year; Kansas City Cncl of Youth Development, Leadership Award, 1991; Missouri Municipal League, Distinguished Service Award, 1991; AME, Black Women Portraits Award, 1992; YouthNet, Leadership Award, 1992. **Business Addr:** Community Outreach Officer, UMB Financial Corp, 1010 Grand Ave, Kansas City, MO 64106, (816)860-7959.

COLLINS, KENNETH L.
Attorney. **Personal:** Born Aug 23, 1933, El Centro, CA; married Beverly Jean Sherman; children: Kevin, Leslie. **Educ:** UCLA, BA 1959; UCLA, JD 1971. **Career:** LA Co, probation ofcr 1957-68; San Fernando Valley Juvenile Hall, acting dir; Fed Pub Defenders Office, pub defender 1972-75. **Orgs:** Mem Langston Law Club; CA Attys for Criminal Justice; CA State Bar; chmn bd dir Black Law Journal; past pres Kappa Alpha Psi Upsion 1957-58; co-founderBlack Law Journal; distinguished serv. **Honors/Awds:** UCLA Chancelors Award 1971. **Military Serv:** AUS corpl 1953-55. **Business Addr:** 3701 Wilshire Blvd, Ste 700, Los Angeles, CA 90010.

COLLINS, LAVERNE FRANCIS. See COLLINS-REID, LAVERNE FRANCIS.

COLLINS, LAVERNE VINES
Federal official. **Personal:** Born Feb 3, 1947, Livorno, Italy; daughter of Myrtle Elizabeth Coy Vines (deceased) and Thomas Fulton Vines (deceased); married Alfred Collins, Jun 21, 1969 (divorced 1985); children: Alfred (deceased), Anthony, McAllister. **Educ:** Univ of Michigan, Ann Arbor, MI, 1964-66; Western Michigan Univ, Kalamazoo, MI, BA, 1968, MA, 1971. **Career:** Western Michigan Univ, Kalamazoo, MI, dean of students staff, 1969-71; US Census Bureau, Suitland, MD, statistician, 1971-72; Office of Management and Budget, Washington, DC, statistician, 1972-82; US Census Bureau, Atlanta, GA, survey statistician, 1982-83; US Census Bureau, Los Angeles, CA, assistant regional director, 1983-85; US Census Bureau, Philadelphia, PA, regional director, 1985-91, Washington, DC, supervisory social science analyst, 1992-94; Chief, Public Information Office 1994-. **Orgs:** member, Alpha Kappa Alpha Sorority, 1965-; board of directors, Budget Federal Credit Union, 1980-82; member, American Statistical Association, 1973-83; member, American Population Association, 1985-86; board of directors, United Way of Southeastern PA, 1987-90; member, Coalition of 100 Black Women of Southern New Jersey, 1989-90. **Honors/Awds:** US Census Bureau, Equal Employment Opportunity Award, 1991. **Business Addr:** Chief Public Information Office, US Census Bureau, Room 2705-3, Washington, DC 20233-0900, (202)457-3100.

COLLINS, LENORA W.
Consultant. **Personal:** Born Feb 25, 1925, Fayette, MS; married Joe H. **Educ:** Univ Sarasota EdD 1977; Governors State Univ, MA 1974; Xavier Univ, BS 1946; DePaul U, advance study. **Career:** Lorman Comm Devel Org Lorman MS, exec dir; Dept of Public Aid State of IL, economics cons; Bur of & Home Economics Cook County Dept Public Aid, asst chief 1964-73; spr home economics 1962-63; supv caseworker 1959-61; Chicago Bd of Educ, home economics teacher 1948-54. **Orgs:** Life mem Am Home Economics Assn; life mem IL Home Economics Assn; v chmn Human Serv Section; chmn Health & Welfare Sect IL Home Econ Assn 1968-69; pres Chicago Home Econ Assn; 1970-71; Chicago Nutrition Assn; Am Public Welfare Assn; bd mem Chicago Met Housing Council Tenant Proj; trustee Jefferson Co Hosp; sec Jefferson Co Hosp 1979-80; mem Nat Negro Bus & Professional Women's Club; mem Delta Sigma Theta; Wacker Neighborhood Assn Chicago Urban League; NAACP. **Honors/Awds:** Recipient Finer Womanhood Award Zeta Phi Beta 1967; Silver Jubilee & Alumnus Award Xavier Univ 1971; listed Chicago Almanac & Reference Book 1973.

COLLINS, LEROY ANTHONY, JR.
City official. **Personal:** Born Jan 13, 1950, Norfolk, VA; son of Thelma Taylor-Collins and Leroy Collins; married; children: Kisten Collins, Lyndsey Collins. **Educ:** Howard Univ, 1967-70; Rutgers Univ, BS, 1973; Temple Univ School of Business, 1980-81. **Career:** City of Newark, NJ, asst budget dir, 1974-78; City of Miami, FL, asst to city mgr, 1978-80; Penn Mutual Life Insurance Co, sr investment analyst, 1980-83; City of Tampa, FL, mgr of econ devel, 1983-86; City of St Petersburg, FL, dir of econ develop, currently; Promethens Innovations, Inc, pres. **Orgs:** Chairman, Black Business Investment Board, 1988-; board member, Operation PAR; board member, Suncoasters; FL Export Finance Authority; Tampa Bay Defense Transition Task Force; Tampa Bay Partnership; Enterprise FL Capital Devt Bd; Bennett Bank of Pinellas County, bd of dirs; Enterprise FL Intl Trade and Economic Development Bd; Tampa Bay Partnership, vice chair of mktg comm; Tampa Bay Partnership, bd mem. **Honors/Awds:** Focus Development, Penn Mutual Life, 1982; Leadership Tampa, Tampa Chamber of Commerce, 1985; Service Award, City of Tampa, 1986. **Military Serv:** USMC E-4, 1970-73; Amer Spirit of Honor Award, 1971. **Home Phone:** (813)360-5670. **Business Addr:** President, Prometheus Innovations, PO Box 40011, St Petersburg, FL 33706, (813)560-4153.

COLLINS, LIMONE C.
Educator. **Personal:** Born Aug 14, 1921, Gonzales, TX; married Billye J Peters; children: Cheryl M Anderson, Limone C Jr, Tyrone J. **Educ:** Prairie View A&M Univ, BS 1947, MS 1953; Univ of Iowa, PhD 1961. **Career:** OJ Thomas HS, head sci dept 1947-49; Prairie View A&M Univ, instructor of biol 1953-59, prof/head of biol dept 1961-73; Johnson C Smith Univ, vp for academic affairs 1973-84; Davidson Coll, prof of biology 1984-. **Orgs:** Bd of dirs Goodwill Industries of Amer 1982-; bd of dirs Amer Red Cross; fellow TX Acad of Science; sr warden St Francis Episcopal Church TX; consultant and proposal reviewer NIH & NSF. **Honors/Awds:** Danforth Fellowship; publications Amer Journal of Physiol 1962, TX Journal of Science 1972, Jour Amer Oil Chem Soc 1973. **Military Serv:** AUS T/5 1943-45, 1950-51. **Home Addr:** 8310 Knights Bridge Rd, Charlotte, NC 28210.

COLLINS, MARVA DELORES NETTLES
Educator. **Personal:** Born Aug 31, 1936, Monroeville, AL; daughter of Bessie Maye Knight Nettles and Alex L Nettles; married Clarence Collins, Sep 4, 1960; children: Cynthia Beth, Eric, Patrick. **Educ:** Clark Coll, BA 1957; Northwestern Univ. **Career:** Monroe Co Training Sch Monroeville, AL, tchr 1958-59; Delano Elem Sch, tchr 1960-75; Westside Prep Sch, founder/dir 1975-; Delano School, teacher 13 years; Westside Preparatory School 1975-. **Orgs:** Dir Right to Read Found 1978; Sunday sch tchr Morning Star Bapt Ch 1978-79; mem President's Commn on White House Fellowships 1981-; mem Alpha Kappa Alpha, NAACP; President's Citizens' Group 1989-. **Honors/Awds:** Fred Hampton Image Award Fred Hampton Found 1979; Watson Washburne Award Reading Reform Found 1979; Educator of the Year Award Phi Delta Kappa 1980; Endow a Dream Awd 1980; Jefferson Natl Awd 1981; Amer Public Serv Awd Amer Inst for Public Serv 1981; featured on TV's "60 Minutes"; subject of a made-for-TV movie "The Marva Collins Story" 1981; publs including Marva Collins' Way 1982; Honorary Degrees from: Washington Univ, Amherst, Dartmouth, Chicago State Univ, Howard Univ, Central State Univ. **Business Addr:** Director, Westside Prep School, 4146 Chicago Ave, Chicago, IL 60651.

COLLINS, PATRICIA HILL
Educator. **Personal:** Born May 1, 1948, Philadelphia, PA; married Roger L Collins; children: Valerie Lisa. **Educ:** Brandeis Univ, AB 1969, PhD 1984; Harvard Univ, MAT 1970. **Career:** Harvard UTTT Program, teacher/curriculum spec 1970-73; St Joseph Community School, curriculum specialist 1973-76; Tufts Univ, dir African Amer Ctr 1976-80; Univ of Cincinnati, assoc prof of African-American Studies 1987-94, prof, 1994-, assoc prof of Sociology 1988-. **Orgs:** Chair Minority Fellowship Program Comm 1986-1989; mem Amer Sociological Assn; vp Great Rivers Girl Scouts Council 1992-94. **Honors/Awds:** Career Woman of Achievement Award, YWCA of Cincinnati, 1993. **Special Achievements:** C Wright Mills Award for "Black Feminist Thought," 1990. **Business Addr:** Prof of African-American Studies, Univ of Cincinnati, Dept of African-American Studies, ML 370, Cincinnati, OH 45221.

COLLINS, PAUL
Artist. **Personal:** Born Dec 11, 1936, Muskegon, MI. **Career:** Paintings Children of Harlem 1976-78; Joseph P Kennedy Found, spl olympics drawings & paintings 1976-79; paintings & book Great Beautiful Black Women 1976-78; mural Famous Moments in Black Amer History 1978-80; paintings Working Americans 1980-83; mural & book Gerald R Ford, A Man in Perspective 1976; paintings-Voices of Israel 1986-89; paintings, drawings and book- Black Portrait of an African Journey 1969-71. **Orgs:** Bd of trustees Robeson Players 1972-80; mem Amer Indian Movement 1972-84; adv bd John F Kennedy Ctr for the Perf Arts 1976-80; co-chrmn for Western Michigan - United Negro College Fund 1989-90. **Honors/Awds:** Designer Martin Luther King Jr Non-Violent Peace Prize Medal 1979-80; Mead Book Awd 1972; Paul Collins Humanist Am Artist 1976; St named "Rue Monsieur Paul Collins" Govt of Senegal Africa 1977; Official Naming Ceremony Pine Ridge SD "Bright Eagle" 1977; 20 Outstanding Figure Painters & How They Work 1979; Arts Council Awd Grand Rapids Arts Council 1979; Black Achievement Awd 1979; People's Choice Awd Amer Painters in Paris 1976; 40th Anniversary Symbol for Israel 1988-89; American Woman Commemorative Plaque 1983. **Business Addr:** Collins Fine Art, 615 Kent Hills Rd NE, Grand Rapids, MI 49505.

COLLINS, PAUL L.
Cleric. **Personal:** Born Apr 19, 1931, Shreveport, LA; son of Willie Mae Adams Collins (deceased) and Paul Collins (deceased); married Shirley Alexander; children: Paula, Darryl. **Educ:** Southern Univ, BA & MEd 1958; GWU, EdD 1976. **Career:** Nazarene Outpost Ministries, executive director, 1990-; professional counselor, 1978-; American Association for Counseling and Development, associate executive, 1970-83; Office of Human Rights, asso exec intl relations, governmental reseach policy & analysis-registered lobbyist for Profnl Develop Prgms; Non White Concerns, dir; Wash Tech Inst, asso prof 1968-71; Roosevelt HS, dir guidance 1965-68; Wash Jr HS, tchr 1962-65; BTW HS, prof Military Sci 1959-62; Carver Jr HS, 1958-59. **Orgs:** President, Association of Specialists in Group Work, 1985-86; president, Capitol Hill Kiwanis Club, 1981-82; chairman of the board, Prepare Our Youth, 1987-; dean, Mt Bethel Baptist Educational Congress, National Baptist Convention, 1984-92; associate pastor, New Order Christian Fellowship, 1987-90; community advisory board of directors, Washington CTR for Aging Services, 1988-; president, DC Mental Health Counselors Association, 1992-93; assistant to chief prot chaplin, DC General Hospital, 1989-92; certified crisis intervener, ABECI, 1990; American Evangelistic Association, 1992-; Mt Bethel Baptist Assn, field missionary, 1994-. **Honors/Awds:** Outstanding tchr award 1960; outstanding leadership award 1962; outstanding leadership vocational guidance 1970; Christian Leadership 1967; United Nations USA Award, 1971-72; National Counselor Certification, National Board of Certified Counselors, 1983-88; Certificate of Excellence in Spiritual Aims, 1988, Outstanding Club Leadership Award, 1982, Capitol Hill Kiwanis Club; Clinical Pastoral Education Certificate, 1990. **Military Serv:** 1st lt 1954-56. **Business Addr:** Executive Director, Nazarene Outpost Ministries, PO Box 4412, Washington, DC 20017.

COLLINS, PAUL V.
Educator (retired). **Personal:** Born Sep 7, 1918, Philadelphia, PA; married Margaret Anne Chambers; children: Paula L, Pamela E, Richard Paul, Margaret Nicole. **Educ:** Livingstone Coll Salisbury NC, BA 1941; NY Univ New York, MA sociology 1948; TN State Univ Nashville, MS Health & PE 1958; NY Univ New York, Doctoral Studies 1968-69. **Career:** CA State Univ Hayward, assoc prof Educ & coordinator multi cultural Educ 1973-93; Weaver High School, Hartford CT Bd of Educ, prin 1970-73; US Office of Educ, Washington DC, educ program specialist 1969-70; NY Univ, instr in Educ 1968-69; IS 201 Manhattan, New York City Bd of Educ, master teacher 1966-68; JHS 139 Manhattan, NY Bd of Educ, dean of boys 1965-67; Wiley Coll, Marshall TX, head basketball coach & asst prof Sociology 1961-65; Lane Coll, Jackson TN, head basketball coach & assoc prof Health & Physical Educ 1960-61; Mississippi Valley State Coll, Etta Bena, MS, head basketball coach, asst football coach and scout, Assoc prof Sociology, 1957-60; SA Owen Jr Coll, Memphis TN, head basketball coach, 1955-57. **Orgs:** Dir Pacific Center Educ Reserach & Devel Castro Vally PA 1974-; multicultural educ adv com CA State Dept of Educ 1977-78; ad hoc com Racial Isolation in Sch CA State Dept of Educ 1977-78. **Honors/Awds:** Superior serv Award & HEW Office of Educ 1972; Phi Delta Kappa Hartford CT 1973; various papers pub. **Military Serv:** USN amm 3/c 2 years served.

COLLINS, ROBERT FREDERICK
Judge. **Personal:** Born Jan 27, 1931, New Orleans, LA; son of Irma Anderson and Frederick Collins; married Aloha M; children: Francesca McManus, Lisa Ann, Nanette C, Robert A. **Educ:** Dillard Univ, BA (Cum Laude) 1951, LA State Univ, JD; Univ of NV Natl Judge Coll, 1973. **Career:** Augustine Collins Smith & Warren New Orleans, partner 1956-59; So Univ, instr law 1959-61; Collins Douglas & Elie New Orleans, sr partner 1960-72; New Orleans Police Dept, asst city attny, legal adv 1967-69; Traffic Court New Orleans, judge ad-hoc 1969-72; State of LA, asst bar examiner 1970-78; Housing Auth New Or-

leans, attny 1971-72; Criminal Dist Court Orleans Parish LA, judge magistrate sect 1972-78; US Dist Court, judge 1978-; instructor Southern Univ Law School, Baton Rouge LA 1959-61, 1981-90. **Orgs:** Trustee Loyola Univ 1977-83; mem LA Bar Assoc; mem ABA; mem Alpha Phi Alpha, Sigma Pi Phi, Phi Alpha Delta. **Honors/Awds:** Passed Bar, LA 1954; Alpha Kappa Mu, Honor Society 1950; Hon LLD, Dillard Univ, 1979. **Military Serv:** AUS 1954-56.

COLLINS, ROBERT H.

Cleryman, educator. **Personal:** Born Jul 10, 1934, Chicago, IL; children: Robert, Pamela. **Educ:** Wilson Jr Clg Chicago IL, AA 1954; Michael Resse Sch of Med Tech, MT 1955; Roosevelt Univ Chicago IL, BS 1957; Concordia Theology Smnry Springfield, IL,BD 1964, MDiv 1965; Concordia Smnry St Louis, Master of Sacred Theology 1974. **Career:** Univ of IL R&E Hospital, medical tech 1955-56; Northwestern Univ, research chemist 1956; Lab of Vit Tech, chem quality control 1957-59; Concordia Seminary, Springfield IL, 1959-63; Bethlehem Lutheran Church, Col GA, pastor 1963-73; St James Lutheran Church, Bakersfield CA, pastor 1973-77; Northern IL Dist LC-MS, missionary-at-large; Corcordia Theological Seminary, Ft Wayne IN, prof of prctl theology counseling 1977-85. **Orgs:** Mem Scan 1982-; vacancy pstr Shepherd of the City Luth Ft Wayne 1983-; mem Resolve; vol chpln Parkview Meml Hosp Ft Wayne, IN; part-time chpln Cnty Jail; vacancy pastor Mount Calvary Luth Church; consultant cross-cultural ministry Trinity Luth Church. **Honors/Awds:** Meritorious Serv City of Col GA 1971, 72-73; Cert of Aprctn Pres Nixon GA State Advsr Com on Edc 1972; Cert of Aprctn TB Assc, Legal Aid Soc, Sr Citizens; mem Bd of Dir 1972-73.

COLLINS, ROSECRAIN

Dentist. **Personal:** Born Feb 14, 1929, Nashville, TN; married Elizabeth; children: Michelle, Adrienne. **Educ:** TN State U, BS 1952; Meharry Med Coll, DDS 1958. **Career:** Chicago Child Care Soc, Dentist 1976-; Chicago Dept Pub Aid, dental consult 1977-; Martin Luther King Hlth Ctr, dentist 1971-74; Kennedy, Ryan & Monigal Realtors, asso 1973-. **Orgs:** Treas Great Western Investment Ltd 1969-; dir Intl Sporting Club 1974; partner Forestry Recycling Mill 1975-; mem Dental Hlth Screening Chicago Pub Sch 1961-63; mem Lincoln Dental Soc 1959-; memChicago Denatl Soc treas 1970-74; IL Dental Soc 1959-; Am Dental Soc 1959-; Nat Dental Soc 1959-; Acad Gen Dentistry 1974-. **Honors/Awds:** Citation pub serv City Chicago 1962-63. **Military Serv:** AUS sgt 1952-54. **Business Addr:** 1525 E 53rd St #903-R, Chicago, IL 60615.

COLLINS, SYLVIA DURNELL

Registered nurse. **Personal:** Born Nov 17, 1934, Philadelphia, PA; daughter of Catherine Sanford and Frank Durnell; children: Dawn Catherine. **Educ:** Episcopal Hospital, RN 1955; Univ of PA, BSN 1959; Temple Univ, MEd 1973. **Career:** Children/Youth Prog, chief project nurse 1970-72; Southeast Philadelphia Neighborhood Health Ctr, dir of nursing 1972-76; Philadelphia Health Plan, consultant 1976-79; Lutheran Home, instructor insvcs educ 1977-79; ACT Drug Rehab, staff nurse 1981-82; Comm Coll, vstg lecturer 1978-80; Philadelphia Corp for Aging, consultant/health prom 1981-. **Orgs:** Dir North Central YWCA 1976-86; dir Black Alumni Soc Univ of PA 1982-86; chairperson Professional Adv Comm Opportunity Towers Philadelphia 1982-86; faculty Nursing East Continuing Educ 1983,84; mem vice chairperson Ethnic Nurses of Color 1984-86; sec Gratz St Neighbors 1984-86; mem prof ed comm Amer Cancer Soc 1985-86; mem Council of Neighborhoods 1985; mem Public Educ Comm Arthritis Assn; mem Alpha Kappa Alpha Sor, Omega Omega Chapt, Amer Public Health Assn, Chi Eta Phi Sor Theta Chapt; life mem NAACP; member American Cancer Society; bd of directors Keys to Living Unit; member, American Cancer Society; prof educ comm, Keys to Living Unit; member, Survivor's Day, American Cancer Society, 1990; committee, Philadelphia Division; board of trustees YWCA of Philadelphia; board of directors Charles DrewMen Health/Mental Retardation Center. **Honors/Awds:** Author article University of Pennsylvania 1986, BAS Newsletter; Sigma Theta Tau, Kappa Chi Nursing Honor Society 1988; 12 appearances radio & tv; Pennsylvania Health Educators Institute, Special Population Health Education/Promotion Award, 1996. **Home Addr:** 6245 No Gratz St, Philadelphia, PA 19141. **Business Addr:** Consultant, Health Promotion, Philadelphia Corp for Aging, 642 North Broad St, Philadelphia, PA 19130-3409.

COLLINS, TESSIL JOHN

Creative director, producer, multimedia consultant. **Personal:** Born Aug 29, 1952, Boston, MA; son of Evelyn A Gill Collins and Tessil A Collins; children: Dionna Collins. **Educ:** Boston Latin Sch, 1971; Tufts Univ, BA English 1975; Boston Univ, Exec Prog Cert Small Bus Dev Prog 1985. **Career:** Spectrum Management, owner, 1984-; Boston Public Schools, Madison Park Technical-Vocational High School, instructor, Communication Arts/Television Production, 1984-; Beantown Music, natl sales/promotions; RCA/A&M/Arista Records, field merchandiser, 1981-83; WILD Radio, Boston, acct exec, 1975, 1980-81; Rep Melvin H King, campaign mgr, 1978-79; WBCN Radio, acct exec, 1978-80; WBZ Radio, producer, 1973-78. **Orgs:** Prince Hall Grand Lodge F& AM; board member Dimock Community Health Center, Project Africa; board member, Berklee Coll of Music Community Advisory Committee. **Honors/Awds:** Cert Media Technology MA Dept of Educ Div of Occup Educ 1985; position at Beantown announced in Black Enterp May & Feb 1984; producer video on student diversity "I'm Different, You're Different, We're All Okay" Tufts Univ 1985; producer of video for Mrs Black Boston Pageant 1986; Grand Prize Florida Citrus Commission Music Video Competition 1987; Writer/Producer, "It's Christmastime Again," recorded by TSOC, 1994; Producer, "The Beat," A Street Smarts Collaborative Video Project, Boston Police Dept, 1995; producer, "The Voice," WBPS-AM, Boston. **Home Phone:** (617)739-3552. **Business Addr:** President, Spectrum Management, PO Box 1045, Roxbury Crossing Station, Boston, MA 02120, (617)945-4413.

COLLINS, THEODICIA DEBORAH

Attorney. **Personal:** Born Feb 19, 1959, Brooklyn, NY. **Educ:** SUNY Old Westbury, BA 1981; Univ of Bridgeport, JD/MBA 1986. **Career:** Univ of Bridgeport, acctg dept accts asst 1983-84, sch of law legal rsch asst 1984-85, sch of business grad rsch asst 1985-86, tax clinic legal intern 1986. **Orgs:** Mem Black Entertainment & Sports Lawyers Assoc 1985, NY Investors Network 1985. **Honors/Awds:** Certificate of Awd Bd of Educ Bridgeport CT 1985; Certificate of Awd Outstanding Young Women of Amer 1986. **Business Addr:** Entertainment Attorney, 401 Broadway, Suite 300, New York, NY 10013.

COLLINS, WILLIAM, JR.

Clergyman. **Personal:** Born Jul 3, 1924, St Louis; married Margaret Elizabeth Brown; children: Sylvia, Deirdre, William, III. **Educ:** St Louis U, BS 1956; Colgate Rochester Div Sch, BD 1960; Univ Rochester, MEd 1960; Colgate Rochester Div Sch, MDiv 1972; E NE Christian Coll , DD 1972; St Louis U, PhD 1973. **Career:** Antioch Bapt Ch St Louis, pastor 1961-; Bluefield State Coll, dir pub relations & asst registrar 1961; Antioch Bapt Ch St Louis, minister christian educ 1960-61; Second Bapt Ch Leroy NY, student pastor 1959-60; US Postal, employee 1951-56; MO Dept Welfare St Louis, caseworker 1948-51. **Orgs:** Bd trustees St Louis Jr Coll Dist elected 6 yr term 1975; mem Am Bapt Conv; Task Force; Intl Ministries Africa 1971-; bd mem Annie Malone Childrens Home St Louis 1970-; bd Health & Hosp St Louis 1968-; St Louis Municipal Nurses bd 1970-; Landmark & Urban Design Commn St Louis 1968- 72; Adult Welfare Commns St Louis 1970-; Eagle Scout 1939; Alpha Phi Alpha Frat 1947; Preaching Mission Am Bapt El Salvador & Nicaragua Latin Am 1966; Missionary Involvement Tour; Am Bapt W Africa 1972. **Military Serv:** AUS sgt 1943-46. **Business Addr:** 4213 W North Market, St Louis, MO 63113.

COLLINS, WILLIAM KEELAN, SR.

Dentist. **Personal:** Born Oct 30, 1914, Seat Pleasant, MD; married Eleanore; children: William Jr, John. **Educ:** Howard U, BS 1935; Howard U, DDS 1939; Georgetown Univ Coll Dnstry, DSc 1974. **Career:** Pvt Pract, dnstry 1939-. **Orgs:** Past pres Am Assoc Dntl Exmnrs 1976-77; mem exec coun AADE 1972-; sec treasr N E Regnl Bd & Dentl Exmnrs 1969-; chmn bd dir Untd Natl Bnk WA 1964-; bd trustee Howard Univ 1968-. **Honors/Awds:** Harry Struther Aw NY Univ Coll Dnstry 1972; dnst of yr DC Dntl Soc 1970. **Military Serv:** AUS 1st lt. **Business Addr:** 4645 Burroughs Ave NE, Washington, DC 20019.

COLLINS-BONDON, CAROLYN R.

Educational fiscal analyst. **Personal:** Born Mar 30, 1949, Jackson, MS; daughter of Mr & Mrs Roma Collins; children: Celeste. **Educ:** Western Michigan Univ, BS 1971, MA 1980, EdD 1983. **Career:** Grand Rapids Public Schools, teacher 1972-74; Fairfax Co School, lang arts res teacher 1974-79; Western Michigan Univ, administrator 1981-84, lobbyist 1984-87; Higher Educ Fiscal Analyst, 1987-. **Orgs:** Mem bd dirs YWCA 1980-86; WMU Black Caucus Western MI Univ 1981-; mem Amer Soc Trainers and Developers 1983-; pres Training/Learning/Development/Design 1983-; speaker NCEOA Chicago 1985, Washington DC 1986; speaker Evaluation Conference ENET; mem Alpha Kappa Alpha, Natl Assoc Women's Deans & Admin. **Honors/Awds:** Charles Stewart Mott Fellowship Mott Foundation 1981-82; Award for Achievement and Excellence in Educ Natl Assoc of Negro Business & Professional Women 1985.

COLLINS-EAGLIN, JAN THERESA

Psychologist/professor. **Personal:** Born Dec 2, 1950, New York, NY; daughter of Naomi Fraser Collins and John E Collins; married Fulton Eaglin, Jun 1979; children: Christopher, Jennifer, Jessica. **Educ:** California State Univ, Dominguez Hills, BA, 1977; University of Michigan, Ann Arbor, MI, MS, 1980, EdS, 1980, PhD, 1983. **Career:** University of Michigan, Ann Arbor, MI, lecturer, 1983-85; Eastern Michigan University, Ypsilanti, MI, psychologist, 1985-87, coordinator, 1987-90, professor, 1990-. **Orgs:** Member, American Psychological Assn, 1983-; member, Michigan College Personnel Assn, 1987-; member, Links Inc, 1988-; regional foundation officer, Jack and Jill of America, 1988-; member, Alpha Kappa Alpha Sorority, 1975-. **Honors/Awds:** American Psychological Assn Fellow, 1978-82; National Institute for Mental Health Fellow, 1977-81; Research and grants obtained concerning college retention of black students: Select Student Support Services, State of Michigan, 1987-90; Summer Incentive Program, Dept of Labor, 1987-90. **Business Addr:** Psychologist/Professor, Eastern Michigan University, 234 Boone Hall, Ypsilanti, MI 48197.

COLLINS-GRANT, EARLEAN

State Senator. **Personal:** Born Sep 4, Rollingfork, MS; married John Grant; children: Dwarrye. **Educ:** Univ of IL, BS Soc & Ed. **Career:** Collins Realty & Ins Agency, self employed 1969-72; State of IL Dept of Children & Famlty Svcs, soc serv admin 1972-76; State of IL, senator, currently. **Orgs:** Westside Business Assn; Natl Assn Soc Workers; Natl Conf State Leg; Conf of Women Leg; Intergovernmental Coop Council. **Honors/Awds:** Best Legislator Awd Independent Voters of IL; IL Business & Professional Women's Award; IL Ed Assn Award; Amvet's Award. **Business Addr:** Senator, District 4, Illinois State Senate, 5943 W Madison St, Chicago, IL 60644.

COLLINS-REID, LAVERNE FRANCIS (LAVERNE FRANCIS COLLINS)

Government official. **Personal:** Born Sep 8, 1946, San Angelo, TX; daughter of Veora Washington Francis and George Franklin Francis Jr; married A Robert Reid, Mar 26, 1988; children: Andrew Collins Jr (deceased), Kevin Michael Collins (deceased). **Educ:** Univ of Alaska, BS, business, 1977; Univ of Southern CA, masters, public admin, 1980. **Career:** Federal Aviation Adm, Anchorage, AK, realty specialist, staff appraiser, 1975-79, special asst to reg dir, 1979, Washington, DC, international aviation analyst, 1980-81; Anchorage, AK, petroleum analyst, 1981-88; Seattle, WA, human resources specialist, 1989-90; airports prog officer, 1990-92; FAA Academy, airports program instructor, 1992-. **Orgs:** Natl pres, Business & Professional Women of USA, 1989-90; chm, bd of trustees, Business & Professional Women Foundation, 1989-90; US Small Business Natl Advisory Cnl, 1989-93; chair, Alaska USA Federal Credit Union Supv Comm, 1986-88; bd mem, Anchorage 1994 Olympic Organizing Comm, 1987-88; commissioner, State of Alaska Real Estate Commission, 1983-88. **Honors/Awds:** Administrative law judge trng, Natl Judicial College, 1988.

COLLONS, FERRIC JASON

Professional football player. **Personal:** Born Dec 4, 1969, Bellville, IL. **Educ:** Univ of California, attended. **Career:** New England Patriots, defensive end, 1995-. **Business Addr:** Professional Football Player, New England Patriots, 60 Washington St, Foxboro Stadium, Foxboro, MA 02035, (508)543-7911.

COLLYMORE, EDWARD L.

Educational administrator. **Personal:** Born Jan 5, 1938, Cambridge, MA; son of Eulah M Johnson Collymore and Percival E Collymore; married Marcia L Burnett; children: Sandra Collymore Coleman, Edward Jr. **Educ:** Villanova Univ, BS, Econ, 1959, MA, Counseling, 1971; Univ of PA, EdD Admin, 1984. **Career:** Cambridge Public Sch, Substitute teacher, 1963; Liberty Mutual Ins Co, casulty underwriter, 1963-66; Third Dist Ct Cambridge; juvenile probation officer, 1966-69; Office Soc Action Program, Villanova Univ, 1969-; Office of Multicultural Affairs, executive director, currently. **Orgs:** Bd Rosemont Optimist 1983; bd pres Comm Action Agency Delaware CO 1995. **Honors/Awds:** Co-holder, World Record, 60yd dash, AAU Track, 1957; All-Amer 220 yard dash NCAA Track 1957-59; rep US Track Europe, Russia AAU, 1957-58; Soc Action Award VU, 1978; Hall of Fame, VU Alumni Assn, 1980; Distinguished Alumnus Black Cultural Soc, 1982; Rosemont Optimist Man of the Year, 1985; Comm Action Agency of DE County Bd, Mem of the Year, 1985. **Military Serv:** USMCR col, retired. **Business Addr:** Executive Director, Office of Multicultural Affairs, Villanova, PA 19085, (610)519-4077.

COLON, HARRY

Professional football player. **Personal:** Born Feb 14, 1969, Kansas City, KS. **Educ:** Univ of Missouri. **Career:** New England Patriots, defensive back, 1991; Detroit Lions, 1992-94, 1997-; Jacksonville Jaguars, 1995. **Business Addr:** Professional Football Player, Detroit Lions, 1200 Featherstone Rd, Pontiac, MI 48342, (248)335-4131.

COLSON, JOSEPH S., JR.

Telecommunications executive. **Personal:** Born Sep 27, 1947, Washington, DC; son of Bernice Brett Colson and Joseph S Colson Sr; married Rosemary Elizabeth Rogers, Jul 18, 1969 (divorced); children: Angela, Joseph Michael, Timothy; married Sharon L Harrison, May 10, 1995. **Educ:** North Carolina State University, BSEE, 1968; Stanford University, MSEE, 1969. **Career:** AT&T Bell Labs, Greensboro, NC, MTS, 1968-71, Columbus, OH, supvr, 1971-77, Naperville, IL, supvr, 1977-79, dept head, 1979-82, dir, 1982-87, exec dir, 1987-90, Lisle, IL, vp of switching systems, 1990-93; vp of communications services applications, Lisle, IL, 1993-96; Lucent Technologies, AT&T Customer Business Unit, president, 1996-97, International Regions & Prof. Services, president, 1997-. **Orgs:** Executive Advisory Council, International Communications Forum 1987-; IEEE, North Carolina Agricultural & Technical State University, School of Engineering, industry advisory group; bd of trustees, North Carolina State University, brd of visitors. **Honors/Awds:** Phi Eta Sigma, 1964-68; Eta Kappa

Nu, 1964-68; Tau Beta Phi, 1964-68; Phi Kappa Phi, 1964-68; Black Enterprise Mag, one of top 25 Black executives in US, 1988; Black Engineer of the Year for Professional Achievement, Black Engineer Magazine 1989. **Business Addr:** President, International Regions & Prof Svcs, Lucent Technologies, 283 King George Rd, Rm C4A15, Warren, NJ 07059.

COLSON, LEWIS ARNOLD
Community activist, educator. **Personal:** Born Aug 3, 1947, Miami, FL; son of Arthur Mae Ross and Booker T Colson (deceased); married Glendoria Saine, May 14, 1982; children: Doria Arne, Lewis Arnold Jr, Roviere Jordan, Charles, Lewis Armand, Michelle. **Educ:** Wayne State University, political science, 1973-75; Mercy College, criminal justice, 1976. **Career:** Detroit Police Department, 1972-82; Tru-Vue Restaurant, co-owner, 1982-86; Guardian Police Association, executive director, 1986-89; National Black Police Association, administrative assistant, 1986-88; Upward Entrepreneurial Consultant Services, Inc, senior partner, 1986-; Detroit Underground Restaurant, Inc, 1988-90; Southern Corner Caterers, co-owner, 1986-; Doty Multiservice Center Inc, founder, executive director, 1990-92; Detroiters Organized to Train Youth, Inc, founder, director, 1992-. **Orgs:** Black Men Inc, Youth Committee, chairperson, 1992-; NAACP, Economic Committee, 1991-; New Detroit, Anti-Violence Program, chairperson, 1992; Urban League, By Our Own Hands, 1991; Youth Commission, lead agency head, regional chairperson, 1991-; National Black Police Association, chairperson, 1973-91; Guardian Police Association, Peoplemakers Project, executive director, founder, 1978-89; SOSAD, volunteer, trainer; UAW & University of Detroit, youth instructor, 1991. **Honors/Awds:** Detroit City Council, Spirit of Detroit, 1992; Mayor of City of Detroit, Anti-Crime Week, 1991; National Crime Prevention Council, Certificate of Achievement, 1989; REACH Community Organization, Certificate of Appreciation, 1991. **Special Achievements:** Solutions to the Detroit Drug Problem, 1978; Creation of Detroit/ Peoplemakers Project, 1979; Establishment of First Police Department Drug Education-Prevention Program in Nation, 1976; First Crime Prevention Consultant Firm in Michigan, 1990; First African Centered Management Program, 1991. **Military Serv:** US Army, 1966-69; Honor Guard/Military Police-European Headquarters. **Home Addr:** 16231 Princeton Ave, Detroit, MI 48221, (313)863-9190. **Business Addr:** Founder/ Director, Detroiters Organized To Train Youth Inc, 1600 Lawrence Ave, Detroit, MI 48206, (313)863-9190.

COLSTON, FREDDIE C.
Educator. **Personal:** Born Mar 28, 1936, Gretna, FL; married Doris Marie; children: Deirdre, Charisse. **Educ:** Morehouse Clg, BA 1959; AT Univ, MA 1966; OH State Univ, PhD 1972. **Career:** So Univ Baton Rouge, LA, assc prof pol sci 1972-73; Univ Detroit Detroit, MI, assc prof pol sci & blk stds 1973-76; Dillard Univ New Orleans, LA, chrm div soc sci 1976-78; Delta Clg Univ Cntr, MI, asst prof pol sci 1978-80; Exec Semnr Cntr US Ofc Prsnl Mgmt, assoc dir 1980-87; prof and coordinator of graduate studies Inst of Govt, TN State Univ 1987-88; professor and coordinator of graduate studies NC Central Univ 1988-89; dir public admin prog NC Central Univ 1989-91; Dept of History & Political Science, Georgia Southwestern State Univ, Americus, GA, prof, 1992-97. **Orgs:** Mem Natl Conf Blck Pol Sci 1971-, Natl Forum Blck Pblc Admn 1984-, Am Pol Sci Assc 1968-, Ctr for the Study of Presidency 1976-, Am Soc Pblc Admn 1983-, Omega Psi Phi Frat 1956; bd mgmt YMCA Metropolitan Detroit 1976; rptr & mem Govt Subcmt Task Force 2000 Midland, MI 1979; mem Amer Assn for Higher Educ 1987-; mem Amer Mgmt Assn 1988. **Honors/Awds:** Intntl stds summer fellow Ford Found Duke Univ 1967; tchg assc Dept of Pol Sci OH State Univ 1968-71; fellow So Flwshp Fund Atlanta, GA 1968-71; mem Pi Sigma Alpha Natl Pol Sci Hon Soc 1958-; mem Alpha Phi Gamma Natl Jrnlst Hon Soc 1958-. **Home Addr:** 126 Hazleton Ln, Oak Ridge, TN 37830.

COLSTON, MONROE JAMES
Business executive. **Personal:** Born Sep 5, 1933, Richland, TX; married Frances V Brown; children: Rhonda Wardlow, Marietta. **Educ:** Univ MN, AA; Nat Exec Inst, Grad; Univ CO. **Career:** Urban Affairs Gtr Des Moines C of C, mgr; Boy Scouts of Am, exec dir 1968-71. **Orgs:** Real estate commr State of IA; bd dir IA Soc for Mgmt Nat; mem & Metro Assistance Team; Nat Alliance of Businessmen; mem Brain Trust to Congressional Balck Caucus; chmn co-founder Blacks in Mgmt; council mem Boy Scouts of Am; Kappa Alpha Psi; com person IA Career Edn; Civilian Serv Club; mem Am C of C. **Honors/Awds:** Dist scouter of year; IA All Am Family 1970; outst serviceman AUS 1 954. **Military Serv:** AUS corpl 1954-56. **Business Addr:** 800 High, Des Moines, IA 50307.

COLSTON BARGE, GAYLE S.
Business executive. **Personal:** Born Jun 9, 1951, Columbus, OH; daughter of Geneva Laws Colston and Ervin M Colston; married Carlos H Barge, Jul 24, 1971; children: Darron Barge, Mario Barge. **Educ:** Ohio Univ, 1970-71; Wright State Univ, 1972; Minot State Univ, BA, 1981. **Career:** City of Columbus, public education specialist, 1976-78; KBLE of Ohio, administrative manager, 1978-79; JC Penney Insurance Co, customer service representative, 1979-80, underwriter, sr underwriter, 1980-82; JC Penney Co, systems project coordinator, 1982-83, market public affairs coordinator, 1983-88, field public affairs coordinator, 1988-90, field public affairs manager, 1990-; The Barge Group, president, 1995-. **Orgs:** Leadership Dallas, class mbr, 1992-93; Dallas Black Dance Theatre Gala Cmte, co-chair, 1990-; The 500 Inc, montage and auction cmte chairs, 1988-; The Links Inc, Plano Chapter, exec comm, 1995-; Delta Sigma Theta Sorority, natl comm mem, 1993-97, local chap bd, 1994-; Bryan's House, bd mem, 1995-; Dallas Women's Foundation, bd, 1998-; M L King Performing Arts Center, bd of dirs, 1986-88; State of Ohio Job Training Partnership Act Commission, commissoner, appointed, 1987-88; numerous others. **Honors/Awds:** Ohio Univ, Outstanding Black Woman Alumnus, 1980; One of Ten Most Influential Women in Dallas, 1993; Columbus Jaycees, Ten Outstanding Citizens Award, 1984; She Knows Where She's Going Award, 1997; Community Relations Report, Bellringer Award of Excellence, 1992; numerous others. **Special Achievements:** Co-editor of Focus 2000, JC Penney's first diversity publication, 1993. **Business Addr:** President, The Barge Group, 19002 Dallas Parkway, No 1025, Dallas, TX 75287, (972)930-9569.

COLTER, CYRUS J.
Attorney, author. **Personal:** Born Jan 8, 1910, Noblesville, IN; married Imogene Mackay (deceased). **Educ:** Chicago Kent Coll of Law, 1940; Univ of Chicago Circle Campus, Hon Litt D 1977. **Career:** State of IL, commerce commissioner 1951-73; Northwestern Univ, prof of humanities 1973-78; attorney/ writer. **Orgs:** Bd trustees Chicago Symphony Orch; served with Adminis Conf of US for Study of Exec Agencies of Fed Govt; IL Res Planning Comm; Railroads Comm of Natl Assn of Reg & Utility Commrs; mem Friends of Chicago Schs Comm; Kappa Alpha Psi. **Honors/Awds:** Novelist and short story writer, "The Beach Umbrella" (awarded the Univ of IA Sch of Letters Award 1970); "The Rivers of Eros" 1972; "The Hippodrome" 1973; "Night Studies" 1980; City of Light, Thunder Mouth Press, 199 3. **Business Addr:** 190 S LaSalle St, Ste 2062, Chicago, IL 60603.

COLTRANE, ALICE TURIYA
Musician. **Personal:** Born Aug 27, 1937, Detroit, MI; married John Coltrane (deceased); children: John (deceased), Ravi, Oran, Michelle. **Educ:** Attended, Detroit Inst of Technology. **Career:** Jowcol Music, owner. **Orgs:** Director/founder The Vedantic Ctr 1976-; owner Avatar Book Inst 1978-. **Honors/ Awds:** Record albums ABC, MCA, Warner Bros 1968-78; books, audio, video tapes 1978-. **Business Addr:** Owner, Jowcol Music, 23123 Ventura Blvd. #106, Woodland Hills, CA 91364-1104.

COLVIN, ALEX, II
Government official/power engineering instructor. **Personal:** Born Nov 17, 1946, Birmingham, AL; son of Alex & Novella Colvin; divorced; children: Atiba, Jawanza, Kimba, Alex III, Marc, Taylor. **Educ:** UCLA, attended, 1972-74; University of the District of Columbia, attended, 1974-78. **Career:** DC Government, chief boiler inspector, 1972-. **Orgs:** National Assn Black Scuba Divers, recording scy, 1993-; National Assn Power Engineers, instructor, 1974-; National Bd of Boiler & Pressure Vessel Inspectors, 1993-; American Society of Mechanical Engineers, 1981-. **Honors/Awds:** National Association Power Engineers, Educator of the Year, 1997; National Association Black Scuba Divers, Outstanding Service, 1997. **Special Achievements:** Author of book of poetry, "To the People," 1978. **Military Serv:** US Navy, 1963-66; US Marine Corps, 1967-71, E-5, Purple Heart, 1968. **Home Addr:** 1183 Neal St, NE, Washington, DC 20002.

COLVIN, ALONZA JAMES
Elected official. **Personal:** Born Jul 8, 1931, Union Springs, AL; married Charlene A Bacon; children: Judy Webb, James E, Jimmie, Chris, Mark, Elizabeth. **Educ:** GED only. **Career:** General Motors, general labor 1950-75; Saginaw Model Cities Inc, chmn 1967-71; Valley Star News, editor-publisher 1967-73; Buena Vista Charter Township, trustee 1980-. **Orgs:** Mem Natl Newspaper Publishers Assn 1967-73; producer/dir Autumn Leaves Pageant 1967-73; bd of dirs Police-Comm Relations Comm 1970-83; bd of dirs Saginaw Economic Development Corp 1971-72; bd of dirs Big Brothers of Saginaw 1972-76; vice pres Miss Saginaw Co Pageant 1970-. **Business Addr:** Trustee, Buena Vista Char Twnshp, 1160 S Outer Dr, Saginaw, MI 48601.

COLVIN, ERNEST J.
Dental surgeon. **Personal:** Born Jan 20, 1935, Chester, SC; son of Alberta Moffett Colvin and Alex Colvin; married Shirley Beard (divorced); children: Ernest J II. **Educ:** Morgan State Coll, BS 1956; Howard Univ Sch Dentistry, DDS 1968. **Career:** Howard Univ Sch Dentistry, taught part time 1968-71; Self-employed, dr dental surgery. **Orgs:** Bd dir Horseman's Benevolent Protective Assn WV; Chi Delta Mu Frat; Am Dental Assn; MD State Dental Assn fin sec; Baltimore City Dental Soc; Am Indodontic Soc; Am Dental Soc Anesthesiology; Am Soc Gen Dentistry; Kappa Alpha Psi Frat; Columbia Chap Jack & Jill Am Inc; Columbia NAACP Am Cancer Soc; Com Health Council Baltimroe City; bd dir NW Baltimore Community Health Care; St Johns Evangelist Roman Cath Ch. **Honors/ Awds:** Chairman, Maryland Racing Commission 1988-91; member, MD Racing Commission 1977-. **Military Serv:** AUS pfc 1956-58. **Business Addr:** 4413 1/2 Park Heights Ave, Baltimore, MD 21215, (410)664-1900.

COLVIN, WILLIAM E.
Educator, educational administrator. **Personal:** Born May 27, 1930, Birmingham, AL; son of Lucille White Colvin and Lucius Will Colvin; married Regina A Bahner, Jun 9, 1956; children: Felicia Imre, Gracita Dawn. **Educ:** AL State Univ, BS 1951; IN Univ, MS 1960; Academic Affairs Conf of Midwestern Univs, Cert of Administration; IL State, EdD 1971. **Career:** Stillman Coll, Department of Art, chair 1958-69; Illinois State Univ, dir of ethnic studies 1974-78, prof of art 1971-91; Eastern Illinois Univ, professor of art, 1987-, chair Afro-American studies, 1991-. **Orgs:** Elected rep to US/Brazilian Mod Art Soc 1981-; dir career program IL Comm on Black Concerns in Higher Educ 1983-; mem Natl Conf of Artists; mem Natl Art Educ Assn; mem Phi Delta Kappa Hon Soc in Educ. **Honors/ Awds:** Rockefeller Fellow 1973-74; Phelps-Stokes Fund Grant 1973; publs exhibitions in field; Martin Luther King BLM Normal Human Relations 1983; Outstanding Artist in the Field AL State Univ 1985; Outstanding Service Awd IL Committee on Black Concerns in Higher Educ 1985; Fulbright Lecture/Rsch Fulbright Brazil 1981-85; univ grant to Belize for research, 1989. **Home Addr:** 507 N Grove St, Normal, IL 61761. **Business Addr:** Professor of Art, Eastern Illinois University, Charleston, IL 61920.

COLYER, SHERYL LYNN
Personnel, training, labor relations. **Personal:** Born Dec 20, 1959, Portsmouth, VA; daughter of Lubertha Alexander Colyer and Joshua Colyer. **Educ:** Howard University, Washington, DC, 1981; Columbia University, New York, NY, MA, 1983; George Washington Univ, Washington DC, PhD, 1996. **Career:** Internal Revenue, Washington, DC, personnel psychologist, 1983-84; Technology Applications Inc, Falls Church, VA, consultant, 1984-85; General Motors, Fort Wayne, IN, 1985-88, H R specialist; Federal Home Loan Mortgage Corp, training and dev consultant, 1988-90; Pepsico, KFC, Hanover, MD, division manager, 1990-92; Hechinger Co., director, 1992-95; Hardees Food System, vice pres, 1995-96; Independent management consultant, 1996-. **Orgs:** President, Alpha Chapter, Delta Sigma Theta, 1980-81; American Psychological Association; American Society for Training and Development; Society for Industrial and Organizational Psychology Inc; American Society for Personnel Administration. **Honors/Awds:** 100 Most Promising Black Women in Corporate America, 1991; Outstanding Young Women of America, Ebony Magazine. **Home Addr:** 507 E Indian Spring Dr, Silver Spring, MD 20901.

COMBS, JULIUS V.
Medical management company executive, physician. **Personal:** Born Aug 6, 1931, Detroit, MI; son of Everlee Dennis Combs and Julius Combs; married Alice Ann Gaston, Dec 27, 1956; children: Kimberly A, Julius G. **Educ:** Wayne State Univ, BS 1953; MD 1958 Wayne State Univ Affilated Hospital, 1964; Am Bd Ob-Gyn, diplomate 1967; fellow AGOG. **Career:** Vincent & Combs Bldg Corp, pres ; Wayne State Univ School Med, clinical asst, 1976-; Omni Care Health Plan, dir 1973-; chairman of the board 1980-92, exec comm; Associate Med Develop Corp, vice pres 1979-81; United American Health Corp., chairman, chief executive officer, currently. **Orgs:** Detroit Med Soc; chmn Region IV NMA 1975-77; mem Am Fertility Soc; NMA; Detroit Med Soc; MI State Med Soc; Wayne Co Med Soc; Am Assn Gyn Laparoscopists; Am Coll Ob-Gyn; Detroit Inst Arts Founders Soc; life mem NAACP; life mem Kappa Alpha Psi Frat; mem House Del NMA 1967-. Board member, Music Hall Center of Performing Arts; board member, Oakland University; board member, United Way of Southeastern Michigan. **Honors/ Awds:** Michiganian of the Year The Detroit News-1994. **Business Addr:** Chmn/CEO, United American Healthcare Corporation, 1155 Brewery Park Blvd #200, Detroit, MI 48207.

COMBS, SEAN J. (PUFFY)
Record co. executive, rapper. **Personal:** Born Nov 4, New York, NY; son of Janice & Melvin Earl Combs; children: Justin Dior, Christian Casey. **Educ:** Howard University, 1988-90. **Career:** Uptown Entertainment, vice pres A&R, 1990-91; Bad Boy Entertainment, Chief Executive Officer, currently. Justin's Bar and Restaurant, Manhattan, owner, 1997-; Daddy's House Recording Studios. **Orgs:** American Federation of Television & Radio Artists, 1994-; American Federation of Musicians, 1993-; Daddy's House Programs. **Honors/Awds:** ASCAP, Rhythm & Soul Award "Juicy", 1995; Gavin, Rap Indie (Dist. by a Major) of the Year, 1995; 3M, Visionary Award for Producing, 1994; Impace, Award of Merit for Creative Excellence, 1994; Grammys, Award for Best Rap Performance By a Duo or Group, with Faith Evans and 112, Best Rap Album, 1998. **Special Achievements:** Produced songs, directed videos for: Jodeci, Mary J. Blige, Craig Mack, the Notorious B.I.G., Faith Evans and others; released album as Puff Daddy & The Family, No Way Out 1997; released song, "I'll Be Missing You," with Faith Evans and group 112, 1997. **Business Addr:** Chief Executive Officer, Bad Boy Entertainment, 8-10 W 19th St, 9th Fl, New York, NY 10011, (212)741-7070.

COMBS, SYLVESTER LAWRENCE
Educator (retired). **Personal:** Born Nov 15, 1919, Bristow, OK; married Willa Ryan. **Educ:** Langston University, BA; Oklahoma State University, MA. **Career:** Stillwater Middle School, OK, teacher, industrial arts, education chairman, faculty council, 1967 until retirement; Slick High School, OK, teacher, coach, principal, 1957-67; L'Overture High School, OK, principal, 1955-57, teacher, coach, 1946-55; Mutual Funds & Life Insurance Co, registered representative. **Orgs:** OK Education Assn; Natl Education Assn; Stillwater Education Assn; Iota Lambda Sigma; executive bd, Stillwater YMCA; United Supreme Council Sovereign Grand Inspectors; 33rd Degree, Ancient & Accepted Scottish Rite of Free Masonry, Prince Hall Affiliation; Alpha Phi Alpha; Stillwater Evening Fraternity; Stillwater Kiwanis Club; Believers Baptist Church; offered membership, Phi Beta Kappa.

COMBS, WILLA R.
Educator (retired). **Personal:** Born Aug 11, 1925, Oklahoma City, OK; married Sylvester. **Educ:** Langston Univ, BS 1947; Oklahoma State Univ, MS 1955; Colorado State Christian Coll, PhD 1973; Oklahoma State Univ, EdD 1974. **Career:** Attucks High School, Vinita OK, vocational home economics teacher 1947-49; Chandler High School, Chandler OK, 1949; L'Overture High School, Slick OK, home economics teacher 1949-57; Southern Univ, Baton Rouge LA, home economics, home mgmt instructor 1960-61; Slick High School, Slick OK, teahcer 1957-66; Human Resource Devel Cooperative Extension Serv, Oklahoma State Univ, Stillwater OK, cooperative extension specialist 1966-76; Langston Univ Study Tour of W African Countries Liberia Ivory Coast Chana via Portugal Canary Islands, prof & chmn 1972-73; Langston Univ, prof, chmn home economics, agr research 1976-82, prof emeritus 1982-; Oklahoma State University, professor emeritus, 1993-. **Orgs:** Chmn Reactor Panel Natl Educ Leadership Conf, Tuskegee Inst AL 1971; mem Central Coord Com on Amer Home Econ Issues, Pres EEO Com Oklahoma State Univ 1967-76; group leader Oklahoma Coalition for Clean Air 1970; mem Payne-Noble Co Health Advisory Com; trainer Head Start Program Oklahoma State Univ 1966-70; Natl 4-H Club Congress Chicago IL 1968; chmn State Home Econ Family Econ Home Mgmt Sect 1968-70; chmn Family Home Econ Home Mgt Sec of Amer Home Econ Assn Com on World Food Supply; vice pres Prog Phi Upsilon Omicron 1975-76; sec AAUW Stillwater Branch; Anti-Basileus 1970-75; NAACP; Langston Univ Alumni Assn; alumni council & treas Langston Univ Home Econ; Oklahoma State Univ Alumni Assn; charter mem, vice pres Langston/Coyle Business & Professional Women'sClub 1984-85; Black Heritage m Oklahoma Historical Soc 1984-95; citizen review comm Library Improvement Program 1985-88; Chr, Oklahoma Dept of Libraries, 1993-94; Payne County Retired Educators Assn, Oklahoma and National Assn; bd of dirs, Payne County Health Dept Eldercare; bd of dirs, Project HEART, Inc, 1994-95; Church Women United, Stillwater. **Honors/Awds:** Outstanding Alumnus 1975; Distinguished Women's Club Award; Farm Found Scholarship, Colorado State Univ; cum laude Langston Univ OK; Two Thousand Women of Achievement 1970; Named to Natl Register of Prominent Amers & Intl Notables 1975; Named Outstanding Educator of the Year, Prince Hall Grand Lodge 1978-80; Named Outstanding Woman of the Year, AAUW Stillwater Branch 1978; Septima Poinsette Clark Award, Beta Omicron Omega Chapter of Alpha Kappa Alpha 1986. **Business Addr:** Professor Emeritus, Oklahoma State University, Stillwater, OK 74078.

COMEGYS, DAPHNE D. See HARRISON, DAPHNE DUVAL.

COMER, JAMES PIERPONT
Psychiatrist, educator, educational administrator. **Personal:** Born Sep 25, 1934, East Chicago, IN; son of Maggie Nichols Comer and Hugh Comer; married Shirley Ann Arnold (deceased); children: Brian Jay, Dawn Renee. **Educ:** Indiana Univ, AB 1956; Howard Univ Coll of Med, MD 1960; Univ of MI Sch of Pub Health, MPH 1964. **Career:** St Catherine Hospital, E Chicago, Intern 1960-61; US Public Health Service DC, Intern 1961-63; Yale University School of Medicine, psychiatry residency, 1964-74, associate dean, 1969-, Child Study Center, asst prof 1968-70, co-dir Baldwin-King Program, 1968-73, assoc prof, 1970-75, dir School Development Program, 1973-, prof of psychiatry, 1975-, Maurice Falk Prof of Child Psychiatry 1976-; National Institute of Mental Health, staff member, 1967-68; Parent's Magazine, columnist, 1978-. **Orgs:** Dir Conn Energy Corp 1976-; trustee Conn Savings Bank 1971-91; dir Field Foundation 1981-88; trustee Hazen Foundation 1974-78; trustee Wesleyan Univ 1978-84; trustee, Albertus Magnus Coll, 1989-; trustee, Carnegie Corp of NY, 1990-; trustee, Conn State Univ, 1991-94; co-founder 1968, vp 1969-72, pres Black Psychiatrists of Amer 1973-75; Amer Psych Assn 1970-; Ad Hoc Com Black Psychiatrists of APA 1970-71; Natl Med Assn 1967-; Am Orthopsychiatric Assn 1968-; chmn Council on Problems of Minority Group Youth 1969-71; chmn Adolescent Comm 1973-77; Institute of Med of the Natl Academy of Sciences, 1993; Natl Academy of Educ, 1993; Laureate Chap of Kappa Delta Pi, 1993. **Honors/Awds:** Distinguished Alumni Award Howard Univ 1976; Outstanding Serv to Mankind Award Alpha Phi Alpha E Region 1972; Rockefeller Public Serv Awd 1980; John & Mary Markle Scholar in Acad Med 1969-74; Vera Paster Award, American Orthopsychiatric Association 1990; Solomon Carter Fuller Award, American Psychiatric Association 1990; Harold W McGraw, Jr, Prize in Education 1990; Dana Prize in Education, 1991. **Special Achievements:** Author: Beyond Black and White, 1972; School Power, 1980; co-author: Black Child Care, 1975; Maggie's American Dream, 1988; developed Comer Process, a school improvement program now used in numerous schools in eight states, Yale Child Study Center; Waiting For a Miracle: Why Schools Can't Solve Our Problems—And How We Can, 1997. **Military Serv:** USPHS Lt Col 1968. **Business Addr:** Maurice Falk Prof of Child Psychiatry, Child Study Center, Associate Dean, School of Medicine, Yale University, PO Box 207900, New Haven, CT 06520-7900.

COMER, JONATHAN
City official. **Personal:** Born Mar 21, 1921, Eufaula, AL; son of Beatrice Sanders Comer and Jesse Comer; married Emma Mount Comer, Jul 28, 1942; children: William, Joseph, Kathy. **Career:** LTV Steel, East Chicago, IN, first helper, 1948-69; Local Union 1011, USWA, East Chicago, IN, president, 1967-68; United Steelworkers of America, Pittsburgh, PA, assistant director, civil rights dept, 1969-83; Gary Human Relations Commission, Gary, IN, executive director, 1989-. **Orgs:** Steering committee/chairperson, A. Philip Randolph Inst, 1977-79; member/chairman/labor & industry, 1965-70, executive secretary, Indiana conference of branches, 1983-89, State/NAACP. **Honors/Awds:** Ovington Award, NAACP, 1987; Labor Man of the Year, State/NAACP, 1981; Labor Man of the Year, East Chicago Branch, NAACP, 1984; Distinguished Service Award, District 31, USWA, 1972; Distinguished Service Award, Labor Union/Virgin Islands, 1985. **Military Serv:** US Army, T-5, 1942-45; Good Conduct Medal, Sharpshooters Medal. **Home Addr:** 2575 W 19th Ave, Gary, IN 46404.

COMER, MARIAN WILSON
Educational administrator. **Personal:** Born Nov 26, 1938, Gary, IN; daughter of Mary Shuler and Ernest T Bryant; married Richard Comer; children: Lezlie Jo Thompson, Samuel Grady Wilson, Denise Dillard. **Educ:** Roosevelt University Chicago, BS 1966; IN University Bloomington, MAT 1969; University of IL Urbana, PhD 1975; Natl Inst of Health, postdoctoral study; Purdue University, master gardner 1991. **Career:** St Margaret Hospital Hammond, IN, clinical chem medical technical 1964-66; Public School System Gary, IN, teacher 1966-68; University of IL Circle Campus, teaching asst 1970-74; IN University NW, assoc faculty member 1972-74; American Council on Education, Chicago State University, post doctoral fellow 1974-84; NIH, extramural assoc 1978; Chicago State University, asst to vice pres research & development 1978-79, acting dean of student development 1979-81, assoc vice president of academic affairs 1981-84; Institute of Transition Gary IN, president 1984-94; Chicago State University, prof of biology 1984-; Chicago Alliance for Minority Participation, 1994-. **Orgs:** American Inst of Biological Scientist; Botany Society of America; Alpha Kappa Alpha; Horticultural Society; Save the Dunes Council; Gary Public Library, board member; Rotary Intl, board member, 1991-92; Sickle Cell Foundation, board member. **Honors/Awds:** Distinguished Minority Speaker Univ of CA Berkeley Devel Program Grad Level; Dr Marian Wilson Scholarship, Chicago State Univ, Biological Soc; Acad Execellence Award, IN Univ. **Business Addr:** Professor of Biology, Chicago State University, 95th St at Dr M L King Drive, Chicago, IL 60628.

COMER, NORMAN DAVID
Educational administrator. **Personal:** Born Dec 8, 1935, East Chicago, IN; married Marilyn Gaines; children: Norman, Karen. **Educ:** Northwestern Univ, BS 1958; IN Univ, MS 1965; Loyola Univ, EdD 1974. **Career:** E Chicago Public Schools, english teacher 1960-66; Army Medical Corps, chief wardmaster 1961-62; E Chicago Public Schools, asst prin 1966-70, asst supt 1970-. **Orgs:** Evaluator "Princeton Desegregation Plan" (Jackson MI Bd of Educ) 1973; chmn N Central Assn Evaluations (Gage Park & Hirsch HS Chicago) 1973-74; consult Chicago Pub Sch (Yr Round Sch Study) 1974; mem Alpha Phi Alpha 1958; mem Phi Delta Kappa 1972; mem Assn of Supervision & Curriculum Develop (ASCD) 1972; mem Rockefeller Eval Task Force (E Chicago Pub Sch); various articles published. **Military Serv:** AUS m sgt E-8 1960-65. **Business Addr:** Assistant Superintendent, East Chicago Public Schools, 210 E Columbus Dr, East Chicago, IN 46312.

COMER, ZEKE
City councilman. **Personal:** Born Sep 12, 1938, Hertsboro, AL; married Louise. **Educ:** Purdue University, AA, elect tech. **Career:** Inland Steel Co, Electrical Dept, 1976; Third District Precinct Organization, former treasurer, advisory council; Gary 3-9 Precinct, precinct committeeman, 4th two-year term, serving currently; Gary Common Council, council member, currently. **Orgs:** NAACP; Urban League; Local 1010 US Steel Workers of America; Teamsters Union 142; former pres, Evening Star Missionary Baptist Church Choir, 10 years. **Honors/Awds:** Man of the Year, Invahoe Tennant Council 1977; Employee of the Month, Electrical Dept, Inland Steel Co 1976; community service awards during 4-yr term as Precinct Committeeman; elected by Precinct Council to serve out term of previous 3rd District council person. **Business Addr:** Councilmember, Gary Common Council, Municipal Bldg, 401 Broadway, Rm 209, Gary, IN 46402.

COMPTON, JAMES W.
Business executive. **Personal:** Born Apr 7, 1939, Aurora, IL; married Marilyn; children: Janice H, James, Jr. **Educ:** Morehouse Coll, AB 1961; Univ of Grenoble Grenoble France; Loyola Univ Grad Work, 1969; Chicago Tchrs Coll. **Career:** Broome Co Urban League Binghamton NY, exec dir 1969-70; Opportunities for Broome Broome Co Urban League & Bingham NY, interim exec dir 1970; W Side Project Urban League, dir 1968-69; Comm Serv Dept Chicago Urban League, dir 1968-69; Specialist-in-charge W Side Office Employment Guidance Dept Chicago Urban League, 1967-69; On-the-job Training Rep Chicago Urban League, 1965-67. **Orgs:** Teacher, Upper Grade Social Studies, Chicago Bd of Educ; pres, Chicago Urban League; dir, Chicago Com Urban Opportunities; dir Chicago Regional Purchasing Council; dir Comm Fund of Chicago; dir Leadership Council for Metro Open Comm; dir Roosevelt Univ Coll of Educ; dir Union Nat Bank of Chicago Chicago & Alliance for Collaborative Effort, Steering Com; Chicago Manpower Area Planning Council; adv bd WNUS AM/FM; deans adv bd Coll Educ Roosevelt Univ; Chicago Press Club; The Chicago Forum; Citizens Com for Employment; Citizens Com of Greater Chicago Inc; Com on Foreign & Domestic Affairs; Mayor's Commn on Sch Bd Nominations; Concerned Citizens for Police Reform; Congressional Blue Ribbon Panel; TheGroup; Nat Conf on Social Welfare; NE IL Plan Ning Commn; WBEE Radio Comm Needs Comm; WGN Cinental Broadcasting Co; DePaul Univ, bd of trustees. **Honors/Awds:** 10 outstanding young men award Chicago Jr Assn Commerce & Industry 1972; S End Jaycees certification of Appreciation 1972; S End Jaycees Chicago 10 & outstanding young men award; merrill schollar 1959-61; student mem Cultural Exchange Program. **Military Serv:** US & USSR 1959. **Business Addr:** CEO, Chicago Urban League, 4510 S Michigan Ave, Chicago, IL 60653.

COMVALIUS, NADIA HORTENSE
Obstetrician, gynecologist (retired). **Personal:** Born Jan 21, 1926; daughter of Martha James and Rudolf B W Comvalius. **Educ:** Univ Utrecht, MD 1949; Bd Certified Ob Gyn 1970. **Career:** Jewish Memorial Hospital, dir of Gyn present; Lenox Hills Hosp NYC/Beth Israel Hosp NYC, attending Ob-Gyn; Hahnemann Med Coll, cancer rsch 1959-61; Planned Parenthood Westchester, med dir 1970-72; Private Practice USA, retired; Petromin Medical Ctr Yeddah K Saudi Arabia, consultant Ob/Gyn; White Mountain Community Hospital, director of obstetrics/gynecology. **Orgs:** President, Zonta Internal; mem, Business & Professional Women; mem, Mt Sinai Alumni Association.

CONAWAY, MARY WARD PINDLE
City official. **Personal:** Born Jan 26, 1943, Wilson, NC; married Frank M Conaway; children: Frank M Jr, Belinda, Monica. **Educ:** NC Central Univ, BA 1964, 1970; Juilliard School of Music, 1966; Coppin State Coll, MEd 1975; Univ of MD College Park, Spec Advanced Stud Clinical Psy 1978; Wesley Theological Sem, MDiv. **Career:** Yonkers Bd of Ed, music teacher 1970-71; Martin Luther King Jr Parent & Child Ctr, coord 1971-72; Baltimore City Schools, music teacher 1972-74, spec teacher 1974-81; prof singer; Democratic St Central Comm rep; Baltimore City, register of wills; John Wesley - Waterbury United Meth Chrch, pastor, currently. **Orgs:** Life mem NAACP; Alpha Kappa Alpha Sor, Epsilon Omega chpt; Ashburton Neighborhood Assoc, NC Central Univ Alumni Assoc, pres & founder Woman Inc, The United Order of Tents of J.R. Giddings and J.U.; vip panelist Cerebral Palsy Telethon; chartered bd mem at-large Natl Political Congr for Black Women; exec mem MD Assn of Register of Wills; past exec treas Polytechnic Inst; past policitcal action comm chrperson to Natl Conv of United Order of Tent; mem So Christian Leadership Conf; mem Amer Bus Wms Assc; WBJC radio reader for visually impaired; mem Baltimore Urban League; mem of advisory bd of secr and ofce sci, Comm Coll of Baltimore. **Honors/Awds:** Women of the Month Ebeneezer Baptist Church Wilson NC; Afro-Amer Cert of Apprec for Outstanding Serv to the Student Population of Baltimore City; Baltimore City Mayor's Citation of Merit & Appreciation; Baltimore City Council Special Achievement Awd; Amer Business Women's Assoc Inner Harbor Chapt; Citation of Appreciation, Speaker of the Year 1983 Awd of Merit; Awd for Demonstrating Outstanding Courage HUB Inc; Honoree Natl United Affiliated Beverage Assoc Convention Baltimore City; Delegate Democratic Natl Convention 1984; City Councl oustanding accomp resl; Humanitarian Serv Awd, United Cerebral Palsy; Negro Nat Coll Fund Recog; NAACP Stalwarts and Achievers; Democr Nat Conv Citations. **Home Addr:** 3210 Liberty Heights Ave, Baltimore, MD 21215. **Business Addr:** Register of Wills, Baltimore City, 111 N Calvert St #344, Baltimore, MD 21202.

CONE, CECIL WAYNE
Educational administrator. **Personal:** Born May 21, 1937, Bearden, AR; married Juanita Fletcher; children: Cecil Wayne, Leslie Anita, Charleston Alan. **Educ:** Shorter Clg, AA 1953-55;

Philander Smith, BA 1955-57; Garrett Theological Sem, MDiv1958-61; Emory Univ, PHD 1969-74. **Career:** Union AME Little Rock, pastor 1964-69; OIC Little Rock, exec dir 1964-69; Turner Theological Seminary, dean 1969-77; Edward Waters Coll, Jacksonville FL, pres 1977-. **Orgs:** Mem Soc for Study of Blck Rel, Blck Theology Proj of Theology of the Am, NAACP, Alpha Phi Alpha Frat, Natl Urban League, Etc; bd of govr Cof C Jax FL 1978-81; St ethics cmsn State of FL 1979-81; bd of dir Jacksonville Symphny Assc 1984-85, Mayor's Cmsn on High Tech 1984-85. **Honors/Awds:** Author The Identity Crisis in Blck Thelgy 1975; Distnghd Serv Awrd United Negro Clg Fund 1984; Otstndg Edctr of Yr Jacksonville Jaycees 1985; Hon Doctorates Temple Bible Clg Sem & Philander Smith Clg. **Home Addr:** 8787 Southside Blvd, #415, Jacksonville, FL 32256. **Business Addr:** President, Edward Waters College, 1658 Kings Rd, Jacksonville, FL 32209.

CONE, JAMES H.
Educator. **Personal:** Born Aug 5, 1938, Fordyce, AR; widowed. **Educ:** Philander Smith Coll, BA 1958, LLD 1981; Garrett Theol Seminary, BD 1961; Northwestern Univ, MA 1963, PhD 1965; Edward Waters Coll, LLD 1981. **Career:** Philander Smith Coll, asst prof 1964-66; Adrian Coll, asst prof 1966-69; Union Theol Seminary, prof of theology 1969-. **Orgs:** The Journal of the Interdenominational Theological Ctr; Sojourners; The Journal of Religious Thought; mem Soc for the Study of Black Religion, Amer Acad of Religion, Ecumenical Assoc of Third World Theologians. **Honors/Awds:** American Black Achievement Award, in the category of Religion, 1992. **Special Achievements:** 10 book publications including, "Black Theology & Black Power" 1969; "Martin & Malcolm & America: A Dream or a Nightmare," 1991. **Business Addr:** Professor of Systematic Theol, Union Theological Seminary, 3041 Broadway, New York, NY 10027.

CONE, JUANITA FLETCHER
Medical doctor. **Personal:** Born Nov 13, 1947, Jacksonville, FL; married Cecil Wayne Cone PhD. **Educ:** Howard Univ, BS 1968, MD 1974. **Career:** Private Practice, medical doctor. **Orgs:** Mem Amer College of Physicians, Jacksonville Medical Dental and Phar Assoc, Natl Medical Assoc; mem Jacksonville Chamber of Commerce, Natl Council Negro Women, Jacksonville Chapter Links Inc. **Honors/Awds:** Diplomate Amer Bd of Internal Medicine 1979. **Home Addr:** 2955 Ribault Scenic Dr, Jacksonville, FL 32208. **Business Addr:** 580 W Eighth St #610, Jacksonville, FL 32209-6553.

CONEY, LORAINE CHAPELL
Educator. **Personal:** Born Feb 8, 1935, Eustis, FL; son of Julia M Graham and Francis Coney (deceased); married Bettye Jean Stevens; children: Gessner, Melodi. **Educ:** FL A&M U, BS 1958. **Career:** Sumter Co Bd of Pub Instrn, band & choral dir present; Sumter Co Music Tchrs, chmn 1973-77; Streep Music Co, sales rep 1964-69; Omega Psi Phi, bas Gamma Tau 1965-67. **Orgs:** Chmn FL Band Dirs 1963-67; chmn Music Educs Nat Conf 1958-77; Sumter Co Educ Assn NAACP; Omega Psi Phi; Masonic Lodge; guest woodwind tutor LCIE Univ FL 1971, 1974. **Honors/Awds:** 1st Award Winning Co Band Dir 1959; Orgnzd Band & Prod Superior Performers;1st Black Instrument Salesman FL 1964-69; known as the Sch Band Man of Sumter Co 1959-77; FL Bandmasters Assn Adjudicator 1986. **Business Addr:** PO Box 67, Bushnell, FL 33513.

CONGLETON, WILLIAM C.
Counselor. **Personal:** Born Feb 13, 1935, Mt Sterling, KY; married Norma Peterson. **Educ:** Marshall Univ. **Career:** Huntington Post Office, EEO counselor present; NAACP, pres 5 yrs, vice pres chmn labor com; Parish Council, St Peter Claver Cath Ch, pres 1972-73, adv 1974; Cabell County Parks & Recreation Commn, vice pres 1974-; Community Coll, adv 1975; Marshall Univ, com 1975, speaker 1976 & 79; Huntington High Sch, speaker 1977-78. **Orgs:** Mem Huntington Human Rights Commn 1979; commodore Ship of State WV 1979; bd of dirs Action Inc; mem Region II Planning & Devel Council - 6 Co Area; voice Black History WGNT Radio 4yrs; loan officer Nat Alliance of Businessmen; main speaker & chmn Hal Greer Blvd Dedication; chmn Huntington Human Rights Commn 1980; active in Little League. **Military Serv:** AUS corpl 1953-56.

CONGREAVES, ANDREA
Professional basketball player. **Personal:** Born Jun 3, 1970. **Educ:** Mercer, bachelor's degree in human services. **Career:** Charlotte Sting, forward-center, 1997-. **Business Addr:** Professional Basketball Player, Charlotte Sting, 2709 Water Ridge Pkwy, Ste 400, Charlotte, NC 28217, (704)424-9622.

CONLEY, CHARLES S.
Attorney. **Personal:** Born Dec 8, 1921, Montgomery, AL; son of Fannie T Conley and Prince E Conley; married Ellen M Johnson, Aug 8, 1987. **Educ:** Ala State Univ, BS, 1942; Univ of MI, AM, educ, 1947, AM, histroy, 1948. **Career:** FL A&M College of Law, prof, 1956-60; AL State U, 1962-64; Dr Martin Luther King SCLC, counsel; Recorder's CT, judge 1968-73; Macon County CT Common Pleas, 1972-, Macon County attorney, 1986; Alabama District Court, judge, 1977. **Orgs:** Am Nat AL Bar Assns. **Business Addr:** 315 S Bainbridge St, Montgomery, AL 36104.

CONLEY, ELIZABETH-LUCY CARTER
Educational administrator (retired). **Personal:** Born Sep 26, 1919, Indianapolis, IN; daughter of Adah Carter and John Carter; married John E Conley. **Educ:** Butler Univ, BS 1940, MS 1950, MS 1973; IN State Dept of Public Instruction, Adult Educ Certificate 1967. **Career:** Kokomo IN Public Schools, teacher 1941-42; Indianapolis Public Schools, teacher 1942-64, asst principal 1964-73, principal 1973-82. **Orgs:** Educ comm tutoring program 1987, mem Mt Zion Baptist Church 1938-; mem Alpha Kappa Alpha Sor 1939-; life mem Central IN Retired Teachers Assoc 1982-; treasuer, Marion Co Retired Teachers 1983-84; mem NAACP 1986; program committee, Crispus Attucks Alumni Class of 1936, 1986-87; sustaining mem Fall Creek YMCA. **Honors/Awds:** Man of the Year Fall Creek YMCA 1962; SFIE Principal Awd 1977; Certificate for Distinguished Serv Indianapolis Assn of Elementary School Principals 1982.

CONLEY, EMMITT JEROME
Mayor. **Personal:** Born Jun 16, 1922, Arkansas. **Educ:** Attended AR Baptist Coll. **Career:** Southwestern Veneer Co; Warwick Electronics (now Sanyo); Hallett Construction Co, truck driver; City of Cotton Plant AR, mayor. **Orgs:** Consultant, Planters Bank & Trust Co; mem of bd, White River Planning and Devel; Northern AR Human Serv; appointed by Governor Clinton to AR Industrial Commn 1982; member, Woodruff County Hospital Bd; accomplished as mayor, three housing projects, water and sewer projects, an industrial park, street and drainage projects, medical complex and community center; USDA Citizens Advisory Commn Equal Opportunity Federal; bd of dir, Woodruff County Hospital & Nursing Home; White River Revolving Loan; White River Nurses Inc. **Honors/Awds:** Oldest black Republican mayor in the US; Man of the Year Award, Black Mayors Assn of AR, 1984. **Military Serv:** USN 1944-46. **Business Addr:** Mayor, City of Cotton Plant, Town Hall, Cotton Plant, AR 72036.

CONLEY, HERBERT A.
Government official. **Personal:** Born Oct 4, 1942, Monroe, LA; daughter of Eunice R and Lavelle; married Elmira Tucker; children: Mark Warren, Starling David Hunter, Eric Wendell Hunter. **Educ:** Univ of Washington, BA 1973, MBA 1975, PhD 1980. **Career:** State of FL, dir div of treasury. **Orgs:** Mem Amer Mgmt Assn 1970-, Amer Mktg Assn 1970-, Sales & Mktg Execs Assn 1970-, Southern Mktg Assn 1980-; general chairperson United Negro Coll Fund Phoenix AZ 1982-; mem Telecommunications Task Force Public Utilities Comm 1983-84; mem FL Govt Finance Officers Assn 1984-, Intl Foundation of Employee Benefit Plans 1984-, Natl Assn of Securities Professional 1985-; mem Rotary 1986-. **Honors/Awds:** Faculty Grant-in Aid Program 1981-82; publications Proceedings NE Aids Conference San Diego CA 1982, Proceedings NE Aids Conference Boxton MA 1984. **Business Addr:** Dept of Mktg, Howard Univ, 2400 6th St, NW, Washington, DC 20059-0001.

CONLEY, JAMES MONROE
Educational administrator (retired). **Personal:** Born Aug 18, 1915, Livingston, AL; married Ellie M Banks; children: Eddie R, Judy Conley Goldthree, James R, Janis Conley Perry. **Educ:** Tuskegee Inst, BS 1941; TN State Univ, MEd, 1963. **Career:** TN State Univ, res counselor 1963-69; Metropolitan Nashville Public Schools, guidance counselor, 1970-72, vocational program dir, 1972-80. **Orgs:** Deacon, Mt Olive Baptist Church, Nashville, TN 1964-, Sunday school supt 1978-81; basileus Gamma Phi Chapter, Omega Psi Phi Fraternity, 1974-76; pres Optimist Club Central Nashville, TN 1980-81; lt governor TN Dist Optimist Intl 1983-84, Chaplain, 1987-89; Counselor, 5th Dist Omega Psi Phi Fraternity, 1983-88. **Honors/Awds:** Omega Man of the Yr Omega Psi Phi Fraternity, Gamma Phi Chapter, Nashville, TN, 1976, 1982; Honor Club Pres, Optimist Intl, 1988; Outstanding Sec/Treasurer, TN Dist Optimist Intl, 1985. **Military Serv:** USAF major, 1942-63. **Home Addr:** 912 38th Ave N, Nashville, TN 37209.

CONLEY, JAMES SYLVESTER, JR.
Business executive. **Personal:** Born Jun 7, 1942, Tacoma, WA; son of Vera F Dixon and James S Conley; married Eileen Louise Marrinan, Jun 30, 1990; children: Kimberly, Kelli, James III, Ward James W Martin Jr, Erin, Matthew. **Educ:** Univ of Puget Sound, Tacoma, Washington, 1960-61; US Military Academy, West Point, NY, BS, Engineering, 1961-65; New York Univ, GBA, New York, NY, MBA, Finance 1976-82. **Career:** General Motors Corporation, Detroit, MI, dir, Raw Materials Group, Worldwide Purchasing, 1995-, dir, minority supplier devt, 1992-95, Automotive Components Group, technology and planning, 1992, North American Truck Planning, 1990-92; Delco Moraine, Dayton, Ohio, dir marketing and planning, 1989-90, dir technical services, 1988-89, plant mgr, 1985-88, various positions, 1982-85; Avon Products, New York, NY, dir sales coordination 1981-82, various positions 1974-81; CEDC, Inc, Hempstead, NY, vice pres, 1972-74; Capital Formation, New York, NY, exec dir 1970-72. **Orgs:** Bd of dir, Natl Devel Council, 1973-80; trustee, bd of dir, emeritis, Assn of Graduates, US Military Academy, 1975-; lifetime mem, West Point Society of New York; Society of Automotive Engineers, 1986-. **Military Serv:** US Army, captain, 1965-70; Bronze Star for Valor, 1966; Bronze Star Meritorious, 1967; Army Commendation Medal, 1970; Presidential Unit Citation, 1967, Airborne and Ranger, 1965. **Business Addr:** Director, Raw Materials Group, Worldwide Purchasing, General Motors Corporation, 16 Judson St, Pontiac, MI 48342-2230.

CONLEY, JOHN A.
Attorney, educator. **Personal:** Born Mar 10, 1928, Springfield, IL; married Beverly J. **Educ:** Univ of Pgh, BS 1952, JD 1955, MSW 1961. **Career:** Univ of Pittsburgh, prof 1969-; housing developer. **Orgs:** Mem Hill House Assn 1955-69; Neighborhood Ctrs Assn 1963-65; Allegheny Co, PA Bar Assns; bd dirs Pgh Public Schs; Freedom House Enterprise Inc; chmn bd Neighborhood Rehab Inc. **Business Addr:** Department of Social Work, 2201 C1, University of Pittsburgh, Pittsburgh, PA 15260.

CONLEY, MARTHA RICHARDS
Business executive, attorney. **Personal:** Born Jan 12, 1947, Pittsburgh, PA; married Charles D Conley; children: David, Daniel. **Educ:** Waynesburg Coll, BA 1968; Univ of Pittsburgh School of law, JD 1971. **Career:** School Dist of Pittsburgh, asst solicitor 1972-73; Brown & Cotton, attny 1973-74; US Steel Corp, asst mgr labor rel, arbitration, asst mgr compliance 1984-85, compliance mgr 1985-87, atty 1987-93, gen attorney, 1993-. **Orgs:** Mem Homer S Brown Law Assoc, Allegheny Cty Bar Assoc; life mem NBA, Amer Bar Assoc, Alpha Kappa Alpha; bd dir Louise Child Care Ctr 1973-77; commiss Prog to Aid Citizen Enterprise 1973-78; bd dir Health & Welfare Planning Assoc 1978-84; mem NAACP; former mem Intl Toastmistress Club inc; pres Aurora Reading Club of Pittsburgh 1984-85; admitted to practice before bar of Supreme Ct of PA 1972, Supreme Ct of US 1977; Shooting Star Review, bd of dirs. **Honors/Awds:** Consortium of Doctors Award, 1993. **Business Addr:** General Attorney, US Steel Corp, 600 Grant St Room 1580, Pittsburgh, PA 15230.

CONLEY, MIKE
Athlete. **Personal:** Born Oct 5, 1962, Chicago, IL. **Career:** Olympic athlete, triple jump, 1984, 1992. **Honors/Awds:** World Championships, long jump, third place, triple jump, fourth place, 1983; World University Games, triple jump, second place, 1983; Olympic Games, triple jump, silver medal, 1984, gold medal, 1992. **Business Addr:** Gold Medalist, 1992 Games, c/o US Olympic Training Center, 1 Olympic Plaza, Colorado Springs, CO 80909, (719)578-4500.

CONLEY, STEVEN
Professional football player. **Personal:** Born Jan 18, 1972, Chicago, IL. **Educ:** Univ of Arkansas. **Career:** Pittsburgh Steelers, linebacker, 1996-. **Business Addr:** Professional Football Player, Pittsburgh Steelers, Three Rivers Stadium, 300 Stadium Circle, Pittsburgh, PA 15212, (412)323-1200.

CONNALLY, C. ELLEN
Judge. **Personal:** Born Jan 26, 1945, Cleveland, OH; daughter of Gwendolyn J Connally and George L Connally; children: Seth George. **Educ:** Bowling Green State Univ, BS 1967; Cleveland Marshall Law School, JD 1970; Natl Judicial Coll, Reno, NV, 1980-93; Ohio College of Judicial Education, 1980-94; Cleveland State Univ, MA, 1997; Case Western Reserve Univ, PhD candidate. **Career:** Cuyahoga County Court of Appeals, law clerk for Judge Krenzler 1971-73; Cuyahoga County Court of Common Pleas, general trial referee 1973-79; Cleveland Municipal Court, judge 1979-. **Orgs:** Bowling Green State Univ Alumni Assn, 1977-78; pres, Black Women Lawyers Assn of Cleveland, 1977-79; PUSH 1979-; Cuyahoga County Bar Assn, 1979-; advisory committee, Cleveland Bd of Education 1981-; bd of trustees, Community Action Against Drug Addiction 1983-; OH delegate, Natl Judicial Conf on Rights of Victims 1983; Natl Bar Assn; Natl Conference of Black Lawyers; American Judges Assn; pres bd trustees Cleveland Public Theatre 1984-; bd of trustees, Cleveland Soc of the Blind OH Judges Assn; Bowling Green State Univ, bd of trustees, pres, 1988-94, pres, 1994-. **Honors/Awds:** Supreme Court Excellent Judicial Service 1980, 1982; Supreme Court Outstanding Jucicial Service 1981, 1983; Awarded Certificate of Achievement Amer Academy of Jucicial Education 1982. **Special Achievements:** First African American to head the University's Bd of Trustees, Bowling Green Univ, 1994. **Business Addr:** Judge, Cleveland Municipal Court, PO Box 94894, Cleveland, OH 44101-4894.

CONNELL, CAMERON
Business executive. **Personal:** Born Sep 13, 1944; married Barbara. **Educ:** St Anthony's Coll, 1963. **Career:** Hudson-W Radio Inc, vice pres bus mgr 1974-; Harlem Savings Bank, head teller 1971-74; Freedom Nat Bank, teller 1969-71; Barbados WI, tchr 1963- 68; Coco Cola NY, asst ofc mgr 1973-74. **Orgs:** Mem New Rochelle Cricket Club 1970-75.

CONNER, DARION
Professional football player. **Personal:** Born Sep 28, 1967, Macon, GA. **Educ:** Jackson State, attended. **Career:** Atlanta Falcons, defensive end, 1990-93; New Orleans Saints, 1994; Carolina Panthers, 1995; Philadelphia Eagles, 1996-. **Business Addr:** Professional Football Player, Philadelphia Eagles, 3501 S Broad St, Philadelphia, PA 19148, (215)463-2500.

CONNER, GAIL PATRICIA
Law enforcement officer. **Personal:** Born Mar 20, 1948, Detroit, MI; daughter of Alice Conner and George Conner. **Educ:** Exchange student to Bates College, 1967; Wilberforce Univ, BA 1969; Antioch College, MA 1970. **Career:** Detroit Public Schools, teacher 1971-73; State of MI, state probation/parole 1973-77; US Courts-Detroit, US probation/parole officer 1977-. **Orgs:** Quinn AME Church 1948-; member NAACP 1971-; Fed Probation Officers Assoc 1977-; Erma Henderson re-election steering comm 1978; vice president Wilberforce Alumni Assn 1978-82; board member YWCA Detroit 1983-; natl dir for education 1983-, natl dir for membership 1987-, Natl Assn Negro Bus & Prof Womens Club, Inc 1983-; Natl Assn of Black Alumni Steering Comm; parliamentarian, Alpha Kappa Alpha Sorority Inc 1990-. **Honors/Awds:** Spirit of Detroit City of Detroit 1981; Scroll of Distinction Negro Business & Prof 1982; Appreciation Award Jr Achievement 1982; NANBPW Yellow Rose Awd Natl 1982; Appreciation Awd Mott Comm Coll 1983; Natl Black Monitor Hall of Fame 1985; MI Women Resource Guide 1785-1985; Wilberforce Univ Dist Alumni Serv Award 1985; NANBPW Club Woman of the Year 1982; AOIP Hall of Fame 1985; Outstanding Alumni of WU 1985. **Home Addr:** 2082 Hyde Park Dr, Detroit, MI 48207. **Business Addr:** Probation/Parole Officer, US Justice Department, 415 Federal Building, Detroit, MI 48226.

CONNER, LABAN CALVIN
Library director. **Personal:** Born Feb 18, 1936, Ocala, FL; son of Dorothy Helen Todd Conner and Laban Calvin Conner. **Educ:** University of Nebraska-Omaha, Omaha, NE, B Gen Ed, 1959; Emporia State University, Emporia, KS, MSLS, 1964; Nova University, Ft Lauderdale, FL, EdS, 1979; Pacific Western University, Los Angeles, CA, PhD, 1980. **Career:** Dade County Public Schools, Miami, FL, teacher, librarian, 1959-68, cord library services, 1968-70, teacher, librarian, 1973-81; Miami Dade Community College, Miami, FL, asst prof, library science, 1970-73; Florida Memorial College, Miami, FL, library dir, 1981-. **Orgs:** Member, American Library Assn, 1965-; member, Florida Library Assn, 1963-; member, Dade County Library Assn, 1963-; member, African Methodist Episcopal Church, 1936-; board member, Cooperative College Library Center, 1986-. **Military Serv:** US Air Force, A/2C, 1956-59. **Business Addr:** Library Director, Florida Memorial College, 15800 NW 42nd Ave, Miami, FL 33054, (305)623-4149.

CONNER, LESTER ALLEN
Professional basketball player. **Personal:** Born Sep 17, 1959, Memphis, TN. **Educ:** Los Medanos College, Antioch, CA, 1978-79; Chabot College, Hayward, CA, 1979-80; Oregon State Univ, Corvallis, OR, 1980-82. **Career:** Golden State Warriors, 1982-86; Houston Rockets, 1987-88; New Jersey Nets, 1988-93; Los Angeles Clippers, 1993-94; Indiana Pacers, 1994-. **Business Addr:** Professional Basketball Player, Indiana Pacers, 300 E Market St, Indianapolis, IN 46204.

CONNER, MARCIA LYNNE
City manager. **Personal:** Born Feb 26, 1958, Columbia, SC; daughter of Joan Delly Conner and Edward Eugene Conner. **Educ:** Talladega Coll, Talladega, Alabama, B.A. 1980; Univ of Cincinnati, Cincinnati, Ohio, M.C.P., 1982. **Career:** City of Opa-Locka, Opa-Locka, FL, asst city mgr, 1985-87, city mgr, 1987-; Metropolitan Dade County Miami, FL, mgmt intern 1982-83, budget analayst, 1983-85. **Orgs:** Mem, American Society for Public Administrators, 1982-; mem, Intl City Manager's Assn, 1982-; mem, Leadership Miami, 1986-; sec/bd mem, Greater Miami YWCA, 1987-; bd mem, Big Brothers & Sisters of Miami, 1987-; bd mem, Natl Forum for Black Public Administrators, 1987-. **Honors/Awds:** Outstanding Young Professional, South Florida American Society for Public Admin, 1982; One to Watch in '88, South Florida Magazine, 1988; Up & Comers Award, South Florida Business Journal, 1989. **Business Addr:** City Manager, City of Opa-Locka, 777 Sharazad Blvd, Opa Locka, FL 33054.

CONNOR, DOLORES LILLIE
Entrepreneur. **Personal:** Born Sep 15, 1950, Mineral Wells, TX; daughter of Alpearl Sadberry Connor and Walter Malone Connor. **Educ:** Univ of Texas at Arlington, TX, BS 1975; Amber Univ, Garland, TX, MS 1989. **Career:** Vought Systems Div of LTV, Dallas, TX, material control analyst 1969-76; Recognition Equipment, Irving, TX, buyer, 1975-77; Texas Instruments, Dallas, TX, buyer, 1977-78, small/minority business liaison officer, 1978-87, intl officer, 1978-80; mgr, small business programs 1987-89; Texas Instruments, small business programs manager, 1985-89, manager, corporate minority procurement, 1989-91; ''A Piece of Mine'' Corp, president, currently. **Orgs:** Mem, Zeta Phi Eta Honor Fraternity/Communications, 1975; Ft Worth Negro Business & Professional Women's Club 1975-77; bd mem, Dallas Urban League, 1979-80; mem, Richardson Business & Professional Women's Club, 1979-86; mem, Leadership Dallas, 1980-; Leadership Texas Alumni, 1991-92; bd chmn, D/FW Minority Purchasing Council, 1980-83, mem, Texas Governor's Committee for Employment of Disabled, 1981; bd mem, Mayor's Committee for Employment of the Disabled, 1981-85; exec dir, Loan-D/FW Minority Purchasing Council, 1983; captain, Neighborhood Watch, Richardson, TX, 1983-87; Delta Sigma Theta Sorority Inc, 1970-. **Honors/Awds:** Young Careerest, Richardson Business & Professional Women's Club, 1980; sponsor of the largest fund raiser viewing party for the United Negro Coll Fund, 1982-86; Youth Motivator, Natl Alliance of Business, 1983; Supporter of Entrepreneurs, Venture Magazine & Arthur Young, 1987; Entrepreneurs Hall of Fame, 1988; Top 100 Black Women in America, Dollars and Sense Magazine, 1991; published article ''Winning Ways for Women Managers'' in Hispanic Engineer and US Black Enterprise, Fall 1990; Iota Phi Lambda Sorority, Outstanding Businesswoman of the Year, 1995; Dallas Black Chamber of Commerce, Quest for Success Winner, 1996-97; St Luke Community United Methodist Church, Business of the Year, 1997. **Business Addr:** President, A Piece of Mine Corp, Ethnic Greeting Cards & Gifts, P.O. Box 201338, Arlington, TX 76006-1338.

CONNOR, GEORGE C., JR.
State official. **Personal:** Born May 18, 1921, Baldwin, LA; married Marjorie Breard; children: Jan, George, Terri. **Educ:** Xavier U, BS 1950; Bradley U; VA State Coll; Dillard U; Lamar U. **Career:** LA, state rep. **Orgs:** Mem Crescent City Coaches 1952-65; Nat HS Coaches Assn; Alpha Phi Alpha Frat; Holy Name Soc; Knights of Peter Claver; mem So Reg Educ Bd; Educ Commn for States; bd dirs YMCA; St Bernard Area Community Ctr; Interracial Counsel for Business Opportunities; bd trustees Narconon New Orleans. **Military Serv:** AUS 1942-46. **Business Addr:** 2647 Havana St, New Orleans, LA 70119.

CONNOR, HERMAN P.
Printing company executive. **Personal:** Born Aug 27, 1932, Garfield, GA; son of Melvina Connor and George Connor; divorced; children: Sharon, Gregory, Stephanie, Leigh, Donna. **Career:** Consoar Corp, vice pres, currently. **Home Addr:** 49 Cedar Ave, PO Box 161, Montclair, NJ 07042. **Business Addr:** Vice Pres, Consoar Corp, 18 Central Ave, PO Box 132, West Orange, NJ 07052.

CONNOR, JAMES RUSSELL
Business manager. **Personal:** Born Oct 30, 1940, Lima, OH; son of Esther M Rowe Connor and Russell T Connor; married Beryl Dixon, Aug 25, 1973; children: Steven Eric Connor, Jeffrey Allan Connor. **Educ:** Bowling Green State Univ, Bowling Green OH, 1969-71; Defiance Coll, Defiance OH, BS in Business 1972; Indiana Univ, Bloomington IN, MBA (consortium fellowship) 1974; Massachusetts Institute of Technology, Cambridge, MA, senior exec program, 1989. **Career:** Ford Motor Co, Lima OH, quality control superintendent 1980-81; Kelsey-Hayes Co, Marlette MI, manufacturing manager, 1981-82, plant manager 1982-84; General Motors Corp, New Departure Hyatt Div, Sandusky OH, director quality assurance 1984-88, director engine powertrain systems 1988-89, Saginaw Div, Saginaw MI, director engine drive systems, 1989-92, director quality assurance, production control and logistics, 1992-. **Orgs:** Bd mem, Fireland Community Hospital, 1986-87; bd mem, Community Action Program 1986-87; co-chairman, United Way Fund Drive, 1987; chairman, selection committee LEADS, 1988. **Honors/Awds:** Beta Gamma Sigma, Bowling Green State Univ, 1971; Consortium Fellowship, Consortium for Graduate Study in Management, 1973. **Military Serv:** USMC, sgt E5, two meritorious promotions (pfc in 1961, corporal in 1963) 1961-66. **Home Addr:** 504 N Race St, Van Wert, OH 45891-1347.

CONNOR, ULYSSES J., JR.
Educator, educational administrator. **Personal:** Born Dec 13, 1948, New Orleans, LA. **Educ:** Adelphi Univ, BA 1970; Syracuse Univ, JD 1974. **Career:** Syracuse Univ, programs coord 1974-75, dean of students 1975-82; Univ of MD, asst to vice chancellor 1982-85, dir/dev educ 1985-; assistant to the dean/ undergraduate studies, 1988-91; director, Freshman Year Prog, 1991-92; Kutztown University, professor, College Of Education, 1993-. **Orgs:** Bd of dirs Syracuse Ctr for Dispute Settlement 1976-81; allocations comm mem DC United Way 1986-; Zeta Beta Tau Fraternity. **Honors/Awds:** Blue Book of Greater Syracuse 1981; Omicron Delta Kappa Honor Soc 1986; Center for Teaching Excellence, University of Maryland, Teaching Excellence, 1991. **Military Serv:** USAF capt. **Home Addr:** 719 8th St, NE, Washington, DC 20002.

CONRAD, CECILIA ANN
Educator. **Personal:** Born Jan 4, 1955, St Louis, MO; daughter of Eleanor N and Emmett J Conrad; married Llewellyn Miller, May 26, 1984; children: Conrad. **Educ:** Wellesley Coll, BA, 1976; Stanford Univ, MA, 1978, PhD, 1982. **Career:** Federal Trade Commission, economist, 1978-79; Duke Univ, asst prof, 1981-85 ; Hunter Coll, visiting asst prof, 1984-85; Barnard Coll, assoc prof, 1985-; Black Enterprise Magazine, bd of economists, 1993-; Pfizer Inc, consultant, 1992-. **Orgs:** Natl Economics Assn, Coll Board, past pres, chair, Test Devt Comm, advanced placement exam in economics; Committee on Status of Women in Economics Profession, pat bd mem. **Honors/Awds:** Phi Beta Kappa, 1976; Bell Laboratories Cooperative, Research Fellowship, 1976-81; Gladys Brooks Junior Faculty Excellence in Teaching Award, 1990. **Special Achievements:** Publications: ''The Economic Costs of Affirmative Action: A Review of the Evidence,'' The Economics of Affirmative Action, 1995; ''Why Black Economists?,'' Review of Black Political Economy, 1994; ''Pay Now or Later,'' Black Enterprise Magazine, Sept 1994; numerous others; Speeches and Public Addresses: ''The Role of Government in Dependent Care,'' Barnard Coll, 1994; ''Where's My Forty Cents?,'' Barnard Business and Professional Women, 1994; numerous others.

CONRAD, EMMETT J.
Physician. **Personal:** Born Oct 6, 1923, Baton Rouge, LA; married Eleanor; children: Cecila. **Educ:** So Univ, BS 1944; Meharry Med Coll, 1948. **Career:** Private practice, gen surgeon. **Orgs:** Mem Dallas Ind School Bd Tst 1967-77; chmn Career Ed Comm State TX.

CONRAD, JOSEPH M., JR.
Business executive. **Personal:** Born Jan 16, 1936, New Orleans; married Bernadine Barard; children: 3. **Educ:** Xavier U, BS 1962. **Career:** Office of Prog Planning & Control US Small Bus Adm, 1968-. **Orgs:** Mem bd dir Black Sec Catholic Archdiocese of Washington Bdc; permanent deacon Catholic Archdiocese 1971. **Honors/Awds:** Recip 24th An Wm A & Jump Meml Awd 1973; SBA Med for Meritorious Serv 1970. **Military Serv:** AUS 1955-58.

CONTEE, CAROLYN ANN
Dentist. **Personal:** Born Feb 14, 1945, Washington, DC; married Dr James E Lassiter Jr; children: Lisa C Butler. **Educ:** Howard Univ, BA (Cum Laude) 1969, MEd 1973, DDS 1981. **Career:** DC Public Schools, elem tchr 1969-77; Private Dental Practice, dentist 1981-86; Upper Cardozo Comm Hlth Ctr, staff dentist 1982-86; Shaw Comm Health Ctr, staff dentist 1982-86; Fairleigh Dickenson Coll of Dentistry, asst prof 1987; Airport Dental Ctr, asst dir 1986-. **Orgs:** Dir of continuing educ exec bd Robert Freeman Dental Soc 1982-84; house of delegates 1982-86, exec comm 1986, asst treas 1986 Natl Dental Assoc; bdof trustees Natl Dental Assoc Foundation 1983-, Potomac Chap of Links Inc 1984-. **Honors/Awds:** Outstanding Serv Robert T Freeman Dental Soc 1984; Outstanding Serv Capital Headstart Certificate 1985. **Business Addr:** Assistant Dir, Airport Dental Center, Newark Intl Airport Bldg 51, Newark, NJ 07101.

CONWAY, CURTIS LAMONT
Professional football player. **Personal:** Born Mar 13, 1971, Los Angeles, CA; married Leoria; children: Cameron, Kelton. **Educ:** University of Southern California. **Career:** Chicago Bears, wide receiver, 1993-. **Special Achievements:** NFL Draft, First round draft pick, 1993. **Business Addr:** Professional Football Player, Chicago Bears, Harris Hall at Conway Park, 1000 Football Dr, Lake Forest, IL 60045-4829, (847)295-6600.

CONWAY, WALLACE XAVIER, SR.
Museum curator (retired). **Personal:** Born Jun 11, 1920, Washington, DC; son of Jessie Taylor Conway and Ewell Lucas Conway Jr; married Jessie Elizabeth Dedeaux; children: Dianne Pettie, Wallace X Jr, Stephanie Victorian. **Educ:** Miner Teacher Coll, BS, 1941; Cooper Union Sch of Arts & Sciences, 1942; US Dept of Agr Grad School, 1953; Trenton State Coll, 1953; Mercer Community Coll, 1977-79; Paris-American Academy, Univ of Paris, 1977; New York Univ, MA, 1987; Venice, Italy, Painting, 1988; Chicago University, Art Institute, painting, 1989. **Career:** Co-Art Studios (Visual Communications), owner/dir 1950-64; US Weather Bureau, graphic artist, 1964-65; Smithsonian Inst, graphic supvr, 1965-69; Afro-Amer Museum Assoc, Washington DC, advisor 1980-; NJ State Museum, curator, chmn exhibits, 1969-88 (retired); self-employed artist, museum consultant, educator, lecturer, currently. **Orgs:** Consultant, Dept of Educ, NJ, 1962-82; adjunct faculty, Trenton State Coll, NY, 1978-80; chmn, cultural comm Cable TV Network, NJ 1983-85; consultant, Afro Amer Museum, Philadelphia, PA 1981-83, NJ Civil Serv Comm 1981-84, Afro-Am Museum Assn, 1981-85, Bedford-Stynt Hist Assn Brooklyn, NY; chrtr mem Beta Kappa Chap KAU 1945-85; mem Rotary Intl 1975-; artist, author, lecturer, 1970-; validating comm Presbytery of New Brunswick NJ, YWCA Comm Cultural Enrichment Prog Trenton; tech consultant Martin Luther King Natl Holiday Memorial Mural unveiled on site Martin Luther King Library, Washington DC 1986; artist Don Miller making of mural traveling exhibit, 1986-87; consultant, Rouse Associates, 1987-88; consultant, Church & Dwight, 1988-89; consultant, Merrill Lynch, 1987-88; bd of dir, Trent YMCA, 1988-; advisory bd, Minority Arts Assembly, 1988-; member, Trenton Artists Workshop Association, 1980-91; member, District of Col Art Assn, 1970-90; member, National Conference of Artists, 1970-91; Art Students League, Col Springs, CO, bd mem, chair, membership comm, 1994; mem, advisory bd, Colorado Springs Museum. **Honors/Awds:** Major Art Retrospective Exhibit, City of Trenton Museum, 1989; 19 Black Artists of Mercer City Exhibit, Mercer County Coll, 1989; fellowship, Kellogg Found, Field Museum, Chicago, 1987; Black Dimensions in Art, one man exhibit, Schenectady Museum, NY, 1990; Best of Show award, 2 honorable mentions, First Place, Print category, Art Students League. **Military Serv:** USCG seaman 1/c; Honorable Discharge. **Home Addr:** 2119 Olympic Drive, Colorado Springs, CO 80910-1262.

CONWILL, GILES
Educator. **Personal:** Born Dec 17, 1944, Louisville, KY. **Educ:** University of San Diego, BA, philosophy, 1967; Emory University, PhD, cultural studies, 1986; Athenaeum of OH, MDiv, 1973. **Career:** Barona & Santa Ysabel Missions, religious education instructor, 1965-67; Miramar Naval Air Station, chaplain's assistant, 1966-67; St Henry's School, elementary school teacher, 1967-68; Verona Fathers Seminary, choir director, assistant organist, 1968-69; St Rita's Church, associate pastor, 1973-76; San Diego Religious Vocations Office, diocesan coordinator, pre-marriage instructor, 1975; National Office of Black Catholics, Department of Church Vocations, director, 1976-80; St Anthony's Church, Atlanta, associate pastor, 1980-85; St Joseph's Cathedral, San Diego, associate pastor, 1985-86; Morehouse College, Department of History, asso professor, 1987-; Inst for Black Catholic Studies, Xavier Univ, New Orleans, assoc prof, 1990. **Orgs:** Southeast San Diego Interdenominational Ministerial Alliance, vp, 1975; Black Catholic Clergy Caucus, 1975; Assn for the Study of African American Life & History, 1987-; Southern Conference of African Amer Studies, Inc, 1987-; Ass of Southern Historians, 1992-; Georgia Assn of Historians, 1992; Amer Anthropological Assn, 1994; Black Catholic Theological Symposium, 1990. **Honors/Awds:** City of Selma, Alabama, Key to the City, first city-wide Black Catholic revival; Upper Room Publishing Co., interdenominational sermon contest winner; numerous other awards. **Special Achievements:** Author, "The Word Becomes Black Flesh: A Program for Reaching the American Black," What Christians Can Learn from One Another, Tyndale House Publishers, 1988; workshop presenter: "Understanding Transitions: How to Relate to Candidates from Various Backgrounds," Seventh Annual Formation Workshops, Bergamo Center, July 8-10, 1988; African-American history lecture, Shrine of Immaculate Conception, Jan 1991; "Blackology vs Ecology," Leadership Council of the Laity Conference, Feb 1991; Liturgical Sensitivity to the Black Aesthetic, in The Critic, Summer, 1986; Tell It Like It Is: A Black Catholic Perspective on Christian Educ, Natl Black Sisters Conference, 1983; Black Music: The Spirit Will Not Descend Without Song, Pastoral Life, Vol XXXII, June 1983; Blackology vs Ecology, Leadership Council of the Laity. **Business Addr:** Professor, Department of History, Morehouse College, 830 Westview Dr SW, Brawley Hall, Ste 204, Atlanta, GA 30314.

CONWILL, KINSHASHA
Museum administrator. **Career:** Studio Museum in Harlem, dir, currently. **Business Addr:** Director, Studio Museum in Harlem, 114 W 125th St, New York, NY 10027, (212)864-4500.

CONWILL, WILLIAM LOUIS
Psychologist, educator, consultant. **Personal:** Born Jan 5, 1946, Louisville, KY; son of Mary Luella Herndon and Adolph Giles Conwill (deceased); married Faye Venetia Harrison, May 17, 1980; children: Giles Burgess, Leonart Mondlane, Justin Neal. **Educ:** University of San Diego, BA, philosophy, 1968; California State University, San Jose, MA, experimental psych, 1973; Stanford University, PhD, counseling/research clinical, 1980. **Career:** Santa Clara Co Juv Prob Department, sr training counselor, 1969-72; Richmond & San Francisco Police Department, trainer, 1972-73; University of California, psychologist, 1974-76; Co of San Mateo, California, coordinator/chief consult & educ, 1980-82; University of Louisville Department Psychiatry, director, pain program, 1983-88; City of Louisville, Department of Human Svcs, com statis research associate, 1988-90; State of Tennessee, Department of Mental Health/Mental Retardation, psychologist, chief psych, Children & Youth Svcs, 1990-97; Family Stress Institute, president, currently; Minority Male Consortium, prevention specialist; Amer Psychological Assn, trainer; HIV Office for Psychology Ed (HOPE) Program. **Orgs:** American Psychological Association; American Pain Society; Association of Black Psychologists; Tennessee Psychological Association; Kentucky Society of Psychologists; NAACP; Behavioral Medicine Society. **Honors/Awds:** Stanford University, Grad Fellowship, 1973-79; University of Louisville School of Medicine Grant, 1984; numerous other grants. **Special Achievements:** 16-Session videotaping of chronic pain group as therapist, 1984; pre-post filming of rheumatoid arthritic group as co-therapist, 1983; actor: Learning to CARE, behavioral therapy movie, 1978; dissertation: A Conceptual Analysis of Black Family Instability, 1980; Chronic Pain Conceptualization & Religious Interpretation, Journal of Religion & Health, 1986; "Training Parents in Child Behavior-management Skills: A Group Approach," Journal of Negro Education, 1986; "The Inheritance of IQ and Scholastic Achievement: Further Comments on the Jensen Article," Journal of Negro Education, 1980. **Home Addr:** 351 S Waccamaw Ave, Columbia, SC 29205, (803)779-5906.

CONYERS, CHARLES L.
Educational administrator (retired). **Personal:** Born Sep 8, 1927, Cyrene, GA; son of Ella Brown Conyers and Luther H Conyers Sr; married Mary Foster Conyers, Jun 11, 1952; children: Charles C, Andrei B, Brian K. **Educ:** Savannah State Coll, BS 1949; VA State Coll, BS, MS 1952-58; Univ of IL, Grad Study; Univ of VA, Grad Study. **Career:** G W Carver High School, Culpeper, VA, teacher, 1949-51; Mary N Smith HS, VA, 1952; AG Richardson High School, Louisa, VA, teacher, 1952-61; Central Academy School, Fincastle, VA, principal, 1961-63; John J Wright School, Snell, VA, principal, 1963-66; State Department of Education, Richmond, VA, asst super title I, 1966, supervisor, title I and migrant education, 1972, associate director, title I, 1979, director, division of compensatory education, 1981, director, division of special & compensatory programs, 1987, education lead specialist, grants administration, 1992. **Orgs:** Member, National Education Assn; member, Virginia Education Assn; life member, Iota Sigma Chapter; Phi Delta Kappa; first president, National Assn of State Directors of Migrant Education; pres, National Assn of State of Directors of Chapter 1; member, National Advisory Council for Neglected or Delinquent Programs; Phi Beta Sigma Fraternity. **Honors/Awds:** Outstanding Educator Award, Phi Delta Kappa, 1976; State Superintendent's Award, 1989; Literacy Award, International Reading Assn, 1989; Distinguished Alumni Award; National Assn for Equal Opportunity in Higher Education, 1990. **Business Addr:** Education Lead Specialist/Grants Administration, Virginia Department of Education, PO Box 60, 101 N 14th St, James Monroe Bldg, 23rd Floor, Richmond, VA 23216.

CONYERS, JAMES E.
Educator. **Personal:** Born Mar 6, 1932, Sumter, SC; son of Crenella Conyers and Emmett Conyers; divorced; children: Judy, Jimmy, Jennifer. **Educ:** Morehouse Coll, AB 1954; Atlanta Univ, MA 1956; WA State Univ, PhD 1962. **Career:** IN State Univ, prof 1968-; Atlanta Univ, assoc prof 1964-68; IN State Univ, asst prof 1962-64; WA State Univ, teaching asst 1958-61; Lemoyne Coll, teacher, 1955-56. **Orgs:** Chmn, Caucus of Black Sociologists in Amer 1973-74; pres, Assn of Social and Behavioral Scientists, 1970-71; mem, Selection Comm for Natl Fellowship Fund Graduate Fellowships for Black Amer, 1973-78; mem, Advisory Panel for Sociology NSF, 1975-77; mem, Council North Central Sociology Assn, 1991-93; mem, Young Men Civic Club Terre Haute, 1970-; life mem, NAACP; mem, NAACP Natl; comm chmn, Participation & Status of Racial & Ethnic Minorities in the Prof of the Amer Sociological Assn, 1971-72. **Honors/Awds:** Various articles published in Sociology & Social Research; Sociol Inquiry/Journal of Negro Educ; Co-editor, Sociology for the Seventies, 1972; Co-author, Black Elected Officials, 1976; WEB Dubois Award, Assn of Social & Behavioral Scientists, 1981; Distinguished Scholar Award, Assn of Black Sociologists, 1994. **Military Serv:** US Army, E-3, 1956-58. **Business Addr:** Professor of Sociology, Indiana State University, Terre Haute, IN 47809.

CONYERS, JEAN L.
Association executive. **Personal:** Born Nov 10, 1932, Memphis, TN; daughter of Marshall D & Jeffie Ledbetter Farris; married Dr James E Conyers, Jun 4, 1956 (divorced); children: Judith, James Jr, Jennifer. **Educ:** Lemoyne/Owen College, BA, 1956; University of TN, School of Social Work, 1958-59; Atlanta University, School of Business, MBA, 1967. **Career:** Vigo County Community Action, planner, 1968-78, director, 1978-79; United Way of Genessee & Lapeer Counties, sr associate executive, 1980-82; GFOTC, prog coord, 1982-86; Metropolitan Chamber, president/CEO, 1980-; USDOT of LOSP office of Small Business, regional director, 1994-. **Orgs:** Alpha Kappa Alpha (Zeta Beta Omega) Basileus, 1992-; Opportunity Network, president-elect, 1997. **Honors/Awds:** Community Coalition, Community Activist Awd, 1996; National Association of Negro Business & Prof Women, Meritorious Svc, 1994; Black Caucus Foundation of Michigan, Partner in Community Svc, 1994; Boy Scouts of America, Community Svc Awd, 1996. **Special Achievements:** Designed Special Entrepreneurial Curriculum and had it licensed by the Michigan Department of Education; Developed Kidpreneur Training Prog for 5th & 6th Graders. **Business Addr:** President/CEO & Regions V & VII Director of LOSP, Metropolitan Chamber of Commerce/US DOT, 3306 Flushing Rd, Flint, MI 48504.

CONYERS, JOHN, JR.
Congressman. **Personal:** Born May 16, 1929, Detroit, MI; son of Lucille and John; married Monica Ann Esters, Jun 1990; children: John III. **Educ:** Wayne State Univ, BA 1957, JD 1958. **Career:** Congressman John Dingell, legislative asst 1958-61; Conyers Bell & Townsend, sr partner 1959-61; MI Workman's Compensation Dept, referee 1961-63; US House of Reps, representative, 1964-. **Orgs:** Vice chmn Natl Bd of Amer for Dem Action; vice chmn Natl Adv Bd Amer Civil Liberties Union; dir educ Local 900 UAW; exec bd mem Detroit br NAACP; mem Wolverine Bar Assn; gen council Detroit Trade Union Ldrship Council; mem Tabernacle Baptist Ch; Kappa Alpha Psi Frat; publs in field. **Honors/Awds:** Rosa Parks Awd 1967; Wilberforce Univ, Hon LLD, 1969. **Military Serv:** US Army, 1950-54. **Business Addr:** Congressman, US House of Representatives, 2426 Rayburn House Office Bldg, Washington, DC 20055, (202)225-5126.

CONYERS, NATHAN
Publisher. **Career:** Milwaukee Times, publisher, currently. **Business Addr:** Publisher, Milwaukee Times, 2216 N Dr Martin Luther King Jr Dr, Milwaukee, WI 53212, (414)263-5088.

CONYERS, NATHAN G.
Automobile dealer. **Personal:** Born Jul 3, 1932, Detroit, MI; married Diana Callie Howze, 1956; children: Nancy, Steven, Susan, Ellen, Peter. **Educ:** Wayne State University, Detroit, MI, LLB, 1959. **Career:** Attorney in private practice, 1959-69; Small Business Administration, closing attorney, 1963; Veteran's Administration, closing attorney, 1964-65; State of Michigan, Attorney General's Office, special assistant, 1967-70; Keith Conyers Anderson Brown & Wahls, sr partner 1969; Conyers-Riverside Ford Inc, Detroit, MI and Supreme Ford Inc, Mason, MI, president, 1970-. **Orgs:** Life mbr, NAACP; American Civil Liberties Union; YMCA; bd mbr, Greater Detroit Chamber of Commerce; bd mbr, Blue Cross/Blue Shield of Michigan; bd mbr, treasurer, Diversitech; Wolverine Bar Assn; National Lawyers Guild; Detroit Board of Police Commissioners, 1987-89; bd mbr, Black Ford Lincoln/Mercury Dealers Assn, 1979-; bd of dirs, PUSH International Trade Bureau; Rivertown Auto Dealers Assn; Greater Detroit Area Hospital Council, 1972-73; United Negro College Fund, 1972-75; United Foundation Advisory Bd, 1973-75; State Canvassers, bd mbr, 1968-74; State of Michigan, Commerce Department, Minority Business Advisory Council, 1986-. **Special Achievements:** Dealership recognized for commitment to excellence by: Howard Univ School of Business, former President Jimmy Carter, former Atlanta Mayor Andrew Young with the Key to the City. **Military Serv:** US Army, 1953-55. **Business Addr:** President, Conyers-Riverside Ford Inc, 1833 E Jefferson Ave, Detroit, MI 48207.

COOK, ANTHONY ANDREW
Professional football player. **Personal:** Born May 30, 1972, Bennettsville, SC. **Educ:** South Carolina State, attended. **Career:** Houston Oilers, defensive end, 1995-96; Tennessee Oilers, 1997-. **Business Addr:** Professional Football Player, Tennessee Oilers, c/o Baptist Sports Park, 7640 H 70-5, Nashville, TN 37221.

COOK, CHARLES A.
Physician, consulting firm executive. **Personal:** Born Jun 19, 1946, Biloxi, MS; son of Eleanor Posey Shelby and Norman Cook, Sr; married Shirley A Bridges Cook, Oct 23, 1967; children: Timothy, Tamotha, Torryhe. **Educ:** Tougaloo Coll, Tougaloo MS, BA 1971; Tufts Univ School of Medicine, Boston MA, MD 1975; Harvard Univ School of Public Health, Boston MA, MPH, 1975; Univ of North Carolina, Chapel Hill NC, Government Executive Business Certificate, 1982. **Career:** State of MA, Boston MA, special asst, mental health 1974-75; State of Mississippi, Jackson MS, asst chief, disease control 1979-80; Univ of Mississippi Medical Center, asst prof of medicine, 1979-80; State of North Carolina, Raleigh NC, chief adult health, 1980-85; Univ of North Carolina at Chapel Hill, School of Public Health, adjunct-assoc prof, 1987-; Assoc Resources Consulting Group, pres, currently. **Orgs:** Bd mem, Amer Heart Assn of North Carolina, 1980-89; bd mem, Amer Cancer Society of North Carolina, 1980-85; pres, Associated Resources Consulting Group, 1984-89; mem, North Carolina Insurance Trust Commission, 1988-89. **Honors/Awds:** Airman of the Month, US Air Force, 1965; Doctor of the Year, Hinds County Medical Society, 1979; Tarheel of the Week, Raleigh News & Observer 1983; Honored Volunteer, NC Diabetes Assn 1983; Volunteer of the Year, State Baptist Convention, 1984; author of "Anti-Hypertensive Drug Compliance In Black Males," Journal of the Natl Medical Assn 1984, "Hypertensive Therapy in Blacks," Journal of Clinical Hypertension, 1986, "Pathophysiologic and Pharmacotherapy Considerations-Black Hypertension," Amer Health Journal, 1988. **Military Serv:** USAF, sgt, Airman of the Month (April 1967), 1964-68. **Business Addr:** President, Assoc Resources Consulting Group, 3414 Six Forks Road, Park Place, Raleigh, NC 27609.

COOK, ELIZABETH G.
University sports information administrator. **Personal:** Born Jun 30, 1960, Lexington, KY; daughter of Betty L Lillard and Roy L Lillard; married Robert B Cook, Jun 6, 1986; children: Casey A. **Educ:** The Ohio State University, Columbus, OH, BA, 1983. **Career:** Columbus Call & Post Newspaper, Columbus, OH, sports writer, 1986-88; State of Ohio, Columbus, OH, public info officer, 1983-88; Ohio State Univ, assistant sports information director, 1988-. **Orgs:** Member, College Sports Information Directors of America, 1988-. **Business Addr:** Assistant Sports Information Director, Ohio State University Athletic Department, 410 Woody Hayes Dr, St John Arena, Room 124, Columbus, OH 43210.

COOK, FRANK ROBERT, JR.
Attorney, accountant. **Personal:** Born Aug 19, 1923. **Educ:** BS 1945, JD 1949, LLM 1955, BCS 1963, MCS 1964, PhD 1951, DD 1967. **Career:** Frank R Cook Jr, attny pub acct & mngmt cnslt, real property appraiser 1950; Chldrn of Ch of Christ, minister 1966-; RE Broker, bus chance broker 1945-; Integrity Adjustment Co, owner 1944-49. **Orgs:** Mem WA Bar Assn; Nat Soc Pub Acct Adm Planned Parnthd & Sex/Mar Cnslng Prog 1967. **Business Addr:** 1715 Eleventh St NW, Washington, DC 20001.

COOK, HANEY JUDAEA
Clergyman. **Personal:** Born Nov 5, 1926, Little Rock, AR; son of G C Cook; married Osa L Jones; children: Cecilia Cook Pryor, Millicent, Hancy Jr, Veda. **Educ:** AR Baptist Coll, BS 1958, DDivinity 1962; TN Baptist School of Religion, Hon Doctor of Letters 1974; Intl Bible Inst & Seminary Orlando FL,

MBible Theology 1983. **Career:** Gideon Missionary Baptist Church, pastor, currently. **Orgs:** Organizer of North Shore Baptist Ministers Alliance 1962; trustee Waukegan Twp 1977-85; founder & sponsoring committee Lake Cty Urban League; life mem NAACP; bd of dir EC Morris Inst Little Rock AR, Bethlehem Bapt Dist Assoc of IL; vice pres United Bapt State Convention of IL; large faculty mem McKinley Theological Seminary North Shore Extension; board of directors, National Baptist Convention, USA Inc; president, North Shore Baptist Ministers Alliance, 1995-97. **Honors/Awds:** Freedom Awd Alpha Phi Alpha Frat Inc Kappa Chi Lambda Chap 1979; Cert of Recognition IL House of Rep 1980. **Military Serv:** USN 2nd class petty officer 4 yrs; 4 Battle Stars, 2 Campaign Ribbons, Asiatic & Phillipine Liberation. **Home Addr:** 2833 Tyler St, Waukegan, IL 60087. **Business Addr:** Pastor, Gideon Missionary Baptist Church, 1500 Ridgeland Ave, Waukegan, IL 60085.

COOK, HAROLD J.
Administrative judge. **Personal:** Born Feb 2, 1946, Richmond, VA. **Educ:** Howard Univ, BA 1968; Attended, Amer Univ Law Sch; Howard Univ Law Sch, JD 1971. **Career:** HUSA Howard Univ, vice pres 1967-68; Val Viola Memorial Found Washington, dir 1973; JCD Enterprises Inc, dir 1973; Pace Assoc Inc, dir 1974; Coll & Comm Consult Inc, 1975; administrative judge. **Orgs:** Natl exec sec Omega Psi Phi Frat Inc; mem Phi Alpha Delta Law Frat Inc 1972; officer Omega Psi Phi Frat Inc Wash DC; mem Howard Alumni Assn 1974; life mem Omega Psi Phi Frat Inc 1972; mem NAACP; Natl Legal Aid Defender's Assn 1968; mem Natl Leadership Conf on Civ Rights; NE Comm Orgn Kappa Psi Chap Omega Psi Phi Frat; mem Lamond-Riggs Civic Assn 1975; mem Big Bros; mem Boy and Girls Clubs; mem DC Alumni; Operation Crossroads Africa. **Honors/Awds:** Keys to Cities of Bossier 7 Shreveport LA 1977, Norfolk 1975, Birmingham 1975; Appreciation Awd 1972; participant Operations Crossroads Africa Ghana 1967; Hon Cit Spartanburg SC 1974; six time winner CORE Scholarship 1965-71; Grad Basileus of the Yr Third Dist Omega Psi Phi Frat Inc 1971; Alpha Chap Omega Psi Phi Frat Inc Man of the Yr Awd 1967; Kappa Psi Chap Omega Psi Phi Frat Inc Man of the Yr Awd 1969; Vol of the Yr Bureau of Rehab 1982; Big Brother of the Yr Natl Capital Area 1983; Region III Big Brother of Yr 1983; Pan Hellenic Citizen of Yr 1983; Omega Psi Phi Frat Inc Washington DC Citizen of the Yr 1983; City Council Resolution 1984; tribute Congressional Record 1984; vice pres Shiloh Branch Boys an d Girls Clubs 1986-89; pres Skill ShotRacquetball Club 1988-.

COOK, HENRY LEE, SR.
Dentist. **Personal:** Born Sep 7, 1939, Macon, GA; married Mamie R Richmond; children: Cathy L, Henry L II. **Educ:** Tuskegee Univ, BS 1962; Meharry Medical Coll, DDS 1969. **Career:** Private Practice, dentist. **Orgs:** Chairman of bd Minority Asst Corp 1977-87; mem Col Bd Health 1978-87; pres Alpha Phi Sigma, Phi Beta Sigma 1980-87, L & L Sports Unlimited 1980-87; vicechmn bd YMCA 1982-87; treas GA Dental Soc 1983-87; natl vice pres Tuskegee Natl Alumni 1985-87; natl trustee Natl Dental Assoc 1986-87. **Honors/Awds:** Cited in Who's Who Among Amer Colls & Univs; Outstanding Young Man of Amer; Civil Rights Awd Natl Dental Assoc; Governor apptd Statewide Health Coord Council. **Military Serv:** USAF 1st lt 1962-65. **Business Addr:** 1190 Martin L King Blvd, Columbus, GA 31906.

COOK, JAMES E.
Clergyman, dean. **Personal:** Born Mar 25, 1925, Lancaster, SC; son of Mr & Mrs Neely; married Mildred C Washington; children: Diaon, Gloria, Roslyn. **Educ:** Livingstone Coll, AB 1948; Hood Theological Seminary BD, 1951; AL St Univ; VA, Union Theol Sem; Alabama State University Med, 1975, Livingstone College, DD, 1976. **Career:** Butler Ch AME Zion, minister 1961-; Lomax-Hannon Jr Coll, acad dean 1967-84, dean of religion 1961-67; Warner Temple AME Zion Ch Lancaster, pastor 1950-51; Baum Temple AME Zion Ch Summerville, pastor 1951-61; Moore's Chapel AME Zion Ch, asst pastor 1949. **Orgs:** Acting presiding elder of Greenville Dist S AL Conf; mem Bd Trustees Lomax-Hannon Jr Coll; mem of bd Christian Educ AME Zion Ch; mem Bd of Evangelism AME Zion Ch; mem Ministers & Laymen Assn AME Zion Ch; mem 33 Degree Mason; United Supreme Council Class of 1972; Wingfiled Lodge #23a & Consistory #19; Chancellor Comdr Eagle Lodge KP; Omega Psi Phi; mem bd dir Recreation City of Greenville; Organized Comm Action Program. **Honors/Awds:** Many certificates for outstanding work in religion Daniel Payne Coll 1966; Many plaques for outstanding works in local church & community. **Business Addr:** Lomax Hannon Jr Coll, Greenville, AL 36037.

COOK, JOYCE MITCHELL
Educator, writer (retired), philosopher. **Personal:** Born Oct 28, 1933, Sharon, PA; daughter of Mary Bell Christman Mitchell (deceased) and Isaac William Mitchell (deceased); divorced. **Educ:** Bryn Mawr Coll, AB 1955; Oxford U, BA 1957, MA 1961; Yale U, PhD 1965. **Career:** White House Staff, staff asst 1977-81; Howard Univ, spec asst for communications, 1981-89, dir of honors prog, mem dept of philosophy 1966-68, 1970-76; CT Coll, dept of philosophy 1968-70; Office of Economic Opportunity, publ Head 1965-66; US Dept of State, foreign serv reserve officer 1964-65; Wellesley Coll, dept of philosophy 1961-62; Yale Univ, dept of philosophy 1959-61. **Orgs:** Mng editor Review of Metaphysics 1959-61; consult Inst for Serv to Educ 1972-76; mem Am Philosophical Assn; Com on Blacks in Philosophy 1970-76; prog com Eastern Div 1974-76. **Home Addr:** 429 N St SW, Washington, DC 20024.

COOK, JULIAN ABELE, JR.
Judge. **Personal:** Born Jun 22, 1930, Washington, DC; son of Ruth Elizabeth McNeill Cook and Julian Abele Cook; married Carol Annette Dibble; children: Julian Abele III, Peter Dibble, Susan Annette. **Educ:** PA State Univ, BA, 1952; Georgetown Univ, JD, 1957; Univ of Virginia, LLM, 1988. **Career:** Judge Arthur E Moore, law clerk, 1957-58; private practice, attorney, 1958-78; State of MI, special asst, attorney general, 1968-78; Univ of Detroit-Mercy, adjunct prof of law, 1970-74; East Dist of MI, US Courthouse, Detroit, US Dist Judge, 1978-, chief judge, 1989-96, sr judge, 1996-; Trial Advocacy Workshop, Harvard Univ, instructor, 1988-. **Orgs:** Amer & Natl Bar Assns; Am Bar Found; co-chmn, Prof, Devel Task Force, MI Bar Assn; MI Assn of Black Judges; Fed Bar Assn; Oakland Univ Proj Twenty Comm, chmn, bd of dirs, 1966-68; Pontiac Area Urban League, pres, 1967-68; MI Civil Rights Comm, chair, 1968-71; Todd Phillips Children's Home, bd of dirs, 1968-78; Amer Civil Liberties Union, bd of dirs, 1976-78; Amer Inn of Court, pres, master of the bench, chap XI, 1994-96; Cont Legal Educ Comm, Oakland County Bar Assn, 1968-69, judicial liaison, Dist Court Comm, vice chair, 1977; Cont Legal Educ Comm, 1977; Unauthorized Practice of Law, 1977; MI Supreme Court Defense Serv Comm, 1977; exec bd of dir, past pres, Child & Family Serv of MI; chmn, Sixth Circuit Comm on Standard Jury Instruction; bd of dirs, Amer Heart Assn of MI; Amer Bar Assn, fellow, 1981-; Detroit Urban League, bd of dirs, 1983-85; Brighton Health Svcs Corp, 1985-92; Georgetown Univ Alumni Assn; Judicial Conference of the US, chmn, 1990-93; Harvard Univ, trial advocacy workshop, instructor, 1988-; life mem, NAACP; PA State Univ, Alumni Assn, alumni coun, 1986-92; Hutzel Hosp, bd of dirs, 1984-95; Georgetown Univ, bd of visitors, 1991-; NY Univ Root Tilden Snow Scholarship Prog, screening panel, 1991-; Mediation Tribunal Assn; Third Judicial Circuit of MI, bd of dirs, 1992-; Amer Law Inst, 1996-; Judicial Coun of the Sixth Circuit, sr judge personnel comm, 1996-97; MI Bar Foundation, fellow, 1987-, chair, 1993-. **Honors/Awds:** Distinguished Citizen of the Year, NAACP, Oakland Co, MI, 1970; Citation of Merit, Pontiac, MI Area Urban League, 1971; chmn, Civil Rights Commn, achieved resolution, State of MI, House of Representatives, 1971; Boss of the Year, Legal Secretary Assn, 1973-74; Pathfinders Award, Oakland Univ, 1977; Serv Award, Todd-Phillips Home Inc, 1978; Focus & Impact Award Oakland Univ, 1985; Distinguished Alumnus Award, Pennsylvania State Univ, 1985; Distinguished Alumnus Award, John Carroll Award, Georgetown Univ, 1989; Augustus Straker Award, 1988; Absalom Jones Award, Union of Black Episcopalians, Detroit Chapter, 1988; Bench-Bar Award, Wolverine, Detroit Bar Assn, 1987; Presidential Award, North Oakland Co, NAACP, 1987; Honor Soc, Univ of Detroit School of Law, 1981; B'nai B'rith Barrister, 1980; Federal Bar Assn, 1978; MI Lawyers Weekly, voted 1 of 25 Most Respected Judges in MI, 1990, 1991; Detroit Monthly, voted 1 of the best Judges in the Metro Detroit area, 1991; Georgetown University, Doctor of Law, Honoris Causa, 1992; Jewish Law Veterans of the US, Brotherhood Award, 1994; MI State Bar, Champion of Justice Award, 1994; Univ of Detroit-Mercy, Doctor of Laws, Honoris Causa, 1996; Wayne State Univ, Doctor of Laws, Honoris Causa, 1997; Georgetown Univ, Paul R Dean Award, 1997; Pontiac, MI, City Wide Choir Union, Humanitarian Award. **Special Achievements:** Published: Jurisprudence of Original Intention, co-author, 1986; A Quest for Justice, 1983; Some Current Problems of Human Administration, co-author, 1971; The Changing Role of the Probation Officer in the Federal Court, article, Federal Sentencing Reporter, vol 4, no 2, p 112, 1991; An Overview of the US District Court for the Eastern District of Michigan, article, Inter Alia, vol 28, no 1, winter 1990; Rule 11: A Judicial Approach to an Effective Administration of Justice in the US Courts, 15 Ohio N U L 397, 1988; ADR in the United States District Court for Eastern District of Michigan, Michigan Pleading and Practice ADR, Section 62A-405-62A-415, 1994; Thurgood Marshall and Clarence Thomas: A Glance at Their Philosophies, Michigan Bar Journal, March 1994, Vol 73, No 3, p298; George A Googasian-58th President of the State Bar of Michigan, Michigan Bar Journal, Oct 1992, Vol 71, No 10; ''Family Responsibility, Federal Sentencing Reporter,'' 1995; Federal Civil Procedure Before Trial: Sixth Circuit, 1996; ''Dream Makers: Black Judges on Justice,'' Univ of MI Law Review, 1996; ''Death Penalty,'' co-author Cooley Law Review, 1996; ''Closing Their Eyes to the Constitution: The Declining Role of the Supreme Court in the Protection of Civil Rights,'' co-author, Detroit Coll of Law, 1996. **Military Serv:** US Army Signal Corps, 1st lt, 1952-54. **Business Addr:** Chief Judge-US District Court, Eastern District of Michigan, 718 Theodore Levin United States Courthouse, 231 W Lafayette, Detroit, MI 48226.

COOK, KEITH LYNN
Banking executive. **Personal:** Born May 24, 1963, Chicago, IL; married Tia Cook, Feb 1, 1996. **Educ:** Roosevelt University, 1989-92. **Career:** Citibank ISB, mortgage acct executive, 1986-92; Harris Trust & Savings Bank, residential mortgage specialist, 1992-95, assistant manager, 1995-, manager, business development, currently. **Orgs:** Cosmopolitan Chamber of Commerce, 1996-; Urban Bankers of Chicago, 1996-; Dearborn Real Estate Board, 1994; Network of Black Real Estate Professionals, 1993; South/Southwest Board of Realtors, affiliate mem, 1992; Chicago Real Estate Fund, 1994; National Association of Black Accountants, 1990. **Honors/Awds:** Harris Bank, Community Reinvestment Act Awd, 1992, 1993.

COOK, LADDA BANKS
Business executive (retired). **Personal:** Born Aug 22, 1935, Lancaster, SC; married Jessie Lee Oliver; children: Anita, Deborah. **Educ:** Johnson C Smith Univ, BS 1957; Amer Coll of Life Underwriters, CLU 1972, CHFC 1986. **Career:** New York City Dept of Hosp & Health, asst chemist 1960-65; Gen Agents & Mgrs Assoc Brooklyn Chapt, pres 1976; NY Life Ins Co, gen mgr 1965-93, managing partner, 1994. **Orgs:** Bd of dirs Natl Assoc of Life Underwriters 1977, Amer Soc of Chartered Life Underwriters 1972-93; mem 100 Black Men 1977, NAACP 1979, Kiwanis Club 1971; bd of disting visitors Johnson C Smith Univ 1979; pres Johnson C Smith Univ Alumni Assoc 1969; dir Reg I 1969; 2nd vice pres Natl Alumni Assoc 1977; basileus Omega Psi Phi, Alpha Upsilon Chap 1984; elder Siloam Presbyterian Church 1977-97; bd of trustees Claflin Coll 1984; board of directors, NY Chapter of General Agents and Managers Association. **Honors/Awds:** Robert Brown Mem Scholarship Awd 1957; Black Achievers in Industry Awd, YMCA of Gr NY 1971, NY Lifes Pres Trophy 1972. **Military Serv:** AUS 1958-60. **Home Addr:** 228-03 139th Ave, Jamaica, NY 11413.

COOK, LEVI, JR.
Company executive. **Career:** Advantage Enterprises Inc., chief executive officer, currently. **Special Achievements:** Company is ranked #45 on Black Enterprise's list of top companies, 1994. **Business Addr:** CEO, Advantage Enterprises Inc., 5030 Advantage Dr., Toledo, OH 43612, (419)727-0027.

COOK, MARY MURRAY
Educator. **Personal:** Born May 7, 1936, Winston-Salem, NC; married Rev Payton B Cook; children: Pamela, Lisa, Melanie. **Educ:** Winston-Salem State Univ, BSN 1958; Univ of MD, MS 1970. **Career:** Comm Hosp Wilmington NC, instructor 1958-59; DC General Hosptial, head nurse pediatrics 1959-62; Central State Hosp Milledgeville, instructor inservice 1965-68; GA Coll, assoc prof nursing. **Orgs:** Pres 1978-80, treasurer 1980-14th Dist GA Nurses Assoc; bd of ed Baldwin Cty 1984-; sr cadette Girl Scout Leader; undergrad advisor Delta Sigma Theta-Sor. **Honors/Awds:** Mem Alpha Kappa Mu Hon Soc, Alpha Phi Sigma Hon Frat, Sigma Theta Tau Hon Soc; Nurse of the Year 14th Dist GA Nurses Assoc 1980. **Home Addr:** 1100 Dunlap Dr, Milledgeville, GA 31061.

COOK, NATHAN HOWARD
Educator. **Personal:** Born Apr 26, 1939, Winston-Salem, NC; married Thelma Vernelle Upperman; children: Carlene Y, Erika Y. **Educ:** NC Central Univ, BS 1961, MA 1963; Univ of NC Greensboro, 1964; NC State Univ, Grad Credit 1965; OK State Univ, PhD 1972. **Career:** Barber-Scotia Coll, asst prof of biology 1962-68; Wica Chemicals Inc, faculty intern 1968; OK State Univ, grad teaching asst 1968-69; Lincoln Univ, prof & head of biology dept. **Orgs:** Chmn Sickle Cell Adv Comm MO Div of Health 1972-79; eval panelist Natl Science Found 1976; mem bd of dirs Amer Cancer Soc Cole Unit 1981-85; consultant/review panelist Natl Institutes of Health/div of Rsch Resources 1982; mem Environ Quality Comm 1981-; pres elect MO Acad of Science 1984-85; presSunrise Optimist Club of Jefferson City 1984-85. **Honors/Awds:** Ford Found Fellow 1969-71; Blue Tiger Awd US Army ROTC Unit Lincoln Univ 1982. **Home Addr:** 2908 Sue Dr, Jefferson City, MO 65101. **Business Addr:** Prof of Biology, Lincoln Univ, 820 Chestnut St, Jefferson City, MO 65101.

COOK, RALPH D.
Justice. **Career:** Supreme Court of Alabama, justice, currently. **Business Addr:** Justice, Alabama Supreme Court, 300 Dexter Ave, Montgomery, AL 36104-3741, (205)242-4609.

COOK, RUFUS
Attorney, investor. **Personal:** Born Nov 22, 1936, Birmingham; divorced; children: Bruce. **Educ:** Talladega Coll, BA 1956; Univ Chgo, LLD 1959. **Career:** Judge Luther M Swygert US Dist CT, law clerk 1959-60; Private Practice, Lawyer 1963. **Orgs:** Pres bd chmn Continental Inst Tech Inc; pres Phoenix Realty Inc; partner Cook Apts Assos; pres Pinnacle & Graphics Corp; chmn bd Hyde Park -Kenwood Comm Conf 1966-68; bd mem Chicago Fedn Settlements 1967-69; Daniel Hale Williams U; mem Nat Moot Ct Team Univ Chicago 1958-59. **Honors/Awds:** Prize Univ Chicago 1958; USAF Commendation Medal 1963. **Military Serv:** USAF capt 1963-66. **Business Addr:** 180 N La Salle St, Ste 3018, Chicago, IL.

COOK, SAMUEL DUBOIS
University president. **Personal:** Born Nov 21, 1928, Griffin, GA; son of Mary Beatrice Daniel Cook and Manuel Cook; mar-

ried Sylvia Merelene Fields, Mar 18, 1960; children: Samuel Jr, Karen Jarcelyn. **Educ:** Morehouse Coll, AB 1948; OH State Univ, MA 1950, PhD 1954. **Career:** Southern Univ, prof 1955-56; Atlanta Univ, chmn 1956-66; Univ of Illinois, visiting prof 1962-63; Duke Univ, prof 1966-74; The Ford Foundation, program officer 1969-71; Dillard Univ, pres 1975-97. **Orgs:** Bd of trustees Martin Luther King Ctr for Soc Change 1969-; editorial bd Amer Polit Sci Rev; editorial bd Jour of Politics; editorial bd Jour of Negro History; bd of dir So Christian Ldrsp Conf; bd dir Amer Cncl of Library Resources; bd of tst Cncl on Religion in Intl Affairs; past pres So Polit Sci Assn; mem Mayor's Charter Revision Comm; bd of dir Inst for Serv to Educ; mem Exec Council Amer Polit Sci Assn; past vice pres Amer Polit Assn; mem Phi Beta Kappa; Pi Sigma Alpha; mem Natl Cncl for Humanities, Omicron Delta Phi, Omega Psi Phi, Sigma Pi Phi; trustee Duke Univ. **Honors/Awds:** Outstanding Prof Awd Duke Univ; Disting Achvmt Awd St Augustine's Coll; Citation of Achvmt Awd OH State; Torch of Liberty Awd Anti-Defamation League; contrib articles to professional journals and anthologies; honorary degrees: Morehouse College, 1972; Ohio State Univ, 1977; Duke Univ, 1979; Illinois College, 1979. **Military Serv:** AUS 1953-55. **Business Addr:** Former President, Dillard University, 2601 Gentilly Blvd, New Orleans, LA 70122.

COOK, SMALLEY MIKE
Writer, producer. **Personal:** Born Mar 10, 1939, Chicago, IL. **Educ:** Univ of Massachusetts, MA 1972; Union Grad Sch, PhD 1977. **Career:** Image Alliance, writer/producer 1974-; Univ of Iowa, professor of drama 1987-. **Orgs:** Consultant Chicago Urban League 1973-; consultant Chicago Dept of Cultural Affairs 1983-; founder Dramatic Arts Repertory Ensemble for Youth 1986-. **Honors/Awds:** Writer-producer "Drums of the Night Gods," staged, Los Angeles Cultural Ctr 1981; Goodman Theatre Chicago 1983, Chicago Cultural Ctr 1983; writer-producer "The Fire and the Storm" Lindblom Park Dist Chicago 1986. **Military Serv:** AUS spl/4 3 yrs; European Svcs.

COOK, TOI FITZGERALD
Professional football player. **Personal:** Born Dec 3, 1964, Chicago, IL. **Educ:** Stanford. **Career:** New Orleans Saints, defensive back, 1987-93; San Francisco 49ers, 1994-95; Carolina Panthers, 1996-. **Business Addr:** Professional Football Player, Carolina Panthers, 800 Mint St, Ericsson Stadium, Charlotte, NC 28202, (704)358-7000.

COOK, VERNICE WILHELMINA BARNES
Educator (retired). **Personal:** Born Apr 17, 1919, Charlottesville, VA; daughter of Eliza Frances Cosby Barnes and Clarence William Timothy Barnes; married Cleophas Darrow Cook, Aug 28, 1949 (died 1972); children: Dwight Roderick Bartlet, Evangeline LaTonya Cook-Earle. **Educ:** South Carolina State, Orangeburg, SC; Virginia Union University, Richmond, VA, BA, 1945; Connecticut College, New London, CT. **Career:** Smoaks Elementary School, Smoaks, SC, 4th and 5th grade teacher, 1939-40; Carlton County Elementary School, SC, head teacher, 1941-42; Appomattox Elementary School, Appomattox, VA, 6th grade teacher, 1945-54; Saltonstall Elementary School, New London, CT, 6th grade teacher, 1954-70; Nathan Hale Elementary School, New London, CT, 6th grade teacher, 1970-81. **Orgs:** President, Shiloh Baptist Church Good Samaritan Club; branch secretary, NAACP, New London Branch; secretary, NAACP, Northeastern Region; life member, NAACP; life member, state convener, Natl Council of Negro Women; founder, president emeritus, Natl Council of Negro Women, New London Chapter; chairperson, bd of dirs, New London Community Resources Commission, currently; vice chairperson, bd of dirs, Region I national auxiliary representative, OIC; active past loyal daughter ruler, Daughters of the Improved Benevolent Protective Order of Elks of the World; president, Hempstead Neighborhood Advisory Council; charter member, vice pres, Socialite Social Club; member, Circle 6; member, WFSR-TV Minority Advisory Bd; member, Civil Rights Coordinating Committee of the Commission on Human Rightsember, bd of dirs, YWCA; member, Federation of New London County Black Democrats. **Honors/Awds:** Woman of the Year, National Council of Negro Women, Connecticut State Chapter, 1978; First Annual National NAACP Women's Conference Service Award in Recognition of Outstanding Services in the Promotion of NAACP Branch Programs, 1980; 10Year Service Award as Vice Chairperson, New London County OIC, Board of Directors, 1980; In Memory of Mary McLeod Bethune Plaque: Founder and Organizer of the New London County Section, presented, 1980.

COOK, WALLACE JEFFERY
Clergyman, dentist. **Personal:** Born Jul 14, 1932, El Reno, OK; married Martha; children: Cheryl, Jeffery, Jeryl. **Educ:** AZ State U, BA 1954; Howard U, DDS Coll of Dentistry 1957; Crozer Theol Sem, MDiv 1964; Union Theol Sem Richmond VA, D Ministry 1978; VA Union U, DD 1973. **Career:** Ebenezer Bapt Ch Richmond VA, pastor 1971; Providence Public Schs, dentist dept of health 1970; Joseph Samuels Dental Clinic, dentist 1969; Ebenezer Baptist Church Providence RI, pastor 1964-71; 1st Baptist Church Yardley PA, pastor 1963-64; USAF, Dentist 1957-61. **Orgs:** Richmond Comm Sr Center 1975; Urban League 1970; Urban Coalition 1970; Richmond Oppty Indus Ctrs 1976. **Military Serv:** USAF capt 1957-61. **Business Addr:** 216 W Leigh St, Richmond, VA 23220.

COOK, WILLIAM WILBURT
Educator. **Personal:** Born Aug 4, 1933, Trenton, NJ; son of Frances Carter Cook (deceased) and Cleve Cook (deceased). **Educ:** Trenton State Coll, BS, valedictorian, 1954; Univ of Chicago, MA (w/Honors) 1976. **Career:** Trenton Public Schools, teacher of English/social studies 1954-61; Princeton Regional Schools, teacher of English/chair of English Dept 1961-73; Dartmouth Coll, dir African and Afro-Amer studies 1977-84, 1985-90, assoc prof of English, prof of English 1973-; Israel Evans, prof of oratory and belles lettres, 1991-; English Dept, Dartmouth Coll, chair, 1994-. **Orgs:** Humanities consultant Natl Faculty of Arts & Scis 1976-; bd of dirs Amer Folk Theater 1982-; patron/dir North Country Theater 1983-; chair adv comm on minority affairs Conf on Coll Comp & Communications 1983-85; children's media consultant Natl Endowment for the Humanities 1984-; adv bd Natl Civil Rights Museum 1986-88; asst chair 1990, assoc chair 1991, program chair 1991, chair 1992, Convention Coll Comp and Communications. **Honors/Awds:** Disting Alumni Citation Trenton State Coll 1977; Danforth Assoc 1979-85; has published poetry, literary criticism; edited 3 books; Dartmouth Distinguished Teaching Award 1989; author, Hudson Hornet and other Poems 1989; Israel Evans Professor of Oratory and Belles Lettre Dartmouth College 1991; Council for the Advancement & Support of Educ, New Hampshire Professor of the Year, 1993; Rivier Coll, Doctor of Humane Letters, 1994. **Military Serv:** AUS sp-4 1957-59. **Business Addr:** Chair, Department of English, Dartmouth College, PO Box 6032, Hanover, NH 03755, (603)646-2318.

COOK, YVONNE MACON. See POWELL, YVONNE MACON.

COOKE, ANNA L.
Librarian (retired). **Personal:** Born in Jackson, TN; daughter of Effie Cage Lee and Thurston Lee; married James A Cooke; children: Elsie Cooke Holmes. **Educ:** Lane Coll, BA 1944; Atlanta Univ, MLS 1955. **Career:** Douglas Jr High School Haywood County TN, principal 1944-46; Jackson City School, teacher 1947-51, librarian 1951-63; Lane Coll, catalog librarian 1963-67, PR & Alumni dir 1966-69, head librarian 1967-88 (retired); Metro Forum, Jackson Sun, freelance writer, 1990-. **Orgs:** Mem Amer Library Assn 1964-; bd of dir Amer Cancer Soc 1967-73; sec bd of dir Jackson Arts Council 1974-76; bd dir Reelfoot Girl Scout Council 1974-86, 1st vice pres 1983-86; bd trustees Jackson Madison Co Library 1984-93; TN Library Assn; West TN Library Assn; American Library Association; Delta Sigma Theta Sorority Inc; Links, Inc; NAACP; bd of dirs Jackson Volunteer Ctr, 1988-90; chairman, women's advisory board, HCA Regional Hospital of Jackson, 1990-96; Jackson/Madison County Historic Zoning Comm, 1993-96. **Honors/Awds:** Library Sci Lane Coll 1966; Hon Fellow Philosophical Soc of England 1969; Alumni Plaque Lane Coll 1975; Action Awd Radio Station WJAK 1982; Serv Plaque City of Jackson 1972; Girl Scout Friendmaker Awd 1985; Serv Plaque Delta Sigma Theta Sor; author "History of Lane College," 1987; Distinguished Service Award, State of Tennessee 1988; Diamond Jubilee Service Award, Delta Sigma Theta Sorority 1988; Certificate of Merit, Lane Coll 1988; Presidential Citation, National Assn for Equal Opportunity in Higher Education, 1989; Distinguished Service Award, City of Jackson, 1992; Honorary Degree, Doctor of Humane Letters, Lane Coll, 1993; Metro Forum Service Award, 1991-97; Published poem God's Love in Dark Side of the Moon: The Natl Library of Poetry, 1994; Distinguished Service Plaques, Delta Sigma Thete Sorority, 1994-95; Jackson/Madison County Board Service Award, 1993; Alpha Kappa Alpha Community Affairs, Hall of Fame, 1995; Delta Sigma Theta, Service Award, 1995; Housing Historic Zoning Commission, Service Award, 1996; Jackson City Community, Treasure Award, 1997.

COOKE, LEONARD
Law enforcement official. **Personal:** Born in Weldon, NC. **Career:** City of Washington, DC, police officer; City of Eugene, Oregon, chief of police, 1992-. **Orgs:** FBINAA; NOBLE; OCPA; IACP. **Honors/Awds:** IACP, Fellowship, 1988. **Business Addr:** Chief of Police, Eugene Police Department, 777 Pearl St, Rm 107, Eugene, OR 97401.

COOKE, LLOYD M.
Former organization executive. **Personal:** Born Jun 7, 1916, LaSalle, IL; son of Anna Maria Miller and William Wilson Cooke; married Vera; children: Barbara Anne, William E. **Educ:** Univ WI, BS 1937; McGill Univ, PhD 1941. **Career:** McGill Univ, lectr, 1941-42; Corn Prods Refining Co Argo IL, sect leader, 1942-46; Films Packaging Div Union Carbide Corp Chgo, grp leader, 1946-49, dept mgr, 1950-54, asst to mgr tech div, 1954-57, asst dir rsch, 1965-67, mgr planning 1967-70; New York City, dir urban affairs, 1970-78, corp dir univ relations, 1973-76, corp dir comm affairs, 1976-77, sr consult, 1978-81 (retired 1983); LMC Associates White Plains, New York, president, 1987-. **Orgs:** Natl Sci Bd 1970-82; consult, Office of Tech Assessment US Congress 1972-79; vice chmn, Econ Devel Council of NY 1978-81; pres, Natl Action Council on Minorities in Engrg 1981-83, pres emeritus 1983; contrib articles to professional journals; Comm Conf Bd Downers Grove IL 1968-70; trustee, McCormick Theol Sem 1976-80; NY Acad Scis; Amer Chem Soc; AAAS; Sigma Xi; Phi Kappa Phi; Beta Kappa Chi; Chicago Chemists Club; NY Chemists Club; trustee, New York State Science & Technology Foundation 1986-96. **Honors/Awds:** Proctor Prize Sci Sci Rsch Soc Amer 1970; Fellow Amer Inst Chemists (honor scroll Chicago); College of Ganado, LLD (hon). **Home Addr:** 1 Beaufort St, White Plains, NY 10607.

COOKE, NELLIE
Educator. **Personal:** Born Dec 17, 1948, Brighton, AL; daughter of Loudelia Freed Cooke and Prentis Cooke; married Robert Jefferson, Oct 18, 1990; children: Derek Vincent. **Educ:** Bethune-Cookman College, Daytona Beach, FL, 1965-67; District of Columbia Teachers College, Washington, DC, BA, 1973; VPI-Virginia Tech, Blacksburg, VA, Masters, 1988. **Career:** Shaw Junior High School, Washington, DC, teacher/dean of students, 1974-. **Orgs:** Chair, National Junior Red Cross; member, advisory committee, WHMM-TV, Washington, DC, currently; member, advisory board, Young Writers Contest Foundation. **Honors/Awds:** Woman of the Year, Shiloh Baptist Church, 1989; Torchlighter Award, The Potomac LINKS, Washington, DC, 1989; cover story, Washington Post Magazine, January, 1989; educational consultant, Nightwatch, CBS. **Business Addr:** Asst Principal, Bertie Backus Middle School, 5171 S Dakota Ave, NE, Washington, DC 20017.

COOKE, PAUL PHILLIPS
Consultant, educator. **Personal:** Born Jun 29, 1917, New York, NY; son of Mamie K Phillips Cooke and Louis Philip Cooke; married Rose Clifford, Aug 22, 1940; children: Kelsey C Meyersburg, Paul C, Anne, Katherine. **Educ:** Miner Tchrs Coll, BS (cum laude), 1937; NY Univ, MA 1941; The Cath Univ of Am, MA 1943; Columbia Univ, EdD 1947. **Career:** Miner Teachers College & DCTC, prof of English 1944-74; District of Columbia Teachers College, president 1966-74; Amer Assn of State Colleges & Univs, dir of intl programs 1974-75; AASCU, special consultant 1974-90. **Orgs:** Consultant, World Peace through Law Ctr 1974-78; consultant, Amer Bar Assn Standing Committee on World Order under Law 1975-77; consultant, Howard Univ Dept of Physics 1976, 81; consultant, School of Education 1979, 1988; consultant, Anacostia Neighborhood Museum (Smithsonian) for 4 exhibits 1979-92; special asst to the pres of the Univ of the District of Columbia for Historical Rsch 1982-83; vp, academic affairs, Beacon College 1984-85; participant, World Veterans Federation General Assemblies, numerous times; life mem NAACP; life mem Kappa Alpha Psi Fraternity. **Honors/Awds:** Am Vet Com Bessie Levine Award 1960; Nat Sor of Phi Delta Kappa Award 1975; 202 publications & papers, numerous publications including, "The Centennial Drama, A History of Miner Teachers College," "Civil Rights in the United States," "The Cooke Lecture Series;" Educ of the Disadvantaged in the Model Sch Div 1965; 22 articles in the Journal of Negro Education 1949-82 and other articles in the Negro History Bulletin 1958-82, Negro Educational Review, Mid-West Journal; establishment of the Paul Phillips Lecture Series 1979, Paul Phillips Scholarship 1984, at the Univ of the District of Columbia; Pope John Paul II Papal Medal, Pro Ecclesia et Pontifice 1984; Thomas Wyatt Turner Award, Office of Black Catholics, Washington DC; Kappa Alpha Psi Fraternity Laurel Wreath Designate; Doctor of Laws Degree, Honoris Causa, Univ of District of Columbia 1986; Editor-In Chief, 1988 Assn for the Study Afro Life & History Kit. **Military Serv:** USAF corpl 1945-46.

COOKE, THOMAS H., JR.
Business development executive. **Personal:** Born Oct 13, 1929, Camden, SC; married Audrey E Wilson; children: Bonnye A Jefferson, Julie L, Michael W Thomas III. **Educ:** NY Univ, BS, 1954; Montclair State College, MA, 1974. **Career:** US Veterans Admin Hosp, corrective therapist, 1957-58; Newark Bd of Educ, Victoria plan coord, 1958-77; City of East Orange, mayor, 1978-85; McLaughlin PivenVogel Inc, sr govt bond specialist, 1986-87; Maintenance Mgmt Specialists Inc, pres, 1987-. **Orgs:** Bd of dirs, 2nd vice pres, Natl Conf of Black Mayors, 1978-85; govt relations comm, Natl United Way, 1979-; bd of dirs, exec comm, US Conf of Mayors, 1981-85; bd of dirs, finance comm, Natl League of Cities, 1981-85; commissioner, NJ Martin L King Commemorative Comsn, 1983-; commissioner, NJ Drug Adv Comsn, 1983-; bd of dirs, NJ Multi Housing Industry, 1987-; life mem, NAACP; Natl Council of Negro Women; Natl Council of Jewish Women. **Honors/Awds:** Completion of Downtown Renewal Prog, 40 yrs in the making, 1981-85. **Military Serv:** US Navy Reserves, asst psychologist, 1954-56; Honor Man Grad Co, 1954. **Home Addr:** 74 Hawthorne Ave, East Orange, NJ 07018. **Business Addr:** President/Managing Partner, Maintenance Mgmt Specialists, 576 Central Ave, Ste LL-7, East Orange, NJ 07018, (201)672-7624.

COOKE, WILCE L.
City official. **Personal:** Born Jun 18, 1939, Benton Harbor, MI; son of Elizabeth Walker; married Beverly. **Educ:** Oakland Comm Coll School of Practical Nursing, 1968; Inst for Adult Ed Instr, Ed Prof Devel Act 1970; Lake Michigan Coll, AA 1975; Western MI Univ, BS 1976, MA 1985. **Career:** City of Benton Harbor, mayor. **Orgs:** Adv bd Tri-Can; former suprv comm Peoples Comm Fed Credit Union; former bd of dir, org Self-Help Co-Operative; former charter revision commiss BentonHarbor Charter Commiss; treas mercy Hosp Staff Council

1977-82; mem Phi Theta Kappa; Benton Twp Black Coalition; bd of dir Berrien Cty Heart Unit MI Heart Assoc; trustee bd, asst sunday school supt Bethlehm Temple Pentecostal Church; mem Alpha Kappa Delta. **Honors/Awds:** Natl Upper Div Scholarship Competition 1976; Outstanding Serv Awd Benton Harbor Concerned Citizens; Berrien Cty Medical Soc for spearheading drive in retaining Open Heart Surgical Unit at Mercy Hosp in Southwestern MI 1978. **Home Addr:** 1130 Salem, Benton Harbor, MI 49022. **Business Addr:** Mayor, City of Benton Harbor, 200 East Wall St, Benton Harbor, MI 49022.

COOKE, WILLIAM BRANSON
Cartographer. **Personal:** Born Mar 11, 1927, Spencerville, MD; married Theresa M Johnson. **Educ:** Miner Tchr Coll, BS 1951; Am U. **Career:** Geological Survey Interior Dept, supr cartographer. **Orgs:** Mem Antarctican Soc; mem Nat Congress on Surveying & Mapping; pres DC Br NAACP. **Honors/Awds:** Presidential award for outstanding serv DC Br NAACP. **Military Serv:** AUS pfc 1946-47. **Business Addr:** Geol Survey Interior Dept, 1925 Newton Sq E, Reston, VA 22090.

COOLEY, ARCHIE LEE, JR.
Assistant football coach, educator. **Personal:** Born Mar 18, 1939, Sumrall, MS; son of Bernice Cooley and Archie Lee Cooley Sr; married Georgia Ester Reed, Dec 28, 1962; children: Dwight A, Lisa R. **Educ:** Jackson State University, BS, 1962; University of Southern Mississippi, MS, 1972; Tennessee State University; State Department of Education, AAA certification. **Career:** Mississippi Valley State University, head football coach, 1980-86; Arkansas Pine Bluff, athletic director, head football coach, 1987-91; Southern University, Baton Rouge, offensive coordinator, 1992-93; Norfolk State University, head football coach, beginning 1993; Texas Southern Univ, asst football coach, currently. **Orgs:** National Oak Park School Alumni Assn; Golden Lions Booster Club; Pine Bluff Community College; American Alliance of Health, Physical Education, Recre Dance; Mississippi Alliance for Health, Physical Education, Recreation, and Dan Mississippi Assn of Educators; Mississippi Coaches Assn; American Football Assn Optimist International; M W Stringer Master Mason. **Honors/Awds:** Selected as one of ''Arkansas' Most Influential People,'' 1990-91; Jackson State University, Football Hall of Fame, 1985; Greeenwood Voters League, Distinguished Service Award, 1984; Southwest Athletic Conference, Co-Coach of the Year, 1980, Coach of the Year, 1983; numerous others. **Special Achievements:** Television appearances: ''The Archie Cooley Show,'' 1988-90; CNN Sports, 1985, 1989, 1990; ESPN Sports, 1989; ''NFL Today,'' CBS, 1984; WJTV; WLBT; KARK; KATV; KTHV; KLRT; KASN; various national and local television stations; radio programs: ''Talking with Archie Cooley,'' 1990; ''The Archie Cooley Show,'' 1981-82. **Military Serv:** US Army, spc-4, 1962-64. **Home Addr:** 3600 Rosewood, No 1312, Houston, TX 77004. **Business Phone:** (713)313-1907.

COOLEY, JAMES F.
Clergyman, civic worker, educator. **Personal:** Born Jan 11, 1926, Rowland, NC; son of Martha Buie Cooley (deceased) and Rev James F Cooley (deceased); married Carolyn Ann Butler; children: Virginia M Cooley Lewis, Gladys M Cooley Taylor, James Francis, Franklin Donell, Stephen Lamar, Stetson Laron. **Educ:** Johnson C Smith Univ, AB Soc Sci 1953, BD Theol 1956; Interdenom Theol Center, DM 1973; World Univ Tucson, AZ, PhD Soc Sci 1982; Life Science Coll, DD 1972; St John Univ NE, MA Sociology 1972; Law Enforcement Official, certified; Law Enforcement Instructor of Jail Opers and Jail Admin, certified. **Career:** Grant Chapel Presb Ch, minister 1956-57; St Andrews Presb Ch, minister 1957-69; Forrest City Spec Sch Dist #7, 1957-69; St Francis Co, juv prob ofcr 1959-68, assoc juv judge 1963-64; Shorter Coll, polit sci dir/minister of svc/dean of men/acad dean 1969-73; State Rep Art Givens Jr, chf legisl on comm affairs; 5th Div Circ Ct for Judge Jack Lessenberg, prob ofcr; Tucker Prison, first black chaplain in AR 1971; Attorney Genl's Office, agent consumer protection; Pulaski County, deputy registrar; County Contact Comm Inc, founder/exec dir. **Orgs:** Police commr Wrightsville PD 1984; chaplain Pulaski Co Sheriff Dept 1985; AR Cncl on Human Rel; Natl Hist Soc; Urban League; Early Amer Soc; Natl Conf of Christians and Jews Inc; Postal Commem Soc; Natl Black Veterans Organ Inc; major genl Natl Chaplains Assn; foot distrib for the poor AR Food Bank Network; Amer Legion, Natl Sheriff's Assn; sr warden, comm mem 33rd Degree Mason; Boy Scouts of Amer; bd of dirs AA AWARE Drug and Alcohol Prevention Prog; Worshipful Master, Welcome Lodge #457 masonic 1987-; life member, Disabled American Veteran; life member, Veteran of Foreign Wars. **Honors/Awds:** Dr J F Cooley Month in N Little Rock 1977; Hon DD Shorter Coll No Little Rock; Hon D Civil Law E NE Christian Coll; Order of the Long Leaf Pine by Gov of NC 1986; Medallion of Honor by AR Gov Bill Clinton 1986; Cert of Appreciation Natl Chaplain's Assoc 1987; Certificates of Merit and letters of highest Commendation from Atty Genl Steve Clark, Sheriff C Gravett, Sec of State Bill McCuen; State Auditor Julia Hughes, Co Clerk Carolyn Staley, Sen Dale Bumpers, US Congressman Tommy Robinson; Dr. J. F. Cooley Day in Arkansas 1988 by Gov Bill Clinton; NAACP Community Service Award Jacksonville AR NAACP Chapter 1989; had a street in Rowland, NC, named in his honor, 1990. **Military Serv:** AUS 1944-46; several decorations and 2 Battle Stars, 6 Bronze Stars; WWII Victory Medal 1985; Good Conduct Medal; ETO Campaign Medals; ATO Campaign Medals. **Business Addr:** Minister, County Contact Comm Inc, PO Box 17225, North Little Rock, AR 72117.

COOLEY, KEITH WINSTON
Engineering executive consultant. **Personal:** Born Oct 7, 1945, Ann Arbor, MI; son of Hyacinth Holmes Cooley and Roy Van Cooley; married Yvonne A Smiley, May 21, 1977; children: Brett Winston, Todd Lloyd, Ross Allyn, Erin Blair. **Educ:** University of Michigan, College of Engineering, BSE, physics, 1967, MSE, nuclear, 1972. **Career:** Knolls Atomic Power Lab, experimental physicist, 1968-69; University of Michigan, College of Engineering, minority program office director, 1969-72; General Motors, research engineer, 1972-73, Environmental Activities Staff, staff project engineer, 1973-78, Cadilac Motor Car, staff project engineer, 1978-83, program mgr, future car line, 1983-86, engineering department head, 1986-94, dir of strategic planning & issues manager, 1994-96; Principia, Inc, business consultant, pres, 1997-. **Orgs:** Big 10 Athletic Conference, Big 10 Championship Gymnastics Team, 1966; GM University Relations Team, coordinator, 1979-96; Engineering Society of Detroit, 1980-; Tennessee Squire Association, 1981-; University of Michigan Alumni Society, 1988-; University of Michigan College of Engineering, Dean Search Committee, 1988-; University of Michigan Engineering Alumni Association, board of directors, 1991-93. **Honors/Awds:** General Motors, ''Best of the Best,'' 1995; Dollars and Sense Magazine, Outstanding Business and Professional Award, 1991; Tau Beta Pi Engineering Honorary Society, Eminent Engineer, 1989. **Special Achievements:** Plasma Nitriding of Ferrotic Material, GM Research Memorandum, 1974; Plasma Hardening of High Chromium Steel, Journal of Vacuum Science Technology, 1974; Dependence of Plasma Nitriding on Discharge Current, GM Research Report, 1974. **Business Addr:** President, Principia, Inc, Business Consultants, 1868 Squirrel Valley Dr, Bloomfield Hills, MI 48304-1146.

COOLEY, NATHAN J.
Artist, educator. **Personal:** Born Aug 24, 1924, Indianapolis, IN. **Educ:** Ball State Univ, BS 1951, MS 1955; IN Univ NW, grad study; educational tour of Europe 1969; Univ of Ghana, studied 1970. **Career:** AL A&M Univ, prof of art 1951-55; City of Gary, educ 1955; IN Univ NW, assoc prof of art; City of Gary, dir of beautification, beginning 1955; Marquette Park Pavilion, art teacher, currently. **Orgs:** Designer Life Membership Pin Kappa Alpha Psi; bd of dir N Cent Prov Kappa Alpha Psi Frat, mem bd of dir Save the Dunes Coun; mem bd of dir Lake MI Fed; mem NAACP; Kappa Alpha Psi; Phi Delta Kappa; 32 Degree Mason; Amer Fed of Tchrs; IN Fed of Tchrs; Black Merit Acad Educators to Africa Assn; Amer Soc of Planning Officials; Kiwanis Intl; vice pres, pres, Greater Gary Art Council. **Honors/Awds:** Kappa Man of the Yr 1968-69; C Leon Wilson Awd 1964; Serv to the Comm Awd NAACP 1972; Kappa of the Year 1974; Serv Awd IFTA 1976; Outstanding Citizen Awd Art Council 1984-85; Kappa Alpha Psi, Elder Watson Diggs Award. **Military Serv:** AUS s/sgt 1943-45. **Business Addr:** Art Teacher, Marquette Park Pavilion, 1 North Grand Blvd, Gary, IN 46407.

COOLEY, WENDY
Judge, television producer & hostess. **Personal:** Born Jan 1, 1949, Birmingham, AL; daughter of Bessie Crenshaw and Louise Cargill; divorced. **Educ:** Eastern Michigan University, education, 1968; University of Michigan, higher education, 1972; University of Detroit, JD, 1980. **Career:** 36th District Court, judge, 1984-; ''Winning Ways'', television/radio show, host, producer, 1990-. **Orgs:** Michigan District Judges Association; Association of Black Judges; Michigan State Bar Association; Natl Bar Assn; National Association of Negro Business and Professional Women's Club Inc; Coalition of 100 Black Women; Delta Sigma Theta; Gamma Phi Delta; Michigan Martin Luther King Jr Holiday Commission. **Honors/Awds:** Michigan's Outstanding Volunteer; National Leadership Program of America; Little Rock Baptist Church, Golden Heritage Award; Top Ladies of Distinction, Judical Excellence Award; Foremost Woman of the 20th Century; Governor Jim Blanchard, Michigan Correctional Officer Training Council. **Special Achievements:** Host and producer, ''Winning Ways,'' television and radio shows; founder and president, Women Who Win. **Home Addr:** PO Box 07158, Detroit, MI 48207. **Business Addr:** Judge, 36th District Court, 421 Madison Ave, Ste 5072, Detroit, MI 48226, (313)965-8718.

COOLIO (ARTIS IVEY)
Vocalist. **Personal:** marrIed. **Career:** Rap artist, currently. **Special Achievements:** Songs include: ''Gangsta Paradise'', ''1,2,3,4'', ''Fantastic Voyage'', ''Mama, I'm in Love'''; Album: My Soul, 1997; TV: ''Sabrina, the Teenage Witch''. **Business Addr:** Rap artist, Tommy Boy Music Inc, 902 Broadway, 13th Fl, New York, NY 10010, (212)388-8300.

COOMBS, FLETCHER
Business executive, retired. **Personal:** Born Jul 8, 1924, Altanta, GA; son of Pearl Magnolia Floyd Coombs (deceased) and Fletcher Coombs (deceased); married Helen Grimes, May 21, 1955; children: Toni, Kei. **Educ:** Morehouse Coll, AB; Atlanta Univ School of Bus Admin, MBA; Indiana University Bloomington, Ind, Graduate School of Savings & Loan, Certificate 1971. **Career:** Mutual Fed Savings & Loan Assn, various positions 1953-73, pres 1973-90, vice chm, bd of dirs, 1990-97. **Orgs:** Fin chmn, bd mem Sadie G Mays Nursing Home; Butler Street YMCA. **Honors/Awds:** Boss of the Year Golden Dome Chap Amer Bus Women Assoc; Butler Street YMCA. **Military Serv:** 2nd lt reserves, t/sgt active duty.

COOMBS, HARRY JAMES
Business executive. **Personal:** Born Sep 19, 1935, Washington, DC; married Barbara Ann Parrish. **Educ:** Armstrong High Sch, 1952. **Career:** Philadelphia Intl Records, exec vice pres 1971-; Tangerine Records Corp, natl field rep 1970-71; Capitol Record Dist Corp, e coast regional prom rep 1969-70; CBS Records Inc, e coast regional promo rep 1969-69; Ramsel Productions, dir 1968-68; Schwartz Bros Whis Rec Dist, local promotions mgr 1965-67. **Orgs:** Mem exec council Black Music Assn 1978. **Military Serv:** AUS spec 4 1954-56.

COOMBS, ORDE
Writer, editor. **Educ:** Yale U, BA 1965; Clar Coll 1965-66; NY U, MA 1971. **Career:** NY Mag, writer contbs editor; Mccall Pub Co, sr editor 1969-71; Doubleday & Co, asso editor 1966-69; Black Conversations WPIX-TV, co-host 1975; NY U, adj lectr 1973. **Honors/Awds:** Alicia Patterson Award PRSA 1974; media award for pub serv reporting 1974; edited ''Is Massa Day Dead?'' 1974; ed ''What We Must See, Young Black Storytellers'' 1971; ''We Speak as Liberators, Young Black Poets'' 1970; ''Do You See My Love For You Growing'' 1974. **Business Addr:** 444 Madison Ave, New York, NY 10022-6903.

COOPER, ALBERT, SR.
Construction company executive. **Personal:** Born Sep 22, 1934, Americus, GA; son of Mr & Mrs Anderson Cooper; married Josephine Wiggins; children: Albert Jr, Booker Alphonse, Jerel Boyd. **Educ:** Sumter Cty Comprehensive High School, night school 1984-85; Georgia Southwestern College, Americus, GA, 1987. **Career:** Cooper's Groc & Mkt, 1979-83; Cooper's Const Co, owner 1970-85. **Orgs:** Councilman Americus GA 1979-91; elected mayor protem 1982, 1985; mem Early Bird Ctn 1980; bd of governors Chamber of Comm 1981; zoning bd City of Americus1978-85. **Honors/Awds:** Excellence in Business Awd Ed Bryant 1978; Disting Serv Male Awd Oscar Marwell 1979; Men Bus League Awd 1984; Volunteer work providing housing for the poor 1984; Community Service Award, Black Business Achievement Award, 1988; Certificate of Appreciation, Chamber of Commerce, 1989; Thurgood Marshall Award, United Holiness Church, 1991.

COOPER, ALMETA E.
Attorney. **Personal:** Born Dec 27, 1950, Durham, NC; daughter of Patricia Carter Cooper and Horton Cooper; married Herbert A Nelson, Jul 1984; children: Elise Adele Nelson. **Educ:** Wells Coll, BA 1972; Northwestern Univ Sch of Law, JD 1975. **Career:** Vedder Price Kaufman & Kammholz, assoc 1975-77; Amer Med Assn, asst dir of health law div 1977-82; Tuggle Hasbrouck & Robinson, partner 1980-82; Meharry Medical Coll, corporate secretary & general counsel, 1982-88; St Thomas Hospital, Nashville, TN, general counsel, 1988-; College of St Francis, Nashville, TN, adjunct faculty, 1989-. **Orgs:** Lecturer Joint Comm on Accreditation of Hospitals; lecturer Amer College of Hospital Administrators; lecturer New England Hosp Assembly; mem Amer Soc of Hospital Attorneys; bd of dir Minority Legal Educ Resources; alternate mem Hines Veterans Admin Cooperative Studies Prog Human Rights Comm; pres bd of dir IL Family Planning Council; mem Renaissance Women; appointed mem Nashville Private Industry Council; fin comm League of Women Voters Nashville; mem Leadership Nashville 1986-87, Music City Chap of the Links, TN Bar Assn, Napier-Looby Bar Assn, Amer Acad of Hospital Attorneys. **Honors/Awds:** Chicago Urban League; Alumnae Assns of Wells & Spelman Colleges; Outstanding Alumna Spelman Coll; Outstanding Volunteer Chicago Urban League; Natl Finalist White House Fellowship 1982; publications have appeared in Journal of the Amer Med Assn and in St Louis Univ Law Journal.

COOPER, AUGUSTA MOSLEY
Association executive. **Personal:** Born Aug 8, 1903, Wilmington, NC; daughter of Ida Chestnut Mosley and Levie McKoyand Mosley; widowed. **Educ:** Howard Univ, BS 1930; Catholic Univ of Amer, grad study 1939. **Career:** NC Pub Schs, tchr 1924-25; Emergency Relief Admin of Phila, caseworker 1931-32; Emergency Relief Admin of New Hanover Co, supvr 1932-36; New Hanover Co Social Serv Dept, caseworker 1936-63; New Hanover Co Social Serv Dept, supvr 1963-66. **Orgs:** NC Conf of Social Serv 1939-;chrtr mem Delta Sigma Theta 1940-; Natl League of Women Voter 1959; mem Amer Pub Welfare Assn 1957-; PACE First Coord Com 1967; organizer Homeowners Improvement Assn of Wilmington 1968-; trustee Chestnut St United Prebyterian Ch 1968-72; mem Redevel Commn Adv Com 1968; mem SE Regional Commn Inc Cape Fear Council of Govts 1972-; mem Blue Cross Blue Shield NC Subscriber Adv Council 1975; mem NAACP; Mayor's Preservation Task Comm of Wilmington NC; Gr Wilmington Chamber of Comm Govt Affairs Comm; Preservation Preservation Net Work 1987; New Hanover County Museum Foundation, Inc,

1985; bd Pine Forest Cemetery 1982. **Honors/Awds:** Certificate of merit NC Caseworkers Assn 1960, Citizen of Yr Delta Sigma Theta 1968 & Omicron Alpha; Citizen Adv Comm for a Workable Prog for Wilmington Comm Improvement 1968-70; first Black woman candidate City Council Wilmington NC 1969; first woman Wilmington Human Relations Commn 1971-; first vice chwmn New Hanover Co Dem Party 1972; Distingushed Serv Prince Hall Grant Lodge Free & Accepted Masons of NC 1972; Gr Wilmington C of C New Hanover Wilmington Human Relations Commn Outstanding Cit 1973; Golden Life mem Delta Sigma Theta 1973; Hist Preservations of Amer 1977; Comm Leaders & Noteworthy Amer Amer Biog Inst 1976-77; Zeta Phi Beta Awd for Outstanding Comm Serv 1983; New Hanover Co Democratic Party Awd for Distingushed Serv 1984; Susan B Anthony Awd forLifetime Achievement sponsd by New Han over Co Natl Org for Women, 1984; award for outstanding service (preservation), Pine Forest Cemetery.

COOPER, BARBARA J.
Federal government official. **Personal:** Born in North Carolina; daughter of Ezola Cooper Britt and Jasper Cooper. **Educ:** Hampton Univ, BS (highest honors); Michigan State Univ, MBA; Stanford Univ, Graduate Certificate. **Career:** Portsmouth VA School System, teacher; Central Intelligence Agency, special asst to the deputy director, deputy dir of personnel; deputy inspector general for investigations, deputy dir of financial management, dir of financial mgmt. **Orgs:** Exec Women in Govt; Alpha Kappa Alpha Sorority; Natl Hampton Alumni Assn; vice pres Northern VA Chapter Natl Hampton Alumni Assn 1984-86. **Honors/Awds:** Public Affairs Fellowship, Stanford Univ. **Business Addr:** Director of Financial Management, Central Intelligence Agency, Washington, DC 20505.

COOPER, BARRY MICHAEL
Screenwriter. **Career:** William Morris Agency, screenwriter, currently. **Special Achievements:** Film credits include: Sugar Hill; New Jack City; Above the Rim. **Business Addr:** Screenwriter, c/o The William Morris Agency, Attn: James Stein or Ron Mardigan, 151 El Camino Dr, Beverly Hills, CA 90212, (310)274-7451.

COOPER, BOBBY G.
Educator. **Personal:** Born Nov 3, 1938, Bolton, MS; married Della M Larkin; children: Christopher, Demetria, LaCarole. **Educ:** Tougaloo Coll Touglaoo, MS, BS 1961; Univ of IL Urbana, MS 1970; Univ of CO Boulder, EdS 1971; Univ of CO Boulder, EdD 1977. **Career:** Humanitites Div Utica Jr Coll, Utica MS, chairperson 1972-; Special Educ Opportunity Univ of IL Urbana, counselor 1969-70; Camp Tree Tops, Lake Placid NY, counselor 1968-69; E T Hawkins High School, Forest MS, music tech 1961-68. **Orgs:** Mem Music Educators Nat Conf; mem Am Choral Dirs Assn; mem Music Com Meth Ch 1976; Fmem Phi Delta Kappa; organist Asbury United Meth Ch Bolton, MS 1961-; trustee Asbury United Meth Ch Bolton, MS 1975-. **Honors/Awds:** Music scholarship Tougaloo Coll 1958; leadership devel grant Ford Found 1968; music scholarship Univ of IL 1969; grant Office of Educ 1971. **Business Addr:** Utica Jr College, Utica, MS 39175.

COOPER, CANDACE D.
Judge. **Personal:** Born Nov 23, 1948, Los Angeles, CA; daughter of Eunice Cooper and Cornelius Cooper. **Educ:** Univ of Southern CA, BA 1970, JD 1973. **Career:** Gibson Dunn & Crutcher, atty 1973-80; Los Angeles Municipal Court, judge, 1980-88; Los Angeles Superior Court, judge 1988-. **Orgs:** Mem CA Assoc of Black Lawyers 1975-87, Black Woman Lawyers of Los Angeles 1975-87, Natl Assoc of Women Judges 1980-87; life mem Natl Bar Assoc; mem NAACP; bd of dir Watts/Willowbrook Boys & Girls Club 1982-87, Exceptional Childrens Found 1982-87. **Honors/Awds:** Outstanding Alumni Ebonics, Univ of S CA 1982; Woman of Achievement Bus & Professional Women Los Angeles Sunset Chap 1985; Bernard S Jefferson Judge of the Year Awd 1986; Beta Pi Sigma Sor Inc Alpha Chap Outstanding Black Achievement Awd 1986; Women lawyers, A Los Angeles Ernestine Stalhut Award, 1990; Los Angeles County Bar Association, Criminal Justice Section, Judge of the Year 1990, 1992; Century City Bar Association, Criminal Judge of the Year, 1992; Los Angeles YWCA, Silver Achievement Award, 1991. **Business Addr:** Judge, Los Angeles Superior Court, 111 No Hill St, Los Angeles, CA 90012.

COOPER, CANDACE LUCRETIA
Public relations officer. **Personal:** Born Jan 27, 1961, Akron, OH; daughter of Mary Carson Cooper (deceased) and Charles Cooper Jr. **Educ:** University of Akron, Akron, OH, BA, communications, 1985. **Career:** M O'Neil Company, Akron, OH, adminstrative assistant, 1985-89; Akron Summit Community Action Agency, Akron, OH, public relations officer, 1989-. **Orgs:** Member, Fair Housing Contact Service Board of Directors, 1991; member, Youth Motivation Task Force for Private Industry Council, 1990-; treasurer, Akron Assn of Blacks in Communications, 1989-; Delegate member, Cuyahoga Valley Assn Board of Directors, 1989-; member, Summit County Democratic Central Committee, 1990-; member, Alpha Kappa Alpha Sorority Inc, 1980; campaign manager, Ohio State Representative Vernon Sykes, Akron, OH, 1989-; Conducts public relations worksops nationally.

COOPER, CARDELL
City official. **Personal:** married. **Career:** City of East Orange (NJ), mayor, 1995-. **Business Addr:** Mayor, City of East Orange, 44 City Hall Plz, East Orange, NJ 07019, (201)266-5151.

COOPER, CECIL
Professional baseball player (retired). **Personal:** Born Dec 20, 1949, Brenham, TX; married Octavia; children: Kelly, Brittany, Tori Camille. **Educ:** Attended, Blinn Jr Coll, Prairie View A&M Coll. **Career:** Boston Red Sox, infielder, 1971-76; Milwaukee Brewers, infielder 1977-87, director of player dev, 1996-; Coordinated Sports Management Co Inc, vp, sports operations/owner, currently. **Orgs:** Milwaukee Brewers Baseball Club. **Honors/Awds:** MVP and Wisconsin Sports Personality of Yr 1980; named AL Player of the Month in August and Player of the Week in Sept 1980; set World Series record with 10 assists by a first baseman 1982; Distinguished Athlete Awd 1982; Roberto Clemente Awd 1982; earned team MVP & HR Awd 1983; named AL Player of the Week twice and Player of the Month in August 1983; 3 Silver Bat Awds from Sporting News; 3 time winner Harvey Kuenn Awd; named club's MVP 1985; Athlete for Youth's "Good Guy" Awd 1985; 2 Golden Glove Awds; American League All-Star Team, 1979, 1980, 1982, 1983, 1985; elected to Texas Baseball Hall of Fame, 1992.

COOPER, CHARLES W.
Physician. **Personal:** Born Jun 13, 1929, Hayti, MO; son of Louise Black Cooper and Roy Cooper Sr; married Bobbye Jean Hollins; children: Terri Lyn, Janis Kaye, Karyl Jean, Daryl Dean, Alan Jeffrey. **Educ:** Lincoln Univ MO, BS 1951; Univ of Wichita, grad study 1956; Meharry Med Coll, MD 1964. **Career:** Physician, currently. **Orgs:** Pres Lincoln Univ Found 1972-73; trustee Quinn Chapel AME Ch 1967-. **Honors/Awds:** Natl Meth Scholar Meth Ch 1962-63; Mead Johnson Award Mead Johnson Pharm Co 1966; dipl, 1973, fellow, 1977, Am Acad Fam Phys. **Military Serv:** USAF s/sgt 1951-55; Good Conduct Medal, 1954. **Business Addr:** 300 E Dunklin St, Jefferson City, MO 65101.

COOPER, CLARENCE
Judge, attorney. **Personal:** Born May 5, 1942, Decatur, GA; married Shirley; children: Jennae, Corey. **Educ:** Clark Coll, BA 1960-64; Emory Univ Sch Law, JD 1965-67; MIT Comm Flws Prgm, flwsp 1977; Harvard Univ John F Kennedy Sch Govt Pub Admin, 1977-78. **Career:** Atlanta Legal Serv Prog, atty 1967-68; Fulton Co GA, asst dist atty 1968-76; Atlant Muncpl Ct, assoc judge 1976; Fulton County Superior Ct, judge; US District Court, judge. **Orgs:** Mem Natl Bar Assn, Gate City Bar Assn, Natl Conf BLack Lawyers, State Bar GA, Atlanta Bar Assn; mem exec bd Atlanta Br NAACP; mem Natl Urban League; bd dir Amistrad Prod, EOA's Drug Prog; past mem Atlanta Judicial Commm. **Honors/Awds:** Schlrsp Clark Coll 1960-64; publ "The Judiciary & It's Budget an adminstrv hassle". **Military Serv:** AUS E-6 1968-70; Bronze Star, Certificate of Commendation. **Business Addr:** Judge, US District Court, Northern District of GA, 1721 US District Court, 75 Spring St, SW, Atlanta, GA 30303.

COOPER, CLEMENT THEODORE
Attorney. **Personal:** Born Oct 26, 1930, Miami, FL; son of Louise Bethel Cooper and Benjamin Leon Cooper; married Nannie Coles; children: Patricia, Karen, Stephanae, Bridgette, Stacey. **Educ:** Lincoln Univ, AB 1952; Boston Univ, attended 1954-55; Howard Univ Sch of Law, JD 1958; CO State Christian Coll, Hon PhD 1973; Hastings Coll of Law Univ of CA, first natl coll of advocacy 1971. **Career:** Private Practice, attorney-at-law 1960-. **Orgs:** Mem MI State Bar 1960; mem DC Bar 1960; mem US Sup Ct Bar, US Ct Appeals, DC & Tenth Cir CO, US Ct Mil Appeals, Third Cir Phila, US Ct of Claims, US Second Circuit Ct of Appeals, US Fourth Circuit Ct of Appeals, US Sixth Circuit Ct of Appeals, US Ct of Appeals for Federal Circuit; mem Natl Bar Assn; Amer Bar Assn; Amer Trial Lawyers Assn; mem Amer Judicature Soc; Amer Civil Liberties Union; Pub Welfare Adv Council 1966-68; mem Ch of the Ascension & St Agnes Wash DC; life mem Alpha Phi Alpha; arbitrator, Natl Assoc of Securities Dealers. **Honors/Awds:** Author "Sealed Verdict" 1964; author "Location of Unpatented Mining Claims" CA Mining Journal Jan-May 1975 Vol 44; contrib editor Natural Resources Section Amer Bar Assn "Significant Adminis Legislative & State Court Decisions Affecting the Petrol Ind in States E of the MS River" 1979-80. **Military Serv:** US Army, 1952-54; Adjunct Prof, Business Law & Bus Ethics; Strayon College, Washington DC. **Business Addr:** Attorney, Law Offices of Clement T Cooper, PO Box 76135, Washington, DC 20013-6135.

COOPER, CONSTANCE MARIE
Educator. **Personal:** Born Dec 16, 1952, Lorain, OH; married Hewitt J Cooper; children: Candace, Adrienne, Hewitt Jr. **Educ:** Univ of MI, BBA 1975, MBA 1977. **Career:** Univ of Cincinnati, assoc prof of acctg, acting assistant dean of business & finance. **Orgs:** Mem bd of dirs Victory Neighborhood Serv Agency 1981; mem bd of trustees Goodwill 1986; mem metro bd of dirs YMCA Hamilton Co 1986. **Honors/Awds:** CPA Ohio 1984. **Business Addr:** Assoc Prof of Accounting, Univ of Cincinnati, University Coll ML #47, Clifton Ave, Cincinnati, OH 45221.

COOPER, CURTIS V.
Business executive. **Personal:** Born in Savannah, GA; son of Joshua Cooper; married Constance Hartwell; children: Custis, Allyson. **Educ:** Savannah State Coll, BS 1955; Savannah State Coll, Spectal Studies Chem 1965-66; Armstrong State Coll, Entomology 1966; Univ of MI Ann Arbor, MPH 1977. **Career:** Guaranty Life Ins Co, debit mgr 1955; Toomer Realty Co, RE salesman & rents mgr 1957; USDA, rsch asst 1959; Westside Comprehensive Health Center, exec dir 1972; Westside Urban Health Ctr, exec dir 1980. **Orgs:** Dir Savannah Port Authority 1976-82; dir bd trustees Memorial Med Center 1979-; mem Natl Assoc of Comm Health Centers; past dir Savannah Area Chamber of Commerce 1980-84; pres Savannah Branch NAACP 1976-; CCFC & 33 mason Most Worshipful Prince Hall Grand Lodge GA 1977-. **Honors/Awds:** Founding dir Westside Urban Health Center 1972; Alpha Man of the Year Beta Phi Lambda Chapter Alpha Phi Alpha Fraternity Comm Serv Award GA Council of Deliberation Prince Hall Masons; Freedom Award Savannah Chapter NAACP. **Business Addr:** Executive Dir, Westside Urban Health Center, Inc, 115 E York St, PO Box 2024, Savannah, GA 31401.

COOPER, CYNTHIA
Professional basketball player. **Personal:** Born Apr 14, 1963, Chicago, IL; daughter of Mary Cobbs. **Educ:** USC. **Career:** Segovia team, Spain, 1986-87; Parma team, Italy, 1987-94; Alcamo team, Italy, 1994-96; Houston Comets, WNBA, guard, 1997-. **Honors/Awds:** NCAA Final Four, All-Tourney Team, 1986; European League, All-Star Game, MVP, 1987; US Olympics, women's basketball, gold, 1988, bronze, 1992; WNBA, Player of the Week, 1997, All-WNBA First Team, 1997, MVP, 1997, Championship MVP, 1997. **Special Achievements:** Won city championship, 300 Hurdles; NCAA Championship, 1983, 1984; European League, Three Point Contest winner, 1988, 1992; European Cup, leading scorer, 1996; WNBA, set individual game scoring record twice, scored 30 points or more in eight games, placed in top ten of seven categories including: scoring, assists, steals, shooting accuracy, three-point shooting accuracy, free-throw shooting accuracy, minutes, 1997; played Europe with group of WNBA players, 1997; General Motors spokeswoman, 1997. **Business Addr:** Professional Basketball Player, Houston Comets, 2 Greenway Plz, Ste 400, Houston, TX 77046, (713)627-9622.

COOPER, DANEEN RAVENELL
Engineer. **Personal:** Born Oct 27, 1958, St Albans, NY; daughter of Carrie Ravenell and James Ravenell; married Maurice N Cooper; children: Elana Simone, Kellen Marsalis. **Educ:** Columbia Univ Sch of Engrg and Applied Science, BSEE 1980. **Career:** Bell Labs, sr tech assoc 1976-79; New Jersey Bell, engr 1980-86; United Parcel Service, Wireless Date Dept mgr 1986-. **Orgs:** Counselor Sponsors for Educ Oppty 1982-84; pres Council of Action for Minority Professionals 1983-87; mem Consortium of Telecommunications Execs 1985-86; mem Coalition of 100 Black Women 1985-; pres Council of Action for Minority Profls 1984-85; mem Black Data Processing Assoc 1989-; mem IEEE 1989-; Maplewood/So Orange, Parents Advisory Council, 1993-; pres, YMCA Jaguar Track Club Parents' Association. **Honors/Awds:** Bell Laboratories Engrg Scholarship Program 1976-80. **Home Addr:** 25 Highland Ave, Maplewood, NJ 07040.

COOPER, DRUCILLA HAWKINS
Police officer. **Personal:** Born Dec 27, 1950, Riverside, CA; daughter of Thelma Anthony Williams and Alton Hawkins; married Aubery J Cooper (divorced 1976); children: Alton C Strickland, Crusetta A Cooper. **Educ:** City Coll, San Francisco, CA, 1969-70; Los Med Amos Coll, Pittsburg, CA, Basic Law Certificate, 1970; Contra Costa Coll, San Pablo, CA, AA (with honors), 1982. **Career:** Plaza Hotel, San Francisco, CA, maid, 1966; Sutter Hotel, San Francisco, CA, maid, 1969-70; Blue Shield Ins Co, San Francisco, claims examiner, 1973-78; Contra Costa County, Martinez, CA, deputy sheriff, 1978; Dr C Stephens, Richmond, CA, billing clerk, 1979-80; City of Berkeley, Berkeley, CA, police officer, 1980-. **Orgs:** Natl delegate, Natl Black Police Officers Assn, 1984-; star point, Order of the Eastern Star, 1990-; mem, Berkeley Black Police Officers Assn, 1981-; mem, Women's Peace Officers Assn, 1989-. **Honors/Awds:** Basic Intermediate & Advance Certificate, State of CA Dept of Justice, 1981, 1985, 1989; Certificate of Completion (3) Juvenile Law & Procedures, Univ of Southern CA, 1985-86; Certificate of Training, Sexual Assaults Warrants, Dom Viol, Leandro Police Dept, 1985-85; (6) Certificates, Criminal Justice Admin, NBPA, 1985-90. **Business Addr:** Patrol Officer, Berkeley Police Dept, 2171 McKinley St, Berkeley, CA 94703.

COOPER, DUANE (SAMUEL)
Professional basketball player. **Personal:** Born Jun 25, 1969, Benton Harbor, MI. **Career:** Los Angeles Lakers, 1992-93; Phoenix Suns, 1993-. **Business Addr:** Professional Basketball Player, Phoenix Suns, 201 E. Jefferson St, Phoenix, AZ 85004, (602)379-7900.

COOPER, EARL, II (SKIP)
Management consultant. **Personal:** Born Feb 4, 1944, Oakland, CA; son of Martha Cooper and Earl Cooper. **Educ:** Merritt Coll Oakland CA, AA 1968; Golden Gate Coll San Francisco, BA

1970; Univ of So CA, MBA 1973. **Career:** IMPAC, business analyst 1972-74; Jim Dandy Fast Foods Inc, mkt rep 1974; Los Angeles Economic Develop Corp, exec deputy dir 1974-83; EC II & Assocs, pres 1979-; Councilman Gilbert W Lindsay, Los Angeles, CA, special consultant, 1983-86. **Orgs:** Mem Natl Black MBA Assoc LA Chap 1974-, US Small Business Admin Region Adv Comm 1978-; pres Black Business Assoc of Los Angeles 1979-; mem Los Angeles Co Private Industry Cncl 1979-84; mem Mayor's Office of Small Business Assistance 1980-; commissioner Housing Auth of Los Angeles 1984-86; vice pres NAACP Los Angeles Branch 1986-88. **Honors/Awds:** CA delegate to the White House Conf on Small Business 1980,86; Resolution from CA speaker of the assembly for exemplary service to the comm & state for promoting the growth & develop of business 1981; Natl Educ for Business Develop Awd 1983; Natl Awd of Excellence from SBA 1983; US Small Business Admin Minority Business Advocate of the Year for the State of CA 1985. **Military Serv:** AUS spl 4 1965-67; Natl Defense Service, Vietnam Service Medal, Combat Medical Badge, Marksman Rifle 10/S Bar 1965-67. **Business Addr:** President, EC II & Associates, 727 S Ardmore Ave Ste 1006, Los Angeles, CA 90005.

COOPER, EDWARD SAWYER
Educator. **Personal:** Born Dec 11, 1926, Columbia, SC; son of Dr and Mrs H H Cooper Sr (deceased); married Jean Marie Wilder; children: Lisa Cooper Hudgins, Edward S Jr (deceased), Jan Cooper Jones, Charles W. **Educ:** Lincoln Univ PA, AB 1946; Meharry Med Coll, MD 1949; Univ of PA, MA (honors) 1973. **Career:** Philadelphia Gen Hospital, internship medical residency 1949-54, fellow in cardiology 1956-57, pres of medical staff 1969-71, chief of medical serv 1972-76; Univ of PA, prof medicine 1973-. **Orgs:** Certified and recertified Amer Bd of Internal Medicine 1957-74; Master Amer Coll of Physicians 1960; co-dir Stroke Research Center Philadelphia Gen Hospital 1968-74; chmn & member exec comm Stroke Council Amer Heart Assn 1982-; chmn talent recruitment council & member editorial bd journal of Natl Med Assoc 1959-77; member of the council Coll of Physicians of Philadelphia 1970-84, 1994-; member bd of dir Blue Cross of Greater Philadelphia 1975; member bd of dir Amer Foundation Negro Affairs 1977; president American Heart Association 1992-93. **Honors/Awds:** Hartley Gold Medal highest honors Meharry Medical Coll 1949; Distinguished Alumnus Award Lincoln Univ PA 1959; Distinguished Alumnus Award Meharry Medical Coll 1971; Alpha Omega Alpha Honor Medical Soc 1962; Charles Drew Award for Distinguished Contributions to Medical Educ 1979; Amer Heart Assn, award of merit 1986; Gold Heart Award, 1997; Strittmatter Award, Phila, Co Med Soc. **Military Serv:** USAF captain 1954-56; Chief Medial Serv, 6208 USAF Hospital. **Business Addr:** Professor Emeritus of Medicine, Univ of Pennsylvania, Univ of Pennsylvania Hospital, 3400 Spruce St, Philadelphia, PA 19104.

COOPER, EMMETT E., JR.
Postmaster. **Personal:** Born Jun 3, 1921, Cleveland; married Ermelda Mohr; children: Emmett, Gerald, Hewitt. **Educ:** Harvard Univ Adv Mgmt Prog, grad, BS 1951, MS 1954. **Career:** Cleveland Post Office, supt training 1954; Wage & Salary Admin, supt 1956, office personnel dir 1957; Cuyahoga Comm & Coll, teacher 1958-66; Postal Mgmt Br USPS HQ, dir 1970; Detroit Postal Dist, mgr 1971; Chicago Post Office, post master 1973-77; Eastern US Reg, postmaster gen 1977-78; Southern Region Memphis TN, retired postmaster gen 1978-83; Harte-Hanks Direct Mktg Group, dir postal affairs. **Orgs:** Mem Chicago Fed Exec Bd Campaign for Chicago Area; mem bd dirs Highland Comm Bank; Nat Assn Postmasters US Mem Chicago Assn Commerce & Industry; Chicago Urban League; Chicago Br NAACP; Christmas Seal Campaign; Chicago Lung Assn. **Honors/Awds:** Postmaster of Year 1974. **Military Serv:** AUS 1944-47. **Home Addr:** 11050 Embassy Drive, Cincinnati, OH 45240.

COOPER, ERNEST, JR.
City planner, educator. **Personal:** Born Jun 19, 1941, Toone, TN; son of Pauline Anderson Cooper and Ernest Cooper; married Marva Harper; children: Jeanine, Ernest III, Keita. **Educ:** Lincoln Univ, BS 1963; Howard Univ, MA, city plnng 1970; Univ of PA, ABD, city plnng. **Career:** Nia Group, pres; Adult & Vocational School Cairo IL, math instr 1965-68; Washington Tech Inst, asst prof, math 1968-70; Washington Tech Inst Conceptualized Urban Plnng Tech Prog, train para-prof; Urban Inst, consult to eval staff 1971; University of District of Columbia, Department of Urban and Regional Planning, chmn, professor of urban planning, currently. **Orgs:** American Planning Assn; Natl Assn Planners; Amer Assn Univ of Prof; board of directors, Metropolitan Washington Planning & Housing Association. **Honors/Awds:** ML King Jr Study Grant Woodrow Wilson Found 1969-70, 1971-72; Grad Asst in Rsch & Recruit Howard Univ 1969; Urban Trans Ctr Fellow 1970; Voorhees School Natl Cap Area by AIP 1970; Fontaine Fellow Univ of PA. **Business Addr:** Chairman, Dept of Urban & Regional Planning, University of the District of Columbia, 4200 Conn Ave NW, Bldg 52, Rm 7920, Washington, DC 20008.

COOPER, ETHEL THOMAS
Educator (retired). **Personal:** Born Mar 2, 1919, Abbeville Co, SC; daughter of Janie Delvin Thomas and Simon M Thomas; married Rev B J Cooper; children: Joethel, Sandra. **Educ:** Allen U, AB 1939. **Career:** Greenville Co, teacher 1964-82 (retired); basketball coadh: Charleston County, 1959-64; Spartanbury County, 1957-59; Dillon County, 1948-57; Marion County, 1947-48; Williamsburg County, 1944-46; Florence County, 1940-44; Edgefield County, 1939-40. **Orgs:** Pres Greenvl Co & Assn of Classroom Tchs 1973; exec bd SC Educ Assn 1975; bd of dir SC Educ Assn 1974; bd of dir NEA; chmn Credentials Comm SCEA; basileus Epsilon Iota Zeta; basileus Gamma Zeta; antapokritis SE reg ZOB Sor 1972-76; Greenvl Co Friends of Educ 1974-76; lay spkr United Meth Ch; mem NAACP; National Council N Women; chmn, Hilda Machling Fellowship Comm for NEA, 1979-82. **Honors/Awds:** Runner-up Citz of Yr Greenvl Co; Zeta Phi Beta Awd; ACT pres Awd; Greenville Co ACT Awd; NEA Retirement Award; Hall of Fame, Z0B Sorority, 1997. **Home Addr:** 203 Daisy Dr, Greenville, SC 29605.

COOPER, EVELYN KAYE
Judge. **Personal:** Born Jun 23, 1941, Detroit, MI. **Educ:** Univ of Detroit, BBA 1968; Wayne State U, post grad Math; Wayne State Univ Law Sch, JD 1973. **Career:** Recorder's Ct, judge 1978-; Detroit Traffic Ct, traffic ct referee 1977-78; Self-employed, atty law office 1974-77; Detroit Jr High Sch, bd of educ 1966-70. **Orgs:** Mem Nat Assn of Women Judges; mem MI State Bar Assn; mem MI Judges Assn; mem Womens Lawyers Assn; mem Women's Conf of Concerns; mem NAACP 1976-;mem March of Dimes; Mem Delta Sigma Theta Sorority; judicial mem Nat Bar Assn 1974-; mem Wolverine Bar Assn. **Business Addr:** Recorders Court, 1441 St Antoine, Detroit, MI 48226.

COOPER, GARY T.
Physician. **Educ:** Marquette Univ, BS 1970; Howard Univ Coll of Medicine, MD 1975; Loyola Coll of Md, MBA, 1996. **Career:** Planned Parenthood of Washington, med dir, 1979-80; Howard Univ Hospital, resident coordinator 1980-87; instructor, 1980-86; asst prof 1986-87; Private Practice, physician Ob/Gyn, 1979-92; Prudential HealthCare Mid Atlantic Region, medical director, currently. **Orgs:** Mem, Amer Coll of Ob/Gyn 1978-; Diplomate, Amer Bd of Ob/Gyn 1983-; mem, Washington Gynecological Soc 1981-, Kappa Alpha Psi Fraternity, Mem, Med Soc of the District of Columbia, 1979-; Southern Medical Assn. **Business Addr:** Ob/Gyn, 2800 N Charles St, Baltimore, MD 21218.

COOPER, GORDON R., II
Attorney. **Personal:** Born Mar 22, 1941, Wallisville, TX; married Barbara Ellison; children: Gordon R III. **Educ:** Texas So U, BA 1965; JD 1970. **Career:** Humble Oil Co, labor relations dept; Ins Underwriter Pvt Practice. **Orgs:** Mem TX Am Houston Jr Bar Assn; regional dir Nat Bar Assn; Alpha Phi Alpha Frat; Phi Alpha Delta Legal Frat; Harris County Crim Lawyers Assn. **Business Addr:** 2614 Two Houston Ctr, Houston, TX 77002.

COOPER, IRIS N.
Educator. **Personal:** Born Oct 30, 1942, Ahoskie, NC. **Educ:** NC Central U, BA 1964; Howard U, grad study; Univ of VA; Coll of William & Mary. **Career:** Portsmouth School System, instructor; Norfolk State Evening Coll, instructor 1968-69; Palmer Memorial Inst, instructor 1964; Project Upward Bound, Norfolk St Coll, instructor 1968-71. **Orgs:** Mem NEA; VA Educ Assn; Portsmouth Educ Assn; VA Assn Fof Classroom Tchrs; Portsmouth Assn of Classroom Tchrs; Am Assn of Women; Tidewater Alliance ofBlack Sch Educators; Am Assn of Tchrs of Spanish & Portuguese; mem Ebenezer Bapt Ch; NCCU Alumni Assn; Norfolk Players Guild; Portsmouth Chap Delicados Inc; Gamma Delta Omega Chpt; Alpha Kappa Alpha. **Honors/Awds:** Outstanding young woman of America 1974. **Business Addr:** Churchland High School, 5601 High St, Portsmouth, VA 23703.

COOPER, IRMGARD M.
Company executive. **Personal:** Born Jun 29, 1946, Teisendorf, Germany; daughter of Ruth St Ville Carter and Senator Richard A Carter. **Educ:** DePaul University, Chicago, IL, BS, 1968; Northern Illinois University, DeKalb, IL, MS, 1976. **Career:** Jones Metropolitan High School, Chicago, IL, teacher/coordinator, 1970-82; IMC Services Inc/IMC Automation, Chicago, IL, president, 1985-; IMC Associates Inc, Muskegon, MI, president, 1990-. **Orgs:** Board of directors, Streeterville Chamber of Commerce, Chicago, 1991, second vice president, 1990-; secretary/treasurer, Chicago Executive Network, Chicago, 1986-; member, North Michigan Ave, BPW, Chicago, 1989-. **Honors/Awds:** Nominee, Ernst & Young Entrepreneur, 1990; Nominee, Chicago Women's Hall of Fame, 1989; Nominee, Small Business Administration Minority Small Business of the Year, 1989; Awardee, Top 100 Business & Professional Women, Dollars & Sense, 1988. **Business Addr:** President, IMC Services Inc/IMC Automation, 333 E Ontario, 307B, Chicago, IL 60611, (312)664-0622.

COOPER, J. CALIFORNIA (JOAN)
Writer. **Personal:** Born in Berkeley, CA; daughter of Maxine Rosemary Cooper and Joseph C Cooper; children: Paris A Williams. **Educ:** Attended various colleges. **Career:** Author, Homemade Love, 1986, A Piece of Mine: A New Short Story Collection, 1984, Some Soul to Keep, 1987, Family, 1990, Center Stage, anthology (plays); The Matter is Life, 1991; In Search of Satisfaction, Doubleday, 1994; Some Love, Some Pain, Some Time, Doubleday, 1995. **Honors/Awds:** ALA Literary Lion; American Book Award; James Baldwin Award; Notable Book Award. **Business Addr:** Author, In Search of Satisfaction, c/o Doubleday, 1540 Broadway, New York, NY 10036.

COOPER, JEROME GARY
Military officer (retired). **Personal:** Born Oct 2, 1936, Lafayette, LA; son of Gladys Catherine Morton Cooper (deceased) and Algernon Johnson Cooper (deceased); married Beverly; children: Patrick C, Joli, Gladys Shawn. **Educ:** Univ of Notre Dame, BS, 1958; George Washington Univ, grad study; Harvard Sch of Bus, attended 1979. **Career:** State of Alabama Department of Human Resources, Montgomery, AL, commissioner, 1974-78; David Volkert and Associates, Mobile, AL, vice president, 1981-89; US Marine Corps, Washington, DC, director of personnel procurement, 1988; US Department of Defense, Washington, DC, assistant secretary of the Air Force, 1989-. **Orgs:** Member, AFCOMAP, 1990-; member, Air Force Association, 1990-; member, National Image, 1991-; life member, Reserve Officers Association; life member, Montford Point Marine Association; member, Marine Corps Reserve Association. **Honors/Awds:** 1st Black to lead infantry co into combat USMC 1967; apptd Commanding Officer of 4th Battalion 14th Marines Headquarters Birmingham AL; Man of Yr Nonpartisan Voters League 1977; Highest Award Given by Sec USN for Public Serv 1978; MO Beale Scroll of Merit for Good Citizenship, Mobile Assn, 1979; John J. Cavanaugh Award, Alumni Assn of Univ of Notre Dame, 1987; Benjamin Hooks Meritorious Service Award, 1990, Roy Wilkins Meritorious Service Award, 1989, NAACP; Honorary LLD, Troy State University, 1990; Distinguished Service Medal, 1991. **Military Serv:** US Marine Corps, Major General, active 1958-69, reserves 1969-91; Silver Star; Legion of Merit; Bronze Star with Combat V; Purple Heart (2); Vietnam Cross of Gallantry with palm & two stars; numerous others. **Business Addr:** Assistant Secretary of the Air Force, Department of Defense, SAF/MI, 4E1020, Pentagon, Washington, DC 20330-1660.

COOPER, JOSEPH
Attorney. **Personal:** Born Dec 20, Hemingway, SC; son of Mary Cooper and Harmon Cooper; children: Kenneth. **Educ:** Univ of Utah Sacramento City Coll, AA 1965; University of the Pacific, McGeorge Law School, JD (honors), 1969. **Career:** Pres, First Capital Real Estate; atty gen pract 1969-; Joseph Cooper Court Corp, president, currently; Northwestern California University, School of Law, dean of academic affairs. **Orgs:** Former mem, board of directors, California Trial Lawyers Assn; member, American Trial Lawyers Assn; Success Institute of America Inc, pres/founder. **Honors/Awds:** City of San Francisco, Distinguished Service Award. **Military Serv:** AUS 1960-62. **Business Addr:** 1310 H St, Sacramento, CA 95814.

COOPER, JOSEPHINE H.
Educator. **Personal:** Born Apr 7, 1936, Salinas, CA; married. **Educ:** BA MA MA PhD; US CA Univ of San Francisco, research. **Career:** Educ Svcd Inst, asst dir; Programs for Mentally Handicapped, head teacher; Meritt Coll, GED prgm 1968; Low Income Housing Program in Vocational Counseling; Peralta Coll Dist, presently dean of educ occupation. **Orgs:** Mem CA Tchrs Assn; mem NAACP; United Taxpayers & Voter's Union CA; Alameda Co Contra Costa Co Com for Equal Oppor in Apprenticeship Tng; Berkeley Dem Club; Nat Council Negro Women Inc. **Honors/Awds:** Numerous scholarships grants for further study; mem CA Comm & Jr Coll Assn on "Minorities and the Voc Disadv in Occupational Prgms in CA Comm Coll Trade Tech Schs". **Business Addr:** Laney Coll, 900 Fallon St, Oakland, CA 94607.

COOPER, JULIUS, JR.
Law enforcement official (retired). **Personal:** Born Jan 8, 1944, Sarasota, FL; son of Johnnie Mae Jones Ramey and Julius Cooper, Sr; married Barbara Irene Campbell; children: Julius, Julian, Adrienne, Tara, Taheim. **Educ:** Essex County Coll, A 1977; Natl Crime Prevention Inst, attended 1983; Security Mgmt & Admin Inst, attended 1984; Rutgers Univ, BS 1985; Seton Hall Univ Masters 1990. **Career:** Essex County Police Dept, breathalyzer oper, affirmative action officer, supervisor 1983-84, instructor 1983-85, crime prevention coord 1983-86, sergeant, currently; Newark, NJ Board of Education, substitute teacher, 1991; Essex County College, professor, 1992; Rutgers Univ, guest professor, 1991; Zion Missionary Baptist Church, deacon, 1996-. **Orgs:** Vice pres Ebony Six Cooperation; life mem NAACP; mem PBA. **Honors/Awds:** Certificate Awd US Dept of Health & Human Serv 1985; Achievement Awd Essex Co PBA Conference 1985; Achievement Awd Essex Co Bd of Freeholders 1986; Valor Award Essex Co Bd of Freeholders 1987.

COOPER, KENNETH JOSEPH
Journalist. **Personal:** Born Dec 11, 1955, Denver, CO; son of Maxine Marie Cooper and George Howard Cooper Jr; married Lucilda Loretta Dassardo, Jun 10, 1985. **Educ:** Washington University, BA, 1977. **Career:** St Louis American, associate editor, 1977; St Louis Post Dispatch, staff writer, 1977-80; Boston Globe, staff writer, 1980-86; Knight Ridder Inc, national reporter, 1986-89; Washington Post, national reporter, 1989-95, South Asia bureau chief, 1996-, foreign correspondent, 1996-. **Orgs:** National Association of Black Journalists, 1978-; Omega Psi Phi Fraternity, 1983-. **Honors/Awds:** Columbia University, Pulitzer Prize, Special Local Reporting, 1984; NABJ, Print Journalism, Honorable Mention, 1984; UPI, Public Service, 1984. **Special Achievements:** Director, Minority Journalism Workshop sponsored by the Washington Association of Black Journalists, 1990-95. **Business Addr:** Foreign Desk, Washington Post, 1150 15th St, NW, Washington, DC 20071.

COOPER, LAMOYNE MASON
Educator, foreign service officer (retired). **Personal:** Born Aug 8, 1931, Emporia, VA; son of Theresa Mason and Edgar Mason; married William Franklin Cooper, Nov 26, 1988; children: Derrick Matthews, Yvette Matthews, Kevin Matthews. **Educ:** Morgan State Univ, AB 1951; Howard Univ, MSW 1961; Univ of MD, PhD 1976. **Career:** Baltimore City Dept of Soc Svcs, 1954-65; MD State Dept Soc Svcs, 1965-68; Montebello Chronic Disease & Rehab Hosp, 1968-69; Morgan State Univ, 1969-82; Foreign Svc, US Dept of State, 1987-91. **Orgs:** Mem Acad of Cert Soc Workers 1961-; member, Delta Sigma Theta 1950-; member, Baltimore Museum of Art; member, Baltimore Zoo, Chesapeake Audubon Society, Tucson Desert Museum. **Honors/Awds:** Natl Teaching Fellow 1973-74; Univ of MD Grad School Fellowship 1973-75; Educ to Africa Study Grant 1974; 100 Outstanding Baltimore Women Delta Sigma Theta 1974; Baltimore County Bd of Ed 1979-84.

COOPER, LARRY B.
Communications company manager. **Personal:** Born Jul 25, 1946, Fordyce, AR; son of Brucella Cooper and Charles Cooper; children: Sherri Jean. **Educ:** Univ of AR at Pine Bluff, BS 1969; Southern Methodist University, MBA 1996. **Career:** Kansas City Schl Dist, teacher/coach 1969-72; Southwestern Bell Tele Co, mgmt trainee 1972-73, engineer 1973-74, sr engineer 1974-77, mgmt dev supv 1977-79, dist stf mgr-pers/budgets 1979-81, stf mgr mgmt dev 1981-83; dist stf mgr Res Serv 1983-85; dist manager Res Serv 1985-87; Southwest Bell, Little Rock, AR, district manager of business services, 1987-89, division manager of education and economic development, beginning 1989-, St Louis, MO, general manager, operator svcs; Competitive Provider Account Team, gen manager, currently. **Orgs:** Exec bd of directors, Boy Scouts of America, 1985-; bd of directors, Southwest City Civitan, 1985-; mem, Kappa Alpha Psi Alumni Assn, 1972-; president, Tall Timber Home Owners, 1978-79; commissioner, Tall Timber Imp Dist, 1986; Member, Arkansas Advocate for Family & Children, 1990-; board member, Arkansas State Council on Economic Education, 1991-92; advisory bd, Vocational Technical Education, 1989-92; chairman, Arkansas Regional Minority Purchasing Council, 1986-92; United Way Planning and Allocation Committee, 1982-84; Dallas Downtown Improvement District. **Honors/Awds:** Distinguished Alumni Awd NAFEO 1986; Distinguished Achievement Award Kappa Alpha Psi 1985; Black Corporate Executives Award, NAACP, 1991; Bernard De La Harde Award for Community Leadership, Little Rock Chamber of Commerce, 1989-91. **Business Addr:** General Manager, CPAT, Southwestern Bell Telephone Co., 4 Bell Plz, Rm 800, Dallas, TX 75202.

COOPER, LINDA G.
Entrepreneur. **Personal:** Born Jun 1, 1954, Jacksonville, FL; daughter of Freddie Lang Groomes and Benjamin H Groomes. **Educ:** FL State Univ, BS 1974; Indiana Univ, MBA 1977. **Career:** Hallmark Cards Inc, budget analyst 1977-81, mktg budget mgr 1981-85, dir minority affairs 1985-92; LGC & Associates, president & owner, currently. **Orgs:** Alpha Kappa Alpha Sor 1972-, Defense Adv Comm on Women in the Serv 1984-87; pres bd of trustees Greater KC Black Economic Union 1984-92; Greater KC Chamber of Commerce; past president, Central Exchange, mem Natl Assoc of Market Developers 1985-91; mem Natl Black MBA Assoc; bd mem YMCA 1987-90; Urban League of GKC, vice chair. **Honors/Awds:** Up and Comers Award, 1996; YWCA Hearts of Gold Award, 1993; SCLC, Black Achiever in Business and Industry, 1984; Black Chamber of Commerce of Kansas City, President's Award, 1988. **Special Achievements:** "100 Most Promising Black Women in Corporate America," Ebony Magazine, 1991; "100 Most Influential African-American in KC," KC Globe Newspaper, 1997. **Business Addr:** President, Owner, LGC & Associates Inc, 4601 Madison, Ste 201, Kansas City, MO 64112.

COOPER, LOIS LOUISE
Transportation engineer (retired). **Personal:** Born Nov 25, 1931, Vicksburg, MS; widowed; children: Wyatt E, Christopher. **Educ:** Tougaloo Coll MS, 1949; CA State Univ Los Angles, BA Math 1954; Post Graduate Civil Engineering CA State Univ 1975-81. **Career:** Div of Hwys (Caltrans), eng aid 1953-58, jr civil eng 1958-61; Caltrans, asst transp eng 1961-84, assoc transportation engineer 1984-88; Sr Transportation Engineer 1988-91. **Orgs:** Past Brd of dir sec Los Angeles Council of Eng of Sci; adv brd Minority Eng Pgm CSULA; past co-ch career guidance Scty of Women Engrs 1985; pres LA Cncl of Black Professional Engrs 1975-76, v pres 1974-75, sec/treas 1972-74; ASCE, NSPE. **Honors/Awds:** Trail Blazer Natl Asso Negro Bus & Prof Womens Inc 1964; fellow Inst for the Adv of Engr 1982; First Black Woman to attain a Professional Engineers License in Civil Engineering in CA 1978; First Black Woman to achieve all positions at Caltrans 1983; Fellow, Society of Women Engineers 1989. **Home Addr:** 14324 Clymar Ave, Compton, CA 90220.

COOPER, MATTHEW N.
Psychologist, educator. **Personal:** Born Oct 29, 1914, Macomb, IL; married Ina B; children: Matthew, John. **Educ:** Western IL State Tchr Coll, BEd 1940; Univ of IL, MA 1946; NY U, PhD 1955. **Career:** TX So U, prof 1947; Lovejon IL Sch Dist, 1941-46; Riverside Gen Hosp Drug Abuse Clinic, 1972-; Private Practice, psychologist 1958-. **Orgs:** Mem Am Psychol Assn; Am Personnel & Guidance Assn. **Business Addr:** 2601 Prospect St, Houston, TX 77004.

COOPER, MAUDINE R.
Association executive. **Personal:** Born Sep 30, 1941, Benoit, MS; divorced; children: Maria Teresa. **Educ:** Howard Univ Coll of Liberal Arts, BA Business Admin 1964; Howard Univ Sch of Law, JD 1971. **Career:** Natl Urban League, deputy dir 1976-79, asst vice pres public policy 1979, vice pres for Wash Oper 1980-83; DC OHR & Minority Business Oppor Commn, exec dir; DC Officeof Human Rights, dir 1983-89; staff director, Office of the Mayor; Greater Washington Urban League, currently. **Orgs:** Mem bd of dirs Natl Bar Assn 1979-80; mem bd of dirs Centennial One Inc 1982-87; vice pres for legislative affairs Black Women's Agenda 1983-; legal advisor MCAC/Delta Sigma Theta Sor 1985-88; treas Washington Chap Natl Assn of Human Rights Workers 1986-87; mem several bar Associations; mem bd of dirs, The Doug Williams Foundation; board of dir, DC Private Industry Council, 1993; board of dir, Bell Atlantic, Washington, DC, Inc, 1994. **Honors/Awds:** One of the Women to Watch in the 80's Ebony Magazine 1982; Alumna of the Year Howard Univ Law Alumni Assn 1984; Woman of the Year Capitol Hill Kiwanis Club 1985; America's Top 100 Black Business & Professional Women Dollars and Sense Magazine 1986; chair, DC Govt's 32nd One Fund Drive, 1986; Judge For The First Ms Black USA Scholarship Pagent, 1987; Awarded the Natl Assn of Minority Political Women's Diamond award for Outstanding Service, 1988. **Business Addr:** President and CEO, Washington Urban League Inc, 350114th St NW, Washington, DC 20010.

COOPER, MERRILL PITTMAN
Business executive. **Personal:** Born Feb 9, 1921, Charlestown, WV. **Educ:** Storer Coll, 1938. **Career:** TWU, intl exec bd 1965-68; Local 234, sec, treas, vice pres 1968-77; Transport Workers Union, intl vice pres. **Orgs:** Mem Negro Trade Union Ldrsp Cncl; NAACP; vice pres Philadelphia AFL-CIO 1977-; intl vice pres Transport Workers Union 1977-; mem Urban League. **Honors/Awds:** Outsdng Man of Comm 1977. **Business Addr:** Vice President, Transport Workers Union, 80 West End Ave, New York, NY 10023.

COOPER, MICHAEL GARY
County government administrator. **Personal:** Born Jan 11, 1954, Cleveland, OH; son of Fletcher Lee Bailey Cooper and Clifford Cooper Sr; married Corrinne Crockett, May 26, 1984; children: Stacy, Michael Fletcher, Malik. **Educ:** Univ of Pittsburgh, BA 1975; Atlanta Univ, MA History 1979, MSW Social Work 1979. **Career:** Young Men's Christian Assn, asst dir 1975-76; Atlanta Univ, admin intern 1977-79; City of Atlanta, field coord 1979; DeKalb Co Commission Office, affirmative action officer 1979-80; Fulton County Govt, director/contract compliance/EEO, Atlanta GA, 1988-. **Orgs:** Mem Amer Assoc for Affirmative Action Workers 1982-; mem Natl Forum for Black Public Adminis 1983-; treas Region IV Amer Assoc for Affirmative Action 1983-; mem Natl Assoc of Human Rights Workers 1986; American Assn for Affirmative Action, regional director. **Honors/Awds:** Governor's Intern Program 1978; Disting Serv Awd Univ of GA Extension Serv 1985; Community Involvement Award, Black Pages Magazine, 1990. **Business Addr:** Director, Deptartment of Contract Compliance/EEO, Fulton County Government Center, 141 Pryor St, Suite 2034, Atlanta, GA 30303.

COOPER, MICHAEL JEROME
Professional basketball player (retired), administrator. **Personal:** Born Apr 15, 1956; married Wanda; children: Michael Jr, Simone. **Educ:** Pasadena City Coll; Univ of NM, 1978. **Career:** Los Angeles Lakers, professional basketball player, 1979-90, asst coach, currently. **Orgs:** NAACP; NM State chairperson for sickle cell anemia; Junior Blind Foundation, board member; NM Red Ribbon Campaign Nationwide, state spokesperson; Coops Kids for Kids, founder; Call Coop Hotline for Youth, founder. **Honors/Awds:** Walter J Kennedy Award for Outstanding Community Work; NBA, Defensive Player of the Year, 1987. **Special Achievements:** professional basketball player: Five NBA world championship rings; 9 times selected 1st Team All Defense in NBA; holds championship record, with 2 others, for most 3-point shots (6) in one game; leader in many Lakers statistical catagories.

COOPER, ROBERT N.
Company executive. **Personal:** marrIed Marcia; children: Robin, David. **Educ:** Oakland Univ, BA; Michigan State Univ, MBA. **Career:** Michigan Bell, technician, beginning 1973; Ameritech-MI, sr dir of distribution services, 1989-93; Ameritech Cellular, human resources, vp, 1993-96; Ameritech-MI, pres, 1996-. **Business Addr:** President, Ameritech - Michigan, 444 Michigan Ave, Detroit, MI 48226, (313)223-9900.

COOPER, RONALD LOUIS
College football coach. **Personal:** Born Feb 11, 1961, Huntsville, AL; son of Martha B Cooper and Wilbert H Cooper; married Kim, Jun 3, 1989. **Educ:** Jacksonville State University, BS, education, 1983; Appalachian State University, MA, 1984. **Career:** University of Minnesota, assistant coach, NG; Austin Peay State University, assistant coach, recruiting coordinator, linebackers; Murray State University, defensive coordinator, defensive backs; East Carolina University, assistant coach, linebackers; University of Nevada at Las Vegas, defensive coordinator, linebackers; University of Notre Dame, assistant head coach, defensive backs; Eastern Michigan University, head football coach, beginning 1992; Univ of Louisville, head coach, currently. **Orgs:** American Football Coaches Association, 1983-; Black Coaches Association, 1989-; Kappa Alpha Psi Fraternity Inc, 1982-; Fellowship of Christian Athletes, 1980-; Masonic Order, 1983-. **Honors/Awds:** Cotton Bowl, Notre Dame vs Texas A&M, 1993; Sugar Bowl, Notre Dame vs Florida, 1992. **Special Achievements:** Teaching films: Deep Coverage, 2 vols; Coverage, 3 vols; Punt-Block; drill film: UNLV Defensive Team and Position Drills; manual: Techniques of Defensive Backs. **Business Addr:** Head Football Coach, Univ of Louisville, Football Complex, Louisville, KY 40292-0001, (502)852-5555.

COOPER, SAMUEL H., JR.
County official. **Personal:** Born Feb 2, 1955, Nassawadox, VA; son of Margaret C. Cooper and Samuel H. Cooper, Sr.; married Sandra; children: Cedrick, Shenae. **Educ:** Norfolk State Coll, 1973-75; John Tyler Coll, AAS 1975-77. **Career:** CC Humbles Funeral Servs, mortician 1977-83; Accomac County Circuit Court, clerk. **Orgs:** Mem, Macedonia AME Church; Macedonia Lodge #19; Virginia Court Clerks Assn. **Business Addr:** Clerk Circuit Court, Accomac County Circuit Court, PO Box 126, Accomac, VA 23301.

COOPER, SYRETHA C.
Social worker, educator. **Personal:** Born Nov 15, 1930, Youngstown, OH; married Murray A Cooper; children: Carole Cooper Walker, Frances Cooper Polite, Corrine Cooper Byrd, Louise, Murray Jr, Marvin. **Educ:** Youngstown Coll, BA 1952; Western Reserve University, Mandell Sch Applied Soc Sciences, MSSA, 1954, PhD, 1988. **Career:** Fam Serv Soc Youngstown, caseworker, 1954-55; Woodside Receiving Hospital, psychiatric social worker 1957-61; Adult Mental Health Center psychiatric, social worker 1961-71; Youngstown State Univ, asst prof of social work 1971-83, associate professor of social work, 1983-91, professor of social work, 1991-, coordinator of social work, 1989-92. **Orgs:** Nat Assn Social Workers; Acad Certified Social Workers; registered in Clinical Social Work Registry 1976; NEA; Youngstown OH Alumnae Chap Delta Sigma Theta Sor; case consult Youngstown Pub Sch Home Visitation Prog; McGuffey Centre Bd Trustees; chrtrd bd mem P & C Prod of Youngstown; life mem United Counc of Negro Women; Youngstown State Chapter Ohio Education Association; Council on Social Work Education; Licensed Independent Social Workers of Ohio; Ohio College Association of Social Work Educators, 1992. **Honors/Awds:** Chi Omega Alumnae Award, outstanding soc sciences student, Youngstown College, 1952; St Andrews AME Ch, Woman of the Year, 1976; Price Memorial AMEZ Church, Woman of the Year, 1977; 1981 Iota Phi Lambda Woman of the Year; McGuffey Centre, Hall of Fame Award in Education, 1981; Phi Kappa Phi 1984; Black United Students, Outstanding Teacher, 1987; NASW Region 4, Social Worker of the Year, 1992. **Business Addr:** Professor of Social Work, Youngstown State University, 410 Wick Ave, Youngstown, OH 44555-3442.

COOPER, WALTER
Research associate, chemist. **Personal:** Born Jul 18, 1928, Clairton, PA; son of Lula Cooper and Alonzo Cooper; married Helen E Claytor; children: Robert B, Brian P. **Educ:** Washington & Jefferson Coll, BA 1950; Univ of Rochester, PhD 1956; Washington & Jefferson Coll, ScD, 1987. **Career:** Eastman Kodak Co, research chemist 1956, sr research chemist 1964, research associate 1965; Action for Better Comm, assoc dir 1964-65; Rsch Assoc, 1966; US Small Business & Admin Special Consultant to Admin, 1968-69; Easman Kodak Co Rsch Assoc, 1969; Sigma Xi, 1956; ACS, 1959; AAAS, 1960; NYAS, 1970; APS, 1974; NY State Adv Comm to US Civil Rights Commn 1966; Eastman Kodak Co, mgr, Office of Tech Communications, 1984-86, Retired 1986; Consultant, 1987-; University of The State of New York, board of regents, 1988. **Orgs:** Bd trustees Washington & Jefferson Coll 1975; bd of Governors Genesee Hosp 1966; bd dir Rochester Area Found 1975; Genesee Regional Health Planning Council 1974; Urban Suburban Pupil Transfer Program 1973; Urban League of Rochester 1965-71; NAACP 1960-65; Celanese Corp of Am Fellow 1952-54; Nat

Sci Found Fellow 1955-56; NY State Bd of Regents, 1988. **Honors/Awds:** Rochester Jr Chamber of Commerce Leroy E Snyder Award 1966; Outstanding Achievement Award & Rochester Club of Natl Negro Professional & Business Women Inc 1966; Rochester Chamber of Commerce Devel Award, 1966; Washington & Jefferson Coll Distinguished Alumni Award 1968; Achievement Award Intl Org of Eastern Stars 1974; Knight of the Natl Order of the Republic of Mali, 1982; Rochester Chamber of Commerce Intl Relations Award; 3 patents in Photographic Science & Technology; 25 scientific & technical publications; Univ of Rochester, Hutchinson Medal, 1994; Mimett Professor, Rochester Institute of Technology, 1996-97. **Business Addr:** Consultant, 68 Skyview Lane, Rochester, NY 14625.

COOPER, WILLIAM B.
Business executive. **Personal:** Born Sep 5, 1956, Washington, DC; married Sandra F Burrus. **Educ:** Control Data Institute, 1975-76; University of Maryland, 1978-80. **Career:** Control Data Corp, systems analyst 1974-79; TYMSHARE, Inc, applications consultant 1979-80; CGA Computer Assoc, Inc, 1980-84; Cray Research, Inc, analyst-in-charge 1984-. **Orgs:** Precinct chairman Montgomery County Republican Party 1979-80; member Association for Computing Machinery 1979-; member natl Panel of Consumer Arbitrators 1980-; deacon Plymouth Congregational UCC 1981-; cubmaster Cub Scout Pack 340 1981-; president Cooper & Associates 1982-. **Honors/Awds:** Commissioner Advisory Neighborhood Commission 1982-85; delegate DC Statehood Constitutional Convention 1982-85; Outstanding Young Men of America 1983.

COOPER, WINSTON LAWRENCE
Advertising executive. **Personal:** Born Oct 27, 1946, Port-of-Spain, Trinidad and Tobago; married Jeanne A Cox-Cooper; children: Zara. **Educ:** Trinity Coll WI, GCE 1963; Univ of the West Indies, BA 1967. **Career:** Ogilvy & Mather Inc, acct suprv 1970-77; Case & McGroth Adv Inc, mgmt suprv 1977-79; Uniworld Group Inc, vice pres mgmt suprv 1982-85. **Home Addr:** 510 E 86th St, New York, NY 10028.

COOPER-FARROW, VALERIE
Risk manager. **Personal:** Born Oct 18, 1961, Stamford, CT. **Educ:** Morgan State Univ, BS 1983; Columbia Univ Grad Sch of Business, MBA 1987. **Career:** The Travelers Co, computer programmer 1983-85; Goldman, Sachs & Co, vice pres, currently. **Orgs:** Mem Alpha Kappa Alpha Sor Inc 1980-, Natl Black MBA Assoc 1985-, The Network Inc 1986-. **Honors/Awds:** COGME Fellowship 1985. **Business Addr:** Vice Pres, Goldman, Sachs & Co, 85 Broad St, New York, NY 10004.

COOPER-GILSTRAP, JOCELYN
Music industry executive. **Personal:** daugHter of Andrew W Cooper. **Educ:** Hampton Univ, 1986. **Career:** Polygram Records, asst, Urban-Promotion Dept; Warner Chappell Music Inc, creative mgr, creative dir; Midnight Music Inc, pres, 1993-; Universal Music Group, sr vp, special asst to the chairman, currently. **Business Addr:** President, Senior VP & Special Assistant to the Chairman, Universal Music Group, 1755 Broadway, 7th Fl, New York, NY 10019, (212)373-0731.

COOPER-LEWTER, NICHOLAS CHARLES
Educator, consultant, psychotherapist, author, cleric. **Personal:** Born Jun 25, 1948, Washington, DC; children: Michelle Marie, Sonia Renee, Sean Darcy, Nicholas Jr,. **Educ:** Ashland Coll, BA 1970; Ecumenical Ctr, African-American church studies, adv studies, DMin prog 1978; Univ of MN, MSW 1978; CA Coast Univ, PhD 1988. **Career:** Univ of MN, teaching asst, 1974-75; City of St Paul Human Rights Dept, field investigator, 1974; consultant, various Christian churches, 1976-; Cooper Lewter Hypnosis Ctr NB, dir owner 1978-83; New Garden of Gethsemane, pastor, 1985-90; CRAVE Christ Ministries Inc, founder, psychotherapist, author; Bethel College and Seminary, professor of social work, visiting instructor of cross cultural counseling, 1990-95; Cooper-Lewter Rites of Passage, founder, 1995-; Committed by Choice Ministries, president, 1996-; McKnight Multi Cultural Grant, coordinator, 1991-95. **Orgs:** Founder, 1st basileus, Xi Theta Chap, Omega Psi Phi, 1966-70; rsrch specialist, Ctr for Youth Devel Rsrch, Univ of MN, 1972-73; bd dir, American Academy of Med Hypnoanalysis, 1977-; NASW; NUL; NAACP; AAMH; ACSW; board member, Adoptive Families of America Inc; TURN Leadership Foundation: Salvation Army. **Honors/Awds:** University of MN School of Social Work, Deans Grad Fellowship, 1974; Teamer School of Religion, Honorary LHD, 1978; Bethel College and Seminary, Distinguished Faculty Service Award, 1992; St Paul Urban League, SE Hall Community Service Award, 1992; Society of Medical Hypnoanalysts, Outstanding Contributor to the Field of Medical Hypnoanalysis, 1983; Los Angeles Olympic Committee, Judgeship, 1984. **Special Achievements:** Author, works include: ''Concerns of Working Youth,'' People Human Svs MN, 1974, ''Working Youth: Selected Findings from Exploratory Study,'' Jrnl Youth & Adolescence, 1974, ''Sports Hypnotherapy: Contenderosis & Self Hate,'' Jrnl of Med Hypnoanalysts, 1980; ''The Initial Environmental Experience: A Powerful Took for Psychotherapy & Hypnotherapy,'' Journal of Medical Hypnoanalysts, 1981; ''Keep On Rollin' Along: The Temptations and Soul Therapy,'' The Journal of Black Sacred Music, vol 6, num 1, Spring 1992; co-author: Soul Theology: The Heart of American Black Culture, Harper and Row, 1986, re-published, Abingdon Press, 1991; consultant: various Olympic Team members, 1980-; US Junior Olympic Team NRA, 1983-; California State Fullerton Football Program, 1983-84; UCLA Basketball Program, 1984-85; lecturer: Bishop College; LK Williams Institute, 1985; SMU Perkins School of Theology, 1986. **Home Phone:** (612)290-7768. **Business Addr:** President, Cooper-Lewter Rites of Passage, 253 E 4th St, Ste 201, St Paul, MN 55101, (612)638-6045.

COPAGE, MARC DIEGO
Performer. **Personal:** Born Jun 21, 1962, Los Angeles, CA. **Educ:** Attended college, 1 yr. **Career:** Actor singer comedian TV & stage since age 5; Metromedia Records, rec artist; Avco Records & Sussex Records, rec artist, currently. **Orgs:** Mem Screen Actors Guild; mem AFTRA. **Honors/Awds:** Nominated Best Actor NAACP Image Awards 1971; Human Rights Award NEA 1970; Communications Award CA Tchrs Assn; award BSA; award Goodwill Indus; award Salvation Army; numerous others.

COPE, DONALD LLOYD
Government official. **Personal:** Born May 16, 1936, Kansas City, KS; married Eddie L. **Educ:** Weber St Coll, BS 1973. **Career:** Gov Scott M Mattheson, ombudsman, pres; Ogden City Police Dept, comm relat ofcr 1971-72. **Orgs:** Consult & lectr, race rel Weber St Coll, Cont Ed Dept 1973; govt intern prog Brigham Young U; Univ of UT Soc Dept; Weber St Coll Black Std Union; NAACP; Ogden Brkfst Exchng Clb; pres League of UT Consumers 1974-75; mem dinner com 7th Anual Congsnl Black Caucus Dinner 1977; past mem, adv NewsBd for KTUX, Chan 4 1974; mem Gov Policy Standard & Goals Task Force; bd of dir St Girl Scout Cncl Comm. **Honors/Awds:** Serv award NAACP 1975; comm achvmt award Ogden Comm Action Agency 1977; publ brochure Govs Black Adv Cncl; Black Resource Cat On Blacs in UT; orgnzr Black Coll Std Intern Prog. **Business Addr:** 110 State Capitol, Salt Lake City, UT 84114.

COPELAND, BARRY BERNARD
Accountant. **Personal:** Born Jan 8, 1957, Paterson, NJ; son of Levonia Copeland and Albert Copeland; married Canary Gasaway; children: Eric, Antoine, Elise, Timothy, Malcolm. **Educ:** Prairie View A&M Univ, BBA 1979. **Career:** Internal Revenue Serv, IRS agent 1979; AUS, accountant 1980-82; Corpus Christi Army Depot, auditor 1982-85; Beeco Acctg Svcs, owner/accountant 1985-; Defense Contract Audit Agency, supervisory auditor 1985-; Barry B Copeland, certified public accountant 1988-. **Orgs:** Mem Alpha Phi Omega 1977-, NAACP 1986-; Assn of Govt Accountants 1988. **Honors/Awds:** Exceptional Performance Award Corpus Christi Army Depot 1985. **Military Serv:** AUS SP/4 E-4 2 yrs; Army Commendation Medal. **Home Addr:** 16327 Dew Drop Lane, Houston, TX 77095-1507. **Business Addr:** Supervisory Auditor, Defense Contract Audit Agency, 8876 Gulf Frwy, Ste 500, Houston, TX 77017-6544.

COPELAND, BETTY MARABLE
Health services consultant. **Personal:** Born Aug 31, 1946, Durham, NC; divorced; children: Abosede O. **Educ:** NC Central Univ, BA, Psych 1975; NCCU, MA, Psych 1980. **Career:** Durham Tech Inst, part-time instructor, 1978-80; Mental Retardation & Substance Abuse Durham County, forensic screening examiner, 1980-; Rural Day Care Assoc of Northeastern NC Div of Mental Health, training consultant, 1983-; Durham County Community Mental Health Ctr, psychotherapist, 1969-96; Durham Public Schools, family specialist, 1996-. **Orgs:** Chairperson NC Assoc of Black Psych, 1980-; mental health consultant, various organizations, 1982-; mem, NC Test Study Commn, 1982-; mem, NC Black Leadership Caucus, 1982-, Natl Black Child Devel Inst Durham Affiliate, 1982-; co-chair health comm Durham Comm on Affairs of Black People 1983; mem Durham NC City Bd of Educ 1983-; advisory bd mem Creative Arts in Public Schools 1984-; mem NCNW Durham Affiliate 1984-; state treas natl Council of Negro Women NC 1984-; serv unit mgr central unit Durham Cty Pines of Carolina Girls Scouts 1984-; founder & coord Coalition for Prevention of Adolescent Pregnancy 1984-; mem Natl Org for Legal Problems in Educ 1984-, Natl Assoc of Female Executives 1985-, bd nominating comm YWCA Durham, 1987; mem, Greater Durham Chamber ofCommerce Human Relations EdComm, 1985-87; vice chmn, Durham City Bd of Educ, 1987-present; mem, National Organization of Legal Problems in Education, 1985-90; mem/board of directors, Child and Parent Support Services, 1987; advisory board member, Creative Arts in Public Schools, 1984-90. **Honors/Awds:** Advocate of the Year Admin Category NC School Counselors Assoc 1984; Woman in Leadership Durham Comm on Affairs of Black People Natl Council of Negro Women 3rd Annual Bethune Recognition Luncheon 1984; Service Awd Durham Comm on Affairs of Black People 1987; Certificate of Advanced Achievement, NC School Bd Acad, 1987; Outstanding Leadership & Service as Black Elected Official, NC Leadership Conf, 1986; Serv Award, Interdenomination Health & Human Services, 1988; Certificate of Appreciation, Dedication and Services Rendered, Durham Child Advocacy Commission, 1986. **Home Addr:** 2138 S Roxboro St, Apt D, Durham, NC 27707. **Business Addr:** Psychotherapist, Durham County Community Mental Health Center, 414 E Main St, Durham, NC 27701.

COPELAND, DANNY RAY
Business owner. **Personal:** Born Apr 15, 1960, Booneville, MS; son of Carolina Copeland and Ezell Copeland; divorced; children: Taylor L, Dannilla. **Educ:** North Iowa Community Coll, AA, bus adm, 1981; Univ of Arizona, hospital administration, 1984. **Career:** Tucson Warehouse & Transfer Co, manager, 1984-85; Copeland Moving & Storage Co, owner/operator, 1985-93; Copeland Corporation Co, pres/CEO, 1992-; Tucson Minority Business Ctr, pres/founder, 1993-. **Orgs:** Pima County MBE Committee, Small Bus Adv Council; Natl Small Business Committee, advisor; Sign Code Advisory Committee; CODAS Comittee, bd mem; Yacht Club, bd mem; Omega Psi Phi. **Honors/Awds:** MBE, Businessman of the Year, 1987; Entrepreneur of the Year, 1990; Outstanding Young Man of America, 1987; Tucson Minority Bus Development Ctr, Young Minority Entrepreneur of the Year, 1988.

COPELAND, ELAINE JOHNSON
Educator. **Personal:** Born Mar 11, 1943, Catawba, SC; daughter of Lucille Hawkins Johnson and Aaron J Johnson; married Robert M Copeland; children: Robert M Jr. **Educ:** Livingstone Coll, BS (with honors) 1964; Winthrop Coll, MAT 1971; Oregon State Univ, PhD (with high honors) 1974; Univ of IL Urbana-Champaign, MBA 1987. **Career:** Wilson Jr High School, biology teacher 1964-65; Jefferson High School, biology teacher 1966-70; Oregon State Univ, counselor/instructor 1970-74; Univ of IL, associate dean/associate prof 1975-, associate vice chancellor, academic affairs. **Orgs:** Pres Girls Club of Champaign County 1977; pres Univ of IL YWCA 1979; pres Univ of IL Chap Honor Soc of Phi Kappa Phi 1982; pres Champaign-Urbana Alumnae Chap Kappa Phi Delta Sigma Theta Sor 1984-86; affirmative action rep Div E counseling and devel Amer Educ Rsch Assoc 1984-86; vice pres Assoc Relations Natl Assoc for Women Deans Administrators & Counselors 1985-87; president National Association for Women Deans, Administrators and Counselors 1988-89. **Honors/Awds:** Distinguished Service Award College of Agriculture 1979; ''Cross-Cultural Counseling and Psychotherapy, An Historical Perspective, Implications for Research and Training,'' Personnel and Guidance Journal 1983; Distinguished Alumni Presidential Natl Assoc for Educ Oppor in Higher Educ 1986; co-authored The Production of Black Doctoral Recipients, A Description of Five States Title IV Regulation, Problem and Progress, Teachers College Press 1988; Univ of IL Mother's Assn Medallian of Honor, Outstanding Leadership & Service, 1993; Univ of IL MBA, Students of Colon Award for Breaking Down Barriers & Daring to Dream, 1994, 1997. **Business Addr:** Professor, Department of Psychology, Clinton Junior College, Educational Emeritus Psychology, 1209 Crawford Rd, Rock Hill, SC 29730.

COPELAND, EMILY AMERICA
Educator, business executive. **Personal:** Born Apr 12, 1918, Tifton, GA. **Educ:** Spelman Coll, AB 1937; Atlanta U, BSLS 1942; Columbia U, MSLS 1948; NY U, attended; Columbia U, attended; Univ So CA, Attended. **Career:** Tift Co Independent High School, teacher 1937-38; Finly High School, librarian 1938-40, 1942; Spelman Coll Library, asst 1941-42; Gamon Theological Seminary, head librarian 1942-44; Atlanta Univ, librarian, asst ref 1944-46; NY Pubkuc Library, ref, school work asst 1945-46; SC State Coll, Dept of Library Science, head 1946-51; FAMU, library serv 1951-71. **Orgs:** Fndr, pres Black Res Inf Coord Svc, Inc 1942-; mem numerous off & coms Am Libr Assn; FL Libr Assn; Nat Small Bus Assn 1977-. **Honors/Awds:** Carnegie Grant to study at Atlanta Univ 1948; awards by gen educ bd to conduct orkshps in Library Sci at SC St Coll; Spellman Coll Merit Achiev Award 1968; Alumni Citation, Columbia Univ 1970; Rosalyn Carter Cert 1978; Cert of Recognition, Nat Alumnae of Spelman Coll 1978; Cert of rec for Cntrbtn to Afro-Am Heritage; sec of State FL 1979; Cert of Appreciation, Std Parents & Friends 1979. **Business Addr:** PO Box 6353, Tallahassee, FL.

COPELAND, HORACE NATHANIEL
Professional football player. **Personal:** Born Jan 2, 1971, Orlando, FL; married Tangela; children: Christopher Alan. **Educ:** Miami (Fla.), attended. **Career:** Tampa Bay Buccaneers, wide receiver, 1993-. **Business Addr:** Professional Football Player, Tampa Bay Buccaneers, One Buccaneer Place, Tampa, FL 33607, (813)870-2700.

COPELAND, JOHN
Professional football player. **Personal:** Born Sep 20, 1970, Lanett, AL. **Educ:** Univ of Alabama, attended. **Career:** Cincinnati Bengals, defensive end, 1993-. **Business Addr:** Professional Football Player, Cincinnati Bengals, One Bengals Dr, Cincinnati, OH 45202, (513)621-3550.

COPELAND, KEVON
Sr. economic development specialist. **Personal:** Born Mar 29, 1953, Pittsburgh, PA; son of Mary Jo Boxley Copeland and Edward S Copeland Jr; married Valire Renaye Carr Copeland, Aug 18, 1990. **Educ:** Connecticut Coll, BA 1976; Univ of Pgh Sch of Business, MBA Finance 1980. **Career:** Urban Redevelopment Authority of PGH, sr bus development specialist; PNC Bank, acct officer for China Hong Kong Singapore Malaysia Indonesia Thailand India 1981-86, acct officer for Japan Korea China 1986-90, asst vice president, foreign direct investment,

1987-91, assistant vice pres, credit policy division, 1991-93, asst vice pres, Affiliate National Banking, 1993-. **Orgs:** Pres vice pres sec Natl Black MBA Assoc Pgh Chapt; Founding mem One Hundred Black Men of Western PA; Alumni Committee CT Coll 1987-96; exec bd Alumni Assn CT Coll 1987-96; board of trustees, Sewickley Academy, 1991-95; board of trustees, Connecticut College, 1991-96; President of the Board, The Fund for the Advancement of Minorities Through Education (FAME), 1992-97; advisory bd, Summerbridge Pittsburgh, founding member, 1992-96. **Honors/Awds:** Robert L Hampton Award, Unity Alumni Council at Connecticut College. **Home Addr:** PO Box 23031, Pittsburgh, PA 15222-6031.

COPELAND, LEON L.
Educator. **Personal:** Born Sep 14, 1945, Portsmouth, VA; married Mary B; children: Leon, Jr. **Educ:** Norfolk St Coll, BS 1968; VA St Coll, MEd 1973; VA Tech, EdD 1977. **Career:** Univ of MD, asst prof 1977-; VZ Tech, co-op counselor 1975-77; Oscar Smith High School, Chesapeake VA, teacher 1968-75. **Orgs:** Mem Ind Arts Assn 1973-; mem Phi Delta Kappa 1977-79; mem Am Vocatnl Assn 1977-; mem Kappa Alpha Psi Frat 1968-; mem Emergency Sch Aid Adv Com 1978-79; mem Salisbury Housing Rehab Com 1980. **Honors/Awds:** Recp Outstng Young Men of Am Award; US Jaycees 1979; Dept Instr of the Yr, Univ of MD 1979; pub journal article Nat Assn of Indsl Tech Tchr Educ 1979; cited One of Ten Nat Leaders in Ind Arts VA Tech 1979. **Business Addr:** U of MD Eastern Shore, Princess Anne, MD 21853.

COPELAND, RAY
Music educator. **Personal:** Born Jul 17, 1926, Norfolk; married Edna E Garrett; children: Keith, Darrin. **Educ:** Wurlitzer Sch of Music NY. **Career:** Kaercea Music Enterprise, Inc, pres; Nassau & Suffolk County Schools, fac artist & clinician; NJ High Schools, fac artist & clinician; Jazz Workshops, Wilmington DE, fac artist & clinician; NY State School Music Assn, lect, demos; NY Brass Conf, lect, demos; The Creative Art of Jazz Improvisation, cond seminar, lect, & demos 1975; Wilson Concert Hall, cond classes, clinics 1975; Monterey & Newport Jazz Festivals, jazz soloist, featured in US & Europe, jazz tours in 14 countries. **Honors/Awds:** Composer "Classical Jazz", "Ste in Six Movements"; author "Ray Copeland Meth & Approach to Creative Art of Jazz Improvisation"; commnd by Nat Endowment for Arts; underscore strings, woodwind, precussion accomp to Jazz Suite, Cape Cod MA 1975; commnd Hedgerow, E Sandwich MA. **Business Addr:** Kaercea Music Enterprises, PO Box 62, Jamaica, NY 11422.

COPELAND, RICHARD ALLEN
Construction company executive. **Personal:** Born Aug 5, 1955, Minneapolis, MN; son of Laura Copeland and John Copeland; divorced; children: Leo, Laura, Derick. **Educ:** University of Minnesota, BS. **Career:** Mr Rib, manager; Lincoln Deli, cook; Flyers Bar & Deli, owner; Copeland Cartage, vice pres; Thor Construction, president, 1983-; Copeland Tru-King Inc, chief executive officer, 1985-. **Orgs:** National Association of Minority Contractors, president, 1990-92; Minneapolis Minority Purchasing Council; Minority Business Enterprises Input Committee; African-American Chamber of Commerce, co-founder, board member; Rotary, 1992; Pacesetters, 1985-90. **Honors/Awds:** MEDA, Charles W Poe Entrepreneur of the Year, 1992; MMPC, Minority Supplier of the Year, 1990; National Minority Supplier Development Council Conference, Supplier of the Year, 1992; US DOT, Administrators Minority Business Enterprise Award, 1990. **Special Achievements:** MMPC Supplier of the Year, Insight, 1990; Making Do in '92, Star Tribune, 1991; Local Suppliers Receive Awards, Insight, 1992. **Business Addr:** CEO, Copland Truc-King, Inc, 5400 Main St NE, Ste 201, Minneapolis, MN 55421-1132, (612)572-0505.

COPELAND, ROBERT M.
Educator, administrator. **Personal:** Born May 12, 1943, Hendersonville, NC; son of Florie Jeter Copeland and Aggie McDaniel Copeland; children: Robert McDaniel Copeland, Jr. **Educ:** Livingstone Coll, BS, 1964; Oregon State Univ, MS, 1971; Oregon State Univ, PhD, 1974. **Career:** Coll of Liberal Arts & Sciences, Univ of IL, assoc dean, 1986-96, asst dean, 1974-86; exc and senior assoc dean, 1996-; Oregon State Univ, teacher, counselor, 1971-74; Ebenezer Ave School Rock Hill SC, teacher, 1968-70; Sunset Park School, Rock Hill, SC, teacher, coach, 1964-68. **Orgs:** Mem, Natl Science Teacher's Assn, Natl Educ Assn, Assn for Educ of Teachers of Sci, Urbana Council Comm for Training of Teachers of Science, Alpha Phi Alpha, Phi Delta Kappa Hon Soc, Amer Coll Personnel Assn, Assn for Council & Devel; member, National Academic Advisory Association, 1988-. **Honors/Awds:** fellow, Natl Science Found, 1970-71, Ford Found, 1971-72, Natl Fellowships Fund, 1972-74; Pres, Natl Assn of Acad Affairs Administrators 1987. **Home Addr:** 34 Ashley Lane, Champaign, IL 61820. **Business Addr:** Associate Dean, University of Illinois at Urbana/Champaign, College of Liberal Arts and Sciences, 702 S Wright Street, Urbana, IL 61801.

COPELAND, RUSSELL
Professional football player. **Personal:** Born Nov 4, 1971, Tupelo, MS. **Educ:** Memphis State, attended. **Career:** Buffalo Bills, wide receiver, 1993-96; Philadelphia Eagles, 1997-. **Business Addr:** Professional Football Player, Philadelphia Eagles, 3501 S Broad St, Philadelphia, PA 19148, (215)463-2500.

COPELAND, TERRILYN DENISE
Speech pathologist. **Personal:** Born May 2, 1954, Toledo, OH. **Educ:** Kent State Univ, BS, 1976; Bowling Green State Univ, MA, 1980. **Career:** Lucas Co Bd of Mental Retardation, instructor and speech pathologist, 1978-81; contract home health speech pathologist, 1981-86; St Francis Rehab Hospital, staff speech pathologist, 1986-88, Flower Memorial Healthplex, 1988-89, staff speech pathologist; St Francis Rehabilitation Hospital, dir of speech pathology and audiology, 1989-94; Toledo Mental Health Center, speech pathologist, 1985-89; Rehab America, rehabilitation coordinator, 1994-95; Mercy/St Charles Hospitsla, in-patient coord, 1995-. **Orgs:** Mem, Delta Sigma Theta Sor, 1973-; Amer Speech & Hearing Assn, 1980-; Aphasiology Assn of OH, area representative, 1987-90, legislative representative, 1990-92; Amer Assn of Univ Women, 1986-89; League of Women Voters, 1986-; OH Speech & Hearing Assn, 1980-93; Mem, Amer Business Womens Assn, 1989-93; The National Head Injury Foundation, 1986-90; board of directors, League of Woman Voters, 1990-92; The Junior League, 1989-. **Honors/Awds:** Certificate of Clinical Competence (CCC), Amer Speech & Hearing Assn. **Business Addr:** Inpatient Coordinator, St Charles Hospital, 2600 Navarre, Toledo, OH 43605, (419)698-7205.

COPELIN, SHERMAN NATHANIEL, JR.
Legislator/businessman. **Personal:** Born Sep 21, 1943, New Orleans, LA; son of Marie Armant Copelin and Sherman N Copelin Sr; married Donna Sorapuru Copelin, Sep 21, 1990; children: Sherman Nathaniel III, Michon Jarel, Shane Nathan Copelin. **Educ:** Dillard University, BA, 1965; Loyola University at New Orleans, advanced study in psychology, 1966, advanced study in real estate investment, 1978. **Career:** 107 Group, Inc, pres, currently; EST Inc, chair of bd, currently; Gateway South Travel Agency, sec/trea, currently; Pro Tempore, speaker, 1993-; Superdome Services Inc, president/CEO, 1973-; Marketing Services Inc, president/CEO, 1978-; State of Louisiana, state representative, 1985-; Health Corporation of the South, chairman/CEO, 1989-. **Orgs:** Natl Business League, 1977, vice chairman of board, 1984-92, president, 1992-; co-chairman, Louisiana Council for Policy Review, 1985-; chair, Louisiana Bus League; chair, Natl Council for Policy Review; trea, Louisiana Legislative Black Caucus; exec comm, Natl Black Caucus of State Legislators; Southern Legislative Conference, exec comm; Natl Democratic Committeeman; State Central Committeeman; US Chamber of Commerce, Small Bus Council. **Special Achievements:** Author: How Can the US & Local Chamber Encourage and Support the Emerging Minority-Owned Business?; US Chamber of Commerce Small Bus Council Task Force on Emerging Business, 1992. **Business Addr:** President, Natl Business League, 107 Harbor Circle, New Orleans, LA 70126.

COPES, RONALD ADRIAN
Insurance company executive. **Personal:** Born Dec 1, 1941, Hartford, CT; son of Mamie Weaver Bailey and Aelix Copes; married Melva Washington Copes, Jun 12, 1964; children: Ronald A II, Rodney A. **Educ:** Lincoln University, Jefferson City, MO, BS, 1963; Atlanta University, Atlanta, GA, MBA, 1973. **Career:** US Army, Vietnam; district senior advisor, 1970-71; US Army, Fort Leavenworth, KS, author/instructor, 1973-77; US Army, 1st armored division, squadron executive officer, squadron commander, 1977-82; US Army, Baltimore, MD, professor of military science, 1982-85; US Army, St Louis, MO, director of information management, 1985-90; MassMutual, Springfield, MA, 2nd vice president, 1990-. **Orgs:** Vice Basileus, Omega Psi Phi Fraternity Inc, 1989-90. **Honors/Awds:** Honor Society, Delta Mu Delta, 1971-73. **Military Serv:** United States Army, Colonel, 1963-90; Silver Star, Bronze Star, Air Medal, Parachute Badge. **Home Addr:** 54 Blueberry Ridge, Westfield, MA 01085. **Business Addr:** Second Vice President, Massachusetts Mutual Life Insurance Co, Corporate Communications Division, 1295 State St, F 084, Springfield, MA 01111.

COPPEDGE, ARTHUR L.
Artist, lecturer. **Personal:** Born Apr 21, 1938. **Educ:** Brooklyn College; Brooklyn Mus Art School; Pratt Graphic Art Center; Art Stu League. **Career:** Amer the Beautiful Fund, artist in resd; teacher art classes, private studio; Brooklyn Mus Art School, teacher; Walden School NYC, teacher; NY Soc for Ethical Culture, teacher adult ed; Brooklyn Coll, Cornell Univ, Natl Conf of Artists, Amer Assoc of Mus Waldoft Astoria Hotel, lecturer; Inst of Jamaica, painting & drawing teacher. **Orgs:** Bicentennial Proj US Dept of Interior, Univ of PA; commiss Art in Embassies Prog US Dept of State; mural Servo-Mation Corp; publ NY Times, Washington Post, Cultural Post, Amer 1976, Black Enterprise, Essence, Attica Black, Viking Press; crit reviews NY Times, Wash Post, Art Worker News, The New Yorker,Art News; board member Hilton Hotel; founder, pres Brooklyn Consortium for Artists & the Arts; founder, established Brooklyn Artists Coalition; 1st dir exhibition ept New Muse Comm Mus; art consult The Gallery NYC; hon chmn Com to Honor Judge Bruce Wright; former chmn BACA Re-Grant Bd; chmn Ed Comm 8; mem comm Brooklyn Comm Plnng Bd; estab art dept NY Soc for Ethical Culture; establ artists series, slide collection New Muse Mus; art consultant African-American Caribbean Cultural Center, Brooklyn, NY; board member, BrooklyY; board member Brooklyn Downtown Development Corp. **Honors/Awds:** Exhibits Mus of Mod Art NYC, Brooklyn Mus, Smithsonian Inst, Inst of Contemp Art Boston, Fogg Mus Boston, Randall Gallery NYC, Natl Acad Galleries NYC, Hudson River Mus Yonkers, Allied Artists NYC, Amer Acad of Arts & Letters NYC, NY Cultural Ctr, Hunter College; Awds Judge Wash Sq Art Exhibit NYC; numerous publications.

CORAM, WILLIE MAE
Educational administrator. **Personal:** Born Apr 20, 1934, Fayetteville, NC; daughter of Mary Helen Council Walker and Willie Clayton Walker; divorced; children: Lynn D Coram-Allen, Bruce Allan Coram Sr. **Educ:** Boston Univ, BA, 1955; Univ of Med & Dentistry of New Jersey, PhD, 1983. **Career:** Grassland Hospital, research technician, lab supvr, 1955-63; Montefiore Hospital, lab supvr, 1963-64; GEIGY Chem Corp, res scientist, supvr of autonomic pharmacology group, 1964-71; CIBA-GEIGY Corp, numerous positions, 1971-89; Univ of Med & Dentistry of New Jersey, asst dean of students and alumni affairs, 1989-. **Orgs:** Natl Assn of Graduate Admissions Professionals; Sigma Xi; Amer Assn for the Advancement of Science; NY Acad of Sciences; MSACRAO; AACRAO; numerous other past memberships. **Honors/Awds:** Natl Assn of Negro Business and Professional Women's Clubs Inc, Achievement Award, 1985; Jersey City State College, Outstanding Leaders in Business, Education, and Industry, 1988; Natl Urban League, Certificate of Recognition, 1986; CIBA-GEIGY TWIN Award, 1986. **Special Achievements:** Restoration of Normal Tissue K Levels in Heart, Aorta and Skeletal Muscle of Furosemide-Treated Rats on Mg-Deficient Diet, 1988; Effects of CGS 10078B on Catecholamine Content of Brain, Heart, Uterus and Plasma in Conscious Rats, 1986; numerous others. **Home Addr:** 1651 Springfield Ave, PO Box 445, New Providence, NJ 07974-0542, (908)665-1634. **Business Addr:** Asst Dean, Student & Alumni Affairs, University of Medicine & Dentistry of New Jersey, 30 Bergen St, ADMC 1, Ste 110, Newark, NJ 07103, (201)982-4511.

CORBETT, DORIS R.
Educator. **Personal:** Born Jun 9, 1947, Elizabethtown, NC; daughter of Isadora Beatty Corbett White and Henry Edward Corbett; married William Johnson, Oct 20, 1982. **Educ:** North Carolina College, Durham, NC, BS, 1969; North Carolina Central University, Durham, NC, MS, 1972; University of Maryland, College Park, MD, PhD, 1981. **Career:** Camp Curtin Junior High School, Harrisburg, PA, high school teacher, 1969-70; John Harris Senior High School, Harrisburg, PA, high school teacher, 1970-71; Howard University, Washington, DC, associate professor, 1972-. **Orgs:** President, AAHPERD, 1990-91, chairman of the board of governors, 1990-91, president, Eastern District Association, 1987-88, American Alliance for Health, Physical Education, Recreation & Dance; international vice president, International Council for Health, Physical Education & Recreation, 1988-91; president, National Association for Girls & Women in Sports, 1980-81. **Honors/Awds:** Ethics Scholar, University of Rhode Island Institute for International Sport, 1990-91; Mabel C. Robinson Lecturer Award, Alabama State Association for HPERD, 1990; R. Tait McKenzie Award, American Alliance for HPERD, 1989; Honor Award, Eastern District Association, HPERD, 1984; Honor Award, District of Columbia Association for HPERD, 1979. **Business Addr:** Professor, Dept of Physical Education & Recreation, Howard University, 6th & Girard St NW, Washington, DC 20059.

CORBIE, LEO A.
Educational administrator. **Career:** Medgar Evers College, Brooklyn, NY, acting pres, currently. **Business Addr:** Acting President, Medgar Evers College, Brooklyn, NY 11225.

CORBIN, ANGELA LENORE
Physician. **Personal:** Born Nov 19, 1958, Washington, DC; daughter of Ruby Corbin and Maurice C Corbin. **Educ:** Howard Univ, BS 1980; Meharry Medical Coll, MD 1984; Univ MD Hospital resident 1984-87; Univ MD Hospital nephrology 1987-89. **Career:** Univ of MD Hospital, resident 1984-. **Orgs:** Mem Amer Coll of Physicians, Amer Medical Assoc. **Honors/Awds:** Mem Alpha Omega Alpha Medical Honor Soc 1984; National Medical Association. **Home Addr:** 11304 Classical Ln, Silver Spring, MD 20901.

CORBIN, EVELYN D.
Administrator (retired). **Personal:** Born Sep 25, 1923, New York, NY; daughter of Beulah Talbot Dixon and Eustace Augustus Dixon; married Eustace E, Dec 31, 1948; children: Pamela Joy, Patricia Jill. **Educ:** Westchester School of Nursing Valhalla NY, RN 1948; Hunter Coll CUNY, BE 1961; Queens Coll CUNY, MLS 1972. **Career:** Elmont Public Library, Adult Services Program Coordinator 1986-89; Lakeview Pub Lib, Nassau Co, Long Island NY, founding dir 1975-86; Elmont Pub Library Nassau Co, adult serv librarian 1973-75; Franklin Gen Hosp Valley Stream NY, RN 1967-68; St Albans Naval Hosp, RN labor & del 1958-59; LI Jewish Hosp, nurse ob serv 1954-56; Beth-El Hosp, Brooklyn NY, head nurse labor & del 1952-54; head nurse labor & delivery, very, Greenpoint Hosp 1948-50. **Orgs:** 4-H Leader 1960-67; PTA 1960-67; Girl Scouts 1960-67; Church board of Trustees 1960-67; editor Church Newsletter 1961-63; chmn Friends of the Lake View library 1963-71; chmn Lakeview NAACP 1965-67. **Honors/Awds:** L

Marion Moshier Award, NY Lib Assn 1976; Community Service Award, Central Nassau Club of Natl Assn of Negro Business & Professional Women's Clubs Inc 1977. **Military Serv:** WAC pvt 1943-44.

CORBIN, SEAN
Professional basketball referee. **Career:** NBA official, currently. **Business Addr:** NBA Official, c/o National Basketball Association (NBA), 645 5th Ave, 15th Fl, New York, NY 10022-5986.

CORBIN, STAMPP W.
Company executive. **Career:** Resource Computer Systems One, CEO, currently. **Special Achievements:** Company is ranked number 88 on BE's List of Top 100 Companies, 1994. **Business Addr:** CEO, Resource Computer Systems One, 4900 Blazer Pkwy, Dublin, OH 43017.

CORBIN, TYRONE KENNEDY
Professional basketball player. **Personal:** Born Dec 31, 1962, Columbia, SC; married Dante; children: Tyjha, Tyrell. **Educ:** DePaul Univ, BS, computer science. **Career:** San Antonio Spurs, forward, 1985-86, Cleveland Cavaliers, 1986-87, Phoenix Suns, 1988-89, Minnesota Timberwolves, 1989-91, Utah Jazz, 1991-94; Atlanta Hawks, 1994-95; Sacramento Kings, 1995-96; Miami Heat, 1996; Atlanta Hawks, 1996-. **Business Addr:** Professional Basketball Player, Atlanta Hawks, One CNN Tower, Ste 405, Atlanta, GA 30335, (404)827-3800.

CORBITT, JOHN H.
Clergyman. **Personal:** Born Aug 24, 1941, Salley, SC; son of Thelma Corbitt and John Corbitt; married Betty Starks; children: Bruce, Terry. **Educ:** SC State Coll, BA 1962; Interdenominational Theol Ctr, MDiv 1966; Vanderbilt Univ Div Sch & Yale Div Sch; McCormick Theol Sem, DMin 1979. **Career:** Bells Chapel Baptist Church, pastor 1966-67; Owen Coll, coll minister & prof of religion 1966-67; Arkansas Bapt Career, interim dean of religion; Philander Smith Coll, coll chaplain & prof of religion & philosophy 1970-74; Mt Pleasant Baptist Church Little Rock, pastor 1967-74; Springfield Baptist Church, pastor, currently. **Orgs:** Consult Natl Student Ministries So Bapt Conv 1969-87; mem Natl Assn of Coll & Univ Chplns; Ministries to Blacks in Higher Educ; pres Interdenominational Ministerial Alliance of Greater Little Rock; natl dir Natl Baptist Student Union Retreat 1973-; mem NAACP; bd of adv Little Rock Urban League; mem Foreign Mission Bd Natl Baptist Convention USA Inc 1968-74; dean Natl Baptist Congress of Christian Educ 1984; apptd by Gov Rockefeller to Gov's Comm on First Offenders State of AR 1969; apptd Gov Dale Bumpers to Bd of Pardons & Parole State of AR 1971; apptd by Gov James B Edwards to Greenville Area Bd of Mental Health; pres Enoree River Congress of Christian Educ 1975-79; pres Gr Greenville Ministerial Assn 1980-81; attended World Baptist Alliance meeting in Toronto Canada 1980, Los Angeles CA 1985, Seoul Korea 1990, Buenos Aires Argentina 1995; attended Baptist World Youth Congress Buenos Aires Argentina 1984; pres SC State Congress of Christian Educ 1986-90; attended Baptist World Youth Conference, Glasgow, Scotland, 1988; Harare, Zimbabwe, 1993; attended Baptist World Alliance, Seoul, Korea, 1990; member, Preaching Teams, Africa, 1979, Soviet Union, 1988; natl dir, NH Bapt Student Union Retreat, 1973-96; former pres, Greater Greenville Ministerial Assn; mem, Phi Beta Sigma Fraternity Inc, former chap pres; mem, Commission on Evangelism & Education, Bapt World Alliance; mem, Religions Education Assn of the US and Canada. **Honors/Awds:** Alumnus of the Year, McCormick Theological Seminary, 1991; Order of the Palmetto, Governor of SC, 1988; Honored by Morehouse College, 1992; Named to Martin Luther King, Jr bd of preachers, Morehouse Coll, 1992; author, Black Churches Reaching Coll Students, 1995. **Business Addr:** Pastor, Springfield Bapt Church, 600 E McBee Ave, Greenville, SC 29601.

CORDELL, LADORIS HAZZARD
Judge. **Personal:** Born Nov 19, 1949, Bryn Mawr, PA; daughter of Clara Jenkins Hazzard and Lewis R Hazzard; divorced; children: Cheran, Starr. **Educ:** Antioch Coll, BA 1971; Stanford Law School, JD 1974. **Career:** NAACP Legal Defense & Educ Fund, staff attorney 1974-75; attorney private practice 1975-82; Stanford Law School, asst dean 1978-82; State Court of Appeal Sixth Dist, justice pro tem 1986-87; Municipal Ct Santa Clara Co, judge 1982-88; Superior Ct Santa Clara Co, judge 1988-. **Orgs:** Mem Natl Bar Assn; mem American Bar Assn; mem NAACP; mem CA Judges Assn; mem CA Women Lawyers; chairperson bd of dirs Manhattan Playhouse East Palo Alto 1980; bd of dirs & steering comm Natl Conf on Women and the Law 1980, 1984-85; policy bd Center for Rsch on Women Stanford Univ 1980-82; chairperson bd of dirs East Palo Alto Comm Law Project 1984-87; bd of trustees, United Way of Santa Clara County 1987-; bd of dir, Police Activities League (PAL), San Jose Chapter 1987-89, Natl Conf of Christians & Jews Inc, Santa Clara County 1988-; bd of trustees, Mills College, Oakland, CA, 1996-; bd of dir, Lucik Packard Fndtn for Children, Stanford, CA, 1997-; mem Silicon Valley Forum Council, Commonwealth Club of CA 1997-; bd of dir, Asian Law Alliance, San Jose, CA, 1997, mem Advisory bd, Healthy Alternatives for African American Babies, San Jose, CA, 1994-; mem American Law Institute, 1996-. **Honors/Awds:** Black History Award Tulip Jones Womens Club 1977; nominated for Black Enterprise Magazine Annual Achievement Award in under 30 category 1977, 1978; Comm Involvement Award East Palo Alto Chamber of Comm 1982, 1983; Public Serv Awd Delta Sigma Theta 1982; Public Serv Awards Natl Council of Negro Women 1982; Outstanding Mid-Peninsula Black Woman Award Mid-Peninsula YWCA 1983; Political Achievement Award CA Black Women's Coalition & the Black Concerns Assn 1982; Featured in Ebony Magazine 1980, 1984; Implemented a minority recruitment program at Stanford Law School as asst dean; First Black Woman Judge in Northern CA; elected presiding judge of the Municipal Court 1985-86 term; author of "Before Brown v Bd of Educ—Was It All Worth It?" Howard Law Journal Vol 23 No 1 1980; co-author, "The Appearance of Justice: Judges' Verbal and Nonverbal Behavior in Criminal Jury Trials" Stanford Law Review Vol 38, No 1, 1985; "Black Immigration, Disavowing the Stereotype of the Shiftless Negro" Judges' Journal Spring 1986; Co-author, "Musings of a Trial Court Judge," Indiana Law Journal, vol 68, No 4, 1993; Achievement Award, Western Center on Domestic Violence 1986; Santa Clara County Woman of Achievement Award 1985; Recipient of first Juliette Gordon Lowe Award for Community Serv 1987; first black woman on Superior Court in Northern California 1988-; Distinguished Citizen Award, Exchange Club 1989; Don Peters Outstanding Volunteer Award, United Way of Santa Clara County, 1991; Baha'i Community Service Award, 1992; Special Recognition Award, Human Relations Commission of Santa Clara County, 1994; Youth Service Award, Legal Advocates for Children & Youth, 1996; Unsung Heroes Award, Minority Access Committee, Santa Clara County Bar Assoc, 1996; Social Justice award, San Fran Women's Center, 1996; Legal Impact Award, Asian Law Alliance, 1996, Advocate for Justice Award, Legal Aid Society of Santa Clara County, 1996. **Business Addr:** Judge, Superior Court, 191 N First St, San Jose, CA 95113.

CORDERY, SARA BROWN
Educator (retired). **Personal:** Born Feb 4, 1920, Chester, SC; daughter of Frances Halsey Brown and William Brown; married Albert Theodore Cordery, Mar 30, 1947 (deceased). **Educ:** Brainerd Institute, Chester, SC, 1938-39; Barber-Scotia College, Concord, NC, 1939-40; South Carolina State College, Orangeburg, SC, BS, 1940-42; Columbia Univ, New York, NY, MA, 1946, EdD, 1955. **Career:** US Government, Washington, DC, statistical analyst, 1942-45; Barber-Scotia College, Concord, NC, teacher, professor, department chair, division chair, director inst research, special asst. to president, vice president for academic affairs, 1946-74; Morgan State Univ, Baltimore, MD, professor, dean of school of business & mgmt, 1975-85. **Orgs:** Elder, Presbyterian Church, USA, 1978-; moderator, Presbytery of Baltimore, 1989-90; president, Presbyterian Women, Presbytery of Baltimore, 1985-88; mem, 1978-84, chair, 1983-84, Natl Com of Self-Development of People, Presbyterian Church, USA; member, Coordinating Team, Presbyterian Women, Synod of Mid-Atlantic, 1988-93; moderator, Presbyterian Women Churchwide, Presbyterian Church, USA, 1991-94. **Honors/Awds:** President's Award, Barber-Scotia College, 1985; Outstanding Alumna, Barber-Scotia College, 1989; Meritorious Service, Barber-Scotia College, 1967; Promoter of the Present, Grace Presbyterian Church, 1990; Honorary Life Membership, Presbyterian Women, Grace Presbyterian Church, 1988. **Special Achievements:** First African-American woman to moderate the Presbyterian Women Churchwide. **Home Addr:** 8820 Walther Blvd, Apt 2008, Baltimore, MD 21234.

CORINALDI, AUSTIN
Hospital executive (retired). **Personal:** Born Mar 31, 1921, New York, NY; son of Claris Corinaldi and Oswald Corinaldi; married Dorothy; children: Dyhann, Greg. **Educ:** Columbia Univ, MS, hosp admin, 1969; MPH, 1964; NYU, BA, 1949; Coll of City of NY, attended 1942. **Career:** US Coast & Goedetic Survey, topographical draftsman, 1941-43; Riverton Labs, NYC, lab tech, detailman 1945-55; New York City Bd of Educ, teacher, health educ, 1955-67; Public Health Sanitarian NYC, Dept of Health, 1950-69; Harlem Hosp Cntr, admin resident 1968-69, dep asst commr planning 1969-70, dep asst commr operations 1970, assoc exec dir 1970-74, acting exec dir 1974-77; Coler Mem Hosp, retired deputy exec dir, 1977-85. **Orgs:** Mem Am Coll of Hosp Admin; Am Hosp Assn; Am Pub Health Assn; The Royal Soc of Health, England, Fellow; Nat Assn Of Hlth Serv Execs; Black Caus of Harlem Hlth Wrkrs; Nat Environ Hlth Assn; Assn of the Alumni of the Columbia Univ Sch of Pub Hlth; NY Univ Alumni Assn; Smithsonian Assoc; mem NY NAACP; NY Urban League; YMCA of Gr NY, Harlem Br; pres Harlem Neighborhds Assn; Beta Lambda Sigma Hon Soc Biology. **Military Serv:** USAF acting s/sgt 1943-46. **Home Addr:** 2600-7 Netherland Ave, Bronx, NY 10463.

CORLETTE, EDITH
Attorney. **Personal:** Born Oct 19, 1942, Oklahoma City, OK; daughter of Gwendolyn Parker and Stephen Parker. **Educ:** Hampton Inst, BS 1964; NW Sch of Law, JD 1974; UCLA, MS 1975. **Career:** Self-employed, atty. **Orgs:** Mem Delta Sigma Theta Sor 1962; Alpha Kappa Mu Hon Soc 1963-64; Langston Law Clb 1974; SW Bar 1974; LA Co Bar 1975; Nat Conf of Black Lwyrs 1975; pres Women's Div of NBA; sec CA Assn of Black Lwyrs; past mem at large NBA; sec Black Women Lwyr of So CA 1975; Nat Bus Assn 1976; Beverly Hills Law Assn 1977; bd dir NAACP, Hollywood Br; bd dirs Proj HEAVY. **Honors/Awds:** Woodrow Wilson Fellowship 1964; Outstanding Young Women of America 1966; NW Urban Fellow 1973-74. **Business Addr:** PO Box 8692, Los Angeles, CA 90008-0692.

CORLEY, EDDIE B.
Automobile dealer. **Career:** Grants Ford Lincoln-Mercury, Inc, CEO, currently. **Special Achievements:** Co. is ranked #100 on Black Enterprise magazine's list of top 100 auto dealers, 1992. **Business Addr:** CEO, Grants Ford Lincoln-Mercury Inc., PO Box 908, Grants, NM 87020, (505)285-4695.

CORLEY, LESLIE M.
Investment banker. **Personal:** Born May 1946, Chicago, IL; son of Leslie T & Lorena Turner Corley; married Freddie Corley, Sep 1995; children: John F J Clark III. **Educ:** Aeronautical & Astronautical Engineering, University of IL, BS with high honors, 1969; Harvard Graduate School of Business Administration, MBA, 1971. **Career:** Exxon, Inc, financial analyst, 1969-71; Fidelity Investments, senior securities analyst, 1972-77; Norton Simon Inc, mgr acquisitions strategic planning, 1977-81; Kelso & Co, general partner, 1981-88; LM Capital Corp, president/CEO, 1988-; Convenience Corp of America, Inc, chmn, 1995-96. **Orgs:** Urban League of Palm Beach County, dir, 1996-97; d'essence Designer Fragrances, LLC, dir, 1996-; LM Capital Corp, president/CEO, 1988-; Tri-West, Inc, dir, 1986-88; American Sterilizer, Inc, dir, 1984-86; Manhattan Community Board 9, treasurer, 1991-92; Aaron Davis Hall, treasurer/dir, 1986-95. **Honors/Awds:** Tabernacle Missionary Bapt Church, Businessman of the Year, 1997; Phi Eta Sigma, Freshman Collegiate Honorary Society, 1965; Sigma Gamma Tau, Engineering Honorary Society, 1967; University of IL, Edmund J James Honors Program, 1965-69. **Special Achievements:** Formed largest minority owned convenience store operator, 1995; Company is ranked #8 on Black Enterprise's 1997 list of Top 100 Black businesses. **Business Addr:** President/CEO, LM Capital Corp, 515 N Flagler Dr, West Palm Beach, FL 33401, (561)833-9700.

CORLEY-SAUNDERS, ANGELA ROSE
Government official. **Personal:** Born Jun 9, 1947, Washington, DC; divorced. **Educ:** Howard U, BA 1975. **Career:** The White House, spec asst 1977-77; USDA Ofc of the Asst Sec for Rural Dev, spec asst 1977-79; USDA Rural Economic & Community Devel, civil rights staff, equal employment specialist, 1987; Equal Opportunity Specialists 1986-; USDA Farmers Home Admin mgmt analyst 1979-. **Orgs:** Mem Natl Council of Negro Women 1978-; bd mem Unity of Washington DC, 1983-. **Business Addr:** Equal Employment Specialist, US Dept of Agric, Rec'd Civil Rights Staff, 14th & Indep Ave SW Ag Box 0703, Washington, DC 20250, (202)245-5528.

CORMIER, LAWRENCE J.
Business executive. **Personal:** Born Sep 26, 1927, San Benito, TX; married Helen Jones; children: Patricia Watkins, Janet, Lawrence. **Educ:** Pace Univ, 1965-72. **Career:** US Merchant Marine, 3rd officer 1950-55; Ebony Oil Corp, bd chmn, CEO 1955-87; Cormier & Ebony Trucking Inc, bd chmn, ceo 1964-87; The Inner-City Mgmt Co, CEO, bd chmn 1977-85; The Cormier Group Ltd, Jamaica, NY, CEO and bd chair, 1990-. **Orgs:** Charter mem, bd mem, Assoc of Minority Bus Enterprise NY Inc; bd mem, past vice pres Gr Jamaica C of C; past pres, Intl Kiwanis, Jamaica Club; past pres Gr Jamaica Devel Corp; past pre, bd mem, charter mem United Black Men of Queens Cty Inc; Jamaica NAACP, St Albans, NY, branch pres. **Honors/Awds:** Bus & Comm Serv Awd Omega Psi Phi 1965; NY State Small Businessman of the Year US Small Bus Adm 1967; Spec Recog Awd NAACP 1968; Outstanding Serv Awd Jamaica C of C 1970; Business Man of the Year Jamaica C of C 1974; Delta Sigma Theta outstanding community serv award, 1974; Assn of Minority Enterprise serv award, 1979; NY Urban League community serv award, 1981; NY State Dept of Commerce outstanding leadership award, 1982; Queens Fedn of Churches outstanding leadership award, 1983; Natl Cancer Soc outstanding community serv award, 1984; Businessman of the Year, St Albans Cham of Commerce, 1985; Benjamin S Rosenthal Humanitarian Award, B'nai B'rith, 1985; Regl Minority Mfr of the Yr Award, US Dept of Commerce, 1986; Natl Minority Mfr of the Yr Award,US Dept of Commerce, 1986; US Small BAdmin outstanding bus achieve award, 1986. **Military Serv:** US Merchant Marines. **Business Addr:** Chief Exec Officer, Bd Chmn, Mont Blanc Limousine, The Cormier Group Ltd, 107-35 Merrick Blvd, Jamaica, NY 11433, (718)657-1144.

CORMIER, RUFUS, JR.
Attorney. **Personal:** Born Mar 2, 1948, Beaumont, TX; married Yvonne Clement; children: Michelle, Geoffrey, Claire. **Educ:** So Meth Univ, BA 1970; Yale Univ, JD 1973. **Career:** Paul Weiss Rifkind Wharton & Garrison, attny 1973-74; US House of Reps Judiciary Comm, spec asst to counsel 1974; Baker & Botts, attny. **Orgs:** Mem Amer Bar Assoc, Houston Bar Assoc, Houston Lawyers Assoc. **Honors/Awds:** Avella Winn Hay Achievement Awd 1970; One of Five Outstanding Young Texans selected by Texas Jaycees 1981. **Business Addr:** Attorney, Baker & Botts, LLP, 3000 One Shell Plaza, Houston, TX 77002.

CORNELIUS, CHARLES HENRY
Insurance executive. **Personal:** Born Nov 13, 1955, Bronx, NY; son of Melvin & Dolores Cornelius; married Sheila Harris Cornelius, May 12, 1984; children: Charles Jr, Michael. **Educ:** University of Hartford, BA, 1977. **Career:** Allstate Ins Co, manager, 1977-84; Chubb Group Ins Co, vice pres, 1984-96; Atlanta Life Ins Co, president/CEO, 1996-. **Orgs:** Atlanta Action Forum, 1996-; National Insurance Association, dir, mem, 1997-; 100 Black Men of Atlanta, 1996-; NAACP, lifetime, 1997-; Albany Inst of Art/History, director, 1993-96; Urban League of NE NY, director, 1994-96; Inroads, volunteer; Jr Achievement, volunteer. **Honors/Awds:** YMCA Harlem Branch, Black Achievers in Industry, 1991; National Insurance Ind Association, Honoree, 1996. **Business Addr:** President/Chief Executive Officer, Atlanta Life Insurance Co., 100 Auburn Ave, NE, Herndon Plz, Atlanta, GA 30303-2527, (404)659-2100.

CORNELIUS, DON
Television host. **Personal:** Born Sep 27, 1936, Chicago, IL; married Delores Harrison, 1956; children: Anthony, Raymond. **Career:** Golden State Mutual Life, insurance salesman, 1956-66; WVON, announcer, 1966; WCIU-TV, sports anchor, 1968; Soul Train, host/producer, 1970-. **Honors/Awds:** Album, The Soul Train Gang. **Special Achievements:** Soul Train Records, founder, 1975; Soul Train Music Awards, creator, 1987; Soul Train Comedy Awards, creator, 1993. **Military Serv:** US Marines, 1954-55. **Business Addr:** Founder, Don Cornelius Productions, 9255 Sunset Blvd, Ste 420, Los Angeles, CA 90069.

CORNELIUS, ULYSSES S., SR.
Clergyman. **Personal:** Born Dec 12, 1913, Waskom, TX; married Willie Hicks; children: Ulysses Sidney, Jr. **Educ:** Bishop Coll, BA 1947, MEd 1952, Hon DD 1975; Miami U, grad; VA U. **Career:** Mt Sinai Bapt Ch, Dallas, pastor, TX pastor; LA, pastor; Waskom,TX, instr pub schs; Interracial Bapt Inst, Dallas, instr; Bishop Coll, instr. **Orgs:** Vp Nat Bapt SS & Bapt Training Union-Congress USA, Inc; pres BM&E St SS & BTU Congress of TX; fin Sec-treas LK Williams Ministers Inst;mem Interdnmntnl Ministerial All of Dallas; mem trustee bd BM&E Conv of TX; mem bd dir Interracial Bapt Inst of Dallas; mem 32 deg Prince Hall Masons; past mem bd trustees Bishop Coll; past mem bd dir Black C of C of Dallas; mem bd dir TX Fed of Garden Clubs. **Honors/Awds:** Recip "Big Boss" Ldrshp Award, YMCA; cert of Appreciation for Dedicated Ldrshp in Advancemnt of Bishop Coll 1969-75; Alumni Citation Award, Bishop Coll 1968; srv Award Bethlehem Bapt Ch, Bonham TX 1971; srv Award Mt Sinai Bapt Ch, Dallas 1973; srv Award NW Dist Bapt Assn 1974. **Military Serv:** AUS t/sgt 1943-46. **Business Addr:** 1106 Pemberton Hill Rd, Dallas, TX 75217.

CORNELIUS, WILLIAM MILTON
Educational administrator. **Personal:** Born Dec 4, 1936, Hinds Co; son of Annie Louise Mellon Cornelius Fortner and Lawrence Milton Cornelius. **Educ:** S Tougaloo College, BA, 1959; Indiana University, MA, 1972; Kansas State University, PhD, 1979. **Career:** Saints Jr College, instructor, dean, 1962-65; Wilkinson County Public Schools, instructor, assistant principal, 1965-69; Hinds Community College, Utica Campus, director, student support services, 1969-. **Orgs:** Mem Nat Geo Soc; mem So Historical Assn; mem So Sociological Soc; mem Academic of Art & Sciences; mem Nat Council of Social Studies; mem MI Educators Assn; mem Nat Tchrs Assn; mem Nat Assn of Geography Tchrs; mem Hinds Co Tchrs Assn; mem Nat Assn of Coll & Univ Prof; mem IN Univ Alumni; mem KS State Univ Alumni; mem Tougaloo Coll Alumni; mem Am Mus of Nat History; mem Nat Assn of Curriculum & Supervision; mem MS Assn of Educ Opportunity Prog Personnel; mem Southeastern Assn of Educ Opportunity Prog Personnel. **Honors/Awds:** Dean's Honr List, 1959; grant, Merrill-Palmer Inst, 1960; grant, Wayne State Univ, 1960-61; Most Cooperative Tchr Award, 1963; summer grant, Hampton Inst, 1965; grant, IN Univ, 1967; grant, Univ of Southwestern LA, 1968; grant, Norfolk State Coll, 1969; grant, Howard Univ, 1970; St John's of Santa Fe, Outstanding Educators of America, 1974; Faculty Devel Grant, 1974-79. **Business Addr:** Director, Student Support Services, Hinds Community College, Utica Campus, Utica, MS 39175.

CORNELL, BOB
Company executive. **Personal:** Born Dec 21, 1938, Jersey City, NJ; son of Sylvia Cornell and Frank Cornell; children: Patricia, Valerie, Robert, Andrew, David. **Educ:** Arapahoe Community College, AAS, 1975; Metropolitan State College, 1976-79; Colo Sales Training Institute, certificate, 1970. **Career:** Colo Sales Training Institute, consultant, 1970-72; US Federal Protective Service, training officer, 1974; Littleton Police Department, police officer, 1972-74, 1975-78; People Skills Institute, president/chief executive officer, 1978-. **Orgs:** American Society for Training and Development; Worksmart International; Minority Enterprise Inc. **Honors/Awds:** Colorado Black Leaders Profile, 1990; E E Van Stee Scholarship, University of Wisconsin, Business Management Seminar; Rocky Mountain & National Small Business Supplier of the Year, 1993; President's Award, Motel 6. **Special Achievements:** Selected as program Evaluator for Community Coalition for Minority Males Grant; Certified Professional Consultant to Management; Certified Professional Development Trainer; Certified Vocational Instructor, State of Colorado. **Military Serv:** Vietnam Veteran; US Air Force, tsgt, 1958-70; recipient of two Air Force Commendation Medals. **Business Addr:** President/CEO, People Skills Institute, PO Box 348, Sedalia, CO 80135-0348, (303)688-2152.

CORNELY, PAUL B.
Educator (retired), physician. **Personal:** Born Mar 9, 1906, Pointe a Pitre, Guadeloupe; son of Adrienne Mellon Cornely and Eleodore Cornely; married Mae Stewart, Jun 23, 1934; children: Paul B Jr. **Educ:** Univ of MI, AB 1928, MD 1931, Dr PH 1934, DSc (Hon) 1968; Univ of Pacific, D Public Service (Hon) 1972. **Career:** Dep of Bacteriology, Preventive Med & Public Health, Harvard Univ, assoc prof, 1934-47, chairman, 1943-47; Freedmen's Hosp Wash DC, med dir 1947-58; Department Community Health and Family Practice Howard University, prof & chmn 1955-73; Agency Intl Devel, Washington DC, consultant 1960-74; System Sciences Bethesda MD, sr med consultant 1971-82; Howard University College of Medicine, Washington, DC, prof emeritus, 1974-. **Orgs:** Pres Technical Assn Inc 1977; chmn Board of Dir Prof Exam Serv 1978-82; pres Phys Forum 1960-61; pres Community Group Health Found 1968-73; mem Pres Committee on Popl & American's Future 1970-72; pres John Carroll Society Wash DC 1971-73. **Honors/Awds:** Pres, Physicians Forum, 1954; Pres American Public Health Assn 1971-72; fellow Amer Coll of Preventive Med fellow Amer Board of Preventive & Public Health; fellow (Hon) Amer Coll of Hospital Admin; Sedgwick Mem Awd Amer Public Health Assn 1972; Awarded Honorary degree DSc by Howard University, 1991.

CORNISH, BETTY W.
Educational administrator. **Personal:** Born Jul 10, 1936, New York City, NY; daughter of Edna Charles Williams and John A Williams; married Edward H Cornish (deceased). **Educ:** Boston Univ, BFA (Cum Laude) 1958; Univ of Hartford, MEd 1962, MAEd 1980. **Career:** Hartford Neighborhood Ctrs, youth group leader 1959-63; Bloomfield Publ Schools, teacher 1958-68; Central CT State Coll, asst prof, art ed 1966-83; Gemini User Group Inc, exec dir 1983-91, education consultant, 1991-92; Saint Joseph College, director of intercultural affairs, 1992-. **Orgs:** Mem CT Ed Assoc 1960-74; coord Afro-Amer Studies Prog 1969-73; mem NAEA; pres & exec bd CT Art Ed Assoc 1975; mem Amer Assoc of Univ Prof 1976-; exec bd New England Art Ed Conf 1977-79; pres affirm action comm Central CT State Univ 1978-80; co-chair Central CT State Univ Pres Comm Race Relatations; mem Soc CT Craftsmen, Hartford Reading Is Fundamental Comm; presentations to civic school & adult groups; chmn student-faculty comm Afro-Amer Studies Prog CCSC; mem Council Unitarian Soc of Hartford; Literacy Volunteers of America; CT Coll Personnel Association. **Honors/Awds:** Delta Sigma Theta Scholarship Awd 1954-55; Boston Univ Full-Tuition Scholarship Awd 1954-58; Outstanding Art Ed in CT Awd 1979; implemented art ed maj CCSC; Black Alumni CCSU Serv Awd.

CORNISH, JEANNETTE CARTER
Attorney. **Personal:** Born Sep 17, 1946, Steelton, PA; daughter of Anna Elizabeth Stannard Carter and Ellis Pollard Carter; married Harry L Cornish, Dec 24, 1970; children: Lee Jason, Geoffrey Charles. **Educ:** Howard Univ, BA 1968; Howard Univ Law Sch, JD 1971. **Career:** Office of Gen Counsel USDA, law clerk 1968-71; Newark-Essex Jt Law Reform Proj, attorney 1971-72; Equal Employment Opportunity Comm, attorney 1972-73; BASF Corp (formerly Inmont Corp), sr atty, 1974-. **Orgs:** Mem Amer Bar Assn; mem Natl Bar Assn; mem Amer Corp Counsel Assn; bd mem Paterson YWCA; bd mem Lenni-Lenape Girl Scout Council; trustee, Barnert Hospital, Paterson, NJ. **Honors/Awds:** Scholarship Alpha Kappa Alpha Sor 1964-65; Scholarship Delta Sigma Theta Sor 1964-66. **Business Addr:** Sr Attorney, BASF Corp, 3000 Continental Dr, N, Budd Lake, NJ 07828, (973)426-3241.

CORNWALL, SHIRLEY M.
Dentist. **Personal:** Born Dec 8, 1918, Panama, Panama; married Jerlene; children: Howard, Caral, Cedric, Rupert, Vicount, Francis. **Educ:** BS 1946; MS 1947; DDS 1952. **Career:** Charlotte Nc, intern & residency 1952;DDS prvt practice 1955; real estate bus, 1960. **Orgs:** Mem N MS Med Dental Pharm & Nurses Soc; mem Kappa Alpha Psi Frat; St & Francis Cath Ch. **Honors/Awds:** First black receive MA NC Coll Durham NC. **Business Addr:** 125 W Johnson St, Greenwood, MS 38930.

CORNWELL, W. DON
Business executive. **Personal:** Born Jan 17, 1948, Cushing, OK; son of Lelia and Felton; married Saundra Williams; children: Don, Samantha. **Educ:** Harvard U, MBA 1971; Occidental Coll, AB 1969. **Career:** Corporate Finance, vp; Goldman, Sachs & Co, vp; Hartford Comm Capital Corp Hartford Nat Corp, mgr 1970; Granite Broadcasting Corp, Chairman, CEO, currently. **Orgs:** Trustee Natl Urban League; Zeta Boule. **Honors/Awds:** Nat Merit Achvmt Schlrshp 1965. **Business Addr:** Chief Executive, Granite Broadcasting Corp, 767 3rd Ave, 34th Fl, New York, NY 10017.

CORNWELL, WILLIAM DAVID
Attorney. **Personal:** Born Sep 28, 1960, Washington, DC; son of Shirley Mae Nims Cornwell and Edward Eugene Cornwell, Jr. (deceased). **Educ:** American University-Cairo, Cairo, Egypt, 1981-82; Tufts University, Medford, MA, BA, History, 1982; Georgetown University Law Center, Washington, DC, JD, 1985. **Career:** Whitman & Ransom, New York, NY, associate, 1985-87; National Football League, New York, NY, assistant counsel and director of equal employment, 1987-. **Honors/Awds:** 40 under 40, Crains New York Business Magazine-One of the top 40 executives under 40 in New York City, 1990. **Business Addr:** Assistant Counsel and Director of Equal Employment, National Football League, 410 Park Ave, New York, NY 10022.

CORPREW, CHARLES SUMNER, JR.
Educator (retired). **Personal:** Born Feb 14, 1929, Norfolk, VA; married Bertha Delois Bryant; children: Jovandra Stacey Sanderlin, Charles Sumner III. **Educ:** WV State Coll Inst WV, AB 1951; NY Univ, MA 1963; Kent State Univ Old Dominion Univ, postgraduate study. **Career:** Norfolk City School Bd, adv council vice chmn 1965; Norfolk City Schools, elem principal 1967-69; Educ Assn of Norfolk, pres 1969-70; Norfolk City Schools, asst prin in admin 1969-71, principal secondary 1971-93, personnel coordinator, 1993-94, retired, 1994. **Orgs:** Pres, Norfolk Teachers Assn Federal Credit Union 1978-; classroom tchrs state pres Norfolk City Sch 1960; eastern regional dir Natl Council of Urban Educ Assn NEA 1964-67; educ com chmn Chamber of Commerce, Norfolk 1969; keeper of records & seals Omega Psi Phi Fraternity, 1954-55; mem Phi Delta Kappa Educ Fraternity, 1970; music dept chmn First Baptist Church, Norfolk 1978-80; Optimist Club, Norfolk Chapter, 1992; First Baptist Church Norfolk, trustee, finance comm, 1990-; Retired Teachers Assn-District L, mem; Natl Ed Assn, life mem; Omega Psi Phi Fraternity, Inc, life mem. **Honors/Awds:** Outstanding Contributions in Field of Educ Award, Omega Psi Phi Frat Norfolk VA Lambda Omega Chap 1971; Outstanding Contributions in Field of Educ Award, VA Educ Assn Minority Caucus 1977; NAACP, Thurgood Marshall Service Award, for participation "In The Trenches" of the Civil Rights Struggle, 1994. **Military Serv:** AUS maj 1951-69; Medal of Honor.

CORPREW, WILBERT E.
Educational administrator. **Educ:** Virginia Union Univ, BA, 1964; Crozier Theological Seminary, 1964-65; Rutgers Univ, 1971-72; SUNY-Binghamton, MA, 1990. **Career:** J J Newberry, asst manager, 1965-68; Rutgers Univ, assistant registrar, 1968-73; SUNY-Binghamton, associate registrar, 1974-94; Broome Community Coll, registrar, 1994-. **Orgs:** Alpha Phi Alpha Fraternity; Middle States Assn, Collegiate Registrars and Officers of Admission, vice pres, 1992-94, pres elect, 1996-97, pres, 1997-. American Association of Registrars and Admissions Officers, 1968-; State of Univ of NY Registrars Assn, vice pres, pres; New York State United Teachers, 1974-; United Univ Professions, pres, 1974-94; American Federations of Teachers, 1974-. **Honors/Awds:** SUNY-Binghamton Univ, Award for Excellence in Professional Services, 1985. **Business Addr:** Registrar, Broome Community College, PO Box 1017, Binghamton, NY 13902, (607)778-5527.

CORRIN, MALCOLM L.
Association executive. **Personal:** Born Jun 12, 1924, Sea Bright, NJ; widowed; children: Weldon, Lois, Linda. **Educ:** Morehouse Coll, AB 1950; Univ PA, MBA 1953; Am Coll Of Life Underwriters, 1960; Stanford U, Grad Sch Bus Admn, 1972. **Career:** Bishop Coll bus mgr 1952-54; great lakes mutual life ins co agency dir 1954-56; CT gen life ins co estate & analyst ins sp1 1966-67; Interracial Council For Bus Opportunity NJ Br exec dir natl pres 1974; rutgers grad sch bus adminstrn vis prof. **Orgs:** Mem E Orange Bd Educ 1972, Pres 1974; E Orange Fire Commr 1971-72; mem NAACP; Urban League. **Honors/Awds:** Commendation, Pres Richard Nixon 1970. **Military Serv:** 1st lt 1943-47. **Business Addr:** President & CEO, Interracial Cncl for Bus Oppor, 800 2nd Avenue, Ste 307, New York, NY 10017.

CORTADA, RAFAEL LEON
Educational administrator. **Personal:** Born Feb 12, 1934, New York, NY; son of Yvonne Cortada and Rafael Cortada; married Selonie Head, Jun 24, 1961; children: Celia, Natalia, Rafael. **Educ:** Fordham Coll, AB 1955; Columbia U, MA 1958; Fordham Coll, PhD 1967; Harvard Grad Sch Bus, cert 1974. **Career:** Wayne County Community College, pres, 1990-; Univ of the District of Columbia, pres, 1987-90; Pepperdine Univ, adjunct prof, 1983-87; Community Coll of Baltimore, pres, 1977-82; Metropolitan Community Coll, pres, 1974-77; Hostos Coll, vice-pres 1971-74; Medgar Evers Coll, dean 1970-71; Federal & City Coll, assoc prov 1968-70; Smith Coll, dir 1969-72; US Dept of State, foreign serv 1966-69; Univ of Dayton, asst prof 1964-66; New Rochelle High School, 1957-64, bd of governors 1964-66. **Orgs:** Mem Overseas Liaison Comm 1970; vice pres Wash Task Force On African Affrs 1969; Consult Media Sys Corp 1976; Nat Adv Comm Danforth Foun; comm E Harlem Experimental Coll 1971-75; adv KTCA TV Minneapolis 1976; accr visitor Middle States Assn; ed bd "Current Biblio on African Affrs" 1973; Univ of Guyana, bd of governors, 1971-; American Council on Educ Commission on Minorities in

Higher Educ, 1982-. **Honors/Awds:** Publ 88 articles & reviews In Caribbean, Afro-Amer, Latin Amer; history publ ''Black Studies, An Urban & Comparative Curriculum'' 1974. **Military Serv:** AUS 1st lt 1955-57. **Business Addr:** President, Wayne County Community College, 801 W Fort St, Detroit, MI 48226.

CORTEZ, JAYNE

Poet. **Personal:** Born May 10, 1936, Arizona; married Melvin Edwards, 1975; children: Denardo Coleman. **Career:** Poet and lecturer. **Orgs:** Organization of Women Writers of Africa; Poetry Society of American; Pen American Center. **Honors/Awds:** Rockefeller Foundation grant, 1970; Creative Artists Public Service poetry award, New York State Council on the Arts, 1973, 1981; National Endowment for the Arts fellowship in creative writing, 1979-80, 1986; New York Foundation for the Arts award, 1987; American Book Award, 1980. **Business Addr:** c/o Bola Press, PO Box 96, Village Station, New York, NY 10014.

CORTOR, ELDZIER

Painter, printmaker. **Personal:** Born Jan 10, 1916, Richmond, VA. **Educ:** Attended, Art Inst of Chicago, Inst of Design, Columbia Univ. **Career:** Taught at Centre D'Art, Port-au-Prince & Pratt Inst; various exhibitions, Art Inst of Chicago, Metro Museum of Art, Martha Jackson Gallery, Howard Univ, Carnegie Inst, Assoc Amer Artists, The Studio Museum of Harlem, Museum of Nat Cntr of Afro-Amer Artists Boston. **Orgs:** Mem Soc Amer Graphic Artists. **Honors/Awds:** Carnegie Awd; Bertha Aberle Florsheim Awd, William H Bartels Awd; Amer Negro Exposition Awd; Rosenwald Fellowship 1944-45; Guggenheim Fellowship 1950. **Business Addr:** 35 Montgomery St, New York, NY 10002.

CORYATT, QUENTIN JOHN

Professional football player. **Personal:** Born Aug 1, 1970, St Croix, Virgin Islands of the United States. **Educ:** Texas A&M. **Career:** Indianapolis Colts, linebacker, 1992-. **Business Addr:** Professional Football Player, Indianapolis Colts, PO Box 535000, Indianapolis, IN 46253, (317)297-2658.

COSBY, CAMILLE OLIVIA HANKS

Actress, Philanthropist. **Personal:** Born 1945, Washington, DC; daughter of Guy and Catherine Hanks; married William Henry Cosby, 1964; children: Erika, Erin, Ennis (deceased), Ensa, Evin. **Educ:** Univ of Maryland, psychology, attended; Amherst College, MA, education, 1980, PhD, education, 1993. **Career:** Cosby Company, vice pres; speaker; producer, Broadway Play, Having Our Say, 1995. **Honors/Awds:** Honorary membership, Delta Sigma Theta sorority; commencement speaker, Howard Univ, 1987, Spelman College, 1989; has (with spouse, Bill Cosby) provided financial support to schools and institutions, including Spelman College, Fisk Univ, Meharry and Bethune-Cookman Colleges, and Harlem Hospital Center for Women and Children; has worked (with Judith Rutherford James) on a Winnie Mandela film project; serves on corporate boards; appeared on PBS-TV's MacNeil-Lehrer News Hour; Natl Coalition of 100 Black Women, Candace Award, 1992; Tony Award Nomination, Having Our Say: The Delany Sisters' First 100 Years. **Business Addr:** c/o The Cosby Show, attn: Wayne, Astoria Studios, 34-12 36th St, Astoria, NY 11106.

COSBY, WILLIAM HENRY

Entertainer, comedian, actor. **Personal:** Born Jul 12, 1937, Germantown, PA; son of Anna C and William Henry Cosby; married Camille Hanks Cosby, Jan 25, 1964; children: Erika, Erinn, Ennis (deceased), Ensa, Evin. **Educ:** Temple Univ, BA; Univ of MA, MA, EdD. **Career:** Comedian, appearing in numerous night clubs; guest appearances on TV shows: The Electric Co, 1972, Capt Kangaroo, co-star, I Spy, 1965-68, The Bill Cosby Show, 1969, 1972-73; records: Revenge, To Russell, My Brother, With Whom I Slept, Top Secret, 200 MPH, Why Is There Air?, Wonderfulness, It's True, It's True, Bill Cosby Is a Very Funny Fellow, Right, I Started Out as a Child, and numerous others; has appeared on several TV commercials; film: Hickey and Boggs, Man and Boy, 1972, Uptown Saturday Night, 1974, Let's Do It Again, 1975, Mother Jugs and Speed, 1976, Aesop's Fables, A Piece of the Action, 1977, California Suite, 1978, Devil and Max Devlin, 1979, Leonard Part VI, 1987, Ghost Dad, 1990; star and producer, The Cosby Show, 1984-92; You Bet Your Life, 1992; The Cosby Mysteries, 1995; Cosby, 1996-; Kids Say The Darnedest Things, 1997. **Orgs:** Pres, Rhythm and Blues Hall of Fame, 1968-; bd dirs & natl chmn Sickle Cell Foundation; United Negro College Fund; NAACP life mem; Operation PUSH. **Honors/Awds:** 8 Grammy Awards; 4 Emmy Awards; NAACP Image Award; author: The Wit and the Wisdom of Fat Albert 1973, Bill Cosby's Personal Guide to Power Tennis, Academy of TV, Arts & Sciences, Hall of Fame, 1992. **Special Achievements:** Author: Fatherhood, 1986; Time Flies, 1987, Love and Marriage, 1989, Childhood, 1991, Little Bill Books for Beginning Readers, 1997. **Military Serv:** USNR 1956-60. **Business Addr:** PO Box 4049, Santa Monica, CA 90404.

COSE, ELLIS

Journalist, author. **Personal:** Born Feb 20, 1951, Chicago, IL; married Lee Llambelis. **Educ:** Univ of IL Chicago, BA Psych 1972; George Washington Univ, MA Sci Tech & Publ Policy 1978. **Career:** Chicago Sun-Times, columnist/reporter/editor 1970-77; Joint Center for Polit Studies Washington, sr fellow/dir energy policy studies 1977-79; Detroit Free Press, edit writer/columnist 1979-81; Natl Acad Scis, resident fellow 1981-82; USA Today, spec writer 1982-83; Inst Journalism Education, pres, 1983-86; Newsweek Magazine, contributing editor, essayist, 1993-; Gannett Ctr for Media Studies, Columbia Univ, 1987; Time Magazine, contributing editor, essayist, 1989-90; New York Daily News, editorial bd chairman, 1991-93. **Orgs:** Natl Assn of Black Journalists; Env Adv Comm, Dept of Energy, 1978-79 Natl Urban League Energy Proj 1979-80. **Honors/Awds:** Author, ''Energy and Equity, Some Social Concerns'' 1978; ''Energy and the Urban Crises'' 1978; The Rage of a Privileged Class, 1993; named Outstanding Young Citizen of Chicago Jaycees 1977; 1st Place Newswriting Award, IL UPI, 1973; Stick-o-Type Award, Chicago Newspaper, Guild, 1975; Best Polit Reporting, Lincoln Univ Natl Unity Award 1975, 1977; Decentralizing Energy Decisions: The Rebirth of Community Power, 1983; The Press, 1988; A Nation of Strangers, 1992; A Man's World, 1995; Fellowships: The Ford Foundation; Andrew Mellon Foundation; Rockerfeller Foundation Grant; Aspen Institute for Humanistic Studies; Myers Ctr Award, Human Rights in North America; numerous others. **Business Addr:** Contributing Editor/Essayist, Newsweek Magazine, 251 W 57th St, New York, NY 10019.

COSHBURN, HENRY S., JR.

Oil company executive. **Personal:** Born Mar 15, 1936, NYC, NY; son of Dorothy Coshburn and Henry Coshburn; married Veanna G Ferguson; children: Williams S Coshburn. **Educ:** Univ of PA, BS 1957; Columbia Univ, MS 1964. **Career:** US Army Signal Corps, chem engr 1958-60; Yardney Elec Corp, sales engr 1960-63; Mobil Oil, sr engr 1964-68; Esso Eastern, mktg analyst 1968-71; Exxon Intl Co, acct exec 1973-82; First Natl Crude Oil, vice pres. **Orgs:** Mem Alpha Phi Alpha, Alpha Chi Sigma, Amer Inst of Engrs, Amer Electrochem Soc, ACS, Amer Soc Lub Engrs, Princeton Club; NY Admission Rep Univ PA; visiting prof mktg Southern Univ Bethune Cookman Coll, Wilberforce Univ, Miles Coll, Norfolk St Coll; instr ICBO Mktg mem Harlem Hosp Bd; pres Harlem Civ Imp Counc; vice pres Penn/Princeton Club NYC; bd dirs Univ of PA Alumni Assn; patents hardware greases. **Honors/Awds:** Cert Recog Amer Inst Chem Engr NY Sect 1970; Cert Apprec Urban League 1971-74; Vol Serv Award ICBO 1971-74; Citation Univ PA 1974; Alumni Award of Merit Univ of PA. **Business Addr:** Vice President, First Natl Crude Oil, 148 East Ave, Norwalk, CT 06851.

COSTA, ANNIE BELL HARRIS

Journalist. **Personal:** Born Oct 24, 1943, New Madrid, MO; married Ernest Antone Costa, Mar 4, 1972; children: Kara Ann, Todd Bernard. **Educ:** Michigan State University, (cum laude) BA, Journalism, 1978; University of California, Berkeley/ Institute for Journalism Educations Minority Reporting Program, 1985. **Career:** Michigan Dept of Corrections, public information specialist, 1978-80; Michigan Employment Security Commission, publications editor, 1980-85, 1987-91; Lansing State Journal, staff writer/reporter, 1985-87; Michigan Office of Community Corrections, public information officer, 1991-. **Orgs:** Institute for Journalism Education Alumni Assn; Natl Assn of Black Journalists; Natl Assn of Govt Communicators. **Honors/Awds:** Selected for the University of California, Journalism Education Minority Reporting Program at Berkeley, 1985. **Special Achievements:** Intl Assn of Business Communicators, Detroit chptr, External Newsletter, Honorable Mention, 1990; Torch Drive United Fund, Award of Merit Special Publication, 1981. **Home Addr:** 3781 W Outer Drive, Detroit, MI 48221. **Business Addr:** Public Information Officer, Michigan Officer of Community Corrections, PO Box 30003, Grandview Plaza, Lansing, MI 48909, (517)373-9527.

COSTEN, JAMES H.

Educational administrator. **Career:** Interdenominational Theological Ctr, pres, currently. **Orgs:** Assn of Theological Schools, pres, currently. **Business Addr:** President, Interdenominational Theological Ctr, 671 Beckwith St, SW, Atlanta, GA 30314, (404)527-7702.

COSTEN, MELVA WILSON

Theological educator. **Personal:** Born May 29, 1933, Due West, SC; daughter of Azzie Lee Ellis Wilson (deceased) and John Theodore Wilson Sr (deceased); married James Hutten Costen, May 24, 1953; children: James, Jr., Craig Lamont, Cheryl Costen Clay. **Educ:** Harbison Jr Coll, Irmo SC, 1947-50; Johnson C Smith Univ, Charlotte NC, AB Educ 1950-52; Univ of North Carolina, Chapel Hill NC MAT Music 1961-64; Georgia State Univ, Atlanta GA, PhD Curriculm and Instruction/Music 1973-78. **Career:** Mecklenburg County School, Charlotte NC, elementary teacher, 1952-55; Edgecombe County, Rocky Mount Nashville NC, elementay teacher, 1956-57; Nash County, Nashville NC, elementary and music teacher 1959-65; Atlanta Public Schools Atlanta GA, intinerant music teacher 1965-73; Interdenominational Theological, Atlanta GA, Helmar Emil Nielsen Professor of Worship and Music, 1973-. **Orgs:** Regional director, Natl Assn of Negro Musicians 1973-75; co-chair, choral div, District V Georgia Music Educators Assoc 1981-82; mem of bd Presbyterian Assn of Musicians 1982-86; chairperson, Presbyterian Church Hymnal Committee 1984-1990; mem of bd Liturgical Conference 1985-91; mem of bd Mid-Atlanta Unit, Cancer Society of America, 1985-87; artistic dir, Atlanta Olympics, 1996-99; Atlanta University Ctr Choruses, 1996. **Honors/Awds:** Conducted 500-voice elementary chorus, Music Educators Natl Conference 1970; Teacher of the Year, Slater School, Atlanta Ga, 1973; Teacher of the Year, Interdenominational Theological Center, 1975; Golden Dove Award, Kappa Omega Chapter, Alpha Kappa Alpha Sorority 1981; conducted 800-voice adult choir, Reuniting Assembly of Presbyterian Church 1983; Two Doctor of Humane Letters, Erskine Coll, Due West SC, 1987 and Wilson College, Chambersburg PA; chairperson, Presbyterian Hymnal Committee, 1985-90. **Special Achievements:** Published book African-American Christian Worship, Nashville, Abingdon press, 1993. **Home Addr:** 225 East Court Dr, SW, Atlanta, GA 30331. **Business Addr:** Helmar Emil Nielson Professor of Worship & Music, Interdenominational Theologicat Ctr, Music/Worship Office, 700 Martin Luther King Jr Dr, SW, Atlanta, GA 30311.

COSTON, BESSIE RUTH

Association executive (retired). **Personal:** Born Nov 29, 1916, Jackson, GA; daughter of Nannie J Harkness Bivins (deceased) and Elbert Bivins (deceased); married Floyd Thomas (died 1997); children: Lynn Ruth Phillips. **Educ:** Wilberforce U, BS 1939; OH State U, MA in Soc Adm 1941; Youngstown U, Grad Study; Westminster Coll, Grad Study. **Career:** Phyllis Wheatley YWCA Indianapolis, IN, dir older girls activities 1941-44; Neighbor House Columbus, OH, prog dir 1944-46; Bureau of Employment Sec Youngstown, OH, interviewer/cnslr/supr 1947-63; YWCA, prog dir 1963-68, asst exec dir 1968-70, exec dir 1970-74. **Orgs:** Commr Youngstown Metro Housing Bd 1974-78; mem Advisory Council Soc Serv 1972-74; mem/sec bd Doris Burdman Homes 1973-76; natl pres Iota Phi Lambda Sor Inc 1969-73, natl 1st vice 1968-69, natl 2nd vice 1966-68, northern regional dir 1954-58; pres/vp/sec/dean of pledges Alpha Nu Chap Iota Phi Lambda Sor Inc 1949-57; mem Acad Certified Social Workers 1972-77, 1989-; mem Natl Assn Social Workers 1972-77, 1989-; White House Conf Children Wash, DC 1970; White House Conf on Aging 1971; hon mem Gamma Phi Chap Delta Kappa Gamma; life mem NAACP; mem/former state convenor Natl Council of Negro Women; mem Youngstown Area Urban League; mem McGuffey Centre; mem St Andrew's AME Ch; mem American Assn of Retired Persons, 1985-; mem Natl Council of Senior Citizens 1985-; mem Advisory Bd, Retired VolunteServ, 1985-88; Iota Phi Lambda Sorority, Inc; Alpha Nu Chapter; League of Women Voters; National Association of Social Workers; Academy of Certified Social Workers; honorary bd mem, YWCA; National Council of Negro Women Inc; National, State & Greater Youngstown Association of Parliamentarians; NAACP; National Urban League, the McGuffey Center. **Honors/Awds:** Honorable Mention Intl Assn Personnel Employment Sec Chicago 1963; Achievement Award Natl Bus & Prof Women 1971; Mayors Proclamation City of Youngstown 1973; Civic Award Jr Civic League 1970; Merit Award WKBN Radio 1963; Outstanding Serv Award McGuffey Centre 1963; Woman of the Yr Alpha Nu Chap Iota Phi Lambda 1963; Mother of the Yr W Fed YMCA 1963; This Is Your Life Natl Council of Negro Women 1958; Recognition Luncheon, Natl Council of Negro Women, 1995; Mahoning County Commissioners, Proclamations; The Congress of the United States; Congressman James A Traficant, Jr, Ohio, Official Proclamation. **Home Addr:** 1940 McClure Ave, Youngstown, OH 44505.

COTHARN, PRESTON SIGMUNDE, SR.

Retired government official. **Personal:** Born Jan 29, 1925, E St Louis, IL; son of Lula Whitenhill Cotharn (deceased) and Robert Provina Cotharn (deceased); married Berteal Whitehead, 1964 (deceased); children: Preston Jr, Cynthia, Titus, Christopher. **Educ:** Lincoln U, BS 1946; Gov State U, MA 1973; DePaul U, MEd 1975; Univ Sarasota, EdD 1977; 9 acad degrees; law degree; hon DD Degree; ordained minister 1978. **Career:** Illinois Dept of Labor, Bureau of Employment Security, mgr, interstate benefits, exec IV, exec III, office mgr II, office mgr I, claims supervisor, adjudication supervisor, adjudicator, supervising claims examiner; IL Dept Labor-cons, free lance mgmt; Fuller Elem Sch, tchr; Grant Elem Sch, tchr; ISTSB HS Div; asst asst dep warden; Armour & Co, correction supr admin assst to night supt; Armour & Co, toured US & abroad. **Orgs:** Fisk Jubilee Singers with Mrs James A Myers. **Honors/Awds:** Recipient voice tng, Dr O Anderson Fuller & Frank Laforge. **Home Addr:** 11601 S Aberdeen, Chicago, IL 60643.

COTHORN, MARGUERITE ESTERS

Social worker (retired). **Personal:** Born Dec 23, 1909, Albia, IA; daughter of Nellie Esters and Arthur Esters; divorced; children: John A. **Educ:** Drake Univ, Des Moines IA, BA 1930; Drake Univ, MA 1932; Univ of IA School of Social Work, MSW 1954. **Career:** Polk Co Juvenile Ct, Des Moines, probation officer 1930; Baltimore Emergency Relief, caseworker 1933-41; Willkie Hse (Settlement & Rockford IL), dir 1941-52; VA Hosp Knoxville IA, caseworker (psych) 1954-56; Des Moines United Way, planning div 1956-65, dir of planning div 1965-73; 1965-73; United Way Central Ins, retired social worker ACSW. **Orgs:** Mem (ACSW) Natl Assn, Social Workers Charter; mem, Natl Conf Social Workers; Mem, NAACP, broadlawns med center psychiatric advisory com, 1975-; various offices, Delta Sigma Theta Sorority 1927-; camp vistor Amer Camping Assn, 1957-60; various capacities League of Women Voters, 1983-. **Honors/Awds:** Plaque for leadership Black Comm 1973; Alice Whipple Award, Outstanding Serv in Health & Welfare S IA Central Federation of Labor (AFL-CIO); Key to City Mayor & Voter Bureau 1973; Distinguished alumni Drake Univ, 1974; Club Women's Comm Award PL Culture Club 1974; Distinguished serv IA Civil Rights Comm 1983; elected IA Women's Hall of Fame 1986; Governor's Volunteer Award, 1990. **Home Addr:** 48211 Bayshore Dr, Belleville, MI 48111.

COTMAN, HENRY EARL
Physician. **Personal:** Born Apr 13, 1943, Archer, FL; married Jacqueline Nickson. **Educ:** FL A&M U, BA 1965; Univ FL; Harvard Peter Bent Brigham Hosp, externships; MD 1970. **Career:** Gulf Coast Oncology Center, pvt prac; Univ AZ Hlth Div Sci Ctr Div Radiation Oncology, asst prof 1975-77; Wm Beaumont Army Hosp Med Ctr Div Radiation Oncology, chf 1975; Univ of MN, resd 1971-74; Union Meml Hosp, med internship 1970-71; MI State U, asso clinical prof. **Orgs:** Mem Am Coll of Radiology; Am Soc of Therapeutic Radiology; Nat Med Assn; Ingham Co Med Soc; mem Alpha Phi Alpha Frat Inc; clinical flw Am Cancer Soc 1971-74; chf resd Radiation Oncology 1974. **Honors/Awds:** One of the first blacks to grad Univ of FL Coll of Med; publ "The Usage of The Bipedal Lymphogram As A Guide During Laparotomy in Hodgkin's & Non-Hodgkin's Lymphomas" ACTA Radiologica; "Combination Radiotherapy & Surger in the Mgmt of Squamous Carcinoma of the Head & Neck" Radiology Soc meeting 1976. **Military Serv:** Med Corp maj 1975. **Business Addr:** Gulf Coast Oncology Center, 701 Sixth St South, St Petersburg, FL 33701.

COTMAN, IVAN LOUIS
State government official. **Personal:** Born Apr 4, 1940, Detroit, MI; son of Marguerite Caine Cotman and Louis Richard Cotman; married Jeanetta Hawkins; children: Ivan Louis, Jr, Arthur Robert, Amir Charles. **Educ:** KY State U, BA English, Soc Sci 1958-62; Atlanta U, MA Social Work 1962-64; Univ of MI, Schl Public Hlth Medical Care Org 1969-70; Univ Of Manchester (England), Cerifiticate in New Town Planning 1972; Wayne State Univ, EdD Curriculum & Admin 1975; Univ Oklahoma, Advanced Studies 1983; Harvard University JFK School of Government. **Career:** Detroit Bd of Educ, schl social worker 1964-69; United Co Serv Detroit, agcy prog consul/assist budget dir 1969-72; Detroit Bd of Education, electee, 1971-73; New Detroit Inc, dir of employment 1972-73; MI Dept of Ed Disability Deter Serv, area admin 1973-79; MI Dept of Education, assoc superintendent 1979-, intern, registered lobbyist, 1989-, direct services, deputy superintendent, 1992-97; Cotman & Associates, CEO, 1997-. **Orgs:** Mem Acad of Certif Social Workers, Natl Assoc of Disablility Exams, Natl Assoc of Social Workers, Natl Rehab Assn, MI Civil Serv Oral Appraisal Bd, MI Occupational Info Statutory Comm; Past Natl Vice Pres Alpha Phi Alpha Frat, Inc; past bd mem United Neighborhood Ctr of Amer; life mem NAACP; adjunct prof Michigan State Univ; State Credit Union Supervisor Committee; Past board of governors University of Chicago, Meadville/Lombard Theological School. **Honors/Awds:** Resolution of Tribute MI Senate 1973; Dist Alumni KY State Univ 1975; Dist Citizen MI House of Rep 1977-80; Regional Commissioner's Citation Social Sec Adminstration 1979; Order of KY Colonels; board of directors, United Community Service, 32 Degree Prince Hall Mason; Disting Alumni Awd KY State Univ, Natl Assoc for Equal Oppor in Higher Educ; cited for Leadership by US Sec of Educ; 6 week exec placement in Washington based Commn on Excellence, U.S. Dept of Education; articles on Leadership published in MI Sch Bd Journal, Waterloo (Ontario) Press, Detroit News, Michigan Chronicle, Congressional Record; Board of Governors, Meadville Lombard Theology School (Univ of Chicago); Resolution of Merit, MI House, 1989. Israel Study Mission, 1994. **Business Addr:** Cotman & Associates, 20141 McIntyre, Detroit, MI 48219.

COTTON, ALBERT E.
Director. **Personal:** Born Oct 6, 1939; married Kathleen; children: Christopher, Eric B. **Educ:** San Francisco State University, BA 1970, MBA 1977. **Career:** Shaklee Corp, dir benefits & compensation 1979-; Shaklee Corp, dir ind relations 1978-79; Shaklee Corp, personnel mgr 1975-78; Hunt Wesson Corp, personnel mgr 1974; City of Richmond CA, CETA dir 1972-74; Schlage Lock Corp, mfg supr 1964-71. **Orgs:** Bd of dir N CA Ind Relations Council 1974-; mem Am Soc of Personnel Adminstr 1974-; mem Am Compensation Assn 1979; Beta Gamma Sigma Nat Chap 1969. **Honors/Awds:** Scholarship Award, No CA Ind Relations Council 1970. **Business Addr:** Director of Benefits & Compensation, Shaklee Corp, 444 Market St, San Francisco, CA 94111.

COTTON, GARNER
Civil engineer. **Personal:** Born Nov 10, 1923, Chicago, IL; son of Pearl Little Cotton and Deleon Cotton (deceased); children: Garner T, Atry S. **Educ:** Lincoln Univ, BS, bldg engineering, 1943; Drexel Univ, civil engineering, 1951; Edison Technical School, basic electronics, 1960; Temple Univ, naval architecture and metallurgy, 1961. **Career:** General Industries Engineers, structural designer and checker, 1947-54; City of Philadelphia, Water Dept, structural designer and checker, 1954-56; United Engineers and Construction Co, 1956-58; Frederick Massiah Concrete Contractor, asst construction superintendent, 1958-59; Boeing Aircraft Co, facilities and structural engineer, 1959-60; United Engineers and Construction Co, 1960-62; New York Shipbuilding Corp, Scientific Group, structural engineer, 1962-65; Allstate Engineer & Development Co, structural engineer, 1965-67; School District of Philadelphia, staff construction engineer & structural designer, 1967-88; G Cotton Engineering Associates Inc, founder, 1976-. **Orgs:** American Society of Civil Engineers; Natl Society of Prof Engineers; Assn of School Administrators; American Arbitration Assn. **Honors/Awds:** Citizen Award of the Year, New Jersey Soc of Professional Engineers 1977; Citizen Award, Lawnside Democratic Club 1970; Registered Professional Civil Engineer New Jersey; Registered Professional Planner New Jersey; Fellow, Amer Soc of Civil Engineers 1988; Registered Professor Civil Engineer, PA; Honarary Doctor of Humane Letters, Lincoln University, 1997. **Home Addr:** 505 N Warwick Rd, Lawnside, NJ 08045.

COTTON, JAMES
Professional basketball player. **Personal:** Born Dec 14, 1975. **Educ:** Long Beach State. **Career:** Seattle SuperSonics, guard, 1997-. **Business Addr:** Professional Basketball Player, Seattle SuperSonics, PO Box 900911, Seattle, WA 98109, (206)281-5850.

COTTON, KENYON (KENYON)
Professional football player. **Personal:** Born Feb 23, 1974, Bossier City, LA. **Educ:** Southwestern Louisiana, attended. **Career:** Baltimore Ravens, running back, 1997-. **Business Addr:** Professional Football Player, Baltimore Ravens, 11001 Owings Mills Blvd, Owings Mills, MD 21117, (410)654-6200.

COTTRELL, COMER J.
Business executive. **Personal:** Born Dec 7, 1931, Mobile, AL; married Isabell Pauloing; children: Renee, Comer III, Aaron. **Educ:** Univ of Detroit, 1952. **Career:** Sears Roebuck, sales mgr, 1964-69; Pro-Line Corp, chmn, pres, 1970-; African Heritage Network, partner; Universal Packaging Co, co-owner. **Orgs:** Dir Republic Bank, Southwest Dallas Hosp Corp, Western Pacific Indust, Dallas Financial Corp, Pro-Ball Inc; Sigma Pi Phi Boule; Texas Rangers Baseball Inc, partner. **Honors/Awds:** Bishop College, Doctor of Laws; Northwood University, Doctor of Laws; City University of Los Angeles, Doctor of Laws. **Business Addr:** Chairman/CEO, Pro-Line Corp., 2121 Panoramic Circle, Dallas, TX 75212.

COTTROL, ROBERT JAMES
Educator. **Personal:** Born Jan 18, 1949, New York, NY; son of Jewel Gassaway Cottrol and Robert W Cottrol; married Susan Lemmerbrock Cottrol, Jun 20, 1987; children: John Marshall II. **Educ:** Yale Univ, BA 1971, PhD 1978; Georgetown Univ Law Ctr, JD 1984. **Career:** CT Coll, instructor 1974-77; Emory Univ, asst prof 1977-79; Georgetown Univ, lecturer 1979-84; Boston Coll Law School, asst prof of law 1984-87, assoc prof of law, 1987-90; Rutgers School of Law, Camden, NJ, assoc prof, 1990-. **Orgs:** Consult GA Commn on the Humanities 1978-79; mem Amer Historical Assoc 1974-, Amer Soc for Legal History 1982-, Amer Bar Assoc 1985-; mem Law and Society Assoc 1985-. **Honors/Awds:** Author The Afro Yankees, Providence's Black Community in the Antebellum Era publ by Greenwood Press 1982; Outstanding Academic Book, Choice, 1983. **Military Serv:** AUS (Reserve) capt 1971-81; USAFR capt 1981-87, major 1987-; Air Force Commendation Medal, Joint Service Commendation Medal. **Business Addr:** Professor, Rutgers School of Law, Fifth and Penn Sts, Camden, NJ 08102.

COUCH, JAMES W.
Community health ctr executive. **Personal:** Born Oct 15, 1934, Ingram Branch, WV; son of Richard Couch & Daisy Hall-Couch; married Eileen Couch, Aug 22, 1981; children: Kevin Turney, Jamir Couch, Sasha Couch. **Educ:** State University of New York at Stoneybrook, MA. **Career:** Florence High School Dept, chair, teacher of social studies, 1963-69; Patterson Task Force, executive director, 1969-70; Nassau Economic Opportunity Comm, executive director, 1970-74; Long Island Sickle Cell Corp, executive director, 1974-88; Suffolk County, assistant deputy executive, 1988-92. **Orgs:** GAPHC, pres-elect, 1998-99, chmn of legislative comm, 1997-; NACHC, chmn of the bd, 1996-97; Suffolk Cty Gov't, founder/organizer, 1988-92; Suffolk Cty Caucus of Black Democrats, chmn, 1974-92; Black Health Advocates Network, chmn, 1978-88; Vision 2020, mem, 1992-; The Atlanta Project, mem, 1992-. **Honors/Awds:** NACHC, Chmn Achievement Award, 1997; Quality of Life Health Svcs, CHC Programs Award, 1997; State of Georgia, Comm Svc Award, 1996; People of Colour, Achievement Award, 1994; Rev MLK Jr Holiday Commission, Humanitarian Award, 1989. **Special Achievements:** Published work in Atlanta Business Chronicle, 1995; CNN Talk Back Live, 1995, 1996; gave keynote addresss in Montgomery, AL, 1996; appeared before Congressional Black Caucus, 1997; keynote address at Martin Luther King Jr Anniversary, 1997. **Military Serv:** Air Force, airman 1st class, 1953-57. **Business Addr:** Senior VP/COO, West End Medical Ctrs Inc, 34 Peachtree St NW, 1 Park Tower Bldg, Ste 780, Atlanta, GA 30303, (404)524-6798.

COUCH, LUDIE
Food company executive. **Personal:** Born Apr 19, 1918, Monticello, GA; son of Hattie Couch and Tommie Couch; married Dorothy Couch, Sep 8, 1941 (deceased). **Educ:** State Teachers & Agriculture College. **Career:** Couch's Country Style Sausage, Inc, president, currently. **Honors/Awds:** Crain's Cleveland Business, Small Business Award, 1992; State of Ohio, Equal Opportunity Center Entrepreneur of the Year, 1992. **Business Addr:** President, Couch's Country Style Sausage Inc, 4750 Osborn Rd, Garfield Heights, OH 44128, (216)587-2333.

COUCHE, ROBERT
Educational administrator (retired). **Personal:** Born Dec 18, 1918, Gainesville, GA; married Ruby Sherman. **Educ:** GA State Coll, attended 1938-41; NYU, BS 1952; NYU, MA 1953; Queens Coll, professional cert in couns 1965; St John's U, attended 1967-69; NY State Secondary Sch, Pring Cert 1969. **Career:** Prospect Hts High Sch Brooklyn, principal 1973-79; Andrew Jackson High Sch Queens, asst principal 1969-73; Guidance Serv Big Sister's Educ Family Serv, dir counseling 1967-69; Out-of-Sch Youths Bd of Educ NYC, guidance counselor 1963-64; Newtown High Sch & Springfield Gardens High Sch, guidance counselor 1962-69; NYC, tchr 1952-62. **Orgs:** Pres Distributive Educ Assn 1958-62; mem Nat Assn of Secondary Sch Prin 7 yrs; mem High Sch Prin Assn New York City 6 yrs; mem numerous educ assns for prins & couns; co-founder Springfield Gardens Comm Day Care Center Springfield Gardens NY; founder & bd chmn Springfield Gardens St Albans Sr Citizens Center 1973-; various offices NAACP brs; mem various dem coms; bd mem & chmn exec com Allied Fed Savings & Loan Assn Jamaica NY; youth adv & bd mem Nat Conf of Christians & Jews; orgn mem & treas New Dimensions Day Care Center; mem St John's Univ Chpt; Phi Delta Kappa Frat; bd of dirs, exec comm, publications chair, Carver Savings and Loan Bank, until 1994. **Honors/Awds:** Pub numerous educ articles 1961-68; various educ awards sororities clubs & assns; various comm serv awards frats & chs; Martin Luther King Jr Award, Wilmington DE Martin Luther King Jr Com; One-In-A-Million Award, Citizens of Queens & Nassau Co NY; Dedicated Serv Award, NY Assn of Black Educators; Brotherhood Award & Cert of Recognition, Nat Conf of Christians & Jews; Purple Heart Inf 1945. **Military Serv:** Inf 1st lt 1941-46.

COUCHE, RUBY S.
Educator. **Personal:** Born Dec 10, 1919, Whigham, GA; married Robert Couche. **Educ:** Savannah State Coll, BS 1941; Hunter Coll, MA 1952; Long Island Univ, Hofstra, Puerto Rico Univ, Plattsburg Univ, Pottsdam Univ, Adv Study; York College City of New York, computers in business, certificate, 1989. **Career:** Todd Grant High School, Darien GA, teacher 1941-43; New York City School Dist 28, teacher 1950-59, school comm coord 1959-68, asst principal 1968-71, dep to supt 1971-72, curriculum adm comm 1972-77 (retired); Western IL Univ, adjunct prof 1980. **Orgs:** Mem Assoc of Suprv & Curriculum Devel 1972-; mem chmn, 3rd vp, 2nd vp, concert chmn Jamaica Comm Concert Assoc; mem bd of dirs S Queens Choral Assoc; mem bd dirs Merrick-Queens Co Comm Ctr; mem Ed Comm Queens Reg Natl Conf Christians & Jews; mem Steering & Coord Comm, SE Queens Emancipation Proclamation Centennial Auth; mem Phi Delta Kappa, Beta Omicron Chapt, Jamaica Br NAACP, Tri-Comm Council, St Albans Comm Council, Abyssania Bapt Church, Protestant Teachers Assoc of NYC, School-Comm Coord Assoc, 103rd Police Precinct Youth Council, Urban League, Adm & Suprv Assoc NYC, Amer Women in Ed, Queensboro Teacher Assoc, Natl School Publ Rel Assoc; ldrshp conf Civil Rts; chtr mem Phi Delta Kappa, Beta Omicron Chapt; tour Madrid, Paris, London, Rone1978 and 1986; study tour West Africa 1980; l pres Phi Delta Kappa 1981-85; mem 1st Pres Ch; vp Laurelton Springfld Day Care Ctr; coord Human Rel Inst Natl Body; Phi Delta Kappa, Perpetual Scholarship Foundation, president, 1987; 1st Presbyterian Church of Springfield Gardens, 1984-, organizer of Presbyterian Women of Springfield Gardens, 1987; Laurelton Springfield Comm Day Care Center, bd of dirs, 1979-. **Honors/Awds:** Supreme 2nd Anti-Basileus Natl Acheivement Awd 1969-; Nom for Supreme Basileus of Natl Sor of Phi Delta Kappa 1977-81; Participant IDEA Fellows Prog Kettering Found; NAACP Humanitarian Awd 1986; PTA Abyssian Baptist Church Christian Family, Certificate of Recognition, 1985; Jamaica Branch NAACP Humanitarian Award, 1988; AOIP Hall of Fame Community Building Award, 1988; Phi Delta Kappa, Beta Omicron Chapter, Certificate of Appreciation, 1989; AOIP Trustee, Certificate of Recognition, 1990; NYS Assembly for Community Service, Citation, 1996; Phi Delta Kappa Frat, Hofstra Univ Chap, Hempsted, NY, Educator of the Year Award, 1997. **Home Addr:** 178-02 136th Ave, Jamaica, NY 11434.

COULON, BURNEL ELTON
Educator (retired). **Personal:** Born Jul 6, 1929, New Orleans, LA; married Sylvia; children: Michele, Angela, Burnel II, Sylvia II. **Educ:** Tuskegee Inst, BS 1953; NC A&T State U, MS 1960; Bulter U/Ball State U/IN U, grad work. **Career:** Indianapolis Public Schools, dean of students 1979-, chmn industrial arts 1976-79; Shortridge Press & Indianapolis Public Schools, instr & mgr 1964-76; Paramount Graphics, pres 1970; Louisville Public Schools, instructor graphic arts 1961-64; MS Valley State Univ, dir public relations 1953-60. **Orgs:** Bd of dirs MS State Negro Fair 1957-59; pres Indianapolis Fedn of Tchrs

1973-76; sec Indianapolis Chap Phi Delta Kappa 1978-79; sec Marion Co Graphic Arts Assn 1968-70; first v grand basileus Omega Psi Phi Frat 1978-79; grand basileus Omega Psi Phi Frat 1979-82. **Honors/Awds:** Honor grad, Tuskegee Inst 1953; Outstanding Grad Alumnus, NC A&T 1975; Omega Man of the yr, 10th Dist Omega Psi Phi Frat 1976; Cert of Merit, Mayor New Orleans 1980.

COUNTEE, THOMAS HILAIRE, JR.
Business executive, attorney (retired), state official (retired). **Personal:** Born Aug 7, 1939, Washington, DC; son of Arrieanna C T Countee and Thomas H Countee Sr; divorced; children: Mekela I J. **Educ:** Amer Univ, Washington, DC, BA, 1963; Georgetown Univ Law Center, JD, 1967; Harvard Business School, MBA, 1971. **Career:** Countee, Countee & Assoc, Inc, chmn, CEO, 1988-; chief exec officer, 1978-88; MD, Natl Capital Park & Planning Commn, gen counsel, 1977-78; Office of Mat & Budget, legislative counsel; exec offce of pres, 1975-76; MODEDCO Inv Co, pres, 1971-75; Howard Univ, Washington, DC, prof, 1973; Fed City Coll, prof, 1973; Poloroid Corp, Cambridge MA, asst general counsel, 1971; Roxbury Small Business Devel Center, Boston, consultant, 1970; Securities & Exchange Commn, Washington, DC, attorney, 1969. **Orgs:** Mem, DC Bar; Practiced before US Dist Court, DC, US Court of Appeals for DC, and US Court of Mil Appeals; mem, bd of dir, New Life, Inc 1972-; National Council for Therapeutic Riding, 1980-; alumni recruiter, Phillip's Acad, 1979, Harvard Business School, 1971; mem, Kappa Alpha Psi. **Honors/Awds:** Harvard Univ Scholarship, 1956-58; Harvard Business School Fellowship, 1969-71; Georgetown Law School, Lawyers Co-op Publishing Co Prizes; Published History of Black-Owned & Operated Finance Institutes, 1968; State of Maryland Disabled Person of the Year, 1980. **Home Addr:** 2100 Washington Ave, #9C, Silver Spring, MD 20910.

COUNTS, ALLEN
Company executive. **Career:** Citibank World Corp, head, shipping group, 1973-80; Pryor, McClendon, Counts & Co, partner, currently. **Special Achievements:** Firm is ranked second among the nation's African-American investment banks, Black Enterprise, 1992. **Business Addr:** Partner, Pryor, McClendon, Counts & Co, 17 State St, 31st Fl, New York, NY 10004, (212)952-1919.

COUNTS, GEORGE W.
Physician, educator. **Personal:** Born Jun 14, 1935, Idabel, OK; children: George IV, David, Philip. **Educ:** Univ OK, BS 1957, MS 1960; Univ IA, MD 1965; OH State Univ Hosp, intern resd 1965-68; Infectious Diseases Univ WA, fellowship 1968-70. **Career:** DHHS/PHS/NIH, assoc dir Clinical Res Activities, Div Microbiology & Infectious Disease, dir, Off Res Minority & Women's Health, NIAID, 1994-97; CRMB, Div of AIDS, chief, 1989-94; Univ of WA, professor of med, 1985-89, associate prof of med 1975-85; Harborview Med Ctr, chf div infectious diseases 1975-84; Univ Miami Sch of Med, asst prof pathology 1972-75; Jackson Meml Hosp, dir clinical microbiology sect 1972-75; Jackson Meml Hosp, dir infection control dept 1972-75; Univ of Miami, asst prof med 1970-75. **Orgs:** Bd dir Assn for Practitioners in Infection Control 1977-85; pres, 1983; Am Fed for Clinical Rsrch; Soc Hosp Epidemiol of America; licenses to practice in IA OH WA FL MD; fellow Infectious Diseases Soc of Am 1974; Nat Med Flwsp 1961-65. **Honors/Awds:** PHS Sup Serv Award, 1992; Leopold Schepp Found Schlrsp 1961-65; diplomate Am Bd of Internal Med 1970; flw Am Coll of Physicians 1971; Leinfelder Award, Univ IA 1965; mem Alpha Omega Alpha 1965; publ num jour & books; fellow Amer Acad Microbiology, 1996. **Business Addr:** Dir Office of Research on Minority & Women's Health, Natl Inst of Allergy & Infectious Diseases, Natl Inst of Health, 6003 Exec Blvd, Solar Bldg, Rm 4B04, Bethesda, MD 20892-7600, (301)496-8697.

COURTNEY, CASSANDRA HILL
Educational administrator. **Personal:** Born Feb 8, 1949, Newport News, VA; daughter of Mary S Hill and Marion Alton Hill; married Vernon Stanley Courtney, Sep 28, 1974; children: Aliya Diane. **Educ:** Wilson Coll, AB (Cum Laude) 1971; Penn State Univ, MS 1974, PhD 1980. **Career:** Middlesex Co School Bd Saluda VA, dir federal projects 1974-76; Pennsylvania State Univ, academic counselor 1979-81; Wilberforce Univ, social science div chairperson and asst prof psychology 1982-83, vice pres academic affairs 1983-1988, exec asst to the pres, 1989-91, vp adult and continuing education 1991-94; Fund for the Improvement of Postsecondary Education (FIPSE), US Dept of Educ, program officer, 1994-. **Orgs:** Mem Academic Dean's Task Force of the Council of Independent Colls 1983-85; mem Adv Comm Campus Trends of the Amer Council on Educ 1985-91; mem Amer Educ Rsch Assoc; Phi Delta Kappa; Amer Assoc for Higher Educ; mem Jack & Jill of Amer Inc; Cooperative Educ Assoc; Natl Assoc for Women in Education; Alpha Kappa Alpha; pres, Springfield, OH Chapter of Links Inc; 1989-93; mem Amer Assn of Univ Women; mem Accreditation Review Council of the North Central Association. **Honors/ Awds:** Natl Achievement Scholar 1967-71; Phi Beta Kappa 1971-; Fellowship Natl Fellowships Fund 1973-74, 1977-80; Harvard Inst for Educ Mgmt, 1989. **Business Addr:** Program Officer, FIPSE, Rm 3100-ROB 3, 7th & D Sts, NW, Washington, DC 20202, (202)708-5750.

COURTNEY, STEPHEN ALEXANDER
Senior engineer. **Personal:** Born Nov 16, 1957, Philadelphia, PA; son of Olga Viola Facey Squires Courtney and Archie Lee Courtney; married Jennifer Williams Courtney, Jun 26, 1988. **Educ:** Drexel Univ, BSEE 1980; American Univ, MBA 1987. **Career:** IBM Corp, customer engr 1979; E-Systems, elec engr 1980-82; Booz Allen & Hamilton, sr consultant 1982-85; Contel Corp, sr engr 1985-. **Orgs:** Career develop coord Black Data Processing Assoc 1985; convention coord Washington DC Black Data Processing Associates 1985; mem Black MBA Assoc 1987, Inst of Electrical and Electronic Engrs 1987.

COUSIN, PHILIP R.
Clergyman. **Personal:** Born Mar 26, 1933, Pittston, PA; married Joan; children: Philip Jr, Steven, David, Michael, Joseph. **Educ:** Central State Univ; Boston Univ, ThM; Colgate Rochester Divin Sch, PhD Ministry. **Career:** Pastored churches in NC/ VA/FL; Kittrell Coll, pres 1960-65; AME Church, bishop of AL; Edward Waters Coll, pres; AME Church, bishop 11th Episcopal Dist. **Orgs:** Pres bd governors Natl Council of Churches of Christ; chmn bd Edward Waters Coll; natl bd SCLC; chmn Human Relations Commn Durham 1968-69; chmn NC Voter Educ Proj 1968-; trustee Lincoln Hosp Durham 1966-72; trustee Fayetteville State Univ 1972-; chmn Polit Comm Durham Comm on Affairs of Black People 1966-; mem Durham Co Bd of Soc Serv 1970-; mem Durham Co Bd of Educ 1972-. **Honors/Awds:** Kellogg Fellowship 1965; Martin Luther King Fellow in Black Ch Studies 1972; conducted Days of Dialogue Germany for AUS in Europe 1973; 1985 Honoree The Religion Award for achievements as pres of Natl Cncl of Churches, and for leadership as a bishop of the AME Church. **Military Serv:** AUS 2nd Lt 1953. **Business Addr:** Natl Cncl Chs of Christ USA, 475 Riverside Dr, New York, NY 10115.

COUSINS, ALTHEA L.
Educator. **Personal:** Born Nov 5, 1932, New York, NY; married Carl M Cousins; children: Kimberly, Karen. **Educ:** Fisk U, BA 1953; Columbia U, MA 1955; Temple U, MA 1957; Univ of PA Elementary Principal's Certificate 1963; Univ of PA, Comprehensive Principal's Certificate 1969; Temple U, post graduate program 1972-73; Temple U, Superindendents Certificate 1975; Walden U, doctoral program 1976-. **Career:** Div of Pupil Personnel & Counseling, School Dist of Philadelphia, dir 1974-; Childs Elementary School, prin 1972-73; Compers Elementary School, prin 1970-71; elementary school prin, admin asst to dist supt 1967-70; Wagner Jr High School, asst to prin 1966-67; Sartain Elementary School, counseling teacher 1957-66, teacher 1954-57; Barratt Jr High School, teacher 1953-54; Gideon Summer School, teacher 1960; headstart counselor summer 1966; Miller School, outreach counselor 1966; Friends Neighborhood Day Camp, supvr 1958 -59. **Orgs:** Mem Nat Assn of Pupil Personnel Adminstr; Nat Educ Assn; Am Personnel & Guidance Assn; Am Sch Counselors Assn; PA Sch Counselors Assn; Nat Assn of Coll Admissions Counselors; Philadelphia Assn of Sch Adminstr; Women in Educ 1974-; has served on numerous com councils; bd dir Main Line Day Care Center 1973-; exec bd Ithan Elem Sch 1969-71; mem Rotary Ann's Group 1973-; Golden Circle Women 32 degree Masons 1975; Mt Hebron Friends & Neighbors Comm Group 1973-; Women's Aux; Am Vet Med Assn; various alumni groups; Links, Inc; Delta Sigma Theta Sor; Zion Bapt Ch; Women's Aux; Alpha Phi Alpha Frat; League of Women Voters. **Honors/ Awds:** Recipient Philadelphia Sch Adminstr Assn Recognition Award; Chapel of the Four Chaplins Award; Philadelphia Home & Sch & Council Award; Dist Two Supt Recognition Award; article photograph Nat Assn of Pupil Personnel Adminstr Journal & PA Sch Counselors Assn Journal; author of num publs & articles. **Business Addr:** 21 Parkway, Philadelphia, PA 19103.

COUSINS, FRANK
Law enforcement official. **Career:** Newbury Port City council; MA State Legislature, 1993-96; Essex County, sheriff, currently. **Special Achievements:** First African-American sheriff in Massachusetts. **Business Addr:** Sheriff, Essex County Sheriff's Dept., PO Box 807, Middleton, MA 01949, (508)687-7136.

COUSINS, JAMES R., JR.
City official. **Personal:** Born Apr 29, 1906, Washington, DC; married Ethel Boatwright; children: James R. **Educ:** Morgan State Coll, BS 1973. **Career:** Glenarden MD, contractual commn liaison advisor councilman 1974-; Town Council Bd, chmn 1973-74; Glenarden, mayor 1941-70; Glenarden, chief of police 1939-41. **Orgs:** Chmn Prince Georce Co Municipal Assn 1969; mem exec bd MD Mun League 1973; mem bd Visitors Bowie State Coll 1972; mem Pr George Co Adv Com on Aging 1974; chmn Deacon Bd First Bapt Ch Glenarden 1950-74; moderator Bapt Assn of So Md 1972-74; pres Glenarden Civic Assn 1939-41; chief Glenarden Fire Dept 1936-39; chmn of Incorp Com for Glenarden. **Honors/Awds:** Trophy Outstanding Mayor for 1968; award Outstanding Service as Mayor 1941-70; award Glenarden Civic Assn, testimonial by citizens of Glenarden 1970. **Business Addr:** 9171 Central Ave, Capitol Heights, MD 20743.

COUSINS, WILLIAM, JR.
Attorney, alderman, judge. **Personal:** Born Oct 6, 1927, Swiftown, MS; son of Drusilla Harris Cousins and William Cousins; married Hiroko Ogawa, May 12, 1953; children: Cheryl, Noel, Yul, Gail. **Educ:** Univ of IL, BA 1948; Harvard Univ, LLB 1951. **Career:** Chicago Title & Trust Co, atty 1953-57; Cook Co, asst state's atty 1957-61; Private Practice, law 1961-76; 8th Ward Chicago, alderman 1967-76; DePaul Law School, lecturer 1981-84; Circuit Ct Cook Co, judge 1976-92; Illinois Appellate Court, justice 1992-. **Orgs:** Asst moderator, United Church of Christ 1981; admitted to practice before IL, US Dist, Fed Ct of Appeals & US Supreme Ct; IL Supreme Ct appointee to exec comm, IL Judicial Conf 1984-; mem, Amer, Chicago, Illinois, Natl, Cook Co Bar Assns; mem, Delta Sigma Rho; mem, Kappa Alpha Psi; chair-elect, Judicial Council, National Bar Assn, 1994-95; former bd member, Judicial Council, NBA, 1992-93; former trustee, Lincoln Memorial United Church of Christ; former pres, Chatham Avalon Pk Comm Council; former vice pres, Independent Voters IL; former bd mem, PUSH; former bd mem, Chicago Chapter NAACP; former bd mem, Planned Parenthood Assn; Parkway Comm House; Ams Dem Action; chairman, IL Judicial Council, 1987-88; chairman, Illinois Judicial Conference, 1989-90. **Honors/Awds:** Edward N Wright Award Cook Co Bar Assn 1968; William R Ming Jr Civil Rights Award 1974; Kenneth E Wilson Award, IL Judicial Council 1992; National Bar Assn Hall of Fame, 1994; Outstanding Judge of Yr Award John Marshall Chapter Black Law Students Amer 1980; delegate Dem Natl Convention 1972; Outstanding Layman of Year Lincoln Mem Church 1958; author, A Judges View of Judicial Selection Plans, Illinois Bar Journal, 1987; Thurgood Marshall Award, IIT Chicago-Kent, 1985; Outstanding Jurist Award, John Marshall Law School, 1989. **Military Serv:** AUS lt 1951-53; lt col JAG (res) 1975-. **Home Addr:** 1745 E 83 Place, Chicago, IL 60617.

COVIN, DAVID L.
Educator. **Personal:** Born Oct 3, 1940, Chicago, IL; son of Lela Jane Clements Covin and David Covin; married Judy Bentinck Smith; children: Wendy, Holly. **Educ:** U Univ of IL, BA, 1962; Colorado Univ, MA, 1966; Washington State Univ, PHD, 1970. **Career:** California State Univ, Sacramento, asst prof, Govt & Ethnic Studies, 1970-74, assoc dean, general studies, general studies, 1972-74, assoc prof, govt & ethnic studies, 1975-79, prof, govt & ethnic studies, 1979; Union Graduate School, adjunct prof 1979-; State of CA, consultant, 1979; California State Univ, Sacramento, dir, Pan African studies. **Orgs:** Contributing editor, Rumble, 1973-; commr, CA Educ Evaluation & Mgmt Commn 1977-81; Black Caucus Criminal Justice Brain Trust, 1977-; vice-chmn, Sacramento Area Black Caucus, 1978-83; consultant, Sacramento City United School Dist, 1980; co-chair, Sacramento Chapter of Natl Black Independent Political Party, 1981-85; political/educ chair, Sacramento Area Black Caucus, 1983-; educ chair, Black Comm Activist Comm, 1985-; mem, Sacramento Chapter, Natl Rainbow Coalition Org Comm; delegate, Natl Party Congress, Natl Black Independent Political Party; mem, The Natl Faculty, 1988-; acting chair, Black Science Resource Center, 1987-present; exec bd, Women's Civic Improvement Club, 1987-present; chair, Sacramento Area Black Caucus, 1988-90, 1994-96; newsletter editor, Sacramento Area Black Caucus, 1992-97; steering committee, Cooper-Woodson College, 1988-; mem, The National Faculty, 1988-; participant, The American Assembly, 1990. **Honors/ Awds:** Community Serv Award, Sacramento Area Black Caucus, 1976; grant recipient, CA Council for Humanities Public Policy, 1977; Sacramento Community Serv Award, Sacramento Kwanzaa Comm, 1978; Man of the Year, Omega Psi Phi, 1982; Community Serv Award, All African People, 1986; novel, Brown Sky, 1987; Meritorious Performance Award, California State Univ, Sacramento, 1988; Short Story, The Walk, 1988; Article, "Towards A Pan African Vision of the Caribbean," 1988; "Afrocentricity in O Movimento Negro Unificado," The Journal of Black Studies, 1990; John C Livingston distinguished faculty lecture, CSU Sacramento, 1992; Publications in The Western Journal of Black Studies; Ethnic Studies Journal; The Journal of Third World Studies; Natl Political Science Review; The Black Literture Forum; Chap in Dilemmas of Black Politics, Impuruzu; Amer Philosophical Society Grant, 1992; NSF Grant, 1993. **Business Addr:** Dir of Pan African Studies, California State University, 6000 J St, Sacramento, CA 95819.

COVINGTON, DAMIEN
Professional football player. **Personal:** Born Dec 4, 1972, Berlin, NJ. **Educ:** North Carolina State. **Career:** Buffalo Bills, linebacker, 1995-. **Business Addr:** Professional Football Player, Buffalo Bills, One Bills Dr, Orchard Park, NY 14127, (716)648-1800.

COVINGTON, H. DOUGLAS
Educational administrator. **Personal:** Born Mar 7, 1935, Winston-Salem, NC; son of Fannie Covington and Henry Covington; married Beatrice Mitchell, Jun 14, 1958; children: Anthony Douglas, Jeffrey Steven. **Educ:** Central State Univ, BS 1957; OH State Univ, MA 1958, PhD 1966. **Career:** Montclair NJ Public Schools, deputy supt of schools 1972-74; Tuskegee Univ, vice pres development affairs 1974-77; Winston-Salem State Univ, chancellor 1977-84; Alabama A&M Univ, pres 1984-. **Orgs:** Bd dirs Council for Advancement & Support of Educ, Amer Assn of State Colls & Univs; bd trustees Faulkner

Univ; chmn HBCU Adv Comm US Dept of Interior; bd dirs Amer Heart Assn, Huntsville Chamber of Commerce; state chmn Africatow n Comm. **Honors/Awds:** Distinguished Alumnus Award OH State Univ; Distinguished Alumnus Award Central State Univ; Academic Scholarship Jessie Smith Noyes Foundation; various other awards. **Business Addr:** President, Alabama A&M University, PO Box 285, Normal, AL 35762.

COVINGTON, JAMES ARTHUR
Clergyman, administrator. **Personal:** Born Aug 4, 1927, Hernando, MS; married Mary Ella Blackwell. **Educ:** MS Indsl Coll Holly Springs, BA 1950; Univ of OR, MA 1953; Pacific Sc of Religion Berkley CA, MTh 1957; Mount Hope Bible & Theol Sch Houston, Hon DMin 1979. **Career:** Bebee Tabernacle CME Ch Houston, pastor 1978-; Phillips Chapel CME Ch Tucson, pastor 1970-78; Phillips Meml CME Ch Phoenix, pastor 1966-70; Phillips Temple CME Ch San Diego, pastor 1962-66; AK Dist Christian ME Ch, presiding elder 1959-62. **Orgs:** Chmn bd of dirs Pima Co AZ CEO 1975-76; Thirty-three dgr mason, Prince Hall Affiliation 1957; organizer CMECh AK 1959. **Honors/Awds:** Recipient Ford Fellowship Grant for Study in Urban Ministry, Univ of Chicago 1968-69. **Business Addr:** Bebee Tabernacle CME Church, 822 W Dallas, Houston, TX 77019.

COVINGTON, JOHN RYLAND
Physician. **Personal:** Born Mar 27, 1936, Philadelphia, PA; son of Verlie Covington and John Covington; married Delores E; children: Deidra. **Educ:** St Joseph Coll, BS 1964; Philadelphia Coll of Osteopathic Med, DO 1971. **Career:** Osteopathic phys pvt prac; analytical chemist rsrch; Covington Medical Group, pres. **Orgs:** Mem Am Osteopathic Assn; Ethics Com St of PA; Am Coll of Emerg Room Phys; Sigma Sigma Phi Nat Hon Osteopathic Soc; mem Omega & Psi Phi Frat; NAACP. **Honors/Awds:** Grad in top ten percent of Med Sch Class; winner 3 of top 5 gradn awds; publ 2 sci papers. **Military Serv:** AUS.

COVINGTON, KIM ANN
News reporter. **Personal:** Born Mar 30, 1964, Centreville, IL; daughter of Delores Collins Covington and Wendell Covington Sr. **Educ:** University of Missouri, Columbia, MO, broadcast journalism, 1986. **Career:** KYTV, Springfield, MO, news reporter, 1986-88; KPLR-TV, St. Louis, MO, director of public affairs, 1988-89, news reporter, 1989-. **Orgs:** Member, Communications Committee, Urban League of Greater St. Louis, 1987-90; member, Delta Sigma Theta Sorority Inc, 1984-; member, National Association of Black Journalists, 1986-. **Honors/Awds:** Investigative Reporting, Lincoln University Unity Award, 1988; Horace Mann Award, PSA, 1989; Arkansas Associated Press Award Investigative Reporting, 1988; Investigative Reporting, Missouri Associated Press Award, 1988; Investigative Reporting, National Associated Press Honorable Mention; Distinguished Service Award, Sigma Delta Chi, Reporting, 1988; Won Local Emmy, for Spot News Coverage. **Business Addr:** News Reporter, KPLR-TV, 4935 Lindell, St Louis, MO 63108.

COVINGTON, M. STANLEY
Attorney (retired). **Personal:** Born Apr 25, 1937, Langhorne, PA; son of Madalyn Johnson Covington and Marlow O Covington (deceased); married Laura Aline; children: Lisa, Eric (deceased), Scott. **Educ:** Bloomsburg U, BS 1955-59; Rutgers U, 1960; Howard Univ School of Law, JD 1962-65. **Career:** NJ Dept of Labor, field rep, 1965-66; Allstate Ins Co, sr trial attorney 1966-96. **Orgs:** Alternate mem Governing Board, Dist Of Columbia Assign Claim Bureau 1984-86; mem bd of Dir Alumni Assoc Bloomsburg Univ 1978-80; mem Natl Bar Assn 1972-; mem Amer Bar Assn, Washington 1972-; mem Bar Assn Dist of Columbia Br 1972-; mem Maryland Bar Assn 1985-, Montgomery Cnty Bar Assn; Fellowship of Christian Athletes 1981-; mem, Prince George's County MD Bar Assn; adv bd mem, Inverness Custom Plastics, Inc; mem, Sigma Delta Tau Legal Front. **Honors/Awds:** Achievement award, Kiwanis Langhorne, PA 1955; Little All Amer Football End hon men by Asso Press 1957-58; elected to Neshaminy High School Football Hall of Fame, Langhorne Pennsylvania 1987; Certificate of Excellence, Allstate Insurance Company. **Home Addr:** 16001 Amina Dr, Burtonsville, MD 20866, (301)421-1631.

COWAN, JAMES R.
Physician, business executive. **Personal:** Born Oct 21, 1919, Washington, DC; married Juanita G; children: James Jr, Jay, Jill. **Educ:** Howard U, BS 1939; Fisk U, MA 1940; Meharry Med Coll, MD 1944; Harlem Hosp, intern 1944-45; Freedmen's Hosp, res 1945-48; Howard U, flw 1948-50. **Career:** Blue Cross & Blue Shield of Grtr NY, sr vice pres 1976-; Hlth & Envir, asst sec of defense 1974-76; Ofc of the Asst Sec of Defense, consult 1974; NJ St Dept of Hlth, commr 1970-74; pvt prac 1953-70. **Orgs:** Mem Am Med Assn; Am Coll of Preventive Med; Essex Co Med Soc; Interns & Residents Assn; Howard U; Am Assn of Pub Hlth Phys; Am Assn of Univ Profs; Acad of Med of NJ; Acad of Med of Washington DC; Mental Hlth Assn of Essex Co; Assn of Mil Surg of US; Am Hosp Assn; Am Pub Hlth Sci; Nat Cancer Adv Bd; Interagy Drug Rev Task Force of White House Domestic Counc; Nat Commn on Arthridtis & Related Musculoskeletal Diseases; Armed ForcesMed & Policy Counc; Nat Counc on Intl Hlth; Strat Counc on Drug Abuse; Nat Adv Counc on Alcohol Abuse & Alchol; Nat Adv Mental Hlth Counc; Nat Adv Dental Rsch Counc; Nat Adv Allergy & Infect Diseases Counc; Nat Arthritis Metabolism & Digestive Diseases Adv Counc; Nat Adv Child Hlth & Human Devel Counc; Nat Adv Eye Counc; Nat Adv Gen Med SciCounc; Nat Heart & Lundv Counc; Nat Adv Neurol Diseases & Stroke Counc; Nat AdvRsch Resrcs Counc; Sickle Cell Disease Adv CounF Hyperten Info & Educ Adv Com; pres Com on Mental Retardation. **Military Serv:** AUS chief of surgery battalion surgeon 1950-53. **Business Addr:** President, United Hosp Med Center, 15 S 9th St, Newark, NJ 07107.

COWAN, LARINE YVONNE
Civil rights activist, educational administrator. **Personal:** Born Mar 25, 1949, Kensett, AR; daughter of Ola Mae Cowan and William Cowan; children: Alexander Milton Omar, Christopher Alvin Lamar. **Educ:** Univ of AR, Pine Bluff, BA 1971; Univ of AR, Little Rock, MSW 1973; Management and Training Develop Workshops, 1974-. **Career:** City of Champaign, Community Relations Dept, dir, 1974-79; Univ of IL Urbana-Champaign, Affirmative Action Nonacademic Office, equal opportunity officer, 1982-85, director, 1984-91, Office of the Vice Chancellor, Affirmative Action director, assistant vice chancellor, 1991-92, assistant chancellor, associate director, 1992-94, asst chancellor, dir, 1994-. **Orgs:** American Association of Affirmative Action; American Association for Higher Education; American Association of Univ Women, Champaign-Urbana Chap; Champaign Cty Urban League, board of directors, past chair; Executive Women's Club-Champaign Cty; Illinois Affirmative Action Officers Assn, Educational Initiative Comm, Conference Comm, co-chair, 1989-90; Illinois Comm for Black Concerns in Higher Educ; Natl Assn for Female Execs, 1993; NAACP; National Coalition Building Institute (NCBI), Prejudice Reduction Team, campus coord, 1987-93; Private Industry Council-Champaign, Ford, Iroquois and Piatt Counties, Prog Services Comm; Savoy Rotary Club, charter mem, 1990-92; Illinois State Council of Opportunities Industrialization Centers of America, Inc (OIC), 1983-87, state coord; State of Illinois Job Service, Employment Comm; Southern Poverty Law Center & Klanwatch Project; Univ of IL Black Faculty & Professional Staff Caucus and Advisory Comm, mem, 1991-93. **Honors/Awds:** Outstanding Achievement in Volunteerism, United Way of Champaign Cty, 1992; Special Award, Martin Luther King, Jr., presentation, presented by Major General Lawrence Day, Center Commander, Chanute Air Force Base, 1990; United Way Gold Award, United Way of Champaign Cty, 1989; Chancellor Morton W. Weir's Award of Appreciation for Outstanding Service as Chair of Campus Charitable Fund Drive, 1988; "The Very Best Campaign at Any State University" Award, United Way of Champaign Cty, 1988; Proclamation-Special Achievements in Human Rights, presented by Mayor Joan Severns, City of Champaign, 1979; Outstanding Services in Human and Civil Rights, Champaign Human Relations commission, 1979; Outstanding Contributions in the Field of Human Rights, City of Urbana Mayor Jeffrey Markland and the Urbana Human Relations Commission, 1979; Boss of the Year Awd, Champaign-Urbana Jaycees, 1978. **Special Achievements:** Co-author: The Human Rights Ordinance for the City of Champaign, IL; "Police Community Relations: A Process, Not a Product," The Police Chief's Magazine, 1976. **Business Addr:** Asst Chancellor & Director, Affirmative Action, University of Illinois at Urbana/Champaign, 601 E John Street, 100A Swanlund Admin Bldg, Champaign, IL 61820.

COWANS, ALVIN JEFFREY
Certified credit union executive. **Personal:** Born Jun 15, 1955, Alexandria, VA; son of Jessie M Cowans and Willie L Cowans; married Shirley Mae Smith, Dec 18, 1976; children: Alvin Jeffrey II, Marcus Adrian. **Educ:** Univ of Fl, BS 1977; Inst of Financial Educ, supervisory training cert 1979; graduate of Florida Credit Union Management Institute, graduate of the Certified Credit Union Executive Program. **Career:** US Pipe & Foundry, sales rep 1977-78; Pioneer Federal Savings & Loan, asst vice pres, office mgr, admin asst 1978-83; McCoy Federal Credit Union, sr vice pres 1983-85, pres 1986-. **Orgs:** Mem Central Florida Urban Bankers Assn; mem, Credit Union Executive Society; mem and past president Univ of Florida Lettermens Association; director, mem Gator Booster Board; former board member Central Florida Kidney Foundation; National Association of Federal Credit Unions, regional director; Federal Reserve's Consumer Advisory Council; Southeast Federal Credit Union, director; Boy Scouts of America; Central Florida AAU; Orange County Schools Partners in Education. **Honors/Awds:** Grad of the Chamber of Commerce Leadership Orlando Prog 1980; Outstanding Young Men in America 1981; Citizen of the Year, Chi Tau Chapter, Omega Psi Phi Fraternity. **Business Addr:** President, McCoy Federal Credit Union, PO Box 593806, Orlando, FL 32859-3806.

COWARD, JASPER EARL
Marketing manager. **Personal:** Born Nov 21, 1932, Kinston, NC; married Josephine Stuldivant; children: Renee, Natalie. **Educ:** Howard U, BA 1960. **Career:** Joseph Schlitz Brewing Co, mgr spl markets/Dixie Div 1963-; Carling Brewing Co Atlanta, rep 1962-63; Johnson Pub Co Atlanta, mdse rep 1960-62. **Orgs:** Mem Nat Assn of Marketing Developers 1958-80; mem DAV; mem NAACP. **Honors/Awds:** Recipient Good Conduct Medal/UN Serv/Korean Serv/Nat Defense Serv Awards. **Military Serv:** USAF airman 2nd class 1953-56. **Business Addr:** Joseph Schlitz Brewing Co, PO Box 614, Milwaukee, WI 53201.

COWARD, ONIDA LAVONEIA
Journalist. **Personal:** Born Sep 26, 1964, Panama City, Panama; daughter of Marcia E Pitter and Ricardo E Coward. **Educ:** Buffalo State College, Buffalo, NY, BA, 1986. **Career:** Paragon Cable Manhattan, New York, NY, public and leased manager, 1987-89; Brooklyn Community Access Television, Brooklyn, NY, director, 1989-. **Orgs:** Board member, American Cancer Society, Harlem Unit, 1991; board member, Harlem YMCA "100 Years of Basketball", 1991; member, National Assoc of Black Journalists, 1988; New York chapter secretary, National Assoc of Minorities in Cable, 1987; member, One Hundred Black Women, 1988. **Honors/Awds:** Community Service Award, Community Bd #11, Manhattan, 1989; Creator/Exec Producter PAL Awards, Paragon Cable Manhattan, 1988-89; Open Doors Award, Board of Education, 1988. **Home Addr:** 5810 Beverly Rd, Brooklyn, NY 11203.

COWDEN, MICHAEL E.
Educator. **Personal:** Born Jul 17, 1951, Louisville, KY. **Educ:** Shoreline Commun Coll, AA 1971; Univ Washington, BA, American ethnic studies. **Career:** Louisville Public Schools, martial arts instructor, chinese boxing 1975-; actor; poet; playwright. **Honors/Awds:** United States Achievement Academy's All American Scholar, 1993-94.

COWELL, CATHERINE
Nutritionist. **Personal:** Born Nov 13, 1921, Norfolk, VA. **Educ:** Hampton Inst, BS 1945; Univ of CT, MS 1947; Univ of CT, grad asst in nutrition 1945-47. **Career:** Metabolism Clinic Mt Sinai Hosp NYC, lab techn 1947-49; pub health nutrionalist 1969; Bur Nutrition, acting dir 1971; NY Med Coll Flower Fifth Ave Hosp, asst clin instr preventave med pub health indsl & hygiene 1953-55; Albert Einstein Sch of Med Yeshiva Univ NYC, instr nutrition environmental med 1962-69; NY U, vis lectr; Montclair State Tchr; Coll Rep to NY Nutrition Council 1963-; Nutrition Bur New York City Dept of Health, dir. **Orgs:** Mem White House Conf on Food Nutrition & Health 1969; adv council Ch Human Ecology, Cornell Univ 1970-72; mem Manhattan Br; Nat Council Negro Women; fellow, Am Pub Health Assn; mem Am Home Econ Assn; NY State Home Econ Assn; chmn health & welfare section 1961-62; pres 1971-; mem St George Assn of New York City Health Dept; Royal Soc Health; mem Hampton Alumni Assn; Lambda Kappa Kappa Mu natl pres 1961-65; Order Eastern Star Club. **Honors/Awds:** Recipient Nutritional Award, New York City Pub Health Assn 1960; JF Goodwin Scholarship, Reading PA; contrib articles to professional jours. **Business Addr:** 93 Worth St, Room 714, New York, NY 10013.

COWENS, ALFRED EDWARD, JR.
Professional baseball player (retired). **Personal:** Born Oct 25, 1951, Los Angeles, CA; married Velma; children: Purvis, Dante, Trinetta. **Career:** Kansas City Royals, outfielder 1974-79; California Angels, outfielder 1980; Detroit Tigers, outfielder 1980-81; Seattle Mariners, outfielder 1982-86. **Honors/Awds:** Royals' Player of the Year 1977.

COX, ARTHUR JAMES, SR.
Social work educator. **Personal:** Born Jun 15, 1943, Avon Park, FL; married Deloris Murray; children: Arthur Jr, Travis J, David I. **Educ:** Howard Univ, AB 1965, MSW 1970; Columbia Univ, DSW 1978. **Career:** FL State Univ, asst prof 1975-78; East TN State Univ, chmn/assoc prof 1978-83; Southern IL Univ, dir & assoc prof 1983-86; Salem State Coll, dean & prof 1986-. **Orgs:** Adv panel mem CONTACT 1978-83; chmn Human Serv Goals Directions 2000 Program 1980-83; secty/treas Inst of Children Resources 1980-82; steering comm mem Southeast Child Welfare Training Resource Ctr Univ of TN Sch of Social Work 1981-82; treas Assoc of Baccalaureate Prog Dirs 1981-83; pres Natl Assoc ofSocial Workers TN Chap 1981-82; mem Publications Comm Cncl on Social Work Educ 1981-84; mem Alcohol Treatment Serv Adv Bd Jackson County Comm Mental Hlth Ctr Carbondale IL 1984-; mem editorial review bd Journal of Social Serv Rsch GWB Sch of Social Work Washington Univ St Louis 1985-88; mem Natl Assoc of Black Social Workers, Natl Assoc of Social Workers, Cncl on Social Work Educ, Natl Conf of Social Welfare; elected delegate TN Governor's State Conf onFamilies, White House Conf on Famili Minneapolis. **Honors/Awds:** NIMH Fellowship for Doctoral Study 1973-74; Teacher of the Year Lehman Coll of CUNY 1973, FSU Sch of Social Work 1977; Jaycees Man of the Year 1979; ACE Fellow 1979; TN Chap NASW Social Worker of the Year 1980; numerous papers presented, workshops, special lectures,TV appearances, chapters in books and articles published. **Home Addr:** 1282 Lake Lotela Dr, Avon Park, FL 33825-9737.

COX, BRYAN KEITH
Professional football player. **Personal:** Born Feb 17, 1968, East St Louis, IL; married LaTonia; children: Lavonda, Brittani, Chiquita, Bryan Jr. **Educ:** Western Illinois, bachelor's degree in mass communications. **Career:** Miami Dolphins, linebacker,

1991-95; Chicago Bears, 1996-. **Honors/Awds:** Pro Bowl, 1992, 1994, 1995; National Football League, Extra Effort Award, 1994. **Business Addr:** Professional Football Player, Chicago Bears, Halas Hall at Conway Park, 1000 Football Dr., Lake Forest, IL 60045-4829, (847)295-6600.

COX, CORINE
Editor. **Personal:** Born May 31, 1944, Mansfield, LA; married Doyl Cox; children: Dwayne E. **Educ:** Texas Southern U, 1962-63; Univ Bus Coll, cert sec training 1964. **Career:** Society and Women's Ed Forward Times Pub Co, compositer supr newswriter soc ed 1964-. **Orgs:** Mem adv bd Ct Calanthe; Eta Phi Beta; Mt Rose Missionary Bapt Ch tchr Mission I; ch sec Prairie View A&M U. **Honors/Awds:** Award media coverage 1974; outstanding Neophyte Awd 1974-75; woman of year awd at Ch. **Business Addr:** 4411 Almeda Rd, Houston, TX 77004.

COX, DIANNE FITZGERALD
Sales executive. **Personal:** Born Aug 12, 1951, Memphis, TN; daughter of Lillian Johnson and Harry Fitzgerald Jr; married Harold Louis Cox, Apr 12, 1975; children: Kelle Nikole, Erika Patrice, Kyle Fitzgerald. **Educ:** Memphis State University, BBA, 1974. **Career:** Xerox Corp., 1974-, sales planning manager, 1982-83, sales manager, BPD, 1983-84, sales operations manager, 1984-85, branch marketing manager, 1985-86, major account sales manager, 1986-88, document systems manager, 1988-89, Memphis area manager, 1989-. **Orgs:** Memphis Urban League, board of directors; Mississippi Boulevard Christian Academy, board of directors; The Links, Inc, board of directors; Memphis in May, Inc, board of directors; Greater Memphis Area Award for Quality, board of directors. **Honors/Awds:** Girls, Inc of Memphis, She Knows Where She's Going Award, 1992; Ebony Magazine, 100 Most Outstanding Corporate Females, 1991. **Business Addr:** Memphis Area Sales Manager, Xerox Corporation, 6555 Quince Ave, Ste 500, Memphis, TN 38119, (901)753-3200.

COX, DUBOIS V.
Investment banker. **Personal:** Born Mar 24, 1950, St Louis, MO; son of Christine Y Willis Cox and Roland Cox; divorced; children: Mercedes Nicole Cox. **Educ:** Southern Illinois Univ, Edwardsville IL, BS 1973; Southeastern Univ, Washington DC, MS Study Intl Business, 1981; Johns Hopkins Univ, Washington DC, MS Study Intl Business, 1981. **Career:** Calvert Group, Washington DC, investor relations 1980-82; US Army Europe, West Germany, logistician 1982-86; Congressman W E Fauntroy, Washington, DC, 1986-87; Daniels & Bell, branch mgr, 1987-88; WR Lazard & Co, Inc, Washington, DC, vice pres, currently. **Orgs:** Pres, bd of trustees Invest America Capital Fund 1988-; mem Natl Assn of Securities Professionals; mem Kappa Alpha Psi Fraternity; mem Urban League, Washington DC. **Honors/Awds:** Author of several financial planning articles in community newpapers, professional conference materials and army publications while in Europe. **Business Addr:** Vice President, WR Lazard & Co, Inc, 655 15th St NW, Ste 300, Washington, DC 20005.

COX, EUOLA WILSON
Educator. **Personal:** Born in Muskogee, OK; children: Daryl E, Vodra E Dorn. **Educ:** Langston Univ OK, BA English; Univ of Albuquerque, Univ of NM, College of Santa Fe, MA Ed Admin; Univ of NM, additional training 1978. **Career:** Hoover Middle School, teacher 1970-71; Highland HS, teacher 1971-73; Univ of Albuquerque, part-time prof 1973 & 1975; Albuquerque HS, teacher 1973-75; Wilson Middle School, asst principal 1975-80; Eastern NM Univ, assoc prof emeritus 1980-. **Orgs:** Sponsored Y-Teen Group Albuquerque YWCA 1962-69; mem bd of dir South Braodway Oppty Ctr 1964-67; coord, organizer Black Voices Comm Choir 1965; initiated 1st Black Heritage Observance in Albuquerque Public Schools 1969; conducted Black History Seminars in Model Cities Neighborhood 1970-71; sponsor Youth Group NAACP 1972; Univ of NM Schl of Pharm Minority Recruitment Comm 1973-75; recruiter of Minority Youth NM Employment Sec Comm 1973-75; mem bd of trustees Bernalilillo Cty Mental Hlth Ctr 1974; consult Farmington Pub Schl Syst Initiation of Ethnic Studies Prog for the Syst 1974; recruited 25 minority students for SSandia Corp Pilot Prog 1974; recruiter Alb Pub Schls 1976; mem Albuquerque Urban Coaltion 1976; pres bd of dir Cntrl Cities Consult Coop 1976;David King's Political Action CoNAACP 1976; cochrprs United Negro Coll Fund Telethon 1978; title IX wkshp consult Univ of NM & Alb Pub Schls 1978-79; spsr Concrnd-Women for Chg ENMU Weusi Choir 1980-82; adv Blk Stdnt Union ENMU 1980-82; adv bd NM Eth Hrtg Tchr Training Proj 1981; Phi Delta Kappa; Delta Sigma Theta. **Honors/Awds:** Multiple publ, lectures & papers incl "Multicultural Ed" TX Tech Jrnl of Ed 1982 Fall, Title I Reg III Workshop Eastern NM Univ "Barriers to Conferencing with Parents of Minority Students" 1982, Natl Black Family Conf "A Model for Community Involvement" 1983; assoc prof emeritus Eastern NM Univ 1985.

COX, GEORGETTA MANNING
Educator. **Personal:** Born Sep 16, 1947, Washington, DC; married Walter Bishop Cox Jr; children: Malakia Iman. **Educ:** Hampton Inst, BA 1970; Howard Univ Coll of Dentistry, DDS 1976; Johns Hopkins Univ, MPH 1979. **Career:** Howard Univ Coll of Dentistry, prog coord 1977-78, asst prof 1979-86; assoc prof. **Orgs:** Presentor/mem Intl Assoc for Dental Rsch; mem Sigma Xi Rsch Soc, Amer Public Health Assoc; consultant United Planning Org Health Adv Comm 1982-; managing editor NDA Journal Natl Dental Assoc 1983-; vice pres 1984, pres 1985 Omicron Kappa Upsilon Natl Dental Honor Soc; vice pres Howard Univ Dental Alumna Assoc 1985. **Honors/Awds:** President's Awd Natl Dental Assoc 1984; Outstanding Service Awd Natl Dental Assoc 1986; articles published "Pathological Effects of Sickle Cell Anemia onthe Pulp," Journal of Dent for Children 1984, "Oral Pain Experience in Sickle Cell Patients," Oral Surgery, Oral Medicine, Oral Pathology 1985; "The Psycho Social Aspects of Pregnant Adolescents, A Dental Perspective," Journal of Dentistry for Children 1986. **Business Addr:** Associate Professor, Howard Univ Coll of Dentistry, 600 W St NW, Washington, DC 20059.

COX, JAMES L.
Business executive. **Personal:** Born Dec 11, 1922, Birmingham, AL; married Marjorie; children: Adria, Chandra, James III. **Educ:** Lincoln Univ, AB 1949; Atlanta Univ, MSW 1952. **Career:** Salvation Army, USO dir 1952-54, Forrest Neighborhood House, social group worker 1954; Malone Comm Center, exec dir 1955-62; Univ of NE Sch of Social Work, lecturer 1957-62; Community Welfare Council of Buffalo & Erie County, comm planning dir 1962-64; Catholic Univ of America, Natl Catholic Sch of Social Service, asst prof 1964-69; People's Comm Services of Metropolitan Detroit, pres. **Orgs:** mem, Natl Assn of Social Workers; NAACP; Natl Conf on Social Welfare; Natl Fed of Settlements & Neighborhood Centers; Acad of Certified Social Workers; mem, Alpha Phi Alpha Fraternity; Intl Assn of Lions Clubs. **Honors/Awds:** WOMC Metro Media Radio Brotherhood Awd 1975; Cert of Honor Amer Red Cross of Lancaster Co 1962; Comm Headstart Inc of Catholic Social Serv 1975. **Military Serv:** AUS 1943-45. **Business Addr:** President, People's Comm Serv of Detroit, 412 W Grand Blvd, Detroit, MI 48216.

COX, JESSE L.
Newspaper executive. **Personal:** Born Jun 1, 1946, Bay Minette, AL; son of Artensie Wesley Cox and Jesse Cox Sr; married Mary Walker Cox; children: April, Anwar, Tasia. **Educ:** AL A&M Univ, BS 1969; Mercy College, BS 1979. **Career:** Alexander's Dept Stores, mgr 1971-83; Buffy Merchandising Corp, general mgr, 1983-86; Gannett Weschester Rockland Newspaper, cir dist mgr, currently. **Orgs:** Mem, Kappa Alpha Psi Fraternity, 1965-; consultant, Clitee Assocs, 1979-; Jamaican Amer Varieties, Lewis Security Corp, 1986-; Legislative advisory Comm, NY City Council 1985-. **Honors/Awds:** Articles published on business & drugs Parkchester News 1985. **Military Serv:** AUS E-4 2 years; Bronze Star. **Business Addr:** Circulation Distribution Manager, 1 Gannett Drive, Gannett Weschester Rockland Newspapers, Bldg #1, White Plains, NY 10604.

COX, JOHN WESLEY
Assistant vice president-community affairs. **Personal:** Born Aug 2, 1929, College Park, GA; married Marian E. May, Jul 3, 1960. **Educ:** Morehouse College, Atlanta GA, BA, 1952; Atlanta University, Atlanta GA, MSW, 1957; Western Reserve University, Cleveland OH, 1961. **Career:** Butler Street YMCA, Atlanta GA, branch director, 1947-52, youth director, 1952, asst program director, 1952-54, program director, 1956-58, president, 1969-75; Goodric Bell Social Settlement, Cleveland OH, director, 1958-65; US Department of Labor, manpower specialist, 1965-66, executive asst manpower administration, 1966-68; City of Atlanta, director youth council, 1968-69; self-employed consultant, 1975-78; Delta Air Lines, Inc, Atlanta, consultant, 1978-82, director of community affairs, 1982-83, asst vice pres of community affairs, 1983—. **Orgs:** NAACP, Urban League, Georgia Epilepsy Foundation, United Youth Adult Conference, Georgia Commission on Higher Education, Martin Luther King, Jr., Center for Nonviolent Social Change, Atlanta Mental Health Association. **Honors/Awds:** Awards from National Association of Social Workers, United Youth Adult Conference, YMCA, Job Corps, City of Atlanta, City of Cleveland. **Military Serv:** US Army, 1956.

COX, JOSEPH MASON ANDREW
Writer, poet. **Personal:** Born Jul 12, 1930, Boston, MA; son of Edith Henderson Cox and Hiram Cox. **Educ:** Columbia University, BA, 1949, LLB, 1952; World University, Hong Kong, Ph D, art psychology, 1972. **Career:** New York Post, New York NY, reporter and feature writer, 1958-60; Afro-Asian Purchasing Commission, New York NY, president, 1961-68; New York City Board of Education, Brooklyn NY, consultant, 1969-71; Manhattan Community College of the City University of New York, New York NY, lecturer, 1972-73; Medgar Evers College of the City University of New York, Brooklyn NY, asst prof of English, 1973-74; Cox & Hopewell Publishers, Inc, New York NY, president, 1974; poet and writer; professor at City University of New York, Manhattan Community College, Bronx Community College, Medgar Evers College, New York City Univ Research Center, 1975-83; Federal Government Crime Insurance, 1983-88. **Orgs:** International Poetry Society, International Poets Shrine, United Poets Laureate International, World Literature Academy, Authors League of America, Poetry Society of America, Phylaxis Society, NAACP; member, International Academy of Arts, Science and Letters. **Honors/Awds:** International Essay Award, Daniel S Mead Agency, 1964; "Great Society" writer's award from President Lyndon B Johnson, 1965; Master Poets Award, American Poet Fellowship Society, 1970; World Poets Award, World Poetry Fellowship Society, 1971; PEN grant, 1972; Humanitarian Award and Gold Medal for poetry from International Poets Shrine, both 1974; American Book Award nomination, 1979, for New and Selected Poems; "Statue of Victory" World Culture Prize from Accademia Italia, 1985; Gold Medal, American Biographical Assn, 1987; United Poet Laureate International Gold Crown, 1976; Asbury Park Neptune NAACP Medal of Distinction, 1984; American Biographical Assn Gold Medal, 1988; International Academy of Arts, Science and Letters Bronze Statue, 1985. **Special Achievements:** Author, Unfolding Orchid 1847-1993, 1993.

COX, KEVIN C.
State representative. **Personal:** Born Dec 1, 1949, Oklahoma City, OK; son of Martina Cox and Frank Cox; married Carlise Ann Washington; children: Kenny. **Educ:** Florida A&M Univ, BS Polit Sci 1972; Univ of GA, M Public Admin 1974. **Career:** State of OK, field monitor 1974-77; Energy Conservation & Housing Foundation, minority business develop 1977-80; State of OK, state representative, 1980-. **Orgs:** Life member, Florida A&M Alumni Assn; bd of dirs Eastside YMCA; life mem Kappa Alpha Psi Frat Inc; life mem NAACP; mem bd dir Urban League; chmn Ins Comm; 33 Degree Prince Hall Mason; Prince Hall Shriner. **Honors/Awds:** Eastside YMCA Volunteer of the Year; Set Club Citizen of the Year; Hon Alumnus Langston Univ. **Home Addr:** 5909 N Terry, Oklahoma City, OK 73111. **Business Addr:** State Representative, State of Oklahoma, 537-A State Capitol, Oklahoma City, OK 73105, (405)521-2711.

COX, M. MAURICE
Beverage company executive. **Personal:** Born Dec 20, 1951, Dover, NC; son of Nicy Chatmon Cox and Earl E Cox; married Earlene Hardie Cox, Jul 1, 1978; children: Michelle Hardie, Michael M. **Educ:** Univ of North Carolina, Greensboro NC, BA Economics, 1974. **Career:** Greensboro News Co, Greensboro NC, reporter, 1973-74; Associated Builders & Contractors, Washington DC, editor, 1975-78, dir communications, 1979-81; Pepsi-Cola Co, Somers NJ, manager public relations, 1981-86, dir government affairs, 1987-91, vice pres of corp development & diversity, 1991-. **Orgs:** Black Managers Assn, mem, 1986; White Plains Youth Council, mentor, 1988-; Food Patch, Executive Leadership Council. **Honors/Awds:** Community Hero Award, National Urban League, Ebony Magazine list of powerful executives.

COX, OTHA P.
Business executive. **Career:** Educational Technologies Inc, president, currently. **Orgs:** City of Key West, FL, utility board; American Public Power Association, board of directors. **Special Achievements:** First African-American elected to the board of directors for the American Public Power Association. **Business Addr:** Board Member, American Public Power Association, 2301 M St NW, Washington, DC 20037, (202)467-2900.

COX, OTIS GRAHAM, JR.
Government official. **Personal:** Born Oct 29, 1941, Winston-Salem, NC; son of Geraldine Cox and Otis Cox (deceased); married Wanda Woodlon; children: Wendi, Kevin, Keith. **Educ:** Savannah State Coll GA, BSIA 1963; FBI Academy Quantico VA, law enforce cert 1969; Suffolk Univ Boston, MPA 1980. **Career:** Baltimore Co MD, sch teacher 1963-67; Westinghouse Elec Corp, engr writer 1967-69; FBI, special agent investigator 1969; FBI Boston, supr civil rights 1977; FBI Washington DC, adminstr pub 1979, special agent supr pub 1979-, asst section chief. **Orgs:** Mem Alpha Phi Alpha Frat 1960-80; mem Natl Police Assoc 1972-78; treas mem MA Assoc of Afro Amer Policemen 1976-78; mem Amer Soc for Public Admin 1979; mem NOBLE, Urban League, Black Exec Exchange Prog; assoc mem Int Assn of Chiefs of Police Inc; deacon Peace of Mind Baptist Church; Rotarian; board of directors, United Hospital Center; executive bd, Boy Scouts of America. **Honors/Awds:** Toland Collier Meml Awd Savannah State Coll 1961; A A Leadership Awd Alpha Phi Frat Delta Eta 1963; Cert of Bravery MA Assn of Afro Am Policemen 1975; Cert of Accomplishment Assessment & Designs Inc 1975; 1992 Achievement Award Order of Eastern Star; 1992 Exceptional Accomplishment Award, The Mountain State Bar Association; Executive of the Year, Fraternal Order of Police, 1992. **Business Addr:** Asst Section Chief, FBI, Criminal Justice Information Services Division, Clarksburg, WV 26301.

COX, ROBERT L.
Business executive. **Personal:** Born Mar 14, 1933, Jonesboro, NC; married Audrey L Revis; children: Lorecia, Kenneth, Brian, Gerald. **Educ:** Columbia U, 1973; Adelphi U, MBA 1972; Adelphi U, BA 1956. **Career:** National Westminister Bank USA, vp; Co of Nassau NY, dep sheriff; Franklin Natl Bank, admin asst; Equitable Life Assurance Soc of US, underwriter. **Orgs:** Assoc mem Natl Bankers Assn; dem candidate for public office 1959, 67; treas Great Neck March of Dimes; youth adv NAACP; pres regional dir Natl Credentials Com Emancipa-

tion Centennial Dinner Chmn 1957-64; adv com commr Nassau Co Com for Human Rights 1962-65; trustee exec comm pres sec to bd of trustees Adelphi Univ Alumni 1972-80; asst treas dir exec com vice pres LI YMCA 1971-80; mem NY Governor's Policy Advisory Comm LI Sound Crossing; chmn LI Chap American Diabetes Assn 1978-; mem Natl Council of YMCA's; mem, Urban Bankers Coalition; chmn, ADL "A World of Difference" Coalition 1989-; chmn, Town of North Hempstead Minority Affairs Council. **Honors/Awds:** Hall of Fame Adelphi Univ Sch of Bus Admin; Man of the year YMCA; Small Business White House Conf; Friend of Westinghouse, George Westinghouse HS, Brooklyn 1988. **Business Addr:** Vice President, National Westminister Bank USA, 97-77 Queens Blvd, Rego Park, NY 11374.

COX, RONALD
Professional football player. **Personal:** Born Feb 27, 1968, Fresno, CA. **Educ:** Fresno State. **Career:** Chicago Bears, linebacker, 1990-95, 1997-; Green Bay Packers, 1996. **Business Addr:** Professional Football Player, Chicago Bears, 1000 Football Dr, Halas Hall at Conway Park, Lake Forest, IL 60045-4829, (847)295-6600.

COX, SANDRA HICKS
Attorney. **Personal:** Born Apr 28, 1939, Baton Rouge, LA; daughter of Eleanor Victorine Frazier Hicks and Henry Beecher Hicks Sr; married Ronald Virgil Cox; children: Michelle Louella, Damien Monroe. **Educ:** Howard Univ, BA 1959; OH State Univ Coll of Law, JD 1962. **Career:** Donald P McCullum, Oakland, CA, counsel, 1965; Dixon & White, & William C Dixon & Associates, Oakland, CA, counsel, 1965-67; San Francisco Neighborhood Legal Assistance Foundation, Domestic relations counsel, 1967-69; San Francisco Legal Assistance Foundation, chief of domestic relations department, 1969-72; State of California Public Utilities Commission, Legal Assistant to public utilities commissioner, 1972-73; Kaiser Foundation Health Plan, Inc, Counsel, 1973-84; Kaiser Foundation Hospitals/Kaiser Foundation Health Plan Inc, vice president and regional counsel, 1984-. **Orgs:** Mem OH State Bar 1963-, CA State Bar 1964-; mem Agency Relations Council United Way Inc 1985-86; mem National Bar Association; member, Los Angeles County Bar Association; member, Jack & Jill of America, Inc, 1990-93. **Honors/Awds:** Parliamentarian, Delta Sigma Theta Sorority, Inc, 1986-87, 1991; Black Women of Achievement Award, NAACP Legal Defense & Educational Fund Inc, 1987; House Counsel of the Year, John M Langston Bar Association, 1990; President's Compass Award, National Bar Association, 1990, Sr Advisor to President, Langston Bar Assn, 1994. **Business Addr:** Vice President and Regional Counsel, Kaiser Foundation Health Plan Inc, Walnut Center, 393 E Walnut St, Pasadena, CA 91188, (818)405-5630.

COX, TAYLOR H., SR.
Accountant, manager (retired). **Personal:** Born Feb 28, 1926, Clarksburg, WV; son of Matilda Cox (deceased) and Wade Cox (deceased); married Betty Leftridge, 1947 (died 1963); children: Taylor Jr, Patricia Conner, Nancy Willis; children: Annette Austin, Lamont Seals. **Educ:** WV Wesleyan Coll Buckhannon, BS Business Econ (Cum Laude) 1953; IN Univ Bloomington, MBA 1954. **Career:** Home Fed Savings & Loan Assoc, Detroit (only African-American owned & oper in state), general mgr 1954-59; Detroit Coca-Cola Bottling Co, asst to sales mgr (1st African-American mgr) 1959-64; Motown Records Detroit, dept head-artist mgmt 1964-72; Invictus Records Detroit, vice pres artist mgmt 1972-73; MI Bell Telephone Co, dist mgr minority econ devel. **Orgs:** Life mem Detroit Crime Comm NAACP 1955-; columnist MI Chronicle 1955-79; publ issues task force Urban League Detroit 1975-79; mem affirmative action comm United Comm Serv Detroit 1975-79; mem Natl Business League 1976-80; proj mgr New Detroit Inc 1978-79; exec bd mem Amer Bridge Assn 1979-80; mem Detroit Assn of Business Econ 1979-80. **Honors/Awds:** Numerous Certificates of Appreciation & Plaques NAACP, Urban League, New Detroit Inc, United Comm Serv 1955-79; listed Natl Top 50 List Amer Bridge Assn 1979-80. **Military Serv:** US Army, sgt, 1944-46, 1948-49; Bronze Starr ETO.

COX, TYRONE Y
City official, accountant. **Career:** Ty Cox Accounting and Business Services, Inc., pres/CEO, currently; Durham City Council, councilman, currently. **Orgs:** First Cavalry Baptist Church Boy Scout Troop 108, scout leader; First Cavalry Baptist Church Cub Scout Pack 108, scout leader; North Carolina Public Allies, board member; Natl Assoc of Black Accountants, Inc, natl bd mem. **Special Achievements:** Youngest person ever elected to the Durham City Council. **Business Addr:** Councilman, Durham City Council, 101 City Hall Plz, Durham, NC 27701, (919)956-5555.

COX, WARREN E.
Attorney. **Personal:** Born Apr 26, 1936, Brookhaven, MS; son of Pinkie Cox; married Alpha Whiting Cox, Apr 20, 1957; children: Diethra D, Reggie R. **Educ:** Alcorn A&M Coll, BSEd 1957; So IL U, MEd 1966; Univ of MS, JD 1969. **Career:** US DOL/OFCCP, Jackson, MS assistant district director, 1987-91; US Equel Employ Opp Commn, dist counsel; EEOC, sr investigator 1973; Holly Springs, staff atty 1969-72; Univ Law Sch, research asst 1966-69; Lincoln's Attendance Cntr, teacher band dir 1964-69; Gentry HS, teacher band dir 1957-64. **Orgs:** Mem NAACP; MS Dem Pary MS Bar Assn; Nat Bar Assn; Am Bar Assn; Magnolia Bar Assn; MS Lawyers Assn; Federal Bar Assn; Am Judicate Soc. **Home Addr:** 5238 Cloverdale Dr, Jackson, MS 39212.

COX, WENDELL
Dentist, broadcasting executive. **Personal:** Born Nov 7, 1914, Charleston, SC; married Iris; children: Wendell Haley, Iris Marie. **Educ:** Talladega Coll, AB; Meharry Coll, DDS 1944; Fisk Univ & Boston U, grad courses. **Career:** PrivPrac Inkster, dentist 1946-; radio stations KWK St Louis WCHB-AM & wjzz-FM Detroit, vp. **Orgs:** Mem Am & Nat Dental Assns; mem Mayor's Com on Human Realtions; bd mem New Detroit Com; Detroit C of C; Detroit Inst of the Arts; Meharry Med Coll. **Business Addr:** 32790 Henry Ruff Rd, Inkster, MI 48141.

COXE, G. CALIMAN
Illustrator (retired). **Personal:** Born May 8, 1908, Carlisle, PA; son of Ama Della Caliman Coxe and Rev Philip John Augustus Coxe; widowed. **Educ:** Univ Louisville, BS art. **Career:** Ft Knox KY 1 man exhibit Louisville, retired illustrator 1968. **Orgs:** Founded Louisville Art Workshop 1966. **Honors/Awds:** Many 1 man & major group exhibits. **Military Serv:** USN.

COXE, WILLIAM HADDON
Architect, director (retired). **Personal:** Born Oct 12, 1920, Mebane, NC; son of Ama Della Coxe and P J Agustus; married Laurice Young; children: Karen Lynn, William H Jr. **Educ:** Attended, Johnson C Smith Univ; Howard Univ, BArch 1953; Univ of No CO, Landscape Arch, Natural Urban Sys. **Career:** George M Ewing Co Architects-Engrs Washington DC, priv industry 15 yrs, Philadelphia office 1953-66; US Post Office Dept, engrg & res div 1958-61; DC Public Schs, architect facilities planner dir div of buildings & grounds (retired). **Orgs:** Mem Assn of Sch Bus Ofcls of MD & DC; Building Code Adv Council of DC; Metro Sch Facilities Planners; mem All Comm Sch Planning Comm; Anthony Bowen Br YMCA DC. **Honors/Awds:** 1st place medal Architectural Design Howard Univ 1953; represented Howard Univ in Intl Arch Design Competition Sao Paulo Brazil 1952. **Military Serv:** AUS WW II; Italian Campaign 1942-45.

COX-RAWLES, RANI
Educator (retired). **Personal:** Born Nov 9, 1927, Buffalo, NY; daughter of Robuty G Hale and George Hale; married Cornelius Milton, Nov 28, 1959. **Educ:** Univ of Paris Sorbonne, BA, MA 1948-54; Univ of Buffalo, PhD 1965. **Career:** E HS, teacher 1957-70, improve prog 1970-79; Buffalo Bd of Ed, proj admin; Buffalo Vocational Tech Ctr, occupational spec 1979-90. **Orgs:** Adv Future Teachers of Amer, Girls Charm Club Yearbook 1957-62; Aspire instr Proj Able 1964-66; commencement speaker Kleinhans 1970; serv Future Health Planning Career Council Syracuse 1974; dir CAC Youth Employement 1974; bd of dir Girls Scouts of Amer 1977-81; mem Black Educ Assn, Comm Adv Council, Notary Publ Officer, Natl Educ Assn, Sr Citizens Adv; community consultant to TV Channels 2, 7 & 29; YOP Buffalo Psych Ctr; mem Mayors Heritage Comm, Archit Historians Preserv Soc, Amer Museum of Natural History, Soc for Provention Cruelty to Children; educ comm Emmanuel Temple;mem VEA Comm for Erie Community Coll 1980-90. **Honors/Awds:** Outstanding Citizen Awd Bethel AME Church 1973; Woman of the Year Awd SUNY Buffalo Urban Ctr Div 1973; Yearbook Dedication for E HS 1974; Omicron Soc Awd 1974.

COY, JOHN T.
Police officer. **Personal:** Born Oct 5, 1939, Princeton, NJ; son of Alice Jeanette Douglas Coy and John I Coy (deceased); married Faithe Suzanne Parago, Jan 31, 1959; children: Barrie A (deceased), Wendy D, David S, Dhana P, Dawn C. **Educ:** Trenton State Coll, Ewing Township NJ, 1972-73; Mercer County Community Coll, West Windsor NJ, 1983-86; Atlanta Univ, Criminal Justice Institute, 1983-88. **Career:** Trenton Police Dept, Trenton NJ, patrolman, 1964-70, detective, 1970-78, sergeant, 1978-82, detective sergeant, 1982-. **Orgs:** Charter mem, past pres, Brother Officers Law Enforcement Society, 1968-; mem, Trenton Superior Officers Assn, 1978-; mem, Mayor's Advisory Committeee on Affirmative Action, 1981-; bd of dir, Carver Youth & Family Center, 1983-; mem, Roga Golf Club, 1983; mem delegate, Natl Black Police Assn, 1983-; pres, Carver Century Club, 1984-; information officer, New Jersey Council, Natl Black Police 1985-; mem, NAACP, 1985-; information officer, Northeast Region, Natl Black Police Assn, 1987-; mem bd of dir, Natl Black Police Assn 1987-. **Honors/Awds:** Author of article on police/community relations in The Police Chief, 1974; author of Police Officer's Handbook for the Trenton Police Division 1980, 1986; Valor Award, Trenton Police Division, 1980; founder & current pres, Carver Century Club, 1984; founder & current editor, Vanguard ANJ Publication for Black Police Officers, 1984; superior office of the year, City of Trenton, 1985; founder & current editor, Northeast Regional News, Natl Black Police Assn 1985; superior officer of the year, City of Trenton, 1985; mem of the year, Natl Black Police Assn Northeast Region, 1986. **Home Addr:** 513 Eggerts Crossing Road, Trenton, NJ 08638.

COYE, DENA E.
Entrepreneur. **Personal:** daugHter of Kathleen Coye (deceased) and Ruel Coye (deceased). **Educ:** Fordham Univ, MA, social science, 1978; New School for Social Research, MA, human resource management, 1982; postgraduate courses in business management and television production. **Career:** Dena Coye Productions, founder/president, currently; producer/host, tv series, Dena Coye Money Matters, currently. **Orgs:** The Mosaic Council Inc, founder/pres, 1990-; National Association of Black Journalists, 1989-; Natl Association of Female Executives, 1981-89; National Association of Women Business Owners, 1991; Jackie Robinson Foundation, Jazz Committee, 1980-. **Honors/Awds:** Video Center of Arts Performers, Business Award, 1991; BBI Productions, Rubenesque for Career Achievement, 1990. **Business Addr:** President, Dena Coye Productions, 163 Third Ave, Suite 133, New York, NY 10003.

COYLE, MARY DEE
Association executive. **Personal:** Born Apr 6, 1916, Wichita Falls, TX; widowed; children: Doris, Paul, Luther, Larry, Charles. **Educ:** Tex Thcr Coll Harrison Tchr Coll Eden Theol Sem. **Career:** Union Sarah Corp, dir contact worker; Community Corp Chap (LAW), con league for adequate wflr; Mo Natl wlfr Right Org, rep. **Orgs:** Mem NAACP; Foundation Area & Neighborhood Assn; Parents for Progress; Anna Malone Children Hm. **Honors/Awds:** Mother of yr Chick-Finney awd 1973; community services awd 1974.

COZART, JOHN
Judge. **Personal:** Born Aug 31, 1928, Birmingham, AL; married Powell L Hairston; children: Rhonda, Steven. **Educ:** Howard Univ Wash DC, BS 1950; Wayne State Law School Detroit, JD 1955. **Career:** Wayne Cty Dept of Social Welfare, soc worker 1952-54; Cozart Real Estate Co, real estate broker 1955-; Common Pleas Ct Detroit, judge. **Orgs:** Founder Med Professional Bldg Complex 1967; mem Alpha Phi Alpha; trustee Greater New Mt Moriah Bapt Church. **Business Addr:** Judge 36th District Court, Madison Center Building, 421 Madison Ave, Detroit, MI 48226.

CRABLE, DALLAS EUGENE
Government official (retired). **Personal:** Born Mar 31, 1927, Brownsville, PA; married Galena Mae Woodson; children: Woodson Dillard. **Educ:** Huchtinson Community Junior College, AA 1971; Sterling College, BA 1975; Wichita State University, MEd 1978. **Career:** Kansas Board of Tax Appeals, beginning 1979; personnel dir, Krause Plow Corp, 1976-79; dir, Title IV, Upward Bound & ASC College Cntl, KS, 1974-76; Title IV, Special Service Hutchinson Junior College, counselor, 1971-74; Shadduck Park Community Center, dir, 1969-71. **Orgs:** Fleet Reserve Association; NAACP; AARP; USGA Public Committee, 1992-93; mem, Amer Legion; Kansas Bd Tax Appeals, 1979-87; counselor, Hutchinson Comm College, 1987-89. **Honors/Awds:** Elected to Hutchinson City Commission, 1971-73. **Military Serv:** US Navy, petty officer (retired), 1944-46, 1950-68. **Home Addr:** 309 East Avenue A, Hutchinson, KS 67501.

CRAFT, E. CARRIE
Nurse, educator (retired). **Personal:** Born Feb 16, 1928, Jeffersontown, KY. **Educ:** Harlem Hosp Sch Nursing, RN 1952; Hunter Coll, BS 1959; Hunter Coll, MS 1962; attended workshops & seminars nursing; Univ of AL Birmingham, Post-Masters Cert as Nurse Educator in Oncology 1980-81. **Career:** New York City Dept Health, pub health nurse 1953-59; Misericordia Hosp Sch Nursing Bronx, 1959-60; Rutgers Univ, Newark NJ Coll Nursing, instr 1962-64; St Mary & Elizabeth Sch Nursing Louisville, instr 1965-66; Montifiori Hosp Bronx, summer staff nurse 1969; St Lukes Hosp NYC, supr 1971-72; Mt Holly Nursing Home Lou, summer part time staff nurse 1974-76; IN Univ School of Nursing, Southeast Campus, assoc prof 1966-92, assoc prof emeritus, 1996-. **Orgs:** Treas IN State Nurses Assn 1974, 1976-; mem Amer Nurses Assn; mem Nat League for Nurses; mem KY League for Nurses; bd mem Clark Co Cancer Soc 1979-81; mem First Bapt Ch Jeffersontown, NAACP, Urban League; bd mem Louisville Lutheran Home 1983-; sec & mem bd of dirs Louisville Lutheran Home 1985-86; mem Southern IN Heart Assoc 1986-87; chairperson, Scholarship comm, First Baptist Church of Jeffersontown, 1989-92; volunteer, Hospice of Louisville, KY, 1993-95; ombudsman, KY Home for Aged, 1993-96; Tutor for Elem School Children, Bd of Education. **Honors/Awds:** Certificate 10 yrs serv 1977, 15 yrs 1982, 20 yrs 1987 IN Univ School of Nursing, Southeast Campus; IN School of Nursing, Certificate for 25 Years of Service; Good Samaritan Center, Certificate for Volunteer Service, 1995. **Business Addr:** Associate Professor, Indiana Univ Southeast Campus, 4201 Grantline Rd, New Albany, IN 47150.

CRAFT, GUY CALVIN
Library director. **Personal:** Born Oct 19, 1929, Atlanta, GA; son of Josie Hubert Glass and Guy Craft; married Martha Broadwater Craft, Sep 1972; children: Guy Jr, Audrey, Anthony, Gayle, Scott. **Educ:** Morehouse College, Atlanta, GA, AB, 1951; Atlanta University, Atlanta, GA, MSLS, 1961; Southern Illinois University, Carbondale, IL, PhD, 1976. **Career:** Florida Memorial College, St Augustine, FL, head librarian, 1957-63; Elizabeth City State University, Elizabeth City, NC, chief cata-

loger, 1963-65; Albany State College, Albany, GA, head librarian, 1965-85; Atlanta University Center/Robert W Woodruff Library, Atlanta, GA, library director, 1985-. **Orgs:** Mem, Kiwanis, 1987-; mem, Metropolitan Atlanta Red Cross, 1986-87; pres, Community Relations Council, 1976-78; chairman, Chehaw Council Boy Scouts, 1976-80; mem, Board of Directors/CCLC, 1977-. **Honors/Awds:** Resolution Commendation, Georgia House of Representatives, 1986; Honor Certificate & Plaque, Boy Scouts, 1978; Honor Certificate, Job Corps, 1977; Honor Cerrtificate, Morehouse College, 1976; Boss of the Year, ABWA, 1988. **Military Serv:** Air Force, captain, 1951-56. **Business Addr:** Library Director, Atlanta University Center, Robert W Woodruff Library, 111 James P Brawley Drive, SW, Atlanta, GA 30314.

CRAFT, SALLY-ANN ROBERTS (SALLY-ANN ROBERTS)
Journalist. **Personal:** Born Feb 14, 1953, Chandler, AZ; married Willie Jerome. **Educ:** Univ of So MS, BA 1976; Univ of So MS, MS 1977. **Career:** WWL-TV New Orleans, reporter 1977-; WDAM TV Sta Hattiesburg MS, weathercaster/Reporter 1977; WXXX Radio Sta Hattiesburg MS, radio announcer 1976. **Orgs:** Mem MS Press Women 1977; mem AFTRA; big sister Big Sisters of Greater New Orleands; program com mem St Mark's United Meth Ch. **Honors/Awds:** 1st place Gen Reporting MS Press Women 1977; 2nd place Gen Reporting Nat Assn of Press Women 1977; gaines baston meml award AFTRA 1978; TV journalist of the year Physically Limited Assn for a More Constructive Environment (PLACE) 1979. **Business Addr:** WWL-TV, 1024 N Rampart St, New Orleans, LA 70126.

CRAFT, THOMAS J., SR.
Biologist, educator, administrator. **Personal:** Born Dec 27, 1924, Monticello, KY; son of Wonnie Travis Craft and Thomas Marion Craft; married Joan Ruth Hunter, Sep 4, 1948; children: Thomas J Jr, Yvonne Diane. **Educ:** Central State Univ, BS 1948; Kent State Univ, MA 1950; OH State Univ, PhD 1963. **Career:** Central State Univ, Instructor 1950-51, asst prof 1951-59, assoc prof 1959-63, prof 1963-; Wright State Univ, adjunct prof 1973-79; FL Memorial Coll, program dir DOE energy grant 1980, natural sciences & math div dir 1981, institutional planning dir 1982, dean of faculty 1984-87. **Orgs:** Mem Dade Co FL Educ Task Force of the Beacon Council 1984; mem Research Resources Council Natl Inst of Health 1973-76; CSU/NASA 14 CSU/NASA 1972-76; health science admin HEW NIH Div of Rsch Resources Bethesda MD 1977-79; NSF NIH OH State Dept of Health ad hoc consulting; mem chmn Rsch Resources (NIH) Group on Minority Biomedical Research 1976-77; investigator Rsch Projects 1970-77; chmn WSU/Med Sch Anatomy Faculty Search Comm 1976-77; mem exec comm OH Acad of Sci 1975-77; fellow Ohio Academy of Science, mem Advisory Panel, Educ Devel Center, Newton MA, 1984-87; fellow Amer Assn for the Advancement of Sci; consultant Natl Science Foundation, Gujurat Univ, Ahmedebad, India, 1967, Osmania Univ, Hyderabad, India, 1968; member, health subcommittee,Governor's Commission on the Disadvantaged Black Male, 1-90; board of directors, education committee; Xenia, Ohio Area Chamber of Commerce; board of directors, children services board, Greene County, Ohio, 1989-93; Greene Oaks Health Ctr, Xenia OH, board of directors, 1993-. **Honors/Awds:** Tri-Beta Biological Honor Soc; Sigma Pi Phi Boule; Soc of Sigma Xi; AAAS, Fellow; Ohio Academy of Science, Fellow; OH State Univ, Citation for Achievement 1979; Emeritus Professor of Biology, Central State University, Ohio. **Military Serv:** USMCR corporal, 1943-46; company (recruit) Honor Man; Central State Univ, Achievement Halll of Fame, 1993. **Home Phone:** (937)372-5006.

CRAIG, CHERYL ALLEN
Judge. **Personal:** Born Dec 16, 1947, Pittsburgh, PA; daughter of Corrine Davis Allen and Robert Allen; married Frederick S Craig, Jun 17, 1978; children: Jason, Justin, Frederick. **Educ:** Pennsylvania State Univ, Pittsburgh, PA, BS, elementary education, 1969; Univ of Pittsburgh, Pittsburgh, PA, graduate studies, 1971-72, JD, 1975. **Career:** Pittsburgh Public Schools, Pittsburgh, PA, teacher, 1969-72; College of Arts and Sciences, Univ of Pittsburgh, academic advisor, 1973-75; Neighborhood Legal Services, Northside Office, staff attorney, 1975-76; Pennsylvania Human Relations Commission, assistant general counsel, 1976-77; Allegheny County Law Department, assistant county solicitor, 1977-90; self-employed lawyer, 1980-90; Allegheny County Disadvantaged and Women's Business Enterprise Appeal Board, administrative hearing officer, 1988-90; Allegheny County Common Pleas Court, Criminal Division, judge, 1990-. **Orgs:** Board member, Community Service Center; board member, Stanton Heights Recreation Association; member, Pittsburgh Chapter NAACP; member, Mayor's Task Force on Women; member, National Association of Negro Business & Professional Women, Pittsburgh Club. **Honors/Awds:** Black Women of Achievement, Alpha Kappa Alpha Sorority, 1987; Greater Pittsburgh Achievers, Negro Business & Professional Womens Club, 1987; Pennsylvania Women of Distinction, Pennsylvania Women's Campaign Fund, 1986; Professional Woman of the Year, Triangle Corner Ltd, 1991. **Business Addr:** Judge of Common Pleas Court, Family Div, Juvenile Sec, Allegheny County, Pennsylvania, 3333 Forbes Avenue, Pittsburgh, PA 15213.

CRAIG, CLAUDE BURGESS
Elected government official. **Personal:** Born Dec 17, 1946, Atlantic City, NJ; married Dawn; children: Tamikio, Claude II. **Educ:** Hampton Inst, BS 1970. **Career:** Newark Bd of Ed, hearing officer; East Orange City Council, chmn. **Honors/Awds:** Outstanding Young Man of Amer Jaycees 1980. **Business Addr:** Chairman, East Orange City Council, 44 City Hall Plaza, East Orange, NJ 07019.

CRAIG, ELSON L.
Physician. **Personal:** Born Nov 27, 1933; divorced; children: Joellyn, Carlton. **Educ:** OH State U, BS 1955; OH State U, MS 1961; OH State U, MD 1966f. **Career:** Aff Coll of Medicine OH, opthalmologist, asst dean for students 1970-. **Orgs:** Mem Acad of Me of Columbus & Franklin Co; Am Assn of Ophthalmology; Am Med Assn; bd of dir OH Soc for the Prevention of Blindness 1977; Columbus Assn of Physicians & Dentists; OH State Med Assn; Nat Med Assn; Electron Mocroscope Soc of Am; mem Nu Sigma Nu; Simga XI; Soc of Heed Fellows; Alpha Omega Alpha Med Soc; Landacre Soc. **Military Serv:** AUS 1st Lt 1956-58. **Business Addr:** 456 Clinic Dr, Columbus, OH 43210.

CRAIG, EMMA JEANELLE PATTON
Educator. **Personal:** Born Feb 11; daughter of Sebell Rabon Patton and Eddie D Patton; married Howard James Craig Sr, Dec 22, 1986; children: Howard James Jr. **Educ:** Grambling State Coll, BS 1966; Univ of Scranton, MS 1976, post masters 1982, Grambling State Univ, 1977-79, 1982, LA Tech Univ, 1978, 1979. **Career:** Galveston TX Indus School Dist, teacher 1967-68; Richland Parish School Bd, teacher/dance inst 1966-68; Des Moines Indus School Dist, teacher 1968-70; Bloomsburg State Univ, asst dir of Center for Acad Devel & asst resident dean of student life 1974-76; RCA Serv Co Govt Serv, mgr of educ, voc training & data consultant, 1970-74 & 77-78; Grambling St Univ Lab School, teacher & HS coach (girls Varsity Basketball); Al Nellums & Assoc Inc, consultant 1978-79; Orleans Parish School Bd, teacher & chapter coordinator, 1979-82; St Charles Parish Public Schools, teacher 1982-84; Grambling State Univ, EEO officer & telecomm coordinator, 1984-86, telecommunications liaison officer 1986-89; Alabama State Univ, assoc coordinator freshman orientation program, 1989-. **Orgs:** Mem Alpha Kappa Alpha Sor; mem LA Equal Oppor Assoc 1984-86; mem Assn of Social and Behavioral Scientists Inc 1984-86; mem Energy Mgmt/Telecomm Surveillance and Security Systems Comm Grambling State Univ 1984-; managing editor Journal of Social & Behavioral Scis 1985-86; mem steering comm Cancer Prevention Awareness Grambling State Univ 1985-; mem Amer Assn for Higher Educ 1986-; mem Adv Comm for Telecommunications Grambling State Univ 1986-; research & proposal writer RCA Serv Co Government Services 1971-74 & Bloomsburg State 1975-77; member, Alabama Assn for Developmental Ed, 1990-91; member, Natl Education Assn, 1986-. **Honors/Awds:** Outstanding Award for Serv to Students, Orleans Parish LA 1982; Certificate of Achievement The LA State Dept of Educ 1981-83; Certificate of Achievement United States Dept of Labor; The North LA Consortium for Education Teacher Appraisal & The Improvement of Instructions 1978-79.

CRAIG, FREDERICK A.
Oral surgeon. **Personal:** Born Apr 28, 1933, Selma; married Leslie J Cyrusd. **Educ:** Fisk U, BS 1954; MS 1958; Meharry Med Coll, DDS 1963. **Career:** Fisk U, instr 1956-58; US Post Office, 1958; Private Dental Prictice, 1966-67; Chicago Bd of Health, oral surgeon 1967-70; Private Practtce, oral surgeon; Daniel Hale Williams Neighborhood Health Center, dental dir. **Orgs:** Bd dirs Daniel Hale Williams Heighorhood Health Center; mem Dental Subcom Chicago Heart Assn; mem IL Soc Oral Surgery; Chicago Soc Oral Surgery; Am IL Chicago Dental Socs; Alpha Phi Alpha Frat. **Military Serv:** AUS 1954-56. **Business Addr:** 2011 E 75 St, Chicago, IL 60649.

CRAIG, RHONDA PATRICIA
Administrative law judge. **Personal:** Born Nov 27, 1953, Gary, IN; daughter of Myrtle Glover and William Craig; married Fulton Smith Jr, Jun 28, 1985; children: Andaiye Spencer, Fulton Douglass Smith. **Educ:** Valparaiso Univ, BA 1975, Sch of Law JD 1978. **Career:** Wayne Co Neighborhood Legal Svcs, staff atty 1978-79; Legal Aide and Defender's Office, public defender 1979-80; Wayne Co Corp Counsel, asst corp counsel 1981; State of MI, administrative law judge 1982-. **Orgs:** Legal counsel Soc of Engrs & Applied Scientists 1982-; Wolverine Bar Assn 1982-; Assn of Black Judges of MI 1983-; bd of dirs Legal Aide & Defender's Assn 1987; Augusta D Straker Bar Assn. **Honors/Awds:** Special Achievement Awd SEAS 1984. **Business Addr:** Adminstration Law Judge, State of Michigan, 1200 Sixth St #540, Detroit, MI 48226.

CRAIG, RICHARD
Personnel administrator (retired). **Personal:** Born May 10, 1915, Springfield, OH; son of Arlethia Craig and Mack Craig; married Catherine Elise; children: Donald, Richard. **Educ:** Univ of Toledo, BA 1940; Univ of MI, MA 1962. **Career:** Claflin Coll, coach & athletic dir 1940-42; Univ of Toledo, asst football coach 1943; Ft Valley State Coll, coach & athletic dir 1945-54; Jefferson Jr High School, Pontiac Bd of Educ, teacher 1954-62, prin 1962-68, Pontiac Bd of Educ, dir of personnel 1968-83. **Orgs:** Chmn Rules Com So Athletic conf 1952; mem NAACP; mem Omega Psi Phi; institutional rep BSA 1966; bd dirs ESCRU 1966-67; bd dirs Pontiac Boys Club 1968-75; bd dirs Pontiac Urban League 1969-72; mem Amer Assn of Sch Personnel Adminstrs 1979-; mem Diocesan Commn on Ministry 1980; Governor's Entrepreneurial Small Business Commission, 1990. **Honors/Awds:** First Black Staying on Univ of Toledo Campus 1936-40; First Black from Univ of Toledo to play in All-Star Game 1940; Organizer Black HS State Track Meet in GA 1950; Orgn First Black HS All-Star Football Game in GA 1952; helped 80 HS Grads receive Athletic Scholarships to Coll; Track Facility named "Richard Craig Track Facility" Pontiac Bd of Educ 1978; inducted Hall of Fame Univ of Toledo 1980; inducted into Fort Valley State Coll Hall of Fame as a coach 1982; Alma G Stallworth Award, 1996.

CRAIG, STARLETT RUSSELL
Educational administrator. **Personal:** Born Aug 17, 1947, Asheville, NC; daughter of Mr & Mrs Robert Russell; divorced; children: Kemi, Karma. **Educ:** Spelman Coll, BA Sociology 1969; Bryn Mawr Grad School of Social Work & Social Rsch, MSS 1969-71. **Career:** Univ of NC Asheville, dir office for aging 1978-80; Western Carolina Univ, foreign student adv, asst to the vice chancellor for student devel; Clemson Univ, dir of academic programs, currently. **Orgs:** Mem rsch comm NC Assoc of Women Deans, Counselors & Admin 1982-85; grad advisor Alpha Kappa Alpha Sor 1984-85; mem Natl Assn of Foreign Student Affairs; mem Jackson County Council on the Status of Women. **Honors/Awds:** Field Scholar Spelman Coll 1965-69; Holt-Manley Wilburn Young Scholar Alumnus Awd 1965-67; Outstanding Young Women of Amer 1983; congressional intern, summer 1984. **Business Addr:** Director of Academic Programs, Clemson University, Tillman Hall, G-11, Clemson, SC 29634, (864)656-4720.

CRAIG-JONES, ELLEN WALKER
City official (retired). **Personal:** Born Jun 5, 1906, Franklin Co; daughter of Charles O Bell Walker; married James H Craig (deceased); children: James P, Esterleen Moore. **Educ:** Urbancrest & Columbus Public Schools. **Career:** Village of Urbancrest OH, 12 yr council member, mayor (retired). **Orgs:** Manpower Adv Council; Mid OH Region Planning Commn; Black Women Leadership Council; OH Black Polit Assembly; Central OH Mayor's Council; State OH Mayor's Council; chmn of bd Manpower Advising Council; PIC; CETA; Urbancrest Civil Improvement Assn; Urbancrest Comm Recreation Bd; Black Women Leadership Council; 1st pres CMACAO's Federal Credit Union; dir Men's Chorus Union Bapt Church; Sunday sch teacher Union Bapt Church; pres Urbancrest Housing Bd; Joint Center for Political Studies; African Heritage Studies Assn, 1996; African Council of Elders, 1996. **Honors/Awds:** Bapt Ch Humanity Awd Columbus Metro Ares Comm Action Orgn 1972; Outstanding Achievement Fedn Consumers Council 1974; Ellen Walker Craig Day OH Gov Gilligvan 1974; Humanitarian Awd OH Balck Polit Assembly 1974; Serv to Mankind Awd Grove City Sertoma Club 1975; Ellen Walker Craig Day the City of Springfield OH 1975; Merit Awd Affiliate Contractors Am Inc 1975; Mayor's Medal City of Columbus OH 1978 Tom Moody Mayor; first Black Woman in nation to be elected mayor; YWCA, Women of Achievement, 1993; Ohio Women's Hall of Fame, 1994. **Special Achievements:** First African-American female elected mayor, in the USA, 1972. **Home Addr:** 2870 Walnut St, Urbancrest, OH 43123.

CRAIG-RUDD, JOAN
Government administrator. **Personal:** Born Oct 5, 1931, Flushing, NY; children: Carolyn Hopkins, Michael, Reginald. **Educ:** Attended, Immanuel Lutheran Coll 1948-49, NC Central Univ 1949-50, US Army Logistics Mgmt Ctr 1969; Natl Contract Mgrs Assoc, seminars 1977-78. **Career:** US Air Force Brooklyn, expeditor 1958-64; US Army New York City, purchasing agent contract negotiator 1967-71; Otis Air Force Base, procurement specialist 1971-72; New York City Off Track Betting Corp, contract administrator, contracts compliance officer, mgr contracts 1975-. **Orgs:** Credit union loan commn Off Track Betting Corp 1976-; mem Natl Contract Mgrs Assoc 1976-81; OTBC rep New York City Prevailing Wage Council 1981-; OTBC Informal Hearing Officer 1983-; life mem NAACP 1985; peer counselor NY Chap Natl Multiple Sclerosis Soc 1985-. **Honors/Awds:** Service Awd NY Multiple Sclerosis Society 1986. **Home Addr:** 168-42 127th Ave #2A, Rochdale Village, NY 11434. **Business Addr:** Manager, New York City Off Track Betting Corp, 1501 Broadway, New York, NY 10036.

CRAIGWELL, HADYN H.
Architect, engineer. **Personal:** Born Jun 12, 1907, New York, NY; married Ruth. **Educ:** Swiss Fed Polytech Zurich, 1932; Tech Univ Berlin, MS, cum laude, 1935. **Career:** Private prac, architect-engr 1946-87. **Orgs:** Mem NY State Soc Professional Engrs 1960; Am Inst Architects 1960; Nat Tech Assn 1937; mem Grand Jury NY County 1947; arbitrator Am Abritration Assn 1961; bd dirs Greater NY YMCA 1967-69; mem past pres Lions Intl 1967-69; mem Aircraft Owners Pilot Assn. **Military Serv:** Nat Guard 1937-39.

CRAMER, JOE J., JR.
Educator. **Personal:** Born in Houston; married; children: 3. **Educ:** TX So U, BBA 1959; IN U, MBA 1960; IN U, DBA 1963. **Career:** TX Southern Univ, student asst 1955-57; Wilson & Cooker CPA's, staff accountant 1957-59; IN Univ, Bureau Business Reasearch, asst accountant 1959-60; IN Graduate School of Business, teacher 1960-62; IN Warehouse Inc, accountant 1963; PA State Univ, asst prof 1963-66, assoc prof 1966-69; Arthur Andersen & Co, faculty resident 1968-69; PA State Univ, prof 1969-74; Arthur Andersen Faculty Fellow, prof 1974-; PA State Univ, head dept accounting 1971; FL A&M Univ, visiting prof 1972; AICPA, consultant 1973; Financial Accounting Standards Bd, consultant 1974. **Orgs:** Mem Bata Gamma Sigma; Beta Alpha Psi; Alpha Kappa Psi; Alpha Kappa Mu; Am InstCertified Pub Accuntants; Am Accounting Assn; Com Coordinate Am AccountingAssn; Adv Panel Nat Assn Accountants; Nat Const Com. **Honors/Awds:** Presented many professional & tech Papers; student achievement award Wall St Journal 1959; opportunity fellow John Hay Whitney Found 1959-60.

CRANFORD, SHARON HILL
Executive director. **Personal:** Born Feb 8, 1946, Jaoquin, TX; daughter of Eulalia Hill and Rev Garfield Hill (deceased); married Dr Evies O Cranford; children: Charlton F, Corey M. **Educ:** TX Woman's Univ, BA 1966; Atlanta Univ, MA 1970; Kansas State Univ, PhD 1981. **Career:** TX State Dept of Human Resources, coord volunteer serv 1976-77; Jarvis Christian Coll, dir student union 1977-79; Residential Homes for Boys, dir 1983-84; Wichita State Univ, asst prof 1984-85; Cranford Adult Living-Learning Centers Inc, exec dir 1982-. **Orgs:** Corres sec The Links Inc 1985-87; public relations chair Alpha Kappa Alpha Sor Inc 1985-87; first vice pres City of Wichita Public Library Bd of Dirs 1985-; mem County Coalition for Mental Hlth 1986-; pres Residential Area Providers of Handicapped Serv 1986-; mem KS State Dept Social Serv Bd 1987-89; KS Para Transit Council 1987-; grad advisor Alpha Kappa Alpha Sor Inc 1987-; soprano/soloist Calvary Bapt Church and Choir 1984-. **Honors/Awds:** Title XIX Doctoral Fellowship KS State Univ 1979-81; Service Commendations to Handicapped Elks Training Ctr 1984; Service to Youth Awd Natl Alliance of Business 1985; Public Serv Awd Omega Psi Phi Frat 1986; soprano/soloist Porgy and Bess 1st Natl Black History Soc 1987. **Home Addr:** 2420 N Dellrose, Wichita, KS 67220.

CRAVEN, JUDITH
Association executive. **Career:** School of Allied Health Sciences, Houston, TX, dean; United Way of the Texas Gulf Coast, president, currently. **Special Achievements:** First African-American to head the Texas Gulf Coast office. **Business Addr:** President, United Way of the Texas Gulf Coast, PO Box 924507, Houston, TX 77292-4507, (713)685-2756.

CRAVER, AARON LERENZE
Professional football player. **Personal:** Born Dec 18, 1968, Los Angeles, CA; married Dawn, Jun 29, 1991; children: Jalen, Kyndol. **Educ:** Fresno State. **Career:** Miami Dolphins, running back, 1991-94; Denver Broncos, 1995-96; San Diego Chargers, 1997-. **Business Addr:** Professional Football Player, San Diego Chargers, Qualcomm Stadium, 9449 Friars Rd, San Diego, CA 92108, (619)280-2111.

CRAWFORD, BARBARA HOPKINS
Business executive. **Personal:** Born Feb 4, Aurora, IL; divorced. **Educ:** Drake U, 1942; Northwestern U, 1945; DePaul Univ Law Sch, 1964; Govs St U, BA 1974; Roosevelt U, grad study 1976. **Career:** Dollars & Sense Mag managing ed 1980-; Charles A Davis & Asso, vice pres 1977-79; Dearborn Real Estate Bd, acct exec 1974-77, exec dir 1973-74; Nat Ins Assn, asst dir 1968-73; law firm, exec sec 1947-68; Dollars & Sense Mag, asso editor 1977-79; Issues Unltd WGN-TV panelist 1977; Chicago Chap Nat Assn ofMedia Women, prs 1973-77, natl 1st vice pres 1977-81; NAMU, natl rec sec 1975-77. **Orgs:** Mem Women in Communicatiolns; co-chmn Minority Recruitment Prog 1973-76; dir Pro & Con Screening Bd 1975-; mem Chicago Urban League; NAACP; League of BlackWomen; Nat Hook-up of Black Women Inc; AFRICARE; Chicago Chap Media Woman of Yr; Natl Asso of Media Women 1977-78. **Honors/Awds:** Nat Pres Plaque NAMW 1976; publ Articles Dollars & Sense Mag 1976; Image Bvuilder Awd, Operation PUSH; wrote, prod slide film Natl Ins Assn 1973; wrote, prod slide film Natl Conf of Christians & Jews 1977. **Business Addr:** 840 E 87th St, Chicago, IL 60619.

CRAWFORD, BETTY MARILYN
Program analyst. **Personal:** Born Sep 25, 1948, Philadelphia, PA; daughter of Dolores Fuller Crawford and James Crawford. **Educ:** DC Bible Institute 1985-87; Gayles Theological Seminary, DC 1988. **Career:** Univ of Pennsylvania, receptionist; Internal Revenue Service, temporary clerk/typist acctg dept, account maintenance clker; IRS Washington DC, computer systems analyst 1977-1983; IRS Wash DC program analyst 1983-. **Orgs:** Mem Assoc for the Improvement of Minorities-IRS 1972-; mem Guildfield Baptist Church, Wash DC 1983-; dir District Federation of Young People of DC & Vicinity 1987-; chairman Black Employment Program Managers-IRS 1988-. **Honors/Awds:** Profiled in Black Enterprise magazine for career accomplishments 1987; honored as an outstanding Adopt-A-School Volunteer 1988; employee of the year Internal Revenue Service 1989. **Business Addr:** Program Analyst, Internal Revenue Service, 1111 Constitution Ave NW, Rm 2210, Washington, DC 20024.

CRAWFORD, BRENITA
Hospital administrator. **Personal:** Born in Amory, MS. **Educ:** Jackson State University, bachelor's degree, biology, chemistry; University of Alabama, master's degree, hospital and health administration. **Career:** University of Mississippi, University of North Carolina, joint research team, data collection; LeBonhuer Medical Center, admissions administrator; Regional Medical Center, executive asst position, vp; Henry Ford Hospital, associate administrator, 1987-91; Mercy Hospital, president, CEO, 1991-. **Orgs:** Warren/Conner Development Association; Cancer Foundation; Greater Detroit Area Health Council; Healthy Detroit. **Honors/Awds:** National Council of Negro Women, Detroit Chap, Anti-Defamation League Women of Achievement; National Association of Negro Business and Professional Women, Community Service Award. **Business Addr:** President,CEO, Mercy Hospital, 5555 Conner St, Detroit, MI 48213-3499, (313)579-4210.

CRAWFORD, CARL M.
Educational administrator. **Personal:** Born Nov 14, 1932, Tallahassee, FL; married Pearlie Wilson; children: LeVaughn Harrison. **Educ:** FL A&M Univ Tallahassee, FL, BA 1954; Boston Univ MA, MEd 1965; Univ of Miami Sch of Educ Coral Gables, FL, EdD 1971. **Career:** Battery D 95th Anti-Aircraft Artillery Battalion, Mannheim Germany, exec officer 1954-56; Dillard Elementary School Grades 1-6, Ft Lauderdale FL, art, 1956-60, grade 6 1960-61, grade 5 1961-62, art grades 1-6 1962-65; S FL School Desegregation Consult Center, School of Educ, Univ of Miami, asst consultant 1965-66, assoc consultant 1966-67; Art Center Title III ESEA Proj Broward Co Bd of Public Instr, coord/comm 1967-70; Psychology & Educ Dept, Miami-Dade Comm Coll S Campus, Miami FL, chmn 1970-73, chmn self-study steering comm 1972-73; N Campus Broward Comm Coll, dean 1974-75. **Orgs:** Natl & S Regnl Cncl on Black Am Affairs; Nat Assn of Black Sch Educators; Phi Delta Kappa; FL Assn of Comm Coll; Am Assn of Comm & Jr Coll; NAACP; Urban League; consult The Annual Fest of the Arts Nat YMCA Week NW Branch YMCA Ft Lauderdale, FL 1963-66; consult World of Work Conf Dept of Attendance & Equal Educ Oppor Palm Beach, FL 1966; speaker African Art Spring Fest in Music/Drama & Art Dillard Comp HS Ft Lauderdale, FL 1966; consult Pinellas Co Tchrs Assn Human Rel Cncl Conf on Integration of Sch Fac Chinsegut Hill Univ of S FL 1968; speaker African Art Cult Enrichment Series Allapattah Jr HS Miami, FL 1968; consult African Art for Intro to Afro-Am Studies Palm Beach Jr Coll Palm Beach, FL 1969; consult Miami Springs Jr HS Humanizing the Fac & Stdnts1971; chmn Curriculum Com on S AsVisiting Com for Evaluation of St Thomas HS Ft Lauderdale, FL 1971; reactor Synergy in Med Serv sponsored by SAA at Dupont Plaza Hotel Miami, FL 1971. **Honors/Awds:** Disting Serv Award for Prof Educ Broward Co Tchrs Assn 1967; Outstand Achievement & Serv in the Field of Educ Award Piney Grove 1st Bapt Ch 1971; Awardfor Appreciation Symbolic of Friends of Educ Mrs Susie H Womack Principal Sunland Park Elem Sch 1972; Cert of Recog for Serv as a Resource Bank Vlntr for Enriching the Classroom Exper of Stdnts in Broward Co Sch 1974-75; Appreciation for Outstand Ontrib in Fostering Better Comm Rel in Broward Co Award Broward Co Ofc of Comm Rel 1975; Outstand Educators of Am in Admin Published by a Div of Fuller & Dees Wash, DC 1975; Cert of Appreciation for Educ Achievement The Links Inc 1975; The Johnnie Ruth Clarke Award for Excell in Comm & Jr Coll Serv S Regnl Cncl on Black Am Affairs Richmond, VA 1982; Biography in "BlackPioneers of Broward Co" "A acy Revealed" published by The Links Inc The Ft Lauderdale Chap 1976. **Military Serv:** AUS lt 1954-56. **Business Addr:** Provost, Broward Comm Coll, 1000 Coconut Creek Blvd, Coconut Creek, FL 33066.

CRAWFORD, CHARLES L.
Government executive. **Personal:** Born Apr 3, 1929, Fordwick, VA; married Marion Elizabeth Osborne; children: Charles Preston, Keith Warren, Cynthia Evette. **Educ:** Howard U, BSCE 1956; Catholic Univ of Am, MSE 1964. **Career:** Bur of Design & Engineer Dept of Environmental Svcs, chief engineering div; Federal City Coll Sch of Engineering Washington DC, asso prof 1968-72; Dept of Highways & Traffic Bridge Design Div, structural engr 1961-65; various engineering posts. **Orgs:** Mem Am Soc of Civil Engrs; mem Am Public Works Assn; Nat Soc of Professional Engrs; pres Sousa Jr HS PTA 1973-74; mem Dupont Park Civic Assn; chrmn Public Works Com Far Northeast-Southeast Council 1974; pres Sousa Jr HS Comm Sch Bd 1975. **Honors/Awds:** Author Naval Ship R&D Center Report #2532 "buckling of web-Stiffened sandwiched cylindrical shells" 1967; democratic at-large candidate for DC city Council 1974. **Military Serv:** USAF Corpl 1947-51. **Business Addr:** 415 12 St NW, Washington, DC 20004.

CRAWFORD, CRANFORD L., JR.
Business executive. **Personal:** Born Jan 12, 1940, Marshall, TX; married Jennie Henry Crawford (deceased). **Educ:** Tx So U, BA 1963. **Career:** REECO, sr clerk; Zion Univ Meth Church, black comm developer; Juvenile Ct, probation officer 1970-73; Prot Serv & Juvenile Prob, supr intake units 1973-76; Clark Cty Juvenile Ct Svcs, prog dir 1976-87, div supv detention 1987-. **Orgs:** Vp Las Vegas Br NAACP 1973-77; life mem Alpha Phi Alpha NV Chapt, Natl Assn of Black Soc Workers, Prince Hall Mason, Clark Cty Com on Christian Social Concerns, Westside Athletic Assn, Alpha Kappa Alpha; grand master Most Worshipful Prince Hall; mem MWPH Grand Lodge of NV, F&AM 1985-, Scottish Rite Mason 33 degree; hon past potentate, imperial adviser Ophir Temple #211; mem AEAON-MS Inc. **Honors/Awds:** Serv to Manking Awd 1973; Awd of Merit Las Vegas NAACP 1973; Afro Unity Festival Awd of Merit 1978,80; YMCA Serv Awds 1978,81,82; 100 Most Influential Black in NV 1980; Afro-Amer of the Year SOMBER 1982; Grand Marshal Dr ML King Jr Parade 1985; Serv Awd Sickle Cell Anemia Found of NV 1986. **Business Addr:** Division Supervisor, Clk Co Juvenile Crt Serv, 3401 E Bonanza Rd, Las Vegas, NV 89191.

CRAWFORD, CURTIS J.
Communications company executive. **Educ:** DePaul Univ, MBA. **Career:** AT&T, numerous positions; IBM, numerous positions; Lucent Technologies, Microelectronics Group, pres, currently, Intellectual Property Division, pres, 1997-. **Special Achievements:** Selected as one of Black Enterprise's 25 Hottest Black Managers, 1988. **Business Addr:** President, AT & T Microelectronics, AT & T, 2 Oak Way, Rm 5NC01, Berkeley Heights, NJ 07922, (908)771-2405.

CRAWFORD, DAN
Professional basketball referee. **Career:** NBA official, currently. **Honors/Awds:** IBCA Hall of Fame; Chicago Public Schools, Hall of Fame. **Business Addr:** NBA Official, c/o National Basketball Association (NBA), 645 5th Ave, 15th Fl, New York, NY 10022-5986.

CRAWFORD, DAVID
Operations administrator. **Personal:** Born Mar 12, 1941, Charlotte, NC; son of Margaret Adams Crawford and Rev Columbus Crawford; married Joan McGill Crawford, Jul 31, 1965; children: Davaree Ashenbaum, Darlisa. **Educ:** Johnson C Smith University, Charlotte, NC, BS, 1963; University of Liverpool, Liverpool, England, 1963-64; University of North Carolina, Chapel Hill, NC, MA, 1966; RPI, Hartford, CT, MS, 1983. **Career:** UTC Pratt & Whitney, East Hartford, CT, mgr, manpower phng & dev, 1972-75, divisonal superintendent, machine shop, 1975-78, exec asst to pres, 1978-80, North Haven, CT, prod mgr, 1980-84, Southington, CT, plant mgr, 1984-91, North Haven, CT, plant mgr, 1991-93; Mfg Technology UTC, Pratt & Whitney, director, 1993-. **Orgs:** Board of directors, Connecticut Pre-Engineering Program, 1990-; first vice pres, Cheshire Lion Club, 1981-. **Honors/Awds:** UTC Leadership Award, 1987. **Business Addr:** Director, Manufacturing Technology Operations, Pratt & Whitney, 400 Main St, M/S 118-03, East Hartford, CT 06108, (860)565-1017.

CRAWFORD, DEBORAH COLLINS
Educator. **Personal:** Born Oct 6, 1947, San Antonio, TX; divorced; children: Candice Aundrea. **Educ:** Prairie View A&M Coll, BS 1969; Our Lady of the Lake Univ, MEd, Admin Cert. **Career:** St Philips Coll, dance instr; Union Carbide, accts recv clk 1970; Valhalla Sch Dist, pe instr 1970-71; Summer Camp, White Plains, pe instr 1971; Alamo Community Coll Dist Office Mgmt Workshop, coord insvc, computer literacy instr 1987; City of San Antonio Human Resources, presenter "Why Man Creates"; San Antonio Ind School Dist, summer principal. **Orgs:** Mem AWRT; coord YWCA Seminar; lectr Our Lady of the Lake Univ Black Hist Wk Activity; Bus & Professional Womens Club; co-emcee Miss PV Pageant; res person NAACP State Conv; mem Links Inc; AKA Sor; Miss Black SA Pageant & Choreographer 1977; Ella Austin Comm Ctrs Bd; St Philips Coll Rest Mgmt Prog; Eastside Boys Club; Pine St & Ctr YWCA; Girl Scouts Publicity Com; NAACP publicity com; bd mem Yth Philharmonic; mem Black Expressions Art League; mem City Fine Arts Commission; mem TX State Teachers Assn 1978-; mem Dance Educators of Amer 1988-; mem Jack & Jill of Amer 1988. **Honors/Awds:** Disting Public Serv Awd Prairie View A&M 1974; Awd for Cause of Human Dignity NAACP 1975; nom Outstanding Young Woman in Amer 1976; Serv Awd Sr Oppty Serv Ctr 1975-76; Model Comm Ldrs Awd Miss Black SA Bd 1976; Comm Serv Awd Walker-Ford Gospel Singers; mayoral appointment to Martin Luther King Jr memorial Commission for the City of San Antonio as Media Chairperson 1987; city council appointment to arts & cultural adv bd; citation from Mayor Cisneros & Councilman Webb, for Public Service 1989; dir Debbie's Darlings, Inc 1989. **Business Addr:** Summer Principal, San Antonio Ind Schl Dist, 141 Lavaca, San Antonio, TX 78207.

CRAWFORD, ELLA MAE
Educational administrator. **Personal:** Born Sep 8, 1932, Coffeyville, KS; married Willie E Sr; children: Willie E. **Educ:** WA State U, adminstrn internship for Vocational Educ 1979-80. **Career:** Tacoma Public School #10, occupational information asst & financial aid officer; LH Bates Vocational-Tech Inst, coordinator for disadvantaged 1968-71; Tacoma Urban Coali-

tion, coordinator for secretarial improvement program 1968; City of Tacoma WA, supr res relocation for families & individuals 1960-68; Tacoma Housing Authority, relocation asst 1954-60. **Orgs:** Former mem Spl Educ Task Force (WA State -Spl Needs); former v-chmn WA State Developmental Disabilities Planning Council; former sec Pacific NW Regional Nat Housing & Redevel Ofcls (Puget Sound Chpt); mem WA State Financial Aid Adminstrs; Black Prog Educators for Tacoma Pub Schls; Title IX Sex Equity Adv Com; Educ for all Legislation (WA State DSHS Council); bd mem & chmn of Scholarship Com Tacoma Chap of NAACP 1968-; mem, former pres Tacoma Altrusa Club 1968; mem E B Wilson Civic Club Bethlehem Ch 1975; bd mem Pierce Co Personel Review Bd 1978-81; bd mem City of Tacoma Pub Utilities 1979-85; mem United Good Neighbors Planning Cncl 1967-79; mem UGN Budget Com 1967-79; sec Tacoma Model Cities bd 7 yrs; former mem Hilltop Improvement Council (Study Comfor Poverty Prgm) OEO; mem Minority cerns Task Force; Sat Morning Collective; Civic & Prog Assn; Employment Com for WA State Develpment Planning Council; liaison & 1st vice pres Tacoma Urban League Guild. **Honors/Awds:** Citizen award OEO Poverty Prgm 1964; woman of yr Zeta Phi Beta Sorority (Acad) 1972; outstanding citizen award Tacoma Model Cities Exec Bd 1975; Appreciation Award; Title IX Chmn. **Business Addr:** 1101 S Yakima Ave, Tacoma, WA 98405.

CRAWFORD, H. R.
Housing management executive. **Personal:** Born Jan 18, 1939, Winston-Salem, NC; married Eleanora Braxton; children: Leslie, Hazle, George, Gregory, Lynne. **Educ:** Howard Univ, 1961-63; DC Tchrs Coll, 1963-65; Am Univ, 1967; Chicago St Univ, BA; NC Architectural & Training Univ, hon LLD 1975. **Career:** Crawford/Edgewood Manager's Inc Washington DC, natl housing mgmt exec, bd chmn, pres; Housing Mgmt US Dept Housing & Urban Devel, asst sec; HR Crawford Inc, pres 1972-73; Kaufman & Broad Asset Mgmt Inc, vice pres 1971-73; Polinger-Crawford Corp, vice pres 1969-73; Polinger Co, 1968-69; Frederick W Berens Sales Inc, prop mgr 1966-68. **Orgs:** Mem Inst Real Estate Mgmt, Builders Owners & Mgrs Assn; Nat Assn Housing & Redevel Officials; Professional Property Mgrs Assn; Washington Bd Realtors; Natl Assn Real Estate Brokers, Washington DC Chapter, pres, 1994-96; Washington Planning & Housing Assn; Natl Assn Home Builders; Resident Mgrs Assn; dir Bonabond Inc; Washington DC Adv Bd of Recreation; Anacostia Economic Devel Corp; Frederick Douglass Comm Center; Congress Heights Assn for Serv & Educ; Am Cancer Soc; Jr Citizens Corp Inc; bd mem 1st vp, NAACP Washington DC Chapter, 1995-97; Kiwanis Club. **Honors/Awds:** Numerous awards, honors, special achievements; JW Paletou; IREM Manager of the Year 1973; Natl Real Estate Brokers & Omega Tau Rho Distinguished Serv Awards; Cherokee Indians Goodwill Award. **Military Serv:** USAF sgt 1956-65. **Business Addr:** Former Councilmember, Council of Distict of Columbia, 916 Pennsylvania Ave SE, Washington, DC 20003.

CRAWFORD, JAMES MAURICE
Insurance administrator. **Personal:** Born Jan 8, 1946, Boligee, AL; son of Dollie Crawford and Maurice Crawford; married Patricia Jones, Jun 9, 1973; children: Courtney. **Educ:** Ohio University, BBA, 1968; Yale University, 1970; Occidental College, MA, 1972. **Career:** National League of Cities, sr legislative counsel; US Department of Housing & Urban Development, special asst to secretary; US Department of Health & Human Service, special asst to secretary/deputy executive secretary; The Equitable Life Assurance Society of the US, executive asst to chief financial officer, planning financial manager; The Principal Financial Group, strategic development, government relations, director, currently. **Orgs:** Children & Families of Iowa, board mem, 1991-; Foundation for Children & Families of Iowa, board president, 1990-91; Metro Des Moines YMCA, board mem, 1992-; KAPSI Foundation, board mem, 1991-; Corinthian Gardens Elderly Housing, bd mem, 1994-; Science Bound Development Council, Iowa State University, charter mem, 1996-; West Des Moines Public Library, Friends Foundation, board member, 1996-. **Honors/Awds:** Ford Foundation, National Urban Fellow, 1970; US Department of Health & Human Service, Secretary's Achievement Award, 1981; Des Moines Chamber of Commerce, Leadership Institute, 1984; Des Moines Register Newspaper, Up-and-Comer, 1985. **Home Addr:** 4601 Pleasant St, West Des Moines, IA 50266, (515)224-0514. **Business Addr:** Director, Principal Financial Group, 711 High St, S-6, Des Moines, IA 50392-0220, (515)247-5480.

CRAWFORD, JAMES WESLEY
Foundation executive. **Personal:** Born Jun 5, 1942, Nashville, TN; son of Bessie Harris Crawford and Robert Crawford Jr; married Sheila Simmons Crawford, Sep 7, 1989; children: Conrad. **Educ:** Philander Smith Coll, BA 1960-64; Eastern Montana Coll, 1967-68. **Career:** US Peace Corps Tanzania, volunteer 1964-66; Economic Opportunity Agency, Pulaski City AR, vista supv 1968-70; Action Region 6, Dallas TX, program officer 1970-73; The Pathfinder Fund, program operations dir Africa 1973-79, regional dir Africa/Middle East 1979-87, dir of special projects 1987-92; Massachusetts Legal Assistance Corp., program director, 1993-95. **Orgs:** Mem Alpha Phi Alpha 1962-, Assn of Black Found Execs 1974-, Natl Council for Intl Health, Amer Public Health Assn; consultant Harvard School of Public Health 1983-; mem NAACP. **Business Addr:** Executive Director, Center for Health and Development, 2 Park Plz, Ste 701, Boston, MA 02116, (617)357-0224.

CRAWFORD, JAYNE SUZANNE
Association executive. **Personal:** Born May 11, 1958, Hartford, CT; daughter of Beatrice Crawford and Odell Crawford. **Educ:** Lincoln Univ, BA 1980. **Career:** Inquirer Newspaper Grp, reporter 1980-82; Focus Magazine, assoc editor 1981-83; Crawford-Johnson Assoc, partner 1981-; Comm Renewal Team, indus organizer 1983-84, asst to the exec dir, vice pres for direct service, currently. **Orgs:** Co-chmn Young Executives 1983; bd of dirs Urban League of Greater Hartford 1982-85; pres Urban League Guild of Greater Hartford 1982-85; mem Leadership Greater Hartford Inc; exec chairperson New England Urban League Guild Network 1986-87; member, Key Issues Leadership Forum/The Hartford Conrant, 1989-. **Honors/Awds:** Co-editor "Beyond Ourselves" Comm Renewal Team 1982. **Business Addr:** Vice President for Direct Service, Community Renewal Team of Greater Hartford, 555 Windsor St, Hartford, CT 06103.

CRAWFORD, KEITH
Professional football player. **Personal:** Born Nov 21, 1970, Palestine, TX. **Educ:** Howard Payne. **Career:** New York Giants, wide receiver, 1993; Green Bay Packers, 1995; St Louis Rams, 1996-. **Business Addr:** Professional Football Player, St Louis Rams, One Rams Way, St Louis, MO 63045, (314)982-7267.

CRAWFORD, LAWRENCE DOUGLAS
Mayor, dentist. **Personal:** Born Jun 13, 1949, Saginaw, MI; married Winnie Hill; children: Lawrence D Jr, Alan A. **Educ:** Univ of MI, Pol Sci 1967-70; Univ of MI Dental School, DDS 1970-74. **Career:** LD Crawford DDS PC, dentist 1974-; Town of Saginaw, city councilman, mayor 1981-. **Orgs:** Saginaw Cty Dental Soc, Saginaw Valley Dental Soc, MI State Dental Assoc, Natl Dental Assoc, Amer Dental Assoc, Mid-State Study Club; consult Univ of MI Dental Admiss Hattie M Strong Found; mem bd of dir 1st Ward Comm Ctr; commiss E Central MI Planning Commiss; pres RCA View Devel Corp; mem Frontier's Intl, Black Businessmen's Assoc of Saginaw, Alpha Phi Alpha Frat, East Side Lions Club, Bethel AME Church. **Honors/Awds:** Natl Merit Semifinalist; Public Health Fellowship; 1967 Honor Awd; Frontier's Businessman of the Year Frontier's Intl Saginaw 1980; Family Members United Meritorious Serv Awd 1980; Professional Achievement Awd Zeta Phi Zeta Sor 1981. **Business Addr:** Mayor, Town of Saginaw, PO Box 1746, Saginaw, MI 48602.

CRAWFORD, MARGARET WARD
Elected official. **Personal:** Born Apr 18, 1937, Pontiac, MI; married Samuel Kenneth Crawford Sr; children: Cheryl, Samuel Jr, Gary, Sara Elizabeth, Adrienne Irene. **Educ:** Wayne State Univ, BS. **Career:** MI Dept of Social Svcs, social worker 1960-73; Free Lance Volunteer, counsellor, facilitator, political, social activist 1973-; Schrock Adult Care Homes, admin, asst to the dir 1980-; Lincoln Consult Schools, pres bd of ed. **Orgs:** Mem MI Assoc of School Bds 1974-; trustee Lincoln Schools Bd of Ed 1974-; mem Natl Assoc of School Bds 1975-; instr MI Dist Congress on Christian Ed 1979-; pres Lincoln Schools Bd of Ed 1981-; mem Sumpter Housing Rehab Council 1981-; bd of dir The Corner Health Ctr 1981-82; mem Legislative Comm 1982-84, Washtenaw Cty Black Elected Officials 1983-; designated friend The Corner Health Center 1983-; mem Sumpter Twp Political Action Comm 1984-; trustee, church clerk Mt Hermon Missionary Baptist Church 1984-; mem Resolutions Comm 1985-; ex-officio mem Sumpter Young Women's Assoc 1985-; mem Sumpter NAACP; various committees Gifted & Talented Spec Ed Child Advoc; mem delegate Washtenaw Cty School Officers Assoc. **Honors/Awds:** Speaker & consult Students Rights, Spec Ed, School Boardsmanship, Youth Advocacy, State & Fed Legislation Impacting Youth, Womens Issues 1979-; Key Awd MI Assoc of School Bds 1984; Certif by Twp School Dist & Natl Black Child Devel Council. **Home Addr:** 49372 Arkona, Sumpter Twp, Belleville, MI 48111.

CRAWFORD, MARY GREER
Educator. **Personal:** Born May 28, Marshall, TX; daughter of Lucy Clark Greer and Francis Greer; divorced; children: Margaret, Cranford, Jr. **Educ:** Wiley Coll, BA 1947; New Mexico Highland U, MA 1953; E Texas State Univ 1974, 1980; East TX Baptist Univ, 1985. **Career:** Wiley Coll, head dept bus 1947-70, prof/advisor dept office adm bus educ; prof 1947-. **Orgs:** Coord Div Social Sci & Bus 1967-69; chmn Dept Office Admin & Bus Educ 1970-71; adv 1972; mem Natl Alumni Assn Wiley Coll; sec Pi Omega Pi Natl Frat; Natl Council UNCF; sec chmn Const Commn Pre-Alumn Act Natl Educ Assn; sec Faculty Wiley Coll; mem TX Bus Educ Assn; mem TX Bus Educ Assoc; TX Cong Col, PTA, E TX Soc Cul Civ Educ Dev; asst Juris Conf Central Jur; TX & Gulf Coast Confs; asst sec Del Gen Conf UMC Charter; mem Natl Assn Negro Bus & Professional Women's Clubs Lctr; consult dir workshops in fields; mem Amer Assoc of Univ Profs, Region VIII TX Bus Educ Assoc, Pi Omega Pi Natl Business Teachers Honor Soc, Natl Business Educ Assoc, Mountain Plains Business Educ Assoc. **Honors/Awds:** Woman of the Year Zeta Phi Beta Sor; Alumnus of the Year Pemberton HS Alumni Assoc; Outstanding Citizen of Marshall; Outstanding Educator of Amer, Leading Lady Business Civic and Politics of Marshall; elected/installed TX Black Women's Hall of Fame; Teacher of the Year Dist VIII TBEA; Piper Prof 1986; cited in TV productions as Teacher of Excellence; "Mrs MG Crawford Day" held at Wiley Coll.

CRAWFORD, MURIEL C.
President. **Educ:** Hampton Univ, BS 1956; Cuyahoga Comm Coll, refresher course architectural drawing 1978; Univ of WI Sch of Engrg & Science, attended 1979; Case Western Reserve Univ Weatherhead Sch of Mgmt, course in business planning 1986. **Career:** York Rd Jr HS, art instructor 1956-57; Cleveland Bd of Educ, art instructor 1957-69; Charles Eliot Jr HS, art dept chmn 1967-69; Self-employed, interior designer 1969-75; The Halle Bros Co, interior designer 1975-78; Edith Miller Interiors, interior design 1978-84; Management Office Design Inc, pres 1982-. **Orgs:** Professional mem holding various positions incl vice pres elect 1987 Amer Soc of Interior Designers; Interior Design Educ Tour England Amer Soc of Interior Designers 1978; designer Dining Room Hope House Amer Cancer Soc ASID Benefit 1979; vignette designer March of Dimes Gourmet Gala/ASID Benefit 1984; speaker Natl Endowment for the Arts Recog of Women in the Design Profession 1985; juror Natl Cncl for Interior Design Qualification Qualifying Exam for Interior Design Profession 3 yr appt 1986. **Honors/Awds:** Amer Soc of Interior Designers Presidential Citation Ronald McDonald House 1979, Hope House Designer 1979, Personal Dedication to Ohio North Chap 1985; Natl Endowment for the Arts Women in the Design Profession recognition as Interior Designer 1985. **Business Addr:** President, Management Office Design Inc, 16611 Chagrin-Lee Plaza, #202, Shaker Heights, OH 44120.

CRAWFORD, NATHANIEL, JR.
Clergyman. **Personal:** Born Aug 22, 1951, Tarpon Springs, FL; son of Virginia Crawford and Nathaniel Crawford; married Helen Jones; children: Nathaniel III, Isaac Antonia, Erica Rachell. **Educ:** St Leo Coll, BS 1974; Atlanta Univ, MSW 1976; Interdenominational Theol Ctr, MDiv 1980. **Career:** State of FL, youth counselor 1973-74; Pasco Co Manpower Svcs, job counselor 1975; Whitehead Boys Club, athletics dir 1976-78; Rockdale Co Boys Club, prog dir 1977-78; State of GA Youth Svcs, youth devel worker 1978-; USAF, chaplain 1980-. **Orgs:** Bd mem Faith Ctr 1979-80; Faith COGIC 1979-84; NAACP, 1986-89. **Military Serv:** USAF chaplain major 9 yrs.

CRAWFORD, ODEL
State employment manager. **Personal:** Born Apr 23, 1952, Brownwood, TX; son of Jewel Crawford Danner and Charles Williams; married Catherine Goodwin Crawford, Aug 15, 1972; children: Vanessa Yvonne, Ashanti Monque, Pharren Rene. **Educ:** Abilene Christian University, 1974. **Career:** Mutual of Omaha, sales agent, 1976; KMART Corp., assistant manager, 1976-78; Texas Employment Commission, area manager, 1978-. **Orgs:** Black Chamber of Commerce, Permian Basin, board of directors, president, 1989-; West Texas Adult Literacy Council, board of directors, president, 1991-; Odessa Boys and Girls Club, board member, 1988-; Permian Basin Private Industrial Council, board member, 1989-92; Greater Odessa Chamber of Commerce, board member, 1988-; Junior Achievement, Odessa, classroom consultant, board member, 1990-; Texas Association of Black Chambers of Commerce, board secretary, 1988-; Business Development Board and Enterprise Zone Committee, chairman, board member, 1991-. **Honors/Awds:** National Veteran Training Institute, Dean K Phillips Award, 1988; Black Chamber of Commerce, Ebony Bar Award, 1986. **Special Achievements:** Publications: Minorities are Huge Force in Workplace, 1989; Helps to Employers on Hiring and Firing, 1989; Government Provides Many Services to Local and National Small Businesses, 1989. **Home Phone:** (915)580-4423. **Business Phone:** (915)332-4314.

CRAWFORD, SAMUEL D.
Educator. **Personal:** Born Nov 25, 1936, Dothan, AL; married Naomi Levert; children: Samuel D, Sabrina, Kitamba. **Educ:** Tuskegee Inst, BS 1966; Univ NE, MS 1968. **Career:** Creighton Univ, assoc vice pres student personnel 1972; Tech Jr High School, prin 1971-72; Druid Hill School, prin 1970-71; New Careers Program, dir 1969-70; Franklin Elementary School, teacher 1968-69. **Orgs:** Mem Urban League; NATE; Phi Delta Kappa; Phi Beta Sigma; NAACP. **Honors/Awds:** Co-author Black Language Reader 1973; citizens award Afro-am Culture Cntr 1972; hon adm citation Royal Navy NE Govs Ofc 1974; outstanding educ am award1974-75; black excelence journ award 1975; meritorious serv award Urban League 1975. **Military Serv:** USAR 1959-61; pfc 1961-62. **Business Addr:** 2500 California St, Omaha, NE 68178.

CRAWFORD, VANELLA ALISE
Association executive. **Personal:** Born Nov 25, 1947, Washington, DC; daughter of Dorothy Samella Raiford Patton and James Vance Jackson, Jr; married William Alexander Crawford, Apr 1971 (divorced); children: Kahina B Crawford. **Educ:** Fisk Univ, 1965-67; Federal City College, BA, 1973; Howard Univ, MSW, 1975; Washington School of Psychiatry, Certified, 1983. **Career:** Urban Professional Assoc, dir of outpatient ser-

vice, 1975-79; Lt Joseph P Kennedy Institute, counselor, 1977-79; Howard Univ Hospital, psychiatric social worker, 1980-86; The Congress of Natl Black Churches Inc, project dir, 1986-; Decades Inc, The Body Shaping Shoppe, co-owner, 1992-. **Orgs:** Pres, The Vanella Group, 1988-; Young People's Project 15-24 Clinic, 1985-88; private productions/co-owner, Psychological Resource Center, 1985-87; Consultant, The Congress of Natl Black Churches, 1986; Georgetown Univ Child Devel Dept, 1978; United Way of Amer, 1978; trainer, DCPC, 1985; CNBC, 1985; Natl Assn of Black Social Workers, 1985; Natl Assn of Social Workers, 1979; DC Coalition of Social Work Health Care Providers; dir, Christian Educ North Brentwood AME Zion Church 1982-85; advisory board, Amer Red Cross Adolescent Program; executive board/co-chairperson, Duke Ellington School of the Performing Arts. **Honors/Awds:** Alpha Delta Mu National Work Honor Society. **Special Achievements:** Designed nationally acclaimed parent education program, PRAISE: Parents Reclaiming African Information for Spiritual Enhancement, 1980-93. **Business Addr:** President, The Vanella Group, PO Box 29472, Washington, DC 20017.

CRAWFORD, VANESSA REESE
Correctional facility executive. **Personal:** Born Dec 30, 1952, Petersburg, VA; daughter of Esther Elizabeth Taylor Reese and Richard A Reese Jr (deceased); married Leon Crawford, Jul 11, 1987; children: Latricia, Richard, Roderick, Cornell II, Leon Jr, Courtney. **Educ:** Virginia Commonwealth University, Richmond, VA, BS, 1974. **Career:** Central State Hospital, Petersburg, VA, social worker, 1974-78; Chesterfield Correctional Unit, Chesterfield, VA, counselor, 1978-85, asst superintendent, 1985-87; Dinwiddie Correctional Unit, Church Road, VA, asst superintendent, 1987-89; New Kent Correctional Unit, Barhamsville, VA, superintendent, 1989-91; Pocahontas Correctional Unit, Chesterfield County, VA, superintendent, 1991-. **Orgs:** Bethany Baptist Church, 1961; Natl Assn of Blacks in Criminal Justice, 1980; Amer Bus Women's Assn, 1987; Petersburgh Chap 33 Order of the Eastern Star, 1989; scy, Parent & Dist Advisory Council, Petersburg Schools, 1990; Natl Assn of Female Executives, 1990-; appointed, Dist 19 Community Advisory Board, Petersburg, VA, 1993-; chair, Camelot Neighborhood Watch Asson; Petersberg Symphony Orchestra Women's Committee; mentor, VA Commonwealth Univ; vp, Petersburg High Sch Boosters Club; bd of dirs, Town and Country Nursery Sch Foundation; board of directors, Burger King, Communities in Schools; parent advisory coun, Petersburg High School; teenage pregnancy coun-Southside Regional Med Ctr; Petersburg Public Sch, Character Educ Task Force. **Honors/Awds:** American Business Women's Association, Boss of the Year Award, 1993; National Association of Negro Business & Professional Women's Club, Achievement Award for Outstanding Performance, 1994; WTVR Channel 6, African-American Role Model, 1997. **Home Addr:** 1616 Kings Road, Petersburg, VA 23805. **Business Addr:** Superintendent, Senior Pocahontas Correctional Unit, 6900 Courthouse Rd, Chesterfield, VA 23832, (804)796-4277.

CRAWFORD, VERNON
Professional football player. **Personal:** Born Jun 25, 1974, Texas City, TX. **Educ:** Florida State, attended. **Career:** New England Patriots, linebacker, 1997-. **Business Addr:** Professional Football Player, New England Patriots, 60 Washington St, Foxboro Stadium, Foxboro, MA 02035, (508)543-7911.

CRAWFORD, WILLIAM A.
State representative. **Personal:** Born Jan 28, 1936, Indianapolis, IN; son of Essie L Crouch Crawford and Kenneth C Crawford; married Lennie M Crawford. **Career:** Postal clerk and community organizer; St John's Missionary Baptist Church, Indianapolis IN, youth coordinator, 1972-78; Indiana General Assembly, state representative, 1973-86, currently; Marion County Clerk, administrative asst, 1978. **Orgs:** Mem, NAACP; mem, Urban League; mem, TransAfrica Southern Christian Leadership Conf; mem, Free South Africa Movement. **Military Serv:** US Navy. **Business Addr:** State Representative, Indiana General Assembly, 200 Washington St, Rm 4-2, Indianapolis, IN 46202.

CRAWLEY, A. BRUCE
Business executive. **Personal:** Born Mar 24, 1946, Philadelphia, PA. **Educ:** St Josephs Coll, BS 1967; Charles Morris Price School of Advertising, Adv Cert 1973; Temple Univ, MJ 1983. **Career:** 1st Pennsylvania Bank Corp, br mgmt trainee 1967-69, commercial credit analyst 1969-79, sr officers asst/main office, commercial lending 1970-71, mktg officer 1971-73, asst vice pres br adv 1973-76, vp, dir of adv 1976-79, vp, dir of public & investor relations 1979-. **Orgs:** Vchmn, dir Urban League of Philadelphia; gen chmn Philadelphia United Negro Coll Fund Telethon; past pres, bd mem Natl Assoc of Urban Bankers; past pres, bd mem Natl Assoc of Urban Bankers; past pres Urban Bankers Assoc of DE Valley; dir Philadelphia Indust Devel Corp; mem Public Relations Soc of Amer, Natl Investor Relations Inst; mem corp adv comm Natl Assoc for Equal Oppty in Higher Ed; mem public relations adv comm Adoption Ctr of DE Valley; lay mem Fee Dispute comm Philadelphia Bar Assoc; mem Mktg Comm Exec Intl; mem Japan Karate Assoc, Philadelphia Karate Club, US Karate Team, 1977; campaign chmn Comm to Elect Madaline G Dunn City of Philadelphias 4th Councilmanic Dist; numerous speaking lecturing engagements. **Honors/Awds:** Philadelphia Chap Public Relations Soc of Amer-Pepper Pot Awd Hon Mention 1982; Penny Awd Annual Report Competition Penn-Jer-Del Chap Bank Mktg Assoc 1982; Finalist Outstanding Young Leader of Philadelphia 1981; Outstanding Banker of the Year Urban Bankers Coalition 1976-78; Disting Alumnus Awd Charles Morris Price School of Advertising & Journalism 1977; Selected one of 77 People to Watch in 1977 Philaelphia Mag; Outstanding Serv to Spanish Merchants Assoc Awd 1976; Copywriting Awd Charles Morris Price School 1973; Advertising Media Selection Awd Charles Morris Price School 1973; Co Leadership Awd US Army Basic Training Exercises Ft Campbell KY 1968. **Business Addr:** Vice President, Dir, 1st Pennsylvania Bank & Corp, Centre Sq Bldg, Philadelphia, PA 19101.

CRAWLEY, BETTYE JEAN. **See BROWN, BETTYE JEAN.**

CRAWLEY, DARLINE
Elected government official. **Personal:** Born Sep 3, 1941, St Louis, MO; married Lou E Crawley. **Educ:** Assoc Degree Human Services. **Career:** Real estate entrepreneur; City of Pagedale MO, alderwoman ward 3. **Orgs:** CORO grad; Women in Leadership; deaconess Fifth Baptist Church. **Home Addr:** 1835 Ferguson, Pagedale, MO 63133.

CRAWLEY, GEORGE CLAUDIUS
Government official. **Personal:** Born Mar 19, 1934, Newport News, VA; married Cynthia Hewitt; children: Judith Crawley Johnson, Jason Claudius. **Educ:** VA State Univ, BA 1956. **Career:** Southeastern Tidewater Oppor Project, exec dir 1966-73; City of Norfolk, div of social serv dir 1973-76, dept of human resources dir 1976-83, city mgrs office asst city mgr 1983-. **Orgs:** Dir Legal Serv Corp of VA, United Way of Tidewater, Athletic Foundation of Norfolk State Univ, Darden Sch of Business, Univ of VA Inst of Mgmt, Southeastern Tidewater Manpower Auth, Norfolk Investment Corp, STOP Organization; chmn Hampton Roads Alumni Group of Virginia State Univ; dir Virginia State Univ Alumni Adv Bd; dir Girls & Boys Club of Hampton Roads VA, St John AME Church. **Honors/Awds:** Distinguished Serv Awd Tidewater Conf of Minority Public Administrators 1985; received numerous awds and citations for contributions from govtl, civic, social and religious organizations. **Military Serv:** AUS lt 1957-58. **Home Addr:** 1466 Holly Point Rd, Norfolk, VA 23509. **Business Addr:** Asst City Manager, City of Norfolk, City Hall Bldg, Norfolk, VA 23501.

CRAWLEY, OSCAR LEWIS
Personnel administrator. **Personal:** Born May 19, 1942, Lafayette, AL; son of Katie Crawley and Carlton Crawley; married Clemestine Clausell; children: Deitra Phernam, Oscar Lewis III. **Educ:** AL State U, BS psychology 1963; Univ of S AL, graduate study. **Career:** Westpoint Pepperell Inc Fairfax Towel Operation, personnel dir 1975-; asst pers dir 1972; Marengo High Sch & Dixon Mills AL, tchr 1963-72; West Point Pepperall Inc, industrial relations manager, 1988-; Bath Products, Westpoint Stevens, div human resources dir, 1994. **Orgs:** Mem Alpha Phi Alpha Inc 1974; commr Goodwill Inds 1976; chmn bd of comr Lanett City Housing Auth 1978; dist committeeman George H Lanier Council of Boy Scouts 1975; chmn Indsl Com Chambers Co Mental Health 1978; chmn Aux Com Chambers Co Bd of Educ 1979; gov staff State of AL Gov George C Wallace 1977; board member, Chambers County Heart Association, 1990; Chambers County Library, bd of dirs, 1994. **Honors/Awds:** Amer Heart Assn, Chair of the Year, Jailbail, 1992-93; Valley Crime Stoppers, Bd of Dirs, 1994. **Business Addr:** Boulevard St, PO Box 297, Valley, AL 36854.

CRAWLEY, SYLVIA
Professional basketball player. **Personal:** Born Sep 27, 1972. **Educ:** Univ of North Carolina. **Career:** Portland Power, forward, 1996-. **Honors/Awds:** USA Basketball Player of the Year, 1995. **Business Addr:** Professional Basketball Player, Portland Power, 439 N Broadway, Portland, OR 97227, (503)249-1130.

CRAY, ROBERT
Musician. **Personal:** Born Aug 1, 1953, Columbus, GA; son of Maggie Cray and Henry Cray; married Susan Turner-Cray. **Career:** The Robert Cray Band, leader, 1974-; albums include: Who's Been Talkin', 1980, Bad Influence, 1983, False Accusations, 1985, Strong Persuader, 1986, Don't Be Afraid Of The Dark, 1988, Midnight Stroll, 1990, I Was Warned, 1992, Shame A Sin, 1993, Some Rainy Morning, 1995, Sweet Potato Pie, 1997; home video appearances include: Hail! Hail! Rock 'n' Roll, tribute to Chuck Berry, 1988; Break Every Rule, HBO special with Tina Turner, 1987; 24 Nights, concert video with Eric Clapton, 1991; The Robert Cray Collection, music, videos, live performances, interviews, 1991. **Honors/Awds:** Rolling Stone critics, Best R&B Artist; three Grammy Awards, six additional Grammy nominations; San Francisco Bay Area Muisc Awards, BAMMIE; Northwest Area Music Assn, numerous awards; numerous W C Handy Awards; Blues Hall of Fame, Showdown! inducted, 1989; platinum and gold status albums worldwide. **Special Achievements:** Has appeared on albums with other artists, including: Showdown!, Johnny Clyde Copeland and Albert Collins, 1985; Live in Europe, Tina Turner, 1988; with John Lee Hooker: The Healer, 1989, Mr Lucky, 1991, Boom Boom, 1992; with Eric Clapton: Journeyman, 1989, 24 Nights, 1992; with BB King: Blues Summit, 1993; A Tribute to Stevie Ray Vaughan, various artists, 1996; key live performances include: The Robert Cray Band co-headlined with B.B. King for two months on the Blues Music Festival Tour, Summer/Fall 1997; The Robert Cray Band opened seven concerts for the Rolling Stones' 1995 tour of Europe after Cray made a guest appearance on their Hoodoo U Voodoo live pay per view concert, 1994; Presidential Inaugural Ball, 1993; Guitar Legends in Seville, Spain, 1991; New York's Radio City Music Hall, 1989; Carnegie Hall, 1983, 1986; Rocksummer, Tallin, Estonia, 1989. **Business Addr:** Musician, The Robert Cray Band, c/o Publicist Kathy Johnson, PO Box 1087, Kenwood, CA 95452.

CRAYTON, JAMES EDWARD
Administrator. **Personal:** Born Dec 18, 1943, Thomasville, AL; son of Ernestine Crayton and Bennie Crayton. **Educ:** AL State Univ, BS 1964; Atlanta Univ, MLS 1968; CA State Univ Long Beach, MA 1975; Claremont Grad Sch, PhD Educ/Higher Educ Admin 1980. **Career:** Milton FL Sch Dist, 1964-65; Cobb Co Bd of Educ Austell GA, 1965-67; Anaheim Pub Lib, 1968-70; LA Co Pub Lib, 1970-72; Pasadena City Coll, lib 1972-80, dir of occupational education 1980-, associate dean Community Skills Center. **Orgs:** Mem ALA 1970-; mem council CA Lib Assn 1974-, minority adv 1973-74; chmn Black Caucus Leg Comm 1972-; mem NAACP LA Urban League. **Honors/Awds:** Publ "What Black Librarians Are Saying" 1972; art "Wilson Library Bulletin" Jan 1974; art "Film Library Quarterly" vol 7 1974; travel, Mexico, Europe, N Africa. **Business Addr:** Associate Dean, Pasadena City Coll, Community Skills Center, Pasadena Area Community College District, 325 S Oak Knoll Ave, Pasadena, CA 91101.

CRAYTON, SAMUEL S.
Business executive. **Personal:** Born Feb 15, 1916, Omaha, GA; married Elizabeth Adams; children: 11. **Educ:** Morris Brown Coll, atnd 1935; NY Univ 1938-39; Babson Coll 1942-43. **Career:** Asst to vp; gen mgr corp in Lowell MA 1941-50; SS Crayton & Sons, owner & mgr 1950-. **Orgs:** Past pres Merrimack Valley Br NAACP; bd mem Comm Devel Cit Adv Council; life mem NAACP; chmn; life mem; com Merrimack Valley Br NAACP; mem Gr Lowell Lions Club; mem Contractors Assn of Boston Recip; Community Teamwork, Inc, former chmn of bd; Lowell Human Relations Commission, former chmn; former mem, Lowell City Redevelopment Advisory Comm, Lowell Plan Advisory Bd, Census Advisory Comm, Human Services Bd, Greater Lowell Mental Health Assoc; Univ of Lowell, former parent & student coord for Talent Search Prog; International Institute, former mem bd of dir; mem of bd, Goodwill Industries Merr Valley Rehab Ctr, Board of Educ Found, Inc; Merrimack Valley Hsg Serv, treasurer. **Honors/Awds:** Cert of commendation Gr Lowell Council of Chs 1964; founder originator Black News in Merrimack Valley Over WLLH Radia; cert of commendation Greater Lowell Mental Health Assn 1972; Univ of Lowell Beulah Pierce Memorial Award for outstanding service in the community, 1984. **Home Addr:** 673 School St, Lowell, MA 01851.

CREARY, LUDLOW BARRINGTON
Physician. **Personal:** Born Nov 17, 1930, Kingston, Jamaica; married Lou Jene. **Educ:** Long Island U, BS 1956; Howard U, MD 1960. **Career:** Wayne Co Hosp Detroit, intern 1960-61; Ventura Co Hosp CA, resident family practice 1961-63; Los Angelas, practice med & specializing in family practice 1964-; W Adams Comm Hosp, chief med staff 1971-72; med Dr 1972-; Broadweay Hosp, chief med 1969-72; Div Family Practice, physician in charge continuing educ interim chief; Charles R Drew Postgrad Med Sch; Martin Luther King Jr Hosp Los Angelas 1970-; Univ of CA at Los Angelas, asso prof; Am Bd Family Practice diplomat; am acad gen pratice, fellow. **Orgs:** Mem Am Acad Family Hysicians; mem CA Assn Del; Los Angeles Co Med Assn. **Business Addr:** 11924 S Central, Los Angeles, CA 90059.

CREDITT, THELMA COBB
Nurse. **Personal:** Born Jun 1, 1902, Baltimore, MD; widowed. **Educ:** Cheyney Training Sch, 1919; Provident Hosp Sch of Nursing, 1922; Winston Salem Tchrs Coll, 1948-49; A&T Coll, 1950-52; DePaul U, 1959-62. **Career:** Provident Hosp, dir 1956; Lunsford Richardson Hosp, dir 1950; Kate Bitting Reynolds Hosp, dir 1948; Kate Betting Reynolds Hosp, supr 1946; Winston Salem, pvt duty 1932; Freedman's Hosp, supr 1926; Milwaukee, pvt duty 1924; Vis Nurses Assn 1923; Provident Hosp, supr 1923. **Orgs:** Colored Grad Nurses Assn 1926; Am Nurses Assn 1930; Provident Hosp Alumna 1940; edtrl staff 1st Dist Nurses Jour 1958; Am Soc for Dor of Vol Servs1967; Council for Dir of Hosp Vol; Nat Hlth Council Survey Vol Serv Taylor Homes; mem Epis Ch; Bishops Commn on Metro Afrs; Loop Coll Cert of Completion for Dir Vol Health Care; bd of hlth Model Citites Prgm; Chicago Lassiter Hlth Mgmt. **Honors/Awds:** Pictured NC Nell Hunter Singers Nat Med Assn Jour 1969; requested to sing for Pres FD Roosevelt Chapel Hill; requested to sing for King & Queen of England White House; wrote dir shows for Nat Negro Hlth Wk; pulb poetry 1941;

wrote dir Nurses Prayer & Hym 1959; wrote 8 lullabys 1964; employee of yr Chicago Hosp Council 1968; cert of Recog Chicago Hosp Council 1977. **Business Addr:** 426 E 51st St, Chicago, IL 60615.

CREFT, BRENDA K.
Military officer, nurse. **Educ:** Northwestern State Univ. **Career:** US Air Force, Wilford Hall Med Ctr, colonel/chief nurse, currently. **Military Serv:** US Air Force, currently. **Business Addr:** Colonel/Chief Nurse, Surgical Division, US Air Force, Wilford Hall Medical Center, 2200 Bergquist Dr, San Antonio, TX 78236-5300, (210)670-7100.

CREIGHTON-ZOLLAR, ANN
Educator. **Personal:** Born Sep 16, 1946, Thomasville, AL; daughter of Jimmie A Gordon and Thomas E Creighton; divorced; children: James A, Nicai Q. **Educ:** Univ of IL Chicago, BA 1973, MA 1976, PhD 1980. **Career:** Garfield Park Comprehenisve Comm Health Center, program evaluator 1979-80; VA Commonwealth Univ, asst prof soc 1980-88, assoc professor, 1988-, African American Studies Program, dir, 1993. **Honors/Awds:** "A Member of the Family, Strategies For Black Family Continuity" Chicago Nelson Hall 1985; "The Contribution of Marriage to the Life Satisfaction of Black Adults" Jrnl of Marriage and the Family 1987. **Special Achievements:** Adolescent Pregnancy and Parenthood, Garland, 1990; The Social Correlates of Infant and Reproductive Mortality in the United States, Garland, 1993. **Business Addr:** Assoc Professor of Sociology, Virginia Commonwealth Univ, VCU Dept of Soc/Ant, 923 W Franklin St, Richmond, VA 23284-2509.

CRENNEL, ROMEO A.
Professional football assistant coach. **Personal:** Born Jun 18, 1947, Lynchburg, VA; son of Mary Donigan Crennel and Joseph L Crennel, Jr; married Rosemary, Jan 7, 1967; children: Lisa, Tiffany, Kristin. **Educ:** Western Kentucky Univ, BS Physical Educ, Master's degree 1970. **Career:** Western Kentucky Univ, physical educ instructor/coach 1971-74; Texas Tech Univ, defensive asst 1975-77; Univ of MS, defensive end coach 1978-79; Georgia Tech, defensive line coach 1980; New York Giants, special teams coach 1981-89, defensive line coach, 1990-. **Orgs:** Mem Sigma Delta 1969-70; mem Amer Football Coaches Assoc. **Honors/Awds:** Captain Western Kentucky Football Team 1969; mem Ohio Valley All Conference Football Team 1969; mem NY Giants World and Super Bowl Champions 1987, 1991. **Business Addr:** Assistant Coach, New York Giants, Giants Stadium, East Rutherford, NJ 07073.

CRENSHAW, REGINALD ANTHONY
Research analyst. **Personal:** Born Sep 29, 1956, Mobile, AL; son of Johnnie Mae Crensaw; married Portia LaVerne Johnson. **Educ:** Morehouse Coll, BA Economics 1978; Univ of S AL, MPA Public Admin 1984. **Career:** Mattie T Blount HS, high school instructor 1978-79; City of Prichard, councilman 1980-88; Bishop State Jr Coll, rsch analyst & instructor 1980-. **Orgs:** Mem of adv bd Commonwealth Natl Bank 1982-; bd of dirs Mobile Co Urban League 1983-; vice pres bd of dirs Deaborn St Comm Ctr 1984-; President of Beta Omicran Lambda Chapter of Alpha Phi Alpha Fraternity. **Honors/Awds:** Man of the Yr Awd Alpha Phi Alpha Frat 1980; UNCF Distinguished Leadership Awd 1982 & 1983; Mobilian of the Yr Awd Mobile Chap of Phi Beta Sigma Frat 1983; Comm Leadership Awd Ladies Auxiliary of Knights of Peter Claver #172 1984. **Home Addr:** 1021 Sample St, Prichard, AL 36610.

CRENSHAW, RONALD WILLIS
Attorney. **Personal:** Born Jan 4, 1940, St Louis, MO; son of Rosetta Crenshaw and Willis C Crenshaw; married Jo Ann D; children: Ronald Jr, Candace P. **Educ:** Fist U, BA 1962; Univ of SD Sch of Med, grad; Univ of SD Coll of Law, JD 1971. **Career:** Ronald W Crenshaw & Asso PC, atty 1976-; State of MI, spl asst atty gen 1974-; Elliard Crenshaw & Strong, partner 1973-76; Zechman & Crenshaw, partner 1972-73; US Atty's Ofc, law clrk 1971; Fredrikson Byron & Colborn Law Ofcs, legal intern 1970; Univ of SD Sch of Med, resrch asst 1968; Dept of Aero-Space Med Mcdonnell Aircraft Corp, asso physiologist 1964-67; Dept of Biochemistry Cntrl Resrch Div Monsanto Co, resrch biochemist 1964; Dept of Radiophysics Sch of Med Wash Univ St Louis, resrch asst 1962-64. **Orgs:** Mem State Bar of MI; mem Wolverine Bar Assn; mem Fed Bar Assn; mem Am Bar Assn; mem num other Bar Assn; mem public adv com on jud cands Detroit Bar Assn; chmn of adm com Detroit Bar Assn 1978-79; vice pres bd of dirs Don Bosco Hall Juvenile Home; chmn Kappa Alpha Psi Frat; found & chmn Martin Luther King Jr Meml Scholar Found Univ of SD 1968-71; chmn Martin Luther King Jr Meml Day Activities 1968-70; mem Hon Code Rev Com Univ of SD 1969; memConstl Rules Com 1969-70; pres Vermillion Chap Phi Delta Phi Legal Frat; licensed State Cts of MI; Fed Dist Ct for the E Dist of MI; US Ct of Appeals 6th Cir. **Honors/Awds:** Fellow awd Univ of SD 1967; pub articles "The Vagrancy Statute to be or not to be", "the purposeful inclusion of am indians" 1970-71; contestant Moot Ct 1969; Am Jurisprudence Awd Univ of SD 1970; gunderson seminar awd Univ of SD 1971.

CRENSHAW, WAVERLY DAVID, JR.
Attorney. **Personal:** Born Dec 17, 1956, Nashville, TN; son of Corinne Smith Crenshaw and Waverly D Crenshaw, Sr. **Educ:** Vanderbilt University, Nashville TN, BA, 1978, Doctor of Jurisprudence, 1981. **Career:** Chancery Court, Nashville TN, legal counsel to chancellors 1981-82; US District Judge John T Nixon, Nashville TN, law clerk 1982-84; Tennessee Attorney General, Nashville TN, asst attorney general 1984-87; private law practice, 1987-; Waller, Lawsden, Dortch and Davis, Nashville, TN, attorney, 1990-; Vanderbilt Univ School of Law, adjunct law faculty, 1994. **Orgs:** Mem, Panel for Selection of US Magistrate, 1984; pres, Napier-Looby Bar Assn 1986-87; bd mem, Nashville Bar Assn Young Lawyers Division, 1986; bd mem, Middle Tennessee, Amer Civil Liberties Union, 1986-88; bd mem, Nashville Urban League, 1986-90; mem, Chancellor's Committee on Women & Minorities at Vanderbilt Univ, 1987; bd mem, Tennessee Capital Case Resource Center, 1988-92; mem, Harry Phillips American Inns of Court; mem, American Bar Assn; Nashville Electric Svc Ethics and Audit Comm, 1992-; bd of governors, Nashville Area Chamber of Commerce, 1994-97, legal counsel, 1995-96; bd of dirs, Nashville Bar Assn, 1994-97; chair, Merit Selection Panel for US Magistrate, US District Ct, Middle District of Tennessee, 1997-98. **Honors/Awds:** Sylvan Gatchal Award, Vanderbilt Univ, 1978; Nashville Urban League, Whitney Young Jr Award for Excellence in Legal Svcs, 1996. **Home Addr:** 1105 Seven Springs Ct, Brentwood, TN 37027-4436. **Business Phone:** (615)244-6380.

CRESWELL, ISAIAH T., JR.
Governmental official. **Personal:** Born Aug 16, 1938, Nashville, TN; son of Pearl W Sanders Creswell and Isaiah T Creswell Sr. **Educ:** Amherst College, Amherst, MA, BA, 1960; Vanderbilt University, Nashville, TN, LLB, 1964. **Career:** US Comm on Civil Rights, Washington, DC, assistant staff director, 1969-77; Federal Trade Commission, Washington, DC, director, 1977-80; Kass & Skalet, Washington, DC, attorney, 1980-85; DC Rental Housing Commission, Washington, DC, commissioner, 1985-89; Tennessee Valley Authority, Knoxville, TN, vice president, 1989-. **Orgs:** Member, American Public Power Association, 1990-, District of Columbia Bar Association, Knoxville College Roundtable, 1990-, Diocese of East Tennessee Committee on Racism & Economic Justice, 1990-, Leadership, Knoxville, 1990-. **Business Addr:** Vice President, Minority Resources, Tennessee Valley Authority, 400 W Summit Hill, ET 12F, Knoxville, TN 37902.

CREW, JOHN L., SR.
Educator, psychologist. **Personal:** Born Nov 2, 1926, Westminister, SC; married Brooksie Wilks; children: John L. **Educ:** Morgan St U, BS 1952; Morgan St U, post-grad 1952-53; Am U, grad stud 1953-54; NY U, MA 1955; Univ of MD, PhD 1968. **Career:** Baltimore Public Schools, supt 1976-, interim supt 1975-76, deputy supt & planning res & eval 1973-75; Plan Res & Eval, Baltimore Public Schools, acting assoc supt 1972-73, dir div of special serv 1969-72. **Orgs:** Prof educ & Assn &Dir of Res West Chester Coll 1968-69; st supv Res & Eval MD St Dept of Educ 1966-68; spec asst Educ Testing Balt City Pub Schl 1955-66; educ psychol Balt City Pub Sch 1960-65; psychometrist Balt City Pub Schl 1955-60; consultantships at Model Cit Agcy Econ Dev Prog MD St Dept of Educ Spec Educ Div of Archdiocese of Balt; instruct asst NDEA Inst Univ of MD; res asst Univ of MD; mem Amer Psy Assn Amer Educ Res Assn; mem Er Per & Guid & Assn MD Schl Psy Assn; mem MD Acad of Sci; mem MD Per & Guid Assn; mem MD Assn of Meas & Eval in Guid; mem NatlCoun on Meas in Edn; mem Psi Chi Frat; mem MD Psy Assn Amer Assn of Schl Adm 1974-; mem Bd of Trustees; mem Samuel Ready Sch 1972-73; mem advcomm to the Sec of Personnel St of MD 1971-73; v chmn St Plan &Adv Counc on Develop Disaities to sec of Health & Ment Hygiene; dir of Ment Retard 1970-73; mem Adv Counc on Ment Hygiene to Sec of Health & Commiss of Ment. **Military Serv:** USN 1950-52; AUS res col 1950-. **Business Addr:** 3 E 25th St, Baltimore, MD 21218.

CREW, RUDOLPH F.
Chancellor. **Career:** Tacoma (WA) Schools, superintendent, until 1995; New York City Education Board, chancellor, currently. **Business Addr:** Chancellor, New York City Education Board, 110 Livingston St, Brooklyn, NY 11201, (718)935-2794.

CREW, SPENCER R.
Curator. **Personal:** Born Jan 7, 1949, Poughkeepsie, NY; son of Ada L Scott Crew and R Spencer Crew; married Sandra Prioleau Crew, Jun 19, 1971; children: Alika L Crew, Adom S Crew. **Educ:** Brown Univ, Providence RI, AB, 1967-71; Rutgers Univ, New Brunswick NJ, MA, 1971-73; Rutgers Univ, New Brunswick NJ, PhD, 1973-79. **Career:** Univ of MD Baltimore County, Catonsville MD, assistant professor, 1978-81; Smithsonian Institution, Natl Museum of Amer History, Washington DC, historian 1981-87; Natl Museum of Amer History, curator 1987-89; Natl Museum of Amer History, chair, Dept of Social and Cultural History 1989-91, deputy director, 1991-92, acting director, 1992-94; director, 1994. **Orgs:** Program chairperson, 1985-86, executive bd member, 1986-90, Oral History in the Mid-Atlantic Region; mem Oral History Assn 1988-; 2nd vice pres African Amer Museums Assn, 1988-91; program co-chairperson, Oral History Assn 1988; commissioner (bd mem), Banneker-Douglass Museum, 1989-93; editorial board mem, Journal of Amer History, 1989-93; program chairperson, African Amer Museums Assn, 1989; senior youth group coordinator, St John Baptist Church, 1989, co-editor, Newsletter for the American Historical Assn, 1990-. **Honors/Awds:** Curator for exhibition "Field to Factory: Afro-American Migration 1915-1940"; author of booklet Field to Factory: Afro-American Migration 1915-1940, 1987; Osceola Award, Delta Sigma Theta Sorority, Inc 1988; co-curator: "Go Forth and Serve: Black Land Grant Colleges Enter a Second Century," 1990, "African American Images in Postal Service Stamps," 1992; author, Black Life in Secondary Cities: A Comparative Analysis of the Black Communities of Camden and Elizabeth, NJ, 1860-1920, 1993. **Business Addr:** Director, National Museum of American History, Smithsonian Institution, Rm 5112, Washington, DC 20560.

CREWS, DONALD
Author, illustrator. **Personal:** Born Aug 30, 1930, Newark, NJ; son of Marshanna White Crews and Asa H Crews; married Ann Jonas Crews, Jan 28, 1964; children: Nina Melissa, Amy Marshanna. **Educ:** Cooper Union for the Advancement of Science & Art, New York NY, certificate of completion, 1956-59. **Career:** Dance Magazine, New York NY, asst art director 1959-61; Will Burton Studios, New York NY, staff designer 1961-62; freelance designer for varoius employers; author and illustrator, 1979-. **Honors/Awds:** Caldecott Honor Award for books Freight Train, 1979, and Truck, 1980, American Library Assn; NYT, 10 Best Illustrated Books for Flying, 1986. **Military Serv:** Army, pfc 1962-64.

CREWS, VICTORIA WILDER
State government official. **Personal:** Born Sep 18, 1946, Brownsville, TN; daughter of Eutropia B Wilder and Calvin C Wilder Sr; divorced; children: Christine, Charles, Kara. **Educ:** Franklin University, associate's, bus admin, 1985; Ohio Dominican College, sociology, attended, 1985-87. **Career:** Ohio Department of Health, administrative assistant, 1969-87; Ohio Department of Alcohol and Drug Addiction Services, coordinator Women's Programs, 1987-90, manager, prevention services unit, 1990-. **Orgs:** Governor's National Education Goals, 1991-92; Governor's Head Start Collaborative, 1991-92; Ohio Prevention and Education Resource Center, advisory bd, 1990-92; Governor's Drug-Exposed Infants Task Force, 1989-91; Ohio Credentialing Board for Chemical Dependency Professionals, 1990-92. **Special Achievements:** National Drug Prevention Network Representative for Ohio, 1990-92. **Business Addr:** Manager Prevention Services, Ohio Department of Alcohol and Drug Addiction Services, 2 Nationwide Plaza, 280 N High St, 12th Fl, Columbus, OH 43215-2537, (614)466-6379.

CREWS, WILLIAM HUNTER
Clergyman. **Personal:** Born Mar 18, 1932, Winston-salem, NC; married June; children: William H. **Educ:** Virginia Union U; Newy York U, M Ed; Union Theological Sem of NY; George Coll Downers Grove IL. **Career:** YMCA Highland Park Branch Detroit, exec dir; Shiloh Bapt, pastor 1969-. **Orgs:** Mem bd dir Rotary Intnl Bapt & Pastors Council of Detoit; bd dir Mcih Mental Health Soc; assoc Prof YMCA Dir; Omega Psi Phi. **Honors/Awds:** Outs comm ser award St of Mich 1973; comm ser award from First Bapt Ch 1970. **Business Addr:** 557 Benton, Detroit, MI 48201.

CREWS, WILLIAM SYLVESTER
Business executive. **Personal:** Born Mar 5, 1947, Advance, NC; married Belinda Harden; children: David, Angela, William Jr. **Educ:** Winston-salem State U, BA 1969. **Career:** Wachovia Bank & Trust, audit & control trainee 1969-70, asst local auditor 1970-73, retail credit analyst 1973-75, mgr 1975-, vice pres, bond opers, sr vice pres, currently. **Orgs:** Mem Bankersednl Soc Inc 1978; mem Nat Bankers Assn 1978; mem Omega Psi Phi Frat 1967; treas Nature Sci Ctr 1979. **Business Addr:** Senior Vice President, Wachovia Bank & Trust NA, PO Box 3099, Winston-Salem, NC 27102.

CRIBB, JUANITA SANDERS
County official. **Personal:** Born Nov 18, 1950, Winston-Salem, NC; married Kenneth Cribb, Jun 1969; children: Darrell, Dawn, Kenya. **Educ:** The Carolina School of Broadcasting and Journalism, AAS, 1977. **Career:** Albany Local Development Corporation, Albany, GA, exec dir, 1986-88; Crystal Communications Corporation, Albany, GA, 1988-. **Orgs:** Member, Governor's Advisory Council for Georgia Clean and Beautiful, 1989-; director-at-large, National Assn of Black County Officials, 1989-; secretary, Black County Commisssioners of Georgia, 1988-; board of Directors, Southwest Georgia Community Action Council, 1989-; member, Leadership Albany, 1988-89. **Honors/Awds:** Co-host Hour Magazine Talk Show, Fox Television, 1989; Women Who Make a Difference Award, Minorities & Women in Business Magazine, 1990; Community Leader Award, Delta Sigma Theta Sorority, Albany Alumnae Chapter, 1990; Humanitarian Award, The Holiday Society, 1990; Award of Merit, Albany NAACP, Dougherty Chapter, 1989. **Business Addr:** Consultant/Trainer, Crystal Communications Corp, PO Box 4636, Albany, GA 31706-4636, (912)436-4721.

CRIBBS, THEO, SR.
State legislator. **Personal:** Born Mar 11, 1916, Sulligent, AL; son of Isabella Marchbank Cribbs and Charlie Cribbs; married Vera, Apr 30, 1948; children: Theo Jr, Tommie, Lois. **Educ:** Lamar Co Training School, Vernon, AL. **Career:** Wichita KS, state rep, dist #89, 1972-; mem Public Health & Welfare Comm, Labor & Industry Comm, Insurance Comm; Interstate Cooperation Comm, ranking minority mem. **Orgs:** Mem Chapel AME Church, Noah Well Masonic Lodge #110, Wichita Urban League; treasurer Wichita A Phillip Randolph Institute; mem Wichita Natl Educ Assn Progressive Democratic Quorum, State Democratic Comm. **Honors/Awds:** Outstanding Citizen Award 1978. **Home Addr:** 1551 N Minnesota, Wichita, KS 67214.

CRIDER, EDWARD S., III
Administrative law judge. **Personal:** Born Feb 7, 1921, Kimball, WV; married Verdelle Vincson. **Educ:** WV State Coll, BS 1941; advanced study, Columbia Univ, 1947-49; Brooklyn Law School, JD 1953; Modern Mgmt Tech Long Island Univ, Certificate, 1970. **Career:** Sr public health sanitarian 1947-67; part time practitioner of law 1955-; New York City Dept of Health, regional dir 1967-77; New York City Dept of Health, spl asst to dir pest control 1974-77; Dept of Health NY, admin law judge. **Orgs:** Pres, NY Chapter, WV Coll Alumni Assn 1975-; pres Brooklyn Alumni Chapter, Kappa Alpha Psi 1957-59; Y's Men; sec Westbury Branch NAACP; Urban League; YMCA; Kimball HS Alumni NY Chapter; NY State Trial Lawyers Assn; Nassau Co Bar Assn; NY State Sanitarians Conf; Fellow Food & Drug Law Inst NYU Law School 1959. **Military Serv:** AUS 1st Lt 1941-45. **Business Addr:** Dept of Health, 65 Worth St, New York, NY 10013.

CRIGHT, LOTESS PRIESTLEY
Educational administrator(retired), child care center administrator. **Personal:** Born Dec 3, 1931, Asheville, NC; married George Edward; children: Shaun, Shaniqua, Shannon, George, Wilson. **Educ:** Johnson C Smith Univ, BA 1953; Brooklyn Coll, MS 1980. **Career:** Public School, teacher 1953-69; CUNY NY Tech Coll, reading instr 1969-71, cord of counseling 1971-77, dir special services, beginning 1977; Brooklyn College, dir of student support services, until 1994; Amistad Child Care & Family Center, Administrative Dir, begin 1995. **Home Addr:** 110-15 164th Pl, Jamaica, NY 11433.

CRIM, ALONZO A.
Educator. **Personal:** Born Oct 1, 1928, Chicago, IL; son of Hazel Crim and George Crim; married Gwendolyn Motley; children: Timothy, Susan, Sharon. **Educ:** Roosevelt Coll, BA 1950; Univ of Chicago, MA 1958; Harvard Univ, EdD 1969. **Career:** Chicago Pub Schs, teacher 1954-63, supr 1968-69; Whittier Elem Sch, principal 1963-65; Adult Educ Ctr, 1965; Wendell Phillips HS, 1965-68; Compton Union HS, 1969-70; Compton Unified Sch Dist, 1970-73; Atlanta Pub Sch, 1973-88; GA State Univ, prof, beginning 1988; Spelman College, prof, currently. **Orgs:** Mem various offices and committees, Amer Assn Sch Admin; Natl Alliance Black Sch Superintendents; Natl Alliance Black Sch Educ; Harvard Grad Sch Educ; Jr Achievement Gr Atlanta; So Council Intl & Pub Affairs; Educ Prog Assn Amer; GA Council Economic Educ; Amer Cancer Soc; GA Assn Sch Superintendents; Atlanta YMCA; Natl EdD Prog Educ Leaders; Rotary Club; Atlanta Council for Intl Visitors; Atlanta Area Scout Council's Expo; Phi Beta Kappa; life mem NAACP; mem Amer Assn of Sch Administrators; mem Kappa Alpha Psi, Kappa Boule, Phi Delta Kappa. **Honors/Awds:** Eleanor Roosevelt Key Awd Roosevelt Univ 1974; Vincent Conroy Awd Harvard Grad Sch 1970; Distinguished Educators Awd Teacher's Coll Columbia Univ 1980; Father of the Year Awd in Educ SE Region of the US 1981; Honor of the Yr Awd in Patriotism Military Order of World Wars 1981; Hon life mem IL Congress of Parents and Teachers 1982; One of North Amer 100 Top Execs The Executive Educator magazine 1984; Big Heart Awd GA Special Olympics 1985; The Golden Staff Awd GA State Univ; Volunteer of the Year YMCA of Metro Atlanta; Horace Mann Bond Cup Fort Valley Coll 1985; Abe Goldstein Human Relations Awd Anti-Defamation League 1985; Distinguished Public Relations Awd GA Chap of the Public Relations Soc of Amer 1986; hon DL degree Newberry Coll, hon doctor of public serv degree Gettysburg Coll, Honorary Degree Georgetown Univ; Honorary Degree Princeton Univ; Honorary Degree Harvard Univ; Honorary Degree Tuskege Univ; Honorary Degree Columbia Univ. **Military Serv:** USNR 1945-46. **Business Addr:** Professor, Spelman College, Education Department, Box 360, 350 Spelman Lane, Atlanta, GA 30314.

CRIM, RODNEY
Finance company executive. **Personal:** Born Jun 29, 1957, Chicago, IL; son of Katie Brown Crim and Elisha Crim. **Educ:** Univ of Minesota, Minneapolis, MN, BSB Accouting 1975-80; St Thomas Univ, Minneapolis, MN, MBA, 1991. **Career:** CPA; Pillsbury, Minneapolis MN, internal auditor, 1979-81; The Musicland Group, Minneapolis MN, financial analyst, 1981-82; American Express Financial Services, Minneapolis MN, general accounting supervisor 1982-83, human resources staffing associate 1983-84, manager of financial reporting 1984-87, assistant controller 1987-88, director controller 1988-91, dir of operational audit, 1991-92; Microtron Inc, Minneapolis, MN, chief financial officer, 1992-. **Orgs:** Pres, Alpha Phi Alpha, Minneapolis MN, 1977-78; teacher, Junior Achievement, 1984; Allocation Panel Mem United Way 1985; pres Natl Assn of Black Accounts, MN 1985-87; mem Leadership Minneapolis Program 1987; bd mem YMCA Board, Minneapolis MN, 1988-89; member, Minneapolis Community College Advisory Board, 1991; member, National Assn of Black MBA's; member, National Assn of Black Accountants. **Honors/Awds:** Vita Tax Assistance, State Board of Accountancy 1983; mem of the year, Natl Assn of Black Accountants 1988.

CRINER, CLYDE
Educator, musician. **Personal:** Born Dec 2, 1952, Albany, NY; son of Charlotte M Criner and Clyde Criner Jr; married Aisia De Anthony. **Educ:** Williams Coll, BA Psychology, 1975; New England Conservatory, MM (honors), 1977; Univ of MA at Amherst, EdD Urban Educ, 1978-81; Juilliard School of Music, postdoctoral study, 1984-; private study in composition with Vivan Fine, 1985-. **Career:** Music dir, Western MA Upward Bound Program, 1978-81; lecturer in music, Williams Coll, Williamston, MA, 1983-84; adjunct prof, Coll of New Rochelle, NY, 1983-85; asst prof of music, Long Island Univ, Brooklyn, NY, 1984-; visiting prof of music, Bennington Coll, 1985; debut recording as solo artist, composer, New England, Vanguard Records, 1985; original works performed by Boys Choir of Harlem, Carnegie Recital Hall, New York, NY, 1985; world premier of commissioned work, The Black Swan, Merkin Concert Hall, New York, NY, 1986; visiting lecturer in music, Pace Univ, 1986-; recording artist with Alphonson Johnson, CBS Records, 1977, Archie Shepp, Blue Marge Records, 1980, Chico Freeman, Elektra/Musician Records, 1982, Sanford Ponder, Private Music, 1985,Geoffrey McCabe, Timeless Records,85, Craig Harris, JMT/Polygram, 1988, 1989, Avery Sharpe, Sunnyside Records, 1988, Anthony Davis, Gramavision/Polygram, 1989, Victor Bailey, Atlantic Records, 1989, Hannibal, Atlantic Records, 1989; pianist with Dewey Dedman, Woody Shaw, Reggie Workman, Max Roach, Art Blakey, Kevin Eubanks, Wynton Marsalis, Dizzy Gillespie, Wayne Shorter, Carlos Santana, Noel Pointer, Arthur Blythe, David Murray, James Newton, Marcus Miller, Omar Hakim, St Luke's Orchestra and Chorus with William H Curry conductor; recording artist, BMG/RCA Records, New York, New York, 1987-; composer, pianist, Behind the Sun, RCA/Novus Records, 1988, The Color of Dark, RCA/Novus Records, 1989; Victor Bailey, Atlantic Records, 1990; Andre Jaume, Hat Hut Records, 1990. **Orgs:** Member, Natl Assn of Jazz Educ, 1979-, Black Music Assn, 1980-, Black Music Caucus, 1980-, Amer Jazz Alliance, 1980-. **Honors/Awds:** Phi Kappa Music Honor Soc, 1977; Sack Theater Music Composition Award, 1978; composer, performer, documentary film on community coll sponsored by Exxon Corp, 1981; Natl Endowment of the Arts, 1983, 1985; 125 Alumni to Watch, Univ of Massachusetts, 1988; Keynote Speaker, Williams College Black Alumni Career Weekend. **Business Addr:** Asst Professor of Music, Long Island University, University Plaza, Brooklyn, NY 11201.

CRIPPENS, DAVID L.
Public television executive. **Personal:** Born Sep 23, 1942, Jefferson City, TN; son of Dorothy Crippens and Nathaniel Crippens; married Eloise Crippens, Aug 4, 1968; children: Gerald. **Educ:** Antioch College, Yellow Springs OH, BA, 1964; San Diego State University, San Diego CA, MSW, 1968. **Career:** Free-lance writer/journalist, 1971-73; KCET, Channel 28, Los Angeles CA, director of educational services, 1973-77, vice pres, 1977-90; Educational Enterprises, senior vice president, currently. **Orgs:** California Federation of Employment & Disability, Black on Black Crime, Antioch College Board of Trustees. **Honors/Awds:** Corp for Public Broadcasting fellowship, 1969; distinguished alumni, Graduate School of Social Work, San Diego State University, 1973; named one of Pittsburgh's most influential blacks, Pittsburgh Post Gazette, 1973; service to media award, San Diego chapter of NAACP, 1975; minority telecommunications award, National Association of Educational Broadcasters, 1978; commendation from California State Legislature for Voices of Our People, 1983; outstanding service award, Young Advocates, 1986; honored by National Association of Media Women, 1986; 1990 Euclan Award, School of Education, UCLA; National Sorority of Phi Delta Kappa, National Citation Award, 1992; Frank D Parent PTA, Positive Image Award, 1992; National Sorority of Phi Delta Kappa, Outstanding Educational Leadership Award, 1992; Senior Highschools, Principals Organization Award, 1991; Cal Poly, Excellence in Educational Communications Award, 1991. **Business Addr:** KCET, Channel 28, 4401 Sunset Blvd, Los Angeles, CA 90027.

CRISP, ROBERT CARL, JR.
Educator. **Personal:** Born Apr 17, 1947, Sanger, TX; son of Martella Turner Crisp and Robert Crisp; married Carolyn Tyler Crisp, Jan 31, 1970; children: April Nichole, Adria Camille. **Educ:** Langston University, Langston, OK, BA, 1969; University of Michigan, Ann Arbor, MI, MA, 1971, PhD, 1976. **Career:** Detroit Public Schools, Detroit, MI, band director, 1969-84, department head, 1979-84, music supervisor, 1984-94, dir, Office of Music Education, 1994-. **Orgs:** Board of trustees, Messiah Baptist Church, 1979-; classical roots steering CMT, Detroit Symphony, Orchestra, 1985-88; board of trustees, Detroit Chamber Winds, 1987-; board of trustees, Community Treatment Center, 1989-; national talent co-chairman, Omega Psi Phi Fraternity, 1990-. **Honors/Awds:** Urban Adult Attitudes Towards Busing and Desegration, University of Michigan, 1976; Distinguished Service Award, Wayne County Executive, 1985; Testimonial Resolution, Detroit City Council, 1987; Kappan of the Year, Phi Delta Kappa International, 1987; Service Award, Omega Psi Phi Fraternity, 1990-. **Business Addr:** Dir, Office of Music Education, Detroit Public Schools, 5057 Woodward, Room 850, Detroit, MI 48202.

CRISWELL, ARTHURINE DENTON
Administrator. **Personal:** Born Jan 30, 1953, Memphis, TN; daughter of Celia Hambrick Denton and Arthur Denton; married Gordon Maxwell Criswell; children: Joshua Michael. **Educ:** Park College, BA 1973; Univ of KS, MSW 1981. **Career:** KS Children's Serv League, social work intern 1979-80; KS Dept of Social & Rehab Svcs, grad intern 1980-81, program supervisor 1981-84, area mgr 1984-. **Orgs:** Mem Natl Assoc of Social Workers 1979-; Natl Assoc for Couples in Marriage Enrichment 1983-; bd mem Private Industry Council 1984-85; pres Junior League Wyandotte & Johnson Counties, 1995. **Honors/Awds:** Educational Stipend KS Dept of Social & Rehab Serv 1979-81; Outstanding Alumna, Park College, 1995. **Home Addr:** 2966 N 58th, Kansas City, KS 66104. **Business Addr:** American Family Insurance, 5046 Lamar Ave, Mission, KS 66202-1741.

CRITE, ALLAN ROHAN
Consultant. **Personal:** Born Mar 20, 1910, Plainfield, NJ. **Educ:** Harvard U, BA 1968; Harvard U, cons. **Career:** Liturgical Art, lecturer; Rambusch Dec Co, writer; self-employed; artist 1950; Harard Univ Press, author; Boston Public Library, exam com. **Orgs:** Mem Archaeological Soc of Am; mem Harvard Alumni Assn; Alumni Assn of Boston Mus Sch; Harvard Club; Faculty Club of Harvart U; Mus of Fine Arts Boston ; Mus of Natural Hist of NY; Smithsonian Inst; consult Semitic Mus; lay ldr Episcopal Diocese of MA; adv bd Nat Ctr of Afro Am Artists Sect of Sch Bldg Named For Allan Crite. **Honors/Awds:** Schlrsp Boston Mus Sch. **Business Addr:** Ext Libr, Harvard Univ, Cambridge, MA 02138.

CRITTENDEN, RAY
Professional football player. **Personal:** Born Mar 1, 1970, Washington, DC. **Educ:** Virginia Tech. **Career:** New England Patriots, wide receiver, 1993-96; San Diego Chargers, 1997-. **Business Addr:** Professional Football Player, San Diego Chargers, Qualcomm Stadium, 9449 Friars Rd, San Diego, CA 92108, (619)280-2111.

CROCKER, CLINTON C.
Arts and education consultant. **Personal:** Born Sep 7, 1928, Norfolk, VA; son of Helen Mae Ford Crocker and William L. Crocker; married Doris Hickson; children: Clinton Jr, Leah Kay, Roger, Ronald. **Educ:** Rider University, Trenton, NJ, BMus 1952; Kean Coll, Union, NJ, MA 1967. **Career:** Newark, NJ, public schl tchr 1955-67; Kean College, NJ, adjunct prof 1959-67; Brookdale Comm Coll Lincroft, NJ, exec dean 1969-72; Rutgers Univ, NJ, univ arts admin 1972-85; CC Crocker & Co, NJ, pres, currently. **Orgs:** Fdr & past pres NJ Haiti Partners of the Am 1977-83; fndr Hispanic Arts Inst Rutgers Univ 1975; prdr Rutgers Univ Summer Festvl TV Special 1980; fndg mem & past pres NJ Sch of the Arts 1980; mem Intl Order of St John Knights of Malta; bd of trustees Brookdale Community Coll 1987-91; bd of trustees Brookdale Community Coll Fdn 1988-91; bd of dirs Assn of Community Coll Trustees, 1990; founder, pres, African American Arts & Heritage Festival, Garden State Arts Center, Holmdel, NJ, 1988; bishop election committee, Episcopal Diocese of New Jersey; co-founder, Urban League of Monmouth County, New Jersey; New Jersey State Council on the Arts; bd of directors, Monmouth Council (NJ) Boy Scouts of America, 1995; bd of trustees, Rutgers University, New Burnswick NJ; vice pres, Monmouth Council, NJ, Boy Scouts of America; board of directors, Count Basie Learning Ctr, Red Bank NJ. **Honors/Awds:** Composer & lyrist Alma Mater Brookdale Com Coll 1971; NJ Soc of Architects AIA NJ 1971; United Fund Monmouth Co NJ 1977; Outstanding Public Serv Award Brookdale Comm Coll 1972; dir 200th Commemorative Session NJ State Legislature 1983-84; National Conference of Christians & Jews, Brotherhood Award, 1994; Selected 100 Most Influential and Positive Individuals in New Jersey by City News, Plainfield, NJ. **Military Serv:** AUS E-4 1952-54. **Home Addr:** 120 Willshire Dr, Tinton Falls, NJ 07724. **Business Addr:** President, CC Crocker & Co Inc, 120 Willshire Dr, Tinton Falls, NJ 07724.

CROCKER, CYRIL L.
Educator, physician. **Personal:** Born Aug 21, 1918, New Orleans; married Anna Ruth Smith. **Educ:** Talladega Coll, AB 1939; Howard U, MD 1950; Univ of CA, MPH 1968. **Career:** Natl Bureau of Standards Washington, chemist 1942-46; Obstetrics & Gyneology, Flint Goodridge Hospital New Orleans, dir 1955-56; Howard Univ, instructor 1956-62, asst prof 1962-68; Makerere Univ, lecturer 1968-69; Mulago Hospital, Kampala Uganda, E Africa, consultant 1968-69; Howard Univ, prof 1969-72; Family Planning Serv, Dept of Ob/Gyn Howard Univ, project dir 1970-76; Dept of Ob/Gyn Howard Univ, prof, chmn

1976-. **Orgs:** Mem Alpha Omega Alpha 1975; Kappa Pi Honor Soc; Am Coll of Obstetricians & Gynecologists Am Coll of Surgeons; Nat Med Assn; Med Soc of DC Medico-chirurgical Soc of DC; Am Assn of Planned Parenthood Physicans; Howard Univ Med Alumni AssnRecipient. **Honors/Awds:** Distinguished serv award Chmn DC Met Interagency Council on Family Planning 1975. **Military Serv:** USNR 1945-46. **Business Addr:** Howard Univ Hosp, Georgia Ave NW, Washington, DC 20060.

CROCKER, WAYNE MARCUS
Library administrator. **Personal:** Born May 26, 1956, Petersburg, VA; son of Nancy Cooley Crocker and George Crocker; married Sabrina Tucker Crocker, Oct 15, 1983; children: Shannon Nicole, Courtney Lynn. **Educ:** Virginia State College, Petersburg, VA, BS, 1978; Atlanta University, Atlanta, GA, MSLS, 1979. **Career:** Petersburg Public Library, Petersburg, VA, page/library aide, 1973-78; Atlanta Public Library, Atlanta, GA, library assistant/librarian, 1978-80; Petersburg Public Library, Petersburg, VA, director of library services, 1980-. **Orgs:** Member, American Library Association, 1980-; member, Virginia Library Association, 1980-; member, Alpha Phi Alpha Fraternity, 1985-; member, State Networking Users Advisory, 1989-; president, board of directors, Petersburg City Employees Federal Credit Union, 1987. **Honors/Awds:** Louise Giles Minority Scholarship, American Library Association, 1978. **Home Addr:** 101 South Plains Dr, Petersburg, VA 23805. **Business Addr:** Director of Library Services, Petersburg Public Library, 137 South Sycamore St, Petersburg, VA 23803.

CROCKETT, DELORES LORAINE
Government administration. **Personal:** Born Jun 18, 1947, Daytona Beach, FL; divorced; children: Ayanna T. **Educ:** Spelman Coll, BA Psych (Cum Laude) 1969; Altanta Univ, MA Guidance & Counseling 1972. **Career:** Minority Women's Employment Prog, proj dir 1974-77; Avon Products Inc, employment & commun suprv 1977-79; Natl Alliance of Bus, metro dir 1979; US Dept of Labor, reg dir. **Orgs:** Selected Leadership Atlanta 1977, Leadership GA 1978; bd of dir Big Brothers/Big Sisters 1985-; bd of trustees Leadership Atlanta 198-81; bd of dir Amer Red Cros 1982-; AH Task Force Natl Conf of Black Mayors 1985. **Honors/Awds:** Woman of Achievement Business & Professional Women's Clubs Inc 1977,79; One of the Ten Outstanding Young People of Atlanta 1979; Citation for Outstanding Comm Serv Atlanta Women in Business 1984; Selected by Labor Dept as 1 of 2 reps to serve on Panel III studying Intl Training Prog to Eliminate Sex Imbalances in the Work Place Paris France 1983,84; Outstanding Alumnae Awd Spelman Coll Class of 1969 1984. **Business Addr:** Regional Dir, Women's Bureau US Dept Labor, 1371 Peachtree NE Rm 323, Atlanta, GA 30367.

CROCKETT, EDWARD D., JR.
Physician. **Personal:** Born Aug 26, 1937, Chattanooga, TN; married Mary Alice; children: 3. **Educ:** Amherst Coll, BA 1958; Howard Univ, MD 1962. **Career:** Howard Univ, asst prof, Private Practice, physician internal medicine & pulmonary diseases. **Orgs:** Mem Med Chirugical Soc DC; DC Thoracic Soc; DC Med Soc; asst chmn Undergrad Med Educ Dept Med Howard Univ 1973. **Honors/Awds:** Fellow, Amer Coll Physicians, Amer Coll Chest Physicians. **Military Serv:** USN 1967-69. **Business Addr:** 1827 First St NW #A, Washington, DC 20001.

CROCKETT, GEORGE W., III
Judge. **Personal:** Born Dec 23, 1938, Fairmont, WV; son of Emily Ethelene Jones Crockett and George William Crockett Jr; divorced; children: Enrique Raul. **Educ:** Morehouse College Atlanta, GA, BA 1961; Wayne State University Detroit, MI, 1958-59; Detroit College of Law Detroit, MI, JD 1964. **Career:** Recorders Court for the City of Detroit, judge; Defenders Office Detroit, dep Defender 1970-76; Wayne Co Neighborhood Legal Serv, supv atty 1967-70; asst corp counsel 1967; pvt practice 1965-66. **Orgs:** Natl Bar Assn; MI State Bar; Wolverine Bar Assn; Assn of Black Judges of MI. **Business Addr:** Judge, Recorder's Court for the City of Detroit, 1441 St Antoine, Detroit, MI 48226.

CROCKETT, GEORGE WILLIAM, JR. See Obituaries section.

CROCKETT, GWENDOLYN B.
Attorney. **Personal:** Born Apr 25, 1932, Monroe, LA; daughter of Maggie Duncan Bailey and Isaac Bailey; children: John, Jr, Donald. **Educ:** So U, BA 1954; So Univ Law Sch, JD 1958. **Career:** So Univ Law Sch Baton Rouge, instr Law 1961-67; Legal Aid Soc Baton Rouge, dir 1967-72; US Dept Labor Wash 1972-73; US Consumer Product Safety Commn 1973-; Washington DC Louis A Martinette Legal Soc La, pvt prac & law ofc. **Orgs:** LA State Bar Assn; DC Bar Assn. **Honors/Awds:** Distinguish serv award Legal Aid Soc Baton Rouge 1972; Nat Client Council 1971; CPSC Chmn citation 1977. **Business Addr:** President, Crockett & Johnson, PC, 2021 Brooks Dr, Ste C-2, Forestville, MD 20747.

CROCKETT, PHYLLIS D.
Journalist. **Personal:** Born Jul 14, 1950, Chicago, IL; daughter of Mae Corbin Williams and Leo Crockett; children: Adina Gittens. **Educ:** Univ of Illinois, Chicago, BA, 1972; Northwestern Univ, Medill School of Journalism, Masters, 1979; Stanford Univ, Palo Alto, CA, Knight Fellow, 1990-91. **Career:** WSOC News Radio, producer, reporter, anchor, 1978-79; AP/UPI, Raleigh and Durham, NC, freelance reporter, 1978-80; WFNC/WQSM, producer, reporter, anchor, 1979-80; Johnson C. Smith Univ, visiting instructor, 1979; America's Black Forum, panelist, 1980-83; Fayetteville State Univ, visiting instructor, 1980; Sheridan Broadcasting Network, exec editor/special correspondent, 1980-81; panelist, guest lecturer, Howard Univ, Univ of DC, Stanford Univ, DC Public Schools, Fairfax County Public Schools, 1980-; WTTG-TV, news writer, 1981-82; National Public Radio, reporter, 1981-89, White House correspondent,1989-91, senior correspondent, 1992-; Pacific News Service, freelance reporter, 1984, CNN analyst, 1992-; Black Entertainment Television, analyst, 1987-; C-SPAN Cable TV Network, WHHM-TV, anal, 1987-. **Orgs:** Natl Assn of Black Journalists, 1978-; Sigma Delta Chi, 1979 -; Smithsonian Institution, African American Advisory Committee, 1989-. **Honors/Awds:** Robert F. Kennedy Award for program, ''Black Men: Lost Generation?'' 1990; NEA Award for ''Acting White,'' 1988; Frederick Douglass Award for ''MLK the Prolonged Dream,'' Natl Assn of Black Journalists, 1984; Natl Assn of Black Journalists Award for ''Sickle Cell: Shadow of Death''; consultant to Clark Atlanta University; contributor to book, Split Image: African Americans in the Mass Media, edited by Jannette L. Oats and William Barlow, 1990; has written book reviews appearing in the New York Times, 1988, 1992, and the Los Angeles Times, 1989.

CROCKETT, RAY
Professional football player. **Personal:** Born Jan 5, 1967, Dallas, TX. **Educ:** Baylor, BA in computer science, 1992. **Career:** Detroit Lions, defensive back, 1989-93; Denver Broncos, 1994-. **Orgs:** United Way. **Business Addr:** Professional Football Player, Denver Broncos, 13655 Broncos Pkwy, Englewood, CO 80112, (303)649-9000.

CROCKETT, ZACK
Professional football player. **Personal:** Born Dec 2, 1972, Pompano Beach, FL. **Educ:** Florida State. **Career:** Indianapolis Colts, running back, 1995-. **Business Addr:** Professional Football Player, Indianapolis Colts, PO Box 535000, Indianapolis, IN 46253, (317)297-2658.

CROFT, IRA T.
Mayor. **Personal:** Born Feb 7, 1926, White Hall, AR; son of Effie Croft and Rev E O Croft; married Dorothy Jean Taylor Croft, Feb 10, 1951; children: Sonya Faye Croft, Lisa Juanita Croft. **Educ:** Shorter Coll, North Little Rock AR, BA Sociology, 1951; Fisk Univ, Nashville TN, Advanced Study in Sociology, 1951; Arkansas State Coll, Amer History Inst, Jonesboro AR, 1964; Oklahoma State Univ, Economic Inst, Stillwater OK, 1969. **Career:** West Memphis School Dist, West Memphis AR, teacher and admin, 1957-86; City of Edmonson, AR, mayor, currently; Adult Sunday School Teacher. **Orgs:** Masons. **Honors/Awds:** Appointed chairman of all incorporated towns in Arkansas by the Arkansas Municipal League, 1992. **Military Serv:** Veteran of WW II. **Home Addr:** 400 Harrison, PO Box 65, Edmondson, AR 72332.

CROFT, NORMAN F.
Packaging company executive. **Personal:** Born Nov 5, 1950, Cincinnati, OH; son of Ruth Croft and Paul Croft. **Educ:** University of Cincinnati, BS, 1974. **Career:** Brunswick Corp., inventory analyst; Sun Electric, purchasing manager; Signode Corp., purchasing manager; Service Packaging, Inc, president, currently. **Orgs:** National Association of Purchasing Managers, 1974-81; Chicago Regional Purchasing Council, 1981-; National Minority Business Council, 1985-. **Business Addr:** President, Service Packaging, Inc, 5915 Lincoln Ave, Morton Grove, IL 60053-3348, (847)966-6556.

CROFT, WARDELL C.
Insurance executive. **Personal:** Born in Gadsden, AL; son of Minnie Croft and Thomas Croft; married Theora; children: Bobbie. **Educ:** Stillman Coll; Alexander Inst; Univ MI Extension Div, Loma, Atlanta GA. **Career:** Wright Mutual Ins Co, top mgmt responsibility, 1950-62, CEO, bd chmn, 1962-. **Orgs:** Vice chmn bd of dirs 1st Independence Natl Bank one of founders; mem bd of dirs Physician Drug Center, Detroit Renaissance, New Detroit Inc; mem bd of trustees Stillman Coll; bd mem & chair, Life Insurance Assoc of MI; chmn Detroit Inst of Commerce; vice chmn UNCF Exec Comm of MI. **Honors/Awds:** MI Citizen of the Year MI Chronicle; ''S'' Award Stillman Coll; Citizen Award Phi Beta Sigma Fraternity; Silver Beaver Award Boy Scouts of Amer; CC Spaulding Award Natl Business League; Equal Opportunity in Higher Educ; Focas & Impact Oakland Univ. **Military Serv:** AUS WW II 1st sgt. **Business Addr:** CEO/Board Chairman, Wright Mutual Insurance Co, 2995 E Grand Blvd, Detroit, MI 48202.

CROMARTIE, ERNEST W., II
Attorney. **Personal:** married Raynette White; children: Ernest W, Antionette. **Educ:** MI State Univ, 1968; George Washington Natl Law Ctr, JD (Cum Laude) 1971. **Career:** Cureton & Cromartie, attorney 1974-76; EW Cromartie, II, attorney 1976-; City of Columbia Dist II, councilman. **Orgs:** Life mem NAACP; mem Optimist Club, East Columbia Jaycees, United Way Bd of Trustees, 32nd Degree Mason, Shriners, Midlands Elks, Townmen Club, Columbia Chamber of Commerce, Housing Comm of Greater Columbia Chamber of Comm, United Way Governing Bd, Kiwanis Club; mem Bishop Mem AME Church, past pres usher bd, sunday school teacher, mem bd of trustees, chmn of bldg fund, chmn Men's Day Activities; mem SC Bar Assoc, Richland Cty Bar Assoc, Amer Bar Assoc, SC Trial Lawyers Assoc, Amer Trial Lawyers Assoc; Admitted to practice in SC Supreme Court, US Dist Court, US Court of Appeals 4th Circuit. **Honors/Awds:** Appt by the Mayor to City of Columbia Zoning Bd of Adjustments & Appeals 1976-80, 1980-85; Atty of the Year 1979; chmn Eau Claire Task Force for Comm Ctr 1980-81; Outstanding Serv Awd SC Chap Natl Assoc of Real Estate Brokers; Living Legacy Awd Natl Council of Negro Women; Appt to SC Youth Serv Bd. **Home Addr:** 2213 Lorick Ave, Columbia, SC 29203.

CROMARTIE, EUGENE RUFUS
Association executive. **Personal:** Born Oct 3, 1936, Wabasso, FL; son of Ulysses and Hannah; married Joyce Bell Mims; children: Eugene II, Leonardo, Marcus, Eliseo. **Educ:** FL A&M Univ, BS 1957; Univ of Dayton, MS 1968; US Army Command & Gen Staff Coll, 1970; Natl War Coll, 1977. **Career:** Assignments incl command MP Co, two MP battalions & a criminal invest reg covering 22 states; Univ of Dayton OH, asst prof of military sci; US Army Military Police Sch, staff/faculty mem; Command & Gen Staff Coll, staff/faculty mem; 82nd Airborne Div, provost marshal; Wash, DC, assignment ofcr/ofcr personnel directorate; USACIDC, spec asst to the commanding gen; US Army Criminal Invest Command Fort Meade, MD, commander first reg; US Army Europe & Seventh Army, dep provost marshal, provost marshal; US Army Military Community Mannheim, Germany; US Army Criminal Invest Command, spec asst to the commanding gen, commanding general; International Assn of Chiefs of Police, Arlington, VA, d/exec dir & chief of staff, 1990-. **Orgs:** Exec director, currently, exec com Intl Assn of Chiefs of Police 1983-; mem Intl Fedn of Sr Police Officers 1981-; Natl Cncl Law Enforcement Explorer Boy Scouts of Amer 1983-; mem Alpha Phi Alpha Frat 1954-; mem Natl Org of Black Law Enforcement Exec 1984-; natl chmn Law Enforcement Exploring Comm Boy Scouts of Amer 1986-. **Honors/Awds:** FAMU Meritorious Achievement Award 1982; State of FL Resolution Acknowledged as Outstanding Floridian recorded in State Archives 1982; City of Tallahassee & Leon Co declared May 1, 1982 as Brigadier Gen Eugene R Cromartie Day; Key to City of Tallahassee 1982; featured in Ebony Mag Army's Top Cop 1985; 1st inductee into FL A&M Univ ROTC Hall of Fame 1986; Awd FL A&M Centennial Medallion for Distinguished Serv 1987; Honorary Doctor of Laws, Florida A&M Univ, 1990; NAACP Meritorious Service Award, NAACP, 1989; Public Service Award, National Assn of Federal Investigators, 1989; President's Award, National Sheriffs Assn, 1989. **Military Serv:** AUS Major Gen; served over 30 years; 2 Bronze Star Medals; 3 Meritorious Serv Medals; 2 Army Commendation Medals; Parachutist Badge; Distinguished Service Medal, 1990. **Business Addr:** Exec Dir & Chief of Staff, International Assn of Chiefs of Police, 515 N Washington St, Alexandria, VA 22314-2357.

CROMBAUGH, HALLIE
Business executive. **Personal:** Born Sep 9, 1949, Indianapolis, IN; married Dennis; children: Trenna, Kendra. **Educ:** Porter Coll, 1974; IN Central Coll; St Mary of the Woods Coll. **Career:** Indy Today & Comm, dir, comm affairs, exec producer/host; WISH-TV, asst dir, comm Affairs; 1975-76; Coll/U Corp, auditor, gen accounting dept 1974-75; Am Fletcher Nat Bank, IBM & opr; IN Nat Bank, NCR opr. **Orgs:** Chmn by-laws com Nat Broadcast Assn Comm Affairs; bd dir Comm Servs Council of Greater Indpls; chmn Family Violence Task Force; chmn bd of Dirs Wishard Meml Hosp Midtown Comm Mental Hlth Ctr; adv bd Indianapolis Jr League; vchmn Queens Selection & Coronation Com Indianapolis 500 Festival Asso; bd dirs Indianapolis 500 Assn Inc; mem Gamma Phi Delta Intl Sor Inc; asso min St Paul AMECh; mem IN Conf of 4th Episcopal Dist; ordained deacon AME Ch;chmn adv bd Auntie Mames CDC. **Honors/Awds:** Recpt & outsdng serv award United Award 1975-79; media yr award Marion Co Heart Assn 1975-76; outsdng serv award Indianapolis Pub Sch Operation Catch-up 1977; outsdng serv award Indianapolis Pre-sch Inc 1975-79; outsdng serv award Indy Trade Assn 1977; golden heart award Am Heart Assn 1979 outstanding mental health serv award 1978-79. **Business Addr:** Community Affairs Dir, WISH-TV 8, PO Box 7088, Indianapolis, IN 46207.

CROMWELL, ADELAIDE M.
Educator (retired). **Personal:** Born Nov 27, 1919, Washington, DC; daughter of Yetta M Cromwell and John W Cromwell Jr.; divorced; children: Anthony C Hill. **Educ:** Smith Coll, BA 1940; Univ of PA, MA 1941; Bryn Mawr, Cert in Soc Work 1952; Radcliffe Coll, PhD 1952. **Career:** Hunter Coll, mem faculty 1942-44; Smith Coll, mem faculty 1945-46; Boston

Univ, mem faculty 1951-, dir Afro-Amer studies, prof emerita sociology. **Orgs:** Adv comm Corrections Commonwealth MA 1955-68; adv comm Voluntary AID 1964-80; mem Natl Endowment for the Humanities 1968-70; dir African Studies Assoc 1966-68; adv comm, to dir census 1972-75 IRS; mem Natl Ctr of Afro-Amer Artists 1970-80, African Scholars Council 1971-80; bd mem Wheelock Coll 1971-72; mem Commonwealth Inst of Higher Ed 1973-74; mem Natl Fellowship Fund 1974-75, Bd Foreign Scholarships 1980-84; mem Bd on Sci & Tech for Intl Devel 1984-86; mem African Studies Assoc, Amer Soc Soc, Acad of Arts & Sci, Council on Foreign Relations; Massachusetts Historical Commission, 1993-; Massachusetts Historical Society 1997-. **Honors/Awds:** Mem Phi Beta Kappa; National Order of Ivory Coast 1967; Univ of Southwestern MA LHD 1971; Alumnae Medal Smith Coll 1971; TransAfrica Africa Freedom Awd 1983; Honorary Doctor of Humanities, George Washington University, 1989; Honorary Doctor of Humane Letters, Boston U. 1995. **Business Addr:** Prof Emerita Sociology, Boston University, 138 Mountfort St, Brookline, MA 02146.

CROMWELL, MARGARET M.
Administrator. **Personal:** Born Jan 30, 1933, Bridgeport, CT; daughter of Margaret M Cromwell and McKinley H Cromwell Sr; married McKinley H; children: Marcelina Johnson, Mc Kinley, Jr, Jarrett. **Educ:** Training on family planning in educ & admin, 1966; Training for instructional aide, 1967. **Career:** Screening & Educ Cnrt CT State Dept of Health, coordinator/Counselor sickle cell disease 1972-; CT of Social Work's Summer Inst Training, instructor, 1972; Family Planning/Neighborhood Health Servcs, dir 1968-72; Family Planning Center, coordinator 1966-68; Bridgeport bd educ, instr aide 1967-68. **Orgs:** Past mem Action for Bridgeport Community Devel; past mem Action for Bridgeport Community Devel; exec bd vice-chmn North End Neighborhood Action Coun; past vice pres YWCA; past chmn Cntr for Racial Justice YWCA; past mem bd of Comprehensive Health Planning; past mem Unite Community Services; past co-chmn ParentAdv Coun of Hall Neighborhood House Day Care Cntr; past chmn Dept Children Youth Serv Multi-Serv Cntr; Bridgeport Chap Child Guidance; pres Planned Parenthood Chap Com of Bridgeprot ; past co-chmn Police Community Relations for Urban Coalition; past mem Bridgeport Chap Heart Assn; mem Nat Coun of Negro Women; bd dirs ARC; Channel 8 Minority Adv Com New Haven CT; State Police Coun; NAACP; chmn Youth Outreach Prevention Program HallNeighborhood House; bd dirs Hall Neighborhood House75-78; Gov Planning Com for Criminal Adminstrn Youth Crime & Delinquency sub-com; US Commn on Civil Rights; CT Adv Com; pres Community Awareness Progrma Sickle Cell Anemia; Urban Coalition; vp. **Honors/Awds:** Recipient serv award Action for Bridgeport Community & Devel 1969; volunteer award Parent Adv Com Hall Neighborhood House 1970; serv award 1970; certificateof recognition for Community Serv 1972; serv award Urban Coalition 1972; community serv award 1972; numerous other civic & serv Awards. **Business Addr:** ABCD Inc, 815 Pembroke St, Stratford, CT 06497.

CROPP, DWIGHT SHEFFERY
School administrator. **Personal:** Born Aug 5, 1939, Washington, DC; married Linda Washington; children: Allison, Christopher. **Educ:** Howard U, BA & MA 1965; Yale, Post Master's 1970. **Career:** DC Bd Edn, exec sec; DC Pub Schs, exec asst to supt 1971; DC City Coun, spl Asst Chmn 1971; DC Pub Schs, educ 1965; US Dept of State, research analyst 1964. **Orgs:** Mem Am Assn Sch Adminstrn; mem Urban League, US Office of Educ fello 1969; fellow Yale Urban 1970. **Military Serv:** AUS first lt 1961-63. **Business Addr:** 415 12 St NW, Washington, DC 20004.

CROSBY, EDWARD WARREN
Educational administrator (retired). **Personal:** Born Nov 4, 1932, Cleveland, OH; son of Marion G Naylor Crosby and Fred D Crosby; married Shirley Redding, Mar 17, 1956; children: Kofi M Khemet, Darryl M L, E Malcolm. **Educ:** Kent State Univ, BA 1957, MA 1959; Univ of KA, PhD 1965. **Career:** Educ Resources Inst Inc E St Louis, vice pres program devel 1968; Experiment in Higher Educ SIU, dir of educ 1966-69; Inst for African Amer Affairs Kent State Univ, dir 1969-76; Univ of WA, dir Black Studies Program 1976-78; Kent State Univ, assoc prof 1969-94, chm, dept of Pan-African Studies, 1976-94; Network for Educ Devel & Enrichment, Kent OH, vp, 1988-. **Orgs:** Resident consult Regional Council on Intl Educ; Faculty Inst on the Black World 1970-72; consult Peat Marwick Mitchell & Co 1971-72; pres NE OH Black Studies Consortium 1974; pres OH Consortium for Black Studies 1980-; former board member, Harriet Tubman, African American Museum 1985-. **Honors/Awds:** Hon Leadership Award Omicron Delta Kappa 1976; Hon mem Alpha Kappa Mu; publ The Black Experience, "An Anthology" 1976; published "Chronology of Notable Dates in the History of Africans in the Am & Elsewhere" 1976; publ "The Educ of Black Folk, An Historical Perspective" The Western Journal of Black Studies 1977; publ "The African Experience in Community Devel" Two Vols 1980; Your History, A Chronology of Notable Events 1988. **Military Serv:** SCARWAF corporal 1952-54. **Business Addr:** Chmn Emeritus, Dept of Pan-African Studies, Kent State Univ, Rm 117, Center of Pan-African Culture, Kent, OH 44242.

CROSBY, FRED MCCLELLEN
Furniture company executive. **Personal:** Born May 17, 1928, Cleveland, OH; son of Marion Grace Naylor Crosby and Fred Douglas Crosby; married Phendalyne' D Tazewell, Dec 23, 1958; children: Fred C, James R, Llionicia L. **Career:** Crosby Furniture Co Inc, pres, chief exec officer, 1964-. **Orgs:** Appointee of USA to Advisory Council SBA 1978-80; gov appointee State Boxing Comm 1984-94; bd dirs First Bank Natl, 1974-90; CBL Economic Devel Corp; the Buckeye Exec Club of State of OH; ex bd trustee Greater Cleveland Growth Assn, 1973-; bd dir Auto Club, Ohio Retail Merchants Assn; bd of trustees, Public TV, 1970-; Better Business Bureau, 1996-; Cleveland Cuyahoga County Port Authority, 1986-90; vice chairperson, Ohio Council Retail Merchants Association, 1988-91, chairman, 1994-95; chairman, First Inter-City Banc Corporation, 1988-; board member, Cuyahoga County Loan Review Committee, 1990-; board member, Cuyahoga County Community Improvement Corp, 1990-; trea, Urban League, 1973-74; vice pres, NAACP Cleveland Branch, 1971-72; bd trustee, United Black Fund, 1992-; bd trustee, American Auto Association, 1993-98. **Honors/Awds:** Citizens Award Bel Air Civic Club 1969; Family of Year Metro Club 1969; Businessman of Day WDOK Radio 1970; Family of Year Urban League of Cleveland 1971; Outstanding Civic Leadership YMCA 1971; Outstanding Leadership YMCA; Sustaining Mem Enrollment BSA 1972; Access Dept of Commerce Publication 1972; Black Enterprises 1973; Sojourner Truth Collection Prince George Library 1974; Business Man of the Year, Mirror Mirror Productions, 1982; Certificate of Appreciation, US Department of Commerce, 1985, Minority Enterprises Development Award, Mayor George Voinovich, 1985; United Black Fund, Ebony Club Award, 1990. **Military Serv:** AUS s/sgt 1950-52. **Business Addr:** President, Chairman/CEO, Crosby Furniture Co Inc, 12435 St Clair Ave, Cleveland, OH 44108.

CROSBY, MARGAREE SEAWRIGHT
Educator. **Personal:** Born Nov 21, 1941, Greenville, SC; daughter of Josie Williams Seawright and Mark Seawright; married Willis H Crosby Jr, Jun 24, 1963; children: Anthony Bernard, Anedra Michelle, Erich Garrett. **Educ:** South Carolina State University, BS, 1963; Clemson University, MEd, 1973; University of Massachusetts/Amerst, EdD, 1976. **Career:** School District of Greenville County, headstart tchr, summers, 1965, 1966, elementary tchr, 1964-68, reading resource tchr, 1968-74; University of Massachusetts, teaching asst, CUETEP coordinator, 1974-76; University of South Carolina, Spartanburg, asst professor, 1976-77; Clemson University, associate professor, 1977-. **Orgs:** National Association of Black Educators, 1991-; National Association of Black Reading and Language Arts Educators; Greenville Hospital System Board of Trustees, chairperson, nominating committee, 1991-97; Governor's Blue Ribbon Committee on Job Training, 1985; SC Council of International Reading Association, board of directors, chairperson, conf pro comm, 1992; Sunbelt Human Advancement Resources, Project RISE advisory board, 1988-; Clemson University, university self study committee, 1986; Affirmative Action Committee; Elementary Curriculum Committee, chairperson, 1992, department head search committee, 1985, faculty search committee, chairman, 1988. **Honors/Awds:** SC Pageant, 1992 SC Women Achievement Award, The First Award, 1992; Fifty Most Influential Black Women of South Carolina, 1992; Greenville News/Hayward Mall, Order of the Jessamine Award, 1991; American Association of University Women, Women in History Who Make a Difference, 1982; Greenville Middle School, Outstanding Educator and Service Award, 1992; Regional Positive Image Award, 1993; International Citizen of the Year, Omega Psi Phi Fraternity Inc, 1994, Cleveland, OH; Appointed Woman of Achievement, South Carolina Governor's Office, 1994. **Special Achievements:** Groomed and trained over 1500 young men and ladies for presentation to society in Debutante Cotillion, AKA, Beautillion (Jack & Jill), 1968-; trained and developed over 500 AFDC mothers for gainful employment in the hospitality sector, 1984-88; principal investigator, A Survey of Principal Attitudes Toward Ability Grouping/Tracking in the Public School of So St, 1991; coordinator, Multi-Cultural Enhancement Project, 1992; "Cooperative Learning," "Alternatives to Tracking and Ability Grouping," Natl Council for Teachers of English and the Natl Dropout Prevention Center. **Business Addr:** Associate Professor, Coordinator of Elementary & Early Childhood Education, Clemson University, College of Education, Tillman Hall, PO Box 340709, Clemson, SC 29634-0001, (803)656-5116.

CROSBY, WILLIS HERMAN, JR.
Human services administrator. **Personal:** Born Jul 31, 1941, Anderson, SC; son of Alwille Hardy Crosby and Willis H Crosby; married Dr Margaree S Crosby, Jun 24, 1963; children: Anthony, Anedra, Erich. **Educ:** South Carolina State University, BA, 1963; Furman University, MA, 1972; University of Massachusetts/Amherst, EdD,1977. **Career:** Spartanburg School District 7, social studies teacher, 1963-66; School District of Greenville County, social studies teacher, 1966-70, ombudsman, 1970-73; Ford Foundation Leadership Development Program Fellowship, 1973-74; University of Massachusetts, research assistant, 1974-76; Tri-County Technical College, division chairman, 1976-79; Sunbelt Human Advancement Resources, Inc, executive director, 1979-94, president/ceo, 1994-. **Orgs:** South Carolina Association of Human Service Agencies, president, 1991-93; South Carolina Association of Community Action Agencies, president, 1986-88; Southeastern Association of Community Action Agencies, board mem, 1986-; Greenville Breakfast Rotary Club, vocational committee chairman, 1992-93; Greater Greenville Chamber of Commerce, board mem, 1991-94; South Carolina Education Resource Center for Missing & Exploited Children, board mem, 1990-94; Greater Greenville Pan Hellenic Council, president, 1990-92; South Carolina Social Welfare Forum, president, 1983-85. **Honors/Awds:** Southeastern Association of Community Action Agencies, Exceptional Service Award, 1992; Greater Greenville Pan Hellenic Council, Dedicated Leadership & Service Award, 1992; South Carolina Head Start Association, Humanitarian Award, 1991; Phillis Wheatley Past Fellows Association, Excellence in Leadership, 1988; South Carolina CAP Directors Association, Meritorious Award, 1987; The Greenville Alumnae Chapters, Delta Sigma Theta Sorority, Humanitarian Award for Social Action, 1994. **Special Achievements:** Sunbelt Economic Opportunity Conference, founder, 1988; Greenville MSA Needs Assessment, principal investigator, 1989; Leadership Effectiveness: An Agenda for Developing the African-American Community During the 1990's, 1990; Services to the Changing Faces of Poverty, prinicpal investigator, 1992; Southeastern Region Bank Services Assessment, principal investigator, 1992. **Business Addr:** Executive Director, Sunbelt Human Advancement Resources, Inc, 1200 Pendleton Street, PO Box 10204, Greenville, SC 29603, (803)269-0700.

CROSBY-LANGLEY, LORETTA
Agency administrator. **Personal:** Born Sep 14, 1957, Clover, SC. **Educ:** Lander Coll, BS Psychology 1979; Winthrop Coll, continuing educ. **Career:** SC Dept of Social Servs, generalist/analyst 1982-86; Richmond County Dept of Family & Children Servs, county eligibility consultant 1986; Emory Univ, personnel generalist 1986; Greenville News-Piedmont Co, exec sec 1986-87; SC Develop Disabilities Council, program information coordinator, 1987-. **Orgs:** Vice Pres/Pres Lambda Lambda Chapter, Alpha Kappa Alpha 1977/78; treasurer, Pamoja Club African-Amer; mem, Psych Club Greek Council Entertainment Council review Magazine staff; participant Poetry for the People Workshop, 1981. **Honors/Awds:** First place poetry in Lander Coll Review Literary Magazine 1979; Published poetry in review, Scribblings, The Bears Tale, News & Views Magazine, The Naiad; Published commentary in News & Views Magazine.

CROSLAN, JOHN ARTHUR
Marketing research manager. **Personal:** Born Aug 24, 1939, Henderson, NC; son of Neomia T. Croslan and Emanuel Croslan; married Emogene Barnes, Aug 1964; children: John Jr, Kimberly Rignald. **Educ:** NC Central Univ, BS 1962, MBA 1963. **Career:** NC Dept of Revenue, revenue collector 1965-67; Operation Breakthrough Inc, accountant 1967-68, asst bus mgr 1968-69, exec dir 1969-72; State Dept of Human Resources, consultant 1972-74, dir grant mgmt 1974-76, spec asst to comm 1976-; Croslan and Associates, president, currently. **Orgs:** Pres Parent-Teacher Assn 1981; pres Neighbor Watch Club 1984; mem comm NAACP, 1984; chairman of allocation committee, 1988-89, board member, 1991, United Way; Salem Baptist Church, 1978-; chairman, board of directors, AMEN; member, Georgia Black Elected Officials. **Honors/Awds:** Outstanding Leadership Chamber of Commerce 1980; Outstanding Leadership, General Assembly Resolution, 1985; Administrator of the Year, State of Georgia, 1989; Public Speaker of the Year, Student Government, North Carolina State University, 1990; Distinguished Service Award, NAACP, 1990. **Military Serv:** US Army, Spc 5, 2 years. **Home Addr:** 1908 King Charles Rd, Atlanta, GA 30331. **Business Addr:** Spec Asst To Commissioner, State Human Resources, 47 Trinity St Rm 541, Atlanta, GA 30334.

CROSS, AUSTIN DEVON
Management consultant. **Personal:** Born Jun 8, 1928, Villa Ridge, IL; son of Ada M Cross and George A Cross; married Frances J Dedeaux. **Educ:** Wilberforce Univ (OH), BA 1950; John Marshall Law Schl Attended 1954. **Career:** Amoco Oil Co, mrg-credit & cust serv 1969-71; coord-minority affairs 1971-74; Standard Oil Co, sr coord-merit emply 1974-76, consultant-employee rel 1976-85; Amoco Corp, human resources executive 1985-92; Cross Consulting Co., president, 1992-. **Orgs:** Bd dir Wilberforce Univ Alumni Assoc 1969-; mem NAACP, NUL; oper comm chmn Harbor Hse Condo Assoc 1977; finance chmn Frontier Intl, Inc 1984-; pres Wilberforce Univ Alumni Association 1986-90; bd of trust Wilberforce University 1986-. **Honors/Awds:** Distinguished Alumni Awd Wilberforce Alumni Assoc; Distinguished Serv Awd So IL Reunion Council; Distinguished Serv Awd Natl Alliance of Businessmen; Distinguished Serv Awd Chicago Chamber of Commerce; Distinguished Alumni Awd NAFEO; Honorary Doctor of Humanities 1989, Alumnus of the Year 1990, Wilberforce University, Hall of Fame, 1993. **Military Serv:** AUS sgt major 1950-52; Honor Student-Leadership Schl AUS 1950. **Home Addr:** 3200 N Lake Shore Dr, #401, Chicago, IL 60657, (773)281-5142. **Business Addr:** President, Cross Consulting Co., 3200 N Lake Shore Dr, Ste 401, Chicago, IL 60657, (773)281-5142.

CROSS, DOLORES E.
Educational administrator. **Personal:** Born Aug 29, 1938, Newark, NJ; daughter of Ozie Johnson Tucker and Charles Tucker; divorced; children: Thomas Edwin Jr, Jane Ellen. **Educ:** Seton Hall University, South Orange Newark, NJ, BS, 1963; Hofstra University, Hempstead, NY, MS 1968; The University of Michigan, Ann Arbor, MI, PhD, 1971. **Career:** Northwestern University, Evanston, IL, assistant professor in education & director of master of arts in teaching, 1970-74; Claremont Graduate School, Claremong, CA, assoc prof in education & dir of teacher education, 1974-78; City University of New York, New York, NY, vice chancellor for student aff & spec programs, 1978-81; New York State Higher Education Service Corp, Albany, NY, president, 1981-88; University of Minnesota, Minneapolis, MN, associate provost & assoc vice pres for acad affairs, 1988-90; Chicago State University, Chicago, IL, president, 1990-. **Orgs:** Member, Women Executives in State Government; advisory board member, Assn of Black Women in Higher Education; member, NAACP; member, American Educational Research Assn, 1990-; vice chr, American Association for Higher Education; vice chr, Campus Compact, Senior Consultant South Africa Project. **Honors/Awds:** Honorary Doctorate of Law, Skidmore College, 1988; Honorary Doctorate of Law, Marymount Manhattan, 1984; John Jay Award, New York State Commission of Independent Colleges and Universities, 1989; NAACP, Muriel Silverberg Award, New York, 1987; Honorary Doctorate, Hofstra University, Elmhurst College. **Business Addr:** Head, The GE Fund, 3135 Easton Turnpike, Fairfield, CT 06431.

CROSS, HAMAN, JR.
Clergyman. **Personal:** Born Jan 28, 1949, Detroit, MI; son of Malettor Gause Cross and Haman Cross, Sr.; married Roberta Alexander Cross, Jun 26, 1971; children: Haman III, Gilvonna Corine, Sharryl Lanise. **Educ:** Nyack Missionary College, Nyack, NY, 1967-68; William Tyndale College, BA, 1971. **Career:** Detroit Afro American Mission, Detroit, MI, director youth guidance, 1971-82; William Tyndale College, Farmington, MI, varsity basketball coach, 1973-79; Rosedale Park Bapt Church, founder, sr pastor 1982-. **Orgs:** Board member, Carver Foreign Missions; board member, Christian Research and Development; board member, Here's Life Black America; board of directors, Joy of Jesus, 1983; Victory Christian School, 1984; consultant, Taylor University, 1985; consultant, World Christian Center, 1985; consultant, Cedine Bible Mission, 1986; board of directors, Children's Center of Detroit, 1986; consultant, Justice Fellowship, 1987; board of directors, Center for the Black Church, 1987; board of directors, Black American Response to African Crisis; board of directors, Carver Foreign Missions; board of directors, Detroit Afro-American Mission. **Honors/Awds:** MVP, Basketball Capt of Team William Tyndale, 1969-73; Honorary Citizen of El Paso TX, 1986; author of "Dating and Courtship," "God's Honor Roll of Faith," "The Life of Moses," all in Christian Research and Development; writer of scripts for the videos Tough Talk on Love, Sex and Dating, Parent/Teen Relationships, and How to Reach and Discipline Black Men. **Home Addr:** 14017 Robson, Detroit, MI 48227. **Business Addr:** Senior Pastor, Rosedale Park Baptist Church, 14161 Vaughan, Detroit, MI 48223.

CROSS, HOWARD
Professional football player. **Personal:** Born Aug 8, 1967, Huntsville, AL. **Educ:** Univ of Alabama, attended. **Career:** New York Giants, tight end, 1989-. **Honors/Awds:** New York Giants, True Value Man of the Year, 1995. **Business Addr:** Professional Football Player, New York Giants, Giants Stadium, East Rutherford, NJ 07073, (201)935-8111.

CROSS, JACK
City official. **Personal:** Born Oct 7, 1926, Bessemer, AL; married Vergie Dlee Hooks; children: Deborah, Raymond, David. **Educ:** IN Univ, 1946-47; John Carroll Univ, 1950-55. **Career:** Price Waterhouse and Co, public acct 1951-61; Own Firm, 1961-71; exec asst adminstr 1969-71; city treasurer 1971-; all Cleveland. **Orgs:** Nat Assn Accts; Nat Assn Blak Accts; Black Accts Soc OH; treas YMCA; Boy Scout & United Torch Dr; dist chmn USAAC 2 yrs. **Business Addr:** City Hall, Rm 116, Cleveland, OH 44114.

CROSS, JUNE VICTORIA
Journalist. **Personal:** Born Jan 5, 1954, New York, NY; daughter of Norma Booth Storch and James Cross. **Educ:** Harvard/Radcliffe Coll, BA 1975. **Career:** The Boston Globe Boston, MA, corresp 1975-76; WGBH-TV (PBS) Boston, MA, asst dir 1976-78; WGBH-TV (PBS) Boston, MA, prodn mgr 1977-78; NacNeil/Lehrer NewsHour, reporter urban reg affairs 1978-80, reporter def & natl sec 1980-84, reporter politics 1984-85, producer/corresp 1985-, producer CBS News 1987-. **Orgs:** Judge Electron Journalism Awards Natl Urban Coal 1984; judge Electron Journalism Awards Robt F Kennedy Meml 1983; founding bd mem Harvard-Radcliff Black Alumni Assn NY (1980) & Washington (1983); mem TransAfrica 1979-; council on foreign relations Natl Press Club; mem Natl Acad of TV Arts & Sci; mem Nat'l Assoc of Black Journalists 1988-. **Honors/Awds:** Emmy Award Outstanding Coverage of Breaking News Story (Grenada) natl Acad of TV Arts & Scis 1983; Journalism Fellowship Carnegie-Mellon Sch of Urban/Publ Affairs 1979; Emmy nominee Outstanding Series The 1985 Defense Debate 1986; Joan S Barone Awd for Outstanding Reporting Defense Debate. **Business Addr:** Producer, CBS News, 524 W 57th St, New York, NY 10019.

CROSS, WILLIAM HOWARD
Clergyman. **Personal:** Born Oct 19, 1946, Cincinnati, OH. **Educ:** Univ Cinn, 2 yrs; St Gregory's Sem, Ph B; St Mary's Sem, MDiv. **Career:** Social Justice & New Testament Theol at McNicholas High Sch, tchr 1980; Guardian Angels Ch, asso pastor; Mt St Mary's Sem, student librn 1972-73; St James Cath Sch Dayton OH, religious educ 1973-4; St Joseph Ch & Archdiocese of Cinn, assoc pastor; St Joseph Cath Sch, rel educ coord; St Margaret Mary Church, Cincinnati, OH, assoc pastor; St Andrew Church, Cincinnati, OH, pastor, 1988-. **Orgs:** Mem Archdiocesan Soc Action Commin; 1st degree Knights of Columbus; mem Cinn W End Task Force; Nat Office Black Catholics; Nat Black Catholic Clergy Caucus; board of directors, Jobs for People; board of directors, NAACP, Cincinnati chapter. **Business Addr:** 6531 Beechmont Ave, Cincinnati, OH 45230.

CROSS-BATTLE, TARA
Athlete. **Personal:** Born Sep 16, 1968, Houston, TX; daughter of Ruthie M. Tate and Leo O. Cross, Jr.; married Spencer Battle, Sep 8, 1990. **Educ:** California State University-Long Beach, 1986-89. **Career:** Women's National/Olympic Volleyball Team, 1990-92; Italian Volleyball League, spiker, 1992-. **Honors/Awds:** NCAA, Player of the Year (volleyball) awarded twice, 1988,1989; Amateur Women's Sports Day, Player of the Year (all sports), 1989; Honda, Honda Award (volleyball), 1990; US Women's National Team, Coach's Award (volleyball), 1991; 1992 Olympics, Bronze Olympic Medal (volleyball), 1992.

CROSSE, ST. GEORGE IDRIS BRYON
Attorney, clergyman. **Personal:** Born Sep 16, 1939, St Georges, Grenada; son of Iris Ernest Thomas Crosse and Winston C Crosse; married Delois Bowman; children: Karin Vanessa, Liris Jewel Christina. **Educ:** Univ of MD Eastern Shore, BSc (Magna Cum Laude) 1964; Coppin State Coll, MEd 1975; Wesley Theol Seminary, MDiv 1980; Univ of Baltimore School of Law, JD 1970. **Career:** Calvary United Methodist Church, sr pastor 1975-78; Lewin United Methodist Church, sr pastor 1978-80; Crosse-Henson & Assoc, pres & CEO 1979-83; St Matthew's United Methodist Church, sr pastor 1980-; US Dept of Housing & Urban Devel, special advisor for minority affairs, regional manager of Maryland 1987-89; Morgan State University, Baltimore, MD, asst to the president 1989-; Fallston Federal Hill Charge, United Methodist Church, senior pastor 1989-. **Orgs:** Staff atty MD Human Relations Comm; founder, pres Soc for the Advancement of Families Everywhere 1979-85, Baltimore Coalition Against Crime 1980; natl delegate Natl Republican Convention 1980; founder MD Coalition Against Crime 1981; elected mem MD State Central Comm 1982; ordained elder Baltimore Wash Conf of United Methodist Church 1982; Maryland Housing Policy Council 1987-; Regional Planning Council 1988-. **Honors/Awds:** Alumni Scholarship Univ of MD 1964; Scholar of the Year Omega Psi Phi Frat 1964; Special Ambassador Nation of St Kitts-Nevis 1983; Outstanding Alumnus Univ of MD Eastern Shore 1984; Father of the Year, WEBB Charities 1988; Excellence in Minority Business, Minority Contractors of Maryland 1989. **Military Serv:** AUS spec 4 clas 6 yrs; Marksman, Good Conduct Medal 1964. **Home Addr:** 3509 Kings Point Rd, Randallstown, MD 21133. **Business Addr:** Regional Mgr of Maryland, US Dept of Housing & Urban Devel, 10 N Calvert St, Baltimore, MD 21202.

CROSSLEY, CHARLES R., II
Artist, educator, businessman. **Personal:** Born Oct 11, 1938, McComb, MS; married Freddie L; children: Juan Derke, Charles R. **Educ:** Coronado Sch Fine Arts, grad. **Career:** Studio Frame Gallery, owner; Studio 38, found 1971; E County Fair, Elcajon CA, art juries 1970. **Orgs:** The Fine Arts Cultural Grp 1970; mem San Diego Adult Ed, Spring Valley; mem C of C 1974. **Honors/Awds:** 1st pl Ghetto Bowl Festival 1971; Artist of Yr Award, Fine Arts Culture Grp 1972. **Military Serv:** USN 1956-58. **Business Addr:** 711 S 38 St, San Diego, CA 92113.

CROSSLEY, FRANK ALPHONSO
Metallurgical engineer (retired). **Personal:** Born Feb 19, 1925, Chicago, IL; son of Rosa Lee Brefford Crossley and Joseph Buddie Crossley; married Elaine J Sherman, Nov 23, 1950; children: Desne Adrienne Crossley. **Educ:** IL Inst of Tech, BS ChE Dean's List 1945; IL Inst of Tech, MS PhD, MetE 1947, 1950. **Career:** TN A&I State U, prof dept head 1950-52; IIT Research Inst, sr scientist 1952-66; Lockheed Palo Alto Resch Lbtry, sr mem 1966-74; Lockheed Missiles & Space Co, dept mgr 1974-79; Lockheed Missiles & Space Co, cnltg engr 1979-86; Aerojet Propulsion Rsch Inst, rsch dir propulsion matls 1986-87; Gen Corp Aerojet Tech Systems, dir materials applications 1987-90; Gen Corp Aerojet Propulsion Division, Technical Principal 1990-91. **Orgs:** Chrmn Titanium Comm The Metallurgical Soc -AIME 1974-75; mem Matls Comm Am Inst of Aero & Astro 1979-81; mem Nat'l Materials Advsry Brd Ad Hoc Comm on Welding High Strength Structures 1972-74; Minerals, Metals & Material Soc, 1946-; Sigma XI, 1947-. **Honors/Awds:** Patentee Transage Titanuim Alloys 1976; Flw Am Socty for Metals 1978-; articles 58 published in various technical jnls 1951-90; patents 7 issued 1957-83; prof serv Northern CA Coun of Black Prof Engrs 1978; Gen Corp Aerojet R B Young Technical Innovation Award, in quality & manufacturing, 1990; Trailblazer Award, The Northern CA Council of Black Professional Engineers and the National Society of Black Engineers-Alumni Extension, Silicon Valley Chapter, 1994. **Military Serv:** UNSR lt jg Victory Ribbon WW II, Am Theater, Asiatic-Pacific Theater, 1944-54.

CROSS-MCCLAM, DELORIS NMI (DEE NMI CROSS)
Automotive manufacturer sales & marketing manager. **Personal:** Born Aug 5, 1952, Lake City, SC; daughter of Louis J & Pauline McClam; divorced; children: LaTarcha D Cross. **Educ:** Prince George's Community College, AA, 1987; Columbia Union College, BS, 1991; Mercer University, MBA, 1997. **Career:** Ford Motor Company, area manager remarketing, 1979-. **Orgs:** National Black MBA Association, 1996-; Ford Motor Co, community relations committee, 1989-; Ford Motor Co, Howard University, scholarship committee, 1986-; Dr Ronald E McNair Foundation, 1986-; NAACP, 1978-. **Honors/Awds:** Florence, SC, County School District, Hall of Fame, 1997; SC African American Women's Conference Award, 1994. **Business Addr:** Area Manager, Ford Motor Company, Atlanta Auto Auction, 7205 Campbellton Rd, Atlanta, GA 30331, (404)349-5555.

CROUCH, ANDRAE
Gospel singer/composer/musician. **Personal:** Born Jul 1, 1942, Pacoima, CA; son of Catherine Dorthea Hodnett Crouch and Benjamin Jerome Crouch. **Educ:** Life Bible College, Los Angeles, CA, attended. **Career:** Began singing gospel at age of 12; has recorded over one dozen gospel albums; organizer of gospel group, The Disciples, 1968-; Christ Memorial Church of God in Christ, pastor, 1995-. **Honors/Awds:** Won 5 Grammys and numerous other awds & honors; Gold Record for "Jesus is the Answer"; author "Through It All" 1974; Soul Gospel Artist, Billboard Magazine, 1975, 1977; Grammy Awd for Best Soul Gospel Performance 1984; Daviticus Awards 1979; Dove Award 1978. **Business Addr:** c/o Word Inc, PO Box 141000, Nashville, TN 37214.

CROUCH, ROBERT ALLEN
Government official. **Personal:** Born Aug 9, 1955, St Joseph, MO; son of Arvilla Hughes Crouch and Robert A Crouch Sr. **Educ:** Southwest Missouri State Univ, Springfield, MO, BS, Psychology, 1978. **Career:** Missouri Dept of Public Safety, Jefferson City, MO, program specialist, 1979-81; Missouri Dept of Labor & Ind Rel, Jefferson City, MO, assistant director, 1981-. **Orgs:** Chairman, Black Christian Single Adult Task Force, 1984-; member, NAACP, member, Urban League, 1981, member, National Forum for Black Public Administrators, 1987; member, Alpha Phi Alpha Fraternity. **Home Addr:** 1415 Summity View Dr., Holts Summit, MO 65043.

CROUCHETT, LAWRENCE PAUL
Executive director, historical society. **Personal:** Born Mar 18, 1922, Beaumont, TX; married Lorraine Jacobs; children: Dennis P Handis, Diane L Saafir. **Educ:** Tillotson Coll, AB 1949; Univ of CA-Berkeley, MA 1969, EdD 1973. **Career:** Diablo Valley Coll CA, history prof 1962-68, dean of sp prog 1968-83; Downey Place Publishing House Inc, pres/publisher 1983-88; Northern CA Center for Afro-American History and Life, Exec Dir, Oakland CA. **Orgs:** Mem Sigma Pi Phi Frat 1972-; contributing editor The Boule Journal Sigma Pi Phi 1980-; project dir Visions Toward Tomorrow, The History of the East Bay (CA) Afro-Amer Comm. **Honors/Awds:** Danforth Fellow Univ of CA-Berkeley; William Byron Rumford, The Life and Public Service Career of a California Legislator 1984. **Military Serv:** AUS corpl 1941-46; Good Conduct Medal, Two Bronze Stars.

CROUTHER, BETTY JEAN
Educator. **Personal:** Born Mar 2, 1950, Carthage, MS; daughter of Eugene Garner Crouther and Lee M Crouther; divorced; children: Velsie Dione Pate. **Educ:** Jackson State Univ, BS (Summa Cum Laude) 1972; Univ of MS, MFA 1975; Univ of MO Columbia, PhD 1985. **Career:** Lincoln Univ, asst prof of art 1978-80; Jackson State Univ, asst prof of art 1980-83; Univ of MS, assoc prof of art history 1983-. **Orgs:** College Art Assn; Southeastern College Art Conference; Natl Art Ed Assn; MS Art Ed Assn; Phi Kappa Phi Honor Society; Kappa Pi International Honorary Art Fraternity; Pi Delta Phi Honorary Fraternity; University of Mississippi, University Museum, friends of the museum. **Honors/Awds:** University of Missouri, Superior Graduate Achievement Award, 1985; Stanford University, J Paul Getty Postdoctoral Fellowship, 1986; participant in Fulbright Group Studies program, India, 1989; Southeastern Coll Art Conference, Award for Excellence in Teaching, 1994. **Special Achievements:** Juried exhibition, "Images '84," The Mississippi Pavilion, Louisiana World Exposition, 1984; contributor, exhibition catalogue "Dean Cornwell, Painter As Illustrator," Museum of Art and Archaeology Univ of MO-Columbia 1978; co-moderator with Dr Joanne V Hawks in enrichment program "Uniting Generations Together/The Search for Meaning," 1984; author, "Deciphering the Mississippi

River Iconography of Frederick Oakes Sylvester,'' MUSE, vol 20, pp 81-9, 1986; reader for Jacob K Javit's Fellowship Fund, U S Department of Education 1989-90; invited papers: ''Diversity in Afro-American Art,'' University of Missouri, Columbia, 1990; ''Iconography of a Henry Gudgell Walking Stick,'' Southeastern College Art Conference, Memphis, 1991; ''Iconography in the Art of Contemporary African-Americans: Lawrence A Jones and Roger Rice,'' James A Porter Colloquium, Howard University, 1992; ''Marriage and Social Aspiration in the Art of Rembrandt,'' Mississippi Museum of Art, 1992; ''Images of Peace and African Heritage in the Art of Lawrence A Jones,'' Southeastern College Art Conference, Birmingham, AL, 1992; Betty J Crouther, ''Iconography of a Henry Gudgell Walking Stick,'' SECAC REVIEW, p 187-91, 1993; Southeastern College Art Conference, New Orleans, LA, ''The Hand as a Symbol for African American Artists,'' 1994. **Business Addr:** Assoc Prof of Art & Art History, University of Mississippi, Art Dept, University, MS 38677.

CROUTHER, BETTY M.
Educator. **Personal:** Born Jun 5, 1931, St Joseph, MO; married Melvin Jr; children: Lou-Ann. **Educ:** Lincoln U, BA 1952; NY U, MA 1953. **Career:** Cleveland Bd of Educ, 5th grade enrichment teacher 1985; Moses Cleveland School, teacher 1963-77; Garfield School, Columbus OH, 1961-63; Blewett School, St Louis, 1956-61; AR Baptist Coll, Little Rock AR, 1954-56; Newport School, 1954; Stephens School, Asheville, 1953-54. **Orgs:** Chmn for vars comm,life mem-past pres Nat Assn Negro B&PW Clbs, Inc; past pres Nat Council Negro Women; mem Delta Sigma Theta; Nat Bus League;NOW Cuyahoga Co Coalition; Alpha Wives. **Honors/Awds:** Woman of Yr, Bapt Ch 1972; Ollie C Porter Ldrshp Award 1973; Outstndng Elem Tchr of Am 1974; Cleveland Sr Clb Apprec Award 1976. **Business Addr:** Moses Cleaveland Sch, 4092 E 146 St, Cleveland, OH 44128.

CROUTHER, MELVIN S., JR.
Association executive (retired). **Personal:** Born Nov 22, 1926, Little Rock, AR; married Betty Madison; children: Lou-Ann. **Educ:** Lincoln Univ, BS; Warren Brown Sch Washington Univ, MSW 1960. **Career:** Cleveland Reg Ofc, reg dir 1962-66; Neighborhood Opportunity Cntr, assoc dir 1966-67, dir 1967-68; Cuyahoga Hills Boys Sch, dep supt 1968-71, supt 1971-74; Ohio Youth Commn Review Bd, chmn & chief Institutional Serv 1974-; Council for Econ Opportunities Greater Cleveland, exec dir 1979-retirement; Cuyahoga County Dept Human Svcs, chief, intake Child Abuse & Neglect, retired, 1988. **Orgs:** Pres Warrensville Kiwanis 1975; life mem NAACP; life mem Alpha Phi Alpha; mem Lee Rd Bapt Ch; Nat Assn Soc Wrkrs; Acad Certified Soc Wrkrs; mem Nat Comm Action Agency Exec Dirs Assn; mem OH Assn CAA; Lincoln Univ Alumni; Prince Hall Mason 32 degrees Knights Temp; Shriner; Eastern Star; OH Cts & Correction Assn; Nat Council Crime & Delinq; Police Athletic League. **Honors/Awds:** Highest Drama Award LU 1951; developed 1st state subsidized home for delinquent youth 1964; selective serv sys 1971-74; Dist Serv Award Grand Jury Assn 1973; Spl Recognition Award Case Western Res Medicine-Law Acad 1973. **Military Serv:** USMC 1945-46.

CROW, HIAWATHA MOORE
Educator, elected official. **Personal:** Born Jul 19, 1907, Columbia, MO; daughter of Rosie Elizabeth Johnson Ross (deceased) and Curtis Leon Moore (deceased); married James H Crow (deceased). **Educ:** Lincoln Univ, Teachers Cert 1928; Culver-Stockton Coll, BS Ed 1960; Northeast MO State Univ, MA Elem School Admin 1966. **Career:** Douglass Jr HS, teacher eng & soc studies 1958-60; Monroe City Elem School, teacher, principal 1960-66; Monroe City HS, Jr HS, teacher lang arts 1966-73 (retired); Marion Cty In-Home Svc, coord 1979-83; Hannibal Sr Ctr, coord 1983-84; City Council Hannibal, councilwoman ward 6, beginning 1987. **Orgs:** Historian, coord Restoration Proj 8th & Ctr St Baptist Church, Hannibal, MO 1977-; sec asst to rsvp dir RSVP 1978-80; pres Hannibal Amer Assoc of Univ Women 1979-81; Marion-Ralls Area Retired Teachers Unit 1979-81; mem Univ of MO Extension Council 1980-; chairman Political Action Comm Hannibal NAACP 1984-87; served on Sts & Alleys Commn 1983-89, adv bd Hannibal Industrial Council, Affirmative Action Ad Hoc Comm Fire Bd 1983-88; mem vice pres MO Div AAUW; president NEMO Re Dist 1986-88; mem of nominating committee South West Central Region American Assn of Univ Women 1987-89; bd mem appointed to bd of North East MO Area on Aging 1988; 6th Ward Councilwoman Hannibal City Council, Finance Committee, 1983-88, Bd of Public Works, Advisory Committee Chairman 1989, chair Public Works Advisoryittee 1990-91. **Honors/Awds:** Golden Cert of Recognition Missionary Baptist Convention of MO 1979; Citation for Untiring Serv to the Wellbeing of Retired Persons Natl Retired Teachers Assoc 1981; Recognition of Significant Serv a Named Gift to Amer Fellowships Amer Assoc of Univ Women 1981; 2nd Named Gift by MO State Div Amer Assn of Univ Women 1983-84; Spec Recognition of Women of Distinct by MO Div AAUW 1984; Plaque ''Another Voting Woman'' in apprec for outstanding serv as Regional Dir Coord by MO Women's Vote Project 1984; Cert of Merit The James T Brown President Award for Serv to the Community of Hannibal by Hannibal, MO Branch NAACP; 2nd Place in Recogn of Outstanding Public Serv Activity and Use of the Tools of Communication Resulting in Signif Contrib to the Community andEnhanced Publ Awareness of AAUW 1985;me honored Amer Assoc of Univ Women Educ Foundation 1985-86; This Is Your Life, Honor Marion-Ralls Retired Teachers Unit 1991. **Home Addr:** 2500 Pleasant ST, #124, Hannibal, MO 63401-2600.

CROWELL, BERNARD G.
Educator/executive. **Personal:** Born Nov 3, 1930, Chickasha, OK; married Virginia M; children: Bernard Jr, Christopher L. **Educ:** Langston Univ, BS 1953; Univ of OR, MS 1958; OK State Univ, EdD 1970. **Career:** Langston Univ, exec asst to the pres 1970-75; dir of inst rsch 1973-75, inst rsch consortium 1973-75, dir interdiscip prog coord coll & univ 1973-74; dir for admissions & records 1973-75; TN State Univ, vice pres for academic affairs 1975-84, exec admin for intl affairs 1984-. **Orgs:** Mem President's Council TN State Univ 1975-; chmn Satisfactory Progress Comm TN State Univ 1985-; Faculty Athletics Rep TN State Univ 1986-; pres Optimist Club 1986-. **Honors/Awds:** Boss of the Year TN State Univ Secretaries Assn 1977; Phi Beta Lambda Awd 1981; Disting Service Awd TN State Univ 1984; Resolution/Faculty Senate TN State Univ 1984. **Home Addr:** 861 Stirrup Dr, Nashville, TN 37221. **Business Addr:** Exec Admin for Internl Afrs, Tennessee State University, 3500 John A Merritt Blvd, Nashville, TN 37203.

CROWELL-MOUSTAFA, JULIA J.
Educator, importer. **Personal:** Born Oct 8, 1923, Philadelphia, PA; daughter of Josephine Gaines Lewis (deceased) and James Lincoln Lewis (deceased); married Moustafa Saad Moustafa, Oct 23, 1985. **Educ:** Cheyney State Coll, BS; Univ of MD, MEd; Wayne State Univ, Specialist in Admin. **Career:** MI Educ Assn, professional; traveler, importer of Egyptian artifacts. **Orgs:** First black sec & pres, Area Six Assn Classroom Teachers, 1966, 1967; First black treasurer, president-elect, Region Six MEA, 1968-73; member, evaluating team, Natl Council for Accreditation of Teacher Educ, 1971-74; first woman elected to Clintondale Board of Educ, 1969-73; reg dir, Great Lakes Region Zeta Phi Beta Sorority Inc, 1974; Youth Serv Commn Clinton Township, 1974; sec, pres, Area D Council Urban Renewal; elder deacon, elder commr gen assembly, Peace United Presbyterian Church; admin comm implementing reorganization Detroit Presbyterian; member, MI Acad of Professional Educ; MEA-NEA-R; retired volunteer, Amer Cancer Soc WICS; bd of dir, Selective Serv Bd. **Honors/Awds:** Teacher of the Year, 1969; Woman of Year, 1970; Beta Omicron Zeta Chap Zeta Phi Beta Sponsorship Award, 1972.

CRUDUP, GWENDOLYN M.
Television producer. **Personal:** Born Aug 14, 1961, Lebanon, TN. **Educ:** Univ of Tennessee, Knoxville, TN, BS, communications, 1983; Univ of Missouri, Columbia, MA, journalism, 1987. **Career:** WAND-TV, Decatur, IL, producer, 1987-88; WTEN-TV, Albany, NY, producer, 1988-90; WPVI-TV, Philadelphia, PA, associate producer, 1990-. **Orgs:** Member, National Association of Black Journalists, 1987-; member, Philadelphia Association of Black Journalists, 1990-92, 1994-95; member, National Association of Female Executives, 1991-92; member, Society of Professional Journalists, 1987-88. **Honors/Awds:** Graduate & Professional Scholarship Recipient, 1985-87. **Business Addr:** Associate Producer, WPVI-TV6/Capital Cities, 4100 City Ave, Philadelphia, PA 19131.

CRUISE, WARREN MICHAEL
Attorney. **Personal:** Born Jun 3, 1939, Baltimore, MD; divorced; children: Enid, Wesley. **Educ:** Morgan St U, AB 1963; Howard Univ Law Sch, JD 1970. **Career:** Nat Ed Assn, legal cnsl 1985; Nghbrhd Legal Srv Prg, staff atty. **Orgs:** Vp, bd of dir NEA Credit Union; mem Retirement Bd, NEA Kappa Alpha Psi Frat; Phi Alpha; Delta Law Frat; NAACP; Nat Bar Assn; Conf of BlackLwyrs; Am Bar Assn. **Honors/Awds:** MJ Naylor Meml Award; high acad achvmt in field of Philosophy. **Business Addr:** 1201 16th St NW, Washington, DC 20036.

CRUM, ALBERT B.
Physician, psychiatrist. **Personal:** Born Nov 17, 1931. **Educ:** Univ of Redlands, CA, 1973; Harvard Med Sch, MD 1957; Columbia Univ Div, Bellevue Hosp, internshp 1957-58; Psychiatric Inst of Columbia Presb Med Ctr, NYC, residency. **Career:** Am Inst of Addictive Disorders, chief psychiat cons; Human Behavior Found, med dir; Human & Behavior Pub Co, gen ed. **Orgs:** Mem AMA; Kings Co Med Soc; Delta Alpha Honor Soc; NY St Med Soc; World Med Assn; Duke Hall Camp Harvard Med Soc chrmn; Harvard Clb of NYC; mem Acad of Med Studies, MENSA; Kappa Alpha Psi; bd dir Univ of Redlands Sci Assoc Hon DSc, Redlands CA 1974. **Honors/Awds:** Brooklyn Young Man of the Yr 1966; diplomat Nat Bd of Med Exam; diplomat Pan Am Med Assn. **Military Serv:** USAF capt.

CRUMP, ARTHEL EUGENE
State official, attorney. **Personal:** Born Oct 19, 1947, New York, NY; son of Mary Yeates Crump and Walter Eugene Crump; married Linda Rose Cooke Crump, Oct 10, 1970; children: Kathryn Rose, Eric Eugene. **Educ:** Nebraska Wesleyan Univ, 1965-67; Univ of Nebraska at Lincoln, BA, sociology, 1973; Univ of Nebraska College of Law, JD 1976. **Career:** Legal Service of Southeast Nebraska, attorney, 1976-82; Nebraska Gov Robert Kerrey, legal counsel, 1983-85; Nebraska Dept of Justice, deputy atty general, 1985-91, general counsel, chief deputy tax commissioner, 1991; Nebraska Wesleyan University, Criminal Justice Department, visiting instructor, 1992, 1995, 1998; Central Interstate Low-Level Radioactive Waste Commission, general counsel, executive director, 1991-. **Orgs:** Nebraska State Bar Assn House of Delegates; Natl Assn of Atty Generals; Natl Gov's Assn; Educ Comm of the States; board of directors, Univ of NE Gymnastic Booster Club; board of directors, Family Serv Assn of Lincoln; board of directors, United Way of Lincoln & Lancaster Cos; board of directors, Theater Arts for Youth; board of directors, Malone Comm Ctr; board of directors, Lincoln Comm Playhouse, board of directors, Malone Headstart Program; panel mem Nebraska Arts Council; Touring Artists' Progs; Minority Arts Adv Comm; NAACP; Nebraska Civil Liberties Union; Coalition of Black Men; Univ of Nebraska Booster Club Womens' Athletics; bd of trustees, Nebraska Wesleyan Univ; advs comm, Lincoln Public Schools Gifted Children; advs committee, Lancaster Co Child Care; advs committee, NE Leg Sub-Comm Revision of Licensing Regulations for Child Care Insts; advs committee, Lincoln Public Schools Multi-Cultural Educ; reorganization of cofare advs comms, Lancaster Co Ad Hoc Comm; Malone Area Citizens Council; Lincoln Public Schools Evaluation of Student Health Educ Project; State Dept of Public Welfare Comm to Review Daycare Center Licensing Standards; board of directors, Pinewood Bowl Assn; board of directors, Leadership Lincoln; Nebraska State Bar Assn Ways, Means and Planning Comm, board of directors; Nebraska Supreme Court Judicial Nomination Commission; Lincoln Bar Assn; Midwest Bar Assn; Natl Low-Level (Radioactive) Waste Forum Commission Rep; Lincoln Interfaith Council; Cornhusker Council BSA, board of directors; Crucible Club; Troop 49 Boy Scouts of America, Arborland Dist; Nebraska Urban League; NAACP; Foundation for Educational Funding, board of directors; First Natl Bank/Lincoln, board of directors; Nebraska Wesleyan Univ, board of directors; Newman United Methodist Church; Board of Higher Educ & Campus Ministry, Nebraska United Methodist Church. **Honors/Awds:** Nebraska Law College, scholarship; Kelso Morgan Scholarship; Council on Legal Educ Opportunity Stipend; Alumni Achievement Award, Nebraska Wesleyan University; Silver Key Award, Law Student Division, American Bar Assn; Community Leaders of America; Univ of Nebraska-Lincoln, Maurice Kremer lecturer. **Military Serv:** US Army, sgt, 1967-70; Natl Defense Medal; Good Conduct Medal; Armed Forces Expeditionary Medal. **Business Addr:** Executive Director/General Counsel, Central Interstate Low-Level Radioactive Waste Commission, 1033 ''O'' St, Ste 530, Lincoln, NE 68508.

CRUMP, CAROLYN F.
Physician. **Personal:** Born Jan 27, 1950, Lexington, NC; daughter of Mr and Mrs Theodore Crump. **Educ:** Bennett College, BS, 1972; George Washington Univ School of Med, MD, 1976. **Career:** US Public Service Hospital Output Dept; Center for Disease Control, chief med officer, 1978-82; Medfirst, physician, 1982-92; First Family Care, physician, 1992-. **Orgs:** Southern Medical Assn; Amer Med Assn; Medical Assn of Georgia; Clayton County Chamber of Commerce; asst chief, Family Practice Dept, South Fulton, Atlanta Georgia; South Fulton Hosp, exec comm; Primary Care Physician for Occupational Medicine; South Fulton Hosp, Ad Hoc medical advisory comm; The Amer Board of Forensic Examiners. **Military Serv:** US Public Health Service, 1977-82. **Business Phone:** (404)361-6272.

CRUMP, JANICE RENAE
Community affairs director. **Personal:** Born Aug 9, 1947, Dragaton, UT; daughter of Johnnie Lee Roney Lewis and Jerry Andrew Green Sr; married Maurice Malone Crump Sr, Sep 14, 1968; children: Maurice Jr, Jason Bernard, Toiya Danielle. **Educ:** Tuskegee Institute, Tuskegee, AL BS, home ec, 1969; North Carolina Central Univ, Durham, NC, BA, English, 1981; Simmons Graduate School of Management, cert, 1986. **Career:** AT&T Southern Bell, Atlanta, GA, 1970; Georgia Power Co, Atlanta, GA, customer serv, 1970-72; Delta Airlines, Atlanta, GA, reservationist, 1972-74; Soul City Company, Soul City, NC, public relations, 1975-80; WTVD II/Cap Cities ABC, Durham, NC, community affairs dir, 1981-. **Orgs:** Chairman, Warren County Board of Elections, 1975-82; president, Northside & Norlina & Warren High PTA's; 1976-88; member, Gov Small Business Advisory Council, 1979-81; president, Warren County Democratic Women, 1982-83; vice chair, Z Smith Reynolds Foundation, 1988-91. **Honors/Awds:** Volunteer Award, American Cancer Society County, Community Service Award, WTVDII Advisory Committee, Parent of the Year Award, Soul City Interfaith Council, The Silver Bell Award for Public Service, Ad Council, Total Station Project Award, NBACA. **Home Addr:** PO Box 27, Soul City, NC 27553. **Business Addr:** Community Affairs Director, WTVD II Captial Cities/ABC, 411 Liberty St, PO Box 2009, Durham, NC 27702.

CRUMP, NATHANIEL L., SR.
Engineer (retired). **Personal:** Born Jul 18, 1920, Little Rock, AR; married Ruby M Chappell; children: N Lloyd Jr. **Educ:** Lincoln Univ, BS Chem 1948. **Career:** McDonnell Douglas Aerospace Co, space eng, until 1987; Mercury, Gemini, Apollo,

Sky Lab Shuttle Progs, unit chief 1962-; St Louis Child's Hosp, Cardiol Sec, res asst 1961-62; Hanley Ind, & Pyrotechnics & Explo Chem, proj eng 1959-61; Universal Match R & D Arma Div, lab asst, proj eng 1952-59; DuGood Micro-analytical Lab, St L, micro-analyst 1948-52. **Orgs:** Mem Am Chem Soc; mem Soc Aerospace Mtrls & Process Eng; Am Assn Contam Cont Kappa Alpha Psi Frat; bd mem Coalition for the Environ; vice pres St L Co Chap, Civitan Interntl Civic Org; srvd on 12 man adv com to Vice Pres Humphrey, "Youth Motivation" 1965-68; apptd to bd of Human Rel of Univ City, MO 1972-78; loaned exec, Greater St Louis United Way Drive, 1987-94; loaned exec, Arts & Educ Council Drive, 1988-93; bd mem, Tower Village Nursing Home, 1992-93; advisory bd mem, Mid East Area Agency on Aging, 1992-94, bd mem, 1995; bd mem, ABHF, 1993-. **Honors/Awds:** Author papers on Organic Microanaly, Analytical Chem, Space Sys Contam Cont, Aircraft Hyd Sys Clean Cntrl; Inducted in Greater St Louis Area Amateur Baseball Hall of Fame, 1992; Harris Stowe State Coll, Distinguished Alumnus Award, 1993. **Military Serv:** Res 1942-43; Act Duty 1943-46. **Business Addr:** Unit Chief, McDonnell-Douglas, PO Box 516, St Louis, MO 63166.

CRUMP, WILBERT S.
Business executive. **Personal:** Born in Portsmouth, VA; married Phyllis Lorraine Archer; children: Deborah D, David P. **Educ:** Howard Univ Wash DC, BA (Cum Laude) 1965. **Career:** Pfizer Inc NY, suprv professional placement 1971-73; CUNY LaGuardia Coll, adj lecturer 1972-75; Allied Signal Inc, mgr critical manpower admin 1973-76; Natl Urban League, lecturer, black exec exchange prog 1975-; Allied Signal Inc, dir/EEO 1976-. **Orgs:** Mem Alpha Phi Alpha, NAACP, Edges Group Inc; various business/professional org. **Honors/Awds:** Full Scholarship Howard Univ; recipient, Pres Cup as Outstanding DMG Grad Sr Howard Univ 1965; Black Achiever in Industry Awd 1976. **Special Achievements:** "Executive Accountability," Ensuring Minority Success in Corporate Management, 1988. **Military Serv:** AUS capt 1965-70; Bronze Star Medal, Army Commendation Medal. **Business Addr:** Dir, EEO, Allied Signal, Inc, Box 2245R, Morristown, NJ 07960.

CRUMP, WILLIAM L.
Educational administrator (retired). **Personal:** Born Jul 21, 1920, Enid, OK; divorced; children: Debra C, Utley III, Lisa Kai, Jacquelyn Denise. **Educ:** Lincoln U, BS 1942; Northwestern U, MA 1946; Northwestern U, PhD 1949. **Career:** School of Business & Public Management, Univ of Washington DC, dean; MD State Coll, prof, chmn business admin; TN A&I Univ Div of Business, prof, dir; KY St Coll Dept of Business, chmn; Central State Univ Div of Busubess, chmn; NASA, mgmt cons. **Orgs:** Bd chmn Urban Bus Educ Assn; bd mem DC Municipal Rsrch Bur; vice pres Intl Assn of Black Bus Educators; Kappa Alpha Psi; Delta Pi Epsilon; Pi Omega Pi; Phi Delta Kappa. **Honors/Awds:** Ford Found Fellow IN Univ 1960; Elder Watson Diggs Award Kappa Alpha Psi 1972; Delta Mu Delta, natl honor soc; hon mem Epsilon Sigma. **Special Achievements:** Co-author, The Story of Kappa Alph Psi. **Military Serv:** Armed forces 1942-45.

CRUMPLER, CARLESTER
Professional football player. **Personal:** Born Sep 5, 1971, Greenville, NC. **Educ:** East Carolina. **Career:** Seattle Seahawks, tight end, 1994-. **Business Addr:** Professional Football Player, Seattle Seahawks, 11220 NE 53rd St, Kirkland, WA 98033, (206)827-9777.

CRUMPTON, LESIA
Educator, engineer. **Educ:** Texas A&M University, BS, MS, PhD, industrial engineering. **Career:** Mississippi State University, assoc professor, industrial engineering, developer/director, Ergonomics/Human Factors program, currently. **Orgs:** National Action Council for Minorities in Engineering (NACME); Institute of Industrial Engineers, sr mem; Industrial Ergonomics Technical Group of the Human Factors and Ergonomic Society, newsletter editor; Alpha Pi Mu. **Honors/Awds:** NACME, Black Engineer of the Year, 1997; Mississippi State University, Hearin-Hess College of Engineering Distinguished Professor Award; National Science Foundation (NSF), Early Career Development Award, Presidential Faculty Fellows Award, nominee. **Special Achievements:** First African American woman to earn an engineering doctorate from Texas A&M University; first and only professor from dept of industrial engineering to receive Hearin-Hess Distinguished Professor Award.

CRUSE, HAROLD WRIGHT
Educator. **Personal:** Born Mar 8, 1916, Petersburg, VA. **Career:** Prof emeritus, Univ of MI History/Afro-Amer Studies. **Orgs:** Corr mem European Acad of Arts, Sciences, & Humanities. **Military Serv:** AUS quatermaster staff sgt 1941-45. **Business Addr:** Professor Emeritus of History, Univ of MI, Dept of History, Ann Arbor, MI 48109.

CRUSOE-INGRAM, CHARLENE
Human resources executive. **Personal:** Born 1950, New Albany, MS; daughter of Robert & Virginia Simmons; married Earnest Ingram, Aug 17, 1982. **Educ:** Bradley University, BA, Sociology French, 1972, MA, Personnel Services, 1975. **Career:** American Hospital Supply Corp, safety mgr/sr personnel specialist, 1980-82; Abbott Labs, division personnel mgr/corp recruiter, 1983-86; Enterprise Systems, Inc, vice pres of human resources, 1986-88; The Coca-Cola Co, human resources mgr, 1988-91, dir of human resources, 1991-94, dir of client services, 1994-95, vice pres of organization and people development, 1995-. **Orgs:** Inroads, mem, board of directors, 1995-; Nexus Contemporary Arts Center, bd of dirs, 1996-; Womens Food Service Forum, 1995-; Literacy Council, volunteer, 1994-95. **Honors/Awds:** Dollars & Sense, Very Important Prestigious Women Award, 1995; YWCA, Award of Excellence, 1995. **Special Achievements:** Beverage Industry, pp 23, February 1997. **Business Addr:** Vice Pres, Organization & People Development, The Coca-Cola Co, 1 Coca-Cola Plz, USA 2028, Atlanta, GA 30313, (404)676-2813.

CRUSTO, MITCHELL FERDINAND
Government official. **Personal:** Born Apr 22, 1953, New Orleans, LA; married Ann Marie Walter Crusto; children: Eve Michelle, Mia Elizabeth. **Educ:** Yale University, New Haven, CT, BA, history (magna cum laude), 1975, PhD Candidate, 1975-77, JD, 1981; Oxford University, Oxford, England, BA, jurisprudence, 1980, MA, jurisprudence, 1985. **Career:** Cravath, Swaine and Moore, New York, NY; Donovan, Leisure, Newton and Irvine, New York, NY, 1981; Honorable John M. Wisdom, US Court of Appeals, New Orleans, LA 5th Circuit, advisor, 1981-82; Jones, Walker, Waechter, Pointevent, Carrere and Denegre, New Orleans, LA, attorney, 1982-84; Stifel, Nicolaus and Company, Inc, St Louis, MO, senior vice president and general counsel, 1984-88; Washington University Business School, St Louis, MO, instructor, 1985-89; Webster University, St Louis, MO, instructor, 1986; St Louis University Law School, St Louis, MO, adjunct professor, 1987-88; Crusto Capital Resources, Inc, St Louis, MO, president and CEO, 1988-89; US Small Business Administration, Washington, DC, associate deputy administrator for Finance, Investment, and Procurement, 1989-. **Orgs:** American Bar Association; Federal Bar Association; American Corporate Counsel Association; Illinois Bar Association; Louisiana Bar Association; Missouri Bar Association; Honourable Society of the Middle Temple British Barrister Association; Securities Industry Association, Compliance and Legal Division, 1986-88; vice president, Missouri Mutual Funds Association, 1985-87; arbitrator, National Association of Securties Dealers, 1988-; director, St Louis Economic Development Corporation, 1987-89; director, Big Brothers/Big Sisters, 1985-89. **Honors/Awds:** Author, "Federalism and Civil Rights: The Meredith Incident," the Integration of the University of Mississippi by James Meredith in 1963, Tulane Law School, National Black Law Journal, summer 1989; author, "Reflections on Insider Trading," Sloan Management Review, fall 1987; author, "Blacks Can Shake Off Their Taken-for-Granted Status," LA Times, October 25, 1988; author, "Why Blacks Left the Party of Lincoln," St Louis Dispatch, January 14, 1988; "Mr. Bush and the Plight of Urban African-Americans," Ripon Forum, February, 1989; active in Republican Party. **Business Addr:** Assoc Deputy Administrator for Finance, Investment & Procure, Small Business Administration, 409 3rd St, SW, Washington, DC 20416.

CRUTCHER, BETTY NEAL
Health services administrator. **Personal:** Born Nov 21, 1949, Tuskegee, AL; married Ronald Andrew Crutcher; children: Sara Elizabeth Neal. **Educ:** Tuskegee Institute, BS, 1971; University of Michigan, MPH, 1973. **Career:** University of NC at Greensboro, chancellor's asst, 1980-85; Guilford College, president's asst, starting 1985; Dudley Hair Care Products Manufacturing Co, community relations director, 1989-91; Cleveland Clinic Foundation, community relations director, 1991-. **Orgs:** Humana Hospital, bd of directors, 1981-85; Altrusa Intl, bd of directors, 1984-85; Delta Sigma Theta, Arts and Letters Committee, 1972-; Childen's Home Society, bd of directors, 1986-; Children's Health Museum, bd, 1992-; WUIZ Educational Television Station, bd, 1992-; American Public Health Assn, 1992-. **Honors/Awds:** Natl Council for Negro Women, Outstanding Service, 1974-79; Alumni Leadership Greensboro, 1981-; Loaned Executive, United Way, 1984-85; Advocate for Black Teenage Mothers, Junior League of Greensboro, 1986-. **Business Addr:** Director of Community Relations, Cleveland Clinic Foundation, 9500 Euclid Ave, Cleveland, OH 44195.

CRUTCHER, RONALD ANDREW
Educational administrator. **Personal:** Born Feb 27, 1947, Cincinnati, OH; son of Burdella Crutcher and Andrew Crutcher; married Betty Joy Neal; children: Sara Elizabeth. **Educ:** Miami Univ, BA, BM 1969 (Cum Laude); Yale Univ, MMA 1972; State Acad of Music (Frankfurt W Germany), Diploma 1976; Yale Univ, DMA (with distinction) 1979. **Career:** Bonn (W Germany) School of Music, cello instructor, 1976-79; Wittenberg Univ, asst prof, 1977-79; UNC Greensboro, assistant professor, 1979-83, associate professor and coordinator of string area, 1983-88, associate vice chancellor for academic affairs, 1988-90; The Cleveland Inst of Music, vice pres of academic affairs, dean of conservatory, 1990-. **Orgs:** Consultant NC Arts Council 1981-88; bd dirs Amer Cello Comm Council 1982-88; founder and pres Carolina Cello Club 1983-88; consultant Natl Endowment for the Arts 1986-; bd of dirs Greensboro Cerebral Palsy Assn 1986-88; pres NC Amer String Teachers Assn 1986-88; bd of dirs, Eastern Music Festival 1988; bd of dirs, United Arts Council of Greensboro 1988; university council member, Case Western Reserve Univ, 1990-; member, Community Music Project, 1991-; advisory committee member, Northeast Ohio Jazz Society, 1990-. **Honors/Awds:** Woodrow Wilson Fellow 1969; Phi Beta Kappa; Ford Foundation Fellowship 1969-72; Fulbright Fellow 1972-74; Outstanding Serv to Strings Awd NC Amer String Teachers Assoc 1983; Pi Kappa Lambda; Omicron Delta Kappa; Danforth Fellowship Nominee, Miami Univ, 1969. **Business Addr:** Vice President of Academic Affairs/Dean of the Conservatory, The Cleveland Institute of Music, 11021 E Boulevard, Cleveland, OH 44106.

CRUTCHFIELD, JAMES N.
Newspaper editor. **Personal:** Born Dec 7, 1947, McKeesport, PA; son of Nancy Viola Summers Hill and Charles Crutchfield; children: Rashida Marie Crutchfield. **Educ:** Duquesne University, BA, 1992; Cleveland State University; Oakland University. **Career:** Pittsburgh Press, reporter, 1968-71; Pittsburgh Model Cities Program, public information officer, 1971; Pittsburgh Post-Gasette, reporter, 1971-76; Detroit Free Press, reporter, 1976-79; US Sen Carl Levin, Washington, DC, press secretary, 1979-81; Detroit Free Press, state capital bureau chief, asst city editor, deputy city editor, city editor, metro editor, Detroit managing editor, 1981-89; Akron Beacon Journal, managing editor, 1989-. **Orgs:** Member, Alpha Phi Alpha Fraternity, 1966-; member, National Assn of Black Journalists, 1983-; president, Society of Professional Journalists, 1991-93. **Business Addr:** Managing Editor, Akron Beacon Journal, 44 E Exchange St, Akron, OH 44328.

CRUTCHFIELD, SABRINA DAMES. See DAMES, SABRINA A.

CRUTCHFIELD-BAKER, VERDENIA
Financial administrator. **Personal:** Born Jul 27, 1958, Sylvester, GA; married Joe Thomas Baker. **Educ:** FL State Univ, BS 1976-79, MSPA 1981-82. **Career:** Health and Rehabilitative Svcs, counselor; School Bd St Lucie Co, teacher 1980; Dept of Labor Employment Security, interviewer 1982; Broward Cty Budget Office, budget analyst. **Orgs:** Mem NAACP 1977-79; mem Delta Sigma Theta 1977-; mem Amer Soc of Public Admin 1981-; mem Natl Forum of Black Public Admin 1983-. **Honors/Awds:** Service Awd Delta Sigma Theta 1981; Outstanding Young Women of America 1982; lst Black budget analyst Broward Cty Govt. **Business Addr:** Budget Analyst, Broward County Budget Office, 115 S Andrews Ave, Fort Lauderdale, FL 33313.

CRUTHIRD, J. ROBERT LEE
Educator. **Personal:** Born Dec 10, 1944, LeFlore Cty, MS; son of Mary Florence Black Cruthird and Harvie Cruthird; divorced; children: Robert Lee Jr. **Educ:** Univ of IL, BA, sociology, 1973, MA, sociology, 1976; Chicago State University, 1982; Critical Thinking and Acculturation Inst, University of Chicago, attended 1986; University of Wisconsin at Madison, summer 1983. **Career:** IL Dept of Corrections, correctional counselor 1977-78; Kennedy-King College, dir institutional rsch 1982, asst prof of sociology 1978-; Mayor's Summer Youth Employment Prog City Colleges of Chicago, site coord 1984-86; KKC, Title III basic skills develop 1985-86; City Colleges of Chicago, academic support serv coord 1986-87, coord of coll advisement project 1987, assoc prof of sociology 1987; asst director MSYEP 1987-. **Orgs:** Amer Sociological Assn; Assn for Institutional Rsch; Assn for the Study of the Life and History of Afro-American; consultant Educational Mgmt Assocs 1981-82; sponsor Phi Theta Kappa 1982-; life mem UIC Alumni Assn; Natl Assn for Develop Educ; Alpha Phi Alpha Frat Inc. **Honors/Awds:** Fellowship Crime and Delinquency Rsch Training 1976; fellowship Natl Endowment for the Humanities 1983; visiting scholar Univ of WI 1983; Hall of Honors IL Phi Theta Kappa 1984, 1986, 1988-91; "Black Rural-Urban Migration" ERIC 1984; "Remedial/Developmental Instructions" ERIC 1987; honors scholar 23rd Institute, New York 1990; honors scholar 24th Institute, Minneapolis 1991. **Military Serv:** US Army, specialist E4, 2 yrs; Good Conduct Medal, Letter of Commendation 1967. **Home Addr:** 259 E 107th St, Chicago, IL 60628. **Business Addr:** Associate Prof of Sociology, Kennedy-King College, 6800 S Wentworth Ave, Chicago, IL 60621.

CRUZ, ILUMINADO ANGELES
Physician, associate professor. **Personal:** Born Nov 20, 1936; son of Flora Angeles and Dr Iluminado S Cruz Sr; married Aurora Bunda; children: Danny, Eliza, Loralei. **Educ:** Univ of the Philippines, MD 1962. **Career:** Howard Univ Coll of Med, instr 1968-69, asst prof 1971-76, assoc prof 1977-. **Orgs:** Dir Hemodialysis Unit Howard Univ; fellow Amer Coll of Physicians; mem Amer Soc of Nephrology; Intl Soc of Nephrology; Natl Med Assn; Med Chirurogical Soc DC; DC Med Soc; Amer Heart Assn; Natl Capital Med Found. **Business Addr:** Associate Professor, Howard Univ Coll of Medicine, 2041 Georgia Ave NW, Washington, DC 20060.

CRUZ, VIRGIL
Educator, clergyman. **Personal:** Born Dec 21, 1929, New York, NY; married Margot Cruz-DeNijs; children: Miguel Newcomb,

Isabel DeNijs. **Educ:** Houghton Coll, BA Greek major 1953; Pittsburgh Seminary, MDiv 1956; Vrije Universiteit Amsterdam, Neth, PhD 1973. **Career:** Hebron United Presb Ch, 1956-60; Univ of Dubuque Seminary, prof of New Testament 1966-82; Western Theol Seminary, prof of Biblical studies 1982-86; Louisville Presbyterian Theological Seminary, professor, 1986-. **Orgs:** Moderator Albany Presbtery 1959-60; chair Natl Comm for Ordination Examin 1979-80; mem Gen Assembly Cncl of Presby Ch 1984-; mem The Soc of Biblical Literature 1968-; mem The Soc for the Study of Black Religion 1975-; dir Presbyterians United for Biblical Concerns 1985-; dir Found for Educ & Rsch 1985-. **Honors/Awds:** Purdy Scholarship Pittsburgh Seminary 1954; Lee Church Hist Award Pittsburgh Seminary 1956; Foreign Student Scholarship Vrije Univ 1960; Grant from German Govt for language study 1968; Higgins Fellowship (2 times); Presb Grad Fellowship 1972; author of "The Mark of the Beast, A Study of Charagma in the Apocalypse," "Amsterdam Acad Press 1973; numerous articles and book reviews; Houghton College, LHD, 1991; Westminster College, DD, 1992. **Business Addr:** Prof of New Testament, Louisville Presbyterian Theological Seminary, 1004 Alta Vista Rd, Louisville, KY 40205.

CRUZAT, EDWARD PEDRO
Physician. **Personal:** Born Apr 28, 1926, Chicago, IL; married Mildred Clemon; children: Severa, Edward II, Liza. **Educ:** Univ of IL, AB 1947; Meharry Med Coll, MD 1952. **Career:** Univ of IL, clin asst, prof of surgery; Northwestern Univ, instr in surg; Edward P Cruzat & Assocs, private practice. **Orgs:** Mem Chicago Med Soc,; IL Surg Soc; Amer, Natl Medical Assocs, Cook Cty Med Soc; Am & Coll of Chest Phys; Am Coll of Surg; Intl Coll of Surg; Chic Surg Soc. **Honors/Awds:** Cert Pan-Am Surg Soc Dr; Am Bd of Surg 1961. **Military Serv:** USN lt 1955-57. **Business Addr:** Edward P Cruzat & Assocs, 8501 Cottage Grove Ave, Chicago, IL 60619.

CRUZAT, GWENDOLYN S.
Educator, consultant. **Educ:** Fisk Univ, BA, mathematics, 1951; Atlanta Univ, MLS, 1954; Wayne State Univ, PhD, higher education information science, 1976. **Career:** Fisk University, assistant librarian, 1954-60; Harper Hospital, Detroit, assistant librarian, 1960-64; Wayne State University School of Medicine, research librarian, associate director, Post-Master's Fellowship Program, 1964-70; University of Western Ontario, lecturer, 1970; University of Michigan School of Information, lecturer, 1970, assistant professor, 1971-76, associate professor, 1976-79, professor, 1979-92, prof emeritus, 1992-; University of Hawaii Graduate School of Library and Information Studies, visiting associate professor, 1977; University of Maryland School of Library and Information Studies, visiting lecturer, 1978; National Library of Medicine, regent, 1981-84; Department of Education, Division of Library Programs, consultant, 1987-; numerous editorial, and research positions. consultant, 1987-; numerous editorial, and research positions. **Orgs:** Medical Library Association, 1960-, American Library Association, 1971-90; ALA Committee on Accreditation, 1984-86; Committee on Collective Bargaining, chairman, 1976-80; Michigan Interorganizational Conference for Cont Library Education; Cont Library Education Network & Exchange; American Society for Information Sciences; American Association of University Professors; Special Libraries Association; University of Michigan Student Group, advisor, 1973-90; Metro Detroit Medical Libraries Group; Association of College and Research Libraries; Association for Library and Information Science Education; University of Michigan Alumni Association, director-at-large, 1986-90; Med Lib Assn, Fellow & Distinguished Member, 1993; Univ of MI Co-faculty Rep to Big Ten Intercollegiate Conf, 1981-91. **Honors/Awds:** Atlanta Univ Alumnus in Residence, 1989; Gabriel Awd for Scholarship Fisk Univ; Beta Phi Mu Honor Society, 1954-; Distinguished Serv Awd of the Univ of MI 1977; Janet Doe Lectr Med Lib Assn 1978-79; various rsch activities & funded grant proposals 1964-; num publs 1963-. **Business Addr:** Professor Emeritus, School of Information, University of Michigan, 550 E University, Ann Arbor, MI 48109-1092.

CRYER, LINKSTON T.
Dental surgeon. **Personal:** Born Jul 10, 1933, Mt Hermon, LA; married Elizabeth. **Educ:** Southern Univ, BS 1945; Meharry Medical Coll, DDS 1961; Dade County Research Clinic, post graduate studies in endodontics, oral surgery, minor tooth movement, periodontal surgery. **Career:** FL State Dental Health Dept, 1961-62; Variety Children's Hospital, staff 1966-; Private Practice, dental surgeon 1962-. **Orgs:** Dade County Dental Soc 1961-; pres South Dade Political Action League 1965-80; spres Richmond Enterprises Inc 1965-; vice pres Dunbar Medical Arts Inc 1971-; pres Iota Pi Lambda Chapter Alpha Phi Alpha 1972-; mem Dade County Dental Research Clinic 1980-, The Acad of General Dentistry 1980-; pres Dade County Dental Soc 1985-87; mem Amer & Natl Dental Assns, The Amer Inst of Hypnosis; life mem Alpha Phi Alpha. **Honors/Awds:** Founder of Iota Pi Lambda Chapter of Alpha Phi Alpha. **Military Serv:** AUS 1st lieutenant 1954-56. **Business Addr:** 11350 Dunbar Dr, Miami, FL 33158.

C'SHIVA, OYA. See FORTUNE, GWENDOLINE Y.

CUDJOE, SELWYN REGINALD
Educator. **Personal:** Born Dec 1, 1943; son of Carmen Rose and Lionel Reginald; children: Frances Louise, Kwamena. **Educ:** Fordham Univ, BA 1969, MA 1972; Cornell Univ, PhD 1976. **Career:** Fordham Univ, instructor 1970-72; Ithaca Coll, adjunct asst prof 1973-75; Ohio Univ, assoc prof 1975-76; Harvard Univ, asst prof 1976-81; Wellesley Coll, Marion Butler McLean, Professor in the History of Ideas, prof, African studies. **Honors/Awds:** Resistance and Caribbean Literature Ohio Univ Press 1980; Movement of the People Calaloux Published 1983; A Just and Moral Society Calaloux Published 1984; VS Naipaul: A Materialist Reading, Univ of MA Press, 1988; Caribbean Women Writers: Essays from the First International Conference, Calaloux & University of Massachusetts Press, 1990; Eric E Williams Speaks, ed, 1993; CLR James: His Intellectual Legacies, co-edited with Bill Cain, 1995; Editor "Maxwell Philip, Emmanuel Appadocca," Univ of Massachusetts, 1997; NEH Fellowship, 1991-92, 1997-98; American Council of Learned Societies Fellowship 1991-92; Senior Fellow, Society for the Humanities, Cornell University 1992; Visiting Fellow, WEB DuBois Institute for African-American Research, Harvard University 1991; Visiting Scholar, African-American Studies Department, Harvard University 1992-97. **Business Addr:** Professor, Wellesley College, Africana Studies, Wellesley, MA 02181.

CUFF, GEORGE WAYNE
Clergyman (retired). **Personal:** Born Sep 3, 1923, Chester, PA; son of Lydia Cuff and Theodore Cuff; married Mary Elizabeth; children: Henry Earl Tucker Jr, Selena Cuff Simpson. **Educ:** Lincoln Univ PA, BA 1951; M Div Crozer Theol Sem, 1955. **Career:** Office of Finance & Field Serv, field rep; Bd of Global Ministries United Meth Ch, 1979-; Hillcrest Bellefonte United Methodist Church, Wilmington DE, pastor, 1975-79; Wilmington Dist Peninsula Conf, supt 1973-75; Dover Dist Peninsula Conf, supt 1969-73; NJ/DE/MD, pastor 1955-69; retired 1986. **Orgs:** Bd of trustees Wesley Coll Dover DE 1970-92; bd of govs Wesley Theol Sem Wash DC 1973-80; bd of dir Wilmington Good Will Industries 1973-79; gen bd mem Global Ministries United Methodist Church. **Honors/Awds:** Plaque of Appreciation, Meth Action Program of Wilmington Dist 1975; Good Conduct Medal; WWII Medal; Sharp Shooters Medal. **Military Serv:** USN third class petty officer 1943-46.

CULBREATH-MANLY, TONGILA M.
Broadcasting executive. **Personal:** Born Jun 9, 1959, Atlanta, GA. **Educ:** Univ of Colorado, Boulder, BA 1981; Atlanta Univ, MBA 1987. **Career:** Educ Media Ctr, media tech 1977-81; H Harper's Design Studios, asst mgr 1981-82; Sandusky Broadcasting KNUS-AM, tech producer 1982-84; New City Comm WYAY-FM, acct exec 1984-88; Summit Communications, WVEE/WAOK, acct executive, 1988-89; WEDR Inc, WEDR-FM, sales manager, 1989-90; WRIC-TV, acct executive, 1991-. **Orgs:** NBMBAA, 1986-87; Executive Women International. **Home Addr:** 9240 Tuckerbrook Ln, Alpharetta, GA 30202.

CULLERS, SAMUEL JAMES
Consultant. **Personal:** Born in Chicago, IL; son of Letitia T Cullers and Samuel P Cullers; married Geraldine Lewis, Jan 1, 1950; children: Samuel J, Jr, Mark E. **Educ:** MIT, MCP 1952; Fisk Univ, BA, Sociology, 1950. **Career:** Deputy dir, Hartford Redevel Agency, Hartford, CT, 1952-58; chief of party, Litchfield, Whiting, Bowne & Assoc, New York, consultants to Ministry of Interior, Thailand, 1958-60; city planning advisor, Ministry of Interior, govt of Thailand, Bangkok, 1960-61; dir, Chicago Community Renewal Program, 1961-63; dir, urban renewal study, Metropolitan Toronto Planning Bd, 1963-66; acting dir and chief, urban planning, California Office of Planning, 1966-70; acting dir, office of planning and research, California governor's office, 1970-71; vice pres, environmental and urban planning, Engineering Science Inc, 1971-79; pres, Samuel J Cullers & Assoc, environmental planning and devel consultants, 1971-; lecturer, govt planning, Univ of California Davis, Golden Gate Univ; lecturer, Univ of California Los Angeles, Univ of Toronto, California State Univ Sacramento. **Orgs:** Council of State Planning Agencies, bd of dir 1968-69; Amer Planning Assn, 1st vice pres 1969-70; DHUD, urban fellowship advisory bd 1969-73; Sacramento Symphony Assn, bd of dir 1972-84; Sacramento Metro Chamber of Commerce, bd of dir 1974-78; Sacramento City-County Human Rights Comm, chmn 1975-79; Rotary Intl, mem 1976-; comm on transportation & land devel policy NRC 1977-79; Sacramento Area Comm and Trade Assn, bd of dir 1980-83; Sacramento Metro YMCA, chmn 1980-81; Washington Neighborhood Center, bd of dir 1980-95; Sacramento Urban League, chmn, 1984-85; Alpha Phi Alpha; Rotary Intl, Lambda Alpha, Intl Land Economics Society; Commission on Teacher Credentialing, State of California, 1988-93. **Honors/Awds:** Published, Zoning—A Tool for Renewal, Ontario Housing 1964; publ, An Expl of Planning Relationship to Integration ASPO 1967; contributor, Discoveries on the Civic Design Aspects of Toronto's City Hall, Journal Royal Arch Inst of Canada 1965; MIT Graduate Scholarship, 1950-52; John Hay Whitney Fellowship, 1950-52; Fisk Univ Scholarship, 1948-50. **Home Addr:** 6409 S Land Park Dr, Sacramento, CA 95831.

CULLERS, VINCENT T.
Advertising executive. **Personal:** married Marian; children: Vincent Jr, Jeffery. **Educ:** Art Inst of Chgo, attd; Am Academy of Art; Univ Chgo. **Career:** Am 1st Blk Advertising Agy, founder; Vince Cullers Advertising Inc, Chicago 1956-; Nat Agency of Record for Sears Roebuck and Co. **Business Addr:** Vince Cullers Advertising Inc, 676 N Saint Clair, Chicago, IL 60611.

CULPEPPER, BETTY M.
Librarian. **Personal:** Born Jan 15, 1941, Lynchburg, VA; daughter of Agnes Head Culpepper Witcher and Roosevelt Culpepper. **Educ:** Howard Univ, BA 1963; Kent State Univ, MA 1966; Cath Univ, MS 1969; Howard Univ, MPA 1981. **Career:** Washington DC Public Library, reader's adv 1964-67; Prince George's County Memorial Library, branch librarian 1967-72; Washingtoniana Div DC Public Library, chief 1972-77; Moorland-Spingarn Research Center Howard Univ, bibliographer/head of ref 1977-86, asst chief librarian Technical Service & Automation 1986-90; Library of Congress, Washington, DC, head of social science team, 1990-. **Orgs:** Amer Library Assn; Afro-American Historical & Genl Soc; NAACP; Assn for Study of Afro-American Life & History; ALA Caucus of Black Librarians; Alpha Kappa Alpha; Historical Society of Washington. **Honors/Awds:** Awarded Scholarship Howard Univ; Fellow Kent State Univ; Scholarship MD Library Assn. **Business Addr:** Head of Social Sciences Team, Library of Congress, 1st & Independence, Ave, SE, Washington, DC 20560.

CULPEPPER, DELLIE L.
Traffic court director. **Personal:** Born Mar 24, 1941, Talbotton, GA; daughter of Daisy Culpepper and Willie Culpepper. **Educ:** Dimery's Business College, Atlanta, GA, ABA 1963; Atlanta Law School, Atlanta, GA, LLB 1979. **Career:** Southwest Council Atlanta Chamber of Commerce, member executive comm 1978; Traffic Court, Atlanta, GA, court administrator/director. **Orgs:** Member NAACP 1980; member Ida Prather YWCA 1980; vice president The Cruisers Fund Raising 1984; member Black Public Administrators 1984; member National Association of Trial Court Administrators 1984; member Atlanta Chapter COMPA 1985. **Business Addr:** Director, City Court of Atlanta, 104 Trinity Ave SW, Atlanta, GA 30335.

CULPEPPER, LUCY NELL
Physician. **Personal:** Born Jun 11, 1951, Awin, AL; daughter of Lucy Lee Davis Culpepper and L C Culpepper; married Joseph Williams, Jun 30, 1984. **Educ:** AL A&M Univ, BS 1973; Meharry Medical Coll, MD 1977. **Career:** Martin Luther King Jr General Hosp, intern, resident 1977-80; NHSC, pediatrician medical dir 1980-82; private practice, pediatrician 1982-87; Maude Whatley Health Center, pediatrician, 1988-, medical director, 1989-. **Orgs:** Mem Zeta Phi Beta Sor Inc 1972-; active staff mem DCH Regional Medical Ctr 1980-; mem Tuscaloosa Co Medical Soc 1982-, Medical Assoc of State of AL 1982-; youth dir First Baptist Church 1984-90; mem West AL Pediatric Soc 1984-, West AL Medical Assoc 1985-, AL State Medical Assoc 1985-. **Honors/Awds:** Woman of the Year Christian Study Ctr of AL 1983. **Home Addr:** 4415 Maple Ln, Northport, AL 35476. **Business Addr:** Medical Director, Maude Whatley Health Center, 2731 Martin Luther King Jr Blvd, Tuscaloosa, AL 35401, (205)758-6647.

CULVER, RHONDA
Accountant. **Personal:** Born Nov 18, 1960, Phoenix, AZ; daughter of Rose Culver and Roscoe Culver. **Educ:** Arizona State Univ, BS 1981, MBA 1986. **Career:** Searle Consumer Products Div, asst cost accountant 1983-84; Garrett Airline Serv Div, sr accountant 1984-86, accounting supervisor 1986-. **Orgs:** Bd of dirs/treas Natl Assoc of Accountants Phoenix 1983-; mem Assoc of MBA Execs 1984, Mayor's Citizen Tax Fairness Commn 1986; comm chmn United Negro Coll Fund Phoenix 1986,87; finance comm Alpha Kappa Alpha Sor 1985-87; technical communications coord Focus Software Users Group. **Honors/Awds:** Black Board of Directors Honoree Phoenix 1986; Outstanding Woman 1987. **Home Addr:** PO Box 27786, Tempe, AZ 85282. **Business Addr:** Accounting Supervisor, Garrett Airline Service Div, PO Box 29003, Phoenix, AZ 85038.

CUMBER, VICTORIA LILLIAN
Columnist. **Personal:** Born Feb 5, 1920, San Antonio, TX; daughter of David H Johnson and Lora L Johnson. **Educ:** Phillips Bus Sch 1935-36; Metro Business Sch, attended 1936-38. **Career:** Sepia Hollywood Mag, pub 1941-45; Herald Attractions Agency, mgr 1949-55; Lil Cumber Attractions Agency, theatrical agent 1956-96; SW Wave Newspaper, columnist 1967-86; Scoop Newspaper 1986-; Shirley Wilson & Associates Talent Agency, consultant, currently. **Orgs:** Mem Sec Comm Actions Com 1958-60; mem NAACP Hollywood Beverly Hills Br 1937-; co-organizer Beverly Hills Hollywood Image Awards 1967. **Honors/Awds:** Plaque Bus & Professional Women's Club 1967; Black Filmmakers Hall of Fame 1974; Coorganized the first Commercial Casting Directors/Industry Awds saluting honorees who have been voted as an awardee by their peers 1982; So Calif Motion Picture Council 1987 honoree; Special Pioneer Award, Afro American/Humor Awards, 1990; Beverly Hills/Hollywood 4th Annual Theatre Trailblazer

Award, 1991; Golden Star Halo Award, Motion Picture Council, 1994. **Business Addr:** Consultant, Lil Cumber Management, PO Box 3358, West Hollywood, CA 90048.

CUMMINGS, AEON L.

Banker. **Personal:** Born Jul 5, 1963, Annotto Bay, Jamaica; son of Gladys Cummings and Wilmore Cummings; married Shawn Lawson Cummings, Aug 28, 1993. **Educ:** Hamilton College, AB, econ/govt, 1985; Brooklyn Coll, MA, economics, 1988; Univ of VA, Darden School of Business, MBA, finance, 1991. **Career:** NYC Board of Educ, english teacher, 1985-88; NYC Housing Preservation & Development, analyst, 1989-90; Citibank, NA, vice pres, prod manager, 1991-. **Orgs:** Hamilton Coll, alumni recruiting and fund raising, 1985-; Natl Black MBA, 1993-; Univ of VA, Darden Business School, pres, 1990-91; UNCF Citicorp Mentors, mentor, 1991-93. **Honors/Awds:** Citicorp/Citibank Fellow, one of 10 natl fellows, 1990-91; Brooklyn Coll, Outstanding Student in Economics, 1988; Fairfield County NBMBAA, Achievement Award, 1994. **Special Achievements:** Master Thesis, "The Determinants of Housing Prices in Brooklyn NY," 1988; selected as one of the MBAs of the future by Minority MBA Magazine; speaks fluent Spanish. **Business Addr:** Vice Pres, Citibank, NA, 111 Wall St, 16th Fl Zone 2, New York, NY 10043, (212)657-0113.

CUMMINGS, ALBERT R.

Marketing manager. **Personal:** Born Oct 27, 1940, Fort Scott, KS; son of Cleo Cummings and Booker Cummings; children: Simone, Albert Jr, Valerie. **Educ:** KS State Coll of Pittsburg, BA Math 1962; WA Univ St Louis, MS Appl Math & Comp Sci 1971; Southern IL Univ Edwardsville, MBA 1974. **Career:** Defense Mapping Agency USAF; physical scientist 1962-69; Ralston Purina, oper rsch analyst 1969-75; Southern IL Univ, asst prof mgmt sci 1974-80; Anheuser-Busch, mgr sales & mktg analysis 1975-82; Brand Manager, King Cobra 1982-. **Orgs:** Dir Anheuser Busch Credit Union 1983-; mem Alpha Phi Alpha Frat 1961-. **Military Serv:** AUS E-4 2 yrs. **Business Addr:** Senior Product Manager, Anheuser Busch Inc, One Busch Place, St Louis, MO 63118.

CUMMINGS, CARY, III

Medical doctor. **Personal:** Born Jul 13, 1949, Monticello, FL; children: Lindsey. **Educ:** SUNY Binghamton, BS 1972; Meharry Medical Coll, MD 1976; Univ of Cal at San Francisco, Nephrology Fellowship, 1990-92; Univ of California at San Francisco, Critical Care Fellowship, 1992-93. **Career:** Univ of Rochester, intern 1976-77; US Public Health Svcs, lt commander 1977-79; Harrisburg Hosp, residency; Hershey Emergency Medicine Prog, asst prof dept of internal medicine 1981-83; Memorial Sloan-Kettering of Cornell Univ, fellow in critical care medicine 1983-84; Harrisburg Hosp, asst prof dept of internal medicine 1984-86; Hershey Medical Ctr, asst prof emergency medicine & trauma 1985-86; Private Practice, physician, 1985-. **Orgs:** Dauphin Co Medical Soc, 1985-, PA Medical Soc, 1986-; American Med Assn, 1992-; Pennsylvanis Med Society, 1985-; Dauphin County Med Society, 1985-; Amer Society of Internal Med, 1985-; International Society of Nephrology, 1993-. **Business Addr:** 1617 N Front St, Harrisburg, PA 17102.

CUMMINGS, CHARLES EDWARD

Physician. **Personal:** Born Oct 2, 1931, Richmond, VA; married Mary Quash; children: Charles Jr, Kevin. **Educ:** VA Union Univ, BS 1958; Howard Univ Sch of Medicine, MD 1962. **Career:** Charles E Cummings MD Ltd, president 1964-; 1540 Broadcasting Co, president begining 1977; FM 100 Radio Group, dir, currently. **Orgs:** Bd mem VA State Univ Foundation 1979-86, VA Heart Assoc 1985-86; mem Alpha Kappa Mu Honor Soc Beta Kappa Chi. **Honors/Awds:** Gold Heart Awd Amer Heart Assoc 1980. **Military Serv:** USAF staff sgt 1950-54; Korean Service Medal. **Business Addr:** Director, FM 100 Radio Group, 2809 North Ave, Richmond, VA 23222, (804)321-2572.

CUMMINGS, DONNA LOUISE

Manager. **Personal:** Born Jan 17, 1944, Cleveland, OH; divorced; children: Dahlia Loi. **Educ:** Cleveland State U, BA Psych 1966-77; Baldwin-Wallace Coll, MBA Syst Mgmt 1979-81; Gestalt Inst of Cleveland, Ptgrde Certif Org & Syst Develp 1981-83. **Career:** TRW Inc, various admin pos 1963-74; TRW Inc, comm affairs assist 1974-75; TRW Inc, comm affairs rep 1975-77. **Orgs:** Consult Nbrghd Ctrs Assoc 1982-83; pres Karamu Hse 1981-83; chrmn Assoc of Black Found Exec 1978-79; chrmn Windermere Child Care Ctr 1976-79. **Honors/Awds:** Outsdg Young Wmn of Am 1978; certif of merit YWCA 1977 & 1978; One of Cveland's 80 Most Interesting People Cleveland Magz 1980; Charles L Loeb Outstdng Young Urban League of Grtr Cleveland 1982.

CUMMINGS, E. EMERSON

Educator. **Personal:** Born Jun 17, 1913, Winchester, MA. **Educ:** Bates Coll, BS 1939; MA Inst Tech, grad studies; NH U, tchr. **Career:** Math & Science Dept, Old Orchard Beach, teacher, chmn; town clk; assessor; Police Force, sergeant; Assessment Review, bd chmn ; councilman 7th term; owned & operated Taxi & Bus business; Amusement Co, bookkeeper; MA Savings Bank, corporator; Salvation Army, bd dir. **Orgs:** Mem Lions Club; Am Leg; VFW; chmn Sch Bldg Commn. **Military Serv:** 1st sgt. **Business Addr:** 123 Portland Ave, Old Orchard Beach, ME 04064.

CUMMINGS, ELIJAH E.

Congressman. **Personal:** Born Jan 18, 1951. **Educ:** Howard Univ, BA, 1973; Univ of Maryland, JD, 1976. **Career:** Attorney; Maryland House of Delegates, 1983-96; US House of Representatives, congressman, 1996-. **Orgs:** MD Governor's Commission on Black Males, chair, 1990-; MD Bootcamp Aftercare Program, founder, 1991-; New Psalmist Baptist Church. **Business Addr:** Congressman, US House of Representatives, 1632 Longworth House Office Bldg, Washington, DC 20515-2007.

CUMMINGS, FRANCES MCARTHUR

Educational administrator. **Personal:** Born Feb 2, 1941, Lumberton, NC; children: Isaiah T. **Educ:** Livingstone Coll, BS Bus Ed 1961; NC Central Univ, MS Bus Ed 1974; Univ of NC at Greensboro, Bus & Office Voc Cert 1976. **Career:** NC Assoc of Classroom Teachers 1978-79; Southeast Reg Assoc of Classroom Teachers, pres 1980; Natl Ed Assoc, dir 1980-87; NC Assoc of Ed, pres 1983-84; Lumberton Sr HS, teacher; North Carolina Association of Educators, associate executive director, 1987-89; elected North Carolina House of Representatives, House District 87, 1992-. **Orgs:** Mem Hilly Branch Baptist Church 1970-85; chartered mem Alpha Kappa Alpha 1974; mem Robeson Cty Dem Women 1979-85, NC Council on the Status of Women 1980-85; commiss Ed Commiss of the States Gov Appt 1983; bd of dir NC Ctr for Public Policy Rsch 1983-86; board of directors North Carolina Math & Science Alliance; chairperson, Women & Minority Panel, Gov Appt 1990; Private Industry Council, Lumber River, County Commissioners' Appt 1990. **Honors/Awds:** The Order of the Long Leaf Pine Governor's Awd 1983; Gov's Public School Prog of Excellence Governor's Awd 1983; Outstanding Leader of Robeson Cty RobesonCty Black Caucus 1983; Par Excellence Serv Awd Gen Baptist Conv of NC 1984; Tar Heel of the Week News & Observer Raleigh 1984. **Business Addr:** Assistant Vocational Director, Public Schools of Robeson County, PO Drawer 2909, Lumberton, NC 28359.

CUMMINGS, JAMES C., JR.

Business executive. **Personal:** Born Sep 22, 1929, Indianapolis, IN; married Norma Lewis; children: Cynthia, James III, Cecilia, Ronald, Claudia. **Educ:** IN Central U, BS 1962; IN U, grad work. **Career:** Urban Advance, pres; Oxford Devel Co, asst vice pres 1970-71; Bd For Fundamental Edn, dir of operations 1966-70; Village Mgmt Corp, proj mgr 1960-66. **Orgs:** Chmn Nat Black Rep Council, mem exec com Rep Nat Com; chmn IN Black Rep Council; exec asst chmn IN Rep State Com; del Rep Nat Conv Fdr 1976; pres IN Black Expo 1971-73; former vice-chmn Inst of Industrialized Bldg Oppty; mem Public Works IN; bd mem Zoning Appeals IN; former mem of bd IN NAACP. **Honors/Awds:** Disting Hoosier Award, Gov Edgar Whitcomb; Sagamore of the Wabash IN High Est Award, Gov Otis Bowen; Key to City of Indianapolis, Mayor William Hudnut. **Military Serv:** AUS corpl 1951-53. **Business Addr:** 155 W Market St, Indianapolis, IN 46204.

CUMMINGS, MIDRE ALMERIC

Professional baseball player. **Personal:** Born Oct 14, 1971, St Croix, Virgin Islands of the United States. **Career:** Pittsburgh Pirates, outfielder, 1993-97; Philadelphia Phillies, 1997-. **Business Addr:** Professional Baseball Player, Philadelphia Phillies, PO Box 7575, Philadelphia, PA 19101, (215)463-6000.

CUMMINGS, PAT

Author/illustrator of children's books. **Personal:** Born Nov 9, 1950, Chicago, IL; daughter of Christine Taylor Cummings and Arthur Cummings; married H Chuku Lee, Dec 27, 1990. **Educ:** Pratt Institute, Brooklyn NY, BFA, 1974. **Career:** Free-lance author/illustrator, 1974-. **Orgs:** Graphic Artists Guild; Society of Children's Book Writers; The Author's Guild; The Writers Guild of America; The Center for Multicultural Children's Literature. **Honors/Awds:** Coretta Scott King Award, 1983, for My Mama Needs Me; Black Women in Publishing Illustration Award, 1988; Horn Book Award, Boston Globe, 1992. **Business Addr:** c/o Harper Collins Publishing, 10 East 53rd Street, New York, NY 10022.

CUMMINGS, ROBERTA SPIKES

Librarian. **Personal:** Born May 1, 1944, Angie, LA; daughter of Wanda Coby Collins and William H Collins; children: 1. **Educ:** Grambling State Univ, BS Speech & Drama 1960; Univ of SW LA Lafayette, 1968; LA State Univ Baton Rouge, MSLS Library Sci 1972; S Univ Baton Rouge, Media Broadcasting 1973-77; MS Computer Science 1987. **Career:** Lafayette Parish Sch Bd, librarian 1966-73; East Baton Rouge Parish Public Library, librarian 1973; US Army Reserve, personnel mgmt super 1975-81; Atty Genl's Office State of LA, consultant for the Huey P Long Library 1982; 321st MMC TAACOM, equipment authorization tech 1981-; S Univ Sch of Law, asst law librarian & head of acquisitions 1973-. **Orgs:** Mem of following organs Alpha Kappa Alpha 1964; Grambling State Univ Debate Team against Harvard Univ Debate Team 1965; Istrouma Chap of Scouters of Amer 1979; Spec Librarians Assn; Natl Bar Assn; Southeastern Chap Amer Assn of Law Librarians; Amer Assn of Law Libraries; Southwestern Librarians Assn Natl Educ Assn. **Honors/Awds:** Best Supporting Actress Awd 1962; Alpha Theta Phi Honor Soc; published an article "Many Views" Natl Library Week 1971; co-authored "Black History & Culture" 1972; developed a media pkg "Past, Present, and Future of School Libraries" 1978. **Military Serv:** AUS cw2; Army Achievement Medal; Army Prof Develop Ribbon Level 1; Army Serv Ribbon; Expert Badge. **Business Addr:** Assistant Law Librarian, So Univ Law Center, Law Library, Baton Rouge, LA 70813.

CUMMINGS, TERRY (ROBERT TERRELL)

Professional basketball player. **Personal:** Born Mar 15, 1961, Chicago, IL; divorced; children: Robert Terrell Jr, Sean, Antonio. **Educ:** DePaul Univ. **Career:** Church of God in Christ, ordained Pentecostal minister; San Diego Clippers, forward, 1983-84; Milwaukee Bucks, 1985-89; San Antonio Spurs, 1990-95; Milwaukee Bucks, 1995-96; Seattle Supersonics, 1996-97; Philadelphia 76ers, 1997-98; New York Knicks, 1998-. Cummings Entertainment Group, president, currently. **Honors/Awds:** NBA Rookie of the Year, 1983; NBA All-Star, 1985, 1989. **Special Achievements:** NBA Draft, First round pick, #2, 1982. **Business Addr:** President, Cummings Entertainment Group, 10004 Wurzbach Rd, #367, San Antonio, TX 78230, (210)696-4667.

CUMMINGS, THERESA FAITH

State government administrator. **Personal:** Born Feb 27, Springfield, IL; daughter of Mary Jeanette Irvine Cummings and Nelson Mark Cummings. **Educ:** Winston-Salem State University, BS Educ; So IL Univ, MS Educ. **Career:** St Louis Public School System, teacher 1957-67; Multi-purpose Neighborhood Serv Center System of Springfield/Sangamon Co Comm Action Agency, proj dir 1967-69, exec dir 1969-85; Aband Mine Hands Reclam Cncl, asst dir beginning 1987; Illinois Department of National Resources, chief EEO officer, currently. **Orgs:** Couns/guidance chairperson Human Devel Corp 1965-67; planner/cons Mr Achievers Summer Inst Banneker Dist St Louis Pub Sch 1966-67; mem League of Women Voters; mem Amer Assn Univ Women; mem Natl Council for Negro Women; bd dir Sangamon Co March of Dimes; mem St Paul AME Ch; life mem NAACP; mem various other orgns; mem Illinois Ambulatory Surgical Treatment Ctr Licensing Bd; vice chair, chair & state tres, Natl Woman Political Caucus; DVPE Treas appointed to the Federal Reserve Consumer Adv Cncl; Business & Professional Women's Club; past treasurer, president, District Dir First Vice Pres of Federation BPW, Women In Govt; Women In Mgmt; pres, National Associated Business Women Owners; American Business Women Club; Imperial Credit Union, chair. **Honors/Awds:** Citation Gr Lakes Regional Office of Economic Opportunity for Svc; citation Springfield Ministerial Alliance for Dedication & Devotion to Duty; cert for serv & contrib to Project Mainstream Together Inc; cert Consumer Credit Counseling Serv Bd of Dirs; cert Contrib to Comm Develop OH Chapter of NACD; runner-up plaque Lola M Parker Achievement Award; Medallion for Serv March of Dimes; Fellow SIU Sch of Med 1979; Woman of the Yr Zeta Phi Beta Sor 1982; Springfield Women Policical Caucus, Elizabeth Cady Stanton Awardee; Women In Management Charlotte Danton Award for Government. **Business Addr:** Chief EEO Officer, Illinois Department of National Resources, 524 South 2nd St, Rm 400, Springfield, IL 62701.

CUNDIFF, JOHN HOWARD

Dentist. **Personal:** Born in Roanoke, VA; son of Mildred Cundiff and Arthur Cundiff; married Virginia Radcliffe (deceased); children: Daphne Renee, John Howard Jr. **Educ:** WV State Coll, BS; Howard Univ, graduate student; Howard Univ School of Dentistry, DDS. **Career:** Dentist, currently. **Orgs:** Mem, bd of mgrs Hunton Branch YMCA; former chmn Memorial Comm Omega Psi Phi Fraternity; former parliamentarian Omega Psi Phi Fraternity; former dist chmn Mohawk Dist BSA; mem, bd of dir Delta Dental Plan of Virginia. **Honors/Awds:** VA Dentist of the Year Award 1976; Man of the Year Award, Omega Psi Phi Gamma Alpha Chapter 1976.

CUNNINGHAM, ARTHUR H. See Obituaries section.

CUNNINGHAM, COURTNEY

Government official. **Personal:** Born Feb 17, 1962, Ocala, FL; son of Juanita Perry Cunningham and James Charles Cunningham, Sr. **Educ:** University of Florida, Gainesville, FL, BA, 1983; University of Florida College of Law, Gainesville, FL, JD, 1986. **Career:** Fisher, Rushmer, Orlando, FL, associate, 1986-87; Rumberger, Kirk, Orlando, FL, associate, 1987-89; Republican National Committee, Washington, DC, deputy chief counsel, 1989-90; Interstate Commerce Commission, Washington, DC, attorney/advisor, 1990-91; Office of Congressional and Intergovernmental Affairs, Department of Labor, senior legislative officer, 1991-93; American Trucking Assn, senior legislative representative, Washington DC, 1993; Ryder System, Inc, director, govt relations, Miami, FL, 1994-. **Orgs:** Member, Florida Blue Key Fraternity, 1983-86; vice chairman, Justice Campbell Thornal Moot Court Board, 1986; member, Florida Board of Osteopathic Medical Examiners, 1988; member, American Judicature Society, 1988. **Honors/Awds:** Consultant, National Republican Institute for International Affairs, 1990; Legal Counsel, Florida Republican Convention, 1994-95. **Business Addr:** Government Official, 3600 NW 82nd Ave, Miami, FL 33166, (305)593-3159.

CUNNINGHAM, DAVID S., JR.
Elected official. **Personal:** Born Jun 24, 1935, Chicago, IL; married Sylvia AC Krappel; children: David Srumier III, Leslie, Robyn, Amber. **Educ:** Univ of Riverside, BA; Occidental Coll, MA 1970. **Career:** Cunningham Short Berryman & Assoc, Inc, consultants former partner; Los Angeles City Council, 1973-. **Orgs:** Chmn Grants Housing & Comm Develop; vice chmn Finance & Revenue Comm; mem Police Fire & Public Safety Comm; authored or co-authored many laws among which include the establish of the Mayor's Office of Small Business Assis; reduc of the minimum age fore firefighters from 21 to 18 yrs; pioneered the use of fed block grants for local govt use; created the city's dept of aging; created Vista Montoya Los Angeles' first subsidized condo project for low and median income families; initiated organ of the Mid-Town Chamber of Commerce and Pico-Union Chamber of Commerce; charter mem CA Minority Employ Council; mem Los Angeles Black Agenda; mem Bd of Interracial Council for Business Affairs; mem Urban League; bd of dirs Los Angeles Co Sanitation Dist No 1; chmn Natl BlackUnited Fund; past pres CORlumni Assn; life mem Omega Psi Phi Frat Inc; life mem NAACP; life mem Natl Council of Negro Women; col in the CA Guard; former mem World Affairs Council; chmn LA Brotherhood Crusade 1971-72; S CA Assn of Govts Comm & Economic Develop Comm 1978-79; bd of dirs Natl League of Cities 1981-83. **Honors/Awds:** Man of Tomorrow Omega Psi Phi 1973; Los Angeles Brotherhood Crusade 1973, 1976; Honorary Mayor of Baton Rouge LA 1974; Mid-City Chamber of Commerce 1974; Delta-Sigma Theta 1982,83,84; Dept of the Navy 1984; Boy Scouts of Amer; S CA Fair Housing Congress 1984; Alex Haley Heritage Awd 1984.

CUNNINGHAM, E. BRICE
Attorney. **Personal:** Born Feb 17, 1931, Buffalo, TX; son of Tessie (Roblow) Cunningham and Hattie Cunningham; married Rosie Nell (Portis) Cunningham, Mar 6, 1964; children: LaWanda Kay, Ledner, Michele, Elana Brice. **Educ:** Howard Univ Sch of Law, BA, LLB 1960. **Career:** E Brice Cunningham (Professional Corp), atty/pres; City of Dallas, muni ct judge 1971-72; City of Dallas, appeals judge. **Orgs:** Mem State Bar of TX 1960; former mem of State Bar Com on Coord with Other & Groups; mem State Bar Public Affairs Com; mem State Bar Sub-Com Grievance Com; Dallas Bar Assn; Special Cts Com; Fee Disputes Com Dallas Bar Assn; Courthouse Com; State Board Code of Criminal Pruc Study Com; Nat Bar Assn Inc, Region VI, former regional dir; Am Judicature Soc; past chr, vice chmn, charter mem, S Dallas Br of YMCA; Past Grand legal Adv Most Worshipful Prince Hall Grand Lodge F&AM of TX; bd dirs Children's Aid Soc; Planning Commn for the city of Dallas 1973-76; Alpha Phi Alpha Frat; mem, legal advisor, Paul Drayton Lodge No 9; Dale Consistory No 31, Zakat Temple No 164, AEADNMS, Inc; Elks; mem NAACP; atty metrop br Dallas NAACP, Region VI, past regional dir; Hearing Ofcr Dallas 1974-76; Dallas City Planning Commn 1973-76. **Honors/Awds:** Recip Award in Law Com of 100 1973; Award for Legal Services, Dallas TX NAACP 1977; Black Historical Achievement Award, Aldersgate United Methodist Church; Certificate of Merit, J L Turner Legal Assn; Certificate of Merit, Legislative Black Caucus of the State of Texas 1981; South Central Business & Professional Women's Club, Man of the Year Award, 1986; Six Bar Associations in Dallas, Dr Martin Luther King Jr Justice Award, 1995; TX NAACP, Texas Heroes Award, 1997; and numerous other awards. **Military Serv:** AUS corpl 1948-54. **Business Addr:** President, E Brice Cunningham, A Professional Corp, 777 S RL Thornton Freeway, Ste 121, Dallas, TX 75203.

CUNNINGHAM, ERSKINE
Financial credit manager. **Personal:** Born Oct 3, 1955, Talladega, AL; son of Dorothy Ragland Cunningham and Frank Cunningham. **Educ:** Northwood Inst Midland MI, BA 1977; Rosary Coll River Forst IL, MBA 1981. **Career:** Detroit Bank & Trust, asst branch mgr 1979; Ford Motor Credit Co, accounts rep 1979-84; Rowntree DeMet's Inc, financial credit mgr 1985-. **Orgs:** Mem Chicago Chap Natl Black MBA Assn 1984-; mem Chicago Midwest Credit Manager's Assn 1985-; election comm Rosary Coll Grad Student Business Alumni Assn 1985-86.

CUNNINGHAM, F. MALCOLM
Attorney. **Personal:** Born Jan 27, 1927, Plant City, FL; married Nealia Brookins; children: Karren, Malcolm, Jr, Deneal, Mallorye. **Educ:** FL A&M U, BA 1950; Howard Univ Sch of Law, LLD 1953. **Career:** Cunningham & Cunningham, senior partner 1953-. **Orgs:** Mem FL Bar Assn; Palm Beach Co Bar Assn; Am Trial Lawyers Assn; NBA; Am Arbitration Assn; Am Bar & Assn; Ethic & Circuit Ct Adv Com Palm Beach Co Bar Assn; co-organizer vchmn bd First Prudential Bank of West Palm Beach; vice-chrmn Planning Bd Riviera Beach 1961; elected to City Council 1962 re-elected 1964,66; Dem Candidate for House of Rep 1968; City Atty Riviera Beach FL 1971-73; pres Palm Beach Co Referral Bd & Kindergarten Inc (United Fund Agy) 1956-62; chrmn trustee bd Tabernacle Bapt Ch 1965-67; chmn Comm Action Council of Palm Beach Co 1967-68; past mem Gulfstream Council BSA; Phi Beta Sigma; Vanguard Club; Elk; Mason; bd Palm Beach Co Chap AKC; legal adv local chap NAACP; dir Vis Nurses Assn. **Honors/Awds:** Recipient Harriet T & Dorrah Merit Award FL Assn of Women's Club Inc 1963; citation for Comm Leadership State Voters League 1964; citation Omega Si Phi 1963; solid citizen Award Comm Round Table of W Palm Beach 1967; Comm Leadership Award City of Riviera Beach 1968; family of the year Tampa Urban League 1968. **Business Addr:** 600 Rosemary Ave, West Palm Beach, FL 33401.

CUNNINGHAM, GLENN DALE
Law enforcement official, elected official. **Personal:** Born Sep 16, 1943, Jersey City, NJ; son of Gladys M Green-Cunningham and Lowell J Cunningham. **Educ:** Jersey City State Coll, BA cum laude 1974; Rutgers Sch of Criminal Justice, MA 27 credits. **Career:** Jersey City Police Department, captain, 1967-92, retired; Hudson County, NJ, Board of Chosen Freeholders, elected position, 1975-78; Jersey City State College, adjunct instructor, 1980-81; City of Jersey City, elected council president, 1981-89; Jersey City Housing Authority, manager, housing and security, 1982-84; Jersey City Medical Center, board of managers, 1987-89; Jersey City Alcohol Beverage Control Commission, commissioner, 1992-; Hudson County, NJ, director of public safety, 1992-. **Orgs:** Grad Natl Crime Prevnetion Inst 1976; mem Amer Acad for Prof Law Enforcement 1976-; mem Superior Officers Benevolent Assoc 1977; cert police inst NJ Police Training Comm 1977-; former exec bd mem NAACP 1978-80; bd of school estimates JC Bd of Educ 1981-82, 85-87; grad Security Mgmt & Admin Inst 1984. **Honors/Awds:** Policeman of the Month Detectives Crime Clinic 1972; life fellow NJ Assn of Counties 1978; Muhamed Ali Awd Urban League of Hudson Co NJ 1980; Black Male Achievement Awd Tau Gamma Delta Sor Inc 1980; Alumnus Awd Jersey City State Coll 1982. **Military Serv:** USMC nco 4 1/2 yrs.

CUNNINGHAM, JAMES J.
Educator. **Personal:** Born Apr 19, 1938, Pittsburgh, PA; son of Roberta Cunningham and Steve Cunningham; married Lois Vines; children: Lita Denise, James Jr. **Educ:** BS, 1964; MA, 1967; EdS, 1969; DEd, 1971. **Career:** Elementary school teacher, 1964-66; Washington DC, counselor, prin 1966-68; Fed City Coll, Washington DC, 1968-71; Assoc Cont Res & Analysis Inc, Washington DC, consultant 1969; Fed City Coll, dir of admissions 1971; HEW/DE, Washington DC, consultant 1971; Moton Consortium on Adm & Financial Aid, co-dir 1971-72; TX Southern Univ, dean of students, prof of educ 1972-74; Mankato State Coll, Mankato MN, vice pres student servs, prof of educ 1974; TX Southern Univ Houston, special asst to the pres 1986, prof of graduate educ, vice pres institutional advancement. **Orgs:** Mem Natl Assn for Higher Edn; Personnel Guidance Assn; Assn of Coll Adm Counselors; DC Couns Assn; Elem Classroom Tchrs Assn; Natl Tchrs Assn; TX Personnel Serv Adminstrs; MN State Coll Student Assn; MN Student Serv Adminstrn; NAACP. **Military Serv:** USAF A/1C 1955-59. **Business Addr:** Professor, Graduate Education, Texas Southern University, 3100 Cleburne St, Houston, TX 77004.

CUNNINGHAM, JOHN F.
Clergyman. **Personal:** Born Oct 27, 1941, Homer, LA; married Alva Atkinson; children: Michael, Timothy. **Educ:** Am Bapt Theol Sem Nashville, BA 1965. **Career:** Mt Enon Baptist Church, pastor; Mt Olive Bapt Ch Clarksville TN, former pastor, active leader 1964-; Bd Trustees Am Bapt Coll of Bible Nashville TN, mem; The So & Nat Bapt Conv USA Inc, a joint venture; Clarksville Bapt Extension Unit of Am Bapt Coll of Bible, registrar, treas, instr. **Orgs:** Pres Clarksville Br NAACP 1968-72; chmn Montegomery Co Voter's Council Affiliate of The TN Voter's Council; minority group chmn Clarksville Human Relations Commn 1969-71; mem Citizens Adv Task Force Clarksville; regional pres TN Bapt Educ Congress; mem The Educ Fund Com Lemoyne-Owen Coll Memphis; moderator Stones River Dist Assn 1969-72; mem Clarksville C of C; mem bd dir, treas TN Opportunity Program for Seasonal Farm Workers; mem bd dir Clarksville-Montgomery Co. **Military Serv:** USO; AUS 1959-60. **Business Addr:** Mt Enon Baptist Church, 1501 W Third, Dayton, OH 45407.

CUNNINGHAM, MALENA ANN
Reporter, broadcast journalist. **Personal:** Born Oct 27, 1958, Laurens, SC; daughter of Betty Brummell Cunningham and O'Dell Cunningham. **Educ:** University of Georgia, ABJ, 1980. **Career:** Atlanta Gas Light Co, public relations associate, 1980-82; Cable News Network, writer/producer, 1982-86; WTVQ-TV, reporter, 1986-87; WHTM-TV, reporter, 1987-88; WSAV-TV, anchor, 1988-91; WVTM-TV, anchor/reporter, 1992-. **Orgs:** Natl Assn of Black Journalists, 1992-; Birmingham Association of Black Journalists, vice pres, broadcasting, 1992-; Delta Sigma Theta, 1977-; YWCA, junior board member, 1992-; Birmingham Assoc of Black Journalists, pres, 1994. **Honors/Awds:** United Press International, First Place, Spot News Reporting, 1988; Associated Press, Second Place, Spot News Reporting, 1988; Associated Press, Best Newscast, 1990; Best Newscast, Emmy, 1992; Best Series, Emmy, 1995; Best Special Project, Emmy, 1996. **Business Addr:** News Anchor/Reporter, WVTM-TV, Vulcan Pkwy, Birmingham, AL 35202, (205)558-7325.

CUNNINGHAM, MARGARET. See DANNER, MARGARET ESSIE.

CUNNINGHAM, PAUL RAYMOND GOLDWYN
Surgeon, educator. **Personal:** Born Jul 28, 1949, Mandeville, Jamaica; son of Sylvia F Marsh Cunningham and Winston P Cunningham; married Sydney Keniston, Feb 14, 1987; children: Shawn, Rachel, Lucinda, Tifanie. **Educ:** University of the West Indies, Jamaica, MB, BS, 1966-72; Mount Sinai Medical Center, New York, NY, surgical intern, 1974-75, surgical resident, 1975-79. **Career:** Joint Disease North General Hospital, New York NY, asst dir of surgery, 1979-81; Bertie Memorial Hosptial, Windsor NC, attending physician, 1981-84; East Carolina University, Greenville NC, professor of surgery, 1994-, preceptor for science track enhancement program, 1986-, Pitt County Memorial Hospital, Greenville, NC, chief of medical staff, 1991. **Orgs:** American Medical Association, National Medical Association, Southern Medical Association, American Association for Surgery of Trauma, Eastern Association for the Surgery of Trauma, Transplantation Society. **Honors/Awds:** American College of Surgeons fellow, 1986. **Military Serv:** US Army Reserve, Major, 1990-. **Business Addr:** East Carolina University, Department of Surgery, School of Medicine, Greenville, NC 27834, (919)816-4299.

CUNNINGHAM, RANDALL
Professional football player. **Personal:** Born Mar 27, 1963, Santa Barbara, CA; married Felicity DeJagar; children: Randall II. **Educ:** Univ of Nevada Las Vegas. **Career:** Philadelphia Eagles, quarterback, 1985-96; Minnesota Vikings, 1997-; owner of marble-and-granite business, currently; TNT network, TV studio analyst. **Honors/Awds:** Played in Pro Bowl, 1988, 1989, 1990; holds career rushing record for quarterbacks with 4,482 yards; Washington Touchdown Club, NFC Player of the Year, 1988; Bert Bell Award, 1988, 1990; Pro Football Weekly, Comeback Player of the Year, 1992. **Business Addr:** Professional Football Player, Minnesota Vikings, 9520 Vikings Dr, Eden Prairie, MN 55344, (612)828-6500.

CUNNINGHAM, RICHARD T.
Minister. **Personal:** Born May 30, 1918, Dallas, TX; son of Ida Henry Cunningham and Ed Cunningham; married Jessie Jewel; children: R Theo Jr, Michaela, Carlotta, Carlette, Melanie. **Educ:** Paul Quinn Coll, AB, 1940; Dallas Thological Coll, MDiv. 1945; Mt Hope Bible Coll, D, Min, 1968. **Career:** Mt Hope Bible Coll Houston, fac mem pastor's tsch dirs 1974-; Christian ME Ch Houston, minister 1975-. **Orgs:** Trustee Phillips Sch of Theol Atlanta; mem Com on Episcopacy CME Ch; mem NAACP; mem Prince Hall Masonic Lodge; mem Harris Co Grand Jury Assn; trusteeTX Coll Tyler TX; chmn bd trustees Mt Hope Bible Coll Houston 1974; assoc editor The Christian Index Ofcl Orgn CME Ch; mem Adv comm to Mayor of Houston; mem TX Sheriff's Assoc; exec comm Ministers Conf at Prairie View Univ, TX Southern Univ Chaplaincy Prog; mem Interfaith Judicatory Forum Rice Univ; public relations consultant Houston Police Dept; trustee Houston Grad Sch of Theol. **Home Addr:** 5338 Tidewater Dr, Houston, TX 77045.

CUNNINGHAM, RICK (PATRICK DANTE ROSS)
Professional football player. **Personal:** Born Jan 4, 1967, Los Angeles, CA; married. **Educ:** Texas A&M. **Career:** Indianapolis Colts, tackle, 1990; Orlando Thunder, 1991-93; Arizona Cardinals, 1994; Minnesota Vikings, 1995; Oakland Raiders, 1996-. **Business Addr:** Professional Football Player, Oakland Raiders, 1220 Harbor Bay Pkwy, Alameda, CA 94502, (510)615-1875.

CUNNINGHAM, ROBERT SHANNON, JR.
Company executive. **Personal:** Born Jan 17, 1958, Columbia, SC; son of Dorothy Mae Bell Cunningham and Robert Shannon Cunningham Sr; married Shenita Gilmore, Sep 23, 1989. **Educ:** Johnson C Smith University, Charlotte, NC, BS, 1980. **Career:** Union Carbide, Simpsonville, SC, production supervisor, 1980; IBM Corporation, Charlotte, NC, financial analyst, 1980-89; IBM Corporation, Research Triangle Park, NC, business planner, 1989-91, development programming manager, 1991-. **Orgs:** Vice chairman, Mecklenburg County Personnel Commission Board, 1982-88; member, City of Charlotte Certified Development Board, 1989; secretary, Focus on Leadership Board, 1987; member, United Way Community Resource Board, 1981; member, Urban League, 1985-; numerous positions, Omega Psi Phi Fraternity, 1977. **Honors/Awds:** Man of the Year, Johnson C Smith, Omega Psi Phi Fraternity, RHO Chapter, 1979; Citizen of the Year, Pi Phi Chapter-Omega Psi Phi Fraternity, 1988. **Home Addr:** 1008 Sunny Brae Court, Apex, NC 27502.

CUNNINGHAM, T. J.
Attorney. **Personal:** Born Feb 6, 1930, Plant City, FL; son of Janette Rome Cunningham and Garrison S. Cunningham; children: Belinda C. Palmore, Tequesta C. Alston, Kimberly Cun-

ningham. **Educ:** Florida A&M University, Tallahassee, FL, BS, sociology, 1952; Howard University Law School, Washington, DC, JD, 1957. **Career:** Cunningham & Cunningham, PA, West Palm Beach, FL, owner, 1960-. **Orgs:** The Florida Bar; District of Columbia Bar Assn; American Bar Assn; US Court of Appeals; US Supreme Court; Palm Beach County Bar Assn; National Bar Assn; Florida Academy of Trial Lawyers; founder/member, F. Malcolm Cunningham, Sr. Bar Assn; former member, Florida Bar Grievance Committee, Palm Beach County; World Peace through Law; former board member and vice president, National Bar Association; past president, Florida Chapter, National Bar Association; life member, NAACP; life member, Alpha Phi Alpha; member, Florida Chapter of National Guardsmen Association; charter member, Forum Club of the Palm Beaches; Florida State Action Council; member, National Urban League; former advisory council member, Florida A&M Univ. **Honors/Awds:** Florida A&M University Alumni Leadership Award, Palm Beach County; Leadership Award, 1986, President's Service Award, Florida Chapter of NBA, 1981, President's Award, 1975; F. Malcolm Cunningham Sr. Bar Achievement Award, 1981; Chairman Convention Award, National Bar Assn, 1972. **Military Serv:** US Army, Corporal, 1952-54; received Korea Combat Badge, Purple Heart, Korean Service Award. **Business Addr:** Attorney, Cunningham & Cunningham, PA, 1897 Palm Beach Lakes Blvd, Cross Roads Bldg, Ste 201, West Palm Beach, FL 33409.

CUNNINGHAM, VERENESSA SMALLS-BRANTLEY
Physician. **Personal:** Born Aug 4, 1949, Charleston, SC; married Herman Cunningham. **Educ:** Spelman Coll, BS 1971; Meharry Medical Coll, MD 1975. **Career:** Martland Hosp Newark NJ, resident 1975-76; Monmouth Medical Ctr Long Branch NJ, resident 1976-77, fellowship 1977-79; Perth Amboy General Hosp, dir of nurseries 1980-83; Private Practice, pediatrician 1983-85; Point Pleasant Hosp, dir of nursery 1985-86; Kaiser-Permanente, pediatrician/neonatologist. **Orgs:** Mem Amer Acad of Pediatrics 1983-85, Natl Assoc of Black Business & Professional Women 1985-, Atlanta Medical Soc 1987. **Honors/Awds:** Achievement Awd Natl Council of Negro Women Inc North Shore Area 1985. **Military Serv:** USAR capt 1 yr. **Business Addr:** Pediatrician/Neonatologist, Kaiser-Permanente, 505 Fairburn Rd SW, Atlanta, GA 30331.

CUNNINGHAM, WILLIAM (PETE)
Business owner. **Personal:** Born Nov 7, 1929, Union Co, NC; son of Johnnie Mae Lockhart; divorced. **Educ:** Perry's Bus Coll, 1951; Johnson C Smith U, 1952-54; FL State Univ Extension, 1972. **Career:** NC Mutual Life Ins Co, debit mgr 1957-61; SE Bus Coll, instr 1969-70, vp, admin dean 1970-72; RSL, assoc dir of minority recruiting 1972-73; Hatchett & Cunningham Assoc, partner, 1973-84; Affordable Used Car, owner, 1987-; NC House of Representatives, rep, 1987-, minority leader, 1995-96; HKL Inc, CEO, 1987-. **Orgs:** Mem Charlotte C of C; Charlotte BBB; mem Parkwood Inst CME Ch; YMCA; Retired Veterans Assn; Johnson C Smith Alumni Assn; CLU Civil Liberties Union; contributing mem United Negro Coll Fund; mem Voter Educ Proj; contributing mem Urban League. **Military Serv:** USN 20 yrs active duty. **Business Addr:** Chief Executive Officer, HKL Inc, PO Box 16209, Charlotte, NC 28297.

CUNNINGHAM, WILLIAM DEAN
Educator. **Personal:** Born Aug 9, 1937, Kansas City, MO; divorced; children: Crystal. **Educ:** Univ of KS, BA 1959; Univ of TX, MLS 1962, PhD 1972. **Career:** Federal Aviation Agency, chief library serv 1965-67; Topeka Public Library, head adult serv 1967-68; US Dept of Educ, program officer 1968-71; Howard Univ, dir univ libraries 1970-73; Univ of MD Coll of Library & Information Services, asst prof 1973-. **Orgs:** Mem Amer Library Assn 1970-, Assn for the Study of Afro-Amer Life and History 1974-; bd dirs Soul Journey Enterprises 1974-; mem Natl Black Heritage Council 1984-. **Honors/Awds:** Citations from Dept of Education, FAA, ASALA; books "Blacks in Performing Arts", co-author "Black Guide to Washington". **Military Serv:** USAF t/sgt 1954-60. **Business Addr:** Assistant Professor, University of Maryland, Coll of Library & Info Serv, College Park, MD 20742.

CUNNINGHAM, WILLIAM E.
Physician. **Personal:** Born Apr 6, 1920, Chicago, IL. **Educ:** Northwestern Univ, 1942; Howard Univ Sch of Med, 1945. **Career:** Self-employed, physician; Michael Reese Hospital & Mercy, staff pos. **Orgs:** Mem Am Med Assn; mem IL St Med Soc; mem Chicago Med Soc; mem Nat Med Association; past president Med Association Bldg Corp 1974, 1975. **Military Serv:** USNG brig general retired. **Business Addr:** Physician, 5044 S State St, Chicago, IL 60609.

CUNNINGHAM, WILLIAM L.
Government official. **Personal:** Born Aug 28, 1939, Little Rock, AR; children: Karm Joy. **Educ:** Univ of AR Pine Bluff, BS 1961; St Vincent Med Center Little Rock, Asso 1964; US Dept Of Agriculture Salt Lake City, Mgmt Cert 1967; Univ of Utah Salt Lake City, MA 1972. **Career:** State of UT Anti-discrimination Div, investigator/conciliator, pres; State of UT, lbr econmst 1970-72; Univ of Wash Med Center, lab supr 1968-70; US Dept of Agrl, agr engr 1966-68; Univ of UT Med Center, researcher 1965-66; Univ of AR Med Center, biochemist 1964-65; US Dept of Agrl, field adv 1965-68; Wash Univ Med Center, med consult 1968-69; State of UT, economist adv 1971-73. **Orgs:** Bd mem NAACP 1957-61, 1993-, 3rd vice pres, 1996-; officer Elks 1965-68; bd mem Elks 1966-67. **Honors/Awds:** Special service award USAF 1962; hon mem cert Amer Basketball Assn 1973; spl serv award, Elks 1975; exalted ruler award Elks 1977; outstanding citizen award Elks 1979. **Military Serv:** USAF a/1c 1961-63. **Business Addr:** Sr Investigator, Conciliator, State of Utah, 160 E 300 S, PO Box 146640, Salt Lake City, UT 84114-6640.

CUNNINGHAM, WILLIAM MICHAEL
Investment company executive. **Personal:** Born Jul 16, 1958, Washington, DC. **Educ:** Howard Univ, BA, Econ, 1978; Univ of Chicago, MBA, Finance, 1983, MA in Econ, 1983. **Career:** Data Resources, Inc, mktg rep, 1977-83; Conn Mutual Life, inv analyst, 1983-85; Merrill Lynch, institutional sales, 1985-87; Fed Home Loan Mktg Corp, institutional sales, 1987-88; Creative Investment Research, investment adv, 1989-. **Business Addr:** Investment Advisor, Creative Investment Research, PO Box 55793, Washington, DC 20040-5793.

CURBEAM, ROBERT L.
Astronaut. **Personal:** Born Mar 5, 1962, Baltimore, MD; married Julie Dawn Lein; children: two. **Educ:** US Naval Academy, BS, aerospace engineering; Naval Postgraduate School, MS, aeronautical engineering, 1990, aeronautical and astronautical engineering, 1991. **Career:** US Navy, naval flight officer, 1984-; US Naval Academy, Weapons and Systems Engineering Dept, instructor, 1994; NASA, astronaut, 1994-. **Orgs:** US Naval Academy Alumni Assn; Assn of Old Crows. **Special Achievements:** Mission specialist on STS-85 assignment, shuttle Discovery, 1997. **Military Serv:** US Navy, naval flight officer, 1984-; Fighter Wing One Radar Intercept Officer of the Year, 1989; US Naval Test Pilot School, Best Developmental Thesis (DT-II) Award; two Navy Commendation Medals, Navy Meritorious Unit Commendation, Armed Forces Expeditionary Medal, National Defense Service Medal, Navy Battle Efficiency Award, Sea Service Deployment Ribbon. **Business Addr:** Astronaut, Astornaut Office/CB, NASA, Johnson Space Center, Houston, TX 77058, (281)483-0123.

CURETON, EARL
Professional basketball player. **Personal:** Born Sep 3, 1957, Detroit, MI. **Educ:** Robert Morris Coll; Univ of Detroit. **Career:** NBA career: Philadelphia 76ers, 1980-83; Detroit Pistons, 1983-86; Chicago Bulls, 1986; Los Angeles Clippers, 1987-88; Charlotte Hornets, 1988-91; Houston Rockets, 1993-; Italian League career: Milano, 1983-84; Philips Milano, 1989-90; French League career: Tours, 1991-92; CBA career: Sioux Falls Skyforce, 1993-94. **Business Addr:** Professional Basketball Player, Houston Rockets, PO Box 272349, Houston, TX 77277, (713)627-0600.

CURETON, JOHN PORTER
Human resources director. **Personal:** Born Oct 4, 1936, Oxford, NC; son of Marie Cureton and John Cureton; married Carolyn Bethea; children: Tonya Yvette, John Porter. **Educ:** Johnson C Smith Univ, BS Psychol 1960; Adelphia Univ, postgrad 1960-61; Univ of PA, attended 1962-63; Univ of Hartford, M Orgnl Behavior 1980. **Career:** NY State Dept Mental Hygiene, psychiat soc wrkr 1960-62; Inter-State Staffing Inc, mgmt consult 1962-66; Philco Ford Corp, sr employ rep 1966-68; Tanatex Div Sybron Corp, indus rela mgr 1968-73; US Postal Svcs, reg labor rela exec 1973-75; Heublein Inc Groc Products Grp, mgr empl rela 1975-78; US Tobacco Co, Industrial & Sales Relations, director 1978-. **Orgs:** Mem Natl Assn of Market Developers; mem Employment Mgmt Assoc; mem Inst Rela & Rsch; mem Inst Collective Bargaining & Group Relations; mem Soc for Human Resources Mgmt; mem Amer Soc Training & Develop; bd mem Voluntary Action Ctr; mem Ct UNCF Comm; mem Kappa Alpha Psi; mem Natl Urban League, NAACP mem; mem Western NE Organization Development Network. **Honors/Awds:** Various awards from UNCF, UL, BNA-Personnel Policies Forum, Kappa Alpha Psi, YMCA. **Business Addr:** Director, Industrial & Sales Relations, US Tobacco Co, 100 W Putnam Ave, Greenwich, CT 06830.

CURETON, MICHAEL
Police officer. **Personal:** Born Nov 15, 1955, Cincinnati, OH; son of Dolores J Thomas Rowland and James A Cureton, Sr.; married Jennifer L Horton Cureton, Jun 20, 1987; children: Shana, Mike Jr., Christopher, Angela, Brandon. **Educ:** University of Cincinnati, Cincinnati, OH, AS, 1976. **Career:** City of Cincinnati, Cincinnati, OH, police cadet, 1973-76; Procter & Gamble Co., Cincinnati, OH, security, 1976-78, sales representative, 1978-80; City of Cincinnati, Cincinnati, OH, police officer, 1980-. **Orgs:** President, Sentinel Police Assn., 1986-; chairperson ways & means, National Black Police Assn. Eastern Region, 1989-; member/steerng comm., Dr. Martin Luther King Coalition, 1988-; volunteer chair site/security, National Council of Negro Women Black Family Reunion, Cincinnati Site, 1989-. **Honors/Awds:** Emerging Leaders for the 90's, Applause Magazine, 1990; brought lawsuit against Cincinnati Police Division, which ultimately promoted minorities into upper levels of police command structure, 1988. **Business Addr:** Lieutenant, Cincinnati Police Division, Sentinel Police Association, 1889 W Central Pkwy, Cincinnati, OH 45214.

CURETON, STEWART CLEVELAND
Clergyman, educational administrator. **Personal:** Born Mar 24, 1930, Greenville, SC; son of Martha Henderson Cureton and Santee Cureton; married Claudette Hazel Chapman, Dec 27, 1954; children: Ruthye E Cooley, Stewart C Jr, Santee Charles, Samuel C. **Educ:** Benedict Coll, AB, 1953; Starks School of Theology, BD 1956; Morris Coll, Dr of Divinity, 1982; Benedict Coll, Dir of Divinity 1983. **Career:** North Warren HS, instructor 1956-61; Beck HS, instructor 1965-82; Amer Baptist Theological Seminary, instructor 1961-85; SC Congress of Christian Education, instructor 1965-83. **Orgs:** Moderator Reedy River Baptist Assn 1972-76; state vice pres Natl Baptist Convention 1977-94; commissioner Human Relations 1978-84; vice pres E&M Baptist Convention of SC; honorary state vice pres NAACP 1982-84; member Urban League Board of Directors 1983; treasurer SHARE 1983-85; chrmn, Urban League Bd 1989-90, pres, Bapt Educational & Missionary Convention of SC 1986-91; vice pres At Large, National Baptist Convention, USA Inc, 1994-. **Honors/Awds:** Service Award Martin Webb Learning Center 1980; Outstanding Citizen Human Relations 1983; Outstanding Service Christian Action Council 1984; Outstanding Serv Awd South Carolina State House of Representatives 1986; Man of the Year, Urban League, 1990. **Home Addr:** 501 Mary Knob, Greenville, SC 29607.

CURLS, PHILLIP B.
State senator. **Personal:** Born Apr 2, 1942, Kansas City, MO; son of Velma E. Wagner Curls and Fred A. Curls; married Melba Jean Dudley, 1964; children: Phillip B II, Michael Jay, Monica Joy Bianca, Louis Brandon Audley III. **Educ:** Rockhurst Coll, BS, BA 1965; OH State Univ; Univ of Kansas City; Chicago Univ. **Career:** Jackson Cty Circuit Court, asst clerk 1960-67; Oper Upgrade of Model Cities Prog, chief fin admin 1970-71; Curls, Curls, and Associates, secr, treas; Missouri State House of Representatives, representative, 1972-83; Missouri State Senate, senator 1983-. **Orgs:** Mem Appraisers Inst. **Business Addr:** Senator, Missouri State Senate 9th Dist, State Capitol Building, Jefferson City, MO 65101.

CURRENT, GLOSTER BRYANT. See Obituaries section.

CURRIE, BETTY
Government official. **Career:** Office of the President, executive secretary, currently. **Business Addr:** Executive Secretary to the President, Office of the President, The White House, 1st Fl, W Wing, 1600 Pennsylvania Ave, NW, Washington, DC 20500, (202)456-1414.

CURRIE, EDDIE L. See Obituaries section.

CURRIE, JACKIE L.
City clerk. **Personal:** Born Nov 2, 1932, Casscoe, AR; daughter of Lillie Montgomery Cooper and Dwight Garrison; married Charmie Currie, Dec 1949; children: Michael, Gregory, Charmie III, Allen. **Educ:** Wayne State Univ, Detroit, MI, BS, 1974; Univ of Michigan, Ann Arbor, MI, 1975. **Career:** Wayne State University, Detroit, MI, community service coordinator, 1972-; Wayne County Commission, Detroit, MI, commissioner, 1976-93, chair pro-tem; City of Detroit, city clerk, 1993-. **Orgs:** Past chair, Public Safety & Judiciary Committee; chair, Wayne County Community Advisory Board, 1989-; chair, Committee on Airports, Roads, and Public Service; board member, Detroit East, Inc, 1980-; SHAR House, 1970-; president, Gamma Phi Delta Sorority, Inc, 1990. **Honors/Awds:** Community Development, Detroit Urban Center; Devoted Work, Boy Scouts of America; Golden Heritage Award, Civil Service; Community Service, Eastside Community Slate; Youth Advocacy Programs, CPA Barrow-Aldridge & Co. **Business Addr:** City Clerk, City of Detroit, 200 City-County Bldg, Detroit, MI 48226.

CURRY, CHARLES E.
Business executive. **Personal:** Born Jan 22, 1934, Jackson, TN; married Beverly; children: Charles F, David E, Michael A. **Educ:** Lane Coll Jackson TN, AB 1955; Emory Univ Atlanta GA, 1973; King Meml Coll, Hon Doctorate 1977. **Career:** Quaker Oats Co, mgr comm affairs. **Orgs:** Exec dir Youth Action 1969-70; deputy dir Youth Action 1968; area dir & westside Youth Action 1966-67; dir Chicago Youth Cntr Streetwork Prog 1965; Advisory Com Chicago ALL Of Business 1969-70; Chicago Catalyst 1967-72; Gtr Lawndale Consult Comm 1967-68; Mid-west Vice Pres Nat Urban Affairs Coun 1972-73; pres Urban Affairs Coun 1972-73; mem Public Affairs Coun Wash 1971-; mem Nat Assn Manuf; chairman Urban Affairs Com; exec con Chicago Urban Affairs Coun 1974; So Shore Valley Org 1969-; Mid-west Vice Pres Lane Coll Alumni Assn; Chicago Chap Pres Lane Coll Alumni Assnl; bd dir Chatam YMCA 1972; bd dir Urban Gateway 1973; bd of trustees Lane Coll 1977; adv bd Univ Of Chicago Metro Cntr 1972; Steering Com NAACP Legal & Defense Fund 1972. **Honors/Awds:** Spec Alumni Award for outstand serv 1972-74; Lane Coll WGRT Good Guy Award 1973; a salute to Black bus & pronl Men Leag Of Black Women 1977; Achievement Award for youth serv Inspiration For Youth 1973; Beautiful People Award Chicago Urban League 1974. **Business Addr:** Merchandise Mart Plaza, Chicago, IL 60654.

CURRY, CHARLES H.
Advertising executive. **Career:** Burrell Advertising, president, chief operating officer, until 1993. **Business Addr:** Former President/COO, Burrell Advertising Inc., 20 North Michigan Ave, Chicago, IL 60602, (312)443-8600.

CURRY, CLARENCE F., JR.
Lecturer. **Personal:** Born Aug 15, 1943, Hampton, VA; married Agnes A Mason; children: Clarence III, Candace. **Educ:** Lafayette Coll, BS Met Eng 1965; Univ of Pittsburgh, MBA 1971; Carnegie Mellon U, MS IA 1973. **Career:** Univ of Pittsburgh, 1974-; Westinghouse Elec, engr; Univ of Pittsburgh School of Business, director Small Business Devel Center, vice chancellor, currently. **Orgs:** Panelist Amer Arbitration Assn; several consulting projects for 500 Firms; United Way; Minority Business Opportunity Comm; mem, ICSB; mem, USASBC; mem, SBIDA. **Honors/Awds:** Pennsylvania Minority Business Advocate SBA 1983. **Special Achievements:** International consultant on bsiness development in Brazil, Peru, Poland and Czechoslovakia. **Business Addr:** Vice Chancellor, Student & Public Affairs, Office of the Vice Chancellor, Univ of PA, 3814 Forbes Ave, Pittsburgh, PA 15213.

CURRY, DELL (WARDELL STEPHEN)
Professional basketball player. **Personal:** Born Jun 25, 1964, Harrisonburg, VA. **Educ:** Virginia Polytechnic Institute and State Univ, Blacksburg, VA, 1982-86. **Career:** Utah Jazz, 1986-87; Cleveland Cavaliers, 1987-88; Charlotte Hornets, 1988-. **Business Addr:** Professional Basketball Player, Charlotte Hornets, Hives Dr, Charlotte, NC 28217.

CURRY, ERIC FELECE
Professional football player. **Personal:** Born Feb 3, 1970, Thomasville, GA. **Educ:** Univ of Alabama, attended. **Career:** Tampa Bay Buccaneers, defensive end, 1993-. **Business Addr:** Professional Football Player, Tampa Bay Buccaneers, One Buccaneer Place, Tampa, FL 33607, (813)870-2700.

CURRY, GEORGE E.
Journalist. **Personal:** Born Feb 23, 1947, Tuscaloosa, AL; divorced. **Educ:** Knoxville College, Tennessee, 1970; Harvard University; Yale University. **Career:** St Louis Post-Dispatch, reporter, 11 year; Sports Illustrated, reporter, 2 years; Chicago Tribune, Washington correspondent, New York bureau chief, 10 years; Emerge Magazine, editor-in-chief, 1993-. **Orgs:** St Louis Minority Journalism Workshop, founding director, 1977; Washington Assn of Black Journalists, annual high school journalism workshop, founding director; New York Assn of Black Journalists, workshop initiator, 1990; Youth Communication, bd of directors, elected chairman, 1990; Student Press Law Center, bd member. **Honors/Awds:** Has won over a dozen journalism awards, including: Lincoln University, Unity Media Awards, investigative reporting category, first place, 1990; Natl Urban Coalition, Distinguished Urban Journalism Award, 1982; profiled in Contemporary Authors; Assn for Education in Journalism and Mass Communication, secondary division, Top Annual Award recipient, 1989, newspaper division, Distinguished Service Award, 1992; Southern Press Institute, Distinguished Service Award, 1989. **Special Achievements:** Author, Jake Gaither: America's Most Famous Black Coach, Dodd, Mead & Co, 1977; appeared on numerous tv shows, including: The Today Show, The MacNeil/Lehrer Newshour, Washington Week in Review, America's Black Forum, C-Span, Speaking of Everything.

CURRY, GLADYS J. See WASHINGTON, GLADYS J.

CURRY, JERRY RALPH
Business consultant. **Personal:** Born Sep 7, 1932, McKeesport, PA; son of Mercer Curry and Jesse Curry; married Charlene; children: Charlein, Jerry, Toni, Natasha. **Educ:** Univ of NE, BA 1960; Command and General Staff Coll, 1967; Boston Univ, MA Internatl Relations 1970; Luther Rice Seminary, D Ministry 1978; US Army War College, graduate. **Career:** US Army, major general (highest rank attained), 1950-84 (retired); National Perspectives Institute, president and publisher, 1985; Systems Management America Corporation, vice president, 1987; National Highway Traffic Safety Administration, 1989-92, bus consultant, currently. **Orgs:** Board member, Greater Washington, DC Board of Trade; board member, American Red Cross; federal trustee, Federal City Council; Delta Phi Alpha; The National Honorary German Society; Phi Alpha Theta; International Honor Society in History; National Eagle Scout Assn; chairman, Black Revolutionary War Patriots Foundation. **Honors/Awds:** Distinguished Alumni, University of Nebraska, 1979; Washingtonian of the Year, Washingtonian Magazine, 1982; Oxford Society of Scholars, fellow. **Military Serv:** US Army, Maj Gen, 1950-84; Defense Distinguished Service Medal; Army Distinguished Service Medals; Legion of Merit with Oak Leaf Clusters; Meritorious Service Medals; Bronze Star with V Device; Cross of Gallantry with Palm (Vietnam); Army Commendation Medals; Navy Commendation Medal; Navy Unit Commendation Ribbon; Air Medals; Queen Beatrix of the Netherlands of Orange-Nassau; Combat Infantryman Badge; others. **Business Addr:** Chateau Antioch, PO Box 407, Haymarket, VA 22069.

CURRY, LEVY HENRY
Personnel administrator. **Personal:** Born Feb 3, 1949, Buffalo, NY; son of Cora Marie Curry and Levi Curry; married Dianne Curry; children: Tasha. **Educ:** Morehouse Coll, BA 1971; Atlanta Law Sch, JD 1975. **Career:** Consolidated Manufacturing Co, plant manager, 1970-71; International Harvester, sales manager, 1971-74; Equal & Employment Opportunity Commission, legal research analyst, 1974; Steak & Ale Restaurants of America, director of personnel, 1975-87, director of affirmative action, 1975; National Urban League Beep Program, visiting professor, 1977; Hospitality Industries Inc, board of directors, 1978; American Federal Bank, senior vice president, 1987-. **Orgs:** Mem bd of dir Chain Restaurant Compensation Assn 1978; Morris Brown Coll Sch of Restaurant & Instrumental Mgmt 1977; mem Dallas Personnel Assn/Am Socof Personnel 1977; consult jr Achievement Project Bus 1979; member, Morehouse College Alumni Assn; board of trustees, African Museum of Life & Culture; member, Junior Black Academy of Arts and Letters. **Honors/Awds:** Mary C Miller Scholarship, Nat Urban League 1967; hon degree FL Intern At Univ 1976.

CURRY, MARK
Actor, comedian. **Personal:** Born in Oakland, CA. **Career:** Stand up comedian; Hangin with Mr Cooper, actor, 1992-. **Special Achievements:** Showtime at the Apollo, host; guest appearances on The Arsenio Hall Show, Dinbad and Friends, HBO One Night Stand. **Business Addr:** Actor, Hanging with Mr Cooper, c/o ABC Television, 4151 Prospect Ave, Los Angeles, CA 90027-4524, (213)557-4396.

CURRY, MICHAEL
Professional basketball player. **Personal:** Born Aug 22, 1968, Anniston, AL. **Educ:** Georgia Southern. **Career:** Capital Region Pontiacs (CBA), guard, 1992-93; S Clear (Italy), 1993-94; Philadelphia 76ers, 1993; Valvi Girona (Spain), 1994-95; Omaha Racers (CBA), 1995-96; Washington Bullets, 1996; Detroit Pistons, 1996-97; Milwaukee Bucks, 1997-. **Business Addr:** Professional Basketball Player, Milwaukee Bucks, 1001 N Fourth St, Bradley Center, Milwaukee, WI 53203, (414)227-0500.

CURRY, MICHAEL BRUCE
Minister. **Personal:** Born Mar 13, 1953, Chicago, IL; son of Dorothy A Strayhorne Curry and Kenneth S L Curry; married Sharon Clement; children: Rachel, Elizabeth. **Educ:** Hobart College, BA (with honors), 1975; Yale University Divinity School, MDiv, 1978. **Career:** St Stephen's Episcopal Church, rector, 1978-82; Diocese of Southern Ohio, racism staff, 1982-87; Bethany School, chaplain, 1983-88; St Simon of Cyrena Church, rector/pastor, 1982-88; St James Episcoapl Church, rector/pastor, 1988-. **Orgs:** NAACP; Union Black Episcopalians; College of Preachers Board. **Special Achievements:** "Power in the Word," Sermons that Work II; " Servant Woman," Sermons that Work II. **Business Addr:** Minister, St James Episcopal Church, 1005 W Lafayette Ave, Baltimore, MD 21217, (410)523-4588.

CURRY, MITCHELL L.
Clergyman, psychotherapist. **Personal:** Born Feb 5, 1935, Augusta, GA; son of Ernestine Curry and W L Curry; married Carolyn D; children: Sonja M, Edwards, Reuben B, Rachel M, Michele L. **Educ:** Morris Brown Coll Atlanta GA, BA 1960; Andover Newton Theol Sch Newton Ctr MA, MDiv 1964; Univ of Louisville, Louisville KY, MSSW 1972; Schl of Theol at Claremont CA, PhD 1979. **Career:** Natl Urban League-Western Reg, asst reg dir 1972-75; Lewis Metro Meth Ch LA, minister 1974-76; Florence Ave Presby Ch LA, minister 1976-80; LA Co Dept Mental Htlh, psychotherapist 1976-86; Allen AME Ch San Bernardino, pastor 1985-90; psychotherapist in private practice, currently. **Orgs:** Consult Natl Inst of Mental Health 1972-79; fellow Amer Assn of Pastoral Counselors, 1979-; LCSW State of CA 1975; mem Academy of Certified Social Workers, NASW 1974-; mem bd of govr Natl Council of Ch 1980; mem Alpha Phi Alpha Frat 1959; licensed clinical social worker, Board Certified Diplomate. **Honors/Awds:** LHD Reed Christ Coll Angeles 1976; scholarship Grant Natl Inst of Mental Health 1970-72; scholarship Grant Lilly Found 1961; scholarship Grant Am Missionary Assoc 1960-64. **Military Serv:** AUS, honorably discharged, 1954-56.

CURRY, NORVELLE. See Obituaries section.

CURRY, PHYLLIS JOAN
Government official. **Personal:** Born Apr 5, 1929, Pittsburgh, PA; married Joseph. **Educ:** Hunter Coll of the City of New York, BA; Columbia Univ Sch Of Social Work, MS Social Work 1969. **Career:** NY State Dept of Correction Serv, superintendnt 1977-; NY & State Dept Correction Serv, dep supt for progm 1977; NY State Dept of Correction Serv, regnl training coordinator 1972-77; NY State Div of Parole, parole ofcr/supr 1960-72; Dept of Social Serv, social worker 1955-60. **Orgs:** Mem Nat Council Crime & Delinquency 1979-; mem Am Correction Assn Spt & Wardens Assn 1979-; student/faculty adv com Columbia Univ Sch of Social Work 1967-69; mem Columbia Univ Sch of Social Work Alumni 1969-; mem Coalition of 100 Black Women 1977-; adv council Westchester Community Coll 1977-; adv com Dept Corr Servs-multi-yr Plan 1979-; mem Middle Atlantic States Correction Assn 1980. **Business Addr:** 247 & Harris Rd, Bedford Hills, NY 10507.

CURRY, SADYE BEATRYCE
Educator, physician. **Personal:** Born in Reidsville, NC; daughter of Limmmer P Curry and Charlie Will Curry. **Educ:** Johnson C Smith Univ, BS,(Cum Laude), 1963; Howard Univ College of Medicine, MD, 1967; Duke Univ Med Center, internship, 1967-68. **Career:** VA Hospital, Washington, DC, internal medicine residency 1968-69; Fellowship in Gastroenterology, Duke Univ, 1969-72, instructor in medicine, Duke University, 1969-72; Howard Univ, asst prof of medicine 1972-77; Howard Univ Svc, Washington DC General Hospital, asst chief medical officer 1973-74; Howard Univ Coll of Medicine, asst chief of medicine 1974-78, assoc prof of med, 1978-. **Orgs:** Mem Natl Med Assn; Am Med Assn; Medico-chirurgical Soc of DC; DC Med Soc; Natl Insts of Health-Natl Inst of Arthritis Metabolic & Digestive Diseases Training Grants Com in Gastroenterology & Nutrition 1972-73; mem Am Digestive Diseases Soc; mem Gastrointestinal Drug Adv Com FDA 1975-76; mem Alpha Kappa Alpha; Beta Kappa Chi; Alpha Kappa Mu; US Friendship Force Ambassador to West Berlin, 1980; past pres, Leonidas Berry Society for Digestive Diseases; mem, bd of trustees, Lake Land Or Property Owners Assn, Ladysmith VA; American Society of Internal Medicine. **Honors/Awds:** Recipient student council faculty award for teaching excellence Howard Univ Coll of Med 1975; Kaiser-Permanente Award for Excellence in Teaching Howard Univ Coll of Med 1978; Woman of the Year Award, Howard University College of Medicine Student American Medical Women's Association, 1990. **Business Addr:** Associate Professor of Medicine, Howard Univ Hospital, 2401 Georgia Ave, NW, Washington, DC 20060.

CURRY, VICTOR TYRONE
Pastor. **Personal:** Born Mar 8, 1960, Hollywood, FL; married Cynthia D Baskin (divorced 1990); children: Victoria T Curry, Veronica T Curry. **Educ:** Florida Bible College, Hollywood, FL, 1978-81; Florida Memorial College, Miami, FL, BS, 1986. **Career:** Mt Carmel Missionary Baptist Church, Miami, FL, pastor/administrator, 1984-; Dade County School Board, Miami, FL, classroom teacher, 1987-89; Margolis Broadcasting Co, Miami Beach, FL, radio announcer, talk show host, 1989-. **Orgs:** President, Miami Christian Improvement Association, 1986-; executive committee member, NAACP Miami Dade Branch, 1988-; member, Omega Psi Phi Fraternity, Sigma Alpha Chapter, Miami, FL, 1989-. **Honors/Awds:** Kool's Achievers Award, finalist, Civic Category, 1988; Black Achievers Award, winner of Religious Category, Metropolitan Dade County, 1989; Citizen of the Year, City of Miami, 1989; 1990 Future Leader of America, Ebony Magazine, 1990. **Business Addr:** Pastor, Mount Carmel Missionary Baptist Church, 1745 NW 79th St, Miami, FL 33147.

CURRY, WILLIAM THOMAS
Physician, surgeon. **Personal:** Born Jan 4, 1943, Great Neck, NY; married Katherine E Lum, Dec 23, 1967; children: William Jr, Christian. **Educ:** NY Univ, BS 1964; Howard Univ, MD 1968. **Career:** George Wash Hosp, surgical intern 1968-69; The NY Hosp Cornell Med Ctr, surgical resident 1969-72, chief resident surgeon 1972-73; Cornell Univ Med Coll, asst prof; NY Hosp, attending surgeon. **Orgs:** Practicing gen & vascular surgery with emphasis on cancer; fellow surgery 1969-72; instr surgery 1972-76; clinical asst prof surgery Cornell Univ Med Coll 1976-; diplomate Amer Bd of Surgery 1974; fellow Amer Coll of Surgeons 1976; Kappa Alpha Psi Frat; Reveille Club of NY; mem bd dir Music for Westchester Symphony Orch; Mt Kisco Country Club; vice-chairman, Committee for Insurance Review, New York County Medical Society 1988-; Shinnecock Hills Golf Club. **Military Serv:** AUSR med corps 1972. **Business Addr:** Surgeon, New York Hospital, Cornell Medical Center, 342 E 67th St, New York, NY 10021, (212)628-1681.

CURSON, THEODORE
Musician. **Personal:** Born Jun 3, 1935, Philadelphia, PA; married Marjorie; children: Charlene, Theodore II. **Educ:** Granoff Mus Conservatory, 1952-53. **Career:** PBS TV Show "Jazz Set", Star 1972; NY U, Concerts; Antibes, Lugano, Warsaw, And Others, appearances, radio, tv, clubs, jazz festivals; Max Roach, Philly Joe Jones, Charles Mingus, trumpeter; Jazz Festivals incl, Jazz Yatra in India, Pori Jazz Festival in Finland 1965-, Camden Festival in England, 1965-, Monterey in CA, Bled in Yugoslavia, Vienne in France, Cork in Ireland, Blue Note Jam Session NYC, Le Petit Opportun Paris, Juan Sebastian Club Caracas Venezuela; recording artist, jazz trumpeter & bandleader, currently. **Orgs:** Mem Charles Mingus & Jazz Wrksp 1959-60; pres Nosruc Pub Co 1961-; mem Am Fedn Musicians. **Honors/Awds:** New jazz artist Jazz Podium; Ted Curson & Co winner Down Beat Readers Poll 1978; LI Musicians Soc Awd 1970. **Special Achievements:** Composer: "Tears for Dolphy," 1961; "Fliptop," 1977; "Typical Ted," 1977; albums and CDs: Snake Johnson, Ted Curson & Co, Canadian Concert 1985-86; Mingus at Antibes; Ted Curson Groups; Fire Down Below; Plenty of Horn. **Home Addr:** 130 Arlington Ave, Jersey City, NJ 07305.

CURTIN, JOHN T.
Federal judge. **Personal:** Born Aug 24, 1921, Buffalo, NY; son of Ellen Quigley Curtin and John J. Curtin; married Jane R. Good, Aug 9, 1952; children: Ann Elizabeth, John James, Patri-

cia Marie, Eileen Jane, Mary Ellen, Mark Andrew, William Joseph. **Educ:** Canisius College, BS, 1945; Buffalo University, LLB, 1949. **Career:** Attorney in private practice, Buffalo, NY, 1949-61; US Attorney's Attorney's Office, Western District of New York, US attorney, 1961-67; US District Court, Western District of New York, judge, 1967-, chief judge, currently. **Orgs:** New York State Bar Assn; American Bar Assn; Erie County Bar Assn. **Military Serv:** US Marine Corps, Lt Col, 1942-45, US Marine Corps Reserves, 1952-54. **Business Addr:** Chief Judge, US District Court for the Western District, US District Court 624, US Courthouse, 68 Court St, Buffalo, NY 14202.

CURTIS, HARRY S.
Data processing manager. **Personal:** Born Aug 26, 1934, Springfield, IL; married Sylvia; children: Diana, Harry Jr, Eric, Christopher. **Educ:** Attended Thornton Comm Coll of Harvey; Gov's State Univ, BA Public Admin. **Career:** DKV Estates, real estate salesman 1964-66; RR Retirement Bd, supervisory computer systems analyst. **Orgs:** Bd dirs Natl Caucus Black Sch Bd Mems 1970-; pres Bd of Educ Dist #147 1972-73, 1976-79, 1970-83; chief negotiator Bd of Edn; Vol Police Reserve Harvey 1975-; Scottish Rite Masonic Order AF & AM; Nobles of the Mystic Shrine; Federal Mgrs Assoc, Natl Sch Bd Assoc Federal Relations Network 1982-83. **Honors/Awds:** Nominee Outstanding Supr Employee Fed Employee of Yr. **Military Serv:** IL NG 1956-62. **Business Addr:** Super Computer Sys Analyst, US Railroad Retirement Board, 844 North Rush St, Chicago, IL 60611.

CURTIS, IVERY
Educational administrator. **Career:** Wayne County Community College, pres, currently. **Business Addr:** President, Wayne County Community College, 801 W Fort St, Detroit, MI 48226, (313)496-2500.

CURTIS, JAMES L.
Physician, educator. **Personal:** Born Apr 27, 1922, Jeffersonville, GA; son of Frances Curtis and Will Curtis; married Vivian A Rawls; children: Lawrence, Paul. **Educ:** Albion Coll, AB 1943; Univ of MI, MD 1946. **Career:** State Univ of NY, instructor asst prof 1954-67; Cornell Univ Med Coll, assoc prof 1968-81; Columbia Univ Clinic, prof of psychiatry 1982-; Harlem Hospital Center, director of psychiatry, currently. **Orgs:** Mem Amer Psychiatric Assn; Amer Orthopsychiatric Assn; NY Acad Medicine; Amer Acad Psychoanalysis; AMA; Natl Med Assn. **Honors/Awds:** Published book Blacks Medical School & Soc; many other publications. **Military Serv:** USAF capt 1952-54. **Business Addr:** Dir of Psychiatry, Harlem Hospital Center, 506 Lenox Ave, New York, NY 10037.

CURTIS, JEAN TRAWICK
Library administrator. **Personal:** Born in Washington, DC; daughter of Dannie May Trawick and Ivory Wilson Trawick (deceased); divorced; children: Karen Elizabeth Phoenix, Jeffrey Lynn Phoenix. **Educ:** Howard University, Washington, DC, BA, library science, 1958; University of Maryland, College Park, MD, MLS, 1971, Library Administrators Development Program, 1977. **Career:** DC Public Library, Washington, DC, children's librarian, 1958-65, reader's advisor, 1965-69; University of Maryland, College Park, MD, research assistant, 1969-71; Enoch Pratt Free Library, Baltimore, MD, young adult field worker, 1971-75, regional librarian, 1975-78, chief of extension division, 1978-85; Detroit Public Library, deputy director, 1986-87, director, 1987-. **Orgs:** Member, American Library Association; member, Michigan Library Association; director, University Cultural Center Association, 1987-; director, New Detroit, Inc, 1987-; member, Southeastern Michigan League of Libraries, 1987-; member, Library of Michigan, Library Services and Construction Act Advisory Committee, Task Force on Library Interdependency and Funding, 1987-90; board president, Detroit Associated Libraries Network, 1988-90; member, Michigan Women's Hall of Fame, Historical Honors Committee; member, Xonta International, Detroit Chapter, 1988-90; member, Mayor's Trouble Shooting Task Force, 1985. **Honors/Awds:** Operated campaign to secure community and political endorsements in favor of increase millage to support schools and libraries; reorganized Detroit Public Library administration; speaker at several university seminars on library science; consultant to Information Access Company on strategic planning, 1990. **Business Addr:** Director, Detroit Public Library, 5201 Woodward Ave, Detroit, MI 48202.

CURTIS, JOSEPH F., SR.
Clergyman. **Personal:** Born May 2, 1916, Washington, DC; son of Mary Matilda Kelly Curtis (deceased) and Joseph M Curtis (deceased); married Cora L (deceased); children: Joseph Jr, Wilson T, Mary S. **Educ:** St Augustine Seminary, Postal Inst; St Josephs Seminary, Diaconate Training; DC Gen Hosp, Chaplains Training. **Career:** US Post Office, cleaner/carrier/ clerk, Washington DC, 1941-69; US Post Office, foreman operator, Washington DC 1969-71; Holy Comforter-St Cyprian Church, minister 1971-; DC Gen Hosp, Asst Catholic chaplain 1971-74; Hadley Mem Hosp, Catholic chaplain 1974-83; Archdiocese of Washington. **Orgs:** Mem Greater Washington Catholic Chaplains Assn; Natl Alliance of Postal & Fed Employees; Knights of St John Holy Name Society; St Vincent de Paul Soc. **Military Serv:** USMC cpl.

CURTIS, JUANITA GWENDOLYN
Educator. **Personal:** Born Feb 6, 1920, Chicago, IL; married Norvel W Sr. **Educ:** Phoenix Coll, diploma 1939; AZ St Univ Tempe, BA 1940; AZ St Univ Tempe, MA 1944; AZ St Univ Tempe, EdD 1963. **Career:** Univ of Pacific, prof of educ 1964-; Univ of Washington Seattle, guest lecturer 1969; Berkely Unified School Dist, curriculum consultant 1963-64; Prairie View A&M Coll TX, prof 1950-54; Sam Huston Tillotson Coll, prof 1946, summers 1947-49; Phoenix School Dist #1, teacher 1941-63; Avondale Elementary School AZ, teacher 1940-41. **Orgs:** Soc studies & reading consult State of NV Dept of Educ 1972-75; num professional consult through the country; wrkshps cond for num Sch past 30 yrs; mem Emmanuel Bap Ch/ Stockton Chap of Links Inc/Intl Reading Assn/ASCD/ALPHA Kappa Alpha/Delta Kappa Gamma/Phy Delta Kappa/NEA/ RELATED Professional Orgn; eval bd mem Nat Councl for Accreditation of Coll of Tchr Educ 1974-78.

CURTIS, MARVIN VERNELL
Educator, musician. **Personal:** Born Feb 12, 1951, Chicago, IL; son of Dorothy Marva Curtis and John W Curtis Jr; married Sharon Curry Curtis, Jul 19, 1986. **Educ:** North Park College, Bachelor of Music, 1972; Presbyterian School of Christian Education, Master of Arts, 1974; Westminister Choir College, 1978; The Juilliard School of Music, 1982; University of the Pacific, Doctor of Education, 1990. **Career:** The Graham School, music teacher, 1975-80; the Riverside Church, director of church school music, 1978-80; Emmanuel Baptist Church, minister of music, 1980-84; San Diego State University, director of gospel choir, 1984-86; Morse High School, chairman of music department, 1985-86; California State University, Stanislaus, assistant professor of music education, 1988-91; Virginia Union University, director of choral activities, 1991-94. **Orgs:** American Choral Directors Association, national chair ethnic & minority concerns, 1992-94; San Joaquin County Arts Council, president, 1989-91; National Association of Negro Musicians Inc, assistant treasurer, 1991-; Music Educations National Conference; Central Virginia Faculty Consortium, 1992-; California Arts Council, grants panel member, 1990-; California State University, Stanislaus, faculty senator, 1989-91. **Honors/ Awds:** National Association for Equal Opportunity in Higher Education, Research Award, 1992; University of the Pacific Alumni Association, Young Alumni Award, 1992; University of the Pacific School of Education, Educator Alumnus of the Year, 1991; City of Savannah, Georgia, Key to the City, 1992; San Diego Association of Community Theatre, Aubry Award, Outstanding Musical Director, 1985. **Special Achievements:** Published, 30 choral compositions, Mark Foster Music Co, 1975-; Conductor, Emmanuel Baptist Church Concert, Alice Tully Hall-Lincoln Center, 1983; Conductor, Virginia Union University Concert Choir, Alice Tully Hall-Lincoln Center, 1992; Commissioned by Philander Smith College to compose musical work for Clinton Inaugural Activities, 1992, composed musical work, Clinton Inauguratal Activities, 1993. **Home Phone:** (804)226-6188.

CURTIS, MARY C.
Journalist. **Personal:** Born Sep 4, Baltimore, MD; daughter of Evelyn C Thomas and Thomas E Curtis; married Martin F Olsen, Oct 16, 1976; children: Zane A Curtis-Olsen. **Educ:** Fordham University, New York, NY, BA, communications, summa cum laude. **Career:** The Associated Press, New York and Hartford, CT, editor, writer, freelance nwspaper and magazine reporter, 1977-81; The Travelers Insurance Co, mktg services coord, 1977-81; Arizona Daily Star, Tucson, AZ, copy editor, 1981-83; Baltimore Sun, Baltimore, MD, travel editor, asst features ed, 1983-84, arts & entertainment editor, 1984-85; New York Times, copy editor, Culture Department, 1986-88, deputy editor, Living Arts Section, 1988-90, editor, Living Arts Section, 1990-92, editor, The Home Section, 1992-93, education life editor, 1993-94; The Charlotte Observer, features editor, currently. **Orgs:** Society of Professional Journalists, Sigma Delta Chi, 1972-; National Association of Black Journalists, 1984-; American Association of Sunday and Feature Editors, 1994-. **Honors/Awds:** American Association of Sunday and Feature Editors, Award for Commentary, 1995. **Business Addr:** Features Editor, The Charlotte Observer, 600 S Tryon, PO Box 30308, Charlotte, NC 28230, (704)358-5255.

CURTIS-BAUER, M. BENAY (BENAY CURTIS)
Stockbroker. **Personal:** Born Aug 12, 1948, Berkeley, CA; daughter of Emory C & Dorothy A Curtis; married Jon K Bauer, Jul 4, 1988. **Educ:** University of California, Berkeley, BA. **Career:** Dean Witter, registered representative, 1991-. **Orgs:** St Dominic's Church, Finance Council. **Business Addr:** Dean Witter, 101 California St, San Francisco, CA 94111.

CURTIS HALL, VONDIE
Actor. **Personal:** Born in Detroit, MI; married Kasi Lemmons; children: Henry. **Career:** Actor; writer; director. **Orgs:** Black Filmmaker Foundation. **Honors/Awds:** Audelco Award; National Board of Reviews, Excellence in Flimmaking. **Special Achievements:** Films: Coming to America, Passion Fish, Crooklyn, The Drop Squad, Die Hard 2, Sugar Hill, Romeo and Juliet, Gridlock'd; TV: Chicago Hope, Don King: Only in America, HBO, 1997; Eve's Bayou, 1997. **Business Addr:** Actor, Gersh Agency, PO Box 5617, Beverly Hills, CA 90210, (310)274-6611.

CURTIS-RIVERS, SUSAN YVONNE (SUSAN MANGO CURTIS)
Journalist. **Personal:** Born Jun 27, 1958, Savannah, GA; daughter of William & Lillain Curtis; married James Socrates Rivers, Dec 12, 1992; children: Jasmine DuBignon. **Educ:** Virginia COmmonwealth University, BFA design, 1981. **Career:** National Rifle Association, art dir, 1981-84; NUS Corp, graphic supervisor, 1984-86; Phillips Publishing Inc, art dir, 1986-87; The Washington Post Magazine, assistant art dir, 1987-88; Theimes Journal Newspaper, Springfield, designer, 1988-90; Design's Graphics, assistant managing editor, 1990-. **Orgs:** National Association of Black Journalists; Society of Newspaper Design; National Association of Minority Media Executives, 1991-94; National Association of Hispanic Journalist; Florida A&M University School of Journalism & Graphic Arts, bd of visitors, 1996. **Honors/Awds:** Nomination for a Knight-Ridder Entrepreneurial Excellence Award, 1990; The Associated Press Society of Ohio Award, 1991; Society of Newspaper Design: The Beacon Journal Art Department Staff won 2 Silver Awards, 1 Bronze Award, and 4 Awards of Excellence, 1992; The Cleveland Press Club Excellence in Journalism, 1993; The Pulitzer Prize Gold Medal for Public Service, 1994; National Headliner Award, 1995; Society of Newspaper Design, Staff won 2 Awards of Excellence, 1996; numerous others. **Special Achievements:** Recipient of the Garth C Reeves Sr Chair, Florida A&M University School of Journalism and Graphic Arts, Spring 1996. **Business Addr:** Assistant Managing Editor, Design & Graphics, The Akron Beacon Journal, 44 E Exchange St, PO Box 640, Akron, OH 44309-0640, (330)996-3557.

CURVIN, ROBERT
Educator. **Personal:** Born Feb 23, 1934, Newark, NJ; married Patricia; children: Frank, Nicole. **Educ:** Rutgers, BA 1960; Rutgers, MSW 1967; Princeton, PhD 1975. **Career:** CUNY Brooklyn Coll, assoc prof, until 1978; Rutgers Univ, lecturer comm des spl 1968-74; League for Industrial Democracy, dir training Program 1965-66; Essex City Welfare Bd, supvr case work 1960-65; New York Times, editorial board member, 1978-83; New School for Social Research, Graduate School of Management and Urban Policy, 1984-88; Ford Foundation, director of the urban poverty program, 1988-. **Orgs:** Treas 21st Century Found 1977; trst Princeton Univ 1977; trst Channel 13 WNET 1977; natl v chmn CORE; chmn Newark Essex CORE 1962-63; mem Tri-state RegPlanning Commn 1977; Com for Resp Legis 1977; Wallace Eljabar Flowsp 1971-73; Ford Found Travel Study 1976-77; Victoria Foundation, trustee, 1976-; The Revson Foundation, trustee, 1987-91; Broad National Bank, director, 1985-88. **Honors/Awds:** Outstanding Alumnus, Rutgers, 1991. **Military Serv:** AUS 1st lt 1953-57. **Business Addr:** Director, Urban Policy Program, The Ford Foundation, 320 E 43rd St, New York, NY 10017.

CURWOOD, STEPHEN THOMAS
Author, broadcast producer. **Personal:** Born Dec 11, 1947, Boston, MA; son of Sarah Ethel Thomas Curwood and James L Curwood; married Liza Little; children: Anastasia (Stacy), James, Sadie. **Educ:** AB Harvard Coll, Cambridge, Honors concentration in problems of developing societies, 1969; Westtown School, Westtown PA, 1965. **Career:** Bay State Banner, managing editor, 1971-72; Boston Globe, writer, 1972-76, witer/columnist, 1982-89; WGBH TV, producer/reporter, 1976-79; National Public Radio, reporter/host, 1979-, senior host, "World of Opera," 1990-, exec producer, "Living on Earth," currently. **Orgs:** Harvard Unit, visiting lecturer; Society of Environmental Journalists, bd mem; Pew Science Scholars, advisory comm; Farm & Wilderness Camp, trustee; Civic Educ Foundation, Tufts Univ, trustee. **Honors/Awds:** Pulitzer Prize for public service, part of Boston Globe team, 1975; ANDY Award for radio documentary, 1982; New England Environmental Leadership Award, for work on promoting environmental awareness, 1992. **Business Addr:** Executive Producer/Host, Living on Earth, National Public Radio, PO Box 380639, Cambridge, MA 02238-0639.

CUSHINGBERRY, GEORGE, JR.
County official. **Personal:** Born Jan 6, 1953, Detroit, MI; son of Edna Louise and George Cushingberry Sr; married Maria Hazel Drew; children: George III, Brandon Drew. **Educ:** Wayne State Univ, BA, 1974; Univ of Detroit Law School, graduate. **Career:** Wayne State Univ, Southend News, editor, vice-chmn Assn of Black Students; State of MI, state rep; Wayne County Bd of Commissioners, commissioner, currently. **Orgs:** NAACP, life member; Founders Society, Detroit Inst of Arts; Michigan Ethnic Heritage Center; Museum of African American History, bd of trustees; Michigan Humanities Council. **Honors/Awds:** Superior Cadet Awd Cass Tech High 1971; Young Man of The Year Jaycees 1975; Comm Serv Awd EBONI Women 1975; Young Dem Awd 1st Cong Dist 1975; Together Bros & Sisters Comm Serv Awd 1975; Man of The Year MI Chronicle Newspaper 1977. **Business Addr:** Commissioner, Wayne County Bd of Commissioners, 600 Randolph, Ste 450, Detroit, MI 48226.

CUSHMAN, VERA F.
Manager. **Personal:** Born Jul 28, 1944, Dermott, AR; married John R; children: Christophe Stephen. **Educ:** Grambling Coll, BS Educ 1966; Univ of NM, MA 1974; Univ of MN, MA Pub

Adminstrn. **Career:** BIA Navajo Reservation, teacher 1966-68; EEO Women in Mgmt Minority Women, panelist/cons natl & local workshop leader 1968-; Bur of Indian Affairs-Navajo Reservation, educ spec 1969-71; SW Indian & Polytech Inst, instr 1971-76; Dept of Interior, eeo investigator 1973-76; Natl Council Negro Women, various offices 1973-; Kirtland AFB, discrimination complaints officer 1976-. **Orgs:** Bd mem Albuquerque Montessori Sch 1975-77; del State of MN; Houston Womens Conf 1977; mem Standards & Goals Com Criminal Justice Dept Dtate of MN 1977; locator NM & AZ Contribution of Black Women 1978-79; mem NAACP, NOW, MN WPC; organizer, charter mem, officer Black Comm Forum 1979; pres Nat Council of Negro Women Albuquerque Chap 1980-81; mem Gov Penitentiary MN Blue Ribbon Panel to Monitor Invest of Riot & Advise the Govt on Improvement 1980; organizedlocal ACTSO NAACP 1982; pres Albq Bus & Professional Women 1985-86; youth dir, mem bd of dir Algq NAACP 1986-87; dir Dist I New Mex Fed of Bus & Professional Women 1987-88. **Honors/Awds:** Natl Council Negro Women 1976; Disting Public Serv Awd State of NM highest honor state bestows on a citizen 1985; Outstanding NM Woman 1986; NM Women's Hall of Fame 1986; chair, bicentennial project Pub Book "Profiles in Leadership The Black Woman in Amer". **Business Addr:** Discrimination Compalints Ofcr, Kirtland AFB, 1606 Air Base Wing, Albuquerque, NM 87117.

CUSTER-CHEN, JOHNNIE M.
Attorney, educator. **Personal:** Born Aug 26, 1948, Birmingham, AL; daughter of Willie Lee Robinson Custer and John Custer; divorced; children: Christopher Chen, Michael Chen. **Educ:** Howard Univ, BA 1971; Washington Univ, MEd 1972; Cleveland-Marshall College of Law, JD 1984. **Career:** St Louis OIC, dir of counseling 1974-75; State Comm Coll, career educ counselor 1975-77; Cuyahoga Comm Coll, coord cooperative educ 1980-85; Loop Coll, dir cooperative educ 1986; IL Dept of Children and Family Svcs, attorney 1987-89; Illinois Dept of Professional Regulation, Chicago, IL, attorney, 1989-; private practice, attorney, currently. **Orgs:** Mem Amer, Chicago and IL State Bar Assocs; mem PUSH, Urban League, League of Black Women. **Honors/Awds:** Chicago's Up & Coming Black Business & Professional Women Awd Dollars & Sense Magazine 1986.

CUSTIS, ACE (ADRIAN LLEWELLYN)
Professional basketball player. **Personal:** Born May 24, 1974. **Educ:** Virginia Tech. **Career:** Dallas Mavericks, forward, 1997-. **Business Addr:** Professional Basketball Player, Dallas Mavericks, 777 Sports St, Reunion Arena, Dallas, TX 75207, (214)748-1808.

CUSTIS, CLARENCE A.
Business executive. **Personal:** Born Nov 9, Bridgeton, NJ; married Yvonne; children: Steven, Kim, Jon, Darren. **Career:** Mainline Sales & Serv Co, owner; Moores Super Stores Vineland NJ Br, truckdriver, salesman, asst mgr; farmer 1959-64. **Orgs:** Mem Fairfield Twnshp Bd of Educ 1967-75; Farmers Home Adminstrn Loan Adv Com 1971-74; Cumberland Co Fairfield Vol Fire Co 1959-; chief bd dirs Intl Self Help Hsng Asso 1967-69; vP Cumberland Regional bd of edn. **Honors/Awds:** Recip cert of merit FHA 1967; honored by Fairfield bd of educ 1975; Devoted Serv & Leadership. **Military Serv:** USAF 1955-59.

CUTLER, DONALD
Educator. **Personal:** Born Oct 20, 1943, Tampa, FL; married Rosemary N. **Educ:** Albany State Coll Albany GA, BS 1971; GA State U. **Career:** Dougherty County Public Schools, educator 1972; Goodwill Ind, Albany GA, dir work adj training 1971-72; WJIZ Radio, Albany GA, disc jockey 1969-70; WAYX Radio, Waycross GA, radio announcer 1965-66; Waycross Jour Herald, Waycross GA, news correspondent 1965-66; WALB-TV, Albany GA, sports announcer, weekend anchor 1973-77; Cougherty Co Albany, co commr bd of commrs 1978-. **Orgs:** Vpp Cong of Black Orgn Albany 1977-; org/spokesman Albany Black Caucas 1979-; mem NEA/GAE/DCAE/NAACP; Handicapped Employer of the Year SW; GA Easter Seal Soc 1976; elected mem Dougherty Co Dem Exec Commn elected 1st Black Commr Dougherty Co Commn; elected mem Exec Com SW GA APDC. **Business Addr:** Pine Ave, PO Box 1827, Albany, GA 31701.

CUTLIFF, JOHN WILSON
Attorney (retired). **Personal:** Born Dec 2, 1923, Shreveport, LA; divorced; children: Jennifer C. **Educ:** So U, BA 1945; Lincoln U, LLB 1948; NY U, LLM 1961; Atlanta U, MSLS 1968. **Career:** Retired private practice, atty 1980-90; NC Central U, assoc law libr, assoc prof 1973-79; Media Serv & Fed City Coll, assoc dir, assoc prof 1968-73; Howard Sch of Law, assoc law libr 1965-67; SC State Coll Sch of Law, law libr 1948-65; Chester County Public Library, literacy coordinator, currently. **Orgs:** Mem Amer Bar Assn; Natl Bar Assn; Amer Assn of Law Libraries; SC Bar 1950; life mem NAACP; life mem Kappa Alpha Psi; mem Unitarian Universalist Assn; Ford Fellow, NYU 1959-61. **Home Addr:** 553 Flint St, #L4, Box 406, Chester, SC 29706-1861, (803)581-8808.

CUYJET, ALOYSIUS BAXTER
Physician. **Personal:** Born May 20, 1947, Jersey City, NJ; son of Barbara Baxter Cuyjet and Aloysius Cuyjet; married Beverly M Granger, Sep 15, 1990. **Educ:** Brandeis U, BA 1968; NY U, MD 1972. **Career:** Harlem Hosp Ctr, cardiology flw 1975-77, intern & resd 1972-75; Columbia Univ Coll of Physicians & Surgeons, asst instr 1975-77; United Hospitals Medical Ctr, dir adult critical care medicine, dir of medicine, currently. **Orgs:** Assn of Black Cardiologists; Amer Heart Assn; Society of Critical Care Medicine; Amer Coll of Cardiology. **Honors/Awds:** Fellow Amer Coll of Cardiology 1988; diplomate, American Board of Internal Medicine. **Business Addr:** Director of Medicine, United Hospitals Med Ctr, 15 South 9th St, Newark, NJ 07107.

CUYJET, CYNTHIA K.
Company executive. **Personal:** Born May 16, 1948, Philadelphia, PA; daughter of Esther King Cuyjet and C Jerome Cuyjet. **Educ:** Marymount Coll BA 1970; Jersey City State Coll, MA 1974; NYU. **Career:** Marymount Coll, Tarrytown, NY, admissions counselor 1970-71; Prudential Insurance Co, adult educ instr 1971-72; Jersey City St Coll, asst admission dir 1972-76; Selection & Placement Manager, Supermarkets Gen Corp, mgr 1976-77; Avon Products Inc, supr mgmt devel 1977, mgr, job opportunity, corporate mgr mgmt devel & training 1978-80, div sales mgr 1980-84; Coca-Cola USA, sr project mgr, mgr mgmt trng, 1984-87; Cuyjet Mgmt Consultants Inc, pres, 1987-. **Orgs:** Co-Chairperson, Women in Business Comm Atlanta Business League; mem Atlanta Womens Network; mem Amer Soc for Training/Develop; chair employment comm Coalition of 100 Black Women; exec bd mem Council of Concerned Black Executives 1976-80; exec bd mem NJ Assn for Sickle Cell Anemia; mem Black Merit Academy E St Louis IL; mem Black Executive Exchange Program Natl Urban League; mem, Amer Soc Training & Devel; mem, Atlanta Women's Network, consultant to Inroads/Atlanta, Inroads/Chicago; dir, mgmt training ctr, Kellogg Graduate School Business, Northwestern University; instructor, newspaper mgmt ctr, Northwestern Univ. **Honors/Awds:** Women in Business/Industry Award NCNW 1981; participant White House Conf Women in Work Force 1983; Service Award, Institute for Journalism Education, 1991.

CUYLER, MILTON (MILT)
Professional baseball player. **Personal:** Born Oct 7, 1968, Macon, GA. **Career:** Detroit Tigers, 1990-. **Business Addr:** Professional Baseball Player, c/o Detroit Tigers, 2121 Trumbull Ave, Detroit, MI 48216, (313)962-4000.

D

DABBS, HENRY ERVEN
Television executive, art director. **Personal:** Born Oct 15, 1932, Clover, VA; son of Gertrude Dabbs and Charles Dabbs; married Loretta D Young; children: Lisa DeLane. **Educ:** Pratt Inst, BFA 1955. **Career:** Berton Wink Inc, book designer 1958-62; USN John F Small Adv Agency, creative dir minority adv 1975-78; Henry Dabbs Prod Englishtown NJ, pres 1977; Cinema & Graphic Design Jersey City St Coll, instr 1977; wrote produced and directed "Joshua" a full length feature film shot on location in Charleston SC and Harlem NY 1979; Fitzgerald Sample NYC, art dir producer dancer 1963-. **Orgs:** Painted original 39 paintings of famous Afro-Amer in Amer history permanent collection Frederick Douglass Mus Smithsonian Inst Washington; mem NAACP; created History Fact Pack 1968; First Multi-Media, audio visual prog on Black American. **Honors/Awds:** Author "Afro-Amer History Highlights" 1968; screened "Joshua" at the Cannes Film Festival France along with Steven Spielberg's ET 1982; authored & published "Black Brass" Black generals & admirals in the Armed Forces of the US the first book of its kind ever published 1984; author Black History section NY Times; NAACP, Enhancing the Lives Of Others, Humanitarian Award, 1992. **Special Achievements:** Developed a comprehensive Black History Video program, 1992. **Military Serv:** AUS 1955-58.

DABNEY, DAVID HODGES
Psychiatrist, lobbyist. **Personal:** Born Aug 18, 1927, Washington, DC; divorced. **Educ:** Univ of PA, BA 1949; Howard Med Sch, MD 1955. **Career:** Mass Participation Lobbyists Assn, legal psychiatrist/registered lobbyist (Cong); Forensic Psychiatry Res Consultants, consultant; Harriet Tubman Projects, intl lobbyist, 1993-. **Orgs:** Mem Omega Psi Phi 1946-; expert witness in courts (DC & State, Fed & Military) 1957-; experience in mental homes & prisons since 1957; mem Amer Psychiatric Assn; AMA; Amer Correctional Assn; DC Medical Soc; Washington Psychiatric Soc; Medico-Chirurgical Soc; Natl Medical Assn; consultant Skidmore Owings & Merrill Chicago; pres Chance for a Child Inc; bd dir Tiber Island Condominium 1965-70; SW Comm Assy Health & Welfare Task Force 1965-70; mem Univ of Pennsylvania Alumni Fund-Raising & Secondary Educ Committees. **Honors/Awds:** Natl winner, Elks Oratorical Contest, "The Negro and the Constitution," 1943; author of publication voted Best Paper on Rehabilitation at APA Convention 1963; congressional candidate 1972, 1974; cited by judges of US Dist Ct of Appeals DC in landmark cases (criminal responsibility). **Home Addr:** 1237 Irving St NE, Washington, DC 20017.

DA BRAT
Rapper. **Personal:** Born in Chicago, IL. **Career:** Rapper, currently. **Special Achievements:** Albums include: Funkdafied; ANUTHATANTRUM; rapped with others, songs include: "Da Bomb," with group Kriss Kross; "Ladies Nite," with lil Kim, Missy Elliot and Left-Eye from TLC; appeared on "The Parent Hood;" and Full Court Press, film. **Business Addr:** Rapper, So So Def Recordings, c/o Artistic Control, 685 Lambert Dr NE, Atlanta, GA 30324, (404)888-9900.

DADE, MALCOLM G., JR.
Human resources executive. **Personal:** Born May 7, 1931, New Bedford, MA; son of Esther Clay Dade and Malcolm G Dade Sr; married Kitty L Wallingford; children: Sharon Daniels, Malcolm G III, Karen. **Educ:** Macalester Coll St Paul MN, attended; Wayne State Univ, BA Pol Sci; Wayne State Univ School of Social Work, grad studies; Columbia Univ, Exec Mgmt Prog. **Career:** The Detroit Edison Co, vice pres of human resources, 1989-, vice pres community & govt affairs, 1986-89, manager of local and state govt affairs, 1982-86; Sen Philip A Hart, special asst 1973; Coleman A Young, Mayor, campaign dir 1973, interim office 1973-74; Atty Gen Frank Kelley, State MI, admin asst 1971-73, senate campaign 1972; Off Sch Decentralization, asst decentralization coord 1970-71; Dem Party, dep chmn 1969-70; Dem State Central Com, staff dir 1968-70; Mayor's Com Human Resources Devel, 1968-70; Comm Children & Youth, 1963-67; Dept Pub Welfare, 1956-63. **Orgs:** Member, American Management Assn, 1989; board of directors, American Society of Employers; board of directors, Assn of Governing Boards of Universities and Colleges; member, Kappa Alpha Psi Fraternity; member, Booker T Washington Business Assn; member, Michigan State University Alumni Organization; member, NAACP; member, Society for Human Resource Management, 1989; member, Wayne State University Alumni Organization. **Honors/Awds:** Union of Black Episcopalians Award, 1989; Gold Key Award for Community Service, Greater Opportunities Industrialization Center of Metro Detroit; Wayne State University Alumni Award, 1988. **Military Serv:** USAF s/sgt 1951-55. **Business Addr:** Vice President, Detroit Edison Co, 2000 Second Ave, Detroit, MI 48226.

DAGGS, LEON, JR.
Automobile dealer. **Personal:** Born Feb 12, 1941, St Louis, MO; son of Dorothy Echols Daggs and Leon Daggs; married Saundra Stills Daggs, Apr 19, 1965; children: Christopher. **Educ:** Harris Teachers College, St Louis, MO, BA, 1964; St Louis University, St Louis, MO, MBA, 1969-71. **Career:** St Louis Board of Education, St Louis, MO, teacher, 1963-64; Procter-Gamble, St Louis, MO, sales, 1968-70; McDonnel Aircraft, St Louis, MO, mgr, 1970-71; Ford Motor Co, Dearborn, MI, supervisor, 1971-85; Hub City Ford-Mercury, Crestview, FL, president, 1986-; Walton County Ford-Mercury, Defuniak Springs, FL, president, 1996. **Orgs:** Member, Kappa Alpha Psi Fratrnity, 1961-; board member, Private Industry Council, 1986-; board member, Board of Directors NAACP, 1973-77; director, Chamber of Commerce, Crestview, 1986-; charter member, Crestview Rotary Club, 1988-; special deputy, Okaloosa City Sheriff Dept, 1988-; board of directors, Ford Lincoln-Mercury Minority Dealers Assn, 1994-. **Honors/Awds:** Man of the Year, Kappa Alpha Psi, 1988. **Military Serv:** US Navy, Lt Jg, 1964-68; Naval Flight Officer, 1964. **Business Addr:** President, Hub City Ford Mercury, Inc., PO Box 1118, 4060 S Ferdon Blvd, Crestview, FL 32536.

DAGGS, LEROY W.
Attorney. **Personal:** Born Aug 9, 1924, St Louis; married Harriet; children: LeRoy, III, Leslie. **Educ:** Univ MI, AB 1947; Univ Detroit, LLB 1952. **Career:** Detroit, int rev agt 1950-55; Daggs Ins Agy, owner 1955-68; pract atty Detroit 1953-. **Orgs:** Mem State Bar Of MI 1953-; Am Bar Assn 1953-; Detroit Bar Assn 1955-; Wolverine Bar Assn 1955-, dir 1947 & 75; mem Half Million Dollar Round Table (NIA) 1957; mem student legis Univ MI 1946 & 47; life mem Alpha Phi Alpha Frat; life mem NAACP. **Honors/Awds:** Outstanding Athlete Univ MI 1946-47; Honor Man Company US Navy 1943; outstanding contrb support of bowling basketball & baseball teams Brewster Cntr 1960-63; Univ MI Track Team 1946-47. **Military Serv:** USN 1c 1942-45. **Business Addr:** 1435 Randolph Center, Ste 202, Detroit, MI 48226.

DAILEY, QUINTIN
Professional basketball player. **Personal:** Born Jan 22, 1961, Baltimore, MD. **Educ:** San Francisco, 1981. **Career:** Chicago Bulls, 1982-86, Los Angeles Clippers, 1987-89, Seattle SuperSonics, 1990-. **Honors/Awds:** Named mem NBA First Team All-Rookie Squad 1982-83; owned best rookie scoring mark in 1978-79.

DAILEY, THELMA
Association executive. **Personal:** Born in Baltimore; divorced. **Educ:** BA, AAS. **Career:** Trade Union Women of African Heritage Inc, pres, founder. **Orgs:** Bd mem NCNW; mem Women's Forum Inc; coord Bronx Chap United Nations Assn; Multi-Ethnic Woman Workshop at Fashion Inst Tech; publs The Ethnic Woman Inc; coord Inst of Polit Educ of Black Women; mem IWY Tribune. **Business Addr:** 13 Astor Pl, New York, NY 10003.

DAIS, LARRY (LARRY DEAS)
Education administrator. **Personal:** Born Nov 3, 1945, Columbia, SC; son of Mamie Jeffcoat Dais and Wade Dais; married Olga Carter; children: Landon, Larik. **Educ:** Baruch Coll, BS 1974; Columbia Univ Graduate School of Business, MS 1976; Cornell NYSSILR, and Hofstra Univ School of Law, Certificate, 1986. **Career:** Grumman Engineering, admin 1964-68; State Univ of Farmingdale, admin 1968; Leadership Inst Hofstra Univ, asst dir 1968-69; Columbia Coll, Columbia Univ, dir 1969-81; Columbia Univ, asst vice pres govt relations & dir of community affairs, 1981-. **Orgs:** Pres, Natl Council of Educational Opportunity Progs 1982-84; senior vp, NY Urban League; chairman, board of directors, Harlem YMCA; chairman of education, 100 Black Men; member, American Arbitration Assn; president, council of board, chairperson, National Urban League. **Honors/Awds:** Man of the Year Award, YMCA of Greater NY; Educational Service Award, Marquette Univ; President's Award, Natl Council of Educ Assns; Award of Excellence, Assn for Equality & Excellence in Education; Outstanding Leadership Award, The Leadership Institute, Hofstra University. **Military Serv:** US Army, Sgt, 1960-63. **Business Addr:** Asst Vice Pres of Govt Relations, Columbia University, 301 Lowe Library, 116th St and Broadway, New York, NY 10027.

DALE, CLAMMA CHURITA
Opera singer. **Personal:** Born Jul 4, 1953, Chester, PA; daughter of Clara Robinson Dale and Granvaul Dale; married Terry C Shirk, Dec 19, 1981 (died 1987). **Educ:** Settlement Mus Sch Phila; studied with Alice Howland/Hans Heinz/Corneilius Reed; The Juilliard School, New York, NY, Bachelors degree, Masters degree. **Career:** Houston Opera Co, singer 1976; NY City Opera Co, 1975; performed with Bronx Opera Co/ Brooklyn Opera Theatre/Met Opera's Mini-Met; Houston Grand Opera Co, revival 1976-77; Manhattan Theatre Club, completed successful engagement singing popular works by Ellington/Rodgers & Hart/others 1977; appeared in premiere of Leonard Bernstein's Am Song Cycle "Songfest" 1977; clarinet player; performed with the Paris Opera, Berlin Opera, the New York City Opera and the Opera Company of Philadelphia; DAL Productions Ltd, pres, 1989-. **Honors/Awds:** Cue Golden Apple as Best Broadway Actress for role of Bess in "Porgy & Bess" 1976; recipient 2 Naumburg Awards; recitals at Avery Fischer Hall & Lincoln Cntr. **Business Addr:** President, DAL Productions, Ltd, Ansonia Station, PO Box 898, New York, NY 10023.

DALE, LOUIS
Educator, educational administrator. **Personal:** Born Nov 24, 1935, Birmingham, AL; son of Anne Mae Boykins Dale and Finley Dale; married Gladiola Watts Dale; children: Louis Jr, Valerie Louise, Annice Jeanette, Jonathan David. **Educ:** Miles College, Birmingham, AL, BS, 1960; Atlanta University, Atlanta, GA, MS, 1964; University of Alabama, Tuscaloosa, AL, PhD, 1973. **Career:** Atlanta University, Atlanta, GA, instructor, 1964-66; Miles College, Birmingham, AL, acting dean, 1969-73; University of Alabama at Birmingham, Birmingham, AL, professor, 1974-88, professor, associate dean, 1988-, associate vice president, Academic Affairs, 1991-. **Orgs:** Member, American Mathematical Society, 1975-; president, 1984-88, member, 1978-88, Birmingham Board of Education. **Honors/Awds:** Review, National Science Foundation, 1988-. **Military Serv:** US Army, Corporal, 1954-57. **Home Addr:** 663 Dublin Ave, Birmingham, AL 35212. **Business Addr:** Associate Vice Pres, Academic Affairs, University of Alabama at Birmingham, 901 S 15th St, Room 242, UAB Station, Birmingham, AL 35294.

DALE, ROBERT J.
Advertising agency owner. **Personal:** Born May 2, 1943, Chicago, IL; son of Jessie M Dale and Charles McDearmon; married Shirley J White, Jul 8, 1989; children: Kondo, Yusef, Kareem. **Educ:** Arizona State Univ, Tempe AZ, BS Business, 1971; Stanford Univ, Stanford CA, MBA Business/Mktg, 1973. **Career:** Kaiser Broadcasting, Chicago IL, account exec, 1973-74; Field Spot Television Sales, Chicago IL, natl account exec, 1974-75; R J Dale & Assoc, Chicago IL, consultant, 1976-78; Small Business Admin, Chicago IL, mgmt consultant, 1978-79; Chicago State Univ, Chicago IL, asst prof, 1979-84; R J Dale Advertising, Chicago IL, pres, CEO, 1979-. **Orgs:** Mem, Amer Mktg Assn, 1977-, PUSH Intl Trade Bureau, 1984-, Natl Black United Front-Chicago, 1984-, Amer Assn of Advertising Agencies, 1986-; co-chair, Chicago State Univ Coll of Business Hall of Fame Bd, 1987-; advisory bd mem, Black Public Relations Soc-Chicago, 1988-; bd mem, March of Dimes Birth Defects Found, 1989-; president, Institute of Positive Education, 1989; chair, Black Ensemble Theatre Corp., 1990. **Honors/Awds:** Outstanding Black Businessman Award, Natl Black United Front, 1986; Pinnacle Award, Being Single Magazine, 1989. **Military Serv:** US Air Force, airman 1st class, 1962-66. **Business Addr:** President & Chief Executive Officer, R J Dale Advertising Inc, 500 N Michigan Ave, Suite 2204, Chicago, IL 60611.

DALE, VIRGINIA MARIE
Administrator, educator. **Personal:** Born Aug 8, 1925, Haskell, OK; married Luther William Dale; children: Kenneth Ray Gilmore, Jr, Pamela Kay (McClain), Anita Ray (Harris), Joey Luther Dale. **Educ:** KS State U, BS 1967; KS State U, San Jose State, KC MO U, Grad study. **Career:** Dale's Acad, admin, teacher; teacher in public schools for over 20 yrs; social worker. **Orgs:** Order of Eastern Star; Zeta Phi Beta; Black Econ Union; avd bd Penn Valleycoll; Am Fed of Tchrs; United Trade Group; mem West Paseo Christian Ch; orgnr Bus & Prof Women's Assn of Gr KC; San Mateo Chap Jack & Jill. **Honors/Awds:** Elected Outstanding Woman of Year (Small Bus). **Business Addr:** 7304 Cleveland, Kansas City, MO.

DALE, WALTER R.
Attorney, accountant, educator. **Personal:** Born Dec 23, 1944, Chicago, IL; divorced. **Educ:** University of Illinois, BS, finance, 1966; Governors State University, MBA, 1981; IIT Chicago Kent Law School, JD, 1985; John Marshall Law School, LLM, tax, 1988. **Career:** Small Business Administration, loan servicing officer, 1971-72; Chicago City Bank & Trust Co, commercial loan officer, 1972-75; Jackson Park Hospital, internal auditor and patient accounts manager, 1980-81; Chicago State University, professor of accounting and finance, 1987-; United States Department of the Treasury, Internal Revenue Service, revenue agent, field auditor, tax law researcher, 1981-85; Caldwell & Hubbard, tax attorney, 1985-86; Brown & Porter, entertainment, tax and corporate lawyer, currently. **Orgs:** Alpha Phi Alpha; Chicago Black Attorneys in Sports & Entertainment, president; Black Entertainment & Sports Lawyers Association; National Academy of Recording Arts & Sciences. **Special Achievements:** "A New Approach to Federal Taxation," Midwest Accounting Society, March 1993. **Military Serv:** USAF, capt, 1966-70. **Business Phone:** (312)427-2383.

DALEY, GUILBERT ALFRED
Educator. **Personal:** Born Dec 31, 1923, Washington, DC; married Thelma Thomas. **Educ:** Catholic Univ of Amer, BA 1949, MA 1952; Univ of NC, LDA 1968; So IL Univ, PhD 1978. **Career:** Shaw Univ, Raleigh NC, asst prof 1953-62; NC High School Drama Assoc, exec dir 1953-62; Intercollegiate Drama Assoc, exec dir 1956-60; IDA, pres 1960-62; The Crescent, natl editor 1978-79, 1981-; Coppin State Coll, prof & coord speech/ theatre 1962-. **Orgs:** Mem AAUP; Amer Theatre Assn; Coll Language Assn; Speech Assn of Amer; mem treas Gr Baltimore Arts Council 1966-69, pres 1969-71; pres, immediate past natl dir of educ, Distinguished Service Chap, Phi Beta Sigma; vice pres Baltimore Pan-Hellenic Council; pres Zeta Sigma Chap Phi Beta Sigma Frat Inc; pres Wm T Dorsey Educ Loan Fund 1984; founder, advisor, Delta, Delta Chap, Phi Beta Sigma Frat, Coppin State Coll, Baltimore MD; 100 Black Men of MD; pres, Baltimore Chap, Pan Hellenic Council; editor, The Crescent, 8 years; vp, African Amer Theatre, 1993. **Honors/Awds:** Carolina Playmakers Scholarship 1960; Teaching Fellow SIU Carbondale. **Military Serv:** AAF 1944-46. **Business Addr:** Coordinator Speech Theatre, Coppin State College, 2500 W North Ave, Baltimore, MD 21216.

DALEY, THELMA THOMAS
Educator. **Personal:** Born Jun 17, Annapolis; married Guilbert A. **Educ:** Bowie St Coll, BS; NY U, MA. **Career:** Raleigh & Baltimore County Bd of Educ, prof, counselor; NC Central, Western MD Coll, Univ of WI, Harvard Univ, visiting instructor. **Orgs:** Nat pres Am Sch Counselor Assn 1971-72; natl treas Delta Sigma Theat 1963-67, natl vice pres 1971-75; pres Am Personnel & Guidance Assn 1975-76; mem NAACP; Black Adoption Prog 1968-73; Nat Proj Chrwmn 1967-71. **Honors/ Awds:** MD Personnel & Guidance Achievemt Award 1972; Life Mem Award NAACP 1973; appointed Commn Educ Panel Scholars Career Educ 1972; natl pres Delta Sigma 1975-77. **Business Addr:** Bd Educ, Towson, MD 21204.

DALFERES, EDWARD R., JR.
Medical researcher, educator. **Personal:** Born Nov 4, 1931, New Orleans, LA; son of Ray Dalferes and Edward Dalferes Sr; married Anita Y Bush; children: Edward Rene, Anthony Renard. **Educ:** Xavier Univ, BS 1956. **Career:** St John Parish School Bd, science teacher 1956-57; Louisiana State Univ School of Medicine, med rsch 1957-75, instructor; Tulane Univ Medical Center, instructor, currently. **Orgs:** Mem LA Heart Assn; Amer Assn for Advancement of Sci; So Connective Tissue Soc; Soc of Complex Carbohydrates; in collaboration with others author of numerous publs. **Military Serv:** AUS Med Corps 1950-52. **Business Addr:** Instructor, Tulane Univ Medical Center, 1430 Tulane Ave, New Orleans, LA 70112.

DALLEY, GEORGE ALBERT
Attorney. **Personal:** Born Aug 25, 1941, Havana, Cuba; son of Constance Joyce Dalley and Cleveland Ernest Dalley; married Pearl Elizabeth Love, Aug 1, 1970; children: Jason Christopher, Benjamin Christian. **Educ:** Columbus Coll, AB 1963; Columbua Univ School of Law, JD 1966; Columbia Univ Grad School & Business, MBA 1966. **Career:** Metropolition Appl Res Cntr, assis to the pres 1962-69; Stroock & Stroock & Lavan, assoc cousnel 1970-71; US House of Representatives Comm on the Judiciary, assist counsel 1971-72; Congressman Charles Rangel, admin asst 1973-76; US Dept of State, deputy asst sec of state 1977-79; US Civil Aero Bd, mem 1980-82; Mondale for Pres, deputy camp mgr 1983-84; Cong Charles Rangel, coun and staff dir 1985-1989; senior vice pres Neill and Company Inc, 1989-93; Neill and Shaw, partner, 1989-93; Holland & Knight, partner, 1993-. **Orgs:** Adjunct prof Am Univ Schl of Law 1981-; avat human rights Am Bar Assoc; Intl law comm Nat'l Bar Assoc Fed Bar Assoc 1976-; mem Transafrica, NAACP, Urban League 1974-; Crestwood Comm Assn 1986-; mem bd of dir Africare, Transafrica DC Support Group; consultant, United Nations Devel Program 1989-; American Bar Association; American Bar Foundation; DC Judicial Nominating Commission. **Honors/Awds:** Published art Federal Drug Abuse Enforcement 1974; speeches Dem Corp Select Process 1976; various Mags Articles 1977-. **Home Addr:** 1706 Crestwood Dr, NW, Washington, DC 20011, (202)722-5184. **Business Addr:** Partner, Holland & Knight, 2100 Pennsylvania Ave, NW, Ste 400, Washington, DC 20036, (202)955-3000.

DALTON, RAYMOND ANDREW
Educational administrator, artist. **Personal:** Born Jan 15, 1942, Chicago, IL; son of Dorothy Mitchell Hunter and Ernest Mitchell; married Alfonsa Vicente (divorced); children: Carlos, Julio, Solange. **Educ:** IL State Univ, BS 1964, MS 1966; Univ of San Francisco, doctoral study, 1978; Purdue Univ, West Lafayette, IN, PhD, 1990. **Career:** Antelope Valley High School, instructor 1965-67; Lake Hughes, instructor 1967; Drew Jr High School, instructor 1967-68; Univ of IL, asst dean, asst prof 1971-84; Cornell Univ, Ithaca, NY, senior lecturer of art, 1992-, director of minority educational affairs, 1989-. **Orgs:** Advsr Black Student Organ of Archt & Art 1972-75; co-clrm Art Comm 1972; consul Park Forest Pub Sch Black Art Workshop 1973; co-advsr Orgn of Intl Stud 1975; mem Prof Orgn Academic Affairs Admin Midwest; mem Natl Conf of Artists, Union of Black Artists, Coll Art Assn, Natl Art Educ Assn, Natl Conf of Art Admin; mem Assn of Collegiate Registrars & Counselors; National Organization of Minority Architects; Grad Asstshp IL State Univ 1964-65, Purdue Univ 1984-85; sab lv Univ of Puerto Rico 1977; sab lv Nigeria 1982; member, Gamma Delta Iota Fraternity, 1986-; member, Omicron Delta Kappa Society, 1989-; member, Purdue Circle, 1989-. **Honors/ Awds:** Edwards Medal IL State Speech Contest 1965; Purdue Fellowship 1987-89. **Business Addr:** Director, Minority Educational Affairs, College of Architecture, Art & Planning, Cornell University, B-1 Sibley Dome West, Ithaca, NY 14853.

DALY, FREDERICA Y.
Psychologist (retired). **Personal:** Born Feb 14, 1925, Washington, DC; daughter of Geneva A Sharper Young (deceased) and Samuel P Young (deceased); married Michael E, Mar 15, 1972. **Educ:** Howard U, BS 1947, MS 1949; Cornell Univ PhD 1956. **Career:** Howard U, Instr 1950; Cornell U, teachg asst 1953-55; George Jr Republic, clincal psychology 1955-72; SUNY Empire State Coll, assoc prof 1972-80; UNM Mental Hlth Prog, clinical Psychology 1980-81; Alcohol Prog VA Med Ctr, Coord 1981-88. **Orgs:** Gov's task force mem State of NM 1984; board member Family Serv Agency 1958-60; New Mexico Bead Society; American Psychological Assn; Institute of Noetic Sciences; Society of Layerists in Multi-media. **Honors/Awds:** Grant Fellowship Cornell Univ 1954-55; Cora Smith Fellowship Cornell Univ 1953-54; Perspectives on Native American Women's Racism & Sexism Experiences, paper presented at the American Association for the Advancement of Science, 1990; Poetry published & one poem to be published in a Russian Journal; Feminist Press, CUNY, Challenging Racism & Sexism. **Home Addr:** 526 Hermosa NE, Albuquerque, NM 87108.

DALY, MARIE MAYNARD
Biochemist (retired). **Personal:** Born Apr 16, 1921, New York, NY; daughter of Helen Page Daly and Ivan C Daly; married Vincent Clark, Mar 18, 1961. **Educ:** Queens Coll, BS 1942; NY U, MS 1943; Columbia U, PhD 1947. **Career:** Albert Einstein Coll of Medicine, Yeshiva Univ, assoc prof, 1971-86, asst prof 1960-71; Columbia Univ, assoc 1955-59; The Rockefeller Inst, asst 1951-55, vis invst 1948-51; Howard Univ, instr 1947-78; Queens Coll, fellow, tutor 1942-44; fellow Am Cancer Soc 1948-51; est investigator Am Heart Assn 1958-63; career scientist Health Rsrch Council of NY 1962-72. **Orgs:** Am Chem Soc; fellow AAAS; mem bd of govs NY Acad of Sci 1974-76; Harvey Soc; Am Soc of Biol Chemists; fellow Council on Arteriosclerosis, Am Heart Assn; NAACP; Nat Assn of Negro Bus & Prof Women. **Honors/Awds:** Phi Beta Kappa, Alumni Membership Sigma of New York Queens College, 1989. **Home Addr:** 4 Copeces Lane, PO Box 601, East Hampton, NY 11937.

DALY, RONALD EDWIN
Printing company executive. **Personal:** Born Feb 23, 1947, Chicago, IL; son of Ella McCreary Brown and Edwin W Daly; married Dolores, Jul 28, 1978; children: Dawn, Ronald Jr, Erin. **Educ:** Governors State Univ, University Park IL, BA Business Admin, 1977; Loyola Univ, Chicago IL, MBA Finance, 1980. **Career:** R R Donnelley & Sons, Chicago IL, supvr, 1972-79, mgr, 1980-84, Cherry Hill NJ, gen mgr, 1984-87, Lancaster PA, gen mgr, 1987-88, Chicago IL, div dir, 1988-; RR Donnelley Norwest Inc, sr vp, Portland, OR, 1991-94; Americas Global Software Services, sr vp of operations, beginning, 1994; Telecommunications Business Unit, president, 1995. **Orgs:** Chicago Symphony, trustee; Elliott Donnelley Youth Center, bd mem; Oregon Independent Colleges Foundation Board; Junior Achievement Board, Executive Committee; Environmental Law and Policy Ctr, bd mem; Leadership Greater Chicago, bd mem. **Honors/Awds:** Black Achiever, YMCA, 1977.

DAMES, KATHY W.
Educational administrator. **Personal:** Born Jan 22, 1963, Chicago, IL; daughter of Katie C Williams and Sellers Williams Jr. **Educ:** Western Illinois University, BA, 1984, MA, 1991. **Career:** Illinois State Comptrollers Office, assistant legislative liaison, 1986-88, chief legislative liaison, 1988-90; Board of Governors Universities, lobbyist, 1990-; Chicago State Univ, dir of alumni affairs, 1993-95; Harold Washington Coll, asst to the pres, beginning 1995; Roosevelt Univ, dir of alumni development, currently. **Orgs:** Chicago Women in Government; Illinois Women in Government; Illinois Women Administrators; Women's Legislative Network; Assn of Black Women in Higher Education Inc; Illinois Committee on Black Concerns in Higher Education; Delta Sigma Theta Inc. **Honors/Awds:** Dollars & Sense Magazine, Best & Brightest Business and Professional Women, 1991. **Business Addr:** Director of Alumni Development, Roosevelt University, 430 S Michigan, Chicago, IL 60601, (312)341-3623.

DAMES, SABRINA A. (SABRINA DAMES CRUTCHFIELD)
Broadcast journalist. **Personal:** Born Nov 9, 1957, Washington, DC; daughter of Anita Mae Wilson Dames and Harold Alexander Dames, Sr; married Curtis A Crutchfield, Jun 4, 1988. **Educ:** Howard University, Washington, DC, BA, 1979; Columbia University, New York, NY, MS, 1981. **Career:** WTOP Radio, Washington, DC, news writer, 1981-84; CBS News Nightwatch, Washington, DC, news writer, 1984-85; WJLA-TV, Washington, DC, news writer, 1984-86; Black Entertainment TV, Washington, DC, reporter, producer, 1986-. **Orgs:** National Association Black Journalists, currently; AFTRA, 1981-84; Alpha Kappa Alpha Sorority, 1983-; National Television and Radio Correspondents Association, 1986-. **Honors/Awds:** Cable Ace Award Nominee, News Special "Beyond The End," 1995. **Business Addr:** Reporter/Producer, News Dept, Black Entertainment Television, 1899 9th St NE, Washington, DC 20018.

DAMPER, RONALD EUGENE
Tea manufacturing company executive. **Personal:** Born Sep 18, 1946, Birmingham, AL; son of Ruby Damper and Willie Damper; married Patricia Dianne Ward, Jun 7, 1970; children: Ronald Sean, Shevonn Denise. **Educ:** Knoxville College, BS, matematics, 1967; New York University, 1967-70; University of Connecticut at Bridgeport, MBA, 1977. **Career:** GEEC, marketing manager, 1973-77; Greyhound Leasing, district manager, 1977-79; Bankers Trust, vice pres, 1979-81; Citicorp, vice pres, 1981-84; Visions Entertainment, Blockbuster Video, principal, 1990-; Damron Corp., president, chief executive officer, 1985-. **Orgs:** McDonald's Minority Supplier Council, chairman, 1993-; Montay College, chairman, board of trustees, 1990-; Demico Youth Services, board of directors, 1988-; No Dope Express, board of directors, 1990-; Illinois Department of Community Affairs, board member, 1990-; Community Service Development Committee, board member, 1989-93; Tea Association of the US, 1989-; Alliance of Business Leaders and Entrepreneurs, 1992-. **Honors/Awds:** Industrial Council of NW Chicago, Business Person of the Year, 1990; Ernst & Young, Entrepreneur of the Year, finalist, 1990; Boy Scouts of America, Leadership Member, 1992. **Military Serv:** US Air Force Reserves, ssgt, 1968-74. **Business Addr:** President, CEO, Damron Corp., 4433 W Ohio St, Chicago, IL 60624, (312)826-6000.

DAMPIER, ERICK TREVEZ
Professional basketball player. **Personal:** Born Jul 14, 1974, Jackson, MS. **Educ:** Mississippi State. **Career:** Indiana Pacers, center, 1996-97; Golden State Warriors, 1997-. **Special Achievements:** NBA Draft, First round pick, #10, 1996. **Business Addr:** Professional Basketball Player, Golden State Warriors, 1001 Broadway, Oakland, CA 94607, (510)986-2200.

DANCE, DARYL CUMBER
Educator. **Personal:** Born Jan 17, 1938, Richmond, VA; daughter of Veronica Bell Cumber and Allen W Cumber; married Warren C Dance; children: Warren C Jr, Allen C, Daryl Lynn. **Educ:** VA State Coll, AB 1957, MA 1963; Univ of VA, PhD 1971. **Career:** VA State Coll, asst prof of English 1962-72; VA Commonwealth Univ, asst prof of English 1972-78, assoc prof of English 1978-85; prof of English 1985-92; editorial advisor, Journal of West Indian Literature 1986-; University of California, Santa Barbara, visiting professor of African-American studies, 1986-87; University of Richmond, professor English dept, 1992-. **Orgs:** Danforth Assoc 1964-; adv editor Black Amer Lit Forum 1978-. **Honors/Awds:** Author "Shuckin' & Jivin', Folklore from Contemporary Black Americans" 1978; various fellowships & grants; Folklore for Contemporary Jamaicans 1985; Fifty Caribbean Writers 1986; Long Gone The Mecklenburg Six & The Theme of Escape in Black Literature, 1987; "New World Adams: Conversations with West Indian Writers," 1992; Honey, Hush! An Anthology of African American Women's Humor, 1998. **Business Addr:** Prof of English, University of Richmond, Richmond, VA 23173.

DANCY, WILLIAM F.
Clergyman. **Personal:** Born Nov 6, 1924, Greenville, MS; son of Belle Dancey and William Dancey; married Darnell E Pruitt; children: Antonia M, William, Winnona, Darryl, Kimberly. **Educ:** Roosevelt U; Central Bapt Sem; Robert Terrell Law Sch. **Career:** Allen Chapel, minister, dist supt; Sr Citizens Home, admin; Mt Life, sales rep & election commr; St Peters AME, St Louis, MO, minister; First AME Church, Kansas City KS, pastor, currently. **Orgs:** 3rd Degree Mason; life mem NAACP; real estate broker Chmn Oak Pk Soc Serv Orgn Hon Doctorate Edward Waters Coll, AME Sem. **Military Serv:** USN store keeper 1943-45.

DANDRIDGE, BOB
Professional basketball player (retired). **Personal:** Born Nov 15, 1947, Richmond, VA; married Barbara. **Educ:** Norfolk State, 1969. **Career:** Milwaukee Bucks, 1969-77, 1982, Washington Bullets, 1977-81. **Honors/Awds:** 29th on All-Time Scoring List with 15,248 points; NBA All Star Team 1973, 1975, 1976 & 1979.

DANDRIDGE, RITA BERNICE
Educator. **Personal:** Born in Richmond, VA. **Educ:** VA Union Univ, BA 1961; Howard Univ, MA 1963, PhD 1970; National Endowment for the Humanities Study Grant, 1995. **Career:** Morgan State U, asst prof English 1964-71; Univ of Toledo, asst prof English 1971-74; Norfolk State U, prof English 1974-. **Orgs:** Subscriber Modern Language Assn, Coll Language Assn, Multi-ethnic Lit of US African American Review; mem Natl Women's Studies Assn, Modern Lang Assn; Coll Language Assn. **Honors/Awds:** Selected articles, "But Some of Us Are Brave," Eds Gloria T Hull & Others, Old Westbury, NY, The Feminist Press, 1982; "Louise Meriwether," Dictionary of Literary Biography, Afro-Am Fiction Writers after 1955, Eds Thadious Davis & Trudier Harris, Detroit, Gale Research Co 1984 Vol 33, Pp 182-186; "Josephine Joyce Turpin, Richmond Writer," The Richmond Quarterly 9 Fall 1986 11-13; book "Ann Allen Shockley, An Annotated Primary and Secondary Bibliography," 1987 Greenwood Press Westport CT; book, Black Women's Blues, A Literary Anthology (1934-1988), 1992, GK Hall New York; "Debunking the Beauty Myth" in Terry McMillan's "Waiting to Exhale," Language, Rhythm and Sound, eds Joseph K Adjorpe and Adrienne R Andrews, Univ of Pittsburgh Press, 1997. **Business Addr:** English Professor, Norfolk State Univ, 2401 Corprew Ave, Norfolk, VA 23504.

DANDY, CLARENCE L.
Clergyman, business executive. **Personal:** Born Jan 7, 1939, St Petersburg; married Luagussie; children: Cynthia, Louis, Anthony, Jackie, Korbett. **Educ:** Full Gospel Minister Intl of Dallas, DD; FL A&M U, 1959. **Career:** United Full Gospel Temple (3 Temples in NC), founder, pres; The Prayer Tower Raleigh, NC, dir. **Orgs:** Chmn bd dir Rev C Dandy Evangelistic Assn Raleigh. **Honors/Awds:** Recipient 1st Prize Trophy, Evangelist of the Year, by United Full Gospel Temple 1974. **Military Serv:** AUS pfc 1956. **Business Addr:** 417 S Person St, Raleigh, NC.

DANDY, ROSCOE GREER
Federal official, educator. **Personal:** Born Dec 20, 1946, Los Angeles, CA; son of Doris L Edwards Dandy and Roscoe Conkling Dandy; married. **Educ:** California State Univ, BA 1970; Univ Southern California, MSW 1973; Univ of Pittsburgh, MPH 1974, MPA 1975, DrPH 1981; Harvard Univ, certificate 1981; Univ of Illinois, Urbana, IL, 1965-68; LaSalle Extension Univ, Chicago, IL, 1966-68. **Career:** California State Youth Authority, youth counselor 1971; Colorado State Dept of Health, public health intern, 1974; Green Engineering Corp, health planning intern, 1975; Univ of Pittsburgh, instructor 1977-80; Kane Hospital, admin health intern, 1979; US Public Health Serv, lt commander, assoc dir out-patient clinic 1980-81; Central Michigan Univ, instructor 1981-; Veterans Administration Hospital, asst chief trainee, 1981; Veterans Administration, asst chief medical admin 1983-85, social worker 1985-93; US Public Health Svc, public health analyst, 1993-; Columbia Institute of Psychotherapy, psychotherapist, 1989-91; Columbia Pacific Univ, instructor, 1990; Nova Univ, instructor, 1991. **Orgs:** Consultant Jackson State Univ, Jackson, MS, 1977; mem Southern Christian Leadership Conf 1973-; mem, NAACP, 1987-; mem, Amer Public Health Assn, 1987-; Joint Center for Political Studies, 1986-; mem, Brookings Inst, 1985; mem, Federation of Amer Scientists, 1988-. **Honors/Awds:** Fellow Dr Martin Luther King Jr, Woodrow Wilson Foundation Princeton Univ 1971-73; Outstanding Unit Citation US Public Health Serv Scientist 1981; author, Board and Care Homes in Los Angeles County, 1976; International Directory of Distinguished Leadership Award, 1989, Man of the Year, 1990, 1993, American Biographical Institute, Inc. **Military Serv:** USAF sgt 1965-68; USMC Reserves sgt 1 yr; Air Force/Vietnam Era Veteran Award. **Business Addr:** Public Health Analyst, US Public Health Service, 5600 Fisher Lane, Rockville, MD 20852.

D'ANGELO
Vocalist. **Personal:** chilDren: one. **Career:** Vocalist, currently. **Special Achievements:** Album: Brown Sugar, 1996.

DANIEL, ALFRED IRWIN
Finance company executive. **Personal:** Born Aug 7, 1934, Plainfield, NJ; son of Emilie B Daniel and Leonard I Daniel; married Patricia A Daniel, 1993. **Educ:** Albright Coll, BS Biology/Chem 1957; Seton Hall Univ MBA Marketing/Industrial Relations 1972. **Career:** CIBA/Geigy Pharmaceuticals, sr pharmacologist 1957-69; Ortho Pharmaceuticals, rsch info super 1969-75; ER Squibb, clinical info scientist 1975-77; Stuart Pharmaceuticals Div ICI Americas, invest material coord 1977-88; Pharmaceutical Consultant, Daniel Associates, 1988-94; IDS Financial Services Inc, financial planner, 1989-94; Nations Securities, 1994-95; CPI Financial Services Inc, currently. **Orgs:** Bd Plainfield YMCA 1969-74; bd Plainfield Area United Way 1974; bd Village 2 Civic Assoc 1974-77; bd mem Northeast Area Partners 1979-85; bd mem Christina School Dist 1981-86; chair 1984-85, commissioner 1979-94, DE Human Relations Comm; Montgomery Meadows, bd or dirs, 1993-94. **Military Serv:** AUS sp4 1957-65. **Home Addr:** 1314 Asylum Ave, Hartford, CT 06105.

DANIEL, COLENE YVONNE
Healthcare administrator. **Personal:** Born Apr 23, 1954, Cincinnati, OH; divorced. **Educ:** University of Cincinnati, BS, 1977; Texas Woman's University, 1978-80; Health Care Administration Residency, 1979; Johns Hopkins School of Hygiene & Public Health, Masters of Public Health, and Health Policy, 1996. **Career:** Veterans Administration Medical Ctr, health systems specialist, 1980-82; American Medical Intl Inc, assistant hospital dir, 1982-86, mgt assoc, 1986-87; The University of Chicago Hospitals, assoc dir, 1987-91; John Hopkins Health System, vice pres of corporate and community services, 1991-. **Orgs:** Healthcare Forum; Healthcare Forum Journal; American College of Healthcare Executives; Johns Hopkins Medical Services Corp, bd of trustees, 1995-97; John Hopkins Health System, Dome Circle Associate, 1995-97; Johns Hospkins Medicine/Parking, 1996-98; College of Notre Dame, bd of trustees, 1993-99; Health Educational Resource Organization, bd of trustees, 1996-98; The Historic East Baltimore Community Action Coaltion, Inc, bd of trustees, 1994-98; The Links, Inc, Harbor City Chap, 1997-2000; African-American Committee of the Walters Art Gallery, 1994-97; PULSE Community Program, bd advisor for operations, 1992-96. **Honors/Awds:** Maryland House of Delegates Citation for Excellence in Service, 1996; Maryland's Top 100 Women, Finalist, and Maryland's Leading Women Executives, 1996; Delaware House of Delegates Citation for Excellence in Service, 1996; Winner of Healthcare Forum's Emerging Leaders in Healthcare Award, 1995; National Association of Health Services Executives, Administrator of the Year-Midwest, 1993; Leadership Maryland Fellowship Awarded by the Governor, 1992; numerous others. **Special Achievements:** Healthcare Forum, "Managing Organizational Transition," 1996; American College of Healthcare Executives, "Community-Based Primary Care, Assessment and Program," 1995; National Association of Health Services Executives, "The Role of Total Quality Mgt in Healthcare Reform," 1993. **Home Addr:** 9 E Lake Ave, Baltimore, MD 21212. **Business Addr:** Vice President, Corporate and Community Services, Johns Hopkins Hospital and Health System, 600 N Wolfe St, Admin 312, Baltimore, MD 21287-1812, (410)955-8515.

DANIEL, DAVID L.
Social worker, welfare administrator (retired). **Personal:** Born Jan 2, 1906, Columbia, TN; son of Mahalah Loyd Daniel (deceased) and David Daniel (deceased); married Mary Beatrice Evins Daniel, Aug 4, 1935. **Educ:** Fisk Univ, BA Chem 1928; Univ of Chicago, MA 1954, additional courses in Social Serv Admin 1955-56. **Career:** Licensed social worker; Cook County Bureau of Public Welfare and Cook County Dept of Public Aid, 1933-69, casework supr, asst district super, asst dir public assistance division, dir of services programs, dept dir, 1969-74; IL Dept of Public Aid, asst dir 1974-83. **Orgs:** Mem Natl Assn of Social Workers; Academy of Certified Social Workers; Amer Public Welfare Assn; member, past president IL Welfare Assn; Natl Conference on Social Welfare; bd mem, past pres Natl Assn of County Welfare Directors 1969-76; life mem Alpha Phi Alpha; mem Urban League; life mem NAACP; life mem, pass post commander, Greater Chicago Amvets Post #1; past mem Amer Acad Political and Social Science; mem United Way I & R Committee; mem Exec Service Corps; mem Chicago Commons Bd; mem Youth Guidance Bd; bd mem, past pres City Club of Chicago 1949-; president, The Chicago Umbrian Glee Club, 1936-. **Honors/Awds:** Honors and Awards received from Xi Lambda Chapter Alpha Phi Alpha Fraternity, Greater Chicago Churchmen, City Club of Chicago (past pres), Fisk University, Joint Negro Appeal, United Way/Crusade of Mercy, Greater Chicago Amvets Post #1, Chicago Senior Citizens Hall of Fame, and many others. **Military Serv:** AUS 1943-46; graduated from The Infantry School; Military Police Detachment Commander; US Army Reserve Corps, Civil Affairs/Military Govt Officer, Captain retired 1961; WWII Honors: Good Conduct Medal, Victory Medal, American Theatre Medal, Sharp Shooter Badge, Post Commander's Letter of Commendation for Outstanding Service. **Home Addr:** 5839 S Michigan Ave, Chicago, IL 60637.

DANIEL, EUGENE
Professional football player. **Personal:** Born May 4, 1961, Baton Rouge, LA. **Educ:** Louisiana State Univ. **Career:** Indianapolis Colts, defensive back, 1984-96; Baltimore Ravens, defensive back, 1997-. **Business Addr:** Professional Football Player, Baltimore Ravens, 11001 Owings Mills Blvd, Owings Mills, MD 21117, (410)654-6200.

DANIEL, GRISELDA
Educational administrator. **Personal:** Born Feb 7, 1938, Battle Creek, MI; daughter of Teritha Daniel and Edward Daniel; children: Cornell A, Gary L, Cheri A, Patrick H. **Educ:** Western Michigan Univ, BS (magna cum laude) 1973, MS Admin 1980. **Career:** Borgess Hospital, surgical nurse 1958-66; Kalamazoo St Hospital, attendant nurse 1966-70; Western Michigan Univ, Coll of Gen Studies, counselor/trainer 1970-73, dir Martin Luther King, Jr prog 1975-80, asst to vice pres acad affrs/dir spec prgms 1980-88, asst to dean of the Graduate Coll, and director of Graduate diversity program, 1988-. **Orgs:** WMU designer/devlpr Mentor Program 1980-81; WMU award Invaluable Contribution Upward Bound Program 1982. **Honors/Awds:** Member NAACP, American Assn Univ Administrators, Natl Assn Female Executives, Natl Consortium for Black Prof Devel, received award from Delta Kappa Gamma for Outstanding Contribution to Field of Educ, 1981; Creative Programming Award, Continuing Educ Assn, 1989; Outstanding Leadership and Committment, the Martin Luther King Jr Program, 1989; Committment to Public Serv Award, Van Buren County Dept of Social Serv, 1989. **Home Addr:** 27847 County Road 53, Gobles, MI 49055. **Business Addr:** Assistant to the Dean, Graduate College/Director, Graduate Diversity Program, Western Michigan University, W Michigan Ave, Kalamazoo, MI 49008.

DANIEL, JACK L.
Educator. **Personal:** Born Jun 9, 1942, Johnstown, PA; married Jerlean Colley; children: Omari, Marijata. **Educ:** Univ of Pittsburgh, BS Psych 1963, MA Speech 1965, PhD Speech 1968. **Career:** Central MI Univ, asst prof 1967-68; Univ of Pittsburgh, chmn, assoc prof 1969-73; Univ of Pittsburgh, Coll of Arts & Sciences, assoc dean 1973-78; Stanford Univ, amer council of ed fellow 1974; Faculty of Arts & Sciences, assoc dean 1978-83. **Orgs:** Mem Speech Commun Assoc, Intl Commun Assoc, Soc for Intercultural Ed Training & Rsch; bd mem Red Cross Ed Ctrs. **Honors/Awds:** Publ in Todays Speech, Jrnl of Communications, Speech Teacher, Black Scholar, Black Lines, Crisis. **Business Addr:** Assistant Provost, Univ of Pittsburgh, Pittsburgh, PA 15260.

DANIEL, JAMES L.
Consultant. **Personal:** Born Nov 16, 1945, Brunswick, GA; married Brenda; children: James Jr, Tonya. **Educ:** Tuskegee Inst, 1963-64; Brunswick Coll, AS BA 1976. **Career:** Sears Roebuck & Co, div mgr 1968-76; Brunswick City, city commr, 1972-76; Stripe-A-Lot/Precision Pavement Marking & Maintenance Co, owner 1986-; Southern Bell Telephone, acct exec 1978-80, serv consultant 1980-91, sr acct executive 1991-. **Orgs:** Pres, Founder Leaders of Amer Dem Soc, 1959; ex-officer, Brunswick Chamber of Commerce, 1972-76; bd dir, Am Help Am 1974-76. **Honors/Awds:** Outstanding Serv, Christ Memorial Baptist Church, 1982; Brunswick City Comm, 1976, Frat Order of Police 1973. **Military Serv:** USAF amn 1st cl 4 yrs; Expert Marksman Medal, Vietnam Serv Medal, Natl Defense Serv Medal, Pres, Unit Citation, Airforce Unit Commedation, 1964-68. **Home Addr:** 504 Picabo St, Woodstock, GA 30189. **Business Addr:** Sales Manager, Bellsouth Small Business Svcs, 2305 Parklake Dr, Ste 225, Atlanta, GA 30345.

DANIEL, JESSICA HENDERSON
Psychologist. **Personal:** Born Aug 2, 1944, San Antonio, TX; daughter of Geraldine Thomas Henderson and James E Henderson (deceased); children: Margaret. **Educ:** Fayetteville State Coll, BS 1964; Univ of IL Urbana, MS 1967, PhD 1969; Harvard Medical School, Postdoctoral Clinical Fellow 1974-76. **Career:** Univ of IL, asst prof educ psych 1969-70; Univ of Oregon, asst prof dept of special educ 1970-72; Boston Coll, asst prof educ psych 1972-76; Harvard Medical Sch, instructor in psych 1976-91, asst professor, psych 1991-; Children's Hosp, rsch assoc/psych 1972-; Judge Baker Children's Ctr, psychologist 1976-; Harvard Law School, Cambridge, MA, teaching fellow, 1989. **Orgs:** Mem vice chmn Bd of Registration of Psychologist, State of MA, 1984-89, chrm bd of registration, 1989-93; mem bd Brookline Arts Center 1985-88; mem Tech Adv Comm Robert Wood Johnson Foundation 1986-; psychology consultant Public Schools Brookline, Cambridge MA; mem Charles St AME Church, Coalition of 100 Black Women, Boston Chapter; Amer Psychological Assoc, MA Psychological Assoc; fellow Amer Orthopsychiatric Assoc; chmn, Bd of Registration of Psychologist (MA,) 1989. **Honors/Awds:** Black Achiever Greater Boston YMCA 1984; President's Awd Boston Chap NAACP 1986; Distinguished Alumni Citation of Yr Natl Assoc for Equal Opportunity in Higher Educ 1986; Resource, Harvard Negotiation Project, Harvard Law School, 1989; Woman of Courage & Correction, Greater Boston Section of the Natl Council of Negro Women, 1995. **Home Addr:** P O Box 605, Brookline, MA 02146. **Business Addr:** Senior Staff Psychologist, Judge Baker Children's Ctr, Children's Hospital, 295 Longwood Ave, Boston, MA 02115, (617)232-8390.

DANIEL, LEVI GARLAND
Business executive. **Personal:** Born Jul 28, 1918, Halifax Co, VA; son of Cora Daniel and Charles Daniel; married Elizabeth Francis Barnhart; children: Ervin Stanley, Levi Melvin, William Tyrone, Enzy Raymond, Norma Faye, Carol Louginia, David Garland, George Darnell, Timothy Elisha, Karen L, Letisha. **Career:** United Mine Workers of America (UMWA), intl rep, coord; UMWA, Occup Health & Safety Dept, intl rep 1974; UMWA, dir of field service office 1974, pres Dist 29 1973, intl exec bd mem 1972-73, observer Dist 29 1972; Local Union 5955, rec sec 1953-72. **Orgs:** Bd Gulf Area Housing Assn; bd WV Coal Field Housing; mem NAACP.

DANIEL, MARY REED
Artist. **Personal:** Born in East St Louis, IL; married William J Daniel Sr; children: William J Jr. **Career:** Artist, work shown at museums in numerous states and countries, currently. **Orgs:** Artist Guild of Chicago; Artist League of the Midwest; South Side Community Art Center; Old Town Triangle Art Center Surface Design Assn; Chicago Artists Coalition. **Honors/Awds:** Listed in Afro-American Artists, Boston Public Library; shows: Earl Graves Publishing Co Black Enterprise Mag, Art Institute Sales & Rental Gallery, Milliken Rug Design Competition, Galerie Triangle, Lansburgh Center, Evans-Tibbs Collection, A Montgomery Ward Gallery, Tweed Museum, Paramaribo Suriname South America; publication, Black Dimensions in Contemporary American Art.

DANIEL, SIMMIE CHILDREY
Business education teacher. **Personal:** Born Feb 9, 1934, Shorter, AL; daughter of Ora M Childrey and Luther J Childrey (deceased). **Educ:** Alabama State Univ, BS, 1957; Indiana Univ, MS, 1967; St Louis Univ, Univ of Nevada, special student. **Career:** Albany State Coll, Albany GA, exec sec, 1957-60; St Louis Public Schools, St Louis MO, business teacher, 1963; El Reno Public Schools, El Reno OK, English teacher, 1963; Clark County School District, Las Vegas NV, 1964-. **Orgs:** Natl Business Educ Assn; Clark County Classroom Teachers Assn; Nevada State Educ Assn; Natl Vocational Educ Assn; Professional Coll Women Assn; Natl Sorority of Phi Delta Kappa Inc, 1973; Gamma Phi Delta Sorority, 1975. **Business Addr:** Teacher, Eldorado High School, 1139 Linn Lane, Las Vegas, NV 89110.

DANIEL, WALTER C. See Obituaries section.

DANIEL, WILEY YOUNG
Attorney. **Personal:** Born Sep 10, 1946, Louisville; son of Lavinia Daniel and Wiley Daniel; married Ida Seymour; children: Jennifer, Stephanie, Nicole. **Educ:** Howard Univ, BA 1968; Howard Univ Sch of Law, JD 1971. **Career:** Volunteer legal work; Dickinson Wright McKean Cudlip & Moon, attorney 1971-77; Gorsuch Kirgis Campbell Walker & Grover, attorney 1977-88; Popham, Haik, Schnobrich & Kaufman, partner, 1988-95; US District Court, judge, 1995-. **Orgs:** Mem Natl Bar Assn; pres-elect, 1991-92, pres, 1992-93, CO Bar Assn; trustee, Denver Bar Assn, 1990-93; Amer Bar Assn; Managing Ed Howard LLJ; mem Delta Theta Phi Law Frat, Alpha Phi Alpha Social Frat; Law Journal 1970-71; mem Detroit Coll of Law part-time faculty 1974-77; Univ of CO School of Law 1978-81; mem Iliff Sch of Theology; mem, Colorado State Bd of Agriculture, 1989-95. **Honors/Awds:** 1986 Disting Serv Awd Sam Cary Bar Assoc, Colorado Assoc of Black Attorneys; Fellow, American Bar Foundation; Fellow, Colorado Bar Foundation; USA Speaker Aboard, Nigeria, 1995. **Business Addr:** Judge, US District Court, District of Colorado, 1929 Stout St, Rm C-218, Denver, CO 80294.

DANIELS, A. RAIFORD
Financial executive. **Personal:** Born Dec 13, 1944, Columbia, SC; son of Alma Gordon Daniels and Willie L Daniels. **Educ:** Lincoln Univ, BA 1966; Columbia Univ NY, MBA 1973; Columbia Univ, EdD, 1997. **Career:** Prudential Insurance Cty Newark, mgmt trainee group insurance 1966-67; Citibank, account officer, Natl Bank Group 1968-72; Corning Corp, NY, sr financial analyst, 1973-74; Bank of America, San Francisco, vice pres, N America Div, 1974-78; Prudential Insurance Co, vice pres, Capital Markets Group, 1978-88; The Wilalm Group, managing principal and CEO, currently; Bergen Community College, professor, currently. **Orgs:** Columbia Club; Lincoln Univ Alumni; Minority Interchange NY; The Amer Soc of CLU and ChFC; Naval Reserve Assoc; NAACP; YMCA, Natl Naval Off Assn; Newark Chamber of Commerce; Natl Assn of Review Appraisers. **Honors/Awds:** Calder Fellow Calder Found NY 1972; Licensed Certified General Real Estate Appraiser, real estate and insurance broker; registered investment advisor and general securities representative; Certified Review Appraiser, register mortgage underwriter and broker. **Military Serv:** USNR Captain, 1966-. **Business Addr:** Managing Principal, The Wilalm Group, Ltd, PO Box 1098 (Number Six Bleeker St), Newark, NJ 07101.

DANIELS, ALFRED CLAUDE WYNDER
Educator. **Personal:** Born Mar 22, 1934, Philadelphia, PA; married Ginger Daniels; children: Carmen, David, Jerry. **Educ:** AZ State U, BS 1965; Harvard Law School, JD 1975. **Career:** Harvard Law Sch, asst dean 1975-; NE HH Aerospace Design Co Inc, vice pres. **Orgs:** Mem Nat Assn of Black Mfr; pres Black Corp Pres of New England; mem Urban League; NAACP. **Military Serv:** USAF maj 1952-72. **Business Addr:** Harvard Law Sch, Cambridge, MA 02138.

DANIELS, ANTHONY HAWTHORNE
Clergyman. **Personal:** Born Jun 9, 1950, Kingsport, TN. **Educ:** Morristown Jr Coll, AA 1970; Knoxville Coll, BS 1972; Graham Bible Coll, ABE 1983. **Career:** Knoxville Comm Dev Agency, coord 1972; Boxing Rehabilitation Prog, founder & dir 1976; TN Valley Auth, energy advisor 1977; Bethel Baptist Church, asst pastor 1984; First Baptist Church, pastor 1985. **Business Addr:** Pastor, First Baptist Church, Church & Third St, Barbourville, KY 40906.

DANIELS, ANTONIO
Professional basketball player. **Personal:** Born Mar 19, 1975. **Educ:** Bowling Green State. **Career:** Vancouver Grizzlies, guard, 1997-. **Business Addr:** Professional Basketball Player, Vancouver Grizzlies, 788 Beatty St, Ste 311, Vancouver, BC, Canada V6B 2M1, (604)688-5867.

DANIELS, CECIL TYRONE
Educator. **Personal:** Born Nov 23, 1941, Miami, FL; married Patricia Ann Robinson; children: Lee Ernest, Letitia Nicole, La Keitha Jonise. **Educ:** Univ No CO, MA 1974; FL A&M U, BA Elem Ed, Social Studies, Drivers Ed 1964. **Career:** Dade County Public School System, prin, asst prin 1974-76, teacher 1965-73, human relations coord 1970. **Orgs:** Nat Alliance of Black Sch Educators; Dade Co Schs Adminstr Assn; Dade Co Guidance Assn; consult Univ of No CO 1975-76; FL A&M Alumni Assn; Univ of No CO Alumni Assn; vice pres Lions Club Intl 1977; Phi Delta Kappa; Big Bros Inc jack & jill of am inc. **Honors/Awds:** Serv Award, WJ Bryan Elem PTA 1976; Serv Award, Fulford Elem PTA 1977; Serv Award, Cub Scouts 1977; nom Adminstr of the Year 1976-77; cert for runner-upAdminstr of the Year 1977; Fulford Comm Award 1976-77; Admin of the Year 1978; Ad Hoc Com Dade Co Sch Sys 1980. **Military Serv:** College ROTC 1960-64. **Business Addr:** 3125 NW 176th St, Opa Locka, FL 33056.

DANIELS, CURTIS A.
Sales representative. **Personal:** Born Apr 1, 1941, Italy, TX; married Cynthia A Epps. **Educ:** Bishop Coll, BA 1973. **Career:** Fox & Jacobs, sales rep; Ingham Co Hosp, asst physical therapist 1961-62; Titche-Goettinger, buyer 1961-62. **Orgs:** Mem Fox & Jacobs' "Million Dollar Circle" 1975; lectr Bishop Coll; mem Omega Psi Phi, Mu Gamma Chpt. **Honors/Awds:** Outstanding Airman, USAF. **Military Serv:** USAF. **Business Addr:** 2800 Surveyor Blvd, Carrollton, TX 75006.

DANIELS, DAVID HERBERT, JR.
Physician. **Personal:** Born Sep 1, 1941, Little Rock, AR; married Doris; children: David, Dorothy, Doreen, Danny, Dora. **Educ:** Philander Smith Coll, BS 1968; Univ AR Med Sch, MD 1967; Los Angeles Co Med Ctr 1967-68. **Career:** Cardiac Ctr Dir Cardiac Pulmonary Serv, physician cardiologist; Montclair & Chino Gen Hosp, physician. **Orgs:** Dir cardiac chmn Cardiac Surgery Com Dr's Hosp; mem Am Coll of Cardiology, Am Coll of Physician, Am Coll of Cert Physicians. **Honors/Awds:** Alpha Kappa Mu Nat Hon Soc 1962; Beta Kappa Phi Nat Sch Hon Soc 1962; cert flw Am Coll. **Military Serv:** USAF maj 1968-74. **Business Addr:** 1770 N Orange Grove, Pomona, CA.

DANIELS, EARL HODGES
Journalist. **Personal:** Born May 19, 1963, Tallahassee, FL; son of Betty Daniels and Earl Daniels. **Educ:** Florida A&M University, BS, sociology, 1987; University of South Carolina, Multicultural Newspaper Workshop, post graduate study, 1989. **Career:** Fort Lauderdale Sun-Sentinel, news reporter, 1989-. **Orgs:** National Association of Black Journalists, 1990-; Kappa Alpha Psi Fraternity, Inc, 1982-. **Business Addr:** News Reporter, Fort Lauderdale Sun-Sentinel, 3333 S Congress Ave, Delray Beach, FL 33445, (407)243-6629.

DANIELS, ELIZABETH
Dentist. **Personal:** Born Sep 23, 1938, Sebastian, FL; daughter of Addie Blackshear Daniels and Levi Daniels; married Jesse J Robinson; children: Jennifer. **Educ:** TN State Univ, BS 1958; Howard Univ, MS 1962; Univ of CA, PhD 1968; Univ of Conn Sch of Dental Med, DMD 1977. **Career:** Lockheed Propulsion Co, proposal writer 1963-64; Pfizer Inc, medicinal chemist 1968-73; Private Practice, 1978-; Meharry Med Coll Sch of Dentistry, asst prof 1977-1985, asst dean academic affairs 1985-88; Department of Periodontics, assoc prof 1988-89; private dental practice, 1990-. **Orgs:** Natl Dental Assoc, mem 1978-; American Assoc of Dental Schools, mem 1978-89; NAACP, Golden Heritage mem; TN State Univ Natl Alumni Assoc, vice pres, 1986-88; Howard University Alumni Associate; Church and Community in Action; Portsmouth City School Board, mem, 1996-; NAACP, Portsmouth Branch, pres, 1997-98. **Honors/Awds:** NASA Fellowship at Univ of CA, 1964-68; Outstanding Young Women of America, 1969; Outstanding Men and Women of Science, 1970. **Business Addr:** Dentist, 4259 Greenwood Dr, Portsmouth, VA 23701, (757)488-4776.

DANIELS, FREDERICK L., JR.
Banker. **Personal:** Born Oct 9, 1965, Cleveland, OH; son of Gail M Daniels. **Educ:** Univ of Virginia, BA, Economics/English, 1987. **Career:** First National Bank of Atlanta, credit analyst, 1987-89; Wachovia Bank of Georgia, bus dev mgr, 1989-90, branch mgr/banking officer, 1990-93; First Southern Bank, AVP/comm loan officer, 1993-, vice pres commercial lending, 1996-. **Orgs:** Kappa Alpha Psi, community serv chairperson, 1984-; American Lung Assn, bd of dirs, Dekalb County, 1993-; Dekalb Chamber of Commerce, Small Bus Committee, 1994-96; Lithonia Chamber of Commerce, 1993-95; NAACP, 1989-; Greenforest Baptist Church, 1980-; South DeKalb Business Association, board of directors, 1996. **Business Addr:** Vice Pres, Commercial Lending, First Southern Bank, 2727 Panola Road, PO Box 1019, Lithonia, GA 30058, (770)987-3511.

DANIELS, GEORGE BENJAMIN
Attorney. **Personal:** Born May 13, 1953, Allendale, SC; son of Florence Ellen Morten and Rufus Jacob Daniels; married Stella Marie Stots, Aug 30, 1986. **Educ:** Yale University, BA, 1975; University of California, Berkeley, JD, 1978. **Career:** Legal Aid Society of New York, Criminal Defense Division, trial attorney; California Supreme Court, Chief Justice Rose E Bird, law clerk, attorney; Skadden, Arps, Slate, Meagher & Flom, litigation attorney; US Attorney, Eastern District of New York, assistant US attorney; Brooklyn Law School, adjunct professor of law; City of New York, Criminal Court, judge, Mayor's Office, counsel, currently. **Orgs:** Andrew Glover Youth Program, board of directors, 1982-; Suffield Academy, board of trustees, 1986-. **Business Phone:** (212)788-3143.

DANIELS, GERALDINE L.
Government official. **Personal:** Born Sep 9, Harlem, NY; married Eugene Ray Daniels II (deceased); children: Eugene R III. **Educ:** CUNY Queens Coll, BA Polit Sci; Malcolm-King Harlem Coll, AA. **Career:** The New York State Legislature, former chairperson for standing comm on social svcs, presently chairperson for the steering comm; New York State Legislative Caucus, chairwoman. **Orgs:** Vice pres Inner City Broadcasting Corp; vice chair Harlem Urban Develop Corp; chairperson NY County Democratic Comm; treas Council of Black Elected Democrats of NYS; district leader Martin Luther King Jr Democratic Club in Central Harlem; life mem NAACP. **Honors/Awds:** Sojourner Truth Awd Negro Business & Professional Women of New York; raised monies for preventive health care programs; "Mid-Day-Live" on NY City Cable Television.

DANIELS, JEAN E.
Educator. **Personal:** Born Dec 4, St Louis, MO; daughter of Maurine David Daniels and Chester Daniels; married Dr James Harrison Bracy. **Educ:** Univ of KS, BA 1964; Howard Univ, MSW 1966; UCLA, MPH 1973, DSW 1976. **Career:** Neuropsychiatric Ins UCLA, psych social worker; various local consultations; California State Univ, Northridge, sociology dept, prof 1987-. **Orgs:** Bd mem Am Lung Assn 1976-; chairperson Amer Public Health Assn, Social Work Sect 1984; Natl pgm comm Alpha Kappa Alpha Sor 1982-86; prog dev bd joint policy committee CA Council on Geriatrics and Gerontology; officer, Natl Women of Achievement, Los Angeles Chapter 1987-89; board member, Am Lung Association, 1976-93; board member, American Heart Association, West Valley Region, 1995-96. **Honors/Awds:** Honored Educator Phi Delta Kappa LA 1977; Found Ford Fellowship 1975; American Lung Assn of Los Angeles County Serv Awd 1980; CSUN Faculty Dev Awd 1985; Top Ladies of Distinction, Inglewood Chapter Award 1989; Research Grant, California State Univ, Northridge 1989-90; Tokiwa University, Japan Lecturer 1991; National Science Foundation, Psychology of Aging Awardee, 1992; First International Conference of Black Studies Lecturer, Accra Ghana, 1993. **Special Achievements:** Niigata, Japan, lecturer, International Welfare and Medical College, 1997. **Business Addr:** Professor, California State University, 18111 Nordhoff St, Northridge, CA 91330.

DANIELS, JERRY FRANKLIN. See Obituaries section.

DANIELS, JESSE
Design engineer. **Personal:** Born Oct 14, 1935, Montgomery, AL; son of Prince C Borom Daniels and David M Daniels; married Ella McCreary; children: Jessica, Kenneth, Eric, Adrienne, Diane, Carl. **Educ:** AL State Univ, BS 1961; Graduate Credit, Auburn Univ, Emory Univ, Wake Forest Univ, Clemson Univ, GA Southern Coll. **Career:** Ford Motor Co, design engr. **Orgs:** Mem Engrg Soc of Detroit 1963-78, 1978-83; mem Kappa Alpha Psi Frat 1964-, Prince Hall Masons 1974-, Southeastern MI Acapella Chorus 1982-, Screen Actors Guild 1984-, NAACP 1985-. **Honors/Awds:** 2 Natl TV Commercials Ford Motor Co 1984; 1986 Disting Alumnus AL State Univ 1986; Narrator, Ford College Recruitng Video. **Home Addr:** 11360 Auburn, Detroit, MI 48228.

DANIELS, JOHN C.
University executive. **Personal:** Born Apr 24, Macon, GA; married Bess; children: Leslie, John. **Educ:** Cheshire Acad 1956; Villanova U, 1960; Nat Urban Fellow, Yale U, 1971; Occidental Coll, 1972. **Career:** Yale Univ, mgr Affirmative Action; West Haven High School, teacher 1961-65; EOC, dep dir 1965-67; NH Redevelopment Agency, proj dir 1967-69; Quinnipiac College, asst & pres Urban Affairs 1969-70; Joint Center Political Studies, special asst 1970-72; City of New Haven, CT, aldermen, 14 yrs, mayor, 1990-94; State Senate, CT, president pro tem, 1987-90; Enterprise Plumbing & Heating Inc, president, 1987-. **Orgs:** Trustee Hannah Gray Home; bd dir YMCA; bd dir Dixwell Comm House; bd dir Urban League; bd mem Family Planning; NAACP; adv bd Highland Hts 1969-71; mem Prince Hall Masons; Alpha Phi Alpha; assoc fellow Trumbull Coll; Sigma Fraternity; 33 degree Mason, Prince Hall Masons. **Honors/Awds:** Outstanding Citizens Award 1969; Honorary Degree, University of New Haven in Law, 1992. **Special Achievements:** NCAA College Football Official, Big East Conference, 1986. **Business Addr:** 801 State St, New Haven, CT 06511.

DANIELS, JORDAN, JR.
County government official. **Personal:** Born Nov 26, 1923, Shreveport, LA; married Ellita. **Educ:** Compton Coll, graduate; Political Sci, LA City Coll, 1 yr life underwriting training course; LUTC, ins laws & conts; Attended, Loyola Univ, Xavier Univ 1941-43; CLU Studies, 1 yr. **Career:** Insurance Exec, 25 yrs; Supreme Life Ins Co of Am, state supr; State & Assemblyman, admin asst 6 yrs; Greene's Travel Serv Inc, vp; Henry A Waxman Assemblyman, admin asst 1975; State of CA Dept of Commerce Office of Small Business, bd chmn 1983-86; LA County Commn for Public Social Svcs, commissioner. **Orgs:** Pres Lutheran Human Relations Assn, 1965-71; pres Proj Hope; mem Westside Comm Improvemt Assoc; Consolidated Comm Action Assn; del Lutheran HS Assn; "Men of Tommorow"; chmn bd of trustees St Paul Luth Ch; pres LA Mgmt Assn Black Ins Cos 1972-73; Psi Beta Sigma 25 yrs; class moderator "Staff Mgr's Training Sch" Univ of So CA 1972-73; mem Faifax High Adv Council; mem McBride Sch; Handicap Adv Bd; mem W Hollywood Coord Council; vice chmn Hollywood Wilshire Scouts 1972-73; mem Baldwin Hills Dem Club; mem Dem Co Cent Com; rep Mini-convention KC 1974; State of CA, Dep of Commerce, Office of Small Business, 1982-90; Pacific Coast Regional Small Business Development Corp, chairman of bd, 1990-. **Honors/Awds:** Aware of Merit Lutheran Businessmen's Assoc Long Beach CA 1968. **Business Addr:** Commissioner, Commn for Public Social Serv, PO Box 781015, Los Angeles, CA 90016.

DANIELS, JOSEPH
Medical director. **Personal:** Born Mar 18, 1931, Linden, NJ; married; children: Joan, Jean. **Educ:** Lincoln Univ PA, BA (cum laude) 1953; Howard Univ Coll Med, MD 1957; Med Ctr Jersey City, Intrnshp 1957-58; Worcester City Hosp MA, Res Med 1958-59; Ancora Psych Hosp, Res Psych 1962-65. **Career:** NJ Psychiatric Hospital Ancora, attending psych 1965-66; Salem Out-Patient Clinic, Salem NJ, dir 1966-67; Mental Health Center, Wycksoff WI, dir 1967-70; In-patient Unit Mt Carmel Guild, dir 1970-71; NJ Coll of Medicine, chief outpatient 1971-77; Center Growth & Rcncltn Inc, med dir. **Orgs:** Clnl asso prof psych NJ Coll Med 1970-81; Cnsltnt psych E Orange Bd of Edctrs 1970-75, Newark Bd of Edctrs 1977-85, Victory Hse Inc 1970-77; bddirs Yth Devlp Inc 1968-73, Northside Addict Rehab Ctr 1969-71; bd trustees Nyack Coll Nyack, NY 1973-82; pres bd chmn Mnstry Of Recncltn, Inc 1981-85. **Honors/Awds:** Beta Kappa Chi Natl Scntfc Hnry Scty 1953; Am Coll Stdnt Ldrs 1953; Outstndng Yng Men of Am 1967; Psychodynmcs & Psychopathlgy of Racism Publ 1969. **Military Serv:** AUS Med Corp cptn 1959-62. **Business Addr:** Medical Dir, Ctr Grwth & Recncltn, Inc, 498 William St, East Orange, NJ 07019.

DANIELS, LEGREE SYLVIA
Former government official. **Personal:** Born Feb 29, 1920, Barnwell, SC; married Oscar Daniels; children: two stepdaughters. **Educ:** Attended Temple University and Central Pennsylvania Business School. **Career:** Staff asst, former Senate Minority Leader Hugh Scott; PA State Tax Equalization Bd, Harrisburg PA, chairman, 1979-85; PA Bureau of Elections, Harrisburg PA, commissioner, 1985-86; PA Dept of State, Harrisburg PA, deputy secretary of commonwealth, 1986-87; US Dept of Education, Washington DC, assistant secretary for civil rights, 1987-89; member, Republican Natl Committee Executive committee. **Orgs:** Former chairman, Natl Black Republican Council; chairman, Black Voters for Reagan/Bush; secretary, Republican State Committee of PA; director, PA Council of Republican Women; board member, Natl Endowment for Democracy; US Army Science Board; member of advisory board, US Commission on Civil Rights; Joint Center for Political Studies; board member, Young Women's Christian Association; PA Martin Luther King Commission; past matron, Order of the Eastern Star; Baptist Missionary Society. **Honors/Awds:** DHL, Atlanta University, 1988. **Home Addr:** 1715 Glenside Dr, Harrisburg, PA 17109.

DANIELS, LEMUEL LEE
Company executive. **Personal:** Born Dec 28, 1945, Montgomery, AL; son of Martha Daniels Johnson and Frank Hudson; children: Quintin Daniels. **Educ:** University of Illinois, Chicago Circle, IL, 1963-64; Southeast College, Chicago, IL, 1965-67; Southern Illinois University, Carbondale, IL, BS, communications, 1971. **Career:** Merrill Lynch, Los Angeles, CA, registered representative, 1976-78; A G Becker, Los Angeles, CA, assistant vice president, 1978-84; Drexel Burnham, Los Angeles, CA, vice president, 1984-85; Bear, Stearns & Co, Los Angeles, CA, associate director, 1985-94; Merrill Lynch, 1st vp investments, 1994-. **Orgs:** Treasurer, board of directors, Los Angeles Arts Council, 1989-; vice chair, National Association of Securities Professionals, Task Force Rebuild Los Angeles; trustee, executive committee, Cross Roads Arts Academy, 1990-; board member, WEB DuBois School, 1982-84; chancellor assoc, University California, LA, 1978-80. **Honors/Awds:** Full Scholarship, Southern Illinois University, 1967; Certificate of Appreciation, Merrill Lynch, 1976; One of two minorities chosen to represent Merrill Lunch in their first Affirmative Action recruitment program, 1975-76; Broker of the Year, Bear, Stearns & Co Inc, Special Investment Group, 1985; responsible for BET Holdings going public, the first African-American company listed on the NYSE, 1991. **Military Serv:** US Army, E-5, 1967-69; Platoon Leader, Outstanding Platoon, 1967. **Business Addr:** 1st Vice President Investments, Merrill Lynch, 2121 Ave of the Stars, Los Angeles, CA 90067.

DANIELS, LESHUN
Professional football player. **Personal:** Born May 30, 1974; married Alicia; children: LeShun Jr. **Educ:** Ohio State, attended. **Career:** Minnesota Vikings, guard, 1997-. **Business Addr:** Professional Football Player, Minnesota Vikings, 9520 Viking Dr, Eden Prairie, MN 55344, (612)828-6500.

DANIELS, LINCOLN, SR.
Educational administrator (retired). **Personal:** Born Feb 17, 1932, Hickman, KY; son of Viola Daniels (deceased) and James Daniels (deceased); married Robbie L Davis; children: Karen Lee Trice, Lincoln, Jr, Terence Leon. **Educ:** Philander Smith Coll, BA (cum laude) 1953; Wash U, MA 1969; Wash U, Advanced Studies. **Career:** St Louis Bd of Educ Div of Evaluation, divisional asst 1975-80; St Louis Bd of Educ Div of Evaluation, research statistician 1973-75; St Louis Bd of Educ, elementary teacher 1964-69; Washington Univ, coordinator elementary educ summer 1971, master teacher summer 1970, clinical assoc 1967-70, supvr elementary educ 1970-73; St Louis Co Social Studies Implementation Project, master teacher, 1966-69; Washington Univ, research adv sum 1970; St Louis Board of Education, admin asst, 1980-84, instructional coordinator, 1984-87, elementary principal, 1987-97. **Orgs:** Treas St Louis City Counc Internatl Reading Assn 1976-78; chmn Block Unit #375 Natl Urban League Confederation of Block Units 1976-; vice pres Midwest Region Philander Smith Coll Natl Alumni Assn 1977-79; pres-elect St Louis City Counc Intl Reading Assn, 1978-79, pres, 1980; participant St Louis forum on Fgn Policy co-sponsored by St Louis Counc on World Affairs & the US St Dept of State 1977; research asst St Louis Metro Soc Studies Cntr Wash Univ 1966-69; various activities Wash U; mem Comm Black Recruitment; comm Undergrad Ed Pre-serv Tchr Educ Comm; Kappa Delta Pi Educ Honor Soc 1969; pres, 1970-71, historian-reprtr, 1971-72, Kappa Delta Pi St Louis; mem Phi Delta Kappa Ed LdrshpSoc 1969-; Philander Smith Coll Alumni Chap 1966-68; past pres Metro-st Louis Philander Smith Coll Alumni Chpt; sec ro-st Louis Philander Smith Coll Alumni Chptr 1970-74; pres, St Louis City Council, 1979-80; vice president, Congregations Allied for Community Improvement, 1998-2000; board mem, Metropolitan Congregations United for St. Louis, 1995-; Worshipful Master, Caution Lodge #23, Prince Hall Masons, 1976. **Honors/Awds:** Philander Smith College, Distinguished Alumnus Award, 1980; Iota Phi Lambda Sorority Inc, Alpha Zeta Chapter, Distinguished Service as an American Educator Award, 1990; Alpha Kappa Alpha Sorority Inc, Omicron Omega Chapter, Salute to Black Men for Excellence in Education Award, 1991; National Honor Society, 1948-; Community Leaders and Noteworthy Americans, 1977-; Service Awards: Omega Psi Phi Fraternity, 1968; Prince Hall Masons, Past Master's Council, PHM, Frank J Brown Lodge #80, PHM, Caution Lodge #23, Monsanto YMCA, 1990; United Negro College Fund, Meritorious Service Award, 1985; Phi Delta Kappa, Educational Leadership Society, 1969; Hickey Elementary School Exemplary Service Award, 1997; Administrator's Association, Local 44, AFSA Award for Outstanding Service to the St. Louis Public School and The St. Louis Community, 1997. **Military Serv:** AUS paratrooper para-medic 1953-55.

DANIELS, LLOYD
Professional basketball player. **Personal:** Born Sep 4, 1967, Brooklyn, NY. **Career:** San Antonio Spurs, guard, 1992-. **Business Addr:** Professional Basketball Player, San Antonio Spurs, 600 E Market St, Ste 102, San Antonio, TX 78205, (512)554-7787.

DANIELS, MELVIN J.
Professional athlete, basketball scout, coach. **Personal:** Born Jul 20, 1944, North Carolina; son of Bernice Clemmons Daniels and Maceo Daniels; married Cecilia J Martinez. **Educ:** Attended, Burlington Jr Coll, Univ of NM. **Career:** American Basketball Assn, 1967-75; MN Muskies, forward 1967-68; IN Pacers, center 1968-74; Memphis Sounds, center 1974-75; NY Nets,

center 1976-; Indiana State, asst basketball coach; IN Pacers, asst basketball coach/scout 1981-. **Orgs:** Began Amer Quarter Horse Farm Circle M Ranch, Sheridan IN board, breed, train, show Lady Bugs Moon, American Preview, and Dash for Cash bred stock. Operating since 1972, specializing in barrel racing and pole bending. **Honors/Awds:** Named to ABA All League Team 1968-72; Rebound Leader 1967-71; Team Ctr All Star Game 1968-73; Most Valuable Player All Star Game 1971; Rookie of Yr 1968; Most Valuable Player, ABA 1968, 1971. **Business Addr:** Indiana Pacers, Market Square Arena, Market St, Indianapolis, IN 46204.

DANIELS, PATRICIA ANN
Municipal employee. **Personal:** Born Aug 6, 1940, Kaufman, TX; daughter of Mary Elizabeth Burnett Alexander and James Hiawatha Alexander; married Valjean Daniels, Dec 2, 1964; children: Barry M Alexander, Brette M. **Educ:** Los Angeles Junior Coll of Business, Los Angeles CA, AA, 1964; Univ of San Francisco, San Francisco CA, BS, 1979. **Career:** City of Berkeley, Berkeley CA, supervisor, housing codes, 1968-80, supvr, parking collections, 1981-89, personnel-labor relations trainee, 1989-92, assistant building and housing inspector, 1992-. **Orgs:** National regional dir, first vice pres, Far Western Region, National, 1989-; Gamma Phi Delta Sorority, Volunteer Serv, 1971-; charter mem, Beta Sigma Chapter, 1990-91, Supreme First Anti-Basileus, 1992; California Federation of Business & Professional Women, Bay Valley District, 1983-, president, 1990-91; membership, pres-elect, Diversity Task Force, Bay Valley Dist, 1983-; mem, board of directors, Natl Forum for Black Public Admin, 1985-; charter mem, Natl Council of Negro Women, Alameda County Section; mem, board of directors, Local Black Women Organized for Political Action; mem, Women's Missionary Union, program dir, North Richmond Missionary Baptist Church; Housing Advisory Commission Personnel Board, City of San Pablo, vice pres; Gamma Phi Delta. **Honors/Awds:** Rose Pin Award, Gamma Phi Delta Sorority, Natl, 1976; Woman of the Year, Far Western Region, Gamma Phi Delta Sorority, 1979; Dedicated Serv, Beta Sigma, 1986; Woman of the Year, Outstanding Community Serv, Natl Forum for Black Public Admin, 1987; Local Woman of the Year, District Woman of the Year, Woman of Achievement, California Fedn of Business & Professional Women, 1988; Marks of Excellence, North Richmond Church, 1989; author of two leadership manuals, Gamma Phi Delta Sorority. **Home Addr:** 1810 Hillcrest Rd, San Pablo, CA 94806.

DANIELS, PETER F.
Educator. **Personal:** Born Dec 5, 1928, Pine Bluff, AR; married Ruby; children: Peter Jr, Ronson, Darryl, Connie. **Educ:** AR AM&N Coll, BS 1951; IN U, MSE 1965; State Coll AR; AR State U. **Career:** Linwood School Dist, supt 1969-; Vaster High School, prin 1956-69, instructor Biology & Science 1953-56; Sherrill Jr High School, instructor Biology; Joiner AR, teacher 1951. **Orgs:** Mem Nat Educ Assn; AR Educ Assn; Jefferson Co Educ Assn; Nat Alliance Black Sch Edn; AR Adminstrn Assn; AR Sch Bus Officials; AR Adv Bd, ESAA & Title I; adv bd AR Tech Asst Ctr; Jefferson Co Comprehensive Hlth Bd; Black Children Adoption Cncl; NAACP; Kappa Alpha Psi Frat; deacon,bd mem St Paul Missionary Bapt Ch. **Business Addr:** PO Box 61, Moscow, AR.

DANIELS, PHILLIP BERNARD
Professional football player. **Personal:** Born Mar 4, 1973, Donalsonville, GA. **Educ:** Univ of Georgia. **Career:** Seattle Seahawks, defensive end, 1996-. **Business Addr:** Professional Football Player, Seattle Seahawks, 11220 NE 53rd St, Kirkland, WA 98033, (206)827-9777.

DANIELS, PRESTON
Mayor. **Personal:** marrIed Patty. **Career:** Mayor of Des Moines, IA, currently. **Special Achievements:** First African American mayor of Des Moines, IA. **Business Addr:** Mayor, City of Des Moines, City Hall, 400 E 1st St, Des Moines, IA 50309, (515)283-4500.

DANIELS, REBECCA HAYWOOD
Educator. **Personal:** Born Oct 10, 1943, Columbus Co, NC; married George Daniels; children: Geraldine Renee, Starlin Wynette. **Educ:** Fayetteville State Univ, BS 1966. **Career:** Richard B Harrison, teacher 1966-67; S Lumberton Elem, teacher 1967-69; Acme-Delco Jr Sr High School, teacher 1970-. **Orgs:** Councilwoman 1975-77, mayor pro-tem 1975-, town clerk 1974 Town of Bolton; mem NC Assoc of Classroom Teachers, Bicentennial Comm, NC Ext Homemakers Assoc Inc, NEA, NCEA, PACE, Green Ghapel Missionary Baptist Church, VFW Aux Post 9003.

DANIELS, REGINALD SHIFFON
Chaplain. **Personal:** Born Sep 6, 1963, Newport News, VA; son of Bertha Mae Daniels and Thomas R Daniels. **Educ:** Attended, Christopher Newport Coll 1981-82; Averett Coll, BA 1986; Virginia Union Univ Sch of Theology 1986-89; Presbyterian School of Christian Education, Richmond, VA, MA, 1990. **Career:** Loyal Baptist Church, assoc minister 1983-86; 31st St Baptist Church, assoc minister 1986-87; Pilgrim Baptist Church, Christian education dir 1987-88; Richmond Memorial Hospital, chaplain 1988; Eastern State Hospital, chaplain 1988; Heritage Methodist Home, Richmond, VA, chaplain, 1990-. **Orgs:** Recruiter NAACP 1982-86; scoutmaster Boy Scouts of Amer 1984-86; missionary Intl Assoc of Ministers' Wives 1985; pres Baptist Student Union 1986-87; Peninsula Track Club 1981-85; Richmond Road Runners 1989. **Honors/Awds:** Academic Scholarship Ebony Blazers 1981; Keesee Fellowship 1982-86; West Hampton Baptist Church Scholarship 1982-86; VA Baptist Assoc Scholarship 1982-86; Julian Hodgenson Scholarship 1986; Academic Scholarships Intl Assoc of Ministers Wives 1986, VA Union Univ Sch of Theol 1986; 31st St Baptist Church Scholarship 1987. **Military Serv:** Navy, 1989-; Division Officer for Chaplain Candidate School.

DANIELS, RICHARD BERNARD
Professional sports administrator. **Personal:** Born Oct 19, 1944, Portland, OR; married Gloria; children: Sunde, Whitney. **Educ:** Pacific Univ, attended. **Career:** Defensive back, Dallas Cowboys, 1966-68; Chicago Bears, 1969-70; Miami Dolphins, player, 1971, scout, 1972-75; Tampa Bay Buccaneers, head scout, 1975; San Francisco 49ers, scouting dept, 1976-77; Washington Redskins, dir of player personnel, 1978-84, 1985-89; Los Angeles Express (USFL), vp, player personnel, 1984; San Diego Chargers, asst general mgr, 1990-96; Philadelphia Eagles, dir, football operations, 1996-. **Honors/Awds:** Member of: 1966 Dallas Cowboys NFL Eastern Conference championship team, 1967 Dallas Cowboys NFL Eastern Conference, Capitol Division, championship team. **Business Addr:** Asst General Mgr, San Diego Chargers, Jack Murphy Stadium, 9449 Friars Rd, San Diego, CA 92108.

DANIELS, RICHARD D.
Clergyman. **Personal:** Born Jan 27, 1931, Micanopy, FL; married Doris B Bagley. **Educ:** FAMU, BS 1958. **Career:** St Luke AME, Gainesvl, pastor 1958-59; Silver Spgs 1959-64; St Stephens AME, Leesburg, FL, 1964-71; Mt Zion AME, Ocala, 1971-72. **Orgs:** Del Gen Conf AME Ch 1972; mem NAACP; Masonic Lodge; Blood Bank Assn, Alachua Co; presiding elder AME Ch 1973-. **Military Serv:** AUS, Korean Conflict, 1951-53.

DANIELS, RON D.
Association executive. **Personal:** chilDren: Malik, Sundiata, Jeannette. **Educ:** Youngstown State, BA 1965; Rockefeller School of Public Affairs, MA 1967; Union Institute, Candidate for Doctoral Degree in Pol. Sci, 1976. **Career:** Assn Neighborhd Ctr, Hagstrom House, S Side Ctr, Camp Lexington, boys' prog dir, youth & young adult worker, camp counselor, camp prog dir 1961-64; Youngstown State Univ, educator 1967-69; Kent State Univ, educator, asst prof, African American Affairs & Pan-American studies, 1971, & 1981-86; Cornell Univ, educator, visiting prof, 1979-80; College of Wooster, educator, visiting assoc. prof, black studies, 1993; Hiram Coll, OH, educator 1973, asst prof of Pol Sci & Pan-African Studies, 1974-77; Jesse Jackson for Pres Campaign, Southern Regional mgr, 1988; exec dir, Natl Rainbow Coalition, 1987; moderator & producer, '' Perspectives in Black'' and ''Ron Daniels Show,'' WYTV, Youngstown OH, 1968-87 founder & chairman, Freedom Inc., 1967-75, exec dir, 1969-74; Inst for Community Organization and Development, Youngstown, OH, exec dir; Center for Constitutional Rights, exec dir, 1993-; syndicated columnist; editorial opinion writer, Black media Project of the Progressive Magazine; contributor, the Black Collegion and Z Magazine; Guest Host, Night Talk, the American Urban Radio Network. **Orgs:** Natl co-chairperson, Natl Black Independent Political Party, 1981-83; Pres Nat Black Political Assembly 1974-80 candidate for Mayor 1977; chairperson, 1983-85; exec Cong African People; founding mem African Liberation Day Coord Com, 1972; convener OH delegation Natl Black Polit Conv, Gary, IN, 1972; pres OH Black Pol Assembly; Nat Black Pol Assembly, elected pres 1974; training & proj eval consult Episcopal Ch Gen Conv Spec Prog; co- ordinator Mid-West Regional Coalition; Council of Elders, Fedn of Pan-African Educ Insts; elder Marcus Garvey Sch; adjunct prof & mem bd dir OH Inst of Practical Pol 1973; del No Am Reg Steering Conf, 6th Pan-Africa Conf; Help Us Make A Nation (HUMAN) Training Inst; Natl Economic Development & Law Center; National Jobs with Peace Campaign, board of directors; Greenpeace USA, board of directors; Nation Institute, board of directors; National Malcolm X Commemoration Commission, co-chairperson; African American Institute for Research and Empowerment, board of directors; Ntl. Chairperson, campaign for a new tomorrow 1992-; steering committee, Ntl African American Ldshop summitt, 1994-96, exec council, Ntl Org committee, The Millian March & Day of Action, 1995, founder, the Haiti Support Project, 1995; coordinator, NH State of Race Conference 1994; independent candidate for Pres of U.S., 1992. **Honors/Awds:** Youngstown Black Polit Assembly-Freedom Inc Award 1974; Minority Affairs Dir's Award 1974; Model Cities Citizen Participation Orgn Award 1974; Omega Psi Phi community service award, 1979; McGuffey Center community service award, 1982; African Cultural Weekend Award for dedicated leadership, 1985; Inter-Faith Community Action Committee Award, 1986; Inter-DenominationalClergywomen's Alliance civic award, 1986; First Williams Publishing Co Pioneer Award for outstanding contributions to civil rights in the media, 1988. **Business Addr:** Executive Director, Center for Constitutional Rights, 666 Broadway, 7th Fl, New York, NY 10012.

DANIELS, RUBEN
Administrator. **Personal:** Born Oct 17, 1917, Broken Bow, OK; son of L B French and Richard Daniels; married Elizabeth Chapman; children: Leslie Daniels Echols. **Educ:** Michigan State Univ, 1957. **Career:** Congressman Bob Traxler, aide; First Ward Community Center, exec dir 1965-; Saginaw Police Dept, patrolman & juvenile officer 1947-65; Gen Motors Corp, 1945-47, 1940-43; Grants Wholesale Groc, warehouseman 1939-40; Saginaw Dept of Recreation WPA, recreation leader 1936-39. **Orgs:** Past pres Saginaw Bd of Edn; adv com Social Studies Dept Delta Coll; trustee MI Natl Bank; chmn bd dir Saginaw Osteopathic Hosp; chmn Community Affairs Dept Cath Diocese; dir Saginaw Co Drug Treatment Ctr; mem Statewide Voc Task Force, MI Assn of Sch Bds; mem educ com MI Assn of Sch Bds; mem Human Relations Commn; exec bd OIC; mem Jefferson Meml Scholarship Fund; mem Local 699 Scholarship Fund; lay rep Jr League; mem Nat Alliance of Bus; chmn Law Enforcement Com, Human Relation Commn; pres, Saginaw Board of Education, 1990-92. **Honors/Awds:** Citations Saginaw Police Dept 1947-65; Lions Club Award 1963; NW Kiwanis Award 1966; Frontiersman of the Year, Frontiers Intl Saginaw Chap 1966; Achievement Award Saginaw Club Natl Assn of Negro Bus and Professional Womens Club Inc 1968; Layman of Year, Bethel AME Ch 1968; Distinguished Alumnus Saginaw High Sch 1972; Community Serv Award, Saginaw Chap Frontiers Intl 1979; Bob Alberts Award, C of C; Liberty Bell Award; Recognition Award, NAACP 1979; Recognition Award, Youth Employment Serv; Kwame Nkrumah Award, Black Honors Convocation; Saginaw Image Award, 1989; Honorary Degree, Saginaw Valley State College, 1974; Educator of the Year, Delta College; Building named in his honor: Ruben Daniels Lifelong Learning Center; Saginaw Val State Coll, Hon LlD/LittD, 1974. **Military Serv:** USNR po 3rd class 1943-45. **Business Addr:** 1410 N 12th St, Saginaw, MI 48601.

DANIELS, SIDNEY
Clergyman. **Personal:** Born Jul 28, 1923, Trumbull Co, OH; married Emma Lee Bryant. **Educ:** Youngstown Coll, BA 1945-49; Oberlin Theol Sem, 1949-50; Gammon Theol Sem, 1950-51; Howard Univ Sch Rel, BD 1951-53; John Hopkins Univ, 1970-72; MA 1976. **Career:** Civil Aero Bd, fed govt clerk 1950-52; Fairmont Hill Jr Sr HS, educator 1970-71; Samuel Gompers Jr HS, educator 1971-72; Emanuel C C Ch, minister 1958-; Equal Opportunity Officer. **Orgs:** IDBC; past pres Harlem Park Neighborhood Council Baltimore; chmn Empoyment Com Interdenomination Ministers' All; bd mem Baltimore Adv Council Voc Edn; bd mem founder Opportunities Industrialization Ctr Baltimore; pres Vol Pov War; volunteer work Crownsville Hosp Ctr; served TV & radio on educ & religious topics; established IOU Course given at Comm Coll Baltimore; First black chpln; Baltimore Fire Dept 1973. **Military Serv:** US Army, pvt, 1943-44. **Business Addr:** 1210 W Lanvale St, Baltimore, MD 21217.

DANIELS, TERRY L.
Manager. **Personal:** Born Jul 28, 1951, Shreveport, LA; son of Annie Daniels (deceased) and Louis Daniels (deceased); married Joyce E Hall Daniels, Aug 24, 1972; children: Shemetra Rachel, Nikki Renee. **Educ:** Southern University, A&M College, BS, industrial technology, 1973; Webster College, MA, management, 1977. **Career:** General Electric Co, manager, 1973-88; Eastman Kodak, mgr, manufacturing, 1988-91, mgr, site management, 1991-94; AT&T (GBCS), general mgr, vp, 1994-. **Orgs:** Network Northstar Inc, 1991-; Southern University Alumni Association; Boy Scouts of America, West Section (explorers) Oteciana Council, chairman; International Facilities Management Association, 1992-; National Maintenance Excellence Award, Board of Directors, membership committee, chairman, 1992; Alliance of Black Telecommunications Workers, mem. **Honors/Awds:** National Maintenance Excellence Award, Peak Award, 1992; Black Achievers, Youth Service Award, 1984. **Special Achievements:** Author, Maintenance Technology Magazine, p 24, Jan 1992; Plant Engineering Magazine, p 72, September 1992. **Business Addr:** General Mgr & Vice Pres, Denport Mfg-GBCS, AT&T, 1200 West 120th Ave, Westminster, CO 80030, (303)538-2000.

DANIELS, WILLIAM JAMES
Educational administrator. **Personal:** Born Mar 7, 1940, Chicago, IL; son of Ethel Cora Dent McCoy and William Hector McCoy; married Fannie Pearl Hudson Daniels, Aug 25, 1963; children: Twanda Delois. **Educ:** Upper Iowa University, Fayette, IA, BA, 1962; University of Iowa, MA, 1964, PhD, 1970. **Career:** Union College, Schenectady, NY, assistant professor, 1966-72, associate professor, 1973-81, professor, 1982-88, associate dean, 1983-88; Rochester Institute of Technology, College of Liberal Arts, dean, prof of political science, 1988-. **Orgs:** American Political Science Association, vice president, 1990-91; National Conference of Black Political Scientists, president, 1972-73; Association of American Colleges, board member; American Association of Higher Education; National Urban League of Rochester, chr, bd of dirs. **Honors/Awds:** Schenectady County Bar Association, Liberty Bell Award, 1988; National Conference of Black Political Scientists, Distinguished Service Award, 1972-73; Fulbright-Hayes Fellowship, Japan, 1973-74; Alfred E Smith Fellowship, 1970-71; US Supreme Court, Judicial Fellowship, 1978-79. **Business Addr:** Dean College of Liberal Arts, Rochester Institute of Technolo-

gy, 1 Lomb Memorial Drive, P O Box 9887, Rochester, NY 14623-0087.

DANIELS, WILLIAM ORLAN
Administrator. **Personal:** Born Apr 26, 1944, Rendville, OH; married Lamerial Ann Garrison; children: Leslie Michelle. **Educ:** Fisk U, BS. **Career:** New Eng Terr Dayco Printing Products Co, district mgr 1980; Dayton Urban League Inc, dir educ & employment; Dayton Urban League Inc, adminstr acting exec dir 1974-80; Montgomery Co Childrens Serv Bd, social worker 1972-74; Dayton Pub Sch Dist, tchr 1969-72; Dayton Pub SchESAA Adv Com, chmn 1976-77;Trotwood Madison Sch Dist Capital Univ Without Walls, consult 1976 1978. **Orgs:** Mem Miami Valley Personnel Assn 1980-; mem Kappa Alpha Psi Frat Inc 1965-; mem Miami Valley Reg Planning Commn 1977-; commr City of Dayton Tennis Commn 1978-; founder Dayton Urban League Youth Forum 1974; founder Dayton Urban League Summer Employment Project 1976.

DANIELS, WILLIE L.
Company executive. **Career:** United Daniels Securities Inc, CEO, 1984-. **Special Achievements:** Company is ranked #11 on the Black Enterprise list of top investment banks, 1994. **Business Addr:** CEO, United Daniels Securities Inc., PO Box 617521, Orlando, FL 32861-7521.

DANNER, MARGARET ESSIE (MARGARET CUNNINGHAM)
Poet. **Personal:** Born Jan 12, 1915, Chicago, IL; daughter of Naomi Danner and Caleb Danner; married Cordell Strickland (divorced); children: Naomi. **Educ:** Attended YMCA Coll, Chicago, IL, Roosevelt Univ, and Northwestern Univ; also studied under Karl Shapiro and Paul Engle. **Career:** Poetry magazine, Chicago, IL, editorial asst, 1951-55, asst editor, 1956-57; Wayne State Univ, Detroit, MI, poet in residence, 1961-62; touring poet, Baha'i Teaching Committee, 1964-66; Whitney fellow in Senegal, Africa, and Paris, France, 1966; Virginia Union Univ, Richmond, poet in residence, 1968-69; LeMoyne-Owen Coll, Memphis, TN, poet-in-residence, 1970-75; founder of Boone House (Center for the Arts), Detroit, MI, and of Nologonyu's, Chicago, IL. **Orgs:** Mem, Soc of Afro Amer Culture; Contemporary Artists; Natl Pen Women; Memphis Cable TV; Natl Council of Teachers of English; Poets in a Bottle; dir, Boone House; life mem, Chicago Southside Comm Art Center Nologonias. **Honors/Awds:** Author of Impressions of African Art Forms, Broadside Press, 1960, To Flower: Poems, Counterpoise Series, 1963, Iron Lace, Poets Press, 1968, The Down of a Thistle, Country Beautiful, 1976; editor of anthologies Brass Horses, 1968, and Regroup, 1969; recorded, with Langson Hughes, Writers of the Revolution; John Hay Whitney Fellowship; Amer Writers Award; Harriet Tubman Award; Native Chicagoans Literary Award; Midwestern Writers Award; named Teacher of the Year, LeMoyen-Owen Coll, 1975. **Home Addr:** 626 East 102nd Pl, Chicago, IL 60628.

DANSBY, JESSE L., JR.
Educational administrator, entrepreneur. **Personal:** Born Aug 17, 1942, Bessemer, AL; son of Ora L Martin and Rev Jesse L Dansby Sr; divorced; children: Natasha Lynn, Mischa Anita. **Educ:** TN State Univ, BS 1964; Univ of OK, MA 1973; Industrial College of the Armed Forces, Management Certificate 1975; Air Command and Staff Coll, Management Certificate 1977; Air Force Inst of Tech Intl Logistics, Management Certificate 1977; Univ of OK, Yale Univ, Certificate, Human Resource Mgmt, 1972 -73. **Career:** Intl Logistics Ctr, dir Middle East & African program 1979-80; Defense Electronic Supply Ctr, dir of installation serv 1980-83; Kwang Ju Air Base South Korea, base commander 1983-84; HQ Air Force Logistics Command, dir of inquiries and govtl affairs office of inspector general 1984-; IN Univ, Richmond, IN, college administrator, director of diversity and multicultural affairs, 1989-. **Orgs:** Mem Omega Phi Phi 1962-; mem Greater Dayton Real Estate Investment Assoc 1980-; bd dirs Girl Scouts of Amer 1982-; mem Industrial Relation Assoc 1985-; mem Ancient Egyptian Arabic Order of the Mystic Shrine. **Honors/Awds:** Outstanding Social Actions Officer USAF Europe 1974; Presidential Citation Khartoum Sudan 1979; author handbook on Equal Oppor USAF Europe 1973; co-author handbook "Human Relations in the Military" USAF Europe 1973; 33 Degree Mason 1988. **Military Serv:** USAF lt col 1964-89; Defense Meritorious Serv Medal; Efficiency Medal First Class (Govt of Sudan); Air Force Meritorious Serv Medal w/Two Oak Leaf Clusters; Air Force Commendation Medal. **Home Addr:** 1880 El Camino Dr, Xenia, OH 45385. **Business Addr:** Director, Multicultural Affairs, Indiana University East, 2325 Chester Blvd, Richmond, IN 47374-9979.

DANTICAT, EDWIDGE
Writer, novelist. **Personal:** Born Jan 19, 1969, Port-Au-Prince, Haiti; daughter of Rose & Andre Danticat. **Educ:** Barnard Coll, BA, 1990; Brown Univ, MFA, 1993. **Career:** Clinica Estetico, prod researcher. **Orgs:** Alpha Kappa Alpha. **Honors/Awds:** Essence Fiction Award; The Caribbean Writer Fiction Prize; Seventeen Magazine Fiction Prize. **Special Achievements:** Novel, Breath, Eyes, Memory; published a collection of short stories, Krik? Krak!.

DANTLEY, ADRIAN DELANO
Basketball player. **Personal:** Born Feb 28, 1956, Hyattsville, MD; son of Geraldine Robinson Dantley and Avon Dantley; married DiNitri. **Educ:** Univ of Notre Dame, business, 1977. **Career:** Buffalo Braves, 1976-77; Indiana Pacers, 1977; LA Lakers, 1977-79; Utah Jazz, 1979-86; Detroit Pistons, 1986-88; Dallas Mavericks, 1989-91; Milwaukee Bucks, 19991; Breeze Milano, Italy, currently. **Honors/Awds:** Gold medal team US Olympic basketball, 1976; twice All-American; Rookie of the Yr, 1976-77; leading scorer NBA, 1980-81; NBA Comeback Player of the Year Award, 1983-84; NBA All Star Team 1980-82, 1984-86. **Business Addr:** Basketball Player, Philips Olympia Milano, via Callanissetta 3, 20129 Milan, Italy.

DANZY, LEROY HENRY
Law enforcement. **Personal:** Born May 22, 1929, Wayside, KS; son of Julia Danzy and Henry Danzy; married Velma Lee Ballard; children: Gwenevere, Gail, Leronna, Vance. **Educ:** US Army School, Heavy Equip Maint 1955; IN Vocation Tech, Cert 1969. **Career:** Farmer, 1944-54; US Army, 1954-56; Wheelabrator, shop laborer 1953-65, milwright 1965-; MI Constable & Court Officers Assoc, vp, pres 1987-. **Orgs:** Constable Calvin Twp Cass Cty 1957-; deacon Chain Lake Baptist Church 1962-; steward & guide committeeman United Auto Workers Union 1964-72, 1972-79 Bargaining Committeeman; vice pres educ dir MI Constable & Court Off Assn 1970-; mem & sec Cassopolis Publ Sch Bd 1972-84; fair practice chmn United Auto Workers Union 1972-; pres Cassopolis Public Sch Bd 1984-86; vice pres Cassopolis Publ Schl Bd 1986-88; FruitBelt Electric Co-op, director, 1994-97; Midwest Energy Co-op, 1998-. **Honors/Awds:** Constable of the Year MI Constable & Court Off Lansing 1972. **Military Serv:** AUS spec 3 1954-56. **Home Addr:** 17532 Williamsville St, Cassopolis, MI 49031.

DAPREMONT, DELMONT, JR.
Automobile dealer. **Career:** Coastal Ford, Inc, automobile dealer. **Honors/Awds:** Named one of the top one hundred auto dealers by Black Enterprise in June, 1988. **Business Addr:** Coastal Ford Inc, 7311 Airport Blvd, Mobile, AL 36608.

DARBY, CASTILLA A., JR.
Physician. **Personal:** Born Jul 17, 1946, Anniston, AL; children: Kimberlynne Michelle. **Educ:** AL State Univ, BS 1968; VA Hosp Tuskegee Inst AL, Corrective Physical Therapy 1968-69; Schiff Scout Reservation Teng Ctr Mendham NJ, scout exec 1970; Meharry Medical Coll, MD 1978. **Career:** Woodson HS, biology instructor; Ford Greene Elem Sch Nashville, physical educ instructor 1969-70; Boy Scouts of Amer Middle TN Cncl, dist scout exec 1970-71; TN Valley Authority Nashville, clinical physician; Douglas Memorial Hospital Jefferson TX, medical dir 1980-83; Private Practice, physician; Lake CliffHospital Dallas TX, chief of staff. **Orgs:** Mem NAACP 1986, Meharry Medical Coll Alumni Assoc 1986-87, AMA, Natl Federation of Independent Business 1986-87; mem TX Federation of Sr Citizens 1987; life mem Kappa Alpha Psi Frat Inc; mem TX Medical Assoc. **Honors/Awds:** AL State Univ Freshman Awd for Academic Excellence; tutor Anatomy & Physiology AL State Univ; Jessie S Noyles Scholarship Obstetrics & Gynecology 1978. **Business Addr:** PO Box 150278, Dallas, TX 75315.

DARBY, MATTHEW LAMONT
Professional football player. **Personal:** Born Nov 19, 1968, Virginia Beach, VA; married Cheryl; children: Matthew, Marcus. **Educ:** UCLA, bachelor's degree in Afro-American studies. **Career:** Buffalo Bills, defensive back, 1992-95; Arizona Cardinals, 1996-. **Business Addr:** Professional Football Player, Arizona Cardinals, 8701 S Hardy, Tempe, AZ 85284, (602)379-0101.

DAR DAR, KIRBY DAVID
Professional football player. **Personal:** Born Mar 27, 1972, Morgan City, LA. **Educ:** Syracuse. **Career:** Miami Dolphins, running back, 1995-.

DARDEN, ANTHONY KOJO
Principal community service assistant. **Personal:** Born Jan 10, 1943, Birmingham, AL; son of Annie B Harris & Samuel Darden (both deceased); divorced; children: 2. **Educ:** Wayne County Community College, associate's of arts/liberal arts, 1974; Detroit Institute of Technology, bachelor's of arts/psychology, 1976; Wayne State University, master's/social work, 1984. **Career:** City of Detroit, principal community service assistant, currently. **Orgs:** The 24 Hour Store Marketing Associates, board chairman; Enterprising Business Associates Marketing, board chairman; Shrine of the Black Madonna, member. **Special Achievements:** Wayne State University, real estate, laws & sales, 1973; Omaha Insurance Co, insurance, rules & law, 1975; Amway Corp, networking mkgt, art & science, 1989; Wayne County Community College, Recognition for Organizing first student government structure, president, 1974, co-organizer "The Open Door," managing editor, 1973; Shrine of the Black Madonna, 25 Year of Service. **Home Phone:** (313)868-9021. **Business Addr:** Chairman, Enterprising Business Associates, PO Box 321232, Detroit, MI 48232, (313)927-3245.

DARDEN, CALVIN
United parcel service executive. **Personal:** Born Feb 5, 1950, Buffalo, NY; married Patricia Gail Darden, Aug 21, 1971; children: Ramarro, Tami, Lorielle. **Educ:** Canisius College, BS, 1972; Emory Univ, Executive Development Consortium, 1997. **Career:** UPS, district manager North Jersey, 1984-86, district manager Metro Jersey, 1986-91, district manager Metro DC, 1991-93, vice pres Pacific region, 1993-95, vice pres corporate strategic quality coordinator, 1995-, senior vp of operations, 1997-. **Orgs:** African American Unity Centers, Atlanta Chapter, pres, 1996-; National Urban League, bd of dirs, 1997-; National Urban League Black Executive Exchange Program, bd of dirs; 100 Black Men of Metro Atlanta; WATL Channel 36, bd of dirs; Deliverance Temple of Atlanta, deacon; United Way of Long Beach, CA, bd of dirs; Atlanta Quality Resource Center, bd of dirs; Orange County City Council, commissioner. **Business Addr:** Senior VP, US Operations, United Parcel Service, 55 Glenlake Parkway, NE, Atlanta, GA 30328.

DARDEN, CHRISTINE MANN
Aerospace engineer. **Personal:** Born Sep 10, 1942, Monroe, NC; married Walter L Darden Jr; children: Jeanne Darden Riley, Janet Christine. **Educ:** Hampton Inst, BS (w/high honors), math, 1962; VA State Coll, MS, math, 1967; George Washington Univ, DSc, mech engineering, 1983. **Career:** Brunswick Co Sch, tchr 1962-63; Portsmouth City Sch VA, tchr 1964-65; VA State Coll, math instr 1966-67; NASA Langley Rsch Ctr, data analyst 1967-73, aerospace eng, group leader, sonic boom group, 1989-92, senior project engineer, advanced vehicles division, deputy proj mgr, HSR TU-144 program, currently. **Orgs:** Pres Hampton Roads Chpt, Natl Tech Assn 1984-88; assoc fellow, 1973-, secretary, aerocoustics technical committee, 1990-91, Amer Inst of Aeronautics & Astronauts; elder Carver Mem Presbyterian Ch 1980-; mem Gamma Upsilon Omega Chap of AKA 1960-, Natl Langley Exchange Cncl 1979-; chmn boundaries comm Southern VA Presbyterian Church USA 1983-88; moderator, Synod of Mid-Atlantic Presbyterian Churches, 1989-90; ; chairman, Presbytery Council, Easter VA Presbytery, 1990-; national secretary, National Technical Association, 1990-92. **Honors/Awds:** 20 Year Alumnus Award, Hampton Inst 1982; Dr AT Weathers Tech Achievement Awd, Natl Tech Assoc 1985; Dollars & Sense Mag, 100 Top Black Bus & Professional Women 1986; Black Engineer of the Year in Government, Mobile Oil Council of Eng Deans, 1988; Technology Transfer, NASA, 1990; Technical Achievements and Humanitarian Efforts, North Carolina State Univ, 1990; NASA, EEO Medal, 1991; NASA Langley Research Center, Dual Career Ladder Award, 1991; Women in Science & Engineering, Outstanding Women in Government Award, 1992; Langley Engineering Achievement Award, 1994. **Special Achievements:** Author or co-author of over 54 technical reports and articles. **Business Addr:** Deputy Proj Mgr, HSR TU-144 Program, NASA Langley Research Ctr, MS 412, Hampton, VA 23665.

DARDEN, CHRISTOPHER A.
Law professor. **Personal:** Born Apr 8, 1956, Martinez, CA; son of Jean and Eddie Darden; children: Jenee. **Educ:** San Jose State Univ, BA, administrative justice, 1977; Univ of California-Hastings College of Law, JD, 1980. **Career:** National Labor Relations Board, attorney, 1980-81; Los Angeles County, assistant head deputy, Special Investigations Division, begin 1981; Los Angeles County District Attorney's Office, deputy district attorney; Southwestern Univ School of Law, prof, 1995-. **Orgs:** California Bar, Criminal Law Section, exec comm, 1994-97; National Black Prosecutors Assn, board member, 1989; Loved Ones of Homicide Victims, past pres, bd of dirs, 1987-; Los Angeles County Assn of Deputy District Attorneys, board member, 1986-87; John M Langston Bar Assn, 1995. **Honors/Awds:** San Jose State Univ, Dept of Admin Justice, Alumnus of the Year Award, 1995. **Special Achievements:** The People vs Orenthal James Simpson, BA097211, part of prosecuting team; co-author, In Contempt, 1996; appeared in television movie. **Business Addr:** Law Professor, Southwestern University, School of Law, 625 S. West Moreland Ave., Los Angeles, CA 90005-3905, (213)738-6700.

DARDEN, GEORGE HARRY
Attorney. **Personal:** Born Mar 14, 1934, Cadiz, KY; son of Sammie Darden and Belknap Darden; married Gwen Wright; children: George II, Tiffany, Betsy, Josette. **Educ:** KY State Univ, BS 1955; Salmon P Chase College of Law, JD 1964. **Career:** Hamilton Cnty, OH, asst cnty prosecutor 1964-66; Cincinnati, OH, Hopkinsville, KY, priv pract 1964-69; Legal Serv Proj Ctr OH, chief attny 1967-68; Lincoln Hts, OH, city solicitor 1967-68; EEOC, Washington, DC, staff attny 1969-71, supervisory 1973, chief legal consel div 1973-75; Equal Employment Opportunity Commission, regional attorney, Atlanta, GA, 1975-. **Orgs:** Pres Double Dollar Co 1965-68; chrmn, legal comm Hopkinsville, KY, NAACP 1968-69; chrmn, legal redress comm Denver, CO 1984-. **Honors/Awds:** Citations EEOC Houston Hearings 1972-73, Chief Judge, Cincinnati Muncpl Ct 1968, WCIN Radio Station 1968; Cincinnati Herald Paper 1968.

DARDEN, JOSEPH S., JR.
Educator. **Personal:** Born Jul 25, 1925, Pleasantville, NJ; son of Blanche Paige Darden and Joseph S Darden Sr.; married; children: Michele Irene Darden Burgess. **Educ:** Lincoln Univ, AB 1948; NY Univ, MA 1952, EdD 1963. **Career:** Clark Coll, instructor Biological Science 1952-55; Albany State Coll, asst to prof, Biology & Health Educ 1955-64, chmn science div 1959-60; Wagner Coll, adjunct prof, 1966-88; Rutgers Univ, adjunct prof Sex Educ 1974,75; Montclair State Coll, 1975; Kean Coll of NJ, prof & coordinator, Health Educ 1964-, chair, Health and Recreation Dept, 1979-84, dir, Minority Enrollment, 1988-94. **Orgs:** Pres E Dist Assn AAHPERD 1974-75; vice pres & chmn Health Educ Div E Dist Assn AAHPERD 1971-72; vice pres Health Educ NJ Assn for HPER 1967; mem adv bd ''Health Educ'' AAHPERD 1973-76; editorial bd ''The Journal of School Health'' ASHA 1969-72; governing council Amer School Health Assn 1970-73; author, lecturer, workshop dir, radio & TV panelist in sex educ; bd dir Assn for Advancement of Health Educ 1975-78; E Dist Rep to Alliance Bd, 1979-82; founder NJ Health Educ Council 1967; NJAHPERD; ASHA; SIECUS, AASECT; Fellow ASHA; bd of trustees Planned Parenthood of Essex County 1985-; diplomate, American Board of Sexology, 1990-. **Honors/Awds:** Danforth Found Fellow 1958-59; Distinguished Serv Award, Amer School Health Assoc 1971; Hon Fellow Award, NJ Assoc for Health, Physical Educ & Recreation 1972; Honor Award NJ Health Educ Council 1975; Distinguished Leadership Award, NJ Assoc for Health, Physical Educ & Recreation 1975; District Hon Award, East District Assoc AAHPERD 1976; Distinguished Serv Award, Alpha Alpha Lambda Chapter Alpha Phi Alpha 1975; Alliance Honor Award AAHPERD 1985; Outstanding Coll/ Univ Teacher of the Year Eastern Dist Assn AAHPERD 1983; numerous articles published in state, regional & natl journals, Charles D Henry Award, AAHPERD, 1988; Edwin B. Henderson Award, EMC, AAHPEDD, 1991; Professional Service to Health Education Award, AAHE/AAHPERD, 1990; The Alumni Achievement Award, Lincoln Univ, 1993. **Special Achievements:** Toward A Healthier Sexuality: A Book of Readings, 1996. **Military Serv:** AUS t/sgt 1944-46. **Home Addr:** 1416 Thelma Dr, Union, NJ 07083. **Business Addr:** Kean Coll of New Jersey, Physical Educ, Recreation & Health Dept, Union, NJ 07083.

DARDEN, ORLANDO WILLIAM
Business executive. **Personal:** Born Jun 2, 1930, Washington, DC; married Peggie Hamer; children: Orlando Jr, Michael. **Educ:** Howard U, BA 1953. **Career:** Comm Fed Sav & Loan Assn of Washington, pres 1974-; mort bnkr; real est brkr; OWD Enterprises, president. **Orgs:** Mem bd, PA Ave Devel Corp; Mayor's Econ Devel Com for DC; Adv Com of Pub Serv Commn of DC; mem DC Gambling Study Commn; Devel Sch Found; chmn bd CF Financial Corp; dir Dolphin & Evans Settlements, Inc; vice pres Urban Mgmt Serv Listed Mortgage Banker 1973. **Honors/Awds:** Washington Real Estate Brokers Award, DC C of C. **Military Serv:** USAF 1st lt 1953-55. **Business Addr:** President, OWD Enterprises, Inc, 1511 K Street, NW #319, Washington, DC 20005.

DARDEN, WILLIAM BOONE
Police chief (retired). **Personal:** Born Aug 16, 1925, Atlanta, GA; married Rose M Meyers, Jun 6, 1956; children: Darrell, William Jr, Kimberly. **Educ:** Nova Univ FL, MA Criminal Justice 1977; SE Univ SC, MA Pub Adminstrn 1976; FL Intl U, BS Criminal Justice 1974; Palm Beach Jr Coll, Asso Arts 1971. **Career:** Retired 1983; Riviera Beach Police Dept, chief of police 1971-83; Migrant Leg Serv, chf investgtr 1971; ret Lt 1965; W Palm Beach Police Dept, lt patrol 1960; W Palm Beach Police Dept, sgt patrol 1956; W Palm Beach Police Dept, detect 1952; W Palm Beach Police Dept, walking patrolman 1948. **Orgs:** Chmn affirmative action Dem Parto of FL; mem Nat Dem Com-Nat Rules Com-dem Party; bd of dirs Nat Ofcrs of Black Law Enforcement Execs; mem Alpha Phi Alpha Frat; mem Lambda Alpha Epsilon; Am Crim Justice Assn; Sigma Pi Phi Frat. **Honors/Awds:** Mem, Natl Tranportation Advisory Comm, presidential appointment by Pres Carter, 1978-81. **Military Serv:** Milit Police World War II.

DARE, YINKA
Professional basketball player. **Personal:** Born Oct 10, 1972, Kano, Nigeria. **Educ:** George Washington. **Career:** New Jersey Nets, center, 1994-98; Orlando Magic, 1998-. **Business Addr:** Professional Basketball Player, Orlando Magic, PO Box 76, Orlando, FL 32801, (407)649-3200.

DARITY, JANIKI EVANGELIA
Health administrator. **Personal:** Born Mar 29, Beirut, Lebanon; daughter of William & Evangeline Darity. **Educ:** Spelman College, BA, 1980; Univ of Texas, Austin School of Law, JD, 1983; Harvard Univ, School of Public Health, MPH, 1984. **Career:** Campbell, Davidson & Morgan, law clerk, 1981-82; Bechtel Group, Inc, law clerk, 1982; Southern Union Gas Co, law clerk, 1983; Harper Hospital, admini fellow, hospital admini, 1984-87; Michigan Hosp Assoc, asst dir, legal & regulatory affairs, 1987-89; Henry Ford Hosp, dir urban health initiative, 1989-91; Henry Ford Health Systems, corp dir community health devt, 1992-94; vp community devt, 1994-. **Orgs:** Leadership Amer Alumni Assn, 1994-; United Cerebral Palsy of Metro Der, bd of dirs, 1993-1997; Leadership Oakland, chair race & ethnic diversity steering community, 1993-; In-Site Horizon Field Trips, Inc, first vp board of directors, 1992-; Detroit Rotary Club International, chair, youth services & community svcs, 1992-; Alpha Kappa Alpha Sorority, Inc, 1979-; Natl Assn of Health Svcs Execs, 1984-; Natl Health Lawyers Assn, 1983-; Natl Bar Assn, 1981-; Amer Assn of Univ Women, 1993-; Women's Economic Club, 1992-; Assn of Healthcare Philanthropy, 1994; Junior League of Birmingham, MI, 1996-; Generation of Promise board of directors, 1996-; Detroit United Negro College Fund, Walk-A-Thon, co-chair, 1997-98. **Home Phone:** (810)353-8312. **Business Addr:** VP, Community Devt, Henry Ford Health System, One Ford Place, 5A, Detroit, MI 48202, (313)874-4033.

DARITY, WILLIAM A.
Educator. **Personal:** Born Jan 15, 1924, Flat Rock, NC; son of Elizabeth Smith Darity (deceased) and Aden Randall Darity (deceased); married Evangeline Royall, Dec 23, 1950 (deceased); children: William Jr, Janki Evangelia; married Leonel Grady Smith, Dec 28, 1996. **Educ:** Shaw U, BS 1948; NC Central U, MSPH 1949; Univ of NC, PhD 1964. **Career:** Univ of MA, prof, 1965-, prof pub health and dean, Sch of Health Sci, 1973-89, prof of public health, 1989-91, prof emeritus of public health, 1991-; World Health Orgn, regional advisor, 1953-64, consultant, 1971-80; Peace Corps Training Programs, consult dir, 1962-67; Headstart Training Programs, consult lectr, 1965-67; Univ of NC, vis prof, 1973; Univ of SC, vis prof, 1980; external examiner, Univ of Ibadan, Nigeria, and Univ of West Indies, 1973-; Natl Cancer Inst, dir and principal investigator, Res on Cancer and Smoking in Black Populations, 1986-91; The Population Council, NY, senior associate, posted in Cairo, Egypt, 1991-93. **Orgs:** Fellow Am Pub Health Assn; fellow Soc for Pub Health Educ Inc; fellow Am Sch Health Assn; mem Am Nat Council on Health Edn; mem Intl Union on Health Edn; Delta Omega; asso Danforth Found; mem bd dir Drug Abuse Council Inc 1972-79; bd dir Planned Parenthood Fed of Am Inc 1967-73; bd dir SIECUS 1967-71; pres MA Assn for Mental Health 1967-69; pres Hampshire Public Health Assn 1967-70; bd of trustees, Univ of NC-Chapel Hill, 1985-91; bd of Scientific Counsellors, Natl Cancer Inst, 1986-90; bd of dir, MA Water Resources Authority, 1989-91; Phi Kappa Phi; Sigma Xi; Sigma Pi Phi, 1986-; Omega Psi Phi 1946-; mem & official of many other civic orgns. **Honors/Awds:** Recipient Fellowship World Health Orgn; Hildrus Poindexter Public Health Service Award, BCHW/APHA, 1975; Distinguished Lecture/ Chancellor's Medal, Univ of MA, 1989; Dist Alumnus Awd, Univ of NC, 1996; Shaw Univ, Alumni Achievement Awd, 1997. **Military Serv:** US Army, infantry, 1st lieutenant, 1943-47. **Home Addr:** 105 Heatherstone Road, Amherst, MA 01002.

DARK, LAWRENCE JEROME
Educational administrator. **Personal:** Born Jan 18, 1953, Americus, GA; son of Frances Adrilla Harris Howard and Charlie Dark; married Okianer B Christian; children: Harrison Edward. **Educ:** Denison Univ, BA 1976; Northwestern Univ, JD 1980. **Career:** Frostburg State Coll, asst to the pres 1979-82; Amer Bar Assn Council on Legal Educ Oppor, assoc dir 1982-85; Claflin Coll, dir corporate foundation relations and devel 1985-86; Amer Univ, adjunct faculty mem 1985; Claflin Coll, part-time faculty mem 1985-86; American Red Cross, corporate initiative assoc 1986-88; Virginia Council on Human Rights, dir (appointed by Gov Gerald L Baliles as the first dir for this new state agency), 1988-90; National Institute Against Prejudice & Violence, executive director, 1991; Univ of South Carolina, executive asst to the president for equal opportunity programs, 1992-. **Orgs:** Natl advisory comm mem Natl Inst for Citizen Educ in the Law 1986-; mem Alpha Phi Alpha Fraternity Iota Upsilon Lambda Chapter; bd mem MD Humanities Council 1980-84, MD State Bd for Social Serv 1982-84; comm mem United Way 1988-; field service chair American Red Cross EOH 1988-; comm mem American Red Cross Volunteer Communications Campaign Advisory Comm, Policy Issues Comm 1989-; comm mem Amer Society of Public Admin 1989-; numerous others. **Honors/Awds:** Citation by Sec of the MD Dept of Human Resources for Serv on the State Bd for Social Serv 1984; Citation for Serv on the MD Humanities Council 1984; Natl Scholarship Serv and Fund for Negro Students Award; Woodrow Wilson Natl Fellowship 1985-86; Improved Fundraising Capabilites Program; United Negro Coll Fund Leadership Pin Award 1986; Council on Legal Educ Opportunity Scholarship; Natl Endowment for the Humanities Fellowship 1981; selected to attend American Red Cross Leadership Institute 1987, The Governor's Educational Program, Virginia Executive Institute 1988; selected to attend the 1989/1990 Leadership Metro Richmond Leadership Development Program 1989, Executive Leadership Institute of the National Forum for Black Public Administrators 1989; numerous others. **Business Addr:** President/CEO, The Urban League of Portland, 10 North Russell Street, Portland, OR 97227.

DARK, OKIANER CHRISTIAN
Educator. **Personal:** Born Dec 8, 1954, Petersburg, VA; daughter of Vivian Louise Rier Christian and Marshall Christian Sr; married Lawrence Dark, Jun 20, 1981; children: Harrison Edward. **Educ:** Upsala College, BA (magna cum laude), 1976; Rutgers University School of Law, JD, 1979. **Career:** US Department of Justice, Antitrust Division, trial attorney, 1979-84, Civil Division, trial attorney, 1984; University of Richmond Law School, assistant professor, 1984-87, associate professor, 1987-90, professor, 1990; American University, The Washington College of Law, visiting professor and scholar, 1991-92; Willamette Univ Coll of Law, visitinr professor, 1994-95; US Attorney's Office, asst US attorney, 1995-. **Orgs:** National Bar Association, advisory board of NBA Magazine, 1988-; VA Black Women Attorneys Association, board of directors, 1990-94; The Daily Planet, board member, 1989-95; Saint Paul's College, board of trustees, 1989-; Jewels of Ann Private Day School, board of directors, 1991-92; Saint Paul's Baptist Church, 1989-94. **Honors/Awds:** Rutgers University, Alumni Senior Prize, 1979; Hope for People Award, 1991; University of Richmond, Distinguished Education Award, 1990 and 1993; VA Women Attorneys Association, Foundation Distinguished Faculty Award, 1991; South Brunswick High School, Distinguished Graduate Award, 1994. **Special Achievements:** Is the National Childhood Vaccine Injury Act of 1986 the solution for the DTP Controversy, 19 University of Toledo L Rev 799, 1988; Racial Insults: Keep Thy Tongue From Evil, 24 Suffolk L Rev 559, 1990; Catchin An Attitude About Learning to Respect Persons of Difference, 1990; Videotape -Nationally distributed on Housing Discrimination, 1991. **Home Addr:** 5236 NE Cleveland Avenue, Portland, OR 97211. **Business Addr:** Professor, T C Williams School of Law, University of Richmond, Richmond, VA 23173, (804)289-8197.

DARKE, CHARLES B.
Dentist, educational administrator. **Personal:** Born Sep 22, 1937, Chicago, IL; son of Annie Waulene Tennin-Darke and Paul Olden Darke; married Judith Chew-Darke; children: Charles B Darke II. **Educ:** Wilson Jr Coll, AA 1960; Meharry Medical Coll, DDS 1964; Univ of California, Berkeley, MPH 1972. **Career:** Hospital Appointments: Mt Zion Hospital, St Mary Hospital, San Francisco General Hospital; Career Highlights: Dept of Labor Job Corp Region 9, dental consultant; Univ of California, School of Med, asst clinical prof; Univ California, School of Dentistry, lecturer; San Francisco General Hospital, dir dental serv; San Francisco General Hospital, asst admin, Satellite Health Centers; Operations Officer, San Francisco Health Dept; part time private practice, dentist, currently; California State University, Fullerton, Fullerton, CA, director of student health and counseling center, currently. **Orgs:** State Bd of Dental Examiners California; dir Dental Ser San Francisco General Hospital div of outpatient & comm serv; American Health Care, consult prepaid health plans; bd dirs CA Children's Lobby; field consultant Joint Commn on Accreditation of Hospitals; past president, Northern California, National Dental Assn; Yorba Hill Medical Center, bd of dirs; Chapman Univ, science task force. **Honors/Awds:** Outstanding Young Men of America, 1973. **Military Serv:** USAF Capt 1965-67. **Business Addr:** 2175 Hayes St, San Francisco, CA 94117.

DARKES, LEROY WILLIAM
Electrical engineer (retired). **Personal:** Born Sep 26, 1924, Atlantic City, NJ; son of Isabella Wynder Darkes and William E Darkes; married Mamie Doris Simpson; children: William S, Leroy S, Lois L Bond, Matthew S. **Educ:** Rutgers Univ, BS Elec Engr 1947, MS 1948. **Career:** Atlantic City Elec Co, elec engr 1948, distrib engr 1953, syst planning engr 1958, mgr Var Areas 1965-89. **Orgs:** Mbr IEEE 1948-, Natl Soc of Professional Engineers 1955-, Atlantic Cty Bd of Ed 1969-87, Atlantic County Planning Bd 1972-89. **Honors/Awds:** Licensed NJ Professional Engineer 1955-. **Military Serv:** AUS pfc 1944-46. **Home Addr:** 1915 Grant Ave, Atlantic City, NJ 08401.

DARKINS, CHRISTOPHER OJI
Professional football player. **Personal:** Born Apr 30, 1974, Houston, TX; married Paula; children: Andre. **Educ:** Univ of Minnesota, attended. **Career:** Green Bay Packers, running back, 1997-. **Business Addr:** Professional Football Player, Green Bay Packers, 1265 Lombardi Ave, Green Bay, WI 54304, (414)494-2351.

DARKINS, DUANE ADRIAN. See Obituaries section.

DARLING, JAMES
Professional football player. **Personal:** Born Dec 29, 1974. **Educ:** Washington State, attended. **Career:** Philadelphia Eagles, linebacker, 1997-. **Business Addr:** Professional Football Player, Philadelphia Eagles, 3501 S Broad St, Philadelphia, PA 19148, (215)463-2500.

DARNELL, EDWARD BUDDY
Airport management official. **Personal:** Born Mar 4, 1930, Chicago, IL; son of Mary Darnell and Edward Darnell; married Gwendolyn Wilson, Aug 19, 1953; children: Glenn T, Gary L. **Educ:** Detroit Institute of Technology, BAA, 1968; Wayne State University, MSW, 1971; University of Michigan, specialist in gerontology, 1971. **Career:** Detroit City Airport, deputy director, currently. **Orgs:** Imperial first ceremonial master, Imperial Council Shriners, 1988; grand recording secretary, United Supreme Council, 1977. **Honors/Awds:** Legion of honor, Prince Hall Shriners, 1973; Scottish Rite Hall of Fame, Prince Hall Scottish Rite, 1984. **Military Serv:** US Marine Corps, sergeant; Presidential Unit Citation, 1953. **Home Addr:** 250 E Harbortown Dr, #703, Detroit, MI 48207-5010.

DARRELL, BETTY LOUISE
Beverage company executive. **Personal:** Born Mar 16, 1934, Louisville, KY; daughter of Cleoda Mason McDonald and Jerome McDonald; married Neville T Darrell, Mar 16, 1984; children: Tasha Wiesing, Lew K Olive, Elayna R Olive, Anthony C Olive. **Educ:** Univ of Louisville, Louisville KY, BA, 1955, attended 1955-56; Washburn Univ, Topeka KS, MA, 1969. **Career:** Bd of Educ, Louisville KY, teacher, 1955-56; Kansas Comm on Civil Rights, Topeka KS, educ specialist, 1968-69; Washburn Univ, Topeka KS, upward bound instructor, 1968-69, Natl Bd YWCA, New York NY, Racial Justice Assoc natl dir, 1970-78; Project Equality, New York NY, assoc natl dir, 1978-82; New York/New Jersey Minority Purchasing Council, New York NY, exec dir, 1982-84; Pepsi-Cola Co, MBE program director, dir of supplier devt, 1984-. **Orgs:** Mem, Delta Sigma Theta Sorority, 1954, English Speaking Union, 1964-66, British Amer Women's Assn, 1964-66, NAACP, 1970-74, Teaneck NJ Community Relation Advisory Comm, 1975-78, Ethnic Heritage Comm, Natl Educ Assn, 1975-77, Black Agency Exec, 1975-78; sec, Natl Minority Business Directory, 1985-89; nominating comm, Natl Minority Supplier Devel Council, 1987. **Honors/Awds:** Anglo-Amer Award, British Amer Women's Org, 1966; Community Relations, Teaneck NJ Advisory Council, 1978; Affirmative Action/EEO Project Equality, 1982; Minority Vendor Coordinator's Award, New York/New Jersey Vendor Input Comm, 1985; Black Achievers in Industry, Harlem YMCA, 1986. **Home Addr:** Tonetta Lake Way Dr, Brewster, NY 10509.

DARTON, EDYTHE M.
Educator. **Personal:** Born Nov 6, 1921, Ruffin, SC; married; children: 2. **Educ:** Claflin Coll, AB 1947; Atlanta U, MEd 1948; Central MO State U, specialist 1968. **Career:** Kansas City MO School Dist, elementary school dir; Meservey School, prin 1971-72; Mary Harmon Weeks School, admin cood, instructor 1968-71; Title I Program, reading asst 1965-68; primary teacher 1948-65; Avila Coll, instructor 1972-74. **Orgs:** Mem Assn for Supervision & Curriculum Evelop; Alpha Kappa Alpha; Kansas City Sch Adminstr AssnF Intnl Reading Assn; MO State Tchr Assn; NEA; Assnof Tchr Educators; Atlanta 19 Alumni Assn; Am Bus Women's Assn; Phi Delta Kappa; Nat Assn of Elem Prin; Central MO State Alumni Assn; mem Jack & Jill of Am; NAACP; Nat Council of Negro Women; Ward Parkway Country Club; Girl Scouts of Am; ARR; Carver Neighborhood Cntr Bd Phi Kappa Phi 1972. **Honors/Awds:** Women of Yr, Am Woman's Assn 1972; Certificate of Award, E C Meservey PTA 1972. **Business Addr:** 1211 Mc Gee, Kansas City, MO 64106.

DASH, HUGH M. H.
Financial administrator. **Personal:** Born Feb 19, 1943, Brooklyn, NY; married Patricia Morris; children: Angela, Phillip. **Educ:** Morehouse College, Business Admin 1969; Howard Univ, Executive Management 1974. **Career:** Citizens Trust Bank, commercial lending & credit officer 1972-72; Interracial Council for Business Opportunity, dep exec dir 1972-75; Southern Conf of Black Mayors, sr economic dev 1975-76; Enterprises Now, Inc, executive vice pres 1976-80; Prudential Health Care Plan, Inc, dir of admin & asst cont 1980-. **Orgs:** Member Leadership Atlanta 1978-; board member and president Atlanta Business League 1978-79, 1985; Georgia treasurer White House Conf on Small Businesses 1979-80. **Honors/Awds:** Catalyst Interracial Council for Business Opportunity 1977. **Military Serv:** AUS Sp4/E4; served 3 years. **Home Addr:** 1374 Dodson Drive SW, Atlanta, GA 30311. **Business Addr:** Dir of Administration, Prudential Health Care Plan, 2849 Paces Ferry Road, Ste 400, Atlanta, GA 30339.

DASH, JULIE
Filmmaker. **Personal:** Born in New York, NY; children: Nzinga. **Educ:** City College of New York; American Film Institute; University of California Los Angeles; Studio Museum of Harlem, 1971. **Career:** Filmmaker, screenwriter, films include: Four Women, 1978; Diary of an African Nun; Twelve Women; Illusions, 1983; Daughters of the Dust, 1992. **Honors/Awds:** Natl Coalition of 100 Black Women, Candace Award, 1992; Black Communications Inc, CEBA Award, for Daughters of the Dust, 1991; Fulbright Fellowship, 1992. **Special Achievements:** Daughters of the Dust, Dutton, 1997. **Business Phone:** (212)281-8526.

DASH, LEON DECOSTA, JR.
Reporter. **Personal:** Born Mar 16, 1944, New Bedford, MA; son of Ruth Dash and Leon Dash; children: Darla, Destiny. **Educ:** Howard Univ, BA 1968. **Career:** The Washington Post, reporter 1966-68; Kenya, Peace Corps tchr 1969-70; The Washington Post, reporter/Africa corresp/reporter investig desk 1971-. **Orgs:** Natl Assn of Black Journalist. **Honors/Awds:** Honorable mention, Robert F Kennedy Awd for outstng Coverage of Disadvantaged 1973; George Polk Award Overseas Press Club 1974; Balt-Wash Guild Award for Intl Reporting 1974; Capitol Press Club Intl Reporting Award 1984; First Place, General News Award, Natl Assn of Black Journalists, 1986; President's Award, Washington Independent Writers, 1989; co-author, Shame of Prisons, 1972; author, When Children Want Children, 1989; Rosa Lee, 1996; Africare International Reporting Award, 1984; Distinguished Service Award from Maryland Social Services Administration, 1986; First Prize, Public Service Award, Washington-Baltimore Newspaper Guild, 1987; First Place Award, Investigative Reporters and Editors Organization, 1987; Special Citation, PEN/Martha Albrand Nonfiction for ''When Children Want Children''; Pulitzer Prize, Explanatory Journalism, 1995; 1st Prize for Print, Robert F Kennedy Award, 1995; Emmy Award, National Academy of Televison Arts & Sciences, Washington, DC Chapter, 1996; first prize, Harry Chapin Best Book Media Award, The World Hunger Year Organization; co-winner, Political Book Award, Washington Monthly Magazine; National Coun on Crime and Delinquency, Prevention for a Safer Society Literature Award, 1997; Hon Doctorate, Lincoln Univ, 1996. **Business Addr:** Reporter Investigative Desk, The Washington Post, 1150 15th St NW, Washington, DC 20071, (202)334-4490.

DATES, JANNETTE LAKE
Educator. **Personal:** Born Mar 17, Baltimore, MD; daughter of Moses and Iantha Alexander Lake; married Victor H Dates Sr, Dec 17, 1960; children: Karen, Victor Jr, Matthew, Craig. **Educ:** Coppin State College, BS; The Johns Hopkins Univ, MEd; Univ of Maryland at College Park, PhD. **Career:** Baltimore City Public School System, classroom demonstration teacher, 1958-63, televsion demonstration teacher, 1964-69; Morgan State Coll and Goucher College, instructor, 1970-72; Morgan State Univ, instructor, 1972-77, coordinator of television projects, 1973-80, asst prof, 1977-80; Howard Univ, asst prof, 1981-85, sequence coordinator, 1981-85; Coppin State College, associate prof, 1985-87, video production service dir, 1985-87; Howard Univ School of Communications, associate dean, 1987-92; Howard Univ, associate prof, 1990-; Howard Univ School of Communications, acting dean, 1993-96, dean, 1996-. **Orgs:** Baltimore City Cable Television Commission, commissioner, 1979-81, education task force chairwoman, 1979-81; Baltimore Cable Access Corporation, pres, 1982-86, vice pres, 1986-88; Mayor's Cable Advisory Commission, education task force chairwoman, 1988-90, member, 1990-94. **Honors/Awds:** California State Univ at Dominquez Hills, Young, Gifted and Black Distinguished Resident Scholar, 1991; Freedom Forum Media Studies Center Fellowship, 1992; Gustavus Myer Award, co-editor, best book on human rights, 1990. **Special Achievements:** Co-author: Split Image: African Americans in the Mass Media, 1993; author: ''African American TV Images Shaped By Others,'' Crisis magazine, December 1992; ''Quantity, Not Quality, Suffices for Our TV Images,'' p 8, Sept 30-Oct 6, 1992; ''This TV Season Will Be Blacker, But Will It Be Better?'' September 13, 1992; reviewer: ''A Review of the book Enlightened Racism,'' Journal of Broadcasting and Electronic Media, Fall 1993; ''A Review of Said's Culture and Imperialism,'' Critical Studies in Mass Communications, Fall 1995. **Business Addr:** Dean, School of Communications, Howard University, 525 Bryant St, NW, W2-203-G, Washington, DC 20059, (202)806-7694.

DAUGHTRY, HERBERT DANIEL
Cleric. **Personal:** Born Jan 13, 1931, Savannah, GA; son of Emmie Cheatham Williams and Alonzo Austin Daughtry; married Karen Ann Smith, Apr 28, 1962; children: Leah, Sharon, Dawnique, Herbert Jr. **Career:** African Peoples Christian Org, pres 1982-; Natl Campaign Comm of Rev Jesse Jackson, special asst & confidant 1983-84; The House of the Lord Churches, natl presiding minister, currently. **Orgs:** Bedford Stuyvesant Youth in Action, board of directors, vice chairman, 1968; Operation Breadbasket, vice chairman, 1969; Ministers Against Narcotics, co-chairman, 1969; Commission on African Solidarity, founder, 1977; Coalition of Concerned Leaders & Citizens to Save our Children, founder, president, 1977; Black United Fund NY, board of directors, 1980-; United African-American Churches of NYS, board of directors, 1988-; National Rainbow Coalition, board of directors, 1985-; Randolph Evans Memorial Scholarship Fund, board of directors, 1978-; National Black United Front, chairman, 1979-86, chairman emeritus, 1986-; Association of Brooklyn Clergy for Community Development, chairman, 1991-; African-American Clergy and Elected Officials, founder, chairman, 1991-; Black Leadership Commission on AIDS, commissioner, 1989-. **Honors/Awds:** Hon mem Malik Sigma Psi Fraternity; Doctor of Letters Seton Hall Univ 1980; author, Jesus Christ: African in Origin, Revolutionary and Redeeming in Action. **Special Achievements:** Author, Inside the Storm; No Monopoly on Suffering. **Business Addr:** Natl Presiding Minister, The House of the Lord Churches, 415 Atlantic Ave, Brooklyn, NY 11217.

DAUPHIN, BOREL C.
Insurance company executive. **Career:** Williams Progressive Life & Accident Insurance Co, company executive, currently. **Business Addr:** Executive, Williams Progressive Life & Accident Insurance Co, 348 S Academy, Opelousas, LA 70570.

DAURHAM, ERNEST
Haircare company owner. **Career:** D-Orum Haircare Products, CEO, 1979-. **Special Achievements:** Company is ranked #73 on the Black Enterprise list of Top 100 industrial/service companies, 1994. **Business Addr:** CEO, D-Orum Hair Care Products, 325 W 103rd St, Chicago, IL 60628-2503.

DAUWAY, LOIS MCCULLOUGH
Church administrator. **Personal:** Born Jul 30, 1948, Boston, MA; daughter of Pearl Kathleen Griffith McCullough and Eural Allen McCullough (deceased). **Educ:** Univ of MA, studies in Educational Admin; Manhattanville Coll, BA. **Career:** Career Oppor Prog MA State Dept of Educ, asst dir 1970-72; Project JESI Univ of MA, project site dir 1972-74; Natl Div General Bd of Global Ministries, black comm developer 1974-77; General Bd of Global Ministries United Methodist Ch, sec of mission personnel 1977-82; Natl Council of the Churches of Christ in the USA, asst general sec for justice and liberation. **Orgs:** Natl training staff Black Comm Developers Prog The United Methodist Church 1977-; bd of dirs Natl Black United Fund 1980-83; mem Natl Assoc of Female Execs 1986-; mem Black Women's Concerns Prog Initiative Area; women's caucus Black Methodists for Church Renewal, Natl Council of the Churches of Christ, Theology in the Amers; bd mem Women's Theol Ctr, Anna Howard Shaw Ctr Boston Univ Sch of Theology; guest lecturer New York Theological Seminary; Washington Office on Haiti. **Honors/Awds:** Delegate UN End of the Decade for Women NGO Forum Nairobi Kenya; authored Women's Section of the Report of the Futures Task Force UMC; Intl BPDE Outstanding Leadership in Religious Educ 1977; Outstanding Young Women of Amer 1980. **Business Addr:** Asst General Secretary, Natl Cncl Churches of Christ, Commn on Justice/Liberation, 475 Riverside Dr Rm 866, New York, NY 10115.

DAVALT, DOROTHY B.
Educator. **Personal:** Born Dec 25, 1914, Jacksonville, FL; married Clarence J; children: Clarence J, Vincent P. **Educ:** Florida A&M University, BS 1949. **Career:** College professor, University of Southern Florida, University of Rochester. **Orgs:** President, Escambia Co Teachers Florida Education Assn; Florida Women's Polit Caucus; NEA; NAACP; Natl Council Urban & State Educ Assns; Florida Education & Vocational Assns; Governor's Conference on Education; State Political Action Committee; Keep Florida Beautiful; Common Cause League Arts; Human Rights Committee, Escambia Education Assn; Elks; precinct committeewoman, Pensacola Chamber of Commerce; Mt Zion Baptist Church. **Honors/Awds:** COPE & NEA convs; effected merger, black/white local teacher assn, 1966-68; Governor's Commission Teacher Training Center, 1976. **Business Addr:** Educator, 30 E Texas Dr, Pensacola, FL 32503.

DAVE, ALFONZO, JR.
Government official, real estate broker. **Personal:** Born Apr 2, 1945, St Louis; son of Pearl Dave and Alfonzo Dave, Sr; children: Alfonzo III. **Educ:** University of Colorado, BA, 1967, University of California, graduate study. **Career:** Licensed real estate CA; Al Dave & Asso Realty, broker & owner; CA Employment Devel Dept, Deputy Area Administrator; alternate LA County Area Admin, state administrator for youth employment opportunity program; previous assignments as mgr, asst mgr, staff instructor, case worker, job developer, employment interviewer. **Orgs:** Los Angeles City Private Industry Council, chp Youth/Young Adult Comm, Central City Exec Comm, Summer Youth Employment Training Prog, Youth Opportunity Unlimited Task Force, Performance Evaluation Task Force, New Ad Hoc Progs Comm; Central City Enterprise Zone Business Advisory Council; Southern California Employment Round Table; LA Urban League Data Processing Training Ctr Advisory Bd; Intl Assn of Personnel in Employment Security; Personnel & Industrial Relations Assn Inc; Natl Conf of Christians & Jews; Community Rehabilitation Industries; Alpha Kappa Delta; Alpha Phi Alpha; City of Los Angeles Youth Service Academy; Community Service Center Program; Rebuild Los Angeles Co-Chairperson Education & Training Task Force; LA Demonstration Model for Vocational Education, Workforce Los Angeles Steer Committee; Museum of Afro-American Arts; LA Transportation Commission Job Development and Training Task Force; Rebuild LA Educational/Training/Job, steering committee; Nickerson Gardens Empowerment Program Advisory Council; New Programs Task Force, LA City PIC; Community Projects for Restoration. **Honors/Awds:** Commendation LA Co Probation Dept 1975; N Hollywood Chamber of Commerce, 1977; Selected participant in 21st Annual Wilhelm Weinberg Seminar, Cornell Univ, 1979; Cash bonuses, State of CA Managerial Performance Appraisal Program, 1986, 1988; Certificate in Mgmt, Amer Mgmt Assn, 1974; Certificate in Mgmt, State Personnel Bd, 1970; Selected by US Conference of Mayors to make presentation on ''Remediation in the Inner City,'' 1988; Commendation for completion/instruction of Masters of Executive Excellence through EDD, 1988.

DAVENPORT, C. DENNIS
Attorney. **Personal:** Born Dec 27, 1946, Lansing, MI; married Dr Roselle Wilson; children: Ronald, Charlene. **Educ:** MI State Univ, BA 1969; MI State Univ, MA 1970; Univ of MI, JD 1972. **Career:** General Motors Corp, attorny 1972-; Natl Bar Assoc, mem 1973-; MI State Bar, mem 1973-; Wolverine Bar Assoc, mem 1973-. **Orgs:** NAACP; Kappa Alpha Psi Frat. **Business Addr:** Attorney, General Motors Corporation, 3044 West Grand Blvd, Detroit, MI 48202.

DAVENPORT, CALVIN A.
Educator. **Personal:** Born Jan 15, 1928, Gloucester, VA; son of Carrie Ernestine Brooks Davenport (deceased) and James Robert Davenport (deceased); married Beverly Jean Wills; children: Dean Darnell, Lynn Angela. **Educ:** VA State Univ, BS 1949; MI State Univ, MS 1950; National Univ of Mexico, Mexico City, 1957; MI State Univ, PhD 1963; Univ of California, Berkeley, CA, 1966. **Career:** CA State Univ, prof emeritus, Biology, 1969-92; VA State Coll, prof microbiology 1963-69; MI State Univ, res asst 1957-62; Michigan Dept of Health, Div of Laboratories 1952-53, 1955-56; Letterman Army Hosp San Francisco, lab tech 1953-55; Rancho Santiago Coll, prof, 1993-. **Orgs:** Coord Council for Health Sci Educ 1971-74; chmn 1974; Accreditation Team Wstrn Assn of Schs & Colls 1973-92; Orange Co Long Beach Health Consortium 1973-83; chmn bd trustees 1974-75; Am Soc for Microbiology 1963-; CA State Employees Assn 1973-; Amer Public Health Assn 1968-92; Beta Kappa Chi Natl Scientific Hon Soc 1948-; Kappa Alpha Psi Frat; Iota Sigma Lambda Hon Soc; coord Health Manpower Educ Proj CA Univ Fullerton 1974-75; consult Nat Inst of Health Washington 1973-; Sr Commn of the Western Assn of Sch & Coll 1976-79; evaluation panel in biophysics & biochemistry Natl Sci Found; reading comm Danforth Found 1977-80; sec Acad Assembly of the CA Univ & Coll Med Tech Programs 1978-79; Univ Minority Affairs Council 1981-85;consultant Delst Chem Co 1981-; Univ chm Academic Affirmative Actioomm 1982-84; Univ dir of incentive grants prog, Natl Action Council for Minorities in Engineering 1983-84; dir Univ "Investment in People" prgm 1983-84; Univ AIDS educ 1984-92; Minority Biomed Rsch Support Advisory Comm, Gerontology Rsch Inst, Univ Inst for Health Educ & Training, Univ Health Professions Comm, Dept Long Range Planning Comm, Academic Assembly of the California State Universities & Colleges; chair, CA Public Health Lab Directors Academic Assembly 1990-92; chair, Dept Curriculum Comm 1989-92; Univ Substance Abuse Education Comm 1991-92; Charles Drew, Univ of Med & Sci, mem, bd of trustees, 1994-. **Honors/Awds:** Babcock Fellow, Michigan State Univ 1950-51; awards in recognition of outstanding contributions to the CA St Univ Fullerton Black Organization of Engineers and Scientists 1982, and from the CA St Univ Fullerton Affirmative Action Program 1983, 1984, 1985. **Military Serv:** AUS pfc 1953-55. **Home Addr:** 124 S Carousel, Anaheim, CA 92806. **Business Phone:** (714)564-6690.

DAVENPORT, CHESTER C.
Company executive. **Career:** Envirotest Systems Corp, CEO, 1990-. **Special Achievements:** Company is ranked #11 on the Black Enterprise list of Top 100 Industrial/Service companies, 1994. **Business Addr:** Chairman of the Board, Envirotest Systems Corp, 6903 Rockledge Dr, Ste 214, Bethesda, MD 20817.

DAVENPORT, CHRISTIAN A.
Educator. **Personal:** Born Jun 4, 1965, New York, NY; son of Juliet Seignions & Donn Davenport. **Educ:** SUNY Binghamton, MA, 1989, PhD, 1991. **Career:** University of Houston, assistant professor, 1992-96; University of Colorado-Boulder, associate professor, 1996-. **Orgs:** American Journal of Political Science, editorial board member, 1994-; National Coalition of Blacks for Reparations in America, 1993-; Midwest Political Science Association, 1991-; American Political Science Association, 1991-; National Black Political Science Association, 1992-; Shape Cultural Ctr, instructor, 1993-95; West Dallas Detention Ctr, instructor, 1995; National Popular Culture Association, 1993-; Comparative Politics Center at Univ of Co. **Honors/Awds:** National Science Foundation, Research Development Grant for Minority Scientists & Engineers, 1997; Ebony Magazine, 50 Young Leaders of Tomorrow, 1996; Malcolm X Loves Network, Keeper of the Flame Awd, 1995; National Association of African-American Honors Program, Scholarly Contributions and Leadership, 1996. **Special Achievements:** "Understanding Rhetoric Under The Gun," The Black Panther Party Reconsidered, 1997; "The Political and Social Relency of Malcolm X," The Journal of Politics, 1997; "Constitutional Promises and Repressive Reality," The Journal of Politics, 1996; "The Weight of the Past," Political Research Quarterly, 1996; "Multidimensional Threat Perception & State Repression," The American Journal of Political Science, 1995. **Business Addr:** Assistant Professor, University of Colorado at Boulder, Department of Political Science, Ketchum Hall, Rm 106, Boulder, CO 80309-0333, (303)492-1738.

DAVENPORT, ERNEST H.
Certified public accountant (retired). **Personal:** Born Apr 12, 1917, Lima, OH; son of Emily Kennedy Davenport (deceased) and William E Davenport (deceased); married Lucille M Rosemond, Mar 1, 1944. **Educ:** Morris Brown College, Atlanta, GA, BA 1940; Wayne State Univ Det, MI, 1948; State of MI, certified public accountant 1956. **Career:** Austin, Washington & Davenport, CPAs (Det MI), partner, 1956-71; Office of Econ Opportunity, Washington DC, dir, 1971-73; General Accounting Office, Washington DC, asst dir, 1973-82; Howard Univ, Washington DC, Center for Acct Educ, School of Business, dir, 1983-90. **Orgs:** Council mem Amer Inst of CPAs, 1977-81; pres Mont Pr, Geo Chapter Assn of Govt Accountants, 1978-79; pres, Dist of Columbia Inst of CPAs, 1980-81; pres, Middle Atlantic State Acct Conf, 1982-83. **Honors/Awds:** Outstanding Alumnus Morris Brown Coll 1969; Achievement Award Natl Assn of Black Accountants 1975, M/PG Chapts Assn of Govt Accts 1976,78; Outstanding Serv Natl Assn of Minority CPA Firms 1980; Order of Kentucky Colonels 1985; Laurel Wreath Award Kappa Alpha Psi 1985; Grand Polemarch, Kappa Alpha Psi Fraternity 1967-70. **Military Serv:** AUS, lt col, 1941-46; Air Medal W/3 Oak Leaf Clusters 1945; Licensed Comm Pilot 1946. **Home Addr:** 8201 16th St #605, Silver Spring, MD 20910.

DAVENPORT, HORACE ALEXANDER
Judge. **Personal:** Born Feb 22, 1919, Newberry, SC; son of Julia Davenport and William Davenport; married Alice I Latney; children: Alice D Alexander, Beverly A, Horace Jr, Nina E. **Educ:** Howard Univ, BA 1946; Univ of PA, MA 1947, LLB 1950. **Career:** Gerber, Davenport & Wilenzik, atty, Court of Common Pleas of 38th Judicial Dist of PA, judge. **Orgs:** Former dir Central Montgomery County Bd of Amer Red Cross; former dir GW Carver Comm Center; former dir Central Montgomery County Council of Human Rel; former dir Norristown Comm Concerts; mem Vet of Foreign Wars; mem Historical Soc of Montgomery Cty; mem Norristown Branch NAACP; former mem Norristown Republican Club; former dir Norristown School Bd; dir Citizens Council of Montgomery Cty; former dir Norristown Art League; former dir Montgomery County TB & Health Assc; former Dir Montgomery Hospital; former area cpt Salvation Army; former Norristown Schl Bd Lay Rep to Area Voc-Tech Schl; pres PA School Bd Solicitors Assc 1972-73, dir 1969, 1970, 1971; dir Natl Schl Bds Assc 1969-76; trustee Johnson C Smith Univ Charlotte NC; solicitor Cntrl Montgomeryunty Area Voc-Tech School 1968-76; solicitor Norristown Area School Dist 1966-76; solicitor Norristown Area School Authority 1966-76; solicitor Montgomery Cty Election Bd 1958-76; solicitor Montgomery County Tax Claim Bureau. **Honors/Awds:** Recipient numerous community awards. **Military Serv:** Corps Engr capt. **Business Addr:** Judge, Ct of Common Pleas 38 Judicial Dist, Montgomery Cty Court House, Norristown, PA 19404.

DAVENPORT, J. LEE
Clergyman, social worker, counselor. **Personal:** Born Oct 2, 1935, Mayo, FL; son of Fronie Bell Hadley Davenport and Jesse David Davenport; married Bernice M Webb Davenport, Dec 22, 1958; children: Valarie E Harris, Velina L, Otis, David. **Educ:** Cameron Univ, Lawton OK, BA, 1970; Oklahoma Univ, Norman OK, MSW, 1975. **Career:** St John's Baptist Church, Lawton OK, sr pastor 1965-; Oklahoma Dept of Mental Health, Lawton OK, social worker 1970-85. **Orgs:** Worshipful Master Golden Gate Ldg 1961-63; NAACP; pres Lawton's Chpt; Comm Action bd mem 1965-68; Rotary mem; mem gov adv comm human rel; mem OK Planning Health Comm 1973-74; parole adv; Pastor St John's Baptist Ch; mem Natl Acad Soc Workers; Dean West dist cong Christ educ; disc leader youth disc group Natl Baptist conv Inc USA; 2nd vice pres OK State Conv 1974-78; bd mem Cameron Univ 1981-; state pres One Church, One Child Inc 1988-; bd mem United Way 1985-; pres Coalition for Minority Affairs 1984-. **Honors/Awds:** Oustanding Leadership, NAACP 1986; Humanitarian Award, Alpha Kappa Alpha 1988; Developed Task Force with Justice Dept on Police-Community Relations 1986; Developed a Feed The Hungry Program for Homeless People 1987; King Day Speakers Award, III Corps Artillary, Ft Sill OK, 1990; Human Service, Human Rights Award, Lawton Public Schools, 1990; Humanitarian Service Award, Cameron University, 1991. **Military Serv:** USAF 1953-58, A/1C, Oustanding Marksman Award 1954, GCM 1955. **Business Addr:** Senior Pastor, St John's Baptist Church, 1501 Roosevelt St, Lawton, OK 73501.

DAVENPORT, LAWRENCE FRANKLIN
Educational administrator. **Personal:** Born Oct 13, 1944, Lansing, MI; married Cecelia Jackson; children: Laurence, Anita, Anthony. **Educ:** MI State Univ, BA 1966, MA 1968; Fairleigh Dickinson Univ, EdD 1975. **Career:** Tuskegee Inst, vice pres for develop 1972-74; San Diego Comm Coll Educ Cultural Complex, pres 1974-79; San Diego Comm Coll Dist, provost 1979-81; ACTION, assoc dir for domestic & anti-poverty opers 1981-82. **Orgs:** Comm Martin Luther King Jr Fed Holiday Comm 1985-86. **Honors/Awds:** Outstanding Young Citizen of San Diego-San Diego Jaycees 1978. **Business Addr:** Asst Sec Elem & Secon Educ, US Dept of Education, 400 Maryland Ave SW, Room 2189, Washington, DC 20202.

DAVENPORT, RONALD R.
Company executive. **Personal:** Born May 21, 1936, Philadelphia, PA; son of Beatrice McLemore Davenport and James Davenport; married Judith Loftin Davenport, Aug 4, 1962; children: Ronald R Jr, Judith Allison, Susan Ross. **Educ:** PA State Univ, State College, PA, BS, 1958; Temple Univ School of Law, Philadelphia, PA, LLB, 1962; Yale Law School, New Haven, CT, LLM, 1963. **Career:** Duquesne Univ School of Law, Pittsburgh, PA, prof, 1963-70, dean, 1970-81; Buchanan Ingersoll, PC, Pittsburgh, PA, partner, 1982-84; Sheridan Broadcasting Corp, Pittsburgh, PA, chmn, CEO, 1972-. **Orgs:** Trustee, Comm for Economic Devt, 1975-; bd mem, Allegheny General Hosp; bd mem, Natl Urban League; bd mem, Colgate Univ, 1982-; bd mem, Boys & Girls Club, 1986-. **Honors/Awds:** Honorary Degrees: Point Park Coll, LLD, 1971; Allegheny Coll, LLD, 1978; Distinguished Alumni Award, Penn State Univ, 1975.

DAVID, ARTHUR LACURTISS
Educator. **Personal:** Born Apr 13, 1938, Chicago, IL; son of Annetta David and Carey H David, Sr; married Martha Barham; children: Alexis R Womack, Sean David. **Educ:** Lane Coll, BA 1960; Phillips Sch of Theol, BD 1963; NE U, MA 1970; ITC, MDiv 1971; Middle TN State U, Arts D 1973. **Career:** Soc Sci Div Lane Coll, chmn; Lane Coll, prof of hist 1963-67 69-77; NE Wesleyan Univ, 1967-69; Motlow State Commn Coll, 1972-73; Lane Coll, dean, 1979-93; Prof of History, 1993-. **Orgs:** Mem So Hist Assn; Am Hist Assn; Orgn of Am Historians; mem Pi Gamma Mu Sociol Sci, Hon Soc; Phi Alpha Theta Hist Hon Soc; Sigma Theta Epsilon Hon Soc for Clergymen; Kappa Kappa Psi Hon Band Frat; Alpha Phi Alpha Frat Inc. **Honors/Awds:** Dissertation "The Involvement of the Black Man in the Teaching of Western Civilization a Study of Black Colleges & Univs" 1973; You Can Fool Me But You Can't Fool God, 1976; An Anthology of a Minister's Thoughts, 1977; He Touched Me, 1992. **Business Addr:** Prof of History, Lane College, 545 Lane Ave, Jackson, TN 38301.

DAVID, GEORGE F., III
Business executive. **Personal:** Born Nov 6, 1923, Wilberforce, OH; son of Olivette Poole David and George F David II; divorced; children: George F IV, Lynn David Irby. **Educ:** Wilberforce Univ, BS 1943; St Andrews Univ Scotland, 1946. **Career:** Glidden Co, chemist 1950-52; Oscar Mayer & Co, food technologist, plant mgr 1952-60; Sinai Kosher Sausage Co, plant supt 1960-62; Superior Meat Co, plant supt 1962-63; Superiors Brand Meats, mgr/asst operations mgr 1962-68; Parks Sausage Co, vice pres/dir 1968-88. **Orgs:** Bd mem USO-Central MD 1982-, Girls Scouts-Central MD 1984-; pres Hilltop Comm Orgn, Woodlawn MD 1974-76; bd mem Combined Health Agencies 1986-88. **Honors/Awds:** Achievement Award Eastern Province Kappa Alpha Psi 1976 & 1980; Wm "Box" Harris Award 1986. **Home Addr:** 2110 Meadowview Dr, Baltimore, MD 21207.

DAVID, GERALDINE R.
Elected official. **Personal:** Born Sep 15, 1938, Helena, AR; married Odell Davis Jr; children: Cheryl, Vivian, Odel III, Eva, Darin, Vivian L Ross, Eva Gammon. **Educ:** Univ of Pine Bluff, attended; Rust Coll Holly Springs MS, attended; Phillips Cty Comm Coll, attended. **Career:** Elaine Jr HS, librarian asst 1967; Lake View Coop Assoc, bookkeeper 1970; Lake View Elem School, librarian asst 1974; City of Lake View, sec, treas 1978-. **Orgs:** Bd of dir Cty Ext Comm, Lake View Med Clinic 1980-, East AR Area on Aging 1980-. **Honors/Awds:** Governors Office Volunteer Awd Governors Office 1980; Volunteer Tax Awd Federal Income Tax Office 1980; Tri-Cty Leadership 1980; Mid-Delta Comm Serv Volunteer Awd Comm Serv 1980; Phillips Cty Notary Sec of State Office. **Home Addr:** Rt 2 Box 350-A, Lexa, AR 72355. **Business Addr:** Secretary, Treasurer, City of Lake View, Rt 1 Box 221-A, Helena, AR 72342.

DAVID, KEITH (KEITH DAVID WILLIAMS)
Actor. **Personal:** Born Jun 4, 1956, New York, NY; son of Delores Tittley Dickinson and Lester Williams; married Margit Edwards Williams, Sep 22, 1990. **Educ:** The Juilliard School, New York, NY, BFA, 1979. **Career:** Actor. Films include, Article 99; Voices from Sandover; Marked for Death; Always; Men at Work; Roadhouse; They Live; Bird; Off Limits; Stars and Bars; Hot Pursuit; Platoon; The Thing; television appearances include, Voices from Sandover; Hallelujah Anyhow; Murder in Black and White; Hawk; Christmas in Tattertown; Ladykiller; Roots II; The Equalizer; theatre productions include, The Lady of Dubuque; Titus Andronicus; Coriolanus; Fragments of a Greek Trilogy; Africanus Instructus; Ceremonies in Dark Old Men; La Boheme; The Pirates of Penzance; Alec Wilder: Clues to a Life; Miss Waters to You; A Midsummer Night's Dream; Roar of the Lion Inc, Los Angeles, CA, president, 1990-. **Orgs:** Certified instructor, The Skinner Institute for Speech, 1982-. **Honors/Awds:** Image Award Nomination for appearance in The Thing, NAACP, 1982; Sinclair Bayfield Award for Best Performance in a play by Shakespeare, Actors Equity, 1989.

DAVID, LAWRENCE T.
Chaplain. **Personal:** Born Jan 14, 1930, Cheraw, SC; married Hilda Black; children: Kenneth, Marc, LaDonna, Chapelle. **Educ:** Morris Coll, BA 1954; Gammon Theol Sem, BD 1958; Columbia Bible Coll Grad Sch, 1964-65. **Career:** AUS, chplan 1959-; St John's Bapt Ch Gainesville GA. **Honors/Awds:** Awarded numerous ribbons medals citations including Bronze Star with four clusters; Vietnamese Presidential Citation; US Pres Unit Cit with two Oak Leaf Clusters; Viet Nam Cross of Gallantry. **Military Serv:** AUS 1957-59 promoted to ltc 1974.

DAVIDSON, ALPHONZO LOWELL
Dentist. **Personal:** Born Dec 12, 1941, Fredericksburg, VA; married Carolyn; children: Alphonzo Jr, Stephanie. **Educ:** Howard U, BS 1964; Howard U, DDS 1968; Howard U, cert oral surgery 1973. **Career:** Dept of Oral Surgery Howard Univ, asst prof; Howard Univ Hospital, attending oral surgeon. **Orgs:** Asso staff mem Prince George Co Hosp; mem Am Soc Oral Surgery 1975; Assn Mil Surgeons 1970; DC Dental Soc; Am Dental Soc 1969; Robert T FreedmanDental Soc; Nat Dental

Soc 1969; Chi Delta Mu Frat 1967; Assn of Interns & Residents of Freedmen's Hosp 1972; Dental Soc of Anesthesiology 1978; Oral Cancer Soc 1968-80; pres DC Oral Surgery Soc 1979-80; Omicron Kappa Upsilon Pi Pi Chap 1979-80; mem Sigma Phi Sigma Nat Physics Hon Soc; sec Robert T Freedman Dental Soc; mem Am Bd Oral Surgery 1976. **Military Serv:** USAF capt 1968-70. **Business Addr:** Landover Mall W, Office Ridge 308, Landover, MD 20785.

DAVIDSON, ARTHUR B.
Administrator. **Personal:** Born Dec 5, 1929, Detroit; son of Idella and Arthur B; married Edith. **Educ:** Detroit Inst Tech, BA 1964; Wayne State U, M Pub Adm 1970. **Career:** Human Resources Devel, area adminstrator 1964-68; Butzel Family Ctr Coordinate Serv, dir 1968-70; City Detroit, planning administrator 1970-81, oper & mgmt serv admin 1981-82, dir admin serv & weatherization 1982-88, assistant director, 1988-. **Orgs:** Mem planning exec 1972-; Nat Assn Housing & Redevelopment & Officials 1964-; New Detroit Inc 1970-; OmniCare Health Plan Bd of Trustees, Treasurer, Chmn of Finance, mem of Executive Committee. **Honors/Awds:** Cert excellence Urban League 1965; cert recognition Greater Macedonia Bapt Ch 1965. **Military Serv:** AUS 1951-53. **Business Addr:** Assistant Director, City of Detroit, 5031 Grandy, Neighborhood Serv Dept, Detroit, MI 48211.

DAVIDSON, ARTHUR TURNER
Physician, attorney. **Personal:** Born Jul 30, 1923; son of Rev & Mrs Robert J Davidson; married Ezeria Jennie White; children: Arthur T Jr, Ronald W, Michael G, Kathie E. **Educ:** Howard Univ Sch of Med, MD 1945; St John's Univ Sch of Law, JD 1974. **Career:** Downstate Med Ctr Brooklyn, asst clinical prof of surgery; Columbia Univ Coll of Physicians & Surgeons NY, asst clinical prof of surgery; Albert Einstein Coll of med Bronx, assoc clinical prof of surgery; Private Practice, physician. **Orgs:** Mem AMA; mem Natl Med Assn; mem Amer Bar Assn. **Honors/Awds:** Publ, "Mechanical Small Bowel Obstruction with Gangrene Presenting Narrowing of Pulse Pressure A New Diagnostic Sign" JNMA 56 393 1964; publ "Thymotropic Action of Vitamin A" Federation Proceedings of the Amer Soc of Experimental Biologists 1973; publ "Enhanced Lymphocytic Action on Breast Tumor" JNMA 66 472 1974. **Military Serv:** AUS med corps capt 1951-53. **Business Addr:** Physician, 1378 President St, Brooklyn, NY 11213.

DAVIDSON, CHARLES ODELL
Physician. **Personal:** Born Nov 12, 1935, Pine Bluff, AR; married Fredricka Cooper; children: Harryl, Darryl. **Educ:** Howard Univ Med Sch, MD 1961; Homer G Phillips Hosp, Internship 1961-62; Homer G Phillips Hospital, Resident, Chief Resident, 1962-65. **Career:** The Methodist Hospital of Gary Inc Med Staff, pres 1980-81. **Orgs:** bd trustee, Methodist Hospital of Gary Inc; bd of dirs Gary Bd of Health, 1978-; chmn, Ob-Gyn Gary Merrillville Methodist Hosp; private practice, 1968-77; hosp comdr Malstrom AFB 1967-68; chmn OB-BYN Malstrom AFB 1966-68; supr Ob-Gyn Homer G Phillips St Louis 1965-66; sec-treas Gary Med Specialists Inc; chmn NW IN Planned Parenthood Med Adv Council; mem, Am Fertility Sox; Assn of Amer Gynecological Laparoscopists Diplomat Am; bd of Ob-Gyn 1967; Fellow, Am Coll Ob-Gyn, 1972. **Military Serv:** USAF maj. **Business Addr:** 2200 Grant St, Gary, IN 46404.

DAVIDSON, CHARLES ROBERT
Physician. **Personal:** Born Jan 7, 1922, Lincolnton, NC; married Margaret L Roseboro; children: Margaret D Hayes, Wanda, Charles, Jr, Russell. **Educ:** Johnon C Smith Univ Charlotte NC, BS 1941; BD 1945; Drew Univ Madison NJ, MA 1946; Howard Univ Med Sch Wash DC, MD 1952. **Career:** Pvt Practice Baltimore, physcn 1954; Rural Ch Allen Univ & Benedict Coll Columbia SC, tchr 1947-48; Rural Ch Dept Bishop Coll Marshall TX, tchr 1946-47. **Military Serv:** AUS 2nd lt 1952-54. **Business Addr:** 2034 W North Ave, Baltimore, MD 21217.

DAVIDSON, DONALD RAE
Business executive. **Personal:** Born Jun 9, 1943, Indianapolis, IN; son of Frances Davidson and Fred Davidson; children: Renae, Donald Rae, Dawn, Ingrid. **Educ:** Drake Univ, BA 1964. **Career:** RCA Corp Indianapolis, mgr material coordinator 1965-67; Solar Devel Corp Indianapolis, treas 1967-71; Davidson Hardy & Assocs Indianapolis, sec-treas 1966-68; Dahar Corp Indianapolis, pres 1968-74; FCH Serv Inc Chgo, asst vice pres 1971-73; First Natl Bank of Chgo/Nigeria Lagos, mgr 1973-74; IL Housing Devel Authority, housing devel production admin 1974-77; Salk Ward & Salk Chicago, vice pres 1977-78; Metro Finance Group Ltd Chicago, chmn 1978-; Metro Equities Corp Investment Bankers, pres. **Orgs:** Bd dirs Midwest Assoc for Sickle Cell Anemia; mem IL Mortgage Bankers Assn, Mortgage Bankers of Amer, Real Estate Securities & Syndication Inst; bd dirs IL Serv Fed Savings & Loan Assn, IL Development Finance Authority; bd dir Natl Assn of Securities Profls.

DAVIDSON, EARNEST JEFFERSON
Sculptor, educator. **Personal:** Born Aug 16, 1946, Little Rock, AR; son of Alice Sanders Davidson and Earnest Jefferson Davidson; children: Tamara S, Earnest III. **Educ:** Philander Smith Coll, BA, AR Art Center, 1969; Univ of AR at Little Rock, 1975; Syracuse Univ, MFA 1972; Univ of AR at Little Rock 1986. **Career:** Adventures in Ed Syracuse, NY, woodwork Spclst 1972; Lomax Hanna Jr Coll, teach arts & crafts 1978; Southeast Art & Sci Ctr, teach pottery 1984; AR Art Cntr, teach sculpture 1984; Univ of AR at Pine Bluff, assoc profsr 1972-92, professor, 1992-, Standing Committee on Student Appeals (Adademic Evaluation), chmn; Pine Tech Coll, adjunct profsr, 1994-. **Orgs:** Chrprsn Visual Arts Com Arts & Science Ctr 1985; rep for sw USA FESTAC 77 2nd Wld Black & African Festvl of Arts & Culture; sw rgnl coordntr Natl Conf of Artists 1974-76; Emergency School Aid Act Artist-In-Residence Selection Committee 1976-82; mem Intl Sculpture Assn, 1988-, Amer Foundrymen Soc, 1988-; potter consultant, bd of trustees, SE Arkansas Arts & Science Center, 1990-. **Honors/Awds:** Under grad ad Omega Psi Phi Te 1985-87; Apprentice in the Arts Grant 1982; Gov Award Little Rock Arts & Crafts Fair 1974; Title III Grant Univ of AR at Little Rock 1975; Commissioned to create bronze statue of Martin Luther King, Student Assn of Northern Univ of IL at Dekalb 1985-86; Title III Grant Univ of AR at Little Rock 1986; Pine Bluff Business for the Arts Award 1988; One of three finalists for the Arkansas Vietnam Veterans Memorial 1987; Arkansas Art Registry; Distinguished Faculty Award, Arts & Science, University of Arkansas at Pine Bluff, 1990; Purchase Award, Ceramic Sculpture, Hendrix College, 1990; Golden Citation, Trilogy of South Africa Philander Smith College, 1990; Arkansas State Capitol, Distinguish Arkansas Collection, commissioned work of four ceramic clay busts, Dr Elijah Coleman, 1995, Dr Jerry Jewell, 1995, Dr William Townsend, 1994, Prof Henry Wilkins, 1993; Ancestral Visions Series, Ceramic Sculpture on the Cove of African American Folktales for Young Readers, August House, 1993; Comcast Cable, Studio 14, Learning About Art, talk show host, 1993-. **Business Addr:** Professor, University of Arkansas at Pine Bluff, Fine Art Department, P O Box 53, Pine Bluff, AR 71601.

DAVIDSON, ELVYN VERONE
Surgeon (retired). **Personal:** Born Oct 6, 1923, New York, NY; son of Hattie Olizabeth Hargraves Davidson and John A H Davidson; married Esther M Johnson, Jun 9, 1953 (deceased); children: Pamela D Branner, Evelyne M, Elvyn V II. **Educ:** Lincoln Univ PA, AB 1949; Meharry Med Coll, MD 1953; NYU Post Graduate School Med, certificate in Surgery 1954. **Career:** Univ TE MRC&H Knoxville, instr in surgery 1959-70, asst prof of surgery 1970-; ET Bap Hosp Knoxville, chief of surgery 1974-75; The Amer Soc Abd Surgeon, fellow 1968; Knox County, Deputy Medical Examiner 1979-. **Orgs:** Mem AMA, NMA, KMA, VSMA, TMA, AHA, CSS, SMA, ACS; mem bd dir VIP Home Health Assn 1983; mem Century Club UMCA NAACP; past bas Omega Psi Frat; past grant knight, Knights of Columbus 1982-83; district deputy Knights of Columbus; mem bd of dir Columbus Home. **Military Serv:** AUS tech sgt 1942-46; Purple Heart Combat Inf Award. **Home Addr:** PO Box 14144, Knoxville, TN 37914-1144. **Business Addr:** 710 Cherry St, Knoxville, TN 37914.

DAVIDSON, EZRA C., JR.
Educator. **Personal:** Born Oct 21, 1933, Water Valley, MS; son of Theresa Davidson and Ezra C Davidson Sr; divorced; children: Pamela, Gwendolyn, Marc, Ezra K. **Educ:** Morehouse Coll, BS 1954; Meharry Med Sch, MD 1958. **Career:** LA County Univ of So CA Med Ctr, 1970-80; Martin Luther King General Hospital, chief-of-serv 1971-; Univ of So CA School of Med, prof 1971-80; UCLA, prof 1979-; Drew Univ of Medicine and Science, prof, chmn dept ob/gyn 1971-. **Orgs:** Consult Natl Found March of Dimes 1970-77; mem bd of consult Intl Childbirth Educ Assn Inc 1973-80; mem Natl Med Adv Com Natl Found March of Dimes Inc 1972-77; mem bd dir Prof Staff Assn Found Martin Luther King Jr Gen Hosp 1972-; examiner Amer Bd of Ob/Gyn 1973-; mem Sec Adv Comm for Pop Affairs 1974-77; chmn Serv Task Force 1975-77; mem bd dir Natl Alliance for School Age Parents 1975-80; bd of trustees, 1989-, natl chmn sec, 1975-77, Ob/Gyn Natl Med Assn; pres Assoc of Professors of Gyn and Ob 1987-88; pres Golden State Medical Assn 1989-90; sec 1983-89, pres-elect 1989-90, pres 1990-91 Amer Coll of Ob/Gyn; chm Obstetrical & Gynecological Assn of Southern CA, 1988-89; Food & Drug Administration, chair, advisory committee for fertility and maternal health drugs, 1992; DHHS, chair, secretary's advisory connecticut infant mortality, 1992-; National Academy of Sciences, Institute of Medicine, 1991-. **Honors/Awds:** Fellow Am Coll of Ob-Gyn; fellow Am Coll of Surg; fellow LA Ob-Gyn Soc Inc; num lectures; num articles publ; mem Alpha Omega Alpha Honor Soc; fellow Robert Woods Johnson Health Policy Inst of Med Washington, DC 1979-80; Black Hall of Fame, National Black Alumni Assn, 1990; Alumnus of Year, Chicago Chapter, McHarry Alumni, 1990; Citation of Merit, City of Los Angeles, 1990; first black president of the Amer College of Obstetricians and Gynecologists, 1990; Royal College of Obstetricians-Gynecologists, Fellow ad eundem, 1991. **Military Serv:** USAF captain 1959-63. **Business Addr:** Professor, Chairman Ob/Gyn, 12021 S Wilmington Ave, Los Angeles, CA 90059.

DAVIDSON, FLETCHER VERNON, JR.
Automobile co. planning manager. **Personal:** Born Feb 23, 1947, Portland, OR; son of Stella M Davidson and Fletcher V Davidson Sr; married Rosie Lee Tucker, Sep 10, 1967; children: Fletcher V III, Damion R, Crystal N. **Educ:** Los Angeles City College, AA, technical engineering, 1966; California State University Long Beach, BS, industrial tech, 1972; University Southern California, MS, management science, 1976. **Career:** McDonnell-Douglas Corp, draftsman, 1966-70, sr engineer/system analyst, 1970-73; Toyota Motor Sales USA Inc, planning analyst, 1973-76, systems development mgr, 1977-83, national supply mgr, 1984-90, national logistics planning mgr, 1991-92, North American parts Logistics Division, corporate manager, 1993-. **Orgs:** Council of Logistics Management, 1988-. **Business Addr:** North American Parts Logistics Div, Corp Mgr, Toyota Motor Sales USA Inc, 19001 S Western Ave, #G400, Torrance, CA 90509, (310)783-5301.

DAVIDSON, KERRY
Statewide academic officer. **Personal:** Born May 1, 1935, Water Valley, MS; married Betty Vanover; children: Mary Jaures, Elizabeth Jeanette. **Educ:** Morehouse Coll, attended; Univ of IA, M Pol Sci; Tulane Univ, PhD. **Career:** Southern Univ New Orleans, former chmn dept of history; Fisk Univ, former chmn; LA Bd of Regents, commr acad affairs. **Honors/Awds:** Author of 20th Century Civilization; Danforth Grant. **Business Addr:** Associate Commissioner, Louisianna Bd of Regents, 1 American Pl, Baton Rouge, LA 70816.

DAVIDSON, LURLEAN G.
Director. **Personal:** Born May 3, 1931, West Point, GA; married Ogletree Davidson; children: Marzette, Jerome, John, Darlene, Mary. **Educ:** Case Western Res; OH Univ; Cleveland State Univ. **Career:** Parent Resource Cntrs Cleveland Bd Edn, dir; Sol Victory Mutual Life Ins, 1958-60; medical sec 1951-52; various positions as auditor, intervwr, election clerk; tchrs; asst; Cleveland Bd of Ed, teacher; Davidson's Construction Co, sect, treasure; Inner City Pride, pres. **Orgs:** Mem & Parent Adv Bd YMCA; Precinct Committeewoman 1960-73; mem Glenville Area Coun Phyllis Wheatley Assn NAACP; Urban League; Jewish Council Various PTAs; life membership PTA 1965. **Honors/Awds:** Outstanding serv award to the Comm 1961; outstanding soc award & certificate of merit NAACP 1962; Community Leadership Award, The Council of the City of Cleveland, 1981. **Business Addr:** Joseph F Landis School, 10118 Hampden Ave, Cleveland, OH 44108.

DAVIDSON, RICK BERNARD
Banker. **Personal:** Born Oct 6, 1951, Nashville, TN; son of Beula Jones Davidson and Robert Davidson; married Izola Putnam, Sep 22, 1979; children: Sandra Putnam, Robert Derrick. **Educ:** Tennessee School of Banking, Nashville TN, diploma, 1979-80; ABA Commercial School of Lending (undergraduate & graduate), Univ of Oklahoma, diploma, 1981-83; Graduate School of Banking of the South, Louisiana State Univ, Baton Rouge LA, certificate, 1986-89; Tennessee Commercial Lending School, Nashville TN, certificate, 1988. **Career:** Third Natl Bank, Nashville TN, asst mgr, 1969-78; Commerce Union Bank, Nashville TN, mgr, 1978-80; Commerce Union Bank, Nashville TN, asst vice pres/comm lending officer, 1981-84; Nashville City Bank, Nashville TN, loan review specialist, 1984; Citizens Bank, Nashville TN, first vice pres, 1985-88, pres and CEO, 1988-. **Orgs:** Dir 1985-89, treasurer 1986-88, Bethlehem Center; pres, Middle Tennessee Chapter, Amer Inst of Banking, 1986-87; pres, Amer Inst of Banking, 1986-87; commr, Tennessee Collection Service Bd, 1987-; treasurer, Uptown Nashville, 1989-; dir, Project Pencil, 1989; Legislative Comm, 1989-. **Honors/Awds:** Profiled in Nashville Tennessean Newspaper, 1988, and in Nashville Banner Newspaper, 1989. **Business Addr:** President and CEO, Citizens Savings Bank and Trust Co, 1917 Heiman St, Nashville, TN 37208-2409.

DAVIDSON, ROBERT C., JR.
Paint company executive. **Personal:** Born Oct 3, 1945, Memphis, TN; son of Thelma Davidson and Robert C Davidson, Sr; married Alice Faye Davidson, Jan 5, 1978; children: Robert C Davidson, III, John R Davidson, Julian L Davidson. **Educ:** Morehouse Coll, BA, 1967; Graduate School of Business Univ of Chicago, MBA, 1969. **Career:** Cresap, McCormack & Paget, sr assoc consultant, 1969-72; Urban National Corp, vice pres, 1972-74; Avant Garde Enterprises, exec vice pres, 1974-75; R Davidson & Assoc, consultant, 1975-78; Surface Protection Ind, pres, 1978-. **Orgs:** Board of directors, Los Angeles Chamber Orchestra; board of directors, Children's Hospital of Los Angeles; member, Young Presidents' Organization. **Honors/Awds:** Business listed as #21 in Black Enterprise's list of top 100 black firms, 1989; Black Businessman of the Year, Los Angeles Chapter, Black MBA Association, 1988; Outstanding Entrepreneur, National Association of Investment Companies, 1990.

DAVIDSON, RUDOLPH DOUGLAS
Government official. **Personal:** Born Jul 19, 1941, Louisville, KY; son of Catherine Ruffins Davidson and Nathaniel Davidson; married Jean Slater Davidson, Feb 12, 1988. **Educ:** University of Louisville, Louisville, KY, 1970-72. **Career:** Westinghouse Learning Corp, Louisville, KY, manager, 1966-70; Model Cities Prog, Louisville, KY, director, operation mainstream, 1970-73; City of Louisville, Louisville, KY, director, Lou & Jeff Co, directions to opport, 1973-77, director, Louisville, Jeff Co, WEP, 1977-79, executive director, Lou & Jeff

Co, CAA, 1979-83, director, solid waste mgmt & serv, 1983-. **Orgs:** Member, Lou & Jeff County Community Action Agency, 1983-; member, Jeff County Solid Waste Management Board, 1985-; member, National Forum of Black Public Administrators, 1989-; chairman, Mayor Jerry Abramson's Recycling Committee, 1989-; chairman, Mayor Jerry Abramson's Resource Recovery Project Comm, 1990-; Municipal Waste Management Assn exec comm; pres, Kentucky Bluegrass Chapter, The Solid Waste Association of North America; vice pres, US Conference of Mayors, Municipal Waste Management Association; vice pres, West End Clubs Development Center Board of Directors. **Honors/Awds:** Fleur De Lis Award for Meritorious Serv, Mayor William Stansbury, 1977-82; Certificate of Merit, Louisville, Board of Alderman, 1983; Distinguished Citizen Award, Mayor Harvey Sloane, 1983; Outstanding Community, County Judge, Executive Mitch McConnell, 1983; Commissioned KY Colonel, Governor, John Y Brown, 1983; Black Achiever, 1984. **Military Serv:** Army, E-4, 1963-65, Honorable Discharge, 1965. **Home Addr:** 201 N 46th St, Louisville, KY 40212.

DAVIDSON, TOMMY
Comedian, actor. **Career:** Standup comedian, currently; actor, currently; work includes: Strictly Business, film, 1992; In Living Color, tv show, former cast member; Sitcom star, Between Brothers, 1997-. **Honors/Awds:** Voted one of the Rising Stars of Comedy, 1990. **Business Addr:** Actor, c/o William Morris Agency, 151 El Camino Dr, Beverly Hills, CA 90212, (310)274-7451.

DAVIDSON, U. S., JR.
Educator. **Personal:** Born Oct 28, 1954, Fulton, MS; son of Juanita Davidson and U S Davidson Sr; divorced; children: Brian Anthony. **Educ:** Parkland Community College, AA, univ studies, 1975; North Dakota State University, BS, secondary education, 1978; Eastern Illinois University, Masters, guidance/counseling, 1983, type 75, administration endorsement, 1986. **Career:** Champaign Community Unit District #4, instructional aide, 1978-79, special education teacher, 1979-81, physical education teacher, 1981-85, counselor, 1985-88, dean of students, 1988-90, assistant principal, 1990, prinicpal 1990-. **Orgs:** Kappa Alpha Psi, 1974-; Phi Delta Kappa, 1983-; Association of Illinois Middle School, 1990-; Champaign Human Relations Commission, 1990-; Champaign County Urban League, 1985-; Minority Teacher Recruitment Team, 1989-; Illinois Middle Grades Planning Initiative Committee, 1991-; Committee to Identify Minorities for Boards and Commissions, 1992-. **Business Addr:** Principal, Champaign Community Unit District #4, 817 N Harris St, Champaign, IL 61820, (217)351-3819.

DAVIDSON-HARGER, JOAN CAROLE
Attorney. **Personal:** Born Sep 14, 1946, East Chicago, IN; daughter of Evelyn Ruth Riley-Davidson and Walter Harley Davidson; divorced; children: Scott. **Educ:** University of Michigan, 1965-66; University of Detroit, BA, 1975; Detroit College of Law, JD, 1983. **Career:** Detroit Board of Education, urban adult teacher, math, 1975-76; Ford Motor Co., NAAO, analyst, 1976-89; sole practitioner, attorney, 1987-90; UAW Legal Services, staff attorney, 1990-91; Joan Davidson-Harger, sole practioner, 1991-. **Orgs:** D Augustus Straker Bar Association, 1991-; Oakland County Bar Association, 1987-88; State Bar of Michigan, 1987-; National Bar Association, 1983-; United Methodist Women, vice pres, secretary, 1985-90; Magnolia United Methodist Youth Group, leader/sponsor, 1985-89; Detroit Metropolitan Black United Methodist Scholarshop Fund, 1988-90. **Honors/Awds:** Phi Alpha Theta, Historical Honorary Society, 1974; United Methodist Women, Service Award, 1988. **Business Addr:** Attorney, 17201 W 12 Mile Rd, Southfield, MI 48075, (810)559-3242.

DAVIE, DAMON JONATHON
Automotive agency executive. **Personal:** Born May 8, 1964, Detroit, MI; son of William & Alice Davie; married Ruthanne Davie, May 14, 1988; children: Damon, Daniel. **Educ:** Drake University, 1983-85; Western Illinois University, Communications. **Career:** Pepsi Cola Co, management trainee, 1989-90; Rent-A-Center, account manager, 1990-91; AAA Michigan, 1991-. **Orgs:** Omega Psi Phi Fraternity Inc, Epsilon Beta Chapter, vice pres, 1987; New Detroit Inc, committee mem, 1996. **Business Addr:** Economic Development Coord, AAA Michigan, 1 Auto Club Dr, Dearborn, MI 48126.

DAVIES, LAWRENCE A.
Elected official, clergyman. **Personal:** Born Jul 7, 1930, Houston, TX; son of Autrey Thomas Davies Miller (deceased) and Lawrence A Davies Sr (deceased); married Janice J Pryde; children: Lauren A, Karen M, Sharron L. **Educ:** Prairie View A&M Coll, BS 1949; Howard Univ School of Religion, MDivinity 1957; Wesley Theological Seminary, M Sacred Theology 1961. **Career:** Good Samaritan Baptist Church WA DC, pastor 1956-60; Shiloh Baptist Church WA DC, asst pastor & religious ed dir 1960-62; City of Fredericksburg, 1st black city councilman 1966-76, 1st black mayor 1976-; Shiloh Baptist Church Fredericksburg VA, pastor 1962-. **Orgs:** Pres Fredericksburg Area Ministerial Assoc 1965-66, Fredericksburg Baptist Ministers Conf 1969-70, Rappahannock Citizen Corp 1968-, VA Assoc for Mental Health 1974-76; adv dir Perpetual Amer Bank 1975-88; bd of dir Natl Conf of Black Mayors 1977-86, Natl Kidney Found of VA 1984-86; pres VA Municipal League 1984-85, VA Conf of Black Mayors 1985-; founder Fredericksburg Area Sickle Cell Assoc; mem Fredericksburg Lions Club, Alpha Phi Alpha Frat, Prince Hall Masons, Governor's Commn on Transportation in the 21st Century 1986-88; mem bd of visitors Mary Washington Coll 1986-90; mem, Commonwealth Transportation Bd, 1990-. **Honors/Awds:** Young Man of the Year Fredericksburg Jaycees 1966; Citizen of the Year Omega Psi Phi Frat 1966; Citizenship Awd Fredericksburg Area Chamber of Comm 1976; Man of the Year VFW #3103 1977; Outstanding Serv Awd Natl Assoc for Mental Health 1979; Humanitarian of the Year Awd Mt Bethel Baptist Assoc 1984; Citizen of the Year, Alpha Kappa Alpha Sorority, Mid-Atlantic Region, 1990; Fredericksburg Bible Inst & Sem, DD (honorary), 1985. **Business Addr:** Mayor, City of Fredericksburg, Fredericksburg, VA 22401.

DAVIS, ABRAHAM, JR.
Educator (retired). **Personal:** Born May 14, 1923, Beaufort, SC; son of Everlena and Abraham; married Jennie Howard; children: Silena Davis, Wilkins Garrett Jr, James Wright, Joya Wright. **Educ:** Lancaster Sch of the Bible & Theol, diplomas in Bible & Theol 1949; Houghton Coll, BA 1955; Temple U, MA 1956; Univ of IA, Penn State U, Western Reserve U, 1960; IN Univ Bloomington, PhD 1971. **Career:** Center for Urban Theological Studies, Philadelphia, PA, prof of speech & basic writing, 1986-88; Calvin College, Grand Rapids, MI, visiting prof in the dept of communication arts & sciences, 1986-88. Eastern Mennonite College, Cross Cultural Communication, coordinator/prof, 1980-85; Messiah Coll, Philadelphia PA, prof of comm 1978-80, admin acad dean 1975-78; Asbury Coll, visiting prof 1973-74; Messiah Coll, Philadelphia PA, acting dean 1973-74; sabbatical lecturer & oral inter Afro-Amer Literature & Rhetoric 1972-73; Houghton Coll, assoc prof & prof of Speech 1967-72; IN Univ Bloomington, assoc teacher in public speaking 1965-67; Houghton Coll, instructor Speech & English Composition 1961-65; Greenville Co Negro Public Schools, co speech therpst 1958-61; SC State Coll for Neg, Orangeb SC, speech therpst & instructor 1958-59; Positive Ethnic Models & The Ethnic Integration of the Collegiate Curricula, lecturer, rhetorician, currently. **Orgs:** Volunteers for various organizations. **Honors/Awds:** Speaker & oral interpreter of Afro-Am lit & rhetoric various chs, comm groups, pub assemblies, faculty In Serv; mem & speaker Regional & Nat Professional Speech Comm Assn 1972; mem & spkr Nat Couc of Tchrs of Engl 1973; vis lectr, The Fundamentals of Oral & Written Communication 1976; pub Doctoral Dissertation & Abstract, An Accelerated Spch Curriculum for Selected Educational Disadvtd Negros, Dissertation Abstract, 1971; pub Your God is Too White Journal of Am Sci Affiliation, 1971; pub book review of The Oratory of Negro Leaders 1900-1960 for Ethnic and Minoirty Studies Newsletter of WI State 1972; pub book review Black Jargon in White Am Journal of Am Sci Affiliation; pub article Evangelicals Listen, Please Listen Bridge 1976. **Business Addr:** 1543 North College Ave, Harrisonburg, VA 22801.

DAVIS, ADRIANNE
Elected official. **Personal:** Born Sep 6, 1945, Newark, NJ. **Educ:** Montclair State Coll, MA 1967. **Career:** West Side HS Newark NJ, instr 1967-73; North Ward Ctr Inc Newark NJ, admin 1973-; Essex Cty New Jersey, freeholder at large. **Orgs:** Consult John Hay Whitney Found 1973-74; chrprsn Essex Cty Coll Personnel Comm 1979, Essex Vty Coll Bd of Trustees 1979-80; mem Essex Cty Bd of Freeholders 1982-, Budget Review Comm Essex Cty Bd of Freeholders 1983-, Essex Cty Econ Devel Corp 1983-. **Honors/Awds:** Disting Serv Awd Theatre of Universal Images 1980; Apprec Awd Essex Cty Coll 1980; Citizens Apprec Awd Comm of Womens Concerns Essex Cty 1980; Dr Martin Luther King Recog Awd North Ward Ctr 1983. **Business Addr:** Essex County, 465 High St #560A, Newark, NJ 07102.

DAVIS, AGNES MARIA
Travel agent, registered nurse. **Personal:** Born Jun 3, 1927, Republic of Panama, Panama; daughter of Ellen Taylor (deceased) and Frederick Taylor (deceased); married Samuel Huntley, Mar 17, 1972; children: Alexander Dunker Jr, Ann Maria Dunker. **Educ:** St Francis College, BS, 1984; Long Island University, MS, 1987; School of Nursing, Jewish Hospital and Medical Center of Brooklyn. **Career:** Jewish Hospital and Medical Center of Brooklyn, supervisor, 1961-65; Interfaith Medical Center, full-time assistant director of nursing, 1985-88; Clove Lakes Nursing Home, part-time supervisor, 1992-; Senga Travel Inc, president, currently. **Orgs:** NAACOG, chairperson, three 2-year terms; Nursing Alumnae Board, 1973-; Staten Island Chamber of Commerce, executive board member, 1992-. **Special Achievements:** Author, Fetal Alcohol Syndrome (In The Neonates), 1978. **Business Addr:** President, Senga Travel Inc., 1918 Victory Blvd., Staten Island, NY 10314, (718)816-1608.

DAVIS, ALFRED C., SR.
Commissioner, clergyman, administrator. **Personal:** Born Mar 11, 1938, Vaiden, MS; married Mary L Mack; children: Alfred C Jr, Darlene, Frederick Jerome, Angel Aleeta. **Educ:** NW Training Center OR State, 1968-69; Tacoma Vocational Tech, 1970; Trinity Hall Coll & Seminary York, PA, DD 1980. **Career:** New Jerusalem, asst pastor 1958-61; Altheimer Meml Ch, asst pastor 1961-64; Eastside Comm Church, pastor/founder 1964-; Multi Serv Center (Eastside) ODI, asst dir 1965; Eastside Comm Day Care Center, founder/adminstr 1972-; Tacoma Housing Authority, minister. **Orgs:** Pres & exec ofcr FORCE 1973-; founder majestic Aires Rehab Farm Yelm 1975-; past chmn bd of commr Tacoma Housing Authority 1977-; pres Tacoma Ministerial Alliance 1978-80; bd mem Natl Commn ERS Com of Nahro's 1979-; charter mem The Tacoma Club; mem NAACP; mem Tacoma Urban League; chmn of the Ministrial Alliance; evangelism & mem of the Adv Bd to the TMA Pres. **Honors/Awds:** Service to Mankind Award Puget Sound Sertoma Club 1980; Dist Serv to Mankind Award BC-WA Dist NW Region Sertoma 1980; Key to City of Tacoma, WA from Mayor Mike Parker 1980. **Military Serv:** USAF; Received Good Conduct Medal 1960. **Business Addr:** Minister, Tacoma Housing Authority, 4420 Portland Ave, Tacoma, WA 98404.

DAVIS, ALGENITA SCOTT
Attorney. **Personal:** Born Oct 1, 1950, Houston, TX; daughter of Althea Lewis Scott and C B Scott; married John W Davis III; children: Marthea, John IV. **Educ:** Howard Univ, BBA 1971, JD 1974. **Career:** US Govt Printing Office, clerk-typist 1969-70, 71; Howard Univ Dept of Residence Life, grad fellow 1971-74; US General Accounting Office, legal intern 1972; Shell Oil Co, tax serv mgr, tax compliance dept 1974-77, office of legislation & industry affairs mgr 1977-79, tax atty, tax compliance dept 1979; Burney Edwards Hall Hartsfield & Scott, partner 1975-78; Port of Houston Authority, counsel 1979-89; Texas Commerce Bancshares, vice pres, Community Affairs officer, sr vice pres, community affairs officer, currently. **Orgs:** Mem State Bar of TX, US Tax Court, US Southern Dist Court & Fifth Circuit Court of Appeals, US Supreme Court, Interstate Comm Commn, Fed Maritime Commission; charter mem Natl Bar Inst; political action comm 1975-76, bd dir 1976-77, 1985-88, pres 1988-89 Houston Lawyers Assn; founding mem 1975, bd mem 1975-78, 1986-87, vchair 1983-84, parliamentarian 1986-87 Black Women Lawyers Assoc; Judicial Campaign Worker for Domestic Relations Court Candidate 1976; Judicial Candidates 1978, 1980, 1984, 1986; campaign co-chair Congressional Candidate 1978; co-chair Speakers Bureau Houston Bar Assoc 1978-79; rep Single Mem Dist coalition for Houston Lawyers Assn 1979; sec 1984- NBA Invest Corp 1984-; fundraising chair Committee-to-re-Elect Judson RobinsonCouncilman-at-Large Position 5 1985; Natl Bar n, pres-elect 1989-90, pres 1990-91, vice pres 1988-89, sec 1983-84; NBA Women's Division vice pres 1987-89. **Honors/Awds:** Distinguished Christian Serv Sloan Methodist Church 1977; Distinguished Comm Serv Trinity Methodist Church 1978; Natl Bar Assn Distinguished Serv Awd 1982; One of Houston's Most Influential Black Women Black Experience Magazine 1984; Houston Lawyers Assoc Serv Awd 1985, 1987, 1988; Human Enrichment of Life Program Inc Young Achievers Awd 1986, 1990; Woman of Distinction, Ebony Man Magazine. **Business Addr:** Sr Vice Pres/Community Affairs Officer, Texas Commerce Banchares, 14 TCB-E 93, PO Box 2558, Houston, TX 77252-8093.

DAVIS, ALONZO J.
Artist. **Personal:** Born Feb 2, 1942, Tuskegee, AL. **Educ:** Otis Art Inst, MFA 1973; BFA 1971; UCLA pgrad 1966; pepperdine coll, ba 1964. **Career:** CA State U, instr 1976-; UCLA, lectr 1973 Padasena City Coll, instr 1971; Mt San Antonio Coll, instr 1971-73; La Unified sch dist instr 1962-70; Watts Towers & Art Ctr, consult 1976-; LA Co Mus of Art, consult 1976; Contemporary Crafts Inc, consult 1968-70. **Orgs:** Exec dir Brockman Gallery Prodn 1973-; owner co-dir Brockman Gallery 1967-73; bd mem CA Confederation of Arts 1976-; bd mem Cultural News Serv 1977-; bd mem Comm Arts Devel Group 1976-77; bd mem Artists for Econ Action; editor Neworld Mag 1977; fndr Support The Arts 1976-; exhibits Transition Gallery1976; Bowrs Mus 1975; Just Midtown Gallery 1975; Pomona Pub Libr 1975; Otis Art Inst 1977; LA Muncpl Art Gallery 1977; Studio Mus of Harlem 1977; Craft& Folk Art Mus 1977; Fisher 1976; Mural & Grafiti Exh 1976; number others Grants NEA & 1973-77; Brockman Gallery 1976; Inner City Mural Grant 1974. **Honors/Awds:** Publ ''Black Artists of the New Generation'' 1977; varying Dir of Contemporary Black Artists 1975; Afro Am Artists 1973; Black Artist on Art 1971; Wilson Libr Bull 1969.

DAVIS, AMOS
Psychiatrist. **Personal:** Born Apr 2, 1932, Statesboro, GA; married Beatrice Lacy; children: Amy Louise, Amos Anthony. **Educ:** Meharry Med Coll, MD 1963; Fisk U, BA 1958; Bd Cert Psychiatry 1975. **Career:** Martin Luther Kind Co Hosp LA, staff psychiatrist; Private Prac; LA Co Dept of Mental Health, staff physician 1967-72; Metro State Hosp, residency training. **Orgs:** Mem Charles Drew Med Soc; Am Psychiatric Assn; So CA Psychiatric Soc; Charles Drew Scholarship Loan Fund Inc. **Military Serv:** AUS 1955-57. **Business Addr:** 11665 W Olympic Blvd, Ste 516, Los Angeles, CA 90064.

DAVIS, ANDRE MAURICE
Judge. **Personal:** Born Feb 11, 1949, Baltimore, MD; married Aug 15, 1987; children: Ahmed Jamal. **Career:** District of MD, asst US attorney, 1981-83; University of Maryland, School of Law, assistant professor, 1984-87; District Court of Maryland,

Baltimore City, associate judge, 1987-90; Baltimore City Circuit Court, associate judge, 1990-. **Orgs:** Big Brothers/Big Sisters Central MD, Inc, president; Legal Aid Bureau, Inc, president, 1985-87; Judicial Institute of MD, mem of the board, 1987-90; Judicial Conference of MD, president, executive committee, 1993-94. **Business Addr:** Judge, Circuit Court for Baltimore City, 111 N Calvert Street, Clarence M Mitchell Jr Courthouse, Baltimore, MD 21202, (410)396-5076.

DAVIS, ANGELA YVONNE
Political activist, author. **Personal:** Born Jan 26, 1944, Birmingham, AL; daughter of Sallye E. Davis and B. Frank Davis. **Educ:** Sorbonne, University of Paris, 1963-64; Brandeis University, BA (magna cum laude), 1965; University of Frankfurt, graduate study, 1965-67; University of California at San Diego, MA, 1968, graduate study, 1968-69. **Career:** University of California at Los Angeles, assistant professor, 1969-70; San Francisco State University and San Francisco Art Institute, professor; University of California, Santa Cruz, professor, history of consciousness, currently. **Orgs:** Founder/co-chairperson, National Alliance Against Racist and Political Repression; national board of directors, National Political Congress of Black Women; national board member, National Black Women's Health Project; Che-Lumumba Club; Phi Beta Kappa; Black Panthers; mem of Central Commn, Communist Party. **Honors/Awds:** Lenin Peace Prize, USSR, 1979; Lenin University, PhD; vice presal candidate for the Communist Party, 1980, 1984. **Special Achievements:** Author of numerous works, including: with Ruchell Magee, the Soldedad Brothers et al, If They Come in the Morning: Voices of Resistance, 1971; Angela Davis: An Autobiography, 1974; Women, Race, and Class, 1981; Women, Culture, and Politics, 1989; Angela Davis Speaks; numerous articles. **Business Addr:** Political Activist, 269 Moultrie St, San Francisco, CA 94110.

DAVIS, ANITA LOUISE
County government official. **Personal:** Born Oct 3, 1936, Williamsport, PA; daughter of Jessie Porter and Malcolm Porter; married Morris S, Jun 1962; children: Lynn M, Lyles Jeyious, Wayne D Lyles, Mark E Lyles. **Educ:** Buffalo State Coll, 1954-55, 1977-79; Univ of ND Grand Forks AFB, 1968-69; Univ of NH Pease AFB, 1970-71; Univ of Buffalo 1971-72, 76; Tallahasee Comm Coll; Florida A&M Univ, BS, criminal justice, 1990. **Career:** Health & Rehab Servs Leon Start Center, adminstrv asst sec III 1979-83; Florida Dept of Labor, employment spec, 1983-87, civil rights specialist II, 1987-89; Leon County, commission, former dir of community enrichment, project for Community Task Force on Drugs and Crime, chairman, BSA Swanne Dist st Risk Kids Council, past chairman, Leon County Board of Commissioners, currently; Re-elected Leon City Bd of Commissioners District I 1994; Natl Assn of County Organizations, Elder Services Inc, vice chair; Pride Court of Colanthes' Communit/Civic Committee, vice chair. **Orgs:** Treas & bd of dirs Black Devel Found; former 1st vice pres & com chmn CAO Head Start Overall Policy Council; mem Criminal Justice Com BUILD of Buffalo Inc; criminal justice chairperson NAACP; social dir AD Price & Perry Sr Citizens; coord Masten Dist Block Club Assn; pres, Tallahassee Branch, NAACP, 1981-90; vice pres, Florida State Conference of NAACP Branch, 1986-; past pres, Regional/Local Chapter Philos of Sigma Gamma Rho Sorority, Beta Delta Chapter, 1982-88; Delta Sigma Chapter, reporter, 1992; Delta Sigma Theta; Natl Hookup of Black Women; FSU Leadership Conference; Capital Women's Political Caucus. **Honors/Awds:** Martin Luter King Jr Community Leadership Award, Florida A&M Univ, 1991; Lifetime Achievement Award, Academy of Florida Trial Lawyers, 1987; National Leadership Award, NAACP, 1989, 1990; FL Commission on Human Relations Community Award, 1994. **Business Addr:** Leon County Board of Commissioners, 301 S Monroe, Tallahassee, FL 32301.

DAVIS, ANTHONY D.
Professional football player. **Personal:** Born Mar 7, 1969, Pasco, WA. **Educ:** Utah. **Career:** Seattle Seahawks, 1993; Kansas City Chiefs, 1994-. **Business Addr:** Professional Football Player, Kansas City Chiefs, One Arrowhead Dr, Kansas City, MO 64129, (816)924-9300.

DAVIS, ANTONE EUGENE
Professional football player. **Personal:** Born Feb 28, 1967, Sweetwater, TN; married Carrie; children: Cailyn Marie. **Educ:** Tennessee, attended. **Career:** Philadelphia Eagles, tackle, 1991-95; Atlanta Falcons, 1996-. **Business Addr:** Professional Football Player, Atlanta Falcons, Two Falcon Place, Suwanee, GA 30174, (404)945-1111.

DAVIS, ANTONIO LEE
Professional basketball player. **Personal:** Born Oct 31, 1968, Oakland, CA; married Kendra; children: two. **Educ:** Texas, El Paso. **Career:** Philips Milano (Italian league), 1992-93; Indiana Pacers, forward-center, 1993-. **Business Addr:** Professional Basketball Player, Indiana Pacers, 300 E Market St, Indianapolis, IN 46204, (317)263-2100.

DAVIS, ARNOR S.
Educator. **Personal:** Born Dec 19, 1919, Patterson, GA; married; children: 3. **Educ:** Savannah State Coll Savannah GA, BS; Sch of Religion Howard Univ Wash DC, BD; Religous Educ Sch of Religion Howard Univ Wash DC, MA. **Career:** Inst Relations DC Redevel Land Agency, Washington DC, asst area dir; Antioch Baptist Church, Washington DC, asst minister 1975; New Bethel Baptist Church, Washington DC, dir of religious educ 1960-75; Zion Baptist Church, Washington DC, asst minister 1950-52. **Orgs:** Bd dir local council of Chs; mem Housing Task Force Council of Chs; bd dir Hillcrest Childrens Center 1971-74; bd dir DC Citizens for Better Educ 1970-74; pres bd dir Nat Med Aso Found 1967-74; bd dir Lincoln-Westmoreland Non-Profit Housing Corp; mem Savannah State Alumni Assn DC Chap 1948-74; bd dir Mt Ethel Bapt Training Union 1969-74; mem Bapt Ministers Conf 1960-74; mem Howard Univ Alumni Assn; exec dir Second Precinct Clergymens Assn 1948-74; NAACP 1970-74. **Honors/Awds:** Publs A Guide to Chs & Institutions in the Shaw & Urban Renewal Area 1974; Chs in Shaw 1970; A Guide SAC Area Chs Schs & Non-profit Sponsorships 1975. **Military Serv:** AUS 1941-46.

DAVIS, ARRIE W.
State official. **Personal:** Born Jul 21, 1940, Baltimore, MD; children: Joanne, Aria. **Educ:** Morgan State Coll, BA 1963; New York Univ, MA 1966; Univ Baltimore, JD 1969. **Career:** Baltimore City Public Sch, former English instr, swimming coach, 1964-69; Supreme Bench Baltimore, bailiff, 1968-69; State MD, asst atty gen counsel to div of correction; Baltimore City, asst state's attorney, prof of law, 1970-71; Villa Julie Coll, asst prof; Commercial Law Morgan Coll Grad Sch, asst prof; Private Practioner; City of Baltimore, judge, Court of Special Appeals of Maryland. **Orgs:** Baltimore City Bar Assn; MD State Bar Assn; Am Bar Assn; Nat Bar Assn; Monumental Bar Assn.

DAVIS, ARTHUR, JR.
Educator. **Personal:** Born Apr 17, 1933, Bessemer, AL; married Loretta J; children: Arthur III, Deborah, Sarah. **Educ:** AL A & M, BS 1955; Univ of IL, MA 1968; Univ of IL, PhD 1970. **Career:** Northeastern Univ, dir assoc prof of educ 1976-; KY State Univ, asst prof 1970-76; Univ of IL, asst dir 1966-70; Dept of the Air Force, Chanute Tech Training Center, civilian elec electron training instructor 1963-66; Aero-space Ground Equip Branch, civ aircraft & missle ground suppost equipment repairman tech 1961-63; Aero-space Equipment Branch, civ training instructor ground support 1959-61. **Orgs:** Pres Wrightway Ed Consutl LTD 1972-76; asst coord St Univ of NY 1970-73; consul Urbana Pub Schl 1966; consul Univ of IL Pal Prog; consul Dean of Stud on Loc Urban Commn Needs & Prob 1968-69; c Prgm sul adm of the Clerical Learner Prgm on Design Curr Dev & Eval9 1968-70; consul Rochester NY Model Cities Prog 1971; consul Parents Adv Com on Title I ESEA 1972; consul Univ of IL 1977; consul S IL Univ Coll of Educ 1977; mem Adm Oper & Comm; mem Univ Cabinet; mem Steering Comm on Ath; mem Black Recruit Adv Comm; mem Search Comm for Dean of Coll of Edn; mem Univ Cabinet; mem Task Force on Compensatory Edn; mem Adv Comm on the Arts. **Honors/Awds:** Publ "Racial Crisis in Pub Educ a quest for social order " 1975; presently writing 2 books "the pedagogic of the african am studies" & "the educ of the Am Negro from Slavery to the Presnet" sev articles & ed 2 other books; num art publ. **Military Serv:** AUS 1955-57. **Business Addr:** Coll of Educ Northeastern Univ, 360 Huntington Ave, Boston, MA 02115.

DAVIS, ARTHUR, III
City planner, consultant, educator. **Personal:** Born Nov 12, 1942, Sampson Co, NC; son of Dr & Mrs Arthur Davis; divorced; children: Arthur Paris. **Educ:** Morehouse Coll, BA 1965; Carnegie-Mellon Univ, MA 1966; Univ of Pittsburgh, MPA 1967. **Career:** A&T State Univ, assistant professor 1967-68, 1990-; City of Greensboro, sr planner 1969-; Guilford Coll, lecturer 1975-81; Various Agencies, consultant 1975-; A&T State Univ, asst prof of planning & design, consultant assoc; Carolina Evaluation Research Center, city, corporate, church planner 27 years. **Orgs:** Bd NC Fellows Bd 1971-84; Natl Greene Sertoma pres & bd 1971; bd & pres Greensboro Inter-club Council 1971; pres bd Greensboro Credit Union 1978, BSA Eagle Review Board 1991-; Gnl Greene Council BSA 1980-; bd chmn Greensboro Emp Comem 1978-82; Grimsley PTA bd 1982-86; bd sec Amer Planning Orgn 1981-85; United Arts Council Bd 1983-85; USOA Bd 1985-90; Morehouse Coll Alumni Club; bd mem NC ASPA 1987-; sec, mem NC APA 1980-86; president, American Society for Public Administration, 1991-92; staff advisor, Ole Asheboro Neighborhood Assn, 1989-; County Resource Housing Board 1990-94; Minority/Women Business Development Council 1990-; Committee of 100 1989-; board Human Service Institute 1989-95; Greensboro Visions I & II 1986-92; advisory board GTCC 1989-. **Honors/Awds:** Cmmty Serv Awd A&T 1974, 1975; Univ S Jaycees, Amer Plng Assoc A&T St Univ 1975; Men of Achievement 1976; awd Greensboro YMCA 1978; comm serv Seaoma Intrnl 1981; numerous citations US Dept of Comm, President Leadership Awd 1983; Sertoman of the Year Sertoma International; Greensboro 100 Award 1991; NBFPA Service Award Outstanding Citizen 1992; Outstanding 100 Citizens 1992; Carolina Peacemaker Award, 1993; Technology/Strategic Planning, 1997; Leadership 2000, 1996-98; City Service Award, 1995; ASPA Outstanding Service Award, 1992; Sertoma Award, 1993; Ole Atheles Award, 1994; YPL Award, 1993; NC Credit Union Volunteer, 1994; Comm of 100 Service Award, 1997. **Home Addr:** 910 Ross Ave, Greensboro, NC 27406-2414. **Business Addr:** Planning Research Supervisor, Greensboro Planning and Community Development, City of Greensboro, 300 W Washington St, PO Box 3136, Greensboro, NC 27402-3136.

DAVIS, ARTHUR D.
Musician, educator, psychologist. **Personal:** married Gladys; children: Kimaili, Mureithi. **Educ:** Hunter Coll, BA Psych/Mus (Summa Cum Laude) 1973; City Coll, MA 1976; NY Univ, MA 1976; NY Univ, PhD (w/Distinction) 1982. **Career:** Composer, musician, educator, 1958-; Borough Manhattan Comm Coll, asst adjunct prof 1972-86; Univ of Bridgeport, prof 1979-82; Head Start, consultant, psychologist 1981-82; NY Medical Coll, instr 1983-86; Lincoln Medical & Mental Health Ctr, clinical psychologist 1982-85; Lakeside UFSD, psychologist 1985-86; Orange Coast Coll, faculty, 1987-; private practice, 1986-; psychologist/assoc prof; CA State Univ, Fullerton, prof 1988-90. **Orgs:** Mem Amer Soc of Authors Composers and Publishers 1976-; mem Amer Psychological Assn 1977-; mgr Little League Inc 1979-82; exec bd mem Local 802 Jazz Musicians Found 1984-86; adviser, William Grant Still Museum, 1988-; Orange Co AIDS, 1988; Amer Assn of Black Psychologists, 1983-; New York Acad of Sciences, 1984-; mem Orange County Psychological Assn 1989-; consultant to mental health svcs, consultant to music projects etc; in music gave first double bass concerts in many cities; producer of records and cassettes; numerous lectures workshops clinics both in psychology and music; board of directors, Orange County Urban League, Inc, 1992-; director, Local 47 Musician's Union, Los Angeles, 1993-. **Honors/Awds:** Named No 1 Bassist Downbeat Intl Critics Poll 1962; World's Foremost Double Bassist Dict of International Biogr 1969-; Phi Beta Kappa, Psi Chi Natl Honor Socs; Life Fellow Intercontinental Biographical Assoc 1974-; The Arthur Davis System For Double Bass 1976; Dr Art Davis Live 1984; Reemergence Art Davis, Inter Phi Records, IP7728, 1980; Gold Note Jazz Award LION, Natl Black MBA Assn 1985; cited in NY Times as one of the world's top gourmet chefs; cited for music in Chap 9 of "Music; Black, White & Blue" 1972 Morrow Publ; music album: "Art Davis Quartet, Life" Soulnote 1443 1987; Chancellor's Distinguished Lecturer, University of California, Irvine, 1992-93; Annual Doctor, Art Davis Scholarship; president & CEO, Better Advantages for Students and Society. **Business Addr:** ARKIMU, 3535 East Coast Hwy, Suite 50, Corona Del Mar, CA 92625.

DAVIS, BARBARA D.
Corporate affirmative action officer. **Educ:** St Joseph Calumet Coll, B Sociology, A Social Work; Certificates, Training Counselor IN Univ, Univ of WI Labor Studies, Recruitment and Training Inst. **Career:** Insland Steel Project, officer mgr 1976-77, recruiter-counselor 1977-78, asst project dir 1978-79, dir 1980; Gilbane Building Co, equal employment oppor officer 1982, corporate affirmative action specialist 1984-. **Orgs:** Mem IL Affirmative Action Officers Assoc; chairperson IAAOA Conf 1985; liaison Black Contractors United/Chicago Urban League; consultant World's Fair Plan on Affirmative Action; pres Women in Construction; consultant Intl Women Economic Develop Corp; mem IN Civil Rights Comm; vice pres Fair Share Organization; consultant Women's League State Affiliation NAACP. **Honors/Awds:** Union Counselor Awd AFL-CIO Lake Co Central Labor Union and United Steel Workers of Amer Local 1010; Affirmative Action Officer of the Year Awd Black Contractors United; Dedicated Serv Awd Natl Council of Black Child Develop New York; Special Awd Black Contractors United 1985. **Business Addr:** Corporate Affirm Action Ofcr, Gilbane Building Co, 200 West Madison St, Ste 700, Chicago, IL 60606.

DAVIS, BELVA
Television host. **Personal:** Born Oct 13, 1933, Monroe, LA; daughter of Florence Howard Mays and John Melton; married William Vince Moore; children: Steven Eugene, Darolyn Denise. **Educ:** Oakland City College. **Career:** Sun Reporter Newspaper, San Francisco CA, womens ed, 1963-68; KPIX-TV, San Fancisco, anchor/program host, 1967-77; KQED-TV, San Francisco, anchor/reporter, 1977-81; KRON-TV, urban affairs specialist/program host, 1981-. **Orgs:** Board member Blue Shield of CA 1992-; awards committee SF Foundation 1982-88; natl vice pres Amer Fed of TV & Radio Artist 1984-; board member Howard Thurman Foundation; board mem Black Filmmakers Hall of Fame; mem Links Inc; bd mem, Commonwealth Club of CA, 1991-; bd mem, Metro YMCA. **Honors/Awds:** 5 Emmy's No Cal TV Academy; Natl Journalism Awd Natl Urban Coalition 1985; Natl Journalism Awd Ohio State Univ 1985; Community Service No Cal United Nations Assoc 1984; Outstanding Journalism, Sigma Delta Chi, 1990. **Business Addr:** Program Host, KRON Channel 4, 1001 Van Ness Ave, San Francisco, CA 94109.

DAVIS, BEN JEROME
Professional basketball player. **Personal:** Born Dec 26, 1972, Vero Beach, FL. **Educ:** Kansas; Florida; Hutchinson Comm

College; Arizona. **Career:** Phoenix Suns, 1996-. **Business Addr:** professional Basketball Player, Phoenix Suns, P O Box 1369, Phoenix, AZ 85001, (602)266-5753.

DAVIS, BENJAMIN O., JR.

Business executive. **Personal:** Born Dec 18, 1912, Washington, DC; married Agatha Scott. **Educ:** US Mil Academy, BS 1936. **Career:** City of Cleveland, dir pub safety 1970; Office of Civ Aviation, dir; Dept Trans, sec 1970-71; Trans for Environ Safety & Consumer Affairs, asst sec 1971-. **Orgs:** Mem Bd of Vstrs USAF Acdmy 1970-73; mem bd dir Retired Officers Assn; bd trust Assn of Grads US Mil Academy 1971-74; Natl vice pres Natl Defense Transportation Assn 1972-74; chm Interagency Com Transp Sec; chm Interagency Com on Civ Aviation Sec 1971-74; chm Interagency Exec Gr Mil; asst to Safety & Traffic; mem Citizens Advisory Com to DC Bar; mem bd Pepperdine Univ; mem Natl Com for Educ Ctr Air Force Academy Found; mem Hon Bd Trust; Natl Educ Inst; West Point Academy's Board of Visitors, pres, 1995-. **Honors/Awds:** Hon Degrees: DMilSc, Wilberforce Univ, 1948; DSc, Morgan State Coll, 1963; LLD, Tuskegee Inst, 1963; LLD, Old Wesbury; LL, Daemen College. **Military Serv:** AUS; USAF ltn gen (retired). Military decorations include: Distinguished Service Medal w/2 Oak Leaf Clusters; Silver Star; Distinguished Flying Cross; Legion of Merit w/2 Oak Leaf Clusters; Air Medal w/5 Oak Leaf Clusters; Croix de Guerre w/Palm; Star of Africa; Rep China Cloud & Bnar Medal; 1 Oak Leaf Cluster; Rep Korea Ordr Natl Sec Merit; 2nd cls; many others.

DAVIS, BENNIE L.

Urologist. **Personal:** Born Dec 7, 1927, Muskogee, OK; married; children: Benjamin, Duane. **Educ:** Samuel Huston Coll, BS 1947; Howard U, MD 1952. **Career:** Homer G Philips Hosp St Louis, internship 1952-53; Terre Haute IN, gen practice 1953-54; Homer G Phillips Hosp, surgery resident 1953-55; urology resident 1954-58; Private Practice Indianapolis IN, urologist 1960-. **Orgs:** Mem Am Me Assn; Nat Med Assn; Alpha Phi Alpha Frat; Chi Delta Mu Scientific Frat; Sigma P Phi Frat; Am Urological Assn; instr in Urology IN Univ Med Cntr; mem Indianapolis C of C; Rotarty Club; C of C of the US; vice-pres Our Savior Luthern Ch; chm Div of Urology Meth Hosp Grad Med Ctr 1968-71; chm Urology Sec Natl Med Assn 1974. **Honors/Awds:** Recipient of, Diplomate Am Bd of Urology 1961; fellow Am Coll of Surgeons 1963. **Military Serv:** USAF urologist 1958-60. **Business Addr:** 2615 N Capitol Ave, Indianapolis, IN 46208.

DAVIS, BETTYE J.

State representative. **Personal:** Born May 17, 1938, Homer, LA; daughter of Rosylind Daniel Ivory and Dan Ivory; married Troy J Davis, Jan 21, 1959; children: Anthony B, Sonja Davis-Wade. **Educ:** St Anthony Sch of Practical Nursing, GN 1961; Grambling State Univ, BSW 1971; Univ of Alaska, attended. **Career:** YWCA San Bernardino, asst dir 1971-72; DFYS Anchorage, child care specialist 1975-80; AK Black Leadership Educ Prog, dir 1979-82; Anchorage Youth Serv Div of Family, soc worker 1980; Anchorage Div of Soc Svcs, foster care coord; elected official at large 1982-89; Anchorage Bd of Ed, vp; State of AK Div of Family & Youth Svcs, foster care coord, 1982-87; Alaska State Legislature, Juneau, AK, representative, 1990-. **Orgs:** President Anchorage Chap of Delta Sigma Theta 1979-80, North to the Future BPW Club Inc 1978-79,83, Alaska Black Leadership Conference; treasurer AK Women's Lobby; board of directors March of Dimes 1983-85; mem Blacks in Govt; chairperson AK Black Caucus; Anchorage Br NAACP; member, League of Women Voters; president, National School Board Association, 1989-91; member, Alaska Women's Political Caucus; board member, YWCA of Anchorage, 1989-90; board of directors, National Caucus of Black School Board Members, 1987-89; Winning with Stronger Education, board of directors, 1991-; Anchorage Center for Families, board of directors, 1992-; Alaska 2000, board of directors, 1991-. **Honors/Awds:** Woman of the Year AK Colored Womens Club 1981; Social Worker of the Year Natl Foster Parents Assn 1983; Child Care Worker of the Yr AK Foster Parent Assn 1983; Political Awareness Awd of the Year AK Black Caucus 1984; Outstanding Achievement Awd in Ed AK Colored Womens Club 1985; Outstanding Women in Ed Zeta Phi Beta 1985; Outstanding Serv Awd AK Black Caucus 1986; Outstanding Political Awareness Awd, AK Black Caucus 1986; Comm Serv Awd, AK Black Leadership 1986; Caucus Member of the Year, Alaska Black Caucus, 1987; Boardsmanship Award, 1989, Outstanding Board Member, 1990, Association of Alaska School Boards; Woman of the Year, Alaska Business and Professional Womens Club, 1990; YWCA, Woman of Achievement Award, 1991; Henry Toll Fellowship, Toll Fellow, 1992; California Assembly, Outstanding Leadership Award, 1992. **Home Addr:** 2240 Foxhall Dr, Anchorage, AK 99504.

DAVIS, BILLY, JR.

Professional entertainer, vocalist. **Personal:** Born 1938, St Louis, MO; married Marilyn; children: Steven. **Career:** Professional singer, recording artist, entertainer; original member of the Fifth Dimension, 1965-75; solo artist, 1975-; performed as duet act, Marilyn McCoo and Billy Davis Jr, 1976-80; variety show: "The Marilyn McCoo & Billy Davis Jr Show," CBS-TV, 1977; numerous television and stage appearances. **Honors/Awds:** Grammy Award, with Marilyn McCoo, "You Don't Have To Be A Star," 1977; Tokyo Music Festival, Grand Prize, with Marilyn McCoo; member of 5th Dimension: 6 Grammy Awards; Star on the Hollywood Walk of Fame; 14 Gold Records. **Business Addr:** Singer, c/o Jason Winters, The Sterling/Winters Co, 1900 Ave of the Stars, #1640, Los Angeles, CA 90067.

DAVIS, BRENDA LIGHTSEY-HENDRICKS

Educational administrator. **Personal:** Born Dec 21, 1943, Fairfield, AL; daughter of Flora Lightsey and Guy Lightsey; married William R David MD; children: Tonia D Kelly, William R Jr, Scott, Frank B, Joye Lynn. **Educ:** Harlem Hospital School of Nursing, diploma 1964; Teachers College Columbia Univ, BS 1969, MEd 1972, EdD 1976. **Career:** Riverside Community College, dean grants and contract education. **Orgs:** Mem Natl League for Nurses 1975-; mem CA Comm Coll Administrators 1984-; mem Amer Vocational Educ Assoc 1984-; mem Diamond Bar Black Women's Assoc 1985-; mem Natl Black Nurses' Assoc 1985-; pres Inland Empire Black Nurses' Assoc 1986-; adv comm mem CA State Univ San Bernardino 1986; mem Black History Program Comm/DBBWA 1986-. **Honors/Awds:** Training Grant New York State 1968-69; Minority Scholarship Teachers College Columbia 1970; Training Grant Natl Inst of Mental Health 1971-75. **Home Addr:** 2149 S Indian Creek Rd, Diamond Bar, CA 91765. **Business Addr:** Dean, Grants and Contract, Riverside Community College, 4800 Magnolia Ave, Riverside, CA 92506.

DAVIS, BRIAN

Professional basketball player. **Personal:** Born Jun 21, 1970, Atlantic City, NJ. **Educ:** Duke Univ. **Career:** French League career: Pau Orthez, 1992-93; NBA career: Minnesota Timberwolves, 1993-. **Business Addr:** Professional Basketball Player, Minnesota Timberwolves, 600 First Ave N, Minneapolis, MN 55403, (612)337-3865.

DAVIS, BROWNIE W.

Insurance brokerage executive. **Personal:** Born Mar 13, 1933, Philadelphia, PA; son of Elba and and Brownie; married Elba, Feb 14, 1997; children: Brenda, Bruce. **Educ:** City Coll of NY, BA 1957; Life Underwriter Training Council, grad advanced underwriting & health ins. **Career:** VA Hosp Brooklyn, radioisotope tech; Farmingdale LI Unit, republic aviation supr; Williamsburgh Steel Prod Co, draftsman office mgr; Macy's Rego Park, mgr in charge of housewares; NY Life Ins Co, field underwriter; Guardian Life Ins Co of Amer, dist agency mgr; adjunct prof, Manhattan Community College 1986-; adjunct prof, LaGuardia Community College 1989; Brownie W Davis Agency Corp, pres. **Orgs:** Pres Queens Branch 1st Natl Assn of Life Underwriters; past mem NY Life Agent Adv Council 1973-74; adv bd mem Minority Bus Council; mem Queens Chamber of Commerce; bonding chmn vice pres Assn of Minority Bus Enterprises; pres Cedar Manor Co-op 1967-70; bd mem New York City Housing Auth, Symphony Orchestra; exec vice pres Natl Minority Bus Council. **Honors/Awds:** Natl Quality Awd for Life-Health 1972-75; Centurion 1967-; Group Ins Leader 1973; Health Ins Leader 1967-75; Company Honor Roll over 100 consecutive months; Black Achiever in Industry 1974; speaker Co's Career Conf & Club Meetings also has made video tape training films for Co to help new underwriters; Leader Aetna Life & Casualty Reg; Leadership Award, York College 1989. **Business Addr:** President, Brownie W Davis Agency Corp, PO Box 593, Lawrence, NY 11559.

DAVIS, BUNNY COLEMAN (ELBERTA)

Librarian. **Personal:** Born Mar 21, 1946, New Orleans, LA; daughter of Elberta Plummer Coleman and Joseph Coleman; divorced; children: Sean, Mark. **Educ:** Memphis State Univ, BS Educ 1972; George Peabody Coll of Vanderbilt Univ, MLS 1975. **Career:** Memphis City Schools, librarian 1972-85; State Dept of Educ, evaluator 1985-88; Memphis City Schools, librarian 1988-. **Orgs:** National Education Assn; Alpha Kappa Alpha Sor Inc; Holy Rosary CC Outreach Program; St Peter Auxillary Exec Bd. **Home Addr:** 5020 Pheasant Run Ln, Memphis, TN 38141. **Business Addr:** Librarian, White Station High School, 514 S Perkins Rd, Memphis, TN 38117.

DAVIS, CAL DELEANOR

Company executive. **Personal:** Born Nov 4, 1940, Tulsa, OK; son of Joseph Jr & Retha Davis; widowed; children: Byron, Marvin, Erica. **Educ:** California State Univ, Los Angeles, BS, 1967; Golden Gate Univ, MS, 1987. **Career:** TRW Systems, Inc, sr accountant, 1967-68; FS Moultrie & Co, CPA-auditor, 1968-70; Peat, Marwick & Mitchell, CPA-auditor, 1970-72; Morris, Davis & Co, partner, 1972-; Judie Davis Marrow Donor Recruitment Program, pres & CEO, 1992-. **Orgs:** Bay Area black Consortium for Quality Health Care, bd of dirs, 1991-93; Bank of Oakland, advisory bd mem, 1992; National Marrow Donor Program's Patient Advocacy Committe, advisory bd mem, 1992-93; Chabot College Mentor Program DARAJA Project, 1992-93. **Honors/Awds:** State of CA Assembly woman Barbara Lee, Outstanding Local Small Bus Leader, 1992; Distinguished & Devoted Service From East Bay Area Club, Man of the Year, 1992; Natl Assn of Negro Bus & Pro Women's Clubs Inc, Strong Achiever Award: By Wild 107 FM Radio Station, 1993; Being Single Magazine & Gillette, Pinnacle Award, 1993; Sigma Gamma Rho Sorority, Inc, Sigma Sigma Chapter, Quality of Life Award, 1994. **Special Achievements:** Certified Public Accountant, 1972-. **Military Serv:** US Air Force, airman 2nd class, 1958-62. **Business Addr:** President & CEO, Judie Davis Morrow Donor Recruitment Program, 8393 Capwell Drive, Ste 160, Oakland, CA 94621, (510)430-9249.

DAVIS, CAROLYN ANN MCBRIDE

Senior compensation analyst, supervisor. **Personal:** Born May 28, 1952, Mobile, AL; daughter of Janie Sole McBride and Samuel McBride; married Nolan Davis, Dec 17, 1977; children: Ashley Tamar, Nolan Jarod, Sean Thomas. **Educ:** Wiley Coll, Marshall TX, BA Sociology, 1974; Kent State Univ, Kent OH, graduate program; Univ of South Alabama, Mobile AL, Masters of Public Admin, 1977. **Career:** Natchez Mental Health, Natchez MS, coord, therapist, 1978-79; Texas Dept of Human Serv, Houston TX, social worker, 1979-84; City of Houston, Personnel Dept, Houston TX, compensation specialist, 1984-88; Harris County Hospital District, Houston TX, sr compensation analyst, 1988-. **Orgs:** Mem, pres emeritus, Delta Sigma Theta Sorority, 1971-; founder, exec dir, Christian Debutante Soc of Amer, 1986-; treasurer, bd mem, Houston Youth Chorus, 1986-; Worthy Matron Eastern Star, Bells of Justice Chapter, 1987-; mem, Houston Compensation Assn, 1988-, The Assn of Human Resource Professionals, 1988-, Natl Forum for Black Public Admin, 1989-. **Honors/Awds:** Graduate Assistantship, Kent State Univ, 1975; Graduate Assistantship, Univ of South Alabama, 1976-77; Vernita M Moore Award, Liberty Baptist Church, 1982, 1985; President/Founder, Ambiance Internal, Special Events & Theme Decorating Firm, 1987-.

DAVIS, CARRIE L. FILER

Educator. **Personal:** Born Oct 19, 1924, Marianna, AR; married Wm Davis; children: Arthur, Norma, Helen, Gina. **Educ:** Univ of AR, BA 1948; NE IL Univ, MA 1971; NW Univ, grad study; Univ of Sarasota, EdD 1982. **Career:** Robert Morton High School, educator 1948-55; Crest Finishing School, co-dir 1956-60; Englewood High School Chicago, counselor 1961-72; Chicago Bd of Educ, co-compiler of curriculum guide for drama, admin dist #19, instructional serv coord dist #27, administrator dist #19 1973; Chicago Schools, educational consultant, 1997. **Orgs:** Mem Sigma Gamma Rho 1943-; campus coord Central Region 1972-74 dir 1974; grand epistoleus Sigma Gamma Rho Sor 1980-84; pres Roseland Comm Hosp Aux; chmn Calumet Dist United Charities Educ Comm; mem Good Citizenship Club Inc, Natl Scholarship Comm, Altgeld Urban Prog Ctr Educ Com; com chpsn Afro-Am Family Svcs; mem Quinn Chapel AME Church; mem Southshore YMCA; sub-com White House Conf for Youth; mem St Luke AME Ch; natl pres Natl Women of Achievement Inc; bd of trustees The Univ of Sarasota FL. **Honors/Awds:** Citizenship Awd 1971; Woman of the Yr Crest Finishing Sch 1973; Outstanding Drama Coord 1978; Outstanding Admin 1979; Outstanding Serv to Comm Awd Sigma Gamma Rho Sor; Judge IL Speech Assn Awd; co-author "Curriculum Guide & Activities for Proficiency in Basic Skills" 1977; co-author "Curriculum Guide for Drama Classes" Chicago Bd of Educ; "Proficiency Skills Course" devised for Chicago Bd of Educ for high schools; recipient Governor of Arkansas Awd "Salute to Excellence for Native Arkansans," culminating the Arkansas Sesquicentennial 1986; Robert Moton High School, Marianna, AR, Outstanding Alumni Award, 1997; Roseland Comm Hospital, Comm Service Award, 1997; Mayor Daley, Chicago, Senior Citizen Hall of Fame Award, 1997; LeMoyne College Alumni Award for Comm Ed Service to Youth, 1997. **Business Addr:** Administrator, Chicago Bd of Education, 9912 Ave H, Chicago, IL 60617.

DAVIS, CHARLES

City official. **Personal:** Born Sep 4, 1944, Seattle, WA; married Lonear W Heard; children: Charles II, Jenise A. **Educ:** CA State Univ, BS 1972. **Career:** Hughes Aircraft Co Culver City CA, contract adm accountant 1966-73; City of Compton, clerk. **Orgs:** Mem Intl Inst Municipal Clerks 1973-; Amer Records Management Assn 1973-; Amer Management Assn Advisory bd Compton & Branch Salvation Army; exec bd YMCA; SE Area Planning Council. **Honors/Awds:** Airforce Craftmanship Award Hughes Aircraft Co 1971; Community Serv Award Compton Model Cities 1974; Merit Award Inner City Challenge Inc 1974; council resolution of appreciation 1974-75; first black to receive "Certified Municipal Clerk" designation in the US, 1976. **Military Serv:** USAF 1963-66. **Business Addr:** City Clerk, City of Compton, 205 S Willowbrook, Compton, CA 90220.

DAVIS, CHARLES A.

Business executive. **Personal:** Born Sep 29, 1922, Mobile, AL; son of Clara Davis and Robert Davis. **Educ:** WV State Coll, 1943-44; Roosevelt Univ Chicago, political science 1950-53. **Career:** Dir advertising, dir public relations, city ed, sportswriter, reporter, Chicago Defender 1946-59; Jayson Bldg Assoc, general partner; The Phoenix Group, general partner; Adco Assoc, general partner; ADCO II, partner; Charles A Davis & Assoc Inc, pres. **Orgs:** Economic Club; NAACP, life mem; Chicago Urban League; Alpha Phi Alpha Fraternity. **Honors/Awds:** Honorary Doctor of Human Services, Governor's State Univ, 1967; Citations, Contributor Minority Business Chicago

Comm Human Relations 1974; Gold Oil Can Award Chicago Econ Devel Corp Chamber of Commerce; Spaulding Ins Award Natl Business League. **Military Serv:** US Quartermaster Corps tech sgt 1943-46. **Business Addr:** President, Charles A Davis & Assoc, 2400 S Michigan Ave, Chicago, IL 60616.

DAVIS, CHARLES ALEXANDER
Engineer, educator. **Personal:** Born Aug 20, 1936, Petersburg, VA; son of Bernice Davis and Charles Davis; married Clemetine Johnson (deceased); children: Lisa, Karen, Glen. **Educ:** MI State Univ, BSEE 1959; Univ of MI, MSEE 1963; MI State Univ, PhD 1975; Univ of IL. **Career:** Univ of MI, rsch assoc, 1960-63; Bendix Corp, engr 1963-64; Ford Motor Co, engr 1964-67; Western MI Univ, prof, 1967-94. **Orgs:** Pres, Douglass Comm Assn, 1979-80; commr, General Indus Safety Council 1978-; mem Kappa Alpha Psi, Delta Pi 1958-59; pres delegate Democratic Party 1978; mem Natl Soc of Professional Engr 1976-; mem IEEE, 1984-85. **Honors/Awds:** Book Indus Electronics, 1973; engr, Registered Professional Engrs 1976-; engr honors Tau Beta Pi 1958, Eta Kappa Nu 1957; Phi Kappa Phi, 1991-. **Special Achievements:** Handbook for New College Teachers & Teaching Assistants, 1993; Poems in the Key of Life, 1995. **Home Addr:** 816 Newgate Rd, Kalamazoo, MI 49006.

DAVIS, CHARLES FRANKLIN
Sports administrator. **Personal:** Born Nov 14, 1964, Elizabethton, TN; son of Hildred Davis and Franklin Davis; married Lisa Hales Davis, Nov 24, 1990. **Educ:** University of Tennessee, Knoxville, BA, political science, 1986, MA, history, 1989. **Career:** Southeastern Conference, fellowship, 1988; University of the Pacific, assistant football coach, 1989-90; United States Olympic Committee, assistant to the executive director, 1990, director, United States Olympic Training Center, 1990-94; Stanford Univ, asst athletic dir, 1994-. **Orgs:** Colorado Springs Opera Festival, board of directors, 1991-94; Colorado Springs Non-Profit Center, board of directors, 1992-94. **Business Addr:** Stanford Athletic Dept, Stanford, CA 94305-6150, (415)723-4596.

DAVIS, CHILI (CHARLES THEODORE)
Professional baseball player. **Personal:** Born Jan 17, 1960, Kingston, Jamaica. **Career:** San Francisco Giants, outfielder 1981-87; California Angels, outfielder, 1988-90; Minnesota Twins, outfielder, 1991-92; California Angels, 1993-96; Kansas City Royals, 1997; New York Yankees, 1998-. **Honors/Awds:** All-Rookie Squad, Baseball Digest, 1982; National League All-Star Team, 1984, 1986. **Business Addr:** Professional Baseball Player, New York Yankees, 161st St and River Ave, Yankee Stadium, Bronx, NY 10451, (718)293-4300.

DAVIS, CHRISTINE R.
Business executive. **Personal:** Born in Nashville, TN; married Steve G Davis; children: Pamela E. **Educ:** Fisk U; TN State U; Boston Business Coll; Catholic Univ of Am. **Career:** Washington Bureau Tuesday Publications Inc, dir; US Mem of Congress, admn Asst; Dem Nat Com, exec asst vice chrm, Com on Govt Operations House of & Representatives, staff dir. **Orgs:** Mem Links Inc; Girl Friends Inc; Nat Press Club; Nat Coun of Negro Women; Nat Coun of Women; Delta Sigma Theta Sorority. **Honors/Awds:** Numerous awards from natl organizations, religious, ednl, political, civic & congressional.

DAVIS, CLARENCE
Photojournalist. **Personal:** Born Dec 17, 1939, Atlanta, GA; son of Trudie Goolsby Davis and Clarence Davis; married Carol Venuto Davis, Aug 15, 1968 (divorced); children: Hazel C, Amanda Lael; married Jean Gaffley Chitiva Davis, Dec 30, 1991. **Educ:** City College, New York, NY, 1988; Temple University, Philadelphia, PA, 1958. **Career:** Columbia University, New York, NY, photographers' assistant, 1965-68; Journal News, Nyack, NY, staff photographer, 1968-72; Bergen Record, Hackensack, NY, photojournalist, 1972; New York Daily News, New York, NY, photojournalist, 1972-; Amsterdam News, New York, NY, photo consultant, 1977-79; Rockland Community College, Suffern, NY, photo teacher, 1984-87. **Orgs:** Founder and director, The Africa Project, Inc, 1987-; member, Board of Directors, Arts Council of Rockland, 1989-; member, Board of Directors, Arts in Public Places, 1987-90; member, New York Press Photographers Assn; member, US Senate News Galleries. **Honors/Awds:** First, second, and third place, New York Press Photographers Assn, 1990, third place and honorable mention, 1989, first and second place, 1988, third place, 1987, honorable mention, 1986, 1985; National Black Achievers Award, 1988; The Daily News Photojournalism Award, 1987; New York PBA Award, 1985; first place, New York Daily News Photo Contest, 1977; first place, Bergen Record Insight Award, 1972; honorable mention, New York State AP Award, 1971, first place, 1970. **Home Addr:** 4 Dogwood Pl, Pomona, NY 10970.

DAVIS, CLARENCE
State legislator, educator. **Personal:** Born Sep 25, 1942, Wilkes County, GA; son of Lola M. McLendon Davis and Clement Davis Sr.; married Barbara J. Holder Davis; children: Wayne C, Clarence R, Cherylle M, Dawn T. **Educ:** Morgan State Univ, Baltimore, MD, BA, political science, 1968, MS, history and social science, 1978, currently pursuing doctorate in education. **Career:** Maryland Job Corps Ctr, asst dir 1972-75; Catonsville Comm Coll, coord of vet affairs 1975-79; Vietnam Vet Ctr, dir 1979-82; Maryland House of Delegates, delegate 45th leg dist, 1982-; Essex Community College, assoc professor, 1986-. **Orgs:** Exec dir Hamilton Court Improvement Assoc 1968; suprv St Bernadine Comm Serv Ctr 1971-72; rsch asst Friends of Psychiatric Rsch 1972-75; bd mem Natl Assoc Sickle Cell Disease 1984-87; mem steering comm Natl Assoc Black Soc Wk 1984-86; command council mem Natl Assoc for Black Vets; Dorie Miller Veterans of Foreign Wars Post, IBPOE of W #1043; 1st vice chairman, Maryland Legislative Black Caucus. **Honors/Awds:** Goldseker Fellow. **Military Serv:** USAF E-4 1960-64; colonel, Maryland Line, Md National Guard. **Home Addr:** PO Box 33167, Baltimore, MD 21218. **Business Phone:** (410)841-3257.

DAVIS, CLARENCE A.
Consultant. **Personal:** Born Nov 29, 1941, New York, NY; children: Todd. **Educ:** Long Island Univ, BS Acct 1967. **Career:** Oppenheim, Appel, Dixon & Co, mgr 1976, partnership 1979, audit partner; Clarence A. Davis Enterprises, Inc, founder, 1990-. **Orgs:** Chrmn Amer Inst CPA Minority Recruitment Equal Opport Comm 1977-83; appointed NY State Bd of Public Acct 1984-; appointed Amer Inst CPA Future IssuesComm 1984; fac mem LIU Brooklyn Ctr 1974-80; fac mem NY Inst of Finance 1973-79; fac mem Fnd for Acct Educ; mem NY State Soc of CPA; mem Amer Inst CPA; mem Natl Assc of Black Acct; mem 100 Black Men; mem Kappa Alpha Psi Frat; mem Acct for Public Interest; chrmn schl bd St Brigid's Elem Schl; track coach St Brigid's CYO Track Team 1976-; asst scoutmaster Boy Scout Troop 999 1981-; cubmaster Cub Scout Pack 999 1977-81. **Honors/Awds:** Elected Archbishop Molloy HS Alumni Hall of Fame 1984; article written "Accounting & Auditing Careers" The Black Collegian Magazine 1982. **Military Serv:** USMC corpl 1960-64. **Business Addr:** Clarence A Davis Enterprises, Inc, 885 3rd Ave, Ste 2900, New York, NY 10022.

DAVIS, CLIFTON D.
Educational administrator, actor, singer, cleric. **Personal:** Born Oct 4, 1945, Chicago, IL; son of Irma Davis Langhorn and Toussaint L'Ouverture Davis; married Ann Taylor, 1981; children: Noel, Holly. **Educ:** Oakwood College, degree in theology, 1984; Andrews University, attended. **Career:** Actor; singer; songwriter; minister; Elizabeth City State Univ, interim vic e chancellor, currently. **Orgs:** Member, Actor's Equity, American Federation of Television and Radio Artists, Screen Actors Guild. **Honors/Awds:** Principle television appearances include: Love, American Style, 1971; The Melba Moore-Clifton Davis Show, 1972; That's My Mama, 1974-75; Amen, 1986-; stage appearances include: Scuba Duba, 1967; Horseman Pass By, 1969; Look to the Lilies, 1970; The Engagement Baby, 1970; Two Gentlemen of Verona, 1971; films include, The Landlord, 1970; Gus, Together for Days, 1972; Lost in the Stars, 1974; Scott Joplin, 1977; Theatre World Award for Do It Again, 1971; Tony Award nomination for Two Gentlemen of Verona; Grammy Award nomination for Never Can Say Goodbye, 1971; Gold Record for Never Can Say Goodbye, 1971; Heart Torch Award, American Heart Assn, 1975. **Military Serv:** US Air Force. **Business Addr:** Interim Vice Chancellor, Elizabeth City State Univ, Parkview Dr, Elizabeth City, NC 27909.

DAVIS, CYPRIAN
Educator, clergyman. **Personal:** Born Sep 9, 1930, Washington, DC; son of Evelyn Theresa Jackson Davis and Clarence William Davis. **Educ:** St Meinrad Coll, BA 1953; Catholic Univ of Amer, STL 1957; Catholic Univ of Louvain, Belgium, Lic en Sci Hist 1963, Doctorat en Sci Hist 1977. **Career:** St Meinrad Seminary, St Meinrad, IN, instructor, 1963-68, associate professor, 1971-82, professor, 1982-; St Meinrad Archabbey, archivist 1984-. **Orgs:** Archivist, National Black Catholic Clergy Caucus, 1968-. **Honors/Awds:** John Gilmary Shea Award, for book: The History of Black Catholics in the United States, 1991. **Special Achievements:** Author of several articles, Black Catholic history, Black spirituality; author of textbook on Church History, "The Church a Living Heritage," "Black Spirituality, a Roman Catholic Perspective," review and expositor, "Black Catholics in Nineteenth-Century America," US Catholic Historian "Evangelization in the United States Since Vatican Council II," Catholic Evangelization Today A New Pentecost for the United States (Paulist Press, 1987); "The Holy See and American Blacks, A Forgotten Chapter in the History of the Amer Church", US Catholic Historian 7 157-181, 1988; author, History of Black Catholics in the US, Crossroad, 1990; "The Didache and Early Monasticism in the East and West," in The Didache in Context, Essays on Its Text, History and Transmission, edited by Clayton N Jefford, Leiden: EJ Brill, p 352-367, 1995. **Home Addr:** St Meinrad Archabbey, St Meinrad, IN 47577.

DAVIS, DALE (ELLIOTT LYDELL DAVIS)
Professional basketball player. **Personal:** Born Mar 25, 1969, Toccoa, GA. **Educ:** Clemson University. **Career:** Indiana Pacers, forward, 1991-. **Orgs:** Dale Davis Foundation, founder. **Special Achievements:** Indiana Pacers, first round draft pick, 13th overall, NBA Draft, 1991. **Business Addr:** Professional Basketball Player, Indiana Pacers, 300 E Market St, Indianapolis, IN 46204, (317)263-2100.

DAVIS, DANNY K.
Congressman. **Personal:** Born Sep 6, 1941, Parkdale, AR; son of Mazzie Davis and H D Davis; married Vera Garner; children: 2. **Educ:** AR AM&N Coll, BA, 1961; Chicago State Univ, MS, 1968; Union Institute, PhD, 1977. **Career:** US Postal Serv, clerk, 1961-62; Chicago Bd of Educ, teacher, counselor, 1962-69; Greater Lawndale Conservation Commn, exec dir, 1969; Martin Luther King & Neighborhood Health Ctr, Chicago, dir of training, 1969-71; W Side Health Planning Org, manpower consult, 1971-72; Miles Square Comm Health Ctr, special asst to pres, 1976; W Side Health Planning Org, exec dir, 1972-; 29th Ward City of Chicago, alderman, chmn comm on health, chmn comm on zoning, alderman 1979-90; Cook County, commissioner, 1990-96; US House of Representatives, congressman, 1997-. **Orgs:** Lectr Malcolm X Coll 1972-74; freelance consult 1970-; organizing group W Side State Bank Chicago 1973-; pres Natl Assn of Comm Health Ctrs 1977; pres W Side Assn for Comm Action 1972-; mid-west rep Speaker of House Natl Assn of Neighborhood Health Ctrs; Amer Pub Health Assn; Lawndale People's Planning & Action Conf; commnr Chicago Health Systems Agency. **Honors/Awds:** Achievement Awd Montford Pt Marine Assn 1972; Certificate of Merit Pres Task force on Youth Motivation 1970; featured on "He's A Black Man" Radio Series 1972-73; Comm Serv Awd United Concerned Parents 1973; Chicago Black Sociologists; Afro-Amer Patrolman's League; Austin Business Assoc; Circle Urban Ministries; Northwest Inst; Operation PUSH; Chicago Black United Communities; Best Alderman Awd IVI-IPO; Leon DesPress Award; Appointed by President Clinton, Board of National Housing Partnership. **Business Addr:** Congressman, 7th District Illinois, 3333 W. Arthington, Chicago, IL 60624.

DAVIS, DARLENE ROSE
Legislative staff assistant. **Personal:** Born Mar 9, 1959, New Orleans, LA; daughter of Estelle Cornish Davis and Benjamin Joseph Davis. **Educ:** University of Grenoble, France; University of New Orleans, BA; Tulane University, JD; University of Baltimore, graduate tax program, currently. **Career:** US House of Representatives; Federal Judicial Center; EEO Commission; US District Court of New Orleans, Office of Honorable Louis Moore Jr; Office of Representative Jefferson, legislative staff assistant, 1993-. **Orgs:** Louisiana State Bar Assn; Natl Bar Assn; League of Women Voters. **Honors/Awds:** Moot Court Trial Team Member; Intl Law Jurisdiction, Highest Grade. **Special Achievements:** Contributor: Judicial Evaluations, FJC publication. **Business Phone:** (202)225-6636.

DAVIS, DARWIN N.
Business executive. **Personal:** Born Apr 10, 1932, Flint, MI; married Velmarie Broyles; children: Karen, Dana, Darwin Jr, Derek. **Educ:** AR AM&N Coll, BS 1954; Wayne State Univ, ME 1960; Univ of MI, Additional Study; Ferris State Coll, Univ of AR, Hon Doctorate Degree. **Career:** Detroit Publ School System, math teacher 1956-66; Equitable Life Assurance Soc of US, agent 1966-69, dist mgr 1969-71, agency mgr 1971-74, vp, chief ofmanpower devel 1974-75, div agency vice pres 1975, reg vp, head of external affairs 1980-. **Orgs:** Bd mem Carnegie Mellon Univ; bd dir Boy Scouts of Amer; bd of regents Natl Fund for Med Ed; life mem Alpha Phi Alpha Frat; natl bd Coll Devel All Black Coll; life mem NAACP; mem Natl Urban League; bd of dir Natl Urban Coalition, Stamford Hosp & Girl Scouts. **Honors/Awds:** Natl Builders Trophy 1970; Top 10 Mgrs of over 975 competing; Young Agency Mgr of the Year Natl Equitable Life 1972; Pres Trophy Equitable Life 1972, 73. **Military Serv:** AUS 1954-56. **Business Addr:** Senior Vice President, External Relations Dept, Equitable Life Assurance Society, 1285 Avenue of the Americas, New York, NY 10019.

DAVIS, DENICE FAYE
Health care executive. **Personal:** Born Mar 4, 1953, Flint, MI; daughter of Nita Jean Grier Davis and Raymond Leverne Davis Sr; married Kendall Blake Williams (divorced 1979). **Educ:** Fisk University, Nashville, TN, 1971-72; University of Detroit, Detroit, MI, BA, 1975; University of Michigan, Ann Arbor, MI, JD, 1978; Executive Leadership Program, American Managed Care Review Association, 1992. **Career:** Equitable Life Assurance Soc of the US, Equitable Real Estate Investment and Managing Co, contract specialist, 1979-84, real estate investment trainee, 1982-84; Denice Davis & Assoc, business Consultant, lecturer, 1984-87; Metmor Financial Inc, manager, electronic fund transfer department, 1988-89; United American Healthcare Corp, Detroit, MI, dir planning & dev, 1990-91, vice pres, planning and development, 1991-93, svp, planning & devt, 1993-. **Orgs:** Chaplain, parlamentarian, Pierians, 1990-; founder & member of Theta Tau Chaper, Alpha Kappa Alpha Sorority, 1974-; board member & head of finance committee, Crenshaw Christian Center Alumni Association, 1987-89; Business Policy Review Council; Founder's Society, Detroit Institute of Arts; InRoads of Metropolitan Detroit; Detroit Athletic Club; Planning Forum. **Honors/Awds:** YMCA, Minority Achievers Award, 1992; Executive-on-Campus Program. **Special**

Achievements: Increased productivity, initiated procedural changes to streamline electronic fund transfer system for 7,000 customers, decreasing departmental servicing cost per customer; represented company as member of board of directors for $80 million real estate joint venture. **Business Addr:** SVP, Planning and Development, United American Healthcare Corp, 1155 Brewery Park Blvd, Ste 200, Detroit, MI 48207.

DAVIS, DENYVETTA
Library administrator. **Personal:** Born Jul 26, 1949, Muskogee, OK; daughter of Hattie Bell Shipp Elliott and Denyfeaus Elliott; divorced; children: Melvin, Erma. **Educ:** Central State University, Edmond, OK, BS, 1971; Atlanta University, Atlanta, GA, MSLS, 1974; Central State University, Edmond, OK, MEd, 1977; University of Oklahoma, Norman, OK, 1990-. **Career:** Langston University, Langston, OK, curator, 1974-77; OKC Community College, Oklahoma City, OK, librarian, 1977-82; Ralph Ellison Library, Metro Library System, Oklahoma City, OK, librarian, 1982-84; D'Ermel Enterprises, Oklahoma City, OK, pres, 1984-; Metro Library System, Oklahoma City, OK, director, 1984-; University of Oklahoma, Norman, OK, adjunct, 1990-. **Orgs:** Member, Leadership Oklahoma City, 1987-; president, Literacy Coalition, 1989-90; vice pres, NE Oklahoma City Lioness Club, 1989-91; secretary, Public Library Division, Oklahoma Library Assn, 1990-91; chair, delegate election committee, Governors Conference on Libraries, 1991. **Honors/Awds:** Outstanding Community Service, HARAMBEE, Inc, 1990; Celebrate Literacy Award, International Reading Assn, 1988; John Cotton Dana Public Relations Award, 1986, Young Visionary Leader, 1987, American Library Assn; Finer Womanhood Award, Zeta Phi Beta Sorority, 1988; Outstanding Community Service, Assault on Illiteracy, 1988. **Business Addr:** President/CEO, D'Ermel Enterprises, PO Box 13367, Oklahoma City, OK 73113-3367.

DAVIS, DIANE LYNN
Manager information support services, telecommunications. **Personal:** Born Apr 11, 1954, Detroit, MI; daughter of S Davis and V Davis. **Educ:** Wayne State Univ, Detroit MI, BS, 1981. **Career:** LI Farris Investment, Detroit MI, consultant; Dow Chemical Co, Midland MI, programmer, analyst; Candid Logic, Hazel Park MI, programmer; General Motors Corp, Warren MI, software engineer; Electronic Data Systems, Detroit MI, system engineer mgr; Digital Equipment Corp, Novi MI, information support systems, telecommunication mgr; U of D Mercy, instructor, 1987-. **Orgs:** Mem, Wayne State Univ Alumni Assn, 1981-; national pres, Black Data Processing Assoc, 1992-; mem, CYTCIP Advisory Council, 1988-, Detroit Urban League, 1989-. **Honors/Awds:** Member of the Year, Black Data Processing Assoc, 1987. **Business Addr:** ISS/ Telecommunications Manager, Digital Equipment Corp, 39500 Orchard Hill Place, PO Box 8017, Novi, MI 48376-8017.

DAVIS, DON
Professional football player. **Personal:** Born Dec 17, 1972. **Educ:** University of Kansas. **Career:** New Orleans Saints, linebacker, 1996-. **Business Addr:** Professional Football Player, New Orleans Saints, 5800 Airline Hwy, Metairie, LA 70003, (504)733-0255.

DAVIS, DONALD
Business executive. **Career:** Barclay Limited Development Co, partner, currently; United Sound Systems Recording Studio, owner, currently; First Independence National Bank, chairman, currently . **Business Addr:** Chairman, First Independence National Bank, 44 Michigan Ave, Detroit, MI 48226, (313)256-8250.

DAVIS, DONALD FRED
Educator, artist. **Personal:** Born Jan 14, 1935, Baton Rouge, LA; son of Annabelle Davis and Benjamin Davis; married Anna Mae Eames; children: Anthony, Angela, Derek, Miriam, Michael. **Educ:** Southern Univ, BA 1959, MEd 1966; AZ State Univ, PhD 1983. **Career:** Scotlandville High, art instr 1959-69; Istrouma High, art instr 1969-71; LSU Lab Schl art instr 1972-87, Coll of Ed, 1987-89; Livingston Head Start, dir, 1990-95. **Orgs:** Mbr Natl Art Ed Assoc mem LA Art Ed Assoc; mem Phi Delta Kappa mem gallery II, br, IA; mem NAACP mem United Methodist Church. **Honors/Awds:** Outstanding contrib to arts Links, Inc 1972; numerous art shows Baton Rouge, LA. **Military Serv:** USN pn3 1952-56; Good Conduct, Korean Service, Natl Defense.

DAVIS, DONALD GENE
Air force officer. **Personal:** Born Aug 29, 1971, Snow Hill, NC; son of Mary Patricia Davis & Amos Artis. **Educ:** US Air Force Academy, Bachelor of science, Social Sciences, 1994; Central Michigan University, Master of Science, Administration, 1996. **Career:** Headquarters US Air Force Academy, admissions advisor, 1994-95; Andrews Air Force Base, 89th Services Squadron, plans and force management flight commander, 1995-96, executive officer, 1996-97, 89th Airlift Wing, protocol duty officer, 1997-. **Orgs:** NAACP, 1997; Amer Society for Public Administration, 1997; US Air Force Academy Association of Graduates, 1994-97; Mentor Action Program, air force cadet officer, 1995-97; Democratic National Comm, 1997; Reach for Tomorrow, Inc, prog dir, 1992-97; Metropolitan Admissions Liaison, liaison officer, 1995-97; African Heritage Association, pres, 1994-97. **Honors/Awds:** Ebony Magazine, 50 Top Leaders of Tomorrow, 1995. **Military Serv:** US Air Force, selected for Captain Pin, May 1998, August 1989-; 89th Services Squadron Company, Grade Officer of the Year, 1996. **Home Addr:** 6336 Southlake Court, Bryans Rd, MD 20616, (301)375-7133. **Business Phone:** (301)981-2100.

DAVIS, DONALD W.
Attorney. **Personal:** Born Feb 1, 1934, Oklahoma; married Marjorie D Williams; children: Lawrence, Wayne, Robert, Marjean. **Educ:** Univ CO, BA; Univ WY. **Career:** US Dept of Interior; US Dept of Lbr; Mntn Sts Tel Co Denver; Priv Pract, atty. **Orgs:** Mem Nat Bar Assn Inc; The Nat Bar Fndtn; Crt Mdrnztn Com; gen Pract Sectn; am Bar Assn; Amer Judctr Soc; lwyr Refrl Com; mem Bnkng; Comrcl & Crdt Com OK Bar Assn; v-chrm JJ Bruce Law Soc; mem Masons; NAACP; bd dir Urbn Lgue; Ok Cty; coaltn of Civ Ldrshp; mem Fth; mem Bapt Ch. **Military Serv:** USAF.

DAVIS, DORIS ANN
Public official. **Personal:** Born Nov 5; divorced; children: John, Rick. **Educ:** Attended, Chicago Tchrs Coll BEd, MA Northwestern Univ, Univ of Chicago; Lawrence Univ Santa Barbara, PhD. **Career:** Chicago & LA, teacher; City of Compton, elected city clerk 1965, mayor 1973-77; Heritage Unlimited Inc, owner; Daisy Child Development Ctr. **Orgs:** Mem bd dir Southern CA Cty Clks' Assn; mem CA Tchrs Assn; Southern CA Clrk's Assn, 1967-97; Intl Muncpl Clerk's Assn; mem Dem natl Policy Council; mem St CA Jnt Com for Revsn of Electn Laws; educ rscher SWRL; pres Davis Edgerton Assocs; adv bd Water Reclamation & Resource Recovery State of CA; bd dir Wlfr Infrmtn Serv; mem CA Museum of Sci & Industry; bd dir NAACP, Natl Urban League, Conf Negro Elected Officials, Phi Beta Kappa, Iota Lambda Phi, AKA Sor, PTA; del CA 1972 Dem Conv; mem Links Intl, League of Women Voters, Welfr Information Serv, Med-Dental & Pharmaceutical Aux; mem St CA State Bar Court; mem International Studies Comm; pres LA Chapter, National Congress Black Political Women. **Honors/Awds:** Commission Status of Women, Founder; Inductee Hall of Fame; Ron H Brown Award, African American Trailblazers. **Business Addr:** Heritage Unlimited Inc, 4206 E Rosecrans, Compton, CA 90221.

DAVIS, DUPREE DANIEL
Attorney. **Personal:** Born Mar 18, 1908, Jackson, TN; married Cleo. **Educ:** Morehouse Coll, AB 1930; TN State Univ, BS 1933; LaSalle Univ, LLB 1944; IA State Univ, JD 1944; Harvard Law Sch, post grad 1944-45; Washington Univ, grad work social work 1956. **Career:** TN Public Sch System, taught sch 12 yrs; St Clair Co IL, past 30 yrs atty asst state's atty; State of IL, spec asst atty gen; City E St Louis IL, city atty 14 yrs, corporation counselor. **Orgs:** Mem East St Louis Township Bd Auditors; hold license practice law IA, TN, IL; legal counsel NAACP Hanford Washington area 1944-45. **Business Addr:** City Attorney, E St Louis IL, 19 Collinsville Ave, East St Louis, IL 62201.

DAVIS, EARL S.
Educator. **Personal:** Born in New York, NY; son of Evelyn Bryan Davis and Maurice; divorced. **Educ:** North Carolina Central Univ, Durham, NC, BA, 1951; New York University, New York, NY, MSS, 1957; Long Island Consultation Center, New York, NY, certificate, Psychoanalytical Psychotherapy, 1968. **Career:** Dept of Social Services, New York, NY, supervisor, special family counseling, 1959-62; Travelers Aid Society, New York, NY, airport supervisor, JFK, 1962-64; Lutheran Community Services, New York, NY, caseworker, dir group homes, 1964-68, dir social services, 1968-71; St Christophers School, Dobbs Ferry, NY, director treatment services, 1971-72; New York University, New York, NY, assistant dean, SSW, 1973-79, director IAAA, retired, 1979-94; NYW Shirley M Ehrenkrenz, School of Social Work, consultant special programs, 1995-. **Orgs:** Board of directors, New Federal Theatre, 1990-; board of directors, Carib Arts Festival Ensemble, 1989-; board of directors, Rod Rogers Dance Company, 1986-; member, One Hundred Black Men, New York City, 1973- member, UNESCO, 1982-84. **Honors/Awds:** Outstanding Community Service, Peoples Alliance Community Organization, 1990; Outstanding Service Award, Black Women in Higher Education, 1988; Service and Dedication, New York University Black Faculty, Administrators, 1987; Citation of Appreciation, Community Service, Abyssinian Baptist Church, 1983; Outstanding Faculty, Administrator, Black Student Caucus, New York University, 1981. **Military Serv:** US Army, 1st Lt, 1951-54. **Home Addr:** 401-1st Ave, New York, NY 10010.

DAVIS, EDWARD
Marketing consultant. **Personal:** Born Feb 27, 1914, Shreveport, LA; son of Helen Bryant Davis and Thomas Davis; married Mary Agnes Miller. **Educ:** Alexander Hamilton Inst of Bus, grad; Wayne State Univ, business courses; Cornell Univ School of Labor, certificate. **Career:** Studebaker Corporation, automobile dealer, 1940-56; Davis Motor Sales, pres 1945-55; Floyd Rice Inc, vice pres, 1956-63; Chrysler Corporation, automobile dealer, 1963-71; Ed Davis Inc, owner/pres, 1963-71; City of Detroit Transportation System, gen mgr 1971-73; Ed Davis Assoc, pres, currently. **Orgs:** Life honorary trustee Kalamazoo Coll 1984; vice pres Detroit Econ Club; bd dir exec com Better Bus Bureau; bd dirs Blue Cross-Blue Shield; bd dirs exec com C of C Metro Bd Detroit YMCA, bd trustees, Kalamazoo Coll; Natl Bd of Natl Conf Christians & Jews; Small Bus Adminst; bd of dirs Detroit Sci Cntr 1979; bd of dirs Meth Children Home 1980. **Honors/Awds:** Outstanding Businessman of the Year Award, Small Business Admin, 1966; Natl Bus Man's Award 1964; MI Businessman of the Year Award 1967; Quality Dealer Award Time Mag 1969; First Black automobile dealer in US 1941-70; author autobiography "One Man's Way" 1979; author, A Dilemma of Equality in the World of Work, 1985; Choice of the Year Award Detroit Public Library 1980; Booker T Washington Business Award, 1969; Greater Detroit Chamber of Commerce, 1972; National Museum of American History, Edward Davis Pioneer Award, 1993; Induction into the Automobile Hall of Fame. **Special Achievements:** First African-American to be inducted into the Automobile Hall of Fame, 1996. **Business Addr:** President, Ed Davis Associates, 3000 Book Building, Washington Blvd and State St, Detroit, MI 48226.

DAVIS, EDWARD
Salesman. **Personal:** Born Aug 6, 1935, Germantown, TN; married Henrene Cannon Davis; children: Dara Dene, Debra Donne, Edward Jr. **Educ:** TN State Univ Nashville, 1957. **Career:** Life Ins, salesman 1957; teacher 1960; Edward Davis & Co, ins & real estate broker 1964; TN Dist 33, state senator 1978-. **Orgs:** Mem Kappa Alpha Psi. **Business Addr:** Senator, State of Tennessee, Dist 33, Memphis, TN 38106.

DAVIS, EDWARD D.
Business executive. **Personal:** Born Feb 1, 1904, Thomasville, GA; married Larone Taylor; children: Samuel Edward, Cynthia Marcia. **Educ:** Paine Coll, BA 1928; Northwestern U, MA 1934; Columbia U, Post Grad Work 1939-40. **Career:** Tampa-ocala FL, hs principal 1929-42; real estate & merchandising bus 1942-55; Central Life Ins Co FL, sec 1955-64; pres 1964-. **Orgs:** Co-founder 1st Community Fed Sav & Loan Assn Faculty Ethune Cookman Coll FL A&M U; pres FL Voters League; founder, pres Marion Fed Cr Union; bd governors Tampa C of C; trustee Miles Coll Birmingham; Paine Coll Augusta; pres elect Nat Ins Assn; life mem NAACP; Paine Coll Nat Alumni Assn; pres Business & Professional Mens Club; Frontiers Am Kappa Alpha Psi; mem Christian ME Ch. **Honors/Awds:** Honored educ pioneering FL State Teaches Assn 1958; received citation Ocala Conrtibutions Civil & Human Relations 1958; outstanding achievement voter registration FL Voters League 1963; outstanding service alumni assn & devotion ideals Paine College 1970; numerous other awards. **Business Addr:** 1400 N Boulevard, Tampa, FL 33606.

DAVIS, EDWARD L.
Educator. **Personal:** Born Dec 6, 1943, Union Bridge, MD; married Carol Johnson Davis; children: Tanya Lynn, Brian Patrick. **Educ:** Morgan State Univ, BS 1965; OH Univ, MS 1967; Johns Hopkins Univ, MS 1973; NC State Univ, PhD 1977. **Career:** Morgan State Univ Math Dept, instr 1970-73; Univ of Cincinnati Coll of Business, asst prof 1976-80; Atlanta Univ Graduate School of Business, assoc prof 1980-88; Clark Atlanta University, chmn decision science dept, 1988-95, Business School, acting dean, 1995-. **Orgs:** Mem Operations Rsch Soc of Amer 1974-; mem Transport Rsch Bd 1980-; mem Alpha Phi Alpha Frat 1961-; task force mem Atlanta C of C 1982-; Operations Rsch Soc of Amer 1973-; Amer Inst for Decision Sci 1980-; Transp Rsch Bd 1980-. **Honors/Awds:** MD Senatorial Fellowship 1961-65; Balt Colt Found Scholarship 1961-65; So Fellowship Found 1973-76; Volunteer of the Year City of Raleigh 1974. **Military Serv:** AUS 1st Lt 1967-69. **Home Addr:** 1424 Niskey Lake Tr, Atlanta, GA 30331. **Business Addr:** Interim Dean, Clark Atlanta University, James P Brawley at Fair St, Atlanta, GA 30314.

DAVIS, ELAINE CARSLEY
Educator. **Personal:** Born Apr 15, 1921, Baltimore, MD; daughter of Corinne Baker Carsley (deceased) and Stanley Carsley (deceased); married R Clarke Davis (deceased); children: R Clarke Jr, Lisa. **Educ:** Coppin State Coll, BS 1942; Morgan State Coll, BS 1943; Univ of MD, LLB 1950; Johns Hopkins Univ, MEd 1955, PhD 1958. **Career:** Baltimore City Public Schs, 1942-74; Morgan State Coll, instr 1959-73; Baltimore Jr Coll, instr 1963-68; Loyola Coll, instr 1963-66; Johns Hopkins Univ, instr 1964-, assoc prof dir of educ 1974-86. **Orgs:** Mem chmn bd of trustees of MD State Coll 1967-73; bd trustees Goucher Coll 1972-75; natl vice pres Pi Lambda Theta 1973-78; Delta Sigma Theta; bd trustees Morgan State Coll 1965-67; mem bd dir of the Rouse Co 1978-91. **Honors/Awds:** Elected to Law Review Staff Univ of MD 1948; Fellowships from Amer Assn of Univ Women 1957, John Hay Whitney 1957, George Peabody 1956-57; citations from Iota Phi Lambda 1972; Urban League 1947; Delta Sigma Theta; United Negro Coll Fund 1970; Distinguished Alumni of the Yr Natl Assn for Equal Opportunity Higher Educ 1982; Alumni Awd Coppin State Coll 1965; Phi Beta Kappa, 1958.

DAVIS, EMANUAL
Professional basketball player. **Personal:** Born Aug 27, 1968; children: Jennifer, Tiffany. **Educ:** Delaware State. **Career:** Houston Rockets, guard, 1996-. **Business Addr:** Professional Basketball Player, Houston Rockets, PO Box 272349, Houston, TX 77277, (713)627-0600.

DAVIS, ERELLON BEN
Professional athlete (retired). **Personal:** Born Feb 19, 1912, Pensacola, FL; son of Bell Coker Davis and Ellis Davis; married Ruby Nell Day-Davis, Apr 19, 1952. **Educ:** Attended college 1935. **Career:** Golf instructor 54 years; Rackham Golf Course MI, head professional golfer. **Orgs:** Cotillian Club. **Honors/Awds:** First African-American pro to play on governor's cup, 1974; PGA MI Sectional Sr Champ, 1974; first black Golf Exec Sectional Officer, 1973; first African-American Head Golf Pro at a municipal course in US, 1968; eight hole in ones; course record holder score of 59; course par 71; course rating by USGA 71 = point 5; scholarship fund in his name, Oakland Univ, 1978; testimonial resolution, Common Council, 1986; proclamation, given by Detroit Mayor Coleman Young, 1986; inductee, Black Hall of Fame, 1988; Michigan Golf Hall of Fame, 1992; The Indianwood Country Club, Honorary Life Membership; Placque, Handicappers Club, Detroit Michigan; Honored by the Golf Assn of MI, Detroit Golf Country Club, 1995. **Home Addr:** 1601 Robert Bradby Dr, Apt 413, Detroit, MI 48207, (313)259-5350.

DAVIS, ERIC KEITH
Professional baseball player. **Personal:** Born May 29, 1962, Los Angeles, CA. **Career:** Cincinnati Reds, outfielder, 1984-85, 1986-91; Los Angeles Dodgers, outfielder, 1992-93; Detroit Tigers, 1993-94; Cincinnati Reds, 1996; Baltimore Orioles, 1997-. **Orgs:** Eric Davis Youth Organization; RBI Reviving Baseball in the Inner City. **Honors/Awds:** National League Comeback Player of the Year, 1996. **Business Addr:** Professional Baseball Player, Baltimore Orioles, 333 W Camden St, Baltimore, MD 21201, (410)685-9800.

DAVIS, ERIC WAYNE
Professional football player. **Personal:** Born Jan 26, 1968, Anniston, AL; married Serena; children: Kevin, Nicolas, Daniel, Erica. **Educ:** Jacksonville State. **Career:** San Francisco 49ers, defensive back, 1990-95; Carolina Panthers, 1996-. **Business Addr:** Professional Football Player, Carolina Panthers, 800 Mint St, Ericsson Stadium, Charlotte, NC 28202, (704)358-7000.

DAVIS, ERNESTINE BADY
Nurse educator. **Personal:** Born Apr 8, 1943, Atlanta, GA; daughter of Martha Bady and Henry B Bady; married Luther Davis Jr, Aug 14, 1965 (died 1997); children: Ella Michelle, Luther III. **Educ:** Tuskegee University, BSN, 1965; Medical College of Georgia, MSN, 1973; University of Alabama, EdD, 1979. **Career:** Orange County Medical Center, supervisor, 1969-71; Tuskegee University, pt instructor, 1971-72; JA Andrew, obstetrics, maternal consultant, 1973; Tuskegee University, instructor, 1973-77; University of Alabama Weekend College, asst professor, 1977-80; University of Alabama Capstone, asst professor, 1978-1980; University of North Alabama, College of Nursing, professor, 1980-, RN/BSN coordinator, currently. **Orgs:** American Nurses Association, 1965-; Delta Sigma Theta, 1971-; Alabama State Nurses Association, chairperson of the human rights committee, 1985-89; Phi Kappa Phi Honor Society, banquet committee, 1984-; University of North Alabama, Nursing Honor Society, treasurer, 1986-; Society of Professional Nurses, 1988; Medical College of Georgia Alumni Association, 1973-. **Honors/Awds:** Certificates of Recognition by Alabama Nurses Association, 1988-89; Lillian Harvey Award, 1987; UNA Nursing Honor Society Award, 1992. **Special Achievements:** Awarded Grant, "Students Perceptions of Minority Faculty and Administration in College and Universities in Southeast Region," UNA, 1989-92; author, Integration of Cultural Concepts into Schools of Nursing Curriculum, 1987-90, ASNA, 1990. **Home Addr:** 110 Colonial Dr, Florence, AL 35631, (205)767-5756. **Business Addr:** Professor & RN/BSN Coordinator, University of North Alabama, College of Nursing, Box 5155, Stevens Hall, Florence, AL 35630, (205)765-4583.

DAVIS, ERROLL B., JR.
Utility company executive. **Personal:** married; children: two. **Educ:** Carnegie-Mellon University, BSEE, 1965; University of Chicago, MBA, 1967. **Career:** Wisconsin Power & Light Co, vice pres, finance, 1978-82, vice pres, finance & public affairs, 1982-84, exec vp, 1984-87, president, 1987-, CEO, 1988-; WPL Holdings, president, CEO, 1990-. **Orgs:** Wisconsin Utilities Association, board of directors; American Gas Association, board of directors, 1990-95; United Way Board, 1984-89, chair, 1987, campaign chairman, 1992; Selective Service Appeal Board, 1982-; Wisconsin Association of Manufacturers and Commerce, board member, 1986-, chair, 1994-95; Electric Power Research Institute, vice chair, board of directors, 1990-; Association Edison Illuminating Cos, board of directors, 1993-97; Edison Electric Institute, board of directors, 1995-; Competitive Wisconsin, board member; University of Wisconsin, board of regents, 1987-94; Educational Communications Board, 1992-94; Carnegie Mellon University, life trustee, board of trustees; Sentry Insurance Co., board of directors 1988-97; Amoco Corp., board of directors; PPG Industries, bd of dirs. **Honors/Awds:** Black Engineer of the Year Award, 1988; Univ of Chicago's Graduate School of Business, Distinguished Alumnus Award, 1993; Bronze Medal winner, Financial World's, CEO of the Year, 1993; Sales & Marketing, Exec of the Year, 1995. **Business Addr:** President & CEO, Wisconsin Power & Light Co, 222 W Washington Ave, PO Box 192, Madison, WI 53701-0192.

DAVIS, ESTHER GREGG
Educational administrator. **Personal:** Born Oct 16, 1934, Chicago, IL; married Fred A Cooper. **Educ:** Hofstra U, BS 1966; Northwestern U, MA 1972; Northwestern U, PhD 1974. **Career:** VA Tech, visiting prof Educ 1979-; VA Commonwealth Univ, asst prof Educ 1976-; Blue Cross Assn, dir assessment centers 1974-75; Chicago Bd of Educ, teacher 1970-71; NY Bd of Educ, teacher 1966-67; Richmond Public Schools, ESEA Title I Project, consultant 1976-; Danforth Found, consultant 1976-77; Mgmt Center VA Commonwealth Univ, cons 1977-. **Orgs:** Mem Phi Delta Kappa 1973-; mem Am Mgmt Assn 1979; mem Mat Alliance of Black Sch Educators 1979. **Honors/Awds:** "Intern Perception of Supervisory Support" ERIC 1974; "Classroom Mgmt" Kappa Delta Pi Record 1980-81; "Living Patterns of Urban Sch Adminstrs"; "Lewin's Force Field Theory a model for decision making". **Business Addr:** VA Commonwealth Univ, Richmond, VA.

DAVIS, ETHELDRA S.
Educator (retired), educational administrator, consultant. **Personal:** Born May 11, 1931, Marianne, AR; daughter of Fannie Sampson and Luther Sampson; widowed; children: Andrea, Robert. **Educ:** Los Angeles City Coll, AA 1951; Los Angeles State Coll, BA 1953; Univ of AK, MA 1964; Newport Univ, PhD, 1980. **Career:** Los Angeles Schools, teacher 1953-58; Anchorage Schools, teacher 1958-63, admin intern 1963-65, asst prin 1966, resource librarian; Project Head Start, dir 1966; HEW Region 10, field reader 1967-70; Western Region, OEO consultant 1967-70; Anchorage Schools, Anchorage, AK, principal, 1967-80; Juvenile Diversion Programs, executive director, 1983-, founder. **Orgs:** Alpha Kappa Alpha; NEA; ACPA; NAESP; ISCPP; precinct chmn, Dem 1959-61; pres, Pan-HellenicCouncil of Clubs Anchorage 1960; dir, Child Devel Cntr Anchorage Community Action Agy; tchr arts & crafts YMCA; Boothe Memorial Home for un-wed Mothers; consult Volt & Co; mem Mayor's Adv Bd 1968; mem, Parks & Recreation Bd; mem Camp Fire board of directors; founder of United League of Girls; board member, Boy Scouts of America and Girl Scouts of America; Anchorage Neighborhood Watch, 1982-, cofounder; founder, NAACP Youth Chapter. **Honors/Awds:** Woman of Yr Northern Lights Club 1969; most outstanding in Educ 1970; Certificate of Merit Anchorage Post Ofc 1969; Honor Award, NAACP, for being 1st Black Principal in Anchorage Sch; Volunteer of the Year, National Crime Prevention Council. **Special Achievements:** First black school principal, Anchorage, Alaska. **Home Addr:** PO Box 210127, Anchorage, AK 99521.

DAVIS, EVELYN K.
Entrepreneur. **Personal:** Born Apr 20, 1921, Kansas City, KS; daughter of Nettie Scott and Louis Scott; widowed; children: Donna Jean Lewis-Moore, Robert Lee Lewis, Lawrence M III, Edward, James, Sherrie, Eddie Collier. **Educ:** Area Comm Coll Ames IA, General Educ Certificate 1969; Drake Univ, Cert for Managerial 1969; Iowa State Univ, Cert for Family Environ Course 1969. **Career:** Helped organize Polk County Comm Action Cncl 1965; helped organize Urban Neighborhood Cncl 1970; helped organize Soul Village Learning Ctr 1970; organized initiate the Child Care Barrier Plng Cncl 1976; organized the Black Women's Polit Caucus 1977; organized the Ethnic Minority Women's Cncl 1978; Tiny Tot Child Care Inc, founder/dir 1966-. **Orgs:** Exec bd mem NAACP 1960-; bd mem Iowa Cncl for Children 1976-81; mem Red Cross Exec Comm; director's bd Right to Life Comm; mem Inner Urban Health Ctr Bd; chmn Gateway Oppor Bd; mem State Day Care Adv Bd; state chmn DCCDCA; mem NAEYC, DOVIA; mem Des Moines Child Care Cncl, Polk Co Health Serv Bd. **Honors/Awds:** Dedication Letter from Pres Nixon 1970; Evelyn Davis Health Clinic; George Washington Carver Meritorious Awd Simpson Coll 1979; YWCA Achievement Awd 1983; Iowa Women's Hall of Fame 1983; Black Merit Acad Awd IN Univ; First Eleonor Robinson Awd Cncl of Intl Understanding 1986; Honorary Doctor of Laws, 1992. **Business Addr:** Executive Dir, Tiny Tot Child Care Inc, 1409 Clark St, Des Moines, IA 50314.

DAVIS, EVELYN PAYNE. See Obituaries section.

DAVIS, FRANCE ALBERT
Clergyman, educator. **Personal:** Born Dec 5, 1946, Gough, GA; son of Julia Cooper Davis and John H Davis; married Willene Witt; children: Carolyn Marie, Grace Elaine, France II. **Educ:** Laney Coll, AA Arts and Humanities 1971; Merritt Coll, AA Afro-American Studies 1972; Univ of CA, BA Rhetoric 1972; Westminster Coll, BS Religion & Philosophy 1977; Univ of UT, MA Mass Comm 1978; Northwest Nazarene Coll, Master of Ministry, 1994. **Career:** USAF, aircraft mechanic 1966-70; Univ of UT, instr 1972-76; Calvary Baptist Church, pastor 1973-. **Orgs:** Bd chmn UT Bd of Corr 1982-, bd mem 1975-; bd chmn UT Opportunities Industrialization Cntr 1974-; exec bd DIC/A; 1982 chmn Tribune Common Carrier Editorial Bd 1982; mem Albert Henry Educational Found 1976-; bd mem NAACP Salt Lake Branch 1975-77, 1985-; chmn Martin Luther King Jr Holiday Comm for Utah 1985-86; chmn Mignon Richmond Park Comm 1985-86. **Honors/Awds:** Pres award Salt Lake NAACP 1975; serv award Beehive Elks 1975; torch bearer OIC/A 1979; OIC Torchbearer Awd 1979; civil rights worker Salt Lake NAACP 1984; Black Scholars Outstanding Image Maker 1986; Salt Lake Ambassadors, Salt Lake Convention and Visitors Bureau, 1991; Univ of Utah, Honorary Doctor of Humane Letters, 1993. **Military Serv:** USAF staff sgt commendation award, Vietnam service award 1966-70. **Business Addr:** Pastor, Calvary Baptist Church, 532 E 700 S, Salt Lake City, UT 84102.

DAVIS, FRANCIS D.
Dentist, educator. **Personal:** Born Sep 1, 1923, Macon, GA; son of Carro Appling-Davis and Dr Wanzie A Davis; married Hattimarie; children: Robin, Francis. **Educ:** Morehouse Coll, BS 1947; Howard U, DDS 1951. **Career:** Fairleigh Dickinson Univ Dental Sch, prof chmn dept oral diagnosis; Martland Hosp, oral surgeon; McQuire AFB, chief oral surgeon 1970; McQuire AFB, dir dental asst prgm 1970; Treatment Planning Preventive Dental Radiology, chmn & dept oral diagnosis. **Orgs:** Dir Minority Recruitment Prgm Consult NIH Black Health Providers Task Force 1977; pres Commonwealth Dental Soc 1977-79; bd trustee Nat Dental Assn 1974- 77; mem NDA Liaison Com Am Dental Assn 1974-77; mem bd trustees United Hospitals Med Center of Newark; mem Nat Dental Hon Soc OKU; mem Univ High Blood Pressure Detection Prog 1971-; mem Boul Frat. **Honors/Awds:** Recpt Pres Award Nat Dental Assn 1975; USAF Commendation Medal 1965; Oak Leaf Cluster 1968; 2nd Oak Leaf Cluster; Pres Award Outstanding Serv Nat Dental Assn 1977; fellowship Am Coll Dentists. **Military Serv:** USAF col (ret) 1953-73.

DAVIS, FRANK
Law enforcement officer. **Personal:** Born Mar 22, 1947, Claiborne Cty, MS; son of Mary Lee Barnes Triplett and Green Lee Davis; divorced; children: Tracy, Gary. **Educ:** Alcorn State Univ, BS Physical Ed 1972; Southern Univ, Criminal Justice 1973. **Career:** US Army, 1966-68; Port Gibson MS, dep sheriff 1968-78; Claiborne Cty, civil defense dir 1978-79; Port Gibson Police Dept, asst chief of police 1978-79, sheriff 1980-. **Orgs:** Treas New Zion Lodge 1976; hon mem FBLA 1980; mem Kiwanis Club 1980; professional mem Amer Correctional Assoc 1983; mem, Mississippi Sheriff's Assn; president, NOBLE, MS chap, 1997. **Honors/Awds:** Civil Defense Council MS Civil Defense 1978; Cert of Merit Aide-de-Camp 1979; vice pres, Mississippi Sheriff's Assn 1988; MS Parkway Commission Board, MS Heritage Corridor Board, Governor of the State of MS, 1990; Citizenship Award, 1991. **Military Serv:** AUS E-6 1966-68. **Business Addr:** Sheriff, Claiborne County, PO Box 427, Port Gibson, MS 39150.

DAVIS, FRANK ALLEN
Sales manager. **Personal:** Born Nov 17, 1960, Washington, DC; son of Joan A Johnson Davis and Eugene N Davis; married Elena Labarrere Davis, Sep 25, 1983; children: Michael Allen. **Educ:** Bucknell Univ, BSEE 1982; Univ of AL, Birmingham, AL, MBA, 1989. **Career:** Westinghouse Control Div, div sales engr 1982-85; Westinghouse Industries Marketing, asst sales engr 1985-86, personnel consultant 1985-89, industrial sales engr 1987-89; Honeywell Inc, sr marketing specialist, 1989-92, national distributor sales manager, 1992-93; Siebe PLC Ltd, sr product marketing mgr, 1993-94; Johnson Controls, national end user sales & mktg manager, 1994-95; Delco Ventures, vp, 1994-; Johnson Controls, group gen manager, 1997-. **Orgs:** Mem Alpha Phi Omega 1984-, Natl Black MBA Assoc 1986-, Amer Mktg Assoc 1987-, Open Pit Mining Assoc 1987-89; American Cancer Society, 1990-91; Rockford Association for Minority Management, 1991-97; Northern Illinois Minority Contractors Assn, 1995-97. **Honors/Awds:** William Randolph Hearst United State Senate Youth Scholar; winner Susan Thomas Hensinger Prize; Hon Alpha Mu Alpha Natl Mktg; Johnson Controls Inner Circle Awd. **Home Addr:** 1927 Westover Ln, Kennesaw, GA 30152. **Business Addr:** Johnson Controls, 210 Interstate N Pkwy, Ste 700, Atlanta, GA 30339, (770)980-6741.

DAVIS, FRANK DEROCHER
Personnel consultant. **Personal:** Born Jun 21, 1934, Quitman, GA; son of Shellie Mae Teemer Davis and Arthur James Davis Sr; married Dr Carolyn Brown; children: Farita Denise, Alexria Siglinda, Frank Jr. **Educ:** Tuskegee Inst, BS 1956; Florida A&M Univ, grad studies 1967. **Career:** W R Grace Chemical Co, human relations specialist 1968-71; General Electric Co, minority relations mgr 1971-74; Derocher Assocs Ltd, pres 1974-. **Orgs:** Bd of dirs Bridgeport Regional Narcotics 1976-81, Messiah Baptist Church 1976-86, Bridgeport Public Library 1982-86, Urban Action Grp Bridgeport 1984-86; vice pres The Minority Network 1983-86; member, Kappa Alphi Psi Fraternity, 1968-. **Military Serv:** AUS lt col retired 22 yrs; Army Commendation Medal 1968, Meritorious Serv Medal 1984. **Home Addr:** 2013 Alabaster Dr, Silver Spring, MD 20904. **Business Addr:** President, Derocher Assocs Ltd, PO Box 3714, Silver Spring, MD 20901.

DAVIS, FRED
Clergyman. **Personal:** Born Oct 4, 1934, Chatham, VA; married Juanita; children: Michael, Karen, Donna, Phillip. **Educ:** Rutgers Univ, BA 1967-72; Manhattan Bible Inst, Cert in Divinity 1972-74. **Career:** NAACP Urban League, life mem; Tri-County United Way, exec bd; PA State AFL-CIO Central Labor Council, exec bd; Harrisburg United Negro Coll Fund, exec comm; Shiloh Baptist Church, pastor; Amer Fed of State Cty & Municipal Employees, dir. **Orgs:** Staff rep Textile Workers of Amer 1971-72; dir AFSCME Dist Council 90 1974-. **Honors/Awds:** Personnel dir NJ Health Ctr 1965-70; Rutgers Labor Ctr Spec Program 1963-64; Chosen 1 of 100 most influential young men in NJ to participate in comm actionprog at Rutgers Univ 1400 hours of spec ed & OJT 1963.

DAVIS, FREDERICK D.
Union official. **Personal:** Born Aug 6, 1935, Tulsa, OK; married Patricia; children: Grant Anthony, Frederick Douglass II, Mwindaace N Gai. **Educ:** Oklahoma University. **Career:** McDonnell Douglas Aircraft Corp, 1956-, Equal Opportunity Program, chairman, 1974-75. **Orgs:** President, Tulsa Branch NAACP; pres, bd of dirs, Tulsa Area United Way; public relations dir, Prince Hall Free & Accepted Masons; UAW Constl & Convention Delegate, 1975-; Paradise Baptist Church, 39 years; Coal Creek 88 Masonic Lodge; pres, Tulsa Community Recreation Council, 1972-74; Police/Community Relations. **Honors/Awds:** First Black/minority major developer in the state of Oklahoma.

DAVIS, GENE A.
Business executive. **Personal:** Born Jun 29, 1939, Philadelphia, PA; married Jonna Bjorkefall; children: Peter, Philip. **Educ:** Philadelphia Mus Sch of Art, adv design/undergrad 1958-60; New York City Coll, advertising copy 1964-65. **Career:** CBS Columbia Records, adv prod mgr 1966-68; Westinghouse Group W, mgr 1968-72; WNEW Radio NY, creative dir 1972-74; STOP TV Washington, mgr 1974-76; WMAQTV, mgr 1976-79; Corinthian Broadcasting Corp, vice pres/adv & Pub rel 1979-81; Essence Comm Inc, dir corp crea serv 1983-. **Orgs:** Mem Intl Radio/TV Soc 1978-; treas/sec Broadcasters Promotion Assn Inc 1978-79; BPA Awds (promo); MI State Awds 1974-77; Addy Awds Am Advertising Fed 1977-79. **Honors/Awds:** TV Advt, US TV Commercial Awd 1978; Cable Marketing Awd 1981. **Business Addr:** Director, Corp Creat Serv, Essence Comm Inc, 1500 Broadway, New York, NY 10036.

DAVIS, GEORGE B.
Educator, author. **Personal:** Born Nov 29, 1939, Shepherdstown, WV; married Mary Cornelius, Aug 31, 1963; children: Pamela, George. **Educ:** Colgate Univ, BA, 1961; Columbia Univ, MFA, 1971. **Career:** Washington Post, Washington, DC, staff writer, 1968-69; New York Times, New York, NY, deskman, 1969-70; Bronx Community Coll of the City Univ of New York, Bronx, NY, asst prof, 1974-78; Rutgers Univ, New Brunswick, NJ, asst prof, 1978-; freelance writer for various publications; Columbia Univ and Greenhaven Prison, teacher of writing workshops; Black Swan Communications (design and marketing firm for books, art objects, and creative leisure products), co-founder and pres. **Orgs:** Mem, Author's Guild; Grant New York Council on Arts; Natl Endowment for the Humanities; mem, Authors League of Amer. **Honors/Awds:** Author of Coming Home, Random House, 1971, Love, Black Love, Doubleday, 1978, and (with Glegg Watson) Black Life in Corporate America: Swimming in the Mainstream, Doubleday, 1982; awards from New York State Council on the Arts, Amer the Beautiful Fund, and NEH. **Military Serv:** US Air Force, 1961-68, became captain; received Air Medal. **Business Addr:** Rutgers University, New Brunswick, NJ 08903.

DAVIS, GEORGE NELSON, JR.
Labor union administrator. **Personal:** Born Sep 17, 1936, Somerville, TN; son of Jennie Burr Davis and George N. Davis; married Ruth J. Hayes Davis (divorced 1989); children: Judy Elaine. **Career:** US Postal Service, Memphis, TN, letter carrier, 1960-70; Branch #27 NALC, Memphis, TN, vice president, 1970-78, president, 1978-85; National, NALC, Washington, DC, board of trustees, 1978-85, chairman/board of trustees, 1981-85, director of safety & health, 1986-. **Business Addr:** Director of Safety and Health, National Association of Letter Carriers, 100 Indiana Ave, NW, 6th Floor, Washington, DC 20001.

DAVIS, GLENDELL KIRK
Insurance executive. **Personal:** Born in DeRidder, LA; daughter of Ernestine Simmons Kirk and Claudell Kirk; divorced; children: Monica Katrese. **Educ:** Univ of Hartford, MBA 1981; Rensselaer Polytechnic Inst, MS 1974; Southern Univ, BS (Magna Cum Laude) 1964. **Career:** Natl Science Foundation, teaching asst 1964; Southern Univ, Math prof 1964-65; General Electric Co, scientific programmer 1965-69; Travelers Insurance Co, dir, 1969-91, information systems; Kirk-Davis Assoc Management Consultants, pres and ceo, 1992-93; Aetna Prof Management Corp, vp & chief information officer, 1993-. **Orgs:** Consultant Assoc for the Integration of Mgmt 1975, Natl Youth Motivation Task Force Alliance of Business 1978; v pres New England Telecomm Soc 1980; pres Travelers Toastmistress Club 1973-74; bd of dir, vice pres CT Opera Assoc; advisory bd Economics & Business Dept St Josephs Coll 1984; mem Young Executives, NAACP, Alpha Kappa Alpha Sorority; vice pres & asst treasurer, CT Opera Assn; board of directors, Hartford Symphony Volunteer Assn, 1990; task force member, Connecticut Task Force for the Gifted & Talented, 1990; bd of governors, Hartford Stage Co, 1991. **Honors/Awds:** Nom Woodrow Wilson Fellow 1964; hon soc Pi Mu Epsilon; hon soc Alpha Kappa Mu; Achievers Award 1980; IMPACT Award for Outstanding Performance in the Workplace 1985.

DAVIS, GLORIA-JEANNE
Educational administrator. **Personal:** Born Feb 6, 1945, Gary, IN; daughter of Gloria Lavern Cummings McCarroll (deceased) and Rixie Hardin McCarroll; married Wilbert Douglas Davis; children: Wilbert Douglas II, Rixie Hardin. **Educ:** Eastern KY Univ, BBA 1970, MBA 1971; IL State Univ, PhD 1986. **Career:** Caterpillar Tractor Co, analyst/machine shop training 1974-78; Bloomington City Hall, financial advisor 1978-84; IL Central Coll, instructor/business dept 1986-; IL State Univ, univ affirmative action officer 1984-, asst to pres for affirmative action and equal opportunity, 1988-96; Mitsubishi Motors, dir opportunity programs, 1996-. **Orgs:** ISU Toastmasters, pres, 1990, 1992, mem, 1989-; IL Affirmative Action Officers Assn, pres, 1986-88, mem, 1988-; Assn of Black Academic Employees, pres, 1987-89, 1990-91, mem, 1986-; ISU Recruitment & Retention Committees, chair, 1988-89, mem, 1987-96; Admini Professional Grievance Panel, elected mem, 1985-96; IL Committee on Black Concerns in Higher Educ, steering comm secretary, 1984-93, co chair annual conference, 1993, steering comm mem, 1984-96; IL State Univ Black Colleagues Assn, campus liaison, 1986-96; North Central Assn of Coll & School Self Study, mem, 1993-96; Natl Collegiate Athletic Assn Self Study, mem, 1993-96; McLean Cty AIDS Task Force, bd of dirs, 1993-. 1993-; Institute for Collaborative Solutions, bd of dirs, 1997-; Bloomington Liquor Commission, commissioner, 1997-. **Honors/Awds:** Administrator of the Year Award, Black Student Union, 1987; Educ Administration & Foundations Advisory Council, Recognition Award, 1990; Administrative Professional Distinguished Service Award, Administrative Professional Staff, 1991; MacMurray Coll, NAACP, Civil Rights Award, 1994. **Business Addr:** Director, Opportunity Programs, Mitsubishi, 100 N Mitsubishi Motorway, Normal, IL 61761.

DAVIS, GOLIATH J., III
Law enforcement official. **Career:** St. Petersburg, FL, Police Dept, asst chief of administrative services bureau, until 1997, chief of police, 1997-; Univ of South Florida, adjunct prof of crimology, currently. **Special Achievements:** First African American police chief in St. Petersburg, FL. **Business Addr:** Chief of Police, St Petersburg Police Department, 1300 1st Ave, N, St Petersburg, FL 33705.

DAVIS, GREGORY A.
Broadcasting executive. **Personal:** Born Sep 24, 1948, Fort Smith, AR; son of Rizetta T. Gill Davis and Fred Davis Jr.; married Cheryl Hatchett Davis, Jul 25, 1975; children: Geniece, Michelle, Gregory A Jr. **Educ:** Westark Junior College, Fort Smith, AR, 1968; Lane College, Jackson, TN, BS, 1970; Eastern Michigan University, Ypsilanti, MI, MA, 1973. **Career:** Flint Board of Education, Flint, MI, community school director, 1970-73; London Central High School, London, England, high school counselor, 1972-73; Knight Ridder Publishing Co, Flint, MI, account executive, 1974-78; Field Communications, 1978-79; American Broadcasting, Detroit, MI, account executive & national account executive, 1979-82; Multi-Media Broadcasting Co., Cincinnati, OH, national and general sales manager, 1982-86; Davis Broadcasting Inc, Columbus, GA, president, 1986-. **Orgs:** Board of directors, Water Works, City of Columbus, 1989-91; board of directors, National Association of Black Owned Broadcasters, 1987-; steering committee, Radio Advertising Bureau, 1988-; board of directors, Metro Columbus Urban League, 1987-; board of directors, First Union Bank, 1990-. **Honors/Awds:** Minority Small Business Advocate of the Year for Georgia, 1991; Advocate of the Year Award, Minority Business Development Association, 1990; Small Business of the Month, Columbus Chamber of Commerce, 1990; Public & Community Relations Award, Georgia Association of Broadcasters, 1987; Outstanding Minority Business Award, NAACP, 1989. **Military Serv:** US Army, Sp-4, 1970-73. **Business Addr:** President, Davis Broadcasting Inc, 1115 14th St, Columbus, GA 31902.

DAVIS, H. BERNARD
Auto industry executive. **Personal:** Born Apr 30, 1945, Burnsville, AL; son of Roxie Davis Price and Leslie Holmes; married Delphine Handley Davis, Oct 18, 1964; children: Jason Henry, Jeanine Kianga. **Educ:** Mott Community College, Flint, MI, AD, data processing, 1970; University of Michigan, Flint, MI, BBA, 1976; Michigan State University, E Lansing, MI, MBA, 1984; Penn State University, College Park, PA, exec management program, 1989. **Career:** General Motors Corp Corporate Finance Staff, Detroit, MI, dir product cost analysis, 1979-81; Oldsmobile Division, Lansing, MI, asst divisional comptroller, 1981-84, divisional comptroller (CFO), 1984-88; Powertrain Division B-O-C, Brighton, MI, dir finance & business planning, (CFO), 1988-90; GM Engine Division, Brighton, MI, divisional comptroller, (CFO), 1990-. **Orgs:** Treasurer, member, board of directors, Black Child & Family Institute, 1987-89; sr pastor, Alexander St Church of God, 1988-89; vice chairman, Capital Area United Way, 1987; board of directors, Capital Area Foundation, 1987-89. **Business Addr:** Divisional Comptroller, Finance, GM Engine Division, 100 Powertrain Blvd, Brighton, MI 48116-2365.

DAVIS, HAROLD
Government executive. **Personal:** Born Feb 29, 1932, New Orleans, LA; son of T D Davis & Myrtle L Royal; married Barbara M, Aug 20, 1955; children: Harold Jr, Deborah Davis-Gillespie. **Educ:** Southern Univ, BA, 1952; Univ of CA, MPA, 1957; American Baptist Seminary of The West, LLD. **Career:** Alameda County, CA, Redevelopment Agency, relocation officer, 1961-63, assistant exec dir, 1963-65, exec dir, 1965-68, chief assistant welfare dir, 1968-72; Oakland Housing Authority, CEO, 1972-. **Orgs:** Alpha Phi Alpha, life mem, 1952-; Natl Assn of Housing & Redevelopment Officials, 1962; American Baptist Churches USA, pres, 1988-89; YMCA of the USA, chairman natl bd of dir & pres, 1989-90; Graduate Theological Union, bd mem, 1970 & 1994; Childrens' Hosp & Med Ctr, Oakland, bd chair, 1993-; NAACP life mem; Sigma Pi Phi Boule, Sire Archon, 1994-96. **Honors/Awds:** Alpha Phi Alpha, Distinguished Service, 1987 & 1988; Natl Forum of Black Public Administrators, Outstanding Public Amdinistrator, 1988; American Society of Public Administration, Outstanding Public Administrator, 1989; YMCA/USA, Natl Treasure Award, 1993; Children's Hospital Oakland, Williford Award, 1996; Berkeley California YMCA Legend Award, 1996. **Military Serv:** US Army, 1st Lt, 1952-54, Honorable discharge.

DAVIS, HAROLD R.
Business executive (retired). **Personal:** Born Mar 25, 1926, High Point, NC; married Marva Lane; children: Stpehen, Craig, Brenda, Peggy J Slaughter. **Educ:** US Schl of Admnstrn, CLU, Amer Coll of Life Underwriters 1970; FLMI, Life Office Mgmnt Courses 1976. **Career:** Retired from NC Mutual Life Ins Co, 1988, vice pres mktg svcs, 1984-88, vice pres field operations 1978-84, regnl agency dir 1973-77, asst agency dir 1969-72; dist mgr 1966-69; self employed insurance consultant, Davis Financial Services, 1988-. **Orgs:** Brd of dir Life Ins Mktg & Resch Assn 1982-84; vice pres Natl Ins Ass 1973-; mem Amer Soc of CLU 1970-; brd of dir Durham YMCA 1979-83. **Military Serv:** USNA pfc 1945-46.

DAVIS, HARVEY
Law enforcement official. **Personal:** Born in Wrightsville, GA. **Career:** Springfield Police Dept, numerous positions, beginning 1968, juvenile div supervisor, beginning 1980, asst deputy chief of operations, beginning 1991, deputy chief of investigations, beginning 1993, chief, currently. **Special Achievements:** Only the second African American officer to head the police dept in Illinois' state capital. **Business Addr:** Chief, Springfield Police Dept, 800 E Monroe St, #345, Springfield, IL 62701-1916, (217)788-8311.

DAVIS, HERMAN E.
Business executive. **Personal:** Born Mar 3, 1935, Carlton, AL; married Thelma; children: Millicent, Chiaka, Jennifer, Holly. **Educ:** BEd 1962. **Career:** New Direction Budgeting & Financial Serv Cntr Inc, pres; Assn of Distributive Educ Coords, pres 1966; Dusable HS Chicago , tchr 1962-; Waddell & Reed Inc, rep 1964-. **Orgs:** Pres Bryn Mawr & West Area Council; bd mem South Shore Commn; chrmn Finance Com South Shore Commn; Keeper of Records & Seal, Sigma Omega Chap Omega Psi Phi. **Honors/Awds:** Award of merit US Small Bus Adm & Cosmopolitan C of C 1968; sales champion award Waddell & Reed, Inc 1968; certificate of excellence Cosmopolitan C of C 1969-70. **Military Serv:** AUS security agency sp2 1954-57. **Business Addr:** 2051 E 75 St, Chicago, IL 60649.

DAVIS, HOWARD C.
Dental surgeon. **Personal:** Born May 10, 1928, Washington, DC; married Lorethea; children: Lori, Howard, Jr. **Educ:** Howard Univ, undergrad; Howard Univ Coll of Dentistry, DDS (1st place honors graduate), 1961. **Career:** Coll of Dentistry Howard Univ, instr Dept Oral Surgery 1961-62; Coll of Dentistry Howard Univ, asst prof Dept Oral Radiology 1962-65; self-employed, gen dental practice 1965-; Independence Fed Savings Bank of Washington, vice pres. **Orgs:** Omicron Kappa Upsilon, (National Dental Honor Society); National Dental Association; American Dental Association; Robert T. Freeman Dental Society; District of Columbia Dental Society; National Urban League, former assistant secretary; Omega Psi Phi Fraternity, Inc. **Honors/Awds:** Luther Halsey Gulick Camp Fire Award. **Military Serv:** AUS sgt 1946-48; USAFR 2nd lt 1950-58. **Business Addr:** 5505 5th St NW, Suite 200, Washington, DC 20011, (202)291-2500.

DAVIS, HOWLIE R.
Government and corporate affairs executive. **Personal:** Born Sep 14, 1957, Charlotte, NC; son of Harry and Hattie B Davis; divorced. **Educ:** Morehouse College, BS, business, 1979; At-

lanta University, School of Business, 1979-80. **Career:** Clinton-Gore Presidential Transition Comm, 1992-93; The White House, assoc dir personnel, 1993; US Department of Energy, sr advisor, liaison, 1993-96; Democratic National Convention, dir of security, 1996; Citzenship Education Fund, proj dir, 1996; Presidential Inaugural Comm, dir of special services; Public Private Partnership, Inc, managing partner, 1997-. **Orgs:** Democratic National Comm, consultant; Citzenship Education Fund, consultant; Alpha Phi Alpha Fraternity Inc. **Business Addr:** Managing Partner, Public Private Partnership, Inc, 1000 Thomas Jefferson St NW, Ste 311, Washington, DC 20007, (202)298-7700.

DAVIS, HUBERT IRA, JR.

Professional basketball player. **Personal:** Born May 17, 1970, Winston-Salem, NC; son of Hubert Davis Sr. **Educ:** Univ of North Carolina, bachelor's degree in criminal justice. **Career:** New York Knicks, guard, 1992-96; Toronto Raptors, 1996-97; Dallas Mavericks, 1997-. **Special Achievements:** NBA Draft, First round pick, #20, 1992. **Business Addr:** Professional Basketball Player, Dallas Mavericks, Reunion Arena, 777 Sports St, Dallas, TX 75207, (214)748-1808.

DAVIS, ISAAC

Professional football player. **Personal:** Born Apr 8, 1972, Malvern, AR; married Stephanie; children: Stephen. **Educ:** University of Arkansas. **Career:** San Diego Chargers, guard, 1994-97; New Orleans Saints, 1997-. **Business Addr:** Professional Football Player, New Orleans Saints, 5800 Airline Hwy, Metairie, LA 70003, (504)733-0255.

DAVIS, J. MASON, JR.

Attorney. **Personal:** Born Jul 30, 1935, Birmingham, AL; son of Madeline Harris Davis and J Mason Davis; married June Carolyn Fox; children: Karen M, J Mason III. **Educ:** Talladega Coll, AB 1956; State Univ of NY Law School, JD 1959. **Career:** Univ of AL, School of Law, adjunct prof of insurance and damages 1972-; Sirote and Permutt PC, attorney 1960-, sr partner; Protective Industrial Insurance Co of AL Inc, chmn of the bd of dir, 1988-. **Orgs:** General counsel Natl Ins Assn 1962-77; exec comm mem AL Democratic Party 1970-; exec comm Birmingham Bar Assn 1974-77; sec Birmingham Bar Assn 1978-79; pres Natl Insurance Assn 1978-79; sec AL Democratic Party 1978-; chmn bd of dir Natl Ins Assn 1979-81; mem Alpha Phi Alpha Fraternity, Masons, Elks, NAACP, Sigma Pi Phi, Omicron Delta Kappa; chmn bd of trustees Talladega Coll 1981-88; pres Birmingham Bar Assoc 1985-86; vice chmn Birmingham Airport Authority. **Honors/Awds:** Pres Citation Frontiers of Amer 1962; Man of the Yr Alpha Phi Alpha Fraternity 1973; Outstanding Serv Comm Serv Council 1973; Outdoor Recreation Achievement Award US Dept of Commerce 1975; AL Recreation Parks Soc Lay Award 1975; Outstanding Serv Univ of AL School of Law 1977; Exemplary Dedication to Higher Educ AL Assoc of Colls & Univs 1982. **Business Addr:** Attorney, Sirote and Permutt, 2222 Arlington Ave, S, PO Box 55727, Birmingham, AL 35255.

DAVIS, JACKLEAN ANDREA

Law enforcement official. **Personal:** Born Feb 6, 1957, Cleveland, OH; daughter of Fredrick and LaFrench Davis; children: Christina Katherine. **Educ:** Univ of New Orleans, attended 3 years. **Career:** New Orleans Police Dept, patrol officer, 1981-82, first district, 1982, sixth district, 1982-83, narcotic and drug abuse unit/vice unit, 1983-86, investigator rape unit, 1984-86, investigator homicide unit, 1986-91, sergeant, 1991-. **Orgs:** Black Organization of Police; National Organization of Black Law Enforcement Executive; International Assn of Women Police; International Assn of Chiefs; Martha Grand Chapter to wit Order of Eastern Stars. **Honors/Awds:** Black Organization of Police Officer of the Year, 1989; International Organization of Women Law Enforcement Officer of the Year, 1992. **Home Addr:** 4743 Knight Dr, New Orleans, LA 70127.

DAVIS, JAMES A. See Obituaries section.

DAVIS, JAMES EDGAR

Association executive, engineer. **Personal:** Born Apr 30, 1948, Augusta, GA; son of Sarah N Davis; married Emily Cates, Oct 1994; children: Esa, Veronica. **Educ:** NC State University, Bachelor of Science in Civil Engineering, 1970, Master of Civil Engineering, 1972; University of NC, Master of Regional Planning, 1972; University of Maryland, PhD course Requirements, 1974-76; Federation Executive Institute, 1982, Synectics, 1989, University of Pennsylvania, 1991, Harvard University, 1992. **Career:** Southern Railway Co., management trainee, 1970-72; Barton-Aschman Associates, associate, 1972-73; The MITRE Corp., technical staff, 1973-74; United States Dept of Transportation, chief pre-award review branch, 1974-75, sr program ayalyst, 1976-77, director office of grants assistance, 1978-82, deputy associate administrator for grants management, 1982-83, urban mass transportation administration, 1974-83; Port Authority of New York & New Jersey, assistant director rail transportation, 1983-84; Sea-land Services, Inc, director operations research, 1985-89; American Society of Civil Engineers, assistant executive director, 1989-94, executive director & chief executive officer, 1994-. **Orgs:** Federation Sr Executive Service; Canadian Sr Transportation Management Program, 1980; American Management Association; American Society of Association Executives; Greater Washington Society of Association Executives; Council of Engineering & Scientific Society Executives, American Society of Civil Engineers. **Honors/Awds:** The Secretary of Transportation Silver Medal of Meritorious Achievement; The UMTA Administrator Bronze Medal for Superior Achievement; Represented USDOT in Riyadh, Saudi Arabia, 1978. **Business Addr:** CEO/Executive Director, American Society of Civil Engineers, 345 E 47th St, New York, NY 10017, (212)789-2200.

DAVIS, JAMES F.

Educational administrator. **Personal:** Born Jan 29, 1943, Marion, SC; married Beverly A Hemmingway; children: Shean Askia, Donald Affonso. **Educ:** Johnson C Smith Univ, BA 1964; Pepperdine Univ, MBA 1977. **Career:** EF Hutton & Co Inc, super 1968-71; SC Natl Bank, asst vice pres 1971-78; Rice Coll, faculty mem 1978-79; Benedict Coll, vice pres student affair 1979-. **Orgs:** Mem Columbia Chamber of Commerce 1979; mem US Army Assn 1979; mem Natl Assoc Coll Deans Registrars & Admissions Officers 1984; trustee mem Benedict Coll Fed Credit Union 1979-; mem Amer Assoc College Registrars & Admissions Officers; SCASAA; NASFAA; NAPW. **Honors/Awds:** Outstanding Volunteer Worker Bibleway Child Develop Ctr 1984. **Military Serv:** AUS private 1st class 9 months. **Business Addr:** Dir Admssn Rcrds & Fin Aid, Benedict College, Harden & Blanding Sts, Columbia, SC 29204.

DAVIS, JAMES HAROLD

Clergyman, educator. **Personal:** Born Nov 2, 1932, Tulsa, OK; married Shirley Jean Tucker; children: James H Jr, Jeryl, Kim, Phillip, Byron, Robert, Geri, William. **Educ:** Lincoln Univ, BMus 1961; OK Univ, MSW 1974; Trinity Bible Univ, DD 1974; Central Amer Univ, DMin 1982. **Career:** Langston Univ, vocal pedagogue 1964-66; County Supt of Schools, admin aide 1966-67; Logan County OK, NYC, counselor/asst dir 1967-71; Langston Univ, instructor, political science 1974-75, asst dir dorm life 1975; New Hope Baptist Church, pastor 1975-83; Langston OK School Bd, vice pres 1986; Ward #1 Langston OK, city councilman 1987; Central Amer Univ, Mt Bethel Baptist Church, vice-chancellor/pastor; city councilman, 1987-. **Orgs:** mem, Central Amer Univ Coll Approval Team, 1980-; pres, Congress St Mark Dist Congress Christian Educ, 1984-; lecturer, Natl Baptist Congress Christian Educ, 1972; police chaplain, Wichita P.D., 1979-83; Mayor's Comm, Wichita, 1980-83; charter mem, Sedgwick County Jail Ministry 1981-83; pres, Lions Intl Club of Langston; OK Historical Soc; bd of dir, Assn for Central Oklahoma Govt. **Honors/Awds:** Mem, Smithsonian Inst 1972. **Military Serv:** AUS Field Sgt served 3 yrs; 3rd Army Badge; 3 Star Campaign; Marksman.

DAVIS, JAMES HAROLD

Engineer. **Personal:** Born Jun 19, 1939, Southport, NC; married Mercell Price; children: Rhonda Yvette, Harriette, Jimmy. **Educ:** Durham Tech Inst, Cert Mechanical Draft 1966; Cape Fear Tech Inst, Personnel Supvsn 1967; Drafting & Design Technology 1968; Rec Admin 1970; Southeastern Comm Coll, Bus Law 1974-75; Seneland Real Estate Sch, ICS Civil Engr Professional Real Estate Course 1978-79. **Career:** Carolina Power & Light Co, engr tech; Pfizer Inc, chem plant opr 1975-76; Brown & Root Constr Co, field piping engr 1972-75; Intl Terminal Ops, Stevedore foreman 1970-72; Sterns-Roger Corp, opr tech 1967-70; Babcock & Wilcox Co, draftsman 1966-67; AUS Corps of Engrs Philadelphia Dist, dragtender 1961-66; Rosemont Knitting Mach Philadelphia PA, knitting mach opr fixer 1960-61; NC Licensed Real Estate, broker. **Orgs:** Mem NC Employment Sec Commn 1974-78; mayor Pro-Tem City of Southport 1975-77; adlerman City of Southport 1971-79; chmn Southport Rec Commn 1971-75; v chmn Brunswick Co Planning Commn 1974-79; commr Columbus-Brunswick Co Housing Authority 1980; Southport Br NAACP; NC Minority Rep Conf; Mt Carmel AME Ch Habib Temple No 159; mem Am Soc of Safety Engrs NC Chpt. **Honors/Awds:** Stearns-Roger Corp Safety Award 1968-69; United Way Bronze Plaque Award 1980. **Military Serv:** AUS pvt e-1 1958.

DAVIS, JAMES KEET

Utility company executive. **Personal:** Born Apr 28, 1940, Florence, SC; son of Carrie Barnes Davis and James Keet Davis; married Glenda Gaither; children: James Keet III, Jacquelynn K. **Educ:** Claflin Coll, BS Phys Sci Educ 1962; GA Inst of Tech, MS Urban Planning 1975; GA State Univ Exec Mgmt Sem, 1978; SEE Public Utilities Mgmt Course, 1982; Emory Univ Advance Mgmt Prog, 1984. **Career:** Oconee HS, coach/sci teacher 1963-64; Josten's Jewelry Co, salesman 1964-73; GA Power Co, employed 1972, vice pres corp relations 1982-93, sr vice pres, 1993-. **Orgs:** Chmn Foxhead Develop Corp; Natl Conf of Black Mayors; Amer Assoc of Blacks in Energy; NAACP; mem, founder GA Assoc of Black Elected Officials Corp Roundtable; bd mem Butler St YMCA; Mayor's Task Force on Public Ed, Leadership Atlanta, Leadership Georgia; bd mem GA Dept of Human Resources; bd of trustees Gammon Theol Sem; chmn UNCF Telethon Atlanta 1986-; mem 100 Black Men of Atlanta; bd mem Renaissance Capital Corp; bd mem Southeastern Electric Exchange; comm mem Edison Electric Inst Minority Bus Devel; executive bd mem Atlanta Organizing Committee, 1990-; bd mem Atlanta ORT, 1989-. **Honors/Awds:** Citizenship Awd Omega Chap Men's Club 1976; Young Man of the Year Awd & Citizenship Awd 1976; GABEO Corp Roundtable Corp Leadership Awd; Atlanta Bus League Awd; numerous other awards. **Business Addr:** SVP, Corp Relations, Georgia Power Company, PO Box 4545, Atlanta, GA 30302.

DAVIS, JAMES PARKER

Commissioner. **Personal:** Born Jul 21, 1921, Memphis, TN; married Maurita Burnett; children: JeParker, Daphne, Lezlie. **Educ:** LeMoyne Coll, BS 1943; Washburn U, LLB 1948. **Career:** Wyandotte Co, co commr 1973-, asst pros atty 1951-73; KS House, rep 1959-73; Multi-State Compact, asst minority dir 1969-71. **Orgs:** Chmn bd Omega Psi Phi 1975-76; mem Multi-State Compact 1971-73; gen counsel Cross Line Homes Inc; Bryant Manor Housing Proj; Royal Gardens Hsg Proj; Victory Hills Hsg Proj; past pres Chelsea Pz Homes Democracy Inc; mem NAACP; KS Bar Assn; Am Bar Assn. **Honors/Awds:** Cert of recog Nat Bar Assn KS Econ Oppr Found 1976; Meritorious Govtl Ldrsp OIC 1975. **Military Serv:** AUS 1943-46. **Business Addr:** 1314 N 5th, Kansas City, KS 66101.

DAVIS, JAMES W.

Research administrator. **Personal:** Born Apr 8, 1926, Lexington, VA; married Rosetta; children: James G, Benita J. **Educ:** W VA State Coll, BS 1951; Nashville YMCA Law Sch, JD 1972. **Career:** Meharry Med Coll, rsch admin asst prof genetics & molecular med dir of Sickle cell center school of graduate studies & rsch; Vanderbilt Univ, rsch assoc & lab mgr 1963-73; Case Western Reserve Cleveland OH, rsch tech rsch asst rsch supvr 1954-63. **Orgs:** Mem, soc rsch admin; sec citizens realty & devel co Inc; pres, Nashville Univ; Urban League; deacon, 1st Bapt Ch; mem bd dir WDCN-TV Nashville; pres Eta Beta Sigma Chap Phi Beta Sigma 1973; dir 3rd Dist Frontiers Intl; chmn bd mgrs Bordeaux YMCA, 1972-73. **Honors/Awds:** Man of yr Eta Beta Sigma 1972; frontiersman of yr Nashville Frontier Club 1972; special recognition, Nashville YMCA 1971; honored by WVOL Radio 1966. **Business Addr:** Meharry Med Center, 1005 18th Ave N, Nashville, TN 37208.

DAVIS, JEAN E.

Adviser, attorney. **Personal:** Born in New York, NY; daughter of Cynthia Davis and Martin Davis. **Educ:** Hunter Coll, New York, NY, BS, 1961; Teachers Coll, Columbia Univ, New York, NY, MEd, 1966; Univ of WI Law School, Madison, WI, JD, 1976. **Career:** Lincoln Hosp, Yeshiva Univ, Bronx, NY, coordinator, 1966-67; Maimonides Hosp, Brooklyn, NY, supvr, 1967-69; City Coll, New York, NY, supvr, counselor, 1969-74; Office of the Solicitor, US Dept of Labor, Civil Rights Div, Washington, DC, asst counsel, atty, adv, 1977-88, counsel, interpretations & advice, 1988-90; Drexel Univ, Philadelphia, PA, sr adv to the pres, 1990-. **Business Addr:** Senior Adviser to the President, Affirmative Action and Employment Planning, Drexel University, 32nd & Chestnut Sts, Philadelphia, PA 19104-2884.

DAVIS, JEAN M.

Physical therapist (retired). **Personal:** Born Dec 17, 1932, Natchitoches, LA; daughter of Eddy C Lloyd; married Hayward Jr; children: Raynard T. **Educ:** Howard Univ, BS 1953; Howard Univ Grad School, Zoology 1953-55; Univ of PA School of Phys Therapy, Cert PT 1956. **Career:** Howard Univ Hosp Dept Phys Med & Rehab, staff phys therapist to suprv physical therapist 1956-89. **Orgs:** Mem Amer Phys Therapy Assoc 1956-; lecturer Howard Univ Med School 1975-80; speaker Career Day Progs in HS. **Honors/Awds:** Appeared Network Continuing Med Ed NY 1976, video tape series & on cover Med TV Guide 1976; Cited in article Howard Univ Hosp Publ "Women" 1977; speaker Div of Orthopaedics Annual Continuing Ed Prog. **Home Addr:** 7904 Inverness Ridge Rd, Potomac, MD 20854.

DAVIS, JEROME

Business executive. **Personal:** Born Apr 27, 1950, Eufaula, AL; married Iriam Acevedo; children: Kamille. **Educ:** Yale Univ Law Schl, JD 1976; Oxford Univ England, MA 1973; Princeton Univ, 1971. **Career:** Chemical Bank, v pres/team Ldr 1982-, v pres/calling oper 1980-82. **Orgs:** Trustee Princeton Univ 1978-83; mbr, brd of dir NY Civil Liberties Univ 198-82. **Honors/Awds:** Harlem YMCA Youth Achievers 1983; New Business Award 1982.

DAVIS, JOHN

Professional football player. **Personal:** Born May 14, 1973. **Educ:** Emporia State, attended. **Career:** Tampa Bay Buccaneers, tight end, 1997-. **Business Addr:** Professional Football Player, Tampa Bay Buccaneers, One Buccaneer Place, Tampa, FL 33607, (813)870-2700.

DAVIS, JOHN ALBERT

Educator. **Personal:** Born Jan 6, 1935, La Grange, GA; married Judith Gail; children: Greg, Deanna, Keith. **Educ:** UCLA, BA 1963, MA 1968, PhD 1971. **Career:** Office of Minority Affairs, Univ of Southern CA, 1972; UCLA, asst prof 1968; UCLA

Berkely, visiting prof 1971; Social Action Training Center, dir of rsch 1965. **Orgs:** Mbr of brd Los Angeles Childrens Bureau 1983-, Milton F Williams Fund 1980-; pres Crenshaw Neighbors 1981-83. **Honors/Awds:** Mbr Alpha Sigma Nu Soc Sci Hon Soc 1970; LA Times ''Understanding Black & Chicano Groups'' 1978; jrnl of negro history 1984. **Military Serv:** AUS e-5 1959-61. **Business Addr:** Assistant Professor & Chair, Loyola Marymount Univ, 7101 W 80th St, Department of Afro Am Studies, Los Angeles, CA 90045.

DAVIS, JOHN ALEXANDER
Civil rights activist. **Personal:** Born Jun 2, 1960, Bronx, NY. **Educ:** Columbia Univ NY, BA 1982; Attended, Rutgers Law Sch Newark. **Career:** Century Pacific Investment Corp, law clerk 1985; Cohn & Lifland, law clerk 1985-86; Integrity Life Insurance, paralegal 1986; NAACP, natl youth dir 1986-. **Orgs:** Trustee bd of governors DeWitt Clinton Alumni Org 1978-; natl bd mem NAACP Natl Bd of Dirs 1980-86; alumni officer Columbia Univ 1982-87. **Honors/Awds:** Roy Wilkins Scholarship NAACP 1978; One of Fifty Future Black Leaders Ebony Magazine 1982; Best Legal Brief Frederick Douglass Moot Ct Competition BALSA 1985. **Business Addr:** Dir Youth & College Div, NAACP, 4805 Mt Hope Drive, Baltimore, MD 21215.

DAVIS, JOHN AUBREY
Educator. **Personal:** Born May 10, 1912, Washington, DC; son of Gabrielle Beale Davis and John A Davis Sr; married Mavis E Wormley Davis, Sep 5, 1935 (deceased); children: John A Jr, Smith W. **Educ:** Williams Coll, AB 1933; Univ of WI, AM 1934; Columbia Univ, PhD 1949. **Career:** Howard Univ, lectr 1935-36; Lincoln Univ, asst prof & prof of polit sci 1936-53; Office of Emergency Management, President's Commission on Fair Employment Practice, exec dir, Division of Review & Analysis, Washington, DC, 1943-46; OH State Univ, vis lectr 1950-51; US Dept of State, Office of Personnel, Washington, DC, consultant on Fair Employment, 1951-53; Commissioner for State of New York, commission against discrimination, 1957-61; Center for Adv Study in Behavioral Sci, fellow, 1969-70; City Coll of NY, assoc prof of polit sci 1953-61; City Coll & Grad Faculty CUNY, prof of polit sci & chmn, 1961-80, emeritus, 1980-. **Orgs:** Faculty Fellowship Bd United Negro Coll Fund 1959-61; chf US Delegation World Conf of Black Writers Paris 1956; founder, exec dir, 1957-62, pres, 1962-66, Amer Soc of African Culture; bd of Editors Pres Studies Quarterly 1974-; bd dir Libr of US Presidential Papers 1966-70; adv com Dept Polit Sci Princeton Univ 1966-71; Seminar on Africa, 1967-68; 1964-, Cnl on Foreign Relations; vice pres, 1971-72, cncl & exec com Amer Pol Sci Assn 1957-59 & 1973; bd trustees Williams Coll, MA 1972-77; founder/1st admin The New Negro Alliance 1933; dir Lincoln Univ Conf on Status of the Negro in a Fighting Democracy 1942; asst dir, NY State Comm Against Discrim in Employment (1st in nation) 1942; dir of non-legal rsch for NAACP for Brown vs Topeka 1953-54; consult Gov of NY on adminstrn of a proposed law against discrim in employmnt on account of age 1956-57; life mem NAACP; Phi Beta Kappa; Democratic (Galbraith) adv comm 1959-60; Advisory Committee, Democratic Natl Committee, 1957-60; bd mem, exec comm mem, NAACP, Legal Defense & Education Fund, 1963-75; Pres Johnson's Committee on Domestic Affairs, 1964-66. **Honors/Awds:** Chevalier, Republique Federale du Cameroun, 1964; Commandeur de l'Ordre National, Republique de Senegal, 1966; Pres Medal for Disting Educ Serv to City Coll, 1972; Faculty Fellow of the Fund for the Advancement of Educ, Ford Found 1950-51; LLD, Lincoln Univ, 1983, William College, 1989; numerous publications & articles including, ''Southern Africa in Transition'' JA Davis & JK Baker Eds 1966; ''The Influence of Africans on American Culture'' Annals of the American Acad of Polit and Soc Sciences 1964; ''The Administration of Fair Employment Practices in the United States'' Univ of WI Madison 1951; Review of J Harvie Wilkinson III ''From Brown to Bakke'' Oxford Univ Press 1979, Political Science Quarterly 1980; Regional Org of the Social Security Admin, Columbia Univ Press, 1958, Columbia Univ Stes, #571, reprinted AUS Press, NY, 1968. **Business Addr:** Prof/Chmn Emeritus, The City College of CUNY, 138th & Convent Ave, New York, NY 10031.

DAVIS, JOHN W., III
City official & financial administrator. **Personal:** Born Oct 29, 1958, Cincinnati, OH. **Educ:** Georgetown Univ, BS 1980; Dun & Bradstreet, Financial Analy 1981; ICMA City Mgmt School; Harvard Univ; Indiana Univ, 1986. **Career:** Georgetown Univ, assoc prof 1979-80; City of Cincinnati, contract accountant 1980-82; Queen City Metro, computer programmer 1982-85; SORTA, superintendent of capital; City of Silverton, chief financial officer 1982-87. **Orgs:** Mem Natl Assoc of Accountants 1982-87, Municipal Fin Office Assoc 1982-87, NAACP 1983-87; notary public State of OH 1984-87; bd of trustee OKI 1984-85; mem Natl Budget Review Bd, Natl Cash Mgmt Comm; bd of trustees Cincinnati Branch NAACP. **Honors/Awds:** Bachelor of the Year Ebony Mag 1983; Leader of the Future Ebony Mag 1983; Outstanding Young Person Under 30 Cincinnati Enquirer 1983; Hon Recruiter US Army 1984; Disting Budget Awd 1986.

DAVIS, JOHN WESLEY
Attorney. **Personal:** Born Nov 1, 1943, Detroit, MI; son of Mrs Dorris Miller; married Lorraine F Davis, Mar 30, 1966; children: Aisha, Kiilu. **Educ:** Wabash Coll, AB, 1964; Univ of Denver, JD, 1971. **Career:** Int Assn Human Rights, EEO Program, dir, 1975-76; Natl Bar Assn, EEO Program, exec dir, 1976-78; Howard Univ, Reggie Program, exec dir, 1980-84, law professor, 1978-85; Self Employed, attorney, 1985-. **Orgs:** DC Neighborhood Legal Services, bd mem, 1992-; Natl Bar Assn, life mem, NBA journal editorial board; NAACP, life mem, 1979-, cooperating attorney, 1977-. **Honors/Awds:** NAACP, Award of Merit, 1975, Certificate of Appreciation, 1980; Natl Bar Assn, Equal Justice Award, 1977. **Special Achievements:** Employment Discrimination Litigation Manual, 1977; Law Review Article, NCCU Law Journal, The Supreme Court Rationale for Racism, 1976. **Home Phone:** (703)780-5044. **Business Addr:** Attorney at Law, 601 Indiana Avenue, NW, Ste 1000, Washington, DC 20004, (202)783-3705.

DAVIS, JOHN WESLEY, SR.
Cleric. **Personal:** Born Aug 10, 1934, Laurel, MS; son of Mary Alice Wright Davis and Willie Davis; married Virgie Louise Sumlin, Jul 4, 1958; children: John W Jr, Maurice Benard. **Educ:** Jackson State Univ, BME 1960; America Bible Coll, BPhB 1962-63, MPhB 1965, DD 1968. **Career:** Mt Olive D Congress, past pres 1968-80; The Greater Antioch MB Church, pastor. **Orgs:** Past trustee MI Coll Inst West Point 1975-85; life mem Natl NAACP 1981-; mem SCLC 1981-; mem adv bd Judge Baker 1982; mem bd of dirs Natl Baptist Convention USA, Inc; pres New Educ State Convention; past pres Dist Congress; vice pres, New Educational State Congress; parliametarian, Shiloh District Assn; past mem adv bd Governor of MS Ceta Prog; vice pres Mt Olive Dist Congress Alumni Assn; mem Ministerial Biracial Alliance; mem adv bd MS Cooperative Extension Serv; mem, Interdenominatinal Ministerial Alliance; past mem, Youth Court Advisory Bd; mem, advisory bd, Salvation Army Domestic Violence Shelter; Salvation Army; bd of dirs, Amer Cancer Society; counselor, Youth Prison Ministry; chairperson, President's Council, NBC, USA Inc; pres, Jackson County Interdemominational Ministerial Alliance. **Honors/Awds:** Scholarship Jackson S Univ 1956-60; recording artist known nationally & internationally; Outstanding Minister of the Year, 1994; Volunteer of the Year, 1994; Community Service Award, Jackson County NAACP, 1994; received numerous awards. **Home Addr:** 3401 Westlane Dr, Gautier, MS 39553.

DAVIS, JOHN WESTLEY
Real estate development manager. **Personal:** Born Aug 13, 1933, Birmingham, AL; son of Gertrude Davis-Walker and Richard L Davis; married Shirley A Perry Davis, Jan 2, 1955; children: Cheryle, Paul, Michael, Glenn, Tracy (deceased). **Educ:** Allied Technical Coll, Chicago IL, attended, 1954-56; Chicago Technical Coll/ITT, Chicago IL, attended, 1957-59; Univ of Illinois at Chicago, Chicago IL, attended, 1963-64; Chicago Real Estate Inst Chicago Community Coll, degree, 1970. **Career:** AT&T Teletype Corp, Chicago IL, tool & die maker/designer, 1953-64; Oscar C Brown Real Estate Corp, Chicago IL, vice pres, 1963-66; City of Chicago, Dept of Planning, Chicago IL, supvr of rehabilitation, 1967-72; Dept of Housing & Urban Devel, Washington DC, dir of property disp, 1972-78; Cook County, Chicago IL, deputy accessor, 1981-84; Chicago Transit Authority, Chicago IL, Strategic Planning/Real Estate Devel, mgr, 1984-92; Marjon Realty Corp., president, currently. **Orgs:** Vice president, Chatham Lions Club, 1963-75; commr, Boy Scouts of Amer, 1965-70; mem, Illinois Association of Realtors, 1967-70; dir, bd mem, Natl Housing & Urban Rehabilitation Assn, 1967-72; volunteer, Chicago Urban League, 1970-74; chairman, elder, Stony Island Church of Christ, 1977-; coord, task force, First Congressional Dist Housing Task Force, 1979-82; mem, Illinois Assn of Professional Planners, 1984-88, Amer Public Transit Assn, 1984-88; bd mem, Conf of Minorities in Transit Officials, 1984-. **Honors/Awds:** Winner of the Public High School Oratorical Contest, Birmingham Public High School, 1950; Employee of the Year, AT&T, 1960; Certificate of Appreciation, Boy Scouts of Amer, 1971; Special Honors Achievement, Dept of Housing & Devel, 1974; Honoree for Comm Award, Bud Billiken, 1972; two publications on Public/Private Joint Devel, 1986, 1987. **Military Serv:** US Army Ranger/Airborne, 1st Lt, 1950-53, Honorable Discharge, 1953. **Business Addr:** President, Marjon Realty Corp., PO Box 19029, Chicago, IL 60619-0029.

DAVIS, JOHNETTA GARNER
Educator, educational administrator, speech-language pathologist. **Personal:** Born Nov 1, 1939, Warrenton, VA. **Educ:** Tchrs Coll, BS 1961; George Washington U, MA 1969; Howard U, PhD 1976. **Career:** Univ of Maryland, Coll Park, Office of Graduate Minority Educ, assoc dean, dir, 1993-; Howard Univ, assoc dean, grad prof 1978-96, assoc prof, prof 1972-78; Amer Speech & Hearing Assn, asst sec for prog dev 1971-72; Federal City College, assistant professor, 1970-71; Teachers Coll, instructor 1969-71; Washington DC Public Schools, speech pathologist 1961-68. **Orgs:** Potomac Chapter of Links Inc; American Speech-Language & Hearing Assn 1961-; DC Speech, Language and Hearing, 1963-; task force on intl grad educ Council of Grad Schs Task Force on Minority Education; board of directors Stoddard Bapt Home 1977-82; Sunday sch tchr Mt Sinai Bapt Ch 1977-82. **Honors/Awds:** Howard University, establishment of the Johnetta G Davis Award for Best Mentor of Graduate Students, 1993; Graduate Student Council, Administrator of the Year, 1992, Distinguished Service Awards, 1978-80, 1982, 1986, 1988, 1990; Outstanding faculty citation Students at DC Teachers Coll, 1971; Frederick Douglass Honor Soc Howard Univ Chap 1974; Outstanding Yng Women in Am 1976; Howard University, School of Communications, Outstanding Alumni Award, 1986; DC Teachers College, Outstanding Junior Faculty Award, 1971; US Office of Education, Fellowship, 1967; CCC-SP-L, Amer Speech-Language Hearing Assn, certificate, 1962. **Home Addr:** 519 Brummel Court NW, Washington, DC 20012-1846. **Business Phone:** (301)405-4183.

DAVIS, JOHNNY REGINALD
Former professional basketball coach. **Personal:** Born Oct 21, 1955, Detroit, MI; married Lezli Davis; children: Reginald, Austin. **Educ:** Univ of Dayton, attended; Georgia State Univ, degree in business and community development, 1987. **Career:** Guard: Portland Trail Blazers, 1976-78, Indiana Pacers, 1978-82, Atlanta Hawks, 1982-84, Cleveland Cavaliers, 1984-86, Atlanta Hawks, 1986; Atlanta Hawks, director of community affairs, 1986-89, assistant to the president, 1989-90, assistant coach, 1990-93; Los Angeles Clippers, asst coach, 1993-94; Portland Trail Blazers, asst coach, 1994-96; Philadelphia 76ers, head coach, 1996-97. **Special Achievements:** NBA, Championship, 1977. **Business Addr:** Former Head Coach, Philadelphia 76ers, PO Box 25040, Philadelphia, PA 19147.

DAVIS, JOSEPH SOLOMON
College administrator (retired). **Personal:** Born Apr 8, 1938, Macon, GA; married Sarah Frances Striggles; children: Joan Yvette, Oscar Wendall. **Educ:** Tuskegee Inst, BS, MEd 1960-68. **Career:** Boggs Acad, teacher ind arts 1961-65, guidance dir 1965-67; Stillman Coll, dir financial aid 1967-76, 1981-95, dir counseling serv 1976-81. **Orgs:** Mbr West Tuscaloosa Optimist Club 1980-. **Honors/Awds:** Grad flwshp Southern Assoc of Secondary Schls 1967; Keyman Service, United Way Award, 1978; mem AL Comm on Higher Ed 1984. **Home Addr:** 2608 32nd Street, Northport, AL 35476.

DAVIS, JULIA H.
Organization executive. **Career:** Eta Phi Beta Sorority, national prexy, 1994-. **Business Addr:** National Prexy, Eta Phi Beta Sorority, c/o Julia H. Davis, 2641 NW 16th Ct, Fort Lauderdale, FL 33311-4420, (954)735-0117.

DAVIS, KATIE CAMPBELL
Educator. **Personal:** Born Sep 11, 1936, Lumber City, GA; married Ernest Davis Jr; children: Theresa Lynn. **Educ:** TN State Univ, BA 1957; TN State Univ, MA 1968; Univ IL, PhD 1974. **Career:** Norfolk State Univ, prof, speech, English, theatre arts, currently; teacher various public school since 1951; communication consultant; spiritual, inspirational and motivational speaker. **Orgs:** Mem Speech Comm Assn; mem NAACP; Alpha Kappa Alpha Sorority; American Association of University Women. **Honors/Awds:** National Consortium of Doctors' Perseverance Award, 1992. **Business Addr:** Professor, Norfolk State University, Speech Communication, 2401 Corprew Ave, Norfolk, VA 23504.

DAVIS, L. CLIFFORD
Attorney, judge. **Personal:** Born Oct 12, 1924, Wilton, AR; son of Dora Duckett and Augustus Davis; married Ethel R Weaver, Nov 14, 1955; children: Karen Renae, Avis Janeth. **Educ:** Philander Smith Coll, BA 1945; Howard U, JD 1949. **Career:** Davis Sturns & Johns, atty 1949-; district judge, Fort Worth, 1983-88, 1989-; Johnson, Vaughn and Heiskill, of counsel, 1989-. **Orgs:** Mem Omega Psi Phi Frat; past trustee St Andrews United Methodist Church; past mem bd of Tarrant Cnty Unit Fund; Tarrant Cnty & Prec Worker's Council; charter revision com City of Fort Worth TX; adv coun of TX Legal Serv Corp; YMCA; NAACP. **Honors/Awds:** National Bar Association, Hall of Fame; Silver Gaval Award, Tarrant Cty Bar Association. **Military Serv:** US Army, E-2, 1954-55. **Home Addr:** 2101 Fleming Drive, Fort Worth, TX 76112. **Business Addr:** Attorney, Johnson, Vaughn and Heiskill, 600 Texas St, Fort Worth, TX 76102.

DAVIS, LANCE ROOSEVELT
Food service director. **Personal:** Born Dec 21, 1962, Orange, NJ; son of Joan Henson Roach and Roosevelt Davis Jr. **Educ:** Johson & Wales University, ASc, culinary arts, 1982, BA, food service management, 1984. **Career:** APO Catering, owner/chief operator, 1983-84; Hyatt Regency, New Brunswick, corporate manager trainee, 1984-85, beverage manager, executive steward, 1985-86; gourmet restaurant manager, 1986-88; freelance food and beverage consultant, 1987-89; Hyatt Regency, Kansas City, banquet manager, 1988-89; Harrison Conference Center, asst food & beverage director, 1989-91, food and beverage director, 1991-92; Lackmann Food Service, Food Svc director currently. **Orgs:** Alpha Pi Omega Fraternity Inc, founding father, 1983; Omega Phi Delta Fraternity, founding father, 1984; Distributive Educational Club of America, Stanhope NJ, president, 1979-80; Minority Affairs Board, City Council of

Glen Cove, NY, board mem, 1989-90; Business Volunteers for the Arts, Middlesex County Chamber of Commerce, 1984-85; Glen Cove Citizens Against Substance Abuse Inc, 1989-90; National Association of Black Hospitality Professionals New York Chapter, president, 1992-. **Honors/Awds:** Business Volunteers for the Arts, Central NJ, certification, arts management course, 1985; American Hotel & Motel Association Certification, Human Relations Supervisory Development, 1982; Middlesex County, NJ Health Department, certification, managerial food sanitation, 1985; Nassau County, NY Health Department, certification, food service sanitation, 1992; United Cerebal Palsy of Rhode Island, Certificate of Appreciation, 1984; Roderick & Roderick Development Institute, certification, multiple management course, 1984. **Home Phone:** (516)676-3551. **Business Addr:** Food Service Director, Lackmann Food Service, Dean Witter Discover, 2 World Trade Center, New York, NY 10001, (212)392-8336.

DAVIS, LARRY EARL
Psychologist. **Personal:** Born May 11, 1946, Saginaw, MI; son of Kires and Clara Davis. **Educ:** Attended Delta Coll Bay City MI 1964-66; MI State Univ, BS Psychol 1968; Univ of MI, MSW 1973, MA Psychology 1975, PhD Social Work & Psychology 1977. **Career:** VISTA, New York City, volunteer, 1969-72; Washington Univ, asst prof social work & psychology, 1977-; Univ of Hawaii, sabbatical, 1988-; Norfolk State Univ, adjunct faculty, 1995-97. **Orgs:** Mem Assn Black Psychologists 1977-; mem Natl Assn of Black Social Workers 1977-; mem Natl Assn of Social Workers 1977-; Leadership St Louis, 1986. **Honors/Awds:** Published and co-published numerous articles, including "Racial Composition of Groups," Social Work MA, 1979; "Racial Balance, A Psychological Issue," Social Work With Groups, 1980; "Minority Content in Social Work Educ, A Question of Objectives," Journal of Educ for Social Work, 1983; co-author, Race, Gender and Class: Guidelines for Practice with Individuals, Families, and Groups, Prentice-Hall, 1989; co-editor, Ethnic Issues in Adolescent Mental Health, Newbury Park, CA, Sage, 1990; Black & Single: Finding & Choosing a Partner Who is Right for You, Noble Press, 1994; Too Many Blacks, Too Many Whites: Is There A Racial Balance? Basic and Applied Social Psychology, 1995. **Business Addr:** Prof Social Work/Psychology, Washington University, St Louis, MO 63130, (314)935-6632.

DAVIS, LATINA
Professional basketball player. **Personal:** Born Oct 8, 1974. **Educ:** Univ of Tennessee. **Career:** Columbus Quest, guard, 1996-. **Business Addr:** Professional Basketball Player, Columbus Quest, 7451 State Route 16, Dublin, OH 43016, (614)873-6555.

DAVIS, LAWRENCE ARNETTE, JR.
Educator. **Personal:** Born May 13, 1937, Pine Bluff, AR; married Ethel Louise Grant; children: Sonya, Lawrence III, Catherine. **Educ:** AM&N Coll, BS 1958; Univ of AR, MS 1960; IA State U, PhD 1973. **Career:** Dept of Math & Physics, Univ of AR at Pine Bluff, chmn 1974-; NASA Research Project, Univ of AR, dir 1973-74; Engr Research Inst, IA State Univ, research asst 1971-73; IA State Univ, grad teaching asst 1969-71; NSF In-service Inst, AM&N Coll, dir 1967-68; NASA Office of Advanced Research & Techn summers 1964 1965; AM&N Coll, prof 1961-68; MS Valley State Coll, instructor 1960; Author of 3 papers or writings. **Orgs:** Mem Soc of Indsl & Applied Mathematicians; Math Assn of Am; Nat Assn of Mathematicians; AR Acad of Sci 1966-68; Am Assn for Advancement of Sci; Am Assn of Univ Prof; Am Assn of Physics Tchrs; Beta Kappi Chi; Alpha Kappa Mu. **Business Addr:** Dept of Math & Physics, U of AR, Pine Bluff, AR 71601.

DAVIS, LELIA KASENIA
Business executive. **Personal:** Born Nov 7, 1941, Taft, OK; daughter of Canzaty Smith and Willie Smith; married David Earl Davis, Nov 22; children: Mark, Kasandra, Starla Smith Phillips, Canraty, Derrick. **Career:** Amer Technical Inst, Muskogee OK, admission counselor, 1986-; City of Taft, Taft OK, mayor, 1973-. **Orgs:** Bd of dir, Eastern Oklahoma Devel Dist; pres, LeCon Org; chairwoman, Taft Parade Comm; advisory bd of dir, Dept of Corrections. **Honors/Awds:** First Black Elected Female Mayor, 1973; Amer Ten Outstanding Young Women, 1974; Muskogee League Hall of Fame. **Home Addr:** PO Box 324, Taft, OK 74463.

DAVIS, LEODIS
Educator. **Personal:** Born Sep 25, 1933, Stamps, AK; married N June Wilson; children: Melonie, Leon. **Educ:** Victor Wilson Schl UMKC, BS Chem 1956; IA State Univ, MS Chem 1958, PhD Biochem 1960. **Career:** TN State Univ, asst prof chem 1961-62; Howard Univ Med Coll, asst prof biochem 1962-67, assoc prof biochem 1967-69; IA State Univ, research assoc 1960-61, visit assoc prof 1969, assoc prof biochem 1969-76, prof of chem 1976-, chrmn of chem dept, 1979-87, acting dean, Graduate College, 1988-89, assoc vp, Academic Affairs, 1989-94, director of summer session, 1992-94. **Orgs:** Full memsp Soc of Sigma XI 1960; HEW NIH Min Biomed Supp; biochem study sect Ad Hoc Consult1970-; chem comm on min affairs Amer Soc of Biolog 1973; Aging Rev Comm 1976-80; Natl Res Counc Rev of NSF Grad Fellow 1977-80; NIH Biochem Study Section, 1976-81; Celluar and Molecular Basis of Disease Review Committee, 1986-90; Division of Research Grants Advisory Committee, 1993-97. **Honors/Awds:** One of ten med school fac mem in US awarded Lederle Med Fac Award 1967; Gen Elec Conf for Prof of Chem & Chem Eng 1973; bd of dir Univ of IA Credit Union 1986-; Fogarty Internationsl Research Collaboration Award Special Review Committee, 1992-93. **Business Addr:** University of Iowa, Dept of Chemistry, Dept of Chemistry, Iowa City, IA 52242.

DAVIS, LEON
Business executive. **Personal:** Born May 23, 1933, Chicago, IL; son of Lillian Davis and Henry Davis; married Shirley Pickett, Oct 7, 1988; children: Leon Jr, Daryl, Terrence, Margo. **Educ:** TN A&I Univ Nashville, 1951-1953; Crane Jr Coll Chicago, 1955; Wilson Jr Coll Chicago, 1956. **Career:** Congressman Abner J Mikva, exec asst 1969-71; Operation PUSH, natl exec dir 1971-72; Congressman Ralph H Metcalfe, exec asst 1972-73; The Peoples Gas Light and Coke Co, admin office of vice pres 1973-. **Orgs:** Chmn bd of govs IL State Coll and Univ 1973-; bd of higher educ State of IL 1977-; mem Chicago Bd of Educ 1980; Univ Civil Serv Merit Bd State of IL 1975-77; Community Serv & Continuing Educ Program State of IL 1977-79; bd mem Afro-Am Du Sable Museum 1977; Numerous Published Articles 1971-76; Personal View Column Chicago Sun-Times 1979. **Honors/Awds:** Chicago Sun-Times, Special Black History Month Section "The Political Legacy of Harold Washington" by Leon Davis 1988. **Military Serv:** US Army pvt, 1953-55. **Business Addr:** Superintendent, Peoples Gas Light & Coke Co, 122 S Michigan Ave, Chicago, IL 60603.

DAVIS, LEONARD HARRY
Manager. **Personal:** Born Sep 3, 1927, Indianapolis, IN; married Erla Darling Robinson (deceased); children: Kevin L, Gail D, Janna L, Aaron L (dec), Barry C. **Educ:** Univ of IL School of Fine & Applied Arts Champaign, BS, BA 1949-52. **Career:** Naval Ordinance Facility Indianapolis, asst art dir 1952-57; Indust Arts & Engrg Co San Diego, asst dir 1957-62; Cubic Corp, manager of graphic and promotional arts, currently. **Orgs:** Indus photographer Indus Art & Engrg Co San Diego 1957-62; past sec Kappa Alpha Psi Champaign 1949-52; pres Cubic Mgmt Assoc 1977-79; past pres San Diego Area Council 1980-81. **Honors/Awds:** Numerous 1st through 3rd places for art exhibits 1948-65; Mem of the Year Cubic Mgmt Assoc 1979. **Military Serv:** AUS corpl 1944-48. **Business Addr:** Manager, Cubic Corp, 9333 Balboa Ave, San Diego, CA 92123.

DAVIS, LESTER E.
Engineer, consultant. **Personal:** Born Aug 5, 1918, Tunica, MS; son of Carrie Ruth Jackson Davis and Emanuel Davis; married Annie B Debro; children: Dorothy Wakefield. **Educ:** KS State Univ, BS Arch Engrg 1950; Lincoln Univ, attended 1942 & 1946. **Career:** US Navy Dept Naval Ship Yard, Vallejo, CA, naval architect/structural, 1950-53; St of CA Dept of Transport, bridge engr 1953-75; Bay Area Rapid Transit Dist CA, supr engr structural/civil 1975-86. **Orgs:** Life mem Amer Soc of Civil Engrs; mem No CA Council of Black Prof Engrs; registered prof engr Civil Br State of CA; active in local church & civic assns; life mem Alpha Phi Alpha Frat; mem East Bay Structural Engrs Soc. **Military Serv:** USAF 1943-46. **Home Addr:** 8100 Sunkist Dr, Oakland, CA 94605.

DAVIS, LISA E.
Attorney. **Personal:** Born Feb 6, 1960, Queens, NY; married Anthony Jamison, Oct 15, 1994. **Educ:** Harvard University, AB, 1981; New York University School of Law, JD, 1985;. **Career:** Hon Constance Baker Motley, law clerk, 1985-86; Kramer, Levin, Nessen, Kamin & Frankel, associate, 1986-88; Frankfurt, Garbus, Klein & Selz, associate, 1988-93, partner, 1994-. **Orgs:** National Bar Assn, Intellectual Property Section, 1993-. **Business Addr:** Partner, Frankfurt, Garbus, Klein & Selz, PC, 488 Madison Avenue, New York, NY 10022.

DAVIS, LISA R.
Media relations director. **Personal:** Born Dec 2, 1961, Washington, DC; daughter of Doris & Lorenzo Davis. **Educ:** University of NC at Greensboro, BA, 1983; Howard University, MBA, MPA, 1988. **Career:** Natl Bar Assn, communications dir, 1986-89; Amer Bar Assn, staff dir, media and prof svcs, 1989-93; Democratic Leadership Council, press scy, 1993-96; Clinton/Gore Campaign, natl deputy press scy, 1996; AARP, media dir, 1996-. **Orgs:** Natl Press Club; Public Relations Society of Amer; Delta Sigma Theta, 1983-. **Business Addr:** Media Relations Director, American Associate of Retired Persons, 601 E St, NW, Washington, DC 20049.

DAVIS, LLOYD
Federal government official. **Personal:** Born May 4, 1928, Chicago; married; children: 3. **Educ:** DePaul Univ Chgo, PhB; Loyola Univ Chgo, MSIR; Grad Fed Exec Inst; Westinghouse Mgmt Sch; US Civil Serv Mgmt Sch. **Career:** US Dept of Hsng & Urban Develop Wash DC, dir Ofc of Vol Compliance Ofc of Asst Sec for Fair Hsng & Equal Opp; Cath Interracial Council Archdiocese of Chgo, former dir; Intergroup Relations Ofcr Hsng & Home Finance Agency, former dir; Kennedy Adminstrn, spl asst to post master gen; Dixwell Renewal Proj New Haven CT, former dir; New Haven Redevel Agency, former asst dir; Westinghouse Elec Corp US Defense & Space Cntr Baltimore, former mgr sociol-Economic progs; Model Urban Neighborhood Demonstration Proj Baltimore MD, mgr; MLK Ctr Nonviolent Social Chng, vice pres for govt & intl affairs, exec dir fed holiday commission. **Orgs:** One founder Nat Cath Conf for Interracial Justice; pres Nat Assn of Intergroup Relations Ofcls; mem bd dirs Nat Assn of Human Rights Workers. **Honors/Awds:** Scholarship Achievement Award; recip awards from City of Chicago New Haven Baltimore; Papers Presented to Dillard U. **Military Serv:** AUS bat sgt maj. **Business Addr:** Executive Director, MLK Jr Federal Holiday Commission, Atlanta Office, 449 Auburn Ave, NE, Atlanta, GA 30312.

DAVIS, LOUIS GARLAND
Educator. **Personal:** Born in Danville, VA. **Educ:** Oberlin Coll Conservatory, 1948; New England Conservatory of Music, BMus 1951; Univ of Florence, 1951; Boston U, MMus 1955. **Career:** International Ferienkurse Fur Deutshe Sprache und Germanistik, Salzburg, Austria, 1957 Cert Cum Laude, German Language-Austrian Modern European Music Course; Universite' de Paris, Paris France, 1964, French Language; Bryant College, instructor, 1969-70; Community College of Rhode Island, professor emeritus; University of Rhode Island, summer director of poverty program, 1968; Le Cercle Francais D'Amerique D'Ete L'Academic Internationale Nice, music dir, 1965; Moses Brown School, dir music 1961-68; Phillips Academy & Bradford Jr Coll, instructor 1956-61; Newton Coll Sacred Heart, instructor 1955-56; recitals include: Historic Music Hall, Cincinnati; Cincinnati Chamber Symphony Orchestra, soloist; Boston Univ Symphony Orchestra; Carnegie Hall. **Orgs:** Mem Chopin Club; Nat Assn of Music Tchrs; Taft Museum; RISD Museum; bd trustees bass-baritone soloist Young Peoples Symphony Orch. **Honors/Awds:** Hon doctorate Saengerfest Harvard Univ 1967; Recital career continues since college retirement in 1988-, including Music Mansion Recitals, Providence, Rhode Island. **Home Addr:** 100 Bowen St, Providence, RI 02906.

DAVIS, LUCILLE H.
Educator. **Personal:** Born Aug 14, 1936, Spokane, WA; daughter of Blondine H Jones; married Everett S Davis, Mar 16, 1963; children: Evelyn R, Millicent E. **Educ:** University of Illinois at Chicago, BSN, 1960, MSN, 1965; Northwestern University, PhD, 1971. **Career:** Chicago State Univ, Chicago, IL, assoc prof and dir of nursing educ, 1971-72; Rush College of Medicine, Chicago, IL, assoc prof of sociology, 1972-76, prof of sociology, 1976-77, Rush College of Nursing, assoc prof and coordinator of grad prog in psychiatric nursing, 1972-74, assoc prof and asst dean of grad nursing prog, 1974-76, assoc prof and coordinator of grad prog in geriatric/gerontological nursing, 1976-77; St Xavier College, School of Nursing, Chicago, IL, assoc prof and dean, 1977-81; Northwestern Univ, Chicago, IL, prof and dean of school of nursing, Dept of Community Medicine, 1981-86, dir and prof, Center for Nursing, assoc prof, Dept of Sociology, senior faculty, AIDS Mental Health Educ Project; Univ of Illinois at Chicago, College of Nursing and School of Public Health, research assoc, 1990-; Univ of IL, College of Nursing, asst prof, 1991-93; Health Sciences, Chicago State Univ, prof & dean, 1993-. **Orgs:** Institute of Medicine of Chicago; Sigma Theta Tau, Alpha Lambda Chapter. **Honors/Awds:** Award for Superior Commitment and Dedication to the Nursing Profession, Eta Chi Sorority, Inc, Alpha Eta Chapter, 1980; Young Researcher Award, Association of Black Nursing Faculty in Higher Education, 1990; Certificate of Appreciation for Outstanding and Dedicated Service, Bethany Hospital Board of Directors, 1986; "The Black Church and African-American Elders," Journal of Aging and Judaism, 5(2), 1990; "Interdisciplinary Team: Myth or Reality?," Center on Aging Newsletter, vol 3, no 2. **Home Addr:** 11205 S Longwood Dr, Chicago, IL 60643. **Business Addr:** Professor and Dean, College of Health Sciences Professions, Chicago State Univ, Chicago, IL 60628, (312)995-3987.

DAVIS, LUELLA B.
Librarian. **Personal:** Born Dec 26, 1940, Baton Rouge, LA; daughter of Dolly Jones Butler and Lawrence Butler; married Wayne Davis, Jun 23, 1983; children: Derrick Hemingway, Nicholas Hemingway. **Educ:** San Jose City College, San Jose, CA, AA, 1974; San Jose State University, San Jose, CA, BA, 1976; University of California, Berkeley, CA, MLS, 1977. **Career:** San Jose City College, San Jose, CA, reference librarian, 1977-80; San Jose State University, San Jose, CA, reference librarian, 1978-81; Emory University, Atlanta, GA, reference librarian, 1981-. **Orgs:** Member, American Library Assn, 1981-; member, Assn of College and Research Libraries, 1983-; member, American Library Assn's Black Caucus, 1983-. **Honors/Awds:** Author, Patron Services at the Robert W Woodruff Library, Small Computers in Libraries, 1987; author, A Survey of Academic Library Reference Practices, RQ, 24, 1984; Della J Sister Fellowship, University of California of Berkeley, 1976-77; Ford Foundation Scholarship, San Jose State University, 1974-76. **Business Addr:** Bibliographic Instruction Coordinator, Emory University, Woodruff Library, Reference Dept, Atlanta, GA 30322.

DAVIS, LUTHER CHARLES
Dairy industry marketing consultant. **Personal:** Born Sep 21, 1948, Key West, FL; son of Carol Davis and Earl Davis; married Sharon Ann Williams; children: Jason. **Educ:** Cornell Univ, BA 1970. **Career:** Jewel Companies Inc, buyer 1977; Kraft Inc, Dairy Group, district sales mgr 1984; Mellin Ice Cream Co, vice pres 1985; Wisconsin Milk Marketing Bd, regional marketing mgr. **Orgs:** President, Randallstown Optimist, 1990-91. **Home Addr:** 237 Natanis Ridge Circle, Wells, ME 04090. **Business Addr:** Regional Mktg Manager, Wisconsin Milk Mktg Bd, 8418 Excelsior Dr, Madison, WI 53717.

DAVIS, MAJOR
Administrator. **Personal:** Born Nov 6, 1931, Hartsville, SC; married Elsie M Luck; children: Shynethia Catrice, Trent Damone. **Educ:** Maricopa Tech Comm Coll, AA 1973; Phoenix Coll, AA 1975; AZ State Univ, BA 1979. **Career:** US Air Force, jet test flight engr 1951-72; Alpha Grand Lodge, grand master 1974-75; Miss Black AZ Pageant, dir 1971-; Miss Galaxy Intl Pageant, natl dir 1975-; Youth Together Inc, founder, bd chmn. **Orgs:** Public relations USAF Worlds Southern Hemisphere 1968; editor, publ Phoenix Chronicle Newspaper 1969; mem NAACP 1970-; editor, publ AZ News Mag 1973; mem Phoenix Advertising Club 1976, AZ Newspaper Assoc 1978, Phoenix Chamber of Comm 1978; Founder 1st private state sickle cell anemia found Phoenix. **Honors/Awds:** 33rd Degree Mason Ivanhoe Grand Lodge AF&AM Denver 1964; Commander-In-Chief Jeremiah Consistory Denver 1965; Black & Gold Serv Awd Maricopa Tech Coll 1973; Key to the City Austin TX 1979, Las Vegas NV 1981. **Military Serv:** USAF t/sgt 21 yrs; 15 Decorations. **Business Addr:** Board Chairman, Youth Together Inc, 4310 W Verde Lane, Phoenix, AZ 85031.

DAVIS, MARIANNA WHITE
Educator. **Personal:** Born Jan 8, 1929, Philadelphia, PA; daughter of Laura Bowman White Frederick and Albert McNeil White; widowed; children: Kenneth Renay. **Educ:** SC State College, BA English 1949; NY Univ, MA English 1953; Boston Univ, DEd English 1966. **Career:** SC Pub Sch, tchr, 1949-51, 1955-56, 1986-96; SC State Coll, asst prof, 1956-64; Claflin Coll, prof, 1966-69; Voorhees Coll, vis prof, 1966-68; Boston Univ, vis prof, 1967; Univ of TN, vis prof, 1969; Benedict Coll, English prof & researcher, 1969-82; Upward Bound Tufts Univ; Denmark Tech Coll, acting pres, 1985-86; Davis & Assocs, pres, 1980-; Northeastern University, African-American Literature Teacher Training Project, co-director, 1992-94; Benedict College, special assistant to the president, 1996-. **Orgs:** Bd dir Natl Council of Teachers of English 1958-80; co-founder & sec ABC Devel Corp 1972; chmn Conf on Coll Composition & Comm 1975-76; exec comm ADE Modern Language Assn 1976-79; commr SC Educational TV 1980-95; mem Public Broadcasting System Adv Bd 1981-83; Francis Burns United Methodist Ch; bd chm, Columbia Urban League Bd, 1981-82; Natl Council of Negro Women; YWCA; life mem NAACP; The Moles; coord, Coalition for Concerns of Blacks in Post Secondary Educ in SC; Alpha Kappa Alpha Sor; Order of Eastern Star; Chmn SC Intl Women's Yr Commission; founder VICOS Women's League for Comm Action; TISAWS; The Girl Friends, Inc; Civil Rights Comm Adv Bd 1985-; natl publicity chair, The Moles, 1988-92; bd of educ, S Carolina United Methodist Church 1988-96; board mem, board of visitors, Claflin Coll. **Honors/Awds:** SC State Coll Alumni Scholarship; Crusade Scholar doctoral studies 1964-66; Outstanding Educator of Amer 1970-71; IBM-UNCF Fellowships post doctoral studies 1971 & 1974; Pi Lambda Theta Travel Scholarship for study in Soviet Union 1973; Outstanding Educ Award Kappa Alpha Psi Frat, Athens GA 1974; Contrib to Educ Award SC Comm Affairs 1976; Educators Roundtable Awd 1976; Outstanding Cit Awd Omega Psi Phi Frat 1977; Emory O Jackson Journalism Awd 1978 & 1996; Distinguished Research Award NAFEO 1980; Distinguished Faculty Awd Benedict Coll 1980; Distinguished Serv Award Columbia Urban League 1981; Distinguished Alumni Awd Boston Univ 1981; Distinguished Alumni Award SC State Coll 1981; Par Excellence Award in Educ Operation PUSH 1982; Outstanding Citizen Award, Cleveland, OH, 1984; Kappa Alpha Psi of SC Outstanding Black Woman Award 1987; Jacob Javits Fellowship Bd, Presidential Appointment, 1993; Governor's Award, Outstanding Achievement, 1995; contributed papers to Boston Univ (Mugar Memorial Library), 1989; exec producer, "The Struggle Continues," black history teleconf on PBS, 1986-; author of 18 books & many publ articles. **Business Addr:** PO Box 3097, Columbia, SC 29230.

DAVIS, MARILYN ANN CHERRY
Educator. **Personal:** Born Mar 26, 1951, Aiken, SC; daughter of Sara Wilhelmena Walton Cherry and Council Christopher Cherry; married Charles Douglas Davis, Aug 19, 1975; children: Cheryl Maria Davis. **Educ:** Hampton Institute, Hampton, VA, BA, summa cum laude, 1973; Atlanta University, Atlanta, GA, MA, 1977, PhD, 1979. **Career:** Atlanta Junior College, Atlanta, GA, instructor of political science, 1977-79; Tuskegee Institute, Tuskegee, AL, assistant prof of political science, 1980; Bennett College, Greensboro, NC, assistant professor of political science, 1980-81; Spelman College, Atlanta, Ga, chair, 1984-85, 1988-90, associate professor, political science, 1981-. **Orgs:** Member, American Political Science Association, 1981-; member, Southern Political Science Association, 1981-; member, Georgia Political Science Association, 1981-; member, National Conference of Black Political Scientists, 1981-. **Honors/Awds:** Sears Roebuck Foundation Award, Excellence in Teaching and Campus Leadership, 1990; Valedictorian, Martha Schofield High School, 1969. **Special Achievements:** Contributing author to an anthology: "Dilemmas in Black Politics," HarperCollins, 1991; author "Student Guide to Practicing American Politics," Worth Publishers, 1997. **Home Addr:** 4140 Welcome All Terrace, College Park, GA 30349.

DAVIS, MARILYNN A.
Government official. **Personal:** Born Oct 30, 1952, Little Rock, AR; daughter of Erma Lee Glasco Davis and James Edward Davis. **Educ:** Smith College, BA, 1973; University of Michigan, MA, 1976; Washington University, St Louis MO, MA, 1980; Harvard Graduate School of Business Administration, MBA, 1982. **Career:** State Street Bank, Boston MA, senior credit analyst, 1981; General Motors Corp, Detroit MI, analyst, central office financial staff, 1982-83; General Motors Corp, New York NY, senior financial analyst, overseas borrowing section, 1984, senior financial analyst, financing, investment and financial planning section, 1984, asst to GM group vice president/chief economist, 1984-86; American Express Co, New York NY, vice president, risk financing, beginning 1987; New York Housing Authority, deputy general mgr for finance; US Dept of Housing and Urban Devt, asst secretary for administration, 1993-. **Orgs:** Bd of trustees, Studio Museum in Harlem; chair of committee on residence, Bd of Counselors of Smith College; member of bd of directors, Queensboro Society for the Prevention of Cruelty to Children; management assistance committee, Greater NY Fund/United Way. **Honors/Awds:** Named to 100 Top Black Business and Professional Women list, 1988; Black Achievers Award, Harlem YMCA, 1989. **Home Phone:** (202)364-6943. **Business Addr:** Asst Sec, Administration, US Dept of Housing and Urban Devt, 451 7th St, Rm 10110, Washington, DC 20410.

DAVIS, MARION HARRIS
Director. **Personal:** Born Jul 27, 1938, Washington, DC; married Charles B; children: Alan Edward. **Educ:** Univ of Pittsburgh, MPA Grad Sch of Pblc & Intrntl Affairs 1971; Am Univ Wash DC, Atnd 1966-70. **Career:** US Dept of Hsng & Urban Devel Area Ofc Detroit, deputy dir hsng mgmt div; Co Hsng Ofcr Fairfax VA, exec dir comm devel authority 1972; Deptof Urban Renewal & Economic Devel Rochester NY, dir of program planning 1971-72; Westinghouse Electric Corp, sr mgmt consult 1970-71; FHA Dept of Hsng& Urban Devel Wash DC, hsng prog spclst mgmt asst br div of low & mdrt incm hsng 1969-70; Ofc of the Sec Dept of Hsng & Urban Devel Wash DC, conf asst congr rltns ofcr 1967-69. **Orgs:** Mem Natg Assn of Hsn & Redevel Ofcls; Nat Inst of Real Estate Mgmt; Am Soc of Planning Ofcls. **Honors/Awds:** Recip Carnegie Mid-Career Fellow Grad Sch of Pub & Internatl Affairs Univ of Pittsburgh 1970-71; travel study award $3,000 while attending grad sch Ford Found 1970-71. **Business Addr:** US Dept of Housing & Urb Dev, 660 Woodward Ave, Detroit, MI 48226.

DAVIS, MARK ANTHONY
Professional basketball player. **Personal:** Born Apr 26, 1973, Thibodaux, LA. **Educ:** Howard College; Texas Tech. **Career:** Minnesota Timberwolves, guard-forward, 1995-96; Philadelphia 76ers, 1996-. **Business Addr:** Professional Basketball Player, Philadelphia 76ers, One Corestates Complex, Philadelphia, PA 19148, (215)339-7676.

DAVIS, MARTIN
Brother. **Educ:** Point Park Coll, BA Candidate. **Career:** St Augustine's Capuchin Franciscan Province, brother 1968-; St Brigid/St Benedict, brother The Moor Cath Parish 1970; Lwrncvll Hawks Bsktbll Team, organizer; Black Inner-City Parochial Schs, tchr. **Orgs:** Mem Nat Black Cath Clergy Caucus; Pttsbrgh Dance Council; solemn profession in Capuchin Franciscan Order 1964.

DAVIS, MARVA ALEXIS
Attorney. **Personal:** Born May 19, 1952, Gretna, FL; daughter of Thelma Kenon Robinson & Harold Kenon; married Calvin C Davis, Sep 2, 1973 (deceased); children: Sheletha. **Educ:** Lincoln University, BA, 1974; Florida State University, JD, 1977. **Career:** Public Defender's Office, assistant public defender, 1977-85; CEDO, general counsel, 1986-91; City of Midway, city attorney, 1986-87; Florida A&M University, associate general counsel, 1991; Marva A Davis, lawyer, 1980-. **Orgs:** The Barristers Association, past president; Tallahassee Women Lawyers Association, board member; Big Bend Hospice, board member, 1994-; Children's Home Society, board member, 1993-; Florida Bar Association, 1977-; National Bar Association, 1977-; Academy of Florida Trial Lawyers, 1983-. **Honors/Awds:** Capital Area Community Action Agency, Outstanding Leadership, 1996. **Home Addr:** Rte 1, Box 3045, Havana, FL 32333, (904)539-9951. **Business Addr:** Attorney, Marva A Davis, PA, 100 S Madison St, PO Drawer 551, Quincy, FL 32353, (904)875-9300.

DAVIS, MARY AGNES MILLER
Association executive. **Personal:** Born in Montgomery, AL; daughter of Mollie Ingersoll Miller and George Joseph Miller; married Edward Davis. **Educ:** Wayne State Univ, BA; Univ of Michigan, MSW. **Career:** Catholic Social Services, caseworker/supervisor of students, 1947-48; Wayne County Juvenile Court, foster homes officer, 1953-57; League of Catholic Women Youth Service Bureau, caseworker, 1957-59; City of Detroit Youth Agency, consultant/analyst, 1963; Co-Ette Club Inc, founder natl dir; Metropolitan Detroit Teen Conf Coalition founder-director. **Orgs:** Pres Keep Detroit Beautiful Inc; bd dir Carmel Hall; Franklin-Wright Settlements; chmn Personnel Practices-Bylaws; League of Catholic Women; St Francis Home for Boys; Heartline Inc; Operation Understanding Brewster-Douglas Housing Project; Nominating Com Detroit Chap Amer Red Cross; Natl Council of US Women Inc; mem com Women's Assn of Detroit Symphony Orch; sec, social work administrator, Edward Davis Association Inc, currently; Detroit Area Chmn Meadowbrook Festival Com Oakland Univ; educ com Detroit Opera Assn; chmn ARC Central Region Recognition Ceremony 1980; Merrill Palmer Inst board of directors; Natl Cncl of Women of the US, Inc; Ntl vice pres, prog chmn for USA; Catholic Youth Org board of directors; Alpha Kappa Alpha Sorority; The Girl Friends, Inc. **Honors/Awds:** Greater Detroit Chamber of Commerce Awd; City of Detroit Common Council Leadership Awd; One of Detroit's 12 Most Outstanding Women Awd by Detroit Bicentennial Commission; NCW Woman of Conscious Awd 1984 for Leadership Youth & the Community; One Hundred Most Distinguished Black Women In The USA 1988; National Community Leadership Award, National Council of US Women Inc; Co-Ette Club Alumnus, 50th Anniversary Tribute Luncheon Honoree, 1990; National Volunteer Week Committee, Appointed Member, 1992; United Way Heart of Gold Council, 25th Anniversary Honoree; Top Lady of Distinction Award, Outstanding Civic Leadership, 1993. **Home Addr:** 2020 W Chicago Blvd, Detroit, MI 48206.

DAVIS, MATILDA LAVERNE
Physician. **Personal:** Born Sep 23, 1926, Elizabeth, NJ; daughter of Martha Hilton and James T Davis; married Robert M Cunningham, Aug 15, 1950; children: Robert Davis, Dellena M, William E. **Educ:** Howard Univ Wash DC, BS 1948; Howard U, MD 1951. **Career:** Veterans Administration, Newark, NJ, adjudication physician, currently; FAAFP Cunningham-Davis MD PA, dr 1971-; Karen Horney Horney Clinic, postdoctorate psychiatric 1967-71; Harlem Hosp NYC, intern 1951-52. **Orgs:** AMA; alumni mem Howard Univ Med Sch Present; Nat Med Assn; life mem NAACP; charter mem Howard University Medical Alumni Association; National Carrousels Inc; National Contempo. **Honors/Awds:** First women in the East in tennis 45 yrs & Older, Tennis Players 1979; charter fellow, American Academy of Family Physicians, 1974; physicians recognition award AMA 1980. **Home Phone:** (908)352-7032. **Business Addr:** Adjudication Physician, Veterans Administration, 20 Washington Pl, Newark, NJ 07102, (201)645-3032.

DAVIS, MELVIN LLOYD
Construction company executive. **Personal:** Born Mar 29, 1917, Richmond, VA; son of Adelaide Turner Davis and Thornton F Davis; married Helen Randolph Davis, May 22, 1939; children: Melvin Jr, Langston, Adelaide Flamer, Carolyn Harris, Wendell F, Kermit M, Nancy Elam, Anna Hudson, Leon V, Revell R, Deborah N Davis. **Educ:** John Tyer Community Coll, 1948-49. **Career:** Thorton F Davis, laborer, 1931-35; Thornton J Davis Jr, painter, 1935-42; US Navy, painter, 1942-45; Davis & Myers Building Co, painter, 1945-60; Melvin L Davis General Contractor, owner, 1960-68; Davis Brothers Construction Co, pres, 1968. **Orgs:** Sunday school supt, Troop Providence Baptist Church, 1945-50;. **Business Addr:** Pres, Davis Brothers Construction Co, 2410 Chamberlayne Ave, Richmond, VA 23222.

DAVIS, MELWOOD LEONARD
Research manufacturing company executive. **Personal:** Born Dec 14, 1925, Youngstown, OH; son of Annie Bell Davis (deceased) and Doyle Davis (deceased); married Anne Norris, Dec 28; children: Adrienne Page Davis Dunning, Vikki Anne Davis. **Educ:** A&T State U, BS 1950; Springfield Coll, MsEd 1975; Union Grad Sch, PhD 1978. **Career:** Multi-Devel Enterprises Inc, pres; Nat Bd of YMCA, dir Urban/Africa Affairs 1973-; YMCA asso gen exec 1969-73; arctic av YMCA, exec dir 1967-69; YMCA of Buffalo & Erie Co, asst exec dir 1958-67; Multi-Development Janitorial Supply Co, vice pres mktg. **Orgs:** Dir Youth Urban Serv 1970-73; consult YMCA Career Devel 1970, 72; bd dir NAACP 1973; mem Frontiers Intl 1976; bd dir Tri-Co Mental Hlth 1971; bd dir Sr Citz 1971; Assn Professional Dirs; convener Gov of PA Children & Youth Adv Com 1972; mem Rotary Club of Harrisburg; exec prod "Ride For 24" 1975. **Honors/Awds:** Man of Yr Frontiers Internatl; award for excellence Race Rels 1976; Man of Yr Black Businessmen Assn; Silver Star 1945; A&T St Univ, Sports Hall of Fame; developed Community Urban Program, Harrisburg PA, film, Ride for 24; led fund raiser for Harrisburg Community Hospital. **Military Serv:** AUS corporal, 5 bronze, 1 silver star WWII.

DAVIS, MICHAEL DEMOND
Author. **Personal:** Born Jan 12, 1939; son of John P and Marguerite DeMond Davis; married Jean P Davis, 1978 (divorced 1988). **Educ:** Morehouse Coll, AB, 1963. **Career:** Atlanta Constitution, reporter, 1964-66; Baltimore Afro-American, reporter, 1966-68; Baltimore Sunpapers, reporter, 1968-74; San Diego Union, reporter, 1974-75; Washington Star, reporter, 1975-81; WRC-TV, NBC, metro editor, 1979-, reporter, 1981-84; WETA-TV, commentator; author. **Orgs:** Atlanta Olympic Committee for Women, bd of dirs; Natl Assn of Black Journalists. **Honors/Awds:** NAACP, Award for written coverage of the Vietnam War, 1960's; Newspaper Guild, Front Page Award, 1979. **Special Achievements:** Co-author with Hunter R Clark, Thurgood Marshall: Warrior at the Bar, Rebel on the Bench, Carol, 1992; author, Black American Women in Olympic Track and Field, McFarland, 1992; Our World, Morrow, Avon, 1995. **Home Addr:** 1334 Hamlin St. NE, Washington, DC 20017, (202)635-3033. **Business Addr:** Author, c/o Edward A Novak III, 111 N Second St, Harrisburg, PA 17102.

DAVIS, MICHAEL JAMES
Federal judge. **Personal:** Born Jul 21, 1947, Cincinnati, OH; son of Doris R Smith Davis & Chester L Davis; married Sara Wahl, Sep 6, 1980; children: Michael, Alexander. **Educ:** Macalester Coll, St Paul, BA, 1969; University of Minnesota Law School, Minneapolis, JD, 1972. **Career:** US Department of Health, Education and Welfare, Office of the General Counsel, Litigation Div, atty, 1973; Neighborhood Justice Ctr, criminal defense atty, 1974; Legal Rights Ctr, criminal defense atty, 1975-78; Hennepin Cty Public Defender's Office, criminal defense atty, 1978-83; Hennepin Cty Municipal Ct, judge, 1983-84; Hennepin Cty District Ct, judge, 1984-94; US District Ct, judge, 1994-. **Orgs:** MN Civil Rights Commission, 1977-82; Amer Inns of Ct, 1992-; MN Minority Lawyers Assn, 1980-; Natl Bar Assn, 1990-; Hennepin Cty Bar Assn, 1986; MN State Bar Assn, 1986; MN Lawyers Intl Human Rights Comm, 1983-85; MN Supreme Ct Racial Bias Task Force, 1990-93; MN Supreme Ct, Closed Circuit TV Task Force, 1991; Atty General's Task Force on the Prevention of Sexual Violence Against Women, 1988-89; Hennepin Dist Courts, Fourth Judicial Dist, 1984-; The Intl Academy of Trial Judges, 1996-; The Natl Assn of Public Interest Law Fellowships for Equal Justice, bd mem, 1997-; Eighth Circuit Jury Instruction Comm, 1997-. **Honors/Awds:** Macalester, Outstanding Alumni Award, 1989; WCCO Radio, Good Neighbor Award, 1989; Honorary Black Achievers Award; Minnesota Minority Lawyers Assn, Law Student Scholarship in Judge Michael J Davis' Name. **Special Achievements:** Published "Strategies and Techniques: Court's Role in Promoting Settlement;" Civil Pretrial Practice Inst, MN Inst of Legal Education, 1993; "Jury Challenges Involving Issues of Race," MN Developments and US Supreme Ct Updates, MN State Bar Assn Continuint Legal Education, 1993; "Nominated for appointment: Judge Pamela Alexander," 62 Hennepin Lawyer 11, May-June 1993; MN Supreme Court Closed-Circuit TV Task Force, writer of report adopted by the ct, 1991; "Civil Rights Advocate Doug Hall Retires from Legal Rights Center," 54 Hennepin Lawyer, July-August 1985. **Business Addr:** Honorable Michael J Davis, US District Court, 300 S 4th St, Ste 14E, US Courthouse, Minneapolis, MN 55415, (612)664-5070.

DAVIS, MILTON
Chairman. **Educ:** Morehouse Coll, Graduate; Washington Univ St Louis, Grad Study in Sociology and Economics. **Career:** South Shore Bank in Chicago, chairman 1983-. **Orgs:** Former chmn Chicago Chap Congress of Racial Equality.

DAVIS, MILTON C.
Attorney, association executive. **Personal:** marrIed Myrtle Goore; children: Milton, Warren. **Educ:** Tuskegee University, bachelor's degree; University of Iowa, JD. **Career:** Attorney; Alpha Phi Alpha Fraternity, president, 1993-96. **Orgs:** National Bar Association; Sigma Pi Phi Boule. **Honors/Awds:** American Political Science Foundation, fellow; Ford Foundation, fellow; Herman Lehman Foundation Scholar. **Special Achievements:** First Alabama resident elected as head of Alpha Phi Alpha, the oldest African-American fraternity in the United States. **Business Addr:** 304 N Main St, PO Box 830509, Tuskegee, AL 36083, (205)727-6500.

DAVIS, MONIQUE DEON
State representative. **Personal:** Born Aug 19, 1936, Chicago, IL; daughter of Constance McKay and James McKay; divorced; children: Robert A, Monique C Conway. **Educ:** Chicago State Univ, BS 1967, MS 1975; Graduate Work, Univ of IL, DePaul Univ. **Career:** Chicago Bd of Educ, teacher 1967-86; City Colls of Chicago, teacher 1976-84; Chicago Bd of Educ, coord/administrator 1986-; Illinois General Assembly, state representative, 1987-. **Orgs:** Chmn Southside Chap IVI-IPO 1980-84; chmn Legislative Comm Chicago Area Alliance of Black School Educators 1981-83; coord Chicago Bd of Educ 1986-; bd mem Christian Bd Trinity United Church of Christ; Chicago State University, alumni board, 1992-94. **Honors/Awds:** Teacher of the Year Award Gresham School 1978; Teacher Who Makes a Difference Center for New Schools; coord for election of Mayor Washington 1983, 1987; Excellent Legislator, Operation PUSH, 1989; Excellent Legislator, Dept of Aging, 1988. **Business Addr:** State Representative, Illinois General Assembly, 1234 W 95th St, Chicago, IL 60643.

DAVIS, MORRIS E.
Educator, attorney, mediator. **Personal:** Born Aug 9, 1945, Wilmington, NC. **Educ:** NC A&T State U, BS 1967; Univ IA Coll of Law, JD 1970; Univ CA Sch Pub Health, MPH 1973. **Career:** Dept Housing & Urban Devel San Francisco, atty-adv 1970-72; University of California Berkeley, Inst of Industrial Relations, Labor Occupational Health Prog, executive director, 1974-80; Journal of Black Health Perspectives, managing editor 1973-74; US Merit Systems Protection Board, administrative judge, 1980-85, abritrator and mediator, 1986-. **Orgs:** CA Bar Assn; IA Bar Assn; The Am Arbtrtn Assn; Am Pub Health Assn; fellow Univ CA (San Fran) Schl of Med 1974; fellow Univ CA (Berkeley) Schl Pub Hlth 1972-73. **Business Addr:** American Arbitration Association, 417 Montgomery St, 5th Fl, San Francisco, CA 94104-1113.

DAVIS, MYRTLE HILLIARD
Health care executive. **Personal:** Born Jun 13, 1926, Texarkana, AR; daughter of Thelma Hacker Hilliard and Arthur L Hilliard (deceased); divorced; children: Drew Hillard Davis, JD. **Educ:** Homer G Phillips Hosp, RN 1955; Univ of Cincinnati, MS, health planning admini, 1977. **Career:** Harvard St Health Center Boston, MA, pres 1982-83; St Louis Comp Health Center, admin, 1969-82, pres & CEO, 1983-. **Orgs:** Co-chair finance comm/bd dir St Louis Metro Urban League 1983-; chmn/personnel com/bd dir Tower Vill Geriatric Cntr 1984-; treas/bd dir MO Coalition Amb Care Cntrs 1984-; sec/bd dir, 1983-, chmn, bd of dirs, 1987-, Primary Care Cncl Greater St Louis; Spec Proj Comm St Louis Ambassadors 1985-; Top Ladies of Distinct St Louis Chap 1974-; pres, bd of dirs, Tower Village Nursing Care Center, 1987-; pres, chmn, Health/Medical Advisory Comm, St Louis Urban League, 1987-; secretary, Gateway Chapter, Links Inc, 1986; health, Black Leadership Round Table, 1989. **Honors/Awds:** Cert of Apprec MO Senate; Disting Citizen St Louis Argus Newspaper; Disting Pub Serv Culinary Arts Club; Leadership/Publ Relations Order Eastern Star; Woman of Achievement, Suburban Journals/radio station KMOX, 1989; Black Women Who Make Things Happen Award, Natl Coun Negro Women, Frito Lay, 1988; YWCA Women in Leadersip Award, Non Profit Management, 1993. **Business Addr:** President/CEO, St Louis Comp Health Center, 5471 Dr Martin Luther King Dr, St Louis, MO 63112.

DAVIS, MYRTLE V.
Nurse, educator (retired). **Personal:** Born Aug 23, 1930, Niles, OH; daughter of Willa Mae Smith and Anthony B Smith; married Frank T Davis; children: Robin C. **Educ:** St Elizabeth Hosp Sch of Nursing, Youngstown, OH, RN 1952; Youngstown State U, BS 1957; Kent State U, Kent, OH, MEd; TX Woman's U, MS 1980. **Career:** Youngstown State Univ, instructor 1976-81; Youngstown Bd of Educ, dir 1971-76; RN 1952-54; St Elizabeth Hospital, Youngstown OH, asst head nurse 1954-56, head nurse 1956-62; Choffin School of Practical Nursing, instructor 1963-71; various healthcare agencies, Youngstown, OH, staff nurse, medical surgical nursing 1981-90 (retired). **Orgs:** Mem Youngstown Supvr Personnel Assn; adv Bd St Elizabeth Hosp Sch Nursing; adv com Bd Licensed Pracitcal Nurse Assoc OH; Am Nurses' Assoc; Delta Sigma Theta; Youngstown chap Links Inc; Negro Bus & Prof Women's Club; life mem OH Voc Assoc; Am Voc Assoc; 3rd Baptist Ch. **Honors/Awds:** Appointed first black dir Sch Practical Nursing, State of OH 1971.

DAVIS, N. JUNE (NORMA JUNE WILSON)
Educational administrator. **Personal:** Born May 1, 1940, Jacksonville, FL; daughter of Myra and Maxie; married Leodis; children: Melonie, Leon. **Educ:** Spelman Coll, BA 1961. **Career:** SNCC Atlanta, chmn 1960; IA City Parks & Rec Commn, vice chmn 1972-76; Univ of Iowa, Admin Serv Dept, coord infor 1975-76, coord residence serv, 1976-84; asst dir residence serv 1984-86, acting dir Affirmative Action 1985-86, asst to vice pres of finance 1986-91, assistant vice president of finance and university services, 1991-. **Orgs:** Mem Ad Hoc Commn Racism IA City Sch Bd 1971-72; sec-treas Cedar Rapids Chap Links, Inc 1974-77; University of Iowa African American Council. **Honors/Awds:** Distinguished Achievement Award, University of Iowa, 1996. **Business Addr:** Assistant Vice President, The University of Iowa, 105 Jessup Hall, Iowa City, IA 52242.

DAVIS, NATHAN T.
Educator. **Personal:** Born Feb 15, 1937, Kansas City, KS; son of Rosemary Green and Raymond E Davis; married Ursula Broschke; children: Joyce Nathalie, Pierre Marc. **Educ:** Univ KS, BME 1960; Wesleyan U, CT, PhD Ethnomusicology. **Career:** Club St Germain, Paris, prof debut with Kenny Clark 1963; Donald Byrd, Blue Note Club Paris, 1963; Chat Que Peche, Eric Dolphy, Paris, 1964; toured Europe with Art Blakly & New Jazz Messengers, 1965; Europe & Amer, recorded several albums as leader; total 10 LP's as leader; Belgium Radio-TV, staff composer. **Orgs:** Mem SACEM, Soc of Composers, Paris, France; co-chmn ed com Inst of Black Am Music; mem Afro-Am Bi-Cen Hall of Fame; est & created PhD degree prog in Ethnomusicology, Univ Pittsburgh; created Jazz Program at Univ Pittsburgh; created Jazz Program Paris-Am Acad Paris. **Honors/Awds:** Honorary Doctorate of Humane Letters, Florida Memorial College. **Military Serv:** AUS 298 army band, Berlin, 1960-62. **Business Addr:** Professor, University of Pittsburgh, Music Department, 5th & Bellefield, Pittsburgh, PA 15260.

DAVIS, NATHAN W., JR.
Attorney. **Personal:** Born Dec 24, 1936, Ocean City, NJ; son of Nathan and Louisa Davis; married Emma, Jul 21, 1962; children: Melode, Carla, Nathan III. **Educ:** Rutgers Univ, BA, 1959; Howard Univ School of Law, JD, 1962. **Career:** Self-Employed, attorney, 1974-84; State of New Jersey, deputy public defender, 1984-. **Orgs:** Macedonia Methodist Church, lay leader, 1974-; Egg Harbor Township Board of Education, pres, 1984-; Atlantic County Bar Assn, 1975-; Municipal Utilities Authority, secretary, 1991-. **Honors/Awds:** Egg Harbor Township, Board of Education, Service Award, 1992; Township of Egg Harbor, Service Award, 1991.

DAVIS, NATHANIEL ALONZO
Telecommunications company executive. **Personal:** Born Jan 25, 1954, Fort McClelland, AL; son of Laura M Davis and Jesse Davis Jr; married Al Gene Redding Davis, Jun 11, 1983; children: Taylor, Darren, Jasmine. **Educ:** Stevens Institute of Technology, BE, 1976; Moore School of Engineering, University of Pennsylvania, MSEE, 1982; Wharton School of Business, University of Pennsylvania, MBA, 1982. **Career:** AT&T Telecom Long Lines, engineer, staff supervisor, various other positions, 1976-81; MCI Telecommunications, director, network engineering, 1983-86, vice pres, financial operations, 1986-88, vice pres, systems engineering, 1988-90, sr vice pres, finance, 1990-92, sr vice pres, access svcs, 1992-. **Orgs:** Black MBA Association, 1987-; Black Data Proc Assn, 1988-90; Wharton Alumni Association, 1989-. **Home Addr:** 2609 Geneva Hill Ct, Oakton, VA 22124-1534. **Business Addr:** Senior Vice President, MCI Telecommunications, 1650 Tysons Blvd, Mc Lean, VA 22102, (703)506-6585.

DAVIS, NIGEL S.
Banker. **Personal:** Born Oct 1, 1955, Bastrop, LA; son of Gladys Davis and Charles Davis. **Educ:** Grambling State Univ, Acct 1976. **Career:** Federal Reserve Bank of Kansas City, asst bank examiner 1977-82, bank examiner 1982-86, sr bank examiner and managing examiner 1986-. **Orgs:** Youth task group volunteer for the Full Employment Council, 1990; Women's Employment Network, volunteer. **Home Addr:** 11901 E 77 Terrace, Raytown, MO 64138. **Business Addr:** Senior Bank Examiner, Federal Reserve Bank of KC, 925 Grand Ave, Kansas City, MO 64198.

DAVIS, NORMAN EMANUEL
Association executive. **Personal:** Born Apr 6, 1941, Waycross, GA; married Mineola James Davis; children: Norman, Anthony, Corey V. **Educ:** Tuskegee Inst, 1966. **Career:** Dial-A-Maid Inc, pres 1978-80; Migrant & Seasonal Farmworkers, exec dir 1980-; Young Volunteer in Action, dir; MECRR Activity Center, adjustment instructor; Davis Marketing and Assoc Inc; Children Trust Fund, program asst/planning and econ developments, currently. **Orgs:** Staff planner Planning Commiss; exec dir City of Tuskegee Migrant & Seasonally Employed Farmworkers; city recreation projects City of Tuskegee; mem F&A Mason 32nd Degree, Shriner, Tuskegee Jaycees, Electrolex Club, Elks Lodge, Intl Guild for Resource Devel, Amer Soc of Planning Officials, Amer Legion, Macon Cty Retardation & Rehab Exec Bd; adv bd Macon Cty Medicare & Medicaid; Talent Search Adv Bd; Macon Cty Mental Health Bd; Tuskegee Planning Commiss; Macon Cty Monumental & Historical Soc; Tuskegee-Macon Cty Youth Council; Omega Psi Phi; served 2 yrs as pres of Washington Publ Sch PTA; pres of City Wide PTA; elected 6 yrs to the Macon Co Bd of Edn; Model Cities soc planner for the City of Tuskegee 1969-78; dir & planner for Rec Dept. **Honors/Awds:** Legionnaire of the Year; Social Work Cert for Suprvs; State Mental Health Serv Awd; Youth Council Cert; Red Cross Campaign Fund Raising Cert; Outstanding Achievement Awd City of Tuskegee; Jaycees Scotman Awd; Outstanding Achievement Awd Pro-Plan Intl; Jaycees Outstanding Business Awd Outstanding Young Man of the Year; Macon Cty Council Retardation & Rehab Appreciation Cert; Macon Cty 4-H Leadership Cert; designed, devel & implemented several community programs; Parenting Facilitator. **Home Addr:** 801 Marable Drive, Tuskegee, AL 36083. **Business Addr:** Children Trust Fund, 836 Washington Ave, Montgomery, AL 36103.

DAVIS, OSSIE
Actor. **Personal:** Born Dec 18, 1917, Cogdell, GA; married Ruby Dee; children: Nora, Guy, Hasna. **Educ:** Howard Univ, Class of 1939. **Career:** Actor Rose McClendon Players; dir Cotton Comes to Harlem, Kongi's Harvest, Black Girl, Gordons War, Countdown at Kusini; acted in The Defenders, The Sheriff, Night Gallery, The Scalphunters, The Cardinal, The Hill, The Client, Grumpy Old Men, Let's Do it Again, Gone are the Days; TV appearances: A Menu For Murder, B L Stryker, Evening Shade, Queen, The Ernest Green Story, The Stand; stag e roles Jeb, Wisteria Trees, Purlie Victorious, Green Pastures, Anna Lucasta, A Raisin in the Sun, I'm Not Rappaport; producer of Martin Luther King: The Dream and The Drum, A Walk Through the 20th Century with Bill Moyers, With Ossie and Ruby, Today is Ours. **Orgs:** Masons; NAACP; Grace Baptist Church; Inst of New Cinema Artist, chairman of the bd. **Honors/Awds:** TV Emmy winning Teacher; author Purlie Victorious, Escape to Freedom, The Story of Young Frederick Douglass 1978, Langston 1982; NAACP Image Awards, best

performance by a supporting actor, Do the Right Thing, 1989; NAACP Image Awards Hall of Fame, 1989; Monarch Award, 1990. **Special Achievements:** Published plays include: Curtain Call, Mr Aldredge, Sir Langston, Escape to Freedom; novels include: Just Like Martin, published by Simon and Schuster; interviewed for the Spike Lee film "4 Little Girls," 1997. **Military Serv:** US Army, med corp 1942-45. **Business Addr:** 44 Courtland Ave, New Rochelle, NY 10801.

DAVIS, OSSIE B.
Clergyman. **Personal:** Born May 14, 1922, Starkville, IL; married Ruby Lee Daniels; children: Ethel J, John A, Ossie C, Charles E, Willie J. **Educ:** Rust Coll, AB 1948; Univ of IN, MA 1955; Gammon Theol Sem, post grad 1964; Candler Sch of Theology Emory U, BD 1968; Universal Bible Inst, MBS 1974. **Career:** Minister & ordained deacon 1952; elder 1954; various pastorates since 1950; Pickins Elem Sch, principal 1951-55; Gooddman Jr HS, principal 1955-59; Montgomery Training HS, principal 1959-62. **Orgs:** District sec Evangalism; district dir Youth Work; conf dir Evangelism; delegate 4th Family Life Conf; rep General Conf; part-time exec sec of Christian Edn, Methodist Ch; mem TN-MS Tchrs Assn; State PTA cchaplain; co-chrmn MS Freedom Dem Party; co-chrmn Nat Freedom Rider, SCLC; mem NAACP 1946-; delegate Nat Dem Conv; 32 deg Mason Comm organizer, housing counselor, Economic Opportunity Atlanta Inc; probation counselor Fulton Co Deliquency Treeatment Center; Atlanta Southside Comprehensive Health Center; alcoholic counselor Half Way House. **Military Serv:** AUS 1941-47.

DAVIS, PATRICIA C.
Association executive. **Personal:** Born Jul 25, 1943, Grand Rapids, MI; married Frederick Douglass; children: Grant Anthony, Frederick Douglass II, Mwindaace N' Gai. **Educ:** Detroit Inst Of Commerce, 1969. **Career:** NAACP, exec sec; Amoco Production Co, adminsrv sec 1970-73; UAW Fai Practices & Anti-discrimination Dept, sec 1969-70; League Life Ins Co, stenog 1964-69; US Army Detroit Procurement Dist, clerk stenog 1963; Burroughs Corp, clerk typist 1962-63. **Orgs:** Lay mem Paradise Bapt Ch; Immaculate Conception Christian Bd Of Edn; asst sec OK St Conf of Branches NAACP; asst sec Tulsa Br NAACP; exec sec Tula Br, NAACP, 1970-76.

DAVIS, PATRICIA STAUNTON
Economist. **Personal:** Born Mar 29, 1945, Washington, DC; married James. **Educ:** Howard U, BS 1966; Stanford U, MBA 1973; George Washington U, PhD 1977. **Career:** Fed Res Bd, econnomist; Booz, Allen & Hamilton, mgmt consult 1973-75; Urban Inst, programmer, sr prgmr mktg rep 1970-71; Progm Serv Corp, 1969-70; Serv Bur Corp, 1968-69; Hughes Aircraft Co, 1967-80; White House Fellows Prgm, spl asst sec labor 1967-68; Fed Res Bd, economist 1976-. **Orgs:** Mem Big Sisters Am; recpt shclrsp Howard Univ 1962-66; COGME Flwsp Stanford Univ 1971-73; White House Flwsp Prgm 1975-76.

DAVIS, PHILLIP ALTON
Journalist. **Personal:** Born Jan 9, 1959, Chicago, IL; son of Janet Pilgrim Davis and Paul H Davis. **Educ:** Northwestern University, Evanston, IL, BS, journalism, 1980; Johns Hopkins (SAIS), Washington, DC, MA, international relations, 1989. **Career:** Pittsburgh Post-Gazette, Pittsburgh, PA, city hall reporter, 1980-84; Baltimore Sun, Baltimore, MD, reporter, 1984-91; Congressional Quarterly, Weekly Report, Washington, DC, reporter, 1991-. **Orgs:** Member, National Assn of Black Journalists, 1980-; member, Society of Environmental Journalists. **Honors/Awds:** Golden Quill Award, Journalism, Pennsylvania Press Assn, 1984.

DAVIS, PRESTON A., JR.
Broadcasting company executive. **Personal:** Born in Norfolk, VA. **Career:** Capital Cities/ABC-TV, pres, Broadcast Operations & Engineering, currently. **Business Addr:** Pres, Broadcast Operations & Engineering, Capital Cities, ABC, 47 W 66th St, New York, NY 10023, (212)456-3456.

DAVIS, PRESTON AUGUSTUS
Association executive. **Personal:** Born in Norfolk, VA; son of Mattie E Davis and Charles A Davis; married Mary Pierson; children: Gwendolyn Dyess, Preston A Jr, Karen Heggs, June Kimbrugh. **Educ:** WV State Coll, BS Bus Administration 1949; Command & Gen Staff Coll, MS Exec Mgmt 1965; George Washington Univ, MSA 1974; Post Graduate, Dartmouth and Harvard. **Career:** Fairmicco Industries, vp/gen mgr 1969-70; Morgan State Univ, vice pres for development 1970-71; US Dept of Agriculture, sr mgmt analyst 1971-78, spl asst to asst sec for adminstrn 1978-79, dir of small & disadvantaged business utilization, 1979-87; Grad Sch & No VA Comm Coll, prof 1974-94; Davis & Davis Consultant Assoc 1989-. **Orgs:** Bd dir & com chmn Agr Fed Credit Union 1972-97; mem Masonic Lodge 1949-; mem Omega Psi Phi Frat 1947-; mem Phi Delta Kappa 1978-92; Kiwanis: gov, 1988-89,(1st black in south), international chairman, young children's priority one progs, 1990-93, Kiwanis Intl, UNICEF cabinet chairman worldwide service program, 1993-95; Kiwanis Intl, ambassador worldwide service project, 1995-2000. **Honors/Awds:** Disting Mil Grad WV State Coll 1949; Outstanding Achievement Award Salvation Army Wash, DC 1976; Cert of Merit for Outstanding Performance US Dept of Agr 1979; Publications, "Firepower Chinese Communist Army" & "Signatures of Soviet Nuclear Missle Systems"; NAFEO Distinguished Alumni Award 1983; Hall of Fame, West VA State Coll, Small Business Administration's Award for Excellence 1984; Alumnus of the Year, West VA State Coll, 1990. **Military Serv:** RA Lt Col 1949-70; Bronze Star; Army Commendation Medal; Purple Heart; Army Meritorious Serv Award; 17 other medals & combat ribbons. **Business Addr:** Davis & Davis Consultant Assoc, 600 6th Pl, SW, Washington, DC 20024.

DAVIS, RAOUL A.
Consultant. **Personal:** Born Jul 4, 1931, Crewe, VA; married Waunetta; children: Tierney, Rianna, Raoul Jr. **Educ:** Central State U, BS Psychology 1954; Columbia U, MA Personnel Psychology 1959; Grad Sch of Pub & Intl Affairs U, Urban League Fellow 1965-67. **Career:** Amityville Inst of small Bus Research & Devel, pres; Center for Life Planning & Career Devel, dir; Davis & Davis & Asso/Cons, pres & sr consult 1979; Suffolk Co Youth Bur Suffolk Col Govt Riverhead NY, dep Dir 1975-79; Manhasset Pub Sch Manhasset NY, com serv Dir 1971-74; Wyandanch Pub Sch NY, comm relations consult 1968-71; OIC Pittsburgh PA, exec dir 1967-68; Dept of Pub Safety Pittsburgh 1966-67; Urban League of Long Island, acting dir 1974-75; Gathering of Beautiful People, exec dir 1976. **Orgs:** Bd of dir Suffolk Comm Council 1969-71; bd of dir Urban & League of Ng Island 1975-79; bd of dir Nassau/Suffolk Health Systems Agency 1976-78. **Honors/Awds:** Fellowships (Scholastic & Athletic) 1st Black to Attend Kiski Prep Schl 194950; urban league fellow Univ of Pittsburgh 1965-67; cert of Appreciation Wyandanch OEO Program Wyandanch Day Care Center 1977-78; plaque for Outstanding Serv Urban League of Long Island 1977. **Military Serv:** AUS corpl 1954-56. **Business Addr:** PO Box 774, Amityville, NY 11701.

DAVIS, REGINALD FRANCIS
Journalist. **Personal:** Born Aug 18, 1951, East Chicago, IN; son of Frances Vivian Hyman Ford (deceased) and James William Davis (deceased); married Toni Diane Holliday Davis, May 11, 1980 (divorced 1994); children: Michael, Andrea, Paul. **Educ:** Purdue University, West Lafayette, IN, BA; Northwestern University, Evanston, IL, masters, management, 1997. **Career:** The Times, Hammond, IN, reporter, 1973-76; The Charlotte Observer, Charlotte, NC, copy editor, 1976-78; The Chicago Tribune, Chicago, IL, 1978-, deputy metro editor, 1987-92, assoc managing editor, currently. **Orgs:** Member, Chicago Assn of Black Journalists, 1988-; member, National Assn of Black Journalists; Soc of Newspaper Design. **Honors/Awds:** Graduate with distinction, Purdue University, 1973; Fellow, Management Training Center, Institute of Journalism Education, 1985. **Business Addr:** Assoc Managing Editor for Photo, Art & Graphics, The Chicago Tribune, 435 N Michigan Ave, Chicago, IL 60611.

DAVIS, REUBEN CORDELL
Professional football player. **Personal:** Born May 7, 1965, Greensboro, NC. **Educ:** North Carolina. **Career:** Tampa Bay Buccaneers, defensive end, 1988-92; San Diego Chargers, 1994-. **Business Addr:** Professional Football Player, San Diego Chargers, Qualcomm Stadium, 9449 Friars Rd, San Diego, CA 92108, (619)280-2111.

DAVIS, REUBEN K.
Judge. **Personal:** Born Jul 26, 1920, Columbus, MS; son of Leola H Adkins and Reuben B Davis; married Elizabeth Zangerle; children: Jennifer, Andrea, Mark. **Educ:** VA State Coll, BA 1946; Boston Univ Law School, LLB 1949. **Career:** Hurst Davis & King, attorney 1955-66; City of Rochester, deputy corp consl 1966-68, comm of bldg 1968-72; Stewart & Bennett Inc, gen counsel 1972-74; Assoc Justice, Appellate div New York State Supreme Court, fourth Judicial Dept 1987-. **Orgs:** Trustee Meml AME Zion Church 1958-, Monroe Cty Bar Assoc 1966; chmn Monroe Cty Human Rel Comm 1966-69; Comm Savings Bank, trustee 1969-74; bd of dir YMCA 1976-; mem NY State & Monroe Cty Bar Assoc. **Military Serv:** AUS 1st lt 1943-46. **Business Addr:** Associate Justice, New York State Supreme Court, Appellate Div 4th Dept, Rm 225 Hall of Justice, Rochester, NY 14614.

DAVIS, RICHARD
Musician, composer. **Personal:** Born Apr 15, 1930, Chicago, IL; son of Elnora Johnson and Robert Johnson; children: Robert, Richard, Joshua, Persia. **Educ:** Vandercook Coll Music Chicago, BME 1952. **Career:** Musician bass player freelance; Univ of WI Madison, prof bass & jazz studies; recordings include, "Philosophy of the Spiritual," "Epistrophy & Now's the Time," "Dealin," "With Understanding," "Muses for Richard Davis"; played with Chicago Civic Orch, Natl Orch Assn, Amer Symphony Orch, Orch of Amer, Igov Stravinsky, Gunther Schuller, Leonard Bernstein, Belgium Radio TV Orch, NY Philharmonic, bass prof Univ of WI, Intl Inst of DBL Bass; jazz groups, Ahmad Jamal, Gene Ammons, Thad Jones, Mel Lewis Orch, Kenny Dorham, Eric Dolphy, Charlie Ventura, Miles Davis, Bud Powell, John Tchas, various other groups; adjucator colls in US & France; string bass player 1945-. **Orgs:** Mem NY Bass Choir 1969-; performed in TV specials w/Barbra Streisand "Like It Is", "Black Journal", NET; film soundtrack "Holy Mountain". **Honors/Awds:** Downbeat Critics Poll Awd 1967-74; Downbeat Readers Poll Awd 1967-72; Outstanding Musician's Awd Vandercook Coll 1979; Outstanding Prof Awd Univ of WI Madison 1978-79; grantee Univ WI-WI Arts Board Natl Endowment Arts; ASCAP Awd 1976-79; compositions include, "Dealin", "Julie's Rag Doll", "Blues for Now"; performed at Newport & Monterey Jazz Festivals. **Business Addr:** Professor, Univ of WI, 4415 Humanities Bldg, Madison, WI 53706.

DAVIS, RICHARD
Attorney. **Personal:** Born Sep 12, 1943, Miami, FL; married Doreen D; children: LaRonda R, Richard QuinRo. **Educ:** Univ of AZ, BS Publ Admin (with Distinction) 1969, JD 1972. **Career:** Univ of AZ Coll of Law, lecturer 1973-; Chandle Tullar Udall & Redhair, assoc attny 1972-80, partner 1980-. **Orgs:** Mem Amer Bar Assoc 1972-, AZ Bar Assoc 1972-; bd of dir So AZ Legal Aid Soc 1975-, Tucson Urban League 1975-, Ododo Theatre 1975-; pres Tucson Urban League 1977-78; bd of dir Pima Cty Bar Assoc 1978-80, Amer Red Cross 1980-83, YMCA 1983-. **Honors/Awds:** Woodrow Wilson Natl Fellowship 1969-72; commiss AZ Athletic Comm 1977-81; mem AZ Civil Rights Comm 1977-78; Distinguished Citizen Awd NAACP Tucson 1982. **Military Serv:** US Air Force E-4 4 yrs. **Home Addr:** 5620 E So Wilshire, Tucson, AZ 85711. **Business Addr:** Attorney, Chandler,Tullar,Udall,Redhair, 33 North Stone #1700, Tucson, AZ 85701.

DAVIS, RICHARD C.
Educator. **Personal:** Born Sep 6, 1925, Los Angeles, CA; married Dolores Parks; children: Saundra, Marilyn, Jacqueline. **Educ:** Geo Pepperdine Coll LA, BA 1952; Compton Coll, AA 1949. **Career:** Sacramento County, Office of Educ, Child Welfare & Attendance Servs, cons; Child Welfare & Attend, Compton Unified School Dist, supt 1970-74; Compton Union School Dist 1967-70; Compton Sr High School, vocational educ counselor 1966-67; Tubman High Schooll, continuing educ guidance counselor 1965-66; Ralph Bunche Jr High School, teacher 1957-65; Willowbrook Jr High School 1952-57; Los Angeles Conty Dept of Parks & Recreation, recreation dir 1948-52. **Orgs:** Pres elct CA Assn Suprvrs Chld Wlfr attended CTA; NEA; Compton Sec Ndry Tchrs Assn; CA Cont Educ Assn; Assn Compton Schls Adminstrators; mem many spec coms in professional capacity; mem LA Co Dist Attys AdvCouncil; cit adv com Reg Planning Commn; agcy exec Com Welfare Planning Council; chmnVandalism Prev Task Frc; chmn Feasibility Study YMCA; mem Del Amo Home Owners Assn; mem Comm Orgn to Study Student Behavior; PTA; bd dir Adv Concercened Cit for Neighborhood; pres Grant, UCa LA 1968. **Honors/Awds:** Nat Jr Coll Track & Field Award; All Pacific Island Champ Football Award. **Military Serv:** USMC corpl 1943-46. **Business Addr:** 1623 E 118 St, Los Angeles, CA 90059.

DAVIS, RICHARD O.
Automobile dealer. **Personal:** son Of Katherine Davis and Richard Davis. **Career:** Davis Buick-Jeep Eagle, Inc, chief exec officer; Davis Automotive Inc, pres, currently.

DAVIS, ROBERT E.
Government official. **Personal:** Born Nov 21, 1908, Kenensville, NC; married Bernice Shaw; children: Sandra Roberta. **Educ:** Fayetteville State U, BS 1936. **Career:** State NC, rep 1978-80; David Bros Wholesale Grocers, co-owner 1940; City of Maxton, city councilman 1972-78; Robesou Co Bd of Edn, tchr 1930-43. **Orgs:** Master Masonic Lodge 86 Maxton 1950-54; illustrous potentate Ouda Temple 147 Shriner 1952-56. **Business Addr:** Davis Bros Wholesale Grocers, Wilmington St, Maxton, NC 28364.

DAVIS, ROBERT E.
Business executive. **Personal:** Born Aug 26, 1937, Indianapolis. **Educ:** Assoc Degreee in Bus Mgmt 1963. **Career:** Fun & Travel Inc, pres; NAACP, youth advisor 1970-71; Addison YWCA, youth advisor 1965-67; Lawson's Dairy Store Cleveland, mgr 1963; Cleveland Public Library, purchsng clrk; Delta & Enterprise, talent booking agent 1967; Lorain Sound Recording Co, pub rel 1969; Jetay Music Publ Co, ow Ner 1970. **Orgs:** Mem Black Hist Inst; NAACP; mem Cleveland Bus League; Nat Assn of TV & Radio Announcers; treas Local 1054, Am Fed of State Co & Municipal Empl Oyees. **Business Addr:** Box 20113, Cleveland, OH 44120.

DAVIS, ROBERT N.
Educator. **Personal:** Born Sep 20, 1953, Kewanee, IL; son of Robert Ezekiel & Rose Davis; married Linda M Williams, Aug 28, 1982; children: Robert L. **Educ:** University of Hartford, BA, 1975; Georgetown University Law School, JD, 1978. **Career:** US Department of Education, attorney; United State Attorney, special assistant; CFTC, attorney; University of MS School of Law, professor, currently. **Orgs:** American Arbitration Association, mediator/arbitrator. **Honors/Awds:** Teacher of the Year, 1990. **Special Achievements:** Founder of Journal of National Security Law. **Military Serv:** US Navy, lt cmdr, 1987-. **Business Addr:** Professor, University of Mississippi, School of Law, University, MS 38677, (601)232-6859.

DAVIS, ROLAND HAYES
Administrator (retired). **Personal:** Born in Cleveland, OH; son of Amaza Dewey Weaver Davis and Sylvester S Davis Sr; divorced; children: Jeffrey, Leslie, Kurt. **Educ:** Western Reserve Univ Cleveland OH, 1946; Hofstra Univ Hempstead NY, 1958; Long Island Univ, BA 1961; Adelphi Univ School of Social Work, MSW 1969. **Career:** Nassau Cty Dept of Soc Srvs, asst to deputy comm 1966-79; Hofstra Univ, coord of comm dev 1979-92, Affirmative Action officer 1988-92; Guardian Bank N A, dir 1975-89. **Orgs:** Chmn board of directors Guardian Bank NA 1975-86; pres Assn of Minority Enterprises of NY Inc 1982-86; president Hempstead Chamber of Commerce 1992-; pres 100 Black Men of Nassau/Suffolk Inc 1980-86; dir Health & Welfare Council of Nassau Cty Inc 1983-91; bd dir United Way of Long Island 1982-88; bd trustees Sci Museum of Long Island 1984-85; life mem Hempstead Branch NAACP; treasurer EDGES Group Inc, 1990-. **Honors/Awds:** Unispan Award Hofstra Univ 1979; HUB Summer Career Awareness Prog 1980; Ldrshp Award LI Minority Bus Comm 1981; NYS Legislative Resolution Citation 1983; NOAH Prog Hofstra Univ 1984; Pres Recognition Award for Comm Srv 1984. **Military Serv:** AUS 1st lt 1946-66.

DAVIS, RONALD
Construction company executive. **Educ:** Tri-State Design Construction Co Inc, CEO, 1981-. **Career:** Tri-State Design Construction Co In, CEO, currently. **Special Achievements:** Company is ranked #89 on the Black Enterprise list of Top industrial/service companies, 1994. **Business Addr:** CEO, Tri-State Design Construction Co. Inc., 550 Pinetown Rd., Fort Washington, PA 19034.

DAVIS, RONALD P.
Corporate manager. **Personal:** Born May 29, 1949, Montgomery, AL; son of Princess A Davis and William W Davis; married Tinny B Jones; children: Ronald Prince, Tracye Belinda. **Educ:** Southern IL Univ, BS 1971; MS Coll, MBA 1975. **Career:** South Central Bell, sales mgr 1972-74, mgr emp/coord 1974-77, operations mgr I&M 1977-83; AT&T, district mgr/csso 1983-1987; district manager-training 1987-89, district security mgr, 1989-91; Brookings Institution, congressional fellow, 1992-. **Orgs:** Pres Alpha Phi Alpha/Epsilon Lambda Chap 1977-79; bd mem Metropolitan YMCA 1979-83, Jackson MS Public Schools 1981-83, Hinds Co Human Resources Agency 1981-; mem Sigma Pi Phi Frat 1981-; pres Jackson MS Urban League 1983; exec committee, FIINA. **Honors/Awds:** Service Appreciation Awd Jackson Professional Educators 1983. **Business Addr:** District Security Manager, AT&T, 20 Independence Blvd, Ste 4B08, Warren, NJ 07059.

DAVIS, RONALD R.
Organization executive. **Personal:** Born Feb 5, 1942, New York, NY; son of Lauribel Diana Davis and Stanley A Davis; married Jean Williams Davis; children: Yvette, Pamela. **Educ:** City College, accounting. **Career:** RCA, section mgr; Afro-American Vegetarian Society, New York, president, 1976-. **Business Addr:** President, Afro-American Vegetarian Society, PO Box 46, Colonial Park Station, New York, NY 10039.

DAVIS, RONALD W.
Business executive. **Personal:** Born Sep 16, 1950, Camden, NJ; son of Emma Davis and Arthur Davis; married Willabel; children: Ronald W II. **Educ:** VA State U, BS 1968-72, MED 1973-75. **Career:** San Fran 49ers, football plyr 1972; St Louis Cardinals, football plyr 1972-76; United VA Bank, retail/oper officer 1976-84; Metro Richmond Conven & Visitors Bureau, deputy executive dir, currently. **Orgs:** Pres of bd dir VA State Univ Found 1979-85; bd of dir Metropolitan Business League 1977-84; mem NFL Players Assn 1976-85; Guilfield Church Finance Bd 1985-89. **Honors/Awds:** All Am NCAA Div II 1972; Man of the Yr Hlth Phys Ed & Recreation 1972; Top 10 in Ricmond, Richmond Surroundings Mag; VA State Univ Sports Hall of Fame 1989.

DAVIS, RUSSELL ANDRE
Educational administrator. **Personal:** Born Sep 16, 1958, Wilmington, DE; son of Warren and Alberta Davis. **Educ:** Hampton University, BA, 1980, MA, 1982; University of Maryland, MEd, 1989, EdD, 1992. **Career:** The Washington School for Secretaries, dean of students, 1983-86; Howard University, instructor of English, 1986-88; Bowie State University, adjunct faculty, English department, 1988-, coordinator for psychological services, 1989-90, director of counseling & student development, 1990-92; vice president for student & academic services, currently. **Orgs:** National Council of Teachers of English, 1986-; Maryland Assn for Multicultural Counseling & Development, president, 1988-92; National Education Assn, 1980-; Health Care for the Homeless, 1993-; American College Testing Council, chair, 1986-. **Honors/Awds:** Prince George's Community College, Master Teacher's of English Distinction, 1992; Washington School for Secretaries, Instructor of the Year, 1984; Bowie State University, Outstanding Male Administrator, 1994. **Business Addr:** Vice President for Student and Academic Services, Bowie State University, 14000 Jericho Park Rd., Henry Admin Bldg, Rm 0135, Bowie, MD 20715-9465.

DAVIS, RUTH A.
Educational administrator. **Career:** Foreign Service Institute, director, currently. **Special Achievements:** First African American woman to direct Foreign Service Institute. **Business Addr:** Director, Foreign Service Institute, 4000 Arlington Blvd, Arlington, VA 22204, (703)302-6703.

DAVIS, SAMMY, JR.
Educator, mayor. **Personal:** Born Oct 2, 1930, Ferriday, LA; married Elizabeth A; children: Sammy III, Craig Fenton. **Educ:** Grambling State Univ, BS 1954; Southern Univ Baton Rouge, MA 1967. **Career:** Teacher, Breauybridge LA 1954-57, Ferriday LA 1957; Concordia Parish, principal 1967-74 police juror; Concordia Parish Educ Assn, pres 1971-73. **Orgs:** Mem LEA-NEA; Kappa Alpha Psi; NAACP; Helping Hand; Police Jury Assn; Educ Comm of States; natl Assn of Counties; mem Concordia Parish Civil League; Student Bar Assn; mem, Jamadi Temple #171 (A.E.A.O.N.M.E. Inc); mem, Louis R Price Consistory 32 Prince Hall. **Honors/Awds:** Award for Outstanding Achievements in Politics; Special Award LEA-NEA. **Military Serv:** AUS sgt 1951-53. **Home Addr:** P O Box 444, Ferriday, LA 71334.

DAVIS, SAMUEL C.
Journalist. **Personal:** Born Dec 10, 1959, Baltimore, MD; son of Sam & Mammie Davis; married Gina Marie Davis, Oct 8, 1994. **Educ:** Community College of Baltimore, 1981; Coppin State College, 1983. **Career:** Baltimore Sun, editorial assistant, 1980, sports reporter, 1984, local sports editor, 1992, assistant sports editor, deputy sports editor. **Orgs:** Christian Memorial Church, trustee. **Honors/Awds:** Carver High School, Hall of Fame. **Business Addr:** Deputy Sports Editor, Baltimore Sun, 501 N Calvert St, Baltimore, MD 21278.

DAVIS, SANDRA B.
Librarian. **Personal:** Born Nov 10, 1947, Chicago, IL; daughter of Mattie McGuire Matthews and Aubrey D Matthews; married Ali S Mohammad; children: Nena, Christopher. **Educ:** Chicago State Coll, Chicago, IL, BA, 1971; University of Illinois at Urbana-Champaign, Urbana, IL, MS, 1973. **Career:** The Chicago Public Library, Chicago, IL, librarian I, first asst, 1976-77, librarian I, branch head, 1977-80, librarian I, unit head, 1980-82, librarian II, reference asst, 1982-93, reference, 1993-. **Orgs:** Member, Black Caucus of ALA, 1978-; member 1979-, chair-elect 1981-82, chair 1983, Chicago Chapter, Black Caucus of the ALA. **Business Addr:** Librarian II, The Chicago Public Library, HWLC, 400 S State St, Chicago, IL 60605.

DAVIS, SHEILA PARHAM
Educator. **Personal:** Born Nov 30, 1954, Sumter, SC; daughter of Mattie Mae Garvin Parham and James Franklin Parham Sr; married Dr Melvin Davis, Aug 19, 1973; children: Deia Deneace, Danyetta Denise. **Educ:** University of South Carolina, Columbia, SC, ASN, 1973-75; University of Alabama Huntsville, Huntsville, AL, BSN, 1983-84; University of Alabama Birmingham, Birmingham, AL, MSN (cardiovascular nursing), 1984-85; Georgia State University, Atlanta, GA, PhD in Nursing Education, 1993. **Career:** Huntsville Hospital, Huntsville, AL, critical care nurse, 1983-85; University of Alabama, Birmingham, AL, instructor, 1985-89, assistant prof, 1989-. **Orgs:** Director at Large, South Central Association of Black SDA Nurses, 1988-; education committee chair, Alabama League for Nurses, 1988-90; medical temperance leader, South Park SAC Church, 1988-; publication-communication committee, Association of Black Nurses Higher Ed, 1989-. **Honors/Awds:** Honor Graduate, University of Alabama Huntsville, 1984; Inducted in National Honor Society of Nurses, Sigma Theta Tau, 1984; Faculty Recognition Award, University of Alabama at Birmingham, 1988; Fellowship for PhD, National Consortium for Educational Access, 1989-; Fellowship for PhD, American Nurses Association, 1989-; Young Publisher Award, ABNF; Medical Officer Real Truth Ministries, Inc. **Home Addr:** PO Box 1372, Washington, MS 39190.

DAVIS, SHIRLEY E.
Labor industrial relations manager (retired). **Personal:** Born Feb 23, 1935, New Haven, CT; married Eldridge Davis Jr; children: Annette S Sands. **Educ:** Attended Morgan State Coll Baltimore 1953-54; attended Quinnipiac Coll New Haven 1956-58; attended So CT State Coll. **Career:** US Postal Serv, distrib clerk/postal data systems tech 1958-90; Natl Alliance of Postal & Federal Employees, natl secty. **Orgs:** Dist 8 pres NAPFE 1972-80; mem Natl Exec NAPFE Bd 1972-91; bd of dirs Urban League of Greater New Haven 1974-80; commr Commn on Equal Oppor New Haven 1975-; vice chairperson Commn on Equal Oppor New Haven 1977-80; Civil Service Board, New Haven, CT, 1992-97, chairman, 1992-94. **Honors/Awds:** First Black Female Career Employee New Haven PO 1958; First Female Pres NAPFE Local 811 New Haven 1969; First Female Pres NAPFE Dist 8 1972; First Female Natl Sec NAPFE 1980; One of the Highest Ranking Women US Labor Movement.

DAVIS, STEPHEN
Professional football player. **Personal:** Born Mar 1, 1974, Spartanburg, SC. **Educ:** Auburn, bachelor's degree in vocational education. **Career:** Washington Redskins, running back, 1996-. **Business Addr:** Professional Football Player, Washington Redskins, 13832 Redskin Dr, Herndon, VA 22071, (703)471-9100.

DAVIS, STEPHEN SMITH
Educator. **Personal:** Born Oct 24, 1910, Philadelphia; married Aileen Priscilla Harris; children: Stephen Harris. **Educ:** Howard U, BS in Mech Engineering 1936; Harvard U, MS Mech 1947. **Career:** Howard Univ, faculty, mechanical engineering prof 1938, dept head 1962, dean School of Engineering & Architecture 1964-70; Natl Bureau Standards, mechanical engineer 1943-45; Naval Ordinance Lab, consultant 1953-63. **Orgs:** Mem Washington Acad Sci; Am Soc ME; AAAS; Am Soc Engineering Edn; DC Soc Professional Engrs mem Tau Beta Pi; Cosmos, WA. **Honors/Awds:** Invented with patent Flexible Wing-tunnel Nozzle.

DAVIS, SUSAN D.
Judge. **Educ:** Norfolk State Univ, grad; College of William & Mary, Marshall Wythe School of Law, JD. **Career:** Judge Lawrence M. Lawson, Monmouth County Superior Court, law clerk, 1987-88; Giordano, Halleran & Ciesla, P.C., 1988-96, partner, 1996; City of Asbury Park, public defender, 1989-93; State of NJ, US magistrate, currently. **Orgs:** Dist IX, Ethics Comm, 1991-94, chair, 1995; Supreme Court, Adv Comm on Professional Ethics. **Special Achievements:** First African American female US magistrate in NJ; second woman US magistrate in NJ; youngest judge appointed to federal bench in NJ. **Business Addr:** US Magistrate Judge, 39 Sycamore Ave, Little Silver, NJ 07739, (732)345-5100.

DAVIS, TARA
Professional basketball player. **Personal:** Born Sep 25, 1972. **Educ:** Univ of Washington, bachelor's degree in general studies, 1995. **Career:** Seattle Reign, guard, 1997-98; New England Blizzard, 1998-. **Business Addr:** Professional Basketball Player, New England Blizzard, Hartford/Springfield, 179 Allyn St, Ste 403, Hartford, CT 06103, (860)522-4667.

DAVIS, TERRELL
Professional football player. **Personal:** Born Oct 28, 1972, San Diego, CA. **Educ:** Georgia. **Career:** Denver Broncos, running back, 1995-. **Honors/Awds:** Football Digest, Rookie of the Year, 1995; Pro Football Weekly, All-Rookie Team, 1995; Football News, All-Rookie Team, 1995; Associated Press, NFL Offensive Player of the Year; Sports Illustrated, NFL Player of the Year; UPI, NFL Player of the Year. **Business Addr:** Professional Football Player, Denver Broncos, 13655 Broncos Pkwy, Englewood, CO 80112, (303)649-9000.

DAVIS, TERRY RAYMOND
Professional basketball player. **Personal:** Born Jun 17, 1967, Danville, VA. **Educ:** Virginia Union Univ, Richmond, VA, 1985-89. **Career:** Miami Heat, forward-center, 1989-91; Dallas Mavericks, 1991-97; Washington Wizards, 1997-. **Business Addr:** Professional Basketball Player, Washington Wizards, MCI Center, 601 F St NW, Washington, DC 20071, (301)622-3865.

DAVIS, THEODIS C. (TED)
Marketing executive. **Personal:** Born Aug 19, 1946, Little Rock, AR; son of Tommy B & Matilda Davis; married Faye E Davis, Dec 26, 1966; children: Jessica, Ericka, Alyson. **Educ:** Indiana University, masters, 1976. **Career:** Hankscrafts Motors, general manager; Gerber Products; area manager, Chicago district; director of sales-baby care; director marketing-baby care; vp, baby care marketing, currently. **Orgs:** Urban League, Muskegon, MI, bd chairman; Kappa Alpha Psi Fraternity; Frontiers International Service Club; Kiwanis Intl; West Shore Symphony, bd member. **Honors/Awds:** Numerous service and professional awards. **Military Serv:** US Air Force, staff sgt, 1964-68. **Business Addr:** Vice President, Baby Care-Marketing, Gerber Products Co, 445 State St, Fremont, MI 49413, (616)928-2167.

DAVIS, THOMAS JOSEPH
Educator. **Personal:** Born Jan 6, 1946, New York, NY; son of Alice Rozina McKenzie Davis and Otto Joseph Davis. **Educ:** SUNY at Buffalo, JD 1993; Ball State Univ, MA 1976; Columbia Univ, PhD 1974, MA 1968; Fordham Univ, AB 1967. **Career:** Columbia Univ, instr, 1968; Southern Univ, instr 1968-69; Manhattanville Coll, dir Afro-Amer stud 1970-71; Earlham Coll, assoc/asst prof 1972-76; Howard Univ, prof/assoc prof 1977-87; State Univ of NY at Buffalo, prof, 1986-96; Arizona State Univ, prof, 1996-. **Orgs:** Bd mem New York City Council Against Poverty 1965-67; consultant Natl Endowment for Humanities 1980, Educational Testing Serv 1979-88, US Dept of Labor 1978-79; exec bd St Camillus Church 1983-86, Humboldt Journal of Soc Rel 1980-88, Journal of Negro History 1974-; Pennsylvania History, 1986-88; Law and History Review, 1996-. **Honors/Awds:** Fellow Ford Found 1971, Herbert H Lehman 1969-71; Fulbright 1972, 1994; Francis Cardinal Spellman Youth Award 1962; Newberry Library Fellow 1982; Smithsonian Inst Faculty Fellow 1983; Alpha Kappa Alpha, Gamma Iota Chapter, Educator of the Year, 1982; NY African American Inst, 1986, 1987; Amer Bar Found, Visiting Fellow, 1994-95. **Special Achievements:** Author, A Rumor of Revolt, New York: Macmillian/Free Press, 1985, UMass, 1990; Africans in the Americas, NY, St Martin's Press, 1994. **Business Addr:** Professor, Arizona State University, Dept of History, Box 872501, Tempe, AZ 85287-2501.

DAVIS, THURMAN M., SR.
Government official. **Personal:** Born Oct 11, 1936, Raleigh, NC; son of John C & Elizabeth Davis, Sr; married Loretta White Davis, Jun 24, 1965; children: Thurman Jr, Cynthia, Stephanie. **Educ:** Hampton Univ, 1960. **Career:** US Gen Svcs Admin, proj dir; Dalton Dalton Little Newport, proj mgr, assoc, 1973-79; US Gen Svcs Admin, exec asst to commissioner, PBS, 1979-83, real property operations, 1983-84, asst regional admin, 1984-94, regional admin, 1994-96, deputy admin, 1996-. **Orgs:** Alpha Phi Alpha Fraternity, Inc, life mem, 1958-; National American Society for Pub Admin, 1989-; National Forum of Black Pub Administrators, 1993-; 100 Black Men of Greater Washington, DC, 1995-. **Honors/Awds:** President of US, President Rank of Distinguished Executive, 1997; President of US, President Rank of Meritorious Executive, 1988, 1994. **Military Serv:** US Army, 1st lt, 1960-61. **Home Addr:** 14924 Emory Ln, Rockville, MD 20853, (301)460-1050. **Business Addr:** Deputy Administrator, US General Services Administration, 1800 F St, NW, GS Bldg, Ste 6137, Washington, DC 20405, (202)501-1226.

DAVIS, TRAVIS HORACE
Professional football player. **Personal:** Born Jan 10, 1973, Harbor City, CA; children: David. **Educ:** Univ of Notre Dame, bachelor's degree in psychology, 1997. **Career:** Jacksonville Jaguars, defensive back, 1995-. **Business Addr:** Professional Football Player, Jacksonville Jaguars, One Stadium Place, Jacksonville, FL 32202, (904)633-6000.

DAVIS, TROY
Professional football player. **Personal:** Born Sep 14, 1975. **Educ:** Iowa State. **Career:** New Orleans Saints, running back, 1997-. **Business Addr:** Professional Football Player, New Orleans Saints, 5800 Airline Hwy, Metairie, LA 70003, (504)733-0255.

DAVIS, TWILUS
Clergyman. **Educ:** Friendship Coll Rockhill SC, DD. **Career:** The Promiseland Bapt Church Caldwell St, N Memphis, pastor 1910 friendship baptist church buffalo, pastor 1929; promiseland baptist church buffalo, pastor; Erie Cnty Pen Old Folks Infirmary, fndr. **Orgs:** 1st Negro Poltcl Club Buffalo; 1st Minstrs Conf; 1st Dist Assn Buffalo Sp L & Achvmt Fndr 8th Grade Schl. **Honors/Awds:** Hon plaque Cncl & Empire St Bapt Conv NYC; prsntd key city of memphis. **Business Addr:** Promiseland Bapt Ch, 243 Mulberry, Buffalo, NY 14204.

DAVIS, TYRONE
Professional football player. **Personal:** Born Jun 30, 1972, Halifax, VA. **Educ:** Virginia. **Career:** New York Jets, tight end, 1995-96; Green Bay Packers, 1997-. **Business Addr:** Professional Football Player, Green Bay Packers, 1265 Lombardi Ave, Green Bay, WI 54304, (414)494-2351.

DAVIS, TYRONE THEOPHILUS
Comptroller. **Personal:** Born Dec 10, 1948, Kansas City, KS; son of Sara A Richardson Davis and Morris T Davis; widowed; children: Monette M, Natalie R, Tyrena E. **Educ:** Univ of Cincinnati, BBA 1970; Lexington Theological Seminary, M Divinity 1976. **Career:** Lexington-Fayette Co, exec dir 1972-74; Phillips Memorial CME Church, sr pastor 1972-76; Urban League of St Louis, accountant 1977-82; Parrish Temple CME Church, sr pastor 1976-79; Jamison Mem CME Church, sr pastor 1979-82; CME Church, admin coord 1982-86; Wesley CME Church, sr pastor 1986-88; Congress of Natl Black Churches, comptroller, 1988-. **Orgs:** Life mem Alpha Phi Alpha Frat 1968-; mem Lexington Fayette Co 1973-76; treas KY Council of Churches 1974-76; former treas KY Conf of NAACP Chapts 1975-76; mem Natl Assoc of Black Accountants 1981-91; treas Beloit Branch NAACP 1986-; pres Beloit Cmm Ministers Fellowship 1987-88. **Honors/Awds:** 110% Awd Merit Alpha Phi Alpha Frat 1976; Hon KY Col State of KY 1976; GW Carver Awd Sigma Gamma Rho Sor 1984. **Business Addr:** Comptroller, Congress of National Black Churches, 1225 Eye St NW, Ste 750, Washington, DC 20005.

DAVIS, WALTER JACKSON, JR.
Military officer. **Personal:** Born Aug 1, 1936, Winston-Salem, NC; married Constance Surles; children: Sharon, Kimberly. **Educ:** Naval Postgraduate School, BS, MS, Aeronautical Engineering. **Career:** Commander, Carrier Group Six; Commandant, Naval Dist Washington 1988-90; Naval Flag Officer, 1988; Special Asst to the Chief of Naval Operations, 1987; Commanding Officer of USS Ranger, 1985-87; Exec Asst to the Deputy Chief of Naval Operations, 1983; Commander, USS Sacramento, 1981; Asst Program Mgr, 1977. **Honors/Awds:** Legion of Merit w/two Gold Stars, Meritorious Serv Medal, Air Medal (ten awards); Navy Commendation Medal w/Combat "V"; Meritorious Unit Commendation, Battle "E" Ribbon, Navy Expeditionary Medal w/three Bronze Stars; Natl Defense Serv Medal, Armed Forces Expeditionary Medal with three Bronze Stars; Sea Serv Deployment Ribbon (two awards); Vietnamese Gallentry Cross with Bronze Star; Republic of Vietnam Meritorious Unit Citation; Vietnam Campaign Medal.

DAVIS, WALTER PAUL (SWEET D)
Public relations administrator. **Personal:** Born Sep 9, 1954, Pineville, NC; married Susan Hatter; children: Hillary Elyse, Jordan Elizabeth. **Educ:** Univ of North Carolina, attended 1973-77. **Career:** Guard: Phoenix Suns, 1977-88, Denver Nuggets, 1989-92; Denver Nuggets, community ambassador, 1992-. **Honors/Awds:** Member, Gold-Medal winning US Olympic Basketball Team Montreal, 1976; Rookie of the Year, 1977-78; Pro Athlete of Year, Phoenix Press Box Assn 1979; 5-time member, Western Conf All-Star Team; member, 37th NBA All Star Team. **Business Addr:** Community Ambassador, Denver Nuggets, 1635 Clay St, Denver, CO 80204.

DAVIS, WANDA M.
Educational administrator. **Personal:** Born Nov 9, 1952, Philadelphia, PA; daughter of Viola S Davis. **Educ:** PA State Univ, BS 1974, MPA 1980, Doctorate 1992. **Career:** YWCA, program planning coordinator 1974-75; Lincoln Univ, residential dir 1975-78; PA State Univ, counselor 1978-84, asst dean of students 1984-89, interim dean of students, 1987-89; asst dean of judicial affairs 1989-, sr research associate, 1988-89. **Orgs:** NAFEO, mem 1980-; American Assoc of Higher Educ, mem 1980-; PA Coll Personnel Assoc 1980-; Phi Delta Kappa, vice pres, mem 1982-83; NAACP, chair, Rorbert A Davis Found, 1989-; AAUW. **Honors/Awds:** CWENS, honorary candidate for academic standing 1972; Woodrow Wilson, fellow 1981.

DAVIS, WARREN B.
Educator. **Personal:** Born Sep 16, 1947, Gary, IN; son of Armenta Davis and Richard Davis; children: Kwame Inhatep; Ida Aisha. **Educ:** Bowling Green State U, MA 1971, BA 1970; Defiance Coll, BA 1970; Developmental Educational Specialists, Appalachian State Univ 1984. **Career:** Bowling Green State U, assoc Dir student devel; Student Devel Prog, coord counseling serv 1973; Defiance Coll, instr Afro-am Hist II 1973; Student Devel Prog, counselor 1971-72; Neighborhood Youth Corps, supvr; Mid-town Coffee Hse, Gary Youth Activities, prog dir Trends in Afro-Am Thought, tchr 1969; USS Steel, laborer part time 1967-69; Coordinator University of Toledo Tutorial Services, Supervisor Career Planning Center; asst dir Academic Support Serv. **Orgs:** Mem Am Pers & Guid Assn 1971; Assn of Counselor Educ & Supvision 1971; Minority Educ Serv Assn of OH; Natl Assn for Developmental Education; Bd of directors Coalition for quality Integrated Education. **Honors/Awds:** Recip Serv Award to Minority Students; BGSU 1974; serv BGSU 1977; Administrator of the Year BSU 1983.

DAVIS, WENDELL
Professional football player. **Personal:** Born Jun 27, 1973, Wichita, KS. **Educ:** Univ of Oklahoma, attended. **Career:** Dallas Cowboys, wide receiver, 1996-. **Business Addr:** Professional Football Player, Dallas Cowboys, One Cowboys Pkwy, Irving, TX 75063, (214)556-9900.

DAVIS, WILEY M.
Educational administrator (retired). **Personal:** Born Dec 4, 1927, Meadowview, VA; son of Pearl Fitzsimmons Davis and William Jackson Davis; married Mary Hargrove; children: Wiley Jr. **Educ:** Swift Jr Coll, AA; St Augustines Coll, BA; Springfield Coll, MEd; Brigham Young Univ, DEd. **Career:** Meadowview Elementary School, teacher 1947; History, instructor 1952; Douglas HS, teacher 1953, principal 1956; St Augustine's Coll, dean of students 1960, admin asst to pres 1970, vice pres for admin 1973; vice pres for Student Affairs, 1974-. **Orgs:** Sec Elizabethton Principal Assoc; treas, pres Phi Beta Sigma; mem Raleigh, NC Community Action Council, Govt Comm on Employment of Handicapped, Phi Delta Kappa Hon Soc, NC Cemetery Commn; Hospice of Wake County, Deacon, Martin St Baptist Church. **Honors/Awds:** Honorary mem St Augustines Coll Vet Club; Phi Beta Sigma Achievement Award; Henry Street Settlement's Thomas Higgs Operation Athlete Education Award. **Military Serv:** AUS 1951-53.

DAVIS, WILLIAM AUGUSTA, III
Professional football player. **Personal:** Born Jul 6, 1972, El Paso, TX. **Educ:** Pittsburgh, attended. **Career:** Dallas Cowboys, wide receiver, 1995-. **Business Addr:** Professional Football Player, Dallas Cowboys, One Cowboys Pkwy, Irving, TX 75063, (214)556-9900.

DAVIS, WILLIAM E., SR.
Architect, urban/regional planner. **Personal:** Born Dec 1, 1930, Camden, SC; son of Margaret White-Davis (deceased) and Clarence Davis Sr (deceased); married Jacqueline Hawkins (divorced); children: William, Jr, Victor (deceased), Brian. **Educ:** Howard Univ, BArch 1967; Columbia Univ, Pratt Inst of NY, MIT, grad studies; City & Regional Planning Pratt Inst, MS 1976. **Career:** US Treas Dept, 1958-66; RC Architects & Assocs, des & ofc mgr 1967-68; F&M Shaefer Corp Brooklyn, arch designer 1968-69; Brownsville Adv Planning Agency, planner 1969-70; Urban Consultants Inc, vice pres, 1969-75; Volmer Assocs NY, arch & planner 1971; City of Boston Model City Admin, chief phys planning 1972-75; Boston Model City, asst adminst 1975; Onyx Consultants Inc, pres, 1975-76; Massachusetts Dept of Public Works, Bureau of Transportaion and Planning Development, regional planner, 1976; US Dept of Housing & Urban Develop, loan specialist 1977-80; US Dept of Trans Federal Trans Admin, comm planner 1980-87, program manager 1987-. **Orgs:** Mem Conf MA Planning Dirs 1973-75; mem Amer Soc Planning Officials 1969-77; mem Natl Tech Assn 1968-75; founder, chair of graduate students, Black Planners Network of NY 1970; mem Comm Vol Assn for Educ Adv of our Children 1971; housing chmn Roxbury Neighborhood Devel Counc of Boston 1975; prog mgr SW Corridor Land Develop Coalition Proj in Boston 1971-75; Dedham MA town mem Title I Educ Adv Council 1975-76; Greater Manchester Branch NAACP; mem Greater Manchester Black Scholarship Foundation 1987-; mem Martin Luther King Jr Speakers Bureau 1987-89; president, Levi and Penelopia Kirkland Family Assn, 1990-94; planning bd, Town of Auburn, NH, 1987-89. **Honors/Awds:** Martin L King Fellow 1969-71; Commendation for Urban Planning & Development in Boston; Volpe National Transportation Center, Director's Award for EEO. **Military Serv:** AUS 1955-57. **Business Addr:** Program Manager for Operations & Management, US Dept Trans/Federal Transit Administration, 55 Broadway, Ste 904, Cambridge, MA 02142.

DAVIS, WILLIAM HAYES, SR.
Educational therapist. **Personal:** Born Jun 13, 1947, Richmond, VA; married Ivy P West; children: William Jr. **Educ:** Virginia State Univ, BA 1970; Virginia Commonwealth Univ, MEd 1983. **Career:** Gooehland Public Schools, teacher 1972-73; Commonwealth Psychiatric Ctr, ed therapist 1974-79; St Joseph's Villa, ed therapist 1979-81; Garfield Childs Memorial Fund, prog dir 1983-85; VA State Univ, sp educ coll instructor 1986-; Richmond Public Schools, clinical teacher 1981-. **Orgs:** Mem NAACP 1980-; guide right prog dir 1980-84, asst keeper of records 1984-85, Kappa Alpha Psi Inc Rich Alumni; co-owner Assessment Then Remediation 1986-. **Honors/Awds:** Outstanding Leadership Guide Right Kappa Alpha Psi Rich Alumni 1982; Service to the Frat Ach Awd Kappa Alpha Psi Rich Alumni 1983; Inst for Educ Leadership Awd Rich Public Schs 1984-85. **Military Serv:** ANG sp4 1970-76; Certificate of Training Achievement, Outstanding Performance of Duty 1970. **Home Addr:** 2500 Hawthrone Ave, Richmond, VA 23222.

DAVIS, WILLIAM L.
Association executive. **Personal:** Born Dec 30, 1933, Hopewell, VA; married Glenice Claiborne; children: Kevin, Todd. **Educ:** Morgan State Coll, AB 1955; Howard U, JD 1961. **Career:** United Planning Orgn, exec dir; UPO Washington DC, gen counsel 1970-73; Howard U, prof of law 1972; Neighborhood Legal Serv Prog Inc & Washington, acting exec dir 1969-70; NLSP, desp dir 1968-69; US Atty,asst 1965-68; US Dept of Justice DC, trial atty 1961-65; US Dept Navy, law clerk gen counsel 1960. **Orgs:** Mem Washington Bar Assn; Howard Law Sch Alumni Assn; mem bd of dir Independence Serv Corp; mem bd of dir Natl Children's Island Inc; mem Bd Dir UPO Enterprises Inc; mem bd dir UPO Comm Dev Corp Editor-in-chief; Howard Law Journal 1960-61; Class Pres 1960. **Honors/Awds:** Bureau of Nat Affairs Award; Bancroft-whitney Co & Lawyer's Cooperative Publishing Co Award; Legal Writings 6 How L J 90 1960; 6 How L J 213, 1960; 7 HoW LJ 65, 1961.

DAVIS, WILLIAM R.
Educator. **Personal:** Born Apr 28, 1921, Cincinnati, OH; son of Florence Davis and William Davis; married Gladys Hamilton; children: William R, Jr. **Educ:** Univ of Cincinnati, BS 1950; OH State Univ, MA 1951; Northeastern IL Univ, MA 1969; Loyola Univ, doctoral candidate. **Career:** Cincinnati Public Recreation Commn, 1947-54; Chicago Public Schools, teacher, asst principal; Oldtown Chicago Boys Club, athletic dir & prog dir 1954-68; Loyola Univ of Chicago, dir Project Upward Bound, instructor, Curriculum and Instruction 1969-. **Orgs:** Pres Council for College Attend 1970-74; chmn Chicago Nat Coll Fair (NACAC) 1973-75 & 1978-80; mem bd dir IL Assn of Coll Admission Counselors 1974-76; pres I1L Assn for Non-White Concerns in Pers & Guidance 1977-78; pres IL Assn of Coll Admission Counselors 1981-82; mem Amer Sch Health Assn; Am Assn of Univ Profs; Nat Assn for Higher Edn; Nat Assn of Coll Admiss Counselors; Phi Epsilon Kappa; Phi Delta Kappa; Nat Upward Bound Steering Com 1970-72; Assn for Superv and Curriculum Dev; Am Assn for Counseling and Dev (APGA); midwest reg rep Assn for Non-White Concerns in Counseling and Dev; mem IL State Board of Educ Advisory Bd for Pupil Personnel Svcs. **Honors/Awds:** Presidential Award Mid-Amer Assn of Educ Opportunity Program Personnel 1979; Presidential Awardd IL Assoc of Coll Admissions Counselors 1982; Presidential Citation Assoc for Multicultural Counseling & Devel 1984; Human Relations Award Natl Assn of Coll Admissions Counselors 1984; Hon Degree Doctor of Humanities Monrovia Coll Monrovia Liberia West Africa 1986. **Military Serv:** AUS Corpl 1942-46; USAR 1st Lt 1950-64. **Business Addr:** Dir Project Upward Bound, Loyola University, 6525 N Sheridan Rd, Chicago, IL 60626.

DAVIS, WILLIAM R.
Physician. **Personal:** Born Oct 4, 1934, Newport News, VA; son of Mollie Davis Clarke; married Brenda Lightsay Davis; children: William Jr, Cardis, Tonia Kelly, Frank, Joye. **Educ:** Hampton Inst, BS 1956; Med Coll of VA, MD 1964. **Career:** Fitzsimons Hosp, Denver, intern; Brooke Army Med Cntr, San

Antonio, resident; Johns Hopkins Med Sch, instr pediatrics 1972; Baltimore, pvt prac Pediatrics 1969; Univ of S CA, res fellow, allergy immunology 1985; Howard Univ Coll of Med, asst clincal prof pediatrics 1968-69; DeWitt Army Hosp, asst chief pediatrics 1967-68; Dept of Navy, res chemist 1956-60; Loma Linda Univ Sch of Med, asst prof, currently; VA Hospital, chief, allergy & immunology section, Loma Linda, currently. **Orgs:** Mem Omega Psi Phi Frat; Chi Delta Mu Frat; hon Alumnus Johns Hopkins U; mem Beta Kappa Chi; hon Scienlike Soc; diplomate Nat Bd of Med Examiners; diplomate, Am Bd of Pediatrics; fellow Am Acad of Pediatrics, NMA; fellow, Am Bd of Allergy and Immunology; fellow, Am Assn of Certified Allergists. **Honors/Awds:** Recip Award for Metit Svc; Providtne Comp Health Cntr 1971. **Military Serv:** AUS maj m c 1964-72 (retired). **Business Addr:** Asst Prof of Medicine, Loma Linda University Medical School, 11201 Benton St, Loma Linda, CA 92357.

DAVIS, WILLIAM W., SR.
Computer company executive. **Career:** Pulsar Data Systems Inc, CEO, currently. **Special Achievements:** Company is ranked #14 on The Black Enterprise List of Top 100 Industrial/Service Companies, 1994. **Business Phone:** 800-775-7374.

DAVIS, WILLIE A.
Educator, coach. **Personal:** Born Dec 10, 1948, Marks, MS; married Barbara M Landry. **Educ:** Coahoma Jr Coll, AA; Jackson State U, MS 1967, BA; Western MI Univ MI, MA 1974, MS 1970. **Career:** Neighborhood Youth Core, Jackson MS, summer counselor 1970; Jackson Public Schools, Mar-Jun teacher 1970; Albion Public Schools, Albion MI, teacher, coach Football/Track, summers 1973-74. **Orgs:** Pres NAACP Albion Branch; mem Albion Educ Assn; Educ Assoc; mem Twin Athletic Assn; mem HS Coaches Assn; mem Albion United Fund Bd; mem & pres Albion NAACP; mem US Jaycees; mem Big Brothers Am; mem SS Supt Tchr Behtl Bapt Ch; mem Phi Beta Sigma Frat Inc. **Honors/Awds:** Honor student Quitman Co HS 1961-65; honor student Coahma Jr Coll 1965-67; honor student Jackson State Univ 1967-1970; 1974 Nominee Educ Yr; Albion Distinguished Service Award nominee 1974; Albions Distinguished Serv Award 1975. **Business Addr:** Albion Sr HS, 225 Watson St, Albion, MI 49224.

DAVIS, WILLIE CLARK
Professional football player. **Personal:** Born Oct 10, 1967, Little Rock, AR; married Veronica; children: Tiana, Jeremy, William. **Educ:** Central Arkansas, attended. **Career:** Kansas City Chiefs, wide receiver, 1991-95; Houston Oilers, 1996; Tennessee Oilers, 1997-. **Business Addr:** Professional Football Player, Tennessee Oilers, c/o Baptist Sports Park, 7640 H 70-5, Nashville, TN 37221.

DAVIS, WILLIE D.
Business executive. **Personal:** Born Jul 24, 1934, Lisbon, LA; married Ann; children: 2. **Educ:** Grambling Coll, BS 1956; Univ of Chicago, MBA. **Career:** City of Cleveland, teacher; Cleveland Browns; Green Bay Packers; Joseph Schlitz Brewing co, sales & public relations, 1964; Willie Davis Distributing Co, owner; All-Pro Broadcasting Inc, pres, currently. **Orgs:** Bd of dir, Jos Schlitz Brewing Co; charter mem & dir, Exec Savings & Loan Assn; color analyst, KNBC Football Telecast; public relation & promotion work, Chrysler Corp; LA Co Special Task Force; pres & dir, LA Urban League; dir & bd mem W Adams Comm Hosp; chmn, Central Div LA Explorers, BSA; Career Counseling Group; So CA Businessmen's Assn; adv bd, Black Peace Officers Assn; Bicentennial Black Achievement Exhibit; Spl LA Co Study Commn; speaks on an average of once a week to hs civic or comm groups; toured Vietnam for State Dept, 1966; Sara Lee Corp, board of directors; KMart Corp, board of directors; Dow Chemical, board of directors. **Honors/Awds:** Selected to All-Pro teams 6 yrs; Byron ''Whizzer'' White Awd; Hall of Fame of NAIA; Green Bay Packers Hall of Fame 1975; Man of Yr NAACP 1978; Part of 6 Div Championships, 5 World Championships; Black Enterprise list of Top 100 Black Businesses; NFL Hall of Fame, 1981. **Military Serv:** US Army, spec-5, 1956-58. **Business Addr:** President, All Pro Broadcasting Co, 161 N Le Brea Ave, Inglewood, CA 90301.

DAVIS, WILLIE FLOYD, JR.
Clergyman. **Personal:** Born Sep 16, 1963, Bainbridge, GA; son of Mary Beard & Willie Davis Sr; married Michelle R Davis, Aug 24, 1985; children: Leslie Ann, Ashley LaShae. **Educ:** Monroe Comm Coll, AAS, 1983; State Univ of NY at Brockport, BA, 1986; Rochester Real Estate Training Ctr, certification in real estate sales, 1986; Children's Aid Society, National Training Institute, certification in human/teen sexuality training, 1991; NY State AIDS Institute, certification in HIV/AIDS counseling, 1992; Monroe Cty Health Department, certification in HIV/AIDS Prevention Education, 1993; Univ of NC, certification of continuing education, 1993; Univ of Rochester, certification in crisis management response, 1994. **Career:** Mt Olive Bapt Ch, assoc minister/minister of music, 1985-86; Pentacostal Memorial Bapt Ch, assoc minister/minister of music, 1986-91; Action for a Better Community, proj coord, case mgr, housing coord, 1989-92; Emmanuel Missionary Bapt Ch, pastoral asst/assoc minister, minister of music, dir of Christian education, 1991-; Puerto Rican Youth Development & Resource Ctr, dir of prog operations, sr counselor, 1992-94; Catholic Family Ctr, Catholic youth organization prog dir, resource coord, 1994-95; Baden St Settlement of Rochester, Inc, assoc exec dir, 1995-; Ch of the Covenant United Ch of Christ, sr pastor/teacher, 1996-. **Orgs:** Monroe Council on Teen Pregnancy, chair, pres, CEO, 1989-; Black Leadership Commission on AIDS, pres, chair, 1996-; Zion Hill Foundation, bd of dirs, 1995-; Rochester Area Task Force on AIDS, bd of dirs, 1992-; United Way of Greater Rochester, bd of dirs, 1996-; CHANGE Collaborative, bd of dirs, 1996-; Monroe Cty Health Department, CHHA professional advisory bd, 1995-; John Marshall High School, school health advisory bd, 1994-.

DAVIS, WILLIE J.
Attorney. **Personal:** Born Sep 29, 1935, Fort Valley, GA; married Carolyn Scoggins; children: Kristen, Roland. **Educ:** Morehouse Coll, BA 1956; New England School of Law, JD 1963. **Career:** MA Commiss Against Discrimination, field rep 1963; Commonwealth of MA, asst attny gen 1964-69; Dist of MA, asst US attny 1969-71, former US magistrate; Private practice, attny; Northeastern Univ, law enforcement instr, currently. **Orgs:** Mem Amer Bar Assoc, Amer Judicature Soc, Alpha Phi Alpha; bd of trustees Advent School Boston. **Honors/Awds:** Ten Outstanding Young Men Awd Boston Jr C of C 1971; Hon Deg JD New England School of Law 1972; Hon Deg DSc Lowell Tech Inst 1973. **Military Serv:** AUS sp4 1958-60. **Business Addr:** Law Enforcement Instructor, Northeastern University, 44 School St, Boston, MA 02108.

DAVIS, WILLIE JAMES
Lecturer. **Personal:** Born May 14, 1940, Tyronza, AR; divorced; children: Rasul, Hasam. **Educ:** George Washington Univ 1959; Herschel Rowland, Bass 1958; Lincoln Univ, Chem 1959-61; Art Davis, Bass 1962-67; George Andrea, Bass 1967-71; Juilliard Schl of Music 1967-68; NY Univ, BS Music 1971, MA Music 1972; John Gilbert, Composition 1971-72; Alberto Socarras, Sofegeo 1980-. **Career:** Yardney Electric Co, electrochem engr 1961-63; luthier & free-lance musician arranger composer conductor contractor 1965-; Harlem Philharmonic Orchestra, contractor 1969-; Brooklyn Music Schl for Children, instr 1970-81; Youth Bd Inst of NY, music consult 1972; Bronx Comm Clge Music Dept, lecturer adjunct 1973-74; Rutgers Univ, instr bass lecturer music history 1977-81; Vassar Clge, lectuerer black music 1980-81. **Honors/Awds:** DiscographyTV radio film awards, Freddie McCoy ''Collard Greens'' NY 1965 LP, Donald Williams ''I Won the Race'' & ''Look Down the Road'' Safaria Records 1971 45RPM, Jo Grinage ''Mother's Love Song'' Dakeeta Records 1971, Sun Ra ''Pathways to Unknown Worlds'' Impulse Records ASD 9298 LP, Carnegie Hall ''Voice of America Broadcast'' 1968, Count Basie Radio & TV 1974, ''Folk Music Around the World'' Tri Tone Records NY 1972, Lincoln Univ & Rolla Schl of Mines Orchestra LP 1960, Symphony of the New World ''Anniversary Concert'' NY 1966, Harlem Homecoming CBS TV 1974, Michael Olatunji NBC TV 1968, NY World's Fair Symphony Orchestra ''Six Suites for the World's Fair'' NBC TV & Film 1964, Les & Larry Elgart Radio Canton OH 1966, TV Wash DC 1966, Recording 1966, Miriam Makeba Recording CongoAlgeria Tunis Rome & Film 1969, NY Univ Choir NBC TV 1973 Radio 1970, Sam Rivers ''Shades'' New York City 1970, Harlem Philharmonic Orchestra 1974, Joe Turner PabloRecords 1974, Leroy Jenkins ''For Players Only'' J00a 1010 NY 1975, Mort Lindsey Orchestra ''Merv Griffin Show'' NBC TV 1965-67, Dance Theatre of Harlem RecordingNY 1971, Charles Tolliver ''Jazz Repertory Co'' Carnegie Hall 1974. **Business Addr:** 156 W 132nd St, New York, NY 10027.

DAVIS, WILLIS H. ''BING''
Educational administrator. **Personal:** Born Jun 30, 1937, Greer, SC. **Educ:** DePauw Univ Greencastle IN, BA 1959; Dayton Art Inst, studied ceramics 1963-65; Miami Univ Oxford OH, 1967, M.E.D. Graduate Study, IN State Univ, 1975-76. **Career:** DePauw U, asst prof art 1971-76; Coord of Black Studies 1971; Wright State Univ Dayton OH, art instr 1969-71; ESEA Title & III Living Arts Cntr Dayton OH, art dir 1967-71; Dayton OH Pub Schs, tchr 1957-67; Black Hist & Cultural Workshops German Town OH, visiting artist & lectr series 1968; Bergamo Cntr 1968-69, 70; VISTA Prog; Auburn Univ AL 1969; Miami Univ, Assist Dean of Grad School, Associate Pro of Art, 1976-78; Paul Robeson Cult & Perf Arts Center, Dir, 1978-84; Central State Univ, chair Art Dept, 1978-. **Orgs:** OH Scndry & Sr High Prins Assn Conf Cleveland 1970; Western Arts Assn NAEA Milwaukee 1970; Black Studies Inst Miami Univ 1970; VA State Univ Norfolk 1970; Univ of Cincinnati at Blue Ash Raymond Walters Br 1972; The HEW Inst in Afro-Am Studies Earlham Coll Richmond 1972; Living Arts Prog Dayton 1972; Archdiocese of Cincinnati Dayton Area Cath Schs 1972; Purdue Univ Lafayette IN 1972; Univ of MA 1972; Gov State Univ Nat & Endowment for the Arts Prog 1972; Indianapolis Pub Schs Shortrigde HS IN Arts Council 1972; Lafayette Comm Cntr Summer Arts Prog IN Arts Council 1972; Work shown in group juried competitive exhibitions one-man shows priv collections permanent museum collections; African-American Art Collectors Society, The Dayton Art Institute, 1995; Association of American Cultures, San Antonio, TX, 1994; Center for the Study and Development of Effective Pedagogy for the African-American Learner, Texas Southern University, Houston, TX, 1994; Montgomery County Regional Arts and Cultural District, Trustee, 1990-. **Honors/Awds:** Publications Commns LaRevue Moderne Mag article Paris 1967; Mural Panorama on Black Hist Dayton Daily Newspaper 1968; Cover Design for Educ Booklet on Black Hist Geo A Pflaum Pub 1968; Calendar Illus for Nat Ofc for Black Cath Washington DC 1972; represented in book ''Black Artists on Art'' 1972 Black Artist Documentary ''Color It Black'' Channel 13 WLWI-TV Indianapolis 1972. Depauw Univ., Hon Dr of Fine Arts, 1997; Oh Art Educ Assc, OH Art Ed of Year, 1996; Opus Award, 1996; Walk of Fame Award, Dayton OH, 1996. **Special Achievements:** Ceremony & Ritual: The Art pf Bing-Davis Retrospective Exhibit, Dayton, OH, 1996. **Business Addr:** Central State University, Wilberforce, OH 45384.

DAVIS ANTHONY, VERNICE
Health administrator. **Personal:** Born Jan 10, 1945; daughter of Vernice Bradford Chambers and Leonard Chambers (deceased); married Eddie Anthony (died 1993); children: Dana, Dara, Todd. **Educ:** Wayne State Univ, BS, 1970; Univ of Michigan, Ann Arbor, MPH, 1976. **Career:** City of Detroit, services, chief, public health nursing, field program, 1971-79; State of Michigan, Dev and Evaluation, local health services admn, community health field; Wayne County, county health officer chief, office of policy, 1983-91; State of Michigan, dir of Michigan dept of public health, 1991-95; St John Health System, svp, Urban & Community Health, 1995-. **Orgs:** MI Health Officers Association, 1987-, pres, 1987-88; executive council mem, MI Association for Local Public Health; charter mem, MI Health Policy Forum, committee mem, New Detroit, Inc; board mem, St John Hospital, 1986-91; executive committee mem, Greater Detroit Area Health Council. **Honors/Awds:** Service Award, Michigan Health Officers Association, 1988; Achievement Award, Natl Assn of Counties; Governor's Infant Mortality Task Force, 1986; Director's Task Force on Minority Health Status, 1987; Wayne State Univ, Women of Wayne Headliner Award, 1992. **Business Addr:** Senior Vice Pres, Urban and Community Health, St John Health System, 22101 Moross Rd, Detroit, MI 48236.

DAVIS-MCFARLAND, E. ELISE
City official. **Personal:** Born Oct 18, 1946, Greensboro, NC; married Arthur C McFarland; children: Kira Jihan, William Joseph. **Educ:** Univ of NC, BA 1964-68; Univ of VA, MEd 1969-71; Univ of Pgh, PhD 1973-76; Harvard Univ, visiting scholars program 1975; Univ of WI, european studyprogram 1971. **Career:** VA State Univ, instructor dept of english 1971-73; Univ of Pgh, rsch asst dept of psychology 1973-76; Univ of Houston, asst prof dept of speech pathol 1976-79; College of Charleston, Univ Affiliated Facilities Prog, asst dir 1978-79; CHEC Educ Oppor Ctr, dir 1979-82; Charleston Trident Chamber of Commerce, vice pres 1982-86, 1993-; The Citadel, director of institional research, 1993-; Medical University of SC, associate professor and program director, 1993-. **Orgs:** Commissioner SC Health & Human Services Finance Comm 1984-; sec SC Assoc of Elected and Appointed Women Officials 1984-; bd member Natl Rural Develop Finance Corp 1985-. **Honors/Awds:** First Black Chamber of Commerce Vice Pres in SC 1982; nominations Outstanding Young Women of America 1982-83. **Home Addr:** 204 Grove St, Charleston, SC 29403. **Business Addr:** Associate Professor/Prog Director, Department of Rehabilitation Sciences, Med University of South Carolina, 171 Ashley Ave, Charleston, SC 29425.

DAVISON, EDWARD L.
Attorney. **Personal:** Born May 10, 1943, Akron, OH; son of Marie Mapp Gordon and Edward Davison (deceased); married Willa Rebecca Branham; children: Rebecca Marie, Christopher Larry. **Educ:** Univ of Akron, Assoc Degree 1967, BS Natural Science 1973, JD 1977. **Career:** Westinghouse R&D, lab technician 1963-64; General Tire R&D, lab technician 1964-67; Babcock & Wilcox, perf engineer 1967-76; Babcock & Wilcox CRD, cont mgr 1976-89, sr cont mgr 1989-. **Orgs:** Atty Davison, Greene, Holloway & Walker 1978-83, Davison & Greene 1983-; treasurer United Council of Corvette Clubs 1983-87, pres 1987-91; vice pres planning & allocation Summit County United Way 1984-86, treasurer 1987-89. **Honors/Awds:** Award of Merit Summit County United Way 1980; Outstanding Achievement Summit County Democratic Party 1978; United Council of Corvette Clubs, Outstanding Achievement 1986. **Business Addr:** Attorney, 1562 Beeson St, Alliance, OH 44601.

DAVISON, FREDERIC E.
Military official. **Personal:** Born Sep 28, 1917, Washington, DC; married Jean E Brown; children: Jean M, Andrea S, Dayle A, Carla M. **Educ:** Howard U, BS 1938; Geo Wash U, MS 1940; MA 1963. **Career:** Mil Dist of Wash AUS, comndg gen. **Honors/Awds:** Distinguished alumnis Geo Wash Univ 1971; distinguished alumnus Howard Univ 1973; hon degree LLD Estrn MI Univ 1974. **Military Serv:** AUS maj gen 1941-74. **Business Addr:** HQ US Army Military, District of Washington, Fort McNair, Washington, DC.

DAVISON, JERONE
Professional football player. **Personal:** Born Sep 16, 1970, Picayune, MS; married; children: one. **Educ:** Arizona State Univ. **Career:** Sacramento Gold Miners (CFL), running back, 1994;

Rhein Fire (WFL), 1996; Oakland Raiders, 1996-. **Business Addr:** Professional Football Player, Oakland Raiders, 1220 Harbor Bay Pkwy, Alameda, CA 94502, (510)615-1875.

DAVIS-WILLIAMS, PHYLLIS A.
Chief executive officer. **Personal:** Born Apr 20, 1947, Philadelphia, PA; married Halton Wilbur Williams Jr. **Educ:** Nazareth Coll, BA 1968; Wayne State U, mA 1972. **Career:** Barat Human Serv Detroit, exec dir 1978-; Planned Parenthood Fedn Great Lakes Region, asso regional dir 1976-78; State of MI Macomb Co vocational rehabsupr 1972-76; Wayne Co Projec Prescad, pub health consult 1970-72; State of MI Wayne Co, social worker 1968-70. **Orgs:** Bd of dir Accounting Aide Soc Detroit 1980; mem Nat Rehab Assn 1972-; mem Women's Economic Soc 1978-; mem Nat Com for Prevention of Child Abuse.

DAVIS-WRIGHTSIL, CLARISSA
Professional basketball player. **Personal:** Born Jun 4, 1971; married Jerald Wrightsil. **Educ:** Univ of Texas. **Career:** New England Blizzard, forward, 1996; Long Beach Stingrays, 1997-. **Honors/Awds:** Naismith Player of the Year, 1987, 1989. **Business Addr:** Professional Basketball Player, Long Beach Stingrays, One World Trade Center, Ste 202, Long Beach, CA 90831-0202, (562)951-7297.

DAVY, GLORIA (GLORIA DAVY PENNINGSFELD)
Opera singer, educator. **Personal:** Born Mar 29, 1937, Brooklyn, NY; daughter of Lucy Crick Davy and George Timson Davy; divorced; children: Jean-Marc Penningsfeld. **Educ:** Juilliard School of Music, BS, 1954. **Career:** Little Orch Soc Town Hall, debut 1954; toured Italy, Germany, Sweden, Spain 1955-56; Nice Opera 1957; Metropolitan Opera, 1958-62; Vienna State Opera, 1959; Convent Garden Opera Co, 1961; guest performer La Scala in Milan; San Carlo; Naples; Teatro Communale, Bologna; Teatro Massimo, Palermo; Teatre Reggio, Parma; Deutsche Opera, Berlin, guest contract 1961-69; yearly tours of Italy, Germany, France, Switzerland; Indiana University, School of Music, professor, Emeritus. **Orgs:** National Society of Arts and Letters, honorary member. **Honors/Awds:** Marian Anderson Award 1953; Marian Anderson Special Award 1954; Music Education League, award, New York City, 1954; Music Education League, Town Hall Debut, New York City, 1954; created integral work Karl Heinz Stockhausen's "Momente," Beethoven Hall, Bonn 1972; first performances Festival Hall London/Brussels Opera/Theatre De La Ville Paris/Beethoven Halle-Bonn 1973; created "Vortrag Uber Hu" Stockhausen Donauschingen Festival 1974; first performances London & Paris 1974; Wigmore Hall Recital London 1983; Westminster Abbey performance for Royal Family 1983; Concert: Hommage to Gershwin conductor Giorgio Gaslini Orch 1985-87; American Premiere "Daphne," Strauss, 1960; American Premiere, New York Premiere "Anna Bolena" Donizetti, 1957; "Capriccio," R Straus, Juilliard, 1954.

DAWES, DOMINIQUE MARGAUX
Gymnast. **Personal:** Born Nov 20, 1976, Silver Spring, MD; daughter of Loretta Florence Dawes and Don Arnold Dawes. **Career:** Gymnast, currently. **Orgs:** Hill's Gymnastics, elite, 1988-93. **Honors/Awds:** Hill's Gym, Most Outstanding, 1990-92; Olympic Games, Bronze Medal, Gymnastics, 1992; World Gymnastics Championships Competition, Birmingham, England, Silver Medals (2), uneven parallel bars, balance beam, 1993. **Special Achievements:** One of only two African-American females ever to qualify for the US Olympic Gymnastics team, 1992; amateur athlete; Women's Artistic Gymnast; Stage debut in Grease, 1996.

DAWKINS, BRIAN
Professional football player. **Personal:** Born Oct 13, 1973, Jacksonville, FL; married Connie; children: Brian Jr. **Educ:** Clemson, bachelor's degree in education. **Career:** Philadelphia Eagles, defensive back, 1996-. **Business Addr:** Professional Football Player, Philadelphia Eagles, 3501 S Broad St, Philadelphia, PA 19148, (215)463-2500.

DAWKINS, DARRYL (DUNKS)
Professional basketball player. **Personal:** Born Jan 11, 1957, Orlando, FL. **Career:** Philadelphia 76'ers, 1976-82; New Jersey Nets, 1983-87; Utah Jazz, 1988; Detroit Pistons, 1988-89; Phillips Milan, Italy; Harlem Globetrotters, currently. **Business Phone:** (818)457-7272.

DAWKINS, JOHNNY
Professional basketball player. **Personal:** Born Sep 28, 1963, Washington, DC. **Educ:** Duke Univ. **Career:** San Antonio Spurs, 1986-89; Philadelphia 76ers, 1989-. **Business Addr:** Professional Basketball Player, Detroit Pistons, 2 Championship Dr, Auburn Hills, MI 48326, (810)377-0100.

DAWKINS, MICHAEL JAMES
Engineer. **Personal:** Born Nov 11, 1953, Chicago, IL; son of Willie Mae Dawkins and Willie James Dawkins; married Cornelia A Long; children: Erika Michelle. **Educ:** Univ of IL-Chicago, BS 1978, MS 1979. **Career:** Dow Chemical, rsch eng 1979-83; senior research eng 1983-86, project leader 1986-87; research leader 1987-90, research assoc, 1990-. **Orgs:** Mem AIChE 1976-; adv bd Soc of Black Engrs LSU 1982-; chmn LSU SBE Adv Bd 1982-84; minority liason for Georgia Tech & LSU/Dow 1983-; contact Educ Enhancement/Dow 1984-86; NOBCCHE. **Honors/Awds:** EIT Certification LA 1985. **Military Serv:** AUS spl/5 3 yrs. **Business Addr:** Research Associate, Dow Chemical Co, PO Box 150, Bldg 2513, Plaquemine, LA 70765.

DAWKINS, MILLER J.
City commissioner, educator. **Personal:** Born Mar 10, 1925, Ocala, FL; son of Gertrude Ulmer Dawkins and Miller James Dawkins Sr; married Nancy Sidney; children: Myron. **Educ:** FL A&M Univ, 1953-55; FL Mem College, BS, social science, 1969-71; Univ of North Colorado, MA, social science, 1973-74. **Career:** Miami-Dade Comm Coll, chairperson contin ed dept 1977-78; Dade Cty Correctional Ctrs, dir of ed program 1977-82; Miami-Dade Comm Coll, prof/admin 1978-; City of Miami, city commiss 1981-. **Orgs:** Supvr Aircraft Serv Inc 1966-68; vocational counselor Youth Ind Inc 1966-68; admin officer Dade Cty Model City's Program 1969-71; member, Omega Psi Phi. **Military Serv:** US Army, Private, 1950-52.

DAWKINS, SEAN RUSSELL
Professional football player. **Personal:** Born Feb 3, 1971, Red Bank, NJ. **Educ:** California. **Career:** Indianapolis Colts, wide receiver, 1993-. **Business Addr:** Professional Football Player, Indianapolis Colts, PO Box 535000, Indianapolis, IN 46253, (317)297-2658.

DAWKINS, STAN BARRINGTON BANCROFT
Dentist. **Personal:** Born Jul 11, 1933, Jamaica, WI. **Educ:** City Coll of NY, BS 1959; NY Univ Coll of Dent, DDS & MSD 1963; FACD, 1990. **Career:** Self-employed, dentist; Bird S Coler Metropolitan Hospital, chief of prosthetics; Dept of Prosthetics NY Univ Coll of Dentistry, asst prof, associate prof, currently. **Orgs:** Mem ADA; mem NE Gnathological Soc; Am Radiological Soc; art pub in NY State Journ; co-chair comm Encourage Blacks to Enter Med Prof; capt Cty Coll Track Team 1957-59; capt City Coll Soccer Team 1959; Greater NY Academy of Prosthododtics; Amer Prosthodontic Society; NY Academy of Dentistry; OKU, vp, 1995. **Honors/Awds:** Outstanding Athlete Award CCNY 1959; mem CCNY Hall of Fame 1974; disting serv medal good conduct medal USAF. **Military Serv:** USAF sgt 1952-56. **Business Addr:** 186 W 135 St, New York, NY 10030.

DAWKINS, STEPHEN A.
Physician. **Personal:** Born Feb 27, 1960, Nashville, TN; son of Tinye L Dawkins and Wilbert L Dawkins Sr; married Arnika G Dawkins, Dec 17, 1983; children: Brandon, Morgan-Brien, Paige-Nichette. **Educ:** Georgia Institute of Technology, BS, 1982; Morehouse School of Medicine, MD, 1987; Columbia University, MPH, 1990. **Career:** Consultant, 1987; Occupational Health Service, resident, 1988; New Jersey Department of Health, consultant, 1988-90; New Jersey Bell, medical director, 1989-90; Arkins Corp., owner, 1980-90; Occupational Safety and Health Administration, occupational medicine physician, 1990; Occupational Health Atlanta, physician, 1990-. **Orgs:** American College of Occupational and Environmental Medicine, Georgia Chapter; American Medical Assn; Medical Association of Georgia; American Diabetes Association; Arthritis Foundation; State Board of Worker's Compensation. **Special Achievements:** Presentations: Opportunities in Occupational Medicine, 1991; Asbestos Exposure and Clean Air, 1991; Workplace Drug Testing: Implementation Guidelines for Employers, 1992; The Americans With Disabilities Act: Medical Implications and Employer Considerations, 1992; numerous others. **Business Phone:** (404)897-6800.

DAWKINS, TAMMY C.
Educator. **Personal:** Born Aug 30, 1960, Washington, DC; daughter of Alfreda F Jenkins and Dan Lee Jenkins; married Fitzroy W Dawkins, Apr 4, 1987; children: Danielle Charisse, Ayana Noelle. **Educ:** Howard Univ, BS, pharmacy, 1983; State Univ of NY, Buffalo, Doctor of Pharmacy, 1986. **Career:** Erie County Medical Ctr, staff development pharmacist, 1987-88; Howard Univ, asst prof of pharmacy practice, 1988-, Howard Univ Hospital Pediatric AIDS Clinical Trials Group, pharmacist, 1991-. **Orgs:** American Society of Hospital Pharmacists, 1988-; American Assn of Colleges of Pharmacy, 1989-90. **Honors/Awds:** Assn of Black Hospital Pharmacists, Student Achievement Award, 1985; Rho Chi Natl Pharmacy Honor Society, 1982. **Special Achievements:** Nationally recognized by the American Society of Hospital Pharmacists Research Foundation for clinical research dealing with medication allergy documentation, 1992. **Business Addr:** Asst Prof, Coll of Pharmacy, Howard Univ, Chauncey Cooper Hall, 2300 4th St, NW, Washington, DC 20059, (202)806-7960.

DAWKINS, WAYNE J.
Journalist. **Personal:** Born Sep 19, 1955, New York, NY; son of Iris C McFarquhar Dawkins and Edward H Dawkins; married Allie Crump Dawkins, Apr 29, 1988; children: Carmen Jamila Dawkins. **Educ:** Long Island University, Brooklyn, NY, BA, 1977; Columbia University, Graduate School of Journalism, New York, NY, MS, 1980. **Career:** Trans-Urban News Service, Brooklyn, NY, intern/reporter, 1978-79; The Daily Argus, Mount Vernon, NY, reporter, 1980-84; Courier-Post, Cherry Hill, NJ, reporter, 1984-88, editorial writer, 1988-, columnist, 1991-96; Post-Tribune, Gary IN, deputy south lake editor, 1996-. **Orgs:** Editor, co-founder, Black Alumni Network, 1980-; regional director 1984-89, member 1981-, National Association of Black Journalists; co-founder, president, treasurer, Garden State (NJ) ABJ (NABJ Affiliate), 1988-; Journalism Alumni Association, Columbia University, 1981-84; The Trotter Group, 1992-; Publishers Marketing Assn, 1994; president, August Press, 1997. **Honors/Awds:** Journalism Alumni Award, Columbia University, 1990; Robert Harron Award, Columbia University GSJ, 1980; T Thomas Fortune Lifetime Achievement Awd, Golden State Association of Black Journalists, 1994. **Special Achievements:** Author, Black Journalists: The NABJ Story, August Press, 1993. **Home Addr:** 8590 Polo Club Dr, Apt U-598, Merrillville, IN 46410. **Business Addr:** Deputy South Lake Editor, Post-Tribune, 112 W Clark, Crown Point, IN 46307.

DAWSON, ANDRE NOLAN
Professional baseball player (retired). **Personal:** Born Jul 10, 1954, Miami, FL; married Vanessa Turner; children: Darius. **Educ:** FL A&M Univ, attended. **Career:** Montreal Expos, outfielder, 1976-86; Chicago Cubs, outfielder, 1987-92; Boston Red Sox, 1992-94; Florida Marlins, 1995-96. **Honors/Awds:** National League Most Valuable Player, Baseball Writers' Association of America, 1977, 1987; National League Rookie of the Year, Baseball Writers' Association of America, 1977; National League All-Star Team, 1981-83, 1987-90. **Business Addr:** Professional Baseball Player, Boston Red Sox, Fenway Park, 24 Yawkey Way, Boston, MA 02215.

DAWSON, B. W.
University president. **Career:** Selma Univ, Selma, AL, president, currently. **Business Addr:** President, Selma University, 1501 Lapsley St, Selma, AL 36701.

DAWSON, BOBBY H.
Automobile dealer. **Career:** Freedom Ford Lincoln-Mercury Inc, president, CEO, currently. **Honors/Awds:** Company is #84 on Black Enterprise magazine's list of top 100 auto dealers, 1992. **Business Addr:** President, Freedom Ford Lincoln-Mercury Inc, 149 Woodland Dr, PO Box 3419, Wise, VA 24293, (703)328-2686.

DAWSON, DERMONTTI FARRA
Professional football player. **Personal:** Born Jun 17, 1965, Lexington, KY; married Regina; children: Two. **Educ:** Univ of Kentucky, degree in kinesiology and health promotions. **Career:** Pittsburgh Steelers, center, 1988-; NFL Alumni Assn, Offensive Lineman of the Year, 1996. **Honors/Awds:** Pro Bowl appearances, 1992-96. **Business Addr:** Professional Football Player, Pittsburgh Steelers, Three Rivers Stadium, 300 Stadium Circle, Pittsburgh, PA 15212, (412)323-1200.

DAWSON, ERIC EMMANUEL
Government official. **Personal:** Born Dec 26, 1937, St Thomas, Virgin Islands of the United States; son of Ann Olivia Forbes-Dawson and Joseph E Dawson; married Betty Vanterpool, Jun 11, 1966; children: David, Diane, Eric Jr. **Educ:** New York University, BS, business; Howard University, JD. **Career:** Senate of the VI, executive secretary, 1965-67, 1968-71; Special Assistant to Governor, 1967-68; Sales Executive, 1971-72; Government of the VI, senator, 1973-79, chief legal counsel senate, 1983-84, senator, 1985-87, commissioner eco dev, 1987-. **Orgs:** Caribbean Travel Organization, 3rd vice pres; VI Bar Association, 1982-. **Military Serv:** Army National Guard, col, 1969-; Army Commendation, National Defense, Army Achievement. **Home Addr:** PO Box 3536, St Thomas, Virgin Islands of the United States 00803. **Business Phone:** (809)774-8784.

DAWSON, HORACE G., III
Attorney. **Personal:** Born Oct 23, 1954, Durham, NC; son of Horace G Dawson Jr & Lula Cole Dawson; married Mildred L Dawson, Sep 15, 1985; children: H Greeley Dawson III, Mia Karisa Dawson. **Educ:** Harvard College, BA, 1976; Harvard Business School, MBA, 1980; Harvard Law School, JD, 1980. **Career:** Baker & McKenzie, associate, 1980-82; Summit Rovins & Feldesman, associate, 1982-86; Reliance Group Holdings, staff counsel, 1986-87; Telemundo Group Inc, vp & asst general counsel; Hard Rock Cafe International, Inc, sr director of business affairs, vice president of business affairs, currently. **Orgs:** Council on Foreign Relations, 1989-; ABA, 1980-; NY State Bar, 1980-; NY City Bar, 1980-; FL State Bar, 1994-. **Business Addr:** Vice President of Business Affairs, Hard Rock Cafe International, Inc, 5401 Kirkman Rd, Orlando, FL 32819.

DAWSON, HORACE GREELEY, JR.
Government official (retired), educational administrator. **Personal:** Born Jan 30, 1926, Augusta, GA; married Lula M Cole; children: Horace G III, H Gregory. **Educ:** Lincoln Univ PA, AB

1949; Columbia U, AM 1950; State Univ IA, PhD 1960. **Career:** Southern Univ Baton Rouge, instructor of English, 1950-53; NC Central Univ Durham, assoc prof, dir of public relations, 1953-62; Uganda, cultural affairs officer, 1962; Nigeria, cultural affairs officer, 1964; Univ of Lagos Nigeria, visiting professor, 1966-67; Liberia, public affairs officer, 1967; US Dept of State, Senior Seminar in Foreign Policy, 1970, cultural affairs advisor, 1970-71; USIA/Africa, asst dir, director, 1971-76; Univ of MD, visiting professor, 1971-79; US Dept of State, Botswana, ambassador extraordinary, plenipotentiary, 1979-83; Board of Examiners of the Foreign Service, 1983-85; US Information agency, advisor to the director, Office of Equal Employment Opportunity and Civil Rights, director, 1985-89; Howard University, PACE Program, director, 1989-91, Patricia Roberts Harris Public Affairs Program, director, 19, Center for International Affairs, interim director, 1993-. **Orgs:** NAACP; American Legion; vice chair, Alpha Phi Alpha World Affairs Council; Metropolitan AME Church, senior bd of stewards; Assn of Black American Ambassadors; Council on Foreign Relations; World Affairs Council. **Honors/Awds:** USIA, Superior Honor Award, 1965, 1989. **Special Achievements:** Author: New Dimensions in Higher Education, 1961; Handbook for High School Newspaper Advisors, 1961; "Race As A Factor in Cultural Exchange," Exporting America, 1993; "First Black Diplomat," Foreign Service Journal, Jan 1993; numerous others. **Military Serv:** US Army, ssgt, 1944-46. **Business Addr:** Head, Ralph Bunche Center, Howard University, 2218 6th St. NW, Washington, DC 20059.

DAWSON, LAKE
Professional football player. **Personal:** Born Jan 2, 1972, Boston, MA; married Lori. **Educ:** Notre Dame, degree in telecommunications. **Career:** Kansas City Chiefs, wide receiver, 1994-. **Orgs:** Five Loaves and Two Fish Charitable Foundation, sponsor. **Business Addr:** Professional Football Player, Kansas City Chiefs, One Arrowhead Dr, Kansas City, MO 64129, (816)924-9300.

DAWSON, LAWRENCE E.
Educational administrator. **Career:** Amer Council on Education, dir, mgmt program; Voorhees College, pres, 1985-. **Business Addr:** President, Voorhees College, Voorhees Rd, Denmark, SC 29042-0000.

DAWSON, LEONARD ERVIN
Educational administrator. **Personal:** Born Feb 5, 1934, Augusta, GA; married Laura R Dawson; children: Michael, Randall, Lavinia, Stephanie. **Educ:** Morris Brown College, BS, 1954; Columbia University, MA, 1961, diploma, 1964; George Washington Univ, EdD, 1973. **Career:** Paine College, director, assistant dean, 1967-69, academic dean, 1969-70; US Dept of Education, education program specialist, 1970-71; RR Moton Memorial Institute, senior program director, 1971-77, exec vp, 1977-80; United Negro College Fund Inc, American Council on Education (ISATIM), director of special project, 1980-85; Voorhees College, president, 1985-. **Orgs:** American Council on Education; American Management Assn; United Negro College Fund; American Assn of Higher Education; Association of Episcopal Colleges, bd of trustees; Phi Delta Kappa; Alpha Phi Alpha; NAACP. **Honors/Awds:** Morris Brown College, Distinguished Alumni Award, 1981. **Special Achievements:** Author: "The Role of the Counselor," The Columbia Owl, 1964; "Accountability and Federal Programs," United Board for College Development, 1976; "Goverance and the Small, Liberal Arts College," Moton College Service Bureau, 1977; "Intergrated Management Systems in United Negro College Fund Institutions," 1984; "The Next Ten Years: Who Should Benefit from Federal Support Available for Higher Education," a report prepared for the United Negro College Fund, 1984. **Military Serv:** US Army, pfc, 1956-58. **Business Addr:** President, Voorhees College, 1411 Voorhees Rd, Wright Hall, Rm 205, Denmark, SC 29042, (803)793-3351.

DAWSON, LUMELL HERBERT
Government official. **Personal:** Born Sep 5, 1934, Harrisburg, PA; married Jacquelyn Bourne; children: Anegla Lynn, Jeffrey Bourne. **Educ:** WV State Coll, BA 1961. **Career:** New York City Dept of Human Resources, supr caseworker 1962-65; Vocational Educ & Ext Bd, dir soc serv 1965-70; Nassau Co Comm Human Rights, dir 1970-. **Orgs:** Mem Omega Psi Phi Frat 1958-; voc adv bd mem State Univ of NY at Farmingdale 1979-85; voc adv bd mem Hempstead HS NY 1980-; chair fund raising comm Long Island Coalition for Full Emply 1980-; recruiter WV State Coll 1980-; adv bd mem Leadership Training Inst 1982-; mem The EDGES Group 1985-; elected to session Christ First Presby Church Hempstead NY 1987. **Honors/Awds:** Special Recognition Nassau Co Comm Human Rights 1983; Alumni Awd WV State Coll 1986; Outstanding Contrib & Support Operation Get Ahead 1986; Achievement Awd Natl Assoc of Counties 1986. **Business Addr:** Dir of Job Dev Center, Nassau County Commission on, Human Rights, 320 Old Country Rd, Garden City, NY 11530.

DAWSON, MARTHA E.
Educator. **Personal:** Born Jan 12, 1922, Richmond, VA; daughter of Sarah Eaton and John Eaton; divorced; children: Greer Dawson Wilson, Martina M, James M. **Educ:** VA State Coll, BS 1943; IN Univ, MS 1954, EdD 1956. **Career:** Richmond Public Schools, teacher, supr; Multi-Cultural Educ Center, dir; IN Univ, speaker, writer, cons, numerous publs in field; Hampton Inst, chmn dept of elementary educ 1960-70, vice pres for acad affairs. **Orgs:** Mem, Delta Kappa Gamma Hon Soc 1971, Phi Delta Kappa 1975; president, Indiana University School of Education Alumni Board, 1989-90; member, board of visitors, School of Education, Indiana University, 1990-93; member, board of visitors, Defense Opportunity Management Institute, 1987-90. **Honors/Awds:** Distinguished Tchr Hampton Inst 1967; Cert natl Council of Negro Women 1970; finalist Danforth Found Harbison Distinguished Tchr 1970; Outstanding Women of the 70s 1972; vstg scholar So Univ 1974; paper World Conf on Multicultural Educ 1976; Outstanding Achievement Award in Higher Educ, Zeta Phi Beta Sorority, 1984; Old Masters Honoree, Purdue University, 1984; Distinguished Alumni Service Award, Indiana University, 1980; Brother/Sisterhood Award, The National Conference of Christians and Jews, 1991.

DAWSON, MATEL, JR.
Automobile company worker. **Personal:** Born Jan 3, 1921, Shreveport, LA; son of Bessie Hall Dawson and Mattel Dawson Sr; married Herneta Alberta Davis Dawson, Feb 21, 1942 (divorced 1976); children: Jo Ann Dawson Agee. **Career:** Ford Motor Co, skilled trade rigger, 1940-. **Orgs:** NAACP, life member; Local 600, maintenance and construction, 1990, general council, 1990. **Honors/Awds:** Michiganian of the Year, 1991; Honorary Grand Marshal for the 74th Annual Highland Park, MI Parade, 1991; United Negro College Fund, Distinguished Support Award, 1991; Highland Park Community College, Honorary Degree, 1991; National Society of Fund Raising Executives, Outstanding Philanthropy Award, 1995; International Heritage Hall of Fame Honoree, 1996; Wayne State University, Honorary Degree Doctor of Humane Letters, 1996; National Urban League, Equal Opportunity Day Community Hero Award, 1996; UAW Ford Conference, Founder's Award, 1997. **Special Achievements:** Largest single individual donation ($30,000) to United Negro College Fund of Metro Detroit in 11 years of fund raising, 1990; contributed $400,000 to the United Negro College Fund, 1990-92; contributed $10,000 to Highland Park Community College, 1991; The Mattel Dawson Scholarship Fund, Wayne State University, The Damon J Keith Library, NAACP, Special Donation for the National Office of Peoples Community Church, various donations for special projects over 7 year period, Mother Waddles Mission, 1996; Established scholarship honoring parents Matel & Bessie Hall Dawson LSU-Shreveport Endowed Scholarship Fund, Bethel Baptist Church, 1997. **Military Serv:** US Army, Private, 1943.

DAWSON, PETER EDWARD
Physician. **Personal:** Born Nov 18, 1931, Plaquemine, LA; married Jean Lezama; children: Jonathan, Patricia. **Educ:** Xavier U, BS 1954; Meharry Med Coll, 1962. **Career:** St Joseph Hosp, internship resd. **Orgs:** Charter mem Am Acad Family Physicians; asst dir So Infirmary; asso prof family med LSU Scho of Med; past pres Plaquemine Br; NAACP 1966-76;32nd degree Mason; chmn tst My Syremem BC; mem Alpha Phi Alpha Frat. **Honors/Awds:** Physician Recognition Award 1969, 72, 75. **Military Serv:** AUS sp 2 1954-57. **Business Addr:** 1314 Meriam St, Plaquemine, LA 70764.

DAWSON, ROBERT EDWARD
Physician (retired). **Personal:** Born Feb 23, 1918, Rocky Mount, NC; son of Daisy Wright Dawson and William Dawson; married Julia Davis; children: Dianne Elizabeth, Janice Elaine, Robert Edward, Melanie Lorraine. **Educ:** Clark Coll, BS 1939; Meharry Med Coll, MD 1943. **Career:** Homer G Phillips Hosp St Louis, internship 1943-44, resident 1944-46; Lincoln Hosp Ophthalmology Dept, attending staff 1946-55; Duke Univ, preceptorship 1946; NC Central Univ Health Serv, consult ophthalmology 1950-64; 3310 Hosp Scott AFB, chief ophthalmology & otolaryngology 1955-57; Armed Forces Inst of Pathology, ophthalmic pathology 1956; Lincoln Hosp, chief ophthal & otolaryng 1959-76; NY Inst of Ophthalmology, 1962; NY Eye & Ear Infirmary, 1963; Watts Hosp, attend staff 1966; Duke Univ, clinical instr ophthalmology 1968; Durham Co Gen Hosp, attend staff 1976; DCGH, vice pres of staff 1976-77; Duke Univ, clin asst prof ophthalmology; scholar in residence. **Orgs:** Fellow Amer Coll of Surgeons; deplomate Amer Bd of Ophthalmology; fellow Acad of Ophthalmology & Otolaryngology; Amer Assn of Ophthalmology; diplomate Pan Amer Natl Assn; Natl Med Assn; pres, Chi Delta Mu Sci Frat; Soc of Eye Surgeons; Amer Med Assn; bd trustees Meharry Med Coll; exec com chmn Hosp & Health Affairs Comm; bd trustees Natl Med Assn; bd trustees NC Central Univ; chmn Faculty-trustee Relations Com NC Cent Univ; bd dirs Lincoln Comm Health Cntr; bd trustees Durham Acad 1969-72; NC adv comm on Med Asst; bd dir Natl Soc to Prevent Blindness; bd dir Amer Cancer Soc; adv bd NC State Commn for the Blind 1970-78; regional surgical dir Eye Bank Assn of Amer; bd dirs Better Health Found 1960-66; pres Sigma Pi Phi Frat; President's Comm on Employment of the Handicapped; bd dir NatlSto Pr event Blindness; St Joseph's AME Ch; NAACP; bd of visitors Clark Coll; mem Alpha Omega Alpha Hon Soc; pres AOA NMA; Greensboro College, bd of visitors; 33rd degree Mason. **Honors/Awds:** Distinguished Service Award Natl Assn for Equal Opportunity in Higher Edn; Distinguished Service Award Clark Coll 1983; Recipient Physician of the Year Award 1969; Distinguished Service Award (Natl Med Assn) 1982; Publications, Journal of the Natl Med Assn "Equal Access to Health Care Delivery for Blacks, A Challenge for the NMA" Jan 1981; "Crisis in the Medical Arena, A Challenge for the Black Physician" Dec 1979; "Bedside Manner of a Computer" March 1980; "Federal Impact on Medical Care" June 1980. **Military Serv:** USAF Major 1955-57.

DAWSON, SIDNEY L., JR.
Educational administrator (retired). **Personal:** Born Dec 27, 1920, Kansas City, MO; married Etta Mae Jacksson; children: Sandra Kaye, Sidney L III. **Educ:** Univ of KA, BME 1948; Univ of AZ, MME 1956; Educ Admin Certificate, 1968. **Career:** Tucson Educ Assn, pres 1963-64; AZ Educ Assn, pres 1970-71; HS, principal, 1973-79; Catalina HS, asst principal for student activities 1979-84 (retired). **Orgs:** Phi Delta Kappa 1956; pres Rincon Rotary Intl, 1979-80; polemarch Alumni Chapters, Kappa Alpha Psi 1980-81; chairperson Tucson Police Advisory Comm 1983-. **Honors/Awds:** Pusic Phi Mu Alpha 1948. **Military Serv:** AUS t/sgt 1943-46; Honorable Discharge, 1946.

DAWSON, WARREN HOPE
Attorney. **Personal:** Born Oct 17, 1939, Mulberry, FL; married Joan Delores; children: Wendy Hope. **Educ:** FL A&M Univ, BA 1961; Howard Univ Sch of Law, JD 1966. **Career:** Self Employed, atty. **Orgs:** Pres FL Chap Nat Bar Assn 1979; Nat Bar Assn 1979; vice pres Tampa Chap Frontiers Internat; judicial admin selc & tenure FL Bar Assn 1980; standing com legal asst Am Bar Assn 1980; adv bd of dir Tampa Bay Buccaneers 1980; chmn Hillbro Co Civil Serv Bd. **Honors/Awds:** Whitney M Young Meml Award Tampa Urban League 1979. **Military Serv:** AUS co comdr 1961-63. **Business Addr:** 3556 N 29th St, Tampa, FL 33605.

DAWSON BOYD, CANDY
Educator. **Personal:** Born Aug 8, 1946, Chicago, IL; daughter of Mary Ruth Ridley Dawson and Julian Dawson; divorced. **Educ:** Northeastern Illinois State University, BA, 1967; University of California, Berkeley, CA, MA, 1978, PhD, 1982. **Career:** Overton Elementary School, Chicago, IL, teacher, 1968-71; Longfellow School, Berkeley, CA, teacher, 1971-73; University of California, Berkeley, CA, extension instructor in language arts, 1972-79; St Mary's College of California, Moraga, CA, extension instructor in language arts, 1972-79; Berkeley Unified School District, Berkeley, CA, district teacher trainer in reading and communication skills, 1973-76; St Mary's College of California, Moraga, CA, lecturer to assistant professor, 1976-83, chair of reading leadership elementary education, and teacher effectiveness programs, 1976-87, tenured associate professor, 1983-91, professor, 1991-94; Masters Programs in Reading & Special Educ, chair, 1994-. **Orgs:** Member, St Mary's College Rank and Tenure Committee, 1984-87; member, multiple subjects waiver programs committee, review committee, State of California Commission on Teacher Credentialing, 1985-, advisory committee for multiple subject credential with an early childhood emphasis, State of California Commission on Teacher Credentialing, 1986-87. **Honors/Awds:** First Distinguished Professor of the Year, St Mary's College, 1992; author, Circle of Gold, Scholastic, 1984; Coretta Scott King Award Honor Book for Circle of Gold, American Library Association, 1985; author, Breadsticks and Blessing Places, Macmillan, 1985, published in paperback as Forever Friends, Viking, 1986; Outstanding Bay Area Woman, Delta Sigma Theta, 1986; author, Charlie Pippin, Macmillan, 1987; author, Chevrolet Saturdays, Macmillan, 1993; Author, Fall Secrets, Puffin, 1994; A Different Beat, 1994; Author, Daddy, Daddy, Be There, Philomel, 1995; Spotlight on Literature Program, McGraw-Hill, 1995. **Home Addr:** 1416 Madrone Way, San Pablo, CA 94806. **Business Addr:** St Mary's College of California, School of Education, Box 4350, Moraga, CA 94575, (510)631-4700.

DAY, BURNIS CALVIN
Artist, educator. **Personal:** Born Dec 27, 1940, Hepzibah, WV; son of Willie E Day Porter and Jeff M Day. **Educ:** Center for Creative Studies, Detroit, MI, 1966; Famous Artists School, Westport, CT, certificate, 1968; Oakland Community College, Farmington Hills, MI, associates degree, 1969. **Career:** Freuhauf Corporation, Detroit, MI, keyliner and photostat operator, 1970-71; Carl Summers' House of Art, Detroit, MI, art associate, 1971-77; Urban Screen Process, Detroit, MI, art director, 1972-73; Pittman's Gallery Inc, Detroit, MI, art instructor, 1973-74; self-employed artist, 1977-; Wayne County Community College, Detroit, MI, art instructor, 1985-; Institute for Survey Research, field videographer, 1992-93; Chrysler-UAW National Training Center, art instructor, in drawing & painting, 1993-; St Scholastica Summer Day Camp, Detroit, MI, art instructor, 1994-. **Orgs:** Barden Cablevision, Comcast Cable TV, Public Access Program, Detroit, MI, 1988-. **Honors/Awds:** Exhibitions: International Platform Assn, Washington, DC, 1989, Gallery Tanner, Los Angeles, CA, 1984, various others; Semi-Finalist, UAW 50 Year Anniversary Poster, United Auto Workers, 1986; Mural Finalist, Detroit Recreation Dept, Amtrak, 1980; First & Second Place, Tank Automotive, Community Art Show, 1977; Certificate of Recognition, FESTAC '77, US Zone Committee, 1977; First & Second Place, Mural, People's Art &

Detroit Recreation Dept, 1976, 1977; recognized as the world's originator of an innovative painting style known as Neogeometric. **Special Achievements:** Established a school of art on the neogeometric style; exhibits in many numerous collections across US and other countries. **Business Addr:** Artist, PO Box 0255, Detroit, MI 48231, (313)961-0829.

DAY, DANIEL EDGAR
Government official (retired). **Personal:** Born Dec 10, 1913, Montgomery, AL; son of Gertrude Day (deceased) and Thomas Day (deceased); married Sanone Nickerson (deceased); children: Sandra Ann, Gregory Alan (deceased). **Educ:** Crane Jr Coll Chicago, attended 1932-33; Amer Univ, attended 1946, 1962, 1964; Univ of Chicago, attended 1958. **Career:** Robt S Abbott Pub Co Chicago, cartoonist, 1929-35; asst city editor, 1936-40; War Dept Washington, chief negro interest sect bureau public relations 1943-46; FL A&M Univ Tallahassee, prof military sci 1955-61; Natl Newspaper Pub Assn Washington, 1961-66; USDA, admin officer 1966, dept housing & urban devel Wash 1966-68, dep dir pub info div 1968-70, pub info officer 1970-84. **Orgs:** Mem Capital Press; Natl Press Club, membership comm 1997; Pigskin Club. **Honors/Awds:** US Department of Housing & Urban Dev (HUD), Certificate of Merit, 1984. **Military Serv:** US IL Nat'l Guard 1938-41; AUS 1941-61; Grade Lt Colonel, AUS. **Home Addr:** 1316 Fenwick Ln, Apt 915, Silver Spring, MD 20910-3505.

DAY, DONALD K.
Labor official. **Personal:** Born Aug 1, 1936, Cleveland, OH; son of Lillian Reeves Day and Orlie Day; divorced; children: Deneen. **Educ:** Kent University, BS, govt admin, 1962. **Career:** OH AFSCME & AFL-CIO, asst dir & reg lobbyist, 1971-; hospital career devel program, center mgr, 1969-71; county probation officer, 1966-69; teacher, 1963-66; firefighter, 1962-63. **Orgs:** vice pres, OH AFL-CIO; elected office & Jud Comp Comm for OH, Serv Study Comm, 1973-74, Govt Advisory Comm to Intergovern Personnel Act, 1973-74; Found of OH Cit Unit Against Sickle Cell Disease, 1973-74; pres, OH Chapter of the Coalition of Black Trade Unionist; sec-treas, Franklin County Chapter, A Philip Randolph Inst; bd of trust, Woman's Resource & Political Devel Center; bd of trust, Central OH Multiple Sclerosis Soc; Kappa Alpha Psi; exec comm, Franklin County Democratic Party; Carter delegate, Democratic Natl Convention, 1976; exec comm, Central Ohio's United Negro College Fund; OH Ethics Commission; pres, Columbus Center State Theatre. **Honors/Awds:** Man of the Year Award, OH Chap of Public Personnel Assn, 1973. **Military Serv:** US Army Reserves, 1960-66. **Business Addr:** Secretary-Treasurer, Ohio AFL-CIO, 271 E State St, Columbus, OH 43215.

DAY, ERIC THERANDER
Law enforcement coordinator. **Personal:** Born Dec 15, 1952, Mobile, AL; son of Ruby James Day and Joseph Day; married Valerie Jones, Mar 30, 1974; children: Eric Therander Jr, Joaquin Kyron. **Educ:** Univ of South Alabama, Mobile AL, BA, 1977, MEd, 1979. **Career:** Mobile County Sheriff Dept, Mobile AL, asst dir work release, 1977-79, dir work release, 1979-80, asst warden, 1980-81, asst planning officer, 1981-84, dir victim witness program, 1984-85, deputy sheriff, 1985-88; US Attorney's Office, Mobile AL, Law Enforcement, Victim Witness, coord, 1988-. **Orgs:** Mem, Southern States Correctional Assn, 1975-, Lambda Alpha Epsilon, 1977-, Alpha Phi Sigma, 1977-, Alabama Peace Officer Assn, 1979-, Amer Correctional Assn, 1980-; vice pres, Fellowship of Christian Law Enforcement Officers, 1984-; bd mem, 2nd vice pres, Gulf Coast Federal Credit Union, 1985; chaplain, Southern Region Natl Black Police Assn, 1987; bd mem, Epilepsy Chapter of Mobile and Gulf Coast, 1988; mem, Mobile United, 1989, Coalition for a Drug Free Mobile, 1990, Challenge 200-, 1990; vice chmn, Summit to Advance Values & Ethics (SAVE), 1990; vice pres, Blacks in Government, 1987; president, Mobile County Criminal Justice Society, 1984-88; Mobile United, 1989-, Human Resources Committee, chairman, 1992; Coalition for a Drug Free Mobile, 1992, Youth Concerns Committee, chairman, board member; Summit to AdvanValues & Ethics, chairman, 1992-93. **Honors/Awds:** Man of the Year, Alpha Phi Alpha Frat, 1977; Charter Mem, Omicron Delta Kappa, Univ of South Alabama, 1977; Highest Academic (Scholastic), Southwest Alabama Police Academy, 1983; Outstanding Victim Advocate, Alabama, 1990, 1992; Department of Justice, Office for Victims of Crimes, Outstanding Service to Victims Commendation, 1992. **Military Serv:** US Army, sergeant, 1972-74; Natl Defense Medal, 1972; Good Conduct Medal, 1974. **Home Addr:** 2800 Ramada Dr W, Mobile, AL 36693.

DAY, JOHN H., JR.
Physicist. **Personal:** Born Jun 5, 1952, Savannah, GA; son of John H & Elsie M Day; married Agnes A Day, Mar 10, 1973; children: Teresa. **Educ:** Bethune-Cookman Coll, BS, physics, 1973; Howard Univ, MS, physics, 1976, PhD, physics, 1982. **Career:** Martin Marietta Corp, engineer, laser optics div, 1973; Dept of Commerce, physicist, natl bureau of standards, 1974-78; Dept of the Interior, physicist, US Geological survey, 1979-82; NASA, Goddard Space Center, engineer, energy conversion section, 1982-88, section head, energy conversion section, 1988-90, asst branch head, space power branch, 1990-92, branch head, space power branch, 1992-. **Orgs:** Interagency Advanced Power Group; Amer Inst of Aeronautics & Astronautics; Inst of Electrical & Electronic Engineers; Amer Assn for the Advancement of Science; Amer Physical Society; Natl Society of Black Physicists; Sigma Pi Sigma Physics Honor Society; Alpha Kappa Mu, National Honor Society; Phi Beta Sigma Fraternity. **Honors/Awds:** NASA Performance Management & Recognition System Awards, 1989-94; NASA Outstanding Performance Awards, 1984, 1985 & 1987; Goddard Exceptional Achievement Award, 1993; Natl Science Foundation Fellowship, 1976-78; Howard Univ Terminal Fellowship Award, 1980-82; X-Ray Timing Explorer Team Award, 1996; Landsat 7 Design Review Streamlining Team Awd, 1995; Global Geospace Sci Satellite PSE Review Team Awd, 1994; Hubble Space Telescope Servicing Mission Group Award, 1994; Geostationary Operational Environmental Satellite Group Award, 1994; Upper Atmosphere Research Satellite Achievement Award, 1993; Gamma Ray Observatory Group Award, 1992; International Sun Earth Explorer Group Award, 1987; International Cometary Explorer Group Award, 1985. **Special Achievements:** Presentations and publications include: Intersociety Energy Conversion Engineering Conference, 1987; NASA Space Photovoltaics Research & Technology Conference, 1983 & 1994; Institute of Electrical & Electronic Engineers Photovoltaics Conference, 1987; Amer Inst of Aeronautics & Astronautics Small Satellite Symposium, 1993. **Home Addr:** 9711 Bald Hill Road, Mitchellville, MD 20721, (301)577-1821. **Business Addr:** Branch Head, Space Power Applications Branch, NASA Goddard Space Flight Ctr, Mail Code 734, Greenbelt, MD 20771, (301)286-5845.

DAY, MORRIS
Musician, actor. **Personal:** Born 1957; married Judith; children: Evan, Derran, Tionna. **Career:** Musician with the group, The Time; solo performer; actor. **Honors/Awds:** Albums: The Time, What Time Is It?, Ice Cream Castle; movie appearances: Purple Rain, Grafitti Bridge; co-star of TV series A New Attitude. **Business Addr:** Actor/Singer, c/o Reprise Records, Warner Bros, 3300 Warner Blvd, Burbank, CA 91510.

DAY, TERRY
Professional football player. **Personal:** Born Sep 18, 1974. **Educ:** Mississippi State, attended. **Career:** New York Jets, defensive end, 1997-. **Business Addr:** Professional Football Player, New York Jets, 1000 Fulton Ave, Hempstead, NY 11550, (516)560-8100.

DAY, TODD FITZGERALD
Professional basketball player. **Personal:** Born Jan 7, 1970, Decatur, IL. **Educ:** Arkansas. **Career:** Milwaukee Bucks, guard/forward, 1992-95; Boston Celtics, 1995-97; Miami Heat, 1997-. **Special Achievements:** NBA Draft, First round pick, #8, 1992. **Business Addr:** Professional Basketball Player, Miami Heat, 721 NW 1st Ave, Miami Arena, Miami, FL 33136, (305)577-4328.

DAY, WILLIAM CHARLES, JR.
Business executive. **Personal:** Born Sep 17, 1937, Houston, TX; married Evelyn Shaw; children: Margaret Ann, Stephen Brian. **Educ:** TX So U, BA 1966. **Career:** First Harlem Securities Corp, exec Vp 1971-; Shearson Hammill Co Inc, account exec 1968-71; Armour Grocery Prods, sale rep 1967-68. **Orgs:** Chmn of bd First Harlem Mgmt Co; chmn of bd Colonial Quilting Co Inc; mem NY Stock Exchange. **Business Addr:** First Harlem Sec Corp, 32 Broadway, New York, NY 10004.

DAYE, CHARLES EDWARD
Educator. **Personal:** Born May 14, 1944, Durham, NC; son of Addie R Daye and Eccleasiastes Daye; married Norma S; children: Clarence L Hill III, Tammy H Roundtree. **Educ:** NC Central Univ, BA high honors 1966; Columbia Univ, JD honors 1969. **Career:** UNC Chapel Hill School of Law, prof 1972-81; NCCU School of Law, visiting prof 1980-81; dean & prof 1981-85; UNC Chapel Hill School of Law, prof 1985-; Henry P Brandis Dist Professor, 1991-. **Orgs:** Law clerk Hon Harry Phillips 6th Cir 1969-70; assoc Covington & Burlington 1970-72; NC Assoc of Black Lawyers, pres 1976-78, exec sec 1979-; mem bars of, US Supreme Ct, NY, DC, NC; chmn Triangle Housing Devel Corp, 1979-91, mem, 1977-; bd dir United Way of Greater Durham 1984-88; president Law School Admission Council 1991-93; mem Amer Bar Assn, NC State Bar, NC Bar Assn. **Honors/Awds:** Lawyer of the Year NC Assn Black Lawyers 1980; Civic Award Durham Community Affairs Black People 1981; co-author Casebook Housing & Comm Devel 1981; co-author NC Law of Torts; author articles in professional journals; Order of the Coif. **Home Addr:** 3400 Cambridge Rd, Durham, NC 27707. **Business Addr:** Professor of Law, University of North Carolina, School of Law, CB#3380, Chapel Hill, NC 27599-3380, (919)962-7004.

DAYS, DREW SAUNDERS, III
Government official. **Personal:** Born Aug 29, 1941, Atlanta, GA; son of Dorothea Jamerson Days (deceased) and Drew S Days Jr (deceased); married Ann Ramsay Langdon; children: Alison Langdon, Elizabeth Jamerson. **Educ:** Hamilton Coll, Clinton, NY, BA, cum laude 1963; Yale Law School, New Haven, CT, LLB, 1966. **Career:** SUS Dept of Justice, asst atty gen, solicitor general; Yale Law School, Alfred M Rankin Prof of Law, currently; NAACP Legal Defense & Educ & Educ Fund Inc, first asst counsel 1967-77; Temple Univ & Philadelphia, asso prof of Law 1973-75; Comayagua Honduras, peace corps volunteer 1967-69; Cotton Watt Jones King & Bowlus Chicago IL, law asso 1966-67; IL Civil Liberties Union, volunteer atty 1966-67; Agency for Internal Devel Honduras, consult program writer 1968-69; Rockefeller Commn to Latin Am, interpreter 1969. **Orgs:** Congressional Black Caucus & Nat Conference on Educ for Blacks 1972; publ ''Materials on Police Misconduct Litigation''; Reginald Heber Smith Lawyer Fellowship Program; co-editor ''Federal Civil Rights Litigation'', Practising Law Inst 1977; trustee, Edna McConnell Clark Foundation, 1988-93; John D. and Catherine T. MacArthur Foundation, mem bd of dir; Hamilton Coll, trustee; Petra Foundation, mem, bd of dirs. **Honors/Awds:** Judge Robert F Kennedy Memorial Human Rights Award, 1990. **Business Addr:** Alfred M. Rankin Professor, Yale University Law School, PO Box 208215, New Haven, CT 06520-8215.

DAYS, MICHAEL IRVIN
Journalist. **Personal:** Born Aug 2, 1953, Philadelphia, PA; son of Helen Boles Days and Morris Days; married Angela P Dodson, Apr 17, 1982; children: Edward, Adrian, Andrew, Umi. **Educ:** College of Holy Cross, BA, 1975; University of Missouri School of Journalism, MA, 1976. **Career:** Rochester Gannett Newspaper, reporter, 1978-80; Louisville Courier-Journal, reporter, 1980-84; Wall Street Journal, reporter, 1984-86; Philadelphia Daily News, city hall, education reporter, 1986-88, assistant city editor, 1988-89, business editor, 1989-91, assistant managing editor, 1991-. **Orgs:** Louisville Association of Black Communicators, president, 1983; Philadelphia Association of Black Journalists, president, 1982-83; National Association of Black Journalists, national board member, 1985-87; PA Society of Newspaper Editors, board of directors, 1991-. **Business Addr:** Assistant Managing Editor, Philadelphia Daily News, 400 N Broad St, PO Box 7788, Philadelphia, PA 19101, (215)854-5984.

DAYS, ROSETTA HILL
Education administrator. **Personal:** Born in Gibsland, LA; married James Days; children: Yanise, Regiuel. **Educ:** Grambling Coll, BS 1957; Univ MI, MS 1965. **Career:** Wilerson's Homesrv Inst, home economics lecturer 1957-60; Webster Parish Schools, teacher 1960-65, counselor 1965-67; Grambling Coll, chief counselor 1967, asst prof & acad counselor 1967-70, asst prof & dir, prof Rescue 1970-; LA & US Colleges, grants admin & Equal Opportunity Officer; Grambling State Univ, chmn Counseling & Testing Dept 1972-73; LA Assn Student Asst Progs, 1974-75. **Orgs:** Bd of dir SW Assn Stdnt Asst Progs 1974-75 V chmn LA State Adv Cncl on Mental Hlth; mem bd dir Nat Assn of Women in Criminal Justice; reg adv cncl Emergency Med Serv System; mem Amer Prsnnl gdnce Assn; Assn for Cnslr Ed & Suprvsn; Assn for non-white cncrns; Amer Coll Prsnnl Assn; LA Educ Assn; LA Assn for Msrmnt & Eval in Gdnce Aldrmn, Grambling, LA; sec-treas Legue of Womn Vtrs 1972; chap vP Mntl Hlth Assn 1973-74, pres 1974-75; Chap pres Delta Sigma Theta Inc 1971-73; sec Grambling C of C 1974-75; mem Nat Cncl of Negro Wmn; Bd Dir Lincoln Sickle Cell Assn1974-75; vP Lincoln Parish Blk Elcted Coordntg Com 1974-75. **Honors/Awds:** Scroll of Honor Omega Psi Phi Frat 1973, 74; Lewis Templle CME Ch Womn's Day Citn 1972; mem Alpha Kappa Mu Nat Hon Soc. **Business Addr:** Project Dir, Grambling State University, PO Drawer 8, Grambling, LA 71245.

DEAN, CLARA RUSSELL
Educational administrator. **Personal:** Born Sep 11, 1927, Greenville, SC; married Miles Dean; children: Miles Jr, Angela, Jacquelynn, Barbara, Wanda, Patricia. **Educ:** Essex County Coll, AAS 1968-70; Rutgers, BA Psychology 1970, MA Education 1972; Felician Coll, ASRN 1972; Jersey City State, nursing school 1973. **Career:** College Hosp Council, bd mem & chair affirm action 1975-79; CMDNJ, supv implimented dental clinic 1977; Essex Co, long range planning bd 1983-; Weequahic Multipurpose Center, dir/prin 1984-. **Orgs:** Mem 100 Black Woman 1982; life mem NAACP-NB; chairperson Three City Wide Health Fairs 1982-83-84; pres Clara Dean Civic Assoc 1976-; mem Bus & Prof Women 1978-; ed comm Greater Abyssian Ch 1980-. **Honors/Awds:** Achievement Awd PATCH-Newark 1981; Recogn Award Newark Br NAACP 1983; Recogn Award NJ State Commn for the Blind 1985. **Business Addr:** Dir, Weequahic Multi Purpose Center, 146 Clinton Ave, Newark, NJ 07114.

DEAN, CURTIS
Hotel manager. **Career:** Philadelphia Marriott Hotel, hotel manager; Los Angeles Marriott Hotel, manager, currently. **Business Addr:** Manager, Los Angeles Marriott Hotel, 5855 West Central Blvd, Los Angeles, CA 90045, (310)641-5700.

DEAN, DANIEL R.
Business executive. **Personal:** Born Jan 23, 1941, Atlantic City, NJ; son of Cora L Harris Dean and Edward Dean; married Edna Geraldine Jeter; children: Tracey, Kevin. **Educ:** WV State Coll, BS in Business Admin 1963; Rutgers Univ, 1967-68; Pace Univ, 1976-77; Stonier Grad School of Banking, 1980-83. **Ca-**

reer: Citicorp USA Inc Atlanta, relationship team mgr 1984-; Citibank, NA New York, NY, oper head 1978-84, oper mgr 1976-78, oper officer 1972-76. **Orgs:** Chmn bd of dir Frederick Douglas Liberation Library 1969-75; treas Somerset Cnty Comm Action Prog 1973-76; trustee Franklin Township Library Bd 1975-78; pres Superior Golf Assoc 1983-84; pres Southern Snow Seekers Ski Club 1985-88. **Military Serv:** AUS 1st/lt 1963-65. **Home Addr:** 2501 Old Sewell Rd, Marietta, GA 30068. **Business Addr:** President, D & E Floor Service Inc, 2501 Old Sewell Rd, Marietta, GA 30068.

DEAN, DIANE D.
Consultant, educator. **Personal:** Born Aug 26, 1949, Detroit, MI; daughter of Ada Spann and Edward Lesley Dean. **Educ:** Michigan State Univ, 1966-68; North Carolina A&T State Univ, BS 1971; Indiana Univ, MS 1973; Univ of California-Los Angeles, 1982-83; Stanford Univ, Summer Institute 1981; Case Western Reserve, certificate, 1991; Harvard Graduate School of Education, 1995. **Career:** Univ of Miami, area coordinator 1973-75; Occidental Coll, dir of housing 1975-78; Univ of Southern CA, asst dir of admissions, assistance & school relations 1978-80; Univ of CA-Los Angeles, asst dir of admissions 1980-81, assoc dir of admissions 1981-85; Leadership Education and Development (LEAD), dir of operations (consultant) 1983-85; Natl Action Council for Minorities in Engineering, dir incentive grants and scholarship programs 1985-90; Girl Scouts of the USA, management consultant, 1990-95; fund development consultant, 1995-. **Orgs:** Co-chair Region VI Natl Assn Student Personnel Admin 1985; co-facilitator mgmt institute, CA Assn of College/ Univ Housing Officers 1975-78; standing comm appointee Natl Assn of Coll Admissions Counselors 1979-86; apptd rep Graduate Mgmt Admissions Council 1981-85; mem Alpha Kappa Alpha; mem Black Womens Forum of Los Angeles 1980-, CA Museum of Afro-Amer Art 1984-, Studio Museum of Harlem 1985-, Schomburg Society, 1986-; Council of Concerned Black Execs 1986; lifetime mem UCLA Alumni Assoc, North Carolina A&T Alumni Assoc, Urban League (BEEP), Cass Tech Alumni Assn, NAACP, Corporate Womens Network; Literary Society 1989-; Coalition of 100 Black Women, 1991-; Natl Society of Fund Raising Executives; ASTD; NAFE; lifetime member, Girl Scouts; Assn of Girl Scouts Executive Staff, bd of dirs, 1994-. **Honors/Awds:** Directory of Minority Personnel Associated with Admissions, Creator and Editor 1979-; Paddington Corp J&B Winners Circle Award 1984. **Business Addr:** Fund Development Consultant, 420 Fifth Ave, New York, NY 10001.

DEAN, JAMES EDWARD
Educator, social worker, state government official. **Personal:** Born Mar 14, 1944, Atlanta, GA; son of Dorothy Cox Dean and Steve Dean, Sr; married Vyvyan A Coleman; children: Sonya V, Monica A. **Educ:** Clark College, BA, 1966; San Francisco City College, 1966; Fisk University, 1967; Atlanta University School of Social Work, MSW, 1968; University of Georgia, postgraduate studies, 1968; Emory University, postgraduate studies, 1975-76. **Career:** Economic Opport Atlanta Inc, human resource 1965-66; Georgia General Assembly, state representative, 1968-75; Clark College, Atlanta, GA, director of alumni affairs, 1971-78; MBO, contract procurement specialist, 1978-80; National Urban League, Inc, assistant director, 1980-82; BMC Realty Company, Atlanta, GA, management representative, 1982; State of Georgia Department of Transportation, equal employment opportunity officer, 1982-88, equal employment opportunity review officer, 1988-. **Orgs:** Atlanta Daily World Newspaper 1960-70; Atlanta Inquirer Newspaper 1962-68; vice pres Community Services Inc, Atlanta GA, 1982-89; sec/governing bd mem, Pine Acres Town & Country Club 1989; mem, Center for Study of Presidency, New York, 1988-89; mem, Amer Federation of Police; member, National Association of Social Workers; member, National Technical Association; member, Southern Center of International Studies; member, Academy of Certified Social Workers; member, Leadership Georgia Program Foundation; Friendship Baptist Church; Alpha Phi Alpha Inc, life mem; HR Butler Lodge, Prince Hall Masonic Order; Atlanta Area Technical School Off-Campus Advisory Committee; Atlanta Historical Society; Frontiers International Inc; Clark Atlanta Univ Alumni Assn, Atlanta Chapter; Clark Atlanta Univ National Alumni Assn; Minority Worker Training Program Clark Atlanta Univ; Joymen Club; board of directors, Atlanta Chapter United Nations Assn. **Honors/Awds:** Natl Urban League Fellowship; Atlanta Univ Multi-Purpose Schlrshp Award; Alpha Kappa Delta Natl Soc Hnr Soc, 1968; Council of Religion & Intl Affairs Flwshp; Outstanding Young Men of Atlanta Atlanta Jaycees; Souther Cntr for Interntl Studies, Atlanta Black/Jewish Coalition; Special Achievement Award, Dept of Transp State of GA, 1986, 1988; A Study of Community Organizaton Techniques Utilized by Three Self-Help Projects in Securing Low-Income Involvement 1968; Award for Political Leadership, Price High School; Presidential Citation, Clark College; Social Action Leadership Award, North Georgia Chapter, National Assn of Social Workers, Inc; Honorary State Trooper; Governor of Georgia, Lieutenant Colonel Aide de Camp, 1979, 1983, 1991; Governor of Georgia, Admiral of the Georgia Navy, 1971. **Home Addr:** 87 Burbank Dr NW, Atlanta, GA 30314-2450.

DEAN, VYVYAN COLEMAN
Educational administrator, educator. **Personal:** Born Jun 11, 1945, Fort Benning, GA; daughter of Dorothy Sims Coleman and Clarence Coleman; married James Dean, Jun 12, 1966; children: Sonya V, Monica A. **Educ:** Palmer Memorial Institute, Sedalia, NC, diploma, 1962; Clark College, BA, 1966; Atlanta University, MA, 1973; Georgia State University, postgraduate-advanced studies, 1983-87; Atlanta University, postgraduate-advanced studies, 1983-87. **Career:** Atlanta Public School System, Atlanta, GA, teacher, 1966-, Atlanta Metropolitan College, GED teacher, 1966-, John B Gordon Elementray School, Charles R Drew Elementary School, curriculum specialist, 1992-; City of Atlanta Parks and Recreation, Atlanta, GA, summer reading program director. **Orgs:** Vice-president, Decatur/DeKalb Chapter, The Drifters Inc, 1989-91, president, currently; National Association for Education of Young Children; International Reading Association; Georgia Association of Educators; National Association of Educators; Atlanta Association of Educators; Curriculum and Supervision/Development Association; Pals, LINKS Interest Group; treasurer, Atlanta Chapter, Circle Lets Inc, 1982-91; corresponding secretary, The Inquirers Literary Club, 1983-91; Delta Sigma Theta Sorority, 1969-, sgt of arms; member, AAE, AFT and Georgia Adult Literacy Association, 1970-. **Honors/Awds:** Outstanding Teacher of Children, Atlanta Public School, 1990; Special Recognition for Outstanding Teaching of Adults, 1989; Special Recognition, DeKalb Housing Resources Committee; Governor's Staff Appointment, Lieutenant Colonel, Aide De Camp, Governor's Staff, Outstanding Elementary Teaching in America, 1975. **Home Addr:** 87 Burbank Dr, NW, Atlanta, GA 30314.

DEAN, WALTER R., JR.
Educational administrator. **Personal:** Born Dec 12, 1934, Baltimore, MD. **Educ:** Morgan State Coll, BA, 1962; Univ of MD, MSW 1969. **Career:** Baltimore City Community College, chairperson, social and behavioral sciences, affairs, coord human serv asst, 1969-; Health & Welfare Council Baltimore, associate of soc res, 1968-69; St Club Worker Bur of Recreation, 1964-66; Afro-Amer Newspapers Baltimore, reporter, 1962-64. **Military Serv:** US Air Force, airman 1st class.

DEAN, WILLIE B.
Association executive. **Personal:** Born Mar 15, 1951, Potts Camp, MS; son of Mattie Delyta Brown Dean and Eddie B Dean; married Pamela Williamson Dean, Oct 25, 1985; children: Cedric Lamont, Jarrod Wilberforce, Matthew Alexander. **Educ:** Memphis State Univ, Memphis TN, BS Education, 1974; Univ of Texas, Arlington TX, attending, 1977-. **Career:** Glenview YMCA, Memphis TN, program dir, 1974-75; McDonald YMCA, Ft Worth TX, exec dir, 1975-81; Mondanto YMCA, St Louis, MO, vice pres, exec dir, 1981-. **Orgs:** Mem, Jennings-North St Louis Kiwanis Club, 1981-89, pres, 1985; program chmn, 100 Black Men of Metro St Louis, 1983-89; mem, Omega Psi Phi Frat Inc, 1983-89. **Honors/Awds:** Father of the Year, 100 Black Men of St Louis, 1985; Yes I Can Award, Metro Sentinel Newspaper, 1988. **Business Addr:** Vice President, Urban Services, YMCA of Greater St Louis, 5555 Page Blvd, St Louis, MO 63112.

DEANDA, PETER
Actor. **Personal:** Born Mar 10, 1938, Pittsburgh, PA; married Fatima; children: Allison, Peter. **Educ:** Actors' Workshop. **Career:** Pittsburgh Playhouse, actor; Weslin Prodn, actor; Nasara Prodn Labor & Ind Com Beverly Hills, fndr. **Orgs:** Mem NAACP; mem AEA; Image Awards Com Publ Black Drama Anthology 1971; New Am Library; written articles for NY Times & other maj publs; prod OnBdwy, Off-bdwy & TV; films "Lady Liberty" 1971, "The New Centurions" & "Come Back Charleston Blue" 1972; TV "Cannon"; title role "Cutter", "Joe Forrester", & "Police Woman". **Military Serv:** USAF 1955-59. **Business Addr:** 3721 Weslin Ave, Sherman Oaks, CA 91403.

DEANE, MORGAN R.
Dentist (retired). **Personal:** Born Sep 17, 1922, Lawrenceville, VA; son of Dr & Mrs Robert Deane; married Lela W; children: Frances, Judith, Morgan Jr. **Educ:** WV State Coll, BA 1949; Howard U, DDS 1953. **Career:** Cincinnati Health Dept, 1953-74; Health Serv Dir West End Health Center, Dental dir 1975; Dentist, private practice. **Orgs:** OH Valley Dental Soc; Cincinnati Dental Soc; OH State Dental Assn; Am Dental Assn; Am Soc Clinical Hypnosis. **Honors/Awds:** Omega Psi Phi Frat; Westley Smith Lodge; Kentucky Colonel. **Military Serv:** World War II active 3 yrs, inactive 8 yrs. **Home Addr:** 6186 Lakota Dr, Cincinnati, OH 45243.

DEANE, ROBERT ARMISTEAD
Physician (retired). **Personal:** Born Jul 5, 1919, Lawrenceville, VA; son of Otelia Virginia Russell Deane and Robert Armistead Deane; married Miriam Iris Thompson, Jun 24, 1942 (deceased); children: Sharon Deane, Linda Geneva Deane Gordon, Marjel Virginia Deane Thomas. **Educ:** VA State Coll, BS 1940; Howard Univ, MD 1944. **Career:** Freedmen's Hospital Howard Univ, intern, 1944-45, resident Ob/Gyn 1945-48; Walter Reed Army Medical Center Gynecology & Obstetrics Clinic, chief civilian out-patient physicians; Private Practice, gynecolo-

gist; medical examiner Ob/Gyn Walter Reed Army Medical Center, Washington DC 1963-90. **Orgs:** Mem Amer Bd of Ob/Gyn 1959; Hon Science Soc Beta Kappa Chi 1939; mem Chi Delta Mu Fraternity 1941. **Honors/Awds:** Article "Primary Carcinoma of the Vagina" Medical Assn of Washington DC Vol 30 No 7 co-authored with Chas M Cabaniss, MD 1961; article "From Physician to Inpatient at Howard Univ Hospital" Journal Natl Med Assn 1984. **Military Serv:** AUS Reserve 2nd lieutenant 1940-44. **Home Addr:** 6505 14th St, NW #401, Washington, DC 20012.

DEARMAN, JOHN EDWARD
Judge. **Personal:** Born Mar 28, 1931, Troy, TX; son of Jessie Mae Banks-Evans (deceased) and Melvin Dearman; married Ina Patricia Flemming, Dec 22, 1960; children: Tracy, Kelly, Jonathan, Jason. **Educ:** Wiley Coll, BA Social Studies 1950-54; Wayne State Law School, JD 1954-57; Univ of CA, Cert Labor Arbitrator 1973. **Career:** City of Detroit, social worker 1957-58; Private Practice, attorney 1957-59, 1961-77; State of CA, judge 1977-. **Orgs:** NAACP; dir Golden Gate Bridge Bd 1966-70; commissioner metropolitan Transportation Comm 1970-75; dir vice pres Family Serv Assoc of Amer 1968-72; pres of bd Family Serv Agency of SF 1968-72. **Honors/Awds:** Judge of the Year SF Trial Lawyers Assoc 1984; Humanitarian Judge of the Year CA Trial Lawyers Assoc 1984. **Home Addr:** 217 Upper Terrace, San Francisco, CA 94117. **Business Addr:** Judge, State of California, Department 20, 400 McAllister St, San Francisco, CA 94102.

DEAS, LARRY. See DAIS, LARRY.

DEBARGE, EL (ELDRA)
Vocalist. **Personal:** Born Jun 4, 1961, Grand Rapids, MI. **Career:** DeBarge Musical Group, vocalist, 1978-86, solo career, 1986-. **Special Achievements:** Albums include: "El Debarge," "In the Storm," "Heart, Mind, and Soul.". **Business Addr:** Vocalist, Heart, Mind & Soul, c/o Warner Bros, 4000 Warner Blvd, Burbank, CA 91522, (818)954-1744.

DEBAS, HAILE T.
Surgeon, educator. **Personal:** Born Feb 25, 1937, Asmara, Eritrea; married Ignacia Kim. **Educ:** Univ Coll of Addis Ababa Ethiopia, BS 1958; McGill Univ Montreal Canada, MD 1963; Ottawa Civic Hosp, Internship 1963-64; Vancouver Gen Hosp, Surgical Residency 1964-69. **Career:** Univ of British Columbia, rsch fellow 1965-66, 1969-70, asst prof of surgery 1971-75; Univ of CA Los Angeles & Wadsworth VA Med Ctr, rsch fellow 1972-74, prof of surgery 1981-85; Univ of British Columbia, assoc prof of surgery 1976-80; Univ of WA Seattle, prof of surgery, chief of gastrointestinal surgery 1985-87; UCSF, AOA visiting prof, 1989; Univ of CA, professor & chmn surgery, 1987-93; Univ of Texas Medical Branch, Galveston, visiting prof, 1980; Univ of California, San Francisco, dean, School of Med, 1993-. **Orgs:** Fellow Royal Coll of Physicians & Surgeons of Canada 1969-; Amer Coll of Surgeons 1984-; member, American Gastroenterological Assn, 1974-; member, Pacific Coast Surgical Assn, 1982-; member, Society Black Academic Surgeons, 1987-; member, Society of Surgical Chairman, 1987-; dir, American Board of Surgery, 1990-; member, Institute of Medicine, 1990-, foreign assoc, 1990-; pres International Hepato-Biliary-Pancreatic Assoc, 1991-92; fellow, American Academy of Arts & Science, 1992. **Honors/Awds:** British Columbia Surgical Soc Essay Awd 1965; Med Rsch Council of Canada Fellowship 1972-74; William H Rorer Rsch Prize for Original Rsch So CA Soc of Gastroenterology 1973; Golden Scalpel Awd for Teaching Excellence Div of General Surgery UCLA School of Med 1981; Kaiser Award for Excellence in Teaching, UCSF School of Medicine, 1991. **Business Addr:** Dean, School of Medicine, Univ of California, San Francisco, 513 Parnassus Ave, S-224, San Francisco, CA 94143-0410, (415)476-2342.

DEBERRY, LOIS MARIE
State legislator. **Personal:** Born May 5, 1945, Memphis, TN; married Charles Traughber; children: Michael Boyer. **Educ:** Lemoyne-Owen Coll Memphis. **Career:** TN House of Representatives, state representative 1972-. **Orgs:** Pres, Nat Black Caucus of State Legislators; bd of dirs, State Legislative Leaders Foundation; Natl Conference of State Legislators; founder & chairman, Annual Legislative Retreat at TN Black Caucus; NAACP; Delta Sigma Theta Sorority. **Honors/Awds:** The Kansas City Globe 100 Most Influential African-Americans, 1997; The Harold Bradley Legislative Leadership Award, 1997; National Political Congress of Black Women, Inc, Pioneer Award, 1996; NBCSL Legislator of the Year, 1994; Martin Luther King Drum Major Award, 1990; Shelby State Community College Outstanding Woman in Corrections Award, 1979 ; "The Lois DeBerry Correctional Institute for Special Need Offenders" named in her honor, 1977; Outstanding Women in Community Service Award by Epsilon Epsilon Chapter of Alpha Kappa Alpha Sorority, 1975; Memphis Chapter of LINKS Social Service Award, 1975; Glorification of the Image of Black Woman-Hood Award, 1975; Outstanding Woman of the Year, KWAM Gospel, 1973; Tri State Woman of the Year 1972. **Business Addr:** State Representative, Tennessee House of Representatives, Legislative Plaza, Ste 15, Nashville, TN 37243-0191.

DEBNAM, CHADWICK BASIL
Management marketing consultant. **Personal:** Born May 10, 1950, Clayton, NC; son of Madie Debnam and Clarence Debnam; married Mauria Fletcher, May 1, 1979; children: Andrea Dione. **Educ:** Pacific Univ, Forest Grove OR, BS Political Sci 1972; Portland State Univ, Post Grad Studies 1972-73. **Career:** Mary Acheson House, prog dir 1972-75; Urban Redevelopment Corp, mktg dir 1976-78; Three Sixty Degree Publishing, pres 1979-82; B Chadwick Ltd, pres 1982-. **Orgs:** Bd mem Multnomah Co Charter Review 1982-84; chmn Adv Steering Comm Inner NE YMCA 1983-85; mem Albina Lions Club 1983-; pres The Oregon Business League 1984-87; mem Amer Mktg Assoc 1986-87; chmn Black Republican Council of OR 1986-88. **Honors/Awds:** Keynote speaker Annual Banquet Scottish Rites Masons 1984; Century Awd Portland Metro YMCA 1984-85; Businessman of Month MBE Torch Awd Amer Contractor Pub 1985; guest lecturer Camp Enterprise Downtown Rotary 1986.

DEBRACY, WARREN
Attorney, educator. **Personal:** Born Mar 28, 1942, Chicago, IL; son of Amanda Eluira Jones and Warren Jones, Sr; married Marilyn Ann Forger; children: Valerie, Justin, Catherine. **Educ:** Loyola Univ Chicago, BS Soc Sci 1964; Rutgers Univ New Brunswick, NJ, MA Pol Sci 1966; Cornell Univ Ithaca, NY, JD Law 1971. **Career:** Rutgers Univ NJ, asst inst 1966; Loyola Univ Law Sch New Orleans, asst prof 1971-72; Univ of Detroit Law Sch, asst prof 1972-73; Univ of Toledo Law Sch, assoc prof 1973-79; Loyola Univ, New Orleans, LA, visiting prof, 1986; Valparoiso Univ, Valparoiso, IN, visiting prof, 1988-89. **Orgs:** Mem MI Democratic State Central Comm 1985-89; treas 2nd Cong Dist Dem Comm MI 1983-85, vice-chair 1979-81; mem, Rules Comm, Democratic Natl Convention, 1988; delegate, 1980 Democratic Natl Convention. **Honors/Awds:** 1st yr moot court champion Cornell Law Sch 1969; best affimative debator Gennett Newpaper Tournament Rochester 1962; supplement to law, How Years and Social Change, 1978; Legality of Affirmative Action, Journal of Urban Law, 1974-75. **Military Serv:** AUS 1st lt 1966-68; Vietnam Service Metal. **Business Addr:** North Carolina Central, School of Law, Durham, NC 27707.

DEBRO, JOSEPH ROLLINS
Business executive. **Personal:** Born Nov 27, 1928, Jackson, MS; married Anita English; children: Keith, Karl, Kraig. **Educ:** Univ CA Berkeley, AB, MS 1953-59. **Career:** Model Cities, Oakland, CA, dir; Oakland Small Business Devel Cntr, dir; NASA, research scientist; Producers Cotton Oil Co, chem engr; Nat Asso Minority Contractors, exec dir. **Orgs:** Pres Reca Inc; pres Housing Assistance Council; pres JDA Consulting Group Inc; pres Gaylor Construction Co; chmn minority Bus Enterprise Task Force Inc; vice pres Trans Bay Engrs & Builders Sigma Xi; Alpha Phi Alpha; publication, More Than 25 Articles Scientific Bus Jounals. **Business Addr:** World Trade Center, Ste 275 C, San Francisco, CA 94111.

DEBRO, JULIUS
Educational administrator. **Personal:** Born Sep 25, 1931, Jackson, MS; son of Seleana Debro and Joseph Debro; married Darlene Conley; children: Blair, Renee. **Educ:** Univ of San Francisco CA, BA Pol Sci 1953; Univ of San Fran Law Sch, 1957; San Jose State U, MA Sociology 1967; Univ of CA Berkeley, Doctorate of Crim 1975; Narcotic and Drug Research, Inc, postdoctoral research associate, 1989-90. **Career:** Inst of Crim Justice/Criminology Univ of MD College Pk MD, asst prof 1971-79; Joint Commn on Criminology/Criminal Justice Edn/Standards Wash DC, prin investgtr 1978-79; Dept of Public Admin, chrmn 1979-80; The Dept of Criminal Justice Atlanta U, chrmn 1979-, dir 1979-; Atlanta U, prof of criminology, chmn 1985-86 criminal justice/sociology, chmn criminal justice admin, 1986-91; University of Washington Graduate School, Seattle, WA, associate dean, 1991-, acting assistant provost, 1992; Justice Quarterly deputy editor. **Orgs:** Dir Specl Oppor Prgm UC Berkeley 1968-70; bd mem Metropolitan Atlanta Crime Comm 1984-; mem Cncl of Higher Educ in Crim Just; mem Alpha Phi Alpha; mem Citizen's Review Bd Atlanta GA 1985-; mem Central Atlanta Progress Study Commn 1986-87, Atlanta Anti-Crime Bd 1987; chmn Metropolitan Atlanta Crime Commn 1987-88; chmn, Drug Task Force, Fulton County, GA; mem, Chief Justice's Commission on Professionalism, Supreme Court of Georgia, 1989; mem, investigative panel, Georgia Bar Association, 1988-90. **Honors/Awds:** Fellow Nat Inst of Hlth 1969-70; fellow Ford Found 1971; Editorial Bd Crim Justice Review, 1979-; Western Society of Criminology Fellow, 1989; Inter-University Seminar on the Armed Forces and Society Fellow, 1989; Herbert Bloch Award, American Society of Criminology. **Military Serv:** US Army, col; Korean Victory Medal. **Business Addr:** Assoc Dean, Univ of Washington Graduate School, The Graduate School, 200 Gerberding Hall, Box 351240, Seattle, WA 98195.

DECARAVA, ROY RUDOLPH
Photographer, educator. **Personal:** Born Dec 9, 1919, New York, NY; son of Elfreda and Andrew; married Sherry F DeCarava, Sep 4, 1970; children: Susan, Wendy, Laura. **Educ:** Harlem Art Center, 1938-40. **Career:** Berman Studios, illustrator, 1943-58; free-lance photographer, 1958-65; Cooper Union, adjunct professor of art, 1970-73; Sports Illustrated Magazine, photographer, 1965-75; Hunter College, CUNY, distinguished professor of art, 1975-. **Orgs:** PSC/CUNY, 1975-. **Honors/Awds:** Wesleyan University, Honorary DFA, 1992; The Maryland Institute, Honorary DFA, 1986; Rhode Island Institute of Fine Arts, Honorary DFA, 1985; Friends of Photography, Distinguished Career in Photography Award, 1991; American Society of Magazine Photographers, Special Citation for Photographic Journalism, 1991. **Special Achievements:** Publications: The Sound I Saw, book of jazz photos, 1983; Roy DeCarava-Photographs, 1981; exhibition, "The Sweet Flypaper of Life," Roy DeCarava and Langston Hughes, shown throughout the US and overseas.

DECLUE, ANITA. See Obituaries section.

DECOSTA, HERBERT ALEXANDER, JR.
Business executive. **Personal:** Born Mar 17, 1923, Charleston; married Emily Spencer; children: Gail D. **Educ:** IA State U, BS 1944. **Career:** Nat Adv Com for Aeronautics Langley Field, architectural Engr 1944-47; HA DeCosta Co Gen Contractors, vice pres 1948-60, pres 1960-, bd dirs 1969-75. **Orgs:** Nat Assn Minority Contractors 1974-75, 79-; bd dir Nat Assn Home Builders 1973-75; bd dir mem Home Builders Assn of Greater Charleston; active Boy Scouts of Am; bd visitors C State C of C 1971-74; mgmt com Armed Forces YMCA 1972-75; bd dirs St John's Episcopal Mission Center 1965-75; sr warden St Mark's Episcopal Ch 1975, 80; Kiwanis Intl Charleston Chap Bd Dirs 1974-75; Charleston Area Community Relations Com 1970-75; Charleston Planning & Zoning Comm 1970-75; v chmn PA Comm Serv Inc Beaufort SC; mem SC State Bd for Tech & Comprehensive Edn; life mem NAACP; bd trustees Benedict Coll 1972-80; mem Sigma Ph Phi Frat 1978-; mem Bd of Architectural Review City of Charleston SC. **Honors/Awds:** Man of yr Alpha Phi Alpha Frat 1970; silver beaver award Coastal Carolina Council Boy Scouts of Am 1972. **Business Addr:** 93 Spring St, Charleston, SC 29403.

DECOSTA-WILLIS, MIRIAM
Educator. **Personal:** Born Nov 1, 1934, Florence, AL; daughter of Beautine Hubertt DeCosta and Frank A DeCosta; married Archie W Willis Jr, Oct 20, 1972 (deceased); children: Tarik Sugarmon, Elena S Williamson, Erika S Echols, Monique A Sugarmon. **Educ:** Wellesley Coll, BA 1956; Johns Hopkins Univ, MA 1960, PhD 1967. **Career:** Owen Coll, instructor 1960-66; Memphis State Univ, assoc prof of Spanish 1966-70; Howard Univ, assoc prof of Spanish 1970-74, prof & chmn of dept 1974-76; LeMoyne-Owen Coll, prof, Romance Languages, prof of Spanish & dir of DuBois program, 1979-88. **Orgs:** Mem, Coll Language Assn; bd of dirs, MSU Center for Rsch on Women; chair TN Humanities Council; bd Federation of State Humanities Councils; editorial bd Sage & Afro-Hispanic Review; life mem NAACP; chmn, Exec bd/mem, TN Humanities Council, 1981-87; chmn & founding mem, Memphis Black Writers' Workshop, 1980-. **Honors/Awds:** Phi Beta Kappa 1956; Johns Hopkins Fellowship 1965; editor Blacks in Hispanic Literature Kennikat Pr 1977; articles in CLAJ, Journal of Negro History, Black World Negro History Bulletin, Revista Interamericana, Caribbean Quart; Sage Afro-Hispanic Review; Outstanding Faculty Mem of the Year, LeMoyne-Owen Coll, 1982; Homespun Images: An Anthology of Black Memphis Writers & Artists, 1988; editor, The Memphis Diary of Ida B Wells, Beacon Press, 1994. **Home Addr:** 585 S Greer, #703, Memphis, TN 38111. **Business Addr:** Visiting Commonwealth Prof of Spanish, Dept of Foreign Languages & Literature, George Mason Univ, Fairfax, VA 22030.

DEE, MERRI
Newscaster, talk show host, announcer. **Personal:** Born Oct 30, 1936, Chicago, IL; daughter of Agnes Blouin and John Blouin; children: Toya Dorham. **Educ:** St Xavier Univ, major in bus adm. **Career:** WBEE Radio, news hostess of talk-music prog women's ed 1966-72; WSDM-FM radio, hostess "The Merri Dee Show" 1968-69; Women's Ed & staff announcer; WSNS-TV, hostess of TV talk show 1971-72; Cont Bank, spokesperson 1972-76; WGN-TV & WGN-Radio, news announ edit spokesperson 1972-76; Hillman's Foods, consumer adv 1974-75; Kraft Foods, nutrit spokesperson 1975-76 & 1979-80; WGN Broadcasting, newscaster/announcer; WGN-TV, host of "Heart of Chicago" talk show/director of community relations, currently. **Orgs:** Sec & exec bd mem Am Cancer Soc appearances at num Cancer soc-related events; charter trustee & dir Athletes for Better Edn; bd dir Mayors Open Land Project; personal appearances for Amer Cancer Soc, March of Dimes, Men Health Assoc, Chic Park Dist, Urban Leag, Chic Chamber of Comm Mayor Daley's Youth Found YWCA & YMCA, Chic Boys Clubs, univs, Chs, Schs; public speaker; general chmn United Negro Coll Fund; host of UNCF Telethon Chicago 15 yrs; board member, National Assn for the Prevention of Child Abuse; executive board member, Little City Foundation; board of directors, American Federation of Television and Radio Announcers; member, League of Black Women; board of trustees, Easter Seals Foundation; board of advisors, American Foundation for the Blind. **Honors/Awds:** Muscular Dystrophy Fundraising Trophy; National Assn of Media Women Award; National Assn of Black Accountants Recognition Award; Woman of the Year, Chicago Church Women'sderation; Frederick D. Patterson Award, United Negro College Fund, 1990; Little City Foundation Award, Outstanding Volunteer Efforts & Generosity to Children & Adults with Retardation & Other Developmental Challenges, 1995; Natl Assn of Negro Business & Prof Women's Club Inc, President's Award, Outstanding Services & Commitment to Excellence, 1995; Bethany Christian Service Award, Outstanding Dedication of Behalf of Children & Families, 1995; YWCA, Gary Indiana, Capital Campaign Commitment,1994; Camp Fire Boys & Girls Club of Chicago, In Support of Children's Excellence, 1994; US Marine Corp, for Public Service, 1994; Royalties Social & Charity Club, Outstanding Women in Communications & Arts, 1994. **Business Addr:** Director, Community Relations, WGN Broadcasting, 2501 W Bradley Pl, Chicago, IL 60618.

DEE, RUBY (RUBY ANN WALLACE)
Actress. **Personal:** Born Oct 27, Cleveland, OH; married Ossie Davis; children: Nora, Guy, Hasna. **Educ:** Hunter Coll, BA 1945; Amer Negro Theatre, apprentice 1941-44. **Career:** Actress appearing in numerous TV plays and motion pictures; Broadway productions, all black cast of "Arsenic & Old Lace," "John Loves Mary," "Anna & Lucasta," 1946, "A Raisin in the Sun," 1959, "Purlie Victorious," 1961, "Boesman & Lena," 1971, "The Imaginary Invalid," 1971, "Wedding Band," 1972, role of Queen Gertrude in "Hamlet," 1975; motion pictures, "The Jackie Robinson Story," 1950, "St Louis Blues," 1957, "A Raisin in the Sun," 1960, "Buck & the Preacher," 1971, "Go Tell It On the Mountain," "Long Days Journey Into Night," "To Be Young Gifted and Black," "Cop and a Half," "The Stand," "Reading Rainbow," "The World of Sholom Aleichem," "Do the Right Thing," "Glass Menagerie," "Flyin' West," "Tuesday Morning Ride," "Just Cause"; collaborated with Jules Dassin & Julian Mayfield "Uptight," "Wedding Band," by Alice Childress, 1973; 3 yrs with Ossie Davis & Ruby Dee Story Hour over Natl Black Network; edited an anthology of poems "Glow Child and Other Poems"; formed a production company, Emmalyn Enterprises, with husband Ossie Davis; narrated the PBS special "God's Gonna Trouble the Waters," 1998. **Orgs:** Mem NAACP, SCLC; Delta Sigma Theta. **Honors/Awds:** Obie Award 1971; Martin Luther King Jr Award Operation PUSH 1972; Frederick Douglass Award NY Urban League 1970; Drama Desk Award 1974; Theater Hall of Fame, 1988; Best Performance by an Actress, Do the Right Thing, NAACP Image Award, 1989; NAACP Image Awards Hall of Fame, 1989; Literary Guild Award, 1989; Monarch Award, 1990; Emmy Award, Best Supporting Acress, Decoration Day, 1991. **Special Achievements:** Author: Take It From the Top; My One Good Nerve; Two Ways to Count to Ten; Tower to Heaven; Glowchild. **Business Addr:** The Artist Agency, 10000 Santa Monica Blvd, Los Angeles, CA 90067.

DEESE, DERRICK
Professional football player. **Personal:** Born May 17, 1970, Culver City, CA. **Educ:** USC, attended. **Career:** San Francisco 49ers, tackle, 1994-. **Business Addr:** Professional Football Player, San Francisco 49ers, 4949 Centennial Blvd, Santa Clara, CA 95054, (415)562-4949.

DEESE, MANUEL
City official. **Personal:** Born Nov 8, 1941, Toomsboro, GA; married Jean Matthews; children: Eric, Byron. **Educ:** Morgan State Univ, BA Pol Sci; Amer Univ School of Govt & Publ Admin, MPA. **Career:** Natl League of Cities DC, policy analyst 1969-71; City of Alexandria, asst to city mgr 1971-74; City of Richmond, asst city mgr admin 1974-77, asst citymgr operations 1977-79, city mgr 1979-. **Orgs:** Mem governing bd Amer Assoc for Public Admin; bd of dir Richmond Reg Criminal Justice Training Ctr; bd mem Intl City Mgmt Assn. **Honors/Awds:** Alumnus of the Year Morgan State Univ 1981; Recipient of numerous awds for leadership in govt & civic affairs. **Business Addr:** City Manager, City of Richmond, 900 E Broad St, Richmond, VA 23219.

DE FOSSETT, WILLIAM K.
Association executive. **Personal:** Born May 7, 1920, New York, NY; son of Lucille De Fossett and Kenneth De Fossett; married Gloria Green De Fossett (deceased); children: William Jr. **Career:** New York Black Yankees, Pittsburgh Crawfords, Baltimore Elite Giants, Alex Pompez's Cuban Stars, professional baseball player, Negro Baseball League; Veterans Administration, New York, NY, 1946-47; New York Police Dept, New York, NY, officer, 1947-50, Bureau of Special Services, detective, 1950-63, retired from Police force in 1969; US Dpt of State, security officer, 1963-80. **Orgs:** National president emeritus, 369th Veterans' Association, currently; vice chairman, board of directors, Sickle Cell Disease Foundation of New York; past member, Board of Directors, New York State American Negro Emancipation Centennial Authority; past vice chairman, Manhattan Council, Boy Scouts of America; member, NAACP; member, New York Urban League. **Honors/Awds:** First black State Department Security Officer, 1963; Boy Scout Family of the Year, Boy Scouts of America, 1962; citation for preventing the assassination of Chiang Kai Shek's son, 1970; citation for the release of Soviet sailor Simas Kudirka, 1978; under DeFossett's leadership, the 369th Veterans' Association received numerous awards, including the Frederick Douglass

Achievement Award from the New York Urban League, 1980 and a Federal Charter from the US Government, 1984. **Military Serv:** US Army, chief warrant officer, 1936-46. **Business Addr:** President Emeritus, 369th Veterans' Association, One 369th Plaza, New York, NY 10037.

DEFRANTZ, ANITA L.

Association executive. **Personal:** Born Oct 4, 1952, Philadelphia, PA; daughter of Anita P DeFrantz and Robert D DeFrantz (deceased). **Educ:** Connecticut College, BA (with honors), political philosophy, 1974; University of Pennsylvania Law School, JD, 1977. **Career:** Juvenile Law Center of Philadelphia, attorney, 1977-79; Princeton University, administrator, 1979-81; The Corp. for Enterprise Development, counsel, 1980-81; Los Angeles Olympic Organizing Committee, vice pres, 1981-85; Intl Olympic Committee, 1986, executive board, 1992, vice pres, 1997; Amateur Athletic Foundation, president, currently. **Orgs:** Intl Olympic Committee, 1986, executive board, 1992-, vp, 1997-; Connecticut College, trustee, 1974-88, 1990-; US Olympic Committee, board of directors, executive committee; International Committee for Fair Play; Academie des Sports; Salt Lake City Olympic, organizing comm, bd of dir; Women's World Cup 1989, comm tv of SC; Children NOW, Federation Intl Societes d'Aviron, vp. **Honors/Awds:** NAACP Legal Defense and Educational Fund, Black Women of Achievement Award; Essence Magazine, Award for Sports; The Sporting News, one of the 100 Most Powerful People in Sports, 1991-97; Los Angeles Times Magazine, one of Southern California's "Rising Stars," 1988; Ladies Home Journal, one of America's "100 Most Important Women; Los Angeles YWCA, Silver Achievement Award for Public Service; United States Olympic Committee, Olympic Torch Award, 1988; University of Rhode Island, honorary Doctor of Laws, 1989; Connecticut College, Hall of Fame inductee, 1989; Major Taylor Award, 1989; Metropolitan Los Angeles YMCA, Martin Luther King Jr. Brotherhood Award, 1990; National Association of Women Collegiate Athletic Administrators, Honor Award, 1991; US Rowing's Board of Directors, Jack Kelly Award, 1991; Pepperdine University, Doctor of Philanthropy Degree, 1992; Sports Lawyers Association, Award of Excellence, 1992; Turner Broadcasting Trumpet Award, 1993; Billie Jean King, Contribution Award, 1996; Medal of Honor, Intl Softball Federation; numerous others. **Special Achievements:** Rowing Awards: Bronze Medal, Olympic Games, 1976; Silver Medal, World Championships, 1978; Six National Championships; Olympic Order Bronze Medal, 1980; First woman to be named vp of the International Olympic Committee. **Business Addr:** President, Amateur Athletic Foundation of Los Angeles, 2141 W Adams Blvd, Los Angeles, CA 90018, (213)730-9614.

DEGENESTE, HENRY IRVING

Corporate security director. **Personal:** Born Aug 16, 1940, Newark, NJ; son of Olive Pansy Lopes DeGeneste and William Henry DeGeneste; divorced; children: Michelle, Rene, Henry Jr. **Educ:** Fairleigh Dickinson Univ, course work in math & elec engrg 1958-62; Rutgers Univ, certificate Criminal Justice Planning & Rsch 1975; Fed Bureau of Investigation, certificate Exec Management 1976; Columbia Univ, certificate Exec Management of Criminal Justice System 1976; Adelphi Univ, BA Business Admin (cum laude), 1976; John Jay College Grad course work towards MPA. **Career:** Edmond Assocs, draftsman 1962-65; Newark Public Schools, school teacher 1962-65; US Postal Serv, 1965-67; New York-New Jersey, port authority, Law Enforcement, police officer, 1967-74, police sgt, 1974-76, police lt, 1976-78, police capt, 1978-81, supt of police, 1984-88; The Port Authority of New York and New Jersey, director of public safety/superintendent of police, 1988-90; Prudential Securities, sr vice president/director of corporate security, 1990-. **Orgs:** Mem, New Jersey Council on Corrections, 1990; chmn, Tri-State Radio Planning Committee, 1988-90; pres, American Academy for Professional Law Enforcement, 1989-91; pres, Hudson County, New Jersey Chiefs of Police, 1987-88; pres, National Organization of Black Law Enforcement Executives, 1982-83; board mem, New York and New Jersey Cargo Security Council; board mem, New Jersey Special Olympics; board mem, The Mott Hall School of Mathematics, Science, and Technology for Gifted and Talented Students; board mem, Police Executive Research Forum; mem, American Society for Public Administration; mem, American Management Association; mem, Criminal Justice Educators of New York; mem, American Society for Industrial Security. **Honors/Awds:** New Jersey Pride Award, 1986; three Police Commendation Medals; one Meritorious Police Duty Medal; two Port Authority Executive Director's Unit Citations; Whitney M Young Jr Award, National Urban League; Two Black Achievers in Industry Award, Harlem YMCA; United Nations Peace Medal; author, "EMS and the Police Response to Terrorism," The Police Chief, May 1987; author, "Urban Transit Center: Where Crime and the Homeless Meet," Law Enforcement News, February 1987; Author: Policing Transportation Facilities, Charles C Thomas, Publisher, October, 1994. **Home Addr:** 40 Conger St, Bloomfield, NJ 07003. **Business Addr:** Sr Vice President, Director of Corporate Security, Prudential Securities, Inc, 127 John St, 32nd Fl, New York, NY 10292.

DE GRAFF, JACQUES ANDRE

Business executive. **Personal:** Born Nov 11, 1949, New York, NY; son of Beryl Hay De Graff and James Augustus De Graff;

married Jacqueline Riley De Graff, Sep 29, 1974; children: Danielle Janet. **Educ:** Queensborough Community College, Astoria, NY, AA, 1971; Hunter College, New York, NY, BA, 1975. **Career:** New York State Urban Development Corporation, New York, NY, vice president of finance, 1979-83; Packard Press, Inc, New York, NY, national account representative, 1985-86; Securities Press Inc, New York, NY, vice president, 1986-88; De Graff Unlimited Inc, New York, NY, managing partner, 1988-90; Blueberry Treatment Centers Inc, Brooklyn, NY, exec dir, beginning 1990; Rev. Al Sharpton for Mayor, NY, campaign coordinator, currently. **Orgs:** Vice Chairman, Advisory Board, Manhattan Urban League, 1987-; friend, Studio Museum, 1986-; 3rd vice president, National 100 Black Men NY Chapter. **Honors/Awds:** Governor's Citation, Governor of New York, 1982; National Leader Service Award, 1983; Businessman of the Year, DRIVE, 1988; Community Service Award, Caribbean American Legal Institute, 1980. **Home Addr:** 60 Harbor Key, Harmon Cove, Secaucus, NJ 07094.

DEGRAFFENREIDT, ANDREW

Educational administrator (retired), author, farmer. **Personal:** Born Mar 3, 1928, Kansas City, MO; married Eddie Pearl Black; children: Andrew, III, Fredi Grace, Carol. **Educ:** Tougaloo Coll, MS, BS; PA State Univ, MS 1957; FL State Univ, 3 summer NSF program, 1966; FL Atlantic Univ, Univ Miami, certified supvr, admin. **Career:** Broward & Co School Syst, asst admin; Dillard HS Ft Lauderdale, FL, teacher; Everglades Jr HS, teacher chmn sci dept; Broward Co ITV Ctr, devel taught special prog, 1967-70; farmer, author, currently. **Orgs:** Dir CTA; dir FEA; exec council mem FEA; chmn many educ cons; salary chmn BSAA; sch admin Piper HS; elected to the Ft Lauderdale City Comm, 1973-79; Boy Scout Scoutmaster; nghbrhd scout commr; past mem, sub comm Broward Co Chrtr Commn; past bd mem United Way Broward Co; Girl Scout Council Broward Co; Family Serv Agency; Project on aging; chmn Gold Coast League Cities; past chmn NW Boys Club Adv Bd; past mem City Comm Serv & Facilities Bd; past mem Broward Co Health & Planning Council; mem Broward Co Planning Council & pres Brotherhood Org of Piney Grove Church. **Special Achievements:** Author, Grandpa the King; Ft Lauderdale city commission dedicated new building the Andrew DeGraffenreidt Community Center.

DEGRAFFENREIDT, JAMES H., JR.

Utilities company executive. **Educ:** Yale University. **Career:** Maryland, asst people's counsel; Hart, Carroll & Chavers, partner; Washington Gas, beginning 1986, managing attorney, senior vice president, president, currently. **Orgs:** St Matthew's Athletic Association, basketball and soccer coach; Northwood Baseball League, baseball coach. **Business Addr:** President, Washington Gas, 1100 H St NW, Washington, DC 20080, (202)750-4440.

DEHART, HENRY R.

Engineer (retired). **Personal:** Born Nov 11, 1931, Staten Island, NY; married Panzy Hawk; children: Henry, Linda. **Educ:** Polytechnic Inst of NY, BCE 1958. **Career:** New York City Dept of Traffic, dir of hwy design, until 1992. **Orgs:** Licensed professional engr NY; past warden, past dir SS; licensed lay reader St Gabriels PE Church; past pres Staten Island Br NAACP 1965; past commdr Amer Legion 1966; acolyte master St Gabriels Church. **Honors/Awds:** Friend of Howard Adward NY Club, Howard Univ Alumni, 1975; past pres award, Staten Island Branch, NAACP, 1986; Bishop Cross Long Island Diocese, 1987; Meritorious Award for Community Serv 1987. **Military Serv:** USAF 1952-56.

DEHART, PANZY H.

Social worker (retired). **Personal:** Born May 18, 1934, Cleveland County, NC; daughter of Sallie Maude Hawk Owens and Henry Kilgore; married Henry Ross DeHart; children: Henry Jr, Linda. **Educ:** Howard Univ, BA 1956, MSW 1958; George Mercer School of Theology; NYU Graduate School of Social Work, attended. **Career:** DC Dept of Welfare, child welfare social worker 1958-61; Veterans Administration, clinical social worker 1961-65; NY City Dept of Health, consultant 1968-70; Inwood House, supervisor 1966-68, 1970-72; NY Univ Medical Ctr, rehab social worker 1976-96. **Orgs:** Pres Howard Univ Alumni Club of New York City 1970-74; mem bd of dir Parent Preparation Inc 1970-75; mem Queens Chap Jack & Jill of Amer Inc 1973-87; dir Jack & Jill Computer Assisted Lab 1985-87; mem Concerned Citizens of South Queens 1987; Partnership for the Homeless, 1991-; Psychoanalytic Research Society Section VI, American Psychological Association, 1992-; board of directors, Episcopal Charities, 1996-; member, St Gabriel's Episcopal Church, Hollis, Queens. **Honors/Awds:** Service Award Howard Univ Alumni Club 1972; Natl Achievement Award Lambda Kappa Mu Sor 1974; Service Award Jack & Jill of Amer Inc Queens Chap 1986. **Home Addr:** 110-06 214th St, Queens Village, NY 11429.

DEHERE, TERRY (LENNOX DOMINIQUE)

Professional basketball player. **Personal:** Born Sep 12, 1971, New York, NY. **Educ:** Seton Hall University. **Career:** Los Angeles Clippers, guard, 1993-97; Sacramento Kings, 1997-. **Business Addr:** Professional Basketball Player, Sacramento Kings, One Sports Parkway, Sacramento, CA 95834, (916)928-6900.

DEIZ, MERCEDES F.

Judge. **Personal:** Born Dec 13, 1917, New York, NY; daughter of Mary Lopez and Frank Lopez; married Carl H Deiz; children: Bill, Karen, Gilbert. **Educ:** Northwestern Sch of Law, JD 1959. **Career:** WPA Federal Theater, advertising NYC; Bonneville Power Admin Portland, law library asst 1949-53; Portland, legal sec 1954-59; General Practice Portland, trial lawyer 1960-67; OR Workmen's Comp Bd, hearing officer 1968-70; Multnomah Co, dist ct judge 1970-72; State of OR Multnomah Co Courthouse, circuit ct judge, circuit judge, 1979-93, senior judge, 1993-. **Orgs:** Gov's Comm on Judicial Reform & Racial-Ethnic Bias; OR State Bar Com on Pub Serv & Info; former chmn Minor Cts Com; lecturer Family Law Seminar; legal serv to 1967 legislature in OR; former sec-treas Multnomah Bar Assn; mem several bar assns, including NBA; Amer Jud Soc; chmn Status Offenses Comm; Natl Council of Juvenile Ct Judges; chmn of com lectr juvenile & family law race relations rights of minorities Ct Sys serving bd dirs Lewis & Clark Coll; OR Museum of Sci & Industry; OR Symphony; Golden Hrs Inc, CISCO; visiting fellow Woodrow Wilson Prog; dir Natl Assn of Women Judges; founder, Oregon Women Lawyers; dir Assn of Family Conciliation Cts; Amer Inns of Court; Oregon Council for the Humanities; Oregon Bar Diversity Task Force; advisory bd, Community Cts; St Philip the Deacon Episcopal Ch. **Honors/Awds:** Woman of Accomplishment 1969; listed in Mothers Achvmt in Amer History 1776-1976; first Black elected to remunerative ofc in State of OR; First Black Woman Judge in Pacific NW; re-elected to 4th six-year term; Honorary Doctor of Laws, Hunter College, 1997; President Affirmative Action Awd, Oregon State Bar, 1992; Oregon's First African-American Woman Lawyer; Delta's Woman of Excellence, Outstanding Contribution to Children, 1984; Chisholm Awd, To Citizens of Oregon, Distinguished Service to the Bench, 1985; Contribution to African-American Culture, 1991; Outstanding Contribution to Advancement of Minorities, 1991; Bar President Awd, Increasing Diversity in the Profession, 1992. **Business Addr:** Circuit Court Senior Judge, "Of Counsel" Tooze Law Firm, 333 SW Taylor, Portland, OR 97204.

DEJARMON, ELVA PEGUES

Educator. **Personal:** Born Feb 14, 1921, Hartsville, SC; daughter of Jessie Brailey Pegues and Paul Pegues; married LeMarquis, Jun 10, 1942; children: Michelle Renee. **Educ:** Wilberforce Univ, BS, 1941; Western Reserve Univ, MS, 1949; Natl Sci Inst, 1959; NYU, 1961-62; Univ NC, 1974; NCCU, Journalism, 1982-84. **Career:** Dunham Tech Community Coll, adult educ instructor; North Carolina Times, assoc editor, 1970-; Durham Tech Inst, coordinator, training program for disadvantaged, 1965-69; NC Central Univ, asst prof 1960-65; Cleveland Public Schools, teacher 1947-58; Editorial Rsch, 1942-45. **Orgs:** Mem NC Press Women; Am Dietetic Assn nutrition consult (RD); local & state nutrition councils; past pres Nat Barristers' Wives; Alpha Kappa Alpha; Dept of Social Serv 1971-74, mental health 1974-; Oper Breakthrough 1973-; stewardess AME Ch; Sch Adv Bd; NC Heart Assn; YMCA; NAACP; chmn Durham Co Commn Mental Health Cntr; chmn Nominating Com for Mid-Atlantic Reg; Rep to Natl Nominating Com; mem N Central Region Continuing Educ Com for Mental Health Serv-Substance Abuse-Mental Retardation; mem N Central Region Area Bd Chmn Area Dir Assn; Neighborhood advisor Coordinating Council Sr Citizens; bd mem, Widowed Persons Services, 1988-90; Neighborhood Focus Bd, City of Durham, 1988-. **Honors/Awds:** Hon Mid-Atlantic Region Conf, Alpha Kappa Alpha Inc, 1977; Volunteer of the Year Award, 1979; Certificate of Achievement, NC Central Univ, 1983; President's Volunteer Action Award, 1983; Leadership Award, Natl Council of Negro Women, Durham Sect, 1984; Contributions to AME Christian Recorder; Contributions of Black Women to Amer M Davis, YWCA, Women of Achievement Recognition, 1987; Several publications including cookbooks, brochures on Blacks in Durham, History of NCNW Durham Section; Golden Soror, Alpha Kappa Alpha Sorority Inc, 1988; YWCA Women of Achievement, 1988; Leadership Award, Alpha Kappa Alpha Sorority Inc, Alpha Zeta Omega Chapter, 1989; Recognition of Past Basilei, History of Alpha Zeta Omega Chapter, Alpha Kappa Alpha, 1989; Inductee, First Alpha Zeta Omega Chapter-AKA Haof Fame. **Business Addr:** PO Box 3445, Durham, NC 27702-3445.

DEJOIE, CAROLYN BARNES MILANES

Educator. **Personal:** Born in New Orleans, LA; daughter of Alice Milanes Barnes and Edward Franklin Barnes; children: Deirdre Jeanelle, Prudhomme III, Duan Kendall. **Educ:** Universidad Nacional de Mexico, MA 1962; Univ of WI, MSW 1970; Union Grad Sch, PhD 1976; Xavier Univ of LA, BA. **Career:** Southern Univ, instructor 1962-63; VA State Coll, asst prof 1963-66; Univ of WI Ext, admin specialist 1967-68, asst to pres 1970-73, prof of human issues, 1973-, Univ of Wisconsin; Human Relations Counseling Serv, owner, dir 1980-; Sun & Shadows Publishing Co, owner 1987-; Human Relations Counseling Service, Dir and clinician, 1992-; Lectura, 1994-; Itinerant Journalistic Reporter, 1996-; Univ of Havana, Socio-Economic Aspects of Contemporary Cuban Life, investigator, 1996-97. **Orgs:** Foreign language consult Travenol de Mexico Am British Cowdray Hosp Mex 1959-62; exec dir Centro Hispano-Americano Madison 1978-79; psychotherapist Private Practice 1980-; exec bd, NAACP, Madison WI 1987-; author, natl speaker, conference planner; vice president, National Association of Media Women, 1989-90; executive board member, Negro Educational Review, 1988-; editorial advisory board member, Journal of Negro Education, 1985-; crespar, Johns Hopkins University, 1996-. **Honors/Awds:** Fulbright US Gov't 1966; Achievemnt Against Odds WI Humanities Commn Smithsonian Inst Exhibit 1983; Outstanding Contrib to Soc Alpha Kappa Alpha 1984; Outstanding Contrib to Community WI Governor's Award 1984; Natl Assn Media Women Woman of the Year Award 1985; Natl Assn Negro Business & Professional Women Recognition of Serv Award 1986; Bd of Commissioners Genessee County MI Laudatory Resolution 1986; Golden Egg Award, Natl Assn Media Women 1987; Appreciation Award, city of New Orleans 1988; Unsung Heroine Award, NAACP-Madison WI 1988; publications, Students Speak Out: Racial Problems and What Students Can Do About Them; Wisconsin Minority Women's Perspectives on Women's Issues 1989; Etches of Ebony Louisiana Calendar, Forget Me Knots Inc, 1990; Louisiana Black Heritage Award, For Get Me Knots Inc, 1990; Dollars & Sense, Outstanding Professional Woman & Role Model, 1991; Univ of Wis Madison, Certificate of Recognition of Emeritus Status, 1992; State of Wis, Certified Independent Clinical Psychotherapist, 1993; Consortium of Doctor's Award, 1993. **Business Addr:** Dir, Carolyn Dejoie & Associates, 5322 Fairway Dr, Madison, WI 53711, (608)274-2152.

DEJOIE, MICHAEL C.
Communications executive. **Personal:** Born Apr 25, 1947, New Orleans, LA; son of Julia B Dejoie and Constant C Dejoie Jr; divorced. **Educ:** Grinnell College, AB, 1968; Loyola Institute of Politics, fellow, 1970; Columbia University, Graduate School of Business, MBA, 1977. **Career:** WWL-TV, consumer affairs reporter, 1968-70; CBS News, associate producer, editor, 1970-78; AT&T Long Lines, manager, intl & public service advertising, 1978-79, AT&T Long Lines/AT&T Communications, manager, business advertising, 1979-84, AT&T Communications, Southern Region Media Center, manager, 1984-85; MCD Communications Consultants Inc, owner, consultant, 1986-; Southern Christian Leadership Conference, director, communications, 1991-94; Amer Assn of Retired Persons, communications rep, currently. **Orgs:** Atlanta Assn of Black Journalists, 1987, 1992-; IABC, 1987-; AFTRA, 1968-70; Writers Guild of America East, shop steward, 1970-78; Black Public Relations Society of Atlanta, board member, 1988-90; Coordinating Council of Atlanta Public Relations Organizations, board member, 1989. **Honors/Awds:** IABC, Silver Quill for Best Video Production, "Operator," 1985; various advertising awards, 1978-84; Assn of Black Journalist, Best Editorial, 1994. **Special Achievements:** Producer: "What's Going On? with Joseph Lowery," WIGO-TV, 1992-94; editor: SCLC Magazine, 1991-94; Assoc Producer Midwest Bureau, CBS Weekend News with Dan Rather, 1974-76. **Military Serv:** AFROTC, US Air Force Reserves, squadron 1st sgt, 1964-67; Good Conduct, Corps Photographer & Illustrator, Color Guard Commander. **Home Phone:** (404)315-8318. **Business Addr:** Communications Rep, American Assn of Retired Persons, 999 Peachtree St, NE, Ste 1650, Atlanta, GA 30309, (404)888-0077.

DE JONGH, JAMES LAURENCE
Educator. **Personal:** Born Sep 23, 1942, St Thomas, Virgin Islands of the United States; son of Mavis Elizabeth Bentlage deJongh and Percy Leo deJongh. **Educ:** Williams College, BA 1964; Yale Univ, MA 1967; New York Univ, PhD 1983. **Career:** Rutgers Univ Newark, instructor 1969-70; The City Coll of the City Univ of New York (CUNY), prof 1970-; CUNY Inst for Research on the African Diapora in the Americas and the Caribean (IRADAC), interim dir, 1997-. **Orgs:** Mem The Dramatists Guild, Writers Guild of Amer East, Modern Language Assoc, Harlem Writers Guild, Zeta Psi Frat. **Honors/Awds:** Fellow Center for Black Studies Univ of CA Santa Barbara 1981; Outstanding Achievement Awd The Black Action Council of the City Coll of New York 1982; Audelco Recognition Awd Outstanding Musical Creator 1984; Honorary Fellow Brookdale Ctr on Aging of Hunger Coll 1985; Natl Endowment for the Humanities Fellowship for College Teachers 1986; major plays and publications "Hail Hail the Gangs!" w/Carles Cleveland produced by NY Theatre Ensemble Inc 1976; "City Cool, A Ritual of Belonging," w/Carles Cleveland Random House 1978; "Do Lord Remember Me" Off-Broadway Premier Oct 10, 1982 produced by Wynn Handman The Amer Place Theater; "Play to Win, Jackie Robinson" w/Carles Cleveland Natl school tour 1984-86; Vicious Modernism: Black Harlem and the Literary Imagination, Cambridge Univ Press, 1990. **Business Addr:** IRADAC, Y-Bldg 307, City College of the City Univ of New York, English Department, New York, NY 10031.

DEKNIGHT, AVEL
Artist. **Personal:** Born 1933, New York. **Educ:** Ecole des Beaux-Arts, Paris; Pratt Inst; Grand Chaumiere. **Career:** Contemporary Arts Mus, exhibits 1970; SF Mus Art, 1969; Minn Inst Arts; Whitney Mus, 1971; Acad Fine Arts; Larcada Gallery, 1968; num others; Metro Mus Art, collections; Wallcer Art Ctr. **Honors/Awds:** Miles Coll recip Watercolor Soc 1967; Paton Prize, Nat Acad Sch of Fine Arts 1958, 67; Grumbacher Award Audubon Artist Soc 1964; Childe Hassam Fund Purchase, Am Acad of Arts & Letters 1960.

DELANEY, DUANE B.
Government official. **Personal:** Born in Washington DC. **Educ:** Howard Univ, BA, (magna cum laude), sociology, 1977; American Univ, MA, judicial administration; Georgetown Univ Law Center, JD, 1989. **Career:** District of Columbia Superior Court, special assistant to the clerk of court, 1989-90, deputy clerk of the court, 1991; director of Civil Division, 1991-93; acting director of Social Services Division, 1993-94, clerk of the court, currently. **Orgs:** District of Columbia Bar Association; American Bar Association. **Honors/Awds:** Ohi Beta Kappa. **Business Addr:** Clerk of Court, DC Superior Court, 500 Indiana Ave NW, Rm 2500, Washington, DC 20001, (202)879-1400.

DELANEY, HOWARD C.
City official (retired). **Personal:** Born Sep 22, 1933, Lancaster County, NE; married Rosetta Johnson (died 1989); children: Alvin C, Dana E, Ashley W; married Lonni J McNeal. **Educ:** State of CO Cert Bd, "A" Wastewater Oper 1968, "A" Water Works 1969. **Career:** Construction, laborer 1951-66; Denver Sewage Disposal Dist #1, suprv 1966-81; Longmont CO Wastewater Treatment Facility, supt 1981-89. **Orgs:** Sec RMWPCA Personnel Adv Comm 1967-; mem WPCF Plant Oper Comm 1967-; mem Aurora Repeater Assoc 1977-. **Honors/Awds:** 1st black supt of a major CO wastewater facility; 1st black mgr for City of Longmont 1981-.

DELANEY, JOHN PAUL
Journalist. **Personal:** Born Jan 13, 1933, Montgomery, AL; married Anita Jackson; children: John Paul III, David Allen. **Educ:** Ohio State Univ, BA Journalism 1958. **Career:** Atlanta Daily World 1959-61; Atlanta Municipal Ct, probation officer 1961-63; Dayton, OH, Daily News 1963-67; Washington Star, reporter 1967-69; New York Times, corres, Washington Bureau 1969-74, Chicago bureau 1974-77, corres, asst natl editor 1977-80, deputy natl editor 1980-86, chief Madrid bureau 1987-89, senior editor; University of Alabama, chairman, journalism department, currently. **Orgs:** Mem Robert F Kennedy Journalism Awards Comm 1973-75, chmn 1975; founding mem Natl Assn of Black Journalists; bd chmn Publicity Comm, Atlanta Br NAACP 1961-63. **Honors/Awds:** Recipient, Scholarship, Ohio State Univ 1957; First Place, Baltimore-Washington Newspaper Guild, 1968; Lifetime Achievement Award, New York Association of Black Journalists, 1992. **Military Serv:** AUS Corpl 1953-55. **Business Addr:** Chairman, Department of Journalism, University of Alabama, College of Communications, PO Box 870172, Tuscaloosa, AL 35487-0172.

DELANEY, WILLI
Government employee. **Personal:** Born Mar 23, 1947, Washington, DC; divorced; children: Damon. **Educ:** Cath Univ of Am; Atlanta U. **Career:** Women's Bur, spl asst to dir; White House Pres Speechwriting Ofc; Carter Campaign for Pres, natl dir vol; City of Atlanta Ofc of Consumer Affairs, cnslr; Voter Educ Proj of Atlanta, rsrch asst. **Orgs:** Past mem WA Women's Forum 1977; mem Metro Dem Women's Club 1977; Nat Hook-up of Black Women Inc 1977. **Business Addr:** US Department of Labor, Washington, DC 20210.

DELANY, SAMUEL RAY
Writer, educator. **Personal:** Born Apr 1, 1942, New York, NY; son of Margaret Cary Boyd Delany and Samuel Ray Delany; married Marilyn Hacker, Aug 24, 1961 (divorced 1980); children: Iva Alyxander Hacker-Delany. **Educ:** College of the City of New York, 1960-61. **Career:** Author, science fiction, critic; Univ of Massachusetts, prof of comparative literature, 1988-. **Honors/Awds:** World Science Fiction Achievement, Hugo, 1968, 1989; Nebula Award of the Science Fiction Writers of America, 1966-68; Pilgrim Award, Science Fiction Research Assn, Excellence in SF related Scholarship, 1984; William Whitehead Memorial Award, Lifetime Contribution to Lesbian & Gay Writing, 1993. **Business Addr:** Dept of Comparative Literature, University of Massachusetts at Amherst, South College Bldg, Amherst, MA 01003.

DELARUE, LOUIS C.
Clergyman. **Personal:** Born Mar 24, 1939, Orange, TX; son of Ethel Marie Walker and Garrett Louis Delarue. **Educ:** BS, 1974, Lamar Univ; St Joseph Seminary, 1 yr; St Thomas Univ, Houston, TX, MA, Theology; St Marys Sem, M Div; Catholic Univ America, 1 Yr. **Career:** Catholic Charismatic Movement, minister, preaching and healing ministries, 1972-93; Catholic Charismatic Workshops, Baptism of the Holy Spirit; St Mary's, asst pastor, 1st black priest ordained diocese Beaumont, TX, 1975, 1st black diocesan asst pastor to serve a racial mixed parish, St Mary's, Port Arthur, TX; In-home parish serving the black community; 1st black pastor of native parish in the Beamont Diocese, 1986; Interfaith ministry & outstanding black clergyman in greater Orange community; Diocesan dir, Black Catholic Congress, 1987; international preacher and lecturer, Caribbean Islands, 1989-92, Phillipine Islands, 1992; teaches Christian meditation, centering prayer, Afro-American spirituality in the Catholic perspective, Kawanzaa celebrations and other Afro-American celebrations in USA and Caribbean;conts revivals, retreats, mini-workshops on Biblical archaeology and Bible basic studies; provides counseling, drug ministry, preaching, family Catechesis. **Orgs:** Diocesan Emmaus Group, 1987-93; International Spiritual Directors; Renew Team of Diocese of Beaumont; Kiwanis Intl, 1989, TX Catholic Historical Soc, 1985-89, National Black Seminarian Association; National Black Clergy Caucus; NAACP; Association Pastoral Counseling; ecumenical dir, Diocese of Beaumont; Ecumenical Dir of the TX Catholic Conference; spiritual dir, Parish Afro-American Ecumenical Dance Group Henderson Sch of Dance; Diocesan Black Catholic Commn; Greater Orange Ministerial Fellowship; president, Diocesan Presbyteral Council, 1990-91. **Honors/Awds:** Outstanding Afro-Am Worship Award; Only black diocesan priest TX 1975; Outstanding Service Award, NAACP, 1987; Various other Honors/Awards. **Military Serv:** USAF 4 Yrs.

DELAUDER, WILLIAM B.
College president. **Career:** Delaware State Coll, Dover, pres, currently. **Business Addr:** President, Delaware State College, Dover, DE 19901.

DELCO, EXALTON ALFONSO, JR.
Educator (retired). **Personal:** Born Sep 4, 1929, Houston, TX; son of Pauline Broussard Delco and Exalton Delco; married Wilhelmina R, Aug 23, 1952; children: Deborah, Exalton III, Loretta, Cheryl. **Educ:** Fisk Univ, BA 1949; Univ MI, MS 1950; Univ of TX, PhD 1962. **Career:** TX So Univ, instr 1950-55, asst prof 1957-60, rsch asst 1958-62; Huston-Tillotson Coll, assoc prof 1963-66; Prairie View A&M Coll, guest prof 1964; Huston-Tillotson Coll, head, biology dept, prof of biology 1966-68, vice pres for acad affairs 1967-85; Austin Co Coll, vice pres for acad affairs 1985-93. **Orgs:** Fellow AAAS, Amer Inst of Biol Sci; vp, exec sec, mem of council Beta Kappa Chi Sci Honor Soc 1962-68; vp, pres Phi Delta Kappa 1969-72; mem Amer Fisheries Soc, Amer Soc of Ichthyologists & Herpetologists, Amer Soc of Limnology & Oceanography, Soc of Sigma Xi, NY Acad of Sci, TX Acad of Sci, Austin Housing Auth Commiss 1967-69; dist commiss Eagle Dist of Boy Scouts of Amer 1967-68; pres St Vincent de Paul Soc Holy Cross Church 1968; mem Travis Co Grand Jury Assoc, Comm Council of Austin & Travis Co 1968-70; mem 1968-71, pres 1982-85 Family Prac Residency Adv Comm of TX 1968-. **Honors/Awds:** Stoye Prize Amer Soc of Ichthyologists & Herpetologists 1960; Danforth Assoc Huston-Tillotson Coll Campus 1966; Nominated Harbison Awd Danforth Found 1966; Piper Prof 1967; Natl Urban League Summer Fellow Allied Chem Co 1969; Outstanding Educator of Am. **Military Serv:** Surgical tech in 46th MASH unit in Germany 1955-56; rank, SP3.

DELCO, WILHELMINA R.
State government official. **Personal:** Born Jul 16, 1929, Chicago, IL; daughter of Juanita Heath Watson and William P Fitzgerald; married Dr Exalton A Delco Jr, Aug 23, 1952; children: Deborah Diane Agbottah, Exalton A Delco III, Loretta Elmirle Edelen, Cheryl Pauline Delco. **Educ:** Fisk Univ, BA 1950. **Career:** Prov Hosp, rec clerk; IL Bell Telephone, serv rep; Teachers State Assoc of TX, clerk; State of Texas House of Representatives, representative, speaker pro tempore, currently. **Orgs:** Sec, vchmn Citizens Adv Comm to Juv Ct; mem City of Austin Hum Relations Comm, Vol Soc Wkr, Travis Cty Welfare Dept; bd mem Volunteer Bur, Key Trnr; mem Well-Child Conf, Austin League of Women Voters; mem, sec 1972-74 Austin Ind School Dist; mem adv comm TX Employ Comm, TX Comm for Human & Publ Pol; del TX Assoc of School Bds 1973; mem bd trust, sec 1973-74 Aus Comm Coll; del TX Cath Conf 1972-; chmn, leg adv council, mem exec comm Southern Reg Ed; mem steering comm, exec comm Ed Comm of the States; vice chmn of State-Fed Assembly of the Natl Conf of State Legislatures; vchmn, bd of trustees Ed Testing Svc; cchmn Natl Black Caucus of State Legs; mem of commiss Standards of Southern Assoc of Colls & Schools; chrm bd of trustees ETS; chrm assembly on the legislature NatlConf of State Legd of trustees Southern Ed Found; chmn Higher Education Comm TX House of Reps, 1979. **Honors/Awds:** Outstanding Woman Austin Amer Statesman, 1969; Serv Awd 1973 TX Congress of Parents & Teachers, 1973; Liberty Bell Awd Austin Jr Bar Assoc, 1969; Publ School Svc Awd Zeta Phi Beta, 1970; Publ Serv Merit Awd Omega Psi Phi, 1971; Apprec Awd Arthur DeWitty Awd 1971, NAACP 1972; Hon Mem Delta Kappa Gamma 1972; Coronat Med St Edwards Univ, 1972; Appreciation Award Blanton School, 1973; Serv Awd Sakarrah Temple, 1973; Serv Citation Optimist Club of E Austin, 1973; mem TX Women's Hall of Fame, 1986; Huston-Tillotson Coll, Austin, TX; Southwestern Univ, Georgetown, TX; Lee Coll, Baytown, TX; St Edwards Univ, Austin, TX; Wiley Coll, Marshall, TX. **Business Addr:** State Representative, State of Texas, Capitol Bldg, Room 4130, Austin, TX 78769.

DELEON. See RICHARDS, DELEON MARIE.

DELEON, JOSE
Professional baseball player. **Personal:** Born Dec 20, 1960, Rancho Viejo, Dominican Republic. **Career:** Pittsburgh Pirates, pitcher, 1983-86; Chicago White Sox, pitcher, 1986-87; St Louis Cardinals, pitcher, 1988-. **Business Addr:** Professional Baseball Player, St Louis Cardinals, 250 Stadium Plaza, Busch Memorial Stadium, St Louis, MO 63102.

DELEON, PRISCILLA
Convention sales executive. **Personal:** Born Apr 5, 1958, Watsonville, CA; daughter of Federico & Jessie DeLeon; married Douglas Carter, Oct 10, 1987; children: Aaron Carter. **Educ:** San Jose State University, BS. **Career:** Security Pacific Book, operations manager, 1981; Atari, Inc, travel cood, 1982-83; Sheraton Sunnyvale, mtg coord, 1983-86; San Jose Convention & Visitors Bureau, sales research, 1986, sales manager, 1986-96, national sales manager, 1996-. **Orgs:** National Coalition of Black Meeting Planners; Hotel Sales & Mktg Association International. **Business Addr:** National Sales Manager, San Jose Convention & Visitors Bureau, 333 W San Carlos St, Ste 1000, San Jose, CA 95110-2720, (408)295-9600.

DELEON-JONES, FRANK A., JR.
Psychiatrist. **Personal:** Born May 6, 1937, Colon, Panama; married Silvia Cavallaro; children: Karen, Elizabeth. **Educ:** Nat Inst of Panama, BS highest hon 1958; Univ of Rome, Italy, MD Surgery (summa cum laude) 1964; IL State Psychiatric Inst, Psychiatric Residency 1970. **Career:** VA Westside Hosp Chgo, chief of psychiatry; IL State Psychiatric Inst, asso dir research 1973-75, chief metabolic res units 1971-73, res asso 1970-71; Psychiatry Abraham Lincoln Sch of Med Univ of IL, asso prof; prac Psychoanalist; Chicago Inst for Psychoanalysis, grad. **Orgs:** Mem Am Psychiatric Assn; Am Assn for the Advancement of Sci; Am Psychoanalytic Assn; interested psycho pharmacology of depression, schizophrenia, drug addiction, other psychiatric disturbances. **Honors/Awds:** Recip Ginsburg Fellow Troup for the Advancement of Psychiatry 1968-70.

DELIBERO, SHIRLEY A.
Transportation executive. **Career:** New Jersey Transit, executive director, currently. **Orgs:** Newark Performing Arts, advisory bd; Urban League; YMCA Black Achievers; Woman in State Govt; Women in Transit; The American Public Transit Assn, vice chair, bd of dirs. **Honors/Awds:** American Public Transportation Assn, Lifetime Achievement Award.

DELILLY, MAYO RALPH, III
Pediatrician. **Personal:** Born Apr 3, 1953, Los Angeles, CA; son of Irene Wood DeLilly and Mayo R DeLilly Jr; married Carol Covyeau DeLilly, Jun 28, 1986; children: Irene Rose, Lauren Marie. **Educ:** Williams Coll, BA Biology 1974; Howard Univ Coll of Medicine, MD 1974-78. **Career:** Martin Luther King Genl Hosp, intern/resident 1978-81; private practice, pediatrician, currently. **Orgs:** Mem LA Pediatric Soc 1981-, mem Big Brothers of Greater Los Angeles 1981-90; medical advisor, Sheenway Sch Los Angeles 1983-. **Honors/Awds:** Academic Achievement Award Howard Univ Medical School 1976; Medical Alumni Award Howard Univ Medical School 1978; mem Alpha Omega Alpha Honor Medical Society; fellow Amer Acad of Pediatrics 1984; vice chairman Pediatric Committee, California Medical Center 1988-. **Business Addr:** 1828 S Western Ave #22, Los Angeles, CA 90006.

DELK, FANNIE M.
Educator. **Personal:** Born Dec 13, 1933, Lexington, MS; daughter of Inez Mitchell and Theodore R Mitchell; married Frank E Delk Jr; children: Gregory Kevin, Gerald Keith. **Educ:** TN State Univ, AB English (with Distinction) 1956; Memphis State Univ, MEd English, Ed 1971; Univ of Chicago, Natl Endowment for the Humanities Fellow 1980; Ford Foundation Fellow, Univ of Mississippi, 1986-87. **Career:** FL School Memphis TN, teacher English 1956-57; Carver HS, teacher 1957-75; LeMoyne-Owen Coll, prof English 1975-. **Orgs:** Exec bd Alpha Kappa Alpha 1970-; consult Memphis City Schools 1973-; mem Reg Accrediting Teams, Southern Assoc Coll & Schools 1975-; lead volunteer teachert-task prog Memphis Volunteer Placement Prog 1975-; bd of dir Memphis Volunteer Placement Prog 1975-; act-so coord NAACP 1980-84; co-editor Homespun Images, An Anthology of Black Memphis Writers and Artists; pres Memphis Black Writers Workshop. **Honors/Awds:** Humanities Scholar West TN Econ Council 1977; Publ "Toward Stabilization & Survival, The Rural Family in Transition" West TN Econ Council 1977; The Black Pearl Mag "Black Images" 1979, Southern Eye, Southern Mind, A Photographic Inquiry "The South, The Times, The Struggles" 1981; Fifty Yrs of Svc, A History of Beta Epsilon Omega Chap of Alpha Kappa Alpha 1985; AKA Woman of the Year 1982-82; MVP Volunteer of the Year 1982. **Home Addr:** 1556 S Wellington St, Memphis, TN 38106. **Business Addr:** Professor, LeMoyne-Owen College, 807 Walker Ave, Memphis, TN 38126.

DELK, JAMES F., JR.
Automobile dealer. **Personal:** Born Sep 10, 1948, Smithfield, VA; son of Edith Majors Delk and James Delk; married Thelma Garvin Delk, Sep 21, 1985; children: Darlene, Kim, Timothy, James. **Educ:** Temple University, Philadelphia, PA, associates, electrical engineering, 1969. **Career:** IBM, Philadelphia, PA, customer engineer, 1969-71; William H Porter, Newark, DE, salesman, 1971-74; Vans Chevrolet, New Castle, DE, sales mgr, 1974-82; Fairlane Ford Inc, Pottsville PA, chief exec officer. **Orgs:** Member, Alpha Phi Alpha, 1967-; president, Schuylkill County Dealer Assn, 1991-92; regional mgr, Black Ford & Lincoln Mercury Dealers Assn, 1991-93. **Business Addr:** President, Fairlane Ford Sales, Inc, 440 N Claude A Lord Blvd, Pottsville, PA 17901.

DELK, OLIVER RAHN
Educator. **Personal:** Born Feb 4, 1948, Staten Island, NY; son of Mary Dixon Delk and James Delk. **Educ:** Indiana Univ, BA Psychology 1974 honors graduate; GA State Univ, MS Criminal Justice 1976. **Career:** Sears, Roebuck & Co, asst mgr 1974-76; Southeast Branch YMCA Atlanta, comm prog dir 1976-77; Office of the Mayor Atlanta, tech assist specialist 1977-79; Morehouse Coll, dir of govt relations, currently. **Orgs:** Mem Natl Assoc for Equal Oppor in Higher Educ 1979-; pres Assoc for Fund-Raising Officers 1985; chmn Budget and Finance/Water/Waste Water Treatment Operators 1985; mem NAACP 1979-; mem Omega Psi Phi Frat 1979-; mem SCLC 1979-. **Honors/Awds:** Youth Services Awd WAOK Radio 1978; Outstanding Young Man of America awarded by US Jaycees 1979; Public Speaking Awd GA State Univ 1979; three career development program certificates from the YMCA.

DELK, TONY LORENZO
Professional basketball player. **Personal:** Born Jan 28, 1974, Covington, TN. **Educ:** Kentucky. **Career:** Charlotte Hornets, 1996-. **Honors/Awds:** NCAA-Division I, Tournament Most Outstanding Player, 1996. **Special Achievements:** NBA Draft, First round pick, #16, 1996; NCAA-Division I, Championship, 1996. **Business Addr:** Professional Basketball Player, Charlotte Hornets, 100 Hive Dr, Charlotte, NC 28217, (704)357-0252.

DELK, YVONNE V.
Cleric. **Personal:** Born Apr 15, 1939, Norfolk, VA; daughter of Marcus T Delk. **Educ:** Norfolk State College, Norfolk, VA, AB, sociology, 1961; Andover Newton Theological Seminary, Newton Center, MA, master in religious education, 1963; University of Cincinnati, Cincinnati, OH, 1966; New York Theological Seminary, New York, NY, doctor of ministry, 1978. **Career:** United Church of Christ, Board for Homeland Ministries, Boston, MA/Philadelphia, PA, secretary for urban & black church, 1969-76; Harvard Divinity School, Cambridge, MA, visiting lecturer, 1976-77; United Church of Christ, New York, NY, associate for constituency development office for church in society, 1978-79, affirmative action officer, 1980-81, executive director, office for church in society, 1981-90; Community Renewal Society, executive director, currently. **Orgs:** Board of directors, Project Equality, member of program to combat racism, World Council of Churches; advisory commission member, World Council of Churches Convocation on Justice, Peace and Integrity of Creation; member, National Planning Committee on Children in Poverty; coordinating committee member, Choose Peace. **Honors/Awds:** Leadership and Service Award, Project Equality, 1988; Excellence in Field of Religion, Howard University, 1987; Doctor of Divinity, Chicago Theological Seminary, 1986; Doctor of Divinity, Ursinus College, 1986; Antoinette Brown Award, United Church of Christ, 1979. **Business Addr:** Executive Director, Community Renewal Society, 332 S Michigan Ave, Suite 500, Chicago, IL 60604.

DELL, WILLIE J.
City official (retired). **Personal:** Born May 8, 1930, Weldon, NC; daughter of Emma F Grant and Willie Aikens; married Nathan Dell; children: Wayne, Arthur Jones. **Educ:** St Augustines Coll, BA 1952; Richmond Professional Inst Coll William & Mary, MSW 1960. **Career:** Social Serv Bureau, social worker 1953-58; Med Coll VA, med social worker 1961-66; Richmond Public Health Dept, chief med soc worker 1966-68; VA Commonwealth Univ, asst prof 1968-74; JJ & W Assoc, exec dir; City of Richmond VA, mem city council; Richmond Comm Sr Ctr, exec dir 1976-95; adjunct professor Univ of Richmond 1978-. **Orgs:** Pres Richmond Chap Natl Assoc Social Workers 1975; bd mem Commonwealth Psych; cur bd mem Richmond Chapter ARC & Fam & Children Svc, Natl League of Cities; mem VCU Grad School 1978-83, Richmond Comm Hosp 1976-83, Proj Jump St 1975-80; co-owner JJ&W Assoc Consultants, NAACP; sec North Side Civil Assn 1973-75; pres Black Ed Assoc 1973-75; sec St Augustines Chap 1973-75; mem Natl Assoc Black Soc Workers; past chmn Reg III NBC Leo; mem VA Council Soc Welfare Council Human Rel, Del Ver Women Clubs, Delta Sigma Theta; pres Natl Black Presbyterian Caucus; pres Richmond Chap Nat Causes Black Aged 1980-89; pres Adpts 1984-89; pres Richmond Urban Inst 1984-88; Bd Southern Regional Council; Diocese of Richmond, Haitian Commission. **Honors/Awds:** Omega Citizen Year Award 1974; Govt Award Metro Bus League 1975; Delta's Civic & Polit Involvement Award 1975; Distinguished Serv Award St Augustine's Coll, 1982; Outstanding Woman Award in Govt YMCA 1982; Good Govt Award Eta Tau Chapter 1982; Outstanding Volunteer 1988, Powhatan Correctional Center. **Home Addr:** 2956 Hathaway Rd, Richmond, VA 23225.

DELLUMS, LEOLA M. ROSCOE
Attorney. **Personal:** Born Dec 12, 1941, Berkeley, CA; daughter of Esther Lee Higgs and Leo C Higgs; married Ronald V Dellums, Jan 20, 1962; children: Ronald Brandon, Erik Todd, Piper Dellums Ross. **Educ:** San Francisco State University, BA, 1966; California State Teaching Credential, adult education, 1967; Georgetown University Law Center, JD, 1982. **Career:** Institute for Services to Education, consultant, 1976; American Civil Liberties Union, development director/publicist, 1976-1978; Zuko Interior Designs, Public Relations, advertising mgr, 1978-79; Congressman Mickey Leland, special assistant, 1983; Superior Court of District of Columbia, judicial law clerk, 1984-85; Assembly California Legislature, principal consultant, Assembly Office of Research, Washington, District of Columbia, rep, 1985-92; Washington & Christian, attorney at law, 1993-96; US Dept of Commerce, 1996-97; Sole Practioner, attorney at law, 1997-. **Orgs:** National Bar Association; Pennsylvania Bar; California State Society; American Bar Association; The Rainbow Fund; Potomac Links Inc; Alpha Kappa Alpha Sorority; Committee of 21 Human Rights Caucus; Congressional Club; American Society of Composers, Authors and Publishers; San Francisco State Univ Alumni Assn; Berkeley High School Alumni Association; US Supreme Court Bar; District Of Columbia Court of Appeals Bar; US District Court for the District of Columbia Bar; Center to Prevent Handgun Violence, Sasha Bruce Youth Work; Rap Inc Drug Prevention; Minority Breast Cancer Resource Ctr. **Honors/Awds:** The Ella Hill Hutch Award, Black Women Organized for Political Action, 1992; Inductee Berkeley High School Hall of Fame; The Sojourner Truth Meritorious Service Award, National Association of Negro Business and Professional Women's Club Inc, 1991; AT&T Volunteer Activist Award of Washington DC, Area, 1985; Congressional recognition for efforts in attaining passage of HR 1580. **Special Achievements:** Songs published under RREPCO Publishing Company; poetry published in "The Sheet"; prescriptive diagnostic research paper, "Teaching English as a Second Language to Native Born"; hosted "Cloth-A-Thon"; co-hosted "The Place;" hosted local Emmy award-winning television show "Cloth-A-Thon," WGLA; co-hosted local Emmy award-winning television show, "The Place," WRC. **Business Phone:** (202)686-5156.

DELLUMS, RONALD V.
Congressman (retired), civil rights activist. **Personal:** Born Nov 24, 1935, Oakland, CA; son of Willa Dellums and Vernie Dellums; married Leola Roscoe Higgs, Jan 1962; children: Brandy, Erik, Piper. **Educ:** Oakland City College, AA, 1958; San Francisco State College, BA, 1960; University of California at Berkeley, MSW, 1962. **Career:** California Dept of Mental Hygiene, psychiatric social worker, 1962-64; Bayview Community Center, program director, 1964-65; Hunters Point Youth Opportunity Center, assoc director, director, 1965-66; Bay Area Social Planning Council, planning consultant, 1966-67; San Francisco Economic Opportunity Council, Concentrated Employment Program, director, 1967-68; Social Dynamics Inc, sr consultant, 1968-70; Berkeley City Council, 1967-71; US House of Representatives, 9th District of California, democrat, 1971-98. **Orgs:** Ranking mem, House Committee on Natl Security, 1973; Military Procurement Subcommittee; Congressional Black Caucus, former chair; House Committee on the District of Columbia, former chair; House Armed Svcs Committee, former chair; Permanent Select Committee on Intelligence, former mem. **Honors/Awds:** Author, Defense Sense: The Search for a Rational Military Policy, 1983; Wilberforce University, honorary doctor of law, 1975. **Military Serv:** US Marine Corps, active duty, 1954-56.

DELOATCH, EUGENE
University dean. **Career:** Morgan State University, School of Engineering, Baltimore, MD, dean. **Business Addr:** Morgan State University, School of Engineering, Cold Spring and Hillen Roads, Baltimore, MD 21239.

DELOATCH, MYRNA SPENCER
Association administrator. **Personal:** Born in Tarboro, NC; married Johnnie W Deloatch; children: Chris, Tamyra, Ivan. **Educ:** Ag & Tech Univ, BS Home Econ; Purdue Univ, Spec Cert. **Career:** Rural Ed Inst Chillan South Amer, teacher; La Guardia House NY, dir of food serv; Farmers Home Admin, home suprv; Rich Square Training Ctr, home econ teacher; Telamon Corp, employment training specialist; Edgecombe County Department of Social Services, human services coord, currently. **Orgs:** Mem, pres Ebonette Club 1971-; employment interviewer Employment Sec Commiss 1976-81; mem Tarboro Housing & Comm Devel Adv Bd 1979-84; mem Tarboro Arts Council 1981-; mem Tarboro City Sch Bd of Educ 1979-85; Tarboro Community Outreach, board of directors, 1992-; Delta Sigma Theta Sorority, 1959; North Carolina Cooperative Extension Service, advisory board, 1992-. **Honors/Awds:** Outstanding Citizenship East Tarboro Citizen League 1978; Past President Award Ebonette Club 1980; Meritorious Serv East Tarboro Citizens League 1981; spec Serv Awd Black Voices 1982; Meritorious Ser Awd East Tarboro Citizens League 1985. **Home Addr:** 901 E Church St, Tarboro, NC 27886. **Business Addr:** Human Services Coordinator, Edgecomb County Department of Social Services, 301 Fairview Road, Rocky Mount, NC 27801.

DELPHIN, JACQUES MERCIER
Physician. **Personal:** Born Apr 26, 1929, Cape Haitien; married Marlene M; children: Patrick, Barthold, Beverly, Miriam, Matthew, Janice. **Educ:** Graduate of Secondary Studies, BS 1950; Univ of Haiti W Indies, med sch 1957. **Career:** St Cabrini Home W Park, NY, medical dir 1974-; St Francis Hosp Poughkeepsie, NY, attending phys 1968-; Ad Interim, commr of mental health 1973-74; Dutchess Co Dept of Mental Hygiene, psychiatric dir 1969-73; Hudson River Psychiatric Cntr, psychiatric dir 1966-69. **Orgs:** Past pres Mid-hudson Br of Psychiatric Assn 1972; Ffellow APA 1972; med license NY State 1967.

DEL PINO, JEROME KING
Clergyman. **Personal:** Born Sep 12, 1946, Savannah, GA; son of Flossie Mae Childs Del Pino and Rev Jerome Frank Del Pino; married Kathleen Joy Peterson Del Pino, Aug 25, 1968; children: Jerome Curtis, Emily Kathleen. **Educ:** Gustavus Adolphus Coll, BA 1968; Boston Univ Sch of Theology, ThM (cum laude) 1971; Boston Univ Grad Sch, PhD 1980. **Career:** Union United Methodist Church, Boston MA, asst pastor 1968-69; Emerson Coll, Boston MA, lecturer 1971-72; St Andrew's United Methodist Church, Worcester MA, co-pastor 1971-72; Greenwood Memorial United Methodist Church, Dorchester MA, pastor 1973-76; Wesley United Methodist Church, Springfield MA, pastor 1978-; Boston Univ School of Theology, visiting lecturer 1980-82; Luther/Northwestern Theological Seminary, St Paul MN, visiting lecturer 1984-85; Wesley United Methodist Church, Springfield, MA, pastor, 1978-89; Crawford Memorial United Methodist Church, Winchester, MA, pastor, 1989-. **Orgs:** Dir Gen Bd Higher Ed & Min UMC 1980-88; Div of Ordained Min UMC 1980-88; delegate Gen Conf UMC 1976, 1980, 1984, 1988;Northeast Jurisdictional Conf UMC 1976, 1980, 1984; mem Am Soc of Ch Hist 1971-; pres Black Ecumenical Commn of MA 1983-85; mem advisory cncl Word & World Journ 1985-; governor, Gen Bd of Discipleship, United Methodist Church, 1988-; governor, General Council on Ministries, United Methodist Church, 1988-. **Honors/Awds:** Rockefeller Fellowship Fund for Theo Ed Princeton 1971-73; N Am Black Doc Fellowship Fund for Theo Ed 1976-77; fellow Inst Reformation Research St Louis MO 1973; 1st Decade Alumni Achievemnt Award Gustavus Adolphus Coll St Peter MN 1978. **Business Addr:** Pastor, Crawford Memorial United Methodist Church, 34 Dix St, Winchester, MA 01890-2530.

DELPIT, JOSEPH A.
State representative. **Personal:** Born Jan 9, 1940, Baton Rouge; son of Edmae Butler Delpit and Thomas H Delpit; married Precious Robinson; children: Joseph Jr, Thomas, Deidre, Desiree, Derrick. **Educ:** Southern Univ, Baton Rouge. **Career:** Chicken Shack Restaurants, owner/operator 1959-; Gr Baton Rouge Devel Corp, investments In; Gen United Life Ins Co; Sports Unlimited Inc, co-owner; City of Baton Rouge, city councilman, 1968-75; Louisiana House of Representatives, state representative, currently. **Orgs:** Mem bd dirs People's Savings & Loan Co, mem St Francis Xavier Cath Ch; Baranco Clark YMCA Bd Mgmt; bd dirs Baton Rouge Chap NAACP; mem City Parish Bi-racial Com; Cath Lay Congress; Op Upgrade Bd Dirs; Mental Health Soc Bd Mgmt; Capital Region Planning Commn; Mason; Shriner Hon mem John B Frazier Hon Soc 1974. **Honors/Awds:** Outstanding Serv, Southern Univ Alumni Fed, 1973; Businessman of Year, 1973; Outstanding Leadership in Business and Civic Community Service, Omega Psi Phi Frat In, 1971; Outstanding Academic Support, Southern Univ Am Women Soc, 1970; NAACP Natl Freedom Award, 1970; McKinley High Alumni Award for outstanding serv to sch & comm, 1968; Shriver Award for dedicated service to the poor, Office of Economic Opportunity, 1973; Baton Rouge Businessman of Year, News Leader, 1961; Outstanding Serv Award, Baranco Clark YMCA, 1960; first black councilman, Baton Rouge.

DELPIT, LISA DENISE
Educational researcher. **Personal:** Born May 23, 1952, Baton Rouge, LA; daughter of Edmae Butler Delpit and Thomas H Delpit; children: Maya. **Educ:** Antioch College, BA, 1974; Harvard University, MEd, 1980, EdD, 1984. **Career:** Durham Child Development Center, teacher, administrative assistant, 1972-77; North Solomons Provincial Government, consultant, 1982-83; Atari Research Lab, consultant, 1983-84; University of Alaska, assistant professor, reading, language, & literature, 1984-88, Teacher Education Program, coordinator, 1987-88; Michigan State University, School of Education, associate professor, 1988-91; Morgan State University, Institute for Urban Research, sr research associate, 1988-94; Benjamin Mays Chair of Urban Educational Leadership, Georgia State University, 1994-. **Orgs:** National Black Child Development Institute, Baltimore Chapter, research support, 1990-91; Literacy Committee, National Board for Professional Teaching Standards, vice-chairperson; African and African-American Curriculum Infusion Committee for Baltimore PS, co-chair; International Reading Association; Phi Delta Kappa; National Council for the Teaching of English; American Educational Research Association; Center for Collaborative Education, advisory board. **Honors/Awds:** MacArthur Fellow, 1990; National Academy of Education Spencer Fellow, 1988; American Association of University Women Educational Foundation, Dissertation Fellowship, 1984; American Educational Research Assn Raymond Cattell Award for Early Career Achievement, 1994; Harvard Univ, Alumni Award for Outstanding Contribution to Education, 1993. **Special Achievements:** "The Silenced Dialogue: Power and Pedagogy in Educating Other People's Children," Harvard Educational Review, 1988; "Skills and Other Dilemmas of a Progressive Black Educator," Harvard Educational Review, 1986; author, "Other People's Children," The New Press, 1995; winner of several national awards; numerous other articles. **Business Addr:** Benjamin E Mays, Chair of Urban Educational Leadership, Georgia State University, Educational Policy Studies, University Plaza, Atlanta, GA 30303, (404)651-4621.

DEMBER, JEAN WILKINS
Counseling. **Personal:** Born Jan 29, 1930, Brooklyn, NY; daughter of Martha Marie Benson and William H Wilkins Sr; married Clarence Robert Dember; children: Clarence Jr, Judith, Regina, Lila, Theresa, Zelie. **Educ:** Lincoln Schl of Nurses, 1950; Manhattan Bus Inst, cert secy 1952; Empire State College, Old Westbury, 1983; Lincoln Univ, Pennsylvania, MHS, 1988. **Career:** Black History Cultural Prog, presentor designer, 1978-; New York State Delegation Black Political Assem, 1972, pres 1981-82; New York State Commission on Prisons & Genocide, org vol 1982-; Nassau Community College, Black Women Studies, adj prof 1983-92; Dember-Webb African Amer Heritage, curator/co-founder, 1975-; National Urban League of Long Island, career counselor, Structured Educational Support Program, 1989-92. **Orgs:** State Youth Advocacy 1980-84; pres, LI Catholic Interracial Council 1988-91; fnd mem Tri Community Health Council 1974-82; adv bd mem Natl Black Lay Cath Caucus 1970-85; Evangelization Comm Natl Off for Black Catholics 1982-84; Econ Opport Council of Suffolk 1972-84; designer White Racism Mental Health Comm SC Div Mental Health 1977-82; chairperson Long Island Day Care Serv 1986-87; Lincoln Univ Alumni Assoc; NYS Multicultural Advisory Committee, 1984-91; African-American Cultural Center of Los Angeles; National Black Alcoholism Council, 1987-; Uganda Human Rights League, 1982-86; Afrikans United for Sanity Now, 1990-; Reform in Mental Health, to address Racist, White Supremist & Police Brutality & Murders as Psychosocial Pathology; founder, Afrikans United for Sanity Now!. **Honors/Awds:** Natl Off Black Cath Evangelization Award 1982; Martin L King Award Pilgrim State Human Rights Comm 1983; Citizen of Year Chi Rho Chprt Omega Psi Phi Frat Inc 1982; Amer the Beautiful grant for comm prog 1981; vol advocate for African Relief within Cath Church and broader comm; Auburn Prison, NAACP Service Award, 1992; Suffolk County, Jack & Jill Award, 1990; National Assn of Negro Business and Professional Women's Clubs Inc, National Sojourner Truth Award, Meritorious Service, 1991; Natl Black Service Award, Alcohol/Substance Abuse, Long Island Chapter, Cosco Williams, pres; Cert of Svc, Kazi Shule/SHAPE Ctr, 1995-96; Cert of Appreciation, Million Man March LOC, 1996; Cert of Appreciation, Foster Elementary Sch, 1996; various nominations, ABI, 1997. **Business Addr:** Curator, Dember-Webb African-American Heritage, 55 Court St, North Babylon, NY 11703.

DEMBY, JAMES E.
Electrical engineer. **Personal:** Born Dec 24, 1936, Chesapeake, VA; married Mavis A Smith; children: James Jr, Ken, Len. **Educ:** Tuskegee Inst, 1955-57; Howard U, BS 1961. **Career:** Norfolk Naval Shipyard, supervisory electrical engr 1973-; Norfolk Naval Shipyard, advancing positions 1961-. **Orgs:** Mem Naval Civilian Adminstrs Assn; Nat Assn of Naval Tech & Suprs vice pres United Civic League 1963-64; asst dist commr Tidewater Council BSA 1966- 73; mem Chesapeake Chap Nat Tots & Teens. **Honors/Awds:** Superior Performance Award 1971; Beneficial Suggestion Award 1971; Certificate of Merit 1971; Scout Executive's Award 1970; Arrowhead Honor 1971; Scouter's Key1971; Order of the Arrow 1972.

DEMBY, WILLIAM E., JR.
Novelist, educator. **Personal:** Born Dec 25, 1922, Pittsburgh, PA; son of Gertrude Lulu Hendrick and William E Demby; married Lucia Drudi; children: James Gabriel. **Educ:** Fisk Univ, Nashville TN, BA, 1947. **Career:** College of Staten Island, prof of English, 1969-89. **Home Addr:** Box 363, corner of Sag Harbor Tnpke & Deerfield Dr, Sag Harbor, NY 11963.

DEMERITTE, EDWIN T.
Insurance executive. **Personal:** Born Jun 25, 1935, Miami, FL; son of Daisy Demeritte (deceased) and Arnold Demeritte (deceased); married Edith W Dexter; children: Edwin Jr, Kathy Wynn, Deborah Renee, Dianne Marie, Michelle. **Educ:** FL A&M Univ, BS, MEdn; grad work guidance & counseling Barry Coll Miami; grad work admin & supr FL Atlantic Univ; Doc Prog Natl Educ D Prog Nova Univ. **Career:** N Dade Sr HS, teacher 1958-63, dept head 1963-65; Miami NW Sr HS, guidance counselor 1966-67; Miami NW Adult Educ Cent, instructor 1966-69; Miami Edison Sr HS, asst principal guid 1969-70; Hialeah Jr HS, Principal l/2 of Quinmester Prog 1973; Metropolitan Life Ins Co, sales rep sr account executive, currently; Dade County Public School System, Miami, FL, director, 1976-81. **Orgs:** Part Natl Conf Chris & Jews on Violence & Youth 1969; part Natl Inst on Pol & Commun Rel 1970; part Natl Assn Secondary Sch Prin Annual Meeting 1971-73; consult So Reg Educ Bd; mem Million Dollar Round Table 1984-95; trustee, Presbyterian Church USA Foundation, 1991-96; National Assn of Life Underwriters, 1981-; Miami Association of Life Underwiters, 1981-; FL Association of Life Underwriters, 1981-. **Honors/Awds:** Leaders Conf Qualifier Metropolitan Ins Co 1982, 1984; Metro Ins Co policies placed over 200 policy contacts 1983 Awd; 3 Metropolitan SE Territory Awds for Superior Sales Performance 1983; 1984 Qualifying Life Member of the Million Dollar Roundtable; Kiwanis Fellow in Guidance Counseling; Boy Scouting Awd Comm Serv Recog; Dade Co Sch Bd Awd for Commendable Contribution to Educ; pres conf Metropolitan Life 1988, 1994-97; Natl Sales Award NALU 1988, 1994-97; Natl Quality Awards NALU 1988, 1993-97. **Home Addr:** 5301 NW 18 Ave, Miami, FL 33142, (305)696-2677. **Business Addr:** Senior Account Executive, Metropolitan Life Insurance Co, 790 NW 107 Ave, Ste 110, Miami, FL 33172, (305)551-0077.

DEMESME, RUBY B.
Military official. **Career:** Air Force, deputy asst secretary, currently. **Orgs:** Women in Defense; SES Women's Appointees; Subgroup on Women and Children; Senate Black Legislative Staff (Caucus); National Military Family Association; Delta Sigma Theta Sorority. **Honors/Awds:** Superior Civilian Service, 1991; Commanders Award for Exceptional Service, 1984; Outstanding Student Teachers Award, 1968. **Business Addr:** Deputy Asst Secretary of the Air Force, SAF/MIM, 1660 Air Force, Pentagon Rm 5E977, Washington, DC 20330-1660.

DEMILLE, DARCY (WILMA LITTLEJOHN JACKSON)
Journalist. **Personal:** Born Dec 17, Chicago, IL; daughter of Rev R L Littlejohn and Sophia O'Shaw Littlejohn; married Gordon C Jackson; children: Carole Harris, Linda Luten, Shelley Bethay, Jill Jackson Lewis. **Educ:** Univ of MI, BGS 1977; Michigan State U, Certificate 1977; Oakland U, Advanced Study 1975-78; Leadership Flint Training, Certificate 1988. **Career:** ANP, NPI, editor feature writer 1960-65; Sepia Mag, columnist 1963-82; Howard U, guest lecturer 1981; Jordan Coll, instructor 1982-83; Mott Commnty Coll, instructor 1982-85; The Flint Journal, columnist/feature writer 1982-; Univ of MI, guest lecturer 1983-85; "Dear Wilma" columnist 1982-; Travel Consultant/Monarch Travel 1987-; Medi-Rary Literary Service, Editorial Adviser 1987-89; "About Books" Review Service, currently. **Orgs:** Creative consult Gail Mazaraki, Consult 1984-85; consult Manulife Ins Co 1981-82; consult Time Shares, Inc 1982-83; bd mem YWCA Public Affairs 1981-83, NAMW Inc Media Women 1975-85; founder Flint Chap NAMW Inc 1975-85; chartr mem The Links Inc, Flint Area Chptr 1980-85; Phi Delta Kappa Educ Frat 1983-85; mem, bd of dir MI League for Human Services, mem Public Affairs Comm; mem Top Ladies of Distinction, Grand Blanc Arts Guild Paint & Palette Art Group, Univ of MI Alumni Assn, Natl Assoc of Black Journalists; Leadership Flint, mem 1987-89; delegate, Intl Caribbean Conf, Women Aglow 1988; bd mem, Univ of Michigan Alumni Bd Society; CEO, "The Last Word, Inc," pres, "Finders-Keepers, Inc;" Univ of Mich Alumni Society, treas, bd of governors, 1995-97; Eta Phi Beta Sorority, Inc, Delta Tau Chapter, founding chapter/Charter member; treas, Alumni Bd of Gov's, 1997-99. **Honors/Awds:** Woman of Yr Media Women 1976-85; Darcy DeMille Mag Award; Human Rel Award Mayor City of Flint 1982; "Special Tributes" State of MI 1978; Links Service Award 1984; NAMW Communications Award 1989; Honors Award/Community Service, Genesee Area Intermediate School District 1989; conducted: Writer's Workshops, Univ of MI-Flint 1984-89; creative writing seminars, Mott Community Coll 1987-89; YWCA, Nina Mills Women of Achievement Award, nominee, 1994-95; Natl Negro Business & Professor Women Inc, Choice Award, 1997. **Home Addr:** 615 Lippincott Blvd, Flint, MI 48503. **Business Addr:** The Flint Journal, 200 E 1st St, Flint, MI 48502.

DEMILLE, VALERIE CECILIA
Life management consultant. **Personal:** Born Jun 2, 1949, New York, NY; daughter of Annie M. Clark deMille and Arnold C. deMille. **Educ:** North Carolina Central Univ, BS, 1972, MS, 1974, Meharry Medical Coll, MD, 1977; New York Univ/ Bellevue Hospital, forensic psychiatric training, 1987-88; Baruch College, New York, NY, MPA, 1991. **Career:** USAF Sheppard AFB, staff psychiatrist, 1981-83; USAF Vandenberg AFB, chief of mental health serv, 1983-84; Woodhull Hosp, staff psychiatrist, 1985; NY Medical Coll/Lincoln Hospital, New York, NY, unit chief, 1985-87, staff psychiatrist, 1987-88; New York City Department of Mental Health, New York, NY, staff associate anylyst, 1990-91; Upper Manhattan Mental Health Center, executive director, 1992; Life Management consultant, 1993-; Stress Mgmt Assn, Harlem & the deMille Consulting Agency, founder. **Orgs:** Networking Today. **Military Serv:** USAF major 3 yrs. **Business Addr:** 99 Hamilton Place, Ste 100, New York, NY 10031, (212)690-4695.

DEMONBREUN, THELMA M.
Registered nurse. **Personal:** Born Jun 8, 1928, Chicago, IL; divorced; children: Gail Purnell Nutt, Kim Morris Purnell. **Educ:** Thornton Comm Coll, AA 1974; Prairie State Coll, 1981-82. **Career:** Ingalls Mem Hosp, staff nurse 1964-74; Harvey Headstart, nurse coord 1974-. **Orgs:** Chairperson Brownie Troop Adv Comm 1958-62; mem adv Comm Dist 205 1962-66; mem Bd of Educ Dist 147 1965-; founder United Citizen of Dist 147 1968-74; mem IL Assn of Sch Bd 1967-70; mem Natl Caucus of Black School Bd Members 1967-; student mem Student Adv Comm Thorton Comm Coll 1972-74; mem South Suburan Branch of the NAACP 1981-; campaign chmn Damon Rockett for Re-Election of City of Harvey Comm 1983. **Honors/Awds:** First Black Woman Elected to the Bd of Educ Dist 147 South Suburban Leadership Coalition 1980; Appreciation of Support Harvey & US Jaycees 1980; Cert of Achievement completion of all requirements of academy prog AASA Natl Acad for School Execs 1980-83; presided over IL Sch Bd Joint Annual Conf 1983. **Home Addr:** 14730 Lincoln Ave, Harvey, IL 60426. **Business Addr:** Registered Prof Nurse, Headstart Harvey, 15652 Homan Ave, Markham, IL 60426.

DEMONS, LEONA MARIE
College counselor (retired). **Personal:** Born Jan 6, 1928, Townsend, GA; daughter of Rosa Lee Carter Wilson and Stephen Carter; divorced; children: Wynette Hammons, John, Chris, Donna Marie Demons, Clinton Drummond. **Educ:** Savannah State Coll, BS 1949; Atlanta Univ, MA 1962; NDEA Fellow Atlanta, Ga, 1963; Kansas State Univ, NDEA Fellow 1968-69. **Career:** Savannah State College, assist in publ relations 1950-52; Morehouse College, assist in placement 1963-65; Albany State College, counselor/dir of student activities 1965-69; Western Ill Univ, counselor 1970; Lincoln Land Comm Coll, counselor and foreign student advisor, 1971-91 (retired). **Orgs:** NAACP; Urban League; Alpha Kappa Sorority, 1987-; Pleasant Grove Bap Church, Springfield, IL, Mt Carmel Baptist Church, Atlanta GA, counselor, career activities mem, 1997. **Honors/Awds:** NDEA Fellow Dept of Health, Ed & Welfare 1963; NDEA Fellow Dept of Health, Ed & Welfare 1968; Qualified Kansas State (Consortium 1980) Univ (declined due to work obligations). **Home Addr:** 4764 Edwina Ln, SW, Atlanta, GA 30331.

DEMPSEY, JOSEPH P.
Pastor, educational administrator. **Personal:** Born Mar 8, 1930, Nashville, NC; son of Irene Alice Vick Dempsey (deceased) and Sidney H Dempsey (deceased); married Evelyntyne Humphrey, May 31, 1958; children: Denise P, Joseph T, Eric H, Kathy D. **Educ:** Fayetteville State Univ, BS 1958; Shaw Div Sch, BD 1964; NC Cen Univ, MA 1971; Shaw Div Sch, MDiv 1972; Jacksonville Theological Seminary, Florida, DTh, 1982; Faith Evangelical Lutheran Seminary, Tacoma WA, DMin 1988. **Career:** Pastor various locations since 1961; NC Cen Univ, instructor 1971-, assoc dir 1988-; Pine Grove Baptist Church, Creedmoor NC, pastor 1986-87; Elementary & High School, instructor; Worthdale United Baptist Church Raleigh, NC, pastor; NCCU Counseling Ctr, assoc dir, currently; NCCU, Grad School of Education, adjunct assistant professor, 1991-. **Orgs:** Mem Min Bd Wake Baptist Assn 1964; NC Personnel & Guid Assn; Am Personnel & Guid Assn; Exec Com, Wake Co Dem Party; bd dir NC General Baptist Con, bd dir YMCA 1967-; bd dir Comm Day Carde Center; mem Goals for Raleigh Educ Outreach; mem The Raleigh-Wake Martin Luther King Celebration Comm 1989. **Honors/Awds:** Teacher of the Yr 1967; Raleigh, NC Christian Family of the Yr 1972; Outstanding Serv Award NC Central Univ 1973-74. **Home Addr:** 1409 E Martin St, Raleigh, NC 27610-2611. **Business Addr:** Adjunct Assistant Professor, Grad School of Education, NCCU, PO Box 19688, Durham, NC 27707.

DENDY, TOMETTA MOORE
Educator (retired). **Personal:** Born Nov 18, 1932, Ryland, AL; married Fred; children: Frederick, Theresa. **Educ:** AL A&M Coll, BS (cum laude) 1952; Howard U, grad work 1953-54. **Career:** Catholic Univ School of Law, dir of admissions, 1975-95, asst dir admissions 1973-75; US Coast Guard, admin asst 1960-65. **Orgs:** Am Assn of Higher Edn; u & rep Law Sch Admissions Council 1975-; freelance writer; Alpha Kappa Alpha Sor; Cub Scout Ldr 1968-70. **Honors/Awds:** Outstanding performance awards at USCG. **Military Serv:** USCG. **Business Addr:** Educator, The Catholic University, School of Law, 620 Michigan NE, Washington, DC 20064.

DENMARK, ROBERT RICHARD
Information resources security manager (retired). **Personal:** Born Apr 1, 1930, Savannah, GA; son of Gladys Church Denmark and Robert Denmark; married Mamie E Sampson-Denmark, Aug 14, 1971; children: Gladys Denmark-Reed. **Educ:** MTI Business Coll, Certificate Computer Science 1978; American River Coll, AA 1980; Univ of San Francisco, BS 1982. **Career:** Federal Aviation Admin, air traffic control 1969-71; Prudential Insurance Co of Amer, special agent 1971-74; Dept of Interior US Bureau of Reclamation, computer analyst/programmer 1974-84, adp contract administrator 1984-; US Dept of Interior Div of Information Resources, computer consultant, 1980-84; computer security manager, 1988-94. **Orgs:** Chief Rabban Ancient Arabic Order of Nobles of the Mystic Shrine of North and South Amer 1982-; pres Sphinx Club Alpha Phi Alpha Frat Inc 1985; clusterleader Sacramento Area Strategy Team Lutheran Church of Amer 1985-87; Zeta Beta Lambda Chap Alpha Phi Alpha, sec 1987, pres 1988-92; pres First English Lutheran Church Council 1987-; mem, NAACP, Black Data Processing Assn; mem exec bd Div of Aging; 32 Degree Mason of the Ancient Free & Accepted Masonic Congress; executive board member, Sierra Pacific Synod, Evangelical Lutheran Church, 1991-; Sierra Pacific Synod Council, Evangelical Lutheran Church in America, 1991-94; bd of dirs, Sacramento Lutheran High School, 1994-97. **Honors/Awds:** Research project, Univ of San Francisco, A Study of the Potential of Office Automation, 1982; Outstanding Leadership Award Lutheran Church of Amer First English Lutheran Church 1982-84; Special Achievement Award US Dept of Interior 1985-86; Outstanding Serv Award Div of Data Processing Bureau of Reclamation 1987; Meritorious Serv, Zeta Beta Lambda Chapter, Alpha Phi Alpha Fraternity Inc, 1988; Outstanding Serv, Sacramento Area Lutheran Ministry, ELCA, 1988; Performance Award, US Bureau of Reclamation, Dept of the Interior, 1988; Alpha Phi Alpha Man of the Year, Zeta Beta Lambda Chapter, 1990; Outstanding Service Award, Bureau of Reclamation 1991-92. **Military Serv:** USAF master sgt 20 yrs;

Highest Awd, The Air Force Commendation Medal 1969, Outstanding NCO of the Year 1963-64. **Home Addr:** 1043 Lake Glen Way, Sacramento, CA 95822, (916)422-5517.

DENNARD, BRAZEAL WAYNE
Musician, educator, consultant. **Personal:** Born Jan 1, 1929, Detroit, MI; son of Bertha Brazeal and Ezekiel Dennard; married Murdice Vallery Dennard, Oct 10, 1959 (died 1988). **Educ:** Highland Park Junior Coll, Highland Park, MI, 1954-56; Wayne State Univ, Detroit, MI, BS, 1959, M, MUS, 1962. **Career:** Detroit Bd of Education, Detroit, MI, teacher, 1959-71, fine arts dept head, 1971-83, music supvr, 1983-89; Brazeal Dennard Chorale, Detroit, MI, artistic dir, 1972-; Wayne State Univ, Detroit, MI, music instructor, 1984-. **Orgs:** Pres, Detroit musicians Assn, 1974-88; pres, Natl Assn of Negro Mus, Inc, 1975-79; panel mem, chorale panel, Natl Endowment for the Arts, 1985-87; panel mem, Arts in Education, Natl Endowment for the Arts, 1986-88; consultant, Music Educators Natl Conference, 1989-. **Honors/Awds:** Vocal Teacher of the Year, MI School Vocal Assn, 1990; Choral Performance, American Choral Dir Assn, 1989; Distinguished Achievement Award, Arts Foundation of MI, 1989; Outstanding Service Award, Detroit Public Schools, 1989; Distinguished Alumni Award, Wayne State Univ, 1986. **Military Serv:** Army, cpl, 1951-53. **Home Addr:** 4330 Fullerton, Detroit, MI 48238.

DENNARD, DARRYL W.
Broadcast journalist. **Personal:** Born Sep 18, 1957, New York, NY; son of Eleanor Adamson Dennard and Glenn W Dennard; married Darlene Gray Dennard, Jul 13, 1979; children: Autumn Simone Dennard. **Educ:** Fordham Univ, Bronx NY, summer 1985; State Univ Coll at Buffalo, Buffalo NY, BA Broadcasting, 1981. **Career:** US Customs Serv, Buffalo NY, import specialist trainee, 1977-79; WGR-TV, Buffalo NY, production asst, 1980-83; WGRZ-TV, Buffalo NY, news reporter, 1983-87; Johnson Publishing Co, Chicago IL, TV co-host, 1987-. **Orgs:** Mem, Natl Black Media Coalition, 1983-87; bd mem, Buffalo Urban League, 1985-87, SUNY Coll at Buffalo Alumni Assn, 1985-86; lecturer, SUNY Coll at Buffalo, 1987; community advisory bd, Community Dept, SUNY College at Buffalo, 1987. **Honors/Awds:** Best Public Affairs Program, New York State Broadcasters, 1985; Best Newscast of the Year Award, United Press Intl, 1986; Black Leadership Award, 1490 Enterprises, 1986; Young Pioneer Award, Northern Region Black Political Caucus, 1986; Media Award, Buffalo Public Schools, 1987; Special Service Award, Seek/EOP SUNY Coll at Buffalo, 1988; Merit Award, United Negro Coll Fund, 1989. **Business Addr:** Television Co-host, Ebony/Jet Showcase, Johnson Publishing Co, 820 S Michigan Ave, Chicago, IL 60605.

DENNARD, TURNER HARRISON
Physician (retired). **Personal:** Born Oct 12, 1913, Chicago, IL; son of Hattie O Dennard (deceased) and Dr Ernest A Dennard (deceased); married Elizabeth M Dennard, Sep 13, 1940; children: Charles Garrett Dennard (deceased). **Educ:** Univ of MN, BS, pharmacy, 1932-1937, MS, pharmaceutical, 1941; Howard Univ Coll of Med, MD, 1950. **Career:** Howard Univ, Coll of Pharmacy, instructor, 1938-46; part-time pharmacy practice, 1938-40; Cate B Reynolds Hospital, rotating internship, 1950-51, pediatrics resident, 1951-52; Lexington Memorial Hosp, staff member, 1952-57; Freedmens Hosp, pediatrics residency, 1957-59; pediatrics practice and staff member at various hospitals, 1960-90. **Orgs:** Mem Greensboro Med Soc; Old N State Med Soc; Nat Med Assn; bd dir Triad Sickle Cell Anemia Found. **Honors/Awds:** First Black Eagle Scout In South 1929; Natl Honor Soc 1932; currently (1991) first and only black pediatrician in Greensboro, NC. **Military Serv:** USNR seaman 1934-38. **Home Addr:** 2009 Chelsea Ln, Greensboro, NC 27406.

DENNING, BERNADINE NEWSOM
Educational administrator. **Personal:** Born Aug 17, 1930, Detroit, MI; married Blaine; children: Blaine Jr. **Educ:** MI State Normal EMU, BS 1951; Wayne State U, MA 1956, MA & 30 Spclst 1960, EdD 1970. **Career:** Detroit Public Sch, tchr 1951-62, cnslr 1962-70; Univ of MI, asst prof 1970-75; Title IV Civil Rights, dir 1975-77; Office of Revenue Sharing Dept of Treas, dir 1977-79; Detroit Public Sch, asst supt. **Orgs:** Trustee Central MI Univ 1980-; sec MI Atty Discipline Bd 1983-; chrmn MI Women's Commn 1980-; mem YWCA of USA Bd 1973-; vice chrmn Black United Fund 1984-; mem Black Family Devel Bd 1981-; sec Children's Aid Soc 1983-. **Honors/Awds:** Emma V Kelly Award Daughters of IBPOE of W 1983; Disting Award US Coast Guard Acad 1982; Lifetime Achievemnt Award YWCA 1984; Negro Bus & Professnl Award 1978.

DENNING, JOE WILLIAM
Government official. **Personal:** Born Nov 30, 1945, Bowling Green, KY; son of Evelyn Huskey Denning and Marion E Denning; divorced; children: Kita Denning Clements, Larecia Denning Bell. **Educ:** KY State Police Acad, 1970; Western KY Univ. **Career:** Bowling Green Ind School District, member 1975-92. **Orgs:** Mem BG Warren Co Chamber of Commerce; KY League of Cities; National League of Cities; Bowling Green Chamber of Commerce. **Honors/Awds:** City of Bowling Green Elected City Commissioner, 1991.

DENNIS, ANDRE L.
Attorney. **Personal:** Born May 15, 1943, Burton-On-Trent, England; married Julie B Carpenter; children: Matthew. **Educ:** Cheyney University, BA, 1966; Howard University School of Law, JD, 1969. **Career:** Stradley, Ronon, Stevens & Young, associate, 1969-76, partner, 1976-. **Orgs:** Natl Sr Citizens Law Center, bd mem, 1995-; Phila Facilities Management Corp, bd mem, 1994-; PA Capital Case Resource Ctr, pres, 1993-; Philadelphia Bar Assn, chancellor, 1993, Volunteers for the Indigent Program, president, 1990-91, bd of governors, chair, 1986; Community Legal Services, bd of trustees, 1973-84; Pennsylvania Bar Assn House of Delegates, 1988-. **Honors/Awds:** Howard University, Alumni Achievement Award; Salem Baptist Church, ML King Jr Humanitarian Award, 1993; BWEA, Montgomery County Chapter, Appreciation Award, 1992; Community Legal Services, Equal Justice Award, 1992; American Bar Association, Pro Bono Public Award, 1994; Pennsylvania Bar Assn, Pro Bono Service Award, 1991-1992. **Business Addr:** Attorney, Stradley, Ronon, Stevens & Young, 2600 One Commerce Square, Philadelphia, PA 19103-7098, (215)564-8034.

DENNIS, BARBARA RODGERS. See RODGERS, BARBARA LORRAINE.

DENNIS, EDWARD S. G., JR.
Attorney. **Personal:** Born Jan 24, 1945, Salisbury, MD; son of Virginia Monroe Dennis and Edward S Dennis; married Lois Juliette Young Dennis, Dec 27, 1969; children: Edward Brookfield. **Educ:** United States Merchant Marine Academy, BS, 1967; University of Pennsylvania Law School, JD, 1973. **Career:** US Department of Justice, US Attorney's Office, Criminal Division, deputy chief; dep chief, 1978-80, Criminal Division, Narcotic and Dangerous Drug Section, chief, 1980-83, United States attorney, 1983-88, assistant attorney general, 1988-90; US Department of Justice, acting deputy attorney general of the United States, 1989; Morgan, Lewis & Bockius, senior partner, 1990-. **Orgs:** Public Interest Law Center of Philadelphia, board of directors, 1991; American Judicature Society, board of directors, 1990-91; Public Broadcasting Station, WHYY, Inc, board of directors, 1990; Citizens Crime Commission, board of directors, 1990-; International Society of Barristers, fellow, 1991; Amer Coll of Trial Lawyers. **Honors/Awds:** American Jewish Congress, Religious Liberty Award, 1990; attorney general of the United States, Edmund J Randolf Award, 1988; Philadelphia Inter-Alumni Council for the United Negro College Fund, Hobart C Jackson Award, 1988; Educators' Roundtable, Inc, Reverend Dr Martin Luther King Award, 1988; Omega Psi Phi Fraternity, Citizen of the Year, 1987. **Military Serv:** US Naval Reserve, Lt, 1967-82. **Business Addr:** Senior Partner, Litigation, Morgan, Lewis & Bockius, 2000 One Logan Square, Philadelphia, PA 19103-6933, (215)963-5722.

DENNIS, EVIE GARRETT
Educational administrator. **Personal:** Born Sep 8, 1924, Canton, MS; daughter of Ola Brown Garrett and Eugene Garrett; divorced; children: Pia E Dennis. **Educ:** St Louis University, BS, 1953; University of Colorado, MA, 1971; Nova University, EdD, 1976. **Career:** Children's Asthma Research Institute and Hospital, research asst, 1958-63, research associate, 1958-66; Denver Public Schools, Lake Junior High School, counselor, teacher, 1966-71, community specialist, starting 1971; Denver Vocational Guidance Inst, cons, 1971-72; Metro State College, teacher, 1974; Denver Public Schools, superintendent, currently. **Business Addr:** Superintendent, Denver Public Schools, 900 Grant, Denver, CO 80203.

DENNIS, GERTRUDE ZELMA FORD
Law librarian (retired). **Personal:** Born May 19, 1927, Scottsville, VA; daughter of Elizabeth Bentley Ford (deceased) and Bernard C Ford (deceased); married Christopher; children: Ronald, Reginald, Renee, Christine. **Educ:** Washington School of Nursing, diploma, 1967; Federal City College, Washington, DC, BS, 1976, FCC, MA, media science, 1977. **Career:** Naval Medical Center, Bethesda, MD, nurse, 1967-72; District of Columbia General Hospital, Washington, DC, nurse, 1972-74; US Department of Justice, Washington, DC, librarian, 1976-88. **Orgs:** Member, America Library Association Black Caucus, 1977-; member, Armstrong High School Alumni Association, 1980-; University of the District of Columbia Alumni Association, 1977-; corresponding secretary, Association for the Study of Afro-American History, 1986-87, second vice pres, 1997-98; director, My Exhibit I Display, District of Columbia Metro Area Black Authors' Historical Culture; 2nd vp, Assn for the Study of Afro-Amer History, 1994-96; life mem, (UDC), Alumni Univ of the District of Columbia. **Honors/Awds:** Medal of Honor, Lime Stone College, Gaffney, SC, 1976; Scholarship, Federal College Graduate School, 1976-77; Dean's List, Federal City College, 1975-76; meritorious Award, US Dept of Justice, 1979-.

DENNIS, HUGO, JR.
Educator. **Personal:** Born Aug 5, 1936, Tortola, VI; married Carmen Lydia Marrero; children: Tony, Hugh, Jancie, Reynaldo, Alex. **Educ:** Hampton Inst, BS 1959; Univ of CT, 1968. **Career:** Central Labor Council of VI, pres 1976; St Thomas-St

John Fedn of Teacher, pres 1967; VI Public Schools, math teacher 1960; VI Legislature, pres 1983-84; Virgin Islands Govt, acting commissioner of housing 1986-. **Orgs:** Del, 3rd Constl Conv of VI 1978; rep Study Tour of S Afr 1980. **Business Addr:** Acting Commissioner Housing, Virgin Islands Government, P O Box 960, St Thomas, Virgin Islands of the United States 00801.

DENNIS, JAMES CARLOS
Marketing executive. **Personal:** Born Jun 21, 1947, Washington, DC; son of Sadie Dennis; married Tonya Redding Dennis, Jul 1980; children: James Stratford. **Educ:** Fairfield University, Fairfield, CT, BS, Management, 1969; US Navy, Officer Candidate School, Newport, RI, Commission Lt, 1969; Harvard Business School, Soldiers Field, MA, MBA, 1972-74. **Career:** General Foods Corp, White Plains, NY, product mgr, 1974-78; Warner-Lambert Co, Morris Plains, NJ, senior product mgr, 1978-81; Heublein, Hartford, CT, vice president, marketing, 1981-83; Hewlett-Packard, Palo Alto, CA, dir of marketing communications, 1983-89; The Travelers, Hartford, CT, vice president, marketing corporate communications, 1989-. **Orgs:** Board member, Connecticut Special Olympics, 1990-; board member, Hartford Stage Co, 1990-; member, Omega Psi Phi, 1969-. **Military Serv:** US Navy, Lt, 1969-72; received Meritorious Unit Commendation. **Business Addr:** Vice President, Marketing, Corporate Communications Dept, The Travelers Companies, One Tower Square, 4SHS, Hartford, CT 06183.

DENNIS, KAREN
Track coach. **Career:** Univ of Las Vegas-Nevada, track coach, currently. **Orgs:** Black Coaches Assn. **Honors/Awds:** District VIII, Coach of the Year, 1992; USATF Presidents Award, 1993. **Business Addr:** Track Coach, University of Las Vegas-Navada, 4505 Maryland Parkway, Las Vegas, NV 89154, (702)739-3011.

DENNIS, PHILIP H.
Physician. **Personal:** Born Dec 1, 1925, St Louis, MO; son of Nellie Helena Watters Holton Dennis and Herman Dennis; married Patricia; children: Pia Evene, Lisette Marie, Philip Herman, Michael Marion. **Educ:** Attended, Lincoln Univ 1943-47, St Louis Univ 1951-53, Meharry Medical Coll 1953-57, Cook County Graduate School of Medicine, 1972, 1979, 1980, 1982, 1985, 1986, APA (CME), 1988. **Career:** City Hospital St Louis, internship 1957-58; Homer G. Phillips, Renard, & Cochran Hospitals, psychiatric resident, 1972, 1979, 1980, 1982, 1985, 1986; Southern IL Comm Coll, instructor 1971-74; SIU Edwardsville, counselor 1982-; Mental Health Ctr, dir 1980-. **Orgs:** Consultant in psychiatry, Illinois Retirement System, Southern Illinois Univ, Edwardsville; Family Serv Agency; mem Chamber of Commerce, Kiwanis, Amer Soc of Clinical Hypnosis. **Honors/Awds:** NIMH Fellow 1958-59; Lovejoy Award; Golden Rule Award; Host for KATZ radio "Open Mike" 1968-81; Developer Pleasingly Soft Products 1982; Exhibitor one man art & sculpture show. **Business Addr:** Neuropsychiatrist, Med East SC, Windsor Medical Arts Ctr, 100 N 8th St, Ste 200, East St Louis, IL 62201.

DENNIS, RODNEY HOWARD
Psychiatrist. **Personal:** Born Oct 3, 1936, Tampa, FL; son of Gussie Harris Dennis and Huerta W Dennis. **Educ:** NY Univ Coll of Arts/Sci, BA 1958; Howard Univ Coll of Med, MD 1962; Kings County Hosp Brooklyn NY, Rotating Internship 1962-63; NY Sch of Psychiatry Brooklyn State Hosp, Psychiatric Res 1970-73. **Career:** Letterman Genl Hosp, general medical officer 1964-65; Univ of CA, LA Brentwood VA Hosp, psychiatric res 1965-67; Metropolitan State Hosp Norwalk CA, physician 1968-69; Kingsboro Psychiatric Center Brooklyn State Hosp, psychiatrist 1973-83; Woodhull Medical and Mental Health Center, consultation/liaison svcs, attending physician dept of psychiatry 1986-. **Orgs:** Mem Amer Psychiatric Assn; mem The Brooklyn Psychiatric Soc mem The NY Acad of Sci; mem NY Univ Alumni Assn; mem Assn of NY State Mental Hygiene Phys & Dentists; mem AAAS, Acad of Psychosomatic Medicine, Pi Lambda Phi Frat. **Military Serv:** AUS capt medical corps 1962-65. **Home Addr:** 307 Decatur St, Brooklyn, NY 11233. **Business Addr:** Attending Physician, Dept of Psychiatry, Consultation/Liaison Service, Medical Associates of Woodhull PC, 760 Broadway, Brooklyn, NY 11206.

DENNIS, RUTLEDGE MELVIN
Educator. **Personal:** Born Aug 16, 1939, Charleston, SC; son of Ora Jane Porcher Dennis and David Dennis Sr; children: Shay Tchaka, Imaro, Kimya, Zuri. **Educ:** SC State Coll, BS 1966; WA State Univ, MA 1969, PhD 1975. **Career:** VA Commonwealth Univ, coord Afro-Am studies 1971-78, asso prof dept of sociology 1978-; Assoc Chmn, Sociology Dept 1981-83; Commonwealth professor of sociology, George Mason University, 1989-91, prof of sociology, 1992-. **Orgs:** Alpha Kappa Delta Chapter, George Mason Univ, advisor, 1991-; Graduate Program, Sociology Dept, George Mason Univ, co-coordinator, 1991-; Pres Assn of Black Sociologists 1981-83; pres Black Educ Assn 1974-75; Commissioner Richmond Redevelopment & Housing Authority 1979-81; mem NY Academy of Sciences, Am Sociological Assn; mem, Southern Sociological Association. **Honors/Awds:** Sigma Xi Initiation Richmond Chapter Sigma Xi 1980; Reise-Melton Award VA Commonwealth Univ Cultural Award 1981; Boys Club Citizen Award, Richmond Boys Club 1980; Distinguished Community Educ Award, Alpha Phi Alpha Frat 1985; Initiated into Omicron Delta Kappa 1986; The Politics of Annexation: Oligarchic Power in a Southern City (with John Moeser) 1982; Alpha Kappa Delta Founders' Address, Hampton Univ 1985; Distinguished Leadership Award, Afro-American Studies Program, VA Commonwealth Univ, 1991. **Special Achievements:** Co-editor, The Afro-American, 1976; Race & Ethnicity in Research Methods, 1993; editor, JAI Press Series in Race and Ethnic Relations, 1990-; Racial and Ethnic Politics, 1994, The Black Middle Class, 1995, WEB DuBois; The Scholar as Activist, 1996, The Black Intellectuals, 1997. **Military Serv:** AUS sp 4. **Business Addr:** Professor of Sociology, George Mason University, Robinson Hall, Fairfax, VA 22030.

DENNIS, SHIRLEY M.
Government official. **Personal:** Born Feb 26, 1938, Omaha, NE; married William D C Dennis; children: Pamela, Robin, Sherrie. **Educ:** Cheyney State College, 1955-56; Real Estate Institute, 1959; American Institute of Planner, 1970; Temple Univ, AS 1985. **Career:** Tucker & Tucker, Philadelphia, sales & office mgr 1961-67; Redevelopment Authority, Philadelphia, equal opportunity specialist 1967-68; Urban League of Philadelphia, housing dir 1969-71; Housing Assn of Delaware Valley, managing dir 1971-79; Dept of Community Affairs, executive deputy secretary 1979-. **Orgs:** Member Philadelphia Tribune Charities 1978; co-chairperson Philadelphia Housing Task force 1978; chairperson PA Housing Finance Agency 1979-; executive bd member Council State Community Affairs 1980-; executive committee Natl State Housing Finance 1982-; member Coalition of 100 Black Women 1982; member Abington Memorial Hospital 1982; board member Philadelphia Martin Luther King, Jr Assn Inc 1985; board member NAACP Willow Grove Branch; exec bd mem PA State Conferenceof NAACP. **Honors/Awds:** Redbook Magazine one of 12 outstanding women in Penna 1977; Black Journalist Award 1978; Public Service Award PA Federation of Business & Prof Women's Club 1980; Service Award NAACP 1980; Appreciation Award Carlisle OIC 1981; Community Serv Award Natl Assn of Negro Business & Prof Women 1981.

DENNIS, WALTER DECOSTER
Pastor. **Personal:** Born Aug 23, 1932, Washington, DC. **Educ:** VA Coll, BA 1952; NY Univ, MA 1953; Gen Theo Sem, MDiv 1956; Interdeonom Theol Ctr, DD (Honorary). **Career:** Prot Episcopal Church, deacon 1956; St Philips Episcopal Church, curate 1956; Cathedral Church of St John the Divine, asst minister 1956-60; St Cyprians Church, vicar 1960-65; Amer Hist & Const Law Hampton Inst, adjunct, asst prof 1961-65; elected suffragan bishop 1979; CSJD Prog Admin, canon residentiary 1965-79. **Orgs:** Mem Union of Black Epis, Guild of St Ives; corr sec, comm Clergy Deployment; mem The Standing Comm; mem Bishops Comm on Taxation; mem Comm on SocConcerns; fellow in res Univ of the South; mem Epis Church Natl Task Force on Hunger; adj prof Christ Ethics, Gen Theo Sem; convener Black Caucus, Epis Dio of NY Res & Publ Comm; bd mem Sex Info & Ed Council of US; bd mem Juvenile Justice Ctr, Epis Churches Tchg Serv Ethics Vol 1975; bd of dir Manhattanville Comm Ctr Inc, Abort Repeal Assoc, Inst for the Study of Human Resources, Homosexual Comm Couns Ctr, Natl Org for the Reform of Marijuana Laws; lecturer The Div School, Univ of the South 1974-75; mem Christian Ed 1967-68; exam chaplin 1970-72; mem comm on Canons 1974-77; The Standing Commission on the Structure of the Church, 1995-98; vice pres Province II; Presiding Bishop's Council of Advice; bd of editors, Anglican & Episcopal History Journal; Diocesan Episcopal AIDS Committee. **Honors/Awds:** Puerto Rican Neighborhood Awd 1958; Mex Amer Neighborhood 1960; Chap Publ "On the Battle Lines" 1962; arts publ in The Epis New Yorker, The Anglican Theol Rev, The St Lukes Jrnl of Theol; DD The General Theo Seminary; LHD Virginia State Uni & Seminarny of the Southwest L.H.D. **Business Addr:** Episcopal Diocese of New York, 1047 Amsterdam Ave, New York, NY 10025.

DENNISTON, DOROTHY L.
Educator. **Personal:** Born Aug 10, 1944, Springfield, MA; daughter of Irma L Washington Hamer and James H Hamer; divorced. **Educ:** Northeastern Univ, BA 1967; Simmons College, MA 1975; Brown Univ, PhD 1983. **Career:** Secondary Schools, teacher of English, 1967-71; Simmons Coll, asst to dir of admiss, 1971-72, instr of English, 1972-74, assoc dean, 1974-76, 79-80; Univ of TN, asst prof of English, 1983-86; Brown Univ, vstg prof English, 1987-88, asst prof, 1988-94, assoc prof, 1994-. **Orgs:** Nat Assoc Foreign Student Affairs, 1972; Assoc for Study of Negro Life & History, 1972-; Modern Lang Assn, 1975-; Alpha Kappa Alpha Sorority, 1963-67; adv com for scholars-internship prog Martin L King Jr Cntr for Social Change, 1976-; Natl Assoc of Interdiscipliny Ethnic Studies 1977-; standing comm on black studies Coll Lang Assoc 1983-86; SE Lang Assoc, 1984-86; Langston Hughes Center for the Arts, 1988-; NE Lang Association 1991-; college bd, English Composition Test Committee 1984-87; Coll Language Assn, 1984-. **Honors/Awds:** Omega Psi Phi Fraternity Scholarship Boston Chptr 1962; J Rosen Scholarship Award Boston Chptr NE Univ 1965; Fellow Natl Fellowship Fund 1976-79; Brown University, Dorothy Danforth Compton Fellowship, 1981-82, Howard Post-doctoral Fellowship, 1986-87, Wriston Fellowship for Excellence in Teaching, 1990; University of TN, Faculty Rsch Awd, 1985, Faculty Rsch Awd Dept of English, 1984; Ford Foundation, Summer Seminar for Coll Professors, Fellow, 1993. **Special Achievements:** Author, The Fiction of Paule Marshall: History, Culture & Gender, Univ of Tennessee Press, 1995; "Paule Marshall," American Women Writers from Colonial Times to Present, 1980, updated 1992; associate editor, Langston Hughes Review; associate editor, Abafazi: The Simmons College Review of Women of African Descent; "Paule Marshall," Black Women in America: An Historical Encyclopedia, 1992; "Early Short Fiction by Paule Marshall," Short Story Criticism, 1990; "Faulkner's Image of Blacks in Go Down Moses," Phylon, March, 1983. **Business Addr:** Associate Professor, Brown University, Department of English, Box 1852, Providence, RI 02912.

DENSON, DAMON
Professional football player. **Personal:** Born Feb 8, 1975. **Educ:** Univ of Michigan, attended. **Career:** New England Patriots, guard, 1997-. **Business Addr:** Professional Football Player, New England Patriots, 60 Washington St, Foxboro Stadium, Foxboro, MA 02035, (508)543-7911.

DENSON, FRED L.
Attorney. **Personal:** Born Jul 19, 1937, New Brighton, PA; married Catherine; children: Terry, Kelly, Kendra. **Educ:** Rensselaer Poly Inst, BChemE 1959; Georgetown U, JD 1966. **Career:** WOKR-TV ABC, host black dimensions 1972-; Urban League of Rochester, exec dir 1970-71; Eastman Kodak Co, atty 1967-70. **Orgs:** Bd mem NYS Pub Employ Relat Bd; exec dir Nat Patent Law Assn; dir Armarco Mktg; pres Genessee Region Home Care Assn; chmn adv counc NYS Div of Human Rights Am Bar Assn; Nat Bar Assn; Monroe Co Bar Assn; Nat Patent Law Assn; Am Arbitraton Assn. **Honors/Awds:** Author, Know Your Town Justice Court; minority involv in the US Patent Sys; Rochester Comm Serv Awd 1974-76. **Military Serv:** AUS 1st lt 1960-61. **Business Addr:** 14 E Main St, PO Box 801, Webster, NY 14580.

DENT, ANTHONY L.
Senior scientist. **Personal:** Born Apr 19, 1943, Indian Head, MD; married Joyce P Chesley-Dent; children: Antonette, Robert, Christopher. **Educ:** Morgan State Coll, BS 1966; Johns Hopkins Univ, PhD 1970. **Career:** Carnegie Mellon Univ, asso prof Chem Eng 1970-78; DuPont Co, rsch engr 1972; PQ Corp, sr chem, R&D assoc, R&D supervisor, mgr, principal scientist 1979-. **Orgs:** Mem Am Chem Soc; Am Inst Chem Engrs; co-chmn I & EC Annl Chem Engr Sympsm; CMU Fclty Snt 1971-75; sec treas pres elct pres dir Pitts Ctlys Soc 1972-81; chmn sch admsns com Wstrn PA Chap J Hpkns Univ 1972-75, pres Pitts Chap Almn Assn 1976-77; vice chmn 5th N Amer Mtng of Ctlys Soc 1977; Philadelphia Catalysis Club sec-treas, dir 1981-83, chmn elect 1989-90; pres Del Valley Chap of NOBCChE 1983-89, regional chmn 1989-; fellow Amer Inst Chemists 1986; Nat Rsrch Cncl Com; Idntfctn Adv Serv; rcrt wmn & min into engr grad level Sci & Engrs Min Bckgrnds. **Honors/Awds:** Elctd Phi Lambda Upsln 1967, Sigma Xi 1968, Phi Beta Kappa 1969; Beta Kappa Chi Hon Soc 1963; nom Cml & Hnry Dryfs Tchr Schlr Grnt Carnegie- Mellon Univ 1974, 1975; Meritorious Service Award, NOBCChE 1988, 1994. **Business Addr:** Senior Scientist, PQ Corporation, 280 Cedar Grove Rd, Conshohocken, PA 19428, (610)941-2020.

DENT, CARL ASHLEY
Physician (retired). **Personal:** Born May 27, 1914, St Simon's Island, GA; son of Josephine Lillian Green and Earnest Alton Dent; married Lavetta Lucas, Jun 18, 1938; children: Cynthia Jo Kennedy, Patricia Mapp. **Educ:** Pacific Union Coll, BS 1934; Loma Linda U, MD 1939. **Career:** Med Staff Riverside Adventist Hosp, pres 1955-69; Riverside Adventist Hosp, med dir 1950-55; Los Angeles Co Gen Hosp, intern 1938-40; Seventh-day Adventist Health Services Nairobi Kenya, dir 1984-87, 1988, 1990; Physician, retired. **Orgs:** Med Sect, S Central Conf SDA, Fellow, Am Soc Abdominal Surgeons. **Honors/Awds:** Mem Soc Nuclear Med, Refugee relief team leader, Intl Red Cross 1969. **Business Addr:** 617 Nocturne Dr, Nashville, TN 37207.

DENT, CEDRIC CARL
Musician, singer. **Personal:** Born Sep 24, 1962, Detroit, MI; son of Barbara Elouise Carson Dent and Edward Samuel Dent; married Beverly Dawn Hayes Dent, Dec 6, 1987. **Educ:** University of Michigan, Ann Arbor, MI, BM, vocal music education, 1985; University of Alabama, Tuscaloosa, AL, MM, music arranging, theory, 1987. **Career:** Take 6, Nashville, TN, singer, 1985-. **Orgs:** Member, Phi Mu Alpha Sinfonia, 1986-; member, AFTRA/SAG, 1987-; member, AF of M, 1990-; council member, W O Smith Community School of Music, 1991. **Honors/Awds:** Grammy Award, Jazz Vocal Perf Group or Duo, National Academy of Arts & Sciences, 1988; Grammy Award, Soul Gospel Vocal Perf, Group or Duo, 1988, 1989, 1990 ; Six Dove Awards, Gospel Music Assn, 1989, 1990.

DENT, GARY KEVER
Human resources executive. **Personal:** Born Nov 18, 1950, Norfolk, VA; son of Geraldine Brown Dent and Kever H Dent; married Carman Stroud Dent, May 29, 1982; children: Katina Arne, Travis Damon. **Educ:** Norfolk State University, Norfolk, VA, BS, education, 1972; Central Michigan University, Mt. Pleasant, MI, MA, management/supervision, 1983. **Career:** Detroit Diesel Allison-GMC, Indianapolis, IN, service training rep, 1974-76; General Motors Education & Training, Dayton, OH, regional manager, 1977-85; General Motors Personnel Programs & Services, Detroit, MI, manager, 1985-89; General Motors Central Office Personnel, Detroit, MI, manager, 1989-93; City of Detroit, Human Resource Dept, dir, 1994-. **Orgs:** Member, Aircraft Owner and Pilots Association, 1985-; co-chairperson, NAACP, 1980-; president, National Black MBA Association-Detroit; chairperson, Boy Scouts of America-Central Section, 1988-. **Honors/Awds:** Presidential Citation, National Association for Equal Opportunity in Education, 1987; Presidents Award, National Black MBA Association, Detroit chapter, 1990; Outstanding Alumnus, Norfolk State University, 1987; National Quality Section Award, Boy Scouts of America, 1989, 1990; Outstanding Citizen Award, City of Dayton Priority Board, 1985. **Military Serv:** US Army, Capt, 1972-85; Army Commendation Medal, Indiana and Ohio Commendation Medals. **Business Addr:** Director, Human Resources Department, City of Detroit, 316 City-County Bldg, Detroit, MI 48226.

DENT, PRESTON L.
Educator, businessman, psychologist. **Personal:** Born Apr 30, 1939, Philadelphia, PA; son of Alice Livingston Dent and William Preston Dent; married Imelda Velasco; children: David-Preston, Robyn Lynn. **Educ:** PA State Univ, BS Psychology 1961; San Francisco State Univ, MA Psychology 1963; Univ of CA Santa Barbara, PhD Educ Psychology 1971. **Career:** San Francisco City Coll Dept of Psychology, graduate instructor, 1966-67; STIR Facility The Bunker-Ramo Corp, simulator flight control program engineer, 1966-67; TRW Systems Inc Indus Relations Div, trainer, counselor, equal opportunity program office, 1967-68; Pierce Coll, psychology instructor 1967-72; Univ of CA Santa Barbara, asst to chancellor 1969-72; Coll of Letters Arts Science, associate dean, dir of devel & sponsored research; Univ of Southern CA, prof higher educ 1972-86; The Dent-Glasser Corp, president, chief executive officer, 1984-. **Orgs:** International Council of Psychology; Amer Psychology Society; Omega Psi Phi; AAAS; Amer Assn of Univ Admin, NAACP, United Nations Assoc; Golden State Foundation; commr City of Los Angeles 1981-82; fellow Amer Council on Ed 1971-72; dir Los Angeles Child Guidance Clinic; consulant The MacNeal-Schwendler Corp; bd of advisors, American International National Bank; trustee, Paine College. **Honors/Awds:** Outstanding Young Men of Amer Award, US Chamber of Commerce, 1970; Kappa Delta Pi Ed Hon, Phi Delta Kappa Ed Hon; Distinguished Serv Award from City of Los Angeles; Sigma Xi. **Military Serv:** USAF 1st lieutenant 1963-66. **Business Addr:** President, The Dent-Glasser Corp, 606 El Segundo Blvd, Ste A, Los Angeles, CA 90061, (310)516-9604.

DENT, RICHARD LAMAR
Professional football player. **Personal:** Born Dec 13, 1960, Atlanta, GA; married Leslie; children: Mary Francis, Sarah. **Educ:** Tennessee State Univ, attended. **Career:** Chicago Bears, defensive end, 1983-93, 1995; San Francisco 49ers, 1994; Indianapolis Colts, 1996; Philadelphia Eagles, 1997-. **Honors/Awds:** Set TN State record with 39 career sacks; earned NFC Defensive Player of Week honors & game ball; Coll & Pro Ftbl Weekly's 1st team; All-NFC; AP second team; UPI 1st team; Super Bowl XX MVP; played in Pro Bowl, 1984, 1985, 1990, 1993. **Special Achievements:** Bears all-time sack leader with 112; 10.5 playoff sacks is best in NFL history. **Business Phone:** (215)463-2500.

DENT, THOMAS COVINGTON
Journalist, dramatist, poet, essayist. **Personal:** Born Mar 20, 1932, New Orleans, MS; son of Jessie Covington Dent and Albert Dent. **Educ:** Morehouse Coll, BA, 1952; Goddard Coll, MA, 1974. **Career:** Houston Informer, Houston TX, reporter, 1950-52; New York Age, New York City, reporter,1959; NAACP, New York City, public information aide for Legal Defense Fund, 1961-63; Coalition Umbra magazine 1962-63; Free Southern Theater, New Orleans LA, assoc dir, 1966-70; Total Community Action, New Orleans, public relations officer, 1971-73; public lecturer; writer, On Guard for Freedom (political newspaper), 1960; co-founder Southern Black Cultural Alliance, 1971; co-founder of Callaloo (literary magazine), 1978; founder of Congo Square Writers Union, New Orleans, 1974; instructor at Mary Holmes College, 1968-70, Univ of New Orleans, 1979-81; Tulane University, guest instructor, creative writing, 1994. **Orgs:** Mem, African Literature Assn; Oral History Assn., Langston Hughes Society; exec dir, New Orleans Jazz and Heritage Found, 1987-90. **Honors/Awds:** Whitney Young Fellow, 1973-74; author of Magnolia Street (poems), privately printed, 1976, reprinted, 1987; author of Blue Lights and River Songs: Poems, Lotus Press, 1982; author of one-act play, ''Ritual Murder''; author of prose narrative ''The Ghetto of Desire,'' CBS-TV, 1966; author of Southern Journey: A Return to the Civil Rights Movement, William Morrow Co, 1996; co-author of The Free Southern Theater, by The Free Southern Theatre, Bobbs-Merrill, 1969. **Military Serv:** US Army, 1957-59. **Home Addr:** Box 50584, New Orleans, LA 70150.

DENTON, SANDY (PEPA)
Recording artist. **Personal:** chilDren: one. **Career:** Next Plateau Records, producer and member of rap group Salt-N-Pepa; Record- ings include ''Blacks' Magic,'' 1990; ''Very Necessary,'' 1994. **Special Achievements:** First female rapper to have a gold album. **Business Addr:** Rap Artist/Owner, Hollyhood, Around Lenox Shopping Center, 3400 Around Lenox Dr, Ste B-400, Atlanta, GA 30326, (404)848-9030.

DENYE, BLAINE A.
Educator. **Personal:** Born Jun 27, 1933, Chicago, IL; son of Gladys DeNye and Julius DeNye; married Doris L Thornton; children: Paul, Iva. **Educ:** Roosevelt Univ, BA 1960; Chicago Teachers Coll, MEd 1964. **Career:** Teacher 1960-63; counselor 1963-69; Educ Program Planning, dir 1969-70; Model Cities Prog, dir 1969-73; Manley HS Chicago, principal 1973-86; District Ten, superintendent 1986-89. **Orgs:** Chmn Diaconate Bd 1966; mem Trinity United Church Christ chmn exec council 1973-75; chmn Bldg Comm 1974-80; chmn Board Long Range Planning; mem Phi Delta Kappa; vice pres bd of dirs, Trinity; pres, Trinity Community Housing Corp; pres, Trinity Acres Housing Corp. **Honors/Awds:** Phi Delta Kappa Educator of the Year; Ora Higgins Youth Foundation. **Military Serv:** AUS 1st lt 1953-58.

DE PASSE, SUZANNE
Producer, business executive. **Personal:** Born 1948, Harlem, NY; married Paul Le Mat, 1978. **Educ:** Attended Manhattan Community College. **Career:** Assistant executive, Motown Industries, 1968, pres, 1980-; co-author of Lady Sings the Blues; producer, ''Motown 25: Yesterday, Today, Forever''; producer, director, ''Lonesome Dove''; discovered numerous major Motown artists and music stars. **Honors/Awds:** Producer of Emmy-winning television show ''Motown 25: Yesterday, Today, Forever''; signed and polished such famous Motown artists as Lionel Richie, Rick James, Stephanie Mills, Diana Ross and the Jackson Five. **Business Addr:** President, Gordy/de Passe Productions, 6255 W Sunset Boulevard, Los Angeles, CA 90026.

DEPILLARS, MURRY NORMAN
Educator. **Personal:** Born Dec 21, 1938, Chicago, IL; son of Mary Taylor; married Mary L. **Educ:** JC Wilson Coll, AA Fine Arts 1966; Roosevelt Univ, BA Art Educ 1968, MA Urban Studies 1970; PA State Univ, PhD Art Educ 1976. **Career:** Mast Inst, Chicago comm on urban opportunity div of training 1968; Univ of IL Chicago, educ asst program asst dir 1968-71; numerous art exhibits throughout the US; VA Commonwealth Univ Richmond, dean school of art; Chicago State Univ, exec vp for planning and mgmt, currently. **Orgs:** Bd of dir & illustrator 3rd World Press Chicago 1960-; bd of dir & art dir Kuumba Workshop Chicago 1969-; bd of dir & contributing ed Inst of Positive Educ Chicago 1970-; adv bd Journal of Negro Educ Washington 1973-; bd of dir N Amer Zone & co-chmn Upper So Region 2nd World Black & African Festival of Arts & Culture 1973-74; pres Natl Conf of Artists Richmond 1973-77; mem Intl Council of Fine Arts Deans 1976-; hmn of bd Natl Conf of Artists NY 1977; First Sino/Amer Conf on the Arts Taipei Taiwan 1980; arts commission Natl Assoc of State Univ & Land Grant Colls 1981-88; consultant Natl Endowment for the Humanities 1982-84; cons Corp of the Public Broadcasting & the Annenberg School of Communications 1983; OH Eminent Scholars Program Panel OH Bd of Regents1983-84; consult The O Paul GetTrust 1984; Natl Endowment for the Arts Expansion Arts Program 1985-; Natl Jazz Serv Org 1985-; US Info Agency Acad Specialist to Malaysia 1985; Africobra 1985-; arts adv bd Coll Bd 1984-85; chmn, coordinator comm The Richmond Jazz Festival 1984-; art & architectural review bd Commonwealth of VA 1986-. **Honors/Awds:** Elizabeth Catlett Mora Award of Excellence Natl Conf of Artists 1977; Special Arts Awd & Art Educ Award Branches for the Arts 1980; Man of Excellence Plaque Ministry of Educ Republic of China 1980; Excellence in the Educ Preservation & Promotion of Jazz Richmond Jazz Soc 1981; Outstanding Admin Award Black Student Alliance 1982; Outstanding Achievement in the Arts Branches for the Arts 1982; Alumni Fellow Penn State Univ 1989. **Military Serv:** AUS pfc 1962-63. **Business Addr:** Exec VP, Planning and Mgmt, Chicago State Univ, 9501 S King Dr, Chicago, IL 60628.

DEPREIST, JAMES ANDERSON
Orchestra music director and conductor. **Personal:** Born Nov 21, 1936, Philadelphia, PA; son of Ethel Anderson and James Henry DePreist; married Ginette Grenier; children: Tracy Elisabeth, Jennifer Anne. **Educ:** Univ of PA, BS 1958, MA 1961; Philadelphia Conservatory of Music, student 1959-61. **Career:** State Dept, Am specialist music 1962-63; NY Philharmonic, Amer debut 1964; NY Philharmonic Orchestra, asst conductor to Leonard Bernstein 1965-66; Symphony of New World, prin guest conductor 1968-70; Rotterdam Philharmonic, European debut 1969; Natl Symphony Orchestra Washington, assoc conductor 1971-75, prin guest conductor 1975-76; L'Orchestre Symphonique de Que, mus dir 1976-83; Oregon Symphony, conductor 1980-. **Orgs:** Appeared with Philadelphia Orchestra 1972, Chicago Symphony 1973, Boston Symphony, Cleveland Orchestra 1974; conductor Amer premiere of Dvorak's First Symphony NY Philharmonic 1972; trustee Lewis & Clark Coll 1983-; composed ballet scores for, ''Vision of America'' 1960, ''Tendrils'' 1961, ''A Sprig of Lilac'' 1964; concert ''Requiem'' 1965; mem Sigma Pi Phi. **Honors/Awds:** First Prize Gold Medal Dimitri Mitropoulos Intl Music Competition for Conductors 1964; Merit Citation City of Philadelphia 1969; grantee Martha Baird Rockefeller Fund for Music 1969; Medal of City of Que 1983; honorary degrees: Univ of Pennsylvania, LHD, 1976; Laval Univ, DMus, 1980; Univ of Portland, DFA, 1983; Pacific Univ, DFA, 1985; St Mary's Coll, Doctor of Arts & Letters, 1985; Lewis & Clark Coll, Doctor in Humanities, 1986; Linfield Coll, DMus, 1986; Willamette Univ, DFA, 1987; Drexel Univ, DFA, 1989; Reed College, Doctor of Letters, 1990; Oregon State University, DFA, 1990. **Business Addr:** Conductor, Oregon Symphony, 711 SW Alder #200, Portland, OR 97205.

DEPRIEST, DARRYL LAWRENCE
Attorney. **Personal:** Born Sep 23, 1954, Chicago, IL; son of Bertha Williams DePriest and W LaVerne DePriest; married Colleen K Connell, May 19, 1987; children: Brennan Connell, Carlyle Ann. **Educ:** Harvard College, Cambridge, MA, BA, cum laude, government, 1972-76; Harvard Law School, Cambridge, MA, JD, 1976-79; National Institute for Trial Advocacy, Boulder, CO, 1983. **Career:** Honorable Robert E. Keeton, USDJ, Boston, MA, law clerk, 1979-80; Jenner & Block, Chicago, IL, partner, 1980-88; American Bar Association, Chicago, IL, general counsel, 1988-. **Orgs:** American Bar Assn; National Bar Assn; Illinois State Bar Assn; Cook County Bar Assn; Chicago Bar Assn; American Corporate Counsel Assn; American Society of Assn Executives; Chicago Society of Assn Executives; Chicago Board of Ethics; board of directors, Chicago Public Schools Alumni Assn; board of directors, 1981-85, Schools & Scholarship Committee, 1980-, Harvard Club of Chicago; Harvard Club of Boston; Associated Harvard Alumni; board of directors, Leadership Greater Chicago, pres, 1995-96. **Honors/Awds:** Leadership Greater Chicago, 1987-88; 40 Under 40, Crain's Chicago Business, 1989; America's Best and Brightest Young Business and Professional Men, Dollars and Sense Magazine, 1989; Monarch Award for Achievement in Law, Xi Nu Omega Chapter, Alpha Kappa Alpha Sorority, 1989. **Business Addr:** General Counsel, American Bar Association, 750 N. Lake Shore Drive, Chicago, IL 60611.

DEPTE, LARRY D.
Health products company executive. **Personal:** Born Jun 8, 1950, Coatesville, PA. **Educ:** Temple U, BS bus adminstrn 1972. **Career:** Correction Connection, chief executive, currently; Philadelphia Intl Records, pres 1979-, vice pres finance & bus affairs 1975-76; Coopers & Lybrand, auditor 1972-75. **Orgs:** Mem Nat Assn of Black Accountants; com mem Rec Industry Assn of Am; mem Black Music Assn. **Honors/Awds:** Industrial Service 100, Correction Connection, Black Enterprise, 1991.

DERAMUS, BETTY
Columnist. **Career:** Detroit News, columnist, currently. **Honors/Awds:** Pulitzer Prize finalist for commentary, 1993. **Business Addr:** Columnist, Detroit News, 615 W Lafayette, Detroit, MI 48226, (313)222-2315.

DERAMUS, BILL R.
Franchisee. **Personal:** Born Jul 10, 1938, Timpson, TX; son of TJ & Lafayette Deramus; children: William. **Educ:** Prairie View A&M University, BS, 1961; Webster University, MS, 1983. **Career:** Marriott, regional manager, 1991-96. **Orgs:** Alpha Phi Alpha; NAACP: National Black MBA. **Honors/Awds:** Regional Manager of the Year, 1995. **Special Achievements:** First African American franchisee for Marriott Inernational. **Military Serv:** US Army, ltc, 1961-86; Legion of Merit, 1986; Bronze Star, 1967; 3 MSM; 2 ARCOM. **Business Addr:** President, Regent Hospitality, LTD, 4949 Regent Blvd, Irving, TX 75063, (972)929-4004.

DERBIGNY, RHODA L.
Marketing specialist. **Personal:** Born Jul 19, 1960, Hagerstown, MD; daughter of Gloria M Weathers Campher and Maylon A Campher, Sr; married Curtis E Derbigny, Jul 27, 1985; children: Dominique M Derbigny. **Educ:** Hagerstown Jr College, Hagerstown, MD, AA, Business Administration, 1981; Towson State University, MD, BS, Business Administration, 1984. **Career:** Household Finance Corp, Hagerstown, MD, asst mgr, 1984-86; Goodwill Industries, Inc, Hagerstown, MD, dir of community based services, 1986-87; Citicorp, Hagerstown, MD, unit mgr, 1987-89; Corning, Inc, Corning, NY, marketing development specialist, national sales mgr, 1989-. **Orgs:** Board member, Southern Tier Assoc for the Blind, 1990-; member, Society of Black Professionals, 1990-; member, NAACP, 1987-89. **Business Addr:** National Sales Manager, Corning Medical Optics, Corning, Inc, MP 21-2-2, Corning, NY 14831.

DERRICOTTE, C. BRUCE
Business executive. **Personal:** Born Jun 22, 1928, Fostoria, OH; married Toinette Webster; children: Anthony. **Educ:** Defiance Coll, BS; MI U, EE 1955. **Career:** Systems Plng Div The

Chase Manhattan Bank NA NYC, vice pres exec 1973-; Detroit Arsenal Centerline MI instrument engr 1955-60; IT&T NJ labs, product line mgr 1960-68; NY Dist & Control Data Corp, mgr 1968-73. **Orgs:** Mem Am Bankers Assn; Nat'l Planning Assn; Aircraft Owners & Pilots Assn; past mem Nat'l Exec Reserve 1966-68; VP's Task Force for Youth Motivation. **Military Serv:** AUS corpl 1950-52. **Business Addr:** Chase Manhattan Bank, N A 1 New York Plaza, New York, NY 10004.

DERRICOTTE, EUGENE ANDREW
Dentist. **Personal:** Born Jun 14, 1926, Fostoria, OH; son of Bessie M Anderson Derricotte and Clarence C Derricotte; married Jeanne E Hagans; children: Robert. **Educ:** Univ of MI, BS Pharmacy 1950, DDS 1958. **Career:** USAF, dental surgeon/chief dental surgeon various air force bases 1971-79; USAF Acad, command dental surgeon 1979-84; USAF Hosp Chanute AFB, dir dental serv 1984-85; Univ TX Health Sci Ctr at San Antonio, asst prof 1985-. **Orgs:** Mem Amer Dental Assn; mem Alpha Phi Alpha. **Honors/Awds:** University of Michigan, Hall of Honor, 1987. **Military Serv:** US Army Air Corps, 1944-46; US Air Force, colonel, 1962-85; Bronze Star Medal; Meritorious Serv Medal; USAF Commendation Medal w/1 Oak Leaf Cluster; AUS Commendation Medal; Good Conduct Medal; WW II Victory Medal; Natl Def Serv Medal; USAF Longevity Serv Awd w/2 Oak Leaf Clusters; Vietnam Serv Medal w/2 Bronze Serv Stars; Republic of Vietnam Campaign Medal; Legion of Merit 1985. **Home Addr:** 3718 Morning Mist, San Antonio, TX 78230.

DERRICOTTE, TOI
Educator. **Personal:** Born Apr 12, 1941, Detroit, MI; married. **Educ:** Wayne State University, BA, spec education, 1965; NY University, MA, English Literature & Creative Writing, 1984. **Career:** NJ State Council on the Arts & Maryland State Arts Council, master teacher, 1973-88; Columbia University, educational consultant, 1979-82; Old Dominion University, associate professor of English literature, 1988-90; George Mason University, commonwealth professor of English department, 1990-91; The Writers Voice Series of the Manhattan West Side Y, poetry teacher, 1985-86; NY University, Creative Writing Prog, visiting professor, 1992; University of Pittsburgh, associate professor of English department, 1991-; Cave Canem, Historical Workshop & Retreat for African-American Poets, summer 1996, 1997, workshop retreat on Methodology ''Freeing the Voice in a Racist Society,'' sponsored by Goddard College, 1997, founder & implemented with Cornelius Eady, 1996-. **Honors/Awds:** Lucille Medwick Memorial Awd, Poetry Society of America, 1985; Nominated for Pushcart Prize, 1986-89; Pushcart Prize, 1989; Poetry Committee Bood Awd, Floger Shakespeare Library, Washington DC, 1990; Nominated for the Nicholas Roerich Poets' Prize, 1990; Distinguished Pioneering of the Arts Awd, United Black Artists Inc, May 1993; Nominated for Pushcart Prize, 1996. **Special Achievements:** The Black Notebooks, WW Norton & Co., 1997, listed in ''Notable Books of the Year'' 1997, NY Times Book Review; Tender, University of Pittsburgh Press, 1997; Captivity, University of Pittsburgh Press, Oct 1989, 2nd printing, Oct 1991, 3rd printing, Jan 1993, 4th printing, Dec 1995; Natural Birth, The Crossing Press, 1983; The Empress of the Death House, Lotus Press, 1978, 2nd printing, 1989; Creative Writing: A Manual for Teachers, New Jersey State Council on the Arts, 1985; hundreds of poems published in anthologies and journals including: The Garden Thrives: 20th Century African-American Poetry, My Soul Is A Witness, One World Many Cultures, 2nd edition, I Hear A Symphony: African-American Celebrate Love, In Search of Color Everywhere; A Collection of African-American Poetry, Unsettling America: Race and Ethnicity in Contemporary American Poetry; and many others.

DESANDIES, KENNETH ANDRE
Physician. **Personal:** Born Feb 16, 1948, New York, NY; son of Elsie DeSandies and Conrad DeSandies; married Karen Yvonne Grant; children: Kisha, Kanika. **Educ:** Hampton Inst, BA 1969; Meharry Medical Coll, MD 1973. **Career:** Hurley Hosp, intern 1973-74; King's Co Hosp, resident ob/gyn 1974-78; Group Health Assoc, ob/gyn attending 1978-81; Private Practice, dir/owner 1981-. **Orgs:** Mem Amer Assoc of Gynecologic Laparoscopists 1980, Amer Fertility Soc 1980; fellow Amer Coll of Obstetrics & Gynecology 1981; mem National Medical Association 1980-; member, Alfred Street Baptist Church, 1979-. **Honors/Awds:** Bd Certified in Amer Coll of Ob/Gyn 1980; Physician Recognition Awd AMA 1983, 1986, 1991-95; AMA Physician Recognition Award 1989-95; American College OB/GYN Award, 1980, 1991, 1995. **Business Addr:** 4600 Duke St Ste-332, Alexandria, VA 22304, (703)823-5656.

DESASSURE, CHARLES
Computer company executive. **Personal:** Born Apr 19, 1961, Eutawville, SC; son of Moses and Emma Dessesso; married Gloria Sumpter, Apr 26, 1997. **Educ:** Claflin College, BS, 1984; Orangeburg-Calhoun Technical College, AS, 1989; Webster Univ, MA, 1997. **Career:** Compensatory, remedial education teacher, 1984-87; Coordinator, computer instructor, 1988-90; Micro Computer Specialist, programmer, 1990-1993, LAN administrator, 1993-96; Computer Field Technology, analyst, 1996-. **Orgs:** El Center Coll Computer Technology Advisory Comm, bd mem, 1993-; The Assn for Corporate Computing Technical Professionals, 1997-; NAACP; Orangeburg Calhoun Tech Coll Advisory Board, former mem; St Jones Baptist Church, bd or dirs, former mem; Phi Beta Sigma Fraternity, Inc, 1981-; Assn of Records Managers and Administrators, 1997-; Information Systems Audit and Control Assn, 1997-. **Honors/Awds:** Department of SC, American Legion Bronze Medal, 1993; SC NAACP Conference, Presidential Award for Leadership, 1993; Claflin Coll, Creative Writing Contest Award, 1981; Phi Beta Sigma, Leadership Award National, 1982; Clafin Coll, Editor-in-Chief Leadership Award, 1983. **Special Achievements:** Certified Novell Administrator, CNA, 1995; Pres, SC Youth and Coll Conference, NAACP, 1981-83; Outstanding Teacher of the Year, Mansfield Business Coll, Columbia, SC, 1988-89; Editor-in-chief, Les Memoir, College Yearbook Staff, 1982-83; Outstanding Undergraduate of the Year, Southeastern Region, Phi Beta Sigma Fraternity, Inc, 1982-83. **Home Addr:** 1105 Silverwood Dr, Arlington, TX 76006.

DESHIELDS, DELINO LAMONT
Professional baseball player. **Personal:** Born Jan 15, 1969, Seaford, DE. **Educ:** Villanova University. **Career:** Montreal Expos, infielder, 1990-94; Los Angeles Dodgers, 1994-96; St Louis Cardinals, 1997-. **Business Addr:** Professional Baseball Player, St Louis Cardinals, 250 Stadium Plaza, Busch Memorial Stadium, St Louis, MO 63102, (314)421-3060.

DESHIELDS, HARRISON F., JR.
Educational administrator. **Personal:** Born Jan 29, 1927, Philadelphia, PA; married Vivian Watts; children: Carla V, Harrison F III. **Educ:** Wilber Force Univ, BA 1949; Columbia Univ, MA 1957. **Career:** AL A&M Univ, dean of students 1957-61; Volusia Cty Comm Coll, dean of instr 1961-63; Bethume-Cookman Coll, registrar, dir admiss 1963-76; AL State Univ, dean of admiss records 1976-80; Benedict Coll, dir of admiss records 1980-84; Fisk Univ, dir of admiss & records. **Orgs:** Mem Alpha Phi Alpha 1947-; former consult Alfred P Sloan Found 1965-69, Morton Inst of Admiss & Fin Aid 1965-76; 1st black mem Southern Reg of Coll 1967;past pres & admissions officer Natl Assoc of Coll Dean Registrar 1973-74. **Honors/Awds:** James E Davis Admin of the Year Bethune-Cookman Coll 1967,75; Kappa Delta Pi Hon Soc; Phi Delta Kappa Hon Frat; Co-ed on handbook for Admissions & Fin Aid for United Negro Coll Fund 1969; Publ article in Naca Jrnl 1975. **Home Addr:** 4067 Malabar Rd, Montgomery, AL 36116. **Business Addr:** Dir Admissions & Records, Fisk University, 17th Ave North, Nashville, TN 37203.

DESKINS, DONALD R., JR.
Educator. **Personal:** Born May 10, 1932, Brooklyn, NY; married Lois Jackson; children: Sharon, Sheila, Sharlene. **Educ:** Univ of MI, BA 1960, MS 1963, PhD 1970. **Career:** BOR US Dept of the Interior, supervisory recreation resource specialist 1964-68; Univ of MI, faculty counselor 1968-69, lecturer 1968-70, asst prof 1972-74, acting chmn 1974-75, chmn 1975-; Geography & Urban Regional Planning Prog, Univ of MI, assoc prof 1973. **Orgs:** Dir Commn on Geography & Afro-Am 1960-; Assn of Am Georgraphers; mem Commn on Geography & Afro-Am 1968-69; mem Task Force on Minority Research 1970-71; mem editorial bd Professional Geographer 1972-; councilor E Lakes Div 1973-76; chmn E Lakes Div 1975-; Assn of Am Geographers; mem Publ Com 1973-; memexec bd Assn of Social & Behavoiral Sci 1973-; mem GRE Advanced Geography Test Com 1974-; Educ Testing Svc; course dir ChautauguaType Short Courses 1973-76; Nat Sci Found; Am Assn for Advancement of Sci; mem Zoning bd of appeals City of Ann Arbor 1971-73; Assn of Am Geographers; Am Geog Soc; Assn of Social & Behavioral Sci; Population Assn of Am; Regional Sci Assn; Nat Council for Geog Edn; Am Assn for Advancement of Sci. **Honors/Awds:** Sr honors Univ of MI 1959; Fielding H Yost Honor Award 1959; Phi Kappa Phi Honor Soc 1962; Gamma Theta Upsilon 1966; Sigma XI 1974. **Military Serv:** USMC 1953-57. **Business Addr:** Dept of Geography, University of Michigan, Ann Arbor, MI 48104.

DESOUSA, D. JASON
Educational administrator. **Personal:** Born Sep 12, 1964, New York, NY; son of Catherine DeSousa and William DeSousa. **Educ:** Morgan State University, BS, 1987; Bowling Green State University, MA, 1989; Indiana University, pursuing EdD, 1989-. **Career:** Indiana University Department of Afro-American Studies, Ford Foundation fellow, 1990-91; National Pan-Hellenic Council, Inc, assoc executive director, 1991-. **Orgs:** Morgan State University Board of Regents, student regent, 1986-87; Kappa Alpha Psi Fraternity, Inc, national board of directors, 1986-88; American College Student Personnel Association, 1989-. **Honors/Awds:** Ford Foundation, Ford Foundation Fellow, 1990-91; National Collegiate Merit Award, 1988; Kappa Alpha Psi Fraternity, Guy L Grant Medallion, 1988. **Special Achievements:** Co-author, ''Are White Students Really More Involved in Collegiate Experiences Than Black Students,'' Journal of College Student Development, 1992. **Business Addr:** Assoc Executive Director, National Pan-Hellenic Council, Inc, Indiana Memorial Union, Ste 30, Bloomington, IN 47405, (812)855-8820.

DESOUZA, RONALD KENT
Educational administrator. **Personal:** Born Jan 15, 1940, New York, NY; son of Mr & Mrs Winston DeSouza; married Sharon Smith; children: Kelly, Ronald Jr. **Educ:** Hunter Coll, City of New York, 1959; Morgan State Univ, BA, 1960-65, MS, 1965-66. **Career:** Balto Supreme Bench, probation ofcr 1966-68; Balto City Job Corps, cnslr 1968-69; Bowie State Coll, assoc dir or admissions, 1969-71; Coppin State Coll, dir of admissions, 1971-72, vice pres for admin, dir of admissions/records, 1972-74, vice pres, student affairs, 1974-82; vice pres, admin, 1982-, referee Natl Football League, 1980-; supervisor of officials, Natl Football League, 1992-. **Orgs:** Omega Psi Phi Fraternity, 1968-; team mem, Middle States Assn for Accreditation, 1978, 1981, 1987. **Honors/Awds:** Church organist St Phillips Annapolis MD & Holy Nativity Balto MD 1962-74; Cert Appreciation US Army Recruiting 1970. **Military Serv:** AUS major. **Home Addr:** 13 Ridings Parkway, Princeton, NJ 08540. **Business Addr:** Supervisor of Officials, National Football League, 410 Park Ave, New York, NY 10022.

DESSASO-GORDON, JANICE MARIE
Government official. **Personal:** Born Apr 10, 1942, Washington, DC; daughter of Marie E Sheppard and John F Ford (deceased); married Harold J Gordon, Aug 8, 1987; children: Eugene C, Michael A. **Educ:** Univ of the District of Columbia, Washington DC, BA, 1977. **Career:** Various federal govt agencies, Washington DC, sec, 1960-70; US Dept of Commerce, Washington DC, program analyst, 1971-76, Minority Business Devel Agency, program manager, currently. **Orgs:** Annual 30-hour dancer, Washington DC Special Olympics for Mentally Retarded-Dance Marathon, 1983-89; exec vice pres, Holy Comforter-St Cyprian Community Action Group, 1988-; mem, Business & Professional Women's Assn, 1988-; Natl Assn of Female Executives. **Honors/Awds:** Outstanding Performance, US Dept of Commerce, 1973, 1979, 1984, 1986, 1988, 1990-94; Certificate of Appreciation, Natl Minority Supplier Devel Council, 1981; Outstanding Serv Award, Natl Minority Supplier Devel Council, 1985, 1987; Appreciation Award, Nevada Economic Devel Company, 1988. **Business Addr:** Program Manager, US Dept of Commerce/Minority Business Devel Agency, 14th & Constitution Ave NW, Room H-5092, Washington, DC 20230.

DESSELLE, NATALIE
Actress. **Career:** Actress, currently. **Special Achievements:** Appeared in films: BAPS, 1997; Def Jam's How To Be A Player, 1997; TV appearances include: ''Cinderella,'' 1997; ''Built To Last,'' 1997.

DESTINE, JEAN-LEON
Dancer, choreographer, instructor. **Personal:** Born Mar 26, 1928, St Marc, Haiti; son of Lucienne Destine and Leon Destine Sr; children: Gerard, Ernest, Carlo. **Educ:** Lycee Petion Haiti, grad 1940-43; Howard University, Washington DC 1944; Columbia Univ, New York City 1945. **Career:** Haiti's 1st Troupe Nationale Folklorique, dir 1950; Destine Afro-Haitian Dance Co, dir 1951-; New Dance Group Studio NYC, teacher 20 yrs; Lezly Dance Studio, NYC, faculty mem, currently; Destine Dance Found, pres, choreographer, dancer, teacher, lecturer 1975-; New York Univ, School of the Arts, faculty mem, currently. **Orgs:** Mem, Haitian-American Cultural Organization, 1988. **Honors/Awds:** Hon Cultural Attache Rep Haiti; appeared in 2 films; Award of Merit, Haitian-American Society 1970, 1975; Distinguished Visitor, Metropolitan Dade County FL 1986; Officier de l'Ordre National ''Honneur et Merite''; Rockefeller Foundation Scholarship Recipient; Choreography Fellowship, National Endowment for the Arts; founder and director of Haiti's first Troupe Nationale Folklorique.

DEVAUGHN-TIDLINE, DONNA MICHELLE
Health care management administrator. **Personal:** Born Sep 20, 1954, Houston, TX; daughter of Louise Robinson DeVaughn and Canary DeVaughn; married Eric Tidline, Aug 27, 1988; children: Joseph W. **Educ:** Southern Methodist Univ, BBA 1977. **Career:** Prudential Health Care Plan Inc, admin mgr claims 1983-84, dir of admin HMO 1984-86; Prudential Insurance Co Inc, assoc mgr acct 1980-83, dir of health care mgmt 1987-. **Orgs:** Mem Natl Assoc of Female Execs; volunteer Big Brothers/Big Sisters; mem Delta Sigma Theta. **Honors/Awds:** 100 Most Promising Corporate Executives, Ebony Magazine, 1991. **Business Addr:** Dir Health Care Mgmt, Prudential Insurance Co Inc, 845 Crossover Lane, Ste 220, Memphis, TN 38117.

DE VEAUX, ALEXIS
Educator, writer. **Personal:** Born Sep 24, 1948, New York, NY; daughter of Mae De Veaux and Richard Hill. **Educ:** Empire State College, BA, 1976; SUNY at Buffalo, MA, 1989, PhD, 1992. **Career:** New Haven Board of Education, master artist, 1974-75; Sarah Lawrence College, adjunct lecturer, 1979-80; Norwich University, associate faculty, 1984-85; Wabash College, Owen Dutson visiting scholar, 1986-87; Essence Magazine, editor-at-large, 1978-90; SUNY at Buffalo, visiting assistant professor, 1991-92, assistant professor, 1992-. **Orgs:** Organization of Women Writers of Africa, Inc (OWWA). **Honors/Awds:** Drew Child Development Corp., Lorraine Hansberry Award, 1991; American Library Association, Coretta Scott

King Award, 1981, 1988; MADRE, Humanitarian Award, 1984; Medgar Evers College, Fannie Lou Hamer Award, 1984; Lincoln University, Unity in Media Award, 1982, 1983; Brooklyn Museum, Art Books for Children Award, 1974, 1975; numerous others. **Special Achievements:** Author: An Enchanted Hair Tale, 1987, Don't Explain: A Song of Billie Holiday, 1980, Na-Ni, 1973, (all Harper & Row); Blue Heat, Poems, Diva Publishing, 1985; Spirits In The Street, Doubleday, 1973; writer: "Walking into Freedom with Nelson and Winnie Mandela," June 1990, "Forty Fine: A Writer Reflects on Turning Forty," Jan 1990, "Alice Walker: Rebel With A Cause," Sept 1989, (all Essence Magazine); numerous other poems, short stories and plays. **Business Addr:** Assistant Professor, State University of New York at Buffalo, Department of American Studies, 1010 Clemens Hall, Buffalo, NY 14260, (716)645-2810.

DE VEAUX, STUART SAMUEL
Political advisor. **Personal:** Born May 19, 1970, Bronx, NY; son of Jean & Stuart De Veaux. **Career:** Republican Natl Comm, special asst to the co-chair, currently. **Business Addr:** Special Assistant To The Co-Chairman, Republican National Committee, 310 1st St, SE, Washington, DC 20003, (202)863-8600.

DEVEREUEAWAX, JOHN L., III
Former alderman. **Personal:** Born Oct 19, 1953, Flowood, MS; children: Andre, John IV, Marie Janet, Jonathan, Domonique Javelle, Brandi. **Educ:** Jackson State Univ, BA, 1976. **Career:** CETA, mgr; Rockford Comm Assn, exec dir 1981-; City of Rockford, alderman, 1993; Rockford Public Schools. **Orgs:** NAACP; pres, RKF Area MS Club 1980-; assoc mem, Natl Council Negro Women 1984-. **Honors/Awds:** Outstanding Young American 1984.

DEVERS, GAIL
Olympic athlete. **Career:** US Olympic Team, track and field, 1988, 1992. **Honors/Awds:** World Championship Games, Silver Medalist, 1992; Olympic Games, Gold Medalist, 1992. **Special Achievements:** Fought the odds of Graves' Disease to win championship medals that set new records in track and field. **Business Addr:** Olympic Athlete, US Women's Track Team, Olympic Training Center, 1776 E Boulder, Colorado Springs, CO 80909, (719)632-5551.

DEVINE, LORETTA
Actress. **Career:** Actress, currently. **Special Achievements:** Films include: Waiting to Exhale, The Preacher's Wife, Hoodlum; TV include: "A Different World"; Cable include: Clover, 1997; Don King: Only in America, HBO, 1997.

DEVOE, RONNIE
Vocalist. **Career:** New Edition, singer, starting 1983; Bell Biv DeVoe, singer, 1990-; albums include: Poison, 1990. **Honors/Awds:** Number One hit, Billboard Top Ten, "Candy Girl," 1983. **Business Addr:** Singer, Bell Biv DeVoe, c/o MCA Records, 70 Universal City Plaza, Universal City, CA 91608, (818)777-4000.

DEVORE, OPHELIA
Business executive. **Personal:** Born in South Carolina; widowed. **Educ:** NY U; New York City Coll; Vogue Sch of Modeling. **Career:** The Columbus Times, publisher; Ophelia DeVore Assos Inc NY, chmn bd, firm includes model agy, self-devel charm sch, cosmetic co & consult serv in marketing & pub relations. **Orgs:** Mem Am Women in Radio & TV; Nat Assn of Market Developers; Nat Bus League; num other bus leagues. **Business Addr:** Founder, Ophella Devore-Mitchell Charm School, 2230 Buena Vista Rd, Columbus, GA 31906, (706)324-2404.

DEVROUAX, PAUL S., JR.
Architect. **Personal:** Born Oct 4, 1942, New Orleans, LA; son of Freddie Warner Devrouax and Paul Devrouax Sr; married Branda Stallworth, Sep 9, 1972; children: Lesley S. **Educ:** Southern Univ, Baton Rouge LA, Bachelor of Architecture, 1966. **Career:** Nolan Norman & Nolan Architects, New Orleans LA, project architects, 1968-69; Urban Planners Inc, Arlington VA, dir of design, 1969-72; DiSilvestro & Phelps Architects, Miami FL, assoc & designer, 1972-73; Paul Devrouax & Associates, 1973-78; Devrouax & Purnell, Architects-Planners PC, Washington DC, pres, 1978-. **Orgs:** Mem, Mayor's Comm for the Handicapped, Washington DC, 1976-79, The Amer Inst of Architects, 1980-; College of Fellows (FAIA), 1991; pres, The Natl Org of Minority Architects, 1980-81; bd mem, District of Columbia Chamber of Commerce, 1982-; mem, District of Columbia Architectural Review Panel, 1983-, The Amer Arbitration Assn, 1985-; chmn, AIA, Mid-Atlantic Region, 1986-87; sr dir, AIA, Washington Chapter, 1986; mem, District of Columbia Bicentennial Commn, 1987-92; bd of dir, Washington Project for the Arts, 1987-94; Leadership Washington, 1991; Lambda Alpha International, 1991. **Honors/Awds:** Recipient, Historic Preservation and Architectural Design Excellence, AIA, Washington Chapter, #4 Logan Circle, 1981; Recipient, Citation Award, AIA, Washington Chapter, The Iowa Complex, 1981; Recipient, Design Award, The Natl Org of Minority Architects Natl Award Program, Carter Beach House, 1984; Recipient, Professional Serv of the Year, Minority Enterprise Devel Community Award, Washington DC, 1986; Recipient, Architectural Serv Citation, Howard Univ, Washington DC, 1989; features spokesperson, Washington Urban League, Focus: "Design within an Urban Environment.". **Military Serv:** US Army, sergeant, E-5, 1966-68. **Business Addr:** President, Devrouax & Purnell, Architects-Planners PC, 717 D Street, NW, Washington, DC 20004.

DEWBERRY-WILLIAMS, MADELINA DENISE
Human resources professional. **Personal:** Born Oct 18, 1958, Los Angeles, CA; daughter of Johnnie Mae Lemons Dewberry and Clarence Dewberry; married Ja Daun Williams, May 9, 1992. **Educ:** San Jose State Univ, attended 1981. **Career:** San Jose Unified School Dist, teacher 1980-81; Santa Clara Juvenile Hall, counselor 1981; Natl Medical Enterprises, personnel coord 1981-87; American Express TRS, manager, human resources, 1987-. **Orgs:** Vp 1986-87, natl affirmative action 1986-87, natl conf 1987-88 Intl Assoc for Personnel Women; co-chair United Christian Network 1986-; dir Spirit Connections 1986-; Cities in Schools, board mem, 1990-91. **Honors/Awds:** Outstanding Woman in Health Care YWCA 1986. **Home Addr:** 1356 Eagle St, Tracy, CA 95376.

DEWINDT, HAL. See Obituaries section.

DEWITT, FRANKLIN ROOSEVELT
Attorney. **Personal:** Born May 25, 1936, Conway, SC; son of Rebecca Hughes DeWitt and Matthew A DeWitt; married Willa Waylis Johnson; children: Rosalyn Abrevaya, Sharolyn Renee. **Educ:** South Carolina State University, BS Bus Admin 1962, JD 1964; Georgia State Univ, Certificate Housing Mgmt 1973. **Career:** US Justice Dept, summer law clerk 1963; US Civil Serv Comm Washington DC, trial attny 1965-67; Atlantic Beach SC, town attny; Private practice, attny; National Football League Players Association, contract advisor. **Orgs:** Municipal consult Glenarden MD 1965-67; mem Conway SC City Council 1969-84; delegate Natl Dem Party Conv in Miami Beach FL 1972; appt by gov of SC Spec Study Committed on Home Rule 1972; mem US Court of Appeals for Fourth Circuit, Washington DC Bar, US Supreme Court, mem SC State Bar Assoc, Amer Bar Assoc, Fed Bar Assoc; chmn, bd dir Horry-Georgetown Mental Health Clinic; life mem NAACP; contract advisor, National Football League Player Association; Natl Dem Party Conv, delegate, 1980; National Bar Association, life member; Kappa Alpha Psi, life member. **Honors/Awds:** Usher of the Year Cherry Hill Baptist Church 1978. **Special Achievements:** Author of books: Super Redskins Pay Bills in Full, 1992; Washington Just Super, Super Bowl, 1988; History of a Family from Slavery to Freedom, 1985. **Military Serv:** USAF a/1c 1955-59, Active Reserve 1959-61; Good Conduct Ribbon USAF 1957. **Business Addr:** Attorney, 510 Highway 378, Conway, SC 29526.

DEWITT, RUFUS B.
Educational Administrator. **Personal:** Born Dec 1, 1915, Rossville, TN; married Mary Borders; children: Marilyn A, Beatrice Francine. **Educ:** Columbia U, BA, MA, grad studies 1947. **Career:** Elementary school prin 1940-41; Montgomery Branch YMCA, exec dir 1948-55; Dearborn Street YMCA, dir 1955-63; SE Branch YMCA San Diego, dir; Adult Div Community Coll, San Diego Community Coll, vice pres, currently. **Orgs:** Delegate from So area YMCA to Nat Coun YMCA 1949-54; mem So Area Nominating Com for nominating So area bd dir; mem Frontiers Intl 1969-63; mem United Supreme Coun, 33 Degree Masonry & Delegate; CA TB Assn; bd mem Local Draft Bd No 140-B CA 1970; adv to registrants 1973; pres San Diego Community Action Coun 1968; pres SE San Diego Community Theater; pers Zeta Sigma Lambda Chpt; Alpha Phi Alpha Scholarship Frat 1937-74; mem Pi Boule Sigma Pi Phi; Gulf Coast Savings & Loan Assn; sec 3 1/2 million dollar housing project; wrote 1st bldg prog for Model Cities funds. **Honors/Awds:** Received Outst Vol Award 1973. **Military Serv:** Served 1944-45. **Business Addr:** Educational Administrator, 4033 Ruffin Rd, San Diego, CA 92102.

DIAMOND, JOHN R.
Engineer. **Personal:** Born Nov 29, 1905, Houston; married Nathalie Ritchie; children: John R Jr, Russell W. **Educ:** Ford Trade Sch; Wayne State U. **Career:** Ford Motor Co, 1928-31, 1935-46; YMCA, 1932-35; Diamond Elec Co, owner 1946-. **Orgs:** Mem MI Soc Professional Eng; Intl Assn Electrical Inspectors; Nat Fire Protection Assn; Better Bus Bureau; Elec Examiners; Assoc Electricians Inc; mem Nacirema Club Inc; Non-Profit Housing Corp; minority Bus Mens Assoc.

DIANE, MAMADI
Shipping executive. **Personal:** Born May 16, 1947, Conakry, Guinea; son of Nankoria Diane and Ibrahima Diane; married Cynthia Horthense, Jul 16, 1977; children: Mori Diane. **Educ:** Richer College, Houlton, Maine, BA, 1970; George Washington University, Master's, International Business, 1982. **Career:** Amex International Inc, Washington, DC, founder, president, 1983-; St John International, Washington, DC, vice president, 1972-82. **Orgs:** Industry Policy Advisory Committee; US World Cup Organising Committee, board of directors, 1994-; US Industry Policy Advisory Committee, mem, 1995. **Honors/Awds:** Chevalier Odre, National du Leopard, Government of Zaire, 1990; Honorary Member, National Conference of Black Mayors, 1989; Congresional Award, Cong Mervyn Dymally, 1988. **Business Addr:** President, Amex International Inc, 1615 L Street, NW, Suite 340, Washington, DC 20036.

DICK, GEORGE ALBERT
Communications manager. **Personal:** Born Jan 31, 1940, Lloyds, St Thomas, Jamaica; son of Ruby Drummond Dick and Cleveland Dick; married Margaret Wesley, Aug 29, 1981; children: Pete Dick, Dave Dick, Charmaine Dick, Sharon Dick. **Educ:** Bellevue School of Nursing, Kingston Jamaica, RMN, 1959-62. **Career:** Bellevue Hospital, Kingston, Jamaica, student nurse, 1959-62, staff nurse nurse 1962-67; Beverly Hills Hospital, Dallas, TX, staff nurse, supervisor, 1967-77, Southwest Airlines Co, Dallas, TX, ramp agent, 1977-79, flight information agent, 1979-83, flight information supvr, 1983-86 manager, currently. **Orgs:** Mem, Operations Comm Southwest Airlines, 1986-; pres, Third World Sports and Social Assn, 1974-76. **Home Addr:** 732 Havenwood, Dallas, TX 75232.

DICKENS, DORIS LEE
Psychiatrist. **Personal:** Born Oct 12, Roxboro, NC; married Judge Austin L Fickling (deceased). **Educ:** VA Union Univ, BS Chemistry (magna cum laude) 1960; Howard Univ Coll of Med, MD 1966. **Career:** St Elizabeths Hospital, dir mental health, prof for the deaf, psychiatrist 1973-87; Howard Univ College of Medicine, faculty member, 1982-; DC Commission on Mental Health Services, Washington DC, Medical Officer (psychiatrist) 1987. **Orgs:** Mem Amer Psych Assoc 1972-, WA Psychiatric Soc 1972-; bd dir Natl Health Care Found for the Deaf 1973-83; consult Natl Inst of Mental Health 1975-77; mem Mental Health & Deafness Assoc 1980-; faculty mem Howard Univ Coll of Med 1982-; policy adv counc Kendell School; Black Psychiatrists of Greater Washington Metropolitan Area. **Honors/Awds:** Beta Kappa Chi Hon Soc VA Union Univ 1959; Alpha Kappa Mu Hon Soc VA Union Univ 1959; Dept Awds Pediatrics Psychiatry & Neurology Howard Univ Coll of Med 1966; Superior Perf Awd St Eliz Hosp 1976; Dorothea Lynde Dix Awd St Elizabeths Hosp 1980; publ "How and When Psychiatry Can Help You" 1972, "You and Your Doctor" 1973; contrib author "Hearing and Hearing Impairment" 1979, "Counseling Deaf People, Research & Practice" 1985. **Business Addr:** Psychiatrist, Dir, St Elizabeths Hospital, 2700 Martin Luther King Ave SE, Washington, DC 20032.

DICKENS, HELEN OCTAVIA
Physician, educator. **Personal:** Born in Dayton, OH; daughter of Daisy Dickens and Charles Dickens; married Purvis Henderson (deceased); children: Jayne H Brown, Norman S Henderson. **Educ:** Univ of IL, BS 1932; Univ of IL Coll of Med, MD 1934; Univ of PA Grad Sch of Med, MMSc 1945. **Career:** Mercy Douglass Hosp, dir dept of OB-GYN 1948-67; OB-GYN Med Coll of PA, asso clin prof 1954-65; Woman's Hosp Dept of OB, chief of serv 1956-64; Univ of PA Sch of Med, dir teen clinic 1969-, prof emeritus, OB/GYN assoc dean. **Orgs:** Pres Pan Am Women's Alliance 1970-73; Coll of Physicians OB Soc of Phila; Philadelphia Cnty Med Soc; FACS 1950; FACOG 1953; AMA; NMA; AAMC; bd of dir Am Cancer Soc 1963, Children's Aid Soc 1968-, Nat Assn of Med Min Educators 1975-, Devereux Found 1979-. **Honors/Awds:** Distinguished daughter of PA honored by Gov Woman FACS; 1st Negro Recipient 1971; The PA Gimbel Award 1970; Illini Achievement Award, Univ of IL 1982; Med Coll of PA Hon Doctor of Med Sci 1979; Univ of PA Hon Doct of Sci 1982. **Home Addr:** 2 Franklin Town Blvd, Philadelphia, PA 19103. **Business Addr:** Prof Emeritus, Ob-Gyn/Assoc Dean, Univ of Pennsylvania, School of Medicine, 3400 Spruce St, Philadelphia, PA 19104.

DICKENS, JACOBY
Banking executive. **Personal:** Born Jun 19, 1931, Panama City, FL; son of Marie Jackson and Jacoby Dickens; married Eugenia (divorced 1968); children: Karen. **Educ:** Roosevelt University, Chicago, IL, 1952-54. **Career:** Chicago Board of Education, Chicago, IL, engineer, 1959-71; Seaway National Bank, Chicago, IL, chairman, 1979-. **Orgs:** Commissioner, Economic Development Commission-Chicago, 1986-; bd of directo rs, United Way, 1986-; vice chairman, Chicago Urban League, 1986-; bd member, Roundtable Florida A&M Univ, 1987-; executive committee member, Economic Club of Chicago, 1986-. **Honors/Awds:** Hall of Fame, School of Business Chicago State Univ, 1990; Humanitarian of Year, Coalition for United Comm Action, 1984; 20 People Who Made a Difference, Chicago Magazine, 1990; Distinguished American, Dollars & Sense Magazine, 1991; Par Excellence Award, Mayor Harold Washington, 1987. **Military Serv:** Army, Corporal, 1952-54; Battle Star. **Business Addr:** Chmn of the Bd, Seaway Natl Bank of Chicago, 645 E 87th St, Chicago, IL 60619.

DICKENS, SAMUEL
Attorney. **Personal:** Born Apr 5, 1926, Tallulah, LA. **Educ:** BS 1957. **Career:** Juris doctor 1959. **Orgs:** LA St Bar Assn; Baton Rouge Bar Assn; Nat Bar Assn; Am Bar Assn. **Military Serv:** USAF staff sgt 1947-54. **Business Addr:** 8152 Scenic Hwy, Baton Rouge, LA 70807.

DICKERSON, ADOLPHUS SUMNER
Clergyman. **Personal:** Born May 25, 1914, Greenville, GA; son of Mary Dickerson and Dixie Dickerson; married Juanita B. **Educ:** Clark Coll, AB; Gammon Theolo Sem, BD; Atlanta U, MA; Boston Univ Sch of Theol, STM; Clark Coll, DD. **Career:** United Meth Ch Asso, dir Coun of Ministreis; pastor; dist supt sem prof. **Honors/Awds:** 1st black Dist Supt to serve in predom white conf in Un Meth Ch in GA; 1st black man to serve as pres of Chris Coun of Metro Atlanta; minister of year Omega Frat.

DICKERSON, BETTE JEANNE
Educator. **Personal:** Born May 21, 1951, Philadelphia, PA; daughter of Rosa Anthony Dickerson. **Educ:** Morehead State Univ, BA 1972; Univ of Louisville, MEd 1975; Washington State Univ, PhD 1986. **Career:** Louisville/Jefferson Co Bd of Educ, teacher 1972-78; Washington State Univ, rsch asst 1978-81; Natl Urban League, intern/program dir 1981-82; WK Kellogg Foundation, program assoc 1982-86; Delta Sigma Theta Sor Inc, foundation dir 1986-90; assoc prof, American Univ, 1990-. **Orgs:** Amer Sociological Assn; Assn of Black Sociologists; Eastern Sociological Society; Delta Sigma Theta Sor Inc, Phi Kappa Phi Honor Soc; Sociologists for Women in Society; District of Columbia Sociological Society. **Honors/Awds:** George Edmund Haynes Fellowship Natl Urban League 1981; Comm Serv Award Washington Heights Comm Ministeries 1984; Women In Leadership, Junior League of Washington DC 1989; Outstanding Teacher, Office of Minority Affairs, The American University, 1992; Outstanding Educator and Administrator, District of Columbia Council of Administrative Women in Education, 1992. **Business Addr:** Associate Professor, Dept of Sociology, American University, 225 McCabe Hall, 4400 Massachusetts Ave NW, Washington, DC 20016, (202)885-2479.

DICKERSON, DENNIS CLARK
Educator, clergyman. **Personal:** Born Aug 12, 1949, McKeesport, PA; son of Oswanna Wheeler Dickerson and Carl O'Neal Dickerson; married Mary Anne Eubanks; children: Nicole, Valerie, Christina, Dennis Jr. **Educ:** Lincoln Univ, BA 1971; Washington Univ, MA 1974, PhD 1978; Hartford Seminary, additional study; Morris Brown Coll, LHD, 1990. **Career:** Forest Park Comm Coll, part-time instructor 1974; PA State Univ, Ogontz Campus, part-time instructor 1975-76; Williams Coll, asst prof history 1976-83, assoc prof history 1983-85; Rhodes Coll, assoc prof history 1985-87; Carter Woodson Inst Univ of VA, visiting scholar 1987-88; Williams Coll, assoc prof history, 1987-88, prof 1988-; Stanfield professor of history, 1992-; African Methodist Episcopal Church, historiographer, 1988-; Secretary General Officers Council; Payne Theological Seminary, visiting professor, January 1992; Yale Divinity School, visiting prof of amer religious history, Spring 1995. **Orgs:** Pastor, Payne AME Church Chatham NY 1980-85; mem, IBPOEW; Alpha Phi Alpha Fraternity; itinerant elder, AME Church; mem, NAACP; pastor, St Mark AME Church Munford TN 1985-87; board of corporators, Williamstown Savings Bank, 1992-; board of trustees, 1992-95; North Adams State College; GRE History Committee Educational Testing Service, 1990-96; American Society of Church History; Organization of American Historians; American Historical Association; Southern Historical Association; World Methodist Historical Society; Wesley Historical Society; American Bible Study Society, board of trustees, 1995-. **Honors/Awds:** Fellowship Natl Endownment for the Humanities 1982; Moody Grant Lyndon B Johnson Found 1983; Grant-in-aid Amer Council of Learned Soc 1983-84; Fellowship Rockefeller Found 1983-84; articles in New Jersey History, Church History, Pennsylvania Heritage, New York State Journal of Medicine, Methodist History, Western PA Historical Magazine, AME Church Review; Journal of Presbyterian History; contributing author: Encyclopedia of Amer Business History and Biography: Iron and Steel in the 20th Century, Bruccoli Clark Layman Boo, 1994, Historical Dictionary of Methodism, Scarecrow Press, 1996; Blackwell Dictionary of Evangelical Biography, Blackwell Publishers, 1995; Black Apostles at Home and Abroad, GK Hall 1982; Biographical Dictionary of Amer Labor Leaders, Greenwood Press 1984; Encyclopedia of Southern Culture, University of North Carolina Press, 1989; Biographical Dictionary of Amer Social Welfare, Greenwood Press 1986; Life and Labor, SUNY Press 1986. Author "Out of the Crucible, Black Steelworkers in Western Pennsylvania 1875-1980," Alb State Univ of NY Press 1986. **Special Achievements:** Author, Religion, Race and Region: Research Notes on AME Church History, Nashville AME Sunday School Union, 1995; author, Militant Mediator: Whitney M Young, Jr, University Press of Kentucky, 1998. **Business Addr:** Stanfield Professor, Dept of History, Williams College, Williamstown, MA 01267.

DICKERSON, ELLIS L., JR.
Accountant. **Personal:** Born Jul 27, 1934, Los Angeles, CA. **Educ:** Univ So CA. **Career:** State of CA, corp examiner financial analyst 1961-69; Ellis Louis Dickerson Jr, owner, certified public accountant, currently. **Orgs:** Mem Kappa Alpha Psi; various civic & prof soc. **Military Serv:** USAF Air Weather Service.

DICKERSON, ERIC DEMETRIC
Professional football player (retired). **Personal:** Born Sep 2, 1960, Sealy, TX. **Educ:** Attended, Southern Methodist Univ. **Career:** Running back: Los Angeles Rams, 1983-87; Indianapolis Colts, 1987-92; Los A ngeles Raiders, 1992-93; Atlanta Falcons, 1993. **Orgs:** NFL spokesperson for the anti-drug "Just Say No" campaign; natl chmn Natl Lung Assoc. **Honors/Awds:** 1984 NFC Player of Year by UPI, Football News, USA Today, Washington DC Touchdown Club, Atlanta Touchdown Club, Columbus Ohio Touchdown Club and Kansas City Comm of 101; NFL MVP 2 Yrs; Daniel F Reeves Mem Awd; won virtually all Rookie of Yr Honors; played in Pro Bowl, 1982, 1983, 1987.

DICKERSON, ERNEST
Film director. **Career:** Directed Showtime's "Blind Faith," 1998.

DICKERSON, HARVEY G., JR.
Army officer, financial manager and advisor. **Personal:** Born Oct 21, 1926, Prairie View, TX; son of Ada Taminia Kilpatrick Dickerson and Harvey G Dickerson; married Gerthyl Raye Sanders-Dickerson, Jan 13, 1944; children: Glenda Joy, Harvey G III. **Educ:** Prairie View A&M College, BS, 1947; Syracuse University, MBA, 1961. **Career:** US Army, officer, 1948-77; financial advisor, 1977-80, 1985-1990; Corp. for Pubic Broadcasting, vp, 1980-1985; Prairie View A&M University, director of Inst Dev & assistant to president, 1990-. **Orgs:** Association of Syracuse Comptrollers, 1962-; Association of Government Comptrollers, 1963-; American Society of C/U and CHFC, 1985-; The Rocks Inc, president, 1975-; National Business League of Southern Maryland, 1985-90; APA Fraternity Inc, 1975-. **Military Serv:** Army Artillery, colonel, 1948-77; Legion of Merit (w/Oak Leaf Cluster), 1977, nine other citations. **Home Addr:** 12204 Dillard Place, Fort Washington, MD 20744.

DICKERSON, JANET SMITH
Educator, educational administrator. **Personal:** Born Feb 13, 1944, New York, NY; married J Paul Stephens; children: Jill, Karin, Dawn Stephens. **Educ:** The Western Coll for Women, BA 1965; Xavier Univ, MEd 1968; University of PA, further study; Harvard University Institute for Executive Management, certificate, 1982. **Career:** Cincinnati Public Schools, Ach Jr High School, English teacher 1965-68; Sawyer and Bloom Jr High Schools, guidance counselor 1968-71; Univ of Cincinnati Educ Devel Prog, teacher, counselor 1971; Earlham Coll, Richmond, IN, dir supportive serv & asst prof 1971-76; Swarthmore Coll, assoc dean 1976-81, dean of the college 1981-91; Duke University, vice pres for student affairs, 1991-. **Orgs:** Valentine Foundation, board member, 1990-95; North Carolina Equity, board member, 1992-95; Durham Chamber of Commerce, human relations committee; Links Inc, 1993-; Guilford College, board of trustee, 1993-; Reader, HWE proposals 1978-81; Wallingford-Swarthmore School Board, 1988-91; board member Client Security Fund of Commonwlth of PA 1983-88; consultant: Davidson, Oberlin, Scripps, Brown, Barnard, Wesleyan, Haverford, Bowdoin, numerous others. **Honors/Awds:** WASC accreditation teams at Mills, Occidential, UCSD; honorary degrees: Xavier University, LHD, 1990; Swarthmore College, LLD, 1992. **Business Addr:** Vice President for Student Affairs, Duke University, 106 Flowers Bldg, Durham, NC 27706.

DICKERSON, LOWELL DWIGHT
Musician. **Personal:** Born Dec 26, 1944, Los Angeles, CA; son of Ethel Hartie Dickerson (deceased) and Charles Edward Dickerson. **Educ:** CA State Univ, Los Angeles BA Music 1973; Boston Univ Berkley Coll of Music; private lessons from Ray Santisi & Margaret Chaloff; Univ of Southern California Masters in Music 1989; Univ of Southern CA, MM, Jazz Studies, 1990; UCLA, C Ph1, Ethnomusicology, 1995, PhD candidate. **Career:** Three albums: "Sooner or Later," "Windows," and "Dwights's Right's"; performed with Gene Ammons, Conti Condoli, Junior Cook, Freddie Hubbard, Damita Jo, Sergio Mendes, Anita O'Day, Clark Terry, Joe Williams and many others; Los Angeles Musicians Union, piano musician. **Orgs:** Pi Kappa Lambda 1989. **Home Addr:** 308 Westwood PL2 No 349, Los Angeles, CA 90024.

DICKERSON, PAMELA ANN
Business executive, flight attendant. **Personal:** Born Jan 14, 1953, New Orleans, LA; daughter of Catherine Grove Dickerson and I W Dickerson. **Educ:** Southern Univ, New Orleans LA, BS, 1975; Loyola Univ, New Orleans LA, attended, 1979; Georgia State Univ, Atlanta GA, attended, 1984-85. **Career:** Delta Airlines, Atlanta GA, flight attendant, 1976-; X-ceptional Nail Inc, Atlanta GA, president, 1987-92; Sweet Sensations Ltd, president, chief executive officer, 1992-. **Orgs:** Founder, pres, Natl Assn of Negro Business & Professional Women Inc, New Orleans Club, 1982-84; volunteer, Sickle Cell Anemia, 1982-83; past pres, mem, Natl Assn of Negro Business & Professional Women Inc, Decatur-Dekalb Club, 1984-; volunteer, Fund Raising Comm, Amer Cancer Soc, 1987-; volunteer, Democratic Natl Convention, 1988. **Honors/Awds:** Appreciation Award, Natl Assn of Negro Business & Professional Women, New Orleans Club, 1982; Award of Excellence, Amer Cancer Soc, 1987; President's Award, Natl Assn of Negro Business & Professional Women, Decatur-Dekalb Club, 1988.

DICKERSON, RALPH
Association executive. **Career:** United Way of NYC, pres, currently. **Business Addr:** President, United Way of New York City, 99 Park Ave, New York, NY 10016, (212)973-3936.

DICKERSON, RON
College football coach. **Personal:** Born 1948. **Career:** Clemson University Football Team, defensive coordinator, until 1992; Temple University Football Team, head football coach, 1992-. **Orgs:** Black Coaches Association, past president. **Special Achievements:** Only African American head coach in Division I-A football conference, 1992. **Business Addr:** Head Football Coach, Athletic Dept, Temple University Football, Broad & Montgomery Streets, Philadelphia, PA 19121, (215)204-7440.

DICKERSON, THOMAS L., JR.
Television news reporter. **Personal:** Born Mar 1, 1949, Houston, TX; son of Della Dervis Collins and Thomas Dickerson Sr; married Peggy Lou Deale (divorced 1991); children: Traci Lauren, Troy Lewis. **Educ:** Baker University, Baldwin City, BA, journalism, 1971. **Career:** Radio News, KPRC-AM, reporter, KLOL-FM, news dir, KCOH, KWTV-TV, Oklahoma City, news reporter, anchor, 1973-75; KTRK-TV, news reporter, 1975-77; WJLA-TV, Albritton Communications, news reporter, 1977-79; KTRK-TV, Cap Cities ABC, Houston, news reporter outdoors editor, 1979-. **Orgs:** Houston Assn of Black Journalists, 1986-; National Assn of Black Journalists, 1987-91. **Honors/Awds:** Robert F Kennedy (Honorable Mention), Requiem Dying Neighborhood, 1978; Austin Headliner, Parole Series, 1991; International Assn of Firefighters, 1990. **Business Addr:** Outdoors Editor, News, KTRK-TV, PO Box 13, Houston, TX 77001.

DICKERSON, TYRONE EDWARD
Certified public accountant. **Personal:** Born Dec 18, 1943, Abington, PA; married Denise P Dickerson. **Educ:** Central State Univ, BS, 1965; Harvard Graduate School of Business, MBA, 1970. **Career:** Lucas Tucker & Co, CPA's, 1971-74; Urban National, vp, 1974-77; Mitchell/Titus CPA, partner, 1977-80; Tyrone E Dickerson CPA, owner, 1984-. **Orgs:** AICPA, 1974-; VA Society of CPA's, 1980-; New York State Society of CPA's, 1975-; National Assn Black Accountants, 1971-; Kappa Alpha Psi, 1962-. **Business Addr:** Owner, Tyrone E Dickerson, CPA, 2201 E Main St, Room 202, Richmond, VA 23223, (804)783-0701.

DICKERSON, WARNER LEE
Educator (retired), real estate broker. **Personal:** Born Jun 18, 1937, Brownsville, TN; married Arcola Leavell; children: Jarvis, Mechele. **Educ:** TN State Univ, BS Math 1961; Memphis State Univ, MS Math 1969; Univ of Sarasota, EdD Voc Ed 1979. **Career:** Memphis City School, teacher 1961-70; State Tech Inc, teacher 1970-74, dept head devel studies 1974-76, ed admin 1976-78, dir of admin affairs 1978-81, dir 1981-84, Dept of Ed consultant 1984-86; superintendent 1986-91; Prudential Memphis, affiliate broker 1992-94. **Orgs:** Vp NAACP Memphis Br 1977-79; pres OIC Memphis Br 1977-81; NAACP Memphis Br 1979-81; Natl Assoc for the Advancement of Black Amers in Vocational Ed 1982-84. **Honors/Awds:** Distinguished Teacher Awd State Tech Ins 1971. **Business Addr:** Program Director, New Way Inc., 4466 Elvis Presley Blvd #302, Memphis, TN 38116.

DICKEY, ERIC JEROME
Novelist, screenplay writer. **Personal:** Born Jul 7, 1961, Memphis, TN. **Educ:** University of Memphis, BS engineering tech, 1983; UCLA, attended, 1995-97. **Career:** Rockwell Intl, software development, 1983-92; Rowland Unified School District, educator, 1994-97; writer, novelist, 1992-. **Orgs:** Alpha Phi Alpha, 1980-; Intl Black Writers & Artists, (IBWA/LA), 1993-; Project Reach, mentor, 1996-. **Honors/Awds:** City of Pomona, CA, Proclamation, 1998; Edna Crotchfield Founders Award, Commitment as Literary Artist, 1995; Blackboard Bestsellers, "Sister, Sister," 1996, "Friends and Lovers," 1997. **Special Achievements:** Published novels: "Sister, Sister," 1996; "Friends & Lovers," 1997; "Milk in My Coffee," 1998; "Cheaters," 1999; "Cappuccino," screenplay, 1997. **Home Phone:** (213)303-7891.

DICKEY, LLOYD V.
Dentist. **Educ:** Univ CA Univ of Pacific Dental Schs & Presidio of San Fran Army Base, post grad study Oral Surgery, Prosthetics, Radiology; San Fran State Coll, clinical psychology; Meharry Med Coll, DDS; TX Coll, BA. **Career:** Priv Prac, dentist 27 yrs; Life Sci, coll tchr; HS prin; tchr sci math; coach sports. **Orgs:** Pres organizer & founder Golden State Dental Assn; mem Bd Dirs San Fran Dental Care Found; Fillmore-Fell Girl's Home; WsternAdd Proj Area Com; pres N CA Chap Meharry Med Coll Alumni Assn; chmn coord Meharry Med Coll Wstrn Regional Mtng & Fund Raising Event; pres Parents Adv Compacific Heights Elem Sch; chmn Benj Franklin Jr HS Parents Adv Com for Implementing Fresno Plan; chmn Com to Build Schs in Wstrn Add; mem N CA Chap Nat Dental Assn; organizer pres Chater Chpt; N CA chmn state coord Meharry Alumni $88 Million Campaign Fund Drive; organizer Bay Area TX

Coll Alumni Assn; mem Comm Ldrs of Am. **Honors/Awds:** Recip Outstanding Alumnus Award Meharry Med & Moll TX Coll; comm serv Award Bay Area Howard Univ Alumni; author several outstanding scientific papers. **Military Serv:** AUS captain WW II chief surgical tech; Korean War chief oral surgery & Prosthetics. **Business Addr:** 1845 Fillmore St, San Francisco, CA 94115.

DICKINSON, GLORIA HARPER
Educational administrator. **Personal:** Born Aug 5, 1947, New York, NY; daughter of Martha Louis Sinton Harper and Clifford Horace Harper; married Arthur Clinton Dickinson. **Educ:** City Coll of NY, BA European Hist 1968; Howard Univ, MA African Studies 1970, PhD African Stud 1978. **Career:** Caden High School Camden NJ, geography/Social studies teacher 1970-71; English Dept Trenton State Coll, instructor 1971-73; Dept of African-Am Studies Trenton State Coll, chmn asst prof 1973-. **Orgs:** Editorial bd mem Journal of Negro History 1983-93; mem NJ Committee on The Humanities 1984-90; mem ASALH; mem ASA; mem AHSA; mem NCBS; mem NCNW; faculty advisor Zeta Sigma Chptr Alpha Kappa Alpha 1972-; contrib scholar NJ Women's Project 1984; proj dir TSC Summer Study Tours to Africa 1984-; mem NJ Historic Trust 1986-89; chair, International Nominating Committee, Alpha Kappa Alpha Sorority, 1988-92. **Honors/Awds:** NEH summer fellowship for coll fac Univ of IA 1977, NY Univ School of Bus 1979, Univ of PA 1981, Princeton Univ 1984; Fac Mem of the Year Trenton State Coll 1984; Proj Dir NEH Summer Inst in African-Amer Culture Trenton State Coll 1987;Mentor of the Year, Trenton State College Minority Scholars, 1990 Blue Key Honor Society, Trenton State College, 1989. **Business Addr:** Chairman, African-American Studies, Trenton State Coll, CN 550 Hillwood Lakes, Trenton, NJ 08625.

DICKSON, CHARLIE JONES
Educator. **Personal:** Born in Alabama; daughter of Tommie A Jones and Edward Jones; married Joe N Dickson, Apr 2, 1970; children: Jonathan, Chari, Jori. **Educ:** Tuskegee Institute, BS, 1966; Ohio State University, MS, 1969; University of Alabama, EdD, 1984. **Career:** Lawson State Junior College, chair department of nursing, 1969-70; Tuskegee Institute, instructor, 1970-73; University of Alabama at Birmingham, professor, 1973-. **Orgs:** Alabama Board of Nursing, president, 1984-92; Shelby Medical Center, board of directors, 1987-93; Alabama Respiratory Program, board of directors, 1991-; Shelby County Red Cross, board member, 1990-91; National Council of State Boards of Nursing Inc, board of directors, area III director, 1990-91; American Nurse's Association, 1975-; Alabama State Nurse's Association, 1975-; Delta Sigma Theta Sorority, Inc. **Honors/Awds:** Tuskegee University, Class of 87 Award, 1987; University of Alabama School of Nursing, Professionalism Award, 1984, Outstanding Instructor, 1980; Alabama Board of Nursing, Outstanding Leadership, 1992; Fellow, American Academy of Nursing. **Military Serv:** US Air Force Reserve, capt, 1966-68. **Business Addr:** Professor, University of Alabama at Birmingham, UAB Station, Rm 411, Birmingham, AL 35294, (205)934-5476.

DICKSON, DARYL M.
Human resources executive. **Educ:** University of Michigan. **Career:** Quaker Oats Co, vp human resources; Bausch & Lomb, sr vp human resources, currently. **Special Achievements:** First African American on Bausch & Lomb's Mgmt Exec Comm. **Business Addr:** Senior VP Human Resources, Bausch & Lomb, 1 Bausch & Lomb Place, Rochester, NY 14604-2701, (716)338-6000.

DICKSON, DAVID W. D.
Educator (retired). **Personal:** Born Feb 16, 1919, Portland, ME; son of Mary Daly Dickson and David A Dickson; married Vera, 1951 (died 1979); children: David, Deborah, Deirdre; married Barbara, Feb 16, 1981. **Educ:** Bowdoin Coll, AB 1941; Harvard Univ, MA 1942, PhD 1949. **Career:** MI State, assoc prof, 1948-63; Northern MI Univ, prof & head of English Dept 1963-66; School of Arts & Science, Northern MI Univ Marquette, dean 1966-67, vice pres acad affairs 1967-68; Federal City Coll, Washington, provost, vice pres acad affairs, prof 1968-69, SUNY, Stony Brook, dean of continuing & devel educ, 1972-73, prof of English 1969-73; Montclair State Coll NJ, pres 1973-84, distinguished prof 1984-88. **Orgs:** Consultant, Natl Found for the Humanities, 1969-71; Mott Found, 1973-74; bd of trustees, Montclair Art Museum; N Essex Devel & Action Council, Bowdoin Coll, Bloomfield Coll; mem, AAC Comm on Liberal Learning; Policy bd Project Change; Phi Beta Kappa, Sigma Pi Phi, Omega Psi Phi; Rotary. **Honors/Awds:** Rosenwald Fellow; Smith Mundt Fellow; MI State Univ, Distinguished Teaching Award; Distinguished Educ Award, Bowdoin; Hon LHD Bowdoin, 1975, Bloomfield, 1983, Montclair State College 1989. **Military Serv:** SMAC 1st Lt. **Home Addr:** 125 Woodhaven Dr, Palm Coast, FL 32164.

DICKSON, ONIAS D., JR.
Minority rights advocate. **Personal:** Born Jun 18, 1958, Washington, DC; children: Jennifer, O Timothy. **Educ:** Hobart and William Smith, BA (w/Honors) 1981; Univ of Notre Dame, MA (w/Honors) 1983. **Career:** St Martins Parochial Sch, jr hs teacher 1983; American Greetings, biographical researcher 1984; Westat Rsch Corp, freelance investigator 1985; NAACP, natl rsch coord. **Orgs:** Staff writer Herald weekly newspaper Hobart & Wm Sm 1980,81; preime minister Third World Coalition Hobart & Wm Sm 1980; founder Hobart and William Smith Scuba Diving Assoc 1980-81; founder Black Grad Student Org Univ of Notre Dame 1981-83; chmn Govt Grad Student Org Univ of Notre Dame 1982-83; grad student govt rep Univ of Notre Dame 1983; mem Natl NAACP. **Honors/Awds:** Teacher's Assistantship Hobart and Wm Smith 1980-81; Dorothy Danforth-Compton Grad Fellowship Awd 1981,82; Natl Conf of Black Political Scientist Grad Assistantship Awd 1982-83. **Home Addr:** 4805 Mt Hope Dr, Baltimore, MD 21215.

DICKSON, REGINALD D.
Organization executive (retired). **Personal:** Born Apr 28, 1946, Oakland, TN; son of Mildred Smith and Louis Smith; married Illona White; children: Kia, Brandon, Rachel. **Educ:** Univ of MO/Columbia, 1964-66; Harris Teachers Coll, Elementary Educ 1966-69; Washington Univ, Business Admin 1973-78; St Louis Univ, 1975-78. **Career:** St Louis Public Sch System, teacher 1969-73; INROADS, Inc, dir 1973-76, regional dir 1976-80, exec vice pres 1980-83, pres & ceo 1983-. **Orgs:** Co-chairman Salvation Army Tree of Lights St Louis 1977-78; area coord Boy Scouts of Amer 1978; mem Metro Develop Comm for Red Cross 1980; chairman exec comm Child Guidance Ctr 1982-83; bd of dirs First Amer Bank 1981-; bd of dirs Conf on Educ 1982-; mem Statewide Task Force on Educ 1984-; mem Urban League 1986-, CORO Foundation 1986-, Confluence St Louis 1986-; advisory board of trustees, The Foundation for Student Communications; life membership committee member, NAACP. **Honors/Awds:** Participant Danforth Leadership Program St Louis 1978-79; Distinguished Serv Award INROADS Inc St Louis 1984; Distinguished Alumni Award Harris-Stowe State Coll 1985; served as a judge for the Harris-Stowe University's first annual John M. Olin Cup competition, 1989.

DIDDLEY, BO (ELIAS BATES MCDANIEL)
Musician. **Personal:** Born Dec 30, 1928, McComb, MS; son of Ethel Wilson and Gussie McDaniel (adopted parent); married Ethel Mae Smith, 1946 (divorced); children: four. **Career:** Musician/Singer, recordings include: "Bo Diddly," "I'm a Man—Spell it M-A-N," "Who do you Love?," "Say Man," "Mona," "Road Runner," "Hey Bo Diddley," "Crackin' Up," numerous others. **Honors/Awds:** Rock and Roll Hall of Fame; Guitar Player magazine, Editors Award for Lifetime Achievement, 1990.

DIDLICK, WELLS S.
Retired educator. **Personal:** Born Jun 16, 1925, Middletown, OH; son of Lena Didlick and Brack Didlick; married Beverly Chavis; children: four. **Educ:** Miami Univ, BA 1952. **Career:** Campus Inter-Racial Club Miami Univ, pres 1950-51, pres student faculty council 1951-52; Woodlawn Planning Comm, comm 2 yrs; Woodlawn OH, councilman 8 yrs; Cincinnati Bd of Ed, retired teacher. **Orgs:** Mem NAACP; bd mem Zoning Bd of Appeals Village of Woodlawn 1979; appt Gov Task Force on Sch Discipline Cincinnati School Syst 1979; appt Indus Rel Comm Village of Woodlawn 1980, planning commission 1980. **Military Serv:** USN seaman 1/c 1943-46.

DIGGS, ESTELLA B.
State legislator. **Personal:** Born Apr 21, 1916, St Louis, MO; divorced; children: Edward A, Lawrence C, Joyce D. **Educ:** NY Inst of Dietetics, grad; Pace Coll, attended; CCNY, attended; NY Univ, attended; Adult Continuing Ed Queens Coll, attended. **Career:** NY State, committee woman; real estate dealer; freelance writer for various publs; career counselor, catering business, pres; State of New York, legislator,assemblywoman, currently. **Orgs:** Neighborhood chmn Girl Scouts 15 yrs; org Rosary Soc St Augustines Roman Cath Church; chmn March of Dimes 15 yrs; founder & chmn Bronx Cit Comm; bd mem Comm Planning Bd #3, Forest House Day Care, Morrisania Pioneer Sr Citizens; charter mem Professional Women Bronx Chapt, Pride Inc; mem Natl Council of Negro Women, Catholic Interracial Council of the Bronx, Womans Grand Jury Assoc; org better housing comm; bd dir Halfway House for Women; exec mem Prison Rehab Bedford Hills Corr Inst. **Honors/Awds:** Jackson Dem Club Hon Parade Marshal Afro-Amer Day Parade; numerous awds for fund raising BSA; Spec Salesmanship Awds Cushman Baker Co; Confidential Aidto Judge Donald J Sullivan Supreme Ct; Seagram Van Guard Soc Awd 1974; Ecumenical Awd Council of Churches New York City 1973. **Business Addr:** Legislator, Assemblywoman, State of New York, Legislative Office Bldg, Rm 746, Bronx, NY 10456.

DIGGS, IRENE
Educator, anthropologist. **Personal:** Born Apr 13, 1906, Monmouth, IL. **Educ:** Monmouth Coll, Univ of MN, AB 1928; Atlanta Univ, MA 1933; Univ of Havana Cuba, Dr 1945. **Career:** Guest Professor, Bard Coll, Brooklyn Coll, Lincoln Univ, Univ of MD, Univ Coll, Univ of MD Sch of Nursing, Harvard Summer Sch of Arts & Scis & of Educ; Morgan State Univ, prof of anthropology & sociology 1947-76; Amer Anthropological Assn, visiting anthropologist 1964-72; Morgan State Univ, the library rsch & writing. **Orgs:** Fellow Amer Anthropological Assn; assoc in Current Anthropology; fellow Amer Assn for the Advancement of Sci; fellow Amer Assn of Physical Anthropologists; fellow Amer Assn of Applied Anthropology; fellow Evergreen House; mem NY Acad of Sci; mem Amer Assn of Univ Women; mem Intl African Inst; mem Natl Screening Comm Inst of Intl Education; mem Gov's Task Force on Corrections Probation & Parole; chwmn Comm on Correctional Decision Making Rsch & Training 1968; mem Professional Adv Comm of MD Assn for Mental Health; co-founder Phylon; founding mem Women's Comm Baltimore Museum of Art; sec Golden Jubilee Ball Comm Baltimore Museum of Art 1963-64; mem trustee comm Accessions & Deaccessions; mem women's comm Baltimore Museum of Art; mem progcomm Metro Baltimore Assn for Mntl Hlth 1967; mem vadv comm Baltimore City Hosps 1968; mem The Women's Bd of the Peabody Inst; mem Amer Del of the Amer Anthrop Assn; mem Amer Del of the Amer Anthrop Assn 10 36th Congreso Internacional de Americanistas; mem Amer Del AAAS Tokyo 11th Pac Sci Congress. **Honors/Awds:** Portrait of Irene Diggs in bronze & marble by Italian Sculptor Tina Dompe exhibited in Rome Florence Turin Paris; portraits (four) of Irene Diggs by Rivkah Rieger Jerusalem Israel; Roosevelt Fellow Inst for Intl Educ; Exchange Scholar resident in Montevideo Uruguay; Disting Alumni Awd 1964 Monmouth Coll; co-editor "Encyclopedia of the Negro" HW Wilson Co, 1945; author of Black Chronology, From 4000BC to the Abolition of the Slave Trade, G K Hall Publ. **Business Addr:** Professor of Anthropology, Morgan State Univ, The Library Room 338, Baltimore, MD 21239.

DIGGS, LAWRENCE J
Vinegar researcher, educator. **Personal:** Born Nov 2, 1947, Houston, TX; son of Louis Maurine. **Educ:** Antioch Univ, BA, 1987. **Career:** KFRC, announcer, 1968-72; KSFO, announcer/producer/reporter, 1970-72; KSFX, announcer; Quiet Storm Trading Company; Vinegar Connoisseurs International, pres, 1972-. **Orgs:** Peace Corps, medical volunteer, 1979-81; Zen Yukai, pres, 1982-83; Lions Club, 1992-; American Federation of Radio and Television Artists; Media Alliance; Microscopical Society; National Counsel of Returned Peace Corps Volunteers; Soto Zen Mission, bd of directors. **Honors/Awds:** California Senate, Commendation, 1973; California Assembly, Commendation, 1973; San Francisco Board of Supervisors, Commendation, 1973; Beyond War Award. **Special Achievements:** Author: Vinegar, The Standard Reference, 1989; Suihanki Cooking; Introduction to Men's Issues, 1992; Facts About Blacks, 1971. **Business Addr:** President, Vinegar Connoisseurs International, 30 Carlton Ave, Roslyn, SD 57261, (605)486-4536.

DIGGS, ROY DALTON, JR.
Physician. **Personal:** Born Mar 29, 1929, Detroit, MI; married Johnella Smith. **Educ:** Wayne State Univ, 1946-49; Meharry Med School, MD 1953. **Career:** Hurley Hosp, intern 1953-54; KS City General Hospital #2, resd 1954-56; VA Hosp Buffalo NY, resd 1958-61; Lapeer St Home, surgeon 1961-63; Private practice, gen surgeon, currently. **Orgs:** Diplomate Amer Bd of Surgery; fellow Amer Coll of Surgeons; mem Flint Acad of Surgery; fellow Amer Coll of Emergency Physicians; clinical assoc prof of surg MI State Coll of Human Med; mem AMA; life mem NAACP, Natl Urban League; bd dir Foss Ave Christian School; past bd mem Flint Urban League, Omega Psi Phi Frat. **Honors/Awds:** Humanitarian Award Flint Human Relations Comm 1977. **Military Serv:** USMC captain 1956-58. **Business Addr:** General Surgeon, 4250 N Saginaw, Flint, MI 48505.

DIGGS, WILLIAM P.
Clergyman, educator. **Personal:** Born Oct 19, 1926, Columbia, SC; married Clotilda J Daniels; children: Mary Lynne, William jr. **Educ:** Friendship Jr Coll Rock Hill SC, 1943; Morehouse College, AB 1949; Atlanta U, MA 1951; Colgate-Rochester Div Sch, BD 1955; MDiv 1972. **Career:** Friendship Jr Coll, Rock Hill SC, instructor 1950-52; Friendship Jr Coll, instructor Sociology 1955-61; Galilee Baptist Church, York SC, pastor 1955-62; Second Baptist Church, Leroy NY, student pastor 1954-55; Benedict Coll, Columbia SC, asst prof Sociology 1964-74; Trinity Baptist Church, Florence SC & Morris Coll, Sumter SC, minister, asst prof Sociology. **Orgs:** Am Assn of Univ Prof; Alpha Kappa Delta Honorary Sociological Soc; pres Florence Br NAACP 1970-74; life mem NAACP; mem Community Relations Com Relations Florence, SC; chmn Community Action Agency Florence Co; mem Area Manpower Bd; mem Florence Co Bd of Health; mem trustee bd Friendship Jr Coll; mem trustee bd Morrisl Coll. **Honors/Awds:** Valedictorian HS class; honorary DD Friendship Jr Coll 1973; Honorary LHD Morris Coll 1973; honored by Trinity Bapt Ch Florence; recognition of dedicated service ch & community 1969; honored Zeta Phi Beta Sorority Inc; Florence outstanding leadership civic econ comm involvement 1971; citz of the yr Chi Iota Chap Omega Psi Phi Frat 1976; outst achvmt & serv Omega Psi Phi Frat 1976. **Military Serv:** AUS t/5 1945-47. **Business Addr:** 124 W Darlington St, Florence, SC 29501.

DIJI, AUGUSTINE EBUN
Psychiatrist. **Personal:** Born Jun 27, 1932; son of Cecelia Oyeloye Sogo and James Sogo; married Celestine Gavor; children: Augustine, Angela. **Educ:** Queen's Univ Belfast, BS 1958; Queen's Univ Belfast, MD 1961; Royal Victoria Hosp Belfast, intern 1962-63; Queen's Univ Belfast, resd 1963-67.

Career: Ghana Med Sch, instr physiology 1967-69; Erie County Medical Center, special flwsp 1969-70; Erie Co Medical Ctr 1971-; Buffalo General Hosp, staff 1971-; Part-time Pvt Practice, psychiatrist 1971-; State Univ NY at Buffalo, clinical asst prof 1975-; Geneva B Scruggs Comm Health Care Ctr Buffalo, consultant psychiatrist 1985-89; Buffalo Psychiatric Ctr, staff psychiatrist 1970-72, unit chief 1972-78, acting dept clin dir 1978-79, acting dir 1979, medical director 1980-. **Orgs:** Mem British Med Assn 1963-76, Royal Coll of Physicians 1966-, Royal Coll of Psychiatrists 1966-, AMA 1970-, Amer Psychiat Assn 1970-, Natl Medical Assn 1971-, World Assn for Social Psychiatry 1976-; pres Medical & Dental Staff Buffalo Psychiat Center 1976-77; pres medical & dental staff Buffalo Psychiatric Center 1985-88. **Honors/Awds:** Schlrsp Queen's Univ Belfast 1955-61; Milroy Medal Queen's Univ 1957; Hutchinson's Schlrsp Queen's Univ 1957-58; publ "Local Vasodilation Action of Carbon Dioxide on Blood Vessels of Hand" Queen's Univ 1959; "The Local Effects of Carbon Dioxide on Human Blood Vessels" Queen's Univ 1960; dissertation "A Survey of the Incidence of Mental Disorder in the Mentally Subnormal" 1965. **Business Addr:** 1221 Kensington Ave, Buffalo, NY 14215.

DIKE, KENNETH ONWUKA

Educator. **Personal:** Born Dec 17, 1917; married Ona; children: Chinwe, Chukwuemeka, Nneka, Ona, Obiora. **Educ:** Leeds U, 1963; Columbia 1965; Princeton 1965; DLitt Boston U, 1962; Brimingham U, 1964; Ahmadu Bello U, 1965; Ibadan U, 1975; Univ Moscow, DSc 1963; Univ Durham, BA 1943; Univ Aberdeen, MA 1947; LLD 1961; London U, PhD 1950; LLD 1963; Northwestern U, LLD 1962. **Career:** Harvard Univ, prof History 1970-; Comm on African Studies, chmn 1972-, vice chancellor 1960-67, vice prin 1958-60; African Inst Social & Econ, sr rsch fellow 1952-54; Univ Coll Ibadan, lecturer History 1950-52. **Orgs:** Mem Ashby Comm Higher Educ in Nigeria 1957; chmn orgn com Interat Congress Africanists 1962; chmn Negerian Antiquited Commn 1954-67; flw Am Acad Arts & Sci; Royal Hist Soc; Kings Coll; Brit Hist Asn. **Honors/Awds:** Author "Trade & Politics in the Niger Delta 1830-85" 1956; "A Hundred Years of British Rule in Nigeria" 1957; "The Origins of the Niger Mission" 1958. **Business Addr:** Harvard Univ, Widener Lib, Cambridge, MA 02138.

DILDAY, JUDITH NELSON

Judge. **Personal:** Born Mar 28, 1943, Pittsburgh, PA; daughter of Alberta Nelson and Frank Nelson; married James S Dilday, Dec 1972; children: Ayana, Sekou, Zakia. **Educ:** Univ of Pittsburgh, BA 1966; Millersville State Coll, Grad Credits in French; Boston Univ Sch of Law, JD 1974. **Career:** Pittsburgh Bd of Educ, French teacher 1966-70; Boston Model City, educ counselor 1970-71; Suffolk Co District Attorney, asst dist atty 1975; MBA Specialized Training/Advocacy Project, counsel 1977; Stern & Shapiro, attorney 1977-80; Office of the Solicitor US Dept of Interior, atty advisor 1980-81; Private Practice, counselor at law 1981-82; MA Bay Transportation Authority, asst general counsel 1982-89; Burnham, Hines & Dilday, partner, 1989-93; Probate and Family Court of Massachusetts, judge, 1993-. **Orgs:** Bd mem, MA Black Lawyers Assn, 1980-84; steering comm, Lawyer's Comm Civil Rights 1980-; vice pres, Psi Omega Chapter, Alpha Kappa Alpha, 1984-86; bd of dir, Women's Bar Assnm 1984-; delegate, State Democratic Convention, 1986; MA Bar Assn; treasurer, Natl Bar Assn Region I; MA Black Women Attorneys, The League of Afro-Amer Women; first black pres elect, Women's Bar Assn; 1989; delegate, State Democratic Convention, 1987-89; sec of bd of dir, Daniel Marr Boy's Club; president, Women's Bar Association, 1990-91; gen counsel, 100 Black Women, 1992; National Association of Women Judges; MA Black Judges Association; Boston Black Women's Literary Club; eucharistic minister, St Cyprian's Episcopal Church. **Honors/Awds:** First black female Assistant District Attorney Suffolk Co; Hearing Comm Mem Bd of Bar Overseers 1986-89; Woman of the Year, Cambridge, YWCA, 1989; Legal Services Achievement Award, League of Afro-American Women, 1991; Silver Shingle Alumni Award, Boston University School of Law, 1991; Sojourner Truth Legal Service Award, National Association of Negro Business & Professional Women, 1991. **Home Addr:** 9 Larchmont St, Boston, MA 02124.

DILDAY, WILLIAM HORACE, JR.

Business executive. **Personal:** Born Sep 14, 1937, Boston, MA; son of Alease Virginia Scott Dilday and William Horace Dilday; married Maxine Carol Wiggins, Nov 6, 1966; children: Scott, Erika, Kenya. **Educ:** Boston U, BS, BA 1960. **Career:** IBM, supv 1964-68; EG&G Roxbury, 1968-69; WHDH Inc, dir of personnel 1969-72; WLBT-TV, gen mgr 1972-84; WJTV, exec vp, gen mgr, 1985-89; News, Press and Gazette, Broad Div, corporate vice president, 1989-93; Kerimax Communications, pres/CEO, 1994-. **Orgs:** Bd of dir NBC TV Affil Bd; bd of dir Nat Assn of Broadcasters; bd of dir Jackson-Hinds Comprehensive Health Center; bd of dir MS Mental Health Assn City of Jackson; past pres Jackson Urban League 1978-79; bd of dir Private Industry Council; bd of dir Congress Black Caucus' Comm Brain Trust; finance chairperson Boy Scouts of Amer, Seminole Dist, 1988-89; bd mem, Junior Achievement, 1988-89; bd mem, United Way, 1988-89; vice pres, 100 Black Men of Jackson, 1991. **Honors/Awds:** First African-American gen mgr of a commercial TV station; first African-American elected to a TV network affiliate bd of dir; first African-American elected to Natl Assn of Broadcasters Bd of Dir. **Military Serv:** USAR Sp4 1960-62.

DILDY, CATHERINE GREENE

Educator, travel company executive. **Personal:** Born Nov 21, 1940, Dinwiddie, VA; daughter of Cora H Greene and Bruce Greene Sr; married Alvin V Dildy, Jan 1, 1982; children: Jewel D Trotman. **Educ:** Elizabeth City State University, BS, 1964; University of Virginia, 1966-68, 1988-90; Norfolk State University, 1980-81, 1988-89; Old Dominion University, 1970-71, 1976-77, 1978-80, 1986-90. **Career:** Norfolk Public Schools, physical education resource, elementary, 1964-70, health & physical education, junior, 1970-79, health & physical education, 1979-, driver education coordinator, intramural director, city-wide health fair chairman, 1979-92, dance group sponsor, 1979-92; Tri City Tours, vice pres, currently. **Orgs:** Delta Sigma Theta Sorority, president, financial secretary-treasurer, 1960-, chairman budget, May Week Social; Virginia Beach Chapter Pinochle Bugs, financial treasurer, 1980-; Norfolk Chapter National Epicurean, financial secretary, 1988-; Norfolk Chapter Drifters Inc, president treasurer, 1969-; National Education Association, 1964-; Virginia Education Association, 1964-; Norfolk Education Association, 1964-. **Honors/Awds:** Iota Phi Lambda, "Apple For The Teacher", 1990; National Pinochle Bugs Inc, National Champion, 1988. **Special Achievements:** Community Involvement Team for Family Life Education, 1990; contributed to the development of the Curriculum Guide for Family Life; contributed to the development of the Health & Physical Education Guide; Norfolk Public Schools, Health Education Fair, co-chairperson. **Home Addr:** 5524 Connie Ln, Virginia Beach, VA 23462, (804)497-8609.

DILL, BONNIE THORNTON

Educator. **Personal:** Born Oct 5, 1944, Chicago, IL; daughter of Hilda Branch Thornton and Irwin Stanley Thornton; married John R Dill, Nov 29, 1969; children: Allen Richard Kamau, Anika Hillary, Nandi Elizabeth. **Educ:** Univ of Rochester, AB, 1965; New York Univ, MA, 1970, PhD, 1979. **Career:** Office of Equal Opportunity-Northeast Region, field representative, 1965-67; City of New York Community Development Agency, community organizer/program officer, 1967-68; City of New York Human Resources Admin, program developer/field supervisor, 1968-70; New York Univ Ctr for Human Rel, trainer (part-time), 1969-71; Bernard M Baruch Coll Dept of Compensatory Prog, lecturer/counselor, 1970-77; Bernard M Baruch Coll, Black & Hispanic Studies Prog, adjunct lecturer, 1972-73; New York Univ Sociology Dept, teaching assistant, 1974-75, adjunct instructor, 1976-77; Memphis State Univ, asst prof of sociology, 1978-83, dir and founder of Center for Research on Women, 1982-88, assoc prof of sociology, 1983-90, prof of sociology, 1990-91; Univ of Maryland-College Park, prof of women's studies/affateprof of sociology, 1991-. **Orgs:** American Sociological Association; Society for the Study of Social Problems; Association of Black Sociologists; Sociologists for Women in Society; National Women's Studies Association; National Council for Research on Women. **Honors/Awds:** American Sociological Association, Jessie Bernard Award and Distinguished Contributions to Teaching Award, both 1993; Univ of Maryland, Summer Research Award, 1992; Memphis State Univ, Superior Performance in University Research (SPUR) Award, 1984, 1985, 1986, 1987, 1990, Midyear Raise for Merit in Research and Scholarly Productivity, 1985; Memphis Women's Network, Women of Achievement Award for Vision, 1985; National Conference of Christians and Jews, Memphis Chapter, Women's Rights Award, 1984; Alpha Kappa Alpha Sorority, Epsilon Chapter, Outstanding Black Women, 1984; Danforth Faculty Assoc, 1979-; National Fellowship Fund, Graduate Fellowship; numerous others. **Special Achievements:** Co-editor, Women of Color in US Society, Temple Univ Press, 1993; author, Across the Boundaries of Race and Class: An Exploration of Work and Family Among Black Female Domestic Servants, Garland Pub, 1993, "Fictive Kin, Paper Sons, and Compadrazgo: Women of Color and the Struggle for Family Survival," in Women of Color in US Society, Temple Univ Press, 1993, "Race, Gender and Poverty in the Rural South: African American Single Mothers," in Rural Poverty in America, Auburn House, 1992; Co-author, "To Be Mature, Tenured, and Black: Reflections of Twenty Years of Academic Partnership" in Change, 22:2, p 30-33, 1990; numerous others. **Business Addr:** Professor, University of Maryland, Women's Studies Department, 2101 Woods Hall, College Park, MD 20742-5425, (301)405-6878.

DILL, GREGORY

Educational administrator. **Personal:** Born Dec 8, 1958, Flint, MI; son of Charles & Doris Dill. **Educ:** Eastern Michigan University, BBA, 1988, MBA, 1997. **Career:** Catherine McAuley Health Sys, manager, 1989-93; Eastern Michigan University, gen foreman, 1993-95, manager, 1995-. **Orgs:** Alpha Phi Alpha, 1984-. **Business Addr:** Associate Director, McKenny Union, Eastern Michigan Univ, 11 McKenny Union, Ypsilanti, MI 48197, (313)487-3514.

DILLARD, CECIL R.

Pharmacist. **Personal:** Born Dec 28, 1906, Pontotoc, MS; married Alyce M Carter; children: Cecelia. **Educ:** Okolona Jr Coll, instr coach 1933-43; Interlake Chem Corp, production foreman 1943-48; Thompson Med Supply, pharmacist 1949-50; Dillard Professional Pharmacy, owner pharmacist 1950-. **Career:** Dillard Professional Pharmacy, owner pharmacist 1950-; Thompson Med Supply, pharmacist 1949-50; Interlake Chem Corp, production foreman 1943-48; Okolona Jr Coll, instr coach 1933-43. **Orgs:** Mem past pres Chicago Pharmacist Assn 1962; mem past pres Nat Pharmaceutical Assn 1964; mem past pres IL Acad of Preceptors 1973; mem bd IL Pharmaceutical Assn; mem Am Pharmaceutical Assn; elected to membership Am Bd of Diplomates in Pharmacy; mem NAACP; Phi Beta Sigma. **Honors/Awds:** Honored by Phi Beta Sigma & met C of C for work with bd of edn; founder chrmn bd CPA Scholarship Found. **Business Addr:** Pharmacist, Dillard Prof Pharmacy, 67 E 43 St, Chicago, IL 60653.

DILLARD, HOWARD LEE

City official. **Personal:** Born Jan 21, 1946, Clinton, KY; son of Rosie Pearl Smith Dillard and Samuel William Dillard; married Frances Louise Piper Dillard, Aug 20, 1970; children: Wynita M, Christina M, Howard L Jr, Tamra Deann. **Educ:** Draughon's College, Paducah, KY, business administration, 1982. **Career:** Dillard & Hunt, Clinton, KY, partner/manager, 1980-82; Dillard contractors, Clinton, KY, owner, 1982-88; Excel Industries, Fulton, KY, production, 1988-. **Orgs:** Worshipful Master, Prince Hall Masons, 1991-; treasurer, Hickman County Democratic Executive Committee, 1988-; board of directors, Hickman County Senior Citizens, 1988-; executive committee, Hickman County Parks & Recreation Board, 1984; member, Clinton Kentucky City Council, 1988-. **Military Serv:** Army, SP/4; Vietnam Service Medal, Vietnam Campaign Medal, & Vietnam Occupational Medal. **Home Addr:** PO Box 14, Clinton, KY 42031.

DILLARD, JACKIE SMITH

City official. **Personal:** Born Apr 3, 1948, Alexander, AR; daughter of Willene Littlejohn Smith and Alvin Smith; married Lloyd (divorced 1981); children: Lauren, Meredith. **Educ:** Little Rock University, Little Rock, AR; University of Maryland; University of Arkansas, Little Rock, AR. **Career:** City of Alexander, Alexander, AR, mayor, 1982-. **Business Addr:** Mayor, City of Alexander, PO Box 306, Alexander, AR 72002.

DILLARD, JOEY L.

Educator (retired). **Personal:** Born Jun 26, 1924, Grand Saline, TX; son of Thelma J Dillard and M L Dillard; married Mary Lord; children: Kenneth Joseph. **Educ:** So Methodist Univ, BA (Highest Hon) 1949, MA 1951; Univ of TX Austin, PhD 1956. **Career:** Quito Ecuador, fulbright lecturer 1958-59; Bujumbura Burundi, fulbright lecture 1967-68; Yaounde Cameroun, linguist with AID 1964-65; Inst of Caribbean Studies of Univ of PR Rio Piedras, rsch assoc 1961-75; Northwestern State Univ, assoc prof 1975-83; Northwestern State Univ Natchitoches LA, prof of english 1983-89. **Orgs:** Dir Urban Language Study Ctr for Applied Linguistics 1967; visiting lecturer Ferkauf Graduate School Yeshiva Univ 1968-73. **Honors/Awds:** Alumnus Awd Phi Beta Kappa 1964; research grant Amer Philosophical Soc 1986-87; workshop grant Louisiana Endow for the Humanities 1987; Hendrix- Murphy Lecturer, Hendrix Coll, Conway AR, 1989. **Military Serv:** USN yeoman 2nd cl 1942-45.

DILLARD, JUNE WHITE

Attorney. **Personal:** Born Sep 26, 1937, Youngstown, OH; daughter of Dr & Mrs John Ira White; married John Vartoukian, Jul 31, 1988; children: Belinda Louise, Brian Martin, Stephen Jeffrey. **Educ:** Univ of Chicago, AB 1958; Chicago Teachers Coll, MA 1964; Howard Univ Sch of Law, JD (Cum Laude) 1975. **Career:** Chicago Public Schools, teacher 1958-61; Office of Economic Oppor, field rep 1967-70; Securities & Exchange Commn, clerk 1975-76; Taylor & Overby, associate 1978-80; JW Dillard Esquire, attorney 1980-. **Orgs:** Commission for Women of St Mary's County; Business & Professional Women, legal counsel and first vp; Margaret Brent chapter, Minority Business Alliance, legal counsel; past president & trustee, Prince George Arts Cncl; Legal Counsel to Fair Housing Council; NAACP, Prince George's County Branch. **Honors/Awds:** Top Ladies of Distinction; Cable TV Commnr; Service Awd Coalition on Black Affairs; Outstanding Contribution to Legal Comm, Natl Bar Association; Disting Member Awd, Natl Business League of Southern MD; Frederic Douglass Civic Achievement Awd, MD Black Republican Cncl; President's Award, NAACP; Outstanding Service Award, Prince George's County Government. **Business Addr:** 12 Courthouse Dr, PO Box 857, Leonardtown, MD 20650, (301)627-9100.

DILLARD, MARTIN GREGORY

Administrator physician. **Personal:** Born Jul 7, 1935, Chicago, IL; son of Evelyn Farmer Dillard and Manny Martin Dillard; married Patricia Rachelle Cheek; children: Belinda, Brian, Stephen. **Educ:** Univ of Chicago, BA 1956, BS 1957; Howard Univ Med Sch, MD 1965; Michael Reese Hosp Chicago, Internship/Red 1965-69, US Public Hlth Serv Fellowship 1969-70. **Career:** Howard Univ Coll of Med, asst prof of med 1970-74, admin, planning & exec com 1976-, asst dean/clinical affairs 1984-; Howard Univ Hosp, assoc prof of med 1974-; Howard Univ, prof of Med 1987-. **Orgs:** Asst chmn for educ Postgrad Dept of Med Howard Univ Hospital 1973-76; chief

Hemodialysis Unit Howard Univ Hospital 1970-76; bd of dir Hlth Care Coalition Natl Capitol Area 1982-; govr advisory com Am Coll of Phys Wash DC 1980-. **Honors/Awds:** Alpha Omega Alpha Honor Medical Society 1965; Natl Bd of Med Exmnr 1966; Am Bd of Intrl Med 1972; Am Bd of Intrnl Med Nephrology 1978. **Military Serv:** AUS e-4. **Business Addr:** Asst Medical Dir, Howard Univ Hospital, 2041 Georgia Ave N W, Washington, DC 20060.

DILLARD, MELVIN RUBIN
Insurance company administrator. **Personal:** Born Feb 26, 1941, Kendleton, TX; son of Ruby Lee Taylor Dillard and Vellas Dillard; children: Melvin II, Melvia, Melvis. **Educ:** Huston-Tillotson Coll, BA 1964; Prairie View A&M Univ, MA 1973; Life Underwriters Training Council, 1984. **Career:** Life Underwriter Training Council, moderator 1979-86; Natl Western Life, genl agent 1975-81, division mgr. **Orgs:** Mem TX Leaders Round Table 1970-91, Million Dollar Round Table 1977-97, Lone Star Leader 1983-87; natl committeeman, bd mem Houston Assoc Life Underwriters; natl pres Huston-Tillotson Alumni; bd mem TX Comm Corp, United Methodist Church Mission Bd and Pension Bd; pres-elect, San Jacinto Assn of Life Underwriters, 1991-; Division Mgr, 1975-97; Natl Western Life, 1975-97; Regional 4 Director for Texas Assn of Life Underwriters, TALU; United Methodist Ch-South District, district lay leader. **Honors/Awds:** Articles published TX Assoc News Magazine 1979, Salesman Magazine 1980; Presidential Citation Natl Assoc for Equal Opportunity 1983; Doctorate Degree, Huston Tillotson College 1984; LUTCF, Life Underwriters Training Council/National Assn of Life Underwriters, 1984. **Business Addr:** Divisional Manager, Natl Western Life Insur, 2656 South Loop West, Ste 585, Houston, TX 77054.

DILLARD, SAMUEL DEWELL. See Obituaries section.

DILLARD, THELMA DELORIS
Educator, elected official. **Personal:** Born Jan 6, 1946, Macon, GA; daughter of Hester Lou Newberry Bivins; divorced; children: Cartese. **Educ:** Ft Valley State Coll, BS Business Ed 1966; GA Coll, Masters Special Educ 1975, Masters Bus Ed 1978. **Career:** Macon NAACP, sec 1965-, pres, 1995-97; Ft Valley State Coll, teacher 1970; GA State NAACP, asst sec 1978, parliamentarian 1982; Area Planning & Devel Commiss, bd of dir 1980-; Democratic State Comm of GA, appointed mem 1983-; Central High, educator; Bibb Bd of Education, Macon, GA, chmn, special education dept, 1986-. **Orgs:** Mem Zeta Phi Beta 1965-; sec NAACP 1965-; mem GA Coalition of Black Women 1980-; chairperson Rules Comm Macon City Council 1980-; asst sec GA Assoc of Black Officials 1980-; vice chair 1983, chmn 1987-; Public Property Comm, City of Macon, chairman, 1992-; chmn, Cherry Blossom ''Think Pink'' Comm, 1990-91; 1st vice pres, NAACP, 1991; assoc mem, Jack & Jill, 1990-. **Honors/Awds:** 50 Most Influential Women NAACP Macon & Informer Mag 1981; Outstanding Woman of the Year NAACP 1983; 50 Most Influential Women GA Coalition of Black Women 1984; Several Comm Serv Awds from many orgs; mem Jack and Jill of America, 1988.

DILLENBERGER, R. JEAN
Federal official (retired). **Personal:** Born May 6, 1931, Maywood, IL; married John Dillenberger; children: Tsan. **Educ:** San Francisco State Univ, BA 1963, MA 1978. **Career:** San Francisco State Univ, serv to minority students; Ford Found, proj dir; Office for Civil Rights, chief of oper; US Dept of Educ, acting dir higher educ div, dir elementary & secondary educ div regional office for civil rights; deputy regional director, 1987-94. **Orgs:** Director Advocates of Women 1973-77; dir, treas Consumers Coop of Berkeley 1977-83; dir, pres Consumers Group Legal Serv 1973-76; adv bd Women Org for Employment; mem Assn of Fed Women Execs Speaking Engagements, Higher Educ Branch, Office for Civil Rights, HEW. **Honors/Awds:** Published ''70 Soul Secrets of Sapphire,'' ''Toward Viable Directions in Postsecondary Education.''.

DILLIHAY, TANYA CLARKSON
Psychiatrist. **Personal:** Born Aug 8, 1958, Columbia, SC; daughter of Rachel Scott Clarkson and Zack C Clarkson; married Otha R Dillihay Sr; children: Otha R II, Elliot Clarkson, Adam Scott. **Educ:** Spelman Coll, BS Biology 1979; Meharry Medical Coll, MD 1983. **Career:** Wm S Hall Psychiatric Inst, resident in training 1983-87; South Carolina State Hospital, psychiatric service chief, currently. **Orgs:** Treas Afro-Amer Psychiatrists of SC 1986, 1987; chief resident of psycho-social rehabilitation WSHPI 1987; mem Ladson Pres Church Columbia SC; Spelman College Club; Congaree Medical Association; Delta Sigma Theta Sorority. **Honors/Awds:** ''Suicide in Black Children'' published in Psychiatric Forum, 1989.

DILLON, AUBREY
Educator (retired), educational consultant. **Personal:** Born Jan 25, 1938, Prentiss, MS; son of Louella Barnes Quinn. **Educ:** Edinboro State Coll, BS 1961, MEd 1964. **Career:** Playground dir 1961-63; Erie, PA Sch Dist, teacher, guidance cnslr 1961-69; Erie Tech HS, tennis coach 1965-68; basic adult educ coord 1966-68; Edinboro State Coll, assoc dean of men 1969-93, Edinboro University of Penna, professor emeritus, 1993, educational consultant, jazzie bd of dirs, currently. **Orgs:** PA State Educ Assn; dir Human Awareness Lab Edinboro 1965; YMCA asst boy's work dir 1964-66; supr student tchrs; chmn Black Studies Comm Edinboro 1969-72; PA Governor's Justice Commn mem; US SSS Registra; bd of Incorporators WQLN Educ TV; Erie ACT Comm Cntr Bd; Presque Isle Jaycees; Erie Human Rel Educ Com; Erie Urban Coalition; Kappa Delta Phi Natl Educ Frat; Alpha Phi Alpha Soc Frat; bd dir Meadville, PA Unity Cntr; NATO Comm Educ Com; Booker T Washington Comm Cntr Scoutmaster; Citiz Scholarship Found bd dir; Adelphi Univ Drug Inst particip; PA Black Conf on Higher Edn; musician; jazz dj Educ Radio WQLN Erie, PA; Inner-Frat Council Adv; Phi Delta Kappa Edinboro Univ of PA; Edinboro Univ Human Relations Comm; pres Phi Delta Kappa Beta Nu Chapter 1987-88. **Honors/Awds:** Jaycee of the Month 1966; Runner-up Jaycee Man of the Yr 1967; Alpha Kappa Alpha Sor Sweetheart 1971; Freshman Advocate Nominee, First Year Experience, University of South Carolina, 1990-91. **Home Addr:** 222 Beech St, PO Box 506, Edinboro, PA 16412.

DILLON, GLORIA ANN
Educator. **Personal:** Born Feb 6, 1955, Zanesville, OH; daughter of Lillie B Staunton Wade and James E Wade Sr; married Vermon L Dillon, Apr 27, 1990; children: Charles A Wade, Micah Lemar Dillon. **Educ:** Central State University, BSEd, 1977; University of Dayton, MSEd, 1983. **Career:** Zanesville City Schools, teacher, 1977-78; Montgomery County Schools, teacher, 1978-79; Central State University, counselor, 1979-81; Xenia City Schools, teacher, 1981-86, guidance counselor, 1986-90; Louisiana State University, financial aid counselor, 1990-91, academic counselor, 1991-. **Orgs:** Alpha Kappa Alpha Sorority, Anti Grammateus, Grammateus Epitoleus, grad advisor, 1981-90; Alpha Kappa Mu Honor Society, president, vice pres, 1975-77; Louisiana Association of Student Assistance Programs, 1991-; Southwestern Association of Student Assistance Programs, 1991-; Black Faculty and Staff Caucus, president elect, 1992-; Undershepherd Shiloh Baptist Church, community leader, 1991-; Shiloh Baptist Church, Sunday school teacher, 1991-. **Honors/Awds:** Alpha Kappa Mu Honor Society, Charter Member, 1979; LSU Black Faculty and Staff Caucus Outstanding Service, 1992. **Special Achievements:** Guest Speaker, Harvest Day Tea, 1992. **Home Phone:** (513)769-5277.

DILLON, OWEN C.
Orthopedic surgeon. **Personal:** Born Mar 31, 1934, Kingston, Jamaica; son of Clementina Dillon and Noel Dillon; married Pauline Y Titus; children: Denyse Sophia, Paul C. **Educ:** Howard Univ, BS 1961; Howard Univ Med School, MD 1966. **Career:** Howard Univ Coll of Med, instr orthopaedics; several hosp staff appts & privileges, WA Hosp Ctr, WA VA Med Ctr, Providence Hosp; Private practice, orthopedic surgeon. **Orgs:** Mem DC Med Soc, Med Soc of DC Continuing Med Ed, Midico-Chirurgical Soc. **Military Serv:** AUS maj 1969-71. **Business Addr:** 3636 Georgia Ave NW, Ste 102, Washington, DC 20010-1699.

DILLON, VERMON LEMAR
Juvenile probation officer. **Personal:** Born Jun 5, 1958, New Orleans, LA; son of Ruby Mary Cross Dillon (deceased) and Willie L Dillon (deceased); married Gloria Wade, Apr 27, 1990; children: Charles A Wade, Micah Lemar Dillon. **Educ:** Louisiana State University, BS, 1981; Southern University, MS, 1983. **Career:** Nicholls State University, equipment manager of athletics, 1981-82; Southern University, graduate assistant athletics, 1982-83; Bogalusa City Schools, teacher, 1984; Louisiana State University, assistant athletic director, 1984-85; University of New Orleans, department of athletics equipment manager, 1985-86; Central State University, department of athletics equipment manager, 1986-90; Office of Youth Development, baton Rouge Parish, probation officer II, 1990-. **Orgs:** Prince Hall Masons; Kiwanis, president elect, 1992; Phi Beta Sigma Fraternity; Undershepherd Shiloh Baptist Church, community leader, 1991-; Shiloh Baptist Church Brotherhood, 1990-; founder of JC Crump and JJ Piper Memorial, 1979-. **Honors/Awds:** Phi Beta Sigma, Sigma of the Year, 1981. **Special Achievements:** Kool Achiever Awards nominee, 1992. **Home Phone:** (513)769-5277.

DILWORTH, JACQUELYN BREWER
Physician. **Personal:** Born Apr 28, 1961, Washington, DC; daughter of Marlene H Brewer; married Duane A Dilworth, Jun 15, 1985; children: Jacquelyn Marie, Duane Jr. **Educ:** Howard University, BS, 1983; Howard University College of Medicine, MD, 1985. **Career:** Barnes Hospital, internal medicine intern, 1985-86, dermatology resident, 1986-89, private practice, currently. **Orgs:** Mound City Medical Forum, president, 1996-98; St Louis Dermatological Society, president, 1995-97; National Medical Association, Dermatology Section, secretary-treasurer, 1996-97. **Business Addr:** Dermatologist, Jacquelyn B Dilworth, MD, 11125 Dunn Rd, Ste 206, St Louis, MO 63136, (314)355-7111.

DILWORTH, MARY ELIZABETH
Educator. **Personal:** Born Feb 7, 1950, New York, NY; daughter of Martha Lina Williams Dilworth and Tom Dilworth; married Clyde C. Aveilhe. **Educ:** Howard Univ, BA 1972, MA 1974; Catholic Univ of America, EdD 1981. **Career:** Natl Advisory Council on Education Professions Development, education research analyst 1974-76; Natl Inst for Advanced Studies, sr program analyst 1978-82; Inst for the Study of Educational Policy, research assoc 1983-85; Howard Univ Hospital, coord education & training; ERIC Clearinghouse on Teacher Education, dir 1987-; American Assn of Colleges for Teacher Education, Washington, DC, sr dir for research, 1987-; Howard Univ, Washington, DC, adjunct faculty, school of education, 1989-90. **Orgs:** Mem Amer Educ Rsch Assn; bd mem Natl Cnt on Rsch in Teacher Educ; mem Phi Delta Kappa; prog chair Natl Council of Negro Women; mem NAACP Task Force on Teacher Training and Assessment; sec, div k, American Education Research Assn, 1991-92. **Honors/Awds:** NCNW/Frito Lay Black Woman Achiever Awd 1985; Mary McLeod Bethune Recognition Awd 1985; Howard Univ Urban Affairs Outstanding Community Serv Awd 1979, 85; author ''Teachers' Totter, A Report on Teacher Certification Issues,'' 1984; ''Reading Between the Lines: Teachers and Their Racial Ethnic Cultures,'' 1990; Diversity in Teacher Education: New Expectations, editor, 1992; ''Being Responsive to Cultural Differences: How Teachers Learn,'', 1998, editor. **Business Addr:** Senior Director, Research, American Assn of Colleges for Teacher Education, One Dupont Cir, #610, Washington, DC 20036.

DIMRY, CHARLES LOUIS, III
Professional football player. **Personal:** Born Jan 31, 1966, San Diego, CA; married Francine; children: Erin, Carlee, Christopher. **Honors/Awds:** Ed Block Courage Award, 1996. **Business Addr:** Professional Football Player, Philadelphia Eagles, 3501 S Broad St, Philadelphia, PA 19148, (215)463-2500.

DINES, GEORGE B.
Program management officer. **Personal:** Born Feb 28, 1931, Washington, DC; married Dorothy L Baham; children: George Jr, Kedric, Christopher. **Educ:** Yale Univ, exchange student; Howard Univ, graduate studies; Harvard Univ, Graduate School of Business; various short courses, 1972-73. **Career:** Office for Sub-Saharan Africa/Office for Intl Health OASH Dept of Health & Human Services, chief; Office Intl Health Office of the Asst Sec for Health DHEW, program mgmt officer; Div of Org Analysis & Devel Office of Org Devel Bureau of Comm Health Servs DHEW, dir; Div of Health Care Servs CHS DHEW, special asst to dir; Office of Program Evaluation Div of Health Care Servs DHEW, chief; Office of Health Affairs Office of Economic Opportunity, program coordinator; US Peace Corps Sierra Leone W Africa, assoc dir; US Peace Corps No Nigeria, dir; US Dept of Health & Human Servs, Assoc Admin, 1984-. **Orgs:** Amer Public Health Assn, Natl Assn for Comm Devel, Natl Assn of Neighborhood Health Centers, Amer Public Health Assn Intl Section; bd of dir, Boys & Girls Homes of Montgomery County MD; mem, AFRICARE, Blacks in Govt, Assn of Mil Surgeons of the US, Harvard Univ Business School Club of Washington, Natl Assn for Intl Health, Amer Assn for World Health, Natl Assn of Health Serv Execs, DHEW-OASH Exec Intern Program Review Comm, DHEW CHS Task Force on Data Systems for Neighborhood Health Centers, Health & Welfare Council, rep White House Conf on Food Nutrition & Health, CHS Health Center Mgmt Work Group, CHS Task Force on Rural Health, NAACP, Pi Sigma Alpha, White House Task Force on Youth Opportunity, pres, bd of dirs, Woodlawn Cemetary Perpetual Care Assn; chmn, Comm Minority RelationsMonring Comm; Commissioner, Housing Opportunities Commn, Montgomery County, 1986-; Public Management Assn, 1990-91. **Honors/Awds:** Published numerous health books & articles, 1961-77; recipient of Outstanding Student Award, Howard Univ Student Council 1953; Encyclopedia of Leading Negroes in the US, 1956; Special Citation Premier Govt of No Nigeria, 1962; Peace Corps Overseas Staff Dir, 1964; Certificate of Appreciation, Supt Kakuri Prison Kaduna, Nigeria, 1965; Honorary Citizen, State of AZ, 1975; Citation, St Phillips Coll, San Antonio, 1975; Admin Award for Excellence, DHHS, PHS, HRSA, 1987; Mem, US Saudi Arabia Joint Commission on Economic Cooperation Delegation, 1987, Advisory bd, Intl Conf on Emergency Health Care Devel, 1989; Superior Service Award, DHHS, Public Health Service, 1990; Admin Special Citation, Health Resources and Services Adminstrtion, 1984; Citation, Medical Care Development International,1. **Military Serv:** Infantry, captain, 1954-59. **Business Addr:** Associate Administrator, Dept of Health and Human Services, HRSA, 5600 Fishers Lane, Parklawn Bldg, Rm 14-14, Rockville, MD 20857.

DINKINS, DAVID N.
Educator, former mayor. **Personal:** Born Jul 10, 1927, Trenton, NJ; married Joyce Burrows; children: David Jr. **Educ:** Howard Univ, BS 1950; Brooklyn Law School, JD, 1956. **Career:** Dyett, Alexander, Dinkins, Patterson, Michael, Dinkins, Jones, attorney-partner 1956-1975; NY State Democratic Party, district leader 1967-; NY State Assembly, state assemblyman 1966; City of New York, pres bd of elections 1972-73, city clerk 1975-85, Manhattan borough pres 1986-90, mayor, 1990-93; Columbia Univ, prof, 1993-. **Orgs:** NY State Amer for Democratic Action, bd of dir; Urban League, mem; 100 Black Men, bd of dir; March of Dimes, bd of dir; Assn for a Better NY, bd of dir; Manhattan Women's Political Caucus, first male mem; NAACP, life mem; Black-Jewish Coalition, mem; Vera

Institute of Justice, mem; Nova Anorca & NY State Urban Development Corp; Malcolm King Harlem Coll, bd of trustees; Marymount Manhattan Coll, pres advisory council; Assn of the Bar of the City of NY, exec committee. **Honors/Awds:** Pioneer of Excellence, World Inst of Black Communications, 1986; Righteous Man Award, NY Board of Rabbis, 1986; Man of the Year Award, Corrections Guardians Assn, 1986; Distinguished Service Award, Federation of Negro Civil Service Org , 1986; Man of the Year Award, Assn of Negro Bus and Prof Women's Clubs; Father of the Year Award, Metropolitan Chapter, Jack and Jill of America Inc, 1989; first black mayor of New York City. **Business Addr:** Porf, Sch of Intl and Public Affairs, Columbia University, 420 W 118th St, 14th Fl, New York, NY 10027.

DISHER, SPENCER C., III
Banking executive. **Personal:** Born Sep 30, 1957, Florence, SC; son of Georgia G Montgomery and Spencer C Disher, Jr; married Katherine Dowdell Disher, Oct 8, 1989. **Educ:** Univ of WI-Madison, BSCE 1980; JL Kellogg GSM-Northwestern Univ, MBA 1986. **Career:** Mobil Oil Co, project engr 1980-84; Continental Bank, public fin assoc 1985-86; Citicorp Investment Bank, assoc 1986-87; BT Securities, NY, NY assoc 1987-88; Credit Natl, vice pres. **Orgs:** Mem Toastmasters 1984-86, Natl Black MBA Assoc 1985-; mem NAACP; founder Wisconsin Black Engrg Student Soc. **Honors/Awds:** Chevron Fellowship 1985. **Business Addr:** Vice Pres, Credit National, 520 Madison St, 34th Floor, New York, NY 10022.

DISHMAN, CRIS EDWARD
Professional football player. **Personal:** Born Aug 13, 1965, Louisville, KY; married Karen; children: Cris. **Educ:** Purdue, attended. **Career:** Houston Oilers, defensive back, 1988-96; Washington Redskins, 1997-. **Honors/Awds:** Pro Bowl, 1991. **Business Addr:** Professional Football Player, Washington Redskins, 13832 Redskins Dr, Herndon, VA 22071, (703)471-9100.

DISMUKE, LEROY
Educator, educational administrator. **Personal:** Born Aug 18, 1937, Camden, AR; son of Edna Mae Bragg Byrd and Roy Dismuke; married Gladys M; children: Alan Roy. **Educ:** Lane Coll, BA 1960; Eastern MI Univ, MA 1965; Eastern MI Univ, MA 1977, EdS, 1983. **Career:** Flint Educ Assn, 1966-69; United Teachers Flint Exec Bd, 1969-87; Flint Board of Education, Special Education Department, coordinator, currently. **Orgs:** Mem, Flint Educ Assn 1961-69; Professional Negotiation team mem, 1967-73; United Teachers Flint, 1969-87; MI Federation & Teachers, 1969-74; Amer Federation Teachers, 1969-74, represented many educ assn; GRIP; Black Caucus, Natl Educ Assn, 1970-; representative to NEA 1971-91; chmn special educ dept, Flint Bd Educ; treasurer, NAACP 1983-89; Flint Congress of Administrators, 1991-. **Honors/Awds:** 10 & 15 yrs Serv Award, Big Brothers, 1967, 1972; Central Flint Optimist Award, 1985-86; Kappa Alpha Psi, 1985-86; Educator of the Year, Flint Council for Exceptional Children, 1989; Man of the Year, Flint Alumni Chapter, Kappa Alpha Psi Fraternity, 1990; Achievement Award, Phi Delta Kappa, 1992; Achievement Award, Kappa Alpha Psi Fraternity, 1994. **Home Addr:** 1701 Laurel Oak Dr, Flint, MI 48507-2210.

DISMUKE, MARY EUNICE
Association executive. **Personal:** Born Feb 5, 1942, West Point, GA; daughter of Hattie Snow Pelleccitti and Hubert Hazes Moss; married Olin Dismuke (divorced); children: Sonja, Monica. **Educ:** Georgia State University, Atlanta, GA, BS; Wayne State University, Detroit, MI, MSW. **Career:** Detroit, Compact, Detroit, MI, director; Michigan Department of Labor, Detroit, MI, director, urban affairs, Detroit Associate of Black Org, Detroit, MI, executive director. **Orgs:** Executive board member, Detroit Association of Black Social Worker, secretary, Coalition of Black Trade Unionists. **Honors/Awds:** Harriet Tubman Award, A Philip Randolph Institute/Coalition of Black Trade Unionists, 1989; Outstanding Leadership, Detroit Association of Black Social Workers, 1970; Leadership America, 1985. **Business Addr:** Director, Resource Department, Detroit Compact, 600 W Lafayette Blvd, Detroit, MI 48226.

DIUGUID, LEWIS WALTER
Editor. **Personal:** Born Jul 17, 1955, St Louis, MO; son of Nancy Ruth Greenlee Diuguid and Dr Lincoln I Diuguid; married Valerie Gale Words Diuguid, Oct 25, 1977; children: Adrianne Renee, Leslie Ellen. **Educ:** University of Missouri-Columbia, School of Journalism, BJ, 1977; University of Arizona-Tucson, Fellowship, 1984; Institute for Journalism Education, Editing Program for Minority Journalists. **Career:** Kansas City Times, reporter, photographer, 1977-79, general assignment reporter, surburban reporter, 1979-82, Jackson County courthouse reporter, 1982-84, copy editor, automotive editor, 1984-85; The Kansas City Star Co, asst bureau chief, Johnson County, 1985-87, Southland bureau chief and columnist, 1987-92, assistant city editor and columnist, 1993-94; assoc editor, Metro Columnist, 1994-; diversity co-chair, assistant minority recruiter, 1995-. **Orgs:** President 1986-87, secretary 1987-88, member, founder, 1981-, The Kansas City Association of Black Journalists; member, National Association of Black Journalists, 1985-. **Honors/Awds:** Ark of Friends Award for Journalism on mental illness, 1990-92; Urban League, Difference Maker Award, 1992; 100 Most Influential African-Americans in Greater Kansas City, 1992-97, Research Mental Health Services, Media Award, 1992; Missouri Department of Mental Health, Mental Health Award, 1991; Lincoln University, Unity Award, second place investigative reporting, 1979; Harmony Encourages Awareness, Responsibility, Togetherness Award, 1995; Friends of Mental Health, 1994; Ark of Friends of Greater Kansas City Media Professional Award, 1994; 1st Place Opinion Column Award, Kansas City Press Club, 1993; Ark of Friends Media Professional Award, 1993; Missouri Comm Coll, Assn Media Award, 1993; Wayside Waifs Humane Society, Journalism Award, 1993; Mental Health Assn of Kansas City, Mental Health Awareness Award, 1993; Public Affairs/Social Issues Unity Award, Lincoln Univ, 1993; SCLC Evelyn Wasserstorm Award, Commitment to Causes of Freedom, 1996; Project Equality Individual Achievement Award, 1997; Black Achievers in Industry Award, 1997. **Business Addr:** Associate Editor, Editorial Dept, The Kansas City Star, 1729 Grand Ave, Kansas City, MO 64108.

DIUGUID, LINCOLN I.
Science educator, adminstrator. **Personal:** Born Feb 6, 1917, Lynchburg, VA; married Nancy Ruth Greenlee (deceased); children: David, Lewis, Renee, Vincent. **Educ:** WV State Coll, BS Chem magna cum laude 1938; Cornell Univ, MS Chem 1939, PhD Chem 1945, Post Doctorate Organic Chem 1946-47. **Career:** AM&N Coll Pine Bluff AR, head chem dept 1939-43, prof chem 1939-43; Pine Bluff Arsenal, analytical chem 1942-43; Cornell Univ Ithaca NY, research asst organic chem 1945-46, research assc organic chem 1946-47; AM&N Coll, consult in sci 1949-55; Stowe Tchrs Coll St Louis, prof of chem 1949-55; Harris Stowe State Coll, prof chem & chrmn phys sci dept 1955-82; Jewish Hosp, research assc 1959-61; Leukemia Guild of MO & IL, research dir 1961-63; Washington Univ St Louis, visiting prof of chem 1966-68; Harris Stowe State Coll, prof emeritus; Du-Good Chem Lab & Mfrs, dir 1947-, president, currently. **Orgs:** Sigma Xi; Amer Chem Soc; Natl Educ Assc; Phi Kappa Phi; Amer Assc of Univ Prof; MO State Tchrs Assc; Assc of Consult Chem & Chem Engrs Inc; Flw of Amer Inst of Chemists; Omega Psi Phi Frat. **Honors/Awds:** Publ "The Use of Amalgated Aluminum as a Catalyst in the Federal & Crafts Reaction, JACS 63", 1941, Ref, In Organic Reactions Vol III 1946, "Synthetic Organic Chemistry" 1953; "Benzothiazoles II Nuclear Chlorination in the Hertz Process" 1947, "Joint Symposium on Micro Chem & Pet Industry" 1949, "Synthesis of Long Straight Chain Dicarboxylic Acids via the Ketene Synthesis" 1952, "Methods for the Micro Determination of Mixed Halogens & Amide Group" 1952, "Synthesis of Large Carbon Ring Ketones" 1953, "Synthesis of Aliphatic Esters from the Reaction of Olefins & Formaldehyde Condensation" 1957, "Micro Determination of Sulfur & Phosphorus in Organic Compounds by Perchloric Acid Digestion"; Man of Year Award Omega Psi Phi 1960; mem bd dir 1961-, vice pres 1963, Leukemia Guild of MO & IL 19; Carver Civic Award, 1979; US Patent 1985, Burning Efficiency Enhancement Method, Santonic Acid, Pyrazinoindole and Indole 85; St Louis American Newspaper, Merit Award, 1992. **Business Addr:** President, Du-Good Chem Labs & Mfrs, 1215 S Jefferson, St Louis, MO 63104.

DIXON, ARDENA S.
Educator, educational administrator. **Personal:** Born Feb 24, 1927, Baltimore, MD; daughter of Sedonia Parker Simmons and Albert E Simmons Sr; married Daniel E Dixon Jr, Jan 24, 1948 (deceased); children: Deidre I (deceased), Stephanie Dixon-Barnes, Eris I. **Educ:** Coppin State College, BS, 1963; Loyola College, MS, 1971. **Career:** Baltimore City Public Schools, classroom teacher, 1963-69, reading specialist, 1969-73; Baltimore City Department of Social Services, social work asst II, 1965-78, SWAII, supervisor, 1969-71; Baltimore City Public Schools, educational specialist, 1973-74, asst principal, 1974-79, principal, 1979-; Md State Foster Care Review Board, chairman SWII board, 1988-. **Orgs:** Phi Delta Kappa Sorority, Inc, past eastern regional director, 1983-87, eastern region Xinos chairperson, 1992-93; PSASA, 1973-; MAESA/NEA, 1973-; Pinochle Bugs Social/Civic Club, Baltimore Co, vp, 1988-; NANBPWC, 1992-; NCNVV, 1983-; NAACP, life mem, 1987-; ASCD, 1985-; Urban League Guild, 1987-; Perpetnal Scholarship Foundation, pres, 1993-. **Honors/Awds:** National Sorority, Phi Delta Kappa; NAACP, life mem, 1987. **Home Addr:** 1410 N Ellwood Ave, Baltimore, MD 21213, (410)675-1573. **Business Addr:** Principal, Dallas F Nicholas Sr Elementary School, #39, 201 E 21st St, Baltimore, MD 21218, (410)396-4525.

DIXON, ARRINGTON LIGGINS
Business executive. **Personal:** Born Dec 3, 1942, Washington, DC; son of Sallie Dixon and James Dixon; married Sharon Pratt, Jul 7, 1967 (divorced); children: Aimee, Drew. **Educ:** Howard Univ, BA 1966; George Washington Univ, JD 1972; Command and General Stall College, 1989. **Career:** Univ of Dist of Columbia, assoc prof 1967-74; Mgmt Info Systems, pres 1967-74; Council of the Dist of Columbia, chmn, mem 1975-82; The Brookings Inst, guest scholar 1983; Planning Rsch Corp, vice pres 1983-85; Arrington Dixon and Assoc, Inc, pres, currently. **Orgs:** Bd mem Washington Ctr 1983-86; advanced studies, adv comm The Brookings Inst 1983-; bd mem Greater SE Comm Hosp Found 1983-84, Anacostia Museum 1984-. **Honors/Awds:** Congressional Appt US Air Force Acad 1963-65; Software, Statutes & Stare Decisis Howard Univ Law Jrnl 420 1967; Scholarship George Washington Univ Law 1969-72. **Military Serv:** AUS Reserves, LTC, 16 yrs. **Business Addr:** President, Arrington Dixon and Assoc, Inc, 1727 Massachusetts Ave NW, Washington, DC 20036.

DIXON, BENJAMIN
Educational administrator. **Personal:** Born Apr 18, 1939, Hartford, CT; son of Rose Carter Brown and Cue Benjamin Dixon; married Carolyn Holmes; children: Kevin, Kyle, Kimberly. **Educ:** Howard Univ, B Music Educ (Magna Cum Laude) 1962; Harvard Univ, MAT 1963; Univ of MA, EdD 1977. **Career:** Hartford CT Public Schools, teacher 1963-69; Westledge School West Simsburg CT, teacher/advisor 1969-71; Education/Instruction Inc Hartford CT, co-dir 1971-73; Bloomfield Public Schools CT, asst superintendent 1974-87; Capitol Region Educ Council Windsor CT, asst exec dir 1987-89; Capitol Region Educ Council, Windsor, CT, asst exec dir, 1987-89; The Travelers, Hartford, CT, dir Human Resouces, 1989. **Orgs:** Pres CT Assoc of Pupil Personnel Administrators 1983-84; mem bd of dir Univ MA Sch of Educ Alumni Assoc; sec bd of trustees Stowe School; mem CT State Adv Comm on Mastery Testing, Special Educ, Gifted/Talented; treas bd of dir Hartford Dist Catholic Family Services; governor's appointee CT Children's Trust Fund Council; mem bd of dir Educ/Instruction Inc; mem bd of trustees Metro AME Zion Church; mem, Amer Mgmt Assn, 1989; mem, Amer Soc of Personnel Admins, 1989. **Honors/Awds:** Mem Pi Kappa Lambda Natl Honor Soc; Fellow in Exec Leadership Program Ford Foundation 1973-75; Educ Policy Fellow Inst for Educ Leadership 1983-84; Achievement/Service Award Bloomfield Concerned Black Parents for Quality Educ 1987; co-author "Stress and Burnout, A Primer for Special Educ & Special Services Personnel" 1981. **Business Addr:** Dir, Human Resources, AMG-4NB, The Travelers, One Tower Squre, Hartford, CT 06183.

DIXON, BLANCHE V. See Obituaries section.

DIXON, BRENDA JOYCE
Retail company executive. **Personal:** Born Jul 21, 1954, Houston, TX. **Educ:** Univ of Houston, BS 1976. **Career:** K-Mart Apparel, asst apparel mgr 1977-78; K-Mart Corporation, fashion mgr 1977-92; Elegant Plus Sizes, manager, 1992-. **Orgs:** Advisor to the distrib educ program MB Smiley High School 1982-; speaker for annual employer/employee banquet for the Distributive Educ Program Smiley HS 1985; fashion show coord K-Mart Store #4080 1986; store reporter for K-Mart Store #4080 1986; mem Sigma Gamma Rho Sor; Reach to Recovery, American Cancer Society, volunteer visitor, 1988-; mem, Natl Women of Achievement Inc. **Honors/Awds:** Trailblazers Achievement Award, South Central Region, Natl Women of Achievement Inc, Houston Chapter, 1994. **Business Addr:** Manager, Elegant Plus Sizes, 4858 Beechnut St, Houston, TX 77096.

DIXON, DIANE L.
Athlete. **Personal:** Born Sep 23, 1964, New York, NY; daughter of Beverly Dixon and David Dixon. **Educ:** Bernard M Baruch College, BBA, 1988. **Career:** George Steinbrenner, public relations, 1989-91; Fitness consultant, 1993-; People Magazine/Time Inc, special events, 1993-94; CEO/Diane Dixon Inc, Signature Collection, "Woman on the Run". **Orgs:** International Special Olympics, supporter, special guest, 1988-; Multiple Sclerosis Society, supporter, special guest, 1990-; Women's Sports Foundation, special guest, 1986-. **Honors/Awds:** Sportsmen's Club for the City of Hope, Victor Awards, 1991; Jesse Owens Foundation, Jesse Owens Award (nominee), 1986; Metropolitan Atheltics Congress, Athlete of the Year, 1985-91; Wheelchair Charities, Athlete of the Year, 1991; Mobil Corp., Overall Indoor Champion (400m), 1986-91; World Indoor Champion, 400 meters, 1991; National US Indoor Champion, 400 meters, 1982-92; 1988 Olympics, Silver Medal (4 x 400 meter); 1984 Olympics, Gold Medal (4 x 400 meter), American Indoor Record Holder (400 meters), 1991; World Indoor Record Holder (440 yards), 1991. **Business Phone:** (212)802-8797.

DIXON, ERNEST
Professional football player. **Personal:** Born Oct 17, 1971, Fort Mill, SC. **Educ:** South Carolina, bachelor's degree in psychology. **Career:** New Orleans Saints, linebacker, 1994-. **Business Addr:** Professional Football Player, New Orleans Saints, 5800 Airline Hwy, Metairie, LA 70003, (504)733-0255.

DIXON, ERNEST THOMAS, JR.
Cleric (retired). **Personal:** Born Oct 13, 1922, San Antonio, TX; married Ernestin Clark; children: Sherryl D Clark, Ernest R, Muriel Jean. **Educ:** Samuel Huston Coll Austin TX, BA (magna cum laude) 1943; Drew Theol Sem Madison NJ, STM 1945; Huston-Tillotson Coll Austin TX, DD 1962; Southwestern Coll Winfield KS, LHD 1973; Baker Univ Baldwin KS, LLD 1973; Westmar Coll Le Mars IA, LittD 1978; KS Wesleyan Salina, LHD 1980. **Career:** KS area United Meth Ch, bishop beginning 1972; Program Council UM Ch & Dayton OH, asst

gen sec 1969-72; Philander Smith Coll Little Rock AR, pres 1965-69; Div of Local Ch Bd of Educ Meth Ch Nashville, staff mem 1952-64; W TX Conf Bd of Edn, exec sec 1951-52; Tuskegee Inst AL, dir rel extension serv 1945-51; Wallace Chapel AME Zion Ch Summit NJ & E Calvary Meth Ch Harlem NY, pastor & asst pastor 1943-45. **Orgs:** Bd of trustee KS Wesleyan Salina; Baker Univ Baldwin KS; Southwestern Coll Winfield KS; St Paul Sch of Theology KS City MO; So Meth Univ Dallas; UnitedTheol Sem Dayton OH; Wesley Med Center Wichita KS; Lydia Patterson Inst El Paso TX; Mt Sequoyah Assembly Fayetteville AR; Gammon Theol Sem Atlanta GA; mem Alpha Phi Alpha Frat Inc.

DIXON, GERALD SCOTT
Professional football player. **Personal:** Born Jun 20, 1969, Charlotte, NC. **Educ:** Univ of South Carolina, attended. **Career:** Cincinnati Bengals, linebacker, 1993-. **Business Addr:** Professional Football Player, Cincinnati Bengals, One Bengals Dr, Cincinnati, OH 45202, (513)621-3550.

DIXON, ISAIAH, JR.
Business executive. **Personal:** Born Dec 23, 1922, Baltimore; married Miriam Millard. **Educ:** Howard U. **Career:** Gen Assembly MD, ins broker realtor delegate. **Orgs:** Mem Peoples Dem Orgn; NAACP; Kappa Alpha Psi Frat; del Dem Mini-Conv KC MO 1974; del Dem Natl Conv New York City 1976. **Honors/Awds:** Cert of honor NAACP 1970; cert of merit Calverton Jr High Sch 1972; cert of Training & in mgmt Joint Ctr for Polit Studies. **Military Serv:** AUS pfc.

DIXON, IVAN N.
Producer, director. **Personal:** Born Apr 6, 1931, Harlem, NY; married Berlie Ray; children: Ivan IV, N'Gai (deceased), Kimara, Nomathande. **Educ:** NC Central Univ, BA, 1954; Western Reserve Univ, grad studies; Karamu House; Amer Theater Wing. **Career:** Duff Anderson "Nothing But a Man" (Movie), actor; Olly Winter "The Final War of Olly Winter" (CBS Playhouse); Kinchloe "Hogan's Heroes"; Asagai "Raisin In The Sun" Broadway & Movie; Bill Cosby Show, Room 222, Magnum PI, Rockford Files, and many others, director. **Orgs:** Mem Academy of Motion Picturs Arts & Sci; Director's Guild of Am; Screen Actor's Guild. **Honors/Awds:** TV emmy nomination 1967; best black actor First World Black Arts Festival Dakar Africa 1966; best Dir image Award NAACP 1972; best prod Image Award NAACP 1974.

DIXON, JAMES WALLACE EDWIN, II
Cleric. **Personal:** Born Nov 12, 1962, Houston, TX; son of James & Carrol Dixon, Sr; married Linda, Nov 29, 1997. **Educ:** Houston Baptist University; Texas Southern University; Houston Graduate School of Theology. **Career:** Northwest Community Bapt Church, sr pastor, currently. **Orgs:** Fellowship Christian Athletes, bd mem; United Way-Texas Gulf Coast, bd mem; National Bapt Convention-America, pres of ministers conf, pres of social justice comm; NAACP. **Honors/Awds:** Prairie View A&M University, Humanitarian Award, 1986; TX Gospel Music Awards, Outstanding Community Service; Olympic Games Touchbearer, 1996. **Business Addr:** Senior Pastor, Northwest Community Bapt Church, 1023 Pinemount St, Houston, TX 77018.

DIXON, JIMMY
Elected official. **Personal:** Born Dec 9, 1943, Devereux, GA; divorced; children: Glenda, Thaddeus, Taranda. **Educ:** GA Military, 1972, 1974, 1976; Univ of GA, 1975-78; GA Coll, 1976-81. **Career:** Central State Hospital, supr 1964-74; Sparta Parks & Recreation, dir 1975-79; Rheem Air Condition Div, storekeeper 1979-; Hancock Co Board of Ed, chmn 1978-. **Orgs:** Superintendent Jones Chapel AME Sunday School 1971-; mem Jones Chapel AME Steward Bd 1974-, GA School Bd Assoc 1975-, Stolkin Temple #22 1976-, Lebar Consistory #28 1976; GSBA Positions & Resolutions Comm 1979-; committee mem Democratic Party of GA 1982-85. **Honors/Awds:** Appreciation Plaque Blackstone Shrine Club 1977. **Home Addr:** 728 Reynolds Cemetary Rd, Sparta, GA 31087.

DIXON, JOHN FREDERICK
Marketing manager. **Personal:** Born Feb 19, 1949, Boston, MA. **Educ:** Howard U, BA 1971; Columbia Univ Grad Bus Sch, MBA 1973; Columbia Univ Tchr's Coll, PhD Work 1980-. **Career:** Essence Communications Inc, marketing & research serv dir 1978-; Black Sports Magazine, marketing dir 1976-78; Standrad Brands Inc, asst prod mgr 1974-76; Xerox Corp, sales representative 1973-74; US Dept of Agriculture, agriculture marketing specialist 1971. **Orgs:** Consult Africa Mag 1976; consult Horn of Africa Mag 1977-78; mem Am Marketing Assn 1978-; mem Advertising Research Found 1978-; mem Media Research Dirs Assn 1979-; world mem Intl House 1971-; mem African-Am Inst 1973-; mem Alliance Francaise-French Inst 1975-78; mem NAACP 1979-. **Honors/Awds:** Recipient educ fellowship Council on Grad Mgmt Columbia Univ 1971-73; cofounder Red-T Productions 1975-; co-inventor "Claim to Fame" Black History Game 1977; pub "Pony Goes After Young Blacks with 'follow the Leader' Tack" 1977; creator "Battle of New Orleans" 64-page fight Prog (Muhammad Ali vs Leon Spinks) 1978; established In-House Essential Media Ad Agency Essence Mag 1979-; distinguished serv award Harlem Teams for Self-Help 1979. **Business Addr:** Essence Communications Inc, 1500 Broadway, New York, NY 10036.

DIXON, JOHN M.
Business executive. **Personal:** Born Jan 25, 1938, Chicago, IL; divorced; children: Kwane Dubois. **Educ:** Univ MT, BS 1959; New England Sch Law, JD 1966; Boston U, MBA 1976. **Career:** Sonesta NY, regional sales mgr 1968-70; Sheraton Mtr Inns, dir promotion 1970-73; Hyatt Regency O'Hare, exec asst mgr 1973; Burlingame CA, gen mgr 1973; Hyatt Regency, resident mgr 1974-; Hyatt Regency Cambridge, gen mgr 1975-. **Military Serv:** AUS spec 1962-64. **Business Addr:** 575 Memorial Dr, Cambridge, MA 02139.

DIXON, JULIAN C.
Congressman. **Personal:** Born Aug 8, 1934, Washington, DC; married Bettye Lee; children: Cary Gordon. **Educ:** CA State Univ at LA, BS Polit Sci; Southwestern Univ, LLB 1967. **Career:** 49th Dist CA State Assembly, democratic assemblyman 1972-78; 32nd Dist US House of Representatives, member, 1978-. **Orgs:** Congressional Black Caucus, chairman, 1983-84; Democratic Natl Convention Rules Comm, chairman, 1984; US Military Academy, bd of visitors, 1981-86; Appropriations Subcomm; Congressional Black Caucus Foundation, president, 1986-90; Appropriations Subcomm on the District of Columbia, ranking, 1978; CA Assembly Democratic Caucus, chairman; Democratic Steering and Policy Committee, 1993; House Committee on Standards of Offical Conduct, chairman, 1985-91. **Honors/Awds:** California Congressional Recognition Program, cit ed as one of California's Most Effective Legislators, 1992; Pathfinder District of Los Angeles Area Council, Good Scout of the Year Award; SCLC-West, Community and Public Service Drum Major Award; United Teachers of Los Angeles, Legislative Activites of the Year; Politics in America, named one of 12 Unsung Heroes in Congress, 1985. **Special Achievements:** First Black mem in the history of Congress to chair an Appropriations Subcommittee; authored resolutions passed by the House that called for the awarding of the Presidential Medal of Freedom to Dr Benjamin Mays and the declaration of Sept 1983 as "Sickle Cell Anemia Awareness Month"; orig cosponsor of Civil Rights Act; orig cosponsor of Equal Rights Amendment; introduced first economic sanction measures against apartheid in South Africa to be signed into law. **Business Addr:** Congressman, US House of Representatives, 2252 Rayburn HOB, Washington, DC 20515.

DIXON, LEON MARTIN
Medical administrator, physician. **Personal:** Born Nov 12, 1927, Brooklyn, NY; son of Helen Moody Dixon and Leon M Dixon; married Alfonso Baxter; children: Deborah, Carolyn Knight, Cynthia, Suzanne, Leon II. **Educ:** Howard Univ, BS 1949, MD 1953. **Career:** Med/Cardiology Colorado Un Sch of Med, instr 1963-65; US Walson Army Hosp, hosp cmdr 1973-77; Reynolds Metals Co, dir Macmillan Med Ctr, currently. **Orgs:** Cnsltn Disaster Plng Reynolds Metal 1977-, Cardiology Med First Army Area 1965-69; chrmn Pblc Hlth Prvntv Med Richmond Acad of Med 1980-81; mem Chesterfield Cnty Drug Abuse Advsr Com 1979-80. **Honors/Awds:** Phys for Astronant Pgm Gemini Mercury NASA 1965-1969; articles pblchd Physiology of Heart Meningitis, Congenital Heart Disease, Chemotherapy of Tumors. **Military Serv:** AUS col; Legion of Merit Two Oak Leaf Clusters 1969, 71, 77. **Business Addr:** Dir MacMillan Med Ctr, Reynolds Metals Co, 1951 Reymet Rd, Richmond, VA 23234.

DIXON, LEONARD BILL
Juvenile facility executive. **Personal:** Born Aug 1, 1956, Albany, GA; son of Clarence & Ruby Dixon; married Adrian, May 25, 1980; children: Joseph, Rosalind. **Educ:** Southwest Baptist University, BA, 1980; Nova University, masters degree, 1990. **Career:** Department of Health & Rehab Svcs, group leader, 1980-82, supervisor, 1982-85, superintendent, 1985-90; Department Juv Jus Svc, program operations administrator, 1990-95; Wayne County Comm College, adjunct professor, 1995-; Department of Community Justice, executive director, 1995-. **Orgs:** National Juvenile Detention Association; American Correctional Association; Nova University, adjunct staff mem; National Juv Jus Group-Children's Defense Fund; EEOC-Dade County; The Wellington Group; ACA Committee Florida District XI, chr; Community Tree House, Detroit Michigan. **Honors/Awds:** US Congressional Senators, Juv Jus Reform Paper Presentor; Southwest Baptist University, MO, Athletic Scholarship; All American High School Basketball Team. **Business Addr:** Executive Director, Wayne County Juvenile Detention Facility, 1333 E Forest, Detroit, MI 48207-1026, (313)833-2860.

DIXON, LORRAINE L.
City official. **Personal:** Born Jun 18, Chicago, IL; daughter of Edra & Edward Godwin. **Educ:** Chicago State University, BS, 1972. **Career:** Committee on Zoning, chief zoning administrator, 1988-89; Committee on Energy and the Environment, chief of staff, 1989-90; 8th Ward, appointed alderman, 1990; Committee on Human Relations, chair, 1991; City Council, prefabricateds pro tempore, 1993; Sub-comm MBE/WBE/Affirmative Action Matters, chmn, 1994; Committee on the Budget & Government Operations, chmn, 1994; City of Chicago, elected alderman, 8th ward, 1995-. **Orgs:** Christ Temple Cathedral, Ch of Christ Holiness, lifelong mem; Operation PUSH Rainbow Coalition, 1981-; 8th Ward, Regular Democratic Organization, 1972-; Open Hands of Chicago, bd of dirs, 1993; 87th St Chamber of Commerce, bd of dirs, 1993; Democratic National Convention, delegate, 1992; Jackson Park Hosp, bd of dirs, 1992; United Negro College Fund, 1991. **Honors/Awds:** Jackson Park Hosp, Humanitarian of the Year Awd, 1995; Mr Silas Store for Men, Woman of the Year Awd, 1995; 87th St Chamber of Commerce, Exceptional Service to the Community, 1995; The South Shore Ministers Association, Service to the Community, 1995; American Heart Association, Service to the Heart Association & its Mission, 1995. **Special Achievements:** Co-sponsored "Contractor & Vendor Fair for Minority & Women-Owned Business," 1995; first woman elected to chair the Comm on the Budget & Government Operations in Chicago, 1994; first female president pro-tempore of Chicago City Council. **Business Addr:** Alderman, Chicago City Council, 121 N LaSalle, City Hall, Rm 207, Chicago, IL 60602, (312)744-3075.

DIXON, LOUIS TENNYSON
Engineering manager. **Personal:** Born Dec 13, 1941; son of Enid L Dixon and Eitel V Dixon; married Lora M; children: Michael. **Educ:** Howard Univ, BS 1968; Johns Hopkins Univ, PhD 1973. **Career:** Ford Motor Co, principal rsch scientist/sr rsch scientist 1973-76, mgr chemistry dept 1976-78, principal staff engineer 1978-86, engineering associate, 1986-89, mgr, 1989-. **Orgs:** Mem Amer Chem Soc; Soc of Automotive Engrs; Soc of Manufacturing Engrs; Standards Engineering Society, vice pres Intl Club 1966-67; chmn People-To-People 1967-68; pres Phi Lambda Upsilon 1972-73. **Honors/Awds:** Publications, "Infrared Studies of Isotope Effects for Hydrogen Absorption on Zinc Oxide" Journal of Amer Chem Soc 1972; "The Nature of Molecular Hydrogen Absorbed on Zinc Oxide" Journal of Physical Chem 1973; "Infrared Active Species of Hydrogen Absorbed by Alumina-Supported Platium" Journal of Catalysis 1975; "Hydrogen Absorption by Alumina-Supported Supported Platinum" Journal of Catalysis 1975; "Foaming & Air Entrainment in Automatic Transmission Fluids" Soc of Auto Engr 1976; "Fuel Economy -Contributor of the Rear Axle Lubricant" Soc Auto Engr 1977. **Business Addr:** Mgr, Worldwide Materials & Component Standards, Ford Motor Company, Ste 7000, 330 Town Center Dr, Dearborn, MI 48126.

DIXON, MARGARET A.
Organization executive. **Personal:** Born in Columbia, SC; married Octavius; children: three. **Educ:** Allen University; Hunter College, MA; NYU, MA; Fordham University, prof diploma in educational leadership; Nova Southeastern University, EdD. **Career:** New York City Schools, teacher; Brooklyn College Teacher Education program, supervising principal; SC State Department of Education, consultant; Allen University Teacher Education Program, dir; Amer Assn of Retired Persons, pres, currently. **Orgs:** AARP, Minority Affairs Initiative, spokesperson, 1988-92, vice pres, 1992-94, pres-elect, 1994-96, pres, 1996-; AARP Exec and Finance Committee, national legislative council, Andrus Foundation, chair, bd of trustees, board strategic planning committee, chair, board operations committee; National Retired Teachers Assoc Task Force; literacy tutor; Meals-on-Wheels, volunteer. **Honors/Awds:** Delta Sigma Theta, Living Legacy Award for Outstanding Community Service; Ford Foundation Fellowship; US Office of Education Graduate Fellowship; Fordham University, Alumni Achievement Award; Hunter College, Alumni Hall of Fame; National Caucus and Center on Black Aged, Living Legacy Award; National Black Caucus of State Legislators, Nation Builder Award. **Special Achievements:** First African-American president of AARP. **Business Addr:** President, AARP (American Association of Retired Persons), 601 E St, NW, Washington, DC 20049, (202)434-2440.

DIXON, RICHARD CLAY
Mayor. **Career:** City of Dayton, OH, mayor, currently. **Business Addr:** Mayor, City of Dayton, PO Box 22, Dayton, OH 45401.

DIXON, RICHARD NATHANIEL
State official. **Personal:** Born Apr 17, 1938, Westminster, MD; married Grayson Lee; children: Timothy A, Richard N. **Educ:** Morgan State Coll, BS 1960; Morgan State Coll, MBA 1975. **Career:** Provident Hosp, hosp adm 1968-69; Morgan State U, asst prof sch of bus 1976-; Merrill Lynch, delegate/stock broker, asst vice pres; Maryland Dept of Treasury, treasurer, currently. **Orgs:** Mem Bd of Educ 1970-78; pres former stdnt Robert M Sch 1970; sec MD Assn Bd of Educ 1973-74; chair of clinicl finding new ways to finance educ Natl Schl Boards Conv 1974; mem Morgan State Univ Found 1975-; pres and first black Cnty Sch Bd 1975-76; trustee Middle State Assoc of Colls & Schools; mem chmn Budget & Audit Comm, House of Delegates, Maryland House of Pensions; chmn, Joint Committee on Pensions, Maryland House of Delegates. **Honors/Awds:** First black Bd of Educ; 1st blk pres of County Sch Bd Maryland; Future Black Leader in Baltimore, Baltimore Sunpapers 1979; selected top 5 of 50 new delegates 1984; selected to be among top 25 members, House of Delegates; Honorary Doctor of Laws, Western Maryland Coll. **Special Achievements:** First African American state treasurer of Maryland. **Military Serv:** AUS capt med serv corps 1960-68. **Business Addr:** Treasurer, Maryland Dept of Treasury, 80 Calvert St, Baltimore, MD 21202.

DIXON, ROSCOE
State representative. **Personal:** Born Sep 20, 1949, Gilmore, AR; son of Roscoe Dixon, Sr; married Gloria Dobbins. **Educ:** Savannah State Coll, 1971; Univ of Guan Juato, Spanish 1974; Memphis State Univ, BA Political Science 1975. **Career:** Congressman Harold Ford, south office dir 1975; insurance executive 1977-81; Black Merchants Assn, exec dir 1981-; State of TN, state representative. **Orgs:** Capt commander service battery 3-115 field artillery TN Army Natl Guard 1973-; bd mem Mid-South Regional Blood Ctr 1983-85; bd mem Dogwood Village; bd mem Memphis Health Center 1984-85; bd mem Operation PUSH Memphis 1975-. **Military Serv:** AUS spec 5 2 yrs; Good Conduct Medal; Army Commendation. **Home Addr:** 3592 Huckleberry, Memphis, TN 38116. **Business Addr:** State Representative, State of Tennessee, #17 Legislative Plaza, Nashville, TN 37219.

DIXON, RUTH F.
Educator. **Personal:** Born Sep 22, 1931, Camden, NJ; married George Dixon; children: Cheryl Yvette, Brian Duane. **Educ:** BA 1953, MA 1965, EdD 1977. **Career:** Camden City Schools, elementary & secondary teacher 14 yrs, admin 3 yrs; NJ State Dept of Educ, supvr 2 yrs; Rutgers Univ, assoc prof of educ. **Orgs:** Ed consult State Coll 1965-71; mem State Assoc of Adult Ed 1965-; exec bd Black Peoples Unity Movement 1973-; exec bd of ed Oppty Fund Prog 1971-; mayors adv council 1974-; bd of ed Lay Comm 1972-; mem Kappa Delta Pi 1976; bd of trustees Camden Cty Coll 1984; mem council Camden Cty Private Indust 1983, Natl Assoc of Notaries 1984; bd of dir Soc of Ed & Scholars 1984, NJ Assoc of Black Ed 1978-, Our Lady of Lourdes Comm Adv Comm 1984, BPUM Child Devel Ctrs Adv Comm 1983, Dir of Disting Amer in Ed & Comm Serv 1980. **Honors/Awds:** BPUM-EDC Comm Awd 1973; Kappa Delta Pi; BPUM Spec Awd Outstanding Ed 1976; Soc for Ed & Schol Phi Delta Kappa Natl Honor Soc 1975; Pi Lambda Theta Natl Honor Soc 1975. **Business Addr:** Associate Professor of Educ, Rutgers Univ, 311 N Fifth St, Camden, NJ 08102.

DIXON, TAMECKA
Professional basketball player. **Personal:** Born Dec 14, 1975; daughter of Russell ''Boo'' Bowers. **Educ:** Kansas, attended. **Career:** Los Angeles Sparks, guard, 1997-. **Business Addr:** Professional Basketball Player, Los Angeles Sparks, 3900 W Manchester Blvd, Inglewood, CA 90306, 800-978-9622.

DIXON, TOM L.
Educator. **Personal:** Born Jan 29, 1932, Shreveport, LA; married Sarah Hunter; children: Abigail, Cleon. **Educ:** Gramblins State U, BS 1959; Bradley U, MS 1968; Prairie View A&M Univ Northwestern State University, Advance Study. **Career:** Walnut Hill High School, teacher 1959; JS Clark Jr High, teacher 1960-61; Li'near High School; teacher 1961-71; Green Oaks High School, teacher 14 yrs; Caddo Parish School Bd, supr Vocational Educ. **Orgs:** Caddo Educ Assn; LA Educ Assn; Natl Educ Assn; chmn LA Indsl Arts Conf 1976; chmn Banquet LTAA 1975; Indsl Arts Curriculum Plng Com; Am Indsl Arts Assn; 1st blk pres North Shreveport Kiwanis Club 1973-74; pres Phi Beta Sigma Frat; bd dir YMCA. **Honors/Awds:** Am Legion Indsl Arts Tchr Awrd Northwestern State Univ 1968-69; Shreveport Times Edctr of Yr Awrd; outstndng serv prfsn & cmnty 1971; pres Kiwanis Club Awrd Outstndng Ldrshp. **Military Serv:** AUS corpl 1953-55. **Business Addr:** Caddo Parish School Board, PO Box 37000, Shreveport, LA 71103.

DIXON, VALENA ALICE
Public affairs director. **Personal:** Born Jan 11, 1953, Philadelphia, PA; daughter of Alice Dixon and James Dixon; children: James. **Educ:** St Joseph University; University of South Alabama; Westchester State College, BSEd. **Career:** Mobile County Public Schools, educator, 1974-79; Reading School District, educator, 1974-79; Urban League, Philadelphia Chapter, employment counselor, 1979-81; Temple University, community resource specialist, 1981-82; Crisis Intervention Network Inc, administrative & program manager, 1982-87; Greater Media Cable of Philadelphia, community relations manager, 1987-92; Philadelphia Housing Authority, public affairs director, 1992-. **Orgs:** Center for Literacy, board member, 1990-94; Korean and American Friendship Association, board member, 1991-; American Women in Radio and Television, Philadelphia Chapter, president, 1992-; National Forum for Black Public Administrators, 1992-; Public Relations Society of America, 1992-; Philadelphia Public Relations Association, 1990-; Philadelphia Association of Black Journalists, 1990-93; National Black Media Coalition, 1990-92; Linda Creed Breast Cancer Foundation, 1993-. **Honors/Awds:** NAACP, Outstanding Community Service, 1991; WUSL Radio, Community Service Award, 1993; CORPP, Community Service, 1989; United Negro College Fund, Vounteer/Telethon Committee, 1991; Mayor's office of Community Service, Community Service Awards, 1989-91; Natl Political Congress of Black Women, Recognition. **Special Achievements:** Graduate, Leadership Institute, Philadelphia Urban League, 1991; visiting professional, Ohio University, School of Communications, 1990; ''Profile Series,'' C-SPAN, 1992. **Home Addr:** 1224 S Melville St, Philadelphia, PA 19143, (215)222-5434.

DIXON, WILLIAM R.
Musician, composer, educator. **Personal:** Born Oct 5, 1925, Nantucket, MA; son of Louise Wade Williams and William Robert Dixon; divorced; children: William Jr, Claudia Gayle, William II. **Educ:** Hartnette Conservatory Music, diploma 1951. **Career:** UN Secretariat NYC, clk intl civil servant 1956-62; free lance musician composer NYC, 1962-67; Columbia Univ Teachers Coll, mem 1967-70; George Washington Univ, composer-in-residence 1967; Conservatory of Univ of the Streets NYC, dir 1967-68; OH State Univ, guest artist in residence 1967; Bennington Coll VT, mem faculty dept dance 1968-95, chmn black music division 1973-85. **Orgs:** Vis prof Univ WI Madison 1971-72; lectr painting & music Mus Modern Art Verona Italy 1982; Found of UN Jazz Soc NYC; arch Jazz Composers' Guild for Performance of Contemporary Amer Black Music; organizer October Revolution: a Concert Series; recs include Archie Shepp Bil Dixon Quartet 1962; Bill Dixon 7-Tette 1963; Intents & Purposes: The Bill Dixon Orchestra 1967; For Franz 1976; New Music Second Wave 1979; Bill Dixon in Italy 1980; considerations 1 and 2 Bill Dixon 1980, 82; Bill Dixon in the Labrinth 1983; paintings exhibited Ferrari Gallery Verona Italy 1982; exhibited paintings Multimedia Contemporary Art Gallery Brescia Italy 1982; mem Amer Fed of Musicians; panel member, National Endowment for the Arts, 1990-; advisory committee mem, New England Foundation for the Arts, 1988-91. **Honors/Awds:** Honorary member, Duke Ellington Society; recordings: ''November 1981,'' 1981; ''Bill Dixon: 1970-73,'' 1982; ''Collection,'' 1985; ''Thoughts,'' 1987; ''Son of Sisyphus,'' 1990;'' Vade Mecum, '' 1994: ''The Enchanted Messenger,'' 1996; ''Vade Mecum II,'' 1997; Musician of the Year, Jazz Magazine, 1976; Giancarlo Testoni Award for Best Recordings of the Year, 1981; Broadcast Music Inc, Jazz Pioneer Award, 1984; author, L'Opera: A Collection of Writings and Letters, Etc, 1986; Distinguished Visitor in the Arts, Middlebur Coll, 1986; Fellow, Vermont Academy of Arts & Sciences; International Trumpet Guild Recording: VADE MECUm, 1994; Exhibition of Paintings, Ufer Palast, Furth, Nurembert, Germany, 1990; Retrospective of Music Compositions, 1963-91, Radio Station WKCR Columbia Univ; Restrospective of Paintings, Southern VT Coll, 1968-91; Exhibition of Lithographs in Villeurbanne, France, 1994; Exhibition of Lithographs, Chittenden Bank, Bennington VT, 1994-95; Subject in Documentary Film, IMAGINE THE SOUND, Toronto Canada, 1982; Conducted Orchestra Workshop in: Vienna, Austria, 1985; NYC, 1988; Pori Finland, 1991; Israel, 1990; Trumpet Soloist, Celebration Orchestra, Conducted by Tony Oxley, Berlin, 1994; Workshop in Improvisation/Music, Federal Republic of Germany, 1990; Master Class in Improvisation/Music, Villeurbanne, France, 1994; Exhibition of Lithographs, Skoto Gallery, NYC, 1996. **Military Serv:** AUS 1944-46. **Business Addr:** Professor, Music Dept, Dance Dept, Bennington Coll, Route 67A, Bennington, VT 05201.

DIXON, WILLIE
Government official. **Career:** Washington County, AL, commissioner, currently. **Business Addr:** Commissioner, Washington County, PO Box 146, Chatom, AL 36518, (334)246-6670.

DIXON, YVONNE T.
Labor relations executive. **Personal:** Born in Washington, DC. **Educ:** Earlham College, political science, BS (cum laude); NYU, law degree. **Career:** National Labor Relations Board, Office of Appeals, dir, currently. **Special Achievements:** First African-American woman to head NLRB'S Office of Appeals. **Business Addr:** Director, Office of Appeals, National Labor Relations Board, 1099 14th St, NW, Washington, DC 20570, (202)273-3760.

DIXON-BROWN, TOTLEE
Broadcast journalist, television and radio producer. **Personal:** Born Dec 1, New York, NY; daughter of Joyce Levy Dixon and Arthur Stanley Dixon; married John M Brown Sr (divorced 1977); children: J Michael Jr. **Educ:** University of Toledo, BA, theatre/speech, 1968; City College of New York, 1969-70; Institute of New Cinema Artists, New York, NY, 1977-78. **Career:** Syndicated producer, ''For You Black Woman,'' NY State beauty pageants and television specials, 1977-79; ABC-TV, camerawoman, electronic graphics engineer, 1978-86; WWOC Radio, news anchor, community affairs director, 1986-87; National Black Network, radio news anchor, 1987-91; WNYC Radio, news anchor & announcer, 1992-95; media consultant, 1995-. **Orgs:** President/founder, Black Media Women, 1990-; Natl Assn Black Journalists, 1988-90; Delta Sigma Theta, 1968-; Natl Academy of TV Arts & Sciences, 1981-89; NABET, 11 & 16, 1978-. **Honors/Awds:** Emmy Award, NATAS, Summer Olympics, 1984; Media Workshop Award, 1980; Outstanding Community Service, Cotton Club & Intl Youth Leadership Institute, 1991; Outstanding Dramatizer, Ft Benning Dramatizers, 1970; Outstanding Communications, St Ephesus Church, 1991; 2nd Place, Best Director, 3rd US Army Tournament of Plays, 1970. **Business Addr:** PO Box 1143, Ansonia Station, New York, NY 10021, (914)576-5397.

DOANES-BERGIN, SHARYN F.
Employee relations manager. **Personal:** Born in Atlanta, GA; daughter of Mr & Mrs Onzelo Doanes; married Michael Bergin; children: Jennifer, Jessica. **Educ:** Paine Coll, BA 1969; Atlanta Law Sch, JD 1978, ML 1979; Central MI Univ, MPA 1983. **Career:** Honeywell Information Systems, employee relations mgr, 8 yrs; The New York Times Regional Newspaper Group Atlanta, employee relations mgr, currently. **Orgs:** GA Exec Women 1980-87; vice pres Paine Coll Alumni 1982-87; vice pres Georgia Leukemia Soc 1984-87; trustee Paine Coll 1983-88; Odyssey 1985-. **Honors/Awds:** Harlem YMCA, Black Achiever Award, 1992. **Business Addr:** Manager Employee Relations, New York Times Newspaper, 3414 Peachtree St, Atlanta, GA 30326.

DOBBINS, ALBERT GREENE, III
Urban planning executive. **Personal:** Born Jul 25, 1949, Detroit, MI; son of Barbara J Williams Dobbins and Albert Greene Dobbins Sr; divorced; children: Adia Ginneh. **Educ:** Univ of MI, BSME 1971; VA Commonwealth Univ, MURP 1983. **Career:** EI DuPont de Nemours & Co, process engineer 1972-77; City of Richmond VA, sr planner 1977-78; Neuair Inc, sr project engineer 1978-80; Philip Morris USA, rsch engineer 1980-81; Richmond Renaissance Inc, associate director 1983-89; Brooklyn Office New York City Planning, deputy director. **Orgs:** Mem Amer Society of Mechanical Engineers 1972-81; mem Amer Planning Assn 1981-84; dir Greater Richmond Transit Co 1984-89; mem Natl Forum for Black Public Administrators 1984-86; dir Black History Museum and Cultural Center of Virginia Inc 1986-90; mem Richmond Jazz Society 1980-90; mem Concerned Black Men of Richmond VA Inc 1987-89. **Honors/Awds:** Eagle Scout Boy Scouts of Amer 1963; Scholarship Awd Natl Merit 1967; Outstanding Student Amer Inst of Certified Planners 1983; Harvard Univ, Loeb Fellow, 1989-90.

DOBBINS, ALPHONDUS MILTON
Community worker. **Personal:** Born Feb 17, 1924, Corsicana, TX; son of Mr & Mrs Edd Dobbins; married LaVerta Pearl Love; children: Myrna D Ford, Blanche B, Alphondus M II, Cornelius L. **Educ:** Bishops Coll, 1942; Southern Univ, 1945; Prairie View Univ, 1945; TN A&I Univ, BS 1946; St Louis Univ, Soc Work Workshops, 1948; Washington Univ, 1953; Millikin Univ, 1956. **Career:** Smith County School, voc agr teacher, 1946-48; Neighborhood House, boys work dir, 1948-53; A E Staley Mfg Co, process oper 1953-. **Orgs:** Mem, Free & Accepted Masons, 1946-, NAACP 1948-, Antioch Missionary Bapt Church 1953-; driver Bloodmobiles 1953-; chmn of ''Frontiers Comm House'' 1968-; mem bd dir Amer Red Cross 1969-75, 1976-82, 1984-89; chrmn Green Thumb Oper Amer Red Cross 1970-; planning comm Amer Red Cross 1976-79, 1980-81; Chmn, County Devel, 1977-79; Cty Dev Comm 1977-80; bd dir Boys Club of Amer 1977-; Comm Home Environmental Learning Proj 1977-; Public Relations Comm 1980-82, 1983-; adv Blue Book of Macon Cty 1983; Comm Health Serv 1981-82; Sr Citizens Adv Comm Secr of State IL 1983-; chmn African Famine Relief Campaign Northern Territory Amer Red Cross. **Honors/Awds:** Work w/sr citizen's program, 1970-; life mem, IL PTA 1967; leadership bd dir, Amer Red Cross, 1969-75, 1976-82; Sertoma Breakfast & Noon Mankind Award 1975; Frontiers Distg Srv Award 1977; Univ of IL Coop Extention Serv for Comm Serv Helping Others 1978-80; In Recognition of Outstanding Efforts to Frontiers Intl Award Amer Bakeries 1979; IL, WI, IPBO Elks of W Civil Liberties 1979; Heart of IL Div Vol of the Year Award 1979; United Way Comm Civic Culture Award 1980-81; Macon Co Chapter Amer Red Cross Clara Barton Award; Distinguished Serv Award Decatur Jaycees 1986; Outstanding Citizenship Awd Decatur Noon Kiwanis; Special Appreciation for Contribution & Sustaining Efforts Boys Club of Decatur 1986; Commemorative Medal of Honor Amer Biographical Inst 1986; Grand Marshal, Decatur Commun Christmas Parade, 1989; American Red Cross, Certificate of Recognition, Midwestern Operations Headquarters Recommendation for The National Good Neighbor Award, 1989-90; Illinois State Medical Society, Humanitarian Award, 1991; The Clara Barton Honor Award for Meritorious Volunteer Leadership, 1992; Amer Red Cross, Green Thumb Operation, 1992; New Salem Baptist Church, Comm Special Recognition Award, 1993; Omega Pi Phi Fraternity, Citizen of the Year, 1993; Macon County Red Cross- Mr Al M Dobbins Award, 1994; Decatur Club of Frontier Intl Inc, Lifetime of Service Award, 1994; College Futures of Richland Community College, African-American Male Conference Salute, 1995; Al Dobbins. **Home Addr:** 806 W King St, Decatur, IL 62522.

DOBBINS, JOHN STEVE
Utility company executive. **Personal:** Born Mar 29, 1948, Cincinnati, OH; son of Ruth Fields Dobbins (deceased) and John A Dobbins (deceased); married Virginia Ferguson, Dec 11, 1984; children: Charlotte M Martin, Aleisha T, Anthony L Watson (stepson). **Educ:** University of Cincinnati, AS, 1975, BS, 1987; Executive Public Policy Institute, Washington, DC, CC, 1989. **Career:** The Cincinnati Gas & Electric Co., customer services administrator, 1984-86, public affairs representative, lobbyist, 1987-90, community services director, 1990-94, mgr, comm affairs, 1994-. **Orgs:** American Association of Blacks in Energy, 1988-; Sickle Cell Awareness Group of Greater Cincinnati, chairman of the board, 1990-; Ohio Center for The Performing Arts, Cincinnati, board member, 1992-; Citizens Against Substance Abuse, board member, 1991-; Leadership Cincinnati, steering committee member, 1991-; Cincinnati-Hamilton County Community Action Agency, board member; American Gas Association, consumer & community affairs

committee, education committee, 1991-; Edison Electric Institute, consumer affairs committee, educational services committee, utility speakers committee, 1991-; Black Male Coalition, 1990-; NAACP, 1980-; Greater Cincinnati Chamber of Commerce, education committee, chair 1991-; Dan Beard Council Boy Scouts of America, board member; Greater Cincinnati Convention and Visitors Bureau, board member. **Honors/Awds:** NAACP, Cincinnati, Special Award, 1982; YMCA, Cincinnati, Black Achiever, 1980; Greater Cincinnati Chamber of Commerce, Leadership Cincinnati Graduate, 1990; Leadership Ohio Graduate, 1994. **Business Phone:** (513)287-2520.

DOBBINS, LUCILLE R.

Company Executive. **Personal:** married George; children: Diane. **Educ:** Roosevelt Univ, Acctg 1968; IL CPA Cert 1970. **Career:** Hyde Park Fed Savings & Loan, asst treas 1963-69; Blackman Kallick & Co, auditor 1969-73; Harris Trust & Savings Bank, vice pres 1974-84; City of Chicago Dept of Plng, 1st dep commissioner 1984-86; City of Chicago Mayor's Office, chief financial planning officer; Resolution Resources, pres, currently. **Orgs:** Natl Soc of CPA's, IL Soc of CPA's; natl adv Black Career Women Inc, Lambda Alpha Intl Hon Land Econ Soc. **Honors/Awds:** Entrepreneur of the Year, 1994. **Business Addr:** President, Resolutions Resources, 111 W Washington, Ste 1700, Chicago, IL 60602.

DOBBS, JOHN WESLEY

Educator. **Personal:** Born Oct 8, 1931, Grenada, MS; married Mildred; children: Kiley, Kelly. **Educ:** Wstrn MI U, BA 1954; Wayne St U, ME 1960; MI St U, PhD 1975. **Career:** Hempseatd Public Schools, supr of schools; MI Dept of Educ, asst supt; Detroit School System, teacher, counselor, asst prin, prin. **Orgs:** Staff lsn St Adv Cncl for Eql Educ Opp; lsn St Task Frc on Cnsl Guid; coord Task Frc on Out of Sch Out of Wrk Yth; rep MI Commn on Crmnl Jstc; ad com MI Hum Serv Ntwrk; mem AASA; NAACP; Urban Leag; Nat Allnc of Blck Sch Edc; ASCD; grad faculty Eastern MI Univ; bd dir Metro Detroit-Youth Found. **Honors/Awds:** Pres awd Nat Allnc of Blck Sch Educs; outst admin awd Dtrt Soc of Blck Educs; Resolution of Appreciation State of MI Concurrent House of Rep 1983; Outstanding Educ Leader & Humanitarian Awd Hempstead NY Bd of Educ 1986; Disting Educator in Support of Black Children Awd Leadership & Training Inst of Hempstead 1986; Mayor's Proclamation Outstanding Community Leader Village of Hempstead Long Island 1986. **Military Serv:** AUS spec-5 1956-58.

DOBSON, BYRON EUGENE

Journalist. **Personal:** Born Jan 26, 1957, Easton, MD; son of Elizabeth Young Dobson and William Edward Dobson. **Educ:** Bowie State University, Bowie, MD, BA, communications, 1979; University of Arizona, Editing Program for Minority Journalists, graduate fellow, 1985. **Career:** WEMD-Radio, Easton, MD, news assistant, 1979-80; Boca Raton News, Boca Raton, FL, reporter, assistant city editor, city editor, 1980-90; Tallahassee Democrat, Tallahassee, FL, night city editor, 1990-. **Orgs:** Former president/charter member, Palm Beach Association of Black Journalists, 1988-90; member, National Association of Black Journalists, 1990-; member, Kappa Alpha Psi Fraternity Inc, 1984-; member, Blacks in Communications, 1990-. **Honors/Awds:** Featured in The Bulletin, Minorities in the Newsroom, May-June, 1987; Corene J. Elam Communications Award, Bowie State University, 1979. **Business Addr:** Night City Editor, The Tallahassee Democrat, PO Box 990, Tallahassee, FL 32303.

DOBSON, DOROTHY ANN

Social worker (retired). **Personal:** Born May 10, 1934, Chester, VA; daughter of Julia Morton Pryor and Alfred Pryor; married James Dobson, Oct 16, 1957; children: Jacquelyn, Kimberley, Gina. **Educ:** North Carolina A&T State University, Greensboro, NC, BS, 1957. **Career:** Monroe County Department Social Service, Rochester, NY, adult protection caseworker, 1958-89. **Orgs:** President, Jack & Jill of America Inc, 1964-66; president, NC A&T Alumni Association, 1980-82; board of directors, United Way of Rochester, evaluation committee, 1975-; board of directors and other committees of YWCA, 1975-81; board of directors & various committee, Girl Scouts of Genesee Alley, 1970-80; founding member and current president of Greater Rochester AARP, 1989-; elected delegate, New York State, AARP Biennial Convention, San Antonio, 1992; elected delegate, Black Catholic Congress, New Orleans, 1992. **Honors/Awds:** Urban League of Rochester Community Service Award, 1977; Monroe County Human Relations Community Services, 1982; Black Catholic Family Award, 1983; Volunteer Service Award United Way of Rochester, 1984; Dedicated Service Award NC A&T State University, 1987. **Business Addr:** Social Worker, c/o Emmelyn Logan-Baldwin, 171 State St, Rochester, NY 14614.

DOBSON, HELEN SUTTON

Educator. **Personal:** Born Jan 6, 1926, Wheeling, WV; married Robert J Dobson; children: Robert, Leisa. **Educ:** Bluefield State Coll, BS 1959; extra 15 hrs WV Univ Marshall Univ. **Career:** Beckley Jr HS, classroom teacher. **Orgs:** Announcer Trent & Durgan Funeral Home Prog; teacher Raleigh Co Bd of Educ; Delta Sigma Theta Sorority. **Honors/Awds:** Serv Awd Bluefield State Coll; Honor Awd Sec of State A James Manehim; All Coll Achievement Soc NY; WWNR Radio Apprec Awd; 1st black women to sing atGov's Inauguration Gov John "Jay" Rockefeller; invited each year to sing at Dem Jefferson Jackson Day event; Citations from Sen Robt Byrd & Congressman Nick Rahall; Woman of the Year Awd McDowell Cty. **Business Addr:** Beckley High School, South Kanawha St, Beckley, WV 25801.

DOBY, ALLEN E.

Government administrator. **Personal:** Born Oct 26, 1934, Mississippi; son of Mr & Mrs A Doby; married LaFaye Ealy. **Educ:** Calif State Univ Northridge, BS 1973, MPA program. **Career:** County of Los Angeles, district dir 1959-75; City of Compton, dir parks & rec 1975-80; City of Santa Ana, executive dir 1980-. **Orgs:** Member Calif Parks Rec Society 1961-; bd of directors Natl Recreation Parks Assoc 1971-; bd of directors NRPA Ethnic Minority Society 1971-; lecturer Calif Community College System 1973-75. **Honors/Awds:** Administrator of Year, Ethnic Minority Society 1977; California Parks & Recreation Society, Administrator of the Year 1988; elected to Board of Trustees, National Recreation and Parks Association. **Military Serv:** US Army Army E5 1955-57; Good Conduct & Service Medal.

DOBY, LAWRENCE EUGENE, SR.

Professional sports administrator. **Personal:** Born Dec 3, 1923, Camden, SC; married Helyn Curvey; children: Chris, Leslie, Larry Jr, Kim, Susan. **Educ:** Long Island Univ; Virginia Union Univ. **Career:** Cleveland Indians, 1947-55, 1958; Chicago White Sox, 1956-57, manager, 1978; Montreal Expos, coach 1971-73; Cleveland Indians, coach 1974; Montreal Expos, coach 1976; NJ Nets, dir of community relations; Major League Baseball Properties, currently. **Orgs:** Mem State Dept of Japan 1962; US Tour for Pres Council on Physical Fitness 1968. **Honors/Awds:** 1st black in the Am League; played in 2 World Series 1948, 1954; member of the World Series Champion Cleveland Indians, 1948; played in 6 consecutive All Star Games 1949-54; center fielder Baseball Writers Assn of Sporting News 1950; elected to Cleveland Hall of Fame 1955; Baseball Hall of Fame 1977; led the Am League in slugging 1952 Batted 542; honorary doctorates from Montclair State Univ, Long Island Univ; Turner Broadcasting System, Trumpet Award, 1998. **Business Addr:** Major League Baseball Properties, 350 Park Ave, New York, NY 10022.

DOBYNES, ELIZABETH

Personnel advisor. **Personal:** Born Dec 25, 1930, Marion, AL; married Lloyd Sr; children: Barbara, Lloyd Jr, Karl. **Educ:** Miles Coll Birmingham AL, 1951-53; asst degree electronics pending. **Career:** Magnovox Co Fort Wayne IN, employee 21 yrs. **Orgs:** Youth adv & state bd rep IN NAACP 1965-; den leader Cub Scouts 1957-65; treas/coordinator Women's Aux NAACP 1978-; mem PUSH 1980; mem Ft Wayne Urban League 1980; publicity chairwomen Bapt Ministrial Alliance 1979-80; dir Bapt training union Faith Missionary Bapt Ch 1980; missionary tchr & choir mem Faith Missionary Bapt Ch 1980; vacation bible sch dir Faith Missionary Bapt Ch 1980; life mem NAACP Ft Wayne Chpt; public service PUSH Ft Wayne Chap 1975. **Honors/Awds:** Delegate to natl conv NAACP 1967-; A Phillip Randolph Institute for Community Service, Max T Lawrence Award, 1989; Public Service Achievers Award, Black Expo, 1985; Zeta Phi Beta Sorority, Woman of the Year, 1984; NAACP, Indiana State Woman's Auxilliary, Woman of the Year, 1981; NAACP, Loran B Henry Award, 1981. **Business Addr:** NAACP, PO Box 296, Fort Wayne, IN 46802.

DOCKERY, RICHARD L.

Director (retired). **Personal:** married Almeda D; children: Richard L Jr, Eric Richard, Erica Carmen. **Educ:** Dillard U, BA 1950. **Career:** Spalding Bus Coll, instr 1946-59; Cedar Grv Theol Sem, instr 1950-51; City Rec Negroes, dir 1951-52; US Civil Serv, 1952-61; Kelly AFB, procurementdata spl 1961-68; Dockerys Paint Center, owner & mgr 1958-61. **Orgs:** Mem NAACP; Nat Found Fed Employees; TX Adv Com US Commn Civil Rights. **Honors/Awds:** Community serv award KNOK Radio; plaque meritorious serv NAACP 1967; community serv awd Dallas Bock C of C 1975; appreciation award governors awd US Army ROTC Region 1975. **Military Serv:** USN petty officer 2/c 1941-45. **Business Addr:** Regional Dir, NAACP, 4805 Mt Hope Dr, Baltimore, MD 21215.

DOCKERY, ROBERT WYATT

Physician (retired). **Personal:** Born Dec 11, 1909, Charlotte, NC; son of Emma J Patterson and Z A Dockery; married Vera; children: Robert Jr, Glenna. **Educ:** Johnson C Smith U, BS 1931; Meharry Med Coll, MD 1940; Harvard Med School Ch Boston City Hosp Univ Louisville, 1954-57. **Career:** Univ of Louisville, clinical instr 1957-80, assoc clinical prof 1980-; NC, tchr 1931-35; VA Hosp Louisville, ophthalmology consultant 1957-; VA KY, 1970-77. **Orgs:** Mem Louisville Acad Ophthalmology; pres 1969-70; Falls City Med Soc 1957; Jefferson Co Med Soc 1957; KY State Ophthal Soc 1957; AMA 1957; Nat Med Soc 1957; deacon bd tst Plymouth Congr Ch 1964-; mem Alpha Phi Alpha Frat; pres Alpha Lambda Chap Alpha Phi Alpha 1968-71; mem NAACP 1957; Urban League 1957; gov com KY Blind 1970-89; mem Pres Club Johnson C Smith Univ 1976-80, 1988. **Honors/Awds:** Louisville, KY, 25 Year Plaque for starting Preschool Vision Screenings; Desegregated a hospital, 1955; gave African Americans voting rights in North Carolina, 1931-34. **Military Serv:** USAF maj 1943-46; Flight Surgeon Tuskegee Airman swat II.

DOCKETT, ALFRED B.

Business executive. **Personal:** Born Jul 6, 1935, Thomasville, GA; married Erna Rodrigues; children: Alfred III, Michael H, Karen P. **Educ:** IN Inst of Tech, BS 1957. **Career:** Wallace & Wallace Enterprises Inc, pres; Grumman Aerospace Corp, mgmt systems spec 1971-73; Gen Elec/RESD, prgm engr 1966-71; Boeing Co, systems test & mgmt systems engr 1961-66; AUS, intrn of Fire control & missel systems oper. **Military Serv:** AUS 1958-61. **Business Addr:** 200-33 Linden Blvd, Jamaica, NY 11412.

DODD, GERALDA

Steel company owner. **Personal:** Born Jul 4, 1957, Toledo, OH; married T Edward Sellers, 1991. **Educ:** Univ of Toledo. **Career:** Heidtman Steel Products, receptionist, inventory control manager, purchasing manager, vice president of purchasing and administration; Integrated Steel, majority owner and CEO, 1990-; HS Automotive, CEO, 1991-. **Special Achievements:** Company is ranked #59 on the Black Enterprise list of Top industrial/service companies, 1994. **Business Addr:** CEO, Integrated Steel, 12301 Hubbell, Detroit, MI 48227, (313)273-4000.

DODD, JAMES C.

Architect. **Personal:** Born Jan 17, 1923, Texarkana, TX; married Constance M Curry; children: Florenda (Mitchell), James C Jr. **Educ:** Univ of CA, BA 1952. **Career:** Dodd & Asso Architechts & Planners Sacramento, owner 1960-; Urban Construction Co Sacramento, owner 1972-; Barovette & Thomas, project architect 1956-61; State of CA Div of Architecture, designer 1953-56. **Orgs:** Past pres Central Valley Chap AIA 1969; mem bd dir CA Council AIA 1969, 73; vice pres Nat Orgn of Minority Architects 1972-73; mem Am Arbitration Assn; mem AIA; chmn bd governors CA Comm Colleges 1972-73; vice pres Sacrmento Br NAACP 1968-70; mem Coordinatin Council for Higher Educ 1968-70. **Honors/Awds:** Recipient Masonry Honor Award for Architectural Design 1971; architectural achievement award NAACP 1972; merit award Central Valley Chap AIA 1974. **Military Serv:** AUS 1st lt 1943-46. **Business Addr:** James C Dodd & Assoc, 2710 X St, Ste 2, Sacramento, CA 95818.

DODDS, R. HARCOURT

Attorney. **Personal:** Born Jan 11, 1938, New York, NY; son of Beryl Ianthe Archer Dodds (deceased) and Reginald Alexander Dodds (deceased); married Barbara Ann Arrington, Feb 14, 1965; children: Julian I, Jason S, Sarah C. **Educ:** Dartmouth Coll, BA (Magna Cum Laude) 1958; Yale Law School, LLB 1961. **Career:** Ministry of Justice Northern Nigeria, asst comm for native courts 1961-63; US Attny Office Southern Dist of NY, asst US attny 1963-66; Pfizer Inc, legal dept attny 1966-67; New York City Police Dept, dep police comm legal matters 1967-70; New York City Law Dept, exec asst corp counsel 1970-73; Ford Found, prog officer 1973-82; Champion Intl Corp, dir corp responsibility prog 1982-87; Kings County, Brooklyn, NY, exec asst district attorney, 1987-89; St Johns Univ, Jamaica, NY, assoc prof of law, 1990-95. **Orgs:** Mem New Rochelle Council on the Arts 1980-; bd of governors Sound Shore Med Ctr of Westchester, 1983-; consult Clark Phipps Harris Clark, NYC, Rockefeller Found; NY State Organized Crime Task Force; independent drug expert Natl Basketball Assn & Natl Players Assn 1984-87; vice pres CT Bar Found 1984-87; mem NY State Commn on Crim Justice and Use of Force 1985-87; sr consultant, Harlem Educational Activities Fund Inc, 1997-; vice chair, bd of trustees, NY Foundation, 1990-; mem, bd of trustees, New School Univ, 1991-; comm, Black Leadership Comm on Aids. **Honors/Awds:** Trustee Dartmouth Coll 1973-83; overseer Amos Tuck School of Bus Admin 1974-80; mem Phi Beta Kappa. **Military Serv:** NY NG pe5 3 mos. **Home Phone:** (914)235-7144. **Business Addr:** Counsel, Cooper, Liebowitz, Royster & Wright, 3 W Main St, Elmsford, NY 10523, (914)347-5555.

DODDY, REGINALD NATHANIEL

Software engineer. **Personal:** Born Jul 2, 1952, Cincinnati, OH; son of Mildred Peek Doddy and Nathan Doddy. **Educ:** Northwestern Univ, BSEE 1975. **Career:** Eastman Kodak Co, mfg engineer 1975-77; Mead Corp, mfg engineer 1977-79; RCA Corp, assc mem stf engrg 1979-84; Cincinnati Milacron, systems engineer 1984-94; Software Engineering, supervisor, 1994-. **Orgs:** Inst of Elect & Elect Engr, 1977-; Toastmasters Club, 1976-77; tech dir, RCA Minority Engrg Program, 1980-83. **Honors/Awds:** Nomination Outstanding Young Men of Am 1982-83; community serv Indianapolis Center for Leadership Devel 1982. **Home Addr:** 3595 Wilson Ave, Cincinnati, OH 45229. **Business Addr:** Software Engineer Supervisor, Cincinnati Milacron, 4165 Halfacre Rd, Batavia, OH 45103.

DODGE, DEDRICK ALLEN
Professional football player. **Personal:** Born Jun 14, 1967, Neptune, NJ; married Patrice; children: Chante, Dedrick Jr, Nyla. **Educ:** Florida State. **Career:** Seattle Seahawks, defensive back, 1991-92; San Francisco 49ers, 1994-96; Denver Broncos, 1997-. **Business Addr:** Professional Football Player, Denver Broncos, 13655 Broncos Pkwy, Englewood, CO 80112, (303)649-9000.

DODSON, ANGELA PEARL
Editor. **Personal:** Born May 24, 1951, Beckley, WV; daughter of Kira Evelyn Dodson and William Alfred Dodson Sr; married Michael Irvin Days, Apr 17, 1982. **Educ:** Marshall University, Huntington, W VA, BA, 1973; American University, Washington, DC, MA, 1979. **Career:** The Charleston Gazette, intern, Charleston, W.VA, 1972;The Huntington Advertiser, Huntington, W VA, reporter, 1972-74; Gannett News Service, Washington, DC, correspondent, 1974-77, asst news/feature editor, 1977-79; Rochester Times Union, Rochester, NY, asst city editor, 1979-80; The Washington Star, Washington, DC, night slot/features editor, 1980-81; The Courier Journal, Louisville, KY, copy editor, 1981-82; The New York Times, New York, NY, copy editor, deputy editor of the living section, editor of the living section, editor of the style department, 1983-95, senior editor, news administration, consultant/editor, currently; freelance consultant/editor. **Orgs:** Member, The National Assn of Black Journalists, 1977-; former secretary, natl magazine editor, The National Assn of Black Journalists, 1981-83; faculty member & advisory board member, The Editing Program for Minority Journalists, 1982-;director, Editing Program For Minority Journalists, 1985; member, Garden State Association of Black Journalists, 1997-; chapter founder, member, Alpha Kappa Alpha, 1971-75. **Honors/Awds:** Distinguished Alumna, School of Journalism, Marshall Univ, 1989; Black Alumna of the Year, Sons of Marshall, 1988; Black Achiever in Industry, Harlem YMCA, 1990.

DODSON, HOWARD, JR.
Business executive, educator. **Personal:** Born Jun 1, 1939, Chester, PA; married Jualynne E White; children: Alyce Christine, David Primus Luta. **Educ:** W Chester State Coll, BS 1961; UCLA, Additional Study 1964; Villanova Univ, MA 1964; UC Berkeley, ABF 1977. **Career:** Peace Corps, recruiter 1966-67, dir special recruiting 1967-68, training officer 1968; CA State Coll, assoc prof 1970; Shaw Univ, adjunct prof 1975; Emory Univ, lecturer 1976; Inst of the Black World, program dir 1973-74, exec dir 1974-79; Natl Endowment for the Humanities, asst to chmn 1980-82; The Schomburg Center for Rsch in Black Culture, chief 1984-. **Orgs:** Mem Alpha Phi Alpha 1959-64, SC Hist Soc, Peace Corps Vol 1964-66, Oakland Black Caucus 1969-73; consultant Natl Endowment for the Humanities 1979-80; chmn, ceo Black Theology Project 1982-84; mem bd of dir Inst of the Black World, Atlanta Assoc for Intl Ed; mem Ed Brain Trust Congressional Black Caucus, Atlanta Univ School of Soc Work, Natl Comm for Citizens in Ed, GA Assoc of Black Elected Officials, ESEA, Natl Credit Union Fed Ecuador; mem African Heritage Studies Assoc, Assoc for the Study of Afro-Amer History, So Hist Assoc; mem bd of overseers Lang Coll New Sch for Social Rsch; bd of dirs NCBS, AHSA, Caribbean Rsch Ctr. **Honors/Awds:** PICCO Scholarship 1959-61; Grad Fellowship UC Berkeley 1969-73; Rsch Fellowship Inst of the Black World 1970-71; Editor-in-Chief Black World View 1977; Doctor of Humane Letters Widner Univ 1987. **Business Addr:** Chief, Schomburg Center Rsch Black Culture, 515 Malcolm X Blvd, New York, NY 10037-1801.

DODSON, JUALYNNE E.
Educational administrator, educator. **Personal:** Born Jan 4, 1942, Pensacola, FL; daughter of Flora White and Benjamin White; married Howard Dodson; children: Alyce Christine, David Primus Luta. **Educ:** Univ of CA Berkeley, BA 1969, MA 1972, PhD 1984; Warren Deem Inst for Educ Mgmt Columbia Univ Sch of Business, 1985. **Career:** Atlanta Univ Sch of Social Work, instructor 1973-74, rsch project dir 1973-81, dir rsch ctr 1974-80, asst prof 1974-79, assoc prof 1979-82, chair Dept Child & Family Serv 1980-82; Black Theology Project, exec dir 1985-88; Union Theological Seminary, dean of seminary life 1982-87; visiting assoc prof, sociology dept, Hunter Coll, CUNY, 1987-88; sr research assoc, African & African-American Studies, Yale Univ, 1988-90; Ford Foundation, fellow, 1990-91; Princeton University, Center for Studies of American Religion, senior center fellow, 1991-92; University of Colorado, associate professor, religious studies, African-American studies, sociology, currently. **Orgs:** Elected delegate Council on Social Work Educ 1979-82; presentor annual meetings Amer Acad of Religion 1981, 1983, 1984, 1987; Natl Council Convenor Feminist Theol Inst 1982-83; mem Soc for Scientific Study of Religion 1982, 1983, 1986; consult Natl Child Welfare Training Center Ann Arbor, MI 1983-85; chair/bd dirs Black Theol Project 1983-84; keynote speaker Natl Coalition 100 Black Women 1984; NY State Black & Puerto Rican Legislative Caucus Women's Conf 1985; NY State Affirmative Action Adv Council 1985-86; leader Black Church Studies & Student Caucus Retreat Colgate Rochester Divinity Sch spring & fall 1985; mem Soc of Amer Archivists 1986; sponsor, ''I Have a Dream,'' 1988-89; scholar in residence, Irvington Abbott Unified School, 1989. **Honors/Awds:** Research fellow for Applied Sociology Amer Sociological Assoc 1980; gubernatorial appointee White House Conf on Families 1980; Lucy Craft Laney Awd Black Presbyterians United UPCUSA 1982; Spivack Fellow Amer Sociological Assn 1983; adv bd Assoc of Black Women in Higher Educ 1985-88; Medal of Honor Outstanding Comm Serv One Church One Child Prog Indianapolis 1986; delegate Intl Conf ''Ecumenical Sharing'' Nanjing China 1986; bd of dirs New York Council for the Humanities 1986-90; delegate, International Conference ''Racism in the Americas & Caribbean,'' Rio de Janerio, Brazil 1990; delegate, International Conference, ''Kairos Europa,'' Strasbourg, France 1992. **Special Achievements:** Author, ''A Sourcebook in Child Welfare,'' National Child Welfare Training Center, University of Michigan, Ann Arbor 1982; ''An Afro-Centric Educational Manual,'' University of Tennessee Press, Knoxville 1983. **Business Addr:** Associate Professor, Religious Studies, African-American Studies, Sociology, University of Colorado-CSERA, 30 Ketchum, PO Box 339, Boulder, CO 80309-0339.

DODSON, SELMA L.
Broadcasting company executive. **Personal:** Born May 21, 1955, Chicago, IL; daughter of Juanita L Dodson and Robert W Dodson. **Educ:** Northwestern University, BS, 1977. **Career:** WZGC Radio, promotions director/public affairs, 1977-81; KFMK Radio, account executive, 1981-84; KO5HU TV, sales mgr, 1984-86; KMJQ/KYOK, account executive, 1986-88, local sales mgr, 1988-92, general sales mgr, currently. **Orgs:** Houston NAACP, chairperson publicity/comm Annual Freedom Fund Banquet, 1989, 1990, 1991, 1992; Houston Coalition of 100 Black Women, 1989-; American Marketing Association, 1984-85; American Women in Radio/Television, 1981-83; American Women in Radio/Television, historian, 1979-81. **Honors/Awds:** Human Enrichment for Life Program, Young Black Achiever, 1988. **Business Addr:** General Sales Manager, KMJQ/KYOK Radio, 24 Greenway Plaza, #1508, Houston, TX 77046, (713)623-0102.

DODSON, VIVIAN M.
City government official. **Personal:** Born Jan 22, 1934, Washington, DC; daughter of Maefield Wilson Mills and Brevard Mills; married Barke M Dodson, Dec 24, 1958 (died 1991); children: Tangie B, Kaphree A. **Educ:** Washington Coll of Music, Washington DC, AA, 1956. **Career:** Prince Georges County Communications, Upper Marlboro MD, communications operator, 1973-89; Town of Capitol Heights, Capitol Heights MD, councilwoman, 1982-86, mayor, 1986-. **Orgs:** Girl Scouts of America, 1971-; Prince Georges Municipal Elective Women, president, 1992-; Recreation for Capitol Heights, director, 1982-; Prince Georges County Municipal League, board member, 1983-; Mothers On The Move, 1984-; Citizen on The Move, 1986; Mid-County Youth Services; Council of Black Mayors; National Council of Black Women; Prince Georges Municipal Mayors; National Political Congress of Black Women, 1991. **Honors/Awds:** Citizen on the Move. **Home Addr:** 5635 Southern Ave, Capitol Heights, MD 20743.

DODSON, WILLIAM ALFRED, JR.
Church administrator. **Personal:** Born Feb 9, 1950, Beckley, WV; son of Kira E Walthall Dodson and William A Dodson Sr; married Judythe Irene Taylor, Jul 27, 1975; children: Daymon. **Educ:** Marshall Univ Huntington, WV, AB, Sociology, 1973; OH State Univ Columbus, OH, MA Public Admin, 1981; Ohio Real Estate Sales License, 1997. **Career:** Tri-state OIC Huntington, WV, instr 1972-73; ACF Ind Huntington, WV, instrl rel repr 1973-75; Office of Human Serv ODOD, field rep, 1975-77; Office of Appalachia ODOD, housing rep, 1977-82; WCVO-FM New Albany, OH, announcer 1980-; OH Dept of Dev, field rep/devel specialist, 1982-86; Columbus Metro Housing Authority, asst dir of housing programs, 1986-88; Columbus Metro Housing, MIS Mgr, 1988-89, mgmt analyst, 1989-93; Dayspring Christian CDC, exec dir, 1993-. **Orgs:** Elder 1982, exec vp, 1992-, Rhema Christian Center; Neighborhood Services Advisory Council, Columbus, chmn, 1989-90, 1993-94, vp, 1991-93; bd of dirs, 1986-, pres, 1996-97; Directions for Youth, vp, pres, 1992-93; bd mem, 1986-93, Assn for Developmentally Disabled; Natl Assn of Church Bus Admin, pres, 1994-96; Volunters of Amer, bd of dirs, 1995-; Christian Management Assn, 1993-; Christian Comm Dev Assoc, 1993-; Northeast Area Comm, vice chmn, 1993-; Columbus Compact Corp, trustee, 1995-97; Columbus State Comm Coll, vice chmn, 1994-; I-670 Development Corp, 1996-; Urban Concern, 1995-. **Honors/Awds:** Outstanding participant, Natl Alliance of Businessmen Jobs Campaign Huntington Metro, 1975; Natl Achievement Scholar, Natl Merit ETS, 1968; Certified Public Housing Mgr, 1987; Certified Economic Development Specialist, Natl Dev Council, 1984; Comm Achievement Awd, Marshall Univ Alumni Assn, 1996. **Home Phone:** (614)475-1091. **Business Addr:** Exec VP, Rhema Christian Center, 2100 Agler Rd, Columbus, OH 43224, (614)471-0816.

DOGGETT, BILL. See Obituaries section.

DOGGETT, JOHN NELSON, JR.
Clergyman. **Personal:** Born Apr 3, 1918, Philadelphia, PA; son of Winola Ballard Doggett and John Nelson Doggett Jr; married Juanita Toley, Aug 3, 1973; children: Lorraine F, John III, William II, Kenneth Riddick. **Educ:** Lincoln Univ, BA 1942; Union Theol Seminary, MDiv 1945; Saint Louis Univ, MEduc 1969, PhD 1971. **Career:** Union Memorial United Methodist Church, sr pastor 1964-76; Harris-Stowe State Coll, instructor in educ 1973-76; Metro Coll St Louis Univ, assoc prof 1976-78; UM Church St Louis Area, district supt 1976-82; Grace United Methodist Church, sr minister 1982-85; Cabanne United Methodist Church, minister 1985-89; Central Medical Ctr St Louis, chairman bd of dirs 1975-87 chr Emeritus 1987-; CMC Retirement Home, chmn board of directors 1985-; Limelight Magazine, University City, MO, associate publisher/staff writer, 1988-; Med-West Consultants, president, currently. **Orgs:** Staff counselor Pastoral Counseling Inst St Louis 1968-88; pres St Louis Branch NAACP 1973-80; Citizens Comm MO Dept of Corrections 1974-80; board of directors United Way of Greater St Louis 1974-81; board of directors Natl Council of Churches of Christ 1976-80; St Louis Ambassadors & RCGA 1980-90; bd dir Amer Lung Assoc Eastern MO 1985-88, Family Planning Assoc MO 1986-88; ACLU; UNA, 1986-88, Minister's Coalition; founder JN Doggett Scholarship Foundation; Lincoln Alumni Association, St Louis Conference on Education; Confluence National Conference Christians and Jews; bd of trustees, treasurer, exec comm, Missouri Historical Society Inc, 1987-; United Methodist Historical Society, 1988. **Honors/Awds:** Natl Chaplain's Awd Alpha Phi Alpha Fraternity 1973,79,86,87; Outstanding Alumni Awd St Louis Univ 1981; Martin Luther King Awd Alpha & Anheuser-Busch Project 1987; ''Effect of Community School Achievement'' St Louis Univ edition 1971; ''Black Religious Experience'' Gammon Theol Seminary Press GA 1973; Regional Hall of Fame Alpha Phi Alpha Fraternity 1988; Outstanding Service Award, Elijah Parish Lovejoy Society 1989; Job Corp Martin Luther King Excellence Award, 1990; Citizenship Service Certificate, St Louis Public Schools, 1988; Leadership Trainer Award, Kansas City Blacks Against AIDS, 1989; NAACP, Lifetime Achievement Award, 1992; Urban League, Lifetime Achievement Award, 1993; Alpha Kappa Alpha, Lifetime Achievement Award, 1994. **Military Serv:** USNG chaplain 1st lt 1946-50. **Home Addr:** 4466 W Pine Blvd, #2C, St Louis, MO 63108. **Business Addr:** President, Med-West Consultants, 4615 Steinlage Ave, St Louis, MO 63115.

DOGINS, KEVIN
Professional football player. **Personal:** Born Dec 7, 1972. **Educ:** Texas A&M-Kingsville, attended. **Career:** Tampa Bay Buccaneers, center, 1996-. **Business Addr:** Professional Football Player, Tampa Bay Buccaneers, One Buccaneer Place, Tampa, FL 33607, (813)870-2700.

DOIG, ELMO H.
Business executive (retired). **Personal:** Born Aug 14, 1927, Panama, Panama; son of Fortunee Andree and Henry C Doig; married Silvia Doran, Nov 8, 1952; children: Elmo Jr, Yvette. **Educ:** Am Sch, coll prep 1959; CCNY (Baruch) NYC, BBS & MBA 1969. **Career:** Manufacturers Hanover Trust Co, asst vp, until 1986; Manufacturers Hanover Trust Co NYC, branch mgr 1964-; Flower Fifth Ave Hosp NYC, head payroll & accts payable dept 1963-64; Bezozi Corp, supr billing dept 1958-62; Ordnance Corps Panama, supr supply shop 1942-58. **Orgs:** Treas financial sec Bronx Lions Club Bronx NY 1971, delegate, currently; financial com 100 Black Men Inc New York City 1975; treas Mt Kisco Village Condominium 1979; dir, Catholic Youth Org, NYC, 1984-86; dir, Sandpaper Bay Homeowners Assn PSL-FL, 1991-95, pres, 1995-97. **Honors/Awds:** Amer Sch Scholarship Chicago 1960; black achievers in industry Greater NY YMCA 1972; banking & finance Grodon Heights Comm City Tabernacle Church Seventh-day Adventist New York City 1978. **Home Addr:** 2411 SE Morningside Blvd, Port St Lucie, FL 34952.

DOLBY, EDWARD C.
Banking executive. **Personal:** marrIed Dee; children: Ed, Terius, Jarvone. **Educ:** Shaw Univ, bachelor's degree in sociology. **Career:** NationsBank, consumer banking executive, currently. **Special Achievements:** Highest ranking African American line manager for NationsBank.

DOLEMAN, CHRISTOPHER JOHN
Professional football player. **Personal:** Born Oct 16, 1961, Indianapolis, IN; married Toni; children: Taylor Marie, Evan Christopher. **Educ:** Univ of Pittsburgh, majored in administrative justice. **Career:** Minnesota Vikings, defensive end, 1985-93; Atlanta Falcons, 1994-95; San Francisco 49ers, 1996-. **Honors/Awds:** Sporting News NFL All-Star Team, 1989; post-season play: NFC Championship Game, 1987, Pro Bowl, 1987, 1988, 1989, 1990, 1992, 1993, 1995; Miller Lite Lineman-of-the-Year, 1988; hosted: week-long football camp for children, golf tournament to raise funds for Minnesota Center for Independent Living. **Business Addr:** Professional Football Player, San Francisco 49ers, 4949 Centennial Blvd, Santa Clara, CA 95054, (415)562-4949.

DOLEY, HAROLD E., JR.
Business executive. **Personal:** Born Mar 8, 1947, New Orleans, LA; married Helena Cobette; children: Harold III, Aaron. **Educ:** Xavier U, BS; Harvard Univ, Graduate School of Business, DPM. **Career:** Doley Properties, pres; So Univ New Orleans, instr; Bache Halsey Stuart Inc, acct exec; Howard Weil Labouisse & Friedrichs Inc, asst vice pres 1974-75; Minerals

Mgmt Svcs, dir 1982-83; African Development Bank, exec dir 1983-85; Doley Securities Inc, chmn, currently. **Orgs:** NY Stock Exchange; former treas bd mem, Pub Broadcast Sys WYES-TV; Inter-racial Council for Bus & Opp; trustee, African-American Institute; former bd mem, OIC Adv Bd; Lloyds of London; Zeta Boule; NY Options Exchange; Clark-Atlanta Univ, trustee; Shaw University, trustee; LA Weekly Bd; US Africa Chamber of Commerce; Population Resource Center. **Honors/Awds:** Outstanding Stockbrokers by Shareholders Management Co, 1982; Harvard Mgmt Grad Sch of Bus; Wall St Journal, Stock Picker Contest Winner, 1989; Honorary Degrees: Clark-Atlanta University, Bishop College, Shaw University. **Special Achievements:** TV guest appearances: ''The Today Show''; CNN; CNBC; FNN; ''Wall St Week''; ''New York Times Spotlight''. **Business Addr:** Chairman, Doley Secruities Inc, 616 Baronne St, New Orleans, LA 70113.

DOLPHIN, WOODROW B.
Business executive. **Personal:** Born Nov 1, 1912, Boley, OK; married Edwina; children: Michele, Woodrow E, Karl. **Educ:** Wayne State U, BSEE 1937; IL Inst of Tech, 1942-44; Malcolm X Coll, HHD 1970. **Career:** WB Dolphin & Assos, founder & owner; Chicago Nat Tech Assn, consult engrs 1970. **Orgs:** Mem Small Bus of Yr Cosmopolitan C of C 1976. **Business Addr:** W B Dolphin & Assocs, 400 N Wells, Chicago, IL 60610.

DOMINIC, IRWING
Human resources manager. **Personal:** Born Aug 12, 1930, Spartanburg, SC; son of Jessie M Hall Hunt and Irvin Dominic (deceased); married Catherine Virginia Chapman Dominic, Jun 14, 1956; children: Duane, Dwight, Denice, Deirdre, Deland, Damian. **Educ:** Bellevue Univ, BA Sociology 1978; attended Univ of Nebraska-Omaha 1978-79, Creighton Univ Omaha 1979-80. **Career:** US Postal Serv, Omaha NE, mail handler, 1974-79, assoc training & devel specialist eas-14, 1979-80, training & devel spec eas-16, 1980-83, Cleveland manager training, EAS-21, 1983-86, Hicksville NY mgr employment and devel, EAS-23, 1986-88, Akron OH, mgr training and development, 1988-. **Orgs:** Founding mem, Blacks in Govt Omaha NE Chapter, 1981-82; mem, Knights of Columbus, fourth degree 1980, Phoenix Rising Toastmasters, 1982, A-Plus, 1988; educ advisor, Natl Assn Postal Supvr, 1983, Phoenix Postal Supvr, 1983. **Honors/Awds:** US Postal Service, Superior Performance Award, 1979, Managers Recognition Award for Superior Performance in Affirmative Action, 1982, Spot Awards, 1996, Far Exceeds Merit Award, 1997. **Military Serv:** USAF radio operator and electronic analyst, 1949-74; Korean & Vietnam Serv, Sr Crew Mem Badge; Meritorious Service Award. **Home Addr:** 2119 White Oak Dr, Stow, OH 44224-2648, (330)688-5384. **Business Addr:** Mgr, Training, US Postal Serv, 675 Wolf Ledges Pkwy, Akron, OH 44309-9402, (330)996-9535.

DOMINO, FATS (ANTOINE)
Musician. **Personal:** Born Feb 26, 1928, New Orleans, LA; married Rosemary; children: Antoinette, Antoine III, Andrea, Anatole, Anola, Adonica, Antonio, Andre. **Career:** Musician and concert performer, 1950-. **Honors/Awds:** Composer of Let the Four Winds Blow, Walking to New Orleans, Ain't That a Shame, Blue Monday, The Fat Man, I Want to Walk You Home, I'm Gonna Be a Wheel Someday, I'm Walking, and Whole Lotta Loving; hit records include Blueberry Hill, Margie, Lady Madonna, and above compositions; appeared in numerous movies and television shows; awarded more than 20 Gold Records; inductee, Rock and Roll Hall of Fame, 1986; recipient, Grammy Lifetime Achievement Award, 1987.

DONAHUE, WILLIAM T.
City official. **Personal:** Born May 31, 1943, San Antonio, TX; married Monica Lechowick; children: Erin Michelle, Mark Pittman. **Educ:** San Antonio Jr Coll. **Career:** Human Resources & Services, dir 1972-82; City of San Antonio, asst city mgr. **Orgs:** Volunteer US Peace Corps 1965-67; past pres US Conf of City Human Svcs; Official Advisory Comm United Negro Coll Fund; life mem NAACP; co-chair 1980 UNCF Radiothon; delegate Pres Conf on Children & Youth; 1st Black Asst City Mgr City of San Antonio; bd of dir Natl Forum for Black Public Admin1982-; vice chair of the TX Emergency Serv Advisory Council; Commissioned as Admiral in TX Navy; D of Law from Univ TX at San Antonio; mem Intl City Manager's Assn; Achievement Awd, South Central Region of AKA Sorority; mem TX City Mgrs Assn; Outstanding Texan by TX Legislative Black Caucus. **Business Addr:** Assistant City Manager, City of San Antonio, PO Box 9066, San Antonio, TX 78285.

DONALD, ARNOLD WAYNE
Company executive. **Personal:** Born Dec 17, 1954, New Orleans, LA; son of Hilda Aline (Melancon) Donald and Warren Joseph Donald Sr; married Hazel Alethea (Roberts) Donald, May 18, 1974; children: Radiah Alethea, Alicia Aline. **Educ:** Carleton Coll, BA, economics, 1976; Washington Univ, BS, mechanical engineering, 1977; Univ of Chicago, MBA, finance, 1980. **Career:** Monsanto, St Louis MO, sr mktg analyst, 1980-81, mktg research supvr, 1981-82, product supvr, 1982-83, Winnipeg, Canada, round-up product mgr, 1983, mktg mgr, 1983-86, St Louis MO, product dir, 1986, specialty crops dir, 1986-87, lawn & garden business dir, 1987-91, vice pres, Residential Products Division, 1991-92, vice pres/gen mgr, Crop Protection Products Div, 1992-93, group vp & gen mgr, NA Div, beginning 1993, Crop Protection Unit, pres, beginning 1995. **Orgs:** Canadian Agricultural Chemistry Assn, 1983-86; Natl Lawn & Garden Distr ibutor Assn, 1988-91; team captain, 1988-89, bd mem, 1989-91, Monsanto YMCA; participant, 1988-89, Leadership St Louis, bd vice president, 1990-93, pres of bd, 1993; board mem, Theater Project Co, 1989-91; board member, Ecumenical Housing Production Corp, 1990-91; Lindenwood Coll, bd member, 1991-93, exec committee, currently; John Burroughs School, bd member, 1992-93; United Way of Greater St Louis, committee mem, 1991-93; Leadership Center of Greater St Louis, president; British American Project, exec committee; Junior League Advisory Board; Natl Advisory Council for Washington University's School of Engineering. **Honors/Awds:** Natl Achievement Scholar, Carleton Coll, 1972-76; Dave Okada Memorial Award, Carleton Coll, 1976; Washington University School of Engineering and Applied Science, Outstanding Young Alumni Award, 1994; University's Natl Black Alumni Council, National Black Alumni Award, 1994. **Business Addr:** President, Crop Protection Unit, Monsanto Company, 800 N Lindbergh Blvd, C3NA The Agricultural Group, St Louis, MO 63167.

DONALD, BERNICE BOUIE
Judge. **Personal:** Born Sep 17, 1951, DeSoto County, MS; daughter of Mr & Mrs Perry Bowie; married W L Donald. **Educ:** Memphis State Univ, BA Sociology 1974; Memphis State Univ Sch of Law, JD 1979; Natl Judicial Coll, Evidence Certificate 1984. **Career:** South Central Bell, clerk's mgr 1971-79; Memphis Area Legal Svc, attorney 1979-80; Shelby Co Govt Public Defenders Office, asst public defender 1980-82; General Sessions Court, judge 1982-88; US Bankruptcy Court; United States District Judge, currently. **Orgs:** Mem, Memphis Bar Assn; mem TN Bar Assn; mem co-chair courts comm Memphis and Shelby County Bar Assoc; mem Ben F Jones Chap Natl Bar Assn; mem Assn of Women Attorneys; mem 1983-, pres 1990-91, Natl Assn of Women Judges 1983-; mem Amer Judges Assn 1983-; chair General Sessions Judges Conference Educ 1987; bd of dirs Memphis State Univ Law Alumni; chair Comm on Excellence in Legal Educ; mem Zeta Phi Beta Sor, Alpha Eta Zeta Chapt; bd of dirs Shelby State Comm Coll, Criminal Justice Panel, Natl Conf of Negro Women, Business & Professional Women Clubs; assoc mem Natl Ctr for State Courts; mem JAD Div Amer Bar Assn; chair, Commission on Opportunities for Minorities, ABA, Amer Trial Lawyers Assn; mem Conference of Special Court Judges; numerous seminars, conferences, lectures and presentations; pres, Assn of WomenAttorneys, 1990; mem, Natl Conference of Bankruptcy Jes, 1988. **Honors/Awds:** 1st black female in US to serve on Bankruptcy Court; elected first black female judge in the history of the State of TN; Young Careerist Awd State of TN Raleigh Bureau of Professional Women; Woman of the Year Pentecostal Church of God in Christ; Martin Luther King Comm Serv Awd; Citizen of the Year Excelsior Chapter of Eastern Star; 1986 Comm Serv Awd Youth-Natl Conference of Christians and Jews; featured in Essence, Ebony, Jet, Dollar & Sense, and Memphis Magazine; participated on numerous TV shows to discuss legal and judicial issues; participated on numerous panels and forums dealing with legal process and the judiciary.

DONALDSON, JAMES LEE, III
Professional basketball player (retired), business executive. **Personal:** Born Aug 16, 1957, Meachem, England. **Educ:** Wash State, 1979. **Career:** Seattle SuperSonics, 1981-83, San Diego Clippers, 1984, Los Angeles Clippers, 1985-86, Dallas Mavericks, beginning 1986; The Donaldson Clinic, owner, currently. **Special Achievements:** Was one of only two players on the Clippers to have played in all 82 games of the year; set a Clipper club record for highest field goal percentage, hitting on 596 of his shots; earned All Pacific-10 Second Team honors in his senior year at Washington State. **Business Addr:** Owner, The Donaldson Clinic, Physical Therapy, 16030 Bothell-Everett Hwy, Ste 200, Mill Creek, WA 98012.

DONALDSON, JEFF RICHARDSON
Artist, educator. **Personal:** Born Dec 15, 1937, Pine Bluff, AR; son of Clementine Richardson and Frank Donaldson; children: Jameela K, Tarik Jeff. **Educ:** AR State Coll, BS Art 1958; Inst of Design of IL Inst of Tech, MS Art Educ 1963; Northwestern, PhD 1973. **Career:** Howard Univ, Coll of Fine Arts, dean, artist; JAM Recording Co, art dir, 1979-85; Intl Festiv Com 2nd World Black & African Festiv of Arts & Cult, prof of art chmn of art dept vice pres 1975-77; USA Festac '77 Com, chmn/dir 1975-; Howard Univ Wash, dir of galleries of art 1970-76; parttime lectr art hist 1968-69; Northeastern IL State Coll Chgo, asst prof of art 1965-69; Chicago City Coll, asst prof of art 1964-66; John Marshall HS Chgo, chmn art dept 1959-65, teacher, 1958-59. **Orgs:** Mem of numerous bds & assns. **Honors/Awds:** One of the creator of Chgo's orginal ''Wall of Respect'' 1967; recipient of several academic & professional awards; founding mem of AfriCobra Artists Guild 1968-. **Business Addr:** Dean, Howard University, College of Fine Arts, Washington, DC 20059.

DONALDSON, LEON MATTHEW
Educator. **Personal:** Born Aug 16, 1933, Burton, SC; married Merita Worthy; children: Carter, TaJuania. **Educ:** AL State U, BS 1963; So U, MS 1966; Rutgers U, EdD 1973; Auburn U; George Washington U; NC Centrl U. **Career:** Morgan State Univ, assoc prof; Corning Glass Works, chemical engineer 1970-71; TV McCoo High School, teacher 1963-70; Stauffer Chem Corp, chemist; IBM Corp, engineer. **Orgs:** Mem NAACP NEA; Nat Sci Tchrs Assn; Nat Cncl of Tchrs of Math; AL Educ Assn; SC Educ Assn; Civitan Internat; F & AM; Kappa Alpha Psi Frat Inc. **Honors/Awds:** NSF fellow AL State Univ NC Ctrl U; NSF fellow Southern U; EPDA fellows Rutgers U; num articles publ. **Military Serv:** AUS sp5 1957-60. **Business Addr:** Morgan State Univ, Baltimore, MD 21212.

DONALDSON, RICHARD T.
Engineering company executive. **Personal:** Born Jul 2, 1935, St Petersburg, FL; married Charlie M Waller, Aug 2, 1955; children: Jewell, Kimiko, Lisa, Carol. **Educ:** Tri-State Univ, BAD, 1958-62; Emory Univ, advanced mgmt, 1972. **Career:** General Motors Corp, supt mfg, 1972; V.W. of Amer, production mgr, 1979; Chrysler, plant mgr, 1980, general plant mgr, 1983; Environmental Specialists Inc, president currently. **Orgs:** Engineering Soc Detroit, Mgmt Club, Allocation Comm Torch Drive/United Funds; Urban League, Big Brothers, Jr Achievement, NAACP, Trinity Baptist Church; bd of trustees, Tri-State Univ, 1990-. **Honors/Awds:** Distinguished Service Award Tri-State Univ, 1980. **Military Serv:** Army paratrooper, Korean conflict.

DONAWA, MARIA ELENA
Consultant. **Personal:** Born May 13, 1948, Detroit, MI; daughter of Helen Solese and Milton Solese; married John R Lupien. **Educ:** Howard Univ Coll of Pharmacy, BS Pharmacy 1971; Howard Univ Coll of Medicine, MD 1976. **Career:** Marco Pharmacy, pharmacist 1971-72; Peoples Drug Stores Inc, registered pharmacist 1972-73; Howard Univ Hosp, resident 1976-80, chief resident 1979-80; AbelLabs Inc, staff pathologist 1980; Food & Drug Admin Bureau of Medical Devices, special medical consultant 1980-83 to assoc dir for standards 1983-86; Food & Drug Administration Ctr for Devices & Radiological Health, asst dir for device safety & risk mgmt; Metro Laboratory, path dir 1982-83; Donawa & Associates, Ltd, Rome, Italy, international medical device and pharmaceutical consultant, currently. **Orgs:** Precinct chairperson Democratic Party 1978-79; bd of trustees 1979-86, chairperson quality control comm 1983-86, sec & mem exec comm 1985-86 District of Columbia General Hospital; regulatory affairs columnist, Medical Device Technology Magazine. **Honors/Awds:** US Public Health Serv Achievement Awd 1983, Unit Commendation 1985, Serv Citation 1985, Unit Commendation 1986; network TV interview ABC News (World News Tonight) TSS, Tampons & FDA May 2, 1984 and June 21, 1982; selected media interviews; ''The Case of Toxic Shock Syndrome,'' Knowledge Transfer Roundtable US Public Health Serv 1984 Report of Panel Presentations; articles ''Toxic Shock Syndrome, Chronology of State & Federal Epidemiologic Studies and Regulatory Decision Making'' with G Schmid, M Osterholm Public Health Reports Vol 99 No 4 1984. **Home Addr:** via Fonte di Fauno 22, Rome, Italy. **Business Addr:** International Medical Device and Pharmaceutical Consultant, Donawa & Associates, Ltd, via Fonte di Fauno, 22, I-00153 Roma, Italy.

DONEGAN, CHARLES EDWARD
Attorney, educator. **Personal:** Born Apr 10, 1933, Chicago, IL; son of Odessa Arnold Donegan and Arthur C Donegan Jr; married Patty L Harris; children: Carter Edward. **Educ:** Wilson Jr Coll, AA 1953; Roosevelt, BSC 1954; Loyola, MSIR 1959; Howard, JD 1967; Columbia, LLM 1970. **Career:** US Commisson on Civil Rights, legal intern 1966; Poor Peoples Campaign, legal counsel 1968; F B McKissick Enterprises, staff counsel, 1969; SUNY at Buffalo, first asst prof of law 1970-73; Howard Univ, assoc prof of law 1973-77; OH State Univ, visiting assoc prof 1977-78; First US EPA, asst reg counsel 1978-80; So Univ, prof of law 1980-84, visiting professor of law 1992; CE Donegan & Assoc, atty at law; LA State Univ Law Sch, visiting prof 1981; North Carolina Central Univ Law School, visiting prof 1988-89. **Orgs:** Labor arbitrator Steel Inds Postal AAA 1971-; consultant US Dept of Ag 1972; asst counsel NAACP Legal Defense Fund Inc 1967-69; hrng officer Various Govtl Agy 1975-; officer mem Am Natl Dist of Columbia Chicago Bar Assn 1968-; mem NAACP Urban League; Alpha Phi Alpha; Phi Alpha Delta; Phi Alpha Kappa; labor arbitrator FMCS 1985; counsultant Dist of Columbia Govt Dept of Public Works; mem, District of Columbia Consumer Claims Arbitration Bd 1987-; chmn, legal educ committee, Washington Bar Assn, 1984-91; mem, District of Columbia Attorney-Client Arbitration Board, 1990-91; mem, advisory committee, District of Columbia of Education, Ward 4, 1991; moot court judge, Georgetown, Howard, Balsa, 1987-; vp, Columbia Law Alumni Assn, Washington DC, 1994-; pres, vp, mem, Society of Labor Relations Professionals (SFLRP), 1987-; Natl Bar Assn, Arbitration Section, chair; Natl Assn of Securities Dealers, arbitrator, 1994-; Natl Futures Assn, arbitrator, 1994-; New York Stock Exchange, arbitrator, 1996-; Natl Conference of Black Lawyers, founding mem; Washington Bar Assn; Industrial Relations Research Association; Society of Professionals in Dispute Resolution. **Honors/Awds:** Most outstanding Prof So Univ Law Sch 1982; Ford Fellow Columbia Univ Law Sch

1972-73; NEH Fellow Afro Am Studies Yale Univ 1972-73; pub numerous Articals in Professional Journals; contributor Dictionary of Am Negro Bio 1982; Named one of top 45, 42, 56 Lawyers in Washington DC Area, Washington Afro-American Newspaper, 1993, 1994, 1995; Speaker & Participant at National & Regional Conferences; named one of top 45, 42, 56, 61 Lawyers in Washington, DC Area; Washington African-American Newspaper, 1993-96. **Special Achievements:** First Black member elected to the District of Columbia Labor and Employment Law Section, steering comm, 1995-98; Donated papers to Amistad Research Ctr of Tulane Univ, New Orleans, LA. **Home Addr:** 4315 Argyle Terr N W, Washington, DC 20011. **Business Addr:** Attorney and Arbitrator, 601 Pennsylvania Ave NW, Ste 900, S Bldg, Washington, DC 20004.

DONEGAN, DOROTHY
Musician. **Personal:** Born Apr 6, 1922, Chicago, IL; daughter of Ella Day Donegan (deceased) and Donazell Donegan (deceased); married John McClain, 1948 (divorced 1958); children: John; children: Donovan Eady. **Educ:** Chicago Conservatory; Chiacgo Music College, 1942-44; University of Southern California, sociology, 1953-54. **Career:** Classical and jazz pianist, has played in numerous clubs, halls, theaters and festivals throughout the world; recordings include: Piano Boogie, 1942; Dorothy Romps: A Piano Retrospective, 1953-1979; The Feminine Touch; Kilroy Was Here, 1947; DDT Blues, 1953. **Honors/Awds:** Natl Endowment of the Arts, $20,000 fellowship, 1991. **Business Addr:** Jazz Pianist, c/o Charoscuro Records, 830 Broadway, New York, NY 10003, (212)473-0479.

DOOLEY, WALLACE TROY
Orthopaedic surgeon. **Personal:** Born Jun 15, 1917, Conway, AR; married Orealia Clara Robinson; children: Wallace Jr, Orealia L. **Educ:** KS U, AB 1939; KS U, MA 1941; Meharry Med Coll, MD 1947; Geo W Hubbard Hosp, internship, surg resident 1947-51; Mercy Hosp, 1951-53; Children's Hosp, 1953-55. **Career:** State University of Iowa, Meharry Med Coll, assistant prof div ortho surg 1955; Meharry Med Coll, asso & prof, head ortho surg 1965; Riverside Hosp, Taborian Hosp, cons, ortho surg 1963; TN State U, team phys 1963; Meharry Med Coll, dir rehab med 1962; Geo W Hubbard Hosp, dir Crippled Children's Clinic 1955; Nat Med Assn, chmn Ortho Sec 1970-72; RF Boyd Med Soc, exec sec. **Orgs:** Vol State Med Assn; Am Cong of Rehab Med Assn of Ortho chmn; chmn Research Com mem Adv Bd Assn Med Rehab Dir & Coords Inc 1975; Nashville Area C of C; mem, bd dir, chmn Health & Welfare Com Nashville Urban League 1968-73; Nashville Chap of Frontiers Internat; adv Meharry Chap & 19 Kappa Alpha Psi Frat Inc 1974; Nashville Ortho Soc; TN Orthos - Soc; Pride of TN Elks Lodge #1102 BPOE of W mem exec com Black Educators Council of Human Serv 1970; Manpower Devel & Training HEW 1968-71; dir coun of Comm Agency 1961-62; dir Nashville Br NAACP 1958-61; Outlook Nashville 1959-61; Goodwill Ind 1960-62; pres Comm Conf on Employment Oppor 1960-64; Gov Com on Emp of Physcally Handicapped 1965-67; President's Com on Employment of Physically Handicapped 1965-67; Nat Found for Infantile Paralysis Marcf Dimes 1959; chmn Div 'D' United Givers Fund 1961. **Honors/Awds:** Royal Soc of Health (FRSH); ''Outst Serv to Mankind'' Plaque Meharry Med Coll 1972; ''Outst Serv to Mankind'' Plaque Kappa Alpha Frat 1974; Cert of Aprrec, Outst Serv to Mankind, Frontiers Internat, Nashville Chap 1975; Cert of Outst Serv Assn Med Rehab Dir, Coord Inc 1975. **Business Addr:** Prof Emeritus, Meharry Med Coll, 1005 D.B. Todd Blvd, Nashville, TN 37208.

DOOMES, EARL
Educator. **Personal:** Born Feb 8, 1943, Washington, LA; son of Othus Doomes Sr; married Mazie Marie LeDeaux; children: Elizabeth Denise, Edward Earl, Elliot Doyle. **Educ:** So Univ Baton Rouge, BS 1964; Univ of NE Lincoln, PhD 1969. **Career:** Northwestern Univ, post doctoral rsch 1968-69; Macalester Coll, asst prof 1969-74; FL State Univ, rsch assoc 1975-76; Macalester Coll, assoc prof 1974-77; Southern Univ Baton Rouge, assoc prof 1977-82, prof of chemistry 1982-87, chairman, 1987-92, College of Sciences, dean, 1992-. **Orgs:** Reviewer Petroleum Rsrch Fund Grant Prpsl 1970-80; consultant Minority Biomed Rsrch Sprt Pgm of the Natl Inst of Hlth 1979-92; Natl Sci Found Grants Pgm 1985. **Honors/Awds:** Merck Sharpe & Dohme Univ of NE Lincoln 1968; Natl Sci Found Traineeship Univ Of N 1967-68; Natl Sci Found Fclty Sci Flwhp FL State Univ 1975-76; rsrch grnts 8; pblshd artlcls 21; Faculty Excellence in Science and Technology, White House Initiative on HBCU's, 1988; Charles E Coates Memorial Award, 1997. **Home Phone:** (504)774-8284. **Business Addr:** Dean, College of Sciences, Southern Univ-Baton Rouge, P O Box 11513, Baton Rouge, LA 70813, (504)771-5170.

DORMAN, HATTIE L.
Management consultant, associate professor. **Personal:** Born Jul 22, 1932, Cleveland, OH; daughter of Claire Correa Lenoir (deceased) and James Lyman Lawrence (deceased); married James W L Dorman; children: Lydia Dorman, Lynda, James Larry. **Educ:** Fenn Coll, Cleveland State Univ, 1950-58, DC Teacher's Coll 1959-64, Howard Univ, BA, 1987. **Career:** IRS, 1954-79; US Treasury, spl asst to deputy asst sec 1978-79; President's Task Force on Women Business Enterprise, mem 1978-79; Interagency Comm on Women's Business Enterprise US Small Business Admin, deputy dir 1979-83; US Small Business Admin Office of Comm and Govt Support, dir 1983-85; Dorman & Associates, management consultant, and trainer 1985-; Univ of DC, assoc prof continuing educ; Howard Univ, guest lecturer continuing educ; Presidential Transition Team, chief of staff for deputy dir, 1992-93. **Orgs:** Trainer Nation's Capital Girl Scout Cncl 1972-; mem Natl Assoc of Female Execs, Amer Assoc of Black Women Entrepreneurs, Black Career Women Inc, Sr Exec Assoc, Federal Exec Inst Alumni Assoc, Amer Sociological Assoc; life mem Natl Council of Negro Women; golden life mem Delta Sigma Theta Sor Inc; mem Natl Urban League; life mem, Girl Scouts of the USA, bd of dirs; Wider Opportunity for Women; public speaker and trainer field of mgmt and business develop; Amer Society for training & development, Howard Univ Alumni Assn. **Honors/Awds:** Monetary Performance Awds IRS 1970-78; Mary McLeod Bethune Centennial Awd Natl Council of Negro Women; Monetary Performance Awds US Small Business Admin 1980, 1984, 1985; Boss of the Year Awd Amer Business Women's Assoc L'Enfant Chap 1981; other awds and citations from Delta Sigma Theta, PTA's, Amer Assoc of Black Women Entrepreneurs, Natl Assoc of Minority Women; Articles: ''Survey of Support Patterns by Black Organizations for Black Political Appointees'' Benjamin E Mays Monograph series Fall 1988 vol 1, No 2; ''Field of Small Business Develop''. **Business Addr:** Principal, Dorman & Associates, PO Box 1052, Silver Spring, MD 20910.

DORMAN, LINNEAUS C.
Scientist (retired). **Personal:** Born Jun 28, 1935, Orangeburg, SC; son of Georgia Dorman (deceased) and John A Dorman Sr (deceased); married Phae Hubble; children: Evelyn S, John A. **Educ:** Bradley Univ, BS 1952-56; IN Univ, PhD 1956-61. **Career:** No Regional Res Lab, chemist 1956-59; Dow Chem Co, rsch chemist 1960-68, rsch specialist 1968-76, sr rsch assoc 1976-83, assoc scientist 1983-92, senior assoc scientist, 1993-94. **Orgs:** Bd of dir Comerica Bk-Midland 1982-95; Midland sec counselor Am Chem Soc 1971-92; chmn 1984,85 bd of fellows Saginaw Valley State Coll 1976-87, Natl Org of Black Chem & Chem Eng 1978-; pres Midland Rotary Clb 1982-83; chmn Midland Black Coalition 1973, 1977; bd of trustees Midland Found 1981-90; United Negro College Fund; chmn Midland Area Campaign 1981-84; life mem NAACP; vice pres Midland Foundation 1988-90; Elected to Bradley Univ, Centurion Society, 1993; appointed to Bradley Univ Council, 1994; Indiana Univ, Chemistry Dept, appointed to bd of overseers, 1994. **Honors/Awds:** Dow Research Fellow, Indiana Univ, 1959-60; Co-Recipient Bond Awrd Am Oil Chemst Soc 1960; inventor of the yr Dow Chem Central Rsch 1983; patentee in field; cnstribtr to Scientific Journals & Books; Honorary Doctor of Science, Saginaw Valley State Univ 1988.

DORN, ROOSEVELT F.
Judge, minister. **Personal:** Born Oct 29, 1935, Checotah, OK; married Joyce Evelyn Glosson, 1965; children: Bryan Keith, Renee Felicia, Rochelle Francine. **Educ:** University of California School of Law at Berkeley; Whittier College of Law, JD, 1969; California Judicial College; Earl Warren Legal Institute, 1979, 1982. **Career:** Los Angeles County, deputy sheriff/superior court bailiff, 1961-69; City of Los Angeles, asst city atty 1970-79; Inglewood Jud Dist CA, municipal ct judge 1979-80; Los Angeles County Superior Court, judge 1980-. **Orgs:** Founder, 1st pres Inglewood Dem Club 1977-79; mem NAACP, Urban League, LA Co Bar Assn, Langston Bar Assn, CA Black Lawyers Assn, Am Bar Assn, Lions Club; assoc minister Atherton Baptist Church Inglewood, CA; mem CA Judges Assoc, Natl Bar Assn, Los Angeles Trial Lawyers Assn, 100 Black Men of Los Angeles Inc; John M Langston Bar Assn Judges' Division. **Honors/Awds:** Commendation for Outstanding Comm Serv, The Senate CA Legislature 1978; Commendation for Outstanding Serv CA State Assembly 1979; Commendation for Outstanding Achievement New Frontier Dem Club Inglewood Dem Club 1979; Outstanding Serv Awd in the field of Juvenile Justice Natl Sor of Phi Delta Kappa Inc Delta Kappa Chap 1983, John M Langston Bar Assoc 1983, Inglewood Democratic Club, Los Angeles Co Bd of Supervisors 1983, CA State Assembly 1983; Outstanding Contributions Support and Leadership for Youth Awd RDM Scholarship Fund Inc 1984, 1985; Meritorious Serv Youth Awd The Inglewood Teachers Assn 1986; Dedicated Service & Guidance Awd Inglewood High School Student Body; Natl Top Ladies of Distinction Humanitarian Award, 1987; Outstanding Service Award,Prairie View A&M Univ Alumni Assn,89; Los Angeles County, Central District, Most Valuable Judge Certificate, 1991-93; Los Angeles Chief of Police, Willie L Williams, Commendation for Outstanding Leadership, 1992; First African Methodist Episcopal Church, FAME Award, 1992; Distinguished Service Award, Natl Bar Assn Judicial Council; Certificate of Appreciation, Los Angeles Southwest Coll; Natl Honoree, Los Angeles Sentinel's Highest Award; Man of the Year Award, Because I Love You. **Military Serv:** USAF airman 1st class 1954-58. **Business Addr:** Judge, Superior Court Los Angeles County, 110 Regent St, Inglewood, CA 90301.

DORSE, BERNICE PERRY
Government official (retired). **Personal:** Born Apr 5, 1931, West Point, MS; daughter of Statie M Perry and Willie B Perry; divorced. **Educ:** University of Illinois, BS, 1954. **Career:** Dept of Veterans Affairs, Chicago, clinical dietician, 1964-66, dietetic services assistant chief, 1966-72, Salem, VA, dietetic services chief, 1972-74, Cincinnati, dietetic services chief, 1974-76, Boston, dietetic services chief, 1976-82, Washington District of Columbia, dietetic services chief, 1982-87; Department of Veterans Affairs, dietetic services director, 1987-96. **Orgs:** American Dietetic Association, quality management, dietetics education task force, 1992-94; District of Columbia Dietetic Association, career guidance chairperson, 1985-86; American Society for Hospital Food Svc Administration, 1986-96; Illinois Dietetic Association, food administration section co-chair, 1968-69; District of Columbia Dietetic Association, management practices chairman, 1992-93; National Society for Health-care Food Service Management, treasurer, 1994; director, 1991-96. **Honors/Awds:** District of Columbia Public School, Certificate of Appreciation, 1986; Veterans Administration, Certificate of Pride in Public Service, 1989, Honor Award, 1989; Department of Veterans Affairs, Presidential Rank Award, 1992; American Heart Association, American Association of Retired Persons, Certificate of Appreciation, 1991; Exceptional Service Awd, 1996; Health Care Professional of the Year, 1996. **Special Achievements:** Speaker: Dietetic Interns, 1987, 1997; speaker: National Education Conference, NV, 1991, D 1991; Dietetic Interns, MD, 1992; Speaker, American Dietetic Assn, 1993. **Home Addr:** 6121 85th Ave, New Carrollton, MD 20784-2841.

DORSETT, ANTHONY DREW, JR.
Professional football player. **Personal:** Born Sep 14, 1973, Aliquippa, PA. **Educ:** Univ of Pittsburgh. **Career:** Houston Oilers, defensive back, 1996; Tennessee Oilers, 1997-. **Business Addr:** Professional Football Player, Tennessee Oilers, c/o Baptist Sports Park, 7640 H 70-5, Nashville, TN 37221.

DORSETT, KATIE GRAYS
State government administrator. **Personal:** Born Jul 8, 1932, Shaw, MS; daughter of Elizabeth Grays and Willie Grays (deceased); married Warren G Dorsett; children: Valerie. **Educ:** Alcorn State Univ, BS 1953; Indiana Univ at Bloomington, MS 1955; Univ of North Carolina at Greensboro, EdD 1975; State Univ of New York at Buffalo, attended 1981; Univ of Maryland at College Park, attended 1983. **Career:** School of Business & Economics North Carolina A&T St Univ, assoc prof 1955-1987; Greensboro City Council 1983-86; Guilford County Commission 1986-92; Transportation Inst North Carolina A&T, rsch assoc 1983-87; Department of Administration, State of North Carolina, secretary, currently. **Orgs:** Bd mem, Guilford Tech Comm Coll 1978-; exec bd General Greene Council Boy Scouts 1980-; mem Greensboro Citizens Assn; life mem, NAACP; mem League of Women Voters; bd mem, Greensboro Natl Bank; bd mem, MDC Corporation. **Honors/Awds:** 10 publications including ''A Study of Levels of Job Satisfaction and Job Aspirations Among Black Clerical Employees in Greensboro & Guilford Co, North Carolina'' 1976; ''Training & Career Opportunities for Minorities & Women'' Proceedings, 1984; Outstanding Civic Leader Greensboro Interclub Council 1978; TV Citizen of the Week WGHP TV 1978; One Comm Awd Feb One Soc 1982; Outstanding Citizen Award Negro Business & Prof Women 1983; Outstanding Comm Leader Mt Zion Baptist Church 1983; Leader of the Year Omega Psi Phi 1983; Woman of the Year Mt Zion AME Church 1984; Sojourner Truth Award, Negro Business & Professional Women, 1985; Leadership Award, Negro Business & Professional Women, 1986; Distinguished Alumni, NAFEO, 1987; Leadership Award, Sigma Gamma Rho, 1987;Bennett College Comm Servennett Coll, 1988; Silver Anniversary Serv Award, North Carolina Comm Coll, 1989; Woman of Year, NAACP, 1989. **Home Addr:** 1000 N English St, Greensboro, NC 27405.

DORSETT, TONY DREW
Professional football player (retired). **Personal:** Born Apr 7, 1954, Rochester, PA; married Julie; children: Shukura, Anthony Drew Jr. **Educ:** Univ of Pittsburgh, attended. **Career:** Running back: Dallas Cowboys, 1977-87; Denver Broncos, 1988; Southwestern Drilling Mud Co, Midland TX, partner. **Orgs:** Mem Natl Easter Seals Sports Cncl; chmn Amer Heart Assn Jump-Rope-A-Thon 1980; promoted, United Way, United Negro College Fund, TX Dept of Hwys & Public Trans Seat Belt Prog, Dallas Civic Opera. **Honors/Awds:** Heisman Trophy 1976; 1st player in NCAA history with four 1000 yard seasons; established record for longest run from scrimmage (99 yards), 1983; Rookie of the Year, Sporting News, 1977; NFC Player of the Year 1981; holds numerous team (Dallas) records; played in Pro Bowl, 1978-81, 1983.

DORSEY, CAROLYN ANN
Educator. **Personal:** Born Oct 8, Dayton, OH; daughter of Lorana Madeline Webb Dorsey and James J Dorsey. **Educ:** Kent State Univ, BS 1956, MEd 1961; Yale Univ, Danforth Fellow in Black Studies 1969-70; New York Univ, PhD 1976. **Career:** Cleveland Public Schools, teacher 1956-62; Tabora Girls Sch, Tanzania, E Africa, teacher 1962-64; Cleveland Job Corps Ctr, social studies dept chair & teacher 1965-67; Southern IL Univ Exper in Higher Educ Prog, curriculum spec & instructor 1967-69; Yale Univ Transitional Year Program, assoc dir & teacher, 1969-70; NY Univ Inst of Afro-Amer Affairs, jr fellow 1970-

74; IN State Univ, asst prof of afro-amer studies 1976-77; Univ of MO, coord of Black studies & asst prof of higher educ 1977-81, coord of Black studies & assoc prof of higher educ 1981-85, assoc prof of higher educ 1985-, dir of graduate studies, 1986-91. **Orgs:** Stephens Coll Bd of Curators, 1981-91; Amer Assn of Higher Educ, Natl Council for Black Studies; Phi Delta Kappa; Phi Lambda Theta; Assn for the Study of Afro-American Life & History; Alpha Kappa Alpha Sorority; mem of bias panel Amer Coll Testing Program Tests 1982- & The Psychological Corp Stanford Achievement Test, 7th & 8th editions. **Honors/Awds:** Danforth Found Black Studies Fellowship yr spent at Yale Univ 1969-70; Southern Fellowship used for Dissertation Study at New York Univ 1973-74; Danforth Found Assoc 1980-86; resident participant in Summer Inst for Women in Higher Educ Admin, Bryn Mawr Coll, 1989; University of Missouri Faculty Award, 1990; University of Missouri Alumnae Anniversary Award for Contributions to the Education of Women, 1990. **Business Addr:** Associate Professor, University of Missouri, 301 Hill Hall, Columbia, MO 65211.

DORSEY, CHARLES HENRY, JR.
Attorney. **Personal:** Born May 18, 1930, Baltimore, MD; son of Olga Nicholson Dorsey and Charles Henry Dorsey; married Agnes; children: Kathleen, Andrea, Judith, Claire, Charles III, Leonard, Peter, Martin, Nicholas. **Educ:** Epiphany Coll, 1947-48; Loyola Coll, 1949-57; Univ of MD Law Sch, 1957-61. **Career:** US Post Office, clerk 1957-61; Human A Pressman Esq Baltimore, assoc 1961-62; George L Russell Jr, assoc 1962-63; Brown, Allen, Watts, Murphy & Russell Baltimore, assoc 1963-66; Brown & Allen, Dorsey & Josey Baltimore, parnter 1966-69; Baltimore City Solicitor, 1969; Legal Aid Bur, deputy dir 1969-74; Legal Aid Bur Inc, exec dir 1974-. **Orgs:** Mem adv commn Baltimore Dept of Social Serv 1967-69; mem bd dir Assoc Catholic Charities 1969-73; mem Bar Assn of Baltimore City, sec 1972-74, vice pres 1984-85, pres elect 1985-86, pres 1986-87 Monumental City Bar Assn; mem bd governors St Thomas More Soc Mem bd trustees Good Samaritan Hosp 1973; member, bd of trustees, St Joseph Hosp, 1983-91; vice chmn Proj Advisory Group 1976-79; chmn Proj Advisory Group 1979; mem bd of trustees Western MD Coll, Westminister, MD; chairman, Fellows of MD Bar Foundation 1980; chmn judicial appointments MD State Bar Assn 1983-84; MD State Board of Law Examiners, 1972-; chr, 1981-; board of governors, MD State Bar Assn, 1987-89; member, standing comm of legal aid, American Bar Assn, 1985-91. **Honors/Awds:** Papal Order of Knights of St Gregory; Man for all Seasons Awd St Thomas More Soc 1974; Alumni Laureate Awd Loyola Coll 1985; Community Serv Awd Monumental City Bar Assn 1986; John Minor Wisdom Award, ABA Litigation Section, 1990. **Military Serv:** USAF 1st Lt, 1951-56.

DORSEY, CLINTON GEORGE
Educator (retired), cleric. **Personal:** Born Oct 29, 1931, New York, NY. **Educ:** Wilberforce Univ OH, BS Ed 1966; United Theol Sem Dayton OH, MDiv 1970; Wright State Univ Dayton OH, attended. **Career:** AME Church, United Church of Christ, 1962-68; Wright Patterson Air Force Base, Dayton OH, W OH Conf, United Methodist Church, pastor 1969-74; Troy High School, Troy OH, counselor 1975-92. **Orgs:** Pres Clinton G Dorsey Assoc Motivational Human Devel; dist rep OH School Counselors Assoc 1971-76; consult Dem Nom US Rep Fourth Cong Dist OH 1976; bd mem Miami Cty Mental Assoc 1976; adv bd criminal justice comm Edison State Comm Coll 1979; APGA leg prog proj trainer Amer Personnel & Guidance Asn 1980; board member, Miami County Habitat for Humanity, 1992; vice chair, Miami Cty Executive Comm. **Military Serv:** USAF a1/c 1949-53.

DORSEY, DENISE
Graphic artist. **Personal:** Born Apr 24, 1953, Washington, DC; daughter of Lillian Miles Dorsey and Willie K Dorsey. **Educ:** Univ of MD, College Park, MD, BS, 1975. **Career:** YWCA, Baltimore, MD, aerobic instructor, 1981-91; Afro-American Newspapers, Baltimore, MD, graphic artist, 1976-. **Orgs:** Bd of dir, The Charles St Dancers, 1991; sec, treas, United Paperworkers Intl Union, Local 111, 1988-95. **Business Addr:** Graphic Artist, Afro-American Newspapers, 2519 N Charles St, Baltimore, MD 21218.

DORSEY, ELBERT
Attorney. **Personal:** Born Oct 4, 1941, St Louis, MO; son of Juanita Jarrett Green and Velmer Dorsey; married Diane Elaine; children: Elbert Todd, Donielle Elaine, Daniel Christopher, Joseff Alexander. **Educ:** Harris-Stowe State Coll, BA 1966; St Louis Univ School of Law, JD 1973. **Career:** St Louis Comm Coll Dist, asst librarian 1965-66; St Louis Bd of Educ, teacher 1966-70; St Louis Legal Aid Soc, law clerk 1971-72; Small Business Admin, loan officer/attorney 1973-74; Collier, Dorsey, & Williams, attorney. **Orgs:** Historian Mound City Bar Assc; mem Judicial Conf Advy Com for the Eighth Circuit Ct of Appeals; chmn/bd of dir Yeatman/Union-Sarah Jnt Commn on Health; Polemarch St Louis Alumni Chptr Kappa Alpha Psi Frat; chmn/advsry bd St Louis Comprehensive Hlth Cntr Home Hlth Bd. **Honors/Awds:** Ford Fellowship World Conf of Peace 1973; Humanitarian Award St Louis Alumni Chptr Kappa Alpha Psi 1985; Dedication Award Mound City Bar Assn of St Louis 1983. **Business Addr:** Attorney, Law Office of Collier, Dorsey & Williams, 625 N Euclid, Ste 402, St Louis, MO 63108.

DORSEY, HAROLD AARON
Chief executive officer. **Personal:** Born Jun 22, 1933, Louisville, KY; married Julia Anita Willis; children: Michelle, Harold II, Michael. **Educ:** OH Univ Athens, BA Pol Sci 1965; OH State Univ Columbus, MA 1971. **Career:** Community Action Agency, asst dir 1965-69; Grad School OH State Dept Soc, rsch asst 1968-70; Community Action Agency, acting dir 1970; OH State Univ, teaching asst 1970-71; Mansfield OIC, exec dir 1971-. **Orgs:** Past pres Mansfield NAACP 1974; past chmn 9 Cty Manpower Adv Council 1975; bd of dir Mansfield Area C of C 1977-80; pres Natl Black Professional Assoc 1977-80. **Honors/Awds:** Personality of the Week Local Newspaper-Mansfield News Jrnl; Businessman of Week Local Radio Staion; Ed Bd Gerontologist. **Military Serv:** USAF a/1c. **Business Addr:** Executive Dir, Mansfield OIC, 445 N Bowman St, Mansfield, OH 44903.

DORSEY, HERMAN SHERWOOD, JR. (WOODY)
International consultant. **Personal:** Born Apr 5, 1945, Brooklyn, NY; son of Loretta Rosa Kenney Dorsey and Herman Sherwood Dorsey Sr; married Maria Teresa Miller Dorsey, Feb 19, 1966; children: Donna Michelle, Bryan Sherwood. **Educ:** New York City Community College, Brooklyn, NY, AA, mech tech, 1966; Brooklyn Polytechnic Institute, Brooklyn, NY, BS, mech engineering, 1972; New York University, Bronx, NY, BS, mech engineering, 1972; Duke University, Durham, NC, certificate, executive management, 1988. **Career:** Consolidated Edison, New York, NY, technician, 1966-72, engineer, 1972-78, senior engineer, 1978-83, subsection mgr, 1983-86, mgr, steam generation planning, 1986-91, technical superintendent, 1991-93, plant manager, Steam/Electric Station, 1994-; private international consultant, 1992-; motivational speaker, 1995-. **Orgs:** DOE, candidate principle assistant secretary, 1993; IDEA, Natl Planning Committee, 1991-93; US Trade and Development Team, 1995; National Action Council for Minorities in Engineering, liaison, 1989-98; national chairman, American Association of Blacks in Energy, 1996-98; vice pres, board member, Tamiment Resort POA, 1991-94; chairman, Steam Integrated Resource Plan, Consolidated Edison, 1992; member, American Society of Mechanical Engineers, 1972-; National Republican Congressional Comm & Frederick Douglass Republican Coun, 1990-. **Honors/Awds:** Certificate as Visiting Professor, Black Executive Exchange Program, National Urban League & Assn Colleges, 1976, 1977, 1980-89; Black Achiever in Industry, YMCA-Harlem Branch, 1975; three technical papers published internationally, International District Heating and Cooling Assn, 1988, 1989, 1991; Certificate, Shaping the Minds of Young Adults, Consolidated Edison, 1988; Pi Tau Sigma, Scholastic Achievement, Pi Tau Sigma-Honorary Mechanical Engineering Society, 1972; Ms America Pageant judge, 1995; Consultant to Gingdao, China Power Co, 1995. **Business Addr:** Plant Manager, Consolidated Edison of New York, Inc, 850 Twelfth Avenue, New York, NY 10019.

DORSEY, IVORY JEAN
Consultant. **Personal:** Born May 29, 1947, Baton Rouge, LA; daughter of Mary L Wood and Walter E Wood; divorced; children: Edward Douglas. **Educ:** Southern University, BS, bus ed, 1970. **Career:** Xerox Corp, customer representative, Houston, 1974-75, high volume system rep, 1975-76, region program support, Dallas, 1976-77, field sales executive, 1977-79, field sales manager, Atlanta, 1979-81, manager of Xerox store, Atlanta, 1981-84; Golden Eagle Business Services Inc, president/owner, 1984-. **Orgs:** American Society for Training & Development, president, 1992; Atlanta Chamber of Commerce Partners in Bus & Ed, advisory board, 1992; Governor's Small & Minority Business Advisory Committee, vice-chairwoman, 1992; National & Georgia Speakers Association, 1992. **Honors/Awds:** Atlanta Tribune, Annual Salute to Business Owners, 1990. **Business Addr:** President, Owner, Golden Eagle Business Services, Inc, 1401 Peachtree St, NE, Ste 101, Atlanta, GA 30309, (404)881-6777.

DORSEY, JOHN L.
Attorney. **Personal:** Born Sep 24, 1935, New Orleans, LA; married Evelyn. **Educ:** Dillard U, BA 1963; Loyola Univ Law Sch, JD 1969. **Career:** New Orleans Legal Assistance Corp, atty 1968-70; Dorsey & Marks, New Orleans, atty 1970-; John L Dorsey, attorney at law. **Orgs:** Mem Nat Bar Assn; New Orleans Criminal Ct Bar Assn; Am Bar Assn; mem NAACP; New Orleans Urban League; Lower & Ninth Ward Neighborhood Council; Com on Alcholism & Drug Abuse for Greater New Orleans; All Conference Football 1961. **Military Serv:** USAF a/1c 1955-59. **Business Addr:** Attorney, Canal Place One, Ste 2300, New Orleans, LA 70130.

DORSEY, JOSEPH A.
Educational administrator. **Personal:** Born Apr 19, 1932, Baltimore, MD; married Alma K Edmonds; children: Dwain Kevin, Kyle Joseph. **Educ:** Springfield Coll, (cum laude) BS 1954-58; NY U, CAGS 1958-59; Northesastern U, MEd 1964-66; Boston U, DEd 1972-76; Univ of Lowell Dept of Health,prof, chmn 1976-; Boston State Coll & Phys Edn, asso prof, chmn 1968-76; Andover Sch System, tchr coach 1960-68; Wayne Co Gen Hosp Detroit, phys therapist 1959-60; Lawrence Gen Hosp, phys therapist 1960-66; Private Practice, phys therapist 1960-; Andover Bd Health & Sch System, consult pt 1977-78. **Career:** Bd of dir Andover ABC 1977-; com mem Merrimack Valley Health Council 1978-. **Orgs:** Coach of the Year MA Assn Gymnastic Coaches 1967-68; citations State Rep & State Sen 1968 & 1977; Andover Hall of Fame, Andover Sch System 1977; Fellow Am Coll of Sports Medicine 1979; Good Conduct Medal/UN Serv Medal/Korean Serv Medal W/3 Stars/Nat Defense Medal USMC. **Military Serv:** USMC sgt 1951-54. **Business Addr:** 1 Rolfe St, Lowell, MA 01854.

DORSEY, L. C.
Health center executive. **Personal:** Born Dec 17, 1938, Tribbett, MS; daughter of Mary Davis and Abraham Warren; married Hildery Dorsey Sr, Feb 17, 1956 (divorced); children: Cynthia Dorsey Smith, Norma Dorsey, Anita Dorsey Word, Michael Dorsey, Adriane Dorsey, Hildery Dorsey Jr. **Educ:** Mary Holmes Coll, 1969-71; Worker Coll Tel Aviv Israel, 1970; State Univ of NY Stony Brook NY, MSW 1973, Howard Univ, DSW 1988. **Career:** Delta Ministry, asso dir 1977-83; So Coalition on Jails & Prisons Inc, asso dir 1975-83; Washington Co Opportunities Inc, dir social serv 1974; No Bolivar Co Farm Coop, dir 1968-71; Operation Headstart, tchr 1966-67; Delta Health Center Inc, exec dir 1988-95; Univ of Mississippi, research asst prof 1988; Memphis Health Center, asst to the Chief Health Officer 1986-88; Lutheran Social Services of Washington DC, Advocacy & Education, dir 1983-85; Jackson State Univ, Sch of Soc Work, asst prof, 1995-. **Orgs:** MS Conf of Social Welfare 1976-; pres Jackson chap NABSW 1976-78, 80-82; chmn polit action com, Stte NAACP 1979; mem New Bethel MB Ch choir 1975-80; mem First Christian Church, 1988-; writer, board member Jackson Adv 1978-80; poet, founding mem Black Women's Art Collective 1978-80; mem, Presidential Comm, Natl Advisory Council on Economic Opportunities, Washington DC 1978-80; mem, Governor's Commission on Children and Youth, Jackson MS 1980; mem, Governor's Task Force on Indigent Health Care, Jackson MS 1988-89; life mem, NAACP; Natl Coun of Negro Women, 1971-; Amer Public Hth Assn, 1989-; NASW, 1995-; ACLU of MS, 1989-; Southern Regional Coun, 1997-; Pres Clinton's Hth Professionals Commission, Hth Care Reform, 1994-96; chair, Mayor's Task Force on Human and Cultural Service, 1997-. **Honors/Awds:** Meritorious Serv Awards Nat Med Assn, Women's Aux 1970; Woman of the Year New York City Utility Club 1971; Fellowship Black Women's Community Devel Found 1971, 1972; Fannie Lou Hamer Award, Urban League of Jackson 1978; Fellow, MATCH Program, Natl Assn of Community Health Centers 1986-87; The Significance of Jealousy and Addictive Love in Acts of Homicide Among Black Women (Dissertation) 1987; Not In Our Names 1984; Cold Steel 1982; If Bars Could Talk 1980; Freedom Came to Mississippi 1978; Magnolia Bar Assn, Harriet Tubman Award, 1998. **Home Addr:** PO Box 24114, Jackson, MS 39225-4114.

DORSEY, LEON D., SR.
Business executive. **Personal:** Born Feb 10, 1909, Perry, TX; married Althea Fay Hutchings; children: Leon II, Robert. **Educ:** Paul Quinn, 1931-32. **Career:** Dorsey-keatts Funeral Home Inc, owner pres; Independent Funeral Directors Assn, TX Pres Dorsey Funeral Benefit Assn, past chmn bd, past Fpres, past treas; TX Assn Life Ins & Officers, 1st vp. **Orgs:** Marlin City Councilman; finan sec Marlin Miss Bapt Ch; mem exec com Heart TX; Boy Scout Council. **Honors/Awds:** Mortician Yr 1967; 33 deg Mason; Century mem Heart TX Boy Scouts 1973; Past Grand Joshua Heroines Jericho Princ Hall Affiliation 1970-73; v grand Joshua Heroins Jericho of Gen Conf Grand Cts PHA 1976-77; Silv Beaver Aw Scts 1976-77, 1974-75. **Business Addr:** 907 Live Oak St, Marlin, TX.

DORSEY, SANDRA
Association executive. **Personal:** chilDren: Kellee. **Career:** ABC Television; Foundation for Minority Interests in Media, west coast regional office, dir, currently. **Orgs:** American Women in Radio & TV (AWRT), pres, 1997-. **Business Addr:** President, American Women in Radio & TV, 1650 Tysons Blvd, No. 200, Mc Lean, VA 22102, (703)506-3920.

DORSEY, TAFFY ANNE
Physician. **Personal:** Born Mar 20, 1959, Syracuse, NY; daughter of Carrie and J B Dorsey; divorced. **Educ:** Univ of Pittsburgh, BS, 1982; Georgetown Univ Medical School, MD, 1988; Univ of Michigan Hospital Residency in Obstetrics and Gynecology, 1992. **Career:** Univ of Pennsylvania, clinical asst professor, 1992-94; Thomas Jefferson Univ Medical School, clinical asst professor, 1994-; Pennsylvania Hospital, clinical instructor in OB-GYN, 1992-. **Orgs:** Natl Medical Assn, 1988-; Amer Medical Assn, 1988-; Amer College of Obstetrics and Gynecology, 1988-. **Honors/Awds:** Georgetown Univ Medical School, Heniz Bower Award, 1988, Gregory R Thrette, 1987. **Special Achievements:** Fluent in Spanish, studied in Madrid; Spain, 1974. **Business Phone:** (215)829-3198.

DORTCH, HEYWARD
Co. president. **Personal:** Born Jun 25, 1939, Camden, AL; son of Clarence and Alice Dortch; married Amelia, Jul 3, 1966; children: Derrick. **Educ:** Tennessee State Univ, BS, 1966. **Career:** The Diversa Group Inc, president, currently. **Orgs:** Ebenezer AME Church, board of trustees, financial sec, chief fiscal officer, chairperson/insurance and real estate comm of the

board, non-profit housing corp., vice pres; Eastern Michigan Univ, facilities mgt advisory board/college of technology. **Honors/Awds:** Young Men's Christian Assn of Metro Detroit, Minority Achiever in Industry, 1980; Radio Station WJLB, Strong Achiever Award, 1990; Natl Assn of Negro Bus and Prof Women's Club, Outstanding Dedication and Work with Youth, 1990; Detroit City Council, Testimonial Resolution, For Contributions to the City of Detroit, 1991. **Special Achievements:** Michigan Consolidated Gas Company's Annual Jobs and Careers Seminar, founder/chairperson, 1982-94; Serves as a mentor at various schools working primarily with young male students; Author, Preparing for Your Career, A Resource Handbook; Author, How To Start, Operate and Manage A Small Business; founder & coord, Ebenezer AME Church Tutorial Program. **Home Addr:** 15537 Thatcher, Detroit, MI 48235, (313)256-6800. **Business Addr:** President, The Diversa Group Inc, 17515 W 9 Mile Rd, Ste 580, Southfield, MI 48075, (810)559-2066.

DORTCH, THOMAS WESLEY, JR.
State government official. **Personal:** Born Apr 12, 1950, Toccoa, GA; son of Lizzie M Porter Dortch and Thomas Wesley Dortch Sr (deceased); married Carol Warren Dortch, Sep 16, 1985; children: Angelique, Thomas W III. **Educ:** Fort Valley State College, BA, 1972; Atlanta University, MA, 1985. **Career:** Democratic Party of Georgia, Atlanta, GA, associate director, 1974-78; US Senator Sam Nunn, Atlanta, GA, administrative aide, 1978-86, state executive assistant, 1986-90, state director, 1990-. **Orgs:** 100 Black Men of Atlanta, president; GA Association of Minority Entrepreneurs, co-founder, board member; Atlanta Business League, board member; Big Brother Big Sister, board member; Metro Atlanta Mental Health Association, board member; NAACP Special Contibution Fund, trustee; Fort Valley State College Foundation, board member; mem, NAACP; mem, advisory board, GA Assn Blk Elected Officials; chm of the board, Natl Black College Alumni Hall of Fame, Foundation, 1984-; natl vice chm, Assault on Illiteracy Program, 1984-; co-chm, Atlanta Jewish/Black Coalition, 1990-. **Honors/Awds:** Al Knox Award, FVSC 1972; Ford Fellow, GA State Univ, 1972-74; Sears & Roebuck Presidential Found Schlrshp; Good Guy Award, Georgia Women's Political Caucus, 1989; Presidential Citation for Volunteerism, President George Bush, 1990; Humanitarian Award, Georgia Assn of Black Elected Officials, 1989; Fort Valley State College Alumni Hall of Fame, inductee; NAACP, C A Harper Award; NAFEO, Distinguished Alumni Award; Omega Psi Phi, Man of the Year. **Business Addr:** State Director, Office of US Senator Sam Nunn, 75 Spring St, Suite 1700, Atlanta, GA 30303.

DOSS, EVAN, JR.
State official. **Personal:** Born Jul 6, 1948, Lorman, Montserrat; married Emma Ruth Duffin; children: Evan III, Rashida Fayola. **Educ:** Alcorn State U, BS 1970. **Career:** Claiborne Co, tax assessor & tax collector; Claiborne Co Sch System MS, Pt Gibson, MS, history tchr 1970-71. **Orgs:** Assessor Collector Assn; NAACP; Omega Psi Phi Frat. **Honors/Awds:** Port Gibson MS Whitman "Grady" Mayo Scholarship Found Inc. **Business Addr:** Tax Assessor & Collector, Claiborne County, PO Box 653, Port Gibson, MS 39150.

DOSS, JUANITA KING
Clinical psychologist. **Personal:** Born Jan 5, 1942, Baltimore, MD; daughter of Helen King and Charles King; divorced 1975; children: Charles Doss, Lawry Doss. **Educ:** Howard University, Washington, DC, BS, 1963; Wayne State University, Detroit, MI, MSW, 1972; Union Institute, Cincinnati, OH, PhD, 1988. **Career:** Allied Health Services, MI, assoc director, 1972-78; Southwest Detroit Hospital, MI, dir of planning and development, 1978-80; Burdette & Doss Assocs, MI, co-owner, 1980-. **Business Addr:** Psychologist/Consultant, Burdette and Doss Associates, 17336 W. 12 Mile Rd., Southfield, MI 48076.

DOSS, LAROY SAMUEL
Automobile dealer. **Personal:** Born Oct 6, 1936, San Francisco, CA; son of Louvonia Smith Doss and Samuel Doss, Jr; married Mary Joyce Piper; children: Gwendolyn Marie. **Educ:** St Marys Coll, 1955-59. **Career:** Crown Zellerback, warehouseman 1959-61; SF, playground dir 1961-63; Geary Ford, salesman 1963, fleet mgr 1968-69, truck sales mgr 1969-71, used car mgr 1974; Pittsburg Ford Inc, pres 1974-. **Orgs:** 2nd vp, bd dir St Marys Coll Alumni 1963-; Proj Inside/Out San Quentin Prison 1967-71; vice pres Optimist Club 1972-74; pres Pittsburg C of C 1976-; bd dir E Contra Costa YMCA 1977-; dir Sr Citizens Home for Aging Bldg Fund 1977-, Black Political Assn 1975, Pittsburg Rotary Club 1975-, Pittsburg Business & Professional Assn; mem of bd of trustees St Marys Coll 1980-; pres Easter Seals Soc of Contra Costa Solano Cty 1983-84; bd of regents St Mary's Coll Moraga CA 1986-; chmn of the bd, Black Ford-Lincoln-Mercury Dealers Assn 1988-89. **Honors/Awds:** All City Basketball 1955; All League Basketball 1958-59; Most Valuable Player 1959; #92 in 1977, #72 in 1978, #98 in 1997 Black Enterprise Magazine for Most Successful 100 Black Businesses in Amer. **Business Addr:** President, Pittsburg Ford Inc, 2575 Railroad Ave, Pittsburg, CA 94565.

DOSS, LAWRENCE PAUL
Business executive. **Personal:** Born Jun 16, 1927, Cleveland, OH; son of Velma L Kendall Doss and Raymond Doss; married Judith Young Doss; children: Paula, Lawrence, Lawry Seif. **Educ:** Nova Univ, MA; Publ Admin attended; Ohio State Univ, 1947-49; Fenn Coll, 1949-51; Amer Univ 1954. **Career:** IRS, mgmt positions 1949-71; New Detroit Inc, pres 1970-77; Coopers & Lybrand, partner, 1978-89; Doss Ventures Inc, 1989-. **Orgs:** Dir Amer Natural Resources, Hudson-Webber Found; president Coleman A Young Foundation; finance chair, Congressional Black Caucus Found; advisory mem Detroit Black United Fund; board member, exec comm mem Detroit Econ Growth Corp; trustee Harper-Grace Hospital; vice chmn bd & exec comm Martin Luther King Jr Center; president, Detroit First; pres Inner City Bus Improvement Forum 1967-71; chmn State of Michigan Neighborhood Educ Auth 1968-70. **Military Serv:** USN, Seaman 1st class, 1945-46. **Home Addr:** 19391 Suffolk, Detroit, MI 48203.

DOSS, THERESA
Judge. **Personal:** daugHter of Ida Richards Doss and Eddie Edison Doss; married James Tyrone Wahls, Aug 15, 1981; children: James Christopher Doss Wahls. **Educ:** Ohio University, Athens, OH, AB, 1961, JD, 1964. **Career:** Cleveland Public School, teacher, 1961; State of Michigan, law librarian, 1964-65; Archdiocesan Opportunity Program, 1965-66; State of Michigan, assistant attorney general, 1966-76; Detroit Lighting Commission, commissioner, 1974-76; Common Pleas Court, City of Detroit, judge, 1976-81; State of Michigan 36th District, judge, 1981-. **Orgs:** State bar of Michigan, journal advisory commission, 1971-77, representative assembly, 1975-81, Wayne County character & fitness committee, 1971-75; pres, National Bar Assn, Women Section, 1975-76; secretary, Wolverine Bar Assn, 1967-68; pres, Women's Lawyers Assn of Michigan, 1973-74; pres, Michigan District Judges Association, 1991; Wayne County District Judges Assn; Tabernacle Missionary Baptist Church, trustee; NAACP, life member; National Council of Negro Women, life member; Michigan Metro Girl Scouts Council, past member board of directors; Neighborhood Service Organization, board of directors, 1977-87; Michigan Judicial Tenure, commission, 1995-. **Honors/Awds:** Certificate of Distinction, Ohio State University College of Law Alumni Assn, 1983; Natl Council of Negro Women, Outstanding Achievement in Law, 1976; United Methodist Women of Second Grace Methodist Church, Meritorious Achievement of Community Service in Jurisprudence, 1976; Rosa L Gragg Educational & Civic Club, Humantarian Service Award, 1986; honored as Founding Member, Women Division of Natl Bar Assn, 1992. **Business Addr:** Judge, 36th District Court, 421 Madison Ave, #4069, Detroit, MI 48226.

DOTSON, BETTY LOU
Management consultant. **Personal:** Born Jun 29, 1930, Chicago, IL; daughter of Christine Price Dotson and Heber T Dotson. **Educ:** OH Wesleyan Univ, BA 1950; Lincoln Univ, JD 1954. **Career:** Dept of Urban Renewal, 1963; Cook Cty Dept of Public Welfare, caseworker-cons 1964-66; 1st Natl Bank of Chgo, legal serv trust dept 1966-68; US Dept of Agr Food & Nutrition Svc, dir civil rights 1970-75; Dept of Health & Human Services, Washington, DC, dir, office for civil rights, 1981-87; BLD & Associates, pres, currently; Houston Community Coll, instructor. **Orgs:** Asst dir Equal Oppty Action 1975-78; asst to dir Equal Oppty USDA 1978-79; sr staff assoc Joint Ctr for Political Studies 1979-80; chief adjudicationsUSDA Equal Oppty Office 1980-81; bd dir Natl Capital YWCA 1981-84; mem Alpha Kappa Alpha; steeering comm Black Amers for Nixon/Agnew 1968; Arneson Inst of Practical Politics, Ohio Weslegan Univ, advisory bd, 1989-; Ohio Wesleyan Univ, Delaware, OH, trustee, bd of trustees, 1994-. **Honors/Awds:** Admin Asst Office of Pres elect Nixon 1969. **Business Addr:** Pres, BLD & Associates, PO Box 331143, Houston, TX 77233-1143.

DOTSON, EARL CHRISTOPHER
Professional football player. **Personal:** Born Dec 17, 1970, Beaumont, TX; married Janell; children: Jared. **Educ:** Texas A&M-Kingsville, attended. **Career:** Green Bay Packers, tackle, 1993-. **Business Addr:** Professional Football Player, Green Bay Packers, 1265 Lombardi Ave, Green Bay, WI 54304, (414)494-2351.

DOTSON, NORMA Y.
Judge. **Career:** 36th District Court, judge, currently. **Business Addr:** Judge, 36th District Court, 421 Madison Ave, Detroit, MI 48226, (313)965-8728.

DOTSON, PHILIP RANDOLPH
Educator. **Personal:** Born Oct 10, 1948, Carthage, MS; son of Velma Ernest Dotson and Jim O R Dotson; married Judith Kerr Dotson, May 19, 1973; children: Philip T R, Tiffany M, Brian R. **Educ:** Jackson State Univ, Jackson MS, BS Art Ed 1970; Univ of Mississippi, Oxford MS, MFA Painting 1972. **Career:** Memphis Jack & Jill Exhibition, curator, 1983-84; The Spirit of African Art in the South, Memphis State Univ, curator, 1983; LeMoyne-Owen Coll, chairman dept of art, 1972-87, chairman division of fine arts and humanities, 1988-96, prof, currently. **Orgs:** Planning mem, Memphis in May Intl Fest, 1972-73; review mem, Tennessee Arts Commn, 1975-76; mem, Religious Comm Arts & the Amer Revolution, 1976, Chamber of Commerce; arts advisory bd, Mallory Knights Charitable Org, 1976-80; sponsor, Cotton Carnival Assoc, 1972-83; mem, Coll Art Assoc, 1978-80; bd mem, Artist in the Schools Program Arts Council; bd dir, Round Table of Memphis Museum Dir, 1982-; bd mem, Memphis Arts Council, 1986-; bd mem, Memphis Arts Festival, 1989-. **Honors/Awds:** Honorable Mention, Natl Conference of Artists, 1969; Phi Kappa Phi, The Univ of MS, 1972; Art Work Permanent Collection in Nigeria Africa 1981, Permanent Collection Memphis Brooks Museum 1982; Video Tape in Collection State Dept of Archives; illustrations in three med books 1983; oil painting Anthropomorphic Psychosis, permanent collection, Memphis Brooks Museum of Art; co-edited Homespun Images: An Anthology of Black Memphis Writers and Artists. **Home Addr:** 1678 Newsum, Germantown, TN 38138.

DOTSON, SANTANA
Professional football player. **Personal:** Born Dec 19, 1969, New Orleans, LA; married Monique; children: Khari. **Educ:** Baylor, attended. **Career:** Tampa Bay Buccaneers, defensive tackle, 1992-95; Green Bay Packers, 1996-. **Honors/Awds:** The Sporting News, NFL Rookie of the Year, 1992; Defensive Rookie of the Year, 1992. **Business Addr:** Professional Football Player, Green Bay Packers, 1265 Lombardi Ave, Green Bay, WI 54304, (414)494-2351.

DOTSON, WILLIAM S. See Obituaries section.

DOTSON-WILLIAMS, HENRIETTA
City official. **Personal:** Born May 27, 1940, Valden, MS; daughter of Mr. and Mrs. Fred Perteete; married Michael J Williams; children: Angela L Woodson, Earl Dotson Jr, Dennis Dotson, Clifford Dotson. **Educ:** IL Extsn Univ, Sec 1960. **Career:** IL Bell Telephone Co, operator to special eng clerk 1960-68; N IL Women's & Cntr, counsel 1974-; Sec of State, fclty serv clk; "Black Corner" Mntly TV Pgm, frmr moderator; Winnebago Co Bd Dist 12, supr 1972-, elected position. **Orgs:** Pres Winnebago Cty Bd of Hlth 1983-85, IL Assc of Bd of Hlth 1984-86. **Honors/Awds:** Essence Mag Woman of the Month 1978; nominee for Woman of the Yr YWCA 1982 & 1986; Led an Effort to Retain Dr ML King's Birthday as a Legal Holiday for Winnebago County Employees, 800 People Attended Meeting. **Home Addr:** 1202 Kent St, Rockford, IL 61102.

DOTTIN, ROBERT PHILIP
Educator, scientist. **Personal:** Born May 23, 1943, Trinidad, West Indies; son of Lena Dottin and William Dottin; married Gail Dottin, May 1990; children: Melissa, Garreth. **Educ:** Univ of Toronto, BSC 1968, MSC 1970, PhD 1974; MIT, Post Doctoral 1974-76. **Career:** Univ of Copenhagen, visiting prof 1975; MIT, Johns Hopkins Univ, asst prof 1976-82, assoc 1982-87; Hunter College, CUNY, New York, NY, professor 1986-. **Orgs:** Mem Genetics Study Section; grantee Nat'l Inst Health 1984-; mem American Soc for Cell Biology; mem Nat'l Sci Foundation; American Heart Assoc; mem American Soc for Human Genetics 1986; mem American Soc for Biochemistry and Molecular Biology 1985; Coalition for the Advancement of Blacks in Biomedical Sciences, CABBS, A Resource Directory, editor/publisher; Sigma Xi, exec comm. **Honors/Awds:** Governors Generals of Canada Medal 1968; Medical Research Council of Canada Fellowship 1974-76; NATO Travel Fellowship 1991-93; Fogarty Sr Int'l Fellowship, 1991-92; Fogarty Int'l Sr Collaboration Award, 1992-95; Univ of CA, Distinguished Scientist, 1996; Howard Univ, Distinguished Scientist, 1997. **Business Addr:** Professor, City University of New York, Hunter College, Dept of Biological Sciences, 695 Park Ave, Rm 932N, New York, NY 10021.

DOTTIN, ROGER ALLEN
Community relations executive. **Personal:** Born Jul 13, 1945, Cambridge, MA; son of Eunice Dottin (deceased) and Reuben Dottin (deceased); married Marilyn Ames, Apr 9, 1989. **Educ:** Cambridge School of Business, Diploma 1963-65; Grahm Junior College, Honorary Associate. **Career:** Economic Opportunity Atlanta Inc, ctr dir 1970-73; City of Atlanta Comm Relations Commn, asst dir 1974-76; Metro Atlanta Rapid Transit Auth, sr comm relations spec 1976-84, mgr community relations 1984-86; Dallas Area Rapid Transit, mgr customer svcs, 1986-90; Metropolitan Atlanta Rapid Transit Authority, mgr of community relations, 1990-. **Orgs:** Vice chair Sponsor-A-Family Project Atlanta 1983-87; mem Atlanta Public Schools Safety & Emergency Mgmt Adv-Council 1984-86; co-chair Atlanta Branch NAACP Afro-Academic Cultural Tech Scientific Olympics 1984-86; mem Conf of Minority Transportation Officials 1985-; member, International Customer Services Assn (ICSA), past pres; Campbellton/Cascade Y's Men; Local Coordinating Council Fulton County Private Industry Council of ATL, member. **Honors/Awds:** Outstanding Serv Awd John Harland Boys Club Atlanta 1982; Community Serv Awd NAACP Atlanta Branch 1984; Outstanding & Dedicated Serv to the NAACP Atlanta Branch 1986; YMCA Minority Achievers Program, Dallas YMCA 1988. **Military Serv:** AUS E-2 1 1/2 yrs; Honorable Discharge. **Business Addr:** Manager, Community Relations, Metropolitan Atlanta Rapid Transit Authority, 2424 Piedmont Rd NE, Atlanta, GA 30324.

DOTY, ROMEO A.
Aircraft company manager. **Personal:** Born Jan 3, 1938, Kansas City, MO; son of Edna Bradshaw Doty and Romeo Doty Sr (deceased); married Melba Doty (divorced 1983); children: Mari Doty-Theuer, Douglas Doty. **Educ:** Univ of MO, Columbia, MO, BS, Eng, 1960; UCLA, Los Angeles, CA, MBA, 1971. **Career:** TRW, Los Angeles, CA, arrangements operations mgr, 1963-79; Xerox, Los Angeles, CA, microelectronics operations mgr, 1979-88; Hughes Aircraft Co, Los Angeles, CA, asst div mgr, 1988-. **Orgs:** Bd mem, chmn of the bd, Xerox Federal Credit Union, 1981-91; bd mem, Technical Health Career School, 1971-91; bd mem, Industry Advisory Bd, Ctr for Microcontamination Control, Univ of AZ, 1987-88; bd mem, Natl Treas, Society of Logistics Engineers, 1976-77; TRW exec on loan, interracial council for business opportunity, 1970-71. **Honors/Awds:** Sr Mem, American Institute of Aeronautics and Astronautics, 1991. **Business Addr:** Assistant Manager, Processor Division, Radar Systems Group, Hughes Aircraft Company, 2000 E Imperial Highway, El Segundo, CA 90245.

DOUGLAS, ARTHUR E.
Educational administrator. **Personal:** Born Apr 20, 1933, Camden, DE; married Rose Marie Stricklin; children: Daryl. **Educ:** U of Md Eastern Shore, BS 1957; TX A&M 1966; Tarleton State Univ, MA 1980. **Career:** US Air Force, officer 1957-76; Economic Opportunities Advancement Corp, program oper mgr 1976-82; TX State Tech College, grants, dir, human resources, beginning 1982, city manager, currently. **Orgs:** Trustee, pres, Marlin ISD 1979-. **Military Serv:** USAF maj 20 yrs; Meritorious Serv Medal, Air Force Commendation with 3 Oak Leaf Clusters 1957-76. **Home Addr:** 400 Bennett, Marlin, TX 76661. **Business Addr:** City Manager, Texas State Tech College System, Marlin, TX 76661.

DOUGLAS, AUBRY CARTER
Physician, orthopedic surgeon. **Personal:** Born Feb 1, 1943, Onalaska, TX; son of Mary Douglas and Desso Douglas; married Janice Sanchez; children: Mary, Ronald, Jenniffer, Anitra. **Educ:** Fisk U, 1964; Meharry Med Coll, 1968. **Career:** Howard Univ, resident orthopaedics 1973-76; George Hubbard Hosp, resident gen surgery 1970-71; Fisk U, lab asst 1962-63. **Orgs:** Life scout BSA; mem Kappa Alpha Psi; Beta Kappa Chi; Harris & Co Med Soc; mem Houston Medical Forum. **Military Serv:** AUS maj 1971-73. **Business Addr:** 2000 Crawford St, Ste 860, Houston, TX 77002.

DOUGLAS, BOBBY EDDIE
Wrestling coach. **Personal:** Born Mar 26, 1942, Bellaire, OH; son of Belove Johnson and Eddie Douglas; married Jacqueline Davison, Aug 27, 1966; children: Bobby Frederick. **Educ:** Oklahoma State Univ, Stillwater OK, BS, 1966; Arizona State Univ, Tempe AZ, MA, 1980. **Career:** Arizona State Univ, Tempe AZ, coach, 1974-. **Orgs:** Training Camps, dir, 1973-; USA Wrestling, exec comm, 1987-; NCAA (rules), mem, 1989-. **Honors/Awds:** US Olympic Team (wrestling), 1964, team captain, 1968; author, Making of a Champion, 1973, Making of a Champion, Book II, 1975; video, Takedown, 1986; author, Takedown II, 1986; Hall of Fame, USA Wrestling, 1986; Coach of the Year, PAC 10, 1986-89, 1990; Coach of the Year, NCAA, 1988; Man of the Year, Natl Coaches Assn, 1989. **Business Addr:** Head Wrestling Coach, Arizona State University, Athletic Department, Tempe, AZ 85287.

DOUGLAS, BUSTER. See DOUGLAS, JAMES.

DOUGLAS, CARL E.
Attorney. **Career:** Law Offices of Johnnie Cochran, attorney, currently. **Orgs:** State Bar of California; John M Langston Bar Association. **Honors/Awds:** Loren Miller Lawyer of the Year, John M Langston Bar Association, 1994. **Special Achievements:** Attorney of Orenthal James Simpson, 1994-95. **Business Addr:** Managing Attorney, Law Offices of Johnnie L Cochran, Jr, 4929 Wilshire Blvd, Ste 1010, Los Angeles, CA 90010, (213)931-6200.

DOUGLAS, EDNA M.
Educator. **Personal:** Born Jul 22, 1904, Little Rock, AR. **Educ:** Univ of AR Pine Bluff, BA; Atlanta U, Univ of So CA Mills Coll Oakland, CA; Columbia U; Univ of AR; Philander Smith Coll. **Career:** Dunbar High School, Little Rock AR, teacher; Dunbar Jr Coll, teacher; Southwestern Jr High School, Grand Basileus of Sigma Gamma Rho Sorority, teacher; Natl Pan Hellenic Council, chmn. **Orgs:** Past mem bd trustees AM&N Coll; mem Classroom Tchr Assn; AR Tchr Assn; Nat Educ Assn; sponsor Student Christian Assn Dunbar Jr Coll Sec Little Rock Parks & Recreation Com 1952; bd dir ACHR Washington, DC 1952; panel mem Human Rights Day YWCA Radio broadcast 1953; 1st Negro bd dir, mem Greater Little Rock YWCA; chmn Com of Adminstrn Phyllis Wheatley Br YWCA; rep Florence Crittenton Bd of Little Rock, San Francisco 1954; vice pres Little Rock Chap Nat Council of Negro Women 1953-53; Little Rock Com United Nations 1953-55. **Honors/Awds:** Woman of Yr NCNW; Tchr of Yr Social Agency for Comm Participation; chmn Commun Devl Block & Grant S Little Rock 1976-77; Blanche Edwards Award Sigma Gamma Rho 1952; First Ford Found Fellowship offered to Little Rock Pub Sch System 1952-53; Comm Aprreciation Tea for Lengthy & meritorious serv Comm Center Bldg opened in her honor 1954; Residence Hall No 2, The Edna Douglas Hall named in her honor AM&N Coll 1958; mem African Study Tour Council for ChristianSocial Action United Ch of Christ 1961.

DOUGLAS, ELIZABETH ASCHE
Artist, educator. **Personal:** Born Dec 22, 1930, Rochester, PA; daughter of Irma M Edmonds Asche and Charles F Asche; married William R; children: Andrea, Vicki Gaddy, Nanette. **Educ:** Carnegie Inst of Tech, BFA 1947-51; Univ of Pittsburgh, MA 1954-56; Univ of PA, 1979. **Career:** TX Coll, Tyler TX, asst prof 1955-58; Good Publishing Co, Ft Worth, TX, art dir 1958-61; Beaver (PA) Schls, Rochester (PA) Schls, tchr of Art 1962-66; Geneva Coll, Beaver Falls, PA, asst prof, assoc prof, prof, coord of humanities, 1966-96, emerita, 1996-. **Orgs:** Prog chmn Brodhead Cultural Center 1977-78; sec-treas FATE (Foundations in Art, Theory & Educ) 1979-80; art comm Merrick Art Gallery Assoc 1980-; bd mem Christian Scholars Rev 1983-; chair Rochester Area Hum Rel Comm 1973-74; co-chr task force on jvnl delinq SW Regnl Plng Comm Governors Justice Comm 1976-78; mem Assoc for Integrative Studies 1985-; chmn Merrick Art Gallery Assoc Catalog Comm; mem Natl Conference of Artists 1980-; mem College Art Assn 1975-; bd mem Greater Beaver Valley Cultural Alliance 1989-; bd mem Northland Public Library Foundation 1989-92; board member, Christians in Visual Art, 1985-89, 1991-; board member, Association Integrative Studies, 1991-94; bd mem, Merrick Art Gallery, 1992-; bd mem, Sweetwater Ctr for the Arts; bd mem, pres, 1997-, Trinity Episcopal School for Ministry; resource artist, Intergenerational Arts Proj, Butler, Lawrence & Mercer Counties, PA. **Honors/Awds:** Arts rev Christian Scholars Rev 1973-; achvmnt awd Beaver Valley Serv Club 1978; articles published in CIVA (Christians in Visual Arts) numerous times, 1983-; painting exhib awds various locations in country 1960-; papers delivered annual meetings FATE Toronto 1984, Assoc Integrative Studies 1984, Hofstra Univ Conf Avant-Garde Lit/Art 1985; Scholar of the Year, Geneva College Faculty 1985; author/editor Catalogue of the Merrick Art Gallery 1988; article published Leonardo's Last Supper, Christian Scholar's Review 1988; Woman of Distinction in the Arts, Beaver-Castle Girl Scouts Council, 1989. **Home Addr:** 491 McKinley St, Rochester, PA 15074.

DOUGLAS, FLORENCE M.
Physician. **Personal:** Born Mar 26, 1933; married Franklin E Mcfarlane; children: Valerie, Angela, Alychandra. **Educ:** Hunter Coll NYC, BA 1955; Howard Univ Coll of Med, MD 1959. **Career:** Los Angeles Co Gen Hosp, intership 1959-60; Los Angeles Co Gen Hosp, residency gen psychiatry 1960-62; Montefiore Hosp NY, residency gen psychiatry 1972; Los Angeles Co Gen Hosp, residency gen psychiatry 1963; Los Angeles Co Gen Hosp, residency child psychiatry 1963-65; Los Angeles Co Gen Hosp Sch of Nursing, consult 1960-62; Los Angeles Co Juvenile Hall, consult 1960-62; Episcopal Ch Home for Children Pasadena, CA, consult 1963-67; Huntington Meml Hosp Pasadena, consult 1965-66; Los Angeles Co Mental Health Arcardia Sch System, consult 1965-67. **Orgs:** So CA Psychiat Soc; Am Med Assn; Los Angeles Co Med Assn; Am Psychiat Assn; Nat Med Assn; Am Assn for Adolescent Psychiat; Am & Orthopsychiatric Assn; CA Med Assn; Black Psychiat of So CA; Black Psychiat of Am; mem Mental Hlth Devel Commin, United Way; bd mem CA Dept of Rehab; former mem So CA Psychoanalytic Assn; Am Assn for Group Psychotheraphy; Coll of Psychol & Soc Studies bd mem Model Cities Child Care Center; Johnny Tillmon Child Devel Center lectr New Careerists; Inner City Students; Urban Corp Students; Mshauri Students; Medex Program; diplomate Am Bd of Psych & Neurology; bd certified Child & Adolescent Psychiatry; examiner Am Bd of Psychiatry & Neurology; prof of Psychiatry Charles R Drew post-grad med sch UCLA Med Cntr; physician M Edical Staff of DelAmo Hosp, Little Company Mary Hosp, Torrance Meml Hosp; Fellow Am Acad of Child & Psychiatry. **Honors/Awds:** Anna Bartsche Dunne Scholarship, Howard Univ Coll of Med 1956-58. **Business Addr:** 4305 Torrance Blvd, #205, Torrance, CA 90503.

DOUGLAS, HARRY E., III
Educator. **Personal:** Born Nov 8, 1938; children: 2. **Educ:** Univ of Denver, BA 1959; Univ of CA Los Angeles, MPA Personnel 1971; Univ of So CA, MPA Health Serv 1981, DPA Health Admin & Policy 1983. **Career:** Dept of Public Social Servs, proj dir, sr program asst, mgmt trainee, social worker 1960-68; Univ of Southern CA, training officer 1968; Martin Luther King/Charles R Drew Medical Center, personnel officer 1969-71, dir allied health training 1971-73; Cedars-Sinai Medical Center, dir manpower training & devel 1973-74; CA Reg Med Prog, prog dir HS/EP 1974-75; Howard Univ Coll of Allied Health Science, assoc dean, assoc prof 1975-83; Charles R Drew Postgrad Medical School, School of Allied Health, dean 1983-. **Orgs:** External cons/eval Norfolk State Univ; consult DHEW Div of Health Manpower; adv/cons Amer Soc of Allied Health Professions on Natl Data Gathering Proj;conducted zero based budget workshop Dept of Agr; health brain trust mem Cong Black Caucus; mgmt progs nursing personnel George Washington Univ; tech review comm CA Comm on Reg Medical Progs, CA State Dept of Ed; ad hoc adv comm Career Ed in Health Occupations; mem Amer Assoc of Comm & Jr Coll, School of Allied Health Study, Charles R Drew Postgrad Med School, San Francisco Personnel Dept, Natl Inst of Mental Helth, Orange Cty Personnel Dept, UCLA Proj for Allied Health Professions; bd dir DC Coalition on Health Advocates 1976-; treas, bd mem Natl Assoc of Allied Health 1977-; mem Dietetic Manpower DemandStudy 1980-, Child-Find & Advocacdv Comm 1980-; chmn Amer Soc of Allied Prof 1980-, DC Adv Comm Magnet School for Health Careers 1982-; assoc coord Reg Leadership Ctr for Allied Health Ed 1982-; mem Amer Soc for Pub Admin, Amer Pub Health Assoc, Natl Soc of Allied Health. **Honors/Awds:** Numerous presentations & publs incl, "The Declining Enrollment of Minority Group Members in Selected Allied Health Occupations" presentation 1980, "The Learniing Resource Ctr, A Mediating Structure for Reorganizing Allied Health Ed" presentation 1981, "A Systems Approach-Part II" workshop 1982, "Changing the Guard, A Methodology for Leadership in Transition" publ 1983; "Mobility in Health Career Ed" speech 1969; "The San Quentin Report" rsch 1971. **Business Addr:** Dean, Charles R Drew Postgrad Med, School of Allied Health, 2113 S Orange Dr, Los Angeles, CA 90016.

DOUGLAS, HERBERT P., JR.
Consultant. **Personal:** Born Mar 9, 1922, Pittsburgh; married Rozell; children: Barbara Joy Ralston, Herbert III. **Educ:** Xavier U, 1941-42; Univ of Pittsburgh, BS 1945-48; Univ of Pittsburgh, MEd 1950. **Career:** Schieffelin & Somerset Co, vice pres, Urban Market Development, 1977-80, consultant, 1987-; Nat Spl Markets, vice pres beginning 1968- Schieffelin & Co NYC, contl sales rep 1963-65; Nat Spl Markets Mgr, 1965-68; Pabst Brewing Co, sales rep dist mgr 1950-63; managed night business, fathers auto bus 1942-45; Nat Assn of Market Developers, vp. **Orgs:** Mem Track Com Internatl Olympians Track & Field Club; Optimist Club; Philadelphia Pioneer Club; NAACP; Nat Urban League; Omega Psi Phi Frat; Chris Atlete Club; Ebenezer Bapt Ch; Sales Exec Club; International Amateur Athletic Association Inc, president and founder, 1980-. **Honors/Awds:** Black Athletes Hall of Fame 1974; Beverage Ind Award Urban League Guild 1974; selected by Ebony success library as one of top 1000 Successful Blacks in US; played in Olympic Games 1948, currently last athlete from Pittsburgh to win a medal in Olympic Games; Jesse Owens International Trophy Award, 1980; University of Pittsburgh, Lettermen of Distinction Award, 1980-; University Bicentennial Award, 1987; Black Achievement Award, 1987; Western Pennsylvania Sports Hall of Fame, 1988; Pennsylvania Sports Hall of Fame, 1992.

DOUGLAS, HUGH
Professional football player. **Personal:** Born Aug 23, 1971, Mansfield, OH; children: Kayla Rachelle. **Educ:** Central State. **Career:** New York Jets, defensive end, 1995-. **Special Achievements:** 1st round/16th overall NFL draft pick, 1995. **Business Addr:** Professional Football Player, New York Jets, 1000 Fulton Ave, Hempstead, NY 11550, (516)560-8100.

DOUGLAS, JAMES (BUSTER DOUGLAS)
Professional boxer. **Personal:** Born Apr 7, 1960, Columbus, OH; son of Lula Pearl McCauley Douglas (deceased) and William Douglas Jr; married Bertha Paige, Jul 2, 1987; children: LaMar, Cardae. **Educ:** Mercyhurst College; Coffeyville Community College; Dayton Sinclair Community College. **Career:** Professional boxer, heavyweight, 1981-; bouts include: Dan Banks, 1981; David Bey, 1981; Dave Starkey; Jesse "Thunder" Ferguson, 1985; Greg Page, 1986; Tony Tucker, 1987; Pernell Davis, 1988; "Iron" Mike Tyson, 1990. **Orgs:** President, Lula Pearl Douglas Foundation. **Honors/Awds:** Heavyweight Champion of the World, WBA, WBC, IBF, 8 months in 1990.

DOUGLAS, JAMES MATTHEW
Educator. **Personal:** Born Feb 11, 1944, Onalaska, TX; son of Mary L Douglas and Desso D Douglas; married Keryl Douglas; children: DeLicia. **Educ:** TX Southern Univ, BA Math 1966, JD Law 1970; Stanford Univ, JSM Law 1971. **Career:** Singer Simulation Co, computer analyst 1966-72; TX Southern Univ Sch of Law, asst Prof 1971-72; Cleveland State Univ Sch of Law, asst Prof 1972-75; Syracuse Univ Sch of Law, assoc dean assoc prof 1975-80; Northeastern Univ Sch of Law, prof of law 1980-81; TX Southern Univ Sch of Law, dean & prof 1981-95, interim provost and vp academic affairs, 1995; pres 1995-. **Orgs:** State Bar of TX; Houston Jr Bar Assc; Amer Bar Assc Chrmn of Educ Comm of Sci & Tech Section; bd dir Hiscock Legal Soc; fac adv to Natl Bd of Black Amer Law Students; bd of dirs Gulf Coast Legal Foundation; mem Natl Bar Assoc Comm on Legal Educ; mem editorial bd The Texas Lawyer; life mem Houston Chamber of Commerce; bd of dirs, Law School Admission Council; chmn, Minority Affairs Committee, Law Shool Admission Council. **Honors/Awds:** Grad 1st in Law Schl Class; Most Outstanding 3rd Year Student; Winner of 10 Amer Jurisprudence Awards; mem of Sch Moot Court Team; Parlimentarian of Student Bar Assn; adv Alpha Phi Alpha Soc Frat; pres Sophomore Class; pres Student Body; pres Alpha Phi Alpha Soc Frat; publ "Some Ideas on the Computer and Law" TX Souther Univ Law Review 20 1971; work in prog "Cases & Materials on Contracts"; Outstanding Alumnus TX Southern Univ 1972. **Home Addr:** 5318 Calhoun Rd, Houston, TX 77021. **Business Addr:** President, Texas Southern Univ, 3100 Cleburne Ave, Houston, TX 77004.

DOUGLAS, JANICE GREEN
Physician. **Personal:** Born 1944. **Educ:** Meharry Medical School, Nashville, TN, MD; Vanderbilt University, National Institute of Health fellow in endocrinology, 1973. **Career:** National Institute of Health, senior staff fellow; Case Western Reserve University, Cleveland, OH, director of division of Hypertension. **Business Addr:** Case Western Reserve University, 10900 Euclid Ave, Cleveland, OH 44106-4982.

DOUGLAS, JOE, JR.
Government official/fire chief. **Personal:** Born Jun 9, 1928, Topeka, KS; married Nathalia Washington; children: Shelley Jolana Douglas Wilder. **Educ:** Washburn Univ, 1948-49. **Career:** City of Topeka, firefighter 37 yrs, appointed fire chief Sept 1, 1983; USD #501, bd mem 1977-85. **Orgs:** Mem Topeka Council of Churches; 1st Conf Chairperson for KS East Conf Clomm on Religion and Race United Methodist Ch; bd of dir Boys Club of Amer 1971-73; chmn comm Adv Comm on Educ 1975-76; bd pres USD #501 1980-81 & 1983-84; bd of dir Boy Scouts of Amer; mem Mayor's Disaster Adv Cncl, Mayor's Task Force on Illiteracy, Sunset Optimists. **Honors/Awds:** Dean United Methodist Youth Fellowship Inst 1971-73; Presidential Citation for Extraordinary Serv Boys Club of Amer 1972-73; Kansas Friends of Educ plaque winner; Annual Local Govt Official Category 1986. **Military Serv:** AUS pfc 18 mos. **Business Addr:** Fire Chief, City of Topeka, 324 SE Jefferson St, Topeka, KS 66607.

DOUGLAS, JOHN DANIEL
County official, educator. **Personal:** Born Aug 18, 1945, Richburg, SC; son of Alberta Cousar Douglas and James E Douglas; married Mildred Barber Douglas, Feb 12, 1970; children: Maurice, Jermel, GiGi, LaShawn. **Educ:** Morris Coll, BS 1967; Winthrop Coll, MEduc 1976. **Career:** Chester Co Schools, teacher 1967-68; Carolina Comm Actions Inc, Head Start dir 1968-70; York Co Family Court, chief probation officer 1970-75; Charlotte-Mecklinburg School, teacher 1975-80; Rock Hill Sch Dist #3, teacher 1980-; York Co, councilman; Union County Schools, NC, 1988-. **Orgs:** Pres Rock Hill NAACP 1976-81; pol action chmn Menzel Shiner 1980-; councilman York Co Dist #4 1980-; chmn Destinations Human Serv Trans 1982-; chmn Public Works York Co 1982-; financial sec Sterling Elk Lodge 1983-; bd of dirs South Carolina Assoc of Counties 1986; exec admin asst SC Assoc of Elks 1986. **Honors/Awds:** Serv to Mankind Rock Hill NAACP 1979; Comm Serv Awd Elk-Sterling Lodge #344 Rock Hill 1980; Scroll of Honor Omega Psi Phi Frat 1983; Humanitarian Menzel Shiner 1984; Elk of the Year 1986; Man of the Year Rock Grove AME Zion Church 1986; Man of the Year, Elks, 1988. **Business Addr:** Councilman, York County, PO Box 11578, Rock Hill, SC 29731.

DOUGLAS, JOSEPH FRANCIS
Educator, engineer (retired). **Personal:** Born Oct 31, 1926, Indianapolis, IN; son of Marion Elizabeth Brabham Douglas (deceased) and Louis Joseph Douglas (deceased); married Edna J Nichols, Apr 9, 1950; children: Marian E, Joseph Jr, Marie A, Barbara J. **Educ:** Purdue Univ, BSEE 1948; Univ of MO, MSEE 1962. **Career:** Rural Electrification Admin, 1948-56; So Univ, 1956-64; Am Machine & Foundry Co, 1964-66; PA State Univ, engrg instr 1966-70, assoc prof 1970-87; engineering consultant 1987-92; MOEST, after school program, as seventh and ninth-grade teacher. **Orgs:** Mem IEEE 1949-, ASEE 1969-80; reg professional engr 1954-96; mem NAACP, Human Rel Adv Council, York-Adams Area Council, Boy Scouts of Amer, Comm Action Prog; mem bd of dir York Hosp PA 1982-; member, advisory board, Penn State York, 1986-96. **Honors/Awds:** "The Role of the Engineering Teacher" Conf Record Tucson 1972; Lindback Award Distinguished Teaching 1972; Recipient of a Centennial Medal of the IEEE in 1984. **Special Achievements:** Contributor, "Understanding Batteries," technical paper, Volunteers in Technical Assistance Publication (VITA), 1985; special biography, included in various publications on outstanding African-American scientists. **Military Serv:** US Army, Air Corps, aviation cadet 1944-45. **Home Addr:** 2755 Trout Run Road, York, PA 17402.

DOUGLAS, MAE ALICE
Business executive. **Personal:** Born Dec 26, 1951, Rowland, NC. **Educ:** University of NC at Greensboro, BA Sociology 1972. **Career:** Commission on the Status of Women, administrator 1973-74; CIBA-GEIGY Corp, eeo coordinator 1974-77, personnel manager 1978-, mgr human resources 1983-86, dir human resources 1987-. **Orgs:** Leadership Greensboro Chamber of Commerce 1979-80; planning division United Way 1980; professional review committee State Dept of Public Instruction 1981-82; Amer Soc for Personnel Admin 1978-; mem Women's Professional Forum 1985-. **Honors/Awds:** Outstanding Young Women of America 1975; Outstanding Young Woman Greensboro Jaycettes 1978; Outstanding Woman in Business YWCA 1980. **Business Addr:** Dir of Human Resources, CIBA GEIGY Corp, PO Box 18300, Greensboro, NC 27419.

DOUGLAS, MANSFIELD, III
Personnel officer. **Personal:** Born Jun 28, 1930, Nashville, TN; married Barbara Jean Baker; children: Camella Renee, Reginald Mansfield, Karen Rochelle. **Educ:** TN State U, grad. **Career:** Western Electric, personnel ofcr; prev experience in maintenance, accounting, purchasing. **Orgs:** Mem Exec Com Nashville Br NAACP 1962-66; pres Br NAACP 1966-68; pres Davidson Co Young Dem 1967; Vice Pres Exec Bd TN State Labor Council 1963-65; bd dirs S St Comm Cntr; TN Adv Com of US Commn on Rights. **Honors/Awds:** Merit Serv Nashville Urban League 1972; Outstanding Recognition CWA Local 3870 1970. **Military Serv:** AUS Korean Conflict. **Business Addr:** 195 Polk Ave, Nashville, TN.

DOUGLAS, NICHOLAS
Federal official. **Career:** Bureau of Land Management, Bakersfield, CA, division of minerals chief, Anchorage, AK, district manager, currently. **Special Achievements:** First African American district manager for the Bureau of Land Management. **Business Addr:** District Manager, Bureau of Land Mgmt, Anchorage District, 6881 Abbott Loop Rd, Anchorage, AK 99507-2599.

DOUGLAS, OMAR
Professional football player. **Personal:** Born Jun 3, 1972, New Orleans, LA. **Educ:** Univ of Minnesota. **Career:** New York Giants, wide receiver, 1994-. **Business Addr:** Professional Football Player, New York Giants, Giants Stadium, East Rutherford, NJ 07073, (201)935-8111.

DOUGLAS, SAMUEL HORACE
Educator. **Personal:** Born May 10, 1928, Ardmore, OK; divorced; children: Carman Irving, Samuel, Emanuel. **Educ:** Bishop Coll, BS 1950; OK State U, BS 1959; MS 1963; PhD 1967. **Career:** Praire View A&M Univ TX, asst prof Math 1959-63; dept chmn 1962-63; Grambling Coll LA, math prof 1967-; dept chmn 1967-. **Orgs:** MemPanel Spl & Problems Minority Groups; Am Math Soc; London Math Soc; Math Assn Am; consult Com Undergrad Prog Math dir summer & inservice InstsMath, NSF-GRAMBLING Coll 1968-71; vis lectr, vice-chmn, LA-MS sect, Math Assn Am Mem, Pi Mu Epsilon; Alpha Phi Alpha. **Honors/Awds:** Distinguished Service Award, Pi Mu Epsilon 1970; fellow Sci Faculty 1963-67. **Military Serv:** AUS 1943-46.

DOUGLAS, SHERMAN
Professional basketball player. **Personal:** Born Sep 15, 1966, Washington, DC; married Denise; children: Demi. **Educ:** Syracuse Univ, Syracuse, NY, 1985-89. **Career:** Miami Heat, guard, 1989-92; Boston Celtics, 1992-95; Milwaukee Bucks, 1996-97; Cleveland Cavaliers, 1997; New Jersey Nets, 1997-. **Honors/Awds:** NBA All-Rookie First Team, 1990; Miami Heat, Most Valuable Player, 1991. **Business Addr:** Professional Basketball Player, Cleveland Cavaliers, One Center Court, Cleveland, OH 44115-4001, (216)659-9100.

DOUGLAS, SUZZANNE
Actress. **Personal:** Born Apr 12, Chicago, IL; daughter of Lois Mae Douglas and Donald Douglas Sr; married Roy Jonathan Cobb, Feb 11, 1989; children: Jordan, Victoria. **Educ:** Illinois State University, attended, 1975-78. **Career:** Against the Law, series regular; Shadow of Love, tv movie; Three Penny Opera, Broadway, co-star with Sting; Tap, feature, lead with Gregory Hines; Condition Critical, tv movie; I'll Do Anything, movie, with Nick Nolte; George, pilot, lead female; Chain of Desire, independent feature; Search For Grace, TV Movie/ABC; Hallelujah, TV Movie/PBS w/James Earl Jones and Dennis Haysbert; WB's Parenthood, lead role, currently; I'll Fly Away; How Stella Got Her Groove (feature), supporting lead with Angela Bassett; Promised Land, guest star with Gerald McRainey, CBS; Last Weekend, starred in AFI/Lifetime, short film, also exec produced; Jason's Lyric, feature, co-starred with Forrest Whittaker; Inkwell, featured lead, co-starred with Joe Morton. **Orgs:** Camp Giddiup; Athletics Against Abuse; Jackie Robinson Foundation; Starlight Foundation, 1995. **Honors/Awds:** NAACP Image Award, Tap, 1989; Mary Martin Award, 1987. **Business Addr:** Actress, c/o William Blaylock, Manager, 8447 Wilshire Blvd, #206, Beverly Hills, CA 90211, (310)655-0101.

DOUGLAS, WALTER EDMOND, SR.
Association executive. **Personal:** Born Aug 22, 1933, Hamlet, NC; married Retha Hughes; children: Petra, Walter Jr, Mark. **Educ:** NC Cntrl Univ, BS Acctg 1954, MS Bus Admn 1955. **Career:** Intrnl Revenue Serv Data Cntr, brcnh chief 1968-69, asst chief sys div 1969-70, chief mgmt stf 1970-71, asst dir 1971-72; New Detroit, vice pres 1972-78, pres 1978-94; pres, Avis Ford Inc, currently. **Orgs:** Pres part ownr DHT Tranp Inc 1979-; mem Fed Home Loan Bk of Indianapolis 1978-82, YWCA, Channel 56 (PBS), Hlth Alliance Plan, chair, United Way; mem of Bd Detroit Symphony 1980-; Skillman Foundation, bd of dirs; Oakland Univ Foundation, bd of dirs; NCCU Foundation, bd of dirs; AAA of MI, bd of dirs; Henry Ford Health System, bd of dirs; Community Foundation of Southeast Michigan; board, Michigan Sports Hall of Fame. **Honors/Awds:** Grand Jury Invstgtns Pblsh by Detroit Clg of Law 1983; Liberty Bell Awrd Detroit Bar Assc 1975; Awrd from Pres Regan Exemplary Youth Dev Pgm 1984. **Military Serv:** AUS. **Home Addr:** 1189 Lone Pine Wds Dr, Bloomfield Hills, MI 48302. **Business Addr:** President, Avis Ford, Inc, 29200 Telegraph Rd, Southfield, MI 48034.

DOUGLAS, WILLARD H., JR.
Judge (retired). **Personal:** Born Feb 4, 1932, Amherst, VA; married Jane O Eggleston; children: Willard III, Wendelin Janna. **Educ:** VA Union U, AB 1957; Howard Univ Sch of Law, JD 1960. **Career:** Juvenile & Domestic Relations Dist Ct Commonwealth of VA, chief judge 1974-89; Asst Commonwealth Atty, 1969-74; Private Practice, 1965-69; US Commn on Civil Rights, staff atty 1962-65; US Copyright Office, staff atty 1961-62; Teamsters Union, admin asst bd of monitors 1960-61. **Orgs:** Mem Am Bar Assn; VA State Bar; VA State Bar Assn; Old Dominion Bar Assn; Richmond Criminal Law Assn; Richmond Trial Lawyers Assn; VA Trial Lawyers Assn, mem Kappa Alpha Psi Frat Bd Richmond Area Psychiatric Clinic; Richmond Epilepsy Found; Big Bros Ferrum Coll VA Wesleyan Coll; Lay Leader Wesley Memorial United Methodist Church; Asso Lay Leader VA Conf Bd of Laity & Richmond Dist Eastern Province; National Council of Juvenile & Family Ct Judges, bd mem 1986-89; United Methodist Church, Judicial Council, mem 1984-92. **Honors/Awds:** Achievement Award, Richmond Alumni & Petersburg Alumni 1974; Man of Yr, Richmond Alumnae Delta Sigma Theta 1974. **Military Serv:** USMC Sgt 1951-54.

DOUGLASS, JOHN W.
State representative. **Personal:** Born Mar 19, 1942, Princess Anne, MD; son of John Douglass; married. **Educ:** Lincoln U, AB 1964; Johns Hopkins U, MA 1966. **Career:** Morgan State Coll, instr 1966-68; Mutual Funds, salesman 1967-68; RL Johnson Realty Co, 1967-; Baltimore City Council, clerk 1967-68; Balitmore City Planning Dept, consult 1970-71; Maryland House of Delegates, mem 1971-; computer consultant. **Orgs:** New Dem Club, 1968-; mem Adj Neighborhood Improvement Assn 1969-. **Honors/Awds:** Penn Senatorial Scholarship 1960; Rohm & Hass Fellow 1964; Gilman Fellow 1964; Amer Chem Soc Award 1964; Amer Legion Award 1956; Certificate of Achievement Morgan State Coll 1968, 1969; Norman E Gaskin's Prize 1964; Eastern LI Ward 1964.

DOUGLASS, LEWIS LLOYD
Judge. **Personal:** Born Dec 12, 1930, Brooklyn, NY; son of Cornelia and Lloyd; married Doris Wildy; children: David, Lori. **Educ:** Brooklyn Coll, BS 1953; St John's Law Sch LLB 1956. **Career:** Federal Prosecutor's Office, asst US atty 1961-65; Housing Redevelopment Agency, exec dept dir 1965-68; Housing Devel Orgn, general counsel 1968-71; Black Enterprise Magazine, exec vice pres 1971-75; NY State Prison System, exec deputy commr 1975-78; Supreme Court of NY, judge, currently. **Business Addr:** Judge, Supreme Court of New York, 360 Adams, Brooklyn, NY 11201.

DOUGLASS, M. LORAYNE
Educator (retired). **Personal:** Born May 11, 1927, Fort Gibson, OK; daughter of Ollie Nivens and Wallace McNac; married Carlton R Douglas, Jan 30, 1954 (divorced). **Educ:** Langston Univ, BA, 1948; Olkahoma Univ, MEd, 1956. **Career:** Ponca City, Okla Schools, classroom teacher, 1950-54; Oklahoma City Schools, classroom teacher, 1954-63; Los Angeles Unified School Dist, coordinator, consultant, parent education coordinator, and conference planner, curriculum advisor, resource teacher, classroom teacher, 1963-87. **Orgs:** National Sorority Phi Delta Kappa, Far Western, regional director, 1983-87; NAACP, life member, 1987; Founders Church Religious Science, 1965-; United Teachers Los Angeles, 1963-87. **Honors/Awds:** Calif Assn Compensatory Ed, Service Award, 1979; National Sorority, Phi Delta Kappa, Delta Kappa Chapter, Model Excellence Award, 1991; Institute of Religious Science, Associate in Religious Science, 1973. **Home Addr:** 3501 Floresta Ave., Los Angeles, CA 90043, (213)291-1830.

DOUGLASS, MAURICE GERRARD
Professional football player. **Personal:** Born Feb 12, 1964, Muncie, IN. **Educ:** Univ of Kentucky, attended. **Career:** Chicago Bears, defensive back, 1986-94; New York Giants, 1995-; New Image Fitness, owner. **Business Addr:** Professional Football Player, New York Giants, Giants Stadium, East Rutherford, NJ 07073, (201)935-8111.

DOUGLASS, MELVIN ISADORE
Educator, cleric. **Personal:** Born Jul 21, 1948, Manhattan, NY; son of Esther Tripp Douglass and Isadore Douglass. **Educ:** Vincinnes University, AS, 1970; Tuskegee Institute, BS, 1973; Morgan State University, MS, 1975; New York University, MA, 1977; Columbia University, EdM, 1978, EdD, 1981. **Career:** Queensboro Society for the Prevention of Cruelty to Children Inc, child care worker, 1973-75; Public School 401-X, dean of students/teacher, 1973-75; Amistad Child Day Care Center, school age program director, 1976-77; Beck Memorial Day Care Center, administrative director, 1983-84; Department of Juvenile Justice, primary school department chair, 1984-85, ombudsman, 1985-88; John Jay College of Criminal Justice, adjunct instructor, 1988-89; Stimson Middle School, chairperson, boys track head coach, 1988-; College of New Rochelle, instructor, 1993-. **Orgs:** Pres, founder Jamaica Track Club 1973-; bd of dirs Nu Omicron Chap of Omega Psi Phi Day Care Ctr 1984-; mem Prince Hall Masonry; pres bd of dirs New York City Transit Branch NAACP 1984-90; co-chairperson Educ Comm NY State Conf of NAACP 1986-89; chairperson Anti-

Drug Comm Metro Council of NAACP Branches 1986-89; Jamaica East/West Adolescent Pregnancy Prevention Consortium 1986-89; basileus Nu Omicron Chap Omega Psi Phi Frat 1987-88; board of directors, Queens Council on the Arts 1983-86; bd of dirs Black Experimental Theatre 1982-; bf of dirs The United Black Men of Queens County Inc 1986-89; S Huntington Chmns' Assn, 1988-; Queens adv bd, New York Urban League, 1988-93; Amer Federation of Sch Administrators, 1988-; Council of Administrators and Supervisors, 1988-; Natl Black Child Devel Institute, 1982-; National Education Association, 1973-; community adv bd, The City of New York Dept of Correction, The Queens House of Detention for Men, 1991-94; community adv bd, Public School 40, Queens, NY, 1992-; bd of dirs Long Island Tuskegee Alumni Assn, 1986-, vp, 1987-89; bd of dirs, Dance Explosion, 1987-; area policy bd no 12, Subunit 2, 1987-; Ancient Arabic Order of Nobles of the Mystic Shrine. **Honors/Awds:** Grad Scholarship Columbia Univ 1978; Kappa Delta Pi Honor Soc in Educ inducted 1978; Service Awd NY City Transit Branch NAACP 1986; Citation for Comm Serv NYS Governor Mario Cuomo 1986; Citation Awd New York City Mayor Edward Koch 1986; Citation of Honor Queens Borough Pres Claire Shulman 1986; City Council Citation Award, New York City Councilman Archie Spigner 1988; Civil Rights Award, New York City Transit Branch NAACP 1988; Black Winners: A History of Spingarn Medalists 1984; Famous Black Men of Harvard 1988; Jefferson Award, American Institute for Public Service, 1987; Omega Man of the Year Award, Nu Omicron Chapter, 1987; Cert of Ordination, Cross Roads Baptist Church, NYC, 1990; State of New York Legislative Resolution, Senator Alton R Waldon Jr, 1991; Alumni Faculty Citation Award, Vincennes University, 1991. **Special Achievements:** Licensed to preach, Calvary Bapt Ch, Jamaica NY, 1987; written numerous publications, including: "Developing Successful Black Students,'' Feb 5, 1994, "Dr. Gerald W. Deas: More Than Pills,'' Feb 24, 1995, New York Amsterdam News; Social Studies Sixth Grade Teacher's Curriculum Guide, co-written with A. Sheppard, South Huntington School Dist, 1992. **Home Addr:** 108-38 167th St, Jamaica, NY 11433.

DOUGLASS, ROBERT LEE
State senator (retired). **Personal:** Born Jun 23, 1928, Winnsboro, SC; son of Jannie B Stevenson Douglass and John Douglass; married Bernice Viola Sales, 1947; children: Beverly, Ronald K, Eric L, Loren R. **Educ:** Morgan State Coll, BS, math, 1953; John Hopkins U, BS, elect eng, 1962; AmerUniv & Morgan State, M Deg Prog, 1963, 1965. **Career:** Baltimore City Public Schools, teacher, 1955-64; Bendix Corp, electrical design engineer, 1962-64; IBM, systems engineer, 1965-67; Baltimore Electronics Assn, president and founder, 1968-88; Baltimore City Council, councilman, 1967-74; Maryland State Senate, senator, 1974-82. **Orgs:** East Baltimore Community Corp; National Assn of Black Manufacturers; Baltimore Urban Coalition. **Military Serv:** AUS 1st lt 1953-55. **Home Addr:** 2111 Homewood Ave, Baltimore, MD 21218.

DOUTHIT, WILLIAM E.
Business executive. **Personal:** Born Apr 2, 1925, Farrell, PA; married Dorothy; children: William, Jr, Char, Helen. **Educ:** Dillard U, BA 1951; Univ of IL Inst of Labor & Industrial Relations, MA 1953. **Career:** Minneapolis Honeywell Co Aeronautical Div, supr 1962-64; Oklahoma City Urban League, exec dir 1959-62; Industrial Relations Dept St Louis Urban League, sec 1954-59; St Louis Urban League, exec dir. **Military Serv:** AUS 1943-46. **Business Addr:** 3701 Grandel Sq, St Louis, MO 63108.

DOVE, PEARLIE C.
Educator. **Personal:** Born in Atlanta, GA; daughter of Lizzie Dyer Craft and Dan Cecile Craft; married Chaplain Jackson B Dove (deceased); children: Carol Ann Dove Kotcha. **Educ:** Clark Coll, BA 1941; Atlanta Univ, MA 1943; Univ of CO, EdD, 1959. **Career:** Atlanta business & professional secretary, Phyllis Wheatley Branch, YMCA, 1943-45; Clark Coll, dir of student teaching, 1949-62, chmn, Dept of Educ, 1963-85, dist prof, 1975-86; Assoc Chair, Consolidation Steering Comm, Clark Atlanta Univ, 1988-89; Booker T Washington High School, educator, currently; The Atlanta Project, cluster coordinator, 1992-. **Orgs:** GA Stdnt Fin Comm, brd of dir 1981-87; Southern Asssoc of Coll & Schls, elem comm 1975-81; Amer Assoc Coll for Tchr Ed, bd of dir 1972-75; Assoc of Teacher Educators, natl exe comm 1970-73; Clark Coll, Amer Assoc of Univ Prof, pres 1978-80 1983-87; Atlanta Pan-Hellenic Cncl, pres 1960-64; Atlanta Alumnae Delta Sigma Theta Sor, pres 1962-63; advisory council, Fulton High School, Ctr for Teaching, 1990-91. **Honors/Awds:** Distinguished mem, Assn of Teacher Educ, 1983; Chmn's Award, State Comm on the Life & History of Black Georgians, 1979; Serv Award, Atlanta Alumnae, Delta Sigma Theta Sorority, 1963; Woman of the Year in Educ, Iota Phi Lambda Sorority, 1962; Delta Torch Award, Delta Sigma Theta Sorority Inc, 1989; Distinguished Alumni Achievement Award, Clark Coll, 1989; Included in the 1990-1991 Calendar of Atlanta Black History, Southern Bell: A Bell South Co, 1990-91; Honorary Rosalynn Carter Fellow, Inst for Women's Studies, Emory Univ, 1993-. **Business Addr:** Educator, Booker T Washington High School, 45 Whitehouse Dr SW, Atlanta, GA 30314.

DOVE, RITA FRANCES
Educator, poet, writer. **Personal:** Born Aug 28, 1952, Akron, OH; daughter of Elvira E Dove and Ray A Dove; married Fred Viebahn, Mar 23, 1979; children: Aviva Chantal Tamu. **Educ:** Miami Univ Oxford OH, BA 1970-73; Univ Tubingen West Germany, 1974-75; Univ of IA, MFA 1975-77. **Career:** Poet; author; Tuskegee Inst, writer in residence 1982; AZ State Univ, asst prof 1981-84, assoc prof 1984-87, full prof 1987-89; Univ of Virginia, full prof of English 1989-93; VA Commonwealth, prof, 1993-. **Orgs:** Ed bd mem Natl Forum The Phi Kappa Phi Journal 1984-; lit adv panel Natl Endowment for the Arts 1984-86; chair Poetry Grants Panel Natl Endowment for the Arts 1985; bd dir Assoc Writing Progs 1985-88; pres Assoc Writing Progs 1986-87; assoc ed Callaloo Journal of Afro-Amer Arts & Letters 1986-; advisory editor The Gettysburg Review 1987-, TriQuarterly 1988-; mem PEN Club Amer Ctr; advisory editor, The Georgia Review, 1994-; editorial bd, Iris, 1989-; advisory bd, Ploughshares, 1990-; advisory bd, North Carolina Writers' Network, 1991-; advisory bd, Civilization, The Magazine of the Library of Congress, 1994-; Afro-American Studies Visiting Committee, Harvard Univ, 1992-; Council of Scholars, Library of Congress, 1994-; juror, Newman's Own/First Amendment Award, PEN American Center, 1994; consultant, Woman to Woman on Lifetime, Lifetime TV, 1994; senator, Phi Beta Kappa, 1994-; contrib editor, Bellingham Review, 1996-; commissioner, The Schomburg Ctr for Res in Black Culture, 1987-; awards council, Amer Acad of Achievement, 1994-. **Honors/Awds:** Presidential Scholar The Pres of the US of Amer 1970; Fulbright Scholar US Govt 1974-75; Literature Grant Natl Endowment for the Arts 1978, 1989; Guggenheim Fellow Guggenheim Found 1983-84; Lavan Younger Poet Awd The Acad of Amer Poets 1986; Pulitzer Prize for Poetry Pulitzer Bd Columbia Univ 1987; General Electric Foundation Award for Younger Writers 1987; Ohio Governor's Award 1988; Honorary Doctor of Letters, Miami Univ 1988; Bellagio Residency, Rockefeller Foundation 1988; Andrew W Mellon Sr Fellowship, Natl Humanities Center, NC, 1988-89; Honorary Doctorate, Knox Coll, Illinois, 1989; Fellow, Center for Advanced Studies, Univ of Virginia 1989-92; judge, Walt Whitman Award, Acad of American Poets, 1990; judge, Ruth Lilly Prize, 1991; judge, Pulitzer Prize in poetry, 1991; judge, National Book Award, poetry panel, 1991; Literary Lion, New York Public Library, 1991; Induction, Ohio Women's Hall of Fame, 1991; judge, The Anisfield-Wolf Book Awards, 1992-; Commonwealth Professor of English, University of Virginia, endowed chair, 1993-; Phi Beta Kappa Poet, Harvard Univ, 1993; Poetry Reading at The White House, State Dinner in honor of National Medal of Arts recipients, 1993; Speaker at the 200th anniversary celebration of the Capitol, US Congress, 1993; VA Coll Stores Assn Book Award, Through the Ivory Gate, 1993; Woman of the Year Award, Glamour Magazine, 1993; NAACP Great American Artist Award, Natl Assn for the Advancement of Colored People, 1993; US Poet Laureate, 1993-95; Renaissance Forum Award, Leadership in Literary Arts, Folger Shakespeare Library, Washington DC, 1994; Ohioana Award for Selected Poems, 1994; Distinguished Achievement Medal, Miami Univ Alumni Assn, 1994; Golden Plate Award, American Academy of Achievement, 1994; Carl Sandburg Award, International Platform Assn, 1994; Honorary Doctor of Letters, Tuskegee Univ, Alabama, 1994; Univ, of Miami FL, 1994; Washington Univ, St Louis, MO, 1994; Case Western Reserve Univ, Cleveland OH, 1994; Univ of Akron, Akron OH, 1994; Arizona State Univ, 1995; Boston College, 1995; Dartmouth Coll, 1995; The Kennedy Ctr Fund for New American Plays Awd, 1995; Chair of Poetry Jury, Pulitzer Prize, 1996; Heinz Awd in Arts & Humanities, 1996; Charles Frankel prize, The President of the US, 1996; Honorary Doctor of Letters, University of Pennsylvania, 1996; Spelman College, 1996; University of North Carolina/Chapel Hill, 1997; University of Notre Dame, 1997; Sara Lee Frontrunner Award, 1997; Writers for Writers Award, Barnes & Noble, 1997; Disting Woman Award, Natl Assn of Women in Educ, 1997. **Special Achievements:** Author, collection of poems published: Ten Poems, 1977; The Only Dark Spot In The Sky, 1980; The Yellow House on the Corner, 1980; Mandolin, 1982; Museum, 1983; Thomas & Beulah, 1986; The Other Side of the House, 1988; Grace Notes, 1989; Selected Poems, 1993; Lady Freedom Among Us, 1994; Mother Love, 1995; collection of Short Stories published: Fifth Sunday, 1985; novel published: Through The Ivory Gate, 1992; drama published: The Darker Face of the Earth, 1994; essays published: The Poet's World, 1995; Youngest and first African-American Poet Laureate, 1993-95. **Business Addr:** University of Virginia, Dept of English, Wilson Hall, Charlottesville, VA 22903.

DOWD, MARIA
Company executive. **Personal:** chilDren: two. **Career:** African American Women On Tour, exec producer, currently.

DOWDELL, DENNIS, JR.
Human resources administrator. **Personal:** Born Mar 8, 1945; son of Marjorie Dowdell and Dennis Dowdell; married Equinetta Cox, Aug 22, 1970; children: Malaika, Arianne, Cicely. **Educ:** Central State Univ, BS, history/political science, LHD; Cleveland State Univ, Coll of Law, JD. **Career:** Cleveland Bd of Educ, teacher, 1968-71; Legal Serv Org of Indianapolis Inc, staff atty, 1971-72; US Dept of Labor, Office of the Solicitor, Office of the Solicitor, trial atty, 1972-76, asst counsel, OSHA, 1976-78, co-counsel, Black Lung, 1978-80; Amer Can Compa-

ny, Compliance Plans & Litigation, dir, 1980-84; Amer Natl Can, Performance Plastics Div, vice pres human resources, 1985-91; Henry Ford Health System, corp vice pres of human resources, 1991-. **Orgs:** Chmn, president's council, Central State Univ; bd of dir, Natl Urban League, Black Executive Exchange Program; Natl Urban League; NAACP; Amer Bar Assn; Natl Bar Assn; past natl pres, Central State Univ Natl Alumni Assn; exec leadership council, Omega Psi Phi Frat; Central State Univ Foundation; Leadership Detroit; Detroit Urban League; national board of directors, Alzheimer's Disease and Related Disorders Assn Inc; president, 100 Black Men of Greater Detroit; board of directors, Executive Leadership Foundation. **Honors/Awds:** Doctor of Humane Letters, Central State Univ, The Occupational Safety & Health Act of 1970, Practicing Law Inst. **Business Addr:** Corporate VP, Human Resources, Henry Ford Health System, 1 Ford Place, Detroit, MI 48202-3450.

DOWDELL, KEVIN CRAWFORD
Broadcasting company executive. **Personal:** Born Oct 7, 1961, Schenectady, NY; son of Doris Dowdell and Crawford Dowdell. **Educ:** Princeton Univ, BSE 1983; Wharton Business School, MBA 1985. **Career:** Strategic Planning Assocs, senior associate 1985-89; Safe Passage Foundation, Washington, DC, executive director, 1989-93; HBO, vp for new business devt, 1994-. **Orgs:** Pres, Princeton Soc of Black Engineers, 1982-83; vice chmn, Whitney Young Conf at Wharton 1984-85. **Honors/Awds:** Joseph Clifton Elgin Prize for Excellence in Engineering, Princeton 1983; General Electric Co Engineering Fellow 1979-80; Johnson & Johnson Leadership Fellow at Wharton 1983-85; Co-Captain, Varsity Tennis Team, Princeton University, 1982-83. **Business Addr:** VP, New Business Devt, Home Box Office, 1100 6th Ave, New York, NY 10036.

DOWDELL, MARCUS L.
Athlete. **Personal:** Born May 22, 1970, Birmingham, AL; son of Carolyn Dowdell and Robert Dowdell; children: Marsha. **Educ:** Tennessee State University, 1988-91. **Career:** New Orleans Saints, wide receiver, 1992-. **Orgs:** Alpha Phi Alpha Fraternity Inc, 1989-. **Business Addr:** Professional Football Player, New Orleans Saints, 6928 Saints Dr, Metairie, LA 70003, (504)733-0255.

DOWDY, JAMES H.
Business executive. **Personal:** Born Jun 3, 1932, New York, NY; son of Gertrude Dowdy and Edward Dowdy; married Elsia M; children: James Jr. **Educ:** D&B Business School. **Career:** Limosine Serv; Real Estate firm; Vending Co; Contracting Co, 1962; East coast Devel Corp, pres, CEO; Harlem Commonwealth Council, exec dir; Commonwealth Holding Co, pres, CEO 1970-92. **Orgs:** Past chmn Vanguard Natl Bank; bd of dir Freedom Natl Bank NYC; bd mem Harlem Interfaith Counseling Svc; mem Presidential Task Force, 100 Black Men; bd Cathedral Church of St John the Devine; former chmn Boys Choir of Harlem. **Honors/Awds:** 1st Comm Serv Awd Gov of VI; Martin L King Awd. **Business Addr:** President, Eastcoast Dev Corp, 1250 Maryland Ave, SW, Washington, DC 20004.

DOWDY, LEWIS C.
Chancellor. **Personal:** Born Sep 1, 1917, Eastover, SC; married Elizabeth Smith; children: Lewis, Jr, Lemuel, Elizabeth. **Educ:** Allen Univ, AB 1939; Indiana State Univ, MA 1949; Indiana Univ, EdD 1965; Indiana State Univ, LLD 1970; Univ of Maine, PdD 1975; Duke Univ, LLD 1977; Allen Univ, LittD 1964; Indiana Univ, LLD 1981. **Career:** Eastover SC, principal 1939-51; North Carolina A&T State Univ, teacher 1951-56, dean 1956-60; dean of instruction 1960-64, pres & chancellor 1964-80. **Orgs:** Mem Natl Assn of State Univ & Land-Grant Coll; Assn of Amer Coll; Amer Council on Educ; NC Assn of State Univ & Land-Grant Coll; mem Gov Council Aging; NC Atomic Energy Adv Comm 1968-73; Greensboro United Community Serv; C of C; YMCA. **Honors/Awds:** Outstanding Alumnus Award, IN State Univ, 1967; City Greensboro Award, C of C, 1970; short-term study travel grant, Danforth Found, 1970-71.

DOWELL, CLYDE DONALD
City official. **Personal:** Born Aug 19, 1938, Gordonsville, TN; son of Frances & LC Dowell; married Daisy Dowell, Oct 14, 1958; children: Sherry Green, Clyde D II, Marilyn Barnes, Tonja Hale. **Educ:** Wayne State Univ, BS, 1971; MBA, 1975. **Career:** City of Detroit, jr typist, 1962-; jr accountant, 1971-73; sr accountant 1973-74; prin accountant 1974-79; head accountant, 1979-85; accounting manager, 1985-86; deputy budget director, 1986-93; director public works, 1994-. **Orgs:** American Public Works Assn; NAACP, life member, 1981; Detroit Zoological Society; Founder's Society-Detroit Institute of Arts; National Assn of Assessing officers, 1979-85. **Special Achievements:** Ran & Completed 3 Marathons, 1983-85. **Military Serv:** US Army, spec-4, 1958-61. **Business Addr:** Director of Public Works, City of Detroit, City County Bldg, Rm 513, Detroit, MI 48226, (313)224-3901.

DOWELL, OLLIE WILLETTE
Broadcast journalist. **Personal:** Born Mar 7, 1957, St Louis, MO; daughter of Emma Mitchell Dowell and Willie E. Dowell.

Educ: Florissant Valley Community College, associates degree, 1981; University of Missouri School of Journalism, BJ, 1984; University of Toledo, currently attending. **Career:** Harper & Row Publishers, Troy, MO, newsletter editor, 1977-79; KOMU-TV Channel 8, Columbia, MO, anchor/reporter, 1982-83; KMIZ Channel 17, Columbia, MO, anchor/reporter, 1985-89; WTVG-TV, Toledo, OH, anchor/reporter, 1990-. **Orgs:** Vice President, local chapter, National Association of Black Journalists, 1990-; member, Friendship Baptist Church, 1990-; committee member, NABJ Scholarship Fund Raiser, 1990-. **Honors/Awds:** Olive Coates Journalism Scholarship, 1983; Youth Motivational Task Force Appreciation Award, 1988; Unity Journalism Awards Appreciation Award, 1988. **Business Addr:** Anchor/Reporter, WTVG-TV 13, 4247 Dorr, Toledo, OH 43607.

DOWELL-CERASOLI, PATRICIA R.
City official. **Personal:** Born May 13, 1957, Bethpage, NY; daughter of Kathryn Dowell and Norman Dowell; married Paul Cerasoli; children: Justin David. **Educ:** University of Rochester, Rochester, NY, BA, 1978; University of Chicago, Chicago, IL, MA, 1980. **Career:** Dept of Planning, City of Chicago, Chicago, IL, city planner, 1981-86; Mayor's Office, City of Chicago, Chicago, IL, development subcabinet staff director, 1987-89; Department of Planning City of Chicago, Chicago, IL, deputy commissioner, 1989-. **Orgs:** Board member, Midwest Center for Labor Research, 1989-; member, Lambda Alpha Land Economic Society, 1990-; member, National Forum of Black Public Administrators, 1990-. **Honors/Awds:** Leadership Fellow, Leadership Greater Chicago, 1988-89. **Business Addr:** Deputy Commissioner, Dept of Planning, 121 N LaSalle St, Rm 1006, Chicago, IL 60602.

DOWERY, MARY
Educator. **Personal:** Born in Kentucky; divorced. **Educ:** Knoxville Coll, 1950; Atlanta U, MSW 1952; Columbia U, 1963-64; NY U, 1965; Psychoanalytic Inst Training & Rsch, 1974-45; Tulane U, 1975; Union Grad Sch. **Career:** Ball State Univ, asst prof; Arch, 1971-74; Einstein Medical Coll; Comm Mental Coll; Comm Mental Health; Urban Renewal, Mobilization for Youth Inc; Residential Treatment for Adolescent Girls; CA Youth Authority; NY City Bd Educ; NY City, protestant cnc; Social Worker, 1953-65; Personnel By Dowery, founder & operator 1965-71; Black Greeting Card ''Uhuru'', orgnd pub 1968-71. **Orgs:** Mem Delta Sigma Theta; Assn of Personnel Agys NY City 1965-69; Am Mgmt Assn; NASW; Cncl on Social Wk Edn; 100 Black Women 1975-77; Leag Women Voters; NY Society for Sickle Cell Anemia; AU Alumni; Knoxville Coll Alumni Assn; bd mem United Day Care Ctr; Bethel Home for Boys; reviewer Nat Endowment ofHumanities; publ Greeting Card Mag 1970; partcp Mike Wallace Show 1964; publ Et Cetero Mag 1964; Black Enter 1970; Income Mag 1970; Daily News 1972; Bus Wk Peps 1969. **Business Addr:** 710 N Mc Kinley Ave, Muncie, IN 47303.

DOWKINGS, WENDY LANELL
Copy editor. **Personal:** Born Jun 24, 1964, Fort Meade, MD; daughter of Jessie Marbury Dowkings and Bennie Dowkings. **Educ:** University Texas, El Paso, TX, 1982-84; University of Texas, Austin, TX, BA, journalism, 1986. **Career:** Fort Worth Star Telegram, Fort Worth, Tx, intern reporting, 1985; Austin Ameircan Statesman, TX, copy editor, 1985-86; Hartford Courant, Hartford, CT, copy editor, 1986-89; Philadelphia Inquirer, Philadelphia, PA, copy editor, 1989-. **Orgs:** Volunteer fair coordinator, Hartford Neighborhood Housing Association, 1988-89; member, National Assn of Black Journalists, 1986-; member, Connecticut Assn of Black Communicators, 1988-89; member, Philadelphia Association of Black Journalists, 1991-. **Business Addr:** Copy Editor, Neighbors Copy Desk, Philadelphia Inquirer, 400 N Broad St, Philadelphia, PA 19101.

DOWLING, MONROE DAVIS, JR.
Physician. **Personal:** Born Feb 23, 1934, New York, NY; son of Helen Johnson Dowling and Monroe D Dowling; married Judith Ann Prysbeck, Feb 2, 1978; children: Carla Dowling Brown, Monroe D III. **Educ:** Harvard Univ, AB 1956; Howard Univ Coll of Med, MD 1960. **Career:** Good Samaritan Cancer Center of Southeast Ohio, medical dr, 1990-; Good Samaritan Hospital, 1989-; Bethesda Hospital, 1989-; Goldcrest Retirement Center, medical dir, 1987-89; Univ of Nebraska, asst prof of medicine, 1987-89; VA Hospital, Lincoln, Nebraska, consultant, 1977-89; St Elizabeth Comm Hlth Ctr, 1977-89; Bryan Meml Hosp, 1977-89; Lincoln Gen Hosp 1977-89; Meml Hosp Cancer & Allied Diseases, dir Out-Patient Hematology Clinic 1971-77, asst attending physician hematology serv 1971-77, clinical asst physician Dept Med 1968-71, sr clinical trainee 1967-68, clinical rsch trainee Dept Med 1966-67; Cornell Univ Med Coll, fellow med 1966-68, instr 1968-72, asst prof 1972-77; Henry Ford Hosp, resd 1961-61, 64-66; Univ CO Med Ctr, intern 1960-61; Sloan-Kettering Inst forCancer Research,ch fellow 1967-68,rsch assoc 1968-75, assoc 1975-77. **Orgs:** Mem Am Fedn for Clinical Rsch; AMA; Am Soc Clinical Oncology Inc; AAAS; Med Soc, State NY; Med Soc, Co NY; Natl Med Assn; Am Assn for Cancer Rsch; Nebraska Med Assn; Assn of Community Cancer Centers; Lancaster County Medical Assn; Muskingum County Medical Acad; Nebraska Cancer Control Program, chmn Tech Work Comm 1988; Nebraska Lymphoma Study Group. **Military Serv:** USNR lt 1950-66; USN 1962-64.

DOWNER, LUTHER HENRY
Physician. **Personal:** Born Dec 13, 1913, Athens, GA; married Dorothy B. **Educ:** Morehouse Coll Atlanta, BS 1938; Atlanta U, MS 1940; Howard Univ Wash DC, MD 1949. **Career:** Evansville State Hosp, physician-dir of cont care unit 1975-; Physician, pvt prac 1952-75. **Orgs:** Mem AMA; mem IN State Med Soc; mem Vanderbugh Co Med Soc; mem Nat Med Assn; mem Am Acad of Family Prac. **Honors/Awds:** Fellow Am Acad of Family Prac 1979. **Home Addr:** 6613 Arcadia Hwy, Evansville, IN 47715.

DOWNES, DWIGHT
Elected government official. **Personal:** Born Apr 26, 1944, Detroit, MI; son of Mr & Mrs Milton Downes; married Dieadra Ann; children: Damany. **Educ:** Ferris State Coll, ASS Bus Admin 1966; MI Lutheran Coll, BA Bus Admin 1969; Univ of Detroit, Master Bus Admin. **Career:** Highland Park Community College, adult educ instructor, 1969-70; Chrysler Corp, admin trainee/indus relations representative, 1969-71, labor relations representative, 1971-72, labor relations personnel representative, 1972-74, safety admin, 1974-76; Allen Indus Inc, mgr of personnel & labor relations, 1976-79; Highland Park School District, job placement counselor, 1980-84; Stroh Brewery Co, indus relations-personnel specialist, 1984-85; Mains Enterprises, 1985-89; Wayne County Intermediate School District, part-time mgr/placement specialist, 1980-; City of Highland Park, council pres pro tem, currently. **Orgs:** Bd of dirs, Highland Park Caucus Club; bd of dirs, Chrysler Corp; mem, Lions Club; board of directors, Highland Park Men's Forum; life mem, Kappa Alpha Psi; board of directors, Devco Inc; board of trustees, Highland Park Pension Fund; treasurer, Black Caucus; National League of Cities; Black National Caucus of Elected Offices. **Honors/Awds:** Ferris State University, varsity football & track scholarship. **Business Addr:** Council President, City of Highland Park, 30 Gerald, Highland Park, MI 48203.

DOWNEY, AURELIA RICHIE
Educator, co. executive. **Personal:** Born Apr 17, 1917, McKenny, VA; daughter of Aurelia Peterson Lundy and Philip James Lundy; married W Temple Richie (died 1959); children: W Temple Richie Jr, Gloria McCoy Boston, Willistine A Betts. **Educ:** VA State, BS 1939; So Baptist Theological Seminary, MA 1969. **Career:** Nannie Helen Burroughs School Inc, Washington DC, pres, 1969-89; Christian Worship Women's Auxiliary, Program Natl Baptist Convention, instructor 1968-71; Religious Educ Huntington WV, teacher 1940-51; Progressive Natl baptist Convension, USA Inc, Minister's Wives Division, instructor, 1978-84. **Orgs:** Exec bd mem Assn of Independent Schools of Greater Washington DC; mem, Business & Professional Women's League Washington DC; mem Church Women United; mem Women's Dept Program Natl Baptist Convention 1966-; sec/treasurer, Nannie Helen Burroughs Scholarship Fund, Inc, 1978-; treasurer, N Amer Baptist Women's Union, 1987-; World Council of Churches, Churches in Solidarity With Women, 1988-; chair, Resolutions Comm, Women's Convention, NBC, USA Inc; natl speaker for religious & educational occassions; workshop leader, Churches & other religious organizations. **Honors/Awds:** Recip Marshall A Talley Award 1972-73; honorary doctor of humanities award Am Bible Coll 1971; honorary legion of honor award Chapel of 4 Chaplains 1971; serv award Program Natl Baptist Convention 1974; Doctor Humane Letters, VA Seminary & Coll, 1984; Doctor of Humanities, Amer Divinity School, New York, NY, 1972, addressee for Women's Day, 1970. **Special Achievements:** A Tale of Three Women: God's Call and their Response.

DOWNIE, WINSOME ANGELA
Educator. **Personal:** Born Apr 14, 1948, Kingston, Jamaica; daughter of Marie Angela Crarey Downie and Frank G Downie; married Norbert W Rainford, Jun 28, 1980; children: Damien Rainford, Ayana Rainford. **Educ:** Barnard College, New York, NY, AB, 1970; Columbia University, New York, NY, MA, 1977, MPhil, 1977, PhD, 1985. **Career:** Kingsborough Community College, instructor, 1975-78; State University, New York, New Paltz, NY, instructor, 1978; Manhattan College, New York, NY, professor of political science, 1978-. **Orgs:** Member board of directors, Martin Luther King Center, Spring Valley, NY, 1988-92; chair, Church and Society Work Area, United Methodist Church, New City, NY, 1990-; exec board, Jamaican Cultural & Civic Association of Rockland, 1991-; committee mem, Jack & Jill of Rockland County, 1990-; member, chair, Compact Team Viola School, Suffern, Rockland, NY, 1979-. **Honors/Awds:** President's Fellow, Columbia University, 1973-74; Fellowship, Summer Institute Univ of Wisconsin, 1988; Summer Grant, Manhattan College, 1991; Sabbatical Leave (1995-1996) MLK-Center Service Award 1995. **Business Addr:** Professor, Government & Politics, Manhattan College, Manhattan College Parkway, Riverdale, NY 10471.

DOWNING, ALVIN JOSEPH
Entrepreneur, educator (retired). **Personal:** Born Jul 19, 1916, Jacksonville, FL; son of Mary Washington Downing and Ernest Downing Sr; married Edna Bernice Gause, Dec 20, 1944; children: Dierdre Marie Jackson, Evelyn Jean Hamilton, Alvinette Yvonne McCleave. **Educ:** AL State Montgomery, 1934-35; FL A&M Tallahassee, Mus B 1935-39; Catholic Univ Washington, DC, MM Music 1957 & 61; UCLA, 1979. **Career:** Gibbs H Sch St Pete, FL, instr/music 1939-41; Gibbs Jr Coll St Pete, FL, instr/music 1961-65; St Pete Jr Coll Clearwater Campus, instr/music 1965-83; Sharps & Flats Music Ent, pres 1973-74. **Orgs:** Pres/ownr Al Downing Music Entpr, Inc 1970-; pres/leader All Stars Jazz Group 1961-; pres Allegro Music Soc 1973-80; pres Al Downing's FL Jazz Assoc 1981-85; 1st Black Comm St Petersburg Housing Authority 1966-77; Al Downing Tampa Bay Jazz Assn, founder, 1989. **Honors/Awds:** Organist Bethel Bapt/Trinity Presby Church 1966-84; minister of music Bethel AME Church St Pete, FL 1985; 1st black mem St Pete Philharmonic Orchestra 1963; produced oper enjoyment Lockbourne AFB OH 1947; Martin Luther King, Jr Drum Major for Justice Award Southern Christian Leadership Conference 1984; Outstanding Service Award St of St Petersburg FL 1981; composed music & lyrics to ''Tuskegee Airman'' national song of Tuskegee Airman Inc. **Military Serv:** USAF maj, 20 yrs; Bronze Star 1950. **Home Addr:** 2121 25th St S, St Petersburg, FL 33712.

DOWNING, JOHN WILLIAM, JR.
Educator, physician. **Personal:** Born Mar 13, 1936, Phoebus, VA; son of Alice B Downing and John W Downing Sr; married Bessie; children: Kevin, Kimberlynn. **Educ:** Morehouse Coll, BS 1957; Meharry Med Coll, MD 1961. **Career:** Cincinnati Children's Medical Center, fellow, pediatric cardiology 1967-70; Univ of Cincinnati, instructor Pediatrics 1969-70; Howard Univ, asst prof 1970-74, assoc prof 1974-80, prof 1980-, chmn, dept of pediatrics, 1986-. **Orgs:** Dir Pediatric Cardiac Clinic Howard Univ Hosp; consult DC Gen Hosp; chmn prof ed comm Amer Heart Assoc Nations Capital Affiliate; mem DC Med Soc; mem Amer Heart Assoc 1974-; ch cncl Third St Ch of God 1974-; bd dir Amer Heart Assoc Nations Capital Affiliate; diplomate Amer Bd Pediatrics; flw Am Coll Cardiology. **Honors/Awds:** Several publ in med lit. **Military Serv:** US Army, Marine Corp, capt 1964-67. **Business Addr:** Professor, Chairman, Dept of Pediatrics, Howard Univ, 2041 Georgia Ave NW, Washington, DC 20060.

DOWNING, STEPHEN
Assistant athletic director. **Personal:** Born May 28, 1950, Indianapolis; son of Evana Downing and William Downing; married Doris. **Educ:** IN U, BS 1973; IUPUI, MS Counseling & Guidance 1978. **Career:** IN U, adminstrator asst to athletic dir 1978-; Boston Celtics, former bskbll prof. **Orgs:** Active childrens summer groups; first draft Boston 1973. **Honors/Awds:** MVP Big Ten; Converse All-Amer Team; NCAA 3rd place team; HS All-Amer; Indiana Hall of Fame, 1996. **Home Addr:** 6433 Lakeside Woods Circle, Indianapolis, IN 46278.

DOWNING, WILL
Vocalist. **Personal:** Born in New York, NY. **Career:** Singer, currently. **Honors/Awds:** Blues & Soul Magazine, Best Album of the Year, Vocalist of the Year, Best Live Performer, 1992; Soul Train Music Awards, nominated; NAACP Image Awards, nominated. **Special Achievements:** Albums include: Will Downing, 1988; Come Together As One, 1989; A Dream Fulfilled, 1991; Love's The Place To Be, 1993; Moods, 1995; Invitation Only, 1997; Sang background vocals for artists such as: Nona Hendryx, Jennifer Holliday, Najee, Stephanie Mills, David Peaston, Billy Ocean, and Art Porter; sang duets with Rachelle Ferrell, Mica Paris; performed for Prince Charles and Princess Diana at the Prince's Trust Concert. **Business Addr:** Singer, c/o Mercury Records, 825 8th Ave, 19th Fl, New York, NY 10019, (212)333-8000.

DOWNS, CRYSTAL
Writer, editorial consultant. **Personal:** Born Dec 29, 1964, Chicago, IL; daughter of Queen Esta Taylor Downs and Charles Edmond Downs. **Educ:** Chicago State University, Chicago, IL, 1983-87; Columbia College, Chicago, IL, BA, 1989. **Career:** American Journal of Reproductive Immunology and Microbiology, Chicago, IL, editorial intern, 1987-88; Essence Magazine, New York, NY, summer intern, summer 1988; Alpha Kappa Alpha Sorority, Chicago, IL, asst director, assoc editor, 1989-92; self-employed, writer, editorial consultant, 1992-95; Chicago State University, Chicago IL, executive assistant to the president, 1995-. **Orgs:** Member, National Association of Black Journalists, 1990-; member, Alpha Kappa Alpha Sorority, 1984-; mem, CASE; board member, Public Allies; mem, Women's Advisory Group. **Honors/Awds:** Magazine Publishing Procedures Course, Howard University & Magazine Publishers of America, 1990; University of Chicago Publishing Program, 1994. **Home Addr:** 5470 S Harper, Chicago, IL 60615. **Business Phone:** (773)995-3608.

DOWNS, GARY MCCLINTON
Professional football player. **Personal:** Born Jun 6, 1972, Columbus, GA. **Educ:** North Carolina State. **Career:** New York Giants, running back, 1994, 1996; Denver Broncos, 1995; Atlanta Falcons, 1997-. **Business Addr:** Professional Football Player, Atlanta Falcons, Two Falcon Place, Suwanee, GA 30174, (404)945-1111.

DOXIE, MARVIN LEON, SR.
Marketing executive. **Personal:** Born May 15, 1943, Youngstown, OH; son of E Beatrice Boyd Doxie and Melvin; married Feb 27, 1965; children: Monica Yvette, Marvin Leon Jr. **Educ:**

Youngstown State University; Ohio University; Howard University, School of Business and Public Administration, 1975; Prince George's Coll, 1995. **Career:** Greater Washington Business Center, vp, 1973-82; Raven Systems & Research, Business Development, director, 1982-83; DC Government, Minority Business Opportunity Commission, marketing manager, 1983-85; Automated Sciences Group, Inc, marketing support director, 1985-94; M.L. Doxie & Associates, pres, 1994-95; Delon Hampton & Associates, chartered, client relations, dir, 1996-. **Orgs:** Montgomery County High Technology Council, 1989-95; Silver Spring Chamber of Commerce, bd of dirs, 1990-95; AFCEA, 1989-95; DC Chamber of Commerce, 1975-; MD/DC Minority Supplier Development Council, 1989-; American Marketing Association; Architect/Engineering Council, 1996-. **Honors/Awds:** DC Government, Appreciation Award, 1985; White House Conference on Small Business, Certificate of Appreciation, 1986; Montgomery County, MD Government, Cert of Appreciation, 1997. **Home Addr:** 7202 Wendover Dr, Forestville, MD 20747-1742.

DOYLE, HENRY EMAN

Judge. **Personal:** Born Mar 15, 1910, Austin, TX; married Vendya Middleton. **Educ:** Samuel Huston Coll Austin, TX, AB 1933; TX So Univ Law Sch Houston, TX, JD 1950. **Career:** First Court of Civil Appeals of TX, asso justice 1978-; Atty, self-employed 1946-76; Samuel Huston Coll, instr 1946-48; Prairie View A&M Coll, mgr subsistence dept 1942-45; Austin Pub Sch, head math dept 1933-41. **Orgs:** Mem Am Bar Assn; mem TX Bar Assn; mem Houston Bar Assn; Houston Lawyers Assn; Am Judges Assn.

DOZIER, MORRIS, SR.

Insurance executive (retired). **Personal:** Born Nov 30, 1921, Americus, GA; son of Minnie M Dozier and Charlie Dozier; married Mary Lois Strawn; children: Morris Jr, Yolonda Maria. **Educ:** KS State Univ, 1963; Brown Mackie Business Coll, 1965. **Career:** Civilian Conservation Clerk, admin clerk 1941-42; US Army, sr clerk typist 1942-44, command sgt major 1944-51, military personnel off 1951-62; US Govt Ft Riley, independent contractor 1967-78; Universal Insurance Service, owner/operator 1965-; Geary Co, comm 1973-85. **Orgs:** Pres PTA Westwood Elem Sch 1966; vice-pres Kawanis South, Jct City 1970; chmn Advisory Comm Sickle Cell Anemia Educ & Screening Prog 1975-; lay leaderChurch of Our Savior United Methodist 1980-; Geary County Senior Citizens Board of Directors, chmn 1988-; treasurer, Hunger Commission, Kansas East Conference, United Methodist Church 1985-. **Honors/Awds:** Comm Medal 1957, 1st Oak Leaf Cluster 1962 US Army; Disting Citizen of the Yr Awd Omega Psi Phi Frat 1979; Plaque of Recognition for Outstanding Serv of State JTPA Prog Honorable John Carlin Gov State of KS 1983. **Military Serv:** AUS chief warrant officer w3 20 yrs; Good Conduct Medal, Natl Defense Medal, Asiatic Pacific Medal, Philippine Liberation Medal 1943-45; Army Occupation Medals, Japan 1945, Italy 1946. **Home Addr:** 1701 W 17th St, Junction City, KS 66441.

DOZIER, RICHARD K.

Architect, historian, educational administrator. **Personal:** Born Jan 18, 1939, Buffalo, NY. **Educ:** LA Tech Coll, AA 1962; Yale Sch of Architecture, BA 1969, MA 1970; Univ of MI, doctor of architectural history, 1990. **Career:** Historic Preservation Architect Tuskegee Inst AL, prv prac; The Architects Office New Haven, CT, pvt prac; Tuskegee Inst, chmn dept of architecture 1976-79, professor of architectural history, 1979-87; Yale U, prof of architecture 1970-76; Architect with various firms; History of Afro-Am Architects & Architecture, tchng & profl specialization; Morgan State University, professor of architecture, 1987-91; Florida A&M University, associate dean, school of architecture, 1991-96, professor of architecture, 1996-. **Orgs:** Mem Am Inst of Architects; Nat Orgn of Minority Architects. **Honors/Awds:** Yale Univ, Leadership Award, 1969, Honor Award, 1970; Research Fellow, Graham Found 1970; Nat Endowment of the Arts Award; CT Found for the Arts; NEH, Dissertation Award, 1986; FL Hon Grant, Natl Park Services. **Military Serv:** USN, radarman E-5, 1956-60. **Business Addr:** Professor, Florida A&M University, School of Architecture, Tallahassee, FL 32307, (904)599-3894.

DRAIN, GERSHWIN A.

Judge. **Educ:** Western Michigan University, BS, 1970; University of Michigan Law School, JD, 1972; University of Nevada, Reno, National Judicial College, MJS, 1991. **Career:** 36th District Court, Detroit, judge, 1986; Recorder's Court, Detroit, judge, 1987-. **Special Achievements:** One of only two Michigan judges to receive a MJS degree. **Business Addr:** Judge, Recorder's Court, Frank Murphy Hall of Justice, 1441 St Antoine, Detroit, MI 48226, (313)224-2474.

DRAKE, DANIEL D.

Professor of Educational Administration. **Personal:** Born Oct 29, 1931, Memphis, TN; son of Bertha Steverson Calhoune and James Louis Drake, Sr; married Adrienne Carol Moore; children: Daniel, Adriana, Darian. **Educ:** Miami Univ, BS Ed 1955; Cleveland State Univ, M Ed 1971; Univ of Akron, Ed D 1979. **Career:** Cleveland Public Schools, teacher 1955-68, asst principal, 1968-73; Cleveland State Univ, adjunct prof 1971-85, assoc prof, 1991-; Cleveland Public Schools, principal 1973-85; Sioux Falls Public Schools, asst supt 1985-89; Milwaukee Public Schools, community superintendent 1989-91. **Orgs:** Chmn, bd of dir Carroll Inst; chmn of adv bd of dir Community Devel in Sioux Falls SD; vice chmn, bd of dir Amer Indian Serv Inc; mem Zoological Soc; bd dir Great Plains Zoo; vice chair, membership services commission, American Association of School Administrators, 1989-90; vice chair, district administration committee, National Alliance of Black School Educators, 1988-90; president, PDK Chapter of Sioux Falls, South Dakota, 1988-89. **Honors/Awds:** Cleveland State University Distinguished Alumni Award 1990, PDK Dist Serv Awd Phi Delta Kappa Professional Ed Frat 1981; Outstanding Scholastic Achievement 1980; S D Shankland Scholarship Amer Assoc of School Admin 1979; Toward Educational Excellence in an Urban JHS NASSP Bulletin Vol 60 No 401 Sept 1976; Distinguished Alumni Award, Cleveland State University Alumni Association, 1990; PDK Service Key, Phi Delta Kappa Education Fraternity, Cleveland Ohio Chapter, 1985; published articles in various journals, 1977-95. **Business Addr:** Full Professor, Cleveland State Univ, 1983 East 24th Street, Cleveland, OH 44115.

DRAKE, LAWRENCE M., II

Telecommunications executive. **Personal:** Born Jun 10, 1954, Pittsburgh, PA; son of Lawrence M Drake II and Jean Williamson; married Sharon Martin Drake, Sep 3, 1994; children: Kia Nichol, Kory Lawrence. **Educ:** Georgia State University, BS, 1977; Rockhurst College, MBA, 1990. **Career:** Coca-Cola USA, region manager, KC Region, 1985-87, acct group manager, CCE liaison, 1987-88, group director, NY Acct Group, 1990-91; KFC, Div of Pepsico Inc, vp, adm, asst to president, 1990-91, vp, general mgr, N Ctr Div, 1991-93, New Business Development, vp, KFC Express Concepts, 1993-95; Cablevision Systems Corp, senior vp and general manager, 1995-96; Dolman Technologies Group, exec vp, COO, 1996-. **Orgs:** Executive Leadership Council, 1991-; National Black MBA Assn, 1991-; Alpha Phi Alpha Fraternity Inc, 1974-; Georgia State University Alumnae Assn, 1985-; Rockhurst Executive Fellows Assn, 1990-; MAI Inc, board of directors, 1990-; National Conference of Christian & Jews; Leadership Cleveland; Cleveland Business Roundtable. **Business Addr:** Exec VP, COO, Dolman Technologies Group, Inc, 6545 Mercantile Way, Ste 5A, Lansing, MI 48911.

DRAKE, LEONARD

Head basketball coach. **Personal:** Born Jul 16, 1954, Chicago, IL; son of Ruth & Charles Drake; married Rhonda Denise Drake, Apr 19, 1986; children: Jared Leonard, Enjoli Desiree. **Educ:** Central Michigan Univ, BS, education, 1978, MA, phys ed, 1983. **Career:** Central Michigan Univ, asst basketball coach, 1978-79, head basketball coach, 1993-; Xavier Univ, Louisiana, asst basketball coach, 1979-85; Ball State Univ, assoc basketball coach, 1985-93. **Business Addr:** Head Basketball Coach, Central Michigan University, 187 Rose Center, Mount Pleasant, MI 48859.

DRAKE, MAGGIE W.

Judge. **Personal:** daugHter of Arthur & Margaret K Williams. **Educ:** Highland Park College, AA, 1971; Mercy College of Detroit, BSN, 1976; University of Detroit, JD, 1981; Judicial College, DP, 1993. **Career:** Detroit Police Department, sergeant, 1974-92; Corp. Counsel, asst, 1982-92; Detroit Recorders Court, 1992-97; Wayne County Circuit Court, 3rd judicial circuit, 1997-. **Orgs:** Michigan Judges Association, 1993-; Black Judges Association, 1993-; Association Trial Judges, 1993-. **Honors/Awds:** Community Treatment Ctr, Distinguished leader, 1996-97; Blacks in Blue Award, Detroit Police Assn, Distinguished Leader, 1997; BM&E State Convention, Women Auxiliary, Distinguished Leader Award, 1996. **Business Phone:** (313)224-2487.

DRAKE, PAULINE LILIE

Association official. **Personal:** Born Jul 20, 1926, Cliffwood, NJ; daughter of Daisy Etta Brown and Gabriel David Robinson, II; married Howard William Drake; children: Sidney Howard. **Educ:** NY Univ, 1945-46; Brookdale Comm Coll NJ, 1984-85. **Career:** Providence Baptist Church Cliffwood, church clerk 1957-65, youth choir dir 1960-72; Order of Eastern Star AF&AM, worthy matron 1994-97, Monmouth cty dep 1960-71; Order of Sunbeam Youth Dept OES AF&AM, deputy 1972-82. **Orgs:** Pres Matawan Hadassah NJ 1979-81; cert chmn Southern NJ Reg of Hadassah 1981-85; pres Monmouth Cty VFW Aux NJ 1980-81; publicity chmn State of NJ Ladies Aux VFW 1981-82, 1988-89; jr girls unit chmn NJ Ladies Aux VFW 1982-83; safety chmn NJ Ladies Aux VFW 1983-84; voice of democracy & youth activity chmn Ladies Aux VFW 1984-85; safety chmn 1986-87, guard 1986-87, conductress 1987-88 Dept of NJ Ladies Aux VFW; transfer and trackdown chmn, Southern NJ Region of Hadassah 1987-1990; chaplain 1988; jr vice pres, NJ Ladies Aux VFW 1988-1990, rehabilitation chmn 1988-89; JNF chairperson, Southern NJ Region of Hadassah, 1990-91; senior vice pres, NJ VFWA, 1990-91; community activity chairperson, state pres, NJ Ladies Aux VFW, 1991-92; USO, volunteer, 1942-45; Citation for Runner Up State President, 1991-92; Ladies Aux VFW; grand conductress of the Military Order of the Cooties, 1994-95; second vice president, Madison Twp Historical Society, 1994-96; Monmouth County Park Afro American Committee; Aberdeen Twp Community Development Committee; Concerned Citizens of Aberdeen; Southern New Jersey Region of Hadassah, JNF Chair, 1990-96; Ladies Auxiliary MOC, New Jersey grand senior vice pres, 1995-96; Ladies Auxilairy MOC, New Jersey, Grand Pres, 1997-98; Madison Township Historical Society, first vice pres, 1996-98; The Center for Holocaust Studies at Brookdale Community College, Lincroft, bd of dirs, mem, 1996-98. **Honors/Awds:** Woman of the Yr Matawan Hadassah 1979; Citation Bayshore Recreation & Economic Develop 1979; Presidential Awd Natl Hadassah 1981; NJ Publicity 1st Place Natl VFWA Kansas 1982; NJ Jr Girls Unit 2nd Place Natl VFW Kansas 1984; NJ Safety Cert Natl VFW KS 1984; 15 Yr Pin Keyport Aux to VFW NJ 1985; NJ Publicity 1st place Natl VFWA 1988; Runner Up, Rehabilitation National Convention, 1990; Adath Israel Congregation Sisterhood and Men's Club, Humanitarian of the Year Award, 1995. **Home Addr:** 85 Kennedy Ave, Cliffwood, NJ 07721.

DRAKEFORD, JACK

City government official. **Personal:** Born May 14, 1937, Englewood, NJ; son of Margaret Harris Drakeford; married Virginia Finley Drakeford, Sep 16, 1975; children: Gina, Nancy. **Educ:** New York University, New York, NY, business administration; Syracuse University, Syracuse, NY, public administration. **Career:** City of Englewood, Englewood, NJ, firefighter, 1959-73; James E Hanson, Hackensack, NJ, insurance broker/real estate agent, 1973-77; City of Englewood, Englewood, NJ, city clerk, 1977-85, city manager/city clerk, 1985-. **Orgs:** Member, Englewood Hospital Board of Trustees; commissioner, Bergen County Housing Authority; chairman, Northern Valley District Bergen County Boy Scouts; executive board member, Northern Valley Bergen County Boy Scouts, executive board member, Bergen County Girl Scouts. **Honors/Awds:** Received approximately 20 awards from various organizations including: Englewood Chamber of Commerce; Bergen County NAACP; Bergen County Boy Scouts of America; Bergen County Urban League; Bergan County Black Business and Professional Women. **Military Serv:** US Army, Spec/4, 1960-62. **Business Addr:** City Manager, City of Englewood, City Hall, 2-10 N Van Brunt St, Englewood, NJ 07631.

DRAKEFORD, TYRONNE JAMES

Professional football player. **Personal:** Born Jun 21, 1971, Camden, SC; married Cindi; children: Julian James, Justus T. **Educ:** Virginia Tech, bachelor's degree in finance. **Career:** San Francisco 49ers, defensive back, 1994-. **Business Addr:** Professional Football Player, San Francisco 49ers, 4949 Centennial Blvd, Santa Clara, CA 95054, (415)562-4949.

DRAKES, MURIEL B.

State official. **Personal:** Born Nov 25, 1935, Bronx, NY; daughter of Frances Drakes and Alphonso Drakes. **Educ:** DE State Coll, BS 1958; Columbia Teacher Coll, MA 1963. **Career:** NY State Environmental Conservation, dir of EEO, l987-; NY State Office Gen Serv, dir promotion & pub affairs 1976-; Dept Commerce & Ind, dep commr 1974-75; Manpower Devel Commerce Labor Ind Corp, asst vice pres 1972-74; Comm Corp, asso dir prgm 1969-72; Bedford Stuyvesant Comm Corp, dir, educ explt prgm 1965-69; Famingdale Pub Sch, tchr 1958-65; NY City Childrens Aid Soc, vis lctr 1957-60; NY Sch Social Rsch, visiting guest spkr 1968; Dahomey W Africa, visiting guest lecturer 1971; NY State Lottery Public Rels, consult 1976. **Orgs:** Mem Delta Sigma Theta Sor; NEA; vice pres Brooklyn Kings Co Judiciary Sect Comm Bldg; mem C of C Brooklyn Managerial Club; Intl Ind Mktg Club; Albany Women's Press Club; pres Eleanor Roosevelt Educ Action Prgm. **Honors/Awds:** Natl Black Public Admins, l984 Woman of the Year, Albany, YWCA,; l987 Outstanding Leadership by Albany Capital Dist Ethnic Heritage Orgs (28,) l987; Willoughy Walk Tenants Cncl Recpt; distgd citz award Concord Bapt Ch; Outstanding Leadership Civic Assn Jersey City 1974; outsdg effort & Achvmt Inter Ethnic Civic Assn 1975; achvmt excellence Black Photographers Assn 1974; Brooklyn Distinguished Council Negro Women 1975; author ''1965 Proposal of Bedford Stuyvesant Comm Corp on the Homework Study Prgm''. **Business Addr:** NY State, Environmental Conservation, 50 Wolf Rd, Albany, NY 12233.

DRAPER, EDGAR DANIEL

Educator (retired). **Personal:** Born Aug 29, 1921, Brooklyn, MD; son of Anniebelle Saunders Draper and Andrew J Draper Sr; married Emma J Williams Draper, Dec 29, 1948; children: Marie E, Yvonne T, Edgar D, Jr. **Educ:** Howard U, BA 1943; NY U, MPA 1948, PhD 1967. **Career:** TX Southern Univ, dir & instructor 1948-49; Tubman Coll, pres 1949-51; Baltimore Housing Authority, asst mgr 1951-52; Morgan State Coll, business mgr & asst to the pres 1952-60; Conference African Resources NY Univ, asst dir 1960-61; African-American Trade Devel Assn, exec sec 1961-62; UN Inst Public Admin, deputy chief 1962-63; Governor Nelson Rockefeller, program asst 1963-66; Borough Manhattan Comm Coll, assoc dean, dean of college & faculty, 1967-70, pres 1970-84. **Orgs:** Bd mem Met Chap Amer Assoc Pub Adm; NY Plan; Natl Conference Christs Jews 1970-; Council Higher Educ Inst 1972-; Prof Training Com & Mem Com; BSA; Natl African Studies; Natl Ed Assoc;

Comparative Ed Soc; Am Assoc Comm & Jr Coll; Assoc Assist Negro Businesses; Urban Leag; Gov Libr Com; Interstate Compact Ed; Joint Legislative Com; Host Radio WNYC-AM The Open Door 1973-74; chmn 4th Round Table Conference Perspectives Pub Adm Sudan; NY St Gov Com Manpower 1966; member, American Society for Public Administration; member, Baltimore Urban League; member, New York University Alumni Association; life member, NAACP; member, Metropolitan Education Coalition; member, Baltimore Council on Foreign Affairs; task force member, Baltimore City Public Schools. **Honors/Awds:** New York University, Founders Day Award. **Military Serv:** US Army, pfc, 1946-47. **Home Addr:** 2728 Longwood St, Baltimore, MD 21216.

DRAPER, EVERETT T., JR.

Educator. **Personal:** Born Jan 23, 1939, Lochapoka, AL; son of Susie A Wilson Draper and Everett T Draper Sr; married Emma Jeanette Smith; children: Evangeline Hope. **Educ:** Miles College, Birmingham, AL, BA 1960; North Adams State, MA, MEd 1969; Advanced Studies, Yale Univ, Fairfield Univ. **Career:** Housatomic Regional HS, mathematics teacher 1963-69; Harcourt Brace Jovanovich Inc, asst editor, Math 1969-1971; American Book Co, exec editor, Math & Sci 1971-78; LaGuardia Cmmty Coll, adjunct prof of Math 1974-85; Holt Rinehart and Winston, Publishers, sr editor Math 1979-86; Prentice-Hall, Inc, exec edit Math 1986-89, product mgr, 1989-. **Orgs:** Mem Natl Cncl of Teachers of Mathematics, Natl Cncl of Supervisors of Mathematics, ASCD; NABSE; mem Mathematics Assoc of Amer; New Jersey State Mathmatics Coalition-MSEB. **Honors/Awds:** Service Awd United Negro Coll Fund (NYC) 1973-74; first black teacher at Housatonic Reg HS in Connecticut; first black Math Editor at Harcourt Brace 1969, American Book Co 1971, and first black to be named as Math Dept head in publishing industry 1986, marketing mgr 1989. **Business Addr:** Executive Editor Mathmatics, Prentice Hall Allyn & Bacon, Englewood Cliffs, NJ 07632.

DRAPER, FRANCES MURPHY

Newspaper executive. **Personal:** Born Dec 18, 1947, Baltimore, MD; daughter of Frances L Murphy II and James E Wood Sr; married Andre Reginald Draper; children: Kevin E Peck, Andre D, Andrea J, Aaron R. **Educ:** Morgan State Univ, BA 1969; The Johns Hopkins Univ, MEd 1973; Univ of Baltimore, Graduate Certificate in Mgmt 1979, MBA 1981; Loyola College, MS, 1996. **Career:** Baltimore City Public Schools, teacher 1969-73; New Jersey Afro-Amer, mgr 1973-76; Merrill Lynch Pierce Fenner & Smith, acct exec 1976-78; Morgan State Univ, asst vice pres develop 1978-83; Afro-American Newspapers, president, COO, 1986-; national certified counselor. **Orgs:** Mem Delta Sigma Theta Sor Inc 1968-; dir Afro-Amer Newspapers 1976-; vice chair, City of Baltimore's Literacy Foundation 1988-94, chair, 1995-; member, National Coalition 100 Black Women, 1989-; Network 2000; United Way of Central MD, bd mem, 1994-97; Balitmore City Chamber of Commerce, bd mem, 1994-97; Morgan State Univ, bd of regents, 1995-. **Honors/Awds:** Baltimore Magazine, one of the "Area's Most Infuential Women," 1983; USA Today, one of the "People to Watch," 1987; Towson State University, Distinguished Black Marylanders Award; Zeta Phi Beta Sorority Inc, Woman of the Year in Business, 1990; AFRAM, one of 15 women honored, 1992; The New Daily Record, Maryland's Top 100 Women, 1996. **Business Addr:** President, COO, Afro-American Newspapers, 2519 N Charles St, Baltimore, MD 21218, (410)554-8200.

DRAPER, FREDERICK WEBSTER

Educator. **Personal:** Born Jul 10, 1945, St Louis, MO; married Carrie Todd; children: Fred W II, Angela. **Educ:** IN State Univ, BS 1968, MS PE 1969, MS Pers Admin 1972, EdD 1976. **Career:** Project Upswing IN, asst dir 1969; GED Prog for Office of Economic Opportunity, supvr 1972-73; asst physical educ & head crosscountry coach 1969-, dir of ed programs; School of HPER IN State Univ, dir educ opportunity programs, prof; Global Net Solutions, pres/ceo, currently. **Orgs:** Chmn Black Freshmen Orientation Prog IN State Univ 197-74; internship with vice pres IN State Univ for Student Affairs 1972-73; bd vice pres IN State Black Expo; bd dir Hyte Comm Ctr; bd of dir & treas IN Airport; faculty adv Kappa Alpha Psi; mem City Human Rel Comm, School Human Rel Comm, Boy Scout Troup Leader; pres Hulman Reg Airport; bd of dir, mem Civil Rights Commission; chmn of bd IN Black Expo. **Honors/Awds:** Outstanding Black Faculty Awd IN State Univ 1972-73; One of Nations Most Eligible Bachelors Ebony Mag 1969; Dean's List 1968; vice pres Alumni Club; All-conf intrack every year as an undergrad. **Business Addr:** President/CEO, Global Net Solutions, 2626 E 46th Street, Ste 200, Indianapolis, IN 46205.

DRAPER, SHARON MILLS

Educator. **Personal:** Born Aug 21, 1948, Cleveland, OH; daughter of Vick & Catherine Mills; married Larry E Draper, Jul 25, 1970; children: Wendy, Damon, Cory, Crystal. **Educ:** Pepperdine University, BA, 1970; Miami University, MA, 1972. **Career:** Cincinnati Bd of Education, teacher, 1972-97; Mayerson Academy, National Teacher of the Year Program, currently. **Orgs:** National Bd for Professional Teaching Standards, bd of dirs, 1995; Women's City Club; National Council of Teachers of English; Ohio Council of Teachers of English Language Arts; Conference on English Leadership; American Federation of Teachers; Intl Reading Association; Delta Kappa Gamma. **Honors/Awds:** National Teacher of the Year, 1997; Ohio Teacher of the Year, 1997; Excellence in Education Award, 1997; Milken Family Foundation, National Educator Award, 1997; YWCA, Career Women of Achievement, 1997; National Council of Negro Women, Excellence in Teaching Award, 1996; Outstanding High School Language Arts Educator, 1995; American Library Association/Coretta Scott King, Genesis Award for Outstanding New Book, 1995; Fiction Work, "Tears of A Tiger," honored by American Language Association, Best Book for Young Adults, 1995; Ebony Magazine, First Prize in Literary Contest, 1991; Howard Univ School of Education, Dean's Award; Pepperdine Univ, Distinguished Alumnus Award; Marva Collins, Education Excellence Award; Governor of Ohio, Governor's Educational Leadership Award. **Special Achievements:** One of the first teachers in the nation to achieve National Board Certification in English/Language Arts, and is one of only three English teachers in Ohio to be certified; Award winning essay on education was published in: "What Governors Need to Know About Education;" author of numerous works of poetry and fiction, accomplished public speaker.

DRAYTON, TROY ANTHONY

Professional football player. **Personal:** Born Jun 29, 1970, Harrisburg, PA. **Educ:** Penn State. **Career:** St Louis Rams, tight end, 1995-96; Miami Dolphins, 1996-. **Honors/Awds:** Pro Bowl alternate, 1994. **Business Addr:** Professional Football Player, Miami Dolphins, 2269 NW 199th St, Miami, FL 33056, (305)620-5000.

DR. DRE (ANDRE YOUNG)

Rap artist. **Personal:** Born 1966?, Compton, CA. **Career:** Rap group NWA, member; Death Row Records, solo rap artist, currently. **Honors/Awds:** Grammy Award, 1994. **Special Achievements:** Albums include: "The Chronic," 1992; short films inlude: Murder was the Case, director, 1994; recording, "Keep Their Heads Ringing," Priority Records, 1995. **Business Addr:** Rap Artist, c/o Aftermath Entertainment, 15060 Ventura Blvd, Ste 225, Sherman Oaks, CA 91403, (818)385-0024.

DREHER, LUCILLE G.

Association executive. **Personal:** Born Jun 24, 1910, Greenville, SC; daughter of Lucy Hicks; married Frederick D. **Educ:** Claflin Coll. **Career:** Youth Village Center, founder & pres, 1959-66; Youth Village Family Day Care, dir, 1966-76; Bronx, local mayor 1975. **Orgs:** NAACP; Natl Council of Negro Women; NY City Planning Bd #3; Mayor's Vol Action Comm; Bronx Frontier Morrisania Educational. **Honors/Awds:** Scholarship Comm Award, JFK Library Award for Minorities; Natl Council of Negro Women Community Achievement Award.

DRENNEN, GORDON

Auditor. **Personal:** Born Jul 15, 1947, Atlanta, GA; son of Eliza Harris Drennen and Gordon D Drennen Sr; married Diane Hatcher, Mar 17, 1978; children: Kimberly. **Educ:** Fort Valley State Coll, BS 1970; TX Southern Univ, MBA 1971. **Career:** Wolf & Co CPA's, staff accountant 1971-73, sr accountant 1973-78; Tarica & Co CPA's, supervisor 1978-80, mgr 1980-. **Orgs:** Dir Amer Civil Liberties Union of GA 1986-; finance chmn Ft Valley State Coll Alumni Assn 1986-; mem GA State Soc of CPA's; mem/consultant Natl Assn of Comm Health Ctrs, GA Assn for Primary Health Care Inc; mem Kappa Alpha Psi Frat; vice, chair, finance committee, National Black College Alumni Hall of Fame Foundation Inc, 1990-; selection committee, chair, Georgia Assn of Minority Entrepreneurs, 1987-; member, National Assn of Black Accountants, 1973-. **Honors/Awds:** Distinguished Alumni Citation of Year, National Assn for Equal Opportunity in Higher Education; Grad Fellowship, Texas Southern University, 1970-71. **Business Addr:** Manager, Tarica & Co CPA's, 3340 Peachtree Rd, Ste 1776, Atlanta, GA 30326.

DREW, JAMES BROWN

Educator, research physicist (retired). **Personal:** Born Apr 6, 1922, Charlottesville, VA; son of Susan Brown Drew and James William Drew; married Christine Howard, Nov 30, 1944; children: Nataliece, James. **Educ:** Virginia Union University, Richmond, VA, BS, 1943; Virginia State University, Ettrick, VA, 1943; Howard University, Washington, DC, MS, 1947; Rutgers University, New Brunswick, NJ, MS, 1954. **Career:** Howard University, Washington, DC, instructor in physics, 1947-50; Rutgers University, New Brunswick, NJ, graduate research assistant, 1952-54; The Franklin Inst Research Labs, Philadelphia, PA, research physicist, book reviewer, The Journal of the Franklin Inst, 1954-67; Montgomery County College, Blue Bell, PA prof/associate dean, 1967-90. **Orgs:** Executive bd member, Camden Branch NAACP, 1967-70; member/researcher, Camden Branch ASLAH, 1971-81; Assistant District Commissioner, BSA/Camden County, 1958-60; member, National Geographic Society, 1989-; member, National Society of Black Physicists, 1980-83. **Honors/Awds:** Scientific Honor Societies: Sigma X, Sigma Pi Sigma, Beta Kappa Chi, over 20 publications (refereed) in National & International Publications; Lilly Foundation Fellow, Univ of PA, 1980; Lecturer, International Magnetics Conf Stuttgart, Germany, 1960. **Military Serv:** Corp of Engrs, 1st Lt, 1943-; European Theatre & Pentagon Based 2901st Research & Development Training Group. **Home Addr:** 211 Ryans Run, Maple Shade, NJ 08052.

DREW, LARRY DONELLE

Professional basketball player (retired), basketball coach. **Personal:** Born Apr 2, 1958, Kansas City, KS. **Educ:** Univ of Missouri, 1980. **Career:** professional basketball player on various teams: Detroit Pistons, 1980-81, Kansas City Kings, 1982-85, Sacramento Kings, 1986, Los Angeles Clippers, 1987-88, Los Angeles Lakers, 1990-91; Los Angeles Lakers, assistant coach, currently. **Orgs:** Board member, KC K's Red Cross; teacher, basketball camps in Kansas and Missouri. **Honors/Awds:** All Big 8 Honorable Mention; holds all-time record for appearances (117), starts (114), consecutive starts (104), career assists (443), game assists (12), & career field goals (557); 1st-round draft pick, Detroit Pistons, 1980; ranked 9th in NBA in assists, 1984-85; led team in assists, 2nd in scoring, Kansas City Kings 1984-85; 14 double-assist scoring games, 1984-85. **Business Addr:** Assistant Coach, Los Angeles Lakers, 3900 W Manchester Blvd, Forum, Inglewood, CA 90305-2200.

DREW, STEPHEN RICHARD

Attorney. **Personal:** Born May 25, 1949, Detroit, MI; son of Gwendolyn Mae Johnson Drew and Richard T Drew; married Clarice Smith Drew, Apr 22, 1989; children: Richard, Stephen, Anthony, Thomas. **Educ:** Univ of MI, BA 1971; Univ of MI Law School, JD 1974. **Career:** Williams Klukowski Drew & Fotieo, assoc 1974-77, partner 1977-87; Drew, Cooper & Anding, Grand Rapids, MI, partner, 1991-. **Orgs:** Chairperson City of Grand Rapids Comm Relations Commn 1984-85; consultant special investigator Saginaw Police Dept 1985-86; mem Sigma Pi Phi 1985-; judicial merit selection panel mem US Court of Appeals 6th Circuit 1986-; legal redress comm NAACP Grand Rapids Chapter 1987; trustee, 1987, vice pres, 1990-91, president elect, 1991-92, president, 1992-93, mem judicial review committee, Grand Rapids Bar Assn; mem Amer Bar Assn, Natl Bar Assn, MI Trial Lawyers Assn, Amer Trial Lawyers Assn; fellow State Bar of Michigan; pres, Floyd Skinner Bar Assn; member civil justice reform advisory committee, United States District Court. **Honors/Awds:** Chief trial attorney in various civil rights/personal injury cases in MI area, Federal and State Courts 1978-; Outstanding Volunteer Award NAACP Grand Rapids Chapter 1982; Patriotic Serv Award Sec to the US Treasury 1986; Grand Rapids Giant Award Justice; Civil Libertarian of the Year, W Michigan ACLU, 1989. **Business Addr:** Partner, Drew, Cooper & Anding, 125 Ottawa NW, Ledyard Bldg, Suite 300 R, Grand Rapids, MI 49503, (616)454-8300.

DREW, THELMA LUCILLE

Government official. **Personal:** Born May 6, Flushing, NY; married Archer S Drew Jr; children: Richard Michael, Kenneth Edward, Joanne Michelle, Sheryln Liane, Kimberly Terese. **Educ:** Queens Coll, NY, Engish 1946-49; Amer Inst of Banking, Mgmnt 1968-72; Empire State Coll, NY, Pub Admin 1978-80; Hofstra Univ Hempstead, NY, Cert inMuseum Studies 1983-85. **Career:** NY Tele Co, bus off rep 1949-58; Smithtown Townshp, town rec ldr (1st black) 1965-69; Natl Bank of N Amer, baner/mgmnt 1969-73; Suffolk Co Dept ofSoc Svcs, socl welfare examiner 1973-77; Suffolk Cnty Human Rights Comm, sr investgtr 1977-82. **Orgs:** Mbr, NYS Div of Human Rights Cncl 1983-; brd of dir Long Isl Affirmative Act Plan 1980-, Victims Inf Bureau 1980-, Inst of Labor/Mgmnt Studies 1979-;founding mem 100 Black Women of LI 1980-; mem Natl Assn of Female Exec 1982-, Natl Assn of Consumer Prot 1982-; prs/Chrprsn Suffolk Cnty Black Hist Assoc 1982-; pres Sec & fndng mem Long Island Minoritycoalition 1982-; org mem Womens Equal Oppty Cncl 1980-, Womens Equal Rights Congress 1980-82; pres & orgn mem NAACP Smithtown Branch 1966-82. **Honors/Awds:** Womens Equal Rights comm Woman of the Year 1984; comm serv awd Natl Cncl Oppty Cncl/LI 1983; Community Serv Awd Natl Assoc of Cnties/LIAAO 1983; ldrshp Awd Natl Cncl Christ & Jews/LI 1982; comm serv Human Rights Comm/Suffolk Cnty 1981; candidate for pres recog Award for vlnt Rsm/Suffolk 1984. **Business Addr:** Sr Consumer Affrs Investig, Suffolk County Govt, Dept of Consumer Protection, Bldg 340 County Center, Smithtown, NY 11787.

DREW, WELDON

Educator. **Personal:** Born Apr 22, 1935, Silsbee, TX; married Gloria Marie McIntosh. **Educ:** Fisk U, BS 1957; TX So U, MS 1973. **Career:** New Mexico State U, head basketball coach 1975-; Houston Indep Sch District, tchr/coach 1957-75. **Orgs:** Mem & sponsor KAY 1956-; mem NAACP 1957-; mem NABC 1975-80. **Honors/Awds:** TX & HS Coach of the Yr, Houston-austin 1974-75; Houston HS Coach of the Yr 1974-75; Natl Achvmt Award, NABC 1974-75; Coca-Cola Award, Houston 1974-75. **Business Addr:** New Mexico State University, Box 3145, Las Cruces, NM 88003.

DREW-PEEPLES, BRENDA

Attorney. **Personal:** Born Feb 28, 1947, Fresno, CA; daughter of Gladys Drew and Jesse Drew; married Horace Peeples, May 20, 1989; children: Cranford Thomas, Vanessa Leigh. **Educ:**

Des Moines Area Comm Coll, AA 1973; Drake Univ, BS Business Admin 1975; Univ of IA Coll of Law, JD 1978. **Career:** Iowa Cty Atty's Office, legal intern 1978; Aetna Life & Casualty Ins of Des Moines, claim rep 1979; Legal Serv Corp of IA, attorney 1979-81; Polk Co Attorney's Office, asst co atty 1981-83; Davenport Civil Rights Comm, director/attorney. **Orgs:** Mem Iowa State Bar Assn 1980-; moderator Davenport Comm Forum 1985; Quad Cities Vision for the Future; LULAC CLub; NAACP; SLCL; Poor People's Campaign Steering Committee; East Side Advisory Board; National Youth Sports Advisory Board; Quad Cities Merit Employment Council; Women's Encouragement Board; Davenport Civil Service Commission; Iowa Association of Human Rights Agencies; Intl Assn of Official Human Rights Agencies; Natl Assn of Human Rights Workers; Greater Quad Cities Telecommunications Corporation Board; Maternal Health Center Board; Scott County Bar Assn. **Business Addr:** Director-Attorney, Davenport Civil Rights Commission, 226 W 4th St, Davenport, IA 52801.

DREWRY, CECELIA HODGES
Educator. **Personal:** Born in New York, NY; married Henry N. **Educ:** Hunter Coll, AB 1945; Columbia U, AM 1948; Shakespeare Univ of Birmingham, England, Cert 1949; Northwestern U, PhD 1967; Univ of Ghana, Cert 1969. **Career:** Princeton Univ, asst dean, asst prof; Haverford Coll, visiting prof of english 1977; Teachers Coll Columbia Univ, visiting instructor 1968; African & Afro-Amer Studies Prog, chairperson 1969-70; Rutgers Univ, assoc prof 1962-70; High School of Performing Arts NY, teacher 1952-59; Talladega Coll, instrutor 1945-47; Penthouse Dance & Drama Theatre NY, dir of speech 1948-52; Princeton High School, teacher 1959-61; various theatre appearances. **Orgs:** Mem AAVP; AAUW, MLA, SCA; trustee Cedar Crest Coll PA; mem Carnegie Found for Advmt of Tching; NAACP; Nat Council of Negro Women; Princeton Assn of Hum Rights. **Honors/Awds:** Award for excellence in oral interpretation of literature Northwestern Univ Sch of Speech; Alpha Psi Omega Hon Soc; Danforth Assn; Honoree Phi Delta Kappa. **Business Addr:** Princeton University, 408 W College, Princeton, NJ 08540.

DREWRY, HENRY NATHANIEL
Educator, educational administrator. **Personal:** Born Feb 8, 1924, Topeka, KS; son of Bessie Boyd Drewry and Leonard E Drewry; divorced. **Educ:** Talladega Coll, AB 1948; Teachers Coll, Columbia Univ, MA 1949. **Career:** A&T Coll, Greensboro, NC, instructor, 1949-51; Social Security Admin, claims asst, 1952-54; Princeton NJ High School teacher, 1954-60; Princeton High School, History Dept Chmn, 1960-68; Princeton Univ, dir of Teacher Prep & Placement, lecturer, prof, 1968-89; Andrew Mellon Found, program assoc, 1989-94; Andrew Mellon Found, senior advisor, 1994-. **Orgs:** NJ Historical Comm 1977-; mem, bd trustees Talladega Coll 1965-85, Groton School, 1977-91, Manhattan Country School, 1994-96; mem, NY Historical Soc, 1986-89; Council for Basic Educ, 1975-85. **Honors/Awds:** Fellowship, John Hays Fellos Prof, 1964; Distinguished Teacher Award, Harvard Univ, 1964; Oustanding alumnus UNCF, NJ State Org 1978; Honorary Doctorate, Talladega College, 1995, Taugaloo College 1997. **Military Serv:** USAAF corpl. **Business Addr:** Senior Advisor, Andrew W Mellon Found, 282 Alexander St, Princeton, NJ 08540.

DREXLER, CLYDE
Professional basketball player. **Personal:** Born Jun 22, 1962, New Orleans, LA; son of Eunice Prevost Drexler and James Drexler Sr; married Gaynell Floyd Drexler, Dec 30, 1988; children: Clyde Austin, Kathryn Elise, Adam Eugene. **Educ:** Univ of Houston, grad 1983. **Career:** Portland Trail Blazers, forward, 1983-95; Houston Rockets, forward, 1995-98; University of Houston, head coach, 1998-. **Orgs:** Chairman, Blazer/Avia Reading Program, 1988-. **Honors/Awds:** Newcomer of the Year in the Southwest Conf 1981; Houstons MVP as a sophomore; Jr season named Southwest Conf Player of the Year; Won 1st team All-Amer honors on the US Basketball Writers Assn team; NBA All Star, 1986, 1988, 1989, 1990, 1991, 1992, 1993, 1994, 1996, 1997; Honorary Chairman, UNCF, Portland Region, 1988-91; selected as one of the 50 Greatest Players in NBA History, 1996. **Special Achievements:** US Olympic Basketball Team, 1992. **Business Addr:** Head Coach, Basketball, Univ of Houston, Houston, TX 77204-5121, (713)749-1011.

DREYFUSS, JOEL P.
Writer, editor. **Personal:** Born Sep 17, 1945, Port-au-Prince, Haiti; son of Anne-Marie Dreyfuss and Roger Dreyfuss; married Veronica Pollard, Oct 4, 1980; children: Justin. **Educ:** City University of New York, BS. **Career:** New York Post, reporter 1969-71; Washington Post, reporter 1971-73; AP, reporter 1973-76; Black Enterprise, exec editor, 1980-83; Emerge, contributing editor; Fortune, associate editor, 1983-90, Tokyo bureau chief, 1986-88; Business Tokyo, New York, NY, managing editor, 1990-91; PC Magazine, New York, editor, 1991-94; Info Week Magazine, editor-in-chief, currently. **Orgs:** Mem, Council on Foreign Relations, 1986-; mem, Japan Society, 1988-; founding mem, Natl Assn of Black Journalists, 1975-. **Honors/Awds:** Urban journalism fellow, U Chicago 1973; coauthor (with Charles Lawrence III), The Bakke Case: The Politics of Inequality. **Business Addr:** Editor-in-chief, Information Week Magazine, 600 Community Drive, Manhasset, NY 11030.

DRIESSEN, DAN
Professional baseball player (retired). **Personal:** Born Jul 29, 1951, Hilton Head, SC; married Bonnie; children: Dominique, Devon. **Career:** Cincinnati Reds, infielder 1973-84; Montreal Expos, infielder 1984-85; San Francisco Giants, infielder, 1985-86; Houston Astros, infielder, 1986; St Louis Cardinals, infielder, 1987. **Honors/Awds:** Let the NL in 1980 with 93 bases-on-balls; first designated hitter ever used by the NL in World Series play; played in three League Championship and two World Series; finished third in Natl League Rookie-of-the-Year balloting.

DRIESSEN, HENRY, JR.
Elected government official. **Personal:** Born Sep 28, 1927, Hilton Head Isl, SC; married Phoebe; children: Leon, Ann J, Bernard. **Educ:** Savannah State Coll, BA 1957. **Career:** Driessen Groc & Serv Station & Bottle Shop, Merchant 1958; Town of Hilton Head, councilman. **Orgs:** Teacher Screven Ct HS 1957-58; area dir Bank of Beaufort; dir Palmetto Electric Coop Inc; past vice pres Hilton Head Island med Clinic; past master Happy Home Lodge #125; past pres Hilton Head Elem School PTA; past pres McCracken HS; past dir Hilton Head Island Chamber of Commerce. **Honors/Awds:** Islander of the Month Hilton Head Island Chamber of Commerce. **Military Serv:** AUS corpl 2 yrs. **Business Addr:** Councilman, Town of Hilton Head, Box 593 Hwy 278, Hilton Head Island, SC 29928.

DRIGGRISS, DAPHNE BERNICE SUTHERLAND
Educational administrator. **Personal:** Born in New York, NY; married Harvey Driggriss Sr (deceased); children: Harvey William Jr. **Educ:** NY Univ, 1939-41-44; Queens Coll-City Univ of NY, 1949-50; Adelphi Coll-univ, BS 1963; Adelphi Univ, MA 1971; Pace Univ, certif & MS 1973. **Career:** Public Schl #136 Queens, NY, asst prncpl 1970; Public Schl #116 Queens, NY, asst prncpl 1974-78; Public Schl #35 Queens, NY, asst prncpl 1976-77; Public Schl #132 Queens, NY, prncpl 1978-. **Orgs:** Dist 29 treas Cncl of Spvrs & Admnstrs 1976-; New York City Elem Sch Prins Assn 1979-; NAACP-JAMAICA, NY 1950; Beta Omicron Chpts of natl sor of Phi Delta Kappa Inc 1966-; basileus Natl Sor of Phi Delta Kappa Inc Beta Omicron Chpts 1975-77, exec advsr 1977-79; natl coorinator internatl proj Nat Sor PhiDK Inc 1981-, constitution chrpsn Eastern Region 1984-. **Honors/Awds:** Asst Prncpl Achvmnt Awd PTA PS #116 Queens, NY 1977. **Business Addr:** Principal, Public Schl 132 Queens, 132-15 218 St, Springfield Gardens, NY 11413.

DRISKELL, CLAUDE EVANS
Dentist. **Personal:** Born Jan 13, 1926, Chicago, IL; son of Helen Elizabeth Perry-Driskell and James Ernest Driskell Sr; married Naomi Roberts Driskell, Sep 28, 1953; children: Yvette Michele, Isaiah, Ruth, Reginald, Elaine. **Educ:** Roosevelt Univ, BS 1950; Univ of IL Coll of Dentistry, BS, 1952, DDS 1954. **Career:** Lincoln Dental Soc, editor 1966-; Natl Dental Assn, dir publicity 1968-76; Chicago Board of Education, dental consultant, 1972-76; Natl Dental Assn Journal, asst editor; Private Practice, dentist; Chicago State Univ, Illinois Inst of Technology, adjunct prof, 1970-79. **Orgs:** Omega Psi Phi Fraternity 1948-77; fellow Acad General Dentistry 1973; mem Amer Dental Assn, Chicago Dental Soc; vice pres Jackson Park Assn; adjunct prof Minority Students in Pre-Dental Program Chicago State Univ; mem Dean's Com for Black Students Univ IL Coll Dentistry; life mem Chicago Inst Art, Roosevelt Univ, Univ IL; mem Amer School Health Assn, Intercontinental Bio Assn; adjunct off-campus prof for pre-dental students for Chicago State Univ, IL Inst of Technology 1986-87; mem, Int Assn of Anesthesiologists, Inc, 1952-91; mem, Illinois State Dental Society, 1954-; Amer Dental Assn; Chicago Dental Society. **Honors/Awds:** Editorial Award Natl Dental Assn 1968-72. **Special Achievements:** Publications: ''The Seventy-Fifth Anniversary of the Incorporation of the Original Forty Club of Chicago, 1920-1995;'' ''The History of the Negro in Dentistry,'' 1968; ''The Influence of the Halogen Elements Upon the Hydrocarbon & Their Effect on General Anesthesia,'' 1970; ''The Chicago Black Dental Profs 1850-1983;'' Lincoln Dental Soc, 1967-75; Fellowship Acad General Dentistry, 1973. **Military Serv:** AUS, company clerk, 1944-46; European-African-Middle E Campaign Medal; Asiatic-Pacific Campaign Medal; 4 Battle Stars. **Business Addr:** Dentist, 11139 S Halsted St, Chicago, IL 60628.

DRISKELL, DAVID C.
Artist, educator. **Personal:** Born Jun 7, 1931, Eatonton, GA; son of Mary L Cloud Driskell and George W Driskell; married Thelma G Deloatch Driskell, Jan 9, 1952. **Educ:** Skowhegan School of Painting and Sculpture, Maine, certificate, 1953; Howard Univ, AB 1955; Cath Univ, MFA 1962; Ricksbureau Kunsthistoriches Den Haag, Holland 1964. **Career:** Talladega Coll, assoc prof 1955-62; Howard Univ, assoc prof 1962-66; Fisk Univ, prof & chmn dept of art 1966-76; Univ Ife Nigeria, visiting prof 1970; Univ of MD, chmn dept of art 1978-83; Amistad Research Center, curator Aaron Douglas collection 1977-; Univ of MD, prof of art 1977-. **Orgs:** Mem Coll Art Assn Amer; SE Mus Conf; Amer Assn Mus; Amer Fedn Arts; bd dirs National Mus African Art; board of directors, American Federation of Arts. **Honors/Awds:** Afro-Amer Artist 1973; Pubns, monograms, catalogs, film cons; Purchase Awards Birmingham Mus Art 1972; Tougaloo Coll Gallery 1973; num art awards, scholarships, fellowships & grants; foreign study & travel; Honorary Doctor of Humane Letters, Daniel Payne College, 1977, Rust College, 1991; Honorary Doctor of Fine Arts, Tougaloo College, 1977, Bowdoin College, 1989, State Univ of New York, Old Westburg, 1989; Nine honorary degrees; Five fellows; Distinguished University Professor, President's Medal, University of Maryland, College Park. **Military Serv:** US Army, 1st Lieut, 1957-65. **Business Addr:** Professor of Art, Univ of Maryland, College Park, MD 20742.

DRIVER, DAVID E.
Publishing company executive. **Personal:** Born Oct 17, 1955, Chicago, IL. **Educ:** Bradley Univ, BA, 1976; Univ of Chicago, MBA, 1986. **Career:** Arthur Young, mgr, 1977-79; Merrill Lynch, vp, 1979-88; Noble Press, pres, 1988-. **Orgs:** United Way Volunteer Ctr, recruitment chairman, 1990-92; Breakaway, bd mem, 1991-92; Better Boys Foundation, bd mem, 1987-89; Points of Light Foundation, advisory council, 1989-91. **Special Achievements:** Defending the Left, nonfiction book, Noble Press, 1991; The Good Heart Book: A Guide to Volunteering, Noble Press, 1989. **Business Addr:** President, Noble Press, Inc/Black Literary Society, 636 N Orleans St, #2-SO, Chicago, IL 60610.

DRIVER, JOHNIE M.
Engineer, analyst. **Personal:** Born May 8, 1933, Centerville, AL; son of Daisy B Richard and McKelway Driver; married Odessa Wright, Apr 12, 1952; children: Dwaine Stuart, Courtney LaShay. **Educ:** Univ of IL, BS Elec Eng 1961, MS Elec Eng 1963. **Career:** Sperry UT Co Salt Lake City, UT, proj engr 1963-66; Jet Propulsion Lab Systems Div, mem tech staff 1966-. **Orgs:** Pres Salt Lake City NAACP 1965-66; mem UT State Civil Rights Comm 1965; treas Pasadena, CA NAACP; mem/deacon Metropolitan Baptist Church. **Honors/Awds:** 1st Black to address Joint Session UT State Legislature 1965. **Military Serv:** USAF s/sgt 1950-58. **Business Addr:** Member Technical Staff, Jet Propulsion Laboratory, 4800 Oak Grove Drive, Pasadena, CA 91103.

DRIVER, LOUIE M., JR.
Clergyman. **Personal:** Born Mar 18, 1924, LA; son of Myrtle Driver and Louie Driver; married Lillian Stovall; children: Louie III, Brenda, Lamar. **Educ:** Harbor Coll, Certificate 1950; Emmanual Bible Inst, Graduated 1956; Blue Mountain Coll, Psychology Certificate 1963; LTI Biola, Graduated 1975; Univ of Lavern, BA religion 1985; LA Ecumenical Center for Black Church Studies, BA 1985; Graduated 1988 Fuller Theological Seminary MA, 1988; LA Edumenical Center for Black Church Studies. **Career:** Saints Home Church of God in Christ, pastor; Grace Chapel Church, Pendleton OR, pastor; Los Angeles County Sheriff Dapt, Chaplain, 1989-90. **Orgs:** Supt Sunday School Local/Dist; pres Young People Willing Workers, Local, Dist, State; appointed bd dir CH Mason Bible Coll 1977; chmn Bd Elders CA SW; Dist #4 supt CA SW Jurisdiction; mem Exec Bd CA SW Cogic; mem Chas H Mason Theological School, So CA Ext; chapel Chamber of Commerce, Pendleton OR; mem Natl COGIC Pastors Grievance Com; mem Newton St Police Ministers Council Clergy, Los Angeles County Sheriff's Dept Central Jail. **Honors/Awds:** Recipient outstanding pastor of yr CA SW Jurisdiction Religious Workers Guild; hon DD Trinity Hall Coll 1975. **Business Addr:** Church of God in Christ, Saints Home Ch, 7801 So Main St, Los Angeles, CA 90003.

DRIVER, RICHARD SONNY, JR.
Editor, publisher. **Personal:** Born Aug 16, 1926, Philadelphia, PA; son of Helen Birchett Driver and Richard E Driver Sr. **Career:** Free-lance advertising & public relations; Scoop USA, Newspaper editor publisher & owner. **Orgs:** NAACP; consultant, United Black Business Assn; board member, Black United Fund. **Honors/Awds:** NAACP Distinguished Award 1962; Publisher of Scoop USA Newspaper since 1960; Citation Jazz at Home Club of Amer 1971; Advertising Award Lancaster Ave Business Assn 1973; City of Philadelphia Citation, City of Philadelphia 1995; Four Chaplains Legion of Honor Award, Chapel of Four Chaplains 1989; Senator of PA, PA legislative Black Caucus, Service Award, 1992; Philadelphia City Council, Mayor of Philadelphia, Service Award, 1995; US House of Representatives Citation, 1995; PA State House of Representation Citation, 1995. **Military Serv:** US Army, 1944-46. **Home Addr:** 1220 N Broad St, Philadelphia, PA 19121. **Business Addr:** Publisher, Scoop USA, 1220 N Broad St, Box 1111, Philadelphia, PA 19121.

DRIVER, ROGERS W.
Clergyman. **Personal:** Born Jun 14, 1921, Elkton, TN; son of Louetta Driver and Rogers W Driver Sr; married Mackie L Baker; children: John R, William B. **Educ:** Univ of HI, 1944; TN State Univ, BS 1948; TN Univ, Post Graduate 1969; Am Baptist Theological Seminary, BTH 1987. **Career:** Triangle Chem Co, sales rep 1948-66; Pearl Vocational School, instructor 1951-52; General Spec Co, owner mgr 1952-66; Triangle Chem Co, special sales consultant 1966-74, sales mgr 1974, buyer HBA 1978, part time, retired, 1989; pastor, Gladeville Circuit Churches, North Nashville AME, currently. **Orgs:** Past vice pres Nashville Assoc Black Salesmen 1971; mem Natl Assoc Market Devel 1972-, Natl Business League; pres Middle TN Business Assoc; mem NAACP, Nashville Model Cities Cit

Coordinating Comm, Economic Devel Comm, TN State Univ Alumni Assoc, Urban League, Chamber of Commerce; mem Amer Vocational Assoc 1976; charter mem NAABAVE 1977; mem Nashville Job Service Employer Comm State of TN 1973-; mem Inter-Faith Assoc; exec comm mem Nashville Area Rep Lee Chapel AME 1984; minister Lee Chapel AME 1986, ordained elder, AME Church, 1989. **Honors/Awds:** Minority Business Serv Award Frito-Lay Inc 1966; Special Award Business TN State Univ 1968; Outstanding Cit Award WVOL Radio 1953; Cit Month Award Emmas Florist 1962; JC Napier Award Middle TN Business Assoc 1974; Fisk Univ Award 100% Right Comm 1974; appt Hon Sgt-at-Arms of TN House of Rep 1974; Commissioned Hon Dep Sheriff for Davidson Co TN 1975; commissioned to serve as mem TN Advisory Council for Vocational Ed 1975-; Sales Training Course Best Pitchbook Award 1979, inducted in Vintagers Club, TSU 1988, (40 years). **Home Addr:** 3501 Geneva Circle, Nashville, TN 37209-2524.

DRUITT, BEVERLY F.
Attorney. **Personal:** Born Jun 5, 1947, Buffalo, NY; daughter of James and Florence Druitt; divorced. **Educ:** Edna G Dyett School of Practical Nursing, Millard Fillmore Hospital, Buffalo New York, LPN, 1966; State Univ of New York at Buffalo, BA, 1971; Rutgers Univ School of Law, Newark, New Jersey, JD, 1974. **Career:** North Mississippi Rural Legal Services, Oxford, Mississippi, managing attorney, 1975-77; NLRB, field attorney, Memphis TN, 1977-80, sr attorney, Office of Appeals, 1980-. **Orgs:** National Labor Relations Board Professionals Assn, pres, 1990-97; Natl Bar Assn, chairperson, govt lawyers division, 1993-; National Bar Assn, treasurer, labor law section, 1988-97; Natl Bar Assn, vice chair labor law section, 1997-. **Honors/Awds:** NLRB, Special Act Award, 1996. **Business Addr:** Senior Attorney, National Labor Relations Board, 1099 14th Street, NW, Ste 8710, Washington, DC 20570, (202)273-3758.

DRUMMOND, DAVID L., SR.
Clergyman. **Personal:** Born Jan 30, 1918, Hastings, FL; married Evangeline Griffith; children: David, Jr, Reginald, Cheryl, Jonathan. **Educ:** Howard U, 1952; Temple Univ Theol Seminary, STB. **Career:** Sunday Dept, dist supt 1948-53; COGIC, field sec 1953-62; Youth Dept Commonwealth PA, state pres 1970-71; E Diocese, gen supt 1963-70; COGIC Inc, chmn housing & registration 1970-71; City of David Ch & Enterprises, pastor & adminstr; COGIC Inc, vp. **Orgs:** Mem Pastors Fellowship Conf COGIC 1963-70; many other offices Ch God Christ Intnatl Mem Human Relation Dept; Maoyrs spl com asst bd educ 1973. **Honors/Awds:** Hon DD Am Bible Coll; serv award State Youth Dept 1961-67; pastor yr WDAS radio; leading agent award Bankers Life & Casualty Co 1968; Citation Chapel4 Chaplin. **Military Serv:** USN seam 2/c 1943. **Business Addr:** 6035 Ogontz Ave, Philadelphia, PA 19141.

DRUMMOND, THORNTON B., JR.
Police lieutenant. **Personal:** Born Jul 3, 1927, Newport; married Estelle Gaines; children: Donald Thornton, Victoria Pauline, Nancy Ann. **Educ:** BS 1970; Univ RI, MA 1975; Salve Regina Coll, class orator; Babson Coll, Adminstrn Certificate 1968; Bryant Coll, 1966. **Career:** Police Dept, dir community relations 1968-72; Newport Police Dept Newport, lit of police day watch & commander; Newport Neighborhood Youth, counselor 1966-69. **Orgs:** Chmn bd dir Dr Martin Luther King Ctr Newport 1969-73; Frat Order of Police Commissioned Police Officers Assn; bd dir Afro-Bus Leaders Enterprise 1968-73; grand master Prince Hall Mason State of RI 1975 mason 33 Deg; bd dir Child & Family Service Newport 1975; bd dir Newport Hosp Newport 1970-; NAACP; Urban League; State of RI budget panel & special Allocation Com United Ways; Mt Zion AME Ch formerly pastors steward, steward & bd trustee. **Honors/Awds:** Boating, golf, horses State Award Sheriff Dept; E Stars Award service to community; testimonial dinner Martin Luther King Center Cultural Art Com 1973; awards from Police Depts outstanding contribution to police & community; Martin Luther King Center & Ch 20 yrs serv to community; resolution Newport; Masonic Awards service & nomination highs degree 33 service community & masonry. **Military Serv:** 728 Mil Police Batallion corpl 1950-53. **Business Addr:** Marlborough St, Newport, RI.

DRUMMOND, WILLIAM JOE
Educator, freelance journalist. **Personal:** Born Sep 29, 1944, Oakland, CA; son of Mary Louise Tompkins Drummond and Jack Martin Drummond, Sr; married Faith B. Fancher; children: Tammerlin, Sean. **Educ:** Univ of CA, BA 1965; Columbia Univ Grad School of Journalism, MS 1966. **Career:** Courier-Journal, Louisville, KY, staff writer 1966-67; Los Angeles Times, staff writer 1967-79; Natl Public Radio, correspondent 1979-83; School of Journalism, UC Berkeley, prof 1983-. **Orgs:** Spcl correspondent, Christian Science Monitor, 1992-97. **Honors/Awds:** Edwin Hood Awd for dist foreign corr 1983; Natl Press Club Found Awd 1980; Chancellor's Dist Lecturer, UC Berkeley 1983; Sidney Hillman Prize, Sidney Hillman Foundation NY 1986; Jack R Howard Award for Broadcasting Excellence, Scripps Howard Foundation, 1992. **Business Addr:** Prof of Journalism, Univ of California, Berkeley, School of Journalism, Berkeley, CA 94720.

DRYDEN, CHARLES WALTER, SR.
Aerospace company executive (retired). **Personal:** Born Sep 16, 1920, New York, NY; married Marymal Morgan; children: Charles Jr, Keith, Eric, George, Anthony, Kenneth, Cornelia. **Educ:** City College of New York, 1937-40; Hofstra College, BA Pol Sci 1955; Columbia University, MA Public Law & Govt 1957. **Career:** Pepsi-Cola Co, mgr special markets dept 1964-68; Presbyterian Eco Development Corp, executive director 1968-70; Martins-Jamaica, exec asst of president 1972-73; Lockheed-Georgia Co, professional personnel administrator 1975-83, training services officer 1983-88. **Orgs:** Councilman Matawan, NJ 1965-66; president Atlanta Chapter Tuskegee Airman 1983-86; member Military Academies Selection Committee, 5th Congressional District 1983-86; member NAACP Urban League; board of directors, Georgia Aviation Hall of Fame, 1989-; Honorable Order of Kentucky Colonels, 1987; Metro Atlanta Lions Club, order of Dacdalians, 1997-. **Honors/Awds:** Ben Hill United Methodist Church, Atlanta, GA, Man of the Year, 1987; Honorary Doctor of Humane Letters, Hofstra University, 1996; Inductee in Georgia Aviation Hall of Fame, 1998; Order of Gentlemen of the Palmetto, SC, 1997; Outstanding Georgia Citizen, 1997. **Special Achievements:** Autobiography, ''A-Train: Memoirs of a Tuskegee Airman''; University of Alabama Press, 1997. **Military Serv:** US Air Force, command pilot, lt col, 1941-62; Air Medal w/6 Oak Leaf Clusters; Air Force Commendation Medal; Combat missions in WWII, Korea. **Home Addr:** 1273 Oakcrest Dr SW, Atlanta, GA 30311.

DUAL, J. FRED, JR.
Corporate executive, entrepreneur. **Personal:** Born Apr 10, 1942, Chicago, IL; son of Dorothy Marie Bowie Dual and Joseph Frederick Dual; married Joyce Faye Metoyer, 1962 (divorced 1978); children: Leah, Joseph F III, Karen. **Educ:** Northern Virginia Comm College, Annandale, VA, AA, 1972-74; American University, Washington, DC, BA/BS, 1980-81; George Washington University, Washington, DC, 1981-82; Owner-President Management (OPM) Program, Harvard, Cambridge, MA, 1989-91. **Career:** Booz-Allen & Hamilton, Arlington, VA, associate, 1981-85; DUAL Inc, Arlington, VA, president/CEO, 1983-. **Orgs:** Member, Professional Services Council (PSC), 1990-91; member, Navy League of the United States, 1988-95; Natl Training Systems Assn, 1993-; Natl Space Club, 1994-; Amer Defense Preparedness Assn, 1995-. **Honors/Awds:** Entrepreneur of Year Finalist, KPMG Peat Marwick, 1990; EEO Person of Year, Naval Aviation Engineering Services Unit, Philadelphia, 1979; NASA Minority Contractor of the Year, 1989; Black Enterprise, Listed as #75 of Top 100 Black Businesses, 1994. **Military Serv:** US Navy, C Warrant Officer, 1960-79; Navy Commendation, 1978; Navy Achievement Medal, 1977; National Service Medal, 1965. **Business Addr:** President/CEO, DUAL Incorporated, 2101 Wilson Blvd, Suite 600, Arlington, VA 22201, (703)527-3500.

DUAL, PETER A.
Educator. **Personal:** Born Jan 27, 1946, Alexandria, LA; son of Averlee Dual and Peter Dual; married Toni Irene; children: Nikki Averlee, Peter Aaron, Tony Ahmaad, Alfred Michael. **Educ:** Lake Michigan Coll, AA 1966; Western MI Univ, BS 1969, MA 1971; MI State Univ, PhD 1973; Univ of TX, MPH 1975. **Career:** Asst Prof Univ of TX 1973-75; assoc dir African-American Studies 1973-75; Univ of MI, asst prof health behavior, director, Center for Prof Ed of Pub Health Professionals, asst prof of health behavior 1975-80; Eastern MI Univ, dean coll health/human services, prof of health admin, 1980-82; San Diego State Univ, dean of Coll Health, human services, 1982-93; CAP Hannemawn Med Ctr. provost, 1993-95; Cal-Poly, vice pres of academic affairs, Pomona, CA, 1996-. **Orgs:** Mem Amer Assoc of Higher Educ 1980-, Amer Public Health Assoc 1971-; sr consultant to Panama Project Hope 1985; tech consultant Zimbabwe USAID 1986; disting guest lecturer Chinese Med Assoc ROC 1986; lecture presentation in Health/Nursing Beijing PRC 1986; mem Alpha Pi Boule Chap Sigma Pi Phi Frat 1986-; Phi Beta Delta Honor Society for Intl Scholars; American Public Health Assoc 1971; mem bd of dir for Joint-Health Policy, Scripts Research Foundation/Institute SDSU 1988-93. **Honors/Awds:** Natl Public Health Fellowship Univ of TX 1974-75; publications in natl journals in health/human serv 1974-82; Citation Chinese Medical Assoc Republic of China 1986; Martin Luther King/Rosa Parks Vstg Prof Univ MI 1987-88; Confucius Awd Ministry of Education Republic of China; Lecturer Citation Beijing & Health Bureau; first black academic dean in history of Eastern MI Univ 1980; first black academic dean in history of San Diego State Univ 1983; Distinguished Alumnus Award, Lake MI Coll 1986; first black and non MD to deliver keynote address, Chinese Medical Assn 1987; Distinguished Alumnus Award, Coll of Ed, MI State Univ 1988. **Business Addr:** Vice President for Academy Affairs, Cal-Poly Pamona, Pomona, CA 91768.

DUBE, THOMAS M. T.
Educator. **Personal:** Born Dec 25, 1938, Essexvale, Zimbabwe; married Ruth; children: Cengubuqotho, Thina. **Educ:** Univ of Lesotho, BA 1958; Univ of So Africa, UED 1960; CW Post Coll of Long Island U, MS 1963; Univ of Chgo, MA 1972; MI State U, MA 1974; Uof Rochester, EdD 1969; Cooley Law Sch, JD Candidate. **Career:** Western MI Univ, asst prof Social Science; Geneva Coll PA, asst prof; Rochester NY, pre-school teacher; Ministry of African Educ, Rodesia Africa, high school teacher, elementary school teacher. **Orgs:** Mem Rhodesian African Tchrs Assn; vol activities in Black Comm Rochester, Pittsburg, Kalamazoo; mem Assn of African Studies in Am; founder mem JairosJiri Inst for Physically-Handicapped; founder, mem, asst prin Mpopoma African Comm HS. **Business Addr:** 337 Moore Hall, Kalamazoo, MI 49001.

DUBENION, ELBERT
Talent scout. **Personal:** Born Feb 16, 1933, Griffin, GA; married Marilyn Earl; children: Debra Lynn, Carolyn Ann, Susan Marie, Lisa Renee. **Educ:** Bluffton Coll Bluffton, OH, BS 1959. **Career:** Columbus Recreation Dept, 1960-67; OH Malleable Co Columbus, attendance dir 1963-64; Buffalo Bills, professional player 1960-68, college scout. **Honors/Awds:** Voted MVP 3 times for Buffalo; All-AFL; mem Bills Silver Anniversary All-Time team. **Military Serv:** AUS spec serv pfc 1953-55. **Business Addr:** College Scout, Buffalo Bills Inc, One Bills Drive, Orchard Park, NY 14127.

DU BOIS, DAVID GRAHAM
Journalist, social activist, educator. **Personal:** Born Mar 1925, Seattle, WA; son of Shirley Graham Du Bois and William Edward Burghardt (step-father); divorced. **Educ:** Oberlin Conservatory of Music, 1942-43; New York School of Social Work; Columbia Univ; Peking Univ; Hunter Coll, BA, 1950; New York Univ, MA, 1972. **Career:** First Natl City Bank of New York, New York City, clerk-typist, 1950-59; Arab Observer, Cairo, Egypt, editor/reporter, 1960-72; news editor, Egyptian Gazette; reporter and editor, Middle East News and Features Agency; announcer and program writer, Radio Cairo; in public relations for Ghana govt, Cairo, 1965-66; official spokesperson, Black Panther Party; editor-in-chief of Black Panther Intercommunal News Service; editor of Black Panther, 1973-76; lecturer, School of Criminology, University of California, Berkeley, and Cairo Univ; University of Mass, visiting professor, journalism, currently. **Orgs:** Pres, WEB Du Bois Foundation Inc; board member, WEB Du Bois Memorial Centre for Pan African Culture, Accra, Ghana, West Africa. **Honors/Awds:** Author of And Bid Him Sing (novel), Ramparts, 1975. **Military Serv:** US Army Air Force, Infantry, second lieutenant, 1942-46. **Business Addr:** Visiting Professor, Journalism, University of Massachusetts, New Africa House, #324, Amherst, MA 01003.

DUBOSE, CULLEN LANIER
Director. **Personal:** Born Jul 5, 1935, Moss Point, MS; married Helena Joyce; children: Cheri, Cullen, Freddie. **Educ:** Tougaloo Coll, 1954-56; Tri State Coll, BS 1958. **Career:** State of MI, bridge design engr 1958-70; State of MI Housing Devel Authority, civil Engr 1970; dir rehab 1971-72; dir construction 1972- 73; dir mgmt& marketing 1974-. **Orgs:** Mem Tri State Coll Alumni Club; West Side Action Center; Lansing Civic Center Bd; Omega Psi Phi Frat Inc; NAACP; dir housing com; mem Big Bro of Lansing; Model Cities Policy Bd; past pres Gov Milligens Task Force for Operation Break Through 1970-71. **Honors/Awds:** Omega Psi Phi Citizens Award 1966; NAACP Citizen Award 1967. **Military Serv:** Mil serv 1957-58.

DUBOSE, OTELIA
Educational administrator. **Personal:** Born Sep 16, 1949, Winter Haven, FL; daughter of Willie J Dubose; divorced. **Educ:** Florida A&M Univ, Tallahassee FL, BS, 1968; New York Univ, New York NY, MA, 1971; Cornell Univ, Ithaca NY, MRP, 1981, PhD, 1984. **Career:** Community Mental Health Center, West Palm Beach FL, coord (community program), 1974-78; Coconut Grove Health Center, Miami FL, consultant, 1975-85; City of Riviera Beach, Riviera Beach FL, economic devel, 1985-87, asst to the city mgr, 1987-88, city mgr, 1988-; DeBose & Assoc Inc, pres, 1985-; Palm Beach County School Board, minority contract coordinator, 1990-; UTU Inc, treas, 1990-; State of Florida (DJJ), operations management, consultant, currently. **Orgs:** Delta Sigma Theta Sorority Inc, 1975-; mem, Urban League of Palm Beach County, 1985-, NAACP, 1985-; steering comm, Gold Coast Fed Credit Union, 1987-; mem, Democratic Exec Club, 1988-; UNCF, chair, Palm Beach County Advisory Board, planning commission. **Honors/Awds:** Community Serv, Florida A&M Univ Alumni, 1978; American Planning Assn Speaker, 1981, 1987, 1989-90; United Negro College Fund, Distinguished Leadership Award, 1990-91; appointed Palm Beach County Planning Commissioner. **Special Achievements:** Co-author, The Urban Agenda, 1981. **Business Phone:** (561)881-5020.

DU BOSE, ROBERT EARL, JR.
Clergyman. **Personal:** Born Oct 9, 1927, Birmingham, AL; married Angela Grace Edwards; children: Robert III, Audrice, Gerald, Lucy, Angela. **Educ:** St Augustine's Coll Raleigh, NC, BA/BS 1950; Seabury-Western Theol Sem Evanston, IL, LTh 1953; St Augustine's Coll, Hon DCL 1979. **Career:** Historic St Thomas' Episcopal & Ch, rector 1977-; House of Prayer Epis Ch Phila, PA, rector 1966-76; St Barnabas Epis Ch Phila, PA, asso rector 1964-66; St Cyprian's Epis Ch Phila, PA, vicar 1962-64; Historic St Thomas' Epis Ch Phila, PA, curate 1961-62; Ch of the Good Shepherd Montgomery, AL, vicar 1956-61; St Andrew's Tuskegee, AL, vicar 1953-56; Gen Conv of the Epis Ch, spl rep 1970. **Orgs:** Mem Commn on Finance of Prop-

erty Epis Diocese of PA 1974-; mem Bishop's Task Force on Housing Epis Diocese of PA 1979-; active Qparticipant Bus Protest& Sit Ins With Dr M L King Montgomery AL 1956-61; active participant Selective Patronage Prog with Dr Leon Sullivan 1961-64; one of the founders Opport Indsl & Cntrs of Am & Intl 1964 & 67. **Honors/Awds:** Key Award Opport Indsl Cntr Phila, PA 1969; Nat Distinguished Serv Award Alpha Phi Alpha Frat 1970; Outstanding Serv Award Greater W Oak Ln Coordinating Council 1970-71; Service Award The Sch Dist of Philadelphia Wagner Hr HS 1974. **Business Addr:** Historic Saint Thomas' Episcap, Fifty Second & Parrish Sts, Philadelphia, PA 19139.

DUCKETT, GREGORY MORRIS
Health care system executive. **Personal:** Born Jan 26, 1960, Memphis, TN; son of Lavance Harris Duckett and Ocie Duckett; married Brenda Parker Duckett, Oct 11, 1986; children: Stephen Gregory, Kelsey Breanna. **Educ:** Carnegie-Mellon University, Pittsburgh, PA, 1981; Oberlin College, Oberlin, OH, BA, 1982; Memphis State University, Memphis, TN, Doctor of Jurisprudence, 1985. **Career:** US Congressman Harold Ford, Memphis, TN, staff assistant, 1983-84; Shelby County Criminal Court, Memphis, TN, judicial law clerk, 1984-85; US Senator Albert Gore Jr, Memphis, TN, staff assistant, 1985, staff attorney, 1985-86, state counsel, 1986-87; City of Memphis, Memphis, TN, director, division of public service, 1988, director, division of housing and community development, 1988-; City of Memphis, chief administrative office, 1991; Baptist Memorial Health Care System, Community Relations and Risk Management, vice pres, government operations, 1992-; Clinton/Gore Transition Team, apointee, 1992. **Orgs:** Broard member, Leadership Memphis, 1989-; board member, Memphis College of Art, 1990-; board member, Youth Villages, 1988-; board of directors, Memphis Zoological Society; member, Tennessee Advisory Committee to the Lower Mississippi Delta Development Commission, 1989; president, Memphis State University School of Law Student Bar Association, 1985. **Honors/Awds:** Champion Counsel, 1st Place, Memphis State University, Advance Appellate Moot Court Competition, 1983; Outstanding Young Men of America, US Jaycees, 1984, 1985. **Business Addr:** Senior VP/Corporate Counsel, Baptist Memorial Health Care Corp, 899 Madison, Ste 145-UE, Memphis, TN 38146, (901)227-5233.

DUCKSWORTH, MARILYN JACOBY
Publishing company executive. **Personal:** Born in Stamford, CT. **Educ:** Tufts Univ, BA (cum laude) 1978, MA English 1979; Tufts Univ in London England 1976-77. **Career:** Doubleday & Co Inc, publicity asst 1979-80, assoc publicist 1980-82, sr publicist 1982-83, mgr of publicity 1983-85; GP Putnam's Sons, mgr of publicity 1985, dir of publicity 1985-87; GP Putnam's Sons & The Putnam & Grosset Group, executive director of publicity, vp, associate publisher, 1987-. **Orgs:** Mem (hon) College Language Assn 1978-; certified teacher of secondary educ rec'd certification from Tufts in 1978; mem Publisher's Publicity Assoc 1979-, The Women's Media Group 1986-. **Honors/Awds:** Scholastic Achievement Awd Black Educators of Stamford 1974; Natl Honor Soc Hon Soc of Secondary Schools 1974; Dean's List Tufts Univ (every semester) 1974-78; Langston Hughes Literary Awd Tufts Univ 1978; 1st Black Mgr of Publicity at Doubleday & Co Inc 1983-85; First Black exec dir of publicity at GP Putnam's Sons. **Business Addr:** VP, Associate Publisher, Executive Director, Publicity, The Putnam Publishing Group, 200 Madison Ave, New York, NY 10016.

DUDLEY, CHARLES EDWARD
Executive officer, clergyman. **Personal:** Born Feb 27, 1927, South Bend, IN; son of Julia (Talley) Dudley and Joseph Dudley Sr; married Etta Mae Maycock, Dec 28, 1947; children: Bonita Andrea, Charles Edward II, Albert Leroy Sr, Benson Mugemancuro, Seth Bardu. **Educ:** Oakwood Coll, graduated 1947; Emmanuel Mission Coll, 1945; Baptist Theol Seminary, LLD 1969; Union Baptist Seminary, Birmingham AL, Doctor of Divinity; Oakwood College, Huntsville AL, Bachelor of Arts in Religion. **Career:** S Central Conference of 7th Day Adventists, pres 1962-93; Pastor, TN, AL, LA, TX; South Central Conference of Seventh-day Adventists, Nashville TN, pastor 1947-54; pastor, Shelbyville, TN. **Honors/Awds:** Pi Lambda Sigma Awd 1964; Union Baptist Seminary, Honorary Doctor of Laws, 1969; London Institute of Applied Research, Honorary Doctor of Divinity, 1973; Merit of Honor OC Natl Alumni Assn 1977; Andrews University, Institute of Church Ministry Award, 1983; Breath of Life Awd 1984; President George Bush, Citation of Excellence Award; President William Clinton, Citation of Excellence Award; Mississippi Mass Choir, Honorary Leader Award; International Regional Evangelis m Council, Annual Ministers' Conference Award, 1990; Andrews SDA University, Honorary Doctor of Divinity, 1992; Allegheny West Conference, Award of Merit, 1993; NAACP, Golden Heritage Life Membership Award, 1993; Lake Region Conference of Seventh-day Adventists, Award of Distinction, 1993. **Special Achievements:** Publications: Four Volumes, "Thou Who Hath Brought Us.". **Business Addr:** S Ctrl Conf of 7th Day Adv, 715 Youngs Ln, Nashville, TN 37207.

DUDLEY, CRAYTON T.
Clergyman (retired). **Personal:** Born Feb 23, 1928, Atlanta; married Allegra Lewis; children: Angus Clement, Karen Yvette. **Educ:** Clark Coll Atlanta, AB 1950; Gammon Theol Sem Atlanta, BD 1961; MDiv 1973; Univ Pitts, MLS 1965; Atlanta Univ Am U, Grad Study. **Career:** Interdenom Theol Ctr Atlanta, asst lib 1961-64; Rel & Phil Enoch Pratt Free Lib Baltimore, subj splst 1965-68; Coppin State Coll Baltimore, asso dir lib 1968-72; asso prof philos 1972-74; TN St U, collections dev librn 1976; St James Epis Ch Baltimore, worker priest 1968-72; St James, asst priest 1972-74; Montrose Training Sch for Girls State MD, chpln 1968-72; Holy Trinity Epis Ch Nashville, rector; Vicar, St Augustine, 1980-87; St Marks, rector, 1987-93. **Orgs:** Life mem Phi Beta Sigma Frat; mem NAACP; Boy Scouts Am 1972-74; bd mem Grace Eaton Day Ctr 1974; v-chmn Urban Min Diocese of TN 1977; mem counc chpln mem Am Library Assn; Am Theol Library Assn; historiographer Diocese MD 1972-74. **Military Serv:** AUS sgt 1945-46, 1950-53, 1956-62. **Home Addr:** 244 Silver Springs Circle SW, Atlanta, GA 30310.

DUDLEY, EDWARD R.
Supreme court justice (retired). **Personal:** Born Mar 11, 1911, South Boston, VA; married Rae; children: Edward R Dudley Jr. **Educ:** St John's Law Sch, LLB 1941; Johnson C Smith U, BS 1932. **Career:** US Ambassador to Liberia 1948-53; Dom Rel Ct NYC, judge 1955-60; NY Co, boro pres 1960-65; MY State Sup Ct, justice 1965-85. **Orgs:** Asst spec couns NAACP 1943-45, 47-48; asst att gen NY 1942. **Honors/Awds:** Recipient of Honorary LLD's from several universities including Univ of Liberia, Morgan State Coll, Johnson C Smith U. **Special Achievements:** First African-American MS Ambassador. **Home Addr:** 549 W 123 St, New York, NY 10027.

DUDLEY, EUNICE
Company executive. **Personal:** marrIed Joe Louis Dudley Sr; children: Joe Jr, Ursula, Genea. **Career:** Dudley Products, chief financial officer, currently. **Business Addr:** Chief Financial Officer, Dudley Products, 7856 McCloud Rd., Greensboro, NC 27409, (919)282-0570.

DUDLEY, GODFREY D.
Attorney. **Personal:** Born Mar 14, 1944, Newborn, AL; married. **Educ:** Tuskegee Inst, BS 1967; Tuskegee to Univ MI, exchange student 1966; Howard U, JD 1970. **Career:** Tuskegee Inst Community Educ Prog, teacher coordinator 1965; Birmingham Dist Office, equal employment officer 1970; Labor Adv Nat Labor Relations Bd, atty 1970-; DC Office NLRB to Atlanta Regional Office, field atty 1972; instr for new attys & field examiners 1975 & 79; Nat Labor Relations Bd, dep asst gen counsel 1979-. **Orgs:** DC Bar Assn; Bar Assn DC; Am Bar Assn; Nat Bar Assn; AL Bar Asn; Phi Alpha Delta Law Frat NAACP; Urban League. **Honors/Awds:** Certificates commendations Gen Counsel NLRB 1973 & 74; quality work performance awards 1973, 74, 78 & 79. **Business Addr:** 1717 Pennsylvania Avenue NW, Washington, DC.

DUDLEY, HERMAN T.
Government official (retired). **Personal:** Born Apr 4, 1924, Richmond, KY; married Ruth. **Educ:** BS, 1956. **Career:** Detroit Engr Office Bur Archtl, director, 24 years until retirement. **Orgs:** Registered Architect, State of Michigan. **Military Serv:** US Marine Corps, corporal, 1943-46. **Business Addr:** 9th Fl Cadillac Tower, Detroit, MI 48226.

DUDLEY, JOE LOUIS, SR.
Health care company executive, entrepreneur. **Personal:** Born in Aurora, NC; son of Clara and GL Dudley; married Eunice; children: Joe Jr, Ursula, Genea. **Educ:** North Corolina A&T State Univ, business administration, 1967. **Career:** Fuller Products, distributor, 1967; Dudley Products Inc, 1967-; Dudley Cosmetology Univ, founder, 1989; DCU Inn, 1990. **Orgs:** Direct Selling Assn, inner city task force; Joe Dudley Fellows; Dudley Ladies; ComPASS; American Health and Beauty Aids Institute, board of directors; Branch Banking & Trust Financial Corporation, board of directors. **Honors/Awds:** Direct Selling Assn, Vision for Tomorrow Award; President George Bush, 467th Daily Point of Light Award; Maya Angelou Tribute To Achievement Award. **Special Achievements:** "I Am, I Can, I Will" speaking tour; Company is ranked #46 on the Black Enterprise list of Top industrial/service companies, 1994. **Business Addr:** CEO, Dudley Products Inc., 1080 Old Greensboro Rd, Kernersville, NC 27284.

DUDLEY, JUANITA C.
Social worker, human relations commissioner. **Personal:** Born Apr 14, 1929, Talladega, AL; daughter of Fannie Tanner Strickland and Walter Thomas Strickland; married Calmeze Henike Dudley, Jun 30, 1964; children: Rhonda Carroll Le Grice. **Educ:** Talladega College, Talladega, AL, BA, 1950; Atlanta University, Atlanta GA, MSW, 1954; Southwestern University Law School, Los Angeles, CA, 1966-67. **Career:** Govt of Virgin Islands, St Thomas, VI, supervisor of public assistance, 1957-59; Los Angeles County, adoption consultant, 1963-66; Natl Urban League Inc, Los Angeles, asst regl dir, 1966-73; Los Angeles Co Hospital Assn, Los Angeles, Consultant, 1975-76; Los Angeles County Grand Jury, Los Angeles, CA, 1982-83; Dr C H Dudley, Los Angeles, CA, psychiatric soc worker, 1954-. **Orgs:** The Girlfriends Inc, nat'l vp; The Wilfandel Club Inc, The Circlelets Inc. **Honors/Awds:** Woman of Year, Auxiliary of Natl Medical Assn; Woman of Year, Women on Target, 1990. **Business Addr:** Social Worker, 3731 Stocker St, Suite 204, Los Angeles, CA 90019.

DUDLEY, RICKEY
Professional football player. **Personal:** Born Jul 15, 1972, Henderson, TX. **Educ:** Ohio State Univ. **Career:** Oakland Raiders, tight end, 1996-. **Business Addr:** Professional Football Player, Oakland Raiders, 1220 Harbor Bay Pkwy, Alameda, CA 94502, (510)615-1875.

DUDLEY, THELMA
Educator. **Personal:** Born Mar 5, 1923, Columbia, SC. **Educ:** Albany State Coll, BA 1944; Rollins Coll, MAT 1970. **Career:** Advanced Instnl Devel, coord; Valencia Comm Coll, teacher 1970-; Jones High School, teacher 1946-70; Douglass High School, teacher 1944-46; Elbert Co, teacher 1941. **Orgs:** Mem NAACP; FL Assn of Comm Colls; Beta Xi chap Nat & Sor of Phi Delta Kappa; Corinthian Sect Nat Cncl of Negro Women; FL Cncl of Chs gov bd Nat Cncl of Chs; vice pres Women's Missionary Cncl Christian Meth Epis Ch. **Business Addr:** PO Box 3028, Orlando, FL 32802.

DUDLEY-SMITH, CAROLYN J.
Educator. **Personal:** Born Jul 21, 1946, Bessemer, AL; married Aubrey E Smith. **Educ:** Stillman Coll, BA 1968; Howard Univ, MA 1975. **Career:** DC Public Schools, teacher 1969-72, job coord 1972-79, consultant 1980-, counselor 1979-. **Orgs:** Chairperson Title IX/Sex Equity Adv Bd; mem Delta Sigma Theta Sor, Amer Assoc Counsel Develop, Amer School Counselors Assoc. **Honors/Awds:** Author Sex Equity Curriculum Guide published in ERIC 1984; Educational Fellow Inst for Educ Leadership 1985. **Business Addr:** Counselor, DC Public Schools, 55th & Eads Sts NE, Washington, DC 20019.

DUDLEY-WASHINGTON, LOISE
Educator. **Personal:** Born Nov 1, 1944, Ft Lauderdale, FL; daughter of Clara Kirkland Morley and Thomas Dudley; divorced; children: Keith, Renee. **Educ:** CCNY, BS 1978, MS 1980, PhD, 1990-. **Career:** G&S Rsch Analyst, statistician 1981-82; Childrens Circle Daycare Ctr, spec ed coord 1982-88; MLK Health Ctr, mgr/MIS analyst, 1969-89; Children's Circle Daycare Center, director/project Giant Step, 1989-90; St Mary's School, special education teacher, 1990-92; NYC School Board, District 9, pres, 1992-. **Orgs:** Consult Hospital Billing Systems; dir Bronx Youth in Action 1985-. **Honors/Awds:** Outstanding Comm School Bd Mem Bronx Democratic Club 1985; Community Service Award, Montefiore Health Center, 1988; Excellence in Education, NYS Council of Black Republicans, 1986, 1987; Committment to Children and Community, Dist 9 School Board, 1988; elected member of NYC School Board, District 9, 1st vice pres, 1983-92. **Home Addr:** 540 East 169th St, Bronx, NY 10456.

DUERSON, DAVID R.
Entrepreneur. **Personal:** Born in Muncie, IN. **Educ:** Notre Dame, BA, econ, 1983. **Career:** Chicago Bears, 1983-90; NY Giants, 1990; Phoenix Cardinals, 1991-93; McDonald's franchises, owner; Fair Oaks Farms Inc, owner, 1995-. **Orgs:** Chicago Economic Development Corp, pres; Notre Dame College of Business Administration; Notre Dame National Monogram Club; Ronald McDonald House Charities Worldwide Board; Maryville Academy Board; ILAD Board; YPO; Omega Psi Phi Fraternity. **Special Achievements:** Played in two Super Bowls and four Pro Bowls; Company is ranked #48 Black Enterprise magazine's 1997 list of Top 100 Black businesses. **Business Addr:** Owner/CEO, Fair Oaks Farms Inc, 7600 95th St, Kenosha, WI 53142, (414)947-0320.

DUFF, FRED C.
Photographer. **Personal:** Born Jul 6, 1962, Glenridge, NJ; son of Lois & William; married Monica Biondi, Apr 5, 1992. **Educ:** Thomas Edison State Coll, BA, photography, 1995. **Career:** Fred Duff Photography, pres, 1988-. **Orgs:** Natl Assn of Black Scuba Divers, archeology chairperson, 1995-; NABS Archeological Dive Team, head diver. **Honors/Awds:** NABS, Special Service, 1994. **Special Achievements:** Technical Advisor-Middle Passage Exhibit, Field Museum of Chicago, African American Pavillion; Contributing Photographer: NY Newsday Class Magazine; About Time Magazine; The Natl Geographic Society Magazine; Black Enterprise Magazine; Placed Monument on Slave Shipwreck, "Henrietta Marie;" Certified Archeological Research Diver.

DUFF, JAMAL EDWIN
Professional football player. **Personal:** Born Mar 11, 1972, Columbus, OH. **Educ:** San Diego State, attended. **Career:** New York Giants, defensive end, 1995; Washington Redskins, 1997-. **Business Addr:** Professional Football Player, Washington Redskins, 13832 Redskin Dr, Herndon, VA 22071, (703)471-9100.

DUFFOO, FRANTZ MICHEL
Nephrologist. **Personal:** Born Mar 5, 1954, Port-au-Prince, Haiti; son of Leonie Narcisse Duffoo and Franck Duffoo; married Marcia Sylvester; children: Brian Anthony, Christian Jason, Ashley Gabrielle. **Educ:** City Coll of NY, BS, 1977; Meharry Medical Coll, MD, 1979; diplomate, Internal Medicine Amer Bd of Internal Medicine, 1984-; diplomate, subspecialty of nephrology Amer Bd of Internal Medicine 1986. **Career:** Brookdale Hospital Medical Center, resident in internal medicine, 1979-82; Montefiore Medical Center, clinical fellow, 1982-83, research fellow, 1983-84; Woodhull Medical and Mental Health Center, attending physician/consultant nephrology, 1984-92; instructor in medicine, 1985-88, asst prof of medicine, 1988-, SUNY Health Science Center at Brooklyn; Woodhull Medical and Mental Health Center, chief of nephrology/associate director of medicine, 1990-92; New York University, adjunct assistant professor, 1990-; St Mary's Hospital, director of medicine, currently. **Orgs:** Mem, New York Acad of Sciences 1981-88, Amer Coll of Physicians 1985-92, Amer Soc of Nephrology 1985-, Intl Soc of Nephrology 1985-, New York Soc of Nephrology; charter mem, Amer Soc of Hypertension 1986-; charter mem, Intl Soc on Hypertension in Blacks; member, National Kidney Foundtion, 1989-. **Honors/Awds:** Physician's Recognition Award, Amer Medical Assn, 1982, 1988; The Editorial Research Bd, The Physician and Sportsmedicine, 1982; abstract selected for presentation, New York Soc of Nephrology, 1984; Woadhull Medical and Mental Health Center, Secretary of the Medical Staff, 1989, Vice President of Medical Staff, 1990, President of Medical Staff, 1991; Fellow, American College of Physicians, 1992; Secretary, Medical Board, St Mary's Hospital of Brooklyn, 1992. **Home Addr:** 14 Nob Hill Rd, New City, NY 10956.

DUFFY, EUGENE JONES
Business executive. **Personal:** Born Aug 25, 1954, Columbus, OH; son of Helen Jones Duffy and Franklin V Duffy; married Norrene Johnson, Apr 19, 1986; children: Josie Helen, Rosa Patrice. **Educ:** Univ of Ibadan Nigeria; Morehouse Coll, BA 1976. **Career:** Dept Parks Recreation & Cultural Affairs, deputy commissioner; Office of Contract Compliance, director; Office of the Mayor, deputy chief admin officer; H J Russel & Co, Atlanta, GA, sr vice pres, 1990-94; Albritton Capital Management, exec vp, currently. **Orgs:** Natl League of Cities, Natl Conf of Black Public Administrators; trustee Morehouse Coll; YMCA; pres Atlanta Univ Ctr Student Council; founding mem, 100 Black Men of Atlanta; Urban Consortium. **Honors/Awds:** Charles E Merrill Foreign Study Scholar Univ of Ibadan. **Business Addr:** Executive Vice President, Albritton Capital Management, 3 Ravinia Dr, Ste 1470, Atlanta, GA 30346.

DUGAS, A. JEFFREY ALAN, SR.
Physician. **Personal:** Born Aug 6, 1953; son of Laurenetta Dugas and Lester Dugas; divorced; children: Andrea, Jeffrey Jr. **Educ:** Morehouse College, BA, biology, 1972-76; Atlanta University, attended, 1976-77; Roosevelt University, attended 1977-79; Morehouse College School of Medicine, attended 1979-82; Rush Medical College, MD, 1984; Rush-Presbyterian St Lukes Medical Center, internship, 1984-85, residency, 1985-87. **Career:** Michael Reese Hospital and Medical Center, community relations mental health representative, 1978-79; Morehouse School of Medicine, research assistant, 1981-82; Coastal Emergency Services, independent contractor, 1986-87; Provident Medical Center, attending, 1987; Rush-Presbyterian St Luke's Medical Center, instructor in medicine, 1987-, attending, 1987-; City of Chicago Board of Health, physician, 1988-91; Rush Medical College, assistant professor, 1991-; William L Dawson Nursing Center, medical director, 1991-. **Orgs:** Chicago Medical Society; Illinois State Medical Society; American College of Physicians; American Medical Association; National Medical Association, Cook County Physicians Association; Crescent Counties Foundation for Medical Care; Southside YMCA, board of directors, vice-chairman. **Special Achievements:** Dollars and Sense Magazine, Leading Young Black Doctor. **Business Addr:** Physician, Rush-Presbyterian St Luke's Medical Center, 1725 W Harrison, Ste 158, Pro Bldg III, Chicago, IL 60612, (312)733-6968.

DUGAS, HENRY C.
Physician. **Personal:** Born Feb 10, 1917, Augusta, GA; son of Mamie Dugas and Henry Dugas; married June Gordon; children: Denise, Henry. **Educ:** Johnson C Smith Univ, BS 1937; Howard Univ, MD 1947. **Career:** Private practice, physician. **Orgs:** Mem Alpha Phi Alpha, Natl Med Assoc; Amer Academy of Family Physicians. **Military Serv:** AUS capt, mc 1953-54. **Business Addr:** 3737 N Kingshighway, St Louis, MO 63115.

DUGGER, CLINTON GEORGE
Cleric. **Personal:** Born Sep 8, 1929, Beacon, NY; son of Mary Anderson and William; married Virginia McLean, Nov 24, 1962; children: Michael Kerwin. **Educ:** St Augustine's College, BA, 1959; Philadelphia Divinity School, MDiv, 1962; SUNY at Albany, MSW, 1967. **Career:** Trinity Church, curate, 1962-65; Diocese of Albany, diocesan officer, 1965-67; Berkshire Farm For Boys, chaplain, 1967-81; St Luke's vicar, 1973-85; Hoosac School, chaplain, 1981-85; Church of the Redeemer, rector, 1985-. **Orgs:** Lebanon Valley Lions Club; Rensselaer Committee Center Board; Troy Church Home Board; Gould Farm, MA, board of directors; Episcopal Church Counseling Center, board mem, 1986-92; American Legion Post #1683. **Honors/Awds:** Rotary, Man of the Year, 1975; Hoosac School, Chaplain Emeritus, 1987; Diocese, Dean of the Metropolitan Deanery, 1987; Rensselaer, Chaplain of Fire Department, 1992. **Military Serv:** US Army, cpl, 1952-54. **Business Addr:** Rector, Canon, The Church of the Redeemer, 1249 Third St, Rensselaer, NY 12144.

DUGGER, EDWARD, III
Business executive. **Personal:** Born Apr 14, 1949, Dayton, OH; son of Wertha Dugger and Edward Dugger, Jr; married Elizabeth Harris; children: Cyrus Edward, Langston Reid, Chloe D'jenne. **Educ:** Harvard Coll, AB (cum laude) 1971; Princeton U, MPA-UP 1973. **Career:** Irwin Mgmt Co Inc, mgr real estate div 1973-74; UNC Partners Inc, pres chief exec officer 1974-. **Orgs:** Greater Boston YMCA, mem, 1981-92; United Way of MA Bay, 1981-87; Federal Reserve Bank of Boston, corp bd, 1994-; UNC Media Inc, chair, 1991-97; Envirotest Systems Co, corp bd, 1990-; US Radio, LP, advisory comm, 1990-96; Granite Broadcasting Co, corp bd, 1989-; San Francisco Med Ctr, management comm, 1989-; UNC Ventures Inc, corp bd, 1978-97; Boys & Girls Club of Boston, bd of dirs, 1993-; Beth Israel Hosp, Boston MA, bd of dirs, 1991-96; New England Aquarium, bd of dirs, 1988-; The Partnership, bd of dirs, 1988-95; NAACP Legal Defense Fund, New England, bd of dirs, 1985-; The Boston Club, 1994-; MA Bus Roundtable, 1994-; Social Venture Network, 1994-; Students for Responsible Bus, 1994-; The Children's Museum, 1988-95; Harvard Univ, comm on univ resources, 1985-. **Honors/Awds:** Social Venture Pioneer Award, Investor's Circle, 1993; Achievement Award, ONE, 1988; Outstanding Bus Prof, Natl Urban Bankers, 1985; Esquire Register, 1984. **Special Achievements:** Articles: Esquire, 1984; New England Business, 1987; Wall Street Journal, 1983, 1994; Black Enterprise, 1990, 1994; Bay State Banner, 1994; Boston Globe, 1994; Boston Business Journal, 1994; Pension & Investments, 1994. **Business Addr:** President & CEO, UNC Partners, Inc, 711 Atlantic Avenue, Boston, MA 02111.

DUGGINS, GEORGE
Organization executive. **Career:** Vietnam Veterans of America Inc, vice pres, 1995-97, pres, 1997-. **Orgs:** Vietnam Veterans of America Inc., mem, 1985-, natl board of directors. **Special Achievements:** First African American to lead Vietnam Veterans of America Inc. **Military Serv:** Served in Vietnam, 1966-69.

DUHART, HAROLD B.
Project manager. **Personal:** Born Dec 15, 1938, Macon, GA; married Margaret Roberts; children: Bobby, Lori. **Educ:** NC Agr & Tech U, BS 1963; GA Inst of Tech, advance study. **Career:** US Environmental Protection Agy, NC State Project Mgr 1970-; Dept HUD, engineering municipal project mgr 1968-70; US Army Corps of Engrs, space facilities design Engr 1964-68; City of Durham NC, engineering redevelopment officer 1964-65. **Orgs:** Pres Duhart Bros Enterprises of Macon, GA 1974-; mem Federal Water Pollution Control Assn; mem Equal Oppty Com EPA; asso mem ASCE; mem PTA; mem Task force on Minority Bus for EPA prgms; YMCA; SW Atlanta Comm Assn; mem SABFO. **Honors/Awds:** Membership campaign Award YMCA; spl achvmt Award EPA 1973. **Military Serv:** AUS, NATO 1961-63.

DUKE, BILL (WILLIAM HENRY DUKE, JR.)
Actor, director, producer. **Personal:** Born Feb 26, 1943, Poughkeepsie, NY; son of Ethel Louise Douglas Duke and William Henry Duke Sr. **Educ:** Boston University, BA, 1964; New York University, MA, 1968; American Film Institute, MA, 1971. **Career:** Disney Studios, Cemetary Club, director; New Line Cinema, Deep Cover, director; Miramax Films, Rage In Harlem, director; Harpo Productions, Brewster Place, director; American Playhouse, Raisin In The Sun, director; American Playhouse, Killing Floor, director; PBS, The Meeting, director; actor, producer, director, currently. **Orgs:** Artist Against Homelessness, founding member; Directors Guild of America; Writers Guild of America; Screen Actors Guild. **Honors/Awds:** Black American Society, Star Bright Award, 1991; Black Filmmakers Hall of Fame, New Vision Award, 1990; NAACP Image Award, Special Achievement Directing, 1991. **Special Achievements:** An Evening With Bill Duke, American Film Institute, for independent film prod, 1992. **Business Addr:** President/Chief Executive Officer, Yagya Productions Inc, PO Box 55306, Sherman Oaks, CA 91413.

DUKE, GEORGE M. (DAWILLI GONGA)
Recording artist. **Personal:** Born Jan 12, 1946, San Rafael, CA; married Corine Ann Salanga; children: Rashid Amon, John Lee Shiffer. **Educ:** San Fran Conservatory of Music, MusB 1967; San Fran State Coll, MA 1970. **Career:** George Duke Band, Epic Records, leader 1977-; Billy Cobham-George Duke Band, Atlantic, co-leader 1976-77; Julian Cannonball Adderly, Capital & Fantasy, keyboardist/composer/arranger 1971-72; Frank Zappa, Warner Bros, keyboardist 1970-72, 1973-76; Jean-Luc Ponty, United Artists, pianist 1969-70; MPS/BASF Records, recartist (solo) 1973-76; Epic Records, solo recording artist 1976-. **Orgs:** Pres/fdr/mem Mycenae Music Publ Co 1968-; pres/fdr George Duke Enterprises Inc 1976-; consult Contemporary Keyboard Mag 1977-; mem NAACP 1979-; mem BMA 1979-. **Honors/Awds:** Gold Record "Reach For It", RIAA 1978; Gold Record "Dukey Stick", RIAA 1979; Hit Record Awards, ASCAP 1979-80; A Taste of Honey "Twice As Sweet", Capital Records/G Duke Prod 1980. **Business Addr:** Musician, c/o Triad Artists, 151 El Camino Dr, Beverly Hills, CA 90212.

DUKE, LESLIE DOWLING, SR.
Physician. **Personal:** Born Mar 21, 1924, Washington, DC; married Dolores Douglass; children: Leslie Jr, Lori. **Educ:** Howard U, BS 1950; Howard U, MD 1957. **Career:** Walter Reed Gen Hosp, phy 1962-77; Ft Meade, med ofcr 1959-62. **Military Serv:** AUS sgt 1943-46. **Business Addr:** 5223 S Dakota Ave, NE, Washington, DC 20011.

DUKE, RUTH WHITE
Educator (retired), government worker. **Personal:** Born Dec 12, 1927, Hampton, VA; daughter of Lucille Lowry White (deceased) and George David White (deceased); married Everette L Duke, Jun 27, 1953; children: Everette L Jr, Cecil Q. **Educ:** Virginia State University, BS, 1948; New York University, MA, 1951; James Madison University, 1970; Old Dominion University, 1972; Norfolk State University, 1973; Virginia Polytechnic Institute and State University, 1975. **Career:** Lunenburg High School, business tchr, 1949-52; Sumner and Vashon High School, business tchr, 1952-54; Norfolk State University, business tchr, 1955-56; BT Washington High School, business tchr, 1956-57; US Government, civil service worker, 1957-59; Jacox Jr High School, business tchr, 1961-65; Norview High School, business tchr, department chairperson, 1965-86; Old Dominion University, supervisor of social studies student tchrs, 1989-91. **Orgs:** Girls Incorporated of Tidewater, board member, chairman of by-laws, 1975-93; Norfolk Community Hospital, volunteer in administration office, 1990-96; Pinochle Bugs Social and Civic Club, national treasurer, 1988-92, national financial secretary, 1980-84; Bank Street Memorial Church, secretary for church meetings, 1974-94; Meals on Wheels, volunteer for Bank Street, 1987-95; Virginia Beach Pinchole Bugs, has served as president, vp, corresponding secretary, 1972-96. **Honors/Awds:** Certificate for Volunteer Service, Meals on Wheels. **Home Addr:** 1036 Fairlawn Ave, Virginia Beach, VA 23455, (804)461-2908.

DUKE, WILLIAM HENRY, JR. See DUKE, BILL.

DUKES, HAZEL NELL
City government official. **Personal:** Born Mar 17, 1932, Montgomery, AL; daughter of Alice Dukes and Edward Dukes; divorced. **Educ:** AL State Tchr Coll, AA 1950; Adelphi U, advance master prgm Adelphi Univ Grad 1978. **Career:** New York City Off-Track Betting Corp, president, 1990-. **Orgs:** Member, Metro-LINKS; board of directors, Coalition of 100 Black Women; board of directors, State of New York Martin Luther King Jr. Commission; national board, 1977-, pres, 1990-, NAACP; member, board of trustees, State University of New York; Westbury Negro Business and Professional Women's Club; secretary, Council of Black Elected Democrats of New York State; member, Democratic National Committee; pres, New York State NAACP. **Honors/Awds:** Social Action Award Delta Sigma Theta Sor Inc 1976; Sojurner Truth Award Nat Assn of Negro Bus & Professional Women's Clubs Inc 1977; Comm Serv Award New York City OIC 1976; Salute to African American Women, Dollar and Sense Magazine, 1989; Award for Outstanding Contribution to Social Justice, New York City Human Rights Commission, 1985; Award for Promoting Justice and Interracial Harmony, B'nai B'rith, 1990. **Business Addr:** President, New York City Off-Track Betting Corp, 1501 Broadway, New York, NY 10036.

DUKES, JEROME ERWIN
Educational administrator. **Personal:** Born Sep 9, 1938, Albany, NY. **Educ:** Pennsylvania State Univ, Univ Park PA, BA 1961; State Univ of NY at Albany, MA 1971. **Career:** The Psychological Corp, life skills educator 1975; Capital Dist Educ Opportunity Center, Troy NY, coordinator of student personnel serv 1975-; State Univ of NY at Albany, lecturer Afro-Amer studies 1969-75; Mont Pleasant High School, Schenectady NY, teacher 1965-69; Southern Univ, Baton Rouge LA, instructor 1963-64; Rensselaer Polytechnic Inst, visiting lecturer Afro-Amer studies 1970-; Siena Coll, visiting lecturer English; NY Dept of Educ Coll Proficiency Div, consultant 1970-73. **Orgs:** Bd of dir Brewington S Stinney Scholarship Comm 1969-; bd of dir Albany Arbor Hill Interracial Council Inc 1978-; bd of dir NY State Council on the Arts 1979-. **Honors/Awds:** Scholarship Award, C L Hughes Memorial Scholarship Fund, 1960; English Hon Award, Sigma Tau Delta Eng Hon Soc, 1960; Achievement Award, Alpha Phi Alpha Frat, Pennsylvania State Univ, 1961. **Business Addr:** Student Personnel Serv Coord, Educational Opportunity Center, 145 Congress, Troy, NY 12180.

DUKES, OFIELD
Public relations counselor. **Personal:** Born Aug 8, 1932, Rutledge, AL; son of Violet Stringer Dukes (deceased) and Garfield Dukes (deceased); married; children (previous marriage):

Roxi Anica Trapp-Dukes. **Educ:** Wayne State University, BA 1958. **Career:** WCHB Radio, news dir 1958-61; Michigan Chronicle, asst editor, general mgr 1961-64; Information Press Committee on Equal Employment Opportunity & Plans for Progress, dep dir 1964-65; White House Conf to Fulfill These Rights, deputy dir public affairs, 1965-69; Vice Pres Hubert H Humphrey, asst 1966-69; Ofield Dukes& Assoc Inc, pres 1969-; Howard University, instructor, 1972-. **Orgs:** Public Relations Society America; Natl Coalition on Black Voter Participation, board member; Congressional Black Caucus Foundation, board member; Peoples Involvement Corp, board member; Black Public Relations Society of DC, pres, founder. **Honors/Awds:** Outstanding Faculty Award, Howard University School of Communication, 1978; Washington Post, one of top six PR firms in DC, 1971; Silver Anvil Award, PublicRelations Society America, 1974; Frederick Douglass Award, Howard University School of Communication, 1974; Male Decision Maker, Natl Assn Media Women,1971; Eagle Leadership Award, Bethune-DuBois Fund, 1991. **Military Serv:** US Army, 1952-54. **Business Addr:** President, Ofield Dukes & Associates, 1426 Carrollsburg, SW, Washington, DC 20024.

DUKES, RONALD
Executive search consultant. **Personal:** Born Dec 27, 1942, Neelyville, MO; married Albertine A Elliott; children: Barry Girard. **Educ:** Lincoln Univ MO, BS 1964. **Career:** Continental Can Co, training supervisor 1969-71; Emerson Electric Co, sr corporate recruiter 1971-74; Amer Motors Corp, corporate dir of recruiting & mgmt develop 1974-78; Booz Allen & Hamilton, associate 1978-80; Heidrick & Struggles Inc, partner/mem bd of dirs 1980-. **Orgs:** Phi Beta Sigma Fraternity; Chicago Youth Centers and Chariman of the Board, 1995-97; board of directors, executive committee, First Non-Profit Insurance Company; Chicago United Way/Crusade of Mercy Pension Subcommittee. **Honors/Awds:** Listed in the 1990 Harper and Row Book, "The Career Makers: America's Top 100 Recruiters". **Military Serv:** AUS capt 1966-69; Commendation Medal, Combat Badge 1967. **Home Addr:** 1105 Alden Ln, Buffalo Grove, IL 60089. **Business Addr:** Partner/Mem Bd of Directors, Heidrick & Struggles Inc, Sears Tower, 233 South Wacker Drive, Suite 7000, Chicago, IL 60606-6402.

DUKES, WALTER L.
Association executive. **Personal:** Born Jun 23, 1933, Youngstown, OH. **Educ:** Seton Hall Univ, BS Economics 1953; NY Univ, MBA 1956; NY Law Schl, LLB 1959; NY Law Schl, Dr of Law 1968; Hunter Coll, MVP 1981. **Career:** Vista Travel Serv, vice pres 1963-67; US Labor Dept, atrny 1967-69; Civil Disorder, national advisory comm, 1969-70; Kennedy Develmnt Fdn Inc, pres 1970-. **Orgs:** Mbr Natl Mktg Club 1970-; mem NACCP 1951-; mem Urban Planners 1980-; vice pres Natl Org of Boys Scouts 1960-; mem Amer Bar Assoc 1961-; mem MI Bar Assoc 1968-; vice pres Boy's of Yester Year 1975-91. **Honors/Awds:** Dir Natl Youth Dir NAACP 1953-54; charter Life Underwriters Philly PA CLU; Athletic of the Year US Writers Guild 1953; vice pres Alliance Franchise 1975-84; president, National Bar Assn, 1984-91. **Business Addr:** President, King-Kennedy Devt Foundation, PO Box 756, Church St Station, New York, NY 10008.

DULANEY, MICHAEL
Professional football player. **Personal:** Born Sep 9, 1970. **Educ:** North Carolina. **Career:** Chicago Bears, running back, 1995-. **Business Addr:** Professional Football Player, Chicago Bears, 1000 Football Dr, Halas Hall at Conway Park, Lake Forest, IL 60045-4829, (847)295-6600.

DULIN, JOSEPH
Educational administrator. **Personal:** Born Aug 10, 1935, Evansville, IN; son of Charles Dulin & Alberta Cooksey; married Yvonne Dulin, Aug 14, 1976; children: Tierre Porter, Charles Joseph, Joseph II, Doris Fields, Kasner L. Willis. **Educ:** St Joseph's College, BS, 1957; Indiana State University, MS, administration, 1963; Eastern & Western Michigan Universities additional studies. **Career:** St Mary's High School, West Point, IA, teacher-coach, 1958-64; St Martin DePorres High School, principal, 1967-72; Detroit Public Schools, teacher, 1964-67; Neighborhood Svc Organization, community organizer, 1973-74; Friend's School, Detroit, assistant headmaster, 1972-73; Roberto Clemente, Ann Arbor Public Schools, principal, 1974-. **Orgs:** NAAPID, founder, 1995-; NABSE, life mem; MDABSE; Ann Arbor African-American Festival, advisory brd, 1996; Washtenaw County Community Mental Health, vice pres, 1996; The Saturday Academy for African-American Students, president, board of directors, 1992; Ann Arbor Community Foundation, board member, 1993; Cope O'Brien, vice chair, 1996-. **Honors/Awds:** NABSE Hall of Fame; National Parent Day Coalition, Distinguished Achievement Awd in Parenting, 1996; UNCF Eugene Powers Community Svc Awd, 1993; Distinguished Alumni Merit, St Joseph's College, 1969; Black Lay Catholic Caucus Leadership Awd, 1973; United Committee on Negro History Inc, Education & Community Svc, 1971. **Special Achievements:** National African-American Parent Involvement Day, 1995; First African-American Lay Principal of a Catholic School in the Nation, 1967; Founding President, National Black Lay Catholic Caucus, 1970; Consultant-Motivational Speaker, 1996; TV & Press appearances, NBC, CBS, ABC & BET, 1995. **Military Serv:** US Army, private, 1957-58, 1961-62. **Home Addr:** 439 Sumark Way, Ann Arbor, MI 48103, (313)747-6671.

DULIN, ROBERT O., JR.
Cleric. **Personal:** Born Mar 24, 1941, Lawrence, KS; married C Hawice Allen; children: Shannon E, Robert O, III. **Educ:** Anderson Coll, BA 1963; Central Bapt Theol Sem, BD 1967. **Career:** 3rd St Ch God, asso minister 1964-66; 1st Ch God, pastor 1967-69; Nat Bd Christian Edn, asso sec 1969-74; Metropolitan Ch of God, sr minister. **Orgs:** Life mem NAACP 1979. **Honors/Awds:** Alumni Achievement Award Central Bapt Theol Sem 1974. **Business Addr:** Pastor, Metropolitan Church of God, 13400 Schaefer, Detroit, MI 48227.

DUMARS, JOE, III
Professional basketball player. **Personal:** Born May 24, 1963, Shreveport, LA; married Debbie Dumars; children: Jordan Taylor, Aren. **Educ:** McNeese State Univ. **Career:** Detroit Pistons, guard, 1985-. **Honors/Awds:** NBA All-Defensive First Team, 1989, 1990, 1992, 1993; member of NBA championship team, 1989, 1990; NBA Finals MVP, 1989; NBA All-Rookie Team, 1986; NBA All-Defensive Second Team, 1991; All-NBA Second Team, 1993; All-NBA Third Team, 1990, 1991; Six-time NBA All-Star; Walter J Kennedy Citizenship Award, 1994; NBA Sportsmanship Award, 1997. **Business Addr:** Professional Basketball Player, Detroit Pistons, Two Championship Dr, Auburn Hills, MI 48326, (248)377-0100.

DUMAS, FLOYD E.
Cleric. **Personal:** Born Jan 27, 1926, Muskogee; son of Ada and Will; married Grace Lorene Provo; children: Floyd Earl II, Milton, Toya Diana. **Educ:** Langston U, BA 1953; OK Sch of Religion, BTh 1954; Univ of Northern CO, additional study. **Career:** OK Employment Dept Tulsa, employment councellor 1953-55; Univ of OK Hospital, record libarian 1950-53; Gary & Human Relation Commn, field cons; New Hope Baptist Church Okla City, dir of religious ed; Mt Zion Baptist Church, Bethel Baptist Church, Galilee Baptist Church, pastor 1967-. **Orgs:** Sec Northern IN Baptist District Assn; sec Interdenominational Ministerial Alliance; pres Med-Town LCEOC Community Action Coun; life mem NAACP; pres Baptist Minister Conf of Gary & vicinity; presently pastor Met Baptist Church Gary IN; Bapt State Conv, Inc, Congress of Christian Educ, pres; Metropolitan Oasis Corp, Gary IN, pres & CEO. **Military Serv:** USN 1943-47. **Home Addr:** 459 W 20 Pl, Gary, IN 46407. **Business Addr:** Pastor, 1920 Broadway Metropolitan Baptist Church, Gary, IN 46407.

DUMAS, KAREN MARIE
Publicist. **Personal:** Born Oct 22, 1962, Detroit, MI; married Timothy L Look; children: Kirby, Jason. **Educ:** MI State Univ, East Lansing, MI, BS, 1986. **Career:** Marx & Co, Bloomfield Hills, MI, acct asst/media relations, 1986-87; City of Highland Park, Highland Park, MI, dir of public info, 1987-88; Images & Ideas, Detroit, MI, pres, 1988-; Athletes Exclusive Sports Marketing, associate partner, 1996-. **Orgs:** The Adcraft Club of Detroit, 1987-; mem, Civic Searchlight Comm, 1990-; bd of dir, Sickle Cell Detection Comm, 1990-; bd of dir, ALERT, 1987-; mem, NAACP, 1983-; mem, Riverfront Community Org, 1986-; Natl Assn of Black Journalists, Detroit Chapter, 1991-; Black in Advertising, Radio, & Television, 1991-. **Honors/Awds:** State of Michigan, Department of Commerce, MBE, Profiles of Success Award, 1991. **Business Addr:** President, Images & Ideas, 600 River Pl, Ste 6624, Detroit, MI 48207, (313)393-8070.

DUMAS, MICHAEL DION
Professional football player. **Personal:** Born Mar 18, 1969, Grand Rapids, MI. **Educ:** Indiana Univ, majored in sports marketing. **Career:** Houston Oilers, 1991-93; Buffalo Bills, 1994; Jacksonville Jaguars, 1995; San Diego Chargers, 1997-. **Business Addr:** Professional Football Player, San Diego Chargers, Qualcomm Stadium, 9449 Friars Rd, San Diego, CA 92108, (619)280-2111.

DUMAS, RHETAUGH GRAVES
Educational administrator, educator. **Personal:** Born Nov 26, 1928, Natchez, MS; daughter of Josephine Clemmons Graves Bell and Rhetaugh Graves; married Albert W Dumas Jr (divorced 1959); children: Adrienne. **Educ:** Dillard Univ, New Orleans, LA, BSN, 1951; Yale Univ, New Haven, CT, MS, 1961; Union Grad School, Cincinnati, OH, PhD, 1975. **Career:** Community Progress Inc, New Haven, CT, coordinator of interviews, 1964-65; Yale-New Haven Medical Center, New Haven, CT, associate professor/director of nursing, 1966-72; National Institute of Mental Health, Rockville, MD, chief, psych nursing education branch, 1972-76, deputy director of manpower, 1976-79, deputy director, NIMH, alcohol, drug abuse and mental health administration, 1979-81; University of Michigan School of Nursing, Ann Arbor, MI, dean, 1981-94; Health Affairs, Univ of Michigan vice provost, Lucille Cole Prof of Nursing, 1994-. **Orgs:** American Academy of Nursing, president, 1987-89; member, Commission on Future Structure of Veterans Health Care, 1990-91; member, Governmental Affairs Committee, American Association of Colleges of Nursing, 1990-92; member, National Neural Circuitry Database Committee, 1989-91; Natl League for Nursing, pres-elect, 1995-97; President's Natl Bioethics Advisory Comm, 1996-99; Comm to Review the Breast Cancer Research Prog, US Army Med Research & Materiel Command, Inst of Medicine Natl Academy of Sci, 1996-97; WK Kellogg Foundation Ad Hoc Advisory Comm, Healthcare for the Underserved Battle Creek MI, 1996-97; Natl Advisory Council on Nurse Educ & Practice, Division of Nursing; Dept of Health & Human Services, 1993-97. **Honors/Awds:** Honorary Doctor of Humane Letters, Univ of San Diego, 1993; Honorary Doctor of Laws, Dillard University, 1990; Honorary Doctor of Humane Letters, Yale University, 1989; Honorary Doctor of Public Service, University of Cincinnati, 1981; Honorary Doctor of Public Service, Simmons College, 1976; Mentor Award, Sigma Theta Tau, 1989; Women's Honors in Public Service Award, American Nurses Association, 1988; Excellence in Nursing Award, Rho Chapter, Sigma Theta Tau, 1988; Woman of the Year in Leadership, University of Michigan, 1988; President's 21st Century Award, The Natl Women's Hall of Fame, 1994; Honorary Doctor of Public Service, Florida Intl Univ, 1996; Honorary Doctor of Science, Indiana Univ, 1996; Honorary Doctor of Humane Letters, Georgetown Univ, 1996. **Business Addr:** Vice Provost for Health Affairs, University of Michigan, 3088 Fleming Bldg, 503 Thompson St, Ann Arbor, MI 48109-1340.

DUMAS, TONY
Professional basketball player. **Personal:** Born Aug 25, 1972, Chicago, IL. **Educ:** Missouri-Kansas City Coll. **Career:** Dallas Mavericks, guard, 1994-97; Phoenix Suns, 1997; Cleveland Cavaliers, 1997-. **Special Achievements:** NBA Draft, First round pick, #19, 1994. **Business Addr:** Professional Basketball Player, Cleveland Cavaliers, One Center Ct, Cleveland, OH 44115-4001, (216)659-9100.

DUMAS, TROY
Professional football player. **Personal:** Born Sep 30, 1972. **Educ:** Univ of Nebraska. **Career:** Kansas City Chiefs, linebacker, 1996-97; St Louis Rams, 1997-. **Business Addr:** Professional Football Player, St Louis Rams, One Rams Way, St Louis, MO 63045, (314)982-7267.

DUMMETT, CLIFTON ORRIN
Dental educator. **Personal:** Born May 20, 1919, Georgetown, Guyana; married Lois Maxine Doyle. **Educ:** Roosevelt U, BS 1941; Northwestern U, DDS 1941,MSD 1942; Julius Rosenwald Fund Fellow Univ of MI, MPH 1947. **Career:** Meharry Medical Coll, prof, chmn dept periodontics oral diagnosis, chmn dental & admin com 1942-47; School of Dentistry, dean 1947-49; VA Hospital, Tuskegee AL, chief dental serv 1946-65; VA Research Hospital Chicago, 1965-66; Health Center Dir, Watts Health Center, dir 1966-68; School of Dentistry, Univ of Southern CA Los Angeles, prof, chmn dept comm dentistry, assoc dean extramural affairs 1968-. **Orgs:** Diplomate Am Bd Periodontology; diplomate Am Bd Oral Med; fellow AAAS; fellow Am Pub Health Assn; Am Coll Dentists; Intl Coll Dentists; hon mem Am Dental Assn; Intl Assn for Dental Research pres 1969-70; editor, Nat Dental Assn, 1953-75; Assn Emeritus Mil Surgeons of US; Am Acad Dental Med; Acad Perioldontology; mem Air Force Assn; Sigma Xi Omicron Kappa Upsilon Delta Omega; Sigma Pi Phi; Alpha Phi Alpha. **Honors/Awds:** Dentist of the Year Award, Nat Dental Assn 1952. **Military Serv:** USAF 1955-57. **Business Addr:** 925 W 34, Los Angeles, CA 90007.

DUMMETT, JOCELYN ANGELA
Pediatrician. **Personal:** Born Sep 15, 1956, Leicster, England; daughter of Sheila A Waterman Dummett and Kenneth J Dummett; children: Richard Anthony Hunte, Ryan William Hunte. **Educ:** Howard Univ College of Medicine, MD 1980. **Career:** Downstate Medical Ctr, clinical instructor 1983-85; LBJ School Health Program, preceptor 1985-; Health Science Ctr at Brooklyn, asst clinical prof 1985-; Javican Pediatric Assocs, cofounder 1985-87. **Orgs:** Fellow Amer Acad of Pediatrics 1982-, Brooklyn Pediatric Soc 1983-; mem Natl Medical Assoc 1983-; recording sec Provident Clinical Soc 1984-88; medical secty Hanson Place SDA Church 1986. **Honors/Awds:** Howard Univ, Coll of Medicine, Excellence in Pediatrics, 1980; National Health Service Corps, Recoginition Award, 1985. **Home Addr:** 98 Rutland Rd, Brooklyn, NY 11225. **Business Addr:** Physician, 450 Clarkson Ave, Box 49, Brooklyn, NY 11203.

DUMPSON, JAMES R.
Educator, consultant. **Personal:** Born Apr 5, Philadelphia, PA; son of Edythe Francis Smith Dumpson (deceased) and James T Dumpson (deceased). **Educ:** State Teachers Coll, BS 1932; New School for Social Rsch, AB 1947; Univ of PA School of Social Work 1937-38, 1944, 1947; Fordham Univ School of Social Serv 1942-44, New School for Social Rsch, MA 1950; Univ of Dacca, PhD 1955. **Career:** New York City Dept of Welfare, 1st dep commn 1957-59; New York City Dept of Welfare, commn 1959-65; Hunter Coll School of Social Work CUNY, prof assoc dean 1965-67; Fordham Univ Grad School of Soc Svcs, dean, prof 1967-74, prof Chair in Family and Child Welfare 1989-; NYC, commn of social serv & admin of human resources 1974-76; NY Comm Trust, vice pres 1976; City of New York, health services administrator, 1990-94, chair, New York

City Health and Hospital Corp, 1990-94, special asst to the mayor, 1990-94; dir Bur of Child Welfare NYC, consult New York City Welfare Council; cons, supvr Childrens Aid Soc of NYC; supvr Philadelphia Dept of Public Asst; teacher, public school Oxford PA; mem Gov Carey's Task Force on Human Resources; UN adv Chief of Training Soc Welfare to Gov of Pakistan; consult Pakistan to Asia Found. **Orgs:** Chmn Mayor Lindsay Anti-Poverty Council & Anti-Poverty Oper Bd; mem bd Dept Juv Justice NYC, chmn Mayors Task Force on Foster Care; mem pres Kennedy's Commn on Narcotics & Drug Abuses; mem Pres Johnson's Commn on Alcoholism; bd mem Federation of Protestant Welfare Agencies 1987-; chair US Committee Intl Council on Social Welfare 1987-; chair Black Leadership Commn on AIDS 1989-92; mem Governor Cuomo's Advisory Council on AIDS 1989-; bd mem, United Way of New York City, 1986-; bdm, Associated Black Charities, 1984-; United Way of New York City, 1990-; board member, North General Hosp, 1994-; founding president, National Black Leadership Commission on AIDS, 1990-95, commissioner, 1995-. **Honors/Awds:** James R. Dumpson Chair in Family and Child Welfare, Fordham Univ, 1990-; Honorary LLD, Tuskegee Univ; Honorary LLD, Fordham Univ; Honorary LHD, St Peters College; Honorary LLD, Howard Univ; Honorary LHD, City Univ NY. **Business Addr:** Senior Consultant, NY Comm Trust, 2 Park Ave, New York, NY 10017.

DUNBAR, ANNE CYNTHIA
Director. **Personal:** Born Sep 24, 1938, New York City, NY; divorced; children: Christopher. **Educ:** Borough of Manhattan Comm Coll, AA 1967; Brooklyn Coll, BA 1975, MS 1977; Columbia Univ School of Public & Intl Affairs, Cert 1985. **Career:** Citi-Bank/Canal St Training Ctr, asst to master 1968-69; 1st Venture Corp of NY, asst to vice pres 1969-70; Hunter Coll SEEK Fin Aid Prog, dir 1970-76; NYS Dept of Correctional Svcs, dir comm rel 1976-. **Orgs:** Mem Am Personnel & Guidance Assn; founder pres Break Thru in Art; pres NAACP Parkchester Br; adv mem NY City Busmn Coun for employment of ex-offender; educ sponsor Coalition of 100 Black Women; mem bd of dir Bronx Boys Clubs; mem NY State Catholic Conf Criminal Justice Advisory Com; mem Comm SchBd #12; chairperson Special Programs for Handicapped of Comm Sch Bd #12 1977-; mem Brooklyn Coll Alumni Assn; Borough of Manhattan Comm Coll Alumni Assn; Bronx Council on the Arts; Women's City Club of NY; consult Dept HEW Natl Inst of Health Sickle Blood Disease Prog 1977-79; volunteer Women's Div GovOffice 1969-71; chmn bd NY Urban League 1983-; trustee Bronx Museum 1981-. **Honors/Awds:** Citation for Comm Coordination & Devel Northside Center for Child Devel 1972; "Ambassador of Love" Val-to-me Productions 1974; Citation of Achievement Eastern NY Correctional Facility Jaycees 1974; Citation for Activities in Penal Reform Gamblers Anonymous Greenhaven Prison Chap 1974; Certificate of Appreciation Eastern NY Correctional Facility 1975; Claire Joseph King Meml Citation 1975; Each One Teach One Comm Serv Award Harlem Professional & John Hunter Meml Camp Fund1975; founder of Ford-Whitfield-Young Scholarship Fund Hunter Coll CUNY 1975; Outstanding Serv Award Eastern Br NAACP 1975; honoree for Intl Women's Yr Nat Council of Negro Women Inc Flatbush Section 1975; Citation for Distinguished Services to Handicapped Children; Community ServiceAward Schaefer Brewry Co 1978; Citizef the Year Award Bronx Boys Clubs 1979f Humanitarian Award Parkchester Cardiac Diagnostic Med Cntr 1979; Leadership Awd City Council of NY 1983; Disting Community Serv Council of Churches of NY; Commun Serv Awd Consolidated Edison of NY; Congressional Citation Rep Mario Biaggi 1978. **Home Addr:** 1940 E Tremont Ave, Bronx, NY 10462.

DUNBAR, HARRY B.
Educational administrator (retired). **Personal:** Born May 10, 1925, Mineola, NY; son of Rev & Mrs S N Dunbar; married Cora Charlene Whitlow; children: Nona. **Educ:** NY Univ BS, 1949, MA, 1951, PhD, 1961. **Career:** Rust Coll, Holly Springs, MS, instructor 1949-50; Dunbar Jr Coll, Little Rock AR, instructor 1950-54; New York City Public Schools, teacher 1954-60; Nanuet High School, Nanuet NY, dept chmn 1960-65; New York City Community Coll, Brooklyn NY, prof, dean 1965-83; Bergen Community Coll, Paramus NJ, dean of evening div 1983-94. **Orgs:** Free-lance consultant to small business, specializing in travel & hospitality ind; co-chr elec comm Alpha Phi Alpha Frat, Inc, Chgo, IL 1980-; ed chrmn Nyack Branch NAACP, Nyack, NY 1980-; dir United Way of Rockland County 1970-74; trustee Nyack Hosptl, Nyack, NY 1968-74; bd of visitors Rockland Psychiatric Center 1986. **Honors/Awds:** Fulbright Award US Govt 1957; John Hay Whitney flw J H Whitney Fdn 1959; NYC Technical Coll of the City Univ of NY, Prof Emeritus of Humanities, 1983. **Military Serv:** AUS staff sgt 1944-46; Asiatic Pacif Campaign Medal, WW II Victory Medal, EAME Campaign Medal, Good Conduct Medal 1944-46. **Home Addr:** 281 Rose Rd, West Nyack, NY 10994, (914)623-5241.

DUNBAR, JOSEPH C.
Educator, scientist. **Personal:** Born Aug 27, 1944, Vicksburg, MS; son of Henrienne M Watkins Dunbar and J C Dunbar Sr; married Agnes Estorge, Jul 1, 1967; children: Andrea, Erica. **Educ:** Alcorn Coll, Lorman MS, BS, 1963; Texas Southern, Houston TX, MS, 1966; Wayne State Univ, Detroit MI, PhD, 1970. **Career:** Texas Southern, Houston TX, instructor, 1966-67; Sinai Hospital of Detroit, Detroit MI, research assoc, 1970-78; Wayne State Univ, Detroit MI, prof, 1972-, dept of physiology, chmn, 1998-. **Honors/Awds:** Author of 100 publications; Distinguished Faculty Fellow; Outstanding Graduate Mentor; Medical Svc Awd. **Business Addr:** Chairman, Wayne State University, Dept of Physiology, 540 E Canfield, Detroit, MI 48201.

DUNBAR, THOMAS JEROME
Sports manager. **Personal:** Born Nov 24, 1959, Aiken, SC; son of Rosa Lee Dunbar and George Dunbar; married Tjwana Delph Dunbar, Jul 4, 1985; children: Tia, Tyson. **Educ:** Middle Georgia College. **Career:** Texas Rangers, outfielder, 1983-86; Pittsburgh Pirates, 1987; Atlanta Braves, 1988-89; Kansas City Royals, 1989-91; Princeton Reds, manager, currently. **Honors/Awds:** Texas Rangers, Minor League Rookie of the Year, 1984; Oklahoma City, Texas Rangers, American Association Batting Title, 1984; Tulsa, Texas Rangers, All-Decade Team of 1980's, 1982. **Home Addr:** 558 S Palm Dr, Aiken, SC 29803, (803)642-8436. **Business Addr:** Professional Baseball Manager, Princeton Reds, c/o Cincinnati Reds, 100 Riverfront Stadium, Cincinnati, OH 45202, (513)421-4510.

DUNCAN, ALICE GENEVA
Community service worker (retired). **Personal:** Born Mar 9, 1917, Chicago, IL; daughter of Charlotte Harris South and John Hurley South; married Clinton Wesley Duncan, Jul 13, 1945; children: Clifton John Black, Khesha Renee Duncan. **Career:** Helping Hand Baptist Church, Hannibal MO, treasurer, 1976—; Division of Family Services, Foster Home Care, 1972-82; Women in Community Services, job corp screener. **Orgs:** Secretary, NAACP, Hannibal MO branch, 1969-94, life member, member of executive board; member of board, Douglass Community Center; treasurer, Northeast Area Resource Council; secretary-treasurer, Citizens for a New and Better City Government. **Honors/Awds:** NAACP Unsung Heroine, 1985, 1986; NAACP Family of the Year, Hannibal MO branch, 1989. **Home Addr:** 2012 West Gordon St, Hannibal, MO 63401.

DUNCAN, CHARLES TIGNOR
Attorney. **Personal:** Born Oct 31, 1924, Washington, DC; son of Gladys J. Duncan and Todd Duncan; widowed; children (previous marriage): Charles Todd; married Pamela J. Thurber Duncan. **Educ:** Dartmouth Coll, BA (cum laude) 1947; Harvard Law Sch, JD 1950. **Career:** Reeves Robinson & Duncan, partner 1953-60; US Atty for DC, princ asst 1961-65; US Equal Employment Oppor Commn, general counsel 1965-66; corporation counsel DC, 1966-70; Epstein Freidman Duncan & Medalie, partner 1970-74; Howard Univ Sch of Law, dean prof law 1974-78; Peabody Lambert & Meyers Washington, partner 1978-82; Reid & Priest Washington, partner 1982-90, senior counsel, 1990-94; Iran-United States Claims Tribunal, mem, 1994-. **Orgs:** Mem NY Bar 1951, DC Bar 1953, MD Bar 1955, US Supreme Ct Bar 1954, US Seventh Circuit Ct of Appeals Bar 1962; bd of dirs of Nat Bank of Wash 1973-79, Procter & Gamble Co 1982-88, Eastman Kodak Co 1978-95, TRW Inc 1984-95; mem DC Labor Rels Board 1973-75; chmn DC Judic Nomin Commin 1975-80; mem Dartmouth Coll Alumni Counc 1975-78; bd of dir, NAACP Legal Def & Education Fund; mem ABA Nat Bar Assn Wash Bar Assn & Dist of Colum Bar, pres 1973-74; Phi Beta Kappa, Alpha Phi Alpha; Sigma Pi Phi; Delta Theta Phi, Mason; act partic prepar & present of Sch Desegregation cases 1953-55; FAA Lic instr rated comm pilot. **Honors/Awds:** Hon LLD Dartmouth Coll 1986. **Military Serv:** USNR ensign 1944-46. **Home Addr:** 1362 Myrtle Ave, Annapolis, MD 21403-4952. **Business Addr:** Iran-U.S. Claims Tribunal, Parkweg 13, 2585 JH, The Hague, Netherlands.

DUNCAN, GENEVA
Director. **Personal:** Born Aug 21, 1935, Cleveland; married Dave L Sr; children: Jolette, Dave, Jr, Brenda, Darnell, Darlynn, Kevin. **Educ:** Feen Coll; Cleveland State U. **Career:** Ministerial Day Care Assn, dir social serv. **Orgs:** Mem Dem Exec Com; bd Dirs; Crest Found; bd HADC; mem Cuyahoga County Welfare Dept; Fedn for Comm & Plng; Comm Christmas Bureau; dir Pub Relations; Mt Nebo Bapt Ch; Mem Hough Area Council Glenville Area Council; Hough Area Devel Corp; Crest Found. **Business Addr:** 2521 E 61 St, Cleveland, OH 44104.

DUNCAN, JOAN A.
Government official. **Personal:** Born Sep 8, 1939, Butte, MT; daughter of Alyce M Driver Duncan and Dr Walter E Duncan. **Educ:** Syracuse Univ, 1957-58; Carroll Coll, 1958-67. **Career:** Carroll Coll, ast dean of women 1961-67; RDMC Comm Action Agncy, dir Foster Grandparent Prog 1969-75; MT Dept Labor & Indstry, Chief Women's Bureau 1975-81; City of Helena, city commr 1982-86; Montana Legislature, 1983-87; Helena Food Share Inc, exec dir, 1987-91; Hennesys Dept Store, promotions dir and personnal shopper, 1992-. **Orgs:** Dir Helena Area Econ Dvlmnt Inc 1985-87, Rocky Dvlmnt Cncl Inc 1982-86, United Way 1973-89; writer prodcr host Leg 1979-, TV Prog 1979, Women's Window R Dio 52 Stationss 1981, 51% 1976-81, Guardian of the Culch TV Prog 1982-86; mem Last Chance Press Club 1976-, MT Dem Party 1980-, Lewis & Clark Health Brd 1983-86; Lewis & Clark County Tax Appeals Bd; Montana Communities Found; co-chairman, Project Progress, Jobs for Helena's Future 1990-; Montana Food Bank Network, executive director, 1991-92. **Home Addr:** 502 Harrison Ave, Helena, MT 59601-2724.

DUNCAN, JOHN C., JR.
Attorney, military officer. **Personal:** Born Jun 5, 1942, Philadelphia, PA; son of Yvonne A Jackson Duncan and John C Duncan Sr (deceased); married Elizabeth Delores Tunsford Duncan, May 28, 1989. **Educ:** DePauw Univ, BA 1964; Univ of MI, MS, MA 1965-66; Stanford Univ, PhD 1971; Yale Law Schl, JD 1976; Southeastern Univ, MBPA 1985. **Career:** Iraklion AS, Crete, Greece, Staff Judge Advocate 1978-79; Tactical Air Command, Chief Civil Law 1979-81; Hurlburt Field, FL, Staff Judge Advocate 1981-82; AF JAG Career Mgmnt, Chief Military Manpower & Analysis (JAG) 1982-84; Legal Advisor to the Asst to the Secretary of Defense (Intelligence Oversight); Deputy Judge Advocate, United Nations Command, US Forces in Korea, Deputy Staff Judge Advocate, HQ Tactical Ser Command, Langley AFB, VA. **Orgs:** Life mem Alpha Phi Alpha 1968; prof various Univer 1976-; cnslr Marriage Family & Child 1976-; ODO 1976, Amer Assoc of Marriage & Family Therapists 1976; Inter Amer Bar Assoc 1983; ABA, FBA, NBA. **Honors/Awds:** Rector Scholar, DePauw Univ 1960-64; Graduate w/distinction DePauw Univ, Leopold Schepp Found Schlrshp 1965-66; Schlrshp Stanford Univ 1967; Flwshp Richardson Dilworth Fellow Yale 1974-76; Outstanding New Teacher Award, Southeastern Univ 1985. **Military Serv:** USAF Col, 1969-; Meritorious Service medals (4), Air Medals (2); Defense Meritorious Service Medals (2). **Business Addr:** Deputy Staff Judge Advocate, Headquarters Tactical Air Command, Hampton, VA 23665.

DUNCAN, LOUIS DAVIDSON, JR.
Physician. **Personal:** Born Oct 26, 1932, Lancaster, SC; son of Minnie and Louis. **Educ:** Howard U, BS 1954; Howard Univ Sch of Med, MD 1958. **Career:** Private Practice, physician 1960. **Orgs:** Mem Med Surgical Soc DC Inc; mem Nat Med Assn Mem Mt Airy Baptist Church; Phi Beta Kappa. **Business Addr:** 1105 Buchanan St, Washington, DC 20011.

DUNCAN, LYNDA J.
City official. **Educ:** Motlow State Comm Coll, AS 1984. **Career:** Ray Belue & Assocs, model/actress 1974-77; Univ of TN, contract coord 1978-81; City of Tullahoma, court clerk 1982-86; WKQD FM/AM, mktg consultant/copywriter 1986-. **Orgs:** Mem Circle Player, Atlanta 1974-76; fund raiser Comm Action Guild 1977-79; coord youth activities Mt Zion Baptist Church 1977-79; sponsor Black History Club Tullahoma HS 1978-79; treasurer Bd of Dir Tullahoma Day Care Center 1979-81; chairperson C&D Stamps Scholarship Fund 1982-86; bd of dirs TENCO Developments Inc 1986-. **Honors/Awds:** Appeared as principal character in numerous natlly distrib commercials; has appeared as a model in Ebony-Essence-GQ-Madamoiselle 1974-79. **Business Addr:** Mktg Consultant/Copywriter, WKQD FM/AM, Westside Dr, Tullahoma, TN 37388.

DUNCAN, MARVIN E.
Educator, resources center director. **Personal:** Born Nov 23, 1939, Greenville, NC; son of Leroy Duncan (deceased); married Sandra Fields Duncan, Mar 25, 1981; children: Crystal Lynn, Catayah Angelia. **Educ:** North Carolina Coll, Durham NC, BA Math, 1962, MA Educ, 1963; Univ of Virginia, Charlottesville VA, attended, 1969-70; Michigan State Univ, E Lansing MI, PhD Inst Devel/Educ Psychology, 1972. **Career:** North Carolina Central Univ, asst dir, Learning Resources Center, 1963-70, dir, Learning Resources Center, 1972-, prof of educ, currently. **Orgs:** Evaluation consultant, Ohio State Univ, 1971; test consultant, Stanford Research Inst, Menlo Park CA; chmn, Durham Chamber of Commerce Leadership Devel Comm, 1981; planning consultant, North Carolina Schools & Colleges; mem, bd of dir, Edgemont Community Center, Durham NC, 1986-87; bd mem, Child Care Food & Nutrition Network Inc, 1986-87; mem, North Carolina Mental Health Assn 1986-87, Alpha Phi Alpha Frat, Assn for Educ Communication Technology, North Carolina Assn of Educ. **Honors/Awds:** Outstanding Research Award, North Carolina Central Univ, 1988; Distinguished Serv Award, North Carolina Central Univ, 1988; author of 17 publications in the field of educ.

DUNCAN, ROBERT M.
Attorney. **Personal:** Born Aug 24, 1927, Urbana, OH; married Shirley A Duncan; children: Linn, Vincent, Tracy. **Educ:** Ohio State University, BS, 1948, JD, 1952, LLD, 1979. **Career:** General law practice, Columbus OH, 1954-57; State of Ohio, assistant attorney general, 1957-59; Bureau of Workmen's Compensation, attorney examiner, 1959-60; City of Columbus OH, asst city attorney, 1960-63; chief, workmen's compensation section, 1963-65; attorney general of Ohio, chief counsel, 1965-66; Franklin County Municipal Court, judge, 1966-69; Supreme Court of Ohio, justice, 1969-71; US Court of Military Appeals, judge, 1971-74, chief judge, 1974; US District Court for the Southern District of Ohio, Columbus OH, judge, 1974-85; Jones, Day, Reavis & Pogue, Columbus OH, partner, 1985-. **Orgs:** American Bar Assn; Ohio State Bar Assn; Columbus Bar Assn; Columbus Bar Foundation; Federal Bar Assn; Sixth Circuit Judicial Conference; fellow, American College of Trial Lawyers; judicial panel member, Center for Public Resources;

Natl Center for State Courts; past president, Ohio State University College of Law Alumni Assn; board of visitors, Wake Forest Law School; chair, Natl Council of Ohio State University College of Law; US Court of Military Appeals Court Committee; Phi Delta Phi; Kappa Alpha Psi; Sigma Pi Phi. **Honors/Awds:** Franklin Univ Law School Liberty Bell Award, 1969; Ohio State Univ Alumni Centennial Award, 1970; Columbus Urban League Equal Opportunity Award, 1978; Alpha Kappa Alpha Humanitarian Award, 1980; Omega Psi Phi Fraternity Citizen of the Year, 1984; Columbus Education Assn Martin Luther King Award, 1984; Ohio Bar Medal for unusually meritorious service, 1985; Ohio State Univ Ralph Davenport Mershon Award, 1986; ACLU Award, 1986; Christopher Columbus Achievement Award, 1986; HDL, Ohio State Univ, Central State Univ, Wilberforce Univ, and Ohio Northen Univ. **Military Serv:** US Army, 1952-54. **Business Addr:** Jones Day Reavis & Pogue, 41 South High St, 19th Floor, Columbus, OH 43215.

DUNCAN, ROBERT TODD. See Obituaries section.

DUNCAN, ROBIN BARCLAY. See BARCLAY, ROBIN MARIE.

DUNCAN, SANDRA RHODES
Company executive. **Personal:** Born Nov 16, 1944, Chicago, IL; daughter of Doris Millaud and Duplain W Rhodes Jr; divorced; children: Sabrina, Otis Jr, Orrin, Omar, Ashea Duncan. **Educ:** Commonwealth College of Mortuary Science, 1969; Batesville Management Services Seminars, 1976; Louisiana State University, executive management, 1991. **Career:** Duplin W Rhodes Funeral Home, Inc, licensed embalmer, funeral dir, 1962-; Airport Rhodes Transportation Inc, president, 1986-91; Rhodes Enterprises, president, 1991-. **Orgs:** Junior Achievement, chairwoman, 1992-93; Business Council of New Orleans & The River Region; Committee of 21; World Trade Center; Louisiana Council on Fiscal Reform, Amistad Research Center; New Orleans Center for Creative Arts; New Orleans Chapter of Links. **Honors/Awds:** Certificate of Merit for Outstanding Service (City of New Orleans), 1988; National Business League Award, 1988; Humanitarian Award (St Mark Missionary Baptist Church), 1989; Certificate of Appreciation (City of New Orleans), 1986-92; Certificate of Appreciation (The Good Samaritan Committee), 1992; numerous others. **Business Addr:** President, Rhodes Enterprises, 1716 N Claiborne Ave, New Orleans, LA 70116, (504)522-6010.

DUNCAN, STEPHAN W.
Journalist. **Personal:** Born Feb 2, 1924, St Louis, MO; son of Marguerite Turner Duncan and Stephan R Duncan; married Sheila Shields; children: Stephan W. **Educ:** Univ of Illinois, BS 1950; Rutgers Univ Urban Studies Ctr, Urban Fellow 1962-63; Columbia Univ Grad School of Journalism; Interracial Reporting Fellow 1968-69; Drew Univ School of Theology, Madison, NJ, Master of Theological Studies, 1987-89. **Career:** St Louis Argus, 1952-56; Baltimore AFRO-Amer, reporter 1956-57, city editor 1957-58; Afro Amer Newspapers, NJ editor 1958-62; New York World Telegram, asst Brooklyn editor; 1963-66; Region I Office of Econ Opportunity, civil rights officer 1966-68; NY Daily News, asst news editor; New York Daily News, New York, NY, copy editor, 1969-73, Regional Editor, 1973-83; New York Daily News, New York, NY, assistant news editor, 1983-87. **Orgs:** Mem Alpha Phi Alpha Frat; Sigma Delta Chi; adjunct prof of journalism, Columbia Univ Grad School of Journalism, 1970-72; adjunct prof of journalism Brooklyn Coll 1973-75, and 1987-; bd dir Adult School of Montclair NJ 1982-, Urban League of Essex Cty 1961-63, Newark Branch NAACP 1961-63; bd dir, Montclair Sr Housing Corp, 1983-; associate member, National Association of Black Journalists 1987-; Board of Trustees, Day Nurseries Inc, 1990-. **Honors/Awds:** Certificate, Natl Conf of Christians and Jews 1961; Certificate of Appreciation Natl Assn of Business and Professional Women's Clubs 1961; news reporting award Mound City Press Club St Louis MO 1956. **Military Serv:** AUS tech 5th grade; Four Battle Stars European Theatre of Oper 1943-46. **Home Addr:** 120 High St, Montclair, NJ 07042.

DUNCAN, TIM (TIMOTHY THEODORE)
Professional basketball player. **Personal:** Born Apr 25, 1976. **Educ:** Wake Forest, bachelor's degree in psychology. **Career:** San Antonio Spurs, center/forward, 1997-. **Honors/Awds:** NBA All-Star, 1998. **Business Addr:** Professional Basketball Player, San Antonio Spurs, 600 E Market St, San Antonio, TX 78205, (210)554-7773.

DUNCAN, TODD
Editor. **Personal:** Born Sep 3, 1948, Washington, DC; son of Charles T Duncan; married Jennifer Duncan, Apr 22, 1989; children: Lauren, C.D. **Educ:** Cornell Univ, BS, 1972; Univ of Missouri, Grad School of Journalism. **Career:** Ebony Magazine, photographer, 1974-76; Milwaukee Journal, photographer, 1976-79; Self Employed, 1979-83; Newsday NY, editor, 1983-89; The Charlotte Observer, editor, 1990-. **Orgs:** National Assn of Black Journalists; Charlotte Assn of Black Journalists; Society of Newspaper Design; NAACP, legal defense & educational fund-raising committee; Cities in Schools, board of dir; City of Charlotte Parade Commission; Southern Newspaper Publishers Assn of Diversity Comm. **Home Addr:** 304 W 10th St, Charlotte, NC 28202, (704)334-2313. **Business Addr:** Assistant managing editor, graphics, The Charlotte Observer, 600 S. Tryon St., Charlotte, NC 28202, (704)358-5011.

DUNCAN, VERDELL
Elected government official, personnel administrator. **Personal:** Born May 9, 1946, Arkadelphia, AR; children: Constanc Regina, Cameron Chad, Jacobi Edwin. **Educ:** Henderson State Univ, BSE 1964-68; Eastern MI Univ, MA 1972-74, MA 1974-76. **Career:** Greater Flint OIC, dr of training 1972-73; City of Flint, flint police officer 1973-77; City of Flint Retirement, trustee of retirement bd 1977-79; CON-CAM Publishing Corp, owner; City of Flint Hurley Med Ctr, 1st ward councilman, administrator for Culture Diversity/EEO. **Orgs:** Mem Urban League; mem Natl Assoc for the Advance of Colored People; council liason City of Flint Human Relations Comm; mem MI Assn of Hospital PersonnelDirs; bd mem Partner In Progress; sec MI Assoc of Affirmative Action Off; pres/owner Twin & Assoc 1983-; mem Omega Psi Phi Frat; coord Hurley Medical Ctr Employee Assistance Prog; consultant pre-retirement, substance abuse, employee development; chief stockholder PHASE; board member, Community Recovery Center; board member, Community Coalition; board member, Genesee County Federation of the Blind. **Honors/Awds:** Educ scholarships WP Sturges Grant 1964-68. **Military Serv:** US Army, spec 4 1969-71; Combat Medical Badge; Natl Defense Medal. **Home Addr:** 6906 Daryll Dr, Flint, MI 48505. **Business Addr:** Councilmember, City of Flint-Hurley Med Ctr, 1101 S Saginaw, One Hurley Plaza, Flint, MI 48502.

DUNCOMBE, C. BETH
Attorney. **Personal:** Born Apr 26, 1948, Detroit, MI; married Joseph Nuttell Brown. **Educ:** Univ of Michigan, BA 1970, MA 1971; Georgetown Univ Law Center, JD 1974. **Career:** Ed Change Tem Univ of Michigan, asst project dir 1970-71; Fed Trade Commission, law clerk 1972-73; Dickinson, Wright, Moon, Van Dusen & Freeman, partner 1981-. **Orgs:** Pres Nu Chapter Delta Sigma Theta Sorority 1968; mem, City of Detroit Civil Serv Comm 1979-82; mem Senator Donald Riegle's Fed Judicial Merit Selection Comm 1980; pres Wolverine Bar Assn 1980; bd of dir Detroit Symphony Orchestra; mem MI State Bd of Law Examiners 1979-; bd of dir Keep Detroit Beautiful Inc 1978; pres Detroit Chapter Links Inc 1986-88. **Business Addr:** Attorney, Dickinson, Wright, Moon, Van Dusen & Freeman, 800 First National Bldg, Detroit, MI 48226.

DUNGEE, MARGARET R.
Teacher. **Personal:** Born in Richmond, VA; married Winfred A; children: Veronica Dungee Abrams. **Educ:** VA Union U, BA 1962; VA Commonwealth U, MA 1971; Howard U; Univ of VA. **Career:** Fairmount School, teacher 1962-69; John B Caly School, 1969-70; Southampton, resource teacher 1971-72; Westhampton, diagnostic prescriptive teacher 1972-74; Richmond Public Schools, human relations adv specialist 1974-; Thirteen Acres Residential School, special educ 1981-86; Richmond Public Schools Clark Springs, teacher 1986-94; Virginia Union University, reading instructor, 1994-. **Orgs:** Pres & vice pres PTA Fairmont Elem School 1959-61; pres Richmond Educ Assn 1973-74, Delta Sigma Theta; vol McGuire Hosp; advanced gift chmn VA Fund Renewal Conv Am Bapt Ch & Progressive Nat Bapt. **Honors/Awds:** 10 yr trophy PTA Serv 1969. **Business Addr:** Reading Instructor, Virginia Union University, 1500 Lombardy Street, Richmond, VA 23220.

DUNGIE, RUTH SPIGNER
Human resources executive. **Personal:** Born Nov 26, New York, NY; daughter of Fannie Walker Spigner and William M Spigner; married Elias; children: Christopher David. **Educ:** College of New Rochelle, BA 1975; New School for Social Research, MA 1980. **Career:** IBM, personnel prog admin 1981-83, corporate litigation mgr 1983-85, eo prog administrator 1985-86, personnel rsch survey administrator 1987-89; ROLM Company, Norwalk, CT, program manager, employee relations, 1989-; IBM, program manager, HR research, 1991-. **Orgs:** Alpha Kappa Alpha Sor; mem Natl Coalition of 100 Black Women, Natl Black MBA Assoc; mem, Westchester Personnel Mgmt Assoc, 1990; mem, American Society for Personnel Admin, 1990; recording secretary, Greater Hudson Valley Chapter Links, Inc, 1990-; chapter secretary, The Links, Inc. **Home Addr:** 205 Langdon Ave, Mount Vernon, NY 10553.

DUNGY, CLAIBOURNE I.
Physician, educator. **Personal:** Born Oct 29, 1938, Chicago, IL; married Madgetta T; children: Kathryn, Camille. **Educ:** Eastern IL Univ, BS 1962; Univ of IL, MD 1967; Johns Hopkins Univ, MPH 1971. **Career:** Univ of CO, Dept of Pediatrics, 1971-75; Univ of CA, Irvine, Dept of Pediatrics, 1975-88, chief, Div of Gen Pediatrics, 1976-80, 1985-88; Univ of IA, Dept of Pediatrics, 1988-, dir, Division of General Pediatrics, 1988-. **Orgs:** Reg dir Region XIII AAP Head Start Prog 1974-75; mem CA State Child Hlth Bd 1977-82; consult Brookhaven Natl Labs Marshall Islands 1982-; bd mem Urban League Orange Cty Chap 1982-88; consult, KOCE TV, 1980-88; American Public Health Assn, 1971-; American Academy of Pediatrics, 1975-; Ambulatory Pediatric Assn, 1973-; Assn for Academic Minority Physicians, 1991-; co chair, APA Region IX, 1987-88, Region III, 1993-95; Goodwill of Southeast Iowa, bd of dirs, 1993-; American Pediatric Society, 1994-; Amer Academy of Pediatrics, council of pediatric research, 1995-, council on government affairs, 1996-; Ambulatory Pediatric Assn, bd of dirs, 1996-; Archives of Pediatrics and Adolescent Medicine, editorial bd, 1996-. **Honors/Awds:** Distg alumnus Eastern IL Univ 1979; Minority Alumni Hall of Fame, Eastern IL Univ, 1994. **Military Serv:** US Army, 1956-58. **Business Addr:** Pediatrics, University of Iowa, College of Medicine, 200 Hawkins Dr, 2569JCP, Iowa City, IA 52242-1083.

DUNGY, MADGETTA THORNTON
Educational administrator. **Personal:** Born in Lynchburg, VA; daughter of Madge Meadors Thornton and Edgar T Thornton; married Claibourne I Dungy; children: Kathryn, Camille. **Educ:** Cornell College, Iowa, BA, political science, (1st Black female graduate) 1964; University of Colorado, Boulder, MA, education 1974. **Career:** Chicago Urban Renewal Commission, field rep 1964; Chicago School Board, high school teacher-counselor 1964-67; University of Utah, admission counselor 1967-68; Stanford University, financial aids officer 1968-70; Girl Scout Council, dir of membership services 1979-86, counselor/coord summer bridge prog; Univ of CA-Irvine, student affairs officer; University of Iowa College of Medicine, associate, student affairs, director, minority programs, 1988-. **Orgs:** Natl Assn of Medical Minority Educators, Inc, 1989-; Natl Assn of Student Personnel Adminis 1973-; Orange Cty Visiting Nurses Assn 1976-81; citizens advisory council, KOCE TV 1983; advisory board council, Gifted & Talented 1978-; Orange Cty Chapter, charter member, Jack & Jill of America 1980-88; The Links Inc 1982-88; golden life member, Delta Sigma Theta Sorority, Inc, former vice president, Orange Cty Chapter; CA Assn for Counseling & Development 1975-88; Directors of Volunteers in Agencies 1979-86. **Honors/Awds:** Research asst to Lagos Nigeria-Stanford U/U of Lagos Nigeria 1970; What Counselors Need to Know about Health Professions, Awareness Magazine 1974; Meeting the Health Care Crisis, Amer Assn of Higher Education 1975; Concepts in Volunteerism, cable TV program 1981. **Business Addr:** Associate for Student Affairs, Medical College Administration, University of Iowa College of Medicine, College Administration Building, Rm 100, Iowa City, IA 52242.

DUNGY, TONY
Football coach. **Personal:** Born Oct 6, 1955, Jackson, MI; married Lauren; children: Tiara, James, Eric. **Educ:** Univ of Minnesota, 1973-76. **Career:** Pittsburgh Steelers, safety, 1977-78; San Francisco 49ers, 1979; New York Giants, 1980; Univ of Minnesota, defensive backs coach, 1980; Pittsburgh Steelers, defensive asst, 1981, defensive backs coach, 1982-83, defensive coordinator, 1984-88; Kansas City Chiefs, defensive backs coach, 1989-91; Minnesota Vikings, defensive coordinator, 1992-95; Tampa Bay Buccaneers, head coach, 1996-. **Business Addr:** Head Coach, Tampa Bay Buccaneers, 1 Buccaneer Pl, Tampa, FL 33607.

DUNHAM, CLARENCE E.
Communications consultant (retired). **Personal:** Born Aug 29, 1934, Syracuse, NY; son of Leona Shepard and Clarence Dunham; divorced; children: Audrey, Tracey, Joi, Roderick Stubbs. **Educ:** Syracuse U, 1953; AUS Comm Tech Teletype Sch, 1959. **Career:** Western Elec Co Inc, 1953-69; NY Telephone Co, communications cons, 1969-83; AT &T, asistant mgr, 1983-87. **Orgs:** Past coun mem Syracuse Nghbrhd Hlth Ctr; bd dir Dunbar Ctr scl serv & fclty; pres Grand St Boys; adv Jr Achievement Orgn 1972-73; Co Legislator1973; Onondaga Co Legislator Respresenting 23rd Legislative Dist; bd dir PEACE Inc 1974; bd dir WCNY TV 1974; adv bd Bishop Foery Found 1974; bd dir Onondaga Neighborhood Leg Serv 1975; bd dir Metro Syracuse Bus Ind Educ Council 1975; exec com Northern Region Black Pol Caucus; pres Southwest Comm Center, 1989. **Honors/Awds:** Citation from Jr Achievement 1972; 1st runner-up in YMCA Black Achievement Award 1973; YMCA Black Achievement Award 1975. **Military Serv:** AUS 1957-59.

DUNHAM, KATHERINE (KAYE DUNN)
Dancer, actress, writer. **Personal:** Born Jun 22, 1910, Joliet, IL; daughter of Annette Poindexter Dunham and Albert Millard Dunham; married John Thomas Pratt, Jul 10, 1941; children: Marie Christine. **Educ:** Joliet Township Junior College, attended; University of Chicago, PhB; Northwestern University, PhD; MacMurray College, LhD, 1972; Atlanta University, PhDL, 1977. **Career:** A Negro Rhapsody, 1931; Chicago Opera Company, 1933-36; Chicago World's Fair, 1934-35; West Indies dance research, 1937-38; Pins and Needles, dance director, 1937; Tropics, 1938; Le Jazz Hot, 1938; Cabin in the Sky, dancer/choreographer, 1940; toured extensively thoroughout US, Canada, 1940-43; Tropical Revue, toured in US, Canada, 1943-45; Carib Song, co-director/dancer, 1945; Bal Negre, producer, director, star, 1945-48, 1950; Katherine Dunham and Her Company, founder, choreographer, director, performer; Teatro Colon, Argentina, choreographer, 1950; Metropolitan Opera House, Aida, choreographer, 1963; Treemonisha, director/choreographer, 1972; Katherine Dunham School of Cultural Arts, founder, 1943, president, 20 years; Southern Illinois Uni-

versity, Performing Arts Training Center,prssor, director, 1968-; contributor to magazines under pseudonym of Kaye Dunn; author: Las Danzas de Haiti; Journey to Accompong, 1946; La Boule Blanche; L'Agya; A Touch of Innocence, autobiography, 1959; Island Possessed, 1969; Kasamance, 1974; various tv scripts; playwright: Ode to Taylor Jones, 1967-68. **Orgs:** American Guild of Variety Artists; American Federation of Television & Radio Artists; American Society of Composers, Authors, & Publishers; Screen Actors Guild; Actors' Equity Assn; Authors Guild Inc; Black Academy of Arts & Letters; Black Filmmakers Hall of Fame; Sigma Epsilon, Honorary Women's Science Fraternity; Royal Society of Anthropology; American Council on Arts in Education; Advocates for the Arts; adv dance panel, Illinois Arts Council; Arts Worth/ Intercultural Com; Certificate Committee, Doctoral Program, Union Graduate School; Dance Scope; numerous others. **Honors/Awds:** Hatian Legion of Honor & Merit Chevalier, 1950, Commander, 1958, Grand Officer, 1968; laureate, Lincoln Academy, 1968; Key to E St Louis, IL, 1968; Professional Achievement Award, University of Chicago; Dance Magazine Award, 1969; Eight Lively Arts Award, 1969; St Louis Argus Award, 1970; E St Louis Monitor Award, 1970; Katherine Dunham Day Award, Detroit, 1970; Dance Div Heritage Award, American Assn of Health, Physical Education & Recreation, 1971; American Dance Guild Annual Award, 1975. **Business Addr:** Performing Arts Training Center, Southern Illinois University, 532 N 10th St, East St Louis, IL 62201.

DUNHAM, ROBERT
Restaurateur. **Personal:** Born 1932, Kannapolis, NC; married. **Career:** McDonald's Franchise Harlem, pres (3rd most successful of 2,800 outlets in US); NY Waldorf-Astoria Hotel, worked as salad man. **Military Serv:** USAF.

DUNIGAN, MAYME O.
Social planner (retired). **Personal:** Born Oct 4, 1921, Darling, MS; daughter of Corrie Cade Simmons and George W Simmons; married Charles Dunigan; children: 5. **Educ:** Lincoln Univ, attended; Wayne State Univ, attended; Merrill Palmer Inst, Certified Home Mgmt; Wayne State Univ, BS. **Career:** MO Publ School, teacher 2 yrs; Mayors Comm for Human Resources Devel City of Detroit, home mgmt adv 1965-70; Mayors Comm for Human Resources Devel, social planner 1970-76; Neighborhood Service Dept - City of Detroit, counselor. **Orgs:** Founding mem 1st Independence Bank Detroit; mem Womens Guild of 1st Independence Bank; sec Lincoln Univ Alumni Assoc Detroit Chapter 1965-67,l970-72; pres 1972-74, chmn 1973-79 Natl Adv Council Lincoln Univ Alumni Assoc; mem bd of trustees Gr Macedonia Bapt Church 1978-; chmn Budget Comm 1978-79, Scholarship Comm 1978-79, Crime & Justice Task Force, Womens Conf of Concerns 1975-78; mem Equal Justice Council; pres United for Total Comm for Deaf Met Detroit;mem bd trustees Children Hosp of MI; mem Mayors Task Force on Hunger & Malnutrition 1972-75, Interim Comm Nutrition Prog 1973, Womens Conf of Concerns, Greater Macedonia Bapt Church; appt to mem MI State Mental Health Adv Council on Deafness; mem Unity of Hands Deaf Chorale Bd of Dir; mem/bd dir Transformation in Employment, 1989-90. **Honors/Awds:** Cited by NAACP for Achievement in Membership Drive 1972; Recommended MI Chronicle Mother of the Year 1974; nominated for "Heart of Gold" 1984; Distinguished Alumni Award 1976.

DUNLAP, ESTELLE CECILIA DIGGS
Educator (retired). **Personal:** Born Sep 26, 1912, Washington, DC; daughter of Mary F Chasley Diggs (deceased) and John F Diggs (deceased); married Lee Alfred; children: Gladys C Carpenti, Dolly A Sparkman. **Educ:** DC Teachers Coll, BS 1937; Howard Univ, MS 1940; Catholic Univ of America, post grad 1941. **Career:** Garnet-Patterson Junior High Schol, instr & head of math dept 1941-56; MacFarland Junior High School; math sci instr 1956-72; DC Teachers Coll, visiting lecturer of math 1963-64. **Orgs:** Mem Natl Council of Teachers of Math; mem Amer Assn for the Advncmnt of Sci; vice pres Benjamin Banneker Math Club; mem Natl Ed Assn; mem Amer Math Soc; mem Natl Defense Preparedness Assn; mem Soc for Ind and Applied Math; recording sec NW Boundary Civic Assn; mem Smithsonian Resident Assn; founding mem Natl Historical Soc; sponsor Boys & Girls Clubs of Metropolitan Police; treas Petworth Block Club; charter mem WN Performing Arts Soc; Amer Assn of Univ Women; Howard Univ Alumni Assn; Natl Urban League; adv bd Amer Security Council; life fellow Intnl Biographical Assn; advisory bd Am Biographical Rsch Inst; Metropolitan Opera Guild; Amer Film Inst; US Olympic Soc; Natl Assn of Negro Musicians; Amer Assn of Retired Persons; Brunswick Bowling Clubhouse;Natl Council of Sr Citizens; DC Rblican Club; Republican Presidential Task Force. **Honors/Awds:** Fellowship Natl Sci Foundation; Diploma of Honor Intl Inst of Comm Svcs; Certificate of Appreciation Superior Ct of DC; Cultural Doctorate World Univ; Personality of the Yr Awd World Culture Prize Italian Academia 1984; Honorary Doctorate Intl Univ Foundation 1985; Exec Life Rep World Inst of Achievement; Bronze Medal Awd Albert Einstein Intl Acad Foundation 1986. **Home Addr:** 719 Shepherd St N W, Washington, DC 20011.

DUNLAP, KAREN F. BROWN
Journalist, educator. **Personal:** Born Jul 13, 1951, Nashville, TN; daughter of Mary Shute Fitzgerald and Charles Fitzgerald; children: Asim, Christopher, Asha; married Henrry L. Dunlap. **Educ:** Michigan State University, East Lansing, MI, BA, 1971; Tennessee State University, Nashville, TN, MS, 1976; University of Tennessee, Knoxville, TN, PhD, 1982. **Career:** Nashville Banner, Nashville, TN, staff writer, 1969, 1971, 1983-85 (summers); Macon News, Macon, GA, staff writer, 1972-73; Tennessee State University, Nashville, TN, assistant professor, 1976-85; University of South Florida, Tampa, FL, assistant professor, 1985-; The Poynter Institute, St Petersburg, FL, associate professor, 1989-. **Orgs:** Society of Professional Journalists, 1980-; Delta Sigma Theta Sorority, 1982-; National Association of Black Journalists, 1985-; Association of Educators in Journalism and Mass Communications, 1981-. **Honors/Awds:** McKnight Fellow, Florida Endowment Fund, 1986-87; Karl A. & Madira Bickel Fellow, Bickel Foundation, 1979-80. **Business Addr:** Associate, Poynter Institute for Media Studies, 801 3rd St, S, St Petersburg, FL 33701, (813)821-9494.

DUNLAP KING, VIRGIE M.
Educator. **Personal:** Born Oct 9, 1940, Fayette, MS; daughter of Luetter Massie Hunt Dunlap (deceased) and Edward Lee Dunlap; divorced; children: Rufus Daniel King Jr, Jessica Chase King. **Educ:** Jackson State University, Jackson, MS, BS, language arts, 1963; University of Southern California, Los Angeles, CA, MA, education, 1971; University of Alaska, Fairbanks, AK, administrative, 1982. **Career:** FBNSBSD, Fairbanks, Alaska, teacher, 1973-. **Orgs:** National committeewoman, Alaska Democratic Party, 1984-; PGWM Prince Hall Grand Chapter, OES; imperial deputy of the Desert D of I; state loyal lady ruler, Heroines of Jericho; chairperson, FEA Minority Caucus; chairperson, Alaska State Human Rights Commission; chair, NEAT Board; life member, president, NAACP; life member, Jackson State University Alumni. **Honors/Awds:** Williard Bowman Award for Human Rights, NEA-Alaska, 1985; H Councill Trenholm Memorial Award for Human Rights, NEA, Washington, DC, 1985; Martin Luther King, Jr Award, Community Services, Chairperson MLK Committee, 1992. **Home Addr:** 4010 Dunlap Ave, Fairbanks, AK 99709.

DUNMORE, CHARLOTTE J.
Educator. **Personal:** Born Nov 16, 1926, Philadelphia, PA. **Educ:** Univ of PA, BS 1949; Columbia Univ, MSSW 1954; Brandeis Univ Florence Heller School, PhD 1968. **Career:** School of Social Work, Univ of Pittsburgh, prof 1977; Simmons Coll, School of Social Work, assoc prof 1967-77; Episcopal Comm Serv of Philadelphia, social worker 1962-64; Boston Children's Serv Assn, supvr, adoption dept, 1957-62; Mental Health Center, consultant 1974; Natl Inst of Health, consultant 1975. **Orgs:** Bd mem New England Med Center Accreditation commn Council for Social Work Educ 1976-79; review panel Council for Intl Exchange of Scholars 1976-; bd mem Nat Conf of Social Welfare NIMH Fellowship 1964-67; bibliography Black Am Council on Social Work Educ 1970. **Honors/Awds:** Career Scientist Devel Award, Natl Inst of Mental Health, 1972-77; Black Children publ R & E Rsch Assn, 1976. **Business Addr:** Dept of Social Work, Univ of Pittsburgh, 2201 Cathedral/Learn, Pittsburgh, PA 15260-6371.

DUNMORE, GREGORY CHARLES
Journalist, fashion designer. **Personal:** Born Mar 24, 1958, Detroit, MI; son of Jo Thompson-Dunmore and Albert J Dunmore. **Educ:** National University of Mexico, BA, spanish, 1979; Cornell University, BS, industrial and labor relations, 1980. **Career:** Jo Thompson Productions Inc, director, fashion designer, 1985-; Michigan Chronicle Newspaper Agency, columnist, 1987-; Black Entertainment Television, On Line Productions, entertainment reporter, 1989-. **Orgs:** International Institute of Metro Detroit, vice pres of public relations, board of directors, 1990-; Natl Assn of Black Journalists, 1987-; Alpha Phi Alpha, 1989-; Harmonie Park Playhouse, advisory board, 1987-. **Honors/Awds:** Essence Magazine, Bachelor of the Year, 1992; Beefeater Gin's Fashion and Jazz Competition, Michigan Winner; Michigan Opera Theatre, Fellow; Congressman Crockett, Congressional Intern Fellow. **Special Achievements:** Producer, writer, director: "Jo Thompson: This Is My Life-Melodies and Madness!!!" one-woman show, Carnegie Hall, 1991; "Jo Thompson Show," New York's legendary Michael's Pub, 1992; fashion designer: Carlos Nina Haute Couture label. **Home Addr:** 16810 Muirland St, Detroit, MI 48221, (313)874-4734. **Business Addr:** Columnist, Michigan Chronicle, 479 Ledyard St, Detroit, MI 48201, (313)963-5522.

DUNMORE, LAWRENCE A., JR.
Physician. **Personal:** Born May 17, 1923, Georgetown, SC; married Gloria Parker; children: Gwendolyn, Jacquelyn, Lawrence, III. **Educ:** SC State Coll, BS; Howard U, MD; Johns Hopkins U, MPH 1970. **Career:** DC Gen Hospital DC Govt Sec Standard Investments & Standard Ltd Partnership, exec dir. **Orgs:** Mem Health Adv Planning Comm; adv bd Shaw Health Ctr; Health Priorities Subcomm; DC Govt Adv Bd Phys Asst Sch of Allied Health Howard Univ. **Honors/Awds:** Distinguished Pub Serv Award, Govt DC 1973; Outstanding Performance Award Dept Human Resources DC 1974. **Military Serv:** AUS.

DUNN, BRUCE ERIC
Broadcasting executive. **Personal:** Born Jul 23, 1959, Brooklyn, NY; son of Roberta Dunn and Robert Dunn. **Educ:** Ohio University, BS Communications, Associate of Philosophy 1977-82. **Career:** WOUB-TV, producer/director 1977-80; TPC Communications, associate dir 1981; WKID-TV, producer/director 1982, production manager 1983-84; WSCV-TV, operations manager 1985-87; Asst Producer ABC Sports 1987; vice pres One World Entertainment 1987; Black Entertainment Television, sports graphics coordinator, 1987-91; Telemundo Latin Network, operations manager, 1988-89; WPSX-TV, WPSU - FM, dir of program production, 1989-. **Orgs:** Police Benevolent Assn 1982-85. **Honors/Awds:** Floridas Directors Gil Chapter music video award 1984; ABC Sports Olympic Committee for 1984 Summer Olympics National Emmy; 1992 NBC Olympics in Barcelona, Graphics Manager. **Business Addr:** Dir of Program Production, WPSX-TV 3, WPSU - FM 91.5, Wagner Building, University Park, PA 16802, (814)865-7348.

DUNN, DAVID
Professional football player. **Personal:** Born Jun 10, 1972, San Diego, CA. **Educ:** Fresno State, attended. **Career:** Cincinnati Bengals, wide receiver, 1995-. **Business Addr:** Professional Football Player, Cincinnati Bengals, One Bengals Dr, Cincinnati, OH 45202, (513)621-3550.

DUNN, GEORGE WILLIAM
Judge. **Personal:** Born May 16, 1930, New York, NY; son of Helena Isabelle Stephenson and George William Dunn, Sr; married Kristin Ockershauser; children: Leslie Sharon, Darryl Clifford, Nicole Stephanie, Gregory Pascal. **Educ:** OH State Univ, BSE 1956, MA 1958; Univ of Southern CA, JD 1965. **Career:** Legal Aid Found, 1966-67; Private Practice, atty at law 1967-78; California State Univ at Long Beach, professor, 1974-; Long Beach Municipal Ct, judge 1979-88; Los Angeles Superior Court, Long Beach Branch, judge 1988-. **Orgs:** Dir Intl City Bank Long Beach 1984-91, 1996-; Rotary Club. **Honors/Awds:** Moot Ct Honors USC 1963-65; Justice Lassigned Ct of Appeal State CA 1980, 1985; prof, CA Judicial Coll, 1981-86. **Business Addr:** Judge, Long Beach Unified Court, Department 5, 415 W Ocean Blvd, Long Beach, CA 90802.

DUNN, JAMES EARL
Educator. **Personal:** Born Apr 7, 1955, Tunica, MS; son of Helen Dunn and Robert Dunn; married Dorothy Mae Collier. **Educ:** Northwest Jr Coll, 1975; Ft Gordon GA Comm Sch, diploma 1978; Ft Sill Field Artillery Sch, diploma 1981; Delta State Univ, BS 1978, MA 1983. **Career:** Tunica Jr HS, school teacher 1978-; County of Tunica, co supvr, currently. **Orgs:** Mem Natl Guard Assn 1978; mem NAACP 1980; mem Tunica Co PTA 1983; mem MS Assn of Supervisors 1984; mem 1984, bd of dir, 1989, Delta Council; treas Tunica Educ Assn 1983-; bd of dirs, North Delta Planning and Development District 1987. **Honors/Awds:** US Jaycees 1981; Man of the Yr United Voters of Tunica-Tunica Co 1983; Mem of Democratic Executive Committee state of Mississippi, 1988. **Military Serv:** ANG Captain 1986. **Home Addr:** PO Box 1463, Tunica, MS 38676.

DUNN, JASON
Professional football player. **Personal:** Born Nov 15, 1973, Harrodsburg, KY. **Educ:** Eastern Kentucky, attended. **Career:** Philadelphia Eagles, tight end, 1996-. **Business Addr:** Professional Football Player, Philadelphia Eagles, 3501 S Broad St, Philadelphia, PA 19148, (215)463-2500.

DUNN, JERRY MICHAEL
Head basketball coach. **Personal:** Born May 6, 1953, Raleigh, NC; son of Maelene Dunn Leake; married Gwendolyn Dunn, Apr 10, 1977. **Educ:** George Mason University, BS, education, 1980. **Career:** George Mason University, assistant coach, men's basketball, 1979-83; Penn State University, assistant coach, men's basketball, 1983-96, head basketball coach, 1996-. **Orgs:** National Assistant of Basketball Coaches; Black Coaches Association; Second Mile Charity Organizer, board of directors. **Honors/Awds:** NABC Coach of the Year, District #3, 1996. **Special Achievements:** National Clinician, USA Basketball Clinics, 1996; National Camp Speaker, college, 1996. **Business Addr:** Head Basketball Coach, Penn State University, 113 Bryce Jordan, University Park, PA 16802.

DUNN, KAYE. **See DUNHAM, KATHERINE.**

DUNN, MARVIN
Psychologist, educator. **Personal:** Born Jun 27, 1940, Deland, FL; married Linda Irene Lacy; children: Wanda, Fredrick, Kimberly, Jafari, Dierdre. **Educ:** Morehouse Coll, BA 1961; Roosevelt U, MA 1966; Univ of TND phd 1972. **Career:** Miami, psychologist 1970-71; Cultural & Human Interaction Center, dir, founder 1973-; FL Intl Univ, assoc prof 1972-; Acad for Comm Educ, dir. **Orgs:** Mem Nat Assn of Black Phychologists; Dade Co Psychol Assn; vice pres Dade Co Mental Hlth Assn; vice pres Dade-monroe Dist Mental Hlth D; treas FL State Assn of Dist Mental Hlth Bd 1975-76; bd of dir Dade Co Found for Emotionally Disturbed Youth 1975; bd of dir Ctr for Dialogue; mem bd of dir Transition Inc 1976-; pres of bd Driver Imprvmt

Prgm 1976-; mem FL Cncl for Comm Mental Hlth; commr 11th Judicial Circuit Nom Commn 1977; pres bd & Human Interaction Potential Inc; consult HEW/OCD Ford Found Early Admission to Coll Scholarship. **Honors/Awds:** Award KAY SE Reg 1957; acad schlrshp 1969-61; achiever of yr award Achievers of Grtr Miami Inc 1977. **Military Serv:** USN lt 1962-67. **Business Addr:** Dir, Academy for Community Educ, 39 Zamora Ave, Coral Gables, FL 33134.

DUNN, REGINALD ARTHUR
Judge. **Career:** Los Angeles County Superior Court, judge, currently. **Business Addr:** Judge, Superior Court, Los Angeles County, 111 N Hill St, Los Angeles, CA 90012, (213)974-5663.

DUNN, ROSS
Business executive (retired), county official. **Personal:** marrIed Rosa Lee; children: Martin De Rosseau, Rosephanye Tolandra, Kennedy Fitzgerald, Wilfred Julian. **Educ:** Alabama State University, BS, M administrative supervision. **Career:** Dunbar Elementary School, Pine Mtn GA, teacher, 1 year; Johnson Elementary School, Whitesville GA, teacher, 9 years; Laney Elementary School, Waverly Hall GA, teacher 1 year; Johnson Elementary School, West Point GA, principal, 3 years; Macon County School System, asst superintendent, 1 year; Muscogee County School District, administrative asst, 2 years; West Point Pepperell, personnel asst, personnel relations dept, 1974 until retirement. **Orgs:** Natl Education Assn; Muscogee County Assn; GA Education Assn; AL Education Assn; Textile Ind; pres, org, Chambers Cty Valley Br, NAACP; director, president, Huguley Water Systems; dir, Drew Rec Ctr; Goodwill Ind; AL Health Syst Agency; Chattahoochee Valley Area Assn for Retarded Children; bd mem, Chambers Cty Pensions & Security; Jr Achievement; Amer Red Cross; Gov Staff, Montgomery AL; exec bd, George H Lanier Council BSA; co-chmn, Chambers Co Child Abuse; Valley Chamber of Commerce; Valley Chap, AL State Univ Alumni; bd trustees, AL State Univ; org, Chambers Cty Voter Reg, responsible for 75 per cent of Black registered voters; Chambers County Commission, 1988-93, reelected 1992-96. **Honors/Awds:** Responsible for revamping elections, Chambers Cty Comm & Chambers Cty Bd of Ed, 1976; first Black to run for public office in Chambers County Dem Comm; OUtstanding Service, Boy Scouts of America, 1968; Autstanding 4-H Leader, 1969; Man of the Year, 1970, 1971; Essie Handy Award, 1971; Administrative Spirit Award, 1972; NAACP Citation Award, 1973; Democratic Club of Alabama Award, 1974; President's Award, NAACP, 1975; 100 Membership Award, NAACP, 1976-79; BSA Silver Beaver Award, 1978; BSA, Dist Award of Merit, 1977. **Special Achievements:** First Black elected, Chambers County Commission, District 1.

DUNN, W. PAUL
Aerospace engineer. **Personal:** Born Oct 2, 1938, Fort Worth, TX; son of Lillian Dunn and Willie Dunn; married Alnita Frances Rettig; children: Sheri, Brian. **Educ:** Univ of TX Austin, BS Civil Engr 1962; CA State Univ Los Angeles, MS Civil Engr 1969; CA State Univ Dominguez Hills, MBA Business Admin 1976. **Career:** Rocketdyne, research engr 1962-66; TRW Systems Group, mem tech staff 1966-71; Northrop Corp, mgr of engr 1971-77; The Aerospace Corp, 1977-, principal director, currently. **Orgs:** Consult Hi-shear Corp 1970; adv bd mem CA State Univ Los Angeles Minority Engr Prog 1983-86; chm Civil Engineering Visiting Committee, 1987-88. **Honors/Awds:** Public Service Award, Vice Pres US 1966; Manned Space Awareness Award NASA 1968; Award of Rec TRW Systems Group 1969; Special Achievement Award Sickle Cell Anemia Assn of TX 1979; Robert H Herndon Black Image Award 1985; Distinguished Graduate, Univ of Texas, Austin, 1993. **Home Addr:** 5625 Glenford St, Los Angeles, CA 90008. **Business Phone:** (310)336-5648.

DUNN, WARRICK
Professional football player. **Personal:** Born Jan 5, 1975. **Educ:** Florida State, bachelor's degree in information studies. **Career:** Tampa Bay Buccaneers, running back, 1997-. **Special Achievements:** NFL Draft, First round pick, #12, 1997. **Business Addr:** Professional Football Player, Tampa Bay Buccaneers, 1 Buccaneer Pl, Tampa, FL 33607, (813)870-2700.

DUNN, WILLIAM L.
Educator (retired). **Personal:** Born Feb 11, 1919, Birmingham; son of Levonia Dunn and Homer Dunn; married Greta L, Jun 1, 1965; children: Darryl, Michael, William Jr. **Educ:** AL A&M Univ, BS 1947; KS State Coll, MS 1953; FL State Univ, graduate study, 1974. **Career:** St John's Ben Franklin School, principal, 1962-65; Bethune-Cookman Coll, assoc prof of history, 1967-88, track coach, 1982, golf coach, 1994-96. **Orgs:** Family Eagles. **Honors/Awds:** Winner St Thomas Amateur Tournament 1964; plaque, United Negro Coll Fund, 1973; plaque, 1973, Leadership Award, 1987, NAACP; The Christian Community Award, Mt. Bethel Institutional Church, 1990; The Florence Roane and Anthony Hooks Memorial, 1990, King of Westside, 1989-91, Westside Business and Professional Association; B-CC Research Grant, Paramaribo, Surinam, Social Science Division, Bethune-Cookman College, 1982. **Military Serv:** US Army, T5, 1943-46; Good Conduct Medal. **Home Addr:** 823 N Kottle Cir, Daytona Beach, FL 32114.

DUNN-BARKER, LILLIAN JOYCE
Guidance counselor, educator. **Personal:** Born Aug 9, 1938, Robbins, IL; daughter of Margie Moore Wesley and Douglas Ivory Daniels; married Timothy T Barker, Aug 7, 1988; children: Darrin Douglas Dunn. **Educ:** St Augustine's Coll, BA (Phi Delta Kappa Hon Soc) 1960; Chicago State Univ, MS 1976; completed endorsement program in Urban School Admin/Super 1977. **Career:** Mission Union Aid Soc, sec 1956-91; Chicago Bd of Educ, teacher/English & French 1960-76, guidance counselor; Simeon Vocational High School, guidance dept, 1976-; Chicago Board of Educ, chairperson, 1986-. **Orgs:** Certified Vocational Evaluation Specialist; Commission on Certification of Work Adjustment & Voc Evaluation Specialist; mem Phi Delta Kappa Prof Educ Fraternity; pres Chicago State Univ/ St Augustine's Coll Alumni Assoc; Alpha Kappa Alpha Sorority; sec Posen Robbins School Bd 1983-85; sec Robbins Ambulance Fund Comm 1984-85; Pride of Robbins Temple #915 Elks IBPOE of W; dtr ruler, Pride of Tobbins Temple #915, 1988-91; advisor, Chicago Board of Ed, peer counselors 1991; Simeon, Chicago Bd of Ed, Drug Free Schools Program 1991; secretary, Illinois, Wisconsin State Association, IBPOE of W, Election Committee 1991; Illinois Fire & Police Commissioners Assn, Robbins IL, appointed by town of Robbins, 1991-. **Honors/Awds:** Past Grand Daughter Ruler Elks 1974; Teacher's Award Certificate Suburban Fed Credit Union 1977; One of the First Women on School Bd Dist 143 1/2; First Woman Sec 1983; work to form Robbins Park Dist, 1989. **Home Addr:** 13735 S Trumbull St, Robbins, IL 60472. **Business Addr:** Guidance Counselor, Simeon Voc HS, 8235 S Vincennes Ave, Chicago, IL 60620.

DUNNER, LESLIE B.
Symphony conductor. **Personal:** Born Jan 5, 1956, New York, NY; son of Audrey Hemmings Dunner and Lloyd Dunner. **Educ:** University of Rochester, East School of Music, Rochester, NY, BA, 1978; Queens College, New York, NY, MA, 1979; University of Cincinnati, College Conservatory of Music, Cincinnati, OH, DMA, 1982. **Career:** Carleton College, Northfield, MN, asst prof, 1982-86; Dance Theatre of Harlem, New York, NY, princ guest coductor, 1986-; Detroit Symphony, Detroit, MI, assoc conductor, 1987-; Dearborn Symphony, Dearborn, MI, music dir, 1989-. **Orgs:** Bd of directors, American Music Center, 1991. **Honors/Awds:** James Weldon Johnson Award, NAACP, 1991. **Home Addr:** 1300 Lafayette E, #911, Detroit, MI 48207.

DUNNIGAN, JERRY
Educator, artist. **Personal:** Born Jul 28, 1941, Cleveland; married Roberta; children: James, Jerome, Jeffrey. **Educ:** Dayton Art Inst Univ Dayton, BS 1965; Kent State U, MA 1970. **Career:** Linden Center, instructor 1964-65; Akron Art Inst, art instructor 1969-70; E Tech High School Black Acculturation Prog, instructor Black Art 1970-71; Nathan Hale Jr High School, dept chmn. **Orgs:** Mem Nat Conf Artists; numerous exhibitions Com Chmn OH; Div World Festival Black Art 1975. **Honors/Awds:** Scholarships Columbus Coll Art & Design 1960-63; Univ Dayton 1963-65; Martha Holden Jennings Found Tchr Leadership Award 1973. **Business Addr:** 3588 East Blvd, Cleveland, OH 44105.

DUNNINGS, STUART, II
Attorney. **Personal:** Born Oct 29, 1952, Lansing, MI; son of Janet Taylor Dunnings and Stuart J Dunnings; married Cynthia Marie, Oct 22, 1977; children: Courtney R, Coral S M. **Educ:** Amherst College, BA, 1974; University of Michigan School of Law, JD, 1979. **Career:** Dunnings & Frawley PC, attorney, 1980-. **Orgs:** NAACP, Lansing branch, 2nd vice pres, 1993; State Bar of Michigan, standing committee on character & fitness, 1988-. **Business Addr:** Attorney, Dunnings & Frawley PC, 530 S Pine St, Lansing, MI 48933, (517)487-8222.

DUNSON, CARRIE LEE
Educational administrator. **Personal:** Born Apr 19, 1946, Kansas City, MO; daughter of Roberta Dunson and Walter Dunson; divorced; children: Anthony, Darren Harris. **Educ:** Lincoln Univ, Jefferson City MO, BS Psychology 1974; Central MO State Univ Warrensburg, MS Corrections 1975, Educ Spec 1976; Univ of MO at Kansas City, PhD 1990. **Career:** USMC, Kansas City MO, mail clerk supvr, 1967; Washington DC Police Dept, supvr documents, 1971; MO Div of Ins, Jefferson City, sec, test examiner 1973; Central MO State Univ Warrensburg, instructor criminal justice 1975, asst prof indus security 1978, dir of equal employment 1978-. **Orgs:** Sponsor Sigma Gamma Rho Sorority 1975; mem Assn of Black Collegiates 1975, Amer Soc Indus Sec 1978, Order of Eastern Star KS Chapter 1973; Commn on Human Rights, MO Commn on Human Rights, 1976; mem, co-chmn, Commn of MO Affirmative Action Assn, 1979; Assn of Black Women in Higher Educ, 1980. **Honors/Awds:** Honorary Mention in Scholarship, Ford Found 1971; Outstanding Young Women of Amer, Montgomery AL 1978; Certificate of Appreciaiton Jericho Rd Award MLK 1979-80. **Business Addr:** Dir of Equal Employment, Central MO State Univ, Affirmative Action, Warrensburg, MO 64093.

DUNSTON, ALFRED G.
Clergyman. **Personal:** Born Jun 25, 1915, Coinjock, NC; divorced; children: Carol J Goodrich, Aingred G James, Dr Armayne G. **Educ:** Livingstone Coll, 1938; Hood Theol Sem; Drew U; Allen U, DD; Liberia Coll, Monrovia, Liberia, DCL. **Career:** African Methodist Episcopal Zion Ch, bishop; Mother AME Zion, NYC, 1963-64; Big Wesley AME Zion, Phila, 1952-63; Logan Temple AME Zion, Knoxville, 1948-52; Wallace Chapel AME Zion, Summit, NJ, 1946-48; Price Mem AME Zion, Atlantic City, 1941-43; Wallace Temple, Bayonne 1939-41; St John AME Zion,NC 1937-38; Mt Sinai AME Zion, NC, 1936-37. **Orgs:** Tchr Inst for Black Ministries; narrator TV documentaries, "Run From Race" & "The Rising New Africa"; author "Black Man in the Old Testament and Its World" 1974; mem Philadelphia Human Relations Commn 1963; partic Selective Patronage Prgm 1960-63; co-founder OIC 1963; fdr, princ 92nd Inf Div Arty Illiteracy Sch 1943. **Honors/Awds:** Citation for Meritorious Service 92nd Inf Div 1945; 2 Battle Stars. **Military Serv:** AUS chaplain (capt) 1943-46.

DUNSTON, SHAWON DONNELL
Professional baseball player. **Personal:** Born Mar 21, 1963, Brooklyn, NY. **Career:** Infielder: Chicago Cubs, 1985-. **Honors/Awds:** Shares modern major league record for most triples in a game (3), 1990; National League All-Star Team, 1988. **Business Addr:** Professional Baseball Player, Chicago Cubs, 1060 W Addison St, Wrigley Field, Chicago, IL 60613-4397.

DUNSTON, VICTOR
Dentist. **Personal:** Born May 2, 1926, Atlantic City, NJ; son of Florence Lomax Dunston and Walter Rufus Dunston; married Lonnetta Gumbs, May 4, 1963 (divorced); children: Walter, Phillip; children: Victor, Mark. **Educ:** Temple Univ Dental Sch, DDS 1952. **Career:** Private Practice, dentist 1953-89. **Orgs:** Mem, ADA; New Era Dental Soc; bd mem Fellowship House 1961-63; Lower Merion Human Relations Council 1968-72; mem bd of dir Berean Savings & Loan Assn 1977-89. **Military Serv:** USN elctrcns mate 3 class 1945-46.

DUNSTON, WALTER T.
Dentist. **Personal:** Born Jun 3, 1935, Williamsport, PA; children: Walter Jr, Michelle, Connie, Mark. **Educ:** Lycoming Coll, BS 1956; Temple Univ Dental School, DDS 1960. **Career:** Dental Serv Inst of PA Hospital, chief 1968-; Temple Univ Dental School, instructor 1965-67; Univ of PA Dental School, instructor 1967-; private practice, dentist, currently. **Orgs:** Mem bd trustees Lycoming Coll; mem Amer Dental Assoc, Natl Dental Assoc, PA State Dental Assoc; Fellow of Royal Sci of Health London England; mem New Era Dental School of Philadelphia; pres E Coast Investment Corp; apptd commanding officer Naval Reserve Dental Co 4-1; emm Naval Reserve Assoc, Philadelphia Cty Dental Soc. **Military Serv:** USN Dental Corps 31 yrs; navy captain, retired.

DUPER, MARK SUPER
Professional football player. **Personal:** Born Jan 25, 1959, Pineville, LA; married Renee Duper; children: Tracy, Stacey, Mark II, Alexandria, Kirby. **Educ:** Northwestern State Univ. **Career:** Miami Dolphins, wide receiver, 1982-. **Orgs:** Omega Psi Phi Fraternity Inc. **Honors/Awds:** First team All-AFC Choice by UPI, 1984; rated as number one receiver in AFC and number two in NFL by Sportsgrams computer rating system; played in Pro Bowl, 1983, 1984, 1986. **Business Addr:** Professional Football Player, Miami Dolphins, 2269 NW 199th St, Miami, FL 33056, (305)620-5500.

DUPRE, JOHN LIONEL
Psychiatrist, deacon. **Personal:** Born Dec 6, 1953, New Orleans, LA; son of Leverne Boutte Dupre and Antoine Joseph Dupre, Jr; married Yadira Gisella McGrath Dupre, Sep 2, 1984; children: Joya Gabrielle Dupre. **Educ:** Tulane University, New Orleans, LA, BS, 1975; Tulane Medical School, MD, 1979; Univ of California-San Francisco Residency Program, San Francisco, CA, 1979-83. **Career:** San Quentin State Prison, San Quentin, CA, staff psychiatrist, 1983-; Private Practice, Psychiatry, San Francisco, CA, 1983-. **Orgs:** Former president, Black Psychiatrists of Northern California, 1985-89; member, APA; member, NAMA. **Business Addr:** Psychiatrist, 2358 Pine St, San Francisco, CA 94115.

DUPREE, DAVID
Sportswriter. **Personal:** Born May 31, 1946, Seattle, WA; married Gail; children: Bubba (Jondavid). **Educ:** Univ WA, BA 1969. **Career:** WA Post, sportswrtr 1971-; Wall St Jour, stf wrtr 1969-71; Seattle Post-Intelligencer, sportswrtr 1968-69. **Orgs:** Mem Professional Basketball Writers Assn of Am; Baseball Writers Assn; Football Writers Assn; Track & Field Fedn; Nat Urban League 1968.

DUPREE, DAVID H.
Attorney, educator. **Personal:** Born Aug 18, 1959, Knoxville, TN; son of Eloise Edwards Dupree and William F Dupree (deceased). **Educ:** Howard Univ Sch of Business & Public Admin, BBA 1981; Howard Univ Sch of Law, JD 1984. **Career:** Howard Univ Academic Computing Svcs, student rsch asst 1978-84,

systems analyst 1985-87; Self-Employed, rsch methodologist 1979-; Law Offices of David Dupree, attorney 1985-; Howard University School of Business, instructor, 1990-94. **Orgs:** Mem Computer Law Assn 1985-, DC Computer Law Forum 1985-, PA Bar Assn 1985, PA Supreme Ct Bar 1985-; mem Amer Judicature Soc 1986, DC Bar Assn 1986, Tax Court of the US 1986-, Amer Bar Assn 1986, DC Court of Appeals 1986-; bd mem Achievement Scholarship Program 1986-; mem, trustee bd, Greater Mt Calvary Holy Church, 1988-; mem, US District Court, DC, 1989-; mem, Delta Sigma Pi Business Fraternity, 1980-; mem, Phi Alpha Delta Legal Fraternity, 1984-. **Honors/Awds:** Special Serv Awd Howard Univ Comp & Info System Soc 1982; Meritorious Serv Awd Howard Univ Academic Computing 1984; co-author, Affect of Parent Practices on Reading Achievement 1983; Does Rosen Still Live, An Analysis of Gift Tax Income Exclusion on Non-income Producing Property 1984. **Business Addr:** Attorney, 6722 3rd St NW, Ste 103, Washington, DC 20012.

DUPREE, EDWARD A.
Program administrator. **Personal:** Born Mar 24, 1943, Farmville, NC; son of Nellie Fields Lunsford and David Dupree; married Helen Roberts Dupree, Aug 14, 1965; children: Davido M. **Educ:** North Carolina Central University, Durham, NC, BA, 1965; Howard University School of Social Work, Washington, DC, MA, social work, 1968. **Career:** Baltimore City Dept Social Services, Baltimore, MD, casework supervisor, 1968-70; Model Cities Agency, Baltimore, MD, chief, community information division, 1970-80; Urban Services Agency, Baltimore, MD, chief, energy/housing programs, 1980-. **Orgs:** Member, American Association of Blacks in Energy, 1980-; member, Howard University Alumni Association, 1968-; member, National Forum for Black Public Administrators, 1989-; Maryland Energy Directors Association, 1984-; North Carolina Central University Alumni Association, 1966-. **Honors/Awds:** Outstanding Maryland Energy Assistance Prog Director, Maryland Dept of Human Resources, 1987; City Council of Baltimore Resolution, Baltimore City Council, 1982, 1987; House Resolution, Maryland House of Delegates, 1980; Citizen Citation, City of Baltimore, 1990; Vice President's Citation, Vice President of City Council of Baltimore, 1990. **Home Addr:** 2629 Cross Country Blvd, Baltimore, MD 21215. **Business Addr:** Chief, Energy Programs, Urban Services Agency, 501 E Fayette St, Lower Level, Baltimore, MD 21202.

DUPREE, SANDRA KAY
Librarian. **Personal:** Born Jul 17, 1956, Warren, AR; daughter of Erie Ingram and Asibear Dupree; married Paul David Russell, Aug 28, 1982; children: David Dupree Russell. **Educ:** University of Arkansas, Pine Bluff, AR, BA, 1978; Atlanta University, Atlanta, GA, MSLS, 1979; Texas Woman's University, Denton, TX, 1985. **Career:** Public Library of Columbus and Franklin County, Columbus, OH, intern, 1979-80; Bradley County Library, Warren, AR, director, 1980-81; University of Arkansas, Pine Bluff, AR, instructor, 1982; Southeast Arkansas Regional Library, Monticello, AR, specialist, 1982-83; University of Arkansas, Monticello, AR, asst librarian, 1984-. **Orgs:** Member, American Library Assn, 1980-; member, Arkansas Library Assn, 1980-; head of nominating committee, Southeast AR Concert of the Arts, 1987-; board member, Friends of Monticello Branch Library, 1988-; board member, Arkansas Endowment for Humanities, 1986-89. **Honors/Awds:** Honorary Member, Phi Kappa Delta, 1987. **Home Addr:** PO Box 312, Monticello, AR 71655. **Business Addr:** Assistant Librarian, University of Arkansas at Monticello, PO Box 3599, Monticello, AR 71656, (501)460-1080.

DUPREE, SHERRY SHERROD
Librarian, educator, author. **Personal:** Born Nov 25, 1946, Raleigh, NC; daughter of Elouise Heartley Sherrod and Matthew Needham Sherrod; married Herbert Clarence DuPree, Jan 11, 1975; children: Amil, Andre, Andrew. **Educ:** NC Central Univ, BS Voc Home Economics 1968, MA Educ Media 1969; Univ of MI, AMLS Academic Librarian 1974, EdS Instructional Tech 1978. **Career:** Eastern MI Univ, visiting prof educ media 1974; Ann Arbor Public Schools, media specialist 1970-76; University of Florida, associate ref librarian, 1977-83, Institute of Black Culture, project director, 1982-92; Santa Fe Community College, reference librarian, 1983-; Gospel Music Hall of Fame and Museum, Detroit, archivist, 1995-. **Orgs:** Mem Zeta Phi Beta Sor Inc 1967-, NAACP 1977-, Alachua Library League 1977-; pres Univ of FL Library Assn 1981-82; mem Amer Library Assn, Assn of Coll & Rsch Libraries FL Chapt, Black FOCUS, Williams Temple Church of God in Christ; member, Florida Library Assn, 1980-; member, Society for Pentecostal Studies, 1987-; member, Society of American Archivists, 1986-; member, Florida Assn of Community Colleges, 1983-; International Platform Assn, Rosewood Massacre, chairperson, 1994-; Religion Caucus, FL Library Assn, chairperson, 1994-96; Society for Pentecostal Studies, editorial bd, 1994-. **Honors/Awds:** NC Central University, Procter & Gamble Award for Outstanding Student in Home Economics, 1968, Graduate Fellowship, 1968-69; State of Florida, Governor's Award for Outstanding Florida Citizen, 1986; National Endowment for the Humanities, Travel Grant, 1986; Smithsonian Institution, Visiting Research Fellowship, 1987; Southern Regional Education Board, Travel Grant, 1988-92; The Intl Women's Day, The Sojourner Truth Award, 1995; Florida Conference of Black State Legislators, honoree. **Special Achievements:** Author, books/articles including: "Library Media Ctr & Classroom Displays" w/Hertha Jenkins, Media Spectrum 1976; "Mini-Course in Library Skills" Univ of FL 1983; "WhatYou Always Wanted to Know About the Card Catalog But Was Afraid to Ask" 3rd edition revised Displays for Schs Inc 1987; African-American Holiness Pentecostal Movement: An Annotated Bibliography, Garland Publishing, NY, 1996; African-American Good News (Gospel) Music, w/Herbert C DuPree, Middle Atlantic Regional Press, 1993; Exposed !!!: Federal Bureau of Investigation (F.B.I.) Unclassified Reports on Churches and Church Leaders, w/Herbert C DuPree, Middle Atlantic Regional Press, 1993; editor, Biographical Dictionary of African-American Holiness Pentecostals: 1880-1990, 1989. **Business Addr:** Reference Librarian, Santa Fe Comm College, 3000 NW 83rd St, Library P-208, Gainesville, FL 32602.

DUPRI, JERMAINE
Record company executive. **Personal:** Born Sep 23, 1972, Asheville, NC. **Career:** So So Def Recordings, CEO, currently. **Special Achievements:** Label acts include: Kriss Kross, Xscape, Da Brat, Yvette Michele; written and produced for: TLC, Mariah Carey, The Notorious B.I.G., Sylk Times Leather. **Business Addr:** Chief Executive Officer, So-So Def Recordings, 685 Lambert Dr NE, Atlanta, GA 30324, (404)888-9900.

DURAND, HENRY J., JR.
Educator. **Personal:** Born Jun 14, 1948, Griffith, GA; son of Mildred C Durand and Henry J Durand Sr; married Bonita Ruth Cobb, Nov 12, 1979; children: Anitra R, Kendra N, Aprille L, Leroy Alan Larkin. **Educ:** Denison University, BA, sociology, 1971; Xavier University, MEd, 1976; University of Cincinnati, EdD, 1988. **Career:** Cincinnati Board of Education, classroom teacher, reading specialist, 1974-76; University of Cincinnati, instructor, acting director, reading & study skills program, 1976-80, College of Medicine, director, learning resources, 1980-82; Bushido Training Programs, training director, 1982-86; Northern Kentucky University, assistant professor, sociology, 1987-90; SUNY at Buffalo, Center for Applied Public Affairs, senior research associate, 1990-, Center for Academic Development, director, 1990-. **Orgs:** American Educational Research Association; American Association of Higher Education; American Association of University Administrators; American Society for Training & Development; United University Professions. **Home Addr:** 153 Winspear, Buffalo, NY 14215, (716)835-8244. **Business Addr:** Director, Center for Academic Development, Applied Public Affairs Studies Professor, SUNY at Buffalo, 208 Norton Hall, Buffalo, NY 14260, (716)645-3072.

DURAND, WINSLEY, JR.
Consultant. **Personal:** Born Jul 29, 1941, Bunkie, LA; son of Mr & Mrs Winsley Durand, Sr; married Sonya Marie; children: Winsley III, Janay. **Educ:** Southern Univ, BS 1968; Bradley Univ, 1974; USL, 1963; Univ of IL, MBA 1987. **Career:** Western Engr, SALES, Special Assignment employee relations 1973, sales devel engr 1971-72, Acct coordinator 1970-71; Caterpillar Tractor Co, Equal Employment Coordinator 1977-, relations rep mgr 1974-, application engr 1970, jr sales devel engr 1968-70; Mgr Technical Recruiting 1987-; Caterpillar Inc, Peoria IL, annual quality improvement coordinator, 1988. **Orgs:** Civil Rights Movement 1960-65; chmn shop talk auto-mech Tire Rubber & Steel Co 1976; mem So Coll Placement Assn; SW Coll Placement Assn; chmn pres Carver Comm Ctr 1972-77; bd mem Tri Co Labor Educ & Indus Counsel 1977; chmn Voter Reg Drive 1976; pres Peoria Black Political Assembly 1974-75; pres; greater Peoria Big Brother/Big Sister, 1982; bd advisory, Greater Peoria Foundation, 1986; bd mem, Peoria Public Library, 1987; pres, greater Peoria Library Bd, 1992; pres, Greater Peoria Private Industry Council, (PIC), 1993-95. **Honors/Awds:** Outstanding Newmanite for Leadership 1963; Outstanding Marine of Year Award 1965; outstanding marine award, outstanding leadership in civilian work Marines 1969; Dress Blue & Leather Neck Award 1965. **Military Serv:** USM sgt. **Business Addr:** Mgr Reengineering, Caterpillar Inc, 600 NE Washington St, Peoria, IL 61603.

DURANT, ANITA. See MARSHALL, ANITA.

DURANT, CELESTE MILLICENT
Media executive. **Personal:** Born Apr 23, 1947, New York, NY. **Educ:** Columbia Journalism, MSJ 1970; Grinnell Coll, AB Hist 1968. **Career:** KCOP, exec producer, currently; LA Times, staff writer, beginning 1972; Dayton Journal Herald, staff writer 1970-72; Life Mag, publicity asst 1968-70; freelance writer. **Honors/Awds:** Recip LA Press Club Award 1974; OH Newspaper Women's Feature Writing Award 1971. **Business Addr:** Executive Producer, KCOP, 7121 S Olive Way, Englewood, CO 80112-1620.

DURANT, CHARLES E.
Educational administrator. **Personal:** Born Jul 2, 1949, Lynchburg, SC; son of Adeline Durant and William James Durant. **Educ:** State University College, BS, 1971; University of South Carolina, MEd, 1977, EdD, 1985. **Career:** Syracuse City School District, high school teacher, 1971-72; University of Delaware, complex coordinator, 1972-76; University of South Carolina, administrative assistant, 1977-79; The Colorado College, director of residential programs and housing, 1979-82; University of Massachusetts, assistant director of housing services, 1983-89; Indiana State University, dean of student life, 1989-. **Orgs:** Terre Haute Volunteer Action Center, 1992-; Planned Parenthood of Southern Indiana, advisory council, 1990-; Vigo County Public Library, agency bond trainer, 1992-; Covered Bridge Girl Scout Council, accreditation team member, 1991-92; Indiana State University, Student Chapter of the NAACP, faculty advisor, 1992-; Tri-County Youth Services, MA, clerk, board of governors, 1987-89; Association of College & University Housing Offices, journal board, 1988-. **Honors/Awds:** El Dupont Minority Achievers Award, 1976; University of South Carolina, Distinguished Alumni, Educational Administration Program, 1992-93. **Business Phone:** (812)237-3822.

DURANT, KAREN
Music company executive. **Personal:** Born Oct 7, New York, NY; daughter of Frank & Frankie Jackson; divorced; children: Darren Emil Simon. **Career:** CBS Records, manager, 1978-88; Jive Records/Zomba Music, manager, 1988-90; Rondor Music, creative manager, 1992, gen manager, 1994-; EDMI Records, director of A&R, 1992-94. **Orgs:** NARAS. **Business Addr:** Executive Director/General Manager, Rondor Music International, 110 Greene St, Ste 1102, New York, NY 10012, (212)226-5995.

DURANT, NAOMI C.
Clergyman. **Personal:** Born Jun 23, 1938, Baltimore, MD; married Albert; children: George, Victoria, Rodney, Hope. **Educ:** Baltimore Coll of the Bible, DD 1970. **Career:** New Refuge Deliverance Holiness Church Inc, bishop founder 1967-; 4 Churches in Baltimore & Wash Area, overseer bishop; Radio Stations WEBB WSID WUST, gospel disc jockey 1968-73. **Orgs:** Mem Advocates of Bltmr 1971; Ada Chap #1 Order of Eastern Star. **Honors/Awds:** Recipient hon BTH degree MD Bible Coll 1972. **Business Addr:** 1225 E Eager St, Baltimore, MD 21208.

DURANT, THOMAS JAMES, JR.
College professor. **Personal:** Born Apr 9, 1941, Mansfield, LA; son of Lena B Jones Durant and Thomas J Durant Sr; married Mary C Peyton; children: Thomas III, Timothee, Tyrone. **Educ:** Grambling State Univ, BS 1963; Tuskegee Inst, MS 1966; Univ of WI-Madison, PhD 1973. **Career:** US Peace Corps St Lucia Project, agric extension 1963-65; Tuskegee Inst, rsch assoc 1966-68; Virginia State Univ, assoc prof 1972-73; Louisiana State Univ, assoc prof of sociology 1973-95, prof of sociology, 1995-. **Orgs:** International Rsch Ghana West Africa/USAID 1978; Rural Devel Rsch Sierra Leone West Africa/USAID 1983, 84, 86; mem NAACP, Amer Sociological Assoc, Southern Sociological Soc, Rural Southwestern Mid-South and Southern Societies. **Honors/Awds:** Phi Beta Sigma Frat Inc Omicron Beta Sigma 1961-; Gamma Sigma Delta Honor Soc LA State Univ 1979-86; guest editor Sociological Spectrum Sociology Journal 1984, 1995; Omicron Delta Kappa Leadership Soc LSU Chap 1986. **Business Addr:** Prof of Sociology, Louisiana State University, Dept of Sociology, Baton Rouge, LA 70803.

DURANT-PAIGE, BEVERLY
Public relations executive. **Personal:** Born Nov 7, New York, NY; daughter of Eunice Fuller and Wesley Durant; divorced; children: Desiree Spirit. **Educ:** Hunter Coll, 1974. **Career:** CBS Records, NY, mgr publicity, 1978; Howard Bloom Public Relations, NY, sr account exec, 1983; PAIGE ONE Public Relations, NY, pres/CEO, 1985; Polygram Inc, senior director of national publicity; Interscope Records, vice pres, publicity, black music, currently. **Orgs:** Public Relations Soc of New York; life mem, NAACP. **Honors/Awds:** The Lillian Award, Delta Sigma Theta, 1988; Award of Appreciation, New York City Police Dept, 1989; named by Ebony Magazine as one of the industry's top publicists. **Business Addr:** Vice President, Publicity, Black Music, Interscope Records, 540 Madison Ave, New York, NY 10019.

DURDEN, EARNEL
Automobile dealer, coach. **Personal:** Born Jan 24, 1937, Los Angeles; married June Pecot; children: Mike, Kevin, Allan. **Educ:** OR State U, BS 1959; CA State Univ Long Beach, MA 1969; CA State Bd of Edn, Life Diploma. **Career:** General Motors automobile dealer currently; San Diego Chargers, backfield rec, 1974-83; Houston Oilers, off bckfld 1972-73; LA Rams, off bckfld 1971-72; UCLA, off bckfld coach 1969-71; Vrsty Lg Bch CA State U, hd fresh coach asst dfnsv bckfld coach 1968-69; Compton Coll, dfnsv bckfld coach 1966-68; Compton HS, bckfld coach wrstlng coach 1963-66; Jr HS, tchr coach entrprs 1960-63; LA Co Pks & Rec, dir 1959-60; Spl Sprt Prg for Yng Men, spl asst dir & orgnzr; San Diego Chargers, offensive backfield coach. **Honors/Awds:** Recip 1st black Joe Coll OR State 1956-57; 1st black football coach UCLA; 1st black coach CA State Univ Lg Bch; 1st black cch LA Rams; 1st black coach Houston Oilers; 1st team Pcfc Coast Conf 1956-57; All Am 1956; selected to Hula Bowl 1958; played in Rose Bowl Game 1957; tied for lngst contns serv for 13 seasons on Charger Staff. **Business Addr:** Coach, San Diego Chargers, Jack Murphy Stadium, 9449 Friars Rd, San Diego, CA 92108.

DUREN, EMMA THOMPSON
Educator. **Personal:** Born Jun 28, 1925, Macon, GA; married Edward Lee Duren Sr; children: Edward Lee Jr, Timothy Leon. **Educ:** Winston-Salem Teachers Coll, BS Educ 1958; Woman's Coll Univ of NC, MEd 1964; Univ of Minnesota, additional studies. **Career:** Winston-Salem City Schools, teacher 1958-76; Winston-Salem State Univ, coord of intermediate educ, prof of educ 1976-. **Orgs:** Mem NEA, NCAE, ASCD, IRA; mem bd of advisors Student NC Assoc of Educ; pres WSSU-NCAE; coord Intermediate Educ WSSU; mem Alpha Kappa Mu, NAACP, YWCA, NCNW; sec Carolina Conference CME Church; mem bd of dirs Experiment of Self-Reliance. **Honors/Awds:** Teacher of the Year 1975, Reynolds Scholarship Awd 1975 Winston-Salem/Forsyth Sch; one of first women on Judicial Court of the CME Church 1978-86; Excellencein Teaching Awd WSSU 1980. **Home Addr:** 3740 Spaulding Dr, Winston-Salem, NC 27105. **Business Addr:** Coord-Intermediate Educ, Winston-Salem State Univ, PO Box 13207, Winston-Salem, NC 27105.

DURHAM, C. SHELBY
Rehabilitation company executive. **Personal:** Born Jul 25, 1960, Crawl Hill, Bermuda; daughter of Coolidge & Julia L Durham; married Melvin T Jackson, Sep 4, 1993. **Educ:** Bermuda College, general certificates of education, 1977; North Carolina Agricultural & Technical State University, BA, 1981; Howard University, MS, 1983. **Career:** Department of Education, Bermuda, child dev diagnostician, 1981; Ministry of Health & Social Svcs, Bermuda, speech therapy intern, 1983; Howard University, teaching assistant, 1983-84; In Speech, Inc, speech pathologist, 1984-86; Keystone Rehabilitation Systems, speech pathologist, 1986-87, district director, 1987-92; Rehab Options Inc, president/CEO, 1992-. **Orgs:** ASHA, 1983-96; NAWBO, 1995-96; NAFE, 1995-96; NCNW, Inc, 1995-96. **Honors/Awds:** National Coalition of 100 Black Women, Inc, Recognition Awd, 1993; Business Philadelphia & NAWBO, Women to Watch, 1995; African-American Chamber of Commerce, Small Business of the Year, 1995; The Philadelphia Inquirer, 10 Making a Difference, 1996. **Business Addr:** President/CEO, Rehab Options Inc, 111 Presidential Blvd, Ste 101, Bala Cynwyd, PA 19004, (610)617-8775.

DURHAM, EDDIE L., SR.
Government official, publisher. **Personal:** Born Mar 17, 1946, Newellton, LA; son of Annie B Emerson Durham and Rev Albert E Durham; married Fannie Henderson, Dec 14, 1966; children: Eddie Jr, Robert. **Educ:** Southern Univ, Baton Rouge LA, BA English, 1968; Harvard Univ, Cambridge MA, attended, 1967; Univ of Utah, Salt Lake City Ut, MS Admin, 1974. **Career:** Stauffer Chemical Co, Dayton NJ, mgmt trainee, 1969-70; Agway Chemical Co, Yardville NJ, asst plant mgr, 1970-71; New Jersey Dept of Labor, Trenton NJ, claims reviewer, 1971-72, personnel asst, 1972-74, chief of admin, 1974-76, administrative director, 1976-; Red Hot Publishing Co., president, 1989-; Home Income Reporter, nesletter, editor/publisher, 1990-; Success Incorporated, president, 1992-. **Orgs:** Mem, Political Action Comm of Willingboro, 1975-82; pres, Amer Soc for Public Admin (New Jersey), 1976-77; dir, First Peoples Bank of New Jersey, 1977-82; mem, Willingboro Township Council, 1977-82; dir, Saints' Memorial Community Church, 1979-; mem, Blacks in Govt, 1984-, Forum for Black Public Admin, 1986-; dir, Better Day Care Center, 1986-. **Honors/Awds:** Service Award, Saints' Memorial Community Church, 1983, 1984; Service Award, Cathedral of Love, 1989. **Special Achievements:** Editor/pubisher, Home Income Reporter Newsletter, 1990-. **Business Addr:** Administrative Director, New Jersey Department of State, 820 Bear Tavern Rd, 3rd Floor, CN 300, Trenton, NJ 08625.

DURHAM, JOSEPH THOMAS
Educational administrator. **Personal:** Born Nov 26, 1923, Raleigh, NC; son of Serena Hooker Durham and Watt Durham Sr; married Alice Spruill; children: LaDonna D Stamper, LaVerne. **Educ:** Morgan State Coll, AB (honors) 1948; Temple Univ, EdM 1949; Columbia Univ, EdD 1963. **Career:** New Lincoln School, teacher 1956-58; Southern Univ, prof 1958-60; Coppin State Coll, chmn educ 1960-63; Albany State Coll, dean & prof 1963-65; Coppin State Coll, dean of college 1965-68; IL State Univ, assoc dean educ 1968-72; Howard Univ, dean of school of educ 1972-75; Coppin State Coll Baltimore, dean of educ 1975-76; MD State Bd for Higher Educ, dir inst approval; Comm Coll of Baltimore, pres, 1985-90; Morgan State Univ, prof; Coppin State Coll, lecturer, currently. **Orgs:** Mem Phi Delta Kappa; mem Alpha Phi Alpha; visiting prof Univ of New Hampshire 1966. **Honors/Awds:** Fellow General Educ Bd 1953-54; Fellow Danforth Found 1975; "The Story of Civil Rights as Seen by the Black Church" DC Cook Publishing Co 1971; Commissioner Montgomery Co Human Relations 1983-86; Presidential Leadership Medallion, Univ of Texas, 1989. **Military Serv:** USAF sgt 3 yrs; Good Conduct Medal; Philippine Liberation Medal; Pacific Theater Medal. **Home Addr:** 13102 Morningside Lane, Silver Spring, MD 20904. **Business Addr:** Lecturer in Education, Coppin State College, Baltimore, MD 21216, (410)383-5449.

DURHAM, LEON
Professional baseball player (retired). **Personal:** Born Jul 31, 1957, Cincinnati, OH; married Angela; children: Loren. **Career:** St Louis Cardinals, outfielder/infielder, 1980; Chicago Cubs, outfielder/infielder, 1981-88; Cincinnati Reds, infielder, 1988; St Louis Cardinals, infielder, 1989. **Orgs:** Donated $25,500 to Chicago Public HS Athletic Prog. **Honors/Awds:** Ken Hubbs Memorial Award, Baseball Writers Assn of America, Chicago Chapter; National League All-Star Game, 1983; Amer Assn Rookie of the Year 1979. **Business Addr:** Chicago Cubs, 1060 W Addison St, Chicago, IL 60613.

DURHAM, RAY
Professional baseball player. **Personal:** Born Nov 30, 1971, Charlotte, NC. **Career:** Chicago White Sox, infielder, 1995-. **Business Addr:** Professional Baseball Player, Chicago White Sox, 333 W 35th St, Chicago, IL 60616, (312)924-1000.

DURHAM, WILLIAM R.
Federal government official. **Personal:** Born Feb 5, 1945, Woodruff, SC; son of Frances Brewton and Marion Brewton; married Carol Almeda Pearson; children: Kenyatta. **Educ:** South Carolina State Coll, BS 1967; Howard Univ, MBA 1978. **Career:** Federal Power Commn, accountant 1969-79; JIMLA Inc, pres 1982-85; Fed Energy Regulatory Commn, section mgr 1980-89, dir, internal control, 1990-. **Orgs:** Past pres 1981-90, bd of dirs Resources Fed Credit Union; pres Washington DC Chap Natl Black MBA Assoc 1982-84; bd of dirs Natl Black MBA Assoc 1982-83; mem Kappa Alpha Psi Frat, NAACP, Transafrica, Natl Rainbow Coalition, Millwood Waterford Civic Assoc, Blacks in Govt; leader Quality Circle, Federal Energy Regulator Commn. **Honors/Awds:** Meritorious Service and Outstanding Leadership Awds MBA Assoc 1981,83. **Military Serv:** US Army, captain, 2 yrs active, 6 yrs reserve; Bronze Star, Medal for Meritorious Service, Vietnam, 1968-69. **Business Addr:** Director, Internal Control, Federal Energy Reg Commn, 825 North Capitol St, Washington, DC 20002.

DUROJAIYE, PRINCE. See HICKS, WILLIE LEE.

DUSTER, BENJAMIN C.
Consultant. **Personal:** Born Mar 15, 1927, Chicago, IL; son of Alfreda Barnett Duster (deceased) and Benjamin C Duster (deceased); married Murrell Higgins, Aug 22, 1954; children: Alice Duster Pennamon, Benjamin C IV, Karen Duster Reynolds, Muriel Duster DeVore. **Educ:** DePaul U, JD 1954; Grad Sch Bus Univ Chgo, MBA Exec Program 1968. **Career:** Pvt practice, atty 1955-68, Atty 1979-; GH Walker & Co, stockbroker 1968-71; Chicago Comm Ventures Inc, pres chief exec 1971-79; Williams Rux Hill Whitefield Ltd, spec counsel finance invest 1979-80; Cimply Complex Communications Systems Corp, founder/president, 1980-. **Orgs:** Chmn IL Commn on Human Relations 1971-73; vice pres bd trustees Allendale Sch for Boys 1968-; gen counsel Chatham Village Assn 1957-. **Military Serv:** AUS pfc 1951-53. **Home Addr:** 8952 S King Dr, Chicago, IL 60619. **Business Addr:** President, Simply Complex Communications Cystem Corp, 7459 S Cottage Grove Ave, Chicago, IL 60619.

DUSTER, BENJAMIN C., IV
Financial executive. **Personal:** Born in Chicago, IL. **Educ:** Yale Univ, 1981; Harvard Univ, joint graduate degree in law and business, 1985. **Career:** Salomon Brothers, vp, Leveraged Finance Group, currently. **Orgs:** Illinois Bar Assn. **Business Addr:** Vice President, Salomon Brothers, 133 Peachtree Rd, NE, Georgia Pacific Ctr, Ste 5000, Atlanta, GA 30303.

DUSTER, DONALD LEON
Business executive. **Personal:** Born Feb 10, 1932, Chicago, IL; son of Alfreda and Benjamin; married Maxine Porter; children: Michelle, David, Daniel. **Educ:** Univ IL, BS 1953; DePaul U, MBA 1977. **Career:** IL Dept of Bus & Econ Devel, dir 1977-79; Commonwealth Edison Co, exec 1962-87; Chicago Commons Assoc, asst exec dir. **Orgs:** Bd mem, sec Chicago Commons Assn; bd mem USS Africa Leader Exchange Prgm; exec comm Adlai Stevenson Center Univ Chicago; mem Economic Club of Chicago; mem Investment Analyst Soc of Chicago. **Honors/Awds:** Outstanding achievemet award Nat Fed of Settlements 1976; appointed mem Gov Thompsons Cabinet 1977. **Military Serv:** Lt exec officer. **Business Addr:** Assistant Executive Dir, Chicago Commons Assoc, 915 N Wolcott, Chicago, IL 60622, (312)342-5330.

DUSTER, TROY
Educator. **Personal:** Born Jul 11, 1936, Chicago, IL; son of Alfreda M Barnett and Benjamin Cecil Duster; divorced. **Educ:** Northwestern Univ, BS 1957; Univ of CA, MA 1959; Northwestern Univ, PhD 1962. **Career:** Northwestern University, lecturer, 1962; University of California at Berkeley, assistant professor, 1963-66, research sociologist, 1966-71, director of the Institute for Study of Social Change, 1976, professor, 1976-, chairman, Department of Sociology, 1985-; Stockholm University, research sociologist, 1966-67; University of British Columbia, visiting associate professor, 1969; Rose Monograph Series, Amer Sociological Assn, assoc editor, 1968-70, 1974; Comtemporary Sociology, assoc editor 1974-76. **Orgs:** Mem Assembly of Behavioral & Social Sci Natl Rsch Council Wash 1973, Comm on Clinical Eval of Narcotic Antagonists, Natl Acad of Sci 1973; dir Natl Inst of Mental Health Training Grant 1971. **Honors/Awds:** Guggenheim Fellowship London School of Econ 1971; author, The Legis of Morality, 1970; author, Aims & Control of the University's, 1972; author, Some Conditions of Sustained Participation in Governance, 1974; co-author, Patterns of Minority Rel, 1965; author, Backdoor to Eugenics, 1990; contributor to anthologies: Amer Sociologist, 1976; Issues in the Classification of Children, 1975; Social Policy & Sociology, 1975; Sanctions for Evil, 1971; Changing Perspectives in Mental Illness, 1969; The Encyc of Ed, 1971;, Crime in Amer Soc, 1971; The Liberal Univ Under Attack, 1971; Amer Behavioral Scientist, 1968; The State of Univ, 1970; Social Psychiatry, 1968; Our Children's Burden, 1968; Rsch Reports in Sociology; 1963; co-ed with Karen Garrett Cultural Perspectives on Biological Knowledge, 1984. **Business Addr:** Chairman and Professor, Department of Sociology, University of California at Berkeley, Berkeley, CA 94720.

DUTTON, CHARLES S.
Actor. **Personal:** Born 1951, Baltimore, MD; married Debbi Morgan, 1990 (divorced). **Educ:** Junior college courses; Towson State University, BA, theater, drama, 1978; Yale University School of Drama, graduated, 1983. **Career:** Theater appearances include: Ma Rainey's Black Bottom, 1984; Pantomime, 1986; Fried Chicken Invisibility, 1987; Joe Turner's Come and Gone, 1987; Splendid Mummer, 1988; The Piano Lesson, 1990; film appearances include: Crocodile Dundee II, 1988; Q & A; Mississippi Masala, 1992; Alien 3, 1992; Distinguished Gentlemen, 1993; A Low Down Dirty Shame, 1995; Time to Kill, 1996; Blind Faith, 1998; television appearances include: Equal Justice; The Trial of Mary Phagan, 1987; Roc, 1991-95; True Women, 1997; The Fly Guys singing group, manager, currently; First-Time Felon, dir, 1997. **Honors/Awds:** Outer Critics' Circle nomination, 1985; Drama Desk Award, 1985; Theatre World Award, 1985; Tony nomination, Ma Rainey's Black Bottom; Tony nomination, The Piano Lesson, 1990; Yale School of Drama, class marshal, 1983.

DUTTON, MARIE
Literary agent/consultant. **Personal:** Born Oct 4, 1940, Philadelphia, PA; daughter of Josephine Brown Dutton & Benson L Dutton; children: Laini. **Educ:** Penn State Univ, BS, Psych, 1962. **Career:** Wagner High School, PA, teacher, 1962-65; Bronze Books, bookstore mgr, 1970-71; Doubleday & Co, assoc ed, 1972-78, ed, 1978-81, sr ed, 1978-81; Elan Magazine, editor-in-chief, 1981-82; Endicott Bookseller, bookseller/asst buyer/asst mgr, consultant, 1982-84; Marie Brown Associates, pres/literary agent, 1984-. **Orgs:** Council of Literary Magazines & Presses, bd of dirs, 1989-; Frederick Douglass Creative Arts Ctr, bd of dirs, 1979-; Poets & Writers, bd of dirs, 1994; The Studio Museum of Harlem, bd of dirs, 1984-. **Business Addr:** Founder, Marie Brown Associates, 625 Broadway, Ste 902, New York, NY 10012, (212)533-5534.

DUVALL, HENRY F., JR.
Public relations administrator. **Personal:** Born Jan 3, 1949, Washington, DC; son of Ruth C Duvall and Henry F Duvall Sr; married Deborah Hawkins Duvall, Aug 12, 1975; children: Cherie. **Educ:** University of Maryland, BS, 1975. **Career:** Albuquerque Journal, copy editor, 1975-76; University of Maryland, staff writer, 1976-77; Potomac Electric Power Co, writer, 1978; Howard University, editor, 1978-81, media coordinator, 1981-89, information officer, 1989-91; American Red Cross, media relations associate, 1991-92; Council of the Great City Schools, communications director, 1992-. **Orgs:** Natl Press Club, 1993-; Natl Assn of Black Journalists, 1977-; Education Writers Assn, 1993-; Capital Press Club, 1978-; Natl School Public Relations Assn, 1993-; American Society of Assn Executives, 1993-; Institute for Educational Leadership, Communication Executives Group, 1992-. **Honors/Awds:** American Newspaper Publishers Association, scholarship, 1974. **Special Achievements:** Established Communications Dept, Council of the Great City Schools, 1992; launched a national news service, Howard University, 1981. **Military Serv:** US Navy, petty officer, 1968-70 (active), 1970-75 (ready reserve). **Business Addr:** Director of Communications, Council of the Great City Schools, 1301 Pennsylvania Ave NW, Ste 702, Washington, DC 20004, (202)393-2427.

DWYER-CARPENTER, ALETA
Radio station executive. **Personal:** Born Mar 11, 1948, Oakland, CA; daughter of Erlene Vinson Dwyer and Roosevelt Dwyer; married Jesse Carpenter, May 28, 1966; children: Krystal Carpenter, Vincent Carpenter. **Educ:** Laney Jr College, Oakland, CA, AA, sociology, (dean's list); California State University-Hayward, Harward, CA, BS, criminal justice. **Career:** Macy's Dept Store, San Francisco, CA, 1966-69; Arnell of California, San Francisco, CA, 1969-73; Alameda County Probation Dept, Oakland, CA, 1973-80; KDIA Radio, Oakland, CA, vice pres, gen mgr, 1980-; KBHK-TV 44, San Francisco, CA, 1987-89. **Orgs:** Board member, Black Child Adoption, 1989-; board member, Mother Wright Foundation for Homeless, 1990-; board member, United Negro College Fund, 1990-; member, Bay Area Black Media Coalition; member, American

Women in Radio and Television; member, NAACP. **Honors/Awds:** Marcus Foster Institute Award; College Bounders Image Award; American Medical Association Award; Soroptmist Society Award; O'Town Humanitarian Award; Cal Pac Association Award; East Bay African American Women of Achievement Award. **Business Addr:** Vice President, General Manager, KDIA Radio, 384 Embarcadero W, #3RD, Oakland, CA 94607.

DYAS, PATRICIA ANN
Fire inspector. **Personal:** Born Dec 6, 1952, Shreveport, LA; daughter of Martile Jefferson and Henry Jefferson; children: Patrick, Matthew, Elizabeth, William. **Educ:** Southern University, BS, 1976; University of Alabama-Tuskegee, degree, 1976. **Career:** Shreveport Fire Dept, Shreveport LA, firefighter, emergency medical technician and fire inspector, 1981—; licensed realtor. **Orgs:** Red Cross Safety Board; board member, YWCA; Greater Shreveport Optimists Club; Shreveport Black Chamber of Commerce. **Honors/Awds:** Outstanding Young Firefighter, Shreveport, 1987; Outstanding community service award, 1987-88; Outstanding Woman of the Year, Zeta Phi Beta, 1987; Distinguished Black Female award, Traveleers Coalition, 1988; St Abraham Baptist Church Outstanding young Christian woman, 1988. **Military Serv:** US Marine Corps, LCaptain, 1978-80. **Home Addr:** 2526 C E Galloway, Shreveport, LA 71104, (318)424-4335. **Business Addr:** Bureau of Fire Prevention, City Hall, 1237 Murphy St, Room 300, Shreveport, LA 71101-3346.

DYCE, BARBARA J.
Biochemist, educator. **Personal:** Born Feb 17, Chicago, IL; daughter of Carolyn Goin and Webster S Thompson III; divorced; children: Sigidi Abdullah. **Educ:** Loyola Univ, attended; Evansville Coll, attended; Univ of IL, attended; Univ of Chicago, attended; Univ of IL Med School, attended; Univ of So CA School of Med, MSc 1971. **Career:** Central Adult HS, instr; Trade Tech Comm Coll, instr; Univ of So CA Med School, asst prof of pharmacology; Crenshaw Adult School, adult basic educ instructor; Radioimmunoassay Lab of So CA, pres, tech dir. **Orgs:** Mem AAAS; founder, past pres Feminine Touch Inc; mem Urban League, NAACP, Alpha Kappa Alpha Sor, Top Ladies of Distinction Inglewood Branch; bd of dir Crenshaw Adult School, Concerned Citizens Comm. **Honors/Awds:** Numerous papers published in scientific journals; Top Ladies of Distinction Inglewood CA.

DYE, CLINTON ELWORTH, JR.
Association executive. **Personal:** Born Apr 9, 1942, Atlanta, GA; married Myrtice Willis; children: Clinton E III, Trevin Gerard. **Educ:** Morehouse Clge, AB 1965; Atlanta Univ Schl of Soc Work, MSW 1969; Atlanta Univ Schls of Soc Work and Bus Admin, PhD and MBA 1983-. **Career:** Economic Oppor Atlanta, dir drug recov prog 1971-73; Atlanta Regl Comm, coord drug and alcohol plng 1973-76; Atlanta Urban League Inc, dir comm srv 1976-79, deputy exec dir 1979-. **Orgs:** Mem Governor's Adv Coun on Mental Hlth 1975-76, Bd of Visitors Grady Mem Hosp 1983-, Ldrshp Atlanta 1971-; v chrmn bd mem Metro Atlanta Pvt Industry Owner 1983-; bd mem North Cntrl GA Health System Agcy 1981-84, Regl Dev Council 1979-83. **Home Addr:** 2807 Landrum Dr SW, Atlanta, GA 30311. **Business Addr:** Deputy Executive Dir, Atlanta Urban League, Inc, 75 Piedmont Ave NE, Ste 310, Atlanta, GA 30303.

DYE, ERNEST THADDEUS
Professional football player. **Personal:** Born Jul 15, 1971, Greenwood, SC; married Rhonda; children: Ariel. **Educ:** South Carolina. **Career:** Arizona Cardinals, tackle, 1994-96; St Louis Rams, 1997-. **Business Addr:** Professional Football Player, St Louis Rams, One Rams Way, St Louis, MO 63045, (314)982-7267.

DYE, JERMAINE TERRELL
Professional baseball player. **Personal:** Born Jan 28, 1974, Oakland, CA. **Educ:** Cosumnes River College. **Career:** Atlanta Braves, outfielder, 1996-97; Kansas City Royals, 1998-. **Business Addr:** Professional Baseball Player, Kansas City Royals, PO Box 419969, Kansas City, MO 64141-6969, (816)921-2200.

DYE, LUTHER V.
Judge. **Personal:** Born Sep 26, 1933, Winston-Salem, NC; son of Mattie Harpe Dye and Luther William Dye; children: Barry, Bryan, Lisa, Blake. **Educ:** Brooklyn Law Sch, LLB 1960; State Univ, BS NC A&T 1955. **Career:** Chicago Title Ins Co, title officer 1958-69; Demov Morris Levin & Shein, assoc atty 1969-73; NY Life Ins Co, assoc counsel office of gen counsel 1974-86; private law practice 1986-88; Civil Court of City of New York, judge, 1988-94; Justice of Supreme Court, currently. **Orgs:** Mem Macon B Allen Black Bar Assn; NY State Bar Assn; exec mem Real Property Law Sect; Queens Co Bar Assn; mem Real Property Com Civil Rights Com & Admissions Com; Grievance Com; mem Local Draft Bd Selective Serv Sys; Brooklyn Law Sch Alumni Assn; former trustee Housing Devel Corp of Council of Churches. **Honors/Awds:** Admitted to US Supreme Court & US Dist Court, elected to Civil Court 1988, elected to Supreme Court, 1994. **Business Addr:** Justice of Supreme Court, 88-11 Sutphen Blvd, Jamaica, NY 11435.

DYER, BERNARD JOEL
Publisher. **Personal:** Born Mar 23, 1933, Bronx, NY; son of Miariam Samuels Dyer and Joel Dyer; divorced; children: Ethelda, Bertha, Minia, Joel. **Educ:** New York City Community College, technology, 1955-57. **Career:** Executive Director C.D.M. Neighborhood Development Institute; Miami Weekly, Journey Magazine, publisher, currently; Third World Media Corp, president/chief executive officer, currently. **Orgs:** Phi Tau, vice pres, 1955-57. **Honors/Awds:** Dade County Award, 1969; National Council of Churches, Nation's Best Community Organization, 1967; Honorary Doctorate in Community Organization; Ford Foundation, Leadership Fellowship, 1979. **Military Serv:** US Army, private first class, 1953-55. **Business Addr:** President/Chief Executive Officer, Third World Media Corp, 3050 Biscayne Blvd, Ste 220, Miami, FL 33127.

DYER, CHARLES AUSTEN
Computer manager. **Personal:** Born Jul 24, 1936, St Ann's Bay, Jamaica; son of Marjorie Emma Lewis Dyer and Jacob Alexander Dyer; married Edwina Weston; children: M. Hakim, Adam L. **Educ:** Pratt Inst, Bachelor Indust Design 1957; Yeshiva Univ, MS 1962; CUNY, PhD 1980. **Career:** Digital Equip Corp, computers educ, artificial intelligence. **Honors/Awds:** Author of Preparing for Computer Assisted Instruction 1972; Teaching Aid patented 1973; Articles & papers on artificial intelligence & computer-assisted instruction 1980-. **Military Serv:** USAR, Infantry, captain, 1957-66. **Home Addr:** 203 Grove St, Framingham, MA 01701.

DYER, JOE, JR.
Television station executive. **Personal:** Born Sep 24, 1934, Bogalusa, LA; son of Barbara Fletcher Brooks and Joe Dyer Sr; married Doris Dillon, Dec 29, 1960; children: Monica, Kimberly, Karen, Joseph III, Dillon. **Educ:** Grambling Coll, BA. **Career:** KCBS, comm rels dir 1965-; Sickle Cell in LA, 1st telethon co-prodcd; United High Blood Pressure Found, co-fndr; Black TV Commn, org; Avalon Carver Comm Ctr, 1st maj & fundraiser coord; Native Am Awareness Wk Resltn LA City Cncl, asst coord; LA, mayor. **Orgs:** Pres Sickle Cell Disease Rsrch Found; High Blood Pressure Found; exec bd mem KNXT Sugar Ray Robinson Yth Found; pub rels adv Watts Summer Festival;Fstvl in Black; LA Brthrhd Crsd; IMPACT; S Central Area Improv Cncl; bd mem Alchlsm Cncl Grtr LA; corp bd mem Untd Way Region 5; bd mem Avalon-Carver Comm Ctr; Protstnt Comm Serv; adv bd mem SW Coll; bd mem Willing Wrkrs for Mentally Retarded; planning com mem Chinese New Year's Celebr; bd mem Oper PUSH; LA Chap Media Women; LA Urban League; Untd Hgh Bld Pressr Found; Sickle Cell Dss Rsrch Found; Willing Wrkrs for Mentlly Retrdd; Dept Sr Citz; Sch Vol Prgm; Kutania People San Brnrdn; Nat Assn Jr Coll; Alpha Chi Pi Omega Sor; Nat Acad Motion Pictrs & TV; Teen Posts Inc; Comm Btfl Pgnt Com; Annl Fstvl Black Com; Lions;Rotaries; Kiwanis; bd memommunity Youth Gang Services; corporate bd, Corporate Commission on Human Relations; bd mem, Crossroads Academy. **Honors/Awds:** Winner Nat Abe Lincoln Award; citation City Human Rels Commn; award Nat Assn Media Women; John Anson Ford Award, County Human Relations Commission; NAACP Image Award; Chinatown Firecracker Award. **Military Serv:** USAF, Airman 1st Class, 1957-61; Airman of the Month, Airman of the Year. **Business Addr:** Director, Comm Rels, KCBS-TV, 6121 Sunset Blvd, Los Angeles, CA 90028.

DYER-GOODE, PAMELA THERESA
Family practitioner, gynecologist. **Personal:** Born Oct 7, 1950, Philadelphia, PA; daughter of Mabel Clyatt and Kirby; children: Lisa, Shonn, Erica, Brian. **Educ:** Cheyney State Coll, BS Biology, BS Chemistry 1971; Temple Univ Med Sch, MD 1977; Medical Coll of PA, internship 1977-78; Hanaemann Med Coll & Hosp, residency 1978-80; Temple Univ, 1985; Miami Univ, Internal Med Review. **Career:** Planned Parenthood, physician/ambulatory 1978-80; Gruiffree Med Ctr, physician/ambulatory care 1980-82; Broad St Hosp, ambulatory care physician 1982-84; SEPTA, industrial medicine & claims specialist 1986; Private Family Practice, 1986-. **Orgs:** Mem, NOW, Coalition of 100 Black Women, PA Med Soc, Amer Med Assn, Natl Med Assn, Friends of the PA Ballet Co. **Honors/Awds:** Distinguished Alumna Awd Cheyney State Coll 1986; Outstanding Alumna St Maria Goretti High School 1986; Philadelphia New Observer "Women on the Move" editorial presentation. **Home Addr:** 305 Pembree Cir, Bala Cynwyd, PA 19004.

DYKES, DEWITT S., JR.
Educator. **Personal:** Born Jan 2, 1938, Chattanooga, TN; son of Violet T Anderson and Rev De Witt S Dykes, Sr; married Marie Draper; children: Laura Marie Christine. **Educ:** Fisk Univ, BA (Summa Cum Laude) 1960; Univ of MI, MA 1961, PhD candidate 1961-65. **Career:** MI State Univ, instructor Amer Thought & Language 1965-69; Oakland Univ, asst prof of history 1969-73; Oakland Univ, dean's asst for affirmative action 1975-78, coordinator Afro-Amer studies 1975-83; Univ of SC School of Public Health, consultant 1977; Oakland Univ, assoc prof of History 1973-. **Orgs:** African Heritage Studies Assn 1970; life mem Assn for the Study of Afro-Amer Life & History; charter mem Afro-Amer Historical & Genealogical Soc 1978; Alpha Phi Alpha Fraternity; bd of editors Detroit in Perspective, A Journal of Regional History 1978-84; vice chmn Historic Designation Advisory Bd City of Detroit 1980-82, chmn 1982-84; book review editor Journal of the Afro-Amer Historical & Genealogical Soc 1981-85; pres The Fred Hart Williams Genealogical Soc 1980-86; bd of trustees Historical Soc of MI 1983-; summer fellowship Natl Endowment for the Humanities 1985; pres Michigan Black History Network 1986-; bd of trustees, Historical Soc of MI, 1983-89; pres, MI Black History Network, 1986-88. **Honors/Awds:** Published "Mary McLeod Bethune"; "Ida Gray Nelson Rollins DDS" Profiles of the Negro in Amer Dentistry 1979; "Augusta Savage;" "Jerome Cavanagh & Roman Gribbs;" "Amer Blacks as Perpetual Victims, An Historical Overview" Victimization of the Weak 1982; "The Black Population in MI, Growth, Distribution & Public Office, 1800-1983" Ethnic Groups in MI Vol 2 1983; Phi Beta Kappa, Honorary Fraternity, 1969; "The Search for Community: MI Soc and Educ, 1945-80" in MI: Visions of our Past, 1989. **Business Addr:** Oakland University, Dept of History, 378 O'Dowd Hall, Rochester, MI 48309-4401.

DYKES, DEWITT SANFORD, SR.
Architect. **Personal:** Born Dec 16, 1903, Gadsden, AL; son of Mollie Wade Dykes and Henry Sanford R Dykes; married Viola Gertrude Logan Dykes, Dec 14, 1950 (deceased); children: Reida B Gardner, DeWitt Jr. **Educ:** Clark Coll, AB 1930; Gammon Sem, BD 1931; Boston U, STM 1932; Rust Coll, DD 1971. **Career:** DeWitt S Dykes & Asso, architect 1970-; Research & Study, 1968-69; United Methodist Ch, natl div of missions 1955-68, minister 1932-54. **Orgs:** Mem Comm Design Center; mem AIA; mem NAACP; YMCA; Beck Cultural Center; mem bd Elec Exam & Review City of Knoxville TN; Alpha Phi Alpha; trustee Morristown Coll. **Honors/Awds:** Honorary Doctor of Divinity, Rust College, 1970.

DYKES, MARIE DRAPER
Educational administrator, nurse. **Personal:** Born Oct 13, 1942, Detroit, MI; daughter of Hattie Nathan Draper Hall and William Cotrell Draper; married DeWitt Sanford; children: Laura Marie Christine. **Educ:** Wayne State Univ, BS 1964; Univ of CA San Francisco, MS 1967; Univ of Michigan, PhD 1978. **Career:** Detroit General Hospital, staff nurse 1966; Coll of Nursing, Wayne State Univ Detroit, assoc prof 1967-, asst dean acad admin 1971-77; Univ of WI Oshkosh, rsch asst 1976-77; Wayne State Univ, assoc provost for acad programs 1977-. **Orgs:** ANA 1964-; mem-at-large EACT Sec MNA 1969-70; Natl Black Nurses Assn 1971-; treas, Lambda Chap, Sigma Theta Tau 1973-75; Sigma Gamma Rho Sor; NAACP; consultant evaluator, N Central Assn of Schools & Colls, 1982-; bd mem, Detroit Metropolitan Coordinating Comm, 1988; Board of Higher Education and Campus Ministry, chair, 1992. **Honors/Awds:** Helen Newberry Joy Scholarship, Wayne State Univ 1960-64; David D Henry Award, Wayne State Univ 1964; Sigma Theta Tau Natl Honor Soc, Nursing Wayne State Univ 1964; Mortar Bd, Wayne State Univ 1964. **Business Addr:** Associate Provost for Academic Programs, Wayne State University, 4112 Faculty Administration Bldg, Detroit, MI 48202.

DYMALLY, LYNN V.
Elected official. **Personal:** Born Sep 8, 1958, Los Angeles, CA. **Educ:** Univ of CA San Diego, BA Comm, Sociology 1979; Univ of Redlands, MA Bus Mgmt 1987; Whittier Coll School of Law, 1988. **Career:** Network Data Processing, vice pres 1979-80; Drew Postgrad Med School Prog of Intl Health & Devel, admin analyst 1980-81; KBRT Radio, bus mgr 1981-85; Compton Unified School Dist, bd of trustee. **Orgs:** Spec asst CA State Museum of Sci/Summer Break & Indust 1973-78; analyst, consult Aid to Needy Children Mother's Anonymous Inc CA State Social Serv Prog 1979-; mem CA League of Women Voter 1983-; staff Youth for Christ 1983-; statewide co-chmn CA Rainbow Youth Coalition Jackson for Pres 1984. **Honors/Awds:** Co-instr The Presidential Classroom 1985. **Business Addr:** Board of Trustees, Compton Unified School Dist, 604 S Tamarind Ave, Compton, CA 90220.

DYMALLY, MERVYN M.
Congressman (retired), company executive. **Personal:** Born May 12, 1926, Cedros, Trinidad and Tobago; son of Andreid Richardson and Hamid Dymally; married Alice M Gueno; children: Mark, Lynn. **Educ:** Lincoln Univ, 1946; California State Univ, BA 1954, MA 1969; US Intl Univ San Diego, PhD Human Behav 1978. **Career:** Los Angeles, teacher exceptional children, 1955-61; Univ of CA, Davis, Irvine, Whittier Coll, Pomona Coll, Claremont Grad School, lecturer; Golden Gate Univ, adj prof; State of CA, coord, disaster office, 1961-62; State Assembly, mem 1963-67; State Senate, mem 1967-75; State of CA, lt gov 1975-79; Mervyn M Dymally Co Inc, pres, 1981-; US House of Representatives, member, 1981-93. **Orgs:** Chmn Caribbean Amer Rsch Inst; bd mem Joint Center of Political Studies, chmn 31st Congressional Dist Adv Commiss; pres Rsch Inst for Space Sci & Tech; task force on Missing in Action US House of Reps; mem, CA Dem State Central Comm, Arab Amer Affairs Council, Jewish Labor Comm, Japanese Amer Citizens League, Chinese Amer Assoc, Korean Amer Political Assoc, Mexican-Amer Political Assn, Asian Democratic Caucus, Urban League, Amer Civil Liberties Union, NAACP, Wash DC Commiss on Crime Prevention, Amer Assn of Univ Professors, Amer Assn for the Advancement of Sci, Amer Political Sci Assn, Amer Acad of Political Science, Amer Acad of

Political and Social Science, Kappa Alpha Psi Frat; United National Council, advisor; LA County Water Appeals Board. **Honors/Awds:** Hon Soc Phi Kappa Phi; Recip Solomon Carter Fuller Award Black Psychiatrist of Amer 1975; Adam Clayton Powell Award Congressional Black Caucus 1975; Chaconia Medal Class 1 Order of Trinity for Pub Serv Govt of Trinidad & Tobago 1975; Distinguished Citizen Award, Lincoln University; author of The Black Politician: His Struggle for Power, Duxbury Press, 1971; LLD, West Los Angeles Univ, California College of Law, 1976, City Univ of Los Angeles, 1976; Honorary JD, Lincoln Law Univ, Sacramento, 1975; HLD, Shaw Univ, 1981; Honorary Counsul, Republic of Benin; Central State University, Distinguished Presidential Professor. **Business Addr:** President, Dymally International Group, Inc, 9111 LaCienega Blvd, Ste 107, Inglewood, CA 90301, (310)641-3688.

DYSON, MICHAEL ERIC
Educator. **Personal:** Born Oct 23, 1958, Detroit, MI; son of Addie and Everett; married Marcia Louise Dyson, Jun 24, 1992; children: Michael II, Maisha. **Educ:** Carson-Newman, BA (magna cum laude), 1982; Princeton University, MA, 1991, PhD, 1993. **Career:** Princeton University, Mathy College, assistant master; Hartford Seminary, faculty member; Chicago Theological Seminary, instructor, assistant professor; Brown University, assistant professor; Univ of NC, Professor of Comm, currently. **Orgs:** Democratic Socialist of America. **Honors/Awds:** National Association of Black Journalists, National Magazine Award, 1992. **Special Achievements:** Reflecting Black: African-American Cultural Criticism, 1993; Black History Booklet, A Collection of 20 Essays; The Second Coming of Malcolm X, liner notes for RCA Records; Making Malcolm: The Myth and Meaning of Malcolm X, Oxford Univ Press, 1994; Between God and Gangsta' Rap, collection of essays, Oxford Univ Press, 1995; Race Rulels: Navigating the Color Line, Addison Wesley, 1997. **Business Addr:** Dept of Comm Studies, University of North Carolina, CB 3285 Bingham Hall, Chapel Hill, NC 27599, (919)962-4940.

DYSON, WILLIAM RILEY
State representative. **Personal:** Born Jul 12, 1940, Waycross, GA; son of Lula Lorene Williams Dyson and Edward James Dyson; divorced; children: Sonia, Wilfred, Erick, Michael. **Educ:** Morris Coll, BA 1962; So CT St Univ, MA 1976, 6th Year Certificate 1982. **Career:** New Haven CT, tchr; Douglas GA, tchr Blackshear GA, tchr; Connecticut General Assembly, state representative, currently. **Business Addr:** State Representative, Connecticut General Assembly, State Capital, Hartford, CT 06106.

E

EADES, VINCENT W.
Marketing executive. **Personal:** Born Feb 19, 1956, Alexandria, VA; son of Nerissia (Pierce) Eades and Lester Vincent Eades; married Dorri Eades (Scott), Dec 27, 1980; children: Brittany Joy, Vincent Bryan. **Educ:** Trenton State Coll, Ewing NJ, BS, 1981; Kansas Univ, Lawrence KS, Exec Devel Program, 1987. **Career:** FMC Corp, Princeton NJ, personnel asst, 1977-80; ITT Corp, New York NY, sales representative, 1980-82; CISS-Toys, New York NY, product mgr, 1982-84; Hallmark Cards, Kansas City MO, product mgr, 1984-86, sr product mgr, 1986-87, gen mgr, 1987-. **Orgs:** Mem, Strategic Planning Alliance, 1985-, Hallpac Political Action Comm, 1985-, Amer Mktg Assn, 1986-, Natl Assn of Market Developers, 1987-, Kansas City Consensus, 1988-; Rotary Club, 1990-. **Business Addr:** General Manager, Christmas Celebrations, Hallmark Cards Inc, 2501 McGee Trafficway, Mail Drop 128, Kansas City, MO 64108.

EADY, LYDIA DAVIS
Publishing executive. **Personal:** Born May 4, 1958, Indiana; daughter of Ruth V Davis and Henderson S Davis; married Jacques Wayne Eady; children: Andrew Jacques. **Educ:** Howard Univ, BA Broadcast Mgmt (Magna Cum Laude) 1980. **Career:** WRTV ABC Indianapolis IN, news reporter 1980-81; Johnson Publ Co, asst dir of public relations 1981-83; Ebony/Jet Celebrity Showcase, assoc producer; Johnson Publishing Co, dir promotion 1983-85, vice president promotion, 1985-. **Orgs:** Mem Quinn Chapel AME Church Chicago, IL; mem Executives Club of Chicago; mem League of Black Women; mem Women's Advertising Club of Chicago; Chicago Association of Black Journalists. **Honors/Awds:** Cert of Merit Folio Magazine Circulation Direct Mail Award for Johnson Publishing Co $50,000 Sweepstakes; CEBA Awd for Merit. **Business Addr:** Vice President of Promotion, Johnson Publishing Co, 820 South Michigan Ave, Chicago, IL 60605.

EADY, MARY E.
Educational administrator. **Personal:** Born in Waterbury, CT; married Eugene H Eady; children: Mary Vienassa, Alan, Larry, Barry, Audrey, John, Carol. **Educ:** Bridgeport Hospital, lpn 1967; Housatonic Comm Coll, AS Drug & Alc Couns 1977; Sacred Heart Univ, BS Psychology 1977; Southern CT State Coll, MACouns 1978. **Career:** St Joseph's Manor, ward charge nurse 1967-74; Greater Baptist Methadone Ctr, staff nurse 1974-75; Dinan Mem Ctr, ward charge nurse 1975-76; Greater Baptist Mental Health Ctr, counselor 1976-78; Housatonic Comm Coll, proj dir spec serv 1979-. **Orgs:** Mem Professional Staff Assoc Housatonic Comm Coll 1979-, Comm Counselor Assoc 1980-; volunteer counselor St George's Church Mental Health Social Group 1980-;pres Housatonic Comm Coll Alumni Assoc 1982-; volunteer School Volunteer Assoc City of Baptist 1983-; mem New England Assoc of Ed Opport Prog. **Honors/Awds:** Community Awareness Program on Sicle Cell Anemia 1969-73; NAACP Police & Community Relations Comm 1973; Univ of Bridgeport Oper Open Doors Program 1975; Chairperson Bridgeport Sr Citizens Activities Week 1976; NAACP Political Action Comm; Univ of Bridgeport's Ed Spec Team; North End Ed Comm, Citizens Non-partisan Register & Vote Comm; Bridgeport Bar Assoc Support to Improve Correctional Serv Comm; North End Neighborhood Council; NAACP Voter Reg Comm. **Business Addr:** Project Dir Spec Serv, Housatonic Community Coll, 510 Barnum Ave, Bridgeport, CT 06608.

EAGAN, CATHERINE B.
Banker. **Personal:** Born Jan 14, 1954, New York, NY; daughter of Adele Dixon Cartey and Desmond Cartey; married Dr Jay Victor Eagan. **Educ:** Simmons College, Boston, MA, BA, 1975, Graduate School of Management, certificate, 1976; Harvard University, Cambridge, MA, EdM, 1978; American Institute of Banking, Wayne State University, 1980. **Career:** Metropolitan Council for Education, Roxbury, MA, support services director, 1975-78; United Community Services of Detroit, MI, program consultant, 1978-80; National Bank of Detroit, Detroit, MI, commercial credit analyst, 1980-82; Detroit Economic Growth Corp., director, beginning 1982; Michigan National Bank, Private Banking Division, vice pres, 1994-. **Orgs:** Finance chair, United Negro College Fund Walkathon, 1986-; life member, NAACP, 1982-; finance chair, Detroit Area Agency on Aging, 1990-; role model, Detroit Public School Student Motivation Program, 1986-; member, Harvard Club of Eastern Michigan, 1982; member, Women's Economic Club, 1983-; member, Economic Club of Detroit, 1984. **Honors/Awds:** Certificate of National Recognition for Trapper's Alley Project, Award of National Excellence, Virginia Park Shopping Center, US Department of Housing and Urban Development; Certificate of Participation, Business Role Model, Detroit Public Schools Student Motivational Program, 1985, 1987, 1988, 1989, 1990; numerous speaking engagements. **Business Addr:** Vice President, Private Banking Division, Michigan National Bank, 1533 N Woodward Ave, Ste 200, Bloomfield Hills, MI 48304.

EAGAN, EMMA LOUISE
Dental hygienist. **Personal:** Born Oct 12, 1928, Cartersville, GA; married Dr John D; children: 3. **Educ:** Spelman Coll, BA 1948; Meharry Med Coll, diploma 1953. **Career:** Working for Husband, orthodontist hygienist; Dr Earl Renfroe Chgo, hygienist; GA Sch Sys, sch tchr 3 yrs. **Orgs:** Mem Delta Sigma Theta Sor; AAVW; Jack n' Jill of Am; Dental Wives Orgn meharry alumni assn; vol worker MI cancer fund; mem moles sunday Sch TchrOrgn; Spellman Coll Alumni Club; League of Women Voters; Nat Dental Hyg Assn; mem Dental Hygiene Hon. **Honors/Awds:** Recip scholarship achievement Medal Arts Award Meharry Coll; cover girl natl write-up on dental hygiene Jet Mag 1958; honored achievements by Spelman AlumniClub Civic & Professional 1960; mem dental hygiene hon soc Sigma Phi Alpha 1962. **Business Addr:** 1130 Woodward Ave, Detroit, MI.

EAGLE, ARNOLD ELLIOTT
Personnel executive. **Personal:** Born Jul 7, 1941, Brooklyn, NY; son of Gwendolyn Saunders Eagle and Porter Eagle; divorced; children: Todd. **Educ:** VA State Coll, BS 1964; VA State Univ, BS 1964; NY Univ, MA, 1975. **Career:** Mfrs Hanover Trust, personnel interviewer 1966-69; Colgate-Palmolive Co, employment mgr 1969-73; Bristol-Myers International, dir human resources, finance & headquarters admin. **Orgs:** Mem Black Retail Action Group 1974-; Am Mgmt Assn 1974-; Am Council of Intl Personnel 1975-; mem Employment Managers Assoc 1975-; mem bd dir Amer Council on Intl Personnel; vp, bd dir Amer Council on Intl Personnel 1982, pres 1987-; mem bd dir Omega Psi Phi Federal Credit Union 1986; mem, Employee Relocation Council, 1988-; vice pres, Omega Psi Phi Fraternity Federal Credit Union, 1989-. **Honors/Awds:** Omega Citizen of the Yer 1976; Basileus Omega Psi Phi Fraternity Iota Xi Chapter; Mem Business & Industrial Comm Omega Psi Phi; Omega Man of the Year 1983. **Military Serv:** AUS 1st lt 1964-66. **Business Addr:** Dir, Personnel Administration, Bristol-Myers International, 345 Park Ave, New York, NY 10154.

EAGLIN, FULTON B.
Attorney. **Personal:** Born Nov 23, 1941, Ann Arbor, MI; son of Marguerite Davis Eaglin and Simon P Eaglin; married Jan Collins Eaglin, Jun 30, 1979; children: Fulton Christopher, Jennifer Naomi, Jessica Marguerite. **Educ:** Eastern Michigan University, Ypsilanti, MI, BS, 1963; Harvard School of Business, Cambridge, MA, 1968-69; Harvard Law School, Cambridge, MA, JD, 1969. **Career:** Harvard University, Cambridge, MA, 1969-72; self-employed attorney, Ypsilanti, MI, 1975-80; Eaglin & Drukis, Ann Arbor, MI, principal, 1980-. **Orgs:** Member, Michigan Bar Assn; member, Ypsilanti and Washtenaw County Bar Assn; chairman, board of directors, United Way of Michigan, 1988; bd of governors, United Way of America, 1992-; member, Kiwanis International, 1975-; member, board of directors, American Red Cross, Washtenaw County Chapter, 1985-87; treasurer, member, board of directors, Child Family Services of Washtenaw County, 1975-77; member, Alpha Phi Alpha Fraternity, 1961-; treasurer 1987-88, vice pres 1989; Sire Archon 1990-92, Gamma Rho Chapter, Sigma Pi Phi Fraternity. **Military Serv:** US Army, First Lt, 1963-66; Combat Infantryman's Badge, 1965, Airborne, 1963, Ranger, 1964. **Business Addr:** Attorney, 220 E Huron, Ste 705, Ann Arbor, MI 48104-1912, (313)665-5355.

EAGLIN, RUTH
Government official. **Career:** White House Office of Presidential Personnel, exec asst to dir, currently. **Business Addr:** Exec Asst to the Dir, Office of Presidential Personnel, White House, 1600 Pennsylania Ave, NW, Washington, DC 20500, (202)456-6676.

EALEY, MARK E.
Social worker. **Personal:** Born Jun 13, 1926, Oklahoma City, OK; married Ruth Keenan; children: Michael K, Marquetta E, Roger K. **Educ:** Howard U, BS 1950; Howard U, MSW 1952. **Career:** Clinical social worker; Pvt Practice, psychotherapy; Univ of the Pacific, chrmn black studies dept 1969-; Univ of CA Berkeley, instr 1960-69; CA Dept of Corrections, social worker 1953-60; San Diego Co Public Welfare Dept, social worker 1952-53. **Orgs:** Mem Nat Assn of Social Workers 1952; CA Probations Parole & Correctional Assn 1955-72; Nat Council on Crime & Delinquency; Nat Council on Social Work Edn; Am Assn of Univ Profs; Inst on Race Culture & Human Dignity; adv council Comm Affairs Dept of KTVU-TV; Center for African & African-American Studies; mem NAACP 1946-; consult Solano Co CA Probation Office 1971; consult Vallejo Unified Sch Dist 1973; fdr & exec bd mem Nat Council for Black Studies 1975-; dir Univ Travel Tour Courses to W & E Africa 1973, 75, 77, 79 & 81; principal speaker Symposium for By Area Correctonal Workers Oakland 1957. **Honors/Awds:** Recipient richard welling fellowship Howard Univ 1951; faculty fellowship Univ of CA 1966-67; outstanding professional in human serv Am Acad of Human Serv 1974. **Military Serv:** USN steward 3/c 1944-46. **Business Addr:** 333 Maryland St, Vallejo, CA 94590.

EALY, MARY NEWCOMB
Educator, financial planner. **Personal:** Born Aug 26, 1948, Charleston, MO; daughter of Susie M Williams Newcomb and Gussie E Newcomb; married Willie R Ealy, Jun 17, 1978; children: Lisa Denise. **Educ:** Lake MI Coll, AA 1968; Western MI Univ, BS 1972. **Career:** Benton Harbor Area School, dept head, unit coordinator social studies 1973, sec 1970-71; Fox's Jewelry, edt mgr 1969-70; Shifren & Willens Jewelry, office coordinator 1969; Jordan Coll Berrien Campus, adjunct prof 1987-. **Orgs:** Mem Exec Comm MEA 1976-77; mem Andrews Unit Chpter; mem Phi Delta Kappa 1976; pres Essence of Blackness 1974-; mem NAACP; del MI & Natl Educ Assn Rep Assembly 1974-; mem NEA Official Black Caucus 1974-; advisor Excelsior Chapter of Natl Jr Hon Soc 1975-; reviewer MI State Dept of Educ 1975-; researcher School Curr & Educ Leadership; mem Delta Sigma Theta Sorority Inc, BH-SJ Alumnae Chapter 1983-; first vice pres Benton Harbor-St Joseph Alumnae Chapter, Delta Sigma Theta 1987-89; coordinator Close-up Found 1985-. **Honors/Awds:** Outstanding Teacher Award, MI Dept of Educ 1976; Certificate of Merit, MI Dept of Educ 1976; Nunn-Williams Family History 1986; Teacher of the Year, Benton Harbor High School 1987. **Business Addr:** President, F&E Enterprises, PO Box 844, Benton Harbor, MI 49023.

EARL, ACIE BOYD, II
Professional basketball player, company executive. **Personal:** Born Jun 23, 1970, Peoria, IL; son of Acie, Carolyn. **Educ:** Univ of Iowa, BS, 1992. **Career:** Boston Celtics, 1993-95; Toronto Raptors, 1995-96, Milwaukee Bucks, 1996-; Ace Promotion and Marketing, vp,1993-; Venom Productions, vp, 1993-. **Orgs:** Ace Award, vp, 1993-; WAM-JAM basketball camp, camp dir, 1994. **Honors/Awds:** Playboy Magazine, pre-season All American, 1992-93; John Wooden Award, nominee, 1992-93. **Special Achievements:** The Omen/Venom Productions, 1995; NBA Draft, First round pick, #19, 1993. **Business Addr:** Vice President, Venom Productions, 2301 14th Ave Place, Moline, IL 61265, (309)775-5084.

EARL, ARCHIE WILLIAM, SR.
Educator. **Personal:** Born Nov 28, 1946, Suffolk, VA; married Doristine Gause; children: Karen, Archie Jr, Keisha. **Educ:** Norfolk State Univ, BS 1971; Hampton Univ, MA 1976; Coll of William & Mary, EdD 1986. **Career:** Hampton Univ, statistics instructor 1983; Coll of William & Mary, grad asst 1983-85; Family Inns of Amer, night auditor 1985-86; City Colleges of Chicago, math lecturer 1986; Saudi Arabian Govt, Dammam Saudi Arabia, Math instructor 1987; Christopher Newport College, Newport News VA, asst prof of Math 1987-90; Earl's Enterprises Inc, president, chief executive officer, 1990-; Norfolk

State University, assistant professor of math, 1991-. **Orgs:** Deacon/treasurer Mt Pleasant Baptist Church 1983-; mem Assoc for the Study of Higher Educ 1986-, Mathematical Assn of Amer 1988-, Amer Mathematical Soc 1988-. **Honors/Awds:** Co-author "A Preliminary Planning Study for a New College," College of Wm & Mary 1983; author "The Budget Information Systems of Selected Colleges & Universities in the State of VA as Described and Perceived by Budget Managers," College of Wm & Mary 1986; Using Mathematics to Determine Efectiveness of Information System, MAA Section Mtg presenter 1989, Using Time Series Multiple Discriminant Analysis to Predict Bank Failures, Christopher Newport College, Math dept presenter 1989. **Business Addr:** Assistant Professor of Mathematics, Norfolk State University, Norfolk, VA 23504.

EARLES, RENE MARTIN
Physician. **Personal:** Born Oct 31, 1940, New Orleans, LA; married Eve Evans; children: Robert, Andrea. **Educ:** Howard U, BS 1963; Howard Univ Coll of Med, MD 1967. **Career:** Self Employed, dermatologist; Rush Med Ctr, resid 1972-75; Univ WA, preceptorship 1970-72; resident surgery 1968-70; Kemo Health Ctr Chicago IL, chief dermatologist. **Orgs:** Chmn Div of Dermatology Mt Sinai Med Ctr Chicago IL; attending dermatology Ruch Med Center Chicago IL; bd dir Region Four IL; Am Cancer Soc; past pres Howard Univ Alumni Assn of Chicago; frat life mem Kappa Alpha Psi; mem Sigma Pi Phi; mem Chicagoans; mem Saracens. **Military Serv:** USN LCDR 1970-72. **Business Addr:** 2930 S Michigan Ave, Ste 100, Ste 204, Chicago, IL 60616.

EARLEY, CHARITY EDNA
Corporate executive. **Personal:** Born Dec 5, 1918, Kittrell, NC; daughter of Rev & Mrs E A Adams; married Stanley A Earley Jr; children: Stanley III, Judith E. **Educ:** Wilberforce Univ, BA 1938; OH State Univ, MA 1946; Univ of Zurich Switzerland, attended 1950-52. **Career:** TN Univ, dean of student services 1948; GA State Coll, dean of student serv 1949; Dayton Power & Light Co, dir. **Orgs:** Mem chmn Dayton Metro Housing Authority 1964-79; bd of gov Amer Natl Red Cross 1972-78; bd of dir Dayton Power & Light Co 1979-91; bd of dir Dayton Opera Co 1964-74; bd of trustees Sinclair Comm Coll Dayton OH 1977-92; bd of dir Dayton Area Chap ARC; United Way. **Honors/Awds:** Top Ten Women of the Miami Valley Dayton Daily News 1965; Outstanding Citizen Serv to Public Affairs Miami Valley Chapter of Amer Soc for Public Admin 1978; inductee OH Women's Hall of Fame 1979; Black Women Against the Odds by Smithsonian Inst; Senior Citizens, Golden Watch Award, 1987; Author of One Woman's Army: A Black Officer Remembers the WAC, 1989; OH State Senate, service to community, 1989; Honorary Doctorate degrees from Wilberforce University, 1991, University of Dayton, 1991. **Military Serv:** US Army WAC lt col 1942-46.

EARLEY, KEITH H.
Attorney. **Personal:** Born Feb 3, 1952, New York, NY; son of Wilma and Charles; divorced; children: Khary. **Educ:** Cornell University, BA, 1974; Rutgers Law School, JD, 1977. **Career:** Freddie Mac PC, associate general counsel, currently. **Home Addr:** 1640 Martha Terrace, Rockville, MD 20852.

EARLEY, STANLEY ARMSTEAD, JR.
Physician. **Personal:** Born Feb 12, 1919, Wellsville, OH; married Charity Edna Adams; children: Stanley III, Judith Edna. **Educ:** OH State Univ, BA 1941; Lafayette Coll Easton PA, German 1942; Univ of Zurich, MD 1951. **Career:** Bordeaux, intern ob-gyn; Jungian Inst; Kanton Hospital, intern pathology & pediatrics; Miami Valley Hosp, chief family prac 1973-; Dayton Pub Schs, schoolphysician 1955-; Private Practice, physician. **Orgs:** Mem Amer Arbitration Assn; Montg Co med Soc; OH State Med Soc; AMA; past pres Gem City Med Soc; Natl Med Soc; chmn Child Guidance Ctr 1976; bd Drug & Alcohol; bd mem Dayton Art Inst; Dayton Philharmonic Orch Soc; life mem past bd mem NAACP; 2nd vice pres Comm Health & Welfare Cncl; past bd mem Hlth Planning Cncl; past pres Dayton Area Cncl Serv; chtr mem Westmont Chap Optimist Intl & Dayton Racquet Club; mem Sigma Pi Phi Boule'; Alpha Phi Alpha Frat; YMCA; May Co Commr & Comm Citz; moderator State Health & Welfare Regional Meeting; bd mem Dayton Com Boys Club; Alfred Adler Inst Dayton; Mont Co Soc & Cancer Ctr; mem Med Adv Com Planned Parenthood. **Military Serv:** USAF tech sgt 3 1/2 yrs. **Business Addr:** School Physician, Dayton Bd of Educ, 3921 W 3rd St, Dayton, OH 45418.

EARLS, JULIAN MANLY
Association executive. **Personal:** Born Nov 22, 1942, Portsmouth, VA; son of Ida Earls and James Earls; married Zenobia N Gregory; children: Julian Jr, Gregory. **Educ:** Norfolk State Coll, BS 1964; Univ of Rochester, MS 1965; Univ of MI, MPH 1972, DrPH 1973; Harvard Univ Grad School of Bus, PMD Admin 1979. **Career:** Cuyahoga Comm Coll, adj math 1966-; NASA, physicist 1965-67; US Nuclear Regulatory Agency, radiation specialist 1967-68; NASA, physicist 1968-; Cleveland State Univ, adj prof 1973-; Capital Univ, adj prof 1984-; NASA Health Safety & Security Div, chief 1983-88, Office of Health Services, dir, beginning 1988; NASA, Lewis Research Center, Cleveland, Deputy Dir for Operations, currently. **Orgs:** Mem Mayors Council for CETA Funded Program Cleveland 1980-; health phys consultant 1970-; natl pres Natl Tech Assn Inc 1976-77; pres, org Cleveland Chapter NTA Inc 1974-76; mem Amer Health Phys Soc Publ Inform Comm 1966-73, Amer Nuclear Soc 1966-, US Nuclear Reg Comm Radiation Emerg Team 1971-, Environ Pollution Cont Bd NASA 1970-; exec safety bd NASA 1972-; vstg comm Case Western Res 1975-; bd of overseers Case Western Res 1977-; chmn Cleveland Bdof Ed Occup Wk Exp Adv Bd 1975-77; mem OH Environ Manpower Symp Strgn Comm 1974-, Natl Urban League Black Exec Exchange Prog 1973-; chmn Norfolk State Coll Alumni Assoc 1971-72, Kappa Alpha Psi Frat Inc 1965-; bd of dir Oppty Ind Ctr Inc, Natl Black Coll Alumni Hall of Fame 1986-; bd of trustees Inner City ProtestantPar 1974-76, Cuyahoga Commty Coll 1987-. **Honors/Awds:** Disting Alumnus Awd Norfolk State Coll 1974; Resol by state of OH House of Rep for serv to community 1974; US Atomic Energy Fellow 1964; NASA Fellow 1971; OIC Serv Awd 1974; EO Awd & Med NASA 1974; Fed Exec Bd Cert of Merit 1973; Natl Urban League Awd for BEEP 1973-74; Beta Kappa Chi Sci Hon Soc; Alpha Kappa Mu Honor; resolution passed by Cleveland City Council for Serv to Community 1978; Tech Achievement Awd Soc of Black Mfgs Engrs & Tech 1978; Disting Serv Awd Cleveland Jaycees; Disting Serv Awd Natl Tech Assoc 1981; Humanitarian Awd Wittenberg Univ 1983; Disting Serv Awd Natl Assoc of Black Accountants 1984; Nat'l Black College Alumni Hall of Fame 1986; Natl Urban League Black College Graduate of Distinction 1987; Technical Achievement Award, Natl Technical Assn 1987; DistinguishedBk In Science, Africa-Scientific Institute, 1990; Sons of Mandela Award, Cleveland NAACP, 1990; Academic Excellence Commendation, The University of Mississippi, 1989; NASA Medal for Exceptional Achievement 1995; Strong Men and Women Excellence in Leadership 1996; Cleveland All Star Salute, 1997. **Business Addr:** Deputy Dir for Operations, NASA, Lewis Research Center, 21000 Brookpark Rd, Cleveland, OH 44135.

EARLY, EZZARD DALE
Automobile dealer. **Personal:** Born Aug 15, 1953, Memphis, TN; son of Nicula B Early and Johne Early; married Joan, Dec 23, 1977; children: Ashley. **Educ:** University of Tennessee, BS, 1975; University of St Thomas, MBA, 1984. **Career:** Missouri Pacific Railroad, assistant tech mgr, 1976-77; Conoco Inc, rail fleet supervisor, 1978-84; Vista Chemical Co, rail fleet mgr, 1984-85; Deerbrook Forest Chrysler-Plymouth Inc, president, currently. **Orgs:** Retary Club, 1988-. **Business Addr:** President, Deerbrook Forest Chrysler-Plymouth, Inc, 22555 Hwy 59 N, Kingwood, TX 77339, (713)359-4000.

EARLY, GERALD
Writer, educator. **Personal:** Born Apr 21, 1952, Philadelphia, PA; son of Florence Fernandez Oglesby and Henry Early; married Ida Haynes Early, Aug 27, 1977; children: Linnet Kristen Haynes Early, Rosalind Lenora Haynes Early. **Educ:** University of Pennsylvania, Philadelphia, PA, BA, 1974; Cornell University, Ithaca, NY, MA, 1982, PhD, 1982. **Career:** Washington University, St Louis, MO, professor of English & African & Afro-American studies, 1982; Randolph Macon College for Women, Lynchburg, VA, writer in residence, 1990. **Honors/Awds:** Whiting Foundation Writer's Award, Whiting Foundation, 1988; CCLM/General Electric Foundation Award for Younger Writers, 1988; The Passing of Jazz's Old Guard, published in Best American Essays, 1986; University of Kansas Minority Postdoctoral Fellowship, 1985-87. **Special Achievements:** Daughters: On Family and Fatherhood, Addison-Wesley, 1994. **Business Addr:** Professor, African and Afro-American Studies, Washington University, Campus Box 1109, One Brookings Dr, St Louis, MO 63130-4899.

EARLY, IDA H.
Educational administrator. **Personal:** Born Nov 3, 1952, Dallas, TX; daughter of Thalia M Ephraim Haynes and Oscar E Haynes; married Gerald L Early, Aug 27, 1977; children: Linnet Kristin, Rosalind Lenora. **Educ:** University of Pennsylvania, BA, 1974; Cornell University, 1977-79. **Career:** University of Pennsylvania, assistant to the vice provost, 1975-77; Cornell University, administrative assistant to the director, 1980-82; Washington University, special projects, information & foundations, director, 1982-93, alumni & development programs, dir, 1993-. **Orgs:** Junior League of St Louis, vp, fundraising, 1991-93; Emmaus Homes, board member, 1990-92; Childhaven, board member, 1992-95; United Nations Association, board member, 1992-94; Washington University, Campus YMCA/YWCA, board member, 1987-95; United Way of St Louis Allocations Panel, 1992-94; Alpha Kappa Alpha, 1974-; Assn of Junior Leagues Intl Inc, bd mem, 1993-95. **Honors/Awds:** Cornell University, First Year Minority Graduate Fellowship, 1977, Graduate Fellowship, 1978, Research and Teaching Assistantship, 1979. **Special Achievements:** Coauthor, "The Consortium for Graduate Study in Management," Selections, The Magazine of the Graduate Management Admission Council, winter 1986, p 14-17. **Business Addr:** Director of Alumni & Development Programs, Washington University, School of Art, One Brookings Dr, Campus Box 1133, St Louis, MO 63130, (314)935-7127.

EARLY, JAMES COUNTS
Government official. **Personal:** Born Jan 12, 1947, Ocala, FL; son of Altobelle Hampton Flanders and James Tweetie Early; married Miriam Stewart Early; children: Jah-Mir, JaBen. **Educ:** Morehouse College, Atlanta, GA, BA, 1965-69; Canal Zone College, Panama Canal Zone, 1966-67; Howard University, Washington, DC, graduate studies, 1971-76; Georgetown University Advanced Portuguese Institute, Washington, DC, June-July, 1973. **Career:** Antioch College, Washington, DC, associate professor, 1976-77; The Howard University, Washington, DC, WHUR Radio, producer, writer, host, 1978-83; Institute for the Arts and Humanities, National Endowment for the Humanities, Washington, DC, humanist adminstrator, 1978-83; Smithsonian Institution, Washington, DC, executive assistant to the assistant secretary for public service, 1984-88, deputy assistant secretary for public service, 1989-90, acting assistant secretary for public service 1990-91, assistant secretary for education and public service, 1991-95; Asst Provost for Educational and Cultural Programs, 1995-; Cultural Studies & Communication Center for Folklife Programs & Cultural Studies, director, 1995-. **Orgs:** Arena stage outreach board, Arena Stage, 1988-; advisory board member, Textile Museum, 1989-; board of visitors, The Center for Public Policy, The Union Institute, 1988-; board member, The Washington Moscow Citizens Exchange, 1988-; board member, Fondo Del Sol Gallery, 1988-; 651 Kings Majestic Theater, board of directors, 1991-; The Environment Project, Washington, board of directors, 1992-; Africa Policy Information Center, 1992-; Crossroads Magazine, editorial advisory committee, 1990-. **Business Addr:** Director, Cultural Studies & Communication, Smithsonian Institution, 955 Cenfant Plaza, SW, Rm 1406, MRC 923, Washington, DC 20560.

EARLY, NORMAN S., JR.
Attorney. **Personal:** Born 1945. **Career:** City of Denver, district attorney, 1984-. **Business Phone:** (303)640-5176.

EARLY, PAUL DAVID
Military executive. **Personal:** Born Sep 10, 1963, Pittsburgh, PA; married Marilyn Ruth Bronough; children: Micah, Paul, Marcus. **Educ:** Attended, Central TX Coll, KS State Univ. **Career:** Voices of Truth Gospel Group, manager; Echo Co 4th MSB, staff sgt; Victory Records, owner. **Orgs:** Economic develop chmn NAACP Manhattan KS; layman Fellowship Temple COGC; master mason KAW BLUE Prince Hall Lodge #107; coach Fort Riley Boxing Team. **Honors/Awds:** Certificate of Appreciation, Special Olympics, 1987-88. **Military Serv:** AUS staff sgt 5 yrs; Arcom, Army Achievement Medal, Good Conduct Medal; Primary Leadership Development. **Home Addr:** 3132 Shady Trail, Tyler, TX 75702. **Business Addr:** Proprietor, Victory Records, PO Box 1154, Junction City, KS 66441.

EARLY, QUINN REMAR
Professional football player. **Personal:** Born Apr 13, 1965, West Hempstead, NY; married Casandra; children: Quinn Camer, Chance. **Educ:** Univ of Iowa, bachelor's degree in commercial art, 1988. **Career:** San Diego Chargers, wide receiver, 1988-90; New Orleans Saints, wide receiver, 1991-95; Buffalo Bills, wide receiver, 1996-. **Business Addr:** Professional Football Player, Buffalo Bills, One Bills Dr, Orchard Park, NY 14127, (716)648-1800.

EARLY, ROBERT S.
Business executive (retired). **Personal:** Born Nov 10, 1935, New York, NY; son of Rose C Jarrett Early and Robert S Early Jr; married Elizabeth Graham, Jun 7, 1986; children: David, Matthew. **Educ:** Univ of Hartford, BS 1957; Morgan State Coll, 1953-56. **Career:** Columbia Univ, vice pres of human resources, beginning 1978; Champion Intl Corp, dir of personnel 1974-78; Speakman Co, dir of personnel & industria relations 1972-74; Colt Indus, mgr personnel & public affairs 1968-72; RCA Global Comm, personnel admin 1958-68; Paper Tech Found Western Michigan Univ, rep; AMA, instr 1969-70; DE Comm Coll, employee relations instructor. **Orgs:** Chmn of bd, Intercommunity Camp, Westport, CT; bd of dirs, Higher Educ Retirement Community Assn; co-chair, Planned Parenthood of New York City, 1987-. **Military Serv:** AUS 1954-56. **Home Addr:** 158 Stone Oaks Drive, Hartsdale, NY 10530, (914)287-0161.

EARLY, SYBIL THERESA
Business executive. **Personal:** Born Aug 25, 1952, Staunton, VA. **Educ:** Bradley Univ, MBA 1972; Fashion Inst, commun 1974. **Career:** United Airlines, flight attendant; Winston Network TDI Inc, manager, account exec; ET Media Inc, owner, president, currently. **Orgs:** National Association of Female Executives; DuSable Museum. **Honors/Awds:** Outstanding Sales Performance Winston Network 1981; Outstanding Sales Performance 1982; Salesperson of the Year Winston Network 1983; Assoc Mem of the Year Awd for Amer Health & Beauty Aids Inst; Salesperson of the Year Winston Network 1986. **Special Achievements:** First female and African-American-owned independent outdoor advertising firm representing 93% of the out-of-home vendors in the US. **Business Addr:** President, ET Media, Inc, 2951 Sheffield, Chicago, IL 60657.

EARLY LAMBERT, VIOLET THERESA
Educational administrator (retired). **Personal:** Born Sep 24, 1924, New Orleans, LA; daughter of Alphonsine Harris Thompson (deceased) and William Thompson Sr (deceased); married Sylvester Early, Jul 25, 1945 (deceased); married Joseph R Lambert, Dec 16, 1991. **Educ:** YMCA School of Commerce, diploma 1945; Agric Mech & Normal Coll, BS 1964; Henderson State Univ, MS Ed 1977; Univ of Arkansas, LLD, 1993. **Career:** Univ of AR at Pine Bluff, asst registrar 1961-85, foreign student advisor 1965-83, registrar/dir of admissions 1983-90. **Orgs:** Mem AR AACRAO 1960-; mem Amer Assoc Registrars Admission Officers 1960-; adv Alpha Rho Chapter AKA Sor 1960-71; adv Alpha Kappa Mu Honor Soc 1970-89; mem Phi Delta Kappa Frat 1977-; sec Pine Bluff Boys Club 1981-83; mem Kappa Delta Pi Educ Frat 1983-; sec Amer Red Cross Chapter 1985-; sec Phi Delta Kappa Educational Frat 1985-; mem Phi Beta Lampda Business Frat; lector St Peter Catholic Church; vice chmn, Economics Opportunity Commission 1975-88; mem PB Social and Art Civic Club, 1960-; mem EOC, 1975-; mem Golden Lion Foundation; life mem AMAN/UAPB Alumni Assn; mem UAPB Foundation; perpetuator Sylvester Early Endowment Scholarship Fund, 1980-; volunteer American Red Cross; mem, AR RSVP, 1990-. **Honors/Awds:** This is Your Life Plaque Univ of AR PB 1983; Alpha Kappa Mu Plaque (service) 1982-84; Alumni Serv Awd AM&N/UAPB Alumni Assoc; Plaque Kappan of Month Phi Delta Kappa 1986; Hall of Fame, Leadership Pine Bluff 1988; Appreciation Award, Royal Knight Society 1988; Keepers of the Spirit Hall of Fame, Univ of AR PB 1994. **Home Addr:** 706 W 14th St, Pine Bluff, AR 71601.

EASLER, MICHAEL ANTHONY
Professional baseball player (retired). **Personal:** Born Nov 29, 1950, Cleveland, OH; married Brenda Jackson; children: Misty, Shandi, Khyla. **Educ:** Attended, Cleveland State Univ. **Career:** Houston Astros, 1973-75; California Angels, 1976; Pittsburgh Pirates, 1977; Pittsburgh Pirates, 1979-83; Boston Red Sox, outfielder 1984; New York Yankees, outfielder, 1986; Philadelphia Phillies, outfielder, 1987; New York Yankees, outfielder, 1987. **Honors/Awds:** Selected as BoSox Club's Man of the Year for contrib to team & cooperation in comm endeavors; Roberto Clemente Award, Pittsburgh Pirates, 1980; National League All-Star Team, 1981.

EASLEY, BILLY HARLEY
Photojournalist. **Personal:** Born Oct 10, 1925, St Louis, MO; son of Myrtle Easley Edmondson Johnson and William Harley Easley; married Gladys Brown Easley, Jan 29, 1958; children: Cassandra V. **Educ:** Tennessee State University, Nashville, TN, certificate, 1944; Nashville School of Photography, Nashville, TN, certificate, 1949; Nashville Technical School, Nashville, TN, certificate, 1975. **Career:** The Tennessean, Nashville, TN, photojournalist, 1966-. **Orgs:** Member, National Press Association, 1967-; member, National Association of Black Journalist, 1985-. **Honors/Awds:** Carter Goodwin Woodson Award-Negro History, 1969; Gannett Award, Special Olympics Photo Competition, 1987; Gannett Award, Gannett Publishing, 1984; Metro Firefighters Association Award, 1977; National Press Association Award, 1979; numerous other awards. **Military Serv:** US Army, Corporal, 1943-45. **Home Addr:** 1906 15th Ave S, Nashville, TN 37212. **Business Addr:** Photojournalist, The Tennessean, 1100 Broadway Street, Nashville, TN 37203.

EASLEY, BRENDA VIETTA
Association executive. **Personal:** Born Jun 28, 1951, Buffalo, NY; daughter of Lacetta Dixon Easley and James T Easley; children: Cynthia Duncan, Bryon Duncan, Robert Webb. **Career:** Buffalo & Erie County Public Library, Buffalo, NY, principal library clerk, 1968-88; Catholic Diocese of Buffalo, Buffalo, NY, dir, office of black ministry, 1988-. **Orgs:** Membership chairperson, National Assn of Black Catholic Administrators, 1989-; regional coord, National Black Catholic Congress, 1989-; chair, member, communication committee, Buffalo Area Metropolitan Ministers Board of Trustees, 1989-. **Business Addr:** Director, Catholic Diocese of Buffalo, Office of Black Ministry, 795 Main St, Buffalo, NY 14203.

EASLEY, CHARLES F., SR.
Educational administrator. **Personal:** Born May 3, 1935, Dalton, GA; son of Bertha Kenyon Easley & Oscar Easley Sr; married Helen Saxton Easley, Jun 19, 1960 (deceased); children: Charles Jr, Tania Patrice. **Educ:** Knoxville Coll, AB, 1956; Teachers Coll, Columbia Univ, teacher cert, 1959-60; Atlanta Univ, Clark Atlanta Univ, MA, 1965; GA State Univ, Doctoral Candidate, 1972-78. **Career:** Stephens School, counselor, social studies, asst principal, 1958-65; Morris Brown Coll, dean of students & asst prof, 1965-74; Natl Urban League, summer fellowship prog, consultant, 1967-73; Atlanta Jr Metropolitan Coll, vp of student affairs, 1974-. **Orgs:** West Fulton Rotary Club, past pres & secy, 1985-94; West End Rotary Club, 1994-; Leadership Atlanta, 1982-; Phi Delta Kappa Education Frat, 1972-; Warren Memorial Boys Club, 1980-86; Trinity School, bd of trustees, secy, personnel comm chair, 1980-; Natl Council of Presbyterian Men, natl pres, 1992-94; Southwest Atlanta Youth Academic & Athletic Assn, consultant, 1992-. **Honors/Awds:** Georgia Teachers & Educ Assn, State Teacher of the Year, 1963; NAFEO, Distinguished Alumni Award, 1992; Natl Council of Presbyterian Men, Churchman of the Year, 1994; Natl Council of Negro Women, Family of the Year, 1992. **Special Achievements:** "Personnel Selection & Placement in Selected Industries," master's thesis, 1964. **Military Serv:** US Army, sp-5, 1958-60; Reserve Commission, 1962-68. **Home Addr:** 787 Duffield Dr, NW, Atlanta, GA 30318, (404)792-2024.

EASLEY, DAMION
Professional baseball player. **Personal:** Born Nov 11, 1969, New York, NY. **Career:** California Angels, 1992-96; Detroit Tigers, 1997-. **Business Addr:** Professional Baseball Player, Detroit Tigers, 2121 Trumbull St, Detroit, MI 48216, (313)962-4000.

EASLEY, EDDIE V.
Educator. **Personal:** Born Nov 16, 1928, Lynchburg, VA; son of Berta Easley and George Easley; married Ruth Burton; children: Jacqueline, Michael, Todd. **Educ:** VA State Univ, BS 1948; IA State Univ, MS 1951, PhD 1957. **Career:** Drake Univ, chrmn prof 1957-65, 1966-84; Univ of WI Milwaukee, prof 1965-66; Kimberly Clark Corp, mrkt spec 1969-70; Wake Forest Univ, prof of bus, 1984-. **Orgs:** American Marketing Assoc, 1957-; NAACP 1985; Alpha Phi Alpha Fraternity 1948-; Bd of Zoning Adj 1971-73; Sigma Pi Phi 1985. **Honors/Awds:** Outstanding Teacher Award Drake Univ 1968; Outstanding Educ of Amer, 1970. **Military Serv:** AUS sp 3 1954-56; Honorable discharge 1956. **Business Addr:** Professor of Business, Wake Forest Univ, Box 7285 Reynolda Station, Winston-Salem, NC 27109.

EASLEY, JACQUELINE RUTH
Business executive. **Personal:** Born Oct 21, 1957, Ames, IA; daughter of Ruth Burton Easley and Dr Eddie V Easley; married Odell McGhee; children: Carey Lucia. **Educ:** Carleton Coll, BA 1980. **Career:** Amer Republic Ins Co, personnel assoc 1980, asst vice pres 1984-. **Orgs:** Mem Admin Mgmt Soc 1982-, Des Moines Public Schools Career Adv Council 1983-; bd of dir YWCA of Des Moines 1983-, pres 1987; United Way of Central IA 1984-; mem Minority Ed Braintrust 1985-; exec committee, NAACP, 1987-; chairperson, Metropolitan Transit Authority, 1990-. **Honors/Awds:** Woman of Achievement, 1984, Excellence in Leadership, 1990, YWCA of Des Moines 1984; Des Moines Register - "Up & Coming Business Leader" 1986; Board of Education, Des Moines Independent School District, 1990-, President, 1994; Outstanding Young Citizen, Des Moines Jaycess, 1990; Outstanding Young Iowan, Iowa Jaycees; America's Best and Brightest Business Professionals, 1992. **Business Addr:** Asst Vice Pres Prsnl & Education, Amer Republic Ins Co, 6th Ave, Des Moines, IA 50334.

EASLEY, KENNY, JR.
Professional football player (retired), business executive. **Personal:** Born Jan 15, 1959, Chesapeake, VA; married Gail. **Educ:** Univ of California, Los Angeles, BA, political science. **Career:** Seattle Seahawks, safety, 1981-87; Fo-Five Inc (businesses include: Makena Sport, Foster-Easley Sports Mgmt Group, Roller Wheels Inc, Alderwood Olds-Cadillac, Sherm's BBQ Inc), owner, currently. **Orgs:** United Way; United Cerebral Palsy. **Honors/Awds:** NFL Defensive Player of the Year, 1984; Kansas City 101 Club; NFL Alumni Assn, Def Back of the Year; First-team All-NFL; Pro Football Weekly; Sports Illustrated; NFL Films, Sporting News, AP; Pro Football Weekly, Football Digest, College & Pro Football Newsweekly; Seagram Sports Award; First-team All AFC; Pro Football Weekly, UPI; Seahawks Most Valuable Player; AFT Def, co-captain; AFC Def Player of the Week, nine times; AFC Def Rookie of the Year; First-team All-Rookie; First-team All NFL, All AFC; AFC Def Player of the Year; played in the Pro Bowl, 1982-85, 1987; First player in PAC-10 history named all-conference, 4 years; holds UCLA career interception record with 19; voterd to the NFL All-Decade Team, 1980's; voted into the College Football Hall of Fame, 1991; voted into UCLA Athletic Hall of Fame, 1991; UCLA football jersey #5 retired; voted into the Pacific NW Football Hall of Fame, 1994. **Business Addr:** Owner, Fo-Five Inc, 2401 Utah Ave S, #620, Seattle, WA 98134.

EASLEY, PAUL HOWARD, SR.
Clergyman. **Personal:** Born Sep 7, 1930, Charleston, WV; son of Estella Allen Easley and Alexander Pamplin Easley Sr; married Sarita (deceased); children: Paul Jr, Verita Green, David Allen. **Educ:** WV State Coll, BS 1956; Gammon Theological Seminary, BD 1959; Iliff Sch of Theology, MTS 1972; Interdenominational Theological Seminary, MDiv 1974. **Career:** Fairmont Trinity Methodist Church, pastor 1959-61; Roncevert-White Sulpher Charge, pastor 1961; US Army, chaplain 1961-80; Clark College, chaplain 1980-; Clark Atlanta Univ, Atlanta, GA, university chaplain, currently. **Orgs:** Mem Military Chaplains Assn 1962-, Amer Correctional Chaplains 1964-; Correctional Chaplains Assn 1964-, Clinical Pastoral Assn 1977-, Natl Campus Ministers Assn 1980-; charter president Optimist Intl 1984-; pres, PTA Therral HS, 1984-85; Omega Psi Phi Fraternity; Free and Accepted Masons; NAACP; WV Conference, United Methodist Ch; American Legion; Military Chaplains Association. **Honors/Awds:** Garnet High Hall of Fame, Charleston, WVA, 1966, 1996; Correctional Chaplain of Year 1974; Year Book Dedication of the Year Clark College 1981; Hall of Fame ROTC WV State College 1986; Honorary Commander of US Army, Appointed by Sec of Army, Chaplain Regiment, 1993-96. **Special Achievements:** US Army, First Afro-American Colonel of the Regiment of the Chaplains Corps, 1993-96. **Military Serv:** AUS colonel 23 yrs; Legion of Merit, Bronze Star (2), Meritorious Serv Medal, Army Commendation (2). **Business Addr:** University Chaplain, Clark Atlanta University, 240 J P Brawley Dr at Fair St, Thayer Hall #119, Atlanta, GA 30314.

EASON, OSCAR, JR.
Government Official, civil rights organization executive. **Personal:** Born Jun 30, 1930, San Antonio, TX; son of Oscar & Doris Lucille; married Lois Anne Eason, Feb 3, 1961; children: Angela Green, Oscar Eason III. **Educ:** Prairie View A&M, BS, mechanical engineering, 1956; St Mary's University, MS engineering, 1970. **Career:** Pacific Architects & Engineers, Inc, sup general engineer, 1970-72; Environmental Protection Agency, general engineer, 1973-74; US Navy, Trident Missile System, proj mgr, 1974-81; US Army Corps of Engineers, sup mechanical engineer, 1981-91, asst chief engineer div, 1991-. **Orgs:** Blacks in Government, Inc, natl pres, 1994-, bd chair, 1982-90; Northwest Coalition Against Malicious Harrassment, vp, 1983-87; Seattle King Cty Dispute Resolution Ctr, vp, 1983-92; NAACP, Seattle, bd mem, 1983-; Black Leadership Forum, 1995-; Natl Soc of Professional Engineers, 1972-. **Honors/Awds:** US Navy, Trident Weapon System Prog, Appreciation for Contribution, 1981; Seattle federationeral Executive Bd, Employee of the Year, 1990; US Army, Kuwait Emergency Recovery Office, Achievement Medal for Civilian Svc, 1991; Seattle District, Corps of Engineers, Community Svc Award, 1992; Nordstorm Department Stores, Community Svc Award, Outstanding Citizen in the Northwest, 1990. **Special Achievements:** Newspaper articles: Trying to Liberate Whites from Prison of Prejudice, Seattle Times Newspaper; Halt the Cycle of Despair for Young Black Men; Analyzing Remarks By Nakasone; A Look At Changing White Attitudes Toward Black Americans; Nike Needs Push to Change Its Policies, Seattle Post Intelligencer; Total School Integration Remains the Only Answer, Seattle Post Intelligencer. **Military Serv:** US Army, spec-4, 1950-52. **Home Addr:** 5507 S Leo St, Seattle, WA 98178, (206)725-5303.

EASTER, ERIC KEVIN
Publisher, media executive. **Personal:** Born Jan 19, 1961, Baltimore, MD. **Educ:** Howard University, BA, journalism, 1983. **Career:** DC Coalition for the Homeless, executive director, 1984; Easter and Associates, president, 1985-88; Jackson for President, press assistant, 1988; National Rainbow Coalition, press secretary, 1988-90; Wilder for President, press secretary, 1991-92; New African Visions, president, 1989-; One Media, chairman/CEO, 1992-. **Orgs:** National Association of Black Journalists, 1984-; Howard University Communications Alumni Association, vice pres, 1985-86. **Honors/Awds:** Links, Sojourner Truth Award, 1993; City of New York, Mayor's Special Recognition, 1992. **Special Achievements:** Co-creator, "Songs of My People" book and exhibit, 1992; co-producer, Taste of DC Annual Festival, 1991-. **Business Phone:** (202)265-1071.

EASTER, HEZEKIAH H.
State official (retired). **Personal:** Born Oct 16, 1921, Suffolk, VA; son of Jamie Elnora Woodruff Easter and Hezekiah Easter; married Ruth D Lowe; children: Gregory Paul, Michael Curtis, Scott Anthony. **Educ:** Attended, Juilliard School of Music, Metro Music School, NY S Industrial and Labor Relations School, Cornell Univ. **Career:** Nyack Village, trustee 1965, 1967, 1969; Metro Area Apprentice Training, supvr 1968-72; Rockland Co Legislature, 1969-89; NY State Dept of Labor, job training specialist 1972-84, public work wage investigator 1984-90. **Orgs:** Past mem Rockland Acacia Lodge #59; trustee Pilgrim Baptist Church; life mem Nyack branch NAACP; mem Nyack Rotary 1965-77; sec bd vis Letchworth Village 1969, 1974; advisory council BSA Rockland County Council 1965; past pres Hudson Valley Regional Council 1981-82; mem Nyack Hospital Corp 1966; pres Mt Moor Cemetery Assn 1977; mem, bd of dirs Welfare League/Letchworth Village 1984-90; bd. of dirs Abbott House 1990; African-American Historical Society of Rockland County, vice pres, 1987. **Honors/Awds:** Distinguished Serv Award, RC Council of BSA 1962; Citizen of the Year VFW 1967; Rep of the Year, Orangetown Rep Club 1973; Serv Award, Nyack Village Bd 1971; 1st Black elected to public office Rockland Co; Dr Martin Luther King Brotherhood Award, Human Rights Com LVDC 1975; Capitals of the Age of Enlightment Award AFSCI 1976; Outstanding Achievement Kappa Alpha Psi Fraternity 1988; 20 Years Service Award Rockland County Legislature 1989; Lifetime Achievement Award Chamber of Commerce of the Nyacks 1990; Desert Storm for World Peace Medal, 1991; Governor's Medal for Conspicuous Public Service, 1992. **Military Serv:** AUS corpl 1942-45. **Home Addr:** 100 N Franklin St, Nyack, NY 10960.

EASTER, MARILYN
Educator. **Personal:** Born Jan 6, 1957, Oklahoma City, OK; daughter of Delois Ann Pettigrew & William L; married Dr Walter Easter. **Educ:** University of Colorado, BA; Denver University, MA, MSW; University of San Francisco, EdD. **Career:** Marketing By Marilyn, consultant, 1979-82; General Dentistry,

mktg mgr, 1982-; Amador Adult School, instructor, 1983-85; Chabot College, instructor, 1985-87; California State Univ, instructor, 1987-91; St Mary's College, assoc prof, 1991-93; College of Notre Dame, assoc prof, 1993-. **Orgs:** College of Notre Dame, SAFE, chair, 1997-; American Soc of Training & Dev, 1993-97; Phi Delta Kappa Fraternity, 1991-; California State Teachers Association, 1994-; NAACP, 1997-; Natl Assn of Girl Scouts of Amer, 1991-95; Coll of Notre Dame, steering comm, co-chair, 1997-. **Honors/Awds:** Outstanding Dissertation Award, 1993; Outstanding Student Council Leadership Award, 1992; Emmy Nominee, Affirmative Action Pro 209, 1997; NAFEO, Conference Speaker, 1998; Teacher Excellence, Key Note Speaker, 1998. **Special Achievements:** The ABCs of Mktg a Successful Business, 1986; Stress and Coping Mechanism Among Female Dentists, 1991; Evaluation of Higher Education, A Case Study, 1992; Picking the Perfect School, 1993; A Triangulated Reseaarch Design for Studying Stress, 1993. **Business Addr:** Associate Professor, College of Notre Dame, 1500 Ralston Ave, Belmont, CA 94002-1997.

EASTER, RUFUS BENJAMIN, JR.
Educational administrator. **Personal:** Born Oct 5, 1928, Hampton, VA; married Evelyn Wills. **Educ:** NY Univ Hampton Inst; Temple U; Piano Tech Schs. **Career:** Hampton Inst, admin 1950; VA State School for the Deaf & Blind, curr developer, consultant to supt 1954; Hampton Assn of Arts & Humanities, founder, exec dir 1967; WVEC, consultant comm affairs radio & TV stations 1970. **Orgs:** Bd dirs Assn Coll & Univ Concert Mgrs; Peninsula Symphony Orch; Peninsula Comm Theatre; mem of Asso Council Arts; Assn State & Local Hist; Assn Preservation VA Antiquities; mem Bachelor Benedict Club. **Honors/Awds:** Man of yr award Penisula Vol Serv Bur for works of arts & humainities 1969.

EASTER, WILFRED OTIS, JR.
Educational administrator. **Personal:** Born May 26, 1941, New York, NY; son of Mae Smith Easter and Wilfred Otis Easter Sr; married Mary Moore Easter (divorced 1986); children: Allison Garner, Mallory. **Educ:** Harvard College, Cambridge, MA, BA, history, 1964, Univ of Minnesota, Minneapolis, MN, 1974-79. **Career:** Sports Illustrated Magazine, New York, NY, advertising promotion, 1964-66; Windsor Mountain School, Lenox, MA, teacher/coach, 1966-68; Carleton College, Northfield, MN, associate, dean of students, 1968-76; Control Data Corp, Minneapolis, MN, operations manager, 1979-86; University of California, Berkeley, CA, executive director, 1986-. **Orgs:** Member, National Association of PreCollege Directors, 1986-; member, Natl Assn of Minority Engineering Program Administrators, 1986-; member, Northern California Council of Black Professional Engineers,1986-; member, World Wildlife Fund, 1987-; member, East Bay GO Club, 1986-. **Honors/Awds:** Public Speaking Prize, Harvard College, 1964. **Home Addr:** 266 Adams St, Oakland, CA 94610. **Business Addr:** Executive Director, MESA, University of California - Berkeley, Lawrence Hall of Science, Berkeley, CA 94720.

EASTMAN, ELEANOR CORINNA
Scientist. **Personal:** Born Mar 24, New York, NY; divorced; children: Elizabeth Ann. **Educ:** Hunter Coll, AB 1946; Brooklyn Coll, Grad School 1952. **Career:** Dept of Health, chem lab 1949; Dept of Public Works NY, chemist; Dept of General Services Lab, chief of physical testing div. **Orgs:** Exec vice pres Moore Water & Energy Consult Corp; sec, treas Natl Tech Assoc; exec bd, pres Chap 24, bd of del Civil Serv Tech Guild; bd of deacons Riverside Ch 1980-86; lay couns Riverside Church 1977; 5th vice pres 1970, 1st vice pres 1972 Riverside Ch Bus & Professional Womens Club. **Honors/Awds:** Publ Rapid Colorimetric Determination of Formaldehyde in Toxoids, Jrnl of Amer Pharm Assoc 1951. **Business Addr:** Chief of Physical Testing Div, Dept of Public Works, 480 Canal St, New York, NY 10013.

EASTMOND, JOAN MARCELLA
Educator. **Personal:** Born May 10, 1940, Brooklyn, NY; daughter of Lerta Taylor-Eastmond and Evans E Eastmond; children: Brian S Malone. **Educ:** West Virginia State Coll, BS, home economics, 1963; Cornell Univ, summer instructor Afro Amer Studies, certificate, 1969; Lincoln Univ, Master of Human Services, 1988; Union of Experimental Colleges/Univ, PhD, 1988. **Career:** New York City Bd of Educ, teacher, 1963-70; State Educ Opportunity Center, instructor; Afram Assn, asst to pres, 1971-78; Bedford Study Restoration Corp, dir youth employment, 1978-85; Fort Green Sr Citizens Center, dir youth workers, senior center, 1985-; Lincoln Univ, adjunct prof, field study coord, 1988-. **Orgs:** Pres, Soc Unlimited, 1964-; chmn, Cotilion Found Comm, Natl Assn of Business Professional Women's Clubs, 1980-; Fund Raising Comm, New York Council UNCF, 1980-84; chmn, Teens Found Comm, Jack & Jill of Amer, 1983-88; bd mem, Afram Assoc, 1987-, Health Watch, 1988-. **Honors/Awds:** Crisco Award, Home Economic Dept WVSC, 1963; Trophy, Lil' Sisters Soc Unlimited, 1966; Essence Women, January 1971; Afrikan Liberation Day Bibliography (15pp), 1973; Devel Activities (12pp), 1973; Citation, Natl Council of Black Child Devel, 1974; Citation, Greater New York Council, Exploring Div, 1981; Certificate, 88 Precinct Council, 1987; Key Women of America Award; Proclamation NYS Senate. **Home Addr:** 342 Macon St, Brooklyn, NY 11233.

EASTMOND, LEON
Manufacturing company executive. **Career:** A L Eastmond & Sons Inc, president, CEO, currently. **Orgs:** NAACP; Urban League; American Boiler Manufacturers Association; Oil Heat Association; 100 Black Men. **Honors/Awds:** Ernest & Young, Minority Regional Manufacturer of the Year, 1977; MBDA, Minority Manufacturer of the Year, 1996; NYS Governor's Award, 1995; Star Lite, Little League Award. **Special Achievements:** Company is ranked #77 on Black Enterprise magazine's list of top 100 industrial/service companies. **Business Addr:** President, CEO, A L Eastmond & Sons Inc, 1175 Legett Ave, Bronx, NY 10474, (212)378-3000.

EASTON, RICHARD JAMES
Business executive. **Personal:** Born Jul 30, 1934, Chicago, IL; married Iris A Walker; children: Michael, Danitra, Richard Jr, Shawn, Ricarda, Erika. **Educ:** Chicago State U, BS 1962. **Career:** Munic Credit Unoin of NYC, controller; NY State Spl Dep Controllers Ofc, chief analyst 1976-77; Recruitment & Training Prgm, dir 1970-75; Bedford & Stuyvesant Restoration Corp, mgr 1967-70; NYC, tchr 1963-67. **Orgs:** Mem Assn of Accountants; Nat Bus Tchrs Assn; mem Alpha Phi Alpha. **Military Serv:** USN 1952-55. **Business Addr:** 156 Williams St, New York, NY 10038.

EATMAN, JANICE A.
Counselor, program facilitator. **Personal:** Born Mar 3, 1959, Cleveland, OH. **Educ:** Northwestern Univ, BS Communications 1981; Cleveland State Univ, Post Grad Work 1983-. **Career:** Welfare Rights Organization, community relations specialist 1984; Ohio Works, recruiter 1985; Vocational Guidance Servs, employment & training specialist 1985-88; Case Western Reserve Univ, Intervention Asst, 1987; HE Davis Intermediate School, coordinator of youth resource center, 1989-. **Orgs:** Mem Northwestern Alumni Assoc Cleveland Chapter 1981-; public relations consultant Group Dynamics Inc 1982-83; volunteer UNCF 1983-; mem Messengers of Joy Gospel Ensemble 1984-; planning comm Martin Luther King Jr Day Celebration 1984-85; mem Urban League of Greater Cleveland Fund Develop Comm 1984-85; grad advisor Alpha Kappa Alpha Sor Inc 1985-88 (2 terms); publicity co-chair Ways & Mean Comm AKA Program Years 1985, 1986; mem Northwestern Black Alumni Assoc 1986-; presenter, Carver Connection Adopt-A-School Program, 1987-88; presenter, Career Days Cleveland Public Schools, 1987-88. **Honors/Awds:** Volunteer Serv Award HARAMBEE Serv to Black Families 1983; guest panelist Salute to Excellence Scholarship Program 1986; appointed by the headmaster to the Search Committee for the new Director of Upper School, Hawken School 1987; guest panelist, Minority Recruitment Forum, Hawken School, 1987; volunteer award, Cleveland Public Schools, Carver Connection Adopt-A-School, 1988; Workshop presenter, Pittsburgh Civic Garden Center, 1988. **Business Addr:** On-Site Coordinator Youth Resource Center, Harry E Davis Intermediate School, 10700 Churchill Ave, Cleveland, OH 44106.

EATON, JAMES NATHANIEL, SR.
Educator, museum director. **Personal:** Born Sep 14, 1930, Richmond, VA; son of Sarah Elizabeth Cousins Eaton and John Jasper Eaton; married Leathea Denesa Owen Eaton, Jul 29, 1985; children: Jacqueline Eaton-Thomas, Sabrina Elizabeth, James N Jr, Robert H, Samuel Kenyata. **Educ:** Fisk Univ, Nashville TN, BA, 1952, MA, 1953; Duke Univ, Durham NC, 1962-63, 1964-66, research scholar, 1991; Florida State Univ, Tallahassee FL, 1969-70. **Career:** Miles Coll, Birmingham AL, history instructor, 1953-55; Richmond Police Dept, Richmond VA, patrolman, 1956-57; Hanover School for Boys, Hanover VA, asst principal, 1957-58; Florida A&M Univ, Tallahassee FL, prof of history, 1958-, distinguished professor of history, currently; Black Archives, Tallahassee, FL, 1975-; US Department of Defense, research professor, 1992-96. **Orgs:** Life mem, NAACP, Kappa Alpha Psi Frat; bd mem, Natl Historical Publications & Records Bd, 1978-81; fellow, Intl Initiative for Creative Communication, 1979-83; bd mem, Florida Museum Assn, 1984-; mem, African Amer Museums Assn, 1984-; chairman, African-American Study Commission for the State of Florida, 1990-92; State of Florida, Dr Martin Luther King Jr Birthday Celebration Committee, chairman; Florida Commission of Education Task Force on the Teachingof African-American History & Culture in the Public Schools, K-12, chmn, 1994-97. **Honors/Awds:** Danforth Scholar, Danforth Found, 1964-66; Certification in Archives Admin, American Univ, 1976; FSU/Rockerfeller Scholar, Florida State Univ, 1983; FAMU Centennial Medallion, Florida A&M Univ, 1988; James N Eaton Appreciation Day, 1988; cited in over 100 leading magazines and publications including: Time, US News & Report, Art & Auction and Who's Who in the South and Southeast; published numerous articles: Teacher of the Year, Florida A&M Univ, 25 times 1958-96; James Eaton Endowment Fund, 1988-; State of Florida, CASE Professor of the Year, 1991; Capitol City Forum, Man of the Year Award, 1992; Publisher of the world famous "African-American History is the History of America Calendar;" Awarded over $2 million in Historic Preservation Grants. **Business Addr:** Distinguished Professor of History/Director, Black Archives, Black Archives Research Center & Museum, Florida A&M University, Tallahassee, FL 32307.

EATON, LELA M. Z.
Educator. **Personal:** Born Dec 30, 1946, Granville Co, NC. **Educ:** Johnson C Smith U, AB 1968; Columbia U, MS 1971; Univ NC Tchr Kittrell Coll, PhD 1973. **Career:** "Daily Advance", columnist 1970-71; S Granville High School, teacher 1968-70; "W Harlem Spokesman", editor 1971. **Orgs:** Mem Nat Council Tchrs English; Assn Journalism; Granville Improvement & Assn; Nat Council Coll Newspaper Advisors; mem Belton Creek Bapt Ch. **Honors/Awds:** English William Brewer Award 1968; fellowship Knight Newspaper Found 1971; alumni fellow Univ NC 1974-75; (cum laude) Smith Univ 1968.

EATON, MINETTA GAYLOR
Educator. **Personal:** Born Oct 1, 1912, Whitakers, NC; married James W; children: Jeanne Phillips, Faye Yvonne. **Educ:** Morgan State U, BA 1936; NY U, MA 1942; NY Univ Chicago U, additional study tour of Europe. **Career:** Raleigh City Schools NC, prin 1959-73, teacher 1944-59; Spaulding High School NC, teacher, librarian 1938-44; Brick School NC, teacher 1936-38. **Orgs:** State 2nd vice pres mem exec bd NC Adminstrv Women in Edn; mem NC Nat Council of Adminstrv Women in Edn; co-chairperson membership com State Dist & Raleigh-Wake Unit of NC Retired Personnel; mem NC Assn of Educators; Nat Educ Assn; Nat Elementary Prins Assn; bd dir Downtown Housing Improvement Corp 1974-77; bd dir Research Triangle Lung Assn; bd dir Wake Co Mental Health Assn; NC bd dir Mental Health Assn; adv council Inner City Statellite Mental Health Center; State Steering Com; chairperson com for state's 1975 fall forum NC Council of Women's Orgn Inc; mem Nat Council of Negro Women; Com ofAdminsrrn & Mgmt YWCA; Am Assn of Univ Women; Alpha Kappa Alpha Sorrity Inc; Women in Action for Prevention of Violence & Its Causes; Task Force of S Central Comm;RSVP Adv Council Bd 1975-77; Wake Black Dem Cauces; NAACP; Raleigh-Wake Cit Assn; Dem Women of Wake Co; mem Alphabettes of Raleigh; Prestige Club; First Bapt Ch; Notable Ams of Era. **Honors/Awds:** Appointed state co-chairperson of Women in Action for Prevention of Violence's State Chapter Meeting; appointed to Nat Publicity Com of Moles Inc; appointed to Mid-Altantic Regional Nominating Com of Alpha Kappa Alpha Sorority; several awards Alpha Theta Omega Chap of Alpha Kappa Alpha Sorority 1975; honored by Alpha Kappa Alpha Sorority Inc Ilpah Thega Omega Chpt; cert Nat Caucus of Black Aged Inc 1974-75; honored by Radio Station WPTF NC comm leader of Am award 1969.

EATON, PATRICIA FRANCES
Senior program analyst. **Personal:** Born Jun 21, 1944, Washington, DC; children: David Howard. **Educ:** Palmer Mem Inst, Coll Prep, 1959-62; TX Southern Univ, BA Engl 1967; Univ of CA San Diego, African Studies 1967. **Career:** Lesotho Southern Africa, Peace Corps Vol 1967-70; DC Public Schools, teacher 1970-71; DC Dept Human Res, comm relations officer 1971-74; Africare Inc, Comm dir 1974-77; Black Women's Comm Devel Fund, exec dir 1977-79; Overseas Educ Fund, dir for Africa 1979-80; US Peace Corps & USAID Africa, consult 1980-84; African Devel Found, foundation rep, 1984-86; DC Public Schools, teacher, 1986-; DC Public Schools Administration, 1990-; senior program analyst, currently. **Orgs:** Mem bd dir DC Clothing for Kids Inc 1972-, 2nd Genesis Drug Rehab 1980-; life mem Africare 1980-. **Honors/Awds:** Outstanding Teacher, 1990-92; Exemplary Teacher Award, 1994. **Home Addr:** 4418 Eastern Ave NE, Washington, DC 20018.

EATON, THELMA LUCILE
Educator. **Personal:** Born Dec 17, 1928, New Orleans, LA; daughter of Inez Porter and T R W Harris; married William; children: Maurice, Allison. **Educ:** Fisk U, BA 1949; Xavier U, 1950-51; NY U, 1952; Univ of Sthrn CA, MSW 1965; Univ of Sthrn CA, DSW 1973. **Career:** Whittier Coll, prof 1970-; USC Mini-Coll Univ of Sthrn CA, admin off soc wk prog; Dept of Social Serv, staff dev offcr and training & supvis; Suicide Prevent Center, psychiat soc worker; Orleans Parish Sch Bd, tchr nursery sch and elem sch. **Orgs:** Coalition of 100 Black Women; Amer Assn of Univ Prof; State Leason Comm on Human Serv; Natl Assn of Soc Work; Geront Soc; Soc for the Stud of Social Prob; Counc on Social Work Edn; Natl Counc of Negro Women; advis bd Rio Hondo United Way; USC Geront Center Serv to Black Aged; Natl Caucus of Black Aged; Grtr LA Commun Action Agency; bd of dir YWCA; Foster Grdparent Prog; Retired Sr Vol Prog; Rio Hondo Vol Center; pres Awar Women of CA; mem CA Demo State Central Comm LA Co Central Comm; Alpha Kappa Delta; CA State Commiss. **Honors/Awds:** Outstanding Edutr of Amer 1974; Notable Am Award 1976-77; apptd Success to the Ltd Govr of CA; recip Key to Whittier Coll 1976; Outstanding Women of the Year CA; Assembly Black Women's Lawyers Recipient of Community Service Award. **Home Addr:** 1644 Wellington Rd, Los Angeles, CA 90019.

EAVES, A. REGINALD
County official. **Personal:** Born Mar 29, 1935, Jacksonville, FL; son of Gladys Eaves and Cecil Eaves. **Educ:** Morehouse Coll, BA 1956; New England Law School, LLB 1966, JD 1970; Boston Univ, attended; Atlanta Univ, attended. **Career:** City Boston School, guidance couns, teacher; Roxbury Youth Train

& Emp Ctr, exec dir 1963-66; So End Neighborhood Action Prog Inc, exec dir 1966-69;Mayors Office of Human Rights Boston, admin 1969-72; Penal Inst Suffolk Cty & Boston, commiss 1972-74; Boston Univ School of Med, lecturer 1973-74; Commonweath MA, admin asst sent pres; Atlanta Univ, exec asst mayor 1974-; Dept of Publ Safety, commissioner 1974-78; Morehouse Sch of Medicine, lecturer 1983-; Fulton County Govt, commissioner 1979-. **Orgs:** Trustee, bd mem Fulton Cty Bd Health, Natl Assoc Urban Crim Justice Plnng Dir, Amer Dem Action, Advent School, Natl Young Men & Womens Devel Corp, New Breed Teachers, Assoc for Protection Span Spkng; life mem NAACP, Anti-Defamation League; life mem NAACP; mem Natl Org of Black Law Enforcement Execs, NOBLE, IACP, SCLC, Operation PUSH; trustee Fulton County Library; chmn Economic Oppor of Atlanta; chmn GA Assoc of Black Elected Officials; pres Natl Assoc of Black County Officials. **Honors/Awds:** One of Ten Outstanding Young Men of Boston 1970; Outstanding Young Men of Amer 1970; Citation of Merit Graham Jr Coll 1971; Wall St Jrnl Stud AchievementAwd 1956; "Y's" Men Young Man of of the Year Awd 1974; over 350 awards and certificates. **Military Serv:** AUS E-4 1957-59. **Business Addr:** Commissioner, Dept of Public Safety, 260 Peachtree St, Suite 1750, Room 208, Atlanta, GA 30303.

EBBE, OBI N. I.
Educator. **Personal:** Born Jul 8, 1949, Umuobom, Imo, Nigeria; son of Virginia Uduola Ebbe and Ebbe Muoneke Ilonuma; children: Nneka I Ebbe. **Educ:** University of London, London, UK, GCE, A/level, 1967; Western Michigan University, Kalamazoo, MI, BA (honors), 1976, MA, 1977; Southern Illinois University, Carbondale, IL, PhD, 1981. **Career:** Western Illinois University, Macomb, IL, asst prof, 1981; University of Tennessee, Chattanooga, TN, asst prof, 1981-82; Ohio Northern University, Ada, OH, asst prof, 1982-84; Valparaiso University School of Law, Valparaiso, IN, fellow, 1984-85; Delta State University, Cleveland, MS, assoc prof, 1985-87; State University of New York at Brockport, NY, prof, 1987-. **Orgs:** Academy of Criminal Justice Sciences, 1981-; American Society of Criminology, 1981-; International Assn for the Study of Organized Crime, 1985-; Academy of Security Educators and Trainers, 1990-; American Society for Industry Security, 1990-. **Honors/Awds:** Hussel H Seibert, Honors Research Award, Western Michigan University, Kalamazoo, MI, 1975-76; Alpha Kappa Delta, National Sociology Honor Society, 1975; AWGU County Teacher Training College, Valedictorian, 1961. **Home Addr:** PO Box 508, Brockport, NY 14420. **Business Addr:** Professor, Criminology and Criminal Justice, State University of New York College at Brockport, 159 Faculty Office Bldg, Brockport, NY 14420, (716)395-2665.

EBO, SISTER ANTONA (ELIZABETH LOUISE EBO)
Pastoral associate. **Personal:** Born Apr 10, 1924, Bloomington, IL; daughter of Louise Teal Ebo (deceased) and Daniel Ebo (deceased). **Educ:** St Louis Univ, St Louis MO, BS Medical Records Admin, 1962, MHA Hospital Exec Devel, 1970; Aquinas Inst of Theology, Dubuque IA; MTh Health Care Ministry, 1978. **Career:** St Clare Hospital, Baraboo WI, exec dir, 1967-71; St Marys Hospital Medical Center, Madison WI, asst exec dir, 1970-74; Wisconsin Catholic Health Assn, Madison WI, exec dir, 1974-76; St Marys Hospital Medical Center, Madison WI, chaplain, 1978-81; Univ of Mississippi Medical Center, Jackson MS, chaplain, 1981-87; Franciscan Sisters of Mary, St Louis MO, councilor, 1987-91; St Nicholas Church, pastoral associate, currently. **Orgs:** Member first group of sisters participating in "March on Selma"-St Louis Archdiocese, 1965, St Louis Archdiocesan Human Rights Comm, 1965-67; Natl Black Sisters' Conf, mem, 1968-, pres, 1979-81, scy, 1997-; vice chairperson, Madison Urban League Board of Directors, 1972-76, Madison Housing Authority Commr, 1974-76; vice chairperson, Wisconsin Health Facilities Authority, 1976; Natl Assn of Catholic Chaplains, 1979-; Comm on Catholic Health Care Ministry, 1987-88; Leadership Conference of Women Religious, 1987-91; SSM Health Care System Board of Directors, 1987-91, Leadership Conf of Women Religious Task Force on Women's Concerns, 1989-90; St Louis Archdiocesan National Black Catholic Congress, planning committee, 1988-, bd of trustees, 1997-; Cardinal Ritter Institute, bd, 1991-, scy, 1997; St Louis Archdiocesan Human Rights Commission, 1991-; Missouri Catholic Conference Social Concerns Department, 1991-94. **Honors/Awds:** Featured in Catfish & Crystal, Doubleday, Garden City NY, Ernest Kirschten, 1965; Ebony Magazine, "Speaking of People," 1967; Liguori Magazine, "Negro Nun," 1969; Certificate of Commendation, Madison Urban League, Madison WI, 1976; Certificate of Commendation, Governor Patrick Lucey, Wisconsin Health Facilities Authority, 1976; Elected Delegate, Jackson MS Archdiocese, Natl Black Catholic Congress, 1987, 1992, 1997; Pioneer Healers, Health Care, Stepsis & Liptak, 1989; Harriet Tubman Award, National Black Sisters' Conference, 1989; Catholic Health World, 1993, Profile: Moment in History; Loyola University, Chicago, Honorary Doctorate, 1995. **Home Addr:** 8063 Hafner Ct, St Louis, MO 63130. **Business Addr:** Pastoral Associate, St Nicholas Church, 701 N Eighteenth St, St Louis, MO 63103.

EBONG, REGINA U.
Accountant. **Personal:** Born Dec 9, 1953, Jos, Nigeria; daughter of Janet Chinweze and Francis Chinweze; married Ben Ebong, Mar 3, 1973; children: Nne, Ben, Victor, Francis. **Educ:** University of Nebraska, BSBA, 1981, MBA, 1983. **Career:** Enron Corp, senior EDP auditor, 1981-86; Hayes & Associates, partner, 1986-88; Regina Ebong, CPA, owner, 1988-. **Orgs:** AICPA, 1983-; NE Society of CPA's, state & local government accounting committee, 1989-; CISA, 1982; Institute of International Auditors, 1985-; Girls Inc, vice chairman, finance committee, 1988-90; Voices for Children, board member, 1992-. **Honors/Awds:** Omaha Chamber of Commerce, Leadership Omaha, 1991. **Special Achievements:** Omaha Chamber of Commerce, nine months of intensive leadership training program, Class 13, 1991. **Business Phone:** (402)346-1526.

ECCLES, PETER WILSON
Business executive. **Personal:** Born Jan 31, 1936, Lawrence, Long Island, NY; son of Mable Smith Eccles and Wilson Eccles; married Achla Chib; children: Peter Rahul, Radika Elisabeth. **Educ:** Dartmouth, BA magna cum laude 1958; Harvard Law Sch, JD cum laude 1963. **Career:** World Bank, atty 1963-65; Cleary Gottlieb Steen & Hamilton Law Firm, assoc 1965-69; Goldman Sachs & Co, vice pres 1969-74; Ultrafin Internat, vp, mgr corp fin 1974-77; Citibank, vice pres, man. dir, 1977-86; Prudential Bache Capital Funding, dir, investment banking, 1987-90; Eccles Associates, president 1990-; United Nations Development Program, senior advisor 1990-91. **Orgs:** Bd of dir Citizens Com for Children 1967-74; mem exec com, trustees Found for Child Devel 1973-77; mem Econ Club of NY 1979-; charter mem Exec Leadership Council 1986-90; mem bd of visitors Rockefeller Center of Social Sci at Dartmouth 1986-93; mem Council on Foreign Relations, 1993-. **Honors/Awds:** Phi Beta Kappa, Dartmouth Coll 1958; Fulbright Scholar, Cambridge Univ, England, 1959; various publs 1959-79. **Business Addr:** President, Eccles Associates, Inc, International Plaza, 303 E 43rd St, Ste 15-C, New York, NY 10017, (212)682-6064.

ECHOLS, ALVIN E.
Attorney. **Personal:** Born Dec 5, 1930, Philadelphia; son of Rhydine Echols and Alvin Echols; married Gwendolyn G; children: Donna G Echols-Kearse, Alison D Echols. **Educ:** VA Unoin U, BS 1955; Howard U, LLB 1957. **Career:** North City Congress, exec dir 1963-; Priv Law Prac, 1957-63. **Orgs:** Commr Hum Rel Comm 1969-; mem PA chap of Nat Council on Crime & Delinquency 1971-75; Health & Welfare Council 1974-; mem Friends of Free Library 1972-75; Comm Ldrshp Seminar Program 1962-; deputy chairman State Republican Party 1971-75. **Honors/Awds:** Distinguished merit citation Nat Conf of Christian & Jews 1967; achievement award Industrialization Cntr 1966; certificate of appreciation Personnel Dept Philadelphia Med Coll PA 1972-; Grtr Philadelphia Partnership 1974-. **Business Addr:** 1428 N Broad St, Philadelphia, PA 19121.

ECHOLS, DORIS BROWN
Educator (retired). **Personal:** Born Oct 8, 1928, Oakwood, TX; daughter of William P Brown & Tinnie Viola Davis-Brown; married James Jerome Echols, Oct 12, 1950 (died 1974); children: Jennifer Diane Echols; married Richard Alexander, Dec 27, 1975 (divorced). **Educ:** TX Southern Univ, BA, 1954; Univ of CA, Berkeley, masters, 1972. **Career:** Berkeley Unified School District, teacher, 1965-84; World Savings & Loans, acct specialist auditor, 1984-. **Orgs:** Downs United Methodist Church, choir mem, treasure, class leader; Senior Citizen Ctr, volunteer asst, 1985-; NAACP, Berkeley, nominating comm, 1985-; Adult Literacy Prog, Oakland, tutor, 1986-87, planning comm, 1986-; Tutoring for Adult Literacy, board of directors/volunteer, Senior Citizen Center. **Honors/Awds:** Adult Literacy Prog, Outstanding Work, 1986-95; NAACP, Life Membership Award, 1989. **Home Addr:** 1514 Lincoln St, Berkeley, CA 94703-1222.

ECHOLS, IVOR TATUM
Educator. **Personal:** Born Dec 28, 1919, Oklahoma City, OK; daughter of Katie Bingley Tatum and Israel E Tatum; married Sylvester J Echols; children: Kalu Wilcox, Kim A. **Educ:** Univ of KS, AB 1942; Univ of NE, One Year Grad 1945; Columbia Univ, MSSW 1952; Univ of Southern CA, DSW 1968. **Career:** Amer Red Cross Chicago, caseworker 1945-46; Neighborhood Clubs Okla City, dir, Walnut Grove Center, 1949-51; Merrill Palmer Inst, faculty 1951-70; Univ of CT, asst dean 1985-89, prof 1970-89, professor emerita, 1989-. **Orgs:** Teacher Public Schools Geary OK 1943-45, Holderville OK 1942-43; consult Public Schls Columbus OH 1964-66; Scott Paper Co Chester PA; natl chair minority affairs Natl Assn Soc Wrks 1977-79; secr and bd United Neighborhood Ctrs of Amer 1974-85; past pres and bd Hartford Neighborhood Ctrs 1976; Ct Natual Gas/Energy Fnd Hartford CT 1984-87; CT State Historical Commission 1984-86, 1987-96; CT State Advisory Committee, US Commissions Civil Rights, 1989-; natl program committee, National Assn of Social Workers, 1989-92; Natl Assn of Black Social Workers; Delta Sigma Theta Sorority, 1938-. **Honors/Awds:** Sojourner Truth Award Natl Business and Prof Women 1969; Fellowships NIMH 1961, Natl Urban League 1951, Amer Red Cross; Soc Worker of Year CT 1978; publ Paper Journal of Amer Dietetics 1970; civic Achievement Ebonics Award USC 1984; CT Exhibit - Black Women of CT-State Humanities Council; Outstanding Women of Decade United Nations Assn CT, 1987; Citation, Mayor Perry-City of Hartford, 1989; Woman of Year, CT Coalition of 100 Black Women 1989; CWEALF, Maria Stewart Award, 1990; University of Connecticut, Tiffany Jewel Award, 100 years of Women at UConn, 1992; AASWG, CT, Award in Group Work, 1993; Citation, Area Agency on Aging, 1996; CT Historical Commission, 1996; Tribute Fund Honor & IJ Echols Scholarship, University of CT, 1996; Citation, US Civil Rights Commission as Outgoing Chair, 1997. **Home Addr:** 51 Chestnut Dr, Windsor, CT 06095, (860)688-2009.

ECHOLS, JAMES ALBERT
Public relations consultant, marketing. **Personal:** Born Sep 14, 1950, Memphis, TN; son of Vellar C McCraven Echols and Joseph Echols, Jr; married Dorothy Mae Mithcell, Jun 8, 1978; children: Justin Fitzgerald Echols. **Educ:** Central State Univ Edmond OK, BA, 1981. **Career:** Office of the Governor, state affirmative action office 1979-; Nigh for gov Campaign, adminstarn asst minority affairs 1978; Reserve Life Insurance Co, ins agt 1977-78; AUS, sr race relations instr 1976-77; E & C Trades LTD, pres & chmn of bd 1980; Honor Enterprises Inc, chairman of the board; US Army Reserve, career counselor, 1986-. **Orgs:** Mem Urban League of OK City 1977; mem NAACP 1978; vice pres OK Human Relations Assn 1978; mem, Veterans of Foreign Wars; mem, Economic Development Task Force, OK City Urban League. **Honors/Awds:** Commendation medal Bronze Star AUS 1971; vietnamese gallantary cross Rep of Vietman 1972; 2nd AUS commendations (oakleaf cluster) AUS 1977; mem for excellent scholarship Phi Eta Sigma 1978; US Army Recruiting & Retention Non-Commissioned Officers Advanced Course, 1989. **Military Serv:** US Army, sgt 1st class, 1969-.

ECHOLS, MARY ANN
Educational administrator. **Personal:** Born Jan 17, 1950, Youngstown, OH; daughter of Mable Ross Snipes and Otis A. Snipes (deceased); married Robert L. Echols, Oct 25, 1969; children: Robert Jr., Cheri, Michael, Anthony. **Educ:** Youngstown State University, Youngstown, OH, AB, Sociology, 1972, MS, Education, 1977; Kent State University, Kent, OH, Counseling Psychology, 1987-. **Career:** Youngstown Metropolitan Housing Authority, Youngstown, OH, leasing aide, 1973; Youngstown Area Urban League, Youngstown, OH, director of education and employment, 1973-76; Northeastern Ohio Employment and Training Consortium, Youngstown, OH, personnel, equal employment opportunity officer, 1977-80; Youngstown State University, Youngstown, OH, assistant for minority student services, 1980-84, director of special student services, 1984-. **Orgs:** Executive committee member, chair of review committee, Youngstown Area United Way, 1982-; member and second vice president, Associated Neighborhood Centers, 1984-89; board of directors, Help Hotline Inc, 1977-80; bias review panel member, Ohio State Department of Education, 1988-; Cultural Pluralism Task Force member, Lake to River Girl Scout Council, 1983-85; board of directors, Burdman Group Inc, 1988-. **Honors/Awds:** Licensed Professional Counselor, State of Ohio Counselor and Social Worker Board, 1988; Distinguished Service Award, Youngstown State University, 1988; Luke N. Zaccaro Memorial Award, Exceptional Service to Student Body, Youngstown State University, 1987; Outstanding Black Faculty/Staff Award, Black United Students, 1982, 1987; Resolution for Outstanding Community Service, Youngstown Area Urban League, 1976. **Business Addr:** Director, Special Student Services, Youngstown State University, 410 Wick Avenue, Kilcawley Center, Youngstown, OH 44555.

ECHOLS, RUBY LOIS
Nurse, mortician, florist, caterer. **Personal:** Born Oct 21, 1938, Atlanta, GA; daughter of Flora M Powell and George Clements (deceased); married Lamar Echols, Sep 5, 1955; children: Ricky, Sheila D, Dexter B, Kenneth W. **Educ:** Atlanta College of Practical Nursing, LPN, 1968; Gupton Jones College of Funeral Service, Funeral Directors and Embalmers License, 1978. **Career:** Grady Memorial Hospital, registered nurse; Echols Weddings, Flowers and Catering Services, owner, 1983-; Echols Mortuary, owner, 1985-. **Orgs:** Georgia Funeral Service and Practitioners Assn, 1978-; National Funeral Directors and Morticians Assn, 1978-; Epsilon Nu Delta Mortuary Fraternity, Alpha Omega Chapter; Eastern Star; Black Women's Assn; Mother's March of Dimes; US Negro College Fund; Black Women of Atlanta; EOA; Meals on Wheels. **Honors/Awds:** Mortician of the Year, 1993.

ECKSTINE, ED
Recording company executive. **Career:** Mercury Records, president, currently. **Business Addr:** President, Mercury Records, 825 8th Ave, New York, NY 10019, (212)333-8017.

ECTON, VIRGIL E.
Association executive. **Personal:** Born Jul 7, 1940, Paris, KY; married Harriette Morgan-Ecton; children: Virgil, Brian Keith, Blair Christina. **Educ:** Indiana Univ, BS, 1962; Xavier Univ, MEd, 1966; Harvard Univ, Advanced Management Program, 1989. **Career:** Ohio Civil Rights Commission, ast dir of education and community relations, 1968-70; United Negro College Fund, Inc, area development dir, 1970-75, eatern reginal super-

visor, 1975-76, deputy natl campaign dir, 1976-77, natl campaign dir, 1977-79, deputy executive dir of fund-raising, 1979-82, executive vice pres and COO, 1982-90, acting pres and CEO, 1990-91, sr executive vice pres and COO, 1991-. **Orgs:** Natl Society of Fund-raising Executives Foundation, bd mem; Natl Philanthropy Day Steering Committee, founding mem; Boy Scouts of America, Bergen Council, executive bd, vp; Community Access, bd mem; The Intl Parenting Assn, advisory bd mem, Outward Bound, USA and South Africa, advisory bd mem; The Bede School, advisory bd mem; Dwight Englewood School, trustee; Japan Society, advisory bd. **Honors/Awds:** Merit serv award Nat Alliance Businessmen, 1973; Natl Alliance of Bus Men Serv Awd, 1972-74; Blacks in Mgmt Comm Serv Awd, 1975; Natl Tech Assoc Serv Awd, 1974; UNCF Leadership Awd, 1978. **Business Addr:** Sr Executive Vice Pres & COO, The College Fund/UNCF, 8260 Willow Oaks Corporate Dr, PO Box 10444, Fairfax, VA 22031-4511.

EDDINGS, CYNTHIA
Communications manager. **Personal:** Born in Seattle, WA; daughter of Mary Lee Shadrick and Eldridge Eddings. **Educ:** Sorbonne Paris France, French language 1973; CA State Univ at San Jose, BA 1974; New York University, MBA, 1990. **Career:** Essence Mag, assoc editor 1976-77; Fairchild Publications, reporter 1977-79; CBS News, researcher for documentaries including 60 Minutes 1979-82, business & economic news researcher evening news 1982-83; American Express Co, New York, NY, producer/host corporate video programs, dir of employee communications, 1991-. **Business Addr:** Director, Employee Communications, American Express, World Financial Center, New York, NY 10285-4715.

EDDY, EDWARD A.
Educator. **Personal:** Born Feb 27, 1938, Kansas City, KS; married Joyce B Carter; children: Darrell, Duane, Aaron. **Educ:** Pittsburg State Univ, BS 1962; Univ of KS, MA 1966; KS State Univ, PhD 1981. **Career:** Pub Schls KCK, instr 1962-69; Univ of KS, instr 1969-73; Rockhurst, dir spec prog 1973-77; Rockhurst Clge, dean 1977-84; Chicago State Univ, dean; Chevy Chase Nursing Ctr, administrator. **Orgs:** OE regl steering comm TRIO Prog 1973-75; field reader OE Title III Proposals 1982-83; consult educ MLK Jr Hosp KCMO 1975-77; AACD mem Amer Assc Cnslng Dir 1985; natl youth conv staff Church of God 1985; guest soloist Oper PUSH Chicago 1985; mem Higher Educ Commn COG 1986-88. **Honors/Awds:** Key to City Kansas City KS 1984; fnd dir Black Ethos Performing Arts Troupe 1971. **Business Addr:** Administrator, Chevy Chase Nursing Ctr, 3400 So Indiana, Chicago, IL 60616.

EDELIN, KENNETH C.
Physician. **Personal:** Born Mar 31, 1939, Washington, DC; son of Ruby Goodwin Edelin and Benedict F Edelin; married Barbara Evans; children: Kenneth Jr, Kimberley, Joseph, Corinne. **Educ:** Columbia U, BA 1961; Meharry Med Coll, MD 1967; Boston City Hosp, residency ob/gyn 1971-74, chief resident 1973. **Career:** Ob/Gyn Boston Univ Sch of Med, associate dean of student & minority affairs, 1989-; chmn, prof ob/gyn 1979-89, gyn-in-chief 1979-89, dir ob/gyn 1979-, assoc prof 1974-, assist prof ob/Gyn 1976; Boston City Hosp, chf resid ob/gyn 1973-74; Ambulatory Care Boston City Hosp, coord 1974-, instructr ob-gyn 1974-, assoc dir ob-gyn 1974-. **Orgs:** Mem bd of trustees Fuller Mental Health Center; mem bd of trustees Planned Parenthood League of MA; mem bd of trustees NARAL; physic advis Planned Parenthood Leag of Amer; proj dir Boston Sickle Cell Center; mem Amer Assn of Gynecol Laparoscopists; sponsor MA Civ Lib Union; chmn New England Comm NAACP Legal Defense Fund; bd dir NAACP, LDF Inc; pres bd Roxbury Comprehensive Comm Health Center Inc; chairman of the board, Planned Parenthood Federation of America, 1989-. **Honors/Awds:** Dean's List Meharry Med Coll 1963-67; Columbia Univ 1960-61; Alpha Omega Alpha, Honorary Medical Society, 1991. **Military Serv:** USAF capt 1968-71; Commendation Medal USAF 1971; Commendation Medal Army 1971. **Business Addr:** Associate Dean, Student and Minority Affairs, Boston University School of Medicine, 80 E Concord St, Boston, MA 02118.

EDELMAN, MARIAN WRIGHT
Association executive. **Personal:** Born Jun 6, 1939, Bennettsville, SC; daughter of Maggie Bowen Wright and Arthur J Wright; married Peter Benjamin; children: Joshua Robert, Jonah Martin, Ezra Benjamin. **Educ:** Spelman Coll, BA 1960; Yale Law School, LLB 1963; Univ of Geneva Switzerland 1958-59. **Career:** NAACP Legal Defense & Educ Fund, staff atty 1963-64, dir 1964-68; Washington Rsch Project of Southern Center for Public Policy, partner, 1968-73; Center for Law & Educ Harvard Univ, dir 1971-73; Children's Defense Fund, pres 1973-. **Orgs:** DC, MS, Commonwealth of MA, BA Assns; bd of trustees The King Center; adv council M L King Memorial Library; Council on Foreign Relations; Aetna Life & Casualty Found; Yale Univ Corp; chair, bd of trustees Spelman Coll; bd of dir March of Dimes; board member, Center on Budget and Policy Priorities; board member, Citizens for Constitutional Concerns; board member, Joint Center for Political and Economic Studies; board member, NAACP Legal Defense and Educational Fund, Inc; board member, US Committee for UNICEF; board member, Robin Hood Foundation; board member, Aaron Diamond Foundation; Howard Univ Commission; Natl Commission on Children. **Honors/Awds:** Mademoiselle Magazine Award 1 of 4 Most Exciting Young Women of Amer 1965; Honorary Fellow, Univ of PA Law School 1969; Louise Waterman Wise Award 1970; Black Enterprise Magazine Professional Achievement Award 1980; Hon Yale Univ; Hon Smith Coll; Lesley Coll; Lowell Tech Inst; Univ of South Maine; Williams Coll; Coll of New Rochelle; Swarthmore Coll; SUNY; Leadership Award, Natl Women's Political Caucus 1980; Black Womens Forum Award 1980; Medal Columbia Teachers Coll 1984, Barnard Coll; Eliot Award, Amer Public Health Assn; Hubert Humphrey Civil Rights Award, Leadership Council on Civil Rights; John W Gardner Leadership Award of Ind Sector; Public Service Achievement Award, Common Cause; MacArthur Prize Fellow 1985; A Philip Randolph Award, National Urban Coalition 1987; The WilliamP son Award, Congressional Black Caucus, 1987; Radcliffe Medal, 1989; The AFL-CIO Award, 1989; The Fordham Stein Prize, 1989; Gandhi Peace Award, 1989. **Special Achievements:** The Measure of Success, 1992. **Business Addr:** President, Children's Defense Fund, 122 C St, NW, Washington, DC 20001.

EDGAR, JACQUELINE L.
Automobile dealer. **Personal:** Born Nov 27, 1948, Lafayette, LA; daughter of Effie Matthews LeBlanc and Antoine LeBlanc; married Allen L Edgar Sr, Apr 20, 1968 (divorced); children: Rachael Marie, Allen L Jr, Lawrence (deceased). **Career:** Auto Mart Linc-Merc, salesperson, 1973-76; J P Thibodeaux Olds, salesperson, 1976-80; Broussard Pontiac, salesperson, 1980-83; Edgar Chevrolet Inc, president, 1983-87; Edgar Ford Inc, president, 1985-. **Orgs:** Breaux Bridge Chamber of Commerce, treasurer, 1992; Lafayette Catholic Service Center, 1992; Rehabilitaion Center of Acadiana, 1992; Performance Incorporated, 1989-92. **Business Addr:** President, Edgar Ford, Inc, 899 Rees St, PO Box 160, Breaux Bridge, LA 70517, (318)332-2145.

EDGERTON, ART JOSEPH
Administrator. **Personal:** Born Jan 27, 1928, Philadelphia, PA; married Della W; children: Edward. **Educ:** St Joseph Coll, BS 1950; Fordham Coll, MS 1952. **Career:** Univ of Toledo, asst dir for affirmative action/human resources devel 1969-; Community Affairs, produced prog 1968-75, field representative bd of comm relat 1968-69; WTOL-TV, night newsman, editor 1965-68; WTTOL Radio, music dir, disc jockey, announcer 1958-65; Goodwill Indust, public relations 1956-57. **Orgs:** Consult WCWA Radio 1973-; consult WGTE-FM Pub Radio 1976-; Radio & TV News Dir Assn 1966-; pres comm on Employment of the Handicapped; bd mem Toledo Chap Am Red Cross; Yth Adv Com oth the Toledo Bd of Comm Realat; bd mem Goodwill Indust; chmn Radio Reading Serv Com Blind & Physically Handicapped Am Fed of Musicians; state pres OH Citizen's Com for Spcl Educ 1971; served on gov com Employment of the Handicapped; mem Com to Implement the Devel Disabilties Service & Facilities Construction Act of 1970, 1971-74; exec mem Economic Opprty Planning Assn of Grtr Toledo Inc; mem Manpower Com; served Pub Relations Educ & Del Agency Com; mem Educ Com of the OH Civil Rights Commn; bd mem Bd of Comm Relations; mem Educ Com; mem Sigma Delta Chi; former bd mem Toledo Soc forthe Handicapped; past chmnack Am Law Students Assn; chmn Handicapped Avd Com. **Honors/Awds:** Handicapped worker of the yr Toledo Lucas Co 1966; handicapped am of the yr State of OH & USA 1967; OH Super Hall of Fame 1970; reg winn Baldwin-Librace Found Contest 1980. **Business Addr:** U of Toledo, 2801 Bancroft St, Toledo, OH 43606.

EDGERTON, BRENDA EVANS
Food company executive. **Personal:** Born Jun 15, 1949, Halifax, VA; daughter of Bernice Evans and Elmer Keith Evans; married Raymond Edgerton (divorced 1989); children: Lauren, Eric. **Educ:** Pennsylvania State Univ, State College, PA, 1966-69; Rutgers University, New Brunswick, NJ, BA, 1970; Temple University, Philadelphia, PA, MBA, 1976. **Career:** Scott Paper Co, Philadelphia, PA, Mgr money & banking, 1976-84; Campbell Soup Co, Camden, NJ, dir finance, 1984-86, asst treasurer, 1986-88, deputy treasurer, 1988-89, vice pres/treasurer, 1989-94; US Soup, vice pres, 1994-96, vice pres of business devt, 1996-. **Orgs:** Member, Financial Executives Institute, 1989-; member, National Association Corporate Treasurers, 1989; member, Philadelphia Treasurers Club, 1985-; member, YWCA, 1989-; board member, Frontier Corp. **Honors/Awds:** Academy of Women Achievers, YWCA, 1989. **Business Addr:** Vice Pres/Business Devt, Campbell Soup Co., Campbell Pl, Camden, NJ 08103-1799.

EDGHILL, JOHN W. (CHAMP)
Physician, business executive. **Personal:** Born Aug 13, 1921, New York, NY; children: Jaqueline, John W IV, Debbie, Keith. **Educ:** West Coast University, BA, 1948; Howard University Medical College, MD, 1934. **Career:** Champion Associates Ltd, president, 1981-; Flying Fish Boat Co., Barbados, owner; American Tobacco Co., national field/sales manager; Pvt practice, physician; Sydenham Hosp NY, asso vis urologist 1970; NY Med Coll, asst clinical prof urology 1970; Met & Flower Fifth Av, asso visurologist 1964; Harlem Hosp NY, asso vis urologist 1958; Bronx VA Hosp, sr resident urology 1956. **Orgs:** Howard Univ Med Assn; NY Med Coll Urological Soc; pres Chesterfield Bridge Club 1973; pres Cavalier Men's Club 1979; St Phillips Prot Episc Ch; Alantic City Taxi Owners Association, founder, president, 1980-88; Egg Harbor Township Rent Review Board, 1989-. **Honors/Awds:** S G Specialist Urology NY State Workmen's Compensation Bd, 1956; Am Coll of Surgeons, fellow, 1956; Governor Martha L Collins, Commission, Kentucky Colonel, 1989; Egg Harbor Township, Service Award, 1992; AEAON of the Mystic Shrine, Francis M Perdue Memorial Award, 1992. **Special Achievements:** Flyweight Amateur Champion, 1938; Welterweight Champion of Central and South America, 1940. **Military Serv:** US Army MC, capt, 1943-47; Purple Heart; Bronze Star; Silver Star; 3243rd/3244th QM's Leadership Service Awards; Valuable Service Award; Army/Air Force National Guard Bureau, Meritorious Service Award. **Business Addr:** President, Champion Associates, Ltd, 1001 Old Egg Harbor Rd, Ste 10-A, Pleasantville, NJ 08232.

EDLEY, CHRISTOPHER F., SR.
Attorney. **Personal:** Born Jan 1, 1928, Charleston, WV; son of Helen Edley and Phillip Edley; married Zaida Coles; children: Christopher F Jr, Judith Coles. **Educ:** Howard Univ, AB 1949; Harvard Law Sch, LLB 1953. **Career:** Office of Lewis Tanner Moore, attorney 1953-54; City of Phila, asst dist atty & chief of appeals division, 1954-56; Moore Lightfoot & Edley, atty partner 1956-60, 1960-61; US Commn on Civil Rights, chief admin justice div 1960; Fed Housing & Home Finance Region 3, reg counsel 1961-63; The Ford Found, director, govt & law program 1963-73; United Negro Coll Fund, pres & ceo 1973-91, president emeritus, 1991-. **Orgs:** Allstate Ins Co, bd of dirs, 1993-97; Student Loan Corp, bd of dirs, 1993-98; Corporate bd American Airlines 1977-98, The Bowery Savings Bank 1980-85, The Great Atlantic & Pacific Tea Co 1981-, CIT Financial Corp 1975-80, National Bank of North America 1976-79; mem Amer, Natl, NY Bar Assns; numerous civic activities; comm & social affiliations. **Honors/Awds:** 16 honorary degrees; Natl Scholarship Harvard Law Sch 1949; John Hay Whitney Fellow 1950; Howard Univ Alumni Awd 1959; Cert of Appreciation US Commn on Civil Rights 1960; Sigma Pi Phi 1961; Disting Serv Awd Philadelphia Commn on Human Relations 1966; Humanitarian Father of Yr Awd 1974; Outstanding Achievement Awd Ohio State Univ 1977; Distinguished Alumni Award, Howard University, 1979; Howard B Shepard Award, Equitable Life Assurance Society of the US, 1981; Whitney M Young Jr Memorial Award, New York Urban League, 1987; Martin Luther King Center, Salute to Greatness Award, 1991; OIC Humanitarian Award, 1992; Congressional Black Caucus George W Collins Award, 1991. **Military Serv:** US Army Sgt 1946-47, 1950-51. **Home Addr:** 90 Vaughn Ave, New Rochelle, NY 10801.

EDLEY, CHRISTOPHER F., JR.
Government official. **Personal:** Born Jan 13, 1953, Boston, MA; son of Zaida Coles Edley and Christopher Edley Sr; married Tana Pesso, Sep 23, 1983; children: Christopher Edley III. **Educ:** Swartmore Coll, Swartmore PA, BA, 1973; Harvard Law School, Cambride MA, JD, 1978; Harvard Kennedy School, Cambridge MA, MPP, 1978. **Career:** White House Domestic Policy Staff, asst dir, 1978-80; US Govt, Secretary of Housing, Education & Welfare, special asst, 1980; Harvard Law School, prof; Washington Post, part-time editorial page staff, 1982-84; Dukakis for President, natl issues dir, 1987-88; Office of Management & Budget, assoc dir of econ & govt, 1993-. **Orgs:** Bd of managers, Swarthmore Coll, 1980-; bd of dir, Amer Council on Germany, 1981-84; founding trustee, Working Assets Money fund, 1982-84; steering comm, Boston Lawyers Comm for Civil Rights, 1984-87; mem, Comm on Policy for Racial Justice, 1984-; consultant, Joint Center for Political Studies, 1988-; bd of dir, Center for Social Welfare Policy & Law, 1989-; mem, Amer Bar Assn, Natl Bar Assn.

EDMOND, ALFRED ADAM, JR.
Magazine editor, writer. **Personal:** Born Mar 8, 1960, Long Branch, NJ; son of Virginia E Monroe Edmond and Alfred Adam Edmond; married Ruth Stephanie Sanderson Edmond, Sep 20, 1986; children: Monique Marie Brown, Christine Lorraine, David Adam Robeson. **Educ:** Rutgers College, Rutgers Univ, New Brunswick, NJ, BA, 1983. **Career:** Big Red News, Brooklyn, NY, managing editor, 1984-86; MBM/Modern Black Men Magazine, New York, NY, senior editor, 1986-87; Earl G Graves Publishing Co, New York, associate editor, 1987, senior editor, 1987-89, business editor, 1989-90, sr editor/admin, 1990-92, managing editor 1992-95, vice pres, exec editor, 1995-; Rutgers Univ, Dept of Journalism, visiting prof, 1994-95. **Orgs:** Member, American Society of Magazine Editors, 1988-; member, National Association of Black Journalists, 1987-; member, New York Association of Black Journalists, 1985-; board member, Rutgers Alumni Federation, 1990; founding member, Rutgers African-American Alumni Alliance, 1990-; Rutgers Alumni Magazine, editorial board member, 1991-; Society of Amer Bus Editors & Writers Inc, 1994-95; Rutgers Alumni Association, life mem, 1996-. **Honors/Awds:** Recognition of Excellence, Paul Robeson Cultural Ctr, Rutgers University, 1990; Unity Award for Excellence in Media, Lincoln University, MO, 1989-90; Unity Award for Excellence in Media, 1991, 1992; NYABJ Journalism Award, Business Reporting, Magazines, 1992, 1994; Long Branch High School Alumni, Academic Hall of Fame, 1996. **Home Addr:** 309 Pros-

pect Place, Apt 2, Brooklyn, NY 11238-3937. **Business Addr:** Vice Pres/Executive Editor, Editorial Dept, Black Enterprise, 130 Fifth Ave, New York, NY 10011-4399.

EDMOND, PAUL EDWARD
Corporate industrial relations manager. **Personal:** Born May 29, 1944, Shreveport, LA; son of Juanita Brown Allen and Clarence Lee Edmond; divorced; children: Neeve E Samuels, Doran, Oran. **Educ:** Southern Univ, Baton Rouge LA, BS, 1968; Indiana Univ, Bloomington IN, MS, 1973; Univ of Michigan, Ann Arbor MI, 1976. **Career:** State of Indiana, Ft Wayne IN, hospital admin, 1969-71; Lincoln Natl Insurance, Ft Wayne IN, personnel mgr, 1971-76; Miller Brewing Co, Milwaukee WI, corporate industrial relations mgr, 1976-. **Orgs:** Amer Soc Personnel Assn, 1973-; Industrial Relations Mgr Assn, 1979-; Personnel/Labor Relations Assn, 1980-; bd mem, OIC of Amer, 1986-; chairperson, United Way Allocation Comm, 1986-; comm mem, Milwaukee Urban League, Long Range Planning, 1987-; mem, Grambling Univ Accreditation Comm, 1987-; bd mem, Milwaukee Desegregation Comm, 1988-; mem, State of Wisconsin Educ Council, 1988-. **Honors/Awds:** Outstanding Young Men, Ft Wayne Jaycees, 1973; Professional Achiever, Natl Career Center, 1974; Black Achiever, New York YMCA, 1983; President's Award, Miller Brewing, 1984. **Military Serv:** US Army, 1st lt, 1968-70.

EDMONDS, ALBERT JOSEPH
Military officer. **Personal:** Born Jan 17, 1942, Columbus, GA; son of Millie Carter Edmonds (deceased) and Walter Edmonds (deceased); married Jacquelyn McDaniel Edmonds, May 21, 1965; children: Gia Nichelle, Sheri Yvonne, Alicia Josette Leilani. **Educ:** Morris Brown College, Atlanta, GA, BS, 1964; Hampton University, Hampton, VA, MA, 1969; Harvard University, Cambridge, MA, exec program, 1987. **Career:** US Air Force, Pentagon, Washington, DC, major general, beginning 1964; US Air Force, Defense Info Systs Agency, Arlington, VA, director, lt gen, 1993-. **Orgs:** Life member, Kappa Alpha Psi Fraternity, 1963-; life member, Armed Forces Communications-Electronics Assn, 1976-; NAACP, 1991; national 2nd vice pres, Tuskegee Airman, Inc, 1990. **Honors/Awds:** Black Engineer of the Year, 1996; Honorary Doctor of Science, Morris Brown College, 1990; Kappa Delta Pi Honor Society, 1968. **Military Serv:** US Air Force, 1960-; Defense Distinguished Service, Defense Superior Service Medal, Legion of Merit, (3) Meritorious Service Medal, (4) Air Force Commendation Medals. **Home Addr:** 81 Westover Ave, Bolling AFB, DC 20336.

EDMONDS, BEVELYN
Educator. **Personal:** Born Feb 17, 1951, Chicago, IL; daughter of Walter D Edmonds. **Educ:** Tuskegee University, BSN, 1973; Medical College, MSN, 1975; St Xavier, MA, 1990. **Career:** Illinois Central Community Hosp, staff, 1979-86; St Xavier University, assistant professor, 1981-90; St Frances Hospital, instructor, 1990-94; Doctor's Hospital, educator, 1994-95; Jackson Park Medical Ctr, staff, 1986-95; Health Staff, in-house, 1990-; Dimensions Int, staff writer, 1995-. **Orgs:** Association Black Nursing Facility, 1987-; Delta Sigma Theta Sorority, 1969-; Sigma Thetha Tau, 1986-; People United to Save Humanity, 1979-; Community Service Block Club. **Honors/Awds:** St Xavier University, Grant For Adalesent Study, 1982. **Special Achievements:** Mental Health School in System, Need for Laison Service, 1975; RN Working with Chemicals, Dependent Individuals in a Mental Health Setting, 1990. **Home Addr:** 341 Fairview Rd, Ellenwood, GA 30049.

EDMONDS, CAMPBELL RAY
Elected official. **Personal:** Born Jun 9, 1930, Hopewell, VA; married Louise Smith. **Educ:** VA State Univ Trade Sch, 1954; VSU Bus & Mgmt, 1956; Chase Inc Cost/Analysis, 1961. **Career:** Traffic Bd Hopewell, co-chair 1966-76; Blue Ribbon Crime Task Force, chmn 1981; City Council, councilman 1982; Hopewell VA, vice-mayor 1984. **Orgs:** Adjuant gen Albert Mills Post #1387 VFW 1975; bd of dirs C of C 1977-; mem Home Builder's Assn 1980; commr Veterans Affairs of VA 1981; bd mem Hopewell/Prince George Chamber of Commerce; mem bd of dirs Prince George County Heritage Fair; mem Hopewell Voters League; trustee bd 1964-, mem Friendship Baptist Church; aide to VA State Assoc Pres of IBPOE of W. **Honors/Awds:** Outstanding Serv Sunlight Eld Lodge Hopewell 1969; Achievement Awd VA State Assn (Elks) Health Dept 1982; Comm Serv Hopewell Action Council (SCLC) 1985; Certificate of Merit City of Hopewell 1986; Outstanding Citizenship Awd United Fund 1987. **Military Serv:** AUS E-5 1951-53; Korean Conflict. **Home Addr:** 1105 Winston Churchill Dr, Hopewell, VA 23860. **Business Addr:** Vice Mayor, City of Hopewell, Municipal Bldg, Hopewell, VA 23860.

EDMONDS, CURTIS
City official. **Career:** Detroit Fire Dept, chief, currently. **Business Addr:** Chief, Detroit Fire Department, 250 W Larned, Detroit, MI 48226, (313)596-2921.

EDMONDS, JOSEPHINE E.
Artist, art consultant, educator (retired). **Personal:** Born Oct 5, 1921, Cambridge, MA; daughter of Zylpha O Johnson (deceased) and Alexander M Mapp (deceased); married Howard L Edmonds; children: Joel V Bolden Jr. **Educ:** NY City Coll, attended; Amer Art School, attended; Springfield Coll, attended; Univ of Hartford, attended. **Career:** YWCA, art instructor 1965-69; Johnson Publishing, stringer 1957-86; Afro-Amer Cultural Ctr, Amer Intl Coll, art coordinator 1969-81. **Orgs:** Mem 1962-, council mem 1966-68 Springfield Art League 1962-; mem Springfield Library & Museum Assn, Studion Museum in Harlem 1974-, Natl Conf Artists 1973-; co-founder Afro-Art Alliance 1968; mem Urban League; cultural comm Springfield Bicentennial Comm 1973; mem NAACP, Springfield Chap Girl Friends 1958-; natl vice pres Girl Friends Inc 1979-80; trustees comm Springfield Museum of Fine Arts, George Walter Vincent Smith Museum 1980-; corporator Springfield Library & Museum Assoc 1982-; mayoral appt to Springfield Arts Lottery Commn 1986-. **Honors/Awds:** Honor Willia Hardgrow Mental Health Clinic 1974; honored by Alumni Assoc of Amer Intl Coll 1977; Received Exchange Club of Springfields Golden Deed Award, 1983; Proclaimed by Mayor June 3 1983 Josephine Edmonds Day in Springfield MA; Honored by PRIDE a Black Student Org of Amer Intl Coll.

EDMONDS, KENNETH (BABYFACE)
Recording producer, composer, singer. **Personal:** son Of Barbara Edmonds; married Tracey McQuarn, 1992; children: Brandon. **Career:** Singer, producer, currently; Edmonds Entertainment, co-founder; LaFace Records, owner; films: Soul Food, co-producer, 1997; Hav Plenty, co-producer, 1998; television: "Schoolin," co-creator. **Honors/Awds:** Turner Broadcasting System, Trumpet Award, 1998; NAACP, Image Award, Recording Male Artist, 1998; Grammy, Award for Producer of the Year, Nonclassical, 1998. **Business Addr:** Owner, LaFace Inc, c/o Arista Records, 6 W 57th St, New York, NY 10019.

EDMONDS, NORMAN DOUGLAS
Business executive. **Personal:** Born Sep 16, 1938, Suffield, CT; divorced; children: Jeremy, Suzanne, Andrea. **Educ:** Univ of CT, BS 1960. **Career:** Travelers Ins Co, dir mktg 1961-79; Phoenix Mutual Life Ins Co, vice pres 1979-. **Orgs:** Chmn founder CT Savings and Loan Assn 1968-; mem Greater Hartford Chamber of Commerce 1972-; bd of Selectmen chmn Town of Tolland CT 1976-78. **Honors/Awds:** Mem New England Championship Soccer Team 1959; All New England Soccer Team 1959-60; First Black Corporate Officer Travelers Ins Co 1967; distinguished serv award Greater Hartford Jaycees 1971; First Black Chief Elected Official in St of CT 1976. **Military Serv:** Air Natl Guard airman 1961-67. **Home Addr:** 278 Conestoga Way, Glastonbury, CT 06033.

EDMONDS, TERRY
Speech writer. **Personal:** Born 1950, Baltimore, MD; son of Naomi Parker; married Antoinette; children: Maga. **Educ:** Morgan State Univ, BA, 1973. **Career:** Maryland Mass Transit Administration, public relations soecialist, 1978-82; Trahan, Burden and Charles Advertising, dir of public relations, 1982-87; Joint Center for Political Studies, Inc., dir of communications, 1985-87; Office of Kweisi Mfume, press sec, 1987-88; Macro Systems, consultant, 1987-89; Blue Cross Blue Shield of MD, mgr of media relations, 1989-90; University Research Corp, subcontract mgr for public relations work, 1990-91; ROW Sciences, task mgrfor public relations projects, 1991-93; Office of Donna Shalala, US Sec of Health and Human Services, sr speechwriter, dir of speechwriting, 1993-95; President Bill Clinton, dep asst, presidential speechwriter, 1995-97, dep dir of speechwriting, 1997-. **Special Achievements:** First African American speech writer to work in the White House for a President. **Business Addr:** Deputy Director of Speechwriting, The White House, 1600 Pennsylvania Ave NW, Washington, DC 20500.

EDMONDS, THOMAS NATHANIEL
Educator. **Personal:** Born Jun 14, 1936, Suffield, CT; married Joyce Carole Burr; children: Thomas Jr, Allyn, Russell, James. **Educ:** Stanford U, MBA 1972. **Career:** Northwestern Univ School of Law, assoc dean 1975-, dean 1974-75, asst dean, dir 1972-74; Stanford Univ Graduate School of Business, asst dir 1969-72; Lockheed Missiles & Space Co, experimental engineer, planner 1961-69. **Orgs:** Mem, Law Sch Admsn Cncl 1972-; Prelaw Com 1974-77; Ad Hoc Com on Fin Aid 1975-77; Nat Assn for Law Plcmnt 1974-; Am Assn of Coll Regs & Admsns Ofcrs 1973-; Com on Professional Schs 1975-76. **Honors/Awds:** Publ financing grad & grad professional sch Educ 1976; 1st non atty black asso dean maj natl law sch; cert of apprec Oppty Indslzn Ctr W 1970; Herbert Hoover flwshp 1969-70; benkendorf flwshp 1971-72; partic world educ tour 1971. **Military Serv:** USN 2nd class petty ofcr 1956-60.

EDMONDS, TRACEY
Record company executive. **Personal:** marrIed Kenneth "Babyface" Edmonds, 1992; children: Brandon. **Career:** Yab Yum Entertainment, pres, currently; Edmonds Entertainment, pres, currently; films: co-exec prod, Soul Food, 1997; HavPlenty, co-producer, 1998; television: "Schoolin," co-creator. **Orgs:** RIAA. **Honors/Awds:** Black Oscar Awards, three; NAACP Awards, five. **Business Addr:** President, Yab Yum Entertainment, 1635 N Cahuenga Blvd, 6th Fl, Los Angeles, CA 90028.

EDMUNDS, DAVID L., JR.
Attorney. **Educ:** University of Rochester, College of Arts & Sciences, BA, 1975; Case Western Reserve University, Franklin Thomas Backus School of Law, JD, 1978. **Career:** Neighborhood Legal Services Inc, Reginald Herber Smith Community Law Fellow, staff attorney, 1978-81; New York State Department of Law, assistant attorney general, Prison Litigation Bureau, 1981-83, Claims and Litigation Bureau, 1983-86, deputy assistant attorney general-in-charge, Buffalo Regional Office, 1986-. **Orgs:** Minority Bar Association of WNY, president, 1987-91; Erie County Bar Association, Special Task Force on Minorities in the Legal Profession, co-chair; New York State Bar Association, Civil Rights Committee, chairperson; Leadership Buffalo, class of 1989, board of directors; First Shiloh Baptist Church, board of trustees, chairman; Geneva Scruggs Health Center, board of directors, vp; Erie Community College, Citizens Advisory Council, vp; NAACP, life member; Case Western Reserve University Law School, board of governors. **Special Achievements:** Bar admissions: US Supreme Court; US Court of Appeals, second circuit; US District Court, western district of New York; State of New York, all courts. **Business Phone:** (716)847-3375.

EDMUNDS, FERRELL, JR.
Professional football player. **Personal:** Born Apr 16, 1965, South Boston, VA. **Educ:** Univ of Maryland. **Career:** Miami Dolphins, tight end, 1988-93; Seattle Seahawks, 1993-. **Honors/Awds:** Played in Pro Bowl, post-1989 season. **Business Addr:** Professional Football Player, Seattle Seahawks, 11220 NE 53rd St, Kirkland, WA 98033.

EDMUNDS, WALTER RICHARD
Oral surgeon. **Personal:** Born Mar 25, 1928, Philadelphia, PA; son of Waltha Edmunds and McKinley Edmunds. **Educ:** PA State Univ, BS; Howard Univ Coll of Dentistry, DDS; Univ of PA Grad School of Med, attended. **Career:** PA Hospital oral surgeon; Univ of PA School of Dental Med, assoc prof oral pathology; Jefferson Med Coll Thomas Jefferson Univ, clinical asst prof of otolaryngology; Private practice, oral & maxillofacial surgeon. **Orgs:** Mem bd Eagleville Hosp; fellow Amer Coll of Oral & Maxillofacial Surgeons, Soc Hill Club, Amer Bd of Oral Surgeons, Alpha Phi Alpha, Sigma Pi Phi, Chi Delta Mu; bd mem Philadelphia Cty Dental Soc. **Military Serv:** AUS lt.

EDNEY, NORRIS ALLEN, I
Educator. **Personal:** Born Jul 17, 1936, Natchez, MS; son of Elizabeth Grayer Edney and Willie Albert Edney; married Lillian Clark Edney, Jun 5, 1959; children: Norris Allen II, Albert DeFrance, Alvin Darcell. **Educ:** Natchez Junior College, Natchez, MS, AA, 1953-55; Tougaloo, Tougaloo, MS, BS, 1955-57; Antioch College, Yellow Spring, OH, MST, 1962, summer, Michigan Stae Univ, Lansing, MI, PhD, 1969. **Career:** Alcorn State Univ, Lorman, MS, instructor & assist prof bio, 1963-66, professor of biology, 1969, chairman of biology, 1972-79, USDA project director, 1972-, dir of graduate studies, 1975-, dir of arts & sciences, 1973-. **Orgs:** Member, Mycological Society of America, member, American Association for the Advancement of Science, member, American Association of University Professors, member, Mississippi Academy of Sciences, member, Alpha Phi Alpha Fraternity. **Honors/Awds:** First Annual White House Initiative Faculty Award for Excellence in Sci & Tech, 1988; Award, National Assn for Equal Opportunity in Higher Education Research Achievement, 1988; Alumni Award, Natchez Junior College, 1990. **Home Addr:** 302 Eastmoor Dr, Natchez, MS 39120. **Business Addr:** Director, Graduate Studies and Arts and Sciences, Alcorn State University, University Blvd, New Administration Bldg, Room 519, Natchez, MS 39120.

EDNEY, STEVE
Organization executive. **Personal:** Born Jan 10, 1917, Anderson, SC; son of Lena Jenkins and Steve Edney; married Alberta Palmer, Jul 11, 1971; children: Henry. **Career:** Pan Pacific Fisheres Terminal Island, CA filling machine operator; United Cannery & Industrial Workers, business agent, vice pres, pres; United Industrial Workers of SIU, natl dir, 1989-; Seafarers Intl Union, vice pres, 1989-. **Orgs:** Vice pres, Los Angeles County Fedn of Labor, 1989-, California Fedn of Labor, 1989-; mem, Harbor Area Re-Devel Comm, 1989-, Welfare Planning Comm, 1989-, NAACP, 1989-; chmn, Fish-Canners United Industrial Workers Pension & Welfare, 1989-, La Victoria-United Industrial Workers Trust Fund, 1989-, Caribe Tuna-United Industrial Workers Pension Fund, 1989-. **Honors/Awds:** Founder, Fish-Canners-Cannery Workers Union Welfare Trust, 1953; Man of the Year Award, Maritime Trades Dept, 1971, 1977; wrote booklett on the History of the Cannery Workers on Terminal Island. **Business Addr:** Natl Dir, United Indus Workers of the Seafarers Intl Union of N Americ, 510 N Broad Ave, Wilmington, CA 90744.

EDNEY, TYUS DWAYNE
Professional basketball player. **Personal:** Born Feb 14, 1973, Gardena, CA; married. **Educ:** UCLA. **Career:** Sacramento Kings, guard, 1995-97; Boston Celtics, 1997-. **Honors/Awds:** NBA, All-Rookie second team, 1996; Frances Pomeroy Naismith Award, 1995. **Special Achievements:** NCAA-Division I, Championship, 1995. **Business Addr:** Professional Basketball Player, Boston Celtics, 151 Merrimac St, Boston, MA 02114, (617)523-3030.

EDWARDS, ABIYAH, JR. (ED EDWARDS)
Minister. **Personal:** Born Dec 23, 1927, Princeton, KY; son of Ivory Bumpass and Marcles Edwards (both deceased); children: Ed III, Delesa, Carla, Cornell, Yahis, Edwina, Charise, Iva, Philip, SchaKerra, Leonard, Mark. **Educ:** Institute of Divine Metaphysical Research Inc, DD, 1971. **Career:** UAW Local 600-Ford, CIO, 1949-65; Ford Motor Co, Dearborn, MI, 1965-92; Kaiser Jeep; Enjoy Restaurant/Palace, creative consultant/mgr, 1988-89; Third Baptist Church, associate pastor; Institute of Divine Metaphysical Research Inc, recruiter, lecturer; Universal School of Spiritual Awareness, dean, currently. **Honors/Awds:** Project Head Start, Volunteer Service Award, 1992. **Special Achievements:** Foundation of Universal School of Spiritual Awareness; Author, The Beauty of it All, 1995. **Military Serv:** AAF, pfc, 1946-48. **Home Addr:** 5300 Newport Ave, Detroit, MI 48213, (313)822-8415.

EDWARDS, AL E.
State representative. **Personal:** Born Mar 19, 1937, Houston, TX; son of Josephine Edwards and E L Edwards Sr; married Lana Kay Cloth; children: Albert Ely II, Jason Kiamba, Alana Catherine Raquel. **Educ:** Texas Southern Univ, BS, 1966. **Career:** Gen Foods Corp, acct mgr 1958-80; Al Edwards Real Estate, broker 1968-; Al Edwards Publ Relations Advt, pres 1968-; NAACP, publ relations 1976-78; State of TX, state rep, district 85, 1979-82, district 146, 1983-. **Orgs:** Mem Houston Bus & Professional Men; mem Dean of Pledges Alpha Phi Alpha; founder, pres of bd Houston Team Tennis Assn 1976-78; founder TX Emancipation Cultural Assn; chmn Jesse Jackson for President Campaign TX 1984; chmn TX Senatorial Dist 13 Convention 1984; mem Dem Natl Comm 1984, Chm 1995; natl vchmn Mondale for Pres Campaign 1984. **Honors/Awds:** Authored House Bill 1015 Emancipation Day, TX Legal State Holiday 1979; Outstanding Serv in 66th Leg, TX Railroad Passenger Assn 1980; Al Edwards Freedom Heritage Park Dedicated in San Antonio, TX Emancipation Comm 1980. **Business Addr:** Representative, State of Texas, 4913 1/2 Griggs Rd, Houston, TX 77021.

EDWARDS, ALFRED L.
Educator. **Personal:** Born Aug 9, 1920, Key West, FL; son of Kathleen Edwards and Eddie Edwards; married Willie Mae Lewis; children: Beryl L, Alfred L Jr. **Educ:** Livingstone Coll Salisbury NC, BS 1948; Univ of MI, MA 1949; Univ of IA, PhD 1957. **Career:** So Univ, instr 1949-54; Michigan State Univ, asst prof 1957-62; US Dept of Agriculture, deputy asst sec 1963-74; Grad Sch Business Univ of MI, prof & dir of rsch 1974-. **Orgs:** Dir Scrty Bank Corp 1980; consultant Rockefeller Foundation 1976-80; consultant Andrew Brimmer & Co 1975-77; bd of trustees Western MI Univ 1980; Dir Legal Aid & Defenders Assn 1980-83; bd of dir Regal Plastics, Inc, MI Minority Tech Council, Inst for Amer Business, Consortium for Grad Study in Business. **Honors/Awds:** Ford Found Fellow; Danforth Fellow. **Military Serv:** AUS sgt 1943-46; Good Conduct Medal. **Home Addr:** 2448 Adare Cir, Ann Arbor, MI 48104. **Business Addr:** Professor Emeritus of Business Admin, Univ of Michigan, Grad Sch of Bus Adm, Ann Arbor, MI 48109.

EDWARDS, ANTHONY
Professional football player. **Personal:** Born May 26, 1966, Casa Grande, AZ; married Mary Ann; children: Tony, Torrey, Tynette. **Educ:** New Mexico Highlands, attended. **Career:** Philadelphia Eagles, wide receiver, 1989-90; Phoenix Cardinals, 1991-93; Arizona Cardinals, 1994-. **Business Addr:** Professional Football Player, Arizona Cardinals, 8701 S Hardy, Tempe, AZ 85284, (602)379-0101.

EDWARDS, ARTHUR JAMES
Dentist. **Personal:** Born Oct 30, 1902, Talbotton, GA; married Dr Vera Clement Edwards. **Educ:** Ohio State Univ, DDS 1929. **Career:** Shoemaker Health Ctr, clinician 1929-32; Volunteer at Shoemaker Ctr and Public Dental Serv Soc (Emeritus Bd Mem), committees, clinician, consultant, supervisor, educator 1932-84; Private Practitioner, dental practice 1929-. **Orgs:** Mem YMCA 1930-; bd mem, supporter, subscriber United Appeal, Health Fed, Community Action & Change Orgs 1930-; mem Zion Baptist Church, Kappa Alpha Psi, Sigma Pi Phi; life mem NAACP 1935-, Amer Dental Assoc, OH Dental Assoc, OH Valley Dental Assoc, OH State & Natl Dental Assoc; mem Chicago Dental Soc; mem Amer Endodontic Soc 1976-; mem ODA, ADA. **Honors/Awds:** Mem Intl Coll of Dentists; Kappa Alpha Psi 50 Yrs Serv Awd; Zion Baptist Church 50 Yr Awd; Cincinnati Dental Soc 50 Yr Serv Awd; mem Natl Skeet/Trap Shooting Assoc over 100 trophies & awds 1949-; mem & honoree Amistad Black History Assoc 1987. **Home Addr:** 231 Clinton Springs Ave, Cincinnati, OH 45217.

EDWARDS, AUDREY MARIE
Publishing company executive. **Personal:** Born Apr 21, 1947, Tacoma, WA; married Benjamin Williams. **Educ:** Univ of WA, BA 1969; Columbia Univ, MA 1974. **Career:** Fairchild Publication, promotion news editor 1977-79; Black Enterprise Magazine, assoc editor 1978-79, executive editor, vp of editorial operations, 1990-; Family Circle Magazine, sr editor 1979-81; NY Univ, adjunct prof 1982-; Essence Magazine, editor, beginning 1981. **Orgs:** Regional dir Natl Assn of Black Journalists 1981-83; prog chair New York Assn of Black Journalists 1983-. **Honors/Awds:** Unity Awd in Media Lincoln Univ 1985. **Special Achievements:** Children of the Dream: The Psychology of Black Success, 1992. **Home Addr:** 45 Plaza St, Brooklyn, NY 11217.

EDWARDS, BESSIE REGINA
Meeting and conference planner. **Personal:** Born Mar 14, 1942, Gates County, NC. **Educ:** Brooklyn Coll, Special Bacculaurate Degree Program 1975-79; New School of Social Rsch, BA/MA 1979-81. **Career:** Opportunity Industrialization, counselor/teacher 1975-80; Manhattan Cable TV, affirmative action officer 1980-86; Paragon Cable, mgr training and develop. **Orgs:** Bd mem NY Chap Coalition 100 Black Women 1983-; sec Minorities in Cable 1984-; sec Women in Cable 1984-; bd mem EDGES; mem Women's City Club; mem, Brooklyn Chamber of Commerce 1989-90; adjunct lecturer, Borough Manhattan Community College 1988-90. **Honors/Awds:** Cable Careers of the 80's modules in mass communications 1984; Black Achiever selected by Time Inc The Parent Co 1987. **Home Addr:** 195 Willoughby Ave, Suite 1006, Brooklyn, NY 11205.

EDWARDS, BLUE (THEODORE)
Professional basketball player. **Personal:** Born Oct 31, 1965, Washington, DC; married Valerie; children: Brittney, Whitney. **Educ:** Louisburg College, Louisburg, NC, 1984-86; East Carolina Univ, Greenville, NC, 1986-87, 1988-89. **Career:** Utah Jazz, guard/forward, 1989-92; Milwaukee Bucks, 1992-94; Boston Celtics, 1994-95; Vancouver Grizzlies, 1995-. **Honors/Awds:** NBA All-Rookie Second Team, 1990. **Special Achievements:** NBA Draft, First round pick, #21, 1989. **Business Addr:** Professional Basketball Player, Vancouver Grizzlies, 788 Beatty St, Ste 311, Vancouver, BC, Canada V6B 2M1, (604)688-5867.

EDWARDS, CARL RAY, II
Attorney. **Personal:** Born Jul 14, 1947, Detroit, MI; son of Alice Edwards and Carl R Edwards; married Alice Jennings Edwards; children: Patrick Phillips, Kwameena, Tonya Jennings, Ronald G Watters, Saraun, Carl Ray. **Educ:** Michigan Lutheran College, BA, 1970; University of Detroit, MA, 1972; Wayne State University, JD, 1974. **Career:** Philo, Atkinson, Darling, Steinberg, Edwards and Jennings, partner, 1973-82; Edwards and Jennings, PC, president, 1982-. **Orgs:** Association of Trial Lawyers of America, 1976-; Natl Bar Assn, 1985-; Michigan Bar Association, 1975-; Michigan Trial Lawyers Association, executive board member, 1976-, treasurer, secretary, vice pres, president, 1987-88; Natl Conference of Black Lawyers, MI Chapter, co-founder. **Honors/Awds:** National Association for Equal Opportunity in Higher Education, Presidential Citation, 1981; Michigan Trial Lawyers Association, Peoples Law School, Founder's Award, 1989. **Special Achievements:** State Bar of Michigan delegation member of judges and attorneys on legal and constitutional fact-finding mission to USSR and People's Republic of China, 1988; Co-founder of the Michigan Trial Lawyers' Peoples Law School, operating across MI and established by the Assn of Trial Lawyers of America and operating in over 18 states nationwide. **Business Addr:** President, Edwards and Jennings, PC, The Globe Bldg, 407 E Fort St, Ste 605, Detroit, MI 48226, (313)961-5000.

EDWARDS, CECILE HOOVER
Educational administrator. **Personal:** Born Oct 20, 1926, East St Louis, IL; married Gerald Alonzo; children: Gerald Alonzo Jr, Adrienne Annette, Hazel Ruth. **Educ:** Tuskegee Institute, BS, 1946, MS, 1947; Iowa State Univeristy, 1946, PhD, 1950. **Career:** Research Awards, proj dir 1951-; White House Conf Panel on Community Nutrition, chmn 1969; Carver Found Tuskegee Inst, asst prof & rsch assoc 1950-56; Tuskegee Inst, head dept of foods & nutrition 1952-56; NC A&T State Univ, prof of nutrition & rsch dept home economics 1956-71, chmn dept of home economics 1968-71; Howard Univ, chmn, prof of nutrition dept of home economics 1971-74, School of Human Ecology, dean, 1974-87; School of Continuing Educ, dean, 1987-88, prof 1971-. **Orgs:** American Institute of Nutritution, National Institute of Sci, Sigma X; 150 scientific & professional publs in major professional jrnls 1949-; pres Southeastern Conf of Teachers of Foods & Nutrition 1971; mem adv com to dir Nat Inst of Health 1972-75; mem Expert Com on Nitrates Nitrites & Nitrasamines 1975-79; consult Univ of Khartoum Sudan Ford Found 1978; proj dir Training Prog for Residents of Public Housing 1982; chmn Natl Conf on Black Youth Unemployment 1983; prog project dir Nutrition, Other Factors & The Outcomes of Pregnancy 1985-; American Institute of Nutrition; National Institute of Science; Sigma Xi. **Honors/Awds:** Award for Outstanding Achievement Nat Council of Negro Women 1963; Citation for Outstanding Contributions to Edn, City of E St Louis 1964; Award for Achievement in Sci, NC A&T State Univ 1964; Scroll of Hon, Outstanding Achievement in Nutrition & Research The Links Inc 1970; Home Economics Centennial Alumni Award, IA State Univ 1971; Alumni Achievement Award IA State Univ 1972; Alumni Merit Award Tuskegee Inst 1974; Citation from House of Reps State of IL for Devotion to Eliminating Poverty 1980; Awd for Outstanding Unit in Academic Affairs Div Howard Univ 1982; Proclamation by Gov of State of IL April 5 1984 as Dr Cecile Hoover Edwards Day in witness of her contribution, her professional recognition nationally and internationally and the sharing ofher expertise with communities arounde world including East St Louis IL; one of 25 contemporary Tuskegeans honored at Biennial Convention of Alumni Assoc 1984. **Business Addr:** Professor, Department of Nutritional Sciences, College of Allied Health Sciences, Howard University, 2400 6th St NW, Washington, DC 20059.

EDWARDS, CLAUDIA L.
Organization executive. **Personal:** Born in Bronx, NY; daughter of Joshua & Mable Edwards; divorced; children: Damon, Andre. **Educ:** Bronx Community Coll, Associate, 1980; SUNY Purchase, BA, 1983; New York Univ, MA, 1988. **Career:** United Way, vp, 1989-92; Reader's Digest Foundation, executive director, 1992-. **Orgs:** Westchester Medical Ctr, trustee; The Learning Foundation, bd mem; Association of Black Foundation Executives; Women in Communications; Women in Philanthropy. **Honors/Awds:** YWCA, Academy of Women Achievers, 1996; County of Westchester, Distinguished Service Award, 1996; Links, Inc, Meritorious Award, 1997; Bronx Community Coll, Distinguished Alumna, 1997. **Business Addr:** Executive Director, The Reader's Digest Foundation, Reader's Digest Rd, Pleasantville, NY 10570.

EDWARDS, CLAYBON JEROME
Mortician. **Personal:** Born Jul 15, 1929, Peach County, GA; married Mary Nevel; children: Deneise. **Educ:** Morris Brown Coll, grad; Worsham Coll; Ft Valley State NW. **Career:** Edwards Fun Home, mgr; Sup Life Ins Co, home off rep, reg supr, insptr, dist mgr cons, 1st vice pres GA Funer Serv Prctnrs Assn. **Orgs:** Past vice pres Upsilon Nu Delta Morticians Frat; past & mem bd of dir Wabash YMCA; mem, past pres Alpha Phi Alpha Frat Inc; past mem bd of dir Peach Co UCF; sec GFSPA; mem bd of GA Area Plng & Dev Com; treas Citzshp Educ Com mem, Trinity Bapt Ch; mem trustee bd Trinity Bapt Ch; mem C of C Peach Co; mem trustee bd Morris Brown Coll; mem State Bd Dept of Human Rescs; mem NAACP Honored Mort of the Yr 1974; first black elect ofcl City Councmn of GA; Mayor protem, Ft Valley; chmn Police Com. **Business Addr:** PO Box 310, Fort Valley, GA 31030.

EDWARDS, DELORES A.
Journalist, producer. **Personal:** Born Sep 22, 1965, New York, NY; daughter of Lucy Miller Edwards and Nathaniel Edwards. **Educ:** Northeastern University, Boston, MA, BS, cum laude, 1988. **Career:** Columbia University GSAS, graduate advisor, 1988-89; ABC News, production associate, 1989-92, associate producer ABC Children's Special "Prejudice," 1992, "Kids in the Crossfire," 1994, "Live at the White House, President Clinton: Answering Children's Questions," 1994; All- American Television, segment producer, 1992-93; Television Program Enterprises, segment producer, 1992-93; Pacific Rim LTD, research consultant, 1993; Arts & Entertainment Network, associate producer "Biography," 1994, producer, currently; WGBH/GR Productions, associate producer "Surviving the Odds: To Be a Young Black Male in America," 1994; Kelly Films, associate producer "Fighting Destroyer Escorts," "Proudly We Served: The Men of the USS Mason," 1994-; Barwall Productions, producer "Barbara Walters Interviews of a Lifetime," 1994. **Orgs:** Natl Assn of Black Journalists, 1988-; NYABJ, 1988-; SPJ, 1990-; NABET, 1989-. **Home Phone:** (718)601-1302. **Business Addr:** Producer, A & E Network/The History Channel, 235 E 45th St, New York, NY 10017.

EDWARDS, DENNIS, JR.
Judge. **Personal:** Born Aug 19, 1922, New York City, NY; son of Gladys Wilson and Dennis Edwards Sr; married Dorothy Fairclough; children: Lynne Mosley, Denise Young. **Educ:** NY Univ, BA 1941; Harvard Law Sch, JD 1944. **Career:** NY State Supreme Court, law clerk 1948-65; Criminal Court New York City & State Court of Claims, judge 1965-. **Orgs:** Dir NY Co Lawyers Assn 1961-65; Harlem Lawyers Assn 1952; mem Amer Judicature Soc, Amer Bar Assn; dir Speedwell Soc for Children; mem Omega Frat, Elks, Masons, NAACP, Urban League, YMCA. **Business Addr:** Judge, State Court of Claims, 111 Centre St, New York, NY 10013.

EDWARDS, DENNIS L.
Automobile executive (retired). **Personal:** Born Aug 29, 1941, Indianapolis, IN; son of Ella Stange Edwards and Rollin H Edwards; married Judith Johnson Edwards, Jun 15, 1966; children: Camille, Dennis L Jr, Tiffany. **Educ:** Parsons Coll, Fairfield IA, BA, 1964; Central Michigan Univ, Mt Pleasant MI, MA, 1976. **Career:** St Louis Hawks, basketball player, 1964-71; Chrysler Corp, St Louis MO, gen supt, 1978, Detroit MI, gen supt, 1981-, operations mgr, 1982, production mgr, 1983, production mgr, 1985, plant mgr, 1985. **Orgs:** Bd of dir, Goodwill Industries, 1986-, Wayne County Attention Center, 1986-; account executive, United Way; board of visitors, Delaware State College, basketball team advisor, University of Delaware, member, State of Delaware, Adult Literacy Summit; advisor, Ferris School for Boys; member, Detroit Society of Engineers, member, Kiwanis Club of Wilmington, Deleware. **Honors/Awds:** All American Basketball Player, Parsons Coll, 1963, 1964; selected to Participate in Pan-American Games, South America, 1963.

EDWARDS, DIXON VOLDEAN, III
Professional football player. **Personal:** Born Mar 25, 1968, Cincinnati, OH; married Secola; children: Dixon IV, Taylor. **Educ:** Michigan State, attended. **Career:** Dallas Cowboys, linebacker, 1991-95; Minnesota Vikings, 1996-. **Business Addr:** Professional Football Player, Minnesota Vikings, 9520 Viking Dr, Eden Prairie, MN 55344, (612)828-6500.

EDWARDS, DONALD LEWIS, JR.
Professional football player. **Personal:** Born Apr 6, 1973, San Diego, CA. **Educ:** UCLA, degree in political science. **Career:** Kansas City Chiefs, linebacker, 1996-. **Business Addr:** Professional Football Player, Kansas City Chiefs, One Arrowhead Dr, Kansas City, MO 64129, (816)924-9300.

EDWARDS, DONALD PHILIP
Attorney. **Personal:** Born Aug 27, 1947, Buffalo, NY; son of Lorraine V Jarrett Edwards and Robert D Edwards; married Jo Roberson. **Educ:** Morehouse Coll, BA (Cum Laude) 1969; Boston Univ School of Law, JD 1973. **Career:** NAACP Legal Defense Fund, fellow 1973-76; Thomas Kennedy Sampson Edwards & Patterson, partner 1974-92; Law Office of Donald P Edwards, 1992-; Clef Productions Inc, owner, 1993-. **Orgs:** Chmn of bd Hillside Intl Truth Ctr 1980-83; bd of adv Atlanta Legal Aid Soc 1981-85; bd mem Atlanta Volunteer Lawyers Inc 1983-84; pres Northern District Litigation Fund 1984-87; bd mem Natl Bar Assoc 1984, 1985; pres Gate City Bar Assoc 1984; chairman Fulton Cnty Dept of Family and Children Services 1990; dir Nat'l Bar Assn Region XI 1986-87; vice pres, Christian Council of Metro Atlanta 1987-92; bd mem, American Cancer Society, Atlanta Unit 1988-89; trustee, Southwest Hosp & Med Ctr, 1990-; pres, Southwest Hosp Foundation Inc, 1992-95; 100 Black Men of Atlanta Inc; pres, Assn of Metro Atlanta DFCS Bds, 1992-94. **Honors/Awds:** Service Awd Coll Park Voters League 1981; Civil Rights Awd Gate City Bar Assoc 1983; Lawyer of the Year DeKalb Cty NAACP 1984; Top 100 Atlantans under 40 Atlanta Mag 1984; Leadership Atlanta 1985; Black Pages Professional Achievement Award, 1992. **Home Addr:** 954 Willis Mill Rd SW, Atlanta, GA 30311. **Business Addr:** Law Office of Donald P. Edwards, 170 Mitchell St, SW, Atlanta, GA 30303.

EDWARDS, DOROTHY WRIGHT
Educator (retired). **Personal:** Born Jan 13, 1914, Jacksonville, FL; daughter of Julia Peterson Wright and John Wright; married Oscar J Edwards, Jun 8, 1938 (deceased); children: Oscar J Jr. **Educ:** FL A&M Univ, BS 1935; NY Univ, MA 1952; Additional Study, Hampton Inst, Miami Univ, Columbia Univ. **Career:** Physical educ instructor, 1935-40; BTW, business instructor 1940; Miami Housing Authority, cashier-booker 1940-41; Dorsey Jr-Sr High, sec, phys instructor 1941-47, dean of girls 1947-55; Miami Northwestern Sr High, asst prin of guidance 1955-70; Miami Spgs, asst prin of guidance 1970-71; Edward Waters Coll, dean of women 1971-72; Proj Upward Bound, counselor 1972-76; FL Memorial Coll, counselor for women 1976-78; Miami Northwestern Sr High School, jr coll assistance prog adv 1978-retired. **Orgs:** Bd dir OIC; bd dir Dade Mt Zion Fed Credit Union, Amer Assn of Univ Women, Council of Intl Visitors; life mem YWCA, Alpha Kappa Alpha Sor; mem Kappa Delta Pi; fin sec 100 Women for FL Meml Coll; church clerk Mt Zion Baptist Church; Docent at Jackson Meml Hosp Alamo; bd dir Family Health Center Inc. **Honors/Awds:** Outstanding Serv to Youth Phi Delta Kappa; Star Tchr Miami NW Sr HS 1966-67; Certificate of Appreciation YWCA 1975; Alpha Phi Alpha Frat Beta Beta Lambda Chap 1984 Outstanding Citizen Awd 1984.

EDWARDS, DOUGLAS
Professional basketball player. **Personal:** Born Jan 21, 1971, Miami, FL. **Educ:** Florida State Univ. **Career:** Atlanta Hawks, forward, 1993-95; Vancouver Grizzlies, 1995-. **Special Achievements:** NBA Draft, First round pick, #15, 1993. **Business Addr:** Professional Basketball Player, Vancouver Grizzlies, 788 Beatty St, Ste 311, Vancouver, BC, Canada V6B 2M1, (604)688-5867.

EDWARDS, ED. See EDWARDS, ABIYAH, JR.

EDWARDS, ESTHER GORDY
Record, film company executive. **Personal:** Born Apr 25, Oconee, GA; married George H; children: Robert Bullock. **Educ:** Attended, Howard U, Wayne State U. **Career:** Gordy Printing Co Detroit, co-owner genl mgr 1947-59; Motown Record Corp Detroit, sr vice pres sec dir 1959-; Motown Industries Hollywood, CA & Detroit, corporate sec, sr vice pres 1973-. **Orgs:** Detroit Recorders Ct Jury Commn 1960-62; chmn 1961-62; chmn of bd Am Devel Corp; exec dir Gordy Found 1968-; founder, chmn African-Am Heritage Assn 1976-; chmn Wayne Co Dem Women's Com 1956; MI del-at-large Dem Nat Conv 1960; interim asst dep auditor gen MI 1960; bd of dir Bank of the Commonwealth 1973-79; Booker T Washington Bus Assn; Howard Univ Alumni Assn vice pres Metro Detroit Conv & Visitors Bur; mem Wayne State Fund; adv bd sch of mgmtU of MI; Alpha Kappa Alpha. **Business Addr:** Motown Industries, 2648 W Grand Blvd, Detroit, MI 48208.

EDWARDS, G. FRANKLIN. See Obituaries section.

EDWARDS, GEORGE R.
Television broadcasting executive. **Personal:** Born Feb 1, 1938, New York, NY; son of Olga Edwards and John Edwards; divorced; children: Lisa, Veronica, George Drew. **Educ:** City Coll of New York, BA, English 1959. **Career:** British Airways NY, sales mgr 1959-63; Pepsi-Cola Brooklyn NY, gen sales mgr 1964-65; Pepsi-Cola Bronx, gen mgr 1968-70; Venture Mktg Co Heublein Inc, vice pres mktg; Heublein Spirits Div, vice pres, group mktg dir 1974-78; Hartford Graduate Center, visitig prof mktg 1975-78; Natl Black Network, pres/coo. **Orgs:** Chmn mktg comm Greater Hartford Arts Council 1976-78. **Business Addr:** President/COO, Natl Black Network, 505 8th Ave, 9th Fl, New York, NY 10018.

EDWARDS, GERALD DOUGLAS
Plastic manufacturing executive. **Personal:** Born Jul 13, 1950, Chicago, IL; son of Lucille Elizabeth Edwards and William Kenneth Edwards; married Jada Denise Brooks, Nov 18, 1972; children: Candice Rae, Gerald Douglas. **Educ:** Heidelberg College, BA, 1972. **Career:** Ford Motor Co, general supervisor, 1983-86; Detroit Plastic Molding, asst plant manager, 1986-87; Engineered Plastic Products, Inc, ceo, 1987-. **Orgs:** Michigan Minority Business Development Council, Minority Input Commitee, 1989-; Minority Technology Council of Michigan, Director, 1992-; Sumpter Community Church of God, Building Fund Campaign Chairman, 1990-, Board of Directors, 1989-. **Honors/Awds:** Outstanding Young Men of America, 1989. **Business Addr:** CEO, Engineered Plastic Products, Inc, 699 James L Hart Pkwy, Ypsilanti, MI 48197, (313)779-7406.

EDWARDS, GILBERT FRANKLIN
Sociologist, educator. **Personal:** Born Jun 2, 1915, Charleston, SC; son of Bertha Allen Edwards and Gilbert Franklin Edwards; married Peggy Jarvis Edwards, Sep 8, 1946; children: Donalee Marie Wood. **Educ:** Fisk Univ, AB 1936; Univ of Chicago, PhD 1952. **Career:** Fessender Acad FL, teacher social studies 1937-39; Howard Univ, faculty mem 1941-, sociology prof 1960-; Washington Univ, St Louis, visiting teacher 1954; Harvard Univ, visiting prof, 1967-68; consultant, currently. **Orgs:** Public mem Natl Capital Planning Comm 1965-71; mem Pop Assn Amer Sociological Assn; alumni mem Phi Beta Kappa; member, American Sociological Assn; member, White House Historical Society; member, Assn of Black Sociologists; member, Eastern Sociological Society. **Honors/Awds:** Author "The Negro Professional Class" 1959; editor E Franklin Frazier on Race Relations 1968; Public Service Award, University of Chicago, 1980.

EDWARDS, GROVER LEWIS, SR.
Consultant, educational administrator. **Personal:** Born Feb 21, 1944, Henrico, NC; married Lucy Priscilla Moody; children: Reggie Lamont, Telsha Nicole, Kelsey Daneen, Grover Lewis Jr. **Educ:** Elizabeth City State Univ, Associate 1965; Shaw Univ, Bachelors 1976. **Career:** RCA Training Prog, electronics instructor 1969-73, supervisor of instructors 1973-79; Edwards & Assocs Building Contractors, owner/pres 1979; Norfax Real Estate Corp, pres 1983-; Northampton Co Sch Bd, chairman. **Orgs:** Mem past youth adv NAACP 1969; mem past pres Gaston Religious Civic Organ 1971; pres Northampton Housing Assistance Prog 1972; mem NC Home Builders Assn 1980; Northampton Co Sch Bd mem 1972-, chmn 1984-; mem Prince Hall Masonic Lodge 1975-; mem bd of dirs NC Sch Bd 1984-. **Honors/Awds:** Serv Awd Northampton HS West 1980; Serv Awd Athlete Assoc Tri-City Chums 1981; Outstanding Business Awd Northampton Co NAACP 1985. **Military Serv:** USN E4 1965-69; Natl Defense Awd. **Business Addr:** Chairman, Northampton Co School Bd, Star Route Box 52A, Henrico, NC 27842.

EDWARDS, HARRY
Educator. **Personal:** Born Nov 22, 1942, St Louis, MO; married Sandra Y Boze; children: Tazamisha Heshima Imara, Fatima Malene Imara, Changa Demany Imara. **Educ:** San Jose State, BA 1964; Cornell U, MA 1966, PhD 1972. **Career:** San Jose State, instructor Sociology 1966-68; Univ of Santa Clara, instructor Sociology 1967-68; Univ of CA Berkeley, asst prof Sociology 1970-77, assoc prof Sociology, prof Sociology. **Orgs:** Contributed editorials to Los Angeles Times, NY Times, San Francisco Examiner, Oakland Tribune, Chicago Sun-Times, Black Scholar, East St Louis Monitor, Milwaukee Courier, Newsday, Los Angeles Hearld Examiner, Sports Illustrated, Sports & Athletes & Inside Sports; served as consultant with producers of sports relatedprograms on NBC, CBS, ABC and PBS TV networks; sports commentary for Natl Public Radio via satellite to Washington DC; interview/commentary prog on KPFA-Radio Berkeley CA; consulted/appeared on camera for BBC TV (British), CBC TV (Candaian) West German TV for CBS' "60 Minutes", CNN's "Sports Focus", NBC's "Nightly News", ABC's "Sportsbeat" and "Nightline", PBS's "James Michner's World", Turner Sports Nework ESPN "Sports-Forum" and numerous local & relgional TV productions foing on issues relating to sports & society; participated in lecture & consulting fair at Natl Sports Inst Oslo Norway, Natl Sports Inst Moscow USSR; consultant San Francisco 49ers and Golden State Warriors. **Honors/Awds:** NAACP Educ Incentive Scholarship CA State Univ 1960; Athletic Scholarship CA State Univ 1960; Woodrow Wilson Fellowship 1964; Man of Yr Awd San Francisco Sun Reporter 1968; Russwurm Awd Natl Newspaper Publishers Assoc 1968; fellowship Cornell Univ 1968; Dist Scholar in Res fall 1980 OR State Univ; Hon Doctorate Columbia Coll 1981; Miller Scholar in Res fall 1982 Univ of IL Champaign/Urbana Charleston Gazette; Dist Scholar in Res spring 1983 Norwegian Coll of Physical Educ & Sports Oslow Norway; Dist Schlr Spring 1984 Univ of Charleston; Dist Visiting Scholar fall 1984 IN St Univ. **Business Addr:** Professor of Sociology, Univ of CA/Berkeley, 410 Barrows Hall, Berkeley, CA 94720.

EDWARDS, HARRY T.
Judge. **Personal:** Born Nov 3, 1940, New York, NY; son of Arline Lyle and George H Edwards; children: Brent, Michelle. **Educ:** Cornell Univ, BS 1962; Univ of Michigan Law School, JD, 1965. **Career:** Seyfarth, Shaw Fairweather & Geraldson, Chicago, attorney, 1965-70; Univ of Michigan Law School, professor, 1970-75, 1977-80; Harvard Univ Law School, prof 1975-77; Amtrak, bd dir, 1977-80, chmn bd 1979-80; US Ct of Appeals, Washington, DC, judge 1980-94, chief judge, 1994-. **Orgs:** Amer Law Institute; Amer Bar Assn; Amer Academy of Arts & Sciences; Amer Judicature Society; Unique Learning Center, mentor, instructor, bd of directors. **Honors/Awds:** Co-author, Labor Relations Law in the Pub Sector, 1985, The Lawyer as a Negotiator, 1977, Collective Bargaining & Labor Arbitration, 1979, Higher Educ & the Law, 1980; author of more than 75 scholarly articles; Honorary Doctor of Law degress from Williams Coll, Univ of Detroit, Georgetown University, Brooklyn College, State University of New York, John Jay College of Criminal Justice, Lewis & Clark College, St Lawrence Univ; Whitney North Seymour Medal, Amer Arbitration Assn, 1988; Society of Amer Law Teachers Award for distinguished contributions to teaching and public service, 1982. **Business Addr:** Chief Judge, US Court of Appeals - DC Circuit, 5400 E Barrett Prettyman Courthouse, 333 Constitution Ave, NW, Washington, DC 20001-2866.

EDWARDS, HORACE BURTON
Business executive. **Personal:** Born May 20, 1925, Tuscaloosa, AL; divorced; children: Adrienne, Paul, David, Michael. **Educ:** Marquette Univ, BS Naval Sci, Mech Engr 1947, 1948; Iona Coll, MBA 1972; TX Southern Univ, LHD (Hon) 1982; Stillman Coll, LLD (Hon) 1984. **Career:** Atlantic Richfield Co, controller mktg 1968-72, mgr fin & ops analysis 1973-76, mgr planning & control transp div 1976-79; ARCO Transp Co, vice pres planning & control 1978-80; ARCO Pipe Line Co, pres, ceo, chmn of bd. **Orgs:** Trustee Leadership Independence 1984-85, KS Chamber of Commerce Leadership KS 1985-86; dir, pres Independence Ind 1985; mem Assoc of Oil Pipe Lines Exec Comm, Amer Petrol Inst & Central Comm on Pipe Line Transp; pres of bd of dir Jr Achievement of Montgomery Cty Independence KS; mem bd of dir KS Chamber of Commerce & Industry, Independence Community Coll Endowment Bd; trustee Inst of Logopedics Whchita KS, KS Independent Coll Fund, KS Council on Economic Educ, TX Southern Univ Bus School Found; mem Natl Bar Assoc Advisory Comm to its Energy & Environ Law Sect; mem bd of dir Amer Assoc of Blacks in Energy; participant Natl Urban League's Black Exec Exchange Program; mem NAACP, FL A&M School of Business, Industry's Ctr for Entrepreneurial Devel Roundtable. **Honors/Awds:** Marquette Univ Disting Engrg Alumnus Awd 1984. **Military Serv:** USN lt jg 1943-48. **Business Addr:** President, Chmn of the Board, ARCO Pipeline, 15600 John F Kennedy Blvd #300, Houston, TX 77032-2360.

EDWARDS, JAMES FRANKLIN
Professional basketball player. **Personal:** Born Nov 22, 1955, Seattle, WA. **Educ:** Univ of WA, 1973-77. **Career:** Center: Los Angeles Lakers, 1977, Indiana Pacers, 1978-81, Cleveland Cavaliers, 1981-82, Phoenix Suns, 1982-87, Detroit Pistons, 1988-91, Los Angeles Clippers, 1991-92, Los Angeles Lakers, 1992-94; Portland Trail Blazers, 1994-. **Business Addr:** Professional Basketball Player, Chicago Bulls, 1901 W Madison St, Chicago, IL 60612, (312)455-4000.

EDWARDS, JEAN CURTIS
Administrative assistant, teacher. **Personal:** Born May 18, 1929, North Little Rock, AR; son of Laura Bridgette Freeman Edwards and James Wesley Edwards; married Artemeze Redwood Edwards, Nov 24, 1955; children: Marico, Edwin, Jauch, Rhonda. **Educ:** University of Arkansas at Pine Bluff, Pine Bluff, AR, bachelor of science, 1960; Arkansas State College, Conway, AR; University of Arkansas at Fayetteville, Fayetteville, AR; University of Arkansas at Little Rock, AR. **Career:** Self-employed farmer, Sherrill, AR; Sherrill Rosenwald, Sherrill, AR, math teacher, 1960-62; Tucker Rosenwald School, Tucker, AR, principal, 1962-69; Office of Economic Opportunity Commission, Inc, Pine Bluff, AR, coord/dir of neighborhood services, 1969-73; Jefferson County School District, Pine Bluff, AR, principal (Barnes Memorial School), 1973-79; Wabbaseka-Tucker School District, Wabbaseka, AR, administrative asst, teacher; Arkansas State Capitol, state senator, 1990-. **Orgs:** Member, Northside Kiwanis Club, currently; member, AEA and NEA, currently; advisory committee, Arkansas Agricultural & Rural Leadership Program, currently; board chairman, Board of Directors of Wright-Pastoria Water Assn, currently; state member, State Building Service Commission,

1988-. **Honors/Awds:** Service Award, 1988, Justice of the Peace, 1979-88, Jefferson County Quorum Court; Leadership Award, Comprehensive Care Center, 1978-79, 1982-88; Distinguished Achievement Award, Delta Sigma Theta Sorority; Rural Service Award, Sargent Shriver, Office of Economic Opportunity. **Military Serv:** US Air Force, Airman 1st Class, 1951-54; Korean Service Medal, United Nations Service Medal, National Defense Service Medal. **Home Addr:** 8607 Earl Chadick Rd, Sherrill, AR 72152.

EDWARDS, JOHN L.
Educator. **Personal:** Born Oct 18, 1930, Muncie, IN; married Mavis J Jones; children: John, Robert. **Educ:** AZ State U, EdD 1965; AZ State U, MA 1959; Ball State U, BS 1953. **Career:** AZ State Univ, Exten & Prof Coll, asst dean 1973, assoc prof 1969-75, asst prof 1966-69, instructor 1964-66, faculty assoc 1963-64, grad asst 1962-63; Julian Elementary School Phoenix, teacher 1955-62. **Orgs:** Mem Intnl Reading Assn 1963; NEA 1956; AZ Educ Assn; Am Assn of Univ Prof 1964; Phi Delta Kappa 1966; Kappa Delta Pi 1962; has written many articles in his field, faculty Adv Kappa Alpha Psi, AZ State Univ 1962-72 & 1975; bd mem Southwestern Coop End Lab; bd dir Jane Wayland Child Guidance Cntr 1969-75; mem AZ Right to Read Commn 1971; Phoenix Citizens Bond Com 1975; past chmn AZ Educ Assn Instructional & Professional Develop Com; bd dir Assn for Higher Educ 1964; Desert Area reading council 1966. **Honors/Awds:** Outstanding Achievement, Western Provincial Alumni Award, Kappa Alpha Psi 1962; Phoenix Alumni Award, Kappa Alpha Psi 1965, 1963, & 1960; award for Outstanding Achievement Adult Basic Educ Inst 1970. **Business Addr:** U Ex Acad Serv Bldg Rm 110, AZ State Univ, Tempe, AZ 85281.

EDWARDS, JOHN LOYD, III
Foundation executive. **Personal:** Born Feb 18, 1948, Nashville, TN; children: Adrian Joel, Nikita Michelle, Derek Traimain. **Educ:** TN State Univ, attended 1966-68; Univ of TN at Chattanooga, BFA 1980. **Career:** Chattanooga Northstar Newspaper, writer/director advertising 1981-83; Mary Walker Historical and Educational Foundation, exec dir 1983-. **Orgs:** Public relations United States Jaycees 1981-; pres Visual Media Productions 1985-; mem Assoc for the Study of Afro-Amer Life & History 1985-; vice pres Lakeside PTA 1986-; board of directors Joseh Johnson Mental Health Center 1988-; State Department of Tourism task force to develop Black Heritage Site Information for tourist etc. **Honors/Awds:** Outstanding Comm Achievement for Vietnam Era Veteran City of Chattanooga 1979; Public Relations Dir of the Yr TN Jaycees 1983-84; Honorary Life Member United States Jaycees 1987. **Military Serv:** AUS sgt 2 yrs; Bronze Star, Army Commendation Medal, Purple Heart, Vietnam Serv Cross, Combat Infantry Badge 1968-70. **Business Addr:** Executive Dir, Mary Walker Foundation, 3031 Wilcox Blvd, Chattanooga, TN 37411.

EDWARDS, JOHN W., JR.
Physician. **Personal:** Born Apr 9, 1933, Ferndale, MI; son of Josephine Wood Edwards (deceased) and John W Edwards, Sr, MD (deceased); married Ella Marie Law; children: Joella Marie, John W III. **Educ:** Alma College, 1949-50; Univ of Michigan at Ann Arbor, BS, 1954; Wayne State Univ, graduate studies, 1954-56; Howard Univ College of Medicine, MD, 1960. **Career:** Walter Reed Gen Hospital, internship, 1960-61, surgical resident, 1962-63, urological resident, 1963-66; Straub Clinic Inc, urologist, 1970-74, chief dept of surgery, 1973; private practice, urologist, 1974-; asst chief dept of surgery, Queen's Medical Center, 1977-79; chief dept of clinical serv, active staff, Kapiolani Women's & Children's Medical Center, 1981-83; active staff, Kuakini Hospital; consulting staff, Rehabilitation Hospital of the Pacific; consultant in urology, Tripler Army Medical Center; John Burns School of Medicine, Univ of HI, assoc clinical prof, chief of surgery; Queen's Medical Center, Honolulu, vp, medical staff services, 1993-94; The Queens Health Systems, Physician Relations, vp, 1994-. **Orgs:** Certified, Amer Bd of Urology; fellow, Amer Coll of Surgeons; mem, Amer Urological Assn, Western Section Amer Urological Assn, Pan Pacific Surgical Assn, HI Urological Assn, Amer Medical Assn, Honolulu County Medical Soc, HI Medical Assn, South West Oncology Group, Natl Medical Assn, Alpha Phi Alpha, Chi Delta Mu, Waialae Country Club; Pacific Club; life mem, NAACP; fellow, Amer Coll of Surgeons; commr, chmn, City and County of Honolulu Liquor Commn, 1987-89; governor from Hawaii, Amer Coll of Surgeons, 1987-93; pres, Western Section Amer Urological Assn, 1989-90; St Andrews Cathedral, Episcopal. **Honors/Awds:** Alpha Omega Alpha Honor Medical Soc, 1959; The Links Inc, Hawaii Chapter, Hawaii African-American Humanitarian of the Year, 1991; Howard Gray Award, Urology Section, Natl Medical Assn, 1988. **Special Achievements:** Co-author: ''Anuria Secondary to Bilateral Ureteropelvic Fungus Balls,'' Urology, 1974; ''Representive Causes of Ambiguous Genitalia,'' Journal of Urology, 1967; ''Herpes Zoster with Neurogenic Bladder Dysfunction,'' Archives of Dermatology, 1974, Journal of AMA, 1973, 1974. **Military Serv:** US Air Force capt 1959-63; US Army lt col 1963-70; Bronze Star. **Business Addr:** Vice Pres, Physician Relations, The Queen's Health Systems, 1099 Alakea St, Ste 1100, Honolulu, HI 96813-4500.

EDWARDS, JOHN WILSON
Director. **Personal:** Born Feb 17, 1942, Durham County, NC; married Eloise Freeman; children: Brian, Robin. **Educ:** Durham Coll, 1961; NC Fund, Comm Action Tech Training Prgm, 1965. **Career:** State Econ Opp Office NC, dir Present; Institutional Devel Soul City Co, mgr; Alumni Affairs Durham Coll, dir; Voter Educ Proj Atlanta, area coord; NC Voter & Educ Prgm Durham, organizer; Operation Breakthrough Inc Durham, leadership devel coord 1966-67; Winston-salem Boys Club, dir 1965-66; NAACP Durham, field sec-at-large 1962-65; NAACP Youth Workers, field supr, student 1961-62; NAACP, student field worker 1960-61. **Orgs:** Mem Soul City Found Inc; UOCI Fed Credit Union; Durham Con on Affairs of Black People; Durham Opp Found Inc; Durham Coll; Durham Bus & Professional Chain; NC Voter Educ Proj Inc; NC Fed of Child Care Ctrs ; Econ Devel Corp; Durham Coll Alumni Assn pres Pan African Early Educ Ctr; Lincoln Comm Health Ctr; past-chmn adv United Black Officers of Urham, NC consumer credit counseling serv of Wake Co Union Bapt Ct; mem Sr Usher Bd; mem Bd of Trustees. **Business Addr:** PO Box 27687, Raleigh, NC 27611.

EDWARDS, KENNETH J.
Business executive. **Personal:** Born Apr 5, 1947, Beaumont, TX; married Gloria J Holmes; children: Melissa R, Kenitha J, Kenneth J. **Educ:** Lamar U, BS 1970. **Career:** John Deere Co, div sales mgr 1979-, serv mgr consumer prod 1977-79, div serv mgr 1976-77, terrtry mgr 1973-76, sales prom supr 1972-73, serv rep 1971-72; US Govt, reliablty engr 1970-71. **Business Addr:** John Deere & Company, 1400 13th St, East Moline, IL 61244.

EDWARDS, KEVIN DURELL
Professional basketball player. **Personal:** Born Oct 30, 1965, Cleveland Heights, OH. **Educ:** Lakeland Community College, Mentor, OH, 1984-86; DePaul Univ, Chicago, IL, 1986-88. **Career:** Miami Heat, guard, 1988-93; New Jersey Nets, 1993-98; Orlando Magic, 1998-. **Honors/Awds:** NBA All-Rookie Second Team, 1989. **Business Addr:** Professional Basketball Player, Orlando Magic, PO Box 76, Orlando, FL 32801, (407)649-3200.

EDWARDS, LEO DEREK
Composer, educator. **Personal:** Born Jan 31, 1937, Cincinnati. **Educ:** Mannes Coll of Music, BS 1966; Cty Univ NY, MA 1969. **Career:** Shumiatcher School Music, chmn theory dept 1965-; Mannes Coll Music, faculty 1968-; City Univ NY, faculty 1969-75; guest lectures, workshops at: New York University, Centro Colombo-Americano (Bogota), Michigan State University, numerous others. **Orgs:** Soc Black Composers; Phi Mu Alpha Sinfonia (profl music frat); Music Tchrs Nat Assn. **Honors/Awds:** Phi Mu Alpha composition contest winner 1960; Joseph Dillon Award Pedagogy 1966; music tchrs Nat Assn Award 1975; National Endowment for the Arts grant 1976; Compositor Laureado, National Chorus of Colombia, 1985; Faculty Development Grant, New School for Social Research, 1991. **Special Achievements:** Compositions in a wide variety of genres performed throughout the US, Central and South America; works published by Willis Music Co. **Business Addr:** The Mannes College of Music, 150 W 85th, New York, NY 10024.

EDWARDS, LEWIS
Acquisitions administrator. **Personal:** Born May 16, 1953, Philadelphia, PA; son of Margaret Norman and Robert Norman; married Joan Southerland, May 1979; children: Amber G, Ariel D. **Educ:** Penn State University, State College, PA, BS, accounting, 1974. **Career:** Fidelity Bank, Philadelphia, PA, senior auditor, 1974-78; Chrysler First, Inc, Allentown, PA, vice president of acquisitions, 1978-94; Nations Credit Corp, vp/dir, govt affairs, 1994-. **Orgs:** Board member, Big Brothers/Big Sisters, 1986-. **Home Addr:** 308 E Mosser St, Allentown, PA 18103.

EDWARDS, LONNIE
Physician. **Personal:** Born in Asheville, NC; son of Corrie Thomas Edwards and Lonnie Edwards Sr; married Carrie Glover Edwards, Dec 1950; children: Lonnette, Lonnie III. **Educ:** Morehouse College, attended 1945; Howard Univ Sch of Medicine, MD 1948; Provident Hosp, internship 1948-49, residency genl surgery 1949-52; Mt Sinai Hosp, residency 1952-53; Roosevelt Univ, MPA 1974; Nova Univ, MPA 1977-. **Career:** Private Practice, genl surgery 1955-70, family practice 1960; Fantus Health Ctr, assoc med dir 1970-71, dir 1970-71; Cook Co Hospital, dir division of ambulatory serv 1971-73, assoc med dir 1974-83; Fantus Health Ctr, dir employee health serv hospital based coord home health care prog 1974-83; Roosevelt Univ, public admin prog; Abraham Lincoln Sch of Medicine, former clinical asst prof of family prac; Chicago Medical Sch, clinical asst prof dept of family 1974-83; City of Chicago, commissioner of health, 1984-89; Cook County Hospital, deputy medical director, 1989-. **Orgs:** Medical staff Cook Co Hospital Dept of Surgery; mem Scientific Comm Exec Med Staff Cook Co Hosp; mem Medical Audit & Utilization Comm CCH; chmn Outpatient Medical Audit Comm Cook Co Hosp; mem Quality Assurance Comm CCH; mem House of Delegates Amer Hosp Assn; mem Health Serv Develop Grants Study Sect Dept of Health Educ & Welfare; past chmn Governing Council Assembly of Ambulatory & Home Care Serv Amer Hosp Assn; mem Natl Assn of Neighborhood Health Ctrs; mem Prairie State Med Soc; mem Amer Med Assn; mem IL State Med Soc; mem Chicago Med Soc; mem Industrial Med Assn; mem Central States Soc of Industrial Medicine & Surgery; mem amer Assn for the Advancement of Sci; mem Assn of Admin of Ambulatory Svcs; mem Amer Acad of Family Physicians; mem NatlMedical Assn; mem Cook Co Physicians Assn;m Amer Public Health Assn; mem Amer Hospital Assn; member, National Assn of Health Services Executives. **Honors/Awds:** Numerous papers presented to various professional orgns and publications including, Ambulatory Care in a Large Urban Hospital Governors State Univ Seminar March 1978; Oral Cavity Evaluation-A Part of Prenatal Care IL Medical Journal Lonnie C Edwards MD Pedro A Poma MD et al Feb 1979 Vol 155 No 2; Selection of an Organizational Model for Maximizing the Effectiveness of Coordination of the Components of Outpatient Services 1977; Distinguished Service in Hispanic Health, Hispanic Health Alliance, 1985; Community Service Award, National Assn of Health Services Executives, 1986; Community Service Award, Truman College, 1976; President's Award, Illinois Public Health Assn, 1988; Human Service Award, Pilsen Neighbors Community Council, 1988. **Military Serv:** AUS Med Corp capt genl surgeon 1953-55.

EDWARDS, LUTHER HOWARD
City government official. **Personal:** Born Jan 6, 1954, Butler, AL; son of Alma Jackson Edwards and Lee J Edwards Sr; married Geraldine Palmer; children: Ashley Letitia. **Educ:** Livingston Univ, BS 1972, ME 1976. **Career:** James River Corp., Computer Information Services; Town of Lisman, councilman, vice-mayor, currently. **Orgs:** Pres Afro-Amer Soc; vice pres Owen Love Business Assn; mem Student Govt Assn; Collegiate Civilian; mem Men's Housing Council; mem Intramural Sports Assn; mem Yearbook Staff; mem Host & Hostess Comm; mem Phi Mu Alpha Sinfonia Frat; sec Lisman Vol Fire Dept 1980-; sec Pleasant Hill Lodge #950 1980-; sec Edwards Pride Royal Arch Masons 1982-. **Honors/Awds:** Outstanding Man of the Year. **Military Serv:** US Army, reserves, master sgt, 19 yrs; Army Commendation Medal; Desert Storm veteran. **Home Addr:** PO Box 110, Lisman, AL 36912.

EDWARDS, MARVIN E.
Educational administrator. **Personal:** Born Oct 2, 1943, Memphis, TN; son of Edna Henderson Edwards and Rev Simeon Edwards; married Carolyn Johnson Edwards, Jul 30, 1966; children: Belinda, Melissa, Craig, Eric, Derick. **Educ:** Eastern Illinois Univ, Charleston, IL, BS, 1967; Chicago State Univ, Chicago, IL, MS, 1969; Northern Illinois Univ, DeKalb, IL, EdD, 1973. **Career:** Proviso High School, Maywood, IL, teacher, 1967-72; Lockport High School, Lockport, IL, principal, 1972-75; Lockport Fairmont Elementary Schools, Lockport, IL, superintendent, 1975-76; Joliet Township High Schools, Joliet, IL, assistant supt, 1976-78; Richmond Public Schools, Richmond, VA, assistant supt, 1978-80; Joliet Township High Schools, Joliet, IL, superintendent, 1980-85; Topeka Public Schools, Topeka, KS, superintendent, 1985-88; Dallas Independent School Dist, Dallas, TX, general superintendent, 1988-93; Elgin Area School District U-46, Illinois, superintendent, 1993-. **Honors/Awds:** Distinguished Alumnus Award, Northern Illinois Univ, 1987; Distinguished Alumnus Award, Eastern Illinois Univ, 1989; Outstanding Texas Award, Texas Legislative Black Caucus, 1991; The Executive Educator 100 List, The Executive Educator Magazine, 1986, 1992; Illinois Assoc of School Administrators, Superintendent of the Year, 1998. **Business Addr:** Superintendent, Elgin Area School District U-46, 355 E Chicago St, Elgin, IL 60120.

EDWARDS, MATTIE SMITH
Educator (retired). **Personal:** Born Apr 16, 1931, Roxboro, NC; married E Zeno MD; children: Zenia Colette, Tanise Indra. **Educ:** Elizabeth City St Univ NC, BS 1949; NC Cntrl U, MaA 1953; Duke U, EdD 1970. **Career:** Springfield Coll MA, prof of educ 1969-85; Cleveland Co Schools NC, gen supt 1965-69, reading coord 1965-69; Newbold School at Fayetteville State Univ, supr, teacher 1953-58. **Orgs:** Board of trustees, Bay Path Coll MA, 1974-89; adv commn Educ Personnel for St of MA, 1978-81; NAACP, life member; vice pres Auxiliary to Greensboro Medical Society, 1990-. **Honors/Awds:** Links Inc Award of Appreciation, Elizabeth City St Univ 1980.

EDWARDS, MICHELLE
Professional basketball player. **Personal:** Born Mar 6, 1966. **Educ:** Iowa, attended. **Career:** Cleveland Rockers, guard, 1997-. **Honors/Awds:** University of Iowa, Athlete of the Year, 1988; Champion Product Player of the Year, 1988; WBCA, Player of the Year, 1988; Big 10 Conference Player of the Year, 1988. **Special Achievements:** First female athlete at the University of Iowa to have her number retired. **Business Addr:** Professional Basketball Player, Cleveland Rockers, One Center Ct, Cleveland, OH 44115, (216)263-7625.

EDWARDS, MILES STANLEY
Educational administrator. **Personal:** Born Mar 21, 1951, Fort Wayne, IN; son of Wanda L Woods Edwards (deceased) and William Howard Edwards Sr (deceased). **Educ:** Ball State Uni-

versity, BS, 1973, admin cert, 1983; Indiana Univ, MSEd, 1978; Ohio State University, GE Fellow, 1980; University of Akron, PhD, 1994. **Career:** DeKalb GA County School District, math teacher, 1975-76; Operation Breadbasket Learning Academy, teacher, 1985-86; University of Akron, instructor of multicultural education, 1992-93; Ft Wayne Community Schools, teacher, special education 1973-75, competency resource teacher 1976-87, Chapter I resource teacher 1988-90, coordinator of multicultural resource center, 1990-92, Chapter I specialist, 1993-94, assistant principal, 1994-. **Orgs:** Natl Alliance of Black School Educators; Ministerial Alliance Scholarship Found, board mem 1983-86; Homework Hotline, TV host of educational program 1982-85; Alpha Phi Alpha, life mbr, corresponding secretary 1995-97; Phi Delta Kappa, 1985; IN State Teachers Assn, board of minority affairs, 1985-86; Ft Wayne Alliance of Black School Educators, board member-at-large 1983-92; National Education Assn, 1985-94; Intl Reading Assn, dist rep, 1986;MLK Living Memorial Inc, board member, 1986-90; Urban League; NAACP; Assn of Black Communicators 1982-85; Old Fort YMCA, exec bd, 1973-75; Indiana Black Expo-Ft Wayne Chapter, 1982-, president, 1988-90; Pi Lambda Theta Natl Honor and Professional Assn in Ed, 1988-; Natl Cncl of Teachers of English, 1990-96; Assn for Supervision and Curriculum Development, 1989-; Ft Wayne Cinema Center, bd of dirs, 1991-97, vice pres, 1994-95; Allen County-Fort Wayne Historical Society, 1994-; Martin Luther King Montessori Schools, bd of dirs, 1986-, president, 1994-. **Honors/Awds:** General Electric Co, Foundation Fellowship Award 1980; US Jaycees, "Outstanding Young Men of America" 1984; Leadership Fort Wayne, First Vice Pres, 1996. **Home Addr:** 432 Dalman Ave, Fort Wayne, IN 46806.

EDWARDS, MONIQUE MARIE
Attorney, consultant. **Personal:** Born Aug 13, 1961, New Orleans, LA; daughter of Mary Ann B Edwards and Lloyd C Edwards. **Educ:** St Mary's Dominican College, BS, 1982; Southern University Law Center, JD, 1986. **Career:** The Honorable Bernette J Johnson, law clerk, 1986-87; The Travelers Companies, supervisor, 1987-94; Maher, Gibson & Guiley PA, 1994-. **Orgs:** Paul C Perkins Bar Association, vp, 1991-92, secretary, 1990-91; Southern Christian Leadership Conference of Greater Orlando, 1991-, banquet chairwoman, 1991; NAACP, Orange County Branch, executive board, 1991-; Natl Bar Assn, 1990-; Louisiana State Bar Association, 1986-; Florida Bar, 1992; Florida Chapter of the Natl Bar Assn, pres, 1995-96; Academy of FL Trial Lawyers; NAACP, lifemember. **Honors/Awds:** St Mary's Dominican College, Merchandising Student of the Year, 1981; Southern University Law Center, Moot Court Board, 1985. **Business Addr:** PO Box 121, Orlando, FL 32802-0121, (407)647-3304.

EDWARDS, OSCAR LEE
Marketing consultant. **Personal:** Born Dec 8, 1953, Long Beach, CA; son of Susie Belle Edwards and Lewis Allen Edwards; married Anita Grace Johnson; children: Ivan Lewis, Oscar Jr, Christine. **Educ:** UCLA, BA 1978, MBA 1981. **Career:** Crenshaw YMCA, program dir 1977-79; Czand Assocs, vice pres of admin 1981-84; Pacific Serv Inc, consultant, 1984-85; Central News WAVE Publs, dir of mktg 1985-87; TMG/SER, Inc, pres 1987-90; Triaxial Mgmt Service, board of directors, 1989-; Edwards Associates/Media Marketing Network, president, 1990-92; Visionary Marketing Inc, bd or dirs; Edwards Associates, president, 1987-. **Orgs:** Bank credit analyst Bank of Amer 1980; rsch asst Mayor Bradley's Africa Task Force 1981-82; chmn bd of mgrs Crenshaw YMCA 1983-84; pres LA Chapter Natl Black MBA Assoc 1985-86; bd of dirs UCLA Black Alumni Assoc 1986-90; adv bd Drew Health Educ Project 1986-90; program comm UCLA Mgmt Alumni Assoc 1987-; certified NFL Contract Advisor 1987-90; bd of advisors, So CA chapter, United Negro College Fund, 1989-91; prog comm, Amer Marketing Assn, 1993-; Inst of Mgmt Consultants, 1984-; master trainer, United Way, Kellogg Training Center, 1990-. **Honors/Awds:** UCLA, Football All-American, 1977; MBA of the Year NBMBAA Los Angeles 1985; MBA of the Year Natl Black MBA Assn, 1986; Very Special Professional, Congressman Augustus Hawkins 1986; Hon Race Dir Comm City of LA Marathon 1986, 1987, 1988; producer of Outreach Videos, 1986, 1988-89; Comm Service Award, City of Long Beach, 1994; MLK Jr Memorial Fund, Community Service Award, 1997. **Business Addr:** President, Visionary Marketing Inc, 1850 Redondo Ave, Ste 206, Long Beach, CA 90804.

EDWARDS, PRENTIS
Judge. **Educ:** Wayne State Univ. **Career:** Wayne Co, MI, asst county prosecutor; Wayne CO Juvenile Court, chief referee; Court of Appeals and Wayne County Circuit Court Register, visiting judge; Criminal Div, 36th Dist Court, presiding judge; Recorder's Court, judge, currently. **Business Addr:** Judge, Recorder's Court, 1441 St Antoine, Detroit, MI 48226.

EDWARDS, PRESTON JOSEPH
Publisher. **Personal:** Born Jul 3, 1943, New Orleans, LA; married Rosa; children: Preston Jr, Scott. **Educ:** Atlanta U, MBA 1966; Dillard U, BA 1965. **Career:** The Black Collegian Magazine, pub 1970-; Interracial Cncl for Bus Opp vice pres 1976-77; Great Atlantic & Pacific Tea Co, reg mgr 1975-76; So U, Baton Rouge, asst prof 1969-71; 1st Nat City Bank, asst cashier 1966-69. **Orgs:** Bd mem Jr Achvmt; pres Journal Inc; publ, Jrnl of the Natl Tech Assn. **Honors/Awds:** Hon Degree Doctor of Human Letters, Livingstone College. **Business Addr:** Publisher, The Black Collegian Magazine, 140 Corondelet, New Orleans, LA 70130.

EDWARDS, RAYMOND, JR.
Judge. **Career:** San Diego Superior Court, South Bay Branch, judge, currently. **Business Addr:** Judge, San Diego Superior Court, South Bay Branch, 500-C Third Ave, Chula Vista, CA 91910, (619)691-4689.

EDWARDS, ROBERT
Educator. **Personal:** Born Jan 30, 1939, Slocombe, AL; married Barbara J Spalding; children: Randel Keith, Robert Corey. **Educ:** Bethune-Cookman Coll, BS 1965; City Coll of NY, MS 1973. **Career:** Youth Training Acad, dir 1969; Progress Assn for Economic Devel, dir 1972; Opportunity Indus Center, branch mgr 1974; Dade County Public Schools, prin. **Orgs:** Exec council Assn for Study of Afro-Amer Life & History 1971; bd dir Lexia Sch for Young Adults 1974; bd dir OURS Inc 1974; mem Urban League, NAACP, Natl Alliance of Black Sch Educators, Kappa Alpha Psi, Bethune-Cookman Coll Alumni Assn, Assn for Study of Afro-Amer Life & History. **Honors/Awds:** Disting Alumni Awd Bethune-Cookman Coll; OIC NY Supreme Dedication Awd for Altruistic Serv to the Educ of Youth; Awds from Alpha Phi Alpha, alpha Kappa Alpha, City of Miami, OIC NY Disting Serv Awd. **Military Serv:** AUS 1961-63. **Business Addr:** Principal, Dade Co Public Schools, 2349 NW 175th St, Opa Locka, FL 33056.

EDWARDS, ROBERT VALENTINO
Educator. **Personal:** Born Dec 15, 1940, Baltimore, MD; son of Laura Mae Jackson Edwards and Robert Franklin Edwards; married Anne Lindsay. **Educ:** Johns Hopkins Univ, AB Math 1962, MS Chem Engrg 1964, PhD Chem Engrg 1968. **Career:** Case Western Reserve Univ, asst prof 1970-73, assoc prof 1973-79, full prof 1979-; chmn chem engrg dept 1984-90, assoc dean, 1990-94. **Orgs:** Amer Chemical Society; Optical Society of America; Amer Inst of Chemical Engineering; Sigma Xi. **Honors/Awds:** Over 100 scientific papers and talks 1968-85; received more than $1,000,000 in rsch grants 1968-85. **Business Addr:** Professor, Chemical Engineering Dept, Case Western Reserve University, AW Smith Bldg, Cleveland, OH 44106-7217.

EDWARDS, RONALD ALFRED
Business executive. **Personal:** Born Jan 10, 1939, Kansas City, MO; children: Brian. **Educ:** Univ of Syracuse, Cert in Comm Org 1965. **Career:** Nrthrn States Power Co, customer Bus Off 1970-72, coord Envrnmntl Affrs 1972-74, mgr Comm Affrs 1975-78, asst to pres Systms Oprtn 1977-79, asstto vice pres Corp Affairs 1980-83, asst to exec vice pres 1983-84. **Orgs:** V chm Minneapolis Civil Rghts Comm 1968-71; treas Minneapolis Urban League 1972-77; mem Minneapolis Civil Rghts Comm 1978-83, chair 1979-83; pres Minneapolis Urban Leag 1978-; 1st v chair Phyllis Wheatley Comm Ctr 1984-; mem Minneapolis Afrmtv Act Comm 1971; pres Northside Stlmnt Serv 1976-79; bd mem Phyllis Wheatley Comm Ctr 1981-; mem MN St Human Rights Bd 1977-79; mem Jr Chamber of Comm 1972-74; mem Hennepin Co Sntncng Task Force 1977; mem MN Affirmative Act Oversite Comm 1971-. **Honors/Awds:** Otstndng civic serv awd Minneapolis Urban League 1971; comm serv awd Black Women Untd 1979; otstndng civic MN Afrmtv Action Assoc 1983; otstndng vol UntdWay of Minneapolis 1982; otstndng vol WTCN TV 1979; otstndng citzen City of Minneapolis 1978; otstndng civic Minneapolis Urban League Sr Prog 1979; exec prod & host Radio Prog Urban Views/KMOJ Radio Mpls; author Numerous News Stories. **Business Addr:** Assistant to President, Northern States Power Co, 414 Nicollet Mall, Minneapolis, MN 55401.

EDWARDS, RONALD WAYNE
Manager. **Personal:** Born Mar 25, 1958, Birmingham, AL; son of Dorothy Smith Edwards and Carl Edwards; married Barbara Wallace Edwards, Jun 19, 1982. **Educ:** Univ of AL, Tuscaloosa, AL, BS, 1990. **Career:** AL Gas Corp, Birmingham, AL, mgr, community affairs, 1991-. **Orgs:** Vulcan Kiwanis Club; Natl Mgmt Assn; Amer Assn of Blacks in Energy; American Heart Assn; City Stages; pres, Energen Mgmt Assn; pres, American Assn of Blacks in Energy; bd mem, United Way Children's Aid Society; bd of dir, scouting comm, All American Bowl; bd of dir, Birmingham Tip-Off Club; commissioner, Summer Basketball League. **Business Addr:** Manager, Community Affairs, Alabama Gas Corporation, 2101 Sixth Avenue N, Energen Plaza, Birmingham, AL 35203-2784.

EDWARDS, RONDLE E.
Educator. **Personal:** Born Jul 19, 1934, Richmond, VA; son of Irene Taylor Edwards and Alfred M Edwards; married Gloria Twitty; children: Cassandra L, Lanee D Washington, Ronda D. **Educ:** Virginia Union Univ, AB; Virginia State Univ, MA; Ohio Univ, PhD; Ohio State Univ, Columbia Univ, Postdoctoral Study. **Career:** Richmond Public Schools, asst supt for gen admr and pupil personnel 1972-75, asst supt for support serv 1975-76; E Cleveland City Schools, superintendent 1976-84; Portsmouth Public Schools, superintendent 1984-87; Virginia Dept of Educ, asst state supt 1987-92; HarperCollins, vice pres, School Relations Devt, 1992-. **Orgs:** Richmond Rotary Club; trustee Cleveland Scholarship Fund; United Negro College Fund; Phi Delta Kappa Professional Frat, Amer Assoc of School Per sonnel Administrators, Amer Assoc of School Administrators, Ohio Sch Bds Assoc; expert witness before US House of Representatives Comm on Educ and Labor. **Honors/Awds:** Awd for Excellence in Public Educ Delta Sigma Theta Sor; Outstanding Achievement Awd Kappa Alpha Psi Frat, Phi Delta Kappa; Man of the Year Cleveland Club of the Natl Assoc of Negro Business and Professional Women's Clubs; Exec Educator's Recognition One of North America's Top 100 Educators; Ohio Univ Alumni Medal of Merit for Notable Accomplishments in Educ Admin 1986; authored 4 books; numerous presentations. **Business Addr:** VP, School Relations Development, Harper Collins, Scott Foresman Division, 1900 E Lake Ave, Glenview, IL 60025.

EDWARDS, RUPERT L.
Physician. **Personal:** Born Jul 5, 1929, New Amsterdam, Guyana; son of Edith and Robert; married Billie Jean; children: Robert Charles, Geoffrey Taylor. **Educ:** Roosevelt U, 1953-55; IN Univ Sch of Med, 1959. **Career:** Wayne St U, instr 1964-65, clinical asst prof 1965-72, assoc prof 1972-; Edwards & Singal, PC, pres 1978-; chief, Internal Medicine, Harper Hospital, Detroit. **Orgs:** Chief of staff Hutzel Hosp, Detroit 1975-76; mem Detroit Med Ctr Adv Comm 1975-78; life mem NAACP; mem Detroit Athletic Club 1980; mem Detroit Econ Club 1983-; founder-pres Ministerial Phys Hlth Alliance; Detroit Medical Center, board of trustees; Southeast Community Foundation, board of trustees. **Honors/Awds:** Wayne State Univ, School of Medcine, Spirit of Detroit Award, Board of Visitors, 1993. **Business Addr:** Chief, Internal Medicine, Harper Hospital, 4727 St Antoine, Detroit, MI 48201.

EDWARDS, RUTH MCCALLA
Attorney. **Personal:** Born Apr 23, 1949, Cleveland, OH; married Michael M Edwards; children: Ashaunda, Alanna, Kamala. **Educ:** Hiram Coll, BA 1971; Univ of Cincinnati Coll of Law, JD 1974. **Career:** Legal Aid Soc of Cincinnati, atty & office mgr 1974-77; Private Law Practice, atty 1977-79; Hamilton County Public Defender Comm, atty 1979; Univ of Cincinnati, atty, prog coord, paralegal prog 1979-. **Orgs:** Admitted OH State Bar 1974; admitted Fed Bar So Dist of OH 1974; mem bd trustees Cincinnati Tech Coll 1977-; mem Amer, Cincinnati Bar Assns; mem & past pres Black Lawyers Assn of Cincinnati; past bd mem Legal Aid Soc of Cincinnati; bd mem & officer Winton Hills Med & Halth Ctr; bd mem & past officer Comprehensive Comm Child Care; bd mem Cincinnati Tech Coll; mem Alpha Kappa Alpha Sor; arbitrator Better Business Bureau Arbitration Prog; mem Assn of Comm Coll Trustees; sec Central Region Minority Affairs Assembly of the Assn of Comm Coll Trustees; mem Amer Assn for Paralegal Education Inc; chairperson bd trustees Cincinnati Tech Coll 1983-84; past bd mem, officer Winton Hills Med & Health Ctr; arbitrator Amer Arbitration Assoc; chair Central Region MinorityAffairs Comm of the Assoc of Conity Coll Trustees. **Honors/Awds:** Hon Degree of Tech Letters Cincinnati Tech Coll 1985; YMCA Black Achievers Awd 1985. **Business Addr:** Program Coordinator, Univ of Cincinnati, Paralegal Program, Cincinnati, OH 45221.

EDWARDS, SHIRLEY HEARD
Elected official. **Personal:** Born Oct 23, 1949, Doddsville, MS; married Thomas E Edwards; children: Darron, Thomas Jr, Cheryl. **Educ:** MS Valley State Univ, BS 1983. **Career:** Fannie Humer Day Care, sec bookkeeper 1969-79; Sunflower/Humphrey Co Progress, career counselor 1979-83; Sunflower Co Schools, school attendance officer 1983-; City of Ruleville, alderwoman, mayor, 1993-. **Orgs:** Apt mgr Quick Construction 1972-. **Honors/Awds:** Comm Serv Awd NAACP Sunflower Co 1983. **Home Addr:** 113 Vernice Ave, Ruleville, MS 38771.

EDWARDS, SOLOMON
Educator. **Personal:** Born Apr 2, 1932, Indianapolis, IN; married Claudia; children: Gregory D, Risa M. **Educ:** IN Univ, BS 1954, MS 1969, EdD 1984. **Career:** Arts Festival, coord 1956; IN Public Schools, teacher; Purdue Univ, assoc faculty 1971-79. **Orgs:** Mem Omega Psi Phi, NAACP, Phi Delta Kappa IN Univ. **Honors/Awds:** Writers Conf Poetry Awd 1953; dir New York City Dramatic Readers 1957-58; poems published 1959-77; author of "What's Your Reading Attitude?" 1979; "This Day Father" 1979; Discussion moderator Intl Reading Assn Natl Convention 1979; educational game "Freedom & Martin Luther King" 1980.

EDWARDS, SYLVIA
Attorney. **Personal:** Born May 9, 1947, Lackawanna, NY. **Educ:** State Univ Coll at Buffalo, BS 1969; Howard Univ Sch of Law Washington, JD 1973. **Career:** Employment Sect Dept of Justice, trial atty 1973-76; Office of Spl Litigation Dept of Justice Washington DC, sr trial atty; Council of the DC, legislative counsel 1977-79; DC Law Revision Commn, sr atty 1979-. **Orgs:** Mem Adv Commn on Codification Wash DC 1977-79; legislative consult Com on Pub Serv & Consumer Affairs Council of DC 1979; mem NY Bar 1974; mem PA Bar 1974;

mem Natl Assn of Black Women Atty 1978. **Honors/Awds:** Spl Achievement Awd Howard Univ Sch of Law 1972; Intl Moot Ct Awd Howard Univ Sch of Law 1973; Spl Achievement Awd Dept of Justice Wash DC 1975; Resolution of Spl Achievement Council of DC 1979. **Business Addr:** Sr Attorney, DC Law Revision Commn, 1411 K St NW, Ste 1000, Washington, DC 20005.

EDWARDS, TERESA
Professional basketball player, coach. **Career:** Atlanta Glory, player/coach, currently. **Honors/Awds:** USA Basketball, Female Athlete of the Year, 1996; three Olympic gold medals; numerous other awards. **Special Achievements:** Only three-time winner of USA Basketball's Athlete of the Year Award; Only Olympian to appear in four Olympics as a basketball player. **Business Addr:** Coach, Atlanta Glory, 2100 Powers Ferry Rd, Ste 400, Atlanta, GA 30339, (770)541-9017.

EDWARDS, THEODORE ALLEN (TED)
Telecommunications executive. **Personal:** Born Jan 16, 1954, Chicago, IL; son of Theodore & Mary Edwards; married Katheryn Edwards, May 19, 1984; children: Christopher, Cara, Rachael, Casey. **Educ:** Northwestern Univ, BS, 1975; Kellogg Graduate School of Management, MM, 1988. **Career:** Ameritech, various, 1978-90, operations division mgr, 1990-91, mktg public svc, general mgr, 1992, operations carrier svcs, vp, 1993-96, sales, local exchange carriers, vp, 1996-. **Orgs:** Hull House Assoc, bd of trustees, 1990-97; Community Investment Fund, bd of dirs, 1996-97; Pioneer Clubs of America, bd of dirs, 1997. **Honors/Awds:** Chicago YMCA, Minority Achievement Award, 1988. **Business Addr:** Vice Pres, Sales, Ameritech Information Industry Svcs, 350 N Orleans, Fl 3, Chicago, IL 60654, (312)335-6531.

EDWARDS, THEODORE THOMAS
Government official (retired). **Personal:** Born Sep 8, 1917, Bridgeport, CT; son of Maude and Theodore; married Vivian Blackmon, 1956 (died 1987). **Educ:** Quinnipac Coll, Newhaven CT, AA 1941; New York U, BS 1946; Columbia U, MSW 1947; Univ of Chicago, grad work 1957-59; US Public Health Hospital Lexington KY, 1956. **Career:** Goldwater Hospital NY, med social worker 1947-48; NJ Parole Bd, parole officer 1949-55; US Probation-US Parole Commn, probation officer 1955-77, retired. **Orgs:** Youth wrkr, NY Youth Bd 1947; mem, Nat Cncl on Crime & Del 1955-80; mem, Federal Probation Off Assn 1956-80; co-founder, Narcotic Treatment Center 1956; mem, Middle Atlantic St Conf of Correction 1956-80; mem, Rotary International, Paterson NJ 1975-77; mem, Amer Correction Assn 1975-80; life mem Fed Prob Off Assn 1977. **Honors/Awds:** 1st Black Federal Probation Officer, Newark NJ 1955; subject of "The Probation Officer," Newark Sunday News 1957; Certificate Of App, Newark Boys Club 1969; 1st Black Fed Probation Dir, Paterson NJ 1975-77; 4 Battle Stars; Crox De Geurre; co-founder 1st Private Narcotic Treatment Center Newark NJ 1957. **Military Serv:** AUS 1942-45; AUS tch sgt 1942-45.

EDWARDS, THEODORE UNALDO
City government official. **Personal:** Born Sep 18, 1934, New York, NY; son of Mary A Edwards and Joseph Unaldo Edwards (deceased); married Dr Ione L D Edwards; children: Donna M O'Bannon, Esq. **Educ:** St Peter's College, BS 1955; Rutgers Univ, MSW 1962; BARO Clinic, Certificate 1967. **Career:** US Court/Justice Dept, probation officer 1962-69; Harlem Child Guidance Clinic, clinical dir 1969-78; Comm Serv Soc of NY, exec dir 1973-76; Coll of New Rochelle NY, adj prof 1979-; City of New Rochelle Dept of Human Svcs, deputy commissioner 1977-. **Orgs:** Bd mem Catholic Big Brothers of NY 1975-; commissioner Office of Black Ministry Archdiocese of NY 1977-; bd mem Salvation Army of New Rochelle 1985-; exec bd NAACP 1985-; mem Omega (Omicron Iota Chapt). **Honors/Awds:** Community Serv Awd College of New Rochelle NY 1983-85; Spike Harris Serv Awd NY Counselors 1985; publication "Why Bartering," "Budget Time," both 1981 The Voice Magazine; "The City of New Rochelle Senior Population," 1986; Columnist for Tomorrow Newspaper, Westchester NY. **Military Serv:** AUS sgt 2 yrs. **Business Addr:** Deputy Commissioner, City of New Rochelle, Dept of Human Services, City Hall, New Rochelle, NY 10801.

EDWARDS, THOMAS OLIVER
Educational administrator, psychologist. **Personal:** Born Jan 4, 1943, Vanceboro, NC; son of Blanche Ethel Edwards and Calvin Edwards; married Loretta McFadden; children: Tomia, Kuturi, Loretta, Tiffany, Calvin. **Educ:** CCNY, BA 1965; NY Univ, MA 1968; CUNY, MPh 1980, PhD 1981. **Career:** Peace Corps Costa Rica, volunteer 1965-67; Alexander Burger Jr High School, teacher 1967-71; Medgar Evers Coll instructor/lecturer 1971-81, asst professor 1981-84, assoc professor 1984-, assoc dean of admin 1986-88, acting chmn, Social Science Division 1988-89; Medgar Evers College, affirmative action officer, 1992-. **Orgs:** Baseball coach Rochdale Village Little League 1979-; consultant Urban Strategies Inc 1980-; consultant Hale House for the Promotion of Human Potential 1983; board of dir mem Medgar Evers Coll Child Care Ctr 1983-; adjunct professor Coll of New Rochelle 1984-85; board of directors, New York Chapter, Association of Black Psychologists, 1990-92; executive council member, United Partners Association, 1990-92; New York Assn of Black Psychologists, past pres, 1983-; Natl Assn of Black Psychologists, Black Family Task Force, chair. **Honors/Awds:** Pamela Galiber Memorial Scholarship CUNY Grad Div 1977; Communication Skills in the Inner City, Effects of Race & Dialect on Decoding New England Ed Rsch Org Annual Best Papers Monograph 1983; co-organizer of International African-American Cultural & Research Assn; organizer of Annual Conference Focusing on the Black Male, Medgar Evers Coll/CUNY. **Home Addr:** 178-07 137th Ave, Jamaica, NY 11434. **Business Addr:** Associate Professor of Psych, Medgar Evers Coll/CUNY, 1150 Carroll St, Brooklyn, NY 11225, (718)270-4969.

EDWARDS, TONYA
Professional basketball player. **Personal:** Born Mar 13, 1968. **Educ:** Univ of Tennessee. **Career:** Flint Northwestern High School, girl's basketball coach, 1991-94; Columbus Quest, guard, 1996-. **Honors/Awds:** Michigan High School Coach of the Year, 1993. **Business Addr:** Professional Basketball Coach, Columbus Quest, 7451 State Route 16, Dublin, OH 43016, (614)873-6555.

EDWARDS, VERBA L.
Company executive. **Personal:** Born Jul 15, 1950, Boligee, AL; son of Bertha Barker Edwards and George Edwards; married Roberta Mackel Edwards, Aug 25, 1973; children: Keith, Christopher, Raquel. **Educ:** Alcorn State Univ, BS Bus Admin 1973; Central MI Univ, MA Personnel Admin 1977. **Career:** General Motors Corp Chevy Truck Assembly Plant, coord equal employment oppor, general supervisor mfg, supervisor industrial relations, supervisor hourly personnel admin 1973-81; General Motors Corp Chevrolet Central Office, divisional salaried personnel admin 1981-83; General Motors Corp Saginaw Div, asst dir of personnel 1984-87; Wing Tips & Pumps, Inc, pres/CEO, 1987-. **Orgs:** Mem Omega Psi Phi Frat, The Natl Alliance of Business Coll/Industry Relations Div, Natl Assoc for Equal Oppor in Higher Educ; life member, National Black MBA Assn. **Honors/Awds:** Author of "Wing Tips and Pumps". **Business Addr:** President, World Class Executive Search, Wing Tips and Pumps, Inc, PO Box 99580, Troy, MI 48099, (810)641-0980.

EDWARDS, VIVIAN J.
Educator (retired). **Personal:** Born May 19, 1915, Brooklyn, NY; daughter of Helen Louise Gaynor Joseph and Lauchland James Joseph; married Seth Carlyle Edwards, Jun 21, 1943 (deceased); children: Seth C Jr, Jeanne. **Educ:** Brooklyn Coll. Brooklyn, NY, AB, 1936; Teachers Coll, Columbia Univ, NY, MA, 1937, EdD, 1956. **Career:** Barber-Scotia College, Concord, NC, instructor, 1937-44; Cuttington Univ Coll, Suacoco, Liberia, head, English, 1949-60; Univ of Liberia, Monrovia, Liberia, prof, English, 1963-68; Hampton Univ, Hampton, VA, freshman English and literature prof, 1968-71; Univ of Liberia, head, English, 1972-74; Cuttington Univ Coll, Suacoco, Liberia, div head, humanities, 1975-77; Saint Augustin's Coll, Raleigh, NC, visiting prof, 1978-96. **Orgs:** Sponsor, Lambda, Lambda Chapter, Sigma Tau Delta Natl English Honor Soc, 1978-; Wife of pres, Seth Carlyle Edwards, Cuttington Univ Coll, 1949-. **Honors/Awds:** Proposal Study Grant; Booklet, Grassroots Literature, UNCF, 1984-85; Distinguished Prof, 1988, Outstanding Achievement Award, 1987, Saint Augustine's Coll.

EDWARDS, WILBUR PATTERSON, JR.
Attorney. **Personal:** Born Aug 28, 1949, Yokohama, Japan; son of Mary C Edwards and Wilbur P Edwards Sr; married Evelynne Swagerty, Jun 8, 1989; children: Arielle Belson Edwards, Marissa Avery Edwards. **Educ:** Harvard College, BA, 1971; Boston College Law School, JD, 1984. **Career:** Purity Supreme, real estate rep, 1971-73; Grand Union Co, real estate rep, 1973-74; Southland Corp., real estate manager, 1974-79; Toys R Us, real estate manager, 1979-81; Roche, Carens & DeGiacomo, attorney, 1984-88; McKenzie & Edwards, PC, attorney, 1989-. **Orgs:** Massachusetts Black Lawyers Association, 1984-; secretary, 1985; Boston College Law School Black Alumni Network, president, 1990-94; Massachusetts Bar Association, 1984-; Massachusetts Conveyancers Association, 1988-. **Business Addr:** Attorney, McKenzie & Edwards, PC, 1 Bulfinch Pl, Boston, MA 02114, (617)723-0400.

EDWARDS-ASCHOFF, PATRICIA JOANN
Director performing arts. **Personal:** Born Feb 23, 1940, Louisville, MS; married Peter Richard Aschoff. **Educ:** Chadron State Coll, BS 1972; Univ of No IA, MA 1974. **Career:** Dr William J Walker Chicago, dental asst 1963-70; Black Hawk Co, juvenile probation officer 1974-77; Univ of Northern IA, dir ethnic minorities cultural & educ center 1977, human relations instructor 1979-80, special prog asst, div of continuing educ & special progs; Domestic Violence Project Inc, exec dir. **Orgs:** Former bd chmn Minority Alcoholism Action Prog 1976-78; mem Professional & Sci Council 1977; training consult Jesse Cosby Neighborhood Ctr Parent Groups 1978; exec bd mem Family & Children's Council 1978; bd mem/treas Wesley Found 1978; mem Antioch Baptist Church Waterloo IA; bd mem Friends of KHKE/KUNI Pub Radio 1979; mem Alpha Chi #1736 ESA Intl Sorority Oxford MS. **Honors/Awds:** Special Achievement Awd Educ Oppor Prog 1973-74; Outstanding Young Women in Amer 1974; Professional Serv Awd Juvenile Ct Serv 1977; Certificate of Appreciation Kiwanis Club of Oxford MS.

EDWARDS O'BANNON, DONNA M. (DONNA M. EDWARDS)
Administrative judge. **Personal:** Born Jun 26, 1957, New York, NY; daughter of Theodore U Edwards (deceased) & Dr Ione Edwards; divorced; children: Danielle Salone, Dionne Teddie. **Educ:** Wellesley College, BA, 1979; University of Virginia School of Law, JD, 1982. **Career:** Exxon Co USA, tax attorney, 1982-85; Harris County DA, asst DA, 1985-87; Equal Employment Opportunity Commission, trial attorney, 1987-88; sr trial attorney, 1988-89; FDIC, trial attorney, dept head, 1989-94; litigation senior attorney, 1989-94; Equal Employment Opportunity Commission, administrative judge, 1994-. **Orgs:** Links Inc Dallas Chapter, chair, archives committee, 1994-; Thurgood Marshall Recreation Center Advisory Council, vice president, 1994-. **Honors/Awds:** Wellesley College, Freshman Honors, 1975-76; Wellesley Scholar, 1979. **Special Achievements:** Special Achievement Awards from FDIC, 1992-94. **Home Addr:** 2122 Elderoaks Ln, Dallas, TX 75232. **Business Addr:** Administrative Judge, Equal Employment Opportunity Commission, 207 S Houston Street, Hearings Unit, Dallas, TX 75202, (214)655-3341.

EFFORT, EDMUND D.
Dentist. **Personal:** Born Jun 20, 1949, Chicago, IL; son of Beverley Effort and Exzene Effort; married Elaine Leaphart; children: Edmundson David, April Elaine. **Educ:** Univ of IL, BS 1972; Univ of MI, DDS 1977; US Dental Inst, 1986-89. **Career:** Private practice, dentist. **Orgs:** Mem Alpha Phi Alpha, 1969-89; mem Amer Dental Assoc 1977-89; NAACP 1981-89, elected to board of directors 1992; Urban League 1981-89, PA Dental Assoc 1981-89; bd dir Lemington Home for the Aged 1984; mem Lions 1985, Elks 1986; bd dir United Cerebral Palsy 1987, Connely Trade School 1987, Eva P Mitchell Residense 1987, Urban Youth Action 1986-87; coach of little league baseball, Boys Club 1989; board of directors, Boys and Girls Club, 1990-; chairman, Medical Assistance Advisory Committee, PDA; NAACP, Health Affairs, chairman, 1995; Reizenstein Middle School, PTO, pres, 1994; Felix vs Casey, expert witness, 1992-93. **Honors/Awds:** Three articles written for Talk Magazine 1985; Black Achievers News in Print Magazine 1984; PA Air Commendation Medal PA ANG 1986; Community Serv Award Upward Bound Proj 1987; Good Samaritan Award, American Red Cross 1988; Martin Luther King Award, Hand-In-Hand Inc, 1990. **Military Serv:** PA Air Natl Guard maj 20 yrs; Air Commendation Medal 1986; General Stewart Medal 1985; Pennsylvania Air National Guard, 171st ARW Lt Col, 1981-. **Business Addr:** Dentist, Gateway Towers Ste 215, Pittsburgh, PA 15222, (412)765-0199.

EGGLESTON, NEVERETT A., JR.
Association executive, business executive. **Personal:** Born in Richmond, VA; married Jean Deloris; children: Neverett A III, Jayne. **Educ:** A&T Univ, BS 1955. **Career:** Mainstream Inc, pres; Golden Skillet, principal; Silas Lee and Assocs, principal; Eggleston Auto Serv Ctr, president and CEO 1979-; Eggleston's Motel, president and CEO 1960-; The Eggleston Development Corp, president, CEO, 1992-. **Orgs:** Bd mem Natl Business League 1970-, secretary, currently; chmn of bd Minority Supplier Develop Inc 1978-, E and R Janitorial Serv Inc 1978-; bd of mgmt Radiantherm Inc; mem bd of dirs Jefferson Sheraton Hotel; mem adv bd Womensbank; mem Richmond Chamber of Commerce, VA Chamber of Commerce; vice pres Capital Area Innkeepers Assoc; bd of dirs, pres Metro Business League; bd of dirs Richmond Urban League; mem bd of dirs Richmond Comm Action Program; mem bd of dirs Amer Red Cross; chmn People League of Voters; mem bd of dirs Greater Richmond Transit Co; mem of various bds and comms United Givers Fund. **Honors/Awds:** Spoke Awd and Spark Plug Awd Junior Chamber of Commerce; Businessman of the Year Awd Metro Business League; Martin Luther King Comm Learning Week Business Recognition 1982. **Business Addr:** President, CEO, The Eggleston Corp, 604-30 N Second St, Richmond, VA 23219.

EGIEBOR, SHARON E.
Journalist. **Personal:** Born Jun 11, 1959, Kansas City, KS; daughter of Lester Alois Wilborn Patterson and William David Patterson Sr.; divorced; children: Marcus Iyobosa. **Educ:** Dallas County Community College District, Mountain View Campus, AA, liberal arts, 1979; University of Texas at Arlington, Arlington, TX, BA, journalism, 1983. **Career:** Dallas Times Herald, Dallas, TX, reporter, 1983-87, copy editor, 1987, assistant regional editor, 1987-88, assistant city editor, 1988-90, editorial writer, 1990-. **Orgs:** Member, National Association of Black Journalists, 1986-; member, Dallas-Fort Worth Association of Black Communicators, 1985-. **Honors/Awds:** Community Service Award, Black State Employees Association, 1990; School Bell Award, Texas State Teachers Association, 1985; Jack Butler Award, UTA-School of Journalism, 1983; Times Mirror Scholarship, Times Mirror Corp., 1982; Institute of Journalism Education Fellowship for Minority Journalists, 1987.

EGINS, PAUL CARTER, III
Director of player development. **Personal:** Born Sep 22, 1963, Columbus, GA; son of Paul C Egins, Jr (deceased) & Jacquelyn Joy Egins. **Educ:** University of Georgia, BS, biology, 1986; Florida A&M University, attended, 1987. **Career:** Atlanta Braves, Class A, athletic trainer, 1988-89, minor league admin, 1990, asst dir, scouting/player dev, 1991; Colorado Rockies, asst dir scouting, 1992, player dev, 1993-94, asst dir player personnel, 1995-97, dir of player dev, 1997-. **Orgs:** Kappa Alpha Psi Fraternity, 1989-; RBI (reviving baseball in the inner city) Program, 1995-; Bichette Baseball World, bd of dirs, 1996-. **Honors/Awds:** Cystic Fibrosis Foundation, Denver's Fifty Finest, 1997. **Home Addr:** 1200 Galapago St, No 713, Denver, CO 80204, (303)446-0537. **Business Addr:** Director of Player Development, Colorado Rockies Baseball Club, Ltd, 2001 Blake St, Coors Field, Denver, CO 80205-2000, (303)292-0200.

EICHELBERGER, BRENDA
Executive director. **Personal:** Born Oct 21, 1939, Washington, DC. **Educ:** Govs St U, extens grad work in women's std 1976-; Chicago St U, MsS 1973; Eng and Bus Edn, BS; DC Tchrs Coll, 1963. **Career:** Natl Coll of Educ, m equiv school admin and supvr; Natl Allian of Black Feminists, div exec dir; Chicago Public School System, teacher, librarian, counselor 1967-77; Muscatine Community School Dist, teacher 1966-67; Washington DC Public School System, teacher 1964-65. **Orgs:** Found and exec dir, Natl Allian of Black Feminists 1976-; bd mem, Pro and Con Screening Bd 1976-; bd mem, Chicagoland Women's Fed Credit Union 1976-; found, Black Womens's Cntr 1976-; bd mem, treas, Chicago Consort of Women in Educ Prog 1976; fdr, Chrwmn, Chicago Chap Natl Black Feminist Org 1974-76; bd mem, Citz Comm on the Media 1975-76; adv bd mem, Blue Gargoyle Grp Hm for Girls 1975; sec, Dist Ten Tchr Cncl 1974-75. **Honors/Awds:** Writer of artic 1977; Bicent Excell Award, for Black Womanhood, Elite Soc of Amer 1976; Outstndng Elem Sch & Tchr Award, Fuller & Dees 1975; Internatl Yr of the Woman Award, Love Memorial Mission Bapt Ch 1975; Outstndng Yg Woman of Am Award, Fuller & Dees 1975. **Business Addr:** 202 S State St, Ste 1024, Chicago, IL 60604.

EIKERENKOETTER, FREDERICK J., II (REVEREND IKE)
Clergyman. **Personal:** Born Jun 1, 1935, Ridgeland, SC; married Eula Mae Dent; children: Xavier Frederick, III. **Educ:** Am Bible Coll, BTh 1956; DSci of Living Inst 1971; PhD 1969. **Career:** United Christian Evangelistic Assn, found, pres 1962-; United Ch Sci of Living Inst, 1969-; Rev Ike Found, 1973-; Dept Psychiatry, Harvard Med Sch, preacher, vis lectr 1973; Univ AL, 1975; Atlanta Univ Cntr, 1975; Rice U, 1977. **Orgs:** Fdr, Sci of Living Philosophy Church & Inst; life-time mem, NAACP. **Honors/Awds:** Recip, World Serv Award For Outstnd Contributions to Mankind, Prince Hall Masons 1975. **Military Serv:** USAF chapl sect 1956-58. **Business Addr:** 4140 Broadway, New York, NY 10033.

EISLEY, HOWARD JONATHAN
Professional basketball player. **Personal:** Born Dec 4, 1972, Detroit, MI. **Educ:** Boston College, bachelor's degree in communications. **Career:** Minnesota Timberwolves, guard, 1994-95; San Antonio Spurs, 1995; Utah Jazz, 1995-. **Business Addr:** Professional Basketball Player, Utah Jazz, 301 W South Temple, Salt Lake City, UT 84101-1216, (801)575-7800.

EKE, KENOYE KELVIN
Educator. **Personal:** Born Sep 1, 1956, Otari, Abua, Rivers State, Nigeria; son of Nancy Owen Eke and Joseph Eke; married Joy Grimes Eke, Jun 24, 1989; children: Kenoye Kelvin Joseph, Kebbin Henry Joseph. **Educ:** Alabama A&M Univeristy, Normal, AL, BA, highest honors, 1977-80; Atlanta University, Atlanta, GA, MA, political science, 1982, PhD, political science, 1985; Harvard University, Cambridge, MA, post-doctoral studies, 1988, 1990; University of Wisconsin-Madison, Madison, WI, post-doctoral studies, 1989. **Career:** Bethune-Cookman College, Daytona Beach, FL, assistant professor, 1985-89; Savannah State College, Savannah, GA, associate professor & coordinator of political science, 1989-93, dir of intl programs, 1991-93, School of Humanities and Social Sciences, dean and professor, 1993-. **Orgs:** Mem, executive board, African Assn of Political Science, North American Chapter, 1987-; member, benefits advisory board, Chatham County Department of Family and Children Service's 1989-; president, Pan-African Awareness Association, Volusia County, FL, 1988-89. **Honors/Awds:** Nigeria's Foreign Policy under Two Military Governments, 1966-79, The Edwin Mellen Press, 1990; Co-editor, Media Coverage of Terrorism, Sage Publications, 1991; Ja-Flo Davis Faculty Member of the Year Award, Administration and Faculty of Bethune-Cookman College, 1988-89; Harvard Univ, Pew Faculty Fellow in Intl Affairs, 1992-93; American Council on Education, fellow, 1994-95. **Business Addr:** Dean and Professor, Savannah State Coll, School of Humanities and Social Sciences, PO Box 20059, Savannah, GA 31406.

EKECHI, FELIX K.
Educator. **Personal:** Born Oct 30, 1934, Owerri, Nigeria; son of Ekechi Egekeze; married Regina; children: Kemakolam, Chidi, Okechukwu, Chinyere. **Educ:** Holy Ghost Coll Umuahia Nigeria, Gd 2 Tchrs Cert 1955; Univ of MN, BA 1963; KS State Univ MA, 1965; Univ of WI Madison PhD 1969. **Career:** St Dominics Sch Afara-Mbieri, Nigeria, hdmstr 1955-58; Mt St Marys Coll Azaraegbelu, Owerri, tutor 1959-60; Alcon A&M Coll Lorman, MS, inst 1964-65; Univ of Port Harcourt, Alvan Ikoku College of Education, University of Nigeria, visiting prof 1983; Kent State Univ, asst/assoc prof 1969-77, prof, 1978-; Alvan/Ikoku Coll of Education, visiting prof, 1994. **Orgs:** Grad asst KS State Univ 1964-65; grad teaching asst Univ of WI-Madison 1965-69; mem Am Bicentennial Comm, Kent, OH 1976-77; pres Black Faculty & Staff Assoc Kent State Univ 1974; coord African Studies Prog Kent State Univ 1985-; mem African Studies Assn, Amer Historical Assn. **Honors/Awds:** Citation for Meritorious Service, Kent City Council, 1977; IGBO Oral Hist Proj Lily Endwmnt 1975; Am Masns & Educ in Nigeria the Am Philosophical Soc 1979-83; Books, Masonry Enterprises & Rivalry in Igboland (London), 1971 Owerri in Transition, Owerri, Nigeria 1984; Tradition and Transformation in Eastern Nigeria, Owerri and its Hinterland, Kent State Univ Press, 1989; African Market Women & Economic Power: The Role of Women in African Economic Development, Greenwood Press, 1995; numerous articles and reviews in scholarly journals; Summer Seminars for School Teachers, Natl Endowment for the Humanities 1989, 1992, 1996; Distinguished Contribution Award, Kent State Univ, 1997. **Business Addr:** Professor, Kent State Univ, Dept of History, Kent, OH 44242, (330)672-3570.

ELAM, DOROTHY R.
Educator. **Personal:** Born Jul 23, 1904, Philadelphia, PA; divorced; children: 2. **Educ:** Glassboro State Coll, BS 1956; Univ of Rutgers, attended; Glassboro, pursued MA. **Career:** Adult Evening Class Black Studies, teacher; Camden City Bd of Educ, worked on rsch progs; Berlin Township Schools, retired 1964, 37 years of teaching. **Orgs:** Wrote scripts for closed circuit Glassboro Bd Educ Harriet Tubman Dr G W Carver; served as NJ State Rep Assn of Negro Life & Hist; guest spkr ch schP-TA Negro History; assisted in writing radio progs celeb of Negro Hist Week; edited published poetry book "A Slice of Black Living" 1970, 1971 added color sound filmstrip w/record & cassette; aptd exec bd Assn of Study of Negro Life & History 1972; organized Camden Co Intercultural Council 1947; rsch producedrecord album The Hist Interpretations of Negro Spirituals & Lift Every Voice & Sing; founder/dir Conlam Enterprises. **Honors/Awds:** Woman of Yr Local Eta Chapt; Cert of Merit NJ Organ of Teachers; Cert of Appreciation Mt Zion AME Ch of Albion 1966; among first of two blacks to receive Disting Alumnus Awd Outstanding Achievement & Serv in Prof Comm & Fellowman Glassboro State Coll; Plaque NJ State Fed of Colored Women's Club Inc; Plaque Assn of Business a Professional Woman of Camden and Vicinity.

ELAM, HARRIET
Government official. **Educ:** Simmons College, graduated; Tufts Univ, Fletcher School of Law and Diplomacy, master's degree. **Career:** USIA Foreign Service, minister counselor, currently. **Special Achievements:** Highest ranking American woman in all three of the US diplomatic missions in Belgium.

ELAM, HARRY JUSTIN
Judge (retired). **Personal:** Born Apr 29, 1922, Boston, MA; son of Blanche Lee Elam and Robert Elam; married Barbara Clarke; children: Patricia, Harry Jr, Keith, Jocelyn. **Educ:** Attended, VA State Coll 1940-42; Boston Univ Coll of Liberal Arts, AB 1946-48; Boston Univ Law School, LLB 1951. **Career:** Gov's Council MA, exec sec 1960-62; Office of Atty General MA, asst atty general 1964-66; Boston Municipal Ct, assoc justice 1971, chief justice 1978; MA Superior Ct, assoc justice 1983-88. **Orgs:** Chmn bd dir Roxbury Multi Serv Center 1967-70; chmn bd of dir The Advent School 1973-77; chmn bd of dir The Elma Lewis School of Fine Arts 1974-78; chmn Com on EEO & Affirmative Action Trial Ct MA 1978-; mem MA Judicial Council 1978-; pres MA Black Judges Conf 1979-83. **Honors/Awds:** Civil Rights Award Boston NAACP 1968; Comm Serv Award Freedom House 1969; Outstanding Citizen Award Roxbury Multi Serv Center 1974; Citizen of the Yr Omega Psi Phi Frat 1978; Distinguished Public Serv Boston Univ Law School Alumni 1979; Outstanding Public Serv MA Assn of Afro-Amer Police 1979; Alumnus of the Year, Virginia State Univ, 1986. **Military Serv:** USAF sgt 1942-46.

ELAM, HARRY PENOY
Physician, educator. **Personal:** Born Jul 31, 1919, Little Rock, AR; married Sallyann; children: Regina, Bernadette, Joanne, Susanne, Bernard, Christopher. **Educ:** Loyola Univ, BS 1949, MD 1953; Cook Cty Hosp, internship 1953-54, resd 1954-56, rsch fellow pediatric neurology 1957-59. **Career:** Cook County Hospital, attending physician 1956,61, The Children's Neurology Serv Children's Div, assoc dir 1956, assoc dir 1957; St Vincent's Orphanage, attending staff 1957; Mercy Hospital, jr attending staff 1957; Stritch School of Medicine Loyola Univ, asst clinical prof 1957, instructor 1956-58; Mental Health Clinic, Dept of Mental Health, medical dir 1962; Univ of Ibadon Nigeria, sr lecturer 1962; Stritch School of Medicine Loyola Univ, asst prof 1965, assoc clinical prof 1967; Mile Sq Health Center, medical dir 1967; Rush-Presbytery-St Lukes Medical Center, assoc clinical prof 1971; Rush Coll of Medicine, prof of pediatrics, assoc prof preventive medicine 1971-. **Orgs:** Mem med adv bd Good Samaritan School of Mentally Retarded Children 1963-65; mem Handicapped Childrens Council, Chicago Met Interagy Comm, Dept of MentalHlth 1967; professional adv bd United Cerebral Palsy of Gtr Chicago 1966-; mem Amer Acad of Pediatrics, Amer Acad of Cerebral Palsy 1970, Amer Soc of Adlerian Psych, Chicago Pediatric Soc, Alpha Omega Alpha Hon Med Soc 1971, Inst of Med of Chicago 1975. **Business Addr:** Coordinator, Presbyterian St Lukes MC, 1753 W Congress Pkwy, Chicago, IL 60612.

ELAM, LLOYD C.
Educator, physician. **Personal:** Born Oct 27, 1928, Little Rock, AR; married Clara Carpenter; children: Gloria, Laurie. **Educ:** Roosevelt Univ, BS 1950; Univ of WA, MD 1957. **Career:** Univ of IL Hosp, internship 1957-58; Univ of Chicago, residency 1958-61; Univ of Chicago & Billing Hosp, instr of psychiatry 1961; GW Hubbard Hosp, dept of psychiatry 1961-63; Meharry Medical Coll, prof 1963-68, interin dean sch of medicine 1966-68, president, 1968-81, distinguished service prof, psychiatry, currently. **Orgs:** Bd trustees Fisk Univ; bd dir, Premark Int, Merck & Co, Whitehouse Sta NJ; First Union Bank of TN, Nashville, TN. **Honors/Awds:** Religious Heritage of Amer Bus & Professional Leader of Yr Awd in Field of Medicine 1950-52; Hon Degrees DL Harvard Univ 1974, DSc St Lawrence Univ 1974,DHL Roosevelt Univ 1974; Eleanor Roosevelt Key Roosevelt Univ; Citizen of Year Omega Psi Phi. **Business Addr:** Distinguished Service Prof, Psychiatry, Meharry Medical Coll, 1005 18th Ave N, Nashville, TN 37208.

EL-AMIN, SA'AD (JEROYD X. GREENE)
Attorney. **Personal:** Born Feb 10, 1940, Manhattan, NY; married Carolyn Adams; children: Je Royd W III, Nicole, Anissa. **Educ:** Univ Sthrn CA, BA 1965; Yale U, JD 1969, MA 1969. **Career:** World Commun of Islam in the W, natl bus mang 1975-76; Greene and Poindexter, Inc, sr law prtnr 1971-75; Howard U, assit prof of law 1973-74; Sheffield & Greene, assoc in law firm 1969-71. **Orgs:** Amer Bar Assn; Natl Bar Assn; Natl Donfer of Black Lawy; Old Dominion Bar Assn; VA St Bar; VA Trial Lawy Assn; Richmond Criminal Bar Assn; Natl Assn of Criminal Def Lawy bar of the US Sup Ct 1973; fellow, The Urban Cntr Columbia U; Natl Consult & Lectr Cncl on Legal Ed 1974-75; pres, Advis Comm for Amer Muslims Propagat; Fin Assist Fund; mem Iman Consult Bd, Hon Elijah Muhammad Mosque #2. **Honors/Awds:** Lawy of the Yr, Natl Confer of Black Lawy 1974. **Business Addr:** 312 W Grace St, Richmond, VA 23220.

ELCOCK, CLAUDIUS ADOLPHUS RUFUS
Physician. **Personal:** Born Jan 7, 1923; married Annie Bactowar; children: Julia, Claudia. **Educ:** Lincoln Univ, AB 1954; Howard Univ School of Med, MD 1959. **Career:** Mercy Douglass Hosp, med rsd, chief med officer 1960-70, med consult 1973; Presbyterian Hosp, staff mem 1973-77. **Orgs:** Chmn URC; treas Symposium 1943-50; mem Utilization Rev Comm, Quality Assurance Comm, Proj Outreach Comm; nurses adv comm Presb Hosp 1977; mem AMA, PMS, PCMS, PSIM, NMA, MSEP; elder Reeve Meml Presb Church; mem Home & School Assoc of Neighborhood School in Philadelphia 1964-69. **Honors/Awds:** Chapel of Four Chaplains 1975. **Business Addr:** 400 S 57th St, Philadelphia, PA 19143.

ELDER, ALMORA KENNEDY
Educator. **Personal:** Born Jul 4, 1920, Rusk, CO; married Lamar; children: Ferria, Patricia, Wilbert, Barbara, Lamar Jr, Lacetta. **Educ:** Bishop Coll, BS 1947, MA 1956; Prairie View A&M Coll, Attend; Stephen F Austin, 1976; E TX St Commerce TX, Attend. **Career:** Easton, TX, former mayor; Taturn IS Div, estb 1st home making ed dept 1938-39, coach girls bsktbl. **Orgs:** Pres, Taturn Girls Clb Sec 1948-58; mem, Sigma Gamma Rhoc; sec, Eastern Star Chap 1599; life Mem, FSFA; life mem, NEA; life mem CTA; mem, Longview Local Unit TAIR; E TX Cncl of Soc Studies; Aging Com Bapt Honiney Pirtee Kilgore. **Honors/Awds:** Nat Ednr Award of World Books; Kingergarten Cert of Hon, SFA.

ELDER, GERALDINE H.
Government official. **Personal:** Born Sep 13, 1937, Chicago, IL. **Educ:** Morris Brown Atlanta, Attended 1955-57; Loyola Univ Chicago, Attended 1958-59; Emory Univ Atlanta, Attended 1968-69. **Career:** City of Atlanta, commr of parks & rec 1985, dir of comm affairs 1976-77, sec to vice-mayor; Ofc of Mayor City of Atlanta, chief of staff 1977-79, mayor'sexc sec 1974-76; Jackson Patterson Pks & Franklin, legal sec 1970-73; Emory Comm Legal Serv Cntr, ofc mgr 1967-70; Pope Ballard Uriell Kennedy Shepard &Foul, legal sec 1964-65. **Orgs:** Bd mem, Atlanta Conv & Visitors Bur; bd mem, Opp Ind Cntr; fund com chmn, Am Cancer Soc Fulton Co; mem Alpha Kappa Alpha Sorority. **Honors/Awds:** Nominated for Outstndng Young Women of Am. **Business Addr:** Commr of Parks & Recreation, City of Atlanta 260 Central Ave, Atlanta, GA 30303.

ELDER, LEE (ROBERT LEE)
Professional golfer. **Personal:** Born Jul 14, 1934, Dallas, TX; married Rose Harper. **Educ:** PGA Training Sch, 1967-75. **Ca-**

reer: US Army, capt, golf team 1959-61; Lee Elder Enterprises, Inc, dir. **Orgs:** Lee Elder Schlrshp Found; Lee Elder Celebrity Pro-Am Golf Classic 1970; founder, Lee Elder Summer Youth Golf Dev Prog Bd dir Police Boys Clb; Mason; mem natl adv bd, Goodwill Ind; bd dir, Met Wash Police-Boys Clb; life mem, NAACP; dir, PGA Episcopalian; Touchdown Clb, Washington DC; Professional Golfers Assn of Am Ranked on All Time Money Winners List 1968-. **Honors/Awds:** First black to qualify for Ryder Cup Golf Team 1979; first Black Am to prtcpt in multiracial sprts, S Africa; first black to prtcpt in Dunlop Masters, England; May 3 declared Lee Elder Day, Washington DC; received Key to City of Washington 1974; Most Outstndng Ath on a Nat Basis from DC Met Area 1974; received Key to City, Pensacola FL 1975; Charles Bartlett Award, Golf Writers Am 1977; Herman A English Humanitarian Award, City of LA 1977; AG Gaston Award, Nat Bus League 1978; Wash Hall of Stars 1979; Sr PGA Tour winner of the Suntree Classic 1984; Hilton Head Invitational 1984; Champions of Golf 1985; Merrill-Lynch Seniors 1985; Digital Seniors 1985; Citizens Bank Seniors 1985; The Commemorative 1986; Foreign Championships incl Coca-Cola Grand Slam Japan1984, Jamaica PGA Championship gston, Jamaica 1984, Coca-Cola Grand Slam Japan 1986. **Military Serv:** US Army, 1959-61.

ELDERS, M. JOYCELYN
Former Surgeon General. **Personal:** Born Aug 13, 1933, Schaal, AR; daughter of Haller Reed Jones and Curtis L Jones; married Oliver B Elders; children: Eric D, Kevin M. **Educ:** Philander Smith Coll, BA 1952; Brooke Army Med Ctr, RPT 1956; Univ of AR Med Sch, MD 1960, MS Biochem 1967. **Career:** Univ of MN Hosp, intern-pediatrics 1960-61; Univ of AR Med Ctr, resident pediatrics 1961-63, chief res/peds 1963-64, rsch fellow in pediatrics 1964-67, asst prof pediatrics 1967-71, assoc prof peds 1971-76, prof pediatrics 1976-; Arkansas Dept of Health, dir 1987-93; US Dept of Health & Human Services, surgeon general, 1993-94. **Orgs:** Amer Assn for Adv of Sci; Soc for Pediatric Rsch; Acad of Pediatric; Cnrl AR Acad of Pediatrics; Amer Diabetes Assn; Lawson Wilkins Endocrine Soc; Amer Fed of Clinical Rsch; AR Diabetes Assn; The Endocrine Soc; assoc mem FEBS Amer Phys Soc; Amer Bd of Pediatrics 1965; bd mem N Little Rock Workman's Comp Comm 1975-79; AR Sci & Tech Comm 1975-76; Human Growth Found 1974-78; chmn membership comm Lawson Wilkins End Soc 1976; Human Embryologoy & Devel Study Sect 1976-80; Natl Adv Food & Drug Comm 1977-80; pres Sigma Xi 1977-78; Natl Pituitary Agency 1977-80; bd of dir Natl Bank of AR 1979; Maternal & Child Hlth Rsch Comm HHS, NIH 1981-; Editorial Bd Journal of Ped 1981-; sec AR Sci & Tech Comm 1983-; bd mem Noside YMCA 1973-84; 113 publications including, Disorders of Carbohydrate Metabolism is orders of Adrenal Metabolism 1984; "Growth Hormone Effects on B- and T-cell Function, Effect of EGF on Gastrointestinal Mucosal Proliferation" 1984. **Honors/Awds:** Alumni Academic Scholarship Philander Smith Coll 1949-52; Alpha Kappa Mu Natl Honor Soc 1951; BS Magna Cum Laude Philander Smith Coll 1952; USPHS Postdoctoral Rsch Fellow 1964; USPHS Career Develop Awd 1967-72; Alpha Omega Alpha 1972; AKA's Distinguished Women in Amer 1973; Woman of the Year, Arkansas Democrat 1989. **Military Serv:** US Army, 1st lt 1953-56. **Business Addr:** Professor of Pediatric Endocrinology, University of Arkansas, Attn: Dr Elders, 800 West Marshall, Little Rock, AR 72202, (501)320-1431.

ELEAZER, GEORGE ROBERT, JR.
School psychologist. **Personal:** Born Oct 16, 1956, East Patchogue, NY; son of Virginia Lee Conquest Eleazer and George Robert Eleazer Sr; married Cynthia Marie Eleazer, Aug 28, 1983; children: Toshalina, George III. **Educ:** The Choate School, attended 1974; Tufts Univ, BS 1978; Hofstra Univ, MA, 1978, PhD 1984. **Career:** Freeport Public Schs, intern psychologist 1980-81; United Cerebral Palsy of Suffolk, intern psychologist 1981-82; Westbury Public Schs, psychologist 1982-84; William Floyd Public Schs, psychologist 1984; Middle Island School, psychologist; Longwood Central School District, Middle Island, NY, psychologist, 1984-. **Orgs:** Pres of the bd Bellport Local Action Ctr 1980-81; mem South Country School Bd 1982-; adv bd Brookhaven Memorial Hosp 1984-; bd of dirs Bellport Rotary 1985-86; pres, Bellport Rotary Club, 1991-92; mem, South Country School Board, 1982-; mem, Brookhaven Memorial Hospital Advisory Council, 1984-; cochmn, South Country School District, pre kindergarten advisory bd, 1997; South Country School District, budget advisory committee, 1997. **Honors/Awds:** American Legion Award, South Country Schools, 1970; David Bohn Memorial School Award, South Country Schools, 1970; Daniel Hale Williams Award, Tufts Univ 1978; Phi Delta Kappa, 1985. **Home Addr:** 57 New Jersey Ave, Bellport, NY 11713.

ELEWONIBI, MOHAMMED THOMAS DAVID
Professional football player. **Personal:** Born Dec 16, 1965, Lagos, Nigeria. **Educ:** Snow College, 1986-87; Brigham Young Univ, business management major, 1987-89. **Career:** Washington Redskins, guard, 1990-. **Honors/Awds:** Outland Award, 1989. **Business Addr:** Professional Football Player, Washington Redskins, 21300 Redskin Park Dr, Ashburn, VA 22011-6100.

ELEY, RANDALL ROBBI
Company Executive. **Personal:** Born Jan 29, 1952, Portsmouth, VA; son of Melvin & Florence Eley; children: Melisa, Serena, Robin, Kimberly. **Educ:** Yale University, BA, political science, 1974; University of Chicago Law School, JD, 1977. **Career:** Kutak Rock & Campbell, assoc atty, partner, 1977-86; The Edgar Lomax Co, pres, CEO, 1986-. **Orgs:** William & Mary Coll Endowment Assn, trustee, 1997; Norfolk State Univ, Bus School, advisory council, mem, 1996; YMCA, bd of dirs, 1992; DC Bar, 1986. **Honors/Awds:** Dollars & Sense Magazine, "America's Best & Brightest Business Professional Men," 1988; The Wall Street Journal, Dartboard Stock-Picking Contect, 1990. **Business Addr:** President, Edgar Lomax Co, 6564 Loisdale Ct, Ste 310, Springfield, VA 22150, (703)719-0026.

ELIE, MARIO ANTOINE
Professional Basketball Player. **Personal:** Born Nov 26, 1963, New York, NY. **Educ:** American International Univ. **Career:** Milwaukee Bucks, 1985; CBA: Miami Tropics, 1987; Albany Patroons, 1989-91; Youngstown Pride, 1990; Los Angeles Lakers, 1990; Philadelphia 76ers, 1990; Golden State Warriors, 1991; Portland Trail Blazers, 1992; Houston Rockets, 1994-. **Special Achievements:** NBA Championship Team, 1994. **Business Addr:** Professional Basketball Player, Houston Rockets, PO Box 272349, Houston, TX 77277, (713)627-0600.

ELIZEY, CHRIS WILLIAM
Computer co. executive. **Personal:** Born Aug 3, 1947, Brooklyn, NY; son of Dorris Elizey and Hollis Elizey; married Georgia V Robinson, Dec 24, 1972; children: Christopher. **Educ:** University of San Francisco, 1968-70; DePaul University, BS, 1976; University of Oklahoma, ME, 1989; University of Virginia, PhD, 1990. **Career:** AT&T, systems engineer, 1970-76; RCA Communications, vice pres, 1976-80; Centurian Systems, vice pres, 1980-. **Orgs:** Outer City Golf, president, 1990-; National Black Pages, vice pres, 1985-; NAACP, secretary, 1990-; Cleveland Business League, vice pres, 1988-; Black Data Processors Association, president, 1986-88. **Military Serv:** US Navy, e5, 1964-68. **Business Phone:** (216)881-3939.

EL-KATI, MAHHMOUD (MILTON WILLIAMS)
Educator. **Personal:** Born Oct 30, 1936, Savannah, GA; married; children: Erick, Stokley, Kamali. **Educ:** Univ of Ghana, 1969; Univ of Wisconsin, 1964-65; Wilberforce Univ, BA 1960. **Career:** MacAlester Coll Antioch-Minneapolis Coll, instr; lecturer, writer & community activist. **Orgs:** Currently working with black prison inmates regarding educ programs; affiliated with several prison inst since 1966; volunteer, Urban League; NAACP; SNCC; CORE; Creative Ed; dir, The Way Community Center 1967-71. **Honors/Awds:** Page 1 Award, Twin Cities Newspaper Guild 1968; Urban League Award 1969; EROS U-of-the-Streets, Merritt Coll 1969; Recognition Award, Univ of MN; Stillwater Black Inmate Pop 1974. **Business Addr:** 1600 N Snelling Ave, St Paul, MN 55105.

ELKINS, VIRGIL LYNN
Educator. **Personal:** Born Oct 18, 1925, Sarasota, FL; married Argaree; children: Virgil, Sylvia, Kathryn, Angela, Michael. **Educ:** FL A&M U, BS 1946, MS 1959. **Career:** Univ of FL, area prog specialist 1965-, extens dist agent 1961-65, extens agent 1949-61, chair, agr 1948-49; FL School for Boys, teacher 1946-48. **Orgs:** Nat bd of dir, Comm Devel & Soc 1974-76; So Agr Econ Assn; sec, treas, Epsilon Sigma Phi Frat 1976-77; state pres, FL A&M Univ Alumni Assn 1974-;FL Commin on Aging; SER Clb; Kappa Alpha Phi Frat; bd of dir, Bethel AME Ch; Funders, Inc; Tallahassee Citizens Savings Clb; supt, Sun Sch; Rural Devel Goodwill Clb; pres FL A&M Univ Agr Assn; Am Assn of Univ Prof. **Honors/Awds:** Kappa Man of the Yr Award 1975; SER Clb Annual Award 1976; Leon Co Alumni Chap Award 1974; FL A&M Alumni Award 1971. **Business Addr:** Box A-48, FL A&M Univ, Tallahassee, FL 32307.

ELLARAINO
Actress, storyteller. **Personal:** Born Oct 7, 1938, Kilgore, TX; daughter of Lola B Taylor Raino and John Henry Raino (both deceased); divorced; children: Bernard Otis Wright. **Educ:** Los Angeles Metropolitan Coll, AA; John Robert Powers School of Modeling, graduate. **Career:** TV, "Sinbad," "White Shadow", "Police Story", "Sanford & Son", "The Memory of Eva Ryker", "Storytime", "Martin","Beverly Hills 90210", "Saved By The Bell", "Family Matters", "Fox Cubhouse", host; Films, "New York New York", "Big Time", "Mr Ricco"; Stage, "The Crucible" "The Jean London Show", "The Terraced Apartment", "Story of the Blues", "Life Is A Thing", "Hotel Paradiso"; numerous television, motion picture, stage & commercial credits; "Happy Days," asst assoc producer, 1979-82; "The New Odd Couple," assoc producer, 1982-83; Compton Unified School District, Center for Artistically Talented Students, drama/theatre consultant; appeared in TV series, "Father Dowling Mysteries," "Hill Street Blues," "One Day at a Time," "Dan August," "Lucas Tanner," "Search"; featured in films, "House Party," "Vital Signs," "Beaches," "Young Doctors in Love," "New York, New York," "Topaz", "Fire down Below", "Sneakers" ; storytelling/writing, currently; CA Arts Council Artist-In-Residency Summer Program; Consultant & Performance Artist for the International House of Blues Foundation's Educ Tours Program, currently. **Orgs:** Griot Society of So CA; Tellers and Talkers; Natl Storytelling Assn; Natl Assn of Black Storytellers; Screen Actors Guild; Amer Federation of TV & Radio Artists; Founding & charter mem financial sec Kwanza Found Award; OH Close Sch for Boys 1972-74; former mem and secretary, Black Women in Theatre West, 1984-86. **Honors/Awds:** Community Serv Award, Alpha Gamma Omega Chapter, Alpha Kappa Alpha Award; Certificate of Commendation, City of Los Angeles, 1988, 1995; Certificate of Recognition, Jenesse Center; Performance on the Bicentennial of the United States, Shreveport Regional Bicentennial Commission, 1976; Bicentennial Minute Man Award; Co-author of "Another Kind of Treasure: Stories of Dreams Fulfilled"; Official storyteller of Allensworth State Historic Park, California's first town founded by African Americans. **Business Addr:** Storyteller, Ellaraino, PO Box 1420, Studio City, CA 91604.

ELLARD, HENRY AUSTIN
Professional football player. **Personal:** Born Jul 21, 1961, Fresno, CA; married Lillian; children: Henry Austin Jr., Whitney, Christiana. **Educ:** Fresno State, attended. **Career:** Los Angeles Rams, wide receiver, 1983-93; Washington Redskins, 1994-. **Honors/Awds:** Pro Bowl, 1984. **Business Addr:** Professional Football Player, Washington Redskins, 13832 Redskin Dr, Herndon, VA 22071, (703)471-9100.

ELLER, CARL L.
Health services executive. **Personal:** Born Jan 25, 1942, Winston-Salem, NC; son of Ernestine Eller and Clarence Eller; married Mahogany Jaclynne Fasnacht-Eller, Dec 21, 1979; children: Cinder, Regis, Holiday. **Educ:** Univ of MN, Educ 1960-63, Certificate C D Counselor 1982; Metropolitan St Coll, Inst of Chemical Dependency, 1983-. **Career:** MN Vikings, defensive end 1964-78; Seattle SeaHawks, professional football player 1979-80; Viking Personnel, employee consultant 1982; Natl Football League, health consultant; Natl Inst of Sports & Hmnts, founder & dir 1981-; US Athletes Assoc, founder & exec dir 1983-; Triumph Services, executive director, currently. **Orgs:** Mem SAG/AFTRA Actors Talent Assn 1969-; Fellowship of Christian Athletes; bd mem MN Council on Chemical Dependency 1982-, MN Inst of Black Chemical Abuse 1982-; pres NFL Alumni MN Chapter 1982-85; Citizens Advisory Council, State of MN 1984-; bd mem Univ of MN 1984-, Youth Rescue Fund 1983-; Grants comm chair 1983-86; Chemical Dependency Div; State Dept of Health Human Serv; Mayors Task Force on Chemical Dependency 1985-; contributing editor Alcoholism & Addiction Magazine 1985-; executive director, United States Athletes Assn; serves as a consultant to the National Football League on matters of drug and alcohol abuse; president, Univ of Minnesota "M" Club, 1990; vice president, NFL Alumni, Minnesota Chapter, 1986-. **Honors/Awds:** Author "Beating the Odds" 1985; nominee Pro-Football Hall of Fame 1985, 1987, 1991; producer "My 5th Super Bowl" Educ Film 1984; all-pro-football Natl Football League 1969-75; MVP lineman Defense, Natl Football League 1969-71; All American, Univ of Minnesota 1962-63; All Pro, Natl Football League 1969-75; George Halas Award, Best Defensive Lineman 1969; NFLPA Defensive Player of the Year 1971; Key Man Award, Miltipleclerosis Society 1977; Special Task Force Prevention of Chemical Abuse, The White House 1982; Hubert H Humphrey, Minnesota Labor Award 1982; Good Neighbor Award, WCCO Radio 1984; Minnesota Vikings Silver Anniversary All-Time Team, 1985; North Carolina Sports Hall of Fame, 1991; Tribute to Community Enterprise, Dr William Bennett, 1990; Minnesota Sports Hall of Fame, 1989. **Military Serv:** Natl Guard private 1965-71. **Business Addr:** Executive Director, Triumph Services, 3735 Lakeland Ave N, Suite 200, Minneapolis, MN 55422.

ELLERBE, BRIAN HERSHOLT
Basketball coach. **Personal:** Born Sep 1, 1963, Cheverly, MD; married Ingrid; children: Brian Jr, Morgan Ashleigh. **Educ:** Rutgers University, BA in urban planning, 1985. **Career:** Rutgers Univ, graduate asst coach, 1985-86; Bowling Green State Univ, asst coach, 1986-88; George Mason Univ, asst coach, 1988-89; Univ of South Carolina, asst coach, 1989-90; Univ of Virginia, asst coach, 1990-94; Loyola College (MD), head coach, 1994-97; Univ of Michigan, interim head coach, 1997-98, head coach, 1998-. **Business Addr:** Men's Basketball Coach, University of Michigan, Athletic Department, 1000 S State St, Ann Arbor, MI 48109-2201, (313)647-2583.

ELLERBY, WILLIAM MITCHELL, SR.
State representative. **Personal:** Born Sep 19, 1946, Manning, SC; married Sarah Croker; children: Clifford, Andre, Mitchell Jr. **Educ:** Benedict College, Columbia, SC, BA, 1971. **Career:** Sears Roebuck, div mgr 1971-73; Jackson Cty Headstart, admin asst 1973-74; Chevron USA Refinery, refinery oper 1974; State of Mississippi, state representative, 1984-. **Orgs:** Mem Methodist Church, Omega Psi Phi; bd of dir Jackson Cty Area Chamber of Commerce; life mem VFW; Amer Legion; Elks, Evening Lions Club; vice pres Moss Point Boxing Assn; pres Eastside Voting Precinct; city democratic exec comm, former commiss Jackson Cty Port Authority; NAACP. **Honors/Awds:** Host Awareness 1985 WHKS Moss Point. **Military Serv:** US Army, SP-4, 1966-68; Vietnam Campaign Medals 1967-68. **Business Addr:** State Representative, State of Mississippi, PO Box 216, Moss Point, MS 39563.

ELLIGAN, IRVIN, JR.
Clergyman, educator (retired). **Personal:** Born Nov 24, 1915, Chattanooga, TN; son of Annie C Simmons Elligan McDonald and Irvin Elligan Sr; married Florence C Coston Elligan, Jun 23, 1945; children: Rachel A Clark, Irvin III. **Educ:** Knoxville Coll, BS 1938; Pittsburgh-Xenia Sem, MDiv 1944; Union Theological Seminary of VA, postgrad 1966-67; Presbyterian Institute on Industrial Relations, 1968; Columbia Theological Seminary, attended 1972; Urban Training Center, Certificate in Org Devel, 1972, 1976. **Career:** Camden Acad, teacher 1939-41; pastorates in VA & TN, 1944-66; Knoxville Coll, Bible instructor 1952; Presbyterian Church of US, assoc sec of church & soc bd of Christian educ 1963-67; Lakeview Presbyterian St Petersburg, assoc pastor 1967-70; Columbia Theological Seminary, vis instructor 1972; New Covenant Presbyterian Church Miami, pastor; associate professor of Pastoral Ministries, SFL Center for Theological Studies, director of field education, professor emeritus, 1991; pastor emeritus, New Covenant Presbyterian, 1985-. **Orgs:** Moderator of Synod of FL PCUS 1974-; Stillman Coll Board; FL Council Churches, FL Christian Migrant Ministry; moderator Everglades Presbytery PCUS 1980; Synod of FL Mission Council; Presbyterian US Minority Mission Council; bd mem Presbyterian Found; chmn of Racial/Ethnic Task Force Presbyterian Div of Natl Mission; Bd Trustees Presbyterian Church (USA) Foundation; Greater Miami Religious Leaders Coalition; Miami Urban Coalition; Synod C Transition Com; Chmn Black Presbyterian Project of Tropical FL; Program Committee Greater Miami Urban Coalition, 1986-; chmn, Dade County Community Relations Bd, 1980-81; exec comm, Greater Miami Religious Leaders Coalition. **Honors/Awds:** 1st Black Moderator Hanover Presbytery VA 1963; Silver Beaver Award BSA; Outstanding Citizen Award Richmond VA 1962; Key to the City of St Petersburg FL 1970; Black Presbyterian Leadership Caucus Serv Honors 1973; Citizen of the Yr Award Omega Psi Phi Miami 1979; Honors certificates by Metro-Dade County and City of Miami, FL Natl Peace Seekers Award, So Presbyterian Peace Fellowship, 1981; Stillman College, honorary DD, 1965; FL Theological Center, honorary DD, 1991; Essie Silva Community Builder Award, 1992. **Home Addr:** 8431 NW 12th Ave, Miami, FL 33150.

ELLINGTON, BRENDA ANDREA
Advertising executive. **Personal:** Born May 13, 1960, Los Angeles, CA. **Educ:** Stanford Univ, BA Economics 1982; Stanford Graduate School of Business, MBA 1986. **Career:** EF Hutton, stockholders apprentice 1982; Merrill Lynch, marketing intern 1982; Home Box Office, business analyst 1982-84; Salomon Bros, rsch analyst 1985; Leo Burnett Co, asst acct exec 1986-. **Orgs:** Co-pres Black Business Soc Stanford Univ 1981-82; project chair Los Angeles Jr Chamber of Commerce 1984; mem Stanford Grad Sch of Business Alumni Assn 1986-; mem Natl Black MBA Assn Chicago, League of Black Women. **Honors/Awds:** Outstanding Serv Award City of Los Angeles 1980; COGME Fellow 1984; Stanford Graduate School of Business Fellowship 1984-86. **Business Addr:** Alumni Records, PLEASE FORWARD, Stanford Univ, Grad School of Business, Stanford, CA 94305-5015.

ELLINGTON, IDA KAREN
Employment consultant. **Personal:** Born Aug 11, 1954, Gary, IN; daughter of Robert & Thelma Ellington. **Educ:** Indiana University, BS, 1976. **Career:** Snelling & Snelling, consultant, 1979-89; Ellington & Associates, president, 1989-. **Business Addr:** President, Ellington & Associate, 1755 Park St, Ste 200, Naperville, IL 60563, (708)305-0088.

ELLINGTON, MERCEDES
Choreographer, director. **Personal:** Born in New York, NY; daughter of Ruth V Batts and Mercer Ellington. **Educ:** Juilliard Sch of Music, BS 1960. **Career:** Performer/lecturer/demonstrator; June Taylor Dancers Jackie Gleason Show, dancer 1963-70; Sophisticated Ladies, featured performer 1980-83; Balletap America/USA, co-artistic dir 1983-85; choreographer, Blues in the Night 1984,85, Juba 1985,86; asst choreographer for Broadway productions of, No No Nanette, Hellzapoppin, Oh Kay, Happy New Year, The Grand Tour, Sophisticated Ladies, The Night That Made America Famous; DancEllington, artistic dir 1985-93. **Orgs:** Local 802, Songwriters' Guild of Amer; mem Actors Equity Council AEA 1984-85; local bd, natl bd, AFTRA; comm mem, Career Transitions for Dancers; Actors Equity Assn; AGMA; SAG; Society of Stage Dir & Choreographers; Society of Singers. **Honors/Awds:** Symphony Space, ''Wall to Wall Duke Ellington,'' with DancEllington; ''Juba, ''AMAS Production at the Vineyard Theatre; ''No No Nanette,'' St Louis Muny; ''Sophisticated Ladies,'' Birmingham Alabama, Columbus GA, Bring In The Morning-Apollo Theatre; Twist-George St Playhouse; Indianapolis Yuletide Celebration, 7 years; Ain't Misbehavin-Mt Vernon, Columbus, GA, St Louis; Generations Award from the Columbus Times, The Key to the City; 52nd Street American Award; Duke Ellington Memorial Award; Proclamation from Shreveport, Louisiana- Mercedes Ellington Day, also Columbus, GA; Dramalogue Award, San Diego Old Globe - Play on!. **Special Achievements:** St Louis, Eleven MUNY Productions: Peter Pan; Wizard Of Oz; Meet Me In St Louis; Kiss Me Kate; Broadway: Play On!.

ELLIOT, MISSY (MISDEMEANOR)
Rapper, writer, producer, singer. **Career:** Rapper; producer; writer; singer, currently. **Special Achievements:** Albums include: Supa Dupa Fly, 1997; was part of singing group, Sista; Made appearances on: ''Can We,'' SWV, 1997; ''Ladies Nite,'' Lil' Kim, 1997; ''Steelo,'' group 702; Written songs for SWV; 702; Jodeci; Sista; produced songs for Aaliyah; Magoo & Timbaland; MC Lyte; Gina Thompson.

ELLIOTT, ANTHONY DANIEL, III
Concert cellist, conductor. **Personal:** Born Sep 3, 1948, Rome, NY; son of Charlie Mae White Elliott and Anthony Daniel Elliott; married Paula Sokol Elliott, Jun 9, 1975; children: Danielle, Michelle, Marie, Cecille. **Educ:** IN University School of Music, Performer's Certificate 1969, BMusic (with Honors), 1970. **Career:** Aspen Chamber Symphony, principal cello 1970; Toronto Symphony Orchestra, section cello 1970-73; University of MN, instructor 1973-76; Minnesota Orchestra, assoc principal cello 1973-78; MacAlester College, instructor 1974-76; Vancouver Symphony Orchestra, principal cello 1978-82; Vancouver Youth Orchestra, 1982-83; Marrowstone Music Festival, asst music director, 1986-87; Western MI University, assoc prof of cello 1983-87, music dir of: univ opera, univ symphony orchestra; Johannessen Intl School of the Arts, faculty, 1985-93; Univ of Houston, School of Music, Houston, TX, assoc prof, 1987-91, prof, 1991-94; Houston Youth Symphony, Houston, TX, music dir, 1990-94; Univ of MI, professor of music, 1994-; Eastman School of Music, visiting prof, 1994-95. **Orgs:** Asst music dir, Marrowstone Music Festival, 1981-87; conductor, TX Music Festival, 1991-92; adv bd, Music Assistance Fund, NY Philharmonic, 1970-. **Honors/Awds:** CBC Toronto Orch; CO Philharmonic; Indianapolis Philharmonic; Utica Symphony; Aspen Festival; Vancouver Symphony; Debut Recital-Town Hall; St Lawrence Centre for Perf Arts, Toronto CAN 1973; recital appearances in US & CAN; featuring & sponsoring compositions by Black composers; supv, Inner-city Mus Proj, St Paul 1974; string clinician; chamber & ensemble perf; Kraus Meml Prize, IN Univ 1968; semi-finalist, CBC Radio CAN Talent Festival 1973; World Premiere Performance of Concerto for Cello & Orch, Primous Fountain with Stanislav Skrowaczewski & MN Orch 1977; First Black Musician to Maintain Prin Position in Maj Orchestra; only Am Semi-Finalist, Concours Cassado Florence Italy 1979; Grand Prize, Feuermann Memorial Intl Cello Solo Competition, 1987; Solo Appearances with NY Philharmonic, Detroit Symphony, MN Orchestra; Special Resolution Citation from Houston Mayor Kathryn Whitmire and Houston City Council; guest soloist Amer Cello Congress, 1986; recital Carnegie Hall, NY, 1988; compact disc recordings, Koch Intl Classics label, 1991. **Special Achievements:** Master Classes at most of America's leading conservatories including Oberlin, Eastman, Peabody, Rice Univ & Cleveland Inst of Music. **Home Addr:** 2020 Columbia Ave, Ann Arbor, MI 48104. **Business Addr:** Professor, Univ of MI, School of Music, Ann Arbor, MI 48109-2085, (313)764-2523.

ELLIOTT, CATHY
Insurance underwriter. **Personal:** Born Jan 21, 1956, Holly Springs, MS; daughter of Magnolia Newsom Elliott (deceased) and Mamon Elliott Jr. **Educ:** University of Mississippi, Oxford, MS, BPA, 1973-77. **Career:** Hartford Insurance Co., Memphis, TX, casualty underwriter; Nationwide Insurance Co., Memphis, TX, commercial line underwriter; Cigna Corporation, Dallas, TX, production underwriter, 1985-87; Wausau Insurance Co., Dallas, TX, regional casualty underwriter, 1987-.

ELLIOTT, DARRELL STANLEY, SR.
Attorney. **Personal:** Born May 11, 1953, Denver, CO; son of Mattie V Elliott and Frank Elliott; married Diane Elliott, Nov 10, 1991; children: Darrell S Jr, Clarke M. **Educ:** University of Denver, BA, 1975; University of Denver College of Law, JD, 1978. **Career:** Anaconda/Atlantic Richfield, landman, 1978-80; Goldfields Mining Corp, asst counsel, 1980-81; Unocal, regional counsel/mgr, 1981-83; Darrell S Elliott, PC, president/gen mgr, 1984-. **Orgs:** Alfred A Arraj American Inn of Court, vice pres, 1993-; Colorado Bar Association; American Bar Association; Colorado Trial Laywers Association; American Trial Lawyers Association; Denver Bar Association; Rocky Mountain Mineral Law Foundation. **Business Phone:** (303)329-0331.

ELLIOTT, DEREK WESLEY
Educator, historian. **Personal:** Born Oct 3, 1958, Nashville, TN; son of Joan Louise Curl Elliott and Irvin Wesley Elliott Jr. **Educ:** Harvard University, AB, 1980; University of California, Berkeley, MA, 1985; George Washington Univ, PhD, 1992. **Career:** Smithsonian Institution, curator, 1982-92; Tennessee State University, assistant professor of history, 1992-. **Orgs:** American Historical Assn, 1987-; Organization of Amer Historians, 1987-; Society for the History of Technology, 1987-. **Honors/Awds:** Member, Robinson Prize Comm, Society for the Hist of Tech, 1991-94. **Business Addr:** Assistant Professor, Department of History, Tennessee State University, Nashville, TN 37209.

ELLIOTT, FORRISS DUGAS
Judge. **Career:** City of Wellston, 21st Judicial Ct, Municipal Division, judge, currently. **Business Addr:** Judge, 21st Judicial Circuit, Municipal Division, City of Wellston, 5937 W Florissant Ave, Elliott Bldg, St Louis, MO 63136.

ELLIOTT, FRANK GEORGE
Physician (retired). **Personal:** Born Aug 23, 1913, Portsmouth, VA; son of Laura Carr Elliott and Frank G Elliott, II; married Edith Barham; children: Lynne Rosenwald, Alice Smith, Francine Campbell. **Educ:** Lincoln Univ PA, AB 1935; Howard Univ School of Medicine, MD 1940; Freedman's Hospital, Washington DC, rotating internship, 1941. **Career:** US Public Health Serv, Oklahoma State Health Dept, 1942-44; family practice, Bridgeport CT, 1945-67; sr physician emergency dept, Bridgeport Hospital, 1967-78; family practice, primary care, Bridgeport CT, 1978-80; disability claim reviewer, Town of Stratford CT, 1980; emergency physician, Danbury Hospital, 1980-93; Univ of Bridgeport School of Nursing, teacher, emergency and trauma medicine; Housatonic Community Coll, Bridgeport CT, teacher, EMT courses; Town of Stratford, teacher, EMT courses. **Orgs:** Charter mem, Amer Coll of Emergency Physicians 1968; bd of dir, medical advisory comm, CT Blue Cross-Blue Shield; dir & devel, First Methodone Drug Clinic Bridgeport 1973; pres, SW CT EMS Advisory Council 1976-81; chmn, CT State Leg Comm for Emergency Medical Services 1979-80; bd of dir, Bridgeport Area Found 1974-; fellow bd of dir, Peoples Savings Bank 1976; past pres, Bridgeport Medical Soc, Bridgeport Acad of Family Practice; Fairfield County Medical Association; Amer Acad of Family Practice; World Medical Association; Governor's Task Force on Drug Addicition; past president, board director, Family Serv Society of Bridgeport; Governor's Task Force on Venereal Disease; State Advisory Comm on EMS; chmn, State Planning Comm on EMS; Bridgeport Hospital, Devel Comm, Pharmacy andDietary Comm, Patient Care Comm,auma Comm; State of Connecticut House of Delegates from the Fairfield County Medical Soc; member board of directors, Bridgeport Rotary Club 1990-; EMS Advisory Board, data collection committee, chairman, 1992-. **Honors/Awds:** Dr A E Hartzler Knox Award, Conn State Emergency Med Service, 1987. **Home Addr:** 1005 Prospect Dr, Stratford, CT 06497.

ELLIOTT, IRVIN WESLEY
Educator. **Personal:** Born Oct 21, 1925, Newton, KS; son of Leota Jordan Elliott and Irvin Elliott; married Joan Curl, Aug 27, 1952; children: Derek, Karen. **Educ:** Univ of KS, BS 1947, MS 1949, PhD 1952; Harvard Univ, Univ of Copenhagen, postdoctoral. **Career:** Fisk Univ, prof emeritus, 1996-, prof of chem, 1958-96; Howard Univ, visiting prof, 1965-66; Ford Motor Co, visiting scientist, 1964; FL A&M Coll, assoc prof, 1952-57; Southern Univ, instructor, 1949-50; Wellesley College, Wellesley, MA, visiting prof, 1984-85. **Orgs:** Cons, Coll Chem, Amer Chem Soc; chmn, Nashville Section of Amer Chem Soc 1970; bd dir, Nat Adv Bd, CEMREL Inst 1968-74; exec com, Southern Conf of Grad Sch 1971-74; Grad Record Exam Bd 1974-78; mem, Amer Chem Soc; Chem Soc of London; Intl Soc of Heterocyclic Chem; AAAS; Omicron Delta Kappa; Sigma Xi; Beta Kappa Chi; NSF Faculty Fellowship 1957-58. **Honors/Awds:** Syntheses of Isoquinoline Alkaloids; author, Dibenzopyrrocoline Alkaloids, published in The Akaloids, Academic Press, 1987; Consultant, Minority Scholarship Program, DANA Foundation, 1988-91; NOBCChE, Outstanding Teacher Award, 1996; Fisk Univ, Researcher of the Year, 1996. **Special Achievements:** Patent of new anti-HIV compound, US #5,034,544, 1991. **Business Addr:** Professor Emeritus, Dept of Chem, Fisk Univ, Nashville, TN 37208.

ELLIOTT, J. RUSSELL
Mechanical engineer, operations consultant. **Personal:** Born in Chicago, IL; son of Blanche Smith Elliott and J Russell Elliott; married Sharon Lomax. **Educ:** Chicago Tech Coll, BSME 1968; Northwestern Univ, MBA 1975. **Career:** Johnson & Johnson Co, mech engr, suprv 1966-75; Group engineering mgr, Johnson & Johnson Baby Products Co, 1975-80; Ortho Pharmaceutical Div of Johnson & Johnson, dir indus engrg 1980-85; natl mgr package engrg 1986-94; Business Consultant, Operations & Engineering, 1995-. **Orgs:** Bd trustees Chicago Opportunity Industrialization Center 1973-75; bd trustees Sigma Phi Delta Engr Fraternity 1967-69; adv hs youth group Good Shephard Church 1969-75; bd of deacons Good Shephard Congregational Church 1969-75; mem Chicago Urban League 1967-75; mem Alpha Phi Alpha; adv Soc of Black Engineers at Princeton Univ; Bucks County PA, NAACP, 1992-94, executive committee, board of directors; Simon Foundation of PA, board of directors, 1992-94; International Organization of Packaging Professionals, 1986-. **Honors/Awds:** Certificate of Merit Chicago Assn of Commerce & Indus 1973-75. **Business Addr:** 14565 SE 56th St, Bellevue, WA 98006.

ELLIOTT, JOHN
Association executive, educator. **Educ:** Wayne State University, bachelor's degree; University of Michigan, master's degree. **Career:** Detroit School System, teacher, starting 1961; Detroit Federation of Teachers, administrative asst, starting 1966, executive vice president, starting 1968, president, 1981-. **Business Addr:** President, Detroit Federation of Teachers, 7451 Third Avenue, Detroit, MI 48202, (313)875-3500.

ELLIOTT, JOY
Journalist. **Personal:** Born in St Ann, Jamaica. **Educ:** Univ of the West Indies at Mona, BS; Univ of Poitiers Inst de Touraine, diplomas in French; Univ of Paris New Sch for Social Rsch,

MA. **Career:** Associated Press, reporter 1970-72; Reuters News Serv, correspondent 1972-. **Orgs:** Mem, Natl Assn of Black Journalists; Intl Assn for Mass Communication Rsch; Coalition of 100 Black Women; mem Soc of Professional Journalists, NY Sponsoring Comm, NAACP Legal Defense Fund; interim bd of dirs NY Chap Univ West Indies Guild of Gradmakers; bd mem Carib News newspaper NY. **Honors/Awds:** First black woman journalist, Associated Press 1970-72. **Business Addr:** Correspondent, Reuters News, 1700 Broadway, New York, NY 10019.

ELLIOTT, LARRY DOC. **See WORTHY, LARRY ELLIOTT.**

ELLIOTT, LORI KAREN
Attorney. **Personal:** Born May 26, 1959, Patuxent River, MD; daughter of Rhoda Graves-Elliott and Winfred Anthony Elliott. **Educ:** Ohio University, attended, 1977-79; University of Pittsburgh, BA, 1981, School of Law, JD, 1984. **Career:** Legal Aid Society of Cincinnati, staff attorney, senior attorney, 1984-. **Orgs:** Womens City Club; ACLU of Ohio. **Business Addr:** Senior Attorney, Legal Aid Society of Cincinnati, 901 Elm St, Cincinnati, OH 45202, (513)241-9400.

ELLIOTT, SEAN MICHAEL
Professional basketball player. **Personal:** Born Feb 2, 1968, Tucson, AZ; married Akiko Herron. **Educ:** Univ of Arizona, Tucson, AZ, 1985-89. **Career:** San Antonio Spurs, forward, 1989-93; Detroit Pistons, 1993-94; San Antonio Spurs, 1994-. **Honors/Awds:** John Wooden Award, 1989; NBA All-Rookie Second Team, 1990. **Special Achievements:** NBA Draft, First round pick, #3, 1989; NBA, All-Star game, 1993, 1996. **Business Addr:** Professional Basketball Player, San Antonio Spurs, 600 E Market St, San Antonio, TX 78205, (210)554-7773.

ELLIOTT, WILLIAM DAVID
Actor, producer, director. **Personal:** Born Jun 4, 1934, Baltimore, MD; children: David, Damon. **Career:** Films include: Change of Habit 1969, Where Does It Hurt 1972, Coffy 1973, Superdude 1975; TV movies include: Bridget Loves Bernie, That's My Mama, Adam 12, Ironside, Police Story, Celebrity & Sweepstakes, Rookies; musician/singer, CA, MD, NY, 12 years; Elliot Studio Productions, president, currently; actor, director, producer, currently. **Honors/Awds:** Recipient of numerous awards and plaques from various organizations; Key to the City, Newark NJ, 1973; Key to the City, Baltimore MD, 1974; honored, Bill Elliott Day, Baltimore MD, 1974. **Military Serv:** US Navy, radarman seaman.

ELLIS, BENJAMIN F., JR.
Insurance company executive. **Personal:** Born Sep 17, 1939, Philadelphia, PA; son of Tinner F Ellis and Benjamine H Ellis; married Sylvia Ann Simmons; children: Letitia A, Wendy S, Benjamin III, Melanie R. **Educ:** Temple Univ, Assn in Electronics 1967, BS Business Admin (cum laude) 1974. **Career:** Naval Air Eng Ctr, Philadelphia proj adm 1966-73; Penn Mutual Life Insurance Co, bldg supt 1973-76, bldg mgr 1976-79, asst vice pres 1979-81; 2nd vice pres 1981-88; City of Philadelphia, commr of public property, 1988-90; Penn Mutual Life Insurance Co, second vp, Govt and Commun Relations, 1990-. **Orgs:** Corp Financial Comm mem BOMA Intl 1974-; dir BOMA Philadelphia 1978-; mem Toastmasters Intl 1967-73; dir Citizens Coalition for Energy Efficiency 1983-; dir, Philadelphia Center for Older People 1981-; allocations comm United Way of Se PA 1978-. **Honors/Awds:** Outstanding apprentice of yr Naval Air Engr Ctr 1965; 1st Black Vice Pres Penn Mutual Life Insurance Co 1979. **Military Serv:** USN 3rd class petty officer 2 yrs. **Home Addr:** 6702 Wayne Ave, Philadelphia, PA 19119. **Business Addr:** Second Vice President, Govt and Community Relations, The Penn Mutual Life Insurance Company, Independence Square, Rm2G, Philadelphia, PA 19172.

ELLIS, BENJAMIN F., JR.
Military officer (retired), educational administrator. **Personal:** Born Dec 7, 1941, East Palatka, FL; son of Edna Pinkston Ellis and Benjamin F Ellis; married Aaron Robinson Ellis, Sep 8, 1963; children: Eric B, Traci A. **Educ:** Florida A&M University, Tallahassee, FL, BS, 1963; Arizona State University, Tempe, AZ, MA, 1972. **Career:** US Army, Ft Levenworth, KS, intelligence officer, 1973-75, Hawaii, battalion operations officer, 1975-78, Jackson State University, Jackson, MS, senior asst professor of military science, 1978-81, Ft McPherson, GA, asst inspector general, 1981-85, Norfolk State University, Norfolk, VA, comm Army/ROTC, professor of military science, 1985-89; Norfolk State Univ, Norfolk, VA, asst dir/auxiliary enterprises, 1990-91; director, placement and career sevices, Norfolk State University, 1992-. **Orgs:** National Association of Employers & Colleges. **Military Serv:** US Army, Lieutenant Colonel, 1963-89; Legion of Merit, 1989, Meritorious Service Medal, 1985, Silver Star, 1968, Bronze Star for Valor, 1966. **Business Addr:** Director, Placement and Career Services, Norfolk State University, 2410 Corprew Ave, Norfolk, VA 23504.

ELLIS, CALVIN H., III
Educator. **Personal:** Born Jun 9, 1941, Whitesboro, NJ. **Educ:** Glassboro St Coll, BA 1970, MA 1972. **Career:** Atlantic Human Res, training officer 1968-69; Glassboro State Coll, Univ Year for Action, dir 1969-. **Orgs:** Pres, bd trustees, Atlantic Human Res 1975; mem Nat Assn for Comm Dev 1975; Glassboro St Coll Com on Human & Res 1975. **Business Addr:** U Yr for Action, Glassboro State Coll, Glassboro, NJ.

ELLIS, DALE
Professional basketball player. **Personal:** Born Aug 6, 1960, Marietta, GA; married Monique; children: Ashley. **Educ:** Tennessee, 1983. **Career:** Dallas Mavericks, guard-forward, 1983-86; Seattle SuperSonics, 1987-91; Milwaukee Bucks, 1991-92; San Antonio Spurs, 1992-94; Denver Nuggets, 1994-97; Seattle Supersonics, 1997-. **Honors/Awds:** NBA, Most Improved Player, 1987; All-NBA third team, 1989; NBA All-Star, 1989. **Business Addr:** Professional Basketball Player, Seattle Supersonics, PO Box 900911, Seattle, WA 98109, (206)281-5850.

ELLIS, DOUGLAS, JR.
Public administration executive. **Personal:** Born Jul 9, 1947, Chicago, IL; son of Dorothy Mae Rummage Ellis and Douglas Ellis Sr; divorced; children (previous marriage): Anthony Marcus, Chad Dominick, Jonathan Thomas; married Rita M. Ellis; children: Aaron Christopher. **Educ:** Univ of Illinois, Chicago IL, BS, 1976; Roosevelt Univ, Chicago IL, MS, 1979; Certified Public Accountant, Illinois License, 1995. **Career:** Chicago Police Dept, Chicago IL, sergeant, 1972-86; City-Wide Colleges, Chicago IL, instructor, 1984-86; City of Chicago, Bureau of Parking, Chicago IL, dir, 1986-91; Carr & Associates, Public Accounting Firm, managing partner, beginning, 1992-; D Ellis Accounting & Business Svcs, currently. **Orgs:** Certified instructor, Chicago Police Academy, 1976-78; mem, Illinois CPA Soc, 1985-; bd of advisor delegate, Inst of Municipal Parking Congress, 1986-; membership dir, Natl Assn of Black Accountants, 1987-88; Natl Assn of Certified Fraud Examiners, mem, 1995-. **Honors/Awds:** Dept Commendation, Chicago Police Dept, 1981; 1st Degree Black Belt, Taekwondo, 1995. **Military Serv:** US Marine Corps Reserves (retired), E8 Master Sergeant, 1964-68 active duty, 1974- reserve duty, 1974-96; Vietnam Combat Ribbons (various), 1966-68, activated for Persian Gulf War, 1991. **Business Addr:** D Ellis Accounting & Business Svcs, 4574 Oakenwald, Chicago, IL 60653, (773)548-8425.

ELLIS, EDWARD V.
Educator. **Personal:** Born Feb 9, 1924, Louisburg, NC; married Elizabeth Gill; children: Ednetta K, Bruce E, Gary D. **Educ:** Shaw U, BS 1949; NC Coll, MSPH 1950; Univ of NC, PhD 1964. **Career:** Raleigh Public Schools, Wake County Health Dept, health educ, 1950-51; NC Coll, instructor 1951-52; Washingtion DC TB Assn, assoc health educ 1952-55; IN State Coll, faculty mem, school comm & health educ workshop 1963; PA Dept of Health, consultant 1955-63, sect chief 1955-63; PA State Univ, faculty mem 1964-65; Div of Public Health Educ, dir 1964-67; Univ of MN, asst prof 1967-69; PA State Univ, special asst to pres 1970-71, center head 1971-72, acting div dir 1972-74, assoc prof, assoc dean 1969-82; Univ of Maryland Eastern Shore, vice chancellor for acad affairs 1983-. **Orgs:** Numerous Consulting Positions; mem, Various Off; coms, Am Adult Ed Assn; Am Assn Univ Profs; Am Pub Hlth Assn; Prog Dev Bd; Soc Pub Hlth Ed; Nat Univ Extension Assn; Soc Pub Hlth Ed; Coalition of Nat Hlth Ed Orgs; PA Pub Hlth; Cntrl PA Hlth Cncl; Centre Comm Hlth Cncl; Comm on Higher Ed; Adv Com, PA & Dept Publ Hlth; PA Com for Nat Hlth Security; Nat Black Alliance; mem, Vrious Off; Coms, Am Cancer Soc; Cnslng Svc, Inc,of Centre Co; Family Plng Cncl of Cntrl PA, Inc; Family Serv Assn of Am; Human Rel Commn; PA Lung Assn. **Honors/Awds:** Numerous Univ affiliations, Spkng engagements, publs in field. **Military Serv:** USN 1943-46. **Business Addr:** Vice Chancellor for Acad Afrs, Univ of Maryland Eastern Shore, Princess Anne, MD 21853.

ELLIS, ELIZABETH G.
Librarian. **Personal:** Born Nov 6, Raleigh, NC; married Dr Edward V; children: Ednetta, Bruce, Gary. **Educ:** NC Central U, BA 1947, BSLS 1949, MSLS 1962. **Career:** PA St U, head, undergrad libs 1969-; Drexel Univ Grad Sch Lib Sci, adj prof 1965-67; PA St Lib, lib 1956-67, lib 1947-56, univ sen 1975-76. **Orgs:** Chrmnshps & Offs, ALA; PA Lib Assn; mem, Assn Univ Women; League Women Voters; Am Assn Pub Admin Pubs, Lectures. **Honors/Awds:** Librarian Yr, NC Lib Assn. **Business Addr:** Pattee Library, E311, Penn State University, University Park, PA 16802.

ELLIS, ELWARD DWAYNE
Clergyman, chief executive officer. **Personal:** Born Dec 17, 1948, Newark, NJ; son of Dorothy Mae Ward Ellis and Elward Ellis; married E Dawn Swaby Ellis, Oct 9, 1982; children: Dwayne Jonathan Oni Ellis. **Educ:** Shaw Univ, AB History 1966-70; Gordon-Conwell Theological Seminary, MDiv 1970-74; Andover Newton Theological School, 1973; Harvard Divinity Sch, 1974. **Career:** Emmanuel Gospel Center, staff 1971-73; Christian Growth Center, staff 1973-74; Norfolk State Univ, UCCM chaplain 1974-79; Bank St Mem Baptist Church, asst to pastor 1975-79; Friendship Comm Church, minister 1979-80; Inter-Varsity Christian Fellowship, dir of black campus ministry 1980-87; Destiny Movement Inc, pres 1988-. **Orgs:** Mem Optimal Intl 1977; Tidewater Metro Bapt Ministers' Conf Educ Comm 1978-79; chmn Annual Youth Appreciation Week Sunrise Optimist Club 1978-79; adv bd mem Norfolk Public Schools Adv Comm on Spec Educ 1978-79; co-dir "Washington '80" Natl Conf on Ministry in Urban America 1979-80; bd mem Tidewater Big Brothers 1979-80; mem Natl Black Evangelicals Assn 1979-; mem Natl Black Pastor's Conf 1981-; bd mem Justice Fellowship Inc 1984-; bd mem, vice chmn Evangelicals for Social Action 1984-; bd mem Norfolk Comm for the Improve of Educ; mem local committee Georgia Inter-Varsity Christian Fellowship 1986-; bd mem Voice of Calvary Ministry 1988. **Honors/Awds:** VA Baptist Training Union & Sunday School Congress Citation for Outstanding Contributions to Christian Educ; Mt Zion Baptist Church of Norfolk Citation for Yeoman Serv in Campus Ministry 1979; Comm of Christian Students Norfolk State Coll Citation for Outstanding Dedication to Coll Campus Ministry 1979; Bank St Memorial Baptist Church Citation Appreciation for Pastoral Service 1979; The Groove Phi Groove Social Fellowship Spartan Chap The Fellowship and Humanitarian Awd Norfolk State Univ 1978; Executive Dir Destiny '87 Intl Conf on Mission 1987; Silver Anniversary Citation, Natl Black Evangelical Assn 1988; Centennial Award, Gordon-Conwell Theological Seminary 1989.

ELLIS, ERNEST W. (AKBAR KHAN)
Banking executive (retired) musician, composer. **Personal:** Born Dec 4, 1940, New York, NY; son of Mabel and Edmund; married Judy (deceased); children: Anthony, Darius Kenyatta, Edmund Kip. **Educ:** Hartman Inst of Criminology, BS 1963; Am Inst of Banking, advanced degree 1977; Inst for Far Eastern Affairs, Cert 1981. **Career:** United Nations, reporter-general assembly 1962-64; Harmelin Agency, adm asst Ins 1964-66; Prudential, cnslnt ins 1966-69; State Dept CIA, 1967-70; intelligence off; Chase, 2nd vice pres 1970-. **Orgs:** Asst treas Western Hem Life Ins Co 1982-; chief exec off & pres Galactic Intl Ltd 1982-; contributing edtr Assets Protection Mag 1976-; visiting prof Wagner Coll 1976; visiting prof Upsala Coll 1981; v chmn Area Policy Bd 7 New York City 1979-81. **Honors/Awds:** Clifford Brown Mem Music Award New York City 1976; Outstanding Citizen Award, Chase Bank New York City 1972; cert of merit The Assembly St of NY 1981; New Star Vibist Sound of Music 1970. **Home Addr:** 140-55 Burden Crescent, Jamaica, NY 11435.

ELLIS, FREDERIC L.
Business executive (retired). **Personal:** Born Jun 16, 1915, Pensacola, FL; widowed; children: Roberta Jones-Booker, Ettamaria Cooper. **Educ:** Morehouse Coll, AB 1938. **Career:** NC Mutual-Birmingham, dist mgr 1955; NC Mutual-Los Angeles, dist mgr 1963, Retired 1977. **Orgs:** Trustee Second Baptist Church, Kappa Alpha Psi Frat, NAACP. **Honors/Awds:** Oral Review Board, LA Police Dept, 1972; Corp Budget Com, LA United Way, 1977; received resolution, City of Los Angeles, 1977. **Military Serv:** US Army T/3 sgt 1942-46. **Home Addr:** 4323 Don Arellanes, Los Angeles, CA 90008.

ELLIS, GEORGE WASHINGTON
Educator (retired), organization administrator. **Personal:** Born Jan 1, 1925, Arcadia, FL; son of Gussie Staley Ellis and George Edward Ellis; married Alvalia G Jones; children: George, Ruth, Cheryl, Jean. **Educ:** Ind Ed, Florida A&M Univ, BS 1947; Univ of Pittsburgh, EdM 1954; Columbia U, post grad studies 1961; Univ of Pittsburgh, attended 1956-60; Univ of FL, attended 1966-71; Univ of Miami, attended 1969; FL Atlantic Univ, attended 1969-70; FL Int Univ, attended 1975-80; Dade Jr Coll, attended 1974-77, CUT, 1952; MsD. **Career:** Alcorn A&M Coll, tchr, coach 1947-48; FL Memorial Coll, tchr 1948, 1969-70; Carver HS, assist prin & coach 1948-50; Bayview-Bonifay, prin 1950-53; Shadeville HS, prin 1953-56; Richardson HS, prin 1953-56; Monitor HS, prin 1956-57; Westside HS, prin 1960-62; Williston Voc HS, 1962-63; Center HS Waycross, 1963-67; Dade County Schools, asst principal, principal 1967-90. **Orgs:** Pres, Alpha Eta Chapter, Phi Beta Sigma Frat 1946-; pres, Rho Sigma Chap 1970-72; v dir, St of FL 1973-74; dir, FL 1974; v dir, Sthrn Reg 1974-75, dir 1975-77; pres Miami Chap Kappa Delta Pi 1977-78; mem, Orange Blossom Classic Comm 1973-91; vp, Miami Chap FL A&M Alumni 1977-79; pres, Miami Chpt & FAMU Alumni 1980; FL St Chaplain, FL A&M Alumni 1979-80; offcr, NAACP 1972-75; mem, Affirm Act Comm, Minist & Laymen Assn of Miami; chmn, Metro Dade Co Mayor's Advis Bd for Animals; tchr Sun Sch, Church of the Open Door; intl historian, dir so reg Third World Assembly Inc. **Honors/Awds:** Outstanding Principal, Center HS; FL Sigma Man of the Yr 1972, 1977; Phi Beta Sigma's Natl Ed Award; Regl Dir Award, Phi Beta Sigma 1977; FL st treas, Phi Beta Sigma 1977-80; Black Liberation Award 1978, 1981, 1983; Public Health Trust of Dade Co 1984; Presidential Award Natl Alumni FAMU 1984; Goodwill Indust Awards 1982, 1983; Commendation Award Metro Dade Co FL 1978, 1987; Certificate of Appreciation City of Miami FL 1978, 1979, 1984; Martin Luther King Brotherhood Awd 1983, 1984, 1986, The Third World Assembly Inc Award 1990; Florida State Coord Coun Svc Awd, 1990-96; Republican Presidential Legion of Merit, Order of Merit, 1994; Alternative Prog Inc Award, 1995; Florida State Reunion Association Award, 1996; Metropolitan Dade Cty, Certificate of Appreciation, 1997. **Home Addr:** PO Box 510072, Edison Station, Miami, FL 33152.

ELLIS, J. DELANO, II
Clergyman. **Personal:** Born Dec 11, 1944, Philadelphia, PA; son of Lucy Mae-Harris-Ellis and Jesse Ellis Sr; married Sabrina Joyce Clinkscale Ellis, Jan 8, 1982; children: Jesse III, David Demetrius, Lillian Marion, Jessica Delana, Jasmine Delana. **Educ:** Birmingham University, Doctor of Humanities, 1968; Pillar of Fire Seminary, Doctor of Canon Law, 1970; Mason College, Doctor of Divinity, 1984. **Career:** Pentecostal Church of Christ, senior pastor, 1989-. **Orgs:** The United Pentecostal Churches of Christ, presiding bishop; Church of God in Christ, Inc, adjutant-apostolic and chief of protocol, 1970-89; C H Mason Bible College, founding dean, 1969-72; St James COGIC, pastor, 1976-78. **Honors/Awds:** Birmingham University Award. **Special Achievements:** Author, "The Mother Church," 1984; author, "Judicial Administration," 1979; creator and author, The Dress Code for Clergy Church of God in Christ, 1972; founder, the Adjutancy, COGIC, 1970. **Military Serv:** US Air Force, airman fc, 1960-62. **Business Addr:** Pastor, Pentecostal Church of Christ, 10515 Chester Ave, Cleveland, OH 44106, (216)721-5934.

ELLIS, JOHNELL A.
Engineer. **Personal:** Born Sep 28, 1945, New Orleans; married Audrey Baker; children: Kimberly, Sonja. **Educ:** CA St U, BS Engr 1968; Univ of So CA, MBA 1972. **Career:** Getty Oil Co, staff eng 1985; Rockwell Intnl, fin analyst 1974; Dart Ind, acquisitions spec 1972-74; TRW Sys, Redondo Bch, admin asst 1969-72; Bunker-ramo & Westlake, engr 1968; Bambini Stores, Beverly Hills, acct; CA St U, instr. **Orgs:** Mem, Soc of Petro Engr; Inst of Elec & Electronic Engr; mem, Kappa Alpha Psi; Tau Beta Pi; Eta Kappa Nu. **Honors/Awds:** Award of Appreciation, Improvement Act Com. **Business Addr:** 3810 Wilshire Blvd, Ste 410, Los Angeles, CA 90010.

ELLIS, LADD, JR.
Government official. **Personal:** Born Dec 23, 1946, Winnsboro, LA; son of Ladd and Christine Ellis; married Maryetta; children: Kimberlyn, Angela, Stanley, Chris, Sierra. **Educ:** Northeast Louisiana Univ, BBA, accounting, 1972; North Texas State Univ, 1973-75; Syracuse Univ, MPA, 1983; CPA Colorado, 1983; Harvard Univ, 1992. **Career:** US Air Force, air traffic controller, 1965-69; Internal Revenue Service, various positions from revenue agent to director, 1972-. **Orgs:** Assn for the Improvement of Minorities, AIM-IRS, exec comm, 1983-; Internal Revenue Service, Natl Educ Adv Bd, 1994-; Federal Exec Bd, Kansas City, exec comm, 1993-. **Honors/Awds:** Internal Revenue Service, Outstanding Performance, 1992, 1994; President of the United States Rank Award, 1996; AIM-IRS, Meritorious Award, 1992. **Military Serv:** US Air Force, ssgt, 1965-69; Natl Defense Service Medal, AFLSA, AFGCM, 1969. **Business Addr:** Director, Internal Revenue Service, Kansas City Service Center, 2306 E Bannister Rd, PO Box 24551, Stop 1000, Kansas City, MO 64131.

ELLIS, LAPHONSO DARNELL
Professional basketball player. **Personal:** Born May 5, 1970, East St Louis, IL; married Jennifer; children: Elexis, LaPhonso Jr. **Educ:** Notre Dame. **Career:** Denver Nuggets, forward, 1992-. **Business Addr:** Professional Basketball Player, Denver Nuggets, 1635 Clay St, Denver, CO 80204-1743, (303)893-6700.

ELLIS, LEANDER THEODORE, JR.
Psychiatrist. **Personal:** Born May 30, 1929, Summerland, MS; son of Regina Jackson Ellis and Leander Theodore Ellis Sr; married Gettie Thigpen Ellis, Apr 27, 1957; children: Leonard, Lawrence, Laura, Lowell. **Educ:** Hampton Inst, BS 1950; Howard Univ, MD 1954. **Career:** Philadelphia General Hosp, psychiatric residency 1957-60, staff psychiatrist 1960-67; Philadelphia Psychiatric Ctr, attending staff 1962-; Woodhaven Southeastern State Sch & Hosp, staff psychiatrist 1975-77; Private Practice, general psychiatry 1960-. **Orgs:** Diplomat Amer Bd of Psychiatry and Neurology; psychiatric consultant North Central & Comprehensive MH/MR 1981,82; psychiatric consultant Sleighton School 1981-90. **Honors/Awds:** Publication "Stress, A Non-Specific Factor in Emotionality," Journal of Orthomolecular Psychiatry Vol 6 No 4 1977. **Military Serv:** USNR Lt, Medical Corps 1954-57. **Home Addr:** 100 So Swarthmore Ave, Swarthmore, PA 19081, (215)544-2908. **Business Addr:** 2746 Belmont Ave, Philadelphia, PA 19131, (215)477-6444.

ELLIS, LERON PERRY
Professional basketball player. **Personal:** Born Apr 28, 1969, Los Angeles, CA; son of Leroy Ellis. **Educ:** Syracuse Univ. **Career:** Los Angeles Clippers, 1991-92; CBA: Columbus Horizons, 1992-93; Charlotte Hornets, 1993-. **Business Addr:** Professional Basketball Player, Charlotte Hornets, 1 Hive Dr., Charlotte, NC 28217, (704)357-0252.

ELLIS, MARILYN POPE
Educator. **Personal:** Born Jun 24, 1938, Newark, NJ; daughter of Gladys Hillman Pope and James Albert Pope; children: Kristina Pope. **Educ:** CA State Univ Hayward, BA 1969; Univ CA-Berkeley, MA 1972. **Career:** Peralta Community Coll, prof History 1973-76; Skyline Coll, prof History 1973-. **Honors/**

Awds: Third World Artist in the US 1983-84; Crossroads Africa & Parsons African Artists School of Design Ivory Coast & Craftspeople 1984. **Home Addr:** 67 Werner Ave, Daly City, CA 94014. **Business Addr:** Professor of History, Skyline College, 3300 College Dr, San Bruno, CA 94066.

ELLIS, MICHAEL G.
Industrial designer, educator. **Personal:** Born Oct 31, 1962, Detroit, MI; son of Cumire Roberston Ellis and Dave C. Ellis; married Marietta Kearney Ellis, May 25, 1991. **Educ:** Center for Creative Studies, Detroit, MI, BFA, 1984; Wayne State University, MBA program, currently. **Career:** Center for Creative Studies, Detroit, MI, instructor, 1989-91; Wayne State University, Detroit, MI, instructor, 1990; Ford Motor Company, Dearborn, MI, desinger, industrial designer, currently; Ford Motor Company, GHIA, Turin, Italy, designer; Ford of Germany, Cologne, Germany, designer. **Orgs:** Member, Porsche Club of America, 1989-; member, Founder's Society, Detroit Institute of Arts, 1990-. **Honors/Awds:** Concept Showcar Interior, Probe V, 1985; Concept Showcar, Aerostar exterior, 1986; Grand Marquis Exterior, 1991; holds FAA airplane and helicopter pilot license. **Business Addr:** Industrial Designer, Luxury Exterior Design Dept, Ford Motor Company, Design Center, Luxury Car Studio, 21175 Oakwood Blvd, Dearborn, MI 48123.

ELLIS, O. HERBERT
Educator. **Personal:** Born Mar 23, 1916, Chandler, OK; married Virginia Wilson; children: O Herbert Jr, Jeffrey W. **Educ:** Langston U, AB, AM, MPH 1940; Univ of Mi, Attend 1949. **Career:** TB & Health Soc, Detroit MI, sr health educ 1950-56; Michigan Health Council, vice chmn 1954-56; Wayne Co Inter-Agency Council, chmn 1955; Ann Arbor Public Schools, teacher 1985; Washtenaw County TB & Health Assn, pres 1959-61. **Orgs:** Mem, Wash Co Comm-Mental Hlth Bd 1966-; chmn, Wash Co Bd of Commr 1970; mem, Wash Co Bd of Commr 1959-; pres Sr Cit Guild 1974-75; mem, AnnArbor Rotary Clb 1964-; United Meth Ch 1956-. **Honors/Awds:** Recip, Ann Arbor Tchr of Yr Award 1969; 1st Black to serve as chair of Washtenaw Co Bd of Commr; v-chmn, chmn of bd, & various com, Wash Co Bd of Commr; selected as one of five pers to plan altern HS in Ann Arbor 1971. **Business Addr:** Co Bldg, Main at Huron, Ann Arbor, MI 48103.

ELLIS, P. J.
Clergyman. **Personal:** Born Sep 13, 1911, Alabama; widowed. **Career:** Morning Missionary Bapt Ch, minister 1985. **Orgs:** Pres, Bapt Ministers Conf of LA & So CA 1959-62, 1956-; moderator, LA Dist Assn 1959-68; bd dir 28th St YMCA 1957-; life mem, NAACP; parliamentarian, CA St Bapt Conv; mem, Nat Bapt Conv USA, Inc.

ELLIS, RODNEY
State senator, attorney and investment banker. **Personal:** Born Apr 7, 1954, Houston, TX; son of O Theresa Ellis and Eligha Ellis. **Educ:** TX Southern Univ, BA 1975; Univ of TX, MPA 1977; Univ of TX, JD 1979. **Career:** Lt Governor of TX, admin asst 1976-80; US Congress, admin asst 1981-83; Apex Securities Inc, president/chairman, 1987-; State of Texas, senator, currently; McGlinchey Stafford Lang, of counsel, 1995-. **Orgs:** State Bar of TX; Natl Bar Assoc; Amer Leadership Forum; TX Lyceum; board of directors, ARC, United Negro College Fund; Houston International University, Society for the Performing Arts; Houston READ Commission; Mickey Leland Ctr on World Hunger & Peace; mem, NAACP. **Honors/Awds:** Des Porres Scholarship 1972-73; Athletic Scholarship 1973-75; Lyndon B Johnson School of Public Affairs Fellowship 1975-77; Earl Warren Legal Training Fellowship 1977-79. **Business Addr:** Senator, State of Texas, 440 Louisiana, Ste 575, Houston, TX 77002.

ELLIS, TELLIS B., III
Physician. **Personal:** Born Dec 15, 1943, Jackson, MS; son of Lucinda Jenkins Ellis and Tellis B Ellis Jr; children: Tellis IV. **Educ:** Jackson State Univ, BS 1965; Meharry Medical Coll, MD 1970. **Career:** Meharry Medical Coll, straight medical internship 1970-71, internal medicine residency 1971-74; Univ Medical Ctr, cardiology fellowship 1975-77; Private Practice, physician; University of Mississippi Medical Center, Jackson, MS, asst clinical prof of medicine, currently. **Orgs:** Mem Jackson Medical Soc, Natl Medical Assoc, Assoc of Black Cardiologists, Kappa Alpha Psi Frat; past president, Mississippi Med & Surgical Assn. **Honors/Awds:** Fellow, American College of Cardiology; Hall of Fame, Jackson State University, 1987. **Business Addr:** Physician, Jackson Cardiology Associates, 971 Lakeland Dr, Suite 656, Jackson, MS 39216-4607.

ELLIS, ZACHARY L.
Industrial executive. **Career:** Ellis Enterprises, Kenner LA, chief exec. **Business Addr:** The Ellis Company, Inc, PO Box 1009, Kenner, LA 70063.

ELLISON, DAVID LEE
City administrator. **Personal:** Born Oct 11, 1955, Houston, TX; son of Alma L Shelton Ellison and L T Ellison Sr; married

Lethia Fanuiel Ellison, Oct 4, 1977; children: Dayna Leigh, Lyndsay Dalethia, Drew Leslye, Landon David Oran. **Educ:** North TX State Univ, BS, Secondary Educ, 1980; Univ of North TX, MA, Public Admin, 1988. **Career:** City of Denton, TX, urban planner, 1980-83, sr planner,1983-87, asst to the city mgr, 1987-89; City of Mankato, MN, asst city mgr, 1989-. **Orgs:** mem, Natl Forum for Black Public Administrators; Intl City Mgmt Assoc; Natl Trust for Historic Preservation; pres, North TX Chapter of Conf of Minority Public Admin, 1988; exec dir, City of Mankato & Blue Earth County Housing & Redevelopment Authorities, 1989-; Minnesota City Mgmt Assn; board of dictectors, National Community Development Association; board of directors, Greater Mankato Area United Way; board of directors, Mankato Area YMCA. **Honors/Awds:** Distinguished Serv Historical Preservation at the Cty Level TX Historical Comm, 1981. **Business Addr:** Asst City Mgr/ Community Development Dir, City of Mankato, 202 East Jackson, PO Box 3368, Mankato, MN 56003.

ELLISON, JERRY
Professional football player. **Personal:** Born Dec 20, 1971, Augusta, GA; married Loretta. **Educ:** Tennessee-Chattanooga, attended. **Career:** Tampa Bay Buccaneers, running back, 1995-. **Business Addr:** Professional Football Player, Tampa Bay Buccaneers, One Buccaneer Place, Tampa, FL 33607, (813)870-2700.

ELLISON, NOLEN M.
Educator. **Personal:** Born Jan 26, 1941, Kansas City, KS; married Carole; children: Marc, Steven. **Educ:** Kansas U, BS 1963; Hampton Inst, MA 1966; MI State U, PhD 1971. **Career:** Cuyahoga Community Coll Dist, chancellor; Seattle Central Community Coll Washington, pres 1972-74; Metropolitan Jr Coll Dist, Kansas City MO, asst chancellor 1971-72; MI State Univ, East Lansing MI, asst pres 1970-71; Kellogg Found Project, MI State Univ, admin intern; Urban Affairs MI State Univ, assoc dir center 1968-70; University of Missouri, Kansas City, director/professor of urban affairs, currently. **Orgs:** Mem Carnegie Council on Policy Studies in Higher Educ New York City 1973-; bd of overseers Morehouse Med Prog 1975; advisory bd ERIC Clearinghouse Jr Coll UCLA 1973-; bd dir Am Assn Community & Jr Colleges Assn; Governing Boards Univ & Coll; pres adv com 1974-; exec bd N Central Assoc of Coll & Schs 1977; Phi Delta Kappa mem 1968-. **Honors/Awds:** Recipient Nat Jaycees Award; Ten Outstanding Young Men of America 1974. **Business Addr:** Director/Professor of Urban Affairs, Bloch School of Business and Public Administration, University of Missouri, Kansas City, Kansas City, MO 64110.

ELLISON, PAULINE ALLEN
Federal personnel administrator, business executive. **Personal:** Born in Iron Gate, VA; married Oscar Ellison Jr; children: Oscar III, Michele, Karla. **Educ:** Amer Univ, M in Pub Admin; attended Howard Univ, Georgetown Univ, Fed Exec Inst. **Career:** No VA Chap Jack & Jill of Amer, fdr pres 1963-69; Dept of Housing & Comm Develop, dir of personnel DC redevel land agency; Links Inc, natl prog dir 1970-74; Arling Chap Links Inc, vice pres; admin, cons, natl pres 1974-78; Drs Johnson & Ellison Ltd, consultant. **Orgs:** Chmn membership bd of dir Fed Exec Inst Alumni Assn 1972-76; mem bd of dirs Natl Conf of Christians and Jews 1978-87 chmn Ethics Comm and chmn Outreach Comm; sec bd of dir Burgundy Farm Country Day Sch; mem drafting comm Black Econ Summit Meeting; chmn Personnel Policy Com Burgundy Farm Country Day Sch; pres Girls 4-H Club; pres Debating & Literary Club; pres Sr Class; youth leader Baptist Young Peoples Union & Bapt Training Union; mem Amer Soc of Public Admin; Natl Assn of Housing & Redcevel Ofcls; Natl Assn of Suggestion Sys; life mem NAACP; vice pres Arlington Comm TV 1986-87; pres Inter Serv Club Cncl 1986-87; pres Northern VA Chap Minority Political Women 1986-87; adv comm Arlington Hospital, Northern VA Junior League. **Honors/Awds:** Beta Kappa Chi Natl Honor Sci Soc 1949; 1st Black Woman Employee Relat & Mgmt Splst Housing & Urban Devel 1965; 1st Black Woman Dir of Personnel for Fed Agency 1968; Outstanding Grp Performance Awd 1972; Outstanding Perfmc Awd Personnel Admin 1972-76; Disting Achvmt Awd Fed Exec Inst 1974; Disting-Youth Serv Awd 1974; Disting Serv Awd Fed Exec Inst 1974; Outstanding Serv Awd Mayor of Washington 1975; Key to City of Roanoke 1975; Seal to City ofWashington 1976; 100 Most Influential Blacks Ebony Mag 1976-78; Disting Serv Awd Mayor of Washington 1976; Hon Degree Dr of Humanities Wilberforce Univ 1976; commendation Pres of US 1977; Disting Leadership Awd The Links Inc 1978; Leadership Awd Alpha Phi Alpha Frat 1978;Hon Dr of Humane Letters Livingstone Coll 1979; elected Pi Alpha Alpha Hon Somer Univ; One of Eight Civil Rights Leaders to Advise Pres of US; winner State Oratorical Contest; Readers Digest Awd; Danforth Found Awd; numerous scholastic & civic awds; Jack and Jill Awd for Outstanding Serv 1981; apptd commissioner Arlington Civil Serv Commn 1983-87; Woman of the Yr Arlington 1986. **Business Addr:** Consultant, Drs Johnson & Ellison Ltd, 2767 Annandale Rd, Falls Church, VA 22042.

ELLISON, PERVIS
Professional basketball player. **Personal:** Born Apr 3, 1967, Savannah, GA; married Timi; children: Seattle, Aja, Malik. **Educ:**

Univ of Louisville, bachelor's degree in criminal justice. **Career:** Sacramento Kings, forward-center, 1989-90; Washington Bullets, 1990-94; Boston Celtics, 1994-. **Honors/Awds:** Member of NCAA Division I championship team, 1986; Outstanding Player in NCAA Division I tournament, 1986; NBA Most Improved Player, 1992. **Business Addr:** Professional Basketball Player, Boston Celtics, 151 Merrimac St, 5th Fl, Boston, MA 02114, (617)523-6050.

ELLISON, ROBERT A.
Attorney. **Personal:** Born Jan 21, 1915, Winnsboro, SC; children: Robert, Charles. **Educ:** NY City Coll, Ab 1941; Brooklyn Law School, JD 1952. **Career:** NY City Police Dept, detective 1942-61; NY City, private practice, atty 1961-65; Bronx School Dist, teacher 1963-65, prinicpal 1965; Dept of Public Safety VI, asst commr 1965-67; Dept of Law VI, asst atty general 1967-69; Police Science & Business Law Coll VI, instructor 1968-82; Dept of Public Safety VI, commr 1969-71, private practice, atty 1971-78; CA State Univ, instructor 1982-. **Orgs:** Past chmn VI Parole Bd; past commiss VI Publ Serv Commiss; past pres VI Bar Assoc; asst attny gen VI Dept of Law; chief Criminal/Family Law Div; mem Amer Arbitration Assoc, Intl Assoc Chiefs Police, Natl Bar Assoc, Rotary Intl; chmn, parole bd VI Publ Serv Commiss; mem VI Bar Assoc.

ELLISS, LUTHER
Professional football player. **Educ:** University of Utah. **Career:** Detroit Lions, 1995-. **Special Achievements:** Selected in the 1st round/20th overall pick in the 1995 NFL Draft. **Business Addr:** Professional Football Player, Detroit Lions, 1200 Featherstone Rd, Pontiac, MI 48342, (810)335-4131.

ELLOIS, EDWARD R., JR.
Educator. **Personal:** Born May 3, 1922, Ventress, LA; married Evelyn Reese; children: Joseph Bernard. **Educ:** Seattle U, BS; Univ of IL, MA; Univ of OK, Doctorate. **Career:** St Francisville Elementary School LA, prin; Southern Univ Baton Rouge, assoc prof Educ, coordinator elementary student teacher; Coll Educ Southern Univ Baton Rouge LA, prof Educ & assoc dean; Workshops in LA, TX & OK, cons; Southern Methodist Univ Dallas, speaker; Arlington State Coll TX, dir student teaching conf seminars & workshops; SW Center for Human Relations Studies Consultative Center Coll of Continuing Educ, Univ of OK, Norman OK, grad asst. **Orgs:** Asst dir EPDA Inst in English; Alpha Kappa Delta; Kappa Phi Kappa; Phi Delta Kappa; Pi Gammu Mu; Psi Chi; Kappa Alpha Psi Frat; Am Assn Coll for Tchr Edn; Am Asn of Univ Profs; LA Educ Assn; sec Council of Academic Deans So Univ Baton Rouge; Kiwani Interant N Baton Rouge Early Rises Club; second vice pres Kappa Phi Kappa Nat Professional Frat in Educ for Men; Outstanding Educators of Am 1971; Intl & Biography of Educators; Leaders in Black Am; mem Holy Name Soc Immaculate Conception Ch; mem Knights of Peter Claver; St Agnes Council #12 Baton Rouge; vice pres Confraternity of Christian Doctrine Immaculate Conception Parish; Bishop's Adv Council; The Diocese of Baton Rouge LA; mem Lay Council; Diocesan Social Responsibility Bd. **Military Serv:** AUS 1st sgt 1942-46. **Business Addr:** PO Box 9634, Baton Rouge, LA 70813.

ELLSWORTH, PERCY
Professional football player. **Personal:** Born Oct 19, 1974. **Educ:** Univ of Virginia, attended. **Career:** New York Giants, defensive back, 1996-. **Business Addr:** Professional Football Player, New York Giants, Giants Stadium, East Rutherford, NJ 07073, (201)935-8111.

ELMORE, ERNEST ERIC
Attorney. **Personal:** Born Aug 21, 1964, Jamaica, NY; son of Sheila Elmore. **Educ:** Cornell University, AB, 1986; Cornell Law School, JD, 1989. **Career:** Federal Trade Commission, attorney, 1990-. **Orgs:** Alpha Phi Alpha Fraternity, Inc, 1983-; National Bar Association, 1988-. **Home Addr:** 8750 Georgia Ave, #1409B, Silver Spring, MD 20910. **Business Addr:** General Attorney, Federal Trade Commission, 6th & Pennsylvania Ave, NW, Washington, DC 20580.

ELMORE, STEPHEN A., SR.
Auditor. **Personal:** Born Feb 24, 1952, Montgomery, AL; son of Margaret L Elmore and Clinton R Elmore Sr; married Linda J Pryor, Jun 9, 1973; children: Stephen Jr, Dana Pryor, Jonathan Clinton. **Educ:** Morehouse College, BA, 1973. **Career:** Arthur Andersen & Co, staff auditor, 1973-75, sr auditor, 1975-78, audit manager, 1978-80; First Atlanta Corp (acquired by Wachovia Corp in 1985), assistant director of audit, 1980-83, general auditor, 1983-, deputy general auditor, 1987-. **Orgs:** AICPA, 1977-; Georgia Society of CPA's, 1978-; National Association of Black Accountants, 1978-; 100 Black Men of Atlanta, 1991-; American Diabetes Association, director, 1992; University Community Development Corp, director, 1991-; Atlanta-Fulton County Zoo, Inc, finance committee, 1985-91; Institute of Internal Auditors, 1985-. **Business Addr:** Deputy General Auditor, Wachovia Corp., 191 Peachtree St NE, Ste 713, Atlanta, GA 30303, (404)332-5078.

ELMORE ARCHER, JOYCE A.
Nurse, educator. **Personal:** Born Dec 18, 1937, Newton Falls, OH; married Robert A Archer, Sr. **Educ:** Howard U, 1955-56; Freedmen's Hosp Sch of Nursing, Diploma 1958; Santa Monica City Coll, 1959-60; Cath Univ of Am, BSN 1962; Cath Univ of Am, MSN 1965; Cath Univ of Am, PhD 1974. **Career:** Coll of Nursing, Chicago State Univ, dean; Amer Nurses Assn Dept of Nursing Educ, dir; DHHS Office of Family Planning, dir of training 1978-. **Orgs:** Mem ANA; NLN; Howard Univ Alumni Assn; Freedmen's Hosp Scho of Nursing Alumni Assn Inc; Cath Univ Sch of Nursing Alumni Assn; Assn for Educ Communications & Technology; past pres Nurses' Exam Bd of DC; mem Commd Officers Assn; mem Ebenezer AME Ch; pres, Elmore Enterprises Inc 1984-; bd chair Pearl Investors Inc 1986-87; pres, bd chair NorBrooke Knolls Ctr, Inc, 1996-. **Honors/Awds:** Author of various professional articles & publications; recipient of many scholarships for higher edn; "Miss Mecca Temple No 10", 1957; "Miss Capitol Classic", 1957; Comm Serv Award 1973; Chief Nurse Badge USAFR 1978; Commendation Medal USPHS Commd Corps 1980; Outstanding Alumni Achievement Awd, Howard Univ, 1978; Cert of Appreciation, US Dept of Transportation, US Coast Guard, 1983; Plaque of Appreciation, Major General Natl Guard, 1991; Plaque, VA State Univ, Trojan Warrior Battalion Reserve Officer's Training Corps, 1991; Outstanding Nursing Research, Freedmen's Hosp Nurses' Alumni Clubs, Inc, 1991; Public Citation, Howard Univ Coll of Medicine Alumni Assn, 1992; Outstanding Svc Awd, Senegal Friendship Comm, 1992; One of 100 Extra Ordinary Nurses, Sigma Theta Tau Intl Honor Society, 1992; PHS Citation Awd, OASH Awards Prog, 1991; Scholarship & Outstanding Dedicated Avc, McKendree United Methodist Ch, 1991; Community Action Awd, DC Nurses Assn, 1991; Exceptional Sensitivity & Resourcefulness Awd, Howard Univ, 1992; Outstanding Achievements, Alpha Kappa Alpha, 1992; 1st African American Youth Awd, NAAYI, 1992; Outstanding Comm Svc Awd, Alpha Kappa Alpha, 1994; Recognition Plaque, Bureau of Primary Health Carre, 1993-94; Cert of Recognition, Howard Univ Coll of Medicine, 1994; DHHS/PHS Unit Commendation, 1994; Cert of Appreciation, US Public Health Svc, 1994; The Crisis Response Svc Awd, Acting Surgeon General Audrey F Manley, DHHS, PHS, 1996. **Military Serv:** USAFR flight nurse capt-maj 1971-78; USPHS Commd Corps capt, nurse dir 0-6 1986-. **Business Addr:** Sr Program Management Officer, National Health Service Corp., HRSA/BPHC, 4350 East West Hwy, Rm 8-6A-1, Bethesda, MD 20814.

ELZY, AMANDA BELLE
Educator (retired). **Personal:** Born in Pontotoc, MS; daughter of Mr & Mrs Charles Elzy. **Educ:** Rust Coll, AB 1938; IN U, MS 1953; Univ MS, 1968-69. **Career:** Leflore Co Sch, asst supt 1968-, supr 1938-68. **Orgs:** Mem Ford Found Ldrsp Flws Prgm; Talent Search Prgm; Early Childhood Educ Univ TX; mem MS Assn of Edcrs; Nat Cncl of Newgro Women; Am Assn of SchAdminstr; Leflore & Co Tchr Assn; MS Library Assn; State Federated Clubs - Zeta Phi Beta - Sor; Assn of Supr & Curriculum Devel. **Honors/Awds:** Amanda Elzy Sch named in hon Leflore Co Sch Bd of Educ 1959; Zeta Woman of Yr Gamma Gamma Zeta Chap Zeta Phi Beta 1967; Outst Educator of Am 1970; Cert of Achievement, Am Assn of Sch Adminstr 1970; HHD Rust Coll 1973; Distinguished Educator of the Year Phi Delta Kappa 1979; Outstanding Community Service Award MS Valley State Univ 1979. **Home Addr:** 116 Azalea Dr, Columbus, MS 39701-1789.

EMANUEL, BERT TYRONE
Professional football player. **Personal:** Born Oct 27, 1970, Kansas City, MO; married Teri; children: Sydni Brook, Cortni. **Educ:** Rice University, bachelor's degree in business. **Career:** Atlanta Falcons, wide receiver, 1994-. **Business Addr:** Professional Football Player, Atlanta Falcons, Two Falcon Place, Suwanee, GA 30174, (404)945-1111.

EMBREE, JAMES ARLINGTON
Educator (retired). **Personal:** Born Jan 18, 1934, New York City, NY; son of Sylvia Embree and James Embree; married Judith Aasum; children: Karen Secrest, Paul, Leslie Carmichael, Bruce. **Educ:** San Jose State Univ, BA 1960; Sacto State Univ, MA 1984. **Career:** Alameda Co Probation, probation officer 1960-62; CA Youth Authority, parole agent 1962-72, sup/adm 1967-74, superintendent 1976-84; Sacramento City College, professor, 1988-96. **Orgs:** Regional vice pres 1978-80, chair planning & scope 1983-84 CA Probation Parole & Correc Assn; mem San Jose Univ Varsity Basketball Team 1957-60; vol Downs Meml Ch Counseling Prog 1961-64; mem Assn Black Correctional Workers CA 1971-; mem human serv adv comm Amer River Jr Coll 1978-; president, California Probation, Parole Correctional Assn, 1990-91. **Honors/Awds:** Presidential Unit Citation USMC; Credential Jr Coll Lifetime CA Dept of Educ 1978; In Appreciation-Senate Resolution #16 CA Legislature 1980. **Military Serv:** USMC sgt 1st class 1952-56. **Home Addr:** 6423 Puerto Dr, Sloughhouse, CA 95683-9361.

EMBRY, WAYNE, SR.
Professional sports administrator, business executive. **Personal:** Born 1937, Springfield, OH; married Terri; children: Debbi, Jill, Wayne Jr. **Educ:** Miami Univ Oxford OH, BS Educ. **Career:** Cincinnati Royals, professional basketball player 1958-66; Boston Celtics, professional basketball player 1966-68; Milwaukee Bucks, professional basketball player 1968-69, vice pres and genl mgr, vice pres and consultant 1977-85; Indiana Pacers, vice pres and basketball consultant 1985-86; Cleveland Cavaliers, vice pres and genl mgr of basketball opers, currently; Michael Alan Lewis Co, chief executive, currently. **Honors/Awds:** Mem ABU-USA Olympic Basketball Player Selection Comm for US Olympic Team; mem Miami Univ Hall of Fame; first black named to a top front-office position in the NBA and one of the first in professional sports.

EMEAGWALI, DALE BROWN
Researcher. **Personal:** Born Dec 24, 1954, Baltimore, MD; daughter of Johnnie Doris Brown and Leon Robert Brown; married Philip Emeagwali, Aug 15, 1981; children: Ijeoma. **Educ:** Coppin State College, BA, biology, 1976; Georgetown University, PhD, microbiology, 1981. **Career:** National Institutes of Health, postdoctoral fellow, 1981-84; Uniformed Services University of Health Sciences, postdoctoral fellow, 1985-86; University of Wyoming, research associate, 1986-87; University of Michigan, senior research fellow, 1987-88, asst research scientist, 1989-91; University of Minnesota, research associate, 1992-95; Morgan State Univ, 1996-. **Orgs:** Sigma Xi, 1983-; American Assn for the Advancement of Science, 1985-. **Honors/Awds:** Meharry Medical College, Biomedical Fellowship Award, 1974; Beta Kappa Chi and the National Institute of Science, 3rd Place Award, Best Presentation, 1976; Coppin State College, Biomedical Research Award, 1976; National Science Foundation, Postdoctoral Fellowship Award, 1981; American Cancer Society, Postdoctoral Fellowship Award, 1981. **Special Achievements:** Co-author: "Evidence of a Constitutive and Inducible Form of Kynurenine Formamidase," Archives of Biochem Biophysics, 1980; "Sequence Homology Between the Structural Proteins of Kilham Rat Virus," Journal of Virol, 1984; "Purification and Characterization of Kynurenine Formamidase Activity from S Paravulus," Canadian Journal of Microbiology, 1986; "Modulation of Ras Expression by Antisense Non-ionic Deoxyoligonucleotide Analogues," Journal of Gene Research, 1989; "Amplified Expression of Three Jun Family Members Inhibits Erytholeukemia Differentiation Blood," 1990; National Technical Society, Scientist of the Year, 1996. **Home Addr:** 3713 Sylvan Dr, Baltimore, MD 21207-6364.

EMEAGWALI, PHILIP
Educator, mathematician, computer scientist. **Personal:** Born Aug 23, 1954, Akure, Nigeria; son of Agatha I Emeagwali and James N Emeagwali; married Dale Brown, Aug 15, 1981; children: Ijeoma. **Educ:** University of London, general certificate of education, 1973; Oregon State University, BS, mathematics, 1977; George Washington University, MS, civil engineering, 1981, engineer degree, ocean, costal and marine, 1986; University of Maryland, MA, applied mathematics, 1986; University of Michigan at Ann Arbor, PhD, scientific computing, 1993. **Career:** Maryland State Highway Administration, various highway engineering duties, 1977-78; George Washington University, researcher, 1979-82; US National Weather Service/University of Maryland, researcher, 1984-86; US Bureau of Reclamation, civil engineering and research mathematics duties, 1986-87; University of Michigan at Ann Arbor, researcher, 1987-91; University of Minnesota, Army High Performance Computing Research Center, research fellow, 1991-93; Independent Consultant, 1993-. **Orgs:** Institute of Electrical and Electronic Engineers' Computer Society; Association for Computing Machinery; Society for Industrial and Applied Mathematics; National Technical Association, advisory board; American Physical Society; Institute of Electrical and Electronics Engineers; Geoscience and Remote Sensing Society; American Meteorological Society; Natl Society of Black Engineers; Natl Society of Professional Engineers; Professional Communication Society; Society for Technical Communication; Aircraft Owners and Pilots Assn; US Parachute Assn; Balloon Federation of America; Natl Aeronautic Assn; American Inst of Aeronautics and Astronautics; Aerospace and Electronic Systems Society; Natl Air & Space Museum; Underwater Explorers Society. **Honors/Awds:** Institute of Electrical and Electronics Engineers' Society, Gordon Bell Prize, 1989, IEEE Computer Society, Distinguished Visitor, 1993-96; Natl Society of Black Engineers, Distinguished Scientist Award, 1991; Tau Beta Pi Natl Engineering Honor Society, Eminent Engineer, 1994; Natl Technical Assn, Computer Scientist of the Year Award, 1993; Minority Technology Council of Michigan, Intl Man of the Year Award, 1994; Mobil Corp and US Black Engineer Mag, Certificate of Recognition Award, 1991, 1992; Science Museum of Minnesota, Certificate of Appreciation Award, 1994. **Business Addr:** Independent Consultant, 3713 Sylvan Dr, Baltimore, MD 21207-6364.

EMEKA, MAURIS L. P.
Business executive. **Personal:** Born Apr 4, 1941, Fargo, AR; married Sunday A Bacon; children: Amon, Gabriel, Justin. **Educ:** Univ of KS, BA 1961; Univ of WA, MBA 1970. **Career:** Bike Master Inc, Pres; Bicycle Store, owner; Black Econ Union Kansas City, asst dir; Black Econ Reserach Cntr NY, asst dir. **Honors/Awds:** Author of book and articles on Black & Banks. **Military Serv:** USAF capt 1962-67. **Business Addr:** 11 Bennett Rd, Englewood, NJ 07631.

EMMANUEL, TSEGAI
Educational administrator. **Personal:** Born Mar 27, 1940; son of Ghebray Leteyesus and G. Hiwet Emmanuel; married Karen Emmanuel; children: Sarah, Ribka. **Educ:** OK State Univ, BS 1968, MBA 1970; Univ of Missouri, PhD 1978; University of Minnesota, diploma, 1986. **Career:** United Nations Economic Commission for Africa, African Statistical Analysis Department, Addis Ababa, Ethiopia, head, 1960-63; Lincoln University, Jefferson City, MO, assistant professor, 1970-79, director of International Student Affairs, 1974-76. Eastern Washington State University, Cheney, WA, assistant professor, 1976-77, associate professor, 1977-80; Washington State University, Pullman, WA, adjunct professor, 1979-80; Grambling State University, professor/dean of College of Business, 1980-. **Orgs:** American Assembly of Collegiate Schools of Business; Southwest Business Administration Association; Southwest Federation of Administrative Disciplines; Secretary of State Commission on Corporations, State of Louisiana; The Louisiana Council on Black Economic Development; Grambling Chamber of Commerce; Grambling Economic Development Council. **Home Addr:** 708 Hundred Oaks Drive, Ruston, LA 71270. **Business Addr:** Dean, College of Business, Grambling State University, PO Box 848, Grambling, LA 71245.

EMMONS, CARLOS
Professional football player. **Personal:** Born Sep 3, 1973, Greenwood, MS. **Educ:** Arkansas State Univ. **Career:** Pittsburgh Steelers, linebacker, 1996-. **Business Addr:** Professional Football Player, Pittsburgh Steelers, Three Rivers Stadium, 300 Stadium Circle, Pittsburgh, PA 15212, (412)323-1200.

EMMONS, DONALD RAY
Journalist. **Personal:** Born Feb 11, 1965, Gary, IN; son of Genora Darby Emmons and Leander Terry Emmons. **Educ:** Indiana University, Bloomington, IN, BA, Journalism & Sociology, 1983-87. **Career:** Gary Post-Tribune, Gary, IN, sportswriter, 1987; Fort Wayne News-Sentinel, Fort Wayne, IN, reporter, 1987-89; Glendale News Press, Glendale, CA, sportswriter, 1989-. **Orgs:** Member, National Association of Black Journalists, 1990-; secretary/member, Association of Minority Journalists, Indiana University, 1984-87.

EMMONS, RAYFORD E.
Clergyman. **Personal:** Born Jun 25, 1948, Philadelphia, PA. **Educ:** St Charles Seminary, BA 1970; Interdenom Theol, attended. **Career:** Field work experience in parochial schools, hospitals, comm & parish church activities; Atlanta Univ, asst Catholic chaplain 1972; St Patrics Church Norristown, asst pastor 1974-; Most Blessed Sanament Church, asst pastor 1978-80; St Elizabeth Church Philadelphia, asst pastor 1980-. **Orgs:** Mem natl Black Seminarians Assoc 1970-73, Natl Black Catholic Clergy Caucus 1974-; affiliate Natl Black Catholic Lay Caucus. **Honors/Awds:** Several appearances on local & natlTV progs; speaker at civic & religious group affairs; featured in local newspapers; formerly involved in prison, hospital& youth work; 1st black priest ordained for Archdiocese of Philadelphia 1974. **Business Addr:** St Elizabeth Church, Philadelphia, PA 19143.

EMORY, EMERSON
Physician, psychiatrist. **Personal:** Born Jan 29, 1925, Dallas, TX; son of Louise Linthecum Emory and Corry Bates Emory; married Peggy Lillian Herald; children: Sharon, Karon Hutchinson, Emerson Jr. **Educ:** Prairie View A&M Univ TX, 1940-42; Lincoln Univ PA, BA (Cum Laude) 1948; Meharry Medical Coll TN, MD 1952; Univ of TX Sch of Public Health, 1983-84; Southern Methodist Univ Law, 1956-57; Texas Southern Univ Law, 1957-58. **Career:** VA Hospitals Dallas and McKinney, staff physician 1957-60; Terrell State Hosp Terrell, TX, staff psychiatrist 1969-71; Federal Correct Institution Seagoville, TX, chief psychiatric serv 1971-72; Private Practice, physician/psychiatrist; Texas Dept of Human Services, consultant 1988-; Liberty Mutual Insurance Co, Las Colinas, TX, staff physician 1988-; Bridgeport Pre-Release Center, Bridgeport, TX, psychiatrist 1989-92; Paul Quinn College, Dallas, TX, director, student health 1991-94. **Orgs:** Volunteer physician to Viet Nam Agency for Intl Development 1966; founder/past pres Natl Naval Officers Assn 1972; pres Dallas Council USO 1972; candidate for TX State Legislative 1974; candidate for Mayor of Dallas 1975-77; founder/past pres WA/Lincoln Alumni Assn 1976; administrator Forest Ave Comm Hosp Dallas 1983-84; founder/pres Clarence H. Harris Fraternal Order of Elks, Inc. 1987-; mem Prometheaus, Inc. 1945-; perpetual member Military Order of World Wars 1987-; fellow Academy of Psychosomatic Medicine; mem, Secr of Navy Advisory Comm on Retired Personnel, 1992-95; regional coordinator, US Navy Academy Blue & Gold Prog, 1972-75; Dallas Black Living Legend in Medicine, 1987; mem Black Citizens for Justice, Law and Order. **Honors/Awds:** Certified Correctional Health Care Professional, 1993-; Fellow in Psychiatry Univ of TX Southwest Med Sch Dallas 1966-69; Outstanding Alumni Award Lincoln Univ PA 1968; Humanitarian Award Amer Med Assn 1966; Appreciation Award State Dept (Agency for Intl Development) 1966; Publisher/Editor "Freedom's Journal" 1979-; Certificate of Appreciation for service in World War II, President of US and Congressional Black Caucus, 1994; Legacy for Story on Benny Benion; Famous Poets Award, 1996. **Special Achievements:** Appointment to Advisory Committee, Adult Protective Services, Texas Dept of Human Services, 1994. **Military Serv:** US Army Corporal served 3 yrs; USNR Captain 30 yrs; ETO-AP-Philippine Liberation WWII Victory Medal; Armed Forces Reserve Medal with 2 Hour Glass Devices. **Home Addr:** 4931 W Mockingbird Ln, Dallas, TX 75209. **Business Addr:** Psychiatrist, 2606 Martin L King Blvd, Dallas, TX 75215, (214)421-8333.

ENDERS, MURVIN S.
Company executive. **Personal:** Born May 19, 1942; son of Ruth King Enders and Murvin Enders Sr; married Linda; children: Murvin III, Kevin, Erik. **Educ:** Fisk University, Nashville, TN, BA, 1962; University of Indianapolis, IN, MBA, 1981. **Career:** Chrysler Corporation, Indianapolis, IN, various positions, 1962-77, personnel mgr, 1977-81, prod facilities engr manager, 1981-83, shift superintendent, 1983-84, manager of manufacturing engineer, 1984-86, production manager, 1986-89, plant manager, 1989-95; IWC Resources, vice president of administrative affairs, currently. **Orgs:** Goodwill board of directors; Economic Development Commission; Methodist Hospital Foundation, board of directors; Christian Theological Seminary, board of directors; Board of Church Extension, board of directors; NAACP, lifetime member; Circle City Frontiers Service Club; Alpha Phi Alpha Fraternity; Sigma Pi Phi Fraternity; 100 Black Men of Indianapolis. **Honors/Awds:** LWCC Outstanding Achievement Recognition, 1988; Center for Leadership Development Business Achievement Award, 1989; Indianapolis Star Newspaper Family Album Feature, 1989; Children's Museum Generations Exhibit Family Feature, 1990; Frontiers Drum Major Recognition, 1990; Fisk University, Outstanding Alumni Award for Community Service, 1991; Foundry Management and Technology Hall of Honor, inductee, 1992; Living Legend in Black Honoree, 1993; Urban League Family of the Year, 1993; Indiana Academy, inductee, 1997. **Business Addr:** VP of Administrative Affairs, IWC Resources, 1220 Waterway Blvd, Indianapolis, IN 46202, (317)263-6325.

ENGLAND, ERIC JEVON
Professional football player. **Personal:** Born Apr 25, 1971, Fort Wayne, IN. **Educ:** Texas A&M. **Career:** Arizona Cardinals, defensive end, 1994-96; Tennessee Oilers, 1997-. **Business Addr:** Professional Football Player, Tennessee Oilers, c/o Baptist Sports Park, 7640 H 70-5, Nashville, TN 37221.

ENGLAND, RODNEY WAYNE
Physician. **Personal:** Born Jun 24, 1932, Mounds, IL; son of Katie England and Lois England; married Patricia R Shipp; children: Rodney, Michael, Stephen, John, Sarah. **Educ:** Univ of Illinois, BS 1954, MD 1956. **Career:** Univ of Minnesota, clinical assoc prof internal medicine 1978-; Private practice, physician beginning 1962; Health End Clinics-Internal Medicine, 1993-. **Orgs:** Diplomate Amer Bd of Internal Medicine 1964; bd of dirs Health East Corp. **Military Serv:** USAF captain 1957-59. **Business Addr:** 17 W Exchange, St Paul, MN 55102.

ENGLISH, ALBERT J.
Professional basketball player. **Personal:** Born Jul 11, 1967, Wilmington, DE. **Educ:** Virginia Union Univ, Richmond, VA, 1986-90. **Career:** Washington Bullets, 1990-. **Business Addr:** Professional Basketball Player, Washington Wizards, One Harry S Truman Dr, Capital Centre, Landover, MD 20785-4798.

ENGLISH, ALEX
Association administrator. **Personal:** Born Jan 5, 1954, Columbia, SC. **Educ:** University of South Carolina. **Career:** Milwaukee Bucks, 1976-78; Indiana Pacers, 1978-79; Denver Nuggets, 1980-90; Dallas Mavericks, 1990; Italian League, 1991; NBA Players Association, director of player programs and services, 1992-. **Honors/Awds:** NBA All-Star Game 1982, 1983. **Business Addr:** Director, Player Programs and Services, NBA Players Association, 1775 Broadway, Ste 2401, New York, NY 10019.

ENGLISH, CLARENCE R.
City official. **Personal:** Born Sep 11, 1915, Morrilton, AR; son of Lydia Pledger English and William English; married Alpha Talley, Jun 16, 1934; children: Dorothy Brown, Clarence II, Loretta Choate, Joseph, James, Carol Hall, Paul. **Educ:** Black Mayor's Workshops. **Career:** 3M Co, Little Rock AR, mechanic (retired), 1955-80; City of Menifee, mayor, 1979-. **Orgs:** Bd mem, West Central Planning, Bible School teacher, Church of Christ, chaplin, NAACP, 1960's; pres, PTA, 1960's; mem, Black Mayors Assn, 1980's; exec comm, HR Municipal League, 1980-89. **Honors/Awds:** Grants received for City Parks, City Hall, Municipal Water Works, Streets; Certificate of Appreciation, 1955; Outstanding Community Ser, 1966; Distinguished Leadership, City of Menifee, 1986. **Home Addr:** PO Box 8, Menifee, AR 72107-0008.

ENGLISH, DEBORAH
Financial services executive. **Career:** Chrysler First Inc., Allentown, PA, director of operations administration, currently. **Orgs:** General chair, United Negro College Fund, 1991-92; board of directors, American Red Cross, 1986-88; executive committee, Obsidian Inc, 1987-88; member, National Association of Urban Bankers, 1985-; member, American Bankers, 1987-90. **Honors/Awds:** Speaking of People, Ebony Magazine, 1989; On the Move, Black Enterprise, 1989; Management in Service Sector, Wharton School, University of Pennsylvania, 1987. **Business Addr:** Director of Operations Administration, Nations Credit, 225 E John Carpenter Fwy, Ste 800, Irving, TX 75062-2732.

ENGLISH, HENRY L.
Association executive. **Personal:** Born May 27, 1942, West Point, MS; son of Julie Pearl Smith and Flozell English; married Denise Tulloch English, Sep 11, 1989; children: Nkrumah, Kenya, Jumanne, Kamilah. **Educ:** Malcolm X College, Chicago, IL, University of New Hampshire, Durban, NH, BA, 1972; Cornell University, Graduate School of Management, Ithaca, NY, MPA, 1974. **Career:** Kittrell College, Kittrell, NC, asst dir, development director of admission, 1974-75; Jackson Park Hospital, Chicago, IL, assistant administrator, 1975-77; South Chicago Community Hospital, Chicago, IL, director of planning & marketing, 1977-85; Black United Fund of Illinois, Chicago, IL, president/CEO, 1985-. **Orgs:** Co-Chairman, United Black Voters of Illinois, 1977-79; president, COMPRAND Inc, 1981-85; president, Coalition to Save the South Shore Country Club, 1980-84; Calumet District Commissioner, Boy Scouts of America, 1982-84; vice president, South Shore Commission, 1989-. **Honors/Awds:** Fellowship, Woodrow Wilson National Fellowship Foundation, 1972-74; Award for Service to the Community of Retarded Children, Mau-Glo Day Center, 1982; Governor's Service Award, State of Illinois, 1982; Leadership Service Award, Boy Scouts of America, 1983; Leadership Service Award, Coalition to Save the South Shore Country Club, 1983. **Military Serv:** US Marine Corps, CPL, 1961-66; Good Conduct Medal. **Business Addr:** President & CEO, Black United Fund of Illinois, 2302 E 71st St, Chicago, IL 60649.

ENGLISH, KENNETH
Government official. **Personal:** Born Jul 29, 1947, Waycross, GA; children: Crystal Denise, Constance MaryAlice, Kenneth II. **Educ:** Morehouse Coll Atlanta; GA State Univ Atlanta. **Career:** US Dept of Labor, regional rep region IV 1978-. **Orgs:** Pres United Rubber Workers Union Local 887 1969-78; vP GA State AFL-CIO 1972-78; mem Atlanta & Assn of Fed Exec 1978-; mem Indsl Relation Research Assn 1979-; mem of bd So Labor History Assn 1979-; bd of Dir & personnel com Urban League Albany Chap 1970-78; del 1974 Mini-Conv of the Nat Dem Party 1974; sec State Charter Commn GA Dem Party 1974-75; chmn 2nd cong dist Affirmative Action Com GA Dem Party 1975-77; mem GA State Employment & TngCounsel 1975-77; sec Albany-Dougherty Com NAACP Branch 1976-78; mem Dougherty Co Dem Com 1976-78; mem A Philip Randolph Inst Albany Chap 1976-; chmn Auditing Com GA Dem Party 1977-7 8; chmn personnel com Albany Urban League 1977-78; mem GA State Crime Commn 1977-78; mem Nat & Honor Soc Alpha Lambda Delta GSU 1979; mem Select Comon Revision of GA Statenst 1979; vice pres Labor Studies Student Assn GSU 1979-. **Honors/Awds:** Nominated for Who's Who in Am Nat Jaycees 1976.

ENGLISH, MARION S.
Business executive (retired). **Personal:** Born Jul 23, 1912, Jacksonville, FL; married Johnnye P Mitchell; children: Joyce Andrews. **Educ:** NY U, MA; Talladega Coll, BA. **Career:** Consolidated Edison Co, consultant 1978-, personnel mgr 1972-75; Public Affairs Westchester Div, ret asst 1972-78; vice pres Public Affairs Westchester Div Consolidated Edison Co of NY Inc 1972-; Urban Affairs, gen, mrg, former mgr 1969-72; NY State Narcotic Addiction Control Commn, comm relations specialist 1968-69; Civil Rights Compliance & EEO, special asst to commnr on aging in charge 1966-68-; Youth Serv Co Exec Westchester Co, special asst 1962-66; Urban League of Westchester Inc, exec dir 1956-62; Urban League of Greater Boston, exec dir 1954-56; YMCA, Mt Vernon NY, Harrisburg PA, Brooklyn NY, executive 1939-49. **Orgs:** Mem Rotary Club to White Plains; NY C of C; Westchester Clubmen & Found; mem Rotary Club; Zeta Boule Sigma Pi Phi Frat; former asso trustee St Agnes Hosp White Plains NY 1980-88. **Honors/Awds:** Recip Achievement, Annual NY Esquire 1953; White Plains Beautician Achievement Award 1962; bd dirs of the Urban League of Westchester Special Citation; Outstanding Achievements in Field of Human Rights for bldg a stronger Westchester Urban League 1963; Westchester Co Special Serv Award 1966; publications pamphlet "What Is Your Comm Doing for Its Youth? A Primer for Comm Action"; res paper "The Nature & Extent of the Purchase of Cough Medicines for Its Alcoholic & Codeine Kicks", the youth of Westchester; Civil Rights Guidelines for the Adminstrn on Aging HEW. **Home Addr:** 20 Perry Ave, White Plains, NY 10603.

ENGLISH, PERRY T., JR.
Publisher. **Personal:** Born Aug 12, 1933, Blounstown, FL; son of Perry English, Sr; divorced; children: Sharilynn, Lori Laverne. **Educ:** Central State Univ, BS 1956; Faculte de Med Univ de Paris, MD 1965. **Career:** Sainte Antoine Hosp, house phys 1965-71; Friendship Med Center LTD, asst to exec dir 1974-75,

admin 1975-; St Lukes Family Health Ctr Inc, pres 1977; Englewood Med Ctr Inc, pres 1978-; Beverly Hills Convalescent Ctr Inc, pres; Cook Co, phys assoc; Lopere Publishing Co Inc, pres; Blair & Cole, Attorneys at Law, administrator, currently. **Orgs:** Amer Public Health Assn; treas Chicago Investment Corp; vice pres Lake Vista Cntr Inc; pres Lop Re Devel Corp; treas Am Leasing Corp; sec LET Devel Corp; pres Lop Re Intl Inc; treas Madison Mgmt Corp; pres Lorgen Investment & Devel Corp; medl Grp Mang Assn; exec dir AESULAPIUS Soc appt by Gov of State of IL to the ''IL Commission on Economic Development'' mem Health Comm; Chicago Assoc of Commerce and Ind; mem Chicago Counc of Foreign Affairs; treasurer, The Consortium. **Honors/Awds:** Award from 3rd Ward Democratic Party for Dedicated Serv to programs that benefit the less fortunate 1976. **Military Serv:** Pvt 1953-55. **Home Addr:** 8045 South Calumet Ave, Chicago, IL 60619.

ENGLISH, REGINALD
Computer systems executive. **Career:** Intellisys Technology Corp, CEO, currently. **Special Achievements:** Company is ranked #51 on Black Enterprise magazine's 1997 list of Top 100 Black businesses. **Business Addr:** CEO, Intellisys Technology Corp, 11718 Lee Jackson Memorial, Fairfax, VA 22033, (703)691-4717.

ENGLISH, RICHARD A.
Educator. **Personal:** Born Aug 29, 1936, Winter Park, FL; son of Mary English and Wentworth English; married Ireita G W. **Educ:** Talladega Coll, AB 1958; Univ of MI, MA 1959, MSW 1964, PhD 1970. **Career:** Flint Urban League, vocational youth serv dir, 1959-61, acting dir 1961-62; Neighborhood Serv Org Detroit, soc group worker 1963-66; Wayne State Univ, lectr 1965-67; Univ of MI, lecturer 1967-70, asst prof 1970-72; Univ of MI School of Soc Work, asst dean 1971-74; Univ of MI, assoc prof of social work, assoc vice pres for acad affairs 1974-; Univ of TX at Austin, RL Sutherland chair; Howard Univ, dean and professor school of social work 1985-. **Orgs:** Mem, Council on Social Work Educ; Natl Assn of Soc Workers; Natl Assn of Black Social Workers; Am Soc Assn; chmn 1977 Annual Program Meeting Council on Social Work Edn; mem Coun on Soc Work Educ Reaccrdtn Teams for Graduate School of Social Work 1973-; elec & mem House of Dels Coun on Soc Work Educ 1974-77; Annual Program Planning Comm Council on Social Work Educ 1975-78; elec pres Coun on Soc Work Educ 1981-84; Prgm Com of the Sem on Social Work Educ & Human Settlements; Intl Assn of School of Soc Work; vol Operation Crossroads Africa Ghana; mem, bd Amer Civil Liberties Union; mem adv panel Refugee Policy Group; mem Spaulding for Children, member, Emeritus foundation, 1987-; board member, National Assembly of National Voluntary Health Organiztion, 1988-; board member, International Asiation of Social Welfare, 1988-; international committee, Council on Social Work Education, 1989-. **Honors/Awds:** Summer fellowship, Univ of Oslo Norway, 1956; Woodrow Wilson Fellow, Univ of MI 1958-59; co-ed Human Serv Org; Beyond Pathology rsch & theoretical Perspectives on Black Families; Distinguished Serv Award, Natl Assn of Black Social Workers 1983; Certificate of Appreciation Council on Social Work 1984; Distinguished Alumni Award, 1985; Whitney Young Jr Scholar Award for 1988, Western Michigan University, 1987. **Business Addr:** Dean, Howard University, School of Social Work, Washington, DC 20059.

ENGLISH, STEPHEN (JO JO)
Professional basketball player. **Personal:** Born Feb 4, 1970, Frankfurt, Germany. **Educ:** South Carolina Univ. **Career:** Chicago Bulls, 1992; CBA: Tri-City Chinook, 1992-94; LaCrosse Catbirds, 1993-94; Minnesota Timberwolves, 1993; Chicago Bulls, 1993-. **Business Addr:** Professional Basketball Player, Chicago Bulls, 1901 W Madison St, Chicago, IL 60612-2459, (312)943-5800.

ENGLISH, WHITTIE
Company executive. **Personal:** Born Aug 3, 1917, New York, NY; married Lavinia Anderson, Apr 22, 1989; children: Bonita, Joanne. **Educ:** Bergen Coll, attended 1936-38. **Career:** English Enterprises, pres. **Orgs:** Pres English Realty Assoc Inc 1955-, Ebony Builders 1955-, Empire Mortgage Co 1957-80, English Construction 1957-; mem NY State Black Republican Council 1985-; mem NAACP, Urban League; pres NJ State 369 Vets Assn. **Military Serv:** Signal Corps transferred to Air Corps lst Lt 5 yrs, 99th Pursuit Squad, 477 Bomb Group. **Business Addr:** CEO, English Enterprises, 248 Forest Ave, Englewood, NJ 07631.

ENGLISH, WILLIAM E.
Computer services company executive. **Personal:** Born May 18, 1936, Marianna, AR; son of Dan & Lorraine English; divorced; children: William Jr, Romona, Cheryl, Amber. **Educ:** Univ of MI, BS, 1955. **Career:** Group Health Mutual, underwriter, 1959-63; 3M Co, sales mgr, 1963-68; Ceridian, vp, business ventures, 1968-. **Orgs:** Minnesota African American Political Caucus, chair, 1993-; Men Are Responsible for Cultivating Hope, 1994-; Minneapolis Urban League, chair, bd of trustees, 1975-78; Livingstone Coll, trustee, 1986-90; Minneapolis Model Cities Program, chair, 1969-71; Howard Univ Cluster Program, chair, 1988-90; Natl Urban League. **Honors/Awds:** Minneapolis Urban League, President's Award, 1984; Howard Univ Cluster, Outstanding Contribution, 1992; MN Women's Political Caucus, Good Guy Award, 1991. **Business Addr:** VP; Business Ventures, Ceridian, 8100 34th Ave, South, Bloomington, MN 55425.

ENGRAM, BOBBY
Professional football player. **Personal:** Born Jan 7, 1973, Camden, SC; married Deanna. **Educ:** Penn State, attended. **Career:** Chicago Bears, wide receiver, 1996-. **Business Addr:** Professional Football Player, Chicago Bears, 1000 Football Dr, Halas Hall at Conway Park, Lake Forest, IL 60045-4829, (847)295-6600.

ENGS, ROBERT FRANCIS
Educator. **Personal:** Born Nov 10, 1943, Colorado Springs, CO; son of Myrtle Coger Engs and Robert Engs; married Jean Oliver, Dec 20, 1969; children: Robert N. **Educ:** Princeton U, AB (cum laude) 1965; Yale U, PhD History 1972. **Career:** U Univ of PA, assoc prof history 1979-; Univ of PA, asst prof history 1972-79; Princeton U, instr history 1970-72; NJ Black History Inst NJ Dept of Educ, dir 1969-72; Coll of William & Mary, commonwealth visiting prof 1984-85; Univ of PA, Philadelphia, PA, undergraduate chair History, 1986-. **Orgs:** Faculty mem/cons Nat Humanities Faculty 1972-80; adv Nat Humanities Center 1978-80; mem Orgn of Am Historians 1975-; mem Am Hist Assn 1975; mem Assn for Study of Afro-Am Life History 1975; chmn Presidents Forum Univ of PA 1985-87; member Executive Committee Alumni Council of Princeton University, 1989-91. **Honors/Awds:** Short Term Am Grantee, US Dept of State 1971; William Penn Fellow, Moton Cntr for Ind Studies 1976-77; Freedom's First Generation, Univ of PA Press 1979; N&H Summer Fellowship, Natl Endowment of the Humanities 1980; Guggenheim Fellow 1982-83; Lindback Award for Excellence in Teaching, Univ of Pennsylvania 1988.

ENIS, SHALONDA
Professional basketball player. **Personal:** Born Dec 3, 1974. **Educ:** Univ of Alabama. **Career:** Seattle Reign, center, 1997-. **Business Addr:** Professional Basketball Player, Seattle Reign, 400 Mercer St, Ste 408, Seattle, WA 98109, (206)285-5225.

ENNIX, COYNESS LOYAL, JR.
Physician, educator. **Personal:** Born Feb 12, 1942, Nashville, TN; married Katharine; children: Nicole, Kristina. **Educ:** Fisk U, BS 1963; Meharry Med Coll, MD 1967. **Career:** Baylor Coll Med, asst prof surgery; Baylor Coll Med, postdoctoral fellow 1976-77; Cleveland Clinic Educ Found, fellow 1974-76; Cardiovascular Disease Baylor Coll Med, researcher; Methodist Hospital, staff surg; Inst Rehab & Rsch St Joseph Hos; VA Hosp; St Lukes Hosp. **Orgs:** Mem Amer Coll Surg; Michael E DeBakey Intl Cardiovascular Soc; Houston Med Forum; Harris Co Med Soc; TX Med Assn; Houston Acad Med; AMA; Amer Trauma Soc; Houston Surg Soc; Pan Pacific Surg Assn; Denton A Cooley Cariovascular Surgery Soc; dipl Amer Bd of Surgery; diplomate Amer Bd of Thoracic Surgery; Amer Heart Assn. **Honors/Awds:** Most Outstanding Fellow Cardiovascular Surgery, Cleveland Clinic Educ Found 1976. **Military Serv:** USN 1969-71.

ENOCH, HOLLACE J. (SEDONIA)
Federal government official. **Personal:** Born Jul 9, 1950, Mathews, VA; daughter of Gladys Jackson and William Jackson; married Hurley Enoch, Oct 10, 1981 (divorced 1991). **Educ:** Virginia Union University, Richmond, VA, BA, 1972. **Career:** National Labor Relations Board, Baltimore MD, field examiner, 1972-78; US Patent & Trademark Office, Arlington, VA, labor/employee relations specialist, 1978-81; National Labor Relations Board, Washington, DC, labor relations officer, 1981-89, associate exec secretary, 1989-. **Orgs:** Member, Society of Federal Labor Relations Professionals, 1978-89; various leadership positions, Delta Sigma Theta Sorority, 1969-. **Honors/Awds:** Wall Street Journal Achievement Award, 1972. **Business Addr:** Associate Executive Secretary, National Labor Relations Board, 1099 14th St, NW, Rm 11600, Washington, DC 20570, (202)273-1938.

ENOCH, JOHN D.
Publisher. **Career:** Minority & Women in Business, publisher, chairman, editor, currently. **Business Phone:** (919)229-1462.

EPHRAIM, CHARLESWORTH W.
Educator. **Educ:** USAF Tech Sch, radio operations honors 1964; USAF Instr Training Sch, 1964; State Univ of NY, BA honors purchase valedictorian 1973; Yale U, MA, MPhil, PhD 1979; Nat Fellow Ford Found, 1973-78. **Career:** US Air Force, tech instructor, sgt, radio op US & overseas 1964-68; Bankers Trust Co NY, supr 1968-73; State Univ of NY Coll at Purchase, Yale U, instructor; SUNY Empire State Coll, faculty; Mercy Coll, Dept of Philosophy, associate professor, philosophy, currently. **Orgs:** Mem Com for Vets Affairs; mem NY Metropolitan Assoc for Developmental Education; mem Amer Philosophical Assn; mem NAACP; mem Urban League; founder Free Community School of Mt Vernon 1980. **Honors/Awds:** Completed USAF morse-code course in half time; first person in USAF hist to receive 24 GPM while in training, Keesler AFB MS 1964; grad coll in 2 1/2 yrs; rsch being done in Philosophy of the Black Experience; Awarded, Summer Rsch Grant, NY African Amer Inst to study, The Logic of Black Protest, 1988. **Military Serv:** US Air Force, sgt, 1964-68, reserves, 1968-70. **Business Addr:** Associate Professor, Philosophy, Department of Philosophy, Mercy College, 555 B'way, Dobbs Ferry, NY 10522.

EPPERSON, DAVID E.
Educational administrator. **Personal:** Born Mar 14, 1935, Pittsburgh, PA; son of Bessie Lee Tibbs Epperson and Robert N Epperson; married Cecelia Trower; children: Sharon, Lia. **Educ:** Univ of Pittsburgh, BA 1961; Univ of Pittsburgh, MSW 1964; Univ of Pittsburgh, MA 1970; Univ of Pittsburgh, PhD 1975; Univ of the Bosporous & Chinese Univ, attended. **Career:** School of Social Work Univ of Pittsburgh, dean & prof 1972-; Dept of Political Sci Univ of Pittsburgh, Univ fellow in Urban Affairs, consultant 1969-72; Comm Action Pittsburgh Inc, exec dir 1967-69; deputy 1965-67; equal opportunities program univ of Pittsburgh, coordinator 1964-65. **Orgs:** Trustee, Natl Urban League & Natl Center for Social Policy & Practice; vice chairman, Urban Redevelopment Authority of Pittsburgh & YMCA of Pittsburgh; chairman, YMCA of USA/Africa, particapated in Educational & Social Welfare Study Missions To Africa, Asia, Latin America & Western Europe. **Military Serv:** USAF staff sgt 1954-58. **Business Addr:** 2117 Cathedral of Learning, Pittsburgh, PA 15260.

EPPS, A. GLENN
Government employee, attorney. **Personal:** Born Jul 12, 1929, Marshall, TX; divorced; children: David, Lawrence. **Educ:** Univ of MI, BA 1950; Univ of WI, JD 1956. **Career:** MI Employment Sec Commn (MESC), hearing referee 1976-; atty priv prac. **Orgs:** Legal redress chmn Flint Br; Am Civil Libs Union 1960-68; legal redress chmn Flint Br; NAACP 1959-68; asst pros Genesee Co MI 1959-62; past memexec bd Nat Lawyers Guild; Flint Chap Nat Lawyers Guild; mem State Bar of MI; was involved in many civil rights cases in city of Flint. **Honors/Awds:** Recip NAACP Meritorious Award, legal action in pursuit of fair housing; atty for J Merrill Spencer vs Flint Memorial Cemetary, causing integration of cemeteries in MI. **Military Serv:** AUS sgt 1951-53. **Business Addr:** 2501 N Saginaw St, Flint, MI 48503.

EPPS, ANNA CHERRIE
Educational administrator. **Personal:** Born Jul 8, 1930, New Orleans, LA; daughter of Anna Johnson Cherrie and Ernest Cherrie, Sr, MD; married Joseph M Epps, Nov 23, 1968; children: Joseph M Epps, Jr, MD, Grace Epps-Puglisi, PhD. **Educ:** Howard Univ, BS 1951; Loyola Univ, MS 1959; Howard Univ, PhD 1966. **Career:** NIH Clinical Center, blood bank special 1959;Howard Univ School of Medicine, program dir & asst prof of microbiology 1960-69. Tulane Univ School of Medicine, USPHS faculty fellow, 1969, asst prof of medicine, assoc prof of medicine 1971-75, prof, medical dir, 1975-80; asst dean, 1980-86, assoc dean, 1986-, dir, medical rep, student academic support serv. **Orgs:** Prog asst br 1971-75; LA Bd of Health Social & Rehab Serv 1972; bd of regents emeritus, Georgetown Univ 1975-; bd trustees Children's Hospital 1978-79; mem Natl Adv Research Resources Council 1978-; chairperson AAMC GSA/MAS 1979-; mem bd of dir United Federal Savings & Loan Assn 1984-; Louisiana State Health Bd & Human Serv exec dept 1985-; mem Amer Assn of Blood Banks, Amer Assn of Univ Profs, Albertus Magnos Guild, WA Helminthol Soc, Amer Soc of Bacteriologists, Sigma Xi, Amer Soc of Tropical Medical & Hygiene, Musser Burch Soc, Amer Soc of Med Technologists, Amer Soc of Clinical Pathologists; mem Natl Adv Allied Health Professions Council, NIH, Bureau of Health Professions, Educ & Manpower Training Div of Health Manpower. **Honors/Awds:** Award for Meritorious Research Interstate Postgraduate Medical Assn of N Amer 1966; publications ''Fetoprotein Immunoglobulin,'' ''Hepatitis Induced Antigen in Patients with Liver Disease in the New Orleans Area''; 72nd Annual Meeting Amer Gastroenterological Assn 1972; assoc editor ''Medical Educ, Responses to a Challenge''; Merit Scroll, Natl Medical Assn, 1980; author, MEDREP at Tulane, 1984; Distinguished Serv Award, Natl Assn of Medical Minority Educ, 1988. **Business Addr:** Assoc Dean, Offices of Student Serv & Prof of Medicine, Tulane Univ Sch of Medicine, MEDREP Tulane Med Center, 1430 Tulane Ave, Rm M-055, New Orleans, LA 70112.

EPPS, C. ROY
Association executive. **Personal:** Born Jun 6, 1941, Bronx, NY; son of Alice Epps and Clarence Epps; children: Leah, Roy III, Leslye Renee, Camara Rose. **Educ:** Wilberforce U, BS 1963; Rutgers U, MS 1970; MA Inst of Tech, Fellowship 1981-82. **Career:** Civic/Urban League of Greater New Brunswick, comm social worker 1967-68, asst dir, 1968-70, exec dir/pres 1970-. **Orgs:** New Brunswick Tomorrow 1975-; chm/hsng com New Brunswick Dev Corp 1976-94; former pres/ mem New Brunswick Bd of Ed 1976-85; mem Greater Raritan Workforce Investment Board 1983-; co-chair Black Leadership Conference 1986-. **Honors/Awds:** Pres awd Natl Council of Urban League Exec 1978-80; pres awd Eastern Reg Council of Urban League Exec 1977-81; comm fellows prog MA Inst of Tech 1981-82;

Honorary Doctorate, Upsala College, 1994. **Military Serv:** AUS pfc 2 yrs. **Business Addr:** President, Civic League of Greater New Brunswick, 47-49 Throop Ave, New Brunswick, NJ 08901.

EPPS, CHARLES HARRY, JR.
Physician, educational administrator. **Personal:** Born Jul 24, 1930, Baltimore, MD; son of Marjorie Sue Jackson (deceased) and Charles Harry Epps Sr; married Roselyn Payne; children: Charles Harry III, Kenneth Carter, Roselyn Elizabeth, Howard Robert. **Educ:** Howard Univ, BS 1951, MD 1955. **Career:** Howard Univ, prof & chf div orthopaedic surg; Johns Hopkins Hosp, assoc prof orthopaedic surg; Howard Univ Orthopaedic Residency Training Prog, prog dir; ABOS, diplom 1964; Orthopaedic Surg, residency review comm 1971-; ABOS, examiner 1974-92; Amer Bd of Orthotics & Prosthet, examiner 1970-76; Howard University, College of Medicine, dean, 1988-94; Howard Univ, Health Affairs, vp, 1994-. **Orgs:** Comm to study med devices food & drug admin 1972-75; mem, pres Amer Orthopaedic Assoc 1985-86; Gov Health Legisl & Vet Affairs Comm; Amer Acad of Orthop Surg 1976; mem Kappa Alpha Psi Frat Bd of Trustees; Sidwell Friends Sch Wash DC; life mem NAACP; bd of dir Boys Club of Metro Police; gov American Coll of Surgeon 1982-88; mem, Ethical and Judical Council AMA 1982-87; mem, ABOS, 1977-83. **Military Serv:** USAR capt med corps 1956-61; active duty 1961-62; inactive reserv 1962-65. **Business Addr:** Special Assistant to the President, Howard University, Howard University Hospital, 2081 Georgia Ave, NW, Washington, DC 20060.

EPPS, CONSTANCE ARNETTRES
Dentist. **Personal:** Born Feb 8, 1950, Portchester, NY; daughter of Geneva Colbert Gooden and Robert Gooden; married Charles Ray Epps; children: Charles R II, Menika Elyse. **Educ:** Bennett Coll, BS 1971; Howard Univ, DDS 1979; UNC-CH, MPH 1990. **Career:** Blood Rsch Inst Harvard Univ, coagulation technician 1971-72; US Govt Torrejon Air Base Madrid, teacher 1973-74; St Elizabeth Hospital, dental officer 1979-80; NC Dept of Human Resources, public health dentist 1980-86; Guilford Co Health Dept, Greensboro, NC, public health dentist 1986-, dental director 1990-. **Orgs:** Mem ADA, NDA, Acad of General Dentistry, NC Dental Assoc 1979; mem Old North State & Guilford County dental Assocs 1984-; adjunct faculty Univ of NC Chapel Hill 1986-; treas 1986-, vice chairman 1987-, NC Public Health Assoc (Dental); mem High Point Org for Political Educ, Delta Sigma Theta, Guilford Co Headstart Adv Commn; chairman dental section, NC Public Health Assn, 1988-; choir dir, trustee 1988-, chairman/trustee board 1990-, First United Baptist Church; dental dir Greensboro Urban Ministry Medical and Dental Clinic 1989-. **Honors/Awds:** Dr Raymond L Hayes Scholarship Awd Howard Univ Dental Sch 1979; Delta Omega, Natl Public Health Honor Society, Outstanding Coll Students of Amer, 1990; NC Dental Society 3rd District Nominee, Young Dentist of the Year, 1988; Nal Assn of County Health Officials Recognition of Achievement, Homebound Dental Prog, 1988; Author, Homebound Dental Prog, $6,000 Grant Awarded, 1987; A Consortium of Doctors, 1991. **Business Addr:** Dental Director, Guilford County Hlth Dept, 1100 E Wendover Ave, Greensboro, NC 27401.

EPPS, DOLZIE C. B.
Educator. **Personal:** Born Jan 1, 1907, Shreveport, LA. **Educ:** Dillard Univ (New Orleans U), 1929; Wiley Coll Marshall TX, AB 1945; Columbia Univ New York, MA 1950. **Career:** Caddo Parish School System, teacher Health & Physical Educ 1935-73; NAACP/Louisiana State Univ School of Medicine, bd of dir 1976-. **Orgs:** Mem Institutional Review Com on Human Experimentation Shreveport LA; bd of dir Caddo-Bossier Ct Observers 1976-; first vice pres Family Counseling & Children Serv 1976-; bd of dir Shreveport Negro C of C 1976-; bd of dir Phi Delta Kappa Sorority (Beta Alpha Chpt) 1976-. **Honors/Awds:** Community Serv Award, Nat Council of Negro Women 1976; Ann Brewster Community Serv, NAACP 1978; Vacation Bible Sch Award, Galilee Bapt Ch 1979; Branch Serv Award, NAACP 1980. **Business Addr:** 1859 Milam St, Shreveport, LA 71103.

EPPS, EDGAR G.
Educator. **Personal:** Born Aug 30, 1929, Little Rock, AR; son of Odelle Epps and Clifford Epps; married Marilyn Miller; children: Carolyn, Raymond. **Educ:** Talladega Coll, AB 1951; Atlanta Univ, MA 1955; WA State Univ, PhD 1959. **Career:** TN State Univ, asst, assoc prof 1958-61; FL A&M Univ, prof 1961-64; Univ of MI, rsch assoc, assoc prof 1964-67; Tuskegee Inst, assoc dir Carver Rsch Found, chmn div of soc sci, prof of sociology 1967-70; Univ of Chicago, Marshall Field IV prof of Urban Educ 1970-. **Orgs:** Visiting prof Harvard Univ 1969; faculty mem Salzburg Seminar in Amer Studies Salzburg Austria 1975; mem bd of ed Chicago 1974-80; ed of books, "Black Students in White Schools" 1972, "Race Relations, Current Perspectives" 1973, "Cultural Pluralism" 1974; Southern Education Foundation, board of directors, 1976-88. **Honors/Awds:** Co-author "Black Consciousness, Identity & Achievement" 1975; co-editor: College in Black and White: African-American Students in Predominantly White and in Historically Black Public Universities, State University of New York Press, 1991; Restructuring the Schools: Problems and Prospects, McCutchan Publishing Co, 1992. **Business Addr:** Marshall Field IV Professor, Univ of Chicago, 5835 S Kimbark Ave, Chicago, IL 60637.

EPPS, GEORGE ALLEN, JR.
Company executive. **Personal:** Born Jul 3, 1940, Fallas, OK; son of George Ellen Doak-Epps and George Allen Epps Sr; married Linda Edwards, May 26, 1979; children: Gregory Allen, Michael Conrad. **Educ:** Kansas City Junior Coll, Kansas City KS, 1957-58; Rockhurst Coll, Kansas City MO, 1968-71. **Career:** Bendix Manufacturing Co, electronic technician, 1962-65; Southwestern Bell, Kansas City MO, lineman, 1965-68, facility engineer, 1968-71, installation supvr, 1971-76, St Louis MO, plant mechanization supvr, 1976-79, dist mgr-I&M, 1979-85, dist mgr, admin serv, 1985-; Gundacker Realty, sales, 1985-. **Honors/Awds:** Black Achiever in Indus, Southern Christian Leadership Conf, 1976; Optimist of the Year, Optimist Intl, 1987. **Military Serv:** US Navy, E3, 1958-61.

EPPS, OMAR
Actor. **Career:** Actor, currently. **Special Achievements:** Starred in films including: Juice; Higher Learning; "First Time Felon," HBO, 1997.

EPPS, PHILLIP EARL
Professional football player (retired). **Personal:** Born Nov 11, 1958, Atlanta, TX; married Janice; children: Rachel Renee, LaShaunta Nicole. **Educ:** Texas Christian Univ, BS, criminal justice. **Career:** professional football player, wide receiver: Green Bay Packers, 1982-88; New York Jets, 1989-90; Damon Labs, currently. **Honors/Awds:** Rookie of the Year 1982; 9th ranking punt returner in Natl Football Conf; #6 punt returner in the NFC with a 90 yard average for 36 runbacks, 1983; during 1982 off-season he starred in track and field at Texas Christian running the 5th fastest 60 yard dash ever, .607 seconds.

EPPS, ROSELYN PAYNE
Physician, pediatrician. **Personal:** Born Dec 11, Little Rock, AR; daughter of Mattie Beverly Payne (deceased) and Dr William Kenneth Payne Sr (deceased); married Dr Charles H Epps Jr; children: Charles H III (deceased), Kenneth C, Roselyn E, Howard R. **Educ:** Howard Univ, BS (w/Honors) 1951, MD (w/Honors) 1955; Johns Hopkins Univ, MPH 1973; Amer Univ, MA 1981. **Career:** Private Practice, sickle cell rsch 1960-61; DC Govt, med officer, dir to mental retardation clinic, c&y project, infant & pre-school, maternal & child health, clinical programs, act commr of public health 1961-80; Howard Univ Coll of Med, prof of pediatrics/dir child devel center, 1981-88; rsch assoc, Natl Insts of Health 1989-, medical officer. **Orgs:** Consultant US Dept of Health & Human Serv 1965-; bd of dirs Washington Performing Arts 1971-; consultant PSI Inc to Govt of Liberia 1984, United Nations Fund for Population Activities 1984; pres bd of dirs Hosp for Sick Children 1986-89; president, Girls Incorporated, 1990-92; president, American Medical Women's Assn, 1991; president, DC Chapter, American Academy of Pediatrics, 1988-91; Medical Society of DC, president, 1992. **Honors/Awds:** Distinguished Public Serv Award District of Columbia Govt 1981; Recognition Resolution & Day Council of the District of Columbia 1983; DC Women's Hall of Fame, DC Commission on Women, 1990; Community Service Award, DC American Medical Women's Assn, 1990; Community Service Award, DC Hospital Assn, 1990; Elizabeth Blackwell Award, American Medical Women's Association, 1992. **Home Addr:** 1775 North Portal Dr NW, Washington, DC 20012. **Business Addr:** Natl Cancer Institute, DCPC, Natl Insts of Health EPN-241, 9000 Rockville Pike, Bethesda, MD 20892-7333.

EPTING, MARION
Artist. **Personal:** Born in Forrest, MS. **Educ:** Los Angeles City Coll, grad; Otis Art Inst LA Co, MFA 1969. **Career:** Otis Art Inst, rep permanent collections ; Univ CA; San Jose State Coll; Denison U; Seattle Art Mus; pvt collections of Bernie Casey, Dorothy Chandler, Claude Booker, Ruth Stoehr, James Bates. **Honors/Awds:** Recipient num awards; 1st San Diego Nat Invitational Print Exhibition; Otpotsdam Prints; Northwest Printmakers; Del Mar; Portland Art Mus. **Military Serv:** USN. **Business Addr:** Dept of Art, California State Univ, Chico, CA 95926.

ERNST, REGINALD H.
Physician. **Personal:** Born Aug 4, 1928, Detroit, MI; son of Edna Ernst and Clifford Ernst; children: Linda, Michael, Janis, Steven. **Educ:** Univ of MI, BS 1950; Wayne State Univ, MD 1957; Wayne County General Hospital internal medicine 1957-61. **Career:** Wayne State Univ, asst prof of medicine 1962-; Boulevard Gen Hospital, chief of medicine 1963-74; Detroit Medical Society, pres 1970-71; Southwest Detroit Hospital, chief of medicine 1976-77; Harper Hospital, physician. **Orgs:** Chmn Scholarship Black Graduates Univ of MI 1979-80; mem Natl Med Assn 1961-, NAACP 1961-, Amer Soc of Internal Med 1962-, Amer Coll of Physicians 1964-, Detroit Inst of Art 1965-; board member, Wayne State University Alumni Assn, 1987-90. **Military Serv:** AUS sgt 1951-53.

ERSKINE, KENNETH F.
Educational administrator. **Personal:** Born in New York, NY; married Maria; children: Clarke S Lewis F. **Educ:** City Coll NY Convent Ave Campus, BS 1950; Columbia Univ Sch of Soc Wk, MSW 1952; variety of certs & advanced practice credits from various insts, schools & colls 1956-94. **Career:** Vets Adm Psych Out Patient Clinic Bk; psych soc wkr M H Clinic supv 1955-62; Col Univ Sch of Soc Work, asst prof Field Inst 1962-69; Vol in Serv to Amer Col Univ, consult trainer 1964-65; Columbi Univ Sch of Soc Work, asst dir of field work 1969-74; Col Univ C P & S Affil Harlem Hosp, asst dir for social work in Psychiatry, 1974-85; Edupsych Assocs, cons; New York Urban League, Brooklyn Service to Families, consultant/supervisor, 1989-. **Orgs:** Partner Edu Psych Assoc 1962-; mbr, mem Bod Natl Assn of Social Workers; mem Assoc of Black Social Workers; mem Acad of Certified Social Workers; vice pres BOD Manhattan Cntry Sch 1974-; mem BOD Spence Chapin Serv for Children & Families 1974-90; mem sec vice pres, president, H & G Alum Man Chap 1970-; officer 4-D-O Coop 1983-90; member, 100 Black Men Inc, 1979-. **Honors/Awds:** NY State certified social worker NYS Dept of Ed 1972-. **Military Serv:** USAAF OCS cadet/pfc 3 Yrs. **Business Addr:** Consultant, Edupsych Assocs, 224 RSD, New York, NY 10025, (212)332-0036.

ERVIN, DEBORAH GREEN
Educational administrator. **Personal:** Born Apr 4, 1956, Greenville, SC; daughter of Annie V Williams-Green and David Green Jr; married Larry Don Ervin (divorced); children: Sean Deon, Elanda Deliece. **Educ:** Berea Coll, BA 1977; Clemson Univ, MEd 1986. **Career:** Clemson Child Develop Ctr, head teacher 1978-81; Clemson Univ, admissions counselor 1981-86, asst dir admissions 1986; Winthrop University, asst dir admissions, 1987-92, associate director of admissions, 1992-. **Orgs:** Mem Carolina's Assoc of Collegiate Registrars and Admissions Officers 1981-, sec 1989-90, SC vice pres, 1991-93; mem Southern Assoc of College Admissions Officers, Home Economics Adv Comm D W Daniel HS, Clemson Univ Day Care Comm, Clemson Univ Coll of Educ Faculty Selection Comm; member Central City Optimists 1990-. **Home Addr:** 1061 Cypress St, Rock Hill, SC 29730. **Business Addr:** Associate Director of Admissions, Winthrop University, 505 Eden Terrace, Rock Hill, SC 29733.

ERVIN, HAZEL ARNETT
Educator. **Personal:** Born Dec 19, 1948, Washington, GA; daughter of Gladys Anthony Arnett and Harrison M Arnett; divorced; children: Kevin, Erica. **Educ:** Guilford Coll, AB 1980; North Carolina A&T State Univ, MA 1985; Howard Univ, PhD, 1993. **Career:** Nite Line Report, reporter 1982-85; Reidsville Jr HS, English teacher 1980-81; Hancock Co Sch, English/Journalism teacher 1981-82; Montgomery Co Schools, English teacher 1983-85; Shaw Univ, assoc prof of English 1985-, dept head, Dept of English, humanities, & foreign languages, 1993, critic & lecturer, 1992-. **Orgs:** Mem Langston Hughes Review Soc 1985-, Black Scholar 1985-, Natl Geographic 1985-, Obsidian II 1986-, Callaloo 1987-; sec Faculty Senate Shaw Univ 1986-87; assoc mem, Smithsonian Institute 1988; member, Black American Literature Forum, 1988-; member, College Language Assn, 1988-. **Honors/Awds:** Review of works by Langston Hughes 1981, When Harlem Was in Vogue 1982, Rainbow Roun Mah Shoulder 1984, All God's Children Need Traveling Shoes 1986, Fatherhood 1987; over 20 feature stories for now defunct Nite-Line Report Greensboro NC 1982-85; founder Enrichment Camp for Black Youth which focuses on black heritage through literature and song 1982; United Negro College Fund's Educ Grant to pursue PhD in English 1987-88; summer internship as copy editor of American Quarterly 1989, Smithsonian Institute; one of many compilers for Callaloo's bibliography on works by African-Americans, 1988-90; interview with author Ann Petry scheduled for publication 1992; UNCF, Andrew Mellon Fellowship, 1990-91, 1991-92; Ann Petry: A Bio-Bibliography, GK Hall & Co, 1993; Articles on the life and works of Ann Petry in the forthcoming Oxford Companion of African American Literature, 1996.

ERVING, JULIUS WINFIELD (DR. J)
Sports administrator, Professional Basketball Player (retired). **Personal:** Born Feb 22, 1950, Roosevelt, NY; married Turquoise; children: four. **Educ:** Massachusetts Univ, degree 1972. **Career:** Virginia Squires, 1971-73, New York Nets, 1973-76, Philadelphia 76ers, 1976-87; appeared in film "The Fish That Saved Pittsburgh," 1979; DJ Enterprises, dir; Orlando Magic, exec vp, 1997-; RDV Sports, vice pres, 1997-; The Erving Group Inc, president. **Orgs:** Proffitts, bd of dirs, 1997-; Clark Atlanta Univ, trustee. **Honors/Awds:** Rookie of the Yr 1972; Lupus Found Award; NBA All Star Game 1977-80; MVP American Basketball Assn, 3 times, NBA 1980-81; Father Flanagan Award; scored 25,000 career point & became the 9th player in NBA-ABA history to do so, 1983; twice winner of Seagrams Seven Crown of Sports Award as the most productive player in the NBA; NBA Hall of Fame, 1993. **Business Addr:** Executive VP, Orlando Magic, 1 Magic Pl, Orlando, FL 32801, (407)649-3200.

ERWIN, CLAUDE F., SR.
Educator. **Personal:** Born May 6, 1906, Morganton, NC; married Ruby Forney; children: Claude F, Jr. **Educ:** Johnson C U, BS 1931. **Career:** Teacher, retired; Gamewell-Collettsville High School, 1965-71; Freedmon High School, 1937-65; McAlphine High School, 1932-37; Lenoir City, councilman, mayor pro-tem 1974-75. **Orgs:** Mem Humanities Com Calwell Co; v chmn Lenoir Nurse Day Care; trustee steward St Paul AME Ch; 2nd v chmn Dem Party of Caldwell Co. **Honors/Awds:** Layman of yr 1969; distinguished serv award Prince Hall Grand Lodge 1971.

ERWIN, JAMES OTIS
Clergyman, educator. **Personal:** Born Apr 28, 1922, Marion, NC; married Adeline Comer; children: Jo Nina Marie (abram), Janet Ann (Hall), Judith Kathryn. **Educ:** Johnson C Smith U, BA 1943; Garrett Theol Sem, MDiv 1946; Iliff Sch Theology, MRE 1953, STM 1979; Rust Coll, LLD 1971; WV Wesleyan U, LLD 1972. **Career:** United Methodist Church, ordained to ministry 1946; Morristown Coll TN, chaplain, instructor 1946-48; Wiley Coll TX, pres 1970-72, chmn dept religion, philosophy, chaplain 1948-53; Lincoln Univ MO, asst prof 1953-66; Wesley Found Univ of IA, founder 1966-67; Philander Smith Coll AR, dean of students, chaplain 1967-70; Wesley United Methodist Church, pastor 1968-70; St James United Methodist Church Chicago, pastor 1972-76. **Orgs:** Mem Douglas-Cherokee Ofc Econ Opportunity 1970-72; dist supt The United Meth Ch; mem Cherokee Guidance Center Morristown 1970-72; vice-chmn Little Rock BSA 1968-70; mem Intl Platform Assn; Alpha Phi Omega; Phi Beta Sigma. **Honors/Awds:** Contrib articles to professional jours. **Business Addr:** 77 W Washington St, Ste 1806, Chicago, IL 60602.

ERWIN, RICHARD C.
Attorney. **Personal:** Born Aug 23, 1923, Marion, NC; married Demerice Whitley; children: Aurelia, Richard. **Educ:** Johnson C Smith U, BA 1947; Howard U, LLB 1951. **Career:** Erwin & Beaty, partner 1951-. **Orgs:** Mem Found Com; Office Wachovia Bank & Trust Co; pres Forsyth Co Bar Assn; mem State Bd Edn; pres Urban Coalition; chmn Bennett Coll; mem NC Penal Study Commn; mem United Meth Ch Divinity Sch Duke U. **Honors/Awds:** Man of yr Kappa Alpha Frat 1965-66; Silver Cup Urban Coalition 1974; Gen Asembly NC 1975. **Military Serv:** 1st sgt 1943-46. **Business Addr:** 1223 Wachovia Bldg, Winston-Salem, NC 27101.

ESCO, FRED, JR.
City official, insurance company executive. **Personal:** Born Sep 13, 1954, Canton, MS; son of Ida M Hudson Esco and Fred Lee Esco; married Fleta Marie Jones, Aug 7, 1982; children: Freda Noel, Kristi Marie. **Educ:** MS Valley State Univ, BS 1978. **Career:** Esco's Insurance Agency, owner & pres 1979-; City of Canton, alderman, 1979-. **Orgs:** 32 Degree Mason Prince Hall Affiliation 1979-85; mem Elk Club of Canton 1979-85; mem Natl Business League 1979-85; vice pres NAACP of Canton 1983-84; secretary/treasurer Optimist Club of Canton 1984-85. **Honors/Awds:** Outstanding Sales Achievement Costal State Life Ins Co 1977. **Business Addr:** Alderman Ward 5, City of Canton, City Hall, Canton, MS 39046.

ESCOTT, SUNDRA ERMA
State representative. **Personal:** Born Feb 21, 1954, Birmingham, AL; married David Russell. **Educ:** AL State Univ, BS, 1977, Secondary Educ Certificate 1977; Troy State Univ, MBA, 1966. **Career:** Governor State of AL, admin asst 1976-80; self-employed Fashion Boutique 1976-80; Financial Assoc Inc, pres owner 1979-; AL Williams Marketing Firm, service pres 1980-; State of AL, state rep, currently. **Orgs:** Bd of dirs Sickle Cell Birmingham 1980; sec AL Legislative Black Caucus 1980; state legislature AL House Rep 1980-86; Banking AL House of Rep 1982; co-chair local govt AL House of Reps 1982; co-chair political action comm Delta Sigma Theta Sor 1984; bd of dirs YWCA Birmingham Office 1984; bd of dirs Positive Maturity United Way Agency 1984. **Honors/Awds:** Bd of Trustees Israel Methodist Church 1980; President's Council AL Williams Marketing Firm 1984 & 1985.

ESKRIDGE, JOHN CLARENCE
Educational administrator, educator. **Personal:** Born Jun 6, 1943, Pittsburgh, PA; son of Constance Mary Rideout Eskridge and John William Eskridge; children: Aziza, Mark. **Educ:** Duquesne Univ Pittsburgh, BA 1966, MA 1971; Pacific So Univ CA, PhD Philosophy 1978. **Career:** Comm Coll, prof philosophy 1978-; Carlow Coll, dir turial instructor 1973-74; Comm Coll Allegheny County, philosophy faculty 1969-; ''Le Sacre Corps'' Dance Co, artistic dir 1969-79; Pittsburgh Child Guidance Clinic, program dir, creative recreational arts program 1969-70; Comm Coll Allegheny County Campus, dir black studies 1969-71, coll speakers bureau 1978-88; First Baptist Church Pittsburgh, bd of deacons 1970-73; Pittsburgh High School of Creative & Performing Arts, adv bd 1979-90; Community College Allegheny County, department chairman, 1983-; Hot Lix Concert Jazz Band, leader/producer, 1978-89; Orpheo Concert Latin Band, leader/producer, 1989-. **Orgs:** Mem Soc for Phenomenology & Existential Philosophy 1967-80; mem Am Philos Assn 1969-80; founding chmn Hermeneutic Circle 1977-80; bd dirs Inst For Collective Behavior & Memory 1980-87; vice pres, African American Federation of the Americas, 1983-89; member, Pittsburgh Musicians Society, 1967-. **Honors/Awds:** NDEA study fellowship Duquesne Univ 1967-70; faculty spl serv award Comm Coll Allegheny Co Student Union 1978; College Blue Ribbon Faculty Award, Community College Allegheny County, 1981-82. **Business Addr:** Chairman, Comm Coll of Allegheny Cty, Dept of Phil & Foreign Lang, 808 Ridge Ave, Pittsburgh, PA 15212.

ESOGBUE, AUGUSTINE O.
Educator, engineer. **Personal:** Born Dec 25, 1940, Kaduna, Nigeria. **Educ:** Univ of CA LA, BS 1964; Columbia U, MS 1965; Univ of So CA LA, PhD 1968. **Career:** Com of Minority Career Advisors; Industrial & Systems Engineering, School of Health Systems, GA Inst of Technology Atlanta, prof; Morehouse Coll Atlanta, adjunct prof of community med; Atlanta Univ GA, adjuct prof of mathematical science; Operations Rsch & Mem Systems Rsch Center, Case Western Reserve Univ Cleveland, asst prof 1968-72; Engineering & Med, Univ of Southern CA, rsch assoc 1965-68; Water Resources Rsch Center, Univ of CA Los Angeles, devel engr 1966-67; Univ Assoc Inc & Environmental Dynamics, consultant 1968-72; GA Inst of Technology, chmn 1975, prof. **Orgs:** Mem several panels of the Nat Rsrch Counc, Nat Acad of Sci Engring; councillor, chmn ORSA; vis lctr Operations Rsrch & Mgmt Sci; adv editor Intl Jour on Fuzzy Sets & Systems; asso editor ORSA Hlth Applications Tech; mem US Subcom Intl Ctr on Systems & Cybernetics; mem Beverly Hills Rotary Club; faculty adv GA Tech Soc of Black Engrs 1976-; exec bd mem Environment Adv Group Atlanta Reg Commission 1980-; bd dir Atlanta Council of Black Professional Engrs 1981-. **Honors/Awds:** Sigma Xi Fellow AAAS; num sci publ in various tch journals. **Business Addr:** Professor, GA Inst of Tech, Sch of Indsl & Sys Engineering, Atlanta, GA 30332.

ESPOSITO, GIANCARLO
Actor. **Personal:** Born Apr 26, 1958, Copenhagen, Denmark. **Career:** Actor, television experience includes: Go Tell It on the Mountain; The Exchange Student; Finnegan Begin Again; Miami Vice, 1985; Rockabye, 1986; Spenser: For Hire, 1987; Relentless: Mind of a Killer, 1993; theater experience includes: Maggie Flynn; Miss Moffet, 1974; The Me Nobody Knows; Seesaw; Zooman and the Sign, 1980; Keyboard, 1982; Do Lord Remember Me, 1984; Balm in Gilead, 1984; Don't Get God Started, 1987; One for Dexter, 1991; Distant Fires, 1992; film experience includes: Trading Places, 1983; Cotton Club, 1984; Sweet Lorraine, 1987; School Daze, 1988; Do the Right Thing, 1989; Mo' Better Blues, 1990; Night on Earth, 1992; Bob Roberts, 1992; Amos and Andrew, 1993. **Orgs:** Screen Actors Guild. **Honors/Awds:** OBIE Award, for Zooman and the Sign, 1981. **Home Addr:** Actor, c/o 40 Acres and a Mule Filmworks, 124 DeKalb Ave, #2, Brooklyn, NY 11217, (718)624-3703. **Business Addr:** Actor, Amos and Andrew, ATTN: Tood Noonan, DRGW, 1501 Broadway, Ste 703, New York, NY 10036, (212)382-2000.

ESPREE, ALLEN JAMES
Educator. **Personal:** Born May 4, 1941, Lake Charles, LA; married Clara G; children: Glenn Aldric, Gary Allen, Bernice Jeanine. **Educ:** Univ of NE, BS Business 1970; Command & Gen Staff Coll, Master Military Science 1979; Univ of MO, Master Public Admin 1980. **Career:** RCPAC Enlisted Personnel Directorate, deputy dir 1980-83; Bishop Coll, prof of military science. **Orgs:** Consultant A&C Carpet Co 1984-85; superintendent Sunda6y Sch Faith Comm Lutheran Church 1984-85; mem Military Affairs Comm Dallas Chamber of Commerce 1984-85; mem/policy council Dallas Head Start Prog 1985. **Honors/Awds:** Eagle Scout Calcasieu Area Council Lake Charles LA 1957-58. **Military Serv:** AUS lt col 23 yrs; Bronze Star; Purple Heart; Army Commendation; Vietnam Service CIB. **Business Addr:** Professor of Military Science, Bishop College, 3837 Simpson Stuart Rd, Dallas, TX 75241.

ESPY, CECIL EDWARD
Professional baseball player. **Personal:** Born Jan 20, 1963, San Diego, CA. **Career:** Outfielder: Los Angeles Dodgers, 1983, Texas Rangers, 1987-90, Pittsburgh Pirates, 1991-92, Cincinnati Reds, 1992-. **Business Phone:** (513)421-4510.

ESPY, HENRY
Mayor. **Career:** Clarksdale, MS, mayor, 1990-. **Orgs:** National Conference of Black Mayors, president. **Business Addr:** Mayor, City of Clarksdale, City Hall Bldg., Clarksdale, MS 38614, (601)627-8438.

ESPY, MICHAEL
Former agriculture secretary, former congressman. **Educ:** Howard Univ; CA Univ of Santa Clara Law School. **Career:** Law Practice Yazoo City, attorney; Central MS Legal Servs, manager; State Secretary's Office, dir public lands and elections div 1980-84; State Attorney General's Office, chief of consumer protection div 1984-85; US House of Representatives, member, 1986-93; US Dept of Agriculture, secretary, 1993-94. **Special Achievements:** First African-American secretary of agriculture, 1993-94. **Business Addr:** Former Secretary, US Dept of Agriculture, 14th & Independence Ave SW, Washington, DC 20250.

ESQUERRE, JEAN ROLAND
Aerospace consultant. **Personal:** Born Dec 28, 1923, Yonkers, NY; son of Marie Bates Esquerre and Jean B Esquerre; married Maria Elisabet Edman; children: Johanna Maria, Malin Elisabet. **Educ:** Coll of City of NY; NYU; Republic Aviation Corps Staff Engr School; Gruman Aerospace Corp, Training & Devel Ctr; Empire State College SUNY. **Career:** Opportunity Devel Dept Grumman Aeorspace Corp, asst to corp pres, dir 1969-89; price analyst 1969; Lunar Modular #4, engr supr, test dir, cognizant engr 1963-69; Republic Aviation Corp, principal designer 1953-63; NY Transit Authority, mechanical engr draftsman 1952-53; Specialty Assembling & Packing Co, draftsman 1949-52. **Orgs:** Mem, Soc of Automotive Engr; ETA Chapter Alpha Phi Alpha Fraternity, mem 1949-, pres 1951; pres, Planned United Devel Task Force for Huntington; pres & instructor, Grumman Martial Arts Club; mem, Huntington Branch NAACP; Labor & Ind Comm 1949-, chmn 1970; chmn, Sub-Comm for feasibility of Minority Enterprise Small Business Invest Corp; vice chmn, Nathan Hall Dist BSA; pres, Urban League of Long Island; bd dir, Grumman Aerospace Corps, Grumman Ecosystem Corp; bd dir, YMCA; mem, Family Serv Assn; mem, Girl Scouts of Suffolk Co; pres, N Atlantic Karate Assn, 1976; CCNY Varsity Club, 1952; CCNY Boxing Alumni Club, 1948; sec, LI Branch NY Karate Assn, 1961-; mem, Huntington Township Comm on Human Relations, 1961-; Huntington Freedom Ctr, 1963-; former mem CitizensAdvisory Comm on Capital But for Huntington; former mem, Planned United Devel Task Force for Huntington; Huntington C 1 C Human Devel Comm. **Military Serv:** USAAF sgt WW II.

ESQUIVEL, ARGELIA VELEZ
Educator. **Personal:** Born Nov 23, 1936, Havana, Cuba; married Dr Ricardo R; children: Raul P Rodriguez, Argelia M Rodriguez. **Educ:** Univ of Havana Cuba, BS BA 1954; Sch of Sci, Univ of Havana, DSc, Mathematics 1960; Math Inst Univ of wi, NSF Post Grad 1965; TX Chris U, Poast Post Grad 1967-68; SW Ctr for Adv Studies Dallas, Post Grad 1968. **Career:** Bishop Coll, dir, coord Educ Prof Devel Act-Teachers Training Devel 1970-73, prof & dept head Math Science 1968-, instructor Modern Math NSF In-Serv Inst for Secondary School Teachers 1964-68, lecturer NSF Summer Program Advanced High School Students of Math 1964; TX Coll, asst prof Math, chmn of dept 1962-64; Marianao Inst, Havana Cuba, instrutor to asst prof of Math & Physics 1957-61; Bishop Coll, dir, coord Coop Coll School of Science-Natl Science Found Math Proj for Jr High School Teachers 1972-74; Univ of Houston-Bishop Coll Coop Doc Program in Math Educ Houston, assoc dir 1973-74. **Orgs:** Mem Am Assn for the Advancement of Sci DC Am Mathe Soc Providence; Nat Coun of Tchrs of Mathe DC TX Academy of Sci Austin; Mathe Assn of Am DC; dir NSF Minority Inst Sci Improvement Proj 1976-78; dir NSF Pre-coll Tchr Develop Math Proj 1977-78; mem com on Affirmative Acton of the Conf Bd of Math Sci; Am Assn of Univ Profs DC; m Assn of Univ Women DC; Young Women Christ Assn Dallas; Cuban Cath Assn Dallas; Mem bd dirs Dallas Br Am Assn of Univ Women 1973-; chmn Intl Rel Com of am assn of Univ Women 1973-; speaker Annual Conv of Nat Coun of Tchr of Math NC Sec Nov 1972. **Honors/Awds:** Recip natl sci found fellow summer 1965; computer assisted instr fellow for Coll & Univ Profs 1967-68; bishop coll liason rep to the & Am Assn of Univ Women 1970-72. **Business Addr:** 3837 Simpson Stuart Rd, Dallas, TX 75241.

ESSIEN, FRANCINE
Educator. **Personal:** Born in Philadelphia, PA. **Educ:** Temple Univ; Yeshiva Univ, Albert Einstein Coll of Medicine, PhD, genetics. **Career:** Rutgers Univ, Off of Minority Undergrad Science Programs, dir, 1986-, Dept of Biological Sciences, biology prof, currently. **Honors/Awds:** Carnegie Foundation for the Advancement of Teaching, US Professor of the Year, 1994-95. **Special Achievements:** First African-American to receive the 14-year old award of US Professor of the Year. **Business Addr:** Biological Sciences Prof/Dir Off of Min Undergrad Sciene Programs, Rutgers University, Dept of Biological Sciences, Nelson Lab, PO Box 1059, Piscataway, NJ 08854, (908)445-4145.

ESSIET, EVALEEN JOHNSON
Educator, nurse. **Personal:** Born Jun 21, 1933, Roxboro, NC; children: Aja, Bodie. **Educ:** Montefiore Hosp Schl of Nurs, DIPLOMA 1955; Univ of Pgh BS Nursing 1965; Univ of Pgh MSW 1971; Univ of Pgh PhD Higher Ed 1983. **Career:** George Washington Univ Hospital, Washington DC, staff nurse psy 1955-58; Allegheny County Health Dept, supvr of public health nurses 1958-1963; Monefine Hospital School of Nursing, nursing fac 1963-66; Homewd/Bruston Center, St Francis Hospital CMHC, dir 1968-1969; Clinic Hempsted Hospital CMHC, dir of out-patient 1971-73; Comm Coll of Allegheny County, prof of nursing 1973-. **Orgs:** Pres/cons E Johnson Essiet Corp 1983-84; elder Presby Church USA 1985-; mbr/publ chr Chi Sta Phi Nursg Sorrority 1981-85. **Honors/Awds:** Interpation of Nursg 1983; Prog (BS) Curric (Nat'l Study Pub) 1983; Poems publ Am Poetry Assoc 1981-84; Book Rev of Nursg for NLN 1980; Int'l Book ofHnr 1983. **Military Serv:** USAFR capt 1962-68; Flight Nrs Wings From Schl of Aerospa Med 1963. **Home Addr:** 827 Bell Ave, Braddock, PA 15104. **Business Addr:** Prof of Nursing, Comm Coll of AC, 1850 Old Chairton Rd, Rt 885, West Mifflin, PA 15122.

ESSOKA, GLORIA CORZEN
Associate professor. **Personal:** Born May 25, 1938, Philadelphia, PA; daughter of Thelma S Corzen and William B Corzen; married Modi Essoka, Sep 11, 1965; children: Jonathan Dumbe, Ndome Lynette. **Educ:** Jefferson Hospital School of Nursing, diploma, 1959; Univ of Pennsylvania, BSN, 1962; Univ of Pennsylvania, MSN, 1964; New York Univ, PhD, nursing, 1981; Hunter College, post masters practitioner certificate program, 1996. **Career:** Virginia State Coll, instructor, 1964-65; Hunter Coll, instructor, 1971-73; Seton Hall Univ, assoc prof, 1973-82; Hunter Coll, assoc prof, 1982-93; certified pediatric nurse practitioner, 1997. **Orgs:** Association of Black Nursing Faculty in Higher Education, 1988-; National League for Nursing, 1982-; American Nurses Association, 1973-; Sigma Theta Tau, 1967-; New York Alumnae Association, 1981-; Univ of Pennsylvania Alumnae Association, 1962-; Thomas Jefferson Univ Alumnae Association, 1993; St Mary's Hospital, bd of trustees, 1981-89. **Honors/Awds:** Sigma Theta Tau, Research Grant, 1980; Concerned Black Nurses, Newark, Research Award, 1991; Association of Black Nursing Faculty in Higher Education, Young Publisher's Award, 1990. **Special Achievements:** Author, "Homeless Families," 1990; "Disorders of Pregnancy," 1990; "Family Planning and Contraception," 1990; "Nursing Care of the Infant and Neonate," 1991; visiting professor at Univ of Malawi, 1991-93; author: "Children's Ideas of Health," 1998; author: "Pain Perceptions of Korean-American and Euro-American Women;" researched pain as a mental experience for nurses, patients and families in Blautyre and Liongwe, Malawi. **Military Serv:** US Army Reserve/Army Nurse Corps, major, 1983-93. **Business Addr:** Professor, Hunter-Bellevue School of Nursing, 425 E 25th St, New York, NY 10010, (212)481-4335.

ESTEP, ROGER D.
Educator. **Personal:** Born Mar 2, 1930, Clarksville, MD; married Romaine V Cook; children: Frederic. **Educ:** MD State Coll, BS 1951; PA State Univ, MS 1957; Tuskegee Inst, DVM 1962. **Career:** PA State Univ, instructor 1957-58; Tuskegee Inst, DVM 1958-62; Howard Univ, rsch & vet instr 1962-67, vet & asst prof of physiology 1967-70, exec asst to vice pres Health Affairs 1970-71, exec asst to pres 1971; NIH, dir div of rsch 1971-72; Howard Univ, vice pres 1972-. **Orgs:** Chmn publicity comm Amer Assn for Lab Animal Sci 1967; vice pres Natl Capital Area Br Amer Assn for Lab Animal Sci 1964-65, pres 1965-66; bd dir Amer Assn for Lab Animal Sci 1967, exec com 1967-; mem com on rsch Howard Univ 1963-69; chmn Com on Rsch Howard Univ 1969-70; asst gen chmn publicuty sub-com chmn Intl Com on Lab Animals 1969; mem sub-com Natl Acad of Sci 1962-63; mem Intergovtl Ad Hoc Com 1966-67; mem Amer Assn for the Accreditation of Lab Animal Care; mem Natl Adv Allergy & Infectious Diseases Council; pres elect, pres Amer Assn for Lab Animal Sci 1970, 1971; mem Long Term Radiation Effects Adv Com of Pub Health Svc; mem bd dir Natl Soc of Fund Raisers; mem Amer Vet Med Assn; DC Vet Med Assn; Amer Assn for Lab Animal Sci; assoc mem Amer Coll ofLab Animal Sci num papers. **Honors/Awds:** Sch of Veterinary Medicine of Tuskegee Inst The Alumni Recognition Awd 1970; Tuskegee Inst Alumni Merit Awd 1980; NAFEO Distinguished Alumni of the Year Citation 1980; Tuskegee Veterinary Medical Alumni Assn Distinguished Alumni Awd 1981; Univ of MD Eastern Shore Hall of Fame for Distinguished Alumni 1986. **Military Serv:** USAF staff sgt 1951-55. **Business Addr:** VP for Dev & Univ Rels, Howard Univ, 2400 6th St NW, Room 405, Washington, DC 20059.

ESTERS, GEORGE EDWARD
Educator. **Personal:** Born May 30, 1941, Bowling Green, KY; married Bettie Jean; children: Delmer. **Educ:** AR AM&N Pine Bluff, Hist 1964; Western KY Univ Bowling Green, MPS 1978; Western KY Univ Bowling Green, 1980. **Career:** Bowling Green City School Bd, dir of adult educ 1979-, coord of adult learning center, counselor & supr WIN 1972-73, teacher jr high 1971, teacher & high school coach 1964-70,. **Orgs:** Mem KEA-nEA-aGEA; charter KY Comm Educ Assn; mem KACE bd chmn Big Brothers & Sisters 1975-78; adv bd mem Bowling Green Bus Coll 1977;chmn of personnel com Head Start 1979. **Honors/Awds:** Outstanding alumni achievement S Central Provincial KY 1977; outstanding young men of am US Jaycees-Montgomery AL 1978; outstanding citizen Human Rights Commn Bowling Green KY 1979; outstanding leadership AWARE Bowling Green KY 1980. **Business Addr:** Bowling Green City Sch Sys, 224 E 12th St, Bowling Green, KY 42101.

ESTES, ELAINE ROSE GRAHAM
Librarian (retired). **Personal:** Born Nov 24, 1931, Springfield, MO; daughter of Zelma Mae Smith Graham and James McKinley Graham; married John M Jr. **Educ:** Drake Univ, BS 1953, Teaching Certificate 1956; Univ of IL, MS 1960. **Career:** Public Library of Des Moines, dir of library system 1956-95. **Orgs:** Mem past pres IA Library Assn, past pres Des Moines Metro Library Assn, Amer Library Assn; bd mem IA Soc for Preservation of Historic Landmarks; past bd trustees Des Moines Art Ctr; past bd mem Des Moines Comm Playhouse; past adv council Dept on Adult Ed; past bd adv Natl Trust for Historic Preservation; past mem Mayors Sister City Comm; past bd mem Des Moines Civic Ctr; mem Polk Cty Historical Soc; past state vice pres Questers Inc; past president, mem bd Terrace Hill Soc, Gov Comm for Restoration of Govs Mansion; past pres DM Chap Links Inc; past basilius Alpha Kappa Alpha Sorority Beta Phi Mu Hon Libr Scholastic Soc; past chairperson City of Des Moines Historic Dist Commn; mem State of IA Natl Reg Nominations Review Comm; mem adv council Iowa Dept of Cultural Affairs; Rotary 1987-; Natl Commn on the Future of Dr Unake Univ, Task Force on Libraries and Learning Resources 1987-88; president IUPLA 1991; Des Moines Sesquicentennial Committee, chair, history committee, 1992-94; board Wallace House Foundation 1989-95; Proteus, Iowa Antique Association; pres Wilson Alexander Scott, Chapter of Questers. **Honors/Awds:** Des Moines Leadership Awd 1975; Distinguished Alumni Awd Drake Univ 1979; Outstanding Contribution to the Quality of the Built Environment, De Moines Architects Council Community Reward 1981; Award of Merit for Historical Preservation, Iowa State Historical Soc 1984; Women of Achievement Award YWCA 1989.

ESTES, JOHN M., JR.
Mortician/proprietor (retired). **Personal:** Born Dec 6, 1928, Joplin, MO; married Elaine Graham. **Educ:** Univ if IA, 1946-48; Drake Comm Coll, 1950,51,53; KS City Coll of Mortuary Sci, 1952; Chicago Resorative Art, Post Grad Work 1952. **Career:** Estes & Son Funeral Home, retired owner, 1952-97. **Orgs:** Bd mem BSA, Rep Party, Kappa Alpha Psi, NAACP, March of Dimes, Des Moines School Bd, United Comm Svc, Greater Des Moines United Way, Comm Action Council, Gr Oppty Bd, C of C, Gr United Way, Comm Survey Inc, Simpson Coll Trustee, Des Moines Public Housing Authority, Wilkie House Inc, Des Moines Symphony, Tiny Tots Inc, IA Civil Liberties. **Honors/Awds:** Black Athlete Awd 25 yrs; Des Mones Human Rights Comm Recognition; 3 awds March of Dimes Natl Found; Univ of IA Alumni Assoc Awd; IA Employment Security Comm Awd; Des Moines Adult Ed Council Awd; Polk Cty Rep Party Awd; KSO Great Cty Awd; Des Moines Publ School Awd; Little All Amer League Awd; Natl Black Merit Acad Awd; National Council of Christians and Jews Awd. **Business Addr:** Mortician/Proprietor, Estes & Son Funeral Home, 1216 Forest Ave, Des Moines, IA 50314.

ESTES, SIDNEY HARRISON
Educational administrator. **Personal:** Born Jan 18, 1932, Atlanta, GA; married Barbara Ann Brown; children: Sidmel, Edward, Cheryl, Chris. **Educ:** Lincoln U, BA 1953; Atlanta U, MA 1959; IN U, EdD 1967. **Career:** Instructl Planning & Devel, Atlanta Public Schools, asst supt; Doctor Prog in Educ Admin, Atlanta Univ, dir 1971-73, exec dir educ & improv proj 1969-71, assoc dir educ improv proj; Atlanta Public Schools, Ralph Robinson Elementary, prin 1963-68, Slater Elementary, teacher 1957-63; Amer Assn of School Admin; Phi Delta Kappa Prof Frat; Natl Soc for the Study of Educ; Assn for Supvrs and Curriculum Devel, Alpha Phi Alpha Soc Frat BSA, exec Bd. **Orgs:** Mem Camp of Congressmn Andrew J Young 1972; mem Class Leadershp Atlanta 1975-76; mem advis bd Atlanta Counc for Children's TV. **Honors/Awds:** Silver beaver award BSA 1973; publ "The Plight of Black Parents" 1972; " Instruction-inner City where it's really at" 1975; contribut co-auth booklet "Impact of Decentralization on & Curriculum" 1975. **Military Serv:** AUS milit intellig aerial photointerpret 1953-55. **Business Addr:** 2930 Forrest Hill Dr SW, Atlanta, GA 30315.

ESTES, SIMON LAMONT
Opera singer. **Personal:** Born Feb 2, 1938, Centerville, IA. **Educ:** University of Iowa; Juilliard School of Music, scholarship to study. **Career:** L-Beck Opera Company, singer; Hamburg Opera Company, singer; opera singer, bass baritone; Juilliard School of Music, professor, currently. **Orgs:** Old Gold Singers, University of Iowa; American Opera Society; Simon Estes International Foundation for Children; Simon Estes Educational Foundation; Simon and Westella Estes Educational Foundation. **Honors/Awds:** First Intl Tchaikovsky Vocal Competition, Moscow; San Francisco Opera; San Sebastian Festival, Spain; performed all four of the Hoffman roles in Offenbach's Tales of Hoffman, Macbeth's Banquo, The Magic Flute, The Marriage of Figaro; grant, Martha Bard Rockefeller Foundation; Tchaikovsky Medal, 1985; honoree, Fine Arts Award, career achievements; acclaimed appearance, Porgy, Metropolitan Opera's first production of Porgy and Bess; Honorary Doctorates at Siena College, Drake University, University of Tulsa, Luther College; Honorary Colonel, Iowa National Guard. **Business Addr:** Columbia Artist Mgmt, Inc, c/o Laurence Tucker, 165 West 57th St, New York, NY 10019.

ESTES-SUMPTER, SIDMEL KAREN
Television station executive. **Personal:** Born Nov 27, 1954, Marysville, CA; daughter of Emellen Mitchell Estes and Sidney Harrison Estes; married B Garnett Sumpter, Aug 27, 1983; children: Joshua Khalid, Sidney Rashid. **Educ:** Northwestern University, BSJ, 1976, MSJ, 1977. **Career:** Chicago Daily Defender, reporter, 1974; Chicago Daily News, desk assistant, 1975; Gram Cable TV, reporter/anchor, 1977-79; WAGA-TV, news producer, planning manager, assg editor, executive producer, currently. **Orgs:** National Association of Black Journalists, immediate past president, 1991-93, president, 1993-95, regional director, 1987-91; Atlanta Association of Black Journalists, president, 1985-87; Leadership Atlanta, committee member, 1988-; Atlanta Chapter of NAACP, president of youth council, 1970-72; Society of Professional Journalists, board member, 1991; Atlanta Exchange, board member, 1987-89; Ben Hill United Methodist Church, section leader, 1989-91. **Honors/Awds:** Crisis Magazine, Lifetime Achievement, 1992; Outstanding Atlanta, Top Young People of Atlanta, 1991; Atlanta Association of Black Journalist, Pioneer Black Journalist Award, 1990; National Association of Professional & Business Women, Communications Award, 1989, Iota Phi Lombdo, Bronze Woman of the Year, 1989; National Association of Media Women, Media Woman of the Year, 1988. **Special Achievements:** Proclamation of Sidmel Estes-Sumpter Day in Atlanta, 1989; YWCA Award for Women of Achievement, 1988; American Women in Radio and TV, Producer of the Year, 1986; Atlanta Association of Black Journalists, Chairperson's Award, 1985; AABJ, Excellence in Community Science in Television, 1983. **Business Addr:** Executive Producer, WAGA-TV, 1551 Briarcliff Rd, NE, Atlanta, GA 30306, (404)898-0133.

ESTILL, ANN H. M.
Vocalist. **Personal:** Born in Washington, DC; daughter of T Christine Smith-Estill and Dr Don V Estill. **Educ:** Western MI Univ, BMusic; Columbia Univ Teachers Coll, MA; Professional Diploma; New York Univ, DA Voice Performance. **Career:** Kalamazoo Jr Symphony, performed violin four years; JCSC, researched & developed three courses in African & Afro-Amer Classical music; Jersey City State Coll, prof of music. **Orgs:** Numerous recitals in NYC, Washington, Atlanta, WLIB Radio NYC, NBC TV; WOR-TV Joe Franklin Show 1980; St Barthlomew's Church Chorus NYC performed over 60 Oratorios; Bernstein Mass, Kennedy Center; Scott Joplan's Treemonisha, Wolf Trap Farm for Performing Arts Vienna VA; Washington Choral Arts Chamber Choir; Protege Mm Luisa Fraceshi; Amer Inst of Music Studies Graz Austria; Sigma Alpha Iota Professional Hon Frat for Women in Music, NY Alumnae Chapter, president; Al-Past Phi C, province officer; Phi Delta Kappa Educ Hon; Kappa Phi Methodist Women; National Assn Teachers of Singing. **Honors/Awds:** European debut 1983-84 Rome Festival Orchestra 'La Regina della Notte Mozart's Il Flauto Magico; dissertation, "The Contributions of Selected Afro-Amer Women Classical Singers 1850-1955"; guest appearance, "Talent Hunters," Channel 10 Fairfax VA, 1988; Amahl in Gian-Carlo Menotti's Amahl and the Night Visitors, Essex County NJ Opera Co, 1988-89; Recital Concert, Vienna, Austria, 1995, "The Coloratura Sisters" with Sister Jeni Estill.

ETHEREDGE, JAMES W.
Government administrator. **Personal:** Born Jun 6, 1941, Leesville, SC; married Vanetta Bing; children: Lorna V, William Craig. **Educ:** SC State Coll, BS 1963; IN State Univ, Soc 1966; Winthrop Coll, Pol Sci 1973; Univ of SC, MPA 1973. **Career:** City of Rock Hill, social prog spec 1969-70; Winthrop Coll, part time instr 1973-79; City of Rock Hill, dir of admin serv 1971-80; City of Charleston, dir of admin serv 1980-. **Orgs:** Mem SC City & Cty Mgmt Assoc, SC Municipal Assoc, Amer Soc for Public Admin, Omega Psi Phi Frat, Charleston United Way Agency, Charleston Bus & Professional Assoc. **Business Addr:** Director Department of Administrative Svcs, City of Charleston, PO Box 304, Charleston, SC 29402.

ETHRIDGE, JOHN E.
Contractor. **Career:** J E Ethridge Construction Inc, Fresno CA, chief exec. **Business Addr:** J E Ethridge Construction Inc, 5270 E Pine Ave, Fresno, CA 93727.

ETHRIDGE, RAYMOND ARTHUR, JR.
Professional football player. **Personal:** Born Dec 12, 1968; son of Vernolia Walker; married Wanda Yvette; children: Rayven. **Educ:** Pasadena City College, attended. **Career:** Baltimore Ravens, wide receiver, 1996-. **Business Addr:** Professional Football Player, Baltimore Ravens, 11001 Owings Mills Blvd, Owings Mills, MD 21117, (410)654-6200.

ETHRIDGE, ROBERT WYLIE
Educational administrator. **Personal:** Born Nov 12, 1940, Monroe, MI; son of Hazel Johnson Ethridge and Claude Ethridge, Sr (deceased); married Elizabeth Sneed; children: Stephan, Tracy, Michael. **Educ:** Western MI Univ, AB 1962, AM 1970; Univ of MI Ann Arbor, PhD 1979. **Career:** Detroit Public Schools, teacher 1962-69; Western MI Univ, area coordinator housing 1969-72, admin asst to pres 1972-79, sec bd of trustees 1979-81; Emory Univ, coordinator of equal opportunity programs, 1981, asst vice pres 1982-92, associate vp, 1992-, adjunct asst prof, 1982-. **Orgs:** Mem CUPA, NACUBO 1981-, NAACP 1981-; 2nd vice pres 1981-82, 1st vice pres 1982-84 Amer Assoc for Affirmative Action; bd mem Natl Assault on Illiteracy Program 1983-; financial subcomm United Way 1984-; pres Amer Assoc for Affirmative Action 1984-88; bd mem American Contract Compliance Assn; mem Leadership Conference on Civil rights; United Way-Health Services Council 1984-; United Way-Admissions Panel 1984-; AAAA Natl Conf Planner 1982-84; mem Natl Inst for Employment Equity 1986-; chairman of the bd, Amer Contract Compliance Assoc, 1987-89; pres, Onyx Society of Western Michigan Univ, 1989-91; president, American Assn for Affirmative Action, 1990-92; bd of dirs, Western MI Univ Alumni Assn, 1989-, vp, 1993-94, pres, 1994-96; Community Friendship Inc, bd of dirs, 1994-96, treas, 1996-97; Georgia Nursing Foundation, bd of dirs, 1994-

95; WMU Onyx Society, pres, 1994-96, 1997-; 100 Black Men of Dekalb, bd of dirs, 1997-98; Leadership Atlanta, membership comm, 1997-98; Race Relations Comm, 1997-98. **Honors/Awds:** Achievement Award Northern Province KAY 1961-62; Community Bldg Award Black Monitor 1985; Citation for Public Service-Kalamazoo 1979; GA Public Relations Assn 1985; 2nd annual Civil and Human Rights Award-Intl, 1988; Proclamation State of Michigan House of Representatives, 1988; Assn of Official Human Rights Agencies. **Business Addr:** Associate VP, Emory Univ, 110 Administration Bldg, Atlanta, GA 30322, (404)727-6017.

ETHRIDGE, SAMUEL B.
Association consultant (retired). **Personal:** Born Dec 22, 1923, Brewton, AL; son of Lillian Foster Solomon and Frank Ethridge; married Cordia Baylr; children: Samuel David, Sherman George, Camille LaVerne, Steven Edsel. **Educ:** Stillman Jr Coll; Howard Univ, AB 1948; Univ of Cincinnati, MEd 1957. **Career:** Mobile Public Schools, teacher, principal, supvr 1948-58; March of Dimes, assis dir Intergroup Rel 1958-61; United Negro Coll Found, sau reg sec 1962-64; Nat'l Ed Assoc, dir of Civil Rights Exec Asso 1964-84; Natl Ed Assoc, retired (asst to dir). **Orgs:** Nat sec Reading Is Fund 1970-89; mem of bd Martin Luther King Jr Center for Soc Change 1975-89; mem of bd Shillman Coll 1979-85. **Honors/Awds:** Cit Am Teachers Assn 1966; cit Ft Worth UNCF 1969, AL State Teacher 1969, MS State Teacher 1972; Hum Rel awd NEA also NC Ed Assoc 1984; Ed Serv awd Nat Urban League 1984. **Military Serv:** USNA T/5 1943-46. **Home Addr:** 1602 Allison St, NW, Washington, DC 20011.

EUBANKS, DAYNA C.
Journalist. **Personal:** Born Jun 7, 1957, Wichita, KS; married. **Educ:** Univ of KS, BS, journalism, 1979. **Career:** KAKE-TV Wichita KS, psa actress 1975; KJHK Radio News Univ of KS, reporter vice pres Mondale trip 1977; KJHK Radio Univ of KS, newscaster, news editor 1977-78; Audio-Reader Univ of KS, newscaster, broadcaster/reader 1977-78; WREN-AM Topeka KS, legislative reporter 1978; WIBW-TV-AM-FM Topeka KS, newscaster, reporter, photographer, weekend news anchor,TV & radio 1978-79; KOOL-TV Phoenix AZ, weekend news anchor, gen assignment reporter 1979-81; WXYZ-TV ABC Detroit MI, weekendnews anchor, field anchor, Good Afternoon Detroit, gen assignment reporter beginning beginning 1981; WJBK-TV, Detroit, MI, anchor, host of weekday talk show Dayna, until 1992; WKRC-TV, Cincinnati, 1994-. **Orgs:** Amer Women in Radio & TV, Natl Assn of TV Arts & Sci, Natl Assn of Black Journalists, Sigma Delta Chi, Women in Commun, SAG, Amer Fed of TV & Radio Artists, Delta Sigma Theta; lifetime mem NAACP; co-chair & co-org Detroit Black-Jewish Leaders Forum; volunteer teacher & counselor "Who Said I Can't" Program; natl convention chairperson, natl exec bd mem IAWS 1979; advisor Judicial Bd GSP-Corbin Hall, Acad Success for KU Students; ku rep to the IAWS Natl Conv; rep Assoc of Univ Residence Halls. **Honors/Awds:** Apprec Awd NAACP for Generosity to People & Community; Apprec Awd Black History Week 82nd Flying Training Wing Williams AFB 1981; Awd for Contribs to Broadcasting Hartford Mem Baptist Church; Outstanding Achievement in Commun Alpha Kappa Alpha 1981; Awd for Outstanding Achievement as an Anchorwoman Journalist Public-Minded Citizen & Patron of the Arts 1982; Outstanding Woman in Broadcast News Amer Women in Radio & TV 1982; Golden Heritage Awd for Outstanding Achievment in Commun Little Rock Missionary Baptist Church; Robert L Powell Lecturer NAACP Oakland Univ; Outstanding Minority in Industry YMCA 1984; Detroit Emmy Awd Nominee Behind the Best 1985; Ebony Mag Thirty Future Black Leaders 1985. **Business Addr:** WKRC-TV, 1906 Highland Ave, Cincinnati, OH 45219.

EUBANKS, EUGENE E.
Educator. **Personal:** Born Jun 6, 1939, Meadville, PA; married Audrey J Hunter; children: Brian K, Regina A. **Educ:** Edinboro St U, BA 1963; MI St U, PhD 1972. **Career:** University of Missouri-KC, School of Education, prof, currently, dean 1979-89; Univ of DE, prof of educ admin 1972-74; Cleveland Pub Schs, tchr & admnstr 1963-70. **Orgs:** Consult Cleveland Found; consult KC Pub Schs; consult MO St Dept Edn; consult NAACP Sch Desegregation Suit in Cleveland OH; Nat Allinc Blk Sch Edctrs; Natl Conf Profs Educ Admin; Phi Delta Kappa; Am Assn of Univ Profs; NAACP; PUSH; Urban League; pres, AACTE, 1988; mem, Natl Policy Bd of Educ Admin, 1988. **Honors/Awds:** Articles published: A Study of Teacher Perception of Essential Teacher Attributes, 1974; Big-City Desegregation since Detroit, 1975; Rev Jesee L Jackson & PUSH Program for Excellence in Big-City Schools, 1977. **Military Serv:** USAF Sec Serv 1956-60. **Business Addr:** Professor, University of Missouri-KC, School of Education, 5100 Rockhill Rd, Kansas City, MO 64110.

EUBANKS, JOHN BUNYAN
Educator (retired). **Personal:** Born Feb 28, 1913, Clinton, LA; children: Judith, John Jr, David. **Educ:** Howard U, Th B 1935, AB 1936; AM 1938; Univ Chicago, PhD 1947; Northwestern U; Univ MO 1977. **Career:** Howard Univ, prof, until 1970 (retired); Jackson State Coll, 1955-60; Laos & Iraq, comm devel offcr 1953-55; Jarvis Coll, 1949-53; Morris Brown & Coll, prof 1946-49; YMCA, sec 1937-41; Rust Coll, consult 1966, 1975; Am Cncl on Educ, evaluator 1977. **Orgs:** Council on Rel & Pub Educ; council on Anthrop & Educ; soc for Hlth & Human Values Schlr Univ Chicago; gen educ bd fellow; Harvard Inst fellow; EPDA inst Grantee; Amer Museum of Natl History, assoc mem; Wilson Ctr Assoc; Natl Geographic Society. **Honors/Awds:** Fellowship (Comparative Rel.) General Ed Board 1943-44. **Home Addr:** 21 Kathleen Dr, Andover, MA 01810-1901.

EUBANKS, KEVIN
Jazz musician. **Personal:** Born 1958. **Educ:** Berklee Coll of Music. **Career:** NBC-TV, The Tonight Show, musical dir, currently. **Special Achievements:** Author, Creative Guitarist, Hal Leonard; recordings include: "Turning Point," "Spirit Talk," "Spirit Talk 2, Revelations". **Business Phone:** (818)840-4444.

EUBANKS, RACHEL AMELIA
Educator, musician, composer. **Personal:** Born in San Jose, CA; daughter of Amelia Eubanks and Joseph Eubanks; divorced. **Educ:** Univ of CA Berkeley, BA 1945; Columbia Univ NY, MA 1947; Pacific Western Univ, DMA 1980; Fontabl, France, Eastman Schl of Music, UCLA, USC, additional studies. **Career:** Wilberforce Univ, chmn Music Dept 1949-50; Albany State Coll, hd of Music Dept 1947; Eubanks Conser of Music, pres, founder, 1951. **Orgs:** Southeast Sym Assoc; LA County Art Mus; comm Afro-American Museum 1984-; Crenshaw Chamber of Commerce; mem, Natl Guild of Piano Teachers 1959-, Intl Congress on Women in Music 1984-, Musicians Union, Local 47, 1951-, Music Teacher's Natl Assn, Natl Assn of Negro Musicians 1949-; Ethnomusicology Society; American Musicological Society. **Honors/Awds:** Mosenthal flwhp Columbia Univ 1946; Musicianship: Vols I II and Tapes, Symphonic Requiem, Oratorio, Trio, & others; Alpha Mu Honor Society, Univ of CA Berkley 1946; Composition Award, Natl Assn Negro Musicians 1948; Symphonic Requiem, Korean Philharmonic, Los Angeles 1982; three songs, Res Musica, Baltimore 1985; Interlude #5, National Women's Music Festival, Bloomington, Indiana, 1988. **Special Achievements:** Sonata for Piano, premiered by Helen Walker-Hill, Sonneck Society, 1993; Five Interludes for Piano, Vivace Press, 1995; The First & Fifth Interludes on CD, Leonarda Records. **Business Addr:** President, Eubanks Conservatory of Music, 4928 Crenshaw, Los Angeles, CA 90043.

EUBANKS, W. RALPH
Editor/publisher. **Personal:** Born Jun 25, 1957, Collins, MS; son of Warren R & Lucille Eubanks; married Colleen Delaney Eubanks, Apr 22, 1989; children: Patrick Warren, Aidan Joseph, Delaney Marie. **Educ:** University of Mississippi, BA, 1978; University of Michigan, MA, 1979. **Career:** American Geophysical Union, copy editor, 1979-1984; American Psychological Association journals manager, 1984-89; Taylor & Francis, managing editor, 1989-90; American Psychological Association, director, APA books, 1990-95; Library of Congress, director of publishing, 1995-. **Orgs:** Washington Book Publishers, president, 1996-97; Washington Edpress, 1979-; University of Virginia Publishing, adjunct faculty, advisory board member, communications program, 1993-; Howard University Book Publishing Institute, student advisor, 1992-93. **Special Achievements:** "Ole Miss is Still Torn 25 Years After Meredith," Washington Post, Sept 23, 1987. **Home Addr:** 664 E St, NE, Washington, DC 20002, (202)544-5276. **Business Addr:** Director of Publishing, Library of Congress, 101 Independence Ave SE, LM602, Madison Bldg, Washington, DC 20540-4980, (202)707-3892.

EUGERE, EDWARD J.
Pharmacologist, educator. **Personal:** Born May 26, 1930, New Orleans; married Yolanda Rousseve; children: Edward, Jan, Gail, Lisa. **Educ:** Xavier U, BS 1951; Wayne State U, MS 1953; Univ CT, PhD 1956; Baylor Coll Med, Postdoctoral Study Myocardial Biology 1973. **Career:** Numerous Companies, pharmacist 1951-57; Wayne State Univ, grad teacher asst 1951-53; Univ of CT, 1953-56; Highland Park Jr Coll, lecturer; Detroit Inst of Technology, asst prof 1956-57; TX Southern Univ, prof 1957-; School of Pharmacy, dean 1968-70. **Orgs:** Mem numerous offices coms Harris County Pharm Assn; pres Houston Pharm Assn; Am Heart Assn; Lone Star State Pharm Assn; pres Houston Area Chi DeltaMu Professional Frat; Am Assn Coll Pharmacy; Am TX Pharm Assns; Houston Pharmacologists; Sigma Xi Soc; Rho Chi Pharmacy Honor Soc; pres 1977; bd Educ Diocess Galveston-houston 1974-77; pres Grand Jury Assn Houston-harris County; pres Cath Interracial Council Houston; Gulf Coast Area Child Devel Ctr Inc; Am Assn of Colls of Pharmacy Chi. **Honors/Awds:** Consult natl inst of health adv group serv certificate Nat Inst Health HEW 1973; leadership award Houston Pharm Assn 1971; guidance and leadership award Sr Class TX So Univ 1968; Fesler Research award Univ CT 1954-56; travel award Detroit Inst Tech 1957; faculty deve award TX So Univ 1973; researcher Fungal Fungal Toxins Pharmacology. **Business Addr:** Texas So Univ Sch Pharmacy, 3201 Wheeler Ave, Houston, TX 77004.

EURE, DEXTER D., SR.
Community relations executive. **Personal:** Born Nov 20, 1923, Suffolk, VA; son of Sarah Eure and Luke Eure; married Marjorie A; children: Dexter Jr, David, Philip. **Educ:** WV State Coll, BSME 1946. **Career:** PRAC Associates, vice pres 1960-61; Bradlee Div Stop & Shop, advertising product mgr; Boston Globe, asst to circulation mgr 1963-68, asst to editor 1968-70, dir of comm relations 1972-88 (retired). **Orgs:** First act dir Boston Comm Media Comm; mem Public Affairs Council Greater Boston Chamber of Commerce; mem Boston Globe Foundation, 1980-90; former member at large United Way of MA Bay; mem Congressional Black Caucus Comm Braintrust Comm; advisory com Crisis magazine NAACP; panelist Nieman Found for Journalism Harvard Univ Media Racism. **Honors/Awds:** First undergraduate elected to Omega Psi Phi Fraternity Supreme Council; Distinguished Serv Award Union United Methodist Church 1984; President's Award for Meritorious Serv to the Greater Boston Comm NAACP 1986; MA Black Legislative Caucus Eight Annual Award for energizing the black community to make positive and political changes 1986; Dean Dexter Roast & scholarship Benefit by Boston Assn of Black Journalists, 1988. **Military Serv:** AUS sgt 1st class 1948-50. **Business Addr:** Dir of Comm Relations, The Boston Globe, 135 Morissey Blvd, Boston, MA 02107.

EURE, HERMAN EDWARD
Animal parasitologist, educator. **Personal:** Born Jan 7, 1947, Corapeake, NC; children: Lauren Angela, Jared Anthony. **Educ:** MD St Coll, BS 1969; Wake Forest U, PhD 1974. **Career:** Wake Forest U, professor of biology 1974-. **Orgs:** Mem British Soc Parasitology; mem Inst of Ecology Univ of GA; mem Sigma Xi; mem NAACP; mem Alpha Phi Alpha Frat Inc. **Honors/Awds:** Fellow, Ford Found; Fellow, NSF; Oustnd Alumnus MD St Coll 1980; Beta Kappa Chi Nat Hon Soc; Man of the Yr Awd MD St Coll 1968. **Special Achievements:** First African-American to receive PhD, Wake Forest Univ; one of two, first full-time African-American faculty member, Wake Forest Univ; first African-American tenured, Wake Forest Univ. **Business Addr:** Box 7325, Reynolda Station, Winston-Salem, NC 27109, (919)759-5571.

EURE, JERRY HOLTON, SR.
Administrator (retired). **Personal:** Born Mar 4, 1923, Burdette, VA; son of Russie Bell Williams Eure and Rev Alexander Holton Eure; married Anna Blackwell Eure, Jun 6, 1948; children: Dianna, Geraldine, Jerry Jr, Sherri. **Educ:** West VA State College, Institute, WV, pre-eng, 1942; Rutgers University, New Brunswick, NJ, BS, 1951; University of Pennsylvania, Philadelphia, PA, MGA, 1970. **Career:** State of NJ, US Govt, RCA, NAF Inc, Trenton, NJ, various professional titles, 1949-72; State of NJ, Trenton, NJ, supervising planner, 1972-80; US Govt, New York & Newark, NJ, community planner, 1980-81; State of NJ, Trenton, NJ, supervising program development specialist, 1981-85; Coalition for Nuclear Disarmament, Trenton, NJ, educational coordinator, 1985-90. **Orgs:** Mercer County Office on Aging Commission, chair, 1994-; Human Civil Rights Association; Mercer County United Way, bd of trustees; New Jersey Black Issues Convention, board of directors, 1982-; Mercer Street Friends, board member, 1994-. **Honors/Awds:** Appreciation Award, Boy Scouts of America, 1978; Meritorious Award, Kappa Alpha Psi Fraternity, 1990; Certificate of Merit, Trenton Public School, 1989; Service & Community Outreach, Trenton Ecumenical Area Ministry, 1988; Certificate of Honor, Mercer County Board of Chosen Freeholders, 1988; Assembly Resolution, NJ General Assembly, 1987; Father of the Year, Bronzettes, Inc, 1984; Life Membership Award, NAACP, 1992; recipient (as father & husband) of award from National Federation of Colored Women's Club, both State and National Awards; Family of the Year Award, 1992. **Military Serv:** Air Force, Aviation Cadet, 1941-45. **Home Addr:** 924 Edgewood Avenue, Trenton, NJ 08618, (609)396-3279.

EVAIGE, WANDA JO
Educator, mayor. **Personal:** Born Jul 9, 1935, Frederick, OK; daughter of Lenora Oliver-Evaige (deceased) and Sam Evaige. **Educ:** Huston-Tillotson Coll, BA 1955; Univ of OK, current. **Career:** AME Church Rep, gov bd dir NCC USA 1973-76; Boyd Alumni Assn, natl pres 1973-75; Tillman Co Classroom Teachers, pres 1973; NEA, congressional contact 1983; City of Frederick, vice-mayor 1986, mayor, 1987-; Frederick Economic Dev Authority, vice chmn 1987; Frederick Public Schools, music specialist. **Orgs:** Pres TUO Chap Alpha Kappa Alpha Sor 1969-76; pres Frederick classroom Teachers 1973-74/1979-81; city council mem Ward III Frederick OK 1st woman elected 1983; legislative comm OK Municipal League 1984; lobbyist OK Educ Assn 1978-86; mem, Oklahoma Constitution & Revision Commission, State of Oklahoma 1988-. **Honors/Awds:** Teacher of the Year Frederick Teacher/Frederick OK 1st Black 1981; Teacher of the Year Tillman Co Teachers 1st Black 1981; 1st Black & 1st female mayor in the 85 Year History of City of Frederick 1987-89. **Home Addr:** 400 S 3rd St, Frederick, OK 73542.

EVANS, ADA B.
Former mayor, educator. **Personal:** Born Jun 9, 1932, Langley, SC; married Ray Allen; children: Cheri, Rachelle. **Educ:** Benedict Coll, BS (magna cum laude) 1955. **Career:** Park County Schools, teacher 1966-; IDS Marketing & Life Insurance, registered representative, Aiken County Schools, teacher 1955-60. **Orgs:** Mem CO Educ Assn NEA; CO Commn on Status of Women 1974-77; mem NAACP; Southeastern CO Health Systems Agy; Pikes Peaks Are as Council of Govt. **Business Addr:** 500 Front St, Fairplay, CO 80440.

EVANS, AKWASI ROZELLE
Publisher, editor. **Personal:** Born Oct 17, 1948, Dayton, OH; son of Geraline Dale and Garfield Evans; divorced; children: Sherilyn Ronetta Scott. **Educ:** University of Kentucky, BA, 1978; Texas Southern University, graduate school, 1980-82. **Career:** Austin Area Urban League, job developer/instructor, 1983-84; Capitol City Argus Newspaper, reporter, 1983-85; The Villager Newspaper, reporter, 1985-87; NOKOA-The Observer, publisher/editor, 1987-. **Orgs:** National Newspaper Publisher Association, 1986-; Texas Publisher Association, 1986-, vp, 1991-; National Business League, pres board of directors, 1986-91; African-American Improvement Corp, president, founder, 1986-; Multicultured Action Project, board of directors, 1990-; Black Arts Alliance, 1984-87, vp, 1986-87; Save Austin's Neighborhoods and Environments, board of directors, 1984-87. **Honors/Awds:** NAACP, Dewitty Overton Human Rights Award, 1990; Texas Mental Health Mental Retardation, Media Award, 1991; Sankhore Holistic Health Institute, Honorary Doctorate, 1982; Abbie Hoffman Memorial Award, 1990; Delta Sigma Theta, Leadership in Human Rights, 1990; Friends of the Phoenix, Phoenix Award, 1990. **Special Achievements:** Poetry Anthology: "Periplum Austin," 1990; "Seem Southern to Me," 1977; "Perfect Circle," 1974. **Business Addr:** Publisher/Editor, NOKOA-The Observer Newspaper, 1154-B Angelina St, PO Box 1131, Austin, TX 78767, (512)499-8713.

EVANS, ALBERT
Ballet dancer. **Personal:** Born in Atlanta, GA. **Educ:** School of American Ballet. **Career:** New York City Ballet, corps member, soloist, 1991-; ballet performanes include: Phlegmatic in Four Temperaments, Episodes, Ash. **Honors/Awds:** School of American Ballet, full scholarship. **Business Addr:** Dancer, New York City Ballet, 20 Lincoln Center Plaza, New York, NY 10023, (212)870-5656.

EVANS, ALICIA
Public relations director. **Personal:** Born May 28, 1960, Brooklyn, NY; daughter of Magnolia Ballard Evans and Simon Levan Evans. **Educ:** Hofstra Univ, Hempstead NY, BA Communications, 1982; New York Univ, New York NY, Business Mgmt Certificate, 1984. **Career:** Fortunoff's (upscale retail outlet), Westbury NY, promotional sales asst, 1977-84; CBS News, New York NY, program transcriber, 1981; Lockhart & Pettus Advertising Agency, New York NY, account exec, 1982-87; All Ways Natural Hair Care, Brooklyn NY, dir public relations, 1987-. **Orgs:** Mem, Natl Assn for Female Exec, 1988, Public Relations Soc of Amer, 1988; member, New York Black Public Relation Society, 1990-. **Honors/Awds:** News & Feature Editor, "The Satellite," Hofstra Univ, 1981, 1982; pruducer/copywriter, Con Edison, NY Utility Co (radio commercial), 1984; copywriter (brochure), Minority & Women's Div, New York Chamber of Commerce, 1984; producer/copywriter, Dark & Lovely Hair Care Products (radio commercial), 1987; senior editor, "Homecoming," Army ROTC Publication, 1984-87; African-American Achievement Award for Outstanding Serv & Commitment to the Business Community, New York Million Dollar Boys Club, 1988; 1000 Notable Business & Professional Women, American Biographical Institute, 1990. **Home Addr:** 4 First Ave, Westbury, NY 11590.

EVANS, AMOS JAMES
Association executive. **Personal:** Born May 11, 1922, Rayne, LA; married Carolyn S; children: Winnfred, Adrian J, Wendell P, Donald R. **Educ:** Lasalle Bus Coll 1946. **Career:** Port Arthur Br NAACP TX, pres 1972-80; Gulf Oil Corp, operator no 1 1946-80; Ch Sch, couns 1964-80; 7th St Br YMCA, pres 1973-77. **Honors/Awds:** Recipient serv award & membership 7th Br YMCA 1970; outstanding serv to youth award St Paul United Meth Ch 1971; comm serv award Negro BPW Port Arthur TX 1976; meritorious award Port Arthur Br NAACP 1977; cong comm award Golden Gate Civic ZOB Sorority Man 1977. **Military Serv:** USN petty officer 1944-46. **Business Addr:** Port Arthur Branch NAACP, PO Box 1583, Port Arthur, TX 77640.

EVANS, ARTHUR L.
Educator. **Personal:** Born Jul 26, 1931, Macon, GA; married Hattie Fears; children: Ivan Hugh. **Educ:** Morehouse Coll, AB 1953; Columbia Univ, MA 1957; Univ of Miami, PhD 1972; Union Theological Seminary School of Social Music, attended. **Career:** Ballard-Hudson High School Macon, 1953-54; Miami Northwestern Sr High School, 1957-69; Miami-Dade Jr Coll, prof of humanities 1967-69; Hialeah-Miami Lakes Sr High School, chmn, choral dir 1970-72; SC State Coll Orangeburg, dir of concert choir, chmn dept of visual & performing arts. **Orgs:** Chmn humanities, music ed, dir Men's Glee Club Concert Choir; chmn Fine Arts Lyceum Comm 1973; conductor Coll Concert Choir 1974-75; mem Kappa Delta, Phi Mu Alpha Sinfonia, Natl Mus Eds Conf, The Amer Choral Dir Assoc, SC Music Ed Assoc, Phi Beta Sigma. **Honors/Awds:** Ed Awd Phi Beta Sigma 1972; Outstanding Achievement Awd Phi Beta Sigma 1987. **Military Serv:** AUS pfc 1954-56. **Business Addr:** Chmn Visual & Performing Arts, South Carolina State Coll, PO Box 1917, Orangeburg, SC 29117.

EVANS, BILLY J.
Educator, researcher. **Personal:** Born Aug 18, 1942, Macon, GA; married Adye Bel; children: William, Carole. **Educ:** Morehouse Coll, BS (summa cum laude) 1963; Univ of Chicago, PhD 1968. **Career:** Univ of Manitoba, post-doctoral fellow dept of physics 1968-69; Howard Univ, asst prof chemistry 1969-70; Univ of MI, asst prof 1970-73, assoc prof dept geol & mineral 1973-75; Natl Bureau of Standards Alloy Physics Section, consultant 1971-; BASF Wyandotte, consult 1976-78; Univ of MI, assoc prof chem 1975-79, prof of chem 1979; Univ of Chicago, research assoc; US Geological Survey, consultant, 1980-84; Noud Research Labortory, consultant, 1986-. **Orgs:** Mem Amer Phys Soc; Amer Chemical Soc; Mineral Soc of Amer; Canadian Mineral Assn; Amer Geophysical Union; Minorities of the Amer Geophysical Union; advisory committee, Los Alamos, Natl Lab. **Honors/Awds:** Early admission to college, Merrill Scholar Morehouse Coll 1959-63; Phi Beta Kappa; Woodrow Wilson Fellow 1963-; Sigma Xi, 1968-; Natl Rsch Council of CAN Postdoctoral Fellow Univ of Manitoba 1968-69; Alfred P Sloan Rsch Fellow 1972-75; Humboldt Sr Fellow 1977-78; Danforth Assoc 1977-83; Amer Soc of Engineering Educ, Distinguished Faculty Fellow, 1988; Phi Kappa Phi, 1991; Chemical Manufacturer's Assoc, Catalyst Medalist, 1995; ACS Award for Encouraging Disadvantaged Students into Careers in the Chemical Sciences, American Chemical Society, 1996; Gallery of Inventors, Tubman Museum, Inductee. **Business Addr:** Prof of Chemistry, Univ of MI, Dept of Chemistry, 930 N University Ave, Ann Arbor, MI 48109-1055, (313)747-2851.

EVANS, CAROLE YVONNE MIMS
Judge. **Personal:** Born Oct 1, 1951, Hendersonville, NC; daughter of Mary Louise Valentine Mims and Evans King Mims; married Michael Duaine Evans, Sep 5, 1991; children: Tracey Renee Evans, Michael Thomas Evans, Karen Michelle Evans. **Educ:** Wellesley Coll, BA 1973; Duke Univ Sch of Law, JD 1976. **Career:** Chambers Stein Ferguson & Becton, attorney 1976-88; Children's Law Center, 1989-92; 26th Judicial District, NC, district court judge, 1992-. **Orgs:** Bd of dirs Charlotte Assn YWCA 1978-80; bd of dirs Planned Parenthood Charlotte Affiliate 1979-80; bd of dirs Charlotte Mecklenburg Urban League Org 1979-81; Charlotte Speech & Hearing Center 1983-89; NC Bar Assn Bd of Governors 1986-89; mem of bd Bio-Ethics Resources Group 1988-; mem of bd Leadership Charlotte 1988-; Charlotte Mecklenburg Planning Commission, 1980-83; Foundation for the Carolinas, board of directors, 1992-. **Business Addr:** Judge, District Court, 700 E Fourth St, Suite 3304, Charlotte, NC 28202.

EVANS, CHARLOTTE A.
Business executive. **Personal:** Born in Providence, RI. **Educ:** NY Inst of Credit. **Career:** First Nat City Bank, switchboard operator, platform customer rep, official asst, asst mgr 1954-. **Orgs:** Mem Nat assn of Bank Women Inc; Urban Banders Coalition; former bd mem Hamilton Center Day Care Inc; former mem Manhattanville Comm & Center Inc; former mem Scitarnard Players of Providence RI; mem Black Achievers YMCA; original mem Am Negro Theatre of NY; honorary mem Iota Phi Lambda Sorority; vice pres Corr sec NY Rinkeydinks Inc. **Honors/Awds:** Recipient 1970 luncheon Award Iota Phi Lambda Sorority 1971; one of first black achievers 1968; first black women officer of any bank in NY. **Business Addr:** 125 St at Old Broadway, New York, NY 10027.

EVANS, CHERYL LYNN
Banker. **Personal:** Born May 24, 1950, Gary, IN; daughter of Charleston Fullerton Evans and William Henry Evans; married Eldridge Anthony, 1990 (divorced); children: Jeffrey W Anthony, Shonda Y Anthony. **Educ:** Omega The Bank Training Co, San Francisco, CA, certificate, 1982; Dun & Bradstreet Business Educational Services, New York, NY, certificate, 1984. **Career:** Crocker Bank, San Francisco, CA, consumer loan product manager, 1972-80; Sumitomo Bank, San Francisco, CA, vice president compliance officer loan administration, 1980-. **Honors/Awds:** Community Involvement Award, Ella Hill Hutch Community Center, 1984. **Home Addr:** 3 Mabrey Ct, San Francisco, CA 94124-2485.

EVANS, CHUCK
Professional football player. **Personal:** Born Apr 16, 1967, Augusta, GA; married Etopia; children: Clarke. **Educ:** Clark Atlanta, attended. **Career:** Minnesota Vikings, running back, 1993-. **Business Addr:** Professional Football Player, Minnesota Vikings, 9520 Viking Dr, Eden Prairie, MN 55344, (612)828-6500.

EVANS, CLAY
Cleric. **Personal:** Born Jun 23, 1925, Tennessee; married Lutha Mae; children: Diane (deceased), Michael, Ralph, Claudette, Faith. **Educ:** No Bapt Theol Sem, attended; Univ Chicago School of Div, attended; AR Bapt Coll, DD. **Career:** Bapt Ministers Conf, pres 1964-66; WCFL-AM Radio & TV, ministry; Fellowship Bapt Church, pastor, 1950-. **Orgs:** African American Religious Connection, founder/pres, currently. **Business Addr:** Founder/President, African American Religious Connection, 45 Princeton Ave, Chicago, IL 60609.

EVANS, CRECY ANN
Educator. **Personal:** Born Apr 17, 1915, Benton, LA; married John W; children: Christine A Bates. **Educ:** Wiley Coll, BA 1945; Bishop Coll, EdM 1952; Northeast State U, Addl Study; LA Tech U; Univ of CA Berkeley. **Career:** Retired public school admin; elementary school, prin 1934-45; jr & sr high school, asst prin 1945-74; Caddo Parish School Bd, Basileius Sigma Gamma Rho, 1966-74; Esquirett Soc Club, pres. **Orgs:** Life mem PTA NEA; LEA Sponsors Drop-n Serv for Harmony House Nursing Home; mem Scott A Lewis Chap 22 Order of Eastern Star; chair person Scholarship Com; warder amarantha YMCA; Comm Action Club; mem sec Rosa of Sharon No 149; various other activieties. **Honors/Awds:** Trophy outstanding serv Sigma Gamma Rho 1967; sigma of yr 1972; trophy sigma of yr SW Reg 1972; adv of yr Undergrad Chap Sigma Gamma Rho 1974; trophy for serv rendered Valencia Jr HS 1974; develop functional program in Guidance & Reading for Slow Learners Disadvantages Youth.

EVANS, DAVID LAWRENCE
Educator. **Personal:** Born Dec 27, 1939, Wabash, AR; married Mercedes L Sherrod; children: Daniel, Christine. **Educ:** TN State Univ, BS 1962; Princeton Univ, MS Engrg 1966. **Career:** Boeing Com, electrical engineer 1962-64; Lockheed, electrical engineer 1964; Princeton Univ, teaching asst 1964-66; IBM Corp, electrical engineer 1966-70; Harvard Univ, admin officer, asst dean 1970-. **Orgs:** Mem bd trustees St Georges Sch; mem Gov Bd Princeton Grad Alum Assn; mem Inst of Elec & Electronic Engrs, Amer Audlgy Soc; mem Natl Assn ofColl Admiss Couns; mem Alpha Phi Alpha Frat; Harvard Club of Boston; mem Assn of Black Princeton Alumni; Princeton Alumni Assn of New England; select com Natl Merit Corp; prd film Unique Afr Rebels of Surinam 1975; Natl Sci Found Traineeship 1965-66. **Honors/Awds:** Outstanding Young Men of Amer 1971; TN State Univ Alum of the Yr 1972; publ "Making It as a Black at Harvard/Radcliffe" NY Times 1976; "On Criticism of Black Student" Ebony 1977; "School Merit Pay System Gone Awry" LA Times 1984; "An Appeal to Black Alumni" Newsweek 1984.

EVANS, DEBORAH ANN
Librarian, archivist. **Personal:** Born Sep 30, 1959, Detroit, MI; daughter of Irene Parks Evans and Thomas Evans. **Educ:** University of Michigan, AB, 1981, AMLS, 1983; Wayne State University, certificate in archival administration, 1992; Preservation Intensive Institute, University of California, Los Angeles, 1994. **Career:** Dickinson, Wright, et al, law librarian, 1983-84; Wayne County Library, librarian, 1985-88; Detroit Public Library, field archivist, 1988-95; Detroit Public Library, librarian/specialist III, 1995-. **Orgs:** American Library Association, 1992-94; Oral History Association, 1988-89; Fred Hart Williams Genealogical Society, 1989-; Michigan Library Association, 1987-88; American Association of Law Libraries, 1983-84; Special Libraries Association, 1983-84; Deborah Evans Associates, president, 1990-; Detroit Assn of Black Storytellers, 1994-; Fred Hart Williams Genealogical Society, board member at large, 1995-96, 1st vice pres, 1996-97; International Platform Association, 1995-. **Honors/Awds:** University of Michigan, School of Information and Library Studies, Margaret Mann Award, 1983, Edmon Low Award, 1983; Michigan Genealogical Council, Certificate of Appreciation, 1991; Library of Michigan, Librarian's Professional Certificate, 1991; Scholarship form California State Library to attend Preservation Intensive Institute, 1994. **Special Achievements:** Presented paper: "Michigan in Perspective," Local History Conference, 1991; Michigan Archival Association Spring Conference, panelist, 1992; published video reviews, Library Journal, 1992; Michigan African-American Symposium, Detroit Michigan, conference co-chair, 1995; Developer & presenter: African-American Internet Resources Workshops, Detroit Public Library, 1996-97. **Business Addr:** Librarian/Specialist III, Detroit Public Library, 121 Gratiot Ave, Detroit, MI 48226, (313)224-0580.

EVANS, DONALD LEE
Professional football player. **Personal:** Born Mar 14, 1964, Raleigh, NC; son of Novella Scott Evans and Rhuben Evans; married Debra Jeffers Evans, Mar 27, 1988; children: Donald Lee II, Novella Leeann, Jessica Nicole. **Educ:** Winston-Salem State University, BS, health & physical education, 1993. **Career:** Los Angeles Rams, 1987-89; Pittsburgh Steelers, 1990-94; New York Jets, 1994-. **Orgs:** Project Bundle Up, 1987-; United Way, 1987-; Life of Life Mission, 1987-; Share the Warmth, The Hunger Project, Donald Evans Schlorship Fund, Black Arts Supporter. **Honors/Awds:** Winston-Salem State University, All CIAA Football Champions, 1986; Pittsburgh Steeler Fan Club, Black and Gold Barae Player of the Month, 1992. **Special Achievements:** Winston-Salem State University, Dean's List, 1992; Los Angeles Rams, Number One Draft Pick, 1987. **Business Addr:** Professional Football Player, New York Jets, 1000 Fulton Ave, Hempstead, NY 11550-1099.

EVANS, DONNA BROWDER
Educational administrator, educator. **Personal:** Born in Columbus, OH; daughter of Margaret Browder and Clarke Browder; divorced; children: Jocelyn Michelle Brown-Smith. **Educ:** OH State Univ, BSc 1958, MS 1964, PhD 1970. **Career:** Univ of Cincinnati, asst prof 1969-73; Univ of Maine, prof/grad dean

1973-83; Skidmore Coll, prof/chair dept of educ 1983-87, Wayne State Univ, prof/dean of educ 1987-91; University of North Florida, professor/dean, 1991-. **Orgs:** Mem Alpha Kappa Alpha Sor Detroit Chapt; mem Coalition of 100 Black Women Albany 1984-87; mem Amer Assoc of Univ Women Saratoga Springs 1984-87; mem Links Inc Jacksonville Chap 1987-; bd of dirs Assoc Black Educators/Profs 1985-87; bd of dirs Soroptomist Intl 1985-87; bd dir Lake George Opera Festival; bd dir Task Force Against Domestic Violence Saratoga Spngs; Sophisticates Savannah Chap 1988-, Carrousels, Detroit Chap 1988-; Junior Achievement, Jacksonville, board of directors, 1991-. **Special Achievements:** Reviewer Brooks Cole Publishing Co 1980-; editorial bd Journal of Reality Therapy 1984-; publications "Success Oriented Schools in Action" 1981, "A Conversation with William Glasser" 1982, "Opening Doors to the Future Through Education" 1984, "Reality Therapy, A Model for Physicians Managing Alcoholic Patients" 1984, "Curriculum Not Either-Or", 1991. **Business Addr:** Dean, College of Education and Human Services, University of North Florida, 4567 St John's Bluff Rd, Room 2543, Jacksonville, FL 32224.

EVANS, DORSEY
Attorney. **Personal:** Born Dec 7, 1930, Kansas City, KS; married Ruth Wilson; children: Dorsey Delwin, Velma, Elizabeth, Gary C. **Educ:** Univ of KS, B 1952; Howard Univ, JD 1958. **Career:** Howard Univ, legal aid soc; Turner Memorial AME Church, cons; Local Funeral Home, cons; Pride Econ Devel Inc, cons; Storage Co, cons; Westinghouse ElectCorp, cons; Congressman Walter E Fauntroy's Camp Comm, former treasurer 1972-; Delco Settlement Co, pres; Delwin Realty Co, pres; Private practice,attny; Howard Univ, legal counsel. **Orgs:** Mem Natl, Wash DC, Amer, Bar Assocs; mem Amer Judicature Soc, Amer Arbitration Assoc, Supreme Ct US, Supreme & State Ct KS; mem, adv comm Superior Ct Rules Civil Procedure DC; mem Info Ctr for Handicapped Children, Turner Mem Meth Church; former vp, pres Homemaker Svc; past pres Young Dem Clubs, Woodridge Civic Assoc, Young Adult Club; past vice pres Fed Civic Assoc; past chmn 12 Precinct Police Crime Council. **Honors/Awds:** Outstanding Trial Counsel Chief Judge Bazelon. **Military Serv:** US Army, 1953-55. **Business Addr:** Attorney, Howard Univ, 1301 Pennsylvania Ave, N W, Washington, DC 20004.

EVANS, DOUGLAS EDWARDS
Professional football player. **Personal:** Born May 13, 1970, Shreveport, LA; married Myria; children: Aymmara. **Educ:** Louisiana Tech, bachelor's degree in finance. **Career:** Green Bay Packers, defensive back, 1993-. **Business Addr:** Professional Football Player, Green Bay Packers, 1265 Lombardi Ave, Green Bay, WI 54304, (414)494-2351.

EVANS, DWIGHT
State representative. **Personal:** Born May 16, 1954, Philadelphia, PA; son of Jean Odoms Evans and Henry Evans. **Educ:** Philadelphia Community College, gen, 1973; La Salle College, 1975; Temple Univ, 1976-78. **Career:** State of Pennsylvania, state representative, dist 203, currently. **Orgs:** Tutorial program, admissions procedure comm, La Salle College; chm, Black Student League; 10th Ward Dem Exec Comm; City-Wide Polit Alliance; Northwest Polit Coalition; Philadelphia Cnl Neighborhoods; consultant, North Cent Community Mental Health Center, House of Umoja, Coun Labor and Indust; Stenton Food Co-Op Program. **Honors/Awds:** Community Service Award, La Salle College, Urban Studies Center, 1981, Dept of Public Welfare, 1980; Citizen of the Year, Philadelphia Tribune, Pepsi Cola, 1979. **Business Addr:** State Representative, District 203, Pennsylvania State House of Representatives, 7174 Ogontz Ave, Philadelphia, PA 19138.

EVANS, EDGAR E.
Educator. **Personal:** Born Jan 20, 1908, Pittsview, AL; married Zelia V Stephens. **Educ:** Fisk Univ, AB 1930; Univ of MI, MA 1948. **Career:** Apopka FL, Winter Garden, Starke, Siluria AL, Waynesboro VA, principal 1931-48; AL State Univ, prof 1949-72; Royal Soc of Health, ret fellow 1965-. **Orgs:** Mem The Pres Club; life mem Phi Delta Kappa, Phi Beta Sigma Frat, Amer Soc for the Study of Ed, Amer Acad of Pol Sci, Amer Sociol Assoc; dep Shaaban Temple 103; trustee St John AME Church; mem So Pride Elks Lodge 431; 3rd vice pres 9th Episcopal Dist AME Church; life mem NAACP, 33 Deg Mason. **Honors/Awds:** Plaque Shaaban Temple 103; Cert of Apprec, Cty Dist Attny 15th Jud Circuit, Ret Sr Vol Prog of the US of Amer, Dexter Ave Bapt Church, Cleveland Ave YMCA; Man of the Year Awd St John AME Church 1977; The Amer Public Health Assn pays Tribute to Edgar E Evans 1986; Phi Beta Sigma Man of the Year 1987. **Military Serv:** Corpl 1942-45.

EVANS, ELINOR ELIZABETH
Marketing executive. **Personal:** Born Mar 6, 1948, Detroit, MI; daughter of Evelyn & Harold Evans; divorced; children: Tracey Dorsey, Candace Rush, Kevin Dorsey. **Educ:** Wayne County Community College, AA, 1989; Wayne State University, BS, 1997. **Career:** City of Detroit, Transportation Dept, auto mechanic, 1974-77, sr clerk, 1977-83, principal clerk, 1983-84; City of Detroit, Cobo Convention Center, event coordinator, 1984-87, asst sales mgr, 1987-93, sales mgr, 1993-96, asst dir of mktg, 1996-. **Orgs:** National Coalition of Black Meeting Planners, 1993-; International Association of Exhibit Managers, 1995-; Religious Conference Management Association, 1993-; American Society of Association Executives, 1987-; Optimist Club of Central Detroit, 1995-; NAACP, 1965-. **Honors/Awds:** High School of Commerce & Business Administration, Community Svc Award, 1996; Distributive Education Clubs of America, Certificate of Appreciation, 1994; Wayne State University, Otto Finestein Writing Excellence Award, 1997. **Business Addr:** Assistant Director of Mktg, Cobo Convention Ctr, 1 Washington Blvd, Detroit, MI 48226, (313)877-8777.

EVANS, EVA L.
Educational administrator. **Educ:** Wayne State University, bachelor's degree; Michigan State University, master's degree, doctorate degree. **Career:** East Lansing Public Schools, deputy superintendent, currently. **Orgs:** Alpha Kappa Alpha, board of directors, national committee chairman, chapter officer, vice president, international president, currently. **Special Achievements:** First vice president of the Alpha Kappa Alpha sorority, 1990. **Business Addr:** Deputy Superintendent, East Lansing Public Schools, 519 W Kalamazoo, Lansing, MI 48933, (517)337-6459.

EVANS, FAITH
Vocalist. **Personal:** married Christopher Wallace (deceased); children: China, Christopher, Jr. **Career:** Singer, currently. **Special Achievements:** Albums include: Faith Evans; Songs include: "You Used to Love Me", "Soon As I Get Home", "Love Don't Live Here Anymore" duet with Mary J. Blige. **Business Addr:** Vocalist, c/o Bad Boy/Arista Records, 8 W 19th St, New York, NY 10011.

EVANS, GREGORY JAMES
Recreation director. **Personal:** Born Feb 15, 1954, Chicago, IL; son of Willie Evans and Johnnie Evans. **Educ:** Wilbur Wright Jr Coll, AA 1975; Southern IL Univ, BA Phil 1977; Southern IL Univ, MS Health Ed 1979; De Paul Univ, Chicago, IL, PhD candidate, philosophy, 1986-. **Career:** Amer Cancer Soc, public ed, coord 1980-82; Oak Park YMCA, phys ed instr 1982-84; Amer Cancer Soc, publ ed dir 1982; Health & Sports Productions, dir 1982-84; Randolph Tower Fitness Ctr, mgr 1983-84; Village of Oak Park, manager adult educ 1986-; Special Event Entertainment Group 1989. **Orgs:** Free-lance amateur photography; black belt karate, Ahn's Tae Kwon Do Assoc 1978; ice hockey coach volunteer, Oak Park Hockey Assoc 1980-81; gen mem, IL Interagency Council on Smoking & Disease 1980-83; vice pres, IL Soc of Publ Health Ed 1981-82; mem, Oak Park Area Jaycees 1984-; general mem, IL Park & Recreation Assoc 1984-; Amer Assn of Physical, Health & Recreation 1989; mem, Chicago Convention of Bureau and Tourism, 1990; mem, 1991, Board of Regents, 1992-95, School of Sports Management, North Carolina State University; mem, TAC of Illinois, Long Distance Running Comm, 1990. **Honors/Awds:** Natl Publ Ed Ctr Amer Cancer Soc 1980; Basic Fitness Cert Oak Park YMCA 1981; Semi-Pro Football Champs Cook Cty Cowboys 1981; Publ Coach & Athlete Playing Tall with Pylons 1981; Articles & Rsch Innovative Factors on Player Performance Preparation & Conditioning Factors 1981; 10 days training Natl Ctr for Comm Educ 1986; Cultural Arts Awd Jack & Jill Assoc of Amer West Suburban Chap 1986; Revenue Source Mgmt School 1988; Natl Youth Sport Coach Assn 1987; Amer Coaches Effectiveness Program 1985. **Home Addr:** 18 Woodsorrel, Woodridge, IL 60517. **Business Addr:** Manager, Adult Education Programs, Park District of Oak Park, 218 Madison, Oak Park, IL 60302.

EVANS, GROVER MILTON, SR.
City councilman & consultant. **Personal:** Born Mar 6, 1952, Jonesboro, AR; son of Georgia Lee Evans & William Evans (deceased); married Pamela Evans, Jun 7, 1981; children: Grover Evans Jr. **Educ:** Arkansas State Univ, BA, 1992; LaSalle Univ, PhD, 1995. **Career:** Jonesboro Sun, journalist, 1974-77; KXRQ, news dir, 1982-83; City of Jonesboro, city councilman, 1984-; Self employed, consultant & motivational speaker, 1992-. **Orgs:** AR State Spinal Cord Comm, chairman, appt by governor, 1989-99; AR Martin Luther King Jr Comm, commissioner, appt by governor, 1993-; Early Childhood Comm, commissioner, appt by governor, 1989-93; AR Child Placement Advisory Committee, appt by governor, 1987-; Consumer Advisory Council For Rehab Services, appt by governor, 1986-92; Natl Org on Disabilities, liaison for city of Jonesboro, 1986-; Jonesboro Chamber of Commerce, educ committee, 1995; US Water Fitness Assn Inc, vice chairman, 1993-. **Honors/Awds:** Natl Wheelchair Championships, Swimmer of the Year, 1993; Methodist Hosp, Jonesboro, Volunteer of the Year, 1993; Paralympics, US Disabled Swim Team, 1992; State of AR, Ambassador of Goodwill, 1992-; US Postal Service, Outstanding Black Citizen Award, 1989. **Special Achievements:** First Black American to swin in any Olympic Event, 1992; First Black American to swim in a World Championship, 1994; Keynote Speaker at 7th Annual I Have a Dream, Natl Youth Assembly, 1994; Hold 10 American Records in Swimming, sponsored by Martin Luther King Jr Federal Holiday Commission, 1991-95. **Home Addr:** 1613 Jennifer Dr, Little Rock, AR 72212-3827, (501)932-9724.

EVANS, GWENDOLYN
Business executive. **Personal:** Born in North Carolina; daughter of Talmadge Whitley Evans and James L Evans. **Educ:** Essex Coll of Business, Certificate 1965; Rutgers Univ, BS 1973; New School Soc Res, Post Graduate Work 1975-77. **Career:** Prudential Insurance Co, vice president, agency career development, various admin, technical & clerical assigments, 1962-74; College Relations, assoc mgr 1974-75; Equal Opportunity specialist 1975-76; assoc mgr corporate personnel admin 1976; mrg field serv personnel 1976-78. **Orgs:** Dir serv personnel Prudential Insurance CO 1978-, dir field office planning 1982-; instructor Coll in Co Prud Essex County Coll 1973-75; mem Hampton Inst Cluster Proggram VA 1975-77; charter mem Educ Center Youth Newark; exec comm, bd mem Natl Comm Prevention of Child Abuse New Jersey Chapter 1983-88; mem Amer Soc of Devel New Jersey Chapter 1984-85. **Honors/Awds:** Certificate of Appreciation, Amer Soc Training Devel 1984; YWCA Black Achiever Award, Newark NJ 1981. **Business Addr:** Executive, Prudential Insurance Co, 213 Washington St, Newark, NJ 07102.

EVANS, HUGH
Professional sports official. **Personal:** Born 1943. **Career:** NBA, referee, currently. **Business Addr:** NBA Official, National Basketball Association, 645 5th Ave, 15th Fl, New York, NY 10022-5986, (212)826-7000.

EVANS, JACK
College president. **Career:** Southwestern Christian Coll, Terrell TX, pres, currently. **Business Addr:** President, Southwestern Christian College, PO Box 10, Terrell, TX 75160.

EVANS, JAMES CARMICHAEL
Government official. **Personal:** Born Jul 1, 1900, Gallatin, TN; married Roselline; children: James Carmichael, Rose E. **Educ:** Roger Williams U, AB 1921; MA Inst Tech, BS 1925, MS 1926; VA State Coll, LLD 1955; Central State Coll, 1956; Argl & Tech Coll NC, LHD 1961. **Career:** Miami FL, elec eng cnstr 1926-68; Booker T Wash HS Miami, tchr 1927; Trade & Tech Div WV State Coll, prof tech industries dir 1928-37, admnstrv asst to pres 1937-42; Sec War, asst civilian aide 1943-47, civilian aide 1947-48; Sec Def, adv 1947-49, asst 1947, couns Ellor mil & cvln affrs 1964-70; Howard U, adj prof elec engr 1946-70; Afro-Am Life Ins Co, vice pres 1954-; Indsl Bank Washington, dir; Council Nat Def War Mnpwr Com Wash, 1941-43. **Orgs:** Mem Nat Inst Sci; Am Inst Elec Engr; IRE; Am Assn Univ Profs; Nat Educ Assn; Nat Tech Assn, Exec Sec, 1932-57; mem Tau Beta Pi; EpsilonPi Tau; Sigma Pi Phi; Alpha Kappa Mu; Alpha Phi Alpha; Bapt; Adelphian; Miami Club; Musolit; trustee FL Meml Coll Miami; regent Marymount Coll VA. **Honors/Awds:** Cosmos Washington recipient Harmon award in Sci Research in Electronics 1926; Dorie Miller Meml Fnd Award 1953; career serv award Nat Civil Serv League 1959; Sec Def Meritorius Civillian Serv Medal 1970; Patent Holder for Utilization of Exhaust Gases to Prevent Icing on Aircraft.

EVANS, JAMES L.
Broadcast co. administrator. **Personal:** Born Nov 11, 1954, Columbus, OH; son of Darlene Evans; children: Erika Briana, Alonzo James. **Educ:** University of Kentucky, BS, 1976. **Career:** Ohio Secretary of State, press secretary, 1983-87; Franklin County Democratic Party, executive director, 1987-90; WVKO Radio, news director, 1990-. **Orgs:** Sigma Delta Chi; Ohio Association of Broadcasters; Natl Assn of Black Journalists, Central Ohio Chapter. **Honors/Awds:** Associated Press, Best Enterprise Reporting, 1991, 1992. **Business Addr:** News Director, WVKO, 1580 AM Radio, 4401 Carriage Hill Ln, Columbus, OH 43220, (614)451-2191.

EVANS, JOE B.
City official. **Personal:** Born Dec 26, 1929, Fair Bluff, NC; son of Cora Barden Evans and Henry P Evans Sr; married Carrie Bullock Evans, Aug 12, 1956; children: Debra, Rocky, Anthony, Natalie. **Career:** Addis Cates Co Inc; Fair Bluff City, mayor, 1993-. **Orgs:** Mem Fair Bluff Sch Adv Council 1967-; Evans Subdivision Fair Bluff; Columbus Co Civic League; NAACP; City Councilman 1970-; past master Oak Grove Lodge 775 1971-72; Past Worthy Patron Pleasant Plain Chapter 275 1969-; dir United Carolina Bank; dir Telephone and Data Systems; pres Inter Government Commn; bd of director Carver Community Center. **Honors/Awds:** United Masonic Com of Columbus Co twenty-fourth dist award 1972. **Military Serv:** US Army, Sergeant, I951-56. **Business Addr:** Mayor, City of Fair Bluff, Barden St, Fair Bluff, NC 28439.

EVANS, JOSH (MIJOSHKI ANTWON)
Professional football player. **Personal:** Born Sep 6, 1972, Langdale, AL. **Educ:** Alabama-Birmingham, attended. **Career:** Houston Oilers, defensive tackle, 1995-96; Tennessee Oilers, 1997-. **Business Addr:** Professional Football Player, Tennessee Oilers, c/o Baptist Sports Park, 7640 H 70-5, Nashville, TN 37221.

EVANS, LEE
Professional athlete. **Personal:** Born Feb 25, 1947, Madera, CA. **Career:** Nigerian Natl Team, phys fitness couns, coach 1975-80; professional athlete 1973-. **Orgs:** Mem Olympic Track Team 1968,72. **Honors/Awds:** Won 2 Olympic Gold Medals Mexico 1968; won AAU 440 yrd 1966,67,69,69,70; won 400m gold medal Pan-Amer Games 1967; achieved world 400m dash & 1600m relay records Olympics 1968; won AAU 450 1968,72; won AAU 400m 1972.

EVANS, LEOMONT
Professional football player. **Personal:** Born Jul 12, 1974, Abbeville, SC; married Felicia. **Educ:** Clemson, attended. **Career:** Washington Redskins, defensive end, 1996-. **Business Addr:** Professional Football Player, Washington Redskins, 13832 Redskin Dr, Herndon, VA 22071, (703)471-9100.

EVANS, LEON, JR.
Insurance company manager, consultant. **Personal:** Born Jan 8, 1953, Union Springs, AL; son of Annie Ruth Beasley Evans and Leon Evans, Sr.; married Nyle Denise Hallback; children: Andrea Lactrice, Carlos LaRoy. **Educ:** Tuskegee Univ, BS 1977; Samford Univ, MBA 1985. **Career:** New England Bankcard Assoc, mgr trainee 1973-75; John Hancock Ins Co, life underwriter 1977-80; Blue Cross/Blue Shield of AL, consultant/mgr 1980-. **Orgs:** Team leader Big Brothers/Big Sisters Fund Drive 1985; vice pres Groove Phi Groove Graduate Chapter 1985; consultant Junior Achievement of Birmingham 1985-86; certified instructor Ren Advanced Office Controls 1986; mem NBMBAA, 1986-; fellow Life Office Mgmt Assn 1987; member Leadership Development Assn 1988-; member Birmingham Urban League 1988-. **Honors/Awds:** Awd for Outstanding Leadership Junior Achievement 1986. **Business Addr:** Manager, Performance Services, Blue Cross/Blue Shield of AL, 450 River Chase Pkwy East, Birmingham, AL 35298.

EVANS, LEON EDWARD, JR.
Banker. **Personal:** Born Dec 28, 1942, Chicago, IL; married Doris J Davis; children: Aaron Gerard, Sheila Rene. **Educ:** Wilson Jr Coll, Park Coll, attended. **Career:** Continental IL Natl Bank of Chicago, bookkeeping clk, 1963-67; Independence Bank of Chicago, asst cashier, 1967-69; Exchange Natl Bank of Chicago, asst cashier, 1969-70; Gateway Natl Bank of Chicago, vice pres cashier, 1970-72 Douglas State Bank, vice pres, cashier, 1972-75; Comm Bank of NE, pres/CEO, 1975-88; City of Omaha, Office of the Mayor, economic development aide, 1988-89; Business Consulting Specialists, consultant, 1989-90; American State Bank, executive vp, 1990-92, pres/CEO, 1992-. **Orgs:** American Bankers Association, Community Bankers Council; Boys Town, bd mem; Metropolitan Tulsa Chamber of Commerce, bd mem; Oklahoma Bankers Association, bd mem; American State Bank, bd mem; Conn Graduate School of Community Banking, Oklahoma City University, bd mem. **Business Addr:** Pres and CEO, American State Bank, 3816 N Peoria Ave, Tulsa, OK 74106.

EVANS, LEROY W.
Attorney. **Personal:** Born Dec 15, 1946, Houston, TX; married Robbie Moore; children: Anana Salisha. **Educ:** Boalt Hall Sch of Law Berkeley, JD 1972; Univ of Houston, BA 1969. **Career:** Small Farm Devel Corp, admin dir 1979-; Consortium for the Devel of the Rural So East, exec dir 1977-79; Emergency Land Fund, att, gen, couns 1974-; Shearman & Steal, asso 1972-74. **Orgs:** Asst sec, treas, bd mem Riverfront Enterprises Inc; mem Nat Conf of Black Lawyers; mem LABA; bd mem So E YMCA; mem Dekalb Co Young Dem; memDekalb Co NAACP; CA Bar Assn; NY Bar Assn; mem Practicing Law Inst. **Honors/Awds:** Recipient EE Worthing Scholarship 1965; Sigma Iota Epsilon; Martin Luther King Fellowship 1969; Distinguished Military Graduate 1969. **Business Addr:** 836 Beecher St SW, Atlanta, GA 30310.

EVANS, LILLIE R.
Realtor. **Personal:** Born Mar 23, 1913, Chattanooga, TN; married William D; children: William D III. **Educ:** TN A&I State Coll Nashville, 1931-32; UCLA, 1962-63. **Career:** Realtor, private practice, currently. **Orgs:** Mem Consolidated Realty Bd 1956; second vp, dir Consolidated Realty Bd 1962-64; charter mem Los Angeles Club of Nat-Assn of Negro Bus & Professional Women'sClub Inc 1960-; couns W Coast real estate; AME Zion Ch; initiator Comm Swimming Pool Proj 1970-71. **Honors/Awds:** First black woman realtor; first black LA Bd of Realtors 1962; first black dir LA Bd of Realtors 1971-73; recipient Outstanding Contributions in Field of Bus Award, Nat Assn of Negro Bus & Professional Women's Club 1963; Key to City of Chattanooga 1972. **Business Addr:** Realtor, 7315 S Normandie, Los Angeles, CA 90044.

EVANS, LIZ
Broadcast company executive. **Personal:** Born Jun 6, 1941, Augusta, GA; daughter of Geraldine Payne and Robert D Sherard; divorced; children: Tina, Emmet, Ida. **Educ:** Capital University. **Career:** WTVN-AM, WBUK-FM, assistant to public affairs director, 1970; WTVN-TV, WTVN-AM, WBUK-FM, community relations director, 1973; WTVN-AM, Q FM 96, director, public affairs, 1989-. **Orgs:** Mothers Against Crack, Inc, founder, 1989; African American Cancer Support Group, founder, 1992; United Way Project Diversity, 1988; Black Family Connections Adoption Advisory Board, chair, 1987; Direction for Youth Service Board, 1992; Women's Health Month Advisory Committee, 1988; American Cancer Society Reach to Recovery, volunteer, 1992; Cols Aids Task Force Coalition, Media, 1989; Ohio Breast & Cervical Cancer Coalition; Columbus Breast & Cervical Cancer Project; The BEST Program Bd; The National Black Leadership Initiative Against Cancer, Ohio Chap. **Honors/Awds:** Comin Home Community Foundation, Media Awardee, 1992; Black Family Connections, Volunteer Service, 1992; American Cancer Society, Volunteer Service, 1992; The Ohio Commission on Minority Health Award, 1992; The Ohio Governor's Citation, 1989; YWCA Woman of Achievement, 1996; Inductee, Ohio Women Hall of Fame, 1996. **Business Addr:** Director, Community Affairs, Jacon Columbus Communications, 1301 Dublin Rd, Columbus, OH 43215, (614)487-2519.

EVANS, LORENZO J.
Clergyman, educator (retired). **Personal:** Born Feb 21, 1909, Marion, AL; married Louise Bachlor; children: Eddie E Griffin, Stacy M Duke. **Educ:** Clark Coll, AB; Atlanta U, MA; Gammon Theol Sem, BD. **Career:** Disciples of Christ Indianapolis, natl dir of christian educ 1947-; Second Christian Church Muskogee, pastor 1941-42; YMCA Atlanta, sec 1945-47; US Army, chaplain 1942-45; Christian Educ Nation Christian Missionary Conv, dir 1947-60; UCMS & DHM, dir field prog, dir minority groups 1966-74. **Orgs:** Mem Leadership Com, Nat Council of Ch NY 1948-54. **Honors/Awds:** Hon DD TX Christian Univ 1974. **Military Serv:** US Army capt 1942-45.

EVANS, MARI
Educator, writer. **Personal:** Born in Toledo, OH; divorced; children: William Evan, Derek Reed. **Educ:** Attended Univ of Toledo; Marian College, LHD, 1975. **Career:** Indiana Univ-Purdue Univ at Indianapolis, instr in black literature and writer-in-residence, 1969-70; Indiana Univ at Bloomington, asst prof of black literature and writer-in-residence, 1970-78; Northwestern Univ, visiting asst prof, 1972-73; Purdue Univ, West Lafayette, visiting asst prof, 1978-80; Washington Univ, St Louis, visiting asst prof, 1980; Cornell Univ, visiting asst prof, 1981-83, assistant professor, distinguished writer, 1983-85; State Univ of New York-Albany, assoc prof, 1985-86; Miami Univ, Coral Gables, visiting distinguished writer, 1989; Spelman College, Atlanta, writer-in-residence, 1989-90. **Orgs:** Consultant, Discovery Grant Program, Natl Endowment for the Arts, 1969-70; consultant in ethnic studies, Bobbs-Merrill Co, 1970-73; chmn lit adv panel, Indiana State Arts Commission, 1976-77; chmn, Statewide Committee for Penal Reform; mem bd mgmt, Fall Creek Pkwy YMCA, 1975-81; bd dirs, 1st World Found; mem, Indiana Corrections Code Commission; mem, African Heritage Studies Assn; mem, Authors Guild; mem, Authors League of Amer. **Honors/Awds:** Producer, director, and writer for television program "The Black Experience," WTTV, Indianapolis, 1968-73; author of poetry volumes I Am a Black Woman, Morrow, 1970, and Nightstar, Center for African Amer Studies, UCLA, 1980; author of books for juveniles, including J.D., Doubleday, 1973, I Look at Me, Third World Press, 1974, Singing Black, Reed Visuals, 1976, Jim Flying High, Doubleday, 1979, and The Day They Made Beriani; playwright of "River of My Song," 1977, "Eyes" (musical), 1979, 1989, 1995; "Boochie," 1979, "Portrait of a Man," and "Glide and Sons" (musical); editor of Black Women Writers, 1950-1980: A Critical Evaluation, Doubleday-Anchor, 1984; contributor of poetry to textbooks, anthologies, and periodicals;John Hay Whitney fellow, 1965-66; Woodrow Won Foundation grantee, 1968; Indiana Univ Writers Conf Award, 1970; 1st Annual Poetry Award, Black Academy of Arts and Letters, 1970; MacDowell Fellow, 1975; Copeland Fellow, Amherst Coll, 1980; Natl Endowment for the Arts Grantee, 1981-82; DuSable Museum Award, 1989; Hazel J Bryant Award, Midwest African-American Theatre Alliance; Zora Neale Hurston Society Award, 1993; Alainhocke-Gwen Brooks Award, US Inc, 1995; Gwen Brooks Award, 1989, 1996; Zora Nealst Hurston-Paul Robeson Award, National Council for Black Studies, Inc, 1996.

EVANS, MARY ADETTA
Educator. **Personal:** Born Jun 13, 1909, Coldwater, VA; married Warren A; children: James W, Warren, David. **Educ:** VA State Coll, BS 1948; Columbia U, MA 1958. **Career:** King & Queen, teacher of public schools 1931-39; Nottoway Training School, 1941-48; Baker Elementary School, 1948-50; Albert V Norrell Elementary School, 1950-74. **Orgs:** Bldg rep VA Tchrs Assn; mem Richmond Tchrs; NEA; Richmond Retired Tchrs; VA Nat Retired Tchrs Assns; Richmond Nat Assns Univ Women; past pres, sec, Nat Council Negro Women; past supt jr dept Rapahannock River Southside Bapt Assn; vice pres Area C Woman's Aux; Bapt Gen Conv of VA; 1st vice pres Bapt Woman's Aux, Rappahannock River Southside Assn; mem Delver Woman's Club; YWCA; Crusade for Voters; vA Museum Fine Arts; Jr Red Corss sponsor 1972-73; mem Alpha Kappa Alpha Sor; chap pres, sec exec bd VA Minister's Wives Assn; mem Bapt Ch.

EVANS, MATTIE
Educator, consultant. **Personal:** Born Nov 22, 1935, Pascagoula, MS; daughter of Laura Mae Brooks Thompson and Charlie Thompson; divorced; children: Robert, Kenneth, Michael. **Educ:** Fisk Univ, BA (magna cum laude), 1959; TX Southern Univ, MA, 1963. **Career:** Univ of California at Davis, learning skills counselor, 1975-79; American River College, instructor, 1979-80; Sacramento & San Joaquin County Schools, consultant, standard English programs, 1980-84; California State Univ at Sacramento, instructor, 1983-86, Circle Project, consultant, 1986-89; Mississippi Gulf Coast Community College, 1995-96; consultant, human resources training, personal growth workshops and curriculum development, 1989-. **Orgs:** Fisk University General Alumni Association; Girl Scouts of the USA; Natl Council of Negro Women. **Honors/Awds:** Tierra del Oro Girl Scout Council, Girl Scout Role Model Award, nominee; Natl Council of Negro Women, Mary McLeod Bethune Award, 1988. **Special Achievements:** Author: The Untold Story of the Black Man in America, 1971, 1972, 1973; Stetches, 1974; IMAGES: A Workbook for Enhancing Self-esteem and Promoting Career Preparartion, 1988; Booker T Washington: Revisited, 1989; Martin Luther King: 1929-1968, 1995; columnist, "Issues in Education," Sacramento Observer, 1982-83. **Military Serv:** WAC splst 3rd class 1954-56. **Home Addr:** 911 Ridgepoint Ct #78, Baton Rouge, LA 70810-2877.

EVANS, MILTON L.
Chief executive officer. **Personal:** Born Oct 9, 1936, Snowhill, NC; son of Lola Vines Evans and Herbert Evans Jr; married Alice Corella Brown; children: Milton Jr, Alan, Glenn, Warren, Kenneth. **Educ:** Shaw Univ, BS Chem 1960; Tuskegee Inst, MS Chem 1964. **Career:** General Electric, r&d mktg mgmt 1964-73, section mgr compacts 1974-78, section mgr strategic planning, general manager, specialty elastomers, 1980-82; High Tech Biology Systems Inc, pres/CEO, currently. **Orgs:** Dir Siena Coll Business Council, Outreach Inc, Schenectady Private Industry Council, NY Head Injury Assn. **Honors/Awds:** Gold and Silver Medallions GE Inventors Awds; Author: My Sentiments Exactly. **Business Phone:** (518)283-8072.

EVANS, MYRA LYNN. See LAPEYROLERIE, MYRA EVANS.

EVANS, PATRICIA E.
City official, educator. **Personal:** Born Feb 13, 1946, New Orleans, LA; daughter of Grace Medley Evans and Andrew James Evans Jr; married Perker L Meeks Jr, Dec 22, 1973; children: Perker L Meeks III, Alicia Nicole Meeks. **Educ:** Xavier University of Louisiana, New Orleans, LA, BS, 1967; Loyola University School of Medicine, Maywood, IL, MD, 1971; University of California-Berkeley, Berkeley, CA, MPH, 1974. **Career:** East Oakland Family Health Center, Oakland, CA, medical director, 1977-79; private medical practice, San Francisco, CA, 1980-85; Alameda County Health Care, Oakland, CA, consultant for CHDP, 1982-86; San Francisco Dept of Services Agency, San Francisco, CA, medical consultant, 1985-86; San Francisco Department of Public Health, San Francisco, CA, medical consultant, CCS, 1985-86, associate medical director, 1986-91; University of California Department of Pediatrics, associate clinical professor, 1990-; San Francisco Department of Public Health, clinical director of perinatal care, 1991-. **Orgs:** Advisory council member, Alcohol, Drug Abuse and Mental Health Administration, 1988-91. **Honors/Awds:** Fellowship in Tropical Medicine & Public Health, Louisiana State University School of Medicine, 1970; Fellowship in Neonatology, American Lung Association of San Francisco, 1974-76. **Business Addr:** Clinical Director, Perinatal/MCH Substance Abuse Services, San Francisco Dept of Public Health, 101 Grove St, Rm 102, San Francisco, CA 94102.

EVANS, PATRICIA P.
Educator. **Personal:** Born in Topeka, KS; daughter of Lucille Mallory Phelps and C Kermit Phelps; divorced; children: Langston Phelps, Kimberly Dawn, Kristina Ann. **Educ:** Avila Coll, Kansas City MO, BSCh, 1961; Columbia Univ, New York NY, 1971-72. **Career:** St Mary's Hospital, Kansas City MO, medical technologist, 1962-68; Univ of Illinois Medical Center, Chicago IL, clinical teaching asst, asst supvr hematology, 1968-71; Mount Sinai Hospital, New York NY, asst supvr abnormal hematology, 1971-72; Veterans Admin Hospital, Mdison WI, medical technologist, 1974-75; St Mary's Hospital Madison WI, medical technologist, 1977-81; Methodist Hospital, Madison, WI, medical technologist, 1981-82; Univ Hospital & Clinics, Madison WI, project specialist oncology research 1982-86; Univ of WI, sr lecturer, dept of pathology & laboratory medmedical sch, 1986-. **Orgs:** Mem, Amer Soc for Medical Technologists, 1961-, Amer Assn of Blood Banks, 1962-, Amer Soc of Clinical Pathologists, 1962-, Amer Assn for Advancement of Science, 1968-, Wisconsin Assn for Medical Technology, 1972-, Madison Soc for Medical Technology, 1977-; co-chr, membership comm, WI Soc for Medical Technologists, 1988-90; Shorewood League Bd, mem, 1977-94, vice pres of bd, 1990-91, pres, 1991-92, nom-chair, 1994; chp, bd mem, Jack & Jill of Amer Inc, 1979-84; Girl Scout leader, Girl Scouts of Amer, 1982-88; parent mem, Boy Scouts of Amer, 1983-90; bd mem, West High School PTSO 1989-93; parent advisory comm, West HS, 1989-93; publicity chairman, Wisconsin Soci-

ety for Med Tech State Convention, 1990; University Committees: Center for Health Science Minority Affairs Committee, 1988-94, Biological/Medical Science Area Review Committee, 1990-93, Center for Health Sciences Commission on Woms Issues, 1992-95; Women in Science, engineering & math comm, 1994-; Amer Assn of Univ Women, 1995-; Univ of WI Madison Academic Advancement Selection Comm, 1995-; Student Appeals Comm for Undergraduate Prog in the Medical School, 1997-; bd of trustees, Amer Soc for Clinical Laboratory Science Education & Research Fund, Inc, until 1998. **Honors/Awds:** Faith Dravis Award, Wisconsin Soc for Medical Technologists, 1989; Omicron Sigma Recognition, Wisconsin Soc for Medical Technologists, 1989, 1990. **Business Addr:** Senior Lecturer, University of Wisconsin-Madison Campus, 1300 University Ave-Medical Science Center, Madison, WI 53706.

EVANS, PHILLIP L.
Industrial relations company executive. **Personal:** Born Mar 18, 1937, Cincinnati, OH; son of Mildred Thompson Evans and Eddie Evans; married Constance Beckham, Jun 27, 1959; children: Phillip L Jr, Damon A. **Educ:** Univ of Cincinnati, Cincinnati OH, BA, 1959, MA, 1963. **Career:** Cincinnati Public Schools, Cincinnati OH, work/study coord, 1962-68; RCA Corp, Indianapolit IN, industrial relations mgr, 1968-76; Miller Brewing Co, Milwaukee WI, Industrial Relations-Breweries, corporate mgr, 1976-. **Orgs:** Amer Soc of Personnel Admin; bd mem, Milwaukee Area Technical Coll. **Honors/Awds:** Black Achievement Award, Harlem YMCA, 1987; Silver Ring Merit Award, Philip Morris Corp, 1988. **Business Addr:** Corporate Manager, Industrial Relations-Breweries, Miller Brewing Company, 3939 W Highland Blvd, Milwaukee, WI 53208.

EVANS, ROBERT ORAN
Basketball coach. **Personal:** Born Sep 7, 1946, Hobbs, NM; son of Gladys Evans and Oscar Evans; married Carolyn Ann Marshall, Jul 25, 1970; children: Damon LaMont, Amber ShaRon. **Educ:** Lubbock Christian, Associate in Arts and Sciences, 1966; New Mexico State Univ, BS, education, 1968. **Career:** New Mexico State University, asst basketball coach, 1968-75; Texas Tech University, asst basketball coach, 1975-90; Oklahoma State University, asst basketball coach; University of Mississippi, head basketball coach, 1992-98; Arizona State Univ, Men's Basketball, head coach, 1998-. **Orgs:** Texas High School Coaches Assn; New Mexico High School Coaches Assn; Oklahoma High School Coaches Assn; Mississippi High School Coaches Assn; Coaches vs Cancer; South Plains Children's Shelter; Texas Boy's Ranch; Natl Assn of Asst Basketball Coaches. **Honors/Awds:** Inducted to Lubbock Christian University Hall of Fame, 1990; inducted to New Mexico State University Hall of Fame, 1989; Lubbock Christian University, Valley Forge Honor Certificate; Texas Tech University, Outstanding Achievement Award, 1986-87; Distinguished Alumni Field of Educ, New Mexico State Univ, 1994; Associated Press, Southeastern Conf Coach of the Year, 1996; College Hoops Insider, Natl Coach of the Year, 1996. **Home Addr:** 113 River Birch Ln, Oxford, MS 38655, (601)234-0180.

EVANS, ROXANNE J.
Journalist. **Personal:** Born Jun 6, 1952, Omaha, NE; daughter of Margaret L. Steele Martin and James W. Martin Jr.; married Kelly Randolph Evans, Apr 4; children: James, Imani, Askia, Joshua. **Educ:** Howard University, Washington, DC, 1975-76; Drake University, Des Moines, IA, BA, 1982. **Career:** National Urban League, Washington, DC, research assistant, 1975-76; Des Moines Register, Des Moines, IA, reporter, 1978-83; Austin American-Statesman, Austin, TX, reporter, 1983-88, chief editorial writer, 1988-. **Orgs:** President, Austin Association of Black Communicators, 1989-. **Honors/Awds:** Texas School Bell Award, Texas State Teachers Association, 1985-88; Phoenix Award, Friends of Phoenix, 1984. **Business Addr:** Editorial Writer, Austin American-Statesman, 166 E Riverside Dr, PO Box 670, Austin, TX 78767.

EVANS, RUTHANA WILSON
Educator (retired). **Personal:** Born Mar 26, 1932, Roxie, MS; daughter of Lueberta Wilson (deceased) and James Wilson (deceased); married Lit Parker Evans Jr, Mar 22, 1957; children: Cedric Glenn, Valerie Denise. **Educ:** Tougaloo Coll, BS 1955; Univ of IL, Postgrad 1965; NC Coll, 1967; Delta State Coll, MS 1971; Delta State Univ, MS Psychometrist 1977, AAA Counseling 1981; Administration Coursework, AA. **Career:** Shaw School, elem teacher 1955-57; Nailor Elem School, teacher, curriculum chmn 1957-60, teacher, librarian 1960-62, librarian 1963-64; Preschool Story Hour, librarian 1964-66; Bolivar County Dist 4; library supvr 1965-67; Ed TV Jackson, curriculum resources teacher 1968-70; Parks & Pearman Elem Schools, librarian 1968-70, org elem school libr prog 1969; Greenville Elem School, consult 1970; MS Head Start, educ dir 1970-79; Bolivar County Dist 4 Schools Titles I, counselor 1979-; Bolivar County Headstart, psychometrist 1985-; Bolivar Schls, psychometrist; Cleveland Schools testing coord 1986-. **Orgs:** Consult Indianola Preschool Activities 1971; org inventory, classification systems Head Start 1970; mem PTA 1955, MS Personnel & Guid Assoc, MS Library Assoc; job trainer Neighborhood Youth Corps Cleveland 1969; trainer manpower prog STEP 1970-, CETA 1977; sec Negro's Citizens Comm Cleveland 1957-61; active BSA; mem Baptist Training Union Cleveland 1972-, Negro Voters League; treas E Side HS Band Booster 1972; treas 1971, pres 1973 Athena Soc Club; sec Womens Club 1970; mem Natl Council Black Child Devel 1975-78; MS Counselors Assoc; Nat'l Educ Assoc; mem, sec, St Paul Baptist Church; lay bd member of the Jake Ayers Case; American Counseling Assn; Delta Sigma Theta Sorority, Inc. **Honors/Awds:** First runner-up to Miss Tougaloo Coll, 1955. **Home Addr:** 816 Cross St, Cleveland, MS 38732. **Business Addr:** Counselor-Test Coordinator, Cleveland Schools, 305 Merritt Dr, Cleveland, MS 38732.

EVANS, SAMUEL LONDON
Educational administrator. **Personal:** Born Nov 11, 1902, Leon County, FL; married Edna Hoye; children: Retha EB Kelly. **Educ:** Columbia Univ, attended 1948; NY Univ, integrated concepts science philosophy & educ 1951-53; Combs Coll, MusD (Hon) 1968. **Career:** US Div of Physical Fitness, coordinator 1941-45; Philadelphia Chamber Orchestra, impressario 1961-71; S London Publishing Co, publisher; PA State AthleticComm, secretary; Bicentennial Corp, exec vice pres 1971-; AFNA Natl Educ and Rsch Fund, pres/chairman of the board. **Orgs:** Comm member in celebration of the US Constitution 200 year anniversary; Columbia Univ World Study Tour 1948; concept and founder African American Hall of Fame Sculpture Garden 1984; founder, pres, natl chmn Amer Found for Negro Affairs 1968-; mem Mayors Comm on Municipal Svc; bd dir Amer Trauma Soc, Amer Heart Assoc; bd dir, prodn gen mgr Philadelphia Coffee Concerts Com; mem Natl Trust for Historic Preservation, Amer Pub Health Assoc. **Honors/Awds:** Philadelphia Academy of Science Awd sculptured bronze bust by Zenos Frudakis 1981; Sister Clara Muhammad School Annual Education Awd 1983; Philadelphia Miniversity Citizens Awd 1985; USN Awd for Extraordinary Leadership 1976; Charles R Drew Awd 1978; Black Expo Awd 1972; Serv Awd 3rd World 76' Inc 1972; Achievement AwdPhiladelphia Cotillion Soc 1972; Community Serv Awd Philadelphia Oppty Indust Ctrs 1972; Achievement Awd NAACP Reg II 1972; author "The AFNA Plan, A Projection for the Year 200 and Now in Medicine, Law, Business & Commerce, Science Tech" 1974, "Nothing to Fear", "Second Phase of Democracy An Amer Manifesto". **Business Addr:** President, American Foundation for Negro Affairs, 117 S 17th St, Suite 1200, Philadelphia, PA 19103-5025.

EVANS, SLAYTON ALVIN, JR.
Educator. **Personal:** Born May 17, 1943, Chicago, IL; son of Corine M Thompson Evans and Slayton A Evans Sr; married Tommie A Johnson, Jul 15, 1967 (deceased); children: Slayton A Evans III, Amy R Evans. **Educ:** Tougaloo Coll, BS Chemistry 1965; Case Western Reserve Univ, PhD Chemistry 1970; Univ of Texas at Arlinton, postdoctoral fellow, 1970-71; Univ of Notre Dame, post doctoral fellow 1971-72; Illinois Institute of Technology, 1965-66. **Career:** Univ of NC, Kenan Prof of Chemistry 1974-; Dartmouth Coll, research instr 1972-73. **Orgs:** Mem Am Chem Soc 1968; Soc of Sigma Xi; Alpha Xi Sigma; committee chairman, Louisiana State Board of Regents, 1990; advisory board, NSF Chemistry, 1990-95; International Organinzing Committee for the International Conference on Phosphorus Chemistry, 1995, 1998; chair, NSF's Chemistry Division's Advisory Committee, 1993-94; National Committee for the International Union of Pure and Applied Chemistry; the Advisory Board, the journal, "Phosphorus, Sulfur, and Silicon"; Advisory Board, International Council on Main Group Chemistry; NIH National Advisory Council. **Honors/Awds:** Kenan Research Leave, Univ of NC 1984-85; Fulbright 1984-85; NATO Grant for Collaborative Research, NATO 1987-89; over 85 scientific publications in organophosphorus and organo sulfur chemistry; Chmn of NIH BI-4 Study Section; chmn, Regional Review Committee for Academic Programs in Chemistry, Louisiana State Board of Regents, 1990; The Ralph Metcalfe Jr Lectureship Chair (chemistry) at Marquette University, 1993-94; Science Skills Center "Minds in Motion Award," A Tribute to Outstanding African-American Scientists, Jun 7, 1992; National Science Foundation Crativity Awd, 1994; Howard University, Outstanding Achievement Awd. **Business Addr:** Kenan Professor of Chemistry, The University of North Carolina, Department of Chemistry, CB 3290, Chapel Hill, NC 27599-3290.

EVANS, THERMAN E.
Physician, health director. **Personal:** Born Aug 20, 1944, Henderson, NC; son of Constine Evans and Irvin Evans Sr; married Bernetta Jones, Jul 30, 1966; children: Thomas E Evans Jr, Clayton Evans. **Educ:** Howard Univ, BA 1966, MD 1971. **Career:** Operation PUSH, natl health dir; East of the River Health Ctr Washington, phys; CT General Ins Co, 2nd vice pres/corp med dir; CIGNA, asst med dir 1979-83, corp med dir 1983-87, vice pres/corp med dir 1987-. **Orgs:** Natl bd of dirs Operation PUSH 1983, review & adv comm for various agencies of Fed Govt; pres Washington DC Bd of Educ; clinical faculty Howard Univ; pres Operation PUSH, Philadelphia Chapter 1983-86; bd of dirs Southeastern PA Wellness Council 1987-88, Philadelphia Health Mgmt Corp 1988-. **Honors/Awds:** Visiting Regent's Scholar-Lecturer at the Univ of CA; published over 25 articles on various health related subjects in journals & magazines; guest expert on numerous natl & local radio and TV health oriented progs; Alumnae of the Year, Howard Univ Alumnae Assn, Philadelphia Chapter 1988; Stress and the College Student, The Black Collegian Magazine 1989; Being Black in America is Hazardous to Your Health, Journal of the Natl Medical Assn 1989. **Business Addr:** Vice President & Corporate Medical Dir, CIGNA Corporation, One Logan Square, Philadelphia, PA 19103-6930.

EVANS, THOMAS
Cleric. **Personal:** Born Aug 11, 1925, Ramer, AL; married Irene Parks; children: Tommie, Deborah. **Educ:** AL U, Wayne State U, BS Edn, MEd 1953, 1971; Selma U, studied; Theiol & Bible Moody Bible Inst. **Career:** Ch of Our Father Bapt, minister 1957-; Barbour Jr HS Detroit Bd Edn, reading coord; Christ Educ Galilee Dist Conv, minister 1946-51. **Orgs:** Mem Wayne & Co Reading Assn; past pres Dexter-Joy Home Improvement Assn; mem NAACP; mem 11th Percent Police Comm Relation Council. **Military Serv:** WW II 1943-46; Korean War 1950-52. **Business Addr:** 5333 E Seven Mile Rd, Detroit, MI 48234.

EVANS, TIMOTHY C.
Attorney. **Personal:** Born Jun 1, 1943. **Educ:** Univ of IL, BA, 1985; John Marshall Law School, JD, 1965. **Career:** Chicago Dept Investigations, former dep cmr; Secretary of State Office (Cook County, IL), chief hearing off, 1973; Chicago, IL, city alderman, 4th ward, 1973-91; attorney, private practice, 1991-. **Honors/Awds:** Unsuccessful bid for mayor, Chicago, IL, general election, Harold Washington Party, 1989. **Business Addr:** Attorney, 5040 S Ellis Ave, Chicago, IL 60615.

EVANS, VERNON D.
Auditor, accountant. **Personal:** Born Mar 7, 1950, Ft Worth, TX; son of Thelma Evans and Rev Dellie Evans; married Viola Ruth Cross (divorced); children: Victor, Vinikka, Vernessa. **Educ:** N TX State U, BBA, MBA 1972; Cert Public Accountant, 1973; Cert Mgmt Accountant, 1980; Cert Internal Auditor, 1985; Cert Fraud Examiner, 1989. **Career:** Dallas/Fort Worth Intl Airport Bd, deputy exec dir for admin services, 1994-, dir of audit services, 1986-94; Fort Worth Independent Schol Dist, chief internal auditor, 1982-86; Ernst & Whinney, audit mgr and supr, 1972-82; Evans McAfee & Co, mnging partner 1976-78; Ernst & ErnstCPAs, staff accountant, sr accountant, 1972-76. **Orgs:** Texas State Board of Public Accountancy, vice chmn, 1991-98; TCU Accounting Advisory bd, 1992-; Professional Development Institute, bd of trustees, 1992-; Assn of Airport Internal Auditors, founder and past president, 1989-91; So Regional Dir, 1987-90, North American Regional Directors Committee dir-at-large, chmn, 1991-94; Inst of Internal Auditors; Mem Nat Assn Accountants 1974-80; state dir, TX Soc of CPA's, 1988-90; vice pres, 1979-81, pres 1981-83, Nat Assn of Black Accountants; Assn of Govt Accountants; Govt Finance Officerts Assn; Natl Forum of Black Public Administrators; accounting dept advisory bd, North TX State Univ; chair, United Way Allocation Com III 1979-80; chmn McDonald YMCA 1980; treas Metro Economical Devel Corp, 1980; bd of dir, Ft Worth Black Chamber of Commerce; bd of dir, Day Care Assn. **Honors/Awds:** Natl Assn of Black Accountants, Natl Achievement Award, 1989; Institute of Internal Auditors, Inc, Outstanding Regional Dir Award, 1990; Fort Worth Chapter of Texas Society of CPA's, CPA of the Year Award, 1990; Dallas/Fort Worth Chapter Natl Assn of Black Accountants, Outstanding Professional Achievement, 1992; United Negro College Fund, Outstanding Leadership, 1994; McDonald YMCA, Earnest Anderson Award, 1994; Outstanding Achievement Award, Sickle Cell Anemia Assn of TX 1979; Outstanding Achievement Award, Nat Assn of Black Accountants 1979, 1987; Greek Image Award, Pan-Hellenic Coun, 1983; Henry A Meadows Volunteer of the Year Award, YMCA-MFW, 1983; outstanding service awards, McDonald YMCA, 1985, United Negro Coll Fund, 1986; Chi Rho Award, YMCA-MFW, 1988; F M Miller Award, McDonald YMCA, 1989. **Business Addr:** Deputy Exec Dir for Admin Services, Dallas/Ft Worth International Airport Board, PO Drawer DFW, Dallas, TX 75261.

EVANS, WARREN CLEAGE
Government official, lawyer, educator. **Personal:** Born Dec 30, 1948, Detroit, MI; son of Gladys H Cleage Evans and E Warren Evans; divorced; children: Erikka N, Nikki Lynn. **Educ:** Madonna College, Livonia, MI, BA, 1975; University of Detroit, Detroit, MI, MA, 1980; Detroit College of Law, Detroit, MI, JD, 1986. **Career:** Wayne County Sheriffs Dept, Detroit, MI, undersheriff, 1970-90; Wayne County Board of Commissioners, Detroit, MI, dir of administration, 1990-91; Office of County Executive, director of community corrections, 1991-. **Orgs:** Vice pres, Detroit Board of Water Commissioners, 1989-; parlamentarian, nati; advisory board, Criminal Justice Comm, WCCC, 1990-; advisory board, Criminal Justice Comm, U of D, 1988-; advisory board, BCN Law Center, 1986-. **Honors/Awds:** Distinguished Corrections Service Award, 1988; Spirit of Detroit Award, Detroit City Council, 1987. **Business Addr:** Director of Community Corrections, Office of County Executive, 640 Temple St, Ste 210, Detroit, MI 48215.

EVANS, WEBB
Association executive. **Personal:** Born Nov 20, 1913, Greensboro, AL; married Cora Golightly. **Educ:** TN State Coll, 1936-37; Cortez Peters Bus Sch, 1943. **Career:** House of Saunders Chgo, mgr 1974-; Evans Food Mart Chgo, owner 1949-74;

Wells Consumers Coop Inc Chgo, mrg 1945-47. **Orgs:** Pres United Am Progress Assn 1961-; treas Forrestville Civic Improve League 1963-74; treas Fellowship Bapt Dist Assn1971-73; pres Layman Dept Prog Bapt State Convention of IL 1966-68; bd of dir Southside Comm Com for Juv Delinq Prevention 1949-65; bd dir Cosmop C of C 1961-65; pres 41st & 42nd Wells St Block Club; trustee Cathedral Bapt Ch 1964-. **Honors/Awds:** Recipient Top Male Volunteer Award, Vol Bur of Met Chicago 1961; award Outstanding Serv to Civil Rights Movement, Christian Religious Builders 1964; Civil Progress Award, Inter-Denom Min Civ League of IL 1964; Citizen of Week, WBEE Radio 1969; Hon Citizen of State of TN, Gov Frank Clement, 1966; citation, United Am Prog Assn 1972. **Business Addr:** President, United American Progress Assn, 701 E 79th Street, Chicago, IL 60619.

EVANS, WILLIAM C. See Obituaries section.

EVANS, WILLIAM E.
Educational consultant (retired). **Personal:** Born Nov 28, 1931, Mebane, NC; son of Mozelle Evans; married Gloria Battle Evans. **Educ:** Hampton Inst, BS, 1954; Southern Connecticut State Coll, MS, 1961; Bridgeport Univ, sixth year certificate, 1964; Southern Connecticut State Coll, further study; Yale Univ, Drug Educ, 1970-71; Univ of Connecticut, PhD, 1985. **Career:** Laurel Ledge School, Beacon Falls CT, teacher, 1957-58; Barnard School, Waterbury CT, teacher, 1958; elementary physical educ instructor, 1958-59; Wilby High School, Waterbury CT, phys ed/biol instructor, 1958-67; Project Upward Bound, Univ of Hartford, reading instructor, 1966-67, curriculum coord & reading instructor, 1967-68, asst project dir, 1968-72; Community Action Agency, Waterbury, 1967; Waterbury School System, supvr health & physical educ, 1967-72; Waterbury Public Schools, drug coord, 1971; Mattatuck Community Coll, Psychology Department, 1971-72; Waterbury Dept of Educ, dir educ grants, 1972-90; Waterbury Tercentennial Inc, student coord; New Opportunities for Waterbury, CT, education consultant, beginning 1990; Univ of CT, educ consultant. **Orgs:** NAACP, life mem; bd of incorporators Boy's Club of Amer; deacon, Grace Baptist Church, 1985-. **Honors/Awds:** Hampton Alumni Fellowship 1967; Outstanding Alumnus Award, Hampton Inst, 1974; Univ of CT Foundation Fellowship 1984. **Military Serv:** US Army, artillery officer, 2nd lt, 1954-56, 1st lt, 1956-57. **Home Addr:** 1632 Abingdon Ln, Bena, VA 23018.

EVANS-DODD, THEORA ANITA
Educator, administrator. **Personal:** Born Sep 11, 1945, Chicago, IL; daughter of Lucille Jackson Evans and Theodore Evans; divorced; children: Victor Cortez, Theodore Artez, Kimberly Toirelle, Karetha Anita. **Educ:** Loyola Univ, Chicago IL, BS, 1976, MSW, 1978; Univ of Illinois, Chicago IL, MPH, 1987. **Career:** Univ of Chicago Hospitals, Chicago IL, project dir, 1980-81; Merrill, Lynch, Pierce, Fenner & Smith, Chicago IL, account exec, 1981-89; Rush Presbyterian St Luke's Medical Center, Adolescent Family Center, Chicago IL, unit coordinator/faculty, 1984-86; Northeastern Illinois Univ, Chicago IL, visiting lecturer, 1985-87; Illinois MCH Coalition, Springfield IL, exec dir, 1987-; Univ of Iowa, Iowa City IA, clinical asst prof, 1988-. **Orgs:** Mem, Chicago Chapter, Natl Assn of Black Social Workers, 1976-; vice pres, Iowa State Bd, Natl Assn of Social Workers, 1980-89; mem, Natl Urban League, NAACP; sec, Chicago Loop Bd, YWCA, 1982-86; mem, soror, Alpha Kappa Alpha Sorority, 1983-; comm mem, Chicago Plan Advisory Commn, 1985-86; mem, Women Health Exec Network, 1986-, Amer Public Health Assn, 1986-; consultant, Natl Healthy Mothers, Healthy Babies, 1988; bd mem, Mayor's Youth Employment Program, 1989-; board member, Institute for Social and Economic Development, 1990-; board member, Iowa Geriatric Education Center, 1990-. **Honors/Awds:** Fellowship Award, Loyola Univ of Chicago, 1976; Merit & Achievement Award, Chicago Bd of Educ, 1978; Fellowship, Iowa Geriatric Education Center, 1989.

EVANS-MCNEILL, ELONA ANITA
Consultant, government official. **Personal:** Born Nov 22, 1945, Washington, DC; daughter of Angelisa Stewart Evans and Julius Wilherspoon Evans; divorced. **Educ:** Howard Univ, attended 1963-64; Graduate School US Agricultural Dept, attended 1965-66; Amer Univ, attended 1969-72. **Career:** Community Govt Relations, consultant 1983-85; Washington Healthcare Man Corp, comm/govt relations consultant 1981-86; Washington Hospital Center, ambulator services ombudsperson 1986-; DC Government, Washington, DC, dir, mayor's office on bds & commissions, 1991-. **Orgs:** Mem Ward One Democrats 1978-; mem vice chair Bd of Trustee Public Defender Serv 1979-85; vice chair/past chair Adv Neighborhood Comm 1979-86; mediator Citizens Complaint Ctr 1979-; bd mem My Sister's Place Shelter for Battered Women 1980-82; bd mem Calvary Shelter for Women 1982-83; mem DC Democratic State Comm 1984-88; mem Student Non-Violent Coord Comm; Red Cross volunteer Washington Hosp Ctr psychiatric ward; mem DC Women's Political Caucus 1979; past pres & past treas Natl Steering Comm; mem, Natl Real Estate Educators Assn; mem, Natl Assn of Real Estate License Law Officials, 1988-91; commissioner, DC Real Estate Commission, 1988-91; chair, education comm, DC Real Estate Comm, 1989-; dir, Natl Assn of Real Estate Law License Officials, 1990-. **Honors/Awds:** Gettysburg Symposium Rep "Panorama"; Amer Univ Repres 1970 Gettysburg Symposium; recipient Scholastic Excellence Awards Amer Univ 1970-71; recipient Outstanding Comm Volunteer Award Black Policemen's Assn 1980.

EVANS-TRANUMN, SHELIA
Educational administrator. **Personal:** Born Aug 19, 1951, Durham, NC; daughter of Eunice Allen Evans and George Watts Evans Sr.; married Howard James Tranumn Jr, Sep 3, 1988; children: DeAnna. **Educ:** North Carolina Central University, Durham, NC, BA, 1973; Long Island University, Brooklyn, NY, MS, 1977; New York University, New York, NY, currently. **Career:** New York City Board of Education, Auxiliary Services for High Schools, director, 1973-. **Orgs:** Founder/director, Educators for Christ, AME Church, 1988-; president, New York Alliance of Black School Educators, 1986-; chairperson, Multicultural Advisory Board, New York City Board of Education, 1988-; minister to education, Bridge Street AME Church, 1988-; Chancellor's Advisory Committee to Promote Equal Opportunity, 1987-. **Honors/Awds:** High Professional Achievement, Key Women of America, 1985; Trailblazer Award, Administrative Women in Education, 1990; Richard Green Educational Leadership Award, NAACP, 1989; Risk Taker Award, New York Alliance of Black School Education, 1988; Mary McLeod Bethune Award, 1989; African Heritage Award, Association of Black Educators, 1989; Leadership New York, fellow, 1992-93. **Home Addr:** 316 E 57 St, Brooklyn, NY 11203. **Business Addr:** Director, Auxiliary Services for High Schools, New York City Board of Education, 198 Forsyth St, 5th Flr, New York, NY 10010.

EVANZZ, KARL ANDERSON (KARL EVAN ANDERSON)
Editor, author, journalist. **Personal:** Born Jan 16, 1953, St Louis, MO; son of Bernice & Adolphus Anderson; married Alexandra Jane Hamilton Evanzz, Jan 1, 1977; children: Aqila, Aaron, Kanaan, Arianna, Adrian. **Educ:** Westminster College, BA, 1975; American University, Washington College of Law, 1975-77. **Career:** St Louis Argus, national correspondent, 1974-80; Law Offices of Lowe, Mark & Moffitt, law clerk, 1975-76; Harry T Alexander, law clerk, 1977-80; The Washington Post, news aide, 1980-86, on-line editor, 1986-. **Orgs:** National Newspaper Guild, 1980-; National Association of Black Journalists, 1992-95. **Honors/Awds:** Fund for Investigative Journalism, Grant, 1991. **Special Achievements:** Poetry published in "Crevice of Illusion," 1975; "The Judas Factor: The Plot to Kill Malcolm X," 1992; "Elijah Muhammad: A Biography," Pantheon, 1997; Poetry published in Southern Exposure Magazine, 1971; 1st Place Prize, for poetry, Proud Magazine, St Louis, MO, 1970, 1971. **Home Addr:** PO Box 296, Ashton, MD 20861-0296. **Business Addr:** On-Line Editor, The Washington Post, 1150 15th St NW, 4th Fl - News, Washington, DC 20071.

EVE, ARTHUR O.
Elected government official. **Personal:** Born 1933, New York, NY; married Lee Constance Bowles; children: Arthur Jr, Leecia Roberta, Eric Vincent, Martin King, Malcolm X. **Educ:** Erie Comm Coll, Associate; WV State Coll, BS. **Career:** NY State Assembly, assemblyman 1966-. **Orgs:** Estab First School Health Demon Project; chmn NY State Black & Puerto Rican Leg Caucus 1975,76; 1st black to win a major party's primary for Mayor 1977; Deputy Speaker of the Assembly 1979; founded the Black Develop Found and the Black Business Development Corp; formed the Minority Coalition. **Honors/Awds:** Hunters College, Legislator of the Decade Award, 1984; SUNY at Buffalo, President's Distinguished Service Award, 1982; African People's Christian Organization, Malcolm X Leadership Award, 1991; NY Association of School Psychologists, Leadership Legislative Award, 1992; ET Marshall Scholarship Foundation, Leadership Award, 1986; New York State Minorities in Corrections Inc, Achievement Award, 1992; Kennedy Center, Distinguished Leadership in Arts-In-Education Award, 1988; NY State Martin Luther King Jr Institute, Commission, 1992. **Military Serv:** US Army 1953-55. **Business Addr:** Assembly Member District 141, New York State Assembly, 498 Northland Ave #400, Buffalo, NY 14211.

EVE, CHRISTINA M.
Educator. **Personal:** Born Mar 18, 1917, Gainesville, FL. **Educ:** Shaw Univ Raleigh NC, AB 1940; NYU, MA 1958; Univ Miami, Postgrad. **Career:** Treasure Island Elementary School, Miami Beach FL, prin; Dade Co, dist reading teacher, owner-operator, public steno serv, 1st black prin, white school; 1969; Egelloc Civic & Soc Club, founder. **Orgs:** Mem Sigma Gamma Rho; anti basileus AAUW; Meth Ch; FL Adminstrv & Supr Assn; Assn Supr & Curric Dev; Dade Co Sch Adminstrs Assn; FL prins FL Elem Sch; Dept Elem Sch Prins Citizen of Day Local Radio Sta 1969. **Honors/Awds:** Outstanding serv awards Egolloc Club & Sigma Gamma Rho 1970; award Univ Miami TTT Proj 1971; award dept elem prins dedicated serv 1973. **Business Addr:** 7540 E Treasure Dr, Miami Beach, FL 33141.

EVEGE, WALTER L., JR.
Educator. **Personal:** Born Jan 13, 1943, Jackson, MS; son of Cletora Carter Evege (deceased) and Walter L Evege Sr; married Dorthy Ruffin Evege, Mar 1, 1974; children: Daryl, Dietrich, Daphine. **Educ:** Tougallo Coll, Tougaloo MS, BS, 1964; Atlanta Univ, Atlanta GA, MBA (one semester), 1969. **Career:** Jackson Public Schools, Jackson MS, math teacher, 1964-66; Tougaloo Coll, Tougaloo MS, dir financial aids, 1966-69; The Univ of Akron, Akron OH, asst dir, 1970-80; Community Action Agency, Akron OH, assoc dir, 1980-82; Allstate Insurance Co, Akron OH, sales agent, 1982-87; The Univ of Akron, Akron OH, acting dir, 1987-. **Orgs:** Bd Dir, Alpha Phi Alpha Homes Inc, 1974-85; advisory bd, Cuyahoga Street Area Block Club, 1983-; mem, Music Boosters, Copley-Fairlawn Schools, 1987-, chmn, Levey Comm, 1988-, The Ohio Consortium of Blacks in Higher Educ, 1989-. **Honors/Awds:** Outstanding Young Men of Amer, Natl Jaycees, 1978; Youth Motivational Task, Akron Jaycees, 1979; Top New Sales Agent, Allstate Insurance Co, 1983; Service Award, Alpha Phi Alpha Frat (Eta Tau Lambda), 1980; Black History Brochure, Univ of Akron, 1988; Students at Risk Workshops, 1988-89; Volunteer Ser, Crosby Elementary School, 1989. **Business Addr:** Acting Director, Black Cultural Center, University of Akron, 202 E Hall, Akron, OH 44325-1801.

EVERETT, CARL EDWARD
Professional baseball player. **Personal:** Born Jun 3, 1971, Tampa, FL. **Career:** Florida Marlins, outfielder, 1993-94; New York Mets, 1995-97; Houston Astros, 1998-. **Business Addr:** Professional Baseball Player, Houston Astros, PO Box 288, Houston, TX 77001-0288, (713)799-9500.

EVERETT, CYNTHIA A.
Attorney, government official. **Educ:** Florida State University; National Law Center at George Washington University, 1982. **Career:** Dade County State Attorney's Office, supervising attorney; Assistant US attorney, Miami, currently. **Orgs:** Florida Bar Assn, board of governors, 1994-; Florida Chapter of the NBA, treasurer; Women Lawyers Division, Dade County Chapter, past president. **Business Addr:** Asst US Attorney, Civil Division, 99 NE 4th St, Miami, FL 33132, (305)536-4471.

EVERETT, J. RICHARD
Attorney. **Personal:** Born Oct 2, 1936, Montezuma, GA; married Bernice Knowings; children: Jocelyn, Jeannenn. **Educ:** Morehouse Coll, BS 1960; St John's Univ Law Sch, LLB 1967; Patent Offices Patent Academy, US 1968. **Career:** Food & Drug Admin, analytical chemist 1961-66; Food & Legal Officer, 1966-77; Eastman Kodak Co, admin asst, 1974-76; US Patent Office, patent exam, 1967-69, patent attorney, 1969-79, sr patent attorney, 1980-. **Orgs:** American Intellectual Property Association; NY State Bar; Monroe Co Bar Assn; Rochester Patent Law Assn; Nat Bar Assn; Nat Patent Law Assn Volunteer, Volunteer Legal Project; Rochester Bus Oppor Corp & Urban League; panel mem, NY State Public Employees Bd; co-dir Patent Awareness Program; former pres of bd Urban League of Rochester; former v chmn United Comm Chest. **Military Serv:** USN E-5 1954-57. **Business Addr:** 343 State St, Rochester, NY 14650-2201.

EVERETT, KAY
City official. **Personal:** Born Jul 25, 1941, Detroit, MI; daughter of Zipporah Trice Washington and King Washington; married Walter L Everett Jr, Jun 25, 1966; children: Walter L III, Bradford, Taffeda Kay. **Educ:** Wayne State Univ, BA, 1963, post-degree work, communications/speech pathology. **Career:** Detroit Bd of Educ, teacher, 1963-73, Everett & Little MD, PC, Detroit, MI, office mgr, 1981-91; Detroit Bd of Educ, mem of district 5, 1987-91; City of Detroit, city council mem, 1991-. **Orgs:** Mem, Detroit Bd of Educ, district 5, 1987-91; mem, Univ District Assn Bd, 1991; Detroit Carats Inc; life mem, NAACP; chair, Bd of Innovative Home Health Care, 1985-86; Booker T Washington Businessmen's Assn, 1986-; TULC, 1986-; American Cancer Soc, 1984-86; chair, Detroit Chapter, Auxiliary to the Natl Med Assn, 1979; pres, Auxiliary to the Detroit Med Society Inc, 1979-80; mem, Bd of Dirs for Homes for Black Children, 1973-76; pres, Ortho-Med Mgmt Inc, 1981-87. **Honors/Awds:** Certificate of Appreciation, Keynote Speaker, Hampton Middle School, Detroit, MI; Certificate of Appreciation, Detroit Lafayette Park Kiwanis Club; Organizational Award, Sip-In Committee; Certificate of Appreciation, Payne-Pulliam School of Trade; Certificate of Appreciation, For Women Only. **Business Addr:** City Council Member, City of Detroit, City-County Bldg, #1340, Detroit, MI 48226.

EVERETT, PERCIVAL L.
Dentist. **Personal:** Born Aug 1, 1933, Columbia, SC; married Dorothy L; children: Percival II, Vivian. **Educ:** Allen Univ, BS 1955; Meharry Med Coll, DDS 1962. **Career:** State Park Health Center Columbia, stf dntst 1962-68; Self Employed, dentst. **Orgs:** Am Dental Assn; SC Dental Assn; Central Dist Dental Soc; Congaree Med Dental & Phar Soc; Palmetto Med Dental & Pharm Soc City of Columbia bd of Health; Greater Columbia C of C; Civilian Military Liason Com mem trustee Capital City Devel Found; SC Commn on Human Affairs; United Way Agency Relations bd; SC C of C; Alpha Phi Alpha Frat. **Military Serv:** AUS spec first class 1956-58. **Business Addr:** 2124 Washington St, Columbia, SC 29204.

EVERETT, RALPH B.
Attorney. **Personal:** Born Jun 23, 1951, Orangeburg, SC; son of Alethia Hilton Everett and Francis G S Everett Jr; married Gwendolyn Harris, Jun 22, 1974; children: Jason G. **Educ:** Morehouse Coll, BA 1973; Duke Univ Law School, JD 1976. **Career:** NC Dept of Justice, assoc attorney general 1976; NC Dept of Labor, admin asst for legal affairs 1976-77; Senator Fritz Hollings, spec asst 1977-78, legislative asst 1978-83; US Senate, Comm on Commerce, Sci & Transportation, attny, democratic chief counsel, staff dir 1983-86; US Senate, comm on sci & transportation chief counsel and staff dir 1987-89; Paul Hastings, Janofsky and Walker, partner, 1989-. **Orgs:** Mem NC & DC Bars; admitted to US Dist Court for DC; US Court of Appeals for DC Court; US Tax Court; US Court of Claims; US Supreme Court; mem Amer Bar Assoc, Alpha Phi Alpha; mem, Alumni Board of Visitors, Duke Univ Law School; trustee, Natl Urban League; bd of dir, Ctr for Natl Policy. **Honors/Awds:** Phi Beta Kappa; Phi Alpha Theta Intl Hon Soc in History; Earl Warren Legal Scholar. **Business Addr:** Partner, Paul, Hastings, Janofsky and Walker, 1299 Pennsylvania Avenue, NW, Washington, DC 20004-2400.

EVERETT, THOMAS GREGORY
Professional football player. **Personal:** Born Nov 21, 1964, Daingerfield, TX. **Educ:** Baylor Univ, attended. **Career:** Safety: Pittsburgh Steelers, 1987-92, Dallas Cowboys, 1992-94; Tampa Bay Bu ccaneers, 1994-. **Business Addr:** Professional Football Player, Tampa Bay Buccaneers, 1 Buccaneer Pl, Tampa, FL 33607.

EVERS, JAMES CHARLES
Former mayor. **Personal:** Born Sep 11, 1922, Decatur, MS; divorced; children: Pat, Carolyn, Eunice, Sheila, Charlene. **Educ:** Alcorn State U, BS 1951. **Career:** Fayette, MS, mayor 1969-89; Mississippi State Senate, cand, 1975; Mississippi, cand, gov, 1971; US House Reps, candidate, 1968; Mississippi NAACP, field secy, 1963-69; Medgar Evers Fund, pres, 1969-, founder. **Orgs:** Mem Dem Nat Com; adv bd Black Enterprise Mag; exec com MS Municipal Assn; bd dirs SW MS Planning & Devel Dist; Govs Manpower Conf 1974-; NAACP Recipient Nine Hon Degrees Humanities; Social Sci; Philosophy Jurisprudence. **Honors/Awds:** EVERS Author 1970; man of yr award NAACP 1969; MS Lectr Colls Univs Sociology & Humanities 1964-. **Special Achievements:** Author, Have No Fear: The Charles Evers Story, Wiley & sons, 1997. **Military Serv:** AUS sgt maj 1946. **Business Addr:** President, Medgar Evers Funds Inc, PO Box 158, Fayette, MS 39069.

EVERS-WILLIAMS, MYRLIE
Association executive. **Personal:** marrIed Medgar Evers (died 1963); children: three; married Walter Edward Williams, 1975 (died 1995). **Career:** Claremont Coll, asst dir of educ opportunity, beginning 1967; Seligman & La tz, vp; Atlantic Richfield Co, natl dir for community affairs; Los Angeles Bd of Public Works, commissioner. **Orgs:** NAACP, chairwoman, 1995-. **Honors/Awds:** Author, For Us the Living, 1967. **Special Achievements:** First female to chair the NAACP, 1995. **Business Addr:** Chairwoman, NAACP, 4805 Mt Hope Drive, Baltimore, MD 21215.

EWELL, RAYMOND W.
Legislator. **Personal:** Born Dec 29, 1928, Chicago, IL; married Joyce Marie; children: David, Marc, Raymond. **Educ:** Univ IL, BA 1949; Univ IL, MA 1950; Univ Chgo, LLB 1954. **Career:** IL Gen Assembly 29th Dist, legislator 1966-; Chgo, practicing atty; Chgo, tchr pub shcs. **Orgs:** Mem Cook Co Bar Asn; mem bd Chicago Conf to Fulfill These Rights; Fed Pub & Defender Program; mem NAACP; YMCA. **Business Addr:** 9415 S State St, Chicago, IL 60619.

EWELL, YVONNE AMARYLLIS
Urban education consultant. **Personal:** Born Sep 19, 1927, Frankston, TX; daughter of Majorie Morris and Valcris Ewell. **Educ:** Prairie View A&M, BA, 1947; University of Colorado, MA. **Career:** DISD, elementary consultant, 1965-70, coordinator, curriculum development, 1970, deputy assistant, superintendent instr serv, 1975, assistant superintendent East Oak Cliff Sub, 1976, associate superintendent, East Oak Cliff Sub, 1978; Urban Education, consultant, 1984; DISD, board member, 1987-. **Orgs:** Intergovernmental Coordinating Council for Children and Youth; Commission on Substance Abuse; Dallas Together; The Council of the Great City Schools, National Leadership Group; Alliance of Black School Educators, honorary life member, National Council of Negro Women, legacy life member; National Political Congress of African American; Phi Delta Kappa. **Honors/Awds:** 1990 Distinguished Alumni Citation Award; Freedom Journal, Humanitarian Award; Houston Alliance of Black School Educators, Award of Gratitude; Martin Luther King Community Service Award; Bishop College, Honorary Doctor of Laws. **Special Achievements:** Honors for outstanding contribution to the city of Dallas; University of Texas in Austin, Outstanding Leadership in Education Award; NAACP, First Annual National Distinguished Service Award; the Committee of 100, Woman of the Year; South Dallas Business and Professional Women, Trailblazer Award. **Home Addr:** 4641 Kushla Avenue, Dallas, TX 75216, (214)374-8074. **Business Addr:** Trustee, Dallas Independent School District, 3700 Ross Ave, Administration Bldg, Room 114, Dallas, TX 75204, (214)841-5075.

EWERS, JAMES BENJAMIN, JR.
Educator, educational administrator. **Personal:** Born Sep 29, 1948, Winston-Salem, NC; son of Mildred Jane Holland Ewers and Dr. James B Ewers; married Deborah Leu Froy; children: Christopher, Aaron, Courtney. **Educ:** Johnson C Smith Univ, BA 1970; Catholic Univ of Amer, MA 1971; Univ of MA, EdD 1980; Management Development Program, Harvard University, Certificate, 1996. **Career:** Washington DC Public Schools, teacher 1971-75; Stockton State Coll, asst dir of admissions 1976-1978; Univ of MD Eastern Shore, dir of admin & registrar 1978-84; Livingstone Coll, vice pres for student affairs 1984-87; Dillard Univ, vice president for student affairs, 1987-90; Savannah State College, vice president for student affairs, 1990-94; Liberty County School District, Hinesville, GA, faculty mem; Miami Univ, Middletown, OH, dir of student affairs, 1995. **Orgs:** Mem Ntl Assoc of Personnel Wkrs 1985-; mem Phi Kappa Phi 1983-; mem Amer Assoc for Counseling Devel 1982-; mem Ntl Assoc of Foreign Student Affairs 1981-; mem NAACP 1983-; mem Alpha Phi Alpha 1967-; mem Salisbury/Rowan Human Rel Cncl 1985-87; member, American Assn for Higher Education, 1987; Middletown Civil Service Comm, 1996; bd of dirs, Middletown YMCA, 1996-; bd of dirs, Middletown Red Cross, 1996-. **Honors/Awds:** Using Alumni to Recruit Students Black Issues In Higher Educ, 1986; Winston-Salem High School, Sports Hall of Fame, 1990; M L King Jr, Commendation Day Speaker, Hinesville, GA, 1995; Keynote Speaker, African American Male Symposium, Lake Charles, LA, 1997. **Home Addr:** 4504 Rosewood Ct, Middletown, OH 45042-3862.

EWING, JAMES MELVIN
Government official, engineer. **Personal:** Born Jun 15, 1956, Nashville, TN; son of Cora Lee Ewing; divorced; children: Jonathan Micheal. **Educ:** Tennessee State University, BSCE, 1978. **Career:** Georgia Environmental Protection Division, environmental engineer, 1979-90; Macon Engineering Department, civil engineering manager, 1990-. **Orgs:** American Society of Civil Engineers, 1990; National Society of Professional Engineers, 1990; Peachtree City Water & Sewerage Authority, 1990. **Special Achievements:** Professional Engineer's License. **Home Addr:** 700 Poplar St, Macon, GA 31201, (912)751-7180. **Business Phone:** (912)751-7181.

EWING, JOHN R.
Musician. **Personal:** Born Jan 19, 1917, Topeka, KS; married Vivian. **Career:** Disneyland Teddy Buckner Band, trombonist; Lucy Show with Lucille Ball, 1970-74; Dinah Washington, Sam Cooke, Nancy Wilson, Diane Ross, & Others, recorded with; Cab Calloway Band, 1946; Jimmie Luncford, 1943-45; Earl Hinesband, 1938-41.

EWING, MAMIE HANS
Government administrator. **Personal:** Born Aug 15, 1939, Houston, TX; married Robert; children: Steve, Perry. **Educ:** Univ of TX Austin, BA 1960; Prairie View A&M U, MEd 1974. **Career:** TX Dept of Human Resources, regl admnstr 1978-; TX Dept of Human Resources, fld liason ofcr 1977-78; TX Dept of Human Resources, dir Civil Rights 1975-77; TX Dept of Human Resources, dir & EEO 1973-75; Austin Neighborhood Youth Corps, div exec dir 1972-73; TX Dept of Human Resources, supr Child Welfare div 1969-71. **Orgs:** Bd dir Tarrant Co United Way 1979-80; mem Nat Assn of Social Workers; mem Assn of Black Social Workers; mem Alpha Kappa Alpha Sorority; mem Jack & Jill; mem NAACP; mem, Missouri City Links, 1985-. **Honors/Awds:** Recipient Meritorious Serv Award Travis Co Child Welfare bd 1971; trailbazer of the yr award Bus & Professional Womens Assn of Tarrant Co 1979; achievement award Assn of Black Social Workers 1979; Outstnding Women in TX Government, Governor's Comm on Women in Government, 1987; Outstanding African American Alumnus, Univ of Texas at Austin, Ex-Students Assn, 1990; Houston Works Member of the Year, 1994; Mayor's Public Private Partnership Award, 1996. **Business Addr:** Regional Administrator, Texas Dept of Human Services, 5425 Polk St, Houston, TX 77023, (713)767-2401.

EWING, PATRICK ALOYSIUS
Professional basketball player. **Personal:** Born Aug 5, 1962, Kingston, Jamaica; married Rita; children: Randi, Corey, Patrick Jr. **Educ:** Georgetown Univ, BA 1985. **Career:** New York Knicks, center, 1986-. **Orgs:** New York City Bd of Educ "Drop Out Prevention Program," 1985; NBA Players Assn, president, 1997-. **Honors/Awds:** US Olympic Gold Medal winning basketball team, 1984, 1992; NCAA Most Valuable Player 1984; Big East Conf Co-player of the Year 1984-85; NBA first draft choice 1985; NAISMITH 1985; Kodak Award 1985; Rupp Trophy 1985; 3 time All-Amer Basketball Select 1983-84; UPI, AP First Team All American; named "Met Life" Knick of the Year; 36th NBA All Star Team; Shaw Univ, Doctor of Humane Letters, 1991. **Business Addr:** New York Knicks, Madison Square Garden Center, 2 Pennsylvania Plaza, New York, NY 10121, (212)465-5867.

EWING, SAMUEL DANIEL, JR.
Company executive. **Personal:** Born Aug 9, 1938, Topeka, KS; son of Jane Elizabeth Smith and Samuel Daniel Ewing Sr; married Brenda Jean Arnold Ewing, Jul 29, 1985. **Educ:** Univ of Cincinnati, Cincinnati, OH, BSEE, 1961; Univ of CT, Storrs, CT, MSEE, 1964; Harvard Univ, Boston, MA, MBA, 1968. **Career:** Salomon Brothers, New York, NY, sr assoc, 1969-75; Bankers Trust Co, New York, NY, vice pres, dir, 1975-78; Federal Savings & Loan Corp, Washington, DC, dir, 1978-80; Broadcast Capital Fund, Inc, Washington, DC, pres, 1980-81; Ewing Capital, Inc, Washington, DC, pres, 1981-. **Orgs:** Fellow, Fin Analyst Federation; mem, The Washington Society of Investment Analyst; mem, DC Securities Advisory Comm; mem, Natl Assn of Securities Dealers, Inc, Business Conduct Comm; trustee, The Annuity Fund for Ministers & the Retirement Fund for Lay Workers; trustee, Pension Boards, United Church of Christ, Inc; dir, United Church Bd for Assets Mgmt; mem, United Church Bd for Ministerial Assistance, Inc; mem, Comm on Corporate Social Responsibility; mem, Washington, DC Kiwanis Club, mem, Harvard Club of Washington, DC; mem, Harvard Business School Club of Washington, DC; board member, Natl Assn of Securities Professionals; board member, Greater Southeast Community Hosp (subsidiary-Health Delivery Systems Ltd); board member, Washington, DC Convention Pension Fund; board member, Shaw Heritage Trust Fund. **Business Addr:** President, Ewing Capital, Inc, 727 15th St NW, #700, Washington, DC 20005.

EWING, WILLIAM JAMES
Attorney. **Personal:** Born Sep 10, 1936, New York. **Educ:** Seton Hall Law Sch, LLB 1963. **Career:** Essex County Prosecutors Office, atty; CBS Aspen Systems Corp, legal cmptrs corp exec. **Orgs:** Mem NJ State Am Nat Bar Assns; Concerned Legal Asso of NJ; reg dir Young Lawyers Sect Nat Bar Assn; mem Attys for Montclair; NAACP; exec bd Montclair Urban Coalition. **Honors/Awds:** Outstndng Man Of Yr 1973. **Business Addr:** 363 Bloomfield Ave, Montclair, NJ.

EXUM, THURMAN MCCOY
Business executive, educator. **Personal:** Born Mar 29, 1947, Seven Springs, NC; married Wanda R Edwards; children: Thurman Jr, Jermaine. **Educ:** A&T State Univ, BS Auto Tech 1965-69; CO State Univ, 1983-84; NIASE, Auto Service Excellence ID#23880-3862 1985, MS Indust Ed 1987. **Career:** Buick Div GM, dist ser mgr 1971-78; GM Training Ctr, instructor 1978-79; Pat Mullery Buick, dir of service 1979; No VA Comm Coll, instructor/auto 1980-81; Metro Auto Emission Serv Inc, pres 1981-85; A&T State University, School of Technology, instructor, 1985-. **Orgs:** Consultant Natl Home Study Council 1981-82; consultant NJ Comm Coll 1981; consultant Texaco Oil Co 1981; vice pres Council Auto Apprent Coord 1982-83; consultant CO State Univ 1983-84; coord Natl Auto Dev Assoc 1983; mem MD Quality Assurance Moratorium 1984; consultant DC Dept Transportation 1981-; consultant St of VA 1982-; mem No Amer Emissions Control Conf 1982-; coord St of MD Vehicle Admin 1984-; Society of Automotive Engineers, 1986-. **Honors/Awds:** Instr Certification Dept State Police VA 1981; Cert of Achievement MD State/EPA 1983; "Making It" article Black Enterprise Magazine 1984; dev course curric DC and State of MD for emissions train current use; NASA HL20 PLS Project, 1990-91. **Home Addr:** 1818 Sharpe Road, Greensboro, NC 27406.

EXUM, WADE F.
Physician administrator. **Personal:** Born Jan 31, 1949, Clayton, NC; son of Alfred D & Lucille E Exum; married Carolyn Jan, Aug 1, 1970; children: Daniel E, Adam B, Cord H. **Educ:** Ottawa University, BS, biology, 1971; University of Colorado Med Ctr, MD, 1977; University of Colorado Grad School of Business Administration, MBA, 1986. **Career:** Reynolds Electric & Engineering Co (REECO), industrial hygenist, 1971-73; US Public Health Svcs, general med officer, 1977-80; Colorado State University, student health physician, 1980-81; IMB Corp., sr managing physician, 1982-90; US Olympic Committee, usoc director, DCA, 1991-. **Orgs:** American Med Association, mem, 1980-; National Med Association, mem, 1980-; American Occupational Med Association, mem, 1982-90; Colo Springs Chamber of Commerce, board of directors, 1996; Colo Springs Downtown YMCA, board of directors, 1993-; Athletes Against Drugs, board of directors, 1992-; Shaka Foundation, board of directors, 1997; NCAA Sports Sciences Subcommittee, mem, 1992-94. **Honors/Awds:** USA Olympic Team Delegation, mem, 1992, 1996; USA Pan American Games Team Delegation, mem, 1991, 1995; Goodwill Games Anti-Doping Commission, 1994, 1998; Alumni Hall of Fame Inductee, W J Palmer HS, 1993. **Special Achievements:** Editor: Athletic Drug Reference Book, annual, 1993-96; Author: USOC Drug Education Handbook, annual, 1991-96. **Military Serv:** US Public Health Svcs, commander, 1977-80. **Business Addr:** USOC DCA Director, US Olympic Committee, 1 Olympic Plz, Colorado Springs, CO 80909, (719)578-4574.

EZELL, WILLIAM ALEXANDER
Veterinarian. **Personal:** Born Nov 18, 1924, Kansas City, MO; married Ina; children: William, Ruth, Wayman, Paul. **Educ:** KS State Coll, Univ of NE; Michigan State University, DVM, 1946; Cornell Univ, post graduate work. **Career:** Inkster Animal Hosp, owner, 1950-; Detroit Health Dept, sr veterinary inst, 1948-50; Tuskegee Coll Veterinary Med, head dept, Physiology, Pharmacology, 1947; Animal Care Ctr, owner, 1976-; Allied Veterinary Emergency Svc, stockholder; licensed veteri-

narian in Michigan, Indiana, California. **Orgs:** Past Secretary, pres, Bd of Educ, 1954-75; Inkster Lib Commn, 1957-75; Life mem, past pres Alpha Phi Alpha Fraternity, 1966-; exec bd, Wayne County School Bd Assn, 1967-73; mem/past pres SE MI Vet Med Assn 1972-; honorary mem, Amer Animal Hosp Assn; Vet Alumni Council MI State Univ, 1973-77; bd of dir, MI Humane Soc United Found/African Art Gallery, Detroit Inst of Arts; Lay Reader Episcopal Church Diocese MI; mem Am Veternary Med Assn/Am Animal Hosp; Assn/life mem, MI Vet Med Assn-Found Soc of Detroit Inst of Arts; life mem, golden heritage, NAACP; Resolution of Recognition, State of MI House of Legislature 1972; Recognized Am Heritage Rsch Assn Lib of Human Resources 1975; dist mem Editorial bd; appointed Michigan Bd of Veterinary Examiners, Gov Milliken, 1980-84; appointed Gov Blanchard, 1984-88. **Honors/Awds:** Dr Wm Ezell Educ Day City of Inkster, 1976; Certificate of Appreciation, William Milliken, 1976; Special Tribute Michigan State Senate, 1976; Oustanding Community Serv Award SE MI Veterinary Med Assn, 1977; Published articles in Veterinary Journal, Parke-Davis Journal. **Special Achievements:** First veterinarian to serve two consecutive terms under two governors, chmn, 1984. **Military Serv:** Army, 1944-45. **Business Addr:** Veterinarian, 28438 Michigan Ave, Inkster, MI 48141.

EZIEMEFE, GODSLOVE AJENAVI
Coal transfer company executive. **Personal:** Born Dec 10, 1955, Ilue-Ologbo, Nigeria; son of Margaret and Felix; married Carolyn Fay Brown; children: Edita, Nicole, Ajenavi. **Educ:** Maritime Coll SUNY, B Engrg 1979; Univ of New Orleans, MBA 1981. **Career:** Electro-Coal, asst mgr of maint 1981-85; Ace Enterprises, consultant/proprietor 1985-87; Electro-Coal Transfer, mgr of maint 1985-88; International Marine Terminal, mgr of maintenance & engineering 1988-. **Orgs:** Mem Amer Inst of Plant Engrs 1986-; mem Assoc of Nigerian Profls 1986-; mem New Orleans Anti-Aparthied Coalition 1986-. **Home Addr:** 2028 Sugarloaf Dr, Harvey, LA 70058.

F

FADULU, SUNDAY O.
Educator. **Personal:** Born Nov 11, 1940, Ibadan, Nigeria; married Jacqueline F; children: Sunday Jr, Tony. **Educ:** OK, BS, MS, & PhD 1969. **Career:** TX Southern Univ, asst prof 1972-; Univ of OK School of Medicine, res assoc Hematology 1970-71; Univ of Ife Nigeria, rsch drug unit 1969-70; Univ of Nigeria, lecturer pharmaceutical microbiology 1969-70. **Orgs:** Mem Sigma Xi 1968; Beta Beta Beta Biol Hon Soc 1973; Med Mycological Soc of Ams 1974; mem Intl Soc for Hum & Animal Mycology 1975; mem Friends of Youth Houston TX 1975; Nat Inst of Sci Beta Kappa Chi; mem Nat Geog Soc 1973; Smithsonian Inst Recip Fac Res Grant Urban Resources Cntr Sickle Cell Research; Minority Biomedical Res Nat Inst of Health. **Business Addr:** Biol Dept TX So Univ, 3201 Wheeler Ave, Houston, TX 77004.

FAGBAYI, MUTIU OLUTOYIN
Business research analyst. **Personal:** Born Jan 9, 1953, Lagos, Nigeria; married Patricia Ann Russell; children: Jumoke, Yinka. **Educ:** Univ of Dayton, BChE (Cum Laude) 1976; Penn State Univ, MSChE 1978. **Career:** Eastman Kodak Co, rsch scientist 1978-85, sr business rsch analyst 1985-. **Orgs:** Mem Webster Rotary Club 1982-; sec Webster Rotary Club 1983-84; pres Rochester Chap Natl Org for the Professional Advancement of Black Chemists and Chem Engrs 1983-; bd of trustees Webster Montessori Sch 1984-86; mem exec bd NOBCChE 1986-; mem Tau Beta Pi Engrg Natl Honor Soc; admin NOBCCHE Long-Range Strategic Plan 1987-92. **Honors/Awds:** United Way Volunteer Service Excellence Awd NOBCChE 1986 (presented to Rochester Chap for its Adopt-a-School Science Prog). **Home Addr:** 15 Old Westfall Rd, Rochester, NY 14625. **Business Addr:** Sr Business Rsch Analyst, Eastman Kodak, 343 State St, Rochester, NY 14650.

FAGIN, DARRYL HALL
Management official. **Personal:** Born May 18, 1942, Washington, DC; married Susan; children: Elizabeth Peggy, Adam Vincent. **Educ:** Olivet Coll, BA 1968; GWU Nat Law Cntr, JD 1971. **Career:** US Treas Dept of Treas, asst; US House of Reps, leg asst subcom On employ oppt 1978-79; Equal Employ Oppt Commn, law clk 1977-78; Am Security Bank, legal rsrchr for asso counsel 1975-77; Judge Sorrell,Superior Ct DC, law clk 1974-75; Indsl Bank of WA, loan ofcr & asst cshr 1973-74; Black Students Union Olivet Coll, chrtr pres 1968. **Orgs:** Mem Lawyers Com DC Arts Commn 1971; mem Pub Protection Com Met Bd of Trade 1976. **Honors/Awds:** Legal fellowship award; Reginal Huber Smith community law fellowship Washington DC 1971. **Business Addr:** Dept of the Treas, 15th & PA Ave NW, Washington, DC 20220.

FAIN, CONSTANCE FRISBY
Educator. **Personal:** Born Feb 11, 1949, Philadelphia, PA; daughter of Dorothy Frisby and William Frisby; married Herbert Fain, Feb 4, 1972; children: Kimberly K. **Educ:** Cheyney University, BS, education, 1970; Texas Southern University, JD, 1974; University of Pennsylvania, LLM, 1981. **Career:** US Attorney, Department of Justice, law clerk, 1972-74; Funchess, Charles, Long & Hannah Law Firm, attorney-at-law, 1975-76; Texas Southern University, Thurgood Marshall School of Law, instructor, assistant professor, associate professor, professor of law, 1976-, director, analysis, research and writing program, 1978-90; CLEO Program, instructor, 1977, 1978; Glanville Publishers, consultant, reviewer of law books, 1987-. **Orgs:** State Bar of Pennsylvania, 1981-; State Bar of Texas, 1975-; US District Court, Southern District of Texas, currently; US Court of Appeals, 5th Circuit, currently; US Court of Appeals, 11th Circuit, currently; American Society of Writers on Legal Subjects; Phi Alpha Delta Law Fraternity; Black Women's Lawyers Association. **Honors/Awds:** Moot Court Board, Recognition and Service, 1988, Dedicated Service, 1991, Outstanding Service, 1992; Student Bar Association, Professor of the Year, 1988; Women's Legal Society, Professor of the Year, 1989. **Special Achievements:** Author: "Wrongful Life: Legal and Medical Aspects," Kentucky Law Journal, vol 75, no 2, pp 585-631, 1986-87; "Assault and Battery," Matthew Bender and Co Inc, vol 1a, pp 1-206, 1990; "Conjugal Violence," Michie Co, 2nd ed, pp 121-122, 1991; "Professional Liability," Matthew Bender and Co, Inc, vol 5a, pp 1-247, 1991; "Clergy Malpractice," Mississippi Col Law Rev, vol 12, pp 97-141, 1991. **Business Addr:** Professor of Law, Thurgood Marshall School of Law, Texas Southern University, 3100 Cleburne Ave, Houston, TX 77004, (713)527-7393.

FAIR, DARWIN
Association executive. **Career:** Wolverine Bar Assn, president-elect, 1991, president, 1992-. **Business Addr:** President, Wolverine Bar Association, 645 Griswold, Detroit, MI 48226.

FAIR, FRANK T.
Minister. **Personal:** Born Oct 19, 1929, Clinton, SC; son of Vetda Thomas (Fair) Bell (deceased) and Leo Fair (deceased); married Thelma Belton, Dec 22, 1956; children: Frank Thomas II, Tamera Lee, Donna Machelle Conn, Selwyn Tyrelle. **Educ:** Benedict Coll, 1950; Crozer Sem, M Div 1955; Gammon Sem, STM 1959; Eastern Baptist Seminary Philadelphia, DMin 1979. **Career:** New Hope Bapt Church, pastor 1961-; Farrow-Croft Mental Hosp, chaplain 1959-61; JJ Starks Schl of Theol, tchr 1957-61; Benedict Ext Serv for Min, tchr 1957-61; Royal Bapt Church, pstr 1955-61; SC Area Trade Sch, chaplain & teacher 1951-52; Gethsemane Assn of Natl Bapt Conv Inc, ordained to minister; Am Bapt Conv, min 1961-; Montco OIC, exec dir, resigned 1991. **Orgs:** Deputy dir of Montgomery Cnty Oppor Indsl Ctr Inc 1973-80; exec dir Montgomery County Oppor Indsl Cntr 1980-; past pres Norristown Area Coun of Churches 1970-72; mem bd of dir Dept of Pub Assist 1971-; lay adv Cent Montgomery Tech Schl 1972; mem Norristown Area Schl & Discipline Comm 1973-, Norristown Area Manpower Coun 1974-, Masons; chairperson bd of dirs Selective Service System #107 1982-89; chairperson Interdenominational Clergy Energy Council 1985-; bd of dirs Habitat for Humanities, Norristown PA 1988-. **Honors/Awds:** Author "Orita for Black Youth" 1977.

FAIR, TALMADGE WILLARD
Association executive. **Personal:** Born Jan 15, 1939, Winston-Salem, NC. **Educ:** Johnson C Smith Univ, BA Sociology 1961; Atlanta Univ School of Social Work, MSW 1963. **Career:** Urban League of Greater Miami Inc, assoc dir 1963, pres & ceo 1964-; Bethune Cookman College, Florida Intl Univ, adjunct professor, currently. **Orgs:** Pres Miami Varsity Club 1978-; mem Miami Citizens Against Crime Exec Comm 190-; pres Comm Blacks in Org Labor 1981-; mem FL Reg Coord Council for Vocational Ed 1984-88, Beacon Council Organizational Task Force 1985; bd of trustees, Florida Intl Univ; chm, bd of dir, Bayside Foundation; chm, bd of dir, Visitors Industry; bd of governors and exec committee, Greater Miami Convention and Visitor's Bureau; mem, City of Miami Civil Service Bd; Dade/Monroe WAGES Coalition's Evaluation Committee; bd of governers and exec committee, Miami Coalition for a Safe & Drug-Free Community; co-founder, Liberty City Charter Schl. **Honors/Awds:** Outstanding Dedicated Serv Troop 40 Boy Scouts of Amer 1984; Appreciation Awd Martin Luther King Dev Corp 1984; Gratitude Valuable Contrib Econ Oppty Family Health Ctr 1984; Appreciation Awd Progressive Firefighters Assn 1985; Certificate of Appreciation for Outstanding Service, City of Miami; Greater Miami Chamber of Commerce Leadership Award; Outstanding Citizen Service award, State of Florida. **Special Achievements:** Author of numerous published articles in the Miami Herald, Miami Magazine, Tropic Magazine; host of both radio and television programs; interviewed by 60 Minutes, Tom Brokaw, Ebony Magazine and National Geographic. **Business Addr:** President/Chief Executive Ofcr, Urban League of Miami, Inc, 8500 NW 25th Ave, Miami, FL 33147.

FAIRLEY, RICHARD L.
Government official. **Personal:** Born Jul 16, 1933, Washington, DC; son of Gladys and Richmond; married Charlestine Dawson, Mar 25, 1989; children: Ricki Louise, Sharon Rene. **Educ:** Dartmouth Coll, BA 1956; Stanford U, MA 1969; Univ Massachusetts, EdD 1974. **Career:** Office Ed, regional dir 1965-67, broad chief 1967-69, assoc commr 1969-80; Dept Ed, depty assist scty 1980-82, dir inst spt 1982-84, dir mgt serv, dir higher educ prog 1987-. **Orgs:** Ed prog splt USO E/Dept Defense 1961-65; tchr DC Public Schls 1955-61; ed comm Natl Urban League 1968-84; mem Maryland Advisory Comm 1970; US Civil Rghts Comm; mem Kappa Alpha Phi 1975-. **Honors/Awds:** USOE flw 1976; superior serv awd USOE 1968; Bill Cosby awd Univ MA 1982; Doctor of Humane Letters Rust College 1988; Doctor of Humane Letters St. Pauls College 1989. **Military Serv:** USAR capt 13. **Business Addr:** Dir Higher Education Prog, US Dept Education, 400 Maryland Ave SW, Washington, DC 20202.

FAIRMAN, J. W., JR.
Corrections superintendent. **Personal:** Born May 20, 1948, Cleveland, MS; married Jeanne Arthur Hester; children: Bridgette, Darrin, Victor. **Educ:** Coahoma Jr Coll, AA 1967; Hardin-Simmons Univ, BS, 1970; Chicago State Univ, MS, 1975; Harvard Univ, Cambridge, John F Kennedy School of Government, prog for sr execs in state & local government, 1994; Harper and Row Publishing Company, Hostage Negotiations, 1980; Amer Abritration Assn, labor management, 1977; State of IL, Dept of Personnel, administrative & organizational behavior, 1974. **Career:** Chicago DART Work Release, counselor 1971-72, center supvr 1972-77; IL Dept of Corr Work Release, dep supt 1977-79, comm corr ctr supervisor, 1972-77, correctional counselor, 1971-72; Stateville Correct Center, asst supt, 1979; Pontiac Correct Center, warden 1979-82; Joliet Correct Center, warden 1982-91; Cook Cty Dept of Corrections, Chicago IL, exec dir, 1991-; IL Dept of Corrections, Sheridan Correctional Ctr, warden, 1991. **Orgs:** Mem IL Correct Assn 1979-; mem Amer Correct Assn 1980-; mem Natl Assn Blacks in Criminal Justice 1976-; Circuit Court of Cook County Principal's Comm, 1991-; IL Attorney Gen Comm on African-American Males, 1992-94; Chicago Salvation Army Corr Services, advisory bd, 1993-; Office of the Cook Cty State's Attorney Gay & Lesbian Task Force, 1993-; Will Cty Police Chiefs Assn; City of Joliet, IL Task Force for Gangs; Natl Assn of Blacks in Criminal Justice; Assn of State Correctional Administrators; IL Correctional Assn; Amer Correctional Assn; Amer Jail Assn. **Business Addr:** Exec Dir, Cook County Dept of Corrections, 2700 S California Ave, Chicago, IL 60608.

FAIRMAN, JOHN ABBREY
Health care executive. **Personal:** Born Jun 28, 1949, Cleveland, MS; son of Luberta Holmes Fairman and Jimmy W Fairman; divorced; children: Antonio, Tanzala, BeVona, Johnny Abbrey, Quentin Sherrod. **Educ:** Hardin-Simmons Univ, Abilene, TX, BS, 1972; Trinity Univ, San Antonio, TX, MHA, 1974; Univ of Houston, Houston, TX, Certificate, 1975-77. **Career:** Hendrick Mem Hosp, Abilene, TX, business office clerk, 1970-72; Bexar County Hosp, San Antonio, TX, purchasing clerk, 1972-73; Nueces County Hosp, Corpus Christi, TX, admin resident, 1973-74; Harris County Hosp Dist, Houston, TX, asst admin, 1974-76, dep chief admin, 1976-87; Denver Health & Hospitals, Denver, CO, mgr/CEO, 1987-90; JFC Inc, pres, 1990-. **Orgs:** Bd mem, Gulf Coast Hospital Finance Authority Bd; appointee, Grand Jury; mem, Mayor's Cabinet, city of Denver; mem, Greater Denver Chamber of Commerce; mem, Colorado Hospital Assn; mem, Amer Hospital Assn; mem, Natl Assn of Public Hospitals; mem, Natl Assn of Health Services Executives; bd mem, Samaritan House Homeless Shelter.

FAISON, DEREK E.
Company executive. **Personal:** Born Jul 14, 1948, Newport News, VA; son of Carmena Gantt Faison and Edgar Faison; married Wilma A Faison (divorced 1990); children: Natalye, Marcus. **Educ:** University of Colorado, Denver, CO, BS, business administration, 1970; Colorado State University, Fort Collins, CO, 1972. **Career:** Penn Mutual Life Ins Co, Denver, CO, sales representative, 1970-72; IBM, Boulder, CO, copier planning mfg, 1972-81; Faison Office Products Co, Denver, CO, president, 1981-. **Orgs:** Board member, Big Brother, 1988-; board member, Colorado Black Chamber of Commerce, 1990-; board member, Greater Denver Chamber of Commerce, 1990-; board member, Dean's Advisory Board CU Business School, 1990-; board member, Denver Broncos Active Rooster, 1990-. **Honors/Awds:** Certificate of Special Congressional Recognition Dan Schefer, 1991; Graduate Wisconsin Minority Mgmt School, Minority Enterprise Inc, 1990; Business of the Year, Minority Enterprise Inc, 1990. **Business Addr:** President, Faison Office Products Company, 3251 Revere St, #200, Aurora, CO 80011-1816.

FAISON, FRANKIE
Professional actor. **Personal:** Born Jun 10, 1949, Newport News, VA; son of Carmena Gantt Faison and Edgar Faison; married Jane Mandel Faison, Nov 26, 1988; children: Blake, Amanda, Rachel. **Educ:** Illinois Wesleyan University, Bloomington, IL, BFA, 1971; New York University, New York, NY, MFA, 1974. **Career:** Self-employed actor, New York, NY, 1971-. **Orgs:** Local spokesperson, Organization for the Prevention of Child Abuse, 1991; member, Screen Actors Guide, 1974-; member, American Federation of TV and Radio, 1974-; member, Actors Equity Association, 1972-. **Honors/Awds:** Tony Nomination, 1988; Drama Desk Nomination, 1988; Audelco Award, 1989. **Business Addr:** c/o Gersh Agency, 124 W 42nd St, New York, NY 10036.

FAISON, HELEN SMITH
Educator. **Personal:** Born Jul 13, 1924, Pittsburgh, PA; married George. **Educ:** Univ Pgh, AB 1946, MEd 1955, PhD 1975. **Career:** Pittsburgh Public Schools, asst supt; Allegheny County, bd asst, social caseworker, teacher, girls adv, activites dir, conselor, vice prin, prin. **Orgs:** Mem Nat Cncl Negro Women; past bd mem YWCA; mem Pi Lambda Theta; Admin Women in Edn; Am Assn Univ Women; past chmn State Implementation; past mem bd Tst Univ Pittsburgh; Educ TV Sta WQED; Negro Educ Emergency Drive; mem Harriet Tubman Guild Inc. **Honors/Awds:** Bapt Temple Ch Recpt courier top hat award; educator yr award Guardians; Helping Women Advance Professionally AASA/FORD Found 1977; Supt Work Conf Columbia Univ 1971. **Business Addr:** Deputy Supt School Management, Pittsburgh Public Schools, 341 S Bellefield Ave, Pittsburgh, PA 15213.

FAISON, SHARON GAIL
Office products company marketing executive. **Personal:** Born Nov 21, 1955, Newport News, VA; daughter of Carmena Gantt Faison and Edgar Faison; married Melvin E Bryant (divorced 1985); children: Sharonda M, Jai R. **Educ:** Norfolk State University, Norfolk, VA, BA, math, 1982. **Career:** IBM Support Ctr, Boulder, CO, PSR, 1983-86; Faison Office Products Co, Denver, Co, vice president, 1986-. **Orgs:** Member, Zeta Phi Beta, 1984-; member, Minority Enterprise Inc, 1986-; member, Greater Denver Black Chamber of Commerce, 1986-; member, National Office Products Assn, 1982. **Honors/Awds:** Graduate of Fast Track Program, Minority Enterprise Inc, 1990; Certificate of Appreciation, Total Quality Management, 1990; Colorado Business of the Year, Minority Enterprise Inc, 1990. **Business Addr:** Vice President, Faison Office Products Company, 3251 Revere St, #200, Aurora, CO 80011.

FAKHRID-DEEN, NASHID ABDULLAH
Educator. **Personal:** Born Feb 24, 1949, Monticello, AR; son of Mary Thompson and N T Thompson; married Pauline Rashidah Williamson; children: Jashed, Ayesha, Yasmeen. **Educ:** Grand Valley State Univ, BA 1978; Western MI Univ, grad work 1978-79; Univ of Baltimore, School of Law, JD 1984-88. **Career:** Nation of Islam, minister 1975-79; Grand Valley State Univ, asst dir of talent search 1980-83, asst dir of admissions 1979-83; Bowie State Univ, coordinator of recruitment, assoc dir of admissions 1988-90; Kentucky State University, Frankfort, KY, exec asst to the pres 1990-91; Kentucky State Univ, exec asst to the pres, 1990-91; Ohio Univ, coordinator minority student affairs, 1992-94; Univ of Kentucky Commun Coll System, coordinator minority affairs community college system, 1994-. **Orgs:** General business mgr Nation of Islam 1972-76; mem bd dirs Climbing Tree School 1977-78; mem bd dirs Family Services Outreach 1982-83; mem Mid-America Assn of Educ Oppor Program Personnel; Exec Council Black Law Students, Univ of Baltimore; Admissions/Retention Committee; Moot Court Board, 1986-88; Developer/presentator of CARE (motivational workshop), Baltimore/Washington Metro Area; pres, Black Law Students Assn, Univ of Baltimore School of Law 1987-88. **Honors/Awds:** Outstanding Community Service World Community of Islam 1981, 1982; Grand Valley St Univ, Outstanding Service Talent Search Prgm 1983; Office of Admissions, Outstanding Service Award 1983; Outstanding Community Service, 1980-82; Charles Hamilton Houston Award, Univ of Baltimore Black Law Students Assn 1988; Freedom Fighter Award, NAACP, Bowie State University Chapter, 1991. Ohio Univ, Asante Award, 1993, Romeo Award, 1993; Hopeville Community Coll, Significant Contribution Award to Project PARADE, 1995. **Military Serv:** USAF E-4 Sgt 3 1/2 years. **Home Addr:** 4344 Calavares Dr, Lexington, KY 40514.

FALANA, LOLA
Singer, entertainer. **Personal:** Born Sep 11, 1943, Camden, NJ. **Career:** Dancing jobs on the East Coast; recorded for Frank Sinatra's Reprise Label & Motown Records; Sammy Davis Jr's broadway musical Golden Boy, dancer; ABC TV, 2 specials; appeared in several films; Las Vegas, singer, currently. **Honors/Awds:** She has smashed nearly every Las Vegas nightclub attendance & box office record & is recognized as the First Lady of Las Vegas; author of a book.

FALES, SUSAN
Television producer, writer. **Personal:** Born in Rome, Italy; daughter of Timothy Fales and Josephine Premice. **Educ:** Harvard University, BA (with honors), history, literature, 1985. **Career:** The Cosby Show, apprentice writer, 1985-86; A Different World, story editor, 1986-87, co-producer, writer, 1987-93.

FALKNER, BOBBIE E.
Automobile dealer. **Career:** Harvey Chrysler Plymouth (formerly Falkner Enterprise Inc), Harvey, IL, chief executive, currently.

FANAKA, JAMAA
Writer, producer, director. **Personal:** Born Sep 6, 1942, Jackson, MS; son of Beatrice Gordon and Robert L Gordon; children: Tracey L, Michael, Katina A, Twyla M. **Educ:** Compton Jr Coll, AA 1971; UCLA, BA (summa cum laude) 1973; UCLA, MFA 1978. **Career:** Jamaa Fanaka Prodns Inc, writer/producer/dir (motion pictures) "Penitentiary", "Penitentiary II", "Penitentiary III," "Emma Mae", "Welcome Home Brother Charles" 1974; IBM Corp, customer engr 1968-70; Bethlehem Steel, engineering clk 1964-68. **Orgs:** Pres Black Filmmakers Alliance 1975-79; mem Big Brothers of Am 1980. **Honors/Awds:** Ford Found Grant, Ford Found 1972; Rockefeller Grant, Rockefeller Found 1973; UCLA Chancellor's Grant, UCLA 1973; Am Film Inst Grant, Am Film Inst 1976. **Military Serv:** USAF a/1c 1960-64. **Business Addr:** MGM Studios, Culver City, CA 90230.

FANCHER, EVELYN PITTS
Librarian. **Personal:** Born in Marion, AL; daughter of Nell Pitts and D C Pitts; married Charles B; children: Charles, Jr, Mark, Adrienne. **Educ:** AL State Univ, BS; Atlanta Univ, MSLS 1961; Peabody/Vanderbilt Univ, EdS 1969; Peabody/Vanderbilt Univ, PhD 1975. **Career:** Lincoln High, librarian, 1951-56; AL A&M Univ, librarian 1956; TN State Univ, librarian, 1962-75, prof library Sci, 1975, dir libr 1976-89; Vanderbilt University, Kelly M Smith Res Collection, librarian, 1991-96. **Orgs:** Lib consult (USAID) Swaziland, Africa 1982; pres TN Library Association 1984-85; board member TN Advy Council Lbrs 1983-89; Girl Scout brd dir Cumberland Vly 1980-84; SE Library Association; American Library Association; Mdl TN Lbry Association; TN Higher Educ Committee Library Tech Council; Tennessee Long Range Planning Committee, 5 yr plan for libraries; Southern Association of Colleges and Schools (SACS), reviewer. **Honors/Awds:** One of the first women inducted into Phi Delta Kappa Ed Fraternity; recognitions received from Secretary of State and Mayor; Congregational Church, Outstanding Community Service, 1991; St Luke AME Church, Outstanding Community Service, 1991; Nashville Volunteer of the Year, 1992; Good Neighbor Award, 1992; TN Historical Commission Merit Award, 1994. **Special Achievements:** Author: "Educational Technology A Black Perspective" Eric 1984; "Edtg Ethric Minorities" Negro Ed Rev XXV 1974; "College Adm Practices & the Negro Student" Negro Ed Rev XXII 1971; "Merger of TN State Univ & the Univ of TN Libraries" TN Librarian Vol 32 Winter 1980; A Study Guide for Discovering and Preserving African-American Church History Documents, 1991; A Directory of African-American Churches in Nashville, Tennessee, 1991. **Business Addr:** Librarian for the Kelly Miller Research Collection, Vanderbilt University Library, 419 21st Ave S, Nashville, TN 37240.

FANN, AL LOUIS
Actor, educator. **Personal:** Born Feb 21, 1925, Cleveland, OH; son of Beulah Fann and Albert Louis Fann; divorced; children: Tracey King, Shelley Peterson, Melanie, Albert, Kacie, Scott. **Educ:** Cleveland Institute of Music, 1959; Living Ministries International, DD, 1981. **Career:** Actor, 1950-; Al Fann Theatrical Ensemble, executive director, 1965-; Actor, "Bodies of Evidence," television series. **Orgs:** Screen Actors Guild, 1965-; American Federation of Television & Radio Artists, 1965-; Academy of Artists & Sciences, blue ribbon panel judge, 1987; NAACP, life-time honorary member, 1979; Institute for Artistic Development, Higher Mind Training, founder, 1986. **Honors/Awds:** National Cable TV Association, Best Play of the Year, 14 Awards, 1971. **Special Achievements:** Emmy Award Nomination, 1989; Drama as a Therapeutic Tool, 1978; King Heroin, 1967; The World's No 1 Performing Unit, 1967; founded The Institute For Artistic Development, 1986. **Military Serv:** US Army Aircorp, pvt. **Business Addr:** Executive Director, Al Fann Theatrical Ensemble, 6051 Hollywood Blvd, Ste 207, Hollywood, CA 90028, (213)464-0187.

FANN, CHAD FITZGERALD
Professional football player. **Personal:** Born Jun 7, 1970, Jacksonville, FL. **Educ:** Florida A&M, attended. **Career:** Arizona Cardinals, tight end, 1994-95; San Francisco 49ers, 1997-. **Business Addr:** Professional Football Player, San Francisco 49ers, 4949 Centennial Blvd, Santa Clara, CA 95054, (415)562-4949.

FARLEY, WILLIAM HORACE, JR.
City government official. **Personal:** Born Feb 20, 1950, Skowheegan, ME; son of Laura C Farley and William H Farley, Sr; married Gale Foster Farley, Nov 27, 1982; children: William Foster, Royal Chase. **Educ:** Yale Univ, BA (cum laude) 1972; Oxford Univ England, Hons BA 1974; Yale Law School JD 1977. **Career:** McDermott, Will & Emery, atty (partner) 1977-86; City of Chicago, First Asst Corp Counsel 1987-89; Chicago Transit Authority, Gen Counsel 1989-; Jenner & Block, partner, 1992-. **Orgs:** Constitutional Rights Foundation, board of directors; Public Interest Lw Initiative, board of directors; Lawyers' Trust Fund of Illinois, board of directors; Urban Gateways, board of directors; Chicago Bar Association; American BAR Association; Cook County Bar Association; Markey Inns of Court; Committee on Transit & International Transportation Law, Transportation Research Board; American Public Transit Association, legal affairs committee, chairman; Affirmative Action for the Cook County Board of Commissioners, legal committee, chairman. **Honors/Awds:** Rhodes Scholarship 1972; contributing author, Architect and Engineer Liability: Claims Against Design Professionals, Cushman & Bottom, ed, Contributing author, 1995. **Business Addr:** General Attorney, Chicago Transit Authority, 429A Merchandise Mart Plz, Chicago, IL 60654.

FARMER, BRUCE ALBERT
Business executive. **Personal:** Born Mar 25, 1957, Rochester, PA. **Educ:** Univ of Pittsburgh, 1975-79; St Vincent Coll, BA 1980; Temple Univ, attended 1982-83. **Career:** Marriot Inn, bus coord 1979; Hill Refrigeration, prod schedular 1980-81; William H Rorer, mgr 1981-86; Stadium Enterprises, vice pres 1986-; Transitions Inc,asst program dir 1986-. **Orgs:** Bd mem Amer Forestry Environ 1981; pres consult PA Minorities About Change 1981,82,83,84; reporter/editor Philadelphia Org Devel 1982; pres Cultural Awareness Comm 1983-84; bd mem Montgomery Zoning Commiss 1984-85; mem NAACP, Alpha Phi Alpha, GABT, UNCF. **Honors/Awds:** Pres Rochester HS 1972-75; vice pres Alpha Phi Alpha 1978; Brother of the Year Alpha Phi Alpha 1978; Man of the Year Montgomery Cty Comm on Human Rights 1982. **Home Addr:** 754 Tennyson Dr, Warminster, PA 18974.

FARMER, CLARENCE
Business executive. **Personal:** Born Jun 19, 1920, Rochester, PA; son of Margaret Artope and Frank Farmer; married Marjorie Nichols, Apr 17, 1943; children: Clarence Jr, Franklyn. **Educ:** Geneva Coll, Beaver Falls, PA, AB 1940. **Career:** Commn on Human Rel, chmn 1967-82; Commn on Human Rel, exec dir/chairman 1967-82; Philadelphia Police Adv Bd, exec sec 1965-67; Self-employed, business consultant, 1982; Stadium Enterprise, Inc., president; Center for Adult Training, president; Farmer Communications, Inc., president. **Orgs:** Chmn, founder, Greater Philadelphia Enterprise Devel Corp; pres First Loan Co & Farmer Press Inc; board Philadelphia Urban Coalition Inc; bd dir Wissahickon Boys' Club; bd dir Founders' Club; Greater Phila Chamber of Commerce; United Fund; Phila Housing Devel Corp; pres, Options for Women Inc; Philadelphia Civic Ballet Co; Cape May Tennis Club; St Paul Epis Ch; NAACP; Urban League of Phila; Geneva Coll Alumni Assn; Alpha Phi Alpha; Benjamin Lodge F & A M; bd of trustees Geneva Coll, Beaver Falls, PA; chmn, emeritus, bd of dirs, Afro-American Historical and Cultural Museum; Phila Housing Devel. Corp, chairman. **Honors/Awds:** Recip North City Congress Awd 1965; Bapt Ministers Conf 1965; Travelers' Club Awd 1967; Gardian Civic Leag Awd 1967; Legion of Cornelius 1967; Geneva Coll Distng Serv Awd 1969; Vare Jr High Sch Awd 1969; Philadelphia Bar Assn Achmnt Awd 1969; Coun of Clergy Awd 1972; 100000 Pennsylvanians Awd for Comm Serv 1972; Cardinal's Commn on Human Rel Awd 1972; Alpha Phi Alpha Distng Serv Awd 1971; Richard Allen Awd; Mother Bethel AME Ch 1974; USAAF 1943-45; Chamber of Commerce Award, 1991; TX Coll, DHL, 1989. **Military Serv:** USAAF Sgt, 1943-45. **Business Addr:** President, Clarence Farmer Association Inc, 260 S Broad St, Ste 1600, Philadelphia, PA 19102.

FARMER, FOREST J.
Company executive. **Personal:** Born Jan 15, 1941, Zanesville, OH; son of Leatha D Randolph Farmer and William J Farmer; married Rosalyn Farmer McPherson, Dec 1966; children: Forest, Jr, Christopher M. **Educ:** Purdue Univ, Lafayette, IN, BS, 1965. **Career:** Chrysler Motors Corp, Detroit MI, Jefferson Assembly Plant plant mgr, 1981, Newark DE assembly plant mgr, 1983, Sterling Heights MI plant mgr, 1984, dir, advance mfg planning, 1986-87, Highland Park MI gen plant mgr, 1987-88; Acustar, Inc, Troy, MI, pres, 1988-95; Regal Plastics Co, CEO, 1995-. **Honors/Awds:** Outstanding Businessman of 1989; 100 Black Men of America 1989. **Business Addr:** Chrysler-Acustar, 6565 E. 8 Mile Rd., Warren, MI 48091-2949.

FARMER, HILDA WOOTEN
Banker. **Personal:** Born Apr 25, 1950, LaGrange, NC; daughter of Janie Wooten (deceased) _ and Elbert Wooten; married William E Farmer, Aug 11, 1972; children: William Jr, Courtney. **Educ:** NC Central University, Durham, NC, BS, 1972. **Career:** Wachovia Bank, Goldsboro, NC, dealer credit manager, asst vice pres, 1973-. **Orgs:** Treasurer, American Cancer Society, 1986-91. **Honors/Awds:** Service Awards, American Cancer Society, 1988-89. **Home Addr:** Route 4, Box 90, Goldsboro, NC 27530.

FARMER, JAMES
Educator, lecturer. **Personal:** Born Jan 12, 1920, Marshall, TX; son of Pearl Marion Houston Farmer and James Leonard Farmer; married Lula Peterson (deceased); children: Tami Farmer Gonzales, Abbey Farmer-Levin. **Educ:** Wiley Coll, BS 1938; Howard Univ, BD 1941. **Career:** NAACP, program dir 1959-60; Congress of Racial Equality, founder 1942, natl dir 1961-66; US Dept Health Education & Welfare, asst sec 1969-70; Coalition of Amer Public Employees, exec dir 1977-82; Antioch Univ, distinguished prof 1983-84; Mary Washington Coll, distinguished visiting prof, 1985-94, distinguished coll prof, 1994-; A Living History of the Civil Rights Movement, lecturer. **Orgs:** Chmn of the bd Fund for an Open Society 1974-95; mem adv bd ACLU 1984-. **Honors/Awds:** Numerous awards including Omega Psi Phi Award 1961, 1963; First Citizen Award Queens Region Hadassah 1969; American Humanist Award 1976; Author of "Freedom-When?" 1966, "Lay Bare the Heart" 1985; author of numerous other articles and essays; received 22 honorary doctorates; Presidential (Clinton) Medal of Freedom, 1998. **Business Addr:** Distinguished Coll Professor of History & American Studies, Mary Washington College, 1301 College Ave, Fredericksburg, VA 22401.

FARMER, KAREN BATCHELOR
Corporate litigation attorney. **Personal:** Born Jun 8, 1951, Detroit, MI; daughter of Alice Vivian Dickinson Batchelor and Thomas Melvin Batchelor; married Charles Southall Farmer II (divorced 1980); children: Charles Southall Farmer III. **Educ:** Fisk Univ, Nashville, TN, 1969-71; Oakland Univ, Rochester, MI, BA, Psychology, 1980; Wayne State Univ Law School, Detroit, MI, JD, 1985. **Career:** Wayne County Probate Court, Detroit, MI, clerk, 1980-82; Dykhouse Wise & Marsac, PC, Detroit, MI, law clerk, 1984-85, assoc attorney, 1985-87; Standard Federal Bank, Troy, MI, vice pres, assoc counsel, 1987-91; MI Consolidated Gas Co, Detroit, MI, staff attorney, 1991-. **Orgs:** First black mem, Natl Society of the Daughters of the American Revolution, 1977-; mem, American Bar Assn, 1985-; steering comm, bd mem, D Augustus Straker Bar Assn, 1989-; bd mem, Consumer Bankruptcy Assn, 1989-; co-fndr, Fred Hart Williams Genealogical Society, 1979-82; mem, Links Inc, Detroit Chapter, 1984-; Minority In-House Counsel Organizational Task Force, chairperson, objectives committee, 1992-. **Business Addr:** Staff Attorney, Office of the General Counsel, Michigan Consolidated Gas Co, 500 Griswold St, Detroit, MI 48226.

FARMER, NANCY
Judge. **Career:** 36th District Court, Detroit, judge. **Business Addr:** Judge, 36th District Court, 421 Madison Ave, Detroit, MI 48226, (313)965-8720.

FARMER, RAY
Professional football player. **Personal:** Born Jul 1, 1972, White Plains, NY; married Vernet. **Educ:** Duke Univ, bachelor's degree in sociology. **Career:** Philadelphia Eagles, linebacker, 1996-. **Business Addr:** Professional Football Player, Philadelphia Eagles, 3501 S Broad St, Philadelphia, PA 19148, (215)463-2500.

FARMER, ROBERT CLARENCE
Physician. **Personal:** Born Jan 1, 1941, Rochester, PA; son of Ora Juanita McClain Farmer and Francis Alexander Farmer Sr; married Linda Kay Hill Farmer, Aug 4, 1983; children: Saundra, Robert, James, Wendy. **Educ:** Howard Univ, BS 1963, MD 1967. **Career:** Univ of Pittsburgh, instructor pediatric radiology 1973-74; Howard Univ, asst prof radiology 1974-75, asst prof pediatrics 1974-77; St Anthony Hosp, dir radiology 1977-81; Fayette Co Hospital, dir radiology 1978-83; Ft Stewart Hospital, dir radiology 1980-81; Connellsville State General Hosp, dir radiology 1982-85; Highlands Hospital & Health Ctr, dir radiology 1985-; FDIS Inc, president, 1992-. **Orgs:** Life mem NAACP 1953-; life mem Alpha Phi Alpha Frat; mem Radiology Soc of North Amer 1973-, Natl Medical Assn 1977-, Amer College of Radiology 1973-; mem Amer Cancer Soc 1983-, Bd of Health 1984-; bd dirs Amer Lung Assn 1985-; bd of dirs Comm Housing Resource Bd of Fayette Cty PA; mem FROGS Club of Pittsburgh; pres Fayette County NAACP 1989-92; president, Gateway Medical Society NMA 1994-96; 2nd vice president, Pennsylvania State Conference of NAACP Branches, 1989-91; president, Rotary Club of Connellsville; 1st vice president, Pittsburgh Lay Conference AME Church; president Chi Delta Mu Fraternity Pi Chapter, 1995-; board member Blue Cross of Western Pennsylvania, 1996-; board member High-Mark Corp, 1996-. **Honors/Awds:** Publications "Carcinoma of the Breast; A Clinical Study," NMA Journal 1969; "Immunological Responses in Infantile Cortical Hyperostosis," Pediatric Rsch Vol 10 1976; "Immunological Studies in Caffey's Cortical Hyperostosis," Pediatrics 1977; Black Achiever of SW Pennsylvania 11th dist Debora Grand Chapter OES 1988. **Military Serv:** US Army, capt 1966-68. **Business Addr:** Dir of Radiology, Highlands Hospital & Health Center, 401 East Murphy Ave, Connellsville, PA 15425.

FARMER, SHARON
Photographer, government official. **Career:** The White House, staff photographer, currently. **Business Addr:** Photo Office, The White House, 1600 Pennsylvania Ave, W Wing, Washington, DC 20500, (202)395-4050.

FARR, D'MARCO
Professional football player. **Personal:** Born Jun 9, 1971, San Pablo, CA. **Educ:** Univ of Washington. **Career:** St Louis Rams, defensive tackle, 1995-. **Business Addr:** Professional Football Player, St Louis Rams, One Rams Way, St Louis, MO 63045, (314)982-7267.

FARR, HERMAN
Clergyman. **Personal:** marrIed Bruetta Dupre; children: 4. **Educ:** Detroit Bible Coll. **Career:** Clien Air Bacteria Service, proprieter; Ford Motor Co, former employee; Lien Chemical Co, former salesman; Oak Hill Bapt Ch Chmn of Equal Employment Com, presently pastor; Interdenominational Ministerial Alliance, corresponding sec; Mt Herman Bapt & District Assn, treas; Bapt Ministers Fellowship, pres; Shreveport Chap of NAACP, publicity chmn 1-74; NAACP, exec sec 1968-71. **Orgs:** Mem YMCA; coordinator Weekly Radio Broadcast for Ministerial Alliance. **Honors/Awds:** Comm service award AKA Sorority during 41st Central Regional Conf 1973; appreciation award NAACP 1972; certificate of appreciation for service Kiwanis Club 1973; comm service award Negro C of C 1973. **Business Addr:** 190o Milan St, Shreveport, LA 71103.

FARR, LLEWELLYN GOLDSTONE
State official. **Personal:** Born Sep 6, 1928, Kingston, Jamaica; married Edna Rogers; children: Siobhan. **Educ:** St Georgeas Coll Jamaica, diploma 1946; Brooklyn Coll, BS 1959; City Univ NY, postgrad 1959-64. **Career:** NY State Labor Dept, economist 1960-62, sr economist 1962-68; NY State Commerce Dept NYC, asso economist 1968-69. **Orgs:** Asso bus consult 1969-70; dir Job Incentive Bur 1970-; exec sec NY State Job Incentive Bd 1970-; bd dir Bushwick Hylan Comm Center, Brooklyn 1967; pres Local 1473 Am Fedn State Co & Municipal Employees 1966-68; mem Am Statis Assn; mem Am Econ Assn NAACP; Grand Central Athletic Club NYC. **Military Serv:** AUS 1951-53. **Business Addr:** 230 Park Ave, New York, NY 10017.

FARR, MELVIN, SR.
Automobile dealer. **Personal:** Born Nov 3, 1944, Beaumont, TX; son of Miller Farr Sr and Dorthea Farr; married Mae R Forbes; children: Mel Jr, Michael A, Monet A. **Educ:** UCLA, 1963-67; Univ of Detroit, BS 1971. **Career:** Detroit Lions, professional football player 1967-73; Mel Farr Ford Inc, pres 1975-; Mel Farr Lincoln Mercury, pres, 1986-; Mel Farr Imports, pres, 1986-; Mel Farr Ford-Ohio, pres, 1991-; Mel Farr Ford of Grand Blanc, pres, 1993-; Mel Farr Lincoln Mercury-Ohio, pres, 1995-; Mel Farr Ford-Houston, pres, 1996-; Flint, MI 7-Up franchise, co-owner (1st 100% Black-owned major soft drink franchise), 1985-87. **Orgs:** Minority Ford-Lincoln Mercury Dealers Assn, co-founder; National Associatio n of Minority Auto Dealers, director; Sinai Hospital Health Care Foundation, bo ard member, 1993-; Better Business Bureau of Detroit and SE Michigan, board of directors; Public Advisory Committee on Judicial Candidates; NAACP, life member ; Metropolitan Detroit YMCA, board of directors, 1992-; Oak Park, Michigan Cham ber of Commerce. **Honors/Awds:** All-American Football UCLA 1965-66; All Pro Nat Football League Detroit Lions 1967-68; UCLA Sports Hall of Fame, 1988; Michigan Black MBA Assn, Entrepreneur of the Year, 1992; Mercy High School, Meg Mallon Sportsmanship Ac hievement Award, 1992; Black Enterprise Magazine, Auto Dealer of the Year, 1992 ; Oakland County Executive of the Year, 1993. **Business Addr:** President, CEO, Mel Farr Automotive Group, Executive Office c/o Advertising Dept, 24750 Greenfield Rd, Oak Park, MI 48237, (810)967-3700.

FARRAKHAN, LOUIS
Clergyman. **Personal:** Born May 11, 1933, New York, NY; married Betsy; children: 9. **Educ:** Winston-Salem Teachers College, attended. **Career:** Natl Rep and Minister, Nation of Islam, currently. **Special Achievements:** Independent Black Leadership in America, 1991. **Business Addr:** Minister, Nation of Islam, 734 West 79th St, Chicago, IL 60620.

FARRELL, CHERYL LAYNE
Banking and financial services executive. **Personal:** Born Sep 10, 1955, Los Angeles, CA; married Wendell Charles Farrell, May 19, 1985; children: Nia Grace, Alexander Layne. **Educ:** UCLA, Los Angeles, CA, BA, 1987; USC, Los Angeles, CA, MA, 1999. **Career:** Bullocks Dept Store, Los Angeles, CA, dept mgr, asst buyer, 1977-1979; Union Bank, Los Angeles, CA, credit mgr, 1979-81, college recruiter, ops trainee, 1981-82; Bank of America, Los Angeles, CA, asst vice pres, 1982-84, vice pres, Cash Management & Government Services, mgr, 1984-95, communications vp, 1995-96; ADP Electronic Banking, Glendale, CA, natl account mgr, 1997-. **Orgs:** Director of public relations, Los Angeles Urban Bankers, 1986-89; moderator, Morningside United Church of Christ; mem, Bank of America Speaking Club; volunteer, Big Sisters of Los Angeles. **Honors/Awds:** "100 Most Promising Black Women in Corporate America," Ebony Magazine; CINDY Award, Faces of Diversity Video, 1996; Million Dollar Sales Club, Bank of America; Certified Cash Manager Designation, National Cash Mgt Assoc; Suggestion Award, $5,000, Union Bank. **Business Addr:** National Account Manager, ADP Electronic Banking Services, 1146 N Central Ave, No 454, Glendale, CA 91202, (818)247-8330.

FARRELL, HERMAN DENNY, JR.
State official. **Personal:** Born Feb 4, 1932, New York, NY; son of Gladys & Herman Sr; married Theresa, 1958; children: Monique, Herman III. **Educ:** New York Univ, 1954-55. **Career:** Supreme Court Judge Confidential Aid, 1966-72; Mayor John Lindsay, asst dir local neighbor government, 1972-74; NYS Assembly, Ways & Means Comm, assemblyman/chair, 1974-. **Orgs:** Tioga Carver Comm Foundation, honorary mem, 1989-95. **Honors/Awds:** State Parole Officers, Distinguished Legislator Award; NY Affirmative Action Council's Award; Boricua College, Appreciation Award; Childs Memorial Church Award; NY State Court Clerks Assn Award; Amer Legion Certificate of Appreciation; Tioga Carver Comm Foundation. **Military Serv:** US Army, sergeant, 1952-54.

FARRELL, ODESSA WRIGHT
Educator. **Personal:** Born Oct 26, 1908, Kansas City, MO. **Educ:** Stowe Tchrs Coll, grad; IA U, IMA; PA; Washington; St Louis U. **Career:** Dunbar Elementary School, teacher; Vashon High School; Hadley Technical High School. **Orgs:** Dept head Sumner HS; lectr State Coll CA, Hayward; presently asst dir Audiovisual Serv Curriculum Svcs; St Louis Pub Schs Bd Educ Del & Govs Conf Educ 1966, 1968; mem Planning Com 1970; White House Conf St Louis 1972; pres Bd trustees Ferrier-Harris Home Aged; del Gen Conf AME Ch; officer mem Exec Bd Fifth Episcopal Dist Lay Orgn AME Ch; mem bd control MO Council Social Studies; sec trustee bd St James AME Ch; rep participant educ confs & meetings chmn Legislative Research Com; mem bd dir Council Press Women's Nat Orgns; mem Welfare Com MO State Tchrs Assn; mem exec bd Greater St Louis Council Social Studies; treas St Louis Div CTA MO State Tchrs Assn; sec bd dir Heritage House Redevel Corp; appointed Govs Com Children & Youth; appointed Commrs Comauthorized MO State Bd Edn; mem St LouBrs Am-Assn Univ Women; pres bd of control Aid to Victims of Crime Inc; vice pres Ret Sch Employees of St Louis; mem Hist Assn of Greater St Louis; Nat Assn Univ Women.

FARRELL, ROBERT C.
Government official. **Personal:** Born Oct 1, 1936, Natchez, MS. **Educ:** UCLA, BA 1961. **Career:** CA Eagle Newspaper, reporter; Los Angeles Sentinel Newspaper, reporter; Jet Magazine, correspondent; Star Review News in Watts, publisher. **Orgs:** Dep to city councilman Billy C Mills 1963-71; adminstrv coordinator for S Los Angeles on Mayor Bradley's & staff 1969 73; Los Angeles City Councilman 8th Dist 1974-; mem Sigma Delta Chi; Radio & TV News Assn of So CA; Pub Relations Soc of Am NAACP Legal Defense & Educ Fund; NAACP; UCLA Alumni Assn; Urban League. **Military Serv:** USN 1954-59. **Business Addr:** City Hall Rm 236, 200 N Spring St, Los Angeles, CA 90012.

FARRELL, SAMUEL D.
Business executive. **Personal:** Born Oct 7, 1941, New York, NY; children: Samuel Jr, Ronette. **Career:** DNR Assoc, chmn and CEO, currently. **Orgs:** Pres, Alumni Varsity Assoc, 1982-83; mem bd dir, CCNY Alumni Assoc Dem. **Business Addr:** Chairman & Chief Exec Officer, DNR Assoc, 3333 Broadway, D32C, New York, NY 10031.

FARRINGTON, THOMAS ALEX
Business executive. **Personal:** Born Nov 12, 1943, Chapel Hill, NC; son of Mary Farrington and O T Farrington; married Juarez Harrell; children: Christopher, Trevor, Tomeeka. **Educ:** NC A&T State Univ, BS 1966; Northeastern Univ Grad School, attended. **Career:** RCA Corp, 1966-69; IOCS Inc, president 1969-. **Orgs:** Member Council on Foreign Relations, 1989-; director, Boston Private Industry Council; director, Minority Business Enterprise Legal Defense Fund. **Honors/Awds:** Minority Contractor of the Year Dept of Transportation 1984; Natl Minority Serv Industry Firm of the Year US Dept of Commerce 1986; Top 100 Businesses, Black Enterprise; Special Achievement, Black Corporate Presidents of New England, 1988. **Business Addr:** President, Input Output Computer Service, 460 Trotten Pond Road, Waltham, MA 02154-1906.

FARRIOR, JAMES
Professional football player. **Personal:** Born Jan 6, 1975. **Educ:** Virginia. **Career:** New York Jets, 1997-. **Special Achievements:** NFL Draft, First round pick, #8, 1997. **Business Addr:** Professional Football Player, New York Jets, 1000 Fulton Ave, Hempstead, NY 11550, (516)560-8100.

FARRIS, DEBORAH ELLISON
Attorney. **Personal:** Born Dec 29, 1950, Williamsburg, VA; daughter of Ethel C Ellison and John M Ellison Jr; married J Randolph Farris, Sep 15, 1978; children: James R II. **Educ:** Delaware State College, BA, 1972; Antioch Graduate School, MAT, 1973; Howard University School of Law, JD, 1976. **Career:** Private practice, attorney, currently. **Orgs:** Jack n Jill of America, Inc, local financial secretary; National Coalition of 100 Black Women; National Carrousels, Inc, national president, 1990-92; Governor's Task Force for Tuberculosis; Dallas Youth Orchestra Board; Natl Bar Assn; Black Women Attorney's Association; Girl Friends Inc; J L Turner Legal Society; Dallas Youth Orchestra Board. **Home Addr:** 4136 High Summit Dr, Dallas, TX 75244, (214)484-2895.

FARRIS, JEROME
Judge. **Personal:** Born Mar 4, 1930, Birmingham, AL; son of Elizabeth Farris and Willie Joe Farris; widowed; children: Juli Elizabeth, Janelle Marie. **Educ:** Morehouse Coll, BS 1951; Atlanta Univ, MSW 1955; Univ of WA, JD 1958. **Career:** Weyer Roderick Schroeter & Sterne, assoc 1958-59; Weyer Schroeter Sterne & Farris, partner 1959-61; Schroeter & Farris, partner 1961-63; Schroeter Farris Bangs & Horowitz, partner 1963-65; Farris Bangs & Horowitz, partner 1965-69; WA State Court of Appeals, judge 1969-79; US Court of Appeals 9th Circuit, circuit judge 1979-. **Orgs:** WA State Jr Chamber of Commerce, president, 1965-66; Pacific NW Ballet, trustee, 1978-83; ABA Appellate Judges' Conf, chmn, 1982-83; State Fed Judicial Council of WA, chmn, 1983-87; Natl Ctr for State Courts Appellate Justice Project, adv bd, 1978-81; Univ of WA Law Sch Foundation, 1978-84; Tyee Bd of Adv, adv bd, 1984-; Univ of WA Regent 1985-; American Bar Foundation, board of directors, 1987-, executive committee, 1989-; Harvard Law School, visiting comm, 1996-; US Supreme Court, judicial fellows

comm, 1997-; Intl Judicial Relations, judicial conf comm, 1997-. **Honors/Awds:** Clayton Frost Awd Jaycees 1966; Honorary LLD Morehouse Coll 1978; Order of Coif Univ of WA Law School. **Military Serv:** US Army Signal Corps 1952-53. **Business Addr:** Circuit Judge, U S Court of Appeals 9th Cir, 1010 Fifth Ave US Courthouse, Seattle, WA 98104.

FARRIS, VERA KING
Educational administrator. **Personal:** Born Jul 18, 1940, Atlantic City, NJ; widowed; children: King. **Educ:** Tuskegee Inst, BA, biology, (magna cum l aude), 1959; Univ of MA, MS, zoology, 1962, PhD, zoology, parasitology 1965; Univ of MI, postdoctoral fellowship 1965-68. **Career:** Oak Ridge Natl Lab, rsch asst 1958-59; Univ of MA, rsch asst 1963-64; Univ of MI, rsch assoc 1965-66, instr 1967-68; SUNY Stony Brook, lecturer biol 1968-71, asst prof 1970-72, dean of spl programs 1970-72, assoc prof 1972-73, asst to vice pres acad affairs 1969-70, dir inst on innovative teaching & counseling 1968-73; SUNY Brockport, prof biol sci 1973-80, various admin positions 1973-80, chairperson dept women's studies 1975, acting dean liberal studies 1976, acting dean social programs 1977, acting vp academic affairs 1977-79, vice provost academic affairs 1979-80; Kean Coll of NJ, vice pres acad affairs 1980-83, prof biol sci 1980-83; Richard Stockton Coll of NJ, prof biol sci 1983-, pres 1983-. **Orgs:** Flagstar Companies Inc, bd of dirs, chair public affairs comm, 1993-; Natl Utility Investors Corp, 1994-; NUI Executive Compensation Committee; American Council on education, bd of dirs, 1988-91; Comittee on Excellence and Accountability of the NJ Council of Coll Pres, chair, 1995-; Middle States Assn of Colleges and Secondary Schools, bd of trustees, 1991-, immediate past pres, 1994; American Assn of State Colleges and Universities, 1984-; Commission on Recognition of Post-secondary Accreditation, 1994-; Council on Post-secondary Accreditation, immediate past pres, 1993; Natl Advisory Group for Learning Matters, 1992-; Woodson Found Bd, 1986-; NJ State Bd of Examiners, 1984-; Legal Committee, chair, 1988; Regents Commission on Higher Ed, NY State Bd of Regents, 1992-93; Commission for Advisory Council on Holocaust ED in NJ, 1982-; Natl Conference (formerly Natl Conf of Christians and Jews), South Jersey Chapter, exec committee; NJ-Israel Commission, 1989-; Governor's School of NJ, bd of overseers, 1988-; Governor's Award Academy, founding mem, 1986-; Martin Luther King Jr Commemorative Commission of NJ, 1984-. **Honors/Awds:** People of the Year Award Galloway Twp Educ Foundation 1988; Cosmos Club, Washington DC; Outstanding Comm Serv Award, Jewish War Veterans, Carr-Greenstein Post No 39, 1994; NJ Women Policymaker of the Year, Exec Women of NJ, 1994; Dr Mary McLeod Bethund Achievement Award, Natl Concil of Negro Women, 1994, Dr Ellen Carter-Watson Section, Women of Achievement Award, 1994; New Jersey's "Best" Recognition Award, New Jersey Woman Mag 15th Anniversary, 1994; Myrtle Wreath Award, Southern NJ Region of Hadassah, 1993; Recognition Award, US Holocaust Memorial Council, 1993; Recognition of Appreciation, Richard Stockton Coll of NJ Bd of Trustees, 1993; Woman of the Year Achievement Award, B'Nai B'rith Women's Reg Conf, 1993; NJ Assembly Commendation for Outstanding Achievement in Education, presented by the women of the 205th State Legislature, 1993; Myrtle Wreath Award, Camden Co NJ Chapter of Hadassah Hospital of Israel, 1992; NJ Woman of the Year Award, NJ Woman Mag, 1992; Education Award, The Washington Ctr for Internships and Academic Seminars, 1992; Cert of Appreciation Bermuda HS for Girls, 1991; Outstanding Leadership Award, Am Assn of Minority Veterans Prog Adm, 1991; Janicz Karazak Award, Natl Assn for Holocaust Ed, 1991; Father Thom Schiavo Brotherhood Award, Religious Community of Greater Atlantic City, 1990; Charles D Moody Cert of Appreciation, NJ Alliance of Black School Educators, 1990; Woman of Distinction Award, Soroptimist Intl of the Americas, 1990; numerous others. **Business Addr:** President, Stockton State College, Jimmy Leeds Rd, Pomona, NJ 08240.

FARROW, HAROLD FRANK
Dentist. **Personal:** Born May 10, 1936, Pensacola, FL; married Virginia; children: Heather, Vance. **Educ:** TN State U, BS 1959; Howard U, DDS 1970. **Career:** Dentist pvt prac 1972-; Wayne Co Hlth Dept, proj prescad 1971-72; Children's Hosp, Detroit, staff mem 1970-71. **Orgs:** Sec Wolverine Dental Soc 1974; pres Wolverine Dental Soc 1976; Wolverine Dental Soc 1977; mem ADA; MDA; DDDA; NDA; Chi Delta Mu Frat 1970; 32nd degree Mason Unity Lodge #28 1974; noble Marracci Temple #13 Mystic Shrine 1974; life mem NAACP 1976; tst New Prospect Bapt Ch 1977; pres's club Howard Univ 1977; recpt N15 Metabolism Edsel Ford Inst 1964. **Honors/Awds:** Achvmt hon award Wolverine Dental Soc 1974. **Military Serv:** AUS 1960-62. **Business Addr:** President, 334 Livernois, Ferndale, MI 48220.

FARROW, SALLIE A.
Attorney. **Personal:** Born Dec 31, 1942, Plainfield, NJ; daughter of Sallie Mitchell Rivera and James R Rivera; divorced; children: Richard H Staton Jr. **Educ:** Denver Univ, Denver CO, BA (with Honors), 1974; Univ of Nebraska, Lincoln NE, JD, 1976. **Career:** Mutual of Omaha, Omaha NE, asst gen counsel, 1977-87; New York Life Insurance Co, New York NY, assoc counsel, 1987-. **Orgs:** Mem, Kappa Delta Pi, 1973-; cousultant, ACE Counselor SBA, Omaha, 1980-85; panelist, US Office of Educ, Washington DC, 1981; chairperson, Boys Scouts of Amer, Omaha, 1982; organizer, adviser, Metro Science and Engineering Fair Inc, 1982-87; moot court judge, Creighton Univ, 1983-87; consultant, Omaha Public Schools, Career Awareness, 1983-87; dir, Girls Club of Omaha, 1985-87; editor, bar-journal, Natl Bar Assn, 1986-; comm mem, Omaha Bar Assn, 1986-87; volunteer, general council, National Counsel of Negro Women of Greater NY, 1993; mentor, Legal Outreach, 1992-. **Honors/Awds:** Natl Bar Assn Memoirs and Legal Journal, 1986, 1988; Outstanding Achievement, Girls Club of Omaha, 1987. **Business Addr:** Associate Counsel, New York Life Insurance Company, 51 Madison Ave, Room 10SB, New York, NY 10010.

FARROW, WILLIAM MCKNIGHT, III
Financial services executive. **Personal:** Born Feb 23, 1955, Chicago, IL; son of Ruth Katherine Haven Farrow and William McKnight Farrow Jr; married Sandra High Farrow, Feb 7, 1981; children: Ashley Marie, William McKnight IV, Justin Matthew. **Educ:** Augustana College, Rock Island, IL, BA, 1977; Northwestern University, Evanston, IL, master of management, 1979. **Career:** Arthur Andersen & Co., Chicago, IL, senior consultant, 1979-83; G.D. Searle & Co., Skokie, IL, manager of acquisitions, 1983-85; Dart & Kraft Inc, Northbrook, IL, director of strategy, 1985-86; First National Bank of Chicago, Chicago, IL, vice president, head of marketing, 1986-88; First Chicago Capital Markets, Chicago, IL, managing director, 1988-92; NOW, senior vp, 1992; First Chicago Corporate and Institutional Bank, head of marketing, 1992-96; First Chicago NBD Corp, senior vp, prog executive, 1996-. **Orgs:** Regional facilitator, LEAD, 1979-91; member, Chicago Bond Club, 1989-; board of directors, Community Mental Health Council, 1986-88; board of directors, Ancilla Hospital Systems Inc, 1985-89; Leadership Greater Chicago, fellow, 1994; Inroads Inc, board of directors, 1992-; Cabrini Green Tutoring, board of directors, 1995-; United Way/Crusade of Mercy, West Region, chairman for new account development, 1993-; Court Theatre, 1996-; Life Directions, Inc., 1995-. **Honors/Awds:** Best & Brightest Young Businessman, Dollars & Sense Magazine, 1988; Most Significant Marketing Achievement, G.D. Searle & Co., 1984. **Business Addr:** Senior VP/Program Executive, First Chicago NBD Corp, 1 First National Plaza, Ste 0464, Chicago, IL 60670-0453.

FARROW, WILLIE LEWIS
Military officer (retired), pilot, educator. **Personal:** Born Nov 26, 1941, Wetumpka, AL; married Oneita Boyd; children: Stephen Michael. **Educ:** Knoxville Coll, BS 1965; Central MI Univ, MA 1979. **Career:** Dover AFB, squadron training mgr 1974-75, operations exec officer 1975-76, aircraft maint officer 1976-77, pilot resource mgr 1977-79, wing flying training mgr 1979-81; Lt Col C-5 pilot/air operations staff officer; Budget/Financial Advisor, 1981-87; St Jude High School, assistant principal, currently. **Orgs:** Mem Omega Psi Phi Frat; master mason Prince Hall; mem Sigma Iota Epsilon Hon Mgmt Frat; mem Chi Gamma Iota Hon Mgmt Frat. **Honors/Awds:** Recipient Distinguished Flying Cross USAF 1967; USAF Meritorious Serv Medal; USAF Commendation Medal; USAF Air Medal; featured Ebony Magazine 1979. **Home Phone:** (334)277-1680. **Business Addr:** Assistant Principal, Saint Jude High School, 2048 W Fairview Avenue, Montgomery, AL 36108, (334)264-5376.

FATTAH, CHAKA
Government official. **Personal:** Born Nov 21, 1956, Philadelphia, PA; son of Falaka Fattah and David Fattah; married Patricia Renfroe; children: Three. **Educ:** Philadelphia Community College, 1976; Univ of PA, Wharton School, 1978, Fels Center Gvt; Harvard Univ, JFK School of Gvt. **Career:** State of Pennsylvania, state representative, dist 192, 1982-88, state senator, dist 7, 1988-94; US House of Representatives, Second Congressional District of Pennsylvania, congressman, 1994-. **Orgs:** Democratic Congressional Campaign Committee; Congressional Black Caucus. **Honors/Awds:** Ebony Magazine, One of 50 Future Leaders, 1984; Pennsylvania Public Interest Coalition, State Legislator of the Year Award; outstanding leadership in Time Magazine's roster of America's most promising leaders, 1994. **Special Achievements:** Created the Jobs Project which links employers with the unemployed; founded the Graduate Opportunities Conference which offers guidance, resources and scholarships to hundreds of Pennsylvania minority students; founded the American Cities Conference and Foundation which examines the fiscal, infrastructure and social problems of the nation's cities. **Business Addr:** Congressman, US House of Representatives, 1205 Longworth Bldg, Washington, DC 20515, (202)225-4001.

FATTAH, FALAKA
Organization executive, writer. **Personal:** Born Dec 28, 1931, Philadelphia, PA; daughter of Louise C Somers West and Percy Brown; married David Fattah, Jan 26, 1969; children: Stefan, Robin, Kenneth, Chaka, Nasser, David. **Educ:** Course Whitern New School Mse, Course Completed 1949; Fleischers Art School, Course Completed 1949; Temple Univ, English for Writers, Course Completed 1953; Junto Evening School, Course Completed, 1956. **Career:** Philadelphia Bulletin Tribune Afro-Amer Newspaper Pittsburgh Courier, journalist, 1952-68; Umoja Magazine, editor 1968-; Arthur A Little Assoc Ofc Jrvl Jstc, consultant 1982-83; Eisenhower Found, Control Data, consultant, 1982-83; House of Umoja Boystown, chief executive officer 1968-91, president, currently; self employed free lance writer, 1950-91; self employed urban consultant 1970-91. **Orgs:** Exctr comm Urban Affair Partnership, 1980-91; bd dir exec Com Eisenhower Foun 1983-; brd dir Mayonb Comm Wmn; comm Mayor's Drug Alcohol Comm 1982-83; sec, Natl Center Neighborhood Enterprise, 1982-; life mem, Historical Soc PA 1983-; vice chmn, West Philadelphia Youth Counseling Ctr 1981-91; consultant Portland House of UMOJA, 1989-91; consultant Wilmington House of UMOJA 1987-91. **Honors/Awds:** Reduction of Gang Deaths in Philadelphia via vol; coordinator of "IV Gang War in 1974 Campaign"; Presidential Recognition, Temple Award for Creative Altruism, Inst of Noetic Sciences, 1990; Secretary's Award, US Dept of Health & Human Services 1989; Grace B Flandnau Award, National Council on Crime & Delinquency, 1981. **Home Phone:** (215)473-5893. **Business Addr:** President, House of Umoja, Inc, 1410 N Frazier St, Philadelphia, PA 19131.

FAUCETT, BARBARA J.
Educational administrator. **Personal:** daugHter of Reonia Armstead Murphy and Wesley Murphy; married Michael; children: Cynthia Mock, James Mock. **Educ:** Univ Of WI Milwaukee, BS Soc Welfr 1968; Univ Of WI Milwaukee, MS Ed 1973. **Career:** Univ Of WI Milwaukee, acad adv relts 1971-72, dir fld exp hmn relts 1972-76, asst dean of ed 1976-79, depy asst chnlr 1979-80, dir human resources. **Orgs:** Phi Kappa Phi, 1985-; American Red Cross, Milwaukee, board; Natl Forum of Black Public Administrators; TEMPO, 1981-, president 1991; YWCA in Milwaukee, board. **Honors/Awds:** Academic Staff Outstanding Performance Award, Univ of WI 1989; report: Assessment of Affirmative Action in the City of Milwaukee 1988; Black Achievement Award, YMCA, 1988. **Business Addr:** Dir of Human Resources, U of WI Milwaukee, P O Box 413, Milwaukee, WI 53201.

FAULCON, CLARENCE AUGUSTUS, II
Educator. **Personal:** Born Aug 8, 1928, Philadelphia, PA; son of Addie Robinson Faulcon and Leroy C Faulcon; married Jacqueline Beach; children: David Clarence. **Educ:** Lincoln U, 1946-48; Univ PA, BMus Ed 1950; Univ PA, MMus Ed 1952; Philadelphia Conservatory of Music, MusD in Musicolgy 1962-. **Career:** Chairperson Sulzberger Jr Hi (Phila), music teacher, chairperson 1951-63; Cazenovia Coll (Cazenovia, NY), asst prof, chairperson 1963-68; Morgan State Univ (Balt), prof, chairperson 1968-79; Morgan State Univ, prof 1979-. **Orgs:** Delegate, Intl Biographical Centre Arts & Communication Congresses, 1981-. **Honors/Awds:** Morgan State Univ Promethan Soc Faculty Award, 1983; Intl Biographical Cong Medal of Cong, Budapest, Hungary, 1985; Afro Amer Music in Health Promotion Disease Prevention and Therapy, Montreal, Canada, Conf Natl Medical Assn 1984; recital accompanist & artist accompanist in various countries, 1982-88; accompanist, voice concert, and conducted plenary session interviews of eight delegates, International Biographical Centre Congress on Arts and Communications, Nairobi, Kenya, 1990; received IBC Silver Medal struck at the mint of the Queen of England. **Business Addr:** Prof of Music, Morgan State Univ, Baltimore, MD 21239.

FAULDING, CHARLES
Union official. **Personal:** Born Feb 26, 1916, Fredericksburg, VA; married Lorraine Hocker; children: George, Edward. **Educ:** Cornell Sch of Labor & Empire State Coll, 1970. **Career:** United Motormen's Div of TWU, shop steward 1948, vice chmn 1951, chmn 1965; Transport Workers Union Local 100; vice pres & Intl vice pres 1969, full time organizer, recording sec 1974, sec treas 1979. **Orgs:** Pres BMT Surface Operators Club Inc; regl vice pres Union Label & Serv Trade Dept State of NY; pres emeritus Black Trade Unionists Ldrshp Com of New York City Labor Council; adv council Empire State Coll; bd mem NY Urban League; bd mem New York City Central Labor Rehab Council; bd mem Health Care Inst Inc Occupational Safety & Health Office. **Honors/Awds:** A Philip Randolph Institute & Black Trade Unionists Leadership Comm; Guy R Brewer United Democratic Club, Inc NY City Central Labor Council, AFL-CIO; Arthritis Foundation.

FAULDING, JULIETTE J.
Financial advisor. **Personal:** Born Aug 2, 1952, Jackson, MS; daughter of Vannette Johnson and Luella B Tapo. **Educ:** Tougaloo Coll, BA 1974; Columbia Univ, MBA 1976. **Career:** Mobil Oil Corp, banking analyst 1976-77, financial analyst 1977-79, short term investor 1979-81, sr financial analyst 1981-88, financial advisor 1989-. **Orgs:** Comm mem Boy Scout Troop 75 1982-87; assoc advisor Explorer Post 75 Queens NY 1982-87; participant Black Exec Exchange Prog; Black MBA Assn. **Honors/Awds:** Distinguished Grad Awd NAFEO 1984. **Home Addr:** 6168 Hidden Canyon Rd, Centreville, VA 22020. **Business Addr:** Financial Advisor, Mobil Oil Corporation, 3225 Gallows Rd, Fairfax, VA 22037.

FAULK, ESTELLE A.
Educator. **Personal:** Born in Chicago, IL; divorced; children: Lalita, Gina. **Educ:** Chicago State Univ, BE; DePaul Univ, MA; Univ of IL Chicago, PhD; DePaul Univ, Roosevelt Univ & Chicago State Univ, addl study. **Career:** Malcolm X Coll, instructor part-time; Gladstone School, principal. **Orgs:** Mem Samuel B Stratton Assn; Chicago Prin Assn; Natl Assn of Elem Sch Prin; Natl Assn of Supervision & Curriculum Develop; Natl Alliance of Black Sch Educators; Phi Delta Kappa; Amer Assn of Sch Admins; Near West Side Council Chicago; imm past pres Chicago Area Alliance Black Sch Educators; pres DePaul Univ Education Alumni Bd. **Honors/Awds:** Commendation Awd Univ of IL Coll of Educ 1984; Outstanding Leadership Chicago Area Alliance of Black Sch Educators 1983. **Business Addr:** Principal, Gladstone Sch, 1231 S Damen Ave, Chicago, IL 60608.

FAULK, MARSHALL WILLIAM
Professional football player. **Personal:** Born Feb 26, 1973, New Orleans, LA. **Educ:** San Diego State. **Career:** Indianapolis Colts, running back, 1994-. **Honors/Awds:** NFL Offensive Rookie of the Year, 1994; Pro Bowl, 1994, 1995. **Business Addr:** Professional Football Player, Indianapolis Colts, PO Box 535000, Indianapolis, IN 46253, (317)297-2658.

FAULKNER, CAROLYN D. (CAROLYN D. DIXON)
Wedding, travel and cruise consultant. **Personal:** Born Aug 30, 1938, Mullins, SC; daughter of Rembert Gerald & Ollie Mae Smith; married Melvin Faulkner, Sep 15, 1962; children: Lenora, Leonard, Tasheba. **Career:** Shirlon Industries, bookkeeper, 1958-63; J H Taylor Mgmt, bookkeeper, 1964-75; Oak Hill Industries, bookkeeper, 1976-80; Harry Zelenko, bookkeeper, 1981-91; Wedding Plan Plus, pres, consultant, 1966-. **Orgs:** H & R Block, 1984-86; Brooklyn Chamber of Commerce, 1990-93; Assn of Bridal Consultants, 1989-; Block Assn, pres, 1987-. **Honors/Awds:** Brooklyn Borough Pres, Proclamation, 1984; State Assemblyman, Edward Griffith, Award, 1985; Assn of Bridal Consultants, Certificate of Achievement, 1990-91. **Special Achievements:** Congressman Ed Towns, profiency, 1990' Brides Magazine, Performance, 1993; Cruise Line Intl Assn, accredited cruise counselor, 1990; Sobelsohn School of Travel, certified travel agent, 1985. **Business Addr:** President, Wedding Plan Plus Inc, 935 Schenck Ave, Brooklyn, NY 11207, (718)272-3705.

FAULKNER, GEANIE (JEANNE)
Performer, professional singer, producer. **Personal:** Born in Washington, DC; daughter of Mildred James Faulkner and Ernest Faulkner; children: David Michel Dabney. **Educ:** Catholic Univ, BM 1963, MM 1964. **Career:** New Jersey Symphony, soloist 1971; New York City Opera/Opera Theatre, soloist 1972-78; Alvin Ailey Dance Theatre, soloist 1973; Brooklyn Philharmonia Orchestra, soloist 1976, 1979-82; New York Jazz Rep Orchestra, soloist 1976, 1979, 1982; Harlem Opera Soc, principal soloist 1969-; NY City Rep Opera Theatre, soloist 1986; New York Foundation for the Arts, artist-in-residence; Harlem Cultural Council, pres; producer, Amer Black Festival, Palermo Italy, 1985-; Harlem Week in Madrid Spain, 1989; NY Bd of Education, dir of special events & projects, currently; NY premiere, Gian-Carlo Menotti "Remembrances," soloist, 1990; Harlem Festival Orchestra, soloist, 1993; Concerto di Natale, Assisi, Italy, televised Eurovision, soloist, 1996. **Orgs:** Vice pres 1984-85, mem/trustee 1971-pres Schomburg Corp; producer/dir Dancemobile Project 1971-; mem Whitney Museum 1977-84 (1st black mem); pres Harlem Performance Ctr 1978-; mem Bellevue Hospital Art Advisory Bd 1978-84; music consultant Arts/Humanities Project Teacher Corps Hunter Coll 1979-81; mem vice pres Fine Arts Federation; cultural consultant NY State Council on the Arts 1985-, New York City Dept of Cultural Affairs 1985, 1987. **Honors/Awds:** Critical Reviews, New York Times, New York Post, Village Voice, Chicago Daily News, Boston Globe, Houston Post, San Francisco Chronical, Amsterdam News, Am News, High Fidelity/Musica America, Music Journal, Newsweek, Opera News, Porter Andrew "Music of Three Seasons". **Home Addr:** 317 W 98th St, Apt 6BR, New York, NY 10025. **Business Addr:** Dir, Special Events & Projects, NYC Bd of Educ, 110 Livingston St, Rm 406, Brooklyn, NY 11201.

FAUNTROY, WALTER E.
Consulting firm executive. **Personal:** Born Feb 6, 1933, Washington, DC; son of Ethel Vine Fauntroy and William T Fauntroy; married Dorothy Simms, Aug 3, 1957; children: Marvin Keith. **Educ:** VA Union Univ, BA cum laude 1955; Yale Univ Divinity Schl, BD 1958. **Career:** New Bethel Bapt Church, pastor 1959; Wash Bureau of Southern Christian Ldrshp Conf, dir coord of Selma to Montgomery March 1965; DC City Council, 1st appointed vice chrmn 1967-69; Poor People's Campaign, natl dir 1969; House of Representatives, DC delegate 1971-90; pres Walter E Fauntroy & Associates, currently. **Orgs:** Pres Natl Black Ldrshp Roundtable; chrmn bd dir Southern Christian Ldrshp Conf; vice pres Govt Affairs MLK Jr Cntr for Soc Change; natl dir 20th Aniv March on Wash for Jobs Peace & Freedom 1983; former dir founder Model Inner City Community Org Inc Washington; chm Congressional Black Caucus 1981-83; chm DC Coalition of Conscience 1965; co-chm Free South Africa Movement. **Honors/Awds:** Hubert H Humphrey Humanitarian Award Natl Urban Coalition 1984; hnry degrees, Georgetown Univ Law Schl, Yale Univ, VA Union Univ. **Business Addr:** Pres, Walter E Fauntroy & Associates, 1025 Connecticut Ave NW, Washington, DC 20036.

FAUST, NAOMI FLOWE
Educator, author, poet. **Personal:** Born in Salisbury, NC; daughter of Ada Luella Graham Flowe and Christopher Leroy Flowe; married Roy Malcolm Faust. **Educ:** Bennett Coll, AB; Univ of MI-Ann Arbor, MA; New York Univ, PhD. **Career:** Public School System Gaffney SC, elem teacher; Atkins High School Winston-Salem NC, English teacher; Bennett Coll & Southern Univ Scotlandville LA, instr of English; Morgan State Univ Baltimore MD, prof of English; Greensboro Public Schools & New York City Public Schools, teacher; Queens Coll of CUNY, prof of English/Educ. **Orgs:** Mem Amer Assoc of Univ Profs, Natl Council of Teachers of English, Natl Women's Book Assoc, World Poetry Soc Intercontinental, NY Poetry Forum, NAACP. **Honors/Awds:** Publications "Speaking in Verse," a book of poems 1974; "Discipline and the Classroom Teacher," 1977; "All Beautiful Things," poems 1983; also contributes poetry to magazines and newspapers and gives poetry readings; named Teacher-Author by Teacher-Writer 1979; Certificate of Merit Cooper Hill Writers Conf; Certificate of Merit Poems by Blacks; Honored by Long Island Natl Assoc of Univ Women for High Achievement; poetry book "And I Travel by Rhythms and Words," 1990; International Poets Academy, International Eminent Poet. **Home Addr:** 112-01 175th St, Jamaica, NY 11433.

FAVORS, ANITA
City official. **Personal:** Born Feb 8, 1951, Kansas City, KS; daughter of Abraham and Barbara Franklin; married Wayman Walter Favors, Sep 6, 1970; children: Jocelyn, Wayman Jr, Ahmad Khalil. **Educ:** Park Coll, Parkville, MO, BA, 1977; Central MI Univ, MA, public admin, 1981. **Career:** Area Agency on Aging, Kansas City, KS, 1973-82; City of Kansas City, asst city administrator, 1982-83; KS State Dept of Social and Rehab Services, Adult Services, commissioner, begin 1983; City of Tallahassee, dep city mgr, 1990-95, sr asst city mgr, 1995-97, city mgr, 1997-. **Honors/Awds:** Park Coll, Presidential Scholar, 1977; YWCA, Yates Branch, Black Woman of Distinction, 1982; Panhellenic Council, Kansas City, In Service to Kansas City Award, 1983. **Special Achievements:** First African American and first woman to become city manager in Tallahassee, FL. **Business Addr:** City Manager, City of Tallahassee, City Hall, 300 S Adams St, Tallahassee, FL 32301, (850)891-8200.

FAW, BARBARA ANN
Educational administrator. **Personal:** Born Jul 27, 1936, Cullen, VA; daughter of Edna Wilkes Lindsey and Bernard Lindsey; married Joseph A. **Educ:** Morgan State Univ Baltimore, BA 1965; Howard Univ Wash DC, MA 1966. **Career:** Community Coll of Baltimore, vice pres of admin 1988-90, dean of coll 1977-, dean of student activities 1973-77, admin asst to pres 1971-73, chmn dept of business administration 1970-71, prof business administration 1965-71; coordinator & sponsor small business inst 1967-70, chairwoman Conf "Know your Rights" 1973. **Orgs:** Mem Natl Econs Assoc, Sales & Marketing Assn, Amer Assn of Univ Prof, W Arlington Community Org, Mayor's Vol Cadre on Educ, Task Force for Role Scope & Commitment; co-author Study of Unemployment & the Inner City Baltimore Dept of C of C Wash DC 1967-68; mem Natl Council on Black Amer Affairs of the Amer Assoc of Community & Jr Colls 1985-; presidential search comm Comm Coll of Baltimore 1985-86; panelist Conf on Women's Career Paths Univ of Baltimore 1986; bd of review comm Middle States 1987-. **Honors/Awds:** Outstanding Educator of Am 1975; Senate of MD Resolution As First Chancellor of Community College of Baltimore 1986; The City Council of Baltimore Resolution As the Chancellor of Community Coll of Baltimore 1986. **Business Addr:** Dean, Community College of Baltimore, 2901 Liberty Heights Ave, Baltimore, MD 21215.

FAX, ELTON C.
Artist, author, lecturer. **Personal:** Born Oct 9, 1909, Baltimore, MD; son of Willie Estelle and Mark Estelle; widowed; children: 2. **Educ:** Syarcuse Univ, BFA 1931; Rockefeller Found Study & Research Center Bellagio, Italy, scholar-in-residence 1976. **Career:** Claflin Coll, teacher 1935-36; A&T Coll, teacher 1935-36; New York City Harlem Art Center, 1936-40; free lance since 1940; illustrated children's books 1943-. **Orgs:** PEN Am Center; Author's Guild of Amer; partic in Intl Writers' Conf on World Peace Sofia, Bulgaria Bharati Cent Celebration, India 1982. **Honors/Awds:** Recip Coretta Scott King Award 1970; Louis E Seley MACAL Award for best oil painting 1971; author pub & distrib of portfolio of 10 prints from original Fax-Drawings 1969; honored by Arena Players 1972; Key Women of Amer 1974; author of "HASHAR" impressions of life in Soviet Central Asia Progress Publ Moscow USSR1980; author of "ELYUCHIN" impressions of Soviet Transcaucasia Moscow USSR 1984 Progress Publ; writer in residence Langston Hughes Library Queens NY 1987 grant from NY State Council on the Arts; "Soviet People as I Knew Them" (illust by author) Progress Publ Moscow 1988; Syracuse Univ, Chancellor's Medal, 1990. **Business Addr:** Box 2188, Astoria Station, Long Island City, NY 11102.

FAY, TONI G.
Media & entertainment executive. **Personal:** Born Apr 25, 1947, New York, NY; daughter of Allie Smith Fay and George Fay. **Educ:** Duquesne Univ, BA 1968; Univ of Pittsburgh, MSW 1972, MEd 1973. **Career:** New York City Dept of Social Svcs, caseworker 1968-70; Dir Planning & Devel, Natl Cncl of Negro Women 1977-81; Exec VP, D Parke Gibson Assoc 1981-82, dir, Pittsburgh Drug Abuse Ctr Inc 1972-74; commissioner, Governors Cncl on Drug & Alcohol Abuse 1974-77; director Corp Community Relations, Time Warner, 1981-92, vp & officer, 1992-. **Orgs:** US Committee for UNICEF; Congressional Black Caucus Foundation; Franklin & Eleanor Roosevelt Inst; NY Coalition 100 Black Women; Exec Leadership Council Foundation; Natl Council of Negro Women, vp; LINKS, Inc Alpha Kappa Alpha Sorority. **Honors/Awds:** Dollars & Sense-100 Black Women in Business 1986; YWCA of America Twin Award, 1987; NAACP Corporate Award, 1989; New York Women's Foundation Award, 1991; NY Women's Award, 1996; Congressional Black Caucus Foundation Presidents Award, 1996. **Business Addr:** VP, Community Relations, Time-Warner Inc, 75 Rockefeller Plaza, New York, NY 10019.

FEARING, JOHN T.
Business executive (retired). **Personal:** Born Oct 21, 1916, New York; son of Ada and John; married Clara Neblett; children: Susan, Marilyn. **Educ:** Coll of the City of NY, 1939-40; Univ of Bridgeport, 1968-69. **Career:** Exmet Corp, admin research & devel 1949-; Edison Tech, Mt Vernon, 1950-53; New York City Transit System, post office clerk, motorman 1940; FO Reconcilliation MRA & Harlem Chris Youth Council, 1930. **Orgs:** Active NAACP; CORE Cath Inter-racial Council; chmn bd Norwalk Museum Zoo 1973-; chmn Proj Intergroup 1974-; bd Norwalk Drug Abuse Commn 1970. **Honors/Awds:** Recipient Honor Man Great Lakes Naval Training Center 1941. **Military Serv:** USN seaman 1/c 1946. **Home Addr:** 115 William St, Norwalk, CT 06851.

FEARN, JAMES E., JR.
Attorney. **Personal:** Born Feb 2, 1945, Chattanooga, TN; son of Kayte Marsh Fearn and James E Fearn; married Karen Edmunds, Jul 29, 1968; children: Jeremy Kahlil, Jonathan Kyle. **Educ:** Antioch College, BA, 1968; University of Chicago Law School, JD, 1971. **Career:** Seattle Legal Services, staff attorney, 1971-76; Department of Housing and Urban Development, associate regional counsel, 1976-78; Seattle City Attorney's Office, assistant city attorney, 1978-85, Land Use Division, director, 1985-89; Tousley Brain, Land Use Section, head, 1989-93; Seattle Commons, special counsel, 1993-94; Institute for Local Government and Public Service, 1994-. **Orgs:** Washington State Bar Association, 1972-; Washington Association of Municipal Attorney's, 1978-90; Washington State Bar Association, trustee, land use and environmental law section, 1985-88; Evergreen Legal Services, board of directors, 1981-88; Legal Foundation of Washington, board of trustees, 1989-93. **Honors/Awds:** Reginald Heber Smith Fellow, 1971; Law Students Civil Rights Research Council, Fellowship, 1969; Antioch College, Faculty Nomination, Woodrow Wilson Fellowship, 1968. **Special Achievements:** "Preserving Seattle's Rental Housing," Greater Northwest Law Use Review, 1985; "Trusters of Development Rights," Washington Association of Municipal Attorney's Legal Notes, 1979; Tenants Rights: A Guide for Washington State, 1976, 3rd edition, 1991. **Business Addr:** Deputy Director, Institute for Local Govt and Public Service, Huvosvoigyi Ut 54, H-1021, Budapest, Hungary.

FEARN-BANKS, KATHLEEN
Publicist, educator. **Personal:** Born Nov 21, 1941, Chattanooga, TN; daughter of Dr Kayle M Fearn and Dr James E Fearn; divorced. **Educ:** Wayne State Univ, BA, Journalism, 1964; UCLA, MS, Journalism, 1965; University of Southern California, Los Angeles, CA, ABD for PhD, 1978-81. **Career:** NBC Publicity Dept, mgr, media relations, 1969-90; KNXT-TV News LA, newswriter, producer, 1968-69; Los Angeles Ctn Coll, instructor, Journalism, English, Creative Writing, 1965-; Los Angeles Times, Feature Writer, 1968; University of Washington, Seattle, WA, asst professor, 1990-; freelance motion picture publicist, currently. **Orgs:** Member, Public Relations Society of America 1989-; mem, Writers Guild Amer; mem, Publicists Guild; member, Acad of TV & Sciences; bd of dir, vice pres, Neighbors of Watts; mem, Delta Sigma Theta Sorority, chapter vp; member, Association for Education in Journalism & Mass Comm, 1990-. **Honors/Awds:** CA Sun Magazine writers Award, UCLA 1965; Will Rogers Fellowship, UCLA, 1964-65; Numerous freelance magazine & journal articles; 3 Textbooks, The Story of Western Man, co-authored w/David Burleigh; Woman of the Year, Los Angeles Sentinel (newspaper) 1986; Author: Crisis Communications; A Case Book Approach; Teacher of the Year, School of Communications, University of Washington, 1993, 1995. **Business Addr:** Associate Professor, School of Communications, University of Washington, DS-40, Seattle, WA 98101.

FEARS, EMERY LEWIS, JR.
Educator (retired). **Personal:** Born Jul 23, 1925, Tuskegee Institute, AL; son of Evadne Angers Fears and Emery Fears; married Jeanette Johnson Fears, Aug 11, 1951 (died 1979); children: Cheryl; married Cheryl Perry Fears, Jul 31, 1981;

children: Jason, Ashlyn. **Educ:** Howard Univ, BMusED, 1951; Old Dominion Univ, 1974; Univ of MI at Ann Arbor, MMUS, 1962. **Career:** J S Clarke High School, New Orleans, LA, band director, 1951-52; I C Norcom High School, Portsmouth, VA, band director, 1952-72; Manor High School, Portsmouth, VA, band dir and curriculum specialist, 1972-74; Norfolk State Univ, Music Department, associate professor of music, dir of bands, 1974-91, prof emeritus of music, 1992-. **Orgs:** Charter member, 1960-, bd of dirs, 1978-82, 1984-86, National Band Assn; life member, 1985-; president, southern div, 1980-82, College Band Directors National Assn; Phi Beta Mus Nat Schl Bandmaster Frat, 1985-; American Bandmasters Assn, 1981-. **Honors/Awds:** Citation of Excellence, National Bank Association, 1970; Proclamation, City of Portsmouth, VA, 1987, 1991; Roy A Woods Outstand Teacher Award, Norfolk State University, 1989; Great Citizen of Hampton Roads, Cox Cable TV, 1990; Proclamation, City of Portsmouth, VA, 1987, 1991; Proclamation, City of Chesapeake, VA, 1991; Certificate of Recognition, Commonwealth of VA, 1991; Distinguished Service to Music Medal, Kappa Kappa Psi Band Fraternity. **Military Serv:** US Navy, musician, 2nd class, 1944-46. **Home Addr:** 2605 Cecilia Terrace, Chesapeake, VA 23323.

FEASTER, BRUCE SULLIVAN
Law education director, attorney. **Personal:** Born Jul 13, 1961, Flint, MI; son of John Alfred & Lillian Battle Feaster; married Deborah Mallory Feaster, Aug 21, 1993. **Educ:** MI State Univ, BA, 1983; Univ of TX Law School, JD, 1986. **Career:** WCNLS Children's Ctr for Justice and Peace, dir, currently. **Orgs:** Alpha Phi Alpha; Metro Detroit Optimist. **Honors/Awds:** National Mens Scholar. **Business Addr:** Director, WCNLS Children's Center for Justice & Peace, 3400 Cadillac Towers, Detroit, MI 48226, (313)962-0466.

FEASTER, LAVERNE WILLIAMS
Educator (retired). **Personal:** Born Oct 14, 1926, Cotton Plant, AR; daughter of Alma Dorthea Chism Williams and James Waldred Williams Sr; married William Douglas Feaster, Jun 9, 1953; children: Sammie Lee Hart. **Educ:** Swift Memorial Jr. College, Rogersville, TN, diploma, 1947; Tennessee State University, Nashville, TN, BSE, 1949; University of Arkansas, Fayetteville, AR, MEd, 1966. **Career:** Swift Jr. College, Rogersville, TN, home econ teacher, 1949-50; Carver High School, Augusta, AR, home econ teacher, 1950-53; University of Arkansas Extension, Arkadelphia, AR, county extension agent, home econ., 1961-71; University of Arkansas Extension, Little Rock, AR, state 4-H specialist, 1971-77, district program leader, 1977-86, state leader, 4-H, 1986-90 (retired). **Orgs:** President, Epsilon Sigma Phi, 1979-80; member, Arkansas Home Economists Assn. 1950-; member, Ark Assn. Extension 4-H Agents, 1975-; member, Extension Committee on Organizational Policy, 1975-79; member, Commission on Arkansas' Future, 1989-; member, Gamma Sigma Delta, 1988. **Honors/Awds:** Distinguished Service, Ark Assn. Extension 4-H Agents, 1976; Distinguised Service, Epsilon Sigma Phi, 1983; 25-Year Award, Ark Assn. Extension 4-H Agents, 1987; State Service Award, Arkansas Home Econ Assn., 1984; Delta of the Year, Delta Sigma Theta, 1990; First Black Female State 4-H leader, Arkansas; National Association Extension 4-H Agents, American Spirit Award, 1992; University of Arkansas, Emeritus Professor Status, 1991; AR Writer's Project, named as one of the top 100 Women in AR, 1995; Top 100 Women in Arkansas, 1995. **Home Addr:** One Fay Court, Little Rock, AR 72204.

FEATHERSTONE, KARL RAMON
Law enforcement official. **Personal:** Born Oct 13, 1964, Indianaola, MS; son of Charles Edward & Jessie Mae Featherstone. **Educ:** Texas Southern University, BS computer science, 1985. **Career:** United States Marine Corps, special forces; St Clair Shores Police Dept, police officer, currently; Lakeview High School, varsity football asst coach, 1997-. **Orgs:** Alpha Phi Alpha Fraternity, Inc, mem. **Military Serv:** USMC, sgt, 1985-1995; Navy Achievement Medal, 1987; Arm Forces Expeditionary Medal, 1986; Marine Expeditionary Force Medal, 1986. **Business Addr:** Police Officer, St Clair Shores Police Dept, 27665 Jefferson, St Clair Shores, MI 48081, (810)445-5300.

FEDDOES, SADIE C.
Bank executive (retired). **Personal:** Born in St Vincent, West Indies. **Educ:** Pace Univ NY, BA, business. **Career:** Citibank, vice pres, community and govt relations officer, beginning 1955; New York Amsterdam News, columnist, 1972-. **Orgs:** Chairperson of the bd, Billie Holiday Theater of Bedford Stuyvesant Restoration Corp; chairperson: Bedford Stuyvesant Restoration Corp; Brooklyn Economic Devel Corp; Kings County Overall Econ Devel Program Comm; Overall Economic Devel Program for Brooklyn; Coalition of 100 Black Women; Natl Women in Communications; New York Women in Communications; Caribbean Cable TV Co; New York Regional Panel of President Reagan's Commn on White House Fellowships, 1984-85. **Honors/Awds:** Outstanding Performance Award, First Natl City Bank, 1970; Community Serv Award, Brooklyn Club of Natl Assn of Negro Business & Professional Womens Clubs; Journal Award, Brooklyn Chapter Natl Assn of Key Women; The Intl Womens Year Award, Natl Council of Negro Women, Anemia, Journalism Award from Bethany United Meth Church 1973; Journal Award, Empire State Fed of Womens Clubs; Distinguished Citizen Award, Boy Scouts of Amer; Woman of the Year, Bd of Mgr Brooklyn Home for Aged People, 1982; Woman of the Year, Brooklyn Branch NAACP, 1984; recognized as one of 60 outstanding mem, New York Women in Communications, 1984; citation, 25 years with Citibank, presented by borough pres Howard Golden on behalf of the people of Brooklyn; 30 years with Citibank,entered in Congressional record by Conssman Edolphus Towns; awards, Salvation Army, Amer Red Cross, New York State Black and Puerto Rican Legislative Caucus, Natl Urban League, Lions Intl, Natl Conf of Christians and Jews, Coalition of 100 Black Women, Navy Yard Boys and Girls Club, Church Women United of Brooklyn; Congressional Black Caucus of the 102nd Congress, Chairman's Award for Distinguished Service. **Special Achievements:** Television apperances: "Today show," NBC-TV; "Black Pride," WPIX-TV; "Face the Women," cable televison show, alternate guest panelist; West Indian-American Labor Day Parade, grand marshal.

FEELINGS, THOMAS
Artist, educator. **Personal:** Born May 19, 1933, Brooklyn, NY; son of Anna Nash Morris and Samuel Fellings; married Muriel Grey (divorced); children: Zamani, Kamili. **Educ:** George Westinghouse Voc Schl, High Schl Dimp 1948-51; Cartoonist & Illist Sch, 1951-53; Schl Visval Arts, 1958-61. **Career:** Ghana Govt Publshg Hse Ministy of Ed, tchr consult 1964-66; Guyana (SA) Minstry of Ed, tchr consult 1971-74; Self Empld, Freelance Illust; University of South Carolina, associate professor of art, 1989-. **Orgs:** Commissioner, Schomburg Center for Research, Harlem, NY, 1986-. **Honors/Awds:** 2 Caldecott Hnr Bk Moja Means One - Jambo Means Hello 1972-74; otsdg alum awd Sch Vsl Arts 1974; Boston Globe Horn Bk awd Jambo Means Hello 1973; Am Bk awd nomtn Jambo Means Hello 1981; Coretta Scott King awd Something On My Mind, NEA Visl Arts Flwshp Grant 1982; The University of South Carolina Black Faculty Association Award for Distinguished Service to Children through Art, 1991; Multicultural Publisheres Exchange, 1991 Book Award of Excellence in the Children's Book Art Category, First Place Award in Literacy for "Tommy Traveler in the World of Black History;" Soul Looks Back in Wonder, Coretta Scott King Award, 1994. **Special Achievements:** Author: Tommy Traveler in the World of Black History; Soul Looks Back in Wonder, Dial Books, 1994. **Military Serv:** USAF airmen 1st class 1953-57; Good Conduct Mdl 1953-57. **Home Addr:** 180 Wateree Ave, Columbia, SC 29205-3041.

FEEMSTER, JOHN ARTHUR
Physician. **Personal:** Born Sep 9, 1939, Winston-Salem, NC. **Educ:** Knox Coll, BS 1959; Meharry Med Coll, MD; Am Coll Surgeons, physician self flw 1977; Am Coll Angiology; Thorocic-Cardiovascular Surgery, bd cert 1975 wayne state u, resd 1974-75; bd cert gen surgery 1971; u mN, gen surg resd 1970. **Career:** Kirwood Gen Hosp, chf dept surg. **Orgs:** Mem Nat Med Soc; Am Coll Emergency Physicians; v pres Detroit Med Soc; mem Detroit Surg Soc; Detroit Surg Assn; mem Omega Psi Phi Frat; Alpha Omega Alpha Hon Med Soc; NAACP; Founders Soc Detroit Ints Arts. **Honors/Awds:** Founders Soc Detroit Symphony Orch Young Investigator's Award, Am Coll Cardiology 1969; Flwsp, Oak Ridge Inst Nuclear Studies. **Military Serv:** AUS mc col 1970-72. **Business Addr:** Detroit Medical Society, 580 Frederick Douglass Ave, Detroit, MI 48202-4119.

FELDER, CAIN HOPE
Educator, cleric. **Personal:** Born Jun 9, 1943, Aiken, SC; son of Lula Mae Landy Felder (deceased) and James Felder (deceased); married Annette Hutchins, Nov 15, 1973 (divorced 1982); children: Akidah H. **Educ:** Howard University, Washington, DC, BA, 1966; Oxford University, Oxford, England, dip theol, 1968; Union Theological Seminary, New York, NY, MDiv, 1969; Columbia University, New York, NY, MPhil, 1978, PhD, 1982. **Career:** Black Methodists for Church Renewal, Atlanta, GA, national executive director, 1969-72; Morgan State University, Baltimore, MD, director of federal relations/associate professor of philosophy, 1972-74; Grace United Methodist Church, New York, NY, pastor, 1975-78; Princeton Theological Seminary, Princeton, NJ, instructor, 1978-81; Howard University School of Divinity, professor, 1981-. **Orgs:** Member, Society of Biblical Literature; member, Society for the Study of Black Religion; member, American Academy of Religion; member, Middle East Studies Association; member, board of directors, 1978-, executive committee, 1984-86, chair, 1985, 1986, National Convocation Planning Committee, Black Theology Project; board member, Interreligious Foundation for Community Organization, 1970-72; founder, Enterprises Now, Inc; founder, Narco House (drug rehabilitation center), Atlanta, GA; member, 1987-89, alternate member, 1985-87, Council of University Senate, Howard University; chair, Theology Search Committee, Howard University School of Divinity, 1987; founder, chair, the Biblical Institute for Social Change, Washington, DC. **Honors/Awds:** Fellowships awarded by the National Fellowship Fund, The Crusade Fellowship, Union Theological Seminary Graduate Fellowship and Minority Fund, The Rockefeller Brothers Fund-Protestant and Doctoral Fellowships, Columbia University Faculty Fellowship; has received numerous scholarships; Outstanding Leadership Citation, Black Methodists for Church Renewal, The Black Caucus of the Methodist Church, 1973; Martin Luther King, Jr., Scholar-Service Award, Providence and Vicinity Council of Churches; Progressive Natl Baptist Convention, Martin Luther King Jr Freedom Award; AME, 2nd Episcopal Dist, Excellence in Scholarship Award, 1995; editor and author, Stony the Road We Trod: African American Biblical Interpretation, Fortress Press, 1990; author, Troubling Biblical Waters: Race, Class, and Family, Orbis Books, 1989; author, "Cost of Freedom in Urban Black Churches," Vision of Hope, 1989; author, "The Bible and Re-contextualization," African-AmericanReligious Studies: Anthology, 1989; author, "The Holy Spirit in Jesus' Formative Years," Pacific Theological Review, 1988; author, The Season of Lent, 1993; general editor, The Original African Heritage Study Bible, Winston Derek Publishing Co, 1993; editor, Journal of Religious Thought; author of numerous other articles and book reviews; public speaker at institutions of higher learning. **Business Addr:** Professor of Biblical Studies, School of Divinity, Howard University, 1400 Shepherd St, NE, Washington, DC 20017.

FELDER, HARVEY
Symphony conductor. **Personal:** Born Nov 2, 1955, Milwaukee, WI; son of Emma Bell Felder and Harvey Felder Jr. **Educ:** University of Wisconsin, Madison, WI, BS, 1977; University of Michigan, Ann Arbor, MI, MA, 1982. **Career:** Eastern Michigan University, Ypsilanti, MI, visiting lecturer, 1983-84; Haverford College, Haverford, PA, college lecturer, 1984-88; Johns Hopkins University, Baltimore, MD, university symphony conductor, 1987-90; Milwaukee Symphony Orchestra, Milwaukee, WI, assistant conductor, 1988-. **Business Addr:** Assistant Conductor, Milwaukee Symphony Orchestra, 212 W Wisconsin Ave, Milwaukee, WI 53203-2307.

FELDER, LORETTA KAY
Dentist. **Personal:** Born Apr 19, 1956, Sumter, SC; daughter of Lorraine Perry Felder and Daniel DeLeon Felder Sr. **Educ:** Old Dominion Univ, BS 1978; Howard Univ, DDS 1982. **Career:** US Public Health Svcs, lt 1982-85; Ruskin Migrant Health Care Inc Hillsborough Co FL, dentist 1982-84; Midlands Primary Health Care Inc, dental dir 1984-87; private practice 1988-; Carolina Tribune Newspaper, "Minority Health", associate publisher, 1992-. **Orgs:** Consultant/mem SC Richland Co Governors Primary Health Task Force 1984; mem Natl Dental Assn, 1985-87; bd of dirs YWCA of Sumter Area 1986-88; mem Natl Council of Negro Women, NAACP; bd of dirs Big Brothers/Big Sisters Inc of Greater Columbia; mem SC Dental Assoc, American Dental Assoc; bd of dirs SC Women's Consortium, 1996. **Honors/Awds:** Columbia NCNW, Living the Legacy Award, 1993. **Home Addr:** 6110 Hampton Leas Lane, Columbia, SC 29209. **Business Addr:** Dentist, 2329 Devine St, PO Box 50664, Columbia, SC 29205, (803)252-8101.

FELDER, THOMAS E.
Chief executive. **Career:** Victory Savings Bank, Columbia, SC, chief exec. **Business Addr:** Victory Savings Bank, 1545 Sumter St, Columbia, SC 29201.

FELDER, TYREE PRESTON, II
Educational administrator. **Personal:** Born Oct 6, 1927, Mound Bayou, MS; son of B Ottowiess Felder; married Muriel Diggs; children: Gladys Washington, Frankie O, Deborah Schorlemmer, Marva Carter, Muriel T Rogers. **Educ:** Tuskegee Univ, BS ComInd 1948; VA Cmmnwlth Univ, MS Bus 1970. **Career:** Univ S Army, quartermaster 1948-68; VA Cmmnwlth Univ, EEO manager 1970-. **Honors/Awds:** Board mem VA Div Amer Cancer Soc 1982-, Richmond Div 1981-; board mem Adult Dev Cntr for Handicapped 1972-; Citizen of the Year Omega Psi Phi (Phi Phi Chapt) 1981; Public Educ Awd VA Div ASC 1983; Outstanding Serv (treasurer) Amer Assoc for Affirm Action 1976-78; Presidents' Promotional Service Awd AAAA 1980. **Military Serv:** AUS quartermaster 1st Lt 1948-68; Bronze Star 1968.

FELDER-HOEHNE, FELICIA HARRIS
Educator, librarian. **Personal:** Born in Knoxville, TN; daughter of Geraldine Celestine Harris and Boyd S. Ivey (deceased); married Paul Arthur Hoehne, Jan 2, 1979. **Educ:** Knoxville Coll, BS, Atlanta Univ, MSLS 1966; Univ of TN, 1974-78. **Career:** SCLS, sec 1958; McMinn County Schools (TN), English teacher; Knoxville College, asst in admin offices, 1960-63, asst to dir of public relations 1963-65; Atlanta Univ, Trevor Arnett Library, graduate library asst, 1965-66; Knoxville Coll, circulation libr 1966-69; Knoxville Coll Admin Office, admin asst; Athens, Tennessee secondary schools, teacher; Univ of TN, prof/reference librarian 1969-. **Orgs:** American Library Association; Knoxville Roundtable, Natl Conf Christians & Jews 1971-; Alpha Kappa Alpha Sorority; Publ Rels Comm TN Libr Assn, SE Libr Assn, E TN Libr Assn, Intl Womens Yr Decard, NAACP, YWCA, YMCA, Knoxville Planned Parenthood, Knoxville Coll Alumni Assn; Knoxville Black Official Coalition 1976-79; Beck Cultural Exchange Ctr, charter member 1976-; Knoxville Nativity Pageant Choir 1975-, Payne Adv Bapt Church Choir; mem & mem bd of dirs Knoxville Comm Chorus; pres Spring Place Neighborhood Assn 1980-; mem religious task force 1982 World's Fair; bd of dirs UT Federal Credit Union 1984-89; charter mem Natl Museum of Women in the Arts 1985-; hon comm Diva Foundation 1987-88; dir of public

relations, Concerned Assn of Residents East;Tennessee Valley Energy Coalition, 1988-. **Honors/Awds:** Chancellor's Citation Extraordinary Comm Serv 1978; Citizen of the Year Awd Order of the Eastern Star Prince Hall Masons 1979; Public Service University of Tennessee National Alumni Association, 1984; Certificate of Appreciation, Radio Station WJBE, 1978; Religious Service Award, National Conference of Christians and Jews, 1976; Citizen of the Year Award, Order of the Eastern Star, Prince Hall Masons, 1979; UT Federal Credit Union, Certificate of Appreciation, 1989; Habitat for Humanity, Plaque, 1992; Knoxville Mayor, Merit Award, 1994; University of TN Libraries, Humanitarian Award, 1994; University of Tennessee, African American Hall of Fame, 1994; Bridge Refugee Sponsorship and Services, Certificate of Appreciation, 1996. **Special Achievements:** Author "Doubt I You-Nevermore," National Poetry Press, 1975; "Parents Without Partners, The Single-Parent Family ," a Bibliography , 1978; "A Selected List of Sources on Student Fin Aid/Asst," 1978, 1983, 1990-; "A Brief Historial Sketch of Payne Ave Baptist Church, 1930?-83"; A Subject Guide to Basic Reference Books in Black Studies, 1978; "Honorable Norma Holloway Johnson," "Actress Cicely Tyson," Notable Black American Woman, 1992; An Assessment of the African American Collection, The John C. Hodges Library, University of Tennessee, The Melungeons: A Selected Bibliography, 1993; contributor, A Bicentennial Tribute to Tennessee, 1796-1996, A Biographical Directory, 1996; poetry anthologies, The Ebbing Tide, 1995; Silence of Yesterday, 1996; Dance Upon the Shore, 1997; Winds of Freedom, 1998. **Home Addr:** 5413 Spring Place Cir NE, Knoxville, TN 37924-2174. **Business Addr:** Professor/Reference Librarian, The University of Tennessee at Knoxville, 145 Hodges Library, 1015 Volunteer Blvd, Knoxville, TN 37996-1000.

FELICIANA, JERRYE BROWN
Educational administrator. **Personal:** Born Aug 20, 1951, Bethesda, MD; daughter of Katie Glean McNair Brown and James Dudley Brown; married Albert Feliciana; children: Wayne, Jaison, Kyanna. **Educ:** George Washington Univ, BA 1974; Trinity Coll, MA 1976; Maple Springs Baptist Seminary, 1994. **Career:** Georgetown Univ, asst dir upward bound 1977-78; US Dept of Agr, consultant 1981; Trinity Coll, asst dir for minority affairs 1983-84; Trinity Coll, dir upward bound 1978-89; asistant director, Student Support Services, Howard Univ 1989-; vice president for administration, Maple Springs Baptist Bible College and Seminary, 1991-. **Orgs:** Chairwoman DC Consolidation for Ed serv 1983-89; mem of exec bd Mid-Eastern Assoc of Educ Oppty Prog 1983-; member board of directors, Ethel J Williams Scholarship Committee 1989-; Amer Assn of Christian Counselors. **Honors/Awds:** National Dean's List, 1992; Graduated Summa Cum Laude, 1994. **Home Addr:** 5200 Vienna Dr, Clinton, MD 20735. **Business Addr:** Assistant Director, Student Support Services, Howard University, PO Box 313, Carnegie Building, Room 201, Washington, DC 20059.

FELIX, DUDLEY E.
Educator. **Educ:** London Univ, London England; Royal Faculty of Physicians and Surgeons, Scotland; Howard Univ, Washington DC; Univ of Pennsylvania Medical and Dental Colleges; Philadelphia General Hospital. **Career:** Univ of Pennsylvania Gen Hospital, Otorhinolaryngology and Temporo-Mandibular Joint Clinic, resident and attending physician; Philadelphia Gen Hospital, Dept of Oral/Internal Medicine, resident; Howard Univ, clinical instr oral and maxillofacial surgery, 1969-73; Howard Univ, Div of District of Columbia Gen Hospital, dir of senior students, 1974; Meharry Medical Coll, faculty mem school of dentistry, dir of didactic program in oral diagnosis and oral medicine, head of section on oral medicine. **Orgs:** Attending consultant, Hubbard Hospital; lecturer and attending consultant, Dept of Pediatric Medicine, Meharry Medical Coll; guest lecturer and attending consultant, Tennessee State Univ; fellow Royal Soc of Health, United Kingdom; Amer Acad of General Dental Surgery 1979; diplomate Amer Specialty Bd of Oral Medicine 1981; mem Intl Acad of Preventive Medicine 1982; fellow Intl Acad of Medical Preventics 1983; mem Amer Cancer Soc; mem Amer Soc of Regional Anesthesia; mem Intl Assn for Pain Study; mem Amer Assn for Pain Study; mem Intl Soc for Advanced Educ; co-chmn faculty eval comm 1987, mem grievance comm 1987, faculty rep of faculty senate 1988, mem faculty council 1988, mem curriculum comm 1988, Meharry Medical Coll; mem Amer Assn for the Study ofHeadache. **Honors/Awds:** Academic Fellowship, Amer Acad of Oral Medicine; Outstanding Teacher Award, Howard Univ and Meharry Medical Coll; Outstanding and Dedicated Serv Award of Oral/Maxillofacial Surgery, Howard Univ; Clinical Prof of the Year, Meharry Medical Coll; Expertise in Medical Lectures, Meharry Medical Coll; guest of Dr Siaka Stevens, president of Sierra Leone, 1983; guest lecturer in West Africa, Canada and USA; publications include "Oral Symptoms as a Chief Sign of Acute Monoblastic Leukemia, Report of Case," JADA, 1986; Instructor of the Year, Meharry Medical Coll, 1988. **Business Addr:** Head, Section on Oral Medicine, Meharry Medical College, 1005 D B Todd Blvd, Nashville, TN 37208.

FELKER, JOSEPH B.
Clergyman. **Personal:** Born Nov 25, 1926, Chicago, IL; married Ruthie Crockrom; children: Cordelia, Jacquelyn. **Educ:** Univ Chgo, CBI 1953; IL Barber Coll, MA 1952; No Bapt Theol Sem, BTH 1956; McKennley Theol Sem. **Career:** Mt Carmel Baptist Church, pastor 1957-; Vet Barber Shop, pres 1957-. **Orgs:** Moderator Grtr New Era Dist Assn of Chicago 1968-; treas JH Jackson Lib; mem NAACP; The Urban League; treas MI Towers S; chmn of moderators, Bapt Gen State Conv 1973-. **Honors/Awds:** CBI Cert of Achvmt 1971; Outsdng Ldrsp as Moderator, Chs, Grtr New Era Dist Assn 1973; Most Outsdng & Prog Moderator Yr, Midwestern Bapt Layman Flwsp Inc 1974; Civic & Rel Work Hon, Fgn Mission Bd of MB Conv 1976; cert of recg, Gen State Conv IL 25 Yrs of Denominational Christian Serv 1977. **Military Serv:** USN petty ofcr 3rd class. **Business Addr:** 2978 S Wabash Ave, Chicago, IL 60616.

FELTON, JAMES A.
Educator, administration. **Personal:** Born Jun 20, 1945, New York, NY. **Educ:** Tufts, MA 1969; Bradley, BA 1967. **Career:** Univ MA, dir financial aid; Univ MA, asst dir financial aid; Metro Mus Art NYC, intern treasury dept; One Yrs Tour Europe, Germany, Africa, Egypt, Nigeria, Mali; MA Assn Coll Minority Adminstrs;Howard U, Phi Mu Alpha Sinfonia, Foreian Affairs & Scholar.

FELTON, JAMES EDWARD, JR.
Business executive. **Personal:** Born Dec 1, 1932, New York, NY; married Elizabeth Madison; children: Robin Felton Leadbetter, James E III, Cynthia, Corey. **Educ:** Robert Louis Stevenson Inst & the NY School of Tech, 1956; Rutgers University, courses in the principles of supervision 1974. **Career:** General Service Administration grade level of WC-l0, 1957-72; United States Post Office, 1972-77; United Custodial Serv Armed Forces, 2 years; Ebon Serv Intl Inc, sr vp. **Orgs:** Founder United Custodial Service 1969; founder EBON Services Intl 1973; member Bldg Service Contractors Assoc Intl, Essex County Private Industry Council, Human & Civil Rights Assoc of NJ; vice president and Chairman of the Bd EBON Service Intl 1985; mem Bethany Baptist Ch Newark, NJ; co-founder NJ United Minority Business Brain Trust. **Honors/Awds:** Dedicated services award Young Man's Christian Assn 1983; appreciation award Area 9 Essex County Special Olympics 1983; certificate of appreciation Muslums United for Social and Political Change Award 1984; advocacy award Nwk Minority Business Development Center 1984. **Military Serv:** AUS pvt first class 2 yrs; Honorable Discharge 1955. **Business Addr:** Senior Vice President, Ebon Services Intl Inc, Newark International Airport, Terminal "B", Newark, NJ 07114.

FELTON, OTIS LEVERNA
Bank official. **Personal:** Born Jun 8, 1946, Monroe, LA; divorced; children: Lawrence Dwayne, Chloe Queana. **Educ:** Southern Univ, BS 1968; Natl Univ, MS 1976; Grossmont Coll, Special Courses in Real Estate. **Career:** Security Pacific Bank, branch exam off 1970-75; San Diego Trust & Svgs Bank, asst mgr 1975-77; Gibraltar Svgs, vice pres & mgr. **Orgs:** Pst bd mem East Co Bd United Way 1980-82; charter mem treas San Diego Urban Bankers 1980-82; mem Los Angeles Urban Bankers 1985; past mem & pres Rotary Intl. **Military Serv:** AUS E-5 spec; Bronze Star; Army Commendation Medal; Commendation Medal w/Oak Leaf Cluster; Vietnam Serv Medal; Good Conduct Medal.

FELTON, ZORA BELLE
Educator (retired). **Personal:** Born Jun 22, 1930, Allentown, PA; daughter of Josephine Elizabeth Cobbs Martin and James William Martin; married Edward P Felton Jr, Jul 12, 1975; children: stepchildren: Erica Booker, Eric, Edward. **Educ:** Moravian Coll, Bethlehem PA, BA, 1952; Howard Univ, Washington DC, MEd, 1980. **Career:** Sleighton Farm School for Girls, Media PA, field counselor, 1952; Dayton YWCA, Dayton OH, dir teenage dept, 1952-58; Southeast Neighborhood House, Washington DC, dir educ and group work, 1958-67; Anacostia Museum, Washington DC, chief educ and outreach sevices dept, 1967-94. **Orgs:** African-American Museums Assn; mem, Phi Delta Kappa, Museum Educators' Roundtable; mem, Natl Black Child Devel Inst; bd mem, Anacostia Partnership; Delta Sigma Theta Sorority; sec, Ethel James Williams Scholarship Fund Inc, 1986-. **Honors/Awds:** Outstanding Graduating Sr Award, Moravian Coll, 1952; First Annual Raymond S Haupert Humanitarian Award, Moravian Coll, 1970; American's Top 100 Black Business and Professional Women, 1988; Certificate of Appreciation for service to museums of this country, Inst of Museum Services, 1988; Certificate of Appreciation for service to the Ethel James Williams Scholarship Fund, 1989; Professional Award for Outstanding Accomplishments, National Association of Negro Business and Professional Women's Clubs Inc, 1990; Margaret T Burroughs Award for Exceptional Contribution in Museum Education, African-American Museum Association, 1989; American Association of Museums, Educator of Excellence Award, 1991; Moravian College, Comenius Alumni Award, 1991; Union Temple Baptist Church, Mary McLeod Bethune Education Award, 1992; Named to DC Commission on Women, Hall of Fame, 1994. **Special Achievements:** Author, A Walk Through 'Old' Anacostia, 1991 (reprint), as well as numerous articles, museum education materials and learning packages; Co-author, A Different Drummer; John R Kinard and The Anacostia Museum, 1967-89, 1994.

FELTUS, JAMES, JR.
Minister. **Personal:** Born Apr 16, 1921, Gloster, MS; son of Lillie Packnette Feltus and James Feltus, Sr; married Hazel Luter; children: James III, Elliott, Percy, Erasmus, Riley (deceased), Joan F, Wilson, Gerald, Eunice F Little, Michael. **Educ:** Xavier Univ, EdM, PhB 1946; Campbell Coll, BD 1954, DD 1955; New Orleans Bapt Theol Sem, MRE 1973. **Career:** British Honduras, dist supt dist 8 1953-65, overseer 1955; Orleans Parish Sch Bd, substitute teacher 1954-74; First Church of God in Christ, pastor 28 yrs; The Churches of God in Christ (United) in US London & Jamaica, founder 1974; Jurisdiction #2 Church of God in Christ, bishop. **Orgs:** Pres, Interdenominational Ministerial Alliance, 1987-; mem, District Attorney's Committee Against Drugs, 1988-89. **Honors/Awds:** Honorary Civil Sheriff of Orleans Parish by Paul Valteau, 1983; Civil Sheriff Deputy by Paul Valteau; Colonel of the Staff to Gov Edwin Edwards of the State of Louisiana, 1987; Certificate of Appreciation for Contribuiton to the City of New Orleans, Awarded by Mayor S Bartholomew, 1987, Awarded by Mayor Moreal, 1983; Long career of performing good works that daily benefit the City of New Orleans, adopted by the City Council of New Orleans, 1986; Commended and cited by City Council for contribution to community and leadership exhibited, 1987; proclaimed as Bishop James Feltus Jr's Day in New Orleans; adopted by Mayor S Bartholomew and the City Council of New Orleans, 1987; Accomplishments in Religion, The National Sorority of Phi Delta Kappa, Inc, Alpha Theta Chapter, 1990. **Business Addr:** Bishop, Churches of God in Christ United, 2453 Josephine St, New Orleans, LA 70112.

FENTRESS, ROBERT H.
Publishing company executive (retired). **Personal:** Born Oct 24, 1921, Brownsville, TN; married Alice; children: Robert, Barbara. **Educ:** TN State U, attnd. **Career:** Johnson Pub Co, 1950-92, vice pres, circulation dir, until 1991;.

FENTRESS, SHIRLEY B.
Payroll administrator. **Personal:** Born Nov 16, 1937, Bolivar, TN; daughter of Mammie Bernice Pankey McKinnie and John Lester McKinnie; married Ernest Fentress, Aug 3, 1957 (divorced); children: Sherral Fentress Mitchell. **Educ:** TN State Univ, 1955-57; Cortez Business Coll, 1968. **Career:** Frank Thrifty Grocery, owner 1980-81; Frank Thrifty Liquor Corp, owner 1981-84; City Colleges of Chicago, dir of payroll, 1989-. **Orgs:** Sec New Philadelphia Baptist Courtesy Comm 1972; cochmn 1st Union Baptist Church Pastor Anniv 1985, Chairperson Pastors Anniv 1986-87; capt 1st Union Baptist Church Anniversary 1985; Coordinator Crusade of Mercy City Coll of Chicago 1986-87, financial secretary, Victory Christian Church Baptist, 1986. **Honors/Awds:** Woman of the Week WBEE Radio Station Chicago 1974; Citation of Merit WAIT 820 Radio Station Chicago 1974; Great Gal Awd WJPC Radio Station Chicago 1974. **Home Addr:** 308 Hickory, Glenwood, IL 60425. **Business Addr:** Executive Director of Payroll Services & Records, City Colleges of Chicago, 226 W Jackson Blvd, Room 1226, Chicago, IL 60606-6998.

FERDINAND, KEITH C.
Cardiologist. **Personal:** Born Dec 5, 1950, New Orleans, LA; son of Inola Copelin Ferdinand and Vallery Ferdinand Jr; married Daphne Pajeaud Ferdinand, Feb 16, 1973; children: Kamau, Rashida, Aminisha, Jua. **Educ:** Telluride Scholar, Cornell University, 1968-69; University of New Orleans, BA, 1972; Howard University College of Medicine, MD, 1976. **Career:** US Public Health Hospital, New Orleans LA, intern, 1976-77; LSU Medical Center, New Orleans LA, internal medicine resident, 1977-79, cardiology fellow, 1979-80; Howard University Hospital, Washington DC, cardiology fellow, 1981; Flint Goodridge Hospital, New Orleans LA, chief of cardiology, 1981-85; Medical Associates, New Orleans LA, private practice, 1981-83; Xavier University of New Orleans LA, visiting professor, 1981-82, associate professor, 1982-; Health Corp, New Orleans LA, consultant, 1982-85; Heartbeat Life Center, New Orleans LA, private practice, 1983—; LA State Univ Medical Center, New Orleans LA, clinical instructor, 1986—; United Medical Center, New Orleans LA, chief of cardiology, 1985—, chief of medical staff, 1987-88. **Orgs:** Chm of the bd, 1990-, board member, 1987—, editor of newsletter, 1988-90, Assn of Black Cardiologists; fellow, American College of Cardiology; board member, American Lung Assn of LA, 1987—; vice-president, LA Medical Assn, 1988-; American Heart Assn; Trilateral Committee to End Violence in the Black Community; board member, Greater New Orleans Mental Health Assn, 1985-87; board member, Urban League of Greater New Orleans, 1984; Alpha Omega Alpha; board member of several community service groups; president, Orleans Division American Heart Association, 1989-; member, Louisiana State Board of Medical Examiners, 1990-; member, New Orleans Charity Hospital Board, 1990-; president, Physicians Association of Louisiana, Inc, 1992-. **Honors/Awds:** First Place, Unity Awards in Media, Lincoln Univ of MO, 1982; Outstanding Service Award, LP Nurses of LA, 1983; Black Man of the Year, New Orleans Assn of Black Social Workers, 1985; distinguished service award, Greater Liberty BC, 1987; Frederick Douglass Award, Natl Assn of Negro Business and Professional Womens Club of New Orleans, 1988. **Business Addr:** Heartbeats Life Center, 1201 Poland Ave, New Orleans, LA 70117, (504)943-1177.

FEREBEE, CLAUDE T., SR.
Retired dentist. **Personal:** Born Apr 8, 1901, Norfolk, VA; son of Nanny Ferebee and Charles Ferebee; married Hazel Jones; children: Claude T (deceased). **Educ:** Wilberforce U, BS 1923; Columbia U, DDS 1929. **Career:** Dentist, pvt prac; Howard U, faculty of Dentistry 1929-36; Washington DC, pvt prac 1936-41; AUS, Dental Reserve Corps 1932; RT Freeman Dental Soc Wash DC, past pres; Dental Reserve Corps 428th Inf Reserve Ft Howard MD, active duty training 1932-40; 366th Inf Regt Ft Devens MD, extended active duty 1940. **Orgs:** Mem Nat Dental Assn; Am Dental Assn; Odontochirurgical Soc Philadelphia; Am Acad of Dental Med; Am Endodontic Soc; past pres N Harlem Dental Soc; Omikron Kappa Upsilon Dental Honorary Frat Columbia Univ Chpt; Alpha Phi Alpha Frat; NAACP; Luth Ch; Lectr & Clinician Dental Orgns. **Honors/Awds:** Bronze Star Medal with Citation from SW Pacific Theater of Operations 1945; Robert T Freeman Dental Soc Award Gold Plaque; N Harlem Dental Soc Award; Bronze Plaque; The OKU. **Military Serv:** AUS maj 1932-45.

FERERE, GERARD ALPHONSE
Educator. **Personal:** Born Jul 21, 1930, Cap Haitian, Haiti; son of Marie Leroy and Alphonse M Ferere; married Nancy; children: Magali, Rachel. **Educ:** Naval Acad of Venezuela, Ensign 1953; Villanova Univ, MA 1967; Univ of PA, PhD 1974. **Career:** Haitian Navy, naval officer 1953-58; Haiti, language teacher 1958-63; St Joseph's Univ, prof 1964-. **Orgs:** Translator interpreter SELF 1964-; pres Coalition for Haitian Concerns 1982-; Haitian American commissioner, Pennsylvania Heritage Affairs Commission, 1991-. **Home Addr:** 1206 Division Avenue, Willow Grove, PA 19090-1610. **Business Addr:** Professor, St Joseph's Univ, City Ave at 54th St, Philadelphia, PA 19131.

FERGERSON, MIRIAM N.
Art sales representative. **Personal:** Born Sep 15, 1941, Homestead, PA; daughter of Miriam King Watson and James A Watson; married Cecil Fergerson; children: Melanie, John, Kinte. **Educ:** VA State Univ, BA French/Ed 1964; Azusa Pacific Univ, MA Marriage, Family & Child Counseling 1975. **Career:** CA Superior Court Conciliation Court, family counselor 1977-78; Youth Training Sch, youth counselor 1978-83; SanMar Group Homes, substance abuse social worker, 1983-; Art Educ Consultant Servs, founder/admin, 1974-. **Orgs:** Youth counselor Missionary Dept Messiah Bapt Church 1982-86; mem bd Christian Educ Messiah Bapt Church 1983-; bd chmn Friends Wm Grant Still Arts Ctr1983-; vice pres arts/culture 10th Councilmanic Dist Women's Steering Comm 1984-85; consultant Dr Chas R Drew Historical Exhibit Drew Medical Sch 1984-85; researcher City Watts, Watts Towers Art Ctr 1984-85; mem CA for Drug Free Youth 1984; Rev Jesse Jackson for Pres 1984; vice pres Parent Adv Cncl Fairfax High 1984-85; editor/consultant Watts Towers Jazz Festival Publ 1986; liason 10th Dist Arts Adv Council 1986-87; mem Friends of Geneva Cox for City Council; pres Trinity Mission Circle Messiah Church; founder, Friends of Los Angeles Southwest College Art Gallery, 1991; member, Friends of Kerman Maddox City Council, 1991. **Honors/Awds:** TV Documentary Watts Festival Recounted Univ Jenkins Production 1980; Community Counseling Serv Awd Westminster Presbyterian Church, 1984-85; West Angeles Christian Acad Outstanding Volunteer Serv Awd 1986; Natl Conf of Artists Outstanding Serv Awd 1987; article Golden State Life Ins Travel & Art magazine 1978; publisher, "Artaculture: Masud Kordofan," Los Angeles Southwest College, 1990; publisher, "Tribute of Carter G Woodson," Cal State Dominguez Hills, January 1991; publisher, "Listen Rap Movement," Los Angeles Southwest College, February 1991. **Home Addr:** 1417 So Ogden Dr, Los Angeles, CA 90019.

FERGUSON, ANDREW L.
Automobile dealer. **Career:** Auburn Ford-Lincoln-Mercury Inc, CEO, 1985-. **Special Achievements:** Company is ranked #98 on The Black Enterprise list of Top 100 auto dealers, 1992. **Business Addr:** CEO, Auburn Ford-Lincoln-Mercury Inc., PO Box 2798, Auburn, AL 36830, (205)887-8571.

FERGUSON, CECIL (DUKE)
Graphic artist. **Personal:** Born Mar 13, 1931, Chicago, IL; married Irene; children: Mark. **Educ:** Art Inst of Chgo; Inst of Design, IL Inst of Tech; Am Academy of Art. **Career:** Ebony Mag, asst art dir; "The Ebony Success Library", designer; Johnson Publ, promotional illustrations & layouts. **Business Addr:** 820 S Michigan Ave, Chicago, IL 60605.

FERGUSON, DEREK TALMAR
Publishing company executive. **Personal:** Born Apr 20, 1965, Yonkers, NY; son of Roberta Lewis Pieck and James Ferguson; married Regina Bullock Ferguson, Apr 2, 1988; children: Reginald James. **Educ:** Univ of PA, Philadelphia, PA, BS, Economics, 1985; Harvard Business School, Cambridge, MA, MBA, 1990. **Career:** Coopers & Lybrand, New York, NY, sr accountant, 1985-88; Bain & Co, Cambridge, MA, summer assoc, 1989; Urban Profile Communications, Baltimore, MD, COO & assoc pub, 1988-. **Orgs:** Vice pres, AASO-Harvard Business School, 1989-90; corresponding sec, Black Wharton, 1984. **Honors/Awds:** Intl Mar Corp Entrepreneurs Comp-Honorable Mention, Univ of TX at Austin, 1990; Certified Public Accountant, AICPA, 1988; Maggie L Walker Award, Emma L Higgombothum Award, Black Fac & Admin, Univ of PA, 1985; Onyx Sr Honor Society, Univ of PA, 1985. **Home Addr:** 1900 Patterson Ave, Bronx, NY 10473. **Business Addr:** Chief Operating Officer, Urban Profile Communications, Inc, 519 N Charles St, Baltimore, MD 21208.

FERGUSON, EDWARD A., JR.
Financial administrator. **Personal:** Born Jul 21, 1942, New York, NY; son of Oletha G Higgs Ferguson and Edward A Ferguson Sr; married Cynhia Henderson; children: Edward III, Candace, Derek. **Educ:** Iona Coll, BBA 1965; St John's Univ, MBA 1974; New York Univ, Post Grad 1975-78. **Career:** CitiBank, offcl asst 1965-70; Bankers Trust Co, asst mgr 1970; Bedford Stuyvesant Rest Corp, dir of admin serv 1970-74; Xerox Corp, 1974-78, mgr br control New York City 1978-80; Xerox Corp Rochester NY, mgr sales commn admin, serv consult 1980-84; Xerox Corp Columbus, support mgr dist ops 1984-85; Xerox Corp Akron OH, dist mgr customer serv 1985-88; Xerox Corp, district mgr bus operations 1988-93; Reynolds & Reynolds, dir, CSD Management Systems & Processes, 1993-. **Orgs:** Berkshire Farm & Youth Serv 1976-. **Honors/Awds:** Xerox President's Club, 1985. **Military Serv:** US Army, Col, 29 yrs; Army Achvmnt, Army Accomodation, Good Conduct, Armed Forces Reserve Medal, Natl Def Medal, Army Service Ribbon, Ohio Army National Guard 10 yr Long & Faithful Service Medal; overseas ribbon, Army Reserve Medal, NYS 10 yrs medal. **Business Addr:** Dir, CSD Mgmt systs & processes, Reynolds & Reynolds, PO Box 1005, Dayton, OH 45401.

FERGUSON, ELLIOTT LAROY, II
Sales manager. **Personal:** Born Nov 26, 1965, Spokane, WA; son of Gwendolyn Cooper Williams and Elliott L Ferguson Sr. **Educ:** Savannah State College, Savannah, GA, BA, marketing, 1988. **Career:** Savannah, Economic Development, Authority, director of research, 1988-91; Savannah Convention & Visitors Bureau, director of sales, 1991-92; Atlanta Convention & Visitors Bureau, sales manager, 1992-. **Orgs:** Board member, Rape Crisis Center, 1991-92; South Atlantic 2000 Club, 1991-92; Alpha Phi Alpha, 1988-. **Home Addr:** 3920 Dogwood Farm Rd, Decatur, GA 30034-6435.

FERGUSON, IDELL
Real estate broker (retired). **Personal:** Born Oct 20, Montgomery, AL; daughter of Mary I Harris Lawson (deceased) and Frank Lawson (deceased); divorced; children: Ronald E, Mary K Ferguson Robertson, Dennis E Ferguson. **Educ:** Actual Business Coll MI, attended; Univ of Akron OH, Real Estate Courses; Certificate, Hammel-Actual Business Coll Akron, OH, Certicate, Akron Univ,; Mount Union Coll, Alliance, OH 1977-78, 1980-81. **Career:** Russell Realty Co, sec salesperson, legal sec, mgr; certified appraiser 1955-60; Advance Realty, owner, broker 1960-65; Corp Advance Realty, 1961-66; Natl Assoc Real Estate Brokers Inc, instructor, real estate classes 1965-71; pre-kindergarten teacher 1965; Idell Ferguson Realty, owner, broker 1965-; FHA, appraiser 1969-72; notary public 18 yrs; Lawyers Title Insurance Corp, title plant mgr, 1966-82, retired; License Real Estate Broker Akron, OH 1960-87; Oasis Organization, prog dir, 1987-88; Idell Ferguson Ralty, Akron, OH, broker, currently; licensed real estate broker, 1996-. **Orgs:** Coordinator Jesse Jackson for Pres Comm Summit County 1984; mem OH Assoc RE Brokers Inc, Columbus Assoc RE Brokers 1963-65; 1st sec, pres 1969-71, org 1965 Akron Assoc RE Brokers; chairperson State Conv 1966, State Bd 1965-71; mem Women's Council Akron Area Bd Realtors 1968-, Human Relations Comm Akron Bd Realtors 1970-; bd mem Fair Housing Contact Serv 1965-67; housing comm Urban League 1961-63; bd mem Akron NAACP 1961-62; den mother BSA 1961-62; mem OH Civil Rights Comm 1961-65; YMCA; YWCA; Young Business & Professional Womens Club; Akron Business & Professional Womens League; Akron Club Natl Assoc Negro Business & Professional Womens Clubs Inc; Centenary United Methodist Church; NEFCO 1976-; Womens Council of Realtors of the Natl Assoc of Realtors; bd mem United Church Women Columbus 1963-64, Akron 1964-67; headed program Negro History 1968-69; org, sponsored Akron Young Adult Club Natl Assoc Negro Business & Professional Womens Clubs Inc 1971; dist gov NANBPW 1972-74; org Wesley Serv Guild 1953; bd mem Fair Housing Contact Serv 1979; co-chairperson, admin bd Centenary United Methodist Church 1979; St Phillip Episcopal Ch, volunteer tutor, 1991-92; Akron Canton Regional Food Bank, volunteer clerical, 1993; Stan Hywet Hall & Gardens, volunteer, 1996; Akron Urban League, computer lab volunteer, 1997. **Honors/Awds:** Listed in OH State Newspaper; Achievement Award 1970; Recog Award 1972; Leadership Citation 1973; Safari Excellence 1974; Outstanding Serv Award for Leadership & Serv in Re-Org the Akron Assoc of RE Brokers OH Assoc of RE Brokers; Outstanding Serv to Natl Assoc of Negro Business & Professional Women's Club Kent Area Chap Links Inc 1980; Award Realtist Pioneer Natl Assoc of RE Brokers Inc Akron Assoc 1982. **Special Achievements:** License Real Estate Broker, State of Ohio, 1960-; Notary Public, State of Ohio. **Home Addr:** 1100 Bellevue Ave, Akron, OH 44320.

FERGUSON, JASON
Professional football player. **Personal:** Born Nov 28, 1974. **Educ:** Univ of Georgia, attended. **Career:** New York Jets, defensive tackle, 1997-. **Business Addr:** Professional Football Player, New York Jets, 1000 Fulton Ave, Hempstead, NY 11550, (516)560-8100.

FERGUSON, JOEL
Broadcast company executive, real estate company executive. **Personal:** marrIed Erma; children: five. **Educ:** Michigan State Univ, BA, elementary education. **Career:** WLAJ-TV, president, owner, 1990-; F&S Development, partner, currently. **Orgs:** Michigan State University, trustee, currently. **Special Achievements:** First African American elected to the Lansing City Council, 1967. **Business Addr:** Owner, WLAJ TV Station, PO Box 27307, Lansing, MI 48909, (517)394-5300.

FERGUSON, JOHNNIE NATHANIEL
Banking executive. **Personal:** Born Jan 17, 1943, Washington, DC; son of Viola Cooper (deceased) and James H Ferguson; married Delphine David, Oct 31, 1964; children: Michelle D. **Educ:** Univ of the Dist of Columbia, AAS 1973. **Career:** FBI, fingerprint tech 1967; Riggs Natl Bank, Washington, DC, programmer 1977, data processing supervisor 1979, banking officer/asst manager, 1990-93, baning officer/manager, 1993-. **Orgs:** Pres Orr Elem School PTA 1976-84; mem Washington DC Assn of Urban Bankers 1977-83; pres Riggs Natl Bank Club 1979; treas DC Congress of Parents & Teachers 1982-84; treas Adv Neighborhood Comm 6C 1982-; mem DC Federation of Farmers & Consumers Markets 1983-; treasurer Kiwanis Club of Eastern Branch 1988-; 1st v pres D C Congress of PTA 1989-; vice president, Kiwanis Club of Eastern Branch, 1990-; secretary, D C Commission on Human Rights, 1990-; chairman, Local Board #1 Selective Service System, 1988-; controller, Anacostia/Congress Heights Partnership, 1993-; mem, Anacostia Business & Professional Association, 1994-; mem, Area D Community Mental Health Association, 1995-; mem, Hadley Memorial Hosp Community Board, 1996-. **Honors/Awds:** Cert of appreciation Amer Cancer Society 1980; cert of appreciation DC Advisory Council on Vocational Educ 1980; cert of awd Benjamin G Orr Elem Sch 1980-84; honorary life member National Congress of Parents & Teachers 1987-; life member D C Congress of PTA 1986. **Military Serv:** US Army, sgt, 3 yrs; Army Commendation Medal; Good Conduct Medal. **Home Addr:** 1919 Ridge Place SE, Washington, DC 20020-4626.

FERGUSON, LLOYD NOEL
Educator (retired). **Personal:** Born Feb 9, 1918, Oakland, CA; son of Gwendolyn and Noel Ferguson; married Charlotte Welch Ferguson, Jan 2, 1944; children: Lloyd Jr, Stephen Bruce, Lisa Ferguson Walker. **Educ:** Univ of California Berkeley, BS, 1940; PhD, 1943. **Career:** Univ of California Berkeley, National Defense Project, research asst, 1941-44; A&T College, asst prof, 1944-45; Howard Univ, faculty member, 1945-65, chemistry dept head, 1958-65; California State Univ, prof, 1965-86, chemistry dept chairman, 1968-71. **Orgs:** American Chemical Society; American Assn of University Professors; Sigma Xi; Phi Kappa Phi National Honor Society; American Assn for the Advancement of Science, fellow; Chemical Society of London, fellow. **Honors/Awds:** Oakland Museum Assn Award, 1973; Manufacturing Chemists Assn, Award for Excellence in Teaching, 1974; California State Univ, Outstanding Professor Award, 1974; American Foundation for Negro Affairs, Distinguished American Medallion, 1976; American Chemical Society, Award in Chemical Education, 1978; National Organization of Black Chemists and Chemical Engineers, Outstanding Teaching Award, 1979; California State University and College Trustees, Outstanding Professor Award, 1981; Honorary degrees: D.Sc, Howard Univ, 1970, Coe College, 1979. **Special Achievements:** Author: Electron Structures of Organic Molecules, Prentice-Hall, 1952; Textbook of Organic Chemistry, D Van Norstrand, 1958; The Modern Structural Theory of Organic Chemistry, Prentice-Hall, 1963; Organic Chemistry, Prentice-Hall, 1972; Highlights of Alicyclic Chemistry, Franklin Publishing, 1973; Structural Organic Chemistry, Willard Grant Press, 1975; Lloyd N. Ferguson Young Scientist Award; CibaGeigy Corp "Exceptional Black Scientists" Poster; birthdate in "Milestones in Chemistry" calendar. **Home Addr:** 4477 Wilshire Blvd, Apt 110, Los Angeles, CA 90010.

FERGUSON, RALPH
Automobile dealer. **Personal:** Born Feb 23, 1955, Warner Robins, GA; son of Jordan Georgia Ferguson and Jesse Ferguson. **Educ:** Citadel College, Charleston, SC, 1973-77; Georgia College, Milledgeville, GA, 1982-85. **Career:** Houston Bd of Education, Warner Robins, GA, teacher, 1977-83; 20th Century Realty, Warner Robins, GA, sales, 1981-84; J-Mac Olds, Warner Robins, GA, sales, 1984-85; Eddie Wiggins F-L-M, Warner Robins, GA, sales, 1985-86; Sumter Ford-L-M, Americus, GA, co-owner, vice pres, 1986-. **Orgs:** Mem Black Ford Lincoln Mercury, 1986-91; mem, Citadel Alumni Association, 1977-91, mem, Alumni Football Association, 1977-91; pres, Ferguson Family Foundation, 1990-. **Honors/Awds:** Jerome Hartwell Holland Award, United Holiness Church, 1991; Entrepreneurship Award, Ferguson Family, 1988; Honorable Mention All-American, UPI, 1976; All State, SC, State of SC, 1975, 1976; All Conference, Southern Conference, 1975, 1976.

FERGUSON, RENEE
Journalist. **Personal:** Born Aug 22, 1949, Oklahoma City, OK. **Educ:** IN Univ, BA 1971; IN Univ, MA 1972. **Career:** Indianapolis News, news reporter 1971-72; WLWI-TV Indpls, news reporter 1972-76; WBBM-TV Chgo, news reporter 1976-82; CBS News, news reporter 1982-. **Orgs:** Bd of dir The Assoc for Children 1975-78; bd mem Big Sisters of Amer/Indianapolis 1975-78; mem Kappa Alpha Sor. **Honors/Awds:** Ed Writer of the Year Awd Natl Ed Assoc IN 1977; Assoc Press Newswriters Awd Assoc Press 1977; 4 Time Emmy Awd Winner Chicago Chap Natl Acad of TV Arts & Sci 1978-80. **Business Addr:** CBS News, 524 W 57th, New York, NY 10019.

FERGUSON, ROBERT LEE, SR.
Consultant. **Personal:** Born Feb 18, 1932, Rascon, San Luis Potoci, Mexico; son of Corillea Jackson Ferguson (deceased) and Booker T Ferguson; married Ruby Evelyn Brewer Ferguson, Nov 1, 1953 (deceased); children: Robert Jr, Duane; married Raymonde Bateau-Polk Ferguson, Oct 2, 1993; children: Raymonde Polk-Wilson, Samuel Polk, Pierre Polk, Reginal Polk, Carmel Polk. **Educ:** Bakersfield Coll, attended 1950-51; Southwestern Coll, AA 1969; Naval Postgraduate Sch, BA 1973; Univ of N CO, MA 1975; Pacific Western Univ Los Angeles CA, PhD 1986. **Career:** USN Hawaii, captain's steward 1951-52; Heavy Attack Squadron, aircraft maintenance chief; USN, adv in human/minority relations psychology counseling 1967-77; NAS Miramar CA, asst dept head aircraft maintenance 1973-75; USS Enterprise, asst dept head aircraft maintenance 1975-78; NAS Lemoore CA, officer in charge aircraft maintenance 1978-80; Fighter Squadron 124, dept head aircraft maintenance 1980; Rail Company, sr logistics analyst; systems acquisition mgmt cons; self-employed, 1988-. **Orgs:** Mem Fleet Res Assn 1963-65; mgr Parkview Little League Chula Vista CA 1969-77; mem VFW 1974-; mem Naval Aviation Tailhook Assn 1972-; alumni, Naval Post Graduate School, 1973-; alumni Univ of N CO 1975-; mem Natl Naval Officer Assn 1977-; mem San Diego Museum of Art; corresp chmn African Arts Comm. **Honors/Awds:** Author: The Four-O (4.0) Sailor, self-publish, 1990. **Military Serv:** USN comdr 30 yrs served; Naval Gallantry Cross; Vietnam Service; Korea; Secnav Medal 1967, 1971; Air Medal 1971; Bronze Star; Navy Commendation 1980. **Business Addr:** Consultant/Publisher/Author, Left Brain Press, 604 Mariposa Circle, Chula Vista, CA 91911-2500.

FERGUSON, ROSETTA
Former state representative. **Personal:** Born Jul 1, 1920, Florence, MS; married; children: 4. **Educ:** Detroit Inst of Tech. **Career:** 20th District, Detroit, MI, former state rep; Loyalty Investigation Comm, mem staff mgr real estate firm. **Orgs:** Mem Dem State Central; exec bd & precinct Delegate for 10 Yrs; recording sec 13th Congressional District; mem Wayne Co Dem Rep Human Relations Coun on Civil Rights; Gray Lady for Red Cross; cub scout den mother ofr 3 yrs; mem PTA; NAACP,; TULC; Women's Pub Affairs Com of 1000 Inc; orgn Youth Civic Eagles; founder & finan Sec Peoples Community Civil League; mem Missionary Soc of Peoples Bapt Ch; mem MI Right to Life Com & People Taking Action Against Abortion Com; numerous other civic orgn; Ch sponser of Pub Act 127 of 1966 Fair Textbook Law. **Honors/Awds:** Featured in Ebony Mag as one of the Black Women Leaders in State of MI; Alpha Kappa Alpha Sorority's Heritage Series #1, Black Women in Politics; tribute of honor for Far-sighted vision & dedication to the full maturity of the human family; MI House of Rep 1970.

FERGUSON, ST. JULIAN
Sales associate, educator, musician. **Personal:** Born Apr 13, 1935, South Carolina; son of Irene and Alonzo; married Albertha Simmons; children: Darian, Gerald, Bernard. **Educ:** SC State, BS 1957; Loyola Univ, MEd 1971. **Career:** Lower N Youth Ctr, music dir; Tilden Tech HS, inst music tchr 1965-69; Madison Elem, tchr 1969-71; Chicago Bd of Educ, tchr early remediation 1971; Bryn Mawr Elem Sch, teacher beginning 1971; Coldwell Banker, sales associate, 1993-. **Orgs:** Mem NEA, IL Tchr Assn, Chicago Fed of Musicians Local 10208, Operation PUSH; professional piano & trumpet player. **Military Serv:** USMC pfc 1953-57. **Home Addr:** 9956 S Union Ave, Chicago, IL 60621.

FERGUSON, SHERLON LEE
Energy management firm executive. **Personal:** Born Mar 2, 1949, Richmond, VA; son of Grace Brown Ferguson and William Ferguson Sr; married Brenda Russell Ferguson, Jan 1, 1972; children: Mia, Meaghan. **Educ:** Morgan State University, Baltimore, MD, BS mathematics, 1971. **Career:** Blue Cross/Blue Shield, Baltimore, MD, actuarial assistant, 1971-73; Honeywell Inc, Baltimore, MD, senior sales engineer, 1973-83; FSCO Inc, Baltimore, MD, president/CEO, 1983-. **Orgs:** Member, Building Congress & Exchange of Baltimore, 1973-; member, American Society of Heating, Refrigeration & Air Conditioning Engineers, 1973-; member, USChamber of Commerce, 1988-89; member, Better Business Bureau, 1988-; member, Minority Business Development Council, 1988-; member, Associated Builders & Contractors, 1988-; member, Minority Supplier Development Council, 1988-. **Honors/Awds:** STEP Award, National Safety Committee of the Association of Builders & Contractors, 1990; Outstanding Transportation Projects of the Year, COMTO, 1987-88. **Home Addr:** 919 E Belvedere Ave, Baltimore, MD 21212.

FERGUSON, SHERMAN E.
Educator, musician. **Personal:** Born Oct 31, 1944, Philadelphia. **Educ:** Berklee Coll of Music. **Career:** Professional Musician, appearing on TV & making numerous recordings 14 yrs; Catalyst, member music group; Percussion, teacher. **Business Addr:** PO Box 15593, Philadelphia, PA 19131.

FERGUSON, TERRI LYNETTE
Company executive. **Personal:** Born Jul 18, Miami, FL; married. **Educ:** Grambling State University, BS, marketing. **Career:** Burger King World Headquarters, supervisor, consumer response line, dept supervisor, consumer response line, mgr, consumer relations, currently. **Orgs:** Society of Consumer Affairs Professionals, 1989-; Alpha Kappa Alpha Sorority, Inc, 1990-; National Assn of Female Executives, 1990-. **Honors/Awds:** Dollars & Sense Magazine, A Salute to America's Best & Brightest Business Professionals, 1992. **Home Addr:** 20817 SW 122 Pl., Miami, FL 33177. **Business Addr:** Customer Service Manager, Harman Electronics, 14800 SW 166 Street, Miami, FL 33187.

FERGUSON, WILKIE DEMERITTE, JR.
Judge. **Personal:** Born May 11, 1939, Miami, FL; son of Inez Ferguson and Wilkie Ferguson, Sr; married Betty J Tucker; children: Tawnicia, Wilkie III. **Educ:** Florida A&M Univ, BS 1960; Drexel Univ, 1964-65; Howard Univ, JD 1968. **Career:** Ford-Philco Corp, accountant, 1963-65; McCrary Ferguson & Lee, partner, 1970-73; Judge Industrial Claims, admin law judge, 1973-77; Circuit Court, judge, 1977-81; District Court of Appeals, Miami FL, judge, 1981-. **Orgs:** Mem Amer & Natl Bar Assocs 1970-; bd chmn JESCA 1972-80, Florida Memorial Coll 1982-, United Way of Dade Co FL 1986-; mem Supreme Court Comm Jury Instructions for Civil Cases 1986-; member, St Thomas Univ Inns of Court, 1988-. **Honors/Awds:** SE Region Brother of the Year Alpha Phi Alpha Frat 1982; Leadership Awd United Negro Coll Fund 1984; Community Leadership United Way of Dade Co 1985; Thurgood Marshall Awd for Judicial Gallantry Black Lawyers Assoc Miami 1986; Champion of Higher Education Award, Presidents of Ind Colleges and Univ of Florida, 1985-86; Florida Memorial College, Honorary Degree, Doctor of Humane Letters, 1993. **Military Serv:** US Army Airborne Infantry captain, until 1968. **Business Addr:** Judge, US District Court, for the Southern District of Florida, 299 E Broward Blvd, #207B, Fort Lauderdale, FL 33301.

FERNANDES, JULIE A.
White House official. **Educ:** Univ of Chicago Law School. **Career:** Justice Dept, voting expert; White House Domestic Policy Council, special asst to the President for Domestic Policy, currently. **Business Addr:** Special Assistant to the President for Domestic Policy, White House Domestic Policy Council, Old Executive Office Bldg, Rm 224, Washington, DC 20502, (202)456-2216.

FERNANDEZ, JOHN PETER
Manager. **Personal:** Born Oct 22, 1941, Boston, MA; divorced; children: Michele, Eleni, Sevgi. **Educ:** Harvard U, (magna cum laude) Government AB 1969; Univ of CA, Berkeley, sociology MA 1971; Univ of CA Socio Berkeley, PhD 1973. **Career:** Bell of PA, div mgr customer serv 1978-; AT&T Basking Rioge NJ, mgr mgmt educ & devel 1975-78; Yale U, asst prof 1974-75; AT&T NYC, personnel supr-rsrch 1973-74; YMCA Dorchester MA, prog dir 1965-69. **Orgs:** Mem Am Socio Assn 1973-; mem Council of Concerned Black Exec 1975-. **Honors/Awds:** Outst sophomore Govt Major Northeastern Univ 1967; special careers fellowship, Univ of CA Berkeley 1969-73. **Military Serv:** USN elec tech E-5 1960-64. **Business Addr:** Bell of Pennsylvania, 15 E Montgomery Ave, Pittsburgh, PA 15212.

FERNANDEZ, TONY (OCTAVIO ANTONIO CASTRO)
Professional baseball player. **Personal:** Born Jun 30, 1962, San Pedro de Macoris, Dominican Republic; married Clara; children: Joel. **Career:** Toronto Blue Jays, infielder, 1983-90; San Diego Padres, infielder, 1990-92; New York Mets, infielder, 1992-. **Honors/Awds:** Named the All Star SS for the Carolina League 1981; named IL's All-Star SS 1982; R Howard Webster Awd as Syracuse's MVP 1982, 1983; named team's Rookie of the Year by Toronto Chap of BBWAA 1984; led AL shortstops in assists 1985; Labatt's "Blue" Player of the Month June 1986; named to Sporting News and UPI's Amer League All Star Team and Assoc Press Major League All-Star team; Gold Glove winner; American League All-Star Team, 1986, 1987, 1989.

FERREBEE, THOMAS G.
Police officer. **Personal:** Born Jan 24, 1937, Detroit; married Irma; children: Gregory G, Debra L, Angela M. **Educ:** IA State U, BS 1960; Eastern MI U, MA 1963. **Career:** Detroit Police Dept, cmdr Recruiting Div; Ford Motor Co; Hamtramck HS, tchr; Chrysler Corp. **Orgs:** Bd trustees personnel com Childrens Hosp of MI; Cntr for Criminal Justice & Minority Employment in Law Enforcement; consultant Minority Police Recruiting;mem Optimist Club of Detroit; area activity chmn BSA; MI Pub Personnel Assn; mem Concerned Polic Ofc for Equal Justice. **Business Addr:** 8045 Second Ave, Detroit, MI 48202.

FERRELL, DUANE
Professional basketball player. **Personal:** Born Feb 28, 1965, Baltimore, MD; married Tina; children: three. **Educ:** Georgia Tech Univ, bachelor's degree in industrial management. **Career:** Atlanta Hawks, forward, 1988-89; Topeka Sizzlers (CBA), 1989-90; Atlanta Hawks, 1990-94; Indiana Pacers, 1994-97; Golden State Warriors, 1997-. **Business Addr:** Professional Basketball Player, Golden State Warriors, 1001 Broadway, Oakland, CA 94607, (510)986-2200.

FERRELL, ROSIE E.
Human resources executive. **Personal:** Born May 26, 1915, Clarksdale, MS; daughter of Catherine Weatherspoon Carter and Andrew Carter; married Charlie (deceased); children: Henry (deceased), Joyce, Wilma, Lois, Joseph, Rose, Nathaniel. **Educ:** Delta Comm Coll, AA 1974; Saginaw Val State Coll, BA, 1976. **Career:** Saginaw MI, city directory enumerator 1946-71; Field Enterprises Inc, sales re p 1964-66; Saginaw, sch census taker city & state 1965-67; Saginaw Gen Hosp, ward clk 1967; Comm Action Comm, comm aide 1967-69; Dept Model Cities, team capt; Saginaw Multi-Purpose Serv Ctr, information referral splst 1971-76; Our Image Inc, fdr, pres 1976-; Tri City Service Employer Redevelopment, Jobs for Progress, career resources assistant, career resources administrator, currently. **Orgs:** Bd Saginaw Co Social Serv Club 1974-75; Greater Williams Temple Ch of God in Christ 1934-; personal evangelist 1963; NAACP 1935-; chairlady ch membership drive 1965-75; bd mem CAC 1967; worked in drives for United Fund, March of Dimes, Cancer, Sickle Cell; chairlady Muscular Dyst 1961-75; bd mem, coordntr E Side MD Drive 1974-75; v pres Police Comm Relations 1973-76; chairlady Human Resources League Women Voters 1974-75; pres Saginaw City Council PTA 1975-76. **Honors/Awds:** Comm Serv Award Professional & Bus Women 1972; Woman of Yr Zeta Omega Phi Beta Sor Inc 1975; Honor Dinner Greater Williams Temple Ch of God in Christ 1975; Sailors Regional Award Week 1964; Child Evangelism Tchrs Cert 1963; Am Legion Post 500 Humanitarian Award 1975; treas 8th Dist Co Rep Com; candidate for Saginaw City Council (first black woman to run) 1975-77; Wrote book of Poetry - title prolonged (overdue) copyright, 1982-; Religous Tracks, printed, 1984-. **Business Addr:** 220 N 7 St, Saginaw, MI 48607.

FERRELL, TYRA
Actress. **Personal:** Born in Houston, TX; daughter of Rachel Johnson; married Don Carlos Johnson, Apr 9, 1992. **Educ:** University of Texas at Austin, acting. **Career:** Actress, Broadway experience includes: The Lady and Her Music, Dreamgirls; television experience includes: Thirtysomething; The Bronx Zoo; Better Off Dead, 1993; films include: Jungle Fever, 1990; Boyz in the Hood, 1991; White Men Can't Jump, 1992; School Daze, 1988; Equinox, 1992; Poetic Justice. **Business Phone:** (310)550-3982.

FEWELL, RICHARD
English instructor, government official (retired). **Personal:** Born Feb 2, 1937, Rock Hill, SC; son of Laura Steele Fewell (deceased) and Thomas Fewell (deceased); married Geraldine Whitted (died 1996); children: Renee Lorraine, Ritchard Gerald. **Educ:** Univ of Bridgeport, BA (Magna Cum Laude) 1976, MA 1980. **Career:** US Postal Service, mail classification & requirements/postal services, until 1992; Univ of Bridgeport, part-time English instructor, 1994-; Sacred Heart Univ, Fairfield, CT, adjunct instructor; Housatonic Community & Technical College, adjunct instructor, 1996-. **Orgs:** Pres 1975-76, mem 1975-, Alpha Sigma Lambda; bd mem NAACP 1976-; Frank Silvera Writer's Workshop (Harlem) 1978-90; bureau chief Fairfield County; INNER CITY Newspaper (New Haven and Statewide CT), 1990-; freelance writer Fairfield County Advocate, contributing editor Connecticut Update 1982-83; bd of dirs Bridgeport Arts Council 1982-85; comm mem Action for Bridgeport Comm Develop 1984-86; founding mem New Bridge Ensemble 1986-; editor Natl Alliance of Postal & Federal Employees Newsletter/Local 808; African American Family Forum 1990-91; New England Foundation of the Arts, Advisory Committee, 1992; advisory committee, Artists Trust, Cambridge MA, 1992-. **Honors/Awds:** Bert & Katya Gilden Memorial Short Story Awd 1975; 1st prize article in Writer's Digest Creative Writing Contest 1977; Literature Awd Connecticut Commn on the Arts 1984; published in The Black Scholar, The Greenfield Review, Callaloo, Obsidian, The Anthology of Magazine Verse & Yearbook of Amer Poetry, The South Carolina Review, Okike (Nigeria), others; author "The Other Side of Everything;" Heritage Award/Arts & Humanities, Alpha Kappa Alpha Sorority 1987; actor with Dot Playhouse, played role of "Rev Sykes" in To Kill a Mockingbird 1988; poetry readings (own work) with Stan Nishimura Performance Arts/New Haven, CT 1988-89; excerpts from unpublished novel published in Mwendo (Iowa), Obsidian (NC) & Beanfeast (CT); Grant, Connecticut Commission on the Arts, 1990; Nguzo Saba Award, Kwanzaa Seven Productions, 1996. **Special Achievements:** Played Lead Role in Independent Film, "Good Morning," premiered at Yale University, 1991; play "Coon Dog," was a finalist in Theodore Ward prize for playwriting, 1991; play "Hats" was in five finalist in Theodore Ward prize, 1997-98. **Military Serv:** USAF 1955-61. **Home Addr:** 89A Yaremich Dr, Bridgeport, CT 06606, (203)372-1774.

FIELDER, CECIL GRANT
Professional baseball player. **Personal:** Born Sep 21, 1963, Los Angeles, CA; married Stacey; children: Prince, Ceclyn. **Educ:** Univ of Nevada, Las Vegas, NV, attended. **Career:** Toronto Blue Jays, infielder, 1985-86, 1986-88; Detroit Tigers, infielder, 1990-96; New York Yankees, 1996-97; Anaheim Angels, 1997-. **Honors/Awds:** American League All-Star Team, 1990. **Business Addr:** Professional Baseball Player, Anaheim Angels, PO Box 2000, Anaheim, CA 92803.

FIELDER, FRED CHARLES
Educational Administrator. **Personal:** Born Jun 16, 1933, Hattiesburg, MS; son of Quinnie White Fielder and Ben Fielder; married Vivian Johnson; children: Fred Charles, Jr. **Educ:** Tougaloo Coll, BS (magna cum laude), 1956; Meharry Med Coll, DDS 1960; Hubbard Hosp, intern 1960-61; Univ of MI, MS in Oper Dent 1964; MIT, post grad 1966. **Career:** Meharry Med Coll Dept of Oper Dent, instr 1961-63, asst prof 1964-66, assoc prof 1967-74; Meharry Med Coll Schl of Dent, asst dean beginning 1968, executive associate dean, beginning 1989, interim dean, 1992-; Meharry Med Coll Dent Clinic, supt 1971; Meharry Med Coll Dept Oper Dent, prof/chmn/interim dean, dean, 1974-. **Orgs:** Operative Dentistry of Amer Assoc of Dent Schls; comm mem Manpower & Aux of Amer Assn of Dent Schs 1969-70; councl Intl Assn of Dent Res 1969-73; consul NC St Bd of Dent Exam 1970; vice pres Capital City Dent Soc 1972-74, pres 1974-76; vice pres Omicron-Omicron Chap of Omicron Kappa Upsilon Honor Dent Soc 1970-72, past pres 1972-74; past pres Kappa Sigma Pi Honor Soc 1961-62; past zone vice pres Pan TN Dent Assn 1968-75, state vice pres 1979; clinical consult for commn Dent Accred of Amer Dental Assn 1979-; consult the Quarterly Journal of the Natl Dental Assn. **Honors/Awds:** Most Outstanding Soph Dent Student Meharry Med Coll 1958; Chi Delta Mu Awards 1958; Meth Scholarship Award; Mosby Schol Bk Award; Caulk Prize 1959; Meth Shol Award High Sch Aver for 3 years 1959; number 1 ranking student 1960; honor student 1960; Acad of Dent Med Award 1960; Acad of Gold Foil Award 1960; Donley H Turpin Mem Award 1960; Mizzy Award in Crown & Bridge 1960; Pan TN Dent Assn Award 1960; Jos Frank Dent Award 1960; Mosby Book Award 1960; Caulk Prize 1960; Nashville Dent Supply Prize 1960; Snyder Dent Prize 1960; Alpha Omega Award 1960; Fellow United Health Found 1963; dean's list Tougaloo Coll 1953-55; pres of class 1952-56; Valedictorian Royal St HS 1952; Recog & plaque one of l00 most valuable employees, Meharry Med Coll 1975;Dedication Recip Meharrian yearbook 1964; Recog plaque Growth & Devel Meharry Coll l971; Outstanding Faculty of the Year Natl Alumni Assn l988. **Business Addr:** Dean, School of Dentistry, Meharry Medical College, 1005 D B Todd Blvd, Department Oper Dent, Nashville, TN 37208.

FIELDING, HERBERT ULYSSES
State legislator. **Personal:** Born Jul 6, 1923, Charleston, SC; son of Sadie E Gaillard Fielding and Julius P L Fielding; married Thelma Erenne Stent; children: Julius PL II, Herbert Stent, Frederick Augustus. **Educ:** WV State Coll, BS 1948. **Career:** SC House of Representatives, rep 1971-74, 1983-84; SC State Senate, senator, 1985-; Fielding Home for Funerals, vice president, funeral director. **Orgs:** Former member, SC Comm Vocational Rehabilitation; Trident Chamber of Commerce; USC Budget Bd; Bd McClennan Banks Hosp; SC Human Affairs Comm; SC Coastal Counc, 1987-; chair, Charleston County Senate Delegation, 1989; pres Robert Gould Shaw Boys Club; bd, McClennan Banks Hosp; Trident Council on Alcoholism; Omega Psi Phi Frat; founder & past co chmn Charleston County Political Action Comm. **Honors/Awds:** First recipient Chas Business & Professional Mens Assn Man of Year Awd 1966; 1st Black elected to SC House since Reconstruction 1970; Silver Beaver Awd Boy Scouts of Amer 1971; Mu Alpha Chap Man of Year Awd 1972; SC Legislative Black Caucus Awd 1975; Harvey Gantt Triumph Award, 1985; Citizens Comm of Charleston County Award, 1985; Outstanding Legislator Award, 1987; Royal Arch Masons Award, 1988; SC Farm Cooperatives Award, 1988. **Military Serv:** US Army in American & European Theaters, 1943-46; 500th QM Co. **Business Addr:** State Legislator, Gressette Senate Office Building, Suite 610, PO Box 142, Columbia, SC 29202.

FIELDS, ALVA DOTSON
Educational administrator (retired). **Personal:** Born May 29, 1929, Athens, TN; daughter of Estella Vaught Dotson and Walter E Dotson; married James Henry Fields III; children: Gordon, James, Sherri. **Educ:** Knoxville Coll TN, AB (cum laude) 1958; Univ of TN, MSSW 1966, additional work. **Career:** Chattanooga State Tech Comm Coll, dept head 1978-94, coordinator of minority affairs, counselor; Florence AL City Sch, sch social worker 1976-78; Univ of N AL, instr 1976-78; TN Dept of Human Services, dir (1st black in TN) 1973-75, asst dir 1968-73, caseworker/field supr 1958-68. **Orgs:** Curriculum consultant on ethnic content Univ of N AL UMk-m,; panelist TN Governor's Conf on Families 1980; Title XX Regional Adv Com 1979-82; Comm Serv of Greater Chattanooga Inc 1979-82; bd mem Metro Council of Comm Serv 1980-91; mem bd Chattanooga Area Urban League Inc, Family & Childrens Serv Inc, Presbyterian Homes of Chattanooga, VENTURE, Friends of Black Children; chmn Consortium on Adolescent Pregnancy, Venture Task Force on Adolescent Pregnancy; mem Governors Task Force on Healthy Children, Infant Mortality Subcommittee; mem TN Child Welfare Serv Comm; pres TN Conf on Social Welfare 1984, Delta Sigma Theta; vice pres, Chatt Links, Inc, 1989-91; advisory bd, Univ of Chattanooga SE Institute for Educ in theatre, 1989-; TN Conf on Social Welfare; Natl Assn of Social Workers; presnt, Metropolitan Council of Community Services, 1991-; president, The Chattanooga Links Inc, 1991-. **Honors/Awds:** Nominated Social Worker of the Year, Muscle Shoals NASW 1974; Big Brothers-Big Sisters Internat, Chattanooga Chapter 1975; TN NASW Social Worker of the Year 1984; Delta Sigma Theta Hall of Fame for Outstanding Community Serv 1985; recognized by Knoxville Links Inc as one of Knoxville's Black Achievers 1986; Outstanding AA Woman of Influence, Girls Club of Chatt, 1996; Chattanooga Woman of Distinction, 1996.

FIELDS, BRENDA JOYCE
Educational administrator. **Personal:** Born May 4, Tacoma, WA; daughter of Betty Mewborn. **Educ:** Ohio State University, BA, psychology, 1981; Columbus Chamber of Commerce, Leadership Columbus, leadership certificate, 1989; United Way, Project Diversity, board development certificate, 1989; Ohio State University, College of Business, School of Public Policy & Management, MA, 1994. **Career:** Columbus Recreation & Parks Department, dance instructor, choreographer, 1980-90; Ohio State University, public inquiries assistant, 1983-93, asst dir of student programs, 1993-. **Orgs:** Leadership Columbus, Chamber of Commerce, bd of trustees, pred elect, 1995, class representative, Board Development Committee, chair, Program Committee, chair, Dymanics of Human Relations Session, chair, The Irene Radcliff Minority Scholarship Committee, Resource Development Committee, 1989-; National Assault Prevention Center, board of trustees, 1992-; Ohio State University, CCS, Truth-Douglass Society, co-vice pres, 1992-; United Negro College Fund Walk-a-thon Committee, Ohio State University, 1992-; Delta Sigma Theta Sorority, Inc, Rosemont Committee, chair, 1990-; Ohio State University, Women of Color Consortium, 1984-; Ohio State Univ, Ohio Staters Inc, faculty advisor; Greater Columbus Chamber of Commerce, mem, downtown council program; Ohio Staters Inc, faculty advisor; Walter & Marion English Awards Committee of United Way. **Honors/Awds:** Ohio Unions, Employee of the Quarter, spring 1990; Ohio State Univ, Inducted into Council of Honor, African Amer Student Services, 1994; Honorary Member, Sphinx Senior Honoraries, The Ohio State University, 1994. **Special Achievements:** Featured in Blue Chip Profile. **Business Addr:** Executive Director, Eldon W Ward YMCA, 130 Woodland Ave., Columbus, OH 43203, (614)252-3166.

FIELDS, CLEO
Congressman. **Personal:** Born Nov 22, 1962, Port Allen, LA; son of Isidore and Alice; married Debra Horton; children: one. **Educ:** Southern Univ, BA, JD. **Career:** State of Louisiana, senator, 1986-92; US House of Representatives, congressman, 1992-96; Clinton-Gore presidential campaign, volunteer sr advisor, 1996. **Honors/Awds:** Youngest state senator when elected. **Business Addr:** 700 N. 10th St., Ste. 210, Baton Rouge, LA 70802.

FIELDS, DEXTER L.
Psychiatrist, educator. **Personal:** Born Oct 12, 1944, Detroit, MI; married Margaret L Betts. **Educ:** Wayne State University, BA, 1967; Wayne State Univ, College of Medicine, MD, 1972. **Career:** Operation Hope, Community Mental Hlth Ctr, internal medicine resident, consult psychiatrist, 1976-77,1980; Detroit Bd of Education, consult, 1979-; Recorder's Ct Psychiatric Clinic, consult, 1980-; Kirwood Gen Hosp & Hutzel Hosp, staff physician; Kirwood Mental Hlth Ctr, consult psychiatrist, 1976-80; NE Guidance Substance Abuse Ctr, consult psychiatrist, 1974-76; Boston City Hosp, psychiatric resident, 1972-73; Detroit Psychiatric Inst, psychiatric resident, 1973-75; clinical fellow in psychiatry, Harvard College, 1972-74. **Orgs:** Black Psychiatrists Forum of Boston, 1972-73; Black Psychiatrists of Am, 1973; Solomon Fuller, fellow, 1974. **Business Addr:** 17117 W 9 Mile Rd, Ste 1221, Southfield, MI 48075.

FIELDS, EARL GRAYSON
Consultant, housing & community development. **Personal:** Born Jun 18, 1935, Brooklyn, NY; son of Queena Rachel Grayson Fields and Ralph Allen Fields; married Pauline Hay; children: Cheryl, Mark, Leslie. **Educ:** CCNY, BA 1968. **Career:** US Bureau of Customs, customs inspector 1963-68; US Dept of HUD, multi family/coll housing rep 1968-72, model city rep 1972-74, program mgr 1974-78; US Dept of HUD, Santa Ana CA, manager 1978-94. **Orgs:** Vice chmn Orange County Urban League 1981-82; treasurer/co chmn Bowers Museum Black Cultural Council 1982-; mem Orange County Master Chorale 1983-; chairman policy bd, Los Angeles Federal Executive Board 1988-92; National Assn of Black County Officals. **Honors/Awds:** Cert Assoc of Minority Real Estate Devel 1980; Integrity Knowledge Serv Inland Empire Mortgage Bankers Assn 1981; Volunteer Awd United Way of Orange Cty 1982; Patriotic Serv US Dept of Treasury 1984; US Dept of HUD, Region IX, Manager of the Year, 1989-90. **Business Addr:** EGP & Associates, PO Box 11691, Santa Ana, CA 92711-1691.

FIELDS, EDWARD E.
Cleric. **Personal:** Born Jun 24, 1918, Kirkwood, MO; married Marshan; children: Marshan, Edward. **Educ:** Lincoln Univ, BS 1940; KS State Teachers Coll, MS 1947; Univ of Kansas City, Univ of MO, NYU; Univ of KS, DEd 1959. **Career:** Indus arts teacher, 1945; Lincoln High School & RT Coles Vocational High School, coordinator of Co-op Occupational Educ 1946-47; MO Public School, elementary principal, 1947-56; Coll of St Teresa, instructor, 1959-65; Central Jr High School, principal, 1962-71; Dept Career & Continued Educ, dir 1971-72; Div Urban Edn, asst supt 1972-74; assoc supt instr, 1974-75; School Dist of Kansas City, act supt 1975-78; ret school dist 1979; 5th Dist NW MO Annual Conf AME Church, minister. **Orgs:** Mem, MO State Teachers Assn; bd dir, Kansas City Teachers Credit Union; natl, state local Elementary Principal Assns; past chmn Kansas City Teachers Ins Com; life mem NEA; mem Phi Delta Kappa; Natl Assn for Supervision & Curriculum Devel; MO Assn for Supervision & Curriculum Devel; Natl & State Assn of Secondary Sch Prin; Intl Reading Assn; Intl Indus Arts & Voc Educ Assn; Am Assn of Sch Adminstr; exec bd Kansas City School Admin Assn mem Natl Alliance of Black Educators; Conf of Minority Public Admins; mem KCMO-TV Minority Relations Bd. **Honors/Awds:** Lecturer; Various Citations for contributions as educator and contributions to BSA; Ordained Am Meth Episcopal Minister. **Military Serv:** USN.

FIELDS, EWAUGH FINNEY
Academic administrator. **Educ:** Kentucky State College, Frankfort, KY, BS, mathematics, magna cum laude; West Virginia University, Morgantown, WV, MA, secondary education; Temple University, Philadelphia, PA, EdD, mathematics education. **Career:** US Armed Forces Institute, Yokohama, Japan, algebra instructor, 1956-57; Radio Corporation of America, Camden, NJ, class C engineer, 1959-63; Franklin Institute Laboratories, Philadelphia, PA, research mathematician, 1963; Cinnaminson Junior/Senior High School, teacher and mathematics department head, 1963-69; Rutgers Univ, Camden, NJ, adjunct instructor, 1967; Temple Univ, Philadelphia, PA, staff assistant, 1967; Gloucester County College, Sewell, NJ, adjunct lecturer, 1968-69; Drexel Univ, Philadelphia, PA, assistant professor of mathematics, 1969-72, associate professor of mathematics, 1972-76, assistant vice president for academic affairs, 1973-76, professor of mathematics, 1986-, dean, Evening and University college, 1986-92; Univ of Washington, Seattle, WA, vice president for minority affairs, 1976-77, associate professor of mathematics education, 1976-77; Univ of the District of Columbia, Washington, DC, professor of mathematics, 1981-86, dean, the University College, 1978-86, interim coordinator for academic affairs, 1983-84, acting provost and vice president for academic affairs, 1984-85; Univ of Nairobi, Nairobi, Kenya, exchange professor, 1985; Drexel University, Outreach and Access, vice provost, 1992-96, prof of math, dean emeritus, currently. **Orgs:** National Council of Teachers of Mathematics; National Institute of Science; American Society for Engineering Education; American Association for the Advancement of Science; American Council on Education; American Association of Higher Education; National Association of Remedial and Developmental Education; board of directors, Philadelphia Business Corporation, 1987-. **Honors/Awds:** Cost Reduction Incentive Award, University College, Drexel University, 1988; Pioneer Award, National Action Council for Minorities in Engineering, 1985; Drexel University Black Faculty and Staff Award for Outstanding Service, 1985; "Deficiencies in Basic Mathematics Skills as Identified by the University College's/UDC Placement Testing Progress," Abstract, Proceedings of the Forty Third Annual Meeting of the National Institute of Science, Houston, TX, 1981; "Some Basic Mathematics Skills Gaps," Proceedings of the Forty Second Annual Meeting of the National Institute of Science, Little Rock, AR, 1980; Meritorious Service Award, The National Science Foundation, 1982. Foundation, 1982. **Military Serv:** US Army, Women's Army Corps, lieutenant, 1954-57. **Business Addr:** Professor of Mathematics and Dean Emeritus, Drexel University, 32nd and Chestnut Sts, Philadelphia, PA 19104.

FIELDS, INEZ C.
Attorney. **Personal:** Born Mar 13, Hampton, VA; married F C Scott; children: Fred G Scott. **Educ:** Boston Univ Law Sch, LlD 1921. **Career:** Atty. **Orgs:** Life mem NAACP; hon mem Hampton Woman's Serv League; mem Am Assn of Univ Women; Catherine Fields Lit Club; Women's Forum; Old Dominion Bar Assn; VA State Bar; Mt Olive Tent Lodge; Third Bapt Ch; Harry T Burleigh Comm Chorus. **Honors/Awds:** Recip plaque King St Comm Cntr in apprec of outstanding comm svc; mem 25 yrs Delta Sigma Theta Sor; plaque significant comm svc.

FIELDS, KENNETH
Basketball player. **Personal:** Born Feb 9, 1962, Iowa City, IA. **Educ:** UCLA, BA 1984. **Career:** Milwaukee Bucks, 1984-87, Los Angeles Clippers, 1987-88; CBA: Grand Rapids, Tulsa (currently). **Honors/Awds:** Ranked 6th among UCLA's all-time scoring leaders; started 1st 16 games of his freshman season at UCLA; led the Bruins in field goal percentage.

FIELDS, KIM
Actress. **Personal:** Born May 12, 1969, New York, NY. **Educ:** Pepperdine Univ, broadcast journalism. **Career:** Actress; TV series include Baby I'm Back; The Facts of Life; Living Single, Fox-TV; recorded Dear Michael, He Loves Me He Loves Me Not; starred in several Los Angeles stage productions including, Fight the Good Fight; has appeared in numerous commercials for Slim Fast. **Orgs:** West Angeles Church of God in Christ; American Federation of Television and Radio Artists; Screen Actors Guild. **Honors/Awds:** Youth In Film Award, Best Actress; NAACP Image Award, Best Actress, 1985; Justice Dept Role Model of the Year Award, 1987. **Business Addr:** Actress, Living Single, c/o Fox-TV, 10201 W Pico Blvd, Los Angeles, CA 90035, (310)277-2211.

FIELDS, M. JOAN
Association executive. **Personal:** Born Jul 15, 1934, New Middletown, OH; married Stanley; children: Veta Gabrielle, Scott Grant. **Educ:** Cntrl State Coll, BS 1952-56; Wayne State Univ, 1967-69. **Career:** Neighborhood Serv Organ Relocation Prog, dir 1969-; Grabo Corp, cons, trainer; Detroit Hsng Commn Social Serv Prog 1973-74; MSW, Comm Social Work Sequence. **Orgs:** Mem Program Planning Com, Detroit YWCA 1966-67; mem Urban Alliance of Metro Detroit 1968-69; Assn of Black Social Workers 1969-; field instr, grad & undergrad students from 6 diff U, in social work 1970-; mem bd dirs Professional Skills Alliance 1971-; Nat Pub Relations Council 1974; NAHRO 1974; mem bd dirs Don Bosco Home for Boys 1974-; mem bd Neighborhood Institutional Agency Council 1974-. **Honors/Awds:** Recip Outstanding Comm Serv Award, FAAYM, 1967. **Business Addr:** 909 Woodland, Detroit, MI 48211.

FIELDS, MARK LEE
Professional football player. **Personal:** Born Nov 9, 1972, Los Angeles, CA. **Educ:** Washington State. **Career:** New Orleans Saints, linebacker, 1995-. **Special Achievements:** 1st round/ 13th overall, NFL draft pick, 1995. **Business Addr:** Professional Football Player, New Orleans Saints, 5800 Airline Hwy, Metairie, LA 70003, (504)733-0255.

FIELDS, RICHARD A.
Behavioral health care condultant. **Personal:** Born Apr 18, 1950, Washington, DC; married Sylvia Crisp; children: Kirstyn, Richard. **Educ:** Hampton Inst, BA 1971; Duke Univ Sch of Medicine, MD 1975; Duke Univ, resident in Psychiatry, 1975-78. **Career:** Dept of Psychiatry & Neurology AUS, chief 1979-80; Neuse Mental Health Ctr, clinical dir 1980-82; GA Regional Hospital of Atlanta, superintendent 1982-96; Fields & Associates (Behavioral Health Care Consulting), CEO & sr psychiatric consultant, 1996-. **Orgs:** Vice chair Council of Psychiatric Services, 1994-; pres Black Psychiatrists of Amer 1984-88; president, GA Psychiatric Assoc 1992-93; pres GA Chap Amer Assoc of Admin Psychiatrists 1987-88; Omega Psi Phi Fraternity; NAACP; AME Church; fellow of the American Psychiatric Assns, 1991. **Honors/Awds:** Psychiatrist of the Year, Georgia Psychiatric Physician Association, 1994-95. **Military Serv:** US Army, capt 2 yrs; Army Commendation Medal 1980. **Home Addr:** 3610 Idlecreek Dr, Decatur, GA 30034.

FIELDS, SAMUEL BENNIE
Business executive. **Personal:** Born Dec 24, 1925, St Louis, MO; married Helen Lucille Brown; children: Sharon Hall. **Educ:** St Louis Music & Arts Univ, BA Music Instrumental 1949; Weaver School of Real Estate, Diploma 1950; Mensh School of Real Estate, Cert 1970. **Career:** Model Cities Commiss DC, planning chmn 1969-75; New Model Cities Housing Devel Corp, pres, chmn 1971-73; DC Devel Co, vice pres 1974-77; DC Government, comm1976-; Sam Fields & Assoc, pres. **Orgs:** Planning chmn Shaw Project Committee DC 1975-79; chmn of bd Neighborhood Devel Ctr UPO #1 1975-77; mem East Central Civic Assoc DC. **Military Serv:** USN musician 3/c 1944-46; Amer Theatre Med & Pres Commendations 1946.

FIELDS, SAVOYNNE MORGAN
Education administrator, counselor. **Personal:** Born May 26, 1950, Rocky Mount, NC; daughter of Hazel C Brown Morgan and Charlie Morgan; divorced. **Educ:** North Carolina A&T State Univ, BS Psych 1972, MS Guidance 1979. **Career:** Public Library High Point North Carolina, library asst III 1975-79; Louisiana State Univ Eunice, counselor, coord 1979-82; Lousiana State Univ at Eunice, counselor & minority recruiter, 1982-88; Lousiana State Univ at Eunice, recruiter/career placement coord, 1988-. **Orgs:** LASAP 1979-, LAHSRP 1982-; coord LSUE's Black History Activities 1982-; founding mem LADE 1982-; mem NAUW 1983-; mem ACPA 1984-, AACD 1984; mem NAUW Historian 1986-; mem & past recording & corresponding sec, Chat-A-While, Inc. **Honors/Awds:** 1st Black Recruiter Louisiana State Univ at Eunice 1982-; Matron of the Year Little Zion Baptist Church 1984; Little Zion BC Matrons President's Awd 1985; LADE Developmental Educ of LSUE 1986; recognized by Chat-A-While Club as Outstanding Educator, 1987; selected as Outstanding Developmental Educ at LSUE by LADE 1988; selected NAUW Woman of the Year, 1988. **Business Addr:** Recruiter/Career Placement Coord, Louisiana State Univ at Eunice, Career and Placement Center, PO Box 1129, Eunice, LA 70535.

FIELDS, STANLEY
Insurance agent. **Personal:** Born Sep 12, 1930, Detroit; married Mamie Joan Grant; children: Beta Gabrielle, Scott Grant. **Educ:** Wayne State U, BA 1956, MA 1960. **Career:** Detroit Bd Edn, art instr 1956-; EIT, liaison person 1974; Mayor's Com for Human Resources Devel, project FAST 1967; Am Mutual Life Ins Co, insagt 1970-2; Alexander Hamilton Life Ins Co, agt, registered rep 1970-74; Multivest Inestment Co, rep 1974-75; N Am Life & Casualty Co, agt 1975; World Wide Cycling Assn, Detroit area, dir 1974-75; independent auctioneer 1974-; direct sales, distributorship & world trade 1970-; sub-contractor, hardwood floors 1942-75. **Orgs:** Consult Model Cities Educ Component 1972-; bd dirs Uplift-Harper House 1970-71; Metro Distributors 1972-; bd dirs Detroit Pub Schs Art Tchrs Club 1972-73; vp, bd dirs Wayne State Univ Art Educ Alumni 1973-74; treas 1st Nighter 1970-; mem Friends of Belle Isle 1974-; Chequemates 1970-73; The Set Inc 1955-75;Motor City Yacht Club 1974-; charter mem Family Motor Coach Assn, Detroit chpt, 1974-; judge Detroit Edison MI Chronicle Lighting Contest 1972, Block Club Beautification Contest 1975. **Honors/Awds:** Mem X-Country Team, Wayne, 1948; lectr 1969, 70 Univ Detroit; individual reord holder, Champion X-Country Run, Detroit Pub Schs 1974. **Military Serv:** AUS 1952-54. **Business Addr:** 10235 W Mc Nichols Rd, Detroit, MI 48221.

FIELDS, VICTOR HUGO
Chemist. **Personal:** Born Jul 11, 1907, Milwaukee, WI; divorced; children: Victor Hugo. **Educ:** Fisk U, BA 1931, MA 1935; Marquette U, PhD 1944. **Career:** Fisk U, instr 1935-41, asst prof 1941-57; Kelmer Labs, Milwaukee, consult 1944-46; FL A&M Coll, prof, dept chmn 1947-49; Hampton Inst, prof, chemistry, dept chmn natl sci & math 1949-, dir div sci & math, chem dept chmn 1967-73. **Orgs:** Mem VA Acad Sci; AAAS; Nat Inst Sci; mem Beta Kappa Chi; Omega Psi Phi; Ch of Christ; Bachelor Benedict Club, Hampton.

FIELDS, WILLIAM I., JR. (IKE)
Association executive. **Personal:** Born May 4, 1944, Frankfort, KY; son of Kathryn Fields and William I Fields, Sr; married Faye Ford, Mar 29, 1974. **Educ:** Kentucky State Coll, Frankfort KY, BS, 1966 Univ of Louisville, Louisville, KY, MS l971. **Career:** Community Action Commn, Cincinnati, OH, coordinator field service, l971-72; Community Council, Cincinnati, OH, planning assoc, l972-74; Community Chest, Cincinnati, OH, assoc dir planning, l974-77; United Community Planning Corp, Boston, MA, assoc exec vice pres, l978-81; ATE Mgmt, Ridayh, Saudi Arabia, dir admin/personnel, l981-83; United Way of America, Washington, DC, vice pres/dir, l983-90, regional vice president, 1990-. **Orgs:** Vice pres, Health Planning Council of Greater Boston, l979-81; mem, Natl Forum Black Public Admin, l984-86; mem, Big Brothers of Greater Washington, l985-86; mem, Org for New Equality, l985-; member, Literacy Volunteers of Illinois 1990-. **Honors/Awds:** Outstanding Young Men in America, US Jaycees, l980; Henry M Smith Award, 1990; United Way of America, Quest for Excellence Award, 1992. **Military Serv:** US Army, spec-4, 1967-69. **Business Addr:** Regional Vice President, United Way of America, 560 W Lake St, #624, Chicago, IL 60661-1420.

FIERCE, HUGHLYN F.
Bank executive. **Personal:** Born in New York, NY; son of Helen Fierce and Millus Fierce; married Jewel; children: Holly, Heather, Brooke. **Educ:** Morgan State Coll, BA econ; NY U, MBA finance; NYU, APC finance. **Career:** Chase Manhattan Bank, NYC, vice pres & commercial loan officer, joined bank in 1963; Freedom Nat Bank of NY, pres 1974-77; Chase Manhattan Bank, vp 1972, svp, 1984. **Honors/Awds:** Honorary Doctor of Laws, Morgan State University.

FIERCE, MILFRED C.
Educator. **Personal:** Born Jul 6, 1937, Brooklyn. **Educ:** Wagner Coll, BA, MS; Columbia U, MA, MPhil, PhD. **Career:** Vassar Coll, dir Black Studies 1969-71; Hunter Coll, prof, 1973-81; Brooklyn College (CUNY), professor, 1982-. **Orgs:** Apptd exec dir Assn of Black Found Exec Inc 1976; apptd NY St Coll Proficiency Exam Com in African & Afro-Am History, fall 1976; apptd research dir Study Commn on US Policy toward South Africa 1979; mem African-Am Tchrs Assn; African Heritage Studies Assn; Assn for Study of Afro- Amer Life & History; mem Am Historical Assn; Orgn of Am Historians. **Honors/Awds:** So Hist Assn recipient, NDEA 1965; EPDA 1969; delegate Intl Congress of Africanists 1973; recipient Natl Endowment for the Humanities Fellowship, City Univ of NY, 1976. **Military Serv:** AUS 1960-63. **Business Addr:** 2900 Bedford Ave, Brooklyn, NY 11210.

FIGURES, DEON JUNIEL
Professional football player. **Personal:** Born Jan 20, 1970, Bellflower, CA. **Educ:** Univ of Colorado, bachelor's degree in sociology/criminology, 1993. **Career:** Pittsburgh Steelers, defensive back, 1993-96; Jacksonville Jaguars, 1997-. **Honors/ Awds:** Jim Thorpe Award, 1993. **Business Addr:** Professional Football Player, Jacksonville Jaguars, One Stadium Place, Jacksonville, FL 32202, (904)633-6000.

FIGURES, MICHAEL. See Obituaries section.

FIGURES, THOMAS H.
Attorney. **Personal:** Born Aug 6, 1944, Mobile, AL; son of Augusta Mitchell Figures and Coleman Figures; married Janice; children: Nora, Thomas Anthony. **Educ:** Bishop State Jr Coll, Assoc in Science 1964; AL State Univ, Bachelor of Science 1966; IN Univ, MBA 1968; Univ of IL, Juris Doctor 1971. **Career:** Exxon Corp, atrny & asst sec 1971-75; Westchester Cty, NY, asst dist atrny 1975-76; Mobile Cnty AL, asst dist Atrny 1976-78; Southern Dist of AL,asst US attrny 1978-85; Figures, Ludgood and Figures, partner 1985-87; Thomas H. Figures, attorney at law l987; municipal judge l988-; referee, Mobile County Circuit Court l988-89. **Orgs:** State Bars AL & NY, Fdrl Bars, US Supreme Ct US Court of Appeals, US Dist Court, Bar Assns AL State Bar, Natl Bar Assn Mobile Cnty AL; vice chrmn Mobile Cnty Dem Conf 1976-78, chrmn 1989-; Mobile Comm Action, Inc 1976-80; grad Leadership Mobile 1978; NAACP; Omega Psi Phi; Natl Assn of Bond Attorneys l985-. **Honors/Awds:** Outstanding Young Men of Amer 1973; Community Ldrs & Noteworthy Americans 1977; Outstanding Comm Serv Awd 1977; Christian Comm Award 1984; Citizen of the Year, Omega Psi Phi Fraterity, 1990. **Home Addr:** 6120 Palomino Dr N, Mobile, AL 36693. **Business Addr:** 212 S Lawrence St, Mobile, AL 36602, (334)433-0416.

FIGURES, VIVIAN DAVIS
State senator. **Personal:** widoWed. **Career:** Perfect Print, Inc, pres, owner; Mobile AL, city councilwoman, 1993-97; AL State Senate, senator, 1997-. **Orgs:** Democratic Natl Comm, member-at-large; Democratic Natl Conv, delegate, 1984, 1988; AL St Democratic Exec Comm, elected mem, 1986-; AL New South Coalition; State of AL Hwy Safety Comm; AL Alcoholic Beverage Control Bd, advisory bd; several Senate Committees; Al Women's Comm; Metropolitan Mobile YMCA, Big Brothers/Big Sisters Prog, bd mem; Homeless Coalition of Mibile, Inc, bd mem; Drug Ed Council, bd mem; Green Grove Missionary Bapt Ch. **Honors/Awds:** Minority Business Development Ctr, Business Woman of the Year, 1986.

FILER, KELVIN DEAN
Attorney. **Personal:** Born Nov 25, 1955, Los Angeles, CA; son of Blondell Filer and Maxcy Filer; divorced; children: Brynne Ashley, Kree Donalyn. **Educ:** Univ of CA Santa Cruz, BA 1977; Univ of CA Berkeley, JD 1980. **Career:** Deputy state public defender 1980-82; private practice, atty 1982-; Municipal Court of Compton CA, commissioner. **Orgs:** Compton Chamber of Comm, 1st vice pres; mem bd of dirs Compton Chamber of Commerce 1983-; mem South Central Bar Assn; Compton Branch of the NAACP, life mem; CA State Bar; American Bar Assn; Natl Bar Assn; CA Assn of Black Lawyers; Pres, Compton Chamber of Commerce 1988-89; Compton Unified School District, board of trustees, 1981-93. **Honors/ Awds:** Successfully argued case before CA Supreme Court resulting in a unanimous opinion (People vs Taylor 1982 31 Cal 3d 483). **Business Addr:** Commissioner, Municipal Court of Compton, 200 W Compton Blvd, Compton, CA 90220.

FILLYAW, LEONARD DAVID
Educator, law enforcement official, association executive. **Personal:** Born Jun 25, 1939, Brooklyn, NY; son of Rose Rosalind Fillyaw and John David Fillyaw; married Willie M Tate Fillyaw, Jan 26, 1964; children: Sharon, Denise, Dr Tyrone. **Educ:** John Jay College Criminal Justice, AA, 1972, BA, 1973; Dowling College, MEd, 1980. **Career:** Brooklyn Union Gas Co, co representative, 1962-64; New York City Transit Police, police officer, 1966-; New York City Police Academy, police instructor, Social Science Department, currently; Central Islip School District, teacher, 1979-. **Orgs:** Suffolk County Black History Association, vice pres, Membership Committee, 1983-; Guardians Police Association, 1964-; NAACP, 1984-; UNCF, 1986-; Southern Poverty Law Center, 1984-; Minority Black Catholics, St John of God, pres. **Honors/Awds:** New York City Transit Police, four Meritorious Medals, two Honorable Mentions, Unit Citation Award. **Special Achievements:** Essay, ''Juvenile Deliquency: A Sociological Approach for a Cure,'' New York City Police Academy Social Science Department; Ran for Suffolk County Legislature, polled 32%. **Military Serv:** US Army, sp-4c, 1959-63; Liquid Oxygen Missile School. **Business Addr:** Friends of Fillyaw, PO Box 489, Central Islip, NY 11722.

FINCH, GREGORY MARTIN
Attorney. **Personal:** Born Sep 14, 1951, Madera, CA; son of Deloma Dillard (deceased) and Isaac Finch; married Valerie Michelle Beecher; children: Damon, Megan, Christopher. **Educ:** Univ of CA, BA Soc/Art 1974; McGeorge School of Law, JD 1979. **Career:** Attorney, currently. **Orgs:** Delegate State Bar Convention 1983; pres Wiley Manuel Law Assoc 1994; Active 20/30 Club #1; president, 1989; sec Natomas Planning Advisory Council; chmn Small Business Advocacy Comm, Sacramento Chamber of Commerce; board member, Child and Family Institute 1989-; president, Active 20/30, United States and Canada, 1990; America Regional chairman, World Council of Service Clubs, 1993; Sutter Hospital, foundation board; Rotary Club of Sacramento. **Honors/Awds:** Rookie of the Year Active 20/30 Chapter #1 1985. **Military Serv:** USAF Reserve staff sgt 6 years.

FINCH, JANET M.
Educator. **Personal:** Born Jun 4, 1950, Nashville, TN; daughter of Helen Ardis Mitchell and James W Mitchell; married Harold William Finch; children: Harold, Toria. **Educ:** TN State Univ, BA Math 1972, MA Educ 1977; Vanderbilt Univ, EdD 1985. **Career:** Nashville State Tech, educ specialist 1977-80, project dir 1980-81, dept head develop studies 1981-85, asst dean 1981-; Middle TN State Univ, ACE fellow; Motlow State Community College, Tullahoma TN, dean of academic affairs 1988-; exec assistant to president, 1991. **Orgs:** Sec Temple Child Care Develop Center 1984-85; pres Parent Teacher Fellowship 1985-86; youth choir dir/pianist 15th Ave Baptist Church 1985-; mem, Youth Committee YWCA. **Honors/Awds:** Minority Scholarship Vanderbilt Univ 1981; Leader of the 80's Fund for Improving Post Secondary Educ 1984; ACE Fellowship Amer Council on Educ 1986-87; selected to participate in exec leadership institute-sponsored by League for Innovation 1989; Honorary Member, Phi Theta Kappa, 1989. **Home Addr:** 221 Rising Sun Terrace, Old Hickory, TN 37138.

FINCH, RAYMOND LAWRENCE
Judge. **Personal:** Born Oct 4, 1940, Christiansted, St Croix, Virgin Islands of the United States; son of Beryl E Bough Finch and Wilfred C Finch; married Lenore Luana Hendricks (divorced); children: Fay Allison, Mark, Jennifer. **Educ:** Howard U, BA 1962; Howard Univ Sch of Law, LlB 1965. **Career:** Territorial Ct of the VI, judge 1977-; Municipal Ct VI, judge 1976-77; Hodge Sheen Finch & Ross, partner (law firm) 1971-75; Hodge & Sheen, law clerk 1969-70; Municipal Ct VI, law clerk 1965-66. **Orgs:** Mem Am Bar Assn/Nat Bar Assn/Am Judges Assn/Judicial Ethics Com of Am Bar Assn; mem bd dirs Boy Scouts of Am, St Croix 1976-; bd dirs Boys Club, St Croix 1975-. **Military Serv:** AUS, cpt, 1966-69; Army Commendation Medal; Nat Defense Service Medal; Viet Nam Service Medal; Viet Nam Campaign Medal w/60 Device; Bronze Star Medal; Two Overseas Bars.

FINCH, WILLIAM H.
Educator (retired). **Personal:** Born Apr 10, 1924, Columbus, OH; married June Johnson; children: Lisa, Tina. **Educ:** OH State U, BS 1947; DePaul U, MA 1953; Nova Univ, EdD 1983. **Career:** Chicago Bd of Educ, teacher 1947-58, master teacher 1958-59, asst prin 1959-65, prin 1965-71, dist supt, 1971-86; Loyola Univ, asst dir Upward Bound Project 1966-69; Chicago State Univ, instr 1969-71; Chicago Public Schools, asst supt for curriculum, 1986-87. **Orgs:** Pres St Edmunds Church Credit Union 1972-; treas Men St Edmund's Church; mem Alpha Phi Alpha; bd dir S Central Community Svcs; pres Dist Supt Assn1981-86; mem Phi Delta Kappa, Chicago Area Alliance of Black School Educators, Samuel Stratton Assoc, Chicago Principals Assoc, Amer School Health Assn, Amer Assoc of School Admins, Assoc of Supv and Currciulum Devel. **Honors/Awds:** Resolution Recognition mayor & City Council; Hon Life Mem IL Congress of Parents & Teachers; Outstanding Contrib Awd Chatham Avalon Park Community Council; Medal of Merit Community Relations Council of Brainerd; Serv Awd District 20 Educ Council; Serv Awd Dist 17 Educ Council; Educ Awd PUSH; Appreciation Awd 6th Police Dist Appreciation Awd Englewood Community Serv Center; Community Serv Awd Women's Auxiliary Southtown YMCA; Educ Awd Englewood Community Org; South Side Help Center, July 1994.

FINLAYSON, ARNOLD ROBERT
Attorney. **Personal:** Born Jun 30, 1963, Washington, DC; son of Joseph Arnold Jr and Patricia Glenn Finlayson. **Educ:** Bowie State Coll, BS, 1985; Howard University School of Law, JD, 1989. **Career:** US Dept of State, procurement analyst, 1987-90; Hon George W Mitchell, assoc judge, DC Superior Court; judicial law clerk; 1990-92; Shaw, Pittman, Potts & Trowbridge, govt contracts associate, 1992-. **Orgs:** District of Columbia Bar, 1992; Bar of the Commonwealth of Pennsylvania, 1989; US Court of Appeals for the Federal Circuit, 1993; Amer Bar Assn, 1989; Kappa Alpha Psi Fraternity, Inc, 1983. **Honors/Awds:** Howard University School of Law, Wiley A Branton Leadership Award, 1989, American Jurisprudence Award, Professional Responsibility, 1989, American Jurisprudence Award, Natl Moot Court, 1989. **Special Achievements:** Co-Author, Financing Govt Contracts, 1993. **Home Addr:** 701 Pennsylvania Ave NW, Ste 1209, Washington, DC 20004, (202)737-1787. **Business Phone:** (202)663-8842.

FINLAYSON, WILLIAM E.
Physician. **Personal:** Born Sep 1, 1924, Manitee, FL; married Edith; children: Reginald, James. **Educ:** Morehouse Coll, BS 1948; Meharry Med Coll, MD 1953, intern resd 1953-57; Univ MN, resd 1957-58. **Career:** Physician, self-employed. **Orgs:** Mem Milwaukee Med Soc; House Del WI Med Soc; past pres Milwaukee GYN Soc; mem St Joseph's Hosp; Mt Sinai Med Ctr; tchr Milwaukee Med Complex; mem Deaconess Hosp; Cream City Med Soc; Am Coll Surgery; flw Am Coll OB-GYN; Med Coll WI; bd dirs, chmn N Milwaukee State Bank; bd dirs Southeastern WI Health System Agency; past pres Alpha Phi Alpha; Frontiers Int; life mem NAACP; mem Urban League; We-Milwaukeeans; past pres YMCA local br; mem Grtr Galilee Bapt Ch. **Military Serv:** US Army, 1st Lt, 1943-46. **Business Addr:** 2003 W Capitol Dr, Milwaukee, WI 53206.

FINLEY, BETTY M.
Educator. **Personal:** Born Aug 3, 1941, Edison, GA; married Isaac T Finley Jr; children: Michael. **Educ:** Tuskegee Inst, BS 1962; Framingham State Coll, MEd 1977; Simmons Coll Boston, MA 1986. **Career:** East St Louis School Bd, english teacher 1967-68; Pemberton Township School Bd NJ, english teacher 1968-70; Dept of Public Welfare Div of Child Guardianship Boston, social worker 1970-72; Metropolitan Educ Training Dover MA, coord of minority students 1973-74; Dover Sherbon School Bd, teacher 1974-. **Orgs:** Comm mem appt to Headmaster's Adv Comm 1981-82; mem Natl Council Teachers of English 1984-87; organizor Operation Foodbasket 1984; bd mem Children's Literature Foundation 1987-88. **Honors/Awds:** Apptd mem Evaluation Team of New England Assoc of Schools & Colls 1982,86; Ellen Raskin Fellow Simmons Coll 1985. **Home Addr:** 4 Temi Rd, Holliston, MA 01746.

FINLEY, D'LINELL, SR.
Educator. **Personal:** Born Mar 27, 1948, Gunnison, MS; son of Celestine Hayes Finley and George Finley Sr (deceased); married Janet D Duff Finley, Jun 11, 1983; children: Sharriette, D'Linell Jr, Shakealia, Krystel, Carolyn, Arthur. **Educ:** Jackson State University, Jackson, MS, BA, 1972; Atlanta University, Atlanta, GA, MA, 1974, PhD, 1981. **Career:** Alabama State University, Montgomery, AL, asst professor/coordinator political science program, 1975-88, coordinator, 1985-88; Auburn University at Montgomery, Montgomery, AL, adjunct associate professor of political science, 1988; University of Alabama, Graduate Program, Maxwell AFB, adjunct faculty, 1991. **Orgs:** President, post secondary division, Alabama Education Association, 1990-91; member, board of directors, Alabama Education Association, 1990-91; member, board of directors, Central Alabama Laubach Literacy Council, 1990-93; Alabama Political Science Association, 1980-; National Conference of Black Political Scientists, 1977-; 32nd Degree Mason, Phi Beta Sigma Fraternity Inc; president, Capitol City Civitan, Montgomery, AL, 1990-91. **Honors/Awds:** Ford Foundation Fellow, Atlanta University, 1972-75; Pi Gamma Mu International Honor Society in Social Science, 1978; Kappa Delta Pi Education Honor Society, 1982; Phi Delta Kappa Professional Education Honor Fraternity, 1986.

FINLEY, MICHAEL H.
Professional basketball player. **Personal:** Born Mar 6, 1973, Melrose Park, IL. **Educ:** Wisconsin. **Career:** Phoenix Suns, forward, 1995-96; Dallas Mavericks, 1996-. **Honors/Awds:** NBA All-Rookie First Team, 1995-96. **Business Addr:** Professional Basketball Player, Dallas Mavericks, Reunion Arena, 777 Sports St, Dallas, TX 75207, (214)748-1808.

FINLEY, SKIP
Broadcasting executive. **Personal:** Born Jul 23, 1948, Ann Arbor, MI; son of Mildred V. Johnson Finley and Ewell W. Finley; married Karen M. Woolard, May 6, 1971; children: Kharma Isis, R. Kristin. **Educ:** Northeastern University, Boston MA, 1966-71. **Career:** Skifin Gallery, Boston MA, owner, 1970-71; WHDH-TV, Boston MA, floor director, 1971; WSBK-TV, Boston MA, floor manager, asst director, producer, 1971-72; WRKO-Radio, Boston MA, account executive, 1972-73; Humphrey, Browning, MacDougall Advertising, Boston MA, account manager, 1973-74; Sheridan Broadcasting Corp, sales manager for WAMO AM/FM, 1974-75, general manager for WAMO AM/FM, 1975-76, vice-president/general manager for SBC Radio Division, 1976-77, vice-president, corporate office, 1976-82, eastern sales manager, 1977-79, executive vice-president/general manager, 1979-81, president, 1981-82; Albimar Omaha Ltd Partnership/Albimar Management Inc, Boston MA, president and general partner, 1982-; KEZO AM-FM, Omaha, NE, general partner, 1983-88; KDAB-FM, Ogden/Salt Lake City, UT, generpartner, 1985-90; WKYS-FM, Washington, DC, president/general manager, 1988-95; American Urban Radio Networks, CEO/COO, 1995-. **Orgs:** National Thespian Society; trustee on board of overseers, Vineyard Open Land Foundation; Martha's Vineyard Rod and Gun Club; director, Washington Area Broadcasters Assn; director, National Assn of Broadcasters; director, Radio Advertising Bureau; director, National Assn of Black Owned Broadcasters. **Honors/Awds:** Excellence in Media Award, Natl Assn of Media Women, 1981; Communicator of the Year Award, Washington Area Media Organization, 1982; New Horizons Award, DC General Hospital, 1990; Advocacy in Education Award, DC Public Schools, 1990; author of numerous articles on media related subjects; Best Overall Broadcaster/ Radio, Ink Magazine, 1994. **Business Addr:** CEO/COO, American Urban Radio Networks, 960 Penn Ave, 2nd Fl, Pittsburgh, PA 15222, (412)291-8078.

FINN, JOHN WILLIAM
Educational administrator. **Personal:** Born Apr 30, 1942, Lexington, KY; married Joan Washington; children: Jarell Wendell, Janelle Wynice. **Educ:** BS 1966; MBA 1971; taking courses toward PhD in higher educ. **Career:** Gary IN Schools, teacher, coach, recreation leader 1967-69; Anderson Boys Club, activity dir 1968-69; Univ of MI, asst dir of housing 1969-71, assoc dir housing 1977-86; Diversified Educational Products, president, 1986-, administrative assistant to the Superintendent, Gary, IN, 1991-. **Orgs:** Mem MI Housing & Food Serv Officers; MI Coll Personnel Assn; Natl Assn of Student Personnel Admins; Assn of Coll & Univ Housing Ofcls; Amer Assn for Higher Educ; Amer Assn of Jr Coll; mem United Fund; Boys Club of Amer; NAACP; Kappa Alpha Psi Frat Inc; pres Ann Arbor Sportsmen; Black Faculty & Staff Assn. **Honors/Awds:** All City-All State Football 1968-69; Outstanding Young Men of Amer; First Black in Admin pos in Housing Office Univ of MI. **Business Addr:** 620 E 10th Place, Gary, IN 46402.

FINN, MICHELLE
Athlete. **Career:** Track and field athlete, currently. **Honors/Awds:** Olympic Games, gold medalist, 4 X 100 relay, US track and field team, 1992. **Business Addr:** Gold Medalist, 1992 Games, c/o US Olympic Track and Field Team, PO Box 120, Indianapolis, IN 46206, (317)261-0500.

FINN, ROBERT GREEN
Engineer. **Personal:** Born Jan 24, 1941, Lexington, KY; married Mary E Johson; children: Leatrice, Lezelle, Lechrista. **Educ:** Morehead State U, BS 1963. **Career:** IBM, spl engrng request coord. **Orgs:** Councilman 2nd Dist; past pres PTA; vice pres NAACP; Mason; Shriner; Jaycee; mem exec bd Blue Grass Boy Scouts; mem exec council Morehead Alumnus; mem Nat Honor Soc 1959. **Honors/Awds:** Mem Nat Honor Soc 1959; DAR Award 1959. **Business Addr:** IBM 740, New Circle Rd, Lexington, KY.

FINNEY, ERNEST A., JR.
State Supreme Court Justice. **Personal:** Born Mar 23, 1931, Smithfield, VA; son of Collen Godwin Finney and Ernet A Finney Sr; married Frances Davenport; children: Ernest III, Lynn, Jerry. **Educ:** Claflin Coll, BA (cum Laude) 1952; SC State Coll School of Law, JD 1954; Natl Coll State Judiciary Reno NV, Grad 1977; New York Univ Sch of Law, senior srappellate judges seminar 1985. **Career:** Sumter County Courthouse 3rd Judicial Circuit of SC, resident judge 1976-85; South Carolina Supreme Ct, assoc justice 1985-94, chief justice, 1994-. **Orgs:** Chmn of bd Buena Vista Devel Corp; mem Amer, SC, Natl, Sumter Cty Bar Assocs; mem Amer Judicature Soc, mem NAACP, Alpha Phi Alpha, United Meth Church Gen Council on Fin & Admin Legal Responsibilities Comm; chrmn of bd of trustees Claflin Coll; advisory committee, Univ of South Carolina School of Law. **Honors/Awds:** City of Sumter Disting Serv 1970; SC Council for Human Rights 1972; SC State Coll Alumnus Awd 1973; ACLU Civil Libertarian of the Year 1973; Omega Psi Phi Citizen of the Year 1973; Bedford-Styvesant NY Jaycee Awd 1974; Claflin Coll Politic & Alumni Awd 1974; SC Council Human Rights James M Dabbs Awd 1974; Selected to rep SC at Amer Bar Assoc Criminal Code Revision Conf San Diego 1975; Wateree Comm Action Inc Serv 1975; SC NAACP Native Son 1976; Delta Sigma Leadership Serv 1976; Emmanuel Meth Church Serv of Mankind Awd 1977; HHD (Hon) Claflin Coll 1977; Natl Assoc for Equal Oppt in Higher Ed 1986; Distinguished Alumni of the Year Awd from Claflin Coll, SC State Coll; Alpha Phi Alpha Awd of Achievement 1986. **Business Addr:** Chief Justice, South Carolina Supreme Court, PO Drawer 1309, Sumter, SC 29151.

FINNEY, ESSEX EUGENE, JR.
Government official (retired). **Personal:** Born May 16, 1937, Michaux, VA; son of Etta Francis Burton Finney and Essex Eugene Finney Sr; married Rosa Ellen Bradley; children: Essex E III, Karen Finney Shelton. **Educ:** VA Polytechnic Inst, BS (w/ Honors) 1959; PA State Univ, MS 1960; MI State Univ, PhD 1963. **Career:** Rocky Mt Arsenal Denver CO, branch chief 1963-65; Agricultural Rsch Serv USDA, rsch scientist 1965-77; Agricultural Mktg Rsch Inst, inst chmn 1972-75; Beltsville Agricultural Res Ctr, asst dir 1977-83, assoc dir 1983-87; North Atlantic Area Associate Director, 1987-89; Beltsville Agricultural Research Center, USDA, director, 1989-92; Agricultural Research Service, USDA, assoc admini, 1992-95. **Orgs:** Councilman Town of Glenarden MD 1975; sr policy analyst Office of the Science Advisor to the Pres 1980-81; bd of dirs Prince George's Chamber of Commerce 1983-87; pres Beltsville Org of Professional Employees of the US Dept of Agriculture 1984-85. **Honors/Awds:** CRC Press Handbook of Transportation & Mktg in Agriculture 1981; Fellow Amer Soc of Agricultural Engrs 1983; Awd for Administration Gamma Sigma Delta Univ MD 1985; Outstanding Engrg Alumni Awd Penn State Univ 1985; Elected to Natl Academy of Engineering, 1994. **Military Serv:** US Army, Transportation Corps Captain, 1963-65. **Home Addr:** 11206 Chantilly Lane, Mitchellville, MD 20721.

FINNEY, KAREN
Government official. **Career:** Press Office of the First Lady, deputy press secretary, currently. **Business Addr:** Deputy Press Secretary, Press Office of the First Lady, White House, 1600 Pennsylvania Ave, NW, Washington, DC 20500, (202)456-1414.

FINNEY, LEON D., JR.
Organization executive. **Personal:** Born Jul 7, 1938, Louise, MS; married Sharon; children: Kristin, Leon III. **Educ:** Roosevelt U, BA 1964; Nova U, PhD 1978; Goddard Coll, MS 1974. **Career:** Univ Chicago, faculty lctr, fld instr 1970-; Fisk U, vis lctr 1970-71; chair Luth Sch Theol, 1969, vis Sch Theol, vis prof 1968-70; LA State U, cons; The Woodlawn Organization,

president; WCDC, exec dir, currently. **Orgs:** Mem Chicago United; v chmn, bd dirs Guaranty Bank & Trust Co; mem Chicago Assn of Commerce & Ind; mem Black IL Legislative Lobby 1976-; Chicago Urban League 1970-; Natl Urban Coalition; delegate, White House Conference on Balanced Growth & Small Business; consultant, mem, Urban Development, Chicago Economic Dev Comm. **Honors/Awds:** One of four African Americans invited to Israel to study Israeli- Rels, Israeli govt 1973; Affirmative Action Merit Award, Breadbasket Commercial Assn 1973; PACE Award, Pervis Staples 1973; Outst Alumni Award, Hyde Park HS 1972; Distinguished Educator Award 1972; Cert of Merit, Central State Univ Alumni Assn 1971; Chicago Jr Chamber of Commerce, 10 Most Outst Yng Men of 1970; Ford Found Grant 1970. **Special Achievements:** Author, ''Neighborhood Economic Development-Myth or Fact,'' June 1979; co-author, ''Comm Dev Policy Paper Structural Disinvestment: A Problem in Search of a Policy.''. **Military Serv:** USMC 1959-63. **Business Addr:** President, The Woodlawn Organization, 6040 S Harper Ave, Chicago, IL 60637.

FINNEY, MICHAEL ANTHONY
Accountant. **Personal:** Born Oct 2, 1956, Flint, MI; married Gina Michelle Mickels. **Educ:** Saginaw Valley State Coll, BBA 1979; Central MI Univ, MA Candidate. **Career:** Deloitte Haskins & Sells CPA, admin asst 1978-79; J C Penney Co, merchandise mgr 1979-81; Saginaw Valley State Coll, admin rep 1981-84; City of Saginaw,asst city mgr. **Orgs:** Bd of dirs Big Brothers/Big Sisters of Saginaw Inc 1982-83; bd of dirs Saginaw Valley State Coll Alumni Assn 1981-; mem Saginaw Jaycees 1984-, Intl City Mgrs Assoc, MI City Mgrs Assoc. **Honors/Awds:** President-Student Govt Saginaw Valley State Coll 1978-79; Outstanding Young Men in Amer US Jaycees 1979; State Dir of MI Phi Beta Sigma Frat 1979-80; Outstanding Achievement in Black Affairs SVSC Black Student Assn 1983. **Business Addr:** Assistant Manager, City of Saginaw, 1315 S Washington, Saginaw, MI 48601.

FINNIE, ROGER L., SR.
Football player. **Personal:** Born Nov 6, 1945, Winder, GA; married Debbie; children: Shannon Monique, Rogers Lewis Jr. **Educ:** FL A&M U, 1964-69. **Career:** NY Jets, played offensive tackle, guard, defensive end & tight end 1968-72; St Louis Cardinals, 1973-78; New Orleans Saints, 1979. **Orgs:** Works with various youth orgn; mem NFLPA. **Honors/Awds:** Named Pittsburg All-Am 1968; Defensive Lineman of Yr, Ebony All-Am, Defensive Lineman; received game balls, NY Jets 1969 & 1971; trophy for best offensive line in the NFL for fewer quarterback sacks.

FISCHER, LISA
Vocalist. **Career:** Back-up singer for Luther Vandross; So Intense, debut album, Elektra Records, 1991, solo artist, currently. **Honors/Awds:** ''How Can I Ease the Pain,'' from So Intense, co-winner of Grammy Award, Best R&B Female Vocalist, 1992. **Business Addr:** Singer, So Intense, c/o Sherry Ring Ginsberg, 75 Rockefeller Plaza, 17th Fl, New York, NY 10019, (212)275-4160.

FISCHER, WILLIAM S.
Musician. **Personal:** Born Mar 5, 1935, Shelby, MS; son of Wyllie Fisher and R A Fisher; married Dolores; children: Darius, Marc, Bryan, Paul. **Educ:** Xavier Univ of New Orleans, BS; CO Coll, MA; Univ Vienna, attended Akademie Fur Musik und Darstellende. **Career:** Xavier Univ, assoc prof 1962-66; Newport Coll & Cardiff Coll, lecturer 1966; NY Public Sch, 1967-75; NY, publisher 1967-; Atlantic Records, music dir 1968-70, arranger conductor 1965-, record producer 1973-74; Arcana Records, owner 1971-. **Orgs:** Mem Amer Soc Composers Authors & Publishers 1964; mem MENC 1964, Amer Federation Musicians 1953; exec dir Soc Black Composers 1971-; Grants: Edger Stern Family Fund Commn, 1963-65; Akademischer Austausdienst W Germany 1964; mem NY Council on the Arts 1971, Natl Endowment Arts 1971; Organization of American States; Pan American Grant, 1964; New Orleans Philharmonic Comm, 1964-65. **Honors/Awds:** Fulbright Grant 1965-66; Austrian Govt Grant 1965; Commissioned to write Mass for a Saint, SBS of Bensalem, Pennsylvania, 1988; Commissioned Film Score Elliott, A Feature Film, Backroads of Jackson, WO, 1987; Meditation on Mt St Helens for Orch, Ready Productions, 1990-91; Commission to write MASS, Parish LeBeau Louisiana, First Established, by People of Color, Founded, 1897; New Music for Violin/Saxophone Concertos using computer assimilated orchestra, ''The Cross Bronx Concerto'' and other CD's, 1995-96. **Military Serv:** USMC 1956-57. **Home Addr:** 1365 St Nicholas Ave, New York, NY 10033.

FISHBURNE, LAURENCE JOHN, III (LARRY)
Actor. **Personal:** Born Jul 30, 1961, Augusta, GA; son of Hattie Bell Crawford Fishburne and Laurence John Fishburne Jr; married Hajna Moss Fishburne, Jul 1, 1985; children: Langston Issa, Montana Isis. **Career:** Actor, films include: Searching for Bobby Fischer, Class Action, King of New York, Red Head, Cotton Club, Nightmare on Elm Street 3, School Daze, Apocalypse Now, Boyz N the Hood, Deep Cover, What's Love Got To Do With It, Higher Learning, Bad Company, Just Cause, Fled, Event Horizon, Miss Evers Boys, Hoodlum, 1997, Always Outnumbered, Always Outgunned, 1998; Plays include: August Wilson's Two Train Running; HBO Movie, The Tuskegee Airmen, 1995; Deep Cover; Othello. **Honors/Awds:** NAACP, Image Award, Television Movie, Miniseries or Dramatic Special Actor, 1998. **Special Achievements:** First Black to portray Shakespeare's Othello on silver screen.

FISHER, ALMA M.
Librarian. **Personal:** Born Dec 22, 1945, Learned, MI; married Eugene. **Educ:** Tougaloo Coll, BA english 1967; Rosary Coll, MALS 1970. **Career:** Hinds Community College Dist, Utica Campus, librarian, currently; Utica Jr Coll, librn beginning 1972; Chicago Pub Libr Sysd librn 1970-72; Chicago Public School System, teacher, 1967-69. **Orgs:** Mem Am Libr Assn; mem MI Libr Assn; mem MI Tchrs Assn; mem Black Caucus ALA; mem Urban Leag; mem NAACP; mem Utica Jr Coll Alumni Assn. **Honors/Awds:** Recip Assn of Coll & Res Librs Mellon intnshp Jan 1975; recip IL St Libr Sch Schlshp 1969. **Business Addr:** Librarian, Utica Campus, Hinds Community College District, Utica, MS 39175.

FISHER, DAVID ANDREW
Clergyman, educator. **Personal:** Born Sep 12, 1958, Columbus, OH; son of Jean Otis Peck Fisher and Morgan Cecil Fisher (deceased). **Educ:** Ohio Dominican College, Columbus, OH, BA, philosophy, 1980; Gregorian University, Rome, Italy, STB, theology, 1983, STL, theology, 1985. **Career:** St Paul Church, Westerville, OH, assoc pastor, 1985-87; SS Augustine & Gabriel, Columbus, OH, pastor, 1987-90; Ohio Dominican College, Columbus, OH, prof of philosophy, 1989-; St Joseph Cathedral, Columbus, OH, assoc pastor, 1990-. **Orgs:** Member, board of trustees, Alzhiemer Assn, 1986-89; member, board of trustees, St Stephen Comm House, 1988-90. **Honors/Awds:** Seminar Member, The International Institute for Culture, 1989; Commendation, Ohio House of Representatives, 1989; pastoral work in Sweden, Diocese of Stockholm, 1988; Vicar Forane, Northland Vicariate Diocese of Columbus, 1989-90. **Home Addr:** 212 E Broad, Columbus, OH 43215.

FISHER, DEREK LAMAR
Professional basketball player. **Personal:** Born Aug 9, 1974, Little Rock, AR. **Educ:** Arkansas-Little Rock. **Career:** Los Angeles Lakers, guard, 1996-. **Business Addr:** Professional Basketball Player, Los Angeles Lakers, PO Box 10, Inglewood, CA 90306, (213)419-3100.

FISHER, E. CARLETON
College professor. **Personal:** Born Nov 3, 1934, St Louis, MO; children: Victor, Bruce, Vernon. **Educ:** Howard Univ, BS, MS 1956-57; American Univ; Morgan State Univ, EdD 1986. **Career:** Univ of Chicago, numerical analyst 1957-66; IBM, personnel mgr 1966-72; Univ of MD, exec asst to chancellor for affirmative action 1973-77; Notre Dame, exec dir minorities in engr 1977-78. **Orgs:** Kappa Alpha Psi, mem 1952-; American Guild of Organists, mem 1970-; MD Assoc of Affirmative Action Officers, president/founder 1975-77, 1983-85; Prudential Ins, director, college relations 1978-80; Affirmative Action, prof of mathematics asst to pres 1981-. **Honors/Awds:** Morgan State Univ, goldseker fellow 1983-85. **Business Addr:** Professor, Dept of Math, Anne Arundel Community College, 101 College Parkway, Arnold, MD 21012.

FISHER, EDITH MAUREEN
Librarian, educator, freelance writer, business executive. **Personal:** Born Jul 29, 1944, Houston, TX; daughter of Ruby Jase and Freeman Fisher. **Educ:** University of Illinois, Urbana IL, MLS, 1972; Queens College CUNY, Certificate of Ethnicity and Librarianship, 1975; University of Pittsburgh, PhD 1991. **Career:** University of California, San Diego, La Jolla CA, Central University Library, 1972-90, Contemporary Black Arts Program, adjunct lecturer, 1981-90; University of California, Los Angeles, School of Library and Information Science, lecturer, 1989; Evaluation and Training Institute, Los Angeles, CA, consultant/technical advisor, 1991; Tenge Enterprises, Encinitas, CA, president, currently. **Orgs:** Carleson Learning. **Honors/Awds:** Carnegie fellowship, 1971; PhD fellowship, 1987; Provost fellowship, Univ of CA, San Diego, 1987; Provost fellowship, Univ of Pittsburgh, 1988; Black Caucus of the American Library Association President's Award, 1990; author of numerous publications. **Business Addr:** President, Tenge Enterprises, 204 N El Camino Real, Suite E728, Encinitas, CA 92024, (760)753-8644.

FISHER, EDWARD G.
Surgeon. **Personal:** Born Apr 22, 1932; son of Elisa Howell Fisher Dawes and Guy O D Fisher; married Judy Ann; children: Yvonne, Ronald. **Educ:** Brooklyn Coll, BS 1956; Howard U, MD 1961. **Career:** HU, med offcr 1966-68; Operating Rm Com Hadley Hosp, chmn; Howard Univ Hosp; Freedmens Hosp, instr 1966-68; Greater SE Comm, active staff privileges; Inst of Urban Living Washington DC, medical dir; Hadley Memorial Hosp, active attending physician, currently. **Orgs:** Former mem Med Care Evaluation Com; presently surgeon in private practice; mem DC Med Soc; mem DC Medico-chirugical Soc; mem Nat Med Assn; former mem AMA & Interns & Residents Assn of Freedmens Hosp; mem Nat Assn of Interns & Residents; former mem Political Action Com; life mem Urban League Honor Medical Soc 1961; Diplomate Am Bd of Surgery; former Joint Conf Hadley Hosp; former president Medical Staff Hadley Memorial Hosp; mem bd of trustees Hadley Memorial Hospital; Alpha Phi Alpha. **Honors/Awds:** Author of numerous publications; co-author w/wife, Human Sexuality - Christian Perspective 1984. **Home Phone:** (301)390-0098. **Business Addr:** Physician, 3536 Minnesota Ave SE, Ste 1, Washington, DC 20019, (202)581-0200.

FISHER, GEORGE CARVER
Accountant. **Personal:** Born Dec 12, 1939, Texarkana, AR; son of Naomi Johnson Fisher and Thomas Fisher (deceased); married Annie Kate Carter; children: Anthony Karl. **Educ:** Univ of AR Pine Bluff, BS 1969; Univ of AR Fayetteville, MBA 1974. **Career:** Arkansas Best Corp, accountant 1969-73, supv carrier acctg 1973-84, dir carrier acctg 1984-. **Orgs:** Treas EO Trent Consistory #223 1973-79; dir Arkansas Best Federal Credit Union 1983-; chmn Fort Smith Civil Serv Commn 1983-; mem Amer Inst of CPA's; vice pres Fort Smith Girls Club; mem Sparks Reg Medical Ctr Adv Trustee; treas Sunnymede Elem PTA; CPA Arkansas; mem NAACP; life mem Kappa Alpha Psi; past master Widow's Son Lodge #3; bd of dir, Leadership Fort Smith l989-92; bd of dir, United Way of Fort Smith l988-9l. **Honors/Awds:** Distinguished Service Arthritis Foundation 1986. **Military Serv:** USN storekeeper second class petty officer 1957-60. **Home Addr:** 2007 North 48th Circle, Fort Smith, AR 72904. **Business Addr:** Dir Carrier Accounting, Arkansas Best Corporation, 1000 South 21st St, Fort Smith, AR 72902.

FISHER, JOSEPH
Labor union official. **Personal:** Born Feb 7, 1933, Lawnside, NJ; son of Vera Ann Arthur Fisher and Horace J Fisher; married Barbara Bryant, Apr 1952; children: Joseph Jr, Darlene Still, Barbara Arthur, James Fisher. **Educ:** Temple Univ, Philadelphia PA, BS, 1955. **Career:** Liberty Knitting Mills, Philadelphia PA, office manager 1956-58; Intl Ladies Garment Workers Union, Philadelphia PA, vice pres, and director, Eastern Penna Region 1980-. **Orgs:** Chairperson, PA Advisory Committee, US Civil Rights Commission; bd mem, PA Job Training Coordinating Council; bd mem, Philadelphia Urban Coalition; board member, Variety Club-Children's Charity; United Way, Camden County, board member; Red Cross, Camden County, board member. **Business Addr:** Vice Pres, Regional Director, International Ladies Garment Workers Union, 35 South 4th Street, Philadelphia, PA 19106.

FISHER, JUDITH DANELLE
Physician/psychiatric consultant. **Personal:** Born Feb 17, 1951, Sanford, NC. **Educ:** Howard Univ, Coll of Liberal Arts BS 1974, Coll of Medicine MD 1975. **Career:** Howard Univ Hosp, psychiatric psychiatry 1975-77; Hahnemann Medical Coll, psyciatric resident, 1977-78, fellow, 1978-79; CMHC Hahnemann, medical dir 1979-80; Hahnemann Hosp Phila, asst dir in-patient psych unit, 1980-81; private practice, 1980-; CamCare Health Corp, psych actg med dir, 1981-83; Eagleville Hosp, dir Women's In-Patient Unit, 1983-84; Wake Co MHC, staff psychiatrist 1984-85; NC Disability Determination Svcs, psychiatric consultant 1985-. **Orgs:** General mem Amer Psychiatric Assn 1981-; bd of dirs Women in Transition Philadelphia 1982-84; mem Smithsonian Assn 1984-, Natl Assoc of Disability Examiners 1985-, Amer Film Inst 1986-, State NC Employees Assn 1986-; member, Livingston College Alumni Assn. **Honors/Awds:** NIMH Minority Fellowship Amer Psychiatric Assoc 1976-78; Certificate of Recognition Alpha Kappa Alpha Sor Raleigh 1985. **Home Addr:** PO Box 822, 836 Boykin Ave, Sanford, NC 27330. **Business Addr:** Psychiatric Consultant, NC Disab Deter Div of SS Admin, 1110 Navaho Dr, Raleigh, NC 27602.

FISHER, LLOYD B.
Attorney. **Personal:** Born Jan 13, 1942, Marthaville, LA; married Shirley T Little; children: Jawara M J. **Educ:** Purdue U, BS; Valparaiso Univ Sch of Law, JD 1973. **Career:** Lloyd B Fisher Atty at Law, atty 1979-; Lake Co Government, pub defender 1977-79; City of Gary, asst city atty 1973-76; B002 Allen & Hamiltol, consult 1969-70; Gary & Opportunities Industrialization Center, vice pres bd of dirs, 1975-. **Orgs:** Mem TMLA 1979-80; asst to chmn Criminal Law Sect Nat Bar Assn 1980; Basileus Omega ; mem TMLA 1979-80; asst to chmn Criminal Law Sect Nat Bar Assn 1980; Basileus Omega Psi Phi Frat Alpha Chi Chap Gary IN 1974-76; mem Am Bar Assn 1974-; mem Nat Bar Assn 1974-; pres Lake Co Opportunities Devel Found Inc 1975-; mem Bar Assn of the 7th Fed Cir; mem IN State Bar Assn; pub relations chmn of pack Com Pack 23 Of 23 of Cub Scouts of Am Gary; bd mem Thurgood Marshall Law Assn; mem NAACP 1976-; bd mem Purdue Club of Club of Lake Co 1976-. **Honors/Awds:** Cert of appreciation Tolleston Comm Council 1977; cert of Appreciation NAACP 1977; dedicated serv award Gary Opportunities Industrialtization Center 1980. **Military Serv:** AUS 1st lt 1966-68.

FISHER, ROBERT F.
City official. **Personal:** Born Nov 22, 1936, Canton, OH; married Mary Rose Whitehurst; children: Rod, Myra, Craig. **Educ:** Kent State U, 1961; Akron U, Govt Seminar 1969-70; Kent State U, Grad Courses. **Career:** Canton, dir pub serv 1973;

Budget & Projects Canton, dir 1965-73; State Pection & Supervision of Pub Office; Income Tax & Accountant; Canton Water Dept, commercial accountant. **Orgs:** Mem Goodwill Bd of Trustees; OH Housing Develop Bd; Hosp Bureau Bd; NEFCO; Frontiers Club Intnl; Canton Negro Oldtimers Athltc Assn; Walsh Coll Adv Bd; Stark Wayne Manpower Consortium; sec Stark Council of Govt. **Honors/Awds:** Outstanding young man of Yr Jr C of C 1971. **Business Addr:** 218 Cleveland Ave SW, Canton, OH 44702.

FISHER, RONALD L.
Bank officer. **Personal:** Born May 19, 1951, Hamlet, NC; son of Elizabeth Fisher and William Fisher; married Del Johnson, May 12, 1973; children: Ron Jr, Lacy. **Educ:** North Carolina Central University, BSBA, 1973; University of Wisconsin-Madison, MBA, 1976. **Career:** Cameron Brown Mortgage Co, acting vp, commercial real estate, 1977-80; First Union National Bank, vp, employee relations, 1980-89, vp, community lending, 1990-. **Orgs:** Charlotte Urban League, 1991-; 100 Black Men of Charlotte, 1991-; JC Smith University, Business Advisory Board, 1986-. **Business Addr:** VP, Community Lending, First Union National Bank, 301 S Tryon St, MOB-6, Charlotte, NC 28288-1005, (704)374-6558.

FISHER, RUBIN IVAN
Automobile company executive. **Personal:** Born Sep 25, 1948, Baltimore, MD. **Educ:** Univ of CT, BA 1971. **Career:** Travelers Ins Co, asst dir personnel; adminstr Personnel 1977-78; employment couns 1974-77; Aetna Life & Casualty Ins Co, supr field controllers dept 1972-74; The Travelers, Hartford, CT, ast director, 1974-88; Black Collegiate Services, New Orleans, LA, asst vice president, 1988-90; Saab Cars USA Inc, Orange, CT, manager, employment & training, 1990- . **Orgs:** Mem Am Soc for prsnl Adminstrn; mem Reserve Officer Assn of Am; mem Urban League; mem NAACP; accredited personnel specialist designation Am Soc for Personnel Adminstrn-accreditation Inst 1978. **Military Serv:** AUS capt 1971-72. **Business Addr:** Manager, Employment & Training, Human Resource Dept, Saab Cars USA Inc, One Saab Dr, Orange, CT 06477.

FISHER, SHELLEY MARIE
Educator. **Personal:** Born Jul 2, 1942, Gary, IN; daughter of Mr & Mrs Wendell Brumfield; married Alfred J Fisher; children: Tiffiny, Eric. **Educ:** Indiana Univ, BS 1964, MS 1969. **Career:** Gary Comm School Corp, educator 1964-, principal. **Orgs:** Past bd of dirs Self-Marketing Inc 1981-84; past franchiser Natl Employment Transmittal Inc 1981-84; natl sec Natl Tots and Teens Inc 1981-85; 3rd vice pres Drifting Dunes Girl Scout Council 1986-; mem Alpha Kappa Alpha Inc; past facilitator, Learning Indiana Department of Education. **Honors/Awds:** Reading Fellowship Indiana ST Univ 1976; Short fiction published in Indiana Univ/Literary magazine 1979; authored "Resume Writing Slanting Skills in New Direction," 1981. **Home Addr:** 1700 Taft St, Gary, IN 46404. **Business Addr:** Principal, Gary Community School Corp, PO Box 156, Gary, IN 46402.

FISHER, WALTER
Educator. **Personal:** Born Aug 19, 1916, Baltimore, MD. **Educ:** Howard Univ, AB (Magna Cum Laude) 1936, AM 1937; Univ of PA, Doctoral Studies 1941-42,46-48. **Career:** VA Union Univ, instructor History (summers) 1937-39; Howard Univ, instructor History 1937-38; DE State Coll, instructor Social Science 1938-51; Morgan State Univ, dir library 1966-75, prof History 1949-81, emeritus prof History 1981-. **Orgs:** Dir of prog Annual Meetings Assoc for Study of Negro Life & History 1966-70; exec council Assoc for Study of Afro-Amer Life & History 1969-84; consult Dept of Ed Baltimore City & Cty, Anne Arundel Cty, State of MD; coord Penn-Morgan Consortium Lecture Series Univ of PA 1969; co-adv, coord Natl Endowment for the Humanities Afro-Amer Studies Post-Doctoral Fellowship Prog, Johns Hopkins Univ, Morgan State Coll 1970-73; coord Danforth Found, Post-Doctoral Fellowship, Black Studies, Morgan State Coll 1970-71; coord, editor Morgan State Course Guides in Afro-Amer Studies 1970-71; mem Morgan State Performing Arts Series, Bicentennial Comm, Task Force on Student Life; sec MD Council for Publ Broadcasting; bd dir MD Conf of Social Concern; bdtrustees Baltimore Walters Art Gallery 1972-84 & The le Museum 1967-84; cit comm on Black History, Peale Mus; assoc fellow Ctr for African & Afro-Amer Studies; adv council Natl Archives of US 1975-81; vp, bd dir MD Libr Class & Auto Proj 1972-74; mem bd dir Baltimore Heritage 1983-, Historic Baltimore Soc 1984-; bd trust Friends of Enoch Pratt Free Libr 1981-. **Military Serv:** AUS capt 1942-46, 1951-53.

FITCH, HARRISON ARNOLD
Attorney. **Personal:** Born Jul 4, 1943, Elizabeth, NJ; married Ruth Mckinney; children: Harrison A, Jr, Robin L. **Educ:** Columbia Coll, AB 1965; Columbia U, LLB 1968. **Career:** Boston Legal Assistance Project, atty 1968-69; Boston Univ Sch Law, lectr, beginning 1969; Goodwin Procter & Hoar Trustee Boston Five Cents Savs Bank, atty; Fitch, Wiley, Richlin & Tourse, partner, currently. **Orgs:** Mem Babson & Coll; dir Boston Legal Aid Soc Steering Com Lawyers Com for Civil Rights Under Law; dir MA Law Reform Inst; Boston Legal Assistance Proj;mem Governor's Ad Hoc Adv Com on Judicial Appointments 1972. **Business Addr:** 101 Federal St, #1900, Boston, MA 02110-1800, (617)557-3700.

FITCH, MILTON F., JR.
State representative. **Career:** North Carolina House of Representatives, representative, 1985-. **Business Addr:** State Representative, House Standing Committees, State Capitol, Raleigh, NC 27611.

FITCHUE, M. ANTHONY
Educator, writer. **Personal:** Born Dec 13, 1943, Kansas City, MO; son of Carrie Wilma Witherspoon and Robert Anthony Fitchue; married Leah Gaskin White (divorced 1978); children: Ebony Joy Fitchue. **Educ:** Hampton University, Hampton, VA, BS, 1967; Columbia University, New York, NY, MS, 1971; Harvard University, Cambridge, Mass, Ed M, 1974; Columbia University-Teachers College, New York, NY, EdD, 1990. **Career:** Dept of Labor, Office of Federal Contract Comphance, Washington, DC, special asst to director, 1979-81; US Information Agency, US Embassy, Banako, Mali, attache cultural, 1981-82; US Information Agency, US Consulate, Madras, India, vice consul, 1982-85; Pratt Institute, Brooklyn, NY, asst dean, 1987-88; The Chancellor of NY, New York, NY, consultant, 1988; College of New Rochelle City Univ of New York Iona College, New York, NY, adjunct professor, 1987-1990. **Orgs:** Mem, Harvard-Radcliffe Alumni Against Apartheid. **Honors/Awds:** Author, "Armageddon Bogeyman," Essence Magazine, 1991; "Of Choral Chants and Drum Cadences," The Hindu, 1985; Policy Fellow, George Washington Univ, Leadership Institution in Education, 1974-75; International Fellow, Grad Scho ol of Journalism, Columbia University, 1970-71. **Business Addr:** Dir, Multicultural Affairs, LeMoyne College, 200 Grewen Hall, Syracuse, NY 13224.

FITTS, LEROY
Pastor, educator. **Personal:** Born Jul 6, 1944, Norlina, NC; son of Louise Fitts and Johnnie Fitts; married Alice Louise Alston, Aug 18, 1963; children: Timothy, Leroy, Dietrich E, Angelique L, Leticia A. **Educ:** Shaw Univ, BA 1967; Southeastern Bapt Theo Sem, M Div 1970; VA Sem, D Div 1975, DHL, 1990; Princeton Univ, (NEH Inst) 1984; Baltimore Hebrew University, MA 1985. **Career:** First Bapt Ch of Jacksonville, NC, pastor 1968-72; First Bapt Church, Baltimore, MD, pastor 1972-; Comm Coll of Baltimore, adjunct prof 1978-80; VA Sem & Coll, pres 1981; ad; prof, Black Church History, St Mary's Seminary & University, Baltimore, MD. **Orgs:** Editor Loft Carey Baptist Convention 1975-90; brd of mgrs VA Sem & Coll 1980; mem NAACP, Assoc for the Study of Negro Hist 1978-; bd of mgrs, St. Marys Seminary & University. **Honors/Awds:** Author, Lott Carey First Black Msnry to Africa 1978, A History of Black Baptists 1985; article "The Church in the South & Social Issues", Faith & Mission vol II, No I, Fall 1984. **Home Addr:** 3912 The Alameda, Baltimore, MD 21218. **Business Addr:** Pastor, First Baptist Church, 525 N Caroline St, Baltimore, MD 21205.

FITTZ, SENGA NENGUDI (SENGA NENGUDI)
Artist. **Personal:** Born Sep 18, 1943, Chicago, IL; daughter of Elois Jackson Irons and Samuel Irons; married Ellioutt; children: Sanza, Oji. **Educ:** CA State Univ at LA, BA 1966; Waseda Univ Tokyo, Japan, Foreign Studies Prog 1966-67; CA State Univ at LA, MA 1971. **Career:** Pasadena Art Museum, art inst 1969-71; Childrens Art Carnival NYC, art instructor 1971-74; Watts Towers Art Center LA, art inst 1965, 1978; Comm Artists Program LA, program coordinator 1982-88, arts program developer, 1990-, dance instructor, community and private classes, 1992-; African Dance & the Diaspora, CO Coll & Pikes Peak Comm Coll Colorado Springs, guest dance instructor, 1993-; Univ of Co at Co Springs, Afro Am Art Studies Inst, art history instructor, 1998-. **Orgs:** Curatorial comm perf art, The Woman's Bldg, LA 1984-85; board of directors, 1990-, copresident, 1991-92, Performing Arts for Youth; Business of Arts Center, 1990-92; National Black Women's Health Project; Black Life Support Sisterhood, 1990-; community liaison, Kennedy Center Imagination Celebration, 1992-95. **Honors/Awds:** Dance scholarship Orchesis Cal State Univ at LA 1964; CAPS Grant Sculpture Creative Artists Public Serv Prog 1972; creator & independent radio producer for "Mouth to Mouth Conversations on Being" 1988-; "Art as a Verb" Group Travelling Exhibit 1988-89; "Coast to Coast," Group Travelling Exhibit, A Women of Color Artists Box and Books Exhibit 1988-92; Shaping the Spirit, Exhibit CAP St Project/AVT-Experimental Projects Gallery, San Francisco, CA, 1990; artist-in-residence, Mitchell High School; Bd of Regents Univ of CO, Distinguished Service Award, 1994; Independent Radio Producer, Singing the Circle: Four Women Creating Themselves, 1995; Homecoming Watts Tower Art Center, 25th Anniversary Show, 1995; Artists Space-20th Anniversary Show, New York City, 1993. **Special Achievements:** Curator for "Whisper! Stomp! Shout! A Salute to African-American Performance Art," Colorado Springs Fine Art Center, Co, a festival of video documentation of performing art, 1996; lecture/performance "Making a Scene of Ourselves - The Black Arts: Happy Ruminations on Life in America," University of Colorado, 1996; At Banff Arts Center in Canada, 1996; Solo Exhibit "Wet Night Early Dawn Seat Chant Pilgrims Song," Thomas Erben Gallery, NYC, 1996; Participated in as artist, "Incandescent" part of "Now Here," Intl Art Exhibit, Louisiana Museum of Modern Art, 1996; represented by Thomas Erben Gallery, New York, NY, 1995; solo exhibit "Populated Air" Thomas Erben Gallery, 1997; Univ of Ill at Chicago School of Art and Design, visiting artist, 1997; participated as artist, "Out of Action: Between Performance and the Object, 1949-1979," Museum of Contemporary Art Los Angeles, 1998; "Resonances," Galerie Art'O Paris, France, 1997; Guest artist, Univ of IL at Chicago, School of Art and Design 1997; Guest artist, Maryland Inst, College of Art, 1997. **Home Addr:** 4160 Brigadoon Ln, Colorado Springs, CO 80909-1702. **Business Phone:** (212)966-5283.

FITZGERALD, HERBERT H.
Detective. **Personal:** Born Jul 17, 1928, Trenton, NJ; divorced; children: Darrel A, Denise A. **Educ:** Howard Univ Rider Coll, Bus Adminstrn & Police Adminstrn 1974. **Career:** Detective Mercer Co, prosecutor; Trenton NJ Police Dept, officer & detective. **Orgs:** Mem Co Detectives Assn of NJ Inc; pres Bro Officers Law Enforcement Soc; NJ Narcotic & Enforcement Officers Asn; Intl Narcotic Enforcement Officers Assn; mem Alpha Phi Alpha Zeta Iota Lambda Chpt; NAACP; Trenton Housing Authority Commr 1971; bd mem Model Cities Policy Com 1972; Mercer Co Alcoholism Program 1972; master mason King David Lodge #15 F & AM Trenton NJ 32nd Degree Mason Ophir Consisteory 48, trenton Nj; adv bd mem Union Indsl Home for Boys Trenton NJ; Frontiers Intl Bd of Gov Police Athletic League. **Honors/Awds:** Many certificates of commendation for meritorious serv Trenton Police Dept; Drew Pearson Cultural Achievement Award. **Military Serv:** USN. **Business Addr:** Mercer Co Court House, Office of Co Prosecutor, Trenton, NJ 08607.

FITZGERALD, HOWARD DAVID
Government official. **Personal:** Born Sep 24, 1938, Trenton, NJ; son of Mollie and Charles; divorced; children: Howard D Jr, Wayne. **Educ:** Antioch Univ, BA Human Serv 1976, MA Admin & Suprv 1978. **Career:** NJ Dept of Ed, migrant coord 1970-; Middlesex Cty Schools, dir of CETA proj 1980; NJ Dept of Ed, coord of prog mgmt 1982; Trenton City Council, council-member-at-large, currently. **Orgs:** Chmn comm ed Trenton School Bd 1979; mem bd of ed Trenton School Bd 1979-82; mem Trenton Housing Auth 1982-; bd of dir Henry Austin Health Ctr 1982-; chmn Carver YMCA 1982-; pres We Inc 1983-85. **Honors/Awds:** Outstanding Bd mem Trenton School Bd 1980; Ed Excellence Afrikan Peoples Movement 1980; Up & Coming Politican Candlehight Sports Club 1981; Recognition World Hungry Prince Haile Salassie II 1984. **Military Serv:** US Army squad leader 1957-59. **Business Addr:** Council Member-at-Large, Trenton City Council, 225 N Warren St, Trenton, NJ 08618.

FITZGERALD, ROY LEE
City council member (retired). **Personal:** Born Sep 15, 1911, Hiram, GA; son of Ida Willingham Fitzgerald and Joe Fitzgerald; married Ezma Barnwell, Mar 1937; children: Eugene, Helene, Kathryn Martin, Josie Martin, Margaret Zachery, Donald (deceased). **Career:** Mount Olive Baptist Church, Hiram, GA, minister; City of Hiram, council member, 20 yrs; vice mayor; Board of Education, Atlanta, GA, 15 yrs; Roylins, supervisor. **Orgs:** Mason Lodge. **Honors/Awds:** Outstanding Performance Awards from Post Office, Coca Cola & Bd of Educ. **Home Addr:** 330 Ragsdale St, Hiram, GA 30141.

FITZGERALD, WILLIAM B.
Chief executive. **Career:** Independence Federal Savings Bank, Washington, DC, chief exec. **Business Addr:** Independence Federal Savings Bank, 1229 Connecticut Ave, NW, Washington, DC 20036.

FITZHUGH, KATHRYN CORROTHERS
Law librarian. **Personal:** Born Feb 4, 1950, Warren, AR; daughter of Billie Jean Burns Corrothers and Charles Edward Corrothers; married Benjamin Dewey Fitzhugh, Nov 28, 1970; children: Erica Janine. **Educ:** Univ of Arkansas, Fayetteville, AR, BA, 1971; Univ of Illinois at Urbana-Champaign, Champaign, IL, MSLS, 1976; Univ of Arkansas at Little Rock, Little Rock, AR, JD, 1983. **Career:** Univ of AR, Graduate Inst of Technology, Little Rock, technology librarian, 1977-79; Fitzhugh & Fitzhugh, Little Rock, AR, partner, 1985-87; Univ of Arkansas-Little Rock/Pulaski County Law Library, Little Rock, AR, reference circulation librarian, 1987-89, public services librarian, reference and special collections librarian, currently; US Court of Appeals, 8th Circuit Court, Little Rock, AR, branch librarian, 1980-83, 1989-92. **Orgs:** American Association of Law Libraries, 1982-; Pulaski County Bar Assn; Arkansas Bar Association, 1983-; Society of Southwest Archivists, 1994-; American Bar Assn, 1992-; American Library Assn, 1993-; North Little Rock NAACP; Ouachita Girl Scout Council, 1986-88; Delta Sigma Theta Sorority, 1991-; Society of American Archivists; Pulaski Heights Junior High PTA, 1996-; Mid-America Association of Law Libraries. **Honors/Awds:** Wrote chapter in Handbook on Legal Rights for Arkansas Women, Arkansas Dept of Labor, 1987; "Arkansas Practice Materials: A Selective Bibliography," 81 Law Library Journal, No. 2, 1989. **Business Addr:** Reference/Special Collections Librarian & Professor of Law Librariansh, ip, UALR/Pulaski County Law Library, 1203 McAlmont, Little Rock, AR 72202, (501)324-9444.

FITZPATRICK, ALBERT E.
Publishing executive. **Personal:** Born Dec 30, 1928, Elyria, OH; son of Mary Fitzpatrick and Ben Fitzpatrick; married Derien Lucas; children: Sharon, Karyle, Albert II. **Educ:** Kent State Univ, BA journalism, sociology 1956. **Career:** Akron Beacon Journal, rptr asst news edtr, news edtr, city edtr, mng & exec edtr 1956-84; Knight-Ridder, dir of minrty affrs 1985; asst vp, minority affairs, 1987-. **Orgs:** Chmn of bd Wesley Temple AME Church 1965-84; pres Buckeye Chptr, Sigma Delta Chi 1971; assoc prof Medill Sch of Journalism NW Univ 1979-80; pres Akron Press Club 1981-83; pres Natl Assn of Black Journalists 1985-87; chmn minorities bd mem Amer Cancer Soc, Boy Scouts, Cntr on Economics Educ; chrmn UNCF advisory bd, 1989; chairman, National Association of Minority Media Executives, 1990-. **Honors/Awds:** Outstanding Alumnus Award Kent State Univ (Journalism) 1973; Editor of Year-Freedom Journal Cuyahoga Comm Coll, Cleveland 1978; John S Knight Award Sigma Del Ta Chi, Akron, OH 1980; Frederick Douglass Award Lifetime Achievement Natl Assn Black Jounalists 1984; Ida B Wells Award, National Association of Black Journalists, Nat Conf of Editorial Writers, Natl Broadcast Editorial Assn, 1989; Community Service Award, Kent State University, 1991. **Military Serv:** AUS sgt 2 yrs, USAF stf sgr 4 yrs, Sharpshooters Medal 1946. **Business Addr:** Assistant Vice President of Minority Affairs, Knight-Ridder Inc, One Herald Plaza, Miami, FL 33132.

FITZPATRICK, B. EDWARD
Chief executive. **Career:** Puget Sound Chrysler-Plymouth, Inc, Renton, WA, chief executive, 1986-. **Business Addr:** Puget Sound Chrysler-Plymouth, Inc, 585 Rainier, S, Renton, WA 98055.

FLACK, HARLEY EUGENE
Educational administrator. **Personal:** Born Feb 12, 1943, Zanesville, OH; married Mignon Scott; children: Harley E II, Christophere Farrar, Michael Palmer, Oliver Palmer. **Educ:** OH State Univ, BS Phys Therapy 1965; Kent State Univ, MS Rehab Counsel 1968; State Univ of NY Buffalo, PhD Counselor Ed 1971. **Career:** School of Health Related Prof SUNY AB, asst dean 1971-74; Coll of Allied Health Sci Howard Univ, dean, professor 1974-87; SUNY Buffalo, asst dean, 1971-74, vp, academic affairs, 1987-89; Rowan College of New Jersey; exec vp, provost, 1989-93; Wright State Univ, president, 1993-. **Orgs:** Phys therapist Highland View Hosp 1965-67, Western Reserve Convalescent Home 1967-68; lecturer Counseling Psych Dept Rehab 1969-71; co-chair Health Brain Trust Congressional Black 1979-81; volunteer care giver Omega Hospice & St Agnes Homes 1981-84; pres Natl Soc of Allied Health 1986-88; coord first natl conf Black Perspectives in Biomedical Ethics; American Association of State Colleges and Universities Academic Affairs Resource Center, advisory committee; Middle States Accreditation Association, site visitor; Rowan College of New Jersey, African-American Male Mentoring Program, developer. **Honors/Awds:** 20 Piano Choir Compositions 1968-; dir St John Baptist Youth Choir 1979-84; "Giant Steps" book on sons relationship with father dying of cancer 1982; pianist Martin Luther King Baptist Church Columbia 1984-. **Special Achievements:** Author, "Giant Steps," book on sons relationship with father dying of cancer, 1982; "African-American Perspectives in Biomedical Ethics," Georgetown University Press, 1992; "Case Studies in Allied Health Ethics," 1995; soloist and album producer, "Goree Suite". **Business Addr:** President, Wright State University, 3640 Colonel Glenn, Dayton, OH 45435-0001.

FLACK, ROBERTA
Singer, songwriter. **Personal:** Born Feb 10, 1939, Black Mountain, NC; daughter of Irene Flack and Laron Flack (deceased); married Stephen Novosel, 1966 (divorced 1972). **Educ:** Howard, Univ, BA, music education, 1958. **Career:** Farmville, NC 1959-60 and Washington, DC public schools, teacher, 1960-67; singer/songwriter, 1968-; star, ABC TV special, The First Time Ever, 1973. **Orgs:** Mem Sigma Delta Chi; trustee Atlanta U; mem Delta Sigma Theta. **Honors/Awds:** Albums include: First Take, 1969; Chapter Two, 1970; Quiet Fire, 1971; Killing Me Softly, 1973; Feel Like Makin' Love, 1975; Blue Lights in the Basement, 1977; Roberta Flack, 1978; The Best of Roberta Flack, 1981; I'm The One, 1982; Born To Love, 1983; Hits and History, 1984; Roberta Flack, 1985; Oasis, 1989; Roberta, 1995; writer, TV theme song, Valerie; 2 Grammy Awards, Best Song and Best Record for The First Time Ever I Saw Your Face, 1972, 2 Grammy Awards, Best Record and Best Female Vocalist for Killing Me Soflty With His Song, 1973, Best Pop Duo for Where is the Love (with Danny Hathoway), 1972; City of Washington, DC, Roberta Flack Human Kindness Day, 1972. **Business Addr:** Singer/Songwriter, Magic Lady Inc, One W 72nd St, New York, NY 10023.

FLACK, WILLIAM PATRICK
Government official (retired). **Personal:** Born Mar 19, 1927, Anderson, SC; son of Pinder & Alma Burris Flack; married Thomasenia Mattison. **Educ:** Tuskegee Institute, 1947; Rutgers Univ, 1973; Harvard Univ, 1975. **Career:** RTP Inc, manpower coordinator, 1970-83; Anderson Co Human Resources Commission, exec dir, 1983-84; William Ross & Associates, consultant, 1984; South Carolina Dept of Consumer Affairs, commissioner. **Orgs:** Salem Presbyterian Church, elder and trustee; Anderson County Election Committee, commissioner, 1973-77; National Democratic Party, delegate, 1972. **Military Serv:** US Army, 1945-47. **Home Addr:** 2041 Belt Drive, Anderson, SC 29621, (803)224-1247.

FLAGG, E. ALMA W.
Educator, consultant. **Personal:** Born Sep 16, 1918, City Point, VA; daughter of Caroline E Moody Williams (deceased) and Hannibal G Williams (deceased); married J Thomas Flagg (deceased); children: Dr Thomas L, Luisa Flagg Foley. **Educ:** Newark State Coll, BS 1940; Montclair State Coll, MA 1943; Columbia U, EdD 1955; Newark State Coll, LittD 1968. **Career:** Washington, grade teacher 1941-43; Elem Sch, grade tchr 1943-57, remedial reading tchr 1957-63, vice principal 1963-64, prin 1964-67; Newark State Coll, adjunct instr in English 1964; Sch Bd of Educ Newark, asst supt 1967-83; Montclair State Coll, Rutgers Univ, adjunct instructor 1982-; Educ and Editorial Consultant, 1983-. **Orgs:** Mem NCTM; NCTE; NSSE; American Assn of University Women; Dir YMWCA 1964-73; mem Alpha Kappa Alpha; Soroptimist Intl of Newark; Urban League of Essex Co; NAACP; educ chair Project Pride 1980-; mem Governor's Comm on Children's Serv Plng 1983-87; vice pres, Newark Youth Art Exhibition Inc 1988-; mem Kappa Delta Pi Honor Society in Education 1954-; pres League of Women Voters of Newark 1982-84; member Newark Senior Citizens' Commission; charter member Newark Preservation and Landmarks Committee; vice pres, SHARE, NJ, 1996-; volunteer, NJ Performing Arts Ctr, 1994-. **Honors/Awds:** Distinguished Serv to Educ NSC Alumni 1966; Citizenship Awd Weequahic Comm Council 1967; Hon Degree of Litt D Newark State Coll 1968; Roster of Superior Merit East Side HS Alumni 1969; Disting Serv Awd Cosmopolitan 1970; Adam Clayton Powell Educ Awd NJ Alliance of Black Sch Educators 1981; E Alma Flagg Scholarship Fund establ 1984; E Alma Flagg School Newark dedicated 1985; Sojourner Truth Awd Negro Business and Professional Women 1985; ESHS Disting Alumni Awd 75th Anniversary 1986; Educ Law Ctr Awd 1986; Distinguished Alumna Awd Teachers Coll Columbia Univ 1986; published: Lines and Colors (poetry) 1979, Feelings, Lines, Colors (poetry) 1980, Twenty More With Thought and Feeling 1981. **Home Addr:** 67 Vaughan Dr, Newark, NJ 07103.

FLAKE, FLOYD H.
Cleric, former congressman. **Personal:** Born Jan 30, 1945, Los Angeles, CA; son of Rosie Lee Johnson-Flake and Robert Booker Flake Sr; married Margaret Elaine McCollins; children: Aliya, Nailah, Rasheed, Hasan. **Educ:** Wilberforce Univ, BA 1967; United Theological Seminary, D Min, 1994. **Career:** Miami Valley Child Develop Ctrs, social worker 1967-68; Bethel AME Ch, pastor 1968-70; Xerox Corp, marketing analyst 1969-70; Sec Presb Ch, pastor 1971-73; Lincoln Univ, assoc dean students 1973; Martin Luther King Jr Afro Amer Ctr Boston Univ, univ chaplain marsh chapel & dir 1973-76; Mt Zion AME Ch, pastor 1974-75; Allen Sr Citizen Complex, developer; The Allen Christian School, founder; Allen AME Church, Jamaica, NY, pastor, 1976-86; US House of Representatives, congressman 1986-97; Allen AME Church, NY, pastor, 1997-. **Orgs:** Life mem NAACP; ordained minister African Methodist Episcopal Church; life mem SCLC. **Honors/Awds:** Alfred P Sloan Scholarship Northeastern Univ 1974; Outstanding Admin Lincoln Univ 1972; Richard Allen Fellowship Payne Theol Sem 1967-68; Gilbert Jones Philos Scholarship Wilberforce Univ 1964-66; Ebony's Religion Award; Ebony magazine Black Achievement Award in Religion 1986; Doctor of Humanities Degree, Wilberforce Univ 1987; Doctor of Human Letters, Morris Brown College 1989; Doctor of Divinity, Monrovia College 1984. **Business Addr:** Rev Dr Floyd H Flake, 110-31 Merrick Blvd, Jamaica, NY 11433, (718)206-4600.

FLAKE, NANCY ALINE
Television producer, educator. **Personal:** Born Jul 23, 1956, Detroit, MI; daughter of Margaret E Flake and Thomas M Flake. **Educ:** Howard Univ, BBA acct 1977; DePaul Univ, MS taxation 1981. **Career:** Arthur Andersen & Co, sr tax accountant 1977-80; Laventhol & Horwath, tax accountant supv 1980-81; Coopers & Lybrand, tax accountant mgr 1981-84; Howard Univ, assoc prof of taxation; Howard Univ Small Business Dev Ctr, dir 1984-; Small Business Magazine TV Series, exec producer 1987-. **Orgs:** Advisor Jr Achievement 1979-86; natl conf treas Natl Black MBA Assoc 1983; pres Natl Assoc of Black Accountants 1984-85; bd mem Natl Assoc of Negro Business & Professional Womens Clubs Inc Economic Development Corp 1984-87; bd mem DC Chamber of Commerce 1987-; chairwoman Business Comm DC Chamber of Commerce 1986-87; council mem Mayor Barry's Coord Council Self Sufficiency 1985-, chair Alternatives to Welfare Committee 1989-; comr DC Commiss for Women 1987-90; mem National Assn of Black Accountants. **Honors/Awds:** Cert Publ Accountant 1979-; Minority Bus Advocate of the Year 1987, US Small Bus Admin WA DC 1987; Outstanding Business Leader Bus Exchange Network WA DC 1986; Certificate of Appreciation Amer Assoc of Comm Serv Awd Grad Sch of Business & Public Admin 1987; Delta Sigma Pi Frat 1988-; Executive Producer, Small Business Magazine Television Series 1989-. **Business Addr:** Director, Howard Univ Small Bus Dev, 2600 6th St NW, PO Box 748, Washington, DC 20059.

FLAKES, LARRY JOSEPH
Consulting civil engineer. **Personal:** Born Jan 27, 1947, Birmingham, AL; son of Lurlene Patton Flakes and John Wesley Flakes. **Educ:** Howard U, BSCE 1969. **Career:** DC Hwy Dept Bridge & Traffic Div, engr aide 1965; Water Operations Div, 1968; Wash DC Met Area Govts Dept Sanitary Engr System Planning Div, urban career mgmt intern & urban career student trainee 1967; Lockheed Ga Co Marietta, assoc aircraft engr 1969-70; City of Atlanta, certified position #16, traffic engineer I 1970-71; AL Power Co, high voltage electric power transmission & distribution system constr contract admin engineer 1972-74; So Ry Co, civil engineer 1974-, property tax engineer 1976-81; Atlanta Area Tech Sch, part-time evening inst 1978-82; Norfolk Southern Corp, proj engr mw&s dept, 1981-89; self-employed consulting engineer, currently. **Orgs:** Certified in open competition position #16 Traffic Engineer I City of Atlanta GA 1970-71; reg professional engineer, State of GA 1981; registered professional civil engineer, State of Alabama, 1983; mem Amer Soc Civil Engineering, 1969-; Natl Bapt Convention USA; mem Amer Railway Engineering Assn, 1983-; Natl Soc of Professional Engineers, 1986; NAACP. **Honors/Awds:** Scholarship to atttend Tuskegee Inst, United Negro Coll Fund, 1964; Tuition Scholarship, School of Engineering & Architecture, Howard Univ, 1964-65; Deans List Howard Univ Washington 1967, 1969; Natl Awd ASCE NY 1967; ASCE Awd Natl Student Chap for being editor of "Tel Star" Student Civil Engrs Newsletter; articles written for Tel Star "The Master Builder" origins of civil engrg 1967; ASCE, MD, DC area univs conf & lecture on peaceful uses of nuclear energy and tour of Goddard Space Flight Ctr activities report 1967; Certificate Traffic Eng Inst NW Univ 1970; Cert Mun Adm & Supv Univ GA 1971; Cert Dept of Defense Multi-Protection Design of Structures 1974; Cert Business Law, Mktg 1978. **Military Serv:** USAF ROTC cadet 1964-66. **Home Addr:** 48 18th Court S, Birmingham, AL 35205.

FLAMER, JOHN H., JR.
Educational administrator, association executive. **Personal:** Born Oct 13, 1938, Phila; married Mary E Holder; children: Crystal, Dawn, Melanie, Tedd, Todd, Tamiko, Timothy, John, III, Christopher. **Educ:** Southern Illinois University, BS 1964, MS 1975. **Career:** Job Corps SIU, teacher, coach 1965; IL Youth, prin 1967; Business Affairs SIU, asst to vice pres 1968; Affirmative Action Minority Affairs SIU, asst to pres 1969-; Consult EEO US Civil Svc; Assn Health Recreation & Physical Educ; Alpha Phi Alpha; Natl Affirmative Action Officers, pres 1973; Ethnic Adv Com. **Orgs:** Mem State IL; bd Mem Madison St Clair County Urban League; pres Metro Sickle Cell Anemia; Employment Adv Com Inland Steel; vice pres IL Track & Field Coaches Assn Treas Nat Black Alliance for Grad & Professional Edn.

FLANAGAN, ROBERT B., SR.
Association executive. **Personal:** Born Jan 2, 1929, Atlanta, GA; son of Willie Maude Bales Flanagan and Thomas Jefferson Flanagan, Sr; married Ressie J; children: Robert Jr, Shree, Tracy. **Educ:** Morehouse Coll, AB; NY Univ, safety prog org course; NW Univ, traffic mgmt course; Columbus Coll, police comm rel course; Atlanta GA, urban crisis ctr race relations course. **Career:** NAACP, exec sec Atlanta Br 2 yrs 1967; pres GA conf 1978; field dir natl staff 1968; mem natl bd of dirs 1985; dir field operations Voter Education Project Atlanta GA 1980-84. **Orgs:** Black/Jewish Coalition 1979-87. **Honors/Awds:** Thalheimer State Conf Awd Outstanding Prog Activities Natl NAACP 1973-75 1979; cited by Chief Fulton Co Registrar for voter registration efforts; commendation for leadership and serv as a resource person Pres of GA Assn of Police Comm Rel Officers; cited for work done for rural blacks in GA GA Coun on Human Rel; commended by Chief of Staff USAF for work done a mem of Spec Study Gr Pentagon; While stationed at Maxwell AFB Dr Martin Luter King, Jr, asked him to organize military personnel to participate in Montgomery Alabama Bus Boycott, 1956. **Military Serv:** USAF ret maj. **Home Addr:** 937 Redbud Ln SW, Atlanta, GA 30311.

FLANAGAN, T. EARL, JR.
Dentist. **Personal:** Born Jan 20, 1937, Baltimore, MD; son of Marjorie B Flanagan and Thomas Earl Flanagan Sr; married LaVerne; children: Thomas III, Shelley, Brian. **Educ:** Howard Univ, BS 1959, DDS 1966; St Elizabeths Hosp, intern 1966-67; Howard Univ Hosp, resd 1974-75. **Career:** St Elizabeths Hosp, instr intern prog, chief dental officer 1969-; Private Practice, dentist 1966-. **Orgs:** Mem Natl Dental Assn, Amer Dental Assn, Acad of Gen Dentists, Amer Dental Soc of Anesthesiology, Amer Assn of Hosp Dentists State chmn 1977, RT Freeman Dental Soc, MD Dental Soc of Anesthesiology; life mem NAACP 1976; life mem Urban League 1969-; mem Kappa Alpha Psi, Chi Delta Mu; fellow Amer Dental Soc of Anesthesiology. **Honors/Awds:** American Cancer Society, Harold Krogh Award. **Military Serv:** AUS 1st lt 1959-62. **Business Addr:** 905 Sheridan St, Hyattsville, MD 20783.

FLATEAU, JOHN
Executive director. **Personal:** Born Feb 24, 1950, Brooklyn; married Lorraine Witherspoon. **Educ:** Washington Sq Coll NY U, BA 1972; Baruch Coll, Masters Adm Baruch 1977; US Office of Edn, Pub Serv Educ Fellowship 1975-76. **Career:** NYS

Commn on Hlth Educ & Illness Prevntn, prin resrch analist; Adult Educ Dist Council 37 AFSCME & Hunter Coll CUNY, tchr 1968-74; Program Adminstrn BED-STUY Summer Program, supr 1968-72; NY State Assblymn Albet Vann NY State Legislature, past adminstrv asst; Black & Puerto Rican Caucus Inc of the NY State Legltr, exec dir 1977-78; Nat Black Lay Cath Caucus, past youth chmns natl office black caths, bd dir, Harlem Youth Devel Ctr, past comm wckr 1976; Bedford Stuyvesant Pastoral Planning Program, v pres; Bed-stuyvesant Laymen's Convocation pres past. **Orgs:** Mem Urban Voter Educ Assn; mem Comm Educ Task Force; founding mem Vanguard & Indepdt Dem Assn Inc 56th AD; mem Kings Co Dem Com 1972-; Del NY Judicial Conv 2nd District 1972-; mem NAACP Brooklyn Br; mem Alumni Assos NYU/Baruch Coll; mem MLK Jr Alumn Assn; pres JARM Research Assos Ltd 1979-; political action chmn Convention Planner Black Agenda Conv Brooklyn NY 1980; mem Black United Front NY Met Chpt; mem Macon-macdonough-lewis-stuyvesant Block Assn; former mem 592 Prospect Pl Tenants Assn Recipient. **Honors/Awds:** Life membership award Vannguard Civic Assn; listed Dictionary of Intl Biography 1978; listed Comm Leaders & Noteworthy Am 1978; listed outstanding young men of am 1979. **Business Addr:** C/O Assemblyman Albert Vann, 1360 Fulton St Room 519, Brooklyn, NY 11216.

FLATTS, BARBARA ANN
Attorney. **Personal:** Born Sep 27, 1951, New York, NY; daughter of Amy Morris Flatts and Albert Flatts Sr; children: Albert Paul Peoples, Amy Christina Peoples. **Educ:** Hampton Inst, BA 1972; Am Univ Wash Coll of Law, JD 1974. **Career:** Office of Corp Counsel DC Govt, asst corp counsel 1976-80; US Dept of Labor Benefits Rev Bd, atty-advsor 1975-76; Laborer's Dist & Council Wash DC, law clk 1973-74; US Dept of Justice Environmental Enforcement Section Land & Natural Resources Div, trial atty 1980; New York City Housing Auth Contracts Real Estate & Fin div, atty 1984; New York State Dept of Law, Harlem Regional Office, asst attorney general in charge, 1988-, Employment Security Bureau, asst attorney general, 1986-87. **Orgs:** Bd of dir Girl Scout Council of the Nation's Capital 1977-81; bd of dir Wash Urban League 1977-80; mem Juvenile Justice Adv Com DC 1979-80; mem Alpha Kappa Alpha Sor; mem Washington bar Assn; mem past sec Kappa Beta Phi Legal Assn 1976; exec com bd of dir Council on Legal Educ Opportunity 1973-75; pres Am Univ Chap Black Am Law Student Assn 1974; mem Am Bar Ssn 1975-; mem Alpha Kappa Alpha, Epsilon Pi Omega; connection comm coord Alpha Kappa Alpha; board memeber, Harlem Legal Services, 1990-; United Negro College Fund. **Home Addr:** 8373 Charlecote Rdg, Jamaica, NY 11432-2141. **Business Addr:** Assistant Attorney General in Charge, Harlem Regional Office, New York State Department of Law, 163 W 125th St, Suite 1324, New York, NY 10027.

FLEARY, GEORGE MCQUINN
Judge. **Personal:** Born Sep 6, 1922, Brooklyn, NY. **Educ:** CCNY, BS 1948; Brooklyn Law Sch, LlB 1951. **Career:** City of NY, judge civil ct. **Orgs:** Vp NY State NAACP; bd chmn Brooklyn Urban League 1974-77; pres comus club inc hole in one Clariview Golf Course 1975. **Military Serv:** USAF 1st lt Wwii capt orean war.

FLEMING, ALICIA DELAMOTHE
Business executive, personnel administrator. **Personal:** Born in New York, NY; married John A Fleming. **Educ:** NY Univ, BS 1972, MS 1980. **Career:** NY Univ Med Ctr, office mgr admin 1966-79; Booz Allen & Hamilton, mgr non-exempt personnel 1979-81; Time Inc, employment counselor 1981-85; Non-Exempt Recruiting & Develpmnt, manager 1985-; A D Fleming Group, Inc, pres, currently. **Orgs:** Mem EDGES 1985; mem Women in Human Resources Mgmt 1983. **Business Addr:** President, A D Fleming Group Inc, 392 Central Park W Apt 19K, New York, NY 10025-5676, (212)227-0909.

FLEMING, ARTHUR WALLACE
Cardiothoracic surgeon. **Personal:** Born Oct 1, 1935, Johnson City, TN; son of Vivian Cecile Richardson Fleming and Smith George Fleming, Sr (deceased); married Dolores Caffey-Fleming, Apr 8, 1978; children: Arthur Jr, Robyn, Jon, Mark, Robert, Bernadette, Erik. **Educ:** IL State Normal Univ, attended 1953-54; Wayne State Univ, BA 1961; Univ of MI Medical Sch, MD 1965. **Career:** Detroit Inst of Cancer Rsch, rsch asst 1958-61; Walter Reed Army Medical Ctr, thoracic/cardiovascular surg serv staff 1972-83; Walter Reed Army Inst of Rsch, dept of surgery staff 1974-76, div of experimental surgery chief 1976-77, dir dept of surgery 1977-83; Uniformed Serv Univ of the Health Science, assoc prof of surgery 1978-83; King-Drew Medical Ctr, dir trauma ctr 1983-, prog dir genl surg/chief of surgery 1983-; Charles R Drew Univ of Medicine & Science, professor & chairman, Dept of Surgery, 1983-; MLK General Hospital, chief of surgery, 1983. **Orgs:** Mem Los Angeles County Trauma Directors Cmte 1984-; mem bd of dirs Amer Coll of Surgeons So CA Chap 1986-; pres Soc of Black Academic Surgeons 1986-91; chairman dept of surgery Charles R Drew Univ of Med & Science 1983-; chief of surgery LA County Martin L King Jr/Drew Medical Center 1983-; director Trauma Center LA County King/DreW Medical Center, 1983. **Honors/Awds:** Hoff Medal for Research, 1974; Gold Medal paper, Forum on Progress in Surgery Southeastern Surgical Congress 1977; The Surgeon General's "A" prefix Highest Military Medical Professional Attainment 1981; The Legion of Merit Investigative projects in combat casualty care pioneering of autologous blood transfusions US Army 1983; William Sinkler Award Surgical Section of the National Medical Assn 1990; Friend of the Nurses Award, King-Dew Medical Center Nursing Department 1990; Commendation, Director of the Trauma Center 1989. **Military Serv:** AUS col 17 1/2 yrs; Meritorious Serv Awd USAF 1984. **Business Addr:** Professor and Chairman, Department of Surgery Center, Charles R Drew University of Medicine and Science, King-Drew Medical Center, 12021 S Wilmington Avenue, Los Angeles, CA 90059.

FLEMING, BRUCE E.
Educator. **Personal:** Born Jul 17, 1921, Richmond, VA; married Ruth Lewis; children: Jacqueline, Bruce Jr, Shelia, Gregory. **Educ:** VA St Coll, BS 1942; NY U, MA 1948; IN U, spec 1967; NY U, EdD 1969. **Career:** US Dept of Educ, educ program officer 1974-80; HQ Dept Army, dir instrnl tech 1973-74; Pentagon, EEO officer 1971-73; US Army, educ program officer 1970-71; Ft Lee, EEO offocer 1967-70, educ A-V spec 1954-63; Camp Pickett, 1950-54; NY Univ, consultant 1970-72; IN Univ, assoc prof 1963-65; Washington High School, prin 1949-50; Lucille Hunter School, teacher 1948-49; Walker-Grant High School, 1942-43; VA State Univ, vol counselor career planning & placement office; Intl Educ Serv Inst, vice pres for African Affairs. **Orgs:** Life mem NAACP; Phi Beta Sigma; past v reg dir Eastern Reg Phi Beta Sigma; educ coord VA St Conf NAACP; past mem NEA; mem Nat Urban Leag; past chmn Dist Advancement Com BSA; exec com Petersburg Improvement Assn. **Honors/Awds:** Soc action serv awd Phi Beta Sigma Frat 1956; sev awd human rel Kappa Delta Pi Hon Soc in Educ 1968; educ serv awd Phi Beta Sigma Frat 1974; tchg flw NY Univ 1961; grad asst A-V Cntr IN Univ 1966; OH State Univ Serv Awd 1978; Commanding General Ft Lee VA Public Serv Awd 1986. **Military Serv:** AUSR lt col 30 yrs.

FLEMING, CAROLYN
Editor. **Personal:** Born Jan 11, 1946, Orange, NY; daughter of Helen McCrary Cook and James Ralph Cook; married Ronald Howard Fleming I, Aug 17, 1968; children: Ronald H II, Solomon N J, Jasmin A K, Nimrod M, Jade C, Jewell C, Joy C, Jancka J, Jafrica, Jamaica B. **Educ:** Drake College of Business, 1965; Virginia Union University, 1966. **Career:** Fine Print News, editor; Testing Dept VA Union U1966; Astara Inc Mystery Sch 1976; The Rosicurican Order AMORC. **Orgs:** Dir Fashion Show Blacks Arts Festival 1970; dir Art & Show Black Arts Festival 1970; NRA; Nu-Buff Sportsman Club; Regent Sportsman Club. **Business Addr:** Editor, Fine Print News, PO Box 57, Ellicott Sta, Buffalo, NY 14205.

FLEMING, CHARLES WALTER
Judge. **Personal:** Born Apr 20, 1928, Cleveland, OH; son of Katie Belle and Will B Fleming; married Norma; children: Reginald, Patrice, Charles, Gerald, Carlos. **Educ:** Kent State Univ, BA, 1951; Cleveland Marshall Law LLB, 1955; Cleveland Marshall Law, JD 1968; Cleveland State Univ, DL, 1969. **Career:** Internal Revenue Serv, Intl Revenue, 1954-56; Cuyp County OH, asst rector, 1961-69; OH Attorney General, special asst, 1969-75; Cleveland Municipal Court Judge, 1976. **Orgs:** Pres, John Harlan Law Club, 1971-75; chmn, Criminal Law Section, NBA 1973; bd of dir, NBA 1973; immediate past pres & admin judge, 1982-83; bd of dirs, Natl Assn of Criminal Lawyers, 1970-74; honorary past impl por El Hasa Temp #28; chmn elect, Judicial Council NBA; bd of trustees, Oldo Municipal County Judges. **Honors/Awds:** Outstanding past pres, John Harlan Law; supreme judicial serv, OH Supreme Court cong achive US Congress; 330 mason Prince Holl Eureka #52. **Military Serv:** AUS 1947; Honorable Discharge. **Business Addr:** Judge, Cleveland Municipal Court, 1200 Ontario St, Court Room 14C, Cleveland, OH 44113.

FLEMING, DAVID AARON
Engineer, product designer, architect. **Personal:** Born Aug 21, 1963, Washington, DC; son of Charlotte Ann Long and Alton Leonard Fleming. **Educ:** Stanford University, BSEE, 1986, MSME, 1988; Illinois Institute of Technology, MAr, 1992; Northwestern University, PhD, 1991-. **Career:** Congressional Black Caucus, congressional intern, 1982; IBM, engineer, 1983; Johns Hopkins Applied Physics Lab, engineer, 1985-87; Veteran's Administration Hospital, product designer, 1988; General Electric, product designer, 1989; Amoco Oil, engineer, 1989-92; Walt Disney Imagineering, designer imagineer, 1992-; Tek Designs International, engineer, 1996-. **Orgs:** National Society of Black Engineers, national chairperson, 1989-91, national publications chairman, 1987-89; National Student Support Council for Africa, national co-chairperson, 1991-95; Alpha Phi Alpha Fraternity Inc. **Honors/Awds:** General Electric, Latimer Scholar; Consortium for Degrees for Minorities in Engineering, Fellow, 1985; National Organization of Minority Architects, Scholar, 1989; American Institute of Architect, Roche Traveling Scholar, 1990; Walt Disney Imagineering, Imaginations Design Contest, 1st Place, 1992. **Special Achievements:** Co-designed robotic sign language machine "Dexter, The Fingerspelling Robotic Hand," 1988. **Home Phone:** (410)997-1234. **Business Addr:** Engineer, Tek Designs International, 5214 Thunderhill Rd, Columbia, MD 21045.

FLEMING, ELLIS T.
Business executive. **Personal:** Born Mar 26, 1933, Baltimore, MD; son of Lavanna (Moore) Fleming and Lewis Fleming; married Subenia Mae Pettie, Jun 14, 1953. **Educ:** Brooklyn Coll, Graduated Industrial Relations, 1957; attended CCNY 1958-59; LaSalle Law Correspondence Course, 1963. **Career:** NY Proc Dist, adminstr dir of military personnel prog 1957-62; Haryou-Act, asst exec dir of programs 1963-66; New Breed Ent (1st largest Black clothing mfg in USA), part-owner 1966-70; ETF Assoc Bus Cons, pres; Org & Program Consultants, Bed Stuy Lawyers Assoc, Gov Nelson Rockefeller, White House 1972-73, Jackie Robinson Mgmt Corp 1972; ETF Financial Services, president; consultant to exec dir Natl Bankers Assoc, CUNY Hostos Coll, Bd of Educ Health/Physical Educ Dept; Spanish Amer Merchants Assoc; Congressman Edolphus Towns 11th CD New York, special assistant. **Orgs:** Co-founder, executive director of Marcus Garvey Health Facility 1975-78; consult to Congr E Towns 11th CD (BK) 1984; ex-dir E Flatbush (EF) Ed Proj; chr EF Comm Corp; founder/pres Comm of EF Presidents; EF Urban Planning Study 1978-79; mem Operation Breadbasket; mem Congr Black Caucus Roundtable; co-founder EF Church AV Merch Assn; mem Fed of Block Assn; contrib writer, Consequences of Powerlessness, Youth in the Ghetto; consult clothing mfg & retailers; lectr to bus comm; Planning Bd of Regional Planning Assn for NY, NJ, CT; White House Consultant on programs for Black Americans; gen adv to Natl Youth Movement; adv Opportunity Ind Centers NY; field coord, Brooklyn Boro Pres 1985. **Honors/Awds:** Writer/contributor "Consequences of Powerlessness" authored by Dr Kenneth Clark; author "The Great Deluge"; Man of the Year Awd; Brooklyn Jaycees 1964. **Military Serv:** Korean Conflict 1950-52. **Home Addr:** 2100 N Smallwood St, Baltimore, MD 21216.

FLEMING, G. JAMES
Retired educator. **Personal:** Born Feb 15, 1904, St Croix, Virgin Islands of the United States; son of Ernestine and Alexander; married Hazel L Hampton. **Educ:** Univ of WI, BA 1931; Univ of PA, AM 1944, PhD 1948. **Career:** Journal & Guide, news editor 1931-33; Amsterdam News, news editor 1935-37, exec editor 1952-54; The Amer Dilemma, staff mem 1937-40; Philadelphia Tribune, mgng ed 1939-41; President's Comm Fair Employ Pract, examiner 1941-45; Amer Friends Serv Comm, sec race relations 1945-50; WLIB Radio, news dir 1952-54; Morgan State Univ, prof 1954-74, retired; mem, bd of dir Good Samaritan Hospital of Maryland. **Orgs:** Lecturer to various universities and other organizations; chmn Bd of Regents Morgan State Univ 1976-80; life mem NAACP; mem Hampton Alumni Assn; WI Alumni Assn; former bd mem Florence Crittenton Svc; past-pres MD Assn Pub Adm; former mem Civil Serv Comm. **Honors/Awds:** Author "Who's Who in Colored Amer" 1951; Supervising ed "Who's Who in the United Nations" 1952; Author "All Negro Ticket in Baltimore" 1960; "Why Baltimore Failed to Elect A Black Mayor" 1972; Phi Beta Kappa Univ of Wisconsin; Doctor of Human Letters, Hon, Univ of Maryland.

FLEMING, GEORGE
Educational administrator. **Personal:** Born Jun 29, 1938, Dallas, TX; married Tina Bradley, Mar 2; children: Sonja, Yemi. **Educ:** Univ Washington, Seattle, WA, BA, bus admin. **Career:** Football player, Oakland Raiders, 1961, Winnipeg Blue Bombers, 1963-65; Wash Sec of State, Olympia, WA, examiner foreign corps, 1965-66; Washington-Idaho area Pacific Northwest Bell US West Communications, Seattle, WA, employment assistant, 1966-70, communications cons, Seattle area, 1970-73, personnel sup, Washington-Idaho area, 1973-75, mgr econ develop, Wash-Idaho area, beginning 1975; community develop manager; State of Washington, state representative, 1969-71, state senator, dist 37, 1971-91; US West Communications, Seattle, employee; Seattle Public Schools, exec dir of external relations, 1991-94, director of government relations, 1995-. **Orgs:** American Indsl Devel Cnl; past pres, Pacific Northwest Indsl Devel Cnl; Econ Devel Cnl Puget Sound; bd of dirs, Randolph Carter; adv bd, Urban, Racial, Rural and Disadvantaged Educn; past pres, Econ Devel Cnl of Wash; NAACP; Rainer Valley Enterprise Center; fiscal adv comm, Ntl Conf of State Legislators; bus adv comm, Puget Sound Chamber of Commerce; dir, Econ Devel Execs of Wash; Mason. **Honors/Awds:** LLD, honorary, City Univ, Seattle; Community Service Award, US Justice Dept; UN Human Rights Assn Award; Univ of WA Husky Hall of Fame, 1980; Dem Leader of the Year, 1980. **Business Addr:** Executive Director, External Relations, Seattle Public Schools, 815 Fourth Ave N, Seattle, WA 98109.

FLEMING, JOHN EMORY
Museum director. **Personal:** Born Aug 3, 1944, Morganton, NC; son of Mary E Fleming and James E Fleming; married Barbara Durr; children: Tuliza, Diara. **Educ:** Berea Coll, BA 1966; Univ of KY, 1966-67; Howard U, MA, PhD 1970-74. **Career:** KY Civil Rights Commn, educ specialist 1966-67; Peace Corps, visual aids special 1967-69; USCR Commn, program officer 1970-71; Inst for the Study of Educ Policy, sr fellow 1974-80; Natl Afro-American Museum, dir 1980-. **Orgs:** Mem NAACP 1974-87; bd Assoc Study of Afro-Amer Life and History 1978-93; bd Journal of Negro History 1982-96; vice pres bd Art for Comm Expression 1984-87; panel Columbus Foundation 1986-87; v pres Ohio Museums Assoc 1989-90; board member,

American Assn of Museums, 1990-95; board member, Museum Trustee Assn, 1989-95; president & board member, African-American Museums Assn, 1991-96; White House Conference on Travel and Tourism, 1995; Ohio Becentennial Commission, 1996-2003. **Honors/Awds:** "The Lenghtening Shadow of Slavery," Howard Univ Press 1976; "The Case for Affirmative Action for Blacks in Higher Education," Howard Univ Press 1978; Carter G Woodson Award, Berea College; Martin Luther King Award; OH Library Association Humanities Award. **Business Addr:** Director, National African American Museum, PO Box 578, Wilberforce, OH 45384, (513)376-4944.

FLEMING, JUANITA W.
Educator. **Personal:** Born in Lincolnton, NC; daughter of Bertha Wilson and Joseph Wilson; married William Fleming; children: Billy, Bobby. **Educ:** BS, 1957; MA, 1959, PhD, 1969. **Career:** DC Genl Hosp, head nurse 1957-58; DC Bur of PH, PH nurse 1959-60; Freedman's Hosp Sch of Nursing, instr 1962-65; Howard Univ Dept of Ped, PH nursing consult 1965-66; Univ KY Coll of Nursing, prof nursing assoc dean dir grad studies, assoc vice chancellor academic affairs, special assistant to president, academic affairs and professor of nursing. **Orgs:** Mem Sigma Theta Tau, Amer Nurses Assn Secr 1986-89; mem Council Nurse Rschers 1976-; exec comm MCH Council 1982-85; inducted Amer Acad of Nursing 1975, governing council 1982-84. **Honors/Awds:** Omicron Delta Honr Frat 1983; Women Achievement Awd YWCA 1984; Outstanding Woman Frankfort Lexington Links Inc 1976; ANA Comm Nursing Rsch 1976-80; Fellow Admin Amer Council Educ 1977-78; Outstanding Alumni Awd Hampton Inst 1977; Outstanding Educ Awd KY League for Nursing 1978; Cert of Need and Licensure Bd 1980-84; KY Health Servcs Adv Council appointed by Gov of KY 1979-83, reappointed 1983-85; Maternal Child Health Rsch Grants Review Comm appointed by Sec HEW 1979-84; Great Tchr Awd Alumni Assn Univ of KY 1973; Mary Roberts Fellow 1963, Pre-Doctoral Fellowship 1967-69; Alpha Kappa Mu Hon Soc; Hall of Fame Hampton Univ 1987; Marion McKenna Leadership Award Delta Psi Chapter Sigma Theta Tau, 1988; Inducted, Institute of Medicine, 1990; Lifetime Achievement Award from the Association of Black Nursing Faculty, 1991; Distinguished Membership Award, American Nurses Association, 1994. **Business Addr:** Special Assistant to the President for Academic Affairs, University of Kentucky, 7 Administration Bldg, Lexington, KY 40506.

FLEMING, JUNE H.
City government official. **Personal:** Born Jun 24, 1938, Little Rock, AR; daughter of Ethel Thompson Dwellingham and Herman Dwellingham; married Roscoe L, Mar 11, 1966; children: Ethel, Roscoe Lee III. **Educ:** Talladega Coll, BA 1953; Drexel U, MLS 1954; Stanford U, Cert 1974. **Career:** Brooklyn Public Library, branch librarian 1954-55; Little Rock School Syst, librn 1955-56; Phil Smith Coll, assoc prof 1960-66; Palo Alto Calif, dir librn 1967-81; Palo Alto Calif, city mgr, 1992-. **Orgs:** Adv bd YWCA 1983-; Soroptimsit Club 1980-82; mem Peninsula Links 1986-, Delta Sigma Theta, Rotary 1988-. **Home Addr:** 1101 Hamilton Ave, Palo Alto, CA 94301. **Business Addr:** City Manager, City of Palo Alto, Palo Alto, CA 94303.

FLEMING, MELVIN J.
Business executive. **Personal:** Born Jun 10, 1926, Webster Groves, MO; married Dorothy Adams; children: Barbara, Mel Jr, Kenneth. **Educ:** Lincoln U, BA 1949; UCLA, grad training 1963-64; USC, 1964-65. **Career:** Martin Lutehr King Hosp Los Angeles CA, hosp admin 1973-; Martin Luther King Hosp, asso hosp admin 1970-73; asst hosp admin 1969-70; Dept of Pub Soc Soc Services Los Angeles CA, head prog asst 1967-69; Charles R Drew Postgrad Med Sch Los Angeles, lecturer 1970-; UCLA, preceptor 1972-; USC, preceptor 1972-. **Orgs:** Mem Model Neighborhood Exec Com 1974; Lincoln Univ Los Agneles Alumni Chap 1956-; Lincoln Univ Jeff City MO Alumni Century Club. **Honors/Awds:** Received Achievement Award CA Legislature 1974; man of yr los angeles given by Watts Community 1974; outstanding cit awards from Watts Labor Community Action Com LA Model Neighborhood Prog & Lincoln Univ LA Alumni Chap 1974. **Business Addr:** 12021 S Wilmington, Los Angeles, CA 90059.

FLEMING, PATRICIA STUBBS
Federal government official. **Personal:** Born Mar 17, 1937, Philadelphia, PA; daughter of Marion Turner Stubbs and Dr Fredrick D Stubbs; divorced; children: Douglass, Craig, Harold. **Educ:** Vassar Coll, BA 1957, graduate studies; Univ of PA; Cranbrook Acad of Fine Arts; NY Univ. **Career:** Legislative asst to Representative Augustus Hawkins 1971-73, Representative Shirley Chisholm 1973-75, Representative Andrew Young, Committee on Rules, US House of Representatives 1975-77; special asst to Secretary of Health, Educ & Welfare 1977-79; deputy asst sec for Legislation, US Dept of Educ 1980-81; admin asst to Representative Ted Weiss (D-NY) 1983-86; professional staff mem, Subcommittee on Human Resources and Inter-governmental Relations, US House of Representatives 1986-93; special asst to the secretary, Department of Health and Human Services, 1993-94; Interim Natl Aids Policy, coordinator, 1994; The White House, Natl AIDS Policy, director, 1994-. **Orgs:** Bd mem Minority Legisl Educ Prgm; bd mem Black Student Fund, TransAfrica, Maryland Council on Latin America, Natl Center for Therapeutic Riding. **Honors/Awds:** Educ Policy Fellows Program 1971-72; speeches, panels, related to educ for disadvantaged or minority persons, the AIDS epidemic; articles on same topics in a variety of Publ. **Business Addr:** Director, Office of Natl AIDS Policy, The White House, Washington, DC 20500.

FLEMING, QUINCE D., SR.
Educational administrator. **Personal:** Born Dec 7, 1915, Mt Hope, WV; married Vivian; children: Quince D. **Educ:** Tuskegee Inst, BS 1939; PA State; Univ of WI at River Fall. **Career:** Jefferson County Bd of Educ, admin 1967-72, teacher 1940-67. **Orgs:** Pres Charles Town City Council; pres Jefferson Co Parks & Recreation; mem Jeff Co Bd of Edn. **Honors/Awds:** Achievement award NAACP; serv award Selective Serv USA; 5-10-15 & 20 Yrs Agr Serv Future Farmers of Am.

FLEMING, RAYMOND RICHARD
Educator. **Personal:** Born Feb 27, 1945, Cleveland, OH; son of Ethel Dorsey Fleming and Theodore Robert Fleming; married Nancy Runge, Nov 15, 1969; children: John, Peter, Stephen. **Educ:** Univ of Notre Dame, IN, BA, 1967; Univ of Florence, Italy, 1967-68; Harvard Univ, Cambridge MA, 1968-69, PhD, 1976. **Career:** Univ of Notre Dame, Notre Dame IN, instructor, 1969-72; Univ of CA, San Diego CA, asst prof, 1973-80; Miami Univ, Oxford OH, assoc prof of Italian and asst dean of graduate school, 1980-, assoc dean of graduate school, 1985-87; PA State Univ, Univ Park PA, prof of com lit and Italian, currently. **Orgs:** Dante Society of Amer, Amer Council of Learned Societies. **Honors/Awds:** Ford Foundation Fellowships, 1966, 1972; Fulbright Grant to Florence Italy, 1967; Woodrow Wilson Fellowship to Harvard Univ, 1968; Ingram-Merrill Poetry Award, 1971; Alexander Von Humboldt Fellowship to Germany, 1978; author of Ice and Honey (book), 1979; American Philosophical Society Research Grant, 1982; author of Diplomatic Relations (book), 1982; author of Keats, Leopardi, and Holderlin (book), 1987; Natl Endowment for the Humanities, grant, 1989, endowed professorship, 1991. **Business Addr:** Professor of Comparative Literature and Italian, Pennsylvania State University, 433 N Burrowes Building, University Park, PA 16802.

FLEMING, THOMAS A.
Educator. **Personal:** Born 1933; married; children: three. **Educ:** Detroit Bible College, bachelor degree, religious education; Eastern Michigan University, MA, special education, 1968. **Career:** W J Maxey Boys Training School, teacher, 1968; First Baptist Church, associate minister, currently; Washtenaw County Juvenile Detention Center, head teacher, 20 years; Academic Affairs, Eastern Michigan Univ, assist to the provost, currently. **Orgs:** W J Maxey Boys Training School, volunteer. **Honors/Awds:** Council of Chief State School Officers, Encyclopaedia Brittanica, Natl Teacher of the Year, 1992; State Board of Education, Teacher of the Year, 1991-92; Honorary Doctorate, Eastern MI Univ, Education, 1994; Honorary Doctorate Coll Misericordia, Dallas, PA, Humane Letters, 1994. **Military Serv:** US Army Natl Guard, overseas in France, Germany. **Business Addr:** Natl Teacher of the Year, Council of Chief State School Officers, c/o Director John Quam, PO Box 7982, Ann Arbor, MI 48107.

FLEMING, VERN
Professional basketball player. **Personal:** Born Feb 4, 1961, Long Island City, NY; married Michelle Clarke; children: Vern Jr. **Educ:** Georgia, 1984. **Career:** Indiana Pacers, guard 1984-. **Orgs:** US Olympic gold medal winning basketball team. **Honors/Awds:** Coached Kodak All-Amer team for 1983-84; unanimous selection for AP & UPI first team All-SEC; All-Amer honors, MVP of SEC tourney, All-Tournament Selection; mem of the US Select Team. **Business Addr:** Professional Basketball Player, Indiana Pacers, 300 E Market St, Indianapolis, IN 46204-2603.

FLEMING, VERNON CORNELIUS
Manager. **Personal:** Born Dec 19, 1952, Louisa County, VA; son of Josephine Robinson Fleming and William E Fleming; married Vanessa Doris Seaberry; children: Chanell A, Charmaine A. **Educ:** Hampton Univ, BA 1974; College of William & Mary, MBA 1980; US Army Command & General Staff Coll, diploma 1987. **Career:** US Army (Coll of Wm & Mary), asst prof of military sci 1980-83; US Army Reserves, instructor 1985-95; Procter & Gamble, purchasing manager 1983-95, sr purchasing manager, 1995-. **Orgs:** Chmn bd of dirs Williamsburg Head Start 1982-83; Reserve Officers Association 1983-, Prime Mover, Purchases Black, 1989-94; Kappa Alpha Psi Frat; co-chmn prog cmte Natl Black MBA Assoc; National Hampton Alumni Association; president council, Boy Scouts of America; board of directors, Kappa Alpha Psi Fraternity. **Honors/Awds:** Service Awd Peninsula League of Youth 1982; Officer of the Year Cincinnati Chap Kappa Alpha Psi 1985; Polemarch's Awd Cincinnati Chap Kappa Alpha Psi 1987; Silver Graver, Boy Scouts of America, 1996; Hampton University Alumni Association, Alumni of the Year, 1995. **Military Serv:** US Army Air Defense Artillery, Lt Colonel (retired); Meritorious Service Medal; Army Commendation Medal w/3 Oak Leaf Clusters, Army Achievement Medal w/One Oak Leaf Cluster, Overseas Ribbon, Natl Defense Ribbon, Parachutist Badge, Army Serv Ribbon. **Business Addr:** Sr Purchasing Manager, Procter & Gamble Co., 11520 Reed Hartman Hwy, Cincinnati, OH 45241.

FLEMMING, CHARLES STEPHEN
Diplomat. **Personal:** Born Oct 30, 1948, Castries, Saint Lucia, West Indies; son of Mary Magdalene Whitney Flemming and James Flemming. **Educ:** City College of New York, New York, NY, BA, 1977; New York University, New York, NY, MA, 1979, MPhil, 1984, PhD, 1985. **Career:** Malcolm-King College, New York, NY, instructor, 1979-81; New York Univ, adjunct instructor, 1981-84; Bronx Community College, New York, NY, adjunct instructor, 1981-; Mission of St Lucia to the UN, New York, NY, ambassador, 1980-94. **Orgs:** Member, American Political Science Assn, 1980-; member, International Political Science Assn, 1988-; member, International Studies Assn, 1988-; member, Caribbean Studies Assn, 1987-; member, International Assn of Permanent Representatives, 1989-. **Honors/Awds:** Taraknath Das Prize, New York University, 1983; Pi Sigma Alpha, National Political Science Honor Society, 1980; Commendation, City Government of New York City, 1979. **Home Addr:** PO Box 4254, Grand Central Station, New York, NY 10163-6030.

FLEMMING, LILLIAN BROCK
City official, educator. **Personal:** Born Jul 27, 1949, Greenville, SC; daughter of Lila Mae Martin Brock and James Dennis Brock; married Rev Johnadad M Flemming, Jan 2, 1980; children: Davit, Johnandad II, Emanuel. **Educ:** Furman Univ, BA 1971, MEd 1975. **Career:** Greenville City Council Citizen Advisory, chmn 1979, 1980; Southside HS, math teacher 1971-; Greenville City Council, 1981-, vice mayor pro-tem, council-mem 1981-85, mayor pro-tem, 1989-. **Orgs:** Vice pres Greenville Cty Educ Assoc 1978-79; pres Greenville Cty Educ Assoc 1979-80; bd of dir Sunbelt Human Advancement Resource Ent 1981-88; del Dem Natl Conv, 1984, 1988; Natl Council of Negro Women; NAACP, sustaining member; Ronald McDonald House, director. **Honors/Awds:** Comm Serv Client Council of Western Carolina 1981; Woman of the Year Client Council of Western Carolina 1982; Human Relations Greenville Cty Educ Assoc 1984; Outstanding Comm Serv Epsilon Iota Zeta Chap Sor 1984; Teacher of the Year, Southside HS 1974; Martin Luther King Leadership Award, Phillis Wheatley Leadership Organization, 1990; William F Gibson Service Award, Greenville NAACP, 1991; Community Service Award, Azah Temple #140, 1991; Mt View Baptist Church, Distinguished Service Award, 1992; South Carolina Baptist Educ & Missionary Convention, Political Service Award, 1993; Girl Scouts Blue Ridge Council, Woman of Distinction Award, 1994; Greenville County Human Relations Commission, Cooper White Humanitarian Award, 1994; School District of Greenville County, Third Runner-Up for Teacher of the Year, 1993-94. **Business Addr:** Mayor Pro-Tem, Greenville City Council, PO Box 2207, Greenville, SC 29602.

FLETCHER, ARTHUR ALLEN
Federal government official. **Personal:** Born Dec 22, 1924, Phoenix, AZ; married Bernyce; children: Phyllis, Sylvia, Arthur J, Paul, Phillip, Joan. **Educ:** Washburn U, BA 1950; KS State U, Postgrad Courses; San Fran State Coll. **Career:** US Commission on Civil Rights, chm, 1990-; Pres Ronald Reagan, advisor; Pres Gerald Ford, deputy urban affairs advisor; Pres Richard M. Nixon, Domestic Cncl Cabinet Com, chmn; Nat Urban League, exec dir 1972-73; UN Gen Assembly, US & alternate delegate; US Dept of Labor, asst sec for wage & labor 1969-71; State Of WA, cand for election as Lt Gov 1968; WA, spl asst to Gov 1969. **Orgs:** Member of numerous professional & civic groups. **Honors/Awds:** Recipient of numerous awards. **Business Addr:** Chairman, US Commission on Civil Rights, 330 Independence Ave SW, Washington, DC 20201.

FLETCHER, CLIFF
Broadcast media executive. **Career:** WWWZ-FM, president, currently. **Business Phone:** (803)556-9132.

FLETCHER, GLEN EDWARD
Automobile dealership executive. **Personal:** Born Aug 6, 1951, Auburn, NY; son of Naomi P Fletcher and Merritt W Fletcher; married Donna M Mattes, Jul 21, 1979; children: Kasha B, Garrison A. **Career:** New York State Electric & Gas, laborer, 1970-77; Motorla Communications, 1977-78; Fox Dealership, sales and sales manager, beginning 1978-, partner, general manager, currently. **Orgs:** Minority Ford Lincoln Mercury Dealers Association. **Honors/Awds:** Kappa Alpha Psi, Businessman of the Year, 1992. **Home Addr:** 6 Cherry St Rd, Auburn, NY 13021. **Business Addr:** President/General Manager, Fox Ford Co Inc, 1068 Arsenal St, Watertown, NY 13601, (315)782-7200.

FLETCHER, HOWARD R.
Government employee. **Personal:** Born Dec 24, 1924, Washington, DC; married Eva Irene; children: Carolyn, Howard Jr. **Educ:** Howard Univ, BS 1949, additional studies 1949-50. **Career:** Bureau of the Census Washington DC, computer mgmt 1951-80; United Nations, computer tech adv 1980-81; Washington DC, data processing consult 1981-82; Mt Vernon Coll Washington DC, comp sci faculty 1983; Towson State Univ, computer sci faculty 1984; MCES Univ of MD Coll Park, comp & info syst officer 1984-. **Orgs:** Mem, sr warden 1975, vestryperson 1971-73, 1983-85, convenor convocation 10 1971-73, lay reader 1970-80, Transfiguration Episcopal

Church; past pres DC Chap of the Prometheans Inc 1972-73; mem Kappa Alpha Psi Polemarch 1975-76; mem ACM, Amer Natl Stardards Inst, ANSI SIG on Programming Langs. **Honors/Awds:** US Dept of Commerce Silver Medal Awd for Computer Programming Tech 1967; Episcopal Wash Diocesan Review Bd 1972-75; Kappa Alpha Psi Eastern Province Achievement Awd 1974. **Military Serv:** AUS 1943-46. **Business Addr:** Computer & Info Syst Officer, MCES Comp & Info Systems, University of MD, College Park, MD 20742.

FLETCHER, JAMES ANDREW
Business executive. **Personal:** Born May 8, 1945, Tulsa, OK; son of Edna Katherine Fletcher and Howard Bruce Fletcher; married Karen Kite; children: Howard Bruce, Jamie Katherine, Lancelot Lansing. **Educ:** MIT, BS 1967; Fairleigh Dickinson Univ, MS (Cum Laude) 1973; Harvard Grad Sch of Business Admin, MBA (w/High Distinction) 1972. **Career:** GE Systems, simulation engr 1967-68; General Rsch Corp, systems analyst 1969; IBM Corp, mktg rep 1972-73, financial prog administrator 1974-76, lab controller 1976-78, financial program mgr 1979-81, planning consolidation mgr 1981-83, pricing mgr IPD 1983, dir of plans & controls 1983-85; Unisys Corp, staff vice pres pricing & business analysis 1985-89, vice pres of Finance, Communications Line of Business Marketing Division 1989-90, vice president of Corporate Financial Planning and Analysis, 1990-91, vice pres of business operations, 1991; Howard University, vice pres of business and fiscal affairs/treasurers, 1991-95; University of Colorado at Boulder, vice chancellor of administration and finance, 1995-96; Morehouse College, vice pres for business and finance, 1997-. **Orgs:** Mem Amer Friends Serv Comm 1980-; mem Friends Comm for Natl Legislation; mem NAACP, White House Fellows Assoc. **Honors/Awds:** George F Baker Scholar Harvard Grad Sch of Business Admin 1972; White House Fellow 1973-74; mem AFSC South Africa Trip Delegation 1979, mem, FWCC South Africa Trip Delegation, 1989; author "A Quaker Speaks from the Black Experience, The Life and Collected Works of Barrington Dunbar,"1980; co-author Friends Face the World 1987; elected mem of Harvard Business School Century Club; exec asst to deputy dir Office of Management & Budget. **Business Addr:** Vice Pres, Business & Finance, Morehouse College, 830 Westview Dr, Atlanta, GA 30314.

FLETCHER, JAMES C., JR.
Government official. **Personal:** Born May 20, 1934, Bowie, MD; son of Marguritte Helen Shelton-Fletcher and James C Fletcher; married Vernelle A Hammett Fletcher, Mar 18, 1954; children: Anthony (deceased), Carol Anderson, Andrea Fletcher. **Educ:** Attended Howard Univ, Washington DC. **Career:** Fed Govt (retired), Washington DC, computer analyst; City of Glenarden, Glenarden MD, councilman, 1974-83, mayor, 1985-. **Orgs:** Bd of dir, Prince Georges Municipal Assn, 1986-88, pres, 1988-89; bd of dir, Maryland Municipal League, 1987-. **Military Serv:** US Air Force, Airman 1st class, 1953-57. **Business Addr:** Mayor, Town of Glenarden, 8600 Glenarden Pkwy, Municipal Building, Glenarden, MD 20706.

FLETCHER, LOUISA ADALINE
State official (retired). **Personal:** Born Jan 3, 1919, Independence, KS; daughter of Anna T Wilson Wesley and Charles L Wesley; married Allen T Fletcher, Mar 24, 1938 (deceased); children: Jerold V Fletcher. **Educ:** Amer Technical Society, Chicago IL, Certificate, Business Admin, 1938; several management training certificates, 1970-72. **Career:** US Navy Dept, Bremerton WA, clerk typist, 1944-45; Campbell Grocery Store, Bonner Spring KS, clerk, 1945-52; US Treasury, Kansas City MO, graphotype operator, 1952-53; Dept of Health, Education, and Welfare, Social Security Administration,Kansas City MO, clerk typist, 1954-65, reviewer, 1965-67, computer claims clerk supervisor, 1965-75; manager, Fletcher's Rentals, 1970-; mem, Kansas Public Employees, Relation Board, 1977-85. **Orgs:** Pres, NAACP KS State Conference, 1974-; Natl Assn of Retired Federal Employees, 1977-; NAACP Natl board of dir, 1979-; Natl Comm to preserve Social Security and Medicare, 1988-; pres, PTA Bonner Springs KS School, 1940-42. **Honors/Awds:** Outstanding Performance, SSA, 1964-67; NAACP outstanding service Award, 1964, 1977, 1984; NAACP App Service Award, 1976, 1986, 1989; Louisa A Fletcher Day, Kansas City KS, 1978; Mother of the Year, Church Award, 1979, 1986; Gov First MLK Award, 1985; Plaque, Special Leader for Community, Bonner Springs, 1986; author of articles for Kansas City Call & Globe papers, 1987-1988; Speeches printedfor Tabor Coll, 1987-88.

FLETCHER, MILTON ERIC
Human resources executive. **Personal:** Born Feb 20, 1949, New Orleans, LA; son of Mertis Whittaker and Ervin Fletcher Jr. **Educ:** Southeastern Louisiana, BA, marketing, 1971; University of Detroit, MBA, 1991. **Career:** Detroit Diesel Allison, EEO representative, 1976-79; GM Bldg Division, staff assistant, 1979-81; GM Technical Staffs, supervisor, human resources management, 1981-85, supervisor, recruiting, 1985-87, manager, personnel placement, 1987-92; Saturn Corporation, manager, human resources, 1992-. **Orgs:** Alpha Phi Alpha, Gamma Lambda Chapter, Education Foundation, 1988-; Community Case Management Services, Inc, president board of directors, 1976-92; Southern University Business & Industries Cluster, co-chairman, 1985-; Hartford Memorial Baptist Church, deacon, 1987-92; Spruce St Bapt Church, deacon, 1992-. **Honors/Awds:** Southern University, Honarary Alumni, 1989; HBCU Council of Deans, Black Engineer of the Year - For Affirmative Act in Industry, 1992; Southeastern Louisiana University, Commencement Speaker, 1992; General Motors Corp, Chairman's Award For Excellence in Comm Services, 1987. **Home Phone:** (615)321-5237. **Business Addr:** Manager, Human Resources, Saturn Corporation, 100 Saturn Parkway, MD-E22, PO Box 1500, Spring Hill, TN 37174-1500, (615)486-5758.

FLETCHER, PATRICIA LOUISE
Educator. **Personal:** Born Jun 20, 1938, Stuebenville, OH; daughter of Mr & Mrs Clifford Mayo; married Lawrence Fletcher, Jan 24, 1960; children: Dr Anthony Fletcher. **Educ:** Steubenville School of Cosmetology, 1964; Franciscan Univ, 1969; W Virginia Univ, MA, 1972; Dayton Univ, Educational Adm Specialist, 1979. **Career:** Steubenville City School, 1967-72, high school sup, 1972-80, adm principal, 1980-97. **Orgs:** Fair Housing, pres, 1980-92; Alpha Kappa Alpha Sorority, pres, 1990; United Nations Assn of USA, 1994; Franciscan Univ, pres, bd advisory, 1995; Natl Assn of Colored Women's Club, pres, 1996-98; United Way of Jefferson Cty, pres, 1996; Jefferson Comm Coll, vp, 1997; Assn Childhood Dev, pres; NAACP, life mem. **Honors/Awds:** Cameo Women's Ctr, Outstanding Educator, 1991; Franciscan Univ, Honorary Doc Degree, 1993; African-American Comm Award, 1994; Ohio Women's Hall of Fame, 1994; Steubenville City School, Path Finders, 1996. **Special Achievements:** Developed curriculum for Steubenville City School, 1973. **Business Addr:** President, National Association of Colored Women's Clubs, 5808 16th St, NW, Washington, DC 20011, (202)726-2044.

FLETCHER, ROBERT E.
Photographer, film maker, writer, educator. **Personal:** Born Dec 12, 1938, Detroit, MI; son of Rose Lillian Fletcher and Robert Fletcher; married; children: Kabenga. **Educ:** Fisk Univ, attended 1956-59; Wayne State Univ, BA 1961; Natl Educ TV Film Training Sch, attended 1970; Comm Film Workshop Council TV News Cinematography Prog 1971; Natl Acad of TV Arts & Sci/Third World Cinema Prod Inc 1976-77; New York University School of Law, JD, 1990. **Career:** No Student Movement Harlem, field organizer 1963-64; SNCC Jackson MS, Selma AL Atlanta GA, photographer field coord editorial & air dir 1964-68; freelance photographer journalist & film maker 1968-; Brooklyn Coll, adj prof dept of film studies 1975-76; "Vote for Your Life", prod/dir 1977; "Weatherization, What's It all About?"; Video & TV Prod, summer 1977; WPIX-TV, bi-weekly talk show; "A Nation in View", co-producer; Cravath, Swaine & Moore, attorney, 1991-. **Orgs:** Mem Intl Photographers of the Motion Picture Indus; chmn bd dir Rod Rodgers Dance Co 1973-; photographs pub in Ebony, Essence, Black Enterprises, Tuesday, Life, Redbook, NY Mag; author of publ in MS. **Honors/Awds:** Cinematographer dir "A Luta Continva" 1971; documentary film on liberation struggle in Mozambique "O Povo Organizado" 1975; panelist "Voices of the Civil Rights Movement" Smithsonian Inst 1980. **Business Addr:** Attorney, Cravath, Swaine & Moore, Worldwide Plaza, 825 Eighth Ave, New York, NY 10019-7415.

FLETCHER, SYLVESTER JAMES
Environmental company executive, business executive. **Personal:** Born Apr 24, 1934, Ebony, VA; son of Christeal Bishop Fletcher and Saint Luke Fletcher; married Catherine Moore, Sep 10, 1955; children: Karen Fletcher-Jackson, Keith Errol. **Educ:** Virginia State University, BA, agronomy/soil science, 1956. **Career:** US Department of Agriculture, Soil Conservation Service, supervisory soil scientist, 1956-76; Natural Resource Dynamics Inc, president/mgr, certified professional soil scientist, 1976-; Mother Flercher's Inc, president, 1983-; Energenesis Development Corp, president, 1986-. **Orgs:** Newton Rotary, head various committees, 1976-; Soil Conservation Society of America, 1956-83; NJ Soil Conservation Society of America, president, 1971-72; NJ Association of Professional Soil Scientists, charter president, 1974-76; Soil Science Society of America, Agronomy Society of America, 1956-; American Registry of Certified Professionals in Agronomy, Crops, Soils, 1980-. **Special Achievements:** Outstanding Performance Rating, USDA, Soil Conservation Service, 1963; author, Soil Survey Report of Sussex County, NJ, publisher, USDA, SCS, 1975; author, Soil Survey Report of Warren Co, NJ, publisher, USDA, SCS, 1979; co-founder, president, Fast Food Business: Mother Fletcher's Inc, 1983; inventor, modular-stackable front loading container, patent # D 310.744, 1990. **Home Addr:** 18 Wolf's Corner Rd, PO Box 15, Greendell, NJ 07839, (201)383-5668. **Business Addr:** President, Natural Resource Dynamics Inc, PO Box 333, 100 Sparta Ave, Newton, NJ 07860, (201)383-6111.

FLETCHER, TERRELL
Professional football player. **Personal:** Born Sep 14, 1973, St Louis, MO. **Educ:** Univ of Wisconsin, graduated with a degree in English. **Career:** San Diego Chargers, running back, 1995-. **Business Addr:** Professional Football Player, San Diego Chargers, Qualcomm Stadium, 9449 Friars Rd, San Diego, CA 92108, (619)280-2111.

FLETCHER, TYRONE P.
Educational administrator. **Personal:** Born Mar 5, 1939, River Jct, FL; married Doris M McRae; children: Michael, Jeffrey, Carol, Kim. **Educ:** FL A&M U, BS 1957-61; Central MI U, MPA 1976. **Career:** US Army Command & Gen Staff Coll, instructor 1975-79; US Army ROTC, Ft Valley State Coll, pms 1979-83, dir of recruitment 1983-. **Orgs:** State coord Assault on Illiteracy Pgm 1984; advisory bd mem Columbus GA Times Newspaper 1984; Alpha Phi Alpha 1959; Sigma Pi Phi 1984. **Honors/Awds:** Roy Wilkins Meritorious Award NAACP 1980. **Military Serv:** AUS lt col; Silver Star; Bronze Star; Legion of Merit; Meritorious Serv Medal 1961-83. **Business Addr:** Dir of Recruitment, Fort Valley State College, PO Box 4203 FUSC Fort Valley, Fort Valley, GA 31030.

FLETCHER, WINONA LEE
Educator (retired). **Personal:** Born Nov 25, 1926, Hamlet, NC; daughter of Sarah Lownes Lee and Henry F Lee; married Joseph G Fletcher, Mar 28, 1952; children: Betty Ann Fletcher. **Educ:** Johnson C Smith Univ, Charlotte NC, AB, 1947; Univ of Iowa, Iowa City, MA, 1951; Indiana Univ, Bloomington PhD, 1968; attended 5 Univ in West Africa, Toga, Dahomey, Ghana, Nigeria, 1974. **Career:** Delwatts Radio/Electronics Inst, Winston-Salem NC, sec/teacher, 1947-51; Kentucky State Univ, Frankfort, prof/area coordinator, 1951-78; Lincoln Univ, Jefferson City MO, dir/costumer instructor, summers 1952-60; Indiana Univ, Bloomingtn, prof theatre & afro-amer studies, 1978-94, asoc dean coll of arts and sciences, 1981-84. **Orgs:** Costumer, Michiana Summer Theatre, summer 1956; dir of cultural affairs, Upward Bound, KY St. Univ, 1966-67; adjudicator, Amer Coll Theatre Festival, 1973-; mem, KY Arts Commission, 1976-79; consultant, John F Kennedy Center, 1978-; natl pres, Univ/Coll Theatre Assoc, 1979-80, mem, Natl Commission on Theatre Educ, 1980-85, American Theatre Association; US Natl Commission for UNESCO, 1981-85; coordinator, Kennedy Center Black College Project, 1981-84; advisory bd mem, 1st Intl Women Playwrights Conference, 1987-88. **Honors/Awds:** Elected to Coll of Fellows, Amer Theatre Assn, 1979; co-author, Offshoots: The H F Lee Family Book, 1979; Graduate Natl Service Award, Alpha Kappa Alpha, 1980; US Delegate to 5th World Congress on Drama, 1981; Distinguished Alumna, Johnson C Smith Univ, 1986; Elected to Natl Theatre Conference, NTC,New York City, 1988; Career Achievement Award, ATHE, 1993; BTN Award Named in Honor, 1994. **Home Addr:** 317 Cold Harbor Dr, Frankfort, KY 40601.

FLEURANT, GERDES
Educator. **Personal:** Born Jul 7, 1939, Port-au-Prince, Haiti; son of Fanie Jn-Charles Fleurant and Jacques Fabien Pradel Fleurant; married Florienne Saintil; children: Herve, Maimouna. **Educ:** Univ of Haiti, BA Soc Sci 1964; New England Conservatory of Music, BMus Organ 1968; Northeastern Univ, MA Sociology 1971; Tufts Univ, MMus Composition 1980, Caribbean Culture and Music, PhD, 1987. **Career:** Ecole Ste Trinite Haiti, dir of gen music 1959-64; Coll St Pierre Haiti, social studies teacher 1962-64; Brockton Schools, gen music teacher 1968-70; Brandeis Univ, lecturer in black music 1973-74; Assumption Coll, vstg professor in sociology 1976-77; Wellesley Coll, vstg professor in black music 1985-; Salem State Coll, assoc prof of sociology 1971-89; prof of sociology 1989-; dir of African Amer studies; Brown Univ, visiting professor, 1992. **Orgs:** Consult City of Boston Bilingual/Bicultural Phase II 1976, RI Black Heritage Soc Desegregation Program 1980-81; bd mem Advocacy for Comm Changes 1980-83; mem editorial bd New England Jrnl of Black Studies 1982-; bd mem Cambridge Haitian Amer Assoc 1984-85; mem Cambridge Peace Comm 1984-85; pres Natl Council for Black Studies NE Reg 1984-86; consultant Humanities Inst Belmont MA 1987; Patriotic Coumbite of Haitian Diaspora (pres) 1987-91; board chairman CPDH, 1991-. **Honors/Awds:** Article "Class Conflict in Haiti" in Ethnic Conflict & Power 1973; Disting Serv Salem State Coll 1980, 1985; Professional Devel Grant Salem State Coll 1981, 1985; Article "Ethnomusicology of the Rada Rite of Haiti" Perfiles Tufts Univ 1984; Introductory Readings in African American Culture (ed) Ginn Press 1988; Dancing Spirits; Rhythms & Rituals of Haitian Vodun, Greenwood, pres, 1996. **Home Addr:** 222 Putnam St, Cambridge, MA 02139. **Business Addr:** Assoc Prof of Music, Wellesley College, Wellesley, MA 02181, (617)283-2167.

FLEWELLEN, ICABOD
Historian, consultant, museum administrator, counselor. **Personal:** Born Jul 6, 1916, Williamson, WV. **Educ:** Guyer School of Real Estate, graduate, 1968; Cuyahoga Comm Coll, associate degree, 1974; Case Western Reserve University, BS, 1993. **Career:** Dr James C Evans, director of trade and technical education, WVSC, part-time chauffeur, 1941; African & Afro-Amer history & Black studies, researcher 1943-84; Veteran's Administration, 1948-66; Case Western Reserve University, 1966-81; Comm Develop Block Grant, dir 1983-84; Afro-Amer Cultural & Historical Soc Museum & Rsch Library, founder/dir 1953-; African-American Assiento Memorial Museum, founder, 1985, president, currently. **Orgs:** John Malvin Foundation Inc, founder, 1960; life member: Urban League, NAACP, Association for the Study of Afro-American Life and History, National Council of Negro Women; National Museum of Afro-Amer Culture & History, appointed by Gov John J Gilligan, 1972. **Honors/Awds:** Cert of Appreciation City of Cleveland 1973; grant re-

cipient Natl Endowment for the Humanities 1980; Carter G Woodson Awd of Distinction 1980; Cert of Recognition City of Cleveland 1980; Thomas Jefferson Awd WJKW TV and the Amer Inst of Public Serv 1980; Comm Awd OH Conf of the United Church of Christ 1980; Comm Awd Cleveland Chap of the WV State Coll Alumni; Comm Awd Cuyahoga Bd of Comm 1980; African-American Archives Auxiliary of the Western Reserve Historical Society, Dr Carter G Woodson Heritage Award, 1992. **Special Achievements:** Multiple exhibits including two-day exhibit for City of Cleveland Mayor's Comm on Aging 1975; lecture & slide exhibit at Cleveland's Main Public Library on Alexander S Pushkin & Alexander Dumas Pere; 30 day exhibit at Karamu House "Early Black Church in Cleveland and Its Music," 1980. **Military Serv:** Quartermaster 1942-45. **Business Addr:** President, African-American Assiento Memorial Museum, PO Box 606033, Cleveland, OH 44106-4504.

FLINT, MARY FRANCES
Utility company manager. **Personal:** Born Jan 28, 1950, Rustburg, VA; daughter of Virginia James and Cleveland James; married William B Flint, Jun 29, 1974; children: JeVonda, RaShonda. **Educ:** Florida A&M University, BS, 1974; Xavier University, MBA, 1979. **Career:** American Electric Power Co, accountant, 1974-77, supervisor, planning & budgeting, 1977-86, administrative assistant, office of president, 1986-89, customer services manager, 1989-93, community services mgr, 1993-. **Orgs:** PowerCo Credit Union, treasurer, recording secretary, 1992-; Ohio Society of CPA's, 1985-. **Special Achievements:** Certified public accountant, 1985. **Business Addr:** Community Services Manager, American Electric Power Co, 215 N Front St, Columbus, OH 43215, (614)464-7846.

FLIPPEN, FRANCES MORTON
Association executive, teacher. **Personal:** Born in Point Pleasant, WV; daughter of Mary J Morton and Edward L Morton; married John; children: J Bryan. **Educ:** WV St Coll, BS business admin; NYU, MA; NY Univ & WV U, post-grad. **Career:** Delta Sigma Theta Inc, dep dir, management consltant; Nat Council of Negro Women Inc, program specialist; US Dept of Labor, WICS liaison job corps; Shady HS, counselor; Stratton HS, teacher, currently. **Orgs:** Mem Am Personnel & Guid Assn; NEA; NBEA; former vice pres prgm devel chmn Am Assn of Univ Women; Raleigh Co Educ Assn; Am Assn of United Nations; Nat Congress of PTA; life mem NAACP; bd dir YWCA; Am Leg Aux Post 70; life mem former regl dir Midwest Delta Sigma Theta; life mem Nat Coun of Negro Women; mem Links Inc, Eastern Area Treasurer; mem Raleigh Co Assn of Mental Hlth; Raleigh Co Assn of Arts & Hum; Maids & Matrons Soc Study Club; former bd of religious educ Ebenezer Bapt Ch; Alpha Delta Sigma Honorary Society, mem Women's Committee, Washington Performing Arts Society; mem, Women's Committee for the Natl Symphony; bd of dirs Boys and Girls Clubs of America, Washington DC. **Honors/Awds:** Spec recogn awd vol Comm Welfare Coun & WICS Job Corps.

FLIPPER, CARL FREDERICK, III
Company executive. **Personal:** Born Jan 23, 1948, New Orleans, LA; son of Carl F Jr & Maurine Garrette Flipper; divorced; children: Joseph Simeon III, Monica Lee, Natalie Amanda. **Educ:** Sangamon State Univ, BA, economics, 1977; Univ of IL, MBA, finance & marketing, 1985. **Career:** Peoria Urban League, apprenticesip specialist, 1968-71; Springfield IL Urban League, dir labor affairs, 1971-74; Sangamon State Univ, asst vp for bus & admin, 1974-78; IL Fair Employment Practices Comm, admini mgr, 1978-80; Midwest Broadcasting Co, pres & gen mgr, 1980-84; Deloitte Haskins & Sells, sr bus analyst, 1984-87; Lewis-Clark State Coll, dir bus development ctr, 1987-91; Oregon Enterprise Forum, pres, 1992-. **Orgs:** Omega Psi Phi Fraternity Inc, 1968-; Natl Economic Development & Law Ctr, steering comm chair, 1990-; NAACP Portland Branch, bd, 1994-. **Special Achievements:** Community Economic Development, publication, 1990; Econometric Modeling of Economic Development, co-investigator, 1990; Community Needs Statistical Analysis, Eastern Washington/Northern Idaho, 1990. **Home Addr:** 2538 NE Killingsworth, Apt 4, Portland, OR 97211, (503)281-9605. **Business Addr:** Pres & CEO, Oregon Enterprise Forum, Inc, 2611 SW Third Ave, Ste 200, Portland, OR 97201, (503)222-2270.

FLIPPINS, GREGORY L.
Mayor. **Personal:** Born Jul 2, 1950, Shaw, MS. **Educ:** Valley State U, 2 yrs; Delta State U, Grad 1972. **Career:** Shaw MS, mayor; Internal Revenue, 2 1/2 yrs; Bolivar Co Neighborhood Youth Corp, counselor; Chenault Chevrolet Co, car salesman. **Orgs:** Fellow Inst of Politics. **Business Addr:** 106 Mose Ave, Shaw, MS 38773.

FLONO, FANNIE
Journalist. **Personal:** Born May 4, 1952, Augusta, GA; daughter of Prudence King Flono and Adam Flono. **Educ:** Clark College, Atlanta, GA, BA, Journalism, 1974. **Career:** Greenville (SC) News, asst city editor, 1983-84; Charlotte (NC) Observer Newspaper, asst, state editor, 1984-86, asst political editor, 1986-88, political editor, 1988-90, night metro editor, 1990-91, city editor, 1991-93, editorial writer & columnist, 1993-96, associate editor, 1996-. **Orgs:** Past president, Charlotte Area Assn of Black Journalists, 1988, recording secretary, 1990; program committee, National Assn of Black Journalists, 1990; deputy regional director, Region IV National Assn of Black Journalists, 1990; member, Charlotte Business League, 1987-90; Natl Assn of Black Journalists, national scholarship co-chairperson, 1992-93. **Honors/Awds:** Investigative Reporting, reporter, First Place, United Press International (GA), 1980; Georgia School Bell Award, Georgia Association of Educators 1978; Investigative Reporting Editor 1st Place, North Carolina Press Assn, 1988, 2nd Place, Column Writing, 1994; Fellow, Atlantic Bridge Foundation. **Business Addr:** Associate Editor, The Charlotte Observer, 600 S Tryon St, Charlotte, NC 28202.

FLOOD, EUGENE, JR.
Financial services company executive. **Educ:** Harvard College, BA, economics, 1978; MIT, PhD, economics, 1983. **Career:** Stanford University, Graduate School of Business, instructor, finance, five years; lecturer at executive training programs held by MIT, Nomura School of Advanced Management, Tokyo, International Management Institute, Geneva; Morgan Stanley & Co, research & development group, manager, Derivative Trading Group, manager, 1990-91, mortgage-backed securities area, trader, 1991-95; Morgan Stanley Asset Mgmt, portfolio mgr, 1995-. **Honors/Awds:** National Science Foundation, Minority Fellowship in Economics. **Special Achievements:** Area of specialization: asset-backed securities. **Business Addr:** Principal, Morgan Stanley Asset Management, 1221 Ave of the Americas, 22nd Fl, New York, NY 10020, (212)703-4000.

FLOOD, SHEARLENE DAVIS
Educational administrator. **Personal:** Born May 13, 1938, Jefferson Co, AL; married Ralph; children: Angela Harris, Clinton Harris Jr. **Educ:** Elem Educ & Music AL State U, BS 1958; Fellow Univ of AL Guidance Inst, EDPA 1968-69; Educ Adminstr & Higher Educ Univ of AL Tuscaloosa, EdD 1 976. **Career:** Jefferson State Jr Coll, dir of counseling, career lab, special serv 1969-; Birmingham Public School System, instructor of Speech Art & Music 1963-68; Jefferson County Public School System, instructor of English & Music 1960-63; Opelika Public School System, instructor of Music 1958-60. **Orgs:** Mem Am Assn of Comm & Jr Coll; Council on Black Am Affairs; exec mem Student Personnel Div AL Jr & Comm Coll Assn; mem AL Personnel & GuidanceAssn; mem Advisor Nat Assn of Mental Health; comm devel office City of Birmingham; supr of Comm serv JECCO Comm Serv. **Honors/Awds:** Citizens award of Merit in Field of Psychological Services; Booker T Washington Business Coll Beta Psi accounting honor soc 1971; outstanding faculty mem Jefferson State & Jr Coll; service award Jefferson State Jr Coll 1980. **Business Addr:** Jefferson State Junior College, 2601 Carson Rd, Birmingham, AL 35215.

FLORENCE, JERRY DEWAYNE
Automotive company executive. **Personal:** Born Oct 6, 1948, Wichita, KS; son of Rosa Lee Florence and Alise Lee Florence; married Winifred T Watson-Florence, May 4, 1974; children: Michael Brigham. **Educ:** Wichita State University, BS, chemistry, 1971; Rensselaer Polytechnic Institute, 1975; MIT, 1985. **Career:** General Electric, Silicones Division, manager of RTV industrial marketing, manager of market planning; GMC, Packard Electric Division, manager of business planning, manager of sales, marketing, & business planning, AC Rochester Division, divisional director of marketing strategy, Cadillac Division, director of marketing & product strategy, general director of marketing & product planning. Nissan Motor Corp USA, vice pres of marketing, 1993-. **Business Addr:** VP, Communications and Strategic Devt., Nissan Motor Corp, USA, PO Box 191, Gardena, CA 90248-0191, (310)532-3111.

FLORENCE, JOHNNY C.
City transportatin official. **Personal:** Born Jun 9, 1930, Birmingham, AL; son of Eugenia Franklin Florence and Johnnie Florence; married Lillie M Florence Dowdell, Aug 27, 1949; children: Cynthia Ann Patton, Byron Richie, June Levern Kennedy, Robert Daryln, Cedric Jon. **Educ:** Drake Univ, Des Moines IA, 1948; Temple Univ, Philadelphia PA, 1949-51; Indiana Univ NW, East Chicago IN, court management, 1952. **Career:** Inland Steel Co, East Chicago IN, machinist, 1951-76; Lake County Court, Crown Point IN, probation off, 1968-71; City of East Chicago, IN, recreation dir, 1971-83, transit dir, 1983-. **Orgs:** Vice pres, Conference of Minority Transportation Conference; vice chairman, Indiana Black Expo; NAACP Voters Registration Drive; Indiana State Minority Education Bd. **Honors/Awds:** Indiana Black Expo Award, 1976, 1982, 1984; NAACP Award, 1984. **Business Addr:** Director, East Chicago Public Transit, 5400 Cline Ave, East Chicago, IN 46312.

FLORES, JOSEPH R.
Artist, educator. **Personal:** Born Oct 22, 1935, New York, NY; son of Margaret Saunders Gray and Joseph L. Flores; children: Sam, Monique, Grace, Joe, Sean. **Career:** Model Cities Prog, Rochester, NY, dir of communications, 1968-72; Action for a Better Community, Rochester, NY, artist, 1972-74; self-employed, Rochester, NY, artist, 1974-86; Rochester City School Dist, Rochester, NY, instr aide, 1986-. **Honors/Awds:** First place, Whole World in His Hands, St John Fisher College, 1990; first place, Roots & Wings, Waterfront Art Show, 1989; second place, Tired, Letchworth State Park, 1988; first place, Mother Earth, Joseph Ave Art Show, 1987; first place, Martin Luther King Jr, Black American Artists, Inc, 1987. **Special Achievements:** Paintings in the White House, Oval Office during President Carter Administration; previous shows and Awards, street fair, Ann Arbor MI, Detroit Festival of Arts, 1996; Cornhill Arts Festival, Allentown Festival, Buffalo NY; Commissioned Portraits of Rochester Mayor & Executive Director Monroe County. **Home Addr:** 67 Rosalind St, Rochester, NY 14619.

FLORES, LEO
Banker. **Career:** Falcon Natl Bank, pres, currently. **Business Phone:** (512)723-2258.

FLOURNOY, VALERIE ROSE
Author, editorial consultant. **Personal:** Born Apr 17, 1952, Camden, NJ; daughter of Ivie Mae Buchanan Flournoy and Payton I Flournoy Sr (deceased); divorced. **Educ:** William Smith Coll, Geneva NY, BA History 1974. **Career:** The Dial Books for Young Readers, asst editor 1977-79; Silhouette Books/Pocket Books, sr editor 1979-82; The Berkley Publishing Group/Second Chance at Love, consulting editor 1982-83; Vis A Vis Publishing Co 1985-. **Honors/Awds:** ALA Notable Book American Library Assn Chicago 1985; Christopher Award The Christophers Inc 1985; Coretta Scott King Award for Illustrations ALA/Chicago 1985 all awards for The Patchwork Quilt; First recipient Ezra Jack Keats New Writer Award 1986 sponsored by Ezra Jack Keats Found and The NY Public Library; books published "The Twins Strike Back" The Dial Press 1980; "The Best Time of Day" Random House 1978; "The Patchwork Quilt" The Dial Press/Dutton 1985. **Home Addr:** 505 Arch St, Palmyra, NJ 08065.

FLOWERS, D. MICHELLE
Public relations executive. **Personal:** Born Apr 22, Greensboro, NC; daughter of Thomas & Catherine Flowers. **Educ:** Winston-Salem State University, MA, English, 1976; Northwestern University, MS, Advertising, 1982. **Career:** Integon Insurance Co, communications specialist, 1976-78; Chicago Urban League, communications spec/media rel manager, 1978, director of public relations, 1983; Golin/Harris, account supervisor, 1984; Burrell Public Relations, assistant vice pres, 1986, senior vp, 1987; Flowers Communications Group, president/CEO, currently. **Orgs:** Museum of Science/Industry, Black Creativity Advisory Committee; Alpha Kappa Alpha Sorority; Publicity Club of Chicago; Public Relations Society of America; Black Public Relations Society; Life Directions board of trustees. **Honors/Awds:** Cystic Fibrosis Foundation, Media Award; Carolinas Association, Business Communicators Award; Public Relations Society of America, Two Silver Anvils; Publicity Club of Chicago, One Gold/Three Silver Trumpets Award of Merit. **Business Addr:** President/Chief Executive Officer, Flowers Communications Group, 542 S Dearborn, Ste 1150, Chicago, IL 60605.

FLOWERS, LETHON
Professional football player. **Personal:** Born Jan 14, 1973. **Educ:** Georgia Tech. **Career:** Pittsburgh Steelers, defensive back, 1995-. **Business Addr:** Professional Football Player, Pittsburgh Steelers, Three Rivers Stadium, 300 Stadium Circle, Pittsburgh, PA 15212, (412)323-1200.

FLOWERS, LOMA KAYE
Psychiatrist. **Personal:** Born Feb 27, 1944, Chardon, OH; daughter of Elsie Kaye Brown and Dr George W Brown; married Edgar Flowers Jr; children: George, Brandon. **Educ:** OBK, Sr in Absentia 1964; Western Reserve Univ, AB (magna cum laude), honors biology 1965; Case Western Reserve Univ, MD 1968. **Career:** San Francisco Gen Hosp, internship 1968-69; Stanford Univ Med Center, residency in psychiatry 1969-72; E Palo Alto Comm Health Ctr, dir of mental health 1971-73; VA Hospital San Francisco, chief mental hygiene clinic 1973-77; Various Schools Health Business Org, consultant 1970-; Delaney & Flowers Dream Center, dir 1983-; Univ of CA, assoc clinical prof of psychiatry; Host, BET Cable TV, "Dr Flowers on Call" 1985-86; private practice of Psychiatry, 1977-. **Orgs:** Vice pres 1983-85, chmn of bd of dirs Assn for the Study of Dreams 1984-85; AMA; Amer Psychiatric Assn; Negro Business & Professional Women's Assn; NAACP, Black Psychiatrists of America; SFUSD, PTSA. **Honors/Awds:** Motar Bd 1963; Francis Hobart Herrick Prize 1964; Phi Beta Kappa 1964; Medical School Faculty Awd for Rsch 1968; author, "The Morning After: A Pragmatists Approach to Dreams," Psychiatric Journal, Univ of Ottawa, 1988; author, "Psychotherapy Black & White," Journal of Natl Medical Assn, 1972; "The Dream Interview Method in a Private Outpatient Psychotherapy Practice," New Directions in Dream Interpretation, Suny Press, 1993. **Business Addr:** Director, Delaney & Flowers Dream Center, 337 Spruce St, San Francisco, CA 94118, (415)333-8631.

FLOWERS, RALPH L.
Attorney. **Personal:** Born Jan 23, 1936, Palatka, FL; married. **Educ:** FL A&M U, BS 1957, EdM 1968, JD 1968. **Career:** Private Law Practice; City of Fort Pierce, former judge, prosecutor

1972-73; Riviera Beach, prosecutor ad litem 1971-73; Lincoln Pk Acad, band dir 1959-65; atty 1968. **Orgs:** Bd dir & legal adv Indian Rvr Invstmnt Corp Pioneer Investment Capital Corp; bd dir FL Rural Legal Serv; chmn Judicial Council FL Chap Nat Bar Assn; Exalted Ruler Pride of St Lucie Lodge IBPOE of W 1970; mem Alpha Phi Alpha; Am Bar Assn; FL Assn of Trial Lawyers; mem St. **Honors/Awds:** St Lucie Co C of C Flowers for the living award Radio Station WIRA 1973; pub safety award St Lucie Co Safety Council 1974; Alpha Phi Alpha man of the year 1976. **Military Serv:** AUS 1st lt 1957-59. **Business Addr:** Sunrise Theatre Bldg, Fort Pierce, FL 34946.

FLOWERS, RUNETTE (RUNETTE FLOWERS WILLIAMS)
Physician. **Personal:** Born Apr 2, 1945, Donaldsonville, GA; married W Alphonso. **Educ:** Dillard Univ New Orleans, BA Biology 1967; Tuskegee Inst, MS 1969; Meharry Med Coll Nashville, MD 1973. **Career:** Dekalb Grady Clinic, staff pdtrcn 1976-; Dept of Preventive Medicine Emory Univ & Sch of Med, asst prof 1976-; Emory U, residency 1973-76; Edwood-parent-child Ctr, consult 1977-; Sch of Nursing GA Bapt Hosp, lectr 1978-79; Nurse Practitioner Program Emory, preceptor 1978-79. **Orgs:** Mem Health Systems Agency GA 1980; mem Greater Atlanta Pediatric Assn 1978-; mem Delta Sigma Theta Sorority/Beta Kappa Chi Sci Honor Soc. **Honors/Awds:** Most Outstanding Student in Pediatrics Meharry Med Coll 1973; Grace M James Award in Pediatrics Meharry Med Coll 1973. **Business Addr:** Emory Univ Sch of Med, Atlanta, GA.

FLOWERS, SALLY A.
Dentist. **Personal:** Born Jun 18, 1954, Detroit, MI; daughter of Mary Jane Perry James and Willie Oscar Flowers; children: Krystle Maria, Dawn Amber. **Educ:** Eastern Michigan University, Ypsilanti, MI, 1971-74; Howard University School of Dentistry, Washington, DC, DDS, 1978; Johns Hopkins, Baltimore, MD, MPH, 1980. **Career:** Pimlico Dental Clinic, Baltimore, MD, assoc dentist, 1979-; Dr Roy Baptiste, Silver Springs, MD, assoc dentist, 1980-82; Dr Barbara Johnson, Washington, DC, assoc dentist, 1981-82; Capital Hill Dental Center, Washington, DC, assoc dentist, 1981-82; self employed, Washington, DC, general dentist, 1982-. **Orgs:** Recording sec, Kennedy Street Assoc of Merchants of Professionals, 1989-91; member, Academy of General Dentistry, 1982-; member, DC Dental Society, 1982-; member, American Dental Association, 1982-; president, Pin Pro High Golf Club, 1987-88; Johns Hopkins Alumni; Howard University Alumni. **Business Addr:** Dentist, Dental Office, 250 Kennedy St, NW, Washington, DC 20011.

FLOWERS, SONNY. See FLOWERS, WILLIAM HAROLD, JR.

FLOWERS, WILLIAM HAROLD, JR. (SONNY FLOWERS)
Attorney. **Personal:** Born Mar 22, 1946, Chicago, IL; son of Ruth C Flowers and W Harold Flowers Sr; married Pamela Mays Flowers. **Educ:** Univ of CO, BA 1967, Law School JD 1971. **Career:** Adams County, deputy district attorney; Private Practice, 1979-; Holland & Hart, Denver CO, partner, 1989-97; Hurth Yeager & Sisk LLP, 1997-. **Orgs:** Bd of dirs KGMU Radio Station 1981-84; bd of dirs CO Criminal Defense Bar 1982-83; regional dir Natl Bar Assoc 1984-85, vice pres, 1990-91, bd of governors 1985-; exec bd Boy Scouts of Amer 1983-; pres elect 1986, pres 1987 Sam Cary Bar Assoc; mem Comm Corrections Bd 1984-90; bd of governors, Colo Trial Lawyers Assn, beg 1988, vice pres, 1997-98; mem, Judicial Nominating Comm 1988-; bd of dir, CO ACLU, 1990. **Honors/Awds:** Outstanding Alumnus, Univ of CO Black Students Alliance, 1990; Award in Business-Community Action, Boulder County, CO, 1990; Presidential Award, Natl Bar Assn, 1987. **Business Addr:** Hurth Yeager & Sisk, LLP, 4860 Riverbend Rd, PO Box 17850, Boulder, CO 80308.

FLOYD, CLIFF (CORNELIUS CLIFFORD)
Professional baseball player. **Personal:** Born Dec 5, 1972, South Bend, IN. **Career:** Montreal Expos, infielder, 1993-96; Florida Marlins, 1997-. **Business Addr:** Professional Baseball Player, Florida Marlins, Pro Player Stadium, NW 199th St, Miami, FL 33169, (305)356-5848.

FLOYD, DEAN ALLEN
Physician. **Personal:** Born Mar 10, 1951, Loris, SC; son of Ernestine Floyd and Stephen J Floyd Sr; married Gail Payton; children: Anissa Deanne, Dean Allen II, Allycia Summer. **Educ:** Clemson Univ, BS 1972; Medical Univ of SC, MD 1976; Richmond Memorial Hospital, residency 1977-80. **Career:** Family Health Centers, Inc, medical dir 1980-85; Private Practice, 1985-. **Orgs:** Medical consultant SC State Health & Human Services 1985-. **Business Addr:** 2601 Millwood Ave, Suite H, Columbia, SC 29205.

FLOYD, ELSON
Educational administrator. **Personal:** Born in Henderson, NC; married Carmento; children: two. **Educ:** Univ of North Carolina, BA, political sci, speech, MA, adult education, PhD, higher and adult education. **Career:** Eastern Washington Univ, vp for student services, 1990-91, vp for administration, 1991-92, exec vp, 1992-93; Washington State Higher Education Coordinating Bd, exec dir, 1993-95; Univ of North Carolina, asst dean for student life, judicial programs officer, 1978-81, special asst to the vice chancellor, dean of the Division of Student Affairs, General Coll advisor, asst dean of the Division of Student Affairs and the General Coll, asst dean of the General Coll and the Coll of Arts and Sciences, assoc dean for academic services, 1981-88, asst vp for student services for UNC System, 1988-90, vice chancellor, chief admin and operating officer, 1995-98; Western Michigan Univ, pres, 1998-. **Orgs:** Rotary Intl; United Way of America; Natl Assn of Student Personnel Administrators; Assn for the Study of Higher Education; Education Commissions of the States. **Business Addr:** President, Western Michigan University, Office of the President, Kalamazoo, MI 49008-5134.

FLOYD, ERIC AUGUSTUS (SLEEPY)
Professional basketball player. **Personal:** Born Mar 6, 1960, Gastonia, NC. **Educ:** Georgetown, Political Science, Public Admin, 1982. **Career:** NJ Nets, 1983, Golden State Warriors, 1983-88, Houston Rockets, 1988-93; SanAntonio Spurs, 1993-. **Honors/Awds:** Georgetown's All-Time leading scorer; MVP, NCAA West Region Tourney. **Business Addr:** Professional Basketball Player, San Antonio Spurs, 600 E Market St, Ste 102, San Antonio, TX 78205, (512)554-7787.

FLOYD, JAMES T.
Association executive. **Personal:** son Of Willie J Floyd; married Dr Barbara Floyd; children: James T Jr, Norman V, Kimberly U, Javonda A, Brittaine Nakkole. **Educ:** Allen Univ, BS 1957; Tuskegee Univ, MS 1965. **Career:** Sanders HS, teacher 1957-58, head football coach 1960-64; Beck HS, chmn sci dept 1965-69; Union Carbide Corp, process engr 1969-72; WR Grace & Co, process engr 1972-75, quality assurance mgr 1976-82, group leader engrg, 1983-; F & M Development Enterprises Inc, CEO, currently. **Orgs:** Board of dir, Phillis Wheatly Assn, advisory board, USCG College; advisory board, Dept Mental Health. **Honors/Awds:** Selected to Ebony's 100 Most Influential Blacks in Amer 1985-1987; Entrepreneur of Year, 1990. **Military Serv:** AUS 2 yrs. **Home Addr:** 106 Brandon Way, Simpsonville, SC 29681.

FLOYD, JEREMIAH
Association executive. **Personal:** Born Jan 8, 1932, Laurens, SC; son of Clairender Floyd and Willie James Floyd; married Clara Brown; children: Camille, Edgar. **Educ:** Allen U, BS 1956; Northwestern U, MA 1960, PhD 1973. **Career:** Evanston Public Sch, princpl 1970-73; Nat Sch Bd Assn, dir urban & minority rel 1973-76, asst exec dir 1976-78, assoc exec dir 1978-. **Orgs:** Vp Northwestern Univ Alumni Educ 1973-76; pres NU Chap Phi Delta Kappa 1972-74; mem bd of dir United Way Evanston 1971-76; vice chmn, Montgomery Community Services Partnership 1986-95; mem, Montgomery Coll Gen Educ Advisory Comm 1988-; mem, State Advisory Comm on Adult Educ and Community Service 1986-88. **Honors/Awds:** NSF fellowship Nat Sci Found Northwestern Univ 1959-62; IDEA fellow Rockford Coll 1969; pres Wilmette Sch Dist 39 Bd of Educ 1976; mem Montgomery Cnty Bd of Educ MD 1984; vice pres Montgomery Cnty Bd of Educ MD 1985-86. **Military Serv:** USAF m sgt; Nat Defense Medal; Good Conduct Medal 1955. **Home Addr:** 5909 Aberdeen Rd, Bethesda, MD 20817.

FLOYD, MALCOLM
Professional football player. **Personal:** Born Dec 19, 1972, San Francisco, CA. **Educ:** Fresno State. **Career:** Los Angeles Rams, wide receiver, 1993-95; St Louis Rams, 1996-. **Business Addr:** Professional Football Player, St Louis Rams, One Rams Way, St Louis, MO 63045, (314)982-7267.

FLOYD, MARK S.
Attorney. **Personal:** Born Nov 30, 1958, El Paso, TX; son of Vardrene Bailey Floyd and Columbus Floyd; married Lauren Generette Floyd, Sep 2, 1990. **Educ:** Stanford University, Stanford, CA, AB, music/political science, 1980; Columbia Law School, New York, NY, JD, 1983. **Career:** Squire, Sanders & Dempsey, Cleveland, OH, partner, 1983-. **Orgs:** Executive committee, The Cleveland Ballet, 1989-93; executive committee, legal counsel, Cleveland Baroque Orchestra, 1992-96; steering committee, Cleveland Orchestra; tenor soloist, assistant conductor, Mt Zion Congregational Church; Crains Cleveland Business Top 40 Young Business Leaders Under 40; bd of trustees, Cleveland Bar Association. **Business Addr:** Partner, Squire, Sanders & Dempsey, LLP, 4900 Key Center, 127 Public Sq, Cleveland, OH 44114, (216)479-8500.

FLOYD, MARQUETTE L.
Judge. **Personal:** Born Oct 14, 1928, Winnsboro, SC; son of Mary Brown; married Mildred L Floyd. **Educ:** NYU, BS 1958; Brooklyn Law Sch, LLB 1960. **Career:** Suffolk Co, dist court judge; Pvt Prac NY, atty; Ronek Park Civic Assn, pres; New York State, Riverhead, NY, supreme court justice, 1990-. **Orgs:** Pres N Amityville Rep Club; dir chmn ACE Cntr; OEO; dir Legal Aid Soc; dir Sunrise Psychia Clinic; dir & Key Amityville Youth Orgn; sec Eta Theta Lambda Chpt; Alpha Phi Alpha Frat Inc; mem Suffolk Co Bar Assn; NY State Bar Assn; Dist Ct bd of Judges Suffold Co; Dist Ct bd of Judges of Nassau & Suffolk Co; member, Supreme Court Justices; member, Suffolk County Charter Revision Committee; member, New York State Jury System Management Advisory Committee. **Honors/Awds:** Community Service Award, 100 Black Men Nassau/Suffolk, 1982; Schroll of Honor Award, National Association of Business and Professional Women, 1983; Achievement Award, Babylon Council of Black Republicans, 1985; County Court Judge of the Year, Suffolk County Court Officers Association, 1986; Judge of the Year, Suffolk County Bar Association, 1987; Man of the Year, Suffolk County Police Conference, 1990. **Military Serv:** USAF t/sgt 1948-54; National Service Award. **Business Addr:** Judge, Office of Court Administration, New York State Supreme Court Justice, Griffing Ave, Riverhead, NY 11901.

FLOYD, SAMUEL A., JR.
Educational administrator. **Personal:** Born Feb 1, 1937, Tallahassee, FL; son of Theora Combs Floyd and Samuel A Floyd; married Barbara; children: Wanda, Cecilia, Samuel III. **Educ:** Florida A&M Univ, BS 1957; Southern IL Univ, MME 1965, PhD 1969. **Career:** Smith-Brown HS, dir instrumental music 1957-62; Florida A&M Univ, asst dir bands 1962-64; Southern IL Univ, instructor, assoc prof 1968-78; Fisk Univ, prof 1978-83; Columbia Coll Chicago, dir ctr for black music rsch 1983-90, 1993-, academic dean, 1990-93. **Orgs:** Mem College Music Soc 1970-87, Sonneck Soc 1980-87, Amer Musicological Soc 1986-87. **Honors/Awds:** Publs "Black Music in the United States," Kraus Publications 1983; "Black Music Biography," Kraus Publications 1987; "The Power of Black Music," Oxford University Press, 1995; Natl Assoc of Negro Musicians, Distinguished Service Awd, 1986; Sonneck Society for American Music, Irving Lowens Award for Distinguished Scholarship in American Music, 1991. **Business Addr:** Dir, Columbia College, Center for Black Music Rsch, Chicago, IL 60605.

FLOYD, VERNON CLINTON
Broadcasting executive, engineer, educator. **Personal:** Born Nov 20, 1927, Chickasaw Terrace, AL; son of Ora A Ellis Floyd and Nathan D Floyd; children: Marjorie A, Victor C. **Educ:** Dunbar Trade School, Chicago IL, 1945-46; Industrial Training Inst, Chicago IL, 1945-46; Tuskegee Inst, Tuskegee Inst AL, 1948-52. **Career:** Station WMOZ, Mobile AL, chief engineer, 1953-65; Carver Technical Trade School, Mobile AL, electronics instructor, 1966-68; Community Educ Program, Hattiesburg MS, 1988; Circuit Broadcasting Co, Hattiesburg MS, founder/owner, 1969-; Electrical Contractor, Hattiesburg MS, 1972-; WORV-AM/WJMG-FM. **Orgs:** Advancement chmn, Boy Scouts of Amer, 1971-73; mem, BOAZ Lodge #4, 1980-; electrical bd mem, City of Hattiesburg, 1981-83. **Honors/Awds:** Pioneered & developed station WORV-AM, 1969; One of 10 Most Outstanding Men, Hattiesburg Ministerial Group, 1971; designed, built & made total technical instillation, WJMG-FM, 1982. **Military Serv:** One-hundred fifty-ninth Artillery Batt, T5, 1946-48. **Business Addr:** President, General Manager & Chief Engineer, Circuit Broadcasting Company of Hattiesburg, 1204 Graveline St, Hattiesburg, MS 39401.

FLOYD, VIRCHER B.
Educator, community development administrator (retired). **Personal:** Born Apr 3, 1928; married. **Educ:** Earlham College, BA, 1952, MA, 1954; Univ of Pittsburgh, MSW, 1962. **Career:** Sewickley Community Center, exec dir, 1956-60; Pittsburgh Regional Office of Pennsylvania Dept of Public Welfare, state social worker, 1961-63; Rural Community Devel Unit, Tlaxcala Mexico, AFSC, director, 1963-65; Townsend Community Center, Richmond IN, executive director 1965-68; urban programs rep, Peace Corps, Bogota, Colombia, staff dir, 1968-70; Career Serv Office, Earlham Coll, asst prof, dir 1970-75; field director, Foster Parents, Plan International, Columbia, Nicaragua, Brazil, Liberia, Ecuador and Honduras, 1975-92; Foryth Tech Comm College, teacher, tutor. **Orgs:** Vice pres, Allegheny Co Federation of Settlements; natl bd mem, Amer Friends Serv Committee, 1972-75; Academy of Certified Social Workers. **Honors/Awds:** Author of several publications. **Military Serv:** AUS 1954-56. **Home Addr:** 7300 Oak Park Court, Pfafftown, NC 27040.

FLOYD, WILLIAM ALI
Professional football player. **Personal:** Born Feb 17, 1972, St Petersburg, FL; married Bonita; children: William Andrew. **Educ:** Florida State, attended. **Career:** San Francisco 49ers, running back, 1994-. **Business Addr:** Professional Football Player, San Francisco 49ers, 4949 Centennial Blvd, Santa Clara, CA 95054, (415)562-4949.

FLOYD, WINSTON CORDELL
Physician. **Personal:** Born Nov 13, 1948, Edgefield, SC; married Francena Pinckney. **Educ:** Tuskegee Inst, BS 1969; MD 1973; Cook Co Hosp, intern 1973-74; Meharry Med Coll, resd 1974-77. **Career:** Pvt Prac, internal med; Anderson Meml Hosp, attending staff; Meharry Med Coll, instr internal med 1976-77. **Orgs:** Dipl Nat Bd of Med Exmnrs 1974; Am Bd of Internal Med 1977; mem AMA; mem Alpha Phi Alpha Frat. **Business Addr:** 400-G N Fant St, Anderson, SC 29621.

FLOYD ANDERSON, DIONNE CAMILLE
Journalist. **Personal:** Born Jul 9, 1965, Fort Worth, TX; daughter of Essie Floyd Sanders and Robert Floyd; married Jimmy Anderson, Jun 5, 1989. **Educ:** University of North Texas, Denton, TX, BA, 1988. **Career:** WTWC-TV, Tallahassee, FL, news reporter; WTXL-TV, Tallahassee, FL, news reporter/anchor, 1990-. **Orgs:** Member, National Assn of Black Journalists, 1988-.

FLUELLEN, VELDA SPAULDING
Food company executive. **Personal:** Born Feb 5, 1942, Durham, NC; daughter of Sarah Badie Spaulding White McEachin and John Lee White; married Arthur L Fluellen, Jun 18, 1972; children: Randall, Tanya, Bryan. **Educ:** Hampton Institute, BS, 1963, MS, 1969; North Carolina Central University, Business Administration Certification, 1974. **Career:** Phoenix High School, science department chairman, 1963-70; Hampton Institute, graduate assistant, 1969-70; North Carolina Central University, professor of biology, 1970-75; Fluellen's Seafood House, owner, 1975-78; Tucson Jobs Corps, educational curriculum, 1979-80; IBM Corp., staff position in purchasing, 1981-89; A&B Trading Co, Inc, president & CEO, 1988-96; Vel's Catering Services, 1995-. **Orgs:** Pima Early Rising Executives, board member, 1992-; Resources for Women, 1988-; Chamber of Commerce, 1988-; Arizona Restaurant Association, Tucson Chapter, board member, 1991-; Tucson Metropolitan Convention Center & Visitors Bureau, 1988-; NAACP, 1981-88, golden life member, 1988-; The Links, Inc, 1981-; Alpha Kappa Alpha Sorority, 1967-; Natl Council of Negro Women, 1970-92. **Special Achievements:** Selected as an executive on loan from IBM to teach at Arizona State University, 1988-89; received several distinctions for this service. **Home Addr:** 1230 E Magee Rd, Tucson, AZ 85718-1097. **Business Phone:** (520)388-9295.

FLUKER, PHILIP A.
Association executive (retired). **Personal:** Born Nov 10, 1920, Birmingham; son of Eunice Stanford Fluker and Ernest Herman Fluker; married Jeanette Robinson; children: Billy Ray, Samuel Fuston Andrew, Douglas Allen, Winfred, Willie Ernest, Tracy Lynn, Phyllis Gale Christian Johnson, Eunice Patricia Hicks,; children: Barbara James. **Career:** Association executive, retired; community service volunteer, currently. **Orgs:** Teacher, Sunday school, Superintendent, adult Sunday school, bd of trustees, Chairman, usher bd, First Bapt Church; chairman, Boy Scout Troop 104; delegate, Office of Interior, State of Kentucky; SE Kentucky rep, Negro Leadership Conference; pres, vice pres, Harlan Chapter Rosenwald Heritage Organization; bd dir, Rosenwald Harlanite's Inc; chairman, Housing Committee, Harlan County Fair Housing Affirmative Action Committee; Governor Breathitt Advisory Commission, Hon Order of Kentucky Colonel; chairman, Scholarship for Preservation of Roserwald Heritage; chairman Scholarship for the LondonDist Missionary and Education Assn; treas, Christian Outreach with Appalachian People Inc; secretary treasurer, 1990-91, chairman, weatherization, 1990-91, chairman, Harlan County Community Action Agency; pres, London District Assn Sunday Sch & tist Training Union Congress, 1990-. **Home Addr:** 441 Ray St, Apt 71, Harlan, KY 40831.

FLYNN, H. WELTON
Public accountant. **Personal:** Born Dec 22, 1921, Blackville, SC; son of Inez M Flynn and Welton Flynn; married Dec 4, 1942 (widowed); children: Welton C, Gerald A. **Educ:** Golden Gate University, BA, 1951. **Career:** Self-employed, owner, public accountant, 1949-. **Orgs:** Alpha Phi Alpha Fraternity, Inc, 1967; NAACP, life member, 1984; San Francisco Public Utilities Commission, 1970-91; San Francisco Convention & Visitors Bureau, chairman of the board, 1992-; San Francisco Society of Accountants, 1977. **Honors/Awds:** Alpha Phi Alpha, Man of the Year, 1985, 1995, Humanitarian Medal, 1988; NAACP Legal Defense Fund, Man of the Year, 1989; San Francisco Business & Professional Women, Man of the Year, 1983; State of California, State Board of Accountancy, licensed in 1949. **Special Achievements:** H Welton Flynn Motor Coach Division, $30 million public utilities facility, 1989. **Military Serv:** US Army, master sgt, 1942-46; Good Conduct Medal. **Home Addr:** 76 Venus St, San Francisco, CA 94124. **Business Phone:** (415)775-1255.

FOARD, FREDERICK CARTER
Publisher, owner/operator. **Personal:** Born Mar 10, 1945, Philadelphia, PA; son of Adele Carter Foard and Howard A Foard Sr; married Georgeanne Garrett; children: Nicole, Justin. **Educ:** Lincoln Univ of PA, BA 1967; Capital Univ Columbus, MBA 1976. **Career:** HRB-Singer Div Singer Co, behavioral scientist 1967-69; Schering Labs/Schering-Plough, mkt rsch analyst 1969-71; Bristol Labs/Bristol-Myers Co, sr mkt rsch 1971-73; Warren-Teed Pharm/Rohm & Haas Co, mgr mkt rsch 1973-74, product mgr 1974-77; Smith Kline & French Labs/Smith Kline Beckman Corp, sr product mgr 1977-83, product dir 1983-86, dir mktg comms 1986-88, vice pres, Diuretic Products 1988-91; Advanced Communication Strategies Inc, Cherry Hill, NJ, president/CEO, 1991-. **Orgs:** Ofcr & various comm chairmanships Omega Psi Phi Frat 1963-; mem Amer Mgmt Assoc 1977-89; Pharmaceutical Adv Council 1986-93; mem Natl Black MBA Assoc 1983-; corp mktg rep Pharmaceutical Manufacturer's Assn 1986-91; board member, American Health Association, Philadelphia Affiliate, 1990-94; board member, Health Policy International, 1991-; board vice chairman, National Minority Health Association, 1989-94. **Honors/Awds:** CEBA World Communications 1980; Legion of Honor Chapel of Four Chaplains 1981; MBA of the Year, 1990; Omega Man of the Year, 1992. **Business Addr:** President, Advanced Communications Strategies Inc, 407 Monmouth Drive, Cherry Hill, NJ 08002-2006.

FOBBS, KEVIN
Public relations administrator, management services executive. **Personal:** Born Jan 11, 1954, River Rouge, MI; son of Geraldine Jenna Fobbs and Booker Terry Fobbs; married Patricia Marie Strunck, Apr 3, 1982; children: Katherine Marie Strunck-Fobbs. **Educ:** Eastern Michigan University, BS, 1978; Wayne State University Law School, 1978-80. **Career:** Wayne County Neighborhood Legal Services, community outreach coordinator, 1986-90; Fobbs & Strunck Communications, president, 1989-. **Orgs:** Michigan Enterprise Zone Authority, 1992-; Wayne County Department of Social Services, board member, 1992-; Habitat for Humanity, Metro Detroit Branch, board president, 1986-, International Branch, board member, 1992-; Detroit Association of Black Organizations, executive board member, 1984-; Michigan Governor John Engler's Action Team, 1992-; NAACP, ACT-BE Committee on Jobs, Detroit Branch, 1991-. **Business Addr:** President, Fobbs & Strunck Communications, 20418 Lichfield, Detroit, MI 48221, (313)863-2060.

FOGAM, MARGARET HANORAH
Administrative assistant. **Personal:** Born in Bali, Cameroon; daughter of Freida Fogam and Simon Fogam. **Educ:** Georgetown Univ, Washington, DC, BA, 1979-; Clark-Atlanta Univ, Atlanta, GA, MA, 1985, ABD, 1985-. **Career:** Clark-Atlanta Univ, Atlanta, GA, admin assistant, 1989-. **Orgs:** Member, National Conference of Black Political Scientists, 1987-; member, National Association of Social Scientists, 1988-; member, American Association of Political Scientists, 19871-; member, American Assn of Sociologists, 1985-. **Honors/Awds:** Certficate of Appreciation, Teaching Foreign Language Geography, Ogelthorpe Elementary School, 1986-87; Key to City, Community Service, Tuskegee, Mayor Ford, 1980. **Business Addr:** Administrative Assistant, Atlanta University, International Affairs & Development, James P Brawley Dr, SE, Atlanta, GA 30314.

FOGGIE, CHARLES H.
Retired bishop. **Personal:** Born Aug 4, 1912, Sumter, SC; son of Mamie Foggie and James L Foggie; married Madeline Sharpe; children: Charlene Marietta. **Educ:** AB, AM, STB, STM, DD LLD. **Career:** Third Dist, bishop; AME Zion Church, pres bd of bishops. **Orgs:** served AME Zion Ch; pres NAACP; pres Housing Auth City of Pitts; Pittsburgh Fellowship Univ of Pittsburgh; SW Asso Mayors Comm on Resources World Council of Chs; Nat Council of Chs; Consult Ch Union; Black Concerns WCCsEC bd of Bishops AME Zion Ch; sec bd trustees Livingstone Coll; World Bank Sponsor; chmn N Am Sec Worship Com of World Meth Council; mem Prog Com World Meth Council; Western PA Black Political Assembly; Leadership Conf on Civil Rights; chrmn Home Missions Bd AME Zion Church. **Honors/Awds:** Recip Martin Luther King Award, Pittsburgh Courier Award, evangelism AME Zion Award, Home Mission Award AME Zion Ch; Humanitarian Awd AME Church; First Annual Serv Awd NAACP Pgh Branch; Congressional Record Citation Fifty Years in the Pastoral Ministry; Awd for Natl Black Org Bishop Foggie Pres of Bd of Bishops AME Zion Church. **Business Addr:** Bishop AME Zion Church, 1200 Windermere Dr, Pittsburgh, PA 15218.

FOGGS, EDWARD L.
Clergyman. **Personal:** Born Jul 11, 1934, Kansas City, KS; son of Inez Lewis-Foggs and Eddie Foggs; married Joyce; children: Lynette, Iris, Edward Elliot, Joy, Alycia. **Educ:** Anderson Coll & Ball State U, AB 1958; Anderson Sch of Theol & Christian Theol Sem. **Career:** Exec Council of Church of God, assoc exec sec 1975-88, exec sec/CEO 1988-; Afro-Am Studies Anderson Coll, adj faculty 1968-; Urban Mnstrs Bd Of Ch Ext & Home Missions of Ch of God, dir 1970-75; Sherman St Ch of God Anderson IN, pastor 1959-69; Anderson Univ, adjunct faculty 1968-82. **Orgs:** Past pres & past vice pres Inspirational Youth Convention of Nat Assn of Ch of God 1964-72; mem Family Serv of Madison Co 1964-66; chmn IN Gen Assembly of Ch of God 1967-68; pres Urban League of Madison Co 1969-71; bd mem Nat Conf of Black Churchmen 1971-72; mem Operation PUSH 1974-75; alternate bd mem Urban Training Center for Christian Mission 1974-75; mem Am Mgmt Assn 1976-; mem Black Exec in Denominations Related Orgn & Communions 1977-78; mem Nat Religious Adv Council of Nat Urban League 1978-; Conv Speaker/Conf & Leader/Consult Ch Work; mem Planning Conf for Sixth World Conf of Ch of God in Nairobi Kenya E Africa 1978; Contrib to Nat Ch Publ Building Bridges to Racial Understanding 1967; key speaker 5th World Conf of Ch of God in Oaxlepec Mexico1971; bd mem Community Hospital of ison County 1988-, United Way of Madison County 1989-, Inner City Foundation for Excellence in Education, Los Angeles CA 1988-; mem Anderson Area Chamber of Commerce 1988-, Martin Luther King Jr Memorial Committee 1987-88; convener 1991 World Conference of the Church of God, Wiesbaden, West Germany. **Honors/Awds:** Co-authored Study Guide Andrew Billingsleys Book "Black Families & the Struggle for Survival" 1974; Honorary Degree, Doctor of Divinity, Anderson Univ, Anderson IN 1984. **Business Addr:** Executive Secretary/CEO, Exec Council of Church of God, 1303 W 5th St, PO Box 2420, Anderson, IN 46011.

FOGGS, JOYCE D.
Educator. **Personal:** Born Feb 13, 1930, Indianapolis, IN; daughter of Marry Elizabeth Stone (deceased) and Wilbur Stone (deceased); married Edward L, 1955; children: Lynette, Iris, Edward Elliot, Joy, Alycia. **Educ:** Anderson Coll, BS 1954; Ball State Univ, MA 1967, Adm License 1978. **Career:** Park Place School Anderson IN, teacher grade 6 1970-; Hazelwood School Anderson IN, teacher grade 3 1963-70; Westvale School Anderson IN, teacher grade 4 1959-60; Dunbar Elementary School Kansas City KS, teacher grade 4 1954-55; Anderson Community School Corporation, asst principal, Robinson Elementary School, 1988-89. **Orgs:** 1st Black mem Madison Co Delta Kappa Gamma Honor Soc for Women in Educ 1973-; mem Kappa Delta Pi 1973-; 1st Black mem Madison Co Am Assn of Univ Women 1959-65; Nat Spiritual Life Dir Women of the Church of God; mem exec bd Women of the Church of God 1978-; commr Gruenwald Home Historic Preservation 1977; vp bd of trustees Anderson-Anderson Stoney Creek Lib bd 1967-; bd mem, Urban League of Madison County, 1982-; commissioner, Anderson Housing Authority, 1984-; bd mem, Community Hospital Foundation, 1988-. **Honors/Awds:** Contributor Religious Devotional Books; Contributor to National Church Publication "Building Bridges to Racial Understanding".

FOGGS-WILCOX, IRIS
State official. **Personal:** Born in Anderson, IN; daughter of Edward L & Joyce D Foggs; married Kenneth L Wilcox, Aug 13. **Educ:** Ball State Univ, BS, 1980; Univ of PA, MGA, 1994. **Career:** US Congress, legislative aide, 1980-82; Erie Insurance Group, communications specialist, 1983-85; PA Dept of Corrections, deputy press sec, 1987-89; exec assistant to commissioner, 1989-90; PA Dept of State, press sec, 1990-94; deputy sec of state, 1994-. **Orgs:** Natl Assn of Black Journalist, pres, central PA chpt, 1993-95; United Way of the Capital Region, exec cmte bd, 1993-95; United Cerebral Palsy, bd mem, 1989-93; Junior League of Harrisburg, 1987-92; Women In Crisis, bd mem, 1990-92; United Negro College Fund, advisory bd mem, 1991-95; North 17th St Church of God, 1987-95. **Honors/Awds:** Award for Distinguished Public Service, Mayor, Harrisburg, 1990; Affirmative Action Office Award for Outstanding Professional Contributions, US Postal Service, 1990. **Business Addr:** Deputy Secretary of State, PA Dept of State, 302 North Office Bldg, Harrisburg, PA 17120.

FOLK, FRANK STEWART
Physician. **Personal:** Born Oct 2, 1932, Varnville, SC; divorced; children: 3. **Educ:** Hampton Inst, 1954; Brooklyn Coll, BS, 1957; Howard U, MD, 1961. **Career:** Freedman Hosp, New York, NY, res gen surgery, 1962-66, medical officer, 1969-70; Howard Univ, Washington DC, res gen surgery, 1962-66, inst in surgery, 1969, res fellow, 1969-70; US Public Health Service, Staten Island NY, asst resident, 1964-65, chief resident, 1967-68; DC Gen Hosp, Washington DC, chief resident, 1965-66, medical officer, 1969-70; St Barnabas Hosp, Bronx NY, asst resident, 1966-67, assoc atnd, 1970—, assoc dir of surgery, 1980-82; IBM, Brooklyn NY, med dir 1971-75; Downstate Med Coll, Brooklyn NY, asst instr 1973-76, clinical instr, 1976-86; Hosp for Joint Diseases Med Ctr, New York NY, asst atnd, 1973-79; Brooklyn Jewish Hosp, Brooklyn NY, asst atnd surgeon, 1973-81; NY State Athletic Commission, New York NY, asst med dir, 1980—,acting med dir 1986; NY Med Coll, asprof of surgery 1987; Health/Hospital Corp, dir. **Orgs:** Cert Nat bd of med Examrs 1966; NY State Med bd 1967; Am bd of Surgery 1977; Am Coll of Cardiology; candidate Am Coll of Surgeons; mem Nat Med Assn; NY Cardiological Soc; Assn for Acad Surgery; Manhattan Cntrl Med Soc; Provident Clinical Soc of Brooklyn; AMA; founding mem, Amer Trauma Soc; Bronx Co Med Soc; Howard U Med Alumni Assn; Empire State Med Soc; NY State Med Soc; mem Unity Dem Club; asst former State Senotor Basil Paterson 1970; bd dir NY City Hlth Hosp Corp Legislative Med & Prof Capital; bd Dir Charles A Drew Hlth Clinic 1974-; Goldberg-paterson Election Fin Com 1970; chmn Reg 1 Nat Med Assn 1971-74; v chmn United Dem Mens Club 1971-75; mem exec Com of Unity Dem Club 1972-; exec bd of Provident Clinical Soc 1971-; Kings Co Hosp comm bd for Mr Thomas RFortune 1971-74; Num OthOrgns NG 1962-66. **Military Serv:** DC Natl Guard, 115th Med Bn, 1962-66, OIC Troop and Med Clinic, 1964-66; NY State Natl Guard, 42nd Infantry Div, div surgeon, colonel, 1973—.

FOLKS, LESLIE SCOTT
Record company executive. **Personal:** Born Dec 4, 1955, New York, NY. **Educ:** Purdue Univ, BA, 1977. **Career:** CBS Records, NY, minority intern trainee 1976-77, Indiana, college rep 1976-77, Detroit, field sales merchandiser 1978-80, NY, asst dir of product mgmt 1980-85; Elektra Records, NY, dir of Artist & Repetoire 1985-87; EMI Records, NY, dir of A&R, 1987-88; Capitol Records, CA, vp of A&R Black Music, 1989-92; La-

Face Records, GA, senior vp/GM, currently. **Orgs:** Black Music Assn; NARAS. **Special Achievements:** Involved in Gold or Platinum recording projects by: Luther Vandross; Anita Baker; Sade; The Isley Brothers; Natalie Cole; The O'Jays; MC Hammer; Freddie Jackson; BeBe & CeCe Winans; The Whispers; Tracey Spencer; Young MC; Pieces of A Dream; Starpoint; The Clash; Midnight Star; Eddy Grant; Toni Braxton; TLC. **Business Addr:** Senior VP/GM, LaFace Records, 3350 Peachtree Rd, Ste 1500, Atlanta, GA 30326.

FOLLMER, PAUL L.
Banker. **Career:** El Pueblo State Bank, president, CEO, currently. **Business Addr:** President & Chief Executive Officer, El Pueblo State Bank, PO Drawer E, Espanola, NM 87532, (505)753-2383.

FOLSTON, JAMES EDWARD
Professional football player. **Personal:** Born Aug 14, 1971, Cocoa, FL. **Educ:** Northeast Louisiana. **Career:** Oakland Raiders, linebacker, 1995-. **Business Addr:** Professional Football Player, Oakland Raiders, 1220 Harbor Bay Pkwy, Alameda, CA 94502, (510)615-1875.

FOMUFOD, ANTOINE KOFI
Physician, educator. **Personal:** Born Oct 16, 1940, Ngen-Mbo, Cameroon; son of Ngwabi; married Angelina Hirku; children: Antoine, Ngwabi, Nina B. **Educ:** Univ of Ibadan Nigeria, MD 1967, Residency in Pediatrics 1968-70; Johns Hopkins Univ Sch of Med, Fellowships in Pediatrics 1970-73; Johns Hopkins Univ Sch of Hygiene, MPH 1974. **Career:** Howard Univ, asst prof of pediatrics 1974-78, assoc prof of pediatrics 1978-92, dir, neonatology, 1986-, professor of pediatrics, 1992-. **Orgs:** DC Med Soc 1975-; Am Acad of Pediatrics 1975-; Johns Hopkins Med-Surgical Soc 1974-; sec to bd Asoc of African Physicians in North Amer 1980-; Sect on Perinatal & Neonatal Pediatrics Am Acad of Pediatrics; Affil Fellow Franklin Square Hosp 1971-73; med staff Hosp for Sick Children 1975-77; Southern Medical Assoc 1985-90; Amer Assoc for the Advancement of Sci 1985-90; Southern Perinatal Assoc 1985-90; World Congress of Martial Arts 1986-. **Honors/Awds:** Merit Award Howard Univ Med Student Council 1981; Outstanding Physician Residents Dept of Pediatrics Howard Univ Hosp 1982; Howard Univ Hosp, Medical Productivity Award, 1994; Over 50 papers published in peer reviewed medical journals as of Dec 1994. **Business Addr:** Director of Neonatology, Professor of Pediatrics, Howard University Hospital, 2041 Georgia Ave NW, Washington, DC 20060.

FONROSE, HAROLD ANTHONY
Physician. **Personal:** Born Aug 31, 1925, Brooklyn, NY; married Mary Elizabeth; children: Wayne, Mark, Drew, Ward. **Educ:** Adelphi U, BA 1952; Cornell U, MS 1954; Howard U, MD 1958. **Career:** A Holly Patterson Home, med dir 1970; internist 1962-; A Holly Patterson Home, consult 1962-70; Am Bd Internal Med, diplomate 1968; Mt Sinai med Faculty Elmhurst Campus, attending staff physician. **Orgs:** Past bd dir Vanguard Nat Bank 1972-76; mem NY State & Nassau Co Med Soc; Sigma Pi Phi Frat; Alpha Sigma Boule; Alphi Phi Alpha Frat; Fellow Am Coll of Physicians 1977; Am Coll of Geriatrics 1971. **Honors/Awds:** Publ "Digitalis Withdrawal in Aged" Journal of Geriatrics; "Role of Med Dir in Skilled Nursing Facility". **Business Addr:** Physician, Mt Sinai Medical Faculty, Old Cedar Swamp Rd, Jericho, NY 11753.

FONTAINE, JOHN M.
Physician, educator. **Personal:** Born Apr 6, 1954, Haiti; son of Antoine & Gisele Fontaine. **Educ:** Medical School, College of Med & Dent of NJ/Rutgers Med School, 1975-79; Internal Med Internship-Nassau County Med Center, 1979-80; Internal Med Residency-Nassau County Med Center, 1980-82; Cardiology Fellowship, clinic education, 1982-85. **Career:** Veterans Administration Med Ctr, director, pacemaker clinic, 1985-90, director, cardiac arrhythmia clinic, 1985-90, director, electrophysiology lab, 1985-90; State University of NY, Health Science at Brooklyn, assistant professor of med, 1985-90; Medical College of Pennsylvania, PA, director cardiac, electro physiology service, 1990-96, assistant professor of med, 1990-96; Allegheny University, Hospitals-Med Division, director cardiac arrhythmia service, 1996-, associate professor of med, 1996-. **Orgs:** Journal of Pacing & Clinical Electrophysiology, manuscript reviewer, 1994-; Journal of American College of Cardiology, manuscript reviewer, 1996; AHA Southeastern PA Affiliate, bd of governors, 1996-99; Association of Black Cardiologists, mentor's program, 1992-; National Medical Association, mentor's program, 1996; Association of Black Cardilolgists, board of directors, 1990-; Cardiac Electrophysiology Society, 1987-. **Honors/Awds:** Dollars & Sense Magazine, Outstanding Young Doctor, 1993; Association of Black Cardiologists Inc, Distinguished Service Award, 1992; PA House of Representatives, Certificate of Achievement Award, Mentorship of Minority College Students, 1996. **Special Achievements:** Co-author: "The Optimal Use of Isopruterenol..," Pace; "Double Potentials During Ventricular Tachycardia..," Pace; "The Effects of Transcoronary Ethanol..," J of Invasive Card; "Double Potentials in Ventricular Tachycardia..;" "The Optimal Use of Isopruterenol..". **Business Addr:** Assoc Prof, Medicine, Director of Arrhythmia Service, Allegeny University Hospitals-MCP Divison, 3300 Henry Ave, Heritage Bldg, Ste 803, Philadelphia, PA 19129, (215)842-7455.

FONTAYNE, K. NICOLE
Government official. **Personal:** Born Aug 3, Chicago, IL; daughter of Carole Youngblood Rose and James Rose; married James L Mack, May 20, 1990; children: Cameron J Underwood. **Educ:** Univ of Chicago, Chicago, IL, AS, 1976; Roosevelt Univ, Chicago, IL, BA, 1978; Center for Creative Leadership, Colorado Springs, CO, 1989. **Career:** Intl Harvester Credit, Albany, NY, credit analyst, 1979-80; Farmers Ins Group, Santa Ana, CA, supvr, 1980-81; Amerisure/MI Mutual, Detroit, MI, Jula mgr, beginning 1987; Amerisure Companies, resource productivity mgr, 1991-94; City of Detroit, dir of information technology services, 1994-; Detroit Waldorf School, bd of trustees. **Orgs:** Co-chairperson, Amerisure, United Way Campaign, 1990; Word of Faith, 1985-. **Honors/Awds:** Minority Achievement Award, YMCA, 1990. **Business Addr:** Director, Information Technology Services, City of Detroit, 2 Woodward Ave, Rm 526, Detroit, MI 48226, (313)224-2915.

FONTENOT, ALBERT E., JR.
Office products manufacturing executive. **Personal:** Born Oct 23, 1946, Alexandria, LA; son of Albert E Fontenot, Sr & Fay Scott Fontenot; married Beverly, Nov 20, 1967; children: Kimberly, Michelle, Albert III. **Educ:** DePaul University, BA, 1979, MBA, 1985; Bethany Theological Seminary, Doctor of Ministry, 1993. **Career:** Wiseoldt Inc, buyer, 1967-1975; Playskool Toy Co, vp research and development, 1976-81; Wilson Jones Co, vp of mktg, 1981-85; Eldon Office Products, vp of mktg, 1985-91; Eldon-Rubbermaid Office Products, vp of sales, 1991-93; Atapco Office Products, vp of mktg, 1993-94, senior vp of sales and mktg, 1994-95, president/CEO, 1995-. **Orgs:** United Way of Greater St Louis, bd of dirs, 1995-; 1st Bapt Ch of Baldwin MO, assoc pastor, 1994-; Mt Calvary Bapt Ch, Knoxville, TN, assoc pastor, 1992-94; Antioch Bapt Ch, Long Beach, CA, assoc pastor, 1989-92, deacon, 1986-89; Bethel Bapt Ch, bd of trustees, 1982-85. **Military Serv:** US Army, major, 1968-89; Bronze Star, Army Commendation Medal, Vietnam Service Award, Reserve Service Award. **Business Addr:** President, Atapco Office Products Group, 12312 Olive Blvd, St Louis, MO 63141, (314)542-5452.

FONTENOT, ALBERT PAUL
Professional football player. **Personal:** Born Sep 17, 1970, Houston, TX; married Stephanie. **Educ:** Baylor, bachelor's degree in communications. **Career:** Chicago Bears, defensive end, 1993-96; Indianapolis Colts, 1997-. **Business Addr:** Professional Football Player, Indianapolis Colts, PO Box 535000, Indianapolis, IN 46253, (317)297-2658.

FONTENOT, LOUIS K.
Judge (retired). **Personal:** Born Sep 19, 1918, Alexandria, LA; married Dorothy B Williams. **Educ:** Leland Coll, BS 1940; John Marshall Law Sch, LLB JD 1949. **Career:** Will Co, asso circuit judge 1978-85; Kankakee Co, asso circuit judge 1971-78; Kankakee Co, first asst State's Att 1967-71; Joliet, gen practice of law 1955-67; Will Co, asst State's atty 1955-67; Police Training Inst Div of Univ Extension Univ of IL, lecturer 1955-67; Chicago Loop Firm of Fontenot Power Dixon & Burton, gen practice of law 1950-55; HS math tchr & basketball coach 1939-42. **Orgs:** Mem Cook Co Bar, Will Co Bar, Kankakee Co Bar, Am Bar & Nat Bar Assn; Nat Judicial Coun; IL State Atty Assn; Natl & Intl Assn of Probate Judges;Am Judicature Soc; IL Judges Assn; admitted to prac in Fed Courts including US Tax Court & US Supreme Ct Washington; IL State Invstgtr; legal cncl & adj of VFW post; legal cncl & mem Brown's Chapel Ch; legal cncl of Caterpillar Tractor Credit Un & Joliet PO Credit Un; pres NAACP Ottawa-Streetor Br; chmn Legal Aid Com of Will Co Bar Assn; bd govs Joliet Br YMCA; mem Will Co adv bd; Joliet Mayors Commn of Flood Cntrl; Judicial Rules Com Kankakee Co Bar Assn; Coll Fnd Bd Kankakee Commn Coll; Joliet and Shorewood Police Dept, IL; Will County Bar Assn, Joliet, IL. **Honors/Awds:** First Black Lawyer in the 12th Judicial Circuit, Joliet, Will County, IL; First Black Asst State's Attorney in Joliet, Will County, IL; First Black First Asst State's Attorney in the State of Illinois in Xankakee County; First Black Judge in the 12th Judicial Circuit of Illinois including Will, Kankakee, and Iroqois Counties; upon retiring from the Judiciary, Fontenot was cited by the Chicago Daily Law Bulletin as a "Pioneer.". **Military Serv:** Major, US Army Air Corps(Counter Intelligence Agency) 1942-46; Bronze Star with 3 battle stars, several campaign ribbons. **Home Phone:** (815)741-9336.

FONTENOT-JAMERSON, BERLINDA
Community relations manager. **Personal:** Born Jul 5, 1947, San Fernando, CA; daughter of Velma Kyle Fontenot and Leroy Fontenot; married Michael Jamerson, Jun 16, 1984. **Educ:** Los Angeles CA Trade Technological Coll, AA, 1972; CA State Univ, Los Angeles, BA, 1978; Pepperdine Univ, Los Angeles CA, MBA, 1984. **Career:** Southern CA Gas Co Los Angeles CA, sr prof recruiter, consumer affairs mgr, 1984-87, community relations mgr, 1987-92, personnel relations & diversity mgr, 1992-95, Pacific Enterprises, Corp Diversity mgr, 1995-. **Orgs:** Natl board mem, Amer Assn of Blacks in Energy; bd mem, Women of Color, 1987-; bd mem, Careers for Older Americans, 1987-; bd mem, Museum of African Amer Art, 1988-; vice pres, administration, DATACOM, 1988-; committee chair, NAACP-LDF Black Women of Achievement, 1989; bd mem, Coalition for Women's Economic Development; UNCF Blue Ribbon Committee. **Honors/Awds:** Leadership Award, YWCA, 1985; Gold Award, United Way, 1986; Black Women of Achievement Merit Award, NAACP-LDF, 1986; Merit Award, Amer Assn Blacks in Energy, 1986, 1988; Certificate of Support, LA Urban League, 1988-94; Women in NAALR Merit Award; Coalition Women Economic Development Award, 1992. **Business Addr:** Corporate & Diversity Mgr, Pacific Enterprises, 555 W 5th St, Mail Loc 16E2, Los Angeles, CA 90013.

FONVIELLE, WILLIAM HAROLD
Business executive. **Personal:** Born Dec 18, 1943, Chicago, IL; son of Elizabeth Brown Fonvielle and William B Fonvielle (deceased); married Carole Lynn Sharoff; children: Michelle R, Deanne V, Jonathan W. **Educ:** Shimer Coll, AB (with honors) 1963; Northwestern Univ, Doctoral work in Philosophy 1963-64; Yale Sch of Org & Mgmt, MPPM 1981. **Career:** J Walter Thompson Co, media buyer 1966-68; Vince Cullers Adv Inc, media dir 1968-70; Communicon Inc, pres 1970-75; State of IL, dir motion picture/TV prodn/publ info ofcr 1975-77; Denver Reg Cncl of Govts, dir publ affairs 1977-79; Goodmeasure Inc, vp/dir consulting 1981-86; The Forum Corp, vp 1987-94, sr vp 1995-. **Orgs:** Accred comm Colorado Publ Relations Soc of Amer 1978-80; founder Cncl of City & Co Communicators 1978-79; dir Lovespace Inc 1972-75; dir The Apartment Store Inc 1968-70; elec trustee Vill of Carol Stream, IL 1973-77; trustee Garrett-Evang Theol Seminary 1974-76; dir Northeastern IL Planning Commn 1973-77; dir Homes of Private Enterprise 1973-77; chmn MA Product Develop Corp 1986-; mem MENSA 1987-; founding mem Greater Boston Chapter of the International Customer Service Assn 1987-; Organization Development Network 1988-; dir, Horizons Fund, 1990-94; sec, IL-IN Bi-State Comm, 1976-77; Handel and Haydn Society, overseer, 1992-. **Honors/Awds:** CLIOs for Best Copy Writing US Radio; Best Public Service Commercial, Special Citation 1975; SCLC MLK Jr Award Chicago Suburban Chap 1977; Natl Finalist White House Fellowship Competition 1977; Distinguished Alumni Award Shimer Coll 1975; author "From Manager to Innovator, Using Information to become an Idea Entrepreneur" AMS 1988. **Home Addr:** 27 Old Salem Rd, Gloucester, MA 01930. **Business Addr:** Senior Vice President, The Forum Corporation, One Exchange Place, Boston, MA 02109.

FONVILLE, CHAD EVERETTE
Professional baseball player. **Personal:** Born Mar 5, 1971, Jacksonville, NC. **Educ:** Louisberg. **Career:** Montreal Expos, infielder, 1995; Los Angeles Dodgers, 1995-97; Chicago White Sox, 1997; Cleveland Indians, 1998-. **Business Addr:** Professional Baseball Player, Cleveland Indians, 2401 Ontario, Cleveland, OH 44115, (216)420-4200.

FONVILLE, DANNY D.
State corrections officer. **Career:** California Dept of Corrections, corrections officer, 1981-; Becton Dickinson Public Safety, NIT Narcotics Identification, master trainer; Folsom State Prison, conflict management trainer, trainer of trainers; Equal Employment Opportunity/Affirmation Action, counsler & trainer; Folsom State Prison Youth Diversion Program, Department of Corrections State of California, recruiter. **Orgs:** Blacks in Government, Correctional Peace Officer Foundation. **Honors/Awds:** Correctional Officer of the Year, State of California, 1995; Correctional Officer of the Year, City of Folsom, 1995; International Association of Correctional Officers, Meritorious Svc Awd, 1995; Correctional Peace Officer Foundation, Officer of the Year, 1996. **Business Addr:** Corrections Officer, California Department of Corrections, PO Box W, Represa, CA 95671.

FOOTE, YVONNE
Educational administrator. **Personal:** Born Dec 24, 1949, Philadelphia, PA; daughter of Alma Jenkens Alleyne and Lorenzo L Alleyne; married Nathaniel A Foote; children: Omar Y. **Career:** DE Valley Reg Planning Comm, cost accountant 1975-81; Thomas & Muller Co Inc, bookkeeper 1982-84; Laborers Dist Council Legal Fund, secretary/bookkeeper 1984-; Lawnside Bd of Edn, pres; Rawle & Henderson, Philadelphia, PA, bookkeeper, 1987-. **Business Addr:** President, Lawnside Board of Education, 326 Charleston Avenue, Lawnside, NJ 08045.

FOOTMAN, DAN ELLIS, JR.
Professional football player. **Personal:** Born Jan 13, 1969, Tampa, FL; children: Dantavian Hicks. **Educ:** Florida State. **Career:** Cleveland Browns, defensive end, 1993-95; Baltimore Ravens, 1996; Indianapolis Colts, 1997-. **Business Addr:** Professional Football Player, Indianapolis Colts, PO Box 535000, Indianapolis, IN 46253, (317)297-2658.

FORBES, CALVIN
Professor. **Personal:** Born May 6, 1945, Newark, NJ; son of Mary Short Forbes and Jacob Forbes. **Educ:** New School For Social Research; Rutgers University; Brown University, MFA, 1978. **Career:** Emerson College, Boston, MA, assistant prof of English, 1969-73; Tufts Univ, Medford, MA, asst prof of English, 1973-74, 1975-77; Howard Univ, Washington, DC, writer in residence; Washington College, Chestertown, MD, asst prof of creative writing, 1988-89; Fulbright lecturer in Den-

mark, France, and England, 1974-75; guest lecturer at the Univ of West Indies, 1982-83. **Orgs:** Modern Language Assn, College Language Assn. **Honors/Awds:** Author of Blue Monday, Wesleyan Univ Press, 1974; From the Book of Shine, Burning Deck Press, 1979; Natl Endowment for the Arts fellowship, 1982-83; DC Commission on the Arts fellowship, 1984; New Jersey State Council on the Arts fellowship. **Business Addr:** 73 Arsdale Ter, East Orange, NJ 07018.

FORBES, GEORGE L.
Attorney. **Personal:** Born Apr 4, 1931, Memphis, TN; son of Elnora Forbes and Cleveland Forbes; married Mary Fleming; children: Helen, Mildred, Lauren. **Educ:** Manassas, 1949; Baldwin-Wallace Coll, 1957; Cleveland Marshall Law Sch, JD 1962. **Career:** City of Cleveland, teacher, 1958-62, housing insp, 1959-63; radio talk show host, 1972-75; Cuyahoga Co Dem Party, co-chmn, 1972-78; Cleveland City Council, 1964-89, council majority leader, 1972-73, pres, 1973-89; Baldwin-Wallace College, professor, 1990-; Forbes Fields & Associates, managing partner, 1971-. **Orgs:** Mem Nat Assn Def Lawyers; Cuyahoga, Ohio & Cleveland Bar Assns; Gtr Cleveland Growth Corp & Assn; Council for Econ Opportunity; Legal Aid Soc; NAACP, pres, Cleveland Chapter 1992-, grand jury foreman, 1994; Urban League; John Harlan Law Club; Greater Cleveland Safety Council; National League of Cities; United Negro College Fund; Oversight Board of the Bureau of Worker's Compensation. **Honors/Awds:** Citation of Merit 1967; Humanitarian of Year 1968; Man of Year 1969; Outstanding Political & Civic Efforts 1971; citizen participation 1973; Ohio Assn Commodores 1973; Distinguished Merit Awd 1976; Ohio Gov Awd 1977; Police Athletic League Outstanding Service Award 1978; Black Affairs Council, Outstanding Community Leadership Award, 1983; Black Professional of the Year, 1987; Honorary Doctorate Degrees: Baldwin-Wallace College, 1990, Central State University, 1989; Martin Luther King Jr Crusader of the Year Award, 1989; Cleveland State University, Distinguished Alumni Award, 1990; In Tribute to the Public Service Award, Cleveland State Univ Maxine Goodman Levin College of Urban Affairs, 1994. **Military Serv:** USMC corpl 1951-53. **Business Addr:** Attorney at Law, Forbes, Fields & Associates, 700 Rockefeller Building, 614 Superior Ave, NW, Cleveland, OH 44113.

FORBES, MARLON
Professional football player. **Personal:** Born Dec 25, 1971. **Educ:** Penn State, attended. **Career:** Chicago Bears, defensive back, 1996-. **Business Addr:** Professional Football Player, Chicago Bears, 1000 Football Dr, Halas Hall at Conway Park, Lake Forest, IL 60045-4829.

FORD, AILEEN W.
Educational administrator (retired). **Personal:** Born Apr 28, 1934, Shelby, NC; daughter of Rosa Watson and John Watson; married Charles, Jun 8, 1967; children: Valerie Journeane, Regina Antoinette. **Educ:** Fayetteville State U, BS 1954; Howard U, Western Carolina U, Appalachian U; Univ of NC at Charlotte, MA, 1978, CAS, 1982. **Career:** Shelby City Schools, Shelby, NC, teacher, 1954-80, elementary principal, 1980-89, director of testing/chapter I, 1989-. **Orgs:** Pres local chap NCAE; dist dir NCAE; district pres NCACT; pres Gastonia Chap Delta; organizer & sec Cleveland Co Civic League; active in YMCA; Girl Scouts; youth adv in ch; as tchr served on many com & commn; Delta Sigma Theta Sorority; NC Assn of Ed; NC Assn of Classroom Tchr; Nat Ed Assn; Am Assn of Univ Women; Intl Reading Assn; bd dir Cleveland Co Orgn Drug Abuse Prevention 1974; bd of dir Cleveland Co Comm Concert Assn; Shelby Human Relations Cncl; pres PTA Shelby Jr HS 1974; treas Shelby Negro Woman's Club; pres Audacian Club 1974; NAACP; Nat Coun Negro Women; Sunday sch tchr, Mount Calvary Bapt Ch; president, Piedmont Chapter, Links Inc; president, North Carolina Federation of Negro Women Inc; Shelby City Council. **Honors/Awds:** Citizen of the Year, 1984; Elected Official Award, 1987; Outstanding Service Award, 1989. **Home Addr:** 1303 Frederick St, Shelby, NC 28150.

FORD, ALBERT S.
Educator, dentist. **Personal:** Born Jan 23, 1929, Elizabeth, NJ; son of Bessie M Lewis and William H Ford; married Mary Victoria Burkett; children: Albert S Jr, Stephen D, Teresa D, Kevin M, Richard E. **Educ:** Attended, WV St Coll, Seton Hall Univ; Meharry Med Coll, DDS 1958; Rutgers, Grad Sch of Management, Newark, NJ, 1981-82; New School for Social Research, New York, NY, 1979-81. **Career:** Newark Comm Health Serv Group Dent Serv, dir; private practice, Roselle, NJ, 1962-; Fairleigh Dickinson College of Dental Medicine, Hackensack, NJ, assoc prof, 1980-90; Univ of Med & Dentistry, Newark, NJ, assoc prof, 1990-. **Orgs:** Bd of mgmt Meharry Med Coll; mem ADA; mem vice pres Commonwealth Dent Soc; mem Intl Assoc of Begg Study Groups; mem Amer Endodontic Soc; mem Acad of Gen Dentistry; bd mem NJ State Bd of Dental Examiners NE Regional Bd of Dental Examiners 1979; past pres NAACP; mem exec bd Urban League; vicepres Sr Cit Housing Corp; mem adv bd First Natl Bank of Central Jersey; mem Sigma Pi Phi Mu Boule; mem Omega Psi Phi; past mem NJ State Bd of Dental Examiners; past vice pres assoc prof & chmn Treatment Planning Fairleigh Dickinson Univ Sch of Dentistry. **Honors/Awds:** Fellow Amer College of Dentists; Fellow Royal Soc of Health; Diplomat Natl Bd of Dent Examiners; John Dewey Hon Soc 1952; Omicron Kappa Upsilon, 1990. **Military Serv:** US Army, Sgt, 1947-50. **Business Addr:** 1001 Chestnut St, Roselle, NJ 07203.

FORD, ANTOINETTE
Company executive. **Personal:** Born Dec 14, 1941, Philadelphia; married Melvin W Ford. **Educ:** Laval Univ Quebec, attended 1960; Chestnut Hill Coll, BS 1963; Am U, MS 1966; Stanford Univ, attended 1967. **Career:** Natl Oceanographic Data Center, oceanographer 1966-69; Ogden Corp, oceanographer 1969-71; White House fellow 1971-72; Inst Serv of Edn, devel dir 1972-73; TELSPAN Intl Inc, pres. **Orgs:** Mem, DC City Council 1973-75; exec vice pres B & C Assn Inc; Harvard Univ Fellow Inst of Politics 1975; mem numerous professional & business orgs; bd dirs, several orgs; NSF fellow 1967; mem Pres Clemency Bd 1975. **Honors/Awds:** Outstanding Serv Award, Presidential Classroom 1972; Most Successful Under-30 Woman, New Woman Magazine 1971. **Business Addr:** President, TELSPAN International Inc, 2909 Park Dr SE, Washington, DC 20020.

FORD, AUSBRA
Educator. **Personal:** Born Feb 28, 1935, Chicago, IL; son of Carrie Ford and Thomas Ford; married Thelma Wakefield; children: Rangi, Maji. **Educ:** Ray Vogue Art School, 1956-77; Chicago Art Inst, BAE 1959-64, MFA 1964-66. **Career:** Chicago Public School, art instructor 1964-66; Gary Public School, art instructor 1966-68; Southern Univ Baton Rouge, LA, asst prof Art 1968-69; Chicago State Univ, prof of Art 1969-. **Orgs:** Mem Natl Conf of Artists 1975-; chmn Visual Artists Roundtable 1983-. **Honors/Awds:** Young scholars fellowship Natl Endowment of Humanities 1971-72; Intl Studies Award Black Studies Dept Chicago State Univ 1973; Creative Serv Award Kemetic Inst of Chicago 1985. **Military Serv:** USAAF a/bc 1954-56. **Business Addr:** Professor of Art, Chicago State Univ, 9501 S Dr Martin Luther King, Chicago, IL 60628-1598.

FORD, CHARLES
Educator, elected official. **Personal:** Born Jun 5, 1936, Patterson, LA; son of Maxie Columbus Reels and Charles Ford, Sr (deceased); married Doris Jefferies; children: Bryan, Gwendolyn, Monica. **Educ:** Dillard Univ, BA 1960; Univ of AZ, MEd 1966; Atlanta Univ, DEd 1976. **Career:** Model Cities Program Tucson AZ, ed spec 1970; City of Tucson, city countil mem 1979-; Pima Comm Coll, instr 1977-79; Tucson Unified School Dist, educator, school admin 1970-74, 1976-. **Orgs:** Systems analysis for public schools Tucson Unified School Dist 1970; bd of dir Awarenss House, A Drug Free Community 1972; ford fellowship Washington DC Politics & Ed 1975; seminars Northern AZ Univ, Taft Inst of Govt 1981, Harvard Univ, Kennedy School of Govt 1982; bd mem Amer Cancer Soc 1984; co chair Harvard Black Faculty & Admin Org 1989. **Honors/Awds:** Outstanding Admin of Schools Channel 6 TV 1973; Pre-Doctoral Ford Fellowship Atlanta Univ 1974; Lugman Awd of Outstanding Comm Serv 1982; Community Serv Awd Tucson Urban League. **Military Serv:** AUS pfc 1956-58; Expert Rifleman, Good Conduct, Soldier of the Month 1956-58.

FORD, CLAUDETTE FRANKLIN. See Obituaries section.

FORD, DAVID LEON, JR.
Educator. **Personal:** Born Sep 25, 1944, Fort Worth, TX; son of Vernita V Williams and David Leon Ford; married Joan Sessoms; children: David III. **Educ:** IA State Univ, BS 1967; Univ of WI Madison, MS 1969, PhD 1972. **Career:** Purdue Univ, asst prof of mgmt 1972-75; Yale School of Org & Mgmt, visiting assoc prof 1980-81; Univ of TX at Dallas, prof or org behavior. **Orgs:** Pres DL Ford & Assoc Mgmt Consult 1977-, Assn Social & Behavioral Scientists 1978-79; mem Leadership Dallas Alumni Assoc 1978-, Leadership Dallas Adv Council 1978-80; bd of dir Greater Dallas Housing Oppty Ctr 1978-80; budget comm United Way of Metro Dallas 1979; dir Pro Line Corp 1981-84; chmn, bd of dir NTL Inst for Applied Behavioral Sci 1985-86. **Honors/Awds:** 1st Black Engrg Co-op Student LTV Aerospace Corp 1962-67; Leadership Awd KNOK AM-FM Radio 1966; Outstanding Young Alumnus IA State Univ 1977; Scholarship Achievement Assoc of Social & Behavioral Scientists 1983; Distinguished Service Citation, Univ of Wisconsin-Madison, 1988. **Military Serv:** AUS Reserve capt 1967-76. **Home Addr:** 7636 Mullrany Drive, Dallas, TX 75248. **Business Addr:** Dept of Bus, Univ of Texas at Dallas, Box 830688, Richardson, TX 75083-0688.

FORD, DEBORAH LEE
Educator, counselor. **Personal:** Born Sep 22, 1945, Decatur, IL; married David Franklin Ford; children: Alisa, Bryan, Laquitta. **Educ:** Millikin Univ, Music; Richland Comm Coll, Business. **Career:** AE Staley Mfg Co, messenger & office pool sec (1st black in office) 1964; Day Care Licensed Family Svc, suprv, owned, operated 1972-78; US Dept of Commerce, reserve crew leader 1980; Decatur School Dist 61, noon suprv 1983, school board mem; bd mem Mental Health Assoc of Macon Co Inc 1985; bd mem Family Serv 1985. **Orgs:** Dist sec Title I 1980; dist chairperson Title I 1981,82; task force mem Comm Strategic Planning Group 1984; asst leader pre-school prog Dove Inc 1984; dir Wedding Coord 1984. **Honors/Awds:** Cert of Appreciation for Meritorious Asst in Conduct of the 1970 Census US Dept of Commerce Bureau of the Census; Awd of Recognition Title I 1982; Awd of Appreciation Volunteer in Decatur Public School 1982. **Home Addr:** 846 S Webster St, Decatur, IL 62521.

FORD, DEBRA HOLLY
Physician. **Personal:** marrIed Dr Kevin Michael Ford Sr; children: Two. **Educ:** Howard Univ, BS, zoology; Howard Univ School of Medicine, MD. **Career:** Howard Univ Hospital, chief of general surgery division, currently, head, section of colon & rectal surgery. **Orgs:** American College of Surgeons; American Society of Colon and Rectal Surgery; Surgical Section, National Medical Association. **Honors/Awds:** Kaiser-Permanente Teaching Excellence Award. **Special Achievements:** First African American female to become board certified in the field of colon and rectal surgery; first African American female to become a diplomate of the Board of Colon and Rectal Surgery. **Business Addr:** Chief, Division of General Surgery, Howard University Hospital, 2041 Georgia Ave, NW, Washington, DC 20060.

FORD, DONALD A.
Assistant director. **Personal:** Born May 15, 1928, Philadelphia, PA; married Christina K; children: Donald A, Douglas E, Christel A. **Educ:** Shaw U, BA 1950; Am Intl Coll, attending. **Career:** Westfield State Coll, asst dir of student union; Urban Educ Adv for Third World, Westfield State Coll, asst dir 1971-74. **Orgs:** Bd dir MA Heart Assn Western Chap 1971-73; mem Assn of Coll Unions Intl 1971-; mem Assn of Prof Adminstrn 1973-; Ch decon St John's Congreational Ch 1964-; mem St John's Congreational Ch Choir; chmn Affirmative Action Com, Westfield State Coll 1975; mem Kappa Alpha Psi Frat 1946-; mem Admission Com Westfield State Coll. **Honors/Awds:** Recipient Air Force Commendation Award; 2nd Oak Leaf Cluster 1970. **Military Serv:** USAF smsgt 1950-71. **Business Addr:** Western Ave, Westfield, MA 01085.

FORD, EVERN D.
Human resources consultant. **Personal:** Born Apr 28, 1952, Salem, NJ; son of Mr & Mrs Daniel Ford Sr. **Educ:** Goldey Beacom College, BS. **Career:** EI DuPont Co., human resources personnel supervisor, training manager, diversity consultant and trainer, sexual harassment facilitator/trainer. **Orgs:** New Jersey School Board Association; Salem County Vocational Technical School, board member; United Way of Salem County, vice pres; Dale Carnegie Graduate Assistant. **Home Addr:** 81 Cheney Rd, Woodstown, NJ 08098. **Business Addr:** E I DuPont, Jackson Laboratory, Wilmington, DE 19898.

FORD, FLORIDA MAE
Consultant, cleric. **Personal:** Born Feb 22, 1948, Altheimer, AR; daughter of Ossie Morris Thomas and Henry Thomas (deceased); married Rev Fred Ford; children: Eurika, Sonya. **Educ:** Univ of AR-Pine Bluff, AR, BS (magna cum laude) 1969; Univ of AR-Fayetteville, MS, chemistry, 1972; Howard Univ Divinity School, Washington, DC, MDiv, 1991. **Career:** The Dow Chemical Co, Midland, MI, manager of minority recruiting, 1972-87; National Society of Black Engineers, Alexandria, VA, executive director, 1987-93; Ebenezer AME Church, associate minister, 1987-; US Dept of Energy, consultant, 1993-. **Orgs:** Mem Alpha Kappa Alpha Sor 1968-; dir Christian Educ New Jerusalem Church 1980-; adv comm Natl Assoc Minority Engrg Prog Adm 1982; mem Natl Org ofBlk Chemists & Chem Engrs 1984-; industrial adv bd Natl Soc Blk Engrs 1985-; bd mem Woman to Woman Ministries Inc 1986-; chaplain, National Assn of Black Seminarians, 1990-; member, Washington Urban League, 1988-; member, National Assn of Black Meeting Planners, 1989-. **Honors/Awds:** Special Service Awd New Jerusalem Church 1974, 86; Teacher of the Year New Jerusalem Church 1982; Special Recognition Univ of MI 1985; Outstanding Service Dow Chemical 1985; Ford Foundation Fellow, Howard University, 1989-90; Scholarship, Howard University Divinity School, 1988-90. **Business Addr:** President, Shalom Enterprises, Inc, PO Box 1225, Fort Washington, MD 20744, (301)203-8079.

FORD, FRED, JR.
Musician/composer/arranger. **Personal:** Born Feb 14, 1930, Memphis, TN; son of Nancy Jane Taylor and Fred Ford; divorced; children: Joseph Vallier, Jessica Ann Thomas, Jamil A, Jamal A, Idrees A, Jacob A. **Educ:** Studied Music under Eddie Pete Ware 1943-45. **Career:** Elks Club Band, clarinet player 1945-46; Royal American Shows, clarinet baritone sax 1949-50; Duke/Peacok Records Houston TX, clarinet, sax 1950-54; Fred Ford's Beale St USA, orchestra founder/dir 1977-79; Fred Ford/Honeymoon Garner Trio, leader 1970-. **Orgs:** Co-producer Beale St Music Festival 1977,78; producer Sybil Shepherd album Vanilla 1978; chosen as poster subject TN Homecoming "86" 1985; producer album Bear Water-Beale St Scene Fred Ford/Honeymoon Garner Trio 1985. **Honors/Awds:** Honored for preserving Memphis Music Heritage 1985; declared Colonel of State of TN Gov Lamar Alexander 1985; acknowledgment of Honor Pres & Mrs Ronald Reagan 1985; resolutions City, County, Mayor, State Legislature, Congressman of 8th District 1985. **Military Serv:** AUS Band corpl 1st class 1955-57. **Home Addr:** 1591 Sunset, Memphis, TN 38108.

FORD, GEORGE WASHINGTON, III
Funeral home operator. **Personal:** Born Jan 14, 1924, Columbus, GA; son of Evergreen Thweatt Ford and George Washington Ford Jr; married Josephine Adele Bozman Ford, Jan 14, 1948; children: Evergreen Adele Ford-Reeves. **Educ:** Atlanta College of Mortuary Science, Atlanta, GA, diploma, 1949. **Career:** Progressive Funeral Home, Inc, Columbus, GA, president, 1952-. **Orgs:** Member, Georgia Funeral Services Practitioners Association; member, National Funeral Directors Association; member, 837 Club; member, Modern Club; member, Men's Progressive Club; member, The Pathseekers Civic and Social Club; member, A.J. Branch, YMCA; member, Prince Hall Masons; member, Modernistic Club; member, Spencerian Club; member, Losers and Liars Sport Club; advisor to Controllers Civic and Social Club; member, board of directors, American Family Life Assurance Co, 1986-; member, board of directors, Columbus Bank and Trust Co, 1986-. **Honors/Awds:** Mortician of the Year, State and Local Funeral Services Practitioners Association, 1985; Thomas A. Brewer Award, Columbus Branch, NAACP, 1971; National Trend Award, LINKS, 1983; Citizenship Award, Al Faruk Temple 145, Prince Hall Masons, 1971; Distinguished Service Award, Columbus Chamber of Commerce, 1972; Outstanding Services Award, Georgia State Beauty Culturist League, 1973, Columbus Community Center, 1974; Outstanding Services and Dedicated Leadership in Politics and Community Affairs, Pathseekers Civic and Social Club, 1975; Community Services Award, Columbus-Phoenix City Negro Business and Professional Women's Club, 1975; Appreciation Award, Controllettes Civic and Social Club, 1984, The Black Community of Columbus, GA, 1985, the Boxwood Neighbors, 1985,Lindsey Creek Civic Asiation, 1985, The Turning Point Club, 1983; Distinguished Service Award, Bishop Frederick Talbot Retreat Center of the AME Church of Georgia, 1984; George Washington Ford Week, adopted by the city of Columbus, GA, 1985. **Military Serv:** US Marines. **Business Addr:** President, Progressive Funeral Home, Inc, 4235 St Mary Rd, PO Box 5624, Columbus, GA 31907.

FORD, GERALDINE BLEDSOE
Judge. **Career:** Detroit Recorder's Court, judge, currently. **Honors/Awds:** First black female judge in Detroit. **Business Addr:** Judge, Detroit Recorder's Court, Frank Murphy Hall of Justice Bldg, 1441 St Antoine, Rm 603, Detroit, MI 48226.

FORD, HAROLD EUGENE, SR.
Congressman. **Personal:** Born May 20, 1945, Memphis, TN; son of Vera Davis Ford and Newton Jackson Ford; married Dorothy Jean Bowles, Feb 10, 1969; children: Harold Eugene Jr, Newton Jake, Sir Isaac. **Educ:** John Gupton Coll, AA 1968; TN State Univ, BS 1967; Howard Univ, MBA. **Career:** TN House of Representatives, mem 1970-74; US House of Representatives, congressman (TN, 9th dist) 1975-; Ford & Sons Funeral Home, vice pres and mgr 1969-. **Orgs:** Mem natl adv bd, St Jude Children's Rsch Hosp; bd mem, Metro Memphis YMCA, Alpha Phi Alpha; chmn, Black Tennessee Pol Conv; trustee, Fisk Univ, Rust Univ. **Honors/Awds:** Named Outstanding Young Man of the Year Memphis Jaycees 1976; Outstanding Young Man of the Year TN Jaycees 1977; Named Child Advocate of the Year Child Welfare League of Amer 1987. **Business Addr:** Congressman, US House of Representatives, 2305 Rayburn House Office Bldg, Washington, DC 20515.

FORD, HAROLD EUGENE, JR.
Congressman. **Personal:** Born May 11, 1970. **Educ:** Univ of Pennsylvania, BA, 1992; Univ of Michigan, JD, 1996. **Career:** Consultant; US House of Representatives, congressman, 1996-. **Special Achievements:** Youngest member of the 105th Congress. **Business Addr:** Congressman, US House of Representatives, 1523 Longworth House Office Bldg, Washington, DC 20515-4209.

FORD, HENRY (HANK)
Athletic administrator. **Educ:** Maryland State, 1969. **Career:** Hampton Univ, men's basketball coach; Alfred Univ, athletic dir; Howard Univ, athletic dir, 1996-.

FORD, HENRY
Professional football player. **Personal:** Born Oct 30, 1971, Fort Worth, TX. **Educ:** Univ of Arkansas, attended. **Career:** Houston Oilers, defensive tackle, 1994-96; Tennessee Oilers, 1997-. **Business Addr:** Professional Football Player, Tennessee Oilers, c/o Baptist Sports Park, 7640 H 70-5, Nashville, TN 37221.

FORD, HILDA EILEEN
Business executive. **Personal:** Born Apr 19, 1924, New York, NY. **Educ:** Brooklyn Coll; Coll of St Rose. **Career:** City of Baltimore, dir of personnel; NY St Off of Employee Rels, chief negotiator; NY St Dept of Civil Serv, asst div dir; Youth Opprt Ctr, dir. **Business Addr:** 111 N Calvert St, Baltimore, MD 21202.

FORD, JAMES W.
Physician, minister, politician, funeral director. **Educ:** TN State Univ, BS Zoology; Attended, Amer Baptist Theol Seminary, Columbia Univ Coll of Surgeons, Union Theological Seminary, NY Law Sch, Memphis State. **Career:** Harlem Hosp, residency & internship ophthalmology; NJ Ford & Sons Funeral Home, funeral dir; Fellowship Baptist Ch, pastor; private practice, ophthalmologist; Dist 6 City of Memphis, councilman. **Business Addr:** Councilmember, 655 E Raines Rd, Memphis, TN 38109.

FORD, JAMES W.
State official (retired). **Personal:** Born Feb 3, 1922, Florida; married Catherine Britton; children: Daniel J, Cynthia A. **Educ:** FL A&M Univ, BS 1943; TN Agr & Indust Univ, MS 1948; KS State Univ, MS 1949; WA State Univ, Postgrad 1950; KS State Univ, 1951; Boston Univ, 1959-60; Univ of Pittsburgh, 1965. **Career:** Ft Valley State Coll, head dept animal sci 1949-51; Alcorn A&M Coll, assoc prof 1951-52, head dept animal husbandry; AID State Dept Libya, N Africa, ext spec 1952-59; Ministry of Agr Eastern Nigeria, livestock adv spec 1960-62; Food & Agr Office Washington, asst to food & agri, acting dep food & agr officer, natl livestock adv, tech adv to agr dir of Brazil 1965; NE Brazil Mission, agr officer 1965, reg agi adv 1965-69; AID Missions Ghana, Accra, food & agr officer 1970-75; State Dept AID, agr devel consult 1975-; State Dept AID Consultant, 1975-85. **Orgs:** Mem Omega Psi Phi, Mason. **Honors/Awds:** Aid Study Grantee Johns Hopkins School Advanced Intl Studies 1969-70. **Military Serv:** AUS 1942-46. **Home Addr:** 1414 Missouri Ave NW, Washington, DC 20011.

FORD, JOHN NEWTON
Government official. **Personal:** Born May 3, 1942, Memphis, TN; son of Mr & Mrs N J Ford; divorced; children: Kemba Nyja, Sean, Autumn Leigh, Michelle. **Educ:** TN State U, BA 1964; Memphis State U, MA 1978. **Career:** Memphis, TN, city cnclmn 1971-79; TN Genl Assembly, TN state senator 1974-; TN State Senate, state senator, speaker pro tempore 1987-. **Orgs:** Chrmn Senate Genl Welfare, Health & Human Resources Committee; mem Finance, Ways & Means Committee; pres NJ Ford & Sons Funeral Parlors; pres Ford & Assoc; life mem NAACP; mem Nat League of Cities; mem Nat Black Caucus; bd mem Regional Sickle Cell Anemia Cncl; mem State and Local Govt Comm. **Honors/Awds:** Outstand Citizens Award Mallory Knights Charitable 1974; Outstand Accomplishment Civil Liberty League 1975; Community Achievemnt Lutheran Baptist Ch 1976; Disting Grad Memphis State Univ 1978. **Home Addr:** 981 Villiage Park Cove, Memphis, TN 38120.

FORD, JOHNNY
State representative. **Personal:** Born Aug 23, 1942, Tuskegee, AL; married Romanita Braggs, 1998; children: Johnny, Christopher, Tiffany. **Educ:** Knoxville Coll, BA 1964; Natl Exec Inst, postgrad 1965; Auburn Univ, MA 1977. **Career:** Multi-Man Dist, exec Bronx 1967-68; Sen Robt Kennedy, polit campaign strategist 1968; Tuskegee Model Cities Program, exec coord 1969-70; Atty Fred Gray, campaign mgr 1970; Multi Racial Corp, asst dir 1970-72; US Justice Dept Montgomery, state supr comm rel serv 1971-72; City of Tuskegee, mayor, 1972-96; Alabama House of Representatives, state rep, 1997-. **Orgs:** Founder World Conf of Mayors; NAACP; Kappa Alpha Psi; past pres AL League of Municipalities. **Honors/Awds:** Top Campaigner Award BSA 1967; Young Man of the Year Women's Reserve 1967; Youngest Multi-Dist Exec in Nation BSA 1967; Awarded the key to more than 100 Amer and foreign cities. **Business Addr:** State Representative, Alabama House of Representatives, 605 E Martin Luther King Hwy, Tuskegee, AL 36083, (334)242-7600.

FORD, JUDITH DONNA
Judge. **Personal:** Born Aug 30, 1935, Eureka, CA. **Educ:** Univ of CA at Berkeley, BS 1957; University of California-Berkeley, JD 1974. **Career:** Petty Andrews Tufts & Jackson, assoc atty 1974-79; Consumer Fraud Crime Div SF Dist Atty's Office, dir 1977-79; Fed Trade Comm, dir 1980-82; Oakland-Piedmont-Emeryville Jud Dist, judge 1983-. **Orgs:** CA Judges Assn; Alameda Co Trauma Review Comm; US Magistrate Merit Selection Comm; San Francisco Bar Assn Lawyer Referral Serv Comm 1976; NSF SoftwareAuditing Wkshp 1976; Comm for Admin of Justice 1976-79; delegate from San Fran Bar Assn Lawyer Refrl Serv Comm 1976; chair E Oakland Planned Prnthd Adv Comm 1977-80; spkr Bank Admin Inst 1977; spkr EDP Audit Cntrls Wkshp 1977; spkr CPA Soc 1977; various TV & Radio appearances; spoke to comm groupson consult fraud 1977-79; spkr Joint meeting of IIA and EDPA 1978; dir Planned Prnthd 1978-80; chair Blk Women Lawyers, N CA Finance Comm 1979-80; San Fran Lawyers Comm Urban Affairs 1979-80; chair SF Bar Assn Comm Legal Ed Comm 1979-80; bd mem Consumer Union 1979-82; ref St Bar Ct 1979-82; cnclr Law CntrBd of Cnclrs 1979-83; radio & TV spkr on FTrade Comm 1980-82; SF Bar Assoc Judiciary Comm 1981-82; Chas Houston Bar Assoc 1974-; CA Assoc of Black Lawyers 1978-; bd mem Peralta Serv Corp 1983-, judicial council, 1991-94; chair, CTC Privacy & Access Subcommittee, 1995-96; Judicial Council Court Technology, advisory comm, 1995-98; trustee, Alameda County Law Library; board member, California Judges Association, 1996-98. **Special Achievements:** California Criminal Law Procedure & Practice, (CEB 1994, 2nd Ed), coauthor, chapters 4 & 6. **Business Addr:** Judge Municipal Court, Oakland-Piedmont Emeryville, 661 Washington St, Oakland, CA 94607.

FORD, KENNETH A.
Association executive. **Personal:** Born Aug 10, 1949, Washington, DC; married Shirley Payne; children: Travelle. **Educ:** Howard Univ, BSCE 1972, MCE 1977. **Career:** Limbach Co, project engr, 1972-75; Potomac Electric Power Co, env engr, 1975-77; Parametric Inc, program dir, 1977-82; WA Suburban Sanitary Commission, planning mgr, 1982-84; Natl Assn of Home Builders, mgr of civil eng, currently. **Orgs:** Natl Soc of Professional Engineers, 1977-; advisory bd, Utility Location & Coord Council 1984-; Building Seismic Safety Cncl 1984; bd of dir BlackSci Inc 1984-85; Amer Soc of Civil Engrs. **Home Addr:** 11303 Sherrington Ct, Upper Marlboro, MD 20772. **Business Addr:** Manager of Civil Engineering, National Assn of Home Builders, 15th & M St NW, Washington, DC 20008.

FORD, KISHA
Professional basketball player. **Personal:** Born Apr 4, 1975. **Educ:** Georgia Tech, attended. **Career:** New York Liberty, guard-forward, 1997-. **Business Addr:** Professional Basketball Player, New York Liberty, Two Penn Plaza, New York, NY 10121, (212)564-9622.

FORD, LISA DENISE
Chemist, educator. **Personal:** Born Aug 3, 1965, Memphis, TN; daughter of Rev and Mrs Samuel L Ford. **Educ:** Fisk Univ, BS, chemistry, 1987, MA, chemistry, 1990. **Career:** Barrow-Agee Analytical Laboratory, analytical chemist, 1987-88; Cargill Corn Milling Division, quality control chemist, 1988; Fisk Univ, grad laboratory teacher's assistant, 1988-89; MMES, Oak Ridge Natl Laboratory, grad rsch intern, 1989-90; MMES, Nuclear and Environmental Plant, quality control chemist, supv chemist, tech support chemist, staff chemist, 1990-96; MMES, Gaseous Diffusion and Waste Mgt Plant, chemist, 1993-94; Millington Central High School, teacher, chemist, 1996-. **Orgs:** American Chemical Society, 1987. **Honors/Awds:** Fisk Univ, Univ Academic Scholarship, UNCF Scholarship, Most Princeful Lodge Scholarship, 1983-87; MMES Certificate of Appreciation for the Tennessee Quality Achievement Award; Environmental, Restoration and Waste Mgt Mission Success Award; Y-12 Pathfinder Award, 1994; Intl Hall of Fame, Investors Club of America, Advanced Technology Award, 1993; Second Runner-up to Miss Fisk, Fisk Univ Library, 1986-87. **Special Achievements:** Development of a Simple Screening Spectroscopic Method for Polychlorinated Biphenyls (PCBs), Fisk Univ Library, 1990. **Home Addr:** 3033 Spring Hill Cove, Memphis, TN 38127, (901)358-8038. **Business Phone:** (901)873-8100.

FORD, LUTHER L.
Educator. **Personal:** Born Dec 3, 1931, Florence, SC; married Dr Willie B Ford. **Educ:** Grambling State U, BS 1961; Univ IA, MA 1964; Univ NE, EdD 1974. **Career:** Carthage AR, 1962-63; Tallulah LA, teacher 1963-65; Davenport IA, special educ teacher 1965-66; Evaluation Vocational Rehabilitation, Oakdale IA, teacher 1966-67; Univ of NE, visiting prof 1971; Grambling State Univ, prof 1967-. **Orgs:** Mem Black Educators Council Human Serv; mem Assn for the Study of Afro-Am Life History Inc; Kappa Delta Pi Honor Educ Soc; life mem Phi Delta Kappa; mem Disabled Am Vet; bd of dirs Black Analysis Inc NY 1977; Nat Soc for Study of Edn; LA Educ Assn; LA Philosophy Edn; LA Educ Research Assn; life mem Omega Psi Phi; Ford Found Fellowship 1973-74; TTT Fellowship 1971-73; Doctorate Fellowship Black Analysis Inc 1972-74; trch stipend 1973-74; Danforth Assoc Prof 1976-84; mem NAACP, natl Soc for the Study of Educ, Important Black Man 1987; life mem Grambling Alumni. **Military Serv:** AUS army airborne sgt 1951-58. **Business Addr:** Professor, Grambling State Univ, PO Box 644, Grambling, LA 71245.

FORD, MARCELLA WOODS
Educator. **Personal:** Born in Athens, GA; daughter of Lucy Smith (deceased) and Clem Woods (deceased); married Jesse W Ford (deceased). **Educ:** Shaw Univ, AB, LHD, 1982; Amer Bapt Sem, MA. **Career:** Mather School, teacher; Shaw Univ, asst profl, dir; Oakland CA, dir of release time classes; Berkeley Unified School Dist, teacher; Berkeley Adult Ed, teacher 1962-64; Black History. **Orgs:** Mem Ch Women United; pres Bus & Professional Women, No CA Amer Bapt Church; pres, sponsor Interfaith Intercultural Fellowship of E Bay; pres Amer Bapt Women Oakland Area Assoc; mem, bd of dir Intertribal Friendship House; mem Budget United Crusade Panel & Speakers Bur; resource person Human Rel & Afro-Amer History, Oakland Publ School 1969-; History Docent of Oakland Museum; mem dedication comm Oakland Museum; mem Amer Bapt Church of the W Campus Ministry Stud Found; life mem Natl Council of Negro Women; mem steering comm Shaw Univ Alumni 1968-69; dir Rel Ed Beth Eden Bapt Church; mem Alpha Nu Omega Chap Alpha Kappa Alpha Sor, Amer Assoc of Univ Women, YWCA; co-org E Bay Negro Hist Soc; mem Oakland Museum Assoc; life mem Assoc for the Study of Afro, AmerLife & History; mem CA Retired Thers; life mem NAACP, Natl Retired Teachers Assoc. **Honors/Awds:** Num articles publ Woman of the Year Eden Bapt Church, Marcella Ford Circle of Women's Soc of McGee Ave Bapt Church 1959,69; featured in "Faces Around the Bay" The Post Newspaper 1970; Woman of the Year Comm Serv Amer Assoc of Univ Women; appt by Gov mem Allensworth State Historical

Park Adv Comm 1969; mem Historic Landmarks Preservation Bd appt by Mayor & City Council 1973; Leadership Awd Far Western Reg Conf of AKA Sor 1976; Dedication of Allensworth State Hist Park Comm Serv Awds & Rose Bushs planted by Alpha Nu Ome Chap AKA & Marcella Ford Cir 1976; Christian Womanhood Awd Shaw Divinity School Raleigh NC 1976; Recog & MW Ford Scholarship Shaw Univ, Beth Eden Bapt Church 1977; Oakland Piedmont Chap AAUW Scholarship Honor of Mem M Ford 1977; Comm Serv Awdby Cultural & Ethnic Affairs Gd Oakland Museum 1977; Pre-Kwanza Awd Assoc Africans & African Amer Oakland; Natl Sojourner Truth Awd by the Natl Assoc of Negro Bus & Professional Womens Clubs Inc, East Bay Area Club 1981; Woman of Achievement Women Helping Women Awd Soroptimist Intl of Oakland 1982; Resolution of Honor, California Legislature Assembly, 1989; Letter of Commendation, Lionel J Wilson, mayor of Oakland, 1989; Plaque for 20 years of service, Advisory Comm for the Restoration of Colonel Allensworth State Historic Park, 1989; Oakland Legacy Awards, Trailblazer, 1997; Berkley Repertory Theatre and African American Advocate, African-American Matriarch Honoree, 1997. **Special Achievements:** Creator of Wee Pals, 1995.

FORD, MARION GEORGE, JR.
Dental surgeon, business executive. **Personal:** Born Aug 22, 1937, Houston, TX; son of LaVerne and Marion; divorced; children: Inge, Erika, Marion, III. **Educ:** Univ TX, BS (magna cum laude) 1958; Univ TX Dental Br, DDS (magna cum laude) 1962; Univ Bonn Germany, Fulbright Scholar. **Career:** Cty Houston, hydro-engr 1953-62; Univ TX Dental Br, German-French translator, 1958-62, researcher, 1959-62; dentist, peridontal surgeon, 1962-; Ford International Enterprises Inc, president. **Orgs:** Mem Am Dental Assn; Charles A George Dental Soc; secy NE Houston Sch Bd 1968-; mem NAACP; Urban League. **Honors/Awds:** All state swimmer 1951-54; football all city 1954; most outstndg chem stud 1954; developer Denture Acrylic Resin & Shade Guide 1962. **Business Addr:** 4315 Lockwood Dr, Houston, TX 77026.

FORD, NANCY HOWARD
Educational administrator. **Personal:** Born Jul 29, 1942, Wilmington, DE; children: Sergio Howard, Charis. **Educ:** Central State Univ, BS 1964; Univ of DE, MEd 1972. **Career:** CT State Welfare Dept, welfare home economist 1968; Seattle Public Schools, teacher-home arts 1968-70; Wilmington Public Schools, teacher corps intl 1970-72; Cheyney State Coll assoc dean res life 1972-76; Dept of Public Instruction DE, education specialist, nutrition, education and training, and summer food service program, 1977-. **Orgs:** US Peace Corps volunteer US Peace Corps in Brazil 1964-66; misc vol w/various comm organizations 1970-71; vol teacher DE Adolescent Program, Inc 1971. **Honors/Awds:** Natl Honor Soc Wilmington HS 1960; second highest ranking student in home econ Central State Univ 1964; cert of recognition US Peace Corps Service from the White House 1966; American Cancer Society, National Gold Award/Public Education, 1992; received a Senate and House tribute from the Delaware legislature for outstanding work in the area of child nutrition, 1993; honored by the US Dept of Agriculture for contributions made as participant on the USDA Reg Child Nutrition Task Force to improve the School Lunch Program, 1993; honored by USDA for creating partnerships that promote hiring of 157 disabled persons in the Summer Food Program, 1994; nationally recognized by the Food Research and Action Committee as Delaware's Dir of the Summer Food Program, which was number one for the third year in reaching more eligible children than any other state, 1994; received letter from First Lady Hillary Rodham Clinton exessing appreciation for the Child Advocate Award given by the Delaware Summer Food Service Program, 1994. **Special Achievements:** Appeared on Tom Brokaw's Nightly News Special entitled "Keeping Kid's Out of Harm's Way," 1994; participated as speaker in a natl news conference with leaders of the Children's Defense Fund, Share Our Strength, and American School Food Service Assn, 1994. **Business Addr:** Education Specialist, Dept of Public Instruction, Townsend Building, Dover, DE 19901, (302)739-4717.

FORD, RICHARD D.
Administrator. **Personal:** Born Mar 22, 1935, Birmingham, AL; son of Vivian Henderson Ford and Jesse A Ford; married Nancy Thompson, Sep 9, 1961; children: Robin, Richard T. **Educ:** Miles Coll Birmingham, BA 1959; Johnson C Smith Theological Sem Charlotte, BD 1962; State Univ of NY at Buffalo, MSW 1969. **Career:** Westminster Comm House, dir of comm serv & christian educ 1963-66; School of Social Welfare, State Univ of NY, asst prof 1969-70, dir of admissions 1970-72; CA State Univ School of Health & Social Work, dean 1972-. **Orgs:** Pres BUILD of Buffalo NY 1970-72; pres United Presby Health Educ & Welfare Assn 1975-76; mem Council on Soc Work Educ 1972-; mem Natl Assn of Black Soc Workers; mem Natl Conf of Deans of Soc Work 1972-; mem Fresno Co Planning Commn 1978-; mem Steering Comm for Region IX Child Welfare Trng; mem West Side Planning Group Fresno. **Business Addr:** Dean, School of Health and Social Work, California State University, Fresno, Shaw and Maple Ave, Fresno, CA 93740.

FORD, ROBERT BENJAMIN, JR. See Obituaries section.

FORD, ROBERT BLACKMAN
Dentist. **Personal:** Born Nov 22, 1924, Montgomery, AL; married Katherine Brosby; children: Teri, Wendy, Sondra. **Educ:** Morehouse Coll, BS 1948; Howard U, DDS 1952; Veteran's Hosp Tuskegee, additional study 1952-53; 300 hrs post grad study. **Career:** Pvt practice. **Orgs:** Mem Am Dental Assn; OH State Dental Assn; Dayton Dental Assn coun; 1970-73; Buckeye State Dental Soc, treas; Academy of General Dentistry; elected to Jefferson Twp Bd of Edn; past pres 1968-72; bd of mgmt YMCA; bd mem Community Research Inc; mem Kappa Alpha Psi. **Honors/Awds:** First Black in OH appointed to the State Dentl Bd 1974. **Military Serv:** USMC 1944-46. **Business Addr:** 3807 W Third St, Dayton, OH 45417.

FORD, SARAH ANN
Educator. **Personal:** Born Aug 29, 1951, Gary, IN. **Educ:** Ball State Univ, BS 1973, MA 1974; Keller Grad Sch of Mgmt, MBA 1986. **Career:** Marquette Univ, dir multi-cul ctr 1974-78; Univ of WI Extension, arts consultant 1978-84; Univ of WI, business consultant 1984-; US Army Reserves/Guard, drill sgt/1st lt 1975-; Colorlines Magazine, publisher 1980-; Rowland Financial GR, security agent 1980-82; Small Business Develop Ctr, business counselor/instructor. **Orgs:** Mem Delta Sigma Theta Sor 1970-; Talk show host WISN TV "Look In" 1975-82; pres/performer Heritage Chorale 1984-; sec Council on Minority/Small Bus 1987-; pres Colorlines Foundation for Arts and Culture Inc 1986-. **Honors/Awds:** Most Interesting People in Milwaukee-Milwaukee magazine 1983; Awd of Excellence Colorlines Magazine Milwaukee Art Comm 1983; Outstanding Serv Awd Milwaukee ArtMuseum 1984. **Military Serv:** NG 1st lt 6 yrs. **Business Addr:** Business Counselor/Instruct, Small Business Devel Ctr, UWM 929 No 6th St, Milwaukee, WI 53203.

FORD, STACEY
Professional basketball player. **Personal:** Born Jan 14, 1969. **Educ:** Univ of Georgia, bachelor's degree in early childhood education. **Career:** Columbus Quest, forward, 1996-. **Business Addr:** Professional Basketball Player, Columbus Quest, 7451 State Route 16, Dublin, OH 43016, (614)873-6555.

FORD, VERNON N.
Aluminum company executive. **Personal:** Born Feb 15, 1945, Eupora, MS; son of Nancy E Jones Ford and Robert N Ford; married Angela Graves Ford, Oct 10, 1970; children: Tatia L, Erin K. **Educ:** Central State Univ, Wilberforce, Ohio, BS, 1970. **Career:** Alcoa, Los Angeles, CA, sales rep, 1973-77; Alcoa, Indianapolis, IN, branch sales mgr, 1977-79; Alcoa, San Francisco, CA, sales mgr, 1979-84; Alcoa, Houston, TX, sales mgr, 1984-87; Separations Technology Inc, Warrendales, PA, mgr sales & distributor, 1987-90; Vancouver Extension Co, Vancouver WA, pres, beginning 1990; Alcoa, Halethorpe Extrusions Inc, president, currently. **Orgs:** Member, Executive Leadership Council, 1986-; chairperson, MESO Advisory Bd, 1990-; vice-president, Central State Univ Foundation, 1989-; chairperson, College of Business, Advisory Council, Central State Univ, 1990-; member, Rotary, 1990-. **Honors/Awds:** Achievement Hall of Fame, Central State Univ, 1990. **Military Serv:** USAF, E-5, 1962-66. **Business Addr:** President, Alcoa, Halethorpe Extrusions Inc, 425 Sixth Ave, Alcoa Bldg, Pittsburgh, PA 15219-1850.

FORD, VIRGINIA
Educator (retired). **Personal:** Born Jul 3, 1914, Toledo, OH; daughter of Marie Harter Ford Robinson (deceased) and Russell Ford (deceased). **Educ:** Univ of MI Ann Arbor, PH Cert 1938-42; Catholic Univ of Am Washington DC, BSNE 1950, MSN 1960, PhD 1967. **Career:** US Public Health Serv H Huachuca and Mission to Liberia, public hlth advisor 1941-46; Am Nat Red Cross/Korea/Japan, staff asst 1948-50; UN World Hlth Organ/India/Taiwan, public hlth advisor 1955-59; US Veteran's Admin Chicago, asso chief 1966-67; DePaul Univ Chicago, asso prof 1967-74; Chicago State U, dean & prof emeritus 1974-77. **Orgs:** Bd of dir Infant Welfare Society Chicago 1969-78; member, University of Chicago Service League, 1982-91. **Honors/Awds:** Inactive Delta Sigma Theta 1938; Sigma Tau; pre-doctoral research fellow Nat Inst of Hlth (NIMH) 1960-65; service league Univ of Chicago 1983-. **Military Serv:** US Public Hlth Serv maj 1945-46, 1950-55; Am Campaign Medal; European-African Middle Eastern Campaign Medal; WW II Victory Medal 1963; US Public Health Service, Bronze Medal 1963. **Home Addr:** 5530 S Shore Dr, Apt 14B, Chicago, IL 60637.

FORD, WALLACE L., II
City official. **Personal:** Born Jan 13, 1950, New York, NY. **Educ:** Dartmouth Coll, BA, 1970; Harvard Law Sch, JD, 1973. **Career:** WDCR radio, disc jockey; NY State Supreme Court, law secty; NY State Assembly Committee on Banking, counsel; Amistad DOT Venture Capital Inc, exec vice pres & genl counsel; NY State Dept of Commerce Div of Minority Business Develop, deputy commissioner; State of NY Mortgage Agency, exec officer & CEO; Drexel Burnham Lambert, Inc, 1st vp; City of New York, NY, dept of ports and trade, commissioner, 1990-. **Orgs:** Mem Dartmouth Alumni Council; mem Dartmouth Black Alumni Assn; Malcolm King Coll, bd of trustees; Natl Assn of Securities Professionals, mem; NY Urban League (Harlem Branch), bd of dir. **Honors/Awds:** Listed Ebony Magazine One Hundred Leaders of the Future 1978; listed Time Magazine Fifty Faces of the Future 1979; speaker Dartmouth Bicentennial Commencement Exercises 1970; Nat'l Housing Conference annual awd 1984. **Business Addr:** Commissioner, New York City Dept of Ports & Trade, Battery Maritime Bldg, 4th Fl, New York, NY 10004.

FORD, WILLIAM L., JR.
Vice president. **Personal:** Born Jul 31, 1941, Kayford, WV; married Eleanor Holmes; children: Karen, Valerie. **Educ:** Russell Sage Evening Coll, 1961-66; State Univ of Albany NY, 1967-68. **Career:** Mayfair Inc Albany, ofc mgr 1968-70; WROW-WTEN Albany, chief acct 1970-71; WROW Radio Albany, bus mgr 1971; WKBW-TV & Radio Buffalo, bus mgr 1971-76; WFSB-TV Hartford, vice pres bus & admin affairs 1976-78; Post-Newsweek Stations MI Inc WDIV, vp, sta mgr 1978-83; Cellular Telecommunications, vice pres 1984-. **Orgs:** Bd of dir Better Bus Bur of Met Detroit 1979-, Jr Achievement of Southeastern MI, 1979-, Broadcast Fin Mgmt Assoc 1979-; commiss Detroit Black UnitedFund 1979-; bd of gov Detroit Chap Natl Acad of TV Arts & Sci 1980-; bd of dir MI Assoc of Broadcasters 1980-. **Business Addr:** Vice President, Cellular Telecommunications, 550 Lafayette Blvd, Detroit, MI 48231.

FORDE, FRASER PHILIP, JR.
Business executive. **Personal:** Born Nov 24, 1943, Tuskegee, AL; son of Joyce Nourse Forde and Fraser Philip Forde Sr; married LaVerne; children: Tracey, Fraser III, Erika. **Educ:** Hofstra Univ, BBA 1965; Pace Univ, MBA candidate 1980. **Career:** Morgan Guaranty Trust Co, asst vice pres 1987-89, vp, 1989-, asst treas 1973-87; asst officer personnel rep 1971-73; Money Transfer Dept, asst group head 1970-71; Bank & Operations Dept, educ trainee 1969-70; Dun & Bradstreet Inc, credit analyst 1967-69. **Orgs:** Treasurer, Milford Civic Assn of Central Islip Inc 1980-; delegate, Central Islip School District Budget Advisory Comm 1981-. **Honors/Awds:** Black Achievers In Industry, YMCA of Greater NY, Harlem Branch, 1974; Award Outstanding Trainee; Basic Training; Scout Dog Training; CIB O/S Bar; Vietnam Serv Award; Vietnamese Serv Award. **Military Serv:** AUS sp/4 1965-67. **Business Addr:** Vice President, Morgan Guaranty Trust Co of New York, 60 Wall St, New York, NY 10260.

FORDE, JAMES ALBERT
Health services director. **Personal:** Born Jan 23, 1927, Brooklyn, NY; married Gaille Faulkner Forde; children: Janice Ross, Jacqueline Sullivan. **Educ:** Brooklyn Coll, BA English 1949; CCNY, MPA 1955; NY State Univ, Doctoral Courses 1955-60; Ithaca Coll, Nursing Home Admin 1975. **Career:** Dir Bureau of Mgmt Serv Dept of Mental Hygiene 1963-67; dir Bureau of Budget Serv 1967-68; asst commiss NY State Dept of Mental Hygiene Local Serv Div 1968-71; Office of Program Planning & Coord NY State Dept of Mental Hygiene, assoc commiss 1971-74; Willowbrook Devel Ctr, acting dir 1974-75; Mid-Hudson Reg Dept of Mental Hygiene, reg dir 1975-76; Health Care Agency Cty of San Diego, dep admin 1976-79; San Diego Cty Dept of Health Svcs, dir 1979-86; SD Urban League, exec dir; California Black Health Network, exec dir, 1987-. **Orgs:** Mem Amer Public Health Assoc, CA Black Health Network, State of CA Hypertension Adv Council; consultant Federal Office of Health Affairs 1973; mem Willowbrook Review Panel 1975-78; bd mem CD Reg Center for Devlopmentelly Disabled 1979-86. **Honors/Awds:** JCC Disting Serv Awd 1963; Paper Unified Serv A Shift from Who to How "The Bulletin," 1973; Aid Awd for Med 1980; NAACP Awd for Health 1981; Statewide Black Health Individual Achievement Awd 1982; Hildrus Poindexter Award 1995; APHA Award for Excellence 1993. **Military Serv:** AUS sgt 2 yrs. **Business Addr:** California Black Health Network, 7840 Mission Center Court, #103, San Diego, CA 92108.

FORDHAM, CYNTHIA WILLIAMS
Attorney. **Personal:** Born Dec 6, 1954, Philadelphia, PA; daughter of Ola N Williams and Paul Williams; married Rev Jerome Fordham. **Educ:** PA State Univ, BA 1975; Univ of PA Law School, JD 1979. **Career:** Philadelphia Bd of Educ, substitute teacher 1976; Comm Legal Svcs, law clerk 1977,78; PA Dept of State, asst general counsel 1980-84; PA Human Relations Commn, asst counsel 1984-91; PA Public Utility Commission, special agent, 1991-93, administrative law judge, 1993-. **Orgs:** Amer Bar Assn, 1976-, PA Bar Assn, 1979-, Natl Bar Assn, 1983-; chairperson Greater Philadelphia Health Action 1984-; pres bd of dir TSB Church Com Outreach Corp 1986-. **Honors/Awds:** Chapel of Four Chaplains Awd 1967,81; Outstanding Young Women of Amer Awd 1980. **Business Addr:** Administrative Law Judge, Pennsylvania Public Utility Commission, 1302 State Office Building, Broad & Spring Garden Sts, Philadelphia, PA 19130.

FORDHAM, MONROE
Educator. **Personal:** Born Oct 11, 1939, Parrott, GA; married Freddie; children: Cynthia, Barry, Pamela. **Educ:** Emporia St U, BS 1957; Emporia St U, MS 1962; SUNY, PhD 1973. **Career:** Buffalo St Coll, History teacher; Wichita St U, coordinator of black studies; Wichita Pub Schl, Social Studies teacher; Buffalo State Coll, Chairman History Department 1970-. **Orgs:**

Pres Afro-Amer History Assn of Niagara Frontier. **Honors/Awds:** Appointed NY St Bi-centennial Comm Author "Major Themes in Northern Black Religious Thought 1800-1860", numerous art on Afro-Amer History; Ed Afro-amer in NY Life & Hist; an interdisciplinary journal; African American Presence in NYS History, Editor 1989. **Business Addr:** Dept of His & Soc Sci, Buffalo State College, 1300 Elmwood, Buffalo, NY 14222-1004.

FOREE, JACK CLIFFORD
Business owner. **Personal:** Born Mar 29, 1935, New Castle, KY; son of Etta Foree and Jesse Foree; married Daisy Spencer; children: Julia Foree Burton, Stacey, Etta. **Educ:** Kentucky State University, BA 1959; Catherine Spalding University, BA 1966; Indiana University, MA 1971; Grace Theological Seminary, PhD. **Career:** Math teacher, formerly; Franklin Square West, president, currently. **Orgs:** Pres, Breakfast Optimist; Jefferson Co Educators Assn; Kentucky Educators Assn; Natl Educators Assn; Natl Building Contractors Assn; Natl Assn of Math Educators; State Assn of Math & Science Educators; chairman, KY/TN Sunday School Assns, 1972-85. **Honors/Awds:** Kentucky Colonel. **Military Serv:** US Army, S Sergeant, 2 years. **Business Addr:** President, Franklin Square W, 206 Old Harrods Creek Rd, Louisville, KY 40223.

FOREMAN, CHRISTOPHER H.
Attorney. **Personal:** Born Sep 1, 1925, New Iberia, LA. **Educ:** Univ of Cincinnati, BA high hon 1950; Univ of Cincinnati, MA; Univ of MD, LLB 1957. **Career:** Atty pvt prac; Dept of Economics Univ of Cincinnati, asst; US Ordnance Corps, first lt; Ordnance Training Command, Ordnance & Sch Aberdeen Proving Ground, instr; Hon Emory H Niles, law clerk 1956-57. **Orgs:** Phi Beta Kappa; Order of Coif; Am Judicature Soc; mem Law Firm, Callegary, Bracken, Callegary 1957-60; asst Gen Counsel, Dept HEW 1961-62; mem St Thomas Moore Soc 1957-; former gen counsel BACMONILA Inc.

FOREMAN, DOYLE
Sculptor, educator. **Personal:** Born Jun 17, 1933, Ardmore, OK; married Selma J; children: Doyle, Jr, Maia. **Educ:** CA Coll of Arts & Crafts, BA 1960. **Career:** Oakland Recreation Dept, arts & crafts specialist 1957-60, landscape, gardening & land mgmt 1961-65; Univ of CA, Coll V Santa Cruz, assoc prof of art & sculptor 1968-; CA Coll of Arts & Crafts, 1969; Yardbird Publishing Corp, art editor, art dir, bd dir 1971-. **Orgs:** Mem Santa Cruz Co Art Commn 1972-74; mem City of Santa Cruz Bicentennial Com 1975; com chmn to organize New Perspectives in Black Art, Kaiser Center Gallery Oakland 1968. **Military Serv:** AUS 1953-55. **Business Addr:** Coll V Univ of CA, Santa Cruz, CA.

FOREMAN, GEORGE EDWARD
Professional boxer, minister. **Personal:** Born Jan 10, 1949, Travis County, TX; son of J D and Nancy Foreman; married Joan; children: Micki, Leola, George II, George III, George IV, George V. **Career:** Professional boxer: Heavyweight Champion of the World by defeating Michael Moorer, 1994; started boxing career while on Job Corp training program at Grants Pass, OR conservation camp; won Corps Diamond Belt Tournament; entered Golden Gloves competition 1967; lost by split decision, won a berth on US Olympics Squad; turned professional 1969 after winning 19 of out 22 amateur bouts in 2 years; Church of the Lord Jesus Christ, pastor/preacher/proprietor. **Honors/Awds:** Heavyweight Olympic Gold Medal, Mexico City, 1968; won 37 straight professional bouts when entered ring against Joe Frazier for World's HeavyweightChampionship (won Jan 22, 1973); Boxer of the Year, World Boxing Assn, 1974; Heavyweight Champion of the World, Intl Boxing Federation, World Boxing Assn (defeated Michael Moorer, Nov 5, 1994). **Special Achievements:** Co-author w/Joel Engel, By George, Villard Books, 1995. **Business Addr:** Boxer, c/o George Foreman Community Center, 2202 Lone Oak Rd., Houston, TX 77093-3336.

FOREMAN, JOYCE BLACKNALL
Entrepreneur. **Personal:** Born Jul 6, 1948, Thelma, TX; daughter of Betty Lockhart and Roy Blacknall; divorced. **Educ:** University of Texas at Dallas, sociology; El Centro College, AA. **Career:** Foreman Office Products, Dallas, TX, president, currently. **Orgs:** Member, bd of dirs, TX Commerce Bank; mem, bd of management, Urban League; chairperson, Dallas Independent School District's Minority Business Advisory Committee; mem, National Association of Female Executives; mem, NAACP; mem, Women's Business Connection; memr, bd of dirs, Channel 13; mem, the Dallas Assembly; mem, Dallas Citizens Council; mem, Commission on Educational Excellence. **Honors/Awds:** Vendor of the Year, Dallas/Fort Worth Minority Business Development Council, 1984; Quest for Success Award, Miller Brewing Co/The Dallas Morning News/The Dallas Black Chamber of Commerce, 1985; Dreammaker Award, Southeast Dallas Business and Professional Women's Club, 1985; Business Recognition Award, Iota Phi Lambda, 1987; Spotlighting Your Success for Women Business Owner, 1986; Champion 100 Gran Award, 1984; Up and Comer to Watch, The Dallas Times Herald, 1987; Community Service Award, Sigma Gamma Rho Sorority, 1987; Trailblazer Award, South Dallas Business and Professional Women's Club, 1989; Minority Business Advocate of the Year for State of Texas, Small Business Administration, 1989; Doers Award, 1989; Entrepreneur of the Year, Dallas Weekly, 1994; African Amer Hero Award, KKDA Radio & Coca-Cola, 1994. **Business Addr:** President, Foreman Office Products, Inc, 1507 Main St, Dallas, TX 75201.

FOREMAN, LUCILLE ELIZABETH
Church official. **Personal:** Born Jul 8, 1923, Birmingham, AL; daughter of Alberta Elizabeth Lacy Maxwell and George Maxwell; married James Foreman, May 8, 1945; children: James Jr, Rosalind, Shelia. **Educ:** Miles College, Birmingham, AL, BA, natural sciences; University of California at Los Angeles; California Coast University; Fairleigh Dickinson University; Seton Hall University currently. **Career:** Kaiser Foundation Hospital, Bellflower, CA, outpatient medical laboratory technologist supervisor, 1963-67; Mountainside Hospital, Montclair, NJ, chief medical laboratory technologist and laboratory manager, 1967-73; Hoffman La Roche, Nutley, NJ, in process testing lab, pharmaceutical supervisor, 1973-85; Archdiocese of New Jersey, Newark, NJ, field director for English speaking, 1985-87, St. Ann's School, teacher, 1988-90, director of the Office of Black Catholic Affairs, 1990-. **Orgs:** Troop leader, Girl Scouts of America, 1960-89; grand lady, Knights of St. Peter, Claver Ladies Auxiliary Court 297, 1986-; board member, Neighborhood Center for Child Care, 1984-; life member, Delta Sigma Theta Sorority, 1989-; chairperson and trustee, Parish Council Education, St. Peter Claver Church, 1971-; Health Fair Team of Montclair and Nutley, 1970-; Youth Tutorial and Counseling Services, 1970-; Montclair Commission for Women, 1990. **Honors/Awds:** The Caritas Award, Archdiocese of New Jersey, 1985; Jubilee Medal Pro Meritus, Archdiocese of New Jersey, 1988; Service Award, Christian Foundation for Ministry, 1988; Annual Rev. Martin Luther King, Jr. Award, Black Catholic Coordinating Team, 1990; St. Peter Claver Parish Service Award, St. Peter Claver Parish, 1978, 1989; has conducted numerous workshops and seminars on the Church. **Home Addr:** 92 High St, Montclair, NJ 07042. **Business Addr:** Director, Office of Black Catholic Affairs, Roman Catholic Archdiocese of Newark, 100 Linden Ave, Irvington, NJ 07111.

FOREMAN, PEGGY E.
Attorney. **Personal:** Born Feb 18, 1958, Houston, TX; daughter of Ella & Dave Foreman. **Educ:** Univ of Pennsylvania, 1976-78; Univ of Houston, BBA, 1981; TSU, Thurgood Marshall School of Law, JD, 1985. **Career:** Peggy Foreman, attorney, 1985-89; Burney and Foreman, partner, 1990-. **Orgs:** American Bar Assn; National Bar Assn; State Bar of Texas; Texas Young Lawyers Assn; Harris County Young Assn; Houston Lawyers Assn, Houston Bar Assn, Young Lawyers Assn; National Assn of Bond Lawyers; Texas Trial Lawyers Assn; Gulf Coast Black Women Lawyers Assn; Phi Delta Phi Legal Fraternity Alumni Chap; Thurgood Marshall School of Law Alumni Assn. **Honors/Awds:** Houston Business and Professional Men's Club, Special Recognition; Iota Phi Lambda Sorority Inc, Beta Delta Chapter, Woman of the Year. **Special Achievements:** State Bar of Texas Fifth Annual ADR Institute, speaker; Author/Speaker, "Effective Rainmaking", Women in the Law Section Institute, State Bar of Texas, April 1993; Author/Speaker, Wills and Trusts in Texas, Harris County Young Lawyers Assn and Texas Lawyers Assn, May 1989; Author/Speaker, Client Satisfaction, How to Thrive, Not Just Survive in a Solo/Small Firm Practice, State Bar of Texas, December 1993; numerous others. **Business Addr:** Partner, Burney & Foreman, 5445 Almeda, Ste 400, Houston, TX 77004.

FOREMAN, S. BEATRICE
Teacher, educational administrator (retired). **Personal:** Born Sep 23, 1917, Garysburg, NC; daughter of Susie Ransom and Douglas Ransom; married James W Foreman. **Educ:** Hampton Inst, BS 1939; Western Reserve Univ, MS 1956. **Career:** Murfreesboro TN, public sch teacher 1939-41; Cleveland OH, public sch teacher 1942-61; Stamford CT, public sch teacher 1961-82, bd of educ member. **Orgs:** Past pres Westchester Co Chap Delta Sigma Theta Sor; mem League of Women Voters; mem Retired Teachers Assn; mem Democratic Womens Club; mem Hampton Alumnae Assn; mem Urban League; mem Yerwood Ctr; mem The Girlfriends Inc; mem Interfaith Council of Stamford; mem Catholic Interracial Council; mem St Bridgets RC Church; mem Heart Fund Chmn; mem Amer Red Cross Bloodmobile Aide; mem Fairfield Co Alumnae Chap Delta Sigma Theta Sor Inc; 1st vice pres New Neighborhoods Inc 1969-; bd of trustees first black female Stamford Hosp 1972-83; 1st vice pres NAACP 1979-84; CT Justice Comm 1981-82; pres Business/Educ Alliance 1988-89; Bd of Educ 1st black female 1981-; bd of dirs Wright Tech Sch 1981-; Mayor's Comm on Drugs & Alcohol; member SNET advisory, Southern New England Telephone; member advisory bd, Salvation Army of Stamford; bd of dirs, secretary, CTE Anti Poverty Agency; bd of dirs, secretary, Salvation Army. **Honors/Awds:** Serv Awd Interfaith Council 1972; Educ Awd Stamford Black Educators 1978, Westhill HS 1978, Stamford Educ Assn Outstanding 1978; Outstanding Educ Stamford Educ Assn 1978; top vote getter city primary & regular election 1981 & 1984; Serv Awd CT Justice Comm 1982; Outstanding Educator CT State Ministers Wives & Widows Assn outstanding educator 1983; Serv Awd Stamford Hosp 1984; Outstanding Sor Awd Fairfield Co Alumnae Chap Delta Sigma Theta Sor Inc 1984; Comm Serv Awd Yerwood Womens Club 1984; Ed Awd NAACP 1985; Citizen of Year 1987; Senior Employment Service Award 1989.

FORNAY, ALFRED R., JR.
Editor, author. **Personal:** Born Jun 8, Cincinnati, OH; son of Marguerite Weatherford Fornay and Alfred Fornay Sr. **Educ:** Wilfred Acad of Beauty & Hair Design, 1966; City Univ City Coll of NY, AAS 1968; State Univ of NY/Fashion Inst of Tech, AAS 1971. **Career:** Fashion Fair Cosmetics, beauty/training dir 1973-78; Revlon, Inc, polished ambers creative dir 1978-80; Elan Mag, elan bty editor 1980-82; Ebony Mag, beauty & fashion editor 1982-85; EM Magazine, editor 1985-1988; Essence Mag, assoc beauty editor 1972-73; Clairol Inc, asst ethnic mktng mgr 1971-72; American Visions Magazine, fashion & beauty contributing writer 1989-; Johnson Publishing Co Inc, Fashion Fair Div, beauty/training 1988-; Business Week Careers Mag, contribtng fashion & beauty writer, 1987-88; Procter & Gamble, Cover Girl cosmetic division, consultant, 1992. **Orgs:** Natl Assn of Black Journalists, New York Chapter, 1984, 1991-93; mem Nat Beauty Culturist League 1983; friend/former bd mem Boys Choir of Harlem; New York Association of Black Journalist 1991-92; The Authors Guild Inc 1991-93; personal grooming & development consultant, Girls Choir of Harlem, 1994-95. **Honors/Awds:** Alumni of the Yr Award Fashion Inst of Tech 1976, Mortimer C Ritter Award 1976; judge Miss World Beauty Pageant London, Eng 1982; contributor McGraw Hill Book Co Encyclopedia of Black Am 1981; BBW articles 1984; Awd in Excellence Black Women in Publishing NY 1986; Beauty Book: Fornay's Guide to Skin & Makeup for Women of Color, Simon & Schuster Publishers 1989; contributer Black State of the Arts, Love Child Publishing 1991; East NY Club of Brooklyn National Assn of Negro Business & Professional Women's Club Inc 1981; Black Women in Publishing Connections III 1986; BET Weekend Magazine Article, 1997; Amalgamated Publishers Special Beauty Edition, 1996; BE Magazine Article, 1997. **Home Addr:** PO Box 1321, Grand Central Station, New York, NY 10163-1321, (718)260-8605.

FORNEY, MARY JANE
Social service administrator. **Personal:** Born May 23, 1949, Galesburg, IL; children: James LaMour. **Educ:** Sangamon State Univ, BA Child Family Comm Serv 1977, Grad Student Soc Serv Admin. **Career:** Springfield & Sangamon Co Comm Action, admin asst 1968-74; IL Dept of Children & Family Svcs, child welfare worker & soc serv planner 1974-78; Family Serv Ctr of Sangamon Co, dir of child care svcs. **Orgs:** Council mem Head Start Policy Council 1974-76; mem Natl Assn for the Educ of Young Children vice pres 1981-83; chmn Mother's March-March of Dimes 1984 &1985; mem Natl Assn Black Social Worker 1974-; sec Streetside Boosters Neighborhood Adv Bd of Dirs 1976-; comm mem Springfield Reg Adv Bd Dept Children & Family Serv 1981-; spec projs chmn Delta Sigma Theta Inc 1983-; adv bd Chr Sangamon Cty Dept of Public Aid 1985-; mem DPA Adv Bd 1982-; vice pres exec bd March of Dimes. **Honors/Awds:** Founders Day Awd St John AME Church 1979; Social Worker of Yr Natl Assn of Black Soc Workers 1979; Vol Awd Amer Lung Assn 1981; Hall of Fame Awd Springfield-Sangamon Co Comm Action 1981; Outstanding Young Woman-Outstanding Young Women of Amer 1982; Mother's March Chairperson March of Dimes Awd 1985; YWCA Woman of the Year Awd; March of Dimes 5 Year Service Awd 1987. **Home Addr:** 2033 Randall Ct, Springfield, IL 62703. **Business Addr:** Dir of Child Care Serv, Family Ser Ctr Sangamon County, 1308 S 7th St, Springfield, IL 62703.

FORREST, LEON RICHARD. See Obituaries section.

FORREST-CARTER, AUDREY FAYE
Educator. **Personal:** Born Apr 1, 1956, Greenwood, SC; daughter of Ruth B Forrest and Willie Forrest Sr (deceased); married Ewing Carter III, Sep 6, 1986; children: Channing Kamille, Ewing IV. **Educ:** Bennett Coll, BA 1978; NC A&T State Univ, MA 1979; Miami Univ, PhD 1990. **Career:** A&T State Univ, teaching asst 1978-79; Winston-Salem State Univ, instructor 1979-84, asst prof 1990-91; Miami Univ, doctoral assoc 1984-88; North Carolina A&T State University, assistant professor of English, 1992-96; Courtesy Kids, owner, currently. **Orgs:** Mem NCTE, 1992-; CLA, 1994-; Communities-in-Schools, partner, 1994-; grad comm English dept Miami Univ 1984-85; mem rsch team computers & composition Miami Univ 1985; General Greene Elementary, PTA, bd mem. **Honors/Awds:** Publ poem Worn Out 1982; DAP Awd Miami Univ 1984-88; Faculty Develop Grant Winston-Salem State Univ 1984-88; Silver Poet Awd World of Poetry 1986; Board of Governor's Grant, Univ of North Carolina at Chapel Hill, 1988-89, 1989-90. **Home Addr:** 2001 Larchmont Dr, Greensboro, NC 27409.

FORSTER, CECIL R. See Obituaries section.

FORSTER, CECIL R., JR.
Business executive. **Personal:** Born Nov 11, 1943, New York. **Educ:** Middlebury Coll, BA 1964; St John's Univ, JD 1967. **Career:** Irving Trust Company, lender officers in training program, 1967-68; United States Marine Corps, captain, 1968-71; Pepsico Inc, vice pres/sec, counsel, 1971-74; Westinghouse

Broadcasting Company, Inc, vice pres, 1977-81; Unity Broadcasting Network, Inc, vice pres, 1981-85; Legal Business Adivisor, 1985-89; Pace University School of Law, professor of law, 1985-89; Nutri/System, Inc, senior vice pres and interim administrator of corporate operations, 1989, senior vice pres, law & human resources, 1989-90, senior vice pres, law and govt affairs, 1990-91; Patton, Boggs, & Blow, counsel, 1991-93; Infinity Broadcasting Corporation, vice pres & gen manager, 1993-. **Orgs:** Howard Memorial Fund, board of directors, 1976-; AFTRA Health & Retirement Funds, bd of trustees, 1975-; Black Executive Exchange Program, Natl Urban League, exec advisory committee, 1977-; 100 Black Men; Amer Bar Assn; New York Bar Assn; Phi Alpha Delta Law Fraternity; Sigma Pi Phi Fraternity; Fund for the Improvement of Postsecondary Education, 1989. **Honors/Awds:** YMCA, Black Achievers Award, 1972; Council of Concerned Black Executives, Corporate Achievement Award, 1978; Commandant of the Marine Corps, Meritorious Public Service Citation, 1981. **Special Achievements:** Admitted to the New York State Bar, 1968; Admitted to United States Court of Military Appeals, 1971; Admitted to Pennsylvania State Bar, 1992. **Military Serv:** USMC capt 1968-71. **Business Addr:** VP/Gen Mgr, Infinity Broadcasting Corp, Sportsradio 610 WIP, 441 N. 5th St., Philadelphia, PA 19106.

FORT, EDWARD B.
Education administrator. **Personal:** Born in Detroit, MI; married Lessie; children: Clarke, Lezlie. **Educ:** Wayne State Univ, Bachelors 1954, Masters 1958; Univ of CA Berkeley, Doctorate 1964. **Career:** Detroit MI Public Schools, curriculum coord 1964-67; Inkster MI Public Schools, supt 1967-71; Sacramento CA City Schools, supt, dep supt 1971-74; Univ of WI Ctr System, chancellor 1974-81; NC A&T State Univ, chancellor 1981-. **Orgs:** Vstg prof of ed admin Univ of MI Ann Arbor 1965-66; adj prof urban ed Univ of MI Dearborn 1968-71; vstg prof MI State Univ 1974; bd of adv Fund for Improvement of Post Sec Ed 1979-81; NASA Advisory Council, 1991-; NIEH, board of directors, 1988-92; pres commiss NCAA 1984-86; board of directors Natl Assoc for Equal Oppty in Higher Ed 1984-; mem Greensboro NC Chamber of Commerce Exec Bd. **Honors/Awds:** Press Awd Ed Press Assoc of Amer 1969; Chosen Symposium Participant Dept of Sociology Univ of Pretoria S African 1977; Eighty for the 80's Milwaukee Jrnl Awd 1979; Honorary Doctor of Humanities, Wayne State University. **Military Serv:** AUS corpl 2 yrs; Good Conduct Medal 1955-56. **Business Addr:** Chancellor, North Carolina A&T St Univ, Admin Bldg, 1601 E Market Street, Greensboro, NC 27411.

FORT, JANE
Educational administrator. **Personal:** Born Aug 27, 1938, Nashville, TN; daughter of Geraldine Bennett Fort and William Henry Fort; divorced; children: Sekou Fort Morrison. **Educ:** Fisk Univ, BA (cum laude) 1958; Univ of Mass, MS 1960, PhD 1962. **Career:** City of New York, JOIN, dir of research, psychologist, 1964; City Coll & William Alans White Inst, New York City, research assoc, 1965; Harvard Univ Grad School of Educ, research assoc, 1965-69; Newton MA Schools, Reading Program, consultant/psychologist, 1974-75; Brookline Public Schools (BEEP), Brookline MA, consultant and sr research assoc, 1977-81; Roxbury Comm Coll, Roxbury, MA, staff assoc, program developer, 1979-81; Univ of California-Davis, lecturer, researcher, 1981-83; Clark College, program manager for evaluation/dir, 1984-87; Morehouse School of Medicine, Dept of Comm Health and Preventive Medicine 1987-92; Meharry Medical College, Cancer Control Research Unit, Cancer Prevention Awareness Program, associate director/co-principal investigator, 1995-97, asst dean of student affairs, 1998-. **Orgs:** Mem numerous bds of dirs; lecture seminar/conference coordinator/chair; mem alumni clubs; mem Alpha Kappa Alpha Sorority; mem Assn of Black Psychologists; mem Amer Psychological Assn. **Honors/Awds:** Ford Foundation Fisk Univ early entrant 1953; Founder Award, Assn of Black Psychologist 1987. **Home Addr:** 2712 Meharry Blvd, Nashville, TN 37208-2839. **Business Addr:** Meharry Medical College, 1005 DB Todd Blvd, Nashville, TN 37208-3599.

FORT, WILLIAM H.
Attorney. **Personal:** Born Jul 18, 1915, Tuscumbia, AL; married Ruth Wilson; children: Gailmarie, W Howard Jr. **Educ:** OH State Univ, BS 1940, JD 1946; Univ of KS, undergrad work; Univ of WA, post grad work. **Career:** OH Bell Telephone, former dir; Goodyear Tire & Rubber Co, dir; Private Practice, attorney 1947-. **Orgs:** Exec bd N Central Assn Commn on Higher Educ; mem Akron OH & Amer Bar Assn; past chmn Akron Planning Comm; mem Amer Judicature Soc, Natl Council Juvenile Judges, Akron Barristers Club, Akron Law Library Assn; mem bd trustees Akron Area Council BSA; vice chmn bd trustees chmn Amer Red Cross; past pres Akron Area C of C; mem Akron Gen Hosp; chmn Univ Akron 1974-77; bd dir First Natl Bank of Akron; chmn Akron City Planning Comm; pres Akron Urban League; mem exec com bd of trustees Akron Reg Devel Bd; mem exec com bd of trustees Goals for Greater Akron; mem bd of trustees Natl Alliance of Bus Men; bd trustees Akron Child Guidance Ctr; life mem NAACP; pres Frontiers Intl; knight commr Republic of Liberia; pres Bluecoats Inc 1983-; chmnBoys & Girls Clubs of Summit Co OH1983-84; bd of govs Ameatl Red Cross 1981-. **Honors/Awds:** Peter Bommarito Awd 1969; pres Frontiers Intl Hon D of Laws Central State Univ 1969; Silver Beaver Awd BSA 1971. **Business Addr:** Attorney, 40 East Mill St, Akron, OH 44308.

FORTE, JOHNIE, JR.
Army officer (retired), educational administrator. **Personal:** Born Dec 20, 1936, New Boston, TX; son of Sadie and Johnie; married Dolores Bowles Johnson; children: Mitchell C Johnson, Shermaine L Johnson, Denise M. **Educ:** Prairie View A&M Univ, BA 1956; Auburn Univ, MA 1976. **Career:** AUS, Commd 2nd Lt 1956, advanced through grades to Brig Gen; Dept Army, personnel mgmt officer, dir personnel and insp gen W Germany; Dept Army Washington, dir personnel plans and systems; 8th Infantry Div, asst div commander; Wiesbaden Germany, military community commander; 32nd Army Air Defense Command US Army Europe, dep commanding gen; US Army ODCSPER, brigadier general; asst supt, General Services, Fairfax County, VA Public Schools. **Orgs:** Mem Assn US Army Vice Pres Chap 1977-78; mem Rock's Professional Org; Phi Delta Kappa. **Honors/Awds:** Accelerated promotions to lt col, col & brigadier gen based on performance of duties. **Military Serv:** AUS; Decorated Legion of Merit; Defense Superior Serv Medal; Army Meritorious Serv Medal; Army Commendation Medal; Air Force Commendation Medal. **Business Addr:** General Service Spt Center, Fairfax County Public Schools, 6800B Industrial Rd, Springfield, VA 22152.

FORTE, LINDA DIANE
Banking executive. **Personal:** Born in Cleveland, OH; daughter of Bertha l & Delvin L Forte; married Tyrone M Davenport, Nov 7, 1992; children: Lynette Davenport, Simone Perry. **Educ:** Bowling Green State University, BS, 1974; University of Michigan, MBA, 1982. **Career:** Comerica Bank, compensation analyst, 1977-80, loan analyst, 1980-83, assistant vice pres & manager of credit administration, 1983-87, assistant vice pres & lender, 1987-88, vice pres & sr lender, 1988-92, vice pres & alternate group manager, 1992-95, first vice pres & manager, 1995-. **Orgs:** Urban bankers Forum, past president, 1975-; National Black MBA Association, 1982-. **Honors/Awds:** National Black MBA, H Naylor Fitzhugh Awd, 1995; YWCA, Minority Achiever Awd, 1984; Urban bankers Forum, Banker of the Year, 1988. **Business Addr:** First Vice Pres, Comerica Bank, 500 Woodward Ave, Mailcode 3354, Detroit, MI 48226, (313)222-5076.

FORTE, MINNIE T.
Educator. **Personal:** Born Feb 12, 1916, Goldsboro, NC; children: William, Lonnie, Minnie Mae. **Educ:** Fayetteville State U, BS 1939; NC Central U, MA 1951; NC Central U, PhD 1960; Duke U, additional study; Univ of NC. **Career:** Durham City Sch Sys, tchr 1944-60; Fayetteville State U, 1960-62; Shaw U, 1962-65; Operation Breakthrough Cntr for Children, dir 1965-66; St Augustines Coll, asso prof coordinator Early Childhood Educ 1966-74; Fayetteville State University, professor of elementary education, 1974-83. **Orgs:** Chmn bd of Christian Edn, White Rock Bapt Ch; vice pres New Hoep Bapt Assn; life mem Nat Educ Assn; adv student NEA-nCAE 1966-; spl asst Early Childhood Educ 1974; coordinator Early Childhood Educ 1970; aptd by Nat Council for Accreditation of Tchr Educ to evaluate undergrad & grad elem educ prog of St Francis Coll Fort Wayne IN 1975; aptd by NC Bd Educ to evaluate elem educ prog of Fayetteville State Univ 1975. **Honors/Awds:** Tuition scholarship, Univ of Pittsburgh; study in England summer 1970; study grant Phelps-Stokes Fund, St Augustines Coll, 4 countries in W Africa.

FORTE, PATRICK
Sports administrator. **Personal:** Born Mar 17, 1950, Flint, MI; married Christine; children: Brandi, Jade. **Educ:** Lincoln University. **Career:** General Motors, public relations exec; Honeywell Corp, public relations exec; Philadelphia Eagles, chief operating officer, asst to the pres, chief contract negotiator, 1986-90; New England Patriots, vice pres of administration, 1991-. **Business Addr:** VP of Administration, New England Patriots, Sullivan Stadium, Rt 1, Foxboro, MA 02035, (508)543-7911.

FORTIER, THEODORE T., SR.
Dentist, association administrator. **Personal:** Born Aug 15, 1926, San Diego, CA; married. **Educ:** UCLA, Univ of PA, attended; Howard Univ Coll of Dentistry, DDS 1957. **Career:** Los Angeles, dentist pvt practice; Continuing Dental Educ USC Sch of Dentistry, instr 1968; Dental Assisting School, instructor, 1986-93; The Dentists Co., a subsidiary of California Dental Association, board of directors, currently; VSC School of Dentistry, teaching staff; So California, Health Newsletter, appointed editor. **Orgs:** Staff mem LA Co/USC Med Cntr-Compton PTA Sch Dentist 1959-61; pres Angel City Dental Soc 1968-69; vice pres Dental Found of CA 1971; mem bd dir Los Angeles Dental Soc; Fellowship Exam Committee, 1986-91, Acad of Gen Dentistry; delegate to House of Delegates of CA Dental Assn; chief of Dental Dept of Hollywood Presb Med Cntr 1972-74; pres, Kiwanis Club of Angeles Mesa, 1976; gen chmn Fund-raising Dr for Crenshaw YMCA 1975, 1993; mem Omicron Kappa Upsilon; pres South California Academy General Dentistry, 1987; trustee, California Dental Association, 1986-89; president, Crenshaw Chamber of Commerce, 1993-94; Community Police Advisory Committee. **Honors/Awds:** Dental Honor Soc; recipient US Pub Health Fellowship for study of dental disease unique ot social isolated segment of eastern US population; Surgical Technician; Howard University College of Dentistry, Dental Alumni of the Year, 1987; Southern California Academy of General Dentistry, Dentist of the Year, 1992; Recycling Black Dollars Inc, Speaker of the Year Award. **Special Achievements:** Established a dental seminar course to be given in selected areas on selected subjects in dentistry. **Military Serv:** US Army corpl T/5. **Business Addr:** Dentist, 3701 Stocker #408, Los Angeles, CA 90008.

FORTSON, DANNY
Professional basketball player. **Personal:** Born Mar 27, 1976. **Educ:** Univ of Cincinnati. **Career:** Denver Nuggets, forward, 1997-. **Business Addr:** Professional Basketball Player, Denver Nuggets, 1635 Clay St, Denver, CO 80204, (303)893-6700.

FORTSON, ELNORA AGNES
Poet, composer. **Personal:** Born May 7, 1943, Pittsburgh, PA; married Walter Lamarr; children: Akilah, Ayanna, Anika. **Educ:** Grace Martin Bus Sch, Cert of Com 1961; Univ of Pittsburgh Deliverance Bible Inst, 1977-81, 1992. **Career:** Univ of Pgh, Sch of Social Work, secy 1961-62; Westinghouse Elec Corp, data maintenance & accounting, capital stk clerk, 1962-77; Fuller Ins Agency, 1983-84; ACT II Jewelry Inc, jewelry advisor 1984-86; Watkins Products, 1985-; Temple Christian Academy, secretary, librarian, 1990-94; TOD, Inc, 1994-. **Orgs:** Mem Intl Platform Assoc 1980; mem Chicago Intl Black Writer's 1976; publicity dir Homewood Poetry Forum 1973-75; publicity dir Greater Pgh Christian Temple 1980-; publicity dir Temple Christian Acad 1981-; mem Kuntu Writer's Wkshp 1980-; mem, Wind's Writers, 1993; Bloomfield-Garlfield, Neighborhood Reading Center, poeting inst, 1992-93; founder, instructor, PRAISE Poetry Wrkshp 1984-. **Honors/Awds:** Danae Awd & Pub Clover Intl Poetry Cont, 1974; Homewood Poetry Forum, Poet of the Year, 1975; PA Council on the Arts, Literary Fellowship, 1981; World of Poetry, Golden Poet Award, 1990; August Wilson Poetry Award, 1st Place, Adult Poetry Category, 1992. **Special Achievements:** Fellowship poems on tape recording, ''Jesus Walks the Waters of My Soul'' 1981; poetry anthology ''Love from Black Women to Black Men'' 1976; poetry anthology ''Ridin' On a Good Wind'' 1975; published ''Pre-Natal/Post-Natal'' Essence Mag 1977; poetry anthology ''Voices from the Real World,'' 1991; wrote, directed play ''Pittsburgh, Sought Out.. A City Not Forsaken,'' 1992; Women of the Bible Poetry Book, 1993; Sonwriter Composer; Liturgilcal Worship Poems for Greater Pittsburgh Christian Temple, 1992-. **Home Addr:** 5208 Broad St, Pittsburgh, PA 15224.

FORTSON, HENRY DAVID, JR.
Dentist. **Personal:** Born Sep 11, 1946, Haines City, FL; son of Nancy Fortson and Henry Fortson; married Wilnita Yvette Varner; children: Henry D III, Dennis Gregory, William Christopher. **Educ:** Daytona Beach Jr Coll, AA 1966; Knoxville Coll, BS 1968; Meharry Medical Coll, DDS 1984. **Career:** Holston Army Ammunition Plant, chemist; Private Practice, dentist. **Orgs:** Shriner 32 degree 1976; mem Omega Psi Phi Frat 1967-, NAACP 1985-, Thomasville Dental Study Group 1986, GA Dental Soc 1986, Mason; mem Thomasville Thomas Co Comm Club; mem Bd of Recreation in Thomasville. **Business Addr:** Dentist, 1205 East Jackson St, Thomasville, GA 31792.

FORTSON, WALTER LEWIS
Attorney at law. **Personal:** Born Jul 16, 1951, Hatchechubbee, AL; son of Sallie & Oscar Fortson; children: Walter Lewis II, Clara Alexis. **Educ:** Alabama A&M University, BS, 1973; Atlanta Law School, JD, 1979. **Career:** Fortson & Secret, partner, 1991; Fortson & Assocs, owner, 1979-91, 1992-. **Orgs:** State Bar of Georgia, 1979-; National Bar Assn, past regional dir, 1986-; Gate City Bar Assn, 1979-; Fountain City Bar Assn, 1995. **Business Addr:** Owner, Fortson & Assocs, 1004 Broadway, Columbus, GA 31902, (706)324-6254.

FORTUNE, GWENDOLINE Y. (OYA C'SHIVA)
Educator, writer. **Personal:** Born in Houston, TX; daughter of Mittie McCain Young (deceased) and W Hermon Young; divorced; children: Frederic, Phillip, Roger. **Educ:** JC Smith Univ, BS 1948; SC State Coll, MS 1951; Roosevelt Univ, MPh 1972; Nova Univ, EdD 1979. **Career:** Chicago Public Schools, teacher 1954-66; Dist 68 Skokie IL, team coord 1964-70; Oakton Comm Coll, prof ethnic studies coord 1970-84; Consultant ''Discovery'', dir 1984-. **Orgs:** Exec bd IL Council for Black Studies 1980-83; exec comm IL Consultation on Ethnicity in Educ 1980-84; manuscript chair, Off-Campus Writers' Workshop, 1990-. **Honors/Awds:** Intl Black Writers Conference First Place Non-Fiction 1986; 2 articles Black Family Magazine 1986; non-fiction second place, International Black Writers Conference 1987; poetry reading, Chicago Cultural Center 1988; poem ''Tom Cats'' Korone, 1988; other poems published in InnerQuest & Prairie St Companion; Honorable Mention, Poetry, 2 poems: Womanspace, Korone, 1989; Outstanding teaching effectiveness, Oakton Community College, 1981-82.

FORTUNE-MAGINLEY, LOIS J.
Television producer. **Personal:** Born Mar 16, 1946, New York, NY; daughter of Roland K & Hilda O Fortune; married George H Maginley, Nov 25, 1978. **Educ:** Monteith College, Wayne State University, PhB, 1968; New York University, MAT, 1969. **Career:** Children's TV Workshop, associate producer, international department, 1978-79; Nickelodeon, executive producer, Pinwheel series, 1979-82; Children's TV Workshop, resident producer, the Philippines, 1983, executive producer international department, 1985-87; UNESCO/UNDP (New Delhi, India), ETV producer & consultant, 1987-88; Children's TV Workshop, executive producer, 1988-90; Galaxy Classroom, executive producer, 1990-96. **Orgs:** Academy of TV Arts & Sciences, (judge 1966), 1990-; Women in Film, 1993-; International Film & TV Festival, board member, 1986-; National Academy of Cable Programming (judge 1987-88); National Academy of TV Arts & SCIs, roundtable producer; National Endowment fo r the Arts, advisory panel, 1983; Directors Guild of America, 1975-, council mem, 1977-78; American Film Institute. **Honors/Awds:** Baghdad International TV Festival, Silver Medal, 1988; Philippine Catholic Mass Media Awd, 1983; National Cable TV Association, 2 Ace Awds, 1982; National Catholic Association for Broadcasters & Allied Communications, Certificate of Merit, 1981; National Academy of TV Arts & Sciences, Certificate, 1976-77. **Special Achievements:** For the Galaxy Classroom, Executive Produced three interactive educational series, 1990-96; Co-Executive Produced Arabic Reading Series in Amman, Jordan, 1985-87; Consultant Producer, Philippine "Sesame Street," 1983; Executive Producer, "Pinwheel" for the Nickelodeon Channel, 1979-82; Directors Guild of America Training Program Trainee, 1973-75. **Home Addr:** 515 W Gertruda Ave, Redondo Beach, CA 90277. **Business Phone:** (310)798-0013.

FOSKEY, CARNELL T.
District court judge. **Personal:** Born Dec 7, 1956, Darlington, SC; son of Sadie and Thomas; married Francina Little, Jul 4, 1987. **Educ:** State University of New York, BA, political science and history, 1977; California Western School of Law, JD, 1980; Boston University School of Law, LLM Taxation, 1982. **Career:** Nassau County Department of Social Services, staff attorney, 1982-83; Nassau County Office of the County Attorney, deputy county attorney, 1983-89; Office of the Presiding Supervisor, executive assistant, 1989-90; Department of Planning and Economic Development, interim commissioner, 1990-91; Nassau County District Court, district court judge, 1992-. **Orgs:** Bar Association of Nassau County, 1982-; 100 Black Men Nassau/Suffolk, 1988-; American Inns of Court, 1987-89; NAACP Lakeview Branch. **Honors/Awds:** Nassau Black History Committee, Man of the Year, 1992; Dollars & Sense Magazine, 100 Top Black Professionals, 1992. **Business Addr:** District Court Judge, Nassau County District Court, 99 Main St, Chambers #6, Hempstead, NY 11550, (516)566-2200.

FOSTER, ALVIN GARFIELD
Veterinarian. **Personal:** Born Apr 7, 1934, Preston, MD; married Gertrude Dallis; children: Alvin Garfield Jr, Kerwin, Kelsie. **Educ:** MD State Coll, BS 1956; Tuskegee Inst DVM 1960; WA State U, MS 1967; PhD 1969. **Career:** US Dept of Agr, Meat Inspec Div Spokane, vet meat insp 1963-64; WA State U, NIH postdoctoral fellow 1965-69; Merck Inst for Therapeutic Research Rahway NJ, sr micro-biologist 1969-; Merck & Co Inc Rsch, dir animal sci. **Orgs:** Mem Am Vet Med Assn, Alpha Kappa Mu, Phi Zeta, Sigma Xi, Alpha Phi Alpha, Monmouth County Men's Club. **Honors/Awds:** Black Achiever in Industry YMCA of NY 1974. **Military Serv:** USAF capt 1960-62. **Home Addr:** 27 Old Mill Rd, Tinton Falls, NJ 07724.

FOSTER, CARL OSCAR, JR.
Church program administrator. **Personal:** Born Oct 21, 1926, Greensboro, NC; son of Louise Slade Foster and Carl Oscar Foster Sr; married Lola Alexander Foster, Aug 16, 1965; children: Angela Cheryl Foster. **Educ:** A&T State University, Greensboro, NC, BS, 1948, MS, 1956; University of North Carolina, Chapel Hill, NC, 1968-70; De Sales School of Theology, Washington, DC, 1990. **Career:** Concord City Schools, Concord, NC, music teacher, 1948-55; Guilford County Schools, Greensboro, NC, classroom teacher, 1955-56; Greensboro City Schools, Greensboro, NC, classroom teacher, 1956-68, principal, 1968-74, dir of cultural arts, 1974-86; Catholic Diocese of Charlotte, Charlotte, NC, coord of African-American affairs, 1989-. **Orgs:** Basileus, Tau Omega Chapter, Omega Psi Phi Fraternity, 1971-73; chairman, Parish Council, 1980-82; grand knight, Knights of Columbus, 1985-87. **Honors/Awds:** Band Teachers Appreciation Award, Band Teachers, 1972; Omega Man of the Year, Omega Psi Phi Fraternity, 1973; Cultural Arts Award, Cultural Arts Teachers, 1984; Certificate, African-American Black Congress, 1990; Service to the Mentally Handicapped, State Council, Knights of Columbus, 1991. **Military Serv:** US Navy, Musician 2nd Class, 1945-46; Victory Ribbon, American Theater Ribbon, 1946. **Home Addr:** 4603 Southall Dr, Greensboro, NC 27406-9058.

FOSTER, CECIL A.
Journalist, author. **Personal:** Born Sep 26, 1954, Bridgetown, Barbados, West Indies; son of Doris Goddard and Fred Goddard; married Glenys Cadogan; children: Munyonzwe, Michelio, Mensah. **Educ:** Harrison College of Barbados, University of West Indies, diploma, mass communications; York University, BBA, BA (with honors), economics. **Career:** Caribbean News Agency, senior reporter, editor, 1975-77; Barbados Advocate News, reporter, columnist, 1977-79; Toronto Star Newspaper reporter, 1979-82; Contrast Newspaper, editor, 1979-82; Transportation Business Management, editor, 1982-83; Globe and Mail, reporter, 1983-89; Financial Post, senior editor, 1989-. **Orgs:** Pen Canada, director, 1992-; The Writers Union of Canada, 1992-94; Glen Shield Soccer Club, executive member, fundraiser, 1991-93; Harambee Cultural Centres, 1991-; Canadian Artist Network, Blacks in Action, 1992-. **Special Achievements:** Author, works include: No Man in the House, Ballentine Books, 1992; Distorted Mirror: Canada's Racist Face, Harper Collins Publishing, 1991; Miroir Deformant: Le Visage Raciste du Canada, Harper Collins Publishing, 1991; Anthologised-Voices: 16 Afro-Canadians, Harper Collins Publishing, 1992; "Why Blacks are Mad," Chatelaine Magazine, Toronto, Nov 1992; "Rocking the Boat," Toronto Life Magazine, November 1993; "Can Jean Augustine Deliver?" Chatelane, Nov 1994; "Tough Guys Don't Cuss" Canadian Business Magazine, Feb 1995; Rites of Passage, Hyperion Books for Children, 1994; Around The World, Kendall/Hunt Publishing Company, 1994; Sleep on, Beloved, Ballentine Books, 1995; Caribana-Greatest Celebration, Ballantine Books, 1995. **Home Addr:** 125 Greenbush Cres, Thornhill, ON, Canada L4J 5M3, (416)881-4508.

FOSTER, CLYDE
Business executive. **Personal:** Born Nov 21, 1931; married Dorothy M Harri; children: Anitra, Edith, Clydis, Byron, Carla. **Educ:** AL A&M U, BS 1954. **Career:** Marshall Space Flight Cntr, chief, EEO for Civil Serv Employees 1972, instr training courses; AL A&M U, dir Computer Sci Dept, est Data Processing Lab & undegrad degree prog in Computer Sci, first in State of AL Educ Sys of Higher Learning 1968-70; Marshall Space Flight Cntr, mathematician, instr Computation Lab 1960; Army Ballistic Missile Agency, Redstone Arsenal, 1957; Dallas Co Sch Sys, Selma, AL, sci tchr. **Orgs:** Petitioned Probate Judge, gained rejuvenation of Triana, AL 1964; aptd mayor; helped est first rural water sys in Madison Co; instituted first black-managed fee-free recreation river-front land in TN Valley; est Triana Indus Devel Co (promotes indus for employment of disadvantaged minorities); helped organize Data Processing Asso Inc 1970; fdr, pres Triana Indus Inc, first industry to locate in Town of Triana; provided scndry, post-scndry students with edl & occupational opps; dev proposal to est first adult educ prog for sharecroppers 1967; developed proposal for hard-core head-of-household famales to be taught skills in elec soldering, schematic reading, electronic components 1972; aptd to AL Commn of Higher Educ By Gov Geo Wallace 1974. **Honors/Awds:** Recip awards for conscientious performance from following MSFC/NASA 1968; NASA apollo achvmnt award & MSFC award of achvmnt 1969; NASA fifteen Yr Serv Award 1970; Alpha Kappa Sor Dedicated Pub Serv & Outstanding Leadership Award 1971; Omega Psi Phi Frat Merit Serv Award 1971; Delta Sigma Theta Sor Appreciation& Serv Rendered 1972; TARCOG Appreciation for Outstanding Contribution Toward Grown & Devel 1972; MSFC Commen of Achvmnt Award 1972; Citizens of Triana Comm Outstanding & Dedicated Serv Award 1972; AL A&M Univ Distinguish Serv Award 1973; African Meth Epis Ch, Burningham, Comm Serv Award, 1973; Omega Psi Phi Frat Seventh Dist Man of Yr Award 1974. **Military Serv:** AUS pfc 1954-56.

FOSTER, DEBORAH VALRIE
Financial consultant/broker. **Personal:** Born Oct 5, 1955, Beaumont, TX; daughter of Leona E Collins Valrie and Hardy Valrie; married Willie J Foster Jr; children: Janell, Jaulik, Jasmin. **Educ:** Univ of TX at Austin, BSci 1978; College for Financial Planning, Denver CO, CFP, 1988. **Career:** Sanger-Harris Dallas, asst buyer 1977-80; Gordon's Jewelers Dallas, asst store mgr 1980-82; Deb's Designs, co-owner/mgr 1982-83; DV Foster Consultant/Broker, owner/general mgr 1983-88; Merrill Lynch, Arlington TX, financial consultant/CFP, 1989-. **Orgs:** Finance comm mem, CBCL Business Resource Group, 1986; consultant/preparer, Tax R' Us, 1986; mem, Speaker's Bank, AWED, 1986-; mem, NAACP, 1986-, Lancaster Chamber of Commerce 1986; mem, Duncanville Chamber of Commerce, 1989; mem, AWED, 1989-. **Honors/Awds:** Certificate of Participation, Risk Management Workshop, Dallas Independent School Dist, 1986; Certified Financial Planner, 1988. **Business Addr:** Financial Consultant/CFP, Merrill Lynch, 2221 E Lamar Blvd, Suite 800, Arlington, TX 76006-0457.

FOSTER, DELORES JACKSON
Educational administrator. **Personal:** Born Jan 24, 1938, Halltown, WV; daughter of Mary Frances Taylor and Daniel David Jackson; married James H; children: Mark Darnell Bailey, James Jr, Arthur. **Educ:** Shepherd Coll, BA 1960; Jersey City State Coll, MA 1974. **Career:** Page-Jackson HS, teacher 1960-61; Dickinson HS, teacher 1961-71, teacher coord 1971-73, guidance counselor 1973-84, acting vice principal 1982-83, vice principal 1985-, acting principal 1986, guidance counselor, vice principal 1987; PS #34, principal, 1991-. **Orgs:** Corresponding sec Black Educators United 1975; 1st vice pres Coll Women Inc 1979-81; pres Coll Women Inc 1981-83, 1995-; vchmn cong Park Ave Christ Church Disciples of Christ 1982-84; pres Central Atlantic Conf of United Church of Christ 1984-87; mem Empowerment for Change; leadership training United Church of Christ 1979; adv bd Upward Bound Project St Peter's Coll Kersey City NJ 1975-79; workshop leader NJ Alliance of Black Ed conf 1983; elected lay del 15th Gen Synod OCC Ames IA 1985; lay delegate 16th Gen Synod Cleveland OH 1987; mem of St Mark's AME Church 1988; asst dir bd of Christian Ed; NJ Principal & Supervisor Association; Natl Alliance of Black School Educators, Delta Sigma Theta Sorority; advisory bd, Principal's Ctr for the Garden State, 1994-. **Honors/Awds:** Honored as a lay woman in the United Church of Christ at 15th Gen Synod in Ames IA 1985; Summer Institute for Principals, Geraldine R Dodge Foundation Awd, 1993. **Special Achievements:** Co-author Book Integrating the Classroom with the World of Work, 1980; Featured in documentary, "Quicksand and Banana Peels," Dodge Foundation, 1998. **Home Addr:** 89 Hawthorne Avenue, East Orange, NJ 07018. **Business Addr:** Principal, PS No 34, 1830 Kennedy Blvd, Jersey City, NJ 07305, (201)915-6550.

FOSTER, DOUGLAS LEROY
Psychiatrist. **Personal:** Born Mar 3, 1931, New York, NY; children: 2 sons, 1 daughter. **Educ:** City Coll of NY, BS, 1953; Meharry School of Med, MD, 1957. **Career:** St Margaret Hosp, internship, 1957-58; Fellow, Menninger Sch of Psychiatry, 1961-64; Topeka VA Hospital, residency 1961-64; Jackson Park Hosp, chmn dept of psychiatry 1971-79; Bismarck Hospital, consulting psychiatrist 1983-; St Lawrence Hosp, consulting psychiatrist 1985-; Saginaw Comm Hospital, consulting psychiatrist 1985-; Saginaw private practice, psychiatrist 1986-. **Orgs:** Mem, pres Jackson Park Hospital; pres tech advisory comm Dept of Public Health St of IL; mem bd dir pres Foster & Assn Clinic Ltd Sub Abuse Treat Center Inc; pres Comprhnsv res & Dev 1977-78; mem bd dir Sub Dupage Co Hlth Sys Agcy 1976-77; mem, dir, Safari Train & Hum serv Inc; mem dir Impact Clnc; chmn Tech Adv Comm; mem Dept of Public Health; chmn St of IL Task Force on Training Edn; Meharry Med Sch Alumni Assn; mem IL Psy Soc; IN St Med Assn; Lake Co Med Assn; AMA; Am Assn of Univ Prof; Amer Assn for the Advancement of Science; Natl Med Assn; Chicago Med Soc; Gov Com for Revsn of Mental Health Codes 1975-77. **Honors/Awds:** Fellow APA; Menninger Found Alumni Assn Award 1961; black excellency award Countee Cullen School 1973; Award for Dist Comm Psychiatrist & General Mental Health Serv. **Military Serv:** USNR lt commander 1957; USNR staff psychiatrist; US Naval Hospital 1964-66.

FOSTER, E. C.
Educator, government official. **Personal:** Born Jan 4, 1939, Canton, MS; son of Minnie L Pugh Foster and Hugh D Foster (deceased); married Velvelyn Blackwell; children: Garnet A, Sunyetta M. **Educ:** Jackson State Univ, BS 1964; Carnegie-Mellon Univ, MA 1967, DA 1970. **Career:** Natchez Public School, teacher 1964-65; Brushton Inner City Project, community organizer 1965-66; Pittsburgh Public Schools, teacher 1967-68; Jackson MS City Council, pres 1985-94; Jackson State Univ, prof of history 1969-. **Orgs:** Pres Faculty Senate (JSU) 1974-79; bd mem Farish St YMCA 1976-79; assoc editor Journal of Negro History 1978-; pres Assn of Soc & Behav Scientists 1982; legislative comm chmn Local PTA 1984; city councilman Jackson MS 1985-; member, Chamber of Commerce, 1986-; member, Vicksburg/Jackson Trade Zone Commission, 1987-; MS Municipal Assn, bd of dirs, 1994-; Natl League of Cities Leadership Training Council, vice chair, 1994. **Honors/Awds:** Jackson State Univ Alumni Service Awd 1985; Man of the Year Awd Omega Psi Phi 1985; NAEFO Presidential Citation Awd 1986; Dr Martin Luther King Service Awd JSU/SGA 1986; author of approx 30 publications 1969-85. **Military Serv:** AUS Specialist 4 1961-63; Good Conduct Medal 1963. **Business Addr:** Assoc Grad Dean, Jackson State Univ, Jackson, MS 39217.

FOSTER, EDWARD, SR.
Manager. **Personal:** Born Sep 27, 1945, Maplesville, AL; son of Mamie Foster; married Jacqulyn E Grant; children: Edward, Forrest Cedric. **Educ:** Selma Univ, AS 1967; AL A&M Univ, BS 1971. **Career:** Xerox Corp, prod supv 1972-82; GTE Corp, sr quality supv 1983-86; NCR Corp, prod mgr 1986-. **Orgs:** Pres AL A&M ALumni Assoc 1981-82; vice pres Rochester Chap AL A&M Alumni Assoc 1982-83; mem Amer Mgmt Assoc 1984, Amer Soc Quality Control 1985; 32 degree Lodge 107 Masonic Temple 1985; mem Surface Mount Tech 1986. **Honors/Awds:** Outstanding Work in Higher Ed NAFEO 1983. **Home Addr:** 4234 United St Apt G, Greensboro, NC 27407-1337.

FOSTER, FRANCES HELEN. **See Obituaries section.**

FOSTER, FRANCES SMITH
Educator. **Personal:** Born Feb 8, 1944, Dayton, OH; married Warren R Foster; children: Lisa Ramirez, Krishna, Quinton. **Educ:** Miami Univ, BS, 1964; Univ of South CA, MA, 1971; Univ of CA, PhD, 1976. **Career:** Cincinnati Public Schools, teacher, 1964-66; Detroit Public Schools, teacher, 1966-68; San Fernando Valley State Coll, instructor, 1970-71; San Diego State Univ, asst dean, 1976-79, prof, beginning 1971; Univ of California, San Diego, prof, currently. **Orgs:** Humanities Adv

Council; KPBS; San Diego State Univ, Career Plan & Placemt Ctr, Adv Comm; NAACP, Coll Lang Assn; Modern Lang Assn; Philological Assn of the Pac Coast; West Coast Women's Historical Assn; NEH Rsch Fellowship; CSU Faculty Rsch Fellowship; Phi Beta Kappa; Phi Kappa Pi; Althenoi Phi Kappa Delta; Alpha Kappa Alpha; Children's Literature Assoc; MELUS. **Honors/Awds:** Ford Found Fellowship; San Diego Fellowship; Gen Motors Scholar; articles publ "Changing Concepts of the Black Woman," "Charles Wright, Black Black Humorist," "The Black & White Masks of Franz Fanon & Ralph Ellison," "Witnessing Slavery, The Develop of the Ante-Bellum Slave Narrative," Greenwood Press, 1979; "Voices Unheard Stories Untold, Teaching Women's Literature from a Regional Perspective;" SDSU Outstanding Faculty Awd; numerous articles and reviews on Afro-Amer literature.

FOSTER, FRANK B., III
Musician, educator. **Personal:** Born Sep 23, 1928, Cincinnati, OH; married Cecilia Jones; children: Anthony, Donald, Frank IV, Jardis. **Educ:** Central State Coll, 1946-49. **Career:** Musician, composer, arranger with Count Basie Orchestra 1953-64; professional musician performing with many well-known artists Wilberforce Collegians Band, saxophonist, composer-arranger 1946-49; professional musician performing with many well known artists 1949-51; musician, composer, arranger with Count Basie Orchestra 1953-64; freelance composer, arranger, performer & instructor 1964-71; New York City Public Schools, music consultant 1971-72; Music Dept Rutgers Univ, Livingston Coll, asst prof; arranger Frank Sinatra's "LA is My Lady" album and video; Swing That Music Inc, pres, currently. **Orgs:** Mem ASCAP; AGAC; conductor, mem Collective Black Artists; mem bd dirs Instr Young Musicians Clinic of Jazz Interactions Inc; instr Jazzmobile Wkshp, Ensemb Jazzmobile Inc; hon mem Hartford Jazz Soc; hon mem Jazz at Home Club, Phila; mem Am Fed of Mus 802. **Honors/Awds:** Auth of innumerable published compositions and albums; currently performing with own 23-pc band in US & abroad; author of saxophone exercise book & stage band arrngmnts; recip of many awards & citations including Outstanding Contribution to Jazz Award 1971; Nat Endowment for the Arts grant for Jazz/Folk/Ethnic Composition Fellowships; monetary recognition by Popular Awards Panel of ASCAP for past nine yrs. **Military Serv:** AUS pfc 1951-53. **Business Addr:** President, Swing That Music Inc, 1235 Post Rd, PO Box 262, Scarsdale, NY 10583-2132.

FOSTER, GEORGE ARTHUR
Professional baseball player (retired). **Personal:** Born Dec 1, 1948, Tuscaloosa, AL. **Educ:** El Camino College, Torrance, CA, attended. **Career:** San Francisco Giants, outfielder 1969-71; Cincinnati Reds, outfielder 1971-81; New York Mets, outfielder 1982-86; Chicago White Sox, outfielder, 1986. **Orgs:** Founder, George Foster Home for Disadvantaged Children, Upper Dayton OH. **Honors/Awds:** 48th player in major league history to reach 300 homer plateau, 1984; voted Most Valuable Player All-Star Game 1976; Holds World Series record for most putouts by a leftfielder in one game; major league record for most home runs by a righthand batter 1977; National League Most Valuable Player, Baseball Writers Assn of America 1977; National League All-Star Team, 1976, 1977, 1978, 1979, 1981.

FOSTER, GLADYS M.
Attorney (retired). **Personal:** Born Jul 12, 1927, Brooklyn, NY; married John Skidmore. **Educ:** Barnard Coll Columbia Univ, AB 1949; Columbia Law Sch, JD 1953. **Career:** Workmen's Compensation & Unemployment Ins Appeal Bd, attorney; NY State Div of Human Rights, sr attorney. **Orgs:** Mem Brooklyn Bar Assn; Brooklyn Women's Bar Assn; mem Vocational Adv on Law for Barnard Coll; mem NAACP; mem Barnard Coll Alumni By-Laws Com; mem Crown Heights Assn; past vice pres Natl Assn of Coll Women.

FOSTER, GLORIA
Actress. **Personal:** Born Nov 15, 1936, Chicago, IL; married Clarence Williams III, Nov 1967. **Educ:** Illinois State University, attended; Art Institute of Chicago's Goodman Memorial Theater, graduate; University of Chicago Court Theatre; University of Massachusetts Amherst, MEd 1978. **Career:** Theater appearances include: A Raisin in the Sun, 1961; The Trojan Women, 1965; Medea, 1965-66; Yerma, 1966-67; A Midsummer Night's Dream, 1967; Black Visions, 1972; The Cherry Orchard, 1973; Agamemnon, 1977; Coriolanus, 1979; Mother Courage and Her Children, 1980; Long Day's Journey into Night, 1981; The Forbidden City, 1989; A Hand Is on the Gate, 1966; A Dream Play, 1967; film appearances include: The Cool World, 1963; Nothing But a Man, 1964; The Comedians, 1967; The Angel Levine, 1970; Man and Boy, 1972; Leonard, Part 6, 1987; television appearances include: The Atlanta Child Murders, 1985; Top Secret, 1978; To All My Friends on Shore, 1972. **Orgs:** Actors Equity Assn; Screen Actors Guild; American Federation of Radio & TV Artists; Academy of Motion Picture Arts & Sciences; American Film Institute; life mem, NAACP; Forensics Society. **Honors/Awds:** Village Voice, Off-Broadway Obie Award, best performance, In White America 1963-64; Vernon Rice Award, In White America, 1963-64; Theatre World Award, promising performer of 1965-66 season, Medea; Village Voice Off-Broadway, Obie Award, 1965-66; outstanding contribution in field of arts, Alpha Kappa Alpha Award, 1966; AUDELCO, Black Theatre Award, Agamemnon, 1977; 1st place, women's oratory, IL State Oratorical Contest; elected, IL State Univ, 1st Sweetheart of the Campus; Drama Desk Award, nomination, Best Actress in a Play, The Forbidden City, 1989. **Business Addr:** Actress, c/o Albert L Shedler CPA, 225 W 34th St, New York, NY 10001.

FOSTER, GREG
Hurdler. **Personal:** Born 1958, Chicago, IL; married Karen Marie Houlemard. **Career:** Olympic hurdler, 110-meter hurdles, 1984; USA/Mobil Indoor Track & Field Championships, 1991; Millrose Games, 10 time winner. **Honors/Awds:** Olympic Silver Medalist, 110-meter hurdles, 1984; world outdoor hurdle titles, 1983, 1987, 1991; world indoor title, 60-meter hurdle, 1991; world outdoor hurdle championship winner, Tokyo, Japan; nominated for the Jesse Owens Award, 1987; training, 1996 Olympics.

FOSTER, GREGORY CLINTON
Professional basketball player. **Personal:** Born Oct 3, 1968, Oakland, CA. **Educ:** UCLA; Univ of Texas, El Paso. **Career:** Washington Bullets, center, 1990-92; Atlanta Hawks, 1992-93; Milwaukee Bucks, 1993-94; Chicago Bulls, 1994; Minneapolis Timberwolves, 1995; Utah Jazz, 1995-. **Business Addr:** Professional Basketball Player, Utah Jazz, 301 W South Temple, Salt Lake City, UT 84101-1216, (801)575-7800.

FOSTER, HENRY WENDELL
Educational administrator, physician. **Personal:** Born Sep 8, 1933, Pine Bluff, AR; son of Ivie Hill Watson and Henry W Foster; married St Clair Anderson; children: Myrna, Wendell. **Educ:** Morehouse Coll, BS, 1954; Univ of Arkansas, MD, 1958; Receiving Hosp, Detroit, Intern, 1959; Malden Hospital, residency, surgery 1962; George W Hubbard Hospital, residency, Ob-Gyn, 1962-65. **Career:** US Air Force, med officer, 1959-61; Hubbard Hosp, Nashville, physician, 1962-65; Tuskegee Inst, ob/gyn chief, 1965-70; John A Andrews Meml Hosp, chief ob & gyn, 1970-73; Meharry Medical Coll, prof, chmn of Dept of Ob/Gyn, 1973-90, dean, School of Medicine, vice pres for health affairs, 1990-93, acting pres, 1993-94, prof, OB/GYN, currently; Assn of Acad Health Ctrs, health policy fellow, 1994-. **Orgs:** Macon Co Med Soc; AMA; Natl Med Assn; Natl Acad of Sci Inst Med; Am Bd Ob/Gyn, dipl. **Honors/Awds:** Fellow Am Coll Ob & Gyn; Alpha Omega Alpha. **Special Achievements:** President Clinton's nominee for US Surgeon General, 1995; Sr Advisor to President Clinton, Teen Pregnancy & Youth Issues, 1996. **Military Serv:** USAF capt 1959-61. **Business Addr:** Professor of OB/GYN, Sch of Medicine, Meharry Medical College, 1005 Todd Blvd, Nashville, TN 37208.

FOSTER, JAMES H.
Educator, association executive. **Personal:** Born Jul 20, 1931, Roanoke, AL; married Sallye Maryland Burton; children: James H. **Educ:** Bethune Cookman Coll, BS 1957; Atla U, MA 1963. **Career:** Duval Teachers United, Jacksonville FL, asst exec dir 1974-; The Boeing Co, supvr industrial relations 1973-74; Titusville High School, counselor 1964-72; Frederick Douglas High School , prin 1962-63; Wedowee High School, head coach 1961-62; Randolph Co Training School, head coach 1959-61; Woodville Elementary School, prin 1957-59; FL Theater, mgr 1968-69; Sears Roebuck & CO, part-time sales person; General Electric Co & Bendix Corp, summer employment 1967-71. **Orgs:** Mem Titusville Negro Civic & Voters League 1964-67; exec bd dir & employment offcr Classroom Tchrs Assn; Human Rel Com 1969-72; NAACP 1957-; A Phillip Randolph Inst 1973-4; Nat Urban League 1971-; exec bd Titusville Centennial Inc 1966; bd dir YMCA 1969-73; bd dir Brevard Co United Way 1969-74; chrpsn Titusville Hum Rel Commn 1973-74; pres United Black Front, Brevard Co 1972-74. **Honors/Awds:** Tchr of Yr Titusville Jr C of C 1965; ldrshp award United Black Front, Brevard Co 1973. **Military Serv:** AUS sgt 1st class 1950-53. **Business Addr:** 103k La Salle St, Jacksonville, FL 32207.

FOSTER, JAMES HADLEI
Educator, clergyman. **Personal:** Born Apr 29, 1938, Valdosta, GA; son of Willie Mae Wright Foster and Arthur Foster, Sr; married Delores Jackson, Sep 25, 1982; children: Mark Darnell, Arthur. **Educ:** Morris Brown Coll, Atlanta GA, BA, 1960; Pittsburgh (PA) Theological Sem, 1969-70; United Theological Sem, Dayton OH, MDIV, 1973; Vanderbilt Univ, NashvilleTN, DMIN, 1981. **Career:** Massachusetts Council of Churches, Boston MA, dept pastoral serv, 1962-63; Albany State College, Albany GA, dean of the chapel/instr, 1962-66; Alcorn State Univ, Lorman MS, chaplain/asst prof, 1966-68; Christian Assoc of Metro Erie, Erie PA, assoc dir, 1970-73; Wilberforce Univ, Wilberforce OH, chaplain/assoc prof, 1973-80; Dartmouth Coll, Hanover NH, assoc chaplain/lecturer, 1980-84; A Better Chance, Boston MA, Northern New England regional dir, 1980-82; Mercy Coll, Dobbs Ferry NY, prof of religion, 1984-; St Marks AME Church, East Orange, NJ, associate pastor, 1985-. **Orgs:** Mem, Optimist Club, 1975-; assoc pastor, St Mark's AME Church, East Orange NJ, 1985-; mem, Community Relations Commission, NJ Council of Churches, 1985-88; mem, Special Task Force, E Orange Bd of Education, 1985-86; pres, Jersey Chapter, Morris Brown Coll Alumni Assn, 1988-. **Honors/Awds:** Union Coll, LHD, 1971. **Home Addr:** 89 Hawthorne Avenue, East Orange, NJ 07018.

FOSTER, JANICE MARTIN
Attorney. **Personal:** Born Jun 14, 1946, New Orleans; married John P. **Educ:** Chestnut Hill Coll, AB 1967; Tulane Law Sch, JD 1970. **Career:** Jones Walker Waechter Poitevent Carrere & Denegre Law Firm, atty. **Orgs:** Mem New Orleans, LA & Am Bar Assn; bd dir New Orleans Legal Aid Corp. **Business Addr:** 225 Baroone St & Floor, New Orleans, LA 70112.

FOSTER, JYLLA MOORE
Association executive, career development manager. **Career:** IBM Career Development for the Great Lakes area, branch manager, currently. **Orgs:** Zeta Phi Beta Sorority, Inc, 1973-, national chair of executive board, third vice pres, national director of budget and finance, national treasurer, all former positions, grand basileus, 1992-. **Business Addr:** Grand Basileus, Zeta Phi Beta Sorority, 1734 New Hampshire Ave NW, Washington, DC 20009, (202)387-3103.

FOSTER, KEVIN CHRISTOPHER
Professional baseball player. **Personal:** Born Jan 13, 1969, Evanston, IL. **Educ:** Kishwaukee College, attended. **Career:** Philadelphia Phillies, pitcher, 1993; Chicago Cubs, pitcher, 1994-. **Business Addr:** Professional Baseball Player, Chicago Cubs, Wrigley Field, 1060 W Addison St, Chicago, IL 60613, (312)404-2827.

FOSTER, LADORIS J.
Business executive. **Personal:** Born Oct 31, 1933, St Louis, MO. **Career:** Johnson Pub Co Inc, Chgo, personnel dir 1972-, rec, sec, admnstrv Asst 1957-72. **Orgs:** Bd mem So Side Comm Art Cntr; adv bd Amtrak; mem Women's Div Chicago Econ Devel Corp. **Business Addr:** Personnel Dir, Johnson Publishing Co, 820 S Michigan Ave, Chicago, IL 60605.

FOSTER, LLOYD L.
Scientist, (retired) educator. **Personal:** Born Jul 3, 1930, Austin, TX; married Leatrice Norman; children: Lloyd Jr, Lionel Laird, Lyle Lerone. **Educ:** Huston-Tillotson Coll, BS 1951; Incarnate World Coll, MS 1966; Baylor Sch of Medicine, Cert in Physiology with Modern Instrumentation 1967. **Career:** Brooks, AFB, medical tech 1963-64, biologist 1964-70, research chemist 1970-74, educ tech 1974-76, research chemist 1976-91; St Philip's College, biology instructor, 1966-; Sch of Aerospace Medicine, Brooks AFB; Brooks AFB, chief, equal employment counselor, EEO, collateral duty, 1981-91. **Orgs:** Nat Assn for Equal Opportunity in Higher Educ 1977-91; Am Chemical Society 1974-91. **Honors/Awds:** Academic Achievemnt Huston-Tillotson Coll 1974; Alumni Chap Award Nat Assn of Black Coll 1976. **Business Addr:** Biology Instructor, St Philip's College, 1801 Martin Luther King, San Antonio, TX 78203-2098, (512)531-3545.

FOSTER, MILDRED THOMAS
Educational administrator. **Personal:** Born Nov 20, 1927, Pottsville, PA; married Rufus Herbert Jr; children: Vincente Leon, Kathy Maree. **Educ:** SC State Coll, BS 1949; UN U, MS 1959; Clemson U, EdS 1974. **Career:** Cherokee County School Dist No 1, elementary prin 1969-; Spartanburg Union & Cherokee County School Districts, head start staff trainer 1969; Cherokee County Head Start, dir 1967-68; Cherokee County School Dist No 1, first grade teacher 1954-67; Spartanburg City Schools SC, first grade teacher 1949-54. **Orgs:** Mem Nat Assn of Elem Sch Adminstr; past sec-treas SC Assn of Elem Sch Prin 1975-76; mem SC Assn of Sch Adminstr 1975-76; mem United TeachingProf; Basileus, Lambda Rho Omega Alpha Kappa Alpha Sor 1952-80; mem chmn Cherokee Co Mental Health Assn 1975-80; bd mem Cherokee Co Comm on Alcohol & Drug Abuse 1975-80; bd mem Cherokee Co United Way 1977-80; sec Limestone Coll Bd of Assos; mem SC State Library Bd 1977-81; Ford Found Sci, Bank St Coll 1965. **Honors/Awds:** Pub Article on Head Start in Palmetto Educ Assn Journal 1966; habilitation service award Hablttn Serv Cherokee Co Mentally Retarded 1977; elected woman ofthe year Spartanburg Chap Of Links Inc 1979. **Business Addr:** Cherokee Co Sch Dist No 1, PO Box 460, Gaffney, SC 29340.

FOSTER, PEARL D.
Physician. **Personal:** Born Oct 23, 1922, New York, NY; daughter of Isabel Foster and George Foster; married Charles C Hunt; children: Joanne, Patrice. **Educ:** Queens Coll, BS 1943; Howard Univ Med Sch, MD 1948; CW Post MPA 1985. **Career:** Ft Monmouth, chem tstr 1943; New York City Health Dept, jr bacteriologist 1943; SAM Lab, employee 1943-44; Freedman's Hosp, 1949-50; Harlem Hosp, resd 1950-53, attending physician internal med 1963-, chief ward 1963-68; private medical practice, 1953-; Jamaica Day Nursery, physician-in-charge, 1955-81; United Nations International School, physician-in-charge, 1961-70; Columbia University, assistant med, 1968-69, instructor, 1972-73, associate, 1972-; Division of Social Hygiene, medical consultant; Queens Physicians Association Inc, president, medical director, 1989-. **Orgs:** Harlem Hosp

Ctr Med Bd 1970-90; Asst med Columbia Univ 1968-69; bd trustees UN Intl Sch 1961-64; chmn 1974, vice chmn 1970-74, adv com Home Health Agency 1975-; cont med educ com Hillcrest Gen Hosp 1975; Manhattan & Queens Co PSRO; 1st vice pres Amer Coll Quality Assurance Utilization Review; bd certified Amer Bd Quality Assurance & Utilization Review; Med Bd Hillcrest Gen Hosp 1973-86; adv com Home Hlth Homemaker Serv 1976-88; NMA; AMA; Queens Medical Association; Queens Clinical Society; Association of Former Interns & Residents of Freedman's Hospital; NY Academy of Science; NY Heart Socieety; American Public Health Association; Black Caucus of Harlem Health Workers; Howard University Medical Alumni Association, executive board; Med Bd St Joseph, 1986-; HUMAA, executive bd, vice pres; Board of Professional Medical Conduct, 1988-. **Honors/Awds:** Queens College, Distinguished Alumni Award, 1983; Kappa Pi Alumni Association, Citation, 1958; White House Conference on Youth, 1970-75; Kappa Pi, 1947; Pi Alpha Alpha, 1980; Harlem Hospital School of Nursing Alumni Association, Citation, 1958; Pi Alpha, 1978-; Chattanooga, TN, Key to the City, 1985; Harlem Hospital Auxiliary, Service Award, Citation, 1989; Charles A Walburg MD Award, 1991. **Special Achievements:** Author, publications include: ''Chemotherapy in Neoplastic Diseases''; ''Biochem Changes in Neoplastic Diseases''; ''Hepatitis in the Drug Addict''; ''Hlth & Manpower Devel Corp''; Lost Containment Syllabus for American College of Physicians, 1982. **Business Addr:** Physician, 32 Splitrock Rd, Norwalk, CT 06854-4713.

FOSTER, PORTIA L.
Educator. **Personal:** Born Dec 1, 1953, Gadsden, AL; daughter of Myrtle Davenport Foster and Porter Foster. **Educ:** Sanford University, Birmingham, AL, BSN, 1977-79; Univ of Alabama at Birmingham, Birmingham, AL, MSN, 1979-80, DSN, 1987-89. **Career:** Baptist Hospital, Gasden, AL, nurse, 1974-77; University of Alabama Hospital, Birmingham, AL, nurse, 1977-80; Jacksonville State University, Jacksonville, AL, educator, 1980-. **Orgs:** Numerous positions held, Etowah County Nurses Society, 1980-; president, District 4, Alabama State Nurses' Association; board of directors, Alabama State Nurses' Association; board of directors, Alabama, League for Nursing, 1989-; member, American Nurses' Association, 1980-; member, National League for Nursing, 1980-, member, Phi Kappa Phi, 1989. **Honors/Awds:** Medical Center Fellow, WAB, 1988; Faculty Research Award, Jacksonville State Univ, 1990. **Business Addr:** Associate Professor of Nursing, Jacksonville State University, College of Nursing, Jacksonville, AL 36265.

FOSTER, ROBERT DAVIS
Investigator (retired). **Personal:** Born Sep 2, 1929, Brenham, TX; children: Carol Ann, Robert Jr, Michael L. **Educ:** Univ of San Francisco, BS 1974; MA. **Career:** Ambrose Park, recreation dir/park supervisor 1968-69; Oakland Public Sch, dir JROTC 1969-74; Chuska Sch Bureau of Indian Affairs, pupil personnel dir 1975-78; Contra Costa Co Medical Ctr, psychologist 1978-79; Equal Employment Oppor Commn, investigator, 1988; AmVet Service Officer, 1990-94. **Orgs:** Mem bd dirs Concerted Serv 1982-85. **Military Serv:** AUS MSG E-8; Bronze Star, Air Medal, Purple Heart. **Home Addr:** 146 Clearland Dr, Pittsburg, CA 94565. **Business Addr:** Investigator, Equal Employ Oppor Commn, 1333 Broadway, Wells Fargo Bldg Ste 430, Oakland, CA 94612.

FOSTER, ROBERT LEON
Executive officer. **Personal:** Born Mar 11, 1939, Atlanta, GA; married Ethel Doris Bolden. **Educ:** Morris Brown Coll, BA 1961. **Career:** Center for Disease Control HEW, asst exec officer 1978-, asst to dir 1975-78, EEO officer 1972-75. **Orgs:** Mem Phi Beta Sigma Frat; mem NAACP. **Honors/Awds:** Recipient MBC Athletic Hall of Fame. **Military Serv:** AUS prc 1962-64.

FOSTER, ROSEBUD LIGHTBOURN
Educational administrator. **Personal:** Born Nov 13, 1934, Miami, FL; daughter of Dorothy Bernell Lightbourn and Carol Allenmore Lightbourn; married Harris E; children: Harris Emilio II, Sheila Rosebud, Byron Edward, Lorna Lightbourn. **Educ:** Fisk Univ, Chem & Pre-Nursing 1951-53; Meharry Med Coll Nashville, BSN 1956; Wayne State Univ, MS Nursing Ed 1960; Univ of Miami, EdD Higher Ed Admin 1976; Bryn Mawr Coll, Cert Post Grad Residency Inst 1981. **Career:** Detroit General Hospital, head nurse 1956-58, 1969-72; Henry Ford Hospital School of Nursing, Detroit, instructor 1960-62; Providence Hospital, Southfield MI, asst dir 1962-65; Kirkwood General Hospital, dir of nursing 1967-69; Holy Cross Hospital, asst admin 1960-72; Olivia & Bancroft Extended Care Facilities, consultant 1969-72; Univ of Miami, prof of nursing 1972-73; School of Health & Social Svc, assoc dean 1973-77, dean 1977-78; FL Intl Univ, vice provost Bay Vista Campus, prof, health services administration, 1978-90, project director, area health education center, 1990-. **Orgs:** Bd mem, exec bd sec Fair Havens Nursing and Retirement Center 1974; bd mem & exec bd officer Health Systems Agency of Southern FL 1976; Amer Public Health Assn 1976; Public Health Trust of Dade Cty Citizens Adv Council 1977; Health Educ & Quality of Life Comm N Miami 1980; bd of dir mem Young Men's Christian Assn of Greater Miami, accred visitor Southern Assn of Colleges & Schools 1980;bd mem New Horizons Community Mental Health Center 1981; mem Mayor's Econ Task Force of N Miami 1981; bd of dir Ruth Foreman Theatre 1981; bd of dir N Dade Chamber of Commerce 1982; N Miami Chamber of Commerce 1982; chairpersonDelta Sigma Theta Task Force on Econ Devel of Blk Community 1983; adv bd mem Health Planning Council of Dade & Monroe Counties 1983; dir Culture Fest 1983; mem Art Music, Drama N D Proj 1983; bd mem Concerned Citizens of NE Dade Inc 1983; Amer Public Health Assn 1983; adv council Delta Intl The African Diaspora Natl Planning Comm & Adv Council 1984; comm events grant panel Metro Dade County Council Arts & Sci 1984; bd dir United Home Care Serv; vice president, Alliance for Aging, Area Agency on Aging for Dade and Monroe Counties, 1990-. **Honors/Awds:** JC Holman Microbiology Awd, Meharry Med Coll School of Nursing, 1955; Recognition of Outstanding Serv Certificate, Meharry Med Coll; Pres Awd for 25 Yrs of Outstanding Serv to Mankind, 1956-81; Outstanding Nurse Alumni Awd, Coll of Med Dentistry Nursing, Meharry Coll, 1972; Certificate of Appreciation, Health Syst Agency of S Florida, 1979; Certificate of Appreciation, Amer Hosp of Miami Inc, 1980; Certificate of Appreciation, Lutheran Serv for the Elderly, 1982; Outstanding Professional Achievement Awd, Miami Alumnae Chap, Delta Sigma Theta, 1983; Person of the Year Awd, N Miami Chamber of Commerce, 1984; Public Serv Awd, Outstanding Professional Achievement; Outstanding Women 12 honors1986; Miami Ballet Soc; Amer Council on Educ; Florida Statewide Coordinator for Women Exec in Higheruc; North Dade Chamber of Commerce Outstanding Person for Quarter 1987. **Home Addr:** 11041 SW 128th Ave, Miami, FL 33166.

FOSTER, TONI
Professional basketball player. **Personal:** Born Oct 16, 1971. **Educ:** Univ of Iowa, bachelor's degree in economics, 1993. **Career:** Phoenix Mercury, forward-center, 1997-. **Honors/Awds:** Big Ten Player of the Year, 1993. **Business Addr:** Professional Basketball Player, Phoenix Mercury, 201 E Jefferson St, Phoenix, AZ 85004, (602)252-9622.

FOSTER, WILLIAM K.
Business executive. **Personal:** Born Jun 10, 1933, Pittsburgh, PA; married Dolores J Porter; children: Kimberly Anne, William K. **Educ:** Duquesne Univ Pittsburgh, BA 1963; Univ of WI-MADISON Grad Sch of Banking, 1977; Univ Of WI-MADISON Post Grad Sch of Banking, 1978. **Career:** Franklin Fed Savings & Loan Assn, vice pres 1979-; New & World Nat Bank, pres/CEO 1977-79; Pittsburgh Nat Bank, comm banking off 1967-77; Natl Biscuit Co, sales rep 1963-67. **Orgs:** Treas Homewood-Brushton Medical Cntr 1975-76; bd mem Governor's Council on Small Bus 1977; treas Program to Aide Citizens Enterprise 1978-. **Honors/Awds:** Athlete of the year Pittsburgh Optimist Club 1948; airman of the month USAF 1955; good conduct Nationl Service USAF 1956. **Military Serv:** USAF air 1st class 1952-56. **Business Addr:** Marktg/Business Dev Officer, Seaway Natl Bank, 645 East 87th St, Chicago, IL 60619.

FOSTER, WILLIAM PATRICK
Educator, band director. **Personal:** Born Aug 25, 1919, Kansas City, KS; son of Venetia Highwarden and Frederick Foster; married Mary Ann Duncan, Aug 8, 1939; children: William Patrick Jr, Anthony Frederick. **Educ:** Univ of KS, BMus 1941; Wayne State U, MA, 1950; Columbia U, EdD 1955. **Career:** Lincoln High Sch, dir of bands 1941-43; Ft Valley State Coll, dir of music 1943-44; Tuskegee Inst, dir of bands & orchestra 1944-46; FL A&M Univ, dir of bands 1946-, Music Dept, chairman, currently; G Leblanc Corp, advisory bd 1966-; Intl Music Festivals, advisory bd 1970-; McDonald's All Am HS Band, dir 1980-91; Conducted US Army Band, Navy Band, Air Force Band, Marine Band; combined in-ter svc bands, Constitution Hall, Washington, DC; McDonald's All-American High Band; Guest conductor of bands throughout the country. **Orgs:** Pres Coll Band Dir Nat Assn 1981-83; bd of dir Am Bandmasters Assn 1977-79; pres FL Music Educators Assn 1977-79; bd of dirs, Rotary Club of Tallahassee, 1989-91; bd of dirs, John Philip Sousa Found, 1989-; president elect, American Bandmasters Association, 1993. **Honors/Awds:** Fellowship Genl Educ Bd 1953-55; joint resolution FL House & Senate 1977; Distinguished Serv Award Univ of KS 1973; Distinguished Serv Award Kappa Kappa Psi 1972; Celebrity Roast, Florida A&M Univ Booster Club, 1987; Tallahassee Natl Achievement Award, Easter Seal Soc, 1988; Distinguished Alumni Award, Wayne State Univ, 1988; one million dollar endowed chair named in honor, Florida A&M Univ, 1988; composer of four marches for band, 1987; band featured in the French Bastille Day Parade, Paris, France, 1989; Great Floridian, Florida Historical Associates; Hall of Fame, Natl Band Assn; FAMU Marching Band, Sudler Natl Intercollegiate Assn, honor The Congressional Congress; Director of Bands, 50th Anniversary, Florida A&M Univ, 1950. **Home Phone:** (850)576-3736. **Business Addr:** Dir of Bands/Chmn of the Music Dept, Florida A&M Univ, 1500 Martin Luther King Jr Blvd, Tallahassee, FL 32307.

FOSTER FOULKS, IVADALE MARIE
Elected official. **Personal:** Born Mar 30, 1922, Sidney, IL; daughter of Edwarda C Martin Foulks and Warren T Foulks; married Wardell Foster, Oct 19, 1942 (deceased); children: Wardella Marie Rouse, Christina Jo. **Educ:** Danville Area Comm Coll, BS Elem Educ 1966. **Career:** Laura Lee Fellowship House, jr activities super 1958-66; City of Danville Recreation Dept at Lincoln Park, recreation dir 1968-73; Vermilion Co Health Dept, homemaker/home health aide 1970-73; Sch Dist #118, teachers aide 1973-74; Herb Crawford Multi Agency Inc, sr citizens dir & asst dir 1974-78; East Central IL Area on Aging, reaching out to the elderly trainee 1976-77; East Central IL Area Agency, sr citizen employment spec 1981-82; Vermilion Co, co bd member Dist 8 1980-89, chmn 1988-91; Re-elected to Health & Ed Chaplain Comm, bd of chair, 1994-, Pct 26 Comm Woman, 1996; Health Dept, ver co bd rep, 1996. **Orgs:** Past pres present sec Bradley-Maberry Amer Legion Aux 736 1962-; past sec present bd mem Pioneer Ctr for Substance Abuse 1973-; sec Neighborhood House Inc 1975-; precinct comm woman Precinct 26 1978-; pres of Sr Citizens Adv Group Neighborhood House Inc 1980-90; Vermilion County Council American Legion Auxiliary 1972-90, vice president, 1987-88, pres 1988-89; Vermelion County board representative, East Central Ill, Area Agency on Aging, 1988-94; Vermilion County, bd representative, Vermilion County Health Department Board, 1991-94. **Honors/Awds:** Most Outstanding Church Pianist, Faithful Worker & Pianist-30 yrs Allen Chapel AME Church Union Missionary Baptist Church 1976 & 1984; Honorary Banquet for Letter Writers to the Editorial Page Editor of the Danville Commercial News 1979 & 1980; 10 Most Outstanding Leaders of Danville, Danville Commercial News Series & Pictures 1981; Outstanding Comm Contribs Danville Branch NAACP 1981; One of 3 of Danville's Outstanding Women nominated by readers & sel by comm of Danville Commercial News 1964; First Black woman elected to serve on the Vermilion Co Bd, 1980; re-elected in 1982 for 2 yrs, re-elected in 1984 for 4 yrs; Chaplain of the Vermilion Co Bd in 1981, 1989, 1994; re-elected in 1988 for 4 yrs; re-elected in 1992 for 2 yrs; Present Chaplian of Vermilion County Board; Vermilion County RD, chairman of the Health & Education Committee, 1988-94; bd representative, Vermilion County Health Department, 1991-94. **Home Addr:** 516 Anderson St, Danville, IL 61832.

FOSTER-GREAR, PAMELA
Business executive. **Personal:** Born Feb 20, 1957, Cleveland, OH; daughter of Margaret Foster and Curtis Foster; married Lance Grear, Sep 21, 1991; children: Yejide Hadassah-Noni Grear. **Educ:** Cuyahoga Community College, 1977-79; Columbus State Community College, 1983; Fashion Institute of Technology, certificate, 1987; Minority Business Executive Program, Amos Tuck School, Dartmouth College, certificate, 1990. **Career:** University Property Development, manager, 1973-83; Ohio Department of Youth Svcs, computer literacy instructor, 1983-86; Foster & Associates, Inc, president/chief executive officer, 1986-. **Orgs:** Columbus Area Chamber of Commerce, advisory board chairperson, 1992-; The Light Center, board member, 1989-; Junior Achievement, Ohio State University, Min Student Dev Prg, mentorship program, 1992-; Martin Luther King Jr Center for the Performing Arts, board, 1989-90; The Afrikan Center, supporter, 1987-; Northeast Career Center, supporter/guest speaker, 1992; ''I Know I Can'' Program, supporter, 1990-91; Southern Christian Leadership Conference, supporter, 1991-92. **Honors/Awds:** Small Business Assn, finalist, Small Business Person of the Year, 1992; Ohio Assembly of Councils, Corporate Hall of Fame, 1991; Borden, Inc, Minority Business Entrepreneur Program Scholarship, 1990. **Special Achievements:** Educational Youth Entrepreneur, curriculum pending. **Business Addr:** President/Chief Executive Officer, Foster & Associates, Inc, 3761-63 April Ln, Columbus, OH 43227, (614)239-1064.

FOULKS, CARL ALVIN
Physician. **Personal:** Born Jun 10, 1947, Greensboro, NC; married Deborah Casandra Smith; children: Carl Jr, Dion, Cory. **Educ:** Howard Univ Coll of Pharmacy Washington DC, RPh; Howard Univ Medical School, MD. **Career:** Providence Hospital, chief resident; Cumberland County Medical Clinic, dir; Private Practice, physician. **Business Addr:** 407 Owen Dr, Fayetteville, NC 28304.

FOUNTAIN, WILLIAM STANLEY
Educator (retired). **Personal:** Born Aug 12, 1920, Milford, DE; married Alfredia. **Educ:** BS; BA. **Career:** State Dept of Public Instruction, teacher; City of Milford, vice mayor 10 years. **Orgs:** Pres Emeritas, Tri-State Elks, MD, DE, DC. **Honors/Awds:** 1st black vice mayor State of DE. **Home Addr:** 602 North, Milford, DE 19963.

FOUNTAINE, JAMAL
Professional football player. **Personal:** Born Jan 29, 1971, San Francisco, CA. **Educ:** Washington, attended. **Career:** Carolina Panthers, defensive end, 1995; San Francisco 49ers, 1995; Atlanta Falcons, 1997-. **Business Addr:** Professional Football Player, Atlanta Falcons, Two Falcon Place, Suwanee, GA 30174, (404)945-1111.

FOURNIER, COLLETTE V.
Photojournalist. **Personal:** Born Jul 21, 1952, New York, NY; daughter of Cynthia Hubbard Mann and Alexander Fournier.

Educ: Rochester Institute of Technology, Rochester, NY, AAS, 1973, BS, 1979. **Career:** RAETA TV21 WXXI, Rochester, NY, prod asst, engineer trainee, 1978-81; Malrite Communications, TV 31, WUHF, Rochester, NY, senior film editor, 1981-82; Community Darkroom, Rochester, NY, photography instructor, 1982-88; About Time Magazine, Rochester, NY, photojournalist, 1983-88; Journal, News Gannett, West Nyack, NY, photojournalist, 1988-89; The Bergen Record, Hackensack, NJ, photojournalist, 1989-. **Orgs:** Member, Natl Press Photography Assn., 1988-; member, Natl Assn. Black Journalists, 1984-; member, Women's Caucus for Arts, 1984-; member, New Jersey Press Photographers Assn., 1989-. **Honors/Awds:** Woman of Year Achievement, Arts, American Assn. University Women, 1988; Photography Panelist, NY Foundation for the Arts, Inc., 1989; A Ripple of Thunder, Multi-media, Art in America, review of exhibition, 1988; photography works published, Black Photographers: An Illustrated Bio-Bibliography, by Willis, Thomas, Schomburg, 1988; photography works exhibited, one woman & group shows various galleries, museums, 1983-. **Business Addr:** Staff Photographer, Photography/Graphics Dept, The Bergen Record, 150 River St, Hackensack, NJ 07601-7172.

FOUSHEE, GERALDINE GEORGE
Law enforcement official. **Personal:** Born Aug 14, 1947, Newark, NJ; daughter of Anna Mae Smith George and Clarence M George; married Joseph E Foushee; children: Chere Michele, Kyle Edward. **Educ:** Essex County Coll, AS (Magna Cum Laude) 1976; Seton Hall Univ, Certificate of Business Mgmt 1977; Rutgers Univ, Certificate of Business Mgmt 1977, BA (Magna Cum Laude) 1981; Jackson State Univ, Jackson, MS, Criminal Justice Admin Certificate l988; Atlanta Univ, Atlanta, GA, Criminal Justice Certificate l987; Rutgers State University, MA, social work, 1993. **Career:** Essex County Coll, tech asst/admin asst/acting coord of the learning resource ctr 1968-79; Hartford Insurance Group, field claims investigator/adjustor 1979-81; Newark Police Dept, police officer 1981-84; Office of the Sheriff of Essex County, detective/fugitive warrant squad 1984-86; City of Newark Alcoholic Beverage Control, exec sec 1986-90; City of Newark, NJ, acting deputy mayor, 1990; Essex County Sheriff's Dept, Newark, NJ, detective, 1990-; Red Cross Essex Chapter, East Orange, NJ, HIV AIDS instructor, 1991; Essex County Department of Public Safety, Essex County Jail, warden, chief administrator, 1991-. **Orgs:** Lehigh Ave Block Assn 1969-, Sharpe James Civic Assn 1975-, New Jersey Notary Public Commn 1980-, North NJ Women in Police 1981-, Bronze Shields Inc 1981-, Natl Black Police Assn 1981-, Fraternal Order of Police 1981-, Rutgers Univ Alumni 1981-, Intl Assn of Women Police 1982-, Baton's Inc 1984-; chmn membership comm Essex Co Coll Alumni Assn 1985-; adv mem DYFS Home Placement Adv Comm 1986-; treas Safety Officers Coalition Newark 1986-; NJ Council of Negro Women 1986-, NJ Chap Natl Police Officers Assn of Amer 1987-; bd of dir, League of Women Voters l988-; bd of dir, Dayton Community Corp l988-; bd mem, Catholic Community Services, 1990-; New Jersey Crime Prevention Officers Assn, 1990-; Essex County Central Communication Comm, 1990-. **Honors/Awds:** Outstanding Police Awd Bronze Shields Inc 1981; Merit Awd State of NJ Police Training Commn 1981; Comm Serv Awd Lions Club of Hillside NJ 1984; Police Officer of the Year Central Ward Comm 1984; Law Enforcement Awd Mayor Sharpe James City of Newark 1986; Achievement Awd Bronze Shields Inc 1987; Comm Serv Awd Natl Cncl Negro Women 1987; Achievement Awd Baton's Inc 1987; Distinguished Alumni, Essex County College, 1990; Community Service, University High School, 1990; Outstanding Service, Fraternal Order of Police Lodge 12, 1990.

FOUSHEE, PREVOST VEST
Marketing manager. **Personal:** Born Apr 26, 1952, Pittsburg, NC; son of Cora Cotton and Prevex Foushee; married Trudi McCollum, Oct 1985; children: Prevost Jr, Ashlei. **Educ:** Fayetteville State University, BS, business administration, 1977. **Career:** Pillsbury Co., sales rep, 1978; Anheuser-Busch, Inc, sales rep, 1978-79, area sales manager, 1979-81, district sales manager, 1981-83, project manager, management development, 1983-84, special markets manager, 1984-91, geographic marketing manager, 1991-92, product manager, Budweiser, 1992-94; National Light/Ice/King Cobra, brand mgr, 1994-. **Orgs:** United Negro College Fund, marketing committee, 1992. **Honors/Awds:** Harlem YMCA, Black Achievers Award, 1980; American Sentinel Newspaper, St Louis, Yes I Can Award, 1990. **Military Serv:** US Army, sgt, 1972-75.

FOUTZ, SAMUEL THEODORE
Attorney. **Personal:** Born May 3, 1945, Beaumont, TX; son of Mamie Ballard Foutz and Freddie James Foutz; married DeVonne Desmerries Draughn; children: Dietra Michelle, Fredrick William. **Educ:** Lamar State Coll of Tech, BS 1967; Howard Univ Sch of Law, JD 1972. **Career:** Dallas Legal Serv Found, Inc, atty 1972-74, chief cnsl 1974-76, exec dir 1976-77; Private Law Practice, atty & counselor at law 1978-. **Orgs:** Law clerk Dept of HEW, Office of Gen Coun 1971; Nat Bar Assn 1972-; J L Turner Legal Soc 1972-; Delta Theta Phi Legal Frat 1967-. **Honors/Awds:** Am Jurisprudence Acad Award-property 1972; Smith Fellow, Reginald Heber Smith Fellowship Fdn Inc 1972-75. **Military Serv:** US Army, spec-5, 1967-69; NDSM; VCM; VSM; GCMDL; SPS (M-14); 2 O/S Bars 1967-69. **Business Addr:** Attorney, Private Practice, 401 Wynnwood Prof Bldg, #224, Dallas, TX 75224, (214)941-0568.

FOWLER, BARBARA ANN
Nurse, educator. **Personal:** Born Mar 7, 1945, Cincinnati, OH; daughter of Laura Cavanaugh Montgomery (deceased) and Fred Cavanaugh Sr (deceased); married John Arthur Fowler Sr, Aug 10, 1963; children: Shawn Denise, John Arthur Jr. **Educ:** Courter Technical School of Practical/Vocational Education, LPN, 1968; Raymond Walters General and Technical College, AAS, 1976; University of Cincinnati, BSN, 1981, MSN, 1983; University of Cincinnati, Teacher's College, EdD, 1988. **Career:** University Hospital, staff nurse, 1968-70, 1981-83; Cincinnati Health Department, staff nurse, team leader, 1970-81; Bethesda School of Nursing, instructor, nursing, 1983-84; Northern Kentucky University, assistant professor, nursing, 1984-88; Wright State University, Miami Valley College of Nursing & Health, assistant professor, nursing, 1988-94, director, RN to BSN program, 1991-92, assoc prof, nursing, 1994-. **Orgs:** Association of Black Nursing Faculty in Higher Education; Sigma Theta Tau International; American Nurses' Association; Association of Community Health Nurse Educators; American Public Health Association, (Public Health Nursing Section); Midwest Nursing Research Society. **Honors/Awds:** Wright State University, Nursing Scholar, 1990, 1991, Research Incentive Award, 1989; Association of Black Nursing Faculty in Higher Education, Young Researcher Award, 1989; W K Kellogg Foundation, Community Partnerships Leadership Development program, fellow, 1992-94; Indiana University-Purdue University, Ruth Scott Deters Scholarship in Community Health Nursing and Health Policy, 1992 and 1996. **Special Achievements:** Author, The Relationship of Body Image Perception and Weight Status to Recent Change in Weight Status of the Adolescent Female, 1989; author, Adolescence, 24(95), 557-568; A Health Education Program for Inner City High School Youths: Promoting Positive Health Behaviors Through Intervention, 1992; author, 5(3), 72-76, Prenatal Outreach: An Approach to Reduce Infant Mortality in African-American Infants, The ABNF Journal, 1995; author 5(6), 15-18, Pragmatic Issues of Health Promotion Research in the Workplace, AAOHN Journal, p 12-16, 1995; Ideological Shifts in Primary Health Care Delivery: Removing Barriers Through Reform, The ABNF Journal, p 126-129, 1994; A Health Promotion Program Evaluation In A Minority Industry, The ABNF Journal 5(3), p 72-76, 1994; Health Policy Reform Initiatives to Improve the Health of Black Americans, The ABNF Journal, (5)1, p 22-26, 1993; Cross-training: A rural experience, Mother Baby Journal (in press). **Home Addr:** 1036 Thunderbird Dr, Cincinnati, OH 45231. **Business Addr:** Associate Professor, Nursing, Miami Valley College of Nursing and Health, Wright State University, 3640 Colonel Glenn Hwy, Dayton, OH 45435, (937)775-2607.

FOWLER, JAMES DANIEL, JR.
Business executive. **Personal:** Born Apr 24, 1944, Washington, DC; son of Romay Lucas Fowler and James D Fowler; married Linda Marie Raiford Fowler, May 24, 1968; children: Scott, Kimberly. **Educ:** Howard Univ, Washington DC, 1962-63; US Military Acad, West Point NY, BS, 1967; Rochester Inst Tech, Rochester NY, MBA, 1975. **Career:** Xerox forp, rochester NY, coord of graduate relations, 1971-74, mgr personnel admin, 1974-75; DP Parker & Assoc Inc, Wellesley Ma, sr consul, 1975-76; ITT World Headquarters, new York MY, mgr of Staffing, 1976-78; ITT Aetna, Denver Co, voice pres dir of admin 1978; ITT Consumer Financial Corp, Minneapolis MN, senior vp, dir of admin 1978-84, senior vp, dir admin & mktg, 1984-87; exec vp, dir of admin & mktg, 1987-90, exec vp, director of product management, marketing & administration, 1990-92, exec vp, director of administration, 1992-. **Orgs:** US Military Acad West Point, trustee, 1978-86, 1987-90; Association of MBA Executives, Executive Leadership Council, charter member, board of directors; American Financial Services Association; American Society for Personnel Administration. **Honors/Awds:** Black Achiever Awd, ITT, 1979. **Military Serv:** US Army, capt, 1967-71; Bronze Star w/Oak Leaf Cluster; Army Comm Medal with 2 Oak Leaf Clusters. **Business Addr:** Exec VP, Director, Administration, ITT Consumer Financial Corp, 605 Highway 169 North, Suite 1200, Minneapolis, MN 55441.

FOWLER, JOHN D.
Educator. **Personal:** Born Mar 22, 1931, Clinton, NC; son of Sallie L Howard Fowler and John D Fowler; married Wilma J Butler Fowler, Apr 22, 1984; children: Ronald M, Valerie D Fowler Wall, Christopher E. **Educ:** Winston-Salem Central University, honor student 1954; State University New Paltz, MA 1974; Northeastern University, additional educ studies; NC Central University; University Of VT. **Career:** Mt Pleasant Elementary School, principal 1955-58; CE Perry High School, teacher 1958-63; W Pender School, 1963-64; Dunbar Elementary School, 1964-65; Hudson City School Dist, asst principal, AV coor 1965-; City School Dist, Rochester NY, vice principal, 1985-. **Orgs:** NY State Reg Plan Association; bd of dirs, Columbia County Extension Serv; Omega Psi Phi; life mem, NEA; NAACP; vice pres, Kiwanis of Greater Hudson; chmn, Const By-Laws Com Van Rennselear Div Kiwanis Intl; city councilman, 1980-85; County Supervisor, 1985; Lt Governor, Kiwanis International, 1981-82; bd of dir, Anthony L Jordan Health Center; Maplewood YMCA, board of directors; Eastridge Kiwanis Club. **Honors/Awds:** Alumni scholarship Winston-Salem Central Univ 1950; 1st black chosen from Columbia County to represent Northeast Synod; chairperson of many committees while on city council in Hudson NY, 1980-85; Administrator of the Year, PTO of #6 School, 1988-89; Administrator of the Year Dag Hammarskjold School No 6 1989-90; C E Perry High School, valedictorian, graduated with honors. **Home Addr:** 247 Maplewood Avenue, Rochester, NY 14613.

FOWLER, LEON, JR.
Dentist. **Personal:** Born Apr 28, 1943, Fayetteville, NC; children: Roderic Lloyd, Lauren Onell. **Educ:** Hampton Inst, BA 1965; Howard Univ Coll of Dentistry, DDS 1969. **Career:** Winston Salem, Dentist; Howard Univ Coll of Dent, instr 1969-70. **Orgs:** Mem Am Dental Asso; Natl Dent Asso; Old North St Dent Soc; Am Professional Pract Asso; NC Acad of & Gen Dent; NC Dent Soc; second Dist Dent Soc; Forsyth Cnty Dent Soc; Intl Analgesia Soc; Southeastern Analgesia Soc; Twin Cty Dent Soc; Am Fed of Phys & Dent; mem Better Bus Bur; Forsyth Cnty Econ Dev Corp 1974-75; YMCA 1970-75; bd of dir Salvation Army Boys Club 1974-. **Honors/Awds:** Listed in the directory Dist Amer 1981.

FOWLER, QUEEN DUNLAP
Educational administrator. **Personal:** Born in St Louis, MO; children: Darnell Keith. **Educ:** Harris Teachers Coll, BA 1960; St Louis Univ, MEd 1965, PhD 1974, Admin & Superintendency 1977-79. **Career:** WA Univ St Louis MO, lecturer & instructor 1975-79, coord field studies 1977-78, asst dir of adm coord of rec & pub rel 1969-79; School Dist of Wellston, MO, superintendent 1979-84; Pupil Personnel Svcs, exec dir. **Orgs:** Urban League of Metropolitan St Louis 1965-; bd of dir exec bd Girl Scouts Greater St Louis 1978-; bd of dir United Way of Greater St Louis 1979-; natl prog plan comm Amer Assn of School Admin 1982-83; natl adv bd Amer Psych Assoc 1982-86; bd of curators Lincoln Univ Jefferson City MO 1983-87; vice pres Bd of Dirs Metro YWCA 1984-; bd of dirs Natl Assoc of Christians & Jews 1984-88; exec bd Alpha Pi Chi Business & Professional Sor 1984-; regional dir & bd of dirs Delta Sigma Theta Sor Inc 1986-; YWCA, national task force on retirement, 1990-94, national nominating committee, 1980-94, St Louis Branch, president, 1989-90. **Honors/Awds:** Outstanding Contributions in the Field of Psychology King Fanon Comm Mental Health Awd 1980; Volunteer Serv Girl Scout Council of Greater St Louis 1982; Alpha Phi Alpha Outstanding Educator Awd 1982; Disting Leadership United Negro Coll Fund St Louis MO 1983; Comm Serv City of Wellston MO 1983; Disting Alumni Harris-Stowe State Coll St Louis 1983; St Louis American, Salute to Excellence in Special Education Award, 1991; Dollars and Sense Magazine, America's Top 100 Black Business and Professional Women Award, 1988. **Business Addr:** Executive Director, Pupil Personnel Services, 5031 Potomac, St Louis, MO 63139.

FOWLER, REGGIE
Company executive. **Career:** Spiral Distribution Inc, CEO, 1987-. **Special Achievements:** Company is ranked #98 on Black Enterprise's list of Top 100 companies, 1993. **Business Addr:** CEO, Spiral Distribution Inc., 7100 W. Erie St., Chandler, AZ 85226, (602)940-0441.

FOWLER, WILLIAM E., JR.
Chief judge. **Personal:** Born Nov 4, 1921, Akron, OH; son of Maude Fowler and William E Fowler Sr; married Norma June; children: Claude, John, Diane. **Educ:** Fordham Law Sch, AB LLB. **Career:** US Nat Transp Safety Bd, chief adminstrv law judge; Bd Appeals & Review, US cvl serv comm 1966-69; US Dept Labor, trial exam 1964-66; US Dept Justice, spl asst att gen 1961-64; State OH, asst att gen 1959-61; Akron OH, city prosecutor 1956-59. **Orgs:** Pres Federal Adminstrn Law Judges Conference 1974-75; DC Mental Health Assn 1972-74; mem Federal Bar Assn; toastmasters Club 1970-75; dir Fed Bar Assn 1972-74; Housing Opportunities Council 1970-74; Amer Bar Assn; Nat Bar Assn; Wash Bar Assn. **Honors/Awds:** 1st black pres Judges Conference; chief judge Natl Transp Saf Bd USN 1942-45; Winner 1st Place, University of Akron Public Speaking Contest, 1947; Editor-Campus Newspaper, University of Akron, 1948; Distinguished Service Award, D C Public Schools, 1985; Winner 1st Place, Toastmasters National Speaking Contest, 1980. **Business Addr:** Chief Judge, Natl Transp Saf Board, 800 Independence, SW, Washington, DC 20594.

FOWLKES, DORETHA P.
Real estate administrator. **Personal:** Born Apr 2, 1944, Meherrin, VA; children: Tracey. **Educ:** VA Commonwealth Univ, J Sargeant Reynolds, attended, 1965-82. **Career:** RL Williams, sales assoc office mgr 1975-79; Robinson Harris, sales assoc 1979-81; Fowlkes & Co, broker pres 1981-. **Orgs:** Pres Ebony Ladies 1975-77; pres Richmond Bd of Realtists 1981-84; bd mem N Richmond YMCA 1983; bd mem Zoning Appeals Bd 1984; bd mem Metro Bus League 1985; pres VA Assoc Realtist 1985-; board of directors, Consolidated Bank & Trust. **Honors/Awds:** Business of Year Metro Business League 1982; Business Assoc of Year Amer Business Women 1984; business person Youth NAACP 1984. **Business Addr:** President, Fowlkes & Co, Inc, 2519 Chamberlayne Ave, Richmond, VA 23222.

FOWLKES, NANCY P.
Social worker (retired). **Personal:** Born Aug 26, Athens, GA; married Vester Guy Fowlkes (deceased); children: Wendy Denise. **Educ:** Bennett Coll for Women, AB 1946; Syracuse Univ, MA 1952; Smith Coll School for Social Work, MSW 1963; Pace Univ, MPA 1983. **Career:** Bennett Coll, dir of publ relations 1946-47, 1949-50; VA Ed Bulletin, asst editor 1950-52; Comm Serv Soc NYC, asst ofc mgr 1952-55; W Cty Dept Soc Svc, social caseworker, asst suprv div childrens serv 1959-67; Adoption Svc, suprv 1967-74; Homefinding, suprv 1974-89. **Orgs:** Mem Urban League of W 1960-; bd mem Family Serv of W 1961-71; pres Regency Bridge Club 1963-65; mem Acad of Cert Soc Workers 1964-; pres W Chap Jack & Jill of Amer Inc 1965-67; vice pres Regency Bridge Club 1965-67; sec, treas Eastern Reg Jack & Jill of Amer Inc 1967-71; treas United Meth Women 1969-72; chmn, admin bd, Trinity United Meth Church; pres Womens Soc Christian Serv 1970-72; adv council Adult Ed Ctr White Plains Publ School 1970-74; 1st vice pres E View Jr HS PTA 1970-71; mem Intl Platform Assoc 1971; pres Inter Faith Council of White Plains 1971-74; pres United Meth Women 1972-75; lay speaker Trinity United Meth Church 1972-; trustee Trinity United Meth Church 1973-79; pres 1983-86, United Meth Women, NY Conf United Meth Church; bd of trust NY Conf United Meth Church 1982-90; chairman, Program Division, NY Conference, United Methodist Church, 1989-94; board of directors, Gen Board of Global Ministries, United Methodist Church, 1988-96; president, Northeastern Jurisdiction, United Methodist Church, 1988-92; board of directors, Women's Division United Methodist Church, 1988-96; vp, section of finance, Women's Division, 1992-96; associate lay leader, Trinity United Methodist Church, 1990-. **Honors/Awds:** Schaefer Awd for Distinguished Comm Serv 1963; Recog Plaque Jack & Jill of Amer Inc 1976; Distinguished Service Award, Church Women United, 1994. **Home Addr:** 107 Valley Rd, White Plains, NY 10604.

FOWLKES, NELSON J.
Health care marketing executive. **Personal:** Born Dec 26, 1934, Chattanooga, TN; son of Dorothy F Johnson (deceased) and Edward B Fowlkes, Sr; married Peggy Jackson, Sep 25, 1957; children: Errol A, Janet Fowlkes-Allen, Nelson Joseph. **Educ:** Central State Univ, BS Chem 1957; Univ of TN, MS Biochem 1970; Pacific Lutheran Univ, attended 1971-74; Consortium of CA Univ & Colls, MPA 1982. **Career:** Letterman Army Med Ctr, chief clinical chem 1974-75; MI Biomed Lab, admin asst 1976-78; St Agnes Med Ctr, lab manager 1978-80, planning asst 1980-82, asst dir planning 1982-84, dir rsch & planning 1984-86, dir corporate relations 1986-. **Orgs:** Mem Business Adv Council School of Business 1980-89; treas Alumni Trust Council FSU 1984-89; pres Twentieth Century Golf Club 1985-88; exec dir, Harrison Bryant Kearney Boulevard Plaza, Inc; vice chairman Valley Small Business Devel Corp. **Honors/Awds:** "Corporate Health Risk Mgmt: An Employer's Journal of Health Care Newest Tool to Reduce Health Care Costs" Marketing, March, l989. **Military Serv:** AUS Medical Service Corps ltc 20 yrs; 1st Oak Leaf Cluster to Army Commendation Medal. **Business Addr:** Director, Corporate Relations, St Agnes Medical Center, 1303 E Herndon Ave, Fresno, CA 93710.

FOX, CHARLES WASHINGTON, III
Government official. **Personal:** Born Jun 14, 1945, Clarksburg, WV; son of Charles W Fox Jr & Lucille Eleanor Penister; married Judy Delores; children: Charles W Fox IV, Renee Ann, Lori Michelle. **Educ:** Johns Hopkins Univ, MA, 1973. **Career:** MPTV, Owings Mills, PBS, writer, 1972-75; WCVB-TV, producer, 1975-79; Quick Brown Fox Productions, owner, producer, 1979-90; WNEV-TV, CBS, producer, 1981-85; WRC-TV, NBC, producer, 1985-86; American Univ, assoc prof, 1987-89; Maryland Film Commission, dir, 1990-93; Worldnet Television & Film Service, dir, currently. **Honors/Awds:** Academy of TV, Arts & Scis, Emmy, 1973, 1976, 1977, 1979, 1986; Natl Assn on TV Prog Execs, Iris Award, Look Show, 1982-; Religion in Media, Angel Award, 1981. **Special Achievements:** Established Mid-Atlantic Warner Bros Writers Workshop, 1990; Established Multicultural Filmmakers Think Tank, 1990; Developed the Roc Dutton Youth Leadership Summit, 1993. **Military Serv:** US Air Force, staff sgt, 1963-67. **Business Addr:** Director, Worldnet Television & Film Service, 601 D St NW, Ste 5000, Washington, DC 20547, (202)501-7806.

FOX, EVERETT V. See Obituaries section.

FOX, JEANNE JONES
Educator. **Personal:** Born Aug 17, 1929, Chicago; daughter of Helen Duckett Robinson and John Jones; married Richard K Jr; children: Jeanne A, Jane E, Helen K. **Educ:** Rosary College, 1947-49; Roosevelt College , 1949-50; Univ MN, BS 1961; Fgn Serv Inst, lang training 1965-68. **Career:** Buchanan Elementary School, teacher 1961-62; Washington DC Public Schools, substitute teacher 1962; Petworth Public Library, supvr, library asst 1962-64; US Information Agency, foreign serv & limited reserve officer 1964-65; Radnor Elementary School, teacher 1970-71; Mark Battle Assos Mgmt Cons, sr assoc 1971-73; Joint Center for Political Studies, assoc dir research 1973-77; Funders Committee for Voter Registration, Washington, DC, staff consultant, 1983-87; Committee for Study of American Electorate, Washington, DC, project manager, 1987-89; Food Research and Action Council, Washington, DC, director development, 1989-91. **Orgs:** Mem Urban Mass Transit Adv Panel for The Congress of the US; office tech Assessment 1974; bd mem Meridian Ho Intl 1973; mem, unit leader League Women Voters 1956-60; mem Pi Lambda Theta Hon Educ Assn; bd dirs Am Sch of Madrid; sec, scholarship chmn Madrid Spain 1968-70; am chmn Spanish Red Cross Drive Madrid 1969; mem Scholarship Com Am Women's Club Madrid 1965-66.

FOX, RICHARD K., JR.
Ambassador (retired). **Personal:** Born Oct 22, 1925, Cincinnati, OH; son of Kathryn Lynch Fox and Richard K Fox Sr; married Jeanne Jones (deceased); children: Jeanne Fox Alston, Jane, Helen. **Educ:** Indiana Univ, AB, 1950; Indiana Univ Grad School, 1950. **Career:** Urban Leagues St Louis, St Paul, 1950-56; MN Comm Against Discrimination St Paul, asst dir 1956-61; Dept of State, spec asst to dep asst sec for personnel 1961-63, spec asst to dep under sec for admin 1963-65; US Embassy Madrid, counselor for admin affairs 1965-70; Bur Ed Cultural Affairs, dep asst sec 1973-74; Dept of State, dep dir personnel 1974-76; Sr Semnr in Frgn Policy, mem 1976-77; US Ambassador to Trinidad & Tobago 1977-79; Dept of State, dep inspector gen 1979-83; Meridian International Center, sr vice pres, 1983-. **Orgs:** Bd mem, past pres Luth Human Relations Assoc Amer, 1971-76; v chmn Dist Columbia Bd Higher Ed 1972-76; bd of trustees Univ of DC 1976-77; chmn, bd of dir Wheat Ridge Found Chicago 1979-88; pres Amer Foreign Serv Protective Assoc WA 1979-92; bd mem, Vesper Society, CA; member, Washington Institute of Foreign Affairs; member, The American Academy of Diplomacy; member, board of governors, DACOR Bacon House. **Honors/Awds:** Alpha Kappa Delta Hon Soc Indiana Univ, 1950; Superior Honor Awd Dept of State, 1964, 1983; Meritorious Honor Awd Embassy Madrid, 1970; Doctor of Laws, Valparaiso Univ, 1983; Wilbur Carr Award, Dept of State. **Military Serv:** USN 1944-46. **Business Addr:** Senior Vice Pres, Meridian International Center, 1624 Crescent Place NW, Washington, DC 20009.

FOX, RICK (ULRICH ALEXANDER)
Professional basketball player. **Personal:** Born Jul 24, 1969, Ontario. **Educ:** North Carolina. **Career:** Boston Celtics, forward, 1991-97; Los Angeles Lakers, 1997-. **Honors/Awds:** NBA, All-Rookie second team, 1992. **Business Addr:** Professional Basketball Player, Los Angeles Lakers, PO Box 10, Inglewood, CA 90306, (310)419-3100.

FOX, THOMAS E., JR.
Attorney. **Personal:** Born Jul 22, 1963, Brooklyn, NY; son of Juanita Aquart and Thomas Fox. **Educ:** Jackson State Univ, Jackson MS, BA, 1988; Harvard Law School, Cambridge MA, JD, 1988. **Career:** Natl City Board of Correction, New York NY, asst to counsel, 1985; Harvard Prison Legal Assistance Project, Cambridge MA, student attorney, 1986; Brown & Wood Law Firm, New York NY, summer associate, 1987; Honorable Clifford Scott Green, Philadelphia PA, law clerk, 1988-89; White & Case Law Firm, New York, associate, 1989-. **Orgs:** Natl Conference of Black Lawyers, 1987-; former pres/chairman, Natl Black Law Students Assn, 1987-88; New York State Bar, 1989-. **Honors/Awds:** Allan Locke Scholar, Educational Foundation of Phi Beta Sigma, 1984; Rhodes Scholar Finalist, State of Mississippi, 1984; Agnes Fellow, NAACP, 1985-86; Earl Warren Fellow, Legal Defense Fund, NAACP, 1985-88. **Home Addr:** 178 -25 Leslie Rd, Jamaica, NY 11434. **Business Addr:** Associate, White & Case Law Firm, 1155 Avenue of the Americas, New York, NY 10036.

FOX, VIVICA A.
Actress. **Personal:** Born Jul 30, 1964, Indianapolis, IN; daughter of William Fox and Everlyena Fox. **Educ:** Golden West College, attended. **Career:** Actress; Television appearances: Generations, 1989; Beverly Hills 90210, 1991; In the House, 1991; The Fresh Prince of Bel Air, 1991; Out All Night, 1992; The Young and the Restless, 1994; The Tuskegee Airmen, 1995; Living Single, 1996; Arsenio, 1997; movie appearances: Born on the Fourth of July, 1989; Independence Day, 1996; Set It Off, 1996; Booty Call, 1997; Batman and Robin, 1997; Soul Food, 1997; Solomon. **Business Addr:** Actress, c/o Talent Group Inc, 6300 Wilshire Blvd, Ste 2110, Los Angeles, CA 90048.

FOX, WILLIAM K., SR.
Association executive. **Personal:** Born Sep 25, 1917, Beloit, WI; married Reubena M Sturtz; children: William, Jr, Katherine. **Educ:** TN, A&I U, BS 1940; Univ Chicago, BD 1943; Butler U, MS; Christian Theol Sem, 1963; Tougaloo Coll, DD 1973. **Career:** UCMS, field work war serv 1943; Chicago, asst pastor 1940-43; Religion Ext SCCI Edwards MS, dir 1943-47; TN A & I, dean men, coll chpln, prof history 1947-50; Gay-Les Ch Nashville, pastor 1947-50; Centennial Ch St Louis, pastor 1950-60; Ch Federation Indpls, dir spec studies 1961-65; NJ Council Chs E Orange, asst to gen sec 1965-69; Tri-City Citizens Econ Union Newark, executive director 1969-70; Summit Ch Dayton, pastor 1970-72; Gen Office Christian Ch Disciples Christ, asst to gen minister & pres, 1972-82; United Christian Ch, interim minister, 1983; Park Manor Christian Ch, interim minister, 1983-85; Central Christian Ch, interim minister, 1987; Fellowship Christian Ch, interim minister, 1990; Bador Memorial Christian Ch, interim minister, 1992; Oldtimer's Grapevine, editor, manager, 1990-; consultant,churchd community; freelance writer, 1982-. **Orgs:** Editor Christian Plea 1953-57; asso editor Christian Evangelist 1957-60; interm dir ch planning Ch Fed Indianapolis 1962; Lilly-Endowment Ch Planning Fellow 1961-63; lectr black history Montelar State Coll NJ 1969; mem Panel Urban Ch & Consult Bd Ch Ext Indianapolis 1969-72; adj faculty Urban Ch United Theol Sem Dayton 1971-72; v pres, pres Alumni Council Christian Theol Sem Indianapolis 1974-; Christian Ch in KC, chair, urban strategy committee, 1990-92; Urban League of KC, editorial/writer's board, 1991-92; initiator "Hands On Mission Project", Jarvis Christian College, Hawkins, Texas, 1994-96; moderator, board of elders, Raymore Christian Church, Raymore, MO, 1997; interim minister, Central Christian Church, Kansas City, MO, 1997. **Honors/Awds:** Mem Phi Beta Sigma Frat 1939; Phi Beta Tau Scholastic Hon Soc 1943; Honor Soc CTS 1964; 1969 man of year award Frontiers Intl Club; man of yr Oranges & Maplewood Frontiers Intl Club NJ; first black disciple to receive full fellowship; pres of several local natl regional ch groups 1948-. **Business Addr:** Box 1986, Indianapolis, IN 46206.

FOXALL, MARTHA JEAN
Nurse, educator. **Personal:** Born Mar 17, 1931, Omaha, NE; married Pitmon. **Educ:** Bryan Mem Hosp Sch of Nursing, RN 1952; Univ of NE Omaha, BSN 1954; MA 1961; Univ Of NE Med Cntr, MSN 1976; Univ Of NE Lincoln NE PhD 1979. **Career:** Univ of NE Med Cntr Coll of Nursing Omaha, asso prof 1980-; Div of Nurs Midland & Luth Coll Fremont NE, assoc dir 1975-80; Immanuel Med Cntr OmahaNE, asso dir of nursing educ 1968-75; Immanuel Med Cntr Omaha NE, teaching faculty maternity nursing 1953-68. **Orgs:** Lect "Aging & Sexuality" Midland Lutheran Coll 1979-80; chmn CEU com NE League for Nursing 1979-80; research proj dir Univ of NE Med Cntr 1979; memchairperson Com on Mental Health Delta Sigma Theta Sorority 1980; diabetic screening Omaha Area Ch 1978; immunization prog Midland Luth Coll 1977. **Honors/Awds:** Selected to represent US Great Plains Nursing Leaders People to People 1980; faculty reviewer Student Research Forum Univ of NE Med Cntr 1979; mem Sigma Theta Tau; Nat Hon; Soc of Nursing 1979; certification of spl rec NE Nurse's Assn Comm on Nursing Educ 1979; research grant Univ of NE 1978. **Business Addr:** Associate Professor, University of Nebraska, Medical Center, 4111 Dewey Ave, Omaha, NE 68105.

FOXX, JAMIE (ERIC BISHOP)
Comedian/actor. **Personal:** Born in Terrell, TX. **Educ:** US International Univ San Diego, studied classical music. **Career:** Television includes: "In Living Color," "The Jamie Foxx Show," "Straight From the Foxxhole," 1994; films: The Truth About Cats and Dogs, 1996; Booty Call, 1997; The Player's Club, 1998; album: Peep This, 1994. **Honors/Awds:** NAACP, Image Award, TV Comedy Actor, 1998. **Special Achievements:** TV sitcom is #1 among African-American viewers on WB network. **Business Addr:** Comedian/Actor, King Mgmt, 15445 Ventura Blvd, Ste 790, Sherman Oaks, CA 91403, (818)501-2800.

FOXX, LAURA R.
Organization executive. **Personal:** chilDren: one. **Educ:** Univ of NC-Charlotte, BA, english; UNC-Chapel Hill, MA, education. **Career:** NationsBank Foundation, pres, 1997-. **Special Achievements:** First African American president of NationsBank Foundation.

FOYE-EBERHARDT, LADYE ANTIONETTE
Social worker. **Personal:** Born Aug 15, 1943, Birmingham, AL; daughter of Mary Jean Foye Eberhardt (deceased) and John D Eberhardt; children: adopted daughter, Barbara Strickland, JoShawna Eberhardt. **Educ:** The Univ of Akron, BA Sociology/Social Work 1976, BA Psychology 1978, licensed, 1987. **Career:** The Univ of Akron, proctor-tutor 1972-78; Cuyahoga Valley Psychiatric Hosp, vocational rehab volunteer 1979-80; Dept of Human Svcs, friendly visitor volunteer 1980-, social worker II 1980-; Akron Dept of Human Services Mgmt, EPSDT, Healthcheck, Children's Medical, social worker 1983-89. **Orgs:** Order of Eastern Star, Johnson Beauty Chapter #6; AFSCME. **Honors/Awds:** Department of Human Services, Volunteer Services Award, 1980-90; Teri Kingig, Coord, Patrick McGraft Human Services Dir, County Executive Tim Davis, Highpoint Award. **Business Addr:** Licensed Social Worker, County of Summit, Dept of Human Serv, 47 N Main St, Akron, OH 44308.

FOYLE, ADONAL
Professional basketball player. **Personal:** Born Mar 19, 1975. **Educ:** Colgate. **Career:** Golden State Warriors, center, 1997-. **Business Addr:** Professional Basketball Player, Golden State Warriors, 1001 Broadway, Oakland, CA 94607, (510)986-2200.

FRANCE, FREDERICK DOUG, JR.
Real estate investor. **Personal:** Born Apr 26, 1953, Dayton, OH; son of Waldine M France, Sr and Fred France, Sr; married Lawrene Susan Hind, May 14, 1988; children: Kristin Renee,

Jason Kenneth, Kari Lynn. **Educ:** Ohio State Univ, elem educ major 1971-75. **Career:** Professional football player, Los Angeles Rams, Houston Oilers; real estate agent; actor. **Orgs:** Marathon runner; stain glass artist. **Honors/Awds:** Hon mention All-Am Tight End Time Mag; 2nd team NEA; 1st team All-Bag Ten AP; Sporting News NFC All-Stars 1978; Pro Bowl 1977-78; NFC Championship Game 1975, 1976, 1978, 1979; Superbowl XIV 1980. **Business Addr:** President, A Plus Office Products, 25993 Atherton Ave, Laguna Hills, CA 92653-6262.

FRANCIS, CHARLES S. L.

Government administrator. **Personal:** Born Sep 13, 1943, Kingston, Jamaica; son of Barbara Francis and Claude Francis; married Wilma Smith; children: Charles II, Michael, Erica, Aaron. **Educ:** CA State U, BS 1970; MCRP 1977. **Career:** Fresno Model Cities Program, project devel splst one year; CA State Univ Fresno, adjunct professor; budget analyst City Fresno, Fresno Private Industry Council, executive director, currently. **Orgs:** Regional chm Natl & Assn Planners 1972-75; full mem Am Soc Planning Ofcls 1972-; Central Valley YMCA Board dir 1973-; coordntr State Fed Liason Black Polit Council 1975-; chm Lincoln Elem Sch PTA; Affirmative Action Com Fresno Co Bd Edn; pres Alpha Phi Alpha Frat Iota Nu Lambda Chap 1973-75; chm retired, Senior Volunteer Program 1972-; Executive Officer Fresno Branch, NAACP, sec, currently; bd mem, Natl Assn of County Training & Employment Professionals 1988-90; Leadership Fresno Alumni Assn; Business Advisory Council, CSUF-School of Business and Administrative Sciences; Natl Assn of Workforce Development Professionals, board of dirs; Women to Women Advisory Council. **Honors/Awds:** Assn Students service & leadership award 1970. **Military Serv:** USN 2nd class petty ofcr 1960-64. **Business Addr:** Executive Director, Fresno Private Industry Council, 1999 Toulumne Street, Ste 700, Fresno, CA 93721.

FRANCIS, CHERYL MARGARET

Association executive. **Personal:** Born Sep 7, 1949, New Orleans; daughter of Mr & Mrs Albert Francis Jr; married F Daniel Cantrell. **Educ:** Loyola Univ, BS 1971; Univ of Chicago, PhD 1975. **Career:** City of Chicago, department of human services, project manager, 1981-88, manager, title XX programs, 1985-88; United Way of Chicago, manager, non profit consulting unit, 1988-; Contracting Corp of Amer Educ Admin & Conselors, dir 1979-; Coll of Urban Science, Univ of IL, prof; Natl Com for Cits in Educ, midwest staff; Midwest Admin Center, Univ of Chicago, rsch asst; Supt of Schools, Skokie IL, admin asst 1974; Niles Township Demoraphic Study, consultant 1974; MW Admin Center, rsch asst 1971-74, dir students serv 1972-73; Upward Bound Proj New Orleans, program dir 1968-70; Headstart, recruiter 1970; Scope Program, teacher 1970. **Orgs:** Bd sec bd dirs Chicago Opps Industrialization Ctr Inc; Nat Alliance Black Sch Educs; mem Chicago Focus; Am Assn Sch Adminstrs; League Black Women; S Shore Commn; mem Assn for Supervision & Curric; adv panel Nat Inst for Educ Women's Aux for Mary Bartelme Home for Girls; mem Am Educ Research Assn Ford Flwshp Urban Adminstrs 1971; Nat Flwshps Fund Fellow 1974 1974. **Honors/Awds:** Louis J Twomney award Humanitarian Concern 1971; Cardinal Key Hon Soc. **Business Addr:** Manager, Non-Profit Consulting Unit, United Way of Chicago, 221 N LaSalle, 9th Fl, Chicago, IL 60601-1284.

FRANCIS, DELMA J.

Journalist. **Personal:** Born Dec 16, 1953, Lancaster, KY; daughter of Marie Terry Francis and George Francis Jr (deceased). **Educ:** Eastern Kentucky University, Richmond KY, BA, journalism, 1975; University of Louisville, Louisville, KY, MS, community development, 1978. **Career:** The Lexington Herald, Lexington, KY, reporter, 1975-76; The Louisville Times, Louisville, KY, reporter, 1976-86; The Hartford Courant, Hartford, CT, asst bureau chief, 1986-89; Richmond Times-Dispatch, Richmond, VA, asst city editor, 1989-94; Star Tribune, Minneapolis, MN, asst features editor, currently. **Orgs:** Member, former alternate director, National Association of Black Journalists, 1979-; vice president, Connecticut Association of Black Comunicators, 1987-89; member, Louisville Association of Black Communicators, 1977-86; Twin Cities Black Journalists, vice pres, 1995-; member, Big Brothers/Big Sisters, 1990-91; member, Choral Club of Louisville, 1981-86; director, Ebenezer Baptist Church Orchestra, 1990-94; member, Ebenezer Baptist Church Sanctuary choir, 1990-94; Richmond Festival Chorus, 1992-; Leigh Morris Chorale, 1994-. **Honors/Awds:** Investigative News Award, Kentucky Press Association, 1976; Outstanding Communications Alumnus, Eastern Ky, University, 1994. **Home Addr:** 7401 79th Ave N, Brooklyn Park, MN 55445-2608, (612)898-3274. **Business Addr:** Asst Features Editor, Star Tribune, 425 Portland Ave, S, Minneapolis, MN 55415, (612)673-1717.

FRANCIS, E. ARACELIS

Educator, social worker. **Personal:** Born Dec 2, 1939, St Thomas, Virgin Islands of the United States; daughter of Ethanie Maria Smith Francis (deceased) and Amadeo I Francis (deceased). **Educ:** Inter-am U, BA Magna Cum Laude 1960; Univ of Chgo, Sch of SS Admin, AM 1964; Columbia U, Sch of Soc Wrk, DSW 1979. **Career:** Adelphi U, Sch of Soc Wrk, asst prof 1971-75; Dept of Social Welfare, exec dir 1975-80; US Dept of Hlth & Human Svcs, h h fellow 1980-81; Univ of MD, Sch of Social Wrk & CP, asst prof 1982-85; Council on Social Work Education, dir minority fellowship prog 1986-. **Orgs:** Mem Amer Public Welfare Assoc 1962-, Acad of Cert Soc Wrkrs 1965-; vice chrmn State Manpower Serv Cncl 1976-80; bd of dir League of Women Voters VI 1977-80, Caribbean Studies Assoc 1981-85; pres NASW VI Chap 1978-80; chrmn Comm on Minority Groups, Cncl on Soc Work Ed 1982-85; chrmn Comm on Inquiry NASW Metro DC Chap 1984-86; chairperson Planning Comm NASW 1987 Minority Issues Conference; member nominations comm Virgin Islands Assn 1991-92; recording secretary Union of Black Episcopalians, DC Chapter 1990-92; member 1992 World Assembly Planning Subcommittee 1991-92; board of directors, Metropolitan Washington Chapter of the National Associations of Social Workers, 1992-94; president, Metropolitan Chapter of NASW, 1994-96. **Honors/Awds:** Magna Cum Laude Inter Am Univ 1960; NIMH Schlrshp Columbia U, Sch of Social Work 1967-69, CWS Schlrshp 1969-70; HHS Fellow US Dept of Hlth & Human Serv 1980-81; Ed Black Task Force Report, author "Foreign Labor in the US VI"; "Two Outstanding Black Women in Social Welfare History: Mary Church Terrell and Ida B Wells-Barnett"; Wilma Peebles-Wilkins & E Arcelis Francis AFFILIA, vol 5, no 4, winter 1990; "Black Americans" in Ethnic Minority Soc Wk Mental Health Clinical Training Programs: Assessing the Past-Planning for the Future-NIHM survey 1989; Keynote Speaker "Expectations of Migration" at Conference on Caribbean American Family Brooklyn, NY 1990 Medgar Evers College; The Status of former CSWE Ethnic Minority Doctoral Fellows in Social Work Academic Jonl of Soc Wk, Ed Vol 32, No Winter 96, Jerome Scheele E Aracelis Francis. **Business Addr:** Director, Minority Fellowship Programs, Council on Social Work Education, 1600 Duke Street, Suite 300, Alexandria, VA 22314-3421.

FRANCIS, EDITH V.

Educational administrator. **Personal:** Born in New York, NY; daughter of Iris and James Audain; married Dr Gilbert H Francis; children: Deborah Ann Scott-Martin, Denise Tolbert, Dwayne H Francis. **Educ:** Hunter Coll, BA, MA, childhood educ, MS, guidance; NYU, EdD, admin. **Career:** Ed Dept Media Cntr-Audio Visual Proj Ph I Student Tchr Imp, adj prof 1959-61; Student Tchg, instr suprv 1962-63; Elem Schl, tchr 1963-66; Student Tchg Prog, critic tchr 1963-66; Jr/Sr HS, suprv 1967-68; Campus Schs, asst dir 1968-69; Hunter Coll Elem Sch, princ 1968-69; NY City Bd of Ed, consult 1969-70; Except Gifted Chldrn Proj at PS, coord 1970-71; Princeton Reg Schs, princ 1970-76, act spt of schs 1976-77; Hunter Coll Dept of Curr & Tchg; adj prof 1971-72; US Dept of HEW, consult 1973-; Ed Testing Serv, tech asst consult 1975-; Ewing Twnshp Pub Schs, supt of schs 1977-87; Columbia Univ, Teachers College, professor, practitioner/scholar, 1987-91; Irvington Public Schools, superintendent of schools, 1991-92; East Orange Public Schools, director, community and adult education, 1992-. **Orgs:** Pres Princeton Reg Admin Association 1974-75; chairperson of ed comm Princeton Bicentennial Comm 1974-77; board of directors Public Library 1976-77; Witherspoon Devel Corp 1976-82; legislative comm NJ & Amer Assn of Sch Admin 1977-; board of directors YWCA Trenton NJ, 1977-; intl pres Grand Basileus of Zeta Phi Beta 1980-86; bd of examiners NJ Ed Dept, 1980-; board member & trustee Natl Assault on Illiteracy 1982-86; board of directors Helene Fuld Hosp 1982-86; governors task force Trenton NJ 1982-86; board of directors Natl Merit Scholarship Corp 1982-87; Natl Assn of Suprv & Curriculum Devel, Natl Council of Admin Women in Ed, NJ Council of Admin Women in Ed, CUNY Black Professors & Admin Women in Ed, American Association of Sch Admin, American Association of University Professors, Zeta Phi Beta Board of Directors, Schoolmasters of NJ, NJ Association of School Admin, NJ Ed Association, NJ Council of Ed, Phi Beta Kappa. **Honors/Awds:** Honorary degrees: PhD, Humanity of Art, Amer Bible Univ, 1969, PhD, Arts Phil World Univ, 1973; Intl Women's Achvmnt Awd, Global News Synd, 1970; Woman of the Year, Zeta of the Year, 1971; NAACP Awd, 1978; Outstanding Woman Award, 1980; Life Membership Award, 1982; Honor Awds: NJ Dept of Ed, Rider Coll, Ewing Cmmty & NJ State Fed Colored Womens Club, 1979; Prof Dev Awd Mercer Cty CC 1980; Awd Trenton St Coll 1980; One of Most Infuential Black Amer, Commendation by Hamilton Twp Mayor, Mansfield M Finney Achvmnt Awd, Ed Awd Gamma Rho Sigma 1981-1984; Black Media Inc citation 1982; Natl Black Monitor Hall of Fame Awd 1982; Alpha Kappa Alpha Awd for dedicated service 1982; Friends of United Negro Coll Fund Awd for Outstanding Ldrshp & Commitment to Furthering Higher Education, 1982; Natl Cncl of Women, The US Inc Woman of Conscience Awd, 1982; speaking engagements include: Rider Coll, Mercer Cty Com Col, Trenton St Coll, Leadership Conf, Cleveland OH; publications: "Booker T Washington, Temporizer & Compromiser," "Educating Gifted Children," "Gifted Children As We See Them". **Home Addr:** 875 Bear Tavern Rd, West Trenton, NJ 08628.

FRANCIS, GILBERT H.

Educational administrator. **Personal:** Born May 27, 1930, Brooklyn, NY; married Dr Edith V Francis; children: Dr Deborah Scott Martin, Denise Tolbert, Dwayne H Francis. **Educ:** St John's Univ, BBA, LLD. **Career:** US Dept of Health Educ and Welfare Office of Civil Rights, asst chief elem and secondary educ branch 1967-73; NJ Div of Civil Rights Dept of Law & Public Safety, dir of civil rights 1973-74; Supermarkets Genl Corp, dir equal employ oppor 1974-76; Comprehensive Compliance Svcs, consultant/pres 1976-; US Dept of Educ, asst chief tech assistance, 1976-86; NJ State Dept of Educ, educ prog specialist, 1986-97; NJ State Dept of Treasury, sr mgmt specialist, 1997-. **Orgs:** Lecturer Niagara Univ, Hunter Coll, Trenton State Coll, Lehman Coll, Sweet Briar Coll; mem EDGES Group; natl comm co-chairperson Assault on Illiteracy Prog; bd of dirs, chairperson higher educ prog NJ Conf of Branches NAACP; mem Natl Alliance of Black Sch Educators; life mem NAACP; mem Lions Intl, Frontiers Intl; mem legal comm Intl Assn of Official Human Rights Agencies; mem Natl Assn of Human Rights Workers, Comm of One Hundred; comm affairs advisor Hunter Coll Campus Schools NYC; mem Phi Beta Sigma Frat Inc; president, National Pan-Hellenic Council Inc. **Honors/Awds:** NJ Div on Civil Rights Serv Awd; Natl Pan-Hellenic Council Disting Serv Awd; Distinguished Service Key Award, Phi Beta Sigma Fraternity; Man of the Year Awd Phi Beta Sigma Frat Inc; Zeta Phi Beta Sor Disting Serv Awd; Hon Doctorates World Univ L' Universite Libre, Benedict Coll; Man of the Year Awd, Zeta Phi Beta Sor Inc, Central NJ; Distinguished Humanitarian Awd Phi Beta Sigma Frat Inc; Key to the City of Newark NJ; Dr Alvin J McNeil Outstanding Serv Awd Phi Beta Sigma Frat Inc. **Military Serv:** AUS corpl 2 yrs; Army Service Medal. **Home Addr:** 875 Bear Tavern Rd, Trenton, NJ 08628.

FRANCIS, HENRY MINTON

Consultant. **Personal:** Born Dec 23, 1922, Washington, DC; son of Alice King Wormley and John Richard Francis Jr; children: Marsha, Henry, Peter, Morya Hood, John, Deborah Brockway, Russell Jr, William, Yvette, Renee; married Doris Elizabeth Hall, 1982. **Educ:** Univ of PA, 1940-41; US Military Academy at West Point, BS, eng, 1944; Syracuse Univ, MBA (with honors), 1960. **Career:** Dept of Housing & Urban Development, executive asst to first secretary; Office of the Postmaster General, Office of Planning & System Analysis, deputy for plans; Richmond Organization, executive vice president; AVCO Corp, Printing & Publishing, vice president, 1970-73; Department of Defense, deputy asst secretary, Defense Human Goals Program, 1973-77; Howard University, University Planning Director, University-Wide Self-Study Task Force, executive director, Presidential Search Committee, executive secretary, 1989, special asst to president, Government Affairs Director, 1979-91; US Army, Secretary of the Army, civilian aide, past decade; The Black Revolutionary War Patriots Foundation, president, 1992-96; Howard University, director of university research and planning, currently. **Orgs:** Archdiocese of Washington, Catholic Charities, volunteer; Disabled American Veterans, life member; Veterans of Foreign Wars; Assn of Graduates of the US Military Academy, trustee emeritus; Washington Institute of Foreign Affairs; Washington Historical Society, bd of managers; USO-Metro in Washington, director; Natl Press Club; Army and Navy Club of Washington. **Honors/Awds:** Dept of Defense, Distinguished Civilian Service Medal; Dept of Army, Certificate of Appreciation for Patriotic Civilian Service; Urban League, Certificate of Appreciation; NAACP, Certificate of Appreciation, Distinguished Service Award; LDF, Certificate of Appreciation; Beta Gamma Sigma. **Military Serv:** US Army, lt col, 1944-65; Army Concept Team, Vietnam; commander of artillery troops, Korean Conflict, WWII; staff officer, Comptroller of Army, Secretary of Defense; Knight of the Soverign Military Order of Malta, Sept, 1996. **Home Addr:** 1800 Sudbury Rd NW, Washington, DC 20012-2227.

FRANCIS, JAMES

Professional football player. **Personal:** Born Aug 4, 1968, Houston, TX. **Educ:** Baylor Univ, attended. **Career:** Cincinnati Bengals, linebacker, 1990-. **Honors/Awds:** 1989: All-American first team selection, Poor Man's Guide to the NFL Draft, Sporting News, Kodak, AP, Football News; first team choice, All-Southwest Conference. **Business Addr:** Professional Football Player, Cincinnati Bengals, One Bengals Dr, Cincinnati, OH 45202, (513)621-3550.

FRANCIS, JAMES L.

City official. **Personal:** Born Dec 30, 1943, Cincinnati, OH; son of Marjorie L Murphy and James L Francis; married Melanie Hall Francis, Aug 6, 1966; children: Renee L Francis, Darryl L Francis. **Educ:** Ohio Univ, Athens, OH, BA, political science, 1965; Howard Univ, Washington DC, graduate studies, 1966-67; Wright State Univ, Dayton, OH, 1976; Central Michigan Univ, Mt Pleasant, MPA, 1978. **Career:** Govt Employees Insurance Co, Washington DC, claims examiner; City of Dayton, OH, field rep, human relations council, 1970-71, asst to exec dir, human relations council, 1971-72, superintendent, div of property mgmt, 1972-78, dir of public works, 1978-85, asst city mgr for administrative services, 1985-90, exec asst, clerk of city commission, 1990-. **Orgs:** Mem, Alpha Pi Phi Fraternity, 1963-; mem, Westmont Optimist Club, 1984-; mem, Intl City Managers Assn, 1985-; mem, Sigma Pi Phi Fraternity, 1986-; bd mem, Natl Forum Black Public Admin, 1987-96; bd of trustees, OH Municipal League, 1990-97; OH Advisory Council mem, US Civil Rights Commission. **Honors/Awds:** Readers Digest Foundation, Sister City Technical Assistance Program to Monrovia, Liberia, 1986; Certificate of Merit, Louisville KY,

Board of Aldermen, 1988. **Business Addr:** Executive Assistant/Clerk of City Council, City of Dayton, 101 W 3rd St, City Managers Office, Dayton, OH 45401, (513)443-3636.

FRANCIS, JOSEPH A. See Obituaries section.

FRANCIS, LIVINGSTON S.
Association executive, educator. **Personal:** Born Dec 2, 1929, Brooklyn, NY; son of Ethel Price-Francis and James R Francis; married Helen Owensby; children: Brian, Ronald, Gary. **Educ:** Adelpha Univ, Garden City NY, BS, MSW; Columbia Univ, New York NY, Management Certificate. **Career:** NYC Parks, Recreation & Cultural Affairs, New York NY, asst to commissioner, 1960-69; Community Council of Greater New York, NY, assoc executive dir, 1970-77; YMCA of Greater NY-Harlem Branch, New York NY, executive dir, 1977-80; Greater New York Fund/United Way, New York NY, deputy executive dir, 1980-86; Livingston S Francis Assn, pres, Roosevelt NY,1986-; Assn of Black Charities, New York NY, executive dir, 1988-; NY State Univ at Farmingdale, assoc adjunct prof, 1974-76; Adelphi Univ, Garden City NY, adjunct prof, 1976-80; Fordham Univ, New York NY, adjunct prof, 1980-. **Orgs:** Reveille Club; Omega Psi Phi; North General Hosp, chair, bd of dirs; United Hosp Fund, bd of dirs; State Charities Aid Assn, bd of dirs; trustee Medical Health and Research Association of New York; Helene Fuld College of Nursing, trustee. **Honors/Awds:** Governor's Award for African Americans of Distinction, NY State, 1994; Honorary Doctorate of Humane Letters, St. John's University. **Business Addr:** CEO/President, Livingston S Francis Associates, 65 Bauer Ave, Roosevelt, NY 11575.

FRANCIS, NORMAN C.
University president. **Career:** Xavier Univ, New Orleans, LA, pres, currently. **Orgs:** Chmn bd Coll Entrance Examination Bd 1976-. **Business Addr:** President, Xavier Univ, New Orleans, LA 70125.

FRANCIS, PATRICK JOHN
Association executive. **Personal:** Born Sep 4, 1964, New Orleans, LA; son of Blanche Macdonald Francis and Norman C Francis. **Educ:** University of Notre Dame, South Bend, IN, BA, American studies, 1986; LBJ School of Public Affairs University of Texas, Austin, TX, MPA, public affairs, 1988. **Career:** US Senate Comm on Labor and Human Resources, Washington, DC, intern, 1987; Texas Department of Agriculture, Austin, TX, project consultant, 1988; House Research Organization Texas House of Representatives, Austin, TX, researcher/writer, 1989; Texas State Auditor's Office, Austin, TX, performance auditor, 1990; Texas Association of School Boards, Austin, TX, asst director governmental relations; special asst to lieutenent governor of TX, currently. **Orgs:** Editorial staff, Profiles, quarterly publication, Profiling Minority Alumni of LBJ School of Public Affairs, 1990; volunteer, Austin Meals on Wheels Program, 1989-. **Honors/Awds:** Sloan Fellowship for Graduate Study in Public Affairs, 1986-87. **Home Addr:** 4004 Cherrywood, Austin, TX 78722.

FRANCIS, RAY WILLIAM, JR.
Labor union official (retired). **Personal:** Born Jan 22, 1927, New Orleans, LA; son of Ida M Johnson Francis and Ray William Francis, Sr; married Doris A Gill, Mar 20, 1949; children: Ray III, Gerald, Glenn, Robin. **Educ:** Chicago Univ, Chicago, IL, 1961; Labor Educ. **Career:** USWA, Chicago, IL, mng editor, 1961-62, grievance com, 1963-65; AFL-CIO, Washington, DC, field representative, 1965-80, asst dir, 1980-86, dir, 1986-96. **Orgs:** Mem, Intl Labor Press Assn, 1963-65; pres, Du Sable Alumni Club, 1966-78; exec bd mem, South Shore Comm, 1974; pres, South Shore Little League, 1978-80 vice pres & chmn, Jeffery-Yates Neighbor; nat bd member, A Philip Randolph Institute. **Honors/Awds:** Achievement award, Du Sable Alumni, 1977; A Philip Randolph, Award Muskegan County, 1984, Indiana State A.P.R.I., 1984, Chicago Chapter, 1985, Scott County, Iowa, 1985; Illinois Labor History Society Award, 1989; Chicago APRI Renaissance Award, 1990; National APRI Achievement Awd, 1995; Recipient of Minnesota St AFL-CIO Medallion Awd, 1996; Elected to A Philip Randolph Roll of Honor, 1996; Honorary Admiral of Nebraska Navy, North Dakota St AFL-CIO & Nebraska St AFL-CIO; ND Fed Honor Award, 1994; Omaha AFL-CIO CLC, Honorary Award; IN Sagamore of Wabash, 1997; AFL-CIO, Appreciation Award, 31 years of svc and dedication, 1996; AFL-CIO Union YES Award, 1988. **Military Serv:** Infantry/Quartermaster, Platoon Sgt, ETO, Good Conduct, Infantryman awards. **Home Addr:** 8010 S Clyde Ave, Chicago, IL 60617.

FRANCIS, RICHARD L.
Physician. **Personal:** Born Oct 10, 1919, Millerton, NY; son of Irene Virginia Harris and Champ Carter Francis; married De Wreathe Valores Green (deceased); children: DeWreathe V, Irene D. **Educ:** Howard Univ, BS 1941; Howard Univ Med School, MD 1944; Sydenham Hosp NY, Internship 1945; VA Hosp Tuskegee AL, Psych Residency 1947-49; Harlem Valley Psych Ctr Wingdale NY, Psych Residency 1955-57; Vanderbilt Clinic Columbia Presbyterian Med Ctr, Psych Residency 1958-59; NY State Psych Inst, Post Grad Psych & Neurology 1960; Syracuse Univ, Advanced Mgmt Training or Admin in Public Health Facilities 1970-71. **Career:** NY City Farm Colony Staten Island, resident physician 1945-47; VA Hosp Tuskegee AL, neuropsychiatrist 1947-53; Harlem Valley Psychiatric Ctr Wingdale NY, sr physician 1955; Harlem Valley Psychiatric Ctr, supvr psychiatrist 1955-61; Harlem Valley Psychiatric Ctr, asst dir, 1961-67; Sunmont Devel Center, Tupper Lake, NY, dir 1968-81; Sunmont Devel Center, Tupper Lake, NY, chief of Medical Services 1981-88, psychiatric consultant, 1988-. **Orgs:** 1st black asst dir and first black dir NY State Dept of Mental Hygiene Facility, asst dir Harlem Valley Psych Ctr 1961-67, dir Sunmount Devel Ctr 1968-81; sec Mid-Hudson Dist Branch Amer Psych Assoc 1963-67; mem advisory comm North Cty Comm Coll 1968-77; chmn ethics comm Amer Assoc on Mental Deficiency 1971-72; chmn, Narcotic Guidance Council of Tupper Lake NY 1971-76; 1st vice pres Rotary Tupper Lake NY 1973; mem Natl Med Assoc, Amer Assoc of Psych Admin, NY State Med Soc Franklin Cty Med Soc. **Honors/Awds:** Publ "Further Studies in EKG Changes in Old Age" 1947; NY State Qualified Psychiatrist 1959; Cert by Amer Bd of Psych & Neurology in Psych 1970; Licensed Nursing Home Admin 1971; Community Leaders of Amer Awd 1973. **Military Serv:** AUS Med Corp capt 1953-55; Natl Defense Serv Med, Army Occupation Med Germany. **Home Addr:** South Little Wolf Rd, PO Box 1046, Tupper Lake, NY 12986.

FRANCISCO, ANTHONY M.
City official. **Personal:** Born Jun 30, 1960, Nashville, TN; son of Maurine E Moore Francisco and Anceo M Francisco; married Kimberly Statum-Francisco, Oct 3, 1987; children: Alexandria Morgan Francisco. **Educ:** Univ of Oklahoma, Norman, OK, BA, 1978-81; 1981; Univ of Texas/Austin, Austin, TX, SPPS, 1981; Syracuse Univ, Syracuse, NY, MPA, 1983. **Career:** Syracuse Housing Authority, Syracuse, NY, admin aide, 1983; City of Kansas City, MO, mgmt intern, 1983-84; City of Oklahoma City, ok, mgmt/budget analyst, 1984-86; financial enterprise budget officer, 1986-88, dir of street maintenance, 1988-90; investment officer, 1990-. **Orgs:** Christian Church (DOC), 1962-; local president, Kappa Alpha Psi Fraternity, 1979-; Intl City Mgmt Assn, 1983-88; Ambassadors' Concert Choir, 1985-; local pres, Natl Forum for Black Public Admin, 1987-.

FRANCISCO, JOSEPH SALVADORE, JR.
Educator, physical chemist. **Personal:** Born Mar 26, 1955, New Orleans, LA; son of Lucinda Baker and Joseph Salvadore Francisco, Sr. **Educ:** Univ of TX at Austin, Austin, TX, BS (Honors), 1977; Massachusetts Inst of Tech, Cambridge, MA, PhD, 1983. **Career:** Univ of Sydney, Sydney, Australia, visiting lecturer, 1981; Cambridge Univ, Cambridge, England, research fellow, 1983-85; MA Inst of Tech, Cambridge, MA, provost post doctoral fellow, 1985-86; Wayne State Univ, Detroit, MI, asst prof of chemistry, 1986-90, associate professor, 1990-94; California Institute of Technology, research associate, 1991; CA Inst of Technology, Jet Propulsion Laboratory, Visiting Scientist, 1993-94; Purdue Univ, prof of chemistry & prof of earth & atmosphere sciences, 1995; Sterling Brown Visiting Professor, Williams College, 1998. **Orgs:** Faculty advisor, WSU, Nobcche Student Chapter, 1986-; volunteer, Inst Research Appreticeship for Minority High School Students, 1987-; mem, MIT Corp Visiting Comm, 1987-; mem, NASA HBCU Research Panel, 1987-; consultant, Inst for Defense Analysis, 1988-; mem, Amer Physical Soc; mem, AAAS; mem, Natl Org of Black Chemists and Chemical Engineers; Sigma Xi, 1990-; Naval Research Advisory Committee, Dept of Navy, 1994-96; Army Science Bd, 1996-. **Honors/Awds:** Robert Welch Undergraduate Research Fellow Univ of TX, 1973-76; Jr Fellow, Univ of TX, 1977; HEW Fellow, MIT, 1978-81; Wayne State Faculty Award, Wayne State Univ, 1986; Presidential Young Investigator Award, Natl Science Found, 1188; co-author of book, Chemical Kinetics and Dynamics, 1989; Alfred P Sloan Research Fellow, Alfred P Sloan Foundation, 1990-92; Camille and Henry Dreyfus Teacher-Scholar Award, Dreyfus Foundation, 1990-95; Research Fellow, St Edmund's College, Cambridge University, 1983-85; National Organization of Black Chemists and Chemical Engineers, Outstanding Teacher Award, 1992; California Institute of Technology, Jet Propulsion Laboratory Summer Faculty Fellow, 1991-92; John Simon Guggenheim Fellow, 1993-94; American Assn for the Advancement of Science, Mentor Award, 1994; Sigma XI National Lecturer, 1995-97. **Business Addr:** Professor, Dept of Chemistry, 1393 HC Brown Building, Purdue Univ, West Lafayette, IN 47907-1393.

FRANCO, JULIO CESAR
Professional baseball player. **Personal:** Born Aug 23, 1961, San Pedro de Macoris, Dominican Republic. **Career:** Philadelphia Phillies, infielder, 1982; Cleveland Indians, infielder, 1983-88; Texas Rangers, infielder, 1989-. **Honors/Awds:** American League All-Star Team, 1989, 1990. **Business Addr:** Professional Baseball Player, Cleveland Indians, 2401 Ontario, Cleveland, OH 44115.

FRANCOIS, EMMANUEL SATURNIN
Surgeon. **Personal:** Born Dec 23, 1938, Port-au-Prince, Haiti; son of Fausta Lauren Ceau and Saturnin F Ceau; married Edda Gibbs, Jun 19, 1965; children: Randolph Emmanuel, Herve Daniel, Chantal Claire. **Educ:** Coll St Louis De Gonzague, 1958; Univ of Haiti, 1964; Harlem Hosp Ctr Columbia U, resd 1966-72. **Career:** Pvt Prac, surgeon 1973-; Provident Hosp, 1972-73. **Orgs:** Mem Baltimore Cty Med Soc; Med-Chi Soc of MD; AMA; Nat Med Assn; Assn of Haitian Physician Abroad; mem Am Assn for Automotive Med; Trauma Soc; Smithsonian Inst. **Military Serv:** AUS maj 1969-71. **Business Addr:** 1235 E Monument St, Ste 200, Baltimore, MD 21202.

FRANCOIS, TERRY A.
Judge. **Personal:** Born Aug 28, 1921, New Orleans, LA; married Marion L; children: Wade, Gary, Brian, Eric, Carol. **Educ:** Xavier U, New Orleans, BA 1940; Atlanta U, MA 1942; Hastings Coll of Law, Univ of CA, JD 1949. **Career:** San Fran FEP Commn, mem 1957-59; City & Cntry of San Fran, mem, bd of supr 1964-78; City Coll of San Fran, lecturer political sci 1967-75; San Fran Municipal Ct, judge, pro-tem 1982-. **Orgs:** Mem Panel of Arbitrators, AmArbitration Assn; former pres Charles Houston Bar Assn; former pres Multi Culture Inst; mem bd of dir San Fran Legal Aid Soc 1950; pres San Fran NAACP 1959-63; mem bd of dir San Fran Urban League 1950; mem natl bd Catholic Conf for Interracial Justice 1950. **Honors/Awds:** Author Readers Digest article, "A Black Man Looks at Black Racism" 1969; Acting Mayor of San Fran on numerous occasions; 1st Black to Serve on Cnty Bd of Supr in State of CA 1964. **Military Serv:** USMC platoon sgt 1942-45; 51st Defense Battalion; one of 1st black to ever serve in USMC. **Business Addr:** Attorney, Francois & Francois Attorneys, 870 Market St, Ste 608, San Francisco, CA 94102.

FRANCOIS, THEODORE VICTOR
Clinical psychologist. **Personal:** Born Sep 10, 1938, Brooklyn, NY; son of Sylvia Antonia Froix Francois and Theodore Victor Francois Sr (deceased). **Educ:** Manhattan Coll, BS 1960; Fordham Univ, MA 1968; Woodstock Coll, MDiv 1970; NY Univ, MA 1975, PhD 1977; NY Univ, post-doctoral certificate in psychoanalysis 1985. **Career:** St Francis Acad, guidance counselor 1967-70; NY Univ Med Ctr, intern clinical psych 1973-75; Charity RC Church, assoc pastor 1974; NY Univ Med Ctr, intern rsch psych 1975-76; Coll of Med Downstate Med Ctr SUNY, clinical instr psych 1978-83, clinical asst prof of psych 1983-; Kings Cty Hosp Ctr, sr psych 1978-83, chief psych, psych dir of training 1983-; field supervisor in clinical psychology at Yeshiva Univ 1983-and Pace Univ 1986-; dir of psych serv Kings Cty Hosp Ctr 1988-; SUNY Health Science Center, College of Medicine, clinical associate professor of psychiatry, 1992-. **Orgs:** Consult NY Jesuit Provincial 1971-73; co-dir Assn Black Cath Women of Harlem 1973-75; treas, bd of trust 1974-, mem adv bd of dir 1976-, Dwayne Braithwaite School; consult Natl Black Sisters Conf 1976, Black SJ Caucus; mem of, Natl Assn Black Psych 1977, Amer Psychological Assn 1977-, NY Assn of Black Psychologists 1977-, NY Soc of Clinical Psychologists 1985-, NY State Psychological Assn 1986-, NYU Psychoanalytic Soc 1985-; Health & Hospitals Corp., Council of Psychology Directors, 1988-, chairman, 1990-92; New York State Association of Medical School Directors of Psychology, 1988-; New York State Board for Psychology, board member. **Honors/Awds:** NSF Awd Chem 1958-59; Natl Inst Mental Health Traineeship Clinical Psych 1970-73; NYU Philip J Zlatchin Awd in clinical psychology 1978. **Home Addr:** 507 Macon St, Brooklyn, NY 11223.

FRANK, TELLIS JOSEPH, JR.
Professional basketball player. **Personal:** Born Apr 26, 1965, Gary, IN. **Educ:** Western Kentucky Univ. **Career:** Golden State Warriors, 1987-89; Miami Heat, 1989-90; Minnesota Timberwolves, 1991-. **Business Addr:** Professional Basketball Player, Minnesota Timberwolves, 600 First Ave. N., Minneapolis, MN 55403, (612)337-3865.

FRANKLIN, ALLEN D.
Educator. **Personal:** Born May 25, 1945, Berkeley, CA. **Educ:** Merritt Coll, AA 1966; San Francisco State U, BA 1969; Univ CA Berkeley, MBA 1971; PhD 1974. **Career:** CA State Univ, Hayward School of Business & Economics, pres, assoc dean & asst; Graduate School of Business Administration, Univ of CA Berkeley, instructor 1973-74; Planning Dept City of Hayward, consultant 1973-; Far West Lab, consultant 1972-73; Math & Computing Dept, Lawrence Berkeley Lab, math programmer 1969-71. **Orgs:** Mem Caucus of Black Economists/Nat Econ Assn 1971-; bd dir Minority Bus Assistance Student Develop Found 1974-; institutional Mangmt sci 1972-75; Assn for computing Mach 1972-; adminstrv adv Vol Inc Tax Asst Prog 1973. **Honors/Awds:** Outstanding young man am 1975; cert appreciation The Exchange Club Oakland 1975; cert of hon Bus Majors Assn CA State Univ Hayward 1974. **Military Serv:** USNR petty officer 3c 1967-69. **Business Addr:** Sch of Bus & Econ, CA State Univ, Hayward, CA.

FRANKLIN, ARETHA
Singer. **Personal:** Born Mar 25, 1942, Memphis, TN; daughter of Barbara Siggers Franklin and Clarence L Franklin (deceased); married Ted White, 1961 (divorced); children: Clarence, Edward, Teddy, Kecalf; married Glynn Turman, 1978 (divorced 1984). **Educ:** Julliard School, studied piano. **Career:** Renowned vocalist & recording artist; named "Queen of Soul" by music business and fans; gospel singer, 1952-61; Rhythm and Blues/soul vocalist, 1960-84; Pop Music vocalist, 1985-; gospel singer, currently. **Honors/Awds:** Albums include: Ar-

etha, 1961; Electrifying, 1962; Tender Moving and Swinging, 1962; Laughing on the Outside, 1962; Unforgettable, 1964; Songs of Faith, 1964; Running Out of Fools, 1964; Yeah, 1965; Soul Sister, 1966; Queen of Soul, 1967; I Never Loved a Man, 1967; Once in a Lifetime, 1967; Aretha Arrives, 1967; Lady Soul, 1968; Live at Paris, Olympia, 1968; Aretha Now, 1968; Soul 69, 1969; Today I Sing the Blues, 1969; Aretha Gold, 1969; I Say a Little Prayer, 1969; This Girl's in Love with You, 1970; Spirit in the Dark, 1970; Don't Play That Song, 1970; Live at the Filmore West, 1971; Young, Gifted, and Black, 1971; Amazing Grace, 1972; Hey Hey Now, 1973; Let Me Into Your Life, 1974; With Everything I Feel in Me, 1975; You, 1975; Sparkle, 1976; Sweet Passion, 1977; Almighty Fire, 1978a Diva, 1979; Aretha, 1980; Who's Zoomin Who, 1985; Aretha After Hours, 1987; Love All the Hurt Away, 1987; One Lord, One Faith, 1988; Through the Storm, 1989; Grammy Award for Best Female Rhythm and Blues Vocal Performance, 1967-74 (every year), 1981, 1985, 1987; Grammy Award for Best Rhythm and Blues Recording, 1967; Grammy Award for Best Gospel Performance, 1972; Grammy Award for Best Rhythm and Blues Duo Vocal (with George Michael), 1987; numerous hit singles including world famous Respect; R&B Foundation, Lifetime Achievement Award, 1992.

FRANKLIN, BENJAMIN
Engineer (retired). **Personal:** Born Jan 12, 1934, Pilot Point, TX; son of Gasie Lee Pettis Franklin and L T Franklin; married Mary Kathryn Bryson, Jul 6, 1966 (divorced 1997); children: Keven Dwayne, Karen Bennett, Benjamin II, Ouida Kathryn. **Educ:** Univ of WA, BArch 1969; Prairie View A&M Univ, BArchEng 1957-. **Career:** The Boeing Commercial Airplane Group, senior engineer tool design 1989-95; The Boeing Co, payloads sr engr 1977-95; research engr 1957-71; Seattle Opportunities & Insdl Ctr, dir of operations & programs 1971-74; Seattle Opportunities Indsl Ctr, program mgr 1968-70, instructor 1964-68; Consult Mt Baker Rehab Housing Program. **Orgs:** Life mem, Prairie View A & M Alumni; life mem Univ of WA Alumni; bd mem Masonic Lodge Martin Luther King Jr Lodge #65; bd mem Randolph Carter Indsl Wkshp; mem Rainier Kiwanis; mem Seattle Mental Health; bd mem NW Cncl of Blk Professional Engrs; assoc mem Am Inst of Arch; mem Preparedness; connectional bd mem, chaplain, African Methodist Episcopal Church; bd vice pres Primm Tabernacle AME Church; mem Am Defense Preparedness Assn; Boeing advisor to the Jr Achievement Program, 1988-91; The Boeing Applied Academics Program, 1990; director, Boeing Employees Good Neighbor Fund/Tooling Department, 1991. **Honors/Awds:** Employee Award, 1980, Div Employee of the Quarter, 1985, Group Employee of the Month, 1985, Group Employee of the Year, 1986 & 1988, The Boeing Co, Seattle; lead engr 757-200 Airplane Prog Renton WA The Boeing Co 1979-; Achievement Award AME Ch Denton TX 1977; Man of the Year Award Primm Tabernacle AME & Ch Seattle 1966; Seattle Scout Award 1972; Pride in Excell Award The Boeing Co Seattle 1969; Artist Award Prairie View A&M Univ 1956-57. **Military Serv:** ROTC Prairie View A&M Univ, 2 yrs. **Home Addr:** PO Box 823, Renton, WA 98057-0823.

FRANKLIN, BERNARD W.
Educational administrator. **Career:** Livingstone Coll, pres; St. Augustine's Coll, pres, currently. **Business Addr:** President, St Augustine College, 1315 Oakwood Ave, Raleigh, NC 27610-2247.

FRANKLIN, CLARENCE FREDERICK
Manufacturing educator. **Personal:** Born Jan 30, 1945, Knoxville, TN; son of Geraldine Franklin Waller and Clarence David Shell; divorced; children: Carissa Racquel. **Educ:** Tuskegee Inst, attended 1962-63; Univ of TN, attended 1963-64; Cooper Inst, BS Bus Mgmt 1978. **Career:** Union Carbide Corp, machinist 1968-79; Martin Marietta Inc, foreman, training administrator. **Orgs:** VFW 1962; alumni assoc Tuskegee Inst; Optimist Club of Mechanicsville; past president and member, Optimist Club of Mechanicsville/Lonsdale; CC Russell Masonic Lodge#262; Payne Avenue Baptist Church. **Honors/Awds:** Honor Student Campbell High 1962; Honor Student, Cooper Institute 1975-78. **Military Serv:** US Army, spec-4, 2 yrs; Vietnam Serv Medals. **Home Addr:** 4258 St Lucia Ln, Knoxville, TN 37921, (423)588-0014. **Business Phone:** (615)576-4366.

FRANKLIN, COSTELLA M.
Nurse. **Personal:** Born Mar 14, 1932, Durham, NC; divorced; children: Saadia Ardisa, Kevin Leonard, Michale Bernard. **Educ:** Hampton Sch of Nursing, Grad 1953; Univ of CA. **Career:** Coronary Care Meml Hosp Long Beach, asst chg nurse 1968-71; Daniel Freeman Hosp, asst head nurse 1960-65; Childrens Hosp LA, asst head nurs 1956-60; Childrens Hosp WA, chg nurse 1955-56; Blue Angels Charity Club Inc, fdr orgnzr 1st pres. **Orgs:** Life mem contrb supp co-owner Blue Angels Sch for Except Children 1968-; chrpsn Banneker Alumni Parent Assn for Developmentally Disabled Adults 1977; mem CA Professional Nurses Assn; CA Council for the Retarded; Nat Assn for Retarded Childredn; SW Assn for Retarded Childred; Except Childrens Found Women's Aux; Except Adult Parent Guild; Grtr Carson-Compton Parent Grp; Parent Advocate for Human Civil Legal Rights of the Retarded CA Protection Advocacy Agy. **Honors/Awds:** Distinguished cit award 1977; angel of yr award 1972; cit award for outstand achvmt in comm 1971; merit award Lon Beach Meml Hosp Quality control 1969; CA state senate award Senator James Wedworth 1968; Lane Bryant Vol Citzns Comm Award 1967; LA Press Club Award 1962; Sweetheart of the Yr New Decade 1980; Proclamation from the City of Compton 1980; first vice pres Cultural Affairs Assn of West Indian Am Peoples 1980-81.

FRANKLIN, CURTIS U., JR.
Psychiatrist. **Personal:** Born Oct 30, 1929, Commerce, TX; married Rose Marie Henry; children: Curtis, III, Vicki, Lisa, William, Valerie, Rose Marie, Jr. **Educ:** Prairie View A&M Coll, 2 yrs; Fisk U, AB 1949; Howard Univ Coll of Me D, MD 1953. **Career:** Pvt Prac, psychiatry 1967-; Psychiatric Receiving Cntr KC, residency in psychiatry 1964-67; The Doctor's Clinicl KC, practiced internal med 1960-64; Homer G Phillips Hosp, internship residency. **Orgs:** Psychiatric consult to Swope Parkway Health Cntr; Catholic Family & Comm Svc; Vocational Rehabilitation; Social Security Adminstration; asst clinical prof Univ of MO-kC Med Sch; diplomate of Am Bd of Psychiatry & Neurology; fellow Am Psychiatric Assn; AMA; Nat Med Assn; MO Med Assn; Jackson Co Med Soc; KC Med Soc; Alpha Phi Alpha. **Military Serv:** USAR med corp capt 1955-58. **Business Addr:** 4301 Main Ste 14, Kansas City, MO 64111.

FRANKLIN, DAVID M.
Attorney, business executive. **Personal:** Born Apr 27, 1943, Atlanta, GA; divorced; children: Kai, Cabral, Kali. **Educ:** Morehouse College, BA 1964; Amer Univ Law School, JD 1968. **Career:** David M Franklin & Assoc, pres 1975-; Patterson Parks & Franklin, part 1972-75; Former Mgr & Attorney to Roberta Flack, Richard Pryor, Cicely Tyson, Loretta McKee, Peabo Bryson, Julian Bond, UNAmb, Andrew Young, Maynard Jackson & Miles Davis, mgr invst couns; Franklin L Wilson Airport Concessions, (FWAC), founder, CEO, 1994-. **Orgs:** Consultant, Natl Urban Coalition; Cooperative Assistance Fund; Rockefeller Bros Fund; Ford Found; Field Found; Natl Minority Contractors Conf, 1969-73; Natl Urban Coalition, 1968-70; mem, Natl Bar Assn; Washington DC Bar Assn; Phi Alpha Delta Frat; bd of dir, 20th Century Fund; bd of dir, Emergency Black Land Found; bd of dir, Penn Ctr; bd of dir, Garland Foods; bd of dir, WSOK Radio. **Honors/Awds:** Selected black professional of the Year, Black Enterprise Magazine, 1977; American Black Achievement Award in the Professions, Ebony Magazine, 1979. **Special Achievements:** Only African American business licensed for more than one national retail franchises. **Business Addr:** President, David M Franklin & Assoc, One Atlantic Center, Ste 3145, 1201 W Peachtree St, Atlanta, GA 30309.

FRANKLIN, DOLORES MERCEDES
Dentist/administrator. **Personal:** Born in Washington, DC; daughter of Madeline DeLoach Franklin and Charles Lionel Franklin. **Educ:** Barnard Coll, AB 1970; Columbia Univ Sch of Pub Health, MPH 1974; Harvard Sch of Dental Medicine, DMD 1974. **Career:** NJ Dental Group, dir dental serv 1974-75; NY Coll of Dentistry, asst dean for student affairs 1975-79; Cook-Waite Labs Sub of Sterling Drug Inc, dental dir 1979-80; Job Corps US Dept of Labor, gen dental consult 1981-82, principal dental consult 1982-85; Columbia Univ, NY Univ, NJ Coll of Dentistry, adj asst prof; DC Commn of Public Health dental coordinator 1985-. **Orgs:** Consult dental headstart Dept HEW 1974-77; consult quality assurance proj Amer Dental Assn; pub health serv 1977; consult Colgate Palmolive Co 1974-76; bd trustees Natl Urban League 1977-80; bd dir/sec Barnard Bus & Professional Women Inc 1977-78; dental adv comm Dept HHS Bureau of Health Care Delivery & Assistance 1986; dental section council, Amer Public Health Assn, 1987-90; consultant, Dept DHHS Year 2000 Oral Health Objectives of the Nation. **Honors/Awds:** Kizzy Award for Image & Achievement Womanfest, Chicago, 1979; Voted one of the 50 Leaders of the Future Editors of Ebony 1978; Dr Milleken Award Best Paper in the Field of Dental Health Harvard Univ 1974; Author/Editor of professional publications including one book Author of Articles; 1st Black Woman Grad Harvard Sch of Dental Med; keynote speaker Equal Oppty Day Dinner Hartford Urban League & United Way 1978; woman and 1st Black Dean NYU Coll of Dentistry; Dept HHS Secty's Outstanding Comm Health Promotion Program Awd 1986; Highest Ranking Black Sterling Drug, Inc 1979-80. **Business Addr:** Dental Coordinator, DC Commission of Public Health, 1660 L St, NW, Suite 801, Washington, DC 20036.

FRANKLIN, DON
Actor. **Personal:** Born Dec 15, 1960, Chicago, IL; son of Dorothy Jean Franklin and Donald Franklin; married Sheila Burke Franklin, May 4. **Educ:** Studied acting under Soren Kirk, Zephyr Theatre; Dan LaMarte, Training Center of the Working Actor; studied voice under Robert Berthold, Joel Ewing. **Career:** Actor, currently; film appearances include: The Big Picture, Moving, and Fast Forward; series appearances include: "Young Riders," "Knightwatch," "Nasty Boys," "The Cosby Show"; theatre appearances include: Playboy of the West Indies, The Tempest, Dealing, West Memphis Mojo, The Middle of Nowhere in the Middle of the Night, A Chorus Line, One Shining Moment, Kismet, Life of Bessie Smith, Pippin, Amen Corner. **Orgs:** SAG; AFTRA; AEA. **Honors/Awds:** Joseph Jefferson Nomination, Best Actor, The Middle of Nowhere in the Middle of the Night.

FRANKLIN, EUGENE T., JR.
Association executive. **Personal:** Born Jun 8, 1945, Detroit; married Beverkly King. **Educ:** KY State Coll, BA 1972; Univ Louisville, MEd EPDA Grad 1972. **Career:** KY State U, dir Title III project for tchr educ instr 1972-74; Detroit Urban League, dir educ svcs. **Orgs:** Mem Nat Educ Assn; KY Center for Bio-Psychosynthesis; Assn Tchr Educators; Am Inst Econ Research; Detroits Coalition Peaceful Integration; Com Desegregation; former mem Frankfort-Franklin Co Commn Human Rights. **Honors/Awds:** First black houseparents researchers KYC Child Welfare Research Found; responsible research that led to formation KY Sickle Cell Anemia Found 1971; recip grad flwshp Univ Louisville; butzel scholarship Detroit Urban League 1970; deans list KY State U. **Military Serv:** AUSR 1966-72. **Business Addr:** 208 Mack Ave, Detroit, MI.

FRANKLIN, FLOYD
Attorney, educator. **Personal:** Born Dec 26, 1929, Hot Springs; married Myrtle Christy. **Educ:** KY State Coll, BA 1953; CA State Coll, MA 1957; San Fernando Vly Coll, JD 1969. **Career:** CA Community Coll, instructor in law. **Orgs:** ABA; CA State Bar Assoc; Langston Law Club; CA Parole Assoc NAACP; bd of dir Legal Aid Found; mem Omega Psi Phi Frat; cosmo Golf Club; pres KY State Club LA Chap 1965-71. **Honors/Awds:** Man yr Omega Psi Phi 1966; supporter yr Urban League & YMCA. **Military Serv:** AUS pfc 1950-52. **Business Addr:** 5140 Crenshaw Blvd, Los Angeles, CA 90043.

FRANKLIN, GARROME P. (JERRY)
Government official. **Personal:** Born Apr 27, 1949, Cleveland, OH; son of Lacine Watkins & Palmer Franklin; divorced; children: Tanisha Nakaya, Theron Jason. **Educ:** Longview Community College, AA, 1976; Park College, BA, 1976; Webster Univ, MBA, 1978, MA, management, 1978, MAI, 1983. **Career:** General Motors, labor relations, 1976-77; Federal Aviation Administration, numerous management assignments, central region, 1977-87, various mgt positions in FAA headquarters, 1987-91, spec asst, assoc admin for airway facilities, 1988-89, mgr, inform resources staff, Washington headquarters, 1989-91, deputy regional admin, central, 1991-94, regional admin, Great Lakes, 1994-. **Orgs:** Greater Kansas City Federal Executive Board, agency rep, 1991-94. **Honors/Awds:** FAA, Admin Award for Excellence in EEO, 1993; Natl Black Coalition, Silver Bullet Award for Mgrs, 1993, Mgr of the Year, 1992; FAA, Superior Achievement Award, 1987; Vice Pres of US, National Performance Review Participant, 1994. **Special Achievements:** Served on the Vice President's National Performance Review Committee as a representative from FAA, received recognition and acknowledgement from vice president. **Military Serv:** US Air Force, ssgt, 1968-76; numerous commendations & citation awards. **Business Addr:** Regional Administrator, Great Lakes Region, Federal Aviation Administration, 2300 East Devon, Ste 401, Des Plaines, IL 60018, (708)294-7294.

FRANKLIN, GAYLE JESSUP. **See JESSUP, GAYLE LOUISE.**

FRANKLIN, GRANT L.
Physician. **Personal:** Born Jun 21, 1918, Paul's Valley, OK; married Rita Bruckschlogl; children: Monique, Julie, Grant Jr, Dr Carol Susan. **Educ:** Langston Univ, BS 1941; Atlanta Univ, MS 1947; Meharry Medical College, MD 1951. **Career:** Hubbard Hosp, intern 1951-52; Cleveland Veterans Admin and Case Western Reserve Univ Hosps, genl surgical residency 1952-56; Polyclinic Hosp, chief of surgery; Woman's Hosp, chief of surgery; Case Western Reserve Medical Sch, sr clinical instructor of surgery; Cleveland Wade Veterans Admin Hosp, surgical consultant; Private Practice, surgeon; Huron Road Hosp, assoc chief of surgery. **Orgs:** Cert by Amer Bd of Surgery 1957; mem Amer College of Surgeons 1959-, Cleveland Acad of Medicine, Cleveland Surgical Soc, Pan Amer Surgical Soc, Soc of Abdominal Surgeons, Amer Medical Assoc, Ohio Medical Assoc, Cleveland and Natl Medical Assocs, Natl Alumni Assoc of Meharry Medical Coll; mem surgical staffs Lutheran Medical Ctr, St Vincent's Medical Ctr, St Luke's Hosp; mem adv bd Cleveland Foundation; bd of trustees Summer Music Experience; life mem NAACP; mem PUSH. **Honors/Awds:** Honored as Physician of the Year Polyclinic Hosp Reunion; honors extended from Ohio 21st Dist US Congressman Louis Stokes, Cuyahoga Co Commissioners Office, Virgil Brown, and City of Cleveland Council President George Forbes; as trustee of Forest City Hosp was co-presenter of one and one-half million dollars to Eliza Bryant Ctr which is thought to be the largest contribution from one black charitable instution to another in the city and perhaps the nation 1984. **Military Serv:** USAF 1st lt 4 yrs. **Home Addr:** 13944 Cedar Rd, Box 148, Cleveland, OH 44118. **Business Addr:** Assoc Dir of Surgery, Huron Road Hospital, 5 Severance Center, Ste 215, Cleveland, OH 44118.

FRANKLIN, HARDY R.
Library administrator. **Personal:** Born May 9, 1929, Rome, GA; married Jarcelyn Fields. **Educ:** Morehouse College, BA, 1950; Altanta University, MLS, 1956; Rutgers University, PhD, 1971. **Career:** Rockdale County Board of Education, teacher, librarian, 1950-53; Brooklyn Public Library, librarian, 1956-61, community coordinator, 1961-64, sr community coordinator, 1964-68; HEA, associate director, 1971, 1973; EPDA, advisor, 1972-73, asst professor, 1971-74; District of Columbia Public Library, director, 1974-. **Orgs:** Numerous committees, New York Library Assn; Adv Council to Superintendent of Schools, 1973-; Natl Urban League, 1963-; NAACP, 1963-; director, Library Education Division Board, 1972-75; Office of Library Personnel Resources, 1972-73; White House Planning Committee, 1977-; Commission on Program Evaluation Support, 1979-81; American Library Assn, numerous committees, vice president/president elect, 1992, president, 1993-. **Honors/Awds:** Community Leader Award, Freedom Natl Bank 1968; Man of Yr Award, Prince HallMasons 1965; Brooklyn Friends of the Library Award 1963; Natl Endowment for the Humanities, Grant 1970-71; first individual research grant, Council on Library Resources 1970-71; Distinguished Public Service Award, DC Pub School Libr Assn 1979. **Military Serv:** US Army, 1953-55. **Business Addr:** Director, District of Columbia Public Library, 901 G St NW, Washington, DC 20001, (202)727-1101.

FRANKLIN, HAROLD A.
Educator. **Personal:** marrIed Lilla M Sherman. **Educ:** AL State U, AB; Auburn U, MA Tufts Univ Bradeis U, further study; University of Denver, MA, international studies. **Career:** AL State Univ, teacher 1965; Tuskegee Inst, 1965-68; NC A&T Univ, instructor, visiting prof 1969, 1970; AL Serv Center for Black Elected Officials, dir 1969-70; Talladega Coll, asst prof 1968-, counselor, outreach specialist; Terry's Metro Nortuary, manager, currently. **Orgs:** Pres NAACP; mem E AL Planning Commn; Talladega County Overall Econ Commn; Black Coalition Talladega; AL Dem Conf Boy Scouts Am; Citizen's Conf on Pub Affairs; AL Hist Commn Bd Advisors; AL League for Adv of Edn; mem bd treas Star Zion AME Zion Ch; bd advisors Community Life Inst ; mem AL Crt Higher Edn; AL Council Human Relations. **Honors/Awds:** Sigma Rho Sigma Honor Soc; community leadership & serv award; Herbert Lehman scholarship; Phi Alpha Theta International Honor Society in History. **Military Serv:** USAF 1951-58. **Business Addr:** Manager, Terry's Metropolitan Mortuary, PO Box 162, Talladega, AL 35161.

FRANKLIN, HERMAN
Educational administrator. **Personal:** Born May 1, 1935, Mayslick, KY; son of Margaret Taber Franklin (deceased) and Arthur Franklin (deceased); married LaRaeu Ingram; children: Stephen LaMonte. **Educ:** KY State Univ, BS 1960; Tuskegee Univ, MS 1964; Ohio State Univ, PhD 1973. **Career:** AL Cooperative Extension Serv, asst co agent 1963-64; Tuskegee Inst, dir adult ed res project 1964-66; AL State Office of Economic Oppor, dir AL tech asst corp 1966-70; City of Tuskegee AL, ex dir model cities 1970-71; The Ohio State University Office of Minority Affairs, admin assoc 1971-73; TN State Univ, asst prof ext cont educ 1973-74; Tuskegee Inst, dean of students 1974-77; Southern Assoc of Colleges & Schools, consultant 1976-81; Gene Carter and Assoc, consultant/evaluator 1981-83; Middle States Assn of Colleges & Schools, consultant 1981-; US Dept of Educ consultant 1982-83; Univ of MD, vice pres for student affairs currently. **Orgs:** Charter mem bd of dirs, chair Pub Comm, Optimist Intl; mem Lions Intl 1968-70; mem vice chair of bd JJ Ashburn Jr Youth Center 1970-73; chair of comm to reactivate the Chamber of Commerce of Tuskegee 1970, 1974-77; bd of dir-exec bd-vice pres of Chamber of Comm, 1975-77, 1976; presenter Student Services Inst 1979-80; presenter Natl Assoc for Equal Oppor in Higher Educ, 1979-80; mem of exec bd Boy Scouts of America 1984-. **Honors/Awds:** Graduate Fellowship Tuskegee Inst 1962-63; grad assistantship OH State Univ 1971-73; Patriotic Civilian Awd Tuskegee Inst ROTC 1976; century mem Boy Scouts of Amer 1976, 1977; Outstanding Serv Awd Lower Shore Assoc of Counseling & Develop 1983-84; Boy Scouts of Amer, Honorary Trustee Del-Mar-Va Council, 1985, 1995; Bay Shore Chap, Professional Secretaries Int'l, Boss of the Year, 1991. **Military Serv:** AUS E-4 2 yrs. **Home Addr:** 5181 Morris Rd, Pittsville, MD 21850. **Business Addr:** Vice Pres/Student Affairs, Univ of Maryland Eastern Shore, Backbone Rd Ext, Princess Anne, MD 21853.

FRANKLIN, J. E.
Writer. **Personal:** Born Aug 10, 1937, Houston, TX; daughter of Mathie Randle Franklin and Robert Franklin; children: Olff, Malika. **Educ:** Univ of TX, Austin, TX, BA, 1960; Union Theological Seminary, 1972-73. **Career:** City Univ of New York, New York, NY lecturer, 1969-75; Skidmore Coll, Saratoga Springs, NY, dir, 1979-80; Brown Univ, Providence, RI, resident playwright, 1983-89. **Orgs:** Mem, Dramatists Guild, 1971-. **Honors/Awds:** Drama Desk Award, The Drama Desk, 1971; author of Black Girl (play and film,) 1971; author The Prodigal Sister, 1974; Dramatic Arts Award, Howard Univ, 1974; NEA Award, Natl Endowment, for the Arts, 1979; Rockefeller Award, Rockefeller Found, 1980; Writers Guild Award, Writers Guild of Amer, E, 1981; author of Where Dewdrops of Mercy Shine Bright, 1983; author of Borderline Fool, 1988; author of Christchild, 1989.

FRANKLIN, JOHN HOPE
Educator. **Personal:** Born Jan 2, 1915, Rentiesville, OK; son of Mollie Parker Franklin and Buck Colbert Franklin; married Aurelia E Whittington; children: John Whittington. **Educ:** Fisk Univ, AB 1935; Harvard Univ, AM 1936, PhD 1941. **Career:** Fisk Univ, hist instr 1936-37; St Augustine's Coll, hist prof 1939-43; NC Coll at Durham, hist prof 1943-47; Howard Univ, hist prof 1947-56; Brooklyn Coll, chmn dept hist 1956-64; Cambridge Univ, Pitt Prof Amer Hist 1962-63; Univ Chicago, prof Amer hist 1964-82, chmn of history dept, 1967-70; Duke Univ, James B Duke prof hist 1982-85, emeritus 1985-; Duke University Law School, professor Legal history, 1985-92. **Orgs:** Editorial bd Amer Scholar 1972-76, 1994-; bd dirs Salzburg Seminar Mus Sci and Industry; trustee Chicago Symphony 1976-80; bd trustees Fisk Univ 1947-80; Southern Hist Association, president, 1969; Amen Studies Association, president, 1969; Organization American Historians, 1975; mem, pres, 1978-79, Amer Hist Assn; Assn for Study Negro Life and History; Amer Philos Soc; AAUP; senate, 1966-, pres, 1973-76, Phi Beta Kappa; Phi Alpha Theta; DuSable Mus, 1970-; chmn, advisory bd, President's Initiative on Race, 1997-. **Honors/Awds:** Guggenheim Fellow, 1950-51, 1973-74; author, Militant South, 1956; author, Reconstruction After the Civil War, 1961; author, The Emancipation Proclamation, 1963; author, A Southern Odyssey, 1976; author, Racial Equality in America, 1976; author, George Washington Williams, A Biography, 1985; author, Race and History: Selected Essays, 1938-88, 1990; author, The Color Line: Legacy for the Twenty First Century, 1993; Jefferson Medal, 1993; Clarence Holte Literary Prize, 1986; Bunn Award, 1987; Haskins Lecturer, ACLS; Cleanth Brooks Medal, Fellowship of Southern Writers, 1989; honorary degrees from numerous universities; John Caldwell Medal, North Carolina Council on the Humanities, 1991; University of North Carolina Medal, 1992; Encyclopa Britannica Gold Medal Award, 1990; John Hope Franklin Publications Prize of the American Studies Assn, inaugurated 1986; John Hope Franklin Fellowship, National Humanities Center, Inaugerated, 1992; NC Coun on Humanities, 1992, 1993; Charles Frankel Medal, 1993; NAACP Spingarn Medal, 1995; Bruce catton Award, Soc Am Historians, 1994; Cosmos Club Award, 1994; Sydney Hook Award, Phi Beta Kappa Soc, 1994; Presidential Medal of Freedom, 1995; Named to Oklahoma Hall of Fame, 1978; Sr Mellon Fellow, 1973-74; Smithson Bicentennial Award, Smithsonian Inst, 1997; Oklahoma Historians, Hall of Fame, 1996; Peggy V Helmerich, Distinguished Author Award, 1997; Johnson C Smith, Circle of Honor Award, 1997; Booker T Washington, High School Hall of Fame, 1997. **Special Achievements:** Author: Free Negro in North Carolina, 1943, From Slavery to Freedom, 7th edition, 1994; Co-author: Land of the Free, 1966; Illustrated History of Black Americans, 1970; The Color Line: Legacy of the Twenty-First Century, 1993; Editor: Civil War Diary of James T Ayers, 1947, A Fool's Errand by Albion Tourgee, 1961, Army Life in a Black Regiment by Thomas Higginson, 1962, Color and Race, 1968, Reminiscences of an Active Life by John R Lynch, 1970, Black Leaders in the Twentieth Century with August Meier, 1982, Harlan Davidson's American History Series with Abraham Eisenstadt; Lane Coll, Honorary Degree, 1997; Lincoln Memorial Univ, Honorary Degree, 1997; Elmira Coll, Honorary Degree, 1997; Editor with John W Franklin: "My Life and An Era: The Autobiography of Back Colbert Franklin," LSU Press, 1997. **Business Addr:** Professor Emeritus, Duke Univ, Dept of History, Durham, NC 27706.

FRANKLIN, KIRK
Gospel vocalist. **Personal:** Born 1970, Fort Worth, TX; married Tammy Renee Collins, Jan 20, 1996; children: Kerrion, Carrington, Kennedy. **Career:** Mt Rose Baptist Church, minister of music, 1981; Greater, Stronger Rest MBC, minister of music, 1988; Grace Temple SDA Church, musician, 1988; wrote material and performed on I Will Let Nothing Separate Me, DFW Mass Choir 1991, Live in Indianapolis, GMWA National Mass Choir 1993; Gospo-Centric, released Kirk Franklin and the Family, 1993; performed He Say, She Say But What Does God Say?, 1995; appeared on R Kelly album, 1995; Fo Yo Soul Productions, Inc, founder, 1996-; Kirk Franklin & The Family Christmas album; Whatcha Lookin' 4, 1996; Produced album by gospel group, God's Property, God's Property from Kirk Franklin's Nu Nation, 1997; headlined the Tour of Life. **Business Addr:** Gospel Vocalist, c/o Gospo-Centric Records, 417 E. Regent St., Inglewood, CA 90301.

FRANKLIN, LANCE STONESTREET
Educational administrator. **Personal:** Born Jul 3, 1962, Chicago, IL; son of Lawrence Franklin and Carrene Stonestreet; married Anita Valentina Martin, Jul 3, 1986; children: Lance Jabraan, Ian Jamaal. **Educ:** Wayne State Univ, BA, 1986, MSc, 1988; MSCE, 1996. **Career:** Wayne State Univ, laboratory student asst, 1984-86; Detroit Edison, asst industrial hygiene technician, 1986-87; Wayne County Medical Examiner, chemist, 1987-88; Chrysler Corp, research assoc, 1988; Wayne State Univ, mgr, environmental health and safety, 1988-92, interim dir, 1992-94, dir biosafety officer, 1994-. **Orgs:** Univ District Assn, board member, 1995; Samaritan Non-Profit Housing Assn, board member, 1993; AIHA Toxicology Comm, 1992; Wayne County Interview Board, 1995; NAACP, 1992; Freemason, F&AM, PHA, 1990; ACGIH, 1989. **Honors/Awds:** Omega Phi Psi, Scholarship, 1985; KCP Foundation, Fellowship, 1989; WSU, Quality of Svc (Quest), 1993; Office of Gov (MI), Certificate of Congratulations, 1993; City of Detroit, Spirit of Detroit Award, 1993. **Special Achievements:** Author: "Maudsley Reactive (MR/Har) and Nonreactive (MNRA/Har) Rats: Performance in an Operant Conflict Paradigm" with RL Commissaris, JS Verbanac and HL Altman, Physiology and Behavior, Vol 72, 1992; Certified Hazardous Material Mgr, 1990; Registered Environmental Health Specialist, 1990. **Home Phone:** (313)862-3865. **Business Addr:** Dir, Env Health & Safety, Wayne State Univ, 625 Mullet, Rm 207, Detroit, MI 48226, (313)577-1200.

FRANKLIN, MARTHA LOIS
Senior programmer analyst. **Personal:** Born Nov 14, 1956, Nacogdoches, TX; daughter of Ida Smith Sanders and William Sanders, Jr; divorced. **Educ:** Prairie View A&M Univ, Prairie View, TX, BS, 1980;Amer Inst of Banking, Houston, TX, 1986-87. **Career:** Texaco USA, Houston, TX, programmer analyst, 1980-83; Gulf Oil Corp, Houston, TX, sr business analyst, 1983-85; City of Houston, Houston, TX, sr programmer analyst, 1985-86; TX Commerce Bank, Houston, TX, sr programmer analyst, Software Design, Houston, TX, vice pres, 1989-; Pennzoil Co, Houston, TX, sr system analyst, 1988-. **Orgs:** Mem, Ski Jammers, 1985-89; pres, Black Data Processing Assoc, Houston TX, 1985-89; mem, Houston Educ Assn for Reading and Training, 1987-89; mem, 1987-89, financial secretary, 1990, Alpha Kappa Alpha, Omicron Tau Omega; mem, Prairie View A&M Alumni, 1988-89; mem, Toastmasters, 1989; vice pres, Software Design, 1989; board of director, United Negro College Fund, Houston, TX, 1989-90. **Honors/Awds:** Natl Outstanding Sr, 1975; Black Data Processing , Member of the Year, Black Data Processing Associates, 1990. **Home Addr:** 9822 Paddock Pk, Houston, TX 77065.

FRANKLIN, MILTON B., JR.
Government employee. **Personal:** Born Aug 22, 1950, Cleveland, OH; married Anita Lowe; children: Carla Annette, Milton B. **Educ:** Cuyahoga Comm Coll, Grad. **Career:** VA Regional Ofc, vets benefits counselor. **Orgs:** Pres Cleveland Regional Ofc VA Employees Assn 1973-75; chmn Youth Adv Com 1971-72; mem Karamu House Theatre Cleveland OH 1969-73; mgmt Adv Jr Achievement Glenville area Prog 1972-74; vice pres Am Fedn of Govt Employees Local 2823 VA Regional Ofc Cleveland 1975. **Honors/Awds:** Ten outstanding young cit award Cleveland Joycees for Cleveland Area 1973-; award for outstanding community service VA Cleveland 1973; outstanding performance award VA Regional Office Cleveland 1979. **Business Addr:** 1240 E Ninth St, Cleveland, OH 44199.

FRANKLIN, OLIVER ST. CLAIR, JR.
Investment counselor. **Personal:** Born Oct 30, 1945, Washington, DC; son of Hyla Turner Franklin and Rev Oliver St Clair Franklin Sr; married Patricia E Mikols, Jul 7, 1977; children: Julien K. **Educ:** Lincoln Univ, Lincoln Univ PA, BA, 1966; Edinburgh Univ, Edinburgh Scotland, diploma, 1967; Balliol Coll, Oxford Univ, England, Wilson Fellow, 1967-70. **Career:** Univ of Pennsylvania, Annenberg Center, Philadelphia PA, director, 1972-77; independent film producer & critic, 1977-84; City of Philadelphia, PA, deputy city representative, 1984-89; independent publisher, 1989-; Pilgrim, Baxter, Greig & Associates, Wayne, PA, vice president, 1990-. **Orgs:** Pres, Oxford & Cambridge Society, 1985-; bd mem, Opera Company of Philadelphia, 1985-; bd mem, Afro-Amer Historical & Cultural Museum, 1985-; bd mem, Institute of Contemporary Art, 1986-; vice pres, Intl Protocol Assn, 1987-; bd of advisors, First Commercial Bank of Philadelphia, 1989-; mem, The Franklin Inn, 1989; planning committee member, National Association of Security Professionals, 1990-. **Honors/Awds:** Volunteer of the Year, Volunteer Action Council, 1988; Distinguished Alumni, Natl Assn for Equal Opportunity in Higher Education, 1989. **Business Addr:** Vice President, Pilgrim, Baxter, Greig & Associates, Investment Counsel, 1255 Drummers Lane, Suite 300, Wayne, PA 19087.

FRANKLIN, PERCY
Electronic company executive. **Personal:** Born Jan 1, 1926, Freeport, IL; children: Percy Kevin. **Educ:** Western IL U, BS 1950; DePaul, Bus 1961. **Career:** MBE Purchasing Motorola Inc, mgr training 1967-; Falstaff Brewing Co, sales 1962-67; Gallo Wines Inc, sales 1960-62; Liggett & Meyers Tobacco Co, sales 1957-60; Chicago Defender Newspaper, sales 1957-60; Chicago Bd of Edn, pub instr 1950-57; Johnson Products Co, sales mgr 1967-70; Motorola Inc, sales mgr 1970-. **Orgs:** Dir athletics prog Catholic Youth Orgn 1950-59; dir athletics prog Mayor Daley Youth Found 1959-74.

FRANKLIN, RENTY BENJAMIN
Educator. **Personal:** Born Sep 2, 1945, Birmingham, AL; son of Pinkie Simth Franklin and George Franklin; married Theresa C Langston. **Educ:** Morehouse Coll, BS 1966; Atlanta Univ, MS 1967; Howard Univ, PhD 1972; Harvard Sch of Medicine, Porter Found Rsch Fellow 1974. **Career:** NSF, med educ prog grant reviewer; Morehouse Coll, consultant admission com; Atlanta Univ Center, pre-baccalaureate; Robert Wood Johnson Found, cons; NIH cons St Augustine's Coll, instructor 1967-69; Howard Univ Coll of Medicine, asst prof 1972-77; Univ of MD Dental School, assoc prof, 1980-86, prof, 1986-. **Orgs:** Mem Sigma Xi Soc; Amer Physiology Soc; AAAS; NY Acad of Scis;

Endocrinal Society. **Honors/Awds:** Outstanding Faculty Rsch Awd Howard Univ Coll of Med 1976; Porter Found Fellowship Awd 1974; author of over 80 sci articles & abstracts; NIH Scientific Review Group, chairman. **Business Addr:** Professor, University of Maryland at Baltimore Dental School, 666 W Baltimore St, Rm 4-E-36, Baltimore, MD 21201.

FRANKLIN, ROBERT MICHAEL
Educational administrator. **Personal:** Born Feb 22, 1954, Chicago, IL; son of Robert Michael and Lee Ethel; married Dr Cheryl Diane Goffney; children: Imani Renee, Robert Michael III. **Educ:** Morehouse College, attended; University of Durham, England, BA 1975; Harvard University Divinity School, MDiv 1978; University of Chicago, PhD 1985. **Career:** St Paul Church of God In Christ, asst pastor 1978-84; St Bernard's Hosp, prot chaplain 1979-81; Prairie St College, instr in psych 1981; University of Chicago, instr in rel & psych, field ed dir 1981-83; Harvard Univ, Divinity Sch, assoc dir of ministerial studies, 1984-85, visiting lecturer in ministry and Afro-American religion, 1986-88; Colgate Rochester Divinty School, dean/prof of Black Church Studies, 1985-89; Emory Univ, Candler Sch of Theology, asst prof, 1989-91, dir of black church studies, 1989-, assoc prof of ethics and society, 1991-; Ford Foundation, Rights and Social Justice, prog dir, 1995-; Interdenominational Theological Center, president, currently. **Honors/Awds:** American Acad of Religion; Soc for the Scientific Study of Rel; Assn for the Sociology of Rel; Soc for the Study of Black Rel; Black Doctoral Fellowship FTE 1978-80; BE Mays Fellowship FTE 1975-78; Phi Beta Kappa, Morehouse Coll 1975; Publications, Union Seminary Qtrly Review 1986, The Iliff Review 1985, Criterion 1984; Liberating Visions: Human Fulfillment and Social Justice in African-American Thought, Augsburg Fortress Press, 1990. **Business Addr:** President, Interdenominational Theological Center, 700 Martin Luther King Jr. Dr., Atlanta, GA 30314, (404)527-7700.

FRANKLIN, ROBERT VERNON, JR.
Judge. **Personal:** Born Jan 6, 1926, Toledo, OH; married Kathryn Harris; children: Jeffery, Gary. **Educ:** Morehouse, BA (Cum Laude) 1947; Univ of Toledo, JD 1950; Natl Coll of State Trial Judges, attended; Traffic Inst Northwestern, Univ of Denver, Fordham, attended. **Career:** Private practice, attny 1950-60; Toledo OH, prosecuting attny 1953-59, 2nd asst law dir 1959-60; Toledo Mun Ct, judge 1960-69; Lucas Cty Common Please Ct, admin judge 1973-75, judge 1969-. **Orgs:** Mem exec comm OH Common Pleas Judges Assoc; mem Toledo Bar Assoc, Natl Bar Assoc, Lucas Cty Bar Assoc, OH Bar Assoc, Bd of Mgrs, IN Ave YMCA; vice pres Boys Club of Toledo; past pres OH State Conf NAACP, Toledo NAACP; bd of trustees Morehouse Coll, Defiance Coll, Toledo Auto Club, YMCA, Toledo Zoological Soc, St Lukes Hosp; emeritus publ mem Assoc of the US Foreign Svc, Torch Club; pres Scholarship Fund Inc; mem 3rd Babtist Church. **Honors/Awds:** Outstanding Superior & Excellent Judicial Svc, Supreme Ct of State of OH 1972,73,74,75,76; Phi Beta Kappa, Phi Kappa Phi Natl Honor Socs; The Univ of Toledo Gold "T" Awd 1981; 1st BALSA Awd for Excellency in the Field of Law 1983. **Military Serv:** AUS 1st sgt 1950-52. **Business Addr:** Judge, Lucas Cty Common Pleas Court, Lucas Co Courthouse, Toledo, OH 43624.

FRANKLIN, SHIRLEY CLARKE
Policy advisor. **Personal:** Born May 10, 1945, Philadelphia, PA; daughter of Ruth Lyons White and Eugene H. Clarke; divorced; children: Kai Ayanna, Cabral Holsey, Kali Jamilla. **Educ:** Howard Univ, Washington DC, BA, 1968; Univ of Pennsylvania, Philadelphia PA, MA, 1969. **Career:** US Dept of Labor, Washington DC, contract officer, 1966-68; Talladega College, Talladega AL, instructor, 1969-71; City of Atlanta, Atlanta GA, director/commissioner of cultural affairs, 1978-81, chief administrative officer, 1982-90, executive officer for operations, 1990-91, Atlanta Committee for Olympic Games, senior policy advisor, 1991-96; A Brown Olmstead & Associates, partner, 1996-. **Orgs:** National Black Arts Festival, Spelman College, bd of trustees; Atlanta Life Insurance Co, bd of dirs; United Way of Atlanta, bd of dirs; Atlanta Chamber of Commerce, bd of dirs; Carter Center, bd of dirs. **Honors/Awds:** Distinguished alumni award, National Association for Equal Opportunity in Higher Education, 1983; leadership award, Atlanta chapter of NAACP, 1987; Abercrombie Lamp of Learning Award, Abercrombie Scholarship Fund, 1988; Woman of the Year, Atlanta YWCA, 1996; Community Service Award, Atlanta Boys & Girls Club, 1995. **Business Addr:** Partner, A Brown Olmstead & Associates, 127 Peachtree St, Ste 200, Atlanta, GA 30303.

FRANKLIN, WAYNE L.
Public relations manager. **Personal:** Born Jun 7, 1955, Topeka, KS; son of Barbara W Walker Franklin and Earl L Franklin; married Ethel M Peppers, Sep 12, 1981; children: Wayne Michael Franklin, James Nathaniel Franklin. **Educ:** KS State Univ, Manhattan, KS, BS Political Science, 1978. **Career:** Kansas State Univ, Manhattan, KS, financial aid counselor, 1976-78; Southwestern Bell Telephone Co, Kansas City, KS, asst mgr-residence serv center, 1978-81; Southwestern Bell Telephone Co, Salina, Abilene & McPherson, KS, mgr-comm relations, 1981-83; Southwestern Bell Telephone Co, Topeka, KS, area mgr, of constituency relations, 1983-90; Southwestern Bell Telephone Co, Topeka, KS, area mgr, public affairs, beginning 1990, area manager, external affairs, currently. **Orgs:** Past mem, Shawnee County Advocacy on Aging, 1984-88; past pres, Sunset Optimist Club of Topeka, 1984-85; past bd mem, Topeka Jr Achievement, 1984-85; mem, Topeka Chapter NAACP, 1984-; bd mem/vice chaiman, chairman, Topeka Metropolitan Transit Authority, 1985-92; pastor/founder, St Paul Church of God in Christ, 1985-; past bd mem, Private Industry Council-JPTA, 1986-88; mem/past chmn, Mayor's Literacy Commn, 1986-; bd chmn, KS Found for Partnerships in Educ, 1988-89; distinguished Lt Governor, KS Optimist Org, 1988-89; Topeka School Board, 1991-92. **Honors/Awds:** Appreciation of Serv Award, Salina, KS, 1983; 1985 Leadership Greater Topeka Class, 1989 Leadership Kansas Program.

FRANKLIN, WILLIAM B.
Financial consultant. **Personal:** Born May 2, 1948, Brooklyn, NY; married Barbara J Burton; children: Gerald R, Alyce M. **Educ:** New York City Comm Coll, AAS Acct 1971. **Career:** Bache & Co Inc, supvr 1966-71; Daniels & Bell Inc, operatios mgr 1971-75; WB Franklin & Assoc, owner 1975-80; Davis/Franklin Planning Group, vice pres 1980-83; Franklin Planning Group, pres 1983-. **Orgs:** Mem NAACP 1975-; council mem South Belmar 1982-; mem Intl Assoc of Financial Planners 1982-; bd of dir Monmouth County Black United Fund 1983, Monmouth County Check-Mate Inc Comm Action Agency 1984; pres Kiwanis Club of Belmar 1984; arbitrator, New York Stock Exchange, 1988. **Honors/Awds:** Professional Achievement Award from The Central Jersey Club of NANB & PW Clubs Inc 1985; Outstanding Pres Award Belmar Kiwanis Club 1984; Professional Award for Business Excellence natl Assn of Negro Business and Professional Women's Club of Central NJ.

FRANKS, EVERLEE GORDON
Physician. **Personal:** Born May 11, 1931, Washington; married Ruby H; children: Everlee G Jr, Philip W, Karen J. **Educ:** Howard Univ Coll of Pharmacy, BS 1953; Howard Univ Coll of Medicine, MD 1961. **Career:** Private Practice, physician. **Orgs:** Treas 1980-84 Natl Medical Assoc 1965-; vice pres Medico Chirargical Soc of DC 1965-; mem DC Medical Soc 1965-; mem Amer Soc of Internal Medicine 1968-; mem Gordon's Corner Citizens Assoc 1970-; mem Chi Delta Mu Frat grand pres 1984-86. **Military Serv:** AUS Sp3 2 yrs. **Business Addr:** 3230 Pennsylvania Ave SE, #204, Washington, DC 20020.

FRANKS, GARY A.
Congressman. **Personal:** Born Feb 9, 1953, Waterbury, CT; son of Janery Petteway Franks and Richard Franks (deceased); married Donna Williams Franks, Mar 10, 1990; children: Azia Williams (step-daughter). **Educ:** Yale University, New Haven, CT, BA, 1975. **Career:** GAF Realty, Waterbury, CT, president; US House of Representatives, Washington, DC, member, currently. **Orgs:** Director, Waterbury Chamber of Commerce; dir, Waterbury YMCA; dir, Waterbury American Red Cross; dir, Waterbury Foundation; dir, Waterbury Opportunities and Industrialization Center. **Honors/Awds:** Outstanding Young Man, Boy's Club; Man of the Year, Professional Women's Assn, Waterbury. **Business Addr:** US Congressman, House of Representatives, 1609 Longworth Bldg, Washington, DC 20515.

FRANKS, JULIUS, JR.
Dentist. **Personal:** Born Sep 5, 1922, Macon, GA; son of Nellie Mae Solomon Franks and Julius Franks; children: Daryl, Cheryl, Bobby, Beverly A Grant, Fredrick. **Educ:** Univ of MI, BS 1947, DDS 1951. **Career:** Private practice, dentist. **Orgs:** Exec comm, vp, pres 1951-87, mem Kent County Dental Soc 1951-92; mem MI and Amer Dental Assocs 1951-96; trustee Western MI Univ 1964-82; dir Blvd Memorial Medical Ctr 1974-84; dir United Way Kent County 1987-92; trustee emeritus, Western MI Univ, 1983. **Honors/Awds:** MI Hall of Honor Univ of MI 1983; American College of Dentists, Fellow, 1997. **Home Addr:** 1919 Meadow Field NE, Grand Rapids, MI 49505.

FRASER, ALVARDO M.
Physician. **Personal:** Born Feb 8, 1922, New York City, NY. **Educ:** Long Island U, BS 1949; NY U, AB 1954; Meharry Med Coll, MD 1959. **Career:** CK Post (Alcholica Treatment Cntr) ATC at Centra Islip NY, dir 1979-; Sch Med State Univ NY, asst prof clinical psychiatry; Mercy Hosp, former asst clinical atdg. **Orgs:** Mem Prince Hall Masonic Lodge. **Military Serv:** USAAF 1943-46.

FRASER, GEORGE C.
Author, lecturer, entrepreneur. **Personal:** Born May 1, 1945, Brooklyn, NY; son of Ida Mae Baldwin Fraser and Walter Fraser; married Nora Jean Spencer Fraser, Sep 7, 1973; children: Kyle, Scott. **Educ:** Dartmouth College, Amos Tuck School of Business, MBEP. **Career:** Procter & Gamble, marketing manager, 1972-84; United Way, Cleveland, OH, director of marketing and communications, 1984-87; Ford Motor Company, Detroit, MI, minority dealer development program, 1987-89; SuccessSource, Inc, Cleveland, OH, president, 1988-; For Your Success, radio host, 1989-91. **Orgs:** Ohio Building Authority, board of trustees. **Honors/Awds:** Communicator of the Year Award, Cleveland Chapter, Natl Assn of Black Journalists, 1990; Communicator of the Year Award, Black Media Workers of Cleveland, 1990; Commendation for Outstanding Community Service, Ohio Senate and House of Representatives, 1985; National Volunteer of the Year, UNCF, 1982, 1983; Manager of the Year, Procter & Gamble; First Place Award of Achievement for Community Events, SuccessNet, 1989; Voices of Cleveland, Black Achiever of the Year, 1992; Communication Excellence to Black Audiences Award, 1991; City of Cleveland, George C Fraser Day, Feb 29, 1992; Black Professionals Association of Cleveland, Black Professional of the Year, 1992; City of Cleveland, Minority Business Advocate of the Year, 1991; Upscale Magazine, One of the Top 50 Power Brokers in Black America; numerous others. **Special Achievements:** Author: Success Runs In Our Race: The Complete Guide to Effective Networking in African American Community, William Morrow & Co, 1994; Race For Success: The Ten Best Business Opportunities for Blacks in America, William Morrow & Co, 1998. **Business Addr:** President, SuccessSource, 2940 Noble Rd, Cleveland, OH 44121, (216)691-6686.

FRASER, LEON ALLISON
Physician (retired). **Personal:** Born Nov 15, 1921, Winchester, TN; son of Dora L Seward Fraser (deceased) and Phil E Fraser Sr. MD (deceased); married Elizabeth Louise Smith; children: Leon Jr, Keith. **Educ:** Fisk Univ, BA 1948; Howard Univ Sch of Medicine, MD 1952. **Career:** Homer G Phillips Hosp St Louis, intern 1952-53, resident 1953-56; NJ State Dept of Health, public health physician 1958-72, dir chronic diseases 1972-75; Trenton NJ Public Schools, medical dir 1982-94; Private Practice, internal medicine 1956-93. **Orgs:** Mem Mercer Medical Ctr Hospital Staff 1956-; Mercer Co and NJ Medical Socs 1958-; Natl Medical Assoc 1965-; Amer Public Health Assoc 1970-; mem Harvard-Radcliffe Parent's Assoc 1971-; mem Grand Boule Sigma Pi Phi Frat 1986-; life mem NAACP; Kappa Alpha Psi, life member; trust Father's Assoc Lawrenceville Prep School 1972-75. **Honors/Awds:** Alumni Achievement Awd Kappa Alpha Psi 1968; published article "Huntington's Chorea, Case Study," 1966; singles tennis champion Mercer County Med Soc 1982. **Military Serv:** USN SK 1c 3 yrs. **Home Addr:** 217 Huff Ave, Trenton, NJ 08618, (609)393-7866.

FRASER, RODGER ALVIN
Physician. **Personal:** Born Feb 14, 1944, Kingston, Jamaica; married Lesley Crosson. **Educ:** Tuskegee Inst, BS 1969; Howard Univ Sch of Medicine, MD 1974. **Career:** Hubbard Hosp, residency ob/gyn 1978; Private Practice, ob/gyn. **Orgs:** Fellow Cook County Hospital 1978-79; mem Amer, Natl Medical Assocs; jr fellow Amer Coll of Obstetrics & Gynecology; mem Royal Coll of Ob/Gyn. **Honors/Awds:** Publication "Changes in the Umbilical Cord in Normal & Pre-Eclamptic Pregnancy," Medical News 1975. **Military Serv:** USAF Sgt 2 yrs. **Business Addr:** 377 Roseville Ave, Newark, NJ 07107.

FRASER, THOMAS EDWARDS
Attorney. **Personal:** Born Sep 16, 1944, New York, NY; son of Vera Edwina Fraser and Thomas Augustus Fraser (deceased); married Regina Stewart, Jul 24, 1982; children: Helena, Steven, David. **Educ:** University of Wisconsin, BS, 1969, MS, 1973; University of Wisconsin Law School, JD, 1979. **Career:** Public Service Commission of Wisconsin, legal clerk, 1977-79; United Airlines, senior attorney, 1979-; Stewart Collection Productions, secretary, 1993-. **Orgs:** American Meteorological Society, 1969-74; American Bar Association, 1977-82; State Bar of Wisconsin, 1979-; State Bar of Illinois, 1979-; Black Professional Organization, Inc, legal counsel, 1982-86; Illinois Counsel for College Attendance, 1984-; Jazz Institute of Chicago, 1991-; Chicago Urban League, 1991-; Reserve Officer Association, 1992-; American Corporate Counsel Assn, 1994. **Honors/Awds:** Dollar and Sense Magazine, 1992 America's Best and Brightest, 1992. **Special Achievements:** Counseled 2,000 Illinois high-school students, 1991; managed 500 attendee multi-service education symposium, 1990; graduate of Air Command and Staff College, 1984; distinguished graduate of Squadron Officers School, 1974. **Military Serv:** US Air Force, lt col, 1964-76, active duty, 1978-1991, reserve duty; Meritorious Service Medal, 1991. **Business Addr:** Senior Attorney, United Airlines Inc, PO Box 66100, AMF Ohare, IL 60666, (312)952-5443.

FRASIER, LEROY B.
Insurance executive (retired). **Personal:** Born Mar 6, 1910, Camden, SC; son of Rebecca and Joseph; divorced; children: Leroy, Ralph. **Educ:** SC State Univ, BS 1931. **Career:** NC Mutual, retired vice pres agency dir. **Orgs:** Past vice pres Natl Ins Assn; mem NC Humanities Council; chairman Durham Co Social Serv Bd; past vice pres Durham United Fund; past vice pres NC Symphony; NC United Way; chmn trustee Elizabeth City State Univ; life mem NAACP; life mem Alpha Phi Alpha; mem Sigma Pi Phi Fraternity; trustee emeritus, White Rock Baptist Church; trustee emeritus, John Avery Boys Club; chairman Civic Committee, Durham Committee of Black People. **Honors/Awds:** Man of the Yr Durham Business Chain 1956; Alumnus of Yr SC State 1975; Man of Year, Durham Committee on the Affairs of Black People, 1959. **Home Addr:** 715 Massey Ave, Durham, NC 27701.

FRASIER, MARY MACK
Educator. **Personal:** Born May 17, 1938, Orangeburg, SC; married Richard; children: Deirdre Richelle, Mariel Renee. **Educ:** SC State Coll, BS 1958; SC State Coll, MEd 1971; Univ of CT, PhD 1974. **Career:** Univ of GA, Department of Education, professor, psychology, National Research Center on the Gifted and Talented, associate director, 1974-; SC State Coll, dir special serv for disadvantaged students in insts of higher educ 1971-72; Wilkinson High School, Orangeburg SC, instructor Choral Music 1958-71. **Orgs:** President, GA Federation-Council for Exceptional Children, 1977-78; exec bd, Nat Assn for Gifted Children 1977-81; National Association for Gifted Children, president, 1983-91; bd of govs, The Assn for the Gifted 1978-80; Pi Lambda Theta, 1973; Delta Sigma Theta Sorority Athens Alumnae Chap, 1974-; Phi Delta Kappa, 1979-; Kappa Delta Pi, 1990. **Special Achievements:** Articles pub in "The Gifted Child Quarterly, Journal for the Education of the Gifted Exceptional Children"; chap in book "New Voices in Counseling the Gifted" Kendall-Hunt 1979. **Business Addr:** 325 Aberhold, Athens, GA 30602.

FRASIER, RALPH KENNEDY
Banking executive, attorney. **Personal:** Born Sep 16, 1938, Winston-Salem, NC; son of Kathryn Kennedy Frasier and Leroy B Frasier; married Jeannine Marie Quick-Frasier; children: Karen Denise Frasier Alston, Gail S Frasier Griffin, Ralph K Jr, KeithL, Marie K, Rochelle D. **Educ:** Univ of NC, 1958; NC Central Univ, BS Commerce 1963; NC Central Univ Schl of Law, JD (magna cum laude) 1965. **Career:** Wachovia Bank and Trust Co., legal assistant, 1965-66; assistant secretary, 1966-68; assistant vice president, 1968-69; vice president, counsel, 1969-70, The Wachovia Corp., Parent Co., vice president, counsel, 1970-75; The Huntington National Bank, vice president, general counsel, 1975-76, senior vp, general counsel, 1976-83, secretary, 1981-, exec vp, general counsel, secretary, cashier, 1983-, Huntington Bancshares Inc, (Parent Co.), general counsel, 1976-, secretary, 1981-. **Orgs:** North Carolina Bar Association, 1965-; Natl Bar Assn, 1965-; American Bar Association, 1965-; Ohio Bar Assn, 1976-; Columbus Bar Association, 1976-; Columbus Urban League Inc, director, 1987-94, Greater Columbus Arts Council, trustee, 1986-94; Riverside Methodist Hospitals Foundation Inc, trustee, 1989-90; Winston-Salem Transit Authority, vice-chairman, 1968-74, chairman, 1974-75; trustee, Grant Medical Center; trustee, Grant/Riverside Methodist Hosp, 1996-97; vice chairman, 1995, chrman, 1996, Ohio Board of Regents; vice chairman, North Carolina Central University; trustee, National Judicial College, 1996-; trustee, Ohio Health Corp., 1997-. **Military Serv:** US Army, 1958-60, Reserves, 1960-64. **Business Addr:** Exec VP/General Counsel, The Huntington National Bank, 3412 Huntington Ctr, 41 S High St, Columbus, OH 43287, (614)480-4647.

FRAZER, EVA LOUISE
Physician. **Personal:** Born Jun 30, 1957, St Louis, MO; daughter of Louise J Richardson Forrest and Charles Rivers Frazer, Jr; married Steven Craig Roberts, Nov 24, 1984; children: Steven Craig Roberts II, Christian Frazer Roberts, Darci Roberts. **Educ:** Univ of Missouri, Kansas City MO, BA, MD, 1981; Mayo Grad School of Medicine, Rochester MN, internship, residency 1981-84. **Career:** St Mary's Health Center, St Louis MO, physician, 1984-89; Barnes Care, physician, 1990-. **Orgs:** Mem, Natl Medical Assn, 1984-; Univ of Missouri, Board of Curators, 1984-90. **Honors/Awds:** Kaiser Merit Award; Univ of Missouri Alumni Award, 1985; Univ of Missouri, Alumni Service Award, 1994. **Business Addr:** 401 Pine St, St Louis, MO 63102.

FRAZER, VICTOR O.
Congressman, attorney. **Personal:** Born May 24, 1943, St Thomas, Virgin Islands of the United States; son of Albert and Amanda Frazer; children: Kaaren Frazer-Crawford, Aileene. **Educ:** Fisk Univ, BA, 1964; Howard Univ Law School, JD, 1971. **Career:** Virgin Islands Water and Power Authority, gen counsel, 1987-89; Congressman Mervyn Dymally, administrative assistant, 1989-91; Private Law Practice, 1991-; US House of Representatives, Congressman, attorney, currently. **Orgs:** National Bar Association; American Bar Association; Virgin Islands Bar; State of Maryland Bar; State of New York Bar; District of Columbia Bar; Omega Psi Phi. **Business Addr:** Congressman, US House of Representatives, 601 Pennsylvania Ave, NW, North Bldg, Ste 407, Washington, DC 20004-2610.

FRAZIER, ADOLPHUS CORNELIOUS
Educational administrator. **Personal:** Born in Jacksonville, FL; married Mary Charlene; children: Pamela, Eric. **Educ:** FL A&M Univ, BS 1968; Columbia Univ, MA 1975. **Career:** Denver Broncos Football Team, prof athlete 1960-64; Lookout Mtn School for Boys Denver CO, principal supvr 1964-67; York Coll of CUNY, professor, 1969-;, dir financial aid. **Orgs:** Mem NAACP, Coalition on Higher Ed 1979; bd of dir Community Bd 12 1979-, Rochdale Village Inc 1981, Jamaica Arts Ctr 1982. **Honors/Awds:** Delegate Queens Cty Judicial Convention 1976-84; Sports Hall of Fame FL A&M Univ 1979; Campaign Aide Pres Carter 1980; Community Serv Awd S Ozone Park Women Assoc 1981; elected District Leader 32nd Assembly Dist Queens County NYC. **Military Serv:** AUS pfc 18 months. **Home Addr:** 172-40 133 Avenue, Jamaica, NY 11434.

FRAZIER, AUDREY LEE
Business executive. **Personal:** Born Sep 4, 1927, Charleston, WV; married Edward Paul; children: Dwayne Lewis, Paul Vincent. **Educ:** WV State Coll, 1945-47. **Career:** Audrey Frazier Enterprises Inc, pres 1969-71; Key Creations Inc, vice pres, genrl mgr, 1971-74; Audrey Frazier Inc, pres 1974-81; LABOR Inc, admin asst, stat analyst 1980-82; Greater Broadway Local Dev Cor, exec dir 1982-83; Latimer Woods Local Dev Cor, exec dir 1983-85; Megastate Dev Co Inc, pres 1985-90; Audrey Frazier Inc, currently. **Orgs:** Chairperson women's com Nat Assn Black Mfrs 1978-80; chairperson-com on communications Economic Rights Coalition 1979-80; co-chairperson State of NY White House Conf on Small Bus 1980; asst sec Minority Caucus-White House Conf onSmall Bus 1980; del from State of NY Small Bus Unity Com 1980. **Honors/Awds:** Woman of the Year, The Harlem Mothers Assn 1970; woman of the year Utility Club Inc 1970; outstanding services Women's Com Nat Assn of Black Mfrs 1979; woman of the year NABM 1979. **Business Addr:** 671 West 162nd St, New York, NY 10032.

FRAZIER, CHARLES DOUGLAS
Educator, coach. **Personal:** Born Aug 12, 1939, Houston, TX; son of Rebecca Brown; married Betty Alridge. **Educ:** TX So U, BS 1964; TX So U, MS 1975. **Career:** Houston Independent School District, coach, currently; TX Christian U, receivers coach beginning 1976; Univ of Tulsa, receivers coach 1976; Rice U, receivers coach 1975; Houston Oilers & New Eng Patriots, prof football player 1962-70. **Orgs:** Mem Football Coaching Assn; mem Hiram Clark Civic Club; Houston Coaches, Assn. **Honors/Awds:** Mem Record-Setting US 400-meter Relay Team 1962; mem AFL All-Star Team AFL 1966; mem Helms NAIA Hall of Fame for Track & Field LA 1969. **Business Addr:** Coach, Houston Independent School District, 3830 Richmond Ave, Houston, TX 77027.

FRAZIER, DAN E., SR.
City official, clergyman. **Personal:** Born Dec 23, 1949, Ypsilanti, MI; son of Mattie Frazier and Horace Frazier; married Evelyn Westbrook; children: Dennis, Sharron, Evelyn, Daniel Jr. **Educ:** Linfield College; LaVerne University; Portland State University. **Career:** NY Life Insurance Co, field underwriter, 1976-78; Dorite General Contractors, owner-operator, 1978-80; Carter Memorial Church, assoc pastor, 1981-84; Abundant Life Ministries, pastor/founder, 1984-; City of San Bernardino, city councilman. **Orgs:** Bd mem, San Bernardino Redevelop Agency, 1983-; NAACP San Bernardino; corporate bd mem, San Bernardino Community Hospital; political affairs chair, Inland Empire Interdenominational Ministrial Alliance. **Honors/Awds:** Million Dollar Round Table Club, NY Life Insurance Co; brought first communtiy-based police station to the city of San Bernardino, 1983; comm achiever, A Phillip Randolph Inst, San Bernardino Chapt; chosen Most Influential Black Metropolitan Precinct Reporter in the Inland Empire, 1984. **Business Addr:** City Councilman, City of San Bernardino, 300 N D St, San Bernardino, CA 92418.

FRAZIER, EUFAULA SMITH
Executive director. **Personal:** Born Oct 16, 1924, Dodge County, GA; married Arthur Lee; children: Maurice, Noland, Edwin, Michelle. **Educ:** FL Intl U, BS 1977. **Career:** Tenant Educ Assn of Miami, exec dir; comm orgnzr 1967-77; Little Nook Beauty Parlor, owner 1956-67; Atlanta Life Ins Co, underwriter 1951-53. **Orgs:** Dir FL Tenant's Org; co-author, FL Tenant's Bill of Right; Model Cities Task Force 1971-; consult S FL Hlth Task Force 1973-; consult Natl Welafare Rights Orgn 1969-; exec com mem Metro-Dade Co Dem Com 1974; co-host Dem Nat Conv 1972; People's Coalition 1972-; plng advr Counc for Countinuing educ for Women 1971-74; Brownsville CAA 1964-74; facilitator Radical Relat Inst 1973-74; dir Tenant Educ Info Ctr 1974; comm orgnzr Family Hlth Ctr 1969-72; NAACP 1972-77; Legal Serv of Miami 1974-77; Mental Hlth 1975-77; alternate Nat Dem Party Conv 1976. **Honors/Awds:** Women of yr Miami Time Newspaper 1974; woman of yr Achiever Civil Club 1976. **Business Addr:** Executive Dir, Magic City Develop Assn Inc, 4300 NW 12th Ave, Miami, FL 33142.

FRAZIER, FRANCES CURTIS
State official. **Personal:** Born May 19, 1948, Philadelphia, PA; daughter of Letiticia Patsy Thompson Curtis and William Henry Curtis. **Educ:** Norfolk State University, BS, 1972; Ohio State University, MA, 1973. **Career:** Ohio State University, instructor, graduate school, 1974-75; The Ohio Association for Retarded Citizens, Inc, project coordinator, 1976-79; Columbus Community College, instructor, behavorial sciences, 1981-85; Community Arts Project, Inc, executive director, 1982-84; Ohio Department of Mental Retardation and Developmental Disabilities, developmental disabilities consultant, 1983-87; National Assault Prevention Center, special needs consultant, 1985-87; Ohio Department of Human Services, program administrator for cultural initiatives, 1987-. **Orgs:** Greater Columbus YWCA, co-chair, racial justice committee/policy, 1987-95; A Quality of Sharing, Inc, founder, spokesperson, 1979-84; Women of Color Sexual Assault Committee of Ohio, core group, 1989-94; Grailville/National Women's Task Force, 1992-96; US Civil Rights Commission, Ohio Advisory Civil Rights Commission, 1992-97; Riverside Hospital, black women's health program steering committee, 1990-95; Governor's Interagency Council on Women's Issues, steering committee, 1989-91; National Black Women's Health Project, self-help developer, 1989-, bd of dirs, 1993-; Women's Work as a Ministry, spokesperson, 1990-. **Honors/Awds:** Greater Columbus YMCA, Women of Achievement, 1991; The Ohio State University, Outstanding Community Service, 1992; Ohio Women Inc, Women's Equality Day Award, 1992; Alpha Kappa Alpha Sorority Inc, Salute to Black Women Recognition Award 1983; Norfolk State University, Ruth Winstead Diggs Alumni Lecturer, 1978; Eldon W Ward YMCA, Woman of the Year Award, 1995. **Special Achievements:** Author, Sparkle Anyway, a self-talk book for women, 1982, 1990; delegate to the NGO World Conference on Women, United Nations, Kenya, East Africa, 1985; US delegate to World Congress of Women, Moscow, Russia, 1987. **Home Addr:** 3466 Bolton Ave, Columbus, OH 43227. **Business Addr:** Program Administrator for Cultural Initiatives, Ohio Department of Human Services, 30 E Broad Street, 32nd Fl, Columbus, OH 43215, (614)466-6282.

FRAZIER, HERMAN RONALD
Associate athletic director. **Personal:** Born Oct 29, 1954, Philadelphia, PA; son of Frances and Nathaniel; married Katie Nance (divorced 1982). **Educ:** Arizona State University, Tempe, AZ, BS, Political Science. **Career:** Arizona State University, Tempe, AZ, associate athletic director, 1979-. **Orgs:** Board of directors, Fiesta Bowl, 1988-; advisory board, Department of Economic Security, 1985-; board of directors, United States Olympic Committee, 1984-; board of directors, The Athletics Congress, 1984-. **Honors/Awds:** Gold Medal, Olympic Games, 1976; Bronze Medal, Olympic Games, 1976. **Business Addr:** Associate Athletic Director, Arizona State University, Department of Intercollegiate Athletics, ICA Building, Tempe, AZ 85287-2505.

FRAZIER, JIMMY LEON
Physician. **Personal:** Born Aug 29, 1939, Beaumont, TX; son of Thelma Cooper Frazier and E Leon Frazier (deceased); married Shirley Jolley; children: Andrea, Daveed, Keith. **Educ:** TX So Univ, BS 1960; Meharry Med Coll, MD 1967. **Career:** Beaumont TX, teacher 1960-63; NASA, engr 1964; Family Practice, physician 1971-; Wright State Univ Sch of med, admissions com 1977-8l. **Orgs:** Mem Alpha Phi Alpha, Amer Acad of Family Prac, Natl Med Assn, AMA, OH State Med Assn, Shriners-Prince Hall Mason; selectman Dayton OH Montgomery Co Med Assn; Gem City Med Soc; diplomate Amer Bd of Family Practice; fellow Amer Acad of Family Physicians; mem Dayton Racquet Club; mem NAACP. **Military Serv:** AUS maj 1969-71. **Business Addr:** 1401 Salem Ave, Dayton, OH 45406.

FRAZIER, JOE
Businessman, professional boxer (retired). **Personal:** Born Jan 12, 1944, Beaufort, SC; son of Rubin and Dolly Frazier; married Florence; children: Marvis, Weatta, Jo-Netta, Natasha, Jacqui, Hector, Marcus, Reene, Brandon, Joseph, Joye, Derrick. **Career:** Professional boxer beginning 1965; Heavyweight Champion NY MA IL ME 1968; World Boxing Assn Heavyweight Champion 1970-73; winner fight with Mohammad Ali 1971; mem rock-blues group Knockouts; Smokin Joe's Corner, owner; Joe Frazier & Sons Limousine Serv Phila, owner/pres 1974-; Joe Frazier's Gymnasium Phila, owner/mgr/trainer 1974-; mgr prizefighter Marvis Frazier. **Orgs:** Smokin Joe Frazier Gym. **Honors/Awds:** Olympic Gold Medal 1964; New York Hall of Fame, 1992; Phila Boxing Hall of Fame, 1993; New York Police Dept Award of Honor, 1995; WBA Living Legend Award, 1995. **Special Achievements:** Smokin Joe Frazier Clothing Line, 1995.

FRAZIER, JORDAN
Automobile dealership owner. **Personal:** Born in Screven, GA; married Cora; children: Edward, Shayla. **Educ:** Certified automobile dealer, Las Vegas, NV. **Career:** Afro-American Life Insurance Co; Seaboard Coastline Railroad; Roebuck Chrylser Plymouth, sales, until 1975, used car manager, 1979; Jim Bailey City Car Sales, finance manager; Jim Burke Buick, finance manager, 1980; Midfield Dodge, president, general mananger, 1990-. **Orgs:** Vulcan Kiwanis Club; Boys Scouts of America, bd mem; Miles College, trustee. **Honors/Awds:** Small Business Person of the Year, Birmingham Chamber of Commerce, 1996. **Special Achievements:** Listed 63 of 100 top auto dealers, Black Enterprise, 1992. **Military Serv:** US Army. **Business Addr:** Owner/President, Midfield Dodge, 549 Bessemer Superhighway, Midfield, AL 35228, (205)923-6343.

FRAZIER, JOSEPH NORRIS
Police inspector (retired). **Personal:** Born Jul 5, 1925, New York, NY; son of Hazel Washington Frazier and Joseph Frazier; married Dolores Woodard Frazier, Jun 14, 1946; children: Toni Frazier Gilmore, Derek, Nicole, Wendy. **Educ:** Atlantic Comm Coll, AA; Stockton Coll, BA. **Career:** Atlantic City Police Dept, inspector of police, beginning 1975 (retired); capt, 1974-75; sgt 1970-74; patrolman 1954. **Orgs:** Mem NAACP; Sigma Chi Chi Frat; Police Benevolent Assn; Natl Conf of Police Profls; NOBLE. **Honors/Awds:** William Sahl Meml Award in Law Enforcement 1973; Legion of Honor, Outstanding Community Service, Four Chaplains, 1990. **Military Serv:** USCG, seaman 1st class, 1942-46; Good Conduct, Victory, European Theatre.

FRAZIER, JULIE A.
Chemical engineering assistant. **Personal:** Born Dec 9, 1962, Cleveland, OH; daughter of Mrs Gerald N Frazier. **Educ:** Tuskegee Univ, BS 1986. **Career:** Sherwin Williams Technical Lab, lab technician 1984-85; AT&T Bell Labs, Atlanta, GA, chemical engineering asst 1987-89. **Orgs:** Mem Amer Inst of Chemical Engrs 1985-86; volunteer Greater Cleveland Literacy Coalition 1986-87; mem Assault on Illiteracy Program 1986-87. **Honors/Awds:** Chemical Engineering Honor Society Tuskegee Univ 1985-86.

FRAZIER, LEE RENE
Health services administrator. **Personal:** Born Aug 31, 1946, Washington, DC; son of Doretha Frazier and Charles Frazier; married Deborah Ann Lombard; children: Michelle, Bridgette, Adrienne, Yvette. **Educ:** Delgado Coll, SBA 1969; Loyola Univ, BS 1972; Amer Acad of Orthopedic Surgeons, REMT 1974; Tulane Univ, MPH/MHA 1974. **Career:** Charity Hospital, exec dir 1974; Harlem Hospital Ctr, exec dir 1977; South St Seaport, vice pres 1979; Natl Medical Enterprises, vice pres corporate develop 1984; New Orleans General Hospital, administrator/owner 1980-; The Bryton Group, vice pres; Provident Medical Ctr, pres & ceo; visiting professor, Roosevelt Univ. **Orgs:** Consultant J Aron Charitable Foundation; bd mem/treas Natl Assoc of Health Serv Execs; bd mem YMCA; elected to Louisiana State House of Representatives 1981. **Honors/Awds:** Legislator of the Year Metro Press Club 1984. **Military Serv:** AUS 2nd lt ROTC unit 4 yrs; Honorable Discharge.

FRAZIER, LEON
Educator. **Personal:** Born May 16, 1932, Orangeburg, SC; married Irlene Janet Sharperson; children: Angela, Chris, Celeste. **Educ:** SC State Coll, BS 1954; SC State Coll, Grad Study 1955; Univ of OK, Grad Study 1967; AL A&M U, MS 1969; OK State U, DEd 1970. **Career:** AL A&M Univ, vice pres academic affairs, dir 1971-73, assoc prof, asst dean of grad studies 1971-73; US Army Missile School Redstone Arsenal, educational specialist 1968-69, training admin 1961-68, instructor 1958-61; US Air Force Electronics Training Center, Keesler Air Force Base MS, training instructor 1956-58; Aiken County Public Schools SC, teacher 1954-56; State of AL, licensed psychologist. **Orgs:** Mem AAAS; Am Psychological Assn; Nat Educ Assn; Nat Rehab Assn; Nat Assn of Coll Deans Registrars & Admissions com Chmn; Coun of Academic Deans of the So States; Phi Delta Kappa Intl Educ Frat; AL Educ Assn; AL Psychological Assn; Madison Co Mental Health Bd Professional adv com; dir Huntsville-Madison Co Community Action Com; vice pres Madison Co Mental Health Assn; mem Madison Co Community Coun of Orgn; trustee Huntsville Art League & Museum Assn; mem Madison Co Democratic exec com; Nat Assn for the Advancement of Colored People; state dir of public relations Ch of God in Christ; trustee deacon & dir of finance Gov's Dr Ch of God in Christ. **Honors/Awds:** Numerous community serv awards. **Military Serv:** Army. **Business Addr:** Alabama A&M Univ, Normal, AL 35762.

FRAZIER, PAULINE CLARKE
Educator. **Personal:** Born Nov 4, 1936, Richmond, VA; daughter of Earline S Clarke and James C Clarke; divorced; children: Andrea F Warren, Jacquetta Frazier Craig, Randall J. **Educ:** Virginia State University, BS, 1960, ME, 1975. **Career:** Richmond Public School System, teacher, 1963-65; Chesterfield Public School System, teacher, 1967-68; Richmond Public School System, teacher, 1968-; Armstrong High School, Community of Caring, head teacher, 1988-95, vocational education chairperson, 1992-. **Orgs:** Richmond Teachers Association, 1970-; Virginia Teachers Association, 1970-; National Education Association, 1970-; National Home Economics Association, 1970-; Richmond Home Economics Association, 1970-; Delta Sigma Theta Sorority, 1975-; American Business Women's Association, 1985-; Pinochle Bugs Civic & Social Club, 1982-. **Honors/Awds:** Richmond School System, Outstanding Middle School Vocational Education Teacher, 1984-85, Outstanding High School Vocational Education Teacher, 1988-89; Armstrong High School, Unselfish Service, 1989-90; St Peter Baptist Church, Outstanding and Dedicated Service, 1981; ABWA Woman of the Year, Richmond 21st Century Chapter, 1993.

FRAZIER, RAMONA YANCEY
Business executive. **Personal:** Born Jun 27, 1941, Boston, MA; daughter of Gladys E Springer Yancey and Raymond E Yancey Sr; divorced; children: Pamela Rae Frazier. **Educ:** Howard Univ, 1959-60; Simmons Coll, 1961-62; Pace Univ, BA 1984. **Career:** Brown Bros Harriman & Co, employment mgr 1969-73; Anchor Savings Bank, dir of personnel 1973-74; Boston Univ, personnel officer 1974-77; Raytheon Co, eeo mgr 1977; Anchor Savings Bank, asst vice pres personnel officer 1977-79; GAF Corp, dir eeo 1979-84; FW Woolworth Co, dir of personnel 1984-87, corporate mgr 1987-. **Orgs:** Pres The EDGES Group Inc; mem Friend of the Mayor's Commiss on the Status of Women NYC, Human Resources System Profls; mem Delta Sigma Theta. **Honors/Awds:** Black Achiever in Industry Harlem YMCA 1973-78; Mary McLeod Bethune Recognition Award, National Council of Negro Women 1989. **Business Addr:** Corporate Manager-Human Resources, FW Woolworth Co, 233 Broadway #2766, New York, NY 10279.

FRAZIER, RANTA A.
Business executive. **Personal:** Born Nov 2, 1915, Marlboro County, SC; married Grace Lee Booker; children: Barbara, Brenda, Bonita. **Career:** Society Hill, councilman 1969-74; Grocery Store, owner operator. **Orgs:** Mem Citizens Club of Darlington County; Royal Arch Masons Assn; mem Pee Dee Masonic Lodge #56; Cub Scout leader. **Honors/Awds:** 1st Black councilman in Darlington Co.

FRAZIER, RAY JERRELL
Street commissioner, alderman. **Personal:** Born Jun 27, 1943, Lake Providence, LA. **Educ:** Grambling Univ, attended. **Career:** KLPL Radio, announcer; Town of Lake Providence, councilman 1974-; Town of Lake Providence, So Univ St commr. **Orgs:** MW Prince Hall Grand Lodge F & AM of LA Sunrise Lodge #109; mem NAACP. **Business Addr:** St Commissioner, Town of Lake Providence, PO Box 625, Lake Providence, LA 71254.

FRAZIER, REGINA JOLLIVETTE
Director of pharmacy. **Personal:** Born Sep 30, 1943, Miami, FL; married Ronald E Frazier; children: Ron II, Robert Christopher, Rozalynn Suzanne. **Educ:** Howard Univ, BS Pharmacy 1966; Univ of Miami, MBA 1983. **Career:** Comm Drug Store Inc Miami, pharmacy intern 1966; Peoples Drug Stores Inc Washington, pharmacy intern 1967-68, staff pharmacist 1968-69; Natl Assoc of Retired Tchrs & Amer Assoc of Retired Persons Drug Serv Washington, staff pharmacist 1969-70; Economic Oppor Prog, volunteer coord 1970; Univ of Miami Hosps & Clinics, sr pharmacists 1970-73, dir of pharmacy 1973-. **Orgs:** Natl parliamentarian Assoc of Black Hospital Pharmacists; mem Amer Soc of Hosp Pharmacists, Natl Pharmaceutical Assoc, Pharmacy Adv Comm Shared Purchasing Prog The Hosp Consortium Inc, FL Pharmaceutical Assoc; mem adv comm FL/GA Cancer Info Svcs; mem Women's Chamber of Commerce of So FL Inc, The Miami Forum; mem Metro Dade County Zoning Appeals Bd 1977-; pres The Links Foundation Inc; mem League of Women Voters, Amer Assoc of Univ Women; bd ofdirs United Negro Coll Fund, Natl Coalition of Black Voter Participation; mem Alpha Kappa Alpha Sor Inc Gamma Zeta Omega Chapt; mem The Carats Inc, Zonta Intl Greater Miami I Club. **Honors/Awds:** Devoted Serv Awd The Links Inc 1980; Comm Headliner Awd Women in Communication 1984; Trail Blazer Awd Women's Comm of 100 1984; Salute to Leadership Awd Agricultural Investment Fund Inc 1986.

FRAZIER, REGINALD LEE
Attorney. **Personal:** Born Feb 27, 1934, Smithfield, NC; married Levonia P. **Educ:** North Carolina College, AB; North Carolina Central Law School, LLB. **Career:** SCLC, general counsel; Natl Vet Frat, general counsel; self-employed, attorney, currently. **Orgs:** American Bar Assn; Natl Bar Assn; American Judicature Society; North Carolina Trial Lawyers; New Bern Civil Rights Assn; Elks Zeno Lodge; trustee, AME Zion Church. **Business Addr:** Attorney, General Counsel, 1044 Broad St, PO Drawer 430, New Bern, NC 28560.

FRAZIER, RICK C.
Association executive. **Personal:** Born Jul 11, 1936, Lansing, MI; son of Geraldine Taylor Ewing and James Frazier; divorced. **Educ:** Western Michigan University, Kalamazoo, MI, BS (cum laude), 1975, MPA, 1978. **Career:** Mt Carmel Hospital, Detroit, MI, asst vice pres, 1977-81; Douglass Community Association, Kalamazoo, MI, exec dir, 1981-89; City of Richmond, Richmond, VA, asst to city mgr, 1987-89; Fort Wayne Urban League, Ft Wayne, IN, president, CEO, 1989-. **Orgs:** Chair, board of directors, Drug and Alcohol Consortium, 1990-; member, Mayor's Advisory Committee, 1990; incorporator, Greater Fort Wayne Consensus Committee, 1990; board member, Civic Theatre, 1990; host, producer, Bridging the Gap TV Show, 1989. **Honors/Awds:** Mozelle E Manual Service Award, Metropolitan Business League, 1989. **Military Serv:** US Air Force, SSGT, 1956-68; W C O Prep School Speech Award, 1962, Academic Award, 1962, Outstanding Airman Award, 9th S A C Aerospace Wing, 1962.

FRAZIER, SHIRLEY GEORGE
Business executive. **Personal:** Born Oct 1, 1957, Brooklyn, NY; daughter of Joan Branch & Albert George, Jr; married John Beasley Frazier, Jr, Jun 28, 1980; children: Genesis A. **Educ:** Essex County College, AS, 1990. **Career:** Sweet Survival, pres, 1989-. **Orgs:** Gift Association of America, mem, bd mem, 1992-; Gift Basket Professionals Network, assoc mem, 1996-. **Honors/Awds:** Passaic Cty Comm Coll, Carnie P Bragg Sr, Business Awd, 1997. **Special Achievements:** How To Start a Home-Based Gift Basket Business, 1998; Gift Basket Products Guide, 1998; The Complete Gift Basket Industry Reference Direcoty, 1996; Gift Baskets & Beyond, 1995. **Business Addr:** President, Sweet Survival, PO Box 31, River St Station, Paterson, NJ 07544-0031, (973)279-2799.

FRAZIER, WALT
Commentator, professional basketball player (retired). **Personal:** Born Mar 29, 1945, Atlanta, GA. **Educ:** So IL U, Student. **Career:** NY Knicks, 1967-77, tv analyst, currently; Cleveland Cavaliers, 1978-80. **Honors/Awds:** Named to Nat Basketball Assn All-Defensive Squad for 8 consecutive yrs. **Business Addr:** c/o Public Relations Dept, New York Knicks, Four Pennsylvania Plaza, New York, NY 10001.

FRAZIER, WILLIAM JAMES
Physician. **Personal:** Born Aug 20, 1942, Gary, IN; married Veronica; children: Kevin, Monica, Nicole. **Educ:** Fisk U, 1964; IN Univ Sch Med, 1968; Baylor Univ Med Ctr 1968-70; Barnes Hosp WA U, 1972-75. **Career:** Self, physician. **Orgs:** Mem AMA; Dallas Co Med Soc; Am Coll Surgeon; diplomate Am Bd Urology; mem Am Coll Emergency Physicians; mem CV Roman Med Soc; Nat Med Assn. **Honors/Awds:** Publ "Use of Phenylephrine in the Detection of the Opening Snap of Mitral Stenosis" Am Heart Jour 1969; "Early Manipulation & Torsion of the Testicle" JourUrology 1975; bronze star for Meritorious Serv. **Military Serv:** USAF maj 1970-72. **Business Addr:** 3600 Gaston, Dallas, TX 75246.

FRAZIER, WYNETTA ARTRICIA
Health and human services administrator. **Personal:** Born Jul 21, 1942, Mounds, IL; daughter of Annie L Fite Williams and Willie J Williams; married Sterling R; children: Renee, Tommie, Clifford. **Educ:** Governors St Univ, BS & MA 1975; Univ of IL, CDA; Columbia-Pacific, San Rafael, CA, PhD, 1989. **Career:** Gov for Health Affairs, asst; Hlth Serv Adminstr, sr health planner; Comp Health Planning Sub Area, exec dir; Lloyd Ferguson Health Center, asst adminstr; Health Occupations, dir; Nat Asso Health Serv Exec, vice pres; University of Illinois, assistant director of early intervention, 1985-. **Orgs:** Mem Steering Com Am Pub Health Asso; Nat Assn of Neighbrhd Health Ctrs; Pres Auxiliary Cook Cnty Hosp; Pres Kozminski Sch PTA; Vice pres Sch Com Hyde Park Kenwood Community Conf; mem Independent voters of IL; chmn Health Com; mem Leag of Black Women; bd mem Afro Am Fam & Community Service; mem Chicago Forum; national president, National Hook Up of Black Women Inc, president, Chicago Commission on Women. **Honors/Awds:** Ten Outstanding Young People Award Chicago Jaycees; Grant Chas Gavin Scholarshp; Clinic Awards Chicago Med Soc 1972-74 Citizen of the Wk WJPC & WAIT radio stations. **Business Addr:** Assistant Director, ECRIP, University of Illinois, 1640 W Roosevelt Rd, Chicago, IL 60615.

FRAZIER-ELLISON, VICKI L.
State government agency executive. **Personal:** Born Oct 24, 1963, New York, NY; daughter of Lurine Frazier and Thomas Gerald Frazier; married Alvin Ellison, Jul 3, 1992. **Educ:** Cornell University, BS, 1985. **Career:** Bank of New York, account administrator, 1985-86; Mellon Bank, sales/service supervisor, 1986-88; AT&T Communications, account executive, 1988-89; GTE Mobile Communications, operations/service manager, 1989-91; Maryland Lottery Agency, deputy director, 1991-. **Orgs:** First Baptist Church of Guilford, chairperson, men/women's day, 1992, deaconess, 1996; National Association for Female Executives, 1991; MD Public Finance Officers Association; Government Finance Officers Association. **Honors/Awds:** GTE Mobile Communications, Premier Service Quality Award, 1990; AT&T Communications, Sales Achievement Award, 1988; Mellon Bank, Premier Achievement Award, 1987. **Business Addr:** Deputy Director, Administration, Finance & Operations, Maryland Lottery Agency, 6776 Reistertown Rd, Ste 204, Baltimore, MD 21215, (410)764-4390.

FREDD, CHESTER ARTHUR
Educational administrator. **Personal:** Born in Hale Cty, AL; married Hattie Beatrice Long; children: 3. **Educ:** AL State Univ Montgomery AL, BS Sec Ed; Fisk Univ Nashville TN, summer study; AL State Univ Montgomery, MEd Suprv; State Univ of Buffalo, Doctoral Study in Ed Admin; Selma Univ Selma AL, Litt D. **Career:** Jr High Schools (2), principal; Morgan Cty training School Hartselle AL, principal; Hale Cty Training School Greensboro AL, principal; AL Sunday School & Baptist Training Union Congress, instr; CA Fredd State Tech Coll Tuscaloosa AL, pres, president emeritus. **Orgs:** Pres AL Assoc of Secondary School Principals, AL Leadership Study Council, AL State Teachers Assoc; minister Greater Fourteenth St Bapt Church; mem, bd of dir Benjamin Barnes Br YMCA; dean Sunday School & Baptist Training Union Congress; mem, bd of dir W AL Planning & Devel Council; charter mem, bd of trustees Selma Univ; mem Greensboro Zoning Bd; statistician AL State Baptist Convention; life mem Natl Ed Assoc; mem AL Ed Assoc, AL Leadership Study Council, Assoc for Suprv & Curriculum Devel; retired life mem CA Fredd State Teachers Assoc; mem Amer Vocational Assoc, Masonic Lodge Prince Hall Affil, Omega Psi Phi; mem Hale Co Bd of Educ, West AL Mental Health Bd; chmn Hale Co Democratic Conference. **Honors/Awds:** Recipient of Centennial Anniversary Awd AL State Univ 1974; Recipient of Centennial Anniv Awd AL A&M Univ 1975; Tuscaloosa State Tech Coll was named CA Fredd State Tech Coll in honor of CA Fredd Sr its 1st pres. **Business Addr:** President Emeritus, CA Fredd St Tech Coll, 3401 Martin Luther King Blvd, Tuscaloosa, AL 35401.

FREDRICK, EARL E., JR.
Physician. **Personal:** Born Aug 13, 1929, Chicago, IL; son of Lucille Ray Fredrick and Earl Eugene Fredrick Sr; married Barbara Cartman, Mar 21, 1987; children: Earl E III, Erica E. **Educ:** Univ of IL, BS 1951; Howard Univ, MD 1958. **Career:** Univ of Chicago Food Research Inst, 1953; IL Dept of Public Health, bacteriologist 1953-55; Freedmans Hospital, med lab technician 1956-58; Cook County Hospital, rotating internship

1958-59; residency 1959-61; VA Research Hospital, hematology fellowship 1961-62; Fredrick Ashley Clinic, physician internal medicine & hematology; Anchor Organization for Health Maintenance, physician internal medicine 1974-, Anchor-Park Forest Office, clinical dir 1982-85. **Orgs:** Chicago Medical Society; alt delegate, AMA, 1987-95; delegate, AMA, 1997; IL State Medical Soc, bd of trustees, 1997-; Natl Medical Assn; Cook County Physicians Assn; Clinical Assn Internal Medicine Chicago Medical School 1963-73; bd mem Chicago Found for MedCare 1977-83; bd of trustees Chicago Medical Soc 1977-85; mem Amer Coll of Physicians; attending Physician Cook County Hospital, 1963-73; St Francis Hospital, chmn Dept of Med 1974-76; pres of med staff St Francis Hospital 1978-79; chmn of bd Washington Park YMCA 1977-80; consultation staff Roseland Community Hospital; Provident Hospital; Louise Burg Hospital; vice chmn, bd of trustees Chicago Medical Society 1983-85. **Honors/Awds:** Glucose 6-Phosphate Dehydrogenase Deficiency, A Review J, Natl Medical Assn 1962. **Military Serv:** AUS 1951-53. **Business Addr:** 10830 S Halsted St, Chicago, IL 60628.

FREE, KENNETH A.
Athletic conference commissioner. **Personal:** Born Jun 8, 1936, Greensboro, NC; son of Margaret McMurray Free and Lee W Free; married Carolyn Carter Free, Jun 3, 1967; children: Delana, Kenneth Jr, Benjamin. **Educ:** North Carolina A & T State University, Greensboro, NC, BS, 1970. **Career:** Central Motor Lines, Greensboro, NC, 1964-67; New York Mets Prof Baseball, minor leagues, 1960-64; Greensboro Parks & Recreation, Greensboro, NC, 1967-70; N C Dept of Natural & Economic Resources, Fayetteville, NC, park and rec consultant, 1970-78; Mid-Eastern Athletic Conference, Greensboro, NC, commissioner, 1978-. **Orgs:** Executive committee, National Association of Collegiate Directors of Athletics; National Collegiate Athletic Association Committee on Committees, 1984-86; member, Collegiate Commissioners Association; member, University Commissioners Association; NCAA Division I Basketball East Regional Advisory Committee, 1982-84; secretary/treasurer, vice president, currently, University Commissioners Association; NCAA Division I Basketball Committee; Committee on Basketball Issues; president, Fayetteville Alumni Kappa Alpha Psi Fraternity, 1972-77; president, NC Recreation Parks Society, 1978; Mason/Morning Star Lodge 691. **Honors/Awds:** Certified Recreator, state of NC, 1968; Fellow Award, NC Recreation Parks Society, 1986; Man of the Year, Fayetteville Alumni Kappa Alpha Psi Fraternity, 1976; Jostens Distinguished Service Award, 1992. **Military Serv:** US Army, Sp-4, 1955-58. **Business Addr:** Commissioner, Mid-Eastern Athletic Conference (MEAC), 102 N Elm St, Suite 401, Southeastern Building, Greensboro, NC 27401.

FREE, WORLD B.
Professional basketball coach. **Personal:** Born Dec 9, 1953, Atlanta, GA. **Educ:** Guilford, 1976. **Career:** Philadelphia 76er's, 1976-78, 1987, San Diego Clippers, 1979-80, Golden State Warriors, 1981-83, Cleveland Cavaliers, 1983-86; Houston Rockets, 1988; Oklahoma City Calvary, 1991; Philadelphia 76ers, strength and conditioning coach, 1994-. **Honors/Awds:** Voted MVP by teammates; 4 Player of Week Noms; starting lineup for West All-Star Game in Landover, 1980; Clippers MVP, 2nd team All-NBA honors; led NBA in free throw attempts and free throws made.

FREELAND, ROBERT LENWARD, JR.
Business executive, recorder. **Personal:** Born May 5, 1939, Gary, IN; married Carolyn J Woolridge; children: Robin, Brandon. **Educ:** IN Inst of Real Estate, Cert 1962; IN Univ; Calumet College, Whiting IN, 1980, 1981. **Career:** IN state rep 1973-74; Black Horsemen Liquor Stores, owner 1969-81; Four Roses Distillers Co, mktg rep 1968-71; Len Pollak Buick, salesman 1966-68; Mobil Oil Corp, sales engr 1963-66; Devaney Realtors, salesman 1961-63; city of Gary Common Council, city councilman 1975-79, vice pres 1976, pres 1977-79; city of Gary, police commr 1979-83; Calumet Township Trustee, Gary IN, chief deputy trustee 1988. **Orgs:** NAACP; Urban League; Frontiers Intl; bd mem Northwest Indiana Regional Plan Commission 1975-78. **Honors/Awds:** Recip Legis award NAACP 1973; recog award Precinct Orgn 1973; distinction award IN Div Assn for Study of Afro-Am Life & Hist 1973; Lake Co concerned cit recog award 1973; merit serv award Club Carpetbaggers 1972; patriotic serv award 1964; special recog & commend IN Dept of Civil Defense 1961; friendship award Frat Order of Police 1973; first black from Gary elected state rep; first black to serve on House Ways & Means Com; elected del to First Nat Black Assem 1972; elected del to Dem State Convention 4 Times; served on state dem platform com twice; Black History Commemorative Service, WTLC 105FM, Indianapolis IN 1988. **Business Addr:** Lake County Recorder, Lake County Government Center, 2293 N Main St, Recorder's Office, Crown Point, IN 46307.

FREELAND, RUSSELL L.
Consultant. **Personal:** Born Jul 13, 1929, Lawrenceburg, IN; son of Hulda M. Earley Freeland (deceased) and John H. Freeland (deceased); married Joan M; children: Deborah, Mark, Douglas. **Educ:** DePauw Univ, BA 1951; Butler Univ, MS 1960. **Career:** Intl Harvester Co, mgr mfg oper, 1980-82; Intl Harvester, general plants mgr, 1982-83; Intl Harvester, dir, renew operations, 1983; Intl Harvester, director tech admin, 1983-86; retired, 1986; Navistar, consultant, 1987-92; Engine Operations Intl Harvester, plant mgr 1978-80; Intl Harvester Co, mgr direct labor syst 1978; Indianapolis Plant Intl Harvester Co, mgr mfg operations 1977-78; Indianapolis Plant Intl Harvester Co, mgr production operations 1976-77; Indianapolis Plant Intl Harvester Co, mgr indus engineering 1974-76. **Orgs:** Mem, Amer Inst of Indus Engrs, 1974-82; host TV talk show "Opportunity Knocks" WFBM-TV 1971-76; mem bd of visitors DePauw Univ 1979-85; mem Allocations Comm United Way Metro Chicago 1979-80; Lions Club, 1986-. **Honors/Awds:** Silver Anniversary Team, Indiana High School Basketball 1972; Silver Anniversary Team All-Amer, Natl Assn of Basketball Coaches 1976; Civic Award, Intl Harvester, 1976; DePauw Univ, All Sports Hall of Fame, 1989; Lion of the Year, 1992. **Military Serv:** USAF s/sgt 1951-55. **Home Addr:** 1569 Vest St, Naperville, IL 60563.

FREELAND, SHAWN ERICKA
Promotion director. **Personal:** Born Sep 10, 1968, Jacksonville, FL; daughter of Sharon Conley Freeland and Leonard Harris Freeland Sr. **Educ:** Florida Community College-Jacksonville; Columbia University. **Career:** Gospel Television Video, executive producer, public relations; Streetball Partners International, event director; UNC Media of Jacksonville, promotion director; KJMS/KWAM, clear channel communications, promotions director, currently. **Orgs:** NAACP; Jacksonville Together. **Honors/Awds:** City of Jacksonville, Mayor's Office, Proclamation; Jacksonville Sheriff's Office, Community Service Award. **Special Achievements:** Come Together Day, Metropolitan Park, 1992; Martin Luther King Jr Birthday Celebration, Jax Landing, 1992; Support First Coast First, 1992; Come Together Day, Jam 4 Peace, 1994. **Home Addr:** 5400 Julington Creek Rd, Jacksonville, FL 32258.

FREEMAN, ALBERT CORNELIUS, JR.
Educational administrator. **Personal:** Born Mar 21, San Antonio, TX; married Sevara E Clemon. **Educ:** LA City Coll, 1957; Amherst Univ, MA. **Career:** Actor, 1960-; appeared in: The Long Dream, 1960; Kicks & Co, 1961; Tiger Tiger Burning Bright, 1962; The Living Premise, 1963; Trumpets of the Lord, 1963; Blues for Mister Charlie, 1964; Conversations at Midnight, 1964; The Slave, 1964; Dutchman, 1965; Measure for Measure, 1966; Camino Real, 1968; The Dozens, 1969; Look to the Lilies, 1970; Are You Now Or Have You Ever Been, 1972; Medea, 1973; The Poison Tree, 1973; The Great Macdaddy, 1974; Soldier's Play, dir, actor, Howard Univ; movies include: Torpedo Run, 1958; Dutchman, 1967; Finian's Rainbow, 1968; The Detective, 1968; Castle Keep, 1969; The Lost Man, 1969; My Sweet Charlie, 1970, Malcolm X, 1992; One Life to Live, tv series, 17 years; Howard Univ, College of Fine Arts, instructor, chairman, Dept of Drama, currently. **Honors/Awds:** Russwurm Award; Golden Gate Award; Emmy Award for Outstanding Actor in a daytime series, 1979. **Military Serv:** USAF. **Business Addr:** Chairman, Dept of Drama, Howard University, College of Fine Arts, Washington, DC 20059.

FREEMAN, ANTONIO MICHAEL
Professional football player. **Personal:** Born May 27, 1972, Baltimore, MD. **Educ:** Virginia Tech, attended. **Career:** Green Bay Packers, wide receiver, 1995-. **Business Addr:** Professional Football Player, Green Bay Packers, 1265 Lombardi Ave, Green Bay, WI 54304, (414)494-2351.

FREEMAN, CHARLES ELDRIDGE
Judge. **Personal:** Born Dec 12, 1933, Richmond, VA; son of Jeanette Rena Winston Freeman (deceased) and William Isaac Freeman (deceased); married Marylee Voelker Freeman, Aug 27, 1960; children: Kevin. **Educ:** VA Union Univ Richmond VA, BA 1954; John Marshall Law Schl Chicago IL, JD 1962. **Career:** Cook Cty Dept of Public Aid, prop & ins consult 1959-64; Office of Atty Gen Of IL, asst atty gen 1964; State's Attorneys Office, asst state's atty 1964; Bd of Election Commissioners, asst atty 1964-65; IL Industrial Comm, arbitrator 1965-73; IL Commerce Comm, commissioner 1973-76; Circuit Court Cook Cty, elected 1976; First Dist IL Appellate Court, 1986-90; Illinois Supreme Court, justice, 1990-. **Orgs:** Bd dir Conf to Fulfill These Rights; vice pres Englewood Businessmen & Civic League; mem Cook Cty Bar Assc; bd dir Ralph H Metcalfe Youth Fnd; Third Ward Dem HQ; mem Phi Beta Sigma Frat; bd dir Garfield Park Comm Growth Cntr Inc; bd dir Southern Shores Yacht Club 1982-; mem, Chicago Bar Association, Illinois Judge Association, Judicial Council of Illinois, American Judge Association. **Honors/Awds:** Hnrd by Harold Washington Mayor City of Chicago to admin oath of office during swearing in ceremonies 1983, 1987; numerous civic and organizational awards. **Military Serv:** AUS sp/3 1956-58.

FREEMAN, CLAIRE E.
City official. **Personal:** Born Sep 24, 1943, Cleveland, OH; children: Whitney Blair Morgan-Woods, Shani T'Nai. **Educ:** Univ of California-Riverside, BA, sociology/history; Univ of Southern California, MS, urban & regional planning. **Career:** Dept of Housing and Urban Devt, Community Planning and Devt, deputy asst sec; Office of the Secretary of the Defense/Civilian Personnel Policy, deputy asst sec; Dept of Housing and Urban Devel, asst sec for admin; Cuyahoga Metropolitan Housing Authority, CEO, currently. **Honors/Awds:** US Small Bus Adm, State and Local Small Bus Advocate Award, 1992; Southern Christian Leadership Conf, 4th Annual Martin Luther King, Jr Social Justice Crusader of the Year Award, 1992; NAACP, Meritorious Service Award, 1987; Sec of Defense, Medal for Outstanding Public Service Award, 1987, 1989; Housing and Urban Devt, Distinguished Service Medal, 1984; Univ of Southern California, African American Support Group, Outstanding Alumni, 1983. **Business Addr:** CEO, Cuyahoga Metropolitan Housing Authority, 1441 W 25th St, Cleveland, OH 44113, (216)348-5000.

FREEMAN, DAVID CALVIN, SR.
Funeral director. **Personal:** Born Oct 17, 1942, Colerain, NC; married Mabel Butts; children: David Jr, Demetria, Monique. **Educ:** Elizabeth City State Univ, BS 1966; Hampton Univ, 1970. **Career:** Pasquotank Co Schl System, teacher 1966-70; Elizabeth City Pub Schl Sys, teacher, asst principal 1970-79; Walson Funeral Home, Inc, owner/operator 1980-. **Orgs:** State & Natl Funeral Dir & Embalmers Assn, Board of Dir of Skills Inc 1980-85; Northeastern NC Schoolmasters Club, president 1982; NAACP, 1968; Christian Aid, 1982; Corner Stone Missionary Baptist Church, Deacon 1976; Omega Psi Phi, 1983; Eastern Star Lodge; United Supreme Council; SJ Prince Hall, Golden Leaf Lodge 1985; Elizabeth City State Univ, bd of trustees, The Albemarle Board Commissioners, trustee bd. **Honors/Awds:** Award for Expertise in the field of Business 1982; Outstanding Alumni Award, Business 1984; Presidential Citation by the Natl Assn for Eq Opp in Higher Educ, Awd for Appreciation in Recognition of Continued Dedication & Service to Education. **Home Addr:** 404 Speed St, Elizabeth City, NC 27909. **Business Addr:** 504 South Road St, Elizabeth City, NC 27909.

FREEMAN, DENISE
Educational administrator. **Career:** Lincoln County School Board, board member, currently. **Special Achievements:** Only African American school board member in Lincoln County, GA. **Business Addr:** School Board Member, Lincoln County School Board, Lincolnton, GA 30817, (706)359-3742.

FREEMAN, DIANE S.
Educator, educational administrator. **Personal:** Born in Springfield, MA; divorced; children: Urraca Jorge, Joaquin Arturo, Javier Akin. **Educ:** Central CT State Univ, BA Anthropology 1970; Univ of CT, MSW Casework 1977; Wellesley Coll, Cert Mgmt 1983. **Career:** Univ of Hartford, social work consul 1977, dir sociological & multicultural studies prog 1977-78, asst dir for admin 1978-80; New Hampshire College, Connecticut, instructor, 1979-82; Eastern Connecticut State University, instructor, 1981; Hartford Bd of Educ, therapist, special educ, 1989-91; Trinity Coll, asst dir, career counseling, 1981-84; Greater Hartford Community College, dir, special svcs/ASTRA, 1984-87; Manchester Community & Technical College, Social Division, assistant professor, social service program, coordinator, 1987-. **Orgs:** Students of Color, Trinity College, consultant, 1984-85; New England Minority Women Admin in Higher Ed, 1984-86. **Business Addr:** Coordinator, Assistant Professor, Social Science Division, Manchester Community & Technical College, PO Box 1046, Manchester, CT 06045-1046.

FREEMAN, EDWARD ANDERSON
Cleric. **Personal:** Born Jun 11, 1914, Atlanta, GA; married Ruth; children: Edward Jr, Constance, William. **Educ:** Clark Coll, Ab 1939; Central Bapt Sem, BD 1949; Central Sem, ThM 1950, ThD 1953. **Career:** NAACP Kansas City, chaplain 1949-54; Argonne Post Amer Legion, chaplain 1947-55; Interracial Interdenom Ministerial Alliance, 1955; CCSA, pres 1957-58; Austell Publ School, teacher, principal; First Bapt Church, pastor. **Orgs:** Mem City Planning Commiss 1954-; chmn City Planning Commiss KC 1968-; pres Missionary Bapt State Conv KS 1957-82, Natl Sunday School & Bapt Training Union Congress 1968-83; pastor 1st Bapt Church 1946-; vice pres Baptist World Alliance 1980-85; life mem NAACP; bd mem Oper PUSH; mem Study Comm Ch Doctrines & Coop Bodies World Bapt Alliance; bd mem Natl Council Churches, Natl Bapt Conv USA Inc. **Honors/Awds:** Man of the Year Womans C of C Wyandotte Cty 1950; Natl Bapt Conv India 1955; Law Day Awd 1973; Outstanding Alumnus Awd Central Bapt Sem 1972; publ "Epoch of Negro Bapt & the Foreign Mission Bd" Central Sem Press 1953; "The Eighth Century Prophets" Sunday School Publ Bd 1960, "Bapt Jubilee Advance" 1964, "Bapt Rels with Other Christians" 1974; Doctor of Divinity, OK School of Religion, 1978, Central Baptist Seminary, 1987. **Military Serv:** AUS maj 1941-46; Bronze Stars. **Business Addr:** Pastor, First Baptist Church, 500 Nebraska Ave, Kansas City, KS 66101.

FREEMAN, EDWARD C.
Attorney. **Personal:** Born in Beta, NC; widowed; children: Mrs. **Educ:** Knoxville Coll, AB; TX So Univ Sch of Law, LLB JD; Howard Univ Sch of Law, attnd legal sem; Univ of MI Sch of Law; Univ of TN Law Sch; Harvard Univ Sch of Law. **Career:** Pvt Prac, atty couns 1951-; social worker 18 yrs; TN Valley Auth, mail clerk. **Orgs:** Dir Nat Yth & Adm; dir Social Welfare for Mil Manhattan Dist; mem Nat Bar Assn; mem TN & TX Bar; licensed to prac before all State Cts Fed Ct & Supreme Ct

of US; v chmn Knox Co Tax Equal Bd; Knox Co Dem Primary Bd; deL Dem Nat Conv 1976; mem steering com election of Jimmy Carter; mem TN Voters Coun; charter mem Soc Workers of Am; charter mem Magnolia Fed Savings & Loan Assn; former scout master; mem Sect of Am Bar Assn on Continuing Legal Edn; mem Am Bar Assn; Knoxville Bar & TN Bar Assn; exec bd NAACP; Omega Psi Phi Frat; Elks & Mason; exec com Dem Party; Mount Zion BaptCh; hon trst Juvenile Ct for Knox Co TN.

FREEMAN, EVELYN. See Obituaries section.

FREEMAN, FRANKIE M.
Attorney. **Personal:** Born Nov 24, 1916, Danville, VA; married Shelby; children: Shelbe Freeman Bullock. **Educ:** Howard U, LLB 1947; Hampton Inst, 1933-36. **Career:** US Treas Dept, clerk 1942-44; Office of Price Admin, statistician 1944-45; Coll of the Fingerlakes, instr business law 1947-49; attorney at law, 1949-56; Freeman Whitfield Montgomery Staples and White, partner/attorney. **Orgs:** Mem US Commn on Civil Rights; assoc gen counsel St Louis Housing & Land Clearance Authorities; mem Amer, Natl, Mound City Bar Assns; Lawyers' Assn of St Louis; Natl Assn of Housing & Redevelopment Officials; Natl Housing Conf; League of Women Voters; former pres Delta Sigma Theta Sor; bd dir Natl Council of Negro Women; bd mem St Louis Branch NAACP, United Way of St Louis; mem bd of trustees Howard Univ, Laclede Sch of Law; 1st vice pres Natl Council on the Aging; bd mem St Louis Region Natl Conf of Christians and Jews, The Amer Red Cross, St Louis Bi-State Chapt, St Louis Urban League, Gateway Chap of Links Inc; mem trustee bd Washington Tabernacle Baptist Church. **Honors/Awds:** Recipient of numerous honors including Outstanding Citizen Award Mound City Press Club 1953; Women of Achievement Award Natl Council of Negro Women 1956, 1965; Woman of Achievement Awd in Public Affairs St Louis Globe Democrat; Outstanding Alumni Awd for Distinguished Career Hampton Inst; Outstanding Alumni Awd Howard Univ; Outstanding Achievement Awds Omega Psi Phi Frat, Iota Phi Lambda Sor, Links Inc; Mary Church Terrell Awd Delta Sigma Theta Sor; Hon DL Degree Univ of MO 1975; honored by Dollars and Sense Magazine as one of America's Top 100 Women 1985; Hon DHL Harris-Stowe Coll 1986. **Business Addr:** Attorney at Law, 3920 Lindell Blvd, St Louis, MO 63112.

FREEMAN, GREGORY BRUCE
Journalist. **Personal:** Born Aug 18, 1956, St Louis, MO; son of Doris Bradley Freeman and Frederic William Freeman; married Elizabeth Louise Johnson Freeman, Jul 7, 1979; children: William Gregory. **Educ:** Washington University, St Louis, MO, BA, 1978. **Career:** St Louis American, St Louis, MO, associate editor, 1977-78; Oakland Press, Pontiac, MI, reporter, 1978-79; Belleville News-Democrat, Belleville, IL, reporter, 1979-80; St Louis Post-Dispatch, St Louis, MO, columnist, 1980-. **Orgs:** Regional director, National Association for Black Journalists, 1986-91; president, Greater St Louis Association of Black Journalists, 1983, 1988-89; president, St Louis Society of Professional Journalists, 1989-91; president, Press Club of Metropolitan St Louis, 1991-94; fellow, Multicultural Management Program, 1987, director, 1993-94; chairman, Press Club of Metropolitan St Louis, 1994-96; fellow, Leadership St Louis, 1984. **Honors/Awds:** Excellence Award, Missouri Association for Social Welfare, 1990; Journalist of the Year, Greater St Louis Assn of Black Journalists, 1987; Black Excellence in Journalism, Greater St Louis Assn of Black Journalists, 1982-86, 1991-96; UPI Award, United Press International, 1984. **Business Addr:** Columnist, St Louis Post-Dispatch, 900 N Tucker Blvd, St Louis, MO 63101, (314)340-8157.

FREEMAN, HAROLD P.
Director of surgery. **Personal:** Born Mar 2, 1933, Washington, DC; son of Lucille Freeman and Clyde Freeman; married Artholian C; children: Harold Paul, Neale Palmer. **Educ:** Catholic Univ of Amer, AB 1954; Howard Med School, MD 1958. **Career:** Howard Univ Hosp, intern 1958-59, resd gen surgery 1959-64; Sloane Kettering Cancer Ctr, resd 1964-67; Columbia Presbyterian Hosp, assoc attending surgeon 1974; Harlem Hosp Ctr, attending surgeon 1974-, dir of surgery; Columbia University, professor of clinical surgery, 1989. **Orgs:** Mem Soc of Surgical Oncology 1975-; bd of dir Amer Cancer Soc 1978-; medical dir Breast Examination Ctr of Harlem 1979; chmn Natl Adv Comm on Cancer in the Socio-Economically Disadvantaged Amer Cancer Soc 1986-88; Exec Council of Soc of Surgical Oncology l987-89; Governor of Amer Coll Surgeons l988; natl pres Amer Cancer Soc l988-89; elected to Alpha Omega Alpha (honorary medical soc) l989; member, Executive Committee of American College of Surgeons 1990; President's Cancer Panel, chairman, 1991-94. **Honors/Awds:** Harris Awd for Outstanding Gentlemen Cath Univ 1954; Prize in Psychaitry Howard Univ 1958; Daniel Hal Williams Awd Outstanding Achievement as Chief Resident Howard Univ Hosp 1964; Natl Boys Singles Tennis Champion Amer Tennis Assoc 1948; Honorary Doctor of Science: Albany School of Medicine, 1989, Niagara University, 1989, Adelphi University, 1989; Catholic University, Honorary Doctor of Science, 1989. **Business Addr:** Dir of Surgery, Harlem Hospital Center, 135th & Lenox Ave, New York, NY 10037.

FREEMAN, KENNETH DONALD
Accountant. **Personal:** Born Dec 8, 1912, Oakland, CA; son of Florence Francis Carr and Herbert Reid Freeman; married Amelia Anna Tyler Freeman, Dec 8, 1936; children: Kenneth Melvin, Donald Tyler, Lionel William, Shirley Anna. **Educ:** Attended, Merritt Bus Sch, Lincoln Law Sch, Univ of CA Extension, US Treasury Dept of Accounting Courses 1932-42. **Career:** Ken Freeman's Californiana, orchestra leader 1931-36; IRS, dep collector 1942-51; Self-employed, public accountant 1952-. **Orgs:** Mem Gov Adv Commn on Children & Youth 1964-65; mem bd of dirs CA State Central Comm Exec Bd 1964-70; exec bd mem CA State Dem Central Com 1964-70; mem Alameda Co Instn Commn 1966-70; mem Alameda Co Assessment Appeals Bd 1970-74; mem Alameda Co Commn for Prevention of Juvenile Delinquents 1972-73; former diocese social justice commn Hanna Boys Ctr Sonoma Co 1972-78; pres E Bay Chap Soc of CA Accountants; mem Natl Assoc of Black Accountants Inc; member, California State Board of Accountancy, 1979-85, vice pres, 1981. **Business Addr:** Public Accountant, 3426 Pierson St, Oakland, CA 94619.

FREEMAN, KERLIN, JR.
Educator (retired). **Personal:** Born Sep 24, 1930, Chelsea, MA; son of Lucille and Kerlin Freeman; married E Juanita Maybin; children: Leslie R, Beverly F, Alan K. **Educ:** Metro State Coll Denver Co, BA Elem Ed 1975; Lesley Coll Cambridge MA, MA Computers in Ed 1985. **Career:** NAACP, human relationa com 1976-82, pres 1977-82; Xi Pi Chapter Omega Psi Phi, recorder 1977-81; Colorado Springs Dist #11, elementary school teacher, retired, NEA director, 1990-92; XI Chapter Omega Psi Phi, vice baselius, 1986-90. **Orgs:** Chmn human rel comm City of CO Springs 1983-85; chmn minority caucus CO Ed Assoc 1982-; mem NEA, CEA, CSTA, United Teaching Professional CO Football Officials Assoc, Black Ed Dist 11; del Dem Natl Conv 1976; mem Intl Assoc Approved Basketball Officials 1973-92; Omega Psi Phi, Xi Pi Chapter, basileus, 1991-94; NEA, board of directors, 1990-91; CEA, board of directors, 1990-91; Colorado Springs Education Association, board of directors, 1985-91; CSEA, regional director, 1991-92; CEA, Ethnic Minority Advisory Council, at-large director, 1991-92. **Honors/Awds:** Voted 1 of 10 Most Influential Blacks in CO Springs. **Military Serv:** USAF Msgt 1950-71; Non-Commd Officer of the Year USAF-ADC 1970; Meritorious Serv Medal AF 1971.

FREEMAN, LAURETTA
Professional basketball player. **Personal:** Born Mar 17, 1971; children: Jamie. **Educ:** Auburn Univ, bachelor's degree in business administration. **Career:** Atlanta Glory, forward, 1996-. **Business Addr:** Professional Basketball Player, Atlanta Glory, 2100 Powers Ferry Rd, Ste 400, Atlanta, GA 30339, (770)541-9017.

FREEMAN, LELABELLE CHRISTINE
Physician. **Personal:** Born Oct 27, 1923, Chicago, IL; daughter of Ella Washington Freeman and Henry C Freeman; children: Christine Creary, James E Robinson Jr. **Educ:** Spelman College, BA 1944; Howard Univ Medical School, MD 1949. **Career:** Cook County School of Nursing, pediatrics instructor, 1952; Howard Univ Medical School, pediatrics instructor, 1952-53; private practice pediatrician 1953-77; City of Cleveland Well Baby Clinic, clinic physician, 1953-57; East 35th St Clinic, clinic physician, 1953-63; University Hospitals of Cleveland, medical staff, 1953-; M etropolitan General Hospital of Cleveland, medical staff, 1953-63 ; Health Resources Cleveland, clinic physician, 1975-77; Cuyahoga Co Bd of Health contracting physician, 1977-8?. **Orgs:** Academy of Medicine of Cleveland, Family Practice Liaison Committee, 1964-65; Mt Pleasant Community Ctr, bd of trustees; Cuyahoga Co Bd of Mental Retardation, 1967-73; PTA, Health and Safety, 1961-70; Cedar Branch YMCA, child consultant, 1954-1961; Northern Ohio Pediatric Society, charter member. **Honors/Awds:** Numerous awards and citations including: Consortium of Doctors, Seminole Humanitarian Award, 1993, Relationships Award, 1994. **Special Achievements:** Articles include: ''Erythromycin in Treatment of Pyoderma in Children,'' Journal of Pediatrics, vol 42, no 6, pp 669-672, June 1953; ''Influenzal Meningitis Treated Successfully with Polymyxin B,'' Illinois Medical Journal, vol 102, no 3, pp 205-207, Sept 1952; ''Incidence of 'Subclinical' Trichinosis in Children,'' AMA American Journal of Diseases of Children, vol 87, no 4, pp 464-467, April 1954; ''Gastric Suction in Infants Delivered by Cesarean Sections; Role in Prevention of Respiratory Complaints,'' AMA American Journal of Diseases of Children, vol 87, pp 570-574, May 1954; ''Studies in Sickle Cell Anemia: Effect of Age (Maturation) on Incidence of the Sickling Phenomenom,'' Pediatrics, vol 14, no 3, pp 209-214, Sept 1954; ''Observations on Trichinosis: Report of Community Outbreak,'' AMA American Journal of Diseases of Children, vol 89, no 2, pp 194-198, Feb 1955. **Home Addr:** 16306 Aldersyde, Shaker Heights, OH 44120.

FREEMAN, LOUIS
Pilot. **Career:** Southwest Airlines, chief pilot, currently. **Honors/Awds:** Distinguished Career Achievement Award. **Business Addr:** Chief Pilot, Southwest Airlines, Attn: Personnel, 5700 S Cicero Ave Ste B8, Chicago, IL 60638, 800-435-9792.

FREEMAN, MARIANNA
Women's basketball coach. **Personal:** Born Jul 30, 1957, Wilmington, DE; daughter of Marion L Freeman. **Educ:** Cheyney Univ, BS, 1979; Slippery Rock Univ, pursuing MS. **Career:** Delstate Coll, head coach, 1981-83; Univ of Iowa, asst coach, 1983-93; Syracuse Univ, head coach, 1993-. **Orgs:** Black Coaches Assn; Women's Basketball Coaches Assn; National Council of Negro Women; chairperson, NCAA Rules Committee. **Honors/Awds:** Cheyney Univ, Hall of Fame, 1993. **Business Addr:** Head Coach, Women's Basketball, Syracuse University, Comstock Ave, Manley Fieldhouse, Syracuse, NY 13244, (315)443-3761.

FREEMAN, MCKINLEY HOWARD, SR.
Elected official. **Personal:** Born Aug 27, 1920, Detroit, MI; married Virginia Burgen; children: McKinley Jr, William Randall. **Educ:** Lawrence Tech, diesel engr 1938-40; Slade-Gragg, upholstry school 1946-47. **Career:** US Postal Service, special delivery messenger 1940-42; Great Lakes Ins Co, agent 1945-47; Wyatt & McCullars, real estate sales 1955-58; Dept of Transportation, driver-instructor 1948-78. **Orgs:** AL-#181 post commander 1947-48; consultant Econo Group Travel 1978-; VFW #5315 1982-; vice president Democratic Party Newaygo County 1984-; exec board Democratic Party 9th district 1985-; life mem NAACP, VFW 1986-; Newaygo Cnty Planning Commissioner 1985; State Central Democratic Comm 9th Dist 1987-; co-chmn Newaygo Cnty Sesquicentannial Committee 1986-87; exec committee, Newaygo County Democratic Party 1988; special deputy sheriff, Newaygo County 1989-; commissioner, Newaygo County Planning and Zoning Commission, 1991-93; commissioner, Merrill Township Zoning, 1990-; commissioner, vice chairman, Newaygo County Parks & Recreation, 1991-93. **Honors/Awds:** Certificate Special Award for Political Action from VFW 1984; selected as sr citizen of 9th dist democratic party to attend Jefferson, Jackson dinner 1985. **Military Serv:** USMC 1st sgt 1942-45. **Home Addr:** PO Box 179, Brohman, MI 49312-0179.

FREEMAN, MORGAN
Actor. **Personal:** Born Jun 1, 1937, Memphis, TN; son of Mayme Edna Revere Freeman and Morgan Porterfield Freeman (deceased); married Jeanette Adair Bradshow, Oct 22, 1967 (divorced 1979); children: Alphonse, Saifoulaye, Deena, Morgana. **Educ:** Los Angeles City College, theater arts, 1959-60. **Career:** Actor, stage appearances include: The Nigger-Lovers, 1967, Hello Dolly, 1967, Jungle of the Cities, 1969, The Recruiting Officer, 1969, Scuba Duba, 1969, Purlie, 1970, Black Visions, 1972, Sisyphus and the Blue-Eyed Cyclops, 1975, Cockfight, 1977, The Last Street Play, 1977, The Mighty Gents, 1978, White Pelicans, 1978, Coriolanus, 1979, Julius Caesar, 1979, Mother Courage and Her Children, 1980, Othello, 1982, All's Well That Ends Well, 1982, Buck, 1982, The World of Ben Caldwell, 1982, The Gospel at Colonus, 1983, Medea and the Doll, 1984, Driving Miss Daisy, 1987, The Taming of the Shrew, 1990; film appearances include: Who Says I Can't Ride a Rainbow?, 1971, Brubaker, 1980, Eyewitness, 1980, Harry and Son, 1983, Teachers, 1984, Marie, 1985, That Was Then... This Is Now, 1985, Streetart, 1987, Clean and Sober, 1988, Glory, 1989, Lean on Me, 1989, Driving Miss Daisy, 1989, Johnny Handsome, 1989, Robin Hood: Prince of Thieves, 1991, Unforgiven, 1992; Bopha, dir, 1993; The Shawshank Redemption, 1994; Outbreak, 1995; Seven, 1995; Kiss the Girls, 1997; Chain Reaction, 1997; Deep Impact, 1998. TV: Electric Company, 1971-76, Another World, 1982, Hollow Image, 1979, Attica, 1980, The Marva Collins Story, 1981, The Atlanta Child Murders, 1985, Resting Place, 1986, Flight for Life, 1987, Clinton and Nadine, 1988. **Orgs:** Actor's Equity Assn; Screen Actors Guild; American Federation of Television and Radio Artists. **Honors/Awds:** Clarence Derwent Award, Drama Desk Award, Outstanding Featured Actor in a Play, Tony Award nomination, The Mighty Gents, 1978; Obie Award, Driving Miss Daisy, 1987; New York Film Critics Circle Award, Los Angeles Film Critics Award, National Society of Films Critics Award, Golden Globe nomination, Academy Award nomination, Street Smart, 1987; Obie Awards, Mother Courage and Her Children, Coriolanus, The Gospel at Colonus; Academy Award nomination, Best Actor, Driving Miss Daisy, 1991; NAACP Image Award, Motion Picture Supporting Actress, 1998. **Military Serv:** US Air Force, 1955-59.

FREEMAN, NELSON R.
Educator (retired). **Personal:** Born Dec 30, 1924, Lake Wales, FL; son of Audra McRae Freeman (deceased) and Burley B Freeman (deceased); married Willie Mae Freeman; children: Pickens A Patterson Jr, Albert B Patterson. **Educ:** Savannah State Coll, BS Bus Admin 1948; Columbia Univ, MA Guidance & Student Personnel 1956. **Career:** Savannah State Coll, veterans counselor 1948-53, acting dean of men 1953-54, dean of men 1954-56, personnel dir 1956-65, dean of students 1965-72, placement dir 1972-76, acting dean of students 1976-81, placement dir 1981-84, acting vice pres for student affairs & placement dir 1984-86, vice pres for student affairs, retired. **Orgs:** Chatham Co Bd of Registrars 1973-77; Helpline Vol Counselor 1976-78; Tax Equalization Bd of Chatham Co 1978; Southern Coll Personnel Assn; Natl Assn of Personnel Workers; Natl Assn of Student Personnel Admin; Southern Coll Placement Assn, GA College Placement Assn; GA College Personnel Assn; GA Assn for Counselor Education and Supervision;

Alpha Phi Alpha Frat; Eureka Lodge of Free and Accepted Masons; Butler Presby Church; former mem of Bd of Management, May St YMCA; former mem of Bd of Dir Family Counseling Center of Savannah; former mem Minority Employ Oppor Comm; former comm Savannah Adult Softball League; Southern Assoc for Coll Student Affairs; mem Frogs Inc, Wolves Club, Mules Club, Savannah Guardsmen Inc; bd of dir Rape Crisis Center; volunteer,Victim's Witness, District Attorns Office 1987-. **Honors/Awds:** Kappa Delta Pi Honor Soc 1956; Chap Pres Leadership Awd, Alpha Phi Alpha Frat Inc 1962; Man of the Year Awd, Beta Phi Lambda Chap, Alpha Phi Alpha Frat Inc 1963; Nelson R Freeman Honor Soc, Wayne Co Training Sch Jesup GA 1965, Alumni Leadership Awd 1965; Natl Urban League Fellowship with Chas Pfizer & Co 1966; Alpha Phi Omega Serv Frat 1966; self-study consultant and served on visiting comm for the Southern Assn of Colleges and Schools; Wayne County Training School Alumni Leadership Awd Jesup GA 1965. **Military Serv:** USNR personnel yeoman-in-charge, legal yeoman; 1943-46. **Home Addr:** 626 W 45th St, PO Box 22092, Savannah, GA 31405.

FREEMAN, PAUL D.
Symphony orchestra conductor. **Personal:** Born Jan 2, 1936, Richmond, VA; son of Mr & Mrs L H Freeman; married Cornelia Perry; children: Douglas Cornelia. **Educ:** Eastman School of Music, BMus 1956, MMus 1957, PhD Theory 1963; Hochschule Fur Musik Berlin, additional studies; Orchestral & Operatic Conducting with Prof Ewald Lindemann 1957-59; L'Ecole Monteux with Pierre Monteux; Amer Symphony Orchestra League Workshop with Dr Richard Lert. **Career:** Hochstein Music School, Rochester NY, dir 1960-66; Opera Theatre of Rochester, music dir 1961-66; San Francisco Community Music Ctr, dir 1966-68; San Francisco Little Symphony, music dir 1967-68; Dallas Symphony Orchestra, former assoc conductor 1968-70; Detroit Symphony, conductor-in-residence 1970-79; Saginaw Symphony, music dir; Helsinki Philharmonic Orch, principal guest conductor; Columbia Black Composers Series, artistic dir; numerous guest appearances in the US, Austria, England, Germany, Denmark, Norway, Sweden, Poland, Italy, Russia, Mexico, Israel, Finland/Yugoslavia; numerous recordings; Chicago Sinfonietta, music dir, conductor 1987-; Victoria, BC, Canada Symphony, conductor 1979-89; music dir emeritus Victoria Symphony Orchestra, 1988-; Czech National Symphony Orchestra, Prague, currently. **Honors/Awds:** Winner, Dimitri Mitropolous Intl Conductors Competition, 1967; Special Spoleto Awd to conduct Tristan und Isolde, 1968 Festival of Two Worlds; Distinguished Alumni Citation, Univ of Rochester, 1975; Distinguished Citation Award, United Negro Coll Fund; Koussevitzky Intl Recording Award, 1974; included in Time magazine's Top Five Classical Records Listing, 1974; nominated for Ebony Arts Award, 1989; Dominican Univ, LHD, 1994; Loyola Univ, LHD, 1998. **Business Addr:** Music Director, Chicago Sinfonietta, 105 W Adams St, Chicago, IL 60603.

FREEMAN, PRESTON GARRISON
Educational administrator (retired). **Personal:** Born Apr 12, 1933, Washington, DC; married Jean Marie Hall; children: Jacqueline, Michelle, Nicole, Monica. **Educ:** Morgan State Coll, BS 1955; George Washington Univ, MA 1961; Catholic Univ of Amer, PhD 1974. **Career:** Washington DC Public Schools, asst supt 1975-91, asst supt 1972-74, exec asst 1969-72, dir 1966-69, counselor 1963-66, teacher 1955-63. **Orgs:** Mem, Amer Assn of School Admins; mem Assn for Supvr & Curriculum Devel; mem Phi Delta Kapp; mem Kappa Alpha Psi Fraternity; vice chmn Health & Welfare Council 1965-70; vice chmn Prince Georges Comm Action Com 1967-70; mem Child Day Care Assn 1968-70; Council of the Great Cities Fellow 1970-71; Exec Internship. **Military Serv:** AASA Arlington, VA 1973-74. **Business Addr:** DC Pub Sch 3rd Douglas Sts N E, Washington, DC 20002.

FREEMAN, ROBERT TURNER, JR.
Management consultant (retired). **Personal:** Born Apr 25, 1918, New York, NY; son of Eva Freeman and Robert Freeman Sr; married Mary Frances Jones; children: Veronica Coleman, Robert III. **Educ:** Lincoln Univ, BA 1941; NY Univ Grad Sch, attended 1941-42. **Career:** WPB, statistician 1942-45; United Mut Life Ins Co, vice pres actuary 1945-55; Ghana Ins Co Ltd, founder mng dir 1955-62; Ghana Genl Ins Co Ltd, 1959-62; Providence Ins Co Liberia, consult actuary 1958-59; Gr Nigeria Ins Co Ltd Lagos, dir founder 1960-63; Ghana State Ins Corp Accra, mng dir 1962-65; Nigerian Broadcasting Corp Lagos, 1964-65; Peace Corps, assoc dir for mgmt 1965-66; USA, consult minority affairs 1966-68; Freeman Cole & Assocs Inc, pres 1966-68; Bur Africa AID, dir office capital devel & finance 1968-71; Govt Ethiopia, ins adviser 1971-73; Consumers United Ins Co, pres chmn of the bd 1973-83; Freeman Intl Insurance Co, pres & chmn of the bd 1984-86. **Orgs:** Mem Lafayette Fed Credit Union 1966-; trustee Solebury Sch PA; mem NAACP Task Force on Africa; trustee Lincoln Univ PA; dir & 1st vice pres Girl Scouts of the Nations Capitol; dir Children's Hosp; dir Richardson Bellows & Henry; chairman, Phelps Stokes Fund; mem Lincoln Univ Alumni Assn; mem Alpha Phi Alpha; Rotarian; pres chmn of bd Freeman Intl Ins Co; mem Mayor's Fire Adv Comm DC, Mayor's Intl Trade & Investment Comm; mem Economic Develop Comm Conf of Black Mayors; dir Riggs Natl Bank; trustee Davis Memorial Goodwill Indust 1982-84; executive director, District of Columbia Life & Health Insurance Guaranty Association, 1992-95. **Honors/Awds:** Distinguished Alumni Awd NAFCO 1986; Hon LLD Lincoln Univ PA 1987; Bob Freeman Clinic Bldg, State Insurance Corp of Ghana 1987. **Home Addr:** 3001 Veazey Terr NW, Washington, DC 20008.

FREEMAN, RONALD J.
Judge. **Personal:** Born Aug 17, 1947, Winslow, NJ; married Carmen Martinez. **Educ:** Rutgers Law Sch, JD 1972; Lincoln U, BA 1969. **Career:** Legal counsel, comm legal serv phil 1973; Camden Reg Legal Serv Inc, legal counsel 1972-73; Glassboro State Coll, adj 1973; NJ Dept Law & Pub Safety & Div Civil Rights in coop Rutgers Law Sch Clinic Prog, senior field representative aide 1972; NJ Dept Law & Public Safety Div on Civil Rights in coop Rutgers State Univ Sch Law Clinical Prog, 1971; Rutgers State Univ Coll Cntr, staff asst 1970; New Jersey Supreme Court, State board of bar examiners, 1989-; Superior Court of NJ, judge, currently. **Orgs:** Bar of the Supreme Ct PA 1973; Bar of the US District Ct E Dist PA 1973; Bar of the US Ct Appeals Third Ciruit 1974; Bar of the Supreme Ct NJ 1974; Bar of the US District Ct District NJ 1974; PA Bar Assn; Amer Bar Assn; Nat Bar Assn; Phil Bar Assn; Nat Conf Black Lawyers; Phi Alpha Delta; NJ Bar Assn. **Business Addr:** Judge, Superior Court of NJ, Camden County Hall of Justice, 101 S 5th St, Camden, NJ 08103, (609)428-6600.

FREEMAN, RUBY E.
Registered nurse. **Personal:** Born Apr 10, 1921, Port Arthur, TX; married Charles; children: Charles, III, Cheryl, Stanley. **Educ:** Harlem Sch Nursing, RN 1942; NY U, BS 1945; Lamar U, Post Bacclaureate & Graduate Study. **Career:** Pt Arthur Ind Sch Dist, sch nurse Registered Profl, retired 1982; Pt Arthur Indp Sch Dist, resourcer; Lincoln Hosp, med supr 1945-47; Grasslands Hosp, head nurse 1951-56; Nursing Co-Ed Post, explorer advisor. **Orgs:** Former mem, Youth adv Jack & Jill Am Inc Natl Educ Assn; Texas State Tchrs Assn; Texas Classroom Tchrs Assn; NAACP; Delta Sigma Theta Inc; Three Rivers Council BSA; Ladies Aux Knights of Peter Claver; adv com Manpower Devel Training Act; numerous Mayoral & chamber commerce com; membership com Comm Concert Assn 5 yrs; mem Port Arthur Little Theatre; adv bd TX Artists & Museum 1975-97; Port Arthur Hist Soc; named to Port Arthur's Citizen's Adv Com; charged with formulating recommendations for spending $132 million fed comm devel funds for 1st of 4-yr city project; 1 of 40 Texans appointed to serv on Adv Council of TX Employment Commn 1975-; St James Cath Ch; mem Pt Arthur Centennial Planning Comm, 1996-; volunteer, Museum of the Gulf Coast, 1995-. **Honors/Awds:** Awarded Cert Apprec Women in Comm Serv 1969; Outstanding Comm Leader Delta 1973; cited by Am Black Outreach 1st black woman in TX 1970-74; served 2 yrs TX Employment Commn; among first group black women to appear Woman's World annual. **Business Addr:** 401 W 12 St, Port Arthur, TX 77640.

FREEMAN, RUGES R.
Educator. **Personal:** Born Feb 25, 1917, St Louis, MO; son of Willie C Barr Freeman and Ruges R Freeman; married Maxine Carter; children: Wilatrel. **Educ:** So IL Univ, BE 1935; Univ IL, MA 1936; Washington Univ, PhD 1972; Attended, Stowe Tchrs Coll, Univ Chicago, St Louis Univ. **Career:** Dunbar HS, tchr 1936-38; Chicago Relief Admin, caseworker 1938-40; Vashon HS, tchr 1940-47, boys counselor & admin asst 1947-50; Dunbar Elem, asst/prin 1950-51; Carver Elem, Dumas Elem, Cote Brilliante Elem, principal 1951-64; Sumner HS, asst prin 1964-68; Beaumont HS, principal 1965-66; Harrison Elem, principal 1968-73; Teacher Corps, asst dir 1977-79, dir 1979-82; Secondary Student Teaching So IL Univ, assoc prof & coord 1973-76, prof 1982, emeritus 1983. **Orgs:** Bd dir United Church Men 1972-; vice pres Social Health Assn Gr St Louis 1972-; dir tchr corps Prog Dev Splst 1977-79; mem Dean's Adv Council 1978-81; bd dir Nursery Found 1978-81; mem SW IL Supt Conf 1978-; mem 1979-81, chmn 1981-82 Presidential Scholars; dir Tchr Corps 1979-82; mem Natl Soc Study Educ, Amer Educ Rsch Assn, Natl Educ Assn, Assn Supervision & Curriculum Devel, Phi Delta Kappa, Alpha Phi Alpha, Gaylords, Gnashers; St James AME Ch. **Military Serv:** AUS 1944. **Home Addr:** 8027 Bennett Ave, St Louis, MO 63117.

FREEMAN, SHIRLEY WALKER
Librarian. **Personal:** Born Jun 7, 1951, Jackson, MS; daughter of Louise Luster Walker and Leroy Walker Sr; married N Trent Freeman, Aug 15, 1992; children: Jerry, Lamont, Courtney. **Educ:** Livingstone College, 1968-70; Tougaloo College, bachelor's, mathematics, 1973; University of Illinois, Urbana-Champaign, MLS, 1978. **Career:** Rowland Medical Library, assistant librarian, 1972-76; University of Illinois, graduate teaching assistant, 1976-78; Champaign Public Library, branch manager, librarian, 1977-83; Columbus Metropolitan Library, branch manager, librarian, 1983-. **Orgs:** Delta Sigma Theta Sorority, 1969-; American Library Association; United Methodist Church; Assault on Illiteracy Program, 1989-. **Business Addr:** Branch Manager, Livingston Branch, Columbus Metro Library, 3434 Livingston Ave, Columbus, OH 43227, (614)645-2330.

FREEMAN, THOMAS F.
Clergyman, educator. **Personal:** Born Jun 27, 1920, Richmond, VA; married; children: Thomas, Jr, Carter, Carlotta. **Educ:** Univ of Nigeria, Lagos; Univ of Ghana, Ghana E Africa; VA Union U, BA 1939; Andover Newton Theol Sch, BD 1942; Univ of Chicago, PhD 1948; Howard U, further study; Boston U, further study; Univ of Vienna, Austria, further study; African U. **Career:** Weekend Coll, dean; TX Southern Univ, dir continuing educ; Model Cities Training Ctr TSU, dir 1970-74; Coll of Arts & Sci TSU, asst dean 1968-70, dept head Philosophy 1950-67; Carmel Baptist Church, minister 1944-50; VA Union Univ, prof Practical Theology 1944-49; Monumental Baptist Church Chicago, assoc minister 1942-44; Pleasant St Baptist Church, Westerly RI, minister 1940-44; Concord Baptist Church, Boston MA, asst minister 1939-40; Mt Horem Baptist Church; Rice Univ, visiting prof. **Orgs:** Pres Alpha Kappa Mu Nat Honor Soc 1962-66; alumni dir Alpha Kappa Mu Nat Honor Soc 1966; bd dir Andover Newton Alumni Assn; bd dir Assn of Churches; mem NAACP; mem Boy Scouts; Urban League. **Honors/Awds:** Recip Clarke Scholarship VA Union Univ 1939; turner fellowship Andover Newton 1939-42; fellowship Univ of C 1942-46; Univ Divinty Univ Faculty Mem of Yr 1950-51; TSU-PI CC Award TSU 1974; book Choices of The Pew 1963; Am Press co-author "From Separation to Special Designation" 1975.

FREEMAN, WALTER EUGENE
Manufacturing manager (retired). **Personal:** Born Apr 28, 1928, West Hartford, CT; son of Clara L Taylor Freeman and Walter J Freeman; married Shirley M Davis Freeman, Nov 1, 1952; children: Walter E Jr, Brian M. **Educ:** Virginia State Coll, BS 1950. **Career:** Pratt & Whitney Aircraft Co, supv metalurgical test 1962-70, supv metrology 1970-77, asst chief nondestructive test 1977-83, chief purchase matl insp, beginning 1983. **Orgs:** Mem Alpha Phi Alpha Frat 1946-; sec bd of dirs CT Savings & Loan Assoc 1968-79; mem Windsor Human Relations Commn 1976-80; dir Womens League Day Care Ctr 1977-; mem Sigma Pi Phi Frat 1982-; natl mem chmn Amer Soc for Metals 1984-86. **Honors/Awds:** Black and Hispanic Achievers Awd Hartford CT YMCA 1981; Fund Raiser Awd Beta Sigma Lambda Chap Alpha Phi Alpha 1985. **Military Serv:** AUS Cpl, 2 yrs. **Home Addr:** 4 On the Green, Windsor, CT 06095.

FREEMAN, WARREN L.
Military official. **Personal:** Born in Jackson, GA; son of Sara Freeman; married Barbara Ann; children: Kevin, Brandon. **Educ:** National-Louis Univ, MS; Pacific-Western Univ, BBA. **Career:** US Army, commanding general of DC National Guard, currently. **Orgs:** Kappa Alpha Psi; USAWC Alumni Assoc; NGAUS; AUSA. **Honors/Awds:** COM; NSM (4); ARCOM (4); Outstanding Young Men of America. **Special Achievements:** Youngest DC commander; two-star general who bypassed the rank of a one-star general, which is normally required in the service. **Military Serv:** US Army National Guard, major general. **Business Addr:** Commanding General, DC National Guard, Com General's Office, 2001 E Capital, Washington, DC 20030-1719, (202)433-5220.

FREEMAN, WILLIAM M.
Educator, clergyman. **Personal:** Born Jan 8, 1926, Nashville, NC; son of Roberta Freeman and Fred Freeman; married Ruby Burnette; children: Robin, William III, Robert. **Educ:** DE State Coll, BS 1949; Shaw Univ, BD 1958, MDiv 1970; NC Central Univ, MS 1960; Luther Rice Sem, DMin 1977; UNC, Century Univ, EdD, 1997. **Career:** Lillington NC, asst vocational agr teacher; Fuquay-Varnia HS, guidance counselor; Fuquay Varnia Elementary School, principal; Fuquay Springs Consolidated HS, principal 1973-75; Wake Co Public Schools NC, dir fed program; Wake Co School Raleigh NC, asst supt 1975-77; Nash Co Sch Nashville NC, asst supt for personnel 1977-83; Congressman Ike Andrews 4th Congressional Dist, staff asst; The Fuquay-Varina Independent NC, columnist "The Other Side of Fuquay"; North Carolina General Assembly, House of Representatives Dist 62; AME Zion Church, staff writer for Sunday school publ bd, dist supt presiding elder 1981-. **Orgs:** Mem Phi Delta Kappa; Fuquay-Varina Town Commr 1st Black 1973; Mayor Pro Tem 1st Black 1979-; bd dir Chamber of Commerce; NEA; NC Assn of Educators; mem Omega Psi Phi; Mason; Elk. **Honors/Awds:** Outstanding Serv & Achievement Award in Educ & Govt in 6th Dist Omega Psi Phi; Human Relations Award Wake Co & NCAE Dist 11; Outstanding Dedication Wake Co; NCAE First Newsletter Editor "The Teachers Pet" 1973; 1st place among Newsletters in the state published by local NCAE Units in 1976; Outstanding Contributor to Fuquay-Varina HS & Comm; School Advisory Council Bd Dir Wake Co Opportunities Inc 1975; Citizen of Yr Fuquay-Varina 1973; Omega Man of Yr 1975-76; Honored as one of top ten grads from Delaware State Coll decade of 1940-49 honored in 1983; inducted into Delaware State Athletic Hall of Fame for Football, Boxing and Wrestling 1985. **Military Serv:** USMCR sgt E-5 1953-64. **Home Addr:** 507 Burton St, Fuquay-Varina, NC 27526-1607.

FREEMAN-WILSON, KAREN MARIE
Attorney, judge. **Personal:** Born Oct 24, 1960, Gary, IN; daughter of Myrlin Delores Patterson Freeman and Travis Lee

Freeman; married Carmen Wilson Jr, Feb 17, 1991. **Educ:** Harvard College, Cambridge, MA, AB, 1982; Harvard Law School, Cambridge, MA, JD, 1985. **Career:** Lake Co Prosecutor's Office, Crown Point, IN, deputy prosecutor, 1985-89; Lake Co Defender's Office, Crown Point, IN, public defender, 1989; Indiana Civil Rights Commission, Indianapolis, IN, director, 1989-92; private practice, attorney, civil and criminal litigation; Gary City Judge, currently. **Orgs:** Coalition of 100 Black Women, 1990-; vice pres, Delta Sigma Theta Sorority, 1980-; Natl Council of Negro Women; chair, Israel CME Steward Board, 1985-. **Honors/Awds:** 50 Leaders of the Future, Ebony Magazine, 1990; Bethune Award, National Council of Negro Women, 1990. **Business Addr:** Attorney, 504 Broadway, Ste 1016, Gary, IN 46402.

FREEMONT, JAMES MCKINLEY
Physician. **Personal:** Born Dec 2, 1942, Monroe, LA; married Erma Turner; children: James Jr, Joi Michelle, Jonathan Marcus. **Educ:** Southern Univ, BS 1966; Emory Univ Sch of Med, MD 1973. **Career:** Health First (HMO), sec/treas 1980-82; Southwest Comm Hosp, chief, dept ob/gyn 1985-86. **Orgs:** Mem Omega Psi Phi Frat 1962-; med dir Women Health Ctr 1980-; pres Atlanta Chap Southern Alumni Assoc 1983-; bd mem United Comm Corp 1985-. **Honors/Awds:** Outstanding Alumni NAFEO 1986. **Military Serv:** AUS sgt 1966-68. **Business Addr:** 777 Cleveland Ave, Atlanta, GA 30315.

FREGIA, DARRELL LEON
Administrator. **Personal:** Born Sep 8, 1949, San Francisco, CA; married Deborah Brooks; children: Marque, Akil, Shani. **Educ:** City Coll of San Francisco, AA Gen Educ 1967-69; Stanford U, BA Soc 1970-72; Univ of Wash, MHA 1975-77. **Career:** State of Washington Employment Security Department, risk mgr, 1990-, asst comptroller, 1988-90; Group Hlth Coop of Puget Sound Central Hosp & Med Center, asst hosp adminstr 1979-; Group Hlth Coop Fed Way Med Center, adminstr 1978-79; Group Hlth Coop Eastside Hosp & Med Ctr, adminstr 1977-78; VA Hosp Seattle, adminstr, intern 1976; San Mateo Co Probation Dept Redwood City CA, adult probation officer, 1973-75. **Orgs:** Mem, Guiding Light Youth Mentorship Prgm; mem Stanford Univ Buck Club 1972-; mem Stanford Univ Alumni Assn 1972-; cons/analyst Pioneer Mgmt Inc Seattle 1978-; life mem Alpha Phi Alpha Frat Inc 1977; mem Seattle Comm Coll Curriculum Task Force 1978; sec bd of dirs Ctr for Addiction Servs Seattle 1978-; vice pres bd of dir Paul Robeson Theatre Prod 1980; University of Washington Mentorship Program, 1995-. **Honors/Awds:** Recip player of the yr award San Francisco HS AAA Bsktbll 1967; buck club athletic scholorship Stanford Univ Bsktbll 1970-72; scholarships grad sch Vice Pres for Hlth Affairs Univ of Wash 1975-77; traineeship US Dept of Pub Hlth 1975-77; outst young man of Am award US Jaycees 1979. **Business Addr:** Risk Manager, State of Washington Employment Security Department, 212 Maple Park, PO Box 46000, Olympia, WA 98504-6000.

FREGIA, RAY
Business executive. **Personal:** Born Nov 22, 1948, Beaumont, TX; son of Betty Thomas; married Jewell M Perkins, Apr 17, 1971; children: Ray Jr, Rik. **Educ:** Lamar University, BBA, marketing, 1971. **Career:** Ford Motor Co., regional operations manager; River View Ford, president, currently. **Orgs:** Omega Psi Phi; Chamber of Commerce. **Business Addr:** President, Riverview Ford Inc, 2200 Route 30, Oswego, IL 60543, (708)897-8900.

FREISEN, GIL
Record and film producer, company executive. **Career:** A&M Records, president, currently.

FRELOW, ROBERT DEAN
Educator. **Personal:** Born Aug 1, 1932, Seminole, OK; divorced; children: Robert, Fred, Michael. **Educ:** San Francisco State Coll, BA 1954; San Francisco State Univ, MA 1964; Univ of CA-Berkeley, PhD 1970. **Career:** Oakland Unified Schools, teacher 1960-66; Berkeley Unified Schools, asst to supt 1966-70; Greenburgh Dist 7, asst supt 1970-74, supt 1974-. **Orgs:** Mem Amer Assoc of Sch Admin 1970-; adjunct assoc prof Pace Univ 1973-; bd of dirs Westchester Arts Council 1982-87, Amer Red Cross 1985-86. **Honors/Awds:** Omega Citizen of the Yr Beta Alpha Chap Omega Psi Phi 1984; Proclamation Robert D Frelow Day Westchester Bd of Legislators 1985. **Military Serv:** USAF capt 3 yrs. **Home Addr:** 25A Hillside Terr, White Plains, NY 10601. **Business Addr:** Superintendent of Schools, Greenburgh Central Sch Dist 7, 475 West Hartsdale Ave, Hartsdale, NY 10530.

FRELOW, ROBERT LEE, JR.
Communications executive. **Personal:** Born Jan 13, 1966, New Iberia, LA; son of Ethel L Mouton-Frelow and Robert L Frelow Sr. **Educ:** Howard University, Washington, DC, BA, 1988; University of Houston, Houston, TX, currently. **Career:** The Los Angeles Times, San Diego, CA, staff writer, 1988; Houston Defender, Houston, TX, feature editor, 1989-90; The Galveston Daily News, Galveston, TX, religion editor and county gov't reporter, 1990; Greater Houston Partnership, Houston, TX, communications executive, 1990-91; Robleefre Public Department of Aviation City of Houston, Relations Counsel, president, 1991; Office of the Mayor, Houston, TX, sr assistant director of communications, 1992-96; Media Communications Representative, 1996-; Houston Airport System, Houston, TX, media/communications representative, currently. **Orgs:** Media relations coordinator, Alpha Phi Alpha Fraternity Inc; member, International Assn of Business Communicators; member, Houston Assn of Black Journalists; member, National Assn of Back Journalists; member, Howard University Alumni Association; fellow, John Ben Shepperd Public Leadership Forum; United Negro College Fund Public Realtions Committee; vice pres, Black Public Relations Society of Houston; region V chairman, Howard University Alumni Association; chair, Brentwood Baptist Church Public Relations Committee; mem, United Way of the Texas Gulf Coast (UWTGC) Project Blueprint Advisory Committee; mem, UWTGC African American Marketing Committee; Nominating Committee Chair, W.L. Davis District Sam Houston Area Council Boy Scouts of America; Annie B. Casey Mental Health Initiative, advisory board member. **Honors/Awds:** HABJ Journalism Excellence Award in Special Project Design, News Release Writing and Newsletter Design/Writing, 1996. **Home Addr:** PO Box 23162, Houston, TX 77228-3162, (713)726-1001. **Business Phone:** (281)233-3000.

FRENCH, GEORGE WESLEY
Educator. **Personal:** Born Nov 28, 1928, Philadelphia, PA; married Elene Johnson; children: Andrea Natasha, Geoffrey Wesley. **Educ:** Temple Univ, BS, Educ, MS, Educ, EdD, 1970. **Career:** School Dist of Philadelphia, dir, prin, teacher 1952-; Penn-Susquehanna School Dist, consultant 1969; Pennsauken School Dist, 1969; Fordham Univ, 1975; Kent State Univ, 1975; Dayton School Dist, 1975; McGraw-Hill Pub Soc Student Text, 1975-77; PA State Dept of Educ, 1970-77; Beaver Coll, 1971; Fels Inst of Govt, 1976. **Orgs:** Mem Anti/Defamation Leag 1970-71; mem PA St Dem Com 1970-76; Am Acad of Political Sciences; Am Hist Soc; Asso for Curr Devel & Supervsn; Assn for Black Leadership in Ed; pres Black Ed Forum; mem Law Ed & Part Adv Bd; Nat Hist Soc; Black Pol Forum; Nat Coun for the Soc Studies; Orgn of Hist; PA conf for Black Basic Ed; pres Bd of Alice Rouse Donaldson Self-help Ctr; mem Big Broth Assn; pres Christian Sts Men's Club; pres Bd Florence Crittenton Serv; sec Bd of Germantown Stevens Acad; mem exec bd Northwest NAACP; mem Soc of PA; United Way Review Com. **Honors/Awds:** Black Educ Forum Award 1970-71; OV Catto Elks Award; Educator of the Yr 1974; citation of honor Christian St YMCA 1968; Gov Award for outst leadership in Ed 1974. **Military Serv:** USNA corpl 1946-47. **Business Addr:** 21st Parkway, Rm 330, Philadelphia, PA 19103.

FRENCH, HOWARD W.
Journalist. **Personal:** Born Oct 14, 1957, Washington, DC; son of Carolyn Alverda Howard French and David Marshall French; married Agnes Koffi, Oct 5, 1987; children: William Howard, Henry Nelson. **Educ:** University of Massachusetts, Amherst, MA, BA, 1979. **Career:** Self-employed, Abidjan, Ivory Coast, conference translator, 1979-80; University of Ivory Coast, Abidjan, Ivory Coast, assistant professor, English, 1980-82; The Washington Post, Abidjan, Ivory Coast, West Africa stringer, 1982-86; The News York Times, New York, NY, metropolitan reporter, 1986-90, The New York Times, Miami, FL, Caribbean correspondent, beginning 1990, bureau chief, 1990-94; west african bureau chief, Abidjan, Ivory Coast, 1994-. **Orgs:** Natl Assn of Black Journalists; Institute of the Americas; African Studies Association. **Business Addr:** West Africa Bureau Chief, The New York Times, 229 W 43rd St, New York, NY 10036.

FRENCH, JAMES J.
Editor, publisher. **Personal:** Born Oct 7, 1926, Kansas City, KS; married Olivia Jackson; children: James, Jr, Nanette Maria, Simona Alison. **Educ:** KS Tech Coll, 1949; San Francisco State Coll. **Career:** The Chronicle, editor & publ. **Orgs:** Bd mem SC Counc Human Right; SC Task Force Adminstrv Justice; life mem NAACP; vice pres Ctr Preservation & Cultural Black Arts. **Honors/Awds:** NNPA Award Best Columnist 1973; Presidential Unit Citation; Bronze Star Vietnam Combat Journalist. **Military Serv:** USN chief journalist 1951-71. **Business Addr:** PO Box 2548, Charleston, SC 29403.

FRENCH, JOSEPH HENRY
Physician, educator. **Personal:** Born Jul 3, 1928, Toledo, OH; married Marilyn E Doss; children: Lenore, Joseph, Lisa, John. **Educ:** OSU, AB 1950, MD (cum laude) 1954. **Career:** Johns Hopkins Hospital School of Medicine, fellow 1960-61; Univ of CO School of Medicine, asst prof 1961-64; Albert Einstein Coll of Medicine, 1964-79; Dept of Pediatrics, Norwalk Hospital, chmn 1979-80; Clinical Serv Inst for Basic Rsch in Developmental Disabilities, dep dir 1980-; Rose F Kennedy Center for Child's Evaluation, asst dean dir; Albert Einstein Coll of Medicine, asst prof, prof Pediatric Neurology; Interfaith Medical Center, Brooklyn NY, director of pediatrics. **Orgs:** Chmn Pediatric Neurology Sect; co-editor Intl Reviews of Child Neurology 1982-; exec comm Intl Child Neurology Assn 1980-84; pres Tri-State Child Neurology Soc 1982-83; peripheral & central nervous system drugs adv comm Food & Drug Admin 1980-84; exec comm Child Neurology Soc 1977-79; Kappa Alpha Psi 1947; Phi Beta Kappa 1950; Alpha Omega Alpha 1954; Alpha Epsilon Delta 1950; Phi Delta Upsilon 1950; Sigma Pi Phi 1984. **Military Serv:** AUS t/5. **Business Addr:** Director of Pediatrics, Interfaith Medical Center, ACF Building, 2nd Floor, 1545 Atlantic Ave, Brooklyn, NY 11213.

FRENCH, MARYANN
Journalist. **Personal:** Born Aug 12, 1952, Washington, DC; daughter of Carolyn Howard French and David M French; married Dennis M Marshall, Nov 5, 1988 (divorced 1995); children: French Scott. **Educ:** Attended, Boston Univ 1969-70, Johns Hopkins Univ 1979; Johns Hopkins Sch of Advanced Intl Studies, MA 1982. **Career:** Black Women's Comm Develop Found, dir of program admin 1977-78; The Washington Post, researcher 1981-82; Time Magazine, reporter/researcher 1982-84; The Louisville Courier Journal, reporter 1984-86; St Petersburg Times, Washington corres 1986-; St Petersburg Florida Times, Washington correspondent, 1986-88; Baltimore Sun, Washington correspondent, 1988; The Daily News, St Thomas, Virgin Islands, editor, 1989-90; The Washington Post, Washington, DC, staff writer, 1990-. **Orgs:** Mem Louisville Assoc of Black Communicators 1984-86, Natl Assoc of Black Journalists 1984-, Washington Assoc of Black Journalists 1986-. **Honors/Awds:** Fellowship Modern Media (Poynter) Inst 1982; Metro Louisville Sigma Delta Chi Awd for continuing coverage of the artificial heart experiment 1984; Journalism Awd, Outstanding Coverage of the Black Condition, First Place, Features Natl Assn of Black Journalist, 1996; Fellowship, Duke Univ Ctr for Public Policy, 1993. **Special Achievements:** Co-author 40 Ways to Raise a Nonracist Child, Harper Perennial, 1996. **Business Addr:** Staff Writer, The Washington Post, 1150 15th St NW, Washington, DC 20071.

FRENCH, ROBERT P.
Sociologist. **Personal:** Born Jan 28, 1919, Rankin, PA; son of Josephine Tibbs (deceased) and Robert P French (deceased); married Jeanette Foster, Feb 21, 1954; children: Stacye French Blue. **Educ:** M Litt, BA 1954; Univ of Pittsburgh, BA, M Litt. **Career:** Point Park Coll, former part-time instr sociology; PA State U, part-time inst sociology, cont educ prgm; Seagram Dist Co, salesman (retired); North Carolina Mututal Insurance Co, sales. **Orgs:** Bd mem Youth Devel Ctr of W PA; former pres Counc Braddock Hills Boro; mem exec bd Local #131 AFL-CIO 16 yrs; mem bd dir Braddock General Hosp for past 7 yrs; mem trustee bd Mt Olive Baptist Church; chrmn, Public Safety Branch Braddock Hills Boro. **Honors/Awds:** Appointed to the 7 Member Bd of AIM (Aid to Imprint Municipalities), Comm of Allec County. **Military Serv:** AUS capt.

FRESH, EDITH MCCULLOUGH
Educator, therapist. **Personal:** Born Sep 23, 1942, Quincy, FL; daughter of Edith Anderson McCullough and Harry M McCullough (deceased); married Frederick Anthony Fresh; children: Kevin W, Bradford, Carla, Eric. **Educ:** IN Univ, AB 1960-70; Univ of MI, MSW 1970-72; Gestalt Inst of Cleveland, Diploma 1976-77; GA State Univ, MA 1988, Doctoral grad student Clinical Psych 1985-. **Career:** Project Headline Detroit MI, dir outpatient treatment 1972-73; Public Tech Inc, human resources spec 1973-77; FL A&M Univ FL, asst prof 1977-83; EM Fresh & Assoc FL, sr assoc 1977-83; Morehouse School of Med, clinical social worker, 1983-88; Spelman College, clinical social worker, 1988-90; Gerogia Mental Health Institute, Atlanta, GA, psychology intern, 1990-91; The New Foundation, marriage & family therapist, 1990-; DeKalb College, North Campus, instructor, 1991-. **Orgs:** Mem Acad of Cert Social Workers 1976-, Natl Assoc of Social Workers 1976-; reg coord Natl Hook-Up of Black Women 1980-84; clinical mem Amer Assoc of Marriage & Family Therapists 1980-; site visitor for the Commission on the Accreditation for Marriage and Therapy Educ 1982-; visiting staff Gestalt Inst of Cleveland 1981-; bd mem Mental Health Dist Bd II-B Leon Cty, FL 1982-83; mem Amer Assn of Univ Women 1983-85; chairperson, Georgia Assn of Marriage & Family Therapists Minority Affairs Task Force, 1991-; American Association of Marriage & Family Therapists, ethics committee, 1993-. **Honors/Awds:** Rep Gwen Cherry Memorial Awd for Outstanding Contrib for Women's Rights in the State of Florida Southern Reg Journalists Assoc 1980; Woman of the Year Zeta Phi Beta 1982. **Business Addr:** Licensed Clinical Social Worker, The New Foundation, One Baltimore Place, NE, Suite 165, Atlanta, GA 30308.

FRETT, LA KESHIA
Professional basketball player. **Personal:** Born Jun 12, 1975, Carmel, CA; daughter of Raymond and Linda Frett. **Educ:** Univ of Georgia. **Career:** Philadelphia Rage, forward, 1997-. **Honors/Awds:** Voted National Prep Player of the Year by Parade, USA Today, Boost/Naismith, and Gatorade, 1993; Parade All-America, 1991, 1992, 1993. **Business Addr:** Professional Basketball Player, Philadelphia Rage, 123 Chestnut St, Fourth Flr, Philadelphia, PA 19106, (215)629-1976.

FRETWELL, CARL QUENTION, II
Parole supervisor. **Personal:** Born May 5, 1951, Fort Worth, TX; son of Georgetta Enge and Carl Q Fretwell Sr; married Constance Barron (divorced 1989). **Educ:** Tarrant County Junior College, Fort Worth, TX, AA, 1972; Texas Wesleyan University, Fort Worth, TX, BBA, 1975; University of North

Texas, Denton, TX. **Career:** Texas Youth Council, Crockett, TX, caseworker I, 1975-76; Texas Youth Council, Gainesville, TX, caseworker II, senior dorm dir, 1976-82; Board of Pardons & Parole, Ft Worth, TX, parole officer I, unit supervisor, 1982-88; Texas Youth Commission, Ft Worth, TX, parole officer II, parole officer III, office mgr, 1988-, court liasons officer, 1990, parole supervisor, 1996. **Orgs:** Professional member, Texas Corrections Assn, 1976-97; member, NAACP, 1978-; member 1984-, national board of directors 1988-, asst treasurer 1989, national treasurer 1994, NABCJ; board of directors, Boy Scouts, Fort Worth, 1990; founder, Fort Worth Chapter, NABCJ, 1986. **Honors/Awds:** Gang Unit Award, Fort Worth Mayor's Office, 1984; Management Certificate, Governor of Texas, 1986; Outstanding Supervisor Award, Board of Pardons and Parole, 1988; Eminent Man Award, Phi Delta Kappa, Inc, 1997. **Business Addr:** Parole Supervisor, Texas Youth Commission, 500 W 13th St, Ste 295, Fort Worth, TX 76102.

FRIES, SHARON LAVONNE
Educator. **Personal:** Born Jul 26, 1959, Chattahoochee, GA. **Educ:** Univ of MD-College Park, BS 1981; The OH State Univ, MA 1983; Univ of MD-College Park, PhD, 1994. **Career:** The OH State Univ, asst dir Morrill Tower 1981-82, student develop grad asst 1982-83; Towson State Univ, area coord 1983-85; Univ of MD, asst to vice pres for student affairs, chancellor beginning 1985, asst prof, currently. **Orgs:** Mem Amer Coll and Personnel Associate 1981-; mem rsch bd ACPA 1985; directorate of comm IX assessment for student devel ACPA 1986; membership chair/assoc staff rep Black Fac/Staff Assoc; Full Gospel AME Zion; mem Media and Editorial Bd ACPA; rep multicultural affairs comm ACPA; mem Amer Assoc of Affirmative Action Officers; mem Black Women's Council The Univ of MD-College Park; consultations Univ of MD Campus Programs and Off Campus Presentations. **Honors/Awds:** New Presenters Awd MACUHO 1985; Human Relations Serv Awd State of MD 1986; Associate Staff Outstanding Contibution Award, Univ of MD, 1988; mem of Omicron Delta Kappa 1989; Outstanding Service Award, Black Faculty and Staff 1986-88; Presidents Award, Outstanding Contribution as an Associate Staff Member, Univ of Maryland, College Park, 1988; Outstanding Minority Staff Mem of the Year, Presidents Commission on Ethnic Minority Issues, 1991; Woman of Color Award, Univ of Maryland, President's Commission on Women's Affairs, 1992. **Business Addr:** Assistant Professor, University of Maryland College Park, 3113 Benjamin Building, College Park, MD 20742.

FRINK, JOHN SPENCER
Insurance company executive. **Personal:** Born Sep 7, 1930, Fernandina Beach, FL; married Emmie Mae Williams; children: Bruce Romell, Jaques Rummel. **Educ:** Bethune Cookman Coll, BS 1955. **Career:** Atlanta Life Insurance Co, agent, 1955-58, dist mgr 1958-70, asst vice pres area dir 1970-77, vice pres dir of agencies 1977-83, vice pres dir of agency devel 1984-. **Orgs:** chapter pres, Omega Psi Phi Fraternity, 1960-71; vice pres agency section; bd of dirs, Natl Insurance Assn, 1982-83; bd of trustees, Bethune Coleman Coll. **Honors/Awds:** John S Frink Day City of Daytona Beach 1982; Distinguished Alumni Citation NAFEO 1983; Agency Officer of the Year Natl Ins Assn, 1983; Honorary Doctor of Law Degree, Bethune Coleman Coll, 1992; Bethune Coleman Coll, Pinnacle Award, 1995. **Military Serv:** AUS sgt 1st class 1950-53; NCOIC, Crypto Ctr, FECOM 1951-52. **Home Addr:** 1201 Sunset Circle, Daytona Beach, FL 32117. **Business Phone:** (404)654-8815.

FRINK, SAMUEL H.
Business owner. **Personal:** Born Mar 20, 1944, LaGrange, NC; son of O W Frink and E B Frink; married Juanita Vereen Frink, Jun 8, 1968; children: Ivan, Chaun. **Educ:** North Carolina Central University, Durham, NC, BS, chemistry, 1966; Ford Motor Dealer Training, Virginia Beach, VA, 1986. **Career:** Ford Motor Co., Fairfax, VA, sales representative, 1970-80; Major Lincoln-Mercury, Virginia Beach, VA, sales manager, 1980-86; Conway Ford Inc, Conway, SC, president/owner, 1986-; Bobby Gerald Ford-Lincoln-Mercury, partnership, 1991; Grand Strand Nissan, partnership, 1994; Lay-Fisher Chevrolet/Olds Inc, partnership, 1995. **Orgs:** Executive board member, Boy Scouts of America; member, board of visitors, Coastal Carolina College, 1989-90; president, Conway Area Chamber of Commerce, 1990; advisory council member, Horry County Youth 2000, 1988-90; advisory board, Myrtle Beach Branch National bank of South Carolina, 1991. **Honors/Awds:** Minority Small Businessman of the Year, 7 States of Southeast Region, 1990; Elks Americanism Award, Scouts of America, 1989; Businessman of the Year, Phi Beta Sigma Fraternity, 1988; Man of the Year, Cherry Hill Baptist Church, 1988. **Military Serv:** US Army, Capt, 1966-70; received Army Commendation Medal, 1970. **Business Addr:** President, Conway Ford, Inc., 2385 Hwy 501 W, Conway, SC 29526.

FRINK REED, CAROLIESE INGRID
Educator. **Personal:** Born Dec 24, 1949, Jacksonville, FL; daughter of Catherine Danberg Frink and Neal Frink; married Dwight D Reed Sr (died 1988); children: Kasimu Clark, Kali Reed. **Educ:** Temple University, Philadelphia, PA, BS, 1976; Drexel University, Philadelphia, PA, MS, 1980; Univ of Ghana, summer, 1993. **Career:** Free Library of Philadelphia, Philadelphia, PA, children's librarian, 1980-81; Prince William Co Library, Woodbridge, VA, YA librarian, 1982-84; Nassau County School Board, Fernandina Beach, FL, librarian, 1985-87; School District of Philadelphia, Philadelphia, PA, librarian, 1987-96; Fitzsimons Middle School, librarian, 1996-. **Orgs:** Member, National Association for the Preservation and Perpetuation of Storytelling; media selection & review committee, Pennsylvania School Librarians Association, 1990-91; Natl Assn of Black Storytellers, pres, 1994-96, admin assist, 1986-92; mem Black Caucus of the American Library Association. **Honors/Awds:** 1st Recipient L Valeria Richmond Service Award, National African American Storytellers Retreat, Pine Bluff, NC, 1995. **Home Addr:** 859 N 29th St, Philadelphia, PA 19130.

FRISBY, H. RUSSELL, JR.
Commissioner. **Personal:** Born Dec 28, 1950, Baltimore, MD; son of H Russell Frisby Sr & Kathryn T Frisby; married June J Frisby, Jul 15, 1978; children: H Russell III, James. **Educ:** Swarthmore Coll, BA, 1972; Yale Law School, JD, 1975. **Career:** Cable, McDaniel, Bowie and Bond, assoc, 1975-77; MD Attorney General's Off, asst aty general, 1977-79; Federal Communications Commission, aty, 1979-83; Weil, Gotshal & Manges, assoc, 1983-86; Melnicove, Kaufman, Weiner & Smouse, partner, 1986-89; Venable, Baetjer & Howard, LLP, partner, 1989-95; MD Public Service Commission, chmn, 1995-. **Orgs:** Natl Assn of Regulatory Commissioners, vice chair of communications comm, 1997-; Amer Bar Assn, budget off, admin law sect, 1995-, chair of coordinating group on energy law, 1997; Federal-State Joint Bd on Universal Svc, 1997-; Amer Bar Foundation, fellow, 1992-; MD Bar Foundation, fellow, 1992-. **Honors/Awds:** Minority Business Enterprise Legal Defense & Education Fund, Inc, Charles Hamilton Houston Award, 1989. **Business Addr:** Chairman, Maryland Public Svc Commission, 6 St Paul St, 16th Fl, Baltimore, MD 21202-6806, (410)767-8072.

FRITZ, MOSES KELLY
Executive director. **Personal:** Born Jul 6, 1904, Uniontown, AL; married Johnnie M. **Educ:** Eckels Coll Mortuary Sci, 1925. **Career:** Fritz Funeral Home, prop/operator, currently. **Orgs:** Mem Nat Funeral Dir & Morticians Assn; MI Selected Morticians Assn; MI Funeral Dir & Nat Funeral Dir Assn; mem Adv bd Selective Serv Local Bd 92; vice-chmn bd mgmt Northern Br YMCA; chmn Camping Com Detroit Area Counc Camp Fire Girls; treas Housing Found of MI; mem 13th Congressional Dist Dem Orgn; mem-at-large Detroit DistArea Counc BSA; counc mem Intl Inst; mem Elks; Masonic Order Narracci Temple Shrine #13; Wolverine Consistory#6; 33rd Degree Mason; Omega Psi Phi Frat; Cathedral Ch of St Paul (Episcopalian); vice pres Concord Co-op Townhouses; mem Jolly Old-Timers & Amles Club of Detroit.

FROE, DREYFUS WALTER
Agency director. **Personal:** Born Feb 18, 1914, Bluefield, WV; son of Sallie Ann Anderson and Lucian Charles Froe; married Noreika B Froe; children: Dreyfus L II, Dana A. **Educ:** WV State Coll, BSA 1933; WV U, MS 1944; Marshall U, Adv Study 1948; Boston U, Adv Study 1965. **Career:** Bluefield State Coll, tchr & coach 1936-45; Mercer Cnty Sch, tchr & admin 1945-59; US Dept of State, diplomatic serv 1959-69; Mercer Cnty EOC, exec dir 1969-85. **Orgs:** Asst dir Flanner House; Masons; state dir ed Elks-Civitane 1965-75; sir archon Sigma Phi Pi Frat; basalus Omega Psi Phi. **Honors/Awds:** Layman of the Yr United Meth Ch WN Conf 1980; Outstand Citizen Mountain State Bar Assn 1980; Outstand Leadership NAACP Mercer Cnty Bar 1981; Football Hall of Fame WV State Coll 1983; Bluefield Citizen of Year 1990. **Home Addr:** 314 Belcher, Bluefield, WV 24701.

FROE, OTIS DAVID
Research administrator. **Personal:** Born Dec 24, 1912, Bluefield, WV; son of Sallie Anderson Froe and Charles Lucian Froe; married Otyce Brown; children: Lynne Pamela. **Educ:** Bluefield State Coll, BS Math 1935; Univ of MI, MS Stat 1940; Univ of Chgo, PhD Meas 1947. **Career:** Morristown Coll, dean 1940-47; Central State U, dean 1947-50; Morgan State U, dir inst res 1950-76; Research Svcs, Inc, dir, research svcs. **Orgs:** Pres Nat Media Assoc 1957-76; pres MD State Personnel & Guid Assoc; bd of dir Balto Symphony Orc 1975-77; Phi Delta Kappa Prof Edn; Alpha Phi Alpha Soc Frat; Promethean Kappa Tau Hon Soc. **Honors/Awds:** Research fellow Southern Reg Educ Bd; books & articles regarding human behavior. **Military Serv:** AAF. **Home Addr:** 2301 Ivy Ave, Baltimore, MD 21214. **Business Addr:** Director, Research Services, Research Services, Inc, 2301 Ivy Ave, Baltimore, MD 21214.

FROHMAN, ROLAND H.
Dentist. **Personal:** Born Aug 18, 1928, Detroit; married Alice F Hibbett; children: Roland, Jr, Shelley, Jill. **Educ:** Wayne State U, AB 1951; Howard U, DDS 1955. **Career:** Denstistry, prvt prac 1961-; Dr Robert L Moseley, assoc 1957-61; Harper Hosp Detroit, on staff 1968-. **Orgs:** Mem Am Dental Assn; Wolverine Dental Assn; MI State Dental Assn; Detroit Dist Dental Assn; mem The Moors Club. **Honors/Awds:** Redip Cert of Recognition by Mayor of Detroit for serv in Mayors Youth Employment Prgm 1968. **Military Serv:** AUS capt 1955-57. **Business Addr:** 13026 W Mc Nichols, Detroit, MI 48235.

FROST, HUGH A.
Association executive. **Personal:** Born Sep 29, 1926, Youngstown, OH; married Daisy Lillian; children: Hugh L, Gary L, Neal, & Lynette C. **Educ:** Bluffton Coll, BS Social Sci 1951; W Reserve U, Grad Sch Applied Social Sci 1959-61; Westminster Coll, MA Educ Psychology 1966-67; Univ of Dayton; Youngstown U; Geo Williams Coll; McGee Brokerage Firm. **Career:** Younstown State U, asst to pres 1968-; McGuffey Ctr Inc, exec dir 1956-68; Westlake Playground Assn, playground dir 1947-50; Findlay YMCA, instr physical activities 1950; Bradfield Ctr, vol physical dir 1950; Spring St YMCA, boys work sec 1951-52; Deccamen Co, sec treas 1951-55; West Fed St YMCA, boys work prgm sec 1952-54; Am Motors, part-time car slsmn 1952-55; Senate Ave YMCA, mem sec 1955; Chevrolet, part-time car slsmn 1956-57; Real Estate, slsmn 1960-65; Jackson Realty, br mgr 1961-63; Head Consult Agy, 1962-; Lctr, area colls 1965-. **Orgs:** Vp OH Affirmative Action Ofcrs Assn; bd trustees Youngstown Rotary Club; bd trustees Comm Chest Corp; bd trustees Assn Nghbrhd Ctrs; bd trustees Exec Com Mahoning Co; pres McGuffey Ctr Inc; adv bd Nat Plng Assn for Planners; vice pres Youngstown Boys Clubs of Am; bd trustees Fresh Air Camp; mahoning Co Draft Bd #80; alumni pres adv com bd trustees Bluffton Coll; adv com Youngstown Soc for Blind past bd dirs; adv com Youngstown Hearing & Speech Ctr; mem NAACP; Mahoning Co Cits Adv Com on Comm Devel. **Honors/Awds:** Recip recog for serv rendered as chmn Christmas Shopping Tour Youngstown Jr C of C 1958; man of yr award Youngstown Jr C pf C 1961-62; cert appreciation Hubbard Rotary Club 1962; spl cit judge prosecutor & jurors for outst ldrshp as jury forman of session of Mahoning Co Grand Jury 1963; Educ Award OH Assn of Beauticians 1966; comm ldr award Troop 18 Boy Scouts 1967-68; award for comm involvement & serv Rotary Club 1969; outst alumnus award Bluffton Coll 1970; urban family of yr Youngstown C of C 1971; civic award for serv to co & comm Alpha Kappa Psi 1972; meritorious serv award OH Counc for Vocation Educ 1972; outst civic award Buckeye Elks 1972; cert of appreciation valuable serv contributed to nation & Selec Serv Sys in Admin of Military Selec Serv Act of1967, Pres of US 1973; Younsn State Univ Student Gov Serv Award outst serv 1974. **Military Serv:** USAAF cpl. **Business Addr:** 410 Wick Ave, Youngstown, OH 44555.

FROST, OLIVIA PLEASANTS
Educator, genealogical researcher. **Personal:** Born in Asbury Pk, NJ; daughter of Theresa Mitchell Pleasants and William Henry Pleaseants; widowed; children: Carolyn Olivia Frost Downes, James William, Charles S Jr. **Educ:** Hunter Coll, BA; Columbia Univ, MA 1951; NY Univ, Dept of Human Relations, Sch of Educ, PhD 1972. **Career:** Haryou-Contributor to Youth in the Ghetto, rsch assoc 1963-66; NY Urban League, rsch dir 1965-66; Haryou-ACT, rsch assoc 1969-70; New York City Youth Bd Comm Council of NY, rsch assoc; Columbia Univ, MARC Demonstration Proj on Adolescent Minority Females, rsch consultant 1971-75; CUNY, assoc prof 1972-77; Central SEEK, dir prog devel; licensed real estate broker. **Orgs:** Mem Natl Assn Social Workers, Afro-Amer Historical & Genealogical Soc Inc; dir comm study Harlem A Neglected Investment Oppor; mem NAACP, NY Urban League; trustee Schomburg Corp; trustee, Schomburg Corp., chairman, Genealogy Committee with the Schomburg Center for Research in Black Culture, The New York Public Library. **Honors/Awds:** Warburg Fellowship, Dept of Human Relations, Sch of Educ, NYU, 1968; grant for doctoral dissertation, Dept of Labor, Washington DC; founder, Assn of Black Women in Higher Educ.

FROST, WILLIAM HENRY
Mayor. **Personal:** Born Apr 17, 1930, Maysville, NC; son of Gracie Parlen Perry Frost and Philanders Frost; married Ari Mae Jones Frost, Feb 12, 1934; children: Warren, Leddia Frost Chapman, Aletha, Elroy. **Career:** US Civil Service, Camp Lejeune NC, warehouseman, 1955-65, chauffeur, 1965-68, radio dispatcher, 1968-77, bus driver, 1977-85; Town of Maysville, NC, alderman, 1972-85, mayor, 1985-95. **Orgs:** Warehouseman, Civil Serv, chauffeur, 1965-68, radio dispatch, 1968-77, bus driver, 1977-85; Jone County, Demacrat Party, chairman. **Honors/Awds:** Three Civil Serv Awards for Outstanding work, 1981, 1983-84. **Military Serv:** US Army, E4, 1950-55, 2 Good Conduct Medal, Combat Ribbon with 3 stars, United Nation Ribbon, Koran Ribbon. **Home Addr:** 86 Main St, PO Box 191, Maysville, NC 28555.

FROST, WILSON
City official, attorney. **Personal:** marrIed Gloria Shepard; children: Jacqueline, Baldridge, Rhey Orme. **Educ:** Fisk U, BA 1950; Chicago Kent Coll of Law, JD 1958; DePaul Univ & Lawyers Inst. **Career:** Frost Sherard Howse & Coleman, atty 1958-73; Meyer & Frost, 1973-; Postal Transportation Svc, clerk 1950-52; Provident Hosp, acct statistician 1952. **Orgs:** IL Youth Commn Very active in city govt; mem Originial Forty Club; Kappa Alpha Psi Frat; Phi Alpha Delta Legal Frat; IBPOE Lodge #43; com NAACP; Legal Redress Com; com Chicago Varsity Club; Cook Co Bar Assn; IL Bar Assn; Chicago Fisk Club; Chicago Kent Coll of Alumni Assn; Chicago Idlewilders Club;Original Chicago Idlewilders & Lions Internat; past legal adv & vice pres City Club of Chicago; past mem IL Probation & Parole Assn; mem Epsicopal Ch; elected Alderman 21st Ward 1967; acting Dem Ward Com 34th Ward

1970; committeeman 1972; alderman 34th Ward 1971; pres Protem City Counc 1973; floor ldr Com Chmn on France; delegate ot Nat Dem Conv 2nd Congressional Dist 1972. **Military Serv:** AUS Signal Corps.

FRY, DARRELL
Journalist. **Personal:** Born Apr 16, 1963, Oklahoma City, OK; son of Helen M Holmes Gray and Jay D Fry. **Educ:** Florida State Univ, Tallahassee, FL, BS, 1986. **Career:** St Petersburg Times, St Petersburg, FL, staff writer, 1986-. **Orgs:** National Assn Black Journalists, 1986-; Phi Beta Sigma Fraternity, 1984-. **Honors/Awds:** AP Sports Editors, Honorable Mention, 1988, 1990; First Place, Florida Sports Writers Assn, 1987. **Business Addr:** Staff Writer, Sports, St Petersburg Times, 1000 N Ashley Dr, Ste 700, Tampa, FL 33602-3717, (813)226-3366.

FRY, LOUIS EDWIN, JR.
Architect, business executive. **Personal:** Born Sep 11, 1928, Prairie View, TX; son of Obelia Fry and Louis Fry; married Genelle Wiley; children: Jonisa Oliver, Louis Edwin III, Vicki Lynn Wilson, Alexa Genelle Hawkins. **Educ:** Howard Univ, BA Sociology 1947; Harvard Univ, M Arch 1953; Fulbright Fellowship, Tech Hogeschool, Delft, Holland, 1954-55; Harvard Univ, MA Urban Design 1962. **Career:** Various Arch firm in the Wash DC, draftsman to project mgr 1955-60; Fry & Welch Architect, jr partner 1960-72, pres 1972-. **Orgs:** Fellow Am Inst of Architects 1973; founding mem Nat Organ of Minority Architects; mem Am Inst of Architects Committee on Design 1984; mem Overseers Committee to visit The Grad Sch of Design, Harvard Univ 1984-; mem DC Redevel Land Agency (RLA) Architectural Review Panel, Wash DC 1974-; mem Am Arbitration Assns Panel of Arbitrators 1983-. **Honors/Awds:** Fellow Am Inst of Architects 1973; Fulbright Fellowship to study City Planning in The Netherlands 1954; Cert of Appreciation for serv as pres of The DC Architectural Regis Bd 1982; Cert of Award outstanding professional serv rendered to The Morgan Comm Sch Bd, Wash DC 1981. **Business Addr:** President, Fry & Welch Architect, 7600 Georgia Ave, NW, Ste 401, Washington, DC 20012.

FRY, SIMON. See AGURS, DONALD STEELE.

FRYAR, IRVING DALE
Professional football player. **Personal:** Born Sep 28, 1962, Mount Holly, NJ; married Jacqueline; children: Londen, Irving Jr., Adrianne, Jacqueline. **Educ:** Univ of Nebraska, attended; South Florida Bible College and Theological Seminary, bachelor's degree in bible study. **Career:** New England Patriots, wide receiver, 1984-92; Miami Dolphins, 1993-95; Philadelphia Eagles, 1996-. **Orgs:** Founded the Fryar Foundation, a non-profit organization that helps at-risk youths in the Florida area. **Honors/Awds:** Played in East-West Shrine game; Japan Bowl All Star game; first player selected in the 1984 NFL draft; named AP All-Pro 2nd team; College and Pro Football Newsweekly All-Pro 2nd team; took part in NBC Superteams competition; Pro Bowl, 1985, 1993, 1994, 1996, 1997; New England Patriots 1776 Quarterback Club, Community Service Award, 1988; Philadelphia Eagles, True Value/NFL Man of the Year, 1996. **Business Addr:** Professional Football Player, Philadelphia Eagles, 3501 S Broad St, Philadelphia, PA 19148, (215)463-2500.

FRYE, HENRY E.
Associate justice. **Personal:** Born Aug 1, 1932, Richmond Co, NC; son of Pearl A Frye and Walter A Frye; married Shirely Taylor; children: Henry E, Harlan E. **Educ:** A&T State U, BS 1953; Univ of NC Law Sch, JD 1959; Syracuse Univ Law Sch, summer 1958. **Career:** US aty, NC, asst 1963-65; NCC Univ Law Sch, 1965-67; Frye & Johnson atty; NC House of Rep, mem; NC Senate, mem; Supreme Court of NC, assoc justice 1983-. **Orgs:** Mem Greensboro Bar Assn; Am Bar Assn; NC Bar Assn; North Carolina Association of Black Lawyers; Am Judicature Soc; life mem Nat Bar Assn; mem Kappa Alpha Psi Frat; former mem sec bd mgmt Hayes Taylor YMCA; deacon of Providence Bapt Ch; life mem NAACP. **Honors/Awds:** Elected one of Guilford Co 6 rep in NC House 1968; 1st black in this century elected to NC House; received honorary Doctorate Degree Shaw Univ 1971; Alumni Excellence Award A&T State Univ 1972; R R Wright Award, National Bankers Association, 1983. **Military Serv:** USAF capt 2 Yrs; USAFR. **Business Addr:** Associate Justice, North Carolina Supreme Court, PO Box 1841, Raleigh, NC 27602, (919)733-3717.

FRYE, NADINE GRACE
Nurse, educator (retired). **Personal:** Born in Greensburg, PA; daughter of Virgie Middles Frye Grasty (Adopted) and Charles Frye. **Educ:** Univ of Pittsburgh, BSN 1947, M Lit 1951, PhD, 1987. **Career:** Western Psych Inst & Clinic, Pgh PA, staff nurse/head nurse 1948-50; Detroit Dept of Hlth, Detroit MI, public hlth nurse 1951-53; Northville State Hosp (Nrsg Educ Dept), instructor/dir 1953-56; Lafayette Clinic, Detroit MI, dir nrsg educ 1956-57; Wayne State U, Detroit MI, instructor of nrsg 1957-59; Mercywood Hosp, Ann Arbor MI, dir nrsg educ 1959-61; Univ of MI Sch of Nrsng, asst prof/dir of nrsng 1961-66; Western Psych Inst & Clinic, Pgh PA, assoc dir of cmh/mr nursing 1969-73; Univ of Pgh PA Sch of Nrsng, prof of nrsng 1969-90. **Orgs:** Bd of dir 3 Rivers Youth Pgh PA 1971-77; consult St Agnes Catholic Sch Pgh PA 1971-73; consult Univ of S MS Sch of Nrsg 1976; consult Univ of Pgh Sch of Nrsg 1980-81; Am Nurses Assn 1947-; Alpha Kappa Alpha 1944-; Pgh Club Nat Assn Negro Bus & Professional Women 1973-84; Advisory Community Youth Ministry, Pittsburgh, PA, 1988-; Intl Sigma Theta Tau Honorary Nursing Sorority, 1988-. **Honors/Awds:** Honor Award Kappa Alpha Psi, Pgh PA 1943; Robert L Vann Mem Schlrshp 1943; Alumni Award Univ of Pgh 1980; Alumni Serv Awd Univ of Pittsburgh 1986. **Home Addr:** 6352 Aurelia St, Pittsburgh, PA 15206-4319.

FRYE, REGINALD STANLEY
Construction company executive. **Personal:** Born May 18, 1936, Yakima, WA; son of Elise Garrett and Virgil O Frye; married Mikki Goree, Jun 24, 1956; children: Gregory, Martin, Trana. **Educ:** Los Angeles Community Coll, Los Angeles CA, 1955-56. **Career:** V O Frye Manufacturing, Seattle WA, salesman, 1959-64; Washington Natural Gas, Seattle WA, salesman, 1964-72; 3A Industries Inc, Seattle WA, pres, 1972-. **Orgs:** Pres, Central Contractors Assn, 1976-85; vice-chair, State of Washington OMWBE Advisory Bd, 1983-87. **Honors/Awds:** Martin Luther King Jr Humanitarian Award, The Medium Newspaper, 1974; Community Service Award, United Inner City Devel Found, 1974, 1976; Special Recognition, Port of Seattle, 1983; Special Recognition, Natl Assn of Minority Contractors, 1983. **Business Addr:** Chief Executive Officer, 3A Industries Inc, PO Box 14029, Seattle, WA 98114.

FRYE, ROBERT EDWARD, SR.
Government official. **Personal:** Born Oct 11, 1936, Washington, DC; son of Alberta Edwards Frye and James E Frye, Jr.; married Rotha Isabel Holbert, May 30, 1987; children: Robert Jr, Amanda. **Educ:** Howard Univ, BSc 1958; Amer Univ, MPA 1970; Fed Exec Inst, 1975. **Career:** US Army Map Svc, cartographer 1958-65; Wolf R&D Corp, project mgr 1965-69; Natl Bureau of Standards, computer syst analyst 1969-73; US Consumer Prod Safety Com, dir, injury surveillance div, 1973-77, dir, hazard analysis div, 1977-96, dir, office of Planning and Evaluation, 1997-; Natl School Bd Assn, consult 1985-89; Fairfax Co Sch Bd, mem-at-large, 1978-85, 1989-93, 1996-. **Orgs:** Founding mem Reston Black Focus 1969-; mem Kappa Alpha Psi, Fire Reporting Com NFPA 1972-85; mem bd of dirs Natl Caucus of Black School Bd Mems 1983-85, 1989; mem finance comm, 1982-85, mem legislation comm, 1989-93, VA School Bds Assn; mem Fairfax County Committee of 100 1985-89. **Honors/Awds:** Community Serv Awd Urban League Nova Chap 1982; Commun Serv Awd Natl Council of Negro Women 1985; CPSC EEO Achievement Awd 1986; CPSC Chairman's Award, 1988, 1996; CPSC Distinguished Service Award, 1993; Chairman's Commendation, 1995; Community Service Award, Northern VA Alumni Chap, Omega Psi Phi, 1990; Fairfax County NAACP Community Service Award, 1992. **Military Serv:** US Army lt 1959-61. **Business Addr:** US Consumer Product Safety Commission, Washington, DC 20207.

FRYE, THOMAS JOHN
Entrepreneur. **Personal:** Born Jan 17, 1945, New York, NY; son of Gloria & Thomas Frye; married Linda, May 9, 1987; children: Thomas Jr. **Educ:** Lincoln University, BA, 1969; John Marshall Law School, LLB, 1974. **Career:** Belranie Ins Co, claim adjuster/claim mgr, 1967-73; US Dept of Labor, asst regional administrator, 1973-84; State of Illinois, director, 1984-85; Zenith Ins Co, claim manager, 1985-90; Frye Claims, owner, 1990-. **Orgs:** San Francisco Industrial Claim Assn, president, 1994-95; Minority Claim Association, executive director, 1990-92. **Special Achievements:** Wrote a column, "Managers Corner," California Worker Conspector Enquirer, 3 years. **Military Serv:** US Air Force, sgt, 1963-67; supply man of the month.

FRYE, WILLIAM SINCLAIR
Government official. **Personal:** Born Sep 8, 1924, Montclair, NJ; married Helen. **Educ:** US Army Command & Gen Staff Coll, 1970; Rutgers U, 1972. **Career:** US Postal Serv Montclair NJ, postmaster; US Postal Serv Montvale NJ; postmaster 1977; rutherford NJ postal serv, officer in charge 1976; US Postal Serv Verona NJ, branch mgr 1964. **Orgs:** Asst div comdr 50th Armored Div 1977; comdr State Area Command 1978; mem NAACP;Urban League;Nat Guard Assn;Assn of the AUS Lions Club. **Honors/Awds:** Nominated for ARCOM Comdr, Major Gen 1980; Meritorious Serv Medal; Army Commendation Medal. **Military Serv:** AUS brig gen 35 Yr. **Business Addr:** US Postal Serv, 125 Glen Ridge Ave, Montclair, NJ 07042.

FRYSON, SIM E.
Auto dealership owner. **Career:** Sim Fryson Motor Co Inc, owner, pres, 1995-. **Orgs:** Ashland Rotary-Nissan Dealer Advisory Bd. **Honors/Awds:** Nissan Presidents Circle. **Special Achievements:** Company is ranked #72 on Black Enterprise magazine's 1997 list of Top 100 Black businesses. **Business Addr:** President, Owner, Sim Fryson Motor Co Inc, 2565 Winchester, Ashland, KY 41101, (606)329-2288.

FUDGE, ANN MARIE
Company executive. **Personal:** Born in Washington, DC; married Richard Fudge Sr; children: Richard Jr, Kevin. **Educ:** Simmons Coll, BA (honors) 1973; Harvard Bus Sch, MBA 1977. **Career:** Genl Elec, manpower specialist 1973-75; General Mills, marketing asst 1977-78, asst prod mgr 1978-80, prod mgr 1980-83, marketing dir 1983-94; Kraft Foods, exec vp, Maxwell House Coffee Co, pres, 1994-. **Orgs:** Natl Black MBA Assn 1981-; Jr League 1981-; Exec Leadership Council, pres, 1994-96; Links; Committee of 200; board of directors, Allied Signal, Inc; board of directors, Liz Claiborne; board of directors, Federal Reserve Bank of New York. **Honors/Awds:** COGME Fellow 1975-76; YWCA Leadership Awd 1979; Candace Award, 1992; Glamour Magazine Woman of the Year, 1995; Advertising Woman of the Year, 1995. **Business Addr:** President, Maxwell House Coffee, 250 North St, White Plains, NY 10625.

FUDGE, MARCIA L.
Organization executive, attorney. **Educ:** Ohio State University, Cleveland Marshall College of Law, graduate. **Career:** Cuyahoga County Prosecutor's Office, dir budget and finance/office admin, currently. **Orgs:** Delta Sigma Theta Sorority, pres, 1996-98. **Business Addr:** National President, Delta Sigma Theta Sorority, Inc, 1707 New Hampshire, NW, Washington, DC 20009, (202)986-2400.

FUDGE, MARSHA L.
Organization executive. **Career:** Delta Sigma Theta Sorority, pres, currently.

FUERST, JEAN STERN
Educator. **Personal:** Born Sep 29, 1919, New York, NY; son of Rose S Fuerst and Charles F Fuerst; married Dorothy Braude, Jun 1944. **Career:** Loyola University, School of Social Work, professor, social welfare policy, currently. **Business Addr:** Professor, Social Welfare Policy, School of Social Work, Loyola University, 820 N Michigan Ave, Siedenburg Hall, Chicago, IL 60611, (312)915-7005.

FUFUKA, TIKA N.Y.
Entrepreneur. **Personal:** Born Feb 21, 1952, Cleveland, OH; daughter of Mindoro Reed and Russell Reed. **Educ:** Cuyahoga Community College, AA, AAB, 1973; Michigan State University, BA, 1975; Cleveland State University, international business. **Career:** May Co, assistant personnel director, 1975-78; JC Penny, merchandiser, 1978-80; Joseph Horne, sports manager, 1980-81; Higbee, fashion buyer, 1981-86; Fashion Bug, merchandise executive, 1986-92; Mindy's Return to Fashion, pres/CEO, 1993-; Executive & Professional Protection Services Inc, executive vice pres, 1996-. **Orgs:** Black Focus, chairman of the board, 1989-; 21st Congressional Dist Caucus, chair, business women committee, 1984-; Urban League of Greater Cleveland, former board member, 1984-90; Operation Push, former board member, 1987-90; Ohio Youth Advisory Council, council member (governor appointee), 1987-90; Advisory council participation: Cuyahoga County Women Business Enterprise; Cleveland Female Business Enterprise; Displaced/Single Parent Homemakers Cuyahoga Community Council; Mayor's Census Task Force; National Hook-Up; 100 Black Women Coalition; Black Congressional Caucus Braintrust; Association of MBA Executive; Black Professional Association; National Association of Negro Business/Professional Women; National Association of Female Executives; United Black Fund; Greater East Cleveland Democratic Club; League of Women Voters; Ohio Rainbow Coalition; Network Together (Mid-West Region); Black Elected DemocraticOfials of Ohio; Project MOVE; Cuyahoga Hills Boys Advisory Council; Operation Big Vote; National Council of Negro Women; National Political Congress of Black Women; United Way Centralized Resource & Referral Serv, chair, 1993; United Way, general assembly, 1993-96; Joint Committee on Medical Provider Impact for the State of Ohio, vice chair, 1992-; Women Community Foundation, bd mem, 1993; Career Beginning Program, bd mem, 1991-93; United Way Leadership Dev Prog Committee, 1992; Women in Appointed Office Proj, 1994; WCPN Radio, 1994; Planned Parenthood of Greater Cleveland, 1995; Citizen League of Cleveland, 1995; United Way Appeal Committee, 1996; Playhouse Sq Foundation, 1996; Cleveland Museum of Art, 1996; Greater Cleveland Growth Association-Public Affairs Committee, 1996; United Way Public Policy Committee, 1997. **Honors/Awds:** Cleveland State University Community Award, 1991; United Way Leadership Award, 1991; City of Cleveland Volunteer Leadership Recognition, 1991; Women's Network, Women In Appointed Office, Kinsman Youth Developmment Program and Scholarship. **Business Addr:** Four Commerce Park Sq, 23200 Chagrin Blvd, Ste 600, Beachwood, OH 44122.

FUGET, CHARLES ROBERT
Educational administrator. **Personal:** Born Dec 15, 1929, Rochester, PA; son of Mary Harris Fuget and Clinton H Fuget; married Enid Deane (deceased); children: Craig D; married Andrea Blanding. **Educ:** Geneva Coll, BS, 1951; PA State Univ, MS 1953, PhD 1956. **Career:** Esso Research & Engineering, Linden, NJ, rsch chemist, 1955-56; Callery Chemical Co., Callery, PA, rsch chemist, 1957-63; State Univ of NY, Coll at Buffalo, prof, chem, 1963-64; Geneva Coll, Beaver Falls PA, chmn, prof of physics 1964-71; AUS Ballistic Research Labs, Aberdeen, MD, consultant, 1968-69; Indiana Univ of PA, assoc

dean, School of arts/science, 1971-76, dean, coll natl sci/math 1977-84, acting vp, student univ affairs, 1984-85; Dean, Coll Natl sci/math 1985-88; deputy secretary, PA Dept of Educ, Harrisburg, PA, 1988-91; Indiana University of PA, interim president, 1991-92; PA Department of Education, Harrisburg, PA, retired deputy secretary, commissioner, postsecondary and higher education, 1992-94. **Orgs:** IN Rotary Club, board of directors, 1982-88; IN Hosp Corp 1978-83; bd of governors, General Bd of Higher Educ & Ministry, 1980-88, 1992-; chmn, PA Commn for United Ministries in Higher Educ 1978-80; vice pres, Univ Senate of the United Methodist Church, 1989-92. **Honors/Awds:** Distinguished Serv Award, Alumni Assn, Geneva Coll, 1976; Distinguished Serv Award, Upper Beaver Valley Jaycees 1969; Indiana Univ of Pennsylvania, Pres' Medal of Distinction, 1988; LHD, Hahnemann Univ, 1988; Honorary Doctor of Science, Geneva College, 1990; Honorary Doctor of Public Services, Indiana Univ of Pennsylvania, 1995. **Home Addr:** 301 N Progress Ave, Apt M5, Harrisburg, PA 17109.

FUGET, HENRY EUGENE
Bank president. **Personal:** Born Aug 8, 1925, Rochester, PA; married Gladys Mae Smith; children: Sonja L. **Educ:** Univ of Pittsburgh, BA 1966, MA 1967. **Career:** Upper Fifth Ave Office Mellon Bank, NA, manager 1972-79; Gulf Office, Mellon Bank, NA, avp & manager 1979-82; Mellon Bank, NA, avp & asst mngr 1982-85;New World Natl Bank, president. **Orgs:** Sickle Cell Soc, Inc, treasurer 1983-; Three Rivers Rotary Club, Pgh, mem; Central Baptist Church, Pgh, deacon. **Military Serv:** AUS mst sgt 20 years. **Business Addr:** President, New World Natl Bank, 6393 Penn Ave, Pittsburgh, PA 15206.

FUGETT, JEAN S., JR.
Business executive, lawyer, football player. **Personal:** Born in Baltimore, MD. **Educ:** Amherst College, graduated (with honors); George Washington Law School, JD. **Career:** Dallas Cowboys, football player, 1972; Washington Redskins, tight end, until 1979; Washington Post, intern; CBS Sports, football color commentator; TLC Beatrice International Holdings Co, chairman, until 1994. **Special Achievements:** Participated in Super Bowl X with Dallas Cowboys. **Business Addr:** Former Chair, TLC Beatrice Intl Holdings Inc, 9 W 57th St, 48th Fl, New York, NY 10019, (212)756-8900.

FUHR, GRANT SCOTT
Professional hockey player. **Personal:** Born Sep 28, 1962, Alberta;son of Betty Fuhr and Robert Fuhr; married Corrine (divorced); children: 2 daughters; married Jill; children: Robert. **Career:** Edmunton Oilers, goalie, 1981-90; Toronto Maple Leafs, goalie, 1991-92; Buffalo Sabres, goalie, 1992-95; St Louis Blues, 1995-. **Honors/Awds:** Natl Hockey League, Vezina Trophy, 1987-88; played in 6 NHL All-Star Games; played in Canada Cup, 1984, 1987; named to NHL First All-Star Team, 1987-88. **Business Addr:** Professional Hockey Player, St Louis Blues, 1401 Clark Ave, St Louis, MO 63103, (314)622-2500.

FULGHAM, ROIETTA GOODWIN
Educator. **Personal:** Born Jan 28, 1948, Oakland, CA; daughter of Dovie Juanita Miles Goodwin and Roy Alexander Goodwin; divorced; children: Keia Syreeta. **Educ:** Utah State Univ Logan UT, BS 1971, MS 1977. **Career:** Area Voc Ctr Ogden UT, off occupations supv 1971-75; Yosemite Jr Coll Dist Modesto, instructor 1975-76; Los Rios Comm Coll Dist ARC, business instructor 1976-. **Orgs:** Mem Natl Western CA Business Educ Assoc 1976-; mem Natl Educ Assn/CA Teachers Assn 1976-; sec NAACP Central Area Conf 1976-87; vice pres NAACP California State Conf 1988-; treasurer, NAACP Sacramento Branch, 1991-; state council rep CA Teachers Assn 1979-85; natl teller NAACP 1980-81; sec Utah State Univ Black Alumni Assn 1980-; chairperson NAACP West Coast Region 1982-83, NAACP ACT-SO Prog Sacramento Branch 1982-85; chairperson Outstanding Business Student Program California Business Educ Assn 1983; office mgr IDS Financial Serv 1985-86; support analyst Wang Labs Inc 1986; consultant Westroots Business Writing Systems 1986-; member, Delta Sigma Theta, Inc, 1991-. **Honors/Awds:** Outstanding Program Utah State Univ Alumni Assn 1980; Certified Business Educator Business Educ Certification Council 1976; Certified Professional Sec Professional Sec Intl 1982; Outstanding Young Woman of Amer 1982; NAACP Golden Gavel Award NAACP Northern Area Conf 1984; Outstanding Instructor of the Year Amer River Coll 1986. **Home Addr:** 6600 Branchwater Way, Citrus Heights, CA 95621. **Business Addr:** Instructor, Los Rios Comm Coll Dist, American River College, 4700 College Oak Dr, Sacramento, CA 95841.

FULLER, ALFREDIA Y.
Attorney. **Personal:** Born Jun 19, 1958, Miami, FL; daughter of Willie A and Loraine; divorced. **Educ:** University of Maryland, BSBA, 1982; Antioch School of Law, JD, 1986. **Career:** Skadden, Arps, law clerk, 1986-88; Fidelity Mortgage Company, president, 1990-91; George Washington University, Washington Saturday College, lecturer, 1992-93; Law Offices of Alfredia Y Fuller, attorney, 1988-. **Orgs:** National Bar Association, chairman, Bankruptcy Law Section, 1993-95; National Association of Black Women Attorneys, 1995; District of Columbia Superior Court, certified mediator, 1985-; District of Columbia Bar Association, 1989-; Isle of Patmos Baptist Church WDC, trustee, 1989-91; National Bar Association, board of governors, 1993-; Washington Saturday College, board of trustees, 1992-. **Special Achievements:** Contributing Writer, National Bar Association Magazine, 1994-95. **Business Phone:** (202)508-3394.

FULLER, ALMYRA OVETA
Biomedical research scientist, professor. **Personal:** Born Aug 31, 1955, Mebone, NC; daughter of Deborah Evelyn Woods Fuller and Herbert R Fuller; married Jerry Caldwell, Jun 16, 1984; children: Brian Randolph Caldwell. **Educ:** Univ of North Carolina, Chapel Hill, BA, 1977, PhD, 1983; Univ of Chicago, IL, postdoctoral Study, 1983-88. **Career:** Univ of North Carolina, research assistant, 1980-82; Univ of Chicago, IL, instructor & fellow, 1984-85, research associate, 1987-88; Univ of MI, Ann Arbor, asst prof, 1988-. **Orgs:** Alpha Kappa Alpha, Basileus of Alumni Chapter, 1977-78; Natl Technical Assn, cofounder of Research Triangle 1980-; UNC-CH Summer Apprentice Research Program, asst dir, 1981-82; Sigma Xi Research Society, mem, 1983-; Amer Assn for the Advancement of Science, mem, 1984-; Amer Society of Microbiology, mem, 1984-; DeVeras Inc, consultant, 1987-89; Advisory Committee to Fellows Programs, Lineberger Cancer Research Center, 1989-; Ad Hoc Reviewer, Louisiana bd of regents, 1989; Howard Hughes Doctoral Fellowship Panel, 1991. **Honors/Awds:** NTA Service Award, Research Triangle Chapter of NTA, 1983; author of scientific publications, 1983-; Anna Fuller Fund Postdoc Award, 1983-84; Thornton Professional Achievement Award Chicago chap, NTA, 1984; NIH Postdoctoral Research Award, Nat Inst of Science, 1984-86; Postdoctoral Research Award, Ford Foundation, 1986-87. **Business Addr:** Assistant Professor, University of Michigan Medical Center, 6736 Medical Science Bldg II, Ann Arbor, MI 48109-0620.

FULLER, CHARLES
Playwright, author. **Personal:** Born Mar 5, 1939, Philadelphia, PA; son of Lillian Anderson Fuller and Charles Henry Fuller; married Miriam A Nesbitt, Aug 4, 1962; children: Charles III, David. **Educ:** Villanova University, 1956-58; LaSalle College, 1965-67. **Career:** Radio work includes: The Black Experience, director, 1970-71; Afro-American Arts Theatre, co-founder, codirector, 1967-71; stage writings include: The Village: A Party, 1968, revised as The Perfect Party, 1969; In My Many Names and Days, 1972; The Candidate, 1974; In the Deepest Part of Sleep, 1974; First Love, 1974; The Lay Out Letter, 1975; The Brownsville Raid, 1976; Sparrow in Flight, 1978; Zooman and the Sign, 1980, published in 1981; A Soldier's Play, 1981, 1982, 1983, published in 1982; Sally, 1988; Prince, 1988; We, 1989; film writings include: A Soldier's Story, adaptation of play, 1984; Miles, 1994; television writings include: Roots, Resistance, and Renaissance, 1967; The Sky Is Gray, American Short Story, 1980; A Gathering of Old Men, 1987; Sonnyboy, 1993; Zooman, 1995; The Badge 1995; Love Songs, 1997; The Slave Dancer, 1998; author of short stories for anthologies and magazines. **Orgs:** Chadama Ltd & Chadama II, pres & CEO. **Honors/Awds:** CAPS Fellowship, Playwriting Creative Artist in Public Service, 1975; Rockefeller Grant, Playwriting, 1976-77; Fellowship in Playwriting, Natl Endowment of Arts, 1976-77; Guggenheim Fellow in Playwriting, 1977-78; Obie Award, Best Playwright, 1981; Theatre Club Award, Best Play; Pulitzer Prize for Drama, 1982; New York Critics, Best American Play Award, 1982; Outer Circle Critics Award, Best Play, 1982; Audelco Awards, Best Playwright & Best Play, 1981, 1982; Hazelett Award, Pennsylvania Council on the Arts, Distinguished Artist; nominated, Academy Award, screenwriting, Soldier's Story. **Military Serv:** US Army, 1959-62; Good Conduct Medal. **Business Addr:** Author, c/o George Lane, William Morris Agency, 1350 Avenue of the Americas, New York, NY 10019.

FULLER, COREY
Professional football player. **Personal:** Born May 11, 1971, Tallahassee, FL. **Educ:** Florida State, bachelor's degree in criminology and child development. **Career:** Minnesota Vikings, defensive back, 1995-. **Business Addr:** Professional Football Player, Minnesota Vikings, 9520 Viking Dr, Eden Prairie, MN 55344, (612)828-6500.

FULLER, CURTIS D.
Musician, composer, arranger. **Personal:** Born Dec 15, 1934, Detroit, MI; married Judith Patterson; children: Ronald, Darryl, Gerald, Dellaney, Wellington. **Educ:** Detroit Inst of Arts Univ of Detroit; Wayne State U, BA; Bronx Comm Coll, mus theory; Henry St Settlement Inst, jazzmobile prog under Billy Taylor. **Career:** Dizzy Gillispie Orch; Lester Young; James Moody; Quincy Jones Orch; Art Blakey "Jazz Messengers" Count Basie Orch; John Coltrane, recorded with & many others; LITU Long Island, NY, counselor & Instr. **Orgs:** Mem Local 802 Musicians Union; mem Broadcast Music Inc for writers For 17 yrs. **Honors/Awds:** Downbeat Award; Pittsburg Courier Award; recorded World Award Shaefer Beer Award, recorded musical Cabin In Sky by Vernon Duke with the NY Phil Strings & Brass on ABC Paramount; performed at NY Radio City Jam Session 1973; performed at Tribute to Charlie Parker 1975; performed at Newport Jazz Fest; compositions include "Smokin'", "Jacque's Groove", "Sop City", "People Places & Things", recordings include "Crankin'", "Smokin'", "Kwanza", "Love & Understanding" & "A Caddy for daddy". **Military Serv:** AUS band. **Business Addr:** 1864 7 Ave #52, New York, NY 10026.

FULLER, DEWEY C.
Executive director. **Personal:** Born Apr 4, 1934, Alabama; married Inez. **Educ:** Univ of Cincinnati, BA 1946; MI U, Certificate of Labor & Ind Relations 1966; Univ of Cincinnati, grad work. **Career:** Urban League of Greater Cincinnati, dir 1973-, asst dir 1968-73, dir econ 1964-66; Hamilton Co Welfare Dept, case worker 1960-64; US Postal, clk 1950-60. **Orgs:** Nat Urban League Leadership Group - Process Tng; Univ of Cincinnati Human Relations Seminar in Interpersonal Skills; Red Cross Comm Orgn Workshop; Nat UrbanLeague Conf Tech in Problem Solving; Comm Chest Methods Change Seminar; mem Kappa Alpha Psi Frat; bd trustees PREP; JET; sec OH Valley Council of Urban Lg; Cincinnati Manpower Planning Council; bd trustees Funds for Self-interprise; mem Madisonville Kiwanis Club; Wesley Smith Lodge; Prince Hall Mason; OHAdv Council on Voc Edn. **Military Serv:** Sgt 1943-46. **Business Addr:** 2400 Reading Rd, Cincinnati, OH 45202.

FULLER, DORIS J.
Association executive. **Personal:** Born May 26, 1945, Houston County, GA; daughter of Bertha Mae Clark Fuller and Sim Clinton Fuller Jr. **Educ:** Morris Brown Coll, BS 1966; GA State Univ, MEd 1975; Univ San Francisco, NSF Inst 1969. **Career:** Atlanta Bd of Educ, teacher 1966-78; Southern Bell, asst mgr 1978-94; Atlanta Metropolitan College, adjunct instructor/mathematics and trainer/work shop presenter, currently. **Orgs:** 2nd vice pres Atl Alumnae Chap DST Sor 1977-79; educ vice pres Magic Toastmasters TI 1979, 1983, 1986; nominating comm chairperson Southern Region DST Sor Inc 1978-80; mem Southern Bell Speaker's Bureau 1980-93; state youth leadership coord Dist 14 TI 1981; recording sec MBC Natl Alumni Assoc 1984-88; pres Atl Chap MBC Alumni Assoc 1985-87; co-chairperson Mens & Womens Unity Day Beulah Bapt Church 1985; vice pres, MBC National Alumni Assn 1988-95. **Honors/Awds:** President's Awd Toastmasters Intl 1980; Outstanding Corporate Alumni NAFEO Washington DC 1983; Presidential Citation MBC Alumni Assoc Atl Chap 1985; Outstanding Alumni MBC Student Govt Assoc 1985; Southern Bell Speakers Bureau Achievement Awd 1986; Alumna of the Year, MBC National Alumni Assn 1989; Count On Me, Employee Recognition Program of Southern Bell 1989; Southern Bell Best-of-the-Best Winner (a company-wide Speakers Bureau competition) 1988. **Home Addr:** 2190 Star Mist Dr SW, Atlanta, GA 30311.

FULLER, DR. HAROLD DAVID
Educator. **Personal:** Born Sep 1, 1937, Oklahoma City, OK; son of Tisha Mae Fuller and Andrew Fuller; married Annie Laurie Blood, Aug 26, 1961; children: April Beth Fuller, Jeremy David Fuller. **Educ:** Oklahoma University, Norman, OK, BA, 1959; Arizona State University, Tempe, AZ, MA, 1968; EdD, 1992. **Career:** US Air Force, Luke Air Force Base, airman, 1960-66; Roosevelt School District, Phoenix, AZ, teacher, 1964-68, comm school dir, 1968-71, asst principal, 1971-73; Mesa Public Schools, Mesa, AZ, principal, 1973-; Preside Sirrins Adult Day Health Care Board. **Orgs:** Champaign chairman, Mesa United Way, 1990-91; president of board, Mesa ARC, 1987-89; vice chair of board, Mesa United Way, 1987-89; president of board, Mesa Family YMCA, 1986-87; chairman of board, HEATS Foundation, 1990-; Preside Sirrino Adult Day Health Care, board. **Honors/Awds:** Leadership Award, Mesa United Way, 1990-91; Human Service Award, Mesa Community Council, 1988; Achievement Award, Mesa Public Schools, 1988; Citizen of the Year, Mesa Tribune Newspaper, 1988; Boss of the Year, Jonas Salk School, 1980; Presidential Award, Mesa ARC, 1987-89; Leadership Award, Mesa YMCA, 1986-87; Spirit of America, US Air Force, 1960. **Military Serv:** US Air Force, Airman First Class, 1960-66; received Spirit of America Award. **Home Addr:** 1724 E Hope, Mesa, AZ 85203.

FULLER, GLORIA A.
Librarian. **Personal:** Born May 28, 1952, Brunswick, GA; daughter of Rosetta Frazier Atkinson and Calvin Sinclair Atkinson Sr; married Jimmy Lee Fuller, Aug 23, 1986; children: Gabrielle Amanda Fuller. **Educ:** South Carolina State University, Orangeburg, SC, BS, 1974; Prince George's Community College, Largo, MD, AA, 1980; University of Maryland, College Park, MD, MLS, 1982. **Career:** Florence School District, Florence, SC, media specialist, 1974-75; Federal Law Enforcement Training Center, Brunswick, GA, library tech, 1975-76; Smithsonian Institution, Washington, DC, library tech, 1976-83, librarian, 1983-85; Defense Intelligence Agency, Washington, DC, information services specialist, 1985-92; DIA Classified Library, Database Services Division, chief, 1992-. **Orgs:** Member, American Assn of Law Libraries, 1983-89; member, American Library Assn, 1981-; member, ALA Black Caucus, 1988-89; treasurer, financial secretary, chair audit, chair reg his, Delta Sigma Theta Sorority, Inc, 1971-; member, DC Online Users Group, 1984-; member, FEDLINK Executive Advisory Council, 1991-93; Federal Library and Information Center Committee, 1992-, Budget & Finance Working Group, 1994-95; Federal Librarians Round Table, 1985-; Armed Forces Libraries Round Table, 1991; Intelligence Community Librarians' Com-

mittee (ICLC); Community Open Source Program Office (COSPO) Research Secretariat, 1993-96; Emmanuel Baptist Church; Delta Sigma Theta Sorority, Inc, MD journalist, 1997-. **Honors/Awds:** Letters of Appreciation, 1986, 1987, 1988, 1989, 1994-95, Service Awd, 1985, 1990, 1995, Defense Intelligence Agency; Certification of Award for Exceptional Service, Smithsonian Institution, 1979-80, 1984-85; Certificate of Recognition, Operation Desert Shield/Desert Storm, 1991; Community Open Source Program Office, Certificate of Appreciation, 1995; Defense Intelligence Agency, Special Achievement Awd, 1995; Central Intelligence Agency, Exceptional Performance Awd, 1995; Delta Sigma Theta Sorority Inc, 25 Years of Membership, 1996. **Business Addr:** Defense Intelligence Agency, Database Services Division, Attn: SVI-4, Rm E4-250, Washington, DC 20340-5100.

FULLER, JACK LEWIS
Fashion designer. **Personal:** Born Dec 30, 1945, Toombs County, GA; son of Elvera Gillis Fuller and Mell Fuller. **Educ:** Parsons School of Design, BFA 1965. **Career:** Kasper for Joan Leslie, asst designer; Elliott Bass, Upper Crust Sportswear, Nuance Dresses, designer; Leslie Fay Inc, designer; Jardine Ltd, designer; Bleyle-By Jack Fuller, designer. **Orgs:** Consultant on Harlem Public Schools, New York City Bd of Educ. **Honors/Awds:** Key to City of Cincinnati 1975-76; Pres' Awd, Univ of Cincinnati 1976; Rising Stars Fashion Show, Press Week, Plaza Hotel 1975; Urban League Designer of the Year 1975. **Business Addr:** Designer, Jack Fuller, Ltd, 100 W 15, New York, NY 10011.

FULLER, JAMES J.
Educational administrator. **Personal:** Born Nov 11, 1946, Eutawville, SC; married Ruth Smothers; children: Julian, Mark. **Educ:** Morgan State Univ, BA, history and political science, 1972; Howard Univ School of Divinity, MDiv, 1982, Doctorate of Ministry, 1990. **Career:** Univ of Maryland, Baltimore County, Office of Minority Recruitment, asst dir, 1972-74, Campus activities, dir, 1974-80, Upward Bound Program, counselor, 1990-; New Hope Baptist Church, pastor, 1977-. **Orgs:** Natl Council of Educational Opportunity Assn; Mid-Eastern Assn Opportunity Personnel Program; Maryland Executive Council for Educational Opportunity; NAACP; Natl Urban League; Governor's Commission for Afro-American History and Culture, vice chairman; Baltimore Bd of Ed, African/African-American Curriculum Task Force; Baltimore Baptist Ministers Conf, first and second vp. **Honors/Awds:** Man of Yr Prudential Life Ins 1971; Richard H Hunt meml Fund Resolution 1975; Sons of Prophet Cert; 1975; AUS Good Conduct Medal 1968; Am Legion Serv Award 1963; City of Baltimore, Citizen's Citation; Baltimore Junior Academy Natl Alumni Assn, Humanitarian Award; Mayor's Citation for outstanding contributions to church and community; White House invitation from former President Jimmy Carter. **Military Serv:** US Army, spec-4, 1966-68.

FULLER, NORVELL RICARDO
Industrial minerals company executive. **Personal:** Born Apr 8, 1953, St Petersburg, FL; son of Minnie L Henry Fuller and Hubert L Fuller; children: Nicole Rasheda, Duane. **Educ:** Howard Univ, BS 1976; many company management & skills courses. **Career:** Cargill Inc, resin chemist/sales rep 1976-81; K&N International (Importers), vice pres; Pfizer Inc, regional manager of sales development 1981-. **Orgs:** Federation of Coatings Technology 1979-; Adhesive & Sealants Council 1981-; United Way; SLLC; Transafrica & World Visions; Howard Univ Alumni; Soc of Plastic Inst; Cultured Marble Inst; So CA Coatings Soc; Mile Swimmers Club; Ski Club. **Honors/Awds:** Leader in Western Region Sales for 8 years Pfizer Inc 1982-90; ordained minister Universal Triumph, The Dominion of God 1983; Salesman of the Decade Award. **Business Addr:** Sales Representative, Pfizer Inc, 2800 Ayers Ave, Los Angeles, CA 90023.

FULLER, RANDY LAMAR
Professional football player. **Personal:** Born Jun 2, 1970, Columbus, GA; married Gussie. **Educ:** Tennessee State, degree in criminal justice. **Career:** Denver Broncos, defensive back, 1994; Pittsburgh Steelers, 1995-. **Business Addr:** Professional Football Player, Pittsburgh Steelers, Three Rivers Stadium, 300 Stadium Circle, Pittsburgh, PA 15212, (412)323-1200.

FULLER, THOMAS S.
County government official. **Personal:** Born Oct 18, 1934, Abbeville, SC; children: Hazel Jenkins, Toni. **Educ:** Allen Univ, BPsy; Roosevelt Univ, MPA. **Career:** Amer Hosp Assoc, dir div of comm relations 1969-74; State of IL Equal Employment Oppor Office, dir 1975-77; Cook Co Sheriff, asst 1977-78; Metro Water Reclamation Dist of Gr Chicago, pres, comm, currently. **Orgs:** Mem Amer Public Works Assoc; bd mem Comm & Economic Develop Assoc Cook Co; mem NAACP; mem Operation PUSH Chicago Urban League. **Honors/Awds:** Adjunct professorship Chicago State Univ. **Military Serv:** US Army, 2 yrs. **Business Addr:** President, Commissioner, Metro Water Reclamation Dist of Greater Chicago, 100 E Erie St, Chicago, IL 60611.

FULLER, VIVIAN L.
Athletic director. **Personal:** Born Oct 17, 1954, Chapel Hill, NC. **Educ:** Fayetteville State University, BS; University of Idaho, MEd; Iowa State University, PhD. **Career:** Bennett College; NC A&T University; Indiana University of Pennsylvania; Tennessee State University, athletics dir, currently. **Orgs:** National Collegiate Athletic Association; Black Women's Sports Foundation; National Association of NACDA; Delta Sigma Theta; NACWA; American Alliance of Health, Physical Education and Dance. **Honors/Awds:** NACNAA. **Business Addr:** Director of Intercollegiate Athletics, Tennessee State Univ, 3500 John A Merrit Blvd, Kean Hall, Rm 131, Nashville, TN 37209-1561, (615)963-5034.

FULLER, WILLIAM HENRY, JR.
Professional football player. **Personal:** Born Mar 8, 1962, Norfolk, VA; married Precilla; children: Karen, Krystal, Kimberly. **Educ:** North Carolina, degree in psychology. **Career:** Philadelphia Stars (USFL), 1984; Baltimore Stars (USFL), 1985; Houston Oilers, 1986-94; Philadelphia Eagles, 1995-96; San Diego Chargers, 1997-. **Honors/Awds:** Pro Bowl appearances, 1991, 1994, 1995, 1996. **Business Addr:** Professional Football Player, San Diego Chargers, Qualcomm Stadium, 9449 Friars Rd, San Diego, CA 92108, (619)280-2111.

FULLWOOD, HARLOW, JR.
Food service company executive. **Personal:** Born Jan 26, 1941, Asheville, NC; son of Mr & Mrs Harlow Fullwood Sr (deceased); married Elnora Bassett; children: Paquita Tara, Harlow III. **Educ:** Comm Coll of Baltimore, AA 1973; VA Union Univ, BA 1977; Baltimore Police Academy, 1964; Kentucky Fried Chicken Training Center, 1984. **Career:** Baltimore City Police Dept, police recruiter 1964-86; El Pa Ha Foods Inc, pres 1986-; Fullwood Foods Inc, featuring Kentucky Fried Chicken restaurants, pres, 1984-; Harlow Foods Inc, featuring KFC restaurants, 1990; Penn-North Foods Inc, featuring Kentucky Fried Chicken restaurants, pres, 1988-. **Orgs:** Bd of trustees, Concord Baptist Church; trustee bd, VA Union Univ; dir, Honorary Life Member; The Natl Congress of Parents & Teachers; bd of dirs, Signal 13 Found Inc; Baltimore Symphony Orchestra; life mem, Alpha Phi Alpha Fraternity; Paul Harris Fellow, Rotary Found of Rotary Intl; Goldenn Heritage Life Mem, NAACP; board of directors, Advertising & Professional Club of Baltimore, Inc; charter member, National Coalition of 100 Black Men of Maryland. **Honors/Awds:** The Evening Sun Policeman of the Year Awd 1979; J C Penney Golden Rule Awd 1983; The Jefferson Awd 1983; Man of the Year The Natl Assn of Negro Business & Professional Women's Clubs Inc 1983; Baltimore's Best Awd 1984; Kentucky Fried Chicken Five Star Awd 1985; Kentucky Fried Chicken White Glove & 2 SC Awd 1985; Governor's Citation 1986; Mayor's Citation 1986; Meritorius Service Award, The United Negro College Fund, 1983; The Natl Alliance of Business Commendation, 1984; Optimist International, 1979; Community Service Award 1983; The Vanguard Justice Society, Inc, Police Officer of the Year 1984;Helen O Gattie Memorial AwdContinental Societies, Inc, 1985; VA Union Univ First Distinguished Leader Awd 1982; Afro-American Newspaper Award, 1973; VUU Alumnus of the Year, 1979; Distinguishedrvice Award, Baltimore City Police Dept 1986; Kentucky Fried Chicken Million Dollar Award, 1987 & 1988; Minority Business Advocate of the Year, State of Maryland, US Small Business Admin, 1989; Outstanding Leadership & Service to the Business Community & Education Award, Bowie State Univ, 1989; Community Service Award, Inst for Amer Business, 1989; African-American Exposition, chairman, 1993; Government's Recognition Award for Growth & Development, 1992; African-American Male Excellence Award, 1990; Delta Lambda Chapter, A0A Brother of the Year, 1992; Zeta Phi Beta Sorority Inc, Leadership Award, 1993; Henry G Parks Jr Business Award, 1993; Anheuser-Busch, Outstanding Achievement Award, 1994. **Home Addr:** 13 Country Mill Ct, Catonsville, MD 21228. **Business Addr:** President, Fullwood Foods, Inc, 13 Country Mill Court, Catonsville, MD 21228.

FULTON, ROBERT HENRY
Labor union executive. **Personal:** Born Nov 15, 1926, Philadelphia, PA; son of Carlotta Nixon (deceased) and David Fulton (deceased); married Kathryn Lawson Brown, Aug 29, 1987; children: Eleanor Fulton Price, Vincent, Anthony, Darlene Brown, Marcella, Doreen Brown. **Educ:** Cornell Univ School of Indus & L/R, liberal arts 1974. **Career:** Transport Workers Union Local Local 100, vice pres 1979-90; Transport Workers Union Local 100, staff rep, 1963-79, recording secretary 1990-; Transport workers of America, international vice president, 1989-, equal rights & liberties committee chairman, 1989-. **Orgs:** Vp Rochdale Village Recreation & Org 1974-80; commr Boy Scouts of Am New York City So Dist 1975-80; chmn of training BSA EXPLORER Div Career & Educ 1976-80; exec bd mem Black Trade Unionist Leadership Com 1974-78. **Honors/Awds:** BSA Merit of Honor, Boy Scouts of Am Queens 1976; George Meany Scouting Award, AFL/CIO Washington, DC 1978; RVRO Man of the Year Award Rochdale Village Rec Orgn Queens 1979; St George Assn Chapter II NYCTS, publicity dir, Public Relation Award, 1981; Rochdale Village Spring Festival, Mr Spirit of Rochdale, 1982; The Labor Merit Award, 1988; NY City Transit Authority, recognition for 41 yrs of loyal service, 1988; The Silver Beaver Award, Boy Scouts of Amer, 1981; United Negro Coll Fund, Distinguished Leadership Award, 1984, Meritorious Service Award, 1985; New Queens Council Community Leader, Boy Scouts of America, 1989. **Military Serv:** AAC sgt 1945-46. **Business Addr:** Recording Secretary, Transport Workers Union, Local 100, 80 West End Ave, New York, NY 10023.

FULWOOD, SAM, III
Journalist. **Personal:** Born Aug 28, 1956, Monroe, NC; son of Hallie Bernice Massey Fulwood and Samuel L Fulwood Jr; married Cynthia Marie Bell, Sep 1, 1984; children: Katherine Amanda. **Educ:** University of North Carolina, Chapel Hill, NC, BA, journalism, 1978. **Career:** Charlotte Observer, Charlotte, NC, business reporter, sports writer, police reporter, 1978-83; Baltimore Sun, Baltimore, MD, asst city editor, business reporter, Africa correspondent, editorial writer, 1983-87; Atlanta Journal-Constitution, Atlanta, GA, state political editor, assistant business editor, 1987-89; Los Angeles Times, Washington, DC, correspondent, 1989-; Emerge Magazine, Washington, columnist, 1990-92. **Orgs:** Member, 1981-, Parliamentational Board member, 1989-90, National Association of Black Journalists; member, Alpha Phi Alpha Fraternity, 1976-. **Honors/Awds:** Unity Awards in Media, 1st Economics Reporting Lincoln University, 1988, Unity Awards in Media, 1st Political Reporting Lincoln University, 1988; Women, Men and Media, Break Through Award, 1992; Nieman Fellow, Harvard Univ, 1993-94. **Special Achievements:** Author: "Walking From the Dream: My Life in the Black Middle Class," Anchor Books, 1996. **Business Addr:** Washington Correspondent, Los Angeles Times, 1875 I St, NW, Suite 1100, Washington, DC 20006, (202)861-9243.

FUNDERBURG, I. OWEN
Business executive. **Personal:** Born Aug 21, 1924, Monticello, GA; married Clara C; children: I Owen Jr, Ilon Edward, Douglas. **Educ:** Morehouse Coll, BA 1947; Rutgers Univ Grad Sch of Banking, grad 1959; Univ of MI, attended 1947-48. **Career:** Mechanics & Farmer's Bank Durham, NC, teller; Gateway Natl Bank St Louis, exec vp/ceo 1966-74; Citizens Trust Bank Atlanta, GA, pres 1974-. **Business Addr:** President, Citizens Trust Bank, 75 Piedmont Ave NE, Atlanta, GA 30303.

FUNDERBURK, WILLIAM WATSON
Physician. **Personal:** Born Aug 26, 1931, South Carolina; son of Florence and William L; married Marilyn; children: William, Julie, Christina. **Educ:** Johnson C Smith U, BS 1952; Howard U, MD 1956. **Career:** Howard Medical School and Hospital, 1956-74; Howard Univ, assoc dean student affairs 1970-72; Howard Univ, assoc prof surgery 1971-77; Ctr for Ambulatory Surgery, med dir 1977-84; Self Employed, physician. **Orgs:** Mem AOA 1956-, NMA 1956-, Med Chi Soc 1956-; District of Columbia Medical Society 1989-.

FUNDERBURKE, LAWRENCE DAMON
Professional basketball player. **Personal:** Born Dec 15, 1970. **Educ:** Ohio State, bachelor's degree in business finance (magna cum laude), 1994. **Career:** Sacramento Kings, forward, 1997-. **Business Addr:** Professional Basketball Player, Sacramento Kings, One Sports Parkway, Sacramento, CA 95834, (916)928-6900.

FUNN, CARLTON A., SR.
Educator, exhibitor. **Personal:** Born Jan 29, 1932, Alexandria, VA; married Joan Berry; children: Carlton Jr, Tracye, Marc. **Educ:** Storer Coll Harpers Ferry WV, BA 1953; VA State University Petersburg VA, MEd 1972. **Career:** Fairfax County Public School Syst, teacher, minority relations cons; VA School System, teacher 25 yrs; Washington DC Public School Syst, teacher 3 yrs; The History & Culture of Minorities, dir cultural educ prog; Washington, DC, teacher. **Orgs:** Mem, Natl Educ Assn, VA Educ Assn, Fairfax Educ Assn, WA Urban League, NAACP, Alexandria Bicentennial Comm, PTA 1974, Alexandria Dem Committeeman 1967-69; trustee Alfred St Bapt Church 1967-68; bd mem Alexandria Human Relations Council 1973-; vice pres Alexandria Coun on Human Relations, 1972-73, Alexandria Chamber of Commerce, 1967-68; vice pres, Hopkins House Assn, 1972; member, Omega Psi Phi Fraternity, Inc, 1977-; The Society For the Preservation of Black Heritage, 1996; Alexandria, VA city commissioner for the 250th city anniversary 1997-98. **Honors/Awds:** Human/Civil Awd VA Ed Assoc, VA Min Caucus 1976; Human Relat Awd Fairfax VA Ed Assoc 1976; Citizen of the Year Awd No VA Psi Nu Chap Omega Psi Phi Frat Inc 1976; Carter G Woodson Awd Natl Ed Assoc 1976; Apprec Awd Fairfax Ed Assoc Black Caucus 1977; Citizen of the Year Awd Recog Comm of 3rd Dist Omega Psi Phi Frat Inc 1977; Storer Coll Serv Awds, Certs, Scholarship; Robert F Kennedy Scroll Cincinnati Teachers 1972; Cert of Apprec Hopkins House Assoc 1973; Amer Coll Student Leaders Awd 1953; Natl Defense Serv Medal Good Conduct Medal & Marksman Badge AUS; Human Relations Exhibit 1979; History & Culture of Minorities Exhibit, Natl Shown 169 Times 1980; Natl Trends Awd Arlington VA Chap of the Links Inc 1979; NAACP Awd of Appreciation The Alexandria VA Br 1979; Cert of Apprec Natl Assoc of Human Rights Workers 1979; Omega Man of the Year Omega Psi Phi Frat Inc 1979; Meritorious Serv Awds 3rd Dist Omega Psi Phi Frat Inc 1979-80; DOD sponsored showing at Pentagon Bldg 1975; State Dept Rec Assoc sponsored exhibit 1975; Natl Capitol Parks spon-

sored 15 day showing 1975; taught 10 week course in Black Hist/Human Relat to civ & mil personnel at Vint Hill Farms Mil Post Warrenton VA 1974. **Military Serv:** AUS pfc 1953-55.

FUNN, COURTNEY HARRIS

Library administrator, educator. **Personal:** Born Nov 30, 1941; daughter of Evelyn B Harris (deceased) and Jerry L Harris (deceased); divorced; children: LaMarr T Funn. **Educ:** Fisk Univ, BMus; Columbia Univ, MA, music; Univ of Maryland, MLS; Travel Abroad: United Kingdom, Western Europe, Greece, 1965, 1992, 1996. **Career:** Baltimore Public Schools, music resource teacher (K-6), 1963-66; Columbia Univ, School of Music & Music Eductn, asst to librarian, 1965-67; Provident Hospital, fine arts specialist, 1968-69; Bowie State Univ, asst prof of music, 1967-69, dir of library, 1969-, professor of music, 1984-; Maxima Corp., consultant, 1988-. **Orgs:** Chmn, Prince George's County Human Relation Cmsn, 1985-87; chmn, Library Technical Cmte, Metropolitan Washington Cncl of Govt, 1985-86; Natl Forum for Black Public Administrators, 1987-; chmn, Educ Cmte St Margaret's Parish Cncl, 1977-88; Elderly Abuse Oversight Cmte, 1988; District of Columbia Library Assn, 1988; County Executive's Policy Cmte, 1987; White House Conf on Libraries Task Force, 1988; County Facilities Naming Cmte, 1988; exec cmte, bd of dirs, Amer Red Cross, 1987; County Executive's Policy Cmte, 1987; chair, State Cncl of Library Directors, 1986; Prince George's County Executive Transition Team, 1983-; American Library Assn, 1989-; Governor's Conference on Library Planning & Public Policy, 1990; Bowie State Univ, numerous committees and boards; Prince George's County Economic Deve Comm; vice chair, Bishop McNamara High School, bd of dirs, Forestville, MD; special asst, LEARN Foundation, for the Jack Kent Cooke, Inc, Washington Redskins, for the Prince George's County Executive, Landover Educational, Athletic and Recreational Non-Profit Foundation. **Honors/Awds:** Fisk Univ, Woman of the Year, 1962-63; BSC, Presidential Citation for Outstanding Services, 1977; Alpha Kappa Alpha Sorority, Beta Phi Mu Honor Society; State Senate, Certificate for Outstanding Community Service, 1986; Governor's Conference on Library Planning and Public Policy, Panelist, 1990. **Special Achievements:** Author, works include: Beyond the Work Week: Some Creative Uses of Leisure Time, The Crab, 1974; Acronyms: Alphabet Soup, The Crab-Maryland Library Assn, 1975; A Guide to Libraries of the Maryland State Colleges, 1975. **Business Addr:** Director, Thurgood Marshall Library, Bowie State Univ, 14000 Jericho Pk Rd, Bowie, MD 20715.

FURLOUGH, JOYCE LYNN

Health care administrator. **Personal:** Born Mar 4, 1961, San Francisco, CA; daughter of Geraldine Thompson and Eddie Thompson; married Durrell Furlough, Feb 15, 1986; children: Durrell Jay Jr. **Educ:** California State University, Northridge, BS, health care administration, 1983. **Career:** Norrell, staff coordinator; Pacificare, sales rep, marketing manager, project manager, market analysis, manager, Service & Development, director, Product Development; Corporate Marketing, vice pres, currently. **Orgs:** American Marketing Association; California Association of Health Maintenance Organizations; Natl Female Exec Assn; National Council on Aging. **Business Addr:** Vice Pres of Corporate Marketing, Pacificare Health Systems, 3110 Lake Center Dr, Santa Ana, CA 92704-6921.

FURMAN, JAMES B.

Educator. **Personal:** Born Jan 23, 1937, Louisville, KY. **Educ:** Univ of Louisville, B Music Educ 1958, M Music 1965; Brandeis Univ & Harvard Univ, PhD studies. **Career:** Public School System Louisville KY, teacher 1959-60; Mamaroneck NY Public School System, music teacher 1964-65; Choral director, arranger, pianist; published "Four Little Foxes" a choral suite; "Go Tell It On the Mountain", "Some Glorious Day" & "An Oratorio"; Western CT State Coll, Danbury, prof of music; Western CT State Univ, prof of music 1965-. **Orgs:** Mem ASCAP, Amer Assn of Univ Profs, Phi Mu Alpha, Phi Delta Kappa, Afro-Amer Music Oppor Assn, CT Composers Inc, Amer Fed of Teachers; choral dir BBC Documentary film on the Life of Charles Ives 1966; conductor debut at NY City Town Hall 1967; music dir, pianist, TV & radio appearances throughout the USA, Central Amer, Europe & the Orient; composer-pianist, TV & radio appearances throughout the USA. **Honors/Awds:** Top Music Student Omicron Delta Kappa Award 1958; Award of Merit Natl Fed of Music Clubs 1965-77 & Parade of Amer Music 1967; published "Hehlehlooyuh", "Come Thou Long Expected Jesus" & "The Quiet Life"; 1st place in composition Louisville Philharmonic Society's Student Musicians Competition 1953; 1st place composition competition Brookline Library Music Composition Competition 1964; Composer music publ by Oxford Univ Press, Music 70-80, Hinshaw, Dorn, & Sam Fox. **Military Serv:** AUS Pfc 1960-62; music dir Ft Devens MA 1960-62; conductor 1st place in 1st Army of the All Army Entertainment Contest 1961; music dir, pianist World Touring Army Show "Rolling Along of 1961" 1961-62. **Business Addr:** Professor of Music, Western CT State College, 181 White St, Danbury, CT 06810.

FUSE, BOBBY LEANDREW, JR.

Educator. **Personal:** Born Feb 17, 1952, Americus, GA; married Angela Michelle Lamar. **Educ:** Morehouse Coll, BA 1974; Michigan State Univ, MA 1975. **Career:** College of Urban Develop, grad asst to the dean 1974-75; Martin Luther King Jr Ctr, dir youth component 1974-76; Fulton County Democratic Party, exec dir 1977-78; Atlanta Bd of Educ Frederick Douglass HS, teacher 1976-. **Orgs:** Jr deacon Friendship Bapt Church-Americus 1970-; advisor Douglass HS Student Govt 1977-85; bd of trustees Martin Luther King Jr Ctr for Nonviolent Social Change Inc; youth cncl advisor NAACP; mem St John Lodge #17 F&AM, Holy Royal Arch Lodge #4 Americus, Natl Educ Assoc, Natl Assoc of Secondary School Principals, Assoc for Supervision and Curriculum Develop; mem State Comm Life Hist of Black Georgians; mem MI State Univ Alumni Assoc, Morehouse Coll Alumni Assoc. **Honors/Awds:** John Wesley Dobbs Scholar Prince Hall Masons of Georgia 1970; Georgia Bapt Conv 1970-74; Scholarship Alberta Williams King Fund 1977; Century Club Butler St YMCA 1981; faculty member Martin Luther King Ctr Institute of Non-violence 1987. **Home Addr:** PO Box 90583, Atlanta, GA 30364-0583. **Business Addr:** Teacher, Atlanta Public Schools, Frederick Douglass HS, 225 Hightower Rd NW, Atlanta, GA 30310.

FUTCH, EDWARD

Sports trainer. **Personal:** Born Aug 9, 1911, Hillsboro, MS; son of Laura Anderson Futch and Valley Futch; married Eva Marlene, Mar 21, 1996; children: Yvonne, Edwina, Loretta, Edward, Ronald. **Career:** US Postal Service, 1964-69; self-employed, Las Vegas, NV, boxing manager/trainer, 1932-. **Honors/Awds:** James J Walker Memorial, Boxing Writers Association of America, 1982; Al Buck Memorial Award, Boxing Writers Association of America, 1975; International Boxing Hall of Fame, 1994; Michigan Sport Hall of Fame, 1997. **Home Addr:** 5025 Eastern Ave, #16-314, Las Vegas, NV 89119-2318.

FUTRELL, MARY HATWOOD

Educator. **Personal:** Born May 24, 1940, Altavista, VA; daughter of Josephine Austin; married Donald Futrell. **Educ:** Virginia State Univ, BA; George Washington Univ, MA, EdD; Maryland Univ, Univ of VA Polytechnical Inst & State Univ, graduate work. **Career:** Alexandria's George Washington HS, head-ed bus ed dept; Ed Assoc of Alexandria, pres 1973-75; NEA VA Ed Assoc, pres 1976-78; NEA, bd dir 1978-80, sec-treas 1980-83, pres 1980-89; George Washington Univ, Dept of Educational Leadership, senior fellow, 1989-92, Grad School of Ed & Human Development, dean, 1995-. **Orgs:** Bd advisors Esquire Register 1985; mem Task Force on Teaching Carnegie Forum on Educ and the Economy 1985; mem Natl Comm on the Role and Future of State Colls and Univs; mem editorial bd Pro Education magazine; mem Educ Adv Council Metropolitan Life Insurance Co; bd trustees Joint Council on Economic Educ; mem NEA's Special Comm on Attacks on Public Educ; co-convener 20th Anniversary Celebration of the Historic March on Washington led by Dr Martin Luther King; mem Select Comm on the Educ of Black Youth; mem US Natl Comm for the United Nations Educ Scientific and Cultural Organization; mem exec comm World Confederation of Organizations of the Teaching Profession; Education Intl, pres; Carnegie Foundation for Improvement of Teaching, bd mem; Kettering Foundation. **Honors/Awds:** Human Relation Awards, Natl Conference of Christians & Jews 1976, 1986; Outstanding Black Business & Professional Person, Ebony Magazine 1984; One of the Country's 100 Top Women, Ladies Home Journal 1984; One of 12 Women of the Year Ms, Magazine 1985; One of the Most Influential Blacks in Amer, Ebony Magazine 1985, 1986; Anne & Leon Schull Awd Americans for Democratic Action, 1986; Honorary Doctorates: George Washington Univ, VA State Univ, Spelman Coll, Adrian Coll, Central CT State Univ, Eastern Michigan Univ, Lynchburg Coll, N Carolina Central Univ, Univ of Lowell, Xavier Univ; Certificate of Appreciation United Nations Assoc/Capital Area Div; named to Academy of Women Achievers Young Women's Christian Assn; NAACP President's Award. **Business Addr:** Dean, George Washington University, Graduate School of Education & Human Development, 2134 G St, NW, Washington, DC 20052.

G

G, WARREN (WARREN GRIFFIN, III)

Rap artist, producer. **Personal:** Born in Long Beach, CA. **Career:** Rap artist, producer, currently. **Special Achievements:** Album: "Regulate... G Funk Era"; Top 10 song: "Regulate"; Contributed songs to the movie soundtracks of "Poetic Justice" and "Above the Rim". **Business Addr:** Rap artist, "Renegade", c/o Death Row, 10900 Wilshire Blvd., Ste. 1240, Los Angeles, CA 90024.

GABBIN, ALEXANDER LEE

Educator. **Personal:** Born Sep 6, 1945, Baltimore, MD; son of Dorothy Johns and John Gabbin; married Joanne Veal; children: Jessea Nayo. **Educ:** Baltimore City Coll, HS 1963; Howard U, BA 1967; Univ of Chicago, MBA 1970; Temple Univ, PhD 1986. **Career:** Tech Constr Co, asst to pres 1968-70; Touche Ross & Co, staff auditor 1970-72; Chicago Urban League, dep exec dir 1972-74; Price Waterhouse & Co, auditor 1974-75; Lincoln Univ, assoc prof 1975-85; James Madison Univ, assoc prof 1986-. **Orgs:** Mem IL Soc of CPA'S 1978; mem Chicago Urban League, Kappa Alpha Psi, Amer Accounting Assn, Amer Inst of Cert Public Accountants; Natl Assn of Accountants, 1990-. **Honors/Awds:** Grad Fellowship Humble Oil & Refining Co 1968-69; Builder's Award Third World Press 1978; Accounting Educators Award Nat Assn of Minority CPA Firms 1979; Lindback Disting Teaching Awd 1982, School of Accounting Outstanding Teacher 1986, 1988, 1990. **Business Addr:** Associate Professor, James Madison Univ, Harrisonburg, VA 22807.

GABBIN, JOANNE VEAL

Educator. **Personal:** Born Feb 2, 1946, Baltimore, MD; daughter of Jessie Smallwood Veal and Joseph Veal; married Alexander L Gabbin, Jul 2, 1967; children: Jessea Nayo. **Educ:** Morgan State Univ, Baltimore MD, BA, 1967; Univ of Chicago, Chicago IL, MA, 1970, PhD, 1980. **Career:** Catalyst for Youth Inc, Chicago IL, prog dir, instructor, 1973-75; Lincoln Univ, University PA, asst prof of English, 1977-82, assoc prof of English, 1982-85; James Madison Univ, Harrisonburg VA, assoc prof of English, 1985-86, dir, Honors Program, 1986-, professor of English 1988-. **Orgs:** Langston Hughes Soc, Zora Neale Hurston Soc; Middle Atlantic Writer Assn Inc, the MAWA Journal; mem, Coll Language Assn; chair, Student Emergency Fund, First Baptist Church, 1989-; Board of the Virginia Foundation for the Humanities and Public Policy, chair. **Honors/Awds:** Outstanding Achievement Award, Black Conf on Higher Educ, 1982; Distinguished Teaching Award, The Christian R & Mary F Lindback Found, 1983; Creative Scholarship Award, Coll Language Assn, 1986; Women of Color Award, James Madison Uni, 1988; Honorary Mem, Golden Key Natl Honor Soc, 1988; Chairperson, Toni Morrison & The Supernatural, panel at the Middle Atlantic Writers Assn, 1988; Speaker, Creating a Masterpiece, Freshman Convocation James Madison Univ, 1988; publications: Sonia Sanchez: A Soft Reflection of Strength, Zora Neale Hurston Forum, 1987; A Laying on of Hands: Black Women Writers Exploring the Roots of their Folk & Cultural Tradition; Walk Together Children: Color and the Cultural Legacy of Sterling A Brown, 1988; Sterling A Brown: Building the Black Aesthetic Tradition, 1985 "A Laying on of Hands" Wild Women in the Whirlwind, Rutgers Univ Press, 1990, reprinted by Univ Press in VA, 1994; Outstanding Faculty Award, VA State Council of Higher Educ, 1993; George Kent Award, Gwendolyn Brooks Ctr, Chicago State Univ, 1994. **Business Addr:** Professor of English, Dir of the Honors Program, James Madison University, Hillcrest, Harrisonburg, VA 22807.

GABRIEL, BENJAMIN MOSES

Business executive. **Personal:** Born Sep 17, 1931, Brooklyn, NY; married Rebecca; children: Shirley Ann, Janice, Brenda, Benjamin Jr. **Educ:** Cornell U, 1931; Empire State U, BS. **Career:** New York City Transit Authority, supt 1976, contract compliance officer 1973, mgr training ctr 1971, supr 1968, rr porter 1957. **Orgs:** Mem 100 Black Men; trustee Luth Hosp 1976-; bd dir Brooklyn TB & Lung Assn 1975-; chmn Labor & Industry, ENY NAACP, 1976-; v chmn, bd dir Asso Transit Guild; training coord, Asso Transit 1971-; candidate, dist leader 40th AD Dem Party 1976; campaign mgr Local Sch Bd Elections 1973, 75. **Honors/Awds:** Doswell Meml Award, Asso Transit Guild 1977; Comm Serv & Transit Accomplishments, Elite Benevolent Soc 1975; Comm Serv Award, Grace Bapt Ch 1974. **Military Serv:** USAF 1949-53. **Business Addr:** NYCTA 370 Jay St, Brooklyn, NY 11201.

GACHETTE, LOUISE FOSTON

Funeral home executive. **Personal:** Born Apr 17, 1911, Clarksville, TN. **Educ:** A&M Coll, 1938 Huntsville, AL; Gupton & Jones Sch, mortuary; Nashville, Eckels Coll, embalming degree, mortuary tech. **Career:** Public School Huntsville AL, teacher 1938-42; Foston Funeral Home, mgr & owner. **Orgs:** Mem Natl Embalmers & Funeral Dir Assn; Middle Tennessee Embalmers & Funeral Dir; Tennessee State Funeral Dir & Moriticians Assn Inc; Natl Business & Professional Women, Nashville TN; Cosmopolitan Art & Study Club; mem Women Interested in Community Affairs, Clarksville TN; mem Clarksville Montgomery Co C of C; mem Adv Comm of the Mayor of Clarksville; mem Montgomery Co Citizens Adv Comm; mem United Charities Bd, Clarksville TN; mem Gov's Adv Comm, State of Tennessee; mem Memorial Hospital Auxiliary; bd dir USO; sec United Givers Fund Campaign; co-chmn Cerebral Palsy Fund; bd dir Clarksville High School; mem United Church Women. **Honors/Awds:** "Miss A&M College," Huntsville AL, 1937; Woman of the Year Award, Funeral Dir & Morticians 1972; trustee, stewardess, former clerk & treas for 25 years, Wesley Chapel CME Church. **Business Addr:** President, Foston Funeral Home, 816 Franklin St, Clarksville, TN 37040.

GADDY, BEATRICE

Organization executive. **Personal:** Born Feb 20, 1933, Wake Forrest, NC; daughter of Novella Davis Young and Mottie Fowler Sr; married Lacy Gaddy, Sep 1, 1977; children: Sandra Elaine Fowler, Johnnie Fowler, Cynthia Brooks, Michael Brooks, Pamela Brooks. **Educ:** NI Vocational, Wake Forest, NC, 1955-58; Calvert Educational Center, 1968-69; Antioch University, Baltimore, MD, BA, 1977. **Career:** Sinai Hospital,

Baltimore, MD, nursing asst, 1964-68; Police Department, Baltimore, MD, crossing guard, 1970-74; Voluntary Employment, Baltimore, MD, advocate, 1981-. **Orgs:** Executive director, Patterson Park Emergency Ctr, 1981-; executive director, Bea Gaddy Social Development Ctr, 1989-; executive director, Bea Gaddy Home Renovation Fund, 1989-; executive director, Bea Gaddy Lead Program, 1989-; executive director, Bea Gaddy Drug Prevention Program, 1989-; Bea Gaddy Furniture Bank, executive director, 1992. **Honors/Awds:** Champion of Courage, BG&E & WBFF-TV Ch 45, 1989; Meritorious Service Award, National Assoc of Negro Business Womens Club, 1989; Community Service Award, Johns Hopkins Hospital, 1990; Distinguised Black Marylanders, Towson State Univ, 1990; Mother of the Year Award, 1990; President's Citation, City Council, City of Balitmore, 1991; 695th Point of Light, President George Bush, 1991; United States Postal Service Recognition, 1992; 39th Legislative District Recognition, 1991; Bea Gaddy Day Award, Baltimore County, 1992; Congressional Achievement Award, Top Woman Achievers, Congr Mfume, 1992; Girl Scouts of Central Maryland Distinguished Woman of the Year Award, 1992; Citizen Citation, City of Baltimore, Kurt Schmoke, 1992. **Business Addr:** Executive Director, Patterson Park Emergency Food Center, 140 N Collington Ave, Baltimore, MD 21231.

GADSDEN, EUGENE HINSON
Judge. **Personal:** Born Feb 4, 1912, Savannah, GA; married Ida Jenkins; children: Greer Larned, Geoffrey E. **Educ:** Savannah State Coll GA, AB 1934; Lincoln Univ Oxford, PA, BS 1937; NC Central Univ Law Sch Durham, LlB 1953. **Career:** Eastern Jud Circuit of GA, judge superior ct 1979-; GA State Bd of workmen's Comp, admin law judge 1974-79; Self Employed, atty 1953-74; Housing Authority of Savannah, asst mgr 1941-50; Lee Co Bd of Educ Sanford, NC, sci tchr 1937-39. **Orgs:** Dir (Sec) Toomer Realty Co Inc 1966-; dir Carver State Bank 1971-; pres Legal Aid Soc of Savannah 1966-74; dir So Regional Council Inc 1970; chmn ofbd Westside Comprehensive Health Cntr 1972. **Honors/Awds:** RR Wright Award of Excellence Savannah State Coll 1973; Citizen of the yr Mu Phi Chap Omega Psi Phi Frat. **Business Addr:** Judge, Chatham County Courthouse, Room 20, Savannah, GA 31401.

GADSDEN, NATHANIEL J., JR.
Educational administrator. **Personal:** Born Oct 3, 1950, Harrisburg, PA; son of Rosetta Robinson Gadsden and Nathaniel Gadsden; married Carol L, Aug 3; children: David L, Nathaniel J III. **Educ:** West Chester Univ, BS 1973, grad sch 31 credits; Columbia Pacific Univ, MA 1984; NJ Bible Inst; Hershey Med Center, clinical pastoral education; Harrisburg Hospital Clinical Pastoral Educ; Columbia Pacific Univ PhD 1986. **Career:** WCU, resident hall dir 1973-77; Child Abuse Hotline, case worker 1977-80; PA Dept of Education, equity coord beginning 1980; planner for alternative sentencing of PA, beginning 1985; HelpHouse Inc., Harrisburg, PA, counselor 1989. **Orgs:** Bd of dirs Multi-Disciplinary Team Dauphin Co Children & Youth; bd of dirs Multi-Disciplinary Team PA Dept of Children & Youth; bd mem Comm Home Care Services Inc; pres Central PA Black Social Workers 1982-84; dir The Writers Wordshop 1978-; host WMSP-FM radio 1979-; host WHP TV Channel 21 1982-; bd of dirs Metro Arts 1982-; bd of dirs Susquhanna Arts Council 1982; black advisory bd WITF-TV; bus assoc Central PA Guidance Associate 1984-; columnist The City News Harrisburg PA weekly 1984-; mem Intl Org of Journalists; Harrisburg dir of PA Black United Fund; bd dir Children's Playroom Inc; minister Community Chapel Church of God in Christ, Harrisburg, PA. **Honors/Awds:** Mem Natl Alliance of Third World Journalists 1980-; interviewed Yasser Arafat, Prime Minister Maurice Bishop of Grenada; named Comm Worker of Yr by conference on Black Basic Educ; Harrisburg Chap of Frontiers Intl; published poet and writer. **Home Addr:** 2209 N 2nd St, Harrisburg, PA 17110.

GAFFNEY, FLOYD
Educator (retired). **Personal:** Born Jun 11, 1930, Cleveland, OH; son of Bertha Caldwell Gaffney (deceased) and George Gaffney (deceased); married Yvonne; children: Michelle, Antione, Brett, Monique. **Educ:** Adelphi Univ, BA 1959, MA 1962; Carnegie Inst of Tech, PhD 1966. **Career:** Gilpin Players Karamu House, actor 1945-49; Pearl Primus African Dance Co, dancer 1950-51; Jerome School of Dancing, teaching asst 1960-62; Adelphi Univ, graduate teaching assistant of dance 1961; Waltann School of Creative Arts, teacher of dance & drama 1961; Clark Coll, asst prof, Speech 1961-63; William Balls Amer Conservatory Theatre, guest artist 1965; Univ of Pittsburgh, guest dance instructor 1966; OH Univ, asst prof in theatre 1966-69; FL A&M Univ, dir of fine arts project upward bound summer 1968; Univ of CA Santa Barbara, assc prof drama 1969-71, co-chmn of Black Studies dept. UC Santa Barbara. **Orgs:** UCSD Black Fac & Staff Assn 1979-94; Intercampus Cultural Exch Comm 1979-81; Third Clge Fac Comm UCSD 1980-94; Performing Arts Sub-Comm 1972-74; Fac Mentor Prog UCSD 1982; Pres Chair Search Comm UCSD 1982; San Diego Div of Acad Senate UCSD; bd dir Free Southern Theatre 1963-65; Amer Soc for Theatre Research 1966-69; Natl Humanities Fac 1974-75, 1994-; bd dir Combined Arts & Educ Council of San Diego Cty 1982-84; Amer Theatre Assn Black Theatre Prog 1966; artistic dir Southern CA Black Repertory Theatre Inc San Diego 1980-83; Confederation for the Arts 1983-; Steering Comm State & Local Partnership of San Diego Cty 1982-; bd dir, Educ Cultural Complex Theatre, 1981-83; bd mem, Horton Plaza Theatre Fnd, 198384, 1995-; panel mem, Natl Research Council for Minority Fellowship, 1984-87; Phi Lambda Rho Frat, 1958; Theatre Assn, 1966-85; Amer Assn of Univ Prof; Education Committee, Escondido Center of the Performing Arts 1995; Commissioner, Horton Plaza Theatre Foundation 1996-. **Honors/Awds:** Andrew Mellon Fellowship Drama 1964-65; OH Univ Bd Trustees Grant 1968; Fac Senate Grant Univ of CA Santa Barbara 1970; Ford Fnd Grant 1970; Faculty Sen Grant Univ of CA 1971-73; US Info Srv Cultural Exch Prof to Brazil 1972; Natl Humanities Fac 1974-75; grant Univ of CA Creative Arts Inst Grant 1974; Outstanding Educ of Amer Award; special proj grant Natl Endowment for the Arts 1977; Fulbright Scholar to Brazil 1979; Instr Improvement Grant 1979-81, 1984; participant Intl Congress of Black Communication Univ of Nairobi Kenya 1981; moderator Realism To Ritual, Form & Style in Black Theatre ATA Black Theatre Prog Panel 1982; Black Achievement Award forDrama Action Interprises Inc, 1984; Chancellor's Assocs, Merit Award; Outstanding Community Serv, Univ of California, San Diego, 1983; Natl Endowment for the Arts; US-Japan Alliance Best Director of Drama, 1986; NAACP Creative Arts Awards, 1986; UCSD Faculty Senate Research, Japan, Summer, 1987, 1988; Oxford Univ, Oxford, English, Summer; Institute for Shipboard Educ, Semester at Sea, Professor, Spring, 1992; mem, the National Faculty, 1990-93, reappointed 1994; Honorary mem, Golden Key National Honor Society, 1990; UCSD Faculty Senate Research Grants; England Summer 1990, 1993, 1994; UCSD Humanities Center Grant, Teatro Mascara Magica, 1998-. **Special Achievements:** Contributing Editor: Theatre Forum Journal, 1992-; Editorial Advisory Board-Lenox Avenue: A Journal of Interartistic Inquire, 1994-96; Associate Artistic Director, Teatro Mascara Magica; A Common Ground Theatre, 1994. **Military Serv:** AUS 3rd class petty ofc 1951-55. **Business Addr:** Emeritus Professor of Drama, Univ of California-San Diego, PO Box 0344, La Jolla, CA 92093.

GAFFNEY, LESLIE GALE
Electronics company executive. **Personal:** Born Feb 21, 1951, Cleveland, OH; daughter of Lucille Miller Gaffney and George Douglas Gaffney; married Kenneth Wilson Sr, May 19, 1989. **Educ:** Kent State University, BS, 1972. **Career:** R H Macy's, vendor inquiry manager, 1980-84; Sony Corp of America, Corp Controllers, A/R project manager, 1984-85, Components Prod Co, operation manager, 1985-86, accounts payable manager, 1986-87, Consumer Co Mid-Atlantic, operation manager, 1987-88, Peripheral Products Co, administration manager, 1988-89, director, community affairs, 1989-. **Orgs:** NSF, Southern California ACCESS Center, chair, advisory bd, 1989-; KSU Alumni Bd of Dirs, 1993-; New Jersey Institute of Technology, precollege advisory board, 1992-; Greater Monvale Business Association, board of directors, 1992-; National Urban Affairs Council, New Jersey, 1991-; The EDGES Group, executive committee, 1989-; National Urban League Corp, assoc advisory committee, 1995; Kent State University Alumni, bd of directors, 1993. **Honors/Awds:** Kent State University Alumni Association, Special Achievement Award, 1992. **Business Addr:** Director, Community Affairs, Sony Electronics Inc, 1 Sony Dr, Park Ridge, NJ 07656, (201)930-7538.

GAFFNEY, MARY LOUISE
Health services technician. **Personal:** Born Jul 30, Beaufort, SC. **Educ:** VA Union Univ, BS 1966; George Washington Univ, grad study; Faith Grant Coll, LLD, 1994. **Career:** Adv Neighborhood Commn, commr, 1976-; Mather School Alumni, natl pres 1978-; Benedict Coll, trustee 1978-; VA Union Univ, financial sec 1984-; George Washington Univ Hospital, radiation safety tech, currently. **Orgs:** Society of Nuclear Med, 1983, Delta Sigma Theta Sorority Inc; Washington Inter-Alumni Council; Benedict Coll Alumni; Far-Northeast Civic Assn; sr choir, bowling league, New Bethel Baptist Church; Amer Public Health Association; Health Physics Society; Marshall Heights Community Development inc., board member; Watts Branch Patrol, captain; Boys & Girls Club, Eastern Region, bd mem; Ward 7 Democrats. **Honors/Awds:** University of Virginia, Basic Radiation, 1980; Georgetown University, St Law; George Washington University Medical Center, Employee of the Week, 1985. **Special Achievements:** Author: Isolation & Partial Characterization of the Most Immunologically Reactive Antigen From Mycobacterium Tuberculosis H37Ra Culture Filtrate. **Business Addr:** Radiation Safety Technologist, George Washington University Hospital, 2300 I St NW, B-32, Washington, DC 20037.

GAFFNEY, THOMAS DANIEL
Government official. **Personal:** Born Jun 19, 1933, Laredo, TX. **Career:** San Antonio ISD School Bd, vice pres; US Govt, 23 yrs. **Orgs:** Mem AFRES; San Antonio Museum Assn;Ruth Taylor Theater; mem NAACP; 433 TAW/EEOC; 2851 ABGP/WELFARE Fund; LCL Adv Council; Ex Com UNCF; pres PovertyAgency Bd; vice pres sch bd 1973-77; mem San Antonio Rive Com; mem Black Unity Coordination Council; life mem BT Washingotn PTA; mem AFA; ACLU; Nat Caucus of Black - School Bd; mem NCOA. **Military Serv:** USAF 4 yrs. **Business Addr:** 141 Lavaca, San Antonio, TX.

GAILLARD, BERNARD
Attorney. **Personal:** Born Mar 27, 1944, Charleston, SC; married Joyce Anita Williams; children: Lisa, Khari. **Educ:** Columbia Univ, Cert 1966; SC State Univ, AB 1967; Emory Univ Sch of Law, JD 1970. **Career:** So Regional Council, legis asst 1968; OEO, law clerk to regional counsel 1969; ICC, atty adv 1970, dir small bus assistance office 1977, assoc dir compl and consumer asst 1984-, dir compl and enforcement 1985-. **Orgs:** ICC rep vol serv to WA lawyers com for civil rights under the law 1972-75; mem ABA; mem SC, Natl, DC Bar Assns; mem Fed Senior Exec Science 1981;mem Com on Equal Employment in the Surface Transportation Indus 1972; ICC rep Minority Bus Oppor Com 1975-; pres Student Govt Assn 1966-67; pres Interfraternity Council 1966-67. **Honors/Awds:** Sigma Rho Sigma Hon Soc Sci Frat. **Business Addr:** Dir, ICC, 12th & Constitution Ave NW, Washington, DC 20423.

GAILLARD, RALPH C., SR.
Tobacco company executive. **Personal:** Born Dec 24, 1943, Chicago, IL; son of Adele Chilton Gaillard and Julius F Gaillard Jr; married Mary Washington, Dec 31, 1964; children: Ralph Jr, Sean, Nicolle, Courtney. **Educ:** Chicago City Jr Coll, Chicago IL, attended, 1962-64. **Career:** R J Reynolds Tobacco Co, Los Angeles CA, asst div mgr, 1969-71, div mgr, 1971-78, San Francisco CA, chain acct mgr, 1978-80, Winston-Salem NC, vending/military sales mgr, 1980-84, natl military sales mgr, 1984-88, dir military sales, 1988-94; US Military/Duty Free Sales, vp, 1994-. **Orgs:** Pres, Southern California Candy & Tobacco Table, 1977; bd mem, Amer Logistics Assn, 1984-89, convention chmn, 1987, pres, 1988-89; mem, Diocese of Charlotte NC, Bd of Educ, 1984-85, pres, 1985. **Business Addr:** VP, US Military/Duty Free Sales, 401 N Main St, Winston-Salem, NC 27102.

GAINER, ANDREW A.
Utilities company executive. **Personal:** Born Jul 28, 1919, Gracevill, FL; son of Bessie Smith Gainer and Ally Gainer; married Ruth Gainer; children: Patricia, Kim, Janet. **Educ:** Attended one room grad sch Tallavast, FL; Booker High School, Sarasota FL, Graduated 1939; Tuskegee Institute 1938. **Career:** NY Gas Maintenance Co Inc, pres 1950-; Gain-robin Assn, pres 1977; AUCOA Contractors of Am, exec vice pres 1965; US Navy, aviation metalsmith 1st class 1944. **Orgs:** Bd mem COM 1975; mem 100 Black Men Inc 1978; bd & mem Comm Bd #9 1980; bd mem, Uptown Chamber of Commerce 1989. **Honors/Awds:** Good Conduct Medal USN; Pacific Area WW I Ribbon; Unsung Hero Award Ballantine 1965; Bus Award Nat Assn of Negro Bus & Professional Women's Club 1969; Special Recognition, Williams Church, 1991. **Military Serv:** USN Aviation Metalsmith 1st class 1942-45, Good Conduct, Asian Pacific.

GAINER, FRANK EDWARD
Coordinator. **Personal:** Born Jun 18, 1938, Waynesboro, GA; son of Edith Gainer and Walter Gainer; married Alice M Ingram; children: Edward, Ervin, Todd. **Educ:** Morehouse Coll, BS 1960; Tuskegee Inst, MS 1962; IA State Univ, MS 1964, PhD 1967. **Career:** Antibiotic Analytical & Quality Control, mgr 1978; Eli Lilly & Co, sec treasurer; JCG&M. **Orgs:** Asso chmn Amer Chem Soc 1975; chancellor Amer Chem Soc 1977; Sigma Xi; Beta Kappa Chi Hon Sci Soc; NAACP; Urban League; sec Mary Riggs Neighborhood Ctr 1976, treas 1977, bd of dir 1975-; published science journal. **Business Addr:** Lilly Corporate Center, Eli Lilly & Company, Indianapolis, IN 46285.

GAINER, JOHN F.
Educator, musician, composer, choral conductor. **Personal:** Born Aug 8, 1954, East Orange, NJ; son of Stella Wynn Gainer and Benjamin Franklin Gainer. **Educ:** AZ State Univ, BA 1980; University of Oregon, School of Architecute & Allied Arts, 1986-87. **Career:** Various church and comm choirs, dir/musician 1968-; AZ State Univ Gospel Ensemble, founder/dir 1975-80; Lane Comm Coll, music instructor 1984-85; Univ of OR, adjunct faculty 1983-; founder/director, Inspirational Sounds Community Choir 1983-. **Orgs:** Amer Soc of Composers Authors and Publishers 1972-; minister Church of God in Christ Inc 1979-; OR/Lane County Rainbow Coalition 1983-88; precinct comm person Central Democratic Comm 1984-88; Edwin Hawkins Music & Arts Seminar 1984-; chapter rep and national mass choir music committee, Gospel Music Workshop of Amer 1986-. **Honors/Awds:** First African-American gospel artist to perform at the Hult Center for the Performing Arts 1983; invited to teach original compositions in the New Song Seminar at the Natl Conventions of the Gospel Music Workshop of Amer Inc; Honorary DD, Church of God, 1986; Inspirational Sounds one of 4 gospel choirs nationwide which performed at the Great American Gospel Gala at Alice Tully Hall of the renown Lincoln Center for the Performing Arts, 1987; invited to perform at World's Fair 1992; invited to conduct master class and perform, Central Europe, 1992-93. **Home Addr:** 118 High St, Eugene, OR 97401-2306, (541)343-3100. **Business Addr:** School of Music, 1225 Univ of Oregon, Eugene, OR 97403, (541)346-3771.

GAINER, RUBY JACKSON
Educator (retired). **Personal:** Born Mar 9, Buena Vista, GA; daughter of Mr & Mrs W B Jackson; married Herbert P Gainer,

Jun 3, 1946 (deceased); children: James, Ruby, Cecil. **Educ:** AL State Univ, attended 1939; Atlanta Univ, MA 1953; Selma Univ, Hon HHD 1970; B'ham Bapt Coll, LLD; Daniel Payne Coll, Dr of Humane Letters; CO State Christian Coll, PhD; Faith Coll B'ham AL, LLD 1976; Bishop Coll Dallas, Dr of Humane Letters 1977. **Career:** Jefferson County School System, teacher 12 years; Santa Rosa Public School System, teacher 1 year; Escambia County Public School System, teacher English, guidance counselor 49 years; William J Woodham High School, admin dean (retired). **Orgs:** Pres Escambia Classroom Tchr; pres FL State Classroom Tchr; vice pres FL State CTA; vice pres Assn of Classroom Tchr NEA; exec com ACT-NEA; Natl Ed Assn; FL Ed Assn; FUSA; Escambia Ed Assn; Amer Assn of Univ Women; League of Women Voters; life mem NAACP; pres City Assn of Federated Clubs Pensacola; pres Past Grand Daughter Rulers Council of FL; pres Delta Iota Omega Chap of Alpha Kappa Alpha Sor; NACW; Mary McLeod Bethune Fed Club; cand reg dir S Atlanta Region Alpha Kappa Alpha Sor; basileus Delta Iota Omega Chap Alpha Kappa Alpha; NW Chap Phi Delta Kappa; Escambia Co Dem Com exec bd AL State Univ Natl Alumni Assn; vice pres FL Assn of Women's Clubs; New Idea Art & Study Club; Human Relations Council; City Fed of Clubs; chmn, Escambia Ed Human Relations Com; dir of ed Orange Blossom Temple Daughters of Elks; State Daughter Rules Coun; pres FL Assn of Women's Clubs; pres AL State Alumni Assn Pensacola Chapt; deputy supvsr Election Club; life mem Natl Cncl of Negro Women, Natl Assn of Colored Women's Clubs; Natl Women of Achievement; Ladies of Distinction Federated Club. **Honors/Awds:** Shriners Woman of Yr 1946; Zeta Woman of Yr 1947; Zeta's Finer Womanhood Awd; Tchr of Yr 1965; Mother of Yr 1966; Band Mother of Yr 1966; Cit of Yr 1967; Leader of Yr 1968; Outstanding AKA Sor 1969, 1973; Outstanding Ed of Yr 1970; Regional Achievement Awd 1970; Most Aggressive Black Woman 1973; Humanitarian of Yr 1974; voted Pensacola's Top Lady of the Yr; nom Dau Isis of the Yr Comm Serv; elected Com Woman Dem Com; Lady of the Decade Awd Top Teens; Comm Serv Awd 5 Flag Fiesta 1980; runner-up Top Lady of Yr Natl Top Ladies of Distinction Inc 1980; Serv Awd FL Assn of Women's Clubs; Biographical Hall of Fame; Woman of the Yr 1984; Harriet Dorrah Federated Awd; WEAR Making a Difference Awd Channel 3 1984; AL State Univ Alumni of the Year 1986; IBAFellow; Women of Achievement Award, Natil Women of Achievement, 1990; 1st Pres, organizer, Ladies of Distinction, 1979; Women of the Year, ABA, 1990.

GAINES, ADRIANE THERESA
Communications executive. **Personal:** Born Aug 27, 1947, Mt Vernon, NY; daughter of Dorothy McCoy and James McCoy. **Educ:** Fordham Univ, BA (cum laude), 1978. **Career:** Marine Midland Bank, sec & safekeeping deputy 1965-68; State Natl Bank of El Paso, investment & sec deputy 1968-71; Rochester Inst of Tech, asst info specialist 1971-72; Culinary Inst of Amer, asst librarian 1972-73; Unity Broadcasting Network, dir of corp admin 1973-82, corporate vice pres NBN Broadcasting, Inc beginning 1995; WWRL-AM, pres/gen mgr, 1995-. **Orgs:** Co-founder bd mem The World Inst of Black Comm CEBA Awards, 1978-; acting gen mgr KATZ AM/WZEN FM Radio 1982; comm bd of dir Coalition of 100 Black Women, 1984-85; mem Women in Cable 1985; mem Adv Women in Radio & TV 1982-; bd of trustees Apollo Theater Hall of Fame 1986-; advisory comm mem, Schomburg Ctr for Research in Black Culture; bd mem, Aaron Davis Hall; bd mem, The Joan Mitchell Foundation. **Honors/Awds:** Media Woman of the Year, Natl Assn of Media Women 1985; Leadership Award, NAACP, 1995. **Business Addr:** President & Gen Mgr, WWRL-AM, 41-30 58th St, Woodside, NY 11377.

GAINES, AVA CANDACE
Mortuary services administrator. **Personal:** Born Feb 19, 1963, Madison, WI; daughter of Zelma Hamilton Gaines and George Gaines. **Educ:** University of District of Columbia, Washington, DC, 1982-83; University of Texas at Dallas, Dallas, TX, BA, 1991. **Career:** Jones, Day, Reavis & Pogue, Dallas, TX, docket clerk, 1985-86; Black & Clark Funeral Home, Dallas, TX, chaplain, assistant to funeral director, 1987-. **Orgs:** Chaplain, Dallas Ladies Funeral Directors Assn 1988-; member, Black Political Scientist Assn, 1986-; member/recruiting committee, NAACP, 1984-; member, Order of Eastern Stars, 1984-; member, National Ladies Funeral Directors Assn, 1989-. **Honors/Awds:** Author, Anybody Can Get the Holy Ghost, CME Church, 1986; Ordained Elder, CME Church, 1989. **Home Addr:** 7830 Mirage Valley Dr, Dallas, TX 75232.

GAINES, CLARENCE E., SR.
Educator, coach. **Personal:** Born May 21, 1923, Paducah, KY; son of Olivia Bolen Gaines and Lester Gaines; married Clara Berry; children: Lisa Gaines McDonald, Clarence E Jr. **Educ:** Morgan State College, Baltimore, MD, BS, 1945; Columbia Univ, New York, NY, MA, 1950. **Career:** Winston-Salem State Univ, athletic dir/coach, 1948-90; Winston-Salem State Univ Parochial School, coordinator. **Orgs:** Mem AAHPER; NEA; NC Assn for Hlth Physical Educ & Recreation; Nat Assn for Collegiate Dir of Athletics; dist chmn Nat Assn of Intercollegiate Athletics (NAIA) 1966-72; bd of mgmt Patterson Ave YMCA 1968-71; pres Central Intercollegiate Athletic Assn (CIAA) 1972-74; chmn AAHPER Publ Com 1972-74; pres CIAA Bsktbll Coaches Assn 1972-76; coordinator Modern Concepts of Hlth Fitness & Leisure for Senior Citizens Winston-Salem State U; mem Forsyth Co Heart Assn; mem US Olympic Com; bd of mgmt Winston-Salem Boys Club; mem Bsktbll Games Com of the US CollegiateSports Counc; bd of dir Winston-Salem Found; pres, National Assn of Basketball Coaches, 1989-90. **Honors/Awds:** Football coach of the yr CIAA 1948; bsktbll coach of the yr CIAA 1957, 61, 63, 70, & 75; bsktbll Coach of the yr NCAA 1967; hall of fame NAIA Helms 1968; family of the yr award Winston-Salem Urban League 1973; sports hall of fame Morgan State Coll 1973; honor award NC AAHEPR 1974; hall of fame CIAA 1975; outst coach award NAIA Dist 26 1975-78; nominated for NC Sports Hall of Fame 1978; CIAA Tournament Outst Coach Award; Naismith Hall of Fame; Lifetime Achievement Award, Larry Bird Charities, 1990; National Sport Hall of Fame, AAHPER, 1990. **Business Addr:** Professor/Basketball Coach, Winston-Salem State University, 601 Martin Luther King Dr, Winston-Salem, NC 27101.

GAINES, CLARENCE L.
Judge. **Personal:** Born Mar 9, 1914, Dallas, TX; married Pearl; children: Pearl, Delaney, Clarence III, George. **Educ:** Western Reserve U, BBA 1950; Cleveland Marshall Law Sch, LLB 1955. **Career:** City Council, elected 1963, 65; City of Cleveland, dir of Hlth & Welfare 1966-68; Gaines Rogers Horton & Forbes, sr partner; Cleveland Municipal Ct, judge. **Orgs:** Mem Coun on Human Relations; NAACP; Boy Scouts; Urban League; Welfare Fedn; Alcoholic Control Ctr; and others. **Military Serv:** WW II officer. **Business Addr:** Cleveland Municipal Court, 1200 Ontario St, Cleveland, OH 44113.

GAINES, COREY YASUTO
Professional basketball player. **Personal:** Born Jun 1, 1965, Los Angeles, CA. **Educ:** Univ of California at Los Angeles, Los Angeles, CA, 1983-86; Loyola Marymount Univ, Los Angeles, CA, 1987-88. **Career:** Quad City Thunder, 1988-89; New Jersey Nets, 1988-89; Omaha Racers, 1989-90; Philadelphia 76ers, 1989-90; Denver Nuggets, 1990-91; New York Knicks, 1993-94; Phoenix Suns, 1994-. **Business Addr:** Professional Basketball Player, Phoenix Suns, 201 E Jefferson St, Phoenix, AZ 85004, (602)379-7900.

GAINES, EDYTHE J.
Nonprofit corporation director, educator, government official. **Personal:** Born Sep 6, 1922, Asheville, NC; daughter of Mrs Jennie Verina Dillard Jones and Rev Jacob Richard Jones; married Albert (deceased); children: Richard Denis Gaines, Mallory Dillard Gaines. **Educ:** Hunter Coll, AB 1944; NY Univ, MA 1947; Harvard Univ, EdD 1969; Montclair State, LLD 1977. **Career:** New York City Public Schools, teacher, assistant principal 1945-67; NY School Dist #12, comm supervisor 1967-71; Learning Coop, dir 1971-73; New York City Public Schools, exec dir educ planning & support 1973-75; Hartford CT, supt of schools 1975-78; Gr Hartford Consortium for Higher Education, consultant to bd of govs 1978-79; State of CT, Public Utilities Control Authority, commr 1979-91; St Monica's Development Corp., chief executive officer, currently. **Orgs:** State of Connecticut, Higher Education Board of Governors; corporator Mt Sinai Hosp, Hartford Hosp and The Inst for Living; board of directors Hartford Hosp; dir CT Natl Bank & Hartford Natl Corp; bd of dir Kaman Corp; board of directors Hartford Stage Co; chairman of the board CT Opera Assn; chair Comm on Ministry Episcopal Diocese of CT; Gov's Task Force on South African Investment Divestiture Policy; dir Old State House Association. **Honors/Awds:** Honoree CT Black Women Achievement Against the Odds; Recipient of numerous honors & awds including the Family of Man Medallion Awd for Excellence in Education. **Home Addr:** 275 Kenyon St, Hartford, CT 06105-2239.

GAINES, ERNEST J.
Author. **Personal:** Born Jan 15, 1933, Oscar, LA. **Educ:** Attended Vallejo Jr Coll; attended San Francisco State Coll; Denison Univ, DLitt (hon). **Career:** Univ Southwestern LA Dept of English, prof and resident writer; author. **Honors/Awds:** Recip Gold Medal Commonwealth Club of CA 1972, 1984; LA Libr Assn Award 1972; Black Acad Arts and Letters Award 1972; Award for Excellence of Achievement in field of lit San Francisco Arts Comm 1983; Author of books, "Catherine Carmier" 1966; "Of Love and Dust" 1968; "Bloodline" 1968; "The Autobiography of Miss Jane Pittman" 1971; "A Long Day in November" 1971; "In My Father's House" 1978; "A Gathering of Old Men" 1983. **Business Addr:** Professor/Resident Writer, Univ Southwestern LA, Dept of English, PO Box 44691, Lafayette, LA 70504.

GAINES, HERSCHEL DAVIS
Educational administrator. **Personal:** Born Oct 7, 1942, Parkin, AR; married Wilbert Gaines; children: Jacquelyn LaRue, Michelle LaRue, Genee La Rue. **Educ:** Univ of AR at Pine Bluff, BA 1962; AR State Univ, MS 1979. **Career:** Phelix High School, english teacher 1962-69; Marion Sr High School, english teacher 1969-71; McArthur Middle School, chmn english dept 1971-81; Jonesboro High School, asst prin 1981-94; English Instructor, Supervisor of Elem Educ Student Teachers, Arkansas State Univ, 1994. **Orgs:** Bd dirs Jonesboro Classroom Tchrs Assn 1972-; bd dir AR Educ Assn 1976-79; mem affiliate relations com NEA 1977-79; basileus anti-basileus & grammateus Kappa Nu Omega Alpha Kappa Alpha Sor 1976-80; corr sec Alpha Delta Kappa 1979-; apptd by Gov Bill Clinton to Employment Sec Div Adv Coun 1981; nom com Crowley's Ridge Girl Scout Council 1981-83; educ comm Crowley's Ridge Girl Scouts 1981-83; bd dir United Way of Greater Jonesboro 1985-86; Advisory Cncl Upward Bound of AR State Univ 1980-; pres AR State Univ Faculty Women's Club 1985-87. **Honors/Awds:** Educ Awd Alpha Kappa Alpha Sor Jonesboro AR & AR Council of AKA 1976 & 1978; Outstanding Young Educator Awd Jaycees of Jonesboro 1977; Silver Soror-Alpha Kappa Alpha 1985; Alpha Delta Kappa, Pres Nu Chapter, 1994-96.

GAINES, JOHN A., SR.
Attorney. **Personal:** Born May 23, 1941, Rock Hill, SC; son of Ernestine Gaines Moore and John Gaines; divorced; children: John A Jr, Janee Latrice. **Educ:** Friendship Jr College, AA, 1962; Benedict College, BA (with honors), 1964; Howard University Law School, JD, 1968. **Career:** Rock Hill Model Cities Program, advisor and citizen; participation specialist, 1969-70; NAACP Legal Defense Fund Inc, intern, 1970-71; Self-employed, attorney, 1971-. **Orgs:** South Carolina State Bar, 1969-; Natl Bar Assn, 1978-; NAACP Florence, 1971-; Alpha Phi Alpha Fraternity, 1963-; New Life Assembly of God, trustee, legal counsel for Church and prayer coordinator, 1987-; Small Business Management Association, 1976. **Honors/Awds:** Bancroft-Whitney Company, American Jurisprudence Award, 1968; American Biographical Institute, Personalities of the South Award, 1970-71; Reveal Publications, selected as one of the best lawyers in America, 1979; Pineville AME Zion Church Award, 1995; NAACP Legal Defense Fund Inc, awarded internship, 1970-71; Friendship Jr College, award recognizing membership in Friendship 9, 1979; Alpha Kappa Alpha Sorority, award recognizing membership in Friendship 9, 1990. **Special Achievements:** Placed first African-Americans on city council of Florence, SC, via federal law suit and consent decree, 1977; created more equitable election of school board members in Florence School District I, 1981; by federal law suit facilitated change in election procedures allowing African-Americans to be elected to the Georgetown County Council by the African-American Community, 1982; won dismissal of murder charges in highly publicized "American Superette" case, 1982; supplied data and information on voter discrimination to the US Commission on Civil Rights which aided in the extention of the Federal Voting Rights Act of 1965. **Business Addr:** Attorney, 200 West Evans St, Ste 211, Florence, SC 29501, (803)679-3035.

GAINES, LESLIE DORAN. See Obituaries section.

GAINES, MARY E.
Public affairs officer. **Personal:** Born Mar 15, Boligee, AL; daughter of Mattie L Hamilton Gaines (deceased) and Willie Gaines (deceased). **Educ:** Loop City College, Chicago, IL, AA, 1970; Midwestern Broadcasting, Chicago, IL, diploma, 1972; Brewer State Junior College, Fayette, AL, 1974-75; University of Alabama, Tuscaloosa, AL, BA, 1982. **Career:** WCBI-Television, Columbus, MS, anchor/producer/reporter, 1975-77; WNPT-Radio, Tuscaloosa, AL, announcer, 1976-79; Federation of So Co-ops, Epes, AL, administrative assist, 1977-79; Arrington for Mayor, Birmingham, AL, office coordinator, 1982-83; WBRC-TV, Birmingham, AL, reporter/editor, 1978-82; Alabama Public TV, Montgomery, AL, television producer, 1983-93. **Orgs:** Grand lady, Knights of Peter Claver, Ladies Aux, 1990-; state coordinator, Natl Association of Black Journalists, 1983-; founder, Central Alabama Black Media Association, 1988; member, Youth Development & Birmingham Urban League Boards, 1981-82; member, SCLC & NAACP, 1972-75; vice pres, Knights of Delta Clover Ladies Auxiliary, Gulf Coast District; secretary, Emancipation Proclamation Committee; auditor, Archdiocesan Council of Catholic Women; treasurer, Knights of Peter Claver Ladies Auxiliary; co-chair, National Black Catholic Congress. **Honors/Awds:** President & Distinguished SVC AL Poultry/Egg Assn, 1988-86; Media Awards: AL Farmers Federation, Humane Society, 1985-82; Media Awards, Emancipation Association, Alpha Eta Chapter, Iota Phi Lambda, 1982; Fight for Freedom Award, MS, NAACP, 1977. **Business Addr:** Public Affairs Officer, USDA Forest Service, 2946 Chestnut St, Montgomery, AL 36107.

GAINES, OSCAR CORNELL
Physician. **Personal:** Born May 21, 1954, Memphis, TN; divorced. **Educ:** Lambuth Coll, BS 1976; Meharry Medical Coll, MD 1982. **Career:** US Army, capt/physician 1983-87. **Orgs:** Mem Prince Hall Mason Lodge 1986, Alpha Phi Alpha. **Military Serv:** AUS capt 3 yrs. **Home Addr:** 1616 Moss Creek Rd, Waycross, GA 31501. **Business Addr:** Physician, Martin Army Hospital, Emergency Room, Fort Benning, GA 31905.

GAINES, PAUL LAURENCE, SR.
Educator, government official (retired). **Personal:** Born Apr 20, 1932, Newport, RI; son of Pauline P Jackson Gaines and Albert P Gaines Sr; married Jo Eva Johnson, Jul 18, 1959; children: Jena, Patricia, Paulajo, Paul Jr. **Educ:** Xavier Univ of LA, BEd 1951-55; Bridgewater State Coll, MEd in Cnslng 1966-68. **Career:** Newport RI Public Sch, sch tchr 1959-68; Newport RI

Rogers HS, bsktbll coach 1959-68; Newport RI Youth Corps, cnslr 1960-66; Bridgewater State Coll MA, admin 1968-96; Bridgewater State Grad Sch, coll prof 1970-94; Bridgewater State Coll, asst to pres 1983-96. **Orgs:** Mem Newport Branch NAACP; mem Newport Lions Club; mem Cncl #256 Knights of Columbus; Urban League of Rhode Island; commissioner, Rhode Island Ethics Commission 1987-; member Rhode Island Black Heritage Society. **Honors/Awds:** 1st Black Sch Committeeman Since 1900, Newport RI Sch 1969-72; 1st Black City Cnclmn Newport City Cncl 1977-81; 1st Black Mayor in State of RI 1981-83; Citizen of The YrOmega Psi Phi Frat (Sigma Nu Chpt) 1981; recipient George T Downing Award RI 1982; elected to RI Constitutional Convention 1985-86; RI Adv Comm to the US Commn on Civil Rights 1985-87. **Military Serv:** AUS 82nd recon div sp 3 1955-57; 2nd Armored Division. **Home Addr:** 227 Eustis Ave, Newport, RI 02840, (401)846-7222.

GAINES, RAY D.

Surgeon, educator. **Personal:** Born Aug 4, 1932, Minneapolis; married Frances Hunter. **Educ:** Creighton U, BS 1954, MD 1958; Wayne Co Gen Hosp, internship 1958-59; Santa Cruz Co Hosp CA, gen practice residency 1959-60; Wayne Co Gen Hosp, residency in surgery 1960-64. **Career:** St Joseph Hospital, assoc chief emergency serv 1975-78; Douglas Co Hospital NE, chief surg serv 1974-76; VA Medical Center, Omaha NE, assoc chief surg serv; Creighton Univ, asst prof 1973-92, associate professor, 1992-; Public Health Serv Bureau of Health Manpower, consultant 1967-70; Amer Coll of Surgeons, fellow 1966; Amer Bd of Surgery, diplomate 1965; Univ of MI Center, clinical instructor 1965-73; Wayne County General Hospital, staff 1964-73; staff appts at several hospitals. **Orgs:** Mem Nat Med Assn; Metropolitan Omaha Med Soc; NE Med Soc; board of directors NE Division, American Cancer Society; bd dirs Dougals/Sarpy Div Am Cancer Soc 1975-; fellow Southwestern Surgical Congress; mem adv co Med/Am Counc BSA 1975-76; mem Am Burn Assn; mem Creighton Univ Surg Soc; med offcr Gen Daniel James Ct Squad CAP 1976-77; mem Assn of VA Surgns; Assn for Acad Surgery; Omaha Midwest Clinical Soc; u Assn for Emer Medicine; Detroit Surgical Assn; mem Kappa Alpha Psi; Phi Beta Pi; lifemem NAACP; bd dir NE Heart Assn; mem Joslyn Art Mus; Guest Examiner, Am Bd of Surgery Omaha 1974. **Business Addr:** Creighton University Medical Center, Department of Surgery, 601 N 30th St, Omaha, NE 68131.

GAINES, RICHARD KENDALL

Insurance company executive, consultant. **Personal:** Born Apr 11, 1947, St Louis, MO; son of Jewell Gaines Harris and Richard Harris; married Anne-Marie Clarke, Apr 3, 1979; children: Kimberly, Yvette. **Educ:** Coe Coll, BA Sociology 1969; St Louis Univ, Grad School. **Career:** City of Des Moines, deputy dir concentrated employ prog 1969-70; St Louis Bd of Educ, dir of comm educ 1970-73; St Louis Univ, dir of upward bound 1973-76; Urban League of Metropolitan St Louis, dir of educ 1976-77; Richard K Gaines & Assocs; Daniel & Henry Insurance Brokers, vice pres. **Orgs:** Mem Jaycees St Louis 1972-75; mem Amer Personnel & Guidance Assn 1973-76; past pres YMCA Men's Club City North 1979-83; mem Natl Assn of Life Underwriters 1977-; registered rep Natl Assn of Security Dealers 1977-; mem Independent Ins Agents of MO 1984-; mem St Louis Bd of Educ 1983-89; bd of dir YMCA; past pres St Louis Bd of Educ 1987-88; Royal Order of Vagabonds, Inc 1986-, grand pharoah, president, 1992-96; board of directors, Tower Village Nursing Home, 1989-. **Honors/Awds:** Awards salesman-mgr General American Life; presenter Natl Comm Schools Conf 1972; Sales Awd Lincoln Natl Life Ins 1977-. **Business Addr:** Insurance Broker, Consultant, Richard K Gaines & Associates, 2350 Market St, Suite 321, St Louis, MO 63103, (314)444-1969.

GAINES, SAMUEL STONE

Business executive. **Personal:** Born Jan 25, 1938, Fort Pierce, FL; married Theressa Ann Dillard; children: Andre, Arnold, Alwyn. **Educ:** Talladega Coll, BA 1960; McAllister Sch of Embalming, 1961. **Career:** FL Mortician Assn, pres 1979-81; Epsilon Nu Delta Mortuary Frat, natl pres 1982-84; Nat Funeral Dir & Morticians, natl pres 1985-86; St Lucie Co Sch Bd, mem 25 yrs. **Orgs:** Treas Omicron Tau Chap Omega; secy Sunrise Consult #202; treas FL Mortician Assn; mem St Lucic Cnty Sch Bd 1972-; life mem Omega Psi Phi Frat; golden hertigage mem NAACP; Grand Inspector General of the 33rd degree of the Ancient & Accepted Scottish Rite of Free Masonry for the Southern Jurisdiction. **Honors/Awds:** Community Serv Award Club Entre Nous, Ft Pierce 1980; Ft Pierce Chap of Links 1981; FL Mortician Assn 1982; Man of The Yr Alpha Gamma Chap Epsilon Nu Delta 1983; Honorary Doctor of Laws, Faith Grant Coll, 1994. **Business Addr:** 3950 Old Dixie Hwy, Vero Beach, FL 32960.

GAINES, SEDALIA MITCHELL

Educator (retired). **Personal:** Born Mar 31, 1917, Houston, TX; daughter of Sarah Watts Mitchell and William Mitchell; married Dr William Anthony Gaines (deceased); children: William Anthony Jr, Sandra R Gaines Lopes. **Educ:** Tillotson Coll, BS 1939; Temple U, MEd 1947; Intl Sch of Travel, Cert Travel Agent; UNC Greensboro, Cert Early Childhood Training. **Career:** Fessenden Acad, tchr 1940; School District, Ocala, FL, home economics teacher, 1942-46; FL A&M Coll, dir nursery school 1947; School Dist Phila, chmn home econ 1952; HEW, Head Start tchr trainer 1968; UNC Greensboro School Dist Phila, supvr day care 1966-80; Philadelphia School Dist, retired supvr day care. **Orgs:** Mem Assoc Supervision & Curriculum Devel; mem Haven United Methodist Church; mem Delaware Valley Assoc for Educ Young Child; basileus Beta Delta Zeta Chap, Zeta Phi Beta; pres Philadelphia Council, Natl Council of Negro Women; life mem NAACP Natl Council of Negro Women, Zeta Phi Beta; mem bd dir Red Cross; life mem NAEYC; board of directors ARC; mem of bd Theological Educ Consortium; board member, United Methodist Neighborhood Services, 1990. **Honors/Awds:** Ranking student Tillotson Coll; honoree Assn Natl Black Child Devel; Career Woman of the Yr Afro Amer Newspaper; Service Award March of Dimes; Berean Recognition Awd; Four Chaplins Awd; Admin Women in Educ Awd; Resolution Award, City Council, Philadelphia, PA, 1990, 1991. **Home Addr:** 2131 W Master St, Philadelphia, PA 19121.

GAINES, SYLVESTER, JR.

Port director. **Personal:** Born May 13, 1921, Thomson, GA; married Edith Thomas. **Educ:** LaSalle Coll, 2 Yr Study; Nat Training Ctr, US Customs Training Prgm 1972; Baltimore, Labor-Mgmt Seminar 1974. **Career:** Customs at Alexandria VA, port dir 1973-; US Customs Insp, 1958-73; Customs Port Patrol Officer, 1957-58; Custom Files, supr 1956-57; US Customs, cargo handler 1955-56; Railway Mailclerk 1952-54; Naval Aviation Supply Depot Philadelphia, property & supply clerk 1948-52; Postal Clerk, 1947-48. **Orgs:** Co-chmn of capitol funds com Freeway Golf Club Turnersville, NJ; mem Optimist Club of Alexandria; mem Arlington Divots Golf Club; mem Eastern Golfers Assn 1955-; mem Intl Golfers Assn; chmn Entertainment Com Fairview Golf Club 1958-63; chmn Entertainment Com Douglas Golf Club 1966-70; chmn Keystone Open Golf Tournament Douglas Golf Club 1969-70. **Honors/Awds:** Letter of commendation from CO 1944; letter of commendation from CO 5th Engineer Spl Brigade 1944. **Military Serv:** AUS sgt 1943-46. **Business Addr:** GSA Bldg, C/o Port Dir Franklin & Union, Alexandria, VA 22314.

GAINES, THURSTON LENWOOD, JR.

Physician. **Personal:** Born Mar 20, 1922, Freeport, NY; son of Albertha Reubena Robinson and Thurston Lenwood Gaines; married Jacqueline Eleanor Kelly; children: Beverly Doreen, Terrell Lance, William Wesley. **Educ:** Howard U, 1941-43; NY Univ, BA 1948; Meharry Med Coll, MD 1953. **Career:** Hempstead, NY, private practice of surgery 1959-76; South Nassau Comm Hosp, Oceanside, NY, dir prof educ & training 1964-69; Mercy Hosp, Rockville Centre, NY, dir surgical educ 1969-74; Western Mass Hosp, Westfield, MA, chief of prof serv 1977-78; Soldiers Home in Holyoke, med dir 1979-88. **Orgs:** Assoc attending surgeon Nassau County Med Ctr, East Meadow, Long Island, NY 1959-77; mem Kiwanis Club of Hempstead, NY 1963-67; deputy county med examiner Nassau County, Long Island, NY 1964-77; pres Hempstead Community Chest, Hempstead, NY 1965; bd of trustees Catholic Hosp Assn, St Louis, MO 1973-76; asst clinical prof of surgery State Univ of NY at Stonybrook Med Sch 1976-77. **Honors/Awds:** Diplomate Amer Bd of Surgery 1963-; fellow Amer Coll of Surgeons 1965-; fellow Intl Coll of Surgeons 1976-; Diplomate, American Bd of Quality Assurance Utilization Review Physicians, 1987-; Fellow, American College of Utilization Review Physicians, 1987. **Military Serv:** USAAF 1st lt fighter pilot instructor pilot; 332nd Fighter Group Air Medal; 2 Oak Leaf Clusters; Purple Heart 1943-47. **Home Addr:** 14312 Whitewood Dr, Sun City West, AZ 85375-5936.

GAINES, VICTOR PRYOR

University administrator. **Personal:** Born Jul 25, 1939, Staunton, VA; children: Victor P II, Johnathan. **Educ:** KY State Univ, BA 1960; Univ of KY, MA 1969, EdS 1977, EdD 1981. **Career:** Univ of KY, dir of special student programs 1972-74, employee counselor 1974-, employee counselor/acting dir equal oppor 1977-80, acting vice chancellor minority affairs 1984-85, exec dir for minority resource develop and employee counselor 1985-. **Orgs:** Mem bd dirs Lexington Urban League; mem Phi Delta Kappa; bd mem Univ of KY Credit Union 1982-; corporate mem Amer Assoc for Equity & Excellence in Higher Educ 1986-. **Honors/Awds:** Article published "Career Counseling as Experienced by Practicing Black Ophthalmologists," Natl Medical Assoc 1980. **Business Addr:** Exec Dir Minority Resource Dev, Univ of KY, Rm 207 Administration Bldg, Lexington, KY 40506.

GAINES, WILLIAM ALBERT

Professional football player. **Personal:** Born Jun 20, 1971, Jackson, MS. **Educ:** Univ of Florida, attended. **Career:** Miami Dolphins, defensive tackle, 1994; Washington Redskins, 1995-. **Business Addr:** Professional Football Player, Washington Redskins, 13832 Redskin Dr, Herndon, VA 22071, (703)471-9100.

GAINEY, LEONARD DENNIS, II

Association executive. **Personal:** Born Aug 23, 1927, Jacksonville, FL; divorced; children: Leonard III, Derek, Kassandra. **Educ:** Morehouse Coll, BA 1949. **Career:** US Post Office Dept Ft Lauderdale FL, carrier 1953-66; Gaineys Bus Affairs, owner 1953-66; Econ Oppty Coord Group Inc, dep dir, comptroller 1966-73; Stae of FL Ed Dept, fiscal officer 1973-76; Urban League of Broward Cty, pres, ceo 1976-81; Ken Thurston & Assoc Inc, bd mem 1979-80; The Omega Group Inc, mgr mgmt consult br office; North Broward Hosp District, director of minority business affairs, currently. **Orgs:** Pres Ivory Mizell Republ Club; treas FL Black Republ Council; bd mem exec comm Broward Cty Republ Party; mem Omega Psi Phi 1957; mem Ed Comm Ft Lauderdale Broward C of C 1980, Human Affairs Council Natl Council Christians & Jews 1980; chmn Broward Cty Human Relations Adv; American Management Association; National Society of Public Accountants; National Society of Tax Professionals; American Association of Professional Consultants; Florida Association of Minority Business Officials; National Forum for Black Administrators; Omega Psi Phi Fraternity, Inc. **Honors/Awds:** Omega Man of the Year Omega Psi Phi Frat; Citation Broward Cty Human Relations Div 1979. **Military Serv:** AUS corpl 1950-52. **Business Addr:** Director, Minority Business Affairs, North Broward Hospital District, 1608 SE 3rd Ave, Fort Lauderdale, FL 33316.

GAITAN, FERNANDO J., JR.

Corporate counsel. **Personal:** Born Aug 22, 1948, Kansas City, KS. **Educ:** Pittsburgh State Univ, BS 1970; Univ of MO Kansas City, JD 1974. **Career:** Bureau of Prisons; US Justice Dept; Public Defender; Legal Aid Soc; Southwestern Bell Telephone Co, attny 1974-80; Sixteenth Judicial Circuit Jackson Cty Courthouse, circuit court judge. **Orgs:** Mem MO Bar Assoc, Kansas City Bar Assoc, Jackson Cty Bar Assoc, Amer Bar Assoc, Natl Bar Assoc, State & Natl Judicial Conf, St Lukes Hosp, De La Salle Ed Ctr, Ozanam Home for Boys, NAACP, Volunteers in Corrections, Natl Conf of Christians & Jews. **Business Addr:** Corporate Counsel, AT&T, 500 E Eight St, Rm 1344, Kansas City, MO 64106.

GAITHER, ALONZO SMITH

Educator (retired). **Personal:** Born Apr 11, 1903; married Sadie Robinson. **Educ:** Knoxville Coll, AB 1927; Ohio State Univ, MA 1937. **Career:** Henderson Inst Henderson, NC, coach 1927-35; St Paul Jr Coll Lawrenceville VA, 1935-37; FL A&M U, asst coach 1937-44, head coach, prof, Athl dir 1945-69, athletic dir, prof 1970-73; FL A&M Univ, athletic dir emeritus, currently. **Orgs:** Trustee, Am Football Coaches Assn Fellowship of Christ Athletics; mem FL Bd Pardons & Parole Qualifications Com 1974; elder Trinity United Presb Ch; mem Urban League; NAACP; vice chair, ARC; mem Local Assn Charities; mem Sunrioe Optimist Club; Phi Beta Sigma; Sigma Phi Phi Frat; mem Natl Assoc of Intercoll athl; mem Orange Bwl comm; mem Amer Football & Basketball Coaches Assn; mem Natl Negro Coll Football Assn. **Honors/Awds:** College Coach of the Year, American Footbll Coaches Assn 1961; Helmo Hall of Fame NAIA Bethune Medallion 1973; FL Hall Fame & TN Hall of Fame; elected to Nat Football Found Hall of Fame Jan 1975; TN Distinguished Amer Award 1972; Hall of Fame of the Natl Assn of Coll Dir of Athl 1976; Sports Hall of Fame, Florida A&M Univ 1976; Knoxville Coll, Honorary LLD, 1962.

GAITHER, BARRY

Arts administrator. **Career:** Natl Ctr of Afro-American Artists, dir, Museum Div, currently. **Business Addr:** Director, Museum Division, National Center of Afro-American Artists, 300 Walnut Ave, Boston, MA 02119, (617)442-8614.

GAITHER, CORNELIUS E.

Dentist. **Personal:** Born Feb 28, 1928, Philadelphia, PA; son of Edith Albertha Robinson Gaither and Cornelius Hopson Gaither; married Anna Louise Whittaker Gaither, Dec 23, 1952; children: Cornelius, Carmen, Carol, John, Reginald. **Educ:** Meharry Med Coll, DDS 1953; Lincoln Univ, AB 1949. **Career:** Salem Memorial Hospital, chief of dental services; USAF reserves dental corps, 1957-87, retired Lt Col 1987. **Orgs:** Rho Chapter, Alpha Phi Alpha Fraternity; Chi Delta Mu, Medical Dental Pharmaceutical Fraternity; Salvation Army Service Committee 1958-; Aerospace Med Assn; South Jersey Med Dental Assn; Kiwanis Intl: Christ Presb Church, 1970-. **Honors/Awds:** Salvation Army, Others Award. **Military Serv:** USAF 1954-57; USAFR lt col 1957-87. **Business Addr:** Dentist, 128 Kings Hwy, Swedesboro, NJ 08085.

GAITHER, DOROTHY B.

Physician. **Personal:** Born May 27, 1941, St Louis, MO; daughter of Dorothy H Gaither and Alexander D Gaither; married Marion A Randolph; children: Alexander, Michele. **Educ:** Knoxville Coll, BS 1964; Howard U, MD 1970. **Career:** Howard Univ Hosp, intern resident 1970-75, instructor 1975; private practice 1975-, ob gyn; Women's Medical Ctr, medical dir 1985-87; Aunandale Women's Center 1988-. **Orgs:** Treasurer Amer Medical Women's Assn 1983-85 sec l982-83, pres l985-86, Branch I; Arlington Links; sec Northern Virginia Chap Coalition of 100 Black Women 1984-85; mem Natl Medical Assn; DC Medical Society, Medical Chirugical Society, Alpha Kappa Alpha Sor; fellow Amer College Ob/Gyn; mem Physicians Serv Commn Blue Cross/Blue Shield 1985; mem Girlfriends Inc, Jack & Jill of Amer Inc, Carats Inc, Just Us; mem Medical School Admissions Commn Howard Univ 1983-85, Impaired Physicians Commn DC Medical Soc 1983-85; Distinguished

Alumnus, Knoxville College, National Assn Equal Opportunity in Higher Education, 1990. **Honors/Awds:** Articles published in Natl Medical Assn Journal 1968, 1972, 1973; Distinguished Alumnus, Knoxville College, National Assn Equal Opportunity in Higher Education, 1990. **Home Addr:** 9411 Mt Vernon Cir, Alexandria, VA 22309. **Business Addr:** 3230 Pennsylvania Ave SE, Washington, DC 20020.

GAITHER, EDMUND B.
Association executive, artist. **Personal:** Born Oct 6, 1944, Great Falls, SC. **Educ:** Morehouse Coll, BA 1966; Brown U, MA 1968. **Career:** Museum of Fine Arts, spl cons; Museum Nat Cntr of Afro-Am Artists, dir/curator; Elma Lewis Sch of Fine Arts; Spelman Coll, lectr; Boston U, asst prof; Harvard Coll, lectr; NY U, vis critic; Wellesley Coll, lectr; Nat Endowment of the Arts NY State Council on Art & Hum, panelist; Lectures Widely;Piedmont Art Festival Atlanta, judg E 1975; Indpndnc Art Fest Jamaica WI, judge 1971; Afro-Am Artists Musm of Fine Arts, chief organizer. **Orgs:** Mem Nat Conf of Artists. **Honors/Awds:** Insight award Am Assn of Museums RAP 1975.

GAITHER, JAMES W., JR.
Engineer. **Personal:** Born Dec 16, 1954, Battle Creek, MI; son of Marie Elizabeth Stubbs Gaither and James W Gaither Sr; married Susan Lynn Bryant-Gaither, Jun 19, 1982; children: Anika Marie, James Bryant. **Educ:** Michigan State Univ, East Lansing, MI, BS, pkg eng, 1981. **Career:** Revlon Prof Prod, Cincinnati, OH, tech pkg eng, 1982-84; Avon Products, Inc, New York, NY, package dev eng, 1984-89; Revlon, Inc, New York, New York, group leader, package devel, 1989-. **Orgs:** Member, American Management Assn, packaging council, 1990-; member, Institute of Packaging Professionals, 1989-; member, MSU Packaging Society, Alumni, 1987-. **Honors/Awds:** America's Best and Brightest Young Business & Professional Men, Dollars & Sense Magazine, 1989. **Business Addr:** Group Leader, Package Development Dept, Revlon Inc, 625 Madison Ave, New York, NY 10022.

GAITHER, KATRYNA
Professional basketball player. **Personal:** Born Aug 13, 1975. **Educ:** Notre Dame Univ. **Career:** San Jose Lasers, center, 1997-. **Business Addr:** Professional Basketball Player, San Jose Lasers, 1530 Parkmoor Ave, Ste A, San Jose, CA 95128, (408)271-1500.

GAITHER, MAGALENE DULIN
Educator (retired). **Personal:** Born Jul 13, 1928, Mocksville, NC; daughter of Edith Hazel Britton Dulin (deceased) and Leroy Robertson Dulin; married Troy Baxter Hudson (divorced 1960); children: Eric Lynn Hudson Sr, Hazel Shanlon Hudson. **Educ:** Bennett College, Greensboro, NC, BA; North Carolina A&T State University, Greensboro, NC, MS, adult education. **Career:** Buckingham County Training School, Dillwyn, VA, English, reading, 1950-51; Central Davie High School, Mocksville, NC, English, history, 1951-61; Unity High School, Statesville, NC, English teacher, 1961-70; North Iredell High School, Olin, NC, English teacher, 1970-71; Davie High School, Mocksville, NC, English teacher, 1971-83; Davidson County Community College, Lexington, NC, instructor, 1983-87 (retired). **Orgs:** County chairperson, Democratic Party, 1991-; chairperson, Board of Nursing Home Advocacy, 1980-83; member, board of advisors, Milling Manor Home for Handicapped Women, 1985-; NAACP, 1950-; member, board of directors, Davie County Arts Council, 1979-81; National Educators Assn, 1950-; Zeta Phi Beta Sorority; member, Shiloh Baptist Church, 1938-; pres, North Carolina Assn for Educators, Davie County Unit; and numerous others. **Honors/Awds:** Valedictorian, Central Davie High School, 1945; Honor Graduate, Bennett College, 1949; graduate with 4.0 grade point average, Masters Degree, North Carolina A&T State University; selection committee, Davie County Leadership, 1991; Delegate, District & North Carolina State Library Conferences, 1990-91; feasibility committee, YMCA facility; designed course study in gerontology for North Carolina A&T State University; presented music for a reception honoring the late President Lyndon Baines Johnson, Statesville, NC; solicited representation for first black page to serve at North Carolina legislature; Plaque, NAACP Service Award; Zeta Minority Women of the Year; and numerous others.

GAITHER, RICHARD A.
Attorney. **Personal:** Born Oct 28, 1939, Washington, DC; son of Miriam Gaither and John Gaither; married Deanna Dixon; children: Jamala, Marisa. **Educ:** Univ of Dayton, BS Chemistry 1962; Univ of Baltimore, JD 1970; New York Univ, LLM Trade Regulation 1981. **Career:** AUS, officer 1963-65; FDA, research chemist 1963 & 1965-67; US Patent & Trademark Office, patent examiner 1967-72; Lever Brothers Co, atty 1972-74; Hoffmann La Roche Inc, asst gen counsel. **Orgs:** Mem Natl Bar Assn 1970-; mem Amer Bar Assn 1970-; mem Natl Patent Law Assn 1970-. **Honors/Awds:** Black Achiever Newark, NJ YMCA 1980. **Military Serv:** AUS 1st lt 1963-65; numerous letters of commendation. **Business Addr:** Assistant General Counsel, Hoffmann La Roche Inc, 340 Kingsland St, Nutley, NJ 07110.

GAITHER, THOMAS W.
Educator. **Personal:** Born Nov 12, 1938, Great Falls, SC; married. **Educ:** Claflin Coll, BS 1960; Atlanta U, MS 1964; Univ IA, PhD 1968. **Career:** Cong of Racial Equality CORE, field sec 1960-62; Iowa City, forester 1968; Slippery Rock State Coll, assoc prof 1968-. **Orgs:** Mem Botanical Soc Am; mem Mycological Soc Am; Am Assn for the Advancement & Sci; mem Soc Sigma Xi. **Honors/Awds:** Outstanding young mem Am Alpha Kappa Mu Nat Scholastic Hon Soc 1972. **Business Addr:** Dept Biology, Slippery Rock State Coll, Slippery Rock, PA 16057.

GALBRAITH, SCOTT
Professional football player. **Personal:** Born Jan 7, 1967, Sacramento, CA. **Educ:** Univ of Southern California, attended. **Career:** Cleveland Browns, tight end, 1990-92; Dallas Cowboys, 1993-94, 1997-; Washington Redskins, 1995-96. **Business Addr:** Professional Football Player, Dallas Cowboys, One Cowboys Pkwy, Irving, TX 75063, (214)556-9900.

GALBREATH, HARRY CURTIS
Professional football player. **Personal:** Born Jan 1, 1965, Clarksville, TN. **Educ:** Tennessee, bachelors degree. **Career:** Miami Dolphins, offensive guard, 1988-92; Green Bay Packers, offensive guard, 1993-. **Honors/Awds:** The Sporting News, College All-American Team, guard, 1987. **Business Addr:** Professional Football Player, Green Bay Packers, 1265 Lombardi Ave, Green Bay, WI 54304, (414)494-2351.

GALES, JAMES
Government official. **Personal:** Born May 18, 1922, Jefferson Co; married Lucinda Perkins; children: Blanche, AC, Robert, Frank, Mary Ellen, Ronnie, Angela P. **Educ:** Jefferson Co Training Sch; Alcorn A&M Coll, Cert 1949. **Career:** Town of Fayette, mayor pro tem city councilman 1969-; Internatl Paper Co, safety dept 1949. **Orgs:** Bd of dirs Adams Jefferson Franklin Caliborne Comm 1969; bd of dirs Unity Action Agency ARC 1973-; bd of dirs Medgar Evers Comprehensive Health Clinc 1970; bd dir Indl Park for City & Co 1969-. **Honors/Awds:** Faithful worker award NAACP Jefferson Co Chap 1967; faithful worker award AJFC Comm Action Agency 1979; faithful worker award ARC Atlanta GA Chap 1979. **Military Serv:** AUS sgt. **Business Addr:** City Hall, PO Box 98, Fayette, MS 39069.

GALIBER, JOSEPH L.
State senator, attorney. **Personal:** Born Oct 26, 1924, New York, NY; son of Ethel Browser Galiber and Joseph F Galiber; married Emma E Shade, Nov 28, 1946; children: Pamela Susan, Ruby Dianne Wint. **Educ:** College of City of NY, BS 1950; NY Law Sch, JD 1962. **Career:** Youth Counsel Bur Bronx Co Dist Atty Ofc, counselor & borough dir 1950-63; Riverside Hosp NYC, drug abuse counselor recreation dir 1953-59; JOIN, exec-dir 1963-65; Fed Ofc of Econ Oppty, inspector 1966-68; private practice, atty 1965-; NY State, senator 1969-. **Orgs:** Chmn Bronx Co Dem Com 1966-79; del & asst majority leader NY State Constl Conv 1967; del Dem Nat Conv 1968; vice chmn NY State Dem Com 1975; mem St Augustine Presby Ch; life mem NAACP; mem Alumni Assn of CCNY, Bronx Urban League, SE Bronx Nghbrhd Cntrs; mem policy adv council State Legistlative Inst Baruch Coll. **Honors/Awds:** Numerous awards for pub serv; Five Battle Stars AUS 1943-45. **Military Serv:** AUS staff sgt 1943-45. **Business Addr:** Attorney, 840 Grand Concourse, Bronx, NY 10451.

GALL, LENORE ROSALIE
Educational administrator. **Personal:** Born Aug 9, 1943, Brooklyn, NY; daughter of Olive Rosalie Weekes Gall and George Whitfield Gall. **Educ:** New York Univ, AAS 1970; New York Univ Tisch School of Business & Public Admin, BS 1973, Training and Development Certificate 1975; New York Univ SEHNAP, MA Counselor Educ 1977; Teachers Coll, Columbia Univ, EdM 1988; Ed D 1988. **Career:** Ford Foundation, various positions 1967-76; New York Univ Grad School of Business, deputy dir 1976-79; Pace Univ Lubin School of Business, dir of career develop 1979-82; Yale Univ School of Organization and Mgmt, dir of career devel 1982-85; Brooklyn Coll CUNY, asst to the assoc provost 1985-88; asst to the provost 1988-91; Fashion Institute of Technology, asst to the vp of academic affairs, 1991-94; NY City Tech Coll/Cuny, asst provost, 1994-; Natl Assn of Univ Women, northeast sectional dir, 1993-96, natl second vice pres, 1996-; Audience Dev Task Force, Dance Theatre of Harlem, co-chair. **Orgs:** Chairperson bd of dirs Langston Hughes Comm Library 1975-79, 1982-91; first vice pres, awards comm chairperson, Dollars for Scholars 1976-; dir Placement Secretarial Devel Workshops, College Placement Serv 1978-81; asst prof LaGuardia Comm Coll CUNY 1981-95; program chairperson New Haven Chamber of Commerce 1984; mem bd of dirs Assn of Black Women in Higher Educ Inc 1985, pres 1989-93; mem Amer Assn of Univ Women 1985; Natl Assn of Univ Women mem 1986, first vice pres 1982; mem Amer Assn of Univ Administrators 1986; mem Natl Assn of Women in Education; Natl Urban League; first vice pres Natl Council of Negro Women North Queens Section 1987-89, pres, 1989-93. **Honors/Awds:** Mem Educational Honorary Organization Kappa Delta Pi 1986; mem Phi Delta Kappa Columbia Univ Chap 1986; grant/scholarship Jewish Foundation for the Education of Women 1986/87; Sojourner Truth Award, National Assn of Negro Business and Professional Women's Club Inc, The Laurelton Club, 1991; National Honor Roll, Citizen Scholarship Foundation of America, Dollars for Scholars Award; Concerned Women of Brooklyn, Inc, Distinguished Service Award; Natl Assn of Univ Women. **Business Addr:** Asst Provost, NYC Technical College, 300 Jay Street, NAMM-320, Brooklyn, NY 11201.

GALLAGER, MIKE JOHN
Radio station executive. **Personal:** Born Jan 19, 1945, Toledo, OH; married Mary. **Educ:** John Carroll Univ, bus 1967. **Career:** Reams Broadcasting Corp, sr vice pres 1977-80; WABQ, Inc, pres 1980-87. **Orgs:** Mem Alpha Kappa Psi 1968-. **Military Serv:** USA capt 6 yrs. **Business Addr:** President, WABQ Inc, 8000 Euclid Ave, Cleveland, OH 44103.

GALLAGHER, ABISOLA HELEN
Educator, psychologist. **Personal:** Born Oct 13, 1950, Chicago, IL; daughter of Lulla M Jointer and Leroy Gallagher. **Educ:** Northeastern Illinois Univ, BA (w/Honors) 1972; Univ WI-Whitewater, MS 1974; Rutgers Univ, EdD 1983. **Career:** Univ of Wisconsin System Central Admin, educ admin intern 1974-75; Univ of Winconsin-Parkside, counselor-prog coord 1975-78; Douglass Coll Rutgers Univ, asst dean student life 1981-85; Unlimited Potential, management consultant 1985-87; Rutgers Coll/Rutgers Univ, residence dir 1978-81, asst dean office of academic serv 1987-90; Jersey State College, counseling psycholgist, 1990-. **Orgs:** Vice pres 1983-87, pres 1989-, Assn of Black Psychologists New Jersey Chap 1983-87; exec bd mem Coalition of 100 Black Women New Jersey 1985; Assn of Black Psychologists 1985-87, Amer Psychological Assn 1987, New Jersey Psychological Assn 1987; NJ Chapter, Association of Black Psychologists, 1989-91; AIDS consultant, 1990-; Women's Resource Center, executive board mem, 1991-92. **Honors/Awds:** Martin L King Scholarship 1979-80, 1980-81 Rutgers Univ; Outstanding Young Women in Amer 1982,84; Outstanding Service Awd Kappa Alpha Psi Frat 1984; Distinguished Serv Awd Paul Robeson Cultural Ctr Rutgers Univ 1985; publication "Black Women in Group Psychotherapy," Women in Groups Springer Press 1986. **Home Addr:** 175 Slocum Ave, Englewood, NJ 07631-2221. **Business Addr:** Counseling Psychologist, Counseling & Psychological Services Office, Jersey City State College, 54 College Street, Jersey City, NJ 07305.

GALLON, DENNIS P.
Educator. **Personal:** Born in Monticello, FL. **Educ:** Edward Waters Coll, BS 1964; Indiana Univ Bloomington, MS 1969; Univ of FL, PhD 1975. **Career:** Florida Cmmty Coll, professor 1972-1979, business mngr 1979-81, dean of vocational ed 1981-84, dean of instruction 1984-85, dean, College of Liberal Arts and Sciences, 1985-. **Orgs:** Mem Amer Soc for Training & Development; mem Jax Chamber of Comm; mem FL Assn of Cmmty Colleges; mem, Jax Urban League. **Business Addr:** Dean, Liberal Arts & Science, Florida Community College, 501 W State St, Jacksonville, FL 32202.

GALLOT, RICHARD JOSEPH
Elected official. **Personal:** Born Jan 31, 1936, Swords, LA; son of Loretta Gallot and Freddie Gallot; married Mildred Bernice Gauthier; children: Daphne, Loretta, Richard Jr. **Educ:** Tyler Barber Coll, Barber Degree 1961; Grambling State Univ, BS Acct 1975. **Career:** Gallo's Barbershop, barber 1961; Gallo's Grocer & Liquor & Serv, owner 1969-; Town of Grambling, mayor 1981. **Orgs:** Pres Grambling Chamber of Com 1967; dir Grambling Fed Credit Union 1973, Parish Council, St Benedict Church 1975; mem Lion's Club 1983. **Honors/Awds:** Businessman of Year Business Dept Grambling State Univ, 1981; Outstanding Black in LA Teal Enterprise 1982; Appointed to Governor's Com Community Devel 1985. **Military Serv:** AUS Spec 4 1958-62. **Home Addr:** PO Box 148, Grambling, LA 71245. **Business Addr:** Owner, Gallot's Enterprise, 102 South Grand Ave, Grambling, LA 71245.

GALLOWAY, JOEY
Professional football player. **Personal:** Born Nov 20, 1971, Bellaire, OH. **Educ:** Ohio State. **Career:** Seattle Seahawks, wide receiver, 1995-. **Special Achievements:** 1st round/8th overall NFL draft pick, 1995. **Business Addr:** Professional Football Player, Seattle Seahawks, 11220 NE 53rd St, Kirkland, WA 98033, (206)827-9777.

GALLOWAY-BRIGGS, LULA
Paralegal, organization executive. **Personal:** Born Jul 8, 1945, San Bernardino, CA; daughter of Rev David R Briggs & Lillie Chatham Briggs; married Charles E Galloway, Sr; children: Kimberlyne M, Gerald, Cynthia, Sahara, Cia, Charles Jr. **Educ:** San Jose State University, 1987. **Career:** Paralegal Service Co, owner, 1992-; National Association of Juneteenth Lineage, CEO, 1995-. **Orgs:** National Independent Paralegal Association; National Parliamentarians Association. **Honors/Awds:** President Bill Clinton, Contribution of National Juneteenth, 1997; US Congressional Recognition, First National Juneteenth Convention; Mayor, City of Galveston, TX, Special Tribute, 1997; Flint, MI, Bd of Commissioners Resolution, 1997; State

of MI, House of Representatives, 1997. **Special Achievements:** First art exhibition on Juneteenth/Slavery at Rotunda of the Russell Senate Office Bldg, Washington, DC; National Juneteenth Independence Day; Juneteenth Calendar with collectable Black Art; Chair for all festivals & parades, city of San Jose, CA. **Business Addr:** President/CEO, Paralegal Service Co/ National Association of Juneteenth Lineage, 1605 E Remington, Saginaw, MI 48601, (517)752-0576.

GALLWEY, SYDNEY H.
Educator. **Personal:** Born Nov 17, 1921, Manitoba;son of Rebecca and Sidney; married Lucy Newman; children: Steven Lindsay, James Charles. **Educ:** Howard U, BA 1950; Cornell U, Perm Cert Soc Stud 1960-61. **Career:** City Sch, tchr 1964-66, tchr 1969-70; SVC Brockport, tchr 1970-74; City Sch, tchr 1975-76; Rochester City Schools, tutor & instructor, 1980-87; Urban League, bus educ inst, academic instructor 1980-87; NY St Pub Schools, teacher, 1961-. **Orgs:** Dir state branches NYS Assoc for Study Afro Am Life & History 1970; Urban League of Roch 1980-85; lecturer workshops Urban League 1980-85. **Honors/Awds:** Outstanding serv Urban League, Roch NY 1983-84; Research, Publications, History of Black Family in Western New York, 1961-. **Military Serv:** US Army s/sgt 1940-45.

GALTHER, ISRAEL L.
Organization executive. **Career:** Salvation Army, sec for personnel, USA Eastern Territory, chief sec, 1997-. **Special Achievements:** First African American and youngest officer appointed as chief secretary for Salvation Army.

GALVIN, EMMA CORINNE
Educator. **Personal:** Born May 2, 1909, Richmond, VA; married Alx Galvin MD. **Educ:** Shaw U, BA 1924; Univ PA, MA; Cornell U, PhD 1943. **Career:** Ithaca Coll, retired prof; Ithaca School Dist, academic counsultant; Southside Center, teacher; Tompkins Co Med Aux, lecturer, writer past pres. **Orgs:** Mem Ntnl Com Amer Assn Univ Wmn; past pres Pi Lambda Theta & Phi Gamma Delta; mem Alpha Kappa Alpha; mem Citzns Adv Com Envrn Qulty St NY; del Ntnl Conv Lgue Wmn Vtrs; chrprsn Tompkins Cnty Comm Chst; past pres Ithaca PTA; mem Ithaca B & P W Club; bd chmn Sthside Comm Ctr; orgnzr Ithaca Wmn's Comm Bldg. **Honors/Awds:** Comm serv award Black Mem of Ithaca 1974; achvmnt comm for a better Am bk pub Eisenhower Admn; womn of yr Shaw Univ 1924; wmn of yr Ithca B & PW 1959. **Business Addr:** 122 Ashland Pl, #16M, Brooklyn, NY 11201.

GAMBLE, EVA M.
Marketing executive. **Personal:** Born Aug 3, 1952, Providence, RI; daughter of Sarah Gamble and George Andrade. **Educ:** Northeastern University, Boston, MA, 1970-71; University of Rhode Island, Kingston, RI, BA, 1974. **Career:** State of Rhode Island, Providence, RI, employment interviewer, 1974-78; Gulf Oil Co, Providence, RI, clerk/supervisor, 1978-84; Chevron Oil Co, New York, NY, terminal coord, 1984-89; Chevron Oil Co, San Francisco, CA, administration specialist, 1990-. **Orgs:** Asst secretary, American Assn of Blacks in Energy, 1990-. **Business Addr:** Administration Specialist, Marketing, Chevron International Oil Co, Inc, 555 Market St, Rm 719, San Francisco, CA 94120.

GAMBLE, JANET HELEN
Minority specialist, business consultant, nurse, activist (retired). **Personal:** Born May 5, 1917, Dallas, TX; daughter of Thomas G and Nellie Helen Golan; married Toby. **Educ:** Biggers Bus Coll; Oakland Merritt Bus Coll; Univ of AK. **Career:** AK Dept Labor, minority specialist, 1965-80, supr 1944-47; Oakland Naval Supply Depot, minority splst; Alameda Cty Outpatient Dept, minority splst; Ofc of Milo H Fritz MD, ophthalmology and otolaryngology. **Orgs:** Deaconess Shiloh Bapt Ch 1952-; council mem; pres Anchorage Union & Missionary Soc 1971; chmn bd dir Opportunities Indsl Ctr 1974-76; past vice pres Eye-Ear-Nose-Throat Found; AK NAACP; AK Black Caucus; past pres Ch Women United Intl; dir founder Minority Outreach Employment Svc; OES Order of Eastern Star; AK Council on Disabilities and Special Education; immediate past chmn, Older Alaskans Commission; Municipal Senior Advisory Commission, Anchorage. **Honors/Awds:** Hon mem Mothers Christian Fellowship Club; Most Outst in Religion 1974, 1977; P Worthy Matron Alpha Guide #8; Anchorage Br Bestowed Dr of Letters; Grand Dep Worthy Matron of Guiding Light United Grand Chap CA & AK; First Lady of Anchorage, Volunteer of the Year Award; WICS, Rosa Parks Award; White House Conference on Aging, Delegate, 1995. **Special Achievements:** Founder of scholarship program, Shiloh Baptist Church.

GAMBLE, KENNETH
Business executive, musician. **Personal:** Born Aug 11, 1943, Philadelphia; married Dione La Rue. **Career:** Kenny Gamble & Romeos, lead vocal; Gamble Huff Prods, 1968-; Gamble Huff & Bell Prods, 1969-. **Orgs:** Pres/Chmn Philadelphia Intl Records Asso Music Inc; mem BMI; mem AFM; mem NARM; mem NATRA; mem RIAA. **Honors/Awds:** Decade award Top 100 Black Enterprises Record World 1973; prodr of yr NATRA 1968-69; top pub award BMI; songwriter of yr BMI; producer of num gold albums For The Love of Money/Love Train/When Will I See You Again; Many Spl Achievements. **Business Addr:** Chairman, Philadelphia Intl Records, 309 S Broad St, Philadelphia, PA 19107.

GAMBLE, KENNETH L.
City official. **Personal:** Born Apr 24, 1941, Marshall, MO; son of Elizabeth Lane Gamble (deceased) and Rev Ira J Gamble Sr(deceased); married Shiela M Greene, Apr 19, 1969; children: Jerry L Swain, Andrew J Swain, Kendra L E Gamble. **Educ:** Morgan State Coll, Baltimore MD, attended, 1959-62; Youngstown State Univ, Youngstown OH, BA, 1971; Univ of Akron, Akron OH, MA Urban Studies, 1975. **Career:** Univ of Akron, Center for Urban Studies, Akron OH, research asst, 1972-73; Trans Century Corp, Washington DC, consultant, Public Housing, 1973; Canton Urban League, Canton OH, assoc dir, Housing & Community Serv, 1973-77; Toledo NHS, Toledo OH, exec dir, 1977-80; City of Saginaw, Saginaw MI, dir, Dept of Neighborhood Serv; Saginaw Housing Commission, dir, 1991-92, administrative assistant to the assistant city mgr, 1993-. **Honors/Awds:** Dean's List, Youngstown State Univ, 1969-71; Dean's List, Univ of Akron, 1972-73; HUD Fellowship Recipient, 1972-73. **Military Serv:** US Air Force, staff sergeant, 1962-65. **Business Addr:** Administrative Assistant, Department of General Services, City of Saginaw, 1315 S Washington, Saginaw, MI 48601.

GAMBLE, KEVIN DOUGLAS
Professional basketball player. **Personal:** Born Nov 13, 1965, Springfield, IL. **Educ:** Lincoln College, Lincoln, IL, 1983-85; Univ of Iowa, Iowa City, IA, 1985-87. **Career:** Quad City Thunder (CBA), 1987-89; Chicago Express (WBL), 1990; Portland Trail Blazers (NBA), 1987-88; Boston Celtics (NBA), 1988-94; Miami Heat, 1994-95; Sacramento Kings, 1996-. **Business Addr:** Professional Basketball Player, Sacramento Kings, 1 Sport Pkwy, Sacramento, CA 95834, (916)928-6900.

GAMBLE, OSCAR CHARLES
Professional baseball player (retired). **Personal:** Born Dec 20, 1949, Ramer, AL. **Career:** Outfielder: Chicago Cubs, 1969, Philadelphia Phillies, 1970-72, Cleveland Indians, 1973-75, New York Yankees, 1976, Chicago White Sox, 1977, San Diego Padres, 1978, Texas Rangers, 1979, New York Yankees, 1980-84, Chicago White Sox, 1985. **Honors/Awds:** Played in Championship & World Series 1976. **Business Addr:** NY Yankees, Yankee Stadium, Bronx, NY 10451.

GAMBLE, ROBERT LEWIS
City government official. **Personal:** Born Apr 27, 1947, Carroll County, GA; married Lucy Ann Dixon; children: Venus Marie, Athenia Marie. **Educ:** Carver HS, 1966; USMC, data processing 1967. **Career:** USMC, printing press oper 1966; United Parcel Service, feeder driver 1970; City of Whitesburg, mayor. **Orgs:** Chmn Carroll County Pre-health Clinic 1981; vice-chmn Carroll County Vocational Sch 1984. **Military Serv:** USMC sgt 3 yrs; two Purple Hearts Vietnam Service Medal Natl Defense Good Conduct Medal. **Business Addr:** Mayor, City of Whitesburg, PO Box 151, Whitesburg, GA 30185.

GAMBLE, WILBERT
Educator. **Personal:** Born Jun 19, 1932, Greenville, AL; married Zeferene Tucker; children: Priscilla Ann. **Educ:** Wayne State Univ, BS (first in class) 1955, PhD 1960. **Career:** OR State Univ, asst prof 1962-67; Johnson Res Found Univ PA, visiting prof 1967-76; Univ Sci & Tech Kumasi Ghana, Fulbright prof 1971-72; Natl Inst Health, visit res worker 1976-77, 1983-84, IPA investigator 1990-91; OR State Univ, prof of biochemistry 1977-. **Honors/Awds:** NIH Postdoctoral Fellow Cornell Univ 1960-62; Danforth Assoc Danforth Found 1969-; mem Phi Lambda Upsilon Hon Soc 1957; mem Sigma Chi Honor Soc 1960; mem Amer Soc of Bio Chemists; Lehn & Fink Medal for Advancement of Pharm Sci 1955; NIH Predoctoral Fellowship 1959; NIH Postdoctoral Fellowship 1960 & 1968. **Business Addr:** Prof of Biochemistry, Oregon State Univ, Biochemistry & Biophysics, Corvallis, OR 97331.

GAMBLE, WILLIAM F.
Purchasing executive. **Personal:** Born Jan 3, 1950, West Palm Beach, FL; son of Louise Howell Gamble and Johnnie Gamble; married Jacqueline A Butler; children: Kayla, Cameron, Tabitha, Chimere, William Jr. **Educ:** FL A&M University, BS, 1971; SUNY at Albany, MA, public admin, 1976. **Career:** Community Affairs NY State, grants admin 1975-76; John Bryant's & Assocs, deputy dir 1976-77; Broward Co Govt, special project coordinator, 1977-80, Cuyahoga Co Govt Mgmt & Bud, asst dir 1980-82; Cleveland City School Dist, dir purchasing, 1982-92; City of Los Angeles, director of supplies, 1992-. **Orgs:** HIP House, consultant 1976-77; Cuyahoga Co Govt, consultant 1982; bd of dirs, Peoples & Cultures 1981-83; Conf of Minority Public Admin, 1977-; Amer Soc of Public Admin, 1977-; Intl City Mgmt Assn, 1977-; Natl Forum for Black Public Administrators; Natl Institute of Governmental Purchasing; California Assn of Public Purchasing Officers. **Honors/Awds:** Housing Urban Devel State Univ of NY, 1976-77; Natl Urban Fellow Natl Urban Fellows Inc, NY, 1980-81; Outstanding Young Amer, US Jaycees 1981; Executive Leadership Institute, National Forum for Black Public Administrators, 1988.

GAMMON, REGINALD ADOLPHUS
Educator, artist. **Personal:** Born Mar 31, 1921, Philadelphia, PA; son of Martha Gammon and Reginald A Gammon; married Janice Goldberger. **Educ:** Philadelphia Museum Coll of Art, 1949; Temple Univ, Stella Elkins Tyler School of Fine Art, 1950-51. **Career:** Freelance artist; prof, Western MI Univ; Poverty Programs, part-time teacher; US Post Office, advertising artist; WMU, exhibition space gallery; NC Central Univ, exhibition 1977; Acts of Art Gallery, exhibit 1973, 1974; NY Cultural Center, exhibit blacks, 1973; Knauss, Western MI Univ, exhibit floors windows & flks 1947; Knauss Hall Western MI Univ, photo exhibit 1972; Detroit Inst of Art, jazz/Art 1971; Eastern MI Univ, black artist exhibition Still gallery; Western MI Univ, faculty exhibition; Studio Museum in Harlem, exhibition sale; M Jackson Gallery, exhibition sale; SI Museum Coalition 70, exhibit. **Orgs:** Mem, City of Kalamazoo Arts Comm. **Honors/Awds:** Mentioned in Art News, The Spiral Group, Tuesday Magazine, Cue, The Art Gallery, The Evening News, Staten Island Sunday Advance, Sunday News, New York Amsterdam News, Kalamazoo Gazette Jan 24 1991; mentioned in various other newspapers, books and periodicals; Michigan Council for the Arts Creative Artists Grant, 1983; Creative Artist Grant, Arts Fund of Kalamazoo Co, 1988. **Military Serv:** USNR 3rd cl shipfitter 1944-46. **Business Addr:** Educator, Dept of Arts/Fine Arts, Western Michigan University, College of Fine Arts, 1402 Sangren, Kalamazoo, MI 49008.

GANDY, WAYNE LAMAR
Professional football player. **Personal:** Born Feb 10, 1971, Haines City, FL. **Educ:** Auburn. **Career:** St Louis Rams, tackle, 1995-. **Business Addr:** Professional Football Player, St Louis Rams, One Rams Way, St Louis, MO 63045, (314)982-7267.

GANEY, JAMES HOBSON
Dentist. **Personal:** Born Apr 29, 1944, Plainfield, NJ; married Peggy; children: Jayme, Christopher. **Educ:** Howard Univ Coll Pharm, BS 1969; NJ Coll Dentistry, DMD 1974. **Career:** Dental Practice, dentist. **Orgs:** Registered pharmacist Wash DC, NJ; licensed dentist NJ; mem Amer Pharm Assn, NJ Pharm Assn, Natl Pharm Assn; Amer Dental Assn; NJ Dental Assn; Natl Dental Assn, Acad of Gen Dentistry, Union Co Dental Soc, Plainfield Dental Soc, Commonwealth Dental Soc; faculty mem Farleigh Dickinson Univ Dental Sch 1979; mem Health Profls Educ Adv Counc for State of NJ 1979; mem bd dir Planfield Camp Crusade; mem NAACP, Psi Omega Dental Frat; Chi Delta Mu Frat. **Honors/Awds:** Cert of Merit Howard Univ Coll Pharm. **Business Addr:** 108 E 7th St, Plainfield, NJ 07061.

GANT, PHILLIP M., III
Business executive. **Personal:** Born Aug 21, 1949, Chicago, IL; son of Naurice Gant and Phillip M Gant II; married LaJule Steele Gant; children: Kimberli, Lyndsay. **Educ:** Linbloor Technical, Chicago, IL; University of Illinois, Chicago, IL. **Career:** Foote Cone & Belding, Chicago, IL, copywriter to vice pres/creative director, 1971-79; Young & Rubican Adv, New York, NY, sr copy writer, 1979-81; J Walter Thompson Adv, Chicago, IL, vice president/creative director, 1982-84; BBDO Chicago, Chicago, IL, exec vice president/exec creative dir, 1984-. **Orgs:** Board member, Evanston, IL, Community Daycare Ctr; board member, Evanston, IL, School for Little Children. **Honors/Awds:** Honoree, Dollars & Sense Mag-Chicago, 1989; Black Achievers in Industry-New York, 1991; Black Achievers Industry-Chicago, 1988. **Business Addr:** Exec Vice Pres/Exec Creative Director, BBDO Chicago, 410 N Michigan Ave, Chicago, IL 60611.

GANT, RAYMOND LEROY
Educational administrator. **Personal:** Born Jul 7, 1961, Paw Paw, MI. **Educ:** Ferris State Coll, BBA. **Career:** Ferris State Coll, budget analyst 1984-86, dir minority affairs 1986. **Orgs:** Ferris State Coll, mem, alumni bd of dir, minority student scholarship selection committee; Phi Beta Sigma. **Honors/Awds:** Phi Beta Sigma, recipient of Distinguished Service Key Awd. **Business Addr:** Dir of Minority Affairs, Ferris State College, Rankin Center, Big Rapids, MI 49307.

GANT, RONALD EDWIN
Professional baseball player. **Personal:** Born Mar 2, 1965, Victoria, TX. **Career:** Atlanta Braves, outfielder/infielder, 1987-94; Cincinnati Reds, 1994-95; St Louis Cardinals, 1995-. **Business Addr:** Professional Baseball Player, St Louis Cardinals, 250 Stadium Plaza, Busch Memorial Stadium, St Louis, MO 63102.

GANT, TRAVESA
Professional basketball player. **Personal:** Born Oct 10, 1971. **Educ:** Lamar Univ, bachelor's degree in kinesiology. **Career:** Nanya Formosa Plastic (Taiwan), center, 1994-95; Olympiakos Volos (Greece), 1996-97; Los Angeles Sparks, 1997-. **Business Addr:** Professional Basketball Player, Los Angeles Sparks, 3900 W Manchester Blvd, Inglewood, CA 90306, 800-978-9622.

GANT, WANDA ADELE
Federal government official. **Personal:** Born Oct 4, 1949, Washington, DC; daughter of Adela Mills Banks and Monore E Banks (deceased); married Ronald Gary Owens, Jun 24, 1989; children: Richard W Gant V, Ronald Gary Owens II. **Educ:** Central St Univ Wilberforce OH, BS 1971; Southeastern Univ Washington DC MBPA 1982. **Career:** General Services Admin, equal opportunity specialist 1971-78; US Dept Labor, equal opportunity specialist 1978-84; US Info Agency, fed women's prog mgr 1984-89; UISA, international visitors exchange specialist, 1989-93; US Dept of Justice, equal employment opporunity specialist, 1993-. **Orgs:** Member, Outstanding Young Women of America, 1981; Natl Council Negro Women, 1983-; Alpha Kappa Alpha 1983; Federal Women's Interagency Bd 1984; DC-Dakar Sister Cities Friendship Council 1985-; Amer Assn of Univ Women 1986; Business & Prof Women 1986. **Honors/Awds:** Superior Performance of Duty 1971; Outstanding Young Women of Amer 1983. **Home Addr:** 7811 Harder Court, Clinton, MD 20735.

GANTT, GLORIA
Research scientist. **Personal:** Born May 23, 1945, Charleston, SC; married. **Educ:** Hampton Inst Hampton, VA, BA bio (cum laude) 1965f Med Univ of SC Charleston, MS 1972. **Career:** Dept of Neurochem Medicine, Univ of SC Charleston, rsch scientist 1978-; Dept of Med & Dept of Basic Clinical Immunology & Microbiology, rsch scientist 1974-78; Burke High School Charleston, teacher 1969-70; US Naval Research Lab, Washington DC, tech lib 1965-69. **Orgs:** Mem Am Soc of Microbiology; mem Choraliers Music Club Charleston; mem Hampton Alumni Assn Charleston; mem YWCA; mem Morris St Bapt Ch Charleston; mem Alpha Kappa Alpha 1963-. **Honors/Awds:** Pub sci paper on Immunologic Responses Assoc with Thoracic Duct Lymphocytes.

GANTT, HARVEY BERNARD
Architect, politician. **Personal:** Born Jan 14, 1943, Charleston, SC; son of Wilhelmenia Gantt and Christopher Gantt; married Cindy; children: Sonja, Erika, Angela, Adam. **Educ:** Iowa State University, attended, 1961-62; Clemson University, BArch, 1965; Massachusetts Institute of Technology, MA, 1970. **Career:** Architect with various large firms in Charlotte, 1965-70; Soul City, experimental city, planner, 1970-71; University of North Carolina, Chapel Hill, lecturer, 1970-72; Clemson University, visiting critic, 1972-73; City of Charlotte, city council member, 1974-79, mayor pro tem, 1981-83, mayor, 1983-87; Gantt-Huberman Assocs architectural firm, partner, 1971-; US Senate, democratic candidate, 1990. **Orgs:** AIA; American Planning Assn; Charlotte Chapter, NAACP; North Carolina Design Foundation; US Council of Mayors, uncommitted delegate, 1984 Democratic Convention. **Honors/Awds:** Citizen of the Year, Charlotte NAACP, 1975, 1984; Belmont Abbey College, honorary degree; Johnson C Smith University, honorary degree; Clemson University, honorary degree; involved with securing Charlotte Hornets, NBA franchise, for the city. **Home Addr:** 517 N Poplar St, Charlotte, NC 28202.

GANTT, WALTER N.
Educator (retired). **Personal:** Born May 29, 1921, Baltimore, MD; son of Gladys Emily Davis Gantt and Walter Gantt. **Educ:** Coppin State Coll, BS 1942; NY Univ, MA 1949; Univ MD, EdD 1968. **Career:** Baltimore MD, prin & tchr 1942-68; Univ of MD, assoc prof 1968-78; Comm Coll of Baltimore, personnel admin 1978-85; Peace Corps Honduras 1985-87. **Orgs:** Coord Urban Tchr Educ Ctr 1969-70; asst to the chmn Dept Early Childhood Elem Educ 1971-74; mem Proj Aware; Cit Black History Exhibits; Phi Delta Kappa; chmn Career & Occupational Devel Com; mem Assn Supervision & Curriculum Devel; AAUP; NCSS. **Honors/Awds:** Circulus Scholarum Coppin State Coll; Serv Awd Phi Delta Kappa Univ MD 1975; inductee Maryland Senior Citizens Hall of Fame, 1997. **Military Serv:** USAF 1942-46.

GARBEY, BARBARO
Professional baseball player (retired). **Personal:** Born Dec 4, 1957, Santiago, Cuba. **Career:** Detroit Tigers, outfielder/infielder, 1984-85; Texas Rangers, outfielder/infielder, 1988. **Honors/Awds:** Tiger Rookie-of-the-Year, Detroit Sportsbroadcasters Assn, 1984.

GARCIA, KWAME N.
Educational administrator. **Personal:** Born Apr 4, 1946, St Croix, Virgin Islands of the United States; married Grete James; children: Kenny, Sharifa, Khalfani, Gustavo, Luanda, Kwame Jr. **Educ:** Coll of the Virgin Islands, AA 1967; NY Univ, BS 1969; Univ of MA, MBA 1973. **Career:** VI Bd of Ed, elected mem 1978-; Univ of the Virgin Islands, dir coop ext serv 1979-. **Orgs:** Mem Natl School Bd Assoc 1978-; mem bd of trustees VI Public TV Syst 1982-84, Coll of the Virgin Islands 1982-84. **Honors/Awds:** "Learning About the VI Tax System" Coop Ext Serv Coll of the VI. **Home Addr:** PO Box 1307, Kingshill, St Croix, Virgin Islands of the United States 00851. **Business Addr:** Dir Coop Ext Serv, University of the Virgin Islands, RR02, PO Box 10000, Kingshill, St Croix, Virgin Islands of the United States 00850.

GARDENER, DARYL
Professional football player. **Personal:** Born Feb 25, 1973, Baltimore, MD; married Tarnesia, Dec 2, 1995; children: Da'vante. **Educ:** Baylor University. **Career:** Miami Dolphins, defensive tackle, 1996-. **Special Achievements:** NFL Draft, First round pick, #20, 1996. **Business Addr:** Professional Football Player, Miami Dolphins, 2269 NW 199th St, Miami, FL 33056, (305)620-5000.

GARDINER, GEORGE L.
Educational administrator. **Personal:** Born May 3, 1933, Cambridge, MA; married Reida B Dykes; children: Jesse B, Veronica, Lynne, George DeWitt. **Educ:** Fisk Univ Nashville, AB 1963; Univ of Chicago, MA 1967, CAS 1969. **Career:** Oakland Univ, Rochester MI, prof, dean of library science 1972-; Univ of MI School of Library Science, Ann Arbor MI, visiting prof 1975; Central State Univ, Wilberforce OH, dir of library 1970-72; IL State Univ, Normal IL, refrence librarian 1967-70; Am Lib Assn Chicago, asst to exec sec lib admin div 1967. **Orgs:** Mem Am Lib Assn 1967-; mem Am Soc for Infor Sci 1979-; mem Nat Lib Assn 1978-; elctd bd mem Normal Pub Lib Normal IL 1968-70; Afro-Am HistComm IL of C of Supt of Pub Instr 1969-70; Bd Black Coll Program Pontiac MI 1974-; chmn bd MI Lib Consortium 1978-79; chm N MI Council of StateLib Dir 1979-80. **Honors/Awds** Publ A Bibliography of the Pub Writings of Charles S Johnson 1960; 1st prize Nat Essay Contest Am Missionary Assn 1961; lavern noyes schol Univ co Chicago 1963-67; publ The Spirit of Fisk 1866-76, 1968, The Empirical Study of Ref, 1969, Bibliography Section in Role & Contributions of Am Negroes in History of US & IL 1970; Computer Asstd Indexing in Central State Univ Lib 1975. **Military Serv:** AUS corpl 1953-55. **Business Addr:** Oakland University University, Rochester, MI 48309.

GARDNER, AVA MARIA
Convention sales manager. **Personal:** Born Jun 1, 1962, Fort Sill, OK; daughter of John M. Gardner and Essie W. Gardner. **Educ:** Cameron University, Lawton, OK, BS, 1985. **Career:** Oklahoma City Conv & Visitors Bureau, conv sales manager, 1987-93; Denver Metro Conv & Visitors Bureau, conv sales manager, 1993-. **Orgs:** National Coalition of Black Meeting Planners, 1988-, membership comm, 1992-94, conf planning comm, 1996-. **Business Addr:** Convention Sales Manager, Denver Convention & Visitors Bureau, 1555 California St, Ste 300, Denver, CO 80202.

GARDNER, BETTYE J.
Educator. **Personal:** Born in Vicksburg, MS; daughter of Janie Foote Gardner and Glover C Gardner. **Educ:** Howard Univ, BA 1962, MA 1964; George Washington Univ, PhD 1974. **Career:** Howard Univ, instructor 1964-69; Social Sys Intervention Inc, sr rsch assoc 1969; Washington DC Bd of Educ, consultant 1969; Black History Calvert Ct MD, consultant; Washington Technical Inst, asst prof 1969-71; Coppin State Coll, dean of arts & sciences 1981-87, prof of history 1982-, chairperson dept of history 1988-90. **Orgs:** Mem NAACP, Org of Amer Historians, Assoc of Black Women Historians, Assoc for the Study of Afro-Amer Life & History; mem Natl Educ Assn; NCNW, 1980; editorial bd Journal of Negro History; exec counc Asso for the Study of Afro-Amer Life & Hist; vp, Association for Afro-American Life and History, 1993-95, natl pres, 1995-97; publ numerous articles, Educ Licensure Commission, Washington DC, chairperson; Bethune House Federal Commission. **Honors/Awds:** Moton Fellowship, Moton Institute, 1978-79; Danforth Assn, Danforth Foundation, 1980-86; Fellowship, Smithsonian, summer 1988. **Business Addr:** Professor History, Coppin St College, 2500 W North Ave, Baltimore, MD 21216.

GARDNER, CEDRIC BOYER
Attorney. **Personal:** Born Jul 22, 1946, San Antonio, TX; son of Willie Mae Gardner and Tommie L Gardner; married Sylvia Irene Breckenridge, May 7, 1972; children: Zayani Aisha, Bilal Amin, Cedric Ahmed, Saìda Ujima. **Educ:** CA State Univ Los Angeles, BA 1975; Univ of KS, JD 1983. **Career:** Urban League of Wichita, assoc dir 1977-80; Shawnee County Dist Attorney, asst dist attorney 1983-84; Univ of KS, training Mgr 1984-85; KS Dept of Health & Environ, attorney 1985-. **Orgs:** Mem Douglas County NAACP 1978-81, Urban League of Wichita 1980-87; mem Douglas Co Amateur Radio Club 1984-87; mem, Douglas County Assn of Retarded Citizens. **Honors/Awds:** Outstanding Service Wichita NAACP both 1980. **Military Serv:** USAF airman 1st class 4 yrs; Outstanding Airman of the Year 1966. **Home Addr:** 1511 W 26th St, Lawrence, KS 66046. **Business Addr:** Special Asst Attorney General, Kansas Dept of Health, 900 Jackson, Topeka, KS 66612.

GARDNER, EDWARD G.
Business executive. **Personal:** Born Feb 15, 1925, Chicago, IL; married Betty Ann; children: Gary, Guy, Tracy, Terri. **Educ:** Chicago Teachers College, BA; Univ of Chicago, Masters. **Career:** E G Gardner Beauty Products Co, owner; Chicago School System, elem school asst prin 1945-64; Soft Sheen Products, president. **Honors/Awds:** Soft Sheen Prods listed in Black Enterprise Mag in top 10 of 100 Top Black Businesses in the US. **Military Serv:** S/sgt. **Business Addr:** President, Soft Sheen Products Inc, 1000 E 87th St, Chicago, IL 60619.

GARDNER, FRANK W.
Educational administrator. **Personal:** Born Jun 12, 1923, Chicago; married Elaine St Avide; children: Craig M, Glenn P, Susan M. **Educ:** Chicago Tchrs Coll, BA 1948; DePaul U, MEd 1953; Univ of Chicago, Grad Student 1958; Northwestern U, PhD 1975. **Career:** Chicago Public Schools, teacher 1948-54; Betsy Ross Elementary School Chicago, asst prin 1955-65; Ray Elementary School Chicago, prin 1965-68; Bd Of Examiners, Chicago Public Schools, asst sec 1968; Loyola Univ of Chicago, lecturer; Chicago Public Schools, district supt, 1974-83. **Orgs:** Dir wrtng Title III Proposal for Establ of Indep Lrng Cntr for Ray Elem Sch; mem Sch Study Comm of the Archdiocese of Chicago 1970-71; mem Chicago Urban League; mem Phi Delta Kappa; mem Am Assn Sch Personnel Adminstrn; chmn St Clotilde Elem Sch Bd 1966-69; bd dir Faulkner Sch Chicago 1971-72; Bd of Ed, City of Chicago, president, 1984-89. **Honors/Awds:** Harold Washington, Leadership Award; Boys and Girls Club of Chicago; De Paul University, Outstanding Alumnus. **Military Serv:** WWII s/Sgt 1943-46. **Home Addr:** 8426 S Indiana Ave, Chicago, IL 60619.

GARDNER, HENRY L.
City official. **Personal:** Born Oct 29, 1944, Jacksonville, FL; son of Annie B Gardner. **Educ:** University of Illinois, Urbana-Champaign, IL, AB, 1967; Southern Illinois University, Carbondale, IL, MA, 1969. **Career:** City of Oakland, Oakland, CA, asst personnel analyst, 1971-73, administrative asst, 1973-76, asst to city mgr, 1976-78, asst city mgr, 1978-81, city mgr, 1981-. **Orgs:** Member, American Society for Public Administration; member, International City Management Assn; member, Alameda City and County Management Assn; member, National Forum for Black Public Administrators. **Honors/Awds:** Investment in Leadership, Coro Foundation, 1985; Most Valuable Public Official, City and State Magazine, 1990. **Business Addr:** City Manager, City of Oakland, Office of the City Manager, One City Hall Plaza, Oakland, CA 94612.

GARDNER, JACKIE RANDOLPH
Physician. **Personal:** Born Apr 7, 1930, Tampa, FL; son of Georgette Mattox Gardner and Isaac Gardner; children: Adrian Randolph, Pia JoAnna. **Educ:** Fisk Univ, BA (departmental hon) 1948; Univ of MI, Grad Sch Public Health 1949-50; Meharry Med Coll, MD 1955. **Career:** Mercy Hosp Buffalo, internship 1955-56; Sydenham Hosp NY, residency 1958; Kingsbrook Med Ctr Brooklyn, residency 1958-59; Private Practice, physician gen med & fam practice Brooklyn 1961-. **Orgs:** Chmn The Source (civic group) Brooklyn NY 1980; mem Alpha Phi Alpha Frat. **Military Serv:** USN lt (sr gr) 1956-58. **Business Addr:** 678 St Marks Ave, Brooklyn, NY 11216.

GARDNER, LAMAURICE HOLBROOK
Educator, psychologist, psychoanalyst. **Personal:** Born Feb 13, 1936, Morehead, MS; son of Ida Holbrook Gardner Marsh and William Gardner; married Dolores Mallare; children: LaMaurice, Jr, Erika, Victorio, Crystal. **Educ:** Univ Detroit, PhB 1958; Univ Detroit, MA 1960; Loyola U, PhD 1964; Detroit Psychoanalytic Inst, post doctoral educ 1966-70. **Career:** Sinai Hosp Detroit, chief & psychologist & admin asst 1964-68; Childrens Center Wayne Co, dir 1968-74; Wayne State U, part time faculty 1964-74; Met Hosp, consult 1964-66; VA Hosp Allen Pk, consult 1973-; Clinical Psychology, pvt practice 1966-; Wayne State Univ, Detroit, MI, prof/dir, comm psychology; Psychoanalysis & Psychotherapy, pvt practice 1966-; Detroit Osteopathic Hospital, consultant, 1987-. **Orgs:** Mem v chmn Detroit-wayne Co Comm Mental Health Serv Bd 1966-68; Com Children & Youth 1972; mem bd dir Wayne Co Chap MI Soc Mental Health 1966-68;Kappa Alpha Psi; MI Assn Emotionally Disturbed Children, bd dir 1970; TechAdv Research Com State of MI Dept of Mental Health 1979; council agency dirs United Comm Serv Detroit 1971-74; mem bd dir Detroit Urban League 1972; mem bd of dir Mid Western US Div Am Bd of Professional Psychology 1976-86; Am Psychol Assn; Am Acad Psychoanalysis MI Psychol Assn; Detroit Psychoanalytic Soc; Com Ethnocentricity among Psychiatrists Am Psychiat Assn; Council Nat Register of Health Serv Providers in Psychology. **Honors/Awds:** Published books & articles scientific journals; Psi Chi Honor Soc Psychology; diplomate Am Bd Prof Psychology; Fellow, Academy of Clinical Psychology. **Business Addr:** Private Practice, 22250 Providence Dr., Southfield, MI 48075.

GARDNER, LOMAN RONALD
Educator. **Personal:** Born Feb 9, 1938, Detroit, MI; son of Lillian Gardner Barnett and Loman Gardner Sr (deceased); married Aug 6, 1958 (divorced); children (previous marriage): Hansel, Loman III, Toi, Troy; married Kay, Jun 25, 1995. **Educ:** Eastern Michigan University, BFAE, 1964; Michigan State University, MA, 1970, MS, 1976, PhD, 1985; State of Michigan, administrative certificate, endorsed, superintendent, central office and secondary administrative. **Career:** Michigan School System, instructor/counselor, Boys Republic Training School; Detroit Public Schools, instructor, Socially Maladjusted/Special Education; Battle Creek Public Schools, school administrator; Federation Bureau of Investigation, special agent; Detroit Police Department, deputy/acting chief investigator; Tots and Toys Preschools, owner/director; Detroit Public Schools, instructor, Learning Disabled/Special Education, currently. **Orgs:** Kappa Alpha Psi, 1960-; NAACP, lifetime member, 1992;

Mason, Prince Hall, 1972-; Michigan Association of Learning Disabilities Educators, 1990-. **Special Achievements:** Loman Investigations, licensed private investigation agency. **Military Serv:** US Navy, sn, 1956-60. **Home Addr:** 2500 Edison Ave, Detroit, MI 48206, (313)869-2180.

GARDNER, SAMUEL C.
Lawyer, former judge. **Personal:** Born Nov 27, 1931, Detroit, MI; divorced. **Educ:** Wayne St U, BS 1958; Wayne State U, M Educ in guidance & counseling 1960; Wayne State Univ Sch of Law, JD 1965. **Career:** Bell & Gardner, attorney, currently; Frank Murphy Hall of Justice, chief judge of the recorder's ct, beginning 1977, judge of the recorder's ct 1973-77; Bell & Gardner, atty 1972-73; Free Legal Aid Clinic Wayne State U, supervising atty 1969-72; Gragg & Gardner PC, atty 1969-72; NAACP, legal counsel 1968; Wayne State Univ Law Sch legal research instr 1966-68; Dingell Hylton & Zemmol, atty 1966-69; Lawyers Comm for Civil Rights Under Law, staff atty 1966; Hertzberg Jacob & Weingarten, atty 1965-66; Detroit Bd of Educ Craft Elem Sch, sci tchr 1958-65. **Orgs:** Mem Detroit Bar Assn; mem MI State Bar; mem Nat Bar Assn; treas bd mem Nat Bar Found; past pres Wolverine Bar Assn 1970-71; mem Am Arbitration Bd; chmn MI State Bar Grievance Bd, bd mem Legal Aid & Defender; mem Am Civil Liberties Union; tech & com Ct Procedures State of MI; mem spl commn Review Article VI the Jud Article of the Const of MI, Detroit Bd of Educ 1970; referee Civil Rights Comm; mem Wayne Co Jail Adv Comm Sr Class Rep Student Bd of Govs Wayne State Univ Sch of Law; Staff Writer, The Wayne Adv Law Sch Jour; Sr Ed, Wayne State Univ Law Review. **Honors/Awds:** Bronze Award for Achievement Wayne State Univ Law Sch 1965; Article Pub "Constl Law Right of Non-mem of a Race to Raise Systematic Exclusion that Race in Jury Selection" Wayne State Law Review Vol II 1965. **Business Addr:** Attorney, Bell & Gardner, 561 E Jefferson, Detroit, MI 48226.

GARDNER, WALTER
Government official. **Career:** Civil Rights activist; Newton County, MS, board of supervisors, 1991-. **Special Achievements:** First African-American member of Newton County, MS board of supervisors since Reconstruction. **Business Phone:** (601)683-2011.

GARIBALDI, ANTOINE MICHAEL
Educational administrator. **Personal:** Born Sep 26, 1950, New Orleans, LA; son of Marie Brule' Garibaldi and Augustin Garibaldi. **Educ:** Howard Univ, BA (magna cum laude) 1973; Univ of Minnesota, PhD 1976. **Career:** Holy Comforter-St Cyprian DC, elem teacher 1972-73; Univ of Minnesota Coll of Educ, rsch asst 1973-75; St Paul Urban League St Acad, principal 1975-77; Natl Inst of Educ, rsch admin 1977-82; Xavier Univ of Louisiana, Department of Education, chmn, prof of educ, 1982-89, dean, 1989-91, College of Arts and Sciences, vice pres for academic affairs, 1991-96; Howard Univ, provost and chief academic officer, 1996-. **Orgs:** Amer Psychological Assn (Fellow); Amer Educ Rsch Assn; Assn of Black Psychologists; Phi Delta Kappa; Alpha Phi Alpha; Phi Kappa Phi; pres Univ of Minnesota Black Studies Psychological Assn 1974-75; US Army Sci Bd 1979-83; lecturer Howard Univ School of Educ 1981; assoc editor Amer Educ Rsch Journal 1982-84; consultant US Dept of Educ 1983-85; New Orleans Library Bd 1984-93, chairman, 1991-93; Journal of Negro Education, board of directors; co-chmn, Mayor's Foundation for Educ, 1987-90; co-chmn, educ comm, Urban League of Greater New Orleans, 1984-90; American Library Association; Alpha Kappa Mu, Psi Chi; Center for Education of African-American Males, board of directors, 1991-92; Metropolitan Area Committee, board of directors, 1992-96, education fund board, 1991-96. **Honors/Awds:** Author, works include: The Decline of Teacher Production in Louisiana 1976-83; Attitudes Toward the Profession, 1986; Southern Education Foundation monograph, 1986; Educating Black Male Youth: A Moral and Civic Imperative, 1988; editor: Black Colleges and Universities: Challenges for the Future, 1984; "Teacher Recruitment and Retention: With a Special Focus on Minority Teachers", National Education Association, 1989; co-editor: The Education of African-Americans; more than 70 chapters and articles in professional journals and books. **Business Addr:** Office of the Provost, 2400 Sixth Street NW, Room 405, Washington, DC 20059, (202)806-2550.

GARLAND, HAZEL BARBARA
Columnist-consultant. **Personal:** Born Jan 28, 1913, Burnette, IN; married Percy A. **Educ:** Univ of Pittsburgh, 1952-53. **Career:** Retired, 1977; New Pittsburgh Courier, editor in chief 1974-77, city editor 1972-74; Pittsburgh Courier, women's editor 1965-72, entrtnmnt-tv- radio editor 1955-65, feature editor 1954-55, asso magazine editor 1952-54, asst woman's editor 1947-52, gen assgnmnt reporter 1946-47, part-time reporter 1944-46, stringer1943-44. **Orgs:** Pres gateway chap Am Women in Radio-TV 1968-70; pres Pittsburgh Chap Girl Friends Inc 1969-71; vice pres Pittsburgh Comm Found 1975-77. **Honors/Awds:** Nat hon mem Iota Phi-Lambda Sor Wash DC 1969; natl sojourner truth award Bus & Professional Women 1974; editor of the yr award Nat Newspaper Pub Assn 1974; natl headliner award Women in Comm Inc Tulsa OK 1975. **Business Addr:** 315 E Carson St, Pittsburgh, PA 15219.

GARLAND, JOHN WILLIAM
Educational administrator. **Personal:** Born Oct 24, 1944, Harlem, NY; son of John W Garland & Amy Whaley Garland; married Carolyn Farrow, Jan 1975; children: Amy, Jabari. **Educ:** Central State University, BA, 1971; Ohio State University College of Law, JD, 1974. **Career:** Hayes & White, PC, sr attorney, 1983-84; Law Office of John W Garland, attorney, 1984-88; University of the District of Columbia, general counsel, 1988-91; University of Virginia, assoc gen counsel, 1991-93, exec asst to the pres, 1993-96, assoc vp for intellectual property, 1996-97; Central State University, pres, 1997-. **Orgs:** National Association of College & University Attorneys; National Conference of Black Lawyers, bd of dirs; Association of University Technology Managers; Washington Lawyers Committee for Civil Rights Under Law, bd of dirs; National Veterans Legal Svcs Proj, bd of dirs; Journal of College & University Law, editorial bd; US Supreme Ct; Supreme Ct of NC: Supreme Ct of Virginia; Court of Appeals, District of Columbia; US Ct of Military Appeals; LeDroit Park Civic Association, pres, 1974-76. **Honors/Awds:** District of Columbia, Federation of Civic Association, Father of the Year, 1978; TransAfrica Award, 1987. **Special Achievements:** Legal Svcs of the Coastal Plains, founding dir. **Military Serv:** US Marine Corps, cpl E-4, 1967-92; Purple Heart, Combat Infantry Badge, Vietnam Svc Medal, Good Conduct Medal. **Business Addr:** President, Central State University, 1400 Brush Row Rd, Lionel H Newsom Administration Bldg, Wilberforce, OH 45384, (937)376-6332.

GARLAND, PERCY A. See Obituaries section.

GARLAND, PHYLLIS T. (PHYL)
Writer, music critic, educator. **Personal:** Born Oct 27, 1935, McKeesport, PA; daughter of Hazel Hill Garland (deceased) and Percy Garland. **Educ:** Northwestern Univ, BS Journalism. **Career:** Pittsburgh Courier, journalist, writer, feature ed 1958-65; Ebony Mag, asst, assoc contrib ed 1965-77; NY, editor 1969-71; State Univ of NY Coll at New Paltz, asst prof, acting chmn dept of black studies 1971-73; Columbia Univ Grad School of Journalism, asst prof 1973-79, assoc prof 1979-89, professor 1989-; Natl Arts Journalism Prog at Columbia, mentor, 1994-. **Orgs:** Mem Delta Sigma Theta; jazz adv panel Natl Endowment for the Arts, 1976-79; adv bd Columbia Jrnl Review; contrib ed Stereo Review Mag 1977-; board of trustees, Rhythm and Blues Foundation, 1989-; board of directors, Jazzmobile, The Modern School, 1991-; member, Girl Friends Inc, 1970-. **Honors/Awds:** Golden Quill Awd Outstanding Feature Writer 1962; Headliner Awd Outstanding Women in Country in Field of Communications Theta Sigma Phi 1971; Awd for Public Service Reporting, NY Chap of Publ Rel Soc of Amer 1974; Distinguished Scholar of the United Negro Coll Fund, 1985-86; Ralph Metcalfe Prof, Marquette Univ, 1987; author "The Sound of Soul, The Story of Black Music"; contrib of art to books & mags; Writer for documentary film, Adam Clayton Powell, nominated for and Academy Award as best documentary feature, 1990; winner of Erick Barnouw Award from the Organization of American Historians; Award for Excellence In Connumications, Pittsburghers of Washington DC, 1990; Distinguished Visiting Scholar in African-American History, Point Park Coll, 1990-93; Distinguished Achievement Award, Fine Arts Ctr, Univ of Massachusetts, Amherst, 1992. **Business Addr:** Professor, Columbia Univ, Grad School of Journalism, New York, NY 10027, (212)854-3854.

GARNER, CHARLES
Musician, educator. **Personal:** Born Jul 27, 1931, Toledo, OH; married Judith Marie Bonner; children: Kevin, Darchelle. **Educ:** Cleveland Inst of Mus, BMus 1953; Boston U, AM 1957; Yale U, adv stud; Columbia University, New York, NY, EdD, 1991. **Career:** Southern Connecticut State Univ, composer, arranger, prof of music; Hartt Sch of Music, Univ of Hartford, instr 1961-65; East & Midwest, numerous piano & ensemble recitals. **Orgs:** Am Assn of University Prof, mem; Phi Delta Kappa, mem; Kappa Gamma Psi; Kappa Alpha Psi; Am Soc of Composers Authors & Pub. **Honors/Awds:** Recipient Am Fedn of Mus; Mu Phi Epsilon Scholarship 1948; Friends of Mus Award 1949; 1st place OH Mus Tchr Auditions; Ranney Scholarship of Cleveland 1949-52; Charles H Ditson Award of Yale Univ 1968; Frances Osbourn Kellogg prize in counterpoint Yale Univ 1969. **Military Serv:** AUS radio operator 1953-55. **Home Addr:** 190 Corbin Rd, Hamden, CT 06517.

GARNER, CHARLIE
Professional football player. **Personal:** Born Feb 13, 1972, Falls Church, VA. **Educ:** Univ of Tennessee, attended. **Career:** Philadelphia Eagles, running back, 1994-. **Business Addr:** Professional Football Player, Philadelphia Eagles, 3501 S Broad St, Philadelphia, PA 19148, (215)463-2500.

GARNER, CHRIS
Professional basketball player. **Personal:** Born Feb 23, 1975. **Educ:** Memphis. **Career:** Toronto Raptors, guard, 1997-. **Business Addr:** Professional Basketball Player, Toronto Raptors, 150 York St, Ste 110, Toronto, ON, Canada M5H 3S5, (416)214-2255.

GARNER, EDWARD, JR.
Judge. **Personal:** Born Dec 4, 1942, Skippers, VA; married Betty J; children: Erica P, Edward P, Elizabeth P. **Educ:** NC A&T State Univ, BS (Cum Laude) 1967; Squadron Office School USAF 1972; Univ of NC Law School Chapel Hill, JD 1975; Air Command & Staff Coll, 1983; Air War College, 1994. **Career:** Akzo Amer Inc, corp attny 1976-85; NC Dept of Crime Control & Public Safety, asst sec, 1985-89; deputy commissioner, North Carolina Industrial Commission, 1989. **Orgs:** Mem NC Bar, Amer Bar Assn, Air Force Assn, NC Assn of Black Laywers, Aircraft Owners & Pilots Assn, Negro Airmen Intl Inc, Assn of Trial Lawyers of Amer, NC Acad of Trial Lawyers, US Air Force Reserve/NC Air Natl Guard; former chmn of bd of dir Asheville-Buncombe Comm Relations Counc; mem of bd YMI Cultural Ctr Inc; mem Asheville City Personnel Commiss; Govs adv commiss Military Affairs. **Military Serv:** USAF pilot 1968-73; NC Air Natl Guard, 1979-; Disting Flying Cross; Flew C-123 Transport, B-52 Bomber & C-130 Transport; 2 yrs combat duty in Southeast Asia. **Business Addr:** Deputy Commissioner, North Carolina Industrial Commission, Dobbs Bldg, 430 N Salisbury St, Raleigh, NC 27611.

GARNER, GRAYCE SCOTT
Educator. **Personal:** Born Apr 27, 1922, Cambridge, MA; son of Ruby Blackman Garner and Athelohnsend Garner; married Rawle W Garner, Jun 24, 1961. **Educ:** Cambridge Hosp, RN 1944; Simmons Coll, attended 1944-45; Boston Univ, BS Nursing 1954, MS 1956; Columbia Univ, EdD 1963; Boston Univ, post doctoral 1970; Univ RI, post doctoral 1982-83. **Career:** Boston Univ, prof, nursing, faculty mem, 1959-77; Univ of RI, prof of nursing, 1977-85; Univ of MA, prof of nursing & coordinator med health; Prof, Univ of MA, Coll of Nursing, 1985-. **Orgs:** Consult Boston & Worcester St Hosp, Bedford & Brocton VA Hosp, Boston City Hosp; mem Amer Nurses Assn 1977; past bd of dir MA Nurses Assn; mem MA Assn Mental Health; mem Alpha Kappa Alpha Sor. **Honors/Awds:** Merit Awd Mental Health Careers Prog 1974; Navy Merit Awd 1975; Merit Awd Consumer Educ Prog Barbados WI 1975; 1st Black Faculty mem; 1st Black Full Prof; 1st Black Coord of Prog Univ of RI Coll of Nursing; NIMH Rsch Awd; Prog Dir of a 5 yr NIMH grant for grad students in Mental Health Nursing; Several State URI Awds for Devel Grad Program Nursing. **Military Serv:** USAF nurse corps 1st lt 1946-51. **Business Addr:** Prof of Nursing, Univ of Massachusetts, Harbor Campus, Boston, MA 02125.

GARNER, JOHN W.
Academic relations manager. **Personal:** Born Dec 29, 1924, Franklin, TN; married Leslie Olga Abernathy; children: Reginald J, Paul L. **Educ:** Fisk U, BA Chem 1950, MS 1952; IL Inst of Tech MS Physical Chem 1955. **Career:** Percy L Julian Labs, chemist 1952-53; IL Inst of Tech Res Inst, res chemist 1954-66; 3m Co Dental Prod Lab, sr res chemist 1966-70; 3m Co Med Prods Div, sr clinical res coord 1974-75; 3m Health Care Grp, academic reltns mgr 1976-85; Riker Labs Int'l/ 3M Co, mgr licensing adm1985-. **Orgs:** Bd of trustees Fisk Univ 1977-; bd of dir Big Bros/Sis of Greater St Paul 1975-87; ind adv bd Biomed Eng Dept Tulane Univ 1979-; human rel adv comm 3m Co 1978-86; life Mem Alpha Phi Alpha Frat Inc 1976-; mem Omicron Boule Sigma Pi Phi Frat Inc 1979-; MN Metro Golf League 1980; mem Am Chem Soc AAMI Natl Tech Asso 1985; mem Blk Chem Eng Urban League, NAACP, vice pres Sterling Club 1985; bd of dir City Walk Condo Assoc 1985-87; mem licensing exec soc/ USA-Canada. **Honors/Awds:** Distiguished Black Clg Alumnus Awd Fisk Univ (NAFEO) 1983; Christian Father of Yr Awd Trinity United Ch Chicago IL 1966; Natl Life Mbrshp Prog Awd Alpha Phi Alpha Frat Inc 1978; "Think Higher" Awd 3m Health Care Grp 1972. **Military Serv:** AUS staff sgt (field commissioned) 1943-46; 4 Bronze Battle Stars, 2 Invasion Arrow Heads, Europe, Purple Heart 1943-46. **Home Addr:** 66 East 9th St #2105, St Paul, MN 55101. **Business Addr:** Licensing Administration, 3M Health Care Group, 3M Center 225-15-07, St Paul, MN 55144.

GARNER, JUNE BROWN
Columnist (retired). **Personal:** Born Jul 19, 1923, Detroit, MI; daughter of Vela Malone and Simpson Malone; married Warren C Garner; children: Sylvia Mustonen. **Educ:** Wayne State Univ, 2 yrs. **Career:** Detroit News, retired columnist; Michigan Chronicle, classified adv mgr, beginning 1974, retired; Warren Garner Realty. **Orgs:** Founder Let's Read Summer School, A Free Reading Prog for Children 1980; Computer Programming; North Tazewell Elem School, VA, volunteer teacher, currently. **Honors/Awds:** Best columnist Natl Assn of Newspaper Publishers, 1967, 1968; Best Columnist Detroit Press Club 1972, 1973. **Home Addr:** 107 Vernon Ave, Tazewell, VA 24651.

GARNER, LA FORREST DEAN
Educational administrator. **Personal:** Born Aug 20, 1933, Muskogee, OK; son of Fannie M Thompson Garner and Sanford G Garner; married Alfreida Thomas; children: Deana Y, Thomas L, Sanford E. **Educ:** IN Univ School of Dentistry, DDS 1957, MSD 1959, Certificate, Orthodontics, 1961. **Career:** IN Univ School of Dentistry, assoc prof 1967-70; VA Hosp Dental Div, consultant 1979-; James Whitcomb Riley Hospital, orthodontic coordinator, 1979-; IN Univ School of Dentistry, prof & chmn 1970-, associate dean, minority student services, 1987-; Gradu-

ate & Post Graduate Dental Education IUSD, dir, 1994-. **Orgs:** Bd of dir, Visiting Nurses Assn, Indianapolis, 1973-77, Boys Clubs, 1976-; Chmn, Council on Rsch, Amer Assn of Orthodontists, 1976-77; mem, Boule, 1978-; bd of dir, Park Tudor School, Indianapolis IN 1980-; Life Mem, NAACP, 1980-; Chmn, United Way Ancillary Serv 1984-85; pres Amer Assn for Dental Rsch, 1984-85; bd of dir, Indianapolis Zoo, 1987-, bd of dir, Fall Creek Parkway YMCA, 1989. **Honors/Awds:** Natl pres Omicron Kappa Upsilon Natl Dental Scholastic 1974-75; local pres Omicron Kappa Upsilon Local Chapter, 1974-75; fellow of Amer Coll of Dentist 1974; bd of dir Amer Cleft Palate Educ Found 1975-79; mem Sigma Xi 1976. **Business Addr:** Assoc Dean, Indiana Univ, 1121 W Michigan St, Indianapolis, IN 46202.

GARNER, LON L.
Mortician, politician. **Personal:** Born Jul 17, 1927, San Augustine Co, TX; married Vonzella Jones; children: David, Conchita, Alex. **Educ:** Three Yrs Coll. **Career:** Percy Garner & Son, mortician; San Augustine, city alderman serving 3rd 2 yrs term 1969-; Alberta King Day Care Center, dir 1974; San Augustine Fed Credit Union, dir 1972-. **Orgs:** Patron McPhearson Lodge Order Eastern Star 150 San Augustine 1967; mem NFDA 1953; mem Masonic Lodge 1948-; Order Knight Pythian 1947; srvd chmn bd mem Am Red Cross Dr & Chap 1964-; 1st black mem San Augustine C of C; chmn deacon bd True Vine Bapt Ch 1969. **Honors/Awds:** 1st black elected official & 1st elected official San Augustine Co; cert award C of C 1972; outstndng ambul serv only black firm to ever offer serv State TX 1969; 1st credit union soley controlled by black San Augustine Fed Credit Union. **Business Addr:** Manager, Percy Garner & Son Mortuary, 304 Ironosa Rd, PO Box 491, San Augustine, TX 75972.

GARNER, MARY E.
Psychologist. **Personal:** Born in Paterson, NJ; children: Floyd, Jr, Steven. **Educ:** William Paterson Coll, BA Psych 1973; Fairleigh Dickinson Univ, MA Clinical Psych 1976; CUNY, PhD 1983. **Career:** Passaic City Community, prof psych 1983; Fairleigh Dickinson Univ, prof psych summers 1982-84; William Paterson Coll, prof psych 1982-; Paterson Dept Human Resources, spec asst to dir 1982-83, dir 1983-. **Orgs:** Mem & past pres preakness Hospital Bd of Mgrs 1982-84; chairwoman Riverview Towers Tenants Assoc 1973-; mem Coalition for Public Accountability 1982-; mem Zonta Intl (Paterson Area Club) 1983-; mem Black Business & Professional Assoc 1983-; mem NJ Amer Psychological Assoc. **Honors/Awds:** Community serv Social & Economic Change for All Inc 1983, Modern Beautician's Assoc 1983, Black History Month Committee 1984 & 1985; Pres Awd Preakness Hosp Bd Mgrs 1984. **Home Addr:** 85 Presidential Blvd 15C, Paterson, NJ 07522. **Business Addr:** Dir, Paterson Dept Human Resources, City Hall, 155 Market St 2nd Floor, Paterson, NJ 07505.

GARNER, MELVIN C.
Attorney. **Personal:** Born Feb 9, 1941, Philadelphia, PA; son of Freida White Garner and George L Garner; married R Patricia Grant. **Educ:** Drexel Univ, BS 1964; NY Univ, MS 1968; Brooklyn Law School, JD 1973. **Career:** IBM Poughkeepsie NY, jr engr 1964-66; CBS Labs Stamford CT, engr 1966-69; Sequential Inf Sys Dobbs Ferry NY, proj engr 1969-70; Bell Telephone Labs Holmdel NY, mem patent staff 1970-73; Brumbaugh Graves Donohue & Raymond, attny 1973-82; Darby & Darby, attny 1982-. **Orgs:** Mem ABA, NY Intellectual Property Law Assoc, Natl Patent Law Assoc, Eta Kappa Nu (Hon Elect Engrs Soc), Brooklyn Law Review. **Business Addr:** Attorney, Darby & Darby, 805 Third Ave, 27 Fl, New York, NY 10022.

GARNER, NATHAN WARREN
Business executive. **Personal:** Born Dec 25, 1944, Detroit, MI; married Indira S Licht Garner; children: Mark C, Erica D, Vincent C, Warren C. **Educ:** Wayne State Univ, BS 1966; Wayne State Univ Grad School of Ed, MS Ed 1971; Columbia Univ Grad School of Bus, MBA 1975; Stanford Grad Sch of Bus Fin Mgt Prog 1984. **Career:** Scholastic Inc, dir mktg 1969-78; Time Distrib Serv Inc, dir of mktg 1978-80; US Dept of Edn, spec asst to sec of educ 1980-81; Time-Life Films Inc, vice pres 1981-82; Preview Subs TV Inc, pres 1982-83; Manhattan Cable TV Inc, vice pres; Paragon Cable TV Manhattan, pres; USA Networks, vp, 1986-94; The Scholastic Channel, pres, 1995-. **Orgs:** Adv FL A&M Univ Entrepreneurial Devel Ctr 1983-85; mem Cable TV Admin & Mktg Soc 19083-85; mem Assoc for a Better NY 1984-85; bd of dirs East Mid Manhattan Chamber of Comm 1984-85; chmn Natl Assoc of Minorities in Cable 1987-88; steering comm 21st Century Fund; mem Friends of Alvin Ailey Dance Theatre, Alumni Assoc; pres Exec Exchange Program; adv group Columbia Univ Business School Telecommunications Policy Rsch and Information Studies Program. **Honors/Awds:** Black Achievers Harlem YMCA of Greater NY 1983; Andrew Heiskell Awd Time Inc 1986; Excellence in Communications East Manhattan Chamber of Commerce 1987. **Military Serv:** AUS spec 5th class 2 yrs. **Business Addr:** President, The Scholastic Channel, 555 Broadway, New York, NY 10012.

GARNER, THOMAS L.
Executive director. **Personal:** Born Sep 13, 1930, Cincinnati, OH; married Joann Calmeise; children: Stuart, Geoffrey. **Educ:** Cincinnati U, BSE 1952, Grad Work 1975; MI State, Grad Work; OH State, Grad Work. **Career:** Cincinnati Human Relations Comm, exec dir; Model Cities Bd, chair; Better Housing Leag, neighborhood coor 1966-68; Southwestern Reg Council on Alcoholism, assoc dir. **Orgs:** Mem Central Psy Clinic; YMCA; mem Cinti Firearms Comm; Nat Asso Human Rights Workers; Intl Asso Official Human Rights Agencies; Housing Opportunities Made Equal Bd; bd mem Cinti Public Dental Assn; bd mem Union Coll Univ Without Walls; bd mem Seven Hills Schs; founder Prog Unlmtd; mem Comm Ctr Bd. **Military Serv:** USAF reserve 1948-68. **Business Addr:** Associate Dir, SW Reg Cncl on Alcoholism, 830 Main St, Ste 1205, Cincinnati, OH 45202.

GARNER, VELVIA M.
State government official. **Personal:** Born Nov 21, 1941, Halsted, TX; daughter of Mary Elizabeth McKenzie Taylor and Edgar Taylor; married Edward J Garner, Mar 9, 1964; children: Angela, Tonia, Edward. **Educ:** Prairie View A & M Univ, BS, 1963; Univ of Colorado, Denver, CO, 1974; DPA, in progress. **Career:** Ben Taub General Hospital, Houston, TX, team leader, 1963-64; Madigan General Hospital, Tacoma, WA, team leader, 1964-65; St Joseph Hospital, Denver, CO, clinical supervisor, 1965-73; Univ of Colo, Denver, CO, asst professor, 1974-80; Div of Youth Services, dir of medical & psychological services, 1980-87; CO State Parole Bd, vice chair, 1987-92; Lookout Mountain Youth Services Center, asst dir, until 1992; Gilliam Detention Ctr, dir, 1992-. **Orgs:** Chair, Mental Health Corp of Denver, 1985-; mem, CO Community Corrections Advisory Council, 1987-; mem, Rocky Mnt Ctr for Health Promotion and Education, 1987-; mem, NURSES of CO Corp, 1984-, pres, 1988-90. **Honors/Awds:** Community Corrections Advisory Council, 1989; Advisory Council on Adolescent Health, 1982-87; CO Black Women for Political Action, 1986-; Teacher of the Year Award, Students Univ of CO, 1975-76; Community Service Award, CBWPA, 1983; Certificate for Recognition for Outstanding Community Service, Joint Effort Foundation, 1983. **Home Addr:** 13095 E Elk Pl, Denver, CO 80239. **Business Phone:** (303)291-8901.

GARNES, WILLIAM A.
Dentist. **Personal:** Born Jul 6, 1924, New York; married Yvonne Ponce; children: Barbara, Valerie, William. **Educ:** BA 1951; DDS 1955. **Career:** Priv Prac, dentist; New York City Dept of Health, dentist Present; Guggenheim Dental Clinic NY, supvr. **Orgs:** Mem Local Sch Bd #9 Bronx NY 1961-63; Am Dental Assn; NY State Dental Assn; First Dist Dental Soc NY. **Military Serv:** USN, AOM 3/C 1944-46; USAF capt 1955-57.

GARNETT, BERNARD E.
Reporter. **Personal:** Born Nov 18, 1940, Washington, DC; married; children: Cyprian, Malik. **Educ:** Newspaper Inst of Amer, New York, Cert 1966; Howard Univ, Washington DC. **Career:** The Wall St Journal, reporter; Race Relations Information Ctr Nashville, staffwriter audio feed dir 1969-72; Jet Magazine Washington Bureau, assoc editor 1967-69; Washington Afro-Amer, reporter 1965-67. **Orgs:** Past mem Black Perspective 1968; past mem regional coordinator Nat Assn of Black Media Workers 1970. **Business Addr:** 55 Marietta St NW, Ste 1515, Atlanta, GA 30303.

GARNETT, KEVIN
Professional basketball player. **Personal:** Born May 19, 1976, Mauldin, SC. **Educ:** Chicago Farragut High. **Career:** Minnesota Timberwolves, forward, 1995-. **Honors/Awds:** NBA All-Star, 1997, 1998. **Special Achievements:** NBA, First Round Draft Pick, #5 Pick, 1995; Entered NBA Draft directly after high school. **Business Addr:** Professional Basketball Player, Minnesota Timberwolves, 600 First Ave N, Minneapolis, MN 55403, (612)337-3865.

GARNETT, MARION WINSTON
Judge. **Personal:** Born Feb 18, 1919, Jeffersonville, IN; son of Mary Winston and Jerry Garnett; married Juanita Oretta Nogest; children: Marion F, Galda Irma McCants. **Educ:** Univ of Chicago, Bachelor Philosophy 1947, JD 1950; State of IL, admitted to bar 1950; US Court of Appeals 7th Circuit, admitted to bar 1967; US Supreme Court, admitted to bar 1965. **Career:** Wilson & Garnett, partner at law, 1950-52; Hunter, Wilson & Garnett, partner at law 1952-61; Rogers, Strayhorn, Harth, Wilson & Garnett, partner at law 1961-68; Rogers, Garnett, Harth, Vital & Stroger, partner at law, 1968-74; Circuit Court of Cook County, supervising judge. **Orgs:** Exec bd mem, Judicial Council of NBA 1980-; chmn elect, IL Judicial Council 1983-84; chrmn IL Judicial Council 1984-85; grand counselor, Omega Psi Phi Fraternity Inc, 1964-70, first vice grand basileus 1970-73, grand basileus 1973-76. **Honors/Awds:** Keys to city, Birmingham AL, El Paso & Houston TX, Las Cruces, NM, Miami, FL, New Orleans LA, Oklahoma City OK; honorary citizen, New Orleans; Ebony list of 100 most influential Blacks 1974-76; Certificate of Merit Los Angeles; MI House of Rep 339; Commodore Port of Jeffersonville IN. **Military Serv:** USN qmc/2 1942-45. **Business Addr:** Supervising Circuit Judge, Circuit Court of Cook County, 2301 Daley Center, Chicago, IL 60602.

GARNETT, RONALD LEON
Attorney. **Personal:** Born May 27, 1945, Louisville, KY. **Educ:** Central State U, BS 1967; Columbia U, JD 1970. **Career:** Private practice, attorney, currently; New York City, criminal court judge, 1984-86; GTE Corp, senior counsel, 1977-82; US Atty's Office, asst US atty 1974-77; Am Express Co, atty 1973-74; Winthrop Stimpson Putnam & Robts, Atty 1972-73; US Dist Judge Robert McRae, law clk 1971-72. **Orgs:** Am Bar Assn 1973-; NY State Bar Assn 1973; NY Co Lawyers Assn 1973-; Kappa Alpha Psi Inc 1964-. **Business Addr:** Attorney, 299 Broadway, Ste 1601, 26th Fl, New York, NY 10007, (212)587-5159.

GARNETTE, BOOKER THOMAS
Dentist (retired). **Personal:** Born Apr 28, 1930, Norfolk, VA; son of Willie Mae Davidson Wiley (deceased) and Booker S Garnette (deceased); divorced; children: Barbetta Breathwaite, Donna Yvonne Garnette Alexander, Carla Riddick. **Educ:** Howard Univ, BS 1951, DDS 1955. **Career:** Norfolk Gen Hos; St Vincent DePaul Hosp; Norfolk Comm, staff; VA Tidewater Dental Assoc, comm on dental health; VA Dental Assoc, alt house of del; private practice, dentist 1957-95. **Orgs:** Mem Tidewater Dental Assoc, Amer Dental Assoc, John McGriff Dental Soc, Old Dominion Dental Soc, Campbell Lodge #67 F&A Masons Prince Hall, Tux Club, Bachelor Benedict Club; past 3rd dist rep Omega Psi Phi; mem housing auth Omega Psi Phi, Natl Soc Action Comm, Natl Publ Rel Comm; life mem Omega Psi Phi; chmn Natl Recommendations Committee Omega Psi Phi; committee member, National Assault on Illiteracy, Omega Psi Phi, 1990-. **Honors/Awds:** Disting Omega Man Awd Pi Gamma Chap 1977; Omega Man of the Year Lambda Omega Chap Omega Psi Phi 1977; 3rd Dist Omega Man of the Year Omega Psi Phi 1977; 25 Yr Cert Omega Psi Phi; Forty Year Plaque, Omega Psi Phi, 1988; Founders Award, Third District, Omega Psi Phi, 1990; Founders Award, Lambda Omega Chapter, Omega Psi Phi, 1990; first black dentist, Norfolk Gen Hosp, St Vincent DePaul Hosp. **Military Serv:** USNR comrd 1955-75; 1st black naval officer from Norfolk VA; Naval Reserve medal USNR. **Business Addr:** Retired Dentist, PO Box 1823, Norfolk, VA 23501-1823.

GARRAWAY, MICHAEL OLIVER
Educator. **Personal:** Born Apr 29, 1934; son of Isla Marie Garraway and Robert A Garraway; married Annie Marie Watkins; children: Levi Alexander, Isla Pearl, Doris Lorraine. **Career:** McGill Univ Montreal, teaching asst 1959-60, rsch asst 1960-62; Univ of CA Berkeley, rsch asst 1962-66, post doc 1966-68; OH State Univ, asst prof 1968-71, assoc prof 1971-78, prof plant pathology 1978-. **Orgs:** Mem Can Phytopath Soc 1961, Amer Phytopath Soc 1963, Amer Inst for Biol Sci 1964; life mem AAAS 1967; mem OH Acad of Sci 1969; pres Gamma Sigma Delta OH Chap 1977-78; mem Mycological Soc of Amer 1980; consult mildew induced defacement of organic coatings Paint Rsch Inc; mem, Intl Society for Plant Pathology, 1968-. **Honors/Awds:** Author, Fungal Nutrition and Physiology, J Wiley & Sons Inc, 1984; Gamma Sigma Delta, Ohio Chapter, Award of Merit for Research 1989. **Business Addr:** Professor of Plant Pathology, Ohio State Univ, 201 Kothman Hall, 2021 Coffey Rd, Columbus, OH 43210.

GARRETT, ALINE M.
Educator. **Personal:** Born Aug 28, 1944, Martinville, LA. **Educ:** Univ SW LA, BA 1966; Oberlin OH, AM 1968; Univ MA, PhD 1971. **Career:** Univ of Southwestern LA Lafayette, assoc prof Psychology 1971; Univ of MA Amherst, grad res asst; Summer School Faculty USL, teacher 1970 & 1969; Psychometrist Lafayette Parish Schools, summer 1967; Project Head Start, Lafayette LA, teacher 1966. **Orgs:** Mem Am Psychol Assn; mem Nat Assn Black Psychol; mem Soc for Research in Child Devel; mem Psi Chi; mem SE Psychol Assn; mem LA Psychol Assn; mem bd dir Nat Council Black Child Devel; mem com on Acad Affairs & Standards 1972; mem Faculty Senate 1973-; mem Grad Faculty 1971-; mem Equal Employment Opportunity Com 1972; mem council on tchr educ coll educ USL 1974-; mem adv bd SGA-USL Child Care Cntr; mem adv bd Cath Soc Serv 1973; mem Health Adv Bd of Tri-Parish Progress Inc 1974; candidate St Martin Parish Sch Bd 1974; mem Agency Parent Council of SMILE Inc USL Rep 1974; mem byappointment Mayor Willis Soc & Economic Com St Martinville 1974; mem bd dir Lafayette Chap Epilepsy Found; mem Alpha Lambda Delta. **Honors/Awds:** Faculty advisor Nat Honor Soc; outstanding black citizen award So Consumers Educ Found Field of Educ 1975; research grant to do family res HEW Office Child Devel 1974-75; SEPA Visting Women Program 1974-. **Business Addr:** Psychology Dept PO Box 3131 US, Lafayette, LA 70501.

GARRETT, CAIN, JR.
Military officer (retired). **Personal:** Born May 11, 1942, Kilgore, TX; son of Everett V Woods Henry and Cain Garrett Jr (deceased). **Educ:** Univ CO Boulder, BSEE 1968; Naval Post Grad Sch Monterey, MSEE 1973; Naval Post Grad Sch Monterey, elec engr deg 1974. **Career:** US Navy, electrical engr 1974, communications officer 1968-70, operations dept head, 1970-72, lieut comdr flag secretary 1974-77, operational analyst and admi nistrative officer, Navy Operational Test Facility 1977-80. **Orgs:** Mem IEEE; Big Brothers Steering Com Boulder 1964-

68; tournament director, US Chess Federation 1989-. **Military Serv:** USN Lieutenant commander, 1959-80; Commendation Medal; Achievement Medal, Vietnam; 4 unit awards, Vietnam; Sea of Japan, S China Seas Operations; Spirit of Honor Award, Kiwinas 1968; Meritorious Serv Medal, 1980. **Home Addr:** Rte 1, Box 268P, Kilgore, TX 75662.

GARRETT, CHERYL ANN
City official, educator. **Personal:** Born Aug 31, 1946, Bethel Springs, TN; daughter of Jewel Perkins King Smith and Robert Eugene Smith; married Larry Eugene Garrett; children: Larry Eugene II, David Conrad, Cheryl Lynn. **Educ:** Grambling Univ, BS 1969. **Career:** Memphis Park Commiss, community ctr dir 1970-72; Central State Hosp, coord adj therapy 1972-74; Memphis City Schools, sub teacher 1974-; CJH Resources Inc, pres 1983-; Natl Black Republican Council, southern reg vp; Fixit Home Repair, administrative assist 1985; City of Memphis, Memphis, TN, community ctr dir, 1987-. **Orgs:** Commiss Shelby Cty Civil Serv Bd 1979-; v chmn TN Commiss on Status of Women 1980; state president TN Republican Assembly 1980-; treas South Shelby Republican Club 1982-. **Honors/Awds:** Merit Awd Shelby Cty Republican Party 1979; Key to City Chattanooga TN 1981; Family Awd Shelby Cty Republican Party 1983; State Coord Black Vote Div Regan/Bush 1984 Campaign 1984; Key to the City of Memphis, City Government, Mayor Hackett, 1990; TN Rec & Parks Assn, Ethnic Minority Society, Best Program Award, 1991. **Business Addr:** Director, Memphis Parks & Recreation Dept, PO Box 901024, Memphis, TN 38109.

GARRETT, DEAN
Professional basketball player. **Personal:** Born Nov 27, 1966. **Educ:** Indiana, bachelor's degree in criminal justice. **Career:** Minnesota Timberwolves, center, 1996-97; Denver Nuggets, 1997-. **Business Addr:** Professional Basketball Player, Denver Nuggets, 1635 Clay St, Denver, CO 80204-1743, (303)893-6700.

GARRETT, E. WYMAN
Obstetrician, gynecologist. **Personal:** Born May 25, 1933, Newark. **Educ:** Morgan State Coll Balto MD, BS 1955; Howard Univ Coll of Med, MD 1961. **Career:** Newark Mini-Surgi-Site, owner & med dir; Freemdmen's Hosp Wash DC, internship 1961-62; Harlem Hosp NYC, res OB/GYN 1yr; Newark City Hosp, res 2yr; OB/GYN NJ Coll of Med & Denistry, Asso prof. **Orgs:** Mem Newark Bd of Ed 1967-70; All-Am Basketball Morgan State; Beta Kappa Chi; Nat Scientific Soc; Alpha Kappa Mv; orgn dir Drive to Increase Black & Puerto Rican Enrllmnt in NJ Coll of Med & Denistry; Organization of Black Professional & Bus Women. **Honors/Awds:** Nat hon soc Morgan State; Man of Yr Award 1972. **Military Serv:** AUS 1st lt chemical corps 1955-57.

GARRETT, JAMES EDWARD, JR.
State official. **Personal:** Born Feb 26, 1959, Shelbyville, IN; son of Patricia Joan Garrett and James Edward Garrett Sr. **Educ:** Indiana State University, BA, 1981; Indiana University Purdue University, 1989-90. **Career:** Indiana State University, resident assistant, 1979-80; Indiana General Assembly, house staff intern, 1981; Dayton Hudson Corp, Target Store, sales/floor manager, warehouse manager, 1981-85; Indiana Department of Commerce, Div of Energy, program assistant, 1985-89; US Senator Dan Coats, assistant state director, 1989-; city councilman-at-large, City of Shelbyville, IN, 1995-. **Orgs:** Phi Beta Sigma Fraternity Inc, 1978-, past chapter president; Indiana State University, Quality of Life Study Committee, 1979; Council of Black Executives, 1990-; Shelbyville Central Schools, bd of trustees, president, 1985-93; Second Baptist Church, trustee, treasurer, 1986-; Shelby County Community Corrections Bd, 1985-; Bears of Blue River Festival, board member, 1984-; Phi Beta Sigma Fraternity, Inc, IN State dir. **Honors/Awds:** Indiana School Boards Association, Youngest School Board Member, 1985; Ed Simcox, Honorary Indiana Secretary of State, 1981; Indiana State University Rhoads Hall, Rhoads Hall Scholar, 1980; Indiana State Department of Education, Hoosier Scholar, 1977; voice of "Scuffy," Shelby County, 1970. **Special Achievements:** Minority Business and Professional Achiever Center for Leadership Development, 1990. **Home Addr:** 219 Fourth St, Shelbyville, IN 46176-2526, (317)392-1813. **Business Addr:** Assistant State Director, US Senate Office of Senator Dan Coats, 10 W Market St, 1180 Market Tower, Indianapolis, IN 46204, (317)226-5555.

GARRETT, JAMES F.
Engineering executive. **Career:** Sentel Corp, CEO, currently. **Special Achievements:** Company is ranked #75 on Black Enterprise magazine's 1997 list of Top 100 Black businesses. **Business Addr:** CEO, Sentel Corp, 225 Reinekers, Alexandria, VA 22314, (703)739-0084.

GARRETT, JOYCE F.
City official. **Personal:** Born Aug 16, 1931, Detroit, MI; daughter of Mary F Fleming and Thomas A Finley; divorced. **Educ:** Smith Coll, AB 1953; Wayne State Univ, 1959, 1974, MA 1966; Foreign Serv Inst, 1962. **Career:** City of Detroit, director, personnel, 1983-92; Dept of Public Information, dir 1978-83; Detroit News, columnist 1978; Detroit Bicentennial, exec dir 1974-77; Wayne County Office of Human Relations, dir 1969-74; MI Civil Rights Comm asst, dir 1967-69; Oakland Community Coll, pers admin 1965-67; Mayor's Youth Employment Project Detroit, job devel placement specialist 1964-65; Wayne County Civil Serv Comm, personnel tech II 1963-64, personnel tech 1956-61; Dept of State Washington DC & Caracas, Venezuela, for serv ofc 1962; Wayne County Com Coll, educ 1969-72. **Orgs:** Mem Intl Personnel Mgmt Assn; life mem NAACP; bd dir Smith Coll Alumnae Assn 1971-73; pres Neighborhood Serv Org 1974-76; mem Founders Soc Detroit Inst of Arts; mem Detroit Historical Soc; exec com mem Metropolitan Fund; bd mem, Museum of African Amer History; mem, Economic Club of Detroit; life mem, NAACP; Natl Council of Negro Women; Music Hall Center; dir emeritus, bd of dir, Founders Society. **Honors/Awds:** Spirit of Detroit Award 1974; Women of Wayne Headliner 1972; L'Ordre Nat du Merite 1978.

GARRETT, LOUIS HENRY
Educational administrator. **Personal:** Born Jul 16, 1960, Monroe, LA; son of Mattie M Garrett. **Educ:** LA Tech Univ, 1983, Moody Bible Institute; US Army, New Orleans, LA, legal course, 2nd MLC, 1990-91. **Career:** Miss Louisiana Pageant, Inc, dir of advertising; Grambling State University , McCall Dining Hall, manager, currently. **Orgs:** Mem Natl Assn of Miss Amer State Pageants, 1986-87; mem Phi Beta Sigma Frat Inc; faculty advisor GSU Chapter, Phi Beta Sigma Frat; Louisiana State Education Director, Phi Beta Sigma Frat Inc; Ouachita Parish Election Commission, 1988-; Commissioner-in-Charge Ward 10, Precinct 8; commissioner, Monroe City Planning and Zoning Commission, 1990-96. **Honors/Awds:** Mem Sigma Tau Delta Honor Soc in English 1981-83; Phi Alpha Theta Honor Soc in History 1982-83. **Special Achievements:** First African American member of the LA Pageant Board of Dir, 1986-87. **Military Serv:** USAF Reserves 1979-87; Cert Outstanding military performance 1988 at Fort Benning Georgia Infantry Training Center, 1987. **Home Addr:** 1605 Booth St, Monroe, LA 71201-8210. **Business Addr:** First Vice Pres, Leadership Div, PO Box 747, Grambling, LA 71245.

GARRETT, MELVIN ALBOY
Marketing manager. **Personal:** Born Jun 1, 1936, Montclair, NJ; married Maryann Harris. **Educ:** Upsala Coll E Orange NJ, 1956-64. **Career:** United Airlines, mktng mgr; Becker Constrn Co, accountant 1964-65; United Airlines, ticker agt sales rep account exec mktng mgr 1965-; Eisle King Libaire Stout & Co NYSE, asst to mgr 1957-60; Halevy H Simons Architect, pub relations opns coordinator 1962-63; Nat State Bank Newark, banking clk 1963. **Orgs:** Dist co committeman Montclair NJ Essex Cty Dem 1965; NAACP; Urban League; United Airlines Black Employees Assn; The Black Professional Orgn; mem Alpha Kappa Psi Frat. **Honors/Awds:** Interliner of the year 1977 The Detroit Interline Club 1977; mem of hon Detroit Interline Club 1978; ambassador of good will Detroit-Windsor Interline Club Inc; salesman of the year award United Airlines; community serv award United Airlines; leaderhip award United Airlines; black achiever award NY Harlem YMCA 1980; soldier-of-the-month; good conduct medal AUS 1962. **Military Serv:** AUS sp/4 1960-62. **Business Addr:** 1221 Avenue of the Americas, New York, NY 10020.

GARRETT, NAOMI M.
Educator (retired). **Personal:** Born Aug 24, 1906, Columbia, SC; daughter of Anna Maria Threewitts Garrett (deceased) and Casper George Garrett (deceased). **Educ:** Benedict Coll, AB 1927; Atlanta U, MA 1937; Columbia U, PhD 1954. **Career:** High School SC Baltimore, MD, instructor, 1927-41; Project Haiti, US govt English teacher, 1942-44; WV State Coll, prof modern foreign languages, 1947-72; chmn 1958-71; WV State Coll, foreign student adv 1954-72; Denison Univ, Univ prof 1972-74; Denison Univ Granville OH, visiting prof, 1974-79; Univ of Charleston WV, visiting prof, 1980. **Orgs:** Medm CLA; MLA; ACTFL; LASA; League Women Voters. **Honors/Awds:** Rosenwald fellow, 1944-45; Columbia Univ, fellow 1946-47; Ford fellow 1951-52; Fulbright fellow Paris 1958-59; contributing editor, HLAS; author Renaissance of Haitian Poetry; reviews, articles professional jours AAUW; Distinguished West Virginian Award, Gov G Caperton, 1992; Martin Luther King Award, for Scholarship, 1988; African American History Calendar, So Bell Tel, 1992; Denison Univ, hon doctorate, 1979; West Virginia State Coll, hon doctorate, 1981. **Home Addr:** PO Box 111, Institute, WV 25112.

GARRETT, NATHAN TAYLOR
Business executive. **Personal:** Born Aug 8, 1931, Tarboro, NC; son of Julia Garrett and York Garrett; married Wanda June Jones; children: Andrea Mausi, Devron, Nathan Jr. **Educ:** Yale Univ, AB Psych 1952; Wayne State Univ, post grad in Acct & Bus 1960; NC Central Schl of Law, JD 1986. **Career:** Richard H Austin & Co Detroit, acct 1958-62; Nathan T Garrett, CPA Durham, proprietor 1962-75; NC Fund Durham, deputy dir 1964-67; Fnd for Comm Dev Durham, fndr exec dir 1967-72; Garrett, Sullivan, Davenport, Bowie & Grant; Garrett and Davenport, partner currently; NCCU School of Business, tenured faculty. **Orgs:** Bd chair, exec comm NC Mutual Life Ins Co Durham 1977-; bd exec comm Mech & Farmers Bank Durham 1965-78; chrmn investment comm chair Cooperative Asst Fund NY 1970-88; bd exec comm Opport Funding Corp DC 1970-77; bd vice chr of Acad Affairs Comm Duke Univ 1978-90; corp mem Triangle Research Inst Fnd 1980-91; bd president Scarboro Nursery Schl 1989-91; chrmn of People Panel NC 2000 Commission of the Future 1983; NC State Board of CPA Examiners 1986-92; pres, National Assn of State Boards of Accountancy, 1992-93; pres, NC Assn of Minority Business, 1985-88. **Honors/Awds:** Serv as pres Natl Assc of Minority CPA Firms 1978; srv as elect official 25 Civic Grps in Durham & State of NC 1975. **Military Serv:** AUS corpl 1952-54. **Business Addr:** 3923 Northhampton Rd, Durham, NC 27707-5066.

GARRETT, PAUL C.
Attorney, city official. **Personal:** Born Feb 8, 1946, Charlottesville, VA; son of Pauline H Garrett and Dr Marshall T Garrett; married Louise Lawson; children: Matthew L. **Educ:** Brown Univ, AB 1968; Univ of VA Sch of Law, JD 1971. **Career:** USAF, asst staff judge advocate 1972-76; City of Charlottesville VA, asst city atty 1976-80; Charlottesville Circuit Court, clerk 1981-. **Military Serv:** USAF capt 1972-76; USAFR lt col 1976-96. **Business Addr:** Clerk of the Court, Charlottesville Circuit Ct, 315 E High St, Charlottesville, VA 22901.

GARRETT, ROMEO BENJAMIN
Educator (retired). **Personal:** Born Feb 2, 1910, Natchez, MS; son of Pinkie Garrett and Charles Garrett; widowed. **Educ:** Dillard U, AB 1932; Bradley U, MA 1947; New York U, PhD 1963. **Career:** Bradley U, prof Sociology 1947-76; Bradley U, prof emeritus. **Orgs:** Vice pres NAACP 1980-85. **Honors/Awds:** Arno Press published Famous First Facts About Negroes 1972; assoc publishers published The Presidents & The Negro 1982. **Military Serv:** USAF sgt. **Home Addr:** 431 W Fifth St, Peoria, IL 61605. **Business Addr:** Professor Emeritus, Bradley University, Peoria, IL 61606.

GARRETT, RUBY GRANT
Business executive. **Personal:** Born May 13, 1941, Covington, GA; daughter of Lola Price Grant and Robert L Grant; married William H; children: Victoria, Laran. **Educ:** Carver Voc Sch of Practical Nursing, LPN 1960; Atlanta Coll of Art, BFA 1971; GA State U, Masters Pgm 1971-73. **Career:** Ruby G Graphics Design, owner 1969-72; Eric Hill & Assoc Planning, art dir design consult 1971-72; G Designs Inc Adv & PR, pres owner 1972-79; Garrett Comm, pres 1979-; Grant-Garrett Communications, Inc, pres, currently. **Orgs:** Pres NAMD Atlanta Chapter 1982-83; bd mem Enterprise Atlanta 1983-85; comm chmn NAMD Atlanta Chapter 1983-87; bd & comm chm Atlanta Bus League 1983-87; consult speaker Univ of GA Extension Serv 1984; consult Atlanta Jr Coll 1984. **Honors/Awds:** Recognition The Collaborative Inc 1974; recognition Broadcast Enterprise Nat Inc 1984; President Award Nat Assoc of Market Developers ATC Chptr 1984. **Home Addr:** 2121 Beecher Rd SW, Atlanta, GA 30311. **Business Addr:** President, Grant-Garrett Communications, PO Box 53, Atlanta, GA 30301.

GARRETT, THADDEUS, JR.
Business executive, clergyman. **Personal:** Born May 18, 1948, Akron, OH; son of Tommie Garrett and T A Garrett. **Educ:** Univ of Akron, BA; George Washington Univ, grad sch of pub adminis; Howard Univ, grad sch of religion; Allen Univ, DD; ordained African Meth; Wilberforce Univ, DD; Livingstone Coll, DD. **Career:** Wesley Temple African Methodist Zion Church, Akron OH, minister & assoc pastor; chief assistant to former Congresswoman Shirley Chisholm, 1971-75; special assistant to Vice Pres Nelson A Rockefeller, 1975-76; Vice President George Bush, asst at White House 1981-83; Garrett & Co, pres 1983-; special advisor to President George Bush, 1988-92; senior adviser to Republican Natl Comm; visiting prof, Sch of Govt/Politics, Harvard Univ, Cambridge, MA. **Orgs:** OH Civil Rights Commn, commr 1980; former asst Congressman Wm Ayres; spl asst US House Educ & Labor Comm; tchr Akron Buchtel HS & Govt Seminar Univ of Akron; mem US Office of Educ Adv Council on Higher Educ; natl chmn YMCA Youth-In-Govt Prog; vice chmn Akron's Hum Rel Com; mem exec bd March of Dimes; OH Lung Assn; YMCA Youth-In-Govt Prog; Martin Luther King Scholarship Fund; OH Rep Council; NAACP, UMCA; steering comm Natl Black Rep Council; Bd of Trustees, Howard Univ, Kent State Univ; bd of directors First Bank Cleveland, OH; member Livingstone College, bd of trustees, 1988-; Howard Univ, chm of the bd of trustees, 1995-.

GARRETT HARSHAW, KARLA
Newspaper editor. **Personal:** Born Jan 23, 1955, Cleveland, OH; daughter of Bertha C Johnson Garrett and Morgan Garrett; married Timothy C Harshaw; children: Jason D Milton, Vincent V Harshaw, Alexander M Harshaw. **Educ:** Wright State Univ, Dayton, OH, BS, secondary education. **Career:** Dayton Daily News, Dayton, OH, various positions, 1971-90; Springfield News-Sun, Springfield, OH, editor, 1990-. **Orgs:** Board member, American Society of Newspaper Editors; chair, ASNE's Education for Journalism Committee; bd mem, Maynard Institute for Journalism Education; Ohio State University, School of Journalism Advisory Council; founder, Dayton Assn of Black Journalists, 1984; National Association of Black Journalists; National Association of Minority Media Executives; Ohio

Newspaper Women's Association; served on the Pulitzer Prize Nominating Juries in Journalism, 1995, 1996; John S and James L. Knight Foundation Newspaper in Residence Program, Selection Comm, 1997. **Honors/Awds:** Media Award, Montgomery County Mental Health Assn, 1980; Community Service Award, Miami Valley Health Systems, 1982; Dayton's Up & Comers Award, Price Waterhouse & the Muse Machine, 1989; Honor for Religious Writing, Ohio Newspaper Women's Assn, 1981, 1982; Springfield Urban League's Equal Opportunity Day Award, Career Achievement, 1990; Ohio Associated Press, 2nd Place Award, Column Writing, 1995; Ohio Associated Press, Third-Place Award, Editorial Writing, 1997; National Association of Black Journalists Region VI Hall of Fame, inductee, 1997. **Business Addr:** Editor, Springfield News-Sun, 202 N Limestone St, Springfield, OH 45503.

GARRISON, ESTHER F.
Secretary. **Personal:** Born Jul 16, 1922, Ocilla, GA; divorced. **Educ:** Savannah State Coll, attended. **Career:** Sub tchr; sec real estate firms ins firms; AUS; Intl Longshoreman's Assn Local #1414, sec. **Orgs:** Mem Chatham-Savannah Bd Educ 1964-; vice pres & tempore life mem NAACP sec local Br; mem Zion Bapt Ch. **Honors/Awds:** First black woman elected Bd educ S of Mason-Dixon Line; outstanding serv to commn Adult Educ Program 1965; woman of yr Savannah State Coll Chap NAACP 1966; award Prince Hall Mason & Eastern Stars 1975; hon tribute to a black woman Mutual Benevolent Soc 1974; first woman hon in history of 98 yr olf Soc; richard r wright award Svannah State Coll 1974. **Business Addr:** 221 NE Lathrope Ave, PO Box 1262, Savannah, GA 31402.

GARRISON, JEWELL K.
Educator. **Personal:** Born Nov 6, 1946, Dayton, OH; children: Brandon. **Educ:** Central State Univ, BA social work 1969; Atlanta Univ Grad Sch of Social Work, MSW 1972. **Career:** Montgomery Co Juvenile Court, probation counselor 1969-70; Cath Social Serv, sch social worker 1970-71; Atlanta Pub Sch System, sch social worker 1971-72; Montgomery Co Children Serv Bd, dir of staff devel 1972-77; Wright State Univ Dayton, asst prof 1977-84, Dept os Social Work and Medicine in Society, assoc prof/practicum coord 1984-89; Exec Dir of Community Connections, 1989-92; New Futures for Dayton Area Youth, deputy dir, 1992-93; Columbus Foundation, senior program officer, 1993-. **Orgs:** Sec 1976-78, pres 1977-80 Dayton Chap Natl Assn of Black Social Workers; 1st vice pres, OH State Chapter, Natl Assn of Black Social Workers 1978-81; bd dir, Dayton Urban League, 1977-83, 1984-93, bd of dirs chaiperson, 1989-92; reg trustee, Natl Urban League, 1988-91; vp bdof dirs, Community Connections, 1988-89; New Futures for Dayton Area Youth, exec comm, bd of dirs, 1988-89; Dayton Area Council on Youth, bd mem, 1988-90; Human Services Collab, 1993-; Prevent Inst, bd of dirs, 1994-96; United Way of Franklin City-Vision Council, 1996-. **Honors/Awds:** Natl Inst of Mental Health; fellowsip; Alpha Kappa Delta Awd Natl Sociological Hon Soc Alpha Chapt; Leadership Dayton, 1986; The Altursa Soc 1986-89; Zeta Phi Beta, Community Service Award, 1989. **Business Addr:** Senior Program Officer, Columbus Foundation, 1234 E Broad St, Columbus, OH 43205.

GARRISON, JORDAN MUHAMMAD, JR.
Physician. **Personal:** Born Nov 1, 1956, Montclair, NJ; son of Kathleen Wallace and Jordan Muhammad Garrison Sr; married Fitrah Muhammad-Garrison, Jan 24, 1992; children: Khadijah, Naimah. **Educ:** Lehigh University, BS, chemistry, 1978; Rutgers Medical School, MD, 1982. **Career:** University Hospital, UMDNJ, Department of Surgery, surgical intern, 1982-83, chief surgical resident, 1985-89, clinical professor of surgery, 1989-90; Danbury Federal Corrections Institute, U.S. Department of Justice, Federal Bureau of Prisons, chief medical officer, 1983-85; Northern Surgical Associates, surgeon, 1990-. **Honors/Awds:** Surgical Residents Teaching Award, 1983, 1988. **Business Phone:** (804)644-0141.

GARRISON, ROBERT E., JR.
Physician. **Personal:** Born Apr 11, 1923, Columbus, OH; son of Mamie Lambert Garrison and Robert Garrison; married Ruby Doyle; children: Paul M Duffy, Peggy G Drew, Judy G Rodgers, Robert D Saleem. **Educ:** Ohio State Univ, BSc Pharmacy 1948, MD 1957. **Career:** Hackley Hosp, chief of staff 1986; Muskegon Comm Coll, chmn of bd of trustees 1981-85, bd of trustees 1972-. **Orgs:** Bd mem Michigan Consolidated Gas Co 1979-86; bd of trustees, 1st vice pres Assoc of Comm Coll 1981; exec comm New Muskegon 1982-; Exec Comm Bd of Dir 1982-; Pres Assoc of Comm Coll Trustees 1985-86; bd dir First of Amer Bank 1985-89; vice pres New Muskegon Corp 1986-88; bd mem Muskegon County Comm Found 1988-; bd mem Muskegon Economic Growth Alliance 1988-. **Honors/Awds:** Outstanding Citizen Award, United Way of Muskegon County 1987; Johnathan Walker Award, Urban League of Greater Muskegon 1988; Paul Harris Fellow, Rotary Intl, 1990. **Military Serv:** USAF 99th Fighter Squad 1st lt 2 yrs.

GARRISON, ZINA. See GARRISON-JACKSON, ZINA LYNNA.

GARRISON-CORBIN, PATRICIA ANN
Business executive, management consultant. **Personal:** Born Jun 18, 1947, Louisville, KY; married Dr James D Corbin. **Educ:** Western KY Univ, BS 1969; Univ of Louisville, MS Urban Studies & Comm Devel 1970-71; MIT, MS Mgmt 1979. **Career:** MIT, asst to vice pres 1974-78, dir of personnel serv 1979-80; South FL State Hosp, dir human resources 1980-82; State of FL Amer Mgmt Corp, vice pres 1980-82; Greater Philadelphia First Corp, dep exec dir & treas 1982-; Drexel Burnham Lambert Inc, vice pres municipal finance. **Orgs:** 1st dep city mgt City of Philadelphia 1982-84; dep exec dir Greater Philadelphia First Corp 1984-; bd of dir Natl Assoc for Black Public Admin; vice pres PA Coalition of 100 Black Women. **Honors/Awds:** 1st Black Female Sloan Fellow MIT 1979; Urban Ed Fellow Louisville Bd of Ed 1971.

GARRISON-JACKSON, ZINA LYNNA (ZINA GARRISON)
Professional tennis player. **Personal:** Born Nov 16, 1963, Houston, TX; married Willard Jackson. **Career:** Professional tennis player, currently. **Honors/Awds:** Female Amateur Athlete of the Yr US Olympic Committee 1981; ITF Junior of the Year Awd for 1981, won both the Wimbledon Junior and US Open Junior titles; Zina Garrison Day in Washington DC Jan 6, 1982; was First Black Female to be ranked No 1 in Texas region; won European Indoor title in Zurich 1984; winner, US Open Quarter finals, 1988; winner, Chicago Virginia Slims Tournament, 1989; first Black to rank in the top 10 since 1971; winner, Wimbledon semi-finals against Steffi Graff, 1990; finalist, Wimbledon Grand Slam Finals, 1990; Police Athletic League, Woman of the Year, 1991. **Special Achievements:** President't Council on Physical Fitness and Sports, 1994. **Business Addr:** c/o Andrew P Moran, 5625 Milart St, Houston, TX 77021.

GARRITY, MONIQUE P.
Educator. **Personal:** Born Mar 26, 1941; divorced. **Educ:** Marygrove Coll, BA, 1963; Boston Coll, PhD, 1970. **Career:** Univ of MA, assoc prof; Wellesley Coll, asst prof 1970-71; Univ of MA, asst/assoc prof, 1968; Econ Research Unit, instructor; OECD Paris, cons; Metro Area Planning Council Boston, state analyst 1965. **Orgs:** Rengl chmn Caucus of Blk Econ 1971-72; dir Blk Econ Resrch Ctr; Am Scholar Coun; Fulbright Hayes Sr Lectureship Ave Univ of Dakar 1974-75; consult Guinea-Bissau 1978; Senegal 1979. **Honors/Awds:** Research Grant to Haiti, Yale Univ, 1972-73. **Business Addr:** University of Massachusetts, Dept of Econ, Boston, MA 02125.

GARROTT, HOMER L. See Obituaries section.

GARTIN, CLAUDIA L.
Judge. **Career:** 36th District Court, Detroit, judge. **Business Addr:** Judge, 36th District Court, 421 Madison Ave, Detroit, MI 48226, (313)965-8714.

GARTRELL, BERNADETTE A.
Attorney. **Personal:** Born Jun 21, 1945, Plainfield, NJ; daughter of Doryse Laws and Barnett Gartrell (deceased). **Educ:** Howard University, BA, 1967, School of Law, JD, 1970. **Career:** US Department of Housing & Urban Development, atty-advisor, 1970-71; DC Corporation Counsel, ast corp counsel, 1971-73; Mitchell, Shorter & Gartrell, managing partner, 1973-85; Leftwich Moore & Douglas, counsel, 1985-87; Gartrell, Alexander & Gebhardt, managing partner, 1987-92; Gartrell & Associates, managing partner, 1992-. **Orgs:** Trial Lawyers Association of Metropolitan Washington, DC, board of directors; American Trial Lawyers Association; Maryland Trial Lawyers Association; National Association of Black Women Attorneys; NBA, Greater Washington Area Chapter, Women Lawyers Division; Washington Bar Association; J Franklyn Bourne Bar Association; Alpha Kappa Alpha; Maryland Bar Association. **Special Achievements:** Founding partner of largest minority-owned law firm in Maryland, 1987. **Business Addr:** Managing Partner, Gartrell & Associates, Metro Plaza II, Ste 340, 8403 Colesville Rd, Silver Spring, MD 20910, (301)589-8855.

GARTRELL, LUTHER R.
Engineer. **Personal:** Born Aug 20, 1940, Washington, GA. **Educ:** NC A&T St U, BSEE 1964; Old Dominion U, MEEE. **Career:** NASA Langley Res Cntr, res engr. **Orgs:** Mem NAACP; IEEE; AIAA; VA Acad of Sci NASA publ. **Honors/Awds:** Spec achievement award NASA. **Business Addr:** Electronics Engineer, NASA, Langley Station, Hampton, VA 23665.

GARVIN, JONATHAN
Electrician. **Personal:** Born Apr 26, 1932, Jasper County; married Elizabeth Horton; children: Tony Millard, Earl Bernard. **Educ:** Savannah State, attneded 1951. **Career:** Private Practice, electrician. **Orgs:** Chmn Dem Party Jasper County; Band Booster Club; Athletic Club; biracial com Sch Bd Mason; mem choir leader Padgbett Br Bapt Ch; VEP; comm leader. **Military Serv:** USMC 2 yrs.

GARVIN, MILDRED BARRY
Administrator. **Personal:** Born Nov 29, 1929, Chicago, IL; married Ralph Garvin; children: Patricia Barry, Jacquelyn Barry, Ralph Jr, Derrick, Corey. **Educ:** Attended, Univ of IL, Chicago, Paterson State Teachers' Coll, Paterson NJ. **Career:** Rutgers Univ, Urban Studies Center, rsch assoc 1963-71, rsch assoc office of Nwk studies 1971-72; Mayor's Policy & Devel Office, deputy dir review & planning 1972-75; Rutgers Graduate School of Public admin, program coordinator, 1975-. **Orgs:** Exec bd mem, NAACP Orange & Maplewood Chapter; assemblywoman NJ Gehn Assembly Dist 27 Essex 1977; mem Amer Soc for Public Admin; mem Steering Comm NJ State Dem Party; chmn Assembly Educ Comm; vice chmn Assembly Higher Educ & Regulated Professions Comm; co-chmn, Joint Comm on Public Schools; chair Women's Legislative Democratic Caucus; chmn Natl Conf of State Legislators Educ & Labor Comm; state coord legislator Natl Black Caucus of State Legislators; mem NJ Historical Comm; mem YWCA Youth Advisory Bd; mem NJ State Legislative Black Caucus; mem Natl Black Caucus of Local Elected Officials; mem, Essex Co Vocational School Bd Long Range Planning Comm; mem Coalition of 100 Black Women. **Honors/Awds:** First Black to serve on East Orange Bd of Educ; Woman of the Year, Civic Action League of E Orange 1970; co-author "A Revised Policy Concerning Newark's Pequannock Watershed" Rutgers Office of Newark Studies 1971-72; Award for Excellence in Educ Operation PUSH 1979.

GARY, HOWARD V.
Financial company executive. **Career:** Howard Gary & Co, CEO, currently.

GARY, LAWRENCE EDWARD
Educator. **Personal:** Born May 26, 1939, Union Spring, AL; son of Henrietta Mays Gary (deceased) and Ed Gary (deceased); married Dr Robenia Baker, Aug 8, 1969; children: Lisa Che, Lawrence Charles Andre, Jason Edward. **Educ:** Tuskegee Inst, BS 1963; Univ of MI, MPA 1964, MSW 1967, PhD 1970. **Career:** MI Econ Opportunity Prog, staff asst 1964; Univ of MI, lecturer & asst prof 1968-71; Howard U, asst to vice pres for academic affairs 1971-72, dir prof, Institute for Urban Affairs & Research, 1972-90, prof of social work 1985-; Virginia Commonwealth Univ, the Samuel S Wurtzel professor, 1990-92. **Orgs:** Action bd Am Public Hlth Assoc 1973-74; bd of dir DC Inst of Mental Hygiene 1976-84; editorial bd Journal of Social Work 1977-81; Hlth Brain Trust Black Congressional Caucus 1977-87; publications bd Cncl on Social Work Educ 1982-87; consulting editor Jrnl of Social Work 1985-90; social welfare adv bd Natl Urban League 1985-89; bd of mgmt, Howard Univ Press 1987-; youth advisory bd, Lilly Endowment, Inc. Indianapolis, IN 1987-; bd mem, Child Welfare Inst, Atlanta, GA 1988-91; editorial bd, Journal of Teaching in Social Work 1987-; Bd of Trustees, St Paul AME Church, Washington, DC 1984-; advisory bd, DC Commn on Public Health 1984-87; Alpha Phi Alpha Fraternity, Inc; Council on Social Work Education, board of directors, 1992-95; mem visiting comm, School of Social Work, Univ of Michigan, 1991-. **Honors/Awds:** Distinguished Alumni Award Nat Assoc for Equal Opportunity in Higher Educ 1979; Eminent Scholar VA State Univ 1982; Outstanding Publication Nat Assn of Black Social Workers 1983; Labor of Love Award Nat Head Start Assoc 1984; Eminent Scholar Norfolk State Univ 1986; The Henry & Lucy Moses Distinguished Visiting Prof Hunter Coll NY 1986-87; elected delegate, Council on Social Work Eduction, 1988-89; Founder's Medallion Natl Assn of Social Workers 1988; Distinguished Alumni Award Natl Assn For Equal Opportunity in Higher Educ 1988; Tuskegee University Alumni, Merit Award, 1991; The Galt Visiting Scholar, VA Dept of Mental Health, 1994; Distinguished Scholar in Social Work, Albany State Coll, GA, 1994; Distinguished Research Awd, Howard Univ, 1995; Distinguished Recent Contributions to Social Work Awd, Council on Social Work Education, 1996. **Special Achievements:** Author: Black Men, 1981; Mental Health: A Challenge to Black Community, 1978. **Business Addr:** Professor, School of Social Work, Howard Univ, 601 Howard Place, NW, Washington, DC 20059, (202)806-7300.

GARY, MELVIN L.
Psychologist. **Personal:** Born Apr 12, 1938, Brownsville, PA; son of Marie Hood and Joseph Gary; married Juneau Mahan; children: Joseph Tyler. **Educ:** Haverford Coll, AB 1961; OH State U, MA 1964; OH State U, PhD 1967. **Career:** Ctr for Voc & Tech Educ OH State Univ, res assoc 1965; OH State Univ, res assoc 1967; Temple Univ, asst prof psych & ed psych 1968; Livingston Coll, dean of academic affairs, assoc dean of students 1971; Rutgers Univ, assoc for academic prog devel 1975, dean of academic affairs & assoc dean of students, assoc prof of psych, 1977. **Orgs:** Mem Am Assn for Advancement of Science, Am Assn of Univ Profs, Am Psychological Assn, Assn of Black Psychologists, Soc for Psych Study of Social Issues, Amer Assoc of Higher Educ. **Honors/Awds:** Hon men Woodrow Fellowship 1961; Society of Sigma Xi 1968; fellow Am Council on Educ Fellow UCLA 1974. **Business Addr:** Assoc Professor of Psychology, Rutgers Univ, Psychology Dept, New Brunswick, NJ 08903, (732)445-2026.

GARY, WILLIE E.
Attorney. **Personal:** Born in Eastman, GA; son of Mary Gary and Turner Gary; married Gloria Royal Gary; children: Kenneth, Sekou, Ali, Kobie. **Educ:** Shaw University, business administration, 1971; North Carolina Central University Law School, JD, 1974. **Career:** Gary, Williams, Parenti, Finney & Taylor, attorney, senior partner, currently; Gary Enterprises, president, currently. **Orgs:** Shaw University, Board of Trustees, chairman, 1987-. **Honors/Awds:** Shaw University, Honorary Doctor of Laws Degree, 1992; Trumpet Award, 1997. **Special Achievements:** Donated $10 million dollars to Shaw University, the largest cash donation given to an African American university, 1992. **Business Addr:** Attorney/Sr Partner, Gary, Williams, Parenti, Finney, Lewis & McManus, Waterside Place, 221 SE Osceola St, Stuart, FL 34994, (407)283-8260.

GASH, SAMUEL LEE, JR.
Professional football player. **Personal:** Born Mar 7, 1969, Hendersonville, NC; married Kate; children: Samantha Leigh, Samuel Kolby. **Educ:** Penn State Univ, bachelor's degree in liberal arts. **Career:** New England Patriots, running back, 1992-. **Honors/Awds:** Pro Bowl alternate, 1996. **Business Addr:** Professional Football Player, New England Patriots, 60 Washington St, Foxboro Stadium, Foxboro, MA 02035, (508)543-7911.

GASKIN, FRANCES CHRISTIAN
Company executive. **Personal:** Born Feb 7, 1936, New York, NY; daughter of Therese Farrelly Christian and Clement J Christian; married Conrad A Gaskin, Sep 14, 1957; children: Conrad II, Tracy, Troy. **Educ:** Fordham Hospital School of Nursing, Bronx, NY, diploma, 1954-57; Hunter College, CUNY, New York, NY, BS, 1959-62; Adelphi University, Garden City, NY, MS, 1968-70; Fordham University, New York, NY, PhD, 1976-82. **Career:** New York University, New York, NY, adjunct lecturer, 1978-79; Long Island University, Brooklyn, NY, asst prof, 1979-81; Regents College Program, Albany, NY, prof, 1981-82; Hostos Community College, Bronx, NY, prof, director, 1983-85; Frances Christian Gaskin, Inc, founder, pres, Melanin Plus, hair care and skin products, 1986-; NYC Technical College, Brooklyn, NY, adjunct prof, 1991-; Univ of NY at New Patty, assist prof, 1992-95; Brookhaven Natl Lab, research scientist, 1993-. **Orgs:** Sigma Theta Tau, International Honor Society, 1984-; Society of Cosmetic Chemists, 1988-; Fordham Alumni Assn, 1982-; Hunter Alumni Assn, 1962-; Adelphi Alumni Assn, 1970-; Phi Delta Kappa Fraternity, 1982-; Black Nurses Assn of the Capital District; National Black Nurses Assn, 1991-. **Honors/Awds:** Mabel K Staupers (Nursing), Omicron Chapter, Chi Eta Phi Society, 1984; Drum Major for Peace, Justice of Our Lady of Charity RC Church, 1979; presented personal experience as an inventor, State of NY Legislative Resolution, Senator Farlee, 1991; US Patent, protectant composition and method, US Patent and Trademark Office, 1989. **Business Addr:** President, Frances Christian Gaskin, Inc, PO Box 6003, Albany, NY 12206.

GASKIN, JEANINE
Human resource representative. **Personal:** Born Dec 11, 1945, Detroit; married Harry Thomas Gaskinn III. **Educ:** Univ MI, BA 1971. **Career:** Harper-Grace Hosp, hum rsrc rep 1976; Detroit Mem Hosp, persnl asst 1971-74; Detrt Bd of Edn, tchr 1970-71; Detrt News, persnl asst 1966-69. **Orgs:** Mem UWAA 1972-; Univ MI Alum Assn 1971-; Ed Com Coleman Yng Sentrl Conf Com; Secy Blenheim Forest Comm Counc 1973-; mem NW Orgzn Dtrt 1973-; mem Am Prsnl Guid Assn; mem Nat Empl Couns Assn; mem Assn for Non-white Concerns in Persnl & Guid; mem of Fdrs Soc Det Inst of Arts; mem Nat Hist Soc 1975. **Honors/Awds:** Nat Hon Soc Award 1964; Citznshp Award 1964; Schlrshp Award 1964; Archdiocesan Dev Fund Wrtng Award 1964. **Business Addr:** Director, Employment Services, Mt Carmel Mercy Hospital, 6071 W Outer Dr, Detroit, MI 48235.

GASKIN, LEONARD O.
Musician, bassist, composer, educator. **Personal:** Born Aug 25, 1920, Brooklyn, NY; married Mary; children: Leonard Jr, Poppy. **Career:** Bassist, composer, instructor; Louis Armstrong All-Stars, 1950's; Eddie Condon, recordings, including children's songs, with numerous artists, late 1950's; recordings, pop, r&b, gospel, folk, 1960's; Sy Oliver's Rainbow Room Orchestra, 1970's; Savoy Sultans. **Orgs:** International Society of Bassists; American Federation of Musicians; International Art of Jazz; Andy Kirk Foundation, chairman. **Honors/Awds:** President of the Borough of Brooklyn, Citation for Important Contributions to the World of Music; Edinburgh Jazz Festival, 70th Birthday Honoree, 1990. **Special Achievements:** One of the musicians who made 52nd Street famous; has worked with: Charlie Parker, Dizzy Gillespie, Billie Holliday, Thelonious Monk, Lena Horne, Ella Fitzgerald, Erroll Garner, Stan Getz, Miles Davis, Eddie Condon, Louis Armstrong, Charlie Shavers, Billy Taylor, Bob Dylan, Dionne Warwick, Wayne Newton, Little Richard, Rev James Cleveland, Lightnin' Hopkins, Big Sid Catlett, Eddie Haywood, Clyde Hart, Wild Bill Davidson, Cutty Cutshall, George Wettling, Gene Schroeder, Bob Wilber; toured Europe several times; appeared at many jazz festivals; Conducted Symposium on Roots and Development of American Jazz in Senegal, West Africa, December, 1994. **Home Addr:** 170-24 Grand Central Pkwy, Jamaica, NY 11432.

GASKIN, LEROY
Educator, artist. **Personal:** Born Jun 5, 1924, Norfolk, VA; son of Rosa Edwards Osborne (biological parent) and Peter and Carrie Bullock (foster parents); married Nina Mildred Locke, Dec 25, 1953; children: Edwin Leroy. **Educ:** Hampton Inst Hampton VA, BS magna cum laude 1950; Columbia Univ NY, MA 1955, tchrs clge prof diploma 1961; PA State Univ Univ Park PA, Doctor Educ 1972. **Career:** Prince George's Cty Pub Schl MD, art instr 1950-67, supr tchr for students of area clges & univ 1954-74; Letcher's Art Ctr Wash DC, comm art instr 1956-59; Prince George's Cty Pub Schl, helping tchr of sec art 1967-70, supr of art K-12 1976-; lecturer and practicing artist, 1950-. **Orgs:** Spec consult educ Natl Collection of Fine Arts Smithsonian Inst Wash DC 1970-71; eval for summer inst in Art History for hs art tchrs Univ of MD Clge Park MD 1973; eval for Museum & Community Conf for MD Art Educ Assc Baltimore Museum MD 1970; vice pres The Assc for the Preservation and Presentation of the Arts Inc Wash DC 1968-70; pres of DC Art Assc Wash DC 1976-78; pres of MD Art Educ Assc North Englewood MD 1982-84; deacon, Vermont Ave Baptist Church 1959-97. **Honors/Awds:** Museum & Art Tchr Research Prog Natl Gallery of Art & GW Univ 1966; Art Educ Citation Eastern Arts Assc Kutztown PA 1962; Citation Outstanding Contribution Art Educ Smith-Mason Gallery of Art Wash DC 1971; Community Art Award Assc Preservation & Presentation of Art Inc Wash DC 1977; Natl Art Educ Assc Outstanding Contribution to Art Educ Award State MD Atlanta GA 1980; Natl Art Educ Assc Div of Supr & Admin Outstanding Art Educ Award Eastern Region, Dallas, TX, 1985; Prince George's County Arts Council's Artist Grant, 1992. **Military Serv:** USN petty officer 2nd class, 1943-46. **Home Addr:** 1601 Woodhill Ct, Hyattsville, MD 20785-3854. **Business Addr:** Supervisor of Art K-12, Prince George's Cty Pub Sch, Oxon Hill Staff Development Center, 7711 Livingston Road, Oxon Hill, MD 20745.

GASKINS, HENRY JESSE
Educational administrator. **Personal:** Born Feb 27, 1935, Washington, DC; son of Mr & Mrs William Gaskins; married Mary Ann Gaskins, Apr 14, 1961; children: Phyllis, Gregory, Henry J II, Derek J, Kendra L. **Educ:** International University, PhD, 1978. **Career:** Library of Congress, supervisor, 1957-97; Freedom Youth Academy, pres, CEO, 1980-. **Honors/Awds:** President of the US, Honored for After School Program, 1987; Southeast Neighbors Community Awd, Outstanding Community Svc, 1989; President of the US, Volunteer Action Awd, 1990; Mayor Marion Barry, Cert of Commendation, 1990; Washington Space Business Roundtable, Education Awd, 1994. **Business Addr:** President/CEO, Freedom Youth Academy, Inc, 1405 34th St, SE, Washington, DC 20020, (202)584-3012.

GASKINS, LOUISE ELIZABETH
Educator. **Personal:** Born Jun 2, 1930, Raleigh, NC; daughter of Claytae V Hall Watson (deceased) and Joseph B F Cutchin (deceased); children: Pamela, Donna Gaskins-Wetherbee, Eric. **Educ:** NCCU, BS 1951; Fitchburg State, MEd 1972. **Career:** Atkins HS, teacher 1951-54; AEC Germ, teacher 1957-58; Germany, teacher 1959; WA State, teacher 1960-61; Ligon HS, teacher 1961-62; Army Educ Ctr Germany, teacher 1964; Ayer HS, teacher math 1965-72; Ayer Jr HS, guid counselor 1972-75, princ 1975-91; Ayer Public Schools, Administrator/Principal 1975-91. **Orgs:** Mem Ayer's Tchr Assn 1965-91; mem NEA 1965-; mem MA Teachers Assn 1965-; past faculty rep Professional Assn 1966-70; MTAR 1991-; past advr Afro-Amer Culture Club 1967-74; mem N Central MA Guid Assn 1968-75; mem MA Sch Couns Assn 1968-75; past mem Adm Selec Team 1970-73; past mem Professional Negot Team 1970-75; past chmn Supt Sel Com 1971-72; past mem bd dir Adven House 1973-75; mem MA Jr H Midl Sch Prin Assn 1975-91; state del NEA Conv 1975-; dir MA NEA 1976-85; mem Natl Sec Sch Prin Assn; mem New Eng Assn of Black Educators; Black Polit Task Force; MA Dept of Educ Study Com for Jr High/Middle Sch; MA Dept of Educ Evaluation Strategy Group for Handicapped Students; vice pres Montachusett Rgn NAACP 1977-78; bd mem Center for Well Being Inc 1980-. **Honors/Awds:** Natl Sci Found Grant 1967; Human and Civil Rights Award, Massachusetts Teachers Assn, 1988; Teachers Make the Difference, Christa Corrigan McAuliffe Center for Education and Teaching Excellence, 1991. **Home Addr:** 35 Boston Rd, Groton, MA 01450.

GASKINS, MARY ANN
Educational administrator. **Personal:** Born May 18, 1940, Washington, DC; daughter of Mr & Mrs Paul F Brown; married Henry J Gaskins, Apr 14, 1961; children: Henry J II, Derek J, Kendra L. **Educ:** Nova College, BA, education, 1989. **Career:** NASA Headquarters Advisory, comm specialist, 1964-95; Freedom Youth Academy, exec dir, 1980-. **Honors/Awds:** United Planning Organization, Martin Luther King Jr Community Svc Awd, 1996; Questors, Inc, Educational Awd, 1995; DC Commission for Women, Hall of Fame, 1993; President of the US, Volunteer Action Awd, 1990; President of the US, Honored for After School Program, 1987. **Business Addr:** Executive Director, Freedom Youth Academy, Inc, 1405 34th St, SE, Washington, DC 20020, (202)584-3012.

GASKINS, PERCELL
Professional football player. **Personal:** Born Apr 25, 1972. **Educ:** Kansas State. **Career:** St Louis Rams, linebacker, 1996; Carolina Panthers, 1997-. **Business Addr:** Professional Football Player, Carolina Panthers, 800 Mint St, Ericsson Stadium, Charlotte, NC 28202, (704)358-7000.

GASPARD, PATRICE T.
Pediatrician. **Personal:** Born Jun 30, 1954, New Orleans, LA; daughter of Shirley Gaspard and Octave Gaspard; married LeRoy Maxwell Graham; children: Arianne Marie, LeRoy M III. **Educ:** Tulane Univ, BS 1976; Tulane Univ Sch of Medicine, MD 1980. **Career:** Fitzsimmons Army Medical Ctr, pediatric residency; Ft Knox KY, chief of inpatient svcs; Fitzsimmons Army Medical Ctr, fellow in adolescent medicine; Chief, Adolescence Med Clinic, FAMC. **Orgs:** Certified Amer Bd of Pediatrics 1984; mem Amer Acad of Pediatrics; mem American Medical Association, mem National Medical Association, mem Society for Adolescent Medicine. **Honors/Awds:** First black elected to Alpha Omega Alpha Honor Medical Soc at Tulane Univ. **Military Serv:** AUS 1980-; Army Commendation Medal, 1st Oak Leaf Cluster.

GASTON, ARNETT W.
Clinical Psychologist. **Personal:** Born Apr 1, 1938, New York, NY; married Sandra; children: Robyn, Brett. **Educ:** AA 1970; BA magna cum laude 1971; MA 1975, MPh 1977; City Univ of NY, PhD 1981. **Career:** Dept of Correction Prince George's Co MD, dir; Mayor's Crisis Task Force, exec asst commr; Minimum Standards, bd of rev; NY State Standards & Goals for Criminal Justice Plng Com Honolulu Symphony Orchestra 1957; composer author musician conductor; Prison Suicide, recognized as authority; John Jay Coll of Criminal Justice, prof of psychology & forensic studies; New York City Dept of Corrections, former 1st dep commr, commanding officer training acad, clinical psychologist. **Orgs:** Mem 100 Black Men; Nat Assn of Black Psychologists; Nat Assn of Black in Criminal Justice; Am Psychol Assn; Am Correctional Assn. **Honors/Awds:** Num awards professional & pub svc; num articles publ; cited in Am Med Assn Journ; advanced through ranks faster than any man in hist of depart; youngest dep Warden; youngest dep commr. **Military Serv:** USAF 1956-59. **Business Addr:** Clinical Psychologist, New York City Dept of Corr, 100 Centre St, New York, NY 10013.

GASTON, CITO (CLARENCE EDWIN)
Professional baseball manager. **Personal:** Born Mar 17, 1944, San Antonio, TX; married Denise; children: Adrian, Carly. **Career:** Atlanta Braves, 1967; San Diego Padres, 1969-74; Atlanta Braves, outfielder/pinch-hitter 1976-78; Pittsburgh Pirates, 1978; Atlanta Braves, 1978; Atlanta Braves, hitting instructor 1981; Toronto Blue Jays, batting coach, manager, 1989-. **Honors/Awds:** National League All-Star Team, 1970. **Business Addr:** Manager, Toronto Blue Jays, 300 Bremner Blvd W Suite 3200, Toronto, ON, Canada M5V 3B3.

GASTON, JOSEPH ALEXANDER
Educational administrator (retired). **Personal:** Born Jan 3, 1928, Winnsboro, SC; son of Lilla R Gaston and John N Gaston; married Theresa Dutch, Oct 5, 1974. **Educ:** Johnson C Smith University, BS, 1949; Johnson C Smith Seminary, MDiv, 1952; University of Denver, MA, 1960; Michigan State University, PhD, 1970. **Career:** Booneville Edward Webb Presbyterian Church, student pastor, pastor, 1951-52; Board of National Missions (UPCUSA), Sunday school missionary, 1953-56; Johnson C Smith University, director, promotions for univ, assistant dean of men, vice pres, student affairs, executive to president, 1956-85; Catawba Inter-Presbyterian Prog Agency, executive presbyter, 1985-88; Johnson C Smith Seminary, administrative dean, 1988-93. **Orgs:** Presbyterian Church, comm on Mission responsibility through investment, 1989-94, comm on Theological Education, 1988-93; Church Vocation Ministry Unit Committee, 1987-92; Board of Pensions (PCUSA), 1987-89; Urban Mission Support Team Metro/Urban Ministry, 1986-87; Career & Personal Counseling Services Board, Synod of NC, 1986-88; Presbytery of Catawba, stated clerk, 1983, chair, personnel division, 1972-77; Division, Vocation & Professional Development, Piedmont Synod, chair, 1978-80; Catawba Inter-Presbytery Prog Agency, chair, personnel division, 1972-77. **Business Phone:** (404)527-7781.

GASTON, LINDA SAULSBY
Professional association executive director. **Personal:** Born Jun 15, 1947, San Francisco, CA; daughter of Arvis Dixon Harris and Harvey Harris; married James Gaston, Sep 27, 1985; children: Loren Saulsby, Leslie Saulsby. **Educ:** City Coll of San Francisco, San Francisco CA, AA; State Univ of New York, Albany NY, BA. **Career:** Linda Saulsby Mgmt Consulting, Oakland CA, owner; Coopers & Lybrand, Washington DC, Tucson AZ, dir of admin & personnel, 1983-86; Natl Assn of Black Accountants, Washington DC, exec dir, 1986-. **Orgs:** Mem, bd of dir, YWCA, Oakland CA, Tucson AZ, 1981-83, 1985-86; mem, Howard Univ School of Business Advisory Bd, 1987-; pres, Longmead Crossing Homeowners Assn, 1988-; mem, Natl Community Associations Inst, 1988-, Price Waterhouse & Co Minority Recruiting Task Force, 1989-. **Honors/Awds:** President's Membership Council Award, Greater Washington DC Bd of Trade, 1985; articles published: Spectrum (Journal of Natl Assn of Black Accountants), 1987, 1988.

GASTON, MACK CHARLES
Military officer (retired). **Personal:** Born Jul 17, 1940, Dalton, GA; son of Felicia Gilliard Gaston (deceased) and John Gaston (deceased); married Lillian Bonds, Aug 15, 1965 (deceased); children: Sonja Marie. **Educ:** Tuskegee Inst, BS Electronics 1964; US Naval War College, grad level cert 1977; US Industrial Coll of Armed Forces, diploma 1983; Marymount Coll, MBA 1984. **Career:** US Navy, electronic officer/combat information officer USS Buck 1965-67, engineering officer USS O'Brien 1967-69, material officer/squad engr destroyer sqd five staff 1969-71, personal aide/administrative asst navy dir r&d test & eval office of cno 1971-73, exec officer USS Conyngham 1974-76, commanding officer USS Cochrane 1977-79; branch head for off assignment Navy mil pers cmd 1979-81, commanding officer USS Cone 1981-82, head surface warfare tra branch office of cno 1983-84; US Navy, dir equal oppor div; commanding officer battle cruiser USS Josephus Daniels (CG 27) 1986-88; chief of naval operations strategic studies group (CNO Fellow) 1988-89; surface warfare manpower and training dir 1989-90; Defense Nuclear Agency, commander, field command, 1990-92; Naval Training Center, Great Lakes, IL, commander, 1992-. **Orgs:** Jr Deacon & Sunday Sch Tchr Hopewell Baptist Ch 1953-64; Couns & Career Planner Natl Naval Off Assn Washington DC 1977-; Sunday Sch Tchr Greater Zion Bapt Church 1981-85; president, Great Lakes Navy/Marine Corps Relief Society, 1992-; chairman, Great Lakes Combined Federal Campaign, 1992-; chairman, Drug Education for Youth (DEFY), 1992-; United Way of Lake County Exec Bd, 1992-; Northern Illinois Council on Alcoholism and Substance Abuse, 1992-; USO of Illinois, bd of dirs, 1992-; Lake County Economic Development Commission, exec committee, 1992-; Rotary One, 1992-; Federal Executive Board, exec committee, 1992-; US Naval Institute, 1987-; Naval Order of the US, 1992-; Surface Navy Assn; Natl Military Family Assn, 1992-; American Legion, 1993-; Tin Can Sailors, 1993-; Retired Officer's Assn, 1992-; Navy Club of the US, 1993-; Natl Strategy Forum; Navy Memorial Foundation; Flag and General Officer's Mess, 1991-; American Red Cross, bd of dirs, 1992-; North Chicago Citizens Against Drugs and Alcohol Abuse; North Chicago Children of the Future; Saturday Scholars; Partners in Progress; Project White Hat; Tuskegee Alumni Assn; Lake County Learns. **Honors/Awds:** Dalton, Georgia Education Hall of Fame, 1990; Massachusetts Bay Area Navy League, Dalton Baugh Award, 1992; State of Georgia renamed portion of North Dalton Bypass Hwy, Admiral Mack Gaston Parkway, 1992; Natl Image Inc President's Award, 1992; NAACP Wilkins Meritorious Service Award, 1994; Northern Illinois Council on Alcoholism and Substance Abuse James Kemper Humanitarian Service Award, 1994. **Military Serv:** US Navy, rear admiral, 28 years; Defense Superior Service Medal; Meritorious Serv Medal, two awards, Navy Commendation Medal, two awards, one with Combat "V"; Navy Achievement Medal; Natl Defense Serv Medal, two medals; Vietnamese Gallantry Cross; Vietnamese Serv Medal with 4 Campaign Stars; Republic of Vietnam Campaign Medal; Sea Serv Ribbon.

GASTON, MARILYN HUGHES
Physician, educator. **Personal:** Born Jan 31, 1939, Cincinnati, OH; daughter of Dorothy Hughes and Myron Hughes; married Alonzo; children: Amy, Damon. **Educ:** Miami Univ, AB 1960; Univ of Cincinnati, MD 1964. **Career:** Philadelphia Gen Hospital, intern 1965; Childrens Hospital Medical Center, resdent 1967; Community Pediatrics, assoc prof 1968-70; Childrens Hospital Medical Center, asst dir 1968, assoc prof pediatrics 1972-; Cincinnati Comprehensive Sickle Cell Center, dir 1972-; Lincoln Heights Health Center, medical dir 1973-; Howard Univ, asst clinical prof of pediatrics; NIH Sickle Cell Disease Branch Natl Heart Lung & Blood Inst, deputy branch chief; US Public Health Serv, captain commissioned corps; Bureau of Primary Health Care, assistant surgeon general, PHS, director, currently. **Orgs:** Mem Amer Acad Pediatrics, United Black Faculty Assn, Amer Public Health Assn; medical advisory bd State Crippled Childrens Serv; bd of trustees Childrens Health Assn, Pi Kappa Epsilon; medical dir Commissioned Corps US Public health Serv, NMA; Institute of Medicine. **Honors/Awds:** Outstanding Black Women Cincinnati 1974; City's Young Leader Health 1974; Harriet Tubman Woman of the Year 1976; Commendation Medal Public Health Serv Dept of Health & Human Serv; Health Center names Buford-Gaston; Outstanding Service Medal, Univ of Cincinnati; Distinguished Alumnae Award; NIH Directors Award; Marilyn Hughes Gaston Day, City of Cincinnati OH; Gaston H et al-Proph Penicillin in Sickle Cell Anemia, New England Journal 1986; Regular Presentations on Capitol Hill 1989, 1991-96; Inducted into Institute of Medicine. **Business Addr:** Assistant Surgeon General, Bureau of Primary Health Care, 4350 East-West Hwy, 11th Fl, Bethesda, MD 20817.

GASTON, MINNIE L.
Educational administrator. **Personal:** Born Apr 3, 1909, Burkville, AL; daughter of Roberta Carson Gardner and Billy Gardner; married A G Gaston. **Educ:** Tuskegee Inst, BS 1938; New York U; Gregg Coll. **Career:** Cedartown GA School System, teacher; Minnee Cosmetics, pres; Lowndes County School System, prin; Booker T Washington Insurance Co, first vice pres 1939; Booker T Washington Jr Coll of Business, pres, dir 1943-. **Orgs:** Mem Muscular Dystrophy Assoc of Am 1974-82; exec in residence Auburn Univ 1982; dist lecturer Tuskegee Inst 1983; mem dean's advisory cncl Sch of Bus ALState U; mem adv cncl Univ of AL at Birmingham; mem AL Women's Commission; mem Alpha Kappa Alpha; mem Natl Cncl of Negro Women; exec bd Coalition of 100 Black Women; treas Assoc of Independent Coll and Sch; mem Home Economics State (AL) Adv Comm; trustee St John African Methodist Episcopal Church; mem Birmingham Debate '88 Adv Bd, Jefferson Co Child Develop Council. **Honors/Awds:** EDHE Award AL Assoc of Coll & Univ, 1980; appreciation cert, AL NAACP Youth Cncl & Coll, 1982; Rust Coll Shield Rust Coll, 1983; spec awd, SCORE 1984; outstanding achievements, Jefferson Cty Historical Commission 1984; Alumni Merit Award, Tuskegee Inst; Cert of Merit, Natl Alumni Assoc, Booker T Washington Jr Coll of Business; Great Black Alabamian AL Conf of Black Mayors 1985; Presidential Citation, Natl Assoc for Equal Oppor in Higher Educ, 1985; Cert of Appreciation, Fort Valley State Coll, 1985; Meritorious Serv Awd, United Negro Coll Fund, 1986; Appreciation Awd, United Handicap Industries of Amer, 1986; Presidential Award, University of Montevallo, 1987; President's Award for Outstanding Support of Nursing, Sigma Theta Tau, Nu Chapter, 1988. **Business Addr:** President and Director, Booker T. Washington Junior College of Business, 300 18th St, N, Citizen Federal Bank Bldg, Birmingham, AL 35201.

GASTON, PATRICIA ELAINE
Journalist. **Personal:** Born Mar 26, 1959, Kansas City, MO; daughter of Charles & Camille Weems; married Keith A Gaston, Aug 29, 1981; children: Erin Michelle, Jonathan. **Educ:** Kansas City KS, Community Jr Coll, AA, 1979; Univ of Kansas, BA, journalism, 1981. **Career:** Boston Globe, copy editor, 1981; Rochester NY Democrat & Chronicle, copy editor, 1981-86; Dallas Morning News, asst international editor, 1986-. **Orgs:** Journalism & Women Symposium, 1993-95. **Honors/Awds:** Pulitzer Prize, International Reporting, 1994. **Business Addr:** Assistant International Editor, Dallas Morning News, 508 Young St, Dallas, TX 75202.

GATES, AUDREY CASTINE
Educator. **Personal:** Born Dec 9, 1937, Napoleonville, LA; married George M; children: George M, Geoffrey L. **Educ:** Dillard Univ, BA 1958; Dominican College; Drake Univ; Loyola Univ. **Career:** Orleans Parish School System, teacher, dept hd, 1958-68; Urban League of Greater New Orleans, Carrollton Day Care Ctr, dir, First Scholarship Classic, co-dir, Consumer Health Prog, dir, 1970-71; Central City Economic Opportunity Corp, training/techinal asst advisor, 1971-72; Mayors Office of Consumer Affairs, asst dir; 1972-79; Office of Manpower & Economic Development, coord of mayors summer youth prog, 1980-81; City of New Orleans/Civil Service Dept, asst to psychometician for developing exams, 1981-82; City of New Orleans, Public Works, dir of residential parking, 1983-87; City Council Research Staff, principal analyst and asst dir, 1987-94, interim dir, administrator to staff and other research activities, 1994-, dir of research, 1996-. **Orgs:** Federal Consumer Resource Network; Louisiana Dairy Stabilization Board; Better Business Bureau Arbitration Committee; Louisiana State Department of Education, Consumer Education Task Force; Family Service Society, bd mem; WWL & WYES, consumer advisory boards; Mater Dolorosa & St Augustine PTA; Band Parents Club; Palm Air Civic Assn, recording sec/pres-elect; National Forum of Black Public Administrators; Delta Sigma Theta Sorority; First United Methodist Church. **Honors/Awds:** YWCA Role Model, 1997; Women in Government Award, 1997. **Business Addr:** 1 E05 City Hall, New Orleans, LA 70112.

GATES, CLIFFORD E., JR.
Business executive. **Personal:** Born Nov 15, 1946; married Jacqui; children: Angela, Cliff III. **Educ:** Central State Univ, BS 1968; MI State Univ, grad courses in Industrial Mgmt 1971-72; Harvard Univ, MBA Exec Dev Prog 1974. **Career:** Pittsburgh Bd of Educ, teacher 1968-69; Westinghouse Elec Corp Bettis AtomicPower Lab, personnel rep/benefits admin 1968-71; General Foods Corp Battle Creek, MI, personnel spec/sr personnel spec 1971-73; General Foods Corp Corp Hdqtrs NY, assoc mgr equal opp/urban affairs 1971-73; Xerox Corp, asst mgr empl relations/mgr empl relations/mgr group mktg & field operations/ mgr empl rel/ombudsman 1973-77; Executex Inc Mgmt Consulting Firm, pres 1977-78; Revlon Inc NY, corp vice pres 1978-. **Orgs:** Adv bd, Black Exec Exchange Prog, Natl Urban League; bd dir, Negro Ensemble Co; chmn, Business Advisory Council, Central State Univ. **Honors/Awds:** Citation for Outstanding Achievement Natl Alliance of Businessmen; Xerox Special Merit Award for Outstanding Performance. **Business Addr:** Corporate Vice President, Revlon Inc, 625 Madison Ave, New York, NY 10022.

GATES, CLIFTON W.
Business executive. **Personal:** Born Aug 13, 1923, Moscow, AR; son of Mattie and Lance; married Harriet; children: Mark, Lisa. **Career:** CW Gates Realty, pres 1959-; Gateway Natl Bank, chrmn 1964-; Lismark Distributing, pres 1975-. **Orgs:** Bd of dirs Municipal Opera, Cardinal Glennon Hosp for Children, Blue Cross, Boy Scouts of Amer, Boys Town of MO, Convention and Visitors Bureau, President's Cncl of St Louis Univ, Gateway Natl Bank, Local Develop Co, St Louis Comprehensive Health Ctr, Civic Entrepreneurs; chmn St Louis Housing Authority; past police commissioner St Louis. **Honors/Awds:** Management Awd City of Hope Beta Gamma Sigma Univ of MO Chapt; St Louis Argus Public Service Awd. **Military Serv:** AUS 1943-45. **Home Addr:** 5855 Lindell Blvd, St Louis, MO 63112. **Business Addr:** President, Lismark Distributing Co, 1350 S Kingshighway Blvd, St Louis, MO 63110.

GATES, HENRY LOUIS, JR.
Educator, writer/editor. **Personal:** Born Sep 16, 1950, Keyser, WV; son of Pauline Augusta Coleman Gates and Henry-Louis Gates, Sr; married Sharon Lynn Adams, Sep 1, 1979; children: Maude Augusta, Elizabeth Helen-Claire. **Educ:** Yale Univ, BA (summa cum laude), 1973; Clare Coll, Cambridge, England, MA, 1974, PhD, 1979. **Career:** Time, London Bureau, London, England, staff correspondant, 1973-75; Amer Cyanamid Co, Wayne, NJ, public relations representative, 1975; Yale Univ, New Haven, CT, lecturer in English and Afro-American Studies, 1976-79, asst prof of English and Afro-American Studies, 1979-84, assoc prof of English and Afro-American Studies, 1984-85; Cornell Univ, Ithaca, NY, prof of English, Comparative Literature, and Aricana Studies, 1985-88, WEB Du Bois Prof of Literature, 1988-90; Duke University, Durham, NC, John Spencer Bassett Professor of English and Literature, beginning 1990; Harvard Univ, WEB Du Bois prof of the Humanities, chair, African-American Studies, dir, WEB Du Bois Institute for African-American Research, dir, 1991-. **Orgs:** Council on Foreign Relations; board of directors, Lincoln Center Theater and Whitney Museum; European Institute for Literary & Cultural Studies, board of directors, 1990-; American Council for Learned Societies, board of directors, 1990-; American Antiquarian Society; Union of Writers of the African Peoples; Association for Documentary Editing; African Roundtable; African Literature Association; Afro-American Academy; American Studies Association; Association for the Study of Afro-American Life and History; Caribbean Studies Association; College Language Association; Modern Language Association; The Stone Trust; Zora Neale Hurston Society; mem, Pulitzer Prize Board. **Honors/Awds:** Carnegie Found fellowship for Africa, 1970-71; Phelps fellowship, Yale Univ, 1970-71; Mellon fellowship, Yale Univ, 1973-75, 1983-; A Whitney Griswold fellowship, Yale Univ, 1980; Natl Endowment for the Humanities grants, 1980-84, 1981-82; Rockefeller Found fellowship, 1980-81; MacArthur Prize fellowship, MacArthur Found, 1981-86; Whitney Humanities Center fellowship, 1982-84; Afro-Amer Cultural Center Faculty Prize, 1983; Ford Found grant, 1984-85; Zora Neale Hurston Soc Award for Creative Scholarship, 1986; Honorable Mention, John Hope Franklin Prize, Amer Studies Assn, 1988; Amer Book Award, 1989; Anisfield Book Award for Race Relations, 1989; Candle Award, Morehouse Coll, 1989; author, Figures in Black: Words, Signs, and the Racial Self, 1987, The Signifying Monkey: Towards a Theory Afro-Amer Literary Criticism, 1988; Loose Canons: Notes on the Culture Wars, 1991; author, Colored People: A Memoir, 1994; The Future of the Race, 1996; editor, Our Nig, 1983, Black Literature and Literary Theory, 1984, "Race," Writing, and Difference, 1986, The Classic Slave Narratives, 1987; series editor, The Schomburg Library of Nineteenth-Century Black Women Writers, 1988; co-compiler, Wole Soyinka: A Bibliography of Primary and Secondary Sources, 1986; Colored People: A Memoir, Knopf, 1994; editor, The Norton Anthology of African-American Literature, 1996; co-editor, Transition: An International Review; author, editor, and contributor of articles and reviews to periodicals, books, and journals; George Polk Award, 1993; Lilliam Smith Award, Southern Literature, 1994; Chicago Tribune Heartland Award, 1994; 22 Honorary Degrees; Distinguished Editorial Achievement, Critical Inquiry, 1996; Tikkun National Ethics Award, 1996; The Richard Ellman Lectures, Emory University, 1996; Alternative Press Award for Transition, An Intl Review, 1995; Thirteen Ways of Looking At A Black Man, Random House, 1997. **Business Addr:** Chair, Afro-American Studies Dept, Harvard University, 12 Quincy St, Cambridge, MA 02138, (617)495-1443.

GATES, JACQUELYN BURCH
Corporate executive. **Personal:** Born Jul 12, 1951, Brooklyn, NY; daughter of Blanca Knight and Herman Knight; children: Antoinette, Anthony, Jacquelyn Tiffany. **Educ:** Attended Univ of IL Champaign/Urbana; Brooklyn Coll, BA 1973; New School for Social Rsch, MA. **Career:** Agency for Child Develop NY, family counselor 1973-76; NY State Supreme Ct, sec to supreme ct justice 1976-77; JC Penny Corp Headquarters, employment placement rep 1977-79; Revlon Inc, personnel admins/recruiter 1979-81; Paramount Pictures Corp, mgr indust relations NY, NY 1981-82; Pepsi Cola Co, mgr of profession al placement 1982-83; PepsiCo Inc Purchase, NY, mgr of corp relations 1983-; Nynex Mobile Communicators Company, vice pres, Quality and Ethics, Orangeburg, NY, 1990-93; Corporate Cultural Initiatives, director NYNEX, 1994-95; NYNEX Corporation, vp ethics, beginning 1995; Bell Atlantic, vp, Compliance, Diversity, and Organization, currently. **Orgs:** Past president Natl Assn of Negro & Bus & Professional Women Club 1987-91; board of directors, Leadership America; mem NAACP; visiting prof Black Exec Exchange Program Natl Urban League; mem Business Adv Council Central State Univ; past president, NYNEX Multicultural Association; bd of dirs, Martin Luther King Sr, Citizen Center; The Edges Group, past president, 1993-96. **Honors/Awds:** Natl Youth Achvmnt

Award NANBPWC 1980; Achvmnt Award Alpha Cosmetologists of Brooklyn 1979; Outstanding Young Woman 1979; Student Achvmnt Award Brooklyn Young Adults NANBPW 1965; Black Achiever in Industry Harlem YMCA 1984; Sojourner Truth Award East New York Club of Brooklyn NANBPW 1984; 100 Young Women of Promise in 21st Century Good Housekeeping Mag 1985; Top 100 Black Bus & Professional Women in Amer Dollars & Sense Mag 1986; Bus Awd Kings County Club NANBPWC Inc 1986; Young Achiever Award Natl Council of Women of USA 1986; 100 Most Influential Black Americans, Ebony Magazine, 1988-91; New York YWCA, Academy of Women Achievers, 1996. **Business Addr:** VP, Bell Atlantic, 1095 Avenue of Americas, Rm 2308, New York, NY 10036.

GATES, JIMMIE EARL
Journalist. **Personal:** Born Jun 3, 1956, Jackson, MS; son of Birdie Lee Allen Gates; married Pattie Denise Kendrick Gates, Jun 20, 1987; children: April Jimel. **Educ:** Jackson State Univ, Jackson, MS, BS, 1981. **Career:** Jackson Daily News, staff writer, 1983-86; USA Today, Rosslyn, VA, travel & health update line editor, 1986-87; The Clarion-Ledger, Jackson, MS, staff writer, 1987-. **Orgs:** Pres, Jackson Assn of Black Journalists, 1990-91; mem, Jackson Branch of NAACP, 1985-; mem, Society of Professional Journalists, 1990-. **Honors/Awds:** Best of Gannett, The Gannett Corp, 1987; Merit Award, Southern Institute of Journalism, 1985; AP Community Award, Associate Press, 1985; AP Community Award for SE Region, Associate Press 1985. **Business Addr:** Staff Writer, News, The Clarion-Ledger, 311 E Pearl St, Jackson, MS 39205.

GATES, OTIS A., III
Business executive. **Personal:** Born Feb 26, 1935, Chattanooga, TN; married Barbara L; children: George, Theresa, Todd, Khari. **Educ:** Harvard Coll, AB; Harvard Grad Sch of Bus Admin, MBA. **Career:** Kaufman & Boad Homes Inc, asst to gen mgr 1963-64; MI Blue Shield, mgr computer systems & opers 1964-66; Zayre Corp, mgr computer systems devel 1966-68; Arthur Andersen & Co, mgr 1969-76, partner 1976-. **Orgs:** Youth servc com MA Bay United Way Fund 1974-; bd of trustees Univ Hospital 1983-; bd of dirs Jobs for Youth; bd dirs Danforth Museum. **Military Serv:** USAF capt retired reserve. **Business Addr:** Arthur Andersen & Co, 100 Federal, Boston, MA 02110.

GATES, PAUL EDWARD
Oral and maxillofacial surgeon. **Personal:** Born Aug 16, 1945, Keyser, WV; son of Pauline Coleman Gates and Henry Louis Gates Sr; children: Eboni, Jennifer. **Educ:** Potomac State Jr Coll, AA 1964; WV U, BA 1966 WV Univ Sch of Dentistry, DDS 1970; NY Univ Sch of Dentistry, 1971; Harlem Hosp Ctr, Resd 1970-73; Fairleigh Dickinson, MBA, 1992. **Career:** Fairleigh Dickinson Dental School, oral surgeon 1973, asst clinical prof 1973-76, dir minority affairs 1979-86, prof 1986, asst vice pres acad admin 1986-87; acting dean Coll of Dental Medical 1988-89; asst to pres for health planning and policy 1988-89; Bronx-Lebanon Hospital, Bronx, NY, director of oral and maxillofacial surgery, and department of dentistry, 1990-; Assoc Prof Albert Einstein School of Med, 1994-95. **Orgs:** Mem ADA Student 1966-70, 73-77; Xi Psi Phi Frat; WV Univ Alumni Assn; student Am Dental Assn; mem Passaic Co Dental Soc 1973-77; NJ Dept Dentistry 1973-77; bd dir INCAA 1973-74; NJ Dental Soc 1973; Am Bd Oral Surgery Diplomate 1975; Am Soc Oral Surgery 1977; Am Soc Dental Anesthesiology; Am Assn Hosp Dentistry 1977; NJ Soc Dental Anesthesia; Harlem Hosp Soc Oral Surgery; attdg oral surgeon St Joseph's Hosp; NJ Dept Dentistry 1973-77; bd dir INCAA 1973-74; co-chmn Hlth & Nutrition Com Paterson Headstart; vice pres Southside Multiservice Ctr Paterson Task Force; editor Jour Passaic Co Dental Soc; exec com Southside Multiservice Ctr Paterson Task Force; chief of oral & maxillofacial surg & assoc chmn Dept of Dent St Joseph's Hosp & Med Ctr; bdtrustees St Joseph's Hops & Med Ctr 1984-87; N Dental Assn Commonwealth Dental Society; dir of minority scholarship program, National Dental Assn Foundation, 1990-92. **Honors/Awds:** OKU Natl Dental Honor Soc 1980; Amer Council on Educ Fellow 1984-85; publ "Meningitis as a Result of Post Extraction Infection Report of a Case" Jrnl Oral Surgery 1972; publ "Visceral Kaposis's Sarcoma presenting with Gingival Lesions" Oral Surgery Oral Med & Oral Pathology 1980, "Oral Lesions in Crohn's Disease, Report of a Case" NY State Dental Jrnl, "The Dental Cartridge-Its Contents & Clinical Implications" DMD 1980, "Calcium Nutrition & the Aging Process, A Review" Jrnl of Gerodontology 1985, "The Dental Cartridge It's Contents & Clinical Implications" DMD 1985; "Minority Recruitment and Retention at FDU" Journal Natl Dental Assn 1988; Fellow Amer Coll of Dentist 1989; Outstanding Young Men in America, 1970, 1980; Outstanding Oral Surgery Faculty Award, 1977-81; Outstanding Achmnt, Bronx-Lebanon Hosp, Employees of African Descent, 1992-93; Distinguished Practitioner of Dentisty, Nat Academies of Practice, 1997; Sixth Annual Achmnt Award, Nat Pro-Am, Inc, 1997. **Business Addr:** Director, Dept of Dentistry, Bronx-Lebanon Hospital Center, 1770 Grand Concourse, Bronx, NY 10457, (718)960-2018.

GATES, THOMAS MICHAEL
Educator. **Personal:** Born Jan 9, 1943, St Louis, MO; married Doris Atwater; children: Steven A, Genice Arnold. **Educ:** Howard Univ, BFA 1970; CA State Univ Sacramento, MA 1972. **Career:** Economic Opportunity Council, instructor, drama workshop 1971-72; CA State Univ, dir, black theatre program 1972-; CA State Univ, Sacramento, assoc prof, theatre, prof theatre. **Orgs:** Mem Amer Theatre Assoc, CA Black Staff & Faculty Assoc, Sacramento Kwanza Comm; guest dir Black Arts/West Theatre Seattle WA 1975; actor Film "South by Northwest" 1975; dir "The River Nigger"1976; dir five black-one-act plays 1979; directed/produced 40 one-act plays and 17 full length plays at CA State Univ-Sacramento. **Honors/Awds:** Natl Finalist and Awd of Excellence Amer Coll Theatre Festival 1973; Proclamation by Mayor City of Sacramento 1973; Resolution by State Senate; Joint Resolution CA State Assembly & Senate 1985; production "The Sty of the Blind Pig" first black production to be performed in the JFK Ctr for Performing Arts. **Military Serv:** USAF E-4 4 years. **Business Addr:** Professor-Theatre Arts, CA State University, 6000 J St, Sacramento, CA 95819.

GATES, YVONNE ATKINSON
County executive. **Career:** Clark County, Las Vegas, commissioner, chp. **Special Achievements:** First African American female commission, Clark County, Las Vegas. **Business Addr:** Chairperson, Clark County Commission, 500 S Grand Central Pkwy, Las Vegas, NV 89155, (702)455-4431.

GATEWOOD, ALGIE C.
Educational administrator. **Personal:** Born Dec 17, 1951, Wadesboro, NC; son of Bessie M Gatewood and Haywood J Gatewood; married Elaine Thornton, Oct 1973; children: Wendolyn Charmaine, Andrea Marzina, Algie Carver Jr. **Educ:** Livingstone Coll, BA Social Science/History 1970-74; Appalachian State Univ, MA Higher Educ/Coll Admin 1976-77; NC State, Certificate in Guidance & Counseling 1982; UNC-Charlotte, Doctoral Studies, 1988-89; North Carolina State University, EdD; 1988-94; Winthrop Univ, School Administration Licensing. **Career:** Anson Tech, community serv 1974-80, dir of inst research, dir of human resources devel & project dir for community serv 1980-81; Gatewood Motors, owner, currently; Anson Community Coll, acting dean, 1981-82, dean of students, 1982-97; UNC, Gnl Adm, assistant director, 1997-. **Orgs:** Mem Phi Beta Sigma Fraternity 1971-; field reader US Office of Educ 1980-82; task force mem State Dept of Com Coll 1983-84; trustee Ebenezer Baptist Church 1980-; vice pres Professional Video Serv Inc 1985-; NC Foundation for Alternative Health Programs, vice chair, 1997-, secretary, treasurer, 1994-97, board of directors; Anson Regional Medical Services, board of directors; Anson County United Way, board of directors; school bd mem, Anson County Bd of Education, Wadesboro, NC; completed Academy for Com Coll Ldshp Advancement, Innovation & Modeling—Emergency Issues Forum series; Ford Foundation stipend for Ntl Comm Coll Transfer Assembly Panel; presenter, Tech-Prep Conf. **Honors/Awds:** Bd mem emeritus, Anson Regional Medical Services, 1997; bd mem of the year, Anson Regional Medical Services, 1996; nominated John B. Grenzebach Award, CASE, 1996; Martin Luther King Jr. Education Award from NH Association of Univ. Women of Anson; "A Model for Assessing the Fund-Raising Effectiveness of Comm Coll Non-profit Foundations in NC"; "A Comparative Analysis & Evaluation of Comm Coll non-profit Foundations in NC," "The Student Recruitment and Retentio Manual.". **Special Achievements:** Honored by establishment of the Dr. A.C. Gatewood Scholarship, Alpha Pi Chi Sorority & Women Action Club. **Business Addr:** NC State Education Assistance Authority, General Administration, The University of NC, UNC Research Triangle Park Building, 10 Alexander Dr, Research Triangle Park, NC 27709.

GATEWOOD, WALLACE LAVELL
Educator, economist. **Personal:** Born May 31, 1946, West Bend, KY; son of Minnie Lucas Gatewood and Cecil Gatewood; married Sharon JM Oliver, Sep 29, 1985; children: Eboni, Shannon, Ashley. **Educ:** Berea Coll, Berea KY, BS 1968; Oberlin Coll, Oberlin OH, Post-Baccalaureate Certificate 1969; Washington Univ St Louis, MBA 1971; Univ of IL Champaign-Urbana, PhD Labor & Industrial Relations 1975. **Career:** W L Gatewood & Assoc Consulting Firm, pres 1979-; FMCS, labor arbitrator 1980; independent certified financial planner 1980-; Florida A&M Univ Tallahassee, asst prof economics 1974; Florida State Univ Tallahassee, asst prof mgmt labor relations 1974-77; Morgan State Univ Baltimore, assoc prof business & economics 1977-79; Univ of Baltimore, assoc prof mgmt & labor 1980-82; Baruch Coll NYC, asst prof 1982-84; Coppin State Coll Baltimore, assoc prof mgmt science 1984-86; Morgan State Univ, prof business admin & mgmt 1986-, chair 1988-; Long & Foster Real Estate Inc, real estate agent 1987-89; Century 21 Associated Inc, real estate agent 1989-. **Orgs:** Mem Amer Soc for Productivity Improvement; Amer Soc of Training & Devel; Industrial Relations Research Assn; Natl Black MBA Assn; Natl Economics Assn; mem employment advisory comm Baltimore Urban League 1968-; mem NAACP Baltimore 1980; mem Academy of Mgmt, Assn of Human Resources Mgmt & Organizational Behavior; exec bd, pres Maryland Chapter AHRMOB; mem Baltimore Mktg Assn; coord NAACP Lecture Series 1981-82; mem Howard County Commission for Women 1981-84; coord Mgmt Science Serv Coppin State Coll 1984-86; sec Patapsco Valley Regional Council Episcopalian Diocese 1987-88; mem dir Center for Financial Success 1986-. **Honors/Awds:** Scholarship Berea Coll 1964-68; Post-Baccalaureate Fellowship, Oberlin Coll 1968-69; Consortium Fellowship, Washington Univ 1969-71; Fellowship, Univ of Illinois 1971-73; Research Intern, Congressional Budget Office 1978; Faculty Fellow, Social Security Admin 1979; Man of the Year, Soc for Advancement of Mgmt MSU 1980; Advisor of the Year Univ of Baltimore 1981. **Home Addr:** 12 Devlon Ct, Owings Mills, MD 21117.

GATHE, JOSEPH C.
Physician. **Personal:** Born Dec 15, 1929, Scott, LA; married Marion; children: Joseph Jr, Jeffrey, Joy, Julia, Jillian. **Educ:** Xavier U, New Orleans, BS 1949; St Louis U, MD 1953. **Career:** Riverside Surgical Clinic, owner 1960-. **Orgs:** Treas Pan-Texas Mortgage 1970-75; mem State Bd Educ 1972-80; advisory com Univ Savings 1982-; pres Aid to Culturally Deprived Children. **Honors/Awds:** Outstanding citizenship award Urban League 1949. **Military Serv:** USAF capt 1954-56. **Business Addr:** Surgeon, 2914 Blodgett, Houston, TX 77004.

GATLIN, ELISSA L. See Obituaries section.

GATLING, CHRIS RAYMOND
Professional basketball player. **Personal:** Born Sep 3, 1967, Elizabeth City, NJ. **Educ:** Pittsburgh; Old Dominion, 1991. **Career:** Golden State Warriors, forward, 1991-96; Miami Heat, 1996; New Jersey Nets, 1996-. **Special Achievements:** NBA Draft, First round pick, #16, 1991; Golden State Warriors, Jack McMahon Award, 1993. **Business Addr:** Professional Basketball Player, New Jersey Nets, Brendan Byrne Arena, East Rutherford, NJ 07073, (201)935-8888.

GATLING, JOSEPH THEODORE
Legal consultant. **Personal:** Born Mar 11, 1947, Washington, DC; son of Arphelius & Inez Gatling, Sr. **Educ:** Federal City College, 1970-74; Prince Georges Community College, AA, 1987; University of MD, BS, 1988. **Career:** Office Personnel Management, information specialist, 1980-83; Council of the District of Columbia, admin asst, 1984; Arts Commission for DC, arts info coord, 1985; DC Office of Human Rights, prog specialist, 1985-86; Bd of Veterans Appeals, legal technician, 1987, asst chief of hearing section, 1988-89; Disabled American Veterans, national service officer, 1990-95, commander, currently. **Orgs:** Shiloh Baptist Church, teacher, 1982-; Redemption Lodge No 24, PHA, past master, 1986-; Disabled American Veterans, commander, 1968-; NAACP, 1980-; Washington Very Special Arts, staff volunteer, 1995-. **Honors/Awds:** Federal City College, Charles Coleman Award, 1973; Executive Office of Mayor, Outstanding Service, 1985; United Black Fund, Community Service Award, 1986; Combined Federal Campaign, Outstanding Service, 1988-90; Disabled American Veterans, Outstanding Membership Achievement, 1991. **Special Achievements:** Created Geographic Development Art Program in DC, 1985; Honors Graduate, Prince Georges, Comm Coll, 1987; Combined Federal Campaign Fundraising above targeted goal, 1988; appointed Office of General Counsel, Legal Rep, 1990; superintendent of Primary Dept Church School, 1995. **Military Serv:** US Marine Corp, LCpl, Vietnam Era; Good Conduct Medal, 1966. **Business Addr:** Commander, Disabled American Veterans, PO Box 10127, Washington, DC 20018.

GATLING, PATRICIA LYNN
Attorney. **Personal:** Born Jan 16, 1960, Annapolis, MD; daughter of Virginia D Gatling and Luther C Gatling. **Educ:** Johns Hopkins University, BA, international studies, 1979; University of Maryland School of Law, JD, 1982. **Career:** Kings County District Attorney, assistant district attorney, 1983-86; Special Narcotics Court, Sterling Johnson Jr, special narcotics assistant, 1986-87; Special State Prosecutor, New York City Criminal Justice System, special assistant attorney general, 1987-90; Kings County District Attorney, Major Narcotics Bureau, executive asst, district attorney, 1992-96, deputy district attorney, 1996-. **Orgs:** National Black Prosecutors Association, vice pres, 1992-, pres, 1993-94. **Home Addr:** 1175 York Ave, Apt 2T, New York, NY 10021. **Business Phone:** (718)250-2800.

GATSON, WILINA IONE
Administrative assistant (retired). **Personal:** Born Apr 17, 1925, Galveston, TX; daughter of Ina Ivory Sibley Garner (deceased at age 103) and Willie Lee Garner (deceased); divorced; children: Natalie, Kenneth. **Educ:** Sch of Voca Nurs Univ of TX Med Br, 1954; TX So U, 1955-57; Nurs Univ of TX Med Br, BS 1960. **Career:** Moody State Sch for Cerebral Palsied Chold Univ of TX Med Branch, first black nursing supr 1965-; John Sealy Hosp, LVN on psychiatry; St Mary's Hosp US Pub Health Hosp asst night sup; Galveston Coll & UTMB Sch of Nurs guest lecturer, retired. **Orgs:** Mem NAACP-TNA; ANA; Nat Coun Negro Women Inc; held various off in Delta Signa Theta Sor Inc; Ladies Aux Amer Leg; UTMB Alumni Assn; Versatile Dames; Sickle Cell Anemia Found; Jack & Jill of Amer Inc; mem First Union Baot Courts of Calanthes Ch; served on many bds in comm & state during past 20 years coms

in Delta on local & regnl levels; Heroines of Jericho. **Honors/ Awds:** First black to grad from UTMB Deg Nurs Sch 1960; first black to serve as Off in UT Nurs Alumni Assn 1961-62; rec outstndg student of year award from UTMB in 1958; has been honored on various occas by local groups & chs for comm serv; first black to receive Distinguished Alumnus Award Univ of Texas School of Nursing, 1989; Distinguished Alumnus Award, UTMB School of Nursing, 1989; inducted into UTMB Nursing Hall of Fame, 1992.

GATTISON, KENNETH CLAY
Professional basketball player. **Personal:** Born May 23, 1964, Wilmington, NC. **Educ:** Old Dominion Univ, Norfolk, VA, 1982-86. **Career:** Phoenix Suns, 1986-87; played in the Italian league, 1988-89; Phoenix Suns, 1988-89; Quad City Thunder, 1989-90; Charlotte Hornets, 1989-. **Business Addr:** Professional Basketball Player, Charlotte Hornets, Hives Dr, Charlotte, NC 28217.

GAUFF, JOSEPH F., JR.
Educator. **Personal:** Born Apr 20, 1939, Helena, MT; son of Joseph F Gauff Sr; divorced; children: Lisa M, Denise A, Nathan A, Rebecca R. **Educ:** Univ of Washington, BA Business 1971, MBA 1973, PhD 1979. **Career:** Western Washington St Univ, asst prof of mktg 1977; Univ of Denver, asst prof of mkts 1977-80; General Telephone & Electronics, mktg rsch specialist & forecasting 1980-82; Grambling State Univ, prof of mktg 1982-83; California State Univ-Fresno, prof of mktg 1983-86; Florida A&M Univ, prof of mktg 1986-. **Orgs:** Supervisor King County Juvenile Court 1969-77; mem Natl Chap AAS 1974-; partner Business Insight Consulting 1979, 1980; bd of dir mem United Way Denver 1979; bd of dir mem Fresno Madera Counties Chap Red Cross 1984, 1986. **Honors/Awds:** Publications, "Consumer Aspects of Marketing in a Small Health Maintenance Organization," Univ of WA 1979; Hewlett-Packard BASIC, Bellwether Press 1986; "Health Care Marketing," Health Marketing Quarterly Vol 3 No 4 1986; "A Prospectus for a Conceptualization of Preventive Health Behavior Theory," Health Marketing Quarterly Vol 3 No 4 1986. **Home Addr:** 220-8 Belmont Rd, Tallahassee, FL 32301. **Business Addr:** Dept of Bus & Econ Studies, Morehouse College, 830 Westview Dr, SW, Atlanta, GA 30314.

GAULT, MARIAN HOLNESS
Educator. **Personal:** Born Oct 1, 1934, Panama, Panama; children: Taisia Marie, Daryl Justin. **Educ:** St Agnes Med Ctr, Nursing 1952-55; Villanova Univ, 1962; Glassboro Coll, BA Health Ed 1971, MA Ed 1978;; Drexel Univ Philadelphia, Mgmt Cert 1980. **Career:** West Park Hosp, admin suprv 1963-64; Roxborough School of Nursing, nurse ed 1965; SUNY Downstate Med Ctr, teaching, rsch nurse 1966-67; Washington Mem Hosp, dir nursing 1972-78; Einstein Med Ctr, asst dir nursing admin 1979-81; NJ State Dept of Ed, cons, ed of health. **Orgs:** Consult urban ed State Dept Ed 1968; chairperson comm for action NJ Soc Nursing Admin 1978; natl consult jona listing Palpack Entr 1978; seminars, conf, workshops Palpack Entr; bd mem Utopia Youth Mission; mem Natl Assoc Female Exec, Amer Nurses Assoc, Natl League Nursing. **Honors/Awds:** Letter of Commendation for Public Serv US Senator William Cahill 1969; Distinguished Alumnae St Agnes Med Ctr Class, 1955, 1980. **Home Addr:** 11 Yale Road, Atco, NJ 08004. **Business Addr:** Consultant, Educator, Health, New Jersey Dept of Education, 225 West State St, Trenton, NJ 08625.

GAULT, WILLIE JAMES
Professional Football Player. **Personal:** Born Sep 5, 1960, Griffin, GA; son of Willie Mae Roberts and James Gault Jr; married Dainnese Mathis, Jun 11, 1983; children: Shakari Denise, Gabriel James. **Educ:** Univ of Tennessee, Knoxville, TN, Marketing, 1979-83. **Career:** US Olympic Team, track & field 1980; US Natl Team, track & field 1980-83; Chicago Bears, wide receiver; Winter Olympics Bobsleigh, 1988; US Olympic Bobsled Team, pusher, 1990-91; Los Angeles Raiders, pro athlete, currently. **Orgs:** Chmn, Ministry Lay Witnesses for Christ 1983-; public speaker for schools & churches; Lou Garrett commercial 1983; Distonia Commercial 1985; Fair Housing Commerical, City of Chicago; natl spokesperson for AIDS & diabetes associations; spokesperson, Long Beach Ballet Dance Camp, 1990-91; Willie Gault's Youth Enrichment Program. **Honors/Awds:** First man in history of NCAA to win both 60 yards & 60 yard hurdles 1982; MVP Univ of Tennessee Track & Football Team 1983; Athlete of the Year in the Southeastern Conf 1983; NFL All Rookie Team Football Chicago Bears 1983; World record in 4x100 relay track & field 1983; World record 4x110 hurdlers track & field 1982; First Place, Super Stars Competitions, 1989, 1990. **Home Addr:** 7700 Sunset Blvd, #205, Los Angeles, CA 90046.

GAVIN, JAMES RAPHAEL, III
Physician. **Personal:** Born Nov 23, 1945, Mobile, AL; son of Bessie S Gavin and James R Gavin, II; married Dr Annie Ruth Jackson Gavin, Jun 19, 1971; children: Raphael Hakkim, Lamar Kenyon. **Educ:** Livingstone Coll, BS (Magna Cum Laude) 1966; Emory Univ, PhD 1970; Duke Univ Medical School, MD 1975. **Career:** Natl Insts of Health, staff assoc 1971-73; Duke Univ Hospital, pathologist 1975-76; US Public Health Service, commander 2 1/2 yrs active, 11 1/2 yrs reserves; Washington Univ School of Medicine, assoc prof medicine 1979-86; Univ of OK Med Center, prof of medicine 1986-, chief diabetes sect 1987-; OUHSC, OK City, William K Warren prof of Diabetes Studies, 1989-91; Howard Hughes Med Inst, senior scientific officer, 1991-. **Orgs:** Life mem Alpha Phi Alpha 1963-; bd of dirs Amer Diabetes Assn 1983-87; Pres, American Diabetes Assn, 1993-94; bd of dirs Alpha Educ Foundation 1986-; mem Alpha Omega Alpha; natl program dir & sr program consultant, Robert Wood Johnson Foundation, 1987-; trustee, OK Sch Science, Math Foundation, 1992-; member, National Diabetes Advisory Board 1988-92; member, NIDDK Advisory Council, 1995-; trustee, Robert Wood Johnson Foundation, 1996-. **Honors/Awds:** Clinical Teacher of the Year Barnes Hosp Dept Med 1981-82; Wm Alexander Leadership Award Epsilon Lambda Alpha Phi Alpha 1982; St Louis Sentinel Special Achiever St Louis Sentinel 1982; Distinguished Alumnus of HBI NAFEO 1987; Editoral Board, Academic Medicine, 1994-; Outstanding Clinician in Field of Diabetes, Amer Diabetes Assn, 1990; member Amer Assn Academic Minority Physicians, 1988-; member Amer Soc Clin Invest 1985-; member, Amer Assn of Physicians, 1992-; Banting Medal for Distinguished Service, Amer Diabetes Assn, 1994; Institute of Medicine of NAS, 1996-. **Business Addr:** Senior Scientific Officer, Howard Hughes Medical Institute, 4000 Jones Bridge Rd, Chevy Chase, MD 20815.

GAVIN, L. KATHERINE
Educational administrator. **Personal:** Born in Chicago Heights, IL. **Educ:** Chicago State U, BA 1952; Columbia U, MA 1963; Nova U, EdD 1976. **Career:** Prairie State Coll, dir peronalized learning program 1970-, dir child devel progran 1968; Lincoln School, Chicago Heights School Dist #170, prin 1966; Chicago Heights School Dist #170, dean of students, classroom instructor. **Orgs:** Helped found IL Assn of Personalized Learning Programs 1974; mem exec com conducts many workshops/Presenter at many confs/eg SESS-IAPLP-NCTE; mem S Suburban Chicgo Chap of Links Inc; chariperson bd of dirs Dr Chrles E Gavin Meml Found; mem NAACP PUSH. **Honors/Awds:** Outstanding citizens award PUSH; outstanding civic and serv to youth S Suburb Chicago Chap of Links Inc; scholarship image award Fred Hampton Found; lifetime hon ALUMNI Assn Gov State U; mem Hall of Fame Bloom Township High Sch 1980; recognition award outstanding serv Prairie State Coll. **Business Addr:** 202 S Halsted St, Chicago Heights, IL 60411.

GAVIN, MARY ANN
Federal official. **Personal:** Born Aug 8, 1945, Elmhurst, IL; daughter of Evelyn Thomas-Wilford (deceased) and Vernus; married Joeneather Gavin, May 23, 1966; children: Charles A, Darrell E. **Educ:** College of St Francis, Il BA, 1973. **Career:** Social Security Administration, svc rep, 1973-76, claims rep, 1976-79, supervisor, 1979-85, management info specialist, 1985-86, labor relations management analyst, 1986-89, section chief of labor relations, 1989-. **Orgs:** Social Security Black Caucus, 1996; Black Advisory Council, 1994-96; Woman's Advisory Council, 1995-96. **Honors/Awds:** Social Security Administration, Commissioners Citation, 1996, Regional Commissioners Citation, 1995, Excellence In Svc Awd, 1994; Chicago Federal Executive Board, Federal Employee of the Year Nominee, 1995, 1996. **Home Addr:** 1920 Tawny Ct, Joliet, IL 60435. **Business Addr:** Section Chief, Social Security Administration, Labor Employee Relations Team, 600 W Madison St, 3rd FL, Chicago, IL 60601, (312)353-4792.

GAY, BENJAMIN
Clergyman, educator. **Personal:** Born Oct 22, 1916, Valdosta, GA; married Johnnie Morgan. **Educ:** Morris Brown Coll, AB; Turner Theol Sem, BD. **Career:** AME Mem, minister. **Orgs:** Tau Beta Chap Phi Beta Sigma Frat 1974; NAACP; treas GA Ann Conf; bd tsts Morrison Brown Coll; past mem Gen Bd of African Meth Epis Ch; natl secAlumni Assn of Turner Theol Sem. **Honors/Awds:** Ldrsp recog Civil Rights Movement; religious achvmt award Nat Alumni Assn; outsdng pastor of yr Morris Brown Coll 1975; award of the GA Ann Conf forComm Serv; Ann Founder's Day Speaker 1977; dr of humane letters degree AME Ch 1977. **Business Addr:** PO Box 1151, Savannah, GA 31401.

GAY, BIRDIE SPIVEY
Media specialist. **Personal:** Born Mar 13, 1918, Atlanta; married Howard Donald. **Educ:** Morris Brown Coll, Grad 1939; Atlanta Univ Sch of Library Svc, 1962. **Career:** Brooks County, tchr 1939-41; Eatonton, GA, 1941-42; Moutlrie, GA, tchr, librn 1942-45; ER Carter Elem Sch Atlanta, 1946-59; librn & media spec 1959-. **Orgs:** Mem Atlanta GA Assn & Educators; NEA; GA Am Library Assn; mem Com on Adminstrn YWCA; solicitor Cancer Drive, Easter, Retarded Children, Muscular Dystrophy; mem NAACP; UNCF; Morris Brown Alumni Assn; Eta Sigma chpt, Sigma Gamma Rho Sor Beta Phi Mu intl libr4ry sci Hon Frat 1961. **Honors/Awds:** Tchr of yr ER Carter Sch 1960-61; outstanding serv plaque Sigma Gamma Rho Sor 1970. **Business Addr:** E R Carter Sch, 80 Ashby St NW, Atlanta, GA 30314.

GAY, EDDIE C.
Chemical engineer. **Personal:** Born May 13, 1940, Starkville, MS; married Sylvia J; children: Steven E, Richard C. **Educ:** BS 1962; DSc 1967. **Career:** Argonne Nat Lab Battery Prog; mgr 1975; Argonne Natl Lab Battery Prgm, grp ldr 1941-75; Lithium-chalcogen Cell Devel Argonne Nat Lab, problem ldr 1969-71; Lithium & Chalcogen Cell Devel Argonne Nat Lab, asst engr 1968-69. **Orgs:** Mem Electrochemical Soc; Am Inst Chem Engr; sigma xi; pres Nat Orgn Professional Advancement Black Chemists & Chem Engr; mem Faith United Protestant Ch. **Honors/Awds:** Faith United Protestant Ch schlorship Rosalie Tilles Scholarship; resident res Thesis Award Argonne Nat Lab; dist military Student Grad. **Military Serv:** US Army, capt, 1967-68. **Business Addr:** Chem Engineering Div, 9700 S Cass, Argonne, IL 60439.

GAY, HELEN PARKER
City official, caterer. **Personal:** Born Mar 14, 1920, Rocky Mount, NC; daughter of Dillie Virginia Shaw Parker and Frank Leslie Parker Sr (deceased); divorced; children: Leslie Claudius Gay (deceased). **Educ:** Barber-Scotia College; North Carolina State College. **Career:** Employment Security Com of NC, interviewer II 37 years; Rocky Mount City Council, council mem, 1987-, mayor pro tem, 1993; caterer. **Orgs:** Region IV chairperson, 1991, president, 1993-, NC Black Elected Municipal Officials; board member, NC League of Cities, 1990-91; elder, clerk of session, Mt Pisgah Presbyterian Church, Rocky Mount, 1990-91, 1993-; bd mem, Community Shelter for Homeless. **Honors/Awds:** 1st place Merit Awd Emp Sec Com of NC 1950; 2nd place Merit Awd Emp Sec Com of NC 1960; chosen as one of the Outstanding Women of the 20th Century, Honorary Mbr, Sigma Gamma Rho Sor Inc 1986; membership Rocky Mount Moles Inc 1988; honorary life mbr Presbyterian Women Rocky Mt 1989. **Special Achievements:** First African-American female elected council member, Rocky Mount City Council, mayor pro tem, 1985; first African-American member, Rocky Mount Rotary Club; first African-American elected president, NC Chapter, International Assn of Personnel in Employment Sec, 1972-73. **Home Addr:** 1629 Kings Circle, Rocky Mount, NC 27801.

GAY, JAMES F.
Attorney at law, business executive. **Personal:** Born Dec 9, 1942, Norfolk, VA; married Marlynn Miller; children: James F Jr. **Educ:** Norfolk State Coll, BS Chem 1965; Univ of VA Law School, JD 1968. **Career:** Allied Chem Corp, legal adv 1968; Natl Business League, asst to pres 1969; Tidewater Area Business League, past pres; Coastal Pharmaceutical Co Inc, pres 1970-77; Energy Dynamics Inc, pres; Legal Center of Gay & Simmons, sr partner; Aqua Dynamics, pres. **Orgs:** Mem Natl Bar Assn, Natl Platform Soc, VA State Bar, Amer Judicature Soc, Amer Bar Assn, Twin City-Bar Assn, Old Dom Bar Assn; gen council, bd mem Natl Business League; mem Natl Soc for Prevention of Cruelty to Animals, Planned Parenthood, Cancer Assn, Norfolk Comm for Imp of Educ, JCC, Alpha Phi Alpha. **Honors/Awds:** Phi Beta Lambda Business Leadership Awd. **Business Addr:** President, Aqua Dynamics, 1317 E Brambleton Ave, Norfolk, VA 23504.

GAYLE, HELENE DORIS
Physician. **Personal:** Born Aug 16, 1955, Buffalo, NY; daughter of Marietta D Gayle and Jacob A Gayle. **Educ:** Barnard College, New York, NY, BA, 1976; University of Pennsylvania, Philadelphia, PA, MD, 1981; Johns Hopkins University, Baltimore, MD, MPH, 1981. **Career:** Children's Hospital National Medical Center, Washington, DC, pediatric resident, 1981-84; Centers for Disease Control, Epidemic Intelligence Service, 1984-86, Atlanta, GA, medical epidemiologist, 1986-87; Centers for Disease Control, Pediatric and Family Studies Section, medical epidemiologist, 1987-89, Division of HIV/AIDS, asst chief for science, 1989-90, chief, international activity, 1990-92, agency AIDS coordinator and chief, 1992-94; Washington Centers for Disease Control and Prevention, associate director, 1994-95; Natl Center for HIV, STD, and TB Prevention, Centers for Disease Control and Prevention, director, 1995-. **Orgs:** Member, American Public Health Assn; member, American Academy of Pediatrics; member, National Medical Assn; member, International AIDS Society. **Honors/Awds:** Outstanding Unit Citation, 1989, 1990; US Public Health Service, Achievement Medal, 1989; Celebration of Public Service Award, 1990; National Merit Scholar Fellowship Award, 1981; Henrietta & Jacob Lowenburg Prize, 1981; Joel Gordon Miller Award, 1981; Administrators and Black Faculty Merit Award, Univ of PA, 1981; co-author, "Prevalence of Human Immunodeficiency Virus among College and University Students," New England Journal of Medicine, 1990; co-author, "The Epidemiology of AIDS and Human Immunodeficiency Virus Infection in Adolescents," in The Challenge of HIV Infection in Infants, 1991; Colgate-Palmolive Company, Model of Excellence, 1992; US Public Health Service, Outstanding Service Medal, 1992, Unit Commendation Medal, 1992; National Coalition of 100 Black Women, Serwa Award, 1995; US Public Health Service, Poindexter Award, 1996; Columbia University, Medal of Excellence, 1996. **Business Addr:** Director, Natl Ctr for HIV, STD, and TB Prevention, Centers for Disease Control and Prevention, 1600 Clifton Rd, NE, Mailstop E07, Atlanta, GA 30333.

GAYLE, LUCILLE JORDAN
Educational administrator (retired). **Personal:** Born Jun 10, 1920, Leegate, TN; daughter of Ella Brewer Jordan and James Henry Jordan; married Robert E Gayle, Jun 15, 1950. **Educ:** Lincoln Univ, Jefferson City MO, BS Early Childhood Educ, 1942; Teachers Coll, Columbia Univ, New York NY, MA Early Childhood Educ, 1949, Professional Diploma in Guidance, 1954; Digby Coll, London, England, 1967-69; Amer UGWU, Howard Univ, Washington DC; Washington School of Psychology, New York. **Career:** Agee School, Dalton MO, teacher, 1942-43; Washington Elementary School, Jefferson City, MO, teacher, 1942-47; Lowell School, Alton IL, teacher, 1947-48; Attucks School, Kansas City MO, teacher, 1948-54; Grimke School, Washington DC, teacher, 1954-63; Administrative, Washington DC, asst dir guidance dept, 1963-76 (retired). **Orgs:** Awards coord, Amer Bridge Assn, 1962-92; prog planner, scholarship, Northal Portal Civic Assn, 1964-; mem, NAACP, 1970-, Urban League, 1970-, Natl Council of Negro Women, life mem, 1980-; vice pres 1984-88, natl pres 1988-92, Chums Inc; poll worker, Washington DC Bd of Election; mem, Minority Political Women's Assn, 1986-, Black Women's Agenda, 1988-96; Natl Coalition of Black Meeting Planners, 1982-; Clothing for Children, board member, 1980-94. **Honors/Awds:** Publisher/Owner, Agnes Myer Fellowship, Washington Post, 1969; Delegate to White House Conf for Children, 1970; Distinguished Alumni Award, Lincoln Univ, Jefferson City MO, 1974; Commr for the Aging, District of Columbia Mayor Marion Barry, 1988-. **Home Addr:** 8339 E Beach Drive NW, Washington, DC 20012-1008.

GAYLES, FRANKLIN JOHNSON
Government official & educational administrator (retired). **Personal:** Born in Marshallville, GA; son of Marian Richardson Gayles and Franklin Johnson Gayles Sr; married Ruth Teele; children: Michael Perry. **Educ:** Univ of Illinois, AB 1939-42, AM 1946-47; New York Univ PhD (highest honors) 1960. **Career:** Virginia Union Univ, prof pol sci, div dir, academic dean 1948-80; City of Richmond, treasurer, 1979-93. **Orgs:** Mem Treasurers' Assoc of Virginia, Assoc of Constitutional Officers of Virginia; life mem Alpha Phi Alpha, Sigma Pi Phi, Crusade of Voters, NAACP; Serves on Bd of Friends of Housing Opportunities Made Equal. **Honors/Awds:** Founders Day Awd from New York Univ, 1976; Civic Awd from Alpha Phi Alpha, 1983; Civic Awd from Delta Sigma Theta, 1983; Univ of PA, Moton Scholar, 1976; Awarded 1st John Hancock Distinguished Chair, 1977. **Military Serv:** USN 1942-46.

GAYLES, JOSEPH NATHAN WEBSTER, JR.
Corporate official, educator, educational administrator, scientist. **Personal:** Born Aug 7, 1937, Birmingham, AL; son of Earnestine Williams-Gayles and Joseph N Gayles Sr; children: Jonathan, Monica. **Educ:** Dillard Univ, AB (summa cum laude) 1958; Brown Univ, PhD 1963. **Career:** Bur of the Census, demographic stat 1957-58; Brown Univ, rsch assoc 1958-62; OR State Univ, post doc rsch assoc, asst prof; Morehouse Coll, Woodrow Wilson tchg assoc 1963-66; IBM, staff sci & proj dir 1966-69; Morehouse Coll, prof (tenured) 1969-77, assoc prof chem 1969-71; Morehouse School of Med, founder 1975-77; Morehouse Med Ed Prog, founder, prog dir 1972-75; Morehouse Coll, health professions adv 1971-77; Talladega Coll, pres 1977-83; Jon-Mon & Assoc, chairman, ceo 1983-; Morehouse School of Med, vice pres 1983-96; research professor of medicine, 1983-96; Jon-Mon Associates, chairman, currently. **Orgs:** Bd tests Morehouse Coll 1973-77; consult Whitney Found, Ford Found, Woodrow Wilson Found; bd tests Woodrow Wilson Found; National Board Director, NSFRE; consult Natl Inst of Health & DHHS; bd of visitors MIT; mem Alpha Phi Alpha, Reg III chr of brd, Council for Adm and support of education; Amer Chem Soc, Amer Physical Soc, Phi Beta Kappa, Sigma Xi, BXC, AAAS, Amer Assoc of Pol & Soc Sci, GA Conservancy, Sigma Pi Phi; nat assn of fund raising executives. **Honors/Awds:** Andover Full Support Scholarship Phillips Acad 1953; Exchange Cup Scholar 1954; Brawley Writing Awd 1955; Davage Awd; Brown Univ Fellow; Summer European Travel Fellowship 1965; Rhom & Haas Fellow; Woodrow Wilson Teaching Fellow; Drefus Teacher Scholarship; Powers Travel Fellow 1975; Teacher of the Year Morehouse Coll 1976; Disting Alumnus Awd Dillard 1977; Omega Psi Phi Ed Achievement Awd; Comm Serv Awd Elks; Ed Achievement Awd, Emancipation Day Comm Birmingham 1980; Kiwanis Talladega; Morehouse School of Medicine Award, Trustees, 1985; Honorary Degree (LLD), Dillard Univ, 1983; Rotary, Atlanta, 1992-. **Business Addr:** Chairman, Jon-Mon Associates, 1515 Austin Rd, SW, Atlanta, GA 30331-2205.

GAYLES, LINDSEY, JR.
City government official. **Personal:** Born Jul 6, 1953, Memphis, TN; son of Ella Woods and Lindsey Gayles Sr; married Shirley Ann Baines, Feb 17, 0983; children: Chanel Shanta. **Educ:** Univ of Illinois, Urbana IL, Bachelor's of Urban Planning, 1976; Roosevelt Univ, Chicago IL, attending. **Career:** City of Chicago, Chicago IL, sr research asst, 1977-83, city planner, 1983-84, admin asst, 1984-85, Office of Mayor, city council liaison, 1985-; Gayles & Associates Inc, pres, 1986-. **Orgs:** Bd of dir, chmn program comm, Demmicco Youth Serv Inc, 1988-. **Honors/Awds:** Publications: The Cabrini-Green High Impact Program Final Report, City of Chicago, Dept of Planning, 1979; Municipal Security Report: 71st Street Study, City of Chicago, Dept of Planning, 1981; Tournament Coord, Mayor Harold Washington's Holiday (boys and girls) High School Basketball Tournament, 1983-85; Chmn of Mayor Harold Washington's Host Comm for the World Conf of Mayors, 1986; Distinguished Serv Award, Chicago Coalition of Urban Professionals, 1986.

GAYLES-FELTON, ANNE RICHARDSON
Educator. **Personal:** Born Jun 4, 1923, Marshallville, GA; daughter of Marion R Gayles and Franklin J Gayles; married Ambrose M Felton (died 1994). **Educ:** Fort Valley State Coll, BS 1943; Columbia Univ, MA 1949, Prof Diploma, 1953; IN Univ, EdD 1961. **Career:** Stillman Coll, dir student teaching 1952-54; Albany State Coll, 1954-57; FL A&M Univ, dir student teaching 1957-62, head dept of secondary educ 1962-82, prof of secondary educ 1982-; Fort Valley State Coll, instructor, social sciences, 1949-52; Rust Coll Associate Prof of Social Sciences; Arkansas Baptist Coll Head Dept of Sociology 1950-51; Georgia Public Schools, teacher, 10 years. **Orgs:** 1st vice pres Assn of Social & Behavioral Serv 1961-62; exec comm Soc of Prof Educ 1969-70; served on committees Amer Assn in Teacher Educ Coll 1970-80; comm on master teacher Assn of Teacher Educators 1982-85; Delta Sigma Theta; Pi Lambda Theta; Phi Delta Kappa; Kappa Delta Pi; Alpha Kappa Mu; Pi Gamma Mu; Natl Republican Party Presidential Task Force; State of Florida Governors Commemorative Celebration Comm on Dr Martin Luther King, Jr; Governor's Bd of Independent Coll & Univ, State of Florida; Governor's Comm on Quality Educ; Urban League; Republican Party of Florida; United States/China Joint Conference on Education, Beijing, China, invited participant, 1992; United States Military Academy Appointments Board, appointed, several times, by Senator Hawkins (Florida); Citizen Ambassador Program, People to People International, invited participant, 1992. **Honors/Awds:** Florida A&M University, Teacher of the Year, 1989, College of Education, Teacher of the Year, 1991; Fort Valley State College, Alumni Hall of Fame, Inductee, 1984, Division of Social Science, Distinguished Alumni Award; "A Consortium of Doctors: Women of Color in the Struggle," Banquet Honoree, 1991; FAMU Teacher Incentive Award; Assn of Teacher Educators, Distinguished Teacher Educator, 1990; saluted "Living Legend," Florida A & M Univ, 1997. **Special Achievements:** Author: two books; three monograph; co-author of one book and two monographs; 63 articles; 5 research studies; 5 bibliographies; dissertation, editor, writer, reader for first book devoted soley to Multicultural Education; Delivered paper at the 43rd World Assembly of the Intl Council on Education for Teaching in Amman Jordan; chmn of the Lamson Richardson Scholarship Foundation, founded in 1886. **Home Addr:** 609 Howard Ave, Tallahassee, FL 32310. **Business Addr:** Professor of Secondary Education, Florida A&M University, Tallahassee, FL 32307.

GAYLE-THOMPSON, DELORES J.
Physician. **Personal:** Born Feb 28, 1938, Portland, Jamaica; daughter of Lucilda Rebecca Gayle and William Ellison; married Amos F Thompson, Aug 28, 1965; children: Colin, Allison. **Educ:** Howard Univ, Coll of Liberal Arts BS 1963, Coll of Medicine MD 1967; Columbia Univ School of Public Health, MPH 1984. **Career:** Freedmen's Hospital Washington, intern 1967-68; Harlem Hospital, resident in pediatrics 1968-70, physician pediatric clinic 1970-83, assoc dir 1983-; College of Physicians and Surgeons, Columbia University, asst professor of pediatrics, 1990-. **Orgs:** Natl Medical Assn, 1979-; Ambulatory Pediatric Assn, 1979-; Amer Public Health Assn, 1982-. **Honors/Awds:** Citation Howard Univ Century Club 1986; Citation & Membership Howard Univ President's Club 1986; Civic Awd Friends of East Portland Jamaica West Indies 1986. **Business Addr:** Assoc Dir, Ambulatory Pediatric, Harlem Hospital Center, 506 Lenox Ave, New York, NY 10037.

GAYLOR, ADOLPH DARNELL
Senior engineer. **Personal:** Born Apr 26, 1950, Natchez, MS; son of Jessie Beatrice Bland Gaylor and Adolph Gaylor; married Margaret Ann Green, Jun 2, 1973; children: Adrienne Danielle. **Educ:** Southern Univ, Baton Rouge, LA, BSEE, 1972; Alabama A & M Univ, Huntsville, AL, MBA, 1984. **Career:** TN Valley Authority, St Louis, MO, materials eng, 1972-75; TN Valley Authority, Birmingham, AL, materials eng, 1975-82; TN Valley Authority, Bellefonte Nuclear Plt, QA eng, 1982-83; Ballistic Missile Defense Systems Command, Huntsville, AL, PA eng, 1983-85; Southern Co Services, Birmingham, AL, sr eng, 1985-. **Orgs:** Pres, Southern Univ Alumni, 1988-90; financial sec, Alpha Phi Alpha, 1990-; pres, Alpha Phi Alpha, Omicron Lambda Chpt, 1993-95; mem, NAACP, 1985-; mem, Natl Urban League, 1989-; public relations chair, American Assn of Blacks in Energy, 1989-. **Honors/Awds:** Letter of Commendation, 1985; Engineering Service Award, Engineers for Professional Development, 1990.

GAYLORD, ELLIHUE, SR.
Pastor. **Personal:** Born Aug 15, 1922, Center Ridge, AR; married Aurelia; children: Carolyn Riane, Ellihue Jr, Ronald Wayne. **Educ:** AM&N Coll Pine Bluff AR, BS 1950. **Career:** Starlight Baptist Church, pastor 1964-; Farmers Home Admin, asst co supervisor 1965-79, county supervisor 1979-80; Columbia Baptist District Congress, pres. **Orgs:** Mem Omega Psi Phi Frat 1970-; bd mem AR Black Caucus 1978-; AR Farm Land Develop Co 1980-; bd mem Columbia Bapt Dist Assoc 1984-; state pres NAACP 1984-; bd mem Natl NAACP 1985-; bd mem Urban League of AR 1985-. **Honors/Awds:** Outstanding Service Urban League of AR, Senator Donald Pryor, El Dorado, Governor of AR. **Military Serv:** AUS pfc 2 yrs. **Home Addr:** 71 Timberlane Dr, Magnolia, AR 71753.

GAYMON, NICHOLAS EDWARD
Librarian (retired). **Personal:** Born Apr 8, 1928, Pinewood, SC; son of Viola and Rufus; married Clara B. Floyd; children: Renwick, Dara, Warren, Debra. **Educ:** Morehouse Coll, AB 1956; Atlanta Univ, MSLS 1959; FL State Univ, AMD 1973, PhD 1975. **Career:** Lockheed Aircraft Corp, structural assemblyman 1953-59; Atlanta Univ, acquisitions librarian 1959-65, circulation librarian 1965; Dillard Univ, head librarian 1965-69; FL State Univ, adj instr 1974; FL A&M Univ, dir of libraries 1969-. **Orgs:** Mem FL Library Assn; mem SE Library Assn, Amer Library Assn; participant Lawrence Livermore Lab 1977; mem So Assn Visiting Com of Coll & Sch 1971-; mem SE Library Network 1978-; exec bd Dist Adv Counc for Leon Co Sch Bd 1978-; mem Black Caucus of Amer Library Assn; vice pres 1890 Land Grant Colls 1979-. **Honors/Awds:** Ford Found Grant 1967. **Military Serv:** AUS corpl 1951-53.

GAYTON, GARY D.
Attorney. **Personal:** Born Feb 25, 1933, Seattle. **Educ:** Univ of WA, BA 1955; Gonzaga U, JD 1962. **Career:** Stern, Gayton, Neubauer & Brucker, att PS 1965; Western Dist Wash, asst US att 1962-65. **Orgs:** Mem Am Bar Assn; Am Trial Lawyers Assn; King Co Bar Assn; Wash State Bar Assn; Nat Bar Assn; bd mem Universal Security Life Ins Co; Past SeattlePark Comm; mem Seattle Repertory Bd; past mem Seattle Ethics & Fair Camp Comm; mem Seattle King Co Bicentennial Comm; mem bd Salvation Army; mem bd of NW Civic Cultural & Char Orgns; past bd mem NAACP; mem bd inst of black am Music Inc. **Military Serv:** AUS 1955-57. **Business Addr:** Attorney, Sylvester, Ruud, Petrie & Cruzen, 2600 Columbia Center, 701 5th Ave, Seattle, WA 98104.

GEARRING, JOEL KENNETH
Sales and marketing executive. **Personal:** Born May 9, 1936, East Chicago, IN; son of Ruschelle Edwards Gearring and Hollis Gearring; married Carol Rancifer Gearring, Nov 18, 1967; children: Philip, David, Joel R, Timothy. **Educ:** Fisk University, Nashville, TN, 1953-55; Loop City College, Chicago, IL, 1960-64; Loma Institute, Chicago, IL, 1983-. **Career:** Western Electric, Chicago, IL, draftsman, 1955-65; Inland Steel, East Chicago, IN, draftsman, 1966; Prudential, Chicago, IL, agent, 1966-67; Mutual Benefit Life, Chicago, IL, agent, 1967-70; Aetna Life, Chicago, IL, director manager, 1970-81; Supreme Life, Chicago, IL, vice pres/agency, 1981-. **Orgs:** Member/board of trustees, Metropolitan Community Church, 1980-; member/board, Elliott Donnelly Youth Center, 1975-83; president/board, Beacon House Neighborhood Center, 1975-77; member/board, Hyde Park-Kenwood Health Center, 1974-77; founder/chairman, Aetna Life's Black Agents Task Force, 1975-79. **Honors/Awds:** Regionnaire Sales Award, Aetna Life, 1972-75; National Quality Award, National Association of Life Underwriters, 1979-81; Author, Magazine Articles, Insurance Sales Magazine, 1984, 1986, 1990; Certificate of Service, American Hospital Association, 1974-77; Certificate of Service, North Central Accreditation Association, 1990. **Business Addr:** Vice President, Supreme Life Insurance Co of America, 222 Merchandise Mart Plaza #1450, Chicago, IL 60654-1203.

GEARY, CLARENCE BUTLER
Psychiatrist (retired). **Personal:** Born Aug 1, 1912, Steelton, PA; son of Annie Adams Geary and Robert M Geary; married Harriet Williams; children: Steven Craig. **Educ:** Howard Univ Wash DC, BS 1937, MD 1944; Provident Hosp Chgo, Intern in Gen Med 1945-46. **Career:** Cook Cty School of Nursing, instr 1948-53; Cook Cty Hosp, staff psychiatrist 1949-59; Mercy Hosp Clinic, clinic psych 1949-51; Chicago Police Dept, consult psych 1954-61; Chicago Municipal Court, staff psych 1959-63; Cook Cty Hosp, staff psych 1963-78, dir dept of psych 1970-72, dir liaison div 1973-78; Chicago Coll of Osteopathic Med, clinical prof psych 1978; Private practice, psych 1949-96. **Orgs:** Natl Med Assoc 1950-65; AMA 1951-; Amer Psych Assoc 1951-80; diplomate Amer Bd of Psych & Neurology 1951; Natl Assoc of Fed Disability 1969-73; life mem Amer Psych Assoc 1980-, NAACP; Urban League, Druids Mens Club of Chgo; emeritus mem AMA & affiliates 1982; 50 Year Club Howard Univ; life mem, AMA; life mem, APA; 50 Year Club Howard Univ, Med Alumni Assn; retired. **Honors/Awds:** 10 Yrs Recog Awd Howard Univ Coll of Med 1972-84; Physicians Recog Awd AMA 1974-77, 1979-82; Physicians Serv Awd Cook Cty Hosp Chicago 1975; Physicians Recog Awd AMA, APA 1982-85. **Military Serv:** US Army, MAC 2nd lt 1942-44. **Business Addr:** 1137 E 50th St, Chicago, IL 60615.

GEARY, REGGIE (REGINALD ELLIOT)
Professional basketball player. **Personal:** Born Aug 31, 1973, Trenton, NJ. **Educ:** Arizona. **Career:** Cleveland Cavaliers, guard, 1996-97; San Antonio Spurs, 1997-. **Business Addr:** Professional Basketball Player, San Antonio Spurs, 600 E Market St, San Antonio, TX 78205, (210)554-7773.

GEATHERS, JUMPY (JAMES ALLEN)
Professional football player. **Personal:** Born Jun 26, 1960, Georgetown, SC. **Educ:** Wichita State. **Career:** New Orleans Saints, defensive end, 1984-89; Washington Redskins, 1990-92; Atlanta Falcons, 1993-95; Denver Broncos, 1996-. **Business Addr:** Professional Football Player, Denver Broncos, 13655 Broncos Pkwy, Englewood, CO 80112, (303)649-9000.

GECAU, KIMANI J.
Educator. **Personal:** Born Jul 17, 1947; married. **Educ:** Univ of East Africa, BA 1969; McMaster Univ, MA 1970; State Univ of New York, PhD 1975. **Career:** McMaster Univ, teaching asst 1969-70; SUNY Buffalo, teaching asst 1970-72; State Univ Coll Buffalo, instructor 1970-71; Geneseo, instructor 1972-75; Univ of Nairobi, lecturer 1975-. **Business Addr:** Lecturer, Dept of Literature, Univ of Nairobi, Box 30197, Nairobi, Kenya.

GEE, AL (ALBERT GERMANY)
Disc jockey, director. **Personal:** Born Oct 23, 1942, Leeds, AL; married Jessica Khan; children: Mark, Shawn. **Educ:** Univ of Pittsburgh Geo Heide Sch of Announcing, 1964. **Career:** WLIB NY, prgm dir 1973; WLIB NY, 1973; WPIX, 1972; WWRL, 1968-72; Washington Radio, U968; WZUM Pittsburgh, 1966-68; WAMO, 1964-66; Syndicated Radio Show Rap & Rythm; Radio Station ZDK, co-owner; NATRA Natl Assn of radio & TV Announcers, exec dir 1976-77; St Johns Antiqua Professional Black Announcers of NY, West Indies pres. **Business Addr:** 801 2nd Ave, New York, NY.

GEE, WILLIAM ROWLAND, JR.
Engineer. **Personal:** Born Oct 4, 1940, Washington, DC; son of Marietta L Brittain Gee and William Rowland Gee; married Sadie H Phillips; children: Moira G Travis, Morris B, Cathy P Kearney, Julia E, W Rowland III. **Educ:** Howard U, BSME (cum laude) 1962; Oak Ridge Sch of Reactor Tech, Nuclear Eng 1963; Stanford U, MS Applied Mech 1971; Loyola Coll Baltimore MBA 1981. **Career:** US Atomic Energy Commn, project engr 1962-66; GE Breeder Reactor Devel, engr 1966-73; Potomac Electric Power Co, mgr nuclear engineering 1975-77, mgr generating engineering 1981-89, vice pres system engineering, 1989-. **Orgs:** Omega Psi Phi; ASME; ANS; Edison Electric Institute. **Home Addr:** 1006 Coral Berry Ct, Great Falls, VA 22066. **Business Addr:** Vice Pres, System Engineering, Potomac Electric Power Co, 1900 Pennsylvania Ave, NW, Washington, DC 20068.

GELLINEAU, VICTOR MARCEL, JR.
Marketing executive. **Personal:** Born Nov 3, 1942, New York, NY; son of Marcella Gonzalez Gellineau and Victor M Gellineau; married Carole Joy Johnston, Jun 5, 1965; children: Victor M III, Maria M, Carmen E. **Educ:** Howard Univ, BA 1967; Baruch Coll of Business & Public Admin, MBA 1974. **Career:** Burlington Industries, salesman 1967-69; Lever Bros, asst product mgr 1969-71; Amer Home Products, product mgr 1971-73; Zebra Assoc, vice pres dir of acct mgmt 1973-76; Heublein Inc, mktg mgr 1976-83; Ponderosa Inc, dir mktg 1983-85; General Foods Corp, sr product mgr 1985-89; Carol Joy Creations Inc, president. **Orgs:** Mem Amer Mgmt Assn 1970-; visiting prof Natl Urban League Beep Prog 1974-; bd mem pres Artists Collective 1978-83; bd mem pres, Junior Achievement 1978-; mem Natl Black MBA Assn 1983-; facilitator Inroads; bd member, United Way Allocations Committee 1989-. **Honors/Awds:** Black Achiever Awd, Hartford YMCA 1980; State of Conn, Minority Business Develop Awd, 1992; Danbury NAACP, Comm Service Awd, 1993; JC Penney, Minority Supplier Awd, 1994. **Business Addr:** Carole Joy Creations, Inc, 107 Mill Plain Road, Suite 200, Danbury, CT 06811, (203)798-2060.

GENTRY, ALVIN
Professional basketball coach. **Personal:** Born in Shelby, NC; married Suzanne Harris, Sep 22; children: Alexis. **Educ:** Appalachian State Univ. **Career:** Colorado Univ, student assistant coach; Baylor Univ, coach; Colorado Univ, coach; Kansas Univ, assistant coach; San Antonio Spurs, assistant coach/scout; Los Angeles Clippers, assistant coach; Miami Heat, head coach, until 1995; Detroit Pistons, asst coach, head coach, 1998. **Business Addr:** Head Coach, Detroit Pistons, Two Championship Drive, Auburn Hills, MI 48326, (248)377-0100.

GENTRY, ATRON A.
Educator. **Personal:** Born in El Centro, CA; son of Hannah Gentry and Horace Gentry. **Educ:** Pasadena City Clge, AA 1958; CA State Polytechnic Clge, 1959; CA State Univ at Los Angeles, BA 1966; Univ of MA, EdD 1970. **Career:** Apple Creek State Inst OH, asst supr 1975-76; Cleveland State Hosp OH, supr 1976-78; Hull Clge of Higher Educ Hull England, visiting prof 1981; Univ of MA, prof of educ; Visiting Professor in Beijing Tchrs Coll 1986. **Orgs:** Assc dean Schl of Educ Univ of MA 1971-72, 1972-75, dir of the Center for Urban Educ 1968-71; staff mem 1984 Olympic Games L A Olympic Org Comm 1984; Kentucky Colonel 1974; mem Phi Delta Kappa 1971; Dir of Boston Scndry Schls Project, a collaborative prgm between Univ of Mass at Amherst & Boston Secondary Schls. **Honors/Awds:** Citizen of the Year Omega Psi Frat 1967; Urban Srv Award Ofc of Econ Apport US Govt 1966; Urban Educ The Hope Factor Philadelphia Sounder 1972; The Politics of Urban Educ for the 80's Natl Assn of Sec Schl Principals 1980; Dedication & Service, Boston Secondary School Project 1987; The Dr. Carter G. Woodson Memorial Uplift Award Tau Iota Chapter, Omega Psi Fraternity 1988; Crispus Attucks Award, National Committee for Commemoration of America's Revolutionary War Black Patriot, 1991. **Special Achievements:** Author, Learning to Survive: Black Youth Look for Education and Hope; Co-editor, Equity and Excellence in Education. **Military Serv:** AUS sgt 1954-56. **Business Addr:** Professor of Educ, School of Educ, Univ of Massachusetts, Amherst, MA 01002.

GENTRY, LAMAR DUANE
Government official. **Personal:** Born Dec 19, 1946, Chicago, IL; children: Mark J, LaMar P, Carlos D. **Educ:** So IL Univ, BA 1970; Univ of IL, JD 1979. **Career:** Gov Ofc IL, model cities specialist 1970-72, dir model cities 1972-74, dir prog planning & devel 1974-75; Capital Devel Bd IL, regional sch dist analyst 1975-76; City of E St Louis IL, commr comm develop 1981, acting comptroller 1983, dep mayor dir of adminis 1979-. **Orgs:** Bd dir E St Louis Comm Develop Credit Union; bd dir Boy's Club Springfield IN 1973-75; bd dir Springfield Urban League 1973-75; pres Kappa Alpha PsiSpringfield Alumni 1974-76. **Business Addr:** Deputy Mayor/Dir of Adminis, City of East St Louis, #7 Collinsville Ave, East St Louis, IL 62201.

GENTRY, NOLDEN I.
Attorney. **Personal:** Born Aug 30, 1937, Rockford, IL; son of Omega Gentry and Nolden L Gentry; married Barbara Lewis, Apr 24, 1965; children: Adrienne, Natalie, Brian. **Educ:** Univ of IA, BS 1960; IA Coll of Law, JD 1964. **Career:** FBI, special agent, 1964-65; Iowa Assistant Attorney General, 1965-66; Brick, Gentry, Bowers, Swartz, Stoltze, Schuling & Levis, PC, attorney, 1967-. **Orgs:** Former Bd mem Des Moinse Indep Comm Sch Bd; bd mem Greater Des Moines Comm Found; Drake Relays Com; bd mem MidAmerican Energy Holdings Co; bd mem Delta Dental Plan of IA; bd mem Mid-Iowa Health Foundation; bd mem Bankers Trust Company. **Business Addr:** 550-39th St, Suite 200, Des Moines, IA 50312, (515)274-1450.

GEORGE, ALLEN
Attorney. **Personal:** Born Oct 13, 1935, New York, NY; married Valerie Daring; children: Gerald, Kenneth, Johnathan. **Educ:** NYH Univ, BS 1964; NY Univ Graduate School of Business, 1965-68; Howard Univ, 1973; Cleveland State Univ, LLM 1980. **Career:** Pittman George & Copeland Co LPA, pvt practice 1978; Standard Oil Co, atty 1973-77; Lucas, & Tucker & Co, tax accountant 1969-70; IRS revenue agt 1966-69; Bur of Credit Unions, credit union Examiner 1965-66. **Orgs:** Treas Phi Alpha Delta Law Fraternity 1972-73; Nat Bar Assn; Am Bar Assn; OH Bar Assn; Bar Assn Of Greater Cleveland; Cleveland Lawyers Assn; Cuyahoga Co Bar Assn Bd; mem Glenville YMCA 1976; bd mem Catholic Interracial Council; mem Caribbean Comm Cultural Club; mem Knights of Columbus. **Honors/Awds:** Cleveland State Univ Coll of Law 1975-76; published The Tax Treatment of The-cost of Class C Stock Purchases by Farmers' Coop 1971. **Military Serv:** USAF a/1c 1956-59.

GEORGE, ALMA ROSE
Association executive, physician, surgeon. **Personal:** Born in Mound Bayou, MS; daughter of Phillip M George; married Frederick Finch; children: Franklin. **Career:** Detroit General Hospital, internship, beginning 1960; Wayne County: operates three surgical outpatient centers and a patient care management system, currently; medical practitioner, currently. **Orgs:** Detroit Medical Society, president; Wolverine State Medical Society, secretary, president; National Medical Association, board of delegates, elected, 1966, board of trustees, treasurer, president-elect, 1990, president, currently. **Honors/Awds:** Ebony, The 100 Most Influential Black Americans, May 1992. **Business Addr:** President, National Medical Association, 1012 10th St NW, Washington, DC 20001, (202)347-1895.

GEORGE, CARRIE LEIGH
Educator (retired), minister. **Personal:** Born Sep 28, 1915, Winder, GA; daughter of Mattie Olian Owens Leigh and Elijah Leigh; widowed; children: Faith O, Donald T. **Educ:** Clark Coll, (Salutatorian, Cum Laude) AB 1936; Atlanta Univ, MA 1937; Gammon Theological Seminary, MDiv 1954; NYU, EdS 1961; Atlanta Univ, PhD 1970; Famous Writers Sch New Haven CT, Certificate 1976; OH State Univ, 1943; Hartford Seminary Found, 1956-57; Garrett-Northwestern Univ, 1960; Gregg Coll Chicago, Certificate, 1944. **Career:** Clark Coll, assoc prof, math & business educ, 1938-48; Atlanta Public School System, supply teacher, 1948-55; Gammon-Interdenomination Theological Center, assoc prof, religious educ & dir of field exp 1955-64; Archer High School, head math dept, 1956-57; US Dept of Labor, admin asst to Atlanta Concentrated Employee Program Monitor 1967-68; Economic Systems Corp Poland ME, cur dev spclst & sr cnslr 1968; Cross Keys H S, math tchr 1968-70; GA St U, dir of official pub 1970-71; GA State Univ, sr counselor & asst prof of curriculum & instr 1971-80, rsch/asst prof, 1980-86; Atlanta Daily World Newspaper, columnist, 1979-90; George Mem Baptist Church of Faith, pastor, 1981-. **Orgs:** Consultant Educ Dept, Atlanta Job Corp Center, 1980-83; consultant, Center Personnel Morehouse Coll 1981; teaching staff Brown HS Atlanta 1981; Bishop Coll, 1978; pres Friendship Uplifters 1977-79; pres Atlanta Chptr of Natl Assn of Baptist Women Ministers 1984-88; Interdenomination Assoc of Ministers Wives & Widows (Dean of Educ Dept 1980-82); parliamentarian, National Assn of Baptist Women Ministers, 1988-; life member, National Council of Negro Women, 1990; member, Alpha Kappa Alpha Sorority, 1935-; charter member, Societas Docta, 1987-; president, Alumni Assn, Interdenominational Theological Center, 1988-90. **Honors/Awds:** Anglo American Academy, Cambridge, England, elected honorary fellow, 1980; Georgia State University, Women of Excellence Award for Spiritual Devt, 1983; Frontiers Club of America, Community Service Award, 1983; Georgia State University Speakers Bureau, 1984; Burton College and Seminary, honorary EdRD, 1960. **Special Achievements:** Author: ''Some Properties of Algebraic Invariants''; ''Counselor As Person: Philosophical, Theological & Practical Orientations''; Leadership in Action; ''Who Are The Development Studies Students?'' ''What is Counseling''; ''Alternative Schools in Public Educ in GA,'' (co-author); ''A Study Skills Workshop Manual''; ''An Ecumenical Communion Serv for Christian Women''; Leadership Training Series, ''Parlimentary Usage''; ''Communicating Our Faith''; ''Christ in You-The Hope of Glory''; ''The Art of Worship''; ''From the Pen of the Shepherdess''; What Matters Most. **Home Addr:** 1652 Detroit Ave N W, Atlanta, GA 30314.

GEORGE, CLAUDE C.
Educational administrator. **Personal:** Born Nov 22, 1922, Atlanta, GA; married Dr Herma Hightower-George; children: Collette Scott, Yvette, Valeria Hightower, Kimerly Hightower. **Educ:** Tuskegee Inst, BS Ed 1948; NY Univ, MA Ed 1949; Atlanta Univ, EdS 1972, EdD 1981. **Career:** Atlanta Public Schools, dir, student desegregation 1973-77, dir, alternative ed 1978-83, dir, intl exchange, dir, job placement. **Orgs:** Mem Kappa Alpha Psi Frat 1977-85, Atlanta Univ Alumni Assoc 1977-85, CL Harper Mem Fund 1977-85; commiss Atlanta Clean City Commiss 1977-85; chairperson Senate Selection Comm of the Congress Bundstay Youth Exchange; mem Japan-Amer Soc of GA. **Honors/Awds:** Jewish Ed Alliance Achievement Awd NY 1949; Tuskegee Hall of Fame Tuskegee Inst 1975. **Military Serv:** US Army, tech sgt; Good Conduct, European Theater Operation Award, 1943-45. **Business Addr:** Dir Job Placement, Atlanta Public Schools, 551 Houston St NE, Atlanta, GA 30312.

GEORGE, CONSTANCE P.
Cleric. **Personal:** Born May 1, 1931, Farmsville, VA; widowed; children: Otis Jr, Gary, Randall, Lisa George Hamilton, Kirby. **Educ:** College of New Rochelle, BA, 1984; New York Theological Seminary, MDiv, 1988; United Theological Seminary, DMin, 1994. **Career:** Grace Baptist Church, minister for missions; Westchester Medical Center, chaplin consultant; Grace Baptist Church, executive minister, currently. **Orgs:** YMCA of Mount Vernon, board of directors; Westchester Childcare, board of directors; United Black Clergy of Westchester; Mount Vernon Council of Churches, president; Mount Vernon Human Rights Commission, commissioner; National Baptist Convention USA Inc, spiritual life commission; AKA Sorority, Zeta Nu Omega Chapter, Westchester County; NCP. **Honors/Awds:** Black Women's Health Project, Westchester Chapter, Minister of the Year Award, , 1990; Grace Baptist Church, Wall of Honor Citation, 1991; United Black Clergy of Westchester, Recognition of Dedicated and Untiring Service, 1992; Office of County Executive, Westchester County Women's Advisory Board, Certificate of Appreciation, 1988; Westchester County Board of Legislators, Service Award, Proclamation, 1992. **Special Achievements:** Sermon printed, ''Those Preaching Women,'' Ella P Mitchell, editor, 1985; first African-American Baptist ordained clergywoman raised in Mount Vernon, 1986; second African-American Baptist clergywoman ordained in Westchester County, 1986. **Business Addr:** Executive Minister, Grace Baptist Church, 52 S 6th Ave, Mount Vernon, NY 10550, (914)664-2676.

GEORGE, EDDIE
Professional football player. **Personal:** Born Sep 24, 1973, Philadelphia, PA. **Educ:** Ohio State. **Career:** Houston Oilers, running back, 1996; Tennessee Oilers, 1997-. **Special Achievements:** NFL Draft, first round pick, #14, 1996; Heisman Trophy, 1995; NFL Rookie of the Year, 1996; Pro Bowl alternate, 1996. **Business Addr:** Professional Football Player, Tennessee Oilers, c/o Baptist Sports Park, 7640 H 70-5, Nashville, TN 37221.

GEORGE, EDWARD
Business executive. **Personal:** marrIed Cutie Bell; children: 5. **Educ:** Attnd Coll 1 1/2 Yrs. **Career:** Pres & bus agent, Amalgamated Transit Union 1970-72. **Orgs:** Bd mem Legal Aid Soc San Joaguin Co 1969-73; dir Southeast Comm Assn 1972-73; bd mem A Phillip Randolph Institute 1972-73; bd mem KUOP FM Radio Station Univ of Pacific Stockton CA; pres NAACP Stockton; Bd Mem Cit Adv Com San Joaquin Co Planning Assn; adv bd San Joaquin Co Manpower Prog; adv bd mem Child Health Disability Prevention Prog San Joaquin Co. **Honors/Awds:** Achievement award in comm involvement SE Comm Cntr 1971; Cert of App Rec Comm Action Coun; bd dir 1973; service rendered during 1973 Stockton Boy & Girl Drill Team. **Business Addr:** 805 E Webor Ave, Stockton, CA.

GEORGE, GARY RAYMOND
State official. **Personal:** Born Mar 8, 1954, Milwaukee, WI; son of Audrey George and Horace R George; children: Alexander Raymond, Daniel McLean. **Educ:** Univ of Wisconsin Madison, BBA Accounting 1976; Univ of Michigan Ann Arbor, JD 1979. **Career:** Arthur Young & Co, tax atty 1979-80; self-employed, atty 1982-; State of Wisconsin, senator 6th dist 1981-. **Orgs:** Co-chair, Joint Comm on Finance, 1983-; Co-chair Joint Audit Comm 1981-85; mem Uniform State Laws Comm 1981, Ed Block Grant Adv Comm 1981, Ed Comm Bd 1981, Sexual Assault & Child Abuse Study Comm; chmn Park West Redevel Task Force 1981; mem Milwaukee Cty Zoo Bd 1981, Neighborhood Improvement Devel Corp 1982; bd of trustees, mem Family Hosp Inc & Family Hosp Nursing Home Inc 1983; chmn Joint Finance Comm Ed Subcommittee 1983; mem Comm Devel Finance Auth 1983, Alcohol & Drug Abuse Study Comm 1983, State Supported Programs Adv Comm 1983, Mayor's Anti-Gang Initiative Task Force 1984; mem Performing Arts Ctr Bd of Dir 1985; mem WI State Bar, Democratic Party of WI, Natl Caucus of State Legislators, Council on State Govts, Milwaukee Forum, Natl Black Caucusof State Legislators, NAACP. **Business Addr:** Senator Dist 6, Wisconsin State Senate, South State Capitol, PO Box 7882 #119, Madison, WI 53707.

GEORGE, HERMON, JR.
Educator. **Personal:** Born Nov 22, 1945, Tampa, FL; son of Henrene Smith George and Hermon George Sr; divorced; children: Dahren Malcolm, Melissa Niani. **Educ:** Wilkes College, Wilkes-Barre, PA, BA, 1967; Middlebury College, Middlebury, VT, MA, 1968; University of California, Irvine, CA, PhD, 1979. **Career:** Wartburg College, Waverly, IA, instructor of Spanish, 1968-70; Fisk University, Nashville, TN, instructor of Spanish, 1970-71; Spelman College, Atlanta, GA, instructor of Spanish, 1971-73; California State University, Fresno, CA, assistant professor of ethnic studies, 1978-81; SUNY College, New Paltz, NY, assistant professor, Black Studies, 1981-85; University of Northern Colorado, Greeley, CO, associate professor and coordinator, 1985-91; professor, 1991-. **Orgs:** Member-at-large, executive board, National Council for Black Studies, 1980-87; reviewer, Social Science Journal, 1980-81, 1985-; reviewer, Science & Society, 1987-; regional editor, Western Journal of Black Studies, 1991-96; member, National Conference of Black Political Scientists, 1988-89. **Honors/Awds:** American Race Relations Theory, Lanham MD, Univ Press of America, 1984; ''Black Power in Office: The Limits of Electoral Reform'', reprinted in Talmadge Anderson Ed, Black Studies: Theory, Method, and Critical Perspectives 1990; Fellowship, NEH, Summer Institute on African-American Culture, 1987; Faculty Excellence Award, Univ of Northern Colorado, 1987; ''Clarence Thomas: 'Loyal Foot Soldier' for Reaganism''; Court of Appeal: The Black Community Speaks Out on the Racial and Sexual Politics of Thomas vs Hill, 1992. **Special Achievements:** The Black Scholar, advising & contributing editor, 1994; Western Social Science Assn, exec council, 1993-96; The Social Science Journal, assoc editor, 1994-95; Contemporary Authors, V 126, 1989. **Business Addr:** Dept of Africana Studies, University of Northern Colorado, Greeley, CO 80639, (970)351-1743.

GEORGE, LUVENIA A.
Educator, ethnomusicologist. **Personal:** Born Feb 26, 1934, Chicago, IL; daughter of Rev Floyd D Johnson & Sweetie Johnson; married Henry H, Jun 26, 1953; children: Karen Marsha; Adrianne Rose. **Educ:** Howard University, BMEd, 1952; University of Maryland College Park, MEd, 1969; University of Maryland Baltimore County, PhD, 1995. **Career:** District of Columbia Public Schools, music teacher, 1954-92; Smithsonian Institute, research scholar, 1993-94, coordinator DE youth proj, 1994-. **Orgs:** Sargent Presbyterian Church, organist, 1960-, elder, 1991-; District of Columbia Music Education Association, pres, 1970-72; District of Columbia Choral Directors Association, pres, 1978-80. **Honors/Awds:** African-American Museum, Hall of Fame Inductee, 1997. **Special Achievements:** Author: ''Teaching the Music of Six Different Cultures,'' 2nd ed, 1987; Lucie Campbell in ''We'll Understand It Better Bye & Bye,'' 1992; Duke Ellington: ''Composer Beyond Category,'' 1993; ''The Source of African-American Music,'' 1991. **Home Addr:** 7416 14th St, NW, Washington, DC 20012-1502.

GEORGE, PAULINE L.
Cable television executive. **Personal:** Born Apr 9, 1963, Cleveland, OH. **Educ:** Eastern Michigan University, BA, 1985; Michigan State University, MA, 1990. **Career:** WKYC TV-3 News, desk assistant, weekend assoc producer, 1986; Continental Cablevision, telemarketing & sales, 1988-89; CNBC, affiliate relations account exec, Midwest, 1989-90, affiliate relations regional mgr, Midwest, 1990-92, affilate relations regional mgr, Northeast, 1992-93; CNBC/America's Talking, reg dir Midwest & Canada; NBC Cable Networks, regional dir, Midwest & Canada, currently. **Orgs:** National Assn of Minorities in Cable, Detroit Chapter, founding president; Women in Cable & Telecommunications, dir, national bd of dir's, 1995-96, executive committee, 1997; Cable Television Administration and Marketing (CTAM); National Assn of Female Executives; Alpha Kappa Alpha Sorority. **Honors/Awds:** General Electric, Gerald L Phillipe Award for Community Service Nominee, 1994; National Assn of Minorities in Cable, Detroit Chapter, President's Leadership, 1992; Women in Cable, Detroit & NW, OH Chapters, Carla Laufer Achievement Recognition, 1991. **Special Achievements:** The Effects of Race & Gender on Newscaster Believability, Thesis, MSU, 1990; proficient in French. **Business Addr:** Regional Dir, Midwest & Canada, NBC Cable Networks, 2855 Coolidge Hwy, Ste 201A, Troy, MI 48084, (810)643-9033.

GEORGE, RONALD
Professional football player. **Personal:** Born Mar 20, 1970, Heidelberg, Germany; married Julie. **Educ:** Stanford, bachelor's degree in economics, 1992. **Career:** Atlanta Falcons, linebacker, 1993-96; Minnesota Vikings, 1997-. **Business Addr:** Professional Football Player, Minnesota Vikings, 9520 Viking Dr, Eden Prairie, MN 55344, (612)828-6500.

GEORGE, TATE CLAUDE
Professional Basketball Player. **Personal:** Born May 29, 1968, Newark, NJ. **Educ:** Univ of Connecticut, Storrs, CT, 1986-90. **Career:** New Jersey Nets, 1990-93.

GEORGE, THEODORE ROOSEVELT, JR.
Physician. **Personal:** Born Dec 27, 1934, Cincinnati, OH; son of Christine Tatum George and Theodore R George; married Jeanne Sharpe; children: Theodore III, Blair. **Educ:** Howard Univ, BS, 1952-56, MD, 1956-60; Freedman's Hosp, intern, 1960-61, resident, 1963-67. **Career:** DC Gen Hosp, Howard Univ Hosp, WA Hosp Ctr, physician; Howard Univ Coll Med, assistant professor; DC Gen Hosp, sr med officer; physician, currently. **Orgs:** Mem Natl Med Assn, Med Soc DC, Chi Delta Mu Med Soc, Former Interns & Resd of Freedmen's Hosp, Amer Assn of Gynecologic Laparoscopists, Alpha Phi Alpha Frat, WA Gyn Soc, Medico-Chirurgical Soc, Pan Am Med Assn, Urban League, Jr Citizens Corps, NAACP, Police Boy's Club, Cincinnati Club; MD Medical License 1960; DC Med License 1965; Cert Amer Bd Ob & Gyn 1969; chmn Pro Tem St Paul AME Church Trustee Bd; mem, Daniel Hale Williams Reading Club, 1972-; mem, Southern Medical Assn, 1980-. **Honors/Awds:** Natl Competitive Scholarship, 1952-56; Rep Aviation Awd 1954; Dean's list 1952-56; Dean's Cup 1955; Pres's Cup 1956; AFROTC Awd 1956; Outstanding Male Grad Student Council 1956; Grad Cum Laude 1956; Natl Medical Assn Scholarship 1957; Psychiatric Awd 1960; Natl Medical Assn Awd 1967; AMA Physicians Recognition Awd, 1972; Amer Acad of Family Physicians Awd 1974; Howard Univ Med Alumni Assn Awd 1974; Amer Cancer Soc Cert of Merit 1975; Natl Fraternal Order of Police 1976; publ ''Delivery in Elderly Primagravida Following Myomectomy'' 1964; ''Vascular Systems Recovery of Red Blood Cells from the Peritonial Cavity'' 1965; ''Concomittant Use of Stomaseptin & Metronidazole in the Treatment of Trichomonas Vaginalis Complicated by Moniliasis'' 1966; ''Pelvic Exenteration''1967; ''The Changing Role of Crean Section'' 1969. **Military Serv:** USAF capt 1961-63; Commendation Medal. **Business Addr:** Physician, 5505 5th St NW, Ste 200, Washington, DC 20011.

GERALD, ARTHUR THOMAS, JR.
Educational administrator. **Personal:** Born Oct 13, 1947, Boston, MA; married Henrietta; children: Arthur Michael, Alama Michelle. **Educ:** Lincoln Univ, 1965-67; Berkshire Christian Coll, AB Theology 1967-70; Gordon-Conwell Seminary, Masters Degree 1970-72. **Career:** Salem State Coll, advisor to afro-american soc 1972-73, dir of minority affairs 1973-81; assoc dean, academic affairs, 1981-. **Orgs:** Associate minister 12th Baptist Church 1972-. **Business Addr:** Assoc Dean & Academic Affairs, Salem State College, 352 Lafayette St, Salem, MA 01970.

GERALD, GILBERTO RUBEN
Consultant. **Personal:** Born Nov 27, 1950, Panama, Panama; son of Dorothy Whiteman Gerald and Dr Alfred Nelson Gerald. **Educ:** Pratt Inst, Brooklyn, NY, BArch, 1974. **Career:** Georgetown Univ Hospital Office of Planning, Washington, DC, project mgr, 1975-77; Perkins and Will, Washington, DC, designer draftsman, 1977-79; Hennigson Durham and Richardson, Alexandria, VA, project architect, 1979-81; Hellmuth Obata and Kassabaum, Washington, DC, project architect, 1981-82; Arthur Cotton Moore and Assoc Inc, Washington, DC, sr staff architect, 1982-83; Natl Coalition of Black Lesbians and Gays, Washington, DC, exec dir, 1983-86; Natl AIDS Network, Washington, DC, dir of minority affairs, 1986-89; Minority AIDS Project, Los Angeles, CA, exec dir, 1989-90; Gil Gerald and Associates, principal/owner, 1990-. **Orgs:** Americans for Democratic Action, 1986, Natl Minority AIDS Council, 1987; pres, Downtown Shaw Neighborhood Assn, 1980-81, DC Coalition of Black Gays, 1982-83; Los Angeles City AIDS Advisory Panel, 1989-; Los Angeles County/Community HIV Planning Council, 1989-90; Los Angeles County HIV Health Services Planning Council, 1990-; interim steering committee member, Los Angeles County AIDS Regional Board, 1989-90; Gentlemen Concerned, 1991-; AIDS Project Los Angeles, board of directors, 1992-; Metropolitan Community Church of Los Angeles, board of directors, 1992-; African-American Gay and Lesbian Studies Center, founder, president, 1992-. **Honors/Awds:** Certificate of Appreciation, DC Coalition of Black Gay Men and Women, 1985; Gene Frey Award, Whitman-Walker Clinic, 1987; named one of the Advocate 500 important individuals of the gay and lesbian community, Advocate, 1988; Bayard Rustin Award, Natl Black Lesbian and Gay Leadership Conference. **Special Achievements:** Author, ''With My Head Held Up High,'' In the Life: A Black Gay Anthology, 1986; ''What Can We Learn from the Gay Community's Response to the AIDS Crisis?'' Journal of the National Medical Association, 1989; welcoming speech: National Conference on AIDS in the Black Community, National Coalition of Black Lesbians and Gays, Washington, DC, 1986; moderator: AIDS in the Black Community Workshop panel, Joint Center for Political Studies, Fifth National Policy Institute, Washington, DC, 1988; speaker, participant in panel presentations, contributor to numerous publications, 1979-.

GERALD, MELVIN DOUGLAS, SR.
Family physician, association administrator. **Personal:** Born Jul 17, 1942, Cerro Gordo, NC; son of Mattie Vann Gerald (deceased) and Paul Gerald, Sr (deceased); married Lenora Graham Gerald, Dec 24, 1965; children: Sonja Z, Melvin D Jr. **Educ:** Morehouse Coll Atlanta, BS 1964; Howard Univ, MD 1970; Johns Hopkins Univ School of Public Health, MPH 1974. **Career:** Shaw Comm Health Center, med dir 1973-75; Howard Univ, asst prof 1974-, dir family practice 1976-78; Gerald Family Care Assoc, physician 1978-; Providence Hospital, chm dept of family practice, 1989-93. **Orgs:** Bd of dirs MD State Cancer Soc 1979-85; DC Academy of Family Physicians, president, 1992-94; chair, Department of FP, Prince Georges Hosp Ctr, 1994-; president, Howard University Medical Alumni Association, 1996-; president of medical staff, Howard University Hosp, 1996-; board of directors, American Academy of Family Physicians, 1996-. **Business Addr:** President/CEO, Gerald Family Care, PC, 1160 Varnum St NE, Ste 117, Washington, DC 20017, (202)832-7007.

GERALD, WILLIAM
Cleric. **Personal:** Born Dec 15, 1918, Irwin County, GA; son of Bitha Gerald (deceased) and Percy Gerald (deceased); widowed; children (previous marriage): Edmond, Clarence, Frank, Raymond. **Educ:** Eastern Amer Univ, DD 1980; Howard Univ; Cortez Peters Bus Clge. **Career:** Bible Way Church Wash DC, secr to presiding bishop 1948-69; Bible Way Church World Wide Inc, rec secr 1962-83; Lighthouse Church over WBGR, Baltimore, MD, radio minister; former substitute host, ''Spread A Little Sunshine'' channel 9, sub TV host 1969-91. **Orgs:** Clerk typist acct JE Hanger Inc 1978-84; corr rec secr Bible Way Church World Wide 1962-83. **Honors/Awds:** Books publ, ''Coping With & Overcoming Today's Problems'' 1977, ''Divine Basics And Concepts'' 1983, ''The Golden Years'' 1984; co-authored other books of prominence; musician & songwriter; Consecrated Bishop, Bible Way General Convocation, Washington, DC, 1988; Built and Renovated Lighthouse Apostolic Church, 1991-92; Pastor Emeritus, 1997; Certified Semi-Finalist Poem, Written int the NA Open Poetry Contest; Published: The Natl Library of Poetry, Thoughts by Candlelight, 1998; Elected, Intl Poetry Hall of Fame, April 14, 1998 at (www.poets.com). **Home Addr:** 620 Severn Ave, Annapolis, MD 21403.

GERALDO, MANUEL ROBERT
Attorney. **Personal:** Born Dec 20, 1950, Newark, NJ; son of Iria Gouveia Geraldo and Joaquim dos Santos Geraldo; married Cynthia Hart, Jun 9, 1984; children: Manuel R II, Alexander Joaquim. **Educ:** Seton Hall University, BS, 1972; Rutgers University School of Law, JD, 1977; Georgetown University School of Law, LLM, 1984. **Career:** Newark Municipal Council, executive assistant, 1974-77; U.S. Department of of Housing & Urban Development, trial attorney, 1977-79; Robinson & Geraldo, president, 1979-. **Orgs:** Greater Washington Ibero American Chamber of Commerce, director, general counsel, 1988-; Leadership Washington, co-chair, homecoming, 1989-; Portuguese Heritage Scholarship Foundation, director, 1990-; Prince Hall Free & Accepted Mason, 1984-; Prince Hall Shriner, 1985-; First Baptist Church of Suitland, usher, 1990-. **Military Serv:** New Jersey National Guard, e-4, 1970-76. **Business Addr:** Attorney, Robinson & Geraldo, 1316 Pennsylvania Ave SE, Washington, DC 20003, (202)544-2888.

GERAN, JOSEPH, JR.
Designer, educator. **Personal:** Born Nov 23, 1945, San Francisco, CA; son of Clara Geran and Joseph Geran Sr; divorced; children: Paige K, Joseph III. **Educ:** City Coll of San Francisco, AA 1963-66; CA State Univ at San Francisco, BA 1967-70; CA Coll of Arts and Crafts, MFA 1970-72; Univ of RI, 1985-87. **Career:** CA State Univ at San Francisco, lecturer 1969-70; CA Coll of Arts and Crafts, asst prof 1970-74; RI Sch of Design, dean of students 1974-77; Comm Coll of RI, instructor 1980-82; Jewelry Inst Providence, RI, instructor l986-88; Geran Enterprises, designer/modelmaker. **Orgs:** Bd of dir RI Black Heritage Soc 1979-82; mem Black Artists of Rhode Island (BARI), 1985-. **Honors/Awds:** Illinois Sculpture Award, Illinois State Univ 1972; commissioned by the State of Rhode Island to sculpt the bust of Dr Martin Luther King, Jr (bronze), 1986; The Jazz Trumpet (bronze) funded by Black Artists of Rhode Island, 1989; Bird of Hope (bronze) included in the permanent collection of the Smithsonian Inst, Washington, DC, 1973.

GERMANY, ALBERT. See GEE, AL.

GERMANY, SYLVIA MARIE ARMSTRONG
College administrator. **Personal:** Born Jan 10, 1950, New Orleans, LA; married Plenty Morgan Germany Jr; children: Jobyna Joidella, Adam Nathan. **Educ:** Southern Univ in New Orleans, BS 1980. **Career:** Orleans Parish Sch Bd, adm exec sec 1977-80; Pre-Employment Program, business instructor 1980-81; Sidney N Collier Vo-Tech, business instructor 1981-85; Oakwood Coll, personnel assistant 1985-. **Orgs:** Mem LA Vo-Tech Assoc 1981-85; mem Amer Soc for Personnel Administrators 1985-. **Business Addr:** Personnel Administrator, Oakwood College, Personnel Office, Oakwood Rd, Huntsville, AL 35896.

GERVIN, GEORGE (ICEMAN)
Professional basketball coach. **Personal:** Born Apr 27, 1952, Detroit, MI; married Joyce; children: George Jr, Jared, Tia Monique. **Educ:** Eastern MI, attended 1973. **Career:** San Antonio Spurs, 1976-85, Chicago Bulls, 1985-86; Quad City Thunder (CBA), 1989; San Antonio Spurs, asst coach, 1993-. **Honors/Awds:** NBA All Star Game 1977, 1979, 1980; NBA Scoring Champ; All Star 8 times; League's Leading Scorer 4 times; 10th on the all-time points list with 23,746; All-Star Game MVP 1980; Seagram's Crown 1978, 1979.

GEYER, EDWARD B., JR.
Rector. **Personal:** Born Aug 23, 1929, New York City; married Laura E Williams; children: Edward Blaine, III, Ruth Anne. **Educ:** Wash Sq Coll,aB NYU; STB Magna Cum Laude Div Sch Episcopal Ch Phila; Schl Educ NYU, post grad Work. **Career:** St Peter's, NYC, curate 1958-60; St Luke's, New Haven CT, rector 1960-68; St Peter's, Bennington VT 1968-72; Good Shepherd, Hartford CT 1972; Provincial Synod, Del 1974; Greater Hartford Council of Chrs, Vice Pres 1973-78; Capitol Region Conf of Ch 1978-79; Martin Luther King Jr Housing Devel Hartford, Pres 1974. **Orgs:** Mem Exec Council Diocese of Vermont 1970-72; New England Provincial Synod 1971-72; New Eng Prvncl Synod Cncl 1973; Com On State Of Ch 1975; Comm on Ministry 1971-72; Ch Diocesan Liturgical Comm 1971-72; mem Bd trsts Philadelphia Div Sch 1968-73; Gen Theol Sem 1970; vice pres Bennington Cncl Of Chrs 1969-72; mem Bennington Hsng Auth 1970-72; mem bd Bennington-rutland Opp Cncl 1968-72; treas BROC 1971-72; mem bd Phoenix House 1971-72; Bennington Ministerial Assoc 1968-72; Exec Council Diocese of Conn 1965-68; Dept of Christ Educ 1965-68; bd of Dirs New Haven Comm Council 1964-68 ; mem Educ Comm 1964-68; Chaplain New Haven State Jail 1966-68; mem Clergyman's Adv Com CT Planned Parenthood 1965-68; mem Urban Task Force New Haven C of C 1968; bd ReCtr for Mental Retatdation 1965-68; ChildrenCtr Hamden, Ct 1967-68; mem Steering Comm of the NH Young Mother's Prgm 1965-68; Civil Serv Cmmssnr New Haven 1698; mem Christ Ch Cathedral Cathedral Chap Hartford 1968-73; fld Wrk Supr Gen Theol Sem 1958-60 . **Business Addr:** 155 Wyllys St, Hartford, CT 06106.

GHENT, HENRI HERMANN
Concert singer, author, critic. **Personal:** Born Jun 23, 1926, Birmingham, AL; son of Jennie Gantt and Reuben Gantt. **Educ:** New England Conservatory, Boston MA, 1951; Museum School of Fine Arts, Boston, 1952; Longy School of Music, Cambridge MA, 1953; Univ of Paris, France, 1960. **Career:** Cultural news editor, Elegant magazine, New York City, 1964-68; asst dir, Inst of Arts & Sci Brooklyn, 1968-69; dir, Comm Gallery, Brooklyn Museum, 1968-72; New York correspondent, Le Monde de la Musique, Paris; Danser Magazine, Paris. **Orgs:** Consultant, Natl Endowment for the Arts, Washington DC, 1973-74; chief juror, Dayton Art Inst All-Ohio Painting Sculpture Biennial, 1972; chief juror, Grad Students Art & Design, Pratt Inst, Brooklyn NY, 1972; contributed significant articles on visual & performing arts to Le Monde de la Musique Paris, New York Times, Los Angeles Times, Cleveland Plain Dealer, Art Intl (Lugano, Switzerland), Artforum (New York), Art in Amer (New York), Boston Globe, Village Voice (New York). **Honors/Awds:** Hon degree humanities, Allen Univ, Columbia SC, 1966; Art Critics Award, Natl Endowment for the Arts, Washington DC, 1973-74; Ford Found Travel & Study Fellowship, 1974-75; Samuel H Kress Found Award in Arts Research; Martha Baird Rockefeller Fellowship in Music, 1957-58; Achievement in the Arts Award, NAACP, 1973. **Military Serv:** US Army, tech/5th 1945-46; Good Conduct; Good Marksmanship 1946. **Home Addr:** 310 E 75th St, 1-F, New York, NY 10021.

GHOLSON, GENERAL JAMES, JR.
Educator, musician. **Personal:** Born Oct 15, 1944, Norfolk, VA; son of Elsie Gholson and G James Gholson; children: Christopher James. **Educ:** MI State U, BM 1966; Cath U, MM 1970; Cath U, DMA 1975. **Career:** Memphis State Univ, instructor, asst prof, assoc prof of Clarinet 1972-; Catholic Univ, Washington DC, grad asst 1970-72; US Navy Band, Washington DC, section clarinetist & solist 1966-70; Memphis Woodwind Quintet, 1972; Opera Memphis, solo clarinet 1972; Memphis Symphony, solo clarinet 1975. **Orgs:** Faculty adv Kappa Alpha Psi; "Problem Solving in the Clarinet-Studio" Woodwind World 1979; videos "How to Make All West" Jamus 1985, "Kards in the Key of Kroepsch" Jamus 1986, "How to Make All Region a Breeze" Jamus 1986, "Project Solo" Jamus, 1987. **Business Addr:** Associate Professor, Music Department, Memphis State University, Central & Patterson, Memphis, TN 38152.

GHOLSON, ROBERT L.
Company executive. **Educ:** Tennessee State Univ, degree bus adm; University of Memphis, MBA; Life Office Mgt Assn, educational and management credits. **Career:** Universal Life Insurance Co, pres, 1995-. **Orgs:** Memphis Boys Club, bd mem; Junior Achievement, bd mem. **Business Addr:** President, Universal Life Ins Co, 480 Lindea Ave, Memphis, TN 38126, (901)525-3642.

GHOLSTON, BETTY J.
Educational administrator. **Personal:** Born Feb 1, 1942, Wagram, NC; married Willie Gunter; children: Lisa Regina, Betty Cornelia, Saranarda, Willie G Jr. **Educ:** NC Central Univ, BS Commerce 1959-63; NC A&T State Univ, MS Adminis 1977-79; Univ of NC, further study 1978. **Career:** Richmond Cty School, media specialist 1968; Cameron Morrison School, media specialist 1968-77; Cameron Morrison Youth Ctr, project dir/media specialist 1977-83; Richmond Cty Schools, job placement coordinator 1984; NC Dept of Correction, dir of fed proj/educ spec. **Orgs:** Vice pres Cameron Morrison NCAE 1982-83; bd of directors Black Elected Municipal Officials 1983-84; Mayor Pro Tem Wagram Bd of Commissioners 1974-; rep NC Council of Govt-Region N 1982-. **Honors/Awds:** Founder of Wagram Brnch Library 1975; Teacher of the Year NC Dept of Youth Services 1977. **Business Addr:** Dir of Fed Proj/Educ Spec, NC Dept of Correction, Cameron Morrison Youth Ctr, Hoffman, NC 28347.

GIBBES, EMILY V.
Educator. **Personal:** Born Aug 14, 1915, New York, NY; daughter of Genevieve Gibbes and George Gibbes. **Educ:** Hunter Coll, BA (Cum Laude) 1937; NY Univ, MA (Cum Laude) 1951; NY School of Social Work, attended 1952; Attended, Alliance Francaise Paris. **Career:** NY City Council, confidential sec to minority leader, 1941-49; Religious Educ United Presbyterian Church, field dir 1949-57; United Presbyterian Women, general dir educ program 1957-68; Church Educ Africa, consultant 1968-72; Natl Council of Churches, assoc general sec for educ & ministry; NY Theological Seminary, dean of religious educ 1980-. **Orgs:** Conducted study seminars for Church Women to Latin Amer Africa Asia 1953, 1968; consultant in religious education to the Natl Churches Cameroon West Africa, Kenya 1969-72; pres Religious Educ Assoc 1975-78. **Honors/Awds:** Kappa Delta Pi Hon Soc 1950; author of numerous articles study guides training models curricula for church women; Distinguished Alumnae Award School of Educ NY Univ 1978; Church Woman of the Year Award Religious Heritage Assn 1979; Alumnae Hall of Fame Hunter Coll 1981; DHL Mary Holmes Coll 1983. **Business Addr:** Dean of Religious Education, NY Theological Seminary, 5 West 29th St, New York, NY 10001.

GIBBONS, WALTER E.
Electrical engineer. **Personal:** Born May 28, 1952, New York, NY; son of Iris Balfour Gibbons and Eustace Gibbons; married Celeste M Hanson, Jun 5, 1976; children: Adam, Melanie. **Educ:** Massachusetts Inst of Technology, BSEE, 1974, MSEE, 1975; Stanford Univ, MS, mgmt, 1986. **Career:** Bell Lab, Holmdel NJ, technical staff member, 1973-76, Naperville IL, technical staff member, 1976-79; Bell Laboratories, supvr, 1979-86; AT&T, Bell Lab, dept head, 1986-. **Orgs:** Member, IEEE 1987-. **Honors/Awds:** Natl Achievement Scholar, MIT, 1969-73; published article: "Traffic Service Position System No 1 Remote-Trunking Arrangement Hardware & Software Implementation", The Bell-System Technical Journal, vol 58, no 6, 1979; Stanford Sloan Fellow, 1985-86. **Business Addr:** Department Head, AT&T Bell Laboratories, 1200 E Warrenville Rd, Naperville, IL 60566.

GIBBS, ALMA G.
Educator. **Personal:** Born Jul 24, 1914, Dendron, VA. **Educ:** BS 1946; Univ MI & VA State Coll, Grad Study. **Career:** Surey HS, head dept Home Econ 1974; Surey HS, entire teaching career of 29 yrs. **Orgs:** Mem VA Tchrs Assn; past pres Surey Co Ed Assn; VHET; AHEA; AVA; AAUW; Black Caucus; vice president Surry-prince Geo Chap VA State Coll Alumni; memPTA; pres LP Jackson Alumni; Ch Trustee & Clk; VA Lung Assn Southside Reg; bd dor Bicentennial Com; Girl Scouts VA Mun League. **Honors/Awds:** Recipient, Women for Political Action Award, 1970; S Side TB Assn Award, 1970; Recogntion for Outstanding Work w/Youth Bd of VA Lung Assn, 1975; State Coll Alumnae Award 1971.

GIBBS, JACK GILBERT, JR.
Attorney. **Personal:** Born Aug 11, 1953, Columbus, OH; son of Jack Gilbert Gibbs Sr & Ruth Ann Gibbs; married Aloma Gibbs, Jul 27, 1992; children: Jack Gilbert Gibbs III, Anna Louise Gibbs. **Educ:** MI State Univ, BA, 1975; Capital Univ Law School, JD, 1981. **Career:** Columbus Public Schools, teacher, 1976-78; Ohio Attorney General, legal intern, 1980-81; Ben Espy, law clerk, 1982; Self Employed, attorney, 1982-. **Orgs:** Hilltop Civic Council Inc, bd mem, pres, 1987-93; Centenary United Methodist Church, Chairman admin bd, 1987-95; Columbus Bar Assn, 1982-; Ohio State Bar Assn, 1982-; American Bar Assn, 1982-; American Inns of Court, 1994-; Capital Law School Black Alumni, pres, 1990-; UNCF Star Panelist, star panelist, 1993-. **Honors/Awds:** Ohio House of Representatives, resolution, 1983; Columbus Dispatch, Community Service Award, 1988; Capital Law School, Service Award, 1990; Ohio State Univ, Business School, Comm Service Award, 1989; Hilltop Civic Council Inc, Service Award, 1994. **Special Achievements:** Lecture to community groups; Teach one seminar to attorneys a year; testified as an expert witness on Probate Law; Written serveral articles on Probate Law & Estate Planning. **Business Addr:** Attorney At Law, Jack G Gibbs, Jr, Attorney at Law, 233 S High St, Ste 208, Columbus, OH 43215.

GIBBS, JEWELLE TAYLOR
Educator, psychologist. **Personal:** Born Nov 4, 1933, Stratford, CT; daughter of Margaret P Morris Taylor and Julian A Taylor; married James Lowell Gibbs Jr; children: Geoffrey Taylor, Lowell Dabney. **Educ:** Radcliffe Coll, AB (cum laude) 1951-55, Certificate in Business Admin 1958-59; Univ of California, MSW, 1970, MA Psychology 1976, PhD Psychology 1980. **Career:** US Labor Dept Washington, jr mgmt asst 1955-56; Pillsbury Co, Minneapolis MN, market research analyst 1959-61; Stanford Univ, psychiatric social worker 1970-74, 1978-79; Univ of CA Berkeley, prof 1979-. **Orgs:** Clinical psychology private practice consultant, 1983-; consultant Carnegie Corp 1983-; bd of regents Univ of Santa Clara 1980-85; bd of dir Amer Orthopsychiatric Assn 1985-88; task force on special populations Pres Commission on Mental Health WA 1976-78; ed bd Amer Journal of Orthopsychiatry 1980-84; bd of publs Natl Assn of Social Workers 1980-82; adv bd FL Mental Health Inst Univ of South FL at Tampa FL 1985-88; Advisory Board, Natl Center for Children in Poverty, 1987-95; bod, Center for Population Options; bd of trustees, Radcliffe Coll, 1991-95. **Honors/Awds:** NIMH Pre-Doctoral Fellowship, Univ of CA 1979-80; John Hay Whitney Opportunity Fellowship, Radcliffe Coll 1958-59; fellow Bunting Inst Radcliffe Coll 1985; author num professional papers, chapters on adolescent psychopathology, minority mental health & brief treatment; McCormick Award, Amer Assn of Suicidology, 1987; editor, Young, Black and Male in Amer: An Endangered Species, 1988; co-author, Children of Color, with Larke N Huang PhD, 1989; Alumnae Achievement Award, Radcliffe College 1990; elected as fellow, American Psychological Assn 1990; author, Race and Justice: Rodney King and O J Simpson in a House Divided, 1996. **Business Addr:** Professor in Social Policy, Zellerbach Family Fund, School of Social Work, Univ of California, Berkeley, CA 94720.

GIBBS, KAREN PATRICIA
Journalist. **Personal:** Born May 9, 1952, Boston, MA; daughter of James and Bertha Gibbs. **Educ:** Roosevelt Univ Chicago, BSBA 1976; Univ of Chicago Grad Sch of Business, MBA 1978. **Career:** Cont Commodity Serv Inc, intrest rate specialist 1978-82; Harris Trust & Savings Bank, gvt securities rep 1982-83; Dean Witter Reynolds, hedgng & trading strategist 1983-85, sr financial futures analyst 1985-, vice president, 1985-92; CNBC, specialist, anchor, currently. **Orgs:** Sec bd of dirs Henry Booth House 1981-85; bd of dirs Chicago Lung Assoc 1983-86; pres Dorchester Condo Assoc 1984-89; sec Chicago Chap Natl Black MBA Assoc 1985-86; mem Natl Assoc of Security Professionals; Chicago Private Industry Council, 1990-92; Univ of Ill Chicago College of Medicine Corporate Advisory Board. **Honors/Awds:** Quoted frequently in NY Times and Wall St Journal; articles published in CBOT's Financial Exchange; recently selected by pres of Dean Witter's Capital Mkts Group for Natl Ad Campaign to recruit minority employees; Featured Guest on Wall Street Week, 1991. **Business Addr:** Specialist/Anchor, CNBC, 2200 Fletcher Ave, Fort Lee, NJ 07024.

GIBBS, MARLA (MARGARET)
Actress. **Personal:** Born Jun 14, 1931, Chicago, IL; daughter of Ophelia Birdie Kemp Gibbs and Douglas Bradley Gibbs; children: Angela Elayne, Jordan Joseph Jr, Dorian Demetrius. **Educ:** Cortez Peters Business College, 1950-52. **Career:** Service Bindery, receptionist, 1951-56; Kelly Girls, 1956; Gotham Hotel, switchboard operator, 1957; United Airlines, travel consultant, 1963-74; television appearances include: The Jeffersons, 1974-85; Florence; 227, 1985-; You Can't Take It with You; Nobody's Child, 1986; Marla Gibbs Enterprises, president, 1978-; Marla's Memory Lanes, restaurant owner; Hormar Inc, vice president, 1978-. **Orgs:** UGMAA Foundation, treasurer; Science of Mind Church; American Federation of Television & Radio Artists; California State Assembly, 1980. **Honors/Awds:** Award, Natl Academy of Arts & Sciences, 1976; Award, Miss Black Culture Pageant, 1977; Award, United Negro College Fund, 1977; Appreciation Award, LA School District, 1978; Award, Women Involved, 1979; Tribute to the Black Woman Award, WISE, 1979; Image Award, NAACP, 1979-83; Community Service Award, Crenshaw HS, 1980; Award, Paul Robeson Players, 1980; Emmy Award, nominations, Outstanding Performance by Supporting Actress in a Comedy, 1981-85.

GIBBS, ROBERT LEWIS
Circuit court judge. **Personal:** Born Jul 26, 1954, Jackson, MS; son of William & Mary Gibbs; married Debra, Aug 29, 1987; children: Ariana, Justis. **Educ:** Tougaloo College, BA, 1976; Univ of MS, JD, 1979. **Career:** Southeast MS Legal Services, staff attorney, 1979-80; Seventh Circuit District, asst district attorney, 1980; MS Attorney General, deputy attorney general,

1980-90; Hinds County Circuit Court, judge, 1991-. **Orgs:** MS Bar, 1979-; Magnolia Bar Assn, 1979-; Charles Clark Inns of Court, bencher, 1989-; Amer Trial Lawyers Assn, 1993-; Natl Bar Assn, 1992-; 100 Black Men of Jackson, chair, 1990-. **Honors/Awds:** Tougaloo College, Award of Appreciation, 1991; Univ of MS, Award of Distinction, 1988; Magnolia Bar Assn, Government Service Award, 1989; Alpha Kappa Alpha, Community Service Award, 1992. **Special Achievements:** Effective Motion Practice in State Court, Magnolia bar Magazine, 1994. **Home Addr:** 5962 Holbrook Dr, Jackson, MS 39206. **Business Phone:** (601)968-6659.

GIBBS, SANDRA E.
Educator, association administrator. **Personal:** Born Aug 16, 1942, Chicago, IL; daughter of Willa Marie Hurd Gibbs (deceased) and Louis Shelby (deceased). **Educ:** AM & N Coll Pine Bluff AR, AB, AM English 1964; Univ of IL Urbana IL, AM English 1971, PhD English 1974. **Career:** Little Rock AR Public Schools, high school English teacher 1964-70; Univ of IL, teacher of fresh rhtrc 1970-71; Natl Cncl Teacher English, dir of min affairs spec proj 1973-77, dir spec programs, currently. **Orgs:** Con AR Dept Educ Little Rock AR 1969; mem adv bd Prime Time Sch of TV 1975; consult HEW Wmn's Proj Bndct Coll 1978-80; prop rvwr Nat Endwmnt for the Humt 1979; mem Delta Sigma Theta Sor; mem Alpha Kappa Mu Hon Soc. **Honors/Awds:** Tchrs of Engl Flwshp 1971; 4yr Schlr Crst Co 1960-64; 2 NDEA Flwshp 1966-67; pub chap Engl & Min Grps in Engl in the 80's; Consultant Editor for "Tapping Potential, English and Language Arts for the Black Learner," 1984 Natl Council of Teachers of English; Distinguished Alumni Citation, Natl Assn for Equal Opportunity in Higher Education 1986. **Special Achievements:** Publications: co-editor, A Celebration of Teachers, 1986, National Council of Teachers of English; "Black Novels Revisited," New Directions For Women, 1987; "Maria Stewart: Heroic Role Model," New Directions for Women, 1988; "A Symphony of Voices," Maryand English Journal, 1989; "Considering Diversity in Teaching Language and Literature," Michigan English Teacher, 1990; Zelma Watson George biographical sketch, Notable Black American Women. **Business Addr:** Dir, Natl Cncl of Tchrs of English, 1111 Kenyon Rd, Urbana, IL 61801.

GIBBS, WILLIAM LEE
Banker. **Personal:** Born Apr 11, 1945, Hinton, WV; son of Louise A Gibbs and William McKinley Gibbs; married Amporn Mankong, May 25, 1991; children: Vince Visuti (stepson). **Educ:** West Virginia State College, BS, 1972. **Career:** American Fletcher Natl Bank, vice pres, 1972-82; American Bankers Association, associate director, 1982-83; Bank South Corp., senior vp, 1983-92; Citizens Trust Bank, president, chief executive officer, 1992-. **Orgs:** United Way of Metropolitan Atlanta, board member, 1992-; Atlanta Action Forum, 1993-; Central Atlanta Progress Committee, board member, executive committee, 1993-; Stonier Graduate School of Banking, faculty, 1984-; Atlanta Life Insurance Co, board of directors; Atlanta Chamber of Commerce; American Bankers Association Community Bank Council; Board of Councilors, Carter Center. **Honors/Awds:** Atlanta Urban Bankers Association, The Pioneer Award; State of Indiana, Honorary Commissioner of Agriculture. **Business Addr:** President, Chief Executive Officer, Citizens Trust Bank, 75 Piedmont Ave, Atlanta, GA 30303, (404)653-2800.

GIBSON, ALTHEA
Professional tennis player, golfer. **Personal:** Born Aug 25, 1927, Silver, SC. **Educ:** FL A&M Coll, BS 1953. **Career:** US Europe & S Amer, amateur tennis player 1941-58; Lincoln Univ, asst instructor Dept Health & Physical Educ 1953-55; appeared in movie The Horse Soldiers 1958; professional tennis tour w/Harlem Globetrotters 1959; Ward Baking Co, comm relations rep 1959; Ladies Professional Gold Assn, prof golfer 1963; apptd to NY State Recreation Council 1964; Essex Co Park Commn Newark, staff mem 1970, recreation supr 1970-71, dir tennis programs; Valley View Racquet Club Northvale, professional tennis player 1972; City of East Orange, recreation mgr 1980-83; NJ State Athletic Control Board; NJ Governor's Council on Physical Fitness and Sports, special consultant, 1988-. **Orgs:** Mem Alpha Kappa Alpha. **Honors/Awds:** Named to Lawn Tennis Hall of Fame & Tennis Museum 1971; Won World Professional Tennis Championship 1960; Woman Athlete of the Year AP Poll 1957-58; SC Athletic Hall of Fame 1983; author "I Always Wanted to be Somebody" 1958; Monmouth Coll, Honorary DPA degree 1980; FL Sports Hall of Fame 1984; UNC Wilmington, Honorary Littd Degree, 1987. **Home Addr:** PO Box 768, East Orange, NJ 07019.

GIBSON, ANTONIO MARICE
Professional football player. **Personal:** Born Jul 5, 1962, Jackson, MS. **Educ:** Hinds Junior College; Univ of Cincinnati. **Career:** Philadelphia Stars (USFL), 1983-84; Baltimore Stars (USFL), 1985; New Orleans Saints, strong safety, 1986-89; Dallas Cowboys, safety, 1990-. **Honors/Awds:** Speaker at grade schools, Louisiana; post-season play: USFL Championship Game, 1983-85. **Business Addr:** professional football player, Dallas Cowboys, 365 Canal St, Ste 2300, New Orleans, LA 70130-1135.

GIBSON, BENJAMIN F.
Judge. **Personal:** Born Jul 13, 1931, Safford, AL; married Lucille Nelson; children: Charlotte, Linda, Gerald, Gail, Carol, Laura. **Educ:** Wayne State Univ, BS 1955; Detroit Coll of Law, JD (with distinction) 1960. **Career:** City of Detroit, acct 1955-56; Detroit Edison Co, acct 1956-61; State of MI, asst atty gen 1961-63; Ingham County MI, asst pros atty 1963-64; Lansing MI, pvt practice law 1964-; Thomas Cooley Law School, professor, 1979; US Dist Ct Western Dist Grand Rapids MI, judge, 1979-, chief judge, 1991-95, sr judge, 1996-. **Orgs:** Grand Rapids Bar Assn; Michigan Bar Assn; Black Judges of Michigan; Federal Bar Assn; Cooley Law School, bd of dir; United Way, Project Blueprint; Floyd H Skinner Bar Assn; Federal Judges Assn; YMCA, Metropolitan bd of dir; Peninsular Club. **Honors/Awds:** Detroit College of Law, Honorary LLD; Harvard Law School, Program of Instruction for Lawyers, Award of Recognition; Sigma Pi Phi, Outstanding Leadership Award; Distinguished Volunteer Service Award for Community Service; Community of Western District of Michigan, Outstanding Service Award. **Business Addr:** Sr Judge, Michigan Western District, 616 Federal Bldg, 110 Michigan St NW, Grand Rapids, MI 49503.

GIBSON, BETTY M.
University administrator. **Personal:** Born May 15, 1938, New Orleans, LA; daughter of Irene L Hannibal Greene and Jerome G Greene Sr; married Kenneth D Gibson, Aug 22, 1960; children: Tracy Jerome, Tamara Angelique. **Educ:** Kentucky State Univ, Frankfort, KY, BS, 1961; Eastern Kentucky Univ, Richmond, KY, MA, 1974. **Career:** Lincoln Parish Bd of Education, Ruston, LA, music teacher, 1966-67; Franklin County Bd of Education, Frankfort, KY, music teacher, 1967-79; VA Beach Bd of Education, Virginia Beach, VA, music teacher, 1979-84; KY State Univ, Frankfort, KY, asst vp for student affairs, 1984-88; acting vp for student affairs, 1988-; KY State Univ, vp for student affairs, 1991-. **Orgs:** Pres, Frankfort/Lexington The Links Inc, 1990-; dir, Lexington Diocese Commission for Black Catholic Concerns Comm, 1990-; mem, Frankfort Alumni Chap Alpha Kappa Alpha Sorority, 1967-; bd mem, Frankfort Arts Foundation, 1985-; mem, Good Shepherd Church Parish Council, 1986-; Top Ladies of Distinction Inc. **Home Addr:** 5400 Louisville Rd, Frankfort, KY 40601. **Business Addr:** Vice President for Student Affairs, Kentucky State University, East Main St, 103 Hume Hall, Frankfort, KY 40601, (502)227-6671.

GIBSON, CHERYL DIANNE
Physician. **Personal:** Born Oct 10, 1955, Detroit, MI; daughter of Dr George Gibson & Peggy Gibson; married Renzo Fountain, Dec 27, 1996; children: Anne Marie Frances Damron. **Educ:** University of Michigan, 1973-77; Wayne State University, MD, 1987. **Career:** Mercy Hosp, attending physician, obstetrics/gynecology, 1992-93; Detroit Riverview Hosp, attending physician, obstetrics/gynecology, 1993-; Charles C Vincent Continuing Education Ctr, medical director, OB/GYN clinic, 1994-; Macomb Hosp Ctr, attending physician obstetrics/gynecology, 1996-. **Orgs:** National Medical Association, 1984-; American Medical Association, 1984-; American College of Obstetrics/Gynecology, 1984-; Michigan State Medical Society, 1984-; Wayne County Medical Society, 1984-; Detroit Medical Society, 1984-; International Correspondence Society of Obstetricians/GynecologistS, 1988-; Southeastern Michigan Surgical Society, 1989-; Oak Grove AME Church, 1978-; NAACP, 1970-. **Honors/Awds:** American Business Women's Association, Community Svc Awd, 1995. **Special Achievements:** Community Speaker/Women's Health Issues; Michigan Chronicle Newspaper, articles; Established OB/GYN Clinic in Detroit Public Schools for pregnant teens, 1994. **Business Addr:** Ob/Gyn, 15201 W McNichols, Detroit, MI 48235, (313)837-0560.

GIBSON, DONALD B.
Educator. **Personal:** Born Jul 2, 1933, Kansas City, MO; son of Florine Myers Gibson and Oscar J Gibson; married Jo Anne Ivory, Dec 14, 1963; children: David, Douglas. **Educ:** Univ of Kansas City, Kansas City MO, BA, 1955, MA, 1957; Brown Univ, Providence RI, PhD, 1962. **Career:** Brown Univ, Providence RI, instructor, 1960-61; Wayne State Univ, Detroit MI, asst prof, 1961-67; Univ of Connecticut, Storrs CT, assoc prof, 1967-69, prof, 1969-74; Rutgers Univ, New Brunswick NJ, distinguished prof, 1974-. **Orgs:** Coll Language Assn; Modern Language Assn 1964-; editorial bd, African American Review, 1972-; consultant, Educ Testing Serv, 1976-; Natl Council of Teachers of English, 1987-. **Honors/Awds:** Postdoctoral Fulbright, Fulbright Hayes Comm, 1964-66; Study Grant, Natl Endowment for the Humanities, 1970; Research Grant, Amer Council of Learned Socities, 1970; author, The Fiction of Stephen Crane, 1968; editor, Five Black Writers, 1970; editor, Twentieth-Century Interpretations of Modern Black Poets, 1973; author, The Politics of Literary Expression: A Study of Major Black Writers, 1981; author, The Red Bridge of Courage: Redefining The Hero, 1988; editor, W E B Du Bois, The Souls of Black Folk, 1989; National Endowment for the Humanities, fellowship, 1992-93; Stephen Crane, The Red Badge of Courage, Editor, 1996. **Home Phone:** (609)921-1459. **Business Addr:** Professor of English, Rutgers University, Department of English, Murray Hall CN5054, New Brunswick, NJ 08903.

GIBSON, EDWARD LEWIS
Physician. **Personal:** Born Jun 6, 1932, Chicago, IL; married Nannette; children: Joan, Edward Jr, Paula. **Educ:** Roosevelt UL, BS 1953; Howard Univ Coll Med, MD 1957. **Career:** Columbia U, physician, self; asst prof anesthesiology, coll physicians & surgeons; Bellevue Med Ctr, Vis Flw 1962-64; Columbia-presbyn Med & Ctr, asst resd 1958-62; Michael Reese Hosp, intern 1957-58; Princeton Med Ctr, dir anesthesiology 1967-74; Robert R Moton Meml Inst Inc, Tst. **Orgs:** Mem AMA; Am Soc Anesthesiologists. **Honors/Awds:** USAF capt 1958-62. **Military Serv:** USAF capt 1958-62. **Business Addr:** 47 Locust Ln, Princeton, NJ 08540.

GIBSON, ELVIS EDWARD
Consultant (retired). **Personal:** Born Jul 15, 1937, Calvert, TX; married Sylvia M; children: Patricia Elaine. **Educ:** Park Coll, BA Social Work (Cum Laude) 1973. **Career:** Pres KCMO Black United Fund 1976-; Natl Black United Fund, bd of dir 1978-; Charlie Parker Acad of the Arts, chmn 1980-; Black Historical/Genealogy, vice pres 1980-; US Dept of HUD, chief fair housing enforcement, past social engineering consultant. **Orgs:** Chmn Forum for Social Expression Inc 1980; social engr/consultant to private groups; bd of governors, Bruce Watkins Cultural Ctr, 1989-. **Honors/Awds:** Jefferson Awd Taft Broadcasting Corp 1986; Disting Comm Serv Awd; Dr Martin Luther King, Distinguished Community Svc Awd, Governor of Missouri, 1988. **Military Serv:** USAF staff sgt 1955-58. **Home Addr:** 3338 Benton Blvd, Kansas City, MO 64128.

GIBSON, ERNEST ROBINSON
Clergyman. **Personal:** Born Aug 8, 1920, Washington, DC; married Etta; children: Ernest Jr, Dolores, Mark, Bessie Mae, Virginia, Frederick. **Educ:** Howard U, BA 1963; Howard Univ Schl of Religion, BD cum laude 1966. **Career:** Counc of Chs of Grtr Washington, exec dir 1975; Counc of Chs of Grtr Washington, acting exec dir 1975; Inner City Ministry Counc of Chs of Chs of Grtr Washington, dir 1967-75; Neighbrhd Yth Corps Prgm, dir 1966-67; 1st Rising Mt Zion Bat Ch, pastor 1952; Naval Gun Factory, journeyman Molder 1941-56. **Orgs:** Mem bd of dir Model Inner City Comm Orgn 1966-70; Proj Find, chmn 1966-67; Bapt Com on Wider Coop, chmn 1968-70; 1st Rising Mt Zion Bapt Ch Housing Corp, pres 1969; DC Adv Counc for Vocational-edn, chmn 1971-73; Interfaith Assn in Theol Edn, chmn bd of dir 1970; bd mem Redevel Land Agency 1976. **Military Serv:** Armed Servs 1945-46.

GIBSON, HARRIS, JR.
Cardio-thoracic surgeon. **Personal:** Born Nov 19, 1936, Mobile, AL; son of Maude Richardson Gibson and Harris Gibson Sr; married Marva A Boone; children: Michael, Michelle. **Educ:** AL State Univ, BS 1956; Northwestern Univ, MS 1957; Meharry Medical Coll, MD 1961. **Career:** USPHS Hosp NY, internship 1961-62; USPHS Hosp Boston, surgery residency 1962-66; USPHS, asst chief surgery 8 yrs; Boston City Hosp Boston Univ, thoracic surg residency 1966-68; Cardio-Thoracic Assocs Inc, surgeon 1969-; Winchester Hosp, chief thoracic surgery; Boston Univ Medical Sch, asst clinical prof surgery. **Orgs:** Pres New England Medical Soc of NMA 1981-82; pres Middlesex East District Medical Soc of AMA 1983-84; mem Amer Medical Assoc, Soc of Thoracic Surgery. **Honors/Awds:** Mem Alpha Omega Alpha; Fellow Amer Coll of Surgeons, Amer Coll of Chest Physicians; mem Signa Xi. **Business Addr:** Asst Clinical Prof of Surgery, Boston Univ Medical School, 101 George P Hassett Dr, Medford, MA 02155.

GIBSON, HARRY H. C.
Attorney, insurance company executive. **Personal:** Born Oct 8, 1913, Atlanta, GA; son of Alberta A Dickerson Gibson and Truman K Gibson, Sr (deceased); married Mildred C Mickey, Oct 14, 1939 (deceased); children: Edward L Gibson, MD. **Educ:** Univ of Illinois, BA, 1933, JD, 1935. **Career:** Supreme Life Insurance Co of Amer, sr vice pres/general counsel, 1955-; Chicago Burr Oak Cemetery, pres, 1970-. **Orgs:** Natl Bar of Assn; Amer Bar Assn; IL State Bar Assn; Chicago Bar Assn; Bar Assn of the Seventh Federal Circuit; Amer Judicature Society; Amer Cemetery Assn; Sigma Pi Phi Fraternity; Kappa Alpha Psi Fraternity; Royal Coterie of Snakes; Druids Club; NAACP, Chicago Urban League; United Negro Coll Fund; Exec Club of Chicago; Chicago Assn of Commerce and Industry. **Honors/Awds:** Ill State Bar Assn, senior counselor; Chicago Bar Assn, Honoarary Mem; Certificate for dedication and outstanding service to the legal profession for more than 50 years; Univ of IL Coll of law, senior alumnus; Chicago Land Clearance Commission Award, for able and faithful service as a commissioner IL State Bar Assn, privileged member. **Business Addr:** Senior Vice President, Supreme Life Ins Co of America, 3501 South King Drive, Chicago, IL 60616.

GIBSON, JAMES O.
Foundation executive. **Personal:** Born Apr 1, 1934, Atlanta, GA; son of Julia Richardson Gibson and Calvin Harrison Gibson Sr; married Flora Kathryn Defrantz, Jul 18, 1964; children: Tanya Mechelle, Julia Louis, Carl Oliver. **Educ:** Duquesne Univ, Pittsburgh PA, AB, 1956; Atlanta Univ, Atlanta GA, attended, 1959-60; Temple Univ, Philadelphia PA, attended, 1960-61. **Career:** The Potomac Inst, Washington DC, exec assoc, 1966-79; Harambee House Hotel Corp, Washington DC,

CEO, 1975-78; Univ of Southern California, Washington Public Affairs Center, adjunct faculty, 1979-81; Govt of District of Columbia, Planning & Devel, asst city admin, 1979-82; The Eugene & Agenes E Meyer Found, Washington DC, pres, 1983-85; The Rockefeller Found, New York NY, program dir, 1986-. **Orgs:** Mem, bd of dir, Assn of Black Found Exec; mem, assoc of the council, Council on Found; mem, visiting comm, Graduate School of Design, Harvard Univ; mem, bd of dir, Kaiser Permanente Community Health Plan of Mid-Atlantic States; consultant, Natl Planning Found, US Conf of Mayors, White House Conf on Civil Rights; mem, bd of governors, Corcoran Gallery of Art, 1968-72; exec comm mem, Federal City Council, 1971-75; founding mem, Cultural Alliance of Greater Washington, 1977; panel on the underclass, Amer Agenda, 1988. **Military Serv:** US Army, sp7, 1956-59; Honorable Discharge, 1959; mem, US Le Clerc Team, 1957-58.

GIBSON, JOANN
Business owner. **Personal:** Born Jul 2, 1946, Detroit, MI; daughter of Frederick E and Loretta Buckner; married Ronnie L Gibson, Mar 23, 1965; children: Drew Allen, Dayna Harris. **Educ:** Wayne County Community College, 1977; Marygrove College, 1979-84. **Career:** Michigan Bell Telephone, information operator, 1964; Bendix corporation, secretary/customer service coordinator, 1965-84; DynaPath Systems, supervisor, customer service, 1984-91; Matters & More, president, 1995-. **Orgs:** National Association for Female Executives, 1988-; Excel Network, founder and director, 1989-91; National Association of Women Business Owners, 1992-; National Women's History Project, 1990-; Northwest Area Business Association, 1991-; NAACP, 1994-; Strive Network, 1993-; Women on Board Committee, Detroit Womens Forum, 1995; Victory Village Center for Community Youth, bd mem, 1996-. **Honors/Awds:** Northwest Area Business Association, Business Person of the Month, 1992, 1994; Detroit Public Schools, Jewels of Area D, 1992; Michigan Women's Historical Center and Hall of Fame, Michigan Women: Firsts and Founders. **Business Addr:** President, Matters & More, 16634 Greenlawn, Detroit, MI 48221-4912, (313)863-3901.

GIBSON, JOHN A.
Retired law enforcement official, clergyman. **Personal:** Born in Philadelphia, PA; married Eleanor Simmons; children: Sean Edward. **Educ:** Camden County Coll, AS 1979; Glassboro State Coll, BA 1981; Eastern Baptist, MA 1984; Temple Univ Philadelphia PA, PhD candidate. **Career:** Rutgers Univ, mgr 1964-75; Lawnside Police Dept, police lt 1975-; Borough of Somerdale, NJ, councilman, chief of police, 1987-93. **Orgs:** Calvary Baptist Church, Chester, PA, minister, 1987-. **Honors/Awds:** Outstanding Law Enforcement Professional of America. **Military Serv:** AUS Reserves Commission Ofcr. **Home Addr:** 200 Gloucester Ave, Somerdale, NJ 08083.

GIBSON, JOHN THOMAS
Educator. **Personal:** Born Sep 19, 1948, Montgomery, AL; son of L P Gibson and Herman F Gibson (deceased); married Mayme Voncile Pierce; children: John Thomas Jr, Jerard Trenton, Justin Tarrance, Shayla Voncile. **Educ:** Tuskegee Inst, BS EdM (fellowship winner) Disting Military Grad 1971; Univ of CO Boulder, EdS, PhD (fellowship winner) 1973; Harvard Univ, cert in mgmt 1982. **Career:** Tuskegee Inst, instructor of physical educ 1971-72; Smiley Jr High School Denver, admin asst 1971-73; AL State Univ, dir of lab experiences 1973-75, coord of fed rels 1975-76, coord 1976-83, exec asst to pres 1983-86, vice pres of business and finance 1986. **Orgs:** Chmn Affirmative Action Comm Mont Elmore & Autauga Co 1976-; bd mem Bellingrath Exec Council 1976-; treas mem bd of trustees First Congregational Ch1977-; vice polemarch & polemarch Montgomery Alumni Chap Kappa Alpha Psi Inc 1978-; sec IBPOE The Elks Southern Pride #431 1978; Shaaban Temple #103, 330 Mason, Optimist Int'l. **Honors/Awds:** Publs, Public School Finance; 56 publs subj of educ finance & admin FA; Phi Delta Kappa, outstanding education leader 1981. **Military Serv:** Capt 1970-78. **Business Addr:** Vice Pres, Business and Finance, Alabama A&M Univ, PO Box 369, Normal, AL 35762.

GIBSON, JOHNNIE M. M.
Business executive. **Personal:** Born Mar 1, 1949, Caryville, FL; daughter of Rosa Lee Maldon and Alphonso Maldon; children: Tiffany Michele. **Educ:** Chipola Junior College, FL, AA Nursing 1968; Albany State College, GA, BS Health Physical Education 1971; Georgia State University, GA, Med 1976. **Career:** Marianna HS, FL, high school teacher 1971-72; Albany, GA Police Dept, policewoman 1972-76; FBI, FL, special agent 1976-79; FBI, Washington, special agent 1979-82; FBI, White Collar Crime Div, supervisory special agent 1981-82; Office of Congressional and Public Affairs, supervisory special agent 1982-87; Criminal Investigative Division FBI-Detroit, supervisory special agent, 1988-93; Unit Chief Bureau, applicant investigations unit, FBI Head. **Orgs:** Member NOBLE 1981-; member Capital Press Club 1982-; guest lecturer Historical Black Colleges- Universities 1982-; visiting lecturer Urban League Black Executive Exchange Program 1982-; FBI spokeswoman FBI Public Affairs Office 1982-; member IAWP 1984; member-at-large Natl Assoc of Media Women 1985-. **Honors/Awds:** Several letters of commendation from Dir of FBI, 1978, 1980, 1981, 1989; Key to City of Louisville, KY, 1982; Honorary Kentucky Colonel, City of Louisville, 1982; Community Service Award, United Black Fund, Greater Natl Chapter, 1984; Law Enforcement Pioneer Award, North State Law Enforcement Officers Association, 1988; Outstanding Support of Men & Women of the Air Force, The Air Force District of Washington, DC; CBS movie, Johnnie Mae Gibson: FBI, 1986. **Business Addr:** Unit Chief, Federal Bureau of Investigation, Rm 6658, FBI Headquarters, Washington, DC 20535.

GIBSON, KENNETH ALLEN
Mayor. **Personal:** Born May 15, 1932, Enterprise, AL; widowed; children: Cheryl, JoAnn, Joyce. **Educ:** Newark Coll, BS Engrg 1960. **Career:** NJ Hwy Dept, engr 1950-60; Newark Housing Auth, chief engr 1960-66; City of Newark, chief structgural engr 1966-70; City of Newark, mayor 1970-86; Gibson Associates, Inc, construction management firm, president, currently. **Orgs:** Past pres US Conf of Mayors 1976-77; bd dirs Newark Urban Coalition; co-chmn Bus & Indusl Coord Council; bd dirs Newark YMCA-YWCA; mem Amer Soc CE; Frontiers Intl. **Honors/Awds:** Jaycee's Man of the Yr Newark 1964. **Military Serv:** CE, AUS 1956-58. **Business Addr:** Renaissance Towers, 111 Mulberry St, Suite 1G, Newark, NJ 07102, (201)624-2001.

GIBSON, NELL BRAXTON
Church executive. **Personal:** Born Apr 9, 1942, Cordele, GA; daughter of Anne Thomas Braxton and John Thomas Braxton; married Bertram M Gibson II, Apr 10, 1966; children: Erika Anne. **Educ:** Tougaloo College, 1960-61; Spelman College, 1961-62; California State University at Sacramento, 1962-64; Empire State College, BA, 1982. **Career:** General Theological Seminary, pastoral associate, 1982-85; Episcopal Diocese of New York, executive assistant to Bishop, 1983-89; Episcopal Mission Society, Parish Based Services, director, 1989-95; National Council of Churches, program director, 1995-96, associate gen sec for inclusiveness and justice, 1996-. **Orgs:** New York Chapter, UBE (Union of Black Episcopalians), president, 1991-; Metro-Manhattan Chapter, The Links, 1990-; Anglican Consultative Council, alternate, 1988-; Black Diocesan Executives, 1986-; Transafrica, 1984-; General Tehological Seminary, trustee; St Mary's Episcopal AIDS Ctr, vp; Balm in Gilead for the Healing Aids, chairman of bd; Episcopal Church's Standing Committee on Peace With Justice. **Honors/Awds:** Berkeley Divinity School, Yale University, Honorary Doctor of Divinity, 1985; President's Award, Outstanding Service/National Union Black Episcopalians, 1992; Black Ministries Service Award, 1982; General Convention Certificate of Appreciation, 1991. **Special Achievements:** Publications, articles: Journey to Johannesburg, 1987, Namibia, Ground of Hope, 1988, Karibu, 1985, Racism, The Church's Spiritual Death, 1984, Is This Ministry?, 1983; First Woman Elected to Berkeley Divinity School at Yale University, Board of Trustees, 1970. **Business Addr:** Associate General Secretary for Inclusiveness and Justice, National Council of Churches, 475 Riverside Dr, New York, NY 10115, (212)870-2916.

GIBSON, OLIVER DONNOVAN
Professional football player. **Personal:** Born Mar 15, 1972, Chicago, IL. **Educ:** Univ of Notre Dame, degree in economics. **Career:** Pittsburgh Steelers, defensive tackle, 1995-. **Business Addr:** Professional Football Player, Pittsburgh Steelers, Three Rivers Stadium, 300 Stadium Circle, Pittsburgh, PA 15212, (412)323-1200.

GIBSON, PAUL, JR.
Business executive. **Personal:** Born Aug 5, 1927, New York, NY; married Marcia A Johnson. **Educ:** City Coll NY, BA 1953; NY Univ Sch of Law, JD 1952. **Career:** Am Airlines, vice pres gen mgr; City of NY, dep mayor for planning; New York City Bd Educ, educ; Fleary Gibson & Thompson, atty 1954; New York City Housing Auth, comm coord 1955-59; New York City Council, leg couns 1966; NY St Sup Ct, law sec 1969; Am Airlines, dir urban affairs 1969; Urban & Environ Affairs, asst vice pres 1971. **Orgs:** Gen couns NY St NAACP 1962-69; housing chmn NAACP; pres Jamaica NY NAACP; chmn bd dir Jamaica NAACP Day Care Ctr Inc; dir Nat Aerospace Educ Assn; vice pres Jamaica C of C; mem Urban & Reg Affairs Com US C of C; mem Urban Affairs Com Nat Assn Mfgrs; mem corp adv com Nat Urban Coalition; mem bd dir Flagship Intl Inc; pres City Counc 1966-69; chmn Pragmetic Ind NYC; chrmn Intl Trav Ind Exec Com & St John's Epis Ch; mem Queens Co Bar Assn; mem bd trst Niagara U; mem NY St Bar. **Military Serv:** AUS 1946-47.

GIBSON, RALPH MILTON
Educator. **Personal:** Born Oct 5, 1923, Cleveland, OH; son of Audrey Gibson and Milton Gibson; married Rose Cleland Campbell; children: Ralph Jr, John Samuel. **Educ:** Univ of MI, BS 1945, MS 1947, PhD 1959. **Career:** Cleveland Ohio Child Guidance Clinic, chief psychologist 1947-51; Univ of MI Med Sch, asst prof 1962-65, assoc prof 1965-70, prof 1970-, asst dean 1976-83, professor emeritus, 1991-. **Orgs:** Assoc staff mem, Wayne Co Gen Hosp 1963-73; State of MI Comm Cert of Psychologists 1963-65; mem Rotary Club 1965-70; bd dir United Fund 1966-68; mem, 1966-74, pres, 1973-74, bd of trustees, Greenhills School; vice chmn bd in control Intrcoll Att, Univ of Michigan, 1969-74, 1986-87; mem, Natl Advisory Council on Child Health & Human Development, Natl Inst of Health, 1987-91. **Honors/Awds:** 1st black full prof, Univ of Michigan Med School, US Public Health Service, 1952-53; Wade H McCree Jr Distinguished Faculty Award, Univ of Michigan Alumni, 1987; Outstanding Achievement in past 50 years, Rackham Graduate School, Univ of Michigan, 1988; Ralph Gibson Award to be given annually to an outstanding black senior, Univ of Michigan Medical School, established 1991. **Home Addr:** 321 Riverview Dr, Ann Arbor, MI 48104. **Business Addr:** Professor Emeritus, Psychology, Univ of Michigan Med School, 1924 Taubman Health Care Center, Ann Arbor, MI 48109.

GIBSON, REGINALD WALKER
Judge. **Personal:** Born Jul 31, 1927, Lynchburg, VA; son of Julia Ann Butler Gibson and McCoy Gibson; children: Reginald S Jr. **Educ:** Virginia Union Univ, BS, 1952; Univ of Pennsylvania, Wharton Graduate School of Business Administration, 1952-53; Howard Univ School of Law, LLB, 1956. **Career:** Dept of Treasury, Internal Revenue Service, agent, 1957-61; Dept of Justice Tax Division, trial attorney, 1961-71; International Harvester Co, senior tax attorney, 1971-76, general tax attorney, 1976-82; US Claims Court, now called US Court of Federal Claims, judge, 1982-. **Orgs:** Mem District of Columbia Bar Assn; mem Federal Bar Assn; mem Illinois Bar Assn; mem Natl Bar Assn; mem Claims Court Bar Assn; mem J Edgar Murdock Amer Inn of Court Taxation. **Honors/Awds:** Wall Street Journal Award, Ranking student in Business Admin, 1952; Amer Jurisprudence Award, Excellence in Taxation and Trusts, 1956; US Atty General's Certificate of Award, 1969; Special Commendation for Outstanding Service in Tax Division, US Department of Justice, 1970; Distinguished Alumni of the Year Howard Univ School of Law, 1984. **Military Serv:** US Army, Cpl, 1946-47. **Business Addr:** Judge, US Court of Federal Claims, 717 Madison Place NW, Washington, DC 20005.

GIBSON, ROBERT
Sports administrator, professional baseball player (retired). **Personal:** Born Nov 9, 1935, Omaha, NE. **Educ:** Attended Creighton Univ. **Career:** St Louis Cardinals, player 1959-75; NY Mets, coach 1981-82; Atlanta Braves, coach; St Louis Cardinals, announcer; American League, special adviser to the president, 1998-. **Honors/Awds:** Player World Series 1964, 1967-68; Recip Cy Young Award Natl League 1968, 1970; Most Valuable Player Natl League 1968; Baseball Hall of Fame 1981; mem Natl League All Star team 8 times. **Business Addr:** Special Adviser to the President, American League, 350 Park Ave, New York, NY 10022, (212)339-7600.

GIBSON, ROGER ALLAN
Airline executive. **Personal:** Born Jun 9, 1946, Oakland, CA; son of Betty J Gibson; married Patrice Gibson, Oct 21, 1995; children: Terrence, Kai, Jennifer. **Educ:** Merrit College, 1971-73; Chabot College, 1974-76; Saint Mary's College, BA, 1986. **Career:** United Airlines, manager of inventory planning & control, 1979-86, director of MOC supply & system dist, 1986-87, director, inventory planning & control, 1987-89, director, resource planning & control, 1989, director, total quality, 1990-91, general manager, Oakland Aircraft Mod Ctr, 1991-92, vice pres, North America-Mountain, 1992-. **Orgs:** Colorado National Bank, board member, 1995-; Colorado's Ocean Journey, board member, 1996-; Colorado Uplife, board member, 1993-; Denver Area Council Boy Scouts, board member, 1993-; The Denver Foundation, board member, 1996-; Denver Zoological Foundation, board member, 1996-; Metropolitan State College of Denver, board member, 1996-; National Jewish Ctr, board member, 1996-. **Military Serv:** US Navy, 1965-70. **Business Addr:** Vice Pres, North America-Mountain Region, United Airlines, 1225 17th St, Ste 2240, Denver, CO 80202, (303)790-6568.

GIBSON, SARAH L.
Educator, consultant. **Personal:** Born May 8, 1927, Princeton, KY; daughter of Fiercie E Edmonds Gray and Earl N Gray, Sr; children: Piper E Fakir, Kyle C. **Educ:** Wayne Univ, BS 1948; Wayne State Univ, MEd, PhD 1972. **Career:** Bureau of Social Aid, social worker 1949-53; Pontiac School System, teacher 1955-60; Detroit Public School, teacher 1960-68, school admin 1968-84; GECS, educ consultant 1974-. **Orgs:** Mem ASCD, NAACP, MAMSE 1963; assoc prof Univ of Detroit 1965-67; mem & consultant Trade Leadership Council 1967-; sec Metropolitan Detroit Assoc of Black Admin 1969-72; consulting nurse Harper Hospital 1969-72; consultant Marygrove Coll 1970-71. **Home Addr:** 2139 Bryanston Crescent, Detroit, MI 48207.

GIBSON, TRUMAN K., JR.
Attorney, corporation executive. **Personal:** Born Jan 22, 1912, Atlanta; married Isabelle Carson. **Educ:** Univ of Chicago, PhB 1932; JD 1935. **Career:** Chicago, atty 1935-40; War Dept, asst to civilian aide to sec of War 1940-43, acting civilian aide 1943, civilian aide 1943-45; Chicago, atty 1946-. **Orgs:** Mem firm Gibson & Gibson; gen counsel Tuesday Publs Inc; dir mem exec com Supreme Life Ins Co; dir Parkway Hotel Mgmt Inc; apptd mem Pres's AdvCom on Universal Mil Training 1946;

Pres's Com on Morals Character Devel & Religion in Armed Serv 1948;former mem sec Chicago Land Clearance Commn; mem Kappa Alpha Psi; Sigma Pi Phi. **Honors/Awds:** Awarded medal of merit Sec of War Stimson 1945. **Business Addr:** 471 E 31 St, Chicago, IL 60616.

GIBSON, WARREN ARNOLD
Attorney. **Personal:** Born Jul 16, 1941, Gary, IN. **Educ:** IN U, BS 1965; IN Univ 1972; In U, cume laude 1973. **Career:** Dow Chem Co, atty; Exxon Corp, emp Rel Rep 1967-70; Montgomery Wards, supr 1966-67. **Orgs:** Mem Am Bar Assn; Nat Bar Assn; MI Bar Assn; Midland Bar Assn. **Honors/Awds:** Mem Alpha Phi Alpha; bd of dir Midland Jr Achvmt 1976-78; Urban League Black Exec Exchange Prgm.

GIBSON, WAYNE CARLTON
Oil company executive. **Personal:** Born Oct 20, 1958, Fordyce, AR; son of Odis (deceased) & Gertrude Thrower Gibson; married Ruthie N Gibson, Jul 26, 1980; children: Carla Roschelle. **Educ:** Henderson State University, BSBA, 1980; Northwestern University, J L Kellogg School of Business, 1989. **Career:** Murphy Oil Corporation, accountant, 1980-84, senior division order analyst, 1984-86, supervisor, Lease Records & Division Orders, 1986-92, general manager, Corporate Purchasing, 1992-. **Orgs:** El Dorado School Board, board member, 1990-; Barton Library, board of directors, 1989-93; South Arkansas Symphony, board of directors, 1990-; Salvation Army, board of directors, 1985-; National Association of Purchasing Managers, 1992-; American Management Association, 1986-; Arkansas & El Dorado Board of Realtors, 1983-; Union County Literacy Council, board of directors, 1991-94. **Honors/Awds:** Arkansas Department of Parks & Tourism, Community Volunteerism, 1990. **Business Addr:** General Manager, Corp Purchasing, Murphy Oil Corporation, 200 Peach Street, Corporate Headquarters, El Dorado, AR 71730, (501)864-6225.

GIBSON, WILLIAM HOWARD, JR.
Dentist. **Personal:** Born Jan 28, 1941, Memphis, TN. **Educ:** Lincoln U, BS 1961; KS State U, MS 1962; Howard U, DDS 1968. **Career:** Yeatman Hlth Ctr, dentist 1969-77; Metro Med W Univ Park Med Grp, partner/dentist, currently. **Orgs:** Mem Am Dental Assn; Nat Dental Assn; MO Dental Assn; Midwestern States Dental Assn; Grtr St Louis Dental Soc; Mound City Dental Soc; Acad of Gen Dentistry; mem Lincoln Univ Alumni Assn; Howard Univ Alumni Assn; Royal Vagabonds; Rotary Internat; bd dir Univ City MO Club; Chi Delta Mu Frat 1967; Ford Found Flw 1961; pres Alpha Phi Chap 1961; mem Phi Delta Kappa 1962. **Business Addr:** PO box 3055, St Louis, MO 63130-0455.

GIBSON, WILLIAM M.
Clergyman. **Personal:** Born Sep 11, 1934, Hackensack, NJ; son of Evelyn Scott Gibson and James Gibson; married Jean J Gibson, May 2, 1989; children: Monica, Wayne, Wesley, Gibson, Cayce, Jerrell Johnson. **Educ:** Rutgers, BA 1956; Law Review Boston Univ Law, JD 1959; Boston Coll, MSW 1966; Harvard Business School, AMP Certificate 1973; Valordictorian MDiv Virginia Magna Cum Laude 1989. **Career:** US Dept of Justice, asst US Atty 1961-64; Boston Univ Law, dir law & poverty project 1966-70; Boston Univ School Afro Amer Studies, Assoc Prof 1968-71; Office Economic Opportunity, regional counsel 1970-72; FTC, regional dir 1972-78; Fuller Mental Health Center, supt area dir; Boston, Metro Dist, deputy district manager; St Paul's Baptist Church, minister of educ and singles; Medical College of VA Hospital, Richmond, staff chaplain, 1990-91; Saint Stephen's Baptist Church, pastor, currently; VA Union Univ, Criminology & Criminal Justice Dept, instructor, 1993-. **Orgs:** Mem Natl Assoc Social Work 1966; mem Academy Certified Social Worker 1968; mem MA Bar Assoc 1984; Sports Anglers Club, VA; Henrico County Criminal Justice Commission; Richmond Police Citizens Academy Board. **Honors/Awds:** 10 Outstanding Young Men Award Boston Jr CC 1968; Boston Univ Law School, Young Lawyers Chair, 1969; Community Serv Award Roxbury YMCA 1969; Outstanding Performance Award FTC 1972; Outstanding Govt Serv Award NAACP Boston 1975; Outstanding Serv Award Salvation Army 1980; Samuel H James, Sr Theological Award, VA Union School of Theology, 1989. **Military Serv:** USAF Medical Corps staff sergeant, 1959-64. **Home Addr:** PO Box 6102, Richmond, VA 23222.

GIDDINGS, HELEN
State Representative. **Personal:** Born Apr 21, 1943, Dallas, TX; daughter of Arthur and Catherine Warren Ferguson; married Donald Giddings; children: Lizette, Lisa, Stanley. **Educ:** Univ of Texas, BA, business, 1968. **Career:** Sears and Roebuck, training dir, 1975-77, personnel manager, 1977-81, dir of community affairs, 1979-81; Select Personnel, president, 1981-86; Dallas Assembly, elected member, 1981-; Texas state representative, district 109, 1993-; Small business owner, currently. **Orgs:** Leadership Dallas, exec dir, 1985-86; Dallas Alliance, trustee, 1981-, exec dir, 1987; Dallas Symphony, gov, 1980-; District 6 State Bar Grievance Comm; Dallas Theatre Ctr, bd of dirs, 1984-; Dallas Black Chamber of Commerce, president, 1981-92; Dallas Historical Society, secretary, 1983-. **Honors/Awds:** Committee of 100, Woman of the Year, 1980; East Oak Cliff-Dallas Ind Sch Dist, Achieving Against the Odds Award, 1981; Zeta Phi Beta, Woman of the Year Award, 1984; Alpha Phi Alpha, Community Service Award, 1987. **Business Addr:** State Representative, Texas House of Representatives, 1510 North Hampton, Ste. 220, DeSoto, TX 75115.

GIDDINGS, PAULA JANE
Writer, educator. **Personal:** Born Nov 16, 1947, Yonkers, NY; daughter of Virginia Stokes Giddings and Curtis Giddings. **Educ:** Howard University, Washington, DC, BA, 1969. **Career:** Rutgers University, New Brunswick, NJ, Laurie New Jersey chair in women's studies, 1989-; Spelman College, Atlanta, GA, distinguished UNCF scholar, 1986-87. **Orgs:** Treasurer, Author's Guild of America, 1991; Delta Sigma Theta Inc, 1967-; board member, PEN, 1990-; board member, Natl Coalition of 100 Black Women, 1985-; American Historical Assn, 1990. **Honors/Awds:** United Negro Fund Distinguished Scholar, Spelman Coll, 1986-87; Honorary Doctorate, Humane Letters, Bennett College, 1990. **Special Achievements:** Author: When and Where I Enter, 1984.

GIDNEY, CALVIN L.
Dentist. **Personal:** Born Dec 22, 1930, Mt Airy, NC; married Willa Broome; children: Calvin, III, Craig, Evan. **Educ:** Fisk U, AB 1952; Meharry Med Coll, DDS 1959. **Career:** Doctor of Dental Surgery, priv prac present. **Orgs:** Mem Omega Psi Phi; mem Fisk Univ Alumni Assn; trustee Sheridan School. **Honors/Awds:** Alumni of yr Fisk Univ Washington Club 1971. **Military Serv:** AUS 1953-55. **Business Addr:** 511 Kennedy St NW, Washington, DC 20011.

GIDRON, RICHARD D. (DICK)
Automobile dealership executive. **Personal:** Born Oct 10, 1939, Chicago, IL; married Marjorie; children: Bridget, Richard Jr. **Educ:** Bryant and Straton College. **Career:** Cadillac Motors, Chicago, general manager, 1959-72; Dick Gidron Cadillac Inc, owner, president, 1972-; Dick Gidron Ford Inc, president, currently. **Orgs:** Bronx Chamber of Commerce, president; Financial Ctrl Board of City of NY, Fordham University, trustee; Archdiocese of NY, trustee; NAACP. **Honors/Awds:** Doctorate Degree, Pace University; Recognized by President Reagan, Outstanding Business Executive, 1984; numerous others. **Special Achievements:** Company listed #14 on Black Enterprise's list of Top 100 Auto Dealers, 1992. **Home Addr:** Dick Gidron Cadillac Inc, 2030 E Tremont Ave, Bronx, NY 10462-5703, (212)295-3000. **Business Addr:** President, Dick Gidron Ford, Inc, 2030 E Tremont Ave, Bronx, NY 10462, (212)409-4400.

GIFFORD, BERNARD R.
Educator. **Personal:** Born May 18, 1943, Brooklyn, NY; married Ursula M Jean; children: Antoinette, Bernard. **Educ:** Long Island Univ, BS 1965; Univ of Rochester Med Sch, MS 1968; Univ of Rochester Med Sch, PhD 1972. **Career:** Univ of California at Berkeley, prof, currently; Academic Systems Corp, chmn, currently; Russell Sage Found, resident scholar, beginning 1977; New York City Public School System, deputy chancellor & chief of business affairs office 1973-77; New York City Rand Inst, pres 1972-73. **Orgs:** Adv Com, John F Kennedy Inst of Politics, Harvard Univ; bd of visitors, City Coll of NY; bd of trustees, NY Univ; acad adv com, US Naval Academy; consultant, CA Supreme Court, 1978-79; consultant, Asst Sec for Com Planning & Devt, Dept of Housing & Urban Devt, 1979; consultant, Natl Acad of Public Admin, 1979-80; consultant, Natl Inst of Educ; bd of dirs, NY Urban Coalition; bd of trustees, German Marshall Fund of US; editorial bd, Urban Affairs Quarterly; bd of edit advs NY Affairs; editorial bd, NY Educ Quarterly; editorial bd, policy Analysis; appointed adj prof, public admin, Columbia Univ, 1975-77; appointed adj lecturer, Public Policy, John F Kennedy School of Govt, Harvard Univ, 1977-78; appointed adjunct & visiting prof, Dept of Urban Studies &Planning, Hunter Coll, City Univ oY, MA Inst of Tech; US Atomic Energy Comm, Fellow in Nuclear Science, 1965-71. **Honors/Awds:** Phi Beta Kappa. **Special Achievements:** Co-author, "Revenue Sharing & the Planning Process" 1974; author, "The Urbanization of Poverty: A Preliminary Investigation of Shifts in the Distribution of the Poverty Population by Race Residence & Family Structure," 1980; numerous other publications. **Business Addr:** Professor, University of California at Berkeley, Dept of Education, EMST Division, Tolman Hall, Berkeley, CA 94720.

GIGGER, HELEN C.
Attorney. **Personal:** Born Dec 24, 1944, Houston, TX; married Nathan J Gigger. **Educ:** TX South U, BA Pol Sci 1965; TX So U, JD 1968. **Career:** State of OK, OK crime comm, legal coun, planner; Dean of Law Sch, res asst; Houston Leg Found, legal intern; Okla City & Co Comm Act Prog Inc, prog analyst. **Orgs:** Mem Am Nat & OK Bar Assns; sec JJ & Bruce Law Soc; mem Amer Judiccature Soc; EEOC off Okla Crime Comm; mem Nat Spa Courts Plan Org; lect Crim Just OK City U; mem YWCA; Urban League; League of Women Voters Georgia Brown's Demo Women's Club; OK Black Pol Cau; past pres Delta Sigma Theta Sor Inc; sec Local & State NAACP; elected Nat Scholarship & Standards Com 4 yr term; policy making com Delta Sigma Theta Inc 1975. **Honors/Awds:** Grad with Hons in 1961, 1965 & at top of Law Class in 1968; re chrprsn of Reg VI NAACP Conf 1974; Parli; Nat Delta Conv 1973; Delta Cen Reg Parli 1974; mem of Greater Cleves CME Ch; Ch Prog Chrprsn. **Business Addr:** 3033 N Walnut, Oklahoma City, OK 73105.

GIGGER, NATHANIEL JAY
Attorney. **Personal:** Born Jan 1, 1944, Elmore City, OK; son of Katie Wyatt Gigger and Ernest Gigger; married Helen Coleman Gigger, Oct 25, 1968; children: Nikolle Janelle. **Educ:** Langston Univ, Langston OK, BA, 1963; Texas Southern Univ, Houston TX, JD, 1967. **Career:** State of Oklahoma, Oklahoma City OK, asst state atty gen, 1970-79, deputy atty, Dept of Human Resources, 1979; Derryberry, Duncan & Nance Law Firm, Oklahoma City OK, mem, 1979-82; Self-Employed, Oklahoma City OK, atty, 1982-. **Orgs:** Mem, Prince Hall of Masons, 1967-; vice pres, State Conf of Branches NAACP, 1972-77; state legal chmn, Intl Benevolent Protective Order of Elks, 1975-80; mem, Mayor's Comm for Business Devel, 1976-79; exec bd mem, Community Action Agency, 1976-81; mem, Assn of Black Trial Lawyers, 1982-; bd mem, Oklahoma Business & Devel Council, 1984-86; mem, Northeast Oklahoma City Chamber of Commerce, 1987-, J J Bruce Law Soc. **Honors/Awds:** Roscoe Dunjee Humanitarian Award, Oklahoma NAACP, 1975; Outstanding Citizenship Award, Alpha Phi Alpha Frat, 1976; Outstanding Citizen Award, Oklahoma City Set Club, 1981; Outstanding Lawyer Award, NAACP Youth Council, 1986. **Business Addr:** Attorney, 732 NE 36th St, Oklahoma City, OK 73105.

GILBERT, ALBERT C.
Business executive. **Personal:** Born Oct 19, 1924, Carlisle, PA; married Iris Boswell; children: Brenda, Richard, Walda Ann, Albert C III, Charles. **Educ:** Morgan State Univ, Baltimore, MD, BS, 1950; St John Coll, Cleveland, OH, merit, 1966; Cambridge (Center), New York, NY, merit, 1967. **Career:** Continental Can Co, Cleveland, OH, joined in 1950 hourly employee became financial sec then pres of union, supr 1958, supt 1964, first black mgr 1969-, special sales representative, 1974-83; Congressman Louis Stokes, Washington, DC, senior intern, 1985. **Orgs:** Vice chmn Fibre Box Assn; sch bd mem E Cleveland Sch 1971-; mem Natl Black Sch Bd; Natl Safety Council; mem Citizens League Greater Cleveland; mem El Hasa Masonic Shrine 32 degree mason; mem Cleveland C of C; OH Mfgr Assn; former Scout Master; bd dirs Rainey Inst of Music; spec sales rep Continental Group; prs East Cleveland Kiwanis, 1987; Cuyahoga Co, OH, Western Reserve Agency for Senior Citizens, 1987-; board of managers, YMCA, 1988-; governor, Ohio District of Kiwanis International, 1994-95; pres, East Cleveland (FOPA) Fraternal Order of Police Association, 1996-97. **Honors/Awds:** Morgan State Coll Hall of Fame Outstanding Football Player & Wrestler 1974. **Military Serv:** AUS WW II sgt; awarded 4 Bronze Stars. **Home Addr:** 2100 N Taylor Rd, Cleveland, OH 44112-3002.

GILBERT, CHRISTOPHER
Psychologist. **Personal:** Born Aug 1, 1949, Birmingham, AL. **Educ:** Univ of MI, BA 1972; Clark Univ, MA 1975, PhD 1987. **Career:** Judge Baker Guidance Ctr, psychologist 1979-84; Univ of MA Med Sch, psychologist 1979-84; Cambridge Family & Childrens Svcs, psychologist 1983-85; Univ of Pgh English Dept, vstg poet 1986. **Orgs:** Bd of dirs Elm Park Center for Early Educ 1980-84, Worcester Chap Civil Liberties Union of MA 1983-85, Worcester Children's Friend 1983-86. **Honors/Awds:** MA Artists Foundation Fellowship 1981; Walt Whitman Awd Acad of Amer Poets 1983; NEA Fellowship Poetry 1986; Robert Frost Awd 1986.

GILBERT, ELDRIDGE H. E.
Clergyman. **Personal:** Born Oct 27, 1912, New Orleans, LA; married Annie Lee Wilson; children: Eldridge HE Jr. **Educ:** Amer Bapt Theol Sem Nashville, BTh 1944; Rockford Sch Grad Beloit Coll WI, BA 1947; Attended, Virginia Union Univ; Rockford Coll, Hon Doctorate of Humane Letters. **Career:** Rock Valley Jr Coll, tchr the negro in amer history; Rock River Meth Conf Lake Geneva, counselor/tchr; Rock River Bapt Assn Lake Springs, counselor/tchr/pastor; Rockford & Vicinity Bapt Assoc, teacher; Pilgrim Bapt Ch, pastor. **Orgs:** Past pres & sec Ministerial Assn; religious counselor Rockford Coll; past pres Greater Rockford Clergy; past pres Rockford Ministers Fellowship; pub paper "Survey Analysis of Rockford" 1947; pub epilogue "That We Should Know So Little of Men"; guest speaker World Council of Chs Europe 1953; visitor 15 African& Near E Countries 1969; visitor Haiti Missions 1973; mem World Council of Churches; alternate delegate ABC Vancouver BC; bd mem ABC; Comm on Church Unity 4 yrs; Professional Standards Causes of Great Rivers Region 4 yrs. **Honors/Awds:** Citation for Min & Comm Serv Plaque Balthasar 32 Lodge 1974; Citation Natl Council of Negro Women 1975; ordained 4 ministers for pastorate; mem EcumenicalInst Study Confs of the Ministry Salamanca Spain 1977; Citation Winnebago Cty OIC 1975 1977-78; Natl Registry of Prominent Amers 1976-77; Stewardship Awd Protestant Welfare Assn; Alumni of the Yr Awd Beloit Coll. **Business Addr:** Pastor, Pilgrim Bapt Church, 1703 S Central Ave, Rockford, IL 61102.

GILBERT, FRANK
State representative. **Personal:** Born Jun 10, 1934, Greenwood, SC; son of Essie Johnson Gilbert and Thomas James Gilbert; married Ella Lois Robinson, 1960; children: Thomas Wayne, Frank Jr. **Educ:** Benedict College, BA, 1957; Columbia University, Teacher's College, MA, 1964; New York University; University of South Carolina. **Career:** Educator, retired; UniServ,

rep, currently; South Carolina State Senate, senator, district 30, 1983-. **Orgs:** South Carolina Education Association; Florence County Education Association; Alpha Phi. **Honors/Awds:** Benedict College, Distinguished Alumnus Award, 1985. **Special Achievements:** Delegate to Democratic National Convention, 1980, 1984. **Military Serv:** US Army, 1957-59. **Business Addr:** State Senator, State of South Carolina, PO Box 142, Columbia, SC 29202, (803)734-2864.

GILBERT, FRED D., JR.
Higher educational administrator. **Personal:** Born Dec 2, 1947, New Orleans, LA. **Educ:** Dillard Univ, BA Business Admin 1970; Loyola Univ, MEd Educ Admin 1972; IA State Univ Higher Educ, PhD 1978. **Career:** Upward Bound Project, admin dir, 1971-73; Upward Bound & Special Serv Proj Univ, proj dir 1973-75; IA State Univ, rsch asst 1975-76, univ married housing area adv 1976-77, TRIO dir, ast prof 1978-; IA State Univ Coll of Ed, ast dean, 1987-; Des Moines Area Comm Coll, dean of urban campus, 1987-90, executive director of district admin, 1990-92, exec dir or research, foundation, grants and contracts, 1992-94, vp of research & development, 1994-. **Orgs:** Mem/board of directors of the following: Ames School District Foundation, Children & Families of Iowa, Family Enrichment Ctr, IA Comprehensive Manpower Serv & National Council of Research and Development. **Special Achievements:** Book Review of Black Coll in Amer Publishing in Educ Studies 1979; A Study of Power & Authority unpublished PhD Dissertation 1978; Dissertion ranked tenth in nation by Amer Assoc of Higher Educ. **Business Addr:** Vice President, Research & Development, Des Moines Area Comm College, 2006 S Ankeny Blvd, Ankeny, IA 50021.

GILBERT, HERMAN CROMWELL
Publishing executive, author. **Personal:** Born Feb 23, 1923, Marianna, AR; son of Cora Allen Gilbert and Van Luther Gilbert; married Ivy McAlpine; children: Dorthea Gilbert Lassister, Vincent Newton. **Educ:** LaSalle Extension Univ, Corres Law, 1943; Parkway Comm House Chicago, Creative Writing 1952; IBM Educ Cntr, Acct Machines & Computers 1973. **Career:** Packinghouse Wrkrs Union AFL-CIO, asst educ adv 1955-57; Westside Booster Newspaper Chicago, managing edit 1959-60; Citizens Newspapers Chicago, managing edit 1964-66; IL Bureau of Employment Sec, data proc dir 1970-73, asst admin 1973-81; Path Press Inc, exec vp, editorial director, currently. **Orgs:** Vice chrmn Assembly of Black State Exec 1973-77; chrmn Automated Systems Comm Interstate Conf 1974-75; bd mem International Black Writers Conference 1975-; chief of staff Cong Gus Savage 2nd IL 1981-82; exec vp/edit dir Path Press Inc 1982-; Society of Midland Authors 1983-; spec adv Cong Gus Savage 2nd IL 1984-. **Honors/Awds:** Rep William Clay 1st MO, Congressional Commendation, 1984; Rep Mickey Leland 18th TX, Certificate of Special Recognition, 1984; International Black Writers Conference, Alice Browning Award, 1992. **Special Achievements:** Author, novels include: The Uncertain Sound, 1969; The Negotiations, 1983; Sharp Blades in Tender Grass, 1987; This Needs Saying, in progress; The Campaign, in progress; essays: ''Henry Dumas and the Flood of Life,'' Black American Literature Forum, Vol 22, Num 2, 1988, reprinted, Contemporary Literary Criticism, Vol 62, Gale Research Inc; ''Developing An Effective Political Strategy for African-American Empowerment,'' Black Books Bulletin, Vol 8, 1991 Annual. **Military Serv:** AAC staff sgt 1943-46; Unit Citation 1944; Good Conduct Medal 1945. **Home Addr:** 11539 S Justine St, Chicago, IL 60643. **Business Addr:** Executive Vice President and Editorial Director, Path Press Inc, 53 W Jackson Blvd, Suite 1040, Chicago, IL 60604.

GILBERT, JEAN P.
Educator (retired). **Personal:** Born Aug 6, 1928, McDonald, PA. **Educ:** Univ of Buffalo, Ed D 1962; Univ of Buffalo, Ed M 1955; Bluefield St College, BS (cum laude), 1947. **Career:** Brooklyn Coll, counselor, educator 1964-; Univ of IL, counselor, educator 1962-63; Hampton Inst, dir of testing 1957-60; AL A&M Coll, counselor, lecturer 1956-57; SC State Coll, counselor, educator 1964-65. **Orgs:** Mem bd dir DST Telecommunications Inc; Delta Sigma Theta; Pi Lambda Theta; Kappa Delta Pi; Amer Psychlgcl Assn; Amer Persnnl & Guidnc Assn; Natl Voc Guidance Assn; Assn Non-White Concrns; Psychmtrc Dir Educ Prog Eval & Resrch JPG Consltnts Inc; JOB'S Prog; bd grdns bd dir New York City Prtstnt; mem GS Cncl of Grtr NY; mem Bd Gov NY St Prsnl & Guidnc Assn. **Honors/Awds:** Women of Achvmnt Award 1966; John Hay Whitney Fndtn Grnt 1960; James Fndtn Grant 1957; outstndng Edtrs of Amer 1974; Grant, Ford Foundation; author, Counseling Black Inner City Children in Groups.

GILBERT, RICHARD LANNEAR
Engineer. **Personal:** Born Dec 26, 1921, Indianapolis, IN; son of Roberta Wilson Ingram and Robert Howard Gilbert; married Margaret; children: 4. **Educ:** Lain Drafting Coll, attended; Purdue Univ Lafayette IN, attended; Franklin Univ Columbus OH, attended; Youngstown Univ OH, attended; Bowling Green State, attended, OH State Univ Columbus, attended; OH Univ Zanesville, attended. **Career:** US Naval Air Station Port Columbus, engr tech 1951-54; Erdman Anthony & Hosley Consult Engrs Columbus, engr tech 1954-55; Photronix Inc Aerial Photogrammetric & Consult Engrs Columbus OH, consult engr 1956-60; OH State Hwy Dept Div Design & Const Columbus, engr tech 1960-61; Lordstown Military Reservation Warren OH, engr 1961-62; Muskingum Area Tech Inst Zanesville OH, instr, chmn engr dept 1969-82; Inertial Guidance & Calibration Group, civil engr 1962-; City of Zanesville, city councilperson, currently. **Orgs:** Assisted housing problem Urban League, Warren OH 1960-62; comm mem Minority Housing, Citizens Advisory Comm, Zoning Bd of Appeals, Amer Cancer Soc; bd of dirs Zanesville Comm Center 1962-; exec bd mem Muskingum Cty Action Program 1962-; pres Muskingum-Athens/Morgan & WA County NAACP 1962-; mem advisory bd OH Univ Zanesville, OH Black Political Assn, Admission Counselors & Officials 1962-; hon mem Black Caucus of OH 1962-; chmn Muskingum Cty Branch NAACP; tech advisor Coalition of Concerned Citizens; mem Near East Side Area Council & Urban League 1955-75, Muskingum County Drug Council; pres NAACP; lecturer OH Univ Zanesville; devel tech Muskingum Area Tech Ins 1969-70; instructor, various special classes on engineering; coordinator MBE, WBE SE OH; council mem-Zanesville Cty 1982-84; mem O. **Business Addr:** City Councilperson, City of Zanesville, 401 Market St, Zanesville, OH 43701.

GILBERT, SHEDRICK EDWARD
Cleric. **Personal:** Born Jun 21, 1922, Miami, FL; married Wilma Wake, Jan 22, 1947; children: Janelle Gilbert Hall, Stephen, Jeffrey. **Educ:** Hampton University, BS (honors), 1954. **Career:** US Post Office, letter carrier, 1956-78, supervisor, 1978-84; St Agnes Episcopal Church, treasurer, 1967-94, assistant deacon, 1984-. **Orgs:** Algonquin Civic Club, vice pres, head of program committee, 1989-; Omega Psi Phi, 1952-; Overtown Advisory Board, 1991-; Diocese of Southeast Florida, stewardship commission, 1983-85; BTW Class of 1938, president, 1988-; St. Agnes/Rainbow Village Corp, director, 1990-; director, eight week summer recreation program, 1992; Every Member Canvas Campaign, stewardship, chairperson, 1990; Diocese of Southeast Florida, committee on credentials, chairman, 1974-84; Jefferson Reaves Sr Health Ctr Committee; Algonquin Club, president, 1996-97. **Honors/Awds:** Post Office Superior Achievement Award, letter carrier, 1970-84, supervisor, 1982. **Military Serv:** US Army, sergeant t-4, 1943-46. **Home Addr:** 3368 NW 51 Terr, Miami, FL 33142, (305)634-4321.

GILBERT, SHIRL E., II
Educational administrator. **Career:** Indianapolis Public Schools, superintendent, currently. **Orgs:** National Advisory Board for the National Center for Research on Evaluation, Standards and Students Testing. **Business Addr:** Superintendent, Indianapolis Public Schools, 120 E Walnut, Indianapolis, IN 46204, (317)226-4418.

GILCHRIEST, LORENZO
Educator (retired). **Personal:** Born Mar 21, 1938, Thomasville, GA; married Judith Graffman; children: Lorenzo David, Lorena. **Educ:** Newark State Coll, BS 1962; Pratt Inst, MS 1967; Maryland Inst Coll of Art, MFA 1975. **Career:** Towson State Univ, MD, asst prof art dept; Morgan State U, guest artist print workshop summer 1977; Baltimore Museum Art, art tchr adult prgm 1973-74; Cornell U, guest prof 1972-73; Sen Robert Kennedy Proj Bedford Stuyvesant Youth in Action, asst dir 1965-67; prof emeritus. **Orgs:** Mem Am Radio Relay League; Gen Class Amateur Radio Lisc 1976/Advanced Class Amateur Radio Lisc 1980. **Honors/Awds:** Samuel Kress Award 1971; Afro Amer slide depository Samuel Kress Found 1971; Fellow Internatl Artists Seminar 1962; protege of Elaine DeKooning 1963. **Military Serv:** US Army, 1956-57.

GILCHRIST, ROBERTSON
Government official, construction owner. **Personal:** Born Aug 24, 1926, Parksville, SC; married Evelyn Landise Searles; children: Gezetta. **Educ:** Mims HS, diploma 1945. **Career:** Owner construction co; councilmember. **Orgs:** Co-owner operator of restaurant known as Lan's Deli; mem Co Council; mem NAACP; mem Masonic Lodge. **Honors/Awds:** Public Serv & Private Business Awd Comm on Black History 1980; Appreciation Serv & Leadership Awd 4-H Club 1983. **Military Serv:** AUS corpl 18 months. **Home Addr:** PO Box 84, Parksville, SC 29844. **Business Addr:** Councilmember, PO Box 1147, Mc Cormick, SC 29835-1147.

GILCREAST, CONWAY, SR.
Elected government official. **Personal:** Born Feb 1, 1924, West Helena, AR; married Willie Mae Hamner; children: Helen, Conway Jr, Connie, Quiency, Harold, Betty, Carolyn, LaDon, Brenda, Cleopatra. **Educ:** AR Baptist Coll, AA 1951; Phelander Smith Coll, BA 1959. **Career:** Dansby Elementary School, principal 1956-59; Dora E Perkins Elementary School, teacher 1963-68; MM Tate Elementary School, teacher 1968-72; PLM&D Congress, teacher 1966-; City of West Helena, alderman. **Orgs:** Voter registration City of Helena 1978; election judge School Elections state & natl 1948-; pastor Baptist churches 1951-. **Honors/Awds:** Political advisor Political Org for Equal Rights 1979; alderman City of W Helena 1980; political advisor PLM&D, Inc 1981; Teacher of the Year PLM&D Congress 1984. **Military Serv:** AUS t/5 2 1/2 yrs; Good Conduct ATO ETO Marksman Hon Discharge 1943-46. **Home Addr:** 513 W Park, West Helena, AR 72390.

GILDON, JASON LARUE
Professional football player. **Personal:** Born Jul 31, 1972, Altus, OK; married Joy; children: Jason Jr. **Educ:** Oklahoma State. **Career:** Pittsburgh Steelers, linebacker, 1994-. **Business Addr:** Professional Football Player, Pittsburgh Steelers, Three Rivers Stadium, 300 Stadium Circle, Pittsburgh, PA 15212, (412)323-1200.

GILES, ALTHEA B.
Advertising executive. **Personal:** Born Mar 10, 1926, East Orange, NJ; daughter of Beatrice Smith-Banks and Russell Banks; married William R Giles, Jun 15, 1947; children: William R, Sharon Giles-Alexander, Kevin E. **Educ:** Kean Coll, Union NJ, BS, 1951. **Career:** East Orange Board of Educ, teacher, 1952-82; EPC Intl Inc, East Orange NJ, vice pres, beginning 1983, pres, currently; New Day Promotions, consultant, currently. **Orgs:** Consultant, Selig Assoc Inc; pres, Extra Personal Care Inc; consultant, Nancy Wilson Cosmetics; sec, Enterprising Twenty Inc; Arts & Culture Comm, Coalition 100 Black Women; NAACP; Natl Urban League; United Negro Coll Fund; Specialty Advertising Intl Inc; Links Inc; board of directors, Coalition 100 Black Women; co-chairman, New Jersey Lou Rawls Parade of Stars Telethon; board of trustess, Newark Museum; Foundation Board of Kean College. **Honors/Awds:** Community Serv Award, East Orange Mayor Hatcher; Black Heritage Award, City of East Orange; Meritorious Serv Award, United Negro Coll Fund; Outstanding Volunteer Award, United Negro Coll Fund; Citiation, Newark Municipal Council, Newark NJ; Achievement Award, UMD, NJ; Outstanding Service Award, East Orange Board of Education; Community Service Award, National Council Negro Women; Certificate of Appreciation, Essex County, Chapter, Links Inc; Woman of the Year Award, Zeta Phi Beta Sorority Eta Omicron Zeta Chapter. **Home Addr:** 43 Edgemont Rd, West Orange, NJ 07052. **Business Addr:** President, Extra Personal Care, Inc, PO Box 832, East Orange, NJ 07019.

GILES, CHARLOTTE EMMA
Educator. **Personal:** Born Mar 29, 1937, Baltimore, MD; daughter of Phozie Dawson and Samuel Hopkins. **Educ:** Fisk University, BA, 1958; Indiana University, MM, 1960, DM, 1970. **Career:** Tuskegee Institute, instructor, 1958-59; Florida A&M University, assistant professor of music, 1960-65; Knoxville College, associate professor of music, 1968-71; West Virginia State College, professor of music, 1971-. **Orgs:** Association Performing Arts Presenters, 1978-, board mem, 1985-87; Governor's Committee on Arts in Education, 1992. **Honors/Awds:** Sara Maloney Scholarship Award in Music, 1956; Louis Gottschak Music Prize, 4th place, 1970; National Endowment of Humanities Fellow, 1979, 1980. **Special Achievements:** Concert pianist, 1960-92; pianist with Charleston Symphony Orchestra, 1971-82; pianist for West Virginia Opera Theatre, 1972-85. **Business Addr:** Professor of Music, Chair of Concerts & Lectures, West Virginia State College, PO Box 1000, John W Davis Fine Arts Bldg, #203, Institute, WV 25112-1000, (304)766-3194.

GILES, HENRIETTA
Talk show producer. **Personal:** Born Feb 23, 1962, Stanton, TN; daughter of Geraldine Maxwell Giles and Jesse Cornelius Giles. **Educ:** University of Tennessee at Martin, Martin, TN, BS, 1984. **Career:** WTVF-TV, Nashville, TN, associate producer, 1984-85; WSOC-Radio, Charlotte, NC, copy writer, 1985-88; WTVF-TV, Nashville, TN, producer, 1988-. **Orgs:** Member, National Association of Black Journalists, 1990-; member, Nashville Assn of Minority Communicators, 1989-. **Business Addr:** Producer, WTVF-Channel 5, 474 James Robertson Parkway, Nashville, TN 37219.

GILES, JAMES T.
Federal judge. **Educ:** Amherst College, BA, 1964; Yale Univ, LLB, 1967. **Career:** National Labor Relations Board, member, 1967-68; Pepper Hamilton & Scheetz, associate attorney, 1968-79; US Dist Court, Eastern District, Philadelphia, PA, judge, 1979-. **Orgs:** Federal Bar Association; Philadelphia Bar Association. **Business Addr:** Judge, US District Court, Eastern District, 8613 US Courthouse, Independence Mall, W, Philadelphia, PA 19106.

GILES, JOE L.
Company executive. **Personal:** Born Dec 6, 1943, Elrod, AL; son of Pinkie Giles and Jessie Giles; married Sarah Fisher Giles, Dec 29, 1969; children: Alycia, Fredrick, Jolanda. **Educ:** Stillman College, Tuscalusa, AL, BA, 1966; University of Detroit, Detroit, MI, MA, 1976. **Career:** Joe L. Giles and Associates, president, 1980-. **Orgs:** President, Stillman College Alumni Association, 1988-90; director of placement, Kappa Alpha Psi, 1985-87; board of directors, MYFO, 1981-83. **Honors/Awds:** Top Biller, MAPC, 1988; Top Trainer, NAPC, 1988; Man of the Year, Church of the New Convenant, 1990. **Home Addr:** 18105 Parkside, Detroit, MI 48221. **Business Addr:** Owner/President, Joe L Giles and Associates, PO Box 20163, Ferndale, MI 48220, (313)864-0022.

GILES, NANCY
Actress. **Personal:** Born Jul 17, 1960, New York, NY; daughter of Dorothy Aileen Dove Giles and Thomas Jefferson Giles. **Educ:** Oberlin College, Oberlin, OH, BA, 1981. **Career:** Warner Brothers/ABC, Inc, Burbank, CA, actress, "China Beach". **Orgs:** Member, Actors Equity Assn, 1983-; member, Screen Actors Guild, 1984-; member, American Federation of Television and Radio Artists, 1984-. **Honors/Awds:** Theatre World Award, Outstanding New Talent, Theatre World, 1985; Honorary Member, Alliance of Women Veterans, 1989. **Business Addr:** Actress, c/o Bret Adams Ltd, 448 W 44th St, New York, NY 10036.

GILES, WILLIAM R.
Business executive. **Personal:** Born Nov 12, 1925, South Carolina; son of Mattie Giles and Bennie Giles; married Althea; children: William Jr, Kevin, Sharon. **Educ:** Benedict Coll. **Career:** East Orange Genl Hosp, bd of trustees; Cannolene Company, Nancy Wilson Cosmetics, exec vice pres; Evening of Elegance, sponsor; United Negro Coll Fund, major fund raiser; New Hope Bapt Church, chmn bldg fund; 100 Black Men of NJ, pres; Benedict Coll, emeritus, bd of trustees; EPC Intl Inc, founder and chairman. **Orgs:** Chmn, Selig Assoc, Extra Personal Care Inc, Giles Co Inc, Wm R Giles & Co Inc; developer, City Natl Bank; board of directors, E Orange PAL; joint enterprise Trusteeship Corp; bd dir, E Orange Gen Hosp; mem, Kiwanis Club, Premium Mktg Assn, Natl Urban League, Greater Newark Chamber of Commerce, Advtsg Spec Inst, E Orange Chamber of Commerce; board of directors Enterprising Twenty Inc; life member NAACP; assoc mem, Amer Health & Beauty Aid Inst, Spec Advtsg Assn of Greater NY; exec vice pres, OIC's of Amer; board of Governors, Ramapo College; board of directors, 100 Black Men America; board of directors, National MNY Business Council; Community Health Care of New Jersey; director, Lions Clubs International, East OrangeChapter; chairman, advisory committee, UNCF, New Jersey; executive committee, Governor's Economic Conference. **Honors/Awds:** Meritorious Serv Awd, United Negro Coll Fund; Appreciation Awd, Howard Univ Sch of Law; Humanitarian Awd, City of East Orange NJ; Outstanding Awd for the Develop of Minority Youth, Seventh Day Adventist Church; Appreciation Awd, Police Dept, City of East Orange; Honorary Citizen, City of New Orleans; Achievement Awd, Natl Coalition of Black Meeting Planners; Comm Serv Awd, Natl Council of Negro Women; Dedicated Serv in Educ Business & Politics Awd, Mayor John Hatcher; Family Enterprise Awd, Urban League of Essex Co; Black Heritage Awd, City of East Orange; Special Recognition Awd, Minority Interchange Inc; Outstanding Minority Business Awd, Natl Minority Business Council; DHL, Benedict Coll, Columbia SC; Citizen of the Month, Newark, NJ, August 1990;Honorary Citizen Award, State Senate New Jersey; Man of the Year, National Assn of Negro Business and Professional Women's Clubs, 1990; Entrepreneur of the Year, YMWCA of Newark and Vicinity; Distinguished Citizens Award, Ramapo College; Outstanding Business Award, Institute for America Business; Marcus Garvey Award; 100 Black Men of America; St James AME Church, Award of Excellence; Man of the Year, 100 Black Men of New Jersey, 1994; Newark Bd of Education, Dedicated Service Award; Profound Devotion to Youth, AD House Inc, 1994. **Military Serv:** US Army. **Home Addr:** 43 Edgemont Rd, West Orange, NJ 07052. **Business Addr:** Chairman, Extra Personal Care, Inc, PO Box 832, East Orange, NJ 07018.

GILES, WILLIE ANTHONY, JR.
Educational administrator. **Personal:** Born Mar 8, 1941, Conway, AR; married Carolyn Joan Williams; children: Dwayne, Keenon, Dana. **Educ:** AR AM&N Coll, BS 1964; Univ of MI, MA Educ Specialist 1967; Univ of MO Kansas City, Educ Specialist beginning 1986. **Career:** KS City MO School Dist, assoc supt, 1986-, dir of desegregation monitoring, 1985-86, dir of secondary educ, 1981-85, dir of admin servs, 1978-81; NE High KS City MO School Syst, principal, 1976-78; Paseo High KS City MO School Syst, principal, 1971-75; Humboldt High KS City MO School Syst, principal, 1969-70; KS City MO School Syst, teacher, 1968-69; Detroit MI School Syst, teacher, 1964-67. **Orgs:** Bd mem Whatsoever Cir Comm House, currently; bd mem Urban Serv KS City MO, currently; bd mem Paseo Daycare Serv, currently; trustee sec Paseo Baptist Church, currently; mem Citizens Crusade Against Crime, currently; mem Phi Delta Kappa, currently. **Honors/Awds:** Boss of the Year Award Business & Professional Women Starlight Chapter KS City MO 1978; Outstanding Educator Award, Alpha Phi Alpha Fraternity 1980.

GILES-ALEXANDER, SHARON
Business executive, entrepreneur. **Personal:** Born Sep 12, 1951, East Orange, NJ; daughter of Althea B Giles and William R Giles; married Willie L Alexander II, Jun 20, 1982; children: Willie L Alexander III, Jayson A Alexander. **Educ:** Morgan State University, BS, 1973; Rutgers University, MEd, 1975. **Career:** Newark Board of Education, 1973-75; East Orange Board of Education, teacher, 1975-77; EPC International Inc, president, currently. **Orgs:** American Marketing Association; Advertising Specialty Institute; Specialty Advertising Association of Greater New York; Federal Credit Union, board of directors; New Hope Baptist Church, board of directors; New Jersey Coalition of 100 Black Women, vice pres of economic development; National Association of Female Executives; National Minority Business Council; NAACP; White House Conference on Small Business, delegate; Greater Newark Chamber of Commerce, board of directors; East Orange Chamber of Commerce. **Honors/Awds:** WBE, Distinguished Achievement Award, 1989; NBDA, Regional Minority Business Woman of the Year, 1989; One of the Top 100 Black Business Professionals; Congressional Black Caucus Chairman's Award, 1982; Kappa Delta Pi, Honor Society Education; Kizzy Award, 1980; Sharon A Giles Day, West Orange, NJ, Mayor Samuel A Spira City Proclamation, 1981; Outstanding Minority Business Development Award, 1984; Role Model of the Year, 1985. **Business Addr:** President, EPC International, Inc, 34 Woodland Rd, Roseland, NJ 07068, (201)403-2900.

GILES-GEE, HELEN FOSTER
Educator. **Personal:** Born Oct 21, 1950, Fairfield, AL; daughter of Nannette Young Giles and Foster Giles; married Gilford Gee, May 1983. **Educ:** University of Pennsylvania, Philadelphia, PA, BA, 1972, MS, 1973, PhD, 1983, Rutgers University, New Brunswick, NJ, MS, 1977. **Career:** University System of Maryland, Aldelphi MD, associate vice chancellor for academic affairs, director of articulation, 1991-; Towson University, Towson, MD, exec asst to the pres & prof of biology, 1986-92; Cheyney State University, Cheyney, PA, chair of biology, 1983-85, assoc professor, 1975-1986; Rutgers University, New Brunswick, NJ, teaching fellow, 1973-75; Stevens Inst of Technology, Hoboken, NJ, science teacher, Summer, 1974. **Orgs:** VP/President Bd of Dirs, Society for College and University Planning, 1993-94; American Council on Education Maryland and Planning Board; Maryland Association for Higher Education, president, 1989-90; Maryland Associate for Institutional Research, 1987-; National Council of Measurement in Education, 1989-; Omicro Delta Kappa, leadership honor society, 1989-; Phi Delta Kappa, honor fraternity, 1982-; Pi Lambda Theta, honor society, 1982-89; Sigma Xi, scientific honor society, 1988-; University of Maryland System Women's Forum, Steering Committee, treasurer, 1990-91; Fund Raising Committee, 1990-91; American Association for Higher Education, 1986-. **Honors/Awds:** Distinguished Program Award, 1992; Research Award, Maryland Assn for Higher Educ, 1987; Faculty Fellowship, Natl Institutes of Mental Health, 1979-82; Natl Achievement Scholarship Natl Merit Corporation, 1968-72; Biology Club Award/Outstanding Faculty Service Cheyney Univ, 1979. **Business Addr:** Associate Vice Chancellor for Academ, Director of Articulation, University System of Maryland, 3300 Metzerott Rd, Adelphi, MD 20783.

GILFORD, ROTEA J.
Appointed government official. **Personal:** Born Nov 20, 1927, Willis, TX; married Judith Ellen; children: Stephen J, Judy Marie, Chance M. **Educ:** City Coll of San Francisco, AA 1944; SF State Coll, 1954. **Career:** San Francisco Police Dept, inspector of police 1960-78; San Francisco Mayors Office, dep mayor for criminal justice. **Orgs:** Mem Kappa Alpha Psi 1948-, Black Leadership Forum 1970-, Natl Assoc Criminal Justice Planners 1978-, Natl Black Public Admin. **Military Serv:** AUS tech 5th grade 1946-47. **Business Addr:** Deputy Mayor, City of San Francisco, City Hall Room 159, San Francisco, CA 94102.

GILFORD, VERA E.
Company executive. **Personal:** Born Dec 20, 1953, Detroit, MI; daughter of James & Ruby Gilford; divorced. **Educ:** Michigan State University, BA, business, 1975; Texas Southern University, JD, 1978; Mediation International of America, circuit civil mediator, 1995. **Career:** Office of Chief Counsel, attorney, 1978-82; Dept of Justice, special prosecutor, 1983; Office of District Counsel, sr attorney, 1983-87; Pete's Fountain & Bar, president, 1987-; Gilford Broadcasting Co., chief executive officer, 1990-. **Orgs:** National Association of Broadcasters, member, 1993-; The Florida Bar, tax section, 1982-; Florida International University, board member, 1995; Brickell Ave Literary Society, 1993-; Executive Women's Golf League, 1994; The Authors Guild, 1984-; The Miami Civic Chorale, board president, 1995; Conflict Resolution Ctr International, 1995. **Honors/Awds:** St. John Community Dev Corp., Outstanding Business Person, 1988; Texas Southern University, Most Significant Contribution to the Law Review Award, 1978. **Special Achievements:** Accumulated Earnings Tax, 1977; The Constitutionality of No-Fault Auto Ins, 1978; Proclamation, Vera E. Gilford Day, Miami Florida, Oct 1987. **Business Addr:** Chief Executive Officer, Gilford Broadcasting Co., 1925 Brickell Ave, Ste D-1507, Miami, FL 33129, (305)856-9340.

GILKEY, BERNARD (OTIS BERNARD)
Professional baseball player. **Personal:** Born Sep 24, 1966, St Louis, MO. **Career:** St Louis Cardinals, outfielder, 1990-95; New York Mets, 1996-. **Business Addr:** Professional Baseball Player, New York Mets, 126th St and Roosevelt Ave, Shea Stadium, Flushing, NY 11368, (718)507-6307.

GILL, GERALD ROBERT
Educator. **Personal:** Born Nov 18, 1948, New Rochelle, NY; divorced; children: Ayanna E. **Educ:** Lafayette Coll, AB 1966-70; Howard Univ, MA 1974, PhD 1985. **Career:** City School Dist, New Rochelle NY, social studies teacher 1970-72; Inst for the Study of Educ Policy, research asst 1976-78, research fellow 1978-79; Tufts Univ, Department of History, assoc prof, 1980-. **Orgs:** Consult NAACP 1979; consult Ohio Hist Society 1980-85; Office of American Historians; American Hist Assn; Southern Hist Assn; Assn for the Study of Afro-American Life and History; Natl Assn for the Advancement of Colored People. **Honors/Awds:** Massachusetts College Professor of the Year, 1995. **Special Achievements:** Co-author: The Case for Affirmative Action for Blacks in Higher Ed 1978; author Meanness Mania 1980; author: The Rightward Drift in Amer in the State of Black America Natl Urban League 1981; co-editor: Eyes On the Prize Civil Rights Reader, 1991. **Business Addr:** Associate Professor, Department of History, Tufts University, Medford, MA 02155.

GILL, GLENDA ELOISE
Educator. **Personal:** Born Jun 26, 1939, Clarksville, TN; daughter of Olivia Dunlop Gill and Melvin Leo Gill. **Educ:** Alabama A&M University, BS, 1960; University of Wisconsin-Madison, MA, 1964; University of Iowa, PhD, 1981. **Career:** Alabama A&M University, asst professor of English, 1963-69; University of Texas at El Paso, instructor of English, 1970-75; Simpson College, asst professor of English, 1981-82; Tuskegee University, associate professor and department head, 1982-83; Winston-Salem State University, associate professor of English, 1984-90; Michigan Technological University, associate professor of drama, 1990-. **Orgs:** Modern Language Association, 1982-; American Society for Theatre Research, 1984-; The Association for Theatre in Higher Educ, 1987-; World Congress of Theatre, 1989-; Delta Sigma Theta, 1958-; National Council of Teachers of English, 1963-83; Conference of College Composition and Communication, 1963-83; Emmanuel Baptist Church, Winston-Salem NC, 1988-. **Honors/Awds:** National Endowment for the Humanities, Summer Institute, Duke, 1991, Summer Institute, UNC-Chapel Hill, 1989, Summer Seminar, Yale, 1985, Summer Institute, Iowa, 1974; Rockefeller Foundation Grant, 1976, 1977. **Special Achievements:** "The African-American Student: At Risk," CCC, Vol 43, No 2, May 1992; "Canada Lee: Black Actor in Non-Traditional Roles," JPC, Winter, 1991; "View From My Window," Obsidian II, p 41-42, Winter 1990; "White Dresses, Sweet Chariots," Southern Literary Journal, Spring 1990; White Grease Paint on Black Performers, New York: Peter Lang, 1988, 1990; "Rosamond Gilder: Influential Talisman for African-American Performers," Theatre Survey, 1996; "The Alabama A & M Thespians, 1944-1963: Triumph of the Human Spirit," The Drama Review, 1994; "Her Voice Was Ever Soft, Gentle and Low, An Excellent Thing in Ruby Dee," Journal of Popular Culture, 1994. **Home Addr:** 1100 Agate, Apt 5, Houghton, MI 49931-1295, (906)482-4283. **Business Phone:** (906)487-3246.

GILL, JACQUELINE A.
Librarian, educator. **Personal:** Born Jun 4, 1950, New York, NY; daughter of Maude L Flanagan Jones and Nathan S Jones; children: Christopher B Aden. **Educ:** Borough of Manhattan Community College, New York, NY, AA, library tech, 1976; Queens College, Flushing, NY, BA, sociology, 1979; Pratt Institute, Brooklyn, NY, MLS, library science, 1988; City College, New York, NY, MS, educator, 1989. **Career:** Maritime College, Bronx, NY, serials asst, 1976-79; City College, New York, NY, research asst, 1979-83, librarian instructor, 1983-90, asst professor, 1990-, Acquisitions Division, chief, 1996-. **Orgs:** Cognotes reporter, American Library Assn, 1989-91; recording secretary, New York Black Librarians Caucus, 1989-; personnel admin secretary, liaison for JMRT, American Library Assn, 1989-91; systems and service secretary, acquisition system comm member, American Library Assn, 1990-91; CCNY Faculty Senate Elections Committee, 1995-; CCNY Faculty Senate Affairs Committee, secretary, 1995-; North American Serials Users Group, 1995-; New York Library Association, 1996-; Library Association of the City University of New York, 1983-. **Honors/Awds:** Various articles in Cognotes, American Library Assn, Conference Newsletter, 1989-90; book review in Library Resources & Technical Services; PSC-CUNY Research Awd Recipient, 1995-96. **Business Addr:** Chief, Acquisitions Division, Assistant Professor, City College, W 138th St and Convent Ave, New York, NY 10031.

GILL, JOHNNY
Vocalist. **Personal:** Born 1967. **Career:** Albums include: Johnny Gill, Provocative, Chemistry, Perfect Combination (with Stacy Lattisaw), Let's Get The Mood Right, Heartbreak, Home Again with New Edition,1996, LSG with Gerald Levert and Keith Sweat, 1997; singles include: "Super Love," "Tiger Beat," "Rub You the Right Way," "When Something is Wrong with My Baby," "Slow and Sexy" (with Shabba Ranks), My,My,My; motion picture soundtrack contributor: Boomerang, Mo' Money, New Jack City. **Business Addr:** Vocalist, c/o Atlantic Records, 1290 Ave of the Americas, New York, NY 10104, (212)275-2000.

GILL, KENDALL CEDRIC
Professional basketball player. **Personal:** Born May 25, 1968, Chicago, IL. **Educ:** Univ of Illinois, bachelor's degree in speech communications. **Career:** Charlotte Hornets, guard, 1990-93; Seattle SuperSonics, 1993-95; Hornets, 1995; New Jersey Nets, 1995-. **Orgs:** Founded the Kendall Gill House for

working homeless in Charlotte. **Honors/Awds:** NBA, All Rookie first team, 1991. **Special Achievements:** NBA Draft, First round pick, #5, 1990. **Business Addr:** Professional Basketball Player, New Jersey Nets, Brendan Byrne Arena, East Rutherford, NJ 07073, (201)935-8888.

GILL, LAVERNE MCCAIN
Journalist, company executive. **Personal:** Born Oct 13, 1947, Washington, DC; daughter of Mary McCain Williams and Paul McCain; married Tepper Gill, Feb 11, 1977; children: Dylan McDuffie, Tepper M. **Educ:** Howard University, BA, 1969; American University, graduate studies, communications, 1971-73; Rutgers University, MBA, 1977; Princeton Theological Seminary, M Divinity, 1997, Masters of Theology, 1998. **Career:** United States Senate, Senator Alan Cranston, legislative aide, 1970-72; Lassiter & Co, vice pres, 1973-77; University of District of Columbia, associate professor, 1979-82; Federal Reserve Board of Governors, budget analyst, 1983-86; Metro Chronicle Newspaper, editor, co-founder, 1986-90; McCain Media, Inc, president, 1988-. **Orgs:** National Newspaper Publishers Association; Capital Area Chapter, Academy of Arts and Sciences; American Film Television Radio Association; Friends of Rankin Chapel; African-American Media Coalition. **Honors/Awds:** Montgomery NAACP Award, 1987; National Academy of Arts and Sciences, emmy nomination, 1992; Borscht Foundation Fellowship, 1992; Mayor's Community Service Award, 1991; commendation, chmn, Federal Reserve Board of Governors, 1985; Jagou Preaching Award; Excellecne in Homeitics Award, Princeton; numerous others. **Special Achievements:** Author: African American Women in Congress: Forming and Transforming History, Rutgers Univ Press, 1997; Wash Post Article, Princeton Packet, July 8 1997. **Home Addr:** 2309 Glade Bank Way, Reston, VA 22091, (703)476-1026.

GILL, ROBERT LEWIS
Educator. **Personal:** Born Dec 26, 1912, Winnsboro, SC; married Rubye Cordelia; children: Walter, Roberta. **Educ:** Livingstone Coll, AB 1933; Univ of MI, MA 1937; Univ of MI, PhD 1942; Univ of MD Law Sch, 1951-53. **Career:** Morgan State Univ, prof 1945-; Lincoln Univ, teacher 1940-42; Atlanta Univ, teacher 1946; TX Southern Univ, teacher 1948; Univ of DE, teacher 1965; Univ of MA, teacher 1968-69; Univ of MD, teacher 1967-73; State Univ of NY, teacher 1973-74; Univ of MD Far E Div (Japan, Okinawa, Vietnam, Thailand, Taiwan & Korea), teacher 1970-71. **Orgs:** Mem Charter Commn Baltimore City 1963-64; Airport Zoning Bd of Appls 1964-72; splst civil rights educ comm relat US Ofc of Educ 1967-68; dir WilliamRobertson Coe Found 1958-59; exec bd Baltimore Br NAACP 1954-68; Life mem NAACP; bd dir ACLU 1950-70; bd dir Hlth & Wlfr Coun 1958-68; bd dir Untd Nat Assn of MD 1964-70; bd dir Big Bros Inc 1965-73; exec bd Baltimore Urban League 1952-60; bd dir Prisioners Aid Assn of MD 1956-72; author 2book & 95 publ artcls on race & relat & pub law; pres Assn of Soc & Behvrl Sci 1962-63. **Honors/Awds:** Pres hon awd ASBS 1973; Disting Achvmt Awd 1961; spl hon awd ASBS 1975; Life mem Omega Psi Phi Frat; 40 yr Serv Plaque 1970; Disting Alumni Awd 1961. **Military Serv:** USAF 1st lt 1942-45; MD NG maj 1946-48.

GILL, ROBERTA L.
Attorney. **Personal:** Born Jun 25, 1947, Baltimore, MD; daughter of Robert & Rubye Gill; children: Tara Maraj. **Educ:** University of Chicago Law School, 1969-71; University of Maryland Law School, JD, 1972; Johns Hopkins School of Hygiene & Public Health, MPH, 1976. **Career:** Attorney, private practice, 1972-88; East Baltimore Comm Corp, counsel, admin, 1979-83; Sickle Cell Disease Association of Maryland, admin, 1985-88; Office of the Attorney General, asst aty general, 1988-. **Orgs:** Delta Sigma Theta Sorority, 1967-; Cooley's Anemia Foundation, scy, 1988-; Baltimore Cable Access Corp, 1986-; Natl Gill Family Reunion, pres, 1996-. **Honors/Awds:** Sickle Cell Disease Association of MD, Outstanding Contributions, 1996. **Special Achievements:** Member of Rafiki Na Dada, an all female acapella singing group, 1987-. **Home Addr:** 3415 Callaway Ave, Baltimore, MD 21215. **Business Phone:** (410)767-6574.

GILL, ROSA UNDERWOOD
Accountant. **Personal:** Born May 14, 1944, Wake Co, NC; married Jimmie; children: Angie Rosharon, Natalie Denise. **Educ:** Shaw Univ Raleigh NC, BS Math 1968; NC Central Univ Durham, attended 1978-79; NC State Univ Raleigh, attended 1979-80. **Career:** Wake Co Bd of Elections, 1st black female chrpsn present; State Govt Raleigh NC, acct I 1980-; Wake Co Raleigh NC, mat instr 1971-80; Johnson Co Smithfield NC, math instr 1968-70; Nationwide Ins Raleigh NC, acctg clerk 1965-68. **Orgs:** Adv Inter-sch Coun 1978-79; adv Student Coun 1975-80; girl scout ldr Girl Scouts of Am 1974-78; trnd girl scout ldr 1976-78; sec Dem Party Wake Co1974-78; dem 1st black female vice chmn Dem Party Wake Co 1978. **Business Addr:** Wake Co Bd of Elections, 136 Salisbury St, Raleigh, NC 27603.

GILL, SAMUEL A.
Bass violinist. **Personal:** Born Nov 30, 1932, Brooklyn, NY; son of Clarendon Gill and Everton Gill; divorced. **Educ:** Juilliard School of Music; Manhattan School of Music; BA in Music; MD in Music Educ, 1960; Univ of Colorado, D Music, 1989. **Career:** Denver Symphony Orchestra, bass violin; career includes jazz and symphony work; played with Max Roach; Coleman Hawkins; J J Johnson; Harry Belafonte Singers; Randy Weston Trio Master Mason Mt Evans Lodge; 32 Degree Mason Mountain & Plains Consis. **Honors/Awds:** Shriner Syrian Temple Sym Social Award Tilden High 1950; Scholar to Juilliard School of Music 1950; Scholar to Manhattan School of Music 1955; Win of Down Beat Int Crit Award 1955; among first of race to be engaged by major symphony 1960. **Business Addr:** Denver Symphony Soc, 1615 California St, Denver, CO 80202.

GILL, TROY D.
Physician. **Personal:** Born Aug 7, 1937, Chicago, IL; son of Mary Gill and Troy Gill; divorced; children: Eunice, Donald, Mary, Omari. **Educ:** Dillard Univ, BA 1959; Howard Univ Coll of Medicine, MD 1963. **Career:** Little Company of Mary Hospital Illinois, med intern 1963-64; Maricopa Cty Gen Hospital Arizonia, ped res 1964-65; Good Samaritan Hospital Arizonia, chief ped res 1965-66; Univ of Utah Medical Center, adult & child psych fellow 1968-72; Rubicon Intl, phys, public speaker, business owner; Utah State hospital, clinical dir of youth center. **Orgs:** Bd governors Salt Lake Area Chamber of Commerce 1975-78; bd mem Natl Alliance of Business 1977-80; mem Intl Platform Assn 1984-; mem World Medical Assn 1984-; chmn mem Utah State Bd of Mental Health 1976-83; mem Univ of Utah Coll of Nursing Adv Bd 1978-; mental health consultant US Job Corp Clearfield Utah 1972-73; staff mem & consultant Raleigh Hills Hospital 1972-82; mem Utah Medical Assn 1988-; mem Amer Scoiety for Training & Development 1988-. **Honors/Awds:** Black history instr Westminster Coll 1970-74; black history workshop West HS 1970-71; author of chap on creativity in The Management Team, Royal Publ 1984; mem Salt Lake Exec Assn 1972-76; state comm mem White House Conf of Children 1970. **Military Serv:** USN lt comm 1966-68. **Home Addr:** 2024 La Tour Cir, Salt Lake City, UT 84121. **Business Addr:** Clinical Director - Youth Center, Utah State Hospital, Provo, UT 84601.

GILLESPIE, AVON E.
Educator. **Personal:** Born Apr 12, 1938, Los Angeles. **Educ:** IN State U, BS 1960; Memphis State U, MA 1968. **Career:** Schulte High School, teacher 1960-64; Mclean Jr High School, 1964-65; Unitarian Ch Evanston, dir mus 1966-72; Evanston Township High School, teacher 1965-71; Mus Center of N Shore, 1970-71; Barat Coll, guest lecturer 1971-72; Latin School Chicago, teacher 1971-72; Antioch Coll, visiting lecturer 1973-74; Cap Univ, asst prof 1972-. **Orgs:** Bd mem Am Orff Schulwerk Assn 1973-75; mem MENC; Am Choral Dirs Assn; Phi Mu Alpha Sinfonia; bd mem Culture & Worship Com Nat Ofc Black Cath ; numerous appear, lecs, dems, wrkshps for US Sch Dists orgns, grps, convs, confs. **Business Addr:** Capital Univ Conservatory Music, Columbus, OH 43209.

GILLESPIE, BONITA
Business owner, educator. **Personal:** Born Jan 20, 1951, Knoxville, TN; daughter of Hildritn Doris Johnson Gillespie and James Edward Gillespie. **Educ:** East Tennessee State Univ, Johnson City, TN, MA, 1976; Knoxville College, Knoxville, TN, BS, 1973. **Career:** Martin-Maretta Energy System, Oak Ridge, TN, accountant, 1978-86; Knoxville College, Knoxville, TN, assistant professor of accounting & management, 1986-; B G Accounting, Knoxville, TN, owner/accountant, 1987-. **Orgs:** South central regional director, Zeta Phi Beta Sorority Inc, 1986-90; charter member, National Association of Black Accountants, Knoxville Chapter, 1980-; trainer & site coordinator, Internal Revenue Service, Knoxville Office, currently. **Honors/ Awds:** Silver Service Award, IRS, 1990; Presidents Distinguished Service Award, Knoxville College Alumni Association, 1983; Community Service Award, Knoxville Community Action Committee, 1990, 1994. **Home Addr:** 2518 Chillicothe St, Knoxville, TN 37921. **Business Addr:** Owner/Accountant, B G Accounting, 220 Carrick St, Suite 223B, Knoxville, TN 37921.

GILLESPIE, MARCIA A.
Editor, author, consultant. **Personal:** Born Jul 10, 1944, Rockville Centre, NY; daughter of Ethel Young Gillespie and Charles M Gillespie. **Educ:** Amer Studies, Lake Forest Coll, BA 1966. **Career:** Ms Magazine, editor-in-chief, 1993-, exec editor, 1992-93; Ms Foundation for Education and Communications/Times Square, consultant, 1990-92; Ms Magazine, New York, NY, exec editor, editor-in-chief, communications consultant, editor, writer 1980-93; Essence Magazine, editor-in-chief 1971-80; Time-Life Books, Time Inc, New York, div 1966-70. **Orgs:** Nat Coun Negro Women; Amer Soc of Magazine Editors; bd of dirs, Rod Rodgers Dance Co; Arthur Ashe Inst for Urban Health; The Black & Jewish Women in New York City; guest lecturer, Univ of the West Indies School of Communications; advisory to the vice chancellor, Univ of the West Indies, Outreach to North Amer; The Studio Museum, Harlem; Educational Equity Concepts, EEC; advisory comm, Take Our Daughters to Work Day; advisory bd, Feminist Press; bd of dirs, Violence Policy Ctr, Washington DC; advisory bd, Girls Inc, Re-Cast TV; advisory bd, Feminists For Animals Rights Inc, FAR; advisory bd, ISMN. **Honors/Awds:** Outstanding Alumni Awd, Lake Forest Coll 1973; Matrix Awd, NY Women in Communications 1978; Aspen Fellow, The Aspen Inst; Mary MacLeod Bethune Awd, Natl Council of Negro Women; named One of the Fifty Faces for Amer Future Time Mag 1979; March of Dimes Awd, One of Ten Outstanding Women in Mag Publ 1982; NYABJ Life Achievement Awd, Print Journalism. **Business Addr:** Editor in Chief, Ms Magazine, 135 West 50th St, 16th Fl, New York, NY 10020.

GILLESPIE, RENA HARRELL
Educational consultant. **Personal:** Born Oct 26, 1949, Starkville, MS; widowed. **Educ:** MS State Univ, BS 1972, PhD 1981; Univ of Cincinnati, ME 1974. **Career:** Cincinnati Public Schools, resident counselor 1972-74; MS Univ for Women, minority student counselor 1974-78; MS State Univ, residence hall dir 1979-82; Univ of NC at Chapel Hill, assoc dir health careers prog 1983-86; Self-Employed, educational consultant. **Orgs:** Mem United Methodist Local Bd of Ministries 1975-; mem Southern College Personnel Assoc 1979-; mem Amer Personnel & Guidance Assoc 1980-; mem Assoc ofCollege Student Personnel 1980-; mem Natl Minority Health Affairs 1984-; volunteer Outreach Counselor Economic Oppor Atlanta Project Delay, Teenage Pregnancy Prevention Prog 1987-; volunteer Helpline Counselor GA Council on Child Abuse 1987-. **Honors/Awds:** Minority Doctoral Fellowship MS Univ for Women 1978-81; Outstanding Young Woman of Amer 1984. **Business Addr:** Educational Consultant, Educational Solutions Inc, 2007 Candice, Atlanta, GA 30316.

GILLESPIE, WILLIAM G.
Clergyman, educator. **Personal:** Born May 12, 1931, Knoxville, TN; married Martha Cox; children: Vendetta Lambert, William, Harry. **Educ:** Knoxville Coll, BS 1952; Johnson C Smith, BD 1955; Tarkio Coll, DD 1969; Eden Sem, STM & D Min 1970; Univ of MO, LLD 1987. **Career:** Davie St Presb Ch Raleigh, pastor 1955-56; Linwood Coll St Chas, asst prof 1971-73; Eden Sem Webster Groves MO, lectr 1972-74; Maryville Coll St Louis, lectr 1972-74; Cote Brilliante Presby Ch, pastor 1956-. **Orgs:** Pres bd of trustees Johnson C Smith Sem Atlanta 1976-; pres bd of regents Harris-Stowe State Coll St Louis 1978-; bd of trustees Interdenom Theol Ctr Atlanta 1979-; pres bd of dirs Mathews-Dickey Boys Club St Louis 1970-; bd mem Family & Children's Serv St Louis 1978-; bd mem United Way of Gr St Louis 1980. **Honors/Awds:** Citizen of the Yr Awd Sigma Gamma Rho Sor 1975; Disting Citizen Awd Mathews-Dickey Boys Club 1977; Disting Serv Awd St Louis Argus Newspaper 1979; Martin L King Jr Humanitarian Awd St Louis Alliance Against Racial Repression 1980. **Business Addr:** Pastor, Cote Brilliante Presby Ch, 4673 Labadie Ave, St Louis, MO 63115.

GILLETTE, FRANKIE JACOBS
Consultant. **Personal:** Born Apr 1, 1925, Norfolk, VA; daughter of Natalie Taylor and Frank Jacobs; married Maxwell Claude Gillette. **Educ:** Hampton Inst, BS 1946; Howard Univ, MSW 1948. **Career:** Ada S McKinley Comm House Chicago, supr 1950-53; Sophie Wright Settlement Detroit, program dir 1953-64; Concerted Serv Proj, dir 1964-65; Univ of California Soc Welfare Ex, program coord 1965-68; US Comm Serv Admin, spec program coord 1968-81; G & G Enterprises, pres, 1978-. **Orgs:** Dir Time Savings & Loan Assn 1980-90; vice pres San Francisco Handicapped Access Appeals Bd 1982-87; chairperson, bd of dirs NANBPWC Inc 1983-87; commissioner San Francisco Human Rights Commn 1988-92; vice pres Urban Economic Devel Corp, San Francisco 1987-91; member, San Francisco Business and Professional Women, Inc, 1970-; life member, Delta Sigma Theta Sorority; co-chairperson, San Francisco-Abidjan, Cote d'Ivoire Sister Cities Committee; honorary counsel, Cote d'Ivoire; National Association Negro Business & Professional Women's Clubs Inc, president 1983-87; Fine Arts Museums of San Francisco, trustee, 1993-; San Francisco Conventions & Visitors Bureau, bd, 1987-94, 1997-. **Honors/ Awds:** Alumnus of the Year Hampton Inst 1966; Sojourner Truth NANBPWC Inc 1980; publications The Organizer; The Governor NANBPWC Inc 1978 & 1981; ''Women Who Make It Happen'' Frito-Lay and Natl Council of Negro Women 1987; Woman of the Year, Delta Delta Zeta Chapter, Zeta Phi Beta Sorority, 1991. **Business Addr:** President, G&G Enterprises, 85 Cleary Court #4, San Francisco, CA 94109.

GILLETTE, LYRA STEPHANIE
Physician. **Personal:** Born Mar 1, 1930; children: 1 daughter. **Educ:** Barnard Coll, AB 1960; Howard U, MD 1964; Columbia U, MPH 1968. **Career:** Harlem Hosp, vstg clincn & consult 1969; Univ Vienna, guest physician 1969; US PUSH, dep chief ob/gyn 1970; Martin Luther King Jr Hop, dir ambulatory serv ob/gyn 1971; Watts Health Found, chief ob/gyn; Univ So CA, clinical prof ob/gyn 1990; Los Angeles County Dept Health Svcs, md specialist. **Orgs:** Chmn Pub Hlth Com Am Med Women's Assn 1977; consult ob-gyn Device Panel FDA 1976; dip Nat Bd Med Exmnrs 1965; Am Bd OB-GYN 1972; flw Am Coll OB-GYN 1974; Los Angeles OB-GYN Soc 1973; Am Pub Hlth Assn 1971; mem Assn Pub Hlth OB-GYN 1974. **Honors/ Awds:** PHS grant 1968; AMA Physician Rec Awd 1969; publ ''Mgmt of Adenomatous Hyperplasia'' OB World 1977. **Military Serv:** USAF Med Corps maj 1980-83. **Business Addr:** Physician Specialist, LA County, 10616 S Western Ave, Los Angeles, CA 90047, (213)242-6800.

GILLIAM, ARLEEN FAIN
Labor union official. **Personal:** Born Jan 2, 1949, Huntington, WV; daughter of Lorraine Fain and Cicero Fain; married Reginald E Gilliam Jr. **Educ:** MA Inst of Tech, MBA 1976; Skidmore Clge, BS 1970. **Career:** Congressional Budget Office, budget analyst 1976-77; Asst Secr of Labor US Dept of Labor, exec asst 1977-81; AFL CIO Fed Natl Intl Labor Unions, asst dir dept soc sec 1981-84, director of budget and planning 1984-91; Planning and Personnel Policy, director of budget, 1991-; Clinton-Gore transition team, 1992-. **Orgs:** Reston Chapter of Links 1977-87; MIT Sloan School Bd of Governors. **Honors/Awds:** Distg srv award US Dept of Labor 1979. **Business Addr:** Dir, Budget Planning, AFL-CIO, 815 16th St, Washington, DC 20006.

GILLIAM, ARMON LOUIS
Professional basketball player. **Personal:** Born May 28, 1964, Pittsburgh, PA. **Educ:** Independence Junior College, Independence, KS, 1982-83; Univ of Nevada-Las Vegas, bachelor's degree in communications. **Career:** Phoenix Suns, forward, 1987-89; Charlotte Hornets, 1989-91; Philadelphia 76ers, 1991-93; New Jersey Nets, 1993-96; Milwaukee Bucks, 1996-. **Honors/Awds:** NBA All-Rookie Team, 1988; Met Life Net of the Year, 1995. **Special Achievements:** NBA Draft, First round pick, #2, 1987. **Business Addr:** Professional Basketball Player, Milwaukee Bucks, 1001 N 4th St, Bradley Ctr, Milwaukee, WI 53203, (414)227-0500.

GILLIAM, DOROTHY BUTLER
Editor. **Personal:** Born in Memphis, TN; married Sam; children: Stephanie, Melissa, Leah. **Educ:** Sch of Jour, Grad 1961; Lincoln U, BA. **Career:** WA Post, clmnst 1979-, asst ed 1979; Panorama WTTG/TV, brdcstr 1967-72; WA Post, rptr 1961-66. **Orgs:** Lctr Am Univ & Howard Univ 1967-68, wrtr 1967-72; vice pres Inst for Jour Edn. **Honors/Awds:** Publ "Paul Robeson All Am" 1976; grant African-Am Inst 1961; Anne O'Hare McCormick award NY Nwspr Wmn's Club; jour of yr Capital Press Clubs 1967; emmyaward for Panorama; outst alumni Lincoln Univ 1973. **Business Addr:** 1150 15th St NW, Washington, DC 20071.

GILLIAM, EARL B.
Federal judge. **Personal:** Born Aug 17, 1931, Clovis, NM; married Rebecca Prater; children: Earl Kenneth, Derrick James. **Educ:** CA State Univ, BA 1953; Hastings Coll of Law, JD 1957. **Career:** San Diego CA, dep dist atty 1957-62; San Diego Mcpl Ct, judge 1963-74; Superior Ct CA San Diego Cty, judge 1975-80; US Dist Ct CA, judge 1980-. **Business Addr:** Senior Judge, California District Court, 940 Front St, Courtroom 7, San Diego, CA 92189.

GILLIAM, FRANK DELANO
Professional football executive. **Personal:** Born in Steubenville, OH; son of Viola Gilliam and Ed Gilliam; married Velma; children: Frank Jr, Gayle, Michelle. **Educ:** Iowa Univ, BA, 1957. **Career:** Winnipeg and Vancouver Canadian Football League, pro football player; Iowa Univ, asst coach 1966-70; Minnesota Vikings, scouting dir, dir of player personnel 1975-. **Orgs:** NAACP; Iowa Alumni Assc; Iowa Black Alumni Assc; Iowa Lettermans Club. **Honors/Awds:** NEA All-American, 1953; All-Big Ten, 1956; All-American, 1956. **Business Addr:** Director, Player Personnel, Minnesota Vikings, 9520 Viking Drive, Eden Prairie, MN 55344.

GILLIAM, HERMAN ARTHUR, JR.
Communications company executive. **Personal:** Born Mar 6, 1943, Nashville, TN; son of Leola Hortense Caruthers and Herman Arthur Gilliam Sr. **Educ:** Yale University, BA, 1963; University of Michigan, MBA, 1967. **Career:** Universal Life Insurance Co, vice pres, 1967-75; US House of Representatives, administrative aide, 1975-76; Gilliam Communications Inc, president, 1977-. **Orgs:** Memphis Area Radio Stations, past president; Black Bus Assn of Memphis, past chairman of bd; Tennessee Humanities Council, chairman; Lemoyne-Owen College, trustee. **Honors/Awds:** Numerous awards for broadcasting achievement and community service. **Business Addr:** President, Gilliam Communications, Inc, 363 S Second St, Memphis, TN 38103, (901)527-9565.

GILLIAM, JAMES H., SR.
Business executive (retired), consultant. **Personal:** Born Aug 6, 1920, Baltimore, MD; son of Pocahontas Gilliam and James E Gilliam; married Louise Hayley; children: James Jr, Patrice. **Educ:** Morgan State Coll, AB Sociology 1948; Howard Univ Schl of Soc Work, MSW 1950; Yale Univ Summer Schl of Alcohol Studies. **Career:** Greater Wilmington Dev Council Inc, dir neighborhood & housing srv 1965-67; Greater Wilmington Housing Corp, exec dir 1967-70; Leon N Weiner & Assc Inc, vice pres 1970-71; Family Court of the State of DE, admin/dir of treatment srvs, 1971-72; Leon N Weiner & Assc Inc, vice pres 1972-74; New Castle Cty Dev of Comm Dev & Housing, dir 1974-90 (retired); management consultant 1990-. **Orgs:** Dir, Medical Center, DE; Del State, bd of parole; mem NAACP; mem Court on the Judiciary Preliminary Investigatory Comm; Supreme Court of Delaware; mem, Sigma Pi Phi Fraternity; executive committee, Grand Opera House, DE; pres/bd chairman Community Housing, Inc; Kappa Alpha Psi Fraternity. **Honors/Awds:** Distg Delawarean Award State DE 1982; Social Worker of the Year Natl Assc of Social Workers DE Chap 1969; Alumni Award Howard Univ Schl of Soc Work 1952; publns, "The Program Formulation Process of the Maryland Tuberculosis Assn During the Period 1946-1948" Masters Thesis Howard Univ 1950; "The Role of the Area Office in Harlem Park" paper Residential Rehabilitation 1956 Sch of Architecture Univ of MN; NAHRO Natl Ambassador Awd 1985; Regional Ambassador Awd MARC/NAHRO 1985; BPA Achievers Awd for Significant Contribs in Govt 1985; State Ambassador Awd DE NAHRO 1985; Honorary Doctorate, Business Admin Goldey Beacom Coll 1989; Order of the First State, State of DE, Gov P S DuPont 1982; Community Service Award, Kiwanis Club, Wilmington, DE, 1990; Brotherhood Award, 1992; Conf Christian & Jews-Del Region Wallace M Johnson Award for Comm Service, 1986; Castle County Del Chamber of Commerce; Josian Marvel Cup Award, Del State Chamber of Commerce, 1994. **Military Serv:** US Army, capt; Bronze Star with cluster 1945. **Home Addr:** 900 N Broom St, Apt 35, Wilmington, DE 19806-4545.

GILLIAM, JAMES H., JR.
Corporate attorney. **Personal:** Born Apr 21, 1945, Baltimore, MD; son of Louise Hayley Gilliam and James H Gilliam Sr; married Randilyn Woodruff; children: Alexis Randilyn, Leslie Brooke. **Educ:** Morgan State Univ, BA, 1967; Columbia Univ, JD, 1970. **Career:** Paul, Weiss, Rifkind, Wharton & Garrison, New York, NY, associate, 1970-73; Richards, Layton & Finger, Wilmington, DE, associate, 1973-76; State of Delaware, Dept. of Community Affairs and Economic Devel, cabinet sec, 1977-79; Beneficial Corp, Wilmington, DE, vice pres legal, 1979-81, sr vice pres legal, 1982-85, sr vice pres, 1986-89, gen counsel, 1986-, sec, 1987-, exec vice pres, 1989-. **Orgs:** Amer Bar Assn, Natl Bar Assn, Sigma Pi Phi, Kappa Alpha Psi; Delaware Bar Assn; chmn of the bd, Beneficial Natl Bank, 1987-; chmn of the bd, Goldey-Beacom College, 1986-; bd mem, Bell Atlantic Corp, 1989-. **Honors/Awds:** Trustee, bd dirs, Medical Center of Delaware, Howard Hughes Medical Inst. **Business Addr:** Executive Vice President & General Counsel, Beneficial Corp, PO Box 911, Wilmington, DE 19899.

GILLIAM, JOEL
Law enforcement official. **Career:** Decatur Police, chief, currently. **Special Achievements:** First African American police chief in Decatur, AL. **Business Addr:** Police Chief, Decatur Police Dept., 402 Lee St. NE, Decatur, AL 35601-1928, (205)353-2515.

GILLIAM, REGINALD EARL, JR.
Attorney, government official. **Personal:** Born Dec 29, 1944, New York, NY; son of Mary Gilliam and Reginald Gilliam Sr; married Arleen Fain. **Educ:** Lincoln Univ PA, AB (cum laude) 1965; Harvard Law Schl, JD 1968. **Career:** Williams Clge, asst dean lecturer law poli sci 1972-75; US Senator John Glenn, legislative Counsel 1975-80; US Interstate Commerce Comm, v chrmn 1980-83; George Wash Univ, dist visiting prof 1983-85; NY State Dept of Transportation, assistant comm for rail and freight policy, dir freight div 1986-89; Congressman Louis Stokes of Ohio, chief of staff, 1991-93; Hill & Knowlton, Public Affairs World Wide Co, sr vp, 1993-. **Orgs:** Trustee Williams Clge 1979-84; mem NAACP, Omega Psi Phi Frat, Transafrica, Adirondack Mountain Club. **Honors/Awds:** Book New Reality of Natl Black Politics 1985, Black Political Dev 1975; award dist srv Amer Short Line Railroad Assc 1982; award distg srv Minority Trucker Transportation Dev Corp 1980; NAFEO, Distinguished Alumni Citation of the Year Award, 1993. **Special Achievements:** Author, Cases and Materials in Surface Transportation Regulation, 1987.

GILLIAM, ROBERT M., SR.
Attorney. **Personal:** Born Jul 12, 1926, Cleveland, OH; married Elva Ann Hickerson; children: Georgia, Robert, Jr. **Educ:** BBA, 1950; LLB, 1958; JD 1961. **Career:** Legal Aid Soc of Cleveland, atty 1968-; Civ Dir, 1971-73; Sen Staff, atty 1973-; Priv Prac, 1958-61; City of Cleve, asst law dir 1961-68. **Orgs:** Mem Cleveland Bar Assn; Ohio Bar Assn; Cleveland Lawyers Assn; John Harlen Law Club; NAACP; Urban League; NLADA; Kappa Alpha Psi Frat; P Omega P; Hon Bus Frat; bd dir Margie Home for Retarded Adults; bd dir Brdwy YMCA 1945-46. **Business Addr:** 1223 W 6th St, Cleveland, OH 44113.

GILLIAM, ROOSEVELT SANDY, JR.
Educational administrator. **Personal:** Born Sep 9, 1932, Union, SC; son of Lillia Trapp Gilliam and Roosevelt Gilliam; married Bety Davis Gilliam, Dec 24, 1955; children: Roosevelt, Wayne, Sonja Patrice. **Educ:** Allen University, Columbia, SC, BS, physical education; Indiana University, Bloomington, IN, MS, physical education. **Career:** Sims High School, Union, SC, athletic director, head football/basketball coach, 1952-53, 1955-58; Barr Street High School, Lancaster, SC, athletic director, 1960-64; Maryland State College, Princess Anne, MD, head football coach, 1964-69; Empire Sports Company, Denver, CO, professional scout, 1967-75; Springs Industries, Fort Mill, SC, manager, employee relations, 1975-87; State of South Carolina, Department of Social Services, Columbia, SC, executive assistant to the commissioner, 1987-88; South Carolina State College, Orangesburg, SC, vice president for development and industrial relations, 1988-, exec sec, special asst to pres, 1996-. **Orgs:** South Carolina Commission on Higher Education; South Carolina State Development Board; New Horizons Commission of Lancaster, SC; advisory board, Lancaster City Development Board; president, Palmetto Area Council of Boy Scouts of America; board member, Lancaster Children's Home; board member, Adam Walsh Child Resource Center; member, Clinton Junior College Board of Trustees; president, Allen University Yellow Jacket Club; vice president, Lancaster Chamber of Commerce; president, Lancaster East Precinct, 1976-; president, Lancaster Colt League; president, Lancaster Democratic Party; chairman, board of trustees, Mt. Zion A.M.E.Z. Church; chmn, Lancaster County Democratic Party; pres, Washington Baptist Church Men Fellowship; Omega Psi Phi Fraternity; chmn, bd of dirs, Lancaster Comm Center. **Honors/Awds:** Omega Man of the Year, Omega Psi Phi, 1977; Silver Beaver, Distinguished Eagle, Boy Scouts of America; Inductee, The South Carolina Athletic Hall of Fame, 1989; The Order of the Palmetto, Governor of South Carolina; Inductee, Allen University Hall of Fame; has also hosted several televsion shows and been play by play/color analyst for several sports programs. **Military Serv:** US Army, 1953-55. **Business Addr:** Executive Secretary, Special Asst to Pres, South Carolina State College, 1338 Main St, 12th Fl, Ballinger Bldg, Columbia, SC 29201.

GILLIAM, SAM, JR.
Painter, educator, artist. **Personal:** Born Nov 30, 1933, Tupelo, MS. **Educ:** Univ Louisville, BA, MA 1961. **Career:** Whitney Mus Annual, painter, educator, artist 1970; Corcoran Gallery, 1969; Embassies, WA Gallery of Modern Art, art 1967; Martin Luther King Memorial, exhibition mus of modern art 1969; Harlem, exhibited studio mus 1969; 1st World Festival of Negro Arts, 1966; Inst of Contemporary Art, 1965; Venice Biennale, Italy, 1970; Art Inst of Chicago, 1970; WA Gallery of Modern Art, 1964; Pacy Gallery, NY, 1972; Maison de la Culture Rennes France, 1973; Phoenix Gallery, San Francisco, 1974; Philadelphia Museum of Art, 1975; Galerie Darthea Speyer Paris, 1976; Dart Gallery Chicago, 1977. **Honors/Awds:** Norman Walt Harris prize, others. **Business Addr:** 1900 Quincy St NW, Washington, DC 20011.

GILLIAMS, TYRONE
Business executive. **Personal:** Born Mar 8, 1941, Camden, NJ; married Rosalind Louise Lee; children: Tyrone Jr, Haile, Tesemma. **Career:** Careers Inc, pres 1970-; Forrest Ballard Assn, coun 1969-70; Camden Bd of Edn, tchr guidance 1964-69; Fortunes 500, minority recruitment for 100 spl co listed by. **Orgs:** Elected mem Camden Bd Edn; mem bd dir UAME Credit & Housing Corp; chmn Camden City Mayor's Trans Com; chmn Camden Co Mental Hlth Assn United Way Fund Drive; mem bd dir Mental Hlth Assn Camden Co; Camden Educ Assn; part NJEA ldrshp conf; sponsored drug sem 4h Club of Am; rep Black Educ Conf; Camden Educ Assn; mem Personnel Com Camden Co Mental Hlth Assn; Camden City Mayor's Ad Hoc Com; NAACP; part Nat Urban League Ann Conv; BPUM-eDC bd dir; mem exec bd Kappa Alpha Psi. **Business Addr:** Ste 604 Commerce Bldg, Camden, NJ 08103.

GILLIARD, JOSEPH WADUS
Educator. **Personal:** Born Nov 23, 1914, Taylor, SC; son of Anna Durant and Jocephus Gilliard; married Bertha Holder; children: Bernard O, Brenda Lee Gilliard Johnson. **Educ:** Hampton Inst, BS 1941, MA 1952. **Career:** Hampton Inst, faculty, 1941-, asst prof art, 1949-71, asst prof art, 1971-75, prof of art, 1975-; Ceramic Natl Syracuse Museum Fine Arts Richmond Museum Fine Arts, ceramic art exhibit. **Orgs:** Amer Indus Arts Assn; Amer Assn Univ Profs Institutional Rep Dist Comm Peninsula Council, BSA; trustee, Zion Baptist Church, Hampton, VA; Amer Ceramic Society Emeritus. **Honors/Awds:** Recipient Merit Award, 2nd Biennial Showing of Chesapeake Craftsmen Norfolk Mus 1954; Meritoriouis Award Pininsula Jaycees 1958; Walter R Brown Award, Gamma Ita Chapter Alpha Phi Alpha; Outstanding Achievement Award, Gamma Epsilon Chapter Omega Psi Phi 1964; Silver Beaver Award, BSA 1966; Outstanding Achievement Award, Alpha Delta Mu Honor Soc Hampton Inst, 1965-66; Christian R Mary L Lindback Award Distinguished Teaching, 1975; Art of Public Serv, Presidential Citation, Hampton Univ, 1989; art exhibited at Hampton Univ Museum, 1987; art and Invention exhibited, Hampton Univ Museum, 1988. **Military Serv:** USN, Metal Smith 1st class, 1942-45. **Home Addr:** 108 W Cty St, Hampton, VA 23663.

GILLIS, SHIRLEY J. BARFIELD
Educator. **Personal:** Born Oct 2, 1943, Kinston, NC; daughter of Sarah Daughety Barfield and George Barfield; married Harvey Gillis; children: LaChale R. **Educ:** Elizabeth City State University, Elizabeth City, NC, BS, 1970; Eastern Connecticut State University, Willimantic, CT, MS, 1975; Southern Connecticut State University, New Haven, CT, 1990-. **Career:** New London Board of Education, New London, CT, kindergarten teacher, 1970-. **Orgs:** Former president, New London Education Association, 1980-81; membership/chairperson, New London Education Association, 1975-; correspondancy secy, Delta Kappa Gamma, 1989-; member, African American/Latino Co-

alition, 1989-; member, Phi Delta Kappa, 1988-; executive board of directors, New London NAACP; corresponding secretary, Historically Black College Alumni; president, New London Alumni Chapter, Delta Sigma Theta, Inc. **Honors/Awds:** Connecticut Teacher of the Year, State Dept of Education, 1981; Connecticut Educator Award, State Dept of Education & Milken Family Foundation, 1989; Martin Luther King Community Award, NAACP; Community Service Award, National Council of Negro Women, 1990; Alumni Award, Eastern Connecticut State University, 1970; Celebration of Excellence Award, Net & Ct State Dept of Ed, 1995. **Home Addr:** 340 Bayonet St, New London, CT 06320, (860)447-9536. **Business Addr:** Kindergarten Teacher, Harbor Elementary School, 432 Montauk Ave, New London, CT 06320, (860)447-6040.

GILLIS, THERESA MCKINZY
County official. **Personal:** Born Sep 16, 1945, Fort Meade, FL; daughter of Dezola Williams McKinzy and Arthur McKinzy; married Eugene Talmadge Gillis, Dec 23, 1973; children: Reginald, Jarett, Jeraemy. **Educ:** Talladega Coll, BA, 1967; Barry Univ, Miami, FL, MS, 1993. **Career:** Broward Employment and Training Administration, counselor, manager SYEP dir, 1976-82; Broward County Community Development Division, citizen participation coordinator, 1982-84, asst dir, 1984-86, director, 1986-94; Project & Comm Coordination, Public Works Dept, Office of Environmental Services, dir, 1994-. **Orgs:** SSO'SMem past officer, Delta Sigma Theta Sorority, 1968-; of bd, FL Community Development Assn, 1984-; mem, Natl Assn of Counties, 1986-; Home Economics Advisory Bd, Broward School Board, 1987-89; committee mem, Mt Hermon AME Church Credit Union 1988-; bd mem, Code Enforcement City of Lauderdale Lakes, 1988-; mem, Minority Recruitment Broward County School Board, 1989; Coalition of 100 Black Women, Broward County Chapter, charter mem; City of Lauderhill, Economic Dev Agency, bd mem, 1996-; Lauderhill Public Safety, adv bd mem. **Business Addr:** Office of Environmental Services, 2555 W Copans Rd, Pompano Beach, FL 33069.

GILLISPIE, WILLIAM HENRY
Aerospace engineer. **Personal:** Born Jan 8, 1927, Hanna, WY; son of Susie Anderson Gillispie and Nathan Gillispie; married Laura, Dec 21, 1977; children: Vincent, Shiela, Richard. **Educ:** Lincoln Univ, BSME 1950; Washington Univ, Univ of Missouri Rolla & St Louis, grad study. **Career:** USA Aviation Syst Comm, mgr aircraft div 1973-, special asst to commanding gen for pro mgmt USA .1970-73, dep chief it observation helicopter field office USA 1963-70, special asst for R&D USA 1962-63, oper rsch analyst USA 1961-62; A/C Proj Office USA, ch test 1953-61; part in mgt, devel, prod & support of all curr Army fixed & rotary winged aircraft 1953-88; aerospace and management consultant 1989-. **Orgs:** Chmn St Louis Sec AIAA 1977; chmn CFC camp USA Aviation Syst Comm 1974; lectr aerospace St Louis Public Schools; pres Lincoln Univ Missouri State chap 1975-76; mgmt of trans of Aviation Rsch & Devel resp 1960; command work in the act of the AUS Mobility Comm 1963; pres Lincoln Univ Alumni Assn 1979-85. **Honors/Awds:** Army Civilian Merit Award 1971; Award AIAA Sect Leadership Award 1977; Distinguished Alumni Award Lincoln Univ of Missouri 1977; Army Commanders Award for Civil Serv 1980; AIAA Serv Award 1980; President's Award Natl Assn for Equal Opportunity in Higher 1985; Outstanding Serv Award Lincoln Univ 1985; Commanders Award for Meritorious Achievment 1988. **Military Serv:** AUS air corps 1945. **Business Addr:** President, WHG Engineering and Management Counsultants, 1915 Claymills Dr, Chesterfield, MO 63017.

GILLOM, JENNIFER
Professional basketball player. **Personal:** Born Jun 13, 1964. **Educ:** Univ of Mississippi, attended. **Career:** Phoenix Mercury, center, 1997-. **Honors/Awds:** Olympian Magazine, Basketball Sportswoman of the Year, 1985; US Olympic Committee, Basketball Sportswoman of the Year, 1985; Mississippi Sportswoman of the Year, 1986; US Olympic Basketball Team, Gold Medal, 1988; All-WNBA Second Team, 1997. **Business Addr:** Professional Basketball Player, Phoenix Mercury, 201 E Jefferson St, Phoenix, AZ 85004, (602)252-9622.

GILLUM, RONALD M.
State educational administrator. **Personal:** Born May 21, 1939, Gates, PA; son of Edna R Gillum and Roger O Gillum; married Harriette A Coleman, Dec 21, 1963; children: Ronald Jr, Rhonda, Robin. **Educ:** Western MI Univ BS 1963; Wayne St Univ, MEd 1972, EdD 1975. **Career:** MI Dept of State, dir prog devel 1978-80; Detroit Pub Sch, teacher, 1963-70 admin 1969-71; Wayne Co Comm Coll, inst 1969-71; MI O Reg Lab Detroit, demon inst 1967; Detroit Pub Sch, inst 1963-69; Boy's Club of Amer, recreation dir; MI Dept of Educ, Lansing, MI, Adult Educ, deputy dir 1980-83, state dir; Detroit College of Business, executive director, 1996-. **Orgs:** Mem MI Alliance of Black Sch Educators; mem MI Assn of Pub Adult Comm Edn; mem Nat All Black Sch Educators; co-founder Black Tchr Workshops Detroit; mem Urban League Lansing; mem NAACP; mem PTA Lansing; bd of directors, Amer Assn for Adult & Continuing Educ 1987-; policy fellow, Educ Policy Fellowship Program, Natl Inst for Educ Leadership. **Honors/Awds:** Hon mem Sheet Metal Workers Intl Asso; recip Focus & Impact Awd Cotillion Club Inc Detroit; MI State Bd of Educ Distinguished Service Award, 1987; Pres Award, MI Assn of Adult & Continuing Educ 1989; Outstanding Leadership Award in Literacy, US Dept of Educ 1985; ''MI Is Learning How to Close Its Literacy Gap'' Detroit Free Press, 1987; ''Adult Literacy-Can We Handle the Problem'' OPTIONS 1987. **Home Addr:** 2592 Dustin Rd, Okemos, MI 48864-2073. **Business Addr:** State Director, Adult Extended Learning Services, Michigan Dept of Education, PO Box 30008, Lansing, MI 48909.

GILMORE, AL TONY
Educator. **Personal:** Born Jun 29, 1946, Spartanburg, SC; married Beryl Sansom; children: Jack S, Genevieve M. **Educ:** NC Central Univ, BA 1968, MA 1969; Univ of Toledo, PhD 1972. **Career:** Howard Univ, prof of history; Univ of MD, prof of history; Natl Afro-Amer Museum Project, consultant director; ASALH, researcher; Natl Educ Assoc, sr policy analyst, currently. **Orgs:** Bd dirs Assoc for the Study of Afro Amer Life & History 1977-88; consultant dir Natl Afro-American Museum Project Columbus OH 1979-82; mem Organization of Amer Historians, Amer Historical Assoc; Association for Study of African-American Life & History; pres, The Forum for the Study of Educ Excellence; board of directors, Quality Education for Minorities Project; National Council on Educating Black Children; consultant, California Commission on the Status of African-American Males. **Honors/Awds:** Author of several books ''The Natl Impact of Jack Johnson'' 1975, ''Revisiting the Slave Community'' 1979; book reviews and articles have appeared in Washington Post, New York Times, New Republic, American Scholar and others; lectured at over 40 colleges and univs including Harvard, Brown, UCLA, Morehouse and others; editor, African-American Males: The Struggle for Equality. **Home Addr:** 6108 Clearwood Rd, Bethesda, MD 20817-6002. **Business Addr:** Sr Policy Analyst, National Education Association, 1201 16th St, NW, Washington, DC 20036.

GILMORE, ARTIS
Professional basketball player. **Personal:** Born Aug 21, 1948, Chipley, FL; married Enola Gay; children: Shawna, Priya, Tiffany, Otis, James. **Educ:** Jacksonville Coll, BS 1971. **Career:** Chicago Bulls, 1978-82, San Antonio Spurs 1982-87, Boston Celtics, 1988. **Orgs:** Mem Amer Basketball Assn. **Honors/Awds:** All Star Team 1972; Named Rookie of the Yr Amer Basketball Assn 1972; Player of the Yr 1972; All Amer 1971.

GILMORE, CARTER C.
Elected official (retired), business executive. **Personal:** Born May 30, 1926, Grapeland, TX; son of Bertha Gilmore and Payne Gilmore; married Elizabeth Mae Hampton, Dec 26, 1948; children: Carl E, Clifford E, Donald A, Carol E, Rodney C, Janet E. **Educ:** Merritt Coll, attended. **Career:** Granny Goose Foods, bus mgr; City of Oakland, councilman, 1977-97, vice mayor, 1979-81; Gilmore Consultants Ltd, vice pres, 1997-. **Orgs:** Chairperson Rules & Procedures Comm of the Council, Community Action Bd, Personnel & Finance Comm; mem Public Safety Comm of the City Council, Exec Comm & Coord Comm, East Oakland Youth Ctr Bd of Dir, Alameda Cty Fair Bd of Dir, League of CA Cities, League of CA Cities Adv Bd; former chmn Civic Action Comm of the City Council; former mem Legislative Comm of the City Council; mem NAACP, Bethel Baptist Church, Boy Scouts Jr Achievement. **Honors/Awds:** Outstanding Comm Leadership Oakland Comm Org; Civil Rights Leadership Awd NAACP; Outstanding Comm Leadership Awd Granny Goose Foods, Five Year Participant Awd Bay Area Black Cowboys; Outstanding Serv to Youth Awd I Oakland Youth Devel; Delegate to China representing City of Oakland; Delegate to Natl Council of Mayors; Delegate to Japan representing City of Oakland. **Military Serv:** US Navy, petty officer, 1944-46. **Home Addr:** 1953 62nd Avenue, Oakland, CA 94621.

GILMORE, CHARLES ARTHUR
Educational administrator (retired). **Personal:** Born Sep 23, 1919, Columbia, SC; son of Rosa Amelia Scott Gilmore (deceased) and Arthur William Gilmore (deceased); married Josephine Specter; children: Charles A Jr, Michael, Martha, J Andrew. **Educ:** Temple Univ, BS 1949; Univ of PA Philadelphia, MGA 1960. **Career:** City of Phila, admin asst 1957-58, training ofcr 1958-62; NY State Dept Labor, manpower training spec 1963, asst dir 1963-64; US Dept Labor Wash, DC, manpower dev spec 1964, chf div of prgm demonstration 1965-67; Comm Coll of Phila, asst to pres 1967-69, dir div of comm serv 1967-72, dir div ofsoc and behav scis 1969-72; PA Dept Comm Affairs Harrisburg, chf div of municip emp training 1972-74; PA Dept Educ Harrisburg, high educ assoc 1974-79, coord for state-related universities 1979-82, educ and govt administ consultant 1982; retired. **Orgs:** Amer Soc for Training and Dev; Amer Acad of Political and Soc Sci; Amer Soc for Publ Administration; The Academy of Polit Sci; Natl Cncl on Comm Serv for Comm and Jr Colleges; Natl Exec Bd Wharton Grad Sch Alumni; bd dir PA Inst for Law and Justice; mem Center for Study of the Presidency; mem Natl Center for Public Serv Internship Programs; bd dir Wharton Graduate - Philadelphia Chptr; trustee, Harrisburg Area Community Coll, 1988-; trustee emeritus, Harrisburg Area Community College, 1994; trustee bd chairman, 1995, interim president, 1996, Stevens State School of Technology; bd of directors, Tressler Lutheran Svcs, 1996. **Honors/Awds:** Founders Day Award, Harrisburg Area Community College, 1995. **Military Serv:** AUS Lt Col served 9 years. **Home Addr:** 2715 N 4th St, Harrisburg, PA 17110.

GILMORE, EDWIN
Physician. **Personal:** Born Mar 27, 1931, New York, NY; married Dorothy; children: Pamela, Jonathan, Gregory. **Educ:** CCNY, BS 1952; SUNY, MD 1956; Upstate Med Ctr. **Career:** Coll of Med & Dent of NJ, chf serv dept radiology; Montefiore-Morrijania Affliation, asso dir 1964-75; Grasslands Hosp, asst dir 1960-64; Am Bd Radiology, diplomate. **Orgs:** Mem Am Coll of Radiology; Am Trauma Soc; NY Roentgen Soc; Radiol Soc N Am Mem Harlem Lions. **Business Addr:** 65 Bergen St, Newark, NJ 07107.

GILMORE, JOHN T.
Educator. **Personal:** Born Aug 1, 1935, Prescott, AR; married Curley Usher. **Educ:** BS 1957; MSIE 1970; PhD 1971. **Career:** Univ of AR, prof; Boeing Air Co, assoc engineer 1958-60, statistical cons, computer prog cons; Real Estate Broker; Trinity Church, admin asst; Univ of AR Pine Bluff, dir of engineering; Diversified Unlimited Corp Inc, sec bd of trustees. **Orgs:** Mem Am Inst of Indsl Engr Inc; mem Pine Bluff Planning Commn; bd chmn Trinity Ch God Christ. **Honors/Awds:** Beta Kappa Chi Scientific Hon Soc; Alpha Pi Mu Indsl Eng Hon Soc; mem Alpha Kappa M Univ Nat Honor Soc; Outstndg Math Student. **Military Serv:** AUS e3 1962. **Business Addr:** 1116 State St, Pine Bluff, AR 71601.

GILMORE, MARSHALL
Clergyman. **Personal:** Born Jan 4, 1931, Hoffman, NC; married Yvonne Dukes; children: John M, Joan M. **Educ:** Paine Coll Augusta, GA, BA 1957; Drew Theol Sem Madison, NJ, MDiv 1960; United Theol Sem Dayton, OH, DMin 1974. **Career:** Bray Temple CME Chicago, IL, pastor 1960-62; W Mitchell St CME Ch Atlanta, 1962; Allen Temple CME Ch Detroit, 1962-64; Phillips Temple CME Ch Dayton, 1964-; Payne Theol Sem Wilberforce, OH, instr 1972-73. **Orgs:** Pres Dayton NAACP 1971-72; mem bd Phillips Sch of Theol 1966-; Paine Coll 1969-; Gen Conn Bd CME Ch 1966-. **Military Serv:** USAF airman 1-C 1950-54. **Business Addr:** 2050 Germantown St, Dayton, OH 45408.

GILMORE, ROBERT MCKINLEY, SR.
Educator. **Personal:** Born May 14, 1952, Houston, TX; son of Olan Gilmore and Marvin Gilmore; married Letha LaVerne Stubbs; children: Robert Jr, Reshun. **Educ:** TX Southern Univ, BA 1980, MA 1981, MA 1984; Univ of Houston, EdD 1985; Mount Hope Bible Coll, BTh; Houston Graduate School of Theology M.D.V. 1989. **Career:** City of Houston, asst dir 1982-84; Texas Southern Univ, instructor 1981-83; Univ of Houston, grad asst 1982-85; Prairie View A&M Univ, asst prof 1985-89; Houston Graduate School of Theology urban ministry program director; Real Urban Ministry, pres. **Orgs:** Asst to pastor Barbers Memorial Bapt Church 1979-89; radio producer and host KTSU and KPVU 1980-85; pres Real Productions 1980-; consultant Baptist Ministers Assoc 1985-95; mem Phi Delta Kappa Univ of Houston 1985-89; Prairie View A&M Univ 1986-89; dir of Drug Training Programs Independent Missionary Baptist Assn; pres Real Educ Alternatives for Leadership & Learning 1989-91; pres One Church/One Child 1988-90; drug educ consultant City of Houston. **Honors/Awds:** Publication ''Effective Communication a Drug Education Solution,'' 1986; PV Choice Award Prairie View A&M Univ 1989. **Military Serv:** USAF sgt 1971-75; Natl Security Awd 1971. **Business Addr:** Executive Director, Real Urban Ministry, 3253 Winbern, Houston, TX 77004, (713)741-6642.

GILMORE, VANESSA D.
United States district judge. **Personal:** Born Oct 26, 1956, St Albans, NY; daughter of Clifton & Laura Gilmore. **Educ:** Hampton Univ, BS, 1977; Univ of Houston College of Law, JD, 1981. **Career:** Foley's Dept Store, fashion buyer, 1977-79; Sue Schecter & Assoc, attorney, 1985-86; Vickery, Kilbride, Gilmore & Vickery, attorney, 1986-94; US Courts, US district Judge, 1994-. **Orgs:** Houston Bar Assn; NAACP, chairperson for church committee, 1989-93; YWCA, pres, bd of dirs, 1990-92; Links Inc, chairperson for LEAD, 1990-91; Univ of Houston Alumni Bd, 1993-; Texas Dept of Commerce, chairperson, 1992-94; Texans for NAFTA, chairperson. **Honors/Awds:** Houston Defender Newspaper, Citizen of the Month, 1990; National Black MBA Assn, Distinguished Service Award, 1994; Holman Street Baptist Church, Community Service Award, 1994; Human Enrichment of Life, Houston's Young Black Achiever, 1989. **Special Achievements:** Amer Bar Assn, Using Expert Help, 1991; Amer Bar Assn, Motions In Limine, 1993; Amer Trial Lawyers Assn, How to Ethically Dev an Environmental & Toxic Torts Practice, 1990. **Business Phone:** (713)250-5931.

GILOTH-DAVID, KING R.
Clergyman, editor. **Personal:** Born Dec 23, 1940, White Plains, NY; son of Frances Cook Giloth and Henry Giloth; married Mary Lou; children: Laura Lee, Daniel Louis, Matthew David, Jonathan Henry, King David. **Educ:** Univ of Notre Dame, BA

Political Science 1963, MA Teaching 1965. **Career:** The Reformer Newspaper Inc, S Bend IN, editor, publisher 1967-96; Northeast Africa Zion Media, editor, 1995-; Ethiopian Christian Spiritualist Church, founder, pastor, 1997-. **Orgs:** Dir Christian Democratic Center, S Bend IN 1964-87; chmn Christian Democratic Movement 1968-; sec bd of dir St Joseph Co Comm Federal Credit Union 1980-82; dir Reg Fed Anti-Poverty Agency 1980-82; dir Center for Christian Democratic Socialism 1987-; coordinator Christian Democratic Socialist Party 1987-; manager Volkswagen Remanufacturing Cooperative 1988-; member, board of directors, Washington-Chapin African-American Learning Program 1989-94; secretary, St Augustine Church Gospel Choir, 1988-95; member, The Tolton Society, 1987-95; bd of dirs, South Bend Branch NAACP, 1996-97; South Bend Cap Indiana Black Expo, 1997-; St Peter's Lodge #31, F&AM, Prince Hall, master mason, 1995-. **Honors/Awds:** US Delegate of Christian Democratic World Union, Rome, Italy. **Business Addr:** Editor, Northeast Africa Zion Media, 1040 W Jefferson Blvd, South Bend, IN 46601.

GILPIN, CLEMMIE EDWARD
Educator. **Personal:** Born Aug 12, 1942, Beaverdam, VA; children: 5. **Educ:** VA State Coll, AB 1966; OH U, MA 1970. **Career:** Nigeria, Peace Corps volunteer 1966-68; Vista, recruit 1969-71; PA State Univ Capital Campus, instructor 1971-. **Orgs:** Assn for Study Afro-Am Life & History; United Nations Assn Harrisburg; African Liberation Support Com Founder Capitol Campus & Model United Nations. **Business Addr:** PA State Univ, Capitol Campus, Middletown, PA 17057.

GILREATH, COOT, JR.
Educator. **Personal:** Born Jun 3, 1937, Wilkesboro, NC; married Rosalind Delores Petty; children: Greg, Amy. **Educ:** Appalachian St Univ, BT 1978, MA 1981. **Career:** Chatham Mfg, industrial engr 1963-73; Wilkes Comm Coll, dir affirmative action 1973-. **Orgs:** Mem NC Assoc Coordinators of Vet Affairs 1979-, Amer Assoc of Affirmative Action 1984-. **Military Serv:** USAF A/3C 1 yr. **Home Addr:** 3136 White Plains Rd, Roaring River, NC 28669. **Business Addr:** Dir of Affirmative Action, Wilkes Community College, PO Box 120, Wilkesboro, NC 28697.

GILTON, DONNA L.
Librarian, educator. **Personal:** Born Jul 9, 1950, Lynn, MA; daughter of Hattie Franklin Gilton and Charles W Gilton Sr. **Educ:** Simmons College, Boston, MA, BA, 1972, MS, 1975; University of Pittsburgh, Pittsburgh, PA, PhD, 1988. **Career:** Boston Public Library, Boston, MA, librarian, 1972-79; Belize Teachers College, Belize City, Belize, librarian, 1979-81; Western Kentucky Univ, Bowling Green, KY, business ref libn, 1984-88; Pennsylvania State Univ, University Park, PA, business ref libn, 1988-91; University of Rhode Island, library science, assistant professor, 1992-. **Orgs:** American Library Association, 1987-; Special Libraries Association, 1982-83; American Society of Information Sci, 1982-83; Belize Library Association, 1979-81. **Honors/Awds:** The Provost Fund, Univ of Pittsburgh, 1983-84; The Harold Lancour Award, Univ of Pittsburgh, 1983; Title IIB Fellowship, Univ of Pittsburgh, 1981-82. **Business Addr:** Assistant Professor, Library Science, University of Rhode Island, 10 Rodman Hall, Kingston, RI 02881.

GILVEN, HEZEKIAH
Deputy executive director. **Personal:** Born Jul 1, 1927, Birmingham, AL; married Juanita Gilven; children: Ronald, Edwin, Curtis, Phyllis. **Educ:** Evergreen State Coll, BA sociology 1975. **Career:** Tacoma Housing Auth, dep exec dir 1979-; Tacoma-Pierce County Drug Prog, dir drug treat prog 1973-79; Comprehensive Mental Hlth Cntr, mental hlth worker 1972-73; Met Devel Council, mental hlth worker 1971-72; Met Devel Council, bd of dir 1972-73; Health Clinic, bd of dir 1973-74; Citizen Affirmative Action Council, bd of dir 1974-76; Pacific Matrix Soc, bd of dir 1975-76; Tacoma Urban League, bd of dir 1974-79; Oppor Industr Cntr, bd of dir 1976-78. **Orgs:** Mem Gov Adv Council on Drug Abuse 1973-79; commr City of Tacoma Human Relation Comm 1975-78; mem Private Industry Council City of Tacoma 1979-; Tacoma Ministerial Credit Union; CETA Adv Counc; Dept Social & Hlth Serv Adv Counc; Tacoma Sch Dist Affirm Action & Adv Com; Precinet Com person; Black Forum. **Honors/Awds:** Recip Combat Arms; Oak Leaf Cluster; Purple Heart. **Military Serv:** AUS staff sgt 1945-69. **Business Addr:** Tacoma Housing Authority, 1728 E 44th St, Tacoma, WA 98404.

GIOVANNI, NIKKI (YOLANDE CORNELIA JR.)
Poet. **Personal:** Born Jun 7, 1943, Knoxville, TN; daughter of Yolande Watson Giovanni and Jones Giovanni; children: Thomas Watson. **Educ:** Fisk Univ, BA, history (with honors), 1967; Univ of PA, Sch of Soc Work, postgrad 1967; Worcester Univ, LHD, 1972; Ripon Univ, D Litt, 1974; Smith Coll, D Litt, 1975; Columbia Univ School of the Arts. **Career:** Queens College CUNY, asst prof of black studies, 1968; Livingston College, Rutgers Univ, assoc prof of English, 1968-72; Niktom (publishing co), founder, 1970; Ohio State Univ, visiting prof of English, 1984; Mount St Joseph on the Ohio, prof of creative writing, beginning 1985; Virginia Poly Inst and State Univ, Dept of English, currently. **Orgs:** Vol worker, life mem, Natl Council of Negro Women; co-chairperson, Literary Arts Festival, State of Tennessee Homecoming, 1986. **Honors/Awds:** Author, Black Feeling, Black Talk, 1970, Ego Tripping and Other Poems for Young People, 1973, Those Who Ride the Night Winds, 1983, Sacred Cows..and Other Edibles, 1988, numerous others; recorded six albums, including Truth Is On Its Way, 1972, Cotton Candy on a Rainy Day, 1978; tv appearances: Soul!, Natl Educ TV network, the Tonight Show; particip Soul at the Center, Lincoln Center Performing Arts New York City, 1972; Mademoiselle Mag Award Outstanding Achievement 1971; Omega Psi Phi Award; Ford Found Grantee 1967; Woman of the Year, Cincinnati Chapter YWCA 1983; elected Ohio Women's Hall of Fame 1985; keys to numerous cities, including New York, NY (1975) Miami, FL (1982) Los Angeles, CA (1984); Spirit to Spirit: The Poetry of Nikki Giovanni (tv film), PBS, Corp for Public Broadcasg, Ohio Council on the Arts, 1986; NAACP, Image Award, Literary Work, 1998; contributor to numerous anthologies. **Business Addr:** English Dept, Virginia Polytechnic Inst and State Univ, Blacksburg, VA 24061.

GIPSON, BERNARD FRANKLIN, SR.
Surgeon (retired). **Personal:** Born Sep 28, 1921, Bivins, TX; son of Mr & Mrs John Thomas Gipson; married Ernestine Wallace; children: Bernard F Jr, Bruce Edward. **Educ:** Morehouse Clge, BS 1944; Howard Univ Clge of Med, MD 1947; Diplomat of the Amer Bd of Surgery, 1954. **Career:** Private Prac Surgery 1956-95. **Orgs:** Clin assc prof of surgery Univ of CO Schl of Medicine 1985; chrmn Dept of Surgery Mercy Med Ctr 1968; life mem NAACP 1980; chrmn Emancipation Proclamation Schlrshp Fund of Newhope Baptist Church 1974. **Honors/Awds:** Comm srv award Methodist Conf of Western States 1984; article Denver Post 1984; Story of my Life Denver Post Newspaper 1984; Frederick Douglass Award, Esquire Club 1985. **Military Serv:** USAF capt. **Business Addr:** Surgeon, 2375 Monaco Pkwy, Denver, CO 80207.

GIPSON, FRANCIS E., SR.
Federal administrator (retired). **Personal:** Born Apr 25, 1923, Huntington, WV; married Clara; children: Francis, Jr, Linda, Pamela, Teresa, Constance. **Educ:** Kentucky State College, BS, 1950. **Career:** Department of Interior, National Park Service, senior branch chief, youth activites, 1974-; City of East Cleveland, Ohio, former city official, director, Parks & Recreation, vice city manager, 1973. **Orgs:** Former mem E Cleveland bd of edn; mem Lake Erie Assn; Amateur Athletic Union; num other professional orgns; former asst dist mgr Equitable Life Assurance Soc of US. **Military Serv:** US Army, Combat Veteran, WW II, 1943-45.

GIPSON, HAYWARD R., JR.
Company executive. **Educ:** Princeton Univ. **Career:** Playtex Inc, marketing exec; Corning, Vitro Intl, vp/gen mgr, beginning 1989; Playtex, pres, currently. **Business Addr:** President, Playtex, 700 Fairfield Ave, Stamford, CT 06904, (203)356-8000.

GIPSON, LOVELACE PRESTON, II
Dentist. **Personal:** Born Jan 9, 1942, Clarksdale, MS; married Amanda; children: Lovelace III, Tamitha, Teresa, Tinile. **Educ:** AM&N Coll Dd, BS, 1963; St Louis U, 1965; Univ MO, 1966; A&L U, 1967; Univ TN Sch Dentistry, DDS, 1973. **Career:** Pvt Pract, dentist; Hamilton Co Chattanooga Hlth Dept, staff dentist 1974; St Louis & E St Louis Bd Edn, tchr 1965-70; Nashville, AR, bd of Educ 1963-64. **Orgs:** Mem Nat Bus League; pres Professional Corp 1977; mem PK Miller Youth Orgn 1955; Nat Dental Assn; Am Den Assn; Memphis Shelby Co Dental Soc; NAACP; UAPB Alumni Assn; Elks Lodge; Chickasaw Cncl BSA; Urban League; hon del TN Constl Conv; mem Am Endodontic Soc; Fndrs Club The Memphis Goodwill Boy's Club. **Honors/Awds:** Recip Ford Found Flwsp St Louis Univ 1965; NSF Grant Univ MO & Atlanta Univ 1966-67. **Business Addr:** 1216 Thomas, Memphis, TN 38107.

GIPSON, REVE
Consultant. **Personal:** Born Jan 4. **Educ:** Los Angeles Valley College, Van Nuys, CA; UCLA Extension/Workshops, Westwood, CA. **Career:** Freelance writer & editor; KNBC News, Burbank, CA, personal asst & news researcher, 1974-78; Capitol Records, Los Angeles, CA, publicist, 1978-87; Maze Featuring Frankie Beverly, Los Angeles, CA, public relations consultant, 1987-; Los Angeles County Music & Performing Arts Commission, commissioner, currently. **Orgs:** Member, National Academy of Recording Arts & Sciences; member, Alpha Theta Chapter, Beta Phi Gamma. **Honors/Awds:** Distinctive Women of Southern California, City of Los Angeles; Dr. Mary McLeod Bethune Award, County of Los Angeles, Board of Supervisors; Bill of Rights Speaker's Award, Bill of Rights Commendation Committee; County Awards, Los Angeles City Council; organized M C Hammer Day in the City of Los Angeles; founder of the annual "Youth on Parade" program. **Business Addr:** Commissioner, Los Angeles County Music and Performing Arts Commission, 135 N Grand Ave, Los Angeles, CA 90012.

GISSENDANNER, JOHN M.
Educator. **Personal:** Born Aug 13, 1939; son of Plessie M Matthews Gissendanner and Roy L Gissendanner; married Pamela Morgan (divorced 1976). **Educ:** San Francisco State Univ, San Francisco, CA, BA, 1971, MA, 1972; Univ of California, San Diego, PhD, 1982. **Career:** California State University, San Diego, CA, assistant professor, 1972-75; Towson State University, Towson, MD, assistant professor, beginning 1975, associate professor, 1991-98, prof, 1998. **Orgs:** American Association of University Professors, 1972-; National Association for the Advancement of Colored People, 1982-; Middle-Atlantic Writers' Association, 1978-; National Collegiate Honors Council, 1980-; Maryland Writers Council, 1980-. **Honors/Awds:** University Merit Award, Towson State University, 1989; San Diego Fellowship Award, University of California, San Diego, 1971-74; Ford Foundation Fellowship Award, University of California, San Diego, 1973-74. **Business Addr:** Professor, Towson Univ, English Dept, Towson, MD 21204.

GIST, CAROLE ANNE-MARIE
Miss USA 1990, singer. **Personal:** Born in Detroit, MI; daughter of Joan Gist and David Turner. **Educ:** Northwood Institute, marketing, management. **Career:** Midland, Michigan, club singer. **Honors/Awds:** Miss USA Pageant, winner, 1990; Miss Universe Pageant, first runner-up, 1990; Miss Michigan Pageant, winner, 1989. **Special Achievements:** First African American woman to be crowned Miss USA, 1990; first Miss Michigan to be crowned Miss USA, 1990. **Business Phone:** (213)965-0800.

GIST, JESSIE M. GILBERT
Educational administrator. **Personal:** Born Mar 7, 1925, Passaic, NJ; daughter of Annie Iona Nelson Gilbert and David Julian; married James Fredrick Jr (deceased); children: David Allan, Sandra Thorpe, James Fredrick III, Stephanie DuBois. **Educ:** Tombrock Coll, AA 1972; Montclair State Coll, MA 1976. **Career:** Passaic Co Comm Coll, dir of spl prog; Paterson Task Force for Comm Action Paterson NJ, center dir 1965-69; Tombrock Coll W Paterson, NJ, asst to pres for comm affairs 1969-73; Passaic County Comm Coll Paterson NJ, dean of students 1978-80; County Coll of Morris Randolph NJ, dir, Educ Oppty Fund prog. **Orgs:** Life mem NC Negro Women 1977; bd mem & life mem NAACP 1978-80; treas trustee Paterson Regional Devel; chmn Council on Social Serv City of Paterson 1983,84; pres, bd of dir Paterson Task Force for Comm Action Inc 1986-87; treas Natl Council on Black Amer Affairs A Council of the Amer Assoc of Comm &Jr Colls; Council on Comm Serv Am Assn of Jr Comm Coll, pres l975; Commn on Legis, mem; Am Assn of Comm Jr Coll, bd of dir; NJ Educ Oppor Fund Dir Assn, pres l978-80; bd mem, Citizen's Alliance for the Prevention of Drug Abuse l988-; vice pres Coalition of l00 Black Women; bd mem/treasurer Natl Assn of Negro Business & Prof Women's Clubs 1980-86. **Honors/Awds:** Corp Woman of Yr Nat Council on Comm Serv & Continuing Educ Midlantic Region 1976; Community Serv Awd EFA Fitness Center Paterson NJ 1986; Outstanding Serv Awd NJ Educ Oppty Fund Professional Assoc 1986; 20 Year Service Award N.J. Dept of Higher Educ l989; 20 Year Oustanding Service N.J. Educ Opportunity Fund Prof Assn l989; Service Award, Paterson Task Force for Community Action, Inc, 1990; President's Award, NAACP, Paterson Branch, 1991. **Home Addr:** 86-88 17th Ave, Paterson, NJ 07513.

GIST, KAREN WINGFIELD
Educator. **Personal:** Born May 14, 1950, Harrisburg, PA; daughter of Mary Gooden Wingfield and Raleigh Wingfield; divorced; children: Maya Jemelle. **Educ:** Clarion State Univ, BS 1972; Univ of Pittsburgh, MEd 1974; California State Univ, attended 1983. **Career:** Pittsburgh Board of Education, secondary teacher. **Orgs:** Instructor Community Coll of Allegheny County 1974-84; fellow Western Pennsylvania Writing Project 1983-; mem Lambda Kappa Mu Sor Inc Zeta Chapter; mem Pittsburgh Federation of Teachers; mem Natl Council of Teachers of English; mem Urban League. **Honors/Awds:** NHS Fellowship, 1993. **Business Addr:** Secondary Teacher, Pittsburgh Board of Education, 341 S Bellefield, Pittsburgh, PA 15213.

GITE, LLOYD ANTHONY
Journalist. **Personal:** Born Oct 16, 1951, Houston, TX. **Educ:** North TX State Univ Denton, bachelor's degree 1971-74; Southern Methodist Univ Dallas, master's program 1976-77; Univ of MI Ann Arbor, master's/radio-TV-film 1979-80. **Career:** KNOK AM/FM Dallas, news dir 1977-78; Black Forum Dallas, host/producer ABC program 1977-78; Sheridan Broadcasting Network, corres 1980-83; Natl Black Network, corres 1975-83; WTVS TV Detroit, reporter/producer 1981-83; writer for several natl magazines incl Essence, Black Enterprise, USA Today, Gentlemen's Quarterly, Working Woman, Monthly Detroit, 1981-; KRIV TV, reporter/producer 1983-. **Honors/Awds:** Essence Magazine, Essence Man 1976; Press Club of Dallas Media Awd 1977; US Jaycees, one of the Most Outstanding Young Men in Amer, 1978; Ebony Mag, one of the Fifty Leaders of the Future 1978; Natl Assn Black Women Entrepreneurs Mentor of Year Awd 1982; Lincoln Univ, UNITY Awd in Media, 1982, 1983; Houston Press Club Awd for Media 1984. **Business Addr:** Reporter/Producer, KRIV-TV, Channel 26, 3935 Westheimer, Houston, TX 77027.

GITHIGA, JOHN GATUNGU
Chaplain. **Personal:** Born Jul 27, 1942, Muranga, Kenya; son of Joyce Njeri Githiga and Isaac Gitogo Githiga; married Mary N Githiga, Dec 7, 1968; children: Rehema, Isaac Cyprian. **Educ:** Makerere University, theology diploma, 1974; University of the South, MDiv, 1979; International Bible Institute and Seminary, DREd, 1980; University of the South, DMin, 1981. **Career:** Diocese of Nakuru, director of St Nicholars Children Center, five years; St Paul's United Theological College, department head, pastoral theology, 1980-86; African Association for Pastoral Studies and Counseling, founder, president, 1985-88; St Cyprian Church, vicar, 1986-91; Ecumencial Christian Fellowship, founder, president, 1992-; Lakeview Center, telephone crisis counselor, Kairos spiritual director, voluntary, 1992-; Extended Arms Outreach Center, field counselor to juvenile offenders & their parents, 1992; Grambling State University, vicar, chaplain, currently. **Orgs:** University of West Florida Select Committee on Minority Affairs, 1987-92; Martin Luther King Jr Celebration Committee, 1989; Ecumenical and Interfaith Committee, 1987-91; Greater Kiwanis of Pensacola, 1988-92; Association of Theological Institutions in Eastern Africa, 1980-85; National Christian Council of Kenya Youth Department, Nakuru, secretary, 1966-68; Diocese of Nakuru Youth Department, secretary, 1968-71; The First Nakuru Company of the Boys Brigade, captain, 1967-68. **Honors/Awds:** Pensacola Junior College, certificate of appreciation for presentation, 1987; Kiwanis Club of Greater Pensacola, certificate of appreciation for presentation, 1988; Martin Luther King Commemorative Comm, cert of appreciation for planning, 1989; Kiwanis Cert of Appreciation for Spiritual leadership and Service to community, 1989. **Special Achievements:** Author, Christ & Roots, 1988; The Spirit in the Black Soul, 1984; ''The Use of Psychology in Pastoral Counseling in Africa,'' Theological Journal, 1982; ''Family in Transition,'' Beyond, July 1987; co-author, Ewe Ki Jana (Oh Young Man), 1971. **Business Addr:** Vicar/Chaplain, St Luke's Chapel, Grambling State University, PO Box 365, Grambling, LA 71245-0380.

GIVENS, SISTER CLEMENTINA M.
Diocesan office director. **Personal:** Born Nov 15, 1921, Baltimore, MD; daughter of Lavinia Nicholson Givens and James Givens. **Educ:** Webster Grove College, Webster Grove, MO, BS; Catholic University, Washington, DC, MA, 1975. **Career:** Archdiocese of Washington, DC, Washington, DC, elementary teacher, 1956-62; Archdiocese of Miami, Miami, FL, elementary teacher, 1962-73; Archdiocese of Washington, Washington, DC, elementary administrator, 1973-77; Archdiocese of Baltimore, Baltimore, MD, 1977-79; Archdiocese of Washington, DC, Washington, DC, District of Columbia teacher, 1979-81; Archdiocese of Miami, Miami, FL, school admiministrator, 1981-88; Office of Black Catholic Ministry, Rockford, IL, director, currently. **Orgs:** School board member, Archdiocese of Washington, DC, 1958-62; board member, secretariat, Archdiocese of Washington, DC, 1973-77; member, black pastorial council, Archdiocese of Miami, 1981-88. **Business Addr:** Director, Office for Black Catholic Ministry, 617 Lincoln Ave, Rockford, IL 61102.

GIVENS, DONOVAHN HESTON
Physician, educator. **Personal:** Born Dec 31, 1930, Chicago, IL; married Shirley; children: Linda, Rachel, Donna, Elizabeth. **Educ:** Univ PA; Wayne State U; Univ MI Med Sch, MD 1961. **Career:** Oakland Internist Asso, owner; Wayne State U, clinical asst prof 1965-; St Joseph's, resd 1962-65; St Joseph Mercy Hosp, intern 1961-62. **Orgs:** Mem Nat Med Assn; Detroit Med Soc; Wayne Co Med Soc; MI Med Soc; AMA; Am Soc of Internal Med; Am Coll of Phys; mem Vis Com to Med Ctr for Alumniae Univ of MI; Adv Plann Com for Univ Outpaitent Clinic 1971-72; publ ''Urinary Salt Wasting in Chronic Renpl Failure'' Grace Hosp Billiton 1970. **Military Serv:** USAF 1951-55. **Business Addr:** 23077 Greenfield, Southfield, MI 48075.

GIVENS, E. TERRIAN
Business executive (retired). **Personal:** Born Mar 8, 1930, Spartenburg, SC; daughter of Josephine Porter Smith (deceased) and Howard Porter; married Howard; children: Darrick H, Dermot D. **Educ:** Univ of Detroit, BS 1970, MS 1972. **Career:** Mayor's Comm for Human Resources Devel, staff coord 1965-71; Detroit Youth Bd, coord summer activ 1971-73; Detroit Mayor Roman S Gribbs, exec asst 1973-74, admin asst (Grade III) assigned to Detroit Bicent 1974; City of Detroit, principal soc planning & devel asst; City of Detroit, admin asst (Grade IV) in Detroit Planning Dept, retired after 38 years of service. **Orgs:** Established 1st Sub-Center in US under Poverty Prog, Natl Assn Comm Developers; Soc Workers of Metro Detroit, pres 1973-75, 1st vice pres 1972; Detroit Black Coalition; 2nd vice pres Tri-City Business & Professional Women's Club; Citizens Adv Council, Southeastern Michigan Transit Authority; Metro Summer Comm Detroit UCS, 1972-73; mem Women's Econ Club; chairperson Assn of Municipal Professional Women; sec, treas, bd dir Hancock Residential Care Center 1975-88; bd dir St Peter's Home for Boys 1973-88; Natl Round Table of Christians & Jews; NAACP; Natl Drifters Inc; Intl Afro-Amer Museum; Marion Park Civic Club; YMCA; mem, bd dir Detroit Assn for Retarded Children; pres Detroit Jet Setters; vice pres 1967-68, pres 1968-70 National Drifters, Inc; Summit House LTD, co-owner, vp, secy of the bd, 1990-; vice pres, Olympian Palms Owners, bd of dirs, 1995. **Honors/Awds:** WJLB Radio's Citizen of Day 1967; Boy Scouts of Amer, Toppers Club Citation 1970; Optimist Club 1971; Now Black Woman of the Yr, Natl Drifters Inc 1974-75; Woman of the Year, Amer Business Women's Assn 1976-77; Certificate of Appreciation, Detroit Assn of Retarded Citizens 1976; Appreciation Award, Conastoga Coll Kitchner, Ontario, Canada 1979; Notary Public 1972-; Detroit Public Schools Serv Award 1981; Detroit Black United Fund, Certificate of Appreciation 1984-87; Booster Club, United Negro Coll Fund 1987-88; Community Leaders and Noteworthy Americans, Editorial Board of American Biographical Institute 1976-77; Medal for Dedicated Public Service and Proclamation, City of Detroit 1975; resolution, honors over the years, Wayne County Board of Commissioners 1976; Proclamation, Mayor City of Detroit, 1988; Resolution, City Council of Detroit, 1988; Letter of Congratulations from White House, President Ronald Reagan, 1988. **Special Achievements:** First female exec asst to any mayor in the history of Detroit.

GIVENS, HENRY, JR.
College president. **Career:** Harris-Stowe State College, St Louis MO, president. **Business Addr:** President, Harris-Stowe State College, 3026 Laclede Ave, St Louis, MO 63103.

GIVENS, JOSHUA EDMOND
Marketing executive. **Personal:** Born in Norfolk, VA. **Educ:** Northwestern Univ, BS Speech 1975, MS Journalism advertising, 1977. **Career:** WGN-TV, promotional writer 1974, news writer 1974-75; Benton & Bowles Advertising, acct exec 1977-79; Natl Black Network Radio, acct exec 1979-80; Ebony Magazine, acct exec 1980-81; Caldwell Reingold Adv, acct super 1981; Revlon, Inc, dir of marketing 1981-86, vp, dir of mktg ethnic retail markets 1987-93; Lou Roppolo & Associates, ethic marketing specialist, marketing consultant, 1993-. **Orgs:** Mem, Natl Black MBA Assn NY Chapter, 100 Black Men, NY Chapter, Natl Assn Market Devel; NAACP. **Honors/Awds:** Acad Scholarship Northwestern Univ, 1971-75, 1976-77. **Home Addr:** 75 Union St, #2D, Hackensack, NJ 07601.

GIVENS, LAWRENCE
Insurance company executive. **Personal:** Born Nov 30, 1938, Detroit, MI; son of Senia Smith McClain and Timothy Givens; married Delores Clark Givens, May 2, 1959; children: Kimberly, David, Lisa, Stefanie. **Educ:** Wayne State University, Detroit, MI, BS, education, 1962, MBA, 1968. **Career:** Detroit Board of Education, teacher, 1962-64; Chrysler Corporation, vice president of public relations, 1964-82; Detroit Board of Education, assistant to the general superintendent, 1982-84; AAA Michigan, director, corporate relations, 1984-87, assistant vice president, corporate relations, 1987-89, assistant vice pres, human resources, 1989-91, assistant vice pres, corporate relations, 1991-92, vice pres, corporate relations, 1992-. **Orgs:** President, Business Education Alliance, 1989-91; secretary, board of trustees, Horizon Health Systems, 1985-91; chairman of telethon, United Negro College Fund, 1987-89; secretary, board of directors, Efficacy Detroit, 1985-91; board member, Centrum Insurance Company, 1983-91. **Honors/Awds:** Minority Achiever of the Year, Detroit YMCA, 1985; Outstanding Leadership Award, United Negro College Fund, 1989; Sloan Fellow, Nominee, Chrysler Corp., 1968. **Business Addr:** VP, Corporate Relations, AAA Michigan, 1 Auto Club Dr, Dearborn, MI 48126.

GIVENS, LEONARD DAVID
Attorney. **Personal:** Born Sep 10, 1943, Elmira, NY; married Patricia. **Educ:** Mansfield State Coll, BS 1965; Howard Law Sch, JD 1971. **Career:** Miller, Canfield, Paddock & Stone, partner, 1971-; NLRB Wash, law clerk 1970-71; AFSCME Wash, law clerk 1968-69; IBM Owego, NY, admin asst 1965-68. **Orgs:** ABA; NBA; Detroit Bar Assn; Oakland Co Bar Assn; MI State Bar Assn, labor council; Am Judicature Soc; bd dir Homes for Black Children; Greater Detroit Chamber of Commerce; Metropolitan Affairs Corp.; Michigan Biotechnological Institute; Federation of Girls Home; Law Journal invitee Moot Ct Team. **Business Addr:** Miller, Canfield, Paddock and Stone, 150 W Jefferson, Suite 2500, Detroit, MI 48226.

GIVENS, ROBIN
Actress. **Personal:** Born 1965; daughter of Ruth Roper; married Mike Tyson, Feb 7, 1988 (divorced 1988); married Svetozar Marinkovic, 1997. **Educ:** Sarah Lawrence College. **Career:** Actress, entrepreneur; films: A Rage in Harlem, 1991, Boomerang, 1992, Foreign Student, Blankman; television mini-series, The Women of Brewster Place, 1989, On Wings of Fear, The Penthouse and Beverly Hills Madam; television series, ''Head of the Class,'' 1987-91, ''Angel Street,'' 1992, ''Courthouse''; ''Sparks'', 1997-; founder & director, Never Blue Productions, 1990-.

GIVENS, ROCELIOUS (ROY)
Business executive. **Personal:** Born May 21, 1928, Pittsburgh, PA; son of Geneva Burks Givens and Rocelious Givens Sr; married Leora M Stelly, Sep 2, 1952; children: Marsha M Marsh, Sharon A, Rhonda M Brown, Brenda I Hill, Roy A, Craig F, Terri E. **Career:** US Steel, welder, 1947-49; Wagner-Frasier Chrysler Plymouth, bodyfender, 1949-50; Industrial Instrument Supply, panel builder, 1970-74; Pantrol, Inc, owner, vice pres, 1974-78, owner, president, 1978-. **Orgs:** Sunrise East Lions Club, various offices, 1981-; Air Force Sergeants Association, 1992-; Wells Homeowners Association, board member, 1992-. **Military Serv:** US Air Force, smsgt, 1950-70; Air Force Commendation Medal, 1970; various service medals. **Business Addr:** President, Pantrol, Inc, E 2214 Riverside, PO Box 4387, Spokane, WA 99202, (509)535-9061.

GIVHAN, MERCER A., JR.
Business executive. **Personal:** Born Dec 28, 1943, Birmingham, AL; married Annetta Foster; children: Mercer III, Carrie. **Educ:** Morehouse Coll, BA econ 1965. **Career:** Shearson Loeb Rhoades, sr vice pres investments; Shearson Loeb Rhoades, investm broker 1969-. **Orgs:** Pres council Shearson Loeb Rhoades 1975-80. **Military Serv:** A1c a/c 1965-68.

GIVHAN, ROBIN DENEEN
Journalist. **Personal:** Born Sep 11, 1964, Detroit, MI; daughter of Stella Thompson Givhan and Robert Givhan. **Educ:** Princeton University, Princeton, NJ, BA, 1986; Univ of Michigan, Ann Arbor, MI, MA, 1988. **Career:** Detroit Free Press, staff writer, 1988-92, fashion editor, 1993-; San Francisco Chronicle, staff writer, 1992-93. **Orgs:** Member, Detroit Historical Society, Costume Exhibit Committee, 1990-91; member, Detroit Institute of Arts, Founders Society, 1989-91. **Honors/Awds:** Atrium Award, excellence in fashion writing, Univ of Georgia, 1990. **Business Addr:** Fashion Editor, Detroit Free Press, 321 W Lafayette Blvd, Detroit, MI 48226.

GIVINS, ABE, JR.
Government official, insurance consultant. **Personal:** Born Apr 22, 1951, Columbus, MS; son of Corine Givins and Abe Givins Sr; married Linda Sue Robinson Givins; children: Abe III, Ryan Eugene, Christel C. **Educ:** Central State Univ, BS Ed 1974-77. **Career:** Normandy School Dist, teacher 1980-82; City of Pine Lawn MO, alderman 1982-; Insurance Agency, insurance broker 1982-; City of Pine Lawn, alderman; St Louis Public Schools, teacher Biology, 1989-91, special education (Behavior Distributors), 1989-91; Missouri Dept Mental Health, St Louis MO, Residental Therapist, 1991-. **Orgs:** Mem Normandy Municpal League 1982-, MS Municipal League 1982-, Normandy Democratic Club 1982-, Candidate for Mayor, City of Pine Lawn, MO, 1989. **Home Addr:** 2008 Pleasant Valley Dr, St Charles, MO 63303-3867.

GLADDEN, BRENDA WINCKLER
Attorney. **Personal:** Born May 29, 1943, Baltimore, MD; daughter of Grace Lucille Morton Dixon and Raymond McDonald Winckler; married Major Paul Gladden MD; children: Miriam P, Paul B. **Educ:** Cedar Crest Coll Allentown PA, BA 1965; Howard Univ School of Law WA DC, JD 1973. **Career:** NY Hosp NY, chemist 1965-67; US Dept of HUD, Washington, DC, attny 1974-. **Orgs:** Mem Phi Alpha Delta Law Frat 1971-, DC Bar Assoc, PA Bar Assoc, Amer Bar Assoc, 1974-, Delta Sigma Theta, Jack & Jill of Amer Inc, Aux to Medico-Chirurgical Soc DC, Aux to Natl Med Assoc, The Nat'l Bar Assoc, Links Inc, Law Review Invitee Howard 1972. **Honors/Awds:** DC Ct of Appeals 1974; Supreme Ct of PA 1974; US Dist Ct DC 1974; US Ct of Appeals DC Circuit 1980; US Supreme Ct 1980. **Business Addr:** Attorney, US Dept of HUD, 451 7th St SW, Washington, DC 20410.

GLADDEN, MAJOR P.
Orthopedic surgeon. **Personal:** Born Dec 8, 1935, Chester, SC; son of Isabelle Woodward Gladden and Joseph Gladden; married Brenda Winckler; children: Miriam P, Paul B. **Educ:** Morgan State Univ, BS 1957; Howard Univ, MD 1961; Amer Bd of Orthopaedic Surgery, cert 1969, recertified 1983. **Career:** DC Gen Hosp, internship 1961-62; Mt Alto VA Hosp, res training (gen surg) 1962-63; DC Gen Hosp, res ortho 1963-64; Bronx Municipal Hosp, residency ortho 1964-66; Albert Einstein Coll of Med Bronx, instr 1966-68; Howard Univ Coll of Med, asst prof 1969-80; DC Genl Hosp, chief orthopaedic surg1968-80; Howard Univ Coll of Med, assoc prof ortho surg 1980-. **Orgs:** Mem Alpha Phi Alpha Frat 1954-; team physician & ortho consul Howard Univ 1969-; volunteer in Orthopaedics Medico Prog (CARE) Dominican Rep 1978; examiner Amer Bd of Ortho Surg Chicago 1979; vol ortho surg Olympic Training Ctr Colorado Springs 1984; mem bd of dirs Morgan State Univ Found 1984; chief physician DC Boxing & Wrestling Comm 1984. **Military Serv:** AUS maj 1957-71. **Business Addr:** Assoc Prof, Ortho Surgery, Howard Univ Coll of Med, 1140 Varnum St NE, Suite 108, Washington, DC 20017.

GLADMAN, CHARLES R.
City official. **Educ:** National Fire Academy, Executive Fire Officer Program, 1995. **Career:** City of Akron Fire Dept, 1973-, lieutenant/company officer, 1979-85, captain, 1986-89, dist fire chief, 1990-91, dep chief, 1992-96, chief, 1997-. **Special Achievements:** First African American Fire Chief in Akron, OH; One of seven African Americans to integrate Akron's Fire Dept, 1973.

GLADNEY, MARCELLIOUS
Pediatric dentistry consultant. **Personal:** Born May 14, 1949, West Point, MS; son of Annie Gladney and Robert Gladney; married Elizabeth F Jones; children: Scott, Tarik M, Tonia M. **Educ:** St Johns Univ, BS Pharmacy 1972; Univ of Med & Dent of NJ, DMD 1977; Univ of Nebraska, MS, 1993. **Career:** Eli Lilly and Co, pharm sales rep 1972-74; US Public Health Svcs, asst dental surgeon 1977-80; Mercer McDowel Dental Group, pres/founder 1980-; US Public Health Svcs, chief dental officer 1991; Indian Health Svcs, ediatric dentistry consultant, currently. **Orgs:** Mem Amer Dental Assoc 1979-87; mem Princeton WV Civitans 1982-85; pres Southern WV Roadrunners Club 1983-86; Omega Psi Phi, Sigma Pi Phi; National Dental Association; American Academy of Pediatric Dentistry. **Honors/Awds:** Board Certified Pediatric Dentist; PHS Citation Awd, 1980, 1991; PHS Achievement Medal 1988, 1994; PHS Commendation Medal, 1997; American Academy of Pediatric Dentistry, Fellow, 1995. **Home Addr:** 3109 Berwick Dr, Claremore, OK 74017.

GLANTON, LYDIA JACKSON
Educator. **Personal:** Born Jul 11, 1909, Rockvale, TN; married Simon Henry Glanton; children: Thelma Louise Rogers Lawson. **Educ:** TN State Univ, BS (w/honors), 1948; Fisk Univ, Postgraduate 1950; George Peabody Coll, 45 hrs towards Masters degree, 1968. **Career:** Rutherford County Schools, teacher, 1931-38; Rutherford County Schools, Little Hope School, principal, 1938-45; Rutherford County Schools, teacher 1965-74; Rutherford County Bd of Educ, bd mem 1975-84; Rutherford Cty Schools, special educ task force 1986. **Orgs:** life mem, Natl Educ Assn, 1945; pres, Rutheford County Teachers Assn, 1966-67; pres Murfreesboro County Fed, 1970-78, TN Fed Colored Women's Club 1973-77; life mem Natl Assoc CWC 1976-; adv bd Patterson Comm Ctr 1977-; cancer bd 1980; pres Rutherford Cty Retired Teachers 1982-83; bd Local Heart Assoc 1982-84; pres Heart of TN Amer BWS Women Assn 1983-84; judging comm Murfreesboro Chamber of Comm Christmas Parade 1983; vice pres Mid Cumberland Agency Co 1984-85; pres, treas, committees, Criterian Literary & Art Club; mem Dynamic Club; life mem Natl Assoc of Colored Womens Clubs Washington DC; mem League of Women Voters Murfreesboro Chapt, Southeastern Assoc of Colored Womens Clubs; Murfreesboro City Sign Commission 1985; Murfreesboro City Planning Comm1986-89. **Honors/Awds:** Helped write curriculum guide for Rutherford Cty Schools 1965; Head Start Vol Serv head Start Dept of Mid Cumb 1973-78; Outstanding Serv Rutherford County School Bd 1975-84; Hon Staff Mem of TN House of Rep Certificate of Merit 1976; Murfreesboro Masonic Lodge Citizen of the Year Awd 1977; Certificate of Appreciation Mid Cumb Comm Action Agency 1978; Hon Sgt at Arms of TN House of Rep James R McKinney Speaker of House of Rep; Certificate of Award, Kappa Alpha Psi 1978; Outstanding Serv TN School Bd Awd 1982-83. **Home Addr:** 615 East Castle St, Murfreesboro, TN 37130. **Business Addr:** Special Education Task Force, Ruth Co Schools, 467 South Hancock, Murfreesboro, TN 37130.

GLANTON, SADYE LYERSON
Executive secretary. **Personal:** Born Jul 5, 1900, Nashville; widowed. **Educ:** A&I Univ Nashville TN, BS 1918; Univ of Cincinnati, BS 1930; Univ of Cincinnati, grad work. **Career:** Organized Nat Coun of Negro Women, pres 1955-58, 70-74; Zeta Phi Beta Sorority, organizer dir job corps for girls training 1964-68; Springfield NAACP, exec sec; Dramatics Cincinnati Recruiter, dir 1940-48. **Orgs:** Organizer mem Bapt Ch; mem of choir 20 yrs; pres Zeta Phi Beta Sorority 1922-24; pres Nat Coun of Negro Women 1930 & 1954; participent conv Dayton OH. **Honors/Awds:** Citation for comm work Trenton Meth Ch; award of merit for outstanding contribution by Affiliate Contractors of Am Inc 1972; award from YMCA.

GLANVILLE, CECIL E.
Psychiatrist. **Personal:** Born Jan 15, 1925; married Mattie E Lynch; children: Kenneth, Douglas. **Educ:** Teachers Coll Port of Spain Trinidad West Indies, Teachers Diploma 1946; Howard Univ Coll of Liberal Arts, BS (cum laude) 1959; Howard Univ Coll of Medicine, MD 1963. **Career:** Manhattan Psychiatric Center, NY City, unit chief; Harlem Hospital, Manhattan Psychiatric Center, affiliate unit 1967-69; Speedwell Servs for Children, NY City, clinical dir 1969-72; W Harlem Mental Health Council, NY City, medical dir Washington Heights 1973-80; Private Practice; Bergen Pines County Hospital, Paramus NJ, staff psychiatrist. **Orgs:** Gen mem Amer Psychiatric Assn 1967-, Amer Medical Assn 1967-, Natl Medical Assn 1969-; chrmn Youth Guidance Council Teaneck NJ 1974-86; mem Amer Heart Assn 1983-85. **Business Addr:** 185 Cedar Lane, Teaneck, NJ 07666.

GLANVILLE, DOUGLAS METUNWA
Professional baseball player. **Personal:** Born Aug 25, 1970, Hackensack, NJ. **Educ:** Pennsylvania. **Career:** Chicago Cubs, outfielder, 1996-97; Philadelphia Phillies, 1998-. **Business Addr:** Professional Baseball Player, Philadelphia Phillies, PO Box 7575, Philadelphia, PA 19101, (215)463-6000.

GLAPION, MICHAEL J.
Insurance broker. **Personal:** Born May 15, 1947, New Orleans, LA; son of Alma Broussard & Armand P Glapion Jr; married Angeler Robert Glapion, Sep 27, 1969; children: Nicholas, Stacie Rose, Nina Simonne, Christopher. **Educ:** Xavier Univ of Louisiana, BFA, 1969. **Career:** St Paul Fire & Marine Ins Co, commercial property underwriter, 1971-75; Medtronic Inc, mgr, risk management, 1975-78; Graco Inc, mgr of risk management & insurance, 1978-83; Harvest States Cooperatives, dir of risk management, 1983-88; Insurance & Surety Specialist Inc, president & CEO, 1981-. **Orgs:** MN African American Chamber of Commerce, chairman, 1990-95; MN Cultural Diversity Center, co-founder & vice chair, 1991-95; Turning Point Inc, bd member & chair, 1990-95; Natl Assn of Minority Contractors of MN, exec bd, 1993-95; North Community Branch YMCA, bd member & chair, 1979-84; Childrens Home Society of MN, bd member, 1981-84; Richfield Human Rights Commission, commissioner, 1971-74; Risk & Insurance Management Society of MN, bd member & president, 1978-81; Professional Insurance Agents of MN, 1995-, bd mem, pres, 1996. **Honors/Awds:** Natl Assn of Minority Contractors of MN, President's Award, 1994. **Business Addr:** President & CEO, Insurance & Surety Specialist, Inc, 6547 City West Pky, Eden Prairie, MN 55344-3248.

GLASCO, ANITA L.
Educator. **Personal:** Born Oct 24, 1942, Kansas City, KS. **Educ:** U Univ So CA, AB 1964; Harvard Univ Law Sch, JD 1967. **Career:** Univ of Chicago Law Sch, master of comparative law 1970; Southwestern Univ Sch of Law, prof of law 1975-; SW, Asso prof of law 1972-75; Smith & Glascod partner 1971-72; Lewis & Clark Coll, visting prof of law 1975; Univ of Wash, visting prof of law 1974; Univ of TN knoxville, vis prof of law 1980. **Orgs:** Mem CA State Bar Assn 1968-; mem Black Women Lawyers Assn; mem CA Assn of Black Lawyers; chpn Elect of Minority Groups Sect of Assn of Am Law Schs1977; chmn Minority Groups Sect of Assn of Law Schs 1978; fellow Inst French Lang & Civil Univ of Geneva 1968; fellow Inst of French Lang & Civil Univ ofPau 1969; fellow Inst French Lang & Civil Univ of Paris 1969; comparative law fellow Univ of Aix-Marseilles 1969-74. **Honors/Awds:** Outst Young Woman of Am honoree 1971. **Business Addr:** SW Univ School of Law, 675 S Westmoreland, Los Angeles, CA 90005.

GLASGOW, DOUGLAS G.
Educator. **Educ:** Brklyn Coll, BA 1959; Clmb U, MSW 1961; Univ of So CA, DSW 1968. **Career:** Natl Urban League Inc, wash oper; Howard Univ School of Social Work, prof, dean 1971-74; Univ of CA Los Angeles, assoc prof, School of Social Welfare 1970-71; Council on Social Work Educ LA, juvenile delinquency comm 1969-70; The Center for the Stdy of Afro-Amer Historical Culture UCLA, interim dir 1969-70; HEW Office of Juvenile Delinquency Youth Devel LA, prin invest 1968-69. **Orgs:** Mem Nat Assn of Soc Wrks; Intl Coun on Soc Wlfr Inc; The Acad of Cert Soc Wrkrs; Am Acad of Pol & Soc Sci; Nat Assn of Blck Soc Wrkrs; Nat Assn of Soc Wrkrs; bd mem Coun on Soc Wrk Ed; co-chmn Blck Fclty Staff UCLA 1969; CSWE Struc Rvw Com 1971-72, bd dir 1972-74, adv com on Comm Coll Gdlns 1969, Rvw Dsgn Com 1972; v chmn Div Prog NCSW Cntnl Conf 1973; edtrl bd NASW Jrnl of Soc Wrk 1970-73, Gls Comm Jvnl Dlnqncy Adlt Crm 1969-70; US Prog Com ICSW 1973; bd dir Untd Blck Fund Inc Wash; mem adv com Hwrd Univ Inst on Drug Abs & Adctn 1973. **Honors/Awds:** Recip M J Palevsky Fnd Awd 1970; Flwshp Awd Dnfrth Fnd 1971; NIMH Sr Stpnd Awd 1975. **Business Addr:** Howard Univ Sch of Social Work, Washington, DC 20059.

GLASS, GERALD DAMON
Professional basketball player. **Personal:** Born Nov 12, 1967, Greenwood, MS. **Educ:** Delta State Univ, Cleveland, MS, 1985-87; Univ of Mississippi, University, MS, 1988-90. **Career:** Minnesota Timberwolves, 1990-. **Business Addr:** Professional Basketball Player, Minnesota Timberwolves, 600 1st Ave, NW, Minneapolis, MN 55403-1416.

GLASS, JAMES
Labor administrator. **Personal:** Born Jan 27, 1928, Birmingham, AL; married. **Educ:** Miles Coll, Birmingham AL, 1951; Detroit Inst of Technology, Detroit MI, BA Sociology, 1976; Wayne State Univ, Labor School, Detroit MI. **Career:** Chrysler Assembly Plant, 1952-54; Detroit General Hospital, 1952-55; Wayne County Juvenile Court, 1955-81; Todd Phillips Children's Home, 1965-78; AFSCME Council 25, exec vice pres, elected 1981, pres, 1982-. **Orgs:** Mem 1982-, advisory bd mem 1982-, United Foundation, 1982-; chmn, Council 25 Exec Bd, 1982-; exec bd mem, Michigan AFL-CIO, 1982-; vice pres, intl exec bd, AFSCME, 1983-; mem, Coalition of Black Trade Unionists, 1983-; governor's appointee, Michigan Job Training Coord Council, 1983-; bd dir, NAACP, 1983-; exec bd mem, Michigan Trade Union Council for Histadrut. **Honors/Awds:** Dedicated Committeeman, AFSCME Local 409, 1981; Distinguished Service, Coalition of Black Trade Unionists, 1981; testimonial dinner honoree, AFSCME, 1985; Outstanding Leadership, AFSCME Local 1985. **Military Serv:** US Navy, honorable discharge, 1947. **Business Addr:** President, Michigan AFSCME Council #25, 1034 N Washington, Lansing, MI 48906.

GLASS, ROBERT DAVIS
Judge. **Personal:** Born Nov 28, 1922, Wetumpka, AL; son of M E Davis Glass and Isaiah Glass; married Doris E Powell, Dec 9, 1951; children: Robert Jr, Roberta Diane, Rosalyn Doris. **Educ:** NC Central Univ, Durham, NC, BA, 1949, JD, 1951. **Career:** Private pratice, attny, Charlotte, NC, 1951-53, New Bern, NC, attny 1953-60; CT Labor Dept, claims examiner 1961-62; private practice Waterbury CT, attny 1962-66; Asst US Attny Dist of CT, New Haven, CT, 1st black asst US attny 1966-67; 1st black judge CT Juvenile Ct, 1967-78; CT Superior Court, judge 1978-84; Connecticut Judicial District, Waterbury, CT; administrative judge, Superior Court,Waterbury Judicial District, 1984-87; Connecticut Supreme Court, Hartford, CT, associate justice, 1987-92; CT judge trial referee, 1992-. **Orgs:** Eastern NC Counsel NC Conf of NAACP 1953-60, Waterbury Comm on Human Rights 1964; reg vchmn CT Council on Human Rights 1964; mem bd of dir Pearl St Neighborhood House Waterbury 1965-66; pres CT State Fed of Negro Dem Clubs 1965-67; former bd mem of corps Waterbury Savings Bank 1973-84; mem CT Bar, NC Bar, Amer Bar Assoc; life mem Natl Bar Assoc, Amer Judicature Soc, Jucicial Council of Natl Bar Assoc, CT Bar Assoc, Waterbury Bar Assoc, Assoc for Study of Afro-Amer Life & History, Life member, NAACP. **Honors/Awds:** Amer Campaign Medal Asiatic Pacific Campaign Medal; Cert 3 Wks Training Prog Natl Council of Juvenile Ct Judges; Cert 2 Wks Grad Training Natl Coll of Juvenile Judges, 1974; Honorary LLD, NC Central Univ, 1988; Honorary LLD, University of Bridgeport, 1990. **Military Serv:** AUS 1943-46. **Home Addr:** 159 Westmont Dr, Waterbury, CT 06708.

GLASS, RONALD
Actor. **Personal:** Born Jul 10, 1945, Evansville, IN; son of Lethia Glass and Crump Glass. **Educ:** University of Evansville, BA, 1968. **Career:** Television appearances include: Barney Miller series, 1974-82; The New Odd Couple, 1982-83; Shirts and Skins, 1973; Crash, 1978; Rhythm & Blues, 1992; Teen Angel, 1997-; guest appearances, Hawaii Five-O; Maude; Bob Newhart Show; Streets of San Francisco; Sanford & Son, 1972; Good Times; All in the Family; theater appearances include: Tyrone Guthrie Theater, company member, 1968-72; Slow Dance on the Killing Ground, 1972; Day of Absence, 1970; The House of Atreus; The Taming of the Shrew. **Orgs:** Screen Actors Guild; Hollywood Academy of TV Arts & Sciences, Actors Equity Assn; Alpha Psi Omega; American Federation of Television & Radio Artists. **Honors/Awds:** Blue Key Scholastic Honor Society; Alumni Certificate of Excellence, University of Evansville, 1975; Dionysus Award, Hollywood Club Forum Intl, 1977; Communtiy Award, LA Sentinel Entertainment Writer Gertrude Gibson, 1975; Community Award, Phil Wilkes, Freddie Jett, 1976; only student from University of Evansville to win 3 SAMMY's; Pearl Le Compte Award; William A Gumbertz Award, 1968; Medal of Honor, University of Evansville. **Business Addr:** Actor, c/o Lawrence Kubik, PO Box 4669, Los Angeles, CA 90046.

GLASS, VIRGINIA M.
Consultant. **Personal:** Born Dec 14, 1927, Manila, Philippines; daughter of Maria Moreto and Tomas N McKinney; divorced; children: Sidney, Luis. **Educ:** Fordham Univ, undergrad work; Columbia Univ, BA; Columbia Univ School of Library Science, graduate work; Hunter Coll; Queens Coll School, graduate work, Educ, 1977. **Career:** Self-employed consultant in Promotions, Publicity, Community Devel and Educ; pres, Community Tennis Serv, currently; head librarian, LaJolla Country Day School, 1980-81; dir, community serv, City Coll, 1978-80; educ coordinator, San Diego Human Relations Commn, 1974-78; dir, public relations, San Diego Urban League; consultant, Univ of CA, San Diego, 1972-74; consultant, San Diego City Schools, 1970-72; High School Admin, NY City School Dist, 1952-70; librarian, Brooklyn Public Library, 1949-52. **Orgs:** Mem, exec comm USTA, minority participation comm; founder/past pres, Mt. View Tennis Club; past pres, San Diego Dist Tennis Assn; Contemporary Black Arts, UCSD; commr, Chrysler LeBaron Series; coordinator, USTA Volvo League; USTA Umpire and Referee; editor, Black Tennis Magazine; coordinator, Jr Olympic Tennis; Natl Jr Tennis League, Coordinator for San Diego; past pres, Amer Tennis Assn; Executive Board, Phoenix Challenge; Advisory Staff for Yomex and Wilson; bd mem, Black Tennis and Sports Found; bd mem, Southern California Tennis Assn; Natl Conf of Christians & Jews; mem, Natl Assn for Female Execs; advisory bd, Pacific Womens Sports Foundation. **Honors/Awds:** Southeast Community Theatre Award; USTA Community Serv Award, 1977; Mildred Pierce Award for Contribution to Tennis in San Diego; San Diego City Coll Citizens Council Award; Honor Roll, NCCJ; San Diego Dist Tennis Award for Outstanding Serv; California Federation of Black Leadership Serv Award; Ranked #4 in the US Sr Women's Tennis & #2 in Southern California, 1989; Ranked #1 in the World, 1989; Leadership Award for Community Serv, 1985; Elected to Tennis Hall of Fame; Outstanding Community Service to San Diego, 1990.

GLAUDE, STEPHEN A.
Business executive. **Personal:** Born Jul 25, 1954, Washington, DC; son of Phyllis Taylor Glaude and William Criss Glaude; married Rhonda Roland; children: Koya, Shani, Khary. **Educ:** Morgan State Univ, BS 1977. **Career:** Capitol East Children's

Ctr, asst dir 1977-79; DC Assoc for Retarded Citizens, vocational evaluator 1979-80. **Orgs:** Founder/pres Institute for Life Studies 1970-; chairperson/bd of directors Capitol East Children's Ctr 1979; bd member Montgomery Mental Health Assn 1980;mem President's Task Force on Private Sector Initiatives 1981; chairperson/fundraising membership devel cmte Black Child Development Inst 1984; mem Council for Blk Economic Agenda 1985. **Honors/Awds:** President's Second Mild Awd 1977; Mental Health Community Service Awd 1977. **Business Addr:** Executive Dir, Natl Assn of Neighborhoods, 1651 Fuller NW, Washington, DC 20009.

GLEASON, ELIZA
Librarian. **Personal:** Born Dec 15, 1909, Winston-Salem, NC; daughter of Oliona P Atkins and Simon G Atkins; married Maurice F Gleason; children: Joy Carew. **Educ:** Fisk Univ, AB 1926-30; Univ IL, BS 1930-31; Univ CA, MA 1935-36; Univ Chicago, PhD 1937-40. **Career:** Louisville Mun Coll, asst librarian 1931-32, librarian 1932-36; Fisk Univ, asst prof 1936-37; Talladega Coll, dir libraries 1940-41; Atlanta Univ, prof 1941-46; Univ Chicago, guest lecturer 1953; Chicago Tchrs Coll, asso prof 1954-65; IL Tchrs Coll, assoc prof 1965-67; IL Inst of Tech, prof 1967-70; John Crerar Lib, asst librarian 1967-70; Chicago Public Library, asst chief librarian 1970-73; No IL Univ, prof 1974-75; Self Employed, library consultant, currently. **Orgs:** Women's Aux of Cook Co Physicians Assn 1940-; Women's Aux of Meharry Med Coll Alumni Assn 1940-; Hyde Park-Kenwood Comm Conf 1950-; SE Chicago Commn 1952-; Ind Voters of IL 1952-; Women's Aux of Intl Coll of Surgeons 1961-; co-chmn Fisk Univ Centennial Campaign 1963-65; exec comm Fisk Univ Alumni Assn 1964-; mem Phi Beta Kappa, Beta Phi Mu Natl Hon Soc in Lib Sci, Amer Library Assn. **Honors/Awds:** Fellow 1938-40; Fisk Univ Alumni Award 1964; former ALA Counselor; numerous publs.

GLEASON, MAURICE FRANCIS. See Obituaries section.

GLEN, ULYSSES, JR.
Gaming official. **Personal:** Born Aug 11, 1970, Cleveland, OH; son of Janis W & Ulysses Glen Sr. **Educ:** University of Cincinnati, BA, 1993. **Career:** Blue Cross/Blue Shield, sales coord, 1994-96; Total Health Care Plan, mktg manager, 1996; DC Lottery & Charitable Games, chief of staff, 1996-. **Orgs:** NAACP, 1993-; Kappa Alpha Psi Fraternity Inc, vice polemarch, 1996-. **Business Addr:** Chief of Staff/Administrative Officer, DC Lottery & Charitable Games Control Board, 2101 Martin Luther King Jr Dr, Executive Office, 5th Fl, Washington, DC 20024, (202)645-8010.

GLENN, AARON DEVON
Professional football player. **Personal:** Born Jul 16, 1972, Humble, TX. **Educ:** Texas A&M. **Career:** New York Jets, defensive back, 1994-. **Business Addr:** Professional Football Player, New York Jets, 1000 Fulton Ave, Hempstead, NY 11550, (516)560-8100.

GLENN, CECIL E.
Educator. **Personal:** Born Dec 18, 1938, Nashville; married; children: Cecil LaVel, Gerald Glenn. **Educ:** BA; MA; PhD 1975. **Career:** Univ of CO, prof Social Science, head Ethnic Studies; Chicago Dept of Educ, Public Health Serv Civil Rights Envolvement, 10 yrs; teahcer 15 yrs; Higher Educ, area urban sociologist 5 yrs; Mental Health Inc, serv in mental health field chmn 5 yrs. **Orgs:** Chmn Malcolm X Mental Inc; mem NAACP. **Honors/Awds:** Recip awds Nat Alliance of Business 1975; Mt Plains Comm Coll Ldshp 1974; Partners corrective progs 1974. **Business Addr:** 1100 14 St, Denver, CO 80202.

GLENN, DENNIS EUGENE
Automotive manufacturing executive. **Personal:** Born Dec 7, 1948, Detroit, MI; son of Bonnie Beard Glenn and Robert Glenn Sr; married Donna Norman Glenn, Sep 30, 1973; children: Kamara, Kameka, Dennis. **Educ:** Grand Valley State University, Allendale, MI, BS, Business Admin, 1974. **Career:** Digitan Equipment Corp, Salem, NH, buyer, 1976-78; Ford Motor Corp, Dearborn, MI, purchasing administrator, 1978-83; Young Industries, Detroit, MI general manager, 1984-86; Wayne County, Detroit, MI, purchasing agent, 1986-89; Tactictal Truck Corp, Livonia, MI, purchasing agent, 1989; Toyota Motor Manufacturing, USA, Georgetown, KY, development specialist minority supplier, 1989-.

GLENN, EDWARD C., JR.
Senior sales representative. **Personal:** Born Jan 8, 1922, Akron, OH; married Sitella Rodriguez. **Educ:** Wayne State U, attended; MI U, student. **Career:** Superior Life Ins Soc, asst Mgr 1953-57; Mammoth Life Ins Co Detroit, dir training field supr 1957-60; Metropolitan Life Ins Co, sr sales rep. **Orgs:** Bd mem Detroit Asso Life Underwriters; ch educ comm 1972-74; former ch Metropolitan Life's Pres Conf 1972-73; past pres Cotillion Club inc 1970-72, bd ch 1973; pes Bagley Pub Sch PTA 1969; life mem NAACP 1971-. **Honors/Awds:** Cited for prof Ebony & Life Mag 1966, 1972; Nat Quality Awd 1965-73, Detroit News 1970-73; man of yr Metropolitan Life Ins Co 1968, 1969, 1970, 1971, 1972, 1973. **Business Addr:** 28225 Hoover Rd, Warren, MI 48093.

GLENN, PATRICIA CAMPBELL
Mediator. **Personal:** Born Dec 15, 1942, Brandon, MS; daughter of Ewnice Agnes Finch and James Alvin Campbell; divorced; children: Allison, Jennifer, Lee. **Educ:** Ohio State Univ, Columbus OH, BS Educ, 1970; Univ of Illinois, Chicago IL, MS Educ Admin, 1985. **Career:** Gast High School, Columbus OH, teacher, 1971-74; Ohio Civil Rights Comm, Columbus OH, supvr, investigator, 1974-78; US Dept of Justice Community Relations Serv, Chicago IL, sr conciliation specialist, 1978-. **Orgs:** Natl Council Negro Women, 1980-; pres, Major Charles L Hunt VFW Post, 1984-85; dist commr, Boy Scouts, 1987-89. **Honors/Awds:** Humanitarian Award, Columbus Metropolitan Community Action Org, 1980; Outstanding Performance Award, Attorney General, 1984; Human Relations Service Award, 1985; Certificate of Appreciation, Kiwanis Award, 1987; Silver Beaver, Chicago Area Council, 1989.

GLENN, TARIK
Professional football player. **Personal:** Born May 25, 1976, Cleveland, OH. **Educ:** California. **Career:** Indianapolis Colts, guard, 1997-. **Special Achievements:** NFL Draft, First round pick, #19, 1997. **Business Addr:** Professional Football Player, Indianapolis Colts, PO Box 535000, Indianapolis, IN 46253, (317)297-2658.

GLENN, TERRY
Professional football player. **Personal:** Born Jul 23, 1974, Columbus, OH; children: Terry Jr. **Educ:** Ohio State Univ. **Career:** New England Patriots, wide receiver, 1996-. **Honors/Awds:** Fred Biletnikoff Award, 1995; First-team All-American, 1995; Sports Illustrated, Rookie of the Year, 1996. **Business Addr:** Professional Football Player, New England Patriots, 60 Washington St, Foxboro Stadium, Foxboro, MA 02035, (508)543-7911.

GLENN, WYNOLA
Elected official. **Personal:** Born Jan 27, 1932, Farmville, VA; married James L Glenn; children: Denise Mercado, Cheryl Mitchell, Anita Bonet, Delana, Tanya, James L Jr. **Educ:** Baruch Coll CUNY, attended; Coll of New Rochelle, attended. **Career:** Harlem Primary Care Governing Bd, pres 1983-; Zeta Amicac Sor, pres 1984-; Community School Bd #5, pres 1983-. **Business Addr:** School Board President, Board of Education, 433 W 123rd St, New York, NY 10027.

GLOSTER, HUGH MORRIS
Educator. **Personal:** Born May 11, 1911, Brownsville, TN; married Yvonne Arnold King; children: Alice, Evelyn; married Beulah V Harold (divorced); children: Hugh Morris, Jr; married Louis Elizabeth Torrence (divorced). **Educ:** Morehouse Coll, BA 1931 Atlanta U, MA 1933 NY U, PhD 1943. **Career:** Morehouse Coll, pres 1967-87; dean fac 1963-67; Hampton Inst, prof 1946-67; assoc regional exec 1944-46; USO, program dir 1943-46; Morehouse Coll, prof 1941-43; LeMoyne Coll, instructor, assoc prof 1933-41; Hiroshima Univ, Fulbright prof 1953-55; Amer Lit Univ Warsaw Poland, visiting prof 1961-72; lecturer tours 1933-55, 1956, 1959. **Orgs:** Commn on coll adminstrn Assn Am Coll; v chmn GA postsec Educ Commn; President's Councl Am Forum for Intl Studies; Inst European Studie; mem bd nom Am Inst for Pub Svc; exec com Coll Entrance Exam Bd 1967-71; bd dir United Bd for Coll Devel; com on Econ Devel; So Christian Ldrshp Conf; bd dir trustee United Negro Coll Fund; trustee Atlanta Univ Morehouse Coll Interdenominational Theol Ctr Educ Testing Svc; Phi Beta Kappa; Sigma Pi Phi Boule; Alpha Phi Alpha. **Honors/Awds:** Res grant Carnegie Found 1950-51; Disting Contbns Awd Coll Lang Assn 1958; Centennial Med Hampton Inst 1968; Alumnus of Yr Awd LeMoyne Coll 1967; author "Negro Voices in Amer" 1948; co-ed "The Brown Thrush an Anthology of Verse by Negro Coll Students" 1935; "My Life-My Country-My World Coll Readings for Modern Living" 1952; contrib ed "Phylon the Atlanta Univ Review of Race & Culture" 1948-53; Adv Ed Coll Lang Assn Jour 1957; cited among the nations 100 Most Effective College Leaders Jet Dec 15, 1986; Hon Doctorate, Univ of Haiti, 1968, NYU, 1971, Wayne State Univ, 1976, Washington Univ, St Louis, 1977, Morgan State Univ, 1980, Mercer Univ, 1981, St. Paul's Coll, 1982, LeMoyne Coll, 1993. 1987, LeMoyne Coll, 1993. **Business Addr:** c/o Office of the President, Morehouse Coll, 830 Westview Dr SW, c/o President's Office, Atlanta, GA 30314.

GLOSTER, JESSE E.
Educator. **Personal:** Born Apr 15, 1915, Ocala, FL; son of Mattie Gloster and Lorin Gloster; married Norma Robinson. **Educ:** Lincoln U, AB 1941; Univ of Pittsburgh, MA 1947; Univ of Pittsburgh, PhD 1955. **Career:** TX Southern Univ, prof of economics 1948-; NC Mutual Life Insurance Co, Afro-Amer Life Insurance Co, insurance representative. **Orgs:** Organizer TX So Univ Fed Credit Unoin; organizer chrmn bd TX So Financer Corp; co-organizer Riverside Nat Bank. **Honors/Awds:** Author book "Econ of Minority Groups"; publ NC Mutual Life Ins Co Arno Press NY Times subs 1976; authored "Minority Econ Pol & Soc Devel" Univ Press of Am 1978; also numerous publs for professional jour; recip ins research grant 1951f grant TX So Univ 1957; case inst fellow Econ-in-Action 1960; fac research grants TX So Univ 1964, 67; Ford Found Grant 1968-69; author, The Black Prescence in the Texas Sesquicentennial, 1987, America Must Lift Its Cloud of Debt, Houston Post, May 23, 1988, Breaking the Chain of Poverty, Alpha Publ Co, Houston, TX, 1995. **Military Serv:** AUS 1st lt 1942-46. **Business Addr:** Chairman, Texas Southern Investment Corp, 3003 Holman St, Houston, TX 77004.

GLOVER, AGNES W.
Educational administrator (retired). **Personal:** Born Mar 6, 1925, Orangeburg, SC; daughter of Victoria Glover Williams and Benjamin I Williams; married Freddie V. **Educ:** SC State Clge, BS Ed 1956; Hunter Clge, MS Ed E Chhd Ed 1973; Queens Clge, MA Supr and Admin 1983. **Career:** Natl Sor of Phi Delta Kappa Inc Beta Omicron Chapter, 3rd Anti Basileus 1965-67, tamias 1967-69, basileus 1969-71, chrmn of bd of dir Big Sister Educ Action and Srv Ctr 1972-; Hallet Cove Child Dev Ctr, dir. **Orgs:** Dir Grosvenor DC 1968-72; 1st vice pres Flushing Branch NAACP 1982, pres 1974-78; Basileus Natl Sor Phi Delta Kappa Div Beta Omicron Chap 1969-71, chrmn bd dir Big Sister 1972-; life mem, NAACP 1987; mem, South Carolina State College Chapter Phi Delta Kappa 1988. **Honors/Awds:** Srv and dedication Big Sister Educ Action and Srv Ctr 1978; Cert of Appreciation La Guardia Comm Clge 1981, Flushing Branch NAACP 1984; Outstanding Service, Flushing Branch NAACP 1984; for Outstanding Service, The Council of Supervisors and Admin of New York City 1987; Dedicated Service, The National Sorority of Phi Delta Kappa Inc, Beta Omicrom Chapter Big Sister Educational Action and Service Center 1987. **Home Addr:** 1453 Sifly Rd NE, Orangeburg, SC 29115.

GLOVER, ANDREW LEE
Professional football player. **Personal:** Born Aug 12, 1967, New Orleans, LA. **Educ:** Grambling State. **Career:** Los Angeles Raiders, tight end, 1991-94; Oakland Raiders, 1995-96; Minnesota Vikings, 1997-. **Business Addr:** Professional Football Player, Minnesota Vikings, 9520 Viking Dr, Eden Prairie, MN 55344, (612)828-6500.

GLOVER, ARTHUR LEWIS, JR.
Counselor, educator (retired). **Personal:** Born Sep 29, 1912, Los Angeles, CA; son of Lucile Lewis Glover (deceased) and Arthur Glover (deceased); married Beatrice Louise Jones Glover, Sep 10, 1944; children: Beatrice Louise Schine. **Educ:** Univ of CA Santa Barbara, AB 1937; Freedmens Hospital, Certificate of Nutrition 1939; Univ of Southern CA, MA 1952, ME 1956; Nova Cluster Univ, doctoral studies. **Career:** Tuskegee Inst AL, chief dietitian 1939-42; Andersen's Frozen Foods Buellton, product mgr 1946-50; Thomas Jefferson High School, instructor & counselor 1950-69; West LA Community Coll, prof of English & counselor emeritus 1969-84. **Orgs:** Bd dir Culver City Mental Health Clinic; Di Di Hirsch Guidance Clinic; Culver City Police Dept; mem Phi Delta Kappa; past moderator Culver City Educ Comm; mem Mariners Nautilus Ship LA; exec sec, vice pres, DiDi Hirsch Mental Health Center; sec Kayumanggi Lions Club; district chmn Lions World Serv Day; social action chmn Omega Psi Phi Frat; chmn Lords of Inglewood; dist chmn Lions Fundraiser for The City of Hope; NAACP; vice president, Lions Hear, District 413; Lions Club International, District 4L-3, cabinet secretary, 1985-86. **Honors/Awds:** First Black man admitted to Amer Dietitic Assoc 1939; Man of Yr Lambda Omicron 1970; Lion of Yr Culver City Lions Club 1973, Beverly Hills 1980; Counselor of the Year 1982-83 Los Angeles Community Coll Dist (7 colleges). **Special Achievements:** First Black Male Nutritionist Certified by the American Dietetics Assn, 1939. **Military Serv:** AUS med corp sgt 1942-46.

GLOVER, BERNARD E.
Dentist. **Personal:** Born Apr 9, 1933, Suffolk, VA; married Juanita Cross; children: Cheryl, Kevin. **Educ:** Morgan State Coll, BS 1959; Meharry Med Coll, DDS 1963; St Elizabeth Hosp, inter 1964. **Career:** Pvt Prac 1964-. **Orgs:** Mem bd, dir Obici Hosp; mem bd dir Nansemon Credit Unoin; mem Suffolk City Forum; mem John L McGriff Dental Soc; Am Nat & Old Dominoin Dental Assn; Am Endodontic Soc; C of C; Bi-racial Council; Obia Hosp Staff. **Honors/Awds:** E end bapt ch schlshp awd Morgan State Coll 1955-59; Mosby Schshp Awd 1962; man yr Kappa Alpha Si 1974; Elks awd en 1975. **Military Serv:** AUS pfc 1963-65. **Business Addr:** 811 E Washington St, Suffolk, VA 23434.

GLOVER, CHESTER ARTIS
Journalist. **Personal:** Born Sep 3, 1954, Detroit, MI; son of Leona Johnson Glover and Artis O Glover; married Mae Vaughn Glover, May 31, 1977. **Educ:** Valencia Community College, Orlando, FL, AA, 1977; Rollins College, Winter Park, FL, BS, 1982. **Career:** WCPX-TV Channel 6, Orlando, FL, weekend assignment editor, 1980-83; Governor's Press Office, Tallahassee, FL, press aide, 1982; Stetson University, Deland, FL, asst sports info, 1982-84; LAOOC-1984, Los Angeles, CA, asst press chief, 1984; The Orlando Sentinel, Orlando, FL, staff writer, 1984-92; Allen and Associates, Orlando, FL, proofreader/copy editor, 1995-96. **Orgs:** President, Central Florida Press Club, 1990-92; charter member, Central Florida Assn of Black Journalists and Broadcasters, 1988-; education chairman, Sentinel Communications Employees Federal Credit Union, 1990-91; member, National Assn of Black Journalists, 1990-; associate director, Multicultural Resources, Orlando, FL, 1989-. **Home Addr:** 5807 Elon Dr, Orlando, FL 32808-1809, (407)290-0193.

GLOVER, CLARENCE ERNEST, JR.
Educator, educational administrator. **Personal:** Born Apr 19, 1956, Shreveport, LA; son of Elizabeth Bradford Glover and Clarence E Glover, Sr (deceased). **Educ:** Grambling State Univ, BA 1978; Southern Methodist Univ, Master Theology 1982; Harvard Univ, post grad 1985. **Career:** St Duty CME Church, pastor 1974-75; Washington Temple CME Church, pastor 1978-80; Caddo Bossier Assoc for Retarded Citizens, instructor/supervisor 1978-79; El Centro College, campus minister 1979-80; Clarence Glover Ministries, Inc, pres 1981-; Southern Methodist Univ, asst to the chaplain 1980-81, coordinator intercultural education African-American student serv 1980-89; adjunct prof of African-Amer Studies, 1987; Clarence Glover & Assoc, professional lecturing & consulting agency, 1987; dir, Intercultural Educ, 1989;. **Orgs:** African- american cultural consultant Dallas Independent Sch Dist 1980-; mem TX Assoc of Coll and Univ Student Personnel Administrators 1980-; natl coord Natl Black Christian Student Leadership Consultation 1985-; third vice pres TX Assoc of Black Personnel in Higher Educ 1985-; mem NAACP; mem Christian Leadership Conf; mem Natl Assoc of Student Personell Admin; mem American Cancer African-American Task Force; co-host Cable TV Show Religion in Foucus; lecturer & consultant on African-American Religion and Culture; mem Black Male-Female Relations; mem The Life and Time of Dr King the Civil Rights movement andInter-Cultral Relations and Racism. **Honors/Awds:** Outstanding Young Men of Amer US Jaycees 1982-83, 1986; WE DuBois Awd 1980; Advisor of the Year Awd Natl Christian Student Leadership Consultation 1983; consultant/interviewer "In Remembrance of Martin" the First Natl Martin Luther King Jr PBS Natl Documentary 1986; Humanitarian Serv Awd El Centro Coll/Street Acad 1986; Spirituality: An African View, Interview in Essence Magazine, 1987; On Being African-American: The Challenge of a New Generation, Natl Society of Black Engineers Journal, 1988; Honorary Mayor of San Antonio, TX, 1988. **Business Addr:** Director, Intercultural Education, Southern Methodist University, SMU Box 355, SMU Station, Dallas, TX 75275.

GLOVER, DANNY
Actor. **Personal:** Born Jul 22, 1947, California; son of Carrie Glover (deceased) and James Glover; married Asake Bomani; children: Mandisa. **Educ:** San Francisco State University, graduated; studied at, American Conservatory of Theatre; studied at, Black Box Theatre Company. **Career:** San Francisco's Mayor's Office, researcher, 1960s; numerous other local civil positions in the San Francisco Area, early 1970s; actor, 1977-; theater appearances include: Master Harold..and the Boys, 1982; The Island; Sizwe Bansi Is Dead; The Blood Knot; Suicide in B Flat; Macbeth; Nevis Mountain Dew; A Lesson From Alloes; television appearances include: Chiefs, 1978; Lonesome Dove, 1988; A Raisin in the Sun, 1989; A Place at the Table, 1988; John Henry, 1987; How the Leopard Got His Spots, audio-visual, 1989; Dead Man Out, HBO, 1989; Hill Street Blues, guest appearance; Lou Grant, guest appearance; Many Mansions; Paris, guest appearance; BJ and the Bear, guest appearance; American Heroes and Legends, 1992; film appearances include: Escape from Alcatraz, 1979; Chu Chu and the Philly Fh, 1981; Iceman, 1984; Birdy, 1984; Places in the Heart, 1984; Witness, 1985; Silverado, 1985; The Color Purple, 1986; Lethal Weapon, 1987; Mandela, 1987; Bat 21, 1988; Lethal Weapon 2, 1989; To Sleep with Anger, 1990; Predator 2, 1991; Flight of the Intruder, 1991; A Rage in Harlem, 1991; Pure Luck, 1992; Lethal Weapon 3, 1992; Grand Canyon, 1992; Bopha, 1993; Angels in the Outfield, 1994; Gone Fishin, 1997; Buffalo Soldiers, TNT, 1997; Switchback (w/Dennis Quaid), 1997. **Honors/Awds:** Image Award, NAACP; Black Filmmakers Hall of Fame, inductee; Theatre World Award, Master Harold..and the Boys, 1982; Paine College, honorary degree, 1990. **Special Achievements:** PBS, host, Celebrate Storytelling. **Business Addr:** Actor, c/o William Morris Agency, 151 El Camino Dr, Ste 233, Beverly Hills, CA 90212.

GLOVER, DENISE M.
Library administrator. **Personal:** Born Sep 7, 1952, Dayton, OH; daughter of Isabel Rayland Glover and Arthur Glover Jr. **Educ:** University of Cincinnati, Cincinnati, OH, BA, 1974; University of Michigan, Ann Arbor, MI, MALS, 1975, PhD, library science, 1982. **Career:** Central State University, Wilberforce, OH, collection development officer, 1981-83; National Afro-American Museum and Cultural Center, Wilberforce, OH, head, library/manuscript division, 1983-87; Amistad Research Center, New Orleans, LA, assistant dir, 1987-88; University of Maryland University College, College Park, MD, dir, library services, 1988-; Museum of Afro-American History, Detroit, MI, consultant, 1989-90. **Orgs:** Member, American Library Assn, 1988-; member, Society of American Archivists, 1987-88; member, African-American Museum Assn, 1990-. **Honors/Awds:** Beta Phi Mu, National Library Science Honorary Society, 1986-; Award, Minority Museum Professionals, Smithsonian Institution, 1985-; Margaret Mann Award, University of Michigan, 1975. **Business Addr:** Director, Library Services, University of Maryland University College, University Blvd at Adelphi Rd, College Park, MD 20742.

GLOVER, DIANA M.
Personnel executive. **Personal:** Born Apr 19, 1948, Buffalo, NY. **Educ:** Cornell U, BA Sociology 1971; Gen Motors Inst, liberal arts cer 1973. **Career:** GNC Chev Div Tonawanda Motor, supr labor rel 1978-; GMC Che Div Tonawanda Motor, supr salaried pers adm 1976-78; GMC Chev Div Tonawanda Motor, supremployee benefits 1976; GMC Chev Div Tonawanda Motor, EEO rep 1975-76; GMC Chev Div Tonawanda Motor, asst supv employment 1974-75; GMC Chev Div Tonawanda Motor, employment interviewer 1973-74. **Orgs:** Mem Indsl Rela Assn of Western NY 1976-80; dir Center for Women in Mgmt 1978-80; adv coord Jr Achievement 1975-78; mem Buffalo Urban League 1976-; mem NAACP 1978-. **Honors/Awds:** Black achvmt awd 1490 Jefferson Enterpises Inc 1976. **Business Addr:** Assistant Personnel Dir, General Motors, CPC Tonawanda Engineering Plt, PO Box 21, Buffalo, NY 14240.

GLOVER, DON EDWARD
Circuit judge. **Personal:** Born Apr 1, 1944, Dermott, AR; son of Silas Glover Sr & Lucinda Glover; married Dorothy Glover, Aug 17, 1974; children: Dorcedar, Doven. **Educ:** Howard University, School of Law, JD, 1970-73; University of Arkansas at Pine Bluff, BS, business administration, 1965. **Career:** Tulsa County Legal Aid, Baton Rouge Legal Aid, staff attorney, 1973-78; North Louisiana Legal Aid, managing attorney, 1978-80; Jamison & Glover Law Offices, attorney, 1981-83; Law Offices of Don Glover, attorney, 1983-92; Elected Municipal Judge, Dermott, 1986-88, re-elected, 1989-92; Elected Circuit Judge, 10th judicial district, 1993-96, re-elected, 1997-2000. **Orgs:** Peace Corps, volunteer Venezula, SA, 1965-67; St Paul Baptist Chur, treasurer; Dermott Area Chamber of Commerce; Morris Boaker Day Care Ctr, board chair; AR Judicial Council. **Military Serv:** Army, sgt, 1967-70.

GLOVER, HAMILTON
Management officer (Retired). **Personal:** Born Feb 24, 1937, Atlanta, GA; son of Lucile C Glover and Thomas R Glover Sr. **Educ:** Morehouse College, BA, 1957; Atlanta University, MBA, 1958. **Career:** Mutual Federal Savings & Loans, trainee/assistant treasurer, 1958-60, assistant treasurer, starting 1963, secretary/treasurer, vice pres-treasurer, senior vp-treasurer, president, 1994. **Military Serv:** US Army, SP4, 1960-63, (Retired). **Home Addr:** 994 Willis Mill Rd SW, Atlanta, GA 30311, (404)753-0827.

GLOVER, KENNETH ELIJAH
Investment banker. **Personal:** Born Feb 24, 1952, Washington, DC; son of Eunice Washington Glover (deceased) and Elijah B Glover (deceased); married Lauren Dugas, Apr 23, 1988; children: Evan Joseph. **Educ:** Amherst Coll, Amherst MA, BA, 1974; Univ of Maryland, College Park MD, MA, 1976. **Career:** Maryland Gen Assembly, Annapolis MD, staff dir, 1975-76; Prince George's County MD, Upper Marlboro MD, admin asst, 1976-78; Natl League of Cities, Washington DC, project dir, 1978-79; South Shore Bank, Chicago IL, vice pres, 1979-83; Mayor Washington Transit Team, Chicago IL, dir, 1983; Drexel Burnham Lambert, New York NY, managing dir, beginning 1983; First Chicago Capital Markets Inc, first vp/mgr; RJR Nabisco, senior vp, corporate and gvt relations, 1990-. **Orgs:** Dir, Natl Assn of Securities Professionals, 1985-88, pres/bd of directors Natl Black Child Devel Inst, 1987-, Harold Washington Found, 1987-; dir, chmn, Corporate Advisory Council/Natl Forum, 1989; bd member Court Appointed Special Advocates 1991-. **Honors/Awds:** America's Best & Brightest, Dollars & Sense Magazine, 1989. **Business Addr:** Vice Chairman, W R Lazard & Co Inc, 14 Wall St, New York, NY 10005.

GLOVER, KEVIN BERNARD
Professional football player. **Personal:** Born Jun 17, 1963, Washington, DC; married Cestaine; children: Maya Nikkole, Matthew Robert Romeo. **Educ:** Maryland, attended. **Career:** Detroit Lions, center, 1985-97; Seattle Seahawks, 1998-. **Honors/Awds:** Pro Bowl, 1995, 1996, 1997. **Business Addr:** Professional Football Player, Seattle Seahawks, 11220 NE 53rd St, Kirkland, WA 98033, (206)827-9777.

GLOVER, LA'ROI DAMON
Professional football player. **Personal:** Born Jul 4, 1974, San Diego, CA. **Educ:** San Diego State. **Career:** Oakland Raiders, defensive tackle, 1996; New Orleans Saints, 1997-. **Business Addr:** Professional Football Player, New Orleans Saints, 5800 Airline Hwy, Metairie, LA 70003, (504)733-0255.

GLOVER, LINDA F. **See BAILEY, LINDA F.**

GLOVER, NAT
Law enforcement official. **Career:** Duval County, Florida, sheriff. **Special Achievements:** Florida's first African American elected sheriff. **Business Addr:** Sheriff, Duval County, 501 E Bay St, Jacksonville, FL 32202, (904)630-0500.

GLOVER, ROBERT G.
Chemist. **Personal:** Born Jul 4, 1931, Bradley, AR; married Mary; children: Mary, Andrew, Alvin, Shirley, Dedra, Robert. **Educ:** Printing Ink Inst of LeHigh Univ Phila, attended. **Career:** St Clair & Valentine Co; Printing Ink Inst of LeHigh Univ, lab 8 yrs; Quality Printing Ink Co Houston, president. **Orgs:** Mem Litho Club, Craftsman Club, PTA of Houston. **Honors/Awds:** Only black owner of form which mfg printing inks of all types for distrb throughout world. **Business Addr:** President, Quality Color Printing Ink, 1803 Cleburne, Houston, TX 77004.

GLOVER, SARAH L.
Public relations director. **Personal:** Born Apr 27, 1954, Detroit, MI. **Educ:** Shaw Univ, Raleigh NC, BS in Behavioral Science, 1976; Univ of Chapel Hill, Chapel Hill NC, attended, School of Journalism Writing for Publication, 1984; North Carolina Central Univ, Durham NC, Graduate School, Media Educ, 1985-. **Career:** Southland Corp, Raleigh & Durham NC, store clerk, asst mgr, mgr, 1977-79; Bloodworth St YMCA, Raleigh NC, activity asst public relations dir, 1981; Garner Rd Family YMCA, Raleigh NC, public relations dir, 1981-. **Orgs:** Order of Eastern Stars, Detroit, MI, 1974; mem, Public Relations Soc of Amer, 1983-, Natl Professional YMCA Directors, 1985-. **Honors/Awds:** Citizen of the Week Award, WLLE-AM 57, 1982; Chairman's Award, Garner Road Family YMCA, 1984; Citizen of the Week Award, WAUG-AM 750, 1988; National Collegiate Education Award, 1991.

GLOVER, SAVION
Dancer. **Personal:** Born 1974, Newark, NJ; son of Yvette Glover. **Career:** Broadway productions, "The Tap Dance Kid" 1985, "Black and Blue" 1989, "Jelly's Last Jam" 1992, "Bring in 'Da Noise, Bring in 'Da Funk" 1995; film, "Taps" 1988; television, Sesame Street 1991-95, "Dance in America:-Tap," "Black Filmmakers Hall of Fame," "The Kennedy Center Honors.". **Honors/Awds:** Tony Award, best choreography, 1996; Dance Magazine Award, 1996; Nat Endowment for the Arts grant, 1996; Best New Theater Star, Ent Weekly, 1996. **Home Addr:** 000100.

GODBEE, THOMASINA D.
Research associate. **Personal:** Born Apr 10, 1946, Waynesboro, GA; married Cornelius; children: William Jr, Cornelius Tremayne II. **Educ:** Paine Coll, BS 1966. **Career:** Butts Co Bd Educ Jackson GA, chem instr 1966-67; EI du Pont de Nemours & Co, lab tech 1967-69; Grady Meml Hosp, lab tech 1970-71; Univ CA Irvine,staff rsch assoc nuclear physics 1971-. **Orgs:** Mem NAACP; Paine Coll Alumni Club; United Presb Women; Natl Assn of Univ Women; Westminster United Presb Ch Soloist Paine Coll Concert Choir 1966; second vice pres, scrapbook co-chmn, first vice pres, membership com chmn NAUW. **Honors/Awds:** English & Soc Sci Awds 1960 1962; Natural Sci Awd 1961; Outstanding Serv to the Comm Awd NAUW 1977; Special Performance Awd Univ of CA 1984. **Business Addr:** 3501 Stafford, Hephzibah, GA 30815.

GODBOLD, DONALD HORACE
Educational asdministrator. **Personal:** Born Oct 3, 1928, Detroit, MI; son of Alice Virginia Kinney Godbold (deceased) and Eugene Quemado Godbold (deceased); married Delores Roxanna Cofer; children: Michelle Roxanne, Donald Terrence Juan, Monique Toi, Darwyn Eugene. **Educ:** Wayne State Univ, BS 1950, MEd 1956; Univ of MI Ann Arbor, PhD 1967. **Career:** Wayne State Univ, teacher spec educ and supervising teacher 1953-67; Oakland Comm Coll Orchard Ridge Campus, dean of student serv 1967-68, provost & chief exec 1968-70; Univ of No CO, guest prof sociology black history & culture, counselor 1971-74; Community Coll of Denver Auraria Campus, dean of campus & founding chief exec 1970-71, campus dir & chief exec 1971-72, vice pres & chief exec 1972-73; Merritt Coll, pres 1973-77; Peralta Comm Coll Dist, vice chancellor educ serv 1977-80, chancellor 1980-88; independent consultant 1988-; Alameda County Youth Development Inc, George P Scotlan Youth and Family Center, executive director, currently. **Orgs:** Commn mbr Amer Council on Educ Commn on Collegiate Athletics 1977-80; City of Oakland Private Industry Cncl 1978-88; chmn accreditation team Western Assn of Schools & Colls 1979; mem bd of dirs Children's Hospital Medical Ctr 1980-; Convention Adv Comm CA Assn of Comm Colls 1983; Commn on Urban Comm Colls 1983-87, bd mem, 1972-75, Amer Assn of Comm & Jr Colls; adv comm Amer Cncl on Educ 1984-87; Amer Coll Personnel Assn, Amer Personnel & Guidance Assn, CO Assn of Comm Jr Colls, Cncl for Exceptional Children, Natl Assn of Student Personnel Administrators, MI Acad of Sciences Arts and Letters, Natl Vocational Guidance Assn; dir Univ ofMI Chap Phi Delta Kappa; mem Wayne State Univ Coll of Educ Alumni Assn, Wayne State Univ Alumni Assn, Univ of MI Alumni Assn, Assoc of CA Comm Coll Administrato bd mem Urban League of CO Inc; bd of dirs League for Innovation in Commun Colleges 1980-87; bd of dirs, vice pres, secretary New Oakland Committee 1975-87; bd of dirs Bay Area Black United Fund 1981-87; bd of dirs Oakland Society for Prevention Cruelty to Animals, 1978-86; bd of dirs Goodwill Industries of Greater East Bay 1975-86. **Honors/Awds:** Clifford Woody Memorial Scholar Awd for Outstanding Promise in Professional Educ Univ of MI 1966; Comm Coll of Denver Faculty Awd for Outstanding Leadership in the Establishment of the Comm Coll of Denver Auraria Campus 1971; Disting Serv Awd Western Region Cncl on Black Amer Affairs 1976; Meritorious and Unselfish Leadership and Serv Awd as Natl Chairperson (1974-79) in the Founding of the Org Cncl on Black Amer Affairs Natl Chairperson 1980-85; Leonard F Saine Awd Esteemed Black Alumni Awd Univ of MI 1982;

Leadership and Supportive Serv Awd North Central Region Cncl on Black Amer Affairs 1986; recognition The Effective President a natl survey funded by the Exxon Educ Foundation 1986; 13 pulications. **Military Serv:** US Army, pfc, 2 yrs. **Home Addr:** 75 Mission Hills St, Oakland, CA 94605-4612.

GODBOLT, RICKY CHARLES
Military engineer. **Personal:** Born Mar 7, 1959, Buckner, AR; son of Eddie B & Beatrice Godbolt; married Ann, Sep 10, 1990; children: LaKelya, LaChelya, Natasha, Candice, Marcus. **Educ:** Central Texas College, AGS, 1989; Park College, BS (magna cum laude), social psychology, 1993. **Career:** US Army, track mechanic, 1978-80, electrician, 1981-86, mechanic, 1986-90, instructor, 1990-93, chief eng, 1994-. **Orgs:** Pinnacle, 1994-; Fraternal Order Police, 1994-96; Prince Hall Masons, Zedekiah #167, 1994-; Phylaxis Society, 1992-, director of military affairs, 1996-; Eastern Stars, Majorie T Lancaster #84, 1992-95; Retired Officers Assn, 1993-; African Lodge, #459, 1992-; Assn of the US Army, 1992-94; Veterans of Foreign Wars Post 6002, 1996-; US Army Warrant Officer's Association, 1995-96; National Institute for the Uniform Licensing of Power Engineers, first class operator, 1996-; National Society of Black Engineers, 1996-; Citizen's Flag Alliance, charter mem, 1995-; American Legion Post 0368, 1994-; Prince Hall Masons, Samuel T. Daniels Chapter #107, 1991-93, Mount Moriah Commandry #1, 1991-93; Shadrach Jackson Consistory #156, 1992-94; Magnus Temple #3, 1992-94; Charter Member of Howard Bailey McAfee Heritage Society of Park College, 1997-. **Honors/Awds:** Phylaxis Society, Cert of Meritorious Srvice, 1993; Park College, Pinnacle Membership, 1994; Assn US Army, Academic Scholarship, 1992; Education Center ANFB, Honor Roll, 1991-92. **Special Achievements:** First mechanic in history to win instructor of the year, 1992; First African-American to win instructor of the year, 1992; NCO of the Quarter, 1983; First graduate of the school for extended learning to become a member of the Howard Bailey McAfee Heritage Society of Park College. **Military Serv:** US Army, CW2, 1978-; US Army Mechanic's Badge, 1979; Air Assault Badge, 1985; US Army Driver's Badge-Special Equipment, 1991; Certificate of Achievement, 7th Award, 1992; Army Achievement Medal, 9th Award, 1992; Army Good Conduct Medal, 5th Award, 1992; Humanitarian Service Medal, 2nd Award, 1992; US Army Driver Badge-Wheel Vehicle, 1992; National Defense Service Medal, 1992; Army Commendation Medal, 4th Award, 1993; US Army Superior Unit Award, 1993. **Home Phone:** (757)887-0734. **Business Addr:** PO Box 4511, Fort Eustis, VA 23604-0511, (804)878-2500.

GODDARD, ROSALIND KENT
Librarian. **Personal:** Born Mar 7, 1944, Gadsden, AL; daughter of Nettye George Kent Goddard and George Goddard. **Educ:** San Francisco State College, San Francisco, CA, BA, 1965; University of California, Los Angeles, CA, MLS, 1982. **Career:** Los Angeles Public Library, Los Angeles, CA, senior librarian, 1967-92; Los Angeles Community Colleges, executive assistant to the chancellor, 1992-94; Los Angeles Southwest Coll, Los Angeles Comm Colleges, acting assoc dean, 1994; Los Angeles Trade Technical College, acting assoc dean, 1996-97; Los Angeles Community Colleges, Operations Division, Human Resources, assoc director, Recruitment and Training. **Orgs:** Women of Color, Inc, 1989-97; member, California Librarians Black Caucus, 1980-; member, American Library Assn, 1980-; member, NAACP, 1989-; commission member, California Postsecondary Education Commission, 1990-92; mem bd, Friends of Watts Towers, 1997-; Association of California Community College Administrators, 1997-. **Honors/Awds:** Exceptional Leadership Award, LA Brotherhood Crusade, 1973; Los Angeles Public Library, Staff Commendation, 1969; Outstanding Black Leader, LA Communit Colleges, 1993. **Home Addr:** 5268 Village Green, Los Angeles, CA 90016. **Business Addr:** Los Angeles Community College District, 770 Wilshire Blvd, Los Angeles, CA 90017, (213)891-2425.

GODETTE, FRANKLIN DELANO ROOSEVELT
Lawyer. **Personal:** Born Nov 3, 1932, North Harlowe, NC; son of Henderson & Lucinda Godette; married Eunice Godette, Mar 10, 1959; children: Flondezi, Arturo, Felicia. **Educ:** Howard Univ, BA, 1955, JD, 1958. **Career:** Franklin D R Godette, owner/lawyer, 1958-. **Orgs:** North Carolina State Bar, 1958. **Honors/Awds:** Howard Univ Law School, Certificate of Appreciation as assoc editor, Howard Law Journal, 1958; Certificate for Outstanding Accomplishments in Criminal Justice System, Ebenezer Presbyterian Church, 1984. **Special Achievements:** Published articles as assoc editor, Howard Law Journal, 1957-58. **Home Addr:** 1140 Adams Creek Road, Havelock, NC 28532. **Business Addr:** Attorney, Franklin Godette Law Office, 821 Queen Street, New Bern, NC 28560.

GODFREY, RANDALL EURALENTRIS
Professional football player. **Personal:** Born Apr 6, 1973, Valdosta, GA. **Educ:** Univ of Georgia, attended. **Career:** Dallas Cowboys, linebacker, 1996-. **Business Addr:** Professional Football Player, Dallas Cowboys, One Cowboys Pkwy, Irving, TX 75063, (214)556-9900.

GODFREY, WILLIAM R.
Financial administrator. **Personal:** Born May 18, 1948, Gay, GA; son of Iula Godfrey and John W Godfrey; married Joyce Lincoln; children: Runako, Kenan, Nyasha. **Educ:** Clark College, BBA 1970; State Univ of New York, MBA 1973. **Career:** US General Accounting Office, senior auditor 1973-80; US General Serv Adm Office of the Inspector General, senior auditor 1980; Fulton County, assistant finance dir, currently. **Orgs:** Treasurer, Mental Health Assoc of Metro Atlanta, 1984-89. **Home Addr:** 3401 Prince George Dr, East Point, GA 30344.

GOFF, WILHELMINA DELORES
Association administrator. **Personal:** Born Jun 18, 1940, Columbia, SC; daughter of Katie Mae Goff and William Earl Goff. **Educ:** Morgan State Coll, BS 1962; John Carroll Univ, MA 1971; New York Univ, attended; Cleveland State Univ, EdSD. **Career:** Hillcrest Center for Children Bedford Hills, counselor 1962-64; Cleveland Public Schools, music teacher 1964-78, guidance counselor 1971-78; Cuyahoga Community Coll, coord/counselor job corps 1978-, assoc dir access/job corps act 1979-80; Cleveland, asst dean student personnel servs; Natl Council Negro Women, dir prog & devel; Delta Sigma Theta Sorority, Washington, DC, deputy exec dir, 1990-. **Orgs:** Newsletter ed Phi Delta Kappa Reg dir Delta Sigma Theta Sor 1976-; pres OH Assn Non-White Concerns in Personnel & Guidance 1978-80; corres sec/mem at large NE OH Personnel & Guidance 1978-80; bd mem/chmn ed com Cleveland NAACP 1979-80; coord speakers bureau Gr Cleveland Com of IYC 1979; pres, Delta Sigma Theta Tutoring & Nutrition Program, 1986-. **Honors/Awds:** Awd for Congressman Stokes Cleve 1974; Pan-Hellenic Awd Cleveland 1976; Outstanding Serv to Delta New Orleans LA convention 1979; Key to the City Indianapolis IN 1980; Higher Educ Counselor of Yr NEOPGA 1980; Outstanding Serv to Teen Father Prog 1984; Proclamation City of Cincinnati 1982; Outstanding Serv OH Personnel & Guidance Assn; Outstanding Serv to Dyke Coll Student Body 1986; Outstanding Serv to Youth & Educ Cleveland Chap Negro Bus & Profession Women's Club 1986. **Business Addr:** Deputy Executive Director, Delta Sigma Theta Sorority, Inc, 1707 New Hampshire Ave NW, Washington, DC 20009.

GOGGINS, HORACE
Dental surgeon. **Personal:** Born May 14, 1929, Hodges, SC; son of Mattie Butler Goggins and Ulysses Goggins; divorced; children: Horace W. **Educ:** SC State Coll, BS 1950; Howard Univ DDS 1954. **Career:** Self-Employed, dental surgeon Rock Hill SC, currently. **Orgs:** Mem Natl Dental Assn; past pres Palmetto Med & Dental Assn 1973; mem SE Analgesia Soc; mem tri county Dental Soc; mem Piedmont Dental Soc; Beta Kappa Chi Sci Soc; mem Rock Hill Planning Commn; NAACP; Council Human Relations; Mt Prospect Bapt Ch deacon; Alpha Phi Alpha Frat; mem Sigma Pi Phi Frat (Boule); SC Dem Party; American Legion Elks. **Honors/Awds:** Palmetto Dental Association, Doctor of the Year, 1983-84; Rock Hill Chamber of Commerce, Minority Business Person of the Year, 1994; Rock Hill Branch NAACP, Outstanding Service & Leadership 1995; Certificate of Appreciation for Dedicated Service to York County, Delta Sigma Theta, 1992. **Military Serv:** AUS capt dental corps 1954-56; USAR maj. **Business Addr:** 425 S Dave Lyle Blvd, Rock Hill, SC 29730.

GOINES, LEONARD
Educator. **Personal:** Born Apr 22, 1934, Jacksonville, FL; son of Willie Mae LaMar Goines and Buford Goines; married Margaretta Bobo (divorced); children: Lisan Lynette. **Educ:** Manhattan School of Music, BMus 1955, MMus 1956; Fontainbleu School of Music France, Certificate 1959; Columbus Univ, MA 1960, Professional Diploma 1961, EdD 1963; New School for Soc Rsch, BA 1980; New York Univ, MA 1980; Harvard Univ, CAS 1984. **Career:** Leonard Goines Quintet, trumpeter-leader 1960-; Symphony of the New World, trumpeter 1965-76; New York City Bd of Educ, teacher music 1959-65; Bedford Stuyvesant Youth in Action, dir of music 1965-66; Morgan State Coll, assoc prof of music 1966-68; York Coll CUNY, lecturer 1969; Queens Coll CUNY, lecturer; Howard Univ, assoc prof of music 1970-72; NY Univ, lecturer 1970-; DuBois Inst Harvard Univ, postdoctoral fellow 1982-85; Shepard & Goines, partner org & educ arts consultants 1984-; Williams Coll, visiting prof music 1984; Vassar Coll, visiting prof music 1985; Lafayette Coll Easton PA, distinguished visiting prof of music 1986; Manhattan Commun Coll CUNY, prof music, 1969-92. **Orgs:** Folklore consultant Smithsonian Inst 1974-76; jazz consultant Creative Artists Public Serv Program 1980; jazz rsch consultant Natl Endowment for the Arts 1983; music consultant US Info Agency 1984; bd of trustees Natl Assn of Comm School & The Arts 1982-85; chmn special arts sect panel New York State Council on the Arts 1982-85; lecturer NYU 1970-, Manhattanville Coll 1976-; adv bd mem Universal Jazz Coalition Inc; adv bd mem Afro-Amer Music Bicentennial Hall of Fame & Museum Inc; co-exec producer, BAM Majestic Theater, Brooklyn, NY, 1988-96. **Honors/Awds:** Public Serv Award US Dept of Labor 1980; Coll Teachers Fellowship Natl Endowment for the Humanities 1982-83; Faculty Rsch Grants Howard Univ State Univ of NY, CUNY 1971-73; Scholar Incentive Award CUNY 1983-84; Hon Citizenship Winnipeg Canada 1958; writer/contrib articles to Groves Dictionary of Music & Musicians, Black Books Bulletin, 1st World, The Black Perspective in Music, Jrnl of African & Asian Studies, Black World, Downbeat, Music Educ Journal, Allegro; devel series of music filmstrips for Educ Audio Visuals Inc 1975; 1st Annual New York Brass Conf for Scholarships Award 1973. **Special Achievements:** Appointed To Preservation of Jazz Advisory Commission by Secretary of Smithsonian Institute, 1991-93. **Military Serv:** AUS, 1958. **Business Addr:** Professor Emeritus, Borough of Manhattan Community College, CUNY, 199 Chambers St, New York, NY 10007.

GOINS, MARY G.
Educator. **Personal:** Born Sep 8, 1929, Orange, TX; married Lee A Randle. **Educ:** BA, MA. **Career:** Enterpise Jr High School, Compton CA, prin 1974-; various schools, instructor, prin since 1961. **Orgs:** 2nd vice pres Compton Educ Assn 1969-70; pres Assn of Compton Sch Counselors 1970-71; sec Assn of Compton Unified Sch Adminstrs 1971-72; mem Assn of CA Sch Adminstrs; CA Pers & Guid Assn; mem PTA; officer Exec PTA. **Honors/Awds:** Recip finer womanhood awd Xavier Univ 1948; life hon awd PTA 1972. **Business Addr:** 2600 W Compton Blvd, Compton, CA 90220.

GOINS, RICHARD ANTHONY
Attorney, educator. **Personal:** Born Mar 1, 1950, New Orleans, LA; son of James Milton & Vivian Wiltz Goins; married Nannette, Mar 3, 1990. **Educ:** Yale Univ, BA (cum laude), History, 1972; Stanford Univ & Law School, JD, 1975. **Career:** New Orleans Legal Assist Corp, mgr & staff attorney, 1975-77; deputy dir, 1977-78; exec dir, 1978-81; Hon Adrian G Duplantier, law clerk, 1982; Loyola Univ School of Law, asst prof, 1981-84; Adams & Reese, asst attorney, 1984-87; attorney, partner, 1987-. **Orgs:** Thomas More Inn of Court, barrister, 1988-; Loyola Univ Law School, adjunct prof, 1984-; Fed bar Assn, bd of dirs local chapter, 1992-; Merit Selection Panel for the Selection & Appointment of US Magistrate, 1992-96; Amer Bar Assn Conference of Minority Partners in Majority/Corporate Law Firm, 1990-; California State Bar, 1977-; Louisiana State Bar Assn, 1975-. **Honors/Awds:** Stanford Univ, School of Law, Reginald Heber Smith Fellowship, 1975. **Special Achievements:** Leadership Louisiana 1992 Participant; Practical Issues in Class Action Litigation, The Practical Litigator, Vol 6,# 1, Jan 1995, Author; Seminar Presenter, LA Public Retirement Seminar, Baton Rouge, LA 1989, 1990, topic: ''Fiduciary Responsibilities of Trustees of Pension Plans;'' Seminar Presenter, Recent Dev Seminar, Tulane Univ, New Orleans, LA, 1994, topic: ''Recent Dev in Labor & Employment Law.''. **Home Addr:** 4412 Mandeville St, New Orleans, LA 70122, (504)288-1531. **Business Addr:** Attorney, Adams & Reese, 4500 One Shell Sq, New Orleans, LA 70139, (504)581-3234.

GOLDBERG, WHOOPI (CARYN E. JOHNSON)
Comedienne, actor. **Personal:** Born in New York, NY; married Lyle Trachtenberg; children: one. **Career:** Comedienne, actor; Films include: The Color Purple; Jumpin' Jack Flash; Burglar; Fatal Beauty; Clara's Heart; Homer and Eddie; Ghost; The Long Walk Home; Soap Dish, Sarafina, Sister Act, Made in America; Corrina, Corrina; Bogus; Eddie; The Associate; Ghost of Mississippi; television series include: Star Trek: The Next Generation; Baghdad Cafe; Comic Relief seven times; Appearances on Moonlighting; Scared Straight: 10 Years Later; Carol, Carl, Whoopi and Robin; An All-Star Celebration: The '88 Vote; Funny, You Don't Look 200; My Past Is My Own; Hollywood Squares, co-producer, 1998; Broadway: A Funny Thing Happened On the Way To The Forum; Cinderella. **Orgs:** Screen Actors Guild; American Federation of Television and Radio Artists. **Honors/Awds:** Golden Globe Award for Best Performance by an Actress in a Dramatic Motion Picture (The Color Purple), 1985; Academy Award nomination for Best Actress (The Color Purple), 1985; Image Award, NAACP, 1985; Grammy Award for Best Comedy Recording of the Year, 1985; Kid's Choice Award for Favorite Movie Actress, Nickelodeon; Humanitarian of the Year, Starlight Foundation, 1989; Image Award for Best Supporting Actress in a Motion Picture (Ghost), NAACP, 1990; Image Award for Entertainer of the Year, NAACP, 1990; Academy Award for Best Supporting Actress (Ghost), 1991; Amer Cinema Award, 1992; University of Vermont, hon degree, 1997. **Special Achievements:** Hosted her own syndicated late-night talk show, The Whoopi Goldberg Show; HBO specials; ABC's A Gala for the President, Ford's Theatre; Emmy Award nomination for hosting The 66th Annual Academy Awards; Broadway, A Funny Thing Happened on the Way to the Forum, 1997; five Nickelodeon Kid's Choice Awards, Favorite Movie Actress; Book: Alice, 1992; currently writing her second book. **Business Addr:** Actor, Comedienne, c/o Whoop Inc, 9255 Sunset Blvd, Los Angeles, CA 90069.

GOLDEN, ARTHUR IVANHOE
Attorney, insurance executive. **Personal:** Born Jan 14, 1926, New York, NY; married Thelma O Eastmond; children: Thelma Ann, Arthur E. **Educ:** NYU, BS 1959; Brooklyn Law School, JD 1973. **Career:** Golden & Golden Insurance, pres, 1957-; Harlem Branch New York County District Attorney's Office, mem of legal staff 1973-; Mayor's Office of Devel, project dir 1969-70; A Jackson High School, instructor 1966-69; Dept of Licensing NY, 1963-66; Dept Social Services Harlem 1960-63. **Orgs:** Past pres United Insurance Brokers Assn Inc; neighborhood sponser Queens DA Comm Crime Prevention Bureau;

mem Black Amer Law Students Assn; mem Mayor's High School Career Guidance Conf 1966-72; mem advisory council SBA; mem One Hundred Black Men Inc; vice pres, bd of dir, Professional Insurance Agents of NY State; vice pres, bd of dir, Council of Insurance Brokers of Greater NY; state appointed public mem, governing committee, Automobile Underwriting Assn, chairman, Anti-Arson Committee; chairman, Property Management Division, Presbyterian of NY; ruling elder, First Presbyterian Church of Jamaica, treasurer of the session; mem Producer Liaison Committee, Insurance Services Office. **Honors/Awds:** Moot court honor soc Brooklyn Law School 1971-73; Iota Nu Sigma ins hon soc NYU 1959. **Military Serv:** AUS major 1950-54.

GOLDEN, DONALD LEON
Professor, attorney. **Personal:** Born Jan 3, 1940, Walnut Cove, NC; married; children: Donna, Amber. **Educ:** Howard Univ, BA 1972; Howard Univ Law School, JD 1972. **Career:** US Attorney's Office, law clerk 1971; Judicial Panel on Multi-Dist Litigation, temp rsrch asst 1971; Howard Law School Library, 1971-72; US Dist Court, law clerk 1972-73; Covington & Burling, assoc 1973-77; Howard Univ Law School, adjunct prof 1974-81; Asst US Attorney's Office, atty 1977-81; Howard Univ Law School, prof 1981-. **Business Addr:** Professor, Howard Univ Law School, 2935 Uptown St, NW, Washington, DC 20008-1194.

GOLDEN, JOYCE MARIE
Financial executive. **Personal:** Born in Berkeley, CA; married William Paul; children: Shawn Patrick Golden. **Educ:** CA State Univ Hayward, BA, psychology, MBA, accounting & finance. **Career:** Arthur Andersen & Co, sr accountant, 1977-81; Bank of America, vp & financial mgr, vp & planning mgr, vp & financial controller, asst vp & accounting mgr, 1981-86; Citicorp Savings, dir of accounting, 1986-87; San Francisco Newspaper Agency, vp & chief financial officer, 1987-93; Natl Geographic Society, vp of financial planning, currently. **Orgs:** Newspaper Assn of Amer; Amer Women's Society of CPA's; Natl Assn of Urban Bankers; Bay Area Adoption Placement & Research Ctr, bd of dirs, treasurer, 1992-; Bus Volunteers of the Arts, bd of dirs, vp, 1990-93; Oakland Ensemble Theatre, bd of dirs, vp, 1986-89. **Business Addr:** Vice President, Financial Planning, National Geographic Society, 1145 17th Street, NW, Washington, DC 20036-4688, (202)857-7356.

GOLDEN, LOUIE
Educator. **Personal:** Born May 2, 1940, Matthews, SC; married Batty Washington. **Educ:** Claflin Coll, BS 1963; So IL U, MS 1971. **Career:** Sterling High School Greenville, coach, teacher 1963-65; Beck High School, coach, teacher 1965-70; Carolina High School, coach, teacher 1970-72; Riverside High School Greer, athletic dir 1973; Greenville County School Dist, athletic dir. **Orgs:** Coack clinic SC Basketball; SC Educ Assn; Greenville Co Educ Assn; NEA Council Math; SC HS League; master Mason; polemarch Kappa Alpha Psi Frat; Commn on Citizen of week for Co Council; Park & Tourist Commn for Appalachian Council Govt Park & recreation Commn Greenville C of C; mem v chmn trustee bd v chmn fin com chr treas St Matthew United Meth Ch. **Honors/Awds:** First black head coach predominent white sch; first black athletic dir Greenville Co Sch Dist; 750 winning percent basketball for ten yrs; one season 23 wins & no losses. **Business Addr:** Riverside HS, Greer, SC 29651.

GOLDEN, MARITA
Novelist, college professor. **Personal:** Born Apr 28, 1950, Washington, DC; daughter of Beatrice Reid Golden and Fancis Sherman Golden; children: Michael Kayode. **Educ:** Amer Univ, BA, 1972; Columbia Univ, MS, 1973. **Career:** WNET Channel 13, New York NY, assoc producer, 1974-75; Univ of Lagos, Lagos, Nigeria, asst prof, 1975-79; Roxbury Community Coll, Boston MA, asst prof, 1979-81; Emerson Coll, Boston MA, asst prof, 1981-83; author; George Mason Univ, senior writer of the Creative Writing Program, currently; Virginia Commonwealth University, prof in MFA creative writing prg, 1994-. **Orgs:** Inst for the Preservation and Study of African-Amer Writing, exec dir, 1986-87; African-Amer Writers Guild, pres emeritus; president, Zora Neale Hurston/Richard Wright Foundation; president emeritus, African American Writers Guild. **Special Achievements:** Novels: Migrations of the Heart, 1983; A Woman's Place, 1986; Long Distance Life, 1989; And Do Remember Me, 1992; Saving Our Sons, Doubleday, 1994; The Edge of Heaven, 1998; Skin Deep: Black and White Women on Race, edited by Marita Golden and Susan Shreve (Anchor Press). **Business Addr:** Novelist, c/o Carol Mann Agency, 55 5th Ave, New York, NY 10003.

GOLDEN, MARVIN DARNELL
Legal assistant. **Personal:** Born Dec 9, 1955, Chicago, IL; son of Catherine L Golden. **Educ:** DePaul University, Chicago, IL, BA, 1978; University of Illinois Chicago, Chicago, IL, MA, administrative science, 1985. **Career:** Community Relations Service, Chicago, IL, intern, 1978; Solomon, Rosenfeld, et al, Chicago, IL, office service manager, 1979-82; Rosenthal and Schanfield, Chicago, IL, legal assistant, 1982-. **Orgs:** Member, Academy of Political Science, 1983-86; member, American Society of Public Administration, 1982-89; member, Conference of Minority Public Administrators, 1982-89; member, National Young Professional's Forum, 1982-89; member, National Conference of Black Political Scientists, 1991; member, Souvenir Program Committee of Chicago Sinfonietta Annual Benefit, 1991. **Honors/Awds:** An Analysis of the Judicial System as Compared to Contemporary Organization Theory, Graduate Research Project, University of Illinois, Chicago, 1984; Co-Contributing Author of an Analysis Documenting the Legislative History of The Reauthorization of the Community Development Block Grant Programs of 1977; Public Policy Formulation Course, University of Illinois, Chicago, 1981.

GOLDEN, MYRON
Government official. **Personal:** Born Jan 19, 1947, Cleveland, OH; son of Erma N Golden and Joseph E Golden (deceased); children: Malaika Solange. **Educ:** Howard University, BA, 1969, John F Kennedy School, MPA, 1979. **Career:** US Agency for Intl Development, foreign service officer, 1970-; US Operations Mission, Thailand, budget, accounts officer, 1970-71; US Embassy, Bamako, Mali, program officer, 1975-78; USAID, Washington, sahel regional office chief, 1979-80; American Embassy Togo, aid representative, Togo, Benin, 1983-87; American Embassy Jamaica, deputy director, USAID, Jamaica, 1987-89; USAID, Washington, central costal West Africa director, 1989-. **Orgs:** Constituency for Africa, advisory council, 1991-; US Government, Senior Executive Service, 1986-; International Development Society, 1980-; Howard Alumni, 1970-; Harvard Alumni, 1979-; Kappa Alpha Psi Fraternity Inc, 1968-. **Honors/Awds:** US Government, AID, Superior Honor Award, 1978; Government of Mali, Distinguished Service, 1978; Government of Jamaica, National Development Foundation Appreciation, 1989; Jamaican-American Chamber of Commerce, Appreciation Exceptional Service, 1989; Central State University, Service Appreciation, 1992; Republic of Banin, Lifetime Achievement Award for promoting US-African Relations, 1993. **Special Achievements:** Diplomatic service in Southeast Asia, Africa and the Carribean, 1970-; specialist in African Affairs with service in Tanzania, Kenya, Guinea, Mali, Niger, Togo and Benin over a 20 year period. **Business Addr:** Director, Office for Central Costal West Africa, US Agency for International Development, 320 21st St NW, Rm 2733A, US State Department, Washington, DC 20523.

GOLDEN, RONALD ALLEN
Insurance supervisor. **Personal:** Born Feb 6, 1944, St Louis, MO; married Clementina Joyce Thompson; children: Stephanie, Lisa, Ronald. **Educ:** Southwest MO State, BS 1970; Am Educ Inst Inc, casualty claim law asso 1979. **Career:** The Travelers Ins Co, supr casualty prop claims 1968-; St Louis Bd of Edn, pe tchr 1968; McDonnell & Douglas Corp, tool & parts control spec 1966-68. **Orgs:** Mem Am Fed of Musicians Local 2-197 1973-; bus mgr Third World Band 1973-; bus mgr Simply Us Bank 1977-. **Honors/Awds:** First black athlete to win track & field schlshp SMSU 1962-66; outstd freshman awd SMSU Track Team 1962; capt track team SMSU 1966; first black in CP Claim St Louis Office Trav Ins Co. **Business Addr:** Sr Claim Law Associate, The Travelers Companies, 701 Market St, St Louis, MO 63101.

GOLDEN, SAMUEL LEWIS
Fire chief. **Personal:** Born Dec 14, 1921, Althiemer, AR; married Bette R Hall; children: Leslie Freeman, Sammetra L Bircher. **Educ:** St Mary's Coll, BA 1976. **Career:** Oakland Fire Dept, firefighter 1949-58, engr 1958-62, lt of fire 1962-66, capt of fire 1966-73, battalion chief 1973-81, fire chief 1981-. **Orgs:** Mem CA State Bd of Fire Svcs, NAACP, CA Fire Chiefs Assoc, Alameda Co Fire Chiefs Assoc, Intl Assoc of Fire Chiefs, Intl Metro Chiefs Assoc, CA MetroChiefs Assoc, Oakland Black Firefighters Assoc; chairman CA Metro Chiefs Assoc 1984-85; exec vice pres IABPFF. **Honors/Awds:** 1st black pres of a firefighter union; 1st black fire chief; life mem in firefighters union; Outstanding Leadership Awd OBFFA; Affirmative Action Awd WomenFF; Outstanding Leadership Awd Black Amer Women's Movement; Leadership Awd Brothers United San Diego; Appreciation of Serv Oakland Assoc Ins Agents; Certificate of Appreciation CA State Bd of Fire Svcs; Commendation CA State Fire Marshal 1987; Certificate of Special Congressional Recog US Congress 1987. **Military Serv:** AUS tech 5 1943-45. **Business Addr:** Chief, Oakland Fire Department, 2808 Frye St, Oakland, CA 94602.

GOLDEN, WILLIE L.
Law enforcement officer. **Personal:** Born Aug 16, 1952, Miami, FL; son of Louise Smith and Willie S Golden; married Myra E Jones Golden, Dec 19, 1979; children: Bryan, Kyle, Christopher, William Justin. **Educ:** Southeast Florida Inst of Criminal Justice, Miami FL, Certificate of Completion, 1974; Miami-Dade Community Coll, Miami FL, AA, 1978; Biscayne Coll, Miami FL, BA, 1980; St Thomas Univ, Miami FL, MS, 1981. **Career:** Metro-Dade Police Dept, Miami FL, police officer to lieutenant, 1974-; Dade County School System, Miami FL, teacher, 1977-84; Dade County Citizen Safety Council, Miami FL, instructor, consultant, 1984-; Florida Memorial Coll, Miami FL, assoc prof, 1986-; Alexander & Alexander, Miami FL, public relations consultant, 1986-88; Metropolitan Police Inst, Miami FL, instructor, 1987; Metro Dade Police Dept, police lieutenant, currently. **Orgs:** Jr warden, Prince Hall Masons, 1974-; pres, Progressive Officers, 1975-; mem, Dade County Police Ben Assn, 1975-; parliamentarian, Natl Black Police Assn, 1977-; chaplain, Phi Beta Sigma Frat, 1984-; mem, NAACP, 1984-; mem, bd of dir, South Florida Inst of Traffic Safety Unlimited, 1985-; Prince Hall Shriner, temple 149; Police Benevolent Assn; Univ of Miami Medical Advory Board; Natl Organization of Black Law Enforcement Executives. **Honors/Awds:** Planned, Organized and Developed, The Community Oriented Police Unit for the Metro-Dade Police Dept, 1982; Outstanding POC Mem, Progressive Officers Club, 1985; Outstanding Young Man of Amer, Young Americans, 1986; Distinguished Serv Commendation, Metro-Dade Police, 1988; National Black Police Assn's Law Enforcement Award, 1995; National Black Police Assn's WD Cameron Leadership Award, 1994; Proclamation, Dade County Commission, 1995. **Business Addr:** Police Lieutenant, Metro-Dade Police Dept, Northside Station, 2950 NW 83rd Street, Miami, FL 33147.

GOLDSBERRY, RONALD EUGENE
Automobile company executive. **Personal:** Born Sep 12, 1942, Wilmington, DE; children: Ryan, Renee. **Educ:** Central State Univ, BS Chem 1964; MI State Univ, PhD Inorganic Chem 1969; Stanford Univ, MBA Finance/Marketing 1973. **Career:** Univ of CA San Jose, asst prof of chem 1969-71; NASA Ames Rsch Ctr, rsch chemist 1969-72; Hewlett Packard Co, prod mgr 1972-73; Boston Consulting Group, mgmt consultant 1973-75; Gulf Oil Corp, dir corp planning 1975-78; Occidental Chem Corp, vice pres bus develop 1978-81, vice pres gen mgr surface treatment prods 1981-83; Parker Chem Co, pres 1983-87; Ford Motor Company, Plastic Products Division, general manager, 1987-90, North American Automotive Operations, executive director of sales and service strategies, 1990-93, vp, customer services, 1993-. **Orgs:** Bd mem Cranbrook Educ Inst; bd mem MI State Univ Alumni Assn; bd mem Black Exec Exchange Prog; Amer Chem Soc; Natl Black MBA Assn; Natl Org Black Chemists & Chem Engrs; Assn of Consumer Growth; Comm Devt Assn; Amer Mgmt Assn; Economic Club; Greater Detroit Chamber of Commerce; Omega Psi Phi Frat; bd of trustees WTVS Channel 56 Detroit; bd mem Amer Can Co; board member, Rockefeller Foundation; board member, Adrian College; board member, William Beaumont Hospital; board member, Boy Scouts of America; board member, Michigan State Univ Development Fund; board member, ExPrimerica Corporation. **Honors/Awds:** Beta Kappa Chi Hon Soc 1962; Alpha Kappa Mu Hon Soc 1963; Omega Psi Phi Man of the Year 1971; Outstanding Alumnus of MI State Univ 1983; Outstanding Alumnus of NAFEO 1983; patent ''Ultraviolet & Thermally Stable Polymer Compositions'' 1974; Honorary Doctorate of Humane Letters, Central State University; Top 50 Black Executives, Black Enterprise; Excellence in Management Award, Industry Week. **Special Achievements:** Natl Academy of Engineers, 1993; only the 2nd African-American vice president at Ford Motor Company, 1994. **Military Serv:** US Army capt, 1969-71. **Business Addr:** Global Vice President, Ford Motor Co, Customer Service Division, PO Box 43381, Detroit, MI 48243.

GOLDSBY, W. DEAN, SR.
Educational administrator. **Personal:** son Of Ola Lee Ellison Goldsby Lankford and Louis Goldsby; married Laverne Gibson Goldsby, Dec 22, 1980; children: Cathy, Anthony, Ricky, W. Dean Jr., Sandy, Keith Gibson, Kenya, Khaaym, Kelly Eddings. **Educ:** Campbell Jr College, Jackson, MS, AA, 1957; Allen Univ, Columbia, SC, BA, 1959; Univ of Arkansas, Fayetteville, MEd, 1966; Shorter College, Little Rock, AR, DHL, 1977. **Career:** Shorter College, North Little Rock, AR, dean of men, 1960-64, instructor, 1960-67, dean of students, 1964-67, director of fed work-study program, 1966-67, dean of weekend college, 1969, director of student services, vice pres, 1987-88, pres, 1988-. **Orgs:** Sec/treas, Natl Assn for Community Devel, 1973; trustee, Shorter Coll, Natl Community Action Trust Fund, and Bethel AME Church; pre, N Little Rock Coun on Human Rels; pres, AFSCME Local #1934; member, exec bd, AFSCME Coun 38 of AR; member, bd of direcs, Greater Little Rock Chamber of Commerce. **Honors/Awds:** Regional Omega Man of the Year, 1967. **Business Addr:** President, Shorter College, 604 Locust Street, Suite 106, North Little Rock, AR 72114.

GOLDSON, ALFRED LLOYD
Hospital administrator. **Personal:** Born Apr 9, 1946, New York; son of Marjorie Owens Goldson and Lloyd R Goldson; married Amy Goldson. **Educ:** New York U, 1966; Hampton Inst, BS 1968; Coll of Med Howard U, MD 1972. **Career:** Dept of Radiotherapy Howard Univ Hosp, res 1973-75, asst radiotherapist 1976-79, chmn radiation oncolgy department, 1979-, prof of radiotherapy, currently. **Orgs:** Consult Cancer Info Serv Cancer Communication for Met DC 1977; vol lecr smoking rel to teenagers Am Cancer Soc 1977-78; chmn adv com Coll of Allied Health Radiation Therapy Howard Univ 1977-78; mem Nat Med & Am Med Assn 1978-; mem of numerous other civil orgns; bd of trustees DC Div Amer Cancer Soc1979. **Honors/Awds:** Cert of Merit Radiological Soc of N Am 1978; Serv Cit Explorers of Am 1978; Five Yr Serv Cit Howard Univ Hosp 1978; among top 50 sci & res in cancerfor 1978 Am Cancer Soc 21st Annual Seminar for Sci Writers 1979; Alpha Omega Alpha Natl Medical Honor Soc 1987-; Fellow American College of Radiology, 1988. **Special Achievements:** President William Jefferson Clinton, appointed Natl Cancer Advisory Bd, 1994. **Business Addr:** Professor, Howard Univ Hospital, Radiotherapy Dept, 2041 Georgia Ave NW, Washington, DC 20060.

GOLDSON, AMY ROBERTSON
Attorney. **Personal:** Born Jan 16, 1953, Boston, MA; daughter of E Emily & Irving E Robertson; married Alfred L Goldson, Jun 24, 1974; children: Erin, Ava. **Educ:** Smith College, BA (magna cum laude), 1974; Catholic University Law School, JD, 1976. **Career:** Internal Revenue Service, Office of Chief Counsel, Tax Court Litigation Division, attorney, 1976-77; Smothers, Douple, Gayton & Long, attorney, 1977-83; Law Office of Amy Goldson, attorney, 1983-. **Orgs:** Congressional Black Caucus Foundation, general counsel, 1978-; Black Entertainment & Sports Lawyers Assn, bd of directors, 1986-; National Bar Assn, 1976-; American Bar Assn, 1976-; Mayor's Committee on Entertainment, chairperson, 1994; Washington Area Lawyers For the Arts, 1992-; Washington Performing Arts Society, bd of directors, 1987-. **Honors/Awds:** Smith College, Phi Beta Kappa, 1973. **Special Achievements:** Court Admissions: US Supreme Court, 1980; DC Court of Appeals; US Court of Appeals, 1980; US Tax Court, 1978; US Court of Military Appeals, 1978; US District Court for the District of Columbia, 1978; US Court of Appeals for the 4th Circuit. **Business Addr:** Attorney, Law Office of Amy Goldson, 4015 28th Place NW, Washington, DC 20008, (202)966-7531.

GOLDSTON, NATHANIEL R., III
Food service executive. **Personal:** Born Oct 20, 1938, Omaha, NE; son of Mary Burden Goldston and Nathaniel Goldston II; married A Darleen; children: Nathaniel IV, Steven, Kimberly. **Educ:** Univ of Denver, BA 1962. **Career:** Catering Mgmt Inc, food serv dir, dist mgr/regional vice pres 1963-74; Gourmet Serv Inc, pres & chmn of the bd 1975-. **Orgs:** Chmn of the bd Tuskegee Inst Food Service Task Force; bd of dirs Atlanta Regional Commn; natl bd of dirs Amer Business Council; mem Atlanta Chamber of Commerce, Amer Mgmt Assn, Private Industry Council, Natl Restaurant Assn, GA Hospitality and Travel Assn; bd mem School of Hospitality and Mgmt Wiley Coll; mem Univ of Denver Alumni Assn; member, board of trustees, Univ of Denver, 1990-. **Honors/Awds:** Minority Business Person of the Year, Urban Business Devel Center; Catalyst Award Most Outstanding New Business by Interracial Council of Business Opportunity 1976; Black Enterprise Magazine's Annual Achievement Award in the Area of Serv 1977; Columbia MO Restaurateur of the Year 1978; Leadership Atlanta 1980; Minority Business of the Year, Interracial Council for Business Opportunity 1981; Natl Urban League Certificate of Appreciation 1981. **Business Addr:** President, Gourmet Services, Inc, 1100 Spring St Ste 450, Atlanta, GA 30367.

GOLDSTON, RALPH PETER
Professional football scout (retired). **Personal:** Born Feb 25, 1929, Campbell, OH; son of Alice Goldston and Richard Goldston; married Sarah Sloan; children: Ralph Jr, Ursula, Beverley, Monica. **Educ:** Youngstown Univ, BS Educ 1952. **Career:** New England Patriots, scout, 1989-95; Seattle Seahawks, scout, 1975-89; Chicago Bears Club, asst football coach 1974-75; Univ of Colorado, coach 1973; Harvard Univ, 1971-72; Burlington Central High School, Burlington Ontario; Montreal Alouettes, 1966-69; NY Giants, scout 1970; Philadelphia Eagles, played 1952-55; Hamilton Tiger-Cats, 1956-64; Montreal Alouettes, 1965; City of Youngstown & Mahoning Co, surveyor during off-season; City of Philadelphia, rec dir 1952; Burlington Ontario, teacher 1962-67. **Orgs:** First black at Youngstown Univ 1950-51, Philadelphia Eagles 1952-55; pro coach Canadian Football League 1966; coach at Harvard Univ 1971-72; All-Pro def back CFL 1956-63; All-Co HS Mahoning Co Ohio 1945-46. **Honors/Awds:** Letterman & capt, Youngstown Univ 1950-51; athletic scholarship Ind Univ. **Home Addr:** 1599 Ramblewood Ave, Columbus, OH 43235. **Business Addr:** Scout (Retired), Personnel Dept, New England Patriots, Foxboro Stadium, Foxboro, MA 02035.

GOLDWIRE, ANTHONY
Professional basketball player. **Personal:** Born Sep 6, 1971, West Palm Beach, FL; son of Willie and Betty Goldwire. **Educ:** Houston. **Career:** Yakima Sun Kings (CBA), 1994-96; Charlotte Hornets, guard, 1996; Denver Nuggets, 1996-. **Honors/Awds:** CBA, All-Rookie second team, 1995. **Special Achievements:** CBA, Championship, 1995. **Business Addr:** Professional Basketball Player, Denver Nuggets, 1635 Clay St, Denver, CO 80204, (303)893-6700.

GOLIDAY, WILLIE V.
Business executive. **Personal:** Born Feb 22, 1956, Oxford, MS; married Mary Ann Cration. **Educ:** Jackson State Univ, BS 1978, MBA 1980. **Career:** Delta Capital Corp, investment analyst 1980-82; Action Commun Co Inc, pres. **Orgs:** Advisor Jr Achievement 1981; mem JSU Alumni Assoc. **Honors/Awds:** Outstanding Young Man of Amer 1985. **Home Addr:** 64 Milhem, Greenville, MS 38701. **Business Addr:** President, Action Communications Co Inc, PO Box 588, Greenville, MS 38701, (601)335-5291.

GOLIGHTLY, LENA MILLS
Composer, author, poet, radio producer. **Personal:** Born in Horse Cave, KY. **Career:** Author, Premonition of Last Christmas, 1947, Top of the Mountain, 1967, The Seventh Child, 1967; Composer, I Don't Worry, 1955, Sugarpie Tears Easy Now, 1955, Jack is Back, 1957, Mis Bronzeville, 1961, Eternal Flame, 1964, Resurrection City USA, 1968, Do Your Thing & I'll Do Mine, 1969, King Drive, 1969, I Had Too Much To Dream Last Night, 1970; Poems, Golden Chain of Friendship, 1967, America You're Dying, 1969; WXFM-Radio, Chicago, IL, producer, 1966-; WBEE-Radio, Chicago, IL, producer, 1967; Ada S McKinley Comm Svcs, active pub relations, 1967. **Orgs:** Mem Natl Assn Media Women, Chicago Museum Assn; dir Civic Liberty League of IL; mem NAACP, Urban League, AME Church; dir Amer Friendship Club. **Honors/Awds:** Amer Friendship Club Awd 1962-65; Awd of Merit WVON 1965, 1969; Chicago Mus Assn 1965; Awds Chicago No Dist Assn Federated Clubs 1966, WXFM 1966, Carey Temple 1966, WGRT Chicago 1970, Natl Acad Best Dressed Churchwomen 1972, 1973; Humanitarian Awd Baptist Fgn Mission Bur 1973; Dr Martin Luther King Jr Humanitarian Awd Love Meml Missionary Baptist Church 1974.

GOLPHIN, VINCENT F. A.
Writer, educator. **Personal:** Born Aug 7, 1952, Youngstown, OH; son of Charlotte Carter Golpin & Tilmon Golphin. **Educ:** Sacred Heart Seminary, Detroit, MI, BA, history, 1974; University of Dayton, Dayton, OH, MA, theology, 1979; Union Graduate School, PhD, religion/psychology, 1981. **Career:** New York State Assembly, Albany, NY, senior executive asst, 1980-82; National Catholic Reporter, Washington, DC, writer, 1982-87; Charles County Community College, Waldorf, MD, adjunct professor, 1986-87; Herald-Journal, Syracuse, NY, editor/columnist, 1987-95; Onondaga Community College, Syracuse, NY, adjunct professor, 1990-95; Syracuse University, SI School of Public Communications, adjunct professor, 1995-; The Writing Co. Inc, president, currently. **Orgs:** President, Syracuse Press Club, 1989-91; member, Theta Chi Beta (religion honorary), 1990-; member, Phi Delta Kappa (education honorary), 1984-; member, Phi Alpha Theta (history honorary), 1972-. **Honors/Awds:** NISOD, Teacher Excellence Award, 1994.

GOMES, PETER JOHN
Clergyman. **Personal:** Born May 22, 1942, Boston, MA. **Educ:** Bates Coll Lewiston ME, BA 1965; Harvard Univ, STB 1967-68; New England Coll, DD (hon) 1974; Waynesburg Coll, LHD (hon) 1978; Gordon Coll, Hum D (hon) 1985. **Career:** Amer Baptist Church, ordained to ministry 1968; Tuskegee Inst AL, instr history, dir fresmen exptl prog 1968-70; Meml Church Harvard Univ, asst minister, acting minister 1970-74, minister 1974-. **Orgs:** Fellow Royal Soc ARts; mem Royal Soc Ch Music, Colonial Soc MA, MA Hist Soc, Farmington Inst Christian Studies, Amer Bapt Hist Soc, Unitarian HistSoc; pres Signet Soc, Harvard Musical Assn; dir English-Speaking Union; mem Phi Beta Kappa; trustee Pilgrim Soc, Donation to Liberia 1973-, Bates Coll 1973-78,80-, Charity of Edward Hopkins 1974-, Boston Freedom Trail 1976-, Plimoth Plantation 1977-, Rosbury Latin School 1982-, Wellesley Coll 1985-, Boston Found 1985, Jordon Hosp, Plymouth Pub Library 1985-; pres, trustee Intl Fund Def & Aid in S Africa 1977-; natl chaplain Amer Guild Organists 1978-82. **Honors/Awds:** Co-author Books of the Pilgrims; editor Parnassus 1970, History of the Pilgrim Soc 1970. **Business Addr:** Minister, Memorial Church, Harvard University, Cambridge, MA 02138.

GOMES, WAYNE M.
Professional baseball player. **Personal:** Born Jan 15, 1973, Hampton, VA. **Educ:** Old Dominion. **Career:** Philadelphia Phillies, pitcher, 1997-. **Business Addr:** Professional Baseball Player, Philadelphia Phillies, PO Box 7575, Philadelphia, PA 19101, (215)463-6000.

GOMEZ, DANIEL J.
Missionary. **Personal:** Born Nov 26, 1926, Orange, NJ. **Educ:** Seton Hall Univ, BS 1956. **Career:** Capuchin Missionary Zambia C Africa, 1967-; Hse of Novitiate Wilmington DE, confssr 3 yrs; St Ann's Parish Hoboken, asst pastor 2 yrs; Hse of Theology, tchr. **Orgs:** Mem NAACP; mem Order of Cross & Crescent Seton Hall U. **Military Serv:** AUS 6 months; USAF corpl 3 yrs. **Business Addr:** Capuchin-Franciscan Order, PO Box 6279, Hoboken, NJ 07030.

GOMEZ, DENNIS CRAIG
Personnel administrator. **Personal:** Born May 14, 1948, Suffern, NY; son of Elizabeth Gomez and Carlos Gomez; married Henrietta McAlister; children: Camille, Mark, Brian. **Educ:** S IL Univ, BA 1971. **Career:** Chase Manhattan Bank, credit corres 1971-72; Allstate Ins Co, office oper super 1972-73, claim super 1973, div super 1973-74, personnel assist 1974-76, personnel div mgr 1976-79, human resources mgr 1979-80, personnel serv mgr 1980-82, regional personnel mgr 1982-86, human resource director, customer relations dir 1987-88, field human resources director 1989-97, asst vp, 1997-. **Orgs:** Mem ASPA; mem Urban League Phila; mem NAACP North Philadelphia Branch; OIC Fund Raising chmn Montgomery Co, PA 1985; board of directors, CASA Lake County; Parent Council Wake Forest Univ. **Business Addr:** Assistant Vice Pres, Allstate Insurance Company, Allstate Plaza North, Northbrook, IL 60062.

GOMEZ, JEWELLE L.
Writer. **Personal:** Born Sep 11, 1948, Boston, MA; daughter of Dolores LeClaire, John Gomez. **Educ:** Northeastern Univ, BA, 1971; Columbia Univ, Ford Foundation Fellow, MS, journalism, 1973. **Career:** Hunter College, lecturer, 1989-91; NY State Council on the Arts, program assoc, 1983-90, dir of literature, 1990-93; New College, lecturer, 1993-94; Menlo College, visiting writer, 1993; The Poetry Ctr & American Poetry Archives at San Francisco State University, executive director, 1996-. **Orgs:** Open Meadows Foundation, bd mem, 1989-; Coalition Against Censorship, bd mem, 1993-; Cornell Univ Human Sexuality Archives, advisory bd, 1992-; Multi-Cultural Review, editorial advisory bd, 1991-95; Belle Lettres, editorial advisory bd, 1990-96; Gay & Lesbian Alliance Against Defamation, founding bd mem, 1988-90. **Honors/Awds:** Lambda Literary Awards, Fiction & Science Fiction, 1991; Barbara Deming, Money for Women Fund, fiction, 1987; Bead's Fund Award for Fiction, 1985; CA Arts Council, Artist in Residence, 1994, 1995; Fellowship, National Endowment for the Arts, 1997. **Special Achievements:** Author, Don't Explain: Short Fiction, Firebrand Books, 1998; Oral Tradition: Poems Selected & New, Firebrand Books, 1995; Forty Three Septembers, Firebrand Books, 1993; The Gilda Stories, Firebrand Books, 1991; Flamingoes & Bears, Grace Publications, 1986; The Lipstick Papers, Grace Publications, 1980; Playwright "Bones & Ash: A Gilda Story" US tour, 1995-96. **Business Addr:** c/o Frances Goldin - Agent, 305 E 11th St, New York, NY 10003, (212)777-0047.

GOMEZ, KEVIN LAWRENCE JOHNSON
Family support center administrator. **Personal:** Born Nov 27, 1950, Erie, PA; son of Yvonne Johnson Gomez and Lawrence Lucas; married Yvonne Ruth Stepp; children: McKenzie. **Educ:** Univ of CO at Denver, BA 1972; Univ of MI at Ann Arbor, MA equivalency 1973; Univ of CO aT Denver, 1975-. **Career:** US Dept of Interior, envirnmntl protectn spec; Gary W Hart, asst US senator 1978-80; Floyd K Haskell, asst US senator 1975-78; Sam Brown, campaign mgr 1974; Univ of MI, stud advocate 1973; Student Health Conf of SW, Sam Brown for Dir 1975; Denver Affirmtv Action Commn, chmn 1975-77; Denver Dem Cntrl Com, asst sec 1975-79, sec 1979-81; US Dept of Air Force, dir of fam support ctr 1982-. **Orgs:** Bd mem Am Friends Serv Com 1972-; vice pres CO Young Dem 1974-77; adv bd mem Sickle Cell Anemia gubernatorial appt 1976-81; vice pres Denver-Park Hill NAACP 1977-80. **Honors/Awds:** Horace H Rackham Grad Award Univ of MI 1973; Denver Regnl Cncl of Govts Grad Award in Pub Adminstrn Univ of CO 1975; del Nat Dem Midterm Conv 1978; Leadrshp Denver '80 Award Denver C of C 1979-80; Civilian of the Year Candidate, Spangdahlem AB, Germany, 1990. **Business Addr:** Director, Dept of Air Force, Family Support Center, Spangdahlem AB, #47 Ringstrasse, 55 Herforst, Germany.

GONA, OPHELIA DELAINE
Research scientist, educator. **Personal:** Born Jul 4, 1936, South Carolina; daughter of Mattie DeLaine and Joseph A DeLaine; married Amos; children: Shantha, Raj. **Educ:** Johnson C Smith Univ, BS 1957; Yeshiva Univ, MS 1965; City Coll NY, MA 1967; City Univ NY, PhD 1971. **Career:** CCNY, resrch asst, teacher asst 1966-70; Peace Corps Volunteer Ghana, 1961-63; Eastern Dist High School Brooklyn, Biology teacher 1958-61; Cornell Univ Medical School, lab tech 1957-58; Montclair State Coll, asst prof Biology 1970-77; NJ Coll of Medicine & Dentistry, asst prof Anatomy; UMD-New Jersey Medical School, assoc prof of Anatomy 1986-. **Orgs:** Educ consult Hoffman LaRoche Pharms 1972-73; author science publications concrng 1972-77; mem AIBS, AAAS, Am Assn of Anatomists, ARVO, NY Acad of Sci. **Honors/Awds:** Recipient of NIH grants for lens (eye) rsch Golden Apple Award for Excellence in Teaching of Medical Gross Anatomy; author of scientific publications concerning comparative endocrinology of prolactin cataracts of the lens of the eye; developer of computer-based instructional materials for Gross Anatomy. **Business Addr:** Associate Professor, UMDNJ Med School, Dept of Anatomy, Newark, NJ 07103.

GONGA, DAWILLI. **See DUKE, GEORGE M.**

GONZALEZ, CAMBELL
Project engineer (retired), investment advisor, financial planner. **Personal:** Born Aug 26, 1918, Tampa, FL; married Juanita Nash; children: Amelia, Anita, John. **Educ:** Howard Univ, BSEE, 1949; Stevens Inst, graduate courses; Brooklyn Polytechnic Newark Coll of Engineering; College of Financial Planning, Denver, CO, CFP 1983-86. **Career:** RCA, retired proj engr, 1970-82; design devel engr, 1955-70; applied engr, 1950-55; engr training, 1949. **Orgs:** Mem, IEEE; bd dir, YMCA Orange NJ; Alpha Phi Alpha Fraternity; planning bd, adv gr Reading Township; Sewer Adv Commn; teacher elder Flemington Pres Church; pres Inv Club Alumni; Rotary Club of Flemington NJ, 1990-. **Honors/Awds:** Achievement award, Howard Univ, 1957; tech art pub in RCA Engr IRE Trans Electronics; Pat disclosure RCA. **Military Serv:** AUS commanding officer, 1942-52. **Home Addr:** 158 W Woodschurch Rd, Flemington, NJ 08822.

GONZALEZ, TONY
Professional football player. **Educ:** California. **Career:** Kansas City Chiefs, 1997-. **Special Achievements:** NFL Draft, First round pick, #13, 1997. **Business Addr:** Professional Football Player, Kansas City Chiefs, 1 Arrowhead Dr, Kansas City, MO 64129, (816)924-9300.

GONZAQUE, OZIE BELL
City commissioner. **Personal:** Born Jun 8, 1925, Thornton, AR; daughter of Wilie Lee Brown Woods and John Henry Woods; married Roy Sylvester Gonzaque, Mar 15, 1955; children: Frieda Elaine, Barbara Jean, Bernadette, Roy Jr, Janet, Mary Nadene, Joseph Gregory. **Educ:** Southwest College, certificate; USC, certificate. **Career:** Fradelis Frozen Foods, Los Angeles, CA, production supervisor, 1951-63; District Attorneys Evelle Younger, Joseph Busch, and John Von DeCamp, advisory council member, 1969-84; Attorney General Evelle Younger, advisory council member, 1971-83; Bureau of Consumer Affairs, advertising and promotional policy volunteer, 1972-84; Juvenile Justice Center, volunteer, 1977-79; Los Angeles Housing Authority, commissioner, 1985-. **Orgs:** Dir of bd, South Central Social Services Corp; mem, Community Development Commn, County of Los Angeles; pres, Southeast Businessmen's Booster Assn; HACLA, chairperson of board; LA Community Development Bank, board of directors. **Honors/Awds:** Public Service Award, ABLE, 1985; People's Choice Award, People's Choice Inc, 1985; Woman of the Year, State of Calif Legislative Body, 1989; 1990 Achievement Award, NOBLE, 1990. **Business Addr:** Commissioner, Housing Authority Dept, City of Los Angeles, 515 Columbia, Los Angeles, CA 90017, (213)252-1826.

GOOCH, JEFF
Professional football player. **Personal:** Born Oct 31, 1974. **Educ:** Austin Peay State, attended. **Career:** Tampa Bay Buccaneers, linebacker, 1996-. **Business Addr:** Professional Football Player, Tampa Bay Buccaneers, One Buccaneer Place, Tampa, FL 33607, (813)870-2700.

GOOD, WILLA W.
Registered nurse (retired), educator. **Personal:** Born Feb 5, 1915, Pittsburgh, PA; married Dr Edmund E; children: Willa, Phyllis, Sylvia. **Educ:** Harlem Hosp Cntr Sch Nursing, RN; NY U, BS; Iona College, New Rochelle, NY, 1982, BS; College of New Rochelle, New Rochelle, NY, 1985, MS; pursuing PhD, currently. **Career:** Harlem Hosp Cntr Harlem Hosp Svc, various nursg positions; Bellvue Hosp; Dr's Office; Harlem Hospital, Education dept, instructor, currently. **Orgs:** Consult Fed Hosp Cncl; Health Care Faclts Svc; Health Serv & Mental Hlth Adminstrn; Nat Center for Hlth Serv Resrch & Devel; Dept Health Educ & Welfare; commr Mt Vernon Plnng Bd; chr Westchester Rent Guidlns; bd mem numerous offcs; coms Am Nurses Assn; NY State Nurses Assn; Nat League Nursing; Harlem Hosp Center Sch Nursng Alumni Assn; Chi Eta Phi Sor Omicron Chpt; Zeta Phi Beta Sor Gamma Xi Zeta Chpt; Women's Aux Loma Linda Univ Med Sch; Nat Cncl Women of US; Leag Women Voters; Philharmonic Symphony of Westchester Women's Com; Mt Vernon Women's Serv Leag; Intl Inst Women's Studies; Nat Women's Rep Club; sect chmn Mt Vernon Hosp Expansn Pgm Campaign; Hosp Admissns Com Mt Vernon-Eastchester Mental Hlth Cncl; numerous past appntmnts, community activities, pub speaking engagements; first vice pres, Harlem Hospital Centr Auxiliary; mem, friends of Harlem Hospital Centr; Basileus, Omicron Chap, Chi Eta Phi Sorority. **Honors/Awds:** Recip Mt Vernon Housng Authority Distngshd Serv Citation 1965; Mt Vernon United Community Fund Citation 1965; spl award Westchester Lighthse for the Blind 1968; placque Mt Vernon Women's Serv League 1969; Honoree Soror of Yr Chi Eta Phi Sor Omicron Chap 1971.

GOODALL, HURLEY CHARLES, SR.
State representative (retired). **Personal:** Born May 23, 1927, Muncie, IN; son of Dorene Mukes Goodall and Hurley Charles Goodall (deceased); married Fredine Wynn Goodall, May 1, 1948; children: Hurley E, Fredrick. **Educ:** IN Bus Coll, Assoc 1948-49; Purdue U, time & motion courses 1952. **Career:** Muncie Malleable Co, 1944-50, time and motion steward, 1950-58; Muncie Fire Dept, fire fighter 1958-78; Hur Co Inc, owner electrical supplies equipment & devices industrial & commercial; Muncie Board of Education, president, 1974-75; Deleware County, Indiana, assistant county engineer, 1978-80; Indiana House of Reps, state rep 1978-92, assistant floor leader, 1989-92; Middletown Center Ball State University, visiting fellow, currently. **Orgs:** Chair Central Reg, National Black Caucus Schoolboard Members 1972-78; mem Muncie Bd of Educ 1970-78; bd mem WIPB-TV Chan 49 Muncie PBS Sta 1974-80; chmn IN Black Leg Caucus 1979-; mem In Jobs Training Coord Council; mem govs commiss on Minority Bus Devel. **Honors/Awds:** Co-author ''History of Negroes in Muncie'' Ball State Press 1974; Muncie Black Hall of Fame Multi-Serv Cntr of Muncie 1979; Govt Serv Award OIC of Deleware County 1980; Horatio Alger Award, Muncie Boys Club, 1984. **Special Achievements:** Inside the House, published by Ball State Press, 1995. **Military Serv:** AUS pfc 1945-47. **Home Addr:** 1905 Carver Dr, Muncie, IN 47303. **Business Addr:** Visiting Fellow, Political Science Department, Ball State University, Rm 226, Muncie, IN 47306.

GOODE, CALVIN C.
City official. **Personal:** Born Jan 27, 1927, Depew, OK; married Georgie M; children: Vernon, Jerald, Randolph. **Educ:** Phoenix Coll, AA 1947; AZ State Coll, BS 1949; AZ State U, MA 1972. **Career:** Phoenix Union HS Dist, sch comm wrkr 1969-, sch bus mgr, asst proprty contrl dir, asst budget dir 1949-69; Goode & Asso Tax & Accntg Svc, owner & oper 1950-; Phoenix City Cnclmn, 1972-94; Phoenix City V Mayor, 1974, 1984. **Orgs:** Bd mem Comm Council; dir Investmnt Opportnts Inc; past mem CTA, AEA, NEA; past mem United Fund Budget Com; mem Phoenix Urban Leag; mem NAACP; past bd chmn BT Washington Child Devel Cntr Inc; past co-chmn Child Care Project Comm Cncl; mem Omega Psi Phi Frat; past mem Downtown Bkfst Optimist Club. **Home Addr:** 1508 E Jefferson, Phoenix, AZ 85034.

GOODE, GEORGE RAY
Elected official. **Personal:** Born Feb 8, 1930, Clifton Forge, VA; married Doris Hatcher (deceased); children: Cassandra White, George Jr, Ava, Stanley, Kim Rickten, Carren, Stacey, Dana. **Educ:** VA Seminary Ext, Assoc in Religious Educ 1976. **Career:** City of Clifton Forge, city councilman 1974, Mayor. **Orgs:** Chmn Greater Allegheny United Fund 1984. **Home Addr:** 700 Pine St, Clifton Forge, VA 24422.

GOODE, JAMES EDWARD
Clergyman. **Personal:** Born Nov 18, 1943, Roanoke, VA. **Educ:** Immaculate Conceptn Coll, BA 1969; Coll of St Rose, MA 1971; St Anthony Theol Sem, MDiv 1972, MTh 1974; PhD; Univ of Louvain Belgium, post-doctoral studies 1980. **Career:** Our Lady of Charity, pastor 1974-; City Univ NY, adj prof 1975-, chaplain 1975-; Center for Positive Directn, dir 1976-; Black Religious Expernc Inst, co-dir; Directions A Jour of Black Ch/Comm Studies, editor; Black Cath Day, founder; Survival & Faith Inst of NY, cons; Juvenile Justice Task Force of Cntrl Brooklyn, cons; Offc for Black Ministry Diocese of Brooklyn, bd dirs; Bldg a Better Brooklyn, bd dirs; lectr, psychlgy & theology. **Orgs:** Mem New York City Comm Sch Bd; mem Central Brooklyn Yth & Fmly Svcs; mem Juvenile Prevntv Pgms Brooklyn; mem New York City Comm Plnng Bd; mem Culture & Worship Adv Bd Nat Offc for Black Cath; mem Coalition of Concerned Black Eductrs of NY; mem Black Ministers Cncl; mem Nat Black Cath Clergy; Nat Assn of Black Social Wrkrs; Educ Task Force for Positive Direction of NY Urban Commn; ''Catholicsm & Slavery in US'' Labor Press 1975; pub ''Ministry in the 80's in the Black Comm'' Liberation Press 1980; numerous publs. **Honors/Awds:** Dr of Humane Letters VA Theol Sem; Preacher of First Black Cath Revival in US Chicago 1974; Martin Luther King Schlrshp NY Univ 1975-76; Black Cath Leadrshp Awrd; proclmtn declaring Nov 18 1978 Father James E Goode Day New York City 1978; proclmtn declaring Nov 16 1979 Father James E Goode Day Mayor of Brooklyn 1979; Nat Black Cath Clergy Tribute Award 1979; proclmtn NY State Assembly; lead Nat Protest Prayer Serv Against Budget Cuts in Human Servs. **Business Addr:** 1669 Dean St, Brooklyn, NY 11213.

GOODE, W. WILSON
Company executive. **Personal:** Born Aug 19, 1938, Seaboard, NC; son of Rozelar Goode and Albert Goode; married Velma Helen Williams, 1960; children: Muriel, W Wilson Jr, Natasha. **Educ:** Morgan State Univ, BA, 1961; Univ of PA Wharton School, MPA, 1968. **Career:** Probation officer, bldg maintenance supr; insurance claims adjuster; Philadelphia Council for Comm Advancement, pres/CEO 1966-78; PA Public Utilities Commn, chmn 1978-80; City of Philadelphia, managing dir 1980-82; City of Philadelphia, mayor, 1984-92; Goode Group, pres, CEO, 1992-; US Dept of Educ, secretary's regional rep, region III. **Orgs:** Goode Cause Inc, founder. **Honors/Awds:** Numerous honorary degrees, US universities; first black mayor of Philadelphia, PA; conducted investigation into Three Mile Island nuclear disaster and was responsible for ensuring public safety and uninterrupted power flow, 1979. **Military Serv:** AUS, military police, CPT, 1961-63; commendation medal, meritorious service. **Business Addr:** President, CEO, Goode Cause, 2446 No 59th Street, Philadelphia, PA 19131-1208.

GOODEN, C. MICHAEL
Business executive. **Career:** Integrated Systems Analysts Inc, president, currently. **Special Achievements:** Company ranked #34 on Black Enterprise's list of Top 100 Industrial/Service Companies, 1992. **Business Addr:** President, Integrated Systems Analysts Inc, 2800 Shirlington Rd, #1100, Arlington, VA 22206, (703)824-0100.

GOODEN, CHERRY ROSS
Educator. **Personal:** Born Nov 7, 1942, Calvert, TX; daughter of Ludia Beavers Ross and John R Ross; children: Deron LeJohn, DeShaunda Lorraine. **Educ:** Texas Southern Univ, BS 1960-64, MEd 1969-72; Univ of Houston, EdD 1991. **Career:** Houston Independent School District, teacher 1964-76; Texas Southern Univ, associate professor 1976-. **Orgs:** Consultant to various School Districts in State, consultant 1981-; Lockhart Tech Acad, board member 1984-86; Texas Southern Chapter of Phi Delta Kappa; Houston Chapter Jack & Jill of Amer, former treasurer, chaplain 1st vice president & president; Humble-Intercontinental Chapter Top Ladies of Distinction; Houston Chapter Natl Women of Achievement; member, Alpha Kappa Alpha Sorority; member, National Alliance of Black School Educators, 1988-; member, Assn for Teacher Educators, 1986-; member, Assn for Supervision & Curriculum Development, 1987-. **Honors/Awds:** Publication in Texas Tech Journal of Educ 1984; publication in Journal of Educational Equity 1985; appeared in Black History in the Making, Vol 1 Published by Riverside Hospital Houston, TX; Learning Styles of Urban Children, Texas Southern University, 1990. **Business Addr:** Associate Prof of Education, Texas Southern Univ, 3100 Cleburne, Houston, TX 77004.

GOODEN, DWIGHT EUGENE
Professional baseball player. **Personal:** Born Nov 16, 1964, Tampa, FL. **Career:** New York Mets, pitcher 1984-94; New York Yankees, 1996-97; Cleveland Indians, 1998-. **Honors/Awds:** Named Natl League Rookie of Yr by Baseball Writers Assoc of Amer 1984; Led major leagues with 276 strikeouts becoming 1st teen-aged rookie ever to lead either AL or NL in strikeouts; ML record with avg 1139 strikeouts per nine innings; set Mets rookie record with 16 strikeouts in game; broke Natl League record for strikeouts in 2 consec games (32); set major league record with 43 strikeouts in 3 consult nine inning games; establ Mets record with 15, 10-plus strikeout games; established Mets Club mark for victories in season by a rookie righthander with 17-9 mark; youngest player selected to All-Star Game; twice named NL Player of the Week; Topps Major League Rookie All-Star Team; 1st Met pitcher to throw back to back shutouts; led majors by permitting an average of 975 runners per 9 inns; Honoree Jackie Robinson Award for Athletics; 1985 Cy Young Awd winner (youngest pitcher ever to receive awd); Sporting News NL Pitcher of the Year; named Male Athlete of the Year by Associated Press 1985; named New York Athlete of the Year SportsChannel 1985; National League All-Star Team 1984, 1985, 1986, 1988. **Business Addr:** Professional Baseball Player, Cleveland Indians, 2401 Ontario, Cleveland, OH 44115, (216)420-4200.

GOODEN, SAMUEL ELLSWORTH. See Obituaries section.

GOODEN, WINSTON EARL
Educator. **Educ:** Muskingum College, BA; Yale Univ, MDiv, MS, PhD. **Career:** Two Churches in CT, pastored; Unoja Juvenile Program, co-founder & director; Univ of IL at Chicago, asst prof; Fuller Theological Seminary, asst prof. **Honors/Awds:** Published many articles; presented papers across the nation. **Business Addr:** Asst Prof of Psychology, Fuller Theological Seminary, 135 N Oakland, Pasadena, CA 91101.

GOODING, CUBA, JR.
Actor. **Personal:** Born Sep 2, 1968, Bronx, NY; married Sara Kapfer, 1994; children: Spencer, Mason. **Career:** Movies include: Boyz N the Hood; Champion; Lightening Jack; Gladiators; A Few Good Men; Outbreak; Losing Isaiah; Jerry Maguire; Ishmael; What Dreams May Come; A Murder of Crows; television credits include: ''Murder Without Motive: The Edmund Perry Story,'' 1992; ''Daybreak,'' HBO special, 1993; ''The Tuskegee Airmen,'' HBO Movie, 1995. **Honors/Awds:** 69th Annual Academy Awards, Oscar winner, Best Supporting Actor in Jerry Maguire, 1996. **Business Addr:** Actor, c/o William Morris Agency, 151 El Camino Dr, Beverly Hills, CA 90212, (310)556-2727.

GOODLOE, CELESTINE WILSON
Educational administrator. **Personal:** Born May 7, 1954, Brooklyn, NY; married John W Goodloe Jr; children: Jasmine R, Courtney M. **Educ:** Bennett Coll, BS 1976; Miami Univ, MS 1982. **Career:** Bennett Coll, admin counselor 1979-81; Coll of Wooster, asst dir, coordinator of minority 1982-84; Xavier Univ, assoc dir of admin, 1984-. **Orgs:** OH Assn of Coll admin Counselors, mem 1980-; NACAC, mem 1982, panel participant 1985; Amer Personnel & Guidance Assn, mem 1981-82; Greater Cincinnati Alliance of Black School Educators, vp; Natl Alliance of Black School Educators; OACAC Spring Conference, local arrangement committee, 1994; National Association of Foreign Student Advisors, 1994; Region VI, NAFSA Conference, local arrangements committee, 1996. **Honors/Awds:** Miami Univ, graduate assistantship 1981-82; Bennett Coll, Marie Clapp Moffitt scholarship 1975; Xavier Univ, honored at the black student assn banquet for increasing the number of black students 1986; Xavier Univ, Advisor of the Year, 1993-94. **Business Addr:** Assoc Director of Admissions, Xavier University, 3800 Victory Pkwy, Cincinnati, OH 45207-5311.

GOODMAN, GEORGE D.
Association executive. **Personal:** Born Sep 13, 1940, Saginaw, MI; son of Thelma Kaigler Goodman and George V Goodman; married Judith A Mansfield; children: George, Mark. **Educ:** BA 1963; MA 1970. **Career:** Eastern Michigan Univ, instr 1967-68; Univ Michigan, asst dir admissions 1968-73; Opportunity Program, dir 1973-82; City Ypsilanti, mayor 1972-82; exec dir, Michigan Muncipal League, currently. **Orgs:** Chairman, United Way of Michigan Board, 1994-96; National Governing Board, Common Cause, 1990-94; trustee, Starr Commwealth Schools, 1983-92; mem Emanon Club 1967-; life mem Alpha Phi Alpha

Frat; mem United Way of Michigan Bd of Dir 1987-; mem Ann Arbor Summer Festival Bd 1988-96. **Honors/Awds:** Distinguished Serv Award Ypsilanti Area Jaycees 1973; Public Serv Achievement Award Common Cause 1987. **Military Serv:** US Army, capt 1963-67. **Business Addr:** Executive Dir, Michigan Municipal League, 1675 Green Rd, PO Box 1487, Ann Arbor, MI 48105.

GOODMAN, HAROLD
Company executive. **Personal:** Born Jun 3, 1954, Beaumont, TX; son of Harold C Sr & Gloria Lee Goodman; married Jean, Jun 7, 1980; children: Harold P, Winston E. **Educ:** Prairie View A&M Univ, BA, mgt, 1976, MBA, mgt, 1978. **Career:** Federal Express, mgr station ops, 1982-84, sr ramp mgr, Houston Metro Dist, 1985-89, sr district mgr, IAH Dist, 1989-91, managing dir, 1991-. **Orgs:** Oakland Chamber of Commerce, bd of dirs, 1994-; Oakland PIC, bd of dirs, 1991-93; Oakland Convention & Visitor's Bureau, bd of dirs, 1991-93. **Business Addr:** Managing Dir, Federal Express Corp, 1 Sally Ride Way, Oakland, CA 94621.

GOODMAN, JAMES ARTHUR, SR.
Educational administrator. **Personal:** Born Apr 22, 1933, Portsmouth, VA; son of Viola James Goodman and Accie Goodman; married Gwendolyn Jones, Apr 12, 1956; children: James A Jr, Rhonda. **Educ:** Morehouse Coll, Atlanta GA, AB, 1956; Atlanta Univ, Atlanta GA, MSW, 1958; Univ of Minnesota, Minneapolis MN, PhD, 1967. **Career:** Natl Acad of Sciences, Inst of Medicine, Washington DC, sr professional assoc, 1973-75; Univ of Minnesota, School of Social Work, Minneapolis MN, prof, dir, 1975-77; State Dept, Office of Intl Training, Washington DC, dir, 1977-79; Inst of Public Mgmt, Washington DC, exec vice pres, 1979-83; Morehouse School of Medicine, Atlanta GA, exec vice pres, 1980-89, pres, 1989-. **Orgs:** Natl Accreditation Comm, Council on Social Work Educ; Natl Assn of Social Workers; Acad of Certified Social Workers; Council on Social Work Educ; Amer Sociological Assn; mem, bd of dir, Atlanta Urban League, 1981-88, HealthSouth Inc, 1982-88; mem, DeKalb County Hospital Authority, 1984-88, Natl Advisory Council on Educ for Health Professionals, 1985-89, Rotary Intl. **Honors/Awds:** Editorial Advisory Bd Mem, Mental Health Digest, 1971-73; author of ''The Health Community: Perspective for the Future,'' 1973; author of The Dynamics of Racism in Social Work Practice, 1973; author of ''The Social Health of Disadvantaged Black Coll Students,'' Amer Journal of Coll Health, 1974; author of ''Race and Reason in the 1980's,'' Social Work, 1975; Oustanding Achievement, Atlanta Medical Assn, 1985; delivered the Dean Brailsford Brazeal Lecture, Morehouse Coll, 1986; Outstanding Contribution to Medical Educ, Natl Assn of Medical Minority Educ, 1988; Frankie V Adams Award for Excellence, Atlanta Univ, 1988; Fanon Scholar, Charles Drew Postgraduate Medical School. **Business Addr:** President, Morehouse School of Medicine, 720 Westview Dr SW, Atlanta, GA 30310-1495.

GOODMAN, ROBERT O., JR.
Military officer. **Personal:** Born Nov 30, 1956, San Juan, Puerto Rico; son of Marylyn Joan Dykers Goodman and Robert Oliver Goodman Sr; married Terry L Bryant Goodman, Jun 2, 1979; children: Tina, Morgan. **Educ:** US Naval Academy, Annapolis MD, Bachelors Operations Analysis 1978; US Nava l Post Graduate School, Monterey, CA, Masters Systems Technology (Space) 1987. **Career:** US Navy, A6E Intruder Bombadier/Navigator, currently. **Military Serv:** USN, lieutenant commander 1978-.

GOODRICH, HAROLD THOMAS
Educator (retired). **Personal:** Born Aug 1, 1931, Memphis; married Verastine Goodrich; children: Ivan DeWayne, Michael Rene. **Educ:** LeMoyne-Owen Coll, BS 1956; Memphis State Univ, MA 1969; additional studies, 1974. **Career:** Mitchell High School, Memphis, English teacher, 1956-65; coord 1965-67; Adult Basic Ed, teacher 1966; supvr of instructors, 1967-74; Title I Consult & Bolivar City, 1967-70; Adult Basic Educ, supvr 1967-69; Consult AV 1971; Natl Technical Corps, team leader, 1972-74; Capleville Elem, teacher, 1974-76; Ross Elem, teacher, 1976-80; Crump Elem, teacher, 1980-85; retired, 1985. **Orgs:** Chmn mem Vis Com of Southern Assn of Coll & Schls 1974-76; delegate to NEA 1971, 74; mem NEA, TEA, WTEA, SCEA, TASCD, AECT, ASCD, Dem, Omega Psi Phi; vice pres GAIA Investment Club; deacon, mem finance com, mem housing com Mt Vernon Bapt Ch. **Honors/Awds:** Recipient, Phi Delta Kappa Award 1969; Outstanding Educator in Amer for 70's. **Military Serv:** AUS pfc hon gd 1953-55.

GOODRICH, THELMA E.
Insurance broker. **Personal:** Born Apr 19, 1933, New York, NY; daughter of Evelyn Goodrich and James Goodrich; married Lawrence Hill, Jan 24, 1960. **Educ:** Baruch City Coll, New York NY, Assoc Degree, 1952; Coll of Insurance, New York NY, Certificate, 1960; Coll of New Rochelle, New York NY, attended, 1985; Empire State Coll, New York NY, attending. **Career:** Fay Weintraub-Sterenbuck, New York NY, sec, 1953; Thelma E Goodrich, New York NY, owner/mgr, 1959; Goodrich/Johnson Brokerage, New York NY, pres, CEO, 1980-. **Orgs:** Dir, United Mutual Life Insurance Co, 1983-86, New York Porperty Fire Insurance Org, 1983-; treasurer, East Harlem Reinvestment Group, 1985-; dir, Aaron Davis Hall, 1987-, 100 Black Women, 1987-; pres, Harlem Business Alliance, 1989; dir, Professional Insurance Agents, 1989, Council of Insurance Brokers, 1989, Greater Harlem Real Estate Bd, 1989; 1st vp, New York Club, Natl Assn of Negro Business & Professional Women Club Inc, 1989. **Honors/Awds:** Business, Iota Phi Lambda Sorority, 1975; Business, New York City Negro Business & Professional Women, 1978; Insurance Broker, Council of Insurance Brokers, 1980; Community Serv, Insurance Women of New York State; Community Serv, New York City Business & Professional Women, 1988; Community Serv, New York State Black & Public Relations Caucus, 1989.

GOODSON, ADRIENNE M.
Professional basketball player. **Personal:** Born Oct 19, 1966, Jersey City, NJ; daughter of Margo and Ralph Feuker. **Educ:** Old Dominion Univ, bachelor's degree in marketing, 1989. **Career:** Banco de Credito (Brazil), forward, 1991-92; Unimed (Brazil), 1992-94; Ponte Preta (Brazil), 1994-95; Seara (Brazil), 1995-96; Atlanta Glory, 1996-98; Philadelphia Rage, 1998-. **Business Addr:** Professional Basketball Player, Philadelphia Rage, 123 Chestnut St, First Flr, Philadelphia, PA 19106, (215)629-1976.

GOODSON, ANNIE JEAN
Government official. **Personal:** Born in Camp Hill, AL; married Adolph. **Educ:** AL State U, BS (cum laude) 1954; Fisk U, grad study 1956; Howard Univ Sch of Soc Work, MSW 1962. **Career:** Family Serv Adminstrn, acting adminstr 1980-; DC Dept of Human Resrcs, dep bur chief 1976-80; DC Dept of Human Svcs, chief spl serv div 1971-76; Med Eval & Rehab Svcs, chief 1967-71; St Elizabeths Hosp, psychiatric soc wrkr 1962-67; DC Dept of Pub Welfare, caseworker 1958-60; DC Children's Ctr, tchr 1957-58; E Highland HS Sylocauga AL, pub sch tchr 1954-56. **Orgs:** Adv bd Washington DC UpJohn Homemaker Servs; mem Nat Assn of Soc Workers; Acad of Certfd Soc Wrkrs; mem John Wesley AME Zion Ch; Delta Sigma Theta Inc Sor; pres Montgomery Co Alumnae Chap Delta Sigma Theta Inc 1975-77. **Honors/Awds:** Nom Fed Woman's Award 1975; Soror of Yr Award Delta Sigma Theta Sor 1975; Phelps-Stokes Flwshp Cert Grp Therapy St Elizabeths Hosp. **Business Addr:** 122 C St NW, Washington, DC 20001.

GOODSON, ERNEST JEROME
Orthodontist. **Personal:** Born Dec 16, 1953, Concord, NC; married Patricia Timmons, Nov 17, 1984; children: Ernest Jerome Jr (Sonny), Aaron Timmons. **Educ:** Univ of NC Chapel Hill, BSD 1976, Sch of Dentistry DDS 1979; Univ of London Royal Dental Hosp, Fellowship of Dental Surgery 1980; Univ of CA-San Francisco, MS 1984. **Career:** Central Piedmont Comm Coll, faculty 1980; Pasquotank-Perquimans- Cander- Chowan Dist Health Dept, dir of dental servs; Univ North Carolina School of Dentistry, adjunct faculty 1981-82; Elizabeth City State Univ, lecturer math 1981-82; Nash-Edgecombe-Halifak Counties, dir of dental serv, 1984-85; Fayetteville State Univ, lecturer math 1985-86; private practice, orthodontist. **Orgs:** Tutor First Baptist Math-Science Tutorial Prog 1986-; vice pres Minority Health Professionals; Cumberland Co ABC board member appointment 1990-94; foundation board member Fayetteville State Univ; advisory board memeber United National Bank; Leap Community Advisory Board; bd of dir, Fayetteville Museum of Art, 1994-; NC Teaching Fellows Bd, appointed by Governor Hunt, 1994-; Comm of Health Services, Dentist rep, 1993-. **Honors/Awds:** Acad of General Dentistry Scholarship 1985; rsch and publications ''Detection and Measurement of Sensory Illusions'' with Dr Barry Whitsell and Dr Duane Dryer, Dept of Physiology, Univ of NC, School of Medicine and School of Dentistry; ''The London Experience'' Dental Student 1981; ''Dental Education in England'' The Dental Asst 1981; ''Orthodontics for the Public Health Dentist'' NC Dental Public Health 1986. **Business Addr:** Orthodontist, 950 S McPherson Church Rd, Fayetteville, NC 28303.

GOODSON, FRANCES ELIZABETH
Educational administrator, author, poet. **Personal:** Born in Nashville, TN; married David Goodson; children: Shereen, David Hughes. **Educ:** Hofstra Univ, Admin Eval Seminar 1978, Negotiations Seminar 1979; Natl Assn of Educ Negotiators, Negotiations Seminar 1980; Computer Educ, Management Seminar 1980; Natl Sch Bd Journal, Public Relations Seminar 1982-83, Admin Eval Workshops 1983-84. **Career:** Roosevelt Council of PTA's, pres 1973-74; Legislative Liaison for Bd of Educ, NYS 1981-; Adv Council to Gov NYS, state human rights 1984-; Roosevelt Public Schools, bd of educ pres. **Orgs:** Mem Adult Basic Educ Bd 1975; pres Bd of Educ 1977-; mem Natl Caucus Black Sch Bd 1978-; mem bd of dirs NCBSBM 1978-80, chairperson election comm1982; mem Elem Educ Accrediation Comm 1983; regional pres Natl Caucus of Black Sch Bd Members 1983, 1984; Gov's appointment on Comm on Child Care 1984-; mem bd of dirs Natl Caucus Blk Bd members; NY State Liaison representing Roosevelt Bd of Educ 1982-; mem State Human Rights Adv Council 1983-84; vice pres Northeast Region Natl Caucus Black Sch Bd members 1983-84; pres Roosevelt Bd of Educ 1981-82; vice pres Roosevelt Bd of Educ 1983-84; pres Roosevelt Bd of Educ 1984-85; Gov's apptmt NYS Comm on Child Care 1985; mem of Natl Political Congress of Black Women; exec vice pres Natl Caucus of Black School Bd Members1986-87, 1987-88; campaign coordtor, for county executive republican party, 1989; member task force, New York State assembly 18th AD, 1990. **Honors/Awds:** Black Faces in High Places 1979; Outstanding Member Awd NCBSBM 1982, President's Awd of Appreciation 1983; Natl Pres Awd Natl Black Caucus 1983, 1984, 1985; Student Awd Frances E Goodson Awd Est 1980; Democratic Club of Roosevelt Awd 1984; Northeast Region Vice President's Awd NCBSBM 1984; poetry (anthology) Our World's Most Beloved Poems 1985; Natl Woman of the Year Awd 100 Black Men Inc 1985; New York State Senate Commendation Resolution 1985; equalization rate-Roosevelt Public Schools, NYS Legislature law passed, 1988; Nassau Cty proclamation (Ed), Republican Party, 1988; NYS Assembly proclamation for education, 1988. **Home Addr:** 236 Beechwood Ave, Roosevelt, NY 11575.

GOODSON, JAMES ABNER, JR.
Advertising manager. **Personal:** Born Jul 11, 1921, Cuero, TX; married Emma E; children: James III, Theresa Jasper, Johnny L, Jerome K. **Educ:** Metropolitan Coll Los Angeles, 1943; Harold Styles Sch of Radio Announcers, 1952. **Career:** Tire salesman 1940; BF Goodrich, 1944; JAGME Found, pres; Natl Record Newspaper, publisher, pres. **Orgs:** Pres Cosmopolitan Rep Voters Club Inc; mem NAACP 20 yrs, Urban League 25 yrs; mem Hollywood Community Police Council 1977,81, Southside C of C of Los Angeles, Happiness Project, Masonic Lodge, New Hope Baptist Church. **Honors/Awds:** Recipient Exceptional Achievement Awd NAACP 1971; recipient Personal & Professional Achievement Awd Hon Mike Roos 46th Assembly Dist, Hon Maxine Waters 48th Assembly Dist, Hon David Roberts 23rd Senatorial Dist 1980; recipient Cert of Apprec County of Los Angeles 1980; recipient Cert of Commendation Republican Central Comm Los Angeles County 1985; recipient Plaque of Appreciation Young Men's Christian Assoc 1986. **Military Serv:** AUS engr 1945. **Business Addr:** President, Publisher, The Record Publishing Co, 6404 Hollywood Blvd, Hollywood, CA 90028.

GOODSON, LEROY BEVERLY
Physician. **Personal:** Born Feb 11, 1933, Elyria, OH; son of Inez Louise Leach Goodson and Franklin Beverly Goodson; married Evelyn Wimmer Goodson, Aug 27, 1965; children: Earl, Kenneth, Parker. **Educ:** Univ MI, BS 1953-55; Univ MI Med Sch, MD 1955-59; Kenyon Coll, 1951-53. **Career:** St Rita's Hosp, intern 1959-60; Carl S Jenkins, partner 1960-61; Wilberforce Univ, med dir 1960-62; Private Practice, physician 1963-72; Wright Patterson AF Base, 1966-68; Clark Co Drug Control Cnsl, med dir 1971-; Private Practice, physician 1972-; Wright State Univ, consult 1973-; HK Simpson Ctr Maternal Hlth, instr physical diag & anemia 1973-; Wright State Univ, assoc clinical prof family practice 1975-; Alcohol Chem Detox Unit, med dir 1975-83. **Orgs:** Mem Clark Co Med Soc 1960-, sec 1968-70, pres 1971; Comm Hosp Med Staff 1960-, vice pres 1973; OH Acad of Family Physicians 1960-; Hosp Com 1971-; diplomate Amer Bd Family Practice 1973-; mem Operation Big Sister 1968-70, pres bd 1970; Amer Red Cross 1968-71, exec com mem 1969-71; Comm Hosp Bd Mem 1968-71, exec com mem 1969-71; chmn bd Ronez Apt Inc 1972-74; board member, St John's Nursing Home, 1980-; diplomate AMSADD 1989. **Honors/Awds:** Outstanding Serv to Comm Frontiers Intl Inc 1973; Amer Red Cross Serv Awd 1971; Comm Hosp Serv Awd 1971; Alcohol, Drugs & Mental Health, 25 yrs Service Award, 1993. **Military Serv:** AUSMC capt 1961-63. **Business Addr:** Medical Director, Primary Care, PO Box 1228A, Springfield, OH 45501.

GOODSON, MARTIN L., JR.
Educator. **Personal:** Born Feb 14, 1943, Boligee, AL; children: Monique. **Educ:** Stillman Coll, BS 1964; IN State Univ, MS 1970; IN Univ, EdD 1975. **Career:** Rochelle High School, Lakeland FL, biology teacher 1964-65; Druid High School Tuscaloosa, physics teacher 1965-66; Seagrams Distilling Inc, lab technician 1967; IN State Univ, instructor 1970-72; AL A&M Univ Huntsville, assoc prof 1975-77; Delta Coll MI, assoc prof. **Orgs:** Consult Amer Inst Physics 1973-75; outside Coll Univ Ctr MI 1977-; Outside evaluator Proj Impact throughout state of IN 1973-75; consult & evaluator POT Modules 1973-75; keeper of records & seals Omega Psi Phi Frat 1963-64; pres NAACP Terre Haute 1970-72; adv IN State Univ 1968-75; sec Omega Psi Phi Frat 1963-; bd mem Amer Baptist Theol Sem 1978-; mem Phi Delta Kappa 1974-; mem Natl Assn of Rsch in Sci Teaching; Phi Delta Kappa; AL State pres Natl Pres New Farmers Assn 1959-60. **Honors/Awds:** Woodrow Wilson Flwshp 1964; ''The Effect of Objective-Based Diagnostic Test on Physical Science Students'' Journal of Coll Science Tchng 1978. **Military Serv:** ROTC Tuskegee Inst 1959-62. **Business Addr:** Associate Professor, Delta Coll, University Center, MI 48710.

GOODWIN, CURTIS LAMAR
Professional baseball player. **Personal:** Born Sep 30, 1972, Oakland, CA. **Career:** Baltimore Orioles, outfielder, 1995; Cincinnati Reds, 1996-97; Colorado Rockies, 1998-. **Business Addr:** Professional Baseball Player, Colorado Rockies, 1700 Broadway, Ste 2100, Denver, CO 80290, (303)292-0200.

GOODWIN, DELLA MCGRAW

Educator, nurse administator. **Personal:** Born Nov 21, 1931, Claremore, OK; daughter of Allie Mae Meadows and James Edward McGraw. **Educ:** Dunbar Junior College, Little Rock, AR, AA, 1952; Freedmen's Hospital School Nursing, Washington, DC, registered nurse, 1955; Wayne State University, Detroit, MI, BSN, 1960, MSN, 1962. **Career:** Detroit Receiving Hospital, Detroit, MI, hospital head nurse, 1958-60; Boulevard General Hospital, Detroit, MI, director of nursing, 1963-69; Paramedical Services, Detroit, MI, consultant, 1969-70; Wayne County Community College, Detroit, MI, chair, nursing, 1970-82, dean, nursing & health, 1982-86. **Orgs:** President chief executive officer, National Center for the Advancement of Blacks in Health Professions, 1988-; chair, Detroit Substance Abuse Council, 1981-; Health Brain Trust, Michgian Legislative Black Caucus, 1988-; Cabinet on Nursing Education, American Nurses Association, 1984-88. **Honors/Awds:** Induction Academy of Black Women in the Health Professions, 1991; Bertha Lee Culp Human Rights Award, Michigan Nurses Assn, 1985; Headliners Award, Women of Wayne, 1974; Distinguished Educator Award, College Alumni Wayne County Community College, 1980; National African-American Leadership Award, New Detroit Inc, 1992. **Home Addr:** 19214 Appoline, Detroit, MI 48235.

GOODWIN, DONALD EDWARD

Engineer. **Personal:** Born May 5, 1949, Detroit, MI; son of Thelma L Goodwin and James A Goodwin; married Patricia Davis, Mar 25, 1972; children: Malik, Idris, Layla. **Educ:** University of Michigan, BS, mechanical engineering, 1971; University of Michigan-Dearborn, Master's, management, 1978. **Career:** Cummins Engine Corp, product engineer, 1971-72; Chrysler Corp, product engineer, 1972-73; Ford Motor Co, product engineer, brakes & other, 1973-76; Pontiac Division of GM, project engineer, 1976-79; Ford Motor Co, supervisor, powertrain reliability & other, 1979-85; Chrysler Corp, manager, engineering quality & reliability assurance, 1985-89, manager, restraints engineering, 1989-92, executive engineer, LCP interior engineering, 1992-94; Proving Grounds & Durability Testing, exec eng, 1994-. **Orgs:** Engineering Society of Detroit, 1990-; American Society for Quality Control, 1985-91; NAACP, 1989-; bd mem, Washtenaw United Way, 1996-. **Honors/Awds:** Detroit YMCA, Minority Achiever Award, Chrysler Corp, 1989; Dollars and Sense Magazine, America's Best and Brightest Men, 1996. **Business Addr:** Executive Engineer, Chrysler Corp, Chelsea Proving Grounds, CIMS 422-01-03, 3700 South M-52, Chelsea, MI 48118-9600.

GOODWIN, E. MARVIN

Educator. **Personal:** Born Sep 5, 1936, Chicago, IL; married Ann M Hudson; children: Pamela Denise, Eric Winston, Marvin E II. **Educ:** Chicago State Univ, BA History 1970, MA History, Pol Sci 1972; Fulbright Scholar, 1983. **Career:** AB Dick Co, chief admin clerk 1968-72; Kennedy-King Coll, asst prof of history 1972-83, title III coord 1978-81, coll registrar 1985-, history prof, social sci 1984-. **Orgs:** History consult Chicago Metro-History Fair 1976-83; sr consult Ed Mgmt Assoc 1981-85; pres Assoc for the Study of Afro-Amer Life & History 1982-; mem IntlHistory Honor Sco Phi Alpha Theta, Amer Assoc for Higher Ed, Phi Theta Kappa. **Honors/Awds:** Fulbright Scholarship US Dept of Ed 1983; "Black Migration An Uneasy Exodus" publ by ERIC 1984. **Military Serv:** USAF airman 2nd class 1955-58. **Business Addr:** Prof of History, Social Sci, Kennedy-King College, 6800 South Wentowrth, Chicago, IL 60621.

GOODWIN, EVELYN LOUISE

Personnel administrator. **Personal:** Born May 20, 1949, Columbus, GA; daughter of Annie Hinton Goodwin and Alfred Goodwin Jr. **Educ:** Tuskegee Univ, BS 1971; USAF Air Command and Staff Coll, graduate 1982; Webster Univ, MA 1985. **Career:** Military Airlift Command USAF, labor relations officer 1982-84; Air Force Office of Personnel, personnel administrator 1984-85; Secretariate of the Air Force, personnel administrator; USAF Appellate Review Agency, hearings examiner/complaints analyst, currently. **Orgs:** Vice pres Federal Mgrs Assoc Norton AFB Chap 1983-84; public relations officer Tuskegee Airmen Inc San Antonio Chap 1984-85; mem Blacks in Govt; Order of Eastern Star-PHA; Theta Chap Lambda Kappa Mu Sor Inc; pres, Kittyhawk Chapter, Intl Training in Communication, 1989-; mem, Dayton, OH Intergovt Equal Employment Opportunity Council, 1989-. **Honors/Awds:** Martin Luther King Jr Humanitarian Awd; Afro-Culture Workshop Clark AB Philippines 1982.

GOODWIN, FELIX L.

Educator, military officer (retired). **Personal:** Born Nov 24, 1919, Lawrence, KS; son of Lucille Lee Goodwin (deceased) and Felix Goodwin (deceased); married Barbara Gilpin, Aug 15, 1989; children: Cheryl G Washington, Sylvia E, Judith G Barnes. **Educ:** Univ of MD, BS 1958; Univ of AZ, MPA 1965; Univ of AZ, Educ Specialist 1974; Univ of AZ, EdD 1979; School of Journalism, Univ of Wisconsin, Madison, 1961. **Career:** Army 1939-1945; Army Officer 2nd Lt to Lt Col 1945-1969; Univ of AZ, asst prof 1968-69; Univ of AZ, asst to pres 1969-83. **Orgs:** Alpha Phi Alpha; Beta Gamma Sigma business hon; Alpha Delta Delta; Phi Delta Kappa; Kiwanis Intl; NAACP Life Mem; Chmn AZ Bicentennial Comm; past chrmn Pima Cnty Personnel Merit Syst Comm; Pima County Law Enforcement Comm; Natl Urban League; Knights of Columbus Disabled Amer Veterans; Amer Legion; Natl Orig Legal Problem in Educ; Natl Assn Black Schl Educators; Assn of US Army; past chmn Natl Consortium for Black Professional Devel. **Honors/Awds:** 2 Bronze Letters of Appreciation by Mayor/City Council, Tucson; Certificate of Appreciation/plaque Pima Cnty Bd of Supvrs; Honorary Citizen of Sierra Vista, AZ, 1st Sr Distinguished Serv Award, Alpha Phi Alpha Fraternity, Distinguished Serv Awards for Serv in the Western Region; Alpha Phi Alpha Fraternity. **Military Serv:** US Army lt col; Legion of Merit, Meritorious Serv Medal, Army Commendation Medal, Oak Leaf Cluster, Natl Service Defense Medal. **Home Addr:** 5408 N Indian Trail, Tucson, AZ 85715.

GOODWIN, HUGH WESLEY

Clergyman. **Personal:** Born May 6, 1921, Steelton, PA; married Frances Jones; children: Hugh Jr, Paul Kelley, Anna Euphemie, Tom. **Educ:** Howard Univ Wash DC, BA 1939-43; Harvard Law Schl Cambridge MA, LLB 1945-48. **Career:** Private Prac 1949-67; Fresno Cty CA, asst pub def 1967-76; Fresno CA, judge of municipal ct 1976-79; Follow Up Ministries, prison ministries 1979-. **Military Serv:** Infantry Quartermaster 2nd lt 1943-45. **Business Addr:** Minister, 3160 W Kearney Blvd, Fresno, CA 93706.

GOODWIN, JAMES OSBY

Attorney. **Personal:** Born Nov 4, 1939, Tulsa, OK; married Vivian Palm; children: Jerry, Davey, Anna, Jeanne, Joey. **Educ:** Univ of Notre Dame, BA 1961; Univ of Tulsa, JD 1965. **Career:** Atty; OK Eagle Newsppr, publisher. **Orgs:** Chmn Tulsa Human Srvc Agncy 1978-80; bd chmn Tulsa Comprhnsv Hlth Ctr 1973; mem Tulsa City Co Bd of Hlth; mem OK Bar Assn; Am Trial Lawyers; sec, vice pres OK Trial Lawyers; mem Tulsa Co Bar Assn; Tulsa Co Legal Aid; ACLU Award for Serv as Chmn Tulsa City Co Bd of Hlth 1975. **Honors/Awds:** Award for Serv as mem bd chmn Tulsa Comprehensive Hlth Ctr 1973.

GOODWIN, JESSE FRANCIS

City official. **Personal:** Born Feb 7, 1929, Greenville, SC; son of Frances Byrd Goodwin and Jesse Goodwin (deceased); children: Gordon Francis, Paula Therese, Jesse Stephen. **Educ:** Xavier Univ, BS Pharm 1951; Wayne Univ, MS 1953, PhD 1957. **Career:** Wayne State Univ Clge Med, res assc 1958-59; Wayne Cty Gen Hosp; clin biochem 1959-63; Gen Clin Res Ctr Childrens Hosp Wayne State Univ Sch Med, lab dir 1963-73; Detroit Health Dept, dir labs 1973-. **Orgs:** Pres Gamma Lambda Chap Alpha Phi Alpha Frat 1972-76; bd trustees Horizon Health Systems 1982-, Detroit Osteopathic Hosp Corp 1980-, Marygrove Coll 1977-93; 1st vice pres Det Branch NAACP 1982-84, 2nd vice pres 1978-82; commissioner MI Toxic Substance Control Commn 1986-89; bd dirs MI Catholic Conf 1986-89; bd dirs Amer Assoc for Clinical Chemistry 1987-90; board of directors Natl Acad Clinical Biochemistry 1987; Detroit Archdiocesan Educ, advisory comm, 1993-; Loyola High School, bd of trustees, 1993-. **Honors/Awds:** Chrmn MI Section AACC 1964; author 36 Sci Publ 1958-; Distg Serv Award Detroit Branch NAACP 1983. **Business Addr:** Dir of Laboratories, Detroit Health Dept, 1151 Taylor, Room 150C, Detroit, MI 48202.

GOODWIN, KELLY OLIVER PERRY

Clergyman. **Personal:** Born Dec 24, 1911, Washington, DC; son of Martha Gertrude Duncan Goodwin and Oliver Perry Goodwin; married Emmalene E Hart Goodwin, Dec 24, 1940. **Educ:** Howard Univ DC, AB 1935; United Theol Sem, MDiv 1943; Shaw U, DD 1960; NC Bapt Hosp & Bowman Gray, Med Cert 1948. **Career:** Zion Bapt Ch Reading PA, pastor 1936-47; Mt Zion Bapt WS NC, pastor 1946-77; WS St Univ NC, chaplain 1958; WS NC, commissioner of Public Housing 1958-77; WS Human Relations Commission, 1st Chmn 1978-80; Housing Task Force, chm 1984-85; Cedar Grove Bapt Ch, pastor 1970-. **Orgs:** Past pres WS Bapt Min Conf & Asso; past pres Forsyth Ministers Flwshp; A Fdr WS Day Care Asso & Past Pres; adv cncl WS Chronical (Wkly Paper); bd Mem WS Patterson Ave YMCA; bdmem Old Hickory Cncl BSA; A Mem Natl Asso Housing & Redev Officials; A Bd/Mem NAACP Local & St; bd mem Crisis Control Ministry W-S, W-S Industries for the Blind. **Honors/Awds:** Silver Beaver BSA Old Hickory Cncl NC; Ford Fndtn Grant Urban Training Ctr Chicago IL; Lily Fndtn Grant VA Union Univ Richmond PA; WS Dstgshd Citizen Award Sophisticated Gents 1985; Charles McLean Community Service Award, Sara Lee Corp, 1989. **Home Addr:** 501 W 26th St, Winston-Salem, NC 27105.

GOODWIN, MARIA ROSE

Historian. **Personal:** Born Aug 27, 1950, Washington, DC; daughter of Sarajane Cohron & Thomas Cephas Goodwin. **Educ:** George Washington University, MFA, 1974. **Career:** National Endowment for the Arts, prog specialist, 1974-89; US Mint, historian, 1989-. **Orgs:** National Genealogical Society, counselor, 1996-98; Treasury Historical Association, vice pres, 1996-98; Organization of American Historians, 1990-; Smithsonian Institution, volunteer staff, 1974-; Daughters of Dorcas, 1990-; Society for History in the Federal Government, 1991-; African-American Hist & Genealogical Society, guest speaker, 1996-. **Honors/Awds:** Smithsonian Institution, Volunteer Appreciation; Smithsonian/Anacostia, Ujim's Awd. **Special Achievements:** Co-author, Guide to Black Washington, 1989-; Founder, Family Heritage Group, Anacostia Museum, 1988-95; Lecturer & Writer on conducting African-American Geneology Research; author of The Bones-Keeper's Journal, An African-American Geneology Sourcebook; Co-Director "Hidden History Church Proj," Hist Society of Washington DC, 1990-92. **Business Addr:** Historian, US Mint, 633 3rd St NW, 7th Fl, Washington, DC 20220, (202)874-6210.

GOODWIN, MARTIN DAVID

Journalist. **Personal:** Born May 1, 1964, Tulsa, OK; son of Vivian Edwina Palm Goodwin and James Osby Goodwin; married Angela Denise Davis Goodwin, Oct 27, 1990. **Educ:** Benedictine College, Atchison, KS, BA (2), 1986. **Career:** The Oklahoma Eagle, Tulsa, OK, reporter, copy editor, 1983-86; The Ithaca Journal, Ithaca, NY, reporter, copy editor, 1986-88; The Courier-Journal, Louisville, KY, reporter; USA Today, rewrite editor and editorial page asst, 1995-96; The Courier Journal, asst metro editor and Indiana state editor, 1996-. **Orgs:** Scholarship committee member, National Association of Black Journalists, 1986-; president, Louisville Association of Black Communicators, 1988-. **Honors/Awds:** Society of Professional Journalists Award; Best of Gannett Award; Poynter Institute for Media Studies, Fellow, 1992. **Business Addr:** Editor, Metro Desk, The Courier-Journal, 525 W Broadway, Louisville, KY 40202, (502)582-4247.

GOODWIN, MERCEDIER CASSANDRA DE FREITAS

City official. **Personal:** Born in Chicago, IL; daughter of Dr Berneyce de Freitas and Dr Clement de Freitas; married Attorney Quentin J Goodwin, Apr 20, 1957; children: Dr Horace Milano Mellon. **Educ:** Lincoln Univ Jefferson MO, BHE 1944; Chicago Tchrs Clg Chicago IL; De Paul Univ Chicago IL, MA 1961; Northern IL Univ De Kalb, Il, EdD 1974; Harvard Univ, John F. Kennedy School of Govt, summer 1976. **Career:** Central YMCA Comm Clg Chicago, inst in ed 1961-64; Argo, Summit, Bedford Park Summit IL dir of spec ed & principal, 1964-68; IL Tchrs Clg Chicago IL instr, 1965-66; Garfield Sch, Blue Island IL, prin, 1968-69; Graves Sch, Bedford Pk, IL, prin, 1969-71, dir of spec ed, 1970-73; Walker Sch, Bedford Pk IL, prin, 1971-75; Mayor of Chicago, Office of Employment & Training, dep dir, 1975-81; City of Chicago, IL, Dept of Health/Bd of Health, spec asst to commr 1981-90, Chicago Dept of Transportation, asst commissioner, 1990-. **Orgs:** Mem, Exec Women 1981-; chp, Early Outreach, Comm Urban Hlth Prog, Univ of IL Med Ctr Chicago 1978-; mem, Comm of Visitors, Northern IL Univ 1978-; mem, Pres Carter's Youth Motivation Task Force on "Bridging the Gap between Education and Labor" (conduct seminars at major universities); bd mem, Forum for Black Public Administrtors, 1990-; mem, American Public Works Assn, 1990-; Circle - Lets Chicago Chapter, 1959-; mem, Mayors Chicago Comm on Animal Care and Control, 1978-; Mem, 1st Ill State Bd of Ed, 1974-80. **Honors/Awds:** Recipient of & listed in Alive Black Women publ tribute from members of Western Region Iota Phi Lambda Sor Inc Feb 1980; Dist Alum Awd DePaul Univ 1976; selected 2nd woman mem of Spring Conf, 1976; selected to serve on Dept of Labor Comm for selection of CETA Woman of Yr, 1975; recd Intl Woman of Yr Awd in Govt, 1975; Top Black Females of Achievement in Government and Education, Ebony and Black Enterprise Magazines, 1975. **Home Addr:** 601 E 32nd St, #910, Chicago, IL 60616. **Business Addr:** Assistant Commissioner/Director, Community Svcs, Chicago Department of Transportation, 30 N LaSalle, Ste 600, Chicago, IL 60610.

GOODWIN, NORMA J.

Physician, health care administrator. **Personal:** Born May 14, 1937, Norfolk, VA; daughter of Helen Goodwin and Stephen Goodwin. **Educ:** Virginia State Coll, BS 1956; Medical Coll of Virginia, MD 1961. **Career:** Kings County Hospital Center Brooklyn, internship residency 1961-65; Downstate Medical Center, dir clinical asst, asst prof clinical, asst prof medicine 1964-72; Natl Inst of Health, postdoctoral & fellow nephrology 1965-67; Kings County Hospital, Den & State Univ NY, Downstate Medical Center Brooklyn, served; Kings County Hospital, clinical dir hemodialysis unit 1967-69 1969-71; Univ Hospital Downstate Center, attending physician 1968-75; Health & Hospitals Corp, vice pres, sr vice pres 1971-75; Dept Family Practice, clinical asst prof 1972-; Howard Univ School of Business & Public Admin, adjunct prof 1977-; AMRON Mgmt Consult Inc, pres 1976-; Columbia Univ Teachers Coll, adjunct professor. **Orgs:** Mem staff Kings County Hospital Center 1965-; charter mem bd dir NY City Comp Health Planning Agency 1970-72; 2nd vice pres Natl Medical Assn; 1st vice pres Empire State Med Soc State Chapter Natl Medical Assn, sec v speaker & house del 1972-74 exec comm 1974; regional advisory group NY Metro Regional Medical Program; past pres Provident Clinical Soc Brooklyn Inc 1969-72; consultant Dept Health Educ & Welfare; mem Health Serv Research Study Section Dept HEW; chmn com comm med Kings Co Med Soc; 1st vice chmn Bedford Stuyvesant Comp Health Plan Council; mem NY Amer & Intl Soc of Nephrology Amer Public Health Assn; bd trust Atlanta Univ Center; NY Coll of Podiatric Med; bd dir NY Assn Ambulatory Care; NY Heart Assn; Public Health Assn NYC; bd dir mem AmerRed Cross of Greater NY; past mem lth Sci

Careers Advisory Comm; LaGuardia Comm Coll City Univ of NY; mem Natl Assn C omm Health Centers Inc; mem Med Adv Bd on Hypertension New York City Health Dept; mem Leg Comm Med Soc Co of Kings; subcom Hospital Emer Servs Med Soc Co of Kings; mem Task Force Emer Med Care NY St Health Plan Comm; founder & pres, Health Watch Information and Promotion Service Inc, 1987-. **Honors/Awds:** Natl Found Fellow 1958; Jesse Smith Noyes & Smith Douglas Scholarships; mem Alpha Kappa Mu Natl Honor Soc; Beta Kappa Chi Natl Science Honor Soc; Soc Sigma Xi; author or co-author of more than 30 publications; Health Watch News, brochures on cancer and AIDS; Videos on AIDS. **Business Addr:** President, AMRON Mgmt Consult Inc, 3020 Glenwood Road, Brooklyn, NY 11210.

GOODWIN, ROBERT KERR
Association executive. **Personal:** Born Nov 15, 1948, Tulsa, OK; son of Jeanne B Osby Goodwin and Edward L Goodwin; married Harriette Lott Goodwin, Nov 15, 1984; children: Perry, Sean. **Educ:** Oral Roberts University, Tulsa, OK, BA, 1970; San Francisco Theological Seminary, Marin, CA, MA, 1973. **Career:** Oklahoma Eagle Publishing Co, publisher, 1973-81; National University Society, Houston, TX, regional sales mgr, 1981-85; Prairie View A&M University, Prairie View, TX, assoc vice pres, university relations, 1985-87; Texas A&M University System, College Station, TX, asst deputy chancellor for external affairs, 1987-89; US Dept of Education, White House Initiative on HBCU's, exec dir, 1989-92; Natl Points of Light Foundation, exec vp, 1992-95, pres, 1995-. **Orgs:** Steering committee, John Ben Shepperd Public Leadership Forum; board member, Bryan-College Station Chamber of Commerce; campaign co-chair, Brazos Valley United Way. **Honors/Awds:** Honorary Doctorate of Laws, University of Maryland, Eastern Shore, 1990; Honorary Doctorate of Humane Letters, Le-Moyne-Owens College, 1990; Man of the Year, National Council of Christians and Jews, the youngest recipient of that honor. **Business Addr:** President & CEO, Points of Light Foundation, 1737 H Street NW, Washington, DC 20005.

GOODWIN, ROBERT T., SR.
Business executive. **Personal:** Born Nov 25, 1915, Camden, SC; married Neal McFadden; children: Robert, Jr, Myrna. **Educ:** Tuskegee Inst, MEd 1962; SC State Coll, 1938; PA State U. **Career:** GG&F Devel Co Tuskegee Inst, pres 1973-; Consolidated Constrn Co, owned operated 1957-73; Tuskegee Inst, master instr Building Sci 1968-53; BuildingTrades Pub Schs Lancaster, instr 1945-52; Building Trds Pub Schs Moultrie GA, instr 1938-41. **Orgs:** Pres Tuskegee Area Hm Bldrs Assn; mem SE Alabama Self Help Assn; pres Greenwood Cemetery Inc Tusxkegee Inst Ruling elder Westminster Presb Ch Tuskegee; supt Westminister Presb Ch Sch 1960-65; Polemarch Tuskegee Alumni Chap Kappa Alpha Psi 1967-68. **Honors/Awds:** Hon mention Builder of Hse of Yr 1967 sponsrd by AIA & Better Hms & Grdns; submitted in Nat Competition Wade & Hight Architects; co-designed with son Robert T Jr Goodwin Model SEASHA Home model low cost Housing Brochure. **Military Serv:** AUS t/5 1941-45. **Business Addr:** PO Box 1264, Tuskegee Institute, AL 36088.

GOODWIN, STEPHEN ROBERT
Investment banker. **Personal:** Born Jun 3, 1948, New York, NY. **Educ:** Cornell University, BS, economics, 1970. **Career:** Cartwright & Goodwin, Inc, CEO, president, currently. **Orgs:** National Options & Future Society, board of directors. **Business Addr:** CEO & President, Cartwright & Goodwin, Inc, 67 Wall St, New York, NY 10005-3101, (212)809-0877.

GOODWIN, THOMAS JONES (TOM)
Professional baseball player. **Personal:** Born Jul 27, 1968, Fresno, CA. **Educ:** Fresno State University. **Career:** Los Angeles Dodgers, outfielder, 1991-93; Kansas City Royals, 1994-97; Texas Rangers, 1997-. **Business Addr:** Professional Baseball Player, Texas Rangers, 1000 Ballpark Way, Arlington, TX 76011, (817)273-5222.

GOODWIN, VAUGHN ALLEN. See ABDULLAH, SHARIF.

GOODWIN, WILLIAM PIERCE, JR.
Physician. **Personal:** Born Sep 18, 1949, Harrisburg, PA; son of Joan L Robinson-Goodwin and William P Goodwin Sr; married Gloria Baker, Sep 27, 1980. **Educ:** Dillard Univ New Orleans, BA (Magna Cum Laude) 1972; Meharry Medical Coll, MD 1976. **Career:** Univ of OK, assoc prof 1981-85; Martin Army Community Hospital, resident family practice program 1985-88; Reynolds Army Hospital, Ft Sill OK, family practice; family practice, Ellaville, GA, physician, currently. **Orgs:** Mem National, American Medical Assocs; mem Amer Assoc of Family Practice 1985, Amer Geriatrics Soc 1986; mem, American Academy of Family Physicians. **Honors/Awds:** Alpha Chi 1971; Beta Kappa Chi Natl Honor Soc 1971. **Military Serv:** US Army, Lt Col 12 years; Overseas Ribbon, Service Awd, Army Commendation Medal. **Business Addr:** Physician, Goodwin Family Practice, 7 Broad St, Ellaville, GA 31806-0562, (912)937-5333.

GOOLEY, CHARLES E.
Utility company executive. **Personal:** Born Oct 19, 1953, Chicago, IL; son of Anna Williams Gooley and Henry Gooley; children: Justin, Adam. **Educ:** Trinity College, Hartford, CT, BA, 1975; University of Connecticut, Hartford, CT, JD, 1978. **Career:** City of Hartford, CT, Hartford, CT, asst corporation counsel, 1978-79; State of Connecticut, Hartford, CT, asst attorney general, 1979-81; Northeast Utilities, Berlin, CT, counsel, sr counsel, 1981-87, dir, legal & external affairs, 1987-89; Yankee Energy System, Inc., Meriden, CT, vice president & general counsel, 1989-94; Exec VP, 1994-. **Orgs:** Trustee, Julius Hartt Foundation/Univ of Hartford, 1990-; Regent, Univ of Hartford, 1993; Amer Diabetes Assn, dir, ct affiliate, 1991-. **Business Addr:** Exec VP, Yankee Energy System, Inc, 599 Research Pkwy, Meriden, CT 06450.

GOOSBY, ZURETTI L.
Dentist. **Personal:** Born Oct 19, 1922, Oakland, CA; married Jackieline. **Educ:** Univ Ca; BA 1946, DDS. **Career:** Priv practice 30 yrs. **Orgs:** Mem SF Human Rights Commn 1968-70; mem past pres San Francisco Bd Educ 5 yrs; mem Nat, Am, CA, San Francisco Dental Assns; chmn Prgm Com BlackLdrshp Forum; bd dirs TV & Sta KQED 1973, 74; Exploratorium Museum 1970-75; mem State Commn Educ Mgmt Evaluatn 1973, 1974; mem SF Airports Commission, 1977-90; mem SF War Memorial Board of Trustees, 1991-96. **Honors/Awds:** Man of Yr San Francisco Sun-Reporter 1970; Black Chamber of Commerce, Man of the Year, 1981. **Military Serv:** AUS capt 1943-45. **Business Addr:** 2409 Sacramento St, San Francisco, CA 94115.

GORDEN, FRED A.
Military officer. **Personal:** Born Feb 22, 1940, Anniston, AL; son of Mary Ethel Johnson Harper and P J Gordon; married Marcia Ann Stewart; children: Shawn Nicole, Michelle Elizabeth. **Educ:** US Military Academy (West Point), graduate; Middlebury Coll, M Spanish Language & Literature; Attended, Armed Forces Staff Coll, Natl War Coll. **Career:** 7th Infantry Div, asst div commander; Office of the Assistant Sec of Defense for Intl Security Affairs Washington DC, dir; Army Office of the Chief of Legislative Liaison, exec officer; Division Artillery 7th Infantry Div, commander; Eighth US Army in Korea, artillery battalion exec officer; field artillery battalion commander,25th infantry div; 25th Infantry, div inspector general; US Military Academy, commandant of cadets. **Honors/Awds:** Defense Disting Serv Medal; Legion of Merit; Bronze Star Medal with V Device; Meritorious Serv Medal; Air Medal; Army Commendation Medal w/one Oak Leaf Cluster; Honorary Dr of Human Letters, St Augustine Coll, 1988; Candle in the Dark, Morehouse Coll, 1989; Alumnus of the Year, Amer Assn of Community & Junior Coll, Middlebury Coll, 1988. **Military Serv:** AUS brigadier general. **Business Addr:** Commandant of Cadets, United States Military Acad, West Point, NY 10996.

GORDON, AARON Z.
Educator. **Personal:** Born Oct 11, 1929, Port Gibson, MS; divorced; children: Aaron, Jr, Aaryce, Alyta. **Educ:** Univ Mi, BS 1952; Wayne State U, MA 1956; Univ Mi, PhD 1974. **Career:** Ft Monmouth, Assoc Officers Signal Course 1952; Communications Center Qualification Course, 1952; Teletype Operators School, asst officer in charge; Message Center Clk School, officer in charge; SW Signal School Training Center, Camp San Luis Obispo CA; 3rd Infantry Div AFFE Korea, communication center officer, asst cryptographic officer 1953-54; Br Officers Advance Signal Officers Course, 1963; Command & Gen Staff Coll Ft Levenworth; ICAF, 1974; Air War Coll Maxwell Air Force Base; personnel Officer 1965; S1 5064 USAR Garr, 1967-69; 5032 USAR School, branch officer advanced course instructor 1969-71, dir 1971-73. **Orgs:** Mem Hlth & Curriculum Wrkshp Detroit Pub Schs 1963; co-author Guide to Implementation of Unit of Smiking & Hlth 1963; asst dist ldr E Dist & Dist Ldr 1961-63; com chmn Hlth & Phys Ed Tchrs Inst Day E Dist 1964; sch dist rep Last Two Millage Campaigns Educ TV Tchr Channel 56 Detroit Pub Schs 1964; mem Detroit Orgn Sch Admnstrs & Suprs; Phi Delta Kappa; pgm chmn Detroit Sch Mem's Clu Metro; Detroit Sco Black Educ Admn; Natl All Black Ed; MI Assc Elem Sch Admn Region 1; com mem Midwest Dist AAHPR Conv Detroit 1964; mem Pgmd Educ Soc Detroit 1965; speaker Blue Star Mothers Detroit1963; Carter CME Ch Detroit; bd dir mem Troop 775 BSA 1964; participating guest Focus Negro Life & History Six Wk Work Shop 1967; coordntr Annual Spelling Bee 1967; participant Maximizing-Benefits from Testing Workp Test Admn 1968; participant Ed Admn Workshop 1970-73; dir Professional Skills Dev Workshop Metro Detroit Soc Black Ed Admn Ann Arbor 1973; spkr Hampton Sch Detroit 1973; spkr Joyce Sch Grad 1973. **Honors/Awds:** Bronze Star Decoration; co-holder worlds record Outdoor Distance Medley Relay; co-holder world's record Indoor Distance Medley Relay; co-holder am record Indoor Two Mile & Relay 1951. **Military Serv:** USAR col. **Business Addr:** 15000 Trojan, Detroit, MI 48235.

GORDON, ALEXANDER H., II
Sports administrator. **Personal:** Born Jun 13, 1944, Phoenix, AZ; son of Elizabeth DeLouis Davis Gordon and Alexander Houston Gordon I; married Loretta Perry, Jan 28, 1967; children: David Anthony, Ellen Alicia. **Educ:** Marquette Univ, BA Speech/Radio TV, 1962-67; LaSalle Correspondence School, Diploma, Business Admin 1965-67. **Career:** WTMJ AM FM TV, promotion intern and asst, sales promotion & merchandising director, 1965-69; Avco Broadcasting Corporation, corporate advertising writer, 1969-1970; WLWI TV, promotion and publicity director, 1970-71; WPVI TV, audience promotion director, 1971-72; WPVI TV, manager of advertising, 1972-74; WIIC TV, director of advertising, promotion and publicity, 1974-77; WPXI TV, dir of co mmunity relations, 1977-79; Church of God of Prophecy, asst pastor in training, 1978-79, pastor, 1979-93; WPXI TV, account executive, 1979-87; Pittsburgh Pirates Baseball Club, director, community service and sales, 1988-. **Orgs:** Roberto Clemente Foundation, exec dir, 1997; Petra Ministries, elder, 1995-; Mt Ararat Community Ctr, bd mem, 1992-96; Allegheny Trails Council, Boy Scouts of America, bd mem, 1977-93, 1997-; Urban Scouting Committee, vice chariman-programming, 1990-93, Spring Roundup Recruitment Drive, chairman, 1990, 1991, 1992; Cub Scout Day Camp Committee, chairman, 1977-86; Kingsley Assn, treas/bd mem, 1990-92; Neighborhood Ctrs Assn, bd mem/pres, 1977-83; Pittsburgh Advertising Club, bd mem/vp, 1975-77; Rotary Club of Pittsburgh, chaplain, 1977-80; Braodcasters Promotion Assn, bd mem/treas, 1971-77; The Mews of Towne North Home Owners Assn, pres, 1975-83; United Way of Allegheny County, allocations review committee, 1977-81; Wilkinsburg Community Ministry, bd mem, 1983-87; Three Rivers Youth Inc, bd mem/ vp, 1988-92. **Honors/Awds:** Honorable Pastor Church of God of Prophecy PA 1980-81, 1983-84, 1987; Appreciation Award Allegheny Trails Council Boy Scouts of Am 1985; Clio Awards Comm for Advertising 1975; Golden Reel Award Pittsburgh Radio TV Club 1976; Whitney Young Award for work with minority scouts 1986; Silver Beaver Award, Boy Scouts of America, 1988; Salute to Negro League Baseball, The Homestead Grays and the Pittsburgh Crawfords, 1988; California State Coll Alumni Assn, Special Service Award, 1980; Greater Pittsburgh Council, Boy Scouts of America, Special Appreciation Award, 1993. **Military Serv:** US Army, spec-5, 1966-72; Sharpshooter. **Business Addr:** Dir, Community Serv & Sales, The Pittsburgh Pirates, 600 Stadium Circle, Pittsburgh, PA 15212, (412)323-5089.

GORDON, BERTHA COMER
Educator. **Personal:** Born Feb 27, 1916, Louisville, GA; married Carlton. **Educ:** NY U, BS 1945; Hunter Coll, MA 1955. **Career:** Bronx NY, asst supt 1972-74, supt 1974-78; Eli Whitney Vocational High School, dept head 1962-69, counselor 1952-62; Manhattan School, teacher 1950-52; NY City Dept Hospital, registered nurse 1937-50. **Orgs:** Mem NY City Admin Women in Educ 1970; past pres & life mem NAACP Nat Assn Scdry Assn; Scdrry Sch Prin; NY City Supts Assn; Am Assn Sch Admin; Am Vocat Educ Assn; Am NY State NY City Dist 14 Nurses Assn; Doctorate Assn NY City Edn; exec bd Assn Study African Am Life & Hist Hunter Coll NY Univ Alumni Assn. **Honors/Awds:** Hall of Fame Kappa Delta Pi; pres Gr NY Alumni bd; Club Women's City of NY.

GORDON, BRIDGETTE
Professional basketball player. **Personal:** Born Apr 27, 1967. **Educ:** Tennessee, bachelor's degree in political science. **Career:** Sacramento Monarchs, forward, 1997-. **Honors/Awds:** US Olympic Basketball Team, Gold Medal, 1988; NCAA Championship Most Valuable Player, 1989; Broderick Cup, 1990. **Business Addr:** Professional Basketball Player, Sacramento Monarchs, One Sports Parkway, Sacramento, CA 95834, (916)928-3650.

GORDON, BRUCE S.
Company executive. **Personal:** Born Feb 15, 1946, Camden, NJ; son of Violet Gordon and Walter Gordon; married Genie Alston, Feb 20, 1970; children: Taurin S. **Educ:** Gettysburg Coll, Gettysburg, PA, BA, 1968; Univ of Illinois, Bell Advance Mgmt, 1981; Univ of PA, Wharton Exec Mgmt; MIT Sloan School of Mgmt, Boston, MS, 1988. **Career:** Bell Atlantic Corp, Arlington, VA, init mgmt devel, 1968-70, business officemgr, 1970-72, sales mgr, mktg, 1972-74, personnel supvr, 1974-76, market mgmt supvr, 1976-78, mktg mgr, 1978-80, div staff mgr, 1980-81, div operations mgr, 1981, div mgr, phone center, 1981-83, mktg mgr II, 1983-84, gen mgr, mktg/sales, 1985, vice pres mktg, beginning 1988; Bell Atlantic Network Services, group president retail, 1993-. **Orgs:** Founder and past vice-pres, Alliance of Black Mgrs; member, Toastmasters Intl; member, bd of trustees, Gettysburg Coll; direc, Urban League, 1984-86; member, bd of direcs, Inroads of Philadelphia, 1985-88; chair, United Negro Coll Fund Telethon, 1985-86; volunteer, United Way, 1986-88; The Southern Company, bd of dirs, 1994; Bartech Personnel Svcs, bd of dirs, 1995; Bell Atlantic New Jersey, board of directors; Executive LEadership Council, mem; Urban League, director. **Honors/Awds:** Mass Inst of Tech, Alfred P Sloan fellow, 1987. **Business Addr:** Group Pres, Retail, Bell Atlantic Network Services, 1095 Ave of the Americas, New York, NY 10036.

GORDON, CARL RUFUS
Actor. **Personal:** Born Jan 20, 1932, Richmond, VA. **Educ:** Brooklyn College, 1957-59; Gene Frankel Theatre Workshop, 1965-69. **Career:** Theater appearances include: Day of Absence/Happy Ending, 1966-67; Kongi's Harvest, 1968; Trials

of Brother Jero, 1968; Strong Breed, 1968; One Last Look, 1968; The Great White Hope, 1968; Black Girl, 1971; Ain't Supposed to Die a Natural Death, 1971; The River Niger, 1973-74; The Death of Boogie Woogie, 1979; Zooman and the Sign, 1980; In an Upstate Motel, 1981; Do Lord Remember Me, 1983; The Piano Lesson, 1987; Ma Rainey's Black Bottom; Master Harold & The Boys; We; The Great Macdaddy; Nevis Mountain Dew; The Sixteenth Round; The Brownsville Raid; The Sty of the Blind Pig; Versus the IRS; Of Mill and Men; Checkmates, 1997; film appearances include: Gordon's War, 1973; The Bingo Long Traveling All-Stars and Motor Kings, 1976; The Brother from Another Planet, 1984; No Mercy, 1987television appearances include: One Last Look, 1970; Man in the Middle, 1970; Ed Sullivan Show, with cast of Great White Hope, 1970; Love Is a Many Splendored Thing, 1970; Where the Heart Is; The Murder of Mary Phagan, 1988; Roc; Malcolm & Eddie, 1997; Hanging with Mr Cooper, 1996; NY News, 1995; Can't Hurry Love, CBS, 1994; The Piano Lesson, Hallmark Hall of Fame, 1995; Due South, 1994, Burke's Law, 1993; Crossroads, 1993; Disaster on the Coastliner; As the World Turns, 1991; The Practice, 1997; The Wedding, 1997. **Orgs:** AEA; American Federation of Television & Radio Artists; Screen Actors Guild; Project 2000, advisory bd. **Honors/Awds:** NAACP Theatre Awards, Nomination for Best Supporting Actor, 1991; City of Inglewood, CA, Commendation for Commitment to Performing Arts, 1996; Inst of Musical Arts Award, 1996; City of Los Angeles, Certificate of Recognition, 1996; CA State Senate Award, Recognition of Time and Effort for Youth, 1997; County of Los Angeles Commendation, 1997. **Business Addr:** Actor, Roc Live, Krasny Agency, 1501 Broadway, Ste 1510, New York, NY 10036.

GORDON, CHARLES D.
Housing official. **Personal:** Born Aug 10, 1934, Memphis, TN; married Hazel D Mannings; children: Debra, Charles, Jr, Marshall, Kenneth, Derrick, Carlton. **Educ:** Univ WY; TN State; Hampton Inst; Roosevelt U. **Career:** Chicago Hous Auth, clk, mgmt training prog, asst mgr, hous mgr I, hous mgr II 1961-. **Orgs:** Mem NAHRO; mem Cntrl Southside Comm Workers; bd dir Horizon House; lectr various schs; mem Dist Ii Educ Counc; mem Area A Besea Coun Dep commr hit basketball league, hous invitational tour; bd dir Afro-Am touch football league; bd dir housing bowling leadue. **Honors/Awds:** Won commnr flag beautification grounds within CIIA 1971-74; placed 3rd City Chicago beautif grounds mgr Wentworth Gardens 1974; achvmnt plaque for outstndg achvmnt as hous mgr Comm Wentworth. **Military Serv:** USAF s/sgt 1955-61. **Business Addr:** 3640 S State St, Chicago, IL 60609.

GORDON, CHARLES EUGENE
Educator. **Personal:** Born May 31, 1938, Gallatin, TN; married Barbara Gibbs. **Educ:** History Western MI U, BS 1962; Wayne State U, MEd spl educ for emotion disturbed 1970; Univ of MI, PhD higher educ admin 1976. **Career:** Wayne State Univ, dir Office of Special Student Serv Programs 1970-; Project Upward Bound, dir 1968-70; Detroit Youth Home, boys counselor, supvr 1965-67; Detroit Public Schools, secondary teacher Social Studies, Special Educ 1962-65. **Orgs:** Mem ANWC bd dirs; past pres Region V Trio Adv Coun; past pres MI Coun of Educ opp progs; past exec bd mem Nat Alliance ofr grad & professional Edn;exec bd mem Nat Assn of Minority Financial Aid Admin; numerous professional & bus orgns; mem Am Assn of Higher Edn; Am Pers & Guid Assn; Nat Coord Coun of Educ Opp Progs; Nat Vocat Guid Assn; Mid-West Assn of Educ Opp Prog Personnel; MI Coun of Educ Opp Progs; Nat Alliance for Grad & Professional Edn; Am Educ Res Assn. **Honors/Awds:** Recip Region V citation of merit US Ofc of Edn; Distingd Serv Awd MI Coun of Educ Opp Progs; Outstndg Serv Awd The MI Inter-Assn of Black Bus & Engineering Students; Three-yr Appntmt to Nat Adv Coun on Finan Aid to Sutdents, Hon Casper W Weinberger; pres exec dir Cybernetic Res Systems Inc; author Employer Attitudes in Hiring Culturally Different Youth, Careeer Educ Implications for Counseling Minority Students Career Edn; Short Steps on a Long Journey & The Devel Sys Model as a Tool of Prog Adminst & Eval, several art in professional jour. **Military Serv:** AUS radio operator.

GORDON, CHARLES FRANKLIN
Physician. **Personal:** Born Oct 31, 1921, Ward, AL; married Marion; children: Charles Jr, Jacquelyn, Jan. **Educ:** Fisk U, BA 1943; Meharry Med Coll, MD 1947. **Career:** Self, physician; Golden State Med Assn, bd dir 1972-77; Perris Valley Comm Hosp, 1972-77; Riverside Comm Hosp, 1970-73; LA Co Hlth Dept & LA City Hlth Dept, radiology & pulmonary resd; LA City Hlth Dept; Polemarch Riv Alumni Chap KAY Frat; fndr. **Orgs:** Life mem KAY Frat; pres Perris Rotary Club 1971-72. **Honors/Awds:** 25 yr serv awd Meharry 1972; Perris Comm Serv Awd 1975; 30 yr serv awd KAY Frat 1977. **Military Serv:** AUS MC capt 1954. **Business Addr:** 2226 Ruby Dr, Ste 5, Perris, CA 92570.

GORDON, DARRELL R.
Business executive. **Personal:** Born May 18, 1926, Philadelphia, PA; married Joan. **Educ:** Univ of Pennsylvania, BS. **Career:** Gordon Chrysler-Plymouth-Dodge Inc, pres, bd chmn 1989-. **Business Addr:** President/Bd Chairman, Gordon Chrysler-Plymouth-Dodge, Inc, 899 S Delsea Dr, Vineland, NJ 08360.

GORDON, DARRIEN X. JAMAL
Professional football player. **Personal:** Born Nov 14, 1970, Shawnee, OK; children: Jalil Tanyu Gamnje, Najim Tariq Gamnje. **Educ:** Stanford. **Career:** San Diego Chargers, defensive back, 1993-96; Denver Broncos, 1997-. **Business Addr:** Professional Football Player, Denver Broncos, 13655 Broncos Pkwy, Englewood, CO 80112, (303)649-9000.

GORDON, DEREK E.
Arts administrator. **Personal:** Born Dec 6, 1954, Baton Rouge, LA; son of Deasry Jackson Gordon and Wilson Gordon. **Educ:** Louisiana State Univ, Baton Rouge, LA, BM, Music, 1976; MM, Music, 1977. **Career:** Baton Rouge Arts & Humanities Council, Baton Rouge, LA, comm devt dir, 1976-78; Texas Comm on the Arts, Austin, TX, program associate, 1978-80; Cultural Arts Council of Houston, Houston, TX, asst dir, 1980-85; LA Council on tha Arts, Baton Rouge, LA, exec dir, 1985-89; PA Council on the Arts, Harrisburg, PA, exec dir, 1989-. **Orgs:** 2nd vice pres, Natl Assembly of State Arts Agencies, 1989-; bd mem, Natl Assembly of Local Arts Agencies, 1986-90; bd mem, Southern Arts Federation, 1980-88; board member, Mid Atlantic Arts Foundation, 1989-; panelist/consultant, Natl Endowment for the Arts, 1980-. **Business Addr:** Executive Director, Pennsylvania Council on the Arts, 216 Finance Building, Harrisburg, PA 17120.

GORDON, DWAYNE
Professional football player. **Personal:** Born Nov 2, 1969, White Plains, NY; married Melissa. **Educ:** New Hampshire. **Career:** Atlanta Falcons, linebacker, 1993-94; San Diego Chargers, 1995-96; New York Jets, 1997-. **Business Addr:** Professional Football Player, New York Jets, 1000 Fulton Ave, Hempstead, NY 11550, (516)560-8100.

GORDON, ED
Journalist. **Personal:** marrIed Karen; children: Taylor. **Career:** Black Entertainment Television, journalist; "Dateline NBC," correspondent; MSNBC, host, reporter, currently. **Business Addr:** Host, MSNBC, 1 MSNBC Plaza, Secaucus, NJ 07094, (201)583-5010.

GORDON, EDMUND W.
Educator (retired). **Personal:** Born Jun 13, 1921, Goldsboro, NC; married Susan Gitt; children: EdmUnd T, Christopher W, Jessica G, Johanna S. **Educ:** Howard Univ, BS 1942, BD 1945; Amer Univ, MA 1950; Columbia Univ Tchrs Coll, EdD 1957; Yeshiva Univ, Doctor of Humane Letters, 1986; Brown Univ, Doctor of Humane Letters, 1988; Bank Street Coll, Doctor of Humane Letters, 1992. **Career:** Ferkauf Graduate School Yeshiva Univ, chmn dept of special educ 1959-60; Albert Einstein Coll of Medicine Yeshiva Univ, research, asst prof of pediatrics 1961-68; Project Head Start, dir div of rsch & evaluation 1965-67; Ferkauf Univ, chmn dept of educ, psychology & guidance 1965-68; Columbia Univ, chmn dept of guidance 1968-73; Teachers Coll, dir div of health serv science & educ 1970-73; Amer Journal of Orthopsychiatry, editor 1978-83; "Review of Research in Education", editor 1981-84; John M Musser prof of psychology emeritus, 1991-; CUNY Grad School, distinguished prof, educational psychology, 1992-96. **Orgs:** Fellow, Amer Assn for Advancement of Sci; fellow, Amer Psychol Assn; fellow, Amer Psychol Society; fellow, Orthopsychiatric Assn; life mem, Assn of Black Psychologists; mem AERA; trustee, Public Educ Assn; trustee, Svgs Bank of Rockland Co Monsey. **Honors/Awds:** Awd for Outstanding Achievements in Educ Howard Alumni 1973; elected Natl Acad of Educ 1978; Teachers Coll Medal, Distinguished Service to Education, 1993; AERA Plaque Life; Amer Educational Research Assoc, Distinguished Career Contribution Award, 1994. **Home Addr:** 3 Cooper Morris Dr, Pomona, NY 10970-3309.

GORDON, EDWIN JASON
Publishing executive. **Personal:** Born Oct 10, 1952, Cincinnati, OH; son of Willa Harris Gordon and Nathaniel Gordon; married Gloria Holt Gordon, Feb 14, 1978 (divorced 1980). **Educ:** OH State Univ, Columbus, OH, BS, Accounting, 1974. **Career:** South-Western Publishing, Cincinnati, OH, assoc editor, 1974-84; Harcourt Brace Jovanovich, San Diego, CA, sr acquisitions editor, 1984-87; San Diego State Univ Press, San Diego, CA, dir, 1987-89; Howard Univ Press, Washington, DC, asst dir, 1990-94, acting dir, 1994-95, dir, 1995-. **Orgs:** Assn of American Publishers, 1984-; Assn of American Univ Presses, 1989-; Washington Book Publishers, 1992-; Howard University Development Officers Advisory Council, 1991-. **Honors/Awds:** 89 San Diegans for '89, San Diego magazine, 1989; Getting Into College, Mindblast, Inc, 1982. **Business Addr:** Director, Howard University Press, 1240 Randolph St, NE, Washington, DC 20017.

GORDON, ETHEL M.
Educator (retired). **Personal:** Born Nov 16, 1911, Antreville; married Maxie S Gordon; children: Maxie S, Thomas A. **Educ:** Benedict Coll, BA 1939; Temple Univ, MEd 1955; MI State Univ, further study 1966; Harvard Univ, further study 1969. **Career:** Starr SC, public school teacher 1934-38; Pendelton SC, 1938-42, asst librarian, 1944-45, bookstore mgr, 1945-54; Dept of Elementary Educ, chmn 1955-69; Benedict Coll, elementary teacher trainer 1970-. **Orgs:** Mem World Traveler; NEA; SC Reading Assn; Intl Reading Assn; Assn Tchr Educs; SC Educ Assn; Natl Assn Univ Women; SC Coun of Human Relat; League of Women Voters; mem Queen Esther Chap Eastern Star; mem Sigma Gamma Rho Sor; mem Jack & Jills of Amer Inc; historian Woman's Conv Aux; Natl BaptConv USA Inc; fdr SC Assn Ministers Wives pres 4 yrs; instr Natl Sunday Sch & BTU Cong; mem Phi Delta Kappa Univ SC Chap 1977. **Honors/Awds:** Publ book "Unfinished Business" 1976; "Help the Family In Deep Trouble", 1980; Appreciation Plaque Sr Class Benedict Coll 1966, 1975; Women's Conv Aux to Natl Baptist Conv USA Inc 1971; Hon LLD Morris Coll Sumter SC 1975. **Home Addr:** 2221 Marguerite St, Columbia, SC 29204.

GORDON, FANNETTA NELSON
Educator (retired). **Personal:** Born Nov 29, 1919, Hayneville, AL; daughter of Sophia Bailey Nelson and Frank A Nelson Sr; divorced; children: Kelso Jr. **Educ:** Univ of Pittsburgh, BA 1941, MEd 1960; Univ of WA, MA 1967; Franklin & Marshall Coll, 1970. **Career:** PA Dept of Foreign Language Educ, sr adv, st coord of bilingual education 1973-82; PA Dept of Educ, German educ adv 1969-73; Fillion Music Studios, teacher Piano, French & German 1964-69; Pittsburgh Bd of Educ, teacher German, English Language background, English for foreigners 1955-69; State Dept of Welfare Allegheny County Bd of Asst, social worker 1944-45, 1947-50; Dept of Commerce, weather map plottng supvr 1943; City of Pittsburgh YWCA, youth advisor 1941-43; Fannetta Nelson Gordon Music & Dance Studio, owner & operator 1941-69; Cole Tutoring Serv, tutor French, German, English 1960-65; Penn Hall Acad Private School, teacher summer school. **Orgs:** Alpha Kappa Alpha 1938-; Sigma Kappa Phi, for lang honorary, Univ of Pittsburgh, 1941-, st yth adv in PA NAACP 1942-44; mem NAACP 1936-; fdr mem PA Blk Conf on Higher Educ 1971-; liaison with PA Dept of Educ PA Blk Conf on Higher Edn; fdr finan sec, vice pres, mem govrning counc liaison with PA Dept of Educ PA Conf on Blk Basic Edn; mem steering com Natl Blk Alliance on Grad Level Edn; Natl Assn for Blk Child Devel 1976-; Am Counc on the Tchng of Frgn Lang 1969-; Nat Counc of St Supr of Frgn Lang 1969-; PA St Modrn Lang Assn 1960-; Nat Assn on Bilingual Educ 1973-; Tchrs of Eng to Spkrs of Other Lang 1972-; Nat Counc of Negro Wmn; Univ of Pittsburgh Alumna Assn; Univ of WA Alumna Assn; YWCA; Ch of the Holy Cross (Episcpl); mem, Choir Pgh, St Paul Epis Church, Harrisburg; st coord Indochinese Refugee Asst Edn; board member/vice president Harrisburg, PA Branch NAACP, 1983-; mem, Coalition for Cooperation between Harrisburg NAACP Branch & The Jewish Comm, 1994-. **Honors/Awds:** Gold Medal Award, Excellence in French, Univ of PA, 1941; 1 of 22 German tchrs named as Fellows in the Exprncd Tchr Fllwshp Prgm Univ of WA 1966-67; Nat Def Educ Act Flwshp Univ of WA German; Nat Def Educ Act Flwshp Stanford Univ Bad Boll Germany; articles " Articulation in the Tchng of German" 1969; "The Soc Purpose of Lang Lrng" 1974; "The Status of Frgn Lang Educ & What Tchrs Can Do to Improve It" 1973; "Strategies for Improving the Status of Lang Tchng Lrng" 1976; "Is Frgn Lang Educ Necessary" 1977; "Frgn Lang Lrngng an open door to the world" 1976; "frgn lang for the gifted & talented"; citat serv to the cmmnwlth Gov Milton J Shapp PA; schlrshp Dawson MUS Studios, PA; schlrshp Fillion Mus Studios, PA; Citation, Univ of Pittsburgh School of Education for Professional Contributions, 1985. **Home Addr:** 4092 Beechwood Ln, Harrisburg, PA 17112.

GORDON, HELEN A.
Attorney. **Personal:** Born Jul 20, 1923, New York; married Joseph A Bailey; children: Josette, Jonathan, Gordon. **Educ:** Brooklyn Law Sch, LlB, JD 1950; Hunter Coll of City of NY, AB 1947. **Career:** Priv Prac Gordon & Wilkins, atty; AAA, arbitrator. **Orgs:** Mem bd trustees Grahan Sch for Child Hastings on Hudson, NY; mem bd of dir E Tremone Child Care Cntr; mem Bronx & Women's Bar Assn; Gothamettes Inc of NY; lecturer in continuing educ City Coll NY. **Business Addr:** Attorney at Law, Gordon & Wilkins, 304 W 138th St, New York, NY 10030.

GORDON, JOSEPH G., II
Scientist. **Personal:** Born Dec 25, 1945, Nashville, TN; son of Juanita T Gordon and Joseph G Gordon; married Ruth Maye Gordon; children: Perry. **Educ:** Harvard Coll, AB 1966; MIT, PhD 1970. **Career:** CA Inst of Tech, asst prof chem 1970-75; IBM Almaden Research Center, rsch staff mem 1975-, interfacial electrochem mgr 1978-84, interfacial science mgr 1984-86, technical asst to dir of research 1986-88; interfacial chemistry & structure mgr 1988-90, materials science and analysis mgr, 1990-94, batteries and displays mgr, 1994-. **Orgs:** Mem Amer Chem Soc, Royal Soc of Chemistry, Electrochemical Soc, Sigma Xi, Amer Assoc Advanc Science; Caltech Y, bd of dir 1973-75, chmn 1975; treas San Francisco Sect of Electrochem Soc 1982-84, pres 1984-85; sec San Francisco Bay Area Chap of the Natl Orgn for Prof Advancement of Black Chemists & Chem Engrs 1983-86; Gordon Research Conference on Electrochemistry, chmn 1987; mem American Physical Society; mem of exec bd, National Organization for the Professional Advancement of Black Chemists & Chem Engineers 1986-92; Society for Electroanalytical Chemistry, treasurer, 1995-97. **Honors/Awds:** NSF Predoctoral Fellow MIT 1967-70; 3 patents; 70

articles in professional journals; Outstanding Black Engineer for Technical Achievement Award, US Black Engineer & The Council of Engineering, Deans of Historically Black Colleges & Universities, 1990; Percy Julian Award, Natl Orgn for Prof Advancement of Black Chemists & Chem Engineers, 1993. **Business Addr:** IBM Research Division, Almaden Research Center, 650 Harry Rd, D2, San Jose, CA 95120-6099.

GORDON, LANCASTER
Basketball player. **Personal:** Born Jun 24, 1962, Jackson, MS. **Educ:** Louisville, Recreation 1984. **Career:** Los Angeles Clippers, 1984-88; CBA: Pensacola Tornados, 1988-89, La Crosse Catbirds, 1989-. **Honors/Awds:** Named 2nd Team All-Am by The Sporting News & 3rd Team All-Am by Basketball Weekly; voted to the 2nd Team All-Metro Conf for the two seasons; was one of final cuts on Bobby Knight's USA Olympic Bsktbl team, 1984; named to 1984 Mideast Region All-Tournmnt team after scoring 25 pts agnst KY.

GORDON, LEVAN
Judge. **Personal:** Born Apr 10, 1933, Philadelphia, PA; married Vivian J Goode; children: Shari-Lyn L Gordon Pinkett. **Educ:** Lincoln Univ Pennsylvania, AB; Howard Univ Law Sch, LLB; Pennsylvania State Univ. **Career:** Gov Commn Chester, PA, assoc counsel 1964; Philadelphia Housing Info Serv, exec dir 1966-68; Pennsylvania Labor Rel Bd, hearing examiner 1971-74; Municipal Court of Philadelphia, judge, appointed 1974, elected 1975 Court of Common Please of Philadelphia, elected judge 1979; Temple Univ School of Criminal Justice, instructor 1980-; Georgetown Univ Intensive Session in Trial Advocacy Skills, instructor 1984-; Court of Common Pleas, judge, currently. **Orgs:** Mem Alpha Phi Alpha, Zeta Omicron Lambda, Lincoln Univ Alumni Assn, W Philadelphia HS Alumni Assn, Philadelphia & PA Bar Assn, Lawyers Club of Phila, Amer Judicature Soc, Amer Bar Assn, Natl Bar Assn, Pennsylvania Conf of Trial Judges; bd of dir Columbia N Branch YMCA; mem Philadelphia Tribune Charities, Philadelphia Tribune Bowling League, Chris J Perry Lodge Elks IBPOE of W, Natl Bowling Assn, Amer Bowling Congress, AFNA Preceptor Program, Natl Assn of Blacks in Criminal Justice, World Assn of Judges; bd of dir Natl Kidney Found, Men of Malvern; bd of trustees/supr of jr ushers Tindley Temple United Methodist Church; Black Methodist for Church Renewal; Combined Health Appeal of America, bd of dirs. **Honors/Awds:** Distinguished Serv Award Liberty Bell Dist Philadelphia Corcil Boy Scouts of Amer; Community Serv Award Strawberry Mansion Civic Assn Puerto Rican Comm Serv Award; Lincoln Univ Alumni Achievement Award; Man of the Yr Zeta Omicron Lambda Chap Alpha Phi Alpha 1975; The Assn of Business & Professional Women of Philadelphia & vicinity Man of the Year Award 1984; McMichael Home & School Assn Distinguished Serv Award; The Methodist Men Tindley Temple United Methodist Church 1986 Award of Excellence; member, West Philadelphia High School Hall of Fame. **Military Serv:** US Army, 1953-55; USNR Reserve 1958-61. **Business Addr:** Judge, Court of Common Pleas, City Hall, Room 673, Philadelphia, PA 19107.

GORDON, ROBERT FITZGERALD
Dentist. **Personal:** Born Nov 7, 1928; married Mabel Enid Welds; children: Wayne, Gregory. **Educ:** Howard U, BSc 1958, DDS 1964. **Career:** Jersey City Med Cntr, dental intern 1964-66; Somerset, NJ, pvt prac 1966-; Somerset Co Rural Sch Dental Hlth Svc, trustee. **Orgs:** Mem Am Dental Assn; NJ Middlesex Co Commonwealth Dental Soc; mem Alpha Phi Alpha.

GORDON, ROBERT L.
Consultant, psychologist. **Personal:** Born Jun 23, 1941, Lexington, KY; married Mamie R Baker; children: Kimberly; Cedric. **Educ:** Edwards Waters College, BS 1964; Florida A&M Univ, 1965; College of Finger Lakes, MA Psychology 1967. **Career:** Waycross, GA, psychology teacher & baseball coach 1964-65; New York Harlem Astronauts, pro basketball player 1965-67; Ford Motor Co, labor relations 1969-84;Premier Personnel Placement Consultant, Inc, president 1984-85. **Orgs:** Chairman, War Chest Com Natl Assault on Illiteracy, 1984-85; Pres Reagan's Task Force on Priv Sec, 1984-85; board member, Kappa Alpha Psi Foundation, 1984-85, former grand polemarch; co-chairman Labor & Industry Committee NAACP, Ann Arbor Branch 1984-85. **Honors/Awds:** 100 Most Influential Blacks (Ebony) 1982-85; received more than 40 awards throughout the US 1982-85; Honorary Citizen's Award State of Kentucky 1983; Kentucky Colonel State of Kentucky 1983; received more than 200 plaques and awards. **Business Addr:** Former Grand Polemarch, Kappa Alpha Psi Fraternity Inc, Natl Headquarters, 2322 N Broad St, Philadelphia, PA 19132-4590.

GORDON, RONALD EUGENE
Brewing company executive. **Personal:** Born Feb 22, 1946, Springfield, OH; married Felicity Ralph; children: Mark, Rebecca, Ryan. **Educ:** Central State Univ, BS 1973; Xavier Univ, MBA 1976. **Career:** Continental Can Co, production supervisor 1971-77; Formica Corp, production supervisor 1977-79; Miller Brewing Co, production supervisor 1979-. **Honors/Awds:** The Olubandek Dada Award, Dept of Business Admin, Central State Univ, 1973. **Military Serv:** US Air Force, sgt, 4 yrs. **Business Addr:** Production Supervisor, Miller Brewing Co, PO Box 1170, Reidsville, NC 27320.

GORDON, THOMAS
Professional baseball player. **Personal:** Born Nov 18, 1967, Sebring, FL. **Career:** Kansas City Royals, pitcher, 1988-95; Boston Red Sox, 1996-. **Business Addr:** Professional Baseball Player, Boston Red Sox, 24 Yawkey Way, Boston, MA 02215, (617)267-9440.

GORDON, WALTER CARL, JR.
Hospital administrator. **Personal:** Born Oct 25, 1927, Albany, GA; married Suzanne Patterson; children: Walter III, Tia. **Educ:** Hampton Inst, BS 1947; Tuskegee Inst, MS 1948; Meharry Med Coll, MD 1955; Letterman Army Hosp, intern 1956; Walter Reed Army Hosp, resd 1961. **Career:** Phoebe Putney Mem Hosp, surgeon, past chief of staff, past chairman of the board; Fitzsimmons Gen Hosp, chief gen surgeon, 1966-68; Am Coll of Surgeons, fellow. **Orgs:** Mem AMA; Dougherty Co Med Assn; GA State Med Assn; dipl Am Board of Surgery; Sigma Pi Phi; mem Alpha Phi Alpha Frat; bd dir FL A&M; Albany State Coll; mem Criterion Club; Albany C of C. **Honors/Awds:** Recip 3 Commendation Med AUS; Legion of Merit. **Military Serv:** AUS lt col 12 1/2 yrs. **Business Addr:** 401-A S Madison St, Albany, GA 31701, (912)435-6196.

GORDON, WALTER LEAR, III
Attorney. **Personal:** Born Mar 6, 1942, Los Angeles, CA; married Teresa Sanchez; children: Maya Luz. **Educ:** Ohio State Univ, BA 1963; UCLA, MPA 1965, JD 1973, PhD 1981. **Career:** UCLA Law School, lecturer 1978-82; private practice, attorney, currently. **Orgs:** Bd mem SCLC-West 1980-85; mem Langston Bar Assoc 1986. **Honors/Awds:** Published "The Law and Private Police," Rand 1971, "Crime and Criminal Law," Associated Faculty Press 1981; has also published several articles. **Business Addr:** Attorney at Law, 2822 S Western Ave, Los Angeles, CA 90018.

GORDON, WINFIELD JAMES, SR.
Broadcast journalist/anchorman, political staffer (retired). **Personal:** Born Oct 18, 1926, Camden, NJ; son of Tabitha (Payton) Gordon and Rev Winfiled Arandas (deceased); married Genevieve Emily Owens, Jun 1, 1946; children: Brenda Seri Law, Winfield James Jr, James Noble. **Educ:** Graduate of various military schools to qualify as a broadcast journalist, public speaker, reporter/researcher. **Career:** KFMB-TV,TV news report; US Navy, sr chf journ 1965; WHIM, disc jcky 1955-56; WPFM, disc jcky 1955-56, news reader 1953-55; WRIB, disc jcky 1967-68; AFRTS-LA, news annc 1964-66; Ethnic Faces, host prod 1972-75; Interntl Hour, host 1970-72; weekend anchor 1976-81; council and mayoral staff positions 1983-86. **Orgs:** Mem Sigma Delta Chi; mem SD Prof Chptr 1973-; mem SD Cntry Boy Scout Cncl 1974-; mem dir bd Encanto Boys Club 1974-; mem AFTRA, 1992, Fra Br 9, 1972; life mem, Disabled Amer Vets, 1984-; life mem, Vets of Foreign Wars of the US, 1992; Society of Prof Journalists; Highland Park baptist Church, San Diego, CA. **Honors/Awds:** Honor Golden Hill United Pres Chrc 1976; Comm Serv Awd Omega Psi Phi Frat 1978; Comm Serv Awd Pub Comm; nominated for a Bronze Star for service in Vietnam as the NCOIC of the Amer Forces Vietnam Network key station: Saigon. **Military Serv:** USN 1943-69; AF/USMA Vietnam war; nominated for Bronze Star.

GORDON-DILLARD, JOAN YVONNE
Educator. **Personal:** Born Oct 4, 1955, Eglin AFB, FL; daughter of Lois Jackson Gordon and Charles Robert Gordon; married Marvin Clinton Dillard, Aug 29, 1992. **Educ:** Fisk University, BA, 1977; La Sorbonne, Paris, France, Certificate, 1976; The Ohio State University, MA, 1978, PhD, 1982. **Career:** US Department of Labor, educational media specialist, 1979; Ohio State University, coordinator of research, development & support, 1983-94; IBM, information developer, 1984-86, education specialist, 1986-87, account marketing representative, 1988-90, advisory instructor, developer, 1990-94; Lucent Technologies, project manager, distance learning, 1996. **Orgs:** Association for Communications & Technology, 1982-85, 1993; Women in Communications, 1991, 1993; The Doug Williams Foundation, mentoring program, 1988-89; Minority Athletes Networking, Inc, fundraising, 1990-; Crescent Moon Foundation, education & fundraising, 1990-; IBM Aristotle Program, team leader, 1992-; Alpha Kappa Alpha Sorority, Inc, 1978-. **Honors/Awds:** Ohio State University, One-Year Minority Fellowship, 1977; Fisk University & Vanderbilt University, Travel Grant, 1976; Fisk University, Mortar Board, Inc, 1977; Phi Beta Kappa, 1977. **Special Achievements:** Honored during high school graduation ceremony, Grace Dodge Vocational High School, Barbara Bush was keynote speaker, 1991. **Home Addr:** 1 Edgewater Rd, Cliffside Park, NJ 07010, (201)945-6310. **Business Addr:** Project Manager, Lucent Technologies, Inc, 140 Centennial Ave, Piscataway, NJ 08854, (908)457-7301.

GORDON-SHELBY, LURDYS MARIE
Compensation analyst. **Personal:** Born Oct 1, 1963, Rochester, NY; daughter of Ina Eugennie McLeish Scott and George Edgardo Gordon; married Cletis Derand Shelby, May 9, 1987. **Educ:** The Wharton School of the University of Pennsylvania, Philadelphia, PA, BS, organizational behavior, 1985; New York University, New York, NY, MA, psychology, 1989. **Career:** CIGNA Corporation, Hartford, CT, personnel consultant, 1985-87; Pacific Gas & Electric Company, San Francisco, CA, compensation analyst, 1989-. **Orgs:** Member, Amer Assn of Blacks in energy, 1990-; volunteer, San Francisco Volunteers, 1990-. **Business Addr:** Compensation Analyst, Human Resources, Pacific Gas & Electric Company, 123 Mission St, H1748, San Francisco, CA 94106.

GORDY, BERRY, JR.
Business executive, producer, composer. **Personal:** Born 1929, Detroit, MI; married Grace Eaton, 1990; children: Berry IV, Terry James, Hazel Joy, Kerry A, Kennedy W, Stefan K. **Career:** Featherweight boxer; auto worker; record store owner; composer; composer, Reet Petite for Jackie Wilson which became 1st Gordy hit; composer, You Made Me So Very Happy; Tamla Record Label with Smokey Robsinson and the Miracles as first group which recorded Way Over There; Shop Around; Motown Record Corp, founder, pres, 1959-88, sold to MCA; signed stable of little known singers who later became famous including The Temptations, Four Tops, Supremes, Martha Reeves & the Vandellas, Stevie Wonder, Jackson Five (and Michael Jackson) and many others; producer, Lady Sings the Blues, Mahagony, The Wiz. **Orgs:** Dirs Guild Amer; chmn Motown Ind entertainment complex. **Honors/Awds:** Business Achievement Award, Interracial Council for Business Opportunity, 1967; 2nd Annual American Music Award for Outstanding Contribution to Industry, 1975; One of Five Leading Entrepreneurs of Nation, Babson College, 1978; Whitney M Young Jr Award, Los Angeles Urban League, 1980; exec producer film Berry Gordy's The Last Dragon, 1984; elected Gordon Grand Fellow, Yale Univ, 1985; inducted into the Rock and Roll Hall of Fame, 1988. **Special Achievements:** Author, Berry Gordy: To Be Loved, 1994. **Business Addr:** Chairman, Motown Records, 5750 Wilshire Blvd, Ste 300, Los Angeles, CA 90036-3697.

GORDY, DESIREE D'LAURA
Attorney. **Personal:** Born Jul 14, 1956, Long Beach, CA; married Terry J Gordy Sr; children: Terry James Jr, Whitney Jade. **Educ:** San Diego State Univ, BA 1978; Southwestern Univ Sch of Law, JD 1982. **Career:** Work Records a div of MCA Records, outside counsel and business affairs 1987-; Jobete Music Co Inc, Motown Productions Inc, Motown Record Corp, in-house counsel to all three corporations 1983-. **Orgs:** Mem Black Women Lawyers Assoc, John Langston Bar Assoc, CA Women's Lawyers Assoc, Women Lawyers Assoc of Los Angeles; volunteer Bradley for Governor Campaign 1986; volunteer All Africa Games in Kenya 1987; sponsor of children in underdeveloped nations; concert promoter, artist management, songwriter. **Honors/Awds:** Top 100 Black Business and Professional Women 1986. **Business Addr:** In-house Corporate Counsel, Motown Record Corp, 5750 Wilshire Blvd, Ste 300, Los Angeles, CA 90036-3697.

GORE, BLINZY L.
Attorney. **Personal:** Born Jun 13, 1921, Hinton, WV; son of Cora Pack Gore and Isaiah E Gore; married Gloria A Bultman; children: Brian, William. **Educ:** West Virginia State College, Institute, WV, BS, education, 1946; IA Univ, JD 1950; NY Univ, MA 1958, PhD 1967. **Career:** South Carolina State College, Orangeburg, SC, law professor, 1950-66; private practice of law, 1956-; South Carolina State College, Orangeburg, SC, associate professor of social science, 1966; Claflin College, Orangeburg, SC, vice president for academic affairs, 1967-85. **Orgs:** Mem IA Bar & SC Bar; Pi Gamma Mu 1974; life mem NAACP; past pres Assn of Coll Deans, Registrars and Admissions Officers; United Methodist Church. **Honors/Awds:** Founders Day Award NY Univ 1967; Kappa Man of 1975 Orangeburg Alumni Chap Kappa Alpha Psi 1975; Orangeburg Kappa Achievement Award, 1994; Claflin Coll Presidential Citation, 1994. **Special Achievements:** Author of On A Hilltop High, The Origin & History of Claflin College to 1994. **Military Serv:** AUS 1942-46. **Home Addr:** 300 College St, NE Box 7337, Orangeburg, SC 29117-0001.

GORE, DAVID L.
Attorney. **Personal:** Born Dec 17, 1937, Horry County, SC; son of Sadie M Anderson Gore and Samuel B Gore; married Mary L Andrews; children: David Jr, Sheila. **Educ:** Allen Univ, BA 1959; SC State Coll, MEd 1966; Howard Univ Sch of Law, JD 1969. **Career:** Natl Labor Relations Bd, legal asst to chmn 1969-70; Law Office of David L Gore, 1994; United Steelworkers of Amer, asst genl counsel 1970-81, dist counsel 1982-. **Orgs:** Mem IL & PA Bar Assocs, 3rd 6th 7th & 10th and DC Court of Appeals, US Supreme Court; Phi Alpha Delta Legal Frat. **Military Serv:** US Army, sgt, 1960-63. **Business Addr:** District Counsel Dist 7, United Steelworkers of Amer, 155 N Michigan Ave, Chicago, IL 60601, (312)616-4224.

GORE, JOHN MICHEL
Government official. **Personal:** Born Aug 6, 1955, Columbus, OH; son of Rose M Gore and John L Gore; married Judith Ann Jackson Gore, Jun 24, 1978; children: Johnel Marie, Janee Michelle. **Educ:** Bowling Green State University, business administration, 1976. **Career:** Ohio State Auditor, welfare investigator, 1976, assistant auditor, 1978, assistant auditor in charge, 1984, field audit supervisor, 1987, assistant audit manager, 1990, assistant deputy auditor, 1992-. **Orgs:** National Association of Black Accountants; National Association of Certified

Fraud Examiners, 1992-; Free & Accepted Masons; Second Baptist Church, deacon board, finance committee; United Negro College Fund; Alpha Phi Alpha Fraternity, Inc. **Honors/Awds:** National Association of Black Accountants, Columbus, Chapter Member of the Year, 1992-93; Alpha Phi Alpha, Exceptional Service Award, 1989; Second Baptist Church, Man of the Year, 1990. **Home Addr:** 151 Scottsbury Ct, Gahanna, OH 43230.

GORE, JOSEPH A.
Educational administrator. **Personal:** Born in Sypply, NC; married Gloria Gardner; children: Duane K. **Educ:** Livingstone Clge, BS 1952; Univ of MI, MS 1960; Yale Univ, MPH 1970; Univ of MA, EdD 1977. **Career:** Mary Holmes Coll, dean of men and science instructor 1956-58; Mary Holmes High School, prin 1958-59; Mary Holmes Coll, dean of students 1959-62, acad dean 1962-68, dir health servs 1968-70; Tougaloo Coll, acad dean 1970-72; Mary Holmes Coll, pres 1972-. **Orgs:** Mem FAFEO, Amer Pub Assc, Natl Educ Assc, Clay Cty Chamber of Comm, Bd of Dir I M Hosp. **Honors/Awds:** Ped D degree Mary Holmes Clge 1972; LL D degree Lake Forest Clge 1984; Kellogg Fellow St Louis Univ 1964; Natl Sci Fellow Univ NC 1965. **Military Serv:** AUS medic 82nd airborne div 1953-55. **Business Addr:** President, Mary Holmes Coll, PO Drawer 1257, West Point, MS 39773.

GOREE, JANIE GLYMPH
City official. **Personal:** Born Jan 24, 1921, Newberry, SC; daughter of Chaney Hodges Glymph and Orlander Tobias Glymph; married Charlie A Goree; children: Henry L Suber, Denice, Michael, Charles, Winifred Drumwright, Juanita, Darryl. **Educ:** Benedict Coll, BS (magna cum laude), 1948; Univ of CO, MBS 1958; Attended: Univ of SC; Univ of WY; Univ of Notre Dame; SC State Coll. **Career:** Union Cty School, teacher 1948-81; Town of Carlisle, judge 1978-90, mayor, 1978-. **Orgs:** Exec person Democratic Party 1976-82; vice chairperson SC Conf of Black Mayors 1980-; treasurer, 1984-89, board of directors, 1989-, World Conf of Mayors; Delta Sigma Theta Sor, Alpha Kappa Mu Natl Hon Soc; sec Grassroot Rural Devel Advisory Bd; rep & del Natl Conf of Black mayors to Interamer Travel Agents Soc Inc; del Natl Conf of Black Mayors to Japan, China, US, People Republic of China; del World Conf of Mayor in Africa; historian, National Conference of Black Mayors, 1989-; historian, Black Women Caucus of the National Conference Black Mayors, 1990-; president, South Carolina Conference of Black Mayors, 1992; Union County Chamber of Commerce, bd of dirs; Clemson Extension Advisory Committee, 1995. **Honors/Awds:** First elected African-American female mayor of SC, SC Conf of Black Mayors, 1980; Spec Tribute to Black Women Mayors, Natl Conf of Black Mayors, 1983; Natl salutes to 31 Black Female Mayors for Outstanding Political Achievement, Metropolitan Women Democratic Club of DC; Drum Major for Justice, Southern Christian Leadership Conf, 1984; Hon Citizen Liberia, West Africa 1984; Certificate of Award, National Alliance of Business, 1990; SC Commission on Women, Pioneer Award, 1992; Southern Bell's South Carolina African-American History Calendar, 1993; awarded 8 continuing education units from Clark Atlanta University for participating in the National Conference of Black Mayors, Inc Leadership Institute for Mayors, 1987-94; Natl Council Negro Women, Bronx New York Section, Aggressive and Distinguished Leadership Power with a Purpose, 1988; Union Alumni Chapter South Carolina State College, Devoted service in leadership education and to mankind, 1989; Seekwell Baptist Church Award, For service and dedication, 1993; South Carolina Conference of Black Mayors, Charles Ross Leadership Award for outstanding community service and leadership in the state of South Carolina, 1994. **Business Addr:** Mayor, Town of Carlisle, PO Box 305, Carlisle, SC 29031.

GORMAN, BERTHA GAFFNEY
Aviation company executive. **Personal:** Born in Greenville, TX; daughter of Vivian Shoals Gaffney and Bernice Gaffney; married Prentice Gorman (divorced); children: Gregory G, Glen G. **Educ:** Sacramento Community Colleges-City & American River, 1964-69; Sacramento State Coll, Sacramento, CA, BA, 1972; Univ of Upsala, Sweden, 1972-73. **Career:** Sacramento Bee Newspaper, Sacramento, CA, reporter, 1971-79; CA State Dept of Mental Health, Sacramento, CA, public information officer, 1979-80; CA State Assembly, Sacramento, CA, principal consultant in charge of media, 1980-85; Lockheed Corp, Calabasas, CA, dir, issues mgmt, 1985-95; State & Local Government Affairs, Lockheed Martin, dir, 1995-. **Orgs:** Mem, bd of dir, American Cancer Society, CA Div; mem, American Cancer Society Marketing and Communications Comm, CA Div; vice chair, Great Beginning for Black Babies Task Force, Los Angeles, 1990-91; bd chair, Sacramento Regional Assistant District, 1981-85; sec, Black Public Relations Society of CA, Los Angeles, 1986-90; mem, Black Women's Forum, Los Angeles, 1987-. **Honors/Awds:** Columbus Intl Film Festival Chris Plaque, 1988; Black Public Relations Society's Honoree, 1991; IABC Merit Award; PRSA Prism Award, 1994. **Business Addr:** Director, State & Local Government Affairs, Lockheed Martin Corp., 1725 Jefferson Davis Hwy, Ste 300, Arlington, VA 22202-0610, (703)413-5959.

GORMAN, GERTRUDE ALBERTA
Association executive. **Educ:** Case Sch of Applied Sci, cert elec engr 1943; CWRU Cleveland Coll, BA polit phil 1949; Columbia Univ NYC, MA polit sci 1950. **Career:** NAACP, field dir 1949-79; Signal Corps USA War Dept, design & devel ofcr elec engr 1943-45; NAACP Cleveland, sec exec com 1941-43; NPORC NYC, natl pub opinion pollster 1949-51. **Orgs:** Golden heritage life mem NAACP (CONS) 1979-; life mem, Alpha Omega Chapter, Alpha Kappa Alpha 1979. **Honors/Awds:** Nat Distgshed Serv Awd Nat NAACP 1973; NDSA Outstndg Contrib NAACP Convention 1974; hon citizen cert Indianapolis 1975; Cert of Apprec Inter City Sertoma Club 1976.

GOSLEE, LEONARD THOMAS
Physician. **Personal:** Born Aug 5, 1932, Salisbury, MD. **Educ:** Howard Univ, BS; Boston Univ, MS; Meharry Med Coll, MD. **Career:** Detroit Genl Hosp, internship 1958-59; Children's Hosp of MI, residency 1959-62, chief residency 1962-63; Laguardia Med Group Inc, physician 1964-. **Orgs:** Mem Natl Med Assn, Amer Acad of Pediatrics, NY State Med Assn, Queens Co Med Assn, Amer Assn of Pediatrics, Sch Health Planning Program. **Business Addr:** Physician, Laguardia Medical Group Inc, 112-18 Springfield Blvd, Queens Village, NY 11429.

GOSS, CLAYTON
Playwright. **Personal:** Born 1946, Philadelphia, PA. **Career:** Author "Children"; author num plays includ "Homecookin", "Of Being Hit", "Space in Time", "Bird of Paradise", "Ornette", "Oursides", "Mars", "Andrew"; Howard U Wash, DC, playwright-in-residence.

GOSS, LINDA
Storyteller, folk artist, cultural historian, author. **Personal:** Born in Alcoa, TN; daughter of Willie Louise McNair and Willie Murphy McNair; married Clay Goss; children: Aisha, Uhuru, Jamal. **Educ:** Howard University, Washington, DC, BA, drama, 1969; Antioch University, Yellow Springs, OH, ME, education, 1978. **Career:** Professional storyteller; has performed in over 25 states in US & Canada; traveled to Africa, 1981; has performed at several museums at the Smithsonian Institution; has performed at major museums, festivals, universities. **Orgs:** President, Association of Black Storytelling, 1984-; president, Hola Kumba Ya Cultural Organization, 1989-. **Honors/Awds:** Official Storyteller of Philadelphia, City of Philadelphia, PA, 1984; Linda Goss Day, City of Washington, DC, 1983; Lind Goss Day, City of Alcoa, TN, 1986; Talk That Talk, anthology of African-American storytelling, Simon & Schuster, 1989, Best Paperback of 1989, Publishers Weekly, selected by Book of the Month Club for their Quality Paperback Club; coauthor, The Baby Elopard book and cassette, Bantam/Doubleday/Dell, 1989. **Home Addr:** 6653 Sprague St, Philadelphia, PA 19119.

GOSS, THERESA CARTER
Educator, librarian. **Personal:** Born Aug 22, 1932, Latham, AL; daughter of Willie D Carter and Columbus Carter; married James Calvin Goss. **Educ:** AL State Univ Montg, BS; NC Central Univ Durham, MLS; Nova Univ Ft Lauderdale, EdD. **Career:** Jackson State Univ, librarian 1954-55; FL A&M Univ, librarian 1956; Pinellas HS, librarian 1956-66; St Petersburg Jr Coll, librarian 1966-81; MM Bennett Library SPSC, dir 1981-. **Orgs:** Mem League of Women Voters 1957-; mem Amer Assn of Univ Women 1958-; mem NAACP 1964-; mem Amer Assn of Univ Prof 1979-; mem Women's Adv Com Eckerd Coll 1979-; mem FL Library Assn, Amer Library Assn, Southeast Library Assn, FL Assn of Comm Coll, Phi Delta Kappa, Amer Assn of Univ Women; mem Alpha Kappa Alpha Sor, Links Inc, Silhouettes of Kappa Alpha Psi; Clearwater Airport Authority; Pinellas Co Arts Council. **Honors/Awds:** Girl Scout Leadership Awd 1959; PCPTa Awd for Outstanding Serv 1960; Religious Comm Serv Awd 1961; SOUL Awd for Outstanding Serv 1971; Library Bd Mem Awd City of Clearwater 1976; Alpha Kappa Alpha Awd Outstanding Accomplishments 1979; "Model Library Serv for the Hearing Handicapped" Major Applied Rsch Project Ft Lauderdale Nova Univ 1978, various other publications; Kappa Alpha Psi Awd; Links Awd for Outstanding Serv in Library Science; pres Clearwater Adult Adv Comm. **Business Addr:** Dir, MM Bennett Library, 6605 5th Ave N, St Petersburg, FL 33710.

GOSS, TOM
Athletic director. **Educ:** Univ of MI. **Career:** Faygo Beverages, vp of sales; National Beverage Corp, Western Shasco Div, exec vp/general mgr; PIA Merchandising, pres/COO; The Goss Group, managing partner; Univ of MI, athletic dir, 1997-. **Honors/Awds:** All-Big Ten defensive tackle, 1968. **Special Achievements:** First African American athletic director at Univ of MI.

GOSS, WILLIAM EPP
Business executive. **Personal:** Born Feb 3, 1941, Baltimore, MD; married Charlotte; children: Maisha, Zuri, Malaika. **Educ:** Univ Chicago Grad Sch Bus, MBA 1975, MA soc serv admin 1970; Morgan State U, BA 1968. **Career:** Talent Asst Prgm Inc, exec dir 1976-; Minority Bus, mgmt cons; Talent Asst Prgm, asso dir 1975-76; Henry Booth House Settlement-Hull Hse Assn, ctr dir; Univ IL, Jan Addams Sch Sch Work, field instr; Hull House Assn, bd dir. **Orgs:** Mem Nat Assn Soc Workers; Assn Black MBA'S; Assn Black Soc Wrkrs. **Honors/Awds:** Chicago Assn Commerce & Ind Bicentennial Awd Grt Am Excell in Econ 1976; Outsdng Comm Serv Chicago Police Dept 173; Flwsp Univ Chicago Grad Sch Soc Serv Admin 1969-70. **Business Addr:** 19 S La Salle, Chicago, IL 60603.

GOSSETT, LOUIS, JR.
Actor. **Personal:** Born May 27, 1936, Brooklyn, NY; divorced; children: Sate. **Educ:** NYU, BA, drama. **Career:** Actor, made Broadway debut in "Take A Giant Step"; "The Desk Set" Broadway; "Lost in the Stars" Broadway; "Raisin in the Sun" Broadway; "The Blacks"; "My Sweet Charlie"; "Carry Me Back to Morningside Heights"; "The Charlatan"; "Tell Pharoah"; "Roots"; films: The Skin Game, 1971, The Laughing Policeman, 1974, It's Good to Be Alive, 1974, The White Dawn, 1975, Little Ladies of the Night, 1977, The Choirboys, 1977, The Deep, 1977, He Who Walks Alone, 1978, An Officer and a Gentleman, 1982, Jaws 3, 1983, The Guardian, 1984, Finders Keepers, 1984, Iron Eagle, 1985, Enemy Mine, 1985, Firewalker, 1986, The Principal, 1987, Iron Eagle II, 1988, Toy Soldiers, 1991; Diggstown, 1992. **Orgs:** Motion Picture Arts & Sciences Acad; SAG; NAG; AEA; AFM; Alpha Phi Alpha; AGVA; Legal Defense Fund, NAACP. **Honors/Awds:** Starred in TV movie "Sadat" 1983; Emmy Award for role of Fiddler in "Roots"; Oscar Best Supp Actor for role in "An Officer and a Gentleman" (3rd Black to win an acting Oscar); Trumpet Award, 1997; NAACP, Image Award, TV Drama Supporting Actor, 1998. **Business Addr:** c/o NBC-TV, 3000 W Alameda Ave, Burbank, CA 91523.

GOSS-SEEGER, DEBRA A.
Account representative. **Personal:** Born Apr 21, 1958, San Francisco, CA; daughter of Mildred Wilson Goss and Waymond Goss; married Willie Seeger (divorced 1982); children: Justin Seeger. **Educ:** Alameda Junior Coll, AS, Business Admin, 1986; Univ of San Francisco, San Francisco, CA, BS, Business Admin, 1988; Univ of CA, Berkeley, CA, currently attending. **Career:** Xerox Corp, Sunnyvale, CA, exec acct rep, 1975-80; Clorox Corp, Oakland, CA, admin asst, 1980-85; Pacific Gas & Electric Co, Berkeley, CA, major acct rep, currently. **Business Addr:** Major Account Representative, Pacific Gas and Electric Co, 2111 Martin Luther King, Berkeley, CA 94704.

GOTHARD, BARBARA WHEATLEY
Educator. **Personal:** Born Nov 23, 1937, Springfield, IL; married Donald L; children: Donald Jr, Ann Marie. **Educ:** Mt Mary Coll Milwaukee, WI, BA 1959; Long Island Univ Greenvale, NY, MS 1972; MI State Univ E Lansing, MI, PhD stud 1977. **Career:** Utica High School MI, assoc prin 1977-; MI State Univ, instructor 1980; Utica Comm School, art teacher 1973-77; Crimel Oakland Univ, Rochester MI, free lance graphic artist 1972-73; Union Free School Dist #4, Northport NY, art teacher 1966-71; Milwaukee Public Schools, art teacher 1959-64. **Orgs:** Mem Chairprsn publ com MI Assn of Secondary Sch, prin 1977-; mem Nat Assn of Secondary Sch Prin 1977-; mem MI Counc for Women in Sch Admin 1978-; bd of dir Meadowbrook Art Gallery Oakland Univ 1973-76; bd of dir Xochipilli Gallery 1974-76; mem Utica Cultural Arts Counc Exhibits of Paintings include Main Streams "74" Marietta Coll OH, Detroit Artists Market "Woman Works" Univ of MI, Midwest Artists Milwaukee Performing Arts Cntr, Macomb Co Bi-Centennial Exchange Prog Coventry England; solo shows at Delta Coll, Univ City MI, Art Gallery Central MI U, Mt Mary Coll Milwaukee, WI, Xochipilli Gallery MI; newspr reviews prv collections 1972-80. **Honors/Awds:** Outstdng Young Women of Am 1973; edited weekly col "Cultural Arts Events" The Advisor Newspr Utica, MI 1973-75; publ "Art Tchr, Admin" Secondary Educ Today Jour of the MI Assn of Second Sch Prin 1978. **Business Addr:** Utica High School, Utica Community Schools, 47255 Shelby Rd, Utica, MI 48318.

GOTHARD, DONALD L.
Automobile company executive (retired), consultant. **Personal:** Born Dec 2, 1934, Madison, WI; son of William H Gothard (deceased) & Lorraine M Williams Gothard; married Doris M Smith, May 27, 1990; children: Donald Jr, Ann Marie. **Educ:** Univ Notre Dame, BSEE 1956; Graduate ROTC 1956; GMI Tech Staff Management Program, Cert 1974. **Career:** GM AC, Sparkplug Div, jr engineer, production engineering 1956, Electron Div, design sys engineer, Mace Missile Guidance & Navig Equip 1958-62, engineer, Apollo Ground Support Syst, 1962-66; GM Delco, Electron Div, lab supr, Apollo Guidance Sys Lab, 1966-71; GM Auto, Electron Contrl Syst Devel, 1971; GM Instrumentation Sect, Test Dept, supr engineering staff, 1972; GM Engineering Staff, asst manager 1973-76; GM Chevrolet, Motor Div, sr design engineer, 1976-77, asst staff engineer 1977-79, staff engineer 1979-82; GM Truck & Bus Engineering Operations, chief engineer, electrical components 1982-85, exec engineer, adv vehicle engineering 1985-90; GM Research Laboratories, dir res administrative services, 1990-92; GM Design Center, exec prototype & process engineering, 1992-93; GM Manufacturing Center, Prototype Shops, dir quality and mfg eng, 1993-95. **Orgs:** Sec Shelby Township Cable TV Reg Comm 1980-84; Soc of Auto Engineers 1976-; Macomb Co

Comm Coll Citizens Com on Ednl & Finan Needs & Resources 1976; vol, YMCA Youth Basketball Program 1971-87; Meadow Brook Art Gallery Assn 1972-80; asst coach Utica Eisenhower High School Girls Basketball 1985-87; board of directors, Black Alumni of Notre Dame, 1988-94; Univ of Notre Dame Engineering Advisory Council, 1989-; Detroit Science & Engineering Fair, bd of dirs, 1992-. **Honors/Awds:** Certificate of Appreciation Macomb County Comm Coll 1976; Disting Serv Award Utica Educ Assn 1975-76; Certificate of Appreciation Utica Comm Schools 1972-74; NASA Apollo Achievement Award 1969; MIT Cert Commend Apollo Program 1969; name carried to moon on first two lunar landings 1969; Society of Automotive Engineers Excellence in Oral Presentation 1987; lead team that established an intl land speed record with a GMC pickup truck at Bonneville Salt Flats, 194.77 mph, 1989; nominated, Black Engineer of the Year Award, 1991; Univ of Notre Dame, College of Engineering, Honor Award, 1994; Black Alumni of Notre Dame, Rev Edward Williams Service Award, 1994; Black Engineer of the Year Award For Lifetime Achievement-Industry, 1995. **Military Serv:** US Army Ordnance, 1st lt 1956-58; Distinguished Military Graduate Award from Notre Dame 1956. **Home Addr:** 5510 Brookside LN, Washington, MI 48094.

GOUDY, ANDREW JAMES
Educator. **Personal:** Born Apr 15, 1943, Martins Ferry, OH; son of Bertha Goudy and Sidney Goudy. **Educ:** IN Univ of PA, BS 1967, MS 1971; Univ of Pittsburgh, PhD 1976. **Career:** Cameron Cty HS, tchr 1968; Bald Eagle Nittany HS, tchr 1969; Canon Mcmillan HS, tchr 1971; West Chester Univ, prof 1977, chrmn dept chem, 1983-87. **Orgs:** Mem Amer Chem Soc 1976-, Intl Assc Hydrogen Energy 1982, NAACP; Natl Org for the Prof Advancement of Black Chemists & Chem Eng. **Honors/Awds:** Article publ J Less Common Metals 99 1984, J Less Common Metals 91 1983; Research Grants: Petroleum Research Fund, 1982; NSF, 1986. **Business Addr:** Dept of Chemistry, West Chester State Univ, 700 S High St, West Chester, PA 19383-0002.

GOUGH, WALTER C.
Physician. **Personal:** Born Apr 24, 1943, Pittsburgh, PA; son of Kathryn Scott Grinage Gough and Walter C Gough Sr; married May Ella Bailey, Sep 24, 1974; children: Wanda, Marcus, Henry, Lynette, Kathryn, Nora. **Educ:** Tarkio Coll, AB 1965; Meharry Medical Coll, MD 1970; Mercy Hospital Pittsburgh, intern resident 1970-72; Meharry Medical Coll, pediatrics resident, 1973. **Career:** Mound Bayou, MS, medical dir 1974-; Black Belt Family Health Center, medical dir 1973; Taboman Hospital, dir, 1972-75; Delta Comm Hospital & Health Center, physician 1974-; Choctaw Indian Hospital, medical dir 1976-78; Natl Health Serv, medical dir 1978-81; Spectrum ER Care, dir 1981-84; Gough's Family & Ped Clinic, owner 1984-. **Orgs:** Mem Allegheny Co Medical Co 1971-72; AMA, NMA 1973-74; Omega Psi Phi 1967-; mem MS Heart Assn 1974; bd of trustees Delta Health Center 1986-89, WQSZ 1989-. **Honors/Awds:** First black graduate at Tarkio Coll; Man of the Year Award, Pittsburgh Jaycees 1972; Outstanding Alumnus 15 yrs, Tarkio Coll 1974; Distinguished Alumni, Tarkio Coll 1974; Bronze Medal Tarkio Coll 1965; Best Scientific Article, Meharry Coll 1966; Student Christian Med Soc 1967; Jaycee's Man of the Year 1970; Board Certified, American Bd of Physicians, 1977, 1983, 1989; Board Certified, American Bd of Emergency Medicine, 1983, 1989; Man of the Year, Omega Psi Phi 1986; #1 Award Iota Omicron Charter 1986. **Business Addr:** Physician, Gough's Family & Peds Clinic, 189 N Main St, Drew, MS 38737.

GOULBOURNE, DONALD SAMUEL, JR.
Social worker, health care administrator. **Personal:** Born May 5, 1950, New Rochelle, NY; son of Girthel Grayson Goulbourne and Donald Samuel Goulbourne Sr; children: Antoine Donald. **Educ:** Columbia Union Coll, Takoma Park MD, BA, 1973; Columbia Univ School of Social Work, New York NY, MS, 1977; Albert Einstein Coll of Medicine/Yeshiva Univ, Post-Graduate Certificate, 1984. **Career:** New Rochelle Bd of Educ, New Rochelle NY, teachers asst, 1974-75; Washington Heights Community Center, New York NY, social work trainee, 1975-76; Family & Children Serv, Stamford CT, clinical social worker, 1977-79; Natl Health Serv Corps, Einstein Medical Coll, New York NY, social work coord, 1979-84; Dept of Social Serv, Albert Einstein Coll of Medicine, New York NY, 1984-89; Lincoln Ave Clinic, The Guidance Center, New Rochelle NY, dir, 1989-. **Orgs:** US Reserve Officers Assn, 1989; US Commissioned Officers Assn, 1989; Natl Assn of Social Workers, 1989; Soc of Clinical Work Psychotherapists Inc, 1989; volunteer group leader, Minority Task Force on AIDS, 1989; vice pres, Westchester Townhouse Condominium Assn, 1989; professional counselor, Community Adult Patients, 1989. **Honors/Awds:** Letter of Commendation, New York State Dept of Health, 1981; Clinical Assoc Nomination, Dept of Sociology, Herbert H Lehman Coll of the City Univ of New York, 1982; Serv Citation, New York City Dept of Public Health, 1983; Certificate of Appreciation, Yeshiva Univ, 1986, 1987. **Business Addr:** Director, Lincoln Ave Clinic, The Guidance Center, 95 Lincoln Ave, New Rochelle, NY 10801.

GOULD, WILLIAM BENJAMIN, IV
Attorney, educator. **Personal:** Born Jul 16, 1936, Boston; son of Leah Felts Gould and William Benjamin Gould III; married Hilda; children: William, V, Timothy, Bartholomew. **Educ:** Univ RI, AB 1958; Cornell Law Sch, LLB 1961; London Sch Econ, grad study 1963; Univ Cambridge, MA 1975. **Career:** United Auto Wkrs, asst gen counsel 1961-62; Natl Lab Relat Bd Washington, atty 1963-65; Battle Fowler & Stokes, Kheel, NY, asso 1965-68; Wayne State Law Sch, prof law 1968-71; Harvard Law Sch, vis prof law 1971-72; Stanford Law Sch Overseas Fellow Churchill Coll Cambridge, prof law 1975-; Univ Tokyo Law Faculty, vis scholar 1975. **Orgs:** Mem Nat Acad Arbitrat; Labor Law Sect; Am Bar Assn atty; racial discrim class act involving Detroit Edison Co Intl Bro Teamsters; Am Fed Mus; del Dem Party mid-term conv 1974. **Honors/Awds:** Author articles lab law & unions Stanford, Yale, Duke, Cornell, Penn & other law jour; contrib NY Times, Manchester Guard London Econ, Nation, New Rep Commonwealth, New Leader; Endowed Chair Holder, Charles A Beardsley, Prof of Law, 1984; Certificate of Merit, Primer on American Labor Law, 1983. **Business Addr:** Prof, Law, Stanford Law School, Stanford, CA 94305.

GOURDINE, SIMON PETER
Attorney. **Personal:** Born Jul 30, 1940, Jersey City, NJ; son of Laura Emily Rembert Gourdine and Simon Samuel Gourdine; married Patricia Campbell, Aug 1, 1964; children: David Laurence, Peter Christopher, Laura Allison. **Educ:** The City Clge of NY, BA 1962; Fordham Univ Law Schl, JD 1965; Harvard Univ Grad School of Business Cert Prog for Mgmt Develop 1979. **Career:** Southern District of New York, assistant United States attorney, 1967-69; National Basketball Association, New York, NY, assistant to the commissioner, 1970-72, vice president of administration, 1973-74, deputy commissioner, 1974-81; New York City Department of Consumer Affairs, commissioner, 1982-84; The Rockefeller Foundation, secretary, 1984-86; Metropolitan Transportation Authority, New York, NY, director of labor relations, 1986-90; National Basketball Players Association, New York, NY, general counsel, 1990-; TCS-TV, general partner, 1990-93. **Orgs:** Board of directors, Police Athletic League, 1974-, Fresh Air Fund, 1985-, The Fund for the City of New York, 1990-93; member, New York City Civil Service Commission, 1981-82, Governor's Executive Advisory Commission on Administration of Justice, 1981-82, Mayor's Committee on Taxi Regulatory Issues, 1981-82; member, New York State Banking Board, 1979-90; member, New York City Charter Revision Commission, 1988-89; member, New York State Bar, US District Court Bar, US Supreme Court Bar. **Military Serv:** US Army, Capt, 1965-67; Army Commendation Medal, Vietnam. **Business Addr:** General Counsel, National Basektball Players Association, 1775 Broadway, New York, NY 10019.

GOVAN, REGINALD C.
Attorney. **Personal:** Born Dec 2, 1953, New York, NY; son of Gwendolyn Minor and Oswald Govan. **Educ:** Carnegie-Mellon University, BA, 1975; University of Pennsylvania Law School, JD, 1978. **Career:** Squire, Sanders & Dempsey, associate, 1978-79; US Court of Appeals, 6th Circuit, Judge Nathaniel R Jones, sr law clerk, 1979-81; Manhattan District Attorney, assistant district attorney, 1981-83; sole practitioner, federal civil rights and general litigation, 1983-85, 1987-89; US Senate, Committee on the Judiciary, counsel, 1985-87; US House of Representatives, Education & Labor Committee, counsel, 1989-94; Organization Resource Counselors, Inc, sr consultant, 1995-. **Orgs:** District of Columbia Bar, Attorney-Client Arbitration Board, chairman, 1991-94, Disciplinary Review Committee, 1991-93, Task Force on Continuing Legal Education, 1992-94; National Bar Assn, 1984-; Washington Bar Association, 1990-. **Special Achievements:** "Employment Law is a Fishbowl: Coping with Less Privilege and Confidentiality," Employee Relations L.J., Vol. 23, No.3 (Winter 1997); "Honorable Compromises and the Moral High Ground: The Conflict Between the Rhetoric and the Content of the Civil Rights Act of 1991," 46 The Rutgers Law Review 7, 1993; "Framing Issues and Acquiring Codes: An Overview of the Legislative Sojourn of the Civil Rights Act of 1991," 41 The DePaul Law Review 1057, 1992; One Nation, Indivisible: The Civil Rights Challenge for the 1990's, Washington, DC, Citizens' Commission on Civil Rights, 1989. **Business Addr:** Organization Resource Counselors, 1211 Avenue of Americas, 15th Fl, New York, NY 10036, (212)719-3400.

GOVAN, RONALD M.
Research physicist, staff associate. **Personal:** Born Jan 20, 1931, Los Angeles, CA; married. **Educ:** Pacific State Univ Coll of Elec Engr, BSEE 1962. **Career:** USC, physics dept resrch asso; Ryan Aircraft, elec main & calibration tech a; Hughes Aircraft, elec fabric tech a elec main tech a; USN ET2, main of radar, sonar & commun equip; Univ of So CA LA, physics dept asst in resrch 1962-64, chem dept instrument design 1964-66; Rockwell Intl Sci Cntr, staff asso physics 1966-; Univ of CA Santa Barbara Dept of Urban Affairs, conf coord 1969. **Orgs:** Mem Educ Counc of Coll & Univ Ventura Co; chmn local bd 81 selec serv Ventura Co; mem bd dir So CA Comprehen Hlth Plann Bd; vice pres So Area ConfNAACP; vice pres Ventura Co NAACP; lab chmn Educ Chmn; mem Camarillo Jaycees; chmn John C Montgomery Forum on Welfare; mem Camarillo Boys Club bd dir; mem United Fund Ventura Co Budget & Com Task Force chmn; chmn Ventura Co Comm Action Commn; mem Ventura Co Criminal Justice Planning Delegate Conf on Crim Just Sci & Tech Wash, DC 1972; found past pres Camarillo Dem Club; mem Task Force On Excellence in Educ Pomona 1972; CA State Dept of Edn; lectr paid consult Ventura Co Human Relat Comm; Task Force on Housing Ventura Co Plann Dept; Equal Oppor Com; CA State Personnel bd adv com on Career Oppor Devel; memGov's Conf on Law Enforcement Standardsime Control Com; Publs Spectroscopy Grp; Atmospheric Sci Grp. **Honors/Awds:** Recip outstdg Contrib Awd NAACP So Area Conf; recip Comm Serv Awd & 1967 outstdg Comm Interest Awd; Jaycee of Month awd; Distgshd Serv Awd; Commen for High Svc. **Military Serv:** USN electronics tech 2nd class 1949-54. **Business Addr:** 1049 Camino Dos Rios, Thousand Oaks, CA.

GOVAN, SANDRA YVONNE
Educator. **Personal:** Born Jul 28, 1948, Chicago, IL; daughter of Sarah D Wilson Govan and Tanzel Romero Govan. **Educ:** Valparaiso University, Valparaiso, IN, BA, 1970; Bowling Green University, Bowling Green, OH, MA, 1972; Emory University, Atlanta, GA, PhD, 1980. **Career:** Luther College, Decorah, IA, instructor, 1972-75; University of Kentucky, Lexington, KY, assistant professor, 1980-83; University of North Carolina, Charlotte, NC, associate professor, 1983-. **Orgs:** Member, Association for the Study of African American Life and History; member, Modern Language Association, 1980-; member, College Language Association, 1975-; member, Langston Hughes Society; coordinator, Ronald E McNair Postbaccalaureate Achievement Program. **Honors/Awds:** Schomburg Scholar in Residence, NEH, Schomburg Center for Research in Black Culture, 1990-91; Outstanding Alumni Award, Valparaiso University, 1982; National Fellowship Fund Award, Ford Foundation, 1976-80; Emory University Fellowship, 1975. **Business Addr:** Professor of English, University of North Carolina-Charlotte, Charlotte, NC 28223, (704)547-4218.

GOWARD, RUSSELL A.
Government official. **Personal:** Born Aug 25, 1935, St Louis, MO; married Dolores Thorton; children: Russell II, Monika. **Educ:** Hubbards Bus Coll; Harris Tchrs Coll; Univ MO, 1969. **Career:** State rep 1966-; House Com on Soc Serv & Medicade Ins, asst majority floor ldr chmn; broker, real estate broker; R G Lynch & Asso Inc, pres; Freedom Residents, bd dir; Yeatman Corp; Soc Serv Inc. **Honors/Awds:** Legislator of Yr MO Beauticians Assn 1967; merit serv MO Nursing Home Assn 1968, 69, 77; 1 of top 10 legis St Louis Mag; MO Assn of Pub Employ; Outst Legislator 1977. **Military Serv:** USN quarter master 3rd class 1952-56. **Business Addr:** Capitol Bldg, Jefferson City, MO 65101.

GRACE, HORACE R.
Company executive. **Personal:** Born Jan 13, 1943, Timpson, TX; son of Lena Roberts Williams and Robert Grace; married Margaret Richardson (divorced 1979); children: April Grace. **Educ:** Prairie View University, Prairie View, TX, BS, 1966; Virginia State University, Petersburg, VA, MS, 1975. **Career:** Federal Acquisition Consultants, pres, 1982-; The Lawn Barber Landscaping, pres, 1982-; Grace Investments, pres, 1985-. **Orgs:** Vice chairman, Texas Credit Union Commission, 1985-89; member, United Way Board, 1991; member, Christian Farm Board, 1988-; member, Central Texas Alliance of Black Businesses, 1988-; member, board, Private Industry Council, 1989-. **Honors/Awds:** Businessman of the Year Award, CENTABB, 1989. **Military Serv:** US Army, Major, 1970-83; Bronze Star, 1968, Meritorious Medal, 1979, Army Accomodation Medal, 1977. **Business Addr:** PO Box 10065, Killeen, TX 76547-0065.

GRACE, MARCELLUS
Educator, pharmacist. **Personal:** Born Oct 17, 1947, Selma, AL; son of Mary Grace and Capp Grace; married Laura Dunn; children: Syreeta Lynn, Marcellus Jr, K'Chebe M. **Educ:** Xavier Univ of LA; BS Pharm 1971; Univ of MN, MS Hosp Pharm 1975, PhD Pharm Admin 1976. **Career:** Tulane Med Ctr Hosp & Clinic, dir of pharm serv 1976-77; Xavier Univ of LA Coll of Pharm, asst prof & dir of prof exp pro 1976-78; Howard Univ Coll of Pharm & Pharmacal Sci, asst dean for serv ed 1979-82, chmn dept pharm admin 1982; Xavier Univ of LA, dean and professor coll of pharm 1983-. **Orgs:** Mem, board of directors, Urban League of Greater New Orleans, 1996-; mem New Orleans Historical Pharm Commiss 1983-; pres Assoc of Minority Health Professions Schools, 1987-89; pres, Minority Health Professions Foundation; mem, National Heart, Lung and Blood Institute Advisory Council, 1991-93; Board of Directors, American Association of Colleges of Pharmacy, 1992-94; New York Academy of Science, 1991; mem, board of directors, Ernest N Morial Asthma and Respiratory Disease Ctr, 1995-; mem, board of directors, Alton Ochsner Med Foundation, 1996-; mem, The New York Academy of Sciences, 1991. **Honors/Awds:** Eli Lilly Achievement Awd Eli Lilly Co Indianapolis In 1971; Recipient of Fellowship Natl Fellowship Fund Grad Fellowship for Black Amer 1975-76; mem Rho Chi Natl Pharm Honor Soc 1977. **Military Serv:** USN Reserve, captain, 1976-. **Business Addr:** Dean, College of Pharmacy, Xavier University, 7325 Palmetto St, New Orleans, LA 70125, (504)483-7421.

GRACE, PRINCESTON
Automobile dealer. **Career:** Advantage Ford-Lincoln-Mercury Inc, pres, currently. **Special Achievements:** Company is ranked #75 on Black Enterprise magazine's 1997 list of Top 100 Black businesses. **Business Phone:** (317)825-0594.

GRADY, GLENN G.
Company executive. **Career:** Cimarron Express Inc, CEO, currently. **Special Achievements:** Company is ranked #57 on the Black Enterprise List of Top 100 Industrial/ Service Companies, 1994. **Business Addr:** CEO, Cimarron Express Inc., PO Box 185, Genoa, OH 43430.

GRADY, MARY FORTE
Regional coordinator, government official (retired). **Personal:** Born Nov 19, 1921, Chicago, IL; daughter of George Forte and Cyril Forte; married Leonard Grady Jr, Jul 26, 1947; children: Leonard Grady III, Graham C Grady. **Educ:** Wilson Jr Coll; Chicago Conservatory. **Career:** US Dept of Commerce, coord comm serv; US Census Bureau, Chicago, IL, regional coord, retired. **Orgs:** Mem United Way; prog audit comm mem United Negro Coll Fund; assoc bd dir mem Chicago Urban League; Coalition against Crime; Chatham Lions Club Women's Auxiliary; Natl Council Negro Women; Alpha Gamma Pi Sorority. **Honors/Awds:** Bronze Medal, US Dept of Commerce 1974.

GRADY, WALTER E.
Chief executive. **Career:** Seaway National Bank of Chicago, Chicago IL, chief executive. **Business Addr:** Seaway National Bank of Chicago, 645 E 87th St, Chicago, IL 60619.

GRAGG, LAUREN ANDREA
Service relations analyst. **Personal:** Born Dec 20, 1967, Detroit, MI; daughter of LaBarbara A Gragg and J Robert Gragg (deceased). **Educ:** Howard University, BA, 1989. **Career:** Detroit Pistons, Palace Foundation, special project asst, 1990; EDS, service relations analyst, 1990-. **Orgs:** Howard University Alumni Association; NAACP; National Urban League; Delta Sigma Theta. **Home Addr:** 1210 Glynn Ct, Detroit, MI 48202-1457, (313)334-4028. **Business Phone:** (313)696-4800.

GRAHAM, ALBERTHA L.
Educator. **Personal:** Born in Georgetown, SC; married Sam Ellison; children: Kezia Ellison. **Educ:** Morris Coll, 1965; NY Univ, Cert Ldrshp Devel Training 1968; Erikson Inst, MEd 1971; Univ of Pittsburgh, grad stud. **Career:** Chopee High School, teacher 1965-67, summer librarian 1966; Brookhaven HS, head start teacher 1967-68; Cent Brookhaven Head Start Program, dir 1968-70; Suffolk Co Summer Head Start Patchoque NY, dir 1970; Kezia Enterprises, counselor; CA Univ of PA, state training officer, assoc prof, dir of affirmative action/ human relations, counselor. **Orgs:** Mem Nat Assn Educ Young Child; Nat Council Black Child Devel; PA Reg Adv Com Day Care Person Proj conduc EPI 1973; mem Educ Com Pgh Chap NAACP;nat pres Black Women Assn Inc; init & spon "You The Black Woman" in a series of seminars for the Black Wom Assn Inc 1975-; prov training & tech asst toreg Iii agency for Child You & Fam; vol & adv bd mem Nat Cncl of Jewish Women Pgh Sec Friends Indeed Proj 1975-; mem Afric Am Inst; bd mem Inst for Women Ent NAWBO; mem Greater Pgh Commn for Women. **Honors/Awds:** Business Woman of the Year Awd Alleghenians LTD Inc. **Business Addr:** Box 13 LRC, California, PA 15419.

GRAHAM, CATHERINE S.
Director of health & human services. **Personal:** Born Apr 8, 1920, Norfolk, VA; daughter of Irene Stoney and Sye Stoney; married Robert (deceased); children: Antoine. **Educ:** Trenton State Coll, BA 1973, MA 1977; Rider Coll, cert in ins 1968. **Career:** Trenton Ed Devel Corp; Educ Advo Prog City of Trent, form dir; Mercer Co Ct, prin docket clk; St Hm for Girls, supv; City Hall Trenton NJ, health & human serv dir. **Orgs:** Mem Will H Dinkins Real Est; bd dir Unit Prog Inc; mem Foll Through Prog; Hd Start Pol Counc; Spl Educ Adv Counc; Hd Start; Educ Supp Tm;former pres Urb League Met Trenton; past pres NAACP; mem Jack & Jill; bd dirs Nat Counc for Black Child Devel Inc; adv comm Mercer County Human Svcs; mem Mercer County Dem Black Caucus. **Honors/Awds:** Recpt comm spons testim dinner; awds From Omega Phi Psi 1968; frontiersman 1968; Fai Ho Cho Club 1967; City of Trent 1972; Bronzettes 1967; Usher Counc of NJ 1964; Head St Par Action Counc 1974; Carver Cntr YMCA 1972;AKA Recog Achieve 1972; NJ Conf of Christ & Jews Achieve & Awd 1979. **Business Addr:** Dir Health & Human Serv, City Hall, 319 East State St, Trenton, NJ 08608.

GRAHAM, CHARLENE
Fire chief. **Personal:** marrIed Derek; children: Jessica, Jennelle. **Educ:** Ferris State Univ, bachelor's degree. **Career:** Detroit Fire Department, division chief, currently. **Special Achievements:** First woman to hold the rank of division chief in the Detroit Fire Department. **Business Addr:** Division Head, Research & Development Div, Detroit Fire Department, 250 Larned, Detroit, MI 48226.

GRAHAM, CHESTIE MARIE
Educator. **Personal:** Born Nov 7, 1917, Louisburg, NC; married Samuel; children: Samuel Jr, Barbara, Karen. **Educ:** Fayetteville State U, BS 1944; PA State U, MEd 1952. **Career:** Dist of Columbia Bd of Educ, elementary school counselor; teacher 1944-64. **Orgs:** Am Sch Couns; Elem Sch Couns Assn; DC Sch Couns Assn; The Am Personn & Guid Assn; Delta Sigma Theta; YWCA; Nat Counc of Negro Wom; Bus & Prof Wom; Nat Cap Person & Guid Assn; mem NAACP; pres Elem Sch Couns Assn 1974-75; Adv Nghbrhd Commn Wd 6 1976-80; sec DC Sch Couns Assn, 1974-75. **Honors/Awds:** Chpn Human Res & Ag Com in ANC 6b; induct into Pi Lambda Theta Hon Sor; served 5 yrs on Chap Com St Monica's Epis Ch; vol 25 yrs plus With Am Red Cross; served 7 yrs with Girl Scouts; test at hearing on State Plan for DC 1975; part in pres "Mirror Mirror Mirror On The Wall" 1975; outst couns DC Rsrch Club 1975-76; outst achvmt in Advance of Comm & Sch Act James E Coates 1976; outst achvmts Jerry A Moore 1976; reg of atten at Apga Wkshp Am Pers & Guid Assn 1976; cert of apprec serv render Superior Ct 1977; cert of apprec outst serv in DC Empl One Fund Dr; rec cert Assn for one-white conc in person & guid for exemp serv to the assn & the conc of minor in the field of couns & guid 1978; 1st pres DC assn for non-white conc inperson & guid; publ sev art.

GRAHAM, DELORES METCALF
Educator. **Personal:** Born Aug 4, 1929, Frankfort, KY; daughter of Jenny Metcalf and Edward Metcalf; divorced; children: Tanya, Gregory, Derrick. **Educ:** KY State Coll, BS 1952; Georgetown Coll, MA 1982. **Career:** State Of KY, child welfare social work 1957-58; Franklin County Bd of Educ, special reading teacher, classroom teacher. **Orgs:** Mem Franklin Cnty Centr KY Nat Educ Assn; mem Delta Sigma Theta Sor; Nat Counc Negro Wom; mem Alpha Delta Kappa, Foster Care Review Bd; trustSt John AME Church. **Honors/Awds:** Out Elem Tchrs in Am 1973. **Business Addr:** Teacher, Franklin Co Bd of Education, 916 E Main St, Frankfort, KY 40601.

GRAHAM, DERRICK (DETTRICE ANDREW)
Professional football player. **Personal:** Born Mar 18, 1967, Groveland, FL; married Kendra; children: Deltrice. **Educ:** Appalachian State, bachelor's degree in criminal justice. **Career:** Kansas City Chiefs, guard, 1990-94; Carolina Panthers, 1995; Seattle Seahawks, 1996-. **Business Addr:** Professional Football Player, Seattle Seahawks, 11220 NE 53rd St, Kirkland, WA 98033, (206)827-9777.

GRAHAM, DONALD
Banker. **Personal:** Born Jan 28, 1947, Youngstown, OH; son of Morris & Katheryn Graham; married Barbara, Sep 8, 1996; children: Anneke. **Educ:** Youngstown State University, BS, 1970; Xavier University, MBA, 1979; College of Mt St Joseph, Accounting Cert, 1988. **Career:** Pitney Bowes, Inc, sales, 1973; Ford Motor Co, zone manager, 1973-80; Fifth Third Bank, banker, 1980-. **Orgs:** Omega Psi Phi Fraternity Inc, 1968; National Black MBA Association of Cleveland, president, 1990-92; Harambee Svcs to Black Families, board member, 1991-96; Cleveland Childrens Museum, board member, 1993-95; Urban League of Cleveland, trustee, 1994-; American Cancer Society, board member, 1995-; Urban Bankers Association, 1995-. **Honors/Awds:** Cleveland Growth Association, Leadership Cleveland, 1997; Dollar & Sense Magazine, Outstanding Businessman, 1993; YMCA, Black Achiever, 1984. **Military Serv:** US Army, 1971-73; Army Commendation Medal, Vietnam, 1972. **Business Addr:** Sr Vice Pres/Director, Fifth Third Bank of Northeastern OH, 1404 E 9th St, Cleveland, OH 44114, (216)274-5449.

GRAHAM, FREDERICK MITCHELL
Educator. **Personal:** Born Feb 7, 1921, Des Moines, IA; son of Anna Mae Graham and Fred Graham; married Lillian Louise Miller; children: Frederick, Stephen, Anita Wardlaw. **Educ:** Drake U, 1943; IA State U, BS 1948, MS 1950, PhD 1966. **Career:** Prairie View A&M TX, dept civil eng head 1950-59; IA State U, prof of eng sci & mechanics 1961-87. **Orgs:** Consulting engr McDonnell-Douglas & Meredith Publishing Co Etc 1965-; mem ASEE; mem ASCE; former lay reader St John's Episcopal Ch. **Honors/Awds:** Elected Tau Beta Pi IA State U; elected by stdnts Knights of St Patrick; awarded 2 Nat Sci Found Fac Fellowships; chosen Outstand Prof 1978, 1984; pres of local NSPE 1984; elected to Nat GRE Com of Engineering Examiners 1982-86; chosen outstanding prof 1984, 1988; SIRE ARCHON, Gamma Eta Boule. **Military Serv:** USAF m sgt 1943-46. **Home Addr:** 134 S Franklin, Ames, IA 50010. **Business Addr:** Prof of Engineering Sciences, IA State Univ, 209 Lab of Mechanics, Ames, IA 50011.

GRAHAM, GEORGE WASHINGTON, JR.
Government official. **Personal:** Born Feb 16, 1949, Kinston, NC; son of Mattie L Graham and George W Graham Sr (deceased); married Marilyn, Jun 18, 1988; children: Marilyn, George III, Alicia, Brandi. **Educ:** Fayetteville State Univ, BS, 1971; North Carolina State Univ, MS, 1975, doctoral program, currently. **Career:** US Post Office, Fayetteville, NC, mail handler, 1967-71; Simone Jr High School, instructor & athletic coach, 1971-72; Lenoir Community Coll, Kinston, NC, adult basic educ dir, 1972-76, admin asst to the pres & resource devel officer, 1977-79; Dobbs School, Kinston, NC, dir, 1979-. **Orgs:** Mem: Omega Psi Phi, NAACP, St Augustus AME Zion Church, Jaycees, Masons, Kinston Rotary Club, N Carolina Assn of Black Elected Officials, Lenoir County Black Artist Guild; Lenoir County Bd of Commissioners; bd of dirs, Lenoir County Chamber of Commerce; bd of dirs, Lenoir Memorial Hospital; bd of dirs, Untied Way; Lenoir County Commn of 100; Lenoir County Health Bd of Dirs; N Carolina General Assembly Special Legislative Commn on Fairness in Taxation; N Carolina Assn of County Commrs Taxation & Finance Steering Comm; chmn, bldg commn, St Augustus AME Zion Church; bd of dirs, N Carolina Assn of County Commrs. **Honors/Awds:** Teacher of the Year, 1971; Jaycee of the Month, 1973; Outstanding Educ of the Year, 1974; Outstanding Educ of Amer, 1974-75; Outstanding Black Educ, 1976; Jaycee Boss of the Year, 1979; Man of the Year, Omega Psi Phi, 1979; Distinguished Service Award Nominee, Kinston, Lenoir County Chamber of Commerce, 1980; Governor's Award for Excellence Nominee, 1987. **Business Addr:** Dir, Dobbs School, Route 7, Box 180, Kinston, NC 28501.

GRAHAM, GREGORY LAWRENCE
Professional basketball player. **Personal:** Born Nov 26, 1970, Indianapolis, IN. **Educ:** Indiana Univ. **Career:** Charlotte Hornets, guard, 1993; Philadelphia 76ers, 1993-95; NJ Nets, 1995-96; Seattle Supersonics, 1996-97; Cleveland Cavaliers, 1997-. **Business Addr:** Professional Basketball Player, Cleveland Cavaliers, One Center Ct, Cleveland, OH 44115-4001, (216)659-9100.

GRAHAM, HELEN W.
Educator (retired). **Personal:** Born Dec 24, New York, NY; daughter of Pauline and Raymond; married Fitzroy, Jun 26, 1949; children: Rosalyn, Shelle. **Educ:** Howard Univ, Washington DC, BA, 1950; Hunter Coll, New York NY, MS, 1974; LI University, post graduate. **Career:** S Siegel Inc, New York NY, office manager 1950-55; Brooklyn Bd of Educ, Brooklyn NY, teacher, 1962-89. **Orgs:** Treasurer, Natl Sorority of Phi Delta Kappa Inc, Beta Omicron Chapter, 1987-91; vice pres, Key Women of Amer Inc, 1989-92; Protestant Teachers Association; National University Women. **Honors/Awds:** Teacher of the Year, PTA, PS 37Q, 1975; Appreciation of Service, PS 37Q, 1979-81; Appreciation of Outstanding Contributions, Key Women Am Inc, 1990; Appreciation Dedicated Community Service, Jamaica Hospital, 1987-90; Church Affiliations: Grace Episcopal Church fo Jamaica, Social Action Committee, Altar Guild. **Home Addr:** 134-29 166th Place #10A, Jamaica, NY 11434.

GRAHAM, JAMES C., JR.
Association executive. **Personal:** Born Aug 1, 1945, Fort Wayne, IN; son of Marjorie Dickerson Graham and James C. Graham, Sr.; married Cecelia Graham; children: James C III, Joy, Angela, Margie, Audrey. **Educ:** National Urban League Whitney M. Young Executive Program, New York, NY, Diploma, 1984; University of Wisconsin; IBM Executive Development Program; Hillsdale College, Hillsdale, MI, BS, psychology, 1972. **Career:** Metropolitan Human Relations Commission, Fort Wayne, IN, director, 1972-77; Madison Urban League, Madison, WI, executive director, 1977-83; Birmingham Urban League, Birmingham, AL, president and CEO, 1983-. **Orgs:** Chairman, PIC Nomination Committee, Private Industry Council; president, National Urban League, Southern Council of CEOs, 1990-; member, Inclusiveness Committee, Government Relations Committee, United Way; member, Alpha Phi Alpha Fraternity, City of Birmingham Youth Task Force; member, Boy Scouts of America, Leadership/Birmingham; member, Chamber of Commerce Community Relations Committee; member, the Southern Institute on Children and Families; member, Birmingham Youth Task Force. **Honors/Awds:** Martin Luther King Humanitarian Award, Madison, WI. **Business Addr:** President and CEO, Birmingham Urban League, 1717 4th Ave, N, Birmingham, AL 35203.

GRAHAM, JEFF TODD
Professional football player. **Personal:** Born Feb 14, 1969, Dayton, OH. **Educ:** Ohio State. **Career:** Pittsburgh Steelers, wide receiver, 1991-93; Chicago Bears, 1994-95; New York Jets, 1996-. **Business Addr:** Professional Football Player, New York Jets, 1000 Fulton Ave, Hempstead, NY 11550, (516)560-8100.

GRAHAM, JO-ANN CLARA
Educational administrator. **Personal:** daugHter of Clara Polhemus Graham and James Harold Graham. **Educ:** New York Univ, BS 1962, MA 1968, PhD 1982. **Career:** Bronx Comm Coll, prof 1970-, chairperson of communications, division coordinator of humanities. **Orgs:** Exec bd New York State TESOL 1970-73; mem commercial panel Amer Arbitration Assn 1976-; bd of dir Assoc Black Charities 1982-; consultant Mayor's Voluntary Action Center, New York City Bd of Educ, Major New York City Law Firm, McGraw-Hill, Addison Wesley, Macmillan, North Hudson Language Devel Ctr, Haryou-Act; vice pres G/S Associates-Human Communication. **Honors/Awds:** Fellowship Univ of Puerto Rico, New York Univ 1966; co-author The Public Forum, A Transactional Approach to Public Communication, Alfred 1979; chosen 1 of 100 top women in mgmt

nationwide to participate in Leaders for the '80's, 1983. **Business Addr:** Div Coordinator of Humanities, Bronx Community College, 181 St & Univ Ave, Bronx, NY 10453.

GRAHAM, LADELL
Company executive. **Personal:** Born Oct 16, 1957, Shreveport, LA; son of Johnnie Lee & Corine Horton Graham; married Gwendolyn Smith, Dec 14, 1985; children: Justin, Jonathan, Jasmine. **Educ:** Southern Univ, BBS, accounting, 1981. **Career:** Associates Corp, portfolio mgr, 1981-87; Dean Witter, investment mgr, 1987-88; Amer Capital, investment vp, 1988-90; Smith, Graham & Co, pres & chief investment officer, 1990-. **Orgs:** Boy Scouts of America, district enrollment chairman, 1992; Natl Investment Mgrs Assn, 1995; Natl Assn of Securities Professionals, 1995; Amer Diabetes Assn, 1995; Texas Children's Hospital Development Council, 1995. **Honors/Awds:** Houston Black Achiever Award, 1990. **Business Addr:** President & Chief Investment Officer, Smith, Graham & Co, Asset Managers, LP, Texas Commerce Tower, 600 Travis Street, Ste 6900, Houston, TX 77002, (713)227-1100.

GRAHAM, LARRY, JR.
Musician. **Personal:** Born Aug 14, 1946; married Tina. **Career:** Graham Cent Sta Mavimus Prodns, pres 1973-77; Sly & The Family Stone, bass play 1967-73; Dell Graham Jazz Trio, 1951-67. **Orgs:** Mem Jehovah's Witness. **Honors/Awds:** Top star awd; best dress male art 1973; best dress art 1973-74; top big band 1975; ent of yr 1975; #1 black contemp & sing rec all trades cashbox billbd rec wor black rad exclus gavin report jet "One in a Million You". **Business Addr:** Mister I. Mouse, LTD, 920 Dickson St, Marina Del Rey, CA 90292.

GRAHAM, LEROY MAXWELL, JR.
Pediatrician. **Personal:** Born Feb 14, 1954, Chicago, IL; son of Marie C Davis and LeRoy M Graham Sr; married Patrice T Gaspard MD; children: Arianne Marie, LeRoy Maxwell III. **Educ:** St Joseph Coll, BS (cum laude); Georgetown Univ, MD 1979. **Career:** Fitzsimmons Army Medical Ctr, pediatric resd 1979-82; US Army Community Hosp Seoul Korea, asst chief ped svcs, chief newborn nursery 1983-84; Fort Knox KY, chief of ped serv 1984-86; Fitzsimons Army Med Ctr Auora Co, clinical priviledges 1986-; Univ of CO Health Scis Ctr, fellow ped pulmonary med 1986-, clinical instr in ped 1987-, fellow cardiovascular pulmonary rsch lab 1987-; The Childrens Hospital, emergency room attending 1988-; chief, pediatric Pulmonary Serv, dir, pediatric intensive care unit, Fitzsimons Army Medical Ctr 1989-. **Orgs:** Cert Amer Bd of Peds 1983; mem Alpha Phi Alpha; dir of educ Delta Psi Lambda; mem Alpha Omega Alpha Hon Med Soc; mem bd of dirs, Black American West Museum. **Honors/Awds:** First black student to be elected to Alpha Omega Alpha Honor Medical Soc at Georgetown Univ School of Med 1979. **Military Serv:** AUS 1979-; Meritorious Serv Medal; Army Commendation Medal, Army Achievement Medal, Foreign Serv Medal.

GRAHAM, MARIAH
Artist, business executive. **Personal:** Born Nov 3, 1946, South Carolina. **Educ:** The Sch of Visual Arts, cert of grad 1968. **Career:** Mariah Graham Studios, pres/owner 1969-; NY Times, freelance artist, 1968-; Marymount Coll, prof, 1977-; Fashion Inst of Tech, instr 1978-. **Orgs:** Soc of Illust; Graphic Art Guild; Drama & Guild Broadway. **Honors/Awds:** Cert of apprec Baruch Coll 1976; the One Show Merit awd The Art Direct Club 1976; cert of merit The Soc of Illust 1978; cert of merit New York City Coll 1979. **Business Addr:** Mariah Graham Studio, PO Box 425, Jeffersonville, NY 12748.

GRAHAM, MICHAEL ANGELO
Editor, producer. **Personal:** Born Dec 15, 1921, Savannah, GA; married. **Educ:** Savannah State Coll, attended. **Career:** New Observer DC, editor 1973-; Capitol Times DC, 1954-55; Metro-HERALD Beltsville MD, 1972; Afro-Amer Newspaper Natl, theatre writer 1960-; Pittsburgh Courier Natl, 1939-58; AK Spotlight Anchorage, feature writer 1952-54; Savannah Herald, orig staff mem; WA Informer DC, 1969; Black Voice Landover MD, 1973; Vista Raceway MD, pub dir 1970-72; Black & White Scotch DC, 1964-65; Town of Glenarden MD, 1971-72; Theatre Producer Promoter & Publ Lucky Mill Orchest NYC; Howard Theater DC, resident producer & emcee 1956-75; Fun For Fighters Camp Shows DC, dir production 1945-50; Harold Jackson Rad Show. **Orgs:** Mem NAACP; Columbia Lodge of Elks; Prince Hall Mason; Amer Cancer Soc & Pub Comm; Amer Guild of Variety Acts; US Pres Inaugural Entertainment Comm. **Honors/Awds:** Young mem New Orleans Mus Stock Co 1942; recip Red Cross Donors Awd 1962; Q'Pettes Club apprec awd 1969; Bakers Assn honor cit 1974; Nat Negro OperaAwd 1953; ed of the yr awd 1975; VFW Ladies Aux Comm Awd; am Canc Soc Awd; Shriners Awd; Petey Green Theat Awd; Orig Entert of Yr awd 1954. **Military Serv:** US Merchant Marine 1941-42. **Business Addr:** 811 Florida Ave NW, Washington, DC 20001.

GRAHAM, ODELL
Engineer. **Personal:** Born Mar 31, 1931, Chicago, IL; son of Gertha Scott (deceased) and James Graham; married Loretta Harriet Lewis, Jul 17, 1960; children: Karyn, Cynthia, Jessica. **Educ:** Univ of CA Los Angeles, BS, physics, 1961, MS, electrical engineering, 1967, PhD, electrical engineering, 1976. **Career:** Science & Applied Tech, Inc, principal scientist, 1992-; Hughes Aircraft Co, Canoga Park, CA, division chief scientist, 1961-92; Hycon Mfg Co, Monrovia, CA, elec engr, 1960-61; Hughes Aircraft Co, Culver City, CA, resrch & asst 1954-60. **Orgs:** Sr mem Inst of Elec & Elect Engr 1972-; chmn Los Angeles Chap Anten & Prop Soc Inst of Elec & Electron Engr; mem NAACP; executive committee member, engineering dean's council, UCLA, 1987-. **Honors/Awds:** Fellow, Institute for the Advancement of Engineering, 1981; Engineering Merit Award, San Fernando Valley Engineering Council, 1986; Black Engineer of the Year, Outstanding Technical Achievement, 1991. **Military Serv:** USMC corpl 1952-54. **Home Addr:** 3152 W Cumberland Ct, Westlake Village, CA 91362. **Business Addr:** Principal Scientist, Science and Applied Technology, Inc, 21050 Califa Street, Woodland Hills, CA 91367.

GRAHAM, PATRICIA
Educator. **Personal:** Born Mar 9, 1949, Saluda, SC; daughter of Lillian Leo Wertz Graham and Eddie Roy Graham; widowed. **Educ:** Rutgers Univ, BA 1972; Antioch Coll, Med 1974; Univ of Massachusettes, EdD, 1995. **Career:** Morrell School for Girls, group leader 1972-74; Widener Univ, counselor 1974-77; East Stroudsburg Univ, assoc prof/counselor 1977-. **Orgs:** Pres, Pocono Chap, Phi Delta Kappa 1994-95; mem NAACP, Amer Assoc Counseling & Develop, Amer Assoc Univ Professors; president, PA Association Multicultural Counselors, div PA counseing Assn; board of directors, Northeast PA Region, United Negro College Fund. **Honors/Awds:** Appreciation Awd Black Student Assn E Stroudsburg Univ 1981; Chi Alpha Epsilon Honor Society Award, 1994. **Business Addr:** Assoc Prof of Counseling, East Stroudsburg Univ, East Stroudsburg, PA 18301.

GRAHAM, PAUL (SNOOP)
Professional basketball player. **Personal:** Born Nov 28, 1967, Philadelphia, PA. **Educ:** Ohio Univ. **Career:** CBA: Albany Patroons, 1990-91; Philadelphia Spirit, 1991; Altanta Hawks, 1991-. **Business Addr:** Professional Basketball Player, Atlanta Hawks, 1 CNN Ctr NWS Tower, Ste 405, Atlanta, GA 30335, (404)827-3800.

GRAHAM, PRECIOUS JEWEL
Lawyer, social worker. **Personal:** Born May 3, 1925, Springfield, OH; daughter of Lulabelle Malone Freeman (deceased) and Robert Lee Freeman (deceased); married Paul Nathaniel Graham; children: Robert; Nathan. **Educ:** Fisk Univ, BA 1946; Case Western Reserve Univ, MSSA 1953; Univ of Dayton, JD 1979. **Career:** YWCA, prog dir 1946-53; Antioch, other positions 1964-69; 1992-94; Antioch College, prof soc welfare 1969-92; Antioch College, Institute of Human Development, director, 1984-89, social welfare and legal studies, emeritus professor, currently. **Orgs:** Mem OH Bar 1979-; Academy of Certified Social Workers; dir Yellow Springs Instrument Co 1981-; pres Yellow Springs Comm Fnd 1980, Pres, YWCA of USA 1979-85; bd dir, Meadville Lombard Theological Seminary 1983-87; president, World YWCA 1987-91; Boards: Unitarian Universalist Service Committee; Vernay Foundation. **Honors/Awds:** Faculty lecturer Antioch College 1979-80; Soc Wrkr of Year Miami Valley NASW 1975; Danforth Assc Danforth Fnd 1971-; Greene County Women's Hall of Fame Greene Cty OH 1982; Ten Top Women of Miami Valley, Dayton Daily News 1987; Ohio Women's Hall of Fame 1988. **Business Addr:** Emeritus Professor of Social Welfare and Legal Studies, Antioch College, Yellow Springs, OH 45387.

GRAHAM, RHEA L.
Geologist. **Career:** Science Applications Intl Corp, senior scientist, currently. **Special Achievements:** First African American to be nominated as director for the US Bureau of Mines in its 84 year history, 1994. **Business Addr:** Senior Scientist, Science Applications Intl Corp, 2109 Airpark SE, Albuquerque, NM 87106, (505)247-8787.

GRAHAM, RICHARD A.
Dentist. **Personal:** Born Feb 13, 1936, Boston. **Educ:** Norwich U, BS 1956; Howard Univ Dental Sch, DDS 1966. **Career:** Crownsville State Hosp, staff dent 1969-70; Western Hlth Dent Clin Balti, clin dir 1970-. **Orgs:** Md Dental Soc; Am Dental Soc pvt ofce; W Balti Fedn; NAACP. **Military Serv:** AUS lt 1956-60, capt 1966-70. **Business Addr:** 3502 N Rogers Ave, Baltimore, MD.

GRAHAM, SAUNDRA M.
State representative. **Personal:** Born Sep 5, 1941, Cambridge, MA; daughter of Roberta Betts Postell and Charles B. Postell; divorced; children: Carl Jr, Rhonda, Tina, Darryl, David. **Educ:** Univ of Massachusetts, 1971-73. **Career:** City of Cambridge, MA, 1971-77; State of Massachusetts, state representative, 1977-. **Orgs:** Cambridge Community Center; Massachusetts Legislators Association. **Honors/Awds:** Sojourner Truth Award; Distinguished Citizen Award, Natl Assn of Negro Bus & Professional Women's Clubs, 1976; Distinguished Citizen Award, Massachusetts Assn of Afro-American Policeman, 1974; Award for Community Service, Boston Masons, 1974; Citations from Governor and Massachusetts Secretary of State. **Business Addr:** State Representative, Massachusettes Legislators Assn, 580 Massachusetts Ave, Cambridge, MA 02139.

GRAHAM, SCOTTIE (JAMES OTIS)
Professional football player. **Personal:** Born Mar 28, 1969, Long Beach, NY; married Mary; children: Dennis, Marika Skot. **Educ:** Ohio State Univ, bachelor's degree in recreational education, master's degree in Black studies/Black community. **Career:** New York Jets, running back, 1992; Minnesota Vikings, 1993-96; Cincinnati Bengals, 1997-. **Business Addr:** Professional Football Player, Cincinnati Bengals, One Bengals Dr, Cincinnati, OH 45202, (513)621-3550.

GRAHAM, STEDMAN
Marketing entrepreneur. **Personal:** son Of Stedham and Mary; divorced; children: Wendy. **Educ:** Hardin-Simmons Univ, BA, 1974; Ball State Univ, MA, 1979. **Career:** Played basketball in European leagues; B&C Associates; S Graham & Assoc, 1992; Graham Gregory Bozell Inc. (GGB), pres/CEO, 1996-. **Orgs:** Athletes Against Drugs (AAD), founder, exec dir; George Washington Univ, Forum for Sport and Event Mgmt and Marketing, dir, 1994. **Special Achievements:** Author, The Ultimate Guide to Sport Event Management & Marketing, 1995; You Can Make It Happen: A Nine-Step Plan for Success, 1997. **Business Addr:** Pres/CEO, Graham Gregory Bozell Inc, 455 N Cityfront Plaza Dr, 15th fl, Chicago, IL 60611, (312)832-9468.

GRAHAM, TECUMSEH XAVIER
Clergyman. **Personal:** Born Mar 14, 1925, Washington, DC; married Loreda Branch; children: Tecumseh X, Jr, Marjorie Ella. **Educ:** Livingstone Coll, BA 1955; Hood Theol Sem, BD, MDiv 1958, 1974; Xavier U, LlD 1971; Cincinnati Tech Coll, DTL 1973; Cincinnati Bible Coll Seminary, DD 1980; Livingstone Coll, DD 1983. **Career:** Cleveland Co, Shelby NC Pub Schs, Portland OR State Even Coll, Xavier Univ Univ of CT, tchr & lecturer; Sag Horbor Long Island, pastor 1950-53; BelmontNC, pastor 1953-56; Shelby NC, pastor 1956-60; Portland OR, pastor 1960-64; St Mark AME Zion Ch, clergyman 1964-79; Coun of Christ Comm, exec dir 1972-;Broadway Temple AME Zion Church, pastor 1979-. **Orgs:** Vp Local NAACP 1965-66; pres Interdenom Minist Alli 1966-68; Am Assn of Univ Profs 1968-72; pres Bd of Educ 1972; chmn Bd of Trust Cinc Tech Coll 1973; Mem Citizens Com on Yth; mem YKRC-TV Dial Pan 1967-; city councilman Cincinnati OH 1978-79; pres KY Council of Churches 1985-; mem many other civic org. **Honors/Awds:** Outstanding Serv Awd NAACP 1959; Civic Leadership Cit 1959; many other leadership awds and citations. **Business Addr:** Pastor, Broadway Temple AME Zion Ch, 662 South 13th St, Louisville, KY 40203.

GRAMBY, SHIRLEY ANN
Human services specialist. **Personal:** Born Jun 1954, Hartford, CT; daughter of Elizabeth McCall and Sarge McCall Jr; married Charles E Gramby, Aug 16, 1975; children: Talib Eric, Shamar Terrell. **Educ:** BS, elementary, special education, 1977; MA, human resource, management supervision, 1990. **Career:** Ohio Bureau of Workers Compensation, public information assistant, 1979-81; Industrial Commission of Ohio, management analyst, 1981-86; Ohio Department of Human Services, program planner, policy analyst, human services specialist, 1986-; Sunrise Broadcasting, Power 106.3, WCKX Radio, community events, 1992-. **Orgs:** Neighborhood House, board member, fundraising chair, 1989-; United Way, new program committee, 1989-; Leadership Columbus, recruitment committee, 1990-; Delta Sigma Theta, co-chair, arts & letters, 1988-90; I Know I Can, steering committee, 1990-; Wilberforce University Alumnae, Columbus chapter, vice pres, 1991-92; American Cancer Society, Franklin County Breast Cancer Task Force, 1990-91; North East Linden Athletic Association, executive vice pres, 1989-90. **Honors/Awds:** Mayors Award, Outstanding Community Service, 1988; James Penney Cash Award for Outstanding Volunteers, 1987; Columbus Jaycees, Jaycee of the Year, President's Award, 1989; Walter and Marian English Community Service Award, 1990; Delta Sigma Theta, Distinguished Service Award, 1989, 1990. **Special Achievements:** Showcasing Youth in the 90's, Delta Sigma Theta, Columbus Alumnae Project, 1988-89; Afro Fair, 1990; Family Festival, Columbus Urban League, 1990, 1991; Greater Columbus Arts Festival, 1992; Celebrity Waiters, Comedy Night, 1991-92. **Home Addr:** 2424 Delbert Rd, Columbus, OH 43211, (614)475-5868.

GRANBERRY, JAMES MADISON, JR.
Clergyman. **Personal:** Born Apr 29, 1914, Coweta, OK; married Ethel Lee Hymes. **Educ:** Western U, AA 1934; Lane Coll, AB 1936; OK Sch of Rel, 1941-42; Fisk U, grad wk 1954-55; Minist Inst TN State U, 1960-61; Campbell Coll, hon DD 1954; Monrovia Coll, hon LlD 1955; Bethel Ch, ordained Deacon 1940; Ward Chapel AME Ch, ordained Elder 1944. **Career:** Camps Chap AME Ch, pastor; Handy Chapel & AME Ch; Cooper Chapel AME Ch; Bethel AME Ch; Metro AME Ch; St Peters AME Ch; St John AME Ch; St Paul AME Ch. **Orgs:** Sec treas pension dept AME Ch 1964; admitted to ann conf 1939; mem NAACP; mem Comm on struct for Mission 1972; mem Gen Assemb of Nat Counc of Chs 1966; mem IBPOE Pride of TN; Masonic Lodge; Mt Hope 96. **Honors/Awds:** Outst cit of Nash 1960; chart mem Beta Pi Chap of Alpha Phi Alpha 1936; outst minis awd; Payne Sem 1964; cit OK State House of Reps 1970; Chaplain of day Mar 12 1973; gen assemb TN ldrs of Black Am.

GRANDBERRY, NIKKI
Talk show hostess. **Career:** WJBK-TV, general assignment reporter, 1978-86; Detroit Public Schools, substitute teacher; Simons Michelson Zieve Inc, public relations; WXYZ-TV, cohost "Company", 1994-. **Business Addr:** Cohost "Company", WXYZ-TV, Channel 7, 20777 W. 10 Mile Rd., Southfield, MI 48037, (810)827-7777.

GRANGER, CARL VICTOR
Physician. **Personal:** Born Nov 26, 1928, Brooklyn, NY; son of Marie Granger and Carl Granger; married Joanne Ghee (deceased); children: Glenn, Marilyn; married Eloise M Walker, 1995. **Educ:** Dartmouth Coll, AB 1948; New York Univ, MD 1952. **Career:** Yale New Haven Hosp, faculty 1961-67; Tufts New England Medical Ctr, faculty 1967-77; Brown Univ, faculty 1977-83; SUNY at Buffalo, prof 1983-; Functional Assessment Research, director, currently. **Orgs:** American Academy of Physical Medicine & Rehabilitation. **Honors/Awds:** Krusen Award, Zeita Lecturer, Association of Academic Psychiatrists. **Military Serv:** AUS 1st lt to major 1954-61. **Business Addr:** Prof Rehabilitation Medicine, SUNY at Buffalo, UDS 232 Parker Hall, Buffalo, NY 14214, (716)829-2076.

GRANGER, EDWINA C.
Artist. **Personal:** Born Oct 15, Yonkers, NY; daughter of Christina White Weldon Small and Paul Weldon; widowed. **Educ:** New York Univ, Courses & Cert Sculp Ceramic 1952; Caton Rose Inst of Fine Arts, Landscape Anatomy 1958; Art Student League New York, Portrait Fig 1962; Rutgers Univ, Certificate in Real Estate 1978; New Mexico Univ, Composition Abstract 1965. **Career:** Creative Arts McGuire AFB, tchr 1963-64; exhibiting artist throughout USA and Azores 1964-69; Portugal & TTS Colonies People Exhibits, original pen & ink prints 1973-80; Doll Shows Applehead, dollmaker 1976-80. **Orgs:** Festival art consultant 1980, art judge 1984, Garden State Art Center 1980; Meadow Lands Race Track 3 Shows 1979-84; mem, NAACP, 1985; mem, Natl Conf of Artists; mem, Natl League of Amer Pen Women, 1965-81; mem Southern Christian Leadership Conf Women 1988-92. **Honors/Awds:** Alexander Medal of Honor, Walton High School; Outstanding Achievement Art Award, NBPW, Willingboro, NJ; first prize in many art shows, Illinois, New Mexico, New York, New Jersey, Azores. **Special Achievements:** Currently working on Martin Luther King Show/Prints/Oils/Pen/Ink; completed fine are print, "The Spectators," Color Print Limited Edition 500, 1988; 4 print series, Amber, African Mkt Place, Holiday Walk, Caribbean Dancer, 1990; mint print, 3 series, "Girl with Oranges," "The Family," "Lost in the Fog"; Publication: Artist of GA Vol III, cover resume pictures, p 37-38, 1994; Women Artists, p 33, 1990. **Home Addr:** 7145 Chestnut Lane, Riverdale, GA 30274.

GRANT, ANNA AUGUSTA FREDRINA
Educator. **Personal:** Born in Jacksonville, FL; married Thomas Ray Grant; children: Kimberly Anne-Renee, Donna Dianna-Raye. **Educ:** FL A&M Univ, BA; Fisk Univ, MA; WA State Univ, PhD; OD Assn, Cert Orgnl Devel Change Agent. **Career:** WA State Univ, teacher & resch asst 1951-55, counselor 1954-55; Dillard Univ, asst prof & freshman counselor 1956; Grambling Coll, assoc prof sociology 1956-57; Fisk Univ, dean of students & assoc prof 1957-59; LA State Special Educ Team, prof soc & coord of comm studies & psychiatric soc work 1959-63; Morehouse Coll, prof/chair of sociology dept. **Orgs:** Visiting prof & lecturer to numerous sch, coll, univ in Amer & abroad; Amer Personnel & Guidance Assn; GA Psychological Assn; Amer Assn of Univ Prof; So Sociological Soc; mem League of Women Voters; NAACP; Natl Counc of Negro Women; YWCA; YMCA; Delta Sigma Theta; Phi Beta Kappa. **Honors/Awds:** FL Meml Coll Achiev Award 1976; FAMU Alumni Achiev Award 1984; Wash State Univ Alumni Award 1982; Eminent Scholar Norfolk State Univ 1972; NAACP Natl Urban League Black Family Summit 1984; Frederick Douglass Inst Disting Prof Serv Award 1972; Bronze Woman of the Year in Educ Iota Phi Lambda 1972; Dogwood Festival Award 1974; Governor's Award in the Humanities, State of Georgia, 1991; Outstanding Educator, Dollars & Sense Magazine, 1989; Black Heritage Achievement Award, Turner Broadcasting Co, 1986; Fisk Univ, Alumni Achievement Award, General Alumni Assn, 1993. **Business Addr:** Prof of Sociology, Morehouse College, Box 733, Atlanta, GA 30314.

GRANT, ARTHUR H.
Attorney. **Personal:** Born Oct 23, 1930, Louisiana; married Bonnie Connors; children: Arthur H, Jr, Charlotte, Norman. **Educ:** Wilson Jr Coll, 1951; John Marshall Law Sch, JD 1954. **Career:** Arthur H Grant Ltd, attny; Major Lance noted enter, past mgr; Barbara Atklin; Johnny Williams; Profit Publ Co Lucky Labels Inc, pres; Jabita & Co Imprtrs, v p. **Orgs:** Mem NBA; Cook Co Bar Assn; IL Bar Assn. **Military Serv:** AUS spec 4/C 1955-56.

GRANT, BRIAN WADE
Professional basketball player. **Personal:** Born Mar 5, 1972, Columbus, OH. **Educ:** Xavier Univ. **Career:** Sacramento Kings, forward, 1994-97; Portland Trailblazers, 1997-. **Honors/Awds:** NBA All-Rookie First Team, 1995. **Special Achievements:** Appeared in the film "Eddie.". **Business Addr:** Professional Basketball Player, Portland Trailblazers, 700 NE Multnomah St, Ste 600, Portland, OR 97232, (503)234-9291.

GRANT, CHARLES TRUMAN
Business executive. **Personal:** Born Oct 10, 1946, Chicago, IL; son of Mildred Grant and Charles Grant; divorced; children: Jordanna Lynn. **Educ:** DePaul Univ, BA 1969, MBA 1975; Licensed Real Estate Broker 1986; Licensed Mortgage Broker 1987. **Career:** V Mueller Div Amer Hosp Supply Corp, staff accountant, chief accountant, gen acctg mgr, cost acctg mgr 1970-73; Rand McNally & Co, gen credit mgr, dir internal audit 1973-75; Amer Hosp Supply Corp, corp dir, acctg & reporting, div controller officer, 1975-78; Mead Corp, oper admin, vice pres 1978-80; Ft Dearborn Paper Co, ceo, pres 1980-82; Acquisition Mgmt, evp 1982-84; Mid Amer Inc, pres, ceo 1985-; Mergers & Acquisitions, vp; Baird & Warner Inc, 1986-87; Grant-Eaton Ventures, Inc, pres 1985-. **Orgs:** Pres Natl Black MBA Assoc; bd of dir CEDCO Capital Inc, MESBIC Venture Capital; mem NY Credit & Fin Mgmt Assoc; fin adv Jr Achievement. **Honors/Awds:** Article in Ebony Mag 1977, Black Enterprise 1978, Chicago Trib, Crain's Chicago Bus, Chicago Defender, Ebony Mag, Black Enterprise; Ten Outstanding Prof of the Year Blackbook Dollars & Sense Mag 1982; Outstanding Young Man in Amer Jaycees 1982; Outstanding MBA of the Year Natl Black MBA Assoc 1982; DePaul Univ Disting Alumni Awd; publ in Bus & Soc Review Mag 1984-85; Listed in DuSable Museum Chgo. **Military Serv:** AUSR 1968-74.

GRANT, CHERYL DAYNE
Attorney. **Personal:** Born Jan 3, 1944, Cincinnati, OH; married Daniel R (divorced); married Claude H. Audley. **Educ:** Univ of Cin, BA 1966; Univ of Cincinnati Law Sch, 1973. **Career:** Hamilton County Municipal Court, judge; Office of Municipal Investigation, former Chief of Investigation; US Attorney, former assistant; CD Grant & Asso Co LPA, asst OH atty gen 1979-80; Univ of Cincin, asst prof 1976-78; City of Lin Hgts OH, dir legal svcs; Cong Thomas A Luken House of Rep, admin aide of 1974-; Legal Aid Soc, atty 1973-74; Cincinnati Lawyers for Hsing (ABA Proj) 1972; Cin, police Offcr 1968-70; Mem Comm Ctr, soc wrkr 1966-68; ABC'S of Law WCIN-RADIO, co-mod. **Orgs:** Mem bd dir Wom Cty Club; mem bd NAACP; mem bd of Cit Com on Just & Corr; mem pres bd Mem Comm Ctr; mem Alpha Kappa Alpha; mem Cincinnati Bar Assn; OH Bar Assn; ABA; Cin Lawyers Club; Black Lawyers Assn of Cin. **Honors/Awds:** OH Yth Adv Bd 1974-77; appoint OH Juv Just Adv Comm OH 1976-; NAACP scholar 1970-73; Regin Heber Smith fellow Howard U. **Business Addr:** Ste 2125 Krover Bldg, Cincinnati, OH 45202.

GRANT, CLAUDE DEWITT
Educational administrator, educator. **Personal:** Born Dec 20, 1944, New York, NY; son of Rose Levonia Nelson Chenault and Claude Allen Grant; married Gloriana B Waters; children: Damian A, Tahra L. **Educ:** US Armed Forces Inst Germany, 1 yr coll equiv; Bronx Comm Coll, (with Honors) 1970-72; Hunter Coll, BA Social Sci 1972-74; MS in Journalism, Electronic Publishing, IONA College. **Career:** NY Psychiatric Inst, psych intern 1973-74; Yonkers Youth Svcs, adolescent counselor 1974-76; Jamaica Comm Adol Prog assoc psych, sr soc wkr 1976-79; Bronx Comm Coll, coord prog & cultural affairs 1979-1986; Eng Dept, Bronx Comm Coll, adjuct instructor, 1991-; Dir, Business & Professional Development Inst; Consulting Plus, computer/business consulting practice proprietor, 1992-. **Orgs:** Admin ed/fiscal officer, Blind Beggar Press 1977-; spec proj dir, Unity & Strength of BCC 1981-; mem Coll Media Advisors 1982-, Assoc for Ed in Journalism 1983-; exec bd, vp, Bronx Council on the Arts 1983-; Community College Journalism Assoc; 1984; Freelance Contributor to; Essence Magazine, Amsterdam News, etc; "Jazz, Lost Legacy of A People"? (Univ of CA at Berkeley), "Creativity, Imagination Help Preserve Quality Programs on a Limited Budget" (Bulletin of Assoc of College Unions International) Papers presented at BCC, 1986, Pace University 1985, Howard University 1987; Books Published, "Keeping Time" 1981, "Images in a Shaded Light" 1986; exec bd, vp, Mind Builders Creative Arts Center, 1990-; pres, Bronx Council on the Arts Development Corp, 1995-. **Honors/Awds:** Deans List/BCC Bronx CC 1970-72; Serv Awds Bronx CC 1972, 1980, 1981, 1983, 1984; BCC Meritorious Service Awards 1972-86; US Commission on Minority Business Development, Certificate of Appreciation, 1992; Bronx Community College Foundation, Faculty Research Award, 1993. **Military Serv:** AUS corpl 3 yrs; medical technician/medical records clerk Texas, Germany. **Home Addr:** 24 Bowbell Rd, White Plains, NY 10607. **Business Addr:** Dir, Business & Professional Development Inst, Bronx Community College, West 181 St & Univ Ave, Bronx, NY 10453.

GRANT, DARLENE CAMILLE
Lawyer. **Personal:** Born Apr 25, 1959, Jackson Heights, NY; daughter of Leonard & Lucille Grant; married Raymond L Bruce, Nov 30, 1996. **Career:** US District Court for VI, special master, 1996-; National Council on Crime & Delinquency, general counsel, 1994-; Council for DC, assistant gen counsel, 1990-; VI Department of Justice, assistant attorney general, 1989-94. **Orgs:** Delta Sigma Theta Sorority; US Supreme Court; US Courts of Appeals, 3rd circuit, District of Columbia; NY State Supreme Court Appellate Div, 2nd Department; American Bar Association; National Bar Association; Metro Black Bar Assn; VI Bar Association. **Honors/Awds:** VI Department of Justice, Certificate of Appreciation, 1993; Narcotics Strike Force, Certificate of Service, 1993; Earl Warren Legal Scholar, 1981; Council on Legal Education Opportunities, 1981. **Special Achievements:** Should Prison Litigation Be Curtailed?, May 1996, Focus-NCCD; Congressional Study on the DC Department of Corrections, Jan 1996. **Business Addr:** General Counsel, National Council on Crime & Delinquency, 9 East 47 St, Ste 500, New York, NY 10017, (212)371-9150.

GRANT, DEBORA FELITA
Minister. **Personal:** Born Jul 28, 1956, Georgetown, SC; daughter of Lillie M Ward Grant and Rev Joseph J Grant. **Educ:** Clark Coll, Atlanta GA, BA Mass Communications, 1981; Interdenominational Theological Center, Atlanta GA, Master of Divinity Pastoral Care and Counseling, 1987. **Career:** DHR/Div of Youth Serv, Atlanta GA, court serv worker, 1977-85; Flipper Temple AME Church, Atlanta GA, asst minister, 1985-; Morris Brown Coll, Atlanta GA, chaplain, 1987-. **Orgs:** Mem, Black Women In Church and Soc, 1986-89; exec sec, Concerned Black Clergy of Metro Atlanta, 1987-89; mem, NAACP, 1987-89, AME Ministers Union, 1988-89, Natl Assn of College & Univ Chaplains, 1989, Natl Black Campus Ministers Assn, 1989, SCLC Women, 1989. **Home Addr:** 249 Fielding Ln SW, Atlanta, GA 30311. **Business Addr:** Chaplain, Morris Brown College, 643 Martin Luther King Jr Dr, Atlanta, GA 30311.

GRANT, GARY RUDOLPH
Business executive. **Personal:** Born Aug 19, 1943, Newport News, VA; son of Florneza M Grant and Matthew Grant; widowed. **Educ:** NC Central Univ, BA 1965; Shaw Univ, post grad studies attended; NC Wesleyan Coll, post grad studies; Eastern NC Theological Seminary, PhD humanities, 1997. **Career:** Halifax Cty Schools, teacher 1965-79; Tillery Casket Mfg Inc, gen mgr 1979-; Flo-Matt United Inc, pres, currently. **Orgs:** Bd mem Concerned Citizens of Tillery 1979-85; NC Hunger Coalition 1982-86; Halifax Cty Bd of Ed 1982-86; chairperson Committee to Save Black Owned Land 1983-. **Honors/Awds:** Gary Grant Day Tillery Comm 1978; 4-H Club Halifax Cty; Gov Volunteer Awd Gov James B Hunt 1982; Trail Blazer for Environmental Justice, 1996; Halifax County NAACP, Humanitarian Award, 1997. **Business Addr:** President, Flo-Matt United, Inc, PO Box 68, Tillery, NC 27887.

GRANT, GEORGE C.
Library administrator. **Personal:** Born Oct 22, 1939, Memphis, TN; son of Clara Lawson Grant and Willie L Grant Sr; married Alice Morgan Grant, Mar 16, 1963; children: Genine M, Melanie C. **Educ:** Owen Jr Coll, Memphis TN, AA, 1959; Morehouse Coll, Atlanta GA, BS, 1961; Atlanta Univ, Atlanta GA, MSLS, 1962; Univ of Pittsburgh, SLIS, Pittsburgh PA, PhD, 1981. **Career:** Owen Jr Coll, Memphis TN, head librarian, 1962-65; Southern Illinois Univ, Edwardsville IL, E St Louis Campus, chief librarian, 1965-67, assoc dir of library, 1967-76; Morgan State Univ, Baltimore MD, library dir, 1976-81; Stockton State Coll, Pomona NJ, library dir, 1981-86; Rollins Coll, Winter Park FL, dir of libraries, 1986-; Four-G Publishers, pres/CEO, currently. **Orgs:** Amer Library Assn, 1967-; mem, 1971-, exec bd mem, 1980-, editor, newsletter, 1980-, editor, membership directory, 1984-, Black Caucus of ALA; chair, 1982-86, advisory comm, 1982-88, ALA Office of Library Outreach Serv; Florida Library Assn, 1986-; bd of dir, Central Florida Soc of Afro-American Heritage, 1987-89; steering comm, Preserve the Eatonville FL Community, 1988-90; steering comm, Central Florida Library Network, 1988-; advisory comm, Florida State Library, LSCA, 1988-. **Honors/Awds:** Fellowship for PhD Studies, Univ of Pittsburgh, 1974-75; Council on Library resources Acad, Library Internship Yale Univ, 1975-76; Newsletter of the Black Caucus of ALA, 1980-88; Membership Directory, Black Caucus of ALA, 4th edition, 1984, 5th edition, 1986, 6th edition, 1988; Preserve the Etonville Community Inc Serv Award, 1989. **Special Achievements:** Compiler: Directory of Ethnic Professionals in Library and Information Science, FOUR-G Publishers Inc, 1991. **Business Addr:** Director of Libraries, Rollins College, Olin Library, Winter Park, FL 32789.

GRANT, HARVEY
Professional basketball player. **Personal:** Born Jul 4, 1965, Augusta, GA; married Beverly; children: Jerai, Jaren, Jeremy. **Educ:** Clemson Univ, Clemson, SC, 1984-85; Independence Junior College, Independence, KS, 1985-86; Univ of Oklahoma, Norman, OK, bachelor's degree in law enforcement. **Career:** Washington Bullets, forward, 1988-93; Portland Trail Blazers, 1993-96; Washington Wizards, 1996-. **Special Achievements:** NBA Draft, First round pick, #12, 1988. **Business Addr:** Professional Basketball Player, Washington Wizards, MCI Center, 601 F St NW, Washington, DC 20071, (301)622-3865.

GRANT, HORACE JUNIOR
Professional basketball player. **Personal:** Born Jul 4, 1965, Augusta, GA; children: Horace Jr. **Educ:** Clemson Univ, Clemson, SC, 1983-87. **Career:** Chicago Bulls, forward, 1987-94; Orlando Magic, 1994-. **Honors/Awds:** NBA All-Star, 1994. **Business Addr:** Professional Basketball Player, Orlando Magic, 1 Magic Pl, Orlando, FL 32801, (407)649-3200.

GRANT, HOWARD P.
Civil engineer. **Personal:** Born Jul 28, 1925, Houston, TX; married Julia. **Educ:** Univ Of CA, BS. **Career:** City & Cnty of San Franc, civil Eng 1948-. **Orgs:** Mem Natl Soc of Prof Eng; mem North CA Counc of Black Prof Eng; mem Eng Manpower Train Comm; mem Alpha Phi Alpha; mem Commonwealth Club Of CA; bd of dir Bethany Sr CitHm; mem Boy Scout Comm 1970; Mem Big Bros 1965. **Military Serv:** USAF 1944-45.

GRANT, JACQUELYN
Educator. **Personal:** Born Dec 19, 1948, Georgetown, SC; daughter of Lillie Mae Grant and Rev Joseph J Grant. **Educ:** Bennett Coll, BA 1970; Interdenominational Theol Ctr, MDiv 1973; Union Theol Seminary, MPhil 1980, PhD 1985. **Career:** Union Theol Seminary, tutor & relief teacher 1975-77; Harvard Divinity School, assoc in rsch 1977-79; Candler School of Emory/Theol Univ, visiting lecturer 1981; Princeton Theol Seminary, visit lectr 1985; Interdenominational Theol Center, prof 1980-. **Orgs:** Assoc minister Allen AME Church 1973-80; itinerant elder African Methodist Episcopal Church 1976; assoc minister Flipper Temple AME Church 1980-93; Victory AME Church, 1993; founder/dir Black Women in Church & Soc 1981; bd of dirs Black Theology Project in the Americas. **Honors/Awds:** DuBois Fellowship Harvard Univ 1979-80; Dissertation Fellowship Fund for Theological Educ 1979-80; Amer Black Achievement Awd nominee Johnson Publishing Co 1982; Woman of the Year in Religion nominee Iota Phi Lambda Sorority 1984; Martin Luther King, Jr Ministry Award, 1986; Colgate/Rochester Theological Seminary, Outstanding Alumni: Turner Theological Seminary at ITC. **Business Addr:** Professor, Systematic Theology, Interdenominational Theological Center, 700 Martin Luther King Jr Dr, Atlanta, GA 30314.

GRANT, JAMES
Educational administrator. **Personal:** Born Dec 28, 1932, Ruffin, SC; married Maggie Ruth Harrison; children: Christopher, Kevin, Karen. **Educ:** Adelphi Univ, BBA 1959, MBA 1973. **Career:** Adelphi Univ, asst controller 1970-73, controller 1973; CUNY-Medgar Evers Coll, assoc dean of admin 1973-78, dean of admin 1978-79; SUNY-College at New Paltz, vice pres for admin. **Orgs:** Consultant MD State Higher Educl 1984 & 1985; consultant Middle States Assn 1985; pres Auxillary Compus Enterprises Inc 1979-; mem Eastern Assn of Univ & Coll Business Officers 1970-; pres State Univ of NY Business Officers Assn 1983-85. **Military Serv:** AUS sp4 2 yrs. **Business Addr:** Vice President Administration, SUNY/The College at New Paltz, Hab 905, New Paltz, NY 12561.

GRANT, JOHN H., SR.
Manager. **Personal:** Born May 11, 1927, Philadelphia, PA; married Carolyn Sawyer; children: John Jr, Marsha L. **Educ:** Tuskegee Inst, graduated 1949. **Career:** Boeing Vertol, inspector, supervisor, genl supervisor, asst mgr contract maintenance mgr, quality assurance corrective action unit, quality assurance rep, quality control final assembly supervisor, sr product assurance analyst, coord of quality control functions, supervisor dynamic components 1961-. **Orgs:** Mem and past pres Boeing Mgmt Assoc; dir emeritus Northeastern Regional, Tuskegee Inst Alumni Assoc Inc; mem Amer Helicopter Soc Inc; past vice chmn exec bd Natl Tuskegee Alumni Inc; chmn trustee bd New Bethlehem Bapt Church 1975-85. **Honors/Awds:** Deputy/Lecture Awd Outstanding Worshipful Master 1st Dist Prince Hall Masons; 33 Degree Mason, United Supreme Council, Northern Jurisdiction 1988. **Military Serv:** AUS motor sgt 1946-50. **Home Addr:** 267 East Meehan Ave, Philadelphia, PA 19119.

GRANT, KINGSLEY B.
Physician. **Personal:** Born Feb 13, 1931, Central Amer; son of Mina Grant and Barrister E A; married Margaret; children: Ward, Conrad Maxwell. **Educ:** Univ London, BA 1948; Howard Univ, BS 1955, MD 1959; Amer Bd of Pathology, cert 1964; Amer Bd of Pathology & Dermatopathology, cert 1980. **Career:** LA Co Harbor General Hosp, resident anatomic & clinical pathologist, 1962-64, chief resident, 1963-64; St Lukes Hospital, resident anatomic & clinical path 1960-62, assoc path-co-dir path 1970, dir dept pathology & lab serv 1975-88. **Orgs:** Staff St Lukes Hosp 1964-92; bd dir United Way 1966-71; Hawkeye Area Comm Action Prog 1968-69; CR chap Natl Conf Christians & Jews 1969; Am Soc Clin Path Chmn Cedar Rapids Commn Human Rights 1969; pres PTA 1969; clin asst prof Coll Med Univ IA 1973-78; exec comm mem IA Assn Pathologists 1974-89; pres St Lukes methodist Hosp Med/Dental Staff 1981; fellow Amer Coll Pathologists; mem Commn Race & Religion IA United Meth Ch, Rotary Club, Educ Oppor Prog Comm Coll Med Univ IA; mem AMA, NMA, Intl Acad Pathologists; delegate Coll of Amer Pathologists; secty-treasurer/pres, Iowa Assn of Pathologists, 1986-89. **Honors/Awds:** Phi Beta Kappa 1955; Comm Bldr Awd B'nai B'rith 1970; Certificate of Appreciation City of Cedar Rapids 1974. **Business Addr:** 11813 County Road X28, Anamosa, IA 52205-7519.

GRANT, LORRIE
Journalist. **Personal:** Born Jul 27, 1963, Roper, NC; daughter of Curtis Grant and Annie Mae Grant. **Educ:** Iona College, BA, 1985; Univ of Missouri at Columbia, MA, 1987. **Career:** Reuters, correspondent, currently. **Orgs:** National Association of Black Journalist; Society of American Business Editors and Writers; Delta Sigma Theta Sorority Incorporated. **Honors/Awds:** Outstanding Young Women of America, 1989. **Business Addr:** Bureau Chief, Reuters News Agency, 212 S. Tryon St., Ste 1680, Charlotte, NC 28281, (704)358-1202.

GRANT, MCNAIR
Educator. **Personal:** Born Aug 9, 1925, Fort Smith, AR; married Angela I; children: Mc Nair, Jr, Reme, Donna. **Educ:** George Williams Coll, BA 1950; NWU, MA 1955. **Career:** Chicago Bd of Educ, assoc supt 1975-; area assoc supt 1972-75; dist supt 1965-72; prin, teacher 1950-65. **Orgs:** Mem Stratton Educ Assn; Nat Assn of Black Sch Edctrs; Am Assn of Admin; mem NAACP; Urban League. **Honors/Awds:** Class pres George Wms Coll 1950; hon soc Kappa Delta Phi 1950; 1st vice pres Kappa Delta Phi 1970. **Military Serv:** AUS sgt 1943-46. **Business Addr:** 228 N La Salle, Chicago, IL.

GRANT, NATHANIEL
Corporate officer. **Personal:** Born Sep 8, 1943, Washington, DC; married Patricia A; children: Monica D, Nathaniel D. **Educ:** Norfolk State Coll, business admin courses 1964-66. **Career:** Communications Satellite, admin super 1966-69; Amer Assoc of Univ Women, production mgr 1969-73; Natl Public Radio, admin mgr 1973-77. **Orgs:** Mem Natl Forum for Black Public Administrators 1984-87. **Honors/Awds:** Bd Resolution for Outstanding Serv Neighborhood Housing Serv of Amer 1982; Bd Resolution and Monetary Awd Neighborhood Reinvestment Corp 1986,1988. **Military Serv:** USN yeoman 2nd class 4 yrs. **Home Addr:** 13713 Town Line Rd, Silver Spring, MD 20906. **Business Addr:** Dir Personnel & Administration, Neighborhood Reinvestment, 1325 G St NW Ste 800, Washington, DC 20005.

GRANT, STEPHEN MITCHELL
Professional football player. **Personal:** Born Dec 23, 1969, Miami, FL; married Leslie; children: Michael. **Educ:** West Virginia. **Career:** Indianapolis Colts, linebacker, 1992-. **Business Addr:** Professional Football Player, Indianapolis Colts, PO Box 535000, Indianapolis, IN 46253, (317)297-2658.

GRANT, TIMOTHY JEROME
Social worker. **Personal:** Born Aug 6, 1965, Greenville, SC; son of Mamie J Rosemond Grant and John M Grant Sr. **Educ:** Univ of South Carolina, Columbia SC, BS, 1987. **Career:** South Carolina House of Representatives, Cola SC, legislative aide, 1987-89; Richland County Dept of Social Serv, Cola SC, social serv specialist I, 1987-89, social serv specialist II, 1989-90, social serv specialist III, 1990-93, work support specialist, 1993-. **Orgs:** Phi Beta Sigma Frat, 1984-; Notary Public, South Carolina Notary Public, 1987-. **Honors/Awds:** Undergraduate Brother of the Year, Phi Beta Sigma, 1986; Order of Omega Honor Soc, USC Greeks, 1987; Serv Award, South Carolina House of Representatives, 1987. **Home Addr:** 4042 Evergreen Dr, Columbia, SC 29204.

GRANT, WILMER, JR.
Educator. **Personal:** Born Jul 29, 1940, Ahoskie, NC; married Ruth Dale Ford. **Educ:** Hampton Inst, BA 1962; IN U, MS 1967; IN U, PhD 1974. **Career:** Univ of Toledo, asst prof 1973-; Univ of MO, asst dean 1972-73; IN Mil Acad, instructor 1966. **Orgs:** Mem Am Physical Soc; Am Inst of Physics; ctrl OH Black Studies Consortium; Nat Concl of Black Studies; consult DHEW 1976f Assn for the Study of Afro-Am Life & Hist 1976-; mem Alpha Phi Alpha 1961-; Sigma Pi Phi 1977-; Comm Chest Budget Com 1975; bd of tsts Cordelia Martin Ngbrhd Hlth Ctr 1974-76; Toledo Cncl for Bus 1975-77. **Honors/Awds:** Omega Psi Phi talent contest State of VA 1958; comndtn AUS 1961; cert of merit Kappa League 1977f develpr ''Famous Black Symphomic Composers' & Their Works''1976. **Military Serv:** AUS 1st lt capt 1962-64. **Business Addr:** Department of Physics, Landrum Box 8031, Georgia Southern College, Statesboro, GA 30460.

GRANT BISHOP, ELLEN ELIZABETH
Government Official. **Personal:** Born Mar 25, 1949, Buffalo, NY; daughter of Herman & Verba; married George M Bishop Jr, Mar 19, 1983; children: Justin Mason. **Educ:** State University of New York at Buffalo, BA, 1972, MSW, 1974, PhD, 1979. **Career:** Buffalo General Hosp, prog coord, dep dir, asst vp, 1973-83; Community Mental Health Ctr, admin; Buffalo Psychiatric Ctr, social worker, acting team leader, 1975-80; Erie County Medical Ctr, licensed practical nurse, 1968-74; Erie County, Department of Mental Health, commissioner of mental health, 1988-. **Orgs:** Academy of Certified Social Workers, 1974-; NY State Certified Social Workers, 1974-; American College of Mental Health Administration, fellow. **Honors/Awds:** Medaille Coll, Humane Letters, Honoris Causa, 1996; NY State, Social Workers of the Year, 1997; NY State Women's Commissions, Health Award, 1997; NY State Black Psychologists, Nelson Mandela Community Svc Award, 1991; Iota Phi Lambda Sorority, Locam Natl Outstanding Business Woman of the Year Award, Parker Achievement Award. **Special Achievements:** Managing in Black & White: A Guide for the Professional Woman of Color, book; ''Self-Mktg Skills for the New Administration,'' in Comtemporary Directions in Human Resource Management, book chapter. **Business Addr:** Commissioner, Erie County Department of Mental Health, 95 Franklin St, Rm 1237, Buffalo, NY 14215, (716)858-8531.

GRANTHAM, CHARLES
Sports organization executive. **Career:** Natl Basketball Players' Assn, executive director, 1988-95. **Business Addr:** Former Executive Director, National Basketball Player's Association, 1775 Broadway, Ste 2401, New York, NY 10019, (212)333-7510.

GRANTLEY, ROBERT CLARK
Electric utility company executive. **Personal:** Born Aug 30, 1948, Atlanta, GA; son of Edith Clark Grantley and Robert Charles Grantley; married Sandra Prophet Grantley, Nov 22, 1979; children: Michael, Robyn. **Educ:** Howard Univ, Washington DC, BSEE, 1971; Catholic Univ, Washington DC, JD, 1983. **Career:** Challenger Research Inc, Rockville MD, electronics engineer, 1971-73; Potomac Electric Power Company, Washington DC, start-up engineer, 1973-75, site mgr, 1975-78, construction coord, 1978-84, mgr, Energy Use Mgmt, 1974-87, vice pres, Customer Serv, 1987-94, group vice pres, customers & community relations, 1994-. **Orgs:** Mem, Washington DC Bar Assn, 1983-, Maryland Bar Assn, 1983-; board of directors, The American Red Cross, National Capital Chapter; board of directors, The Levine School of Music; board of directors, The Greater Washington Urban League; board of directors, The Latin American Youth Center; board of directors, Leadership Washington. **Business Addr:** Group Vice Pres, Customers & Community Relations, Potomac Electric Power Co., 1900 Pennsylvania Ave NW, Rm 704, Washington, DC 20068.

GRANVILLE, WILLIAM, JR.
Petroleum business executive, educational administrator. **Personal:** Born Dec 6, 1940, Warner Robbins, GA; son of Marian Hicks and William Granville Sr; married Jessica Katherine Hilton; children: Cheryl Lynn, Michelle Marie, William Lamont. **Educ:** Delaware St Coll, BS Math (cum laude) 1962, Doctor of Humane Letters, Honoris Causa 1987. **Career:** Dept of Army, mathematician 1962-65; Mobil Rsch & Develop Corp, res math 1965-69; Mobil Intl Div, intl planning analyst 1969-70, intl rel exec 1970-76; Mobil Oil Corp, mgr Middle East training oper 1976-81, mgr tech transfer Middle East 1981-; Mobil Intl Consulting Serv Inc, exec vice pres 1983-; Granville Academy, founder, 1983-. **Orgs:** Woodrow Wilson Fellow; bd of trustees Rider Coll; bd of dir US Black Engineer and US Hispanic Engineer magazines. **Honors/Awds:** Community Serv Award NAACP 1984; Distinguished Alumnus Award, DE State Coll 1984; Award Natl Assn for Equal Opportunity in Higher Educ Washington; Hon DHL Delaware State Coll; mem Omicron Delta Kappa Honorary Society.

GRATE, ISAAC, JR.
Physician. **Personal:** Born Dec 20, 1952, Georgetown, SC; son of Beulah Grate and Isaac Grate Sr; married Frankie Lee Young; children: Chelsea. **Educ:** Howard Univ, attended 1971-74; Meharry Medical Coll, MD 1978; UCLA School of Public Health, Graduate School 1979-80. **Career:** Martin Luther King Jr General Hosp, intern 1978-79; Johns Hopkins Hosp, resident 1980-82; Texas Tech Univ, instructor surgery/em 1982-84; St Lukes Episcopal Hospital, dir of emergency svcs, 1985-87; Southeast Texas Emergency Physicians, partner, 1987-92; Louisiana Emergency and Trauma, specialist, 1992-. **Orgs:** Mem Univ Assoc of Emergency Physicians 1992-97, Soc of Teachers Emergency Med 1992-97, Amer Coll of Emergency Physicians 1992-97; affiliate faculty, instructor ACLS Amer Heart Assoc 1984-87; mem Houston Medical Forum 1987-92; Southwest Texas Emergency Physicians 1987-92, Natl Medical Assoc 1987-91, NAACP 1996; flight surgeon USAF Reserves 1987. **Honors/Awds:** Dir Medical Educ Texas Tech Univ Sch of Medicine Div Emergency Medicine 1982-85; Fellow Amer College Emergency Physicians 1996-. **Military Serv:** USAF Reserves major 5 yrs. **Home Addr:** 11811 Pepperdine Ln, Houston, TX 77071.

GRAUER, GLADYS BARKER
Artist, educator. **Personal:** Born Aug 15, 1923, Cincinnati, OH; daughter of Maude & Charles Barker; married Solomon Grauer, Dec 27, 1947 (deceased); children: Antoinette Baskerville, Edith, Edward, Leon. **Educ:** Art Institute of Chicago, Rutgers University, attended, 1941-45; attended, 1972-74. **Career:** Essex County Votech High School, teacher, 1974-89; Essex County College, teacher, 1989-92; Neward Museum, 1989-90. **Orgs:** Newark Arts Council, bd mem, 1981-98; City Without Walls Art Gallery, bd mem, 1995-98; Art Institute of Chicago, alumni assoc, 1945-; Black Woman In Visual Perspective, pres, 1980-; Aljira Gallery, 1994-98; National Education Association, 1974-. **Honors/Awds:** James Street Commons, First Prize Watercolor, 1983. **Special Achievements:** New Jersey State Council on the Arts, Fellowship, 1985; Newark Museum Artist in Residence, 1992; Rutgers Innovative Printmaking Fellowship, 1993; art in permanent collections of the Newark Museum, Montclair Museum, Noyes Museum, Newark Public Library, Artist Library of the Victoria & Albert Museum, London, England, Museum of Modern Art, National Museum of American Art Library. **Home Addr:** 352 Seymour Ave, Newark, NJ 07112-2135.

GRAVELY, SAMUEL L., JR.

Naval officer (retired). **Personal:** Born Jun 4, 1922, Richmond, VA; son of Mary George Gravely and Samuel L Gravely Sr; married Alma Bernice Clark; children: Robert (dec), David, Tracey. **Educ:** Virginia Univ, BA History 1948, LLD (hon) 1979; Dr Social Science (hon) 1988. **Career:** US Navy, vice adm (0-9) 1942-80; Third Fleet, commander 1976-78; Defense Communications Agency, dir 1978-80; AFCEA, exec dir educ & training 1984-87; PSE senior corp adv, 1988-. **Orgs:** Vice pres ABSS 1983; vice pres CTEC 1981-82; mem Ruritan Intl 1981-; mem Navy League 1982-; PWC community serv bd 1984-88; NNOA, 1973-; The Rocks 1980-; ECC TAI, 1994-. **Honors/Awds:** Scottish Rite Prince Hall Masonic Bodies of MD Prince Hall Founding Fathers Military Commanders Award 1975; Savannah State Coll Major Richard R Wright Award of Excellence 1974; Alpha Phi Alpha Frat Alpha Award of Merit 1971; Los Angeles Chap Natl Assn of Media Women Inc Communications Award 1972; San Diego Press Club Military Headliner of the Year 1975; Golden Hills United Presb Church Military Service Award 1967; San Diego Optimists Club Good Guy Award; Distinguished Virginian by Governor Holton 1972; VA Press Assn, Virginian of the Year, 1979; Aide-De-Camp to the Governor of VA, 1991. **Military Serv:** USN, vice admiral 38 years; Distinguished Service Medal, Legion of Merit with Gold Star, Bronze Star Medal; Meritorious Serv Medal; Joint Serv Commendation Medal; Navy Commendation Medal; WWII Victory Medal; Naval Reserve Medal for 10 years serv in USN Naval Reserve; Amer Campaign Medal; Korean Pres Unit Citation; Natl Defense Medal with one bronze star; China Serv Medal; Korean Serv Medal with two bronze stars; United Nations Serv Medal; Armed Forces Expeditionary Medal; Antarctic Serv Medal; Venezuelan Order of Merit Second Class; Antartica Support Medal, 1972. **Home Addr:** 15956 Waterfall Rd, Haymarket, VA 22069.

GRAVENBERG, ERIC VON

Educator, educational administrator, consultant. **Personal:** Born May 18, 1950, Oakland, CA; son of Myrtle LeBlanc-Gravenberg and Allen Gravenberg; married Deborah Elaine; children: Roshan, Ashande. **Educ:** California State University, BA, African-American studies, 1972, MPA, public administration, 1974; University of California at Riverside, doctoral candidate. **Career:** California State Univ Chico, dir educ opportunity program 1979-80; Californi a State Univ Hayward, dir educ resource ctr 1980-81; Office of the Chancellor Ca lifornia State Univ, assn dean educ programs 1981-86; Univ of California Riversi de, dir undergrad admissions 1986-; Renaissance Enterprises Private Consulting C ompany, pres 1989-; Institute for Contemporary Leadership, dean of faculty 1989- 91; University of California at Riverside, Saturday Academy, superintendent, dir of undergradua te admissions, 1990-93; Howard Univ, assoc vp for enrollment management, 1993-94. **Orgs:** Affirmative Action Comm Adv Bd Univ of California Irvine 1985-86; board member Western Assn of Educ Opportunity Personnel 1985-86; Natl Council on Access Services College Bd 1985-; organizational development consultant California State Univ-Chico 1986; chmn minority affairs, Western Assn of Coll Admission Counselors 1988-. **Honors/Awds:** Achievers Awd WESTOP Long Beach 1983; President's Award Natl Council of Educ Opportunity Assoc Washington DC 1984; University of California at Riverside, Outstanding Staff Award, 1990; Human Relations Awards, 1990; The Island Consortium for Articulation and Transfer, Educator of the Year, 1992. **Special Achievements:** Author, Learning Assistance Programs, 1986; executive producer, writer, director of theatrical production: "On the Edge of a Dream," 1988; writer, producer, host of over 25 multicultural television productions, 1976-78.

GRAVES, ALLENE

Company executive. **Personal:** Born Jan 5, 1952, Washington, DC; daughter of Eula D Graves and Allen R Graves; children: Kym R Murray. **Educ:** University of District of Columbia. **Career:** United Plannning Organization, secretary, 1972-76; Shaw Project Area Committee, administrative assistant, 1976-79; American Council for Capital Formation, word processor, 1979-83; Academy for Educational Development, executive secretary, 1983-84; Bergson, Borkland & Margolis, legal secretary, 1984-85; Sherman & Lapidus, office manager, 1984-86; The Answer Temps, Inc, president, owner, 1987-. **Orgs:** Metropolitan Washington Temporary Association, 1989; National Association of Female Executives; DC Chamber of Commerce. **Honors/Awds:** Minority Business Women of the Year, Presented by Washington DC Minority Dev Ctr, 1994. **Business Addr:** President, The Answer Temps Inc, 1660 L St NW, Ste 311, Washington, DC 20036, (202)835-0190.

GRAVES, CAROLE A.

Labor union administrator. **Personal:** Born Apr 13, 1938, Newark, NJ; daughter of Jennie Valeria Stafford Anderson and Philip Burnett Anderson; married David Leon Graves, Nov 4, 1962. **Educ:** Kean College, Newark, BA, 1960; Rutger Inst of Labor and Mgmt Rels, labor rels specialist certificate, 1976. **Career:** Newark School System, Newark, NJ, special education teacher, 1960-69; Newark Teachers Union, Local 481, Amer Fedn of Teachers, Newark, NJ, president, 1968-. **Orgs:** Vice-pres, NJ State AFL-CIO; vice-pres, NJ State Indus Union Coun; vice-pres, Essex West/Hudson Central Labor Coun; vice-pres, NJ State Fedn of Teachers; member, Rutgers Lacor Alumni Exec Bd; member, A Philip Randolph Inst; member, Coalition of Labor Union Women. **Honors/Awds:** Named one of Labor's Outstanding Black Women, Natl Org of Black Leaders, 1973; Martin Luther King Award, NJ Labor Press Council, 1973; inducted into NJ Labor Hall of Fame, Newark Community Action Team, 1977; Labor Achievement Award, Women's Affirmative Action Comm, IUC/AFL-CIO, 1983. **Business Addr:** President, Newark Teachers Union, Local 481, 30 Clinton St, Newark, NJ 07112.

GRAVES, CLIFFORD W.

Investment banker. **Personal:** Born Mar 30, 1939, San Francisco, CA; married Anasa Briggs-Graves; children: Sharon, Diane. **Educ:** Univ of CA Berkeley, BA 1961, M City Planning 1964. **Career:** City of Santa Rosa, asst city planner 1961-62; E Sussex Co, town planner & civic designer 1964-66; San Francisco Bay Consult & Dev Commn, assoc planner 1966-69; special projects officer, 1969-70; Comprehensive Planning Asst Div, dir 1970-71; Office of Planning & Mgmt Asst, dir/asst dir 1971-72; Sec for Comm Planning & Mgmt, dep asst 1972-74; Office of Mgmt & Budget, dep assoc dir eval & prog implem; County of San Diego, chief admin officer, 1978-85; San Diego State University, assoc prof, 1979-85; International Technology Corp, Torrance, CA, dir of planning 1986-88; Grigsby/Graves Environmental, San Diego, CA, president 1988-, mng dir 1988-. **Orgs:** Lectr Howard Univ 1970-73; lectr Univ of CA Berkeley 1968-69; mem Amer Inst of Planners; Amer Soc of Planning Ofcl; Amer Soc of Pub Adminstrn; Natl Assn of Planners; commissioner Port of San Diego 1990-. **Honors/Awds:** HUD Disting Serv Award 1972; Wm A Jump Found Award 1972; Student Award Amer Inst of Planners 1972. **Business Addr:** Managing Director, Public Finance, Grigsby Brandford Powell, Inc, 701 B Street, San Diego, CA 92101.

GRAVES, CURTIS M.

Agency official. **Personal:** Born Aug 26, 1938, New Orleans, LA; son of Mabel Haydel Graves and Joseph F Graves; married Joanne Gordon; children: Gretchen, Christopher, Gizelle. **Educ:** Xavier U, atnd; TX So U, BBA 1963; Princeton Univ, Woodrow Wilson Fellow 1984-85. **Career:** Educ & Comm Affairs Br of NASA, chief 1977-87, dep dir civil affairs; Ldrship Inst for Comm Devel in Wash DC, training ofcr tchng state & local govt procedures; Standard Savs Assn of Houston, mgr 1962-66; TX House of Reps, elected 1966-72; National Civil Service League, managing associate, dir of continuing education; NASA, deputy dir of civil affairs of the defense and intergovernmental relations div, deputy dir for academic services in public affairs, chief of community and education services, minority univ program mgr, currently. **Orgs:** Mem steering com Nat Congress of Aerospace Edn; former pres, World AerospaceEduc Org; mem Wash Alumni Chap Kappa Alpha Psi Frat; pres, World Aerospace Education Organization 1983-; bd mem, Kentucky Institute. **Honors/Awds:** Publ book "Famous Black Amers", vol I and II; awards from the Council of Ne gro Women, Delta Sigma Theta Sorority, National Assn of College Women, the City of Los Angeles, Kappa Alpha Psi Fraternity, Texas Southern Univ, New York City School System, National Congress on Aviation and Space Education; two honorary doctorate degrees; Frank G Brewer Trophy, 1989. **Business Addr:** Deputy Dir Civil Affairs, NASA, Code XD, Washington, DC 20546.

GRAVES, DENIQUE

Professional basketball player. **Personal:** Born Sep 16, 1975. **Educ:** Howard Univ, bachelor's degree in teacher education, 1997. **Career:** Sacramento Monarchs, center, 1997-. **Business Addr:** Professional Basketball Player, Sacramento Monarchs, One Sports Parkway, Sacramento, CA 95834, (916)928-3650.

GRAVES, EARL G.

Publisher. **Personal:** Born Jan 9, 1935, Brooklyn, NY; married Barbara Kydd; children: Earl Jr, John Clifford, Michael Alan. **Educ:** Morgan State Coll, BA 1958. **Career:** Senator Robt F Kennedy, admin asst 1965-68; Earl G Graves Ltd, Earl G Graves Pub Co Inc, Earl G Graves Assoc, Earl G Graves Mktg & Rsch Co, Earl G Graves Develop Co; Black Enterprise Magazine, publisher; Pepsi-Cola of Washington, chmn, CEO, 1990-. **Orgs:** Bd dirs Rohm & Haas Corp; Mag Pubs Assn; Natl Minority Purchasing Council Inc; mem Natl Bd Exec Comm Interracial Council for Bus Oppor; mem Natl Bus League; mem NY State Econ Devel Bd; mem exec comm Grtr NY Council BSA; bd selector Amer Inst Pub Svc; trustee Amer Mus Natural History; mem NAACP; SCLC Mag Pub'rs Assn; Interracial Council; Sigma Pi Phi; Statue of Liberty Ellis Island Centennial Comm; visiting comm Harvard Univ's John F Kennedy Sch of Govt; Pres's Council for Business Admin Univ of Vermont; bd mem New York City Partnership; trustee New York Economic Club; bd dirs, New York Urban Development Corp; chmn, Black Business Council; exec comm, Coun of Competitiveness; Stroh's Advisory Coun; natl commissioner and mem exec bd, NatlBoy Scouts of Amer; Natl Minority Business Coun; tree coun, Business Economic Development; bd mem, NY City Partnership. **Honors/Awds:** LLD, Morgan St Univ, 1973, VA Union Univ, 1976, FL Memorial Coll, 1978, J C Smith Univ, 1979, Wesleyan Univ, 1982, Talladaga Coll, 1983, Baruch Coll, 1984, AL St Univ, 1985, Mercy Coll, 1986, Iona Coll, 1987, Elizabeth City St Univ, 1987, Brown Univ, 1987, Lincoln Univ, 1988, Central St Univ, 1988, Howard Univ, 1989, Livingstone Coll, 1989; honorary doctorates, Rust Coll, 1974, Hampton Inst, 1979, Dowling Coll, 1980, Bryant Coll, 1983, St Josephs, NY, 1985, Morehouse Coll, 1986, Suffolk Univ, 1987, Meharry Medical Coll, 1989; Scroll of Honor Natl Med Assn; 1 of 100 Influential Blacks, Ebony Mag; Black Achiever, Talk Mag; 1 of 10 Most Outstanding Minority Businessmen in US, ex-Pres Nixon; 1 of 200 Future Leaders in US, Time Magazine; Broadcaster of the Yr, Natl Assn ofBlack Owned Broadcers; Poynter Fellow, Yale Univ; Recipient of the Boy Scouts Natl Awards, Silver Buffalo 1988, Silver Antelope 1986 and Silver Beaver 1969. **Special Achievements:** Author, "How to Succeed in Business, Without Being White," 1997. **Military Serv:** US Army, Capt. **Business Addr:** Publisher, Earl G Graves Pub Co, Inc, 130 Fifth Ave, New York, NY 10011.

GRAVES, EARL G., JR. (BUTCH)

Publishing company executive. **Personal:** son Of Barbara Graves and Earl G Graves Sr; married Roberta; children: four. **Educ:** Harvard University, Graduate School of Business Administration, MBA. **Career:** Morgan Stanley, investment banker; Earl G Graves Ltd, senior vice president, president, currently. **Business Addr:** President, Earl G Graves Ltd, 130 Fifth Ave, New York, NY 10011, (212)242-8000.

GRAVES, IRENE AMELIA

Educational administrator. **Personal:** Born Feb 22, 1906, St Louis, MO; married Willis M Graves Esq (deceased). **Educ:** Wayne State Univ, AB 1932; McGill Univ, MA 1934; attended Univ of Chicago, CO State Coll, Middlebury Coll, Univ of MN, Univ of MI, Univ of Paris (La Sorbonne); 67 hours beyond MA. **Career:** Detroit Public Schools, teacher 1924-66; Stay-at-Home Camp YWCA, dir 1938; Coll of Ed, dir tchr 1941-47, recruiter 1932-53; Fuller Prod Co Jam Handy Audio Visual Writer, writer in sch serv dept, French translations of English masterpieces 1966-71. **Orgs:** Mem Alpha Kappa Alpha Great Lakes Reg Dir 1938, 1940; chmn social studies teacher Detroit Bd of Ed 1948-60; chmn NAACP 1952; vice chair Cherboneau Condo 1960-62; chair women's comm UNCF 1960; history chair Detroit Branch NAACP 1970-83; 1st black female chair Detroit Windsor Intl Fest Luncheon 1975; chair woman's comm NAACP Life Mem Comm 1976; mem comm Women's Econ Club 1977-85; founder Detroit Chap Barristers Wives, Silhouette Chap Kappa Wives; organizer Largest Group of Inductees Top Ladies of Distinction Inc. **Honors/Awds:** 5 State Awds Governor-Senator 1966-84; 10 City Awds Mayor-Detroit Common Council 1966-84; Carter G Woodson Awd of Distinction Natl Assoc for the Study of Negro Life 1967; Teacher of the Year MI 1975; NAACP Highest Female Seller Life Mem Awd 1978-84; Volunteer of the Week Detroit Free press 1982; Activist on Home Front (one of 3 chosen) 1984; Black Episcopalian Awd Church Comm Activities 1984; Alpha Kappa Alpha Sor of the Year Urban League; 2 Medallions; Highest Award from NAACP for being highest woman salesperson of life membership June 1985; Jefferson Awd Community Serv Nal Organ Medallion 1986; Heart of Gold, United Foundation 1989; Highest Woman Salesperson of Life Memberships in the USA, NAACP 1987-89; United Negro College Fund, Outstanding Award for 50 Years of Volunteer Service, 1994. **Home Addr:** 1585 Cherboneau Condo, Detroit, MI 48207.

GRAVES, JACKIE

Personnel administrator. **Personal:** Born Mar 10, 1926, Santa Anna, TX; married Willie G Clay; children: Roderick L, Sheila R, Jackie A. **Educ:** TX Coll, BA 1948. **Career:** Philadelphia Eagles Football Club, asst dir of player person 1975-; Phil Eagles Football Club, player person scout 1972-75; CEPO, player person scout 1970-72; Boston Patriots Football Club, player person scout 1965-70; AG Spalding Bros, natl sales rep 1965-70; TX So U, asst football coach head golf coach 1950-58; TX Coll, asst head football coach 1958-61; Continental Bowling Lanes Inc, vice pres gen mgr 1961-65. **Orgs:** Mem Almeda Rotary Club; mem Pop Warner Football; mem Almeda Little League Baseball. **Honors/Awds:** Football super scout awd Black Sports Mag 1972; Gentleman of the year Phil Eagles Football Club 1978. **Business Addr:** Veterans Stadium, Broad St & Pattison Ave, Philadelphia, PA 19148.

GRAVES, JERROD FRANKLIN

Dentist. **Personal:** Born Sep 25, 1930, Greensboro, NC; son of Lola Graves and Everett Graves; married Earnestine Ross; children: Jerrod M, Gwendolyn Graves Irowa. **Educ:** Johnson C Smith University, BS, 1951; A&T University, MS, 1955; Meharry Medical College, DDS, 1959. **Career:** Harlem Hosp, intern/resident, oral surgery, 1959-61; self-employed, private practice, dentist, currently. **Orgs:** Omega Psi Phi, 1949-; NAACP; 32 Degree Mason; 369th Veterans Assn; Natl Dental Assn; Academy General Dentistry; Amer Society of Anestheologists; Amer Endodontic Society; Amer Society of Military Surgeons. **Honors/Awds:** Mizzy Award, Best in Oral Surgery. **Military Serv:** Dental Corp, colonel, 15 years, 1952-; US Army Reserves, 1951-; Bronze Star, Army Achievement, Overseas Medal, Army Commendation Medal, Good Conduct Medal, United Nations Ribbon, 1 Oak Leaf Cluster. **Business Addr:** 327 Victory Blvd, Staten Island, NY 10301.

GRAVES, JOHN CLIFFORD
Attorney. **Personal:** Born May 10, 1963, Brooklyn, NY; son of Barbara Eliza Kydd Graves and Earl Gilbert Graves; married Caroline Veronica Clarke Graves, Nov 10, 1990. **Educ:** Colgate Univ, Hamilton, NY, 1981-82; Brown Univ, Providence, RI, BA, 1986; Yale Law School, New Haven, CT, JD, 1989. **Career:** Cleary, Gottlieb, Steen & Hamilton, New York, NY, associate, 1989-. **Orgs:** Student/Sponsor Partnership.

GRAVES, LESLIE THERESA
Attorney. **Personal:** Born Mar 27, 1956, Detroit, MI; daughter of Nora Mallett Graves and Louis Graves. **Educ:** Smith College, Northampton, MA, BA, 1977; Catholic Univ, Washington, DC, JD, 1981. **Career:** State of Michigan, Detroit, MI, workers compensation appeal board member, 1987-91; Wayne County Community College, general counsel; Wayne County Juvenile Court, deputy register, currently. **Orgs:** President, Wolverine Bar Association, 1990-91; State Bar of Michigan Committee for the Expansion of Under-represented Groups in the Law, 1984-91; Women Lawyers Association of Michigan, 1984-; International Visitors Council, 1990-; Brazel Dennard Chorale, bd of dirs, 1988-. **Honors/Awds:** Member of the Year, Wolverine Bar Association, 1985; Private Attorney Involvement Award, WBA, 1990. **Business Addr:** Deputy Register, Wayne County Juvenile Court, 1025 E Forest, Detroit, MI 48207.

GRAVES, RAY REYNOLDS
Judge. **Personal:** Born Jan 10, 1946, Tuscumbia, AL; son of Olga Wilder Graves and Isaac Graves; children: Claire Elise Glass, Reynolds Douglass. **Educ:** Trinity Clge CT, BA 1967; Wayne State Univ, JD 1970. **Career:** Private law practice, atty 1971-81; Lewis, White, Clay & Graves, PC, 1974-81; Univ of Detroit Law School, adjunct prof, 1981-85; US Bankruptcy Court, judge, eastern district, MI, 1982-, chief judge, 1991-95. **Orgs:** Trustee MI Cancer Fnd 1979-83; bd governors Natl Conf of Bankruptcy Judges 1984-87; Sigma Pi Phi Fraternity. **Honors/Awds:** Esquire Magazine's Register, America's Under 40 Leadership, 1986. **Business Addr:** Judge, US Bankruptcy Court, 211 W Fort St, Ste 1900, Detroit, MI 48226.

GRAVES, RAYMOND LEE
Clergyman. **Personal:** Born Jan 3, 1928, Yanceyville, NC; married Pauline H. **Educ:** Winston-Salem State U, BS 1951; NC Central U, MA 1954; Colgate Rochester-Crozier-Bexley Hall Div Sch, MDiv 1968. **Career:** New Bethal CME Ch Rochester NY, rev 1973-; Rochester Econ Oppor Cntr, instr 1969-73; States of VA & GA NY SC, min 1959-80; Sch Bd Danville VA, tchr 1954-62. **Orgs:** Founder Rochester Affiliate of OIC 1978; exec dir Rochester OIC; pres United Ch Ministry; orgn bd mem Action for a Better Comm 1963-65; co-founder FightOrgn 1964; bd mem Push-Excel Rochester Chap 1979-80. **Honors/Awds:** Recip Martin Luther King Prof Chair Awd Colgate Rochester Div Sch 1968; serv awd Urban League of Rochester 1978; Colgate Rochester-Crozier-Bexley Hall achmnt awd Colgate Rochester Div Sch 1980. **Military Serv:** USAF 1951-53. **Business Addr:** New Bethel CME Church, 270 Scio St, Rochester, NY 14606.

GRAVES, RODERICK LAWRENCE
Sports franchise executive. **Personal:** Born Mar 16, 1959, Houston, TX; married Alesia. **Educ:** Texas Tech, BS Economics; Attended, Strake Jesuit Coll Pre Houston. **Career:** Philadelphia Stars USFL, personnel scout, asst dir of player personnel, 1983; Chicago Bears, regional scout, 1984-89, assistant director of player personnel, 1989-; Player Personnel, dir, 1995-. **Business Addr:** Director of Player Personnel, Chicago Bears, 250 N Washington Rd, Lake Forest, IL 60045-2499.

GRAVES, SHERMAN TEEN
Miner. **Personal:** Born Sep 11, 1905, Freeman, WV; married Estella Mae Ward; children: JoAnn, Sherman, Dwight, Debbie, Wanda. **Career:** Miner retired; notary pub 27 yrs; Comm Action, orgnr 1945-46; City of Bramwell, v mayor cnclmn; 1st black mayor; former city judge; Mercer Co, bd of dir. **Orgs:** Indsl Park Devel Assn; chmn Personal Com Rock Dist Clinic Assn; vice pres WV Br NAACP; vice pres Mercer Co OEO; grand rcdr Royal Craft Grand Lodge; F & AAY Masons; pres BHS PTA; treas Mercer Co PTA Cncl; bd of dir Miners Black Lung Hlth Assn; deacon yth adv Bluestone Bapt Ch; rep Black Lung Compensation; Miners Pensions; Unepmt Compensation. **Honors/Awds:** Congressman Nick J Rahall's Adv Com.

GRAVES, VALERIE JO
Business executive. **Personal:** Born Feb 27, 1950, Pontiac, MI; daughter of Deloris Graves and Spurgeon Graves; married Alvin E Bessent; children: Brian. **Educ:** Wayne State Univ, attended 1969-73; NY Univ, Filmmaking Program, 1985-. **Career:** D'Arcy MacManus & Masius Ad Agency, copywriter 1974-75; BBDO Inc Ad Agency, copywriter 1975-76; Kenyon & Eckhardt Boston Ad Agency, copywriter 1977-80; J Walter Thompson USA Ad Agency, sr copywriter 1981-82; Ross Roy Inc, vice pres assoc creative dir, 1982-85; Uniworld Group, vp/assoc creative dir, senior vice president, creative director, 1989-; Clinton/Gore Campaign, creative/media consultant, 1992. **Orgs:** Former mem Harvard Univ Black Comm & Student Theater 1979-80; mem Adcraft Club of Detroit 1982-; consultant 1984-, dir 1984- The Creative Network Inc; mem Natl Assoc Black Women Entrepreneurs 1985; mem, Advertising Club of New York. **Honors/Awds:** Corporate Ad Award Boston Ad Club Francis Hatch Award 1981; Merit Award Art Dirs Club of NY 1982; CEBA Award of Excellence Black Owned Comm Assoc NY 1983; Graphic Excellence Merchandising Graphics Award Competition 1984; Notable Midwest Adwoman Adweek Magazine Chicago 1984; Profile Ebony Magazine Nov 1984; CEBA Award of Excellence, 1987-92; YWCA Academy of Women Achievers, YWCA of New York, 1989. **Business Addr:** Senior Vice Pres, Creative Director, Uniworld Group Inc, 100 Avenue of the Americas, 15th Fl, New York, NY 10013.

GRAY, ANDREW JACKSON
Business executive. **Personal:** Born Jun 20, 1924, Charlotte, NC; married Lucille Jackson; children: Andrew, Jr, Amizie. **Educ:** Morehouse Coll, BA 1946; NC State U, addl studies. **Career:** Andrew J Gray Accounting Firm, acct 1962-; NC Con NAACP Br, auditor. **Orgs:** Mem Nat Soc of Pub Accnt; NC Sor of Accnt; Nat Assn of Enrolled Agents; Nat Assn of Black Accnt; mem Kappa Alpha Psi; NAACP; St Paul Bapt Chl; YMCA. **Honors/Awds:** Charlotte Business League, Hall of Fame Award; Charlotte NC, NAACP, Hall of Fame Award. **Business Addr:** Accountant, Andrew J Gray Accounting Firm, 2202 Beatties Ford Rd, Charlotte, NC 28216.

GRAY, BEVERLY A.
Librarian. **Personal:** Born Aug 3, 1940, Boston, MA; daughter of Mark & Lula Gray. **Educ:** Simmons College, BS, 1962; Columbia Univ, MA, 1964, MLS, 1965. **Career:** Harvard Univ, Africana bibliographer, 1965-67; Boston Univ, librarian, African Studies Library, 1967-72, African section, area specialist, 1972-78; Library of Congress, head, African section, 1978-94. **Orgs:** African Studies Assn; Africana Librarians Council, exec board; Middle East Librarians Assn; Assn of Jewish Libraries; Cooperative Africana Microfirm Project, exec board; American Library Assn; Assn for the Study & Life of African American History. **Special Achievements:** Author, Uganda: Subject Guide to Publications, 1977; Africana Library Resources, In: Ethnic Collections in Libraries, 1983; Liberia During the Tolbert Eval A Guide, 1983; Africana Acquisitions at the Library of Congress, In: Africana Resources & Collections, 1989.

GRAY, BRIAN ANTON
Business owner. **Personal:** Born Apr 13, 1939, Philadelphia, PA; son of Bertha & Cecil Gray; married Linda, Jun 3, 1967; children: Brian, Christian. **Educ:** Cheyney State University, BA, 1964; Howard University, MA, 1972. **Career:** Miller Brewing Co, mgr coll relations, 1975-81; Howard University, dir of personnel, 1982-91; BG & Associates, pres/CEO, 1991-. **Orgs:** Bureau of Rehabilitation, bd chmn, 1985-95; Omega Psi Phi Fraternity, 1962-; Society of Human Resources Management, 1990-; Employment Management Association, 1982-; Nationwide Interchange Svc, 1992-; Nomination Committee, chmn of bd of trustees, 1985-93. **Honors/Awds:** Society Human Resources Management, Senior Professional in Human Resources, 1990; Montgomery County Government, Outstanding Volunteer, 1993; Bureau of Rehabilitation, Outstanding Volunteer, 1993. **Business Addr:** President, BG & Associates, PO Box 34162, Bethesda, MD 20827-0162, (301)365-4046.

GRAY, C. VERNON
Educational administrator, professor, county councilman. **Personal:** Born Jul 30, 1939, Sunderland, MD; son of Virgina Gray and Major Gray; married Sandra Lea Trice; children: Michael, Angela. **Educ:** Morgan State Univ, BA 1961; Atlanta Univ, MA 1962; Univ of MA, PhD 1971. **Career:** Philander Smith Coll, instr 1961-66; Oakland Univ, instr 1970-71; Joint Ctr for Political Studies, Washington DC, 1971-72; Morgan State Univ, assoc dean for soc sci 1974-75; Goucher Coll, visiting prof 1974; Univ of MD, visiting prof 1978-79; Univ of MD College Park, visiting prof 1980-81; Morgan State Univ, chmn political sci 1972-87; Morgan State Univ, dir public serv internship program 1972-87; Morgan State Univ, prof political sci 1972-; Morgan State Univ, chmn political sci & intl studies 1984-87. **Orgs:** Exec council Natl Capitol Area Political Sci Assoc 1976-; pres elect Natl Conf of Black Political Sci 1976-77; chmn Political Action Comm MD State Conf of NAACP 1976-77; bd of dir Meals on Wheels of Central MD 1976; chmn Ad Hoc Contribs Comm Meals on Wheels 1976-77; pres Natl Conf of Black Political Sci 1977-78; nominating comm Southern Political Sci Assoc 1977-78; chmn Ethnic & Cultural Pluralism Award Comm Amer Political Sci Assoc 1977-78; political analyst WJZ, WBAL 1977-; host, producer Politics Power & People 1977-80; speakers bureau United Way of Central MD 1977-78; allocations panel United Way of Central MD 1977-78; adv comm Ctr for Urban Environmental Studies 1977-80; resources bd Minority Energy Tech Asst Program Ctr for Urban Environ Studies 1978; bd of dir Natl Policy Studiesst Goucher Coll 1978; chmn program comm Alpha Phi Alpha 1979-80; dir Educ Activities Alpha Phi Alpha 1979; Election Laws Revision Comm MD 1979-80; chmn county council Howard County MD 1985-87; bd dir MD Assn of Counties, Natl Assn of Counties; bd of dir MD Museum of African Art; bd of dir Howard County Red Cross; chmn United Negro Coll Fund Howard County Campaign, 1990-91; president, Maryland Association of Counties, 1992; health advisory committee, National Association of Counties, 1992-93; board of directors, Howard Health Foundation; board of directors, National Association of Counties, 1986-; Howard County, councilman, 1982-; bd of dirs, NACO Financial Service Ctr; NACO Taxation & Finance Steering Comm; first vice pres, National Association of Counties. **Honors/Awds:** WEAA-FM Awd for Serv 1978; Community Serv Awd United Way of Central MD, 1978; Appreciation Awd Calvert Cty NAACP 1978; Community Serv Admin Certificate of Training 1979; Certificate of Merit Black Women's Consciousness Raising Assoc 1979; Community Serv Awd Howard Community Action 1980, Natl Conf of Black Political Sci 1980; Awd for Distinguished Serv Natl Conf of Black Political Sci 1980; Outstanding Faculty Awd for Community Serv Morgan State Univ 1980; Alpha Man of the Year 1982; mem Pi Sigma Alpha, Ford Found Fellowship, Crusade Scholar, Southern Found Scholar; chmn Educ Comm MD Assn of Counties 1983-84; mem Educ Subcomm/Health and Educ Steering Comm of Natl Assn of Counties; chmn Howard County Council, 1985, 1986, 1990, 1991, 1994; first black elected Howard County Council 1982; Citizen of the Year, Omega Psi Phi Fraternity 1987; Outstanding Service Award, Alpha Kappa Alpha Sorority 1989; Honorary 4-H member; Outstanding Achievement Award, Maryland State Teachers Assn; Amer Lung Assn, Jewish Natl Fund Tree of Life Award, Lawmaker of the Year, 1993. **Business Addr:** Chairman, Political Science, Morgan State Univ, Hillen Rd & Coldspring Ln, Baltimore, MD 21239.

GRAY, CARLTON PATRICK
Professional football player. **Personal:** Born Jun 26, 1971, Cincinnati, OH. **Educ:** UCLA. **Career:** Seattle Seahawks, defensive back, 1993-96; Indianapolis Colts, 1997-. **Business Addr:** Professional Football Player, Indianapolis Colts, PO Box 535000, Indianapolis, IN 46253, (317)297-2658.

GRAY, CAROL COLEMAN
Pediatrician. **Personal:** Born Jun 22, 1946, Wharton, TX; married James Howard Gray MD; children: Nakia, James. **Educ:** Univ of Texas, BS 1967, Medical School MD 1972. **Career:** Walter Reed Army Medical Center, pediatric internship 1972; Univ of MD Hospital, pediatric residency 1977; Dallas Independent School Dist Project Find, medical coord 1979-83; Baylor Univ Medical Center, assoc attending 1981-; Private Practice, pediatrician 1981-. **Orgs:** Mem Amer Medical Assoc, Natl Medical Assoc, CV Roman Medical Soc, NAACP. **Honors/Awds:** Civilian Achievement Award, Walter Reed Army Medical Center 1978; Dallas Independent School Dist Black Women Against the Odds Award; 2nd Annual Salute to America's Top 100 Black Business & Professional Women, Dollars & Sense Magazine 1986; Dream Maker's Award, Southeast Dallas Business and Professional Women; publication "Wednesday's & Thursday's Children, Medical Assessment of the Child with a Handicap" Early Periodic Diagnosis & Treatment Progs. **Military Serv:** AUS capt 1972-73; Internship Certificate 1973. **Business Addr:** Pediatrician, 3600 Gaston Ave #760, Dallas, TX 75246.

GRAY, CHRISTINE
Project director. **Personal:** Born in Cuthbert, GA; married Herman C, 1945 (deceased); children: Dianne Greene, Donna F White. **Educ:** Graduate of Weave High School, 1940; Adminstrv Sch WAAC, 1943; Sch Comptometer, 1944; Exxon, math keypunch 1971. **Career:** Kolodney & Meyers Hartford, payroll clk 1940-46; Hop Equip, customer serv rep 1970-71; Credit Union, sec 1965-67; Thompson & Weinman Co, asst office mgr 1967-70; Union Co OIC, keypunch instr 1971-73; 1975; Union Co Dept Youth Svcs, sec; Union Co OIC, mgr spec; Employment Resource Specialist, 1981-83; Companion Aide, prog dir, 1985-94. **Orgs:** Charter mem NCNW Vauzhall Sect; pres Burnet Jr High PTA; inter club pres YWCA 1942-45; Jr Dgt Ruler Emma V Kelly Elks 1940-42; jr ckl Hopewell Bapt Ch 1941-46; sec Concerned Citizens Vauxhall; sec Citizens Council Vauxhall; pres Jefferson Sch PTA; pres Nat Council Negro Women Vauxhall Sect; chairlady Consumer Educ NCNW; dist ldr Dist 8 Union Co Girl Scout Ldr; bd mem Union Co Anti-proverty bd; sec Calvary Bapt Ch 1959-67, 1970-77; chrtr mem Gary Family Assn; Cancer Soc; Comm Vacation Bible Sch; Calvary Bapt Sunday Sch; Census Bur 1960-70; Calvary Bapt Ch 1973; Historian for Natl Council of Negro Women, Vauxhall Section, 1980-; Mentor Vauxhall & Brookside African-American Youth Literary Club; Time for Teens, sr advisor, 1988-90; Togetherness Assn, sr advisor, 1991-. **Honors/Awds:** Gold pin Girl Scouts; plaque Nat Council Negro Women Vauxhall Sect 1972 & 1973; cert NCNW; guest part Esther Roll Thresa Merritt; Maude Johnson Cultural Awd 1976; Comm Service Award, Natl Council of Negro Women, 1978; Comm Service Award, Bethune Tradition, 1986; Comm Service Award, Vauxhall Homecoming Assn, 1987; Study Commission Union Township, Bd of Educ, 1986. **Military Serv:** WAAC 1943.

GRAY, CLARENCE CORNELIUS, III
Educator (retired). **Personal:** Born Jul 23, 1917, Ridge Springs, SC; son of Maude Gray and Clarence Gray; married Shirley Brown; children: Michele, Clarence, Jennifer. **Educ:** VA State Coll, BS 1943; MI State Coll, MS 1947, PhD 1952; School Adv Intl Studies Johns Hopkins Univ, Certificate 1963; Foreign Serv

Inst US Dept of State, Certificate 1967. **Career:** VA State Coll, asst/assoc/and prof 1948-58; Agency for Intl Dev/US Dept of State, foreign serv officer 1958-70; Rockefeller Foundation, prog off/principal off 1970-83 (retired); Virginia Polytechnic Inst & State Univ, prof 1983-89; prof emeritus 1989. **Orgs:** Trustee/chmn of bd Intl Rice Rsch Inst Philippines 1971-83; consultant United Nations Develop Prog 1973-74; trustee/chmn of bd General Educ Bd 1973-84; mem adv cncl NY Coll of Agr Cornell Univ 1976-82; mem Agr Projects Review Govt of Nepal 1979; mem Governor of Virginia's Intl Trade Adv Cncl 1987-; mem Alpha Phi Alpha, Sigma Pi Phi, National Guardsmen. **Honors/Awds:** Certificate of Merit VA State Coll 1978; Doctor of Laws Morehouse Coll 1979, Virginia State Univ 1982; The W Averell Harriman Intl Serv Awd Intl Ctr Albany 1981; Joseph C Wilson Award, 1990. **Military Serv:** USAR major 25 yrs; Army Commendation Medal 1946, and various serv medals 1943-56. **Business Addr:** CCG Associates, 9945 Great Oaks Way, Fairfax, VA 22030, (703)352-5895.

GRAY, DERWIN LAMONT
Professional football player. **Personal:** Born Apr 9, 1971, San Antonio, TX; married Vicki; children: Presley. **Educ:** Brigham Young, bachelor's degree in sports business management. **Career:** Indianapolis Colts, defensive back, 1993-. **Business Addr:** Professional Football Player, Indianapolis Colts, PO Box 535000, Indianapolis, IN 46253, (317)297-2658.

GRAY, DONNEE L.
Legislative reference assistant, college basketball official. **Personal:** Born Jul 4, 1951, Camp Springs, MD; son of Mattie Gray; married Vedia Thompson-Gray, May 10, 1975; children: Marcus D. **Educ:** St Marys College of Maryland, BA, social science, 1976. **Career:** US Senate Library, head legislative reference assistant, currently. **Orgs:** US Senate Federal Employees Credit Union, chairman board of directors; The Cage Page basketball referee publication, board of directors; IAABO Board #134, president, 1991-. **Honors/Awds:** NCAA Division 1, Tournament, 1989-94, Regional Semi-Final, 1989, 1993-94; NCAA Division 3, Regional Final, 1986, National Final, 1985; Maui Classic, Hawaii, 1989; Japan Classic, Japan, 1990; World Games, Uruguay, South Africa, 1990; Pan Am Trials, Colorado Springs, Colorado, 1991; Portsmouth Invitational Tournament, 1987-93; Great Alaska Shootout, 1993; CIAA Basketball Official of the Year, 1990, 1992; commercials for: NCAA, 1990, ACC, 1992; National Amateur Basketball Association, Head Coach: US National Champions, International Tournament, Mozambique, Africa, 1985. **Special Achievements:** Referee for: Alantic Coast Conference, Alantic Ten Conference, Big East Conference, Colonial Athletic Association, East Coast Conference, Mid-Eastern Athletic Conference, Southwest Conference, USA Basketball (FIBA); US Natl Champions, head coach, 1985. **Home Addr:** 306 Beverly Ct, Fort Washington, MD 20744-5012. **Business Addr:** Head, Legislative Reference Assistant, US Seneate Library, US Capitol Bldg, S-332, Washington, DC 20510.

GRAY, DOROTHY PEYTON
Librarian. **Personal:** Born Jan 22, 1943, Winterville, MS; daughter of Ruth Carter Peyton and A J Peyton; married Oliver J Gray (divorced 1980); children: Nkosi. **Educ:** Southern Illinois University, Carbondale, IL, BA, 1964; Columbia University, School of Library Science, New York, NY, MS, 1972. **Career:** Schomburg Center for Research in Black Culture, New York, NY, librarian, 1974-75; Legislative Analyst, Los Angeles City Council, Los Angeles, CA, 1976-79; UCLA, Graduate School of Education, library/asistant librarian, 1981-83; Los Angeles, Community College District, librarian, 1975-86; Metropolitan Transportation Authority, Library Services, mgr, 1988-. **Honors/Awds:** Education Achievement Award, COMTO, 1990.

GRAY, E. DELBERT
Association official. **Educ:** Tennessee State Univ, BS, industrial education and administration; Michigan State Univ, MA, guidance and personnel services, PhD, administration, commerce, urban development. **Career:** State of Michigan Department of Commerce, Minority Business Enterprise, director, currently. **Orgs:** Spaulding for Children, vice president, executive finance committee, president of board of directors, currently. **Business Addr:** President, Board of Directors, Spaulding for Children, 16250 Northland Dr, Ste 120, Southfield, MI 48075-5226.

GRAY, EARL HADDON
Administrator (retired). **Personal:** Born Apr 19, 1929, Richmond, VA; son of Annie Baker Atkins (deceased) and William Joseph Gray (deceased); married Jane N Harris Gray, Dec 25, 1953; children: Adrienne Anne. **Educ:** Virginia State University, Petersburg, VA, BA accounting, 1970, MA, MEd, 1974. **Career:** Assoc Dir Student Act, Petersburg, VA, assoc dir, 1966-70; Personnel Dir, VSC, Petersburg, VA, pers dir, 1970-71; Dir Model Cities JTPA, Richmond, VA, director, 1971-77; Asst Dir, Planning & Eval, Bal of State, asst dir, 1978-82; Dir Research Div VEC, Richmond, VA, chief director, 1982-85; Imperial Council, Detroit, MI, Imperial Potentate, 1986-88. **Orgs:** Chair of labor & industry committee, NAACP, 1966-70; member, Committee for Elderly, City of Richmond, 1971-74; board member, Gold Bowl Classic, City of Richmond, 1975-; National Assault on Illiteracy, New York, NY, 1984-; Pres, Community Motivators Inc, New York, NY, 1988-. **Honors/Awds:** Honorary Dr of Humane Letters, Virginia Union University, 1988; Seagrams Vangard Award, Seagrams Co, 1985; 100 Most Influential Black American, Johnson Pub Co, 1986-88. **Military Serv:** Navy, Chief Petty Officer, 1946-66; numerous. **Home Addr:** 2930 Seminary Ave, Richmond, VA 23220.

GRAY, EARNEST
Professional football player (retired). **Personal:** Born Mar 2, 1957, Greenwood, MS. **Educ:** Memphis State Univ, attended. **Career:** Wide receiver: New York Giants, 1979-84; St. Louis Cardinals, 1985. **Honors/Awds:** All NFL Rookie Honors, UPI, Pro Football Weekly, Professional Football Writers Assn, and Football Digest; All-American; played in Senior Bowl and East-West Shrine Game.

GRAY, ED
Professional basketball player. **Personal:** Born Sep 27, 1975. **Educ:** Univ of California. **Career:** Atlanta Hawks, guard, 1997-. **Business Addr:** Professional Basketball Player, Atlanta Hawks, One CNN Center, Ste 405, Atlanta, GA 30335, (404)827-3800.

GRAY, EDWARD WESLEY, JR.
Government official. **Personal:** Born Mar 15, 1946, Gary, IN; married Cheryl Bernadette Leggon; children: Robert RL. **Educ:** Univ of Chicago, BA Soc 1967; Columbia Univ Law Schl, Juris Doctor 1970; Parker Schl of Foreign and Corporate Law, Cert 1980. **Career:** Kirkland and Ellis, assc atty 1970-73; RR Donnelley and Sons Co, atty 1973, sr atty, gen atty, Pres Comm on Exec Exch, participant exchange XV 1984-; US Gen Acct Office, spec asst dir gen govt div US gen acct office. **Orgs:** Numrans Bar Assc Amer Arbitration Assc. **Business Addr:** Special Assistant to Dir, US Gen Acct Office, 441 G St NW, Washington, DC 20548.

GRAY, F. GARY
Film director. **Personal:** Born 1969, New York, NY. **Educ:** LA City College, Golden State College, attended. **Career:** Video and film director 1990s-; camera operator, BET, Fox television networks; music videos for W C and the Maad Circle, Coolio, TLC, Ice Cube, Dr Dre; director of films, Friday 1995, Set It Off 1996. **Honors/Awds:** Billboard Music Video Awards, Best Rap Video and Best New Artist Rap Video, 1995; MTV Music Video Awards, four awards including Video of the Year for TLC's "Waterfall" and Best Rap Video for Dr Dre's "Keep Their Heads Ringin'," 1995. **Business Addr:** Bragman Nyman Cafarelli, 9171 Wilshire Blvd, Penthouse Ste, Beverly Hills, CA 90210-5530.

GRAY, FRED DAVID
Attorney, evangelist. **Personal:** Born in Montgomery, AL; son of Nancy Gray Arms and Abraham Gray (deceased); married Bernice Hill; children: Deborah, Vanessa, Fred David Jr, Stanley. **Educ:** Nashville Christian Inst, Diploma; AL State Univ, BS 1951; Case Western Reserve Univ, JD 1954. **Career:** Sr mem of law firm of Gray, Langford, Sapp, McGowan & Gray, with offices in Montgomery & Tuskegee, AL; cooperating attorney with NAACP Legal Defense Fund, Inc; city attorney for city of Tuskegee; Tuskegee Univ, local general counsel; first civil rights attorney for Dr Martin Luther King, Jr and attorney for Rosa Parks in the Montgomery Bus Boycott. **Orgs:** Bar comm 5th Judicial Circuit of AL 1983-86; pres elect Natl Bar Assc 1984-85; pres Natl Assc Cty Civil Attys 1982-83; rep AL State Leg 1970-74; mem Amer Bar Assc, Omega Psi Phi Frat Inc; elder Tuskegee Church of Christ; Natl Bar Assoc, president 1985-86; Southwestern Christian Coll, chairman, bd of trustees. **Honors/Awds:** The Man in the News NY Times 1966; First Annual Equal Justice Award Natl Bar Assc 1977; Drum Major's Award MLK Jr Mem Southern Christian Ldrshp Conf 1980; Pres Award Natl Bar Assc 1982; World Conference of Mayors, the legal awd 1985; Case Western Reserve Univ, law alumni assoc -graduate of the yr 1985, school of law -Society of Benchers 1986; Women at Work of Los Angeles CA & Southwestern Christian Coll, man of the yr awd 1986; WA Bar Assoc, Charles Hamilton Houston Medallion of Merit 1986. **Business Addr:** Senior Partner, Gray, Langford, Sapp, McGowan, Gray & Nathanson, PO Box 830239, Tuskegee, AL 36083-0239.

GRAY, GEORGE W., III (SKIP)
Attorney. **Personal:** Born Sep 28, 1945, Denver, CO; son of Juanita Gray and George W Gray Jr; married Janice Gross; children: Sean Michael, Aaron Christopher. **Educ:** Mesa Coll, AA, 1965; Univ of Denver, BA, 1968, JD, 1985; Univ of Northern Colorado, 1969. **Career:** Job Corps Bureau of Reclamation, youth worker 1965-67; Denver Public Schools, jr high soc studies teacher 1970-73; Metro State Coll Denver, assoc dir financial aid 1973-78; US House of Representatives, First Congressional District, staff aide to Congresswoman Patricia Schroeder, 1977-78; Coloradoans to Re-Elect Richard Lamm Gov, staff aid-constituent groups 1978; Colorado Office of Energy & Conservation of the Gov, mgr IBGP 1978-82; Governor's Office, sr staff aide 1981; Yellow Cab Co, driver 1982-84; Manville Corp, law clerk 1984; Holland & Hart, assoc 1985-88; Gray, Hahn and Browne, managing shareholder, 1989-. **Orgs:** Chmn sub cmte on budgets, Black Educ Adv Cmte, 1974-75, Denver Entry to Energy Education Adv Bd, 1979-82, Denver Public Schools; co-chair, Greater Park Hill Cmte Inc 1974-75; sec, Colorado Assn of Financial Aid Administrators 1975-76; dir, Park Hill Chap Bd, NAACP 1977; Amer Assn of Blacks in Energy 1977-82; incorporator, Natl Assn of Inst Bldgs Grants Prog Administration 1980-82; precinct cmteman 1980-84, capt-at-large, 1982-83, Denver Democratic Party; senator, Student Bar Assn, Univ of Denver Coll of Law 1982-83; hon bd, Univ of Denver Coll of Law 1984-85; Mayor appointed bd mem, Denver Opportunity Inc 1985; Colorado Office of Energy Conservation Adv Cmte, 1985-; dir, chmn nominating cmte ACLU of Colorado 1986-; American Bar Assn, 1986-; Natl Bar Assn, 1986-; Sam Carey Bar Assn, 1986-; Colorado Health Facilities Authority, board member, 1991-. **Honors/Awds:** Mesa College, Freshman Scholarship for Music; USOE, Joint Honor Scholarship; Univ of Denver, School of Education, Fellowship; Sam Carey Bar Assn, Scholarship.

GRAY, JAMES E.
Educational administrator. **Career:** Natchez Junior College, Natchez MS, president, currently. **Business Addr:** President, Natchez Junior College, 1010 N Unionist, Natchez, MS 39120.

GRAY, JAMES HOWARD
Physician. **Personal:** Born May 20, 1943, Kaufman, TX; son of Ocie Bell Blakemore Gray and Wilmer Oscar Gray; married Carol Coleman; children: Nakia, James. **Educ:** North Texas State Univ, B 1966, M 1967; Univ of Texas Medical School, MD 1971; Johns Hopkins Hospital, Wilmer Ophthalmology Inst, attended 1975-78. **Career:** Bexar Co Hospital, internal medicine intern 1971-72; Wilmer Ophthalmology Inst Johns Hopkins Hospital, resident 1975-78; Khalili Hospital Ophthalmology Dept Shiraz Iran, visiting instructor 1978; Baylor Univ Med Ctr, assoc attending 1978-; Southwestern Medical School, clinical faculty 1979-88; TX Instrument & Terrell State Hospital, eye consultant 1979-81; Private Practice, ophthalmologist 1978-. **Orgs:** Fee review comm Dallas County Medical Soc 1985-87; bd mem Good St Baptist Church; mem NAACP, YMCA, Amer Heart Assoc, Soc to Prevent Blindness, Dallas Black Chamber of Commerce; Amer Medical Assoc, Johns Hopkins Hospital Resident's Assoc, Wilmer Resident's Assn; member, American Academy of Ophthalmology; member, Texas Ophthalmological Assn. **Honors/Awds:** Legislative Merit Scholarship; Galaxy of Starts Award, Dallas Independent School District; Social Service Award XZ; First place and best of show awards TX Med Assoc; First place awards Medical Illustration SNMA Wyeth Natl Contest; Fellow, American College of Surgery. **Military Serv:** AUS MC major 1972-75. **Business Addr:** Ophthalmologist, 3600 Gaston Ave #760, Dallas, TX 75246.

GRAY, JERRY
Professional football player. **Personal:** Born Dec 2, 1961, Lubbock, TX. **Educ:** Univ of Texas, attended. **Career:** Los Angeles Rams, cornerback 1985-. **Honors/Awds:** Played in Pro Bowl, 1986, 1987, 1988, 1989.

GRAY, JOANNE S.
Educator. **Personal:** Born Dec 19, 1943, Headland, AL; daughter of Gussie Jones Stovall and Charlie Stoval; married Kenneth Byron Gray; children: Kina Carisse. **Educ:** Chicago City Coll, AA 1965; Chicago State Coll, BS 1970; Governor State Univ, MS 1979; Univ of Chicago, Univ of Illinois, Illinois Institute of Technology, post graduate work. **Career:** Teacher, 1970-; Chicago Board of Education, teacher representative, local school council, 1991-93, dist chairperson science fair, 1983-, chairperson citywide academic Olympics, 1985-86, science dept chairperson 1984-, ECIA coord 1986; Fermi National Laboratory/Chicago State University Summer Institute for Science and Mathematics Teachers, administrative director, 1990-. **Orgs:** Papers-Science Fair Success and Encouraging Females in Science related Activites 1978-; bd of dir Pre-medical and Allied Health Prog Chicago St Univ 1978-81; sec, vice pres Rebecca Circle United Methodist Women 1980-86; Phi Delta Kappa 1984-86; prog chmn Natl Assn of Biology Teachers 1984; coord/facilitator Natl Sci Educ Comm 1984; science curriculum bd of governors St Univ 1986; bd mem Women's Div of Global Ministries 1987; area teen advisor Top Ladies of Distinction Inc 1987-89; chairperson, Volunteers Committee, Chicago Public School Science Fair, 1991-; coordinator, Local School Improvement Plan for Science, 1990-; co-chairperson, Judging Illinois Junior Academy of Sciences State Exhibition, 1991-; board of directors, Chicago Organization for Autism, 1990-;chairperson, Outstanding logy Teachers Awards Subcommittee; executive secretary, board of directors, Chicago State Alumni Association, 1989-; president, National Association of Biology Teachers Section on Role and Status of Women and Minorities in Biology Education, 1992-93. **Honors/Awds:** Celebrated Teacher by Beta Boule' Sigma Pi Phi 1981; Ora Higgins Youth Foundation Award 1981; Exceptional Serv to Students Blum-Kovler Foundation 1981; Principal Scholars Prog Serv Award 1982; Master Teacher Award Governor of IL 1984; Textbook Revision Team Biological Science Curriculum Study 1985; Fellowship Fry Foundation Univ of Chicago 1986;

Outstanding Biology Teacher Natl Assn of Biology Teachers 1986; MidWest Region Excellence in Teaching Award, National Council of Negro Women, 1991. **Special Achievements:** Science curriculum writer, Chicago Bd of Educ, 1985-87; author, ''Motivating Females in Science, Mathematics, and Technolgy Related Careers,'' Zeta Phi Beta Sorority, 1989; curriculum writer, Illinois Institute of Technology SMILE Program, 1989; reader/editor, American Biology Teachers Journal, 1988-; writer of national curriculum standards for science education, with National Research Council/National Science Foundation, 1992-94.

GRAY, JOHNNIE LEE
Professional football player (retired). **Personal:** Born Dec 18, 1953, Lake Charles, LA; married Barbara. **Educ:** Allan Hancock College; California State Univ at Fullerton. **Career:** Green Bay Packers, safety, 1975-83. **Honors/Awds:** Made more than 100 solo tackles during each season, 1977-79; selected All-Conference all four years in college; All-Conference PCAA Honors.

GRAY, JOSEPH WILLIAM
Physician. **Personal:** Born May 31, 1938, Memphis, TN; married Jacquelyn Cooper; children: Joseph IV, Jaylynn, Jeffrey, Jerron, Jerome. **Educ:** St Augustine's Coll, BA; Meharry Med Coll, MD 1963; Santa Monica Hosp, Intern 1963-64; GW Hubbard Hosp, Res 1966-69. **Career:** Physician, 1985-. **Orgs:** Natl Med Assn; AMA; Toledo & Lucas Ped Soc; OH Chap of Amer Acad of Ped; fellow Amer Acad of Pediatrics; certified Amer Bd of Pediatrics; life mem NAACP; Sigma Pi Phi; Alpha Phi Alpha; Alpha Kappa Mu. **Military Serv:** USN 1964-66. **Business Addr:** Physician, 2109 Hughes Dr, Ste 660, Toledo, OH 43606.

GRAY, KAREN G. (KAREN GRAY HOUSTON)
Journalist. **Personal:** Born in Montgomery, AL; daughter of Juanita Emanuel Gray and Thomas W Gray; married. **Educ:** Ohio University, Athens, OH, BA, psychology, 1972; Columbia University, New York, NY, MS, journalism, 1973. **Career:** United Press International, Boston, MA, reporter/editor, 1973-75; WHDH-AM, Boston, MA, reporter/anchor, 1975-76; ABC News New York, NY, radio anchor, 1976-81; NBC News, Washington, DC, radio & tv correspondent, 1981-83; WCBS-TV, New York, NY, writer/associate producer, 1984-87; WTOP Newsradio, Washington, DC, reporter/anchor, 1987-. **Orgs:** Member, National Association of Black Journalists, member, Washington Association of Black Journalists, member, Capitol Press Club. **Business Addr:** Reporter/Anchor, WTOP, 3400 Idaho Ave NW, Washington, DC 20016.

GRAY, KEITH A., JR.
Elected government official. **Personal:** Born Nov 3, 1947, Camden, NJ. **Educ:** Career Ed Inst, Cert 1975; Pierce Jr Coll, Associate 1977; Rutgers Univ, Cert 1983. **Career:** Conrail, customer rep 1982; Juveniles In Need of Suprv, counselor 1984; Cumberland Cty Welfare, intake maintenance 1985; Bayside State Prison, furlough coord, currently; Fairfield Twp Comm, mayor, currently. **Orgs:** Adb bd Fairfield Twp Schools, 1983; leg comm Adv Comm on Women 1984; bd of dir NJ Citizen Action 1985; mem Natl Conf of Black Mayors 1985, NJ Assoc of Mayors 1985, NJ Conf on Mayors 1985. **Honors/Awds:** Cert NJ State Assembly 1984; Cert SCOPE 1984; Placque Concerned Citizens of Fairfield 1984; Cert Concerned Citizens of Fairfield 1984. **Special Achievements:** First African-American Woman to become mayor of Cumberland County. **Military Serv:** USAF E-4 4 yrs. **Business Addr:** Mayor, Fairfield Twp Comm, P O Box 125, Fairton, NJ 08320.

GRAY, KENNETH D.
Military officer. **Personal:** Born in McDowell County, WV; married Carolyn. **Educ:** West Virginia State, BA; West Virginia University, Morgantown, JD, 1969. **Career:** US Army: second lieutenant, 1966, defense counsel, legal assistance officer, Ft Ord, CA, 1969, Vietnam, 1969, Ft Meade, MD, 1971; The Pentagon, Minority JAG Program, Personnel, Plans, and Training Office, personnel management officer; Acting Judge Advocate General, brigadier general, special assistant to acting judge advocate general; US Army Legal Services Agency, commander, 1991-; US Army Court of Military Review, chief judge, 1991-; Trial Judiciary, chief, currently; Secretary of the Army, Procurement Fraud Matters, representative, currently. **Special Achievements:** At one time was only African-American attending West Virginia University's law school and third African-American to graduate, 1966-69; established Summer Intern Program for Judge Advocate General's corps; only commander in JAG; US Army Court of Military Review is the highest court in the Army. **Military Serv:** Decorations include: Legion of Merit, Bronze Star Medal, Meritorious Service Medal, Army Commendation Medal, Army Achievement Medal, and Army General Staff Identification Badge. **Business Addr:** Commander, 2016 White Oak Dr, Morgantown, WV 26505.

GRAY, MACEO
Engineering supervisor. **Personal:** Born Dec 22, 1940, Dallas; married Annie P Hatcher; children: Karen, Kathleen. **Educ:** Prairie View A&M U, BS EE 1963; Univ MO, grad engineering work. **Career:** Bendix Corp, jr engr 1963; Test Equip Design Dept, engineering supr 1969; Electrical Products, engineering supr. **Orgs:** Dir comm proj by Bendix Mgmt Club 1973-74; vice pres spl events Bendix Mgmt Club 1975-76; term vice pres Camp Fire Bowling League; adv Jr Achvmnt Co 1970. **Honors/Awds:** Received numerous outstndg serv awrds Bendix Mgmt Club Work.

GRAY, MARCUS J.
County clerk. **Personal:** Born Sep 22, 1936, Kansas City, MO; married Abbey Dowdy; children: Marcus, III, Sean, Yolanda. **Educ:** BBA. **Career:** Cahoun Co, co clk register 1972-; co clk 1964-72; Eaton Mfg, prod insp chief clk quality con commercial trans clk; Kellogg Co, machine operator. **Orgs:** Mem exec com Calhoun Co Dem Party; Haber & Commn on Polit Reform in Elections; sub-com chmn MI Non-Partisan Election Commn; imm past pres MI Assn of Co Clks; pres Nat Assn of Co Recorders & Clks 1979; mem United Co Officer's Assn; pres Battle Creek Area Urban League; pres Battle Creek Area Council of Ch. **Honors/Awds:** Les Bon Amie Club awd outstd sev; cert of merit Dem Party of MI & Calhoun Co Dem Women's Club; clerk of the yr MI Assn of Co Clks. **Military Serv:** USAF a/2c. **Business Addr:** County Clerk's Office, Calhoun County, Marshall, MI.

GRAY, MARVIN W.
Attorney. **Personal:** Born Aug 12, 1944, Chicago; married Taffy; children: Derek, Jason, Meagan. **Educ:** So IL U, 1966; IL Inst Tech, 1972. **Career:** Chicago Pub Sch, tchr 1966, 1970-72; Aetna Life & Casualty Ins, claims rep 1967-70; Cook Co, asst pub defndr 1972-74; Harth Vital Stroger Boarman & Williams, atty; Braud Warner & Neppl, atty; Firm of Ward & Gray, prtnr; Montgomery & Holland, asso & self-employed 1967-79; Pvt Prac Chgo, atty. **Orgs:** Consult Opera PUSH 1973-74; couns 10 Dist Omega Psi Phi Frat; mem IL Trial Lawyers Assn; mem Phi Delta Phi Intl Legal Frat; mem Nat Cook Co IL & Am Bar Assns. **Honors/Awds:** Moran fund scholarship 1968; IL Inst Tech scholarship 1970. **Business Addr:** Marvin W Gray Ltd, 180 W Washington, Suite 800, Chicago, IL 60602.

GRAY, MEL
Professional football player. **Personal:** Born Mar 16, 1961, Williamsburg, VA; children: Melanie, Devon. **Educ:** Coffeyville (Kan.) Community College, attended. **Career:** New Orleans Saints, running back, 1986-88; Detroit Lions, 1989-94; Houston Oilers, 1995-96; Tennessee Oilers, 1997; Philadelphia Eagles, 1997-. **Honors/Awds:** Pro Bowl, 1990, 1991, 1992, 1994; National Football League Players Assn, Special Teams Player of the Year, 1991. **Business Addr:** Professional Football Player, Philadelphia Eagles, 3501 S Broad St, Philadelphia, PA 19148, (215)463-2500.

GRAY, MOSES W.
Automotive company executive. **Personal:** Born Apr 12, 1937, Rock Castle, VA; son of Ida B Young and Moses Young; married Ann Marie Powell, Nov 22, 1962; children: Tamara Ann, William Bernard. **Educ:** IN Univ, BS Phys Educ 1961; Detroit Diesel Allison Apprentice Training Program, journeyman tool & die maker 1967. **Career:** Indianapolis Warriors, professional football player; DDAD Indianapolis, inspector 1962-63, apprentice tool & die maker 1963-67, journeyman tool & die maker 1967-68, production supervisor 1968-69, supervisor-tool room 1969-73, genl supv tool room 1973-76, asst supt master mechanic 1976-79, dir comm relations 1979-83, mgr mfg serv 1983-88, general supt mfg engineering 1989-. **Orgs:** Bds, Indianapolis Business Develop Found, Black Adoption Comm, Children's Bureau of Indianapolis, Child Welfare League of America, Indianapolis Urban League, Comm Serv Council, IN Vocational Tech Coll, United Way of Greater Indianapolis, NAACP, The Volunteer Bureau, The Office of Equal Oppor-City of Indianapolis, Channel #20 Public Service TV, Black Expo, Indianapolis C of C Corporate Comm Affairs Discussion, Black Child Develop Institute, United Way Agency Relations Adv Comm, Oppor Indus Ctr, Madame Walker Urban Life Ctr, The Wilma Rudolph Foundation; pres, Indianapolis Chapter Sigma Pi Phi Fraternity. **Honors/Awds:** B'nai B'rith Man of the Yr 1974; Gold Medal Winner Genl Motors Awd for Excellence in Comm Serv 1978; Outstanding Achievement in Pub & Comm Serv 1982 Bus & Profls of Indianapolis; Public Citizen of the Year Natl Assoc of Social Workers 1986; Citizen of the Year Omega Psi Phi frat 1986; Moses Gray Awd (first recipient) for Outstanding Service of Special Adoptions 1986. **Business Addr:** General Supt, Mfg Engineering, Detroit Diesel Allison Div, P O Box 894, 4700 West 10th St, Indianapolis, IN 46206.

GRAY, MYRTLE EDWARDS
Educational administrator (retired). **Personal:** Born Nov 20, 1914, Tuscaloosa, AL; daughter of Alabama Bryant Edwards Melton and Burton Edwards; married Samuel Alfred Gray, Mar 13, 1938; children: Myrtle Imogene, Samuel A Jr. **Educ:** Alabama State Univ, BS, MEd 1950; Univ of Alabama, EdS 1971; Wayne State, Marquette Univ, Auburn Univ, Univ of So Alabama, further study. **Career:** Tuscaloosa Cty School Dist, elem teacher 1935-36, 1936-54, principal elem schools 1954-63, suprv principal 1963-80. **Orgs:** Bd dir YMCA 1975-80, Salvation Army 1975-80; chmn Westside Cancer Dr 1979; vice pres Alabama Baptist State Women's Conv; 2nd vice pres Natl Assn Colored Women's Clubs Inc 1980-; pres NW Dist 1981-; mem Alabama Educ Assn, Elem Principals Assn; mem Univ of Alabama Alumni Assn; mem Natl Baptist USA Womens Auxiliary, Nightingale, Cosmos Study; past pres Tuscaloosa City Fed; mem Tuscaloosa C of C; pres Alabama Baptist State Northwest Dist Women's Convention 1981, Natl Assn Colored Women's Clubs Inc 1984-88; chairperson, Alabama Assn Women's Clubs Board; pres, Retired Teachers of Tuscaloosa, 1989-90. **Honors/Awds:** Hon Doct Selma Univ 1986; Past President's Award, NACWC, Inc, 1990. **Home Addr:** 49 Washington Square, Tuscaloosa, AL 35401.

GRAY, NAOMI T.
Business executive. **Personal:** Born May 18, 1924, Hattiesburg, MS. **Educ:** Hampton Inst, BS 1945; IN Univ Sch of Soc Svc, MA 1948. **Career:** Sheltering Arms Children's Serv NY, caseworker 1948-50; Planned Parenthood Fed of Amer NY, director, field consult 1952-61, dir of field serv 1961-68, vice pres field serv 1968-70; Naomi Gray Assoc, president. **Orgs:** Inst of Urban Affairs, pres, 1970-92; Comm Serv Soc 1948-50; bd mem Natl Assn of Soc Workers NY Chap 1969-71; Natl Conf on Soc Welfare 1967-68; Pvt Sch Placement Prog for Disadvantaged Students 1969-71 NY; past pres Educ Access Cable TV Corp of San Francisco 1974-76; Soc Welfare & Health Commn Natl Urban League 1965-69; Amer Pub Health Assn; Natl Assn of Soc Workers; NAACP; Black Leadership Forum of San Francisco; Health Commission, city & county, SF, 1986-93; Golden Gate Natl Recreation Park Service, advisory comm, Natl Park Service, 1994-; Sojourner Truth Foster Family Service Agency, exec dir, 1991-93. **Honors/Awds:** Citation bd dir Natl Assn for Sickle Cell Disease 1973; Citation for Outstanding Achievements in field of bus; Omega Psi Phi SF May 1974; House of Representatives, Congressional Period, 1992; Proclamation, Mayor city & county of SF, Noami Gray Day in SF, 1993; Resolution, CA Legislature, assemby, 1992; Resolution, CA State Senate, 1992; Certificate of Honor, BD of Supervision, city & county of SF. **Business Addr:** President, Naomi Gray Assoc, 1291 Stanyan St, San Francisco, CA 94117.

GRAY, PEARL SPEARS
Educational administrator. **Personal:** Born Aug 19, 1945, Selma, AL; daughter of Jerome Jackson Jones and Hobart William Spears; divorced. **Educ:** Wilberforce Univ, BA Soc 1968; Antioch-putney Grad Schl of Educ, MAT Sec Educ 1970; OR State Univ, PhD, 1986. **Career:** Teachers Corp Project, Providence RI, exec LEA asst coor 1971-73; OR State Univ School of Educ, Portland OR, assc dir 1973-76; OR State Univ, dir of office of affirmative action & asst to pres, 1976-87; Univ of VA, Charlottesville, VA, assoc provost for policy & asst to pres, 1987-. **Orgs:** Bd of dir Natl Human Rel Task Force 1981-; chrprsn bd mem Black Clges Comm Inc 1980-; bd mem Public Health Adv Bd 1985; mem Zonta Intl 1984, Amer Mgmt Assc 1984, Amer Assc of Univ Women, Delta Sigma Theta Inc 1967-; mem, Rotary Intl, 1991-; pres Virginia Assn of Black Faculty & Administrators, 1991-93; mem, American Assn of Univ Admin, 1989-. **Honors/Awds:** Outstanding Srv Award Council of Natl Alumni Assc 1983; Women of Excel Award in Educ Delta Sigma Theta Portland Alumnae 1983; One of 100 Most Influential Persons Black Journal 1976; Boss of Year Natl Assc Educ Secr 1976-77; Rockefellar Family Fund, grant to study & travel in West Africa, 1970; One Hundred Most Influential Persons, Tony Brown's Journal, 1980; Serwa Award for Illustrious Achievement, VA Commonwealth Chapter of Natl Coalition of 100 Black Women, 1989.

GRAY, ROBERT DEAN
Mayor, company executive. **Personal:** Born Jun 30, 1941, Clarksville, TN; son of Willa M Bush Gray and R D Gray; married Gloria Enochs, Aug 19, 1967. **Educ:** Mississippi Valley State Univ, BS, 1964; Texas Southern Univ, courses towards MS, 1968; Chevron Oil Co Business School. **Career:** Bolivar County School Dist #3, tchr, coach 1964-67; TX Southern Univ, asst coach, graduate asst, 1967-68; Bolivar County Headstart Program, dir 1968-70; Shelby Chevron Service Station, owner, operator, 1968-78; City of Shelby, mayor, 1976-; Griffin Lamp Co., president, CEO, 1987-. **Orgs:** Municipal Assn of Mississippi, board of directors, 1978-92; Municipal Assn Service Co Insurance Pool, chairman; Mississippi Institute for Small Town, board of directors, 1979-; Mississippi Delta Council, board of directors, 1986-; National Conference of Black Mayors, 1st vice pres, 1984-86; Mississippi Conference of Black Mayors, president, 1979-86; National Assn of Manufacturers, board of directors, 1989-91. **Honors/Awds:** Mississippi Valley State Univ, Sports Hall of Fame Inductee, 1980. **Business Addr:** President, CEO, Griffin Lamp Co., PO Box 66, US Hwy #61 South, Shelby, MS 38774.

GRAY, ROBERT E.
Armed services officer. **Personal:** Born Oct 18, 1941, Algoma, WV; son of Hattie B Parker Gray and Lloyd Gray Sr; married Annie L Oliver Gray, May 11, 1963; children: Frances D Gray-Warden, Edith D Gray-Negahban, Oliver P. **Educ:** Ohio State University, BA, 1973; US Army Command and General Staff, Leavenworth KS, MMAS, 1977; US Army War College, 1984. **Career:** US Army, Ft Bragg, NC, 35th Signal Brigade, commander, 1986-88, XVIII Airborne Corps, special asst to commanding general, 1988, Ft Gordon, GA, deputy commanding

general, 1988-90, Washington, DC, deputy director for plans and programs, 1990-91, Ft Gordon, GA, commanding general, 1991-. **Orgs:** Armed Forces Communications Electronic Assn, associate director, 1977-; US Army War College Alumni Assn, 1984-; Assn of US Army, 1978-; Officers Christian Fellowship, board member, 1976-. **Military Serv:** US Army, Brigadier General, 1966-; Bronze Star, 2 Legion of Merit awards, 3 Air Medals, 3 Meritorious Service Medals, 3 Army Commendation Medals, Vietnam Service Medal. **Business Addr:** Brigadier General, US Army, Signal Towers, Fort Gordon, GA 30905.

GRAY, ROBERT R.
Government official. **Personal:** Born Jun 13, 1910, Lakeland, MD; married Mildred W. **Educ:** Bowie Normal, 1928-30; Morgan State, BS 1949; NY Univ, MA 1951. **Career:** Talbot Cty, elem schl prin 1930-34; Fairmount Hghts, elem schl prin 1934-70; PGCo Tchrs Assc Fed Credit Union, educ and info offr 1970-76; Town of Fairmount Hghts, mayor 1977-. **Orgs:** Mem County and State Retired Tchrs Assc, NEA, NAACP. **Honors/Awds:** President MD Chap Natl Conf of Black Mayors. **Military Serv:** AUS battalion supply sgt 1942-45. **Home Addr:** 5502 Addison Rd, Fairmount Heights, MD 20743.

GRAY, RONALD A.
Attorney. **Personal:** Born Dec 15, 1952, Blackstone, VA; son of Archie & Mary Frances; married Doris, Aug 31, 1985; children: Avery, Lindsay. **Educ:** Ohio University, BA, economics, 1975; Case Western Reserve University, College of Law, JD, 1978. **Career:** Federal Trade Commission, attorney, 1978-81; American Express, attorney, 1981-85, associate counsel, 1985-87, counsel, 1987-91, senior counsel, 1991-, managing counsel, 1995-. **Orgs:** American Bar Association, 1978-; City of New York Bar Association, vice chair, Committee on Minorities, 1994-; South African Legal Services and Legal Assistance Project, board member, 1993-; Childrens Hope Foundation, board member, 1991-94; MFY Legal Services, board member, 1996-. **Honors/Awds:** Ohio University, Gene Chapin Memorial Award, 1975. **Special Achievements:** Companies Aim for Diversity, New York Law Journal, 1993; Employees at Risk, New York Law Journal, 1994; Chairman, Succeeding in the Business Card Market, Cred Card Institute, Executive Enterprises, 1997. **Business Addr:** Managing Counsel, American Express Co., 200 Vesey Street, World Financial Center, New York, NY 10285-4911, (212)640-5776.

GRAY, RUBEN L.
Attorney. **Personal:** Born Nov 6, 1938, Georgetown, SC; married Jean Dozier; children: Ruben, Jr, Valencia, Valerie. **Educ:** SC Stae Coll, BS 1961; SC State Coll, LLB 1963; Nat Moot Ct Competitor, grad 1st in class. **Career:** Finney & Gray, atty 1973-; Morris Coll, vice pres for devel 1970-73; SC Econ Opp Bd Inc, exec dir 1968-70. **Orgs:** Mem SC State Elections Commn; mem bd trst Sumter Sch Dist 17; mem ABA, NBA; SC Bar Assn; chmn Sumter Co Child Uplift Bd Inc; pres Sumter Br NAACP; mem UMCA; Goodfellows; Sumter Co Black Polit Caucus; Sumter Co Dem Exec Com. **Honors/Awds:** Recip Comm Leader of Am Awd 1968. **Military Serv:** AUS 1963-65f. **Business Addr:** 110 S Sumter St, Sumter, SC.

GRAY, STERLING PERKINS, JR.
Criminal court judge. **Personal:** Born Dec 24, 1943, Nashville, TN; married Kristin Byard; children: Cezanne, Sterling P III. **Educ:** FL A&M Univ, BS 1963; Nashville Law School, JD 1973; Certificate of Completion, Natl Judicial Coll 1984, Harvard Univ 1983. **Career:** Division I Circuit Court, criminal court judge. **Orgs:** Bd of dirs Nashville Symphony Assoc 1978-81, Leadership Nashville 1985-87, Napier Looby Bar Assoc; mem criminal justice comm Nashville Bar Assoc. **Honors/Awds:** Most Disting Grad of the Nashville Law School 1986; commencement speaker Nashville Law Sch 1986. **Business Addr:** Judge of Division I, Circuit Court, 601 Metro Courthouse, Nashville, TN 37201.

GRAY, TORRIAN
Professional football player. **Personal:** Born Mar 18, 1974, Bartow, FL. **Educ:** Virginia Tech, attended. **Career:** Minnesota Vikings, defensive back, 1997-. **Business Addr:** Professional Football Player, Minnesota Vikings, 9520 Viking Dr, Eden Prairie, MN 55344, (612)828-6500.

GRAY, VALERIE HAMILTON
Civil engineer. **Personal:** Born May 10, 1959, Houma, LA; daughter of Lucia T Legaux Hamilton and Allen A Hamilton; married Ian A Gray, Jun 11, 1983; children: Adrienne Theresa, Ian Alexander. **Educ:** University of Notre Dame, Notre Dame, IN, BS, 1981; Corpus Christi State University, Corpus Christi, TX, Computer Science, 1985-87. **Career:** Texaco, USA, Harvey, LA, project engineer, 1980-85; City of Corpus Christi, Corpus Christi, TX, neighborhood improvement division supervisor, 1985-88, engineer II, 1988-89, water construction superintendent, 1989-. **Orgs:** Member, American Water Works Association, 1989-; member, American Society of Civil Engineers, 1981-; mem, Natl Society of Professional Engineers. **Honors/Awds:** Nuects Chapter of The TX Society of Professional Engineers, Young Engineer of the Year, 1994. **Business Addr:** Water Construction Superintendent, Water Div, Dept of Public, City of Corpus Christi, 5352 Ayers, PO Box 9277, Corpus Christi, TX 78469-9277.

GRAY, WILFRED DOUGLAS
Paper company executive. **Personal:** Born Oct 1, 1937, Richmond, VA; son of Lula B Duvall Gray and Richard L Gray; married Shirley M Durant, Nov 23, 1957; children: Alden D, Kathleen Y. **Educ:** Dale Carnegie, Buffalo NY, attended, 1971; State Univ of New York at Buffalo, Buffalo NY, BA, 1974; Printing Industry of Metropolitan Washington, Washington DC, attended, 1981. **Career:** Republic Steel, Buffalo NY, scarfer, inspector, 1962-76; Buffalo Envelope, Buffalo NY, sales representative, 1976-80; Envelopes Unlimited, Rockville MD, sales representative, 1980-81; Gray Paper Products Inc, Washington DC, pres, 1981-. **Orgs:** Mem, District of Columbia Chamber of Commerce, 1984-, NAACP, 1987-; bd of dir, Boys and Girls Clubs of Greater Washington, 1987-; mem, Amer Assn of Retired Persons, 1987-, Natl Assn of Black Public Officials, 1988-, Upper Georgia Ave Business & Professional Assn 1988-, Natl Business Forms Assn, 1988-, Rotary Club of Washington DC, 1988-. **Honors/Awds:** President's Award, Federal Envelope, 1979; Score, Certificate of Training, 1987; Certificate of Appreciation, Browne Jr High School, 1987. **Military Serv:** US Navy, Airman, 1956-60; Honorable Discharge, 1960. **Business Addr:** President, Gray Paper Products Inc, 214 L Street NE, Washington, DC 20002.

GRAY, WILLIAM H., III
Association executive. **Personal:** Born Aug 20, 1941, Baton Rouge, LA; married Andrea Dash; children: William H IV, Justin Yates, Andrew Dash. **Educ:** Franklin & Marshall Coll, attended 1963; Drew Seminary, grad deg 1966; Princeton Theol Sem, grad deg 1970; Univ of PA, Temple Univ, Mansfield Coll of Oxford Univ England, grad work. **Career:** Union Baptist Church Montclair NJ, pastor, 1964-72; Bright Hope Baptist Church Philadelphia, sr pastor, 1972-; Philadelphia Mortgage Plan, helped design; US Congress, representative of Philadelphia PA, 1978-91; United Negro College Fund, president, 1991-. **Orgs:** Dem Steering Com 96th US Congress; sec Cong Black Caucus; mem House Com on Foreign Affairs; mem Com on the Budget; mem Com on the Dist of Columbia; appointed by Pres Carter to US Liberia Presl Commn; vice chmn Congressional Black Caucus; sponsored the emergency food aid bill for Ethiopia 1984; author, the House version of the Anti-Apartheid Acts of 1985, 86. **Honors/Awds:** Man of the Yr, Natl Federation of Housing Counselors, 1980; Martin Luther King Jr Award for Public Serv, 1985, for leadership as chairman of the Budget Committee of the US House of Reps, for contrib as mem of the Congressional Black Caucus, and for political achievements as Dem mem of the House from Philadelphia; National Medal of Honor, Served as Special Advisor to Pres Clinton on Haiti, 1995; Honorary Degrees from more than 50 Colleges; Four Freedoms Award, 1997. **Special Achievements:** Appointed by President Clinton as an envoy to Haiti, 1994. **Business Addr:** President, United Negro College Fund, 8260 Willow Oaks Corporate Drive, Fairfax, VA 22031.

GRAYDON, WASDON, JR.
Educational administrator. **Personal:** Born Sep 22, 1950, Fort Mammoth, NJ; son of Lenora Graydon and Wasdon Graydon; married Veronica Brooks; children: Tremayne, Jasmaine. **Educ:** Abraham Baldwin Agr Coll, AS Sec Educ 1970; GA Southern Coll, BS Soc Sci 1972; Valdosta State Coll, Med History 1974. **Career:** Special Serv Prog, dir 1973-76; Upward Bound Special Serv Prog, dir 1973-76, special serv/min adv prog 1983-87; Tift County, commissioner dist 2 1984-88; G&M Enterprises, partner 1985-87; Abraham Baldwin Agr Coll, dir of Minority Affairs, currently. **Orgs:** Treasurer Georgia Assn of Special Prog Inc 1980-84; consultant mem Georgia Statewide Health Coor Council 1980-83; mem Phi Delta Kappa 1975-83; bd mem SW Georgia Health System Agency Inc 1976-81; mem Tift Co NAACP 1980-87; trustee Everette Temple CME Church 1980-87; mem The PROMISE Club 1983-84; trustee Tifton Tift Co Public Library 1984-88; mem Tift Co Arts Councils 1984-87; bd mem Tifton-Tift Co United Way 1986-88; mem Tifton-Tift Co C of C 1986-87; bd of dir Tifton-Tift Co Main St Prog 1986-87. **Honors/Awds:** GASPP Outstanding Serv Award 1983; SAEOPP Certificate of Recognition 1984; Manager of the Year, 1989-90; Leadership Georgia, 1991. **Home Addr:** 4504 Woodland Drive, Tifton, GA 31794-6553. **Business Addr:** Dir of Minority Affairs, Abraham Baldwin Agr Coll, PO Box 21 ABAC Station, Tifton, GA 31793.

GRAYER, JEFFREY
Professional basketball player. **Personal:** Born Dec 17, 1965, Flint, MI. **Educ:** Iowa State Univ, Ames, IA, 1984-88. **Career:** Milwaukee Bucks, 1988-92; Golden State Warriors, beginning 1992; Sacramento Kings, 1996-. **Honors/Awds:** Member of US Olympic team, 1988. **Business Addr:** Professional Basketball Player, Sacramento Kings, 1 Sport Pkwy, Sacramento, CA 95834, (916)928-6900.

GRAY-LITTLE, BERNADETTE
Psychologist, educator, consultant. **Personal:** Born Oct 21, 1944, Washington, NC; daughter of Rosalie Lanier Gray and James Gray (deceased); married Shade Keys; children: Maura M, Mark G. **Educ:** Marywood Coll, BA 1966; St Louis Univ, MS 1968, PhD 1970. **Career:** Univ of NC, asst prof 1971-76, assoc prof 1976-82, prof 1982-, chair, 1993-, consultant. **Orgs:** Fellow Amer Psychol Assn, Sigma Xi. **Honors/Awds:** Phi Beta Kappa Fulbright Fellow; recipient of grants Social Science Research Council, Carolina Population Center, Spencer Found, Natl Research Council. **Business Addr:** Professor, Univ of NC, Psychology Dept Davie Hall, Chapel Hill, NC 27599-3270.

GRAY-MORGAN, LARUTH H. (LARUTH GRAY)
Educational administrator. **Personal:** Born in Texarkana, TX; daughter of Hazel Johnson and Curtis Hackney; married Norris Gray (deceased); children: Phillip Anthony, Dierdra Alyce Gray. **Educ:** Howard Univ, BA 1954; Columbia Univ, MA 1957; Nova Univ, EdD 1975. **Career:** New Rochelle NY Public Sch, chmn English Dept, principal/ed support center, dir of instructional serv, asst supt 1980-83; Abbott Univ Free School District, Supt of Schools 1983-89; New York University, deputy director, metro center for urban education, 1989-, professor, ed admin, 1990-. **Orgs:** Mem bd comm White Plains YWCA; mem Comm on Aging City of New Rochelle; past chair Urban Affairs Comm NYS Assoc Super & Curr Develop; past vice pres NY State English Council; pres bd of dirs Martin Luther King Child Care Ctr 1980-; mem Council for the Arts 1986-; pres bd of trustees New Rochelle Public Library 1986-90, pres, 1993-95; mem of bd of dir NY State Alliance of Art 1989-91; Westchester (Children's) Assn 1989-95; Westchester Council for the Arts, vp, 1987-94, exec vp, 1996-99; American Association of School Administrators, Committee on Minorities and Women, chair 1990-; Westchester Library System, vp 1996-2000. **Honors/Awds:** Outstanding Educator New Rochelle Branch NAACP and Leadership Advisory Committee, 1973; Outstanding Educator Natl Council of Negro Women 1975; Outstanding Educator Natl Assoc of Minority Bankers 1976; Community Serv Awd West Salute Comm 1984; Cert Recognizing Unique Contribution to Educ US Congressional Black Caucus 1984; 100 Top Educators US and North Amer 1986; Outstanding Supt in the Arts, Kennedy Center DC Arts Alliance 1988; Natl Alliance of Black School Educators Service Leadership Award, 1996. **Business Addr:** Deputy Director, Metro Center for Urban Educ, School of Education, New York University, 82 Washington Sq East, Rm 72, New York, NY 10003, (212)998-5137.

GRAYS, MATTELIA BENNETT
Educational administrator. **Personal:** Born Jul 26, 1931, Houston; married Horace. **Educ:** Dilliard U, BA cum laude; Univ of MI, MA spl edn. **Career:** Will Rogers Research & Devel Center for Houston Independent School Dist, educator admin operator, duties corr to those of school prin, has total resp for acad & curr of enrollees staff devel & mgmt function. **Orgs:** Mem Intl Assn of Childhood Edn; exec bd mem Nat Pan Hellenic Council Inc; natl pres Alpha Kappa Alpha Sor Inc. **Business Addr:** 3101 Weslayan, Houston, TX 77027.

GRAYSON, BARBARA ANN
Educational administrator. **Personal:** Born Oct 10, 1954, Van Buren, AR; daughter of Beatrice Schoate Campbell and Vallard Campbell Sr; children: Lamar. **Educ:** Northeastern State Univ, BA 1976, MEd 1980. **Career:** Alluwe Public Schools, special ed inst 1977; East Central Univ, counselor 1977-80; Connors State College, counselor 1980-. **Orgs:** Member past sec & bd of directors OK Division of Student Assistance 1977-; member/past board Southwest Region Student Assistance 1977-; member-public relations Phi Delta Kappa 1983-; member NAACP.

GRAYSON, BYRON J., SR.
Communications manager. **Personal:** Born Sep 3, 1949, York, PA; son of Hurline V Bridgette and Charles F Grayson Sr; married Jennifer Gibson Grayson, Jan 1, 1985; children: Cortella Jones, Paul Jones, Byron Grayson Jr, Nicolle Grayson. **Educ:** Howard University, Washington, DC, BA, Finance, 1971, MBA, 1978, School of Divinity, MDiv, 1995. **Career:** Bell Atlantic, Washington, DC, mgr, residence serv ctr, 1979-81, mgr, rates & tariffs, 1981-87; Bell Atlantic Corp, Arlington, VA, mgr, affiliated interests, 1987-89; Bell Atlantic Corp, Washington DC, mgr, regulatory matters, external affairs, 1989-; ordained elder, African Methodist Episcopal Church, 1997. **Orgs:** Chairman of the board of directors, Ed in Partnership with Technology Corporation, 1991-96; elected comm, vice chmn, Advisory Neighborhood Comm, 1988-95; elected mem, Washington, DC Ward 3 Democratic Committee, 1988-95; Alpha Phi Alpha Fraternity; Brown Memorial AME Church, assistant to the pastor. **Home Addr:** 20408 Foxwood Terrace, Germantown, MD 20876. **Business Addr:** Manager, External Affairs, Bell Atlantic-Washington, DC, 1710 H St NW, 10th Fl, Washington, DC 20006.

GRAYSON, ELSIE MICHELLE
Counselor. **Personal:** Born May 5, 1962, Fairfield, AL. **Educ:** The Univ of AL-Tuscaloosa, BS; Univ of AL at Birmingham, MA Educ. **Career:** Child Mental Health Svcs, teaching parent 1983-84; AL Dept of Human Resources, social worker 1984-. **Orgs:** Mem Alpha Kappa Alpha Sor Inc Omicron Omega Chapt; mem Eastern Star Corine Chap 257; choir dir/pres/asst teacher New Mount Moriah Bapt Church. **Home Addr:** 322 Knight Ave, Hueytown, AL 35023.

GRAYSON, GEORGE WELTON
State representative. **Personal:** Born Nov 1, 1938, Dixon Mills, AL; son of Martha Harper Grayson and Aaron Grayson; married Lucille Lampkin Grayson, Dec 20, 1963; children: Anthony, Reginald, Deirdre. **Educ:** Alabama A&M Univ, Normal, AL, BS, 1965, MS, 1968; Vanderbilt Univ, Nashville, TN, PhD, 1976. **Career:** Tennessee Valley High School, Hillsboro, AL, teacher, 1966-67, guidance counselor/asst principal, 1967-68; Alabama A&M Univ, biology instructor, 1968-71, department chairman; Alabama House of Representatives, representative, 1983-. **Orgs:** Member, Alabama New South Coalition; member, Synod of Mid-South; member, Presbyterian Council. **Honors/Awds:** Man of the Year, Phi Beta Sigma, 1984; Resolution of Commendation, Michigan State House of Representatives, 1984; Good Government Award, Jaycees, 1985; James Weldon Johnson Freedom Award, 1986; author: Impediments to the Development of Black Scientists in Black American Heritage, Southern Press Inc, 1978, Contributions to the American Culture, Southern Press Inc, 1978. **Business Addr:** Representative, District 19, 3810 Melody Road, NE, Huntsville, AL 35811.

GRAYSON, HARRY L.
Educator. **Personal:** Born Jul 7, 1929, Corinth, MS; married Valeris Maxine Porter; children: 7. **Educ:** Rust Coll, BA 1956; Jackson State Coll, MA 1966. **Career:** Lowe's High School Guntown, teacher, coach 1952-53; Poplar High School Saltillo, prin 1953-60; Green St Elementary School Tupelo, first prin 1960-62; George Washington Carver High School Tupelo, prin 1962-. **Orgs:** Mem Spring Hill Bapt Ch Tupelo; YMCA; United Supreme Council 33rd Mason; First Dist Tchrs Assn MAT Nat; Educ Asnn US; Nat Assn Secondary Schs Prin; Young Dem Club MS; Tupelo Civic Improv Club; Phi Beta Sigma Frat Inc; state off State & Nat Funeral Dirs & Mort Assn; bd mem Comm devel Found; pub rel man Grayson-Porterhs Mortuary; pres Ebony Saving Club; treas Astronaut Saving Club; adv bd BSA; exec sec 1st Dist MTA; chosen as del rep MTA to Nat Educ Assn Atlantic City; past pres 1st Dist Tchrs Assn MTA; past sunday sch supt Spring Hill Ch; past chmn McIntoch Dist BSA; past exalt ruler tst Henry Hampton Lodge 782. **Honors/Awds:** NJ awd outstd ldrshp 1st Dist MTA. **Business Addr:** Principal, George Washington Carver High School, 910 N Green, Tupelo, MS 38801.

GRAYSON, JENNIFER A.
Private industry manager. **Personal:** Born Apr 26, 1949, Union, SC; daughter of Martha Gist Gibson and Cortelyou Gibson; married Byron Grayson, Jan 1, 1985; children: Cortella, Paul, Byron Jr, Nicolle. **Educ:** SC State Univ, Orangeburg, SC, BS, 1972; George Washington Univ, Washington, DC, 1977-78. **Career:** Food & Drug Admin, Brooklyn, NY, consumer safety officer, 1972-74; Food & Drug Admin, East Orange, NJ, consumer safety officer, 1974-77; Food & Drug Admn, Rockville, MD, consumer safety officer, 1977-90, acting branch chief, 1990, branch chief, 1990-, acting assoc div dir, 1993-95; Bio-Reg Associates, senior regulatory affairs specialist, Laurel, MD, 1995-96; Oncor, Inc, sr regulatory affairs apecialist, Gaithersburg, MD. **Orgs:** Mem, Delta Sigma Theta Sorority, 1968-; first vice pres, Alpha Wives of Washington, DC, 1987-90; class leader, St Paul AME Church, 1989-; mem, historian, Missionary Society/St Paul Church, 1990-; first vice pres, Missionary Society/St Paul AME Church, 1991-95; Washington Conference, Ministers Wives, Spouses and Widows Alliance, 1994. **Honors/Awds:** Various service awards from church, 1986-. **Home Addr:** 20401 Foxwood Terrace, Germantown, MD 20876.

GRAYSON, JOHN N.
Business executive. **Personal:** Born Sep 4, 1932, Brooklyn, NY; married Dorothy Lane; children: Lois, Theresa (Wallace), Susan, April. **Educ:** BSEE 1959. **Career:** UNIVOX CA Co, pres; Unified Ind Alexandria VA, dir energy problems proj on minority bus enter 1973; prod line mgr mgr-manu engr test sec; Electronics Harward Operations, sub-proj mgr; Guidance & Nav Lab TWR Sys Redondo Beach CA, bus mgr 1962-71; Hughes Aircraft Co El Segundo CA, proj engr 1955-62. **Orgs:** Mem Nat Assn of Black Manu; Inst of Elec & Electronics Engr Inc; chrtr pres Consolidate Comm Action Assn; mem pres Youth Motivation Task Force; Urban League; NAACP; assisted in organization & devel of comm sel-help group in Mexican Am Comm in E LA; assisted & adv in forming of Oriental-Am Caucus; ruling elder Westminster Presb Ch LA; commr 181st Gen Assembly United Presb Ch 1969; past moderator Synod of So Bca UPCUSA; past chmn com which restructured the Synod of So CA; mem The Gen Assembly Mission Council UPCUSA; cmn The Section on Eval UPCUSA. **Honors/Awds:** Man of Yr Awd Westminister Presb Ch 1972; Outsnd Serv Awd Nat Assn of Black Manuf 1974. **Military Serv:** AUS sgt 1st class 1950-55. **Business Addr:** UNIVOX CA Co, 4505 W Jefferson Blvd, Los Angeles, CA 90016.

GRAYSON, STANLEY EDWARD
Banking executive. **Personal:** Born Sep 11, 1950, Chicago, IL; son of L Elizabeth Smith Grayson and George C Grayson Jr; married Patricia Ann McKinnon Grayson, Jul 4, 1981; children: Lauren Ashley, Stephen Edward. **Educ:** College of the Holy Cross, Worcester, MA, AB, 1972; Univ of Michigan Law School, Ann Arbor, MI, JD, 1975. **Career:** Metropolitan Life Insurance Co, New York, NY, attorney, 1975-84; City of New York, New York, NY, commissioner of financial services, 1984-88, commissioner of finance, 1988-89, deputy mayor for finance and economic development, 1989-90; Goldman Sachs & Co, New York, NY, vice president, 1990-96; Prudential Securities Inc, managing dir, 1996-. **Orgs:** 100 Black Men, 1986-; board of directors, Region of Plan Assn, 1990-95; board of directors, Boys Choir of Harlem, 1987-91; New York State Bar Assn, 1977-; board of directors, March of Dimes of New York City, 1990-96; board of directors, The Museum of the City of New York, 1990-; board of directors, The New York Downtown Hospital, 1991-95; bd of trustees, Coll of The Holy Cross, 1995-; bd of trustees, Management Coll, Tarrytown, 1991-96; bd of dirs, NYC Outward Bound, 1995-. **Honors/Awds:** Crusader of the Year, 1972, Hall of Fame, 1991, College of Holy Cross, 1972; Man of the Year, Brooklyn Chamber of Commerce, 1989. **Business Addr:** Managing Director, Public Finance Department, Prudential Securities, Inc, 1 New York Plz, 14th Fl, New York, NY 10292-2014.

GREAR, EFFIE C.
Educational administrator. **Personal:** Born Aug 15, 1927, Huntington, WV; daughter of Margaret Tinsley Carter and Harold J Carter; married William A Grear; children: Rhonda Kaye, William A Jr. **Educ:** WV State Clge, BMus 1948; OH State Univ, MA 1955; Nova Univ, Doctor of Educ 1976. **Career:** Excelsior High WV, music and band tchr 1948-49; FAMU HS Tallahassee FL, band and chorus tchr 1949-51; Smith-brown HS Arcadia FL, band and chorus tchr 1952-56; Lake Shore HS Belle Glade FL, band and chorus tchr 1956-63, dean 1963-66, asst prin 1966-70; Glades Cnt HS Belle Glade FL, asst prin 1970-75, prin 1975-. **Orgs:** Pres Elite Comm Club Inc Belle Glade 1971-82; pres Belle Glade Chamber of Comm Beautification 1974-80; bd of dirs Mental Health Assc Palm Beach Cty 1984-; pres City Assc of Belle Glade 1984-, mem bd of dirs Palm Beach County Mental Health Agency 1984-; pres Belle Glade City Assoc of Women's Clubs 1985-; bd of governors Everglades Area Health Educ Ctr 1986-; sec, Florida Assn of Women's Clubs 1988-90; bd of dir, Florida High Sch Activities Assn, 1987-88; bd of dir, Glades ACTS, 1987-; scy, Palm Beach Cty Criminal Justice Commission, West Palm Beach, FL, 1997. **Honors/Awds:** Outstanding Comm Ach by FL Atlantic Univ 1977; Woman of Year Elite Comm Club 1979 1982; Outstndng Achmt Hnry Mem Glades Correctional Jaycees Unit 1979; Special Recognition FL Sugar Cane League for Lobbying for Sugar Industry Washington DC 1985; Srv Awd United Negro College Fund Telethon 1985; Zeta Phi Beta Educator of the Yr 1984; Educator of the Yr Phi Delta Kappa Palm Beach Co FL 1986; Hon Chap Farmer of the Future Farmers of Amer local chap 1986; Honored by Gov Bob Graham of FL during first celebration of Martin Luther King Jr Natl observance 1986; Woman of the Yr FL Assoc of Women's Clubs 1986; Citizen of the Yr Belle Glade Chamber of Commerce 1986; Community Service Award, El Dorado Civic Club, 1987; Martin L King, Jr Humanitarian Award West Palm Beach UrbanLeague 1988; Community vice Award Palm Beach County NAACP Branch 1989; Club Woman of the Year, Florida Assn of Women's Clubs, 1989; Citizen of the Year, Kappa Upsilon Chapter, Omega Psi Phi Fraternity, 1990; Florida Association of Secondary School Principals, Principal of Excellence, 1992; Florida Department of Education, Finalist for Ida Baker Distinguised Black Educator, 1992; The Links, Inc, West Palm Beach, FL, Outstanding Educator Award, 1996; Alpha Kappa Alpha Sorority, Mu Rho Omega Chap, Belle Glade, FL, Outstanding Community Svc Award, 1996; Zeta Phi Beta Sorority, Inc, Belle Glade, FL, Outstanding Educator Award, 1997. **Home Addr:** 661 SW 4th St, PO Box 262, Belle Glade, FL 33430. **Business Addr:** Principal, Glades Central High School, 425 W Canal St, Belle Glade, FL 33430.

GREAR, WILLIAM A.
Business owner. **Personal:** Born Sep 16, 1923, Russelville, KY; son of Oretha Williams Grear and Charles C Grear; married Effie Carter; children: Rhonda, William Jr. **Educ:** Palm Beach Jr Clge. **Career:** City of Belle Glade FL, city comm 1968-83; Wee Care Child Dev Ctr, dir 1973-79; City of Belle Glade FL, vice mayor 1974; City of Belle Glade FL, mayor 1975; B and E Rubber Stamps and Trophies, owner mgr 1976-. **Orgs:** Bd of dir Solid Waste Authority Palm Bch Co, Katherine Price Fnd Belle Glade 1985, Habilitation Ctr of Belle Glade. **Honors/Awds:** Man of Year Omega Psi Phi Frat 1969; Citizen of Year Elite Comm Club Inc 1975; Comm Srv Award Eldorado Civic Clb 1980; Community Service Award by Governor Graham during 1st Martin Luther King Jr birthday observance 1986; Alpha Kappa Alpha, Mu Rho Omega Chapter, Distinguished Man of the Glades, 1996, 1997. **Business Addr:** Manager, B & E Rubber Stamps-Trophies, 661 SW 4th St, PO Box 262, Belle Glade, FL 33430.

GREAUX, CHERYL PREJEAN
Government official. **Personal:** Born Jul 30, 1949, Houston, TX; daughter of Evelyn F Jones; married Robert Bruce Greaux. **Educ:** Univ of TX, MA 1973; TX Southern Univ, BA (Magna Cum Laude) 1967. **Career:** NASA Johnson Spacecraft Ctr, procurement spec 1968-71; Dept of Labor, supr compliance officer 1973-80; Allied Corp, corporate manager - EEO Programs 1980-85; Dean Witter Reynolds, Inc, executive recruiter, 1986-88; US Dept of Agriculture, dir of RD Civil Rights Staff, 1995-. **Orgs:** Delta Sigma Theta Sorority 1965-, Coalition of 100 Black Women, 1994 chmn, fund raising NJ Inst of Tech 1981-84; bd mem Morris Cty Urban League 1983-85; Co-founder, Washington Edges Group, Inc. **Honors/Awds:** Ford Found Scholarship; Exec on Loan; Massachusetts Inst of Tech, Presidential Classroom Volunteer Instructor, 1994; President's Leadership Award; Natl Assn of Negro Bus & Prof Women's Clubs, 1993. **Business Addr:** Dir, RD Civil Rights Staff, US Dept of Agriculture, 14th & Independence SW, South Bldg, Rm 6337, Washington, DC 20250, (202)720-9504.

GREAVES, MCLEAN
Company executive. **Personal:** Born Sep 27, 1966, St Thomas, Virgin Islands of the United States; son of Marion & Oswald (deceased). **Educ:** British Columbia Institute of Technology, Journalism, 1986. **Career:** IBM, Delrina Softkey Software, consultant, 1993-96; Paper Magazine, new media editor, 1995-96; CBC TV, correspondent, 1996-; Virtual Melanin Inc, pres, CEO, currently. **Orgs:** Committee of Concerned Journalists, panelist, 1998; Columbia School of Business, lecturer, 1997-98; Pratt Institute, lecturer, 1998. **Honors/Awds:** AT&T Link Award, Web Design, 1997; Friends of Errol T Louis, Brooklyn Innovators Award, 1997; New Yorker Review of Cafe Los Negroes, Website, 1997; selected by Village Voice, One of Top 10 Silicon Alley Entrepreneurs, 1997; selected by New York Times/PC Expo, Top 10 NY Websites, 1996; selected as "Cyber Star," Virtual City Magazine, 1996. **Special Achievements:** Articles published: Essence; The Source; Vibe; BET Weekend. **Business Addr:** CEO/Executive Producer, Virtual Melanin Inc, 300 Quincy St, Ste 1A, Brooklyn, NY 11216, (212)726-1063.

GREAVES, WILLIAM
Film producer, director, writer. **Personal:** Born in New York, NY; son of Emily Muir Greaves and Garfield Greaves; married Louise Archambault, Aug 23, 1959; children: David, Taiyi, Maiya. **Educ:** City College of New York, 1944-45; Film Institute City College, 1950-52. **Career:** Natl Film Bd of Canada, filmmaker 1952-60; United Nations Television, producer, director, 1963-64; Canadian Drama Studio, artistic dir 1952-63; "Black Journal," executive producer, co-host, 1968-70; Lee Strasberg Theatre Institute, instructor, 1968-82; William Greaves Productions Inc, owner, 1964-; Bustin Loose, executive producer; produced, wrote, and directed: The Marijuana Affair; Ali, the Fighter; Symbiopsychotaxiplasm: Take One; "Ida B Wells: A Passion for Justice," PBS; From These Roots. **Orgs:** Actors Studio. **Honors/Awds:** Black Filmmakers Hall of Fame, inductee, 1980; Black American Independent Film Festival, special recognition, 1980; Association of Independent Video and Filmmakers, Indy Special Life Achievement Award; Actors Studio, NY, Dusa Award, 1980; National Academy of Television Arts and Sciences, Emmy, for television series "Black Journal"; over 70 film festival awards. **Special Achievements:** Directed and co-produced a celebration of Paul Robeson's 90th birthday, Shubert Theater; has made over 200 documentary films; has conducted workshops for film directors and screen actors throughout the world. **Business Addr:** President, William Greaves Productions, 230 W 55th St, Ste 26D, New York, NY 10019.

GREEN, A. C., JR.
Professional basketball player. **Personal:** Born Oct 4, 1963, Portland, OR. **Educ:** Attended Oregon State Univ. **Career:** Los Angeles Lakers, forward, 1986-94; Phoenix Suns, 1994-96; Dallas Mavericks, 1996-. **Orgs:** A. C. Green Programs for Youth. **Honors/Awds:** Holds record for most consecutive games played among active players in the NBA; NBA All-Star, 1990. **Business Addr:** Professional Basketball Player, Dallas Mavericks, Reunion Arena, 777 Sports St, Dallas, TX 75207, (214)748-1808.

GREEN, AARON ALPHONSO
Attorney. **Personal:** Born Jul 22, 1946, Gainesville, FL; married Carolyn Speed; children: Ava, Adrienne, April. **Educ:** FL A&M Univ, BS Political Science 1966; Univ of FL, JD 1972. **Career:** Self-employed Aaron A Green Law Office, atty 1973-; Gainesville City Commn, youngest person elect 1975; Gainesville FL, mayor commr 1977-78. **Orgs:** Mem FL Bar Assn; FL Acad Trial Lawyers; Natl Bar Assn 8th Judiciary & Cir Nom Commn; mem chrt class Natl Coll Criminal Defense Lawyers & Public Defenders. **Honors/Awds:** Youngest mayor elected; re-elected for second term of city comm 1978. **Business Addr:** 410 S E 4th Ave, Gainesville, FL 32602.

GREEN, AL
Association executive, judge. **Career:** NAACP, Houston Chapter, pres; Harris County TX, judge. **Business Addr:** Judge, Harris County, 5737 Cullen Blvd, Houston, TX 77021.

GREEN, AL
Clergyman, recording artist, business executive. **Personal:** Born Apr 13, 1946, Forrest City, AR. **Educ:** Lane Coll, Hon BA Music 1976; Lemoyne Owen, Hon BA Music 1977. **Career:** Green Enterprises Inc, owner/pres 1970; Al Green Music Inc, owner/pres/recording artist 1970-; Full Gospel Tabernacle Church, pastor 1976-; formerly recording artist w/Bell then Hi-

Records; songs include Rhymes, Lets Stay Together, Tired of Being Alone, How do You Mend a Broken Heart, Back up Train, Love and Happiness; appeared in Broadway production "Your Arms Too Short to Box with God," 1982; He is the Light, 1986; With Love Is Reality, 1992. **Orgs:** Mem NARAS 1970-, AGVA 1970-; spec deputy Memphis Sheriffs Dept 1976-; hon capt Bolling AFB Washington DC 1976-; pres Lee County Publ Co 1983-; mem Econ & Devel City Hall 1984-. **Honors/Awds:** Tribute in the Music Ind Sullivan Awd 1982; Grammy Precious Lord NARAS 1983; Grammy I'll Rise Again NARAS 1984; Dove Awd Gospel Music Assoc 1984. **Business Addr:** Full Gospel Tabernacle Ministries, PO Box 9485, Memphis, TN 38109.

GREEN, ANGELO GRAY
Financial administrator. **Personal:** Born Sep 20, 1950, Mobile, AL; married Joyce Wright; children: Angela Latifa, Jasmine Niya. **Educ:** Clark Coll, BA Econ 1968-72; Univ of MI, MPP Public Finance 1972-74. **Career:** Cunningham Art Products, cost accountant 1974; City of Atlanta Employment & Training Office, financial analyst II 1974-78; City of Atlanta Fin Dept, financial analyst III 1978-83, fin chief analyst. **Orgs:** Consult United Negro Coll Fund 1979, Southern Ctr for Public Policies Studies 1980,82; mem NAACP 1981-85, Atlanta Urban League 1982-84, Natl Forum for Black Public Admin 1984-85. **Honors/Awds:** Publ "Manpower Devel & Training, An Evaluation" Southern Ctr for Public Policy Studies Clark Coll 1971; Employee of the Year City of Atlanta Employment & Training Office 1977; Manager of the Year City of Atlanta Employment & Training Office 1978. **Business Addr:** Financial Chief Analyst, City of Atlanta, 902 City Hall, Atlanta, GA 30335.

GREEN, ANITA LORRAINE
Banker. **Personal:** Born Jul 18, 1948, Brooklyn, NY; daughter of Queen Esther Carroll and Angus Carroll; children: Corey James. **Educ:** Brooklyn College of the City University of NY, BA, 1980. **Career:** National Urban League, program development specialist, 1972-82; Citicorp Diners Club, marketing communications manager, 1982-88; Citibank FSB, vice pres community relations and CRA officer, 1988-. **Orgs:** Museum Science & Industry, chairperson, black creativity program, 1992-; DePaul University, Center for Urban Education, advisory board, 1990-; Illinois Facilities Fund, board mem, 1993-; Life Directions, bd mem. **Honors/Awds:** Dollars & Sense Magazine, America's Best and Brightest Business, Professional Men & Women, 1991; Mahogany Foundation, Community Relations Award, 1993-; YMCA Black and Hispanic Achievers of Industry Award, 1993; Success Guide, Top Ten To Watch, 1995; Today's Chicago Women, 100 Women Making a Difference. **Business Addr:** Vice Pres, Citibank, 500 W Madison St, Chicago, IL 60661, (312)627-3513.

GREEN, BARBARA-MARIE
Journalist, publisher. **Personal:** Born Mar 21, 1928, New York, NY; daughter of Mae McCarter Green and James Green. **Educ:** Hunter College, New York, NY, BA, 1951; Syracuse University, grad study, 1955; CCNY, New York, NY, MA, 1955; NYU, New York, NY, PhD study, 1965-80. **Career:** New York City Board of Education, New York, NY, teacher, junior high school and high school English, guidance counselor, asst principal, principal, 1952-82; The Creative Record, Virginia Beach, VA, owner, publisher, 1985-. **Orgs:** Eastern region director 1989-91, national board member 1985-89, National Assn of Negro Musicians; Queens Borough wide publicity chair, UNCF, 1986; public relations, National Sorority of Phi Delta Kappa, 1953-56; newsletter editor, 94th St, East Elmhurst, NY Block Assn; Queens advisory board, New York Urban League, 1965-85; Harpers Ferry Historical Society, VA Poetry Society, mem; Induction into African Amer Biographics Hall of Fame, Atlanta GA, for Communications, 1994; Princess Anne Business & Professional Womens Club, mem, 1992-; pres, first vp, corresponding secretary, State Public Relations; chair, VA Federation of Business & Professional Women's Club Inc; Alpha Kappa Alpha Sorority; American Business Women's Association; American Academy of Poets. **Honors/Awds:** Stars Among Stars, Night of a Thousand Stars of the Great American Read Aloud, Queens Borough Public Library, East Elmhurst Queens, NY, 1991; Certification of Appreciation, Outstanding and Dedicated Service in Our Commmunity, Arlene of New York, 1990; Commemorating the First Anniversary of the Good News, adopted in Assembly No. 976, State of New York Resolution, 1986; Citation of Appreciation, Dedicated Service as a Volunteer, Associated Black Charities, 1985; Poetry Books, 1990; Love Pain Hope, anthology 1993; More Poetic Thoughts; Poet Laureute-in-Residence, First Lynnhaven Baptist Church, VA Bch, VA; Hunter College Alumni Assn, Hall of Fame inductee, 1997. **Special Achievements:** Author: poetry, "Dreams and Memories" 1996; "Spirit," 1997; "Keeper of the Flame", 1997; radio show, "Keeping It Real," WPMH-AM, Chesapeake, VA. **Business Addr:** Publisher, Editorial, Bar'JaMae Communications Inc, PO Box 64412, Virginia Beach, VA 23467-4412, (757)479-4127.

GREEN, BRENDA KAY
Educator. **Personal:** Born Dec 7, 1947, Baton Rouge, LA; daughter of Lillian White George and Jackson Willis Green. **Educ:** Southern Univ, Baton Rouge LA, BS, 1969; Northwestern Univ, Evanston IL, MA, 1973; Louisiana State Univ, Baton Rouge LA, post graduate studies, 1980-82. **Career:** East Baton Rouge Parish Schools, Baton Rouge LA, teacher, 1969-89. **Orgs:** Pres, Beta Alpha Chapter, Zeta Phi Beta, 1968; mem, Natl Educ Assn, 1969-, Louisiana Educ Assn, 1969-72, Louisiana Assn of Educ, 1972-, Phi Delta Kappa, 1974-89; 3rd vice pres, Mu Zeta Chapter, Zeta Phi Beta, 1976-80; mem, Natl Council of Negro Women, 1980-; Louisiana State dir, Zeta Phi Beta Sorority Inc, 1980-88; 1st vice pres, Mu Zeta Chapter, Zeta Phi Beta, 1984-88; Natl 2nd vice pres, Zeta Phi Beta Sorority Inc, 1988-; chmn of scholarship, Natl Educ Found, ZOB, 1988-. **Honors/Awds:** Teacher of the Year, Louisiana Educ Assn (local school), 1973, 1974; Outstanding Young Educ, Scotlandville LA Jaycees, 1974; Honorary Dist Atty, East Baton Rouge Parish Dist Attorney's Office, 1983. **Home Addr:** 1423 N 26th St, Baton Rouge, LA 70802.

GREEN, CALVIN COOLIDGE
Educator, clergyman (retired), consultant. **Personal:** Born Jul 19, 1931, Laneview, VA; son of Consula Levallia Deleaver Green (deceased) and James Herman Green (deceased); married Ella Mary Osbourne; children: Robert Caesar, Carroll Anthony, Charles Conrad. **Educ:** VA State Coll Petersburg, BS Biology 1956; A&T Coll of NC Greensboro, MSEd Chem 1965; Grad Sch Med Coll of VA, Physiology 1968-71; Sch of Theology VA Union U, MDiv Theology 1982; Intl Bible Inst & Seminary Orlando, ThD Cnslng 1983; Nova Univ, Ft Lauderdale FL Ed D Program 1987; International Seminary, PhD 1990. **Career:** Downingtown Industrial Sch PA, sci tchr 1956-57; Med Coll of VA Heart Lung Project, surgical Lab Tech 1957-59; Armstrong HS Richmond, tchr of sci 1959-62; Armstrong HS Richmond, prof of military sci/commandant of cadets 1963-69; pastor Lebanon Bapt Church New Kent, VA 1977-82; pastor Calvary Bapt Ch Saluda, VA 1979-91; Thomas Jefferson High School, dept head science 1969-76; Jefferson-Hugeunot-Wythe HS, Dept sci head 1976-80, Chmn Sci Dept 1980-85; Sci Dept Chmn, Thomas Jefferson High School 1985-91 (retired); Church Computer Workshops, self employed consultant, currently; Mt. Carmel Bapt Ch, Richmond, VA, interim pastor, 1997. **Orgs:** Mem VA Acad of Sci Com 1981-85, 1996-; General Board of Baptist General Convention of VA; mem, gen bd of Baptist Gen Convention of VA 1985-89; Chaplain, dept of VA ROA 1983-88; mem Phi Delta Kappa 1988-; mem National Society for the Study of Education 1986-90. **Honors/Awds:** ROTC Hall of Fame VA State Coll 1969-; chaplain VA Dept of Reserve Offcrs Assn (ROA) 1984-88, 1990; honorarium & banquet by New Kent NAACP 1989; plaque from Professional Business Women's Orgn, Middlesix & Vic 1989. **Special Achievements:** Chief plantiff US Supreme Court Decision, "Green v New Kent" 1968; Author, "Counseling, With the Pastor and CPE Stdnt in Mind," Vantage, 1984. **Military Serv:** US Army, Med Serv col 23 yrs; Chaplain Corps col 10 yrs; Occupation Medal (Japan); Korean Svc; Armed Svcs; Armed Forces Reserve 1951-, Adjunct Faculty, Command and General Staff College, 1986; continuous military (USAR) since 1951; officer 1956-; Korean War; enlisted service 1951-53; USAR, Col, 1983-; Two Meritorious Service Awards, 1990; retired col, 1992; Studied Mosow Aviation Institute. **Home Addr:** 5135 New Kent Hwy, Quinton, VA 23141-2519. **Business Phone:** (804)932-4310.

GREEN, CAROLYN LOUISE
Government official. **Personal:** Born Apr 9, 1950, Waterloo, IA; daughter of Madelean Tanner Green and Tommie Lee Green; married Michael Trent Blakeney, Sep 4, 1982. **Educ:** University of Iowa, Iowa City, IA, BM, 1972, 1973; University of California, Berkeley, CA, 1975. **Career:** California Air Resources Board, Sacramento, CA, air quality planner, 1974-77; Jack G Raub Company, Costa Mesa, CA, mgr, policy planning, 1977-82, issues coordinator, 1982-84; Southern California Gas Company, Los Angeles, CA, environmental affairs manager, 1984-87; South Coast Air Quality, El Monte, Ca, deputy executive officer, 1987-.

GREEN, CHARLES A.
Educator, psychologist. **Personal:** Born Oct 17, 1927, Detroit, MI; divorced; children: Iris, Robin Charles. **Educ:** BA 1952; MEd 1957; PhD 1974. **Career:** Detroit Bd of Educ, teacher Special Educ 1953-52; Northville State Hospital, 1958-62; Detroit Bd of Educ, psychology clinic 1962-68; Rsch & Evaluation Dept Detroit Bd of Educ, rsch assoc 1968-. **Orgs:** Fellow-Am Assn on Mental Defieciency; Am Assn Advncmt of Sci; Am Acad of Polit & Social Sci; Phi Delta Kappa; co-fndr & 1st pres MI Assn Tchrs of Emtnlly Dstrbd Children 1960; Alpha Phi Alpha; Bro-Big Sister Orgn 1968-72; Evltn Com New Detroit Inc 1970-; chrmn Thunderbird Dist; chmn Boy Scoutsof Am 1974; chmn MI Assn of Black Psychol, MI Acad of Polit & Social Sci 1978-79; Am Educ Rsrch Assn. **Honors/Awds:** Lstd in ldrs in am sci 1960; comm ldrs of am 1970; men of achvmnt 1974. **Business Addr:** 10100 Grand River, Detroit, MI 48204.

GREEN, CLIFFORD SCOTT
Judge. **Personal:** Born Apr 2, 1923, Philadelphia, PA; son of Alice Robinson Green and Robert Lewis Green Sr (deceased); married Mabel Wood; children: Terri Alice, David Scott. **Educ:** Temple University School of Business, BS (with honors), 1948; Temple University School of Law, LLB (with honors), JD, 1951. **Career:** Norris, Schmidt, Green, Harris & Higginbotham law firm, partner, 1952-64; Commonwealth of Pennsylvania, special deputy atty gen, 1954-55; County Court of Philadelphia, judge, 1964; US District Court, Eastern District of PA, judge 1971-88, senior judge, 1988-. **Orgs:** Bd trustees, Temple University; bd dir, Crime Prevention Assn of Philadelphia; former chairman, White House Fellows Philadelphia Regional Panel; former mgr, Children's Hospital; Sigma Pi Phi, Alpha Boule, 1970-. **Honors/Awds:** Honorary LLD, Temple University; Judge William Hastie Award, NAACP Legal Defense Fund, 1985; J Austin Norris Award, Philadelphia Barristers Assn, 1988. **Military Serv:** US Air Force, 1943-46. **Home Addr:** 2311 N 50th St, Philadelphia, PA 19131. **Business Addr:** Senior Judge, US District Court, Eastern District of PA, 15613-601 Market St, Philadelphia, PA 19106.

GREEN, CLYDE OCTAVIOUS
Physician. **Personal:** Born Oct 6, 1960, St Elizabeth, Jamaica; married Cheryl E Wilson; children: Juliet, Elise. **Educ:** Univ of South Carolina, BS 1982; Howard Univ, MD 1986. **Career:** Student Christian Fellowship, minister 1979-82; Student Natl Medical Assoc, parlimentarian 1982-86; Triumph The Church of New Age, asst pastor 1979-; Medical Center of Central Georgia, physican, currently. **Orgs:** Mem Medical Assoc of GA; rsch asst Howard Univ 1984-86; consultant Natl Council on Aging 1985-86; mem Amer Medical Assoc 1986-. **Honors/Awds:** Dean's List 1981,82; President's List 1981-82; founder/pres Intl Student Professional Assoc 1983-86. **Business Addr:** Physician, Medical Ctr of Central GA, PO Box 794, Gray, GA 31032.

GREEN, CONSUELLA
US Navy officer. **Personal:** Born Mar 14, 1946, New Orleans, LA; daughter of Nancy Mae Green Anderson. **Educ:** Southern Univ, Baton Rouge LA, BS, 1971; InterAmerican Univ, Puerto Rico, MA, 1976. **Career:** US Navy, Great Lakes IL, dir, Race Relations Center, 1973-75, Roosevelt Roads PR, port serv, Base Educ Serv, 1975-77, Navy Reserve Officer Training Corps, asst prof, Naval Science, 1977-80, Washington DC, Devel & Implementation of Navy Training Plans, 1980-83, Little Rock AR, Military Entrance Processing Station, commanding officer, 1984-86, San Diego CA, dir of training & exec officer, Fleet Training Center, 1986-90. **Honors/Awds:** Certificate of Community Serv for the Neighborhood House Assn Head Start Child Devel Program; Community Serv & Professional Achievement Award, Lambda Kappa Mu; Leadership Award, YWCA Tribute to Women In Industry; Young Outstanding Woman of America Award, 1978. **Military Serv:** US Navy, Commander (0-5), 1972-.

GREEN, DARLENE
City official. **Career:** City of St Louis, budget director, comptroller, 1995-. **Orgs:** Zeta Phi Beta Sorority; National Association of Black Accountants; NAACP. **Honors/Awds:** National Association of Black Accountants, National Achievement in Government Award; Young Democrats of St Louis City, Political Leadership Award; various others. **Special Achievements:** First African American female comptroller of St Louis. **Business Addr:** Comptroller, City of St Louis, City Hall, Rm 212, 1200 Market St, St Louis, MO 63103.

GREEN, DARRELL
Professional football player. **Personal:** Born Feb 15, 1960, Houston, TX; married Jewell Fenner; children: Jarrel, Jarod, Joi. **Educ:** Texas A&I Univ, attended. **Career:** Washington Redskins, cornerback, 1983-. **Orgs:** Spokesperson, Big Brother/Big Sisters of America, DC Chapter; honorary chairman, American Red Cross, Northern Virginia Chapter; Darrell Green Youth Life Foundation, founder. **Honors/Awds:** Named to Football Coaches All-American Division II team in college; Lone Star Conference Defensive Player of the Year; selected to AP first team Little All-American; won title of NFL's Fastest Man; named to Football Digest and AP all-rookie first teams; Super Bowl punt return record, 1983; Associated Press, NFL Defensive Rookie of the Year, 1983; played in Pro Bowl, 1984, 1986, 1987, 1990, 1991, 1996; True Value Man of the Year, 1996; Bart Starr Award, 1996; Ken Houston Humanitarian Award, 1996. **Business Addr:** Professional Football Player, Washington Redskins, 13832 Redskin Dr, Herndon, VA 22071, (703)471-9100.

GREEN, DARRYL LYNN
Computer manager. **Personal:** Born Sep 29, 1958, Ypsilanti, MI; son of Clarence & Eleanor; children: Robert Green. **Educ:** Central MI Univ, 1976-78; Computer Learning Center, cert of completion, 1988. **Career:** Alcoa Aluminum, inspector, 1979-91; Packard Bell, project manager, 1991-. **Business Addr:** Manager, Packard Bell Electronics Inc, 8285 West 3500 South, Magna, UT 84044.

GREEN, DEBORAH KENNON
Attorney. **Personal:** Born Aug 14, 1951, Knoxville, TN; daughter of Florence Jones Green and George Green; children: Joshua. **Educ:** Knoxville Coll, BA, 1973; Georgetown Law Ctr, JD 1976. **Career:** David N Niblack Wash DC, law clerk, attny 1976-77; DC Govt Rental Accommodations Office, hearing ex-

aminer 1977-78; Govt Oper Arrington Dixon, DC City Council, comm clerk 1978-79; Council of DC Office Arrington Dixon, leg asst to chmn 1979-80; US Dept of Labor, Arlington, VA, counsel, currently. **Orgs:** Co-chmn 7th Annual Conv Natl Assoc of Black Women Attny 1978-; mem WV Bar Assoc 1979, WA Bar Assoc 1980, Alfred St Baptist Church, 1989. **Honors/Awds:** Tuition Scholarship Georgetown Law Ctr Wash DC 1973-76; Earl Warren Legal Training Scholarship 1973-74; Special Awd of Merit DC Bar 1979; Meritorious Achievement Award, 1985, Federal Women's Program Award, 1990, Department of Labor; Exceptional Secretary's Achievement Award, 1993. **Business Addr:** Attorney, US Dept of Labor, 4015 Wilson Blvd, Rm 428, Arlington, VA 22203.

GREEN, DENNIS
Football coach. **Personal:** Born Feb 17, 1949, Harrisburg, PA; married Margie; children: Patty, Jeremy. **Educ:** Iowa State Univ, BS, educ, 1971. **Career:** British Columbia Lions Canadian Football League, starting tailback; Iowa State, grad asst 1972, quarterbacks/receivers coach 1974-76; Dayton, offensive backs/receivers coach 1973; Stanford Univ, offensive coord 1980, football coach, 1989-; Northwestern Univ, head coach, 1980-85; San Francisco 49ers, receivers coach, 1986-88; Stanford Cardinals, coach, until 1992; Minnesota Vikings, head coach, 1992-. **Honors/Awds:** Big 10 Coach of the Year 1982. **Business Addr:** Head Coach, Minnesota Vikings, 9520 Viking Dr, Eden Prairie, MN 55344.

GREEN, DENNIS O.
Auditor. **Personal:** Born Nov 14, 1940, Detroit, MI; son of Olive May Dean McCaughan and Arthur Salvador Green; married Katherine F, Aug 12, 1961; children: Damon, Leslie. **Educ:** Wayne State Univ, BS 1967; State MI, CPA. **Career:** Arthur Andersen & Co, staff sr accountant, 1967-69, audit manager, 1971-73; Wells & Green Prof Corp, pres 1969-71; finance director, City of Detroit 1974-76; Office of Mgmt & Budget Wash DC, assoc dir exec of the Pres 1977-78; Ford Motor Co, gen auditor, 1978-90; Citicorp, chief auditor, 1990-. **Orgs:** Mem, Amer Inst of CPA's; Natl Assn of Black Accountants; mem, Inst of Internal Auditors, 1984-. **Business Addr:** Chief Auditor, Citicorp/Citibank, 153 E 53rd, 23 Fl, New York, NY 10043.

GREEN, EDDIE L.
Educational Administrator. **Personal:** Born Mar 7, 1942, Houston, TX; son of Matthew & Mary Rose Green; married Jacqueline, Apr 5, 1969; children: Shelley, Bryce. **Educ:** Grambling State University, BS, 1963; Wayne State University, MEd, 1970, EdD, 1993. **Career:** Detroit Public Schools, bus educ dept head, 1979-81, dir, principal, 1981-85, asst dir, 1985-89, area asst superintendent, 1989, area superintendent, 1989-97, interim deputy superintendent, 1997, interim general superintendent & deputy superintendent, 1997-. **Orgs:** AASA, 1989-; ASCD, 1996-; Delta Pi Epsilon, past pres, 1975-; MASA, 1989-; MASSP, 1989-; Michigan Business Education Association, past pres, 1967-; NAPE, consultant, 1984; Phi Delta Kappa - Detroit, newsletter editor, 1980-. **Honors/Awds:** Phi Delta Kappa, Educator of the Year, 1992; Michigan Business Education Association, Distinguished Service, 1981; Detroit Public Schools, Spirit of Detroit Award, 1982, Outstanding Service Award, 1982; National School Volunteering Program, Outstanding Trainee Consultant, 1984. **Special Achievements:** The Effects of Mentoring on Selected Detroit Public Schools Students, 1993; Detroit Public Schools Ninth Grade Restructuring Program, 1992. **Military Serv:** US Army, spec-4, 1964-66; US Quartermaster School, Honor Graduate. **Home Addr:** 3200 Cambridge Rd, Detroit, MI 48221, (313)861-9282.

GREEN, ERIC (BERNARD ERIC)
Professional football player. **Personal:** Born Jun 22, 1967, Savannah, GA. **Educ:** Liberty Univ, BBA, 1990. **Career:** Pittsburgh Steelers, tight end, 1990-94; Miami Dolphins, 1995; Baltimore Ravens, 1996-. **Honors/Awds:** Kodak All-America; All-America, second team AP Div 1-AA; 1990, first Pittsburgh Steeler tight end under coach Chuck Noll's 22-year era to: catch two touchdown passes in a game (early Sept) catch three TD passes in a game (mid-Sept). **Business Addr:** Professional Football Player, Baltimore Ravens, 11001 Owings Mills Blvd, Owings Mills, MD 21117, (410)654-6200.

GREEN, ERNEST G.
Investment banker. **Personal:** Born Sep 22, 1941, Little Rock, AR; son of Lothaire S Green and Ernest G Green, Sr; married Phyllis; children: Adam, Jessica, McKenzie. **Educ:** MI State Univ, BA 1962, MA 1964. **Career:** A Philip RAndolph Educ Fund, dir, 1968-76; US Labor Dept, asst sec of labor 1977-81; Green & Herman, partner 1981-85; E Green & Associates, owner 1985-86; Lehman Brothers, investment banker. **Orgs:** Bd mem Winthrop Rockefeller Foundation; mem Omega Psi Phi; vice-chair, AfriCare; African Dev Foundation, chairman; chair, National Association Securities Professionals. **Honors/Awds:** Rockefeller Public Service Princeton Univ 1976; NAACP Spingarn Awd; Honorary Doctorates, Tougaloo Coll, 1979, Michigan St Univ, 1994. **Special Achievements:** Mem of Little Rock Nine. **Business Addr:** Investment Banker, Lehman Brothers, 800 Connecticut Ave, Ste 1200, Washington, DC 20006.

GREEN, FORREST F.
City official, business executive. **Personal:** Born Feb 2, 1915, E Point, GA; married Mamie E Logan; children: Forrest, Jr, Saul A, Darryl L. **Educ:** Morehouse Coll, BA 1937; Wayne State U, MA 1967. **Career:** City of Detroit, city ombudsman; bus exec 1947-74; social workr 1938-46; Vocational Sch, pres owner. **Orgs:** Mem Intl Bar Assn Ombudsman & Adv Com; Am Arbitrtn Assn; Intl Persnnl Mgmt Assn; Greater C of C; Detroit Rotary Club; first black mem MI Civil Serv Commn 1961-68; first black mem Detroit Parks & Recreation Commn 1962-69; mem Detroit's Charter Revisn Comm 1970-73. **Honors/Awds:** State cert of hon MI Acad of Voltr Ldrshp 1964; outstndg cit awd Detroit Urban League 1965; cert for serv to youth Wayne Univ 1968; liberty bell awd Detroit Bar Assn 1969. **Business Addr:** 114 City Co Bldg, Detroit, MI 48226.

GREEN, FREDERICK CHAPMAN
Physician, educator. **Personal:** Born Oct 7, 1920, Fort Wayne, IN; son of Luretta M Rhodes Green (deceased) and Oliver Green (deceased); married Lucille Ingram Green, Jun 20, 1947; children: Frederick C, Sharman L. **Educ:** IN Univ, BS 1942; IN Univ School of Medicine, MD 1944; Harlem Hospital New York City, internship & residency 1947. **Career:** New York City, private practice pediatrician 1947-67; AUS Hospital, Ft Devene, MA, chief pediatrician 1951-53; Sydenham Hospital NY, dir of pediatrics 1961-71; Pediatric Ambulatory Care Roosevelt Hospital NY, dir 1967-71; US Children's Bureau DHEW, assoc chief 1971-73; Children's Hospital Natl Medical Center, assoc dir 1973-; Child Health Advcy Children's Hospital Natl Medical Center, dir ofc 1973-; Child Health & Devel George Washington Univ School of Medicine & Health Science, prof 1973-; US Nat Commn on the Intl Year of the Child, commr 1979; George Washington Univ School of Medicine, asst dean for prog planning, prof emeritus child health devel. **Orgs:** Chmn Mayor Marion Barry's Interagncy/Interdprtmntl Com on Child Abuse & Neglect 1975-; chmn Mayor Marion Barry's Blue Ribbon Com on Infant Mortality Washington DC 1979-; bd or dirs UNICEF Amer Humane Assn Nat Com for Citizens in Educ 1979-; pres Natl Comm for Prevention of Child Abuse 1986-. **Honors/Awds:** Citation & outstanding serv rendered Job Lewis Smith Award; Am Acad of Ped 1975; distinguished black am fellow Phelps-Stokes Fund 1975-76; guest editor Ped Annuals 1979; pres medal for distinguished comm serv The Catholic Univ of Am & Madison Nat Bank 1979; Hildrus Poindexter Awardee Amer Public Health Assn Black Caucus 1983; Washingtonian of the Year Washingtonian Magazine 1984; Martha M Elliot Award, Maternal & Child Health: American Public Health Assn, 1989. **Military Serv:** US Army, Capt.

GREEN, GEORGIA MAE
Attorney. **Personal:** Born Apr 15, 1950, Knoxville, TN; daughter of Florence Jones Green (deceased) and George Edward Green (deceased). **Educ:** Knoxville Coll, BA (cum Laude) 1972; Howard Univ Sch of Law Washington, DC, JD 1976. **Career:** Dept of Corrections, attorney. **Orgs:** Mem WV Bar Assn 1979-; conv co-chmn Natl Assn of Black Women Atty 1980-; 1st vice pres Amer Fed of Govt Employees Local 1550 DC Dept of Corrections Union 1984; mem District of Columbia Bar Assoc 1985-. **Honors/Awds:** WV Ambassador of Good Will Among All People, WV Sec of State 1979. **Business Addr:** Attorney, District of Columbia, 1923 Vermont Ave, NW, Washington, DC 20001.

GREEN, GERALDINE D.
Attorney. **Personal:** Born Jul 14, 1938, New York, NY; daughter of Lula Chisholm and Edward Chisholm. **Educ:** City Coll of NY Baruch Sch of Bus, BBA 1964; St John's Univ Law Sch, JD 1968. **Career:** Law Offices of Geraldine D Green 1987-; pres Geraldine's Restaurant-Cocktail Lounge 1987-91; Burke, Robinson & Pearman, attorney of counsel 1985-86; Rosenfeld Meyer & Susman, partner 1983-85; CA Corp Comnr 1980-83; Atlantic Richfield Co, sr atty asst corp sec 1972-80; IBM Corp, staff atty 1968-72; Coopers & Lybrand CPA's, tax accountant 1966-68; LA Traffic Commn, commr; Business Law & Finance, Dillard Univ, FL Mem Coll, visiting prof; CA State Bar Comm on Corp 1974-76. **Orgs:** Pres Beverly Hills/Hollywood Br NAACP 1979-82; spec coun LA Urban League; Black Women Lawyers of CA; Langston Bar Assn; Natl Bar Assn; Southern Poverty Law Ctr; Youth Motivation Task Force. **Honors/Awds:** LA Urban League Comm Serv Awd 1973 ; NAACP Freedom Awd Cit 1973; YWCA Cert of Achievement 1976; Geraldine D Green Day in City of Los Angeles, February 1984; Certificate of Achievement California State Legislature 1986; Certificate of Appreciation California State Senate 1984; Certificate of Appreciation City of Los Angeles 1981. **Business Addr:** Attorney-at-Law, Law Offices of Geraldine Green, 500 Shatto Place, #630, Los Angeles, CA 90020-1707, (213)365-0559.

GREEN, GLORIA J.
Attorney. **Personal:** Born Dec 9, 1954, Atlanta, GA; daughter of Mattie Green and Alfred Green Sr; divorced; children: Avery Kelley. **Educ:** Duke University, Durham, NC, BA, 1976; Georgetown University Law Center, Washington, DC, Juris Doctor, 1979. **Career:** Securities and Exchange Commission, Washington, DC, attorney, 1979-82; Securities and Exchange Commission, Atlanta, GA, senior attorney, 1982-86; Federal Home Loan Bank of Atlanta, Atlanta, GA, vice president, deputy general counsel, & director of legal services, 1986-. **Orgs:** Member of board of directors, Wesley Community Centers, 1988-93; member of board of directors, South DeKalb YMCA, 1990-; member of board of directors, DC Express Track Club, 1990-; trustee, Kelley's Chapel United Methodist Church, 1990-; member, National Coalition of 100 Black Women, 1989-93. **Honors/Awds:** Partners With Youth, South Dakalb YMCA, Leadership Award, 1992; DC Express Track Club, Inc, Service Award, 1991, 1992, 1993 & 1994. **Business Addr:** Deputy General Counsel, Legal Department, Federal Home Loan Bank of Atlanta, 1475 Peachtree St, NE, 10th Floor, Atlanta, GA 30309.

GREEN, HUGH
Professional football player. **Personal:** Born Jul 27, 1959, Natchez, MS. **Educ:** Univ of Pittsburgh. **Career:** Linebacker: Tampa Bay Buccaneers, 1981-85; Miami Dolphins, 1985-. **Honors/Awds:** Selected to the Sporting News All-time All-America team; winner of 1980 Lombardi Trophy; runner up, 1980 Heisman Trophy; won four Natl Player of the Year Awards in 1980; selected Player of the Year by touchdown clubs in Cleveland, Columbus, and Washington; first team All-America in 1978, UPI and Walter Camp and second team NEA All-America; as a junior named best defensive player in the country by New York Times; played in Hula Bowl and Japan Bowl; first team All-Pro, The Sporting News, Sports Illustrated, and Football Digest; All-NFC, UPI and Pro Football Weekly; finished 1983 with 138 tackles to lead the team for second straight season; selected All-Pro and St Petersburg Times Buc MVP by media vote; All-Pro, Pro Football Writers, Football Digest, Sports Illustrated,and Pro Football Neeekly; played in Pro Bowl, 1982, 1983. **Business Addr:** Professional Football Player, Miami Dolphins, 2269 NW 199th St, Miami, FL 33056-2600.

GREEN, HYDIA LUTRICE
Banking executive. **Personal:** Born Dec 24, 1963, New Orleans, LA; daughter of Mertis Marie Flanders Coney and Jimmie Lee Coney; married. **Educ:** Louisiana State Univ, Baton Rouge, LA, BS, Management. **Career:** County Savings Bank, Columbus, Ohio, dir of marketing, currently; First Union Natl Bank, asst branch mgr. **Orgs:** Chamber of Commerce 1988-; Civitan, 1989-, Sertoma, 1989-; third vice pres, Zeta Phi Beta Sorority Inc, 1982-; Project Business Inst, Jr Achievement 1989-. **Honors/Awds:** Outstanding Young Women of Amer, 1987; Natl Collegiate Greek Merit Award, 1987; Zeta of the Year, Zeta Phi Beta Sorority Inc, 1986. **Home Addr:** 6621 Pauline Dr, New Orleans, LA 70126-1040.

GREEN, JAMES
Basketball coach. **Career:** Iowa State Univ, asst coach; Univ of Southern Mississippi, head basketball coach, 1996-. **Special Achievements:** First African American head basketball coach at University of Southern Mississippi. **Business Addr:** Head Basketball Coach, University of Southern Mississippi, Box 5017, Hattiesburg, MS 39406, (601)266-7011.

GREEN, JAMES L.
Physician. **Personal:** Born Feb 2, 1945, Hampton, VA; son of Dr and Mrs James L Green; children: Timothy B, Jenifer L. **Educ:** Hampton Inst, BA 1967; Meharry Med Coll, MD 1973. **Career:** Hubbard Hosp, intern 1973-74, resident 1975-77; VA Hosp Tuskegee AL, chief retina sect 1978-79; Univ of IL, asst prof of clinical opthol 1980-; Univ ofIL, fellow vitreous surgery 1979-81, asst prof of opth 1980-; Michael Reese Hospital & Medical Ctr, attending surgeon 1981-; Retinal Vitreal Consultants; Mercy Hospital & Medical Center, chief of retina service, 1986-; University of Chicago, Chicago, IL, clinical assoc prof 1990. **Orgs:** Fellow American Acad of Opthalmology 1979-; certified Amer Bd of Opthalmology 1979-; mem NMA, Chicago Opthalmological Society; Illinois Assn of Ophthalmology. **Honors/Awds:** Rowe Awd in Ophthalmology 1973; Merk Awd 1973; 7 publications. **Business Addr:** Medical Doctor, Retinal Vitreal Consultants, Ltd, 2525 South Michigan Avenue, 8th Floor Eye Center, Chicago, IL 60616, (312)567-2795.

GREEN, JARVIS R.
Steel company executive. **Personal:** Born Feb 20, 1953, Tuskegee, AL; son of Johnnie Lewis and Jerry Green; married Desiree E Green; children: Kawanna. **Educ:** Alabama A&M University, BS, 1976. **Career:** Brandon, Smith & Jones CPA Firm, sr accountant; Atlanta Minority Business Development, construction accountant; Atlanta Housing Authority, programs manager; AGE Industries, exec vp; AGE Enterprises, Ltd, vp, currently. **Orgs:** 100 Black Men Dekalb, financial secretary; Omega Psi Phi Fraternity, finance and budget committee; Dekalb Chamber of Commerce; Georgia Minority Supplier Division Council; Better Business Bureau; US Chamber of Commerce. **Honors/Awds:** Christmas in July Committee, Certificate of Appreciation; US Business Administration, State Small Business of the Year Candidate. **Business Phone:** (404)508-0046.

GREEN, JOHN M.
Historian. **Personal:** Born May 11, 1932, Lawton, OK; son of Johnny M & Jannie McClanahan; divorced; children: John M,

Tiffny E. **Educ:** Lincoln Univ, 1951-53; Wayne State Univ, BA, 1977. **Career:** Santa Fe Railroad, chr car attnd, 1954-55; State of Michigan, mtr veh opr, 1956-64; Automobile Club of Michigan, supervisor-legal, 1964-80; Historical Research Repository Inc, exec dir, currently. **Orgs:** Alpha Phi Alpha, dean of pledges, 1953; Financial Forum, 1966; Museum of African American History, historian, 1984-86; African American Sports Hall of Fame, historian, 1992-94; AAA Housing & Transportation Trust, bd member, 1985-. **Honors/Awds:** Dept of the Army, Suggestion Award, 1957, 1960; Michigan Legislative, Senate Res #233, 1968; House Res #81, 1987; Wayne County, MI, Resolution, 1988; Mich Legislative, Senate #459, 1990. **Special Achievements:** Negroes in Michigan History, 1968, 3rd reprint, 1985; Black Nobel Prize Winners, poster, 1985; International Black Nobel Prize Winners, poster, 1994; African-American Historical Tins; Cake Walk, Come Join Us Bro, Henry O Flipper, 1993-94. **Military Serv:** US Army, spec-4, 1956-58, adjutant general section. **Business Addr:** Executive Director, Historical Research Repository Inc, PO Box 15364, Fox Creek Station, Detroit, MI 48215-0364, (313)822-9027.

GREEN, JOSEPH, JR.
Electrical/logistics engineer. **Personal:** Born Jun 14, 1950, Oakley, SC; son of Anna Bell Evans Johnson and Joseph Green; married Betty A, May 5, 1979; children: Quentin E, Erica R. **Educ:** South Carolina State Coll, BSEE 1973. **Career:** GE/RCA Corp, logistics engr and management coordinator and Logistics Program Plannning for the AEGIS ORDALT Program. **Orgs:** Affiliations w/Philadelphia Regional Introd of Minorities to Engrg 1986-87, Black Exec Exchange Prog 1986-87; mem Soc of Logistics Engrs; mem The Soc of Black and Hispanic Engrs. **Honors/Awds:** Letter of Achievement Recogniton from RAdm Wayne Myers for Successful DDG-51 Logistics Audit 1982; Dale Carnegie Honors 1985; AEGIS Tech Awd for producing several logistics support analysis plans as a mgmt tool for the surface Navy & other representative utilization; development of an intergrated logistics ORDALT Plan for AEGIS ILS Disciplines; member IEEE or International Electrical/Electronics Engineers Society 1990-. **Business Addr:** Logistics Engineer, GE/RCA Corp, Marne Hwy, Moorestown, NJ 08057.

GREEN, LARRY W.
City commissioner. **Personal:** Born Nov 7, 1946, Louisville, KY; son of Alma Vaughn Green and William R Green; married Delmira M Hinestroza Labalsa; children: Larry Jr, Carmen, Diana. **Educ:** Chicago Acad of Fine Art, 1964-66; Univ of KY E'Town Comm, 1971-72. **Career:** Metropolitan Life, rep 1973-82; City of Elizabeth KY, city cnclmn 1974-82; L&D Home Prod Dstrbtrs, pres 1974-84; Rize Unlimited Inc, regional coord; NewHorizons Fin Svc, analyst owner; Elizabethtown Visitors Commission, commissioner, currently. **Orgs:** Legal chrmn Cntrl KY Life Underwriters 1975-80; liason KY Cmrc Cabinet 1972-; oprtng bd Wesley Hilltop Comm Cnt 1972-75; mem Intrntl Platform Assc 1983-; KY State Manpower Comm Reg Crime Comm 1974-78; pres Hardin Cnty Youth Athletic Assc 1974-; regional comm on economic development 1985-; commissioner, Elizabethtown Visitors Commission, 1990-; board member, Helping Hand, 1987-; member, Cabinet 21, 1990-. **Honors/Awds:** Serv Above Self Rotary Clb of Elizabethtown 1981; ''Leadership Elizabethtown'' Chmbr Of Cmrc City 1985. **Military Serv:** USAF stf sgt; Vietnam Era Overseas. **Home Addr:** 119 Pear Orchard Rd, Elizabethtown, KY 42701.

GREEN, LESTER L.
Electrical engineer, business executive. **Personal:** Born Jun 27, 1941, Lynchburg, VA; married Lucille Withers. **Educ:** Howard Univ Sch Archit & Engr Wash DC 1966; BSEE 1966. **Career:** Elect Switching System Western Elect Co, proj engr 1966-; Comm Commun Res Inc, pres 1973-; Am Tel & Tel Co Silver Spring MD, transmsn man 1964-65. **Orgs:** Chmn Cablecommunication Task Force for Develop Reg Learning Cntr Morgan State Coll Baltimore 1973-74; chmn bd dir Comm Commun Sys Inc Baltimore 1970-; indstl mem rep for WE Co Howard Univ Cluster; mem Soc Cable TV Engr; Inst Electrcl & Electrnc Engrs; Alpha Phi Alpha Frat; mem Urban Reg Learning Cntr Policy Bd; exec bd NW Baltimore Corp; charter mem Pk Heights Comm Corp Inc Baltimore; charter mem & vice pres Beacon Hill Tenants Assn Baltimore; charter mem Oxford Manor Tenants Assn Wash DC. **Honors/Awds:** Cost reductn awd WE Co 1974; citznshp & ldrshp awd Howard Univ 1961; author ''The Design and Economics of an Urban Cable & Distrbtn Sys'' 1973. **Home Addr:** 737 Stoney Spring Dr, Baltimore, MD 21210.

GREEN, LILLER
Educational administrator. **Personal:** Born Dec 1, 1928, Atlanta, GA; daughter of Henrietta Parrott and Walter Parrott; married William Clarence Green; children: Pamela A, Jan A. **Educ:** Morgan State Univ, BA (Magna Cum Laude) 1951; Bryn Mawr Coll, MSW 1953. **Career:** Children's Adolescents, Psychiatric Clinic, dir of social work 1957-59; Child Study Center, dir of social work 1959-60; Bryn Mawr Coll, field instr consultant 1963-65; Ivy Leaf School, dir 1965-. **Orgs:** Mem Grace Baptist Church 1952-; golden life mem Delta Sigma Theta 1949-; life mem NAACP 1960-; mem bd dir YWCA 1983-85; mem Elementary Educ Study Group 1985-86. **Honors/Awds:** Eliza Jane Cummings Awd Morgan State Univ 1951; Richard Allen Awd Community Serv Mother Bethel AME 1982; Zeta Outstanding Woman of the Year Beta Delta Zeta 1983; Citizen of the Year Omega Psi Phi 1985; NAACP, Community Service Award, 1990; Minority Enterprise Special Achievement Award, 1991; Morgan State Univ, Outstanding Alumna Award, 1991; Delta Sigma Theta, Sadie T Alexander Community Service Award, 1991; Black Alumnae Coordinating Comm of the Graduate School of Social Work & Social Research, Bryn Mawr Coll Comm Service Award, 1992; Philadelphia Chapter of Natl MBA Assn, Educ of the Year Award, 1992; Natl Kwanzaa Award, Philadelphia area, Kujichagulia, 1994; Phila Council of Clergy, Excellence in Educ Award, Presented at MLK Memorial Service, 1995. **Business Addr:** Dir, Ivy Leaf School, 1196 E Washington Ln, Philadelphia, PA 19138.

GREEN, LISA A.
Law enforcement official. **Personal:** Born in Charleston, SC; daughter of Edward Green Jr & Mary LM Green (deceased). **Educ:** Claflin Univ, BA, 1986. **Career:** Charleston Cty Sheriff's Office, training coordinator sgt, 1997-. **Orgs:** PSLEOA; SCLEOA. **Honors/Awds:** Civitan Intl, Albert T Leppert Memorial Award, 1997. **Special Achievements:** First African American Female Sergeant in Charleston Cty Sheriff's Office, 1996. **Business Addr:** Sergeant - Training Division Supervisor/Coordinator, Charleston County Sheriff's Office, 3505 Pinehaven Dr, Charleston, SC 29405, (803)554-4700.

GREEN, LISA R.
Journalist. **Personal:** Born Nov 2, 1964, Evanston, IL; daughter of Rev Albert W (deceased) & Elease W Green. **Educ:** Eastern Illinois Univ, journalism, 1986. **Career:** Rockford Register Star, reporter, 1986-90, assistant city editor, 1990-91, city editor, 1991-93, assistant business editor, 1993-. **Orgs:** National Assn of Black Journalists, 1988-; Big Brother/Big Sister Program, big sister, 1992-97; YMCA-Booker Washington Center, Black Achievers Steering Committee, 1993-; New Zion Missionary Baptist Church, editor Zion Gazette, 1997; Salter Ensemble, mem. **Honors/Awds:** Black Achievers, Black Achiever of the Year, 1994. **Special Achievements:** Member of one of three training teams for a writing & editing program, Gannett Midwest Newspaper Group, 1994; Served as an editor/mentor for students, working on the daily newspaper produced at the Unity 94 Journalist Convention, Atlanta. **Business Addr:** Assistant Business Editor, Rockford Register Star, 99 E State St, Newsroom, Rockford, IL 61104, (815)987-1379.

GREEN, LITTERIAL
Professional basketball player. **Personal:** Born Mar 7, 1970. **Educ:** Georgia. **Career:** Detroit Pistons, currently. **Business Addr:** Professional Basketball Player, Detroit Pistons, 2 Championship Dr, Auburn Hills, MI 48326, (810)377-0100.

GREEN, OLIVER WINSLOW
Labor union officer. **Personal:** Born Aug 18, 1930, Baltimore, MD; son of Ethel I Gray Green and William S Green; married Loraine E Johnson, Sep 7, 1951; children: Oliver W Jr, Michael G. **Educ:** Attended Morgan State Univ, Baltimore MD. **Career:** Baltimore Tansit Co, Baltimore MD, operator, 1953-69; Mass Transit Admin, Baltimore MD, operator, 1969-70; Amalgamated Transit Union, Baltimore MD, financial sec, 1970-75, Washington DC, vice pres, 1975-. **Orgs:** Bd mem, United Way of Central Maryland, 1972-75, President's Comm on Employment, 1985-; mem operating comm, A Philip Randolph Inst, 1985-; pres, 43/44 Democratic Club, 1986-. **Military Serv:** US Army, staff sergeant, 1951-53.

GREEN, PHA M.
Entrepreneur. **Personal:** Born Feb 10, 1939, Monroe, LA; son of Marteal Green and Willie Green; married Joan Turner, Dec 21, 1990. **Educ:** Prairie View A & M Univ, industrial arts, 1958. **Career:** Pha Green Printing Inc, pres, currently. **Business Addr:** Pres, Pha Green Printing, Inc, 4403 Akard, Houston, TX 77047, (713)734-1251.

GREEN, RAYMOND A.
Government official. **Personal:** Born Aug 18, 1944, Gary, IN; married Lucille McConnell; children: Caleb, Adam. **Educ:** BA, Indus Engineering. **Career:** State of IN, asst state senator 1972-76; Lake Cty Council, asst councilman 1978-85; Lake County Commn, Commn Engr, 1980-85; Govt Center, chief deputy, Lake County recorder 1985-. **Business Addr:** Chief Deputy Lake County Recorder, Govt Center, 2293 N Main St, Crown Point, IN 46307.

GREEN, REUBEN H.
Cleric, educator. **Personal:** Born Jun 14, 1934, Wright City, OK; son of Idella Clark Green (deceased) and Mack Crawford Green; married Mildred Denby; children: Reuben H, Howard D. **Educ:** Bishop Coll, BA 1955; Oberlin Grad Sch of Theo, BD 1959; Iliff Sch of Theo, STM 1969; Vanderbilt Univ Div Sch, DMin 1973. **Career:** Cntrl Bapt Ch Inc, minstr 1968-; Philosy Lemoyne-Owen Coll, asso prof 1968-; Lemoyne-Owen Coll, chapln 1974-; Bells Chapl Bapt Ch, pstr 1964-68;OT OK Sch of Relgn, dean of students instr. **Orgs:** Mem Omega Psi Frat; Knights of Pythians; Prince Hall A F&M; past vice pres Memphis Br NAACP; dean Memphis SS & BTU Congress; mem TN Ldrshp Educ Cong; dean TN Bapt Sch of Rel. **Business Addr:** Dept of Humanities, Lemoyne-Owen College, 807 Walker Ave, Memphis, TN 38126.

GREEN, RICHARD CARTER
Family therapist. **Personal:** Born Oct 28, 1947, Brooklyn, NY; married Florence Elayne Parson; children: Damani Saeed Tale, Taiesha Tene Tale, Khalid Abdu Tale. **Educ:** Central State Univ, BA 1969; Wright State Univ, MS 1983. **Career:** Montgomery County Juvenile Court, probation officer 1969-70; US Army 1st Lt Infantry, instructor of offensive tactics 1970-72; Montgomery Co Juvenile Court, probation counselor 1972-73; Tale Retail and Wholesale Co, owner 1985-; Nicholas Residential Treatment Ctr, family resource counselor 1973-. **Orgs:** Mem Omega Psi Phi Frat Inc 1966-; mem Greater Dayton Jaycees 1972; mem Nguzo Saba Family Educ and Unity Club 1980-; master mason Prince Hall Free MasonryAncient Square Lodge #40 1982-; lecturer Child Discipline and Residential Treatment 1984-; fellow Menninger Foundation 1985. **Honors/Awds:** Certificate of Participation in Seminary on Adolescence Menninger Foundatin 1978; Outstanding Young Men of Amer US Jaycees 1980; Computers Today/Computer Literacy Sinclair Comm Coll/Computer Tech 1983; Gerontological Counseling Wright State Univ 1985; Licensed Professional Counselor OH Counselor and Social Worker Bd 1985. **Military Serv:** AUS Infantry 1st lt 1970-71; Natl Defense Serv Medal 1970, Master Tactician US Army Infantry School 1971. **Home Addr:** 811 Neal Ave, Dayton, OH 45406.

GREEN, RICKEY
Professional basketball player. **Personal:** Born Aug 18, 1954, Chicago, IL. **Educ:** Vincennes Univ, Vincennes, IN, 1973-75; Univ of Michigan, Ann Arbor, MI, 1975-77. **Career:** Golden State Warriors, 1977-78; Detroit Pistons, 1978-79; Hawaii, 1979-80; Billings Volcanos, 1980-81; Utah Jazz, 1980-88; Charlotte Hornets, 1988-89; Milwaukee Bucks, 1988-89; Indiana Pacers, 1989-90; Philadelphia 76ers, 1990-. **Honors/Awds:** Led NBA in steals, 1984. **Business Addr:** Professional Basketball Player, Philadelphia 76ers, Broad St & Pattison Ave, Spectrum, Philadelphia, PA 19148-5288.

GREEN, ROBERT DAVID
Professional football player. **Personal:** Born Sep 10, 1970, Washington, DC. **Educ:** William & Mary. **Career:** Washington Redskins, running back, 1992; Chicago Bears, 1993-96; Minnesota Vikings, 1997-. **Business Addr:** Professional Football Player, Minnesota Vikings, 9520 Vikings Dr, Eden Prairie, MN 55344, (612)828-6500.

GREEN, ROBERT L.
Association executive. **Personal:** Born Nov 23, 1933, Detroit, MI; married. **Educ:** San Francisco State Coll, BA 1958; San Francisco State Coll, MA 1960; MI State U, PhD 1963. **Career:** USOE Grant Chicago Adult Educ Project, Southern Christian Leadership Conf, dir 1967; Southern Christian Leadership Conf, educ dir 1965-66; Cen for Urban Affairs, dir; MI State Univ, prof 1968-73; Coll Urban Devel, dean; MI State Univ, beginning 1973; Univ of Dist of Columbia, former pres; NCJW Center for Research in Educ Disadvantages Hebrew Univ Jerusalem, visiting lecturer 1971; Univ Nairobi Kenya, 1971; Cuyahoga Community College, dir, Center for Urban Education, currently. **Orgs:** Mem Am Psychology Assn; Am Assn Black Psychologists; Am Research Assn; bd dirs Martin Luther King Jr Center for Nonviolent Social Change. **Military Serv:** AUS 1954-56. **Business Addr:** Madison County Urban League, PO Box 8093, Alton, IL 62002.

GREEN, ROLAND, SR.
Transportation executive. **Personal:** Born Aug 26, 1940, Washington, DC; son of Mary Sophie Welch Green and Robert Green Sr; married Elverna Coleman, Dec 31, 1966; children: Rolanda Michelle, Robin Yvette, Roland Green Jr. **Educ:** Univ of Maryland, College Park MD, 1963-64; Bowie State Univ, Bowie Maryland; Univ of Dist of Columbia, Washington DC. **Career:** DC Gen Hospital, Washington DC, physical therapy asst, 1964-66; DC Transit Inc, Washington DC, bus operator, 1966-71; United Planning Org, Washington DC, transportation coord, 1971-77, branch chief,1977-81; Washington Elderly Handicapped Transportation Serv, United Planning Org, Washington DC, gen mgr, 1982-. **Orgs:** Mem, Washington DC Devel Disabilities Council, 1979-81; pres, Owens Rd Elementary School PTA, 1984-86; mem, Conf Minority Transportation Officials, 1984-89; vice pres, Capital Area Community Food Bank, 1985-87; mem, Natl Forum Black Public Admin, 1987-89; mem, Natl Council on Aging, 1989-, Amer Public Transit Assn, 1989-. **Honors/Awds:** Meritorious Serv, Kiwanis Club, Eastern Branch, 1977; Vietnam Vets Award, Natl Black Veterans, 1978; Master Mason of the Year, Prince Hall of Masons, Washington DC, 1979; Appreciation, Washington DC Urban League, 1986. **Military Serv:** US Army Medical Corp, specialist 4, 1958-64, Good Conduct Medals, Overseas Serv.

GREEN, ROY
Professional football player. **Personal:** Born Jun 30, 1957, Magnolia, AR. **Educ:** Henderson State Univ, attended. **Career:** St Louis Cardinals (Phoenix Cardinals after 1988), wide receiver, 1979-. **Honors/Awds:** Tied NFL record for longest kickoff return game (106 yards) against Dallas Cowboys, 1979; named to The Sporting News NFC All-Star Team, 1979; 1983, 1984; played in Pro Bowl, 1983, 1984.

GREEN, RUTH A.
Clinic administrator. **Personal:** Born Feb 2, 1917, Oklahoma; widowed. **Educ:** BS 1936. **Career:** Social worker; probation officer; Step Parent Adoption; Social Service, dir; Sr Citizens Preventive Health Care Serv for Elderly Minority, clinic administrator. **Orgs:** All professional jobs San Diego Pres Comm Hosp of San Diego Aux 1973-74; past reg pres of CA Probtn & Parole Assn; past couns to Youth in Free Clinics as Vol; apptd bd dir by Pres Nixon to Small Bus Bur San Diego; apptd by Bd of Supvs to Charter Review Com; past pres NAACP; 2nd vice pres Urban League; past grand sec of Charity; Order of Eastern Star; orgn San Diego Chap The Links Inc; found Civic Orgn Women Inc; apptd by Mayor of San Diego to Housing Adv Bd; The Gvrn of CA To intergvrnmntl Relations Counc & to the CA State Commn On Aging 1974-75. **Honors/Awds:** Serv awds YMCA, NAACP, Bus & Professional Womens Clubs; Probation Offcr of Yr Awd 1971. **Business Addr:** 446 26 St, San Diego, CA 92102.

GREEN, SAUL A.
Government official. **Personal:** Born 1947; married; children: one. **Educ:** Univ of Michigan, undergraduate degree, U of MI Law School, JD. **Career:** US Attorney's Office, asst, 1973-76; Wayne County, corporate counsel, beginning 1989; Attorney's Office, Eastern District of MI, US attorney, 1994-. **Special Achievements:** Nominated by President Clinton, first African American to hold post of US Attorney in Detroit; top federal prosecutor in the Eastern district of Michigan. **Business Phone:** (313)226-7060.

GREEN, SEAN CURTIS
Professional basketball player. **Personal:** Born Feb 2, 1970, Santa Monica, CA. **Educ:** North Carolina State; Iona. **Career:** Indiana Pacers, guard, 1991-. **Business Addr:** Professional Basketball Player, Indiana Pacers, 300 E Market St, Indianapolis, IN 46204, (317)377-0100.

GREEN, SIDNEY
Professional basketball player. **Personal:** Born Jan 4, 1961, New York, NY; married Dee Dee; children: LaShawn. **Educ:** Univ of NV Las Vegas, 1979-83. **Career:** Forward: Chicago Bulls, 1983-86, Detroit Pistons, 1986-87, New York Knicks, 1987-89, Orlando Magic, 1989-90, San Antonio Spurs, 1990-92, Charlotte Hornets, 1992-. **Honors/Awds:** Ended UNLV career as most honored player; selected first team All-Am by US Basketball Writers Assn; was 2nd team selection by the Sporting News Bsktbl Times after leading team to 28-3 season. **Business Phone:** (704)357-0252.

GREEN, STERLING
Associate executive, clergyman. **Personal:** Born Oct 8, 1946, Washington, DC; married Sophie Ann Pinkney; children: Sterlicia Sophia, Tamika Tamara. **Educ:** Williams Coll MA, 1964-67; USASATC&S Ft Devens MA, 1967. **Career:** United House of Prayer, ordained as elder 1967, asst minister 1971; DC Govt Adv Neighborhood Comm, vice chmn, commr, 1978-85; United House of Prayer, ordained as apostle 1984, dir of special proj for Bishop W McCollough, 1991-. **Orgs:** Elected adv neighborhood Commiss 1978; bd mem SHAW Proj Area Comm 1979; delegate DC Fed of Civic Assn 1979; mem Mayors Commiss on Coop Econ Devel 1980; natl comm mem McCollough Property Invest Comm 1980; asst to ex dir McCollough Scholarship Coll Fund 1984. **Honors/Awds:** Harvard Book Awd Washington DC 1964; Participant White House Briefing on the Cities 1980; Washington Post Article "Remap or Outmap" Census Mapping 1981. **Military Serv:** AUS 1967-69; Vietnam Campaign, Outstanding Trainee. **Home Addr:** 606 Emmanuel Court NW #302, Washington, DC 20001. **Business Addr:** Dir Special Projects, United House of Prayer, 1117 Seventh St NW, Washington, DC 20001.

GREEN, THEODIS GUY
City official, educator, poet, novelist. **Personal:** Born Nov 6, 1930, Wright City, OK; son of Della Green and Mack Green; married Mary Lois Burris; children: Theodis Jr. **Educ:** Langston Univ, BS; OK State Univ, MS. **Career:** City of Langston, mayor, currently; Langston Univ, prof & asst chmn 1977-87. **Orgs:** Life mem Alpha Phi Alpha Frat; mem Prince Hall Masons; pres NAACP; mem OEA, LEDC, NEA; past mem OK Tech Soc; mem bd of trustees Mt Bethel Bapt. **Honors/Awds:** Teacher of the Week, Langston Univ, 1980; Mayor of the Year, OK Conf of Black Mayors; Awarded plaque as a Bronze Ambassador at OSU; Honorary Dr Degree, TN Univ School of Religion; Published poems/novel. **Business Addr:** Professor, Asst Chairman, Langston Univ, Langston, OK 73050.

GREEN, THOMAS L., SR.
State government official. **Personal:** Born Sep 9, 1940, Bronxville, NY; son of Grace Green and Louis T Green; married Patricia S Green, Oct 13, 1963; children: Thomas II, Jennifer. **Educ:** State Univ, Winston-Salem, NC, BS, 1963; AFL-CIO Labor Studies Center, Silver Spring, MD, post grad work, 1971-72; Univ of Utah, post grad work, 1975-76. **Career:** Manufacturer Traders Trust Co, asst mgr 1966-69; Recruitment Training Program, field rep 1969-71; Westchester Affirmative Action Agency, White Plains, NY, exec dir 1970-90; NYS Dept Labor, job training spec 1973-83, assoc employment consultant, 1983-90, deputy director, 1990-. **Orgs:** Relocation dir Urban Renewal Agency 1962-64; resource consult US Dept of HEW 1964-69; proj dir Pres Comm Juvenile Delinquent & Youth Devel 1964-70; prog dir Urban Ed Ctr 1965-68; consult Southern IL Univ 1966-67; cons/proj dir Central State Univ 1967-68; prog dir Urban League of Westchester 1969-70; executive board member, National Assn of Public Sector Equal Opportunity Officers, 1987-; member, International Assn of Personnel in Employment Security, 1983-. **Honors/Awds:** Author 2 years study Juvenile Delinquent & Youth Devel 1965-66; 32 degree United Supreme Council 33 AASR of Free Masonry USA; Community Serv Awd Westchester/Rockland Boy Scouts of Amer. **Business Addr:** Deputy Director, Division of Affirmative Action Programs, New York State Department of Labor, One Main Street, Rm 1109, Brooklyn, NY 11201.

GREEN, VERNA S.
Broadcasting company executive. **Personal:** Born Oct 9, 1947, Columbus, GA; daughter of Evelyn Robinson Crouch and Oscar L Crouch; children: Grant Langston, Jason Wayne. **Educ:** Wayne State Univ, Detroit MI, BS Business Admin, 1973; Michigan State Univ, E Lansing MI, MBA, 1976. **Career:** General Motors Corp, Detroit MI, org devel specialist, 1970-76; Visiting Nurse Assn, Detroit, MI, personnel dir, 1977-78; Detroit Medical Center, Detroit MI, assoc dir public affairs, dir support serv, mgr training & devel, 1979-81; Booth American Co, WJLB-FM, WMXD-FM, Detroit, vice pres, gen mgr, pres, 1982-. **Orgs:** Mem, NAACP, 1982-, Urban League, 1982-; alumni bd, Wayne State Univ Business School; research comm, Natl Assn of Broadcasters; Leadership Detroit, Graduate of Class #7, 1986; bd mem, YWCA of Metro Detroit, 1986-87, Women's Advertising Club, 1986-87, Michigan Assn of Broadcasters, 1987-; advisory bd, Wayne State Univ Journalism Institute for Minorities, 1987-; bd mem, Detroit United Fund, 1987; mem, Michigan Women's Forum, 1987-; bd mem, Children's Aid Soc, 1989; board member, YMCA of Metro Detroit, 1990; Detroit Sports Commission, 1992-; Detroit Economic Growth Corporation, bd, 1994-; Natl Assn of Broadcasters, bd member, 1995-. **Honors/Awds:** General Manager of the Year, Black Radio Exclusive, 1986; Most Outstanding Woman in Radio Management, Detroit Chapter of Amer Women in Radio & Television, 1986; Woman of the 80's Award, J C Penney Co, 1987; Distinguished Alumnus Award, Wayne State Univ Business School, 1988; General Manager of the Year, Young Black Programmer's Coalition, 1988; Corporate Leadership Award, Wayne State Univ, 1989; General Urban Network, Manager of the Year, 1992. **Business Addr:** President/General Manager, WJLB-FM & WMXD-FM, Secret Communications Company, 645 Griswold, 633 Penobscot Building, Detroit, MI 48226.

GREEN, VICTOR BERNARD
Professional football player. **Personal:** Born Dec 8, 1969, Americus, GA. **Educ:** Akron, bachelor's degree in criminal justice, 1993. **Career:** New York Jets, defensive back, 1993-. **Business Addr:** Professional Football Player, New York Jets, 1000 Fulton Ave, Hempstead, NY 11550, (516)560-8100.

GREEN, WALTER
Business executive. **Personal:** Born Sep 5, 1924, Coconut Grove, FL. **Educ:** Miami-Dade Coll Sch of Continuing Educ 1971-72. **Career:** Walt's Laundromat, owner 1972-80; real estate investr 1947-80. **Orgs:** Pres fdr Black Grove Inc; New Frontiers in Envirnmtl Understndg; Human Comm & Social Justice 1970-80; co-author Black Grove a plng model for am Miami Interactn 1973; pres Grove Golfers Assn 1960-70; mem Proj Area Com HUD 1967-70; dir Black Grove Com Design Ctr 1970-76; exec com Intl Optimist Club of Coconut Grove 1972-76; mem Coconut Grove Plng Task Force 1974-76; mem Comm of Man Proj Com 1976. **Honors/Awds:** Conf partic in 1st Nat Seminar on Environmtl Quality & Social Justice in Urban Am The Consrvtn Found 1972; Voice of Am Intervw for W African Nats 1976. **Military Serv:** Pfc WW II 1943-46. **Business Addr:** 3565 Grand Ave, Miami, FL 33133.

GREEN, WILLIAM EDWARD
Educator (retired). **Personal:** Born May 17, 1930, Pittsburgh, PA; son of Willa Lawson Stewart (deceased) and J Edward Green (deceased); married Betty Jayne Garrison, Nov 9, 1950; children: William Jr, Bobbi Brookins, Nancy Hill, Kenneth. **Educ:** Univ of Pgh, BS 1953, MEd 1958, EdD 1969. **Career:** Herron Hill Jr HS, teacher 1955-60; Westinghouse HS, couns 1960-65, vice prin 1965-68, exec asst to supt 1968-69, asst supt 1969-75; Pittsburgh Public Sch, asst supt middle schs 1976-81, asst supt pupil serv 1981-85 retired; W PA Conf United Methodist Church, dir of ethnic minority concerns 1985-93; (retired) Pittsburgh Pist Lay Leader, UM Church, 1990-96. **Orgs:** Prince Hall Mason (Boaz 65) 1959-; Phi Eta Sigma 1949-53; dissertation Sch Coll Orientation Prog 1969; bd dir Need 1969-87; Univ of Pgh Alumni Council 1974-77 1979-; chmn PACE 1974-80; PA State Adv Council on Voc Educ 1974-78; State ESEA Title IV Adv Council 1975-78; mem Alpha Phi Alpha; exec dir Pgh Upward Bound Prog; Omicron Delta Kappa; Phi Delta Kappa; lecturer Carnegie Mellon Univ; treas Warren United Methodist Church 1980-94; chmn Ethnic Minority Local Church Coord Comm Western PA Conf United Methodist Church 1980-84; delegate 1984, 1988, and 1994; United Methodist General/ Jurisdictional Conf; 1988; bd of dirs Need, 1969-90; Pace Board, 1984-90. **Military Serv:** USAF capt 1953-55.

GREEN, WILLIAM ERNEST
Attorney. **Personal:** Born Nov 19, 1936, Philadelphia; married Loretta Martin; children: Billy, Roderic, Nicole. **Educ:** Univ of Pittsburgh, BS 1957; Duquesne Univ Sch of Law, LlB 1963. **Career:** Palo Alto CA, atty pvt prac; CA, NY & US Patent Off, admtd; Palo Alto Area Chptr Am Red Cross, dir. **Orgs:** Mem Palo Alto City Plann Commn; mem Charles Houston Bar Assn; Palo Alto Area Bar Assn; San Mateo Co Bar Assn; Bar Peninsula Patent Law Assn; SF Patent Law Assn; Am Bar Assn; asst gen couns Boise Cascade Corp 1971-73; atty Sybron Corp 1963-71; chemist US Steel Corp; Applied Rsrch Lab PA 1957; past chmn Rochester City Plann Commn five yrs; chmn bd trustees World of Inquiry Sch; rep Co & Regnl Plann Councls; bd dir Rochester Savngs Bank;Comm Chest; Rochester Urban League; Rochester Hlth Serv Corp; Ind Training Sch; Rochester Monroe Co Chap Am Red Cross; Planned Parenthood League of Rochester & Monroe Co; PTA Bd of Sch #1; mng edt Law Review Duquesne Univ Sch of Law. **Honors/Awds:** Rec Folette Greeno Pub Awd 1966; NY State Jaycees Distngshd Serv Awd 1967; cand for NY State Assm 1968. **Business Addr:** William Green & Associates, 550 Hamilton Ave, Palo Alto, CA 94301.

GREEN, WILLIE AARON
Professional football player. **Personal:** Born Apr 22, 1966, Athens, GA. **Educ:** Univ of Mississippi. **Career:** Detroit Lions, wide receiver, 1991-93; Tampa Bay Buccaneers, 1994; Carolina Panthers, 1995-96; Denver Broncos, 1997-. **Business Addr:** Professional Football Player, Denver Broncos, 13655 Broncos Pkwy, Englewood, CO 80112, (303)649-9000.

GREEN, YATIL
Professional football player. **Personal:** Born Nov 25, 1973. **Educ:** Miami. **Career:** Miami Dolphins, 1997-. **Special Achievements:** NFL Draft, First round pick, #15, 1997. **Business Addr:** Professional Football Player, Miami Dolphins, 2269 NW 199th St, Miami, FL 33056, (305)620-5000.

GREENBERG, REUBEN M.
Police chief. **Personal:** Born Jun 24, 1943, Houston. **Educ:** San Francisco State U, BA 1967; Univ CA, MPA 1969; Univ CA, MCP 1975; PhD study. **Career:** City & Co San Francisco, undersheriff 1971-73; first black undersheriff CA hist; CA State Univ Hayward, asst prof sociology 1969-73; City Berkeley, human rel offr 1967-69; Univ NC Chapel Hill, asst prof polit sci; City of Charleston, SC, chief of police, currently. **Orgs:** National Association of Black Law Enforcement Exec; Intl Assn of Chiefs of Police; bd mem, SC Commission on Racial Relations; bd mem, SC Crime Victims Compensation Bd; bd mem, SC Sentencing Commission. **Honors/Awds:** Achievement Award, Foundation for Improvement of Justice, 1989; Justice Professional of the Year, Southern Criminal Justice Association, 1991; Free Spirit Award, Freedom Forum, 1994. **Business Addr:** Chief of Police, Charleston Police Dept, 180 Lockwood Blvd, Charleston, SC 29403.

GREEN-CAMPBELL, DEARDRA DELORES
Financial advisor. **Personal:** Born Jan 21, 1959, Gary, IN; daughter of Harriet L Green and Herman W Green; married Thoman L Campbell, May 24, 1980; children: Evan T. **Educ:** Western Michigan University, attended, 1977; Purdue University, attended, 1978. **Career:** The Stuart James Co., stock broker, 1983-84; Charles Schwab & Co., vice pres, 1984-91; Campbell Planning Associates, president, 1991-. **Orgs:** 100 Black Women, 1991-; Alanta Business League, 1991-; National Association of Female Executives, 1991-. **Honors/Awds:** Charles Schwab & Co., Chairman's Club, 1989, 1990. **Special Achievements:** Columnist, Financial Management Column, The Alanta Tribune, 1991-. **Business Addr:** President, Campbell Planning Associates Inc, 103 Adrian Place NW, Atlanta, GA 30327, (404)355-4040.

GREENE, AURELIA
State representative. **Personal:** Born Oct 26, 1934, New York, NY; daughter of Sybil Russell Holley and Edward Henry; married Jerome Alexander Greene; children: Rhonda, Russell. **Educ:** Livingston at Rutgers, BA 1975. **Career:** Bronx Area Policy Bd #6, exec dir 1980-82; New York State, Assemblywoman, chair of banking standing committee, currently. **Orgs:** District leader 76th Assembly District Bronx 1979-82; mem Comm Sch Bd #9 1985; exec officer Bronx Unity Democratic Club 1986; education advisor Morrisania Educ Cncl 1986; mem NAACP, Urban League. **Honors/Awds:** Woman of the Year

NAACP; Brotherhood Awd NY State Employees; Organizational Impact Awd Alpha Kappa Alpha. **Business Addr:** Assemblywoman, New York State, 1188 Grand Concourse #D, Bronx, NY 10456.

GREENE, AVA DANELLE
Attorney. **Personal:** Born May 13, 1962, Raleigh, NC; daughter of Ruby Powell Greene and George R Greene Sr. **Educ:** Univ of North Carolina-Chapel Hill, BS, Psychology & Criminal Justice, 1984; Howard Univ School of Law, Washington, DC, JD, 1987. **Career:** US Dept of Transportation, Washington, DC, legal intern, 1985; MAXIMA Corp, Rockville, MD, legal intern, 1986-88; District of Columbia Court of Appeals, Washington, DC, judicial law clerk, 1988-89; MAXIMA Corp, Rockville, MD, sr attorney/div legal mgr, 1989-90; Reed Smith Shaw & McClay, Pittsburgh, PA, attorney, 1991-. **Orgs:** Natl chairperson, Natl Bar Assn, 1989-91; board of governors, Natl Bar Assn, 1991-; exec council, American Bar Assn; bd of dir, Washington Bar Assn, 1990-; bd of dir, Vistas at Lake Arbor, 1990-; student mentor, MENTORS, Inc, 1989-. **Honors/Awds:** 100 Most Promising Black Women in Corporate America, Ebony Magazine, 1991; Howard Law Journal, Howard Univ School of Law, 1985-87; American Jurisprudence Award, Howard Univ School of Law, 1986.

GREENE, BEVERLY A.
Clinical psychologist, educator. **Personal:** Born Aug 14, 1950, New Jersey; daughter of Thelma and Samuel. **Educ:** New York University, BA, 1973; Adelphi University, Derner Institute of Advanced Psychology, MA, clinical psychology, 1977, PhD, clinical psychology, 1983. **Career:** New York City Board of Education, school psychologist, 1980-82; Kings County Hospital, Impatient Child and Adolescent Psychology Services, director, 1982-89; University of Medicine and Dentistry of NJ at Newark, supervising psychologist, clinical assistant professor of psychiatry, 1989-91; St John's University, associate clinical professor of psychology, 1991-93, associate professor, 1993-95, professor, 1995-. **Orgs:** American Psychological Assn, fellow, Task Force on Mental Health of Ethnic Minority Women, 1992-, Women of Color Task Force, 1992-, Task Force on Diversity in Clinical Psychology, 1991-92; Continuing Education, co-chair, 1991-93; National Assn of Black Psychologists; American Orthopsychiatric Assn, fellow; Association for Women in Psychology; New York State Psychological Assn, 1984-85; New York Coalition for Hospital & Institutional Psychologists, 1982-91; New York Association of Black Psychologists, 1980-; International Neuropsychological Society, 1979-87. **Honors/Awds:** New York University, Martin Luther King Jr Scholar, 1968-72; Women of Color Psychologies Publication Award, 1991; Distinguished Professional Contributions to Ethnic Minority Issues Award, 1992; Distinguished Humanitarian Award, American Association of Applied & Preventive Psychology, 1994; Awarded Tenure, St John's University, 1995; Psychotherapy with Women Research Award, 1995, 1996; Distinguished Publication Award, 1995; Women of Color Psychologies Publication Award, Association for Women in Psychology, 1995; Outstanding Achievement Awd, Comm on Lesbian, Gay and Bisexual Issues, American Psychological Assn, 1996. **Special Achievements:** Author, works include: ''Psychotherapy with African-American Women: Integrating Feminist and Psychodynamic Models,'' Journal of Training and Practice in Professional Psychology, 1993; ''Human Diversity in Clinical Psychology: Lesbian and Gay Sexual Orientations,'' The Clinical Psychologist: Journal of the Division of Clinical Psychology, 1993; ''Racism and Antisemitism: An African-American Feminist Perspective,'' Catalogue of the Black International Cinema-Berlin, 1992; co-editor: Div 44 American Psychological Assn annual publication series; Psychological Perspectives on Lesbian and Gay Issues, vols, 1-5; ''Women of Color: Integrating Ethnic and Gender Identities in Psychotherapy''; Guilford Press, co-editor, 1994; ''Abnormal Psychology In a Changing World,'' Prentice Hall, co-author, 1994. **Business Addr:** Professor of Psychology, Department of Psychology, St John's University, Marillac Hall, Jamaica, NY 11439, (718)990-1538.

GREENE, CHARLES ANDRE
Business executive. **Personal:** Born May 17, 1939, Blocton, AL; divorced. **Educ:** TX So Univ Sch Bus; Wayne State Univ Sch Mortuary Sci. **Career:** Greene Home for Funerals, v pres. **Orgs:** Mem Nat Funeral Dir & Mortcns Assn; bd dir Greater Flint Oppor Industrl Cntrs Inc; Vehicle City Lodge No 1036 IBPOE of W; bd mem Tall Pine Counc BSA; Epsilon Nu Delta Mortuary Frat; elected fin chmn 5th Ward Charter Revision Commn 1974; appntd asst exec sec Nat Funeral Dir & Mortcns Assn Inc 1974; mem Foss Ave Bapt Ch; found dir Foss Ave Fed Credit Union; mem Wayne State Univ Alumni Assn; TX So Univ Alumni Assn; Urban League Urban Coalition; Centl Optimist Club. **Honors/Awds:** Rec NAACP Achvmnt Awd 1913; v pres Genesee Co Funeral Dir Assn; chmn Educ Com Nat Funeral Dir & Mortcns Assn 1972-73; Youth Splst Nat Funeral Dir & Embalmer Mag; dist gov Dist 4 Nat Funeral Dirs & Mortcns Assn 1973-74; Foss Ave Ldrshp Awd as pres of Credit Union 1973-74; Big Bro & Distngshed Serv Awd 1973; awd mer Flint Fire Dept for saving life of citz 1974.

GREENE, CHARLES EDWARD. See GREENE, JOE.

GREENE, CHARLES EDWARD CLARENCE
Government official. **Personal:** Born Apr 1, 1921, Philadelphia, PA; son of Christine Greene and Raymond Greene; married Julia Castenedes; children: Ruth Gumbs, Martin, Rene, Vincent Cocom, Gamel Bowen. **Educ:** LaSalle Ext, LLB 1940; Univ Church of Brotherhood, DD 1955; TV Southwest Coll, Ref Courses. **Career:** Actor, producer, writer, director, 1937; Negro Cowboys Assn; Rodeo Champ, Natl Pres, 1945-49; Step Inc, Chmn of Bd, 1970-71; Black Political Assn, pres; Independent Prod Assoc, Pres, 1971-72; Casey Coll exec vp; Universal Brotherhood Churches, serge archbishop; Lbr & Indus Comm, NAACP, chmn; Trans-Oceanic Indus Inc, pres; Adelphi Business Coll, public relations consultant; Most Worshipful Prince Hall Grand Lodge F&AM CA & HI Inc, public relations consultant; State of California, senior legislator/ senior senator, currently. **Orgs:** Commr, Los Angeles County Obscenity & Pornography Comm 1980-; pres Sr Coalition Political Action Com 1983-; sr deacon James H Wilson Lodge 68 Pha 1985; very rev asst gr chaplin MW Prince Hall Grand Lodge of CA Inc 1984-; pres Inglewood Southbay Br NAACP 1979-, Independent Producer & Assc. **Honors/Awds:** Graduate inspector general 33rd Degree Supreme Council PHA 1985. **Military Serv:** AUS sgt. **Home Addr:** 2328 West 30th St, Los Angeles, CA 90018.

GREENE, CHARLES LAVANT
Educator. **Personal:** Born Feb 22, 1938, Headland, AL; married Delores Johnson; children: Charles L. **Educ:** Univ of Akron OH, BS Biology 1962; Univ of Pittsburgh PA, MSW 1967; Akron Law Sch OH, JD 1977. **Career:** Kent State Univ, asst prof & asst dean for stud life 1972-, asst prof soc & anthr 1970-, asst prof & coord vol & comm serv 1971-72; CAC Program, Syracuse NY, dep dir for admin 1968-70; E Akron Comm House, coord of comm devel 1967-68. **Orgs:** Vp urban affair Tomorrow's People Inc Consult Firm 1972-; bd mem Alpha Homes Inc Akron OH 1979-; bd sec Ebony Blackstar Broadcast Corp 1980; bd mem Urban League Akron OH 1977-; bd mem Fair Housing Contact Serv Akron OH 1977-; bd mem Mental Hlth Assn of Summit Co Akron OH 1977-80. **Honors/Awds:** Commend medal AUS; US Pub Hlth Scs Scholrshp Univ of Pittsburgh 1965-67; found Law Firm Davison Greene Holloway & Walker 1977; frat awd Kent State 1979. **Military Serv:** AUS capt 1962-65. **Business Addr:** Davidsn Greene Hollowy & Walke, Akron, OH 44308.

GREENE, CHARLES RODGERS
Physician, educator. **Personal:** Born Jul 8, 1926, Lawrence, NY; son of Ada Johnson and Rodgers Greene; married Arlene D Hopkins; children: Allyson Gail, Carla Gay, Wendy Leigh. **Educ:** Howard Univ Coll of Liberal Arts, 1950; Howard Univ Coll of Med, 1954. **Career:** Dept of Family Practice State Univ of NY Downstate Medical Center, assoc prof; Dept of Family Practice, assoc chmn; Coll of Medicine Downstate Medical Center, assoc dean; SUNY College of Medicine, dean of students 1979-. **Orgs:** Mem Comm Adv Bd Kings Co Hosp Ctr; Am Coll of Physicians; Metro Com for Minrty Grps in Med; Hlth Rsrch Counc of City of NY; Downstate Med Ctr Prgm Com. **Honors/Awds:** Diplmt Am Bd of Internal Med NY Acad of Med Allergic Reactns to Dipasis Disease of Chest 1957; Electrocardiogram of Hlthy Adult Negro 1959; Alpha Omega Alpha, SUNY College of Medicine 1978-. **Military Serv:** AUS 1944-46. **Business Addr:** 450 Clarkson, Brooklyn, NY 11225.

GREENE, CLIFTON S.
Business executive (retired). **Personal:** Born Oct 21, 1920, Georgetown, SC; son of Janie Browne Greene and Wally Greene; married Irene (deceased). **Educ:** SC State Coll, 1940. **Career:** Cliff Greene's Wines & Liquors Brooklyn, owner 1948-74; Wally-Thel Inc, pres 1959-69; Greenoung Enterprises, pres 1966; Green-Harris Enterprises, Inc, chmn chief exec ofcr 1966; Ebony Enterprises, Inc, pres 1972. **Orgs:** Pres sole stockholder Nu-way Investors Corp; mem NAACP; Urban League; Prince Hall Mason 32nd Degree; Shriner; Widow's Son Lodge #11; Long Island Consistory #61; Imperial Council; AEAONMS, Inc (Inactive); Amer Legion (Inactive); mem 100 Black Men Inc; Retired Army Officer's Assn; Ft Hamilton Officer's Club. **Honors/Awds:** 1st Black in US to file with FCC for UHF TV station; 1st Black or white to build multi-million dollar housing for elderly in Bedford Stuyvesant, Brooklyn; published ''Unique & Mae'' magazine; various articles, Stock Market Fundamentals 1966. **Military Serv:** AUS Staff Sgt to Captain in 29 mo 1943-45; honorable discharge Nov 1946. **Home Addr:** 1333 President St, Brooklyn, NY 11213.

GREENE, EDITH L.
Government official. **Personal:** Born Oct 29, 1919, Darlington County, SC; daughter of Olivette Mazone Galloway and Cohen Galloway Sr; married Isaac Greene Jr, Apr 22, 1937 (died 1975); children: Doris, Robert Allen, Elouise, Isaac, Frank, Jean, Cohen, Mae, Fred, Gennette, Don. **Career:** Town of Bolton, Bolton, NC, mayor, currently. **Orgs:** Member, Eta Phi Beta, 1980-; member, VFW Ladies Auxilary, 1977-; county council pres, Extension Homemakers Club, 1950-78; member, League of Women Voters, 1976-80; member, leader, 4-H Club, 1970-79. **Honors/Awds:** Outstanding Public Leadership, North Carolinians Against Racist & Religious Violence, 1990; Service Award, NC Chapter of Cystic Fibrosis, 1976; Meritorious Service Award, NC Joint Council on Health and Citizenship, 1978; Leadership Award, Columbus County Extension Homemakers, 1976; Outstanding and Dedicated Service, National Conference on Black Mayors, 1980. **Home Addr:** PO Box 129, Bolton, NC 28423.

GREENE, FRANK S., JR.
Business executive. **Personal:** Born Oct 19, 1938, Washington, DC; son of Irma O Swygert Greene and Frank S Greene Sr; married Carolyn W Greene, Sep 1990; children: Angela, Frank III, Ronald. **Educ:** Washington Univ, BS 1961; Purdue Univ, MS 1962; Santa Clara Univ, PhD 1970. **Career:** Technology Develop Corp, president, board member, 1985-92; ZeroOne Systems Inc, pres chmn bd 1971-87; Sterling Software Inc (subsidary of ZeroOne Systems Group), 1987-89; Networked Picture Systems, chairman of the board, 1989-94; New Vista capital Fund, general partner, 1993-. **Orgs:** Mem Inst of Elec & Electronic Engrs 1960-85; asst chmn, lecturer Stanford Univ 1972-74; mem IEEE Computer Soc Gov Bd 1973-75; bd dir Natl Conf of Christians & Jews 1978-; bd of dir Security Affairs Support Assn 1980-83; bd of regents Santa Clara Univ, 1983-89, trustee, 1990-; mem Amer Electronics Assoc; mem Bay Area Purchasing Council; dir Comsis Corp 1984; mem Natl Cont Mgmt Assn; mem Eta Kappa Nu, Sigma Xi; mem NAACP; member, NCCBPE. **Honors/Awds:** Author of 10 tech articles 2 indl textbooks; 1 patent received. **Military Serv:** USAF capt 1961-65. **Home Addr:** 967 F La Mesa Terrace, Sunnyvale, CA 94086. **Business Phone:** (650)329-9333.

GREENE, FRANKLIN D.
Automobile dealer. **Personal:** Born Jan 23, 1950, Hot Springs, AR; son of Jessie L Muldrow Greene and John H Greene; divorced. **Educ:** The College of the Ozarks Point Lookout, MO, BS 1972. **Career:** Cit Financial Serv, customer serv rep 1972-73; Ford Motor Co, Kansas City, MO, zone mgr 1973-81; Indian Springs Ford Kansas City, MO, pres 1981-83; Republic Ford Inc, pres 1983-; Columbus Ford, Mercury, Columbus, KS, president 1987-; Zodiac Lounge, Springfield, MO, president 1988-90; Quality Ford, Inc, West Des Moines, IA, president/owner, 1989-. **Orgs:** Bd dir Big Brothers and Sisters of Springfield, MO 1985-; pres of bd 1986, volunteer Big Brothers and Sisters of Springfield, MO 1984-; pres School of the Ozarks Springfield Alumni Assn 1986-87; bd mem Metro Credit Union 1987-; bd mem American Red Cross 1987-; past president, Black Ford Lincoln Mercury Dealers Assn, 1991-; board member, Minority Breakfast Club, 1990-; Kappa Alpha Psi Fraternity; Sigma Pi Phi Fraternity, 1994; mem Sigma Pi Phi Fraternity; advisory board member, Bankers Trust of Des Moines; athletic board member, Drake University. **Honors/Awds:** Republic Ford listed as one of Black Enterprise's Top 100 Auto Dealers, 1984-91; Meritorious Achievement Award, College of the Ozarks, 1989; Athletic Hall of Fame, College of the Ozarks, 1986. **Business Addr:** President, Quality Ford, Inc, 1271 8th St, Box 66040, West Des Moines, IA 50265.

GREENE, GABRIELLE ELISE
Capitalist. **Personal:** Born Jun 17, 1960, New York, NY; daughter of Gregory & Patricia Simms; married W Michael Greene, Jun 12, 1988; children: Savannah Elise. **Educ:** Princeton Univ, AB, 1981; Harvard Business, MBA, 1987; Harvard Law School, JD, 1987. **Career:** Bain & Company, consultant, 1982-84; UNC partners, principal, 1987-91; Commonwealth Enterprise Fund, 1991-94; HPB Ventures, general partner, currently. **Orgs:** Boston Partnership Steering Committee, bd mem, 1992-; Boston Children's Museum, bd mem, 1993-; Social Justice for Women, treasurer, 1989-91; Natl Black MBA Assn, 1988-. **Honors/Awds:** National Merit Scholar, 1978; National Black MBA Assn, First Annual Scholarship Recipient, 1985; Roxbury Chamber of Commerce, 100 Most Infulential People in Boston, 1994-95. **Business Addr:** General Partner, HPB Ventures, 888 7th Avenue, Penthouse, New York, NY 10106, (212)664-0990.

GREENE, GRACE RANDOLPH
Elected official. **Personal:** Born Oct 5, 1937, Washington, DC; divorced; children: Denise, Samuel, Michael, Annette, Wayne, Katerina, Grace E, Deloris. **Educ:** Spingarn Sr HS, 1954. **Career:** Dept of Housing & Comm Devel, retired 1982; Advisory Neighborhood Commiss, commiss 1982-84; Friends & Anacostia Library, mem 1984; Central Baptist Church Library, co-chairperson; Central Baptist Church Women's Dept, mem. **Orgs:** Acting mgr-mgmt aide Dept of Housing & Comm Devel 1969-82; volunteer for community; mem Library of Central Baptist Church, Women's Dept of Central Baptist; volunteer Friends of Anacostia Library. **Honors/Awds:** Cert OES Chap #5 Prince Hall 1972; Cert Women's Dept of Central Baptist Church 1984. **Home Addr:** 1924 Naylor Rd SE, Washington, DC 20020.

GREENE, GREGORY A.
Financial services manager. **Personal:** Born Aug 29, 1949, Boston, MA; son of Edna Greene and Harry Greene; married Pearline Booth Greene, Apr 13, 1974; children: Adria. **Educ:** Northeastern Univ, Boston, MA, BS, Business Admin, 1972. **Career:** Authur Andersen, Boston, MA, staff auditor, 1972-75; Arthur Andersen, Cincinnati, Oh, senior auditor, 1976-77; Philip Morris, New York, NY, manager financial services, 1977-; Corp Accounting, dir, 1994-. **Orgs:** Simon Foundation of Penn-

sylvania. **Military Serv:** US Army, SSgt, 1972-78. **Business Addr:** Director, Corp Accounting, Philip Morris Inc, 120 Park Ave, 21st Floor, New York, NY 10017.

GREENE, HORACE F.
Physician, administrator. **Personal:** Born May 5, 1939, Tuscaloosa, AL; married Stephanie Rodgers; children: Amanda, David, Jason. **Educ:** Fisk U, BA 1960; Meharry Med Sch, MD 1964. **Career:** Area C Comm Mental Hlth Cntr, dir adlscnt svc, dir Yth svc, clncl dir, part time stf Psychiatrist, supr Evng Clinic 1970-74; Georgetown Univ Sch Med, asst prof clncl & Psychiatry 1970; VA Hosp Washington, consult Drug Trtmnt & Rsch Prgm 1971; Howard Univ Sch Med, consult Residency Training Prgm 1973; Alexandria Comm Mntl Hlth Cntr, dir 1971-74; Pvt Practice; Bur Mntl Hlth Serv NHA , DC, dep admin chf 1974; VA Hosp, consult dept psychiatry 1974; N VA Prison Aftercare Prgrm, consult 1974-75. **Orgs:** 1975 N ASMHPD Task Force Nat Hlth Ins Adv Cncl; Adv Councl Estrn Area Alcohol Educ & Training Prgrm Inc Beta Kappa Chi Hon Sci; Kappa Alpha Psi Frat Inc; pres ALL Progress Psychiatry; Washington Psychiat Soc; Am Psychiat Assn; Washington Soc & Adlscnt Psychiatry; Psychiat Adv Cncl Mntl Hlth Admin Washington; chmn Professional Adv Com Mntl Hlth Assn Inc; Washington Cncl Child Psychiatry; APA Task Force Psychosurgery; nominating Com Wash Psychiatry Soc 1974; Peer Rvw Comm Wshngtn Psychiatry Soc Nat Med Fnd; WA Hosp Ctr, vchmn of clinical affairs dept of psychiatry 1987-. **Military Serv:** USNL med offcr 1965-67. **Business Addr:** Vice Chairman Clinical Affairs, Washington Hospital Center, 4600 Comm Ave, NW #224, Washington, DC 20008.

GREENE, JAMES R., III
Attorney-at-law. **Personal:** Born Apr 2, 1959, Evreux, France; son of Laura Malvoney-Clay Calhoun Greene and James Russell Greene Jr. **Educ:** Wright State University, Dayton, OH, BA, communications, 1983, BA, political science, 1983; Ohio State University College of Law, Columbus, OH, JD, 1985. **Career:** Public Defender's Office, Columbus, OH, law clerk, 1983-84; City Prosecutor's Office, Columbus, OH, law clerk, 1984; United States Attorney's Office, Columbus, OH, law clerk, 1985; Assistant Attorney General, Columbus, OH, attorney, 1986-88; Dayton Power and Light Co, Dayton, OH, attorney, 1988-93; AT&T Global Information Solutions Law Dept, Litigation Section, 1993-. **Orgs:** President, Thurgood Marshall Law Society, 1990-91; president, Dayton Chapter AABE, 1989-91; first vice-chairman, Concerned Christian Men, Inc, 1990-92; second vice-chairman, American Assn of Blacks in Energy, 1990-92; board of directors, Eastway Corp, 1990-92. **Honors/Awds:** Black Leadership Development, Dayton Urban League, 1988-89; Leadership Dayton, Class President, 1989-90.

GREENE, JEROME ALEXANDER
Educator, public administrator, clergyman. **Personal:** Born Mar 12, 1941, Welch, WV; son of Savannah Eldridge Anderson and Emmanuel A Greene; married Aurel Henry Greene, Apr 18, 1975; children: Rhonda, Russell. **Educ:** City Coll of NY, BA 1964; Brooklyn Coll, grad studies; Attended, Columbia Univ, Univ of Detroit, CCNY; Special Studies, Turtle Bay Sch of Music, Henry St Settlement Sch of Music, MA Bowie State Coll 1983; Liberty Univ, theological studies, currently; Moody Bible Institute, currently. **Career:** Morrisania Comm Corp, dir prog eval educ & training 1967-70; Afro-Amer Ethnic Orientation Soc, exec dir 1970-71; New York City Bd of Educ Dist #9, dir auxiliary personnel & special programs 1971-73; Lehman Coll, instructor & coordinator teacher training 1972-74; Dist #9 Comm School Bd, 10 yrs pres 1975-; New York City Bd of Educ Dist 5, pres dir of funded prog 1975-78; Peoples Devel Corp, exec dir 1979-; Touro College, prof, 1982-86; Bronx Christian Charismatic Prayer Fellowship, Bronx, NY, founder/pastor, 1982-. **Orgs:** Treas Comm Planning Bd #4; pres Morrisania Educ Counc Inc 1970-; co-pres Bronx Educ Alliance; former Bronx chmn NY Assn of Black Educators 1972-74; mem Amer Assn of Sch Admin; pastor & founder Bronx Christian Charismatic Prayer Fellowship Inc; mem Natl Alliance Black Sch Educators; assoc min Morrisania Comm Ch; mem Natl Caucus Black Sch Bd; chmn Area Policy Bd #4; NY State Cert as Sch Admin & Sch Dist Admin; adv bd LaGuardia Comm Coll; former weekly educ columnist Big Red Newspaper; vice chmn Local Draft Bd #133; former Bronx rep NY Assn of Comm Sch Bds; chairperson, Community Board #4, 1986-91; Democratic District Leader, 1988-. **Honors/Awds:** Humanitarian Awd Bronx Counc Bapt Ministers 1972; Man of Yr Bronx NAACP 1973; Outstanding Comm Ldr Awd Morrisania Educ Council 1975; Outst Fed Prog Admin Awd 1977; Outstanding Educator Awd City Tabernacle 1978; Man of Yr E Bronx NAACP 1979; Cited in Resolution NY State Assembly for estab Morrisania Educ Counc; Outstanding Educator Awd 1984; Civic Leadership Award, New York City Mission Society, 1988; Man of the Decade Award, 1985. **Home Addr:** 1248 Teller Ave, Bronx, NY 10456. **Business Addr:** Executive Dir, Peoples Develop Corp, 1162 Washington Ave, Bronx, NY 10456.

GREENE, JEROYD X. See EL-AMIN, SA'AD.

GREENE, JERRY LOUIS
Communication superintendent. **Personal:** Born Mar 30, 1957, Albany, GA; son of Lucius & Ollie Green; married Renee Green, Dec 23, 1987; children: Ashley Renee. **Educ:** Los Angeles Metropolitan College, AA, 1981; Dekalb Community College, 1980-81; University of Maryland, AA, 1986. **Career:** Fort McPherson GA Communication, computer operator, 1984-85; Camp Tango Korea, computer operator, 1984-85; United States Training Mission, Sandi Arabia, computer operator, 1984-86; Defense Intelligence Agency, watch officer, 1986-89; White House Military Office, operation officer, 1989-93; White House Communication Agency, operations officer, 1993-95; Defense Intelligence, superintendent, 1995-. **Special Achievements:** Hand Selected by the White House Support the President; Recognized by Vice Pres Al Gore for Superb Briefing; First NCO to be selected to work in the Presidents Operation Ctr; Top 5% of Army to be Nominated to work at the White House. **Military Serv:** Army, master sgt, 1976-; Defense Meritorious Awd, 1995. **Business Addr:** Superintendent, Defense Intelligence Agency, Pentagon, Rm 1D866, Washington, DC 20040, (202)697-3066.

GREENE, JOANN LAVINA
Educator. **Personal:** Born in Columbus, OH; daughter of Lavina Allen Davis and Lacy Davis; divorced; children: David. **Educ:** San Jose State Univ, BS 1969; Univ of California San Francisco, MS 1970; Univ Southern California, PhD. **Career:** VA Hospital Mental Hygiene Clinic, head nurse 1970-72; San Jose State Univ, instr psych nursing 1972-74; West Valley Coll, instr psych tech program 1974-76; West Valley Mission Coll, dir psych tech program 1976-. **Orgs:** Mem CNA 1972-, ANA 1972-, FACCC, Phi Kappa Phi, Sigma Theta Tau, Alpha Kappa Alpha Sor 1960-62; pres California Assn of Psychiatric Tech Educators 1980-83. **Honors/Awds:** Delta Sigma Theta Scholarship; NIMH Fellowship; Dean's List, President Scholar Phi Kappa Phi; Florence Nightingale Award 2 years; Sigma Theta Tau Natl Nursing Hon. **Business Addr:** Dir, Psychiatric Tech Program, Mission College, 3000 Mission College Blvd, Santa Clara, CA 95051.

GREENE, JOE (CHARLES EDWARD GREENE)
Football coach. **Personal:** Born Sep 24, 1946, Temple, TX; married. **Educ:** North Texas State Univ, attended. **Career:** Pittsburgh Steelers, defensive tackle, 1969-81; CBS-NFL Today, color commentator, 1983; acted and appeared in numerous television commercials; Miami Dolphins, defensive line coach, 1992-. **Honors/Awds:** Named to Sporting News Coll All Stars 1968, Sporting News NFL Eastern Conf All Stars 1969, Sporting News AFC All Stars 1970-74, 1979; played in Pro Bowl, 1970-76, 1978, 1979, 1981; played in all four Steeler Super Bowl victories; named to Natl Football Hall of Fame, 1987. **Business Addr:** Defensive Line Coach, Miami Dolphins, 2269 MW 199th St, Miami, FL 33056.

GREENE, JOHN SULLIVAN
Educator, consultant. **Personal:** Born Oct 27, 1921, Long Branch, NJ; son of Portia Gwathney Greene (deceased) and John J Greene (deceased); married Linda Ray Lichtenstein; children: Lynda Greene Bookhard, Joshua, Benjamin. **Educ:** Boston U, BS 1948; Boston U, MEd 1951. **Career:** Board of Education, NYC, mentor for beginning teachers, 1989-. Dist supt 1973-77; Charles Drew Jr HS, prin 1968-73; asst prin 1962-67; tchr of history 1948-62; Brooklyn Jewish Hosp Sch of Nrsng, Sociology Instr. **Orgs:** Nat Assn of sch adminstrs; Assn of asst Comm supts; Morrisania Educ Cncl; chmn bd dirs Jefferson Twrs Inc. **Honors/Awds:** NAACP Edctr of Yr 1975; Hispanic Ldrshp Conf; Outst Commtmnt & Educ Ldrshp 1975; Morrisania Educ Cncl; Outst Serv in Bronx Comm State Senate 1976; Awd Excptnl Achvmnt JHS Mayor of NY 1969. **Military Serv:** USN 1943-46. **Home Addr:** 700 Columbus Ave, New York, NY 10025.

GREENE, JOSEPH DAVID
Business executive, educator. **Personal:** Born Oct 18, 1940, Emanuel Co, GA; married Barney L Robinson; children: Cathy, J David. **Educ:** Augusta Clg, BBA 1972; Univ GA, MA 1973; Am Clg, CLU 1982. **Career:** Pilgrim Life Insurance Co, salesman 1959-66; Augusta Coll, instructor 1973-84; Pilgrim Life Insurance Co, vice pres 1973-85; Augusta State Univ, prof, currently. **Orgs:** Bd mem McDuffie Cnty Brd of Ed 1972-84; Thomson-McDuffie Chmbr of Comm 1978-81; regent GA Bd of Regents 1984-. **Honors/Awds:** Outstndng Yng Man Thomas Jaycees 1973; man of the yr Thomson Prgrsvc Civic Clb 1974; thesis publd Univ of GA 1973; agcy ofcr of yr Natl Ins Assc 1982. **Military Serv:** AUS e-5. **Home Addr:** PO Box 657, Thomson, GA 30824.

GREENE, LIONEL OLIVER, JR.
Research scientist. **Personal:** Born Apr 28, 1948, Brooklyn, NY; son of Dollie Chapman Greene (deceased) and Lionel Oliver Greene, Sr; children: Tera Ann. **Educ:** CA State Univ Los Angeles, BA 1970; Stanford U, PhD 1978. **Career:** Natl Aeronautics & Space Admn, rsrch scntst 1973-77, 1979-81; MA Inst of Tech, rsrch assc 1977-79; Lockheed Missiles & Space Co, rsrch scntst 1981-84; MacDonnell Douglas Astronautics, sr eng/scntst 1984-85; Univ of Santa Clara, Santa Clara, CA, visiting prof; AT&T Bell Laboratories, sr engr sci human fctrs 1985-; lecturer, Stanford Univ, 1979-84; adjunct professor, Florida A&M Univ; visiting professor, San Jose State Univ. **Orgs:** Mem Soc for Neuroscience 1978-; Mission Spec Astronaut candidate 1978; Aerospace Med Assc 1979-; Assc of Black Psychologists; mem Amer Defense Preparedness Assoc 1986-; FCC Radiotlphn License DJ 6 Yrs; bd of dirs, Goodwill Industries of America, Inc, 1992-. **Honors/Awds:** Ford Found fellow Washingon DC; NASA Predoctoral Fellow Washington DC; NIH Postdoctral Fellow Natl Inst of Hlth Washington DC NRC/NAS Postdoctral Fellow; Natl Rsrch Fellow/Natl Acad of Sci Bethesda MD; 12 research publications 1975-; Ebony Magazine Bachelor, Ebony Magazine, 1980; 20 publications, 1975-; recorded 2 jazz LP's; FAA Pilots License 1972; Reviewer of Papers, NIH, 1988-; Guest Panelist, Our Voices/BETV, 1991; Honor Society, Mensa Society, 1980-; NASA Science achievement award, Top secret Clearance, Defense Investigative Services. **Military Serv:** AUS capt; Air Defense Artillery Co (Hawk Missiles) 1970-82; US Navy High Altitude Test Certification 1975. **Home Addr:** 1937 W 95th St, Los Angeles, CA 90047.

GREENE, MARVIN L.
Educator (retired), consultant. **Personal:** Born Nov 17, 1915, Greenville, AL; son of Julia Rebecca Anderson and Rev Shelly Milton Greene; married Erma Keys, Mar 17, 1948; children: David, Marcia, Glenn. **Educ:** Wayne State Univ, BA 1942, MA 1948, EdD 1968. **Career:** Detroit Public Schools, tchr 1948, dept head 1960, asst prin 1963, supr 1965, asst reg supt 1968, region supt 1970-. **Orgs:** Mem MCTE, NCTE, IRA, MRA, Detroit English Club; Met Linguistics Club pres 1963-69, ASCD, MASCD, AASA, MASA; mem Natl Alliance Black Sch Educators, Metro Detroit Black Educ Admins; Metro Alliance of Black Sch Educators; mem Reserve Officers Assn; Phi Delta Kappa; com mem Boy Scouts Amer; chmn bd dirs Booth Meml Hosp 1975-78; pres Natl Alliance Blk Sch Ed 1981-83; asst supt Curriculum & Staff Dev 1979-83. **Honors/Awds:** Martin Luther King Awd 1972; Nu Omega Man of Yr 1953. **Military Serv:** Lt col 1942-46, 1950-52.

GREENE, MITCHELL AMOS
Educator. **Personal:** Born Nov 2, 1927, Georgetown, SC; children: Charles Myers, Mitchell III, Ann Eileen, Hilliard Dwane, Lois Elizabeth. **Educ:** Dillard Univ, BA 1952; Case Western Reserve Univ, MS 1956; Univ of IA, PhD 1972. **Career:** Orleans Parish Dept of Social Servs, social caseworker 1953-54; Logansport State Hospital, psychiatric social worker 1956-59; Univ of IA, instructor dept of pediatrics 1959-65; IA Office of Economic Opportunity, tech asst 1965-66; IA Wesleyan Coll, asst prof sociology 1966-70; Black Hawk-Grundy Mental Health Center, consultant 1977-; Univ of No IA, assoc prof educator/clinician 1970-. **Orgs:** Mem Baptist Church, Democratic Party, Omega Psi Phi Frat; articles published in professional journals. **Military Serv:** AAF pfc 1946-48.

GREENE, NATHANIEL D.
Chief executive. **Career:** Empire Ford, Inc, Spokane, WA, chief executive, 1986-. **Orgs:** Eastern Washington Univ, Business Advisory Council, pres. **Business Addr:** Chief Executive Officer, Empire Ford, Inc, West 423 Third Ave, Spokane, WA 99204.

GREENE, NELSON E., SR.
Business executive. **Personal:** Born May 20, 1914, Danville, VA; married Gloria Kay; children: Nelson, Jr, Terry F. **Educ:** Shaw Univ, AB 1941; Renourd School of Embalming NY, 1948. **Career:** Greene Funeral Home Alexandria, funeral dir owner; Langston HS Danville, tchr 1941-42. **Orgs:** Mem bd dir, Alexandria Bd of Trade; commr, Alexandria Redevel & Housing & Authority 1966-69; VA bd of Funeral Dir & Embalmers 1972; Natl Funeral Dir Assn; bd dir, VA Mortician Assn; mem NAACP; Urban League, Masons, Elks, Shrine; bd dir Alexandria Hospital 1970; sr warden, Meade Episcopal Church 1969-72, vestry 1974; Virginia City Council, Alexandria, 1979-82; Omega Psi Phi Fraternity, 1938-. **Military Serv:** Military serv major 1942-46, 1951-53.

GREENE, RICHARD T.
Bank chairman. **Personal:** marrIed Virginia Lea; children: Cheryll Greene, Richard T Greene, Jr. **Educ:** Hampton Univ, Hampton, VA, BS, 1938; NY Univ, 1955-64. **Career:** Citizens and Southern Bank and Trust, Philadelphia, PA, former asst treasurer; Associated Pubrs Inc, New York, business mgr, 1945-58; Interstate United Newspapers, sec and business mgr, 1958-60; Carver Federal Savings Bank, New York, exec asst, 1960, mgr of Brooklyn branch office, 1961, asst vice pres, 1963-66, vice pres, 1966-68, exec vice pres, 1968-69, pres and dir, 1969-95, chmn of the bd, 1995-. **Orgs:** Elder, Westminster Presbyterian Church; member, Hampton Alumni Club; member, Omega Psi Phi; member, Pres Coun of Museum of City of NY; former trustee, Citizens Budget Comm; direc, Amer League of Financial Instns; member, One Hundred Black Men Inc; direc, Financial Servics Corp, Thrift Assns Service Corp, Harlem Urban Devel Corp, and Fed Home Loan Bank. **Honors/Awds:** St John's University, Jamaica, NY, Honory Doctor of Commercial Science Degree, 1992. **Military Serv:** US Army, captain, 1941-45; Army commendation medal; Army Res, major. **Business Addr:** Chairman of the Board, Carver Federal Savings Bank, 75 W 125th St, New York, NY 10027.

GREENE, ROBERT CHARLES
Association executive, physician assistant. **Personal:** Born Jul 1, 1951, Los Angeles, CA; son of Rosalie C Greene and Charles H Greene; married Mina Greene, Dec 18, 1973; children: Emmanuel, Angelique. **Educ:** St Stephens College, BS, 1968; Univ of the East, MS, 1976; Univ of Santa Domingo, PhD, 1989. **Career:** US Army Medical Corps, bn cmdr, 1968-92; Missouri Baptist Hospital, house officer, 1992-; Madison County Urban League, pres, CEO, 1992-. **Orgs:** Phi Beta Sigma, 1968; American College of Military Physician Assistants, fellow, 1976; American Academy of Physician Assistants, fellow, 1976; NAACP; Alpha Lambda Mu Honor Society, 1968; American College of Legal Medicine, fellow, 1990. **Military Serv:** US Army Med Corps, lt col, 1968-92; Silver Star 1969; Bronze Star 1969; Distinguished Service Cross, numerous other awards. **Business Phone:** (618)463-1906.

GREENE, RONALD ALEXANDER
Business executive. **Personal:** Born Nov 1, 1945, Greenwood, SC; married Margaret St Mark; children: Ronald Jr, Jennifer. **Educ:** SC St Coll, BS 1965-68. **Career:** Blue Cross Blue Shield, mgr telecommunications 1979; Blue Cross Blue Shield, telecomm Coordntr 1978-79; Blue Cross Blue Shield, mgr data entry 1976-78; Blue Cross Blue Shield, prgrmr analyst 1975-76; prgmr analyst. **Military Serv:** AUS 1974-75; oak leaf cluster; AUS capt 7 yrs. **Business Addr:** I 20 and Alpine Rd, Columbia, SC.

GREENE, SARAH MOORE
Educator, political leader. **Personal:** Born Feb 22, 1917, Madisonville, TN; daughter of Mary Toomey Moore and Isaac Moore; married William J Greene, Oct 3, 1939 (deceased). **Educ:** A & I State Coll, Nashville TN, 1932-34. **Career:** Monroe County School Bd, Sweetwater TN, teacher, 1934-36; North Carolina Mutual Insurance Co, Knoxville TN, special agent, 1936-46; Knoxville TN, private kindergarten proprietor, 1946-66; State of Tennessee, Nashville TN, pardon/parole bd mem, 1967-69; Knox County, Knoxville TN, sec of finance comm, 1971-80; US Government, Knoxville TN, staff aide, 1980-85. **Orgs:** Chairperson, bd of dir, YWCA, 1956-62, KOIC, 1964-88; bd mem, Community Action Comm, 1965-71; mem, Knoxville Bd of Educ, 1969-85; sec, NAACP. **Honors/Awds:** Certificate of Appointment to NCEDC, President Gerald Ford, 1975; Torch Bearer Award, Opportunity Industrial Corp, 1976; Honorary Mem, Alpha Kappa Alpha Sorority Inc, 1976; Civic Serv Award, Greater Knoxville Minority Business Bureau, 1978; Honor Serv Award, Knoxville Opportunity Industrial Corp, 1988; Advocacy Award, 47th Annual NAHRW Conf, 1994; Nation Builder Award, Natl Black Caucus, 1994; Award for Contributions & Accomplishments, The TN Lawyers Association for Women, 1996. **Special Achievements:** 1st black elected to Knoxville City Schools Board of Education, 1969-85; elementary school named Sarah Moore Greene Elementary School, 1972. **Home Addr:** 2453 Linden Ave, Knoxville, TN 37917.

GREENE, WILLIAM
Cleric. **Personal:** Born Sep 13, 1933, Rowland, NC; son of Margaret Brunson Greene and Joe Greene; married Wilhelmenia O. Greene, Dec 28, 1953; children: Wanda Greene. **Educ:** Anchorage Community College, Anchorage, AK, AA, 1982; Alaska Pacific Univ, Anchorage, AK, BA, 1983. **Career:** US Air Force, fuel supt, 1953-80; Shiloh Missionary Baptist Church, Anchorage, AK, chairman, 1974-79, admin, 1979-85; chaplain with state of Alaska, 1980-; Eagle River Baptist Church, Eagle River, AK, pastor, 1985-. **Orgs:** Pres, Interdenominational Ministerial Alliance, 1987-90; pres, Chugiak Food Pantry, 1988-; chair, Black Edn Task Force, 1988-92; chair, Minority Community Rels Police Task Force, 1988-. **Honors/Awds:** Man of the Year Awd, Alaska State Assn of Colored Women, 1987; Outstanding Leadership Awd, Alaska Black Caucus, 1988; military awards include NonCommissioned Officer Academy Graduate Ribbon; Army Good Conduct Medal with Two Devices; Korean Service Medal; AF Longevity Svc Award Ribbon with Five Devices; Natl Defense Svc Medal with One Device; AF Outstanding Unit Awd with Seven Devices; Korean Presidential Unit Citation; United Nations Svc Medal; AF Good Conduct Medal With Five Oak Leaf Clusters; AF Commendation Medal; Meritorious Service Medal With One Oak Leaf Cluster; Honorary Doctor of Divinity, Arkansas Baptist Coll, 1997. **Home Addr:** 7310 E 17th Ave, Anchorage, AK 99504. **Business Addr:** Minister, Eagle River Missionary Baptist Church, 16331 Business Park Blvd, P O Box 775188, Eagle River, AK 99577-5188.

GREENE, WILLIAM HENRY L'VEL
Educational administrator. **Personal:** Born Jul 28, 1943, Richburg, SC; son of Mattie Macon Greene and Malachi Greene; married Ruth Lipscomb Greene; children: Omari, Jamila. **Educ:** Johnson C Smith Univ, BA, 1966; Michigan State Univ, MA, 1970, PhD, 1972. **Career:** Univ of Massachusetts, Amherst, asst prof, 1972-76, director in-service teacher education, Center for Urban Education, 1974-76; Fayetteville State Univ, asst to the chancellor, director of development and university relations, 1976-79; Johnson C Smith Univ, director of career counseling and placement, 1979-83; Livingstone College, president, 1983-89; Gaston College, Dallas, NC, dean of arts and sciences, 1989-. **Orgs:** Member, North Carolina Internship Council, 1986; Mint Museum, Charlotte NC, director; North Carolina Chapter, American Heart Assn; board of directors, Salisbury-Rowan Chamber of Commerce, 1986; Phi Delta Kappa; Omega Psi Phi; Sigma Pi Phi; Salisbury Rowan Symphony Society; Gaston County, YMCA; Salisbury YMCA; First Union National Bank; exec board, Fayetteville Business League, 1986; dir, Gaston County Museum of Art & History; dir, Gaston Coyunty Family Services. **Honors/Awds:** Outstanding Black Educator, Black Caucus, 1976; Advisor of the Year, Fayetteville State, 1978-79; Achievement Recognition Award, American Heart Assn, 1984; Community Service Award, Charlotte North Carolina, Zeta Phi Beta, Delta Zeta Chapter, 1984. **Home Addr:** 1000 Clifton St, Charlotte, NC 28216.

GREENE, WILLIE LOUIS
Professional baseball player. **Personal:** Born Sep 23, 1971, Milledgeville, GA. **Career:** Cincinnati Reds, infielder, 1992-. **Business Addr:** Professional Baseball Player, Cincinnati Reds, 100 Riverfront Stadium, Cincinnati, OH 45202, (513)421-4510.

GREENE-THAPEDI, LLWELLYN L.
Judge. **Personal:** Born in Guthrie, OK; daughter of Fannye M Gaines-Greene and Latimer Hamilton Greene; divorced; children: Severn Latimer Deck, Letha Llwellyn Deck, Sheryl Renee Deck, Andre Martin Thapedi, Anthony Isaac Thapedi. **Educ:** Langston University, OK, BA; University of Saskatchewan, MA; Loyola University, Chicago, IL, JD. **Career:** University of Saskatchewan, Canada, instructor, 1971-72; Amoco Oil Company, Chicago, IL, attorney, 1976-81; Chicago State University, Chicago, IL, instructor, business law, 1977-78; private practice, attorney, 1981-92; Circuit Court, Cook County, IL, judge, currently. **Orgs:** Delivery of Legal Services Standing Committee, Illinois State Bar Association, 1976-85; president, Cook County Bar Association, 1988; member of board of directors, Public Interest Law Internship, 1982-83; member of board of directors, Chicago Bar Association, 1983-85; member of board of directors, Illinois Institute for Continuing Legal Education, 1985-87; member, Citizen's Advisory Committee of the Circuit Court, 1987; member, Illinois Trial Lawyers Association, 1978-88; member of board of directors, National Bar Association, 1987-88; president, Cook County Bar Association, 1987-88; member of hearings committee, Attorney Registration and Disciplinary Committee, 1989-90; member, Urban League; member, NAACP; member, Delta Sigma Theta. **Honors/Awds:** Meritorious Service Award, 1983; National Association for Equal Opportunity in Education Award, 1984; Legal Assistance Foundation Award, 1984; Richard E Westbrook Award for legal excellence, 1986; Kizzie Award for community service, 1987; Martin Luther King Teen Leadership Award, 1988. **Business Addr:** Judge, Circuit Court, Cook County, Daley Center, Chicago, IL 60602.

GREENFIELD, ELOISE
Freelance writer. **Personal:** Born May 17, 1929, Parmele, NC; married Robert J; children: Steven, Monica. **Educ:** Miner Tchrs Coll, 1946-49. **Career:** US Patent Office, clerk typist 1949-56, supv 1956-60; DC Unemploy Compensation Bd, sec 1963-64; Case Cntrl Tch Wrk & Training Oppty & Ctr, 1967-68; DC Dept of Occptn & Profns, admin 1968; DC Writers Workshop, staff mem 1971-74; DC Commn of the Arts, writer in residence 1973; freelance writer. **Orgs:** African Amer Writer's Guild, Authors Guild, Black Literary Umbrella. **Honors/Awds:** Cit Council on Interracial Books for Children; Cit DC Assn of School Librarians; Cit Clbrtns in Lrnng; short stories & articles, for Negro Digest, Black World, Scholastic Scope, Ebony Jr, Negro Hist Bull, num chldrn's Books; Carter G Woodson Book Awd 1974; NY Times Outst Book; Irma Simonton Black Book Awd 1974; Jane Addams Chldrn's Book Awd 1976; Coretta Scott King Awd 1978; Am Library Assn Notable Book; Awd from Natl Black Child Development Inst 1981; producer of childrens recordings 1982; works reviewed & dramatized on publicTV (Reading Rainbow); Awd Black Women in Sisterhood for Action 1983; Wash DC Mayor's Art Awd for Lit 1983; Inst for the Preservation & Study of African Amer Writing 1984; grants DC Comms on the Arts & Humanities. **Special Achievements:** Grandpa's Face, 1988; Night on Neighborhood Street, 1991. **Business Addr:** Author, PO Box 29077, Washington, DC 20017.

GREENFIELD, ROBERT THOMAS, JR.
Physician. **Personal:** Born Jul 8, 1933, Washington, DC; son of Avis Greenfield and Robert T Greenfield Sr; married Wilma Sue Robertson; children: Kimberly, Karyn, Robert III, Richard, Brian, Ashley. **Educ:** Howard Univ, BS 1954; Howard Univ Coll of Med, MD 1958. **Career:** US Army, capt med corps 1958-63; Madigan General Hosp, internship 1958-59; Freedmen's Hosp, res phys ob/gyn 1963-67; Howard Univ Coll Med, clinical instr 1976-; Georgetown Univ, instructor clinical 1978-; Drs Greenfield, Booker Chartered, physician, pres 1969-; Chartered Health Plan, medical dir/founder, 1987-90. **Orgs:** Bd dir Columbia Hospital for Women 1981-85; mem Joint Perinatal Site Visit Task Force for Washington DC 1982-85; chief of staff Columbia Hosp for Women 1983-85; chmn, bd dir Colmesh Inc 1985-86; mem adv bd DC Maternal & Infant Health; mem Joint Venture Medical Staff & Columbia Hospital; vice chmn Washington DC Sect Dist IV Amer Coll of Ob/Gyn; chmn Washington DC Section Dist IV Amer Coll of Obs/Gyn; chmn Perinatal Mortality Comm Dist IV Amer Coll of Ob/Gyn; member, Mayor's Committee on Infant Mortality, 1990; mem Washington, DC Bd of Medicine, 1997-. **Honors/Awds:** Mem Alpha Omega Alpha Med Scholastic Frat. **Military Serv:** AUS capt 5 yrs. **Home Addr:** 2010 Spruce Dr NW, Washington, DC 20012. **Business Addr:** President, Drs Greenfield, Booker Charter, 525 School St, SW, Washington, DC 20024, (202)479-2800.

GREENFIELD, ROY ALONZO
Government official (retired). **Personal:** Born May 7, 1915, Washington, DC; son of Roy Marie Greenfield and Eugene Greenfield; married Mathilde Camille DePoidras. **Educ:** Howard Univ, BS Liberal Arts, MA, PhD Higher Educ Admin; New York Univ, PhD Psychology; New York Univ, postdoctorate courses, Psychology. **Career:** US Federal Govt, first black hospital administrator for Genl Omar Bradley, Veterans Administrator, Washington DC, first black interpreter of French and Spanish WW II under Genl Eisenhower; State College for Colored Students Dover State Delaware, prof of foreign languages; Vet Adm NYRO, psychologist/psychometrist; US Federal Trade Commn, first black chmn dir consumer educ NY regional office (retired). **Orgs:** Mem, Federation National Des Anciens Combattants, NAACP, Urban League, Alliance Francaise, NY Acad of Science, Natl Soc for the Advancement of Ethical Culture; lecturer to staff members at Blair House on how to improve their educ, helping them in their educ programs; consultant to mem of Diplomatic Corps connected with foreign embassies, Washington DC; French and Spanish interpreter at Washington Natl Airport for Delta, Eastern, Piedmont, Pan Am Airlines; USO volunteer, 5 yrs, Washington DC; mem, Natl Assn of Federal Investigators 1958-. **Honors/Awds:** First Black member admitted to NY Acad of Science 1939; only bona fide US Black federal fur expert, textile expert and wool expert in USA trained by US federal government; Outstanding Guest Speaker, Natl Urban League; publication "Speak 5 Languages Instantly for Travellers," 1987. **Military Serv:** Graduated from Camp Ritchie MD Sch of Military Intelligence as an interpreter of French. **Home Addr:** The Blair House, Suite 1016, 9612 Sunset Dr., Rockville, MD 20850.

GREENFIELD, WILLIAM RUSSELL, JR.
Physician. **Personal:** Born Sep 15, 1915, Williamsport, TN; married Mae Rivers Ward; children: William R, Albert, Mae Helaine, Mary Jewel Howard, Theolya Louise, William Ward. **Educ:** TN St U, BS 1938; Meharry Med Coll, MD 1949. **Career:** Physician Prvt Prac Dothan AL 1951; TN St 1937-45. **Business Addr:** 904 DuBoise St, Dothan, AL 36302.

GREENIDGE, JAMES ERNEST
Publicity director. **Personal:** Born Feb 25, 1949, Cambridge, MA; son of M Norma and Beresford. **Educ:** Northeastern Univ, BA 1971. **Career:** Boston Record Amer, news reporter 1971-72; Albany NY Knickerbocker News, sportswriter 1972-73; Rensselaer Polytech, sports info dir 1973-82; Harvard Univ, sports info dir 1982-84; New England Patriots, publicity dir 1984-. **Home Addr:** 17-3 Old Colony Lane, Arlington, MA 02174. **Business Addr:** Publicity Dir, New England Patriots, Sullivan Stadium, Rt 1, Foxboro, MA 02035.

GREENLEAF, LOUIS E.
Investigator. **Personal:** Born Apr 9, 1941, Newark, NJ; married Cynthia Robinson Conover; children: Bridget, Michael, Brectt, Towanna. **Educ:** Essex Co Coll, AS 1973; John Jay Coll of Criminal Justice, BS 1975; Rutgers School of Law, JD 1978. **Career:** Private Law Practice, attorney 1983-86; City of Newark, police dept 1968-86, police director, 1986-88; Essex County Prosecutors Office, chief of investigators, 1988-94; Private Law Practice, 1994-97; Weights and Measures, superintendant, 1997-. **Orgs:** Mem NJ Bar Assoc 1985-; mem Natl Org of Black Law Enforcement Execs; bd of trustees Garden State Bar Assoc; vice chmn bd of trustees NJ Juvenile Insts; Bd of Dir Newark Emr Services for Families. **Military Serv:** AUS E-4 2 yrs; Vietnam Service, Good Conduct 1964-66. **Business Addr:** State Superintendent, Office of Weights & Measures, 1261 Routes 1 & 9 South, Avenel, NJ 07001-1647.

GREENLEE, PETER ANTHONY
Attorney. **Personal:** Born Feb 18, 1941, Des Moines, IA; son of Donna O Graham Greenlee and Archie M Greenlee; married Marcia McAdoo Greenlee, Sep 5, 1965. **Educ:** Univ Wash, BA 1965; Howard Univ Law Sch, JD 1971. **Career:** Univ of OR, instr; Job Corps, 1965-66; US Peace Corps Euthiopia, 1966-68; Reginald Heber Smith Fllw Nghbrhd Lgl Srvcs, Atty 1970-72; Redvlpmnt Lnd Agncy, 1972-74; Dept of Energy, Washington, DC, attorney/advisor, 1974-90; Social Security Administration, Washington, DC, adminstrative appeals judge, currently. **Orgs:** Am Bar Assn; Nat Bar Assn; Delta Theta Phi; US District Court Bar; US Supreme Court Bar. **Business Addr:** Administrative Appeals Judge, Social Security Administration, Office of Hearing and Appeals, 5107 Leesburg Pike, Ste 1305, One Skyline Tower, Falls Church, VA 22041.

GREENLEE, SAM
Author, broadcast journalist. **Personal:** Born Jul 13, 1930, Chicago, IL; married Nienke (divorced); children: 1 daughter. **Educ:** Univ of WI, BS, 1952; Univ of Chicago, grad study, 1954-57; Univ of Thessalonikki, Greece, grad study, 1963-65; Community Film Workshop, 1974. **Career:** Author; US Info Agency, foreign serv officer in Iraq, Pakistan, Indonesia, and Greece, 1957-65; LMOC, deputy dir, 1965-69; University of Djakarta, Indonesia 1960-; WVON-AM, talk show host 1988-; Columbia College, educator, screenwriting, 1990-. **Honors/ Awds:** Author of The Spook Who Sat by the Door, Baron, 1969, Blues for an African Princess, Third World Press, 1971, Baghdad Blues, Bantam, 1976; Ragdale Fondation Fellowship, 1989; IL Arts Cncl Fellowship, Blues for Little Prez 1990; IL PoetLaureate Awd, 1990; contributor of articles & short stories to magazines and journals. **Military Serv:** US Army, first lieutenant, 1952-54.

GREENWOOD, CHARLES H.
Educational administrator. **Personal:** Born Jul 30, 1933, Anderson, IN; son of Lida M Lampkins Greenwood and Huddie Greenwood; married Theresa M Winfrey; children: Lisa Renee, Marc Charles. **Educ:** Ball State Tchrs Coll, BS 1956; CO Coll, 1956-58; Ball State U, MA 1961; IN U, EdD 1972. **Career:** Ball State Univ, graduate asst 1958-59; E Chicago Public Schools, teacher 1959-61; Ball State Univ, instructor 1961-63, assoc prof 1973-; N IL Univ, visiting prof 1973-74; Ball State Univ, asst dean of undergraduate program 1974-84, School of Continuing Educ, asst dean 1984-. **Orgs:** Amer Assn of Higher Educ 1974-; Assn for Supervision & Curriculum Devel 1974-78; Assn of Acad Affairs Admin 1974-78; Adult Educ Assn of IN 1978; Phi Delta Kappa 1976-; evaluator Am Cncl of Educ 1984; vp/pres Kiwanis Club of Muncie IN 1980-81; gov Indiana Dist Kiwanis Intl 1990-91, lt gov Wapahanal Div 1982-83, gov elect; vice pres Jr Achievement 1979-81; sec YMCA Bd 1978; Sigma Iota Epsilon 1986; educational coord Acad Comm Leadership; Washington Center, Washington, DC, liaison officer, Liason Advisor Board, Midwest representative; director of Aerospace Education USAF CAP Aux Indiana Wing; International Chairman Council & Convention Muni, Kiwanas, international bd mem, United Way, 1997. **Honors/Awds:** Natl Bronze Award Jr Achievement 1980; Outstanding Minority Facuty, Ball State; Distinguished Lt Gov Kiwanis Intl 1983; Sagamore of the Wabash, 1991. **Military Serv:** US Army, sp 4, 1956-58; Civil Air Patrol USAF Aux CAP lt col 1989-, Good Conduct; Aerospace Educ Mem 1956-83. **Business Addr:** Assistant Dean, Ball State Univ, 2000 University Ave, Muncie, IN 47306.

GREENWOOD, DAVID
Professional basketball player. **Personal:** Born May 27, 1957, Lynwood, CA; married Joyce; children: Tiffany Crystal Marie. **Educ:** UCLA, BA History 1979. **Career:** Chicago Bulls, 1980-85, San Antonio Spurs, 1986-89, 1990-, Denver Nuggets, 1989, Detroit Pistons, 1990. **Orgs:** Taught basketball clinics Western US 1980. **Honors/Awds:** NBA First Team All Rookie Team 1978-79. **Business Addr:** San Antonio Spurs, 600 E Market, Suite 102, San Antonio, TX 78205-2655.

GREENWOOD, EDNA TURNER
Editorial director (retired). **Personal:** Born in Shiner, TX; daughter of Mamie Koontz and David Koontz; married Wilbert (deceased); children: Ronald Vann Turner; married Norris Greenwood. **Educ:** Tucker Bus Coll St Louis MO, 1953. **Career:** Good Publishing Co (magazines, Jive, Bronze Thrills, Hip, Soul Confessions, Sepia & Soul Teen) Ft Worth TX, editorial dir; circulation mgr, editor 25 yrs. **Orgs:** Mem Baker Chapel AME Ch; mem NAACP; mem Ft Worth C of C; bd mem, Neighborhood Action Comm, Tarrant Action on Aging; bd mem, United Ctrs. **Honors/Awds:** Award Margaret Caskey Women in Commun Ft Worth Professional Chap of Women in Commun 1977.

GREENWOOD, JOHN T.
Educator. **Personal:** Born Feb 2, 1949, Winston-salem, NC; son of Elizabeth Millner Greenwood and Joseph Jackson Greenwood. **Educ:** Cornell, AB 1971; Harvard, JD 1974; Business Admin, Business Law, Criminal Law, Health Law, Civil Rights, Legal Studies. **Career:** Mudge Rose Guthrie & Alexander, atty 1972; Inst of Gov Univ of North Carolina at Chapel Hill, asst prof, asst dir 1974; NC A&T State Univ, asst prof business admin 1975; WS State Univ, asst prof business admin 1976; Barber Scotia Coll, asst prof & dir test-taking & learning skills 1977; Gulton Femco, asst mgr of personnel 1978; WS Urban League, dir of prog 1978; Div of Business Shaw Univ, assoc prof chmn 1979; Mgmt Educ & Real Estate, consulant; JTG Assoc, pres. **Honors/Awds:** Phi Beta Kappa; Alpha Kappa Mu.

GREENWOOD, THERESA M. WINFREY
Writer, musician, educator. **Personal:** Born Dec 28, 1936, Cairo, IL; daughter of Lillian Theresa Williams Winfrey and Hubert Augusta Winfrey; married Dr Charles H Greenwood; children: Lisa Renee, Marc Charles. **Educ:** Millikin Univ, BA music educ 1959; Ball State Univ, EdM 1963, EdD 1976. **Career:** E Chicago Pub Schools, music teacher 1959-61; Muncie Pub Schools, teacher 1962-68; Ball State Univ, acad counselor

1971-72; Ball State Univ Burris Lab School, asst prof educ 1979-, teacher of gifted/talented program 1986-. **Orgs:** Past pres Sigma Alpha Iota 1958; music adjudicator NISBOVA 1961-; bd of dir United Way, ARC, Huffer Day Care, WIPB-TV 1969-75; mem Kappa Delta Pi 1972-73; mem & state sec Natl League Amer Pen Women 1973-78; testified White House Conf on Families 1980; mem Eastern IN Community Choir; ed bd White River State Park 1983; judge Social Study History Days; adv bd Social Studies Council Natl Publ 1982; recipient Ind & MI Electric Co Mini-Grant 1987; Kodak (Newsletter Pub 1985 & Prie Time Newsletter Pub) 1986; editorial bd Natl Soc Studies Journal; speaker HS Young Writers Conf 1986; media volunteer Pan-American Games 1987. **Honors/Awds:** Soc Studies Grant 1982; Commendation IN Gov Orr 1982; NAACP Award 1980; IN All-Amer Family Awd Family Weekly Mag, Eastern Airlines 1972; fellowship Natl Fellowship Funds Emory Univ 1973-76; BSU Minority Achievement Award, minority Student Development, 1989, currently developing "Tap the Gap," a progam for at-risk students; developing innovative elementary parent partnership; Team program "Connections" for Christa McAuliffe Fellowship; Ford Fellowship 1975- 76 for doctorate; Eli Lilly Foundation, 1989; Teacher of the Year, runner-up, Indiana Dept of Educ, 1982-83; Disney Presents The American Teacher Telecast, 1994; Geraldine R Dodge Grant to design and host "A Celebration of Teaching Conf for Minorities," 1994; Indiana Teacher of the Year Finalist, 1994; Video Report Card,developed and innovated for Christa McAuliffe Fellowship; AAUW Round Table Panelist Natl Gender Study "Gender Bias in the Classroom," 1991; "Women of the Rainbow," Indianapolis Minority Chamber of Commerce, 1992; Served on the Search Committee for Superintendent of University Schools, 1994. **Special Achievements:** Feature Story, Ball State University Research Publication Bene Facta; published, Psalms of a Black Mother, Warner Press ,1970, Gospel Graffiti, M Evans, NY, 1978, weekly newspaper column, Muncie Eve Press Poems, "Black Like It Is/Was," 1974, "Break Thru (Upper Room Anthology)," 1972, "Crazy to be Alive in Such a Strange World," 1977; bibliographic, Ladies Home Journal, 1976, Essence Mag, 1975, Church Herald, 1972; article, "Cross-Cultural Educ for Elementary School," The Social Studies Teacher, 1983; published poems in the Saturday Evening Post, 1974; students gained extensive publicity for "Dear-World" letters to Pres Reagan & Gen Sec Mikhail Gorbachev during Washington Summit (exhibited 10 months at World's Largest Children Museum," 1988; writing, "Open Letter to Miss Crawford, Diary of a Black Girl Growing Up in America," Madison County Magazine, March 1991; Published: Technology Horizons Education Journal, "Let's Pop Some Corn and Watch Your Report Card;" Principal Magazine (NAESP), 1995; Inerviewed for Indianapolis Star and Ball State Information Bureau for national wire services for views on "The Status of Minorities in Teaching" and "Black Creativity and Education;" Created and Produced Educational Acess television show, "What's In The Attic?"; Presented at state and national Gifted Conferences, Indianapolis and Salt Lake City, Utah (Young Entrepreneurs Project); Panal for local PBS telecast, "Parents, The Early Years," 1992; Developed a theoretical, Multiple Intelligence Model based on African Proverbs. **Business Addr:** Assistant Professor Primary Education, Ball State Univ, Burris Lab School, 2000 Univ, Muncie, IN 47306, (317)285-1131.

GREER, BAUNITA
Brokerage firm executive. **Career:** Cromwell, Miller & Greer, pres & ceo, currently. **Business Addr:** President, Cromwell, Miller & Greer, 67 Wall, Ste 2411, New York, NY 10005, (212)323-0273.

GREER, CHERIE
Sports professional. **Personal:** Born in Philadelphia, PA; daughter of Hal and Mayme Greer. **Educ:** UVA, bachelors, communications, 1994. **Career:** Lacrosse player; exec assistant, currently. **Honors/Awds:** World Cup Champions, Lacrosse, 1993, 1996, 1997; MVP, 1997. **Special Achievements:** First African American to play on women's world cup lacrosse team, 1993; youngest palyer to be named to team, 1993; first lacrosse player to have shirt retired at Univ of VA. **Business Addr:** Executive Assistant, 2555 S Telegraph, Ste 400, Auburn Hills, MI 48302, (248)745-6200.

GREER, EDWARD
Realtor. **Personal:** Born Mar 8, 1924, Gary, WV; married Jewell Means; children: Gail Lyle, Michael, Kenneth. **Educ:** WV State Coll, BS 1948; George Washington U, MS 1967. **Career:** Greer and Associates Realtors, broker, owner, currently. **Orgs:** Assn of the US Army, Military Order of World Wars; Natl Assn of Uniformed Services, Disabled American Veterans; Alumni Assn, Natl War Coll; Retired Officers Assn, Kappa Alpha Psi Fraternity. **Honors/Awds:** Alumnus of the Year, West Virginia State College. **Military Serv:** US Army, Major General; Distinguished Service Medal; Silver Star; Legion of Merit with Oak Leaf Cluster; Bronze Star with Oak Leaf Cluster; Air Medal; Joint Services Commendation Medal; Army Commendation Medal. **Business Addr:** Greer & Asso Realtors, PO Box 640561, El Paso, TX 79904.

GREER, HAL (HAROLD EVERETT)
Professional basketball player (retired). **Personal:** Born Jun 26, 1936, Huntington, WV. **Educ:** Marshall College, Huntington, WV, attended. **Career:** Guard: Syracuse Nationals, 1958-63, Philadelphia 76ers, 1963-73; Philadelphia Kings, coach, 1980-81. **Honors/Awds:** NBA All-Star Game, 1961-70; NBA All-Star Game MVP, 1968; holds NBA All-Star Game record for most points in one quarter (19), 1968; Naismith Memorial Basketball Hall of Fame, 1981.

GREER, KARYN LYNETTE
Broadcast journalist. **Personal:** Born Jun 20, 1962, Chicago, IL; daughter of Jeanette Brenda Crossley Greer and Ronald Virgil Greer. **Educ:** University of Illinois, Champaign, Il, BA, Broadcast Journ/Speech Comm, 1984. **Career:** WCIA-TV, Champaign, IL, asst dir newscasts, 1983-84; WICD-TV, Champaign, IL, weekend anchor/reporter, 1985-87; WCSC-TV, Charleston, SC, weekend anchor/reporter, 1987-89; WGNX-TV, Atlanta, GA, weeknight anchor/medical reporter, 1989-. **Orgs:** Awards committee, Atlanta Assn of Black Journalists, 1989-; recruiting committee, Dekalb-Decatur 100 Black Women 1989-; Alpha Kappa Alpha Sorority Inc, 1982-. **Honors/Awds:** Revlon Kizzy Award, Black Woman Hall of Fame, 1990; First Place Spot News, (KKK March), Atlanta Assn of Black Journalists, 1990; First Place Feature, (Crack Babies), Atlanta Assn of Black Journalists, 1990; Second Place, Medical Assn of Atlanta, 1990; Emmy Award, National Academy Television Arts & Sciences, Specialty Reporting, 1991. **Business Addr:** News Anchor, WGNX-TV, 1810 Briarcliff Road, Atlanta, GA 30329.

GREER, ROBERT O., JR.
Educator, pathologist, novelist, writer. **Personal:** Born Mar 9, 1944, Columbus, OH; son of Mary A Greer and Robert O Greer Sr; married Phyllis Ann Harwell. **Educ:** Miami Univ Oxford OH, AB 1961-65; Howard U, DDS 1965-69; Boston U, ScD MD 1971-74, MA, creative writing, 1988. **Career:** Dept of Pathology Univ of CO Hlth Sci Cntr, asst prof 1974-77; Dept of Pathology UCHSC, assoc prof 1977-80; Div of Oral Pathology & Oncology Univ of CO Sch of Dentistry, prof & chrmn 1980-; UCHSC, Dept of Pathology and Oncology, prof, chairman, 1984-. **Orgs:** Pres & chief pathologist Western States Regnl Pthlgy Lab; sec Mile High Med Soc 1978-79, pres 1983-85; mem Alumni Bd of Dir Miami Univ 1984-; Editor, High Plains Literary Review. **Honors/Awds:** David Swing Acad Schlrshp Miami Univ 1961-63; tuition schlrshp Howard Univ 1965-69; NIH postdoctoral rsrch flwhsp Boston Univ 1970-74; investigative rsch grants Am Cancer Soc Natl Cancer Inst Smokeless Tobacco Cncl 1980-; three textbooks Tumors of the Head & Neck; author, three medical thriller mysteries, Warner Books. **Military Serv:** USCG lt cmdr. **Business Addr:** Prof/Chmn, Div of Oral Pathology & Oncology, Univ of Colorado Health Science Center, 4200 E 9th St, Box C285, Denver, CO 80262.

GREER, TEE S., JR.
Educational administrator. **Personal:** Born Dec 21, 1936, Miami, FL; son of Florence Lee Greer and Tee Stewart Greer; married Billie Browne Greer, Oct 31, 1958; children: Anita G Dixon, Tee S III, Florence T, Frederick B. **Educ:** Morehouse College, Atlanta, GA, BS, math, chemistry, 1958; Atlanta University, Atlanta, GA, MA, education, 1967; The Union Institute, Cincinnati, OH, PhD, educational adminstration. **Career:** School Board of Dade County, Dade County, FL, assistant superintendent, associate superintendent, deputy superintendent for adminstration, 1987-90; superintendent of schools, 1990; deputy superintendent of federal, vocational & community services, 1990-. **Orgs:** Board member, United Way of Dade County, 1990-92; life member, National Alliance of Black Schools Educators; life member, National Coalition of Title I; life member, Chapter I Parents Morehouse College-Alumni Association. **Honors/Awds:** Distinguished Black Educator of the Year, State of Florida, 1991; Educator of the Year, Phi Delta Kappa, 1990; Educator of the Year, Univ of Miami Chapter Dade County Schools, 1990; Peace and Unity Award, Administrators Association St Martin de Porres Association, 1990; Liberty Humanitarian Award, Liberty Market & Martin Luther King Jr Festival & Parade Inc, 1991. **Business Addr:** Deputy Superintendent, Federal, Vocational, and Community Services, Dade County Public Schools, 1450 NE 2nd Ave, Room 415, Miami, FL 33132.

GREER, THOMAS H.
Newspaper publishing executive. **Personal:** Born Jul 24, 1942, Nashville, TN; son of Eliza S Greer (deceased) and Thomas H Greer (deceased); married Shirley Kasey, Aug 5, 1967; children: Kasey Lynn, Janna W. **Educ:** Dillard University, BA, 1963. **Career:** Chicago-Sun Times, sports reporter; Philadelphia Daily News, sports columnist, writer; New York Daily News, sports columnist; The Plain Dealer, sports editor, managing editor, editor, vice pres/sr editor, 1992-. **Orgs:** American Society Newspaper Editors, 1986-; Cleveland Chapter of Red Cross, board of directors, 1990-; WVIZ, Public Television, board of trustees, 1990-; Greater Cleveland Roundtable, board of trustees, 1991-; Omega Psi Phi Fraternity Inc, 1959-; Natl Assn of Minority Media Executives, 1992-; Cuyahoga Plan, board of trustees; Business Volunteerism Council, bd of trustees; Natl Assn of Black Journalists and the Associated Press

Sports Editors' Assn; Twice served on the Pulitzer Prize Nominating Jury. **Honors/Awds:** Oklahoma State University, Paul Miller Distinguished Journalism Lecturer, 1993; Scripps-Howard Foundation's Walker Stone/Editorial Writing Award, Judge, 1993. **Business Addr:** Vice Pres/Sr Editor, The Plain Dealer, 1801 Superior Ave, Cleveland, OH 44114, (216)344-4700.

GREGG, ERIC
Umpire. **Personal:** married Conchita; children: four. **Career:** Major League Baseball, umpire, National League, 1975-. **Special Achievements:** Third African American umpire in major league history; Author, Working the Plate: The Eric Gregg Story, 1990. **Business Addr:** Umpire, National League, Major League Baseball, 350 Park Ave., 18th Fl., New York, NY 10022, (212)339-7700.

GREGG, HARRISON M., JR.
Attorney. **Personal:** Born Sep 24, 1942, Longview, TX; son of Ola Timberlake Gregg and Harrison Gregg; married Arizona Johnson Gregg, Jun 18, 1963; children: Sherri Kimberly. **Educ:** Texas Southern Univ, BA, 1968, JD, 1971; Master Barber 1958. **Career:** State of Texas, 2nd Admin Region, 4D Master (judge), 1987-; Instructor, Texas Paralegal Sch, 1976-; Gregg Okehie & Cashin, atty, 1972-; barber 14 yrs. **Orgs:** Mem Houston Bar Assn; TX State Bar; Houston Lawyer Assn; TX Crimnal Defense Lawyers; Harris Co Criminal Defense Lawyers; Nat Bar Assn; Am Bar Assn. **Honors/Awds:** Phi Alpha Delta; mem Free & Accepted Prince Hall Mason; volntr UNCF. **Military Serv:** AUS. **Business Addr:** Gregg Okehie & Cashin Law Offices, 49 San Jacinto St #618, Houston, TX 77004-1214.

GREGG, LUCIUS PERRY
Business executive. **Personal:** Born Jan 16, 1933, Henderson, NC; married Doris Marie Jefferson. **Educ:** US Naval Acad, BS 1955; MA Inst Tech, MS 1961; Cath U, doctoral candidate 1961-63; Grinnell Coll, hon DSc 1973; Aspen Inst Exec Prog, 1974; Adv Mgmt Prog Harvard Bus Sch, 1975. **Career:** USAF Office Scientific Rsrch, proj dir in space tech 1961-65; Northwestern U, asso dean of Scis & dir rsrch coord 1965-69; Alfred P Sloan Found, prgm ofcr 1969-71; 1st Chicago Univ Finance Corp, pres 1972-74; 1st Nat Bank Chgo, vice pres 1972-. **Orgs:** Bd dirs Corp for Pub Brdcstng 1975-; acad bd US Naval Acad 1971-; mem Harvard Univ Trsts Visiting Comm in physics 1973-; Pres's Com on White HouseFellows Midwest Reg Selec Com 1974-; mem Nat Acad of Sci Found Com on Human Rsrcs (chmn Com on Minorities in Sci) 1973-; bd mem Fermi (AEC) NatAccel Lab 1967-77f Roosevelt Univ 1976-; Garrett Theol Sem 1974-; Tulane Univ Bd of Visitors 1972-; Chicago Coun on Foreign Rel 1975-; Harvard Bus Sch of Chicago 1977f mem MIT Trsts Visiting Con in Aero & Astronautics; Harvard Club of Chicago 1975-; mem Univ Club Chicago 1972-; Econ Club Chicago 1967-. **Honors/Awds:** Hon mem Sigma Gamma Tau 1969; 1 of 10 outstndg young men of 1966 Chicago Assn Commerce & Indus; outstndg young engr of 1964 Wash Acad Sci. **Military Serv:** USMC pfc 1950-51; USAF 1955-62.

GREGORY, BERNARD VINCENT. See Obituaries section.

GREGORY, DICK. See GREGORY, RICHARD CLAXTON.

GREGORY, FREDERICK DREW
Astronaut, military officer. **Personal:** Born Jan 7, 1941, Washington, DC; son of Nora Drew Gregory and Francis A Gregory (deceased); married Barbara Ann Archer Gregory, Jun 3, 1964; children: Frederick D Jr, Heather Lynn Gregory Skeens. **Educ:** US Air Force Academy, BS 1964; George Washington Univ, MSA 1977. **Career:** USAF, helicopter & fighter pilot 1965-70; USAF/NASA, research test pilot 1971-78, astronaut 1978-; NASA, Office of Safety and Mission Assurance, associate administrator, currently. **Orgs:** Soc of Experimental Test Pilots; Tuskegee Airmen Inc; Am Helicopter Soc; Nat Tech Assn; USAF Acad Assn of Grads; Omega Psi Phi; Sigma Pi Phi; board of directors: Young Astronaut Council, National Capital Area Boy Scouts; Association of Space Explorers. **Honors/Awds:** Distinguished Natl Scientist, Natl Soc of Black Engineers 1979; NASA Outstanding Leadership Award, NASA; Distinguished Alumni Award, George Washington University; Top 20 Minority Engineer 1990; IRA Eaker Fellow, Air Force Association; Honorary Doctor of Science, University of the District of Columbia; Distinguished Service Medal, NASA; three NASA Space Medals; two NASA Space Flight Medals. **Military Serv:** US Air Force, colonel; Defense Superior Service Medal, 2 Distinguished Flying Crosses, Meritorious Service Medal, 16 Air Medals, Air Force Commendation Medal, Defense Meritorious Service Medal. **Business Addr:** Associate Administrator, Code Q, NASA Headquarters, Washington, DC 20546.

GREGORY, KARL DWIGHT
Educator, business executive, economic consultant. **Personal:** Born Mar 26, 1931, Detroit, MI; son of Sybil Gregory and Bertram Gregory; married Tenicia Ann Banks; children: Kurt David, Sheila Therese, Karin Diane. **Educ:** Wayne State Univ, BA Econ 1951, MA Fin 1957; Univ of MI, PhD Econ 1962; Brown Univ, Postdoctoral Micro Econ. **Career:** Detroit Housing Commission, tech aid-acct 1951-53; Federal Reserve Bank St Louis, economist 1959; Office of Mgmt & Budget, Washington DC, economist 1961-64; Wayne State Univ, prof 1960-61, 1964-67; Fed for Self-Determination, exec dir 1968-69; Accord Inc Housing Rehabilitation Detroit, pres, CEO, bd chmn 1970-71; SUNY Buffalo, visiting prof 1974; Congressional Budget Office, exec staff, sr economist 1974-75; 1st Independence Natl Bank, interim pres 1980-81; Karl D Gregory & Assoc, managing dir; Oakland Univ, prof finance & strategic planning, 1968-96, distinguished prof emeritus, 1996-. **Orgs:** Dir Natl Econ Assoc, Black Econ Rsch Ctr 1968-75, Inner City Bus Improvement Forum 1968-87; dir, chief org, chmn of the bd 1st Independence natl Bank 1970-81; bd of trustees Protestant Episcopal Diocese of MI 1972-74, 1984-86, 1989-92; dir Inner City Capital Formation, 1973-86; Detroit Capital Access Ctr 1973-86; adv comm US Census of the Black Population 1976-79, US Trade Negotiations Tokyo Round 1978-81; dir Detroit Br Fed Reserve Bank of Chicago 1981-86; Barden Cablevision of Detroit 1982-94; Detroit Metro Small Bus Investment Corp 1982-85, Detroit Econ Growth Corp 1982-94; bd of trustees Oakland Cty Bus Attraction & Expansion Comm 1983-84; mem Governor Blanchard's Entrepreneurs & Small Bus Comm, 1984-89; vice pres Econ Club of Detroit 1984-89; dir Detroit Urban League, 1989-92; Michigan Governor Engler's Council of Economic Advisors, 1992-94; chmn of board, Greater BIDCO, 1990-96; Detroit Alliance for Fair Banking, 1989; first vice chair, Michigan Minority Technology Council, 1988-. **Honors/Awds:** Num comm serv & acad awds; num publs in acad jrnls; expert witness on econ matters; consult to natl office of the NAACP & other civil rights orgs; Michigan Minority Business Advocate of the Year, US Small Business Administration, 1989. **Military Serv:** AUS artillery 1st lt 1953-56. **Home Addr:** 18495 Adrian, Southfield, MI 48075.

GREGORY, MICHAEL SAMUEL
Employment administrator. **Personal:** Born Dec 25, 1949, Barbourville, KY; son of Dorothy Gregory and Royal Gregory; married Linda Joy McCowan, May 13, 1973; children: Arron K, DaNiel K, Brittany M. **Educ:** Kentucky State University, BS, 1973, MPA, 1974; University of Minnesota, advanced graduate study, 1980-81; Ohio State University, advanced graduate study, 1981-82. **Career:** Kentucky State University, Coop Education, assistant director, 1973-74, director, 1974-77; St John's University, Career Planning, director, 1977-81; Ohio State University, Law Placement, director, 1981-87; Columbus Urban League, Seniors Program, director, 1987-. **Orgs:** Columbus Urban League; NAACP; American Society of Personnel Administrators; Columbus Children's Hospital Development Board; National Urban League; Ohio Society to Prevent Blindness Board. **Honors/Awds:** Kentucky State University, Alpha Mu Gamma Honor Society, 1972; Big Ten Universities, CIC Fellowship, 1980; Ohio State University, Black Law Students Association, 1987; Department of Housing and Urban Development Fellowship, 1973. **Special Achievements:** National Urban League, Senior Job Placement Leader, 1988, Affiliate, 1992. **Home Addr:** 3060 Breed Dr, Reynoldsburg, OH 43068, (614)863-1711. **Business Addr:** Director, Seniors in Community Service Program, 700 Bryden Rd, Bryson Bldg, Rm 225, Columbus, OH 43215, (614)221-0544.

GREGORY, RICHARD CLAXTON (DICK GREGORY)
Civil rights activist, comedian, author, entrepreneur, lecturer. **Personal:** Born Oct 12, 1932, St Louis, MO; son of Lucille Franklin Gregory and Presley Gregory; married Lillian Smith Gregory, Feb 2, 1959; children: Michele, Lynne, Paula, Pamela, Stephanie, Gregory, Christian, Ayanna, Miss, Yohance. **Educ:** Southern Illinois Univ at Carbondale, attended 1951-53 1955-56. **Career:** Entertained at Esquire Club Chicago; opened nightclub Apex Robbins IL; MC Roberts Show Club Chicago, 1959-60; appeared in night clubs in Milwaukee, Akron, San Francisco, Hollywood, numerous other cities 1960-; TV guest appearances Jack Parr Show, others; rec include "Dick Gregory in Living Black & White," "Dick Gregory, The Light Side-Dark Side" others; lecturer univs throughout US; American Prog Bureau, lecturer 1967-; Peace & Freedom Party Presidential Candidate 1968; Dick Gregory Health Enterprises Chicago, chmn 1984-. **Honors/Awds:** Author "From the Back of the Bus," "Nigger," 1964, "What's Happening," 1965, "The Shadow That Scares Me," "Write Me In," "No More Lies," 1971, "Dick Gregory's Political Primer," 1971, "Dick Gregory's Natural Diet for Folks Who Eat Cookin' With Mother Nature," 1973, "Dick Gregory's Bible & Tales with Commentary," 1974, "Up From Nigger" (with Mark Lane), 1976; "The Murder of Martin Luther King Jr," 1977; Winner No Mile Championship 1951 1952; Outstanding Athlete So IL Univ 1953; Ebony-Topaz Heritage & Freedom Awd 1978; Doctor of Humane Letters, Southern Illinois Univ at Carbondale, 1989; numerous other honorary doctoral degrees. **Military Serv:** AUS 1953-55. **Business Addr:** Chairman, Dick Gregory Health Enterprises, PO Box 3270, Plymouth, MA 02361.

GREGORY, ROBERT ALPHONSO
Business executive. **Personal:** Born Jun 21, 1935, Hertford, NC; married Barbara Ann White; children: Alan, Christopher. **Educ:** Elizabeth City State Univ NC, BS 1956. **Career:** Rheingold Breweries Inc, acct sales rep 1963-68; Faberge Inc, acct exec 1968-72; 3M Duplicating Prod Div, area sales rep 1972-74, natl market coord 1974-75; 3M Copying Prod Div, natl sales devel coord 1975-; Office Systems Div 3M, competitive analysis supr 1980-82; System Business Dev Unit OSD/3M, market development supr 1982-83; LES/Ed Markets OSD/3M, natl public sector marketing coord 1983-. **Orgs:** Chap organizer Alpha Phi Alpha Frat Inc 1955-56; presenter St Paul C of C 1974; family mem St Paul Urban League 1975-76; natl coord Copying Prod Div3M 1975-80; finance com spokesman Guardian Angels Parish Counc 1977-80. **Honors/Awds:** Author market resource books 3M Copying Prod Div 1974-75; author awareness bulletins 3M Copying Prod Div 1975-80; author competitive awareness books 3M Copying Prod Div 1977-80; prod VTR Series on Competition 3M Copying Prod Div 1979-80. **Military Serv:** AUS Corpl 1957-60. **Business Addr:** 3M Company, 1101 15th St, NW, Washington, DC 20005.

GREGORY, ROGER LEE
Attorney. **Personal:** Born Jul 17, 1953, Philadelphia, PA; son of Fannie Mae Washington Gregory and George L Gregory; married Carla Eugenia Lewis Gregory, Sep 6, 1980; children: Adriene Leigh, Rachel Leigh, Christina Leigh. **Educ:** VA State Univ, Petersburg, VA, BA, 1975; Univ of MI, Ann Arbor, MI, JD, 1978. **Career:** Butzel, Long, Gust, Klein & Van Zile, Detroit, MI, assoc attorney, 1978-80; Hunton & Williams, Richmond, VA, assoc attorney, 1980-82; Wilder & Gregory, Richmond, VA, managing partner, 1982-. **Orgs:** Pres, Old Dominion Bar Assn, 1990-92; bd of visitors, VA Commonwealth Univ, past rector, 1985-93; bd of visitors, VA State Univ, 1993-; bd of dirs, Richmond Bar Assn, 1989-93; dir, Richfood Holding, Inc, 1994-; dir, Industrial Devt Authority, 1984-91; dir, Richmond Metro Chamber of Commerce, 1989-91; bd of visitors, Left VA State University, 1996; mem, VA State University Foundation Board, 1993-; board of directors, Richfood Holding Inc, 1994-; board of directors, Christian Children's Fund, 1997-. **Honors/Awds:** Honor Society, Alpha Mu Gamma, 1973; Honor Society, Alpha Kappa Mu, 1974; Top 75 Black College Students in America, Black Enterprise Magazine, 1975; 100 Most Influential Richmonders, Richmond Surroundings Magazine, 1990; Proclamation of Achievement, VA State Univ, 1991; National Conference of Christians & Jews, Humanitarian Award, 1997. **Business Addr:** Managing Partner, Wilder & Gregory Law Firm, PO Box 518, Richmond, VA 23204-0518, (804)643-8401.

GREGORY, SYLVER K.
Actress, writer, producer. **Personal:** Born Oct 14, 1973; daughter of China Beauchamp and Claude Beauchamp. **Educ:** Herbert Berghof Studio; New York School for Commercial Music; Alvin Ailey, jazz, ballet; Broadway Dance Center, jazz, modern. **Career:** Actress, television appearances include: The Royal Family, The Cosby Show, Where I Live, It's Secret Weapon, Our House, Little Miss Perfect, The Objects of War, All My Children, Another World; films include: Maid to Order, Crocodile Dundee II, Shakedown; plays include: Life in Six, Romeo and Juliet, Much Ado About Nothing, West Side Story. **Honors/Awds:** Youth in Film Awards, Best Young Actress on a New Television Series, The Royal Family, 1991-92, first Black actress to receive this award in this category. **Special Achievements:** Let It Be Earth Day Every Day, CD and video, RCE label. **Business Addr:** President, Sylver Linings Productions, c/o Shelley Jeffrey Public Relations, 433 N Camden Dr, Ste 600, Beverly Hills, CA 90210, (310)288-1887.

GREGORY, WILTON D.
Clergyman. **Personal:** Born Dec 7, 1947, Chicago, IL; son of Ethel D Duncan Gregory and Wilton D Gregory Sr. **Educ:** Niles College of Loyola Univ, BA 1969; St Mary of the Lake Seminary, STB 1971, MDiv 1973, STL 1974; Pontifical Liturgical Inst Sant'Anselmo Rome Italy, SLD 1980. **Career:** St Mary of the Lake Seminary, teacher; Titular Bishop of Oliva; Archdiocese of Chicago, auxiliary bishop 1983-93; Bishop of Belleville, 1993-. **Orgs:** Mem Catholic Theol Soc of Amer, North Amer Acad of Liturgy, Midwestern Assoc of Spiritual Dirs; mem of NCCB/USCC comms as follows Bishops Comm on the Liturgy, chair, 1990-93, education, 1993, doctrine, 1994; board of trustees, Archdiocese of Chicago Seminaries; member, Catholic Theological Society of America, 1980; member, North American Academy of Liturgy, 1981; member, Midwestern Assn of Spiritual Directors, 1981. **Honors/Awds:** Chicago's First Black Bishop. **Business Addr:** Bishop of Belleville, 222 South Third Street, Belleville, IL 62220-1985.

GRESHAM, DONALD
Videographer. **Personal:** Born Jan 8, 1956, Greenwood, MS; son of Carrie Gresham and Samuel Gresham; married Karen King Gresham, Sep 30, 1989. **Educ:** Illinois State University, Normal IL, BS, communications, 1980. **Career:** WMBD-TV, Peoria, IL, photographer editor, 1980-; WCMH-TV, Columbus, OH, photographer editor, 1982-85, 1988-; WMAQ-TV, Chicago, IL, engineer, 1985-87. **Orgs:** Member, National Press Photographers Association, 1989; member, National Association of Black Journalists, 1989; Alpha Phi Alpha, 1975-. **Business Addr:** Videographer, WCMH-TV, 3165 Olentangy River Road, Columbus, OH 43202.

GRIER, ARTHUR E., JR.
Business executive. **Personal:** Born Mar 21, 1943, Charlotte, NC; married Linda Clay; children: Anthony, Eugene Grier, III. **Educ:** FL A&M U; Central Piedmont Comm Coll; Cincinnati Coll of Mortuary Sci, grad 1969. **Career:** Grier Funeral Svc, pres gen mgr. **Orgs:** Mem Funeral Dirs & Mort Assn of NC; Western Dist Funeral Dirs & Mort Assn of NC Inc; Nat Funeral Dir p Mort Assn of NC Inc; bd mem Nat FD; mem chmn Funeral Dirs & Mort Assn of NC Inc; mem Black Caucus; Big Bros Assn; Epsilon Nu Delta Mortuary Frat; Grier Heights Masonic Lodge #752; Ambassadors Social Club; bd dir Big Bros Assn; vice pres Western Dist Funeral Dirs; Eastside Cncl. **Honors/Awds:** Ousts serv by funeral dirs & mort Assn of NC 1972; professional of yr Western Dist Funeral Dirs & Mort Assn of NC Inc 1974. **Military Serv:** AUS sp/5-e5 1963-66. **Business Addr:** 2310 Statesville Ave, Charlotte, NC 28206.

GRIER, BOBBY
Professional football coach. **Personal:** Born Nov 10, 1942, Detroit, MI; married Wendy; children: Chris, Michael. **Educ:** Univ of Iowa, 1964. **Career:** Eastern MI, coaching staff; Boston Coll, offensive backfield coach; Northwestrn Univ, offensive coord; New England Patriots, college scout, offensive backfield coach, currently. **Honors/Awds:** In coll named honorable mention All-Big Ten as a junior & senior; led the team in rushing as a senior with 406 yds in 98 carries. **Business Addr:** Offensive Backfield Coach, New England Patriots, Schaefer Stadium Route 1, Foxboro, MA 02035.

GRIER, DAVID ALAN
Actor. **Personal:** Born Jun 30, 1956, Detroit, MI; son of Aretas Ruth Dudley and William Henry Grier; married Maritza Rivera, Jul 17, 1991. **Educ:** Univ of MI, BA 1978; Yale Univ Sch of Drama, MFA 1981. **Career:** Films, A Soldiers Story, Corpl Cobb 1982; Streamers, Roger 1982; Beer, Elliot 1984; From the Hip, Steve 1986, Saigon, Rogers 1987, Boomerang, 1992; Theatre, Jackie Robinson, A Soldier's Play, CJ, Memphis Negro Ensemble Company, Dream Girls, James "Thunder" Early; TV, All My Children, In Living Color, Martin. **Honors/Awds:** Tony Award Nomination for The First, 1982; Theatre World Awd for musical, The First, 1981; The Golden Lion for best actor in a film Venice Film Festival for Streamers, 1983.

GRIER, JOHN K.
Business executive. **Personal:** Born May 15, 1950, Charlotte, NC; widowed. **Educ:** Andrews University, MA, 1976. **Career:** Lake Region Office Supply, Inc, president, currently. **Business Addr:** President, Lake Region Office Supply, Inc, 477 Michigan, Ste 155, Detroit, MI 48226, (313)963-2626.

GRIER, JOHNNY
Professional football referee, planning engineer. **Personal:** Born Apr 16, 1947, Charlotte, NC; son of Ruth Minor Grier and Walter Grier; married Victoria Miller Grier, Feb 12, 1966 (divorced 1987); children: Lowell. **Educ:** University of the District of Columbia, Washington, DC, BA, 1987, MA, 1991. **Career:** Chesapeake & Potomac Telephone Co, Washington, DC, engineer; Bell Atlantic Telephone Co., engineer, currently; National Football League, New York, NY, referee, 1981-. **Orgs:** Member of awards committee, Pigskin Club of Washington, DC, 1980-; board of directors, African-American Sports Hall of Fame. **Military Serv:** Air Force, E-5, 1965-69. **Business Addr:** Engineer, Bell Atlantic Telephone Co., 1 E Pratt St, Baltimore, MD 21202, (410)736-6289.

GRIER, MARRIO DARNELL
Professional football player. **Personal:** Born Dec 5, 1971, Charlotte, NC. **Educ:** Tennessee-Chattanooga, attended. **Career:** New England Patriots, running back, 1996-. **Business Addr:** Professional Football Player, New England Patriots, 60 Washington St, Foxboro Stadium, Foxboro, MA 02035, (508)543-7911.

GRIER, MIKE
Professional hockey player. **Personal:** Born Jan 5, 1975, Detroit, MI. **Educ:** Boston University. **Career:** Edmonton Oilers, right wing, 1995-. **Business Addr:** Professional Hockey Player, Edmonton Oilers, 11230-110 S St, Edmonton, AB, Canada T5G 3G8, (403)474-8561.

GRIER, PAMALA S.
Actress. **Personal:** daugHter of Gwendolyn S Samuels and Clarence Ransom Grier; married. **Career:** Film appearances include: The Big Doll House, 1971; The Bird Cage, 1972; Black Mama, White Mama, 1973; Coffy, 1973; Foxy Brown, 1974; Friday Foster, 1975; Sheba Baby, 1975; Greased Lightning, 1977; Fort Apache: The Bronx, 1981; Something Wicked This Way Comes, 1983; Stand Alone, 1986; Posse, 1993; Escape From LA, 1996; Jackie Brown, 1997; television appearances include: "Roots: The Next Generations," 1979; "Miami Vice," 1985; "Crime Story," 1986; "The Cosby Show," 1987; "Fresh Prince of Bel Air," "Martin"; plays: Fool for Love, 1986. **Orgs:** Academy of Motion Picture Arts & Sciences; Screen Actors Guild; AFTRA; Actors' Equity Association. **Honors/Awds:** NAACP, Image Award, Best Actress, 1986.

GRIER, ROOSEVELT. See GRIER, ROSEY.

GRIER, ROSEY (ROOSEVELT GRIER)
Community activist. **Personal:** Born Jul 14, 1932, Cuthbert, GA; son of Ruth Grier and Joseph Grier; married Margie Hanson; children: Denise, Roosevelt Kennedy, Cheryl Tubbs. **Educ:** Pennsylvania State Univ, University Park PA, BS, 1955. **Career:** New York Giants, New York NY, professional football player, 1955-62; Los Angeles Rams, Los Angeles CA, professional football player, 1963-68; National General Corp, public relations director; television and film actor, 1968-77. **Orgs:** Anti-Self-Destruction Program; Soulville Foundation; Direction Sports; Teammates; Giant Step; affiliated with Kennedy Foundation for the Mentally Retarded; Are You Committed?, founder, 1984. **Honors/Awds:** Member of Los Angeles Rams Fearsome Foursome, 1963-67; actor in films, including In Cold Blood, 1968, Skyjacked, 1972, Evil in the Deep, 1977, The Big Push, The Glove; actor on television shows, including The Danny Thomas Show, Kojak, Daniel Boone; host of The Rosey Grier Show and On Campus With Rosey; consultant to numerous committees on youth and senior citizens' affairs; author of The Rosey Grier Needlepoint Book for Men, Walker, 1973; author of autobiography The Gentle Giant, 1986; interviewed in And Still We Rise: Interviews With 50 Black Role Models, Gannett New Media Services, Inc, 1988. **Military Serv:** US Army, 1957-59. **Business Addr:** c/o National Football League, 410 Park Ave., New York, NY 10022.

GRIFFEY, DICK
Company executive. **Personal:** Born Nov 16, 1943, Nashville, TN; children: 3. **Educ:** Attended, TN State Univ. **Career:** Guys & Dolls Night Club, co-owner; Soul Train Records, partner; SOLAR Records, CEO/president, currently; Dick Griffey Productions, chief executive, currently. **Orgs:** Founding mem Black Concert Promoters Assn. **Honors/Awds:** Solar listed 11th in 1986 Black Enterprise List of the Top 100 Black Owned Businesses; Industrial/Service 100, Dick Griffey Productions, Black Enterprise, 1991.

GRIFFEY, KEN, SR. (GEORGE KENNETH)
Sports administrator. **Personal:** Born Apr 10, 1950, Donora, PA; married Alberta Littleton; children: George Jr, Craig. **Career:** Cincinnati Reds, outfielder, 1973-81; NY Yankees, outfielder/infielder, 1982-86; Atlanta Braves, outfielder/infielder, 1986-88; Cincinnati Reds, outfielder/infielder, 1988-90; Seattle Mariners, outfielder, 1990-92, special asst for player development, hitting coach, 1992-. **Honors/Awds:** 1980 Reds MVP & MVP of All-Star game; 1972 named to Eastern League All-Star team and in 1973 to Amer Assc All-Star team; tied Eastern League lead in double plays by outfielders with 6 and tied lead in errors by outfielders with 15 in 1972; National League All-Star Team, 1976, 1977, 1980. **Business Addr:** Special Assistant for Player Development, Seattle Mariners, PO Box 4100, Seattle, WA 98104.

GRIFFEY, KEN, JR. (GEORGE KENNETH)
Professional baseball player. **Personal:** Born Nov 21, 1969, Donora, PA; son of Alberta Littleton and Ken Griffey Sr; married Melissa; children: Trey Kenneth, Taryn Kennedy. **Career:** Seattle Mariners, outfielder, 1989-. **Honors/Awds:** Led American League in double plays (6), 1990; Sporting News American League All-Star fielding team, outfielder, 1990; All-Star Game, 1990; Gold Glove, 1990-96; Baseball Writers Assn of America, American League Most Valuable Player, 1997. **Special Achievements:** Wrote JUNIOR: Griffey on Griffey, 1997. **Business Addr:** Professional Baseball Player, Seattle Mariners, 83 King St, 3rd Flr, PO Box 4100, Seattle, WA 98104, (206)628-3555.

GRIFFIN, ANN WHITE
Government official. **Career:** City of Columbus, Treasurer's Office, city treasurer, currently. **Business Addr:** City Treasurer, City of Columbus, Treasurer's Office, 90 W Broad St, Columbus, OH 43215, (614)645-7727.

GRIFFIN, ARCHIE
Professional football player (retired). **Personal:** Born Aug 24, 1954, Columbus, OH; married Bonita; children: Anthony, Andre, Adam. **Educ:** Ohio State Univ, BS, industrial management, 1976. **Career:** Cincinnati Bengals, running back, 1976-80; Ohio State Univ, Columbus, OH, associate athletic director, currently. **Honors/Awds:** Only player in college history to win Heisman Trophy twice, 1974, 1975. **Business Addr:** Associate Athletic Director, Ohio State University, 410 Woody Hayes Dr, Columbus, OH 43210.

GRIFFIN, BERTHA L.
Business owner. **Personal:** Born Feb 8, 1930, Blythewood, SC; daughter of Lula Woodard Cunningham and Dock Cunningham; married James Griffin, Feb 1, 1947; children: Wayne Griffin, Denise E. Bryant, Geoffrey L. Griffin. **Educ:** Greystone State Hospital, NJ state psychiatric technician training course, 1956; attended Riverton Bio-Analytical Laboratory School, Newark, NJ, 1959. **Career:** Greystone State Hospital, Newark, NJ, psychiatric technician, 1953-56; Drs. Burch and Williams, Newark, office mgr, 1957-63; Girl Friday Secretarial School, Newark, director, 1963-71; Newark Manpower Training, Newark, director, 1971-73; Porterhouse Cleaning, Edison, NJ, president, 1973-. **Orgs:** Sec, Natl Assn of Negro Business and Profl Women, 1961-63; member, Natl Key Women of Amer, 1978-83; sec, Edison, NJ Bd of Edn, 1978-84; delegate, White House Conf on Small Businesses, 1980; member, Small Business Unity Coun and NJ Braint Trust Comm on Small Business; member Minority Business Enterprise Legal Defense Education Fund Inc. **Honors/Awds:** Minority Business Woman of the Year, Newark Minority Business Dev Ctr, 1984; Entrepreneur of the Year, YMCA of NJ, 1987, NJ Black Achievers, 1987, and Venture Magazine, 1988; recognition award, Natl Council of Negro Women, 1987.

GRIFFIN, BETTY SUE
Educator. **Personal:** Born Mar 5, 1943, Danville, KY; daughter of Elise Taylor-Caldwell Richardson and Allen James Caldwell; divorced. **Educ:** Fisk Univ, BS 1965; OR State Univ, MEd 1976, EdD 1985. **Career:** Overbrook HS Philadelphia, teacher 1968-70; Model Cities Portland OR, placement dir 1970-72; OR State Univ, dir, field prog 1972-, prof educ psych, dir tchr training prog; KY Dept of Education, dir beginning teacher internship prog 1986-89; Exec Advisor, KY Dept of Education. **Orgs:** Mem Outstanding Young Women of Ame 1977; ed consult Portland Public Schools 1978-; mem KY Col Assoc 1979, Delta Sigma Theta, Soroptomist; Scholarship committee YMCA Black Achievers; Phi Kappa Phi; Eastern Star. **Honors/Awds:** Bd mem OR Governors Commiss 1978; Danforth Fellow OR State Univ; mem Faculty Networking Stanford Univ 1980; OR Governors Commn on Black Affairs 1985; Governors Scholars Selection Committee 1986; National Forum for Black Public Admin: Eli Fellow.

GRIFFIN, BOBBY L.
Company executive. **Personal:** Born Jan 28, 1938, Prospect, TN; son of Kathleen Hogan Griffin and Frank Griffin; married Betty Wilson Griffin, Mar 15, 1961; children: Barbara, Lindonna, Bobbi. **Educ:** Tennessee State University, Nashville, TN, BS, 1963; Central Michigan University, Mt Pleasant, MI, MA, 1985. **Career:** US Postal Service, Washington, DC, senior accountant, 1958-. **Orgs:** Master mason, Charles Datcher Lodge #15, Prince Hall Affiliation, Washington, DC; member, Sigma Iota Epsilon Business Management Fraternity; member, Tennessee State University Alumni Association; member, Central Michigan University Alumni Association. **Business Addr:** Chairman, Board of Directors, US Postal Service Federal Credit Union, 475 L'Enfant Plaza, SW, Washington, DC 20260.

GRIFFIN, EDNA WESTBERRY
Retired educator. **Personal:** Born Nov 25, 1907, Philadelphia, PA; married William E Griffin (deceased). **Educ:** Univ PA, BS 1931; Columbia Univ, MA 1942; additional study. **Career:** Temple Univ Philadelphia Public Schs, teacher, supr cons; Civic Ctr Museum Univ Akron, presently retired. **Orgs:** Mem Philadelphia Teachers Assn pres 1957-60; chmn 1st of Race; (1st of Race) Classroom Tchrs SE PA; ethics comm PA State Educ Assn; 1st of Race delegate State Natl Convens; numerous coms; Natl Educ Assn; Amer Tchrs Assn; bd dirs CARE; mem Student Welfare Council; 1 of founders of Haesler Fund; mem Alpha Kappa Alpha, AAUW, NAACP; bd Natl Council for Accreditation of Tchr Educ Coll. **Honors/Awds:** Afro-Amer Newspaper Awd; Awd Radio Station WDAS; Awd Natl Sor Phi Delta Kappa, Alpha Kappa Alpha, Natl Council Negro Women, Bus & Professional Women, AME Church, Monumental Baptist Church.

GRIFFIN, ERVIN VEROME
Educational administrator. **Personal:** Born May 15, 1949, Welch, WV; son of Martha Griffin and Roy Griffin; children: Ervin Jr. **Educ:** Bluefield State Coll, BS 1971; Western IL Univ, MS 1974; VA Polytechnic Inst & State Univ, Cert of Advanced Grad Study in Higher Educ 1979, Doctorate of Education 1980. **Career:** McDowell Co Bd of Educ, spec educ teacher 1971-72; Western IL Univ, asst head resident advisor 1972-74; Southwest VA Comm Coll, dir of student financial aid 1974-78 (first Black admin); VA Polytechnic Inst & State Univ, counselor 1978-79; Southwest VA Comm Coll, coord of cocurricular activities 1979-84; Patrick Henry Comm Coll, (first Black admin) dir of student develop 1984-89; West VA State Coll, vice pres of student affairs, 1989-. **Orgs:** Mem Amer College Personnel Assoc; mem Amer Assoc of Non-White Concerns; mem Amer Personnel & Guidance Assoc; elected to Comm XI Directorate Body Amer College Personnel Assn 1984-87; bd of dirs Tazewell Co Helpline 1984-86; Martinsville-Henry Co NAACP 1985-86; Martinsville-Henry Co Men's Roundtable 1985-86; bd of dirs OIC Inc of Charleston, 1991; president West Virginia Association of Student Personnel Adminstrators, 1991-92; National Association of Student Personnel Administrators; Psi Chi National Honorary Society; board of directors, Charleston OIC; WVSC Research and Development Corporation, board of directors; Southeastern Regional Commission Drug and Alcohol, board of advisors; executive board, West Virginia Association of Student Personnel Administrators, 1992-93. **Honors/Awds:** Outstanding Young men of America Jaycees SVCC 1978; multiple publications and presentations including "Educational Opportunity Programs—Educative or Not?" 1980; "The Pareto Optimality Problem" Minority Educ 1981; "Adults Making the Commitment to Return to School" 1985; "Cocurricular Activities Programming,

A Tool for Retention and Collaboration'' 1985; Graduate Fellowship Western IL Univ 1972-74; Innovative Practices and Devel in Vocational Sex Equality, a monograph 1988; The Alliance for Excellence: A Model for Articulation Between the Community Coll and the Black Church 1988; Award of Excellence, Alliance for Excellence, 1989; Meritorious Service Award, Patrick Harvey Comm College, 1989; West Virginia State College, Adminstrator of the Year, 1991-92; Innovative Program Award, West VirginiaAssociation Student Personnel Administrators, 1991-93; Retention Excellence Award, Noel Levitz Center for Student Retention, 1991; Excelsior High School National Alumni Award, 1991; Outstanding Service Award, WVSC SGA, 1989-91. **Special Achievements:** Publications/presentations: Innovative Practices & Developments in Student Mentoring, 1990; Bluefield State College, A Time of Crisis and Reflection, 1991; keynote speaker: The Legacy of the Past and Challenges of the Future, Mingo County EOC, 1992; numerous others. **Home Addr:** 807 Elvira Rd, Dunbar, WV 25064. **Business Addr:** Vice Pres for Student Affairs, West Virginia State Coll, Box 188, Institute, WV 25112.

GRIFFIN, EURICH Z.
Attorney. **Personal:** Born Nov 21, 1938, Washington; son of Lucille and Eurich; divorced; children: Jennifer, Eurich III. **Educ:** Howard U, BA cum laude high honors in economics 1967; Harvard Law School, JD 1970. **Career:** Carlton, Fields, Ward, Emmanueal, Smith, & Cutler PA, atty, currently; US Fifth Cir Court of Appeals Judge Paul H Roneyd, law clerk, 1971. **Orgs:** Mem ABA; Natl Bar Assn; Hillsborough Co FL Bar Assn; pres Harvard Club of the West Coast FL 1974-; mem St Petersburgh Kiwanis Club 1971-74. **Military Serv:** USAF airman 2nd class 1959-63. **Business Addr:** Attorney, Carlton, Fields, Ward, Emmanueal, Smith & Cutler, PA, PO Box 3239, Tampa, FL 33601.

GRIFFIN, FLOYD LEE, JR.
State Senator. **Personal:** Born May 24, 1944, Milledgeville, GA; son of Floyd & Ruth Griffin Sr; married Nathalie E, Jun 15, 1966; children: Brian E, Eric B. **Educ:** Tuskegee Institute, BS, 1967; FL Institute of Tech, MS, 1974; Army Command & General Staff Coll, 1979; National War Coll, 1989. **Career:** US Army, colonel, 1967-90; Slater's Funeral Home, Inc, vp, 1990-; Georgia State Senate, senator, 1995-. **Orgs:** Central State Hosp Foundation Inc, vice chair, 1991-; Omega Psi Phi Fraternity, life mem, 1979-; Sigma Pi Phi Fraternity, 1995-; Prince Hall Free & Accepted Masons, 1985-; American Legion, 1967-. **Honors/Awds:** Milledgeville-Baldwin County Chamber of Commerce Comm Service Award, 1993. **Military Serv:** US Army, colonel, 1967-90; Legion of Merit, 1990. **Business Addr:** State Senator, Georgia Senate, 201 Legislative Office Bldg, Atlanta, GA 30334.

GRIFFIN, GREGORY O., SR.
Attorney. **Educ:** Morehouse College, Atlanta, GA, BA, political science, 1980; University of Pittsburgh School of Law, Pittsburgh, PA, JD, 1983; Boston University School of Law, Boston, MA, LLM, taxation, 1984. **Career:** Chief Prosecutor, Judicial System, Pittsburgh, PA, 1981-83; AG Gaston Enterprises, Inc, Birmingham, AL, assoc gen counsel, 1984-85; private practice, attorney, Birmingham, AL, 1985-86; Legal Services Corp of Alabama, Inc, Selma, AL, 1986-87; Office of the Attorney General, Montgomery, AL, asst attorney general, civil litigation division/utilities litigation division, 1987-; Alabama State University, Montgomery, AL, adjunct prof, income tax accounting, 1989-; AL Bd of Pardons & Paroles, general counsel, 1995-. **Orgs:** Member, State of Pennsylvania Bar Assn; member, District of Columbia Bar Assn; member, State of Alabama Bar Assn; member, Tax Law Review, Boston University School of Law, 1983-84. **Honors/Awds:** Student Body President, Martin Luther King, Jr Scholarship to Europe, Morehouse College, Atlanta, GA; Law School Scholastic Scholarship, winner, First Year Oral Argument, received honors in Oral Advocacy, judge, First Year Arguments, University of Pittsburgh School of Law, Pittsburgh, PA.

GRIFFIN, JAMES STAFFORD
Law enforcement official (retired). **Personal:** Born Jul 6, 1917, St Paul, MN; son of Lorena Waters Griffin (deceased) and William Griffin (deceased); married Edna S; children: Linda Garrett, Helen Anderson, Vianne (dec). **Educ:** Attended St Thomas College, St Paul, MN, WV State College, and MI State Univ, East Lansing, MI; Northwestern Univ, Evanston, IL, 1973; Metro State Univ, St Paul, MN, BA, 1974. **Career:** St Paul Police Dept, patrolman, 1941-54, police sergeant, 1955-68, spec, 1968-70, captain, 1970, station commander, dep chief, 1972-84. **Orgs:** Amer Legion Post 449, Hallie Q Brown Comm Ctr, NAACP; life mem Kappa Alpha Psi; Intl Association of Chiefs of Police; NOBLE, co-founder, 1976-; vestry St Philips Epis Church; chairman, C W Wigington Scholarship Comm; Council of Great City Schools, American History Textbook and Classroom Materials Commission, chairman, 1988-89; Minnesota Historical Society, board of directors, appointed, 1992; St Paul Board of Education. **Honors/Awds:** St Paul Urban League SE Hall Award for outstanding community service; NOBLE (Natl Association of Black Law Enforcement Executives), Natl Walter E Lawson Award for outstanding community service; Significant Contribution to the Social History of St Paul citation, St Phillips Episcopal Church and Kappa Alpha Psi, St Paul/Minneapolis Chapter; MN Association of School Boards, Outstanding School Board Member, 1986; North Central Province of Kappa Alpha Psi, Distinguished Alumni Award, 1986-87; Central High School Stadium, St Paul, renamed James S Griffin Stadium, 1987; Concordia College, honorarydoctor of letters, 1988; Spurgeon Award for outstanding community service and career achievement, 1989; elected to MN High School Football Coaches Hall of Fame, 1989; Nov 1990 received the Dr Richard Greene Leadership Award from the Council ofeat Cities Schools; Man of the Year, Sterling Club, 1988; Outstanding Police Work, US Dept of Justice, 1942-83; Minnesota State High School League, Hall of Fame, 1990; James S Griffin Stadium, bust on display; Elected to WSVA Coll ''W'' Club Hall of Fame, 1993. **Special Achievements:** Author, ''Blacks in the St Paul Police & Fire Department 1885-1976,'' Minnesota History, Fall ed, 1975; HQ Brown Center, volunteer work with youths, 1952; first African-American sgt, captain & deputy chief of police, State of Minnesota; highest ranking African-American officer selected by competitive written civil service examination in metro police department in US, 1972; Police Chief Magazine, article on minority recruitment, 1977. **Military Serv:** USN, Seaman 1st, 1945-46. **Home Addr:** 1592 Western Ave, St Paul, MN 55117.

GRIFFIN, JEAN THOMAS
Educator (retired). **Personal:** Born Dec 26, 1937, Atlantic City, NJ; daughter of Alma Washington and Clifton Washington; married James A Griffin; children: Lillian Hasan, Tallie Thomas, Karen Brondidge, James A IV, Wayne. **Educ:** Temple Univ, BA Psychol 1969, MEd Psychol 1971, EdD Ed Psychol 1973; Natl Training Lab, training internship 1973; Yale Univ, clinical internship 1974-75; Univ of PA, physicians Alcohol Educ Training Prog 1976. **Career:** Yale Univ, asst prof dir 1972-76; Solomon Canter Fuller MHC, clinical dir 1976-77; Union Grad School, core prof 1976-; Univ of Massachusetts-Boston, assoc prof, beginning 1979, prof, 1993. **Orgs:** Comm on racism & sexism Natl Educ Assn 1975; women's career development Polaroid Corp 1977; trainer Natl Training Lab 1977-83; pres of bd Women Inc 1977-84; consultant/ed Univ OK College of Nursing 1978-81; fellow Amer Orthopsychiatric Assn 1978-85; assoc of blk psych Eastern Representative 1979; consultant/training Bank of Boston 1980-84; racism workshop Boston State Coll 1981; adv to dir Roxbury Comm Sch 1981-82. **Honors/Awds:** Grant Prof Growth & Develop 1974; Fellow Mellon Faculty Develop Awd 1982; article West African & Blk Amer Working Women published Journal Black Psychol 1982; chapter in Contemporary Blk Marriage 1984; numerous publications including Exploding the Popular Myths Review of Black Women in the Labor Force Equal Times 1982; Fullbright Fellow to Barbados, 1994; Kelloge Foundation Award, 1993. **Home Addr:** 1927 Kuehnle Ave, Atlantic City, NJ 08401-1703.

GRIFFIN, LEONARD JAMES, JR.
Professional football player. **Personal:** Born Sep 22, 1962, Lake Providence, LA. **Educ:** Grambling State Univ, attended. **Career:** Kansas City Chiefs, defensive end, 1986-. **Business Addr:** Professional Football Player, Kansas City Chiefs, One Arrowhead Dr, Kansas City, MO 64129-1651.

GRIFFIN, LLOYD
Banking executive. **Personal:** Born Apr 24, 1948, Orangeburg, SC; son of Henry L Griffin (deceased) & Minnie L Griffin-Callender; married Judith Griffin, Nov 15, 1974; children: Kimberly A, Jason D. **Educ:** Brooklyn College, BA, economics. **Career:** Morgan Guaranty Trust Co, asistant vp, 1970-87; San Diego Trust & Savings, assistant vp, 1987-90; Danielson Trust Co, vp, 1990-. **Orgs:** National Assn of Urban Bankers, pres; Economic Devt Task Force, treasurer; YMCA of San Diego County, bd of management. **Honors/Awds:** YMCA of Greater New York, Outstanding Black Achiever in Industry; San Diego Museum of Art, 100 African American Role Models. **Business Addr:** VP/Senior Trust Officer, Danielson Trust Co, 525 B St, 16th Fl., San Diego, CA 92101, (619)645-3420.

GRIFFIN, LULA BERNICE
Educator. **Personal:** Born Oct 16, 1949, Saginaw, MI. **Educ:** Tuskegee Inst, BSN 1967-71; Univ MI, Addtl Grad Study 1973-74; Med Clg of GA, MS Nrsng 1976-77. **Career:** Univ AL Hosp B'Ham AL, stf rn psychiatry 1971-73; Comm Hosp Birmingham AL, stf rn; Cooper Green Hosp Birmingham AL, stf rn high risk Nrsng 1982-83; Lawson State Comm Clg Birmingham AL, nrsng instr Level II coord 1974-85. **Orgs:** Mem Chi Eta Phi Sorority Inc 1969; Am Nurses Assc; AL State Nurse Assc; Sixth Ave Bapt Ch; Help One Another Clb Inc 1981; fin sec Tuskegee Inst Nurses Alumni 1982; vol diaster serv Am Red Cross 1984-85. **Honors/Awds:** Certified psychiatric & mental hlth nurse Am Nurses Assc Cert Bd for Psychiatric& Mental Hlth Practice 1985-89. **Business Addr:** Nurse Instructor, Lawson State Comm Clg, 526 Beacon Crest Cir, Birmingham, AL 35209.

GRIFFIN, MICHAEL D.
Automobile company manager, vehicle systems engineer. **Personal:** Born May 11, 1958, McKeesport, PA; son of Thelma Webb Taborn and Wilbur Griffin; married Brenda Olive Griffin, Nov 24, 1990. **Educ:** Rensselaer Polytechnic Institute, Troy, NY, BS, mechanical engineering, 1980; University of Pennsylvania, Wharton School, Philadelphia, PA, MBA, finance/marketing, 1988. **Career:** General Motors-Rochester Products Div, Rochester, NY, senior design engineeer, 1980-88; General Motors Staff, Detroit, MI, senior analyst, North American passenger cars, 1988-90; General Motors Automotive Div, Flint, MI, assistant program manager, vehicle system engineer, 1990-. **Orgs:** Co-chairperson, business/corporate committee, National Black MBA Assoc, Detroit Chapter, 1990-; member, Society of Automotive Engineers, 1980-86, currently. **Honors/Awds:** GM Fellowship, General Motors, 1986-88; US Patents (3 total), US Patent Office, 1984, 1985, 1986. **Business Addr:** Assistant Program Manager, Vehicle Systems Engr, General Motors Corporation, Flint Automotive Division, 4100 S Saginaw St, Flint, MI 48557.

GRIFFIN, PERCY LEE
Administrator. **Personal:** Born Dec 10, 1945, Tougaloo, MS; son of Mary F Perry Gray Griffin and Percy L Griffin; married Andrealene Myles A Griffin, Jul 10, 1969 (divorced); children: Gregory T. **Educ:** Jackson St Univ, BS; IN Univ, MS Recreation Admin. **Career:** Jackson State & Univ Alumni Assn of Indianapolis, vp; Detroit Lions, 1969; Indianapolis Capitols, football player 1969-74; Indianapolis Caps Pro-Football Team, owner, pres 1976-; City of Indpls, administrator Resource Recovery - County. **Orgs:** Mem Small Bus Assn. **Honors/Awds:** Small College All-Amer Pitts Courier. **Business Addr:** Administrator, Department of Public Works, City of Indianapolis, 2700 S Belmont Ave, Indianapolis, IN 46226.

GRIFFIN, PLES ANDREW
Educator. **Personal:** Born Apr 5, 1929, Pasadena, CA; married Lora Lee Jones. **Educ:** Univ CA, BA 1956; USC, MS 1964. **Career:** CA Dept of Educ, chief office intergroup relations; US Office of Educ, consultant 1969-; Pasadena City Coll, counselor 1964-66; Pasadena School Dist, educator, counselor 1960-66; Pasandena Settlement Assn, exec dir 1953-59. **Orgs:** Mem Nat All Balck Sch Educators; Assn CA Sch Adminstr; AssnCA Intergroup Rel Educators; mem NAACP Sacramento Urban League; Alpha Phi Alpha; Episc Ch. **Military Serv:** UAS military intell 1953-55. **Business Addr:** 721 Capitol Mal, Sacramento, CA 95814.

GRIFFIN, RICHARD GEORGE, JR.
Librarian. **Personal:** Born Jun 24, 1927, Tampa, FL; son of Esther Hubert (deceased) and Richard George Griffin; married Dolores, Jul 9, 1965 (divorced 1989); children: Felicia Rene, Eric Hubert. **Educ:** Morehouse College, AB 1949; Atlanta Univ, MLS 1951; Texas Southern Univ, 1954-55, Sch of Law Univ of TN, postgrad 1958; New York Institute of Technology 1963-64. **Career:** TX So U, circulation libr 1950-54, univ libr 1954-57, instr govt 1953-57; Knoxville Coll, asst libr 1957-58; NY Inst Tech Old Westbury, dir libr 1959-79; Wilmington Coll New Castle DE, libr consult 1968-71; US Merchant Marine Academy Kings Point, NY, administrative librarian 1979-80; Fayetteville State Univ, Fayetteville, NC, director of library services, 1981-89; Fitchburg State College, Fitchburg, NC, circulation librarian, 1989-. **Orgs:** Member, NY Libr Assn; member, Am Assn of Univ Prof; member, ALA; member, Assn for Higher Edn; member, Fayetteville Human Services Commission, 1986-88; member, Fayetteville Redevelopment Commission, 1988-89; member/pres, Cumberland County Black Leadership Caucus, 1983-86. **Honors/Awds:** Man of the Year, New York Institute of Technology, 1969. **Military Serv:** US Army, 1946-47; US Maritime Service, Captain, 1979-80.

GRIFFIN, RONALD CHARLES
Educator. **Personal:** Born Aug 17, 1943, Washington; son of Gwendolyn Jones-Points Griffin and Roy John Griffin; married Vicky Lynn Tredway; children: David Ronald, Jason Roy, Meg Carrington. **Educ:** Hampton Inst, BS 1965; Harvard Univ, attended 1965; Howard Univ, JD 1968; Univ VA, LLM 1974. **Career:** Office Corp Counsel Dist of Columbia Govt, legal intern 1968-69, legal clerk 1969-70, asst corp counsel 1970; the JAG School AUS, instructor 1970-74; Univ of OR, asst prof; Notre Dame Univ, visiting prof 1981-82; Washburn Univ, prof of law. **Orgs:** Mem Legal Educ Com Young Lawyers Sect Amer Bar Assn; Young Lawyers Liaison Legal Educ & Admission to Bar Sect Amer Bar Assn; mem Bankruptcy Com Fed Bar Assn; mem OR Consumer League 1974-75; grievance examiner Mid-West Region EEOC 1984-85; mediator NE Kansas Region Consumer Protection Complaints Better Business Bureau 1984-87, pres Central States Law School Assn 1987-88; vice chairperson, Kansas Continuing Legal Education Commission, 1989-90; board member, The Brown Foundation. **Honors/Awds:** Rockefeller Found Grant; Outstanding Young Men of Amer Awd 1971; Outstanding Educators of Amer Awd 1973; Intl Men of Achievement 1976; Outstanding Young Man of Amer Awd 1979; William O Douglas Awd Outstanding Prof 1985-86. **Military Serv:** AUS capt 1970-74. **Home Addr:** 3448 SW Birchwood Dr, Topeka, KS 66614-3214.

GRIFFIN, WARREN, III. See G, WARREN.

GRIFFITH, DARRELL STEVEN
Professional basketball player. **Personal:** Born Jun 16, 1958, Louisville, KY. **Educ:** Univ of Louisville, Louisville, KY, 1976-80. **Career:** Utah Jazz, 1980-. **Honors/Awds:** NBA Rookie of the Year, 1981; NBA All-Rookie Team, 1981; Led NBA in three-point field goal percentage, 1984, 1985. **Business Addr:** Professional Basketball Player, Utah Jazz, 301 W South Temple, Salt Lake City, UT 84101.

GRIFFITH, ELWIN JABEZ
Educator. **Personal:** Born Mar 2, 1938; married Norma Joyce Rollins; children: Traci. **Educ:** Long Island Univ, BA 1960; Brooklyn Law Sch, JD 1963; NYU, LLM 1964. **Career:** Modern HS, teacher 1955-56; Chase Manhattan Bank, asst couns 1964-71; Cleveland Marshall Law Sch, asst prof 1968; Tchrs Ins & Annuity Assn, asst consl 1971-72; Drake Univ, asst dean & asst prof 1972-73; Univ of Cincinnati Coll of Law, assoc dean & prof 1973-78; DePaul Law School, dean & prof 1978-85; FLorida State Univ Coll of Law, prof 1986-. **Orgs:** Barbados Indp Com 1966; Bedford-Stuyvesant Jr C of C 1970-72; mem Black Exec Exchg Prof 1971; mem NY State Bar Assn; Amer Bar Assn. **Honors/Awds:** Publ "Final Payment & Warranties Under the Uniform Commercial Code" 1973; "Truth-in-Lending & Real Estate Transactions" 1974; "Some Rights & Disabilities of Aliens" 1975; "Deportation of Aliens - Some Aspects" 1975; "The Creditor, Debtor & the Fourteenth Amendment Some Aspects" 1977. **Business Addr:** Law Professor, Florida State Univ, College of Law, Tallahassee, FL 32306.

GRIFFITH, EZRA
Physician, educator. **Personal:** Born Feb 18, 1942; son of Ermie Griffith and Vincent Griffith; married Brigitte Jung. **Educ:** Harvard Univ BA 1963; Univ of Strasbourg, MD 1973. **Career:** French Polyclinic Health Center, intern 1973-74; Albert Einstein Coll, chief res psych 1974-77; Yale Univ School of Medicine, asst prof 1977, assoc prof 1982-91, professor of psychiatry & African and African American studies 1991-; Connecticut Mental Health Center, assoc dir 1986-89, director 1989-96; Department of Psychiatry, deputy chairman, 1996-. **Orgs:** Mem Black Psychs of Amer; Amer Psychiatric Assn; Amer Academy Psychiatry and Law; FALK Fellowship; traveling fellow Solomon Fuller Inst 1976; fellow WK Kellogg Found 1980; president, American Academy Psychiatry & Law, 1996-97. **Honors/Awds:** Fellow, American Psychiatric Assn; mem & editorial bd, Hospital and Community Psychiatry; editor-in-chief, Yale Psychiatric Quarterly; Associate Editor, Diversity & Mental Health. **Business Addr:** Professor, Psychiatry & African and African American Studies, Yale University, School of Medicine, 25 Park St, New Haven, CT 06519.

GRIFFITH, GARY ALAN
Marketing and sales executive. **Personal:** Born Sep 27, 1946, New York, NY; son of Martha Allen Griffith and Howard Nelville Griffith; married Bonita Imogene Griffith, Apr 25, 1981; children: David Ward, Blair Adair. **Educ:** Pennsylvania State University, BA, Advertising, 1972; Graduate Work, Broadcasting, 1972-73; University of Southern California, management certificate, 1990; Harvard University, negotiating seminar, 1991. **Career:** Commonwealth of Pennsylvania, press aide to Governor Shapp, 1973-77; Airco, Inc, director of advertising, 1977-78; Merck & Co, Inc, advertising media director, copywriter, district manager, product manager, national account executive, sr region director, 1978-, screenwriter, 1989-; Telecommunications, Inc, dir of mktg and sales, 1995-. **Orgs:** Kappa Alpha Psi, 1965. **Honors/Awds:** United Negro College Fund, Distinguished Service Citation, 1976. **Military Serv:** US Air Force, ssgt, 1966-70; National Service Medal, Good Conduct Medal, Outstanding Airman, Pacific Air Force. **Home Addr:** 6309 Willow Springs Dr, Morrison, CO 80465.

GRIFFITH, HOWARD THOMAS
Professional football player. **Personal:** Born Nov 17, 1967, Chicago, IL; married Kim. **Educ:** Univ of Illinois. **Career:** Los Angeles Rams, 1993-94; Carolina Panthers, 1995-96; Denver Broncos, 1997-. **Business Addr:** Professional Football Player, Denver Broncos, 13655 Broncos Pkwy, Englewood, CO 80112, (303)649-9000.

GRIFFITH, JOHN A.
Utilities manager. **Personal:** Born Dec 14, 1936, Greensburg, PA; married Patricia Cuff; children: Pamela, Gail, Jennifer. **Educ:** IN Univ of PA, BS Educ 1960; Fairleigh Dickinson U, MBA Mgmt 1985. **Career:** Dept of Pblc Asst Beaver Co PA, soc worker 1960-1962; Allencrest Juvenile Detention Cntr Beaver PA, cnslr 1963-64; Nutley Pub Sch NJ, tchr coach 1964-68; Montclair Pub Sch NJ, gdnc cnslr 1968-1969; PSE&G, mgr prsnl dev. **Orgs:** Mem Bd Natl Bnk Advsry Bd 1979-; Intercl Cncl Bus Oprtnts 1985-; Edges Inc 1970-; Am Soc Training & Dev 1980-; mem pres Bd Ed Montclair NJ 1979-85; trustee Urban League of Essex Co NJ 1970-. **Honors/Awds:** 75 achvrs awrd Black Media Inc Corporate Comm Serv. **Military Serv:** AUS sp 4th cls. **Home Addr:** 23 Stephen St, Montclair, NJ 07042.

GRIFFITH, JOHN H.
Educator. **Personal:** Born Aug 28, 1931, Pittsburgh, PA; son of Doris Griffith and Cicero Griffith; married Euzelia Cooper; children: Nell, Ronald (dec). **Educ:** Lincoln Univ PA, BA 1954; Atlanta Univ Atlanta, MA 1964; US International Univ San Diego, PhD 1979. **Career:** Coahoma Jr Coll, Clarksdale MS, instructor, basketball coach 1955-63; Atlanta Univ, instructor summer school 1964; City School Dist of Rochester NY, counselor Manpower Devel & Training Program 1964-66; head counselor 1966-67; dir of testing 1967-68; planning & research dir 1968-71; San Diego City Schools, asst dir planning & research dept 1971-76, dir planning & research 1976-84, dir of research 1984-. **Orgs:** Phi Delta Kappa Educ Frat 1966-; San Diego Sch Admin Assn; Amer Assn of School Administrators; Amer Educ Research Assn; Assn of California School Admin. **Honors/Awds:** Rockefeller Found Suprt Training Internship 1970-71. **Business Addr:** 4100 Normal St, San Diego, CA 92103.

GRIFFITH, MARK RICHARD
News/television producer. **Personal:** Born Apr 12, 1960, Brooklyn, NY; son of Gloria E and Fitzroy Griffith (both deceased); married Lori Lynn Alfred Griffith, Jun 4, 1989. **Educ:** Columbia University, New York, BA, English literature, 1983; Emerson College, Boston, MA, masters candidate, 1983-84. **Career:** WLVI-TV, Boston, MA, assignment editor, 1984-86; CBS News/Radio, New York, NY, senior assistant assignment editor, 1986-87; CBS News/TV, New York, NY, remote producer, 1987-. **Orgs:** New York Assn of Black Journalists, 1986-; member & Program Comm, National Assn of Black Journalists, 1989-; member, Writers Guild of America, 1986-; president CBS news division, CBS Black Enployees Assoc, 1990-; member, convention leader, New York Assoc of Black MBA's, currently; National Association of Black Journalists, mem, 1988-, board member, 1995-; National Black MBA Association, mem, 1991-. **Honors/Awds:** New England Emmy NATAS, 1985; Leadership Award, United Negro College Fund, 1987; Positive Image Award, United Negro College Fund, 1989; Technical Director/Producer, United Negro College Fund, 1989; 45th Annual Dinner w/President Bush, 1991; New York Association of Black Journalists, Service Award, 1994. **Home Addr:** 106 Perez Dr, Glen Ridge, NJ 07028. **Business Addr:** Regional Producer, CBS News, CBS Inc, 524 W 57th St, New York, NY 10019.

GRIFFITH, REGINALD WILBERT
Architect. **Personal:** Born Aug 10, 1930, New York, NY; married Linden James; children: Courtney, Crystal, Cyrice. **Educ:** MCP MIT, 1969; MIT, BA 1960; Inst of Intl Edn, traveling flw in W Africa 1961-62. **Career:** Reg Griffith Asso, owner city planner architech; Am Inst of Planners, 1st vice pres 1977-; Nat Capitol Planning Commn, commr v chmn 1974-; Howard Ud profl1970-; howard u, chmn dept of city reg plng 1971-74; MICCO, dep exec dir 1967-70; boston redevel auth, archt 1962-67. **Orgs:** Bd of dir Am Soc of Planning Ofcls 1974-76; bd od dir AIP Found 1971-; bd dir mem Am Inst of Archt; Georgetown Day Sch 1972; chmn Urban Trans Com of Consortium of Univ 1972-73; mem MIT Educ Cncl 1971-F AIP Bd of Examiners 1972-. **Military Serv:** AUS 1st lt 1956-58. **Business Addr:** 1200 15th St NW, Washington, DC 20005.

GRIFFITH, ROBERT OTIS
Professional football player. **Personal:** Born Nov 30, 1970, Lonham, MD. **Educ:** San Diego State, attended. **Career:** Minnesota Vikings, defensive back, 1994-. **Business Addr:** Professional Football Player, Minnesota Vikings, 9520 Viking Dr, Eden Prairie, MN 55344, (612)828-6500.

GRIFFITH, THOMAS LEE, JR.
Superior court judge. **Personal:** Born Mar 5, 1902, Albia, IA; married Portia Louise Broyles; children: Thomas Lee III, Greta Louise, Liza Jane. **Educ:** Univ So CA, 1922-26; Law Sch, 1925-26; Southwestern U, LLB 1928. **Career:** Admitteed to CA Bar 1931; Pvt prac Los Angeles; Los Angeles, mun ct judge 1953-69; Los Angeles, supr ct judge 1969-. **Orgs:** Mem Am Judicatur Soc; Los Angeles Co Muncpl Ct Presideng Judge 1962; chmn Mun Judge Assn 1968-; Am Bar Assn; Los Agneles Bar Assn; mem Omega Psi Phi; Rep; Bapt. **Business Addr:** 111 N Hill St, Los Angeles, CA 90012.

GRIFFITH, VERA VICTORIA
Educator, city official. **Personal:** Born May 30, 1920, Pittsburgh, PA. **Educ:** Univ of Pittsburgh, BS 1942; Wayne State, MI teaching cert 1943; Univ of MI, MA 1954; Univ of MI, addl stud. **Career:** City of Detroit, deputy dir consumer affairs; Detroit Bd of Educ, elementary school admin 1956-74, elementary school teacher 1943-56. **Orgs:** Dir local sch Headstart Prof Detroit 1967-68; taugh & admin summer sch prog Detroit; thcr Evening Sch for Adults Detroit; asst dir Comm Arts Prog at MI State Fair; Alpha Kappa Alpha; Urban Alliance; Am Civic Liberties Assn; vchmn 13th Dist Dem Orgn; past pres bd trst Detroit Optometric Inst &Clinic. **Business Addr:** Consumer Affairs Dept 312 City, Detroit, MI 48226.

GRIFFITH, YOLANDA
Professional basketball player. **Personal:** Born Mar 1, 1970; children: Candace. **Educ:** Palm Beach Community College; Florida Atlantic Univ. **Career:** Long Beach Stingrays, forward, 1997-. **Business Addr:** Professional Basketball Player, Long Beach Stingrays, One World Trade Center, Ste 202, Long Beach, CA 90831-0202, (562)951-7297.

GRIFFITH JOYNER, FLORENCE (FLO-JO)
Athlete, author, broadcast journalist. **Personal:** Born Dec 21, 1959, Los Angeles, CA; daughter of Florence Griffith and Robert Griffith; married Al Joyner, Oct 10, 1987; children: Mary Ruth. **Educ:** California State University-Northridge; University of California at Los Angeles. **Career:** US Olympic Team, track and field member, 1984, 1988; Flo-Jo International, president, currently; writer, children's stories, currently; sportscaster, color-commentator, currently; Olympic Games, in training for 1996. **Orgs:** Florence Griffith Joyner Youth Foundation, founder; spokesperson for various charities; President's Council on Physical Fitness and Sports, chairwoman, 1993. **Honors/Awds:** James E Sullivan Memorial Award, Most Outstanding Amateur Athlete in America, 1989; UPI, Sportswoman of the Year, 1988; AP, Sportswoman of the Year, 1988; Intl Jesse Owens Award, World's Most Outstanding Amateur Athlete, 1988; Track and Field Mag, Athlete of the Year, 1988; TAC, Jesse Owens Outstanding Track and Field Athlete, 1988; US Olympic Committee, Sports Woman of the Year, 1988; Tass News Agency, Sports Personality of the Year, only American every honored, 1988; Intl Federation of Bodybuilders, Most Outstanding Physique of the 1980's, 1988; Harvard Foundation, Award for Extraordinary Accomplishments in Athletics, 1989; Essence Mag, Sports Award for Extraordinary Accomplishments in Athletics, 1989; Nickelodeon Television, Kid's Choice Award, Favorite Female Athlete, 1989; GermanArtising Industry, Golden Camera Award, 1989; McCall Mag, Outstanding Woman of the 90s, 1991; Trackworld, Greatest Female Track Performer in a Quarter of a Century, 1991; US Olympic Committee, Olympian Award, 1992; Women at Work, Positive Image Award, 1992; Southwestern Christian College, Women of the Year, 1992; Valley Presbyterian Hospital, Women of Vision, 1992; Trumpet Award, 1997. **Special Achievements:** World Cup 4x100m relay, American Record Holder, 1981; 200m, NCAA Collegiate Champion, Record Holder, 1982; 400m, NCAA Collegiate Champion, 1983; Olympic Games, 200m, Silver Medal, 1984; Mobile Grand Prix, Rome, Italy, 100m, Champion, 1985; World Championship Competition, 4x100m relay, Gold Medal, 200m, Silver Medal, 1987; Olympic Games, 100m, Gold Medal, 200m, Gold Medal, 4x100m relay, Gold Medal, 4x400m relay, Silver Medal, 1988.

GRIFFITHS, ERROL D.
Advertising executive. **Personal:** Born Feb 5, 1956, Kingston, Jamaica; son of Canute U Griffiths; married Joan M Nealon, Apr 23, 1988; children: Justin, Jason. **Educ:** College of the City of New York, BA, 1977; Fordham University, MBA, 1988. **Career:** Benton and Bowles, Inc, media planner, 1977-80; Dancer Fitzgerald Sample, account executive, 1980-82; HBO, Inc, affiliate relations, 1982-85; American Visions Magazine, sales rep, 1985-86; Johnson Publishing Co, vp, advertising director, JET, EM, 1986-97; Disney Adventures, eastern ad sales mgr, 1997-. **Business Addr:** Sales Manager, Disney Magazine Publishing, Inc, 114 5th Ave, New York, NY 10011.

GRIFFITHS, PEGGY STRAUSS
Attorney (retired). **Personal:** Born Apr 23, 1925, Roanoke, VA; daughter of Lucile S McKay; married Dr Norman H C Griffiths, Sep 1950 (deceased); children: Stephanie D, Norman D, Michael C, Manel, Peggy M, Arthur A, Jacqueline Deneen. **Educ:** Howard U, 1946; Howard U, JD 1949; Cath U, MA 1958. **Career:** Sen Adlai Stevenson, atty leg asst; Appeals Review Bd US Civil Serv Commn, former member/chmn 1968-77; US Dept of Labor, atty adv 1960-68; VA, spl asst to dir person 1968; Howard U, instr 1947-51, 55-58; Am Univ Cairo Egypt, vis lect 1955-58, in Economics 1966-67. **Orgs:** Mem Nat Bar Assn; Am Bar Assn; chmn Parish Sch Bd of St Francis DeSales Sch for 2 yrs; chrmn Commn on Christian Educ for the DC Archdiocese. **Honors/Awds:** Recip Fellowship in Congress Rel; mem Ph Gamma Mu Nat Honor Soc in Soc Sci.

GRIGGS, ANTHONY
Journalist. **Personal:** Born Aug 13, 1946, Chicago, IL. **Educ:** Eastern IL U, BS 1968. **Career:** Bell Tel Lab, pub rel 1975-; Ebony Mag, jrnlst 1974-75; Nashville TN, rptr 1974-75; Chicago Dailey Defender, 1970-74; Sir George Wms Univ Libr, 1968-70. **Honors/Awds:** Musical achvmt Waukegan-Lake Co Philharmic Soc 1964; 1st place Lincoln Univ 1974; Outstng Yng Man of Am 1977.

GRIGGS, ANTHONY
Professional football player (retired). **Personal:** Born Feb 12, 1960, Lawton, OK. **Educ:** Ohio State Univ, attended; Villanova Univ, degree in communications. **Career:** Linebacker: Philadelphia Eagles, 1982-86; Cleveland Browns, 1986-89; Kansas City Chiefs, 1989.

GRIGGS, HARRY KINDELL, SR.
Educational administrator. **Personal:** Born Mar 26, 1910, Reidsville, NC; son of Alica B Griggs and Jessie P Griggs; married Mary Swan Griggs; children: Harry Kindell Jr, Gary Maurice. **Educ:** Shaw Univ, BS 1934; Univ of MI, MA 1948, 1952. **Career:** Roanoke Inst, teacher 1934-36; Yanceville School, teacher 1936-40; Riedsville City Elementary & High Schools, teacher 1940-48, high school principal 1948-59, retired sr high school principal 1959-74. **Orgs:** Mem bd dir United Fund 1960-70; mem Reidsville C of C 1968-87; mem Natl Lib Trustee Assoc 1968-87; mem NC Public Lib Trustee 1968-87; trust County Publ Lib Prin Section 1987; Boy Scouts. **Honors/Awds:** "The Education of Blacks From Slavery to Covert Enforced Integration" 1987. **Home Addr:** 1713 Courtland Ave, Reidsville, NC 27320.

GRIGGS, JAMES CLIFTON, JR.
Educational administrator. **Personal:** Born Oct 24, 1930, Chicago, IL; married Alice Rebecca Cox; children: Eric James. **Educ:** Roosevelt Univ, BA 1954; IL State Teachers Coll, Master of Educ 1964; DePaul Univ, Doctor of Laws 1977. **Career:** Comm on Youth Welfare City of Chicago, asst dir 1960-65; Chicago Comm on Urban Oppor City of Chicago, dir div of training 1965-68; Univ of IL, dir educ assist pro 1968-77; Malcolm X College, pres. **Orgs:** Mem exec comm Metro Chicago Chapter March of Dimes 1981-83; mem bd of dir Goodwill Industries 1985; mem bd of dir Midwest Comm Council 1985. **Honors/Awds:** Outstanding Leadership and Citizenship Dept of Human Services City of Chicago 1978; Human Relations Comm on Human Relations City of Chicago 1979. **Military Serv:** AUS specialist 3rd class 1954-57. **Business Addr:** President, Malcolm X College, 1900 W Van Buren St, Chicago, IL 60612.

GRIGGS, JOHN W.
Business executive. **Personal:** Born Dec 20, 1924, Birmingham; married Leola Griggs; children: Sylvia, Linda. **Career:** E Linwood Lawnview Dev Corp, pres. **Orgs:** Mem bd trst Cleveland Model Cities 1967-73; chmn Model Cities Housing Com 1967-73; unoin comman Local #188 United Steel Workers Am Jone Laughlin Steel Corp 1970-72; mem past jr sr warden Upper Lawnveiw St Club 19712. **Honors/Awds:** Bd Fundamental Educ Awd 1969; United Steel Workers Educ Awd 1971; Parents of Yr Awd 1971; housing and urban dev cert Cuyahoga Comm Coll 1969; housingspec awd Coyahoga Comm Coll 1970.

GRIGGS, JUDITH RALPH
Educator. **Personal:** Born May 2, 1946, Pittsburgh; married Phillip L. **Educ:** Cheyney State Coll, BS 1968; Carnegie-Mellon U, MA 1969; Univ of Pgh, doc studies. **Career:** Westinghouse HS St & Kieran Elementary School Pittsburgh, teacher 1968; Pittsburgh St Acad Program, teacher 1969-70, head teacher acting dir 1971-72; Counseling & Learning Dept Duquesne Univ, asst dir 1972-75; Learning skills Program Duquesne Univ, assoc dir. **Orgs:** Mem An Psychol Guidance Assn; educ consult Pittsburgh Model Cities; adv bd mem sec adv bd WDUQ Radio Sta & TV Sta Duquesne U; adv bd mem Action Prgm Point Park Coll; fac adv Blck Student Unoin Duquesne Univ Gospel Choir; mem Alpha Kappa Alpha Sor; mem bd dir Harambee Bookstore 1969-71; a founder Together Inc 1967-71. **Honors/Awds:** Richard Humphrey Schlshp Cheyney State Coll; cert schol achvmt Cheyney State Coll; prospective tchr fellwship english Carnegie-Mellon Univ 1968; cert Pub Sch in PA area comp English; & pvt acad schs in PA area english reading educ Dir of pvt acad schs. **Business Addr:** Duquesne Univ Counseling & Learni, Pittsburgh, PA.

GRIGGS, MILDRED BARNES
Educator. **Personal:** Born Mar 11, 1942, Marianna, AR; married Alvin Scott; children: Scott, Paul. **Educ:** AR A M & N Coll, BS 1963; Univ of IL, MEd 1966; Univ of IL, EdD 1971. **Career:** Univ of IL Coll of Educ, assoc prof 1976-; Univ of IL, asst prof 1971-76; Champaign School Dist, teacher 1966-68. **Orgs:** Mem Phi Delta Kappa 1976-; consult Nat Inst of Educ 1979-80; vice pres Am Home Econs Assn 1979-81; mem Delta Sigma Theta Sorority 1960-; mem Urban League; mem NAACP. **Honors/Awds:** Recip outstd undergrad teaching awd Univ of IL 1975. **Business Addr:** University of Illinois, College of Education, 1310 S 6th St, Champaign, IL 61820.

GRIGSBY, CALVIN BURCHARD
Investment banker. **Personal:** Born Dec 24, 1946, Osceola, AR; son of Janever Burch Grigsby and Uzziah P Grigsby; married Cheryl, Feb 24, 1968; children: James, Janene, Calvin Jr. **Educ:** Univ of AZ, BA, 1968; Univ of CA, JD, 1972. **Career:** Pillsburg, Madison & Sutro, San Francisco, CA, corporate lawyer, 1972-75; Univ of San Francisco, San Francisco, CA, securities law prof, 1975-76; Itel Corp, San Francisco, CA, natl mktg mgr, municipal finance, 1975-79; Fiscal Funding, San Francisco, CA, chief exec officer and gen counsel, 1979-; Grigsby, Brandford Powell Inc, San Francisco, CA, chief exec officer and chmn of bd, 1981-. **Orgs:** Member, CA Bar Assn, 1972-; member, Charles Houstion Bar Assn, 1973-; vice chair, Natl Assn of Securities Profls, 1985-; member, Natl Bar Assn, 1987-; member, bd of trustees, San Francisco Symphony, 1987-; member, bd of direcs, Boalt Hall Alumni Assn, 1987-; bd of trustees, UC Berkeley Foundation, 1990-. **Honors/Awds:** Author of "Fiduciary Duties of Bank Trustees," Calif Law Rev, 1972; speaker at Public Admin Conf, New Orleans, 1988; author of "Buy, Borrow or Lease?," 1988. **Military Serv:** US Navy Reserve, 1968-71. **Business Addr:** CEO, Grigsby Brandford Powell Inc, 101 California St. Ste. 200, San Francisco, CA 94111-5852.

GRIGSBY, DAVID P.
Company executive. **Personal:** Born Mar 6, 1949, Greenville, MS; divorced; children: Reginald, Kayla Ann, Jasohn. **Educ:** MS Valley State Univ, BS 1970; AMA Mgmt Acad Saranac Lake NY, Mgmt 1970-71; St Johns Univ Jamaica NY, MBA 1973; Donald T Regan School of Advanced Fin Mgmt, 1984. **Career:** NBC TV NY City, coord, sales devel & promo 1971-73; Metromedia TV Sales NY City, dir, rsch & sales promo 1973-75; Arbitron TV NY City, acct exec, easterntv sales 1975-78; WENZ-AM Drum Commun Inc, pres 1978-81; Merrill Lynch Pierce Fenner & Smith, investment broker, asst vice pres sr finl consultant; Prudential Securities, first vp of investments, 1993-. **Orgs:** 2nd vp, bd of dir Natl Assoc of Black Owned Broadcasters 1979-81; adv bd mem US Small Bus Admin Reg III 1979-81, TV for All Children/Viewer PromoCtr 1979-80; chmn media comm Fed Arts Council 1979-80; publ speaker, broadcasting Temple Univ, Hunter Univ, Union Univ, Howard Univ; mem Manhattan Stockbrokers Club 1984-; adv bd mem US Small Bus Admin Reg II 1984-87; selection comm Small Bus Person of the Year Reg II 1985-87; issues specialist White House Conference on Small Business 1986. **Honors/Awds:** Outstanding Sales US Arbitron TV Sales 1977; Outstanding Serv to Youth Salvation Army Boys Club 1979; March of Dimes Serv Awd Natl Found March of Dimes 1979; Awd of Appreciation "To Be Ambitious Gifted & Black" Hunter Coll 1979; Cert of Appt Small Bus Admin 1979,81; Outstanding Officer Cand, Gov Awd NY Militia Awd; Awd of Appreciation Assoc of Black Accountants 1984; President's Club Merrill Lynch. **Military Serv:** NYARNG 1st lt Gov Awd; NY Militia Awd. **Home Addr:** 360 West 22nd St, New York, NY 10011. **Business Addr:** First VP of Investments, Prudential Securities, 610 5th Ave, 2nd Fl, New York, NY 10020-2403, (212)649-4558.

GRIGSBY, JEFFERSON EUGENE, JR.
Artist, educator (retired). **Personal:** Born Oct 17, 1918, Greensboro, NC; son of Purry Leone Dixon (deceased) and Jefferson Eugene Grigsby Sr (deceased); married Rosalyn Thomasena Marshall, Jun 12, 1943; children: J Eugene III, Marshall C. **Educ:** Johnson C Smith Univ, 1941; Morehouse Coll, BA 1938; OH State Univ, MA 1940; NY Univ, PhD 1963; The Amer Artists School, 1939. **Career:** Johnson C Smith Univ, artist-in-residence 1940-41; Bethune Cookman Coll, art instr, dept head 1941-42; Barber Scotia Coll, art instr 1945-46; Carver High School & Phoenix Union High School, art teacher, head dept 1946-66; AZ State Univ, prof art 1966-88, prof emeritus 1988-. **Orgs:** Vice pres, Natl Art Educ Assn 1972-74; chmn Minority Concerns Comm NAEA 1980-85; consulting editor African Arts mag 1968-80; contrib ed School Arts Mag 1978-83; bd mem, Phoenix Oppty Ind Ctr 1968-; bd mem, Phoenix Arts Coming Together, BTW Child Devel Ctr; bd dir, Phoenix Urban League, Arizona Job Colleges, OIC; bd chmn, Consortium of Black Orgs & others for the Arts 1983-; contrib editor, Arts & Activities Mag 1983-; pres, Arizona Art Educ Assn 1988-; vice president, Garfield Neighborhood Organization, 1989-; president, Booker T Washington Child Dev Center, 1989-; chmn, Artists of the Black Community, Arizona 1990-; Arizona History Makers Hall of Fame, Arizona History Museum, charter member, 1992. **Honors/Awds:** DFA, Philadelphia School of Art 1965; 25th Anniversary Medallion of Merit, Natl Gallery of Art 1966; 75th Anniversay Medallion of Merit, Univ of Arizona; Distinguished Rsch Fellow, Arizona State Univ 1983; Art Educ of the Year, Natl Art Educ Assn 1988; 8th annual Arizona Governor's Award in the Arts for a living individual who has made a signficant contribution to the arts in Arizona 1989; Distinguished Fellow, National Art Education Assn, 1985; Visual Arts Panelist, National Foundation for Advancement in the Arts, 1981-85; Contributions to State & Nation, Delta Beta Omega Chapter AKA, 1990; Morehouse Coll, Bennie Trailblazer Award, 1995; Natl Art Educ Assn, Retired Art Educator of the Year, 1997. **Military Serv:** AUS m/sgt 1942-45. **Home Addr:** 1117 N 9th St, Phoenix, AZ 85006-2734.

GRIGSBY, JEFFERSON EUGENE, III
Educator, urban planner. **Personal:** Born May 30, 1944, Charlotte, NC; son of Rosalind and Jefferson Eugene Grigsby Jr; married Sharon; children: Jefferson Eugene IV, Jenna. **Educ:** Occidental College, AB, sociology, 1966; UCLA, MA, sociology, 1968, PhD, sociology, 1971. **Career:** Los Angeles 2000, staff consultant, 1986-88; 2000 Partnership, staff consultant, 1989-91; UCLA, Grad School of Architecture & Urban Planning, professor, 1971-, Center for Afro-American Studies, acting director, 1991-92, director, 1992-96; The Planning Group, president, 1972-; Advanced Policy Institute, director, 1996-. **Orgs:** Rebuild LA Task Force on Land Use & Transportation, co-chair, 1992; Amer Collegiate School of Planning, executive cmte, 1985-91, bd mbr, 1988-91; Amer Governing Bds of Colleges and Universities, bd mbr, currently; Occidental College, bd of trustees, currently; Journal of the Amer Planning Assn, bd of editors, 1988-92; Journal of Black Studies, bd of editors, 1971-80; HUD Scholars, task force, executive cmte, 1980-81; 1010 Development Corp., bd of dirs, 1991-. **Honors/Awds:** Stanford Univ, United Parcel Services Visiting Scholar Award, 1978; Occidental College, Booker T Washington Outstanding Alumni Award, 1987; Outstanding Book, Residential Apartheid, 1996. **Special Achievements:** Speaker: Assembly Special Cmte on the Los Angeles Crisis, California Legislature, statement about urban planning and transit issues, 1992; House Cmte to the District of Columbia, statement about urban problems in Los Angeles since the Watts Riots, 1981. **Business Addr:** Director, UCLA, Advanced Policy Institute, School of Public Policy and Social Research, 3250 Public Policy Bldg, Box 951656, Los Angeles, CA 90095-1656, (213)825-8886.

GRIGSBY, LUCY CLEMMONS
Educator (retired), editor. **Personal:** Born Dec 27, 1916, Louisville, KY; daughter of Ophelia Bryant Clemmons (deceased) and Clarence Clemmons (deceased); married J Howard Grigsby, Aug 14, 1946; children: Richard Howard Grigsby. **Educ:** Louisville Municipal College, Louisville, KY, BA, 1939; Atlanta Univ, Atlanta, GA, MA, 1941; attended Univ of WI, Madison, WI, 1944-45, 1949-50. **Career:** Atlanta Univ, Atlanta, GA, research fellow, 1941-42, instructor to prof, 1942-87, prof emerita, 1987-, chairperson of English dept, 1969-87, university editor, 1989-; Phylon magazine, assoc editor, 1954-89, interim editor, 1989-. **Orgs:** Consultant, Lang Arts, Phelps-Stokes Fund Project for Improv of Secondary School Instruction, 1956-58; sec, Coll Language Assn, 1969-; direc, curriculum programs at Memphis State Univ, Fisk Univ, and Atlanta Univ, 1970-75; consultant, Inst for Serv to Edn, 1971-75; comm member, Evaluation of Teaching of Writing, Conf on Coll Composition and Communication, 1980-87; member, Coll Language Assn; member, Langston Hughes Soc; member, Zora Neal Hurston Soc; member, NCTE; member, CCCC. **Honors/Awds:** Excellence in Teaching Award, Atlanta Univ, 1963; Award for Disting Serv, Coll Language Assn, 1974; Prof of the Yr Award, Toastmasters Intl; DLit, Atlanta Univ, 1988. **Business Addr:** University Editor, Clark Atlanta University, Atlanta, GA 30314.

GRIGSBY, MARGARET ELIZABETH
Educator, physician. **Personal:** Born Jan 16, 1923, Prairie View, TX; daughter of Lee Hankins Grigsby and John R Grigsby. **Educ:** Prairie Veiw Coll, BS 1943; Univ of MI Med Sch, MD 1948; Homer G Phillips Hosp, intern 1948-49; Homer G Phillips, asst resd med 1949-50; Freedmen's Hosp, 1950-51; Univ of London, Sch of Hygiene & Tropical Med, DTM&H, 1962-63. **Career:** Howard Univ Coll Med, prof med 1966-; Howard Univ Coll Med, adminsitrv asst asso prof med lctr chf infectious deseases sect asst prof med instr med 1952-62; Peace Corps, expert adv 1964-; DC Asian Influenza Adv Com, adv com 1957-58; DC Gen Hosp, atdg phys 1958-; Mt Alto VA Hosp, 1958-64;cons 1964-66; Freedmen's Hosp, phys 1952-63; Univ Ibadan Nigeria, hon vis prof 1967-68; Harvard Med Sch, tchr rsrch flw 1951-52. **Orgs:** Asso mem Am Coll Phys 1957-62; mem AMA; Nat Med Assn; Med Soc DC; Medico-Chirugical Soc DC; Sigma Xi Sci Soc Howard U; Assn Former Interns & Resd Freedmen's Hosp; Pasteur Med Reading Club; Alpha Epsilon Iota Med Sor; Royal Soc Tropical Med & Hygiene; flw Am Coll Phys 1962; Am Soc Tropical Med & Hygiene; Nigerian Soc Hlth; Royal Soc Hlth; Royal Soc Med; Nat Geog Soc; Soc Med Assn; bd gov Medico-Chirugical Soc 1960-62; sec Howard Univ Sigma Xi 1960-62; mem DC Citz for Better Pub Edn; St Luke's Episc Ch; Century Club-Bus & Professional Women's Club; NAACP; Urban League; All-Saints Anglican Ch 1967-68; Ibadan Rec Club 1967-68; Ibadan Motor Club 1968; Alpha Kappa Alpha. **Honors/Awds:** Flwsp Rockefeller Found 1951-52; flw China Med Bd 1956; dip Nat Bd Med Exmrs 1949; Am Bd Internal Med 1956; NIH flwsp 1962-6 USPHS 1966; num honors & publ. **Business Addr:** Professor Dept of Medicine, Howard University, 520 W Street, NW, Washington, DC 20059.

GRIGSBY, MARSHALL C.
Educational administrator, cleric. **Personal:** Born Aug 18, 1946, Charlotte, NC; son of Thomasina Grigsby and Eugene Grigsby; married Germaine A Palmer; children: Rosalyn Kimberly, Michelle Alexandria. **Educ:** Morehouse Coll, BA 1968; Univ of Chicago Div Sch, MTh 1970, DMn 1972. **Career:** Black Legislative Clearing House, exec dir 1970-72; First Unitarian Church of Chicago, assoc minister 1970-75; S Shore Comm Planning Assn, project dir 1972; Assn of Theology Schools, assoc dir 1973-75; Howard Univ School of Religion, asst dean/assoc professor, 1976-85; Benedict College, Columbia, SC, president, 1985-. **Orgs:** Ordained minister Unitarian Universalist Ch 1970-; mem Soc for the Study of Black Religion 1973-; consult Assn of Theol Schs 1975-; natl selection panel Fund for Theol Educ Inc 1976; consult Religion Div of the Lilly Endowment 1977-; mem Natl Counc of Negro Women 1979-; member, Columbia City Board of South Carolina National; member, Junior Achievement of Greater Columbia; board of trustees, ETV Endowment of South Carolina. **Honors/Awds:** Fellowship recipient So Fellowships Fund Inc 1968-71; Fellowship recipient Fund for Theol Educ Inc 1969-71; Regional Finalist White House Fellows Program 1978. **Business Addr:** President, Benedict College, Harden & Blanding St, Columbia, SC 29204.

GRIGSBY, TROY L., SR.
Federal government official. **Personal:** Born Oct 25, 1934, Holly Grove, AR; son of Velma May Ammons (deceased) and Roy Vell Grigsby (deceased); children: Shari, Gloria, Alexis, Troy Jr. **Educ:** Wayne State Univ, BA 1958, MUP 1964. **Career:** State of MI Dept Pub Welfare, soc worker 1959-62; Ypsilanti MI Dept Urban Renewal, asst dir 1962-64; Inkster MI Dept Planning & Urban Renewal, assistant director/director, 1964-66; Greater Cleveland Growth Assn, mgr community dev 1968-71; State of OH Dept Urban Affairs, deputy dir 1971-72; State of OH Dept Econ & Community Devel, dep dir 1971-75; Dept of Community Devel Highland Park, MI, admin 1976-79; US Dept of HUD Omaha, NE, deputy area mgr 1979-82; US Dept of HUD Milwaukee, WI, mgr 1982-86; US Dept of HUD Oklahoma City OK, deputy mgr 1986-. **Orgs:** Mem Amer Soc Planning Officials; mem Cleveland City Club 1969-71; Cleveland Citizens League 1969-71; Mayor's Commn Crisis in Welfare 1968; Mayor's Commn Urban Transportation 1968; bd dirs Plan Action for Tomorrow Housing 1970-71; Cleveland Contractor's Asst Corp 1970-71; mem Mayor's Commn on Trans & Redevelopment 1970-71; sec OH State Bd Housing 1971-75; dir Dayton State Farm Devel Bd 1973-75; Gov Housing & Community Devel Adv Commn 1971-74, staff director; OH Water & Sewer Rotary Commn 1971-75; state rep Appalachian Reg Commn 1971-75; Council Appalachian Govs 1971-75; Council State Housing Finance Agencies Task Force on Natl Housing Policy 1973-74; Council State Comm Affairs Agencies 1974; Govs Conf Task Force on Natl Regional Devel Policy 1973; OH Dept Transportation Adv Comm for Highways, Terminals & Parking 1971-72; OH Comprehensive Health Planning Adv Council 1972-74; Fed Reg Council Task Force Intergovernmental Relations 1974; mem, Oklahoma Governor's Small Business Conference Comm, 1987-90. **Honors/Awds:** Plaque Recognizing Outstanding Service, Mil Federal Officials Association, Wisconsin, 1986; Governors Certificate of Recognition, Oklahoma, 1988; Certificate of Appreciation, Oklahoma Civil Rights Commission, 1990; numerous others. **Business Addr:** US Department of HUD, 500 W Main, Ste 400, Oklahoma City, OK 73102.

GRILLO, LUIS
Professional sports official. **Career:** NBA, referee, currently. **Business Addr:** NBA Official, National Basketball Association, 645 5th Ave, 15th Fl, New York, NY 10022-5986, (212)826-7000.

GRIMES, CALVIN M., JR.
Chief executive. **Career:** Grimes Oil Company, Inc, Boston, MA, chief executive, 1940-. **Business Addr:** Grimes Oil Company Inc, 50 Redfield St, Boston, MA 02122-3630.

GRIMES, DARLENE M. C.
Oil company executive. **Personal:** Born Jul 23, 1960, Boston, MA; daughter of Leah E Christie and Calvin M Grimes. **Educ:** Lesley College, Cambridge, MA, BS, 1983. **Career:** Grimes Oil Co, Boston, MA, vice president of operations, currently. **Business Addr:** Vice President of Operations, Grimes Oil Company, 50 Redfield Street, Boston, MA 02122-3630.

GRIMES, DOUGLAS M.
Attorney. **Personal:** Born Aug 11, 1942, Marshall, TX; married Bernadette. **Educ:** CA St Coll BA 1965; Howard Univ Sch of Law, JD 1968. **Career:** Pvt Practice, Grimes, Barnes & Gill, atty 1971-; Univ of IL Coll of Law, asst prof of Law & dir Comm Involvement 1970-71; Cont IL Nat Bank & Co Chicago, adm asst 1968-70. **Orgs:** Has taught real estate IN U; asst city atty City of Gary; Police Civil Serv Commn; Gary Fire Commn; pres Legal Aid Soc of Gary; pres Thurgood Marshall Law Assn; legal adv Minority Businessmens Steering Com; legal adv Lake Co Corner; mem Gary Jaycees; Urban League of NW IN Inc adv bd NW IN UrbanLeagbue; mem Gary Frontiers Serv Club; sec treas bd mem Gary Leased Housing Corp; mem IN St Black Assembly; mem Gary chap IN St Black Assembly; del Nat Black Assembly Conv 1972-74; bd dir Gary Gus Resource Ctr; past mem Chicago Jaycees, Southend Jaycees; former public dfndr, Gary City Ct; former legal & counsel IN Jaycees. **Business Addr:** 562 Washington St, Gary, IN.

GRIMES, NIKKI (NAOMI MCMILLAN)
Writer, editor. **Personal:** Born Oct 20, 1950, New York, NY; daughter of Bernice McMillan and James Grimes. **Educ:** Rutgers University, Livingston College, New Brunswick, NJ, BA, English, 1974. **Career:** Unique NY Magazine, New York, NY, contributing editor, 1977-78; Cultural Council Foundation, New York, NY, literary consultant, 1978-79; Swedish Educational Radio, Stockholm, Sweden, writer, co-host, 1979-80; AB Exportspaok, Stockholm, Sweden, proofreader, translator, 1980-84; freelance writer, 1984-89; Walt Disney Co, Burbank, CA, editor, 1989-. **Orgs:** Member, Society of Children's Book Writers, 1990-; member, National Writers Union, 1987-88; member, Authors Guild, 1977-88. **Honors/Awds:** Books: Poems, 1970; Growin', 1977; Something on My Mind, 1978; Disney Babies Bedtime Stories; Meet Danitra Brown, 1994; feature articles, editorials, essays, poetry and photographs have appeared in Essence Magazine, Soho News Weekly, Colliers Encyclopedia Year Book, & Confirmation: An Anthropology of African-American Women; co-producer and host of The Kid Show, WBAI FM, New York.

GRIMES, VONI B.
Educational administrator (retired). **Personal:** Born Dec 23, 1922, Bamberg, SC; son of Mittie Grimes and McKinley Grimes; married Lorrayne; children: Johnsie Silas, Edgar Gibson, Naomi Davis, Beverly Devan, Toni Gibson. **Educ:** Penn State Univ, attended 1948-51, certificate 1971-73; Univ of KY, certificate 1982, 1983, 1985. **Career:** Philadelphia Ship Yard, sheet metal mechanic 1942-44; York Hoover Corp, sheet metal worker/oper 1947-49; Cole Steel Equip/Litton Ind, supervisor 1949-70; Penn State Univ/York Campus, dir business serv 1970-88; Golden Personal Care, Inc, president, currently. **Orgs:** Past master Soc Friendship #42 PHA 1956-; mem Nimrod Consistory #9, PHA 1956-; mem Himyar Temple #9 PHA 1951-; bd dirs Indus Mgmt Club since 1965-; lay leader Small Memorial AME Zion Church; advisory bd pres York Co Vocational-Tech School 1985-88; budget chmn York County Red Cross 1978-; bd dir 70001 (for drop-out students); mgr City of York Business Entrepreneur Resource Center 1983-; pres, East York Lions Club 1988-89; 33 degree inspector general The United Supreme Council 1986-. secy, advisory board, White Rose Motor Club, AAA, 1980-. **Honors/Awds:** Honored by Smalls Memorial AME Zion Church School for 20 years service as superintendent 1970; honored by York Recreation Commission 1976; honored by Deborah #26 OES, PHA 1980; October 31, 1984 designated ''Voni B Grimes Day'' by the Mayor of the City of York, PA; renamed gymnasium to ''Voni B Grimes Gym'' by resolution (passed by mayor & council) October 31, 1984; received 33rd Degree inspector general the United Supreme Council PHA 1986; York Yacht Club Honoree. **Military Serv:** Corpl 2 yrs, 4 months, Good Conduct Medal, served in Guam & Siapan. **Home Addr:** 112 Lynbrook Dr So, York, PA 17402.

GRIMMETT, SADIE A.
Psychologist. **Personal:** Born Jan 31, 1932, Talladega, AL. **Educ:** Univ of OR, BA 1952, MA 1962; George Peabody Coll for tchr, PhD 1969. **Career:** Elemtary Portland OR Pub Sch, tchr 1952-66; Early Childhood Educ Ctr Univ Of AZ, research Asso 1969-70; Syracuse U, asst prof 1970-73; IN U, asso prof 1973-; Standard & Rsrch Inst, consult 1969-70; Nat Follow Through, consult 1971-73; Guamanian Project, NW Regional Lab, 1970, Dir Facilitative Environmental Devel, BEH Proj 1974-75. **Orgs:** Mem Educ Adv Bd; Training of Tchr Trainers 1972-73; Am Psych Assn 1971-; Am Educ Rsrch Assn 1965-; Soc for Rsrch in Child Devel 1966; mem Delta Sigma Theta Sor 1950-; Portland OR Urban League Bd 1958-66; Portland OR League Of Women Voters Bd 1963-64; mem Pi Lambda Theta 1952; Pi Delta Phi 1952; DeltaTau Kappa 1975; Delta Kappa Gamma 1966. **Honors/Awds:** Recipient St of OR Schlrshp 1948-50; NDEA Foreign Lang Flwshp 1960; ESEA Grad Training Flwshp 1966-69. **Business Addr:** Inst for Child Study, Bloomington, IN 47401.

GRIMSLEY, ETHELYNE
Consultant. **Personal:** Born Jun 13, 1941, Clayton, AL; married Calvin H Grimsley; children: Kelvin, Karen. **Educ:** NY Comm Coll, AS 1975. **Career:** Staten Island Devel Cntr, social work 1962-80; NJ School Assoc 1980-; Roselle School Board, mem 1980-; Lankmark Travel, travel consultant. **Orgs:** Pres Union Cty School Board Assoc 1983-85; mem NAACP; Union Cty Negro Business & Professional Women's Club. **Honors/Awds:** Women of Achievement Awd Leadership & Community Serv Phileman Baptist Church 1983. **Business Addr:** Travel Consultant, Lankmark Travel, 207 Morris Ave, Springfield, NJ 07081.

GRINSTEAD, AMELIA ANN
Broadcasting company executive. **Personal:** Born Jul 24, 1945, Hopkinsville, KY; daughter of Kate A Chilton Grinstead (deceased) and Scott Edward Grinstead Sr (deceased). **Educ:** Fisk U, BA biology 1967. **Career:** J Walter Thompson Co, print media buyer 1967-68, media planner 1968-71, media supr 1972-74, vice pres assoc media dir 1974-81; Test Mkt Media Planning Advertising Age Media Workshop, faculty 1973-75; The Pillsbury Co, mgr of media serv 1981-85; Miller Meester Adv Inc, vice pres media 1985-86, sr vice pres media dir 1986-88; Televisionaries, Minneapolis, MN, owner, 1988-. **Orgs:** Mem Our Chalet Com World Assn of Girl Guides Girl Scouts 1972-81; dir asst sec Girl Scouts 1972-78, 3rd vice pres 1978-81; US Delegate UNESCO/WAGGGS East-West Cul Conf New Delhi, India 1964; staff mem pub relations GSUSA East-West Cultural Conf Hawaii 1966. **Honors/Awds:** Black Achvrs Awd YMCA Harlem Branch; film subject United Negro Coll Fund 1979.

GRISHAM, ARNOLD T.
Bank executive. **Personal:** Born Dec 3, 1946, Chicago, IL; son of John & Gladys Grisham; married Jane, Jan 18, 1969; children: Kristine, Jonathan. **Educ:** De Paul Univ, BS, mgmt, 1970; De Paul Univ, Graduate School of Bus, MBA, finance, 1972. **Career:** Continental Illinois, second vp, 1975-81; Wells Fargo Corp Services, Chicago, vp & deputy mgr, 1981-82, vp/mgr, 1982-86; Wells Fargo Bank, Oakland, CA, vp & loan team mgr, 1986-88, regional vp, 1988-89, sr vp & regional mgr, 1989-94, exec vp, 1994-. **Orgs:** Hanna Boys Ctr, chair of finance committee, 1992-; Marcus Foster Educational Inst, former pres, 1989-; Holy Names Coll, bd of regents, 1991-; United Negro Coll Fund, East Bay advisory committee, 1991-; East Oakland Youth Development Center, advisory bd; Executive Ldshp Council, mem; Parents Council, Morehouse College, Atlanta, GA, co-chair. **Honors/Awds:** United Negro College Fund, Frederick D Patterson Award, 1992; Watts Foundation Community Trust, Business Award, 1996. **Military Serv:** National Guard, spec-5, 1967-73. **Business Addr:** Exec Vice Pres, Wells Fargo Bank, 420 Montgomery St., 9th Floor, San Francisco, CA 94163, (415)222-6640.

GRISSETT, WILLIE JAMES
Educator/educational administrator. **Personal:** Born Aug 19, 1931, Atmore, AL; married Glender Wilson; children: Frasquita G McCray, Johannice W, Zina E Myers, Tchetha J, Weida S, Deri K. **Educ:** Knoxville Coll, AB 1953; Univ of South AL, MA 1975. **Career:** Clark Co Training School, music inst & choral dir 1953-55; Escambia Co Training School, music inst & choral dir 1955-68; Escambia Co Middle School, administrator 1968-. **Orgs:** Dir Atmore Comm Male Chorus 1971-; mem AL Assoc of School Administrators 1980, AL Middle Level School Administrators 1981, Natl Assoc of School Administrators 1985. **Honors/Awds:** Education and Humaniterian Awd United Civic Clubs 1981; Special Service Awd Gamma Theta Chap Phi Delta Kappa Inc 1981; Special Service Awd Kappa Alpha Psi Frat 1981. **Home Addr:** 171 N 8th Ave, Atmore, AL 36502. **Business Addr:** School Administrator, Escambia County Middle School, P O Box 486, Atmore, AL 36504.

GRISSOM, MARQUIS DEAN
Professional baseball player. **Personal:** Born Apr 17, 1967, Atlanta, GA. **Educ:** Florida A&M University. **Career:** Montreal Expos, outfielder, 1989-94; Atlanta Braves, 1995-97; Cleveland Indians, 1997; Milwaukee Brewers, 1998-. **Business Addr:** Professional Baseball Player, Milwaukee Brewers, County Stadium, 201 S 46th St, Milwaukee, WI 53214, (414)933-1818.

GRIST, ARTHUR L., SR.
Educator (retired). **Personal:** Born Apr 29, 1930, Tampa, FL; son of Eleanor Grist and Edwin Grist; married Nancy Jackson; children: Michelle, Arthur, Michael. **Educ:** Univ of Michigan, MPH; Ohio State Univ, BS. **Career:** Cleveland Div Health, public health sanitarian 1955-61; So Illinois Univ, Carbondale, 1961-; Health Zoning & Housing, comm consult 1961-65; Sol IL Univ, Edwardsville, asst to vice pres 1965-70, asst to pres 1970-76, sp asst to vice pres bus affairs 1976-79, asst prof 1968-82, assoc prof emeritus, 1982-93. **Orgs:** Mem APHA, NEHA, Madison County Red Cross, Edwardsville City Planning Comm, Zoning Bd Appeals 1975-81; YMCA; United Fund; United Way; treasure Metro E Labor Council; vice pres Alliance Reg Comm Health MO & IL, Reg Adv Group IL, Reg Med Program; vice pres, St Clair City Health & Welfare Council 1974-80; mem Black Caucus of Health Workers APHA 1969-71; treasure St Louis Health Systems Agency 1970-78; pres Metro East Health Serv Council Inc 1978-80; City of Edwardsville Park & Recreation Bd 1985-86; Alderman Ward 4 Edwardsville, IL 1986-93. **Honors/Awds:** Serv Award Tri-City Health & Welfare Council 1972; Hildrus A Poindexter Disting Serv Award 1975. **Military Serv:** US Army, 1953-55; OARNG 1955-61; US Army Reserve Medical Serv Corps, Enviromental Science Officer, rank O-6 col, 1961-90, retired; Meritorious Serv, 1983, 1988. **Home Addr:** 1912 McKendree Dr, Edwardsville, IL 62025.

GRIST, RAYMOND
Artist, painter, publisher. **Personal:** Born Jan 31, 1939, New York, NY; son of Ena Francis Grist and Arthur Grist; married Adrienne Daniel, Apr 4, 1986; children: Lisa Grist. **Educ:** School of Visual Arts, New York, certificate of fine arts; attended Baruch School of Business, New York, Poliakoff School of Stage Design, New York, MOK Studio, New York, Printmakers Workshop, New York, New School for Social Research, New York, and Art Students League, New York. **Career:** THE MOORS: An Introduction to the Iberian Empire of the Moors in Al-Andulus; JUMP TV, producer, dir, videographer; East River Houses Research Project, Inc, New York, NY, pres & proj dir; Malcolm/King Harlem Coll Extension, NY, former co-chair, dept of the arts; UN Intl School E Harlem Protestant Parish, Thompsons Rehabilitation Ctr, Grant Day Care Ctr, New Mews, BOCES of Southern Westcherter, NY & with Artists in the Schools Program, NYC, former teacher; JUMP Communications Inc, former pres/publisher; R G TV, NYC, partner; currently. **Honors/Awds:** One man exhibitions at Cinque Gallery, New York, 1970, Shooting Star Gallery, New York, 1971, Metro Applied Research Ctr, New York, 1974, Alaska State Museum, Juneau, AK, 1974, Cellar Gallery, New York, 1984, Studio Museum in Harlem, New York, 1984. **Military Serv:** US Army, 1962-64.

GRIST, RONALD
Corporate finance officer. **Personal:** Born in New York, NY; son of Ena Grist and Arthur Grist; married Joyce. **Educ:** City Coll of NY, New York, BBA. **Career:** Aetna Business Credit, New York, NY, former vice pres; Fidelity Bank, Philadelphia, PA, former sr vice pres; Fidelcorp Business Credit Corp, New York, NY, former exec vice pres; executive vice president/chief financial officer The CIT Group/Credit Finances, Inc. **Home Addr:** 1921 Lark Ln, Cherry Hill, NJ 08003.

GROCE, CLIFTON ALLEN
Professional football player. **Personal:** Born Jul 30, 1972, College Station, TX. **Educ:** Texas A&M. **Career:** Indianapolis Colts, running back, 1995-. **Business Addr:** Professional Football Player, Indianapolis Colts, PO Box 535000, Indianapolis, IN 46253, (317)297-2658.

GROCE, HERBERT MONROE, JR.
Cleric. **Personal:** Born Apr 17, 1929, Philadelphia, PA; son of Gertrude Elaine McMullin and Herbert M Groce Sr; married Linda Jane Rosenbaum; children: Eric H, Cheryl M, Karen D, Herbert M III, Lauren S. **Educ:** La Salle Coll Phila, PA, 1955-60; Gen Theol Sem New York, 1972-74; Inst of Theol Cathedral of St John the Divine, New York City 1975-78. **Career:** Lincoln Center for Performing Arts Inc, dir of operations 1978-; Coll of Medicine & Dentistry of Newark, NJ, vice pres for human resources 1971-78; Delta Found Greenville, MS, exec dir 1970-71; The Singer Co (Link Div) Binghamton, NY, admin 1964-69; Fairchild-Hiller Inc Hagerston, MD, engineering planner 1963-64; Mutual Benefit Fund Newark, dir 1977-; St Stephen's Pearl River, NY, episcopal priest asst 1978-; Trinity Cathedral, Trenton, asst 1980-84; Rector, St Andrews Church, New York City 1984-93; Missionary Diocese of St Paul, bishop, 1994-. **Orgs:** Vice pres/unit Serv Boy Scouts of Amer, NE Region 1978-; mason 33 degree Ancient Accepted Scottish Rite, NY 1979; shriner Mecca Temple, AAONMS NY 1980; MBF-MBL Growth Fund Inc, dir 1982-; MBF-MAP-Government Fund Inc, dir 1982-; Grand Chaplain, Grand Lodge of New York 1984-; Grand Chaplain, Grand Chapter of Royal AR Masons 1986-; director, Frances Federal Halfway House, 1986-89. **Honors/Awds:** Good Conduct Medal, Korean War USAF 1951-55; Law Day Award, Broome/Tioga Bar Assn 1968; Silver Beaver & Silver Antelope Awards, BSA 1975; Whitney M Young Jr/Serv Award, BSA, 1979; Supreme Council 33 degree Ancient Accepted Scottish Rite of Freemasonry, Assoc Grand Prior, 1991-; Northern Masonic Jurisdiction, US of Amer 1989; Honorary Alumnus, Gen Theol Seminary 1983. **Military Serv:** USAF s/sgt 1951-55. **Home Addr:** 875 Berkshire Valley Road, Wharton, NJ 07885.

GROFF, REGIS F.
State senator. **Personal:** Born Apr 8, 1935, Monmouth, IL; son of Fenimore Thomas Groff (deceased) and Eddie Groff (deceased); married Ada Lucille Brooks, 1962; children: Traci Lucille, Peter Charles. **Educ:** Western Illinois Univ, BS, 1962; Univ of Denver, MA, 1972; Urban Affairs Inst, graduate, 1972; Harvard Univ, John F Kennedy School of Government, Program for Senior Executives in State and Local Government, graduate, 1980. **Career:** Cook County Dept of Public Aid, case worker, 1962-63; Denver Public Schools, teacher, 1963-66; Rockford Public Schools, teacher, 1966-67; Univ of Denver, instructor of black history, 1972-73; Metro State College, instructor in black politics, 1972-73; Colorado State Univ, instructor in black history, 1972-73; Univ of Colorado, instructor in black history, 1974-75; Colorado State Senate, senator, 1974-. **Orgs:** Co-founder, member, National Black Caucus of State Legislators; mem, Democratic Planning Bd Gov Commission of Children & Their Families; chmn, Natl Conf of State Legislators Energy Committee, 1986-; Educ Committee, 1988-; bd mem, Amer/Israel Friendship League, 1988-. **Honors/Awds:** Legislator of the Year Award, Associated Press, 1981; Lecture on Democracy, Nigeria, 1980; Presentation of Paper on South African Apartheid, Intl Center, Vienna, 1981; Co-op Educ Workshop, St Johns, Newfoundland, 1988; housing study, West Germany 1983. **Military Serv:** US Air Force, Airman 1st Class, 1953-57. **Business Addr:** State Senator, Colorado Senate, 2841 Colorado Blvd, Denver, CO 80207.

GROFFREY, FRANK EDEN
Educational administrator. **Personal:** Born Dec 23, 1944, Charleston, SC; married Andrea Ollivierra; children: Frank Jr, Marlin, Shannon. **Educ:** St Augustines, BS Bus 1967; TX Southern, MBA 1971; Harvard Univ, MPA 1979, EdD 1983. **Career:** Hampton Inst, instructor 1971-75; NASA, contracting officer 1974-80; St Augustines Coll, dir alumni affairs 1984, chmn div of bus. **Orgs:** Assoc dir Ctr for Minority Bus Devel 1972; adj faculty St Leo Coll 1975-78; rsch asst Harvard Univ 1980-82; bd of advisors Martin Luther King Open School 1982-83; tutor Elliott Congregational Church 1983. **Honors/Awds:** Natl scholar Alpha Kappa Mu 1966; Ford Fellow TX Southern Univ 1969-71; EPM Fellowship NASA/Harvard Univ 1978-79; Whitney Young Fellow 1983. **Military Serv:** AUS Spec 5th Class 2 years; Army Commendation Oak Leaf Cluster 1968. **Business Addr:** Chairman, Div of Business, St Augustines College, Raleigh, NC 27610.

GROOMES, FREDDIE LANG
Educational administrator. **Personal:** Born Sep 2, Jacksonville, FL; married Dr Benjamin H Groomes; children: Linda, Derek. **Educ:** FL A&M Univ, BS 1962, MEd 1963; FL State Univ, PhD 1972. **Career:** Project Upward Bound, coordinator, counselor 1965-68, assoc dir 1968-70; FL A&M Univ, dir inst rsch 1970-72; FL State Univ, exec asst pres & dir human affairs; exec asst to the pres for human resources, currently. **Orgs:** Consult HEW, Univ & Coll Inst for Serv to Educ, State Govt, priv bus & indus, Amer Council on Educ, Coll & Univ Pers Assn; chpsn FL Gov Comm on the Status of Women; mem FL Human Relat Commn; FL Cncl on Indian Afrs; exec bd Amer Assn for Affirm Action. **Honors/Awds:** Rockefeller Fellow 1976; Outstanding Educators of Amer; Kappa Delta Pi Natl Hon Soc. **Business Addr:** Exec Asst to the Pres, Florida State Univ, 201 Westcott, Tallahassee, FL 32306.

GROOMS, HENRY RANDALL
Engineer. **Personal:** Born Feb 10, 1944, Cleveland, OH; son of Lois Pickell Grooms and Leonard D Grooms; married Tonie Marie Joseph; children: Catherine, Zayne, Nina, Ivan, Ian, Athesis, Shaneya, Yaphet, Rahsan, Dax, Jevay, Xava. **Educ:** Howard U, BSCE 1965; Carnegie-Mellon U, MS Civil Eng 1967, PhD Civil Eng 1969. **Career:** DC Highway Dept Wash, DC, hwy engr 1962; Peter F Loftus Corp Pittsgh, PA, structural Engr 1966; Blaw-Knox Co Pittsgh, PA, structural engr 1967-68; Rockwell Intl Downey, CA, structural engr 1969-, engineering mgr. **Orgs:** Mem Tau Beta Pi 1964-; mem Sigma Xi 1967-; mem Kappa Alpha Psi 1963-; mem Am Soc of Civil Engrs 1965-; scoutmaster Boy Scouts of Am 1982-88; coach, Youth Basketball 1984-; coach, Youth Soccer 1985-; tutor, Watts Friendship Sports League, 1990-; co-founder, Project Reach Scholarship Foundation, 1994-. **Honors/Awds:** Engineer of the Yr Rockwell Intl Space Div 1980, Coll Recruiter of the Yr 1979-80; Alumni Merit Award Carnegie-Mellon Univ 1985; Honoree, Western Reserve Historical Society, Cleveland OH, Black History Achives Project 1989; author or co-author of 19 technical papers. **Business Addr:** Engineering Manager, AD 69, Boeing, 12214 Lakewood Blvd, Downey, CA 90241.

GROOMS, KAREN VICTORIA MORTON
Attorney. **Personal:** Born Jun 16, 1956, Plainfield, NJ; daughter of Eva S Morton and Edward N Morton; married Kenneth B Grooms, Oct 10, 1981; children: Kya Nicole, Keenen Edward, Ain. **Educ:** Tufts Univ, Medford, MA, BA, political science, 1977; Northeastern Univ Law School, Boston, MA, JD, 1980. **Career:** City of Boston, assistant corporation counsel, 1980-81; Massachusetts Commission against Discrimination, senior staff attorney, 1981-83; US Equal Employment Opportunity Commission, special assistant/attorney/advisor, 1984-86; Delaney, Siegel, Zorn and Associates, Inc, senior staff counsel/director of training, 1986-87; Dukakis for President, administrative coordinator, 1987-88; John Hancock Mutual Life Insurance Company, assistant counsel, 1988-89, associate counsel, 1990-94, counsel, 1994-. **Orgs:** Member, Massachusetts Black Women Attorneys, 1987-89; board member, Ecumenical Social Action Council, 1988-91; board member, International Institute of Boston, 1991-93; bd mem, American Corp Counsel Assn, Northeast Chapter, 1993. **Honors/Awds:** 100 of the Most Promising Black Women in Corporate America, Ebony Magazine, 1991. **Business Addr:** Counsel, John Hancock Mutual Life Ins Co, PO Box 111, John Hancock Place, Boston, MA 02117.

GROOMS-CURINGTON, TALBERT LAWRENCE, SR.
Government Official. **Personal:** Born Oct 21, 1956, Dayton, OH; son of Lucy M Grooms and James Curington; divorced; children: Talbert L Jr. **Educ:** Sinclair College, AS, liberal arts, 1981; Wilberforce University, BS, management; Univ of Dayton, MEd. **Career:** Wright Patterson AFB, accounting, finance assistant, 1975; Dayton Metropolitan Housing Authority, purchasing agent, 1977; Miami University, Ohio, purchasing manager, 1986; Dayton Metropolitan Housing Authority, finance, purchasing associate director, 1987, asset management director, currently; Wilberforce Univ, prof, currently. **Orgs:** Phi Beta Sigma, Beta Xi Sigma Chapter, president; Citizens Federal Bank, CRA Board; United Way, board member; Kiwanis Club; National Association of Housing and Redevelopment Officials; National Purchasing Council; National Association of Black Accountants; National Association of Blacks in Government; Congressional Advisory Council; NAACP; Phi Beta Sigma Fraternity, vice regional dir. **Honors/Awds:** Phi Beta Sigma, Community Service Award; Black Leadership Recognition Award; Mayor's Proclamation for Outstanding Leadership, 1992; Beta Xi Sigma Chapter, Visionary Award, 1992; Top Ten African-American Males, 1995. **Special Achievements:** Elected into the Purchasing Manager Association. **Home Addr:** 5146 Weddington Dr, Dayton, OH 45426, (513)854-9913.

GROSVENOR, VERTA MAE
Author, journalist. **Personal:** Born Apr 4, 1938, Fairfax, SC; married; children: Kali, Chandra. **Career:** Author of numerous titles including: Vibration Cooking, Doubleday, 1970; Thursday and Every Other Sunday Off, Doubleday, 1970; Plain Brown Rapper, Doubleday, 1975; Amsterdam News, Chicago Courier, writer of food column, currently. **Orgs:** People United to Save Humanity. **Business Addr:** Author, Journalist, Penn Center, PO Box 126, Frogmore, SC 29920.

GROTH, CHAD
Sports executive. **Personal:** Born Apr 25, 1970, Dayton, OH; son of Karl Groth; children: Chazz Marie Groth. **Educ:** Minneapolis Technical College, 1992. **Career:** Minnesota Timberwolves, team attendant, 1988-92; Harlem Globetrotters, mgr of basketball operations, currently. **Military Serv:** Navy, basic training, summer, 1988.

GROVE, DANIEL
Government official. **Personal:** Born Dec 14, 1923, Milport, AL; married Mary E; children: Elbert, Donnie, Robert, Maxie. **Educ:** Stillman Coll, BA; Brook Army Med Ctr, M. **Career:** CO State Bd of Parole, v chmn 1974-; Motor Veh Div, dir 1971-74; Loretto Hts Coll, instr 1971-72; Juvenile Hall, supt 1970-71, asst supt 1966-70; Juvenile Ct, probtn couns 1960-66; Juvenile Hall Boys, 1959-60, supt 1958-59, admns clerk 1958; CO Mil Dist, adminstrv asst 1955-58; Fitzsommons Army Hosp, 1951-55. **Orgs:** Mem CO House of Reps 1965-69; CO Work-Release Prgm; CO Prison Ind Law; CO Chidlren's Code; White House Conf 1966; mem Zion Bapt Ch; bd dirs Curtis Park Comm Ctr 1966-68; Red Shield Comm Ctr 1964-67; Mayor's Commn on Human Rel 1965-68; spl com, Gov 1967; bd dirs Boys Club of Denver 1969-73; Mile High Chap Am Red Cross 1969-74; commr Denver Housing Authority 1969-; bd of tsts Multiple Sclerosis Soc of CO 1971-; liaison rep United Fund City & Co of Denver 1971-72; bd dirs CO Prison Assn 1964-. **Business Addr:** 888 E Iliff, Denver, CO 80210.

GROVES, DELORES ELLIS
Educational administrator. **Personal:** Born Jan 29, 1940, Shelby Co, KY; daughter of Mary Powell Ellis and David I Ellis; married Clyde Groves, Dec 20, 1969; children: Angela D Payden, Robin L Ham. **Educ:** Spalding Coll, BS Ed 1966; John Carroll Univ, MA Ed 1972; Cleveland State Univ, admin certificate, 1976-79; Univ of Akron, EdD, 1996. **Career:** Shaker Heights City School District, elementary principal, currently. **Orgs:** Pres & organizer VIP's Social & Civic Club 1973-75; dean of pledges Phi Delta Kappa 1979-80; mem Phi Delta Kappa 1981-; consultant & workshop leader NAESP Conferences 1982-83; presenter AASA Summer Conf 1983; treas LSAC 1983-85; consultant Cuy Sp Educ Serv Ctr 1983-85; delegate & county rep OAESA 1984-87; health fair coord Shaker Hts Int Group 1985; fund raiser co-chair Delta Sigma Theta 1985-87; delegate to rep assembly NAESP 1985-87; natl nominating chairperson 1986 convention NABSE; treas, Delta Sigma Theta Sor Inc, 1994-97; Links Inc, Cleveland Chap; Olivet Institute Bapt Church; Cleveland Children's Museum, board member, 1992-94. **Honors/Awds:** OAESA, led school to 1st "Hall of Fame" Award 1984-85; Natl Assn of Negro Business & Professional Women Inc, Professional of the Year, 1985; "Salute to Black Women Recognition," Call & Post newspaper, 1989; Intervention Assistance Team Trainer, OAESA & State of OH, 1988-89; workshop planner & leader, Natl Sor PDK, Pre-Conf, 1989; led Woodbury School to recognition by the Ohio Department of Education as an Ohio School of Excellence, 1991-92. **Business Addr:** Elementary Principal, Woodbury Elementary, 15400 S Woodland, Shaker Heights, OH 44120.

GROVES, HARRY EDWARD
Educational administrator (retired). **Personal:** Born Sep 4, 1921, Manitou Springs, CO; son of Dorothy Cave Groves (deceased) and Harry Groves (deceased); married Evelyn Frances Apperson; children: Sheridon Hale. **Educ:** Univ of CO, BA 1943; Univ of Chicago, JD 1949; Harvard Univ, LLM 1959. **Career:** TX So Univ, dean/sch of law 1956-60; Univ of Singapore, dean/faculty of law 1960-64; Central State Univ, pres 1965-68; Sch of Law of Cincinnati, prof 1968-70; NC Central Univ Durham, dean/sch of law 1976-81; Univ of NC, prof sch of law 1981-86; Memphis State Univ, Herbert Heff visiting prof of law, 1989-90; University of Minnesota, visiting professor of law, 1992. US Olympic Committee Ethics Committee Chair, 1993. **Orgs:** Elected mem City Council Fayetteville NC 1951-52; chmn Gov's Task Force on Sec & Privacy 1979-; bd of dir Mutual Svgs & Loan Assn 1979-80; pres NC Prisoner Legal Serv Inc 1979-81; pres Legal Serv of NC 1983-85; mem Sigma Pi Phi, Alpha Phi Alpha Frat; mem NC, TX, OH Bar Assns; vice pres bd of gov NC Bar Assn 1986-87; board of directors, American Bar Foundation, 1986-; member, American Bar Association Council of the Section on Legal Education and Admission to the Bar, 1989-95; board of directors, Law School Admissions Council, 1980-82. **Honors/Awds:** "Comparative Constitutional Law Cases & Materials" Oceana Publs Inc 1963; "The Constitution of Malaysia" Malaysia Publs Ltd 1964; pub more than 30 other books & articles; Phi Beta Kappa; Phi Delta Kappa; Kappa Delta Pi; president, Wake County North Carolina Phi Beta Kappa 1989-90; sire archon, Alpha Tau Chapter of Sigma Pi Phi 1986-88; The Constitution of Malaysia, 4th ed. (with Sheridan) 1979; Malayan Law Journal (PTE.) LTD; Tun Abdul Razak Memorial Lecturer, Kuala Lumpur Malaysia 1983; Judge John J Parker Award, North Carolina Bar Association, 1986; American Bar Association, Robert L Kutak Award, 1997. **Military Serv:** AUS capt 1943-46 1951-52. **Home Addr:** Villa 276, Carolina Meadows, Chapel Hill, NC 27514.

GUDGER, ROBERT HARVEY
Business executive, attorney. **Personal:** Born Nov 17, 1927, Mamaroneck, NY; married Priscilla Kirby; children: Margo T, Gail T, Robin. **Educ:** Univ of Redlands CA, BA Polit Sci 1953; Columbia Univ NYC, MA Psychol 1958; NY Law Sch NYC, JD 1961. **Career:** Xerox Corp, vice pres, Xerox Foundation, 1982-93, mgr higher educ prgms 1971-82; Am Airlines Inc, mgr labor relations 1962-65, 1967-71; Rochester Urban League, exec dir 1965-67; Urban League Westchester, asso dir 1959-62; NY State Dept of Edn, rehab couns 1957-59; NY State

Dept of Labor, employment couns 1955-57. **Orgs:** Bd mem Comm Savings Bank, Rochester 1974-76; bd mem Girl Scouts of Am, Rochester 1974-76; bd mdm Meml Art Gallery Rochester 1975-76; bd mem Jr Achvmnt of Stamford 1979-; bd mem Drug Liberation Inc, Stamford 1979-; bd mem United Way of Stamford 1980; Intl Legal Frat, Phi Delta Phi 1961. **Honors/Awds:** Frederick Douglass Award, Comm Serv Rochester 1966; Black Achievers Award, YMCA New York City 1971. **Business Addr:** 800 Long Ridge Rd, Stamford, CT 06904.

GUFFEY, EDITH A.
Statistician. **Career:** United Church of Christ, sect, exec offices. **Special Achievements:** First African American female and lay person to hold the post of secretary of the 1.5 million-member group of the United Church of Christ. **Business Addr:** Secretary, United Church of Christ, 700 Prospect Ave, E, Cleveland, OH 44115.

GUICE, GREGORY CHARLES
Counselor. **Personal:** Born Nov 13, 1952, Detroit, MI; son of Corrine Bowens and Rufus Guice; married Deena Dorsey, May 5, 1979 (divorced 1991); children: Merrin, Morgan. **Educ:** KY State Univ, Frankfort, KY, BA, 1975; Ctr for Humanistic Studies, Detroit, MI, MA, 1986. **Career:** Vistas Nuevas Headstart; St Theresa School, Detroit, MI, teacher, 1983-86; Black Family Devt Inc, social worker, 1986-88; Don Bosco Home for Boys, Detroit, MI, social worker, 1988-89; Gesu School, Detroit, MI, social worker, 1989-. **Orgs:** Co-founder, Be The Best That You Can Be, 1986-; junior deacon, Prince Hall Masonic Lodge, 1989-. **Honors/Awds:** Mason of the Year, Prince Hall Lodge, 1990; Selected as one of the 10 Best Educators, Ebony Magazine, 1989; several awards form various organizations, churches, etc.

GUICE, LEROY
Judge. **Personal:** Born Dec 12, 1944, Fayette, MS; married Rosemary Thompson; children: Leroy, Cedric. **Educ:** Co-Lin Jr Coll, continuing ed 1974-76; MS Coll, continuing ed 1983-84; Univ of MS, continuing ed 1984-. **Career:** USAF, aircraft frame tech 1964-68; Thomasville Furniture Co, plant production suprv 1972-85; Jefferson Cty, justice court judge 1984-; Business Owner. **Orgs:** Brother, mem United Methodist Church 1972-; mason, brother Jefferson Lodge 1984; judge, Justice Court Judges Assoc 1984-. **Military Serv:** USAF airman 1st class 4 yrs; Vietnam Veteran. **Home Addr:** Rt 2 Box 35, Fayette, MS 39069. **Business Addr:** Judge Justice Court, Jefferson Co Dist 1, PO Box 1047, Fayette, MS 39069.

GUIDRY, ARREADER PLEANNA
Counselor. **Personal:** Born Jan 27, Sour Lake, TX. **Educ:** Xavier Univ New Orleans, 1938; OH State Univ Columbus, 1940-42; Prairie View A&M Univ TX, MS 1958. **Career:** Port Arthur Ind School Dist, counselor 1962; Prairie View A&M Univ, assoc prof 1968, instructor 1959; Port Arthur Ind School Dist, teacher, coach1949; Xavier Univ, Lake Charles LA, instructor 1939. **Orgs:** Com person Nat Merit Scholarship Corp 1980; dir Prairie View Off-Campus Ctr 1976; consult Texas A&M Vocational Doctoral Prgm 1972; mem Delta Sigma Theta Sor Inc/ Nat Educ Assn/Am Personnel & Guidance Assn/TX Classroom Tchrs Assn/TX State Tchrs Assn; sec-treas Assn of Coll Educ & Suprs; pres Delta Sigma Theta Sor 1975; coord guidance & serv Lincoln HS 1962. **Honors/Awds:** Phi Delta Kappa Award; Outstanding Edn, Prairie View A&M Univ 1977. **Business Addr:** Port Arthur Ind Sch Dist, PO Box 1388, Port Arthur, TX 77640.

GUIDRY, DAVID
Metalworking company executive. **Personal:** Born Aug 20, 1957, Opelousas, LA; son of Agnes Guidry and Raphael Guidry; married Brenda Dupuy, Dec 10, 1979; children: Raphael, Amber. **Educ:** Louisiana Tech University, 1975-77; TH Harris Vocational Tech, Associate, 1979. **Career:** Bibbins & Rice Electronics, technician, 1979-82; Guico Machine Works, president & CEO, 1982-. **Orgs:** Gulf South Minority Purchasing Council, board member, 1989-; Harvey Canal Industrial Association, board member, 1991-; Louisiana Regional Vo-Tech Board, 1990-; Governor's Task Force on African Trade & Finance, appointed member, 1992-; Black Economic Development Council, 1990-; Chamber of Commerce, 1989-. **Honors/Awds:** Jefferson Parish Economic Development, Charlet Bus Award, 1994; State of LA, Mfgs; Latern Award, 1994; US Chamber of Commerce, Blue Chip Enterprise Initiative Award, 1993; State of LA, Minority Bus Person of the Year, 1993; SBA, Minority Business Advocate of the Year, 1992; Chamber of Commerce, Small Business Champion, 1991; GSMPC, Minority Business Enterprise Award, 1988; Lincoln Career Center, Employer of the Year, 1987. **Special Achievements:** Featured in Times-Picayune Money Section profiling Guico, 1992; featured by CBS & NBC affiliates on Guico's business Kuwait, 1991. **Business Addr:** President & CEO, Guico Machine Works, Inc, 1170 Destrehan Ave, Harvey, LA 70058-2519, (504)340-7111.

GUILFORD, DIANE PATTON
Librarian. **Personal:** Born Feb 15, 1949, Detroit, MI; daughter of Kathleen Droughn Patton (deceased) and Nesbitt B Patton; married Samuel Guilford, Jun 2, 1973. **Educ:** Kentucky State University, Frankfort, KY, BA, 1970; Atlanta University, Atlanta, GA, MSLS, 1971. **Career:** Atlanta Public Library, Atlanta, GA, asst branch head, 1971-73; Frostproof Public Library, Frostproof, FL, consultant, 1972; Romulus Community Schools, Romulus, MI, media specialist, 1973-77; Fairfax County Public Schools, Springfield, VA, head librarian, 1978-. **Orgs:** Vice pres, Alpha Kappa Alpha/Lambda Kappa Omega Chapter, 1990-91; vice pres, National Council of Negro Women, Reston Chapter, 1982-83; chairperson, Virginia Library Assn, Sch Library Section, 1991-92; chairperson, Southeastern Library Assn, Outstanding Southeastern Authors Committee, 1987-89; Old Dominion Chapter, The Links, Inc, charter mem. **Honors/Awds:** Human Relations Award, 1986, Commendation for Professional Excellence, 1987, Fairfax County Schools; Amer Library Assn Award for Programs for Youth in School and Public Libraries, 1994. **Business Addr:** Head Librarian, Fairfax County Public Schools, Herndon High School, 700 Bennett St, Herndon, VA 20170.

GUILLAUME, ALFRED JOSEPH, JR.
Educator. **Personal:** Born Apr 10, 1947, New Orleans, LA; married Bernice Forrest; children: Alfred III. **Educ:** Xavier Univ of LA, BA 1968; Brown Univ, AM 1972, PhD 1976. **Career:** Xavier Univ, coord of admissions 1977-78, dean of freshman studies 1978-80, dean of arts & sci 1980-. **Orgs:** Bd codofil Council of Devel of French in LA 1976-; asst treas Coll Lang Assoc 1978-81;section chmn South Central Modern Lang Assoc 1978-79; pres LA Collegiate Honors Council 1980-81; mem Amer Conf of Acad Deans, Natl Assoc of Coll Deans Registrars & Admissions Officers, LA Council of Deans of Arts & Sci, Assoc of Amer Coll, Amer Assoc of Teachers of French, Coll Lang Assoc; gov appointee & mem acad advisory council Devel of French in LA; pres LA Collegiate Honors Council 1980-81; Louisianais Athenee; assoc mem Sociedad Nacional Hispanica; reader title III proposals Dept of Ed; presentor & discussion leader Competency Assessment in Teacher Ed; panelist Ed Testing Serv Workshop on Testing Dallas TX; consult Methods of Improving Oral Communication in theTarget Language. **Honors/Awds:** Fulbright-Hays Teaching Assistantship Intl Inst of Ed 1974-75; Baudelaire & Nature, South Central Modern Lang Assoc Convention 1977; ''Conversation with Leopold Sedar Senghor on His Poetry & Baudelaire's'' French Review 1978; ''The Baudelairian Imagination, Positive Approaches to Nature'' Coll Lang Assoc Jrnl 1979; ''To Spring'' (Au Printemps) New Laurel Review 1980; ''Women and Love in the Poetry of the Free People of Color'' South Central Modern Lang Assoc Conv 1980; ''The Emotive Impulse & the Senghorian Response to Nature'' Coll Lang Assoc Conv 1980; ''Literature in Nineteenth Century LA, Poetry & the Free People of Color'' Jambalaya Public Library Lecture Series 1980; ''Jeanne Duval as the Cornerstone of the Baudelairian Imagination'' South Central Modern Lang Assn Convention 1982; ''Love Death &ith in the New Orleans Poets or Color'' Southern Quarterly 1982; ''Joanni Questi, Monsieur Paul'' LA Literature 1984; ''Le Divin Mystere, Religious Fervor in the Literature of the Free People of Color'' Southern Conf on Christianity in Literature 1984. **Military Serv:** AUS sp4 2 yrs; Commendation Medal, Bronze Star 1970. **Business Addr:** Dean of Arts & Sciences, Xavier University of LA, 7325 Palmetto St, New Orleans, LA 70125.

GUILLAUME, ROBERT
Actor, producer. **Personal:** Born Nov 30, 1937, St Louis, MO; married Donna, 1985; children: four. **Educ:** St Louis University, attended; Washington University, attended; studied musical theater and opera. **Career:** Theater appearances include: Fly Blackbird, 1962; No Place to Be Somebody, 1969-70; Fire in the Mindhouse, 1970-71; Purlie, 1971-72; Benito Cereno, 1975-76; Don Juan, 1977; Guys and Dolls, 1976; The Phantom of the Opera, 1990; film appearances include: Seems Like Old Times, 1980; Prince Jack, 1985; Wanted: Dead or Alive, 1987; Lean On Me, 1989; television appearances include: Soap, 1977-79; Benson, 1979-86; roles in numerous episodic shows, 1979-90; Perry Mason: The Case of the Scandalous Scoundrel, 1987; Fire and Rain, 1989; North and South, 1985; appears in many television specials, 1972-; The Kid with the 200 I Q, executive producer, 1983; John Grin's Christmas Special, executive producer/director, 1986; The Robert Guillame Show, executive producer/actor, 1989. **Orgs:** Screen Actors Guild; American Federation of Television & Radio Artists. **Honors/Awds:** Emmy Award, Outstanding Supporting Actor in a Comedy, 1978-79; Emmy Award, Oustanding Lead Actor in a Comedy, 1984-85; recipient, four NAACP Image Awards.

GUILLEBEAUX, TAMARA ELISE
Educator, opera administrator. **Personal:** Born Mar 29, Philadelphia, PA. **Educ:** Robt Joffrey Sch of Ballet, scholarship; Butler Univ IN, BA; NY Univ, MA; PA Ballet Co Sch of Dance; Judimar Sch of Dance; Marion Cuyjet; Essie Marie Dorsey Sch of Dance. **Career:** Metropolitan Opera Lincoln Center, admin devel dept 1986-. **Orgs:** Cultural emissary intl tour to Africa, Syria, Portugal US Intl Communic Agency; mem Alpha Kappa Alpha Sor Inc; bd of dirs Saraband Ltd; dir Scholarship Devel Saraband Ltd 1985-; member, National Assn of Female Executives; Special advisor, board of directors, Robin Becker & Co; New York Foundation for the Arts, panelist, 1992-95; Natl Coalition of 100 Black Women, 1994-96. **Honors/Awds:** Rosenblith Scholarship Awd; soloist 51st Boule AKA Sor 1984; participant Intl Olympics Black Dance Art Festival 1984; co-producer ''Spring Flowering of Arts'' Saraband Ltd Scholarship Prog 1983-; consultant, Career Counseling in the Performing Arts. **Business Addr:** Admin Development Dept, Metropolitan Opera Association, Lincoln Center, New York, NY 10023.

GUILLORY, JULIUS JAMES
Law officer (retired). **Personal:** Born Feb 4, 1927, Opelousas, LA; married Charity Belle Morris. **Educ:** LA State U; So U. **Career:** Opelousas City Court, deputy marshall, currently; Opelousas, LA, asst police chief 1970-96; police capt 1965-70; police lt 1960-65; patrolman 1954-60. **Orgs:** Mem LA Chief Assn; LA Preace Officers Assn; Magnolia State Peace Officers Assn; Municipal Police Officers Assn of LA; Nat Black Police Assn; Nat Org of Black Police Exec; Am Legion; BSA; Foxes Social Club; Frontiers Internat; Holy Ghost Ch Ushers Club; Knights of Peter Claver; NAACP. **Honors/Awds:** KPC Silver Medal Nat Counc, Knights of Peter Claver 1973; KPC Knight of the Year, Knights of Peter Claver 1972; VFW Officer of the Yr 1972; Officer of the Yr, Magnolia State Peace Officers Assn 1970; Nat Black Police Assn Workship 1975-76; Knights of Peter Claver National Council, Gold Medal of Honor, 1988. **Military Serv:** AUS 1945-46.

GUILLORY, KEVEN
Anchor, reporter. **Personal:** Born Feb 20, 1953, Berkeley, CA; son of Emma Crenshaw and Jesse Guillory; married Arleigh Prelow (divorced 1986); children: Alison, Kara; married Donna Barati-Guillory, Mar 24, 1990; children: Maiya. **Educ:** College of Alameda, 1970-72; University of California, Berkeley, CA, 1973-74; Stanford University, Stanford, CA, fellowship 1990-91. **Career:** KSOL, San Mateo, CA, news/public affairs reporter, 1974-75; KBLX, Berkeley, CA, news director, 1976-79; KIOI, San Francisco, CA, public affairs director, 1979-80; Youth News, Oakland, CA, teacher, 1980-82; KQED Inc, San Francisco, CA, producer/reporter, 1985-. **Orgs:** Member, national Association of Black Journalists, 1981-; former president, current member, Bay Area Black Journalists Association, 1983-; member, RTNDA, Radio Television News Directors Association; Bass Anglers Sportsmen Society. **Honors/Awds:** Associated Press News Award for Feature News, Associated Press, 1989, 1990; John Knight Journalism Fellowship, Stanford University, 1990-91. **Business Addr:** Anchor, Reporter, KQED-FM, 2601 Mariposa St, San Francisco, CA 94110, (415)553-2368.

GUILLORY, LINDA SEMIEN
Business owner. **Personal:** Born Oct 4, 1950, Lake Charles, LA; daughter of Adeline Semien and Leo Semien; divorced; children: Tina G, Ashley F. **Educ:** University of Colorado, BA, 1985. **Career:** Mountain Bell, manager, 1970-85; Transformative Management, Inc, president, owner, 1985-. **Orgs:** Mayor's Committee on Employment, 1992-; Denver Victims Service Center, board member, 1989-90; Colorado Black Professionals, vice pres, 1989-90; Colorado Black Chamber of Commerce, board member, 1988-91. **Honors/Awds:** Public Service Co of Colorado, Continued Leadership in Pluralism Award, 1987; US West, Inc, Dedication to Women of Color Project Award, 1989. **Special Achievements:** Published manual, Myth and Methods for Managing a Multi-cultural Workforce, 1989. **Business Phone:** (303)399-1165.

GUILLORY, WILLIAM A.
Educator. **Personal:** Born Dec 4, 1938, New Orleans, LA; children: William Jr, Daniel S. **Educ:** Dillard Univ, BA 1960; Univ CA, PhD 1964. **Career:** Howard Univ, asst prof 1965-69; Drexel Univ, assoc prof 1969-74; Univ of UT, assoc prof Chemistry 1974-76, prof & chmn Chemistry 1976-. **Orgs:** Consult Naval Ordnance Station 1967-76; adv com EPA 1972-75; adv panel NSF 1974-77; natl chmn Professional Black Chemists & Chemical Engrs 1972-; consult Natl Acad Scis 1973-74; author num publs; mem Amer Chem Soc; mem Beta Kappa Chi; mem Sigma Xi, Alpha Chi Sigma, Amer Physical Soc, AAAS, NY Acad Sci, Phi Kappa Phi. **Honors/Awds:** NSF Postdoctoral Fellow Univ Paris 1964-65; Alfred P Sloan Found Fellow 1971-73; Outstanding Educators Amer 1972; Merit Awd City New Orleans 1974; DanfortFound Assn 1975. **Business Addr:** Chairman of Chemistry, Univ Utah, Dept of Chemistry, Salt Lake City, UT 84112.

GUILMENOT, RICHARD ARTHUR, III
Business executive. **Personal:** Born Mar 15, 1948, Detroit, MI; married Melanie Williams. **Educ:** Fisk U, BA 1970; Northwestern U, M BA 1972. **Career:** Ted Bater Adv, acct exec 1972-74; BBDO Adv, acct supr vice pres 1974-77; Mingo Jones Guilmendt, vice pres dir client serv 1977-79; Warner Am Satellite Ent Co, vice pres mktg 1980-82; GCI, pres. **Orgs:** Dir Natl Urban League 1978-81; advsr Amsterdam News 1977-82; barileur Omega Psi Phy 1970-. **Business Addr:** President, GCI, 92 Grandview Ave, Great Neck, NY 11020.

GUINIER, CAROL LANI (LANI)
Attorney, educator. **Personal:** marrled. **Educ:** Radcliffe College, BA, 1971; Yale Law School, JD, 1974. **Career:** US Dis-

trict Judge, Damon Keith, clerk, 1974-76; Wayne County Juvenile Court, referee, 1976-77; US Dept of Justice, Civil Rights Division, 1977-81; NAACP Legal Defense Fund, 1981-88; Univ of Pennsylvania, law prof, 1992-. **Orgs:** Open Society Institute, trustee, 1996-; Commonplace, Inc, founder/president, 1994; Juvenile Law Ctr, Philadelphia, PA, bd of dirs, 1992-. **Honors/Awds:** Univ Penn Law School, Harvey Levin Teaching Award, 1994. **Special Achievements:** Christian Science Monitor, essay, 1991. **Business Addr:** Professor of Law, University of Pennsylvania, 3400 Chestnut St, Philadelphia, PA 19104, (215)898-5000.

GUITANO, ANTON W.
Broadcasting company executive. **Personal:** Born Jul 5, 1950, Brooklyn, NY; son of Blanche Epps Guitano and Whitney J Guitano; married Leslie Marie Ferguson, Jun 15, 1975; children: Jessica Lynn, Jennifer Whitney, Jason Anton. **Educ:** St Peters Coll, Jersey City NJ, BS, 1971. **Career:** Price Waterhouse, New York NY, sr auditor, 1971-78; CBS Inc, New York NY, sr dir auditing, 1978-83; CBS Television Stations, New York NY, controller, 1983-86; CBS Television Network, New York NY, controller, 1986-88; CBS Inc, New York NY, vice pres, gen auditor, 1988-. **Orgs:** Mem, Amer Inst of Certified Public Accountants, 1979-, NYSSCPA, 1979-; pres, Walden & Country Woods Homeowners Assn, 1980-84; mem, Broadcast Financial Mgmt Assn, 1983-, Natl Assn of Broadcasters, 1983-; member, Institute of Internal Auditors; Inst of Internal Auditors, NY State Chapter, bd of governors, 1995-98; mem, Financial Exec Inst, 1995; NY, Internal Audit Industry Comm, 1995. **Honors/Awds:** Certified Public Accountant, New York State Dept of Educ, 1979. **Business Addr:** Vice President & General Auditor, CBS Inc, 51 W 52nd St, Room 2164, New York, NY 10019.

GUITON HILL, BONNIE
Foundation executive. **Personal:** Born Oct 30, 1941, Springfield, IL; daughter of Zola Elizabeth Newman Brazelton and Henry Frank Brazelton; married Walter; children: three. **Educ:** Mills Coll, Oakland CA, BA, 1974; California State Univ, Hayward CA, MS, 1975; Univ of California, Berkeley CA, EdD, 1985. **Career:** Mills Coll, asst dean of students 1974-76; Marcus Foster Educ Inst, exec dir 1976-79; Kaiser Ctr Inc, vice pres & genl mgr 1979-84; US Postal Rate Commn, commissioner 1984-87; US Dept of Educ Washington, DC asst sec 1987-89; US Office of Consumer Affairs, Washington DC, special adviser to the pres & director 1989-90; Earth Conservation Corps, CEO, 1990-91; State of California, State and Consumer Services Agency, sec beginning 1991; University of Virginia, McIntire School of Commerce, dean, professor; The Times Mirror Company, vice pres, currently; The Times Mirror Foundation, pres/CEO, currently. **Orgs:** Northern CA NAACP Legal Defense Fund 1979-84; bd of directors Northern CA Conf of Christians & Jews Assn 1983-86; Natl Urban Coalition 1984-85; Urban Land Inst 1982-84; Natl Assn of Regulatory Utility Comrs 1984-87; Exec Women in Govt 1985-; bd of directors, Natl Museum for Women in the Arts 1988-89; board of directors, Niagara Mohawk Power Corporation, 1991-; RREEF - America LLC, 1992-; Louisiana Pacific Corporation, 1993-; Hershey Foods Corporation, 1993-; AK Steel Holding Corporation, 1994-; Crestar Financial Corporation, 1994-. **Honors/Awds:** Tribute to Women in Intl Industry YWCA 1981; Outstanding Comm Leader & Humanitarian Awd NAACP Legal Defense Fund 1981; CANDACE Awd Natl Coalition of 100 Black Women 1982; Equal Rights Advocate Awd 1984; Distinguished Meritorious Award DC Human Services 1987; Honorary Doctorate Tougaloo Univ 1988; Directors Choice Award, Natl Women's Economic Alliance Council, 1992. **Business Addr:** Vice President, The Times Mirror Company, Times Mirror Square, Los Angeles, CA 90053, (213)237-3700.

GULIFORD, ERIC ANDRE
Professional football player. **Personal:** Born Oct 25, 1969, Kansas City, KS; married Michelle; children: Breanna. **Educ:** Arizona State. **Career:** Minnesota Vikings, wide receiver, 1993-94; Carolina Panthers, 1995; Winnipeg Blue Bombers (CFL), 1996; New Orleans Saints, 1997-. **Business Addr:** Professional Football Player, New Orleans Saints, 5800 Airline Hwy, Metairie, LA 70003, (504)733-0255.

GULLATTEE, ALYCE C.
Physician, educator. **Personal:** Born Jun 28, 1928, Detroit; married Latinee G; children: Jeanne, Audrey, Nat. **Educ:** Univ CA, BA 1956; Howard Univ Coll Med, MD 1964. **Career:** St Elizabeth's Hosp & DC Gen Hosp, rotating intshp 1964-65; St Elizabeth's Hosp, med officer, gen prac 1965-66, Med Officer in Psychiatry 1968-71; St Elizabeth's Hosp & George Washington Univ Hosp, residency psychiatry 1965-68; Howard Univ Coll Med, asst prof psychiatry 1970-, clinical asst prof Family-Practice 1970-; Nat Inst Mental Health, career tchr Addictive Substances Abuse 1974-77. **Orgs:** Mem ed bd Jour Nat Med Assn 1967-; consult Juvenile & Domestic Relations Ct, Arlington Co 1968-; recording sec All Psychiat Progress 1967-70; chiefcons Drug Educ Prgm Juvenile Ct, Arlington 1969; v chmn 1969-70, chmn elect 1970-71, chmn 1971-72 Psychiatry-Neurology Sect, Nat Med Assn; mem Ho of Dels, Nat Med Assn 1968-75; obsvr consult Council Intl Ogrgn, Am Psychiat Assn 1969-73; consult EEO 1969-70; co-coordntr Drug Abuse Seminar, Nat Council Juvenile Ct Judges 1970; chmn ad hoc com HEW, Poor Children & Youth 1969-; rep Am Psychiat Assn Chicago 1970; mem Com Psychiat & Law, Am Psychiat Assn 1973-; chmn Prgm Com, Am Psychiat Assn 1974-75; chmn Grad Com Intl Prgms, Howard Univ 1974-; chief consult Arlington Co Drug Abust Treatment Prgm, Prelude 1969-; Nat-Psychiat Consult & Prgm DevelopNat Council Negro Women 1972-; chmn Com Intl Med, Nat Med Assn, Med-surgical Soc 1974-78; sr adv, co-founder Student Nat Med Assn, Washington; mem Nat Inst Drug Abuse Task Force 1975-. **Honors/Awds:** Outstanding Tchr Award, Howard Univ Coll Medicine 1973; Career Tchr Award, Nat Inst Mental Health 1974-; Academic Honors Zoology, Univ CA 1956; first award Clinical Acumen, Howard Univ Coll Medicine 1964; Magna Cum Laude Internship Award, St Elizabeth Hosp 1965; Citizens Award - Outstanding Contbns to Comm, Santa Monica NAACP 1960; Outstanding Black Woman of 1970, Nat Med Assn; nominee TV Emmy award by Washington Chap Nat Acad TV Arts & Scis, NBC Spl The Disabled Mind; mem by apptmt of Pres of US to Nat Adv Com Juvenile Justice & Delinquency Prevention, US Dept Justice 1975-76; fellow Inst Soc, Ethics & Life Scis Hastings-on-Hudson 1975-77.

GULLEY, WILSON
Business executive, state official. **Personal:** Born Oct 6, 1937, Buckner, AR; married Katherine Richardson; children: Debbie Renee Collins, Wilson Jr, Bruce Edward, Keith Ramon. **Educ:** Everett Comm Coll, AA, 1966; University of Washington, AA, BA, 1968; NYU, post grad 1968-69. **Career:** F & G Constrn Inc, pres 1977-; Omni Homes Inc, pres 1979-; United Inner City Devel Found, pres 1971-75; Nat Bus League Seattle Chpt, pres 1970-79; Central Contractors Association/Washington State Department of Transportation, OJT Supportive Services, project administrator, 1989-92, District I, Operations, contract compliance officer, 1992-94; Washington State DOT, Northwest Region, contract compliance officer, 1994-. **Orgs:** Exec dir Rotary Boys Club, Seattle 1968-70; institutional rep Boy Scouts of Am 1968-70; credit com chmn Central Area Fed Credit Union 1968-73; couns/fdr Youth in Bus Orgn 1971-72; Boys Club (Pres Nixon), Boys Club of Am 1969; comm devel Seattle Police & Fire Depts 1969; Seattle Public Schools, advisory board member; Port of Seattle, advisory board member; Contract Compliance Officers, Region 10; Seattle worker's Center, advisory board member; Washington Department of Labor & Industries, affirmative action committee. **Honors/Awds:** Outstanding Business Proposal, Roxbury Bus Inst, 1972; Special Recognition, Seattle Kiwanis Club, 1971; Scholarship to Univ CA-Berkeley, Nat Council for Equal Business Opportunies, 1972; Scholarship to Univ of Chicago, United Mortgage Bankers of America, 1973; Community Development Award, SER, Seattle Chapter, 1973; Washington State Department of Transportation, On-the-Job Training Program, Recognition Award, 1990; Washington State Joint Apprenticeship Training Council, Committment to Civil Rights Award, 1991; Washington State Employee Combined Fund Drive, Certificate of Performance, 1992. **Military Serv:** US Air Force, airman second class, 1956-60. **Business Addr:** Contract Compliance Officer, Washington State DOT Operations, 15700 Dayton Ave N, PO Box 330310, Seattle, WA 98133-9710, (206)440-4663.

GUMBEL, BRYANT CHARLES
Television broadcaster. **Personal:** Born Sep 29, 1948, New Orleans, LA; son of Rhea Alice LeCesne Gumbel and Richard Dunbar Gumbel; married June Carlyn Baranco, Dec 1, 1973; children: Bradley Christopher, Jillian Beth. **Educ:** Bates Coll, BA 1970. **Career:** Black Sports Magazine, writer, 1971, editor-in-chief, 1972; KNBC-TV, weekend sportscaster 1972-73, sportscaster 1973-76, sports dir 1976-81; NBC's Rose Bowl Parade & coverage, cohost beginning 1975; NBC's Grandstand Show, cohost beginning 1976; Super Bowl XI, co-host 1977; 19-Inch Variety Show, 1977; performer cohost KNBC shows What's Going On, News Conference, Prep Sports World, Brainworks 1977; NBC Today show, cohost, 1982-97; Olympics, Seoul, South Korea, host, NBC, 1988; CBS, host of Public Eye with Bryant Gumbel, 1997-. **Orgs:** Mem AFTRA, SCSBA, NATAS. **Honors/Awds:** Emmy Awd, 1976, 1977; produced, wrote & hosted Olympic Reflections: A Handful of Dreams; Golden Mike Awd, Los Angeles Press Club 1978, 1979; Edward R Murrow Award, Overseas Press Club, 1988; Best Morning TV News Interviewer, Washington Post Journal, 1986. **Business Addr:** Host, "Private Eye", CBS-TV, 555 W 57th St, New York, NY 10019, (212)975-4321.

GUMBEL, GREG
Broadcast journalist. **Personal:** Born May 3, 1946, New Orleans, LA; son of Rhea Alice LeCesne Gumbel and Richard Dunbar Gumbel; married Marcy; children: Michelle. **Educ:** Loras College, BA, 1967. **Career:** American Hospital Supply Co, sales rep, 1968-73; WMAQ-TV, Chicago, sports anchor, 1973-81; ESPN, SportsCenter, co-anchor, 1981-89; CBS Television, NFL Today show, co-host, 1990-94, NFL Preview, host, currently; NFL Live, Olympic Winter Games, host, 1994;. **Special Achievements:** Selected to host 1994 Winter Olympic Games in Lillehammer, Norway. **Business Addr:** Host, NBC Sports, Play-by-Play Announcer, NBC-TV, c/o Scott Cooper, 30 Rockefeller Plaza, New York, NY 10112.

GUMBS, OLIVER SINCLAIR
Physician (retired). **Personal:** Born Oct 31, 1913, Aetna, NY; married Muriel Francene Burruss; children: Mignon, BJ, Carol, John, Oliver, Antoinette. **Educ:** Attended, Cornell Univ, Virginia Union Univ; Meharry Medical School, MD 1941. **Career:** St Martin De Pours Hosp, chief of staff of surgery; Twin Oaks Nursing Home, director/physician; Gateway Drug Prog, director; Private Practice, physician/surgeon 1941-83; Mobile Mental Health Clinic, physician; Searcy Mental Hospital, 1983-86 (retired). **Orgs:** Mem The Utopian Social Club, Florida Guardsmen; mem 32 degree Masons 1946-; mem Mobile Bay Medical Assoc; one of founders Gulf Coast Medical Assoc; one of incorporators State Medical Assoc for Blacks. **Honors/Awds:** State Resolution for Accomplishment AL State Legislature 1980; Ebony's 100 Most Influential Ebony Magazine 1981; Grand Polemarch Kappa Alpha Psi Frat 1981; rec'd Keys to the Cities of Chicago, Indianapolis, Mobile and New Orleans. **Home Addr:** 1113 Sunset Ave, Richmond, VA 23221.

GUMBS, PHILIP N.
Attorney. **Personal:** Born Apr 29, 1923, Perth Amboy, NJ; married Rachel Valentine; children: Robina, Philip Kelvin. **Educ:** Seton Hall U, AA 1948; Lincoln U, JD 1952. **Career:** Township Matawan, councilman 1971-73, mayor 1974; Worker's Compensation Ct NJ Bd Edn, judge 1955-58; Matawan Twp Zoning Bd Admustment, 1964-71. **Orgs:** Bd dirs Monmouth Co United Fund; mem Monmouth Co NJ Bd of Chosen Freeholdes 1974, dir 1975; chmn bd tsts, supt Sunday Sch St Marks AME Ch 1953-;mem Monmouth Co Am, NJ State, Nat Bar Assns chmn Amaricanization & Citizenship Com. **Honors/Awds:** Brotherhood Award, Nat Conf Christians & Jews 1975; Life Fellow, Am Co Govt 1976; Comm Serv Award, The Nat Caucus of the Black Aged Inc 1979. **Military Serv:** AUS sgt 1942-45. **Business Addr:** 1 Ct House Sq, Freehold, NJ 07728.

GUMMS, EMMANUEL GEORGE, SR.
Clergyman & educational administrator. **Personal:** Born Jan 16, 1928, Opelusas, LA; married Shirley Mae Griffen (deceased); children: Emanuel Jr, Salyria, Valenti. **Educ:** Leland College, AB cum laude 1954; Union Seminary, BD 1955; Inter Baptist Theological, ThD 1974, LLD 1976; Universal Bible Institute, PhD 1978; Straigth Business Coll, exec sec 1960. **Career:** West NO Baptist Assn, president 1972-76; LA Cristian Training Institute, president 1973-75; Christian Bible College of LA, academic dean 1976-; First New Testament B C, pastor 1958-. **Orgs:** Supervisor LSU Dental School 1971-77; secretary Jefferson Parish Ministers Union 1973-81; bd chairman Jefferson Parish Voters League 1975-84; general secretary LA Progressive Baptist Assn 1978-; chaplain Veterans of Foreign Wars #2403 1981-. **Honors/Awds:** Outstanding leadership 2nd Congress LBA 1978; communicator West Bank American Muslem 1980; dedicated service ML King Community Center 1981. **Military Serv:** AUS sfc5 6 yrs; OCC MED(J); OCC MED(K); KSM 2 BSS UNSM 1950-56. **Business Addr:** Pastor, First New Testament BC, 6112 W Bank Expressway, Marrero, LA 70072.

GUNDY, ROY NATHANIEL, JR.
Computer analyst. **Personal:** Born Sep 26, 1967, Philadelphia, PA; son of Elizabeth Gundy. **Educ:** Drexel University, BS, commerce, engineering operations management, 1991. **Career:** Channel 6, talk show panelist, 1983-85; Bonatsos, database analyst, 1987-; Devon Systems International Inc, network analyst, 1988-89; Thomas Jefferson University Hospital, micro computer technician, 1987-88, ic analyst, 1992-. **Orgs:** National Society of Black Engineers, region 2 programs chairman, 1986-; Kappa Alpha Psi, guide right chairman, 1990-; Philadelphia Area Computing Society, 1992-; Philadelphia Regional Introduction of Minorities to Engineering, 1982-. **Honors/Awds:** Club Cornucopia, scholarship, 1988-90; Kodak, scholarship, 1987-88; National Black Media Coalition, Achievement in Communication Industry, 1983; Timberland Company, Sales Achievement, 1986. **Home Addr:** 1834 W 73rd Avenue, Philadelphia, PA 19126. **Business Addr:** Analyst, Thomas Jefferson University Hospital, Information Systems, 130 S 9th St, Edison Ste 104, Philadelphia, PA 19107, (215)955-8099.

GUNN, ALEX M., JR.
Educator. **Personal:** Born May 9, 1928, Newkirk, OK; divorced; children: Alexis Lamb, Michael Clay. **Educ:** Langston Univ & Friends U, BA 1953; CA Polytechnic, MA 1962. **Career:** Bureau of Intergroup Relations CA State Dept of Educ, cons; CRA Youth Auth Whittier, dir 1970-71; supvr of acad instruction 1970; Parole & Serv Sacramento, supvr of acad instruction 1969-70; Paso Robles, supvr of acad instr 1965-69, teacher 1965-70, youth auth & teacher 1958-65; boys group supvr 1956-58. **Orgs:** Mem ACIRE; Black Sch Bd mem & Adminstrs; Council of Excptnl Chldrn; chrtr mem ASCA Black Edctrs Assn; past pres CEC Chap 39; NAACP; Assn of CA Sch Adminstr; past pres & vice pres So Co Chap Dist #12 Toastmaster & Intl Gov; pblcty chmn OEO No Co Area Grtr Whittier Fair Hsng Com & Human Rels Com; pres 3 times PRSB Tchr Assn; adv BSA; past membrshp chmn CPPCA; mem Assn of CA Intrgrp Rels Edctrs; CA Council for Intergrated Edn. **Military Serv:** AUS 1950-51. **Business Addr:** CA State Dept of Educ, 721 Capitol Mall, Sacramento, CA 95814.

GUNN, ARTHUR CLINTON
Educator. **Personal:** Born Apr 29, 1942, New Castle, PA; son of Magnolia Hill Murray and John O Gunn Sr. **Educ:** Wilberforce Univ, Wilberforce OH, BS Educ, 1964; Atlanta Univ, Atlanta GA, MS Library Science, 1969; Univ of Pittsburgh, Pittsburgh PA, PhD, 1986. **Career:** Delaware State Coll, Dover DE, librarian, 1969-71; Howard Univ, Washington DC, librarian, 1971-76; Univ of Maryland, College Park MD, adjunct prof, 1972-76; Univ of Pittsburgh, Pittsburgh PA, librarian, 1983-86; Wayne State Univ, Detroit MI, prof, 1986-. **Orgs:** Mem, Amer Library Assn, 1969-, Amer Library and Information Science Educ, 1986-; consultant, General Motors Corp, 1988-; pres, Assn of African-Amer Librarian, 1988-. **Honors/Awds:** Chair, Govt Relations Comm of the Assn for Library and Information Science Educ. **Business Addr:** Wayne State University, Library Science Program, 106 Kresge Library, Detroit, MI 48202.

GUNN, GLADYS
Educational administrator (retired). **Personal:** Born Apr 28, 1937, Columbus, GA; daughter of Jessie Gunn and John R Gunn. **Educ:** Cntrl State U, BS Elem Ed 1959; Miami U, MEd 1964; OH State U, 1971-72. **Career:** Dayton Publ Schls, teacher 1959-66, interviewer for federally funded prgm 1966-69, assoc in personnel 1969-71; OH Youth Cmsn, asst supt 1972-73; CSU W & CSU Training Ins, dir 1973-77; Cntrl Stae U, training & emplymnt pgm 1977-78, crdntr SDIP 1978-80; Dept Hlth & Human Serv, spec asst 1980-81; Dayton Pblc Sch, crdntr evltn 1982-86; Dayton Publ Schls, spec asst for administration & ident of grants 1986-92. **Orgs:** Mem of, Alpha Kappa Alpha Sorority, Soroptimist Intl, Assc Suprvsn & Crclm Dev, Phi Delta Kappa, Subcommittee on Ed of the Ad Hoc Committee on Civil Rights, City of Dayton Comm on Ed; bd mem Daymont Mental Health Prgm; former elected mem Inner West Priority Bd; former bd mem Comprehensive Manpower Training Cntr; mem, Amer Assn of School Admin, 1989-92; League of Women Voters. **Honors/Awds:** Prsdtl apptment Natl Advsry Cncl on Women's Edctnl Pgm 1978-80; presappt Spec Asst for Spec Grps 1980-81. **Home Addr:** 4237 Catalpa Dr, Dayton, OH 45405.

GUNN, WILLIE COSDENA THOMAS
Educator, school academic counselor. **Personal:** Born Dec 24, 1926, Seneca, SC; daughter of Mattie Riley Gideon and Fletcher Gideon; married Willie James Gunn, Dec 24, 1975; children: Dr John Henderson Thomas III. **Educ:** Benedict Coll, BS 1946; Univ of MI, MA Educ 1967, MA Guidance 1970; Urban Bible Coll, Detroit, MI, doctorate, 1987. **Career:** Emerson Jr HS, tchr common learnings & scis 1956-64; Headstart Prog, super 1965; Title I Operation Summer Prog, super 1967-73; MI State Univ, tchr supervisor 1962-64; Emerson Jr HS, guidance counselor 1964-76; Mott Coll, instr social sci 1969-78; Flint Open Sch, guidance counselor 1976-82; Jordan Coll, instr social sci dept 1981; Southwestern HS, guidance counselor 1982-88; Southwestern Acad, guidance counselor, 1988-. **Orgs:** Flint City Adv Comm League of Women Voters; Voter Educ Coalition Drug Abuse Task Force; bd dirs WFBE Pub Radio Station; bd dirs Natl Assn of Media Women; life mem & past pres Zeta Phi Beta Sor; life mem & past pres Natl Sor of Phi Delta Kappa; mem Amer Assn of Univ Women; life mem Natl Assn of Negro Business & Professional Women; mem NAACP, Urban League, Africa Care, Natl Council of Negro Women; Genesee Area Assn of Counseling Devel; United Teachers of Flint; Natl Educ Assn; Michigan Educ Assn; mem, Metropolitan Chamber of Commerce, 1984-; 2nd vice pres, Top Ladies of Distinction, 1985-; public relations dir, Black Panhellenic Council, 1987-. **Honors/Awds:** Woman of the Yr Natl Assn of Media Women 1976; Sepia Awd Natl Assn of Media Women 1978; Zeta Phi Beta Sor Woman of the Yr 1982; Zeta Phi Beta Sor Zeta of the Yr 1969; Panhellenic Woman of the Yr 1972; Educational Awd Natl Sor of Phi Delta Kappa 1974; Achievement Award Rsch Alcoholism Univ WI 1967; March of Dimes Comm Serv Awd 1971; author & counselor consultant Comm Educ Network Proj 1983; Woman of the Year, Natl Assn of Media Women, 1988; Bigger & Better Business Award, Phi Beta Sigma Fraternity, 1989; Hall of Fame, Zeta Phi Beta Sorority, 1989; Counselor of the Year, Genesee Area Assn of Counseling Devel, 1989; author, Black Achievement Register; co-author, "Feelings" (poems), 1971; author, "Countdown to College," 1984; co-author, "Career Planning," 1988. **Home Addr:** 1511 Church St, Flint, MI 48503.

GUNNINGS, THOMAS S.
Educator. **Personal:** Born Feb 8, 1935, Gastonia, NC; married Barbara. **Educ:** Univ of OR, PhD 1969; OR State Univ, DMA 1967; Winston-Salem Teachers Coll, BS 1958. **Career:** MI State Univ Coll of Human Med, adjunct prof psych, prof of psych; G & P Properties, vice pres; Meridian Professional Psych Consult Inc, pres. **Orgs:** Natl consult to many fed state & local agencies; mem Kappa Delta Phi Hon Soc, Natl Inst of Mental Health Training Grants; vstg scientists, vstg psych Amer Psych Assn 1969-72; mem Amer Psych Assn; bd dir Assn of Black Psych mem Natl Assoc of Counseling & Development; editor of a national journal. **Honors/Awds:** Fellow of APA and many other honors. **Business Addr:** President, Meridian Professional Psychol Consul, 5031 Park Lake Rd, East Lansing, MI 48823.

GUNTER, LAURIE
Educator. **Personal:** Born Mar 5, 1922, Navarrow Cty, TX; daughter of Hollie Myrtle Carruthers and Lewis Marion Martin; children: Margo Alyce Gunter Toner, Lara Elaine Bonow. **Educ:** TN A&I State Univ, BS 1948; Univ of Toronto, Cert Nursing Ed 1948-49; Fisk Univ, MA 1952; Cath Univ of Amer, 1956; Univ of CA Berkeley, 1959; Univ of Chicago, PhD 1959. **Career:** George W Hubbard Hosp, staff nurse 1943-44, head nurse 1945-46, suprv 1947-48; Meharry Med Coll School of Nursing, asst instr 1948-50, instr 1950-55, asst prof 1955-57, acting dean 1957-58, dean 1958-61; UCLA, asst prof nursing 1961-63, assoc prof 1963-65; IN Univ Med Ctr, prof nursing 1965-66; Univ of WA, prof 1969-71; PA State Univ, prof of nursing human devel 1971-87. **Orgs:** Mem Amer Nurses Assoc 1948-, Natl League for Nursing 1948-87, Amer Assoc of Univ Prof, 1949-87, Gerontological Soc 1959-91; rsch proj grants 1965-; mem Amer Assoc of Coll of Nursing 1971, Amer Publ Health Assoc 1974-87; consult HRA/Natl Ctr for Health Serv Rsch 1976-89; reviewer HEW 1976-89; mem steering comm PA Nurses Assoc, Council of Nurse Rsch, Amer Nurses Assoc; ad hoc ed, adv comm Div of Geriatric Nursing Pract, Amer Nurses Assoc; proj dir Composite Ed Prog for Geriatric Nursing 1976-77; mem Amer Acad of Nursing 1979-, Inst of Medicine of the Natl Acad of Sci 1980-. **Honors/Awds:** Charles Nelson Gold Medal Meharry Med Coll School of Nursing 1943; Foster Mem Prize Meharry Med Coll School of Nursing 1943; Alpha Kappa Mu Hon Soc TN A&I State Univ 1948; Fellowship Rockefeller Found 1948-49; Rockefeller Found 1953-55; Training Inst in Soc Gerontology Univ of CA 1959; Golden Anniv Citation Spec Competence in Nursing TN Agr & Indust Univ 1963; invitee White House Conf on Food Nutrition & Health 1969; guest lecturer Japanese Nurses First Rsch Conf 1971; author, co-autor num articles & audiovisual prod 1949-. **Business Addr:** 4008 47th Ave, S, Seattle, WA 98118.

GURLEY, DOROTHY J.
Educator. **Personal:** Born Dec 13, 1931, Livingston, AL; daughter of Ethel Conley Johnson and Edward Johnson; married James E Gurley, Jan 2, 1952; children: Dr Marilyn G. Foreman, Beverly G. Lampley, Darryl E, Kenneth A. **Educ:** AL A&M Univ, BS 1951; Tuskegee Univ, MEd 1961; AL A&M Univ, "AA" Certificate 1974; Univ of Alabama, EdD 1988. **Career:** Education Improvement Prog Huntsville City Schs, childhood educ 1966-71; Comprehensive Child Care Prog, program coord 1971-73; Educ Improvement Prog, curriculum specialist 1974-79; Rolling Hills Elem Sch Huntsville, asst principal 1979-88; Alabama A&M Univ, assoc prof 1988-. **Orgs:** Grand dist deputy IBPO of Elks of the World; mem Natl Educ Assoc, Assoc for Supervision and Curriculum Develop, AL Educ Assoc, Huntsville Educ Assoc; vice pres, Alabama Assn for the Educ of Young Children 1983-85; mem, Alabama State Advisory Committee for Early Childhood Educ 1974-; mem, Alabama Public TV Citizen Advisory Bd 1983-85; basileus, Epsilon Gamma Omega Chapter Alpha Kappa Alpha Sorority Inc 1975-77; Phi Delta Kappa; National Association for Elementary School Principals 1988-. **Honors/Awds:** Inducted in to Alpha Kappa Alpha Hall of Fame Epsilon Gamma Omega 1980; Disting Alumni Awd NAEFO 1984; Distinguished Alumni Awd, Natl Assn for Equal Opportunity for Higher Education 1984; Class Achievement Awd, Alabama A&M Natl Alumni Normalite Assn 1986, 1990; Effective Schools Program, Rolling Hills Elementary 1986-88; Teachers' Perceptions Toward Causes of Discipline Problems in the Elementary Grades of Huntsville City Schools 1988; Resolution of Recognition, Huntsville City School Board; Basileus of the Year Award, Southeastern Region, Alpha Kappa Alpha Sorority Inc; Cum Laude Graduate from Alabama A&M Univ; Southern Education Foundation Fellow; Panelist, Tri-State Early Childhood Education Project; Banquet of Doctors Award, A Consortium of Doctors, 1991. **Business Addr:** Associate Professor, Department of Secondary Education, Alabama A&M University, P O Box 357, Normal, AL 35762.

GURLEY, HELEN RUTH
Educational administrator. **Personal:** Born Dec 5, 1939, Ogemaw, AR; daughter of Rev & Mrs Curtis Hildreth (deceased); married Archie Gurley Sr; children: Archie Jr, Thomas Jeffrey, Vallissia Lynn. **Educ:** Natl Univ San Diego, MBA 1975; The Union Institute, PhD. **Career:** Univ of CA, counselor 1971-77; Nueces County MHMR Comm Ctr, service dir 1977-79; City of Corpus Christi, admin human relations 1979-83; Del Mar Coll, EEO/affirmative action officer 1985-95, dir human relations, 1995-. **Orgs:** Consultant Mary McLeod Bethune Day Nursery Inc 1983-85; pres Littles-Martin House Fund Inc 1984-89; pres Corpus Christi Branch NAACP 1984-89; chairperson United Way of the Coastal Bend Agency Council 1984-86; chairperson Coastal Bend Council of Govt Health Adv Comm 1985-95; bd mem Natl Conf of Christians and Jews; treasurer, Amer Assn for Affirmative Action, 1988-95. **Honors/Awds:** Woman of the Year Corpus Christi Alumnae Chap Delta Sigma Theta Sorority 1983-84; Unsung Heroine Natl NAACP 1985. **Military Serv:** USN E-3 seaman 3 yrs; USAR E-8 MSG 17 yrs; Army Commendation; Army Achievement; Humanitarian Service Medal. **Home Addr:** 1322 Southbay Dr, Corpus Christi, TX 78412. **Business Addr:** Director/Administrator, City of Corpus Christi Human Relations, 1201 Leopard St, City Hall, 4th Fl, PO Box 9277, Corpus Christi, TX 78469-9277, (512)880-3190.

GUTHRIE, CARLTON LYONS
Automotive supplier, business executive. **Personal:** Born Sep 15, 1952, Atlanta, GA; married Dr Danille K Taylor; children: Carille, Adam. **Educ:** Harvard Coll, AB (Cum Laude) 1974; Harvard Business School, MBA 1978. **Career:** Jewel Companies Chicago, internal consultant 1978-80; McKinsey & Co Chicago, sr assoc 1980-82; James H Lowry & Assoc Chicago, exec vice pres 1982-85; Trumark Inc, pres & chief executive officer, 1985-. **Orgs:** Ctrs for New Horizons Chicago, director, 1980-, Urban League Lansing MI, 1986-; Joyce Foundation, Chicago Ill, director, 1991-; Single Parent Family Institute, Lansing, MI, chairman of the board, 1987-; Gifted & Talented Education Program, Ingham County Church, director, 1986-. **Honors/Awds:** 1990 Extrapreneur of the Year, Chivas Regal/Seagrams; 1991 Trumark Inc, Michigan Manufacturer of the Year, Impression Fine Science Museum, Lansing, MI; 1992 Trumark Inc: Supplier of the Year, National Minority Supplier Development Council (NMSDC). **Business Addr:** President & CEO, Trumark, Inc, 1820 Sunset, Lansing, MI 48917.

GUTHRIE, MICHAEL J.
Company executive. **Personal:** Born Sep 19, 1950, Lithonia, GA; son of Mary Guthrie and Willie Guthrie; married Valorie C Walker; children: Lauren, Kayla. **Educ:** Harvard Coll, AB 1972; Harvard Law School, JD 1975. **Career:** Sonnenschein, Carlin, Nath & Rosenthal, atty 1975-79; Johnson Products Co Inc, sr atty 1979-83, vice pres corp planning, 1983-85; Trumark Inc, co-owner, exec vice pres 1985-; Guthrie Investment Corp, pres. **Orgs:** Bus adv bd, foundation board Lansing Comm Coll; National Assn of Black Automotive Suppliers, president; Junior Achievement of Mid-Michigan; Physicians Health Plan of Mid-Michigan; Governor's Task Force on Entrepreneurship and Small Business; Michigan Council on Vocational Education, Single Parent Family Institute. **Business Addr:** Executive Vice President, Trumark, Inc, 1820 Sunset Ave, Lansing, MI 48917.

GUTHRIE, ROBERT V.
Educator, psychologist. **Career:** Southern Illinois University, Carbondale, Black American Studies, director, currently. **Business Addr:** Director, Southern Illinois University, Black American Studies, Saner Hall, Carbondale, IL 62901-0000, (618)453-7147.

GUY, ADDELIAR DELL, III
District court judge. **Personal:** Born Nov 1, 1923, Chicago, IL; son of Hattie P Brown Guy and Addeliar D Guy; married Alice Rosalyn Banks Guy; children: Addeliar D IV, Pamela D Guy Anderson, Michael Lawrence. **Educ:** St Norbert Coll, 1941-42; Wilson Jr Coll, 1948; Loyola Univ School of Law, LLB 1957. **Career:** Peterson Johnson & Guy, attorney, 1958-64; City of Chicago asst corp counsel 1960-64; Office of the District Attorney, Clark County, Nevada research asst, 1964, administrative assistant, 1964-66, deputy district attorney, 1966-73, chief deputy district attorney, 1973-75; Eight Judicial District Court, juvenile court judge, 1976-79, chief judge, 1985, judge, 1975-. **Orgs:** Jr Chamber of Commerce; Cosmo Chamber of Commerce; S Side Comm; 3rd Ward Young Dem; 3rd Ward Regular Dem Comm; So NV Human Relat Comm; NAACP; Fitzsimmons House, N Las Vegas Rotary; adv bd AD Guy Boys Club; Clark Cty Dem Cntrl Com; City of Las Vegas Housing Authority, commissioner, 1967-75; Senator Harry Reid's Academy Selection Board, 1986-; executive board: March of Dimes, VFW, Saints & Sinners, Help Them Walk Again, Civilian Mil Council, Boulder Dam Area Council of the Boy Scouts of Amer, 1979-, Judicial Council of the National Bar Assn. **Honors/Awds:** Outstanding Achievement as Judge, NAACP; Silver Lily Award, Easter Seal Soc of Nevada, 1979; Distinguished Achievement Award, Judicial Council of the Natl Bar Assn, 1980; Certificate of Appreciation, Freedom Fund NAACP, 1984; Addeliar D Guy III Law School Scholarship Fund, established 1987; Silver Beaver Award, Boulder Dam Area Boy Scouts of Amer, 1989; Addeliar D Guy Junior High School, 1992; Red Mass honoree, 1992; Distinguished Nevadan, University of Nevada at Las Vegas, 1979. **Special Achievements:** Admitted to practice before: Illinois Bar, 1957; United States District Court for Northern Illinois, 1958; United States Court of Appeals for the Seventh Circuit, 1964; United States Supreme Court, 1964; United States Court of Military Appeals, 1964; Nevada Bar, 1966; United States District Court for Nevada, 1966; United States Court of Appeals, Ninth Circuit, 1973; author: "Is the Criminal Justice System Fair to Minorities?" Howard Law Journal, vol 27, p 115, 1984. **Military Serv:** US Coast Guard, sp3/cw, 1942-46; US Army, lt, 1948-54; Illinois Army National Guard, capt, 1955-64; Nevada Army National Guard, capt1964-66; United States Army Reserve, capt, 1966-68; Nevada Army, lt col, 1968-76; US Army: Purple Heart, 1950, Korean Service Medal with two battle stars, 1950-51, Meritorious Service Award Medal; Combat Infantryman's Badge. **Business Addr:** Judge, Eight Judicial District Court, Clark County Courthouse, 200 S Third St, Dept XI, Las Vegas, NV 89155.

GUY, JASMINE
Actress, dancer. **Personal:** Born Mar 10, 1964, Boston, MA; daughter of Jaye Rudolph Guy and Dr William Guy. **Educ:** Studied at Alvin Ailey Dance Theatre. **Career:** Dancer, Alvin Ailey American Dance Theater, New York; performed with At-

lanta Ballet Junior Co; television appearances: "Fame," "The Equalizer," "Loving," "Ryan's Hope," "At Mother's Request," "A Killer Among Us"; "Touched by an Angel"; stage: The Wiz, Bubblin Brown Sugar, Beehive, Leader of the Pack; films: School Daze, Harlem Nights, Klash; Song Performer, Gremlims 2: The New Batch, 1990; Album, Jasmine Guy, Warner Brothers, 1990; co-star, "A Different World," "Melrose Place.". **Honors/Awds:** NAACP Image Award, Best Actress in a Comedy Series, for A Different World, 1990. **Business Addr:** Actress, c/o NBC Inc, 30 Rockefeller Plaza, New York, NY 10020.

GUY, LYGIA BROWN
Business executive. **Personal:** Born Apr 23, 1952, Charleston, SC; married Peter Steele; children: Aja Steele. **Educ:** Spelman Coll, 1969-72; Fashion Inst of Amer, AA Merchandising/Design 1973; Pepperdine Univ, BA Sociology 1974. **Career:** Chelsa Records, promo coord 1975; Greedy Records, promo coord 1976; ABC Records, promo coord 1977; Connections, dir & owner of co, personnel agent 1984; RCA Records, merchandising mgr, West Coast regional promo. **Orgs:** Mem, NAACP, 1969; mem Acad of Country Music, 1980; mem, AFTRA, 1980; mem, NARAS, 1982; mem, Black Music Assn. **Honors/Awds:** Promo Mgr of the Yr BRE Mag 1984.

GUY, MILDRED DOROTHY
Educator. **Personal:** Born Apr 16, 1929, Brunswick, GA; daughter of Mamie Smith Floyd (deceased) and John Floyd (deceased); married Charles Guy, Aug 8, 1956 (divorced); children: Rhonda Lynn Guy-Phillips. **Educ:** Savannah State Coll, BS 1949; Atlanta Univ, MA 1952; Univ of Southern California, Post Grad Studies 1953; Univ of N Colorado 1960; Foreign Study League-Europe, Post Grad Studies 1977; Colorado University, 1963-79. **Career:** LS Ingraham High School, Sparta GA, chmn soc studies dept 1950-56; N Jr High School Colorado Springs Sch Dist #11, tchr soc studies & English 1958-84, retired teacher. **Orgs:** Originator Annual Minority Student Recognition Prog 1973; trustee Pikes Peak Comm Coll 1976-83; CSTA delegate to Delegate Assembly Colorado Springs Tchrs Assn 1978; life mem NEA, Colorado Council for Soc Studies, ASALH, Friends of Pioneers Museum 1974-; basileus"pres", Iota Beta Omega Chap of AKA 1984-86; local bd mem & life mem NAACP 1979-83; UL 1972-75; NHACS Bd 1984-97; delegate to Dem Pty Assemblys & Conv 1974-94; AAUW; ADK; LWV; Pikes Peak Ctr Fundraiser; CS Fine Arts Ctr; nominating comm Wagon Wheel Council Colorado Springs CO l985-86; bd of managers Women's Educational Society of the Colorado College 1992-98. **Honors/Awds:** Outstanding Soror Award of Mid-Western Region (AKA) 1980; Outstanding Black Educator of Sch Dist #11 1980; Honorable Mention, Colo Tchr of Yr St Bd of Educ 1983; Outstanding Achievemnt in Ed Award; NHACS Award 1984; Iota Omicron Lambda Chap Alpha Phi Alpha Awd 1985; CBWPA Sphinx Awd 1986; Outstanding Grad Chap President Awd Mid-Western Region of Alpha Kappa Alpha 1986; Salute to Women 1986-; Recognition Gazette Telegraph Colorado Springs CO 1986; Distinguished Educator of the Year, Black Educators of District Eleven, 1984; Woman of Distinction, Girl Scouts-Wagon Wheel Council, 1989; Woman of Distinction, Image Productions, 1994; Cert of Appreciation, African-American Youth Conf, Alpha Phi Alpha Chap, 1996. **Home Addr:** 3132 Constitution Ave, Colorado Springs, CO 80909, (719)473-8241.

GUY, ROSA CUTHBERT
Author. **Personal:** Born Sep 1, 1925; daughter of Audrey Gonzalez and Henry Cuthbert; married Warner Guy; children: Warner Jr. **Educ:** New York Univ, attended. **Career:** Author: Bird at My Window 1966, Children of Longing 1969, The Friends 1973, Ruby 1981, Edith Jackson 1979, The Disappearance 1980, Mother Crocodile 1981, Mirror of Her Own 1981, New Guys Around the Block 1983, A Measure of Time 1983, Paris, Pee Wee & Big Dog 1984, My Love, My Love or The Peasant Girl 1985, And I Heard a Bird Sing 1987, Ups & Downs of Carl Davis III, 1989; The Sun, The Sea, A Touch of the Wind, 1995. **Orgs:** Comm mem Negro in the Arts; org Harlem Writers Guild. **Business Addr:** c/o Ellen Levine Literary Agency, 15 E 26th St, Suite 1801, New York, NY 10010.

GUYNES, THOMAS
Professional football player. **Personal:** Born Sep 9, 1974. **Educ:** Univ of Michigan, attended. **Career:** Arizona Cardinals, tackle, 1997-. **Business Addr:** Professional Football Player, Arizona Cardinals, 8701 S Hardy, Tempe, AZ 85284, (602)379-0101.

GUY-SHEFTALL, BEVERLY
Educator, author. **Personal:** Born 1946, Memphis, TN; daughter of Ernestine Varnado Guy. **Educ:** Spelman Coll, BA, 1966; Atlanta Univ, MA, 1968; Emory Univ, PhD. **Career:** AL State Univ, faculty, 1968-71; Spelman coll, prof of English and women's studies, 1971-; Women's Research and Resource Center, Anna Julia Cooper prof of English, 1981; SAGE: A Scholarly Journal on Black women, founding co-editor; speaker. **Honors/Awds:** Kellogg, fellow; Woodrow Wilson, fellow; Spelman College, Presidential Faculty Award for Outstanding Scholarship. **Special Achievements:** Author: Daughters of Sorrow: Attitudes Toward Black Women, 1880-1920, Carlson, 1991; Words of Fire: An Anthology of African-American Feminist Thought; Spelman: A Centennial Celebration, 1981; co-edited Sturdy Black Bridges: Visions of Black Women In Literature, Anchor Books, 1979; Double Stitch: Black Women Write About Mothers & Daughters, Beacon Press, 1992.

GUYTON, ALICIA V.
Pharmacist, government official. **Personal:** Born Nov 12, 1951, Wolfe, WV; daughter of Susie Hayes Guyton and M B Guyton (deceased); children: Mychal B, Erik W (twins). **Educ:** New York City Comm Coll, AS 1974; Brooklyn Coll of Pharmacy of Long Island Univ, BS 1977; Columbia Pacific Univ, MS 1986. **Career:** MCEOC, alcohol counselor 1980-81; Children's Home Soc of WV, asst dir counselor 1981-82; WV Job Service, interviewer 1982-83; Veterans Admin Medical Ctr, pharmacist 1983; Veterans Admin Medical Center, Iowa City, IA, asst chief BMS beginning, 1989; Dept of Veterans Affairs Medical Center, environmental management servie, asst chief, 1991, chief, currently. **Orgs:** Delta Sigma Theta Sor, Bluefield Alumnae Chap; chairperson Comm on Youth Serv, Links Inc, So WV Chap; Berkeley Chap, NAACP; Register official WV Secondary Schools Athletic Commn; Natl Council of Negro Women. **Honors/Awds:** First African-American female USSSA-ASA sanctioned umpire in the State of WV 1978; Outstanding Delta, Bluefield Alumnae Chap, Delta Sigma Theta Sor 1982; first African-American female umpire to work the State Class C Men's slow-pitch softball championships 1982; first black woman to officiate a boys' varsity basketball game in the State of WV 1985. **Business Addr:** Chief, Environmental Management Service, Dept of Veterans Affairs Medical Center, 1601 Kirkwood Highway, Wilmington, DE 19805.

GUYTON, BOOKER T.
Business executive, educational administrator. **Personal:** Born Dec 27, 1944, Clarksville, TX; married Mary Allen Guyton; children: Booker Jr, Roxann, Keisha, Katrina. **Educ:** Univ of the Pacific, BSEd 1971, MA Religion 1972. **Career:** Facilities Mgmt & Inst for Personnel Devel, dir; Humanities & Intercultural Ed Div, chmn; Mgmt Svcs, admin asst to vp; affirm action officer; Johnson & Johnson, suprv mfg; John F Kennedy Ctr, exec dir; Fed Teacher Corps prog, teacher intern; Parks Chapel AME Church, pastor; San Joaquin Delta Comm Coll, instr. **Orgs:** Mem North Stockton Rotary, Assoc of CA Comm Coll Admin, CA Comm Serv Assoc, Natl Ed Assoc, CA School Bd Assoc, Official Black Caucus of Natl Ed Assoc, Kappa Alpha Psi; bd of dir Dameron Hosp Found; pres McKinley Improvement Assoc, State Council Oppty Indust Ctr State of CA. **Honors/Awds:** Numerous awds incl New Educators Awd CA Assoc, Man of the Year Kappa Alpha Psi 1979, Community Serv Awd City of Stockton, Comm Serv Awd Black Teachers Alliance Stockton CA, Cert of Appreciation of Serv CA Black Student Union Assoc, Community Serv Awd League of Black Voters Stockton CA. **Military Serv:** USMC staff sgt 6 yrs. **Home Addr:** 148 W 8th St, Stockton, CA 95207.

GUYTON, SISTER PATSY
Educator, religious sister. **Personal:** Born Jun 16, 1949, Mobile, AL; daughter of Marie Johnson Guyton and Wes Guyton. **Educ:** Bishop State Jr Coll, Mobile AL, Associates in Psychology, 1969; Alabama State Univ, Montgomery AL, BS History, 1971; Springhill Coll, TIPS, Mobile AL, attended, 1979-83; Xavier Univ, New Orleans LA, Masters in Theology, 1989. **Career:** Boca Raton Middle School, Boca Raton FL, teacher, 1971-75; Christian Benevolent Insurance Co, Mobile AL, debit mgr, 1975-76; St Mary's Children Home, Mobile AL, child care worker, 1976-79; Marion Corp, Theodore AL, personnel specialist, 1979-82; Parish Social Ministry, Mobile AL, coord, 1982-88; Most Pure Heart of Mary Church, dir of religious educ, coord of ministries, 1988-92, Religious Education, assoc dir, 1992-. **Orgs:** Alpha Kappa Alpha Sorority, 1970-; bd mem, Valentine Award, Catholic Social Services, 1982-; religious educ consultant, Archdiocese of Mobile AL, 1985-; bd mem, Natl Assn of Lay Ministry, 1985-; interparish council, Black Catholic Congress & National Association of Black Sisters. **Honors/Awds:** Present Presidents' Club, Christian Benevolent Insurance Co, 1975; Outstanding Debit Mgr, Christian Benevolent Insurance Co, 1975; Interparish Council, Catholic of the Year, 1991. **Home Addr:** 2809 Harper Ave, Mobile, AL 36617.

GUYTON, TYREE
Artist. **Personal:** Born Aug 24, 1955, Detroit, MI; son of Betty Solomon Guyton and George Guyton (deceased); divorced; children: Tyree Jr, Towan, Omar, Tylisa. **Educ:** Northern High School Adult Training; Franklin Adult Educ; Center for Creative Studies, Detroit, MI. **Career:** Ford Motor Co, Dearborn, MI, inspector; Northern High School, Master Residence Art Program, Detroit, MI, teacher; Heidelberg Project, Detroit, MI, pres, 1987-; painter, sculptor. **Honors/Awds:** Volunteer Community Service Awd, YOuth Volunteer Corps, 1995; House of Representatives Resolution No 117, State of Michigan, 1995; Humanity in the Arts Awd, Center for Peace and Conflict Studies, Wayne State University, 1992; Michigan Artist of the Year, Governor John Engler, State of Michigan, 1992; Michiganian of the Year, State of Michigan, 1991; Testimonial Resolution Awd, City of Detroit, 1990; Commission Resolution Awd, Wayne County, 1990; Summer Youth Assistance Prog Awd, Detroit, Michigan, 1989; Spirit of Detroit Awd, Detroit City Council, 1989; David A Harmond Awd, City of Detroit, 1989. **Special Achievements:** Solo Exhibitions: The Heidelberg Project, Detroit, MI, 1996; Alexa Lee Gallery, Ann Arbor, MI, 1994, 1995; The Front Room Gallery, Detroit, MI, 1988; Group Exhibitions: Minnesota Museum of American Art, St Paul, 1996; Center Galleries, Detroit, MI, 1995; Urban Institute of Contemporary Art, Grand Rapids, MI, 1994; numerous others. **Military Serv:** US Army, private, 1972. **Business Phone:** (313)537-8037.

GUYTON, WANDA
Professional basketball player. **Personal:** Born Oct 14, 1968; daughter of Johnny Guyton Sr (deceased). **Educ:** South Florida, attended. **Career:** NEC (Japan), forward, 1989-90; Tenerife (Spain), 1990-92; NEC (Italy), 1992-96; Houston Comets, 1997-. **Business Addr:** Professional Basketball Player, Houston Comets, Two Greenway Plaza, Ste 400, Houston, TX 77046, (713)627-9622.

GUZMAN, JUAN ANDRES CORREA (JUAN)
Professional baseball player. **Personal:** Born Oct 28, 1966, Santo Domingo, Dominican Republic. **Career:** Toronto Blue Jays, 1991-. **Business Addr:** Professional Baseball Player, Toronto Blue Jays, 300 Bremner Blvd W, Ste 3200, Toronto, ON, Canada M5V 3B3, (416)341-1000.

GWALTNEY, JOHN L.
Anthropologist (retired). **Personal:** Born Sep 25, 1928, Orange, NJ; son of Mabel Harper and Stanley Gwaltney. **Educ:** Upsala Coll, BA 1952; New Sch Soc Rsrch, MA 1957; Columbia U, PhD 1967. **Career:** Syracuse U, prof anthropology; NE US Urban Afro-Ams, ethnographer 1973-74; Allopsychic Res Proj NY, ethnographer 1961; LI NY, ethnographer among Shinnecock & Poospatuck Indians 1969; Oaxaca Mexico, ethnographer among Highland Chiantec 1963-64; State Univ of NY, assoc prof 1967-71; Ctr Intl Coop Ottawa, sem 1969. **Orgs:** Mem Com on Oppty in Sci & Resource Group; proj on the handicapped in sci AAAS; mem Amer Found for the Blind Sem on Visual Impairment & Ethnicity NY 1977; guest lecturer Smithsonian Inst, Onondaga Public Library, Wellfleet Public Library, 1st Parish Brewster, Amer Found for the Blind, Navser Reg HS, Robt F Kennedy Meml Inst, Amer Red Cross, Boy Scouts of Amer, AAAS, Applied Anthropology Soc, Amer Anthropological Assoc, Amer Folklore Soc, Amer Assoc of Oral History, Brown, Columbia, Northwestern, Univ of MI, Jackson State Univ, Univ of Scranton; bd dir NY Council for the Humanities, Smithsonian Inst Folk Life Council. **Honors/Awds:** Hon DSc Bucknell Univ 1979; Hon Litt D Upsala Coll 1980; Assoc of Black Anthropologists Publ Awd 1980; Robt F Kennedy Book Awd Hon Mention 1981; semi-finalist, 1986 Chancellor's Citation for Exceptional Acad Achievement Syracuse Univ 1983; 13th Annual Unity Awd in Media Educ Reporting, Natl Print Div Lincoln Univ 1983; Best of Show Awd Cultural Resources Council Syracuse NY 1983, 1986; selected publs, Miss Mabel's Legacy Readers Digest 1982, A Native Replies Natural History 1976, Drylongso, A Self-Portrait of Black Amer NY Random House 1980, 1981; The Dissenters, Voices from Contemporary Amer NY Random House 1986; grant-in-aid, Syracuse Univ, 1979, 1981; fellow, Prog in Black Amer Culture, Smithsonian Inst, 1982; fellow, Natl Endowment for the Humanities, 1983-84.

GWIN, WILIVIGINIA FASZHIANATO (CORA)
Educator, administrator. **Personal:** Born Feb 2, 1954, Mobile, AL; daughter of Wiliviginia V Bolden Gwin and Ernest Leslie Gwin (deceased); married Mitchell Hardy Davis, Aug 10, 1990. **Educ:** Bishop State Jr Coll, AS 1974; AL State Univ, BA 1975, MS 1978; Nova University, EdD 1992; Auburn University; University of Alabama. **Career:** Amer Cancer Soc, program dir 1975-79; Upjohn Healthcare Servcs, Service Dir 1979-80; Univ of South AL, admissions counselor 1980-85, dir of minority affairs 1983-85, dir of affirmative action & academic counseling 1985-; Department of Developmental Studies, academic adviser, coord, learning resources center 1987-. **Orgs:** Mem Business & Professional Women's Club 1977; mem Alpha Kappa Alpha Sor Inc 1980; mem Assoc of Admissions Counselors 1980-; bd mem AL Assoc for Counseling &Develop 1985-87; bd mem Univ of So AL Affirmative Action Monitoring Comm 1985-; mem AL New South Coalition 1986-; bd dirs AL Assoc of Counseling & Develop; mem Mobile County Urban League, Mobile Comm Concerts Assoc; board member Friends of the Saenger Theatre. **Honors/Awds:** AL Literary Soc Award 1st place 1973; Alumni Leadership Scholarship AL State Univ 1974; Kappa Delta Pi Natl Honor Soc 1977; Omicron Delta Kappa Natl Honor Soc USA 1984; Abeneefoo Kuo Honor Soc; Pi Sigma Pi Natl Honor Soc.

GWYNN, FLORINE EVAYONNE
Educator, counselor, administrator. **Personal:** Born Jan 16, 1944, Beckley, WV; daughter of Jean Daisy Wright Calhoun and Flauzell Calhoun; married Herman L Gwynn, Aug 5, 1979; children: Towanna M, Catherine S, Alvin, Calvin, Robert. **Educ:** Beckley Coll, AS 1970; Bluefield State Coll, BS 1977; WV Coll Graduate Studies, MS 1982; WV Union Coll of Law, Morgantown WV, attended 1986-88. **Career:** Raleigh County, youth/sr citizens dir 1969-72; Fed Prison for Women, fed correctional officer 1972-75; Nutrition for the Elderly, project dir

1979-80; Raleigh County Comm on Aging, exec dir 1980-81; Social Security Admin, hearing asst 1982-; Bluefield State Coll, asst prof Criminal Justice program 1982-; NCWVCAA, Kingwood WV, counselor/coordinator; Floetta's Inc, president, currently. **Orgs:** Mem Bluefield State Coll Alumni 1977-, WV Coll of Graduate Studies 1979-; bd of dir Domestic Violence Center 1984-; treasurer Raleigh Co Rainbow Coalition 1984-; mem Phi Alpha Delta Law Fraternity 1986-; coordinator Tygart Valley Baptist Assn Sunday School Congress 1988-, Youth Action Inc 1989-; bd mem Sex Equity-Teen Pregnacy Project 1989-; vice pres, Florence Crittenton Home & Svcs, Wheeling, WV; president, Tygart Valley District Baptist Association Women's Convention. **Honors/Awds:** Appreciation for Serv Amer Legion Aux #70 1969; Community Serv Bluefield State Coll Beckly Chapter Alumni 1984; Bluefield State Coll Teacher of the Year 1985; Service Award, Bluefield State Coll Alumni 1986. **Home Addr:** 1401 Anderson Ave, Morgantown, WV 26505.

GWYNN, TONY (ANTHONY KEITH)
Professional baseball player. **Personal:** Born May 9, 1960, Los Angeles, CA; married Alicia; children: Anthony II, Anisha Nicole. **Educ:** San Diego State, attended. **Career:** San Diego Padres, outfielder, 1982-. **Honors/Awds:** Win Clark Award, Top Southern CA Baseball Player, Los Angeles-Anaheim Baseball Writers; voted to start in All-Star Game in Candlestick Park; selected outfielder The Sporting News Nat League All-Star Team; Finished 3rd in balloting for league MVP Award; Northwest Leagues Most Valuable Player Award; Golden Glove winner for Defensive Excellence; mem 1985 and 1986 All Star Team; 3 time winner Padres/Broadway Player of the Month Awd 1986; honored by Hall of Champions as San Diego's Professional Athlete of the Year. **Business Addr:** Professional Baseball Player, San Diego Padres, PO Box 2000, San Diego, CA 92120.

H

HABERSHAM-PARNELL, JEANNE
Educator. **Personal:** Born May 20, 1936, New York, NY; daughter of Paul & Ethel Parnell; divorced; children: Richard Parnell Habersham. **Educ:** Howard Univ, BA, 1958; Columbia Univ, MA, 1972. **Career:** Amsterdam News, Dawn Magazine, Black America, syndicated columnist; Inner City Broadcasting, WLIB/WBLS, producer & host of City Lights; WNYE Bd of Educ Radio & TV, educational programmer & producer; International Magnet School, admin assistant, asst prin, director, 1990-93; IMPACT II, Bd of Educ citywide, director, 1993-. **Orgs:** NYC 100 Black Women; Metropolitan Jack & Jill Alumni; Harlem YWCA, bd member; Opera Ebony, bd member; Lincoln Center, advisory educ committee; American Federation of TV & Radio Artists; Howard Univ Hall Restoration Committee; National Storytelling Assn. **Honors/Awds:** Success Guide, Named one of the top 15 Educators in NYC, 1991; Cultural Educational Curriculum Award, WNET-TV, PBS, 1989; Images in Black, WNYE Award Program for Excellence in Educational Programming; Frank Silvera Writers Award, 1983; Edythe, NBC/TV, Writer & Producer, 1975. **Special Achievements:** Designed & developed the educational curriculum of The International Magnet School; Created & developed professional grant proposal prototype for Dist 2 Perf Arts; Designed & implemented a performing arts program, NYC Public Schools/ Rensulli Method; Directed the NYC International Children's Chorus, which performed nationally; Syndicated Columnist/48 markets nationwide/Dawn Magazines. **Home Addr:** 2301 5th Avenue, New York, NY 10037, (212)234-3417.

HACKER, BENJAMIN THURMAN
Naval officer. **Personal:** Born Sep 19, 1935, Washington, DC; married Jeanne Marie House; children: Benjamin, Bruce, Anne. **Educ:** Wittenberg Univ, BA 1957; US Naval Postgrad School, Engrg Sci 1963; George Washington Univ, MSA 1978. **Career:** US Navy, commd ensign 1958 advanced through grades to rear adm 1980; Naval Facility Barbados WI, commanding officer 1967-69; FL A&M Univ, comdg officer, prof naval sci 1972-73; Patrol Squadron 24 Jacksonville FL, comdg officer 1974-75; US Naval Air Sta Brunswick, comdg officer; US Mil Enlistment ProcessingCommand Ft Sheridan IL, comdr 1980-82; Fleet Air Mediterranean Naples Italy, comdr 1982-84; Navy Dept Washington DC, dir total force training 1984-86; Naval Training Ctr San Diego, commander 1986-. **Orgs:** Mem US Naval Inst, Natl Naval Officers Assoc, Alpha Phi Alpha, F&AM, PHA. **Honors/Awds:** EdD (HS) George Washington Univ 1986. **Military Serv:** USN, rear admiral; Legion of Merit; Defense Superior Service Medal.

HACKETT, BARRY DEAN (DINO)
Professional football player. **Personal:** Born Jun 28, 1964, Greensboro, NC. **Educ:** Appalachian State Univ, criminal justice degree, 1986. **Career:** Kansas City Chiefs, linebacker, 1986-. **Honors/Awds:** Named to play in Pro Bowl, post-1988 season; replaced because of injury. **Business Addr:** Professional Football Player, Kansas City Chiefs, One Arrowhead Dr, Kansas City, MO 64129-1651.

HACKETT, OBRA V.
Educational administrator. **Personal:** Born Sep 9, 1937, Osyka, MS; son of Letha T Williams and James Hackett; married A Carolyn Evans; children: Obra V Jr. **Educ:** Jackson State Univ, BS 1960; Atlanta Univ, MA 1967; attended Mississippi State Univ 1967-68. **Career:** Henry Weathers HS, math teacher 1960-62, asst principal 1962-64; Carver HS, counselor 1965-66; Utica Jr Coll, vocational counselor 1966-69, dean of students 1969-73; Jackson State Univ, dir pub inform 1973-77, dir develop 1977-84; JSU Dev Found, exec sec 1984-87; Jackson State Univ, asst to the dean for career counseling & placement 1987-89, acting dir, career counseling & placement, 1989-91, dir, 1991-. **Orgs:** Charter mem Coll Pub Relations Assn MS 1970; bd of dir Hinds Co Heart Assn 1974-79; sec bd of dir Goodwill Indus MS 1979-; commr of scouting Seminole Dist Andrew Jackson Council BSA 1979-83; pres Callaway HS PTA 1986-87; 3rd vice pres Jackson Cncl PTA 1986-88; key communicator JPS 1986-; 1st vice pres Jackson Council PTA 1988-90; treas Jackson State Univ Natl Alumni Assn 1996-98; pres, Jackson Council PTA, 1990-91; bd mem, Mississippi PTA, 1990-, pres, 1997-99. **Business Addr:** Director, Jackson State University, Career Counseling & Placement, 1400-1600 John R Lynch St, Jackson, MS 39217.

HACKETT, RUFUS E.
Life insurance executive (retired). **Personal:** Born Feb 4, 1910, Baltimore, MD; son of Charlotte and Edward; married Charlotte E Parrott; children: Veronica L Fullwood, Rufus E Jr. **Educ:** Morgan State Coll, BS 1934; Life Ins Agency Mgt Assn Inst, 1962. **Career:** NC Mutual Life Ins Co, comb agt 1934-35, spec ordinary agt 1935-41, asst mgr 1941-61, dist mgr Baltimore 1961-67, asst agency dir 1967-73, reg agency dir 1973-76, retired. **Orgs:** V chmn Meth Bd of Publn Inc NC Christian Advocate Offic Newsp of the United Meth Ch 1980; past pres MD Underwriters Assn; bd mem Atlantic Alumni Assn; past bd mem Provident Hosp; dist chmn BSA; Econ Dev Commn; cochmn Emp Subcom Mayor's Task Force on Equal Rights; bd mem Vol Council on Equal Oppor; bd of mgrs YMCA; life mem NAACP; Morgan State Coll Alumni Assn; Alpha Phi Alpha; bd dir Ret Sr Volun Prgm; coord coun Sr Citizen's; past bd mem Div of Laf Life & Work Durham Dist United Meth Ch. **Honors/Awds:** Life Underwriters Hon Soc Alumnus of Yr Morgan State Coll 1958; Morgan State Coll Athletic Hall of Fame 1972; numerous awards from NC Mutual Life Ins Co.

HACKETT, WILBUR L., JR.
Coordinator. **Personal:** Born Oct 21, 1949, Winchester, KY; married Brenda. **Educ:** Univ of KY, BA 1973. **Career:** Louisville Reg Criminal Justice Commn, comm coord; Gen Elec Louisville, supr 1973; Erwin House, bd dir. **Orgs:** Russel Area Youth Adv Com; adv Urban League Youth Program; vice pres Concerned Young Men of Louisville; adv Project Way-Out; mem Sickle Cell Anemia Found of KY,; Com for Restoration of Black Hist. **Honors/Awds:** First black capt in SFC Univ of KY; hon mention All-SEC Linebacker. **Business Addr:** 400 S 6th St, MSD Bldg, Louisville, KY 40203.

HACKEY, GEORGE EDWARD, JR.
Law enforcement official. **Personal:** Born May 19, 1948, Bethesda, MD; son of Doris Plummer Hackey and George Edward Hackey Sr; married Dory Ann Gray Hackey, Jun 10, 1978; children: Derick, Cari, George III. **Educ:** Montgomery College, Rockville, MD, AA, general education, 1969; Towson State Univ, Towson, MD, BS, sociology, 1971. **Career:** Montgomery County Dept of Recreation, Rockville, MD, playground director, 1962-70; Montgomery County Board of Education, Rockville, MD, building monitor, 1971-73; Montgomery County Dept of Police, Rockville, MD, community relations officer, 1973-. **Orgs:** Treasurer/member, Montgomery County African-American Employees Assn, 1989-; member, Montgomery County Police Association; chaplain, past pres, Montgomery County Coalition of Black Police Officers, 1974-; chaplain, past pres, Great and Respectable Black Organization, 1980-; mentor, Seneca Valley High School-Models and Mentors Program, 1990-. **Honors/Awds:** Dedicated Service, African-American Employees Assn, 1989-91; Dedicated Service, National Black Police Assn, 1988; Member of the Year, Montgomery County Coalition of Black Police Officers, 1978, 1985; Dedicated Service to the Community, Maryland House of Delegates, 1985; Dedicated Service, Montgomery County Board of Education-Headstart, 1987; Community Leadership-Youth Development, Montgomery County NAACP, 1986. **Military Serv:** US Army Reserves, Sergeant First Class, 1971-77. **Home Addr:** 19200 Bonmark Ct, Germantown, MD 20874. **Business Phone:** (301)840-2575.

HACKLEY, LLOYD VINCENT
Educational administrator. **Personal:** Born Jun 14, 1940, Roanoke, VA; son of Ernestine Parker Hackley (deceased) and David W Hackley Sr (deceased); married Brenda L Stewart, Jun 12, 1960; children: Dianna Hackley-Applin, Michael R. **Educ:** MI State Univ of Political Science, BA (Magna Cum Laude) 1965; Univ of CO Dept of Psychology, grad studies in psychology 1966-67; Univ of NC at Chapel Hill Dept of Polit Science, PhD (Honors) 1976; Government Exec Inst, School of Business Admin, Univ of NC Chapel Hill 1980. **Career:** USAF, retired as major 1958-78; Univ of NC General Admin, assoc vice pres for academic affairs 1979-81; Univ of NC at Chapel Hill, faculty govt execs inst sch of business admin 1980-81; Univ of AR at Pine Bluff, chancellor chief exec officer 1981-85; Univ of NC General Admin, vice pres for student serv and special programs 1985-88; USAF Acad, coach track & cross country, 1974-78, assoc prof, course dir political science, 1974-78; Fayetteville State Univ, Fayetteville NC, chancellor 1988-. **Orgs:** Exec comm Triangle World Affairs Center 1978-79; bd dirs United Fund Carrboro-Chapel Hill 1978-80; bd trustees The Village Company Foundation 1980-81; exec comm NC Comm on Intl Educ 1980-81; mem adv bd Natl Ctr for Toxicological Res 1983; adv comm Univ of AR Grad Inst of Tech 1983; chmn subcomm on curriculum & student matters AR Quality Higher Educ Study Comm 1984; chmn subcomm on middle & jr high schs AR Educ Standards Comm for Elementary & Secondary Schs 1983-84; 3rd vice pres United Way of Jefferson Co 1985; vice pres bd dirs AR Endowment for the Humanities 1985-86, 1984-85; chmn AR Adv Comm to the US Commn on Civil Rights 1985; Strategic Planning Team, Cumberland Co Bd of Educ 1989;Fayetteville Area Economic Devel Corp. **Honors/Awds:** Scholastic Achievement Award, Dean's List Award, Univ of MD European Div 1961; Outstanding Young Man in Amer, United States Jaycees 1977; Governor of AR Traveler Award 1982; AR Certificate of Merit 1983; Key to City Flint MI 1984; Resolution of Tribute by MI Legislature 1984; Community Serv Award in Educ, Pine Bluff/Jefferson County AR 1984; also numerous papers and publications; author, "Disadvantaged Students": Testing Education Not Cultural Deprivation, American Middle Sch Education, 1983; "The Agony of Orthodoxy in Education," Congressional Record, Vol 129, Number 161, Part III, 1983; Resolution of Commendation, Arkansas Legislature, 1985. **Military Serv:** US Air Force major (retired), 1958-78; Outstanding Airman Rosas Air Station Spain 1961; Distinguished Military Grad Officer Training Sch 1965; Vietnam Cross of Gallantry 1968; Bronze Star for Meritorious Serv in Combat with Valor Vietnam 1968; Man of the Hour Headquarters Europe 1970; Bronze Star & Meritorious Serv Medal, Europe, 1971; Aircraft Control & Warning School, Honor Grad 1958. **Business Addr:** Chancellor, Fayetteville State Univ, 1200 Murchison Rd, Fayetteville, NC 28301.

HACKNEY, L. CAMILLE
Record company executive. **Educ:** Princeton Univ, bachelor's degree in pre-med and economics; Harvard Business School, MBA. **Career:** Elektra Entertainment Group, sr dir of multimedia marketing and business development, currently. **Orgs:** Time To Read, tutor, mentor. **Business Addr:** Sr Director of Multimedia Marketing, Elektra Entertainment Group, 75 Rockefeller Plaza, 16th Flr, New York, NY 10019, (212)275-4000.

HADDEN, EDDIE RAYNORD
Attorney, pilot. **Personal:** Born May 25, 1943, Many, LA; son of Emma Cross Hadden and Eddie Hadden; married Kay Dupree; children: Eugene. **Educ:** Univ of TX El Paso, BA Journalism 1965; Geo Washington Univ, incomplete MBA 1971; Hofstra Univ Sch of Law, JD 1979. **Career:** JF Small Adv, vice pres 1973-74; Eastern Airlines, pilot 1972-89; US Navy, officer/aviator 1965-72; private practice, lawyer 1980-. **Orgs:** Vice pres Bergen Co NJ NAACP 1980-83; pres Bergen Co NJ Urban League Housing Auth 1981-85; bd of dir Org of Black Airline Pilots Inc 1981-85; city councilman at large City of Englewood NJ 1983-86; board of governors, Englewood , Chamber of Commerce 1990, board of managers, Englewood Community Chest 1990, chmn educational outreach, Alpha Phi Alpha fraternity, Kappa Theta Lambda Chapter 1990-. **Honors/Awds:** Elected official Englewood NJ City Council 1983; Youth Serv Awd Tuskegee Airm Inc Natl Conv 1984; Airline Pilots Association, Rare Bird Award, 1975. **Military Serv:** USN commander 21 yrs. **Business Addr:** Attorney, The Atrium, 80 Rte 4 E, Ste 100, Paramus, NJ 07652.

HADDOCK, MABLE J.
Educator, consultant. **Personal:** Born Jun 20, 1948, Clover, VA; daughter of Mr & Mrs Nephew R Staten; children: Kevin. **Educ:** Mercy Coll, BA 1974; NBC Fellow Kent State Univ, MA 1976; Wharton Bus School, Cert 1982. **Career:** HEOP Mercy Coll, asst dir 1974-76; NBC, writer/rschr 1977-78; Canton Cultural Ctr, urban arts dir 1978-80; Natl Black Programming Consortium, exec dir, 1980-; Ohio State University, Columbus, OH, lecturer, 1988-; Dialogue Magazine, Columbus, OH, contributor; National Video Resources of the Rockefeller Foundation, consultant/curator, 1990-91. **Orgs:** Mem women in Commun, OH Arts Council Minority Arts Task Force 1980-82; consult OH Arts Council 1980-82; bd of dir YWCA 1982; bd mem Columbus Cable Commiss1982-83; mem Columbus Comm Calbe Access 1983-. **Honors/Awds:** YWCA Women of Achievement, 1997; Participated conf on Media in Africa held in Senegal 1981; Co-Produce "Fannie Lou Hamer Story" 1983; Proj Dir "State of Black Amer" 1984, "Forum of Black Amer" 1985, "Mandela" currently in production; selected by the UN as rep on "Seminar on the Intensification of Intl Media Action for the Immediate Independence of Namibia" held in Brazzaville, Congo March 25-29 1985; Unsung Heroes Semi-Finalist, Kool Achievement, 1989. **Business Addr:** Executive Director, National Black Programing Consortium, 761 Oak St, Ste A, Columbus, OH 43205.

HADDON, JAMES FRANCIS
Investment banker. **Personal:** Born Aug 12, 1954, Columbia, SC; son of Ida Beatrice Haddon and Wallace James Haddon; married Sezelle Antoinette Gereau, Sep 25, 1988; children: Madeleine Louise, James Douglass. **Educ:** Wesleyan University, BA, 1976; Stanford, MBA, 1980. **Career:** Mellon National Corp., real estate analyst, 1976-78; Blyth Eastman Paine-Webber, associate, 1980-83; Paine-Webber, vice pres, 1984-87, first vice pres, 1987-89, managing director, 1989-. **Orgs:** National Association for Securities Professionals, board member, 1991-; Sponsors For Economic Opportunity Mentor Program, 1984-. **Business Addr:** Managing Director, Paine-Webber, Inc., 1285 Avenue of the Americas, 10th fl, New York, NY 10019-6093, (212)713-3304.

HADEN, MABEL D.
Attorney. **Personal:** Born Feb 17, Campbell County, VA; married Russell George Smith. **Educ:** Howard U, LLB 1948; Georgetown U, LLM 1956. **Career:** Self-employed atty 1948-; DC, real estate broker 1959-; DC Pub Schs, tchr 1941-50. **Orgs:** Mem ABA; NBA; Washingtion Bar Assn; Nat Assn of Black Women Attorneys; mem Am Civil Liberties Union; Women's Equity Action League; board of governors, Washington Metro Chapter of Trial Lawyers, 1986-91. **Honors/Awds:** Honoree Iota Phi Lambda Sor Gamma Chap 1977; articles Case & Comment Lawyers' Co-operative Pub Co 1975; Charlotte Ray Award, Greater Washington Chapter-NBA, 1991.

HADLEY, HOWARD ALVA, JR.
Physician. **Personal:** Born Jul 14, 1941, Miami, FL; son of Flora Dean Hadley and Howard Alva Hadley Sr; married Cynthia Barnes Hadley, May 31, 1976; children: Howard Alva III, Cynthia Alease. **Educ:** FL A&M U, BS 1963; Howard U, MD 1967. **Career:** Mt Sinai Hosp, intern 1967-68; Dade Co Hlth Dept, gen med clinic 1970; South Dade Community Health Center, emergency room physician, 1975-80; Dept of Family Med Univ Miami, clinical asst prof 1976; private practice, 1980-. **Orgs:** Treasurer, Dade County Chapter, National Medical Assn, 1988-. **Military Serv:** AUS med corps, capt 1968-70. **Business Addr:** Physician, 14654 Lincoln Blvd, Miami, FL 33176.

HADLEY, SYBIL CARTER
Attorney. **Personal:** Born in Dallas, TX; married Roy E Hadley Jr. **Educ:** Univ of VA. **Career:** Swift, Currie, McGhee & Hiers, sr assoc atty; Fulton County Board of Elections and Registration, chair and chief registrar, 1996-. **Special Achievements:** First woman chair and chief registrar of Fulton County Bd of Elections and Registration. **Business Addr:** Sr Associate Attorney, Swift, Currie, McGhee & Hiers, 1355 Peachtree St NE, Ste 300, Atlanta, GA 30309-3238, (404)874-8800.

HADNOT, THOMAS EDWARD
Engineer. **Personal:** Born Jul 23, 1944, Jasper, TX; son of Mertie Shelby Hadnot and Jack Hadnot; married Gay Nell Singleton; children: Wanda Rideau Carrier, Sonja Armstrong, James E Rideau III, Clint D Rideau, Tomi L. **Educ:** Univ of MD, 1967; Prairie View A&M Univ, BS Civil Engrg 1972. **Career:** Exxon Chem Amer, proj engr 1972-73, 1975-76, design engr, 1973-75, start-up engr 1976-77, scheduling engr 1977-79, coord sec supv 1979-81, prod coord/bus planner 1981-83, mfg supr 1983-86, dept mgr 1986-89, quality/productivity adv, 1989-. **Orgs:** Tau Beta Pi; mem, American Society of Quality Control, 1990-. **Honors/Awds:** Phi Beta Sigma Alpha Beta Sigma Chapt; Alpha Kappa Mu Hon Soc. **Military Serv:** USAF E-4 sgt 3 1/2 yrs. **Home Addr:** PO Box 3664, Baytown, TX 77520. **Business Addr:** Quality/Productivity Adviser, Exxon Chemical Company, 5200 Bayway, Baytown, TX 77522.

HADNOTT, BENNIE L.
Business executive. **Personal:** Born Nov 23, 1944, Prattville, AL; son of Flora Hadnott and James Hadnott; children: Danielle, Johnathan. **Educ:** Bernard M Baruch, BBA 1971; Iona Coll, MBA 1976. **Career:** Watson Rice LLP, partner, 1981-. **Orgs:** Am Inst of CPA'S; Assn of Govt Acctnts; NY/NJ Intergovt Audit Forum; Municipal Finance Offcr Assn of the US & Canada; NY State Soc of CPA'S, State & Local Govt & Health Care Comm; AICPA'S Govt Acctng & Auditing Educ Subcommittee; AICPA Fed Acquistion Committee Wash, DC; treas Berger County Br NAACP; treas PIC Council Bergen County; AICPA Future Issues Committee. **Military Serv:** USAF Airman 1st Class 1962-67. **Business Addr:** Managing Partner, Watson Rice LLP, One Park Ave, Fl 10, New York, NY 10016-5802.

HADNOTT, GRAYLING
Mortgage company executive. **Personal:** Born Apr 7, 1950, New Iberia, LA; son of Frances Martina Hadnott and Louie Hadnott; divorced; children: Roxanne. **Educ:** Univ of Southwestern LA, BA 1973, MBA 1980; Attended, Univ of OK, Natl Consumer Credit School. **Career:** St Martin Parish Schools, english teacher 1972-79; Univ of Southwestern LA, english teacher 1973-75; Community Investment Funds, officer/supervisor; Iberia Svgs & Loan Assoc, comm investment funds officer 1980-87; Diversified Mortgage, Inc, senior loan officer, 1989-. **Orgs:** Mem Assoc of MBA Execs 1981-87, NBMBA Detroit Chap 1983-87; bd of dirs Sugarland Optimists' Club 1984-85, Friends of the Library 1985-87; mem LA Assocof Student Aid Administrators 1986-87.

HAGAN, GWENAEL STEPHANE
Cable television executive. **Personal:** Born Oct 9, 1960, Everux, France; son of Suzanne J Boule and Willie D Hagen; divorced; children: Gael Y. **Educ:** Colorado University-Boulder, BS Accounting, 1982; Marquette University, MBA Candidate, 1987-1988; Colorado State University, MBA Candidate, currently. **Career:** KMPG, auditor, 1982-83; Jones Intercable, sr auditor, 1983-85, business mgr, 1985-86, cable television system mgr, 1986-88; director new product development, 1988-90; Mind Extension University, vice pres, business development, 1990-. **Orgs:** National Association Minorities in Cable, committee chairman, vice pres, board mem, 1984-. **Honors/Awds:** Colorado Society of Accountancy, CPA, 1984.

HAGAN, WILLIE JAMES
Educational administrator. **Personal:** Born Dec 17, 1950, Montgomery, AL; son of Dorothy Marie Wright Hagan and Oliver Hagan; married Constance Marie Diaz, Jul 4, 1979; children: Lynea Marie Diaz-Hagan. **Educ:** Mitchell College, New London, CT, AS, 1971; University of Connecticut, Storrs, CT, BA, 1973, MA, 1975, PhD, currently. **Career:** Dept of Higher Education, Hartford, CT, assistant director of legislative services; University of Connecticut, Storrs, CT, director of government relations, 1986-90, acting vice president, 1990, associate vice president, 1990-. **Orgs:** Member, Government Relations and Communications Officers, 1982-87. **Home Addr:** 2908 E Wellesley Ct, Fullerton, CA 92631-2223.

HAGER, JOSEPH C.
Religion instructor. **Personal:** Born Jun 11, 1944, Washington, DC. **Educ:** Marist Coll Poughkeepsie NY, BA 1967; Sherwood Sch of Music Chicago, certificate of music 1960; candidate MA. **Career:** American Univ, camp counselor 1960-61; Family & Child Services; Marist House Formation St Joseph Novitiate, asst dir music; Marist Coll, asst dir music 1965-66; Marist Coll, dir music 1966-67; St Mary Parish Poughkeepsie, CCD instructor 1964-65; Mt St Michael Acad Bronx, secondary educ teacher 1967-70; Emmaculate Concoption Bronx teacher adult educ 1968; Our Lady Perpetual Help Pelham NY, CCD tchr 1968; New Rochelle HS religion, CCD secondary teacher 1968-70; New Rochelle HS religion, CCD training instructor 1968-69; New Rochelle HS religion, CCD curriculum developer 1969-70. **Orgs:** Staff consult Nat Office Black Caths 1970-73; exec dir Nat Black Cath Clergy Caucus 1970-73; dir religious educ St Benedict the Moor Wash DC; 1973-74; Alpha Kappa Psi Frat; DC bicentennial com; Nat Educ Assn; Nat Cath Educ Assn; Nat Black Cath Clergy Causus; bd mem camping programs Family & Child Services; Delta Psi Omega; Nat Office Black Caths; consult DESIGN; Carter G Woodson Com; Nat Black Churchmen Com. **Business Addr:** Woodward Bldg Archdiocese of W, 733 15 St NW #725, Washington, DC 20005.

HAGER, ROSCOE FRANKLIN
Consultant. **Personal:** Born Jul 13, 1941, Gaston Cty, NC; married Anna Evans; children: Roscoe F Jr, Angela, Dorothy R. **Educ:** Elizabeth City State Univ, BS 1963; WI State Univ Eau Claire, MS 1969; Appalachian State Univ Boone NC, MA 1980. **Career:** Anson Cty Bd of Educ, teacher, athletic dir, asst principal 1965; WI State Univ, instructor, counselor 1972; Conner Homes, sales mgr 1973-75; Anson Tech Coll, asst to pres & dir of inst rsch 1976-79; Govt Exec Inst UNC Chapel Hill, 1981; NC Dept of Public Educ Affirmative Action, 1979-. **Orgs:** Manpower chmn Anson Cty Boy Scouts 1976-79; vchmn Anson Cty Grass Roots Art Council 1977-79; chmn Anson Cty Scout Show 1978-79; mem NAACP, Alpha Phi Alpha, NC State Employees Assoc, NC Chap of the Intl Personnel Mgmt Assoc; chmn Wake Forest Comm School Adv Council. **Honors/Awds:** Corpl Elizabeth City State Football Team 1962; NSF Fellowship WI State Univ 1967-69. **Business Addr:** Federal Compliance Consultant, NC Dept of Community Colleges, 114 W Edenton St, Raleigh, NC 27611.

HAGGINS, JON
Fashion designer. **Personal:** Born Sep 5, 1943, Tampa, FL; son of Willie Mae Haggins and John Haggins; divorced. **Educ:** Fashion Inst of Tech, AAS, 1964. **Career:** "Off the Avenue" (first studio), designer 1966; Reno Sweeney in Greenwich Village, Copa, Once Upon a Stove, "Dangerfield's" singer; Jon Haggins Inc, pres/fashion designer, 1980-. **Honors/Awds:** First recognized black designer and one of the youngest designers nominated for The Coty American Fashion Critics Awd; one of designs named "The Dress of the Year" by Bill Cunningham; honored for achievements with 9 other black designers by Harvey's Bristol Cream 1980, 1981, 1983; Black Designer of the Year 1981; Key to the City, Baltimore, MD, 1982; honored by Cornell Univ with an exhibition of his work, 1988; Artist-in-Residence, Cornell Univ, 1988; made numerous TV appearances; clothes featured in magazines & newspapers including Cosmopolitan, Harper's Bazaar, Vogue, Town & Country, New York Times, Essence, Ebony, and many more.

HAGINS, OGBONNA
Independent entrepreuner. **Personal:** Born Feb 22, 1966, Philadelphia, PA; son of Anne & Paul (deceased) Hagins; married Sheena Lester; children: Atamusi Kamau, Atamanu Zaki. **Educ:** Temple University, 1984 1985, 1995, 1996; Community College of Philadelphia, 1987, 1988, 1994. **Career:** Davis, Poole & Sloan, jr draftsman, 1984-87; The Salkin Group, working drawing specialist, 1987-89; Murray Architectural, architectural designer draftman, 1987-94; School Dist of Phila, architectural design & drafting teacher, 1991-96. **Orgs:** Philadelphia Federation of Teachers, 1991-96. **Honors/Awds:** Dobbins/Randolph Alumni Association, Dedication & Leadership, 1995. **Special Achievements:** Developed "Manhood Development/Rites of Passage," at Murrell Dobbins High School, 1993; implementing a private, African-centered educational facility. **Business Addr:** Architectural Design & Drafting Teacher, Dobbins High School, 2243 Gray's Ferry Ave, Philadelphia, PA 19146, (215)545-4892.

HAGLER, MARVELOUS MARVIN
Professional boxer (retired), actor. **Personal:** Born May 23, 1954, Newark, NJ; divorced; children: Gentry, James, Celeste, Marvin Jr, Charelle. **Career:** World Boxing Assn Professional Middleweight Boxer, World Boxing Champion, 1980-88; actor, currently. **Orgs:** World Boxing Assn; US Boxing Assn; World Boxing Council. **Honors/Awds:** Won the Natl Am Middleweight Championship 1973; Outstanding Fighter Awd; Won AAU Championship 1973; became Middleweight Champion 1980; successfully defended his championship 12 times; Honored as Boxer of the Year, World Boxing Council, 1984; 1st in middleweight div to earn a $1 million purse; 1985 Honoree The Jackie Robinson Award for Athletics for accomplishments as simultaneous holder of the World Boxing Assn, World Boxing Council and Intl Boxing Federation middle weight div titles and for successful defense of his titles; Intl Boxing Hall of Fame, 1993. **Special Achievements:** Former undisputed middleweight champion of the world: WBA, WBC, IBF, 1980-87; television commercial appearances include: Pizza Hut, Diet Coke, Gillette Sport Stick; guest appearances include: "Saturday Night Live," "Punky Brewster," "Room 227"; film appearances include: Indio; Indio 2; Night of Fear; established scholarship fund, Massasoit Community College, 1980. **Business Addr:** Former Boxer, c/o Mr Peter De Veber, 112 Island St, Stoughton, MA 02072.

HAGOOD, HENRY BARKSDALE
Real estate developer. **Personal:** Born Aug 19, 1942, Wilson, NC; son of Emmett B Hagood Sr and Aurelia Muir; married Theresa, Nov 26, 1989; children: Gabrielle Toles. **Educ:** Michigan State University, BA, 1965. **Career:** Millender Center Association, developer; Signet Development Company, development manager; Walbridge Aldinger, director of business development; Detroit Housing Department, mayor's executive liaison; Detroit Water & Sewerage Department, administrative assistant, Contract & Grant Division; City of Detroit, Community & Economic Development Department, director; City of Detroit, Mayor's Office, executive assistant to Mayor Young; The Farbman Group, vice president, currently. **Orgs:** Detroit Economic Growth Corporation Executive Committee; Economic Development Corporation; Downtown Development Authority; Detroit Neighborhood Housing Service; Highland Park YMCA, board of directors; Franklin Wright Settlement, board of directors; New Detroit Inc; Housing & Construction Committee, vice-chairman. **Honors/Awds:** Southeastern Michigan Builder's Association, Distinguished Service Award, 1992; University Citizens District Council, Board of Recognition; Detroit Neighborhood Non-Profit Housing Corporation, Outstanding Service Award; Area Council of the Citizens District Council, Outstanding Service Award Leadership. **Business Phone:** (810)351-4357.

HAGOOD, JAY
Professional football player. **Personal:** Born Aug 9, 1973. **Educ:** Virginia Tech, attended. **Career:** New York Jets, tackle, 1997-. **Business Addr:** Professional Football Player, New York Jets, 1000 Fulton Ave, Hempstead, NY 11550, (516)560-8100.

HAILE, ANNETTE L.
Manufacturing company executive. **Personal:** Born Oct 3, 1952, Latrobe, PA; daughter of Edith Hill Haile. **Educ:** John Carroll University, Cleveland, OH, BS, 1974; Baldwin Wallace College, Berea, OH, MBA, 1978. **Career:** IBM Corp, Bethesda, MD, director, 1974-. **Honors/Awds:** Hall of Fame, Negro Business & Professional Womens Clubs, 1990.

HAILE, RICHARD H. See Obituaries section.

HAILES, EDWARD A.
Cleric, association executive. **Personal:** son Of Maggie Hailes and Walter Hailes; married Nettie Drayton; children: Edward Jr, Gregory, Patricia. **Educ:** VA Union Univ, 1950; VA State Coll, Certificate; Harvard & Boston Univs, advanced studies; Howard Univ, Certificate. **Career:** Union Baptist Church New Bedford, pastor 1951-63; Inter-Church Council of Greater New Bedford, supr religious educ 1954-61, exec sec 1963-66; MA Public Sch Syst, substitute teacher 1962-63; DC Branch NAACP, exec sec 1963-66; Opportunity Industrialization Ctr, exec dir; 19th St Baptist Church Washington, DC, assoc pastor 1978-; pastor Mount Moriah Baptist Church. **Orgs:** Comm Adv on Equal Employment 1967-71; bd dir, vice pres 1980-, natl NAACP; pres 1968-72, 1978-, DC Branch NAACP; bd dir

Housing Dev Corp 1969-74; Health & Welfare Council 1969-; mem Commn on Criminal Justice Stand & Goals 1970-71; v chmn Project Build Inc 1972; mem Mayor's Com Project HOME Washington 1973-; adv panel Adult Educ Demonstration Proj 1974-; mem bd dir DC Chamber of Commerce 1983-; pres Charitable Found, United Supreme Council Ancient and Accepted Scottish Rite of Freemasonry Prince Hall Affil 1984-; bd dir United Givers Fund; DC chap US Civil Rights Commn. **Honors/Awds:** Chamber of Commerce Award for role in march on Washington 1963; Created Grand Insp Gen of 33rd Degree The United Supreme Council of the Sovereign Grand Inspector General of the 33rd & Last Degree of the Ancient & Accept Scottish Rite of Freemasonry Prince Hall Affil 1974; Man of the Year Award Shiloh Men's Club Shiloh Baptist Ch 1980; Citizen of the Year Omega Psi Phi Chapters of Washington, DC 1981; Distinguished Serv Award United Supr Coun Ancient & Accept Scottish Rite of Freemasonry Prince Hall Affiliate; Outstand Young Citizen of Yr Jr Chamber of Commerce New Bedford. **Business Addr:** Clergyman, 19th St Baptist Church, 3224 16 St NW, Washington, DC 20010.

HAILEY, PRISCILLA W.
Associate publisher. **Personal:** Born Oct 22, 1947, Georgia; married Howard L. **Educ:** Savannah State Coll, BS 1969. **Career:** The Medium Newspaper Seattle, assoc publisher 1970-; Dublin GA Bd of Educ, tchr 1969-70; Kaiser Gypsum Co, credit sec 1969; Head Start, tchr 1967-68. **Orgs:** Mem bd dir, treas Tilober Publ Co Inc; NAACP; Black Educ & Economics Conf; trainer-supr Seattle Univ Minority Stud Newspaper 1971-73; team capt Neighborhood Cancer Soc; Nat Educ Assn 1969-70; GA Educ Assn 1969-70; vol accountant to inner city residents vol trainer-typesetter Garfield HS Messenger 1970-71. **Honors/Awds:** Recipient Model Cities Citizen Participation Award; Black Comm Unsung Hero Award. **Business Addr:** 2600 S Jackson, Seattle, WA 98144.

HAINES, CHARLES EDWARD
Art director. **Personal:** Born Apr 20, 1925, Louisville, KY; son of Willie M Warfield Haines and William Haines; divorced; children: Charles Jr. **Educ:** IN Univ, AB 1950, MFA 1953, MA 1959. **Career:** Free lance adv art; IN Univ, graduate asst; Sarkes Tarzian Inc, art dir; Avco Broad, art dir; Crosley Broad, art dir; Marian Coll, lecturer; IN Univ/Purdue Univ, Indianapolis, lecturer, 1969-; WTHR TV, Indianapolis, IN, art director, 1959-. **Orgs:** Mem Coll Art Assoc Amer; mem Dean's Select Comm Search & Screen to appt new dean, Herron Sch of Art Indianapolis. **Honors/Awds:** Black Expo Feat in "Ebony Mag" 1957; Exhibitions & Awds various state fairs; art work IN Basketball Hall of Fame; painting Atlanta Univ Collection. **Military Serv:** AUS Corp of Engrg pfc 1944-46; Bronze Star, Rhineland Campaign. **Business Addr:** Art Director, WTHR TV, 1000 N Meridian St, Indianapolis, IN 46204.

HAINES, DIANA
Attorney, government official. **Personal:** Born Mar 4, 1955, Brooklyn, NY; daughter of Minnie Haines. **Educ:** Oberlin College, BA, 1977; George Washington University Law Center, JD, 1980; Antioch University, MA, legal education, 1985. **Career:** Antioch Law School, clinical law professor, 1982-86; Department of Consumer & Regulatory Affiars, chief office of compliance, 1986-92; American University Law School, adjunct instructor, 1986-; DC Government, Civilian Complaint Review Board, executive director, 1992-. **Orgs:** My Sister's Place, Shelter for Battered Women, staff attorney, 1990-; DC Bar, Consumer Affairs Section, steering committee, 1992-; Coalition of 100 Black Women, 1986-; Christian Social Action Committee, United Church of Christ, chairperson, 1991-. **Home Phone:** (202)829-5884. **Business Phone:** (202)535-1716.

HAIR, JOHN
Educational administrator, educator. **Personal:** Born Oct 8, 1941, Gulf Port, MS; son of Julia Frost Hair and John Hair; married Beverly Scott Hair, Dec 22, 1988; children: John Saverson, Melissa Deleon. **Educ:** Wayne State Univ, BS Ed 1969, MS Ed 1971; GA State Univ, EdS 1978; Western MI Univ, EdD 1986. **Career:** Detroit Public Schools, band dir 1969-71; Grand Rapids OIC, exec dir 1973-77; Grand Rapids Job Corps, mgr of educ 1981-82; Davenport Coll, faculty 1982-, dir of minority affairs 1983-88, dean of minority affairs, 1988-90; vice president for student affairs, 1990-; vice pres, cabinet member, 1992-. **Orgs:** Mem Phi Delta Kappa 1980-, MI Academy of Sci Arts & Letters 1983-; higher educ comm mem NABSE 1984-; mem IL Comm Black Concern in Higher Educ 1985-; secondary/higher educ comm AAHE 1986-; adv bd mem Grand Rapids Cable TV 1986-; mem industrial adv council Grand Rapids OIC; mem Grand Rapids Urban League; mem exec adv comm Sara Allen Family Neighborhood Ctr; bd mem, Grand Rapids Public School 1987-90; vice president, Black Educational Excellence Program, 1990-; Sigma Pi Phi, 1992-. **Honors/Awds:** Grad Rsch Asst GA State Univ 1976-77; Band Leader 13 piece band Amway Grand Hotel 1982-85; "GIANTS" Phyllis Scott Activist Award 1988; "HEROES" Hispanic Community Service (non-Hispanic) Award of Merit 1988; chair personnel and Junior College Conn Grand Rapids Public School Board 1988-90. **Military Serv:** AUS pfc 3 yrs. **Home Addr:** 1702 Hiawatha Rd SE, Grand Rapids, MI 49506. **Business Addr:** Vice President for Student Affairs, Student Affairs Dept, Davenport College, 415 E Fulton, Grand Rapids, MI 49503.

HAIRSTON, ABBEY GAIL
Attorney. **Personal:** Born Oct 15, 1955, Chicago, IL; daughter of Horace W & Rosietta Hairston. **Educ:** Drake University, BA, 1976; University of Iowa, College of Law, JD, 1980. **Career:** Florida Rural Legal Svcs, staff attorney, 1980-82, supervising attorney, 1982-84; School Board of Palm Beach County, FL, personal attorney, 1984-88, general counsel, 1988-94; Nova University, adjunct professor, 1984-92; Barry University, adjunct professor, 1991-93; Alexander, Bearden, Hairston & Marks, partner, 1994-. **Orgs:** American Bar Association, 1985-; Association of Trial Lawyers of America, 1996-; Federal Bar Association, 1994; National Bar Association, 1984-. **Special Achievements:** National Employment Law Institute, lecturer, 1993-. **Business Addr:** Partner, Alexander, Bearden, Hairston & Marks, LLP, Lee Plz, 8601 Georgia Ave, Ste 805, Silver Spring, MD 20910, (301)589-2222.

HAIRSTON, EDDISON R., JR.
Dentist. **Personal:** Born Apr 4, 1933, York Run, PA; married Audrey Barnes; children: Eddison, Jr, Robert Eugene. **Educ:** Lincoln U, AB 1954; Howard Univ Dental Sch, DDS 1962. **Career:** Self-employeed dentist 1963-; Howard Univ Comm Dentistry Chronically Ill & Aged Prog, clin asst prof 1967-. **Orgs:** Consult Armstrong Dental Asst Prog 1973-74; mem Robt T Freeman Dental Soc; Am & Nat Dental Assns; DC Dental Soc; Am Soc of Dentistry for Children; Omega Psi Phi; Wash Urban League; NAACP; many other ch, civc & professional orgns. **Military Serv:** AUS dental tech 1954-57. **Business Addr:** 3417 Minnesota Ave, SE, Washington, DC 20019.

HAIRSTON, HAROLD B.
Fire commissioner. **Career:** Philadelphia Fire Department, 32 year veteran, fire commissioner, currently. **Special Achievements:** Philadelphia's first African American fire commissioner. **Business Addr:** Commissioner, Philadelphia Fire Department, 240 Spring Garden St., Philadelphia, PA 19123, (215)686-1300.

HAIRSTON, JERRY WAYNE
Professional baseball player (retired). **Personal:** Born Feb 16, 1952, Birmingham, AL; married Esperanza Anellano; children: Jerry Jr, Justin, Scott, Stacey Lynn. **Educ:** Lawson State Junior College, Birmingham, AL, attended. **Career:** Chicago White Sox, outfielder, 1973-77; Pittsburgh Pirates, outfielder/infielder, 1977; Chicago White Sox, outfielder, 1981-89.

HAIRSTON, JESTER
Actor, singer, composer. **Personal:** Born in North Carolina; married Margaret Lancaster, 1938 (deceased). **Educ:** Attended Univ of Massachusetts; received music degree from Tufts Univ, Boston MA, 1930; attended Juilliard School of Music, New York NY. **Career:** Broadway singer, music instructor, composer, conductor, and actor. **Honors/Awds:** Actor for twenty years on Amos 'n' Andy; composer of Broadway musical Green Pastures; composer of film scores with Dmitri Tiomkin; actor in films including The Alamo, In the Heat of the Night, Lady Sings the Blues, and The Last Tycoon; plays part of Rolly Forbes on television series Amen. **Business Addr:** 5047 Valley Ridge Ave, Los Angeles, CA 90043.

HAIRSTON, JOSEPH HENRY
Attorney. **Personal:** Born May 8, 1922, Axton, VA; son of Julia Hairston and James Hairston; married Anna L Allen; children: Nancy R, Naomi, JoAnn, Victoria M. **Educ:** Univ Maryland, BS 1957; Am U, JD 1960; Georgetown U, LLM 1961. **Career:** Office of Solicitor Dept Labor Wash, atty 1960-61; Operations Div IRS, retired dir 1976-85. **Orgs:** DC Bar Association; American Bar Association; treasurer, Natl Bar Assn; trustee, Baptist Sr Adult Ministries (BSAM); founding mem, Nat Lawyers Club; board of directors, Am Inst Parliamentarians; past pres, vp, bd dirs, Neighbors Inc; past v chmn, moderator, Takoma Park Bapt Ch; founder, pres, Nat Neighbors 1969, 1975; del, Shepherd Park Citizens Assn; exec com, DC Federation Citizens Assns 1970-73; Shepherd PTA; Takoma PTA; Officers Club, Walter Reed Army Med Ctr; Nat Assn Uniformed Serv; commissioner, District of Columbia Advisory Neighborhood Commission; trustee, DC Bapt Foundation; ex-bd, exec comm, DC Bapt Convention; co-chair, DC Postal Advisory Comm; chmn, Washington Gas Co, Citizens Advisory Comm; past pres, DC Chap, American Inst of Parliamentarians; treas, Washington Bar Assn; Coordinating Council, Cooperative Bapt Fellowship. **Honors/Awds:** First black atty apptd sr exec, Office of Chief Counsel, IRS. **Military Serv:** AUS 1940-60. **Home Addr:** 1316 Floral St NW, Washington, DC 20012.

HAIRSTON, OSCAR GROGAN
Physician (retired). **Personal:** Born Jun 8, 1921, Winston-Salem, NC; son of Leanna Grogan Hairston and Jacob Hairston; married Lillian F. **Educ:** Hampton Ins, 1949; Meharry Med Coll, 1958; Harvard Univ, PG 1953; Reynold Hosp, PG surgical residency. **Career:** Geo Washington Carver HS, sci & math teacher 1952-54; physician . **Orgs:** Twin City Med Soc; Oln N St Med Soc; Forsythe Co Med Soc; Amer Academy of Family Practitioners AOA; life mem NAACP. **Honors/Awds:** Fellow Amer Academy of Family Practice. **Military Serv:** USAAC 1942-46.

HAIRSTON, OTIS L.
Clergyman (retired). **Personal:** Born Apr 28, 1918, Greensboro, NC; son of Nancy Wright-Hairston and John T Hairston; married Anna Cheek; children: Mrs Emma Lois Belle, Otis Jr. **Educ:** Shaw Univ, 1940. **Career:** Bapt Informer, ed 1941-56; Shaw Univ, dir publ 1950-51; Brookston Bapt Church, pastor 1952-60; Bapt Supply Store, mgr 1956-58; Shiloh Bapt Church, minister, retired. **Orgs:** Mem PTA, Wake Cty Credit Union, Natl Shaw Univ Alumni Assoc, Shaw Univ Theol Alumni, Raleigh Citizens Assoc, Gen Bapt State Conv, Rowan Bapt Assoc, Org Greensboro Human Rel Comm, Greensboro Ministers Fellowship, Pulpit Forum, Citizens Assoc, Citizens Emergency Comm, NAACP, Hayes-Taylor YMCA; bd mem Industfor the Blind; exec comm Gen Bapt St Convention of NC, Greensboro C of C, United Comm Svc, Comm Plan Council, United Day Care Svc, Comm Christian Soc Ministeries of NC Council Chs, Bd of Ed, Dem Party, Phi Beta Sigma; bd of trustees L Richardson Mem Hosp; adv comm Friends Home; chaplain on call, Wesley Long Hosp; bd of trustees Bennett Coll. **Honors/Awds:** Ford Fellow 1966; Peacemaker Awd 1974; Cert Distinction Lott Carey Bapt Foreign Mission 1973,74; Hon DDiv Shaw Univ 1974; Zeta Phi Beta Sor Awd 1968; YMCA Awd 1971; NAACP Man of the Year Awd 1978; Hayes Taylor YMCA Awd for Leadership to Youth 1971; Citizen of the Year Awd for Meritorius Serv to Greensboro & The Ed Syst Tau Omega Chap of Omega Psi Phi Frat Inc; Brotherhood Citation Awd Natl Conf of Christian & Jews 1983. **Home Addr:** 2 Tipton Ct, Greensboro, NC 27406.

HAIRSTON, RALEIGH DANIEL
Social worker, cleric. **Personal:** Born Nov 15, 1934, Amonate, VA; son of Elsie Wilson Hairston and Samuel Hardin Hairston; married Helen Carol Covington, Dec 22, 1962 (divorced); children: John Lesley Daniel, Karen Nancy. **Educ:** Bluefield State College, BS, 1959; Atlanta University, MSW, 1962; Bexley Hall Episcopal Seminary, MA, 1969; Case Western Reserve University, MA, 1975; Colgate Rochester Divinity School, DMin, 1978. **Career:** Boston University Medical School, Psychiatry Department, adjunct assistant professor, 1970-71; Cleveland Metro Gen Hospital, project administrator, 1972-77; St Simon of Cyrene Episcopal Church, rector, 1977-81; Emmanuel Epicopal Church, interim rector, 1982; Cleveland Municipal Court, probation officer, 1982-85; Veterans Administration Hospital, medical social worker, 1985-88; Calvary Episcopal Church, assistant priest, 1989-91; City of Washington Child & Family Services, social worker, beginning 1989-; Saint Augustine's College, chaplain, 1995-. **Orgs:** NAACP, currently; National Association of Social Workers; Association of Black Social Workers; Union of Black Episcopalians; American Federation of State, Country, and Municipal Employees, currently; Interdenominational Ministerial Association; Diocese of Southern Ohio Commission on Ecumenical Relations, 1979-81; Diocese of Ohio Commission on Ministry, 1975-77; Kappa Alpha Psi Fraternity, 1958-92. **Honors/Awds:** City of Lincoln Heights, Ohio, Human Services Volunteer Award, 1980; Bexley Hall Episcopal Seminary, Firestone Scholarship, 1965; Bluefield State College, Sigma Rho Sigma Hon Fraternity of Social Sciences, 1959. **Special Achievements:** Author, "Blacks and the Episcopal Church in the Diocese of Ohio," unpublished dissertation, May 1978, Colgate Rochester Divinity School, NY; "A Study of Formal Training Provided, Employment, and the Availability of Jobs for Negro High School Graduates in Tampa, Florida," unpublished thesis, June 1962, Atlanta University, Georgia. **Military Serv:** US Army, Specialist 3, 1955-57, Good Conduct, 1957. **Home Addr:** 1505 Oakwood Ave, Raleigh, NC 27610. **Business Addr:** Chaplain's Office, St Augustine's College, 1315 Oakwood Ave, Raleigh, NC 27610, (919)516-4210.

HAIRSTON, ROWENA L.
Examiner. **Personal:** Born Mar 17, 1928, Mohawk, WV; daughter of Rowena L Winfrey and Paul L Winfrey; married Charles B Hairston, Sep 26, 1946. **Educ:** Central Night Sch Columbus OH, 1956-58. **Career:** Bur of Employment Servs, examiner data control 1970-; Bur of Employment Servs Columbus, typist & clk 1961-70. **Orgs:** Nat aux pres Nat Alliance of Postal Fed Employees 1975-; life mem NAACP; natl rep Leadership Conf on Civil Rights 1972-. **Honors/Awds:** Recognition plaque Local #605 Aux NAPFE Columbus 1975; key to city Mayor of Kansas City MO 1977; gold medallion Mayor of Atlantic City NJ 1978. **Home Addr:** 2023 Maryland Ave, Columbus, OH 43219.

HAIRSTON, SAM. See Obituaries section.

HAIRSTON, WILLIAM
Playwright, poet, author, business administrator. **Personal:** Born Apr 1, 1928, Goldsboro, NC; son of Malissa Carter Hairston and William Russell Hairston; married Enid Carey; children: Ann Marie. **Educ:** University of Northern Colorado, Greeley, CO, BA, political science; Columbia, New York, NY; New York University, New York, NY. **Career:** Playwright, actor, director, producer; also, author: The World of Carlos, 1968, Sex and Conflict (story collection), 1993; Playwright, Walk in the Darkness, 1963, Swan-Song of the 11th Dawn, 1962, Curtain Call Mr Aldridge, Sir!, 1964, Black Antigone, 1965, Ira Aldridge, 1988; Phati'tude, lit magazine; Poems pub-

lished: Echoes of Yesterday; Best Poems of 1995; A Voyage to Remember; Forever and A Day; Fields of Gold; Essence of a Dream; Tracing Shadows; The Scenic Route; Journey Between Stars; Scriptwriter, Apollo 11 - Man on the Moon, Media Hora, Festival of Heritage Jules Verne vs Real Flight to the Moon, Operation Money-Wise, English Training - Teaching English as a Second Language, Chicago, Portrait of a City: actor, Take the High Ground, 1953, numerous other appearances; Dir, Jerico-Jim Crow, 1964, Curtain Call Mr Aldridge, Sir!, 1964; recording Jerico-Jim Crow, 1965; The New York Shakespeare Festival, theatre manager and administrator, 1963-66; Democratic National Committee, radio news editor and corpondent, 1968; District of Columbia, Executive Office of the Mayor, Office of Personnel, executive manager, 1970-90; DC Pipeline, Washington, DC, publisher and editor, 1973-79. **Orgs:** The Authors League of America; The Dramatists Guild; executive board, National Capital Area Council, Boy Scouts of America. **Honors/Awds:** Theatre Administration Grant, The Ford Foundation, 1965-66; Literary Study Grant, The National Endowment for the Arts, 1967; Playwrights Festival Award, The Group Theatre, Seattle, WA, 1988; The Silver Beaver Award, The Boy Scouts of America, National Capital Area, 1988; "IRA Aldridge (The London Conflict)" The Group Theatres Multi Cultural Playwrights Festival Winner, 1988; Meritorious Public Service Award, District of Columbia, 1990. **Home Addr:** 5501 Seminary Rd, Falls Church, VA 22041, (703)845-1281.

HAIRSTONE, MARCUS A.
Educational Administrator (Retired). **Personal:** Born Oct 16, 1926, Reidsville, NC; son of Georgia A Hairston and Mack M Hairston. **Educ:** Livingstone Coll, BS 1949; Duquesne Univ, MS 1950; Univ of Pittsburgh, PhD 1956. **Career:** Univ of NE, dir dental res labs 1957-59; Long Island Univ, asst prof, 1959-61; Rockefeller Univ, rsch assoc 1962-64; Columbia Univ, rsch assoc 1964-66; Amer Univ Cairo, prof 1972-74; Natl Institutes of Health, intl health sci admin 1977-95; Cheyney Univ, dean 1986-87; National Institutes of Health, international health scientist administrator; dean 1986-87 (on leave); National Institute of Health, international health scientist administrator; Chief of Party, USAID University Linkages Project, Cairo, Egypt, 1995-96; Director, WorldTech Consulting Group, 1996. **Orgs:** American Assn Adv Sci, 1950-; New York Acad of Sci, 1969-; consultant/prof, Tabriz Univ, Iran, 1971-72; consultant/prof, USAID Addis Ababa Univ, Ethiopia, 1974-75; chair, Africa Comm, Amer Soc Publ Admin, 1978-79. **Honors/Awds:** Fulbright Fellowship Egypt 1966-67, Iran 1969-71; Guest Ed, Scientific Outcomes Apollo II Mission to Moon, AAAS, 1979; Mayor's Adv Comm International Washington DC 1984-86. **Military Serv:** US Army, non-comm officer, 2 yrs. **Business Phone:** (301)882-9078.

HAKIMA, MALA'IKA
Physician. **Personal:** Born Aug 25, 1950, Kansas City, KS; married Larry Linstrome Hodge Hakima; children: Habiibah Nuurah-Salaam, Rabi'a Mala'ika, Mahmoud Abdul, Ihsan-Karim, Yasmin Rahimah, Isa Najm Sulayman. **Educ:** Grinnell Coll, BA 1972; Meharry Medical Coll, MD 1984. **Career:** King/Drew Medical Ctr Los Angeles, intern 1984-85; Self-employed, physician 1985-. **Orgs:** Physician Comm Health Ctr of West Wilcox Co 1986-. **Honors/Awds:** Southern Medical Assoc Scholarship 1980; Alpha Phi Alpha Awd 1981.

HALE, CYNTHIA LYNNETTE
Minister. **Personal:** Born Oct 27, 1952, Roanoke, VA; daughter of Janice Hylton Hale and Harrison Hale. **Educ:** Hollins Coll, Hollins VA, BA Music, 1975; Duke Divinity School, Durham NC, Master of Divinity, 1979; United Theological Seminary, Dayton OH, Doctorate of Ministry, 1991. **Career:** Fed Correctional Institution, Butner NC, Chaplain, 1979-85; Ray of Hope Christian Church, Decatur GA, pastor, 1986-. **Orgs:** Mem, Natl Council of Churches New York, 1978-83; vice pres, bd of dir, Greenwood Cemetery Co, 1979-80; pres, Natl Convocation Christian Church (DOC), 1982-88; mem, General Bd of Christian Church (DOC), 1982-88; vice pres, Concerned Black Clergy Inc, 1987-; board of directors, Christian Council of Metropolitan Atlanta, 1989; Project Impact, DeKalb, 1994-. **Honors/Awds:** Outstanding Young Woman of Amer, 1982, 1986-88; My Story, My Witness, Program for Compelled by Faith, 1983-84; Liberation Award, Natl Convocation CCDC, 1984; The Religious Award for Dedicated Service, Ninety-Nine Breakfast Club, 1990; The Religion Award, DeKalb Branch, NAACP, 1990; Inducted into the Martin Luther Kind Bd of Preachers at Morehouse Coll, 1993. **Business Addr:** Pastor, Ray of Hope Christian Church, 3936 Rainbow Dr, Decatur, GA 30034.

HALE, EDWARD HARNED
Physician. **Personal:** Born Sep 15, 1923, Nashville, TN; son of Harriett Hodgkins Hale (deceased) and William J. Hale (deceased); married Della Ellis Miller; children: Pamela, Deborah, Nancy, Barbara, Rudolph Miller, Maria Miller. **Educ:** TN State Coll, BS 1941; Meharry Med Coll, MD 1945; Univ of IL, MS 1947. **Career:** Harlem Hosp NYC, intern 1945-46; Univ of IL, fellow med 1947-48; Freedman's Hosp, resident 1948-50; West Penn Hosp, staff mem; Howard Univ, instr med 1950-53; VA Hosp Pgh, chief med serv 1955-58; private practice, specializing in internal med and pulmonary disease 1958-92; VA Med Center, staff physician, 1992-96. **Orgs:** Mem Amer Bd Intl Med 1952, 1979-; fellow Fed Clin Rsch; contrib articles to professional jours; treas PA Soc of Intl Med 1976-77; fellow Amer Coll of Physicians 1979; Sigma Pi Phi, 1963-; Research Grants Committee, United Way, chairman, 1971-74. **Honors/Awds:** West Penn Hospital, 18 years Medical Director Home Care Program, 1987. **Military Serv:** US Medical Corps 1953-55; Legion of Merit, 1954. **Home Phone:** (412)682-4305.

HALE, GENE
Construction equipment executive. **Personal:** Born Apr 19, 1946, Birmingham, AL; son of Minnie Hale and Matt Hale; married Cecelia L. Davis Hale, Aug 29, 1978; children: Reginald, Kevin, Crystal. **Educ:** California State University, Dominguez Hills, Carson, CA, BS, Business Administration, 1980. **Career:** G&C Equipment Corporation, Gardena, CA, president and CEO, 1980-. **Orgs:** Co-founder, Fourth Annual Black Business Day Luncheon; chairman, Congressional Task Force in Minority Business Set Asides for the Private Sector; chairman, Greater Los Angeles African American Chamber of Commerce; advisory council chairman, California Department of Transportation; chairman, Century Freeway Employment Advisory Committee; chairman, Federation of Minority Business Associations; co-chairman, California Department of Transportation Employment Committee; director, Gardena Valley Chamber of Commerce; advisory committee member, Entrepreneurial Program for Disadvantaged Youth; member, California Public Utilities Advisory Board; chair, Greater Los Angeles African American, Chamber of Commerce; expert council, Department of Commerce; advisory board, AT&T Technology Board; commissioner, City of Los Angeles; director, Los Angeles Convention & Visitors Bureau. **Honors/Awds:** Certificate of Appreciation, Century Freeway Advisory Committee, 1990; County of Los Angeles Commendation, Supervisor Kenneth Hahn; SBA Recognition Award, Support of Los Angeles Minority Small Business Community, 1990; Supplier of the Year, National Minority Supplier Development Council, 1990; Supplier of the Year, Southern California Purchasing Council Inc, 1990; Community Architect Award, 49th Assembly District, 1989; Bridging the Gap Award, SBE, 1988; Congressional Certificate of Appreciation, 1987; Certificate of Recognition, Los Angeles Area Council, Boy Scouts of America, 1985; Outstanding Minority Business, State of California Minority Enterprise Development Council, 1986;Outstanding Minority Business, State of California, 1985; Black Business of the Year Award, Black Business Aciation of Los Angeles, 1985. **Military Serv:** US Army, Sergeant. **Business Addr:** President and CEO, G&C Equipment Corporation, 1875 W Redondo Beach Blvd., Ste 102, Gardena, CA 90247.

HALE, JANICE ELLEN
Educator, researcher. **Personal:** Born Apr 30, 1948, Ft Wayne, IN; daughter of Cleo Ingram Hale and Dr Phale D Hale Sr; children: Keith A Benson Jr. **Educ:** Spelman Coll, BA 1970; Interdenominational Theol Center, MRE 1972; GA State Univ, PhD 1974. **Career:** Early Childhood Educ Clark Coll, asso prof; Dept of Psychol Yale Univ, rsrch asso; Afro-Am Studies Prog, lecturer 1980-81; Cleveland State Univ, assoc prof; Wayne State University, professor, currently. **Orgs:** Founder, Visions for Children, African-Amer Early Childhood Educ Rsch Demonstration Prog; governing bd mem, Natl Assn for the Educ of Young Children, 1988-92. **Honors/Awds:** Publications "Christian Educ for Black Liberation" in For You Who Teach in th Black Church 1973; "The Woman's Role The Strength of Blk Families" in 1st World, An Intl Jrnl of Black Thought 1977; "De-Mythicizing the Educ of Black Children" 1st World, An Intl Journal of Black Thought 1977; numerous other publications; recipient of grant Spencer Found; numerous presentations on Research for the following institutions and associations: Black Child Devel Inst, Natl Council for Black Child Devel, Natl Assn for the Educ of Young Children, NC Assn for the Educ of Young Children, Univ of SC, SC State Coll, Spelman Coll, Morehouse Coll, GA State Univ, Univ of the West Indies, NY Univ, Head Start Prog of Omaha NE, CO Springs, CO Public Schools; author of Black Children, Their Roots, Culture and Learning Styles, John Hopkins Univ Press, revised edition 1986; 50 Future Leaders, Ebony Magazine, 1978; Distinguished Alumna, College of Educ, Georgia State Univ 1982; author, Unbank the Fire: Visions for the Education of African-American Children, Johns Hopkins University Press, fall 1994; nominated for Pulitzer Prize, 1995. **Home Phone:** (313)661-4339. **Business Addr:** Prof, Early Childhood Educ, Wayne State University, 213 Educ Bldg, Detroit, MI 48202, (313)577-0954.

HALE, KIMBERLY ANICE
Librarian. **Personal:** Born Dec 6, 1962, Champaign, IL; daughter of Margaret I Hale and Emery S White. **Educ:** University of Illinois at Urbana-Champaign, BS, 1985, MS, 1989. **Career:** Columbia College Library, acquisitions librarian/coordinator of collection development, 1989-. **Orgs:** American Library Association, 1989-; Alpha Phi Omega Service Fraternity, life mem, 1983-. **Business Addr:** Acquisitions Librarian/Coordinator of Collection Development, Columbia College Library, 600 S Michigan Ave, 2nd Fl, Chicago, IL 60605, (312)344-7355.

HALE, LORRAINE
Company executive. **Personal:** daugHter of Clara Hale (deceased). **Career:** Hale House, cofounder, CEO, currently. **Business Addr:** CEO/President, Hale House for Infants Inc, 152 W 122 St, New York, NY 10027, (212)663-0700.

HALE, PHALE D.
State legislator, clergyman. **Personal:** Born Jul 16, 1915, Starksville, MS; son of Lee Ellen Hale and Church Hale; married Cleo; children: Phale Jr, Janice Ellen, Marna A, Hilton Ingram. **Educ:** Morehouse Coll, AB; Gammon Theol Sem, MDiv; Cincinnati Bapt Theol Sem, DD; International Theological Center, MDiv; Chapel School of Theology, DDiv. **Career:** OH, Hilton Ingram mem; OH Dist 31, state rep 1966-80; Union Grove Bapt Church Columbus, pastor, 1950-; OH Civil Rights Commission, chmn. **Orgs:** Chmn, past chmn Health & Welfare Com of Ohio Legislature; past chairman of Ohio Civil Rights Commission, 1983-87; Central Ohio Advisory Bd & Campaign Leader, The United Negro College Fund, bd mem, 1966-; CMACAO Economic Development Corp, bd mem, 1970-; Ohio Council of Churches, bd mem, 1976-; Commission on Poverty & Justice of the Ohio Council of Churches, comm mem, 1976-; natl Bd of Dirs of Operation PUSH, bd mem, 1978-; J & L Electric Co, bd mem, 1983-; member, Ohio Democratic Committee, 1995-; vice pres, Columbus Urban Redevelopment Corp; vice pres, Shiloh-Grove Corp. **Honors/Awds:** Inducted, Martin Luther King Jr International Board of Preachers at Morehouse College, 1992; Martin Luther King Humanitarian Award, Columbus Education Association, 1987; Appointed by Pres Clinton, Natl Democratic Comm Member, 1995; Seminar Leader in Seminar I, Natl Baptist USA Congress in Pastors Division; Honorary Citizenship presented by Mayors of Miami, Fl & New Orleans LA. **Home Addr:** 2480 Floribunda Drive, Columbus, OH 43209.

HALES, EDWARD EVERETTE
Attorney. **Personal:** Born Feb 13, 1932, Leechburg, PA; son of Bertha Hales and Charles Hales. **Educ:** Baldwin-Wallace Coll, 1955; Univ of WI Madison Law Coll, 1962. **Career:** Ford Motor Company-United Auto Workers, permanent umpire; Pacific Bell, arbitrator; State of Alaska Public Employees, arbitrator; Hales Hartig, atty 1979-; Hales Harvey & Neu, atty 1973-79; Goodman Hales & Costello, atty 1965-73; City of Racine, asst city atty 1965-67; State of MN, legal asst, atty general 1962-63; Intl Fellowship, consultant; VISTA, consultant; State of MI OEO, consultant; IA Urban Rsch Center, consultant; AIM Jobs, board. **Orgs:** Spec arbitrator Bd of Arbitration US Steel Corp United Steel Workers of Am; spec arbitrator Fed Mediation Serv; spec arbitrator WI Employment Rel Commn; spec arbitrator Bd of Arbitration State of MN NAACP; Urban League; Nat Bar Assn; Am Bar Assn; WI State Bar Assn; WI Council Criminal Justice; WI Higher Educ Aids Bd; WI Univ Merger Implementation Com; Alpha Ph Alpha; chmn Finance Com Bd of Regents Univ of WI System 1975-77; pres Bd of Regents Univ of WI System 1977-79; bd of trustees Assn of Gov Bds of Univ & Coll 1977-; selection com US 7th Circuit & Judicial Court 1978-79; bd of dirs Pub Broadcasting Service 1979-80; bd of trustees Assn for Pub Broadcasting 1979-; arbitrator Am Arbitration Assn 1980-; bd of trustees Ripon Coll Ripon WI 1980-; mem, State of Wisconsin Investment Board, 1987-90; mem, State of Wisconsin Racing Commission, 1988-90; Ford Motor Co & United Automobile Workers, permanent umpire. **Honors/Awds:** Urban Serv Award 1967; effort award Kings Daughter Club 1974. **Military Serv:** AUS 1956-58. **Business Addr:** Attorney, 4089-118 Porte De Palmas, San Diego, CA 92122.

HALES, MARY ANN
Educator, bail bond agent. **Personal:** Born Jul 27, 1953, Fayetteville, NC; daughter of Dorothy M Allen Melvin and Jack E Melvin; divorced; children: Michelle, Mario, Dominique. **Educ:** Fayetteville State Univ, BS Psych (magna cum laude) 1981, masters degree, elementary education & math, 1989; Certification in Educational Admini & Supervision, 1994. **Career:** Foxe's Surety Bail Bonding Co, admin chief 1978-81; Fayetteville Tech Inst, adult basic educ instructor 1981-88; WFBS Radio, radio communications operator 1982-83; HSA Cumberland Psychiatric Hospital, mental health counselor 1985-87; All American Bail Bonding Company, owner/agent 1987-; Long Hill Elementary School, teacher 1989-90; Montclair Elementary School, Fayetteville, NC, teacher, 1990-; Council Real Estate, sales agent, 1994-. **Orgs:** Vice pres Cumberland Co Chapter of Bail Bondsmen 1978-81; notary public State of NC 1980-; mem NC Assn of Adult Educators 1981-; mem NC Bail Bondsmen Assn 1987, Nor Carolina Assn of Educators 1989-, Natl Education Assn 1989-, Assn of Teacher Educators 1989-; North Carolina Council of Teachers of Mathematics, 1988-; member, Fayetteville Jaycees, 1990-; United States Jaycees, 1990-; Fayetteville State Univ, athletic club, 1993-; NC Assn of Realtors, 1994-; Fayetteville Area Bd of Realtors, 1994-; NC Assn of School Administrators, 1994-. **Honors/Awds:** Permanent mem Natl Dean's List 1978-; Alpha Kappa Mu Natl Honor Society 1979; Kappa Delta Pi International Honor Society in Education, 1994. **Home Addr:** 3490 Hastings Dr, Fayetteville, NC 28311-7626. **Business Addr:** Teacher, Montclair Elementary School, 555 Glensford Dr, Fayetteville, NC 28301.

HALES, WILLIAM ROY
Editor, publisher. **Personal:** Born Aug 18, 1934, Girard, GA; married Inez Hales; children: Wilbert R. **Educ:** Univ of Hartford, 1954. **Career:** NAACP, bd mem 1956; Ebony Businessmens League, past pres 1968-71; CT House of Reps, cand ct ho 1968-72; State of CT Justice of Peace, justice of peace 1968-74; Hartford Devel Commiss, commissioner 1984-86; Focus Magazine, editor/publisher; The Inquirer Newspaper Group, editor publisher, currently. **Honors/Awds:** Cert of Appreciation Greater Hartford Jaycees 1971. **Business Addr:** Editor & Publisher, The Inquirer Newspaper Group, 3281 Main St, Hartford, CT 06120.

HALEY, CHARLES LEWIS
Professional football player. **Personal:** Born Jan 6, 1964, Gladys, VA. **Educ:** James Madison Univ, attended. **Career:** Linebacker, defensive end: San Francisco 49ers, 1986-92, Dallas Cowboys, 1992-. **Honors/Awds:** Post-season play: NFC Championship Game, 1988, 1989, NFL Championship Game, 1988, 1989, Pro Bowl, 1988, 1990, 1991. **Business Addr:** Professional Football Player, Dallas Cowboys, 1 Cowboys Pkwy, Irving, TX 75063.

HALEY, EARL ALBERT
Business executive. **Personal:** Born May 18, 1933, Newark, NJ; son of Ada Haley and Earl Haley; married Pearl L Hall; children: Earl Jr, Derek. **Educ:** Fairleigh Dickinson Univ, BS Industrial Engineering 1967. **Career:** Machintronic & Engrg Co, machinist inspector 1951-55; Western Electric Co, detail maker 1955-66, numerous positions 1957-66; Becton Dickinson, mgr special recruiting 1969-71, coord 1973-74, dir EEO, corp staffing & compliance 1985-. **Orgs:** Past chmn Bergen Co Advisory Com; bd of dir, Urban League, NAACP, United Way, Consortium Black Professional Devel; chmn Bergen Co JSIP; bd of dir, Amer Cancer Society, Boy Scouts of Amer, Industry Labor Council, Natl Assoc of Manufacturers, NJ Liaison Group, TWIN, Washington Study Group. **Military Serv:** AUS corpl 1953-55. **Business Addr:** Dir Staffing/Compliance, Becton Dickinson & Co, 1 Becton Dr, Franklin Lakes, NJ 07417-1880.

HALEY, GEORGE WILLIFORD BOYCE
Attorney. **Personal:** Born Aug 28, 1925, Henning, TN; son of Bertha Palmer Haley and Simon Haley; married Doris Elaine Moxley; children: David Barton, Anne Palmer. **Educ:** Morehouse Coll, BA with high honors 1949; Univ of AK, LLB 1952. **Career:** Kansas City KS, deputy city attorney 1954-64; State of KS, KS state senate 1964-68; US Urban Mass Trans Admin, chief counsel 1969-73; US Information Agency, gen'l counsel & congressional liasion 1975-76; George W Haley Prof Corp, president; Postal Rate Commission, chairman, 1990-94, commissioner, 1994-97, vice chmn, 1997-. **Orgs:** Lay-leader Methodist-KS-MO-CO Conference 1956-68; pres, Wyandotte Cty Kansas Young Republicans 1959-60; UNESCO monitoring panel US State Dept 1984; bd of directors Universal Bank 1985; bd of directors Antioch Sch of Law 1985. **Honors/Awds:** Comments editor AR Law Review 1951-52. **Military Serv:** USAF sgt 3 yrs. **Business Addr:** Commissioner, Postal Rate Commission, 1333 H St NW, Ste 300, Washington, DC 20268-0001.

HALEY, JOHNETTA RANDOLPH
Educator. **Personal:** Born Mar 19, 1923, Alton, IL; daughter of Willye Smith Randolph and Rev John Randolph; divorced; children: Karen Douglas, Michael. **Educ:** Lincoln University, BS, 1945; Southern Illinois University at Edws, MM, 1972. **Career:** Lincoln HS, vocal/genl music teacher, 1945-48; Turner Jr HS, vocal music teacher/choral dir, 1950-55; Nipher Jr HS, vocal/gen music teacher/choral dir, 1955-71; Title I Program for Culturally Disadvantaged Children, teacher of black history/music, 1966; Human Devel Corp, program specialist, 1968; St Louis Cncl of Black People, interim exec dir, 1970; School of Fine Arts, S IL Univ at Edwardsville, grad res asst, 1971-72, asst prof of music, 1972-77; TX S U, visiting prof, 1977; So IL Univ, prof of music, 1982-, dir, E St Louis Br 1982-. **Orgs:** Amer Assn of Univ Prof; Coll Music Soc; Music Educators Natl Conf; IL Music Educators Assn; Natl Choral Dir Assn; Mu Phi Epsilon; Assn of Teachers Educators; Mid-West Kodaly Music Educators; Organ of Am Kodaly Educators; Artist Presentations Soc; Pi Kappa Lambda; Alpha Kappa Alpha, supreme parliamentarian; Jack & Jill Inc, past pres, St Louis chapter; Las Amigas Social Club, past pres; Friends of the St Louis Art Museum; Top Ladies of Distinction Inc; United Negro College Fund Inc; Urban League; co-founder St Louis Cncl of Black People; St Louis Mayor's Committee for Protection of the Innocent;initiated Pilot Cnslr Aide Program in St Louis Public School for Delinquent Students; initiated 1st Exhibit of Black-Artist at St Louis Art Museum; advisory bd, Help Inc; chairperson, Illinois Comm on Black Concerns in Her Educ; bd of Trustees, Lincoln Univ 1974-83; bd of Trustees, Stillman Coll, 1984-; bd of Dir, Assn of Governing bds of Univs and Colls; Links Inc. **Honors/Awds:** Woman of the Yr, Greyhound Bus Corp, 1969; Disting Citizen Award, St Louis Argus Newspaper, 1970; Comm Serv Award, Las Amigas Club, 1970; Key to the City, Mayor R Hatcher, 1972; Serv to Music Award, MO Music Educators, 1972; Serv to Educ Award, Kirkwood Sch Dist, 1972; Duchess of Paducah, Award Paducah, KY, 1974; Signel Hon Award for Outstand Comm Serv, St Louis Sentinel Newspaper, 1974; Pi Kappa Lambda Intl Music Hon Soc, 1977; Disting Alumni Award, Lincoln Univ, 1977; Woman of Achievement/Education, KMOX radio & surburban newspaper, 1988; Urban League, Merit Award, 1994. **Home Addr:** 1926 Bennington Common Dr, Saint Louis, MO 63146-2555.

HALFACRE, FRANK EDWARD
Association executive. **Personal:** Born Jun 21, 1936, Youngstown, OH; son of Consuelo Massey Stewart Velar and Walter Melvin Halfacre (Thompson) (deceased); married Mary Tyson; children: Lyle Edward (deceased), Laura Maria Lewis, Keith Russell, Frank Earl II, Mary Consuelo, Madelyn Larue, Walter Allan. **Educ:** Youngstown State Univ, BA, telecommunications, speech, 1981. **Career:** Youngstown Park & Rec Commn, caretaker 1955-65; Kings Records, record promoter, 1965; WWOW-WFIZ, disc jockey, 1965; WFAR, disc jockey, music & program dir, 1966; WNIO & WJMO Radio, disc jockey 1968; James Brown Prod, 1969; African American Music Hall of Fame and Museum Inc, executive director, 1969; Starday King Records, promotions; pub affairs & research positions, 1970-72; Stop 26/Riverbend Inc, vice pres, 1992-; WRBP-FM Radio Station, operations mgr, program dir, 1992-; radio host of shows: Explorations in Jazz 'n Blues, Secret Garden, Lucky's Soul Kitchen, (S)ouldies, Soul Christmas; Shup N Gubble Enterprises, co-founder; T BOB Inc, executive dir, 1995-; WSMZ Radio, program dir, music dir, 1995-. **Orgs:** Natl Assn TV & Radio Announcers (NATRA); FORE; Black Indsl & Econ Union; DAV; PTA; Lexington Players; co-founder 7-11 Club; founder Kleen Teens; vice pres Youngstown Sickle Cell Found; Emanon Jaguars Track Club; co-chmn/coach Youngstown Rayen Girls Track; track coach Rayen Boys Freshman St Edward Jr HS; Youngstown State Univ Track Club; Jack the Rapper Family; Goodwill Games, asst field dir, 1990; Disabled American Veterans; NAACP; Fraternal Order of Record E xecutives; Youngstown Area Urban League. **Honors/Awds:** Man of the Year OH Assn of Beauticians 1968; Disting Serv Award NATRA 1969; Free Lance Writing including, Buckeye Review (Jazz & Sports); Call and Post (Jazz & Sports); The Voice (Jazz & Sports); Hit Kit (Jazz, Rhythm & Blues); Stringer reporter for Jet & Ebony; voted into Youngstown Curbstone Coaches Hall of Fame for Track Field 1987; Youngstown /Hubbard Coalition, Appreciation Day; East/West Network Assn, Award for Community Service. **Military Serv:** US Army, 1951-53. **Home Addr:** 1870 Goleta Ave, Youngstown, OH 44504. **Business Addr:** Executive Director, African-American Music Hall of Fame & Museum Inc, PO Box 5921, Youngstown, OH 44504.

HALL, ADDIE JUNE
Educational administrator, educator, cleric. **Personal:** Born Apr 11, 1930, Houston, TX; daughter of Aniece Clair Ware (deceased) and Milton Gray (deceased); divorced; children: Sharmane C, Dr LeRoy B Jr DVM PhD. **Educ:** Washington Jr Coll, AA 1953; Bethune-Cookman, BS 1955; Columbia Univ, MA 1962; FL State Univ, PhD 1975; Emory Univ, Certificate, Theol 1981; Chandler School of Theology, student, 1996-. **Career:** Agat Guam, instr 1955-58; Escambia Cty School Bd, instr 1959-69, curriculum coord 1969-71, instr coord 1971-73; United Methodist Church, minister, 1971-; FL State Univ, grad instr 1973-74, instr 1974-75; Pensacola Jr Coll, asst prof 1975-78, professor, 1980, dir of adult ed & prof 1978-90, director of Minority Recruitment and Retention, 1990-95, professor of Behavioral Sciences, 1991-95. **Orgs:** Kappa Delta Pi 1972-, Phi Delta Kappa 1974-; parliamentarian FL State Adv Council 1983-; adb bd Dept of Corrections Reg 1983-; NAACP; Tiger Bay Club; FL Admin 1983; TV appearances Adult Educ, Black History 1983, 1984; radio WBOP 1983, 1984; journalist Delta Sigma Theta 1985-; marcher March of Dimes, Arthritis, Leukema Soc; lecturer, counselor Churches Schools Inst; Natl Pol Congress of Blackwomen, AAACE, US Senate Educ Adv Council; president, Pensacola Chapter Links, Inc 1988-92; vice president, Bayside Optimist Club, 1991; Waterfront Mission Board, 1990; Societas Docta, Inc; Code Enforcement Board, 1990-95; Solid Waste Environment Advisory Board, 1990-93. **Honors/Awds:** Pensacola Women 1978; Outstanding Ed Delta Sigma Theta 1982, 1986; Articles publ "The New Amer" 1983, "The Self-Concepts & Occupational Aspiration Level of ABE Students" 1983; Pensacola Leadership Chamber of Commerce 1984-85; Nominee of BIP Prog Chamber of Commerce 1984-85; many certificates of appreciation; certificate from Gov Graham 1986; cert from Senator Hawkins for serving on the US Senate Educ Adv Council 1986; Supervisor of the Year, College Assn of Educ Office Personnel, Pensacola Junior College, 1986; Lady of Distinction, Pensacola Chapter Top Ladies of Distinction, 1987; Community Service Award, and A Believer in the Under Achiever Award, Jordan Street SDA Church, 1987 & 1988; finalist in the Distinguished Black Educator Recognition Award, 1991; Resolution,State of Florida, 1; Deputy Marshall of Martin Luther King Parade, 1990; Proclamation, Pensacola Junior College, 1991; Black Women on the Move Award, Natl Coalition of 100 Black Women Inc, 1994; State of Fla, Department of Corrections, Third Annual Crime Prevention Award, 1994; Many other Awards and Certificates for Community Services, Religious and Political Services. **Special Achievements:** Author "The Wife/The Other Woman;" appeared on National TV religious programs discussing the book. **Home Addr:** 2612 N 13th Ave, Pensacola, FL 32503, (904)438-0250.

HALL, ALBERT
Professional baseball player (retired). **Personal:** Born Mar 7, 1959, Birmingham, AL. **Career:** Atlanta Braves, outfielder, 1981-88; Pittsburgh Pirates, outfielder, 1989. **Business Addr:** Baseball Player, Tucson Toros, PO Box 27045, Tucson, AZ 85726.

HALL, ALFONZO LOUIS
Automobile industry executive. **Personal:** Born Jun 20, 1954, Statesboro, GA; son of Collis and Beaulah Coleman Hall; married Lori-Linell Hall MD, Jul 9, 1988; children: Lyndon, Jordan, Marjani. **Educ:** Brewton Parker Junior College, AA, 1972-74; Indiana Wesleyan Univ, BS, sociology and psychology, 1974-76; General Motors Institute, advanced operation planning, 1984, manufacturing certificate, 1986, MS, 1988; Univ of Pennsylvania School of Business, 1987; Univ of Michigan School of Business, 1989. **Career:** General Motors, general supv of press room and metal assembly, 1982-85, supt of manufacturing, 1985-88, engineer-in-charge of model systems, 1989-92, production mgr, Pontiac luxury car division, 1992, acting plant mgr, 1992-93, loaned exec, 1993-94, plant mgr, 1994-. **Orgs:** PNC Bank Urban Advisory Board; program review board, Agility Forum, Lehigh University; board of directors, Urban League of Pittsburgh; board of directors, Junior Achievement of Southwest Pennsylvania, Inc; executive advisory board, Penn State McKeesport Campus; Engineering Society of Detroit; vice pres, Explorer Scouts of America, Clinton Valley & Oakland County Councils; founding mem, Mission Inc; 32nd Degree Mason, Prince Hall Masonic Order. **Honors/Awds:** Third World Black Caucus, Man of the Year Award, 1978; Marion (IN) Chamber of Commerce, Distinguished Citizen Award, 1985; Dollars and Sense Magazine, Outstanding Business and Professional Award, 1992. **Special Achievements:** Speaker at Black Engineers of the Year Conference, 1990-93; Member of GM Recruiting Team, Historical Black Colleges & Univ, 1990-92; Speaker, Succeeding in Business, Impact Seminar, Detroit Public School, 1992. **Business Addr:** Plant Manager, General Motors Corp., 1451 Lebanon School Rd, West Mifflin, PA 15122, (412)469-6501.

HALL, ALTON JEROME
Computer sales executive. **Personal:** Born Nov 27, 1945, Shreveport, LA; son of Mabel Powell Hall (deceased) and Timothy Hall; married Lois Ann Gregory Hall, Sep 3, 1966; children: Alton Jerome Jr., Lisa Angela. **Educ:** Howard University, Washington, DC, BSEE, 1968; Northeastern University, Boston, MA, 1969-71; Columbia University, Harriman, NY, certificate, executive program in business administration, 1984. **Career:** Honeywell EDP, Waltham, MA, engineer, 1968-70; Raytheon Data Systems, Norwood, MA, senior engineer, 1970-72; Digital Equipment Corp., Landover, MD, regional accounts, sales vice president, 1972-. **Orgs:** Member, Washington Board of Trade, 1987-; committee chair, Advisory Council, Business and Industry, 1989-; board member, Prince George County Public Schools, Regional High Tech Council, 1990-; life member, Prince George/Montgomery chapter, NAACP, 1979-; chairman, Business Advisory Council, Bowie State University, 1989-. **Home Addr:** 12401 Longwater, Mitchellville, MD 20721-2577. **Business Addr:** Sales Vice President, Digital Equipment Corp, 8400 Corporate Dr, Mel 3-1, Landover, MD 20785.

HALL, ANTHONY W., JR.
Elected official. **Personal:** Born Sep 16, 1944, Houston, TX; married Carolyn Joyce Middleton; children: Anthony William, Ursula Antoinette. **Educ:** Howard Univ, BA 1967; Thurgood Marshall School of law, JD 1982. **Career:** Harris Cty Commiss Bray Houston, asst 1971-72; Williamson Gardner Hall & Wiensenthal, partner; State of TX, state rep; City of Houston, city councilmember. **Orgs:** Rules Budget & Fin Coms, TX Dem Party; state dem exec committeeman Senatorial Dist 13; delegate, 1972, 1974, 1976, 1980 Dem Natl Conv; Kappa Alpha Psi, Sigma Pi Phi; Natl Municipal League; mem bd mgrs YMCA Houston; Masons, Shriner, OES, Houston Bus & Professional Mens Club; bd dir, past vp, immed past pres Riverside Lions Club; exec bd mem United Negro Coll Fund, Gr Zion Baptist Church; Natl Bar Assn, TX Bar, Amer Bar, Houston Bar Assn; Houston Lawyers Assn. **Honors/Awds:** Black Achiever Awd YMCA 1972; Cotton Hook of the Year Awd ILA Local 872 1973; Citation for Outstanding Comm Serv NAACP 1972. **Military Serv:** AUS capt 1967-71. **Business Addr:** City Councilmember, City of Houston, P O Box 1562, Houston, TX 77251.

HALL, ARSENIO
Comedian, actor, former talk show host. **Personal:** Born Feb 12, 1956, Cleveland, OH; son of Annie Hall and Fred Hall. **Educ:** Ohio Univ, Athens, OH, attended; Kent State Univ, BA, general speech, 1977. **Career:** Stand-up comedian; films: Coming to America, 1988, Harlem Nights, 1989; television appearances: The Half Hour Comedy Hour, host, 1983, Thicke of the Night, 1984, The New Love, American Style, 1985, Motown Revue, 1985, Solid Gold, 1987, The Late Show, host, 1987, The Arsenio Hall Show, host/executive producer, 1989-93; Arsenio, 1997-. **Business Addr:** Actor, c/o M L Management, 152 W 57th St, 47th Fl, New York, NY 10019.

HALL, BENJAMIN LEWIS, III
Attorney, educator. **Personal:** Born Mar 13, 1956, Laurens, SC; son of Lilease Rogers and Benjamin Lewis Hall II; married Saundra Turner, Apr 18, 1981; children: Benjamin Lewis Hall IV. **Educ:** University of South Carolina, BA (cum laude), 1977; Duke Divinity School, MDiv, 1979; Rheinische Friedrich-Wilheims Universitat, BONN Fed'l Fulbright Rep of Germany Scholar-DAAD, 1980-82; Duke University Graduate School, PhD, 1985; Harvard Law School, JD, 1986. **Career:** South Texas College of Law, adjunct professor of law, 1991; Vinson & Elkins LLP, trial lawyer, special counsel, 1986-92; University of Houston Law Center, adjunct professor of law, 1987-; City of Houston, city attorney, 1992-95; O'Quinn and Laminack, attorney, currently. **Honors/Awds:** Rockefellar Scholar, 1977-78; Benjamin E Mays Scholar, 1978-79; Duke Black Grad Fellow, 1979-80; German Research Fellow, Bonn Universitat, 1980; James B Duke Grad Fellow, 1980-81; DADD Scholar to Germany, 1981-82; Black Doctoral Dissertation Fellow, 1982-83; Shell Fellow to Lambarene, Gabon, Africa, 1982-83; Duke Merit Scholar, 1977-79; Merrill Griswold Scholar, 1986. **Special Achievements:** Bar admissions: Texas, South District of Texas, Fifth Circuit Court of Appeals, District of Columbia, United States Supreme Court. **Business Addr:** Attorney, O'Quinn and Laminack, 2300 Lyric Centre Building, 440 Louisiana, Houston, TX 77002, (713)236-7635.

HALL, BRIAN EDWARD
Transportation company executive. **Personal:** Born May 5, 1958, Cleveland, OH; son of Virginia Hall and William D Hall; married Susan Reed, Mar 14, 1987. **Educ:** University of Cincinnati, Cincinnati OH, BBA, 1980; Baldwin-Wallace College, Berea OH, MBA, 1987. **Career:** Industrial Transport, Cleveland OH, dispatch administrator, 1980-81, operations manager, 1981-83, general manager, 1983-85, president, 1985-; Innovative Restaurant Management Group, (d.b.a. Fuddrucker's Tower City), chairman/CEO, currently. **Orgs:** Ohio Trucking Assn; Michigan Trucking Assn; Council of Small Enterprise and Contractors Assn; Big Brothers of America; Leadership Cleveland; board member, Excel Corp; trustee and treasurer, Cleveland Business League, 1989-90; Kappa Alpha Psi; board member, Convention and Visitor Bureau of Cleveland; board member, Cleveland Chapter, American Red Cross. **Honors/Awds:** Outstanding Men of America, 1982, 1983; Kappa Alpha Psi Award for Entrepreneurship, 1987, Outstanding Achievement Award, 1989; Minority Business Executive Program scholarship, 1988; nominee for business excellence, Crain's Cleveland Business, 1989. **Business Addr:** President, Intrans Inc/Industrial Transport, 2330 East 79th St, Cleveland, OH 44104.

HALL, CHARLES HAROLD
Business executive. **Personal:** Born Mar 10, 1934, Sapelo Island, GA; son of Beulah Hall and Charles Hall; divorced; children (previous marriage): Ronald Charles, Reginald Harold; children: Chuckie, Lori, Reginald, Ronald. **Educ:** Morehouse Clge, BS 1955; DT Watson Schl of Physiat, phys therapy dip 1956; Air Univ USAF, Cert 1957. **Career:** Therapeutic Serv Inc, pres, chf exec ofcr, prof, 1970-; VA Hosp, supv phys therap 1961-69; Total Living Care Inc, admin 1976-; Jefferson Twshp OH Dev Corp, treas 1970-. **Orgs:** First black chmn OH Chptr Amer Phys Therap Assc 1967-69; first black chf deleg OH Chap Amer Phys Therap Assc 1969-71; first black treas pvt pract sect APTA 1975-76; first black pres pvt prac sect APTA 1976-; bd dir BS of Amer 1972-; mem NAACP 1960-; Dayton Metropolitan Housing Authority, commissioner, 1985-. **Honors/Awds:** Sup Perf Award VA Hosp; Outst Srv Award APTA; guest spkr APTA; Delta Sigma Theta Business Man of the Year Award, 1992; National Business League Award, 1992; Robert G Dicus Award, 1st Black, most prestigious award for private practice physical therapist, 1992. **Military Serv:** USAF 1st lt 1957-61; USAFR lt col 1977-. **Business Addr:** President, Prof Therapeutic Services Inc, 45 Riverside Drive, Dayton, OH 45405.

HALL, CHRISTINE C. IIJIMA
University administrator. **Personal:** Born Mar 31, 1953, Colorado Springs, CO; daughter of Fumiko Iijima Hall and Roger Leroy Hall. **Educ:** Los Angeles Harbor Community College, Wilmington, CA, AA, 1972; California State University, Long Beach, CA, BA, 1974; Univ of Calif, Los Angeles (UCLA), Los Angeles, CA, MA, 1975, PhD, 1980. **Career:** Univ of Calif, Irvine, Irvine, CA, student affairs officer, 1979-81, counseling psychologist, 1981-86, director, student development, 1983-86; American Psychological Assn, Washington, DC, director, office of ethnic minority affairs, 1987-89; Arizona State University, West, Phoenix, AZ, asst vice provost, 1989-. **Orgs:** Member, membership chair, board of directors, Asian American Psychological Assn, 1979-; member, Assn of Black Psychologist; member, American Psychological Assn, 1976-; member, Japanese American Citizens League, 1990-; board of directors, American Cancer Society, (Glendale Chapter), 1990-; board of directors, Planned Parenthood of Northern and Central Arizona, 1990-; board of directors, Arizona Humanities Council, 1992-. **Honors/Awds:** Outstanding Alumna, Calif State Univ Long Beach, 1987; Outstanding Black Staff, Univ of Calif, Irvine, 1985; APA Minority Fellow, APA, 1975-80. **Business Addr:** Assistant Vice Provost & Director, Educational Development, Arizona State University-West, 4701 W Thunderbird Rd, Phoenix, AZ 85069-7100.

HALL, DANA ERIC
Professional football player. **Personal:** Born Jul 8, 1969, Bellflower, CA; married Carrie; children: Johnathan, Dana Jr. **Educ:** Univ of Washington, bachelor's degree in political science, 1992. **Career:** San Francisco 49ers, defensive back, 1992-94; Cleveland Browns, 1995; Jacksonville Jaguars, 1996-. **Business Addr:** Professional Football Player, Jacksonville Jaguars, One Stadium Place, Jacksonville, FL 32202, (904)633-6000.

HALL, DANIEL A.
Physician/administrator. **Personal:** Born Nov 16, 1933, Philadelphia, PA; son of Charlotte E Hall and Robert W Hall; married Shirley Louise Conway; children: Joy, Patricia. **Educ:** Howard Univ, BS 1955; Temple Univ, MD 1959; Columbia Sch of Public Health, MPH 1968. **Career:** Gen med Philadelphia 1962-66; Philadelphia Health Dept, resident 1966-69; Health Dist 5, dept dir 1969-72; Temple Univ, assoc prof 1973-78; Prudential Ins Co, dir med serv 1978-. **Orgs:** Finance comm Zion Baptist Church 1967-; mem Philadelphia Boy Scouts Exec Council 1968-72; bd of dirs W Nicetown Neighborhood Health Ctr 1969-71; bd of dirs Temple Univ Med Alumni Assn 1971-73; bd of mgrs N Br YMCA 1972-76; mem Amer Pub Health Assn Awds Comm 1974-77; Med Soc of Eastern PA 1974-; PA Medical Care Found 1984-86. **Honors/Awds:** Scholarship Howard Univ 1951-55, Phi Beta Kappa 1954; Natl Med Fellowship Awards, 1956-59; Charles Drew Awd 1978; Prudential Community Champion Award, 1992; Zion Community Center Service Award, 1992. **Military Serv:** USN capt 1960-62. **Business Addr:** Dir, Medical Services, Prudential Ins Co, 7100 Germantown Ave, Philadelphia, PA 19119.

HALL, DARNELL
Olympic athlete. **Career:** US Olympic Team, track and field, 1992. **Honors/Awds:** Olympic Games, Gold Medalist, 4X400 relay, 1992. **Business Addr:** Gold Medalist, 1992 Games, c/o US Olympic Training Center, 1 Olympic Plaza, Colorado Springs, CO 80909, (719)578-4500.

HALL, DAVID
Educator, educational administrator. **Personal:** Born May 26, 1950, Savannah, GA; son of Ethel Glover Hall and Levi Hall; married Marilyn Braithwaite-Hall, Jun 23, 1990; children: Rahsaan, Sakile. **Educ:** Kansas State Univ, BA political sci 1972; Univ of Oklahoma, MA human relations 1975, JD 1978; Harvard Law School, LLM, 1985, SJD, 1988. **Career:** Federal Trade Commission, staff attorney 1978-80; Univ of Mississippi Law School, asst prof of law 1980-83; Univ of Oklahoma Law School, assoc prof of law 1983-85; Northeastern Univ School of Law, assoc professor of law, 1985-88, associate dean & professor, beginning 1988, sabbatical research, Zimbabwe and South Africa, 1992-. **Orgs:** Natl Conference of Black Lawyers 1978-80; Oklahoma Bar Assn 1978-; attorney, Fed Trade Commn, Chicago, IL, 1978-80; Amer Bar Assn. **Honors/Awds:** Outstanding Senior Award, Oklahoma Bar Assn 1978; Professor of the Year, Oxford Miss Branch of NAACP; Floyd Calvert Law Faculty Award, Univ of Oklahoma Law School 1984; Order of the Coif, Univ of Oklahoma Law School Chapter 1984; Robert D Klein, Northeastern Univ; Floyd Calvert Law Faculty, Univ of OK; professor of the year, NAACP, Oxford, MS; Outstanding KS State Student. **Business Addr:** Professor of Law, School of Law, Northeastern University, 400 Huntington Ave, Boston, MA 02115.

HALL, DAVID ANTHONY, JR.
Dentist. **Personal:** Born Sep 19, 1945, San Francisco, CA; married Pamela C Hall; children: David III, Darryl C. **Educ:** So U, BS 1967; Meharry Med Sch, DDS 1972. **Career:** Dentist 1973-; Health Power Asso, dentist 1972-73. **Orgs:** Louisiana State Board of Dentistry, 1994-. **Honors/Awds:** ADA, NDA pres Pelican State Dental Assn 1980; LDA 6th Dist Dental Assn; Capital & City Dental Assn Scottlandville Jaycees; Baton Rouge Alumni, Kappa Alpha Psi; Mt Zion 1st Bapt Ch; So Univ Alumni Assn; life mem Meharry Med Coll Alumni Assn. **Business Addr:** 1704 Convention St, Baton Rouge, LA 70802.

HALL, DAVID MCKENZIE
Educator. **Personal:** Born Jun 21, 1928, Gary, IN; son of Grace Elizabeth Crimiel Hall and Alfred M Hall; married Jacqueline V Branch, Apr 30, 1960; children: Glen D, Gary D. **Educ:** Howard Univ, BA Business 1946-51, MSEd Soc 1962-66; North Carolina Agricultural and State Univ, Greensboro, NC; MIT, Cambridge MA, Certificate, 1976. **Career:** Scott AFB IL USAF, deputy base cmndr 1974-75, base cmndr 1975-76; Air Force Logistics Cmd USAF, deputy cmptrlr 1976-77, cmptrlr 1977-83; Delco-Remy Div of Gen Motors, dir data prcsg 1983-84; Electr Data Systems Corp, acct manager 1985-88; Electronic Data Systems, Saginaw, MI, regional manager, 1988-93; Northwood Univ, professor, 1993-97; Saginaw Valley State University, College of Business, executive-in-residence, currently. **Orgs:** Mem Air Force Assn 1960-; mem Boy Scouts Am 1942-; vice pres, Saginaw Community Foundation; Life mem, NAACP; Kapa Alpha Psi; member, Community Affairs Committee, 1988-; executive board member, United Way of Saginaw, 1989-93. **Honors/Awds:** Key to city Gary, IN 1981; hon citizen of City Of E St Louis 1976; crtfd systms professional Assn for Systms Management 1984; crtfd cost anlyst Assc of Anlyst 1983; Computers in Combat, AF Comptroller Magazine 1967. **Military Serv:** USAF brigadier gen; Dstngshd Serv Medal 1983; Legion of Merit 1974; Meritorious Serv Medal 1971, 1976. **Home Addr:** 49 West Hannum Blvd, Saginaw, MI 48602-1938, (517)791-1192. **Business Addr:** Curtis 328, SVSU, 7400 Bay Rd, Saginaw, MI 48604, (517)249-1676.

HALL, DELILAH RIDLEY
Educational administrator. **Personal:** Born Aug 23, 1953, Baton Rouge, LA; daughter of Mamie Jones Ridley and Samuel Ridley Sr; married Holmes G Hall Sr; children: Holmes, Byron, Marsha, Michael, Monica. **Educ:** Jarvis Christian Coll, BS 1975; East Texas State Univ, MS 1977. **Career:** East Texas State Univ, coord 1975-77; Longview Independent School Dist, ind instructor 1978; Jarvis Christian Coll, Hawkins, TX, upward bound prog counselor 1978, asst to the dean of academic affairs 1980, asst to the president 1981-; interim vice pres, 1991-, Title III coordinator, assist. to pres, currently. **Orgs:** Mem JCC/SCI Natl Alumni & Ex-Student Assoc 1975; sec Hawkins Elementary PTA 1985-87; mem Zeta Phi Beta Sorority, Inc. **Honors/Awds:** Alpha Kappa Mu. **Home Addr:** P O Box 37, Hawkins, TX 75765. **Business Addr:** Educational Administrator, Jarvis Christian Coll, P O Drawer G, Hawkins, TX 75765.

HALL, DELORES
Actress. **Personal:** Born Feb 26, Kansas City, KS; married Michael Goodstone. **Educ:** Harbor Jr Coll, LACC. **Career:** Broadway Show, "Your Arm's Too Short To Box With God"; "Godspell", "Hair", major roles & night club performer; toured with Harry Belafonte, Tommy Smothers. **Honors/Awds:** Recorded album RCA 1973-74; Antoinette Perry Awd, Best Supporting Actress in a Musical 1977; Toro Awd Young Woman of Am nominee Chs of NJ; music awds; White House performance 1977.

HALL, DOLORES BROWN
Educational administrator. **Personal:** Born in Brooklyn, NY; married Rev Kirkwood M Hall; children: Alexander Chapman. **Educ:** Brooklyn Hosp School of Nursing, RN Diploma 1962; Long Island Univ, BS 1966; Adelphi Univ, MS 1969; NY Univ, PhD 1977. **Career:** Medgar Evers Coll NIMH Rsch Proj, project dir 1975-77; Delaware State Coll, assoc prof 1977-79; Health & Human Serv NIMH St Elizabeth Hosp, dir nursing ed 1979-84; Edison State Coll, dir BSN Prog 1984-. **Orgs:** Workshop leader Delaware Home for the Aged 1976; bd of dir Good Shepard Home Health Aide Prog 1977-79; mem Mental Health Plan Task Force 1978-79; book reviewer Nursing Outlook Addison & Wesley 1980,82; mem USPHS Cont Ed Review Comm 1980-83; consult Charles Drew Neighborhood Health Ctr. **Honors/Awds:** Traineeship Grant Natl Inst of Mental Health 1964-65; EPDA/Southern Fellowship NY Univ 1971-75; Sr Level Rating 14 Fed Govt 1979-84; Postdoctoral Fellowship Gerontological Soc of Amer 1985. **Business Addr:** Dir of BSN Program, Thomas A Edison State College, 101 W State St CN 545, Trenton, NJ 08625.

HALL, ELLIOTT SAWYER
Automobile company executive, attorney. **Personal:** Born 1938; son of Ethel B Hall (deceased) and Odis Hall; married Shirley Ann Robinson Hall; children: Fred, Lannis, Tiffany. **Educ:** Wayne State Univ, Detroit MI, BA, law degrees. **Career:** Govt of Wayne County MI, Detroit, MI, chief asst prosecutor; Dykema Gossett Spencer Goodnow & Trigg, Detroit MI, law partner; Ford Motor Company, Dearborn MI, lawyer, lobbyist, vice pres of govt affairs, 1987-. **Honors/Awds:** Distinguished Alumnus Award, Wayne State Univ. **Business Addr:** Vice President, Washington Affairs, Ford Motor Co, 1350 I St, NW, Suite 1000, Washington, DC 20005.

HALL, ETHEL HARRIS
Educator. **Personal:** Born Feb 23, 1928, Decatur, AL; daughter of Mr and Mrs Harry Harris; married Alfred James Hall Sr; children: Alfred Jr, Donna Hall Mitchell. **Educ:** AL A&M Univ, BS 1948; Univ of Chicago, MA 1953; Univ AL, DSW 1979. **Career:** Jefferson City Bd of Ed, teacher 1955-66; Neighborhood Youth Corps, dir 1966-71; Univ Montevallo, assoc prof 1971-78; Univ of AL, assoc prof 1978-. **Orgs:** Pres AL Personnel & Guidance Assn 1972-73, AL Conf of Child Care 1977; AL Conf of Soc Work 1981-82; AL Assc Womens's Clubs 1984-88; mem Social Work Bd of Examiners; mem AL State Board of Educ 1987-. **Honors/Awds:** Leadership award AL Personnel & Guidance Assn 1974, 1976 , 1977; Alumus of the Yr AL A&M Univ 1975; Serv Award AL Conf of Social Work 1982; fellowship Intrntl Study Dept of State Jamaica, West Indies 1975. **Business Addr:** Associate Professor, Univ of Alabama, PO Box 1935, Tuscaloosa, AL 35486.

HALL, EUGENE CURTIS
City official, urban planner. **Personal:** Born Jan 4, 1958, Monticello, FL; son of Emma Lou Hall Mosley and Henry Hall; children: Eugene Curtis Green, Chelsea Natasha. **Educ:** University of Florida, Gainesville, FL, BA, 1976, MA, 1989. **Career:** Florida A & M Univ, Tallahassee, FL, career counselor, 1983; US Navy, Mayport, FL, operations specialist, 1984-89; State of Florida, Tallahassee, FL, resource planner, 1984-86; City of Monticello, Monticello, FL, city commissioner, 1987-; City of

Tallahassee, Tallahassee, FL, planner II, 1987-, administrative supervisor trainee, 1990-91; Valdosta State University, instructor, currently. **Orgs:** Treasurer, board of directors, Florida Planning & Zoning Association, 1988-; planning committee chairman, Concerned United People, 1990-; member, Apalachee Regional Planning Commission, 1989-90; member, Florida A & M Univ Govern Affairs Board of Directors, 1989-; member, Florida Small Cities CDBG Small Cities Advisory Panel, 1988-89. **Honors/Awds:** Public Service, NAACP, Jeffersn Co Branch, 1989-90; Service Appreciation, City of Monticello Local Planning Agency, 1990-91; Fellowship Award, Alpha Phi Omega, 1977; Academic Honors, Gamma Theta Upsilon, 1982. **Military Serv:** US Naval Reserves, Petty Officer 3rd Class, 1984-89. **Business Addr:** Instructor, Valdosta State, Valdosta, GA 31602.

HALL, EVELYN ALICE (EVELYN MANNING)
Physician. **Personal:** Born Oct 31, 1945, Paterson, NJ; married Dr Macy G Hall Jr. **Educ:** Howard Univ, BS 1967; Howard Univ Clge of Med, MD 1973; Columbia Univ, MPH 1977. **Career:** Rockville Centre Group Hlth Assc, physician if chief 1977-; Columbia Univ, fellow pediatric ambulatory care 1975-77; Roosevelt Hosp, resd 1974-75. **Orgs:** Cand Amer Acad of Pediatrics; bd Elgible Amer Pediatric Bds; DC Med Soc 1977; Howard Univ Med Alumni; Alpha Omega Alpha Med 1973. **Business Addr:** 6111 Executive Blvd, Rockville, MD.

HALL, FRED, III
Market analyst, elected official. **Personal:** Born Feb 9, 1945, St Louis, MO; married Pattie M Burdett; children: Fred IV, Rose M. **Educ:** Sinclair Coll, AS Engrg Tech 1968; Univ of Dayton, BS Engrg Tech 1976; Wright State University, MBA, 1992. **Career:** Delco Prod Div GMC, lab tech 1968-73, sales coord 1973-78, sales engrg 1978-85, mkt analyst, 1985-. **Orgs:** Bd mem Camp Fire Girls 1975-77; city commiss City of Xenia 1977,81-; sec Xenia-Wilberforce Dem Club 1979-82; pres Wilberforce-Xenia Optimist Club 1981-82; chmn bd of zoning appeals City of Xenia 1982,83,85; vice pres Chi Lambda Chap Alpha Phi Alpha 1984-85; president, Chi Lambda Chapter, Alpha Phi Alpha, 1986-87; deputy mayor City of Xenia 1984-; plnng commiss, chmn, City of Xenia 1984, 1992-93; president, city comm, City of Xenia, 1989-90; board mem, Boys and Girls Clubs, 1992-93. **Honors/Awds:** Awd for Excellence in Community Activities General Motors Corp 1979; Omega Psi Phi Fraternity, Citizen of the Year, 1992. **Home Addr:** 3272 Wyoming Drive, Xenia, OH 45385. **Business Addr:** Senior Market Analyst, Delco Chassis Div, GMC, 2000 Forrer Blvd, Dayton, OH 45420.

HALL, HANSEL CRIMIEL
Company executive. **Personal:** Born Mar 12, 1929, Gary, IN; son of Grace Eliz Crimiel Hall (deceased) and Alfred M Hall (deceased); divorced; children: Grace Jean. **Educ:** IN University, BS 1953; Industrial College of the Armed Forces, natl security management certificate, 1971; Blackstone School of Law, B Laws 1982. **Career:** US Dept of Housing & Urban Devel, program specialist 1969-73, dir, F H & E O, div MN, 1973-75, div IN, 1975-79; US Dept of Interior, dir, office of human resources, 1979-88. **Orgs:** Pres, Crimiel Ltd, consulting, 1979-; pres, MN-Dakota Conf, NAACP, 1981-86; pres, bd of dirs, Riverview Towers Homeowners Assn, 1985-87; life mem, Indiana Univ Alumni Assn; Omega Psi Phi; golden heritage mem, NAACP; life member, VFW; elected board of directors, Korean War Veterans Association, 1992-95; President, Minnesota State Association of Parliamentarians 1997-. **Honors/Awds:** Distinguished Toastmaster Award Toastmasters Intl 1986; Outstanding Leadership Award NAACP Region IV 1986; US Parliamentary delegate to Russia & Czechoslovakia, 1992. **Military Serv:** US Air Force Reserve, lt col 25 yrs; United Nations Serv Medal, Korean Serv, ReserveOfficers Assn, Air Force Overseas. **Business Addr:** President, Crimiel Communications Inc, PO Box 14648, Minneapolis, MN 55414-0648.

HALL, HAROLD L.
Chief executive. **Career:** Delta Enterprises, Inc, Greenville MS, chief executive. **Business Addr:** Delta Enterprises Inc, 819 Main St, Greenville, MS 38701.

HALL, HORATHEL
Educator/artist. **Personal:** Born Dec 3, 1926, Houston, TX; married Howard D; children: Kenneth A, Admerle J, Horace D. **Educ:** Prairie View A&M U, BA 1948; NM Highlands Las Vagas, MFA 1962; W African States Art Research, fellowship HISD 1975. **Career:** Houston Independent Sch Dist, art tchr/Artist 1980-; Worthing High Sch, art tchr & dept chmn 1951-80; TX So U, art prof 1964-79; Adept New Am Folk Gallery, crafts consult 1977-79; Eliza Johnson Home for the Elderly, crafts consult 1977-79; Houston Comm Coll, art prof 1975-77. **Orgs:** Affiliated mem Nat Art Educators Assn 1951-80; treas Houston Art Educators Assn 1976-80; affiliated mem Nat Conf of Artists 1976-80; vP Contemporary Handweavers of Houston 1968-69; sec E Sunny Side Civic Club of Houston 1970-80; sec Orgn of Black Artist 1975-80; spl publ Black Artist of the New Generation 1977; The Arts & the Rural & Isolated Elderly Univ of KY 1980. **Honors/Awds:** Pub "Contemporary Concepts of the Liberian Rice Bag Weave" vol 27 no 2 Contemporary Handweavers of TX Inc 1975; Arrowmont Scholarship Pi Beta Alumnae ClubGatlingburg TN 1980. **Business Addr:** Houston Independent Sch Dist W, 9215 Scott St, Houston, TX 77051.

HALL, HOWARD RALPH
Dentist. **Personal:** Born May 1, 1919, Cincinnati; married Dorothy; children: Lillian, Howard, VIII, Juanita. **Educ:** Wilberforce U, BS 1943; Meharry Med Coll, DDS 1947. **Career:** Dover DE, intern 1948-49; Cincinnati Bd Health, 1953-63; pvt practic 1953-; Model Cities Dental Prog KY, proj dir 1970-74. **Orgs:** Mem Nat Am & KY Denatl Assns; bd mem Cincinnati ARC 1973-; mem Kappa Alpha Psi Frat; asst dir pub Nat Dental Assn 1970-. **Honors/Awds:** Outstanding Grad Meharry Coll 1972; Bronze Star Medal 1952. **Military Serv:** AUS capt 1949-53. **Business Addr:** 502 Copplin Bldg, Covington, KY 41011.

HALL, IRA D.
Company executive. **Educ:** Stanford Univ, MBA. **Career:** IBM, numerous positions, treasurer, 1990-. **Special Achievements:** Named as one of Black Enterprise's 25 Hottest Black Managers, 1988. **Business Phone:** (914)766-1900.

HALL, JACK L.
Internal affairs administrator. **Personal:** Born Feb 11, 1941, Cairo, IL; son of Clemmie Lee Hall and J K Hall; married Effie D, Jun 27, 1959; children: Marvin D, Marilyn R Goldwire. **Educ:** Lansing Community College, associates, criminal justice, 1961; Michigan State University, bachelors, criminal justice, 1979; Western Michigan University, MPA, 1992. **Career:** Benton Township Police Department, patrolman, 1962-67; Michigan Department of State Police, captain, 1967-92; Michigan Department of Corrections, Internal Affairs, mgr, 1992-. **Special Achievements:** In 1967 became the first African-American to become a Michigan state trooper. **Business Addr:** Internal Affairs Manager, Michigan Department of Corrections, Michigan at Grand Avenue, Grandview Plaza Bldg, Lansing, MI 48909, (517)335-1412.

HALL, JAMES REGINALD
Military official (retired). **Personal:** Born Jul 15, 1936, Anniston, AL; son of Evelyn Dodson Hall (deceased) and James Reginald Hall Sr (deceased); married Helen Kerr Hall, Jun 25, 1960; children: Sheila A, James R III, Cheryl D. **Educ:** Morehouse College, Atlanta, GA, BA, 1957; Shippensburg State University, Shippensburg, PA, MS, public admin, 1975. **Career:** United States Army, Ft Sheridan, IL, commanding general, 1957-; Morehouse Coll, Campus Operations, vice pres, currently. **Orgs:** Alpha Phi Alpha Fraternity, 1954-; Prince Hall Mason, 1962-. **Honors/Awds:** Hon Doctor of Laws, Morehouse College, 1987. **Military Serv:** US Army, lt general, 1957-; Distinguished Service Medal, Legion of Merit, Bronze Star, Meritorious Service Medal, Combat Infantryman's Badge, Parachute Badge. **Home Addr:** 115 North Dr, Fairburn, GA 30213.

HALL, JEFFREY MAURICE
Hand & microvascular surgeon. **Personal:** Born Oct 31, 1958, Ypsilanti, MI; son of James and Maureen Hall; married Janet R Hall, Aug 24, 1987; children: Elliott Joshua. **Educ:** Univ of MI, BSChE, 1981; Univ of MI Med School, MD, 1985. **Career:** Self-employed, surgeon, currently. **Orgs:** Amer Assn of Surgery of the Hand, 1995; Amer Med Assn, 1991; Amer Coll of Surgeons, fellow, 1996. **Honors/Awds:** Candidate for Chevron Scholarship at the Univ of MI, 1979; Citizen of the Week for WWJ Radio, 1995. **Special Achievements:** Surgeon; Multiple talks on Cumulative Trauma disorders. **Business Addr:** Medical Doctor and Surgeon, Jeffrey M Hall, MD, PC, 21331 Kelly Rd, Ste 100, Eastpointe, MI 48021-3217, (810)776-6661.

HALL, JESSE J.
Educator. **Personal:** Born Dec 16, 1938, Clover, SC; married Nancy Thorne; children: Nathaniel Craig, Yoland Yevette. **Educ:** State Tchrs Clg Fayetteville NC, BS 1962; Univ of NV, MEd Sc Admn 1970; Univ of San Francisco, Doctoral 1984. **Career:** Washoe Co School Dist, Orvis Ring and Sierra Vista Schools, prin 1971-72, Glen Duncan School, prin 1972-80, Lloyd Diedrichsen School, prin 1981-84. **Orgs:** Mem Intrntl Reading Assc 1962; Natl Assc of Elem Sc Prins 1971; NV Assc of Sc Admn 1972; Phi Delta Kappa 1968; Eql Opprtnty Bd UNR 1980; NV StateTextbk Cmsn 1969-79; bd of dir panel chrmn United Way NV 1972-78. **Honors/Awds:** Dist serv awrd Negro Bus & Profsnl Women's Assc 1980; man of the yr Second Bapt Ch Reno 1978; distgshd serv awrd NAACP 1978. **Business Addr:** Principal, Lloyd Diedrichsen Sch, 1735 Del Rosa Way, Sparks, NV 89431.

HALL, JOHN ROBERT
House painter, community activist. **Personal:** Born Jun 29, 1920, Mitford, SC; married Ruth. **Career:** House Painter self-employed. **Orgs:** Mem Deacon Bd, church treas, Sunday school supt Pine Grove Bapt Church; co-organizer Great Falls Br NAACP; organizer Young Men's Council for Political Action; pres Home & Comm Improvement Club; pres Great Falls Br NAACP; organizer Chester Co Voters Assn; pres 1st Vice Pres Chester Co Dem Party; past pres Fairfield Bapt Sunday School Conv of Fairfield Co 1958-62; former mem Chester Co Adv Council on Adult Educ; former mem Carolina Comm Action Bd 1968-70; Gov West's Adv Commn on Human Relations in SC 1970-72; Great Fall Inc Commn; mem Voters Educ Project of SC 5th Congressional Dist; instrumental in getting relief for black citizens treated unjustly in retirement system procedures, helped get black deputy sheriff's policeman jobs for both black & white; mem, Committee to Incorporate the town of Great Falls; mem, Committee to write history of African Americans in South Carolina. **Home Addr:** PO Box 362, Great Falls, SC 29055.

HALL, JOSEPH A.
Educator (retired), consultant. **Personal:** Born May 30, 1908, Chester, WV; son of Lottie Hall and Isaac Hall; married Marguerite L Clemmons; children: JoAnn, Joseph Andrew. **Educ:** Wilberforce Univ, BS, 1931; Western Reserve, MSW, 1944. **Career:** Family Serv Bureau, caseworker, 1933-35; Dept of Public Welfare, caseworker 1935-1940; Juvenile Court Cleveland, OH, probation officer, 1942-45; Cleveland Urban League, industrial rel dir, 1945-46; Urban League of Greater Cincinnati, exec dir, 1946-73; School of Soc Work, Univ of Cincinnati, assoc prof, 1979-92. **Orgs:** Natl Conf of Soc Welfare, 1935-73; pres, Ohio Welfare Conf, 1956; mem Natl Assn of Soc Workers 1949-; pres, Ohio Advisory Council for Voc Educ, 1972; mem Ohio Housing Bd, 1961-72; chmn, Models City, 1973-74, Ohio State Advisory Comm, 1964-70; vice chmn, Childrens Home 1975- . **Honors/Awds:** Man of the Year Cincinnati Prsnl Assn, Cincinnati, OH, 1965; distinguished serv, United Black Comm Orgs, 1969; Man of the Year, Ohio Voc Assn, 1973; Honorary Degree, FFA Ohio Chapter, 1971; Whitney M Young Medallion Award, National Urban League, 1992; Scholarship Award in name of Joseph A Hall, Univ of Cincinnati, School of Social Work, 1994; Greater Cincinnati Chamber of Commerce, Great Living Cincinnatian Award, 1995. **Home Addr:** 3543 Amberacres 409W, Cincinnati, OH 45237.

HALL, JOSEPH CLEMON
Scientist, educator. **Personal:** Born Aug 3, 1955, Philadelphia, PA; son of Lorraine Hall Tunnell and Joseph McPherson; married Carleen Denise Watler Hall, May 1, 1987; children: Vincent, Joseph, Chris, Joel, Carleen. **Educ:** Roanoke College, Salem, VA, BS, biology, 1977; Old Dominion University, Norfolk, VA, MS, biology, 1979; Kent State University, Kent, OH, PhD, chemistry, 1985. **Career:** Norfolk State University, Norfolk, VA, res asst, 1979-80; Kean College of NJ, Union, NJ, asst prof, 1986-87; Indiana University, Bloomington, IN, visiting prof, 1987; Penn State University, University Park, PA, res assoc sci, 1987-88, asst prof, 1988-. **Orgs:** Member, American Institute of Chemist, 1987-; member, American Chemical Society, 1987-; member, American Society for Cell Biology, 1991-; member, American Society of Andrology, 1988-; member, Sigma Xi Sci Res Society, 1988-. **Honors/Awds:** Minority Res Iniation Grant, 1987-90, Creative Extention Grant, 1991-93, National Science Foundation; Leadership Award, Louisville, KY Central Community Center, 1989; Key to City of Louisville, Louisville, KY, 1989; Recipient, Presidential Young Investigator Award, National Science Foundation, 1991. **Business Addr:** Assistant Professor of Biochemistry, Pennsylvania State University, 306 Althouse Laboratory, University Park, PA 16802.

HALL, JULIA GLOVER
Professor. **Personal:** Born in Philadelphia, PA; daughter of Isabel Dickson Glover (deceased) and Harold Heywood Glover (deceased); married William Francis Hall Jr, Nov 28, 1947; children: William Francis III (deceased), Michael David. **Educ:** Temple University, Philadelphia, PA, BA, 1968; Wharton School, University of Pennsylvania, Philadelphia, PA, MA, 1969; University of Pennsylvania, Philadelphia, PA, PhD, 1973; Harvard University, 1976-78. **Career:** Dept of Justice, Governor's Justice Commission, Harrisburg, PA, project evaluator, 1974-79; Drexel University, Philadelphia, PA, assoc prof of psychology & sociology, 1982-91, professor, 1991-; State Correctional Institute, Graterford, PA, coordinator of Concerned Seniors/Gray Panthers, 1986-; Pennsylvania Board of Probation and Parole, trainer, 1988-; Pennsylvania Family Caregiver Support Program, Genontological Society of America, principal investigator & project director, 1988; Natl Institute of Corrections, consultant, 1989-; US Dept of Health & Human Services, principal investigator & project director, 1989-91. **Orgs:** Southern Home Servs, pres/chairman of the board, 1988-90, board of directors/trustee, 1972-; president, Pennsylvania Association of Criminal Justice Educators, 1990-93; convenor, Gray Panther chapter, Graterford, PA, 1989-; board mem, 1st vice-president, Pennsylvania Prison Society; chairperson, Victim Offender Reconcilation Program of Graterford. **Honors/Awds:** Postdoctoral Fellowship in Applied Gerontology, Gerontological Soc of America, 1988; Lindback Award for Distinguished Teaching, 1979; Fellow, Aspen Institute for Humanistic Studies, 1983-; Natl Sci Foundation Fellow, University of Pennsylvania, 1968-73; Woodrow Wilson Fellow, 1968-; Drexel Univ Faculty Scholar Research Award, 1989; Fellowship on The American Judiciary, Freedoms Foundation, Valley Forge, PA, 1989; Legion of Honor, Chapel of The Four Chaplains Award, 1976; Distinguished Service Award, Boy Scouts of America, 1964; Lilly Fellowship, University of Pennsylvania, 1980-84; Natl Sci Foundation, Pyschology of Aging Seminar, Washington University, 1980; Lindback Distinguished Teaching Award, 1979. **Special Achievements:** Producer: TV program Criminal Justice Today, Correcting our Elders, videotape documentary. **Business Addr:** Professor, Dept of Psychology/Sociology, Drexel University, 3141 Chestnut Street, Philadelphia, PA 19104, (215)590-8895.

HALL, KATHRYN LOUISE
Health administrator. **Personal:** Born Jul 19, 1948, Moscow, AR; daughter of Corrine Starks and Chester Hall; children: Kennya Thornburg, Eddie Stokes, Tamu Green. **Educ:** University of California Los Angeles, MPH, 1975, BA, sociology, 1973. **Career:** California State Department of Health, health program advisor, 1975-82; California State Department Serv, regional oper mgr, 1982-83; Family Health Program Inc, Long Beach, administrator, 1983-84; Health Choice Inc, Portland OR, regional mgr, 1984-86; California State Department of Health Serv, health program advisor, 1986-90; Independent Consultant, 1982-; The Center for Community Health and Well Being Inc, executive director, 1988-. **Orgs:** CA Select Committee on Perinatal Substance Abuse, apointee; American Public Health Association; Resources Person's Network, Office of Minority Health, participant; Sacramento YWCA, board of directors; Black Advocates in State Service, chairman of health committee; National Council of Negro Women; Sacramento Black Infant Health Advisory Committee. **Honors/Awds:** HEW, HEW Traineeship in Public Health, 1973; Girl Scouts, Role Model of the Year, 1989; Soroptomist, Women Helping Women Award, 1989; YWCA, Outstanding Woman of the Year, Health Svc, 1989; California State Legislature, Woman of the Year, 1990; California Child Abuse Prevention, Professional of the Year, 1993; CA Public Health Assn, Outstanding Community Service Award, 1993; Essence Magazine, Community Service Award, 1995. **Special Achievements:** The Birthing Project, Founder, 1988. **Business Addr:** Executive Director, The Center for Community Health and Well Being Inc, 1810 S St, Sacramento, CA 95814, (916)442-2229.

HALL, KATIE
Educator, city government official. **Personal:** Born Apr 3, 1938, Mount Bayou, MS; daughter of Bessie Mae Hooper Green and Jeff L Green; married John H Hall, Aug 15, 1957; children: Jacqueline, Junifer, Michelle. **Educ:** MS Valley State Univ, BS, 1960; IN Univ, MS, 1967. **Career:** City of Gary Schs, tchr 1960-; IN 5th Dist, state rep 1974-76; IN 3rd Dist, state senator, 1976-82; US Congress, Congresswoman, IN 1st Dist, 1982-84; City of Gary, IN, city clerk, 1985—. **Orgs:** Pres Gary Cncl for Soc Studs 1972-74; vice chpsn Gary Housing Bd of Commr 1975; House Comm on Afrs of Lake & Marion Cos 1975-76; chpsn Senate Educ Comm 1977; life mem NAACP; Amer Assn of Univ Women; pres, Gary IN branch, Natl Council of Negro Women; Natl Black Political Caucus; Natl Organization for Women; IN State Tchrs Assn; NEA; Amer Fed of Tchrs; US Congressional Black Caucus; US Congressional Caucus on Women's Issues; Alpha Kappa Alpha Natl Sor; exec bd and secretary-treas, Congressional Steel Caucus; chair House sub-comm on census and the US population. **Honors/Awds:** Outstanding Lgsltr Awd NAACP 1975; Outstanding Woman in Politics City of Gary 1975; Outstanding Serv to Comm Gary Com on Status of Women 1976; Outstanding-Women in Politics IN Blk Polit Assn 1975; only Black from IN to serve in US Congress; wrote and served as chief sponsor of the Martin Luther King Jr Natl Holiday Law in 1983; wrote and served as chief sponsor of King Holiday Comm Law in 1984; rec more than 200 awds for serv to religion, educ, politics, civic & comm groups; Gary Branch NAACP's Mary White Irvington Awd 1984. **Business Addr:** Gary City Clerk, 401 Broadway, Gary, IN 46407.

HALL, KENNETH
State government official. **Personal:** Born May 20, 1915, East St Louis, IL; married Anne; children: Kenneth Jr, Maurice, Mark, Thomas. **Educ:** Park Coll. **Career:** Aptd to State Rent Cntrl Bd Gov Adlai Stevenson 1949; St Clair Co Housing Auth E St Louis Park Dist, commnr 1959; St Clair Co Sheriffs & Dept, former investigator; licensed ins broker; Illinois State House of Reps 2 terms; State of Illinois, State Senator, 57th district, 1970-, Appropriations II, chairman; Executive, vice chairman; Education Committee, member; Executive Appointment Committee; Audit Commission, member. **Orgs:** Mem St Clair Co Welfare Serv Com; chmn E St Louis City Dem Cntrl Com; mem NAACP; Knights of Columbus. **Honors/Awds:** Minority Caucus Chair. **Business Addr:** State Senator, Illinois General Assembly, 103 B State House, Springfield, IL 62706.

HALL, KIM FELICIA
Educator. **Personal:** Born Dec 25, 1961, Baltimore, MD; daughter of Vera Webb Hall and Lawrence Harold Hall. **Educ:** Hood College, Frederick, MD, BA (magna cum laude), 1983; Univ of Pennsylvania, Philadelphia, PA, PhD, 1990. **Career:** Democratic Natl Convention, communications coord 1984; Univ of PA, graduate fellow 1985-86; Committee to re-elect Clarence Blount, campaign coord 1986; Swarthmore Coll, visiting instructor; Friends of Vera P Hall, public relations dir 1986-87; Georgetown Univ, Washington, DC, lecturer, 1989-90, assistant professor, 1990-. **Orgs:** Vice pres Grad English Assoc Univ of PA 1985-86; mem Renaissance Soc of Amer; sec Grad English Assoc 1984-85; member, Modern Language Assn; member, Shakespeare Assn of America; member, American Society for Theatre Research. **Honors/Awds:** Hood Scholar 1983; Mellon Fellowship in the Humanities, Woodrow Wilson Natl Fellowship Foundation; Folger Inst Fellowship, Washington DC 1986; Governor's Citation, Gov Harry Hughes MD 1986; Paul Robeson Award, University of Pennsylvania, 1989; Folger Institute Fellowship, Folger Shakespeare Library, 1991; Mellon Dissertation Fellowship, Woodrow Wilson National Fellowship Foundation, 1988-89. **Business Addr:** Assistant Professor, Georgetown University, English Dept, 37 & O Streets, 328 New North, Washington, DC 20057-0001.

HALL, KIRKWOOD MARSHAL
Health official. **Personal:** Born May 13, 1944, Montclair, NJ; son of Alice Chapman Hall and Marshal Eugene Hall; married Dolores Brown; children: Malaika Estelle, Dalili Talika, Alexander Chapman. **Educ:** VA Union Univ, BA Sociology 1967; Pittsburgh Theological Sem, MDiv 1974; Univ of Pittsburgh School of Public Health, MPH 1978. **Career:** Hill Mental Health Team, mental health clinician 1970-74; Western Psych Inst & Clinic, dir 1974-75; NJ Dept of Public Advocate Div of Mental Health, suprv field rep 1975-77; Project SAIL, dir 1977-79; Henry J Austin Health Ctr, clinic suprv mental health. **Orgs:** Asst dir Black Campus Ministries Inc 1971-; chmn Nieghborhood Comm on Health Care 1974; elder Unification Assoc of Christian Sabbath 1976-80; mental health clinician Univ of Med & Dentistry Newark, NJ 1980-82; assoc pastor Union Bapt Church Trenton, NJ 1981-; vice pres Samuel DeWitt Proctor Greater NJ Alumni Chap VA Union Univ 1983-84; assoc pastor, St Paul AME Zion, Trenton NJ 1987-. **Honors/Awds:** Service Awd Neighborhood Adv Bd Mercy Hosp Pittsburgh 1971-75; Cited in Black Amer Writers Past & Present Ed Rush 1975; Publ ''Chapman New Black Voices'' Davis Spectrum in Black, ''Haynes Voices of the Revolution'' Jones & Neal Black Fire, ''Porter Connections'' Univ of Pittsburgh Jrnl of Black Poetry Periodical; Presenter 62nd Annual Meeting Amer Orthopsychiatric Assn ''Suggestions for the Utilization of the Job Training Partnership Act'' NY City April 22, 1985. **Business Addr:** Clinic Supervisor Mental Hlth, Henry J Austin Health Center, 321 N Warren St, Trenton, NJ 08618.

HALL, L. PRISCILLA
Judge. **Career:** New York State Supreme Court, judge, currently. **Business Addr:** Justice, New York State Supreme Court, 360 Adams St, Brooklyn, NY 11201, (718)643-5121.

HALL, LEMANSKI
Professional football player. **Personal:** Born Nov 24, 1970, Valley, AL. **Educ:** Univ of Alabama, attended. **Career:** Houston Oilers, linebacker, 1994-96; Tennessee Oilers, 1997-. **Business Addr:** Professional Football Player, Tennessee Oilers, c/o Baptist Sports Park, 7640 H 70-5, Nashville, TN 37221.

HALL, MELVIN CURTIS
Attorney. **Personal:** Born Jun 2, 1956, Tulsa, OK; son of Eunice Jean Taylor Hall and Isiah Hall; married Alicia Williams Hall, Jul 26, 1980; children: Natasha Marie, Tenia Shanta. **Educ:** Langston University, Langston, OK, BS, 1978; University of Oklahoma, Norman, OK, JD, 1981. **Career:** Cleveland County District Attorney, Norman, OK, assistant district attorney, 1980-83; Oklahoma Human Rights Commission, Oklahoma City, OK, executive director, 1983-87; Chapel, Riggs, Abney, Neal & Turpen, Oklahoma City, OK, attorney, 1988-. **Orgs:** Member, Oklahoma Bar Association, 1982-; member, Oklahoma City Association of Black Lawyers, 1986-; board member, Southwest Center for Human Relations Studies, 1987-; board member, Progress Independence, 1988-; board member, Oklahoma State Chamber of Commerce & Industry, 1989-. **Honors/Awds:** A C Hamlin Tribute, Oklahoma Legislative Black Caucus, 1987; Plaque of Appreciation, A Philip Randolph of Oklahoma, 1990; Certificate of Appreciation, Marion Anderson Middle School, 1987; Certificate of Appreciation, US Dept of Housing & Urban Development, 1986; Blue Ribbon Award, Metropolitan Fair Housing Council of Oklahoma City, 1985. **Business Addr:** Attorney, Chapel, Riggs, Abney, Neal & Turpen, 5801 N Broadway, Paragon Bldg, Suite 101, Oklahoma City, OK 73118.

HALL, NANCY M.
Personnel executive, consultant. **Personal:** Born Feb 17, St Louis, MO. **Educ:** Fisk University, Nashville, TN, BA, business admin & history, cum laude, 1974; Howard University, Washington, DC, MBA, general management, 1977. **Career:** IBM Coporation, Washington, DC, various manufacturing management position, 1977-81, various personnel management positions, 1981-88; IBM Corporation, Purchase, NY, admin assistant to vice pres, personnel, 1989-90; IBM Corporation, Boulder, CO, location personnel manager, 1990-. **Orgs:** Member, Governor's Commission on State Administration, 1990-; natl vice pres of operations, National Black MBA Association, 1988-; member, national board of directors, National Black MBA Assn, 1986-; member, board of directors, Colorado Dance Festival, 1990-; member, board of directors, Organization for a New Equality, 1989-; board of directors, Healthy Transition Inc, 1989-. **Honors/Awds:** MBA of the Year, National Black MBA Assn, Washington, DC chapter, 1987; Outstanding Alumna, Howard Univ School of Business Admin, 1987; Gold Key Honor soc, Fisk University, 1974; Fisk-Morocco Exchange Program, Fisk University, 1971. **Business Addr:** Location Personnel Manager, IBM Corporation, PO Box 1900, DB 400/001-1, Boulder, CO 80301.

HALL, PERRY ALONZO
Educational administrator. **Personal:** Born Sep 15, 1947, Detroit, MI. **Educ:** Univ of MI, BA Psychology 1969; Harvard Univ, EdD Educ & Soc Policy 1977. **Career:** Northeastern Univ, inst 1974; Wayne State Univ, ext prog coord 1974-76, asst prof 1977-80, dir 1980-. **Orgs:** Exec bd mem Natl Council for Black Studies 1978; consultant Chicago Ctr for Afro-Amer Stud & Rsch 1982; consultant State of MI Office of Substance Abuse Serv 1982; Substance Abuse Comm New Detroit Inc 1974-; adv bd mem Equal Oppor Center 1983-. **Honors/Awds:** Doctoral Fellowship Ford Found 1971; listing Outstanding Young Men of America 1980. **Business Addr:** Dir Center for Black Studies, Wayne State University, Center for Black Studies, 5980 Cass Ave, Detroit, MI 48202.

HALL, RAYMOND A.
Administrator. **Personal:** Born Apr 17, 1914, Washington, DC; son of Serina Hall and Edward Hall; married Correne A McDonald; children: Jean M Freeman, Kendall L. **Educ:** Natl Radio Inst Washington DC, grad 1952. **Career:** Dept of Army Bd of Engrs for Rivers & Harbors, retired clk 1940-72; AAF Sch Pueblo CO, airplane mechanic; Rivers & Harbors Dept of Defense, vice pres empls assn bd of engrs for rivers & harbors 1971; City of N Brentwood MD, mayor. **Orgs:** Trustee St Paul CC Ch 1945-; exec bd NCBM vice pres MD Chap 1977-80; pres N Brentwood Citizens Assn 1968; chmn human relations commn exec bd Northwestern HS PG Co 1972; com mem Transp Study PG Co; adv committee chmn, Dept of the Aged PG Co, 1989. **Honors/Awds:** Meritorious Serv Awd Recreat Dept Prince George Co; Outstanding Pub Ofcl MD Intl Rotary Club; cited for 32 yrs serv bd of engrs for rivers & harbors Dept of Def; Golden Anniv Cert of Appreciation MD Natl Park & Planning Commn 1978; President's Award, Natl Conf of Black Mayors, 1991. **Military Serv:** AAF pfc 1944-46; Good Conduct Medal; Amer Theater Ribbon; Victory Ribbon. **Home Addr:** 3907 Windom Rd, Brentwood, MD 20722.

HALL, REGINALD LAWRENCE
Physician, educator. **Personal:** Born Jun 19, 1957, Whiteville, NC; son of Vera Hall and Lawrence Hall; married Ranota Thomas Hall, Jun 17, 1989. **Educ:** Baltimore Polytech Inst, 1975; St Vincent Coll, summa cum laude BS chem 1979; Duke Univ School of Med, 1983; Duke Univ Med Ctr, 1st yr resd 1983-84, jr asst resd 1984-85, resd orthopedic surg 1985-89. **Career:** St Vincent Coll, chem lab asst; Mayor's Coord Council on Criminal Justice Baltimore, work/study alumni devel office intern; Rsch & Plng Dept of Mass Transit Admin Baltimore, intern; Rsch & Plng Dept of Mass Transit Admin, mayor's coord council on criminal justice; St Vincent Coll, chem lab asst, work/study alumni devel office; Duke Med Ctr, phlebotomist, rsch fellow div of ped cardiology, clinical chem lab orthopedic surg resd, assistant professor, currently; Cornell Med Coll, summer fellowship. **Orgs:** Mem Black Student Union, Freshman Orientation Comm, Dean's Coll Subcomm, Resd Adv Council, Alumni Telethon, Duke Univ Med School Admiss Comm, DavisonCouncil Student Govt, Student Natl Med Assoc, Amer Med Student Assoc, Dean's Minority Affairs Subcomm; adv Duke Univ Undergrad Premed Soc. **Honors/Awds:** CV Mosby Book Awd; Analytic Chemistry Award. **Home Addr:** 2819 Hillsdale Rd, Baltimore, MD 21207.

HALL, ROBERT JOHNSON
Educational administrator. **Personal:** Born Jun 5, 1937, Crumrod, AR; married Jerlean. **Educ:** N Coll Pine Bluff AR, BS & AM 1963; UCA Conway AR, MA 1972; UA Fayetteville AR, adminstrv spec 1977. **Career:** Wabbaseka School Dist, supt 1975-; UAPB, assoc dean students 1972-75; AM & N Coll, asst dean of men 1967-72; JS Walker High School, teacher 1967-68; Tucker Rosenwald High School, prin 1966-67, teacher 1963-66. **Orgs:** Phi Delta Kappa Educ Frat; NEA AR Adminstr Assn; Phi Beta Sigma Frat; Royal Knight Soc Deacon Pine Hill Bapt Ch 1969; pres Gamma Psi Sigma Chap Phi Beta Sigma Frat 1974; bd mem OIC 1976. **Honors/Awds:** Outstndg Young Man of Am 1976. **Business Addr:** PO #210, Wabbaseka, AR 72175.

HALL, ROBERT JOSEPH
Physician. **Personal:** Born Dec 21, 1929, Natchitoches, LA; married Ida; children: Wayne, Robi, Krystal. **Educ:** So Univ A&M, BS 1950; Howard Univ Sch of Med, MD 1960. **Career:** Freemans Hosp, intern 1960-61; Freedmans & DC Gen Hosp, resd internal medicine 1961-64; Physician self. **Orgs:** Mem Baton Rouge Alcohol & Drug Abuse Ctr; staff mem Margaret Dumas Mental Health Clinic; mem Phi Beta Sigma Frat, Amer Legion, Mason, Mt Zion First Baptist Church. **Military Serv:** AUS commun sgt 1951-53. **Business Addr:** 8818 Scotland Ave, Ste B, Baton Rouge, LA 70807.

HALL, ROBERT L.
City administrator. **Personal:** Born Apr 1, 1937, Stuart, FL; married Rose Ann. **Career:** City of Stuart, supt of parks & cemetery; City of Stuart, mayor. **Orgs:** Past pres Martin Co Dem Mens Club; past potentate FL St Nursing Home Investigator; chmn Ombudsment Com for nursing home; mem Stuart Volunteer Fire Dept; 32 degree Mason; Shriner; So Assn of Cemeteries; Park Personnel Assn; Mason. **Honors/Awds:** Many awards from Civic & Church Organizations; award for Serving as Commnr & Mayor City of Stuart; award for Voters Registration

Participation Supr of Election. **Business Addr:** Supt of Streets Department, City of Stuart, 121 SW Frazer Ave, Stuart, FL 34995.

HALL, SYDNEY JAY, III
Attorney. **Personal:** Born Feb 27, 1959, Sumpter, SC; son of Loretta Hall and Sidney Hall. **Educ:** Howard Univ, BBA, 1982, JD, 1987. **Career:** Fireman's Fund/American Express, paralegal, 1978-81; American Express, special assistant vice pres of finance, 1982; Travelers Insurance, claims adjuster, 1987; Freistat and Sandler, associate, 1987; Law Office of Jay Hall PC, principal, 1992-. **Orgs:** Natl Bar Assn; American Bar Assn; California State Bar; Maryland State Bar; Pennsylvania State Bar. **Honors/Awds:** International Youth in Achievement Award, Cambridge, England; Leadership, San Mateo, 1992. **Special Achievements:** Founder: Asa T Spaulding Insurance Society, 1990; ATSIS Business Journal, Howard Univ. **Home Phone:** (415)345-2497. **Business Addr:** Attorney, Law Office of Sydney Jay Hall, PC, 1308 Bayshore Hwy, Ste 200, Burlingame, CA 94010, (415)375-8590.

HALL, TIMOTHY
Professional football player. **Personal:** Born Feb 15, 1974, Kansas City, MO. **Educ:** Robert Morris College. **Career:** Oakland Raiders, running back, 1996-. **Business Addr:** Professional Football Player, Oakland Raiders, 1220 Harbor Bay Pkwy, Alameda, CA 94502, (510)615-1875.

HALL, WILLIE GREEN, JR.
Dentist. **Personal:** Born May 23, 1947, Prattville, AL; son of Kattie R Hall and Willie G Hall Sr; married Cheryl F Wesley, Jan 30, 1971; children: Darius, Dashia. **Educ:** Howard Univ, BS 1971, DDS 1978. **Career:** People's Drug Store, pharmacist/asst mgr 1969-72; Standard Drugs, pharmacist 1972-74; Syracuse Comm Hlth Ctr, dentist 1979-80; Southeast Dental Assoc, partner/pres 1984-91; East of the River Health Assoc, dental dir 1980-88; partner, Lake Arbor Dental Assn, 1991; owner, CW Funding; private practice, currently. **Orgs:** Mem Natl & Amer Dental Assocs 1986-, Natl Pharm Assoc 1986-87, Omega Psi Phi Frat 1986-, Robert T Freeman Dental Soc 1986-; Howard Univ Pharmacy & Dental Alumni Assocs; D.C. Dental Society 1988-; Intl Assn for Orthodontics 1988-; mem, Academy of General Dentistry 1989-; Campbell AME Church, Washington DC; Natl Assn of Entrepreneurs, Certified Mortgage Investors. **Honors/Awds:** DC Dept Recreation Special Act Volunteer Awd 1984; Capital Head Start Comm Awd 1984; Washington Seniors Wellness Ctr Awd for Volunteer Serv 1986. **Home Addr:** 4513 Holmehurst Way, Bowie, MD 20720-3455. **Business Addr:** Private Dental Practice, 12164 Central Ave, Ste 221, Mitchellville, MD 20721.

HALL, YVONNE BONNIE (BONNIE)
Social worker. **Personal:** Born in New York, NY; daughter of Rose Reid Bailey and Stanley Bailey; married Leroy Hall, Feb 15, 1951 (divorced); children: Gilda Armstrong, Glenn. **Educ:** Adelphi U, BS 1974; Hunter Sch of Soc Work, MSW 1982. **Career:** Coll for Human Svcs, actg reg 1967-73, asst dir 1974-77, dir of agency devel 1977-83; Jewish Child Care, caseworker, 1984-85; New York City Board of Education, social work coordinator, 1985-; Sadie Amer Lyfe Center, social work coord 1985-. **Orgs:** Chairperson, adv bd, Counseling and Referral Program of the Adoption Assn of Black Social Workers 1979-; adoption spec Lutheran Comm Svcs; corresponding secretary, National Council of Negro Women, 1990-; foster care specialist, Flatbush Family Services Center. **Honors/Awds:** Alvin I Brown Fellowship Aspen Inst 1975; Woman in History Achievement Award, 1982.

HALLIBURTON, CHRISTOPHER
Marketing executive. **Personal:** Born Apr 27, 1958, New York, NY; son of Norman Halliburton & Camille Simonette. **Educ:** Tufts University, BA, history/political sci, 1980. **Career:** Aetna Life Insurance, EBR, 1980-84; Mayer & Meyer Assoc, account executive, 1984-89; Tannenbaum-Harber, account executive, 1982-84; Crossroads Films, sales representative, 1989-91; 900 Frames, executive producer, 1991-93; Ralativity Records, dir of video production, currently. **Special Achievements:** MTV, Video Award, Best International Video, 1991. **Business Addr:** Urban Product Marketing Executive, Relativity Records, 79 Fifth Ave, 16th Fl, New York, NY 10003, (212)337-5317.

HALLIBURTON, WARREN J.
Professor, writer, editor. **Personal:** Born Aug 2, 1924, New York, NY; son of Blanche Watson Halliburton and Richard H Halliburton; married Marion Jones, Dec 20, 1947; children: Cheryl, Stephanie, Warren, Jr, Jena. **Educ:** New York Univ, BS, 1949; Columbia Univ, MEd, 1975, DEd, 1977. **Career:** Prairie View Agricultural and Mechanical College (now Univ), Prairie View TX, English instructor, 1949; Bishop College, Dallas TX, English instructor, 1951, assoc, Inst of Intl Education, 1952; Recorder, New York NY, reporter and columnist, 1953; Brooklyn NY, teacher and dean at high school, 1959-60; coordinator for New York City Board of Education and assoc of New York State Dept of Education, 1960-65; McGraw Hill, Inc., New York NY, editor, 1967; Hamilton-Kirkland Colleges, Clinton NY, visiting prof of English, 1971-72; Columbia Univ, Teachers College, New York NY, editor, research assoc and dir of scholarly journal, govt program, and Ethnic Studies Center, 1972-77; Reader's Digest, New York NY, editor and writer; free-lance edi tor and writer. **Honors/Awds:** Author of Some Things That Glitter (novel), McGraw, 1969; author of The Picture Life of Jesse Jackson, F. Watts, 1972, 2nd edition, 1984; author of Harlem: A History of Broken Dreams, Doubleday, 1974; editor of Short Story Scene, Globe, 1973; contributor of about one hundred short stories, adaptations, and articles to periodicals; writer of fifteen filmstrips and a motion picture titled "Dig.". **Military Serv:** US Army Air Forces, 1943-46. **Home Addr:** 22 Scribner Hill Rd, Wilton, CT 06897.

HALL-KEITH, JACQUELINE YVONNE
Judge. **Personal:** Born Jan 8, 1953, Detroit, MI; daughter of Evelyn V Callaway Hall and William H Hall; married Luther A Keith, Sep 17, 1988; children: Erin Yvonne Hall Keith. **Educ:** General Motors Inst, B Indus Admin 1971-76; Detroit Coll of Law, JD, 1976-80. **Career:** Gen Motors Corp, coll co-op 1971-76; Ford Motor Co, mgmt trainee 1976-78, personnel analyst 1978-80, staff atty 1980-84; State of MI Dept of Labor, admin law judge/magistrate, 1984-94; Michigan Dept of Civil Rights, Dir of the Office of Legal Affairs, 1994-. **Orgs:** Mem, State Bar of Michigan; Wolverine Bar Assoc; mem GMI & DCL Alumni Assoc, Assoc of Black Judges of MI, NAACP; Delta Sigma Theta Sorority, Inc; member, Top Ladies of Distinction; president, 1993-94, board of directors, 1988-91; Association of Black Judges of Michigan; Delsprite Sponsor, Delta Sigma Theta Sorority, 1984-95; Nolan Middle School, mentor, 1993-94; State Bar of Michigan, Alternative Dispute Resolution Section, council member; Fellowship Chapel, Bible Study instructor. **Honors/Awds:** Speaking of People, Ebony Magazine, 1984; Judicial Excellence Award, Top Ladies of Distinction, 1990. **Business Addr:** Dir, Office of Legal Affairs, Michigan Dept of Civil Rights, State of MI Plaza Bldg, 7th Floor, 1200 6th St, Detroit, MI 48226.

HALL-TURNER, DEBORAH
Health services administrator. **Personal:** Born Jun 6, 1951, Detroit, MI; daughter of Herbert & Haroline Hall; married Michael G Turner, Sr, Jan 22, 1978; children: Michael G Turner, Esq. **Educ:** Mercy College of Detroit, BSN, 1973; Case Management Society of America, Certification, 1994. **Career:** Wayne County Pt Care Management, director of quality assurance, 1988-91; Mercy Health Svcs, sr manager of quality management, 1991-93, director of quality svcs, 1993-94, director of accrediation/regulation, 1994-95; MPRO, director of state government programs, 1995-96, director of behavioral health program & managed care evaluation, 1996-. **Orgs:** Association of Managed Care Nursing, past president, bd mem, 1993-; Thea Bowen Wellness Institute, treasurer, 1995-; Black Nurses Association. **Honors/Awds:** Mercy College of Detroit, MaCauley Awd, 1973. **Special Achievements:** Quality Management Program/System for Indigent Managed Care Program-County Care, 1988. **Business Phone:** (313)459-0900.

HALLUMS, BENJAMIN F.
Educator. **Personal:** Born Mar 6, 1940, Easley, SC; married Phyllis; children: Jacqueline, Bernard, Maisha. **Educ:** BA 1970; MEd 1972; 6 Yr Cert 1973. **Career:** Quinnipiac Coll, counselor 1971-75; Allied Health Prgram, counselor 1974; School for the Mentally Retarded, counselor 1972-73; Quinnipiac Coll, asst prof Blk Studies 1973-75, asst prof Fine Arts 1972-75. **Orgs:** Mem Assn Blk People Hghr Educ 1970-75; Estrn Allnc Blk Couns 1974-75; Nat Blk Coll Choir Annl Fest; CT Liason Prgm 1973; Mnrty Coll Couns 1973; rep United Mnstry Hghr Edn; Nat Coll Choirs; sec Coaltn Blk Prnts 1975; vice pres Couples Inc. **Honors/Awds:** Dist Inst Mnrty Coll Couns 1973; citat Mnrty Stdnts 1974; Testmnl 1974; citat Orgn Stdnt Sngng Grp 1974; citat Adv Orgn 1974. **Military Serv:** AUS e5 1961-64. **Business Addr:** College Counselor, Quinniiac College, Mt Carmel Ave, Hamden, CT 06518.

HALYARD, MICHELE YVETTE
Physician. **Personal:** Born Apr 13, 1961, Buffalo, NY; married Paul Edward Leroy Richardson; children: Hamilton. **Educ:** Howard Univ, BS (Summa Cum Laude) 1982; Howard Univ Coll of Medicine, MD 1984. **Career:** Mayo Clinic, fellow radiation oncology 1987-89; Howard Univ Hosp, resident radiation oncology 1984-87. **Orgs:** Mem Natl & Amer Medical Assocs, Phi Beta Kappa Honor Soc, Alpha Omega Alpha Medical Honor Soc, Alpha Kappa Alpha Sor Inc. **Honors/Awds:** Amer Medical Women's Assoc Awd for Scholarship Achievement; Grandy Awd for Internal Medicine; Awd for Clinical Excellence in Psychiatry; Frederick M DRewAwd for Outstanding Performance in Radiation Therapy; article "The Use of Intraoperative Radiotherapy and External Beam Therapy in the Management of Desmoid Tumors," w/JoAnn Collier-Manning MD, Ebrahim Ashayeri MD, Alfred Goldson MD, Frank Watkins MD, Ernest Myers MD in Journal Natl Medical Assoc 1986. **Business Addr:** Office of Information Sevice, Howard University, CB Powell Bldg, 525 Bryant NW, Washington, DC 20059.

HAM, DARVIN
Professional basketball player. **Personal:** Born Jul 23, 1973. **Educ:** Texas Tech. **Career:** Indiana Pacers, forward, 1996-97; Washington Wizards, 1997-. **Business Addr:** Professional Basketball Player, Washington Wizards, MCI Center, 601 F St NW, Washington, DC 20071, (202)661-5000.

HAM, DEBRA NEWMAN
Manuscript historian. **Personal:** Born Aug 27, 1948, York, PA; daughter of Eva Mitchell Newman Owens and Earl F Newman; married Lester James Ham Sr, Apr 29, 1989; children: Lester James Jr. **Educ:** Howard Univ, Washington DC, BA 1970; Boston Univ, Boston MA, MA, 1971; Howard Univ, Washington DC, PhD 1984. **Career:** Natl Archives, Washington DC, archivist/black history specialist 1972-86, currently. **Orgs:** Founding mem Afro-Amer Historial and Genealogical Society 1978-; publications dir, Assoc of Black Women Historians 1987-90; chair, advisory board, Opportunities Industrialization Centers Archival Advisory Board, 1986-90; chair, advisory board, Mt Sinai Baptist Church Outreach Center, 1988-90; exec council, Assn for the Study of Afro-American Life and History, 1990-; editorial board, Society of American Archivists, 1990-. **Honors/Awds:** Coker Prize, Society of Amer Archivists, 1985; Finding Aid Award, Mid-Atlantic Regional Archivists, 1985; Black History, A Guide to Civilian Records in the Natl Archives, 1984. **Business Addr:** Specialist in Afro-Amer History and Culture, Library of Congress, Manuscript Division, Washington, DC 20540.

HAMBERG, MARCELLE R.
Physician. **Personal:** Born Jul 4, 1931, Anderson, SC; son of Pauline Hamlin Hamberg and Robert Clark Hamberg; married Cheryl Jones; children: Marcelle Jr, Gabrielle. **Educ:** Hampton Inst, BS 1953; Meharry Med College, MD 1957. **Career:** Univ of Louisville, instr in urology 1967; Meharry Med Coll, chief div of urology 1976; physician, private practice, currently. **Orgs:** Amer Bd of Urology 1968; Amer Urological Assn, SE 1969. **Honors/Awds:** Newman Van High Spl, Fellow in Cancer Urology, Meml Hosp for Cancer & Allied Diseases, NY, 1962-63. **Business Addr:** Physician, 1916 Patterson St, Suite 603, Nashville, TN 37203.

HAMBERLIN, EMIEL
Educator. **Personal:** Born Nov 8, 1939, Fayette, MS; married Minnie; children: Emiel III, Mark. **Educ:** Alcorn State Univ, BS 1964; Univ of IL, MEd 1978, PhD 1982. **Career:** Chicago Bd of Educ DuSable HS, professor. **Orgs:** Mem Omega Psi Phi Frat 1964-; mem Natl Geographic Soc 1970-; mem Operation PUSH 1972; mem Natl Biology Assoc 1974-; mem Intl Wildlife Federation 1974-; mem IL Teachers Assoc 1975-; mem Phi Delta Kappa 1976-; mem IL Science Teachers Assoc 1978-; hon mem Kappa Delta Pi 1979-; bd mem Ada McKinley Highland for Special Children 1980. **Honors/Awds:** The Governors Awd World Flower Show 1972; Professional Personnel in Environmental Educ IL Environ Educ Assoc 1975; Omega Man of the Year 1977; Those Who Excell Awd State of IL 1977; Illinois Teacher of the Year 1977; Outstanding Educator Awd Lewis Univ 1980; Phi Delta Kappa Educator 1981; IL Master Teacher Governor of IL 1981; Ora Higgins Leadership Awd 1985; Distinguished Alumni of Black Univs Natl Assoc for Equal Oppor in Higher Educ 1986; Outstanding Achievements as an Educ in Horticulture Mayor H Washington 1986; One of the Heroes of Our Time Newsweek 1986. **Home Addr:** 8500 S Winchester, Chicago, IL 60620. **Business Addr:** Professor, DuSable High School, 4934 S Wabash, Chicago, IL 60615.

HAMBRICK, HAROLD E., JR.
Association director. **Personal:** Born Feb 17, 1943, New Orleans, LA; married Margaret; children: Tyra, Jeffery, Sharon. **Educ:** Pepperdine U, BS 1976. **Career:** Western Assn of Comm Hlth Ctrs Inc, exec dir 1974-; Watts Hlth Fdn Inc, sr Acct 1969-75; New Communicators Inc, bus mgr 1967-69; IBM Corp, ofcmgr, Trn 1966-67. **Orgs:** Treas Nat Assn of Comm Hlth Ctrs Inc 1974-76; fndng pres Western Assn of Comm Hlth Ctr Inc 1973-75; v pres Hambricks Mort Inc 1975-; pres Employees Serv Assn 1972-74; bd mem Watts United Credit Union Inc 1974-75; mem Am Soc of Assn Exec 1976-; State of CA Dept of Hlth Advsry Cncl; AmPubl Hlth Assn 1973-; Nat Notary Assn 1972-; Nat Assn of Tax Consult 1972-; CA Assn of Tax Consult 1972-. **Business Addr:** 320 E 111th St, Los Angeles, CA 90061.

HAMBY, ROSCOE JEROME
Attorney. **Personal:** Born Jun 8, 1919, Tupelo, MS; married Mary Lean Farr; children: Roscoe Jr, William. **Educ:** TN A&I State Univ, AB 1944; Kent Coll, LLB 1948. **Career:** Private practice, attny. **Orgs:** Mem TN Bar, Amer Bar, Natl Bar, Fed Bar, Amer Trial Lawyers Assoc; deacon Pleasant Greek Bapt Church; mem IBPOE, Elks, Amer Legion Post #6; past exalted Rulers Council; mem Black Masons Intl Union of Amer 35 yrs; bd of trustees MS Minestineal Inst & Coll. **Honors/Awds:** Dick Slater Awd Cook Cty Trowel Trades Assoc. **Business Addr:** Attorney, 2702 Jefferson St, Nashville, TN 37208.

HAMER, JUDITH ANN
Financial company executive. **Personal:** Born Jan 3, 1939, Brooklyn, NY; daughter of Martha Louise Taylor Thompson and Frank Leslie Thompson; married Martin J Hamer; children: Kim T, Fern S, Jill T. **Educ:** Cornell Univ, BA 1960; Smith Coll, MAT 1961; Columbia Univ, PhD 1984. **Career:** CCNY, instructor 1971-76; Columbia Univ, adjunct instructor 1977-83; Learning Intl, consultant writer 1984-86; Paine Webber Inc, dp trainer beginning 1986, training manager, corporate training dept, division vice pres, currently. **Orgs:** Mem Coalition of 100

Black Women Stamford CT. **Honors/Awds:** Ford Foundation Fellowship for Black Americans 1976-81. **Special Achievements:** Co-editor with Martin J Hamer, Centers of the Self: Short Stories by Black American Women from the Nineteenth Century to the Present, Hill & Wang, 1994. **Business Addr:** Divisional Vice Pres, Corporate Training Dept, Paine Webber Inc., 1200 Harbor Boulevard, 2nd Floor, Weehawken, NJ 07087.

HAMER, STEVE
Professional basketball player. **Personal:** Born Nov 13, 1973, Memphis, TN. **Educ:** Tennessee. **Career:** Boston Celtics, 1996-. **Business Addr:** Professional Basketball Player, Boston Celtics, 151 Merrimac St, 5th Fl, Boston, MA 02114, (617)523-6050.

HAMILL, MARGARET HUDGENS
Educator. **Personal:** Born Mar 9, 1937, Laurens, SC; children: Beatrice Chauntea. **Educ:** Benedict Coll, BA 1958; St Peter's Coll, Ed diploma 1962. **Career:** No 5 Public School, educator 1966-68; Frank R Conwell, educator 1968-74; Joseph H Brensinger, educator 1974-. **Orgs:** School rep NJEA 1985-; advisor Tauette Club 1985-; bd of dirs Bayonne Chap Natl Conf of Christians and Jews 1985-; pres Young Women's League FriendshipBapt Ch 1986-; 1st vice pres Bayonne Youth Ctr Inc 1986-; sgt-of-arms Tau Gamma Delta Sor Psi Chapt. **Honors/Awds:** Comm Serv Awd Bayonne NAACP 1979; Brotherhood Awd Natl Conf of Christians & Jews 1985; Mary McLeod Bethune Awd 1985. **Home Addr:** 42 W 18th St, Bayonne, NJ 07002.

HAMILTON, ART
State legislator. **Personal:** Born in Phoenix, AZ. **Career:** Began as public affairs representative; Arizona State Legislature, Phoenix AZ, state representative, District 22, House Minority Leader. **Special Achievements:** Natl Conf of State Legislatures, first black president. **Business Addr:** House of Representatives, State House, Phoenix, AZ 85007.

HAMILTON, ARTHUR LEE, JR.
Newspaper editor. **Personal:** Born Oct 19, 1957, Detroit, MI; son of Lucy & Arthur Hamilton; married Marilyn, Aug 27, 1992; children: Kyala, Omar, Arlinda, Chineca, Mike. **Educ:** South Western MI, 1979; Northern MI Univ, 1984; Jackson Comm College, associates, 1985-87; Spring Arbor, 1988. **Career:** Oracle Newspaper, staff writer, 1979-81; Huron Valley-Monitor Newspaper, editor, 1985-87; Snow Bird Newspaper, staff writer, 1988-89; Lakeland Pen Newspaper, editor, 1993-. **Orgs:** Fathers Behind Bars Inc, pres & founder, 1993-; NAACP, chairman-press & publicity, 1992-93; Numens Masonic Lodge, 1993-. **Honors/Awds:** NAACP, Member of the Year, 1993; Fathers Behind Bars, Member of the Year, 1994; Southern University of Illinois, Best Prison Paper in Country, 1986-87. **Special Achievements:** Learning to Die, 1981; Caged by the Wolverine, 1995; Rat Race, Poem. **Military Serv:** US Navy, seaman, 1975-77. **Home Addr:** 525 Superior, Niles, MI 49120.

HAMILTON, ARTHUR N.
Judge. **Personal:** Born Jan 21, 1917, New Orleans; married Mary; children: Lisa. **Educ:** Kent Coll Law, JD 1950; Nat Coll Juvenile Ct Judges Univ NV, grad 1973. **Career:** Cook County Circuit Ct, assoc judge 1971-; Chicago Park Dist, 1st asst gen atty; Illinois, special asst atty gen; Cook County, asst states atty; City of Chicago, asst corp counsel. **Orgs:** Mem bd, Augustana Hosp; bd mem, Inter-Relig Conf Urban Affairs; bd mem, Ch Fedn Greater Chicago; bd mem, Pkwy Comm House; delegate, Natl Conv Lutheran Church of Amer 1970. **Honors/Awds:** Advocacy for Children Award Lake Bluff Chicago Homes Children 1974. **Business Addr:** Circuit Court of Cook Co Daley, Chicago, IL 60602.

HAMILTON, AUBREY J.
Company executive, state official. **Personal:** Born Nov 2, 1927, Charlston, SC; son of Rose Maud Langley Hamilton and William C Hamilton; married Elsie Carpenter Hamilton, Oct 1, 1949; children: Catherine H, Beverly H Chandler. **Educ:** St Georges, Kingston, Jamaica, 1936; Brooklyn Coll, Brooklyn, NY, 1943. **Career:** Natl Maritime Union, New York, NY, 1956-70; Seafearers Intl Union, New York, NY, 1945-55; Justice of the Peace; Southeastern Enterprises, Inc, Groton, CT, chief exec officer, 1973-; State of CT, Groton, CT, harbor master, 1980-. **Orgs:** Chmn, Groton City Democratic, CT. **Business Addr:** CEO, Southeastern Enterprises, Inc, 643 North Rd, PO Box 1146, Groton, CT 06340.

HAMILTON, BOBBY
Professional football player. **Personal:** Born Jul 1, 1971. **Educ:** Southern Mississippi. **Career:** New York Jets, defensive end, 1996-. **Business Addr:** Professional Football Player, New York Jets, 1000 Fulton Ave, Hempstead, NY 11550, (516)560-8100.

HAMILTON, CHARLES S. **See Obituaries section.**

HAMILTON, CHARLES VERNON
Educator. **Personal:** Born Oct 19, 1929, Muskogee, OK; son of Viola Haynes Hamilton and Owen Hamilton; married Dona Louise Cooper Hamilton, Oct 5, 1956; children: Valli, Carol. **Educ:** Roosevelt University, Chicago, IL, BA, 1951; Loyola University, School of Law, Chicago, IL, JD, 1954; University of Chicago, Chicago, IL, MA, 1957, PhD, 1964. **Career:** Tuskegee University, Tuskegee, AL, assistant professor, 1958-60; Rutgers University, Newark, NJ, assistant professor, 1963-64; Lincoln University, Oxford, PA, professor, 1964-67; Roosevelt University, Chicago, IL, professor, 1967-69; Columbia, University, New York, professor, 1969-. **Orgs:** Board of trustees, Twentieth Century Foundation, 1973-; board member, NAACP, 1975-; board of editors, Political Science Quarterly, 1975-. **Honors/Awds:** University of Chicago, Alumni Award, 1970; Roosevelt University Alumni Award, 1970; Lindback Teaching Award, Lincoln University, 1965; Van Doren Teaching Ward, Columbia University, 1982; Great Teacher Award, Columbia University, 1985. **Special Achievements:** Adam Clayton Powell Jr, 1991. **Military Serv:** US Army, Private, 1948-49. **Business Addr:** Professor, Columbia University, 420 W 118th St, Room 727, New York, NY 10027.

HAMILTON, DARRYL QUINN
Professional baseball player. **Personal:** Born Dec 3, 1964, Baton Rouge, LA; son of Geraldine Pitts Hamilton and John C. Hamilton Sr.; married Shaun Robinson. **Educ:** Nicholls State University, Thibodaux, LA, 1983-86. **Career:** Milwaukee Brewers, outfielder, 1986-95; Texas Rangers, 1996; San Francisco Giants, 1997-. **Honors/Awds:** Topps Minor League Player of the Month, Topps Baseball Card, 1987; Milwaukee Brewers Player of the Month, Milwaukee Minor League, August, 1986, July, 1987; Milwaukee Brewers Unsung Hero Award, Milwaukee Brewers, 1991; Milwaukee Brewers Good Guy Award, 1992; Team USA, 1985; Nicholls State University Hall of Fame, 1991; Milwaukee Brewers Associate Player Rep, 1992. **Business Addr:** Professional Baseball Player, San Francisco Giants, 3 Com Park, San Francisco, CA 94124, (415)468-3700.

HAMILTON, EDWARD N., JR.
Sculptor. **Personal:** Born Feb 14, 1947, Cincinnati, OH; married Bernadette S Chapman. **Educ:** Louisville Sch Art, 1965-69; Univ Louisville, 1970-71; Spalding Coll, 1971-73. **Career:** Iroquois HS, tchr 1969-72; Louisville Art Workshop, 1972; Louisville Speed Museum, lectr 1974; self-employed sculptor. **Orgs:** Mem Alpha Phi Alpha Frat; mem Nat Conf of Artists 1980; bd mem Renaissance Devel Corp; mem Art Circle Assn; bd mem St Frances HS Louisville; bd mem KY Minority Businessmen. **Honors/Awds:** Award KY Black Achievers 1980; Bronze St Frances of Row, St Frances of Row Ch Louisville; numerous exhibitions group shows pub commns works in private collections including Owensboro Museum of Fine Art, Memphis State University Gallery, Washington Design Center, JB Speed Art Museum and Gibellina Museum in Palermo Italy; National Commission Joe Louis, at Cobo Hall in Detroit, MI, Booker T Washington, at Hampton University in Virginia, and Amistad Memorial, in New Haven, Connecticut; The Spirit of Freedom Memorial.

HAMILTON, EDWIN
Educator. **Personal:** Born Jul 24, 1936, Tuskegee, AL; son of Julia Sullins Hamilton and Everett Hamilton; married Alberta Daniels, Aug 3, 1960; children: Michelle, Stanley, Gina, Carl. **Educ:** Tuskegee Univ, BS 1960, MEd 1963; The Ohio State Univ, PhD 1973. **Career:** Macon County Schools, dir 1965-70; Ohio State Univ, rsch asst 1971-73; FL International Univ, prof 1973-74; Howard Univ, prof 1974-. **Orgs:** Mem AAACE/ASTD 1975-87; presidential assoc Tuskegee Univ 1980-; mem Intl Assoc CAEO/ICA 1984-87; rsch rep Phi Delta Kappa Howard Univ 1986-87; adjunct prof Univ of DC 1986; educ leader Professional Seminar Consultants's (Russia) 1986; adjunct prof OH State Univ 1987; pres, Howard Univ PDK, l989-89; elections judge, P G Bd of Elections, Uppermarlboro, MD, l986-87; chief elections judge, l988-95. **Honors/Awds:** Fulbright Scholar (Nigeria) CIES/USIA 1982-83; Writer's Recognition Univ of DC 1984; Certificate of Appreciation Phi Delta Gamma Johns Hopkins Univ 1986; Certificate of Awd Phi Delta Kappa Howard Univ 1987-89; Distinguished Alumni Citation NAFEO/Tuskegee Univ, l988; President's Award Howard Univ, PDK, l989; designed study-travel to China Tour, l989. **Military Serv:** AUS sp E-4 1954-56; Good Conduct Medal, Honorable Discharge 1956; Active Army Reserve, l956-63. **Business Addr:** Professor of Education, Howard University, School of Education, Washington, DC 20059.

HAMILTON, EUGENE NOLAN
Judge. **Personal:** Born Aug 24, 1933, Memphis, TN; son of Barbara Hamilton Blakey & Thomas E Hamilton; married Virginia, Jun 16, 1956; children: Alexandria, Evanzz, John, James, Eric, David, Rachael, Jeremiah, Michael, Markus. **Educ:** Univ of Illinois, BA, 1955, JD, 1959. **Career:** US Army, judge advocate officer, 1959-61; US Dept of Justice, trial attorney, 1961-70; Superior Court of DC, judge, 1970-; Harvard Law School, lecturer, 1995, teacher, 1985-. **Orgs:** American Bar Assn, executive committee, 1970-; Washington Bar Assn, 1970-; Bar Assn of DC, 1990-; DC Bar Assn, 1970-. **Honors/Awds:** Washington Bar Assn, Ollie Mae Cooper Award, 1993; National Bar Assn, Wiley A Branton Issues Symposium Award; Oldender Foundation Generous Heart Award. **Military Serv:** US Army, captain, 1959-61. **Business Addr:** Chief Judge, Superior Court of District of Columbia, 500 Indiana Ave, NW, Moultrie Courthouse, Washington, DC 20001, (202)879-1600.

HAMILTON, FRANKLIN D.
Educator. **Personal:** Born Oct 30, 1942, Aucilla, FL; son of Esther Hamilton and Verdell Hamilton; children: Kayla, Ebony, Nikki. **Educ:** FL A&M Univ, BS 1964; Univ of Pittsburgh, PhD 1969. **Career:** Univ of Pittsburgh, USPHS pre-doctoral fellow 1964-69; SUNY, USPHS postdoctoral fellow 1969-71; Univ of TN, asst prof 1971-74, assoc prof 1974-79; Univ CA Berkeley, visiting prof 1986-87; Atlanta Univ, assoc prof 1979-88; Univ of CA, Berkeley, CA, visiting prof, dept of biochemistry, 1986-89; FL A&M Univ, dir, div of sponsored research, 1989-. **Orgs:** Vice chair, Sci Adv Comm to the Natl Assn for Equal Opprtunity in Higher Educ; consultant, Natl Inst of Health; consultnt, Robert Wood Johnson Fund; consultant, premed, rev comm, United Negro Coll Fund; AAAS; Amer Soc for Cell Biol; comm mem, MARC Reveiw Comm, NIGMS, NIH; comm mem, NSF Pre-doctoral Fellowship Review Comm; council mem, Amer Soc of Biochem & MSI Biol, 1988-91. **Honors/Awds:** Published, ''Minorities in Sci, A Challenge for Change in Biomedicine'' 1977; ''Proceeding of the Conference on Health Professional Educational Programs'' 1980; ''Participation of Blacks in the Basic Sciences, An Assessment in Black Students in Higher Education in the 70's, Conditions and Experiences'' edited by Gail Thomas, Greenwood Press 1981. **Business Addr:** Div of Sponsored Research, Florida A & M University, Tallahassee, FL 32307.

HAMILTON, H. J. BELTON
Judge. **Personal:** Born Jun 1, 1924, Columbus, MS; married Midori Minamoto; children: Konrad, Camille. **Educ:** Stanford Univ, AB Pol Sci 1949; Northwestern Sch of Law Lewis & Clark Coll, JD 1953; Univ of OR, postgrad studies in pub affairs 1960-61. **Career:** Genl Practice of Law, attorney 1953-54; State Bureau of Labor, asst atty genl state of OR & staff atty 1955-58; US, admin law judge; Social Security Dept, admin law judge. **Orgs:** Sec treas Freedom Family Ltd; pres Alpha Develop Invest Corp; mem OR State, Amer Bar Assns; mem Amer Trial Lawyers Assn; World Assn of Judges; chmn Admin Law Sec of Natl Bar Assn; mem Natl Urban League Quarter Century Club; mem OR State Adv Com to US Commn on Civ Rights; OR State Adv Council; co-founder former chmn legal counsel & Parliamentarian of Intl Assn of Official Hum Rights Agencies; former mem Natl Urban League New Thrust Task Force for institutional reorientation; former pres Urban League of Portland; Boltol-Cedar Oak PTA; Portland chap of Alpha Phi Alpha; TV host of PBL-Spin off; former moderator of radio ''Great Decisions'' prog. **Honors/Awds:** Outstanding Civic Contributions to Comm Alpha Phi Alpha; named in Martindale & Hubbell as atty with high legal skill & ability & highest recommendation; Ford Found Fellow 1960-61; author of legislation atty gen opinion & scholarly articles on wide range of subjects; Book: 33 Years Inside An Interracial Family; guest lecturer at most OR colls & univs. **Military Serv:** US Army, s/sgt, 1943-46.

HAMILTON, HARRY E.
Professional football player. **Personal:** Born Nov 26, 1962, Jamaica, NY. **Educ:** Penn State Univ, BA, pre-law, liberal arts, 1984. **Career:** New York Jets, 1984-87; Tampa Bay Buccaneers, defensive back, 1988-. **Honors/Awds:** Sporting News NFL All-Star Team, 1989. **Business Addr:** Professional Football Player, Tampa Bay Buccaneers, One Buccaneer Pl, Tampa, FL 33607-5794.

HAMILTON, HOWARD W.
Healthcare company executive. **Personal:** Born Jul 21, 1948, Chicago, IL; son of Etta Mae and Howard; divorced; children: Howard, Christina, James, Olivia. **Educ:** Parsons College, BA, 1971; Columbia University, MBA, 1979. **Career:** E R Squibb Pharmaceutical, field sales, 1972-77; Lederle Laboratories, product promotion manager, 1979-80; Schering Laboratories, product manager, 1980-83; Abbott Laboratories, sr product manager, 1984-93; Essilor of America, group marketing mgr, 1994-95; Essilor Thin Films, general manager, 1996-. **Orgs:** Actor's Summer Theater, president, board of trustees, 1989-92; African-American Action Alliance, president, 1991-92; Action Alliance Black Professionals, parlimentarian, 1988-90. **Home Addr:** 10203 Lockwood Pines Lane, Tampa, FL 33635, (813)891-6908. **Business Phone:** (813)572-0844.

HAMILTON, JAMES G.
Consultant. **Personal:** Born Jun 22, 1939, Washington, DC; son of Ruth Aura Lawson Hamilton Proctor and John Henry Hamilton Jr (deceased). **Educ:** Rochester Inst Tech, AAS with Hons 1970; RIT, BS with high Hons 1972; Univ Rochester, MA 1974; Univ Orthodox Coll Nigeria, Hon Doctorate African Hist 1981. **Career:** Rochester, New York Museum & Science Center, comm consultant 1972-74; Eastman Kodak Co, tech sales rep in graphic arts 1975; Aetna Life & Casualty, sr graphic arts consultant 1976-83; SBC Management Corp, pr consultant 1983-85; Freelance Consultant and Lecturer, black history, eth-

nic relations and genealogy; The Melting Pot A Genealogical Publ, ethnic rel consult & assoc ed; genealogical researcher and ethnic relations consultant and coll instructor, Manchester, CT Comm Coll. **Orgs:** Founder/exec dir Ankh-Mobile Proj Inc 1977-81; founder/pres Rochester, NY Branch of the Assn for the Study of Afro-Amer Life & Hist; former mem Amer Film Inst; former mem Connecticut Hist Soc Hartford, CT; life mem Disabled Amer Veterans; life mem NAACP; former mem Natl Geographic Soc Wash, DC; former mem Natl Historical Soc Gettysburg, PA; former mem Natl Trust for Historic Preserv Wash, DC; former mem Smithsonian Inst; former mem Photographic Soc of Amer; former mem Connecticut Computer Soc 1985; mem Natl Huguenot Soc 1984; mem Connecticut Huguenot Soc 1984; former mem Amer Vets Boston MA; former mem Natl Pres Photographers Assoc Wash DC; mem Connecticut Soc of Genealogist; mem Maryland Genealogical Soc; former mem Intl Platform Assoc, Cleveland Heights,OH; former Natl Archives Trustnd Assoc, Washington DC; former mem Camera Club of Fitchburg, MA; former county Committeeman, Monroe County Democratic Committee, Rochester, NY. **Honors/Awds:** Fellowship Social Work Educ NY State Council on the Arts 1972. **Military Serv:** AUS Staff Sgt E-6 1957-67; 3 Good Conduct Medals.

HAMILTON, JOHN JOSLYN, JR.
Government official. **Personal:** Born Dec 16, 1949, New York, NY; children: Issoufou K. **Educ:** Basic Elec & Electronic School, certificate 1969; Sonar Tech School, certificate 1970; Natl Assn of Underwater Instructors, certified scuba diver certificate 1971; College Level Exam Program; Keane Coll, 1972-75; Vol Probation Counselor Training Program, certificate; Dept of Corrections Behavious Modification, staff training certificate; State of NJ, Grantsmanship & Proposal Writing, Dept of Health certificate 1980, comm skills/counseling tech certificate; Amer Legion Leadership Coll, basic & advanced certs 1982; Amer Legion Serv Officers School, certificate 1985. **Career:** First Class Auto Body, payroll & office mgr 1972-74; Musician, performer 1972-80; Kean Coll, audio visual tech 1973-74; Essex County Highway Dept, traffic signal electrician 1975; Private Limousine Serv, mgr chauffeur 1978-80; Beitler Public Relations, acct exec/artist 1978-80; Employment Dynamics, consultant, public relations counselor 1980-81; House of Hope, dir, counselor 1981-84; Veterans Admin Med Center, program specialist, public relations 1984-87; Essex-Newark Legal Services, community legal educ coordinator 1987-, dir Homeless Prevention Program 1987-. **Orgs:** Performed Carnegie Hall, New York All City Chorus 1964; performed world's fair with Bronx Boro Chorus 1964; public relations chmn Third World Organ Keane Coll 1973-75; bd mem co-curricular program bd Keane Coll 1973, 1974; co-founder, public relations chmn, counselor RAPIN 1972-75; vol probation counselor Union Co Probation Dept 1973-82; vol assisting handicapped individual Hand in Hand Inc 1978-79, 1981-82; serv volunteer Veterans Admin 1983-84; commander Amer Legion Post #251 Montclair 1983-; consultant State Program Coordinator N Amer Wheelchair Athletic Assn 1985-; Public speaker, Civic Activist North-East Regional Conference; youngest County Vice Commander Amer Legion 1986-; county chmn NJ POW/MIA Committee 1987-; site coordinator NewarkLiteracy Campaign 1987-; bd mem Newark Transonal Supervised Living Program 1988, Essex Co CEAS Committee 1988. **Honors/Awds:** Hall of Fame Award, St Vincent De Paul New York 1959; Natl Defense Service Medal 1968; Keane Coll Award of Merit 1973-74; Special Commendation for participation in the Intl Conf on Morality & Intl Violence 1974; #1 Artist musician, performer 1978 & 1979; Union Co Volunteer of the Year 1980; ranked #3 in nation by Natl Assn of Volunteers in Criminal Justice 1981; twice recognized & presented resolutions, Essex Co Bd of Chosen Freeholders 1984; Jerseyan of the Week, Star Ledger 1984; 1984 Pride in Heritage Award, Male Volunteer of the Year; Natl Good Neighbor Award, Natl Comm of the Amer Legion Natl Vol of the Year 1984; Federal Distinguished Public Serv Award 1985; IBPOE of W Community Serv Award1986; Citizens' Service Award, Cult-Art Associates 1987; Elected Essex Co Commander, Americaegion 1989; Producer, Host of Community Crisis (Cable TV Show) 1988-. **Military Serv:** US Navy petty officer 3rd class 1968-74. **Home Addr:** 38 Lexington Ave, Montclair, NJ 07042. **Business Addr:** Community Legal Education Coordinator, Essex-Newark Legal Services, 8-10 Park Place, 4th, Newark, NJ 07102.

HAMILTON, JOHN M.
Savings and loan chief executive. **Career:** Washington Shores Savings Bank, FSB, Orlando, FL, chief exec. **Business Addr:** Washington Shores Savings Bank, FSB, 715 South Goldwyn Ave., Orlando, FL 32805.

HAMILTON, JOHN MARK, JR.
Dentist. **Personal:** Born Oct 2, 1931, Washington, DC; son of Mr and Mrs John M Hamilton; married Dorothy Wilson; children: John M III, Sheree R. **Educ:** US Military Academy at West Point NY, BS, 1955; US Army Command and General Staff College, 1964; US Army War College, 1977; Univ of Medicine & Dentistry of New Jersey, DMD, 1982. **Career:** 101st Airborne Division, Vietnam, brigade deputy commander, infantry battalion commander, 1970-71; US Army Command and General Staff College, Fort Leavenworth KS, faculty member, 1971-74; US Military District of Washington DC, chief of human resources division, 1974-75; Office of US Secretary of Defense, military advisor, 1975-78; private practice, dentist, 1982-; JB Johnson Nursing Center, consulting dentist, 1985-; East of the River Health Center, consulting dentist, 1984-; John M Hamilton Jr, DMD, PC, director 1988-; Hamilton Professional Enterprises Inc, president, 1988-. **Orgs:** Mem Kappa Alpha Psi Fraternity 1951-; vice pres Wee Care Youth Academy 1974-; consultant Lawrence Johnson & Assoc 1983; mem Robert T Freeman Dental Soc 1984-; vice pres Investors Consolidated Assoc Inc 1985-87; mem bd of dir Ethel James Williams Scholarship Foundation 1986-; mem bd of dir La Mirage Beauty Enterprises 1986-87. **Honors/Awds:** Harvard Prize Book Award, Harvard Club of Washington DC; Recruiting Award, US Air Force Recruiting Service, 1982. **Military Serv:** AUS Infantry col 23 yrs; Ranger Tab, Parachute Badge, Army Commendation Medal with Oak Leaf Cluster, Vietnam Gallantry Cross with Palm, Legion of Merit, Air Medal with 13th Oak Leaf Cluster, Bronze Star with 1st Oak Leaf Cluster, Vietnam Gallantry Cross with Silver Star, Combat Infantryman Badge. **Home Addr:** 10806 Braeburn Rd, Columbia, MD 21044. **Business Addr:** President, Hamilton Professional Enterprises Inc, 10806 Braeburn Rd, Columbia, MD 21044.

HAMILTON, JOSEPH WILLARD
Manager, educator. **Personal:** Born Mar 12, 1922, Lake Charles, LA; married Lou Wilda Bertrand; children: Joseph W. **Educ:** Leland Coll, BS 1948; Bishop Coll, MEd 1955. **Career:** Hamilton's Enterprise, mgr; Science Dept Plaisance High School, head 1953-76; Plaisance High Sch, head coach 1950-73; St Landry Parish Classroom Teachers, pres 1960-65; Plaisance High School, counselor 1950-60; Elba Elmentary School, prin 1948-50. **Orgs:** Fdr pres St Joseph Cath Ch Counc 1967-77; vice pres Frontiers Internatl Opelousas Club 1976-77; commn BS of Amer 1972-75; dir confirm classes St Joseph Par Cath Ch 1970-77; JW Hamilton Annual Relays Plaisance High Sch 1977; particip Citiz Fgn Pol Forum US Sec of State 1960; Fo. **Honors/Awds:** Coach of Yr CCOA 1959; Expt Rifleman 1943; Good Cond Med 1945; ribbon Pacif Theater of War 1945. **Military Serv:** Sgt mjr 1943-45. **Business Addr:** 948 E Laurent St, Opelousas, LA 70570.

HAMILTON, KEITH LAMARR
Professional football player. **Personal:** Born May 25, 1971, Paterson, NJ. **Educ:** Univ of Pittsburgh, attended. **Career:** New York Giants, defensive tackle, 1992-. **Business Addr:** Professional Football Player, New York Giants, Giants Stadium, East Rutherford, NJ 07073, (201)935-8111.

HAMILTON, LEONARD
Basketball coach. **Career:** Oklahoma State Univ, Stillwater, OK, currently. **Business Addr:** Basketball Coach, Oklahoma State Univ, Stillwater, OK 74078.

HAMILTON, LYNN (LYNN JENKINS)
Actress. **Personal:** Born Apr 25, 1930, Yazoo City, MS; daughter of Nancy Hamilton and Louis Hamilton; married Frank S Jenkins. **Educ:** Goodman Theatre, BA 1954. **Career:** Television appearances: Sanford & Son; Roots II; The Waltons; 227; Golden Girls; Amen; Generations; Dangerous Women; films: Lady Sings the Blues; Buck & the Preacher; Bro John; Leadbelly; Legal Eagles; The Vanishing. **Honors/Awds:** NAACP Image Award. **Business Addr:** PO Box 3612, Los Angeles, CA 90036.

HAMILTON, MCKINLEY JOHN
Clergyman (retired). **Personal:** Born Nov 24, 1921, Lake Charles, LA; son of Jennie Virginia Keys Hamilton and Lincoln Hamilton (deceased); married Mary H Stone, Oct 19, 1957. **Educ:** Butler Coll, Tyler, TX, AA 1943; Bishop Coll, Marshall, TX, BA, 1945; Crozer Theol Sem, Chester, PA, 1945-46; Howard U, Washington, DC, MD, 1958. **Career:** First Bapt Ch Rocky Mt VA, pastor 1958-91; Shiloh Bapt Ch Washington DC, asst to pastor 1947-58; Good Samaritan Bapt Ch, pastor 1955-57; St James Bapt Ch & New Hope Bapt Ch Alto TX, pastor 1942-43. **Orgs:** Bd mem T & C Ministers; vice pres Dist SS Conf 1962-; past pres Fr Cty Ministerial Assn; pres Am Cancer Soc; moderator Bapt Pigg River Assn; bd mem Sheltered Workshop Comm Action of Fr Co; mem Fr Co Hist Soc; Mental Health; pres, local chapter, NAACP; board mem, United Fund; board mem, Cancer Soc; vol Sr Nutrition Program for Sr Citizens. **Honors/Awds:** Plaque for outstanding contribution to Comm of Franklin Co; plaque for being mem of Cneturion Club Ferrum Coll 1975; Honorary Doctor of Humanities Degree, Ferrum College, 1981. **Home Addr:** 80 Patterson Ave SE, PO Box 568, Rocky Mount, VA 24151-1734.

HAMILTON, PAUL L.
Educator (retired). **Personal:** Born Apr 1, 1941, Pueblo, CO; divorced; children: Askia Toure. **Educ:** Univ of Denver, BA 1964, MA 1972; Univ of N CO, EdD 1975. **Career:** Denver Public Schools, teacher 1964-91, principal, 1991-95; State of Colorado, representative 1969-73; Univ of Denver, instructor, 1971, lecturer & rsch asst 1971-72, prof of history, 1982-96; Univ of Colorado, instructor, 1995-96; Hamilton Education Consultants, pres, currently; Power Learning Systems, district dir, 1995-; R A Renaissance Publications, pres, 1993-. **Orgs:** Assn for the Study of Classical African Civilizations; National Alliance of Black School Educators; Univ of Denver National Honor Society; Renaissance Publications, pres. **Honors/Awds:** Denver Assn for Retired Citizens, Educator of the Year, 1991; Univ of Color ado, Black Alumni Award, 1995; Omega Psi Phi Fraternity, Chi Phi Chapter, Citiz en of the Year, 1995. **Special Achievements:** Author: Teacher's Guide for Afro American History; African People's Contributions to World History: Shattering the Myths, Vol 1.

HAMILTON, PHANUEL J.
Government official. **Personal:** Born Aug 3, 1929, Detroit; married; children: Thieda, Deborah, Gregory. **Educ:** Eastern MI U, BA 1951; Northwester U, grad sch speech; DePaul U; Chicago State U; KY Christian U, MA 1973. **Career:** Mayor's Ofc Sr Citizens Chicago, dir field servs 1970-; Human Motivation Inst, consult 1969; OEO, manpower 1966-69; Cook Co OEO, dir 1965-66; Comm Youth Welfare, dir 1964-66; tchr 1956-64. **Orgs:** Mem Am Assn Retarded Persons 1973-75; Cerontological Soc 1975; Nat Coun Aging 1974-75; Nat Assn Soc Wrkrs; Nat Assn Comm Devel; Kappa Alpha Psi; Sigma Phi; Pi Kappa Delta; Urban League; NAACP; Shiloh Bapt Ch Mgmt Devel. **Honors/Awds:** Award 1971; Comm Efford Orgn Cert Merit; achievement award Kappa Alpha Psi. **Military Serv:** USAF 1st lt 1951-56. **Business Addr:** 330 S Wells, Chicago, IL.

HAMILTON, RAINY, JR.
Architect. **Personal:** Born Sep 22, 1956, Detroit, MI; son of Bernice Hodges Hamilton and Rainy Hamilton; married Robbie Lynn Hamilton, Feb 14, 1987. **Educ:** University of Detroit, Detroit, MI, BS, architecture, 1978, bachelors of architecture, 1979. **Career:** Schervish, Vogel and Merz, PC, Detroit, MI, partner, 1979-90; Smith, Hinchman, and Grylls Associates, Inc, associate & project manager, 1990-93; Hamilton Anderson Associates Inc, owner, 1993-. **Orgs:** Member, American Institute of Architects, 1979-; liaison, Minority Resources Committee, American Institute of Architects, 1989-; founding member, Michigan National Organization of Minority Architects; State of Michigan Board of Architects and board of surveyors. **Honors/Awds:** Young Architect of the Year, Detroit chapter, American Institute of Architects, 1988. **Business Addr:** President, Hamilton Anderson Associates, 1435 Randolph St, Ste 200, Detroit, MI 48226, (313)964-0270.

HAMILTON, ROSS T.
Physician. **Personal:** Born Jun 5, 1946, Yonkers, NY; married Toni Plaskett; children: Neil, Ross T, Tonisha. **Educ:** Syracuse U, BA1968; Columbia U, MD 1972; Columbia Univ Internal Med, 1975; Columbia Univ Gastroenterology, 1977. **Career:** Pvt practice internal med gastroenterology; Columbia U, instr, asst clinical prof of medicine; disease control NYC, dir of professional rel; United Harlem Drug Fighters Inc, asst med dir; St Lukes Hosp attending physician; Harlem Hosp attending physician; Hosp for Joint Diseases; sponsor and medical dir Genesis. **Orgs:** Mem Nat Med Assn; mem Nat Assn of Postgrad Physicians; mem Med Soc of State of NY; mem Am Coll of Physicians; mem Manhattan Cental Med Soc; mem American Society for Gastrointestinal Endoscopy; mem American Gastroenterology Assoc; Deacon Abyssinian Baptist Church; mem NYS Bd of Regents; mem Bdof Managers Harlem YMCA. **Honors/Awds:** Publ Esophageal TB a Case Report 1977.

HAMILTON, RUFFIN
Professional football player. **Personal:** Born Mar 2, 1971. **Educ:** Tulane. **Career:** Green Bay Packers, linebacker, 1994; Atlanta Falcons, 1997-. **Business Addr:** Professional Football Player, Atlanta Falcons, Two Falcon Place, Suwanee, GA 30174, (404)945-1111.

HAMILTON, SAMUEL CARTENIUS
Attorney. **Personal:** Born Mar 29, 1936, Hope, AR; married Flora Elizabeth; children: Leslie Terrell, Sydne Carrigan; Patrice Alexan. **Educ:** Philander Smith Coll, BS 1958; Howard U, JD 1970. **Career:** Roy M Ellis & Louise Eighnie Turner Gen Prac of Law Silver Spring MD, asso; Montgomery Co MD, asst states pros atty; Lilver Spring MD, pvt pract of law; Legal Aid Clinic US Dist Attys Off DC; Off of Chief Counsel Fed Highway Adminstrn Litigation Div, legal intern; Ft Detrick MD, res asst. **Orgs:** Mem MD State Bar Assn; Am Bar Assn; Nat Bar Assn; past pres Frederick Co Branch NAACP; vice pres MD State Conference Of NAACP Branches; co-chmn; Comm to Uphold State Pub Accomodationlaw; mem Prince Hall Masons; Kappa Alpha Psi Soc Frat; Phi Alpha Delta Legal Frat; mem bd of dir Comm Action Agency. **Honors/Awds:** Frederick Co Award for Service & Leadership Student Bar Assn Howard Univ Sch of Law; Am Legion Outs Citizen Award; NAACP Outs Ser Award; Prince HallMasons Ser Award. **Business Addr:** 8605 Cameron St, Silver Spring, MD 20910.

HAMILTON, THEOPHILUS ELLIOTT
Educational administrator. **Personal:** Born Feb 6, 1923, Detroit, MI; married Fannie L; children: Millicent. **Educ:** Eastern MI Coll, MusB 1955, MA 1962; Eastern MI Univ, Spec of Arts Degree in Leadership & School Admin 1967. **Career:** Pickford

Public Schools, teacher, dir vocal & instumental music 1955-62; Highland Park Public Schools, vocal music teacher 1962-64, asst principal 1964-67; Eastern Michigan Univ, asst dir of personnel 1967-, asst dir of career planning & placement center 1969-. **Orgs:** Past sec, treas, mem MI Coll & Univ Placement Assoc; admin appt, mem Eastern MI Univ Judicial Bd 1977-78; apptd mem Soc Ministry Comm MI Synod of the Luth Church of Amer 1977-78; assoc mem MI Assoc for School Admin; mem Great Lakes Assoc for Coll & Univ Placement, Coll & Univ Personnel Assoc, School Admin & Prin Assoc, Kappa Alpha Psi, Black Faculty & Staff Assoc at EMU; faculty adv Delta Nu Chap EMU; mem Ypsilanti Twp Plnng Comm; membd of dir Washtenaw Cty Black Caucus Comm, Washtenaw Cty Citizens Comm for Econ Oppty; chmn Ypsilanti Citizens Advising Comm for OEO; affirm action comm Ypsilanti Publ Schools; bd of dirs, Ypsilanti Fed Credit Union, 1996-; Washtenaw County Amer Red Cross Chap, 1988-90. **Honors/Awds:** Alumni Achievement Award, Kappa Alpha Psi, 1974; Dedication & Serv to Comm Award, Kappa Alpha Phi; Best Teacher Award, EMU Personnel; Gold Medallion Award, Division of Student Affairs, 1988; Sustained Superior Svc, Black Faculty and Staff Assoc, 1991; Washtenaw County Metropolitan Planning Commission Chmn Award, 1991-92; International Award, Kappa Delta Pi, 1992; Silver Medallion Award, Division of Marketing and Student Affairs, 1993; Honored for 25 years of Service & 70 years of Inspiration by Career Services, 1993; Operation ABLE, Most ABLE Award, 1994; Honorary Member, Golden Key Natl Honor Society, 1996; Chief's Civilian Award, 1996. **Military Serv:** US Army, 1943-46. **Business Addr:** Asst Dir Career Planning, Eastern Michigan Univ, Career Planning & Placement Cn, Ypsilanti, MI 48197, (313)487-0400.

HAMILTON, VIRGINIA

Author. **Personal:** Born in Yellow Springs, OH; daughter of Etta Belle Perry Hamilton and Kenneth James Hamilton; married Arnold Adoff, Mar 19, 1960; children: Leigh Hamilton Adoff, Jaime Levi Adoff. **Educ:** Attended Antioch Coll, OH State Univ, and New School for Social Research. **Career:** Author of children's books: Zeely, Macmillan, 1967, The House of Dies Drear, Macmillan, 1968, The Planet of Junior Brown, Macmillan, 1971, M C Higgins, the Great, Macmillan, 1974, Paul Robeson, The Life & Times of a Free Black Man, Harper, 1974, Arilla Sun Down, Greenwillow, 1975, Justice & Her Brothers, Greenwillow, 1978, Dustland, Greenwillow, 1980, The Gathering, Greenwillow, 1980, Jahdu, Greenwillow, 1980, Sweet Whispers, Brother Rush, Philomet, 1982, The Magical Adventures of Pretty Pearl, Harper, 1983; A Little Love, Philomel, 1984, Junius Over Far, Harper, 1985, The People Could Fly: American Black Folktales, Knopf, 1985, The Mystery of Drear House, Greenwillow, 1987, A White Romance, Philomel, 1987; Anthony Burns, Philomel, 1988; In the Beginning, HBJ, 1988; The Bells of Christm HBJ, 1989; Cousins, Philomel, 1990; The Dark Way, HBJ, 1990; The All-Jahdu Storybook, HBJ, 1991; Drylongso, 1992; Plain City, Many Thousand Gone, 1993; Jaguarundi, 1995; Her Stories: African American Folktales, Fairy Tales and True Tales, 1995. **Orgs:** Pen; The NAACP Writer's Guild. **Honors/Awds:** Nancy Block Meml Award, Downtown Community School Awards Comm; Edgar Allan Poe Award for Best Juvenile Mystery, 1969, for The House of Dies Drear; Ohioana Literary Award, 1969; John Newbery Honor Book Award, 1971, for The Planet of Junior Brown; Lewis Carroll Shelf Award, Boston Globe-Horn Book Award, 1974, John Newbery Medal & Natl Book Award, 1975, for M C Higgins, the Great; John Newbery Honor Book Award, Coretta Scott King Award, Boston Globe-Horn Book Award, and Amer Book Award nomination, 1983, for Sweet Whispers, Brother Rush; Horn Book Fanfare Award in fiction, 1985, for A Little Love; Coretta Scott King Award, NY Times Best Illus Children's Book Award, & Horn Book Honor List selection, 1986, for The People Could Fly; Boston Globe-Horn Book Award, 1988, Coretta Scott King Honor rd, 1989, for Anthony Burns; Newbery Honor Book Award, 1989, for In the Beginning; Honorary Doctor of Humane Letters, Bank St College of Education, 1990; Reginia Medal, 1990; Hans Christan Andersen Medal, 1992; Laura Ingells Wilder Medal for Body of Work, 1995; Ohio State Univ, Honorary Doctor of Humane Letters, 1994; Honorary Doctor of Humane Letter, Kent State University, 1996; Virginia Hamilton Conf on Multicultural Experiences, established in her name at Kent State Univ, 1981; MacArthur Foundation Fellowship Winner, $350,000, largest of 1995.

HAMILTON, WILBUR WYATT

Business executive. **Personal:** Born Jan 28, 1931, San Antonio, TX; married Joy Coleman. **Educ:** Trinity Jall Sem, DD; Simpson Bible Coll, BTh; San Francisco City Coll, AA; Golden Gate U. **Career:** San Fran Hous Auth, acting exec dir; San Fran Redevel Agy, exec dir 1977-, dep exec dir 1974-77, asst exec dir for adm 1971-74, area dir 1969-71; Am Pres Line, trmnl chf 1965-69. **Orgs:** Sec San Fran Intrdenom Minstrl Allnc; judge field fclty CORO Found; pres No CA Regn NAHRO; pres Pacific SW Regn NAHRO; dir yth serv No CA Ch of God in Christ; past agency commr San Fran Redevel Agy; NAACP; exec counc Am Arbtrn Assn; Intl Lngshrmn/Wrhsmn Union; pastor Hamilton Meml COGIC San Fran; mem St Mary's Hosp Comm Bd; bd trst Univ HS. **Honors/Awds:** Cert of dist Bd of Supvr City & Co of San Fran; chrchmn of yr Nat Conf of Ch of God in Christ; outst grad acad achvmnt Ch of God in Christ Internat. **Business Addr:** San Francisco Housing Authority, 440 Turk, San Francisco, CA 94103.

HAMILTON-BENNETT, MAISHA

Health administrator. **Personal:** Born Sep 20, 1948, Russellville, AL; married Robert E Bennett; children: Kinshasa, Karega, Ayinde. **Educ:** Mt Holyoke Coll S Hadley, MA, BA 1970; Univ of Chicago Chgo, IL, MA 1972, PhD 1973. **Career:** Kennedy King Coll Chgo, IL, cnslr 1971-72, instr 1972-73; IL Sch of Professional Psychlgy, adjnct fclty 1978-; Jcksn Pk Hosp Chgo, IL, dir outpat bhvr med clnc 1974-81, dir bhvrl sci training 1981-82; Private Practice, psychological serv corp 1977-; Chicago Dept of Health, deputy commissioner 1984-87; Hamilton Beyhavioral Healthcare Ltd, CEO, currently. **Orgs:** Cnsltnt STEP Sch Chgo, IL 1982-84, Hlth & Hum Serv Wash, DC 1979-82, Englwd Comm Hlth Org Chgo, IL 1981; Safari Hse Drg Abuse Trtmnt Pgm Chgo, IL 1979-80; pres Natl Assn Blck Psychlgst 1978-79; ofcr Natl Assn Blck Psychlgst 1976-80; chmn Chicago Area Assn Blck Psych 1974-75; bd dir Chicago Area Assn Blck Psych 1973-; mem Am Psychlgcl Assn 1973-; Cngrsnl Blk Caucus Hlth Brain Trust 1977-; ofc bd dir Comm Mntl Hlth Cncl Inc 1983. **Honors/Awds:** Outstndng Srvc Blk Comm Chicago Area Assn Blk Psych 1981; Comm Srvc Awrd Blk Stdnt Psych Assn 1983.

HAMILTON-RAHI, LYNDA DARLENE

Public administrator. **Personal:** Born Oct 22, 1950, Chicago, IL; daughter of Mabel C Clenna Hamilton and Leonard O Hamilton; divorced; children: Mumtaza, Toshmika, Courtney Lyons. **Educ:** Univ of Hawaii, Honolulu HI, 1968-71; Univ of Cincinnati, Cincinnati OH, BS, MPA, 1976; Woodrow Wilson Coll of Law, Atlanta GA, 1979-81. **Career:** City of Cincinnati, Cincinnati OH, program mgr, 1976; Riviera Beach Hsq Authority, Riviera Beach FL, exec dir, 1976-77; City of Marietta, Marietta GA, planner, 1977; Butler Co CAC, Hamilton OH, exec dir, 1977-78; City of Marietta, Marietta GA, planning admin, 1979-83; City of Phoenix, Phoenix AZ, mgmt asst, 1983-, program mgr, 1988-. **Orgs:** Bd mem, Community Serv Bd, 1978; regional coord, Women's Division, Amer Planning Assn, 1981-83; pres, founder, Conf of Minority Public Admin, Arizona Chapter; comm mem, Intl City Mgmt Assn; bd mem, Arizona Governor's 20th Year Civil Rights, 1984; chair, Phoenix Child Care Task Force, 1984, Phoenix Minority Devel Working Comm, 1985; mem, Phoenix Women's Issue Comm, 1985-87; pres, Amer Soc for Public Admin, Arizona Chapter, 1988-89, bd mem, 1989-90. **Honors/Awds:** Talent Show Judge, Marietta Parks Dept, 1980; Outstanding Young Woman of Amer, 1986; Rideshare Coord of the Year, Rapid Public Transit Authority, 1988; Leaderhsip, Amer Soc for Public Admin, 1988.

HAMLAR, DAVID DUFFIELD, SR.

Dentist. **Personal:** Born Sep 27, 1924, Roanoke, VA; son of Maude Smith Hamlar and Robert Hamlar; married Maxine Harbour Hamlar, Apr 16, 1945; children: Jocelyn Hamlar Clark, David Jr, Deidre Diane Hamlar. **Educ:** Hampton Institute, Hampton, VA, 1941-43; Toledo Univ, Toledo, OH, BE, 1948; Howard Univ, Washington, DC, DDS, 1952; Providence Hospital, Baltimore, MD, intern, 1952-53. **Career:** Self-employed, Columbus, OH, dentist, owner, 1954-. **Orgs:** Chairman, Children's Dental Health Week, Columbus Dental Assoc, 1960; chairman, patient care, Children's Hosp, Columbus, OH, 1984-90; president, Columbus Board of Education, 1975-79; basileus, Omega Psi Fraternity, Columbus, OH, 1958; chairman, Committee to Remember the Children, 1990; Columbus Chamber of Commerce Ed Committee, 1990. **Honors/Awds:** Martin Luther King Humanitarian, Columbus Education Assoc, 1980; Equal Opportunity Award, Urban League, 1976; Distinguished Service Award, Columbus Bd of Ed, 1979; Citizen of the Year, Omega Psi Phi Fraternity, 1976; Varsity "T" Hall of Fame, Toledo Univ, 1985. Ohio State Univ, Distinguished Citizen Award; Alpha Kappa Alpha Sorority, Humanitarian Award; Junior League, Outstanding Personal Achievement Award; Franklin Lodge of Elks, Outstanding Service to Community Award. **Military Serv:** US Navy, MoMM 2/C, 1943-45. **Home Addr:** 2626 Kenview Rd S, Columbus, OH 43209.

HAMLAR, JOCELYN B.

Banking executive. **Personal:** Born Jan 8, 1954, Columbus, OH; daughter of Maxine Eloise Harbour Hamlar and David Duffield Hamlar; married Roy Clark, Aug 12, 1978 (divorced 1993); children: Morgan Allison, Sydney Erin. **Educ:** Boston University, MS, 1981, BLS, 1986. **Career:** Bank of New England, asst marketing officer, 1978-80; WNEV-TV, production asst, 1979-81; United Community Planning Corp, communications director, 1982-83; American Hospital Assn, marketing communications specialist, 1982-83; WXRT-FM Radio Station, dir of advertising and promotion, 1983-86; LaSalle National Bank, vp, director of public relations, 1986-91; WBEZ-FM, director of marketing, 1991-93; ABN Amro North America Inc, dir of corp communications, vp, 1993-97, first vp, dir of communications, 1997-. **Orgs:** Child Care Center Assn, board of directors, 1990-; Reman's Theatre, board of directors, 1992-93. **Honors/Awds:** Black Women Hall of Fame Foundation, Kizzy Award, 1987, 1990; Greater Boston YMCA, Black Achievement Award, 1979.

HAMLAR, PORTIA Y. T.

Attorney. **Personal:** Born Apr 30, 1932, Montgomery, AL; children: 1. **Educ:** AL State Univ, BA 1951; MI State Univ, MA 1953; Univ of Detroit School of Law, JD 1972; Univ of MI, Wayne State Univ, Post Grad Studies. **Career:** Univ of MI; acad counselor 1957-58; Pontiac HS, vocal music instr 1963-65; Hyman Gurwin Nachman & Friedman, legal sec 1966-68; MI Appellate Defender Detroit, legal rschr 1971-73; Amer Bar Assoc Lawyers for Housing Prog LA, admin asst 1973; Gr Watts Model Cities Housing Corp LA, legal counsel 1973; Chrysler Corp, atty; DE Law School of Widener Univ, asst prof of law 1980-82; MI State Bar Atty Grievence Commis, assoc counsel 1982-. **Orgs:** Organist, choir dir St Andrews Presby Church 1955-72; vocal music instr Detroit Pub Schools 1953-71; adj prof law Univ of Detroit School of Law; org Resources Counselors Occupational Safety & Health Lawyers Group bd of ed Hazardous Matls Mgmt Jrnl; mem MI State Bar, Detroit Bar Assoc, Delta Sigma Theta, Kappa Beta Pi, Alpha Kappa Mu, Mu Phi Epsilon; law review staff Univ of Detroit 1970-72; mem literature & rsch Amer Bar Assoc Com on Real Prop Law 1971-72; mem ABA Com on OSHA Law 1978-. **Honors/Awds:** Publs "Landlord & Tenant" 1971, "HUD's Authority to Mandate Effective Mgmt of Pub Housing" 1972; "Defending the Employer in OSHA Contests" 1977, "Minority Tokanism in Amer Law Schools" 1983.

HAMLET, JAMES FRANK

Military officer (retired). **Personal:** Born Dec 13, 1921, Alliance, OH; son of Rhoda Hamlet and Frank Hamlet. **Educ:** Tuskegee Univ; St Benedict's Coll; US Army Command & General Staff Coll; US Army War Coll. **Career:** Joint Spl Operations & Spl Weapons Div Ft Leavenworth, project officer later doctrinal devel officer 1963-66; 11th Aviation Group 1st Cavalry Div Vietnam, operations officer 1966; 227th Aviation Battalion, commanding officer, 1966-67; Doctrine & Systems Div Ft Leavenworth, chief airmobility br 1968-69; 11th Aviation Group 1st Cavalry Div Vietnam, Commanding Officer 1970-71; 101st Airborn Div Vietnam, Asst Div Comdr 1971; 3rd Brigade, 1st Cavalry Div, Vietnam, Commanding General, 1971-72; 4th Infantry Div Ft Carson, Commanding General 1972-74; US Army Headquarters, Washington DC, deputy the inspector general, 1974-81; retired, 1981. **Orgs:** Bd dirs Wall St Petroleum Co; bd trustees Rider Univ; JFH Officers & Non-Comm Officers Retiree Counsel at Ft Dix NJ; bd of dirs, Mercer Medical Center; commissioner, Mercer County Community Coll; mem, Governor's Aviation Educ Advisory Council; trustee, AUSA; mem, First Cavalry Div Assn, Fourth Infantry Div Assn, 366th Infantry Veterans Assn; member, Governor's Committee, Employer Support of Guard and Reserve; member, US Army War College Alumni Assn; member, Alpha Boule, Sigma Pi Phi Fraternity. **Honors/Awds:** Distinguished Serv Medal (w/ Oak Leaf Cluster); Legion of Merit (w/2 Oak Leaf Clusters); Distinguished Flying Cross; Soldier's Medal; Bronze Star (w/Oak Leaf Cluster); Air Medal (49 awards); Army Commendation Medal (w/3 Oak Leaf Clusters); Combat Infantryman Badge; Parachutist Badge; Master Army Aviator Badge; Army Aviation Hall of Fame; US Army Infantry Hall of Fame; Toastmaster's Intl. **Military Serv:** US Army, major general, 1942-81. **Home Addr:** 20 Glenwood Avenue, Trenton, NJ 08618.

HAMLIN, ALBERT T.

Attorney. **Personal:** Born Jun 6, 1926, Raleigh, NC; married Jacqueline Peoples; children: Alan C. **Educ:** Shaw U, BS 1944; Howard U, JD with honors 1956. **Career:** Office for Civil Rights Chief Counsel, dir 1977-80; hew Civil Rights Div; Gen Coun for Litigation, dep asst 1966-72; US Dept of Just, exec gbr & leg liaison 1965-66; Off of Alien Prop, chief of litigation 1963-65; Settlement of Societe Internationale Pour Participations Industrielles et Commerciales SA (Interhande IG Chemit vs Kennedy), gov coun; Gen Aniline & Film Corp, sale of Gov's 11,166,438 shares of stock 1963-65; Reeves Robinson Rosenberg Duncan & Hamlin, Ptnr 1960-63; US Dept of Just, tri atty 1956-60. **Orgs:** Mem NAACP Legal Redress Com 1960-63; co-fndr Asst Ed Howard Univ Law Journal; mem Urban Problems Com; Fed Bar Assn. **Honors/Awds:** Outstndg Stud Award Howard Law Sch 1953; Outstndg Atty Award US Dept of Just 1965. **Military Serv:** USN 1944-46.

HAMLIN, ARTHUR HENRY

Educator. **Personal:** Born Jan 4, 1942, Bastrop, LA; son of Augustine Hamlin and Elmore Hamlin; married Deloris E; children: Eric, Erica. **Educ:** Grambling State Univ, BS 1965; Northeast LA Univ, Master 1970, 30 Plus 1975. **Career:** CTA, business oper 1966-67; City of Bastrop, gym super 1973-76; City of Bastrop, councilman 1977-; Morehouse Parish Sch Bd, teacher-coach 1966-; Morehouse Parish Drug Free Schools and Communities, coordinator. **Orgs:** Oper Greenview Club 1971-72; past pres Morehouse Comm Improv Org 1973; past pres Morehouse Concerned Citizens 1979; past secretary Club 21 1981; mem Gents Civic & Social Club. **Home Addr:** 2302 Bonnie Ave, Bastrop, LA 71220.

HAMLIN, DAVID W.

University executive. **Personal:** Born Apr 19, 1952, Pittsburgh, PA; son of Laura McQueen and David H Hamlin; married Lyn Nickens, Jul 6, 1974; children: Brian, Lindsay. **Educ:** Carlow College, BA, business & communication, 1992; Carnegie Mellon, Master Public Mgt. **Career:** Hills Department Store, hardlines merchandise mgr, 1976-80; Equitable Gas Company, buyer, 1980-90; Duquesne Light Company, director of minority business development, 1990-96; Carnegie Mellon University, director of purchasing, 1996-. **Orgs:** National Purchasing Management Association, 1980-; Pittsburgh Regional Minority Purchasing Council, chairman, 1980-. **Honors/Awds:** Black Opinion Magazine, Man of the Year, 1989; Minority Business Opportunity Comm, Excellence Award in Business, 1993. **Business Addr:** Director, Purchasing Svcs & Supplier Management, Carnegie Mellon University, 6555 Penn Ave, Pittsburgh, PA 15206, (412)268-8430.

HAMLIN, ERNEST LEE
Cleric. **Personal:** Born Dec 9, 1943, Sussex County, VA; son of Elma R Hamlin and Arish L Hamlin; married Pamela Diane Carter, May 6, 1978; children: Kevin, Rafael, Cherry. **Educ:** Virginia Union University, BA, 1970, School of Theology, MDiv, 1974; Presbyterian School of Christian Education, 1976; Virginia Commonwealth University, pastoral education, 1976-77. **Career:** Bethesda Baptist Church, pastor, 1981-83; Richmond Virginia Seminary, theology and christian education, professor, 1982-89; Ebenezer Baptist Church, supply pastor, 1984; Union Hill United Church of Christ, pastor, 1986-89; Christian Education Ministries, president, 1990-; Emmanuel-St Mark's United Church of Christ, pastor, 1990-92; Tubman-King Community Church, senior pastor, 1992-. **Orgs:** Habitat for Humanity, board of directors, 1992-; Northeast Ministerial Alliance, executive vice pres, 1991-92; East Side Ecumenical Fellowship, executive secretary, 1990-91, executive vice pres, 1991-92; OIC Metro Saginaw, board of directors, 1990-92; One Church One Child of Michigan, board of directors, 1991-92; SCLC, Virginia State Unit, board of directors, 1982-90, Richmond Chapter, board of directors,1981-85. **Honors/Awds:** Emmanuel-St Mark's UCC, Outstanding Leadership Award, 1992; Richmond Virginia Seminary, Outstanding Service Award, 1986; United Negro College Fund, Honorary Chairperson, 1983. **Special Achievements:** "A True Mother and Christ," published poem, 1990; City-Wide Martin Luther King Jr Christian Unity Service, preacher, 1992; SCLC, Richmond Chapter, Mass Meeting, coordinator, 1984-85; Negro Business and Professional Women's Sisterhood Sunday, preacher, 1991; Women's History Celebration, coordinator, 1991-. **Home Addr:** 148 Springwood Dr, Daytona Beach, FL 32119-1425. **Business Addr:** Senior Pastor, Tubman-King Community Church, 425 N Seneca St, Daytona Beach, FL 32114, (904)258-5683.

HAMM, BARBARA LAWANDA
Media executive. **Personal:** Born Jun 29, 1957, Baltimore, MD; daughter of Ruby E Hamm and Charles O Hamm; children: Tiffany N Hamm. **Educ:** Bennett College, Greensboro, NC, BA, (summa cum laude), 1978. **Career:** WJZ-TV, Baltimore, MD, producer, 1978-84; Black Entertainment Television, Washington, DC, senior producer, 1984-85; WSLA-TV, Washington, DC, consumer producer, 1985-87; WJZ-TV, Baltimore, MD, executive producer, beginning 1987; KYW, news planning manager, currently. **Orgs:** National Assn Black Journalists, 1990-; Assn of Black Media Workers, 1978-. **Honors/Awds:** 1989 Broadcast Awards, Natl Commission Working Women, 1988 American Women in Radio/TV Award "Picture This-Welfare Mom," 1st place winner. **Business Addr:** News Planning Manager, KYW, 101 S Independence Mall, Philadelphia, PA 19106.

HAMMEL-DAVIS, DONNA P.
Physician. **Personal:** Born Oct 6, 1947, New York, NY; daughter of Larcie Cora Levi Davis and George Thomas Davis; married Dr James W Hammel; children: Damien E Hammel, Grant A Hammel. **Educ:** Cornell Univ, BA 1969; Meharry Medical Univ, MD 1973. **Career:** Heffner Medical Clinic, physician 1977-78; CIGNA Health Plan, physician 1978-. **Orgs:** Mem AMA, CMA, AAFP, MADD; supporter NAPCA, Amer Cancer Soc, Amer Heart Assoc. **Honors/Awds:** Community Serv Awd Alpha Kappa Alpha 1984. **Special Achievements:** First African-American female medical officer in US history, 1975, selected as captain, 1992. **Military Serv:** US Navy, commander 10 yrs.

HAMMER, M. C. (STANLEY KIRK BURRELL)
Vocalist. **Personal:** Born 1962, Oakland, CA; son of Louis Burrell Sr; married Stephanie; children: Akeiba Monique, Sarah Brooke, Stanley Kirk. **Educ:** Undergraduate classes in communications. **Career:** Oakland Athletics, bat boy; Holy Ghost Boys (rap group), singer; Bust It Records, founder; solo performer, currently. **Honors/Awds:** Albums, Feel My Power, Please Hammer Don't Hurt 'Em. Grammy Award with Rick James and Alonzo Miller for Best Rhythm and Blues Song, U Can't Touch This, 1990; Grammy Award for Best Rap Solo, U Can't Touch This, 1990; Grammy Award for Best Video Long Form, Please Hammer Don't Hurt 'Em the Movie, 1990. **Military Serv:** US Navy, three years. **Business Addr:** Recording Artist, c/o Capitol Records, Inc, 1750 N Vine St, Hollywood, CA 90028.

HAMMETT, WILLIE ANDERSON
Educator. **Personal:** Born Apr 19, 1945, Sumerton, SC; children: Jamal. **Educ:** Hudson Valley Comm Coll, AAS 1966; WV State Coll, BS 1968; SUNY Albany, MS 1971, EdS 1977. **Career:** Troy School System, guidance counselor 1969-71, basketball coach 1969-71; Hudson Valley Comm Coll, counselor 1971-72, asst basketball coach 1971-72, dir educ opportunity program 1972, vice pres student serv 1972-. **Orgs:** Bd of dir Camp Fire Girls 1969-72; vice pres Troy Jaycees 1969-72; pres NA-MAL Enterprises Inc 1977-79; mem Council on Black Amer Affairs 1977-; bd of trustees Troy YWCA Troy NY 1972-; bd of dir Samaritan Hosp Troy NY 1978-; vchairperson, exec bd NY State Spec Prog Personnel Assoc 1979-. **Honors/Awds:** Listed in Outstanding Young Men of Amer 1972. **Business Addr:** Vice President Student Serv, Hudson Valley Comm College, 80 & Vandenburgh Ave, Troy, NY 12180.

HAMMOCK, EDWARD R.
Government official. **Personal:** Born Apr 20, 1938, Bronx, NY; married Jeanne Marshall; children: Erica, Rochelle, Regina. **Educ:** Brooklyn Coll, BA 1959; St John's Univ Law Sch, LLB 1966. **Career:** NY State Parole Bd, chief exec ofcr/chmn for the div of parole 1976-; NY City Dept of Investigation, dep commr 1973-76; Dept of Law NY State Criminal Investigation Attica Prison Riot, spec asst atty gen 1971-73; Daytop Village Inc, exec dir 1969-72; NY Co Homicide Bur, asst dist atty 1966-69; Supreme Ct Kings Co, probation officer 1963-66; Youth Council Bur, caseworker 1960-63; St John's Univ Sch of Law, adj prof; Nat Inst on Drug Abuse, spec cons; Proj Return Inc, bd dir. **Orgs:** 100 Black Men; NY Co Lawyers Assn; NY State Bar Assn; pres Student Bar Assn St John's Univ Sch of Law. **Business Addr:** 1450 Western Ave, Albany, NY 12203.

HAMMOND, BENJAMIN FRANKLIN
Microbiologist, educator, educational administrator. **Personal:** Born Feb 28, 1934, Austin, TX; son of Helen Marguerite Smith Hammond and Dr Virgil Thomas Hammond. **Educ:** Univ of KS, BA 1950-54; Meharry Med Coll, DDS 1954-58; Univ of PA, PhD 1958-62. **Career:** Univ of PA School Dental Med, inst micro 1958, asst prof micro 1962-65, assoc prof micro 1965-70, prof micro 1970-, chmn of dept 1972-, assoc dean for acad affairs 1984-; Medical College of Pennsylvania, professor of medicine and microbiology, currently. **Orgs:** Historical Society of PA, board member; Museum of Art of Philadelphia; invited stockholder Athenaeum of Philadelphia; American Assoc for Dental Research vice pres, 1977, pres, 1978-79; Racquet Club of Philadelphia; The Union League of Philadelphia; Metropolitan Opera Guild; Philadelphia Museum of Art, board member, American Society for Microbiology. **Honors/Awds:** EH Hatton Intrntl Assc for Dental Rsrch 1959; Lindback Awrd Distngshd Tchng at the Univ of PA 1969; Madaille D'Argent City of Paris France 1976; Pres Lecture Univ of PA 1981; R Metcalf Chair-Distinguished Visiting Prof Marquette Univ 1986; Dean's Lecture Northwestern Univ Med Ctr 1987; Honorary President, International Assn for Dental Research, 1978; Distinguished Speaker, University Paul-Sabatier, Toulouse, France, 1991; Societe Francaise de Parodontologie, Honorary Membership. **Home Addr:** 560 N 23rd St, Philadelphia, PA 19130.

HAMMOND, JAMES A.
Information company executive (retired). **Personal:** Born Nov 11, 1929, Tampa, FL; son of Lucile V Hammond and William Hammond; married Evelyne L Murrell; children: Kevin, Gary, Lisa. **Educ:** Hampton University BS Inds Voc Ed 1951; US Command & General Staff Coll, 1971; Inds Coll of the Armed Forces, 1974. **Career:** Hammond Elect Contracting Inc, pres 1951-65; Comm of Comm Rltns City of Tampa, admn dept head 1965-70; AL Nellum & Assc Inc, vice pres 1969-73; Impact Assc Inc, pres 1972-74; Walter Industries, Inc. dir eo progs 1974-89; Impac Communications Inc, pres & CEO 1983-86; Automation Research Systems Ltd, vice pres, 1990-97. **Orgs:** Dir Comm Fed Savings & Loan Assn 1967-; Tampa Urban League 1967; Am Assc for Affirmative Action 1977-81; mem Kappa Alpha Psi Fraternity; chmn City Civil Serv Bd 1980-87; mem NAACP; Commsn on Access to Legal Syst 1984; Commissioner, Unemployment Appeals Commission-State of Florida. **Honors/Awds:** The Governor Award State of FL 1967; Outstanding Alumnus Hampton Inst 1971; Whitney Young Awrd Tampa Urban League 1978. **Military Serv:** AUS lt col; Distinguished Serv 1951-79. **Home Addr:** 2505 19th Ave, Tampa, FL 33605, (813)248-6225.

HAMMOND, JAMES MATTHEW
Educator. **Personal:** Born Jul 10, 1930, Keanansville, NC; married Carol Howard; children: Endea Renee, Renata Melleri, Rona Meiata, James Matthew Jr. **Educ:** Oakwood Coll, BA 1953; SC State Coll, MSc 1960; Catholic Univ of Amer, MA 1975; Friendship Coll, DDiv 1963; S IL Univ, PhD 1973. **Career:** Atkins HS, guidance counselor 1960-61; Sci Dept Bekwai Teachers Coll, chair 1961-68; Seventh Day Adventist Church of Sierra Leone, pres 1968-70; SDA Church of North Ghana, exec dir 1972-74; Metro Family Life Council, mem 1979; Pan African Develop Coop, bd mem 1981; MD Psychological Assoc, mem 1982-; Columbia Union Coll, chair/prof of psychology. **Orgs:** Mem Metro Family Life Council 1979; bd mem Pan African Develop Coop 1981; mem MD Psychological Assoc 1982; chaplain (maj) Civil Air Patrol 1983. **Honors/Awds:** UNESCO Fellow United Nations Organs 1972; Phi Delta Kappa mem SIU Chap 1972. **Home Addr:** 3200 Fullerton St, Beltsville, MD 20705. **Business Addr:** Chair/Prof of Psychology, Columbia Union College, 7600 Flower Ave, Takoma Park, MD 20912.

HAMMOND, KENNETH RAY
Cleric. **Personal:** Born Jul 28, 1951, Winterville, NC; son of Rev and Mrs Hoyt Hammond; married Evelyn Patrick; children: Kennetta, Brandon. **Educ:** East Carolina Univ, BA, history, 1973, MEd, counselor educ, 1983, CAS, counselor ed, 1985; Shaw Univ, Master's, divinity, 1978; NC State Univ, ABD, 1986-. **Career:** Mendenhall Student Ctr ECU, asst prog dir, 1973-74, prog dir, 1974-85; Cedar Grove Baptist Church, pastor, 1974-79; Mt Shiloh Baptist Church, pastor, 1980-91; East Carolina Univ, asst dir, University Unions, 1985-88, assoc dir, Univ Unions and Student Activities, 1988-91; Union Baptist Church, Durham, NC, sr pastor. **Orgs:** Chmn, Pitt Co Adolescent Sexuality Task Force, 1979-81; Alpha Phi Theta, Honor Hist Soc, 1972-; Assn of College Unions Intl, 1973-91; Natl Assn for Campus Activities, 1973-91; Natl Baptist Convention, 1975-91; bd of dirs, Pitt Co Arts Council, 1984-86; NC Assn for Counseling & Development, 1985-91; Alpha Phi Alpha Fraternity, 1971-; NC College Personnel Assn, 1986; Amer Assn for Counseling and Development, 1987; Amer College Personnel Assn, 1987; Interdenominational Ministerial Alliance of Durham; Area II, Amer Baptist of the South, secretary; East Cedar Grove Baptist Assn, chair, exec bd; Shaw Univ, Divinity School bd of trustees; National Theological Alumni Assn, pres; First Citizens Bank, bd of dirs, 1989-91; Greenville Utilities Comm, bd of dirs, 1989-91; General Bapt State Convention, NC, general bd; Habitat for Humanity, bd of dirs; Downtown YMCA of Durham, bd of dirs. **Honors/Awds:** Coach of the Year, Eastern Carolina Conf, 1973; Joint Council on Health & Citizenship DSA, 1979; Phi Alpha Theta, Honor History Soc, 1972-; Alpha Phi Alpha, ML King Jr Community Service Award, 1986; Phi Kappa Phi, 1988. **Home Addr:** 211 November Dr, Durham, NC 27712-2438. **Business Addr:** Sr Pastor, Union Baptist Church, 904 N Roxboro St, Durham, NC 27701.

HAMMOND, MELVIN ALAN RAY, JR.
Dentist. **Personal:** Born Feb 6, 1949, Austin, TX; son of Helen Bernice Rucke Hannond and Melvin Alan Ray Hammond Sr; married Elloree Sanora Lawson; children: Melvin A R III. **Educ:** Huston-Tillotson Coll, BS 1971; Howard Univ Coll of Dentistry, DDS (w/Honors) 1981. **Career:** Harris Co Hosp Dist, staff dentist 1981-83; Private Practice, dentist 1981-. **Orgs:** Vice pres Charles A George Dental Soc 1984 & 85; pres Gulf States Dental Assoc 1989-90; mem Amer, TX and Natl Dental Assocs, Houston Dist Dental Soc, Gulf States Dental Assoc, Charles A George Dental Soc. **Honors/Awds:** Mem Omega Psi Phi Frat Rho Beta Beta 1976-; Outstanding Young Men of Amer 1982; Estelle Coffey Young Memorial Awd; Robert Hardy Jr Memorial Awd. **Business Addr:** Dentist, 1213 Herman Dr, Ste 840, Houston, TX 77004.

HAMMOND, ULYSSES BERNARD
Court executive. **Personal:** Born Feb 18, 1951, Washington, DC; son of Eliza Jones Hammond and Cleveland Hammond; married Christine Pointer Hammond, May 26, 1979; children: Damon Moore, Shayna. **Educ:** Kenyon College, Gambier, OH, BA, 1973; Wayne State University, Detroit, MI, MPA, 1975; Wayne State University Law School, Detroit, MI, JD, 1980. **Career:** Citizens Research Council of Michigan, Detroit, MI, research assistant, 1974-75; Detroit City Council, Detroit, MI, special projects assistant, 1975-78; Wayne County Circuit Court, Detroit, MI, court executive, 1978-83; Michigan Supreme Court, Lansing, MI, associate state court administrator, 1983-90; District of Columbia Courts, Washington, DC, chief executive officer, 1990-. **Orgs:** President, Optimist Club of North Detroit Foundation, 1980-83; member, National Bar Association, 1991-; vice polemarch, Kappa Alpha Psi, Lansing Chapter, 1989-90, 2nd vice polemarch, Washington chap, 1996-; member, Bar Association of the District of Columbia, 1991-; Conference of State Court Administrators, member 1990-96, bd of dir, 1996-, bd mem, 1995-; board member, Boys and Girls Club of Lansing, 1988-90; Nat Assoc for Court Mgt, bd of dir, 1996-, mem, 1990-, bd mem, 1995; Anthony Bowen YMCA, Washington, DC, bd mem, 1994-; Kenyon Coll, bd of trustees. **Honors/Awds:** Distinguished Alumni Award, Wayne State University, 1989; Pi Alpha Alpha Inductee, National Honor Society for Public Affairs and Administration, 1989; Certificate of Appreciation, Bar Association of District of Columbia, 1990; Award of Appreciation, Family Law Section, Michigan Bar Association, 1988; Outstanding Leadership Award, United Negro College Fund of Michigan, 1987, 1989; National Association of Court Managers, 1992; National Association of Child Support Enforcement, 1992; Measure of a Man Award, United Negro College Fund, 1996; Honorary Doctor of Laws Degree, Kenyon College, 1995. **Special Achievements:** First person to be bd mem of nation's two leading court admin assoc at the same time. **Business Addr:** Chief Executive Officer, District of Columbia Courts, 500 Indiana Ave, NW Suite 1500, Washington, DC 20001.

HAMMOND, ULYSSES S., JR.
Banking executive. **Personal:** Born Jun 16, 1919, Calvert, TX; married Florida M. **Educ:** Huston-Tillotson Coll, BA 1941; Schiff Sch for Scout Execs, grad 1946. **Career:** Tyler, dist scout exec 1946-58; Tyler, field dir 1958-71; Dallas, 1971-; St John Fed Credit Union, manager/treasurer. **Orgs:** Faculty mem Butler Coll 1948-68; pres St John Fed Credit Union 1972-74; bd dirs Downtown Kiwanis Club 1973-74; mem Dallas County Selective Serv Bd 1972-74; basileus Theta Alpha Cpht Omega

Psi Phi 1972-74; Theta Alpha Chap 1974. **Honors/Awds:** Omega Man of Yr SW Region 1964. **Military Serv:** AUS sgt 1941-46. **Business Addr:** Manager/Treasurer, St John Fed Credit Union, 2600 S Marsalis, Dallas, TX 75216.

HAMMOND, W. RODNEY
Psychologist, educator. **Personal:** Born Jan 12, 1946, Hampton, VA; son of Mildred R Cooper Hammond and William R Hammond, Sr; married Andrita J Topps; children: William Rodney III. **Educ:** Univ of IL Champaign/Urbana, BS 1968; FL State U, MS 1970, PhD 1974; Harvard Univ, post-doctoral 1990. **Career:** FL State U, instr 1973; Univ of TN, asst prof Psychology 1974-76; Meharry Med Clg CMHC, asst prof Psychiatry 1976-83, dir chldrns serv 1976-83; Wright State Univ, assoc prof and former asst Dean, School of Professional Psychology; Division of Violence Prevention Centers, Central District, Atlanta, GA, dir, currently. **Orgs:** Mem, Amer Psyclgl Assoc 1975-; pres, TN Behavior Therapy Assoc 1980-81; cnlsltn, Natl Center on Child Abuse 1980; board of trustee, Assn of Psychology, 1991; mem, Ohio Developmental Disabilities Planning Council, 1986-; bd of dirs, Amer Assoc of Gifted Children, 1986; bd of professional affairs, Amer Psychological Assoc, 1988-90; bd of educational affairs, American Psycology Assn, 1991-94; chmn, Montgomery County Bd of Mental Retardation, 1989-. **Honors/Awds:** "100 Outstanding Seniors", Univ of IL at Champaign/Urbana, 1968; Pub Health Sr. Fellow, Natl Inst of Mental Health, 1968-70; Grant Child Youth & Family Serv, NIMH, 1976-82; Grant Matl Center on Child Abuse & Neglect, 1981-83; President's Awd for Outstanding Contribution in Teaching Research and Serv, Wright State Univ, 1986; Fellow and Diplomate, American Board of Medical Psychotherapists, 1987; Fellow, International Society for Research on Agression, 1992; Fellow, American Psychological Association, 1994; Outstanding Article interesting research and policy issues on adolescence, to research in adolescence, 1994. **Home Addr:** 267 Lake Shore Dr., Berkley Lake, GA 30096.

HAMMONDS, ALFRED
Business executive. **Personal:** Born Feb 6, 1937, Gary, IN; married Pearlena J Donaldson; children: Alfred, Jr, Danelle J. **Educ:** Bus Coll Hammond IN, cert accounting 1963; Am Inst Banking, 1968. **Career:** Gary Nat Bank, baker asst vice pres & branch mgr 1963-. **Orgs:** Mem Am Inst Banking; pres Gary Frontiers Serv Club; vice pres Urban League; bd US Selective Serv Bd #44. **Honors/Awds:** 1st Black salesman HC Lyttons & Co Gary 1961-63. **Military Serv:** USAF 1955-59. **Business Addr:** Gary Natl Bank, 1710 Broadway, Gary, IN 46407.

HAMMONDS, CLEVELAND, JR.
Educational administrator. **Personal:** Born Jan 8, 1936, Rayville, LA; son of Louise Buchanan Hammonds and Cleveland Hammonds; married Yvonne Parks Hammonds, Sep 5, 1959; children: Deborah, Rhonda, Marsha. **Educ:** Southern Illinois University, Carbondale, IL, BS, 1958; Southern Illinois University, Edwardsville, IL, MS, 1963; University of Illinois, Urbana, IL, EdD, 1973. **Career:** Champaign Public Schools, Champaign, IL, teacher, couns, 1964-68, assistant superintendent, 1968-75; Inkster Public Schools, Inkster, MI, superintendent, 1975-79; Durham Public Schools, Durham, NC, superintendent, 1979-88; Univ of NC, Chapel Hill, NC, part-time instr, 1984; Birmingham Public Schools, Birmingham, AL, superintendent, 1988-. **Orgs:** Member, American Association of School Administrators; member, Phi Delta Kappa; member, Kappa Delta Pi Honor Society; member, National Alliance of Black Educators; member, Alabama Association of School Administrators. **Honors/Awds:** Superintendent's Award for Excellence in School Communication, North Carolina Public Relations Association, 1984-85; Selected as 1987-88 North Carolina Association of School Administrators; J E Shepard Sertoma Award of Outstanding Community, 1987; The Executive Educator 100 Award, Exec Educ Magazine, 1987, 1990. **Military Serv:** US Army, Specialist 4, 1959-62. **Business Addr:** Superintendent, Birmingham Public School System, 2015 Park Place N, Birmingham, AL 35203.

HAMMONDS, GARFIELD, JR.
Law enforcement official. **Career:** US Drug Enforcement Administration, 1969-94; GA Department of Juvenile Services, head, 1994-95; GA State Board of Pardons and Paroles, bd mem, 1995-96, chairman, 1996-. **Orgs:** 100 Black Men, Atlanta; Kappa Alpha Psi Fraternity; International Association of Chiefs of Police; National Organization of Black Law Enforcement Executives. **Honors/Awds:** Senior Executive Performance; Presidential Meritorious Service Award; US State Department Award for Excellence. **Special Achievements:** First African American parole board chairman in Georgia; first African-American to serve as US Drug Enforcement Regional Director, SE Region. **Business Addr:** Chairman, Georgia State Board of Pardons & Paroles, 2 Martin Luther King Jr Dr SE, Ste 458, East Tower, Atlanta, GA 30334, (404)656-5651.

HAMMONDS, JEFFREY BRYAN
Professional baseball player. **Personal:** Born Mar 5, 1971, Plainfield, NJ. **Educ:** Stanford. **Career:** Baltimore Orioles, outfielder, 1993-. **Business Addr:** Professional Baseball Player, Baltimore Orioles, 333 W Camden St, Baltimore, MD 21201, (410)685-9800.

HAMPTON, CHERYL IMELDA
Journalist. **Personal:** Born in Portsmouth, VA; daughter of Helen Bowen Hampton & George Livington Hampton; divorced; children: Reed Thomas Smith, Adrienne Hampton Smith. **Educ:** Syracuse University, BS, 1973. **Career:** Regional Learning Center, outreach coord, 1981-87; Syracuse Herald Journal/Herald American, editorial asst, 1987-88, staff writer, 1988-89, asst city editor, 1989-90, asst to the managing editor, 1990-91, asst managing editor, 1991-92; The Orange County Register, asst managing editor, 1992-96, deputy editor/nights, 1996-97; Natl Public Radio, dir news staffing and admin, 1997-. **Orgs:** National Assn of Minority Media Executives, 1992-; National Assn of Black Journalists, 1989-; African Cultural Arts Council of the Bowers Museum of Cultural Art, 1993-; Black Chamber of Commerce, 1996-; The Volunteer Center, Syracuse, NY, bd of dirs, 1986-92; New York State Fair Women's Executive Council, 1986-92; Junior League of Syracuse, bd of dirs, 1981-82; League of Women Voters of Central New York, pres, 1983-87. **Honors/Awds:** Rape Crisis Center, Prism Awd, 1991; Syracuse Press Club, Best Investigative Story, Best Series, 1990, Best Story Written Against Deadline, 1989; Urban League of Onondage County, Special Achievement Awd, 1989; Syracuse Post Standard, Woman of Achievement, 1986. **Special Achievements:** Health & Wealth: Poverty and Disease in Onondage County, 1989. **Business Addr:** Director, News Staffing & Administration, National Public Radio, 635 Mass Ave, NW, Washington, DC 20001-3753.

HAMPTON, DELON
Consulting engineer. **Personal:** Born Aug 23, 1933, Jefferson, TX; son of Elizabeth Lewis Hampton (deceased) and Uless Hampton (deceased). **Educ:** Univ of Illinois, Urbana IL, BSCE, 1954; Purdue Univ, West Lafayette IN, MSCE, 1958, PhD, 1961. **Career:** Consulting activities, 1961-; Kansas State Univ, asst prof, 1961-64; Eric H Wang Civil Engineering Research Facility, assoc research engineer, 1962-63; IIT Research Inst, sr research engineer, 1964-68; Howard Univ, Washington DC, prof of civil engineering, 1968-85; Gnaedinger, Banker, Hampton & Assoc, pres, 1972-74; Delon Hampton & Associates, Chartered, Washington, DC, chairman of the board, chief executive officer, 1973-. **Orgs:** Vice president, Housing and Public Facilities, Montgomery County Chamber of Commerce, 1983-85; board of directors, District 5 director, Amer Soc of Civil Engineers, 1991-94; president, Natl Capital Section, 1984-85; assoc mem bd of governors, Amer Public Transit Assn; chmn, exec comm, Amer Soc of Civil Engineers, Engineering Mgmt Div, 1985-89; mem, Transportation Coordinating Comm, Greater Washington Bd of Trade; mem, board of directors, Washington DC Chamber of Commerce, 1985-86; vice pres, Amer Consulting Engineers Council, 1987-89; mem, President's Forum, Montgomery Coll Found, 1987. **Honors/Awds:** National Academy of Engineering; featured in Philadelphia Electric Co's permanent exhibit of 24 outstanding black engineers from 1862-; Edmund Friedman Professional Recognition Award, Amer Soc of Civil Engineers, 1988; Theodore R Hagans Jr Memorial Achievement Award, Outstanding Business Man of the Year, Govt of the District of Columbia, Office of Human Rights, 1988; Award for Outstanding Contributions in the Field of Engineering, Los Angeles Council of Black Consulting Engineers; author, co-author of over 40 publications; Distinguished Alumnus, Civil Engineering Alumni Assn, Univ of Illinois, 1990; Outstanding Journal Paper Award, Journal of Management in Engineering, Amer Soc of Civil Engineers, 1990; President's Award for Special Achievement, DC Council of Engineering & Architectural Societies, 1991; Honorary mem, American Society of Civil Engineers, 1995; Honorary Doctor of Science, New Jersey Institute of Technology, 1996; Honorary Doctor of Engineering, Purdue University, 1994. **Military Serv:** US Army, sp2, 1955-57; US Naval Reserve, lieutenant, 1967-72. **Business Addr:** Chairman of the Board, Chief Executive Officer, Delon Hampton & Associates, Chartered, 800 K St, NW, Suite 720, Washington, DC 20001.

HAMPTON, EDWIN HARRELL
Musician, educator. **Personal:** Born Feb 5, 1928, Jacksonville, TX; son of Lela Barnett and Joe Hampton; married Rosalind, Jun 1, 1951 (deceased). **Educ:** Xavier Univ, 1952; Northwestern Univ, Vandercook Coll, attended. **Career:** St Augustine High School, band dir, 1952-. **Orgs:** Mem LMEA, NCBA, NBA, Musicians Union Local, Alpha Phi Omega, Phi Beta Mu; leader Royal Dukes of Rhythm Band; mem 33rd Army Band 1940; Lay Advisory Board, Josephite Fathers, 1987-; Mayors Advisory Board Mardi Gras, 1986-. **Honors/Awds:** Band Director of the Year, Louisiana, 1967; Key to City, New Orleans, 1969; Doctor of Humane Letters, Baptist Christian College 1988; received another honorary doctorate; Father Hall Award, 1992. **Military Serv:** Med Corps, sgt, 1946-49. **Business Addr:** Band Dir, St Augustine HS, 2600 A P Tureaud Avenue, New Orleans, LA 70119.

HAMPTON, FRANK, SR.
Business executive, city official. **Personal:** Born Jan 2, 1923, Jacksonville; married Willa D Wells; children: Frank, Jr. **Educ:** Edward Waters Coll, 3 1/2 yrs. **Career:** Hampton's Gulf Serv Stn, owner, oper; Hampton's Fuel Oil; Hampton Villa Apts; H & L Adv & Pub Rel; councilman 8th Dist. **Orgs:** Chmn, trust bd Mt Ararat Bapt Ch; pres Duval Co Citizens Bene Corp Char Org; 1st vice pres Donkey Club of Jacksonville; chmn Youth Adv Com ARC; Gov Coun on Crim Just; mem Gator Bowl Assn; NAACP; YMCA; Jacksonville C of C; Boy Scouts of Am; commnr Civil Liberites Elks Lodge IBPOE of W. **Honors/Awds:** Lead the fight for 1st black pol officers 1950; FL's 1st black beverage supr 1953; desegregated Jacksonville's golf courses 1958; filed Omnibus Suit in Fed Ct which desegregated all mun rec facil 1960; placed blacks in city & state offices 1961; apptd by Gulf Oil to vis Africa Angola to invest discrim pract in jobs salary & liv conds; spon Open Golf Tournament annu allproceeds going to indigent familes; num awards for outstndg serv to comm. **Military Serv:** AUS WWII 1943-45. **Business Addr:** 3190 W Edgewood Ave, Jacksonville, FL.

HAMPTON, GRACE
Educator. **Personal:** Born Oct 23, 1937, Courtland, AL. **Educ:** Art Inst Chicago, BAE 1961; IL State U, MS 1968; AZ State U, PhD Dec 1976. **Career:** IL State Univ, prof Art Educ; Northern IL Univ; School Art Inst Chicago; CA State Univ Sacramento; Univ of OR. **Orgs:** Mem Nat Art Educ Assn; Nat Conf of Black Artist; Artist-in-residence Hayden House Phoenix; presented papes local & natl conferences; del Festac 1977.

HAMPTON, HENRY EUGENE, JR.
Film producer. **Personal:** Born Jan 8, 1940, St Louis, MO; son of Veva Gullatte and Henry Eugene Hampton, Sr. **Educ:** Washington University, St Louis, MO, BA, 1961. **Career:** Unitarian Universalist Assn, Boston, MA, director of press and information, 1963-68; Blackside, Inc, Boston, MA, president/founder, 1968-96; Tufts University, Medford, MA, visiting professor, 1988-89. **Orgs:** Chairman of the board, Museum of Afro American History; board member, Children's Defense Fund; member, Massachusetts Film Committee; board member, Boston Center for the Arts; board member, International Documentary Assn. **Honors/Awds:** NEH Charles Frankel Prize, National Endowment for the Humanities, 1990; Loeb Fellowship, Harvard University, 1977; Lyndhurst Fellowship, 1989; Executive Producer of Eyes on the Prize, 1987, 1990; Honorary degrees: Northeastern University, University of Massachusetts, Washington University, St Louis University, Framingham State College, Bridgewater State College, Starr King School, University of California-Berkeley, Roxbury Community College, Suffolk University, Boston College, Brandeis University, Tufts University. **Business Addr:** President, Blackside Inc, 486 Shawmut Ave, Boston, MA 02118.

HAMPTON, KYM
Professional basketball player. **Personal:** Born Nov 3, 1962. **Educ:** Arizona State, attended. **Career:** New York Liberty, forward, 1997-. **Business Addr:** Professional Basketball Player, New York Liberty, Two Penn Plaza, New York, NY 10121, (212)564-9622.

HAMPTON, LEROY
Business executive. **Personal:** Born Apr 20, 1927, Ingalls, AR; married Anne; children: Cedric, Candice. **Educ:** Univ of CO, BS pharmacy 1950; Denver U, MS chem 1960. **Career:** Dow Chem Co Midland MI, mgr issue analysis; analyzes fed & state legis regulatory & other issues as related to health & environment; held positions of devel chemist, devl leader, recruiting mrg, mgr, EEO; Dow Chm Co, 24 yrs promoted to present position 1975. **Orgs:** Mem Am Chem Soc Midland Kiwanis Club; mem Presb Ch.

HAMPTON, LIONEL LEO
Musician. **Personal:** Born Apr 20, 1908, Louisville, KY; son of Gertrude Morgan Hampton and Charles Edward Hampton; married Gladys (died 1972). **Educ:** Univ So CA, studied 1934; Allen Univ, Mus D (hon) 1975; Pepperdine Coll, Mus D (hon); Xavier Univ, PhD Mus (hon) 1975; Howard Univ, PhD Mus (hon) 1979; USC, PhD Music 1982; State Univ of NY, PhD (hon) 1981; Glassboro State Coll, PhD Music 1981; Daniel Hale Williams Univ, Univ of Liege Belgium, PhD. **Career:** Benny Goodman Quartet, 1936-40; Lionel Hampton Orch, organ/dir 1970-; composer conductor entertainer; broke segregation barrier when joined Goodman quartet; recorded with Dizzy Gillespie, Ben Webster, Coleman Hawkins and others; Hampton Band grads include Quincy Jones, Dexter Gordon, Cat Anderson, Ernie Royal, Joe Newman, Charles Mingus, Wes Montgomery, Fats Navarro, Art Farmer, Joe Williams, Dinah Washington. **Orgs:** Chmn bd Glad Hamp Records Glad Hamp Music Pub Co; Swing & Tempo Music Pub Co Lionel Hampton Development Group; Lionel & Gladys Hampton Found; Lionel Hampton Eng; 33rd Degree Mason Imperial Dir of Band; goodwill ambassador for Imperial Shriners; Friars Club; mem Alpha Phi Alpha; grand band master Elks; New York City Culture Com; Lionel Hampton Jazz Endowment Fund; Human Rights Commnr City of New York; chmn New York Republicans for Reagan/Bush; mem Eagles; launched "Who's Who in Jazz" series with artists like Woody Herman, Earl Hines, Dexter Gordon, etc 1982. **Honors/Awds:** Papel Medal from Pope Paul VI; Key to City of New York/LA/Chicago/Detroit; New York City Highest Culture Award Geo Frederick Handel 1966; Appeared London Jazz Expo/Newport Jazz Festival/Carnegie Hall/Town Hall/Avery Fischer Hall; toured Europe/Japan/Africa/Australia/Middle East; compositions, "Hamp's Boogie Woogie," "Airmail Special," "Flyin Home"; films, "Pennies from Heaven," "A Song Is Born," "The Benny Goodman Story"; saluted at

White House by Pres & Mrs R Reagan 1982; Best Rock Instrumental Performance for Vibramatic 1984; Performance by a Big Band for Ambassador at Large 1985; Performance by a Big Band for Sentimental Journey Atlantic 1986; Lionel Hampton Sch of Music established at Univ of ID 1987; Kennedy Center Lifetime Achievement Award, 1992; Natl Medal of Arts Award, 1997.

HAMPTON, OPAL JEWELL
Educator. **Personal:** Born Jul 4, 1942, Kansas City, KS; daughter of Mary Overton Blair and William A Blair; divorced; children: Kenton B Hampton. **Educ:** Emporia State Univ, Emporia KS, BSE, 1966; Azusa Pacific Univ, Azusa CA, MA, 1974. **Career:** Kansas City United School Dist, Kansas City KS, teacher, 1964-66; Pasadena United School Dist, Pasadena CA, teacher, 1966-97, curriculum resource teacher/science resource teacher, 1997. **Orgs:** Usher, First AME Church, 1966-; mem, 1976-, regional dir, 1987-91, Natl Sorority Phi Delta Kappa Inc; mem, Richard Allen Theater Guild, First AME Church, 1987-90; life mem, NAACP. **Honors/Awds:** Mentor Teacher, 1993-96. **Home Addr:** 1030 Chevron Court, Pasadena, CA 91103.

HAMPTON, PHILLIP JEWEL
Educator. **Personal:** Born Apr 23, 1922, Kansas City, MO; son of Goldie Kelley and Cordell Daniels; married Dorothy Smith, Sep 29, 1946 (deceased); children: Harry J, Robert Keith. **Educ:** KS St Clg, 1947-48; Drake U, 1948-49; KS City Art Inst, BFA-MFA 1949-52; KS City U, 1950-52. **Career:** Savannah State Coll, dir art, assoc prof 1952-69; Southern IL Univ Edwardsville, prof of painting 1969-, professor emeritus, currently. **Orgs:** Instr painting Jewish Ed Alliance Savannah 1967-68; bd mem Savannah Art Assc Savannah GA 1968-69; Citizens Advsry Cncl Edwardsville IL 1973-74. **Honors/Awds:** Cert of excellence Savannah Chptr Links 1960; "Schemata of Ethnic & Spec Stds" 1980; Danforth Assc Danforth Found 1980-86; Governors Purchase Award, IL State Fair, 1991; more than 200 works of art in public and private collections; Retrospective Exhibition, King-Tisdell Cottage Foundation Inc, Savannah GA, 1995. **Military Serv:** AUS s/sgt 3 yrs; ETO 5 Campaign Stars 1945. **Home Addr:** 832 Holyoake Rd, Edwardsville, IL 62025. **Business Addr:** Professor Emeritus, Southern IL Univ at Edwardsville, PO Box 1774, Edwardsville, IL 62026.

HAMPTON, ROBERT L.
Educator. **Personal:** Born Nov 18, 1947, Michigan City, IN; son of Annie A Williams Hampton and T L Hampton; married Cathy M Melson; children: Robyn, Conrad. **Educ:** Princeton Univ, AB 1970; Univ of Michigan, MA 1971, PhD 1977. **Career:** Connecticut Coll, asst prof 1974-83; Harvard Med School, lectr of ped 1981-93; Connecticut Coll, assc prof 1983-89, prof 1989-94, dean, 1987-94; professor of Family Studies, professor of Sociology, 1994-; Acad Affairs, assoc provost, dean for undergraduate studies, currently. **Orgs:** Consultant Urban Inst 1975; consultant Women in Crisis 1979-82; consultants Childrens Hospital Boston 1982; mem exec com Peguot Comm Found 1983-86; chr Oprtns Dev Corp 1977-78; pres of bd Child & Family Agency 1987-90; New London County Child Sexual Abuse Task Force; United Way of Southeastern Connecticut, 1992-95; Prince Georges County Superintendent of Schools, advisory comm; Inst for Women's Policy Research, advisory comm. **Honors/Awds:** Danforth Assc Danforth Found 1979; NIMH Post Doc Flwshp 1980; NRC Flwshp Natl Rsrch Cncl 1981; Rockfeller Flwshp Rockefeller Found 1983. **Military Serv:** AUSR, ltc; Army Commendation Medal. **Business Addr:** Associate Provost for Academic Affairs & Dean for Undergraduate Studies, The Univ of Maryland, College Park, MD 20742-5031.

HAMPTON, RODNEY
Professional football player. **Personal:** Born Apr 3, 1969, Houston, TX. **Educ:** Univ of Georgia, attended. **Career:** New York Giants, running back, 1990-. **Honors/Awds:** Univ of Georgia, 1988 season opener: National Player of the Week (Sporting News), ESPN Player of the Game, SEC Player of the Week; 1989 Univ of GA vs Univ of KY, SEC Player of the Week; Pro Bowl, 1992, 1993. **Business Addr:** Professional Football Player, New York Giants, Giants Stadium, East Rutherford, NJ 07073, (201)935-8111.

HAMPTON, RONALD EVERETT
Law enforcement officer. **Personal:** Born Jan 5, 1945, Washington, DC; son of Annie L Hunt-Hampton and Memory J Hampton; married Quintina M Hoban, Aug 27, 1982; children: Candace, Jasmine, Ronald Quinten. **Educ:** American Univ, Washington DC, BS, 1978. **Career:** US Air Force, Dover Air Force Base, staff sergeant, 1968-72; Washington DC Metropolitan Police Dept, Washington DC, police officer, 1972-; Natl Black Police Assn, Washington DC, exec dir, 1987-. **Orgs:** Regional chmn, Eastern Region, Natl Black Police Assn, 1982-84, natl chmn, 1984-86, exec dir, 1987-. **Honors/Awds:** Police Officer of the Year, Eastern Region, Natl Black Police Assn, 1983; writings on Community/Police Relations, 1988; Extended Community Policing, 1989; Outstanding Community Relations Officer, Washington DC Police Dept, 1989. **Military Serv:** USAF, staff seargent, 1968-72, US Air Force Good Conduct Medal, 1970, Vietnam Valor, 1969. **Home Addr:** 303 Allison St NW, Washington, DC 20011. **Business Addr:** Executive Director, National Black Police Association, 3251 Mt Pleasant St NW, Second Floor, Washington, DC 20010.

HAMPTON, THOMAS EARLE
Government official. **Personal:** Born Sep 28, 1950, Greenville, SC. **Educ:** Morgan State Univ, BA Pol Sci & Govt 1973; Univ of Baltimore MPA 1984. **Career:** Baltimore Mayor's Office, administrative aide 1974-83; Maryland Real Estate Committee, sales consultant, 1981-; Mass Transit Administration, Office of Public Affairs, comm relations officer 1983-. **Orgs:** Kappa Alpha Psi Fratenity, 1971-; National Forum for Black Public Administrators, Maryland Chapter. **Honors/Awds:** Outstanding Young Man of the Year Award, 1978; United Way, Community Service Awards, 1978, 1979, 1980, 1981; Two Mayoral Citations, 1980, 1983; Baltimore City Council, Resolution, Recognizing 9 Yrs of Community Service; Maryland State Employees Conference, 1988, 1989, 1990; American Public Transportation Association, Public School Safety Campaign, AdWheel Award, 1992. **Special Achievements:** Host, coordinator: "Inside the Criminal Justice System," public affairs radio show, 1979-83; coordinator logistical arrangements for international visitors touring the Metropolitan Baltimore Area; coordinator logistical arrangements for two regional Mass Transportation Conferences; provided technical assistants to federal grant recipients regarding Federal guidelines & regulations; guest speaker before various community & business groups. **Business Addr:** Community Relations Officer, Baltimore Mass Transit Administration, 300 W Lexington St, 6th fl, Baltimore, MD 21201-3415.

HAMPTON, WANDA KAY BAKER
Consultant. **Personal:** Born in Los Angeles, CA; daughter of Mary Harris and Carter Harris; children: Maury. **Educ:** Univ of So CA, BS Educ 1954, MS 1958, PhD 1971. **Career:** Elem Schl, counselor 1961-67; ESEA Title V Prog, coord 1968; Div of Planning & Research, splst measurement & eval 1969; counselor 1970; Pacific Training & Tech Assist, gen consult 1971; Black Consult Serv, staff trainer 1971; Los Angeles Mgmt & Devel Corp, pres 1971; Model Cities, counselor coord 1973;CA Legislature Assembly Office of Research, consult 1973, prin consult 1974-; HUD administrative assistant to regional administrator, 1978-1981; chief-of-staff to state senator, 1989; Health and Human Services, consultant, 1989-90; Hampton & Associates, private consultant, 1991-. **Orgs:** Intl Youth Oppor Bd 1964; research asst Pacific State Hosp 1960-61; tchr LACUSD 1954-60; mem Los Angeles Assn of Sch Psychologists & Psychometrist; pres Los Angeles City Counselors; adv bd NAACP; Black Alcoholics Assn; volunteer work in mental health agencies; Student Support Syst & Dist Atty; Childrens' Home Society Bd of Directors, Urban League Bd of Directors. **Honors/Awds:** Youth Adv Bd Commendation, Assembly Resolutions, Top Real Estate Producer.

HAMPTON, WILLIE L.
Mortician. **Personal:** Born May 9, 1933, Montgomery Co, TN; son of Geneva L Hampton and G F Hampton. **Educ:** Kentucky School of Mortuary Science, MS 1970. **Career:** Winston Fun Home, licensed fun dir & embalmer, owner & oper 1971-. **Orgs:** Mem So KY Econ Opp Council; Russellville City Council; Cemetary Commr; Asst Police Commr 1971-; mem Men's Welfare League; 32 Deg Mason; mem Am Legion; mem Ra Council Exec Bd; mem, bd dir The Electric Plant Bd. **Honors/Awds:** 1st Black apptd bd dir The Electric Plant Bd; had a city park named in his honor. **Military Serv:** AUS corpl 1953-55. **Business Addr:** 162 S Morgan St, Russellville, KY 42276.

HAM-YING, J. MICHAEL
Physician, educator. **Personal:** Born Mar 16, 1956, Gainesville, FL; son of Dorothy McClellan Ham-Ying and Dr John Russel Ham-Ying; married Franeco Cheeks Ham-Ying, Jun 24, 1989. **Educ:** Oakwood Coll, BA Biology 1977; Meharry Medical Coll, MD 1981; Drew University of Health Sciences, Los Angeles, CA, residency, 1981-84. **Career:** King Drew Medical Ctr, asst medical dir 1984-85; Los Angeles Doctors Hosp, exec staff sec 1984-85; South Eastern Coll of Osteopathic Med, asst clinical prof 1985-96; Hendry General Hospital, attending physician, 1985-96; Clewiston Comm Health Ctr, asst medical dir 1985-87; Florida Community Health Centers, Inc, medical director, 1987-89, chief medical officer, 1989-96; Alpha Health Plan, chief medical officer, currently. **Orgs:** American Medical Assn; Amer Acad of Family Physicians, FL Chapter, 1983; charter member, T Leroy Jefferson Medical Society, 1990-96; Florida Association of Community Health Centers. **Honors/Awds:** Geriatric Fellow Dept of Family Medicine King-Drew Medical Ctr 1985; Regional Health Administrators Award, US Public Health Service, 1987; Certificate of Merit, Everglades AHEC, 1988; American Board of Family Practice, Certification, 1984; Recertificaion, 1995; FACHC, Outstanding Service Award, 1992. **Business Addr:** Alpha Health Plan, 851 Trafalgar Court Ste 225 East, Maitland, FL 32751, (407)475-0909.

HANCOCK, DARRIN
Professional basketball player. **Personal:** Born Nov 3, 1971, Birmingham, AL. **Educ:** Garden City Community Coll; Kansas. **Career:** Maurienne (France), 1993-94; Charlotte Hornets, 1994-96; Atlanta Hawks, 1996-. **Business Addr:** Professional Basketball Player, Atlanta Hawks, 1 CNN Center NW, S Tower, Ste 405, Atlanta, GA 30335, (404)827-3800.

HANCOCK, HERBERT JEFFREY
Composer, musician. **Personal:** Born Apr 12, 1940, Chicago, IL; son of Winnie Belle Griffin Hancock and Wayman Edward Hancock; married Gudrun Meixner, Aug 31, 1968; children: Jessica Dru. **Educ:** Grinnell College, BA, 1960; Roosevelt University, grad work, 1960; Manhattan School of Music, 1962; New School of Social Research, 1967. **Career:** Musician, composer, actor, publisher; television appearances include: Concrete Cowboys, 1981; Saturday Night Live; Sesame Street; Phil Donahue; Late Night with David Letterman; Sun City, 1985; A Jazz Session—Sass & Brass, 1987; Showtime Coast to Coast, host, 1987; Celebrating a Jazz Master: Thelonius Sphere Monk, 1987; The New Orleans Jazz & Heritage Festival, 1988; Grammy Living Legends, 1989; The Neville Brothers: Tell It Like It Is, performer, musical director, 1989; film work includes: 'Round Midnight, actor, music director, composer, 1986; Blow Up, composer, 1966; The Spook Who Sat By the Door, composer, 1973; Death Wish, composer, 1974; A Soldier's Story, composer, 1984; Jo Jo Dancer, Your Life Is Calling, composer, 1986; Action Jackson, co-composer, 1988; Colors, composer, 1988arlem Nights, composer, 1989; keyboardist with various groups including: Coleman Hawkins, 1960; Donald Byrd, 1960-63; Miles Davis, 1963-68; Herbie Hancock Sextet, V S O P Quintet, Chick Corea, Oscar Peterson, 1968-; recording artist, 1963-, recordings include: Mwandishi, 1971; Sextant, 1972; Headhunters, 1973; Thrust, 1974; Man-Child, 1975; Secrets, 1976; V S O P, 1977; Sunlight, 1978; Feets Don't Fail Me Now, 1979; Monster, 1980; Lite Me Up, 1982; Future Shock, 1983; Village Life, 1985; Perfect Machine, 1988; In Concert 1978, with Chick Corea, 1978; Hancock Music Co, founder/owner/ publisher, 1962-; Hancock & Joe Productions, founder, 1989-. **Orgs:** Natl Academy of Recording Arts & Sciences; American Federation of Musicians; Screen Actors Guild; American Federation of Television & Radio Artists; Pioneer Club, Grinnell College. **Honors/Awds:** Downbeat Magazine, Critics Poll Award, Keyboard Player of Year, 1968, 1969, 1970, Composer of Year, 1971; Recording Industry Assn of America, Gold Record Award, Headhunters, 1973; Black Music Magazine Award, Top Jazz Artist, 1974; Grammy Awards, Best R&B Instrumental Performance, "Rockit," 1983, Best R&B Instrumental Performance, Sound-System, 1984, Best Jazz Instrumental Composition, "Call Street Blues," 1987; Academy of Motion Picture Arts & Sciences, Academy Award, Best Original Score, 'Round Midnight, 1986; numerous others, 1963-.

HAND, JON THOMAS
Professional football player. **Personal:** Born Nov 13, 1963, Sylacauga, AL. **Educ:** Univ of Alabama, attended. **Career:** Indianapolis Colts, defensive end, 1986-.

HAND, NORMAN
Professional football player. **Personal:** Born Sep 4, 1972; married Tammy; children: Norman Derrell Jr. **Educ:** Mississippi, majored in criminal justice. **Career:** Miami Dolphins, defensive tackle, 1996; San Diego Chargers, 1997-. **Business Addr:** Professional Football Player, San Diego Chargers, Qualcomm Stadium, 9449 Friars Rd, San Diego, CA 92108, (619)280-2111.

HANDON, MARSHALL R., JR.
Clinical pastoral psychologist. **Personal:** Born Jul 3, 1937, Philadelphia, PA; son of Marshall R Handon; divorced; children: Marcia, Marvette, Mavis, Traci, Maia. **Educ:** Rider Coll, Trenton NJ, BA; New School for Social Research, New York NY, MA; Temple Univ, Philadelphia PA, PhD; Amer Theological Seminary, Milledgeville GA, PhD. **Career:** Ben Hill United Methodist Church, Atlanta GA, minister, 1963-; Arthur Brisbane Child Treatment Center, Farmingdale NJ, dir QA, 1978-79; Ancora Psychiatric Hospital, Hammonton NJ, clinical dir, 1980-82; Physical Mental Health Clinical Ass, College Park GA, clinical psychotherapist, 1982-89; Asbury Park Drug Treatment Center, Asbury Park NJ, psychologist; private practice, Asbury Park NJ, psychologist. **Orgs:** Mem, NAACP, 1960-, Amer Assn of Clinical Pastoral Educ Inc, 1985-; dist dir,Young Adult Ministries, College Park Dist, United Methodist Church, 1985-; mem, Natl Assn of Black Psychologists, 1989-. **Honors/Awds:** Community Leader of Amer, Urban Amer Inc, 1959; Man of the Year, Jaycees, 1960; Gang Members, The Police & Delinquency, 1969; The Microcosm, 1973; Case Work/Case Management, 1979; The Joy of Sharing, 1980; The Real Jesus Christ, 1986; The Ben Hill Phenomena, 1989. **Military Serv:** US Navy, Fleet Marine Force/USMC, lieutenant, 1954-59, 1965-67, Purple Heart.

HANDWERK, JANA D.
Insurance agent, financial planner. **Personal:** Born Nov 22, 1959, Kingston, Jamaica; daughter of Vera M Handwerk; married A Bernard Williams, May 21; children: Zelina. **Educ:** Brown Univ, BS; Wharton School, Univ of PA, MBA. **Career:** Mass Mutual Life Ins Co, agent, currently. **Home Addr:** 242 Ivy Ct, Orange, NJ 07050. **Business Addr:** Independant agent, Massachusetts Mutual Life Insurance Co., 100 Park Ave, Ste 650, New York, NY 10017, (212)661-5252.

HANDY, DELORES
Anchor/reporter. **Personal:** Born Apr 7, 1947, Little Rock, AR; daughter of Myrtle Carr Handy and Rev George G Handy; mar-

ried James Lawrence Brown, Jun 24, 1989. **Educ:** Univ of Arkansas, graduate 1970. **Career:** WTTG-TV Channel 5 Washington DC Ten O'clock News & Black Reflections, anchorperson & host 1978-; Six O'clock News WJLA-TV Channel 7 Wash DC, co-anchor 1976-78; CBS-KNXT-TV, reporter, anchorperson 1974-76; KABC-TV LA, reporter June 1973, April 1974; WHBQ-TV Memphis, reporter, anchorperson 1972-73; FKAAY Radio Little Rock, reporter, announcer 1970-72. **Orgs:** Hollywood-Beverly Hills Chapter Nat Assn of Media Women; Am Women in Radio & TV; Radio & TV News Assn of So CA; charter mem Sigma Delta Chi AR Chapter; bd of dirs Jr Citizens Corps Washington DC; exec comm Natl Capital Area March of Dimes; volunteer Big Sisters of Amer Washington DC Chapter; mem Washington Chapter Amer Women in Radio & TV. **Honors/Awds:** Journalist of the Year Award Capitol Press Club 1977; awards Natl Council of Negro Women/United Black Fund for Excellence in Community Serv; awards Journalistic Achievement Univ of DC; Emmy Award for America's Black Forum Special on Jesse Jackson 1985; Emmy Award for Testing the Class of '87 (Channel 7-Boston) 1987; Honored on 350th anniversary of Black Presence in Boston as one of 350 people who represented Black Presence in Boston 1988. **Business Addr:** WNEV-TV Channel 7, 7 Bulfinch Place, Boston, MA 02114.

HANDY, JOHN RICHARD, III

Saxophonist, composer. **Personal:** Born Feb 3, 1933, Dallas; divorced. **Educ:** City Coll NY, 1960; San Francisco State Coll, BA 1963. **Career:** Modern jazz groups, rhythm & blues bands San Francisco-oakland CA area 1948-58, Charleie Mingus, Randy Westen, Kenny Dorham 1959-62; toured Europe 1961; concerts own band Carnegie Recital Hall 1962, 67 Santa Clara CA Symphony 1967; Newport Jazz Festival 1967; Hollywood Bowl CA 1966; Monterey Jazz Festival 1964-66; Antibes Jazz Festival 1967; head jazz band San Francisco prodn opera ''The Visitation'' 1967; collaborated with Ali Akbar Khan 1970-71; duets tabla players Shandar Ghosh & Zakir Hussein; quest soloist major symphonies coll & univ symphony orchs, concert bands, stage bands, natl. **Orgs:** Mem Jazz Arts Soc mus dir 1960-61; San Francisco Interim Arts Adv Com 1966-67. **Honors/Awds:** Recipient Downbeat Poll Award; 1st Place Award Record World All-star Band 1968. **Business Addr:** 618 Baker St, San Francisco, CA 94117.

HANDY, LILLIAN B.

Information management consulting executive. **Career:** TRESP Associates, Inc, president, CEO, currently. **Orgs:** Minority-Owned Bus Tech Transfer Consortium, chair; Alexandria VA, Hospital Foundation, bd of trustees; Bd of Visitors of NC Agricultural & Tech State Unit, AT&T; Greensboro Delta Sigma Theta Sorority. **Honors/Awds:** Black Engineer of the Year Entrepreneur Award, 1994; Greater Washington Entrepreneur of the Year in the category of Woman-Owned Businesses; Alumna of the Year, Morgan State Univ, 1994. **Special Achievements:** Company ranked 99 of Top 100 African-American owned businesses, Black Enterprise, 1990; Black Enterprise Magazine has repeatedly listed TRESP among the Nation's 100 largest Black-owned companies, most recently in June of 1994; TRESP has been named one of the top 25 women-owned businesses in the Washington metropolitan area by the Capitol area Chapter of the Natl Assn of Women Bus Owners & the Washington Bus Journal. **Business Addr:** Founder, Pres, CEO, TRESP Associates Inc, 4900 Seminary Rd, Suite 700, Alexandria, VA 22311, (703)845-9400.

HANDY, WILLIAM TALBOT, JR.

Bishop. **Personal:** Born Mar 26, 1924, New Orleans, LA; son of Dorothy Pauline Pleasant Handy and William Talbot Handy Sr; married Ruth Odessa Robinson Handy, Aug 11, 1948. **Educ:** Attended Tuskegee Institute, 1940-43; Dillard University, New Orleans, BA, 1948; Gammon Theological Seminary, Atlanta, GA, M Div, 1951; Boston Univ School of Theology, Boston, MA, STM, 1982. **Career:** Newman Methodist Church, Alexandria, LA, pastor, 1952-59; St Mark Methodist Church, Baton Rouge, LA, pastor, 1959-68; The Methodist Publishing House, Nashville, TN, publishing representative, 1968-70; The United Methodist Publishing House, Nashville, TN, vice-president, personnel and public relations, 1970-78; Baton Rouge-Lafayette, LA, district superintendent, 1978-80; resident bishop, 1980-92; Missouri Area, United Methodist Church, bishop; United Methodist Publishing House, chaplain, 1996-; Drew University Theological School, adjunct dir, doctor of ministry program, 1996-. **Orgs:** General bd of publication, 1988-92, past chmn, bd of trustees, St Paul School of Theology; past chmn, bd of trustees, Interdenominational Theological Center; past chmn, bd of trustees, Gammon Theological Sem; past sec, Southern Methodist Univ, bd of trustees; life and Golden Heritage member, NAACP; Hymnal Revision Committee, United Methodist Church, 1984-88; Bishop's Special Committee on SMU, 1986-87. **Honors/Awds:** Honorary DD, Huston-Tillotson College, Austin, TX, 1973; Honorary DD, Wiley College, Marshall, TX, 1973; Honorary DD, Centenary College, Shreveport, LA, 1979; Honorary LLD, Dillard University, New Orleans, LA, 1981; Honorary LHD, Philander Smith College, Little Rock, AR, 1982; Honorary DD, Central Methodist Coll, 1991; Tuskegee University & Dillard University, NAFEO Distinguished Alumnus. **Military Serv:** AUS S/Sgt 1943-46. **Home Addr:** PO Box 210554, Nashville, TN 37221. **Business Addr:** Bishop, The United Methodist Church, 201 8th Ave, S, PO Box 801, Nashville, TN 37202.

HANEY, DARNEL L.

Educational administrator. **Personal:** Born Feb 6, 1937, Phoenix, AZ; son of Pearlie Marie Johnson Haney and Walker Lee Haney; married Marie Packer Haney, Nov 24, 1962; children: Norman Darnel Haney, Keith Lyman Walker Haney, Raven Rebecca Haney. **Educ:** Phoenix Jr Coll, 1959; UT State U, 1960-65; UT State Univ Grad Sch, 1970. **Career:** Weber State Coll Ogden UT, asso dean of students; Inst of Ethnic Studies Weber State Coll, minority vocational counselor; Thiokol Clearfield Job Corps, supvr of counseling 1966-71; Parks & Job Corps Cntr Pleasanton CA counselor 1965-66; Oakland Unified Sch Dist, sub tchr 1962-65; Oakland Rec Dept Oakland, part-time rec dir 1962-65; Oakland Raiders Defensive End, professional football player 1961-62; Black Cultural Arts Group of UT, organizer dir; Lorain County Community College, Elyria, OH, director of student life, 1987-. **Orgs:** Bd dirs Childrens Aid Soc of UT; Black Adv Council to the Gov of the State of UT Coll Com; Affirmative Action; Athletic Com; spl chmnshp City Govt Cultural Washington Terrace; Oddessey Hse Drug Prospective Preventive Progs for Addicts; Human Potential Instr for Positive Behavior; nat consulting with Trinity Univ on Cultural Awareness; bd mem UT Endowment for Humanities; worked with drug & training prog in identifying who are minorities & what they are in the Black experience; Title IV Prog in WY & CO; counseling advising AR Art Cntr in Little Rock African-American Cultural Awareness and Drug training; consult to state of UT Hwy Patrol Title IV Progs Ogden City Sch. **Honors/Awds:** Crystal Crest-William P Miller Friend of Students Award, Associated Students WSC 1982; Whitney M Young Jr Service Award, Boy Scouts of America. **Military Serv:** USCG 1957-59. **Business Addr:** Director, Student Life, Lorain County Community College, 1005 N Abbe Rd, Elyria, OH 44035.

HANEY, DON LEE

Newsman. **Personal:** Born Sep 30, 1934, Detroit, MI; married Shirley; children: Karen Lynn, Kimberly Joy. **Educ:** Wayne State U, Radio-TV Arts Maj 1959; Wayne State U, Polit Sci & Law 1974. **Career:** WXYZ-TV TV Talk Show, host-anchr nwsmn 1968-; WJR, staff announc 1963-68; CFPL-TV, host, wkly pub affairs prog 1967-68; WCHD-FM 1960-63; WQRS-FM & WLIN-FM; WGPR-FM, prog dir 1959-60; CKCR, staff announc 1957-59; WSJM, staff announc 1956-57; free lance exp/motion pict slide films, TV, radio. **Orgs:** Mem New Detr Inc Commun Com; mem bd dir Am Fed of TV & Radio Arts Union; mem bd dir Suddne Infant Death; mem bd Eq Just Counc; chmn Mus Dyst Assn of Am; mem Detr City Airpt Commin. **Business Addr:** 2405 W Mc Nichols Rd, Detroit, MI 48221.

HANEY, NAPOLEON

City government official. **Personal:** Born Oct 1, 1926, Texas City, TX; married Sylvia C; children: Lorraine, Katherine, Angela, Lynette, Napoleon. **Career:** Village of Hopkins Park, mayor, currently. **Honors/Awds:** Award, Men of Progress Kankakee, 1983; Awarded $3,500,000 Sewer Grant for Village, State of Illinois, 1984. **Home Addr:** Rt 4 Box 47Y, St Anne, IL 60964.

HANFORD, CRAIG BRADLEY

Military officer. **Personal:** Born Sep 4, 1953, Washington, DC; son of Doris A Davis Hanford and Lexie B Hanford; children: Craig J Dumas, Ashley F. **Educ:** US Military Acad West Point, BS 1975; Univ of So CA, MSSM 1982; Georgia Tech, MS 1985; Flight School, Army Aviator 1978; Defense System Mgmt Coll, Program Mgr Course 1987. **Career:** US Army, special asst aviation center 1979-81, flight operations officer Korea 1981-82, ch tech transfer office info system eng command 1985-87; PEO Stamis, Ft Belvoir, VA, exec officer, l987-88; A CO, 4-58 AVN, APO, SF, commander, l988-89; chief, contract monitoring, DCA, 1990-91, executive officer, DSSO, DISA, 1991-93. **Orgs:** Comm chmn, Kappa Alpha Psi Inc, 1976, 1980, 1985-87; mem, Tuskegee Airman Inc, 1979-80; mem, Army Aviation Assoc of Amer, 1983-89, Assoc of Computing Mach 1986-89, IEEE 1986-89; comm chmn, Rocks Inc 1986-87; member, Nat's Black MBA Assn, 1983-91. **Military Serv:** US Army, lieutenant colonel, currently; Meritorious Serv Medal, 1979, 1983, l988-89; Army Astronaut Nominee, 1985-87, l989; Army Commendation Medal, 1986; Army Achievement Medal, 1986, 1988. **Business Addr:** Executive Officer, DSSO, DISA, DISSO, JA, 701 S Courthouse Rd, Arlington, VA 22204-2199.

HANKIN, NOEL NEWTON

Marketing, public relations executive. **Personal:** Born Apr 30, 1946, Kingston, Jamaica; son of Iris Penso Hankin and Ivanhoe Hankin; married Gwendolyn Diaz Hankin, Jun 2, 1974; children: Arana, Loren. **Educ:** New York Univ, New York, NY, 1969-70; Fordham University, New York, NY, 1969; Queens College, Queens, New York, NY, BS, 1968; Wharton School of Business, Mktg Cert, 1985. **Career:** Young & Rubicam, New York, NY, account executive, 1970-72; Benton & Bowles, New York, NY, account executive, 1972-74; Hankin & Smith, New York, NY, principal, 1974-76; The Best of Friends, New York, NY, principal, 1970-76; Ogilvy & Mather, New York, NY, vice pres, account supvr, 1976-86; Miller Brewing Co, Milwaukee, WI, director mktg rel, beginning 1986, director ethnic marketing, 1994-96, director, corporate relations, 1996-97; Schieffelin & Somerset Co, vp corporate affairs, 1997-. **Orgs:** Founder, board of directors, secretary and treasurer, Thurgood Marshall Scholarship Fund, 1987-94; bd mem, Literacy Volunteers of America, Inc, 1997-; mem, 100 Black Men. **Honors/Awds:** Black Achievers Award, YMCA-NYC, 1984; Black Book Award to Outstanding Business Person, 1989; CEBA Award, Word Institute of Black Comm, 1985, 1989, 1990; Fundraising Award, UNCF, 1989; NAACP Community Service Award, 1992; Men Who Dare Award from The Family Academy. **Special Achievements:** Appointed by President Clinton to Commission of Historically Black Colleges and Universities, 1994. **Business Addr:** Vice Pres, Corporate Affairs, Schieffelin & Somerset Co, 2 Park Ave, New York, NY 10016.

HANKINS, ANDREW JAY, JR.

Radiologist. **Personal:** Born Jul 15, 1942, Waukegan, IL; son of Julia Lampkins Hankins and Andrew Hankins Sr; married Margaret Roberts; children: Corbin, Trent, Andrea. **Educ:** Univ IA, BA 1960-64; Univ MI Med Sch, MD 1964-68. **Career:** Michael Reese Hosp & Med Cntr, intern 1968-69; Univ of Chicago, resdnt 1971-74; Dept of Radiology Univ Chicago, instr 1974-75; Milton Communit Hosp, stf rdlgst 1975-84; Wayne State Univ, clinical asst prof 1977-85; SW Detroit Hosp, radiologist 1975-80, vice chmn dept radiology 1980-83, chrmn radiology 1984-90; Michigan Health Center, radiologist, 1991; Southwest Detroit Hospital, vice chief of medical staff, 1988-89; Goodwin Ervin Hankins & Associate PC, president, 1988-90; Henry Ford Hospital, sr staff physician, 1991-. **Orgs:** Cnsltnt radio pharmaceutical drug advsry com FDA 1982-84; pres Equip Lsng Firm Hankins Ervin Goodwin & Assc 1984-89; vice pres Goodwin Ervin & Assc PC 1980-87; mem Hartford Memrl Bapt Ch 1984-; mem NAACP; mem Detroit Med Society, Natl Med Assn, & Wayne County Med Society; mem RSNA, SNM, & AIUM; mem Iowa Black Alumni Assn; mem YMCA; Big Ten Conference, Advisory Commission, 1988-94; Univ of Iowa, alumni board of dir, 1994-; Downtown Detroit YMCA, board of governors, 1991-96; Detroit Athletic Club, 1997-. **Honors/Awds:** Distinguished Young Alumni, Univ IA Alumni Assn 1977; Phi Beta Kappa Alpha Chptr IA 1964; Omicron Delta Kappa Univ IA Cir 1963; Big Ten Medal of Honor, Univ of Iowa, 1964; Nile Kinnick Scholar, Univ of Iowa, 1963; Sloan Foundation Scholar, Univ of Michigan Med School, 1964-68. **Military Serv:** USAF capt 1969-71. **Business Addr:** Senior Staff, Diagnostic Radiology & Medical Imaging, Henry Ford Hospital, 2799 W Grand Blvd, Detroit, MI 48202.

HANKINS, ANTHONY MARK

Fashion designer. **Personal:** Born Jan 10, 1968, Elizabeth, NJ; son of Mary Jane & Willie Hankins. **Educ:** Pratt Institute, 1986-89; Ecole de la chambre Syndicale de la Couture, 1989-90. **Career:** Yves Saint Laurent, design assistant, 1989-90; Adrienne Vittadini, design assistant, 1990-91; JC Penney Co., Los Angeles, quality control inspector, 1991-92, Dallas, first in-house designer, 1992-94; Ramone Moya Ltd, fashion director, vice pres, partner, owner, 1994-. **Orgs:** SPCA Texas, board of directors, 1995-; Easter Seals, advisory brd, 1995-; Attitudes & Attire, board of directors, 1995-. **Honors/Awds:** Design Industries Foundation Fighting AIDS (DIFFA), 1996; South Dallas Business & Professional Women's Youth Club, 1996; Honorary Citizen, Jackson, MS, 1996; Good Morning Texas, Channel 8, 1996; MacDill Air Force Base, Black History Committee, 1996; Fabric Of Dreams Fashion Show, MacDill Air Force Base, 1996; Fashionetta, AKA Sorority, Inc, 1996; BRAG, (Black Retail Action Group), 1996; State of Oklahoma Citation, 1996; Turner Broadcasting Trumpet Awd, 1996; Dallas Design Intiative, Absolute Vodka Awd, 1996; Black Retail Action Group, Business Achievement Awd, 1996; National Association Negro Business & Professional Women, Trailblazer Awd, 1995; University of North Texas, Executive in Residence, 1995; New Jersey Education Association, Awd of Excellence, 1995; Trumpet Awards, Young Star Award, 1997; Newsweek's top 100 People to Watch, 1997; Business Week Entreprenur of the Year, 1998; Black Chamber of Commerce, ''Quest for Success,'' Award, 1998;numerous others. **Special Achievements:** ''The Fabric of Dreams,'' Motivational Biography, Dutton Books Publishing, 1998; First In-House Designer, JC Penney Co., 1992-94. **Business Addr:** Design Director/Vice Pres/Owner, Ramone Moya Ltd, 5450 Gaston, Dallas, TX 75214, (214)887-1777.

HANKINS, HESTERLY G., III

Educator, computer analyst. **Personal:** Born Sep 5, 1950, Sallisaw, OK; son of Ruth Faye Jackson Hankins and Hesterly G Hankins II. **Educ:** Univ of California, Santa Barbara, BA, sociology, 1972; Univ of California, Los Angeles, MBA, management information systems, 1974; Golden Gate University, postgraduate study, 1985-86. **Career:** Xerox Corp., application programmer, 1979-80; Ventura College, instructor, 1983-84; Golden Gate Univ, instructor, 1984; Chapman College, instructor, 1985; De Anza College, instructor, 1985; West Coast Univ, faculty, 1987-88; Engineering Division, computer programmer, 1981-84; Naval Air Station, special assistant, 1984-85; PMTC, computer scientist, 1985-88; West Coast University, Dept of Business Management, faculty, 1987-91; Defense Contract Management District, Management Information Systems, senior analyst, 1988-; National University, Department of Computer Science, faculty, currently. **Orgs:** Alpha Kappa Psi, secretary, 1977-, life mbr; Federal Managers Assn; ICTIP; IEEE Computer Society; International Platform Assn; YM/WCA Benefit Jr Rodeo Assn; City of Oxnard United Methodist Church; Combined Federal Campaign Keyperson; Assn of Computer Machinery; Federal Managers Assn; National Univ Alumni Assn; UCSB Alumni Assn; Graduate Student of Management Assn. **Honors/Awds:** International Biographical Centre, Certificate of Merit, 1988; Arthur Young, Entrepreneur of the Year, nomination, 1987; Ernst & Young, Entrepreneur of the Year, nomination, 1991; Alabama Jaycees, Outstanding Young Man of America, 1980. **Special Achievements:** Chief administrative credential, State of California, 1988; US Presidential Task Force, 1990. **Home Phone:** (213)964-2944. **Business Addr:** Faculty, Department of Computer Science, National University, 9920 La Cienega Blvd, #300, Inglewood, CA 90301.

HANKS, MERTON EDWARD
Professional football player. **Personal:** Born Mar 12, 1968, Dallas, TX; married Marva Fuller; children: Maya Angelou, Milan Nicole. **Educ:** University of Iowa, bachelor's degree in liberal arts. **Career:** San Francisco 49ers, defensive back, 1991-. **Honors/Awds:** Pro Bowl, 1994, 1995, 1996. **Business Addr:** Professional Football Player, San Francisco 49ers, 4949 Centennial Blvd, Santa Clara, CA 95054, (415)562-4949.

HANLEY, J. FRANK, II
Attorney. **Personal:** Born Mar 11, 1943, Charlotte, NC; son of Robert D and Frank; divorced; children: Laura Elizabeth, Melinda Lee. **Educ:** Attended Hampton Inst; NC Central Univ School Law, LLB 1968. **Career:** State of IN, deputy atty general 1969-71; Standard Oil Div Amer Oil Co, real estate atty 1971-72; Marion County, deputy prosecutor 1972-73; IN Employment Security Div, mem review bd 1974; private practice, attorney 1974-; public defender 1985-88. **Orgs:** Mem, Marion Co Bar Assn; mem, Indianapolis Bar Assn; National Organization of Social Security Representatives (NOSSCR). **Honors/Awds:** Tennis Doubles Champion, Central Inter-Atlantic Assn, 1965; Tennis Doubles Champion, NCAA Atlantic Coast, 1965. **Business Addr:** J Frank Hanley II, 4277 Lafayette Rd, Indianapolis, IN 46254, (317)290-1800.

HANNA, CASSANDRA H.
Educator, musician. **Personal:** Born Jan 1, 1940, Miami, FL. **Educ:** St Augustines Coll, BA 1961; Univ of Miami, MusM 1971; Univ of Miami, attended; Indiana Univ, attended. **Career:** Episcopal Church St Agnes, organist, choir dir; Miami Dade Comm Choir; concerts on radio & TV, co-dir; Comm Coll in Florida, presented various lecture-recitals; performed with Greater Miami Symphony Soc Orchestra: Grieg piano and concerto, Beethoven 3rd Piano Concerto; pianist-lecturer recitalist; Cassie's Cookies, pres; Miami Dade Comm Coll, assoc prof of music, sr prof of music, currently. **Orgs:** MENC, NEA, FEA, FCME, NFHAS, FHEA, Alpha Kappa Alpha, Phi Kappa Alpha, AABWE, Natl Guild of Organists; Cardiney Corp/Diversified Investments, pres. **Honors/Awds:** Featured performer, Natl Black Music Colloquim & Competition at the Kennedy Ctr 1980. **Business Addr:** Senior Professor of Music, Miami Dade Community College, 11380 NW 27th Ave, Miami, FL 33167-3418.

HANNA, ROLAND
Musician. **Educ:** Eastman School of Music; The Juilliard School. **Career:** Benny Goodman Orchestra, pianist; Charles Mingus, pianist; Thad Jones-Mel Lewis Band, 1970's. **Business Addr:** Abby Hoffer Enterprises, 223 1/2 E 48th St, New York, NY 10017.

HANNAH, BEVERLY K.
Architect. **Personal:** married Carlton Jones. **Educ:** Michigan State University; Lawrence Technological University. **Career:** Hannah & Associates Inc, founder/CEO, 1993-. **Orgs:** Delta Sigma Theta Sorority; The American Institute of Architects. **Special Achievements:** One of only ten licensed African American female architects in the country to head her own firm. **Business Addr:** CEO/Founder, Hannah & Associates Inc, 3011 W Grand Blvd, Ste 1900, Detroit, MI 48202, (313)873-6300.

HANNAH, HUBERT H., SR.
Association executive. **Personal:** Born Jul 6, 1920, Hill Top, WV; married Edith C; children: Hubert, Jr, Dwayne, Judith, Marc, Don. **Educ:** Depaul U, EDP computer uses in accounting 1968; OH State U, MBA 1952; Bluefield State Coll, BS 1942; OH State U, BS 1949. **Career:** J Cameron Wade & Asso Chicago, mgmt consult accountant 1969-72; Statistical Sect Gen Office Intl Harvester Co Chicago, supr & Accounting 1963-69; Steel Div Intl Harvester Co, divisional accountant 1952-63; Antioch Bookplate Co Yellow Springs, chief accounting officer 1949-51; Dept Budget & Finance Health & Hosps Governing Commn Cook Co Hosp Financial Mgmt Assn, bus mgr 1975. **Orgs:** Omega Psi Phi Frat; Trinity United Ch chmn bd trustees 1973-75; Urban League; Beta Alpha Psi Hon Accounting Frat 1951. **Military Serv:** AUS s/Sgt 1942-45. **Business Addr:** 3730 N Lake Shore Dr, Chicago, IL 60613.

HANNAH, JOHNNIE, JR.
Information systems director. **Personal:** Born Nov 20, 1970, Akron, OH; son of Johnnie & Joanne Hannah Sr. **Educ:** Howard University, BBA, information systems, 1993. **Career:** Gen Corp, systems analysis, 1993-96; United Way of Gt Toledo, dir infor systems, 1996-. **Orgs:** Black Data Processing Assoc, vp of mem svcs, 1997; BDPA Toledo Chap, chair, 1996; African-American Christian Fellowship Assoc, bd mem, 1996; NAACP, 1997; Greater Toledo Urban League, 1997; ONYX, 1997; AITP, 1997; InRoads, Alumni Assn, 1993; Upward Bd Program, alumni 1989. **Honors/Awds:** Ebony Magazine, 30 Leaders of the Future, 1996; Leadership Toledo, Distinguished Leadership Award Finalist, 1997; Toledo Jaycees, Twenty Under 40 Award Recipient, 1997; Ghahanian Foundation, Mentor Award for Young Male Palever, 1997; BDPA, President Award, 1997. **Home Addr:** 5366 Glenridge Dr, No 2, Toledo, OH 43614, (419)865-3565. **Business Addr:** Director, Information Systems, United Way of Greater Toledo, 1 Stranahan Sq, Toledo, OH 43604, (419)246-4612.

HANNAH, MACK H., JR.
Savings and loan chief executive. **Career:** Standard Savings Assoc, Houston, TX, chief exec. **Business Addr:** Chief Executive, Standard Savings Assn, PO Box 88026, Houston, TX 77288-8026.

HANNAH, MARC REGIS
Electrical engineer. **Personal:** Born Oct 13, 1956, Chicago, IL. **Educ:** IL Inst of Tech, BSEE 1977; Stanford Univ, MSEE 1978, PhD EE 1985. **Career:** Silicon Graphics, co-founder & mem of the tech staff 1982-85, principal scientist 1986-. **Orgs:** Mem IEEE; ACM, NCCBPE, NTA. **Honors/Awds:** ITT Alumni Assoc Professional Achievement Awd 1987; NTA Professional Achievement Awd 1987. **Business Addr:** Principal Scientist, Silicon Graphics, 2011 Stierlin Rd, Mountain View, CA 94043.

HANNAH, MOSIE R.
Banking executive. **Personal:** Born Jul 11, 1949, Lake City, SC; married Doris Horry; children: Michelle, Brandon. **Educ:** Voorhees Coll, BS, 1967-70; Univ of MI, Grad School & Banking 1980-81; Univ OK, Retail Banking School, 1983. **Career:** Fleet Financial Group, branch mgr, 1973-75, asst vice pres, 1975-79, vice pres, 1979-84, sr vice pres 1984-. **Orgs:** Dir United Nghbrhd Cntrs of Am 1984-; Vstg Nurses Serv Monroe Cnty 1984-; Rochester Bus Oprtnts Corp 1982-; mem allocaties Com United Way of Greater Rochester. **Home Addr:** 31 Crystal Spring Ln, Fairport, NY 14450. **Business Addr:** Senior Vice President, Fleet Financial Group, 1 East Ave, 1 E Ave, Rochester, NY 14638.

HANSBERRY-MOORE, VIRGINIA T.
Educator (retired). **Personal:** Born Jan 26, 1930, Ocala, FL; daughter of Beatrice Thompson (deceased) and L T Thompson (deceased); married Clarence Hansberry (divorced 1977); children: Katrina Veronica Hansberry. **Educ:** Florida Memorial College, St Augustine, FL, BS, Elementary Education, 1947-51; Masters Administration Supervision, Melbourne, FL, 1976-77. **Career:** Broward County School System, Fort Lauderdale, FL, teacher, 1951-84. **Orgs:** Member & youth worker, First Baptist Church Piney Grove, 1951-; Zeta Phi Beta Sorority, 1952-; board of directors, Florida Endowment Fund for Higher Education, 1984-. **Honors/Awds:** Mother of the Year, First Baptist Church Piney Grove, 1974; State Director Award, Zeta Phi Beta, State of Florida, 1978; Zeta of the Year, 1986, Regional Director's Award, 1980; Harriet Dorrah Award, NW Federated Woman's Club, 1973; Teacher of the Year, Sunland Park Elementary School, 1984. **Home Addr:** 3511 NW 23rd St, Fort Lauderdale, FL 33311.

HANSBURY, VIVIEN H.
Educator. **Personal:** Born Feb 5, 1927, Richmond, VA; daughter of Mary Spain Holmes and Arthur J Holmes; widowed; children: Horace A Trent, Sandra Lewis, Vernard Trent. **Educ:** Virginia State University, BS, 1966; Temple University, MEd, 1970, principal certificate, 1972. **Career:** Delaware County Intermediate Unit, teacher, mentally retarded/learning disability, 1966-68, supervisor, special education, 1968-69; Pennsylvania State University, counselor, instructor, 1969-74; School District of Philadelphia, educational advisor, 1974-76, program manager, preschool handicapped, 1976-78, instructional advisor, 1978-80, instructional support teacher, 1980-92; NIA Psychological Associates, educational consultant, currently. **Orgs:** Top Ladies of Distinction, Philadelphia Chapter, president, 1988-93; Zeta Phi Beta Sorority, Black Family, director, 1992-, Civil Rights, national representative, 1986-92; Phi Delta Kappa Fraternity, Univ of PA Chapter, pres, 1990-94; National Association of Colored Women's Clubs, national member-at-large, 1992-; Pinochle Bugs Social & Civic Club, Philadelphia Chapter, secretary, 1992-; Phi Delta Kappa National Sorority, scholarship committee member, 1990-; Virginia State University Alumni Association, Philadelphia Chapter, president, 1993-; Sigma Pi Epsilon Delta, Philadelphia Chapter, Grad Division, president, 1987-; Top Ladies of Distinction, Area II, treasurer, 1993-; Natl Council of Negro Woman, Philadelphia Local. **Honors/Awds:** Top Ladies of Distinction, Appreciation Award, 1990-91, Recognition Award, 1992, Outstanding Achievement Award, 1989; School District of Philadelphia, Achievement & Recognition, 1977, 1983-84, Teacher of the Year, 1988; Zeta Phi Beta Sorority, Zeta of the Year, 1981-82, Recognition & Appreciation, 1985-87, 1991-92; Pan Hellenic Council, Philadelphia Chapter, Recognition & Appreciation, 1981-82; American Red Cross, Outstanding Community Service, 1984, 1986; Dedication to the Community & Outstanding Leadership Among African American Women, Natl Finalist. **Special Achievements:** Diagnostic Prescriptive Teaching, 1979; Educational Assessment, 1978; The Remediation Approach of Hortense Barry, 1970; Is Your Child Ready for First Grade, 1969; Identifying Preschool Handicapped Children, 1969. **Home Addr:** 2246 N 52nd St, Philadelphia, PA 19131.

HANSEN, JOYCE VIOLA
Educator (retired), writer. **Personal:** Born Oct 18, 1942, Bronx, NY; daughter of Lillian Dancy Hansen and Austin Hansen; married Matthew Nelson, Dec 18, 1982. **Educ:** Pace Univ, New York NY, BA English, 1972; New York Univ, New York NY, MA English Educ, 1978. **Career:** New York City Bd of Educ, teacher 1973-95; Empire State College, teacher, 1987-95. **Orgs:** Soc of Children's Book Writers, 1980-; Harlem Writer's Guild, 1982-. **Honors/Awds:** Parent's Choice Award, 1986; Coretta Scott King Honor Book Award, 1987, 1995; African Studies Assn, Children's Book Award, 1995. **Special Achievements:** Author, The Gift-Giver, 1980; Home Boy, 1982; Yellow Bird and Me, 1986; Which Way Freedom?; 1986, Out From This Place, 1988; Between Two Fires: Black Soldiers in the Civil War, 1993; I Thought My Soul Would Rise and Fly, 1997.

HANSEN, WENDELL JAY
Radio/TV executive. **Personal:** Born May 28, 1910, Waukegan, IL; son of Anna Termansen Hansen and Christian Hansen; married Eunice Ervine; children: Sylvia Marie, Dean C. **Educ:** Cleveland Bible Inst, grad 1932; Wm Penn Coll, AB 1938; Univ of IA, MA 1940, PhD 1947. **Career:** Menomonie Broadcasting Co, pres 1952-72; Mid-IN Broadcasting, pres & chmn of bd 1969-; White River Broadcasting Co, pres & chmn of bd 1970-; WESL Inc, pres & chmn of bd 1971-. **Orgs:** Dir St Paul Inter-racial Work Comp 1939; chmn MN Joint Refugee Comm 1940-41; pres dir Great Comm Schools 1956-60; mem East St Louis Kiwanis Club 1981-; dir East St Louis Chamber of Commerce 1982-; advisor Indianapolis Prosecutor 1985 shared platform w/Rev Jesse Jackson. **Honors/Awds:** Awd Natl Religious Broadcasters 1970; Boss of the Year Hamilton Co Broadcasters 1979; awd Women of Faith, Inc 1984. **Home Addr:** 15489 Howe Rd, Noblesville, IN 46060.

HANSFORD, LOUISE TODD
Fine art publisher/distributor. **Personal:** Born Nov 6, 1944, Cincinnati, OH; daughter of James & Josephine Todd; divorced; children: Eric. **Career:** The Andrew Jergens Co, scy, 1963-68; Procter & Gamble, organization effectiveness consultant, 1968-90; Fine Arts by Todd, 1990-. **Orgs:** Valley Forge Federated, 1967-69; National Council Negro Women, 1984-86; Black Aware & Concerned, founder, 1973-78; Atlanta Business League, 1997; National Conf of Artists, 1997; National Black Arts Festival, 1996; Mayor's Masked Ball, co-chair, 1997; Atlanta Chamber of Commerce. **Honors/Awds:** Atlanta Business League, Outstanding Achievement in Business, 1997; Avon Products, Woman of Enterprise Awards, nominated, 1998. **Business Addr:** Owner, Fine Arts by Todd, 1376 Chattahoochee Ave, NW, Atlanta, GA 30318, (404)351-5910.

HANSON, JOHN L.
Radio station executive. **Personal:** Born Aug 5, 1950, Detroit, MI; son of Lavinia Collins; children: Kacey. **Educ:** Huston-Tillotson Coll, 1968-72. **Career:** KHRB-AM Lockhart, disc jockey 1970-71; KUT radio Austin, disc jockey 1974-80, producer In Black America radio series 1980-, executive producer 1984-. **Orgs:** Pres John Hanson & Assoc 1970-; bd of directors Black Arts Alliance 1985; bd of directors Camp Fire 1985; pres Austin Assn of Black Communicators 1986-87; bd of directors, Natl Assn of Black Journalists 1987-89. **Honors/Awds:** Community Service Awards, Greater Austin Council on Alcoholism, Cystic Fibrosis Foundation, Federal Correctional System/TX, Univ of TX; Over the Hill, Inc, Comm Serv Award; Austin Black Art Alliance/The Friends of Phoenix; Phoenix Award. **Business Addr:** Executive Producer, Longhorn Radio Network, Comm Bldg B/UT Austin, Austin, TX 78712.

HAQQ, KHALIDA ISMAIL
Educational administrator. **Personal:** Born Jul 11, 1946, Cape Charles, VA; children: Hassana, Majeeda, Thaky, Hussain, Jaleel, Jameel. **Educ:** Rutgers NCAS, BA Psych, Black Studies (with honors) 1980; Rutgers GSE, MEd Counseling Psych 1983. **Career:** Rutgers Univ, counselor 1976-80; Plainfield Bd of Ed, sub teacher 1980-81; Rutgers Univ, rsch asst 1981-82; New Brunswick HS, career ed intern 1982;Caldwell Coll, counselor 1982-84, coord-eof counseling/tutor 1984-; Rider Coll, eop asst dir, counselor 1985-. **Orgs:** Mem Irvington Parent Teachers Assoc, NJ Assoc of Black Ed 1980-, Assoc of Black Psychologists 1982-, NJ Ed Opportunity Fund Professional Assoc 1982-, Amer Assoc for counseling & Devel 1982-; mem NAACP 1985, Community Awareness Now 1986-, Mercer County Black Dem Caucus 1986; leadership adv bd Rutgers Minority Community. **Honors/Awds:** Martin Luther King Jr

Fellowship Recipient 1982; Soroptimist Scholarship Recipient 1978. **Business Addr:** E O P Asst Dir, Counselor, Rider College, 2083 Lawrenceville Rd, Lawrenceville, NJ 08648.

HARALSON, LARRY L.
Government official. **Personal:** married Irene Williams Haralson; children: Kimberly, Ashley. **Educ:** Memphis State University, Memphis, TN, BBA, 1972. **Career:** National Bank of Commerce, Memphis TN, main office branch manager, 1978-79; First Tennessee Bank, Memphis TN, sales & branch manager, 1979-87; Memphis City Government, Memphis, TN, city treasurer & director, 1988-. **Orgs:** Board member, Whitehaven Community Development Corp, currently; member, 100 Black Men of Memphis Inc, currently; board member, Shelby County Board of Equalizations, 1990-; chairman, Tennessee Jaycees Personal Growth Sweepstakes, 1986. **Honors/Awds:** Volunteer of the Year, Memphis Hemophilia Foundation, 1983. **Military Serv:** US Army, SP5, 1966-68. **Business Addr:** City Treasurer & Director, Memphis City Government, 125 N. Mid-America Mall, Memphis, TN 38103.

HARBIN-FORTE, BRENDA F.
Judge. **Personal:** Born Apr 19, 1954, Meridian, MS; daughter of Woodroc and Sophie Harbin; married Napolean Forte, Sep 2, 1989; children: Ken M. **Educ:** Univ of California, Berkeley, BA, 1976; Boalt Hall School of Law, Univ of California, Berkeley, JD, 1979. **Career:** Legal Aid Society of Alameda County, law clerk, 1977-78; Alameda County Public Defender, law clerk, 1978; Moore & Bell, law clerk, 1978-79; Hastings College of Law, adjunct prof of law, 1983-84; 1981-82; Harris, Alexander, Burris, & Culver, associate, 1982-84; Thelen, Marrin, Johnson, & Bridges, associate, 1984-89, partner, 1990-92; Municipal Court of the State of California, County of Alameda, Oakland-Piedmont-Emeryville Judicial Dist, judge, 1992-. **Orgs:** Alta Bates Medical Center Community Member, associate trustee, 1994-; American Bar Assn; American Bar Found, fellow, 1993-; California Assn of Black Lawyers, president's special assistant judicial, 1992-, vp, north, 1987-89; Charles Houston Bar Assn, exec board member and newsletter editor, 1988, advisory board, 1993-; Edward J McFetridge American Inn of Court, master, 1993-, chair, 1994-95. **Honors/Awds:** Charles Houston Bar Assn, co-recipient, President's Award, 1994; California Assn of Black Lawyers, recipient, Bernard S Jefferson Judge of the Year Award, 1994; ''Judge Brenda Harbin-Forte Day,'' declared in City of Oakland on Nov 19, 1992; Oakland Business and Professional Women, Woman of the Year, 1992; Charles Houston Bar Assn, Commun Service Award, 1991; National Black Law Students Assn Tribute to Black Women in the Legal Profession, Honoree, 1988. **Special Achievements:** First African-American woman President of the Alameda County Bar Assn; First African-American woman to clerk for the Central Staff of the Ninth Circuit; First African-American woman elected Boalt Hall Class President; ''350 Days to Trial, Strategies for Survival Under Trial Court Delay Reduction Programs'', 1988; ''Unfair Media Coverage of Judicial Misconduct Investigations, or Taking Landmark Communications Too Far,'' The San Francisco Attorney, August/Sept, 1987; ''Black Women Pioneers in the Law,'' The Historical Reporter, 1987. **Business Addr:** Judge, Alameda County Municipal Court, 661 Washington Street, Oakland, CA 94605, (510)268-7606.

HARDAWAY, ANFERNEE DEON ('PENNY')
Professional basketball player. **Personal:** Born Jul 18, 1971, Memphis, TN; son of Fae Hardaway. **Educ:** Memphis State Univ. **Career:** Orlando Magic, guard-forward, 1993-. **Honors/Awds:** Schick Rookie Game, MVP, 1994; NBA All-Rookie Team, 1994; NBA All-Star, 1997, 1998; All-NBA First Team, 1995, 1996; All-NBA Third Team, 1996. **Special Achievements:** NBA Draft, first round, third pick, 1993; US Olympics, men's basketball, gold medal, 1996. **Business Addr:** Professional Basketball Player, Orlando Magic, 1 Magic Pl, Orlando, FL 32801, (407)649-3200.

HARDAWAY, ERNEST, II
Oral and maxillofacial surgeon, educator. **Personal:** Born Mar 3, 1938, Col, GA; son of Virginia L and Ernest. **Educ:** Howard Univ, BS 1957, DDS 1966, OSurg 1972; Johns Hopkins Univ, MPH 1973. **Career:** Bureau of Med Svcs, dep dir 1980; Public Health Washington DC, dep commiss 1982; Public Health Wash DC, commiss 1983-84; Federal Employee Occupational Health Prog HHS Region V, dir 1985; Howard Univ, asst prof of oral & maxillofacial surgery 1970-. **Orgs:** Chief policy coord Bur of Med Serv 1978. **Honors/Awds:** PHS Plaque 1980; Commendation Medal USPHS 1973; Meritorious Serv Medal; Outstanding Unit Citation Commendation Medal Unit Commendation Medal, USPHS; Dentist of the Year 1983; Distinguished Dentist of the Year Natl Dental Assoc 1984; Fellow Amer Coll of Dentists Natl Dental Assoc Found; Fellow Intl Coll of Dentists; Fellow Amer Assoc of Oral & Maxillofacial Surgeons; Fellow Acad of Dentistry Intl; Disting Serv Awds. **Military Serv:** USPHS, col 16 yrs.

HARDAWAY, JERRY DAVID
Professional football recruiter. **Personal:** Born Oct 23, 1951, Memphis, TN; son of Bennie Louise Carter and Jerry D Hardaway; married Lisa A Mills, Dec 31, 1986; children: Jason D, Jheri D. **Educ:** Southern Illinois University, BS, speech education, 1973; Grambling State University, MA, sports administration, 1973. **Career:** Memphis State University, assistant football coach, 1978; Grambling State University, assistant football coach, 1984; University of California, Berkeley, assistant football coach, 1986; Arizona Cardinals, professional football team, area scout, east coast, currently. **Business Addr:** Area Scout, East Coast, Arizona Cardinals, 8701 S Hardy, Tempe, AZ 85284, (602)379-0101.

HARDAWAY, TIMOTHY DUANE
Professional basketball player. **Personal:** Born Sep 1, 1966, Chicago, IL; son of Donald; married Yolanda; children: Tim Jr, Nia. **Educ:** Univ of Texas at El Paso, El Paso, TX, 1985-89. **Career:** Golden State Warriors, guard, 1989-96; Miami Heat, 1996-. **Honors/Awds:** NBA All-Rookie First Team, 1990; NBA All-Star, 1991-93, 1997, 1998. **Special Achievements:** NBA Draft, first round pick, #14, 1989. **Business Addr:** Professional Basketball Player, Miami Heat, 721 NW 1st Ave, Miami Arena, Miami, FL 33136, (305)577-4328.

HARDCASTLE, JAMES C.
Educational administrator. **Personal:** Born Aug 20, 1914, Dover, DE; married Edith E; children: Frank J, Carmen E. **Educ:** DE State Coll, BS 1935; NY U, MA 1951; Temple U, U; Univ of DE; DE State Coll, LlD 1979. **Career:** Capital School Dist, Dover DE, dir of personnel 1966-; William W M Henry Jr Sr High School, Dover DE, supt of schools 1954-66; BTW Jr High School, Dover DE School System, teacher, coach 1935-54. **Orgs:** Life mem NEA 1942-; mem DE Assn Sch Adminstrs 1954-; mem Am Assn of Sch Adminstrs 1955-; sec bd of Trustees DE State Coll 1962-; varoius others 1968-; various positions with YMCA 1946-; mem NAACP 1943; mem various frat 1946-; mem barious alumni assns 1954-; various postions United Meth Ch 1972-. **Honors/Awds:** Omega Man of the Year Award Psi Iota Chap Omega Psi Phi Frat Inc 1962 & 1975; Merit Ward Frontierman of Am DE Chap 1694; Outstanding Alumni Award DE Coll 1970; YMCA Outstanding Citizens Award Dover YMCA 1974; various other awards, educators & frats 1978-79; EW Buchanan Distinguished Serv Award C of C 1980. **Business Addr:** Director of Personnel, Capitol School District, 945 Forest St, Dover, DE 19901.

HARDEMAN, CAROLE HALL
Educational administrator. **Personal:** Born in Muskogee, OK; daughter of Rubye Hibler Hall and Ira D Hall; divorced; children: Paula Suzette. **Educ:** Fisk Univ, BA Music; Univ of OK, MA Human Relations 1975, PhD Ed Admin 1979; Harvard Univ, MLE Program, 1988. **Career:** Univ of OK, program devel spec 1975-82; Coll of Educ & Human Relations OU, adj prof 1980-85; Center for Human Relations Studies, exec dir 1982-85; Univ of OK, admin officer 1982-85; Adroit Publ Inc, pres; LeMoyne-Owen College, associate dean of lifelong learning, 1988-90, vice president for academic affairs, 1990-92, vp for research and development 1992-97; Langston University, associate dean of graduate studies, 1997-. **Orgs:** Founder/natl review bd Centerboard Jrnl of OU Ctr 1982; bd of dir United Cerebral Palsy of OK 1983-; exec bd Natl Alliance/Black School Ed 1996-; founder OK Alliance for Black School Educators 1984; cons/speaker NABSE, NAFEO, US Dept of Ed, Natl Conf of Christians & Jews, college bound; HBCU, Natl Faculty Development Symposium, mem Links Inc, Jack & Jill Inc, NABSE, Urban League, NAACP, NAMPW, AASA, ASCD, AERA, Alpha Kappa Alpha, YWCA, Assoc of Women in Math; keynote speaker, Univ of DE, Univ of Pittsburgh, Univ of OK, State Dept of Ed-PA, DC Public Schools, Chicago IL, New Orleans Chap One, Las Vegas; mm Natl Task Force on Multicultural Ed; member, Memphis Arts Council Committee of 100; chair of Research Committee, NABSE, 1989-; bd of dir, Planned Parenthood; bd of dirs, Southern Region of Planned Parenthood, exec bd, 1994-; Memphis in May, Memphis Literacy Council. **Honors/Awds:** Regents Doct Fellow OK State Regents for Higher Ed 1975-79; The Black Student on the White Coll Campus Univ Press 1983; Outstanding Faculty/Staff Univ of OK 1984; Sounds of Sci Curriculum Publ 1984; The Math Connection Math Curriculum Publ 1985; Commiss by Natl Ctr for Ed Stat US Dept of Ed Rsch & Stat Div to write paper addressing policy issues & admin needs of Amer ed syst through the year 2001; Spec Consult for Sci Projects Harvard Univ; publ ''Profile of the Black Coll Student'' Urban League's The State of Black OK; Roscoe Dungee Awd for Excellence in Print Journalism OK Black Media Assoc 1984; num papers, articles publ by US Dept of Ed & Natl Sci Found; co-editor, NABSE Journal, NABSE Research Roundtable Monographs, Editor; Tennessee Higher Education Commission Community Svc Awd, 1997. **Business Addr:** Associate Dean of Graduate Studies, Langston University, 4024 Lincoln Blvd, Oklahoma City, OK 73105, (405)424-4020.

HARDEMAN, JAMES ANTHONY
Corporate employee counselor. **Personal:** Born Feb 2, 1943, Athens, GA; divorced; children: Maria, Brian. **Educ:** Howard Univ, BA 1967; Boston Coll, MSW 1973; Harvard Univ, MPA 1974; Brandeis Univ, PhD, candidate, 1995. **Career:** Dept of Corrections, prison warden 1975-78; Dept of Mental Health, senior social worker 1978-79; Ex-Office of Human Serv State House Boston, deputy dir of planning 1979-83; Polaroid Corp, mgr of corporate employee asst program, 1983-. **Orgs:** Bd mem Boston Coll Bd of Directors 1981-83; pres Boston Coll Grad School of Social Work Alumni Assn, 1981-83; vice pres Natl Assn of Social Work; MA 1982; bd mem Mayflower Mental Health Assn 1983-92, Catholic Charities 1983-85, Crime and Justice Foundation Boston 1985-. **Honors/Awds:** Natl Assoc of Social Workers MA Chap, National Delegate Rep, 1981; Black Achiever Community Service, 1992; Community Service Award, 1991, 1992; Independent Spirit Award, 1992; Greatest Contribution to Social Work Practice, 1997. **Military Serv:** USAF capt 1967-71. **Home Addr:** 128 Bettencourt Rd, Plymouth, MA 02360-4202. **Business Addr:** Manager of Corporate Employee Asst Prog, Polaroid Corp, 750 Main St, Cambridge, MA 02139, (617)386-8288.

HARDEMAN, STROTHA E., JR.
Dentist. **Personal:** Born Oct 26, 1929, Ft Worth; married Willie Mae; children: Sharon Kaye, Keith Dion. **Educ:** VA Union U, BS 1950; Meharry Med Coll, DT 1956; Meharry Med Sch, DDS 1963. **Career:** Gulf State Dental Assn, dentist pres. **Orgs:** Mem NT Wallis Dental Soc; Ft Worth Dental Soc; TX Dental Assn; Am Dental Assn; mem Ambassadore Club; Jack & Jill Am Inc. **Military Serv:** AUS med corp 1950. **Business Addr:** 612 NW 25 St, Fort Worth, TX 76106.

HARDEN, MARVIN
Artist, educator. **Personal:** Born in Austin, TX; son of Ethel Sneed Harden and Theodore Roosevelt Harden. **Educ:** Univ of CA Los Angeles, BA Fine Arts 1959, MA Creative Painting 1963. **Career:** Univ CA Los Angeles, extension instr art 1964-68; Los Angeles Harbor Clge, eve div instr art 1965-68; Univ High Adult Schl, instr art 1965-68; Santa Monica City Clge, eve div instr art 1968; CA State Univ Northridge, prof art 1968-97, prof emeritus, 1997-. **Orgs:** Mem Natl Endowment for Arts Visual Arts Flwshp Painting Panel 1985; mem Los Angeles Municipal Art Gallery Assc Artist's Adv Bd 1983-86; mem bd dir ''Images & Issues'' 1980-86; co-fndr Los Angeles Inst of Contemporary Art 1972; chairman, Los Angeles Cultural Affairs Department, Peer Review Board, Visual Arts Grants, 1990. **Honors/Awds:** Distg Prof Award & Excep Merit Srv Award CA State Univ Northridge 1984; Flw John Simon Guggenheim Mem Fnd 1983; Flw Awards in Visual Arts 1983; Flw Natl Endowment for Arts 1972; selected one man shows, Whitney Museum of Amer Art, Irving Blum Gallery, Los Angeles Municipal Art Gallery, Newport Harbor Art Museum; Eugenia Butler Galleries, James Corcoran Gallery, David Stuart Galleries, Ceeje Galleries, Rath Museum, Geneva Switzerland, The Armory Center for Arts, Pasadena, CA, Brand Library Art Ctr, selected group shows, L A Cty Museum Of Art, Brooklyn Museum, Chicago Museum of Contemporary Art, Equitable Gallery, NYC, Nagoya City Museum Japan, Contemporary Art Assc Houston, Philadelphia Civic Ctr Museum, San Francisco Museum of Art, High Museum of Art, Minneapolis Inst of Arts, Univ of CA Los Angeles, US State Dept tour of USSR, Franklin Furnace NYC, San Diego F Art Gallery. **Home Addr:** PO Box 1793, Cambria, CA 93428.

HARDEN, ROBERT JAMES
Physician. **Personal:** Born Jul 16, 1952, Washington, GA; married Margaret Ellanor Hemp; children: Robert Jr, John Phillip. **Educ:** Univ of IL Chicago, BS 1975; Meharry Medical Coll, MD 1979. **Career:** Weiss Memorial Hosp, medical intern 1980-81; US Public Health Svcs, asst surgeon general 1981-83; Timberlawn Psychiatric Hosp, psychiatry resident 1984-87,child & adolescent fellow 1987-89. **Orgs:** Resident mem of exec council TX Soc of Psychiatric Physicians 1986-87. **Honors/Awds:** S01 W Ginsburg Fellowship Group for the Advancement of Psychiatry 1987-89. **Business Addr:** Resident Staff Psychiatrist, Timberlawn Psychiatric Hosp, 4600 Samuell Blvd, Box 11288, Dallas, TX 75223.

HARDIE, ROBERT L., JR.
Business executive. **Personal:** Born Oct 22, 1941, Portsmouth, VA; son of Janie Norman Hardie and Robert L Hardie, Sr; married Marianne Lowry; children: Levon, Robin, F Gary Lee (stepson). **Educ:** Hampton University, BS 1963; University of MD, Southern IL Univ, Grad Studies for MBA. **Career:** US Army Security Agency Warrenton, chief elect engrg 1964-66; Bunker-Ramo Corp Silver Spring, system integration engr 1966-69; Vitro Lab Automation Ind Inc Silver Spring, proj leader 1969-72; Raytheon Serv Co Hyattsville, sr systems engr 1972-73; Systems Consultants Inc Washington, sr systems engr 1973-75; Scientific Mgmt Assoc Inc, prog mgr 1975-85; sr systems engr Evaluation Research Corp Interntl 1985-86; Sentel Corp, Virginia, CEO, chairman, 1986-. **Orgs:** Mem Amer Soc Naval Engrs 1974-, Navy League 1974-87, Naval Inst, Inst Elec Electronic Engrs 1965-70, 1975-77; pres Greenbelt Jaycees 1973-74; deacon; chmn Greenbelt Comm Relations Adv Comm 1974-76; vice pres Greenbelt Labor Day Festival Comm; bd of dirs Camp Springs Boys & Girls Club 1979-80; mem Greenbelt Rep Transp Citizen Adv Comm Met Washington Council Govts 1975; mem Natl Assn of Minority Business 1984; bd of dirs 1989-91. **Honors/Awds:** Greenbelt Jaycees Keyman Awd 1973, 1975; Jaycee of the Month 1971, 1972; Graduated with dept honors; Distinguished Military Grad; co-authored & publ: ''Let's Design Out EMI,'' 1981; Gold Plaque Award, Letter of Appreciation Naval Sea Systems 1985. **Military Serv:** US

Army, 1st lt, 1964-66. **Business Addr:** Chairman, Chief Executive Officer, Sentel Corporation, 225 Reinekers Ln, #500, Alexandria, VA 22314.

HARDIN, EUGENE

Educator, physician. **Personal:** Born Dec 6, 1941, Jacksonville, FL; widowed; children: Jeffrey, Gregory. **Educ:** FL A&M Univ, BS Pharm 1964; Univ So FL, MD 1977. **Career:** Walgreens, assistant manager, pharmacist, 1964-66; VA Hospital, staff pharmacist, 1966-74; King-Drew Medical Center, Department of Emergency Medicine, physician specialist, 1980-, assistant professor, emergency medicine, 1980-, vice chairman, 1990-93, Residence Training Program, director, 1990-93. **Orgs:** Carson Medical Group, medical director, 1981-; Natl Medical Assn, 1984-92; American Medical Association, 1984-; American College of Emergency Physicians, 1990-; Drew Medical Society, 1985-92; Carson Chamber of Commerce, 1985; SCLC, 1986-; Martin Luther King Hospital, Joint Practices Committee, chairman, 1987; King-Drew Medical Center, Physicians Assistance Program, medical director; California Council of Emergency Medicine Residency Directors, 1991-. **Honors/Awds:** Most Outstanding Residence Internal Medicine Martin Luther King Hosp 1980. **Special Achievements:** Author, paper: ''The Dynamics of Parental Abuse,'' 1987. **Military Serv:** US Army, sp-5, 2 yrs; Foreign Serv Medal 1969. **Home Addr:** PO Box 901, Harbor City, CA 90710.

HARDIN, HENRY E.

Educator, businessman, clergyman. **Personal:** Born 1912, Ft Motte, SC; married Carrie; children: Isadora Wallace, Henrietta Butler. **Educ:** Benedict Coll, BA 1944; Benedict Coll, BD 1945; NY U, MA 1947; NY Univ Union Theol Sem City Coll of NY, pursued addl grad studies. **Career:** St Paul Bapt Ch, pastor; Morris Coll Sumter SC, pres; prof dean of Instr elected by trustees to head Coll 1970; dean dir coll financial aid prog recruited students in large numbers expanded on campus & ext progs; Centennial Celebration of SC Bapt Conv, inst. **Orgs:** Mem numerous professional orgns spl honors include Nat Humanities Flw Duke Univ 1971; mem on Staff of Colgate-rochester Seminar on Black Ch Curr 1969; pres Commn on Equal Opp. **Business Addr:** Morris Coll, Sumter, SC 29150.

HARDIN, JOHN ARTHUR

Educator. **Personal:** Born Sep 18, 1948, Louisville, KY; son of Elizabeth Hansbro Hardin (deceased) and Albert A Hardin (deceased); married Maxine Randle Hardin, Dec 22, 1973; children: Jonathan Rico. **Educ:** Bellarmine College, BA 1970; Fisk Univ, MA 1972; Univ of Michigan, PhD 1989. **Career:** Univ of Louisville, lecturer 1972-84; KY State Univ, asst prof 1976-84, area coord 1978-80; Univ of KY, visiting asst prof 1980-81; Eastern WA Univ, asst prof 1984-90, assoc prof 1990-91; Western KY University, assoc professor, 1991-97, assistant dean, Potter College of Arts, Humanities and Social Sciences, 1997-. **Orgs:** Mem exec comm KY Assoc of Teachers of History 1976-80, 1991-; state dir Phi Beta Sigma Frat Inc 1981-83; club pres Frankfort Kiwanis Club 1983-84; mem KY Historic Preservation Review Bd 1983-84, Publ Advisory Comm Kentucky Historical Soc 1983-84, Natl Council on Black Studies 1984-, KY Historical Soc 1984-; NAACP, 1984-; editorial advisory board member, Filson Club History Quarterly, 1989-92; life member, Phi Beta Sigma, 1980-; member, KY Oral History Commission, 1995-99; member, Phi Alpha Theta History Honor Society. **Honors/Awds:** Lenihan Awd for Comm Serv Bellarmine Coll 1969; Three Univ Fellowship Fisk Univ 1970-72; J Pierce Scholarshp Univ of MI Dept of History 1976; Distinguished Alumni Gallery Bellarmine Coll 1979-80; Pres Awd, Natl Council For Black Studies-Region X (1987); author, Onward and Upward: A Centennial History of Kentucky State University 1886-1986, author, Fifty Years of Segregation: Black Higher Education in Kentucky, 1904-1954. **Business Addr:** Assistant Dean, Western Kentucky University, Potter College of Arts, Humanities & Social Sciences, 1 Big Red Way, Bowling Green, KY 42101-3576, (502)745-2345.

HARDIN, MARIE D.

Equal opportunity administrator. **Personal:** daugHter of Emma Ridley and Harrison Ridley; married Granville N Hardin (deceased); children: Oliver, Alyce Hardin-Cook. **Educ:** Wayne State University; Indiana University; Capital University, 1981-84. **Career:** City of Columbus, division management coordinator, 1970-74, deputy director of CDA, 1974-76, director of division CDA, 1975-77, equal employment opportunity administrator, 1977-; Ohio Senate, legal secretary, 1977-78. **Orgs:** American Association of Affirmative Action; Amethysts, board of directors; Central Ohio EEO Council; Centenary United Methodist Church; Personnel Society of Columbus; Columbus Area College Placement Consortium; Central Ohio Personnel Association; United Methodist Ministers Wives; Interdenominational Ministers' Wives Association; Friend in Action; Century Foundation; NAACP; Natl Council of Negro Women; Columbus Urban League; St Paul Methodist Church; Ebondy House, co-founder; Bethune Center Governing Board; Phillis Wheatley Club; American Association for Affirmative Action. **Honors/Awds:** Outstanding Youth Counselor of the Year; outstanding recognition for advancing the cause of equality in employment and housing; recognition of human rights services; National Management Institute, Executive of the Month. **Special Achievements:** Development of an EEO training manual for supervisors and managers in city government; first EEO administrator to be appointed to serve directly under the office of the mayor; first chosen to represent the city at World Conference Decade for Women; instituted the first Women's Week in Government. **Business Addr:** EEO Administrator, City of Columbus, Ohio, Equal Employment Opportunity Office, 90 W Broad St, Columbus, OH 43215, (614)645-8292.

HARDING, JOHN EDWARD

Port authority director. **Personal:** Born May 28, 1938, Nashville, TN; son of Helen E Harding and James A Harding; married Delores Evon Kelly Harding, Dec 18, 1960; children: Sheri Harding Daley. **Educ:** Tennessee A&I State Univ, Nashville TN, BS Civil Engineering, 1960. **Career:** US Army, Directorate of Civil Engineering, Ohio, civil engineer, 1960-67; Air Force Logistics Command, Ohio, civil engineer, 1967-71; Virgin Islands Dept of Public Works, St Thomas VI, commr, 1971-75; Virgin Islands Port Authority, St. Thomas VI, dir of engineering, 1975-77, exec dir, 1977-. **Orgs:** Mem, Amer Soc Civil Engineers, Airport Operators Council Intl, Amer Assn of Port Authorities, Southeastern Airport Managers Assn, Southeastern and Caribbean Port Authorities, Amer Assn of Airport Executives. **Military Serv:** USAF, 1963-64. **Business Addr:** Executive Director, Virgin Islands Port Authority, PO Box 1707, St Thomas, Virgin Islands of the United States 00801.

HARDING, MICHAEL S.

Food & beverage industry executive. **Personal:** Born Sep 5, 1951, St Louis, MO; son of Derwood & Katie Harding; divorced; children: Lindsey, Michael, Morgan. **Educ:** Central Missouri State Univ, BS, 1973; Univ of North Florida, Post Graduate, 1975-82; Pepperdine Univ, MBA, 1987. **Career:** Anheuser-Busch, production mgr trainee, 1973-74, production supervisor, 1974-80, assistant superintendent, 1980-82, assistant superintendent, 1982-83, superintendent, 1983-85, packaging mgr, 1985-90, senior assistant plant mgr, 1990-91, senior assistant plant manager, 1991-95, plant manager, 1996-. **Orgs:** National Beverage Packaging Assn; National Black MBA Assn, 1991-; Kappa Alpha Psi Fraternity, 1973-; Columbia East Houston Medical Center, board of trustees; Sam Houston Area Council Boy Scouts of America, board of directors. **Honors/Awds:** NJ YMCA, Black Achiever of Business & Education Award, 1988. **Special Achievements:** Completed Production Management Training Program, Anheuser-Busch Inc, 1973. **Business Addr:** Sr Plant Manager, Anheuser-Busch Inc, 775 Gellhorn Dr, Houston, TX 77029-1405, (713)670-1600.

HARDING, ROBERT E., JR.

Former attorney, educator, labor arbitrator. **Personal:** Born May 31, 1930, Danville, KY; son of Olivia (deceased) and Robert Sr (deceased); married Iola Willhite; children: Roberta, Olivia. **Educ:** KY State Univ, BA 1954; Univ KY, JD 1957. **Career:** USPHS, corr officer 1952-58; Natl Labor Relations Bd, atty 1958-74; EEO consultant 1980-86; labor arbitrator 1981-; Univ New Mexico, tchr Afro-Amer studies 1974-87. **Orgs:** Mem KY, NM, Natl, Fed, Albuquerque Bar Assns; New Mexico Black Lawyers Assn; mem US Dist Ct NM; mem US Court of Appeals 10th Circuit; US Ct Appeals DC & Supreme Ct; mem Phi Alpha Delta Legal Frat; pres, Albuquerque Branch NAACP, 1971; pres, bd dir Albuquerque Child Care Centers 1980-81; mem NM Adv Comm to the US Commiss on Civil Rights 1981-97; Better Business Bureau, Albuquerque, volunteer arbitrator, 1983-. **Honors/Awds:** New Mexico Reg Medical Prog, Certificate of Recognition, 1976; Better Bus Bur of New Mexico, Arbitrator of the Year, 1987; Governor of New Mexico Toney Anaya, Certificate of Appreciation, 1984; Sickle Cell Council of New Mexico, Certificate of Appreciation, 1990; Women United for Youth, Certificate of Recognition, 1993. **Military Serv:** US Army, 1946-47. **Business Addr:** PO Box 14277, Albuquerque, NM 87191.

HARDING, VINCENT

Historian, educator. **Personal:** Born Jul 25, 1931, New York, NY; son of Mabel Lydia Broome-Harding and Graham Augustine Harding; married Rosemarie Freeney; children: Rachel, Jonathan. **Educ:** City Coll NY, BA 1952; Columbia, MS 1953; Univ of Chgo, MA 1956; PhD 1965. **Career:** Seventh Day Adventist Church Chicago, sply pastor 1955-57; Woodlawn Mennoite Church Chicago, lay assoc pastor 1957-61; Mennonite Central Com Atlanta, southern rep 1961-64; Spelman Coll Atlanta, asst prof History, dept chmn History Social Sciences 1965-69; Martin Luther King Jr Center, dir 1968-70; Institute of Black World, Atlanta, GA, dir 1969-74; Blackside, Inc, Boston, MA, academic adviser to ''Eyes on the Prize'' documentary, 1985-90; Iliff School of Theology, professor, 1981-. **Honors/Awds:** Author of: must walls divide, 1965, There Is a River, 1981, Hope and History, 1990; cntbg ed, mem, ed bd concern Chrstnty & crisis Chrstn cntry; others, also poems, short stories, articles, sermons to professional publs; Kent fellow Soc Rel in Hghr Edn; Honorary Doctorate, Lincoln University, Swarthmore Coll, 1987; Member, Howard Thurman Trust, 1990; Humanist of the Year, Colorado Council of the Humanities, 1991. **Business Addr:** Professor of Religion and Social Change, Iliff School of Theology, 2201 S University Blvd, Denver, CO 80210.

HARDISON, KADEEM

Actor. **Personal:** son Of Bethann Hardison and Donald McFadden; children: Sophia Milan. **Career:** Television credits include: ''The Cosby Show,'' beginning 1984; ''A Different World,'' beginning 1987; Between Brothers, 1997; films include: School Daze; Def By Temptation, 1990; White Men Can't Jump, 1992; Panther, 1995; video recordings include: The Imagination Machines, 1992: CBS-TV Schoolbreak Special, Word's Up, coexec producer, actor; Showtime special, ''Blind Faith,'' 1998. **Special Achievements:** Has acted as director for ''A Different World.''.

HARDISON, RUTH INGE

Sculptor. **Personal:** Born Feb 3, 1914, Portsmouth, VA; daughter of Evelyn Jordan Hardison and William Lafayette Hardison; children: Yolande. **Educ:** TN State A&I, 1934-35; Art Stdnts League, 1935; Vassar Coll, 1942-44. **Career:** Cmmsnd Sclptrs By Old Taylor Whiskies, ''Ingenious Amers'' 1966; New York City Bd of Educ, ''New Generation'' 1975; New York City Dept Cultural Affairs, Jackie Robinson Portrait 1980; Black Alumni of Princeton Univ, Frederick Douglass Portrait 1982; creator of on-going portrait series ''Negro Giants in History'' begun in 1963 includes, Harriet Tubman, ''The Slave Woman,'' Frederick Douglass, Dr WEB DuBois, Dr Mary McLeod Bethune, 1965; Dr Geo Washington Carver, Sojourner Truth 1968, Dr ML King Jr 1968, 1976, Paul Robeson, 1979; Sojourner Truth head, 1976; Sojourner Truth Pin, 1980; Phillis Wheatley, 1989; new series ''Our Folks'' begun in 1985, collectible sculptures of ordinary people doing ordinary things; Portrait of Al Diop, pres, Local 1549 NYC, commissioned by the Women's Committee, on his 20th year of service; ''Mother and Child,'' 1957, Klingenstein Pavillion, Mt Sinai Hosp, NY. **Orgs:** Presentation, ''Sculpture and the Spoken Word'' with associate Margaret McCaden; founding member, Harlem Cultural Council, 1964; founding member, Black Acad of Arts and Letters, 1969. **Honors/Awds:** Self Discovery Workshops granted by Harlem Cultural Council 1975; school children studio visits Cottonwood Found, 1980; Cultural Achievement Award, Riverside Club of the Natl Business and Professional Women's Clubs, 1987; exhibition of 26 photographs, ''Views From Harlem,'' Portsmouth Museum, Portsmouth, VA, 1988; Sojourner Truth figure presented by New York Governor Cuomo to Nelson Mandela, 1990. **Home Addr:** 444 Central Park W 4B, New York, NY 10025.

HARDMAN, DELLA BROWN TAYLOR

Artist, educator. **Personal:** Born May 20, 1922, Charleston, WV; daughter of Captolia M Casey Brown and Anderson H Brown; married Leon Hardman, Aug 27, 1987; children: Andrea Taylor, Francis Jr, Faith Kinard; married Francis C. Taylor, 1946 (died 1978). **Educ:** WV State Coll, BS 1943; Boston U, MA 1945; MA Coll of Art, addl study; OH U; Kent State Univ, PhD, 1995. **Career:** Senior Center, volunteer art teacher, 1990-; West Virginia State Coll, asso prof 1956-86; real estate broker 1971-; Charleston Gazette & Gazette Mail, art critic 1965-73; Boston Pub Sch, art tchr 1954-56; Cambridge Community Center, arts and crafts director, 1952-54; Fogg Art Mus Cambridge 1950, photo dept asst; 1950. **Orgs:** Mem The Links Inc; Alpha Kappa Alpha; member, National Art Education Assn; The Booklovers. **Honors/Awds:** Mother of Yr Alpha Phi Alpha; WV State Coll Alumnus of Yr 1969; Della Brown Taylor art gallery named in her honor, 1984; numerous awards and exhibitions; Art Educator of Year, National Art Education Association. **Home Addr:** PO Box 2035, DeBettencourt Place, Oak Bluffs, MA 02557.

HARDMAN-CROMWELL, YOUTHA CORDELLA

Educator. **Personal:** Born Jan 10, 1941, Washington, DC; daughter of Esther Willis Jubilee; married Oliver W Cromwell, May 28, 1988; children: Darnell Whitten, Dwayne Whitten, Debra Whitten, Michael Cromwell. **Educ:** George Washington Univ, AA, 1960, BS Math 1963; Troy State Univ AL, MS Ed 1971; Univ of VA; EdS Math, Ed 1984; Howard Univ, MDiv 1986; American Univ, PhD 1992. **Career:** Mountain Home Primary School ID, second grade teacher 1964-67; Garrison Elementary School DC, second grade teacher 1967-68; Fledgling School AL, first grade teacher 1968-70; Misawe Dependents School Japan, chmn Math dept & teacher 1972-75; Elmore County HS AL, math teacher 1975; Stafford Sr HS VA, math teacher 1976-79; Germanna Comm Coll, assoc prof of math 1979-86; Woodlawn United Methodist Church VA Conf, pastor, 1986-89; Howard Univ School of Divinity, coordinator of Field-Based Fellowship Program, 1987-91; lecturer in practical theology, 1989-91; American University School of Education, adjunct faculty, 1989-95; Ford Fellowship Programs, director, 1987-. **Orgs:** Political action chmn Orange County NAACP 1978-86; commission Planning Dist Nine VA 1979-84; bd mem Orange County Recreation Assoc 1979-80; bd mem Orange County Library Bd 1982-84; pres Black Caucus VA Conf UMC 1986-88; Consultant, Secretary, Churches in Transitional Communities, 1987-; Mem, VA Conf Commission on Religion and Race, 1987-; chairperson, Virginia Conference Commission on Religion and Race, 1990-; Vice Chairman SEJ Commission on Religion and Race; board of directors, Edna Frazier Cromwell Scholarship Fund, Inc; board of directors, Hardman-Cromwell Ministries, Inc; board of directors, U Street Theatre Foundation; board of directors, Uplift; board of directors, Reconciling Congregations Program; board of directors, United College Ministries of Northern Virginia; ethics and professional advisory committees, Visiting Nurses Assn; Religion and Race Assn, SEJ. **Honors/Awds:** Outstanding Teacher Dept of Defense Dependent Schools Japan 1974; Serv Awd NAACP Orange County 1982, 1983; Dir 7th Annual Devel Studies Conf VA Community Coll 1983; Benjamin Mays Fellow Howard Univ Divinity School 1984-86; Published Poem "The Sound of Your Laughter" Journal of Religious Thought Fall-Winter 1984-85; Anderson Fellow 1985-86; Deans Award 40 Ave, Henry C Maynard Award for Excellence in Preaching & Ministry, Staff Award for Exceptional Performance, gave welcome address at Howard Univ graduation as rep of all graduates Howard Univ Divinity School 1986; Assistantship American Univ, 1989-90; Women of Color Doctoral Fellowship, 1989-90; Student Graduation Speaker at American University, 1993; National Methodist Fellowship, 1990-91. **Home Addr:** 2015 13th St, NW, Washington, DC 20009. **Business Phone:** (202)265-8252.

HARDMON, LADY (LEJUANA)
Professional basketball player. **Personal:** Born Sep 12, 1970. **Educ:** Georgia, attended. **Career:** Utah Starzz, guard, 1997-. **Business Addr:** Professional Basketball Player, Utah Starzz, 301 West South Temple, Salt Lake City, UT 84101, (801)355-3865.

HARDNETT, CAROLYN JUDY
Librarian. **Personal:** Born Aug 12, 1947, Washington, DC; daughter of Ada West Hardnett and Freddie P Hardnett. **Educ:** Hampton Inst, Hampton VA, 1965-68. **Career:** First & Merchants Natl Bank, Pentagon & Arlington VA, 1968-70; Chicago Tribune, Washington DC, librarian, 1970-85; The Baltimore Sun, Baltimore MD, chief librarian, 1985-. **Orgs:** Sec/treasurer, Special Libraries Assn, News Division, 1982-83, conference planner, 1983-84, chair, 1984-85, dir, Baltimore Chapter, 1986-88, bd of dirs, 1987-89; mem, Natl Assn of Black Journalists, 1985-. **Honors/Awds:** Award of Merit, Special Libraries Assn, News Division, 1985; Certificate of Recognition, Black Enterprise Professional Exchange & Networking Forum, 1989. **Business Addr:** Director of Library Services, The Baltimore Sun, 501 N Calvert St, Baltimore, MD 21278.

HARDWICK, CLIFFORD E., III
Educator. **Personal:** Born Sep 4, 1927, Savannah, GA; son of Mr & Mrs Clifford E Hardwick Jr (deceased); married Beautine Williams Hardwick; children: Clifford IV, Kenneth Allen. **Educ:** Savannah State Coll, BS 1950; Univ of Pittsburgh, LittM 1959; Howard Univ, NC Coll, Atlanta Univ, Univ of GA, Mott Leadership Inst, attended; Morris Brown Coll, LLD 1975. **Career:** Effingham Cty Training School, teacher; instructor, physical science lecturer, gen inorganic chem 1951-52; Springfield Terrace Elementary School, teacher 1952-53; Alfred E Beach High School, chmn biology dept 1953-61; Secondary Educ, supvr 1961-68; Comm Educ Savannah, dir 1968-70; Continuing Educ Program Univ of GA, asst prof, dir 1970-; Coastal Georgia Center for Continuing Ed ASC/SSC, asst to the dean, currently. **Orgs:** 1st black elected to serve as foreman on grand jury 1974; ordained as itinerate elder AME Church 1980; mem Natl Univ Ext Assoc, Natl Comm School Ed Assoc, GA Adult Ed Council; adv comm Adult Basic Ed, Alpha Phi Alpha; pres Greenbriar Children Ctr, Savannah Tribune; dir Carver State Bank; exec bd Savannah Chap NAACP; mem Comm of Christian Ed St Philip AME Church, Savannah State Coll Alumni Assoc; mem Cardiovascular Nutrition Comm; vchmn, bd of dir Amer Red Cross Savannah Chapt; mem Hospice Savannah Bd; mem Amer Heart Assoc; exec comm Coastal Area Council Boy Scouts of Amer, United Way Allocations Panel. **Honors/Awds:** Man of the Year Alpha Phi Alpha 1962; Model Cities Recognition Awd for Leadership 1971; Citizen of Day WTOC 1974; Cirus G Wiley Disting Alumnus Awd Savannah State Coll 1974; Community Serv Awd Savannah Bus League 1976; Honorary Doctor of Laws Degree, Morris Brown College. **Business Addr:** Assistant to the Dean, Coastal Georgia Center for Continuing Education, University of Georgia, Athens, GA 30602.

HARDY, CHARLIE EDWARD
Insurance executive. **Personal:** Born Jan 19, 1941, Montgomery, AL; son of Sarah W Hardy and William H Hardy; married Lillie Pearl Curry; children: Randall Charles, Christa Valencia. **Educ:** AL State Univ, BS Secondary Ed 1962; IN State Univ, attended 1967; Life Underwriters Training, Council Grad 1972. **Career:** Brewton City School System, dir of bands 1962-66; Macon Cty Public School, dir of bands 1966-69; MetLife, sr sales rep, assoc branch mgr 1988, sr acct exec, currently. **Orgs:** Mem Natl Assoc of Life Underwriters 1969, NAACP, Tuskegee Civic Assoc, 33 Degree Mason Shriner; life mem Alpha Phi Alpha Frat Inc; deacon Greenwood Missionary Baptist Church; legislative liason Tuskegee Civic Assn 1989; Finance Committee, City of Tuskegee, 1997; president, Tuskegee Area Chamber of Commerce, 1998; Chairman, MetLife Multicultural Career Initiative in the Southern Territory, 1997. **Honors/Awds:** Outstanding Alumnus AL State Univ 1972; Alpha Man of the Year Alpha Phi Alpha Frat Inc 1975; Salesman of the Year Metropolitan Life Montgomery Dist 1979; Alpha Man of the Year Alpha Phi Alpha Frat Tuskegee 1984; Distinguished Alumnus AL State Univ 1985; Inducted as Veteran for 20 Years of Service, Metropolitan Life & Affiliated Companies 1989. **Business Addr:** Sr Account Executive, MetLife, 4201 W Martin L King Hwy, Seasha Bldg, Tuskegee, AL 36083, (334)727-5584.

HARDY, DARRYL GERROD
Professional football player. **Personal:** Born Nov 22, 1968, Cincinnati, OH. **Educ:** Univ of Tennessee, attended. **Career:** Arizona Cardinals, linebacker, 1995; Dallas Cowboys, 1995-97; Seattle Seahawks, 1997-. **Business Addr:** Professional Football Player, Seattle Seahawks, 11220 NE 53rd St, Kirkland, WA 98033, (206)827-9777.

HARDY, DOROTHY C.
Educational administrator. **Personal:** Born in Town Creek, AL; daughter of Lorean Cal and Odis Cal; children: Althea J Mootry. **Educ:** AL St U, BS; Xavier U, MEd; Univ of Cincinnati, EdD. **Career:** Univ of Cincinnati, Grps & Univ Progams, asst dean stdnts 1973-77; KS St U, asst prof & emp/rcrtmnt Spec; Univ of Cincinnati, instr; Cincinnati Life Adj Inst, pres 1980-83; OH Dept Mental Hlth, comm div bus adm 1983-84; Southeast Missouri State Univ, 1984-89; Hardy Residential Rentals, 1986-96; Single Parent Program, Cape Grardeau Area Vocational Technical School, coord, 1991-95; University of N Alabama, adjunct prof of English, 1997. **Orgs:** Human Invlvmnt Prog 1979; bus act Madisonville Job Training 1982; consult Archdiocese of Grtr Cincinnati 1983; Prog Assoc for Economic Dev; mnrty coord Issues 2 & 3 Ctzns for Gov Richard F Celeste 1983-84; training dir Mondale/Ferraro Camp 1984. **Honors/Awds:** Brodie Rsrch Award #1000 Plus 1975; Otstndg Comm Serv 1976; Otstndng Women NAACP 1981; Background Player "The Jesse Owens Story" Paramount Studio for ABC-TV 1984; Cert of Merit for the Fiction (Writer's Digest) Poetry (Creative Enterprise, World of Poetry) Pebble in the Pond 1985; Golden Poet Award 1986; Fiction published in the Summerfield Journal Castalia Publishers & Ellipsis, Literary Journal; Poetry published in Essence Magazine, 1989, 1991-93; Southwest Missouri State Univ Museum Exhibit, Black Women: Against the Odds, 1996; Alabama State Univ, Alumni of Distinction, 1997. **Home Addr:** 901 Pine St, Florence, AL 35630-3342.

HARDY, EURSLA DICKERSON
Educator, librarian (retired). **Personal:** Born May 5, 1933, Thibodaux, LA; daughter of Albertha Lucas Dickerson and McNeil Dickerson; married McHenry Hardy Jr., Jul 23, 1955; children: Timothy Wayne. **Educ:** Grambling State University, Grambling, LA, BS, 1951-55; Northwestern University & Grambling State University Library of Science, 1967; Prairie View A&M University, Prairie View, TX, MA. **Career:** West Baton Rouge Parish, Port Allen, LA, teacher, 1955-58; Caddo Parish School Board, Shreveport, LA, teacher/librarian, 1958-85. **Orgs:** Founder/organizer, 1990, Sigma Rho Omega Chapter, Alpha Kappa Alpha Sorority, 1990-92, anti-basileus, 1990-92; board member, Allendale Bnch, YWCA, 1991-92; mem, vice grand lady, Lady Auxillary of St Peter Claver; Shreveport Art Guild & Friends of Meadows Museum of Art, Centenary College, executive board member and corresponding secretary, 1994-95; CWW (Celebration of Women Week), steering committee member; charter member, Friends of the Library; board of directors, member, Northwest, Louisiana YWCA, 1992-1996; Volunteer Docent Meadows Museum Centenary College; Mentorship Program, Green Oaks Laboratory High School; Tutorial Program Volunteer, George P Hendrix Elementary School; Esquirettes Social Club, vice president; president, 1996-; Caddo Parish Career Ctr, bd of dirs, 1997-99. **Honors/Awds:** Newton Smith Elementary PTA Service Award, 1985; Recognition of Faithful Service Educator Award, Caddo Association of Educators, 1985; Bookworm Reading Club Librarian Award, 1977-78; Basileus, 1993-94; Sigma Rho Omega Chapter, Alpha Kappa Alpha Sorority Inc; won 1994 Outstanding Graduate Basileus Award, South Central Region, Alpha Kappa Alpha Sorority Inc; 1994 Outstanding Graduate Program Service Award 3rd Place; AKA Education Advancement Fund, 4 Stars Chapter Award, 1994; Hostess Chapter, Area Retreat AKA Certificate Award, 1993; "You are in the News," Outstanding Community Service Recognition by Shreveport Mayor Hazel Beard, 1994. **Special Achievements:** Zeta Phi Beta, Woman of the Year Award, 1997; "You Are in The News," Outstanding Comm Service Recognition. **Home Addr:** 106 Holcomb Dr, Shreveport, LA 71103.

HARDY, FREEMAN
Educator. **Personal:** Born May 22, 1942, Winona, MS; married Cozetta Hubbard; children: Tonya, Tasha. **Educ:** AR AM&N Coll, BS 1964; Howard Univ, DDS 1970; Georgetown Univ, MSc 1974. **Career:** AR AM&N Coll, lab instructor 1964; Howard Univ, instructor 1970-72; Georgetown, post-grad training 1972-74; HUCD, asst prof 1974-77, assoc prof 1977-83, prof 1983-; Howard Univ Coll of Dentistry, prof. **Orgs:** Consult Howard Univ Hosp; Oral Cancer Soc Chi Delta Mu; Omicron Kappa Upsilon; ADA; Robert T Freeman Dental Soc; NDA; Amer Coll of Prosthodontics; AADR; IADR; Sigma Xi; DC Dental Soc; Alpha Phi Alpha; Diagnosis & Treatment Planning for Rem Partial Dentures 1976; Comparison of Fluid Resin & Compression Molding Methods in Processing Dimensional Changes 1977.

HARDY, JOHN LOUIS. **See Obituaries section.**

HARDY, KEVIN
Professional football player. **Personal:** Born Jul 24, 1973, Evansville, IN. **Educ:** Univ of Illinois. **Career:** Jacksonville Jaguars, outside linebacker, 1996-. **Honors/Awds:** Selected to the All-American team as a freshman, 1992; First team All-Big Ten, 1994, 1995; Consensus All-American, 1995; Finalist for the Bronko Nagurski Award, 1995; Butkus Award, 1995. **Business Addr:** Professional Football Player, Jacksonville Jaguars, 1 Stadium Place, Jacksonville, FL 32202, (904)633-6000.

HARDY, MICHAEL A.
Attorney. **Personal:** Born Jul 2, 1955, New York, NY; son of William Hardy & Carmen Sanchez. **Educ:** Carleton College, BA, 1977; New York Law School, JD, 1988. **Career:** NYC Health and Hospital Corp, analyst, 1977-81; NYC Tax Commission, special asst, 1981-83; Natl Alliance Newspaper, exec ed, 1983-88; Intl Law Institute, attorney, 1988-92; Torres, Martinez, & Hardy, attorney/partner, 1992-. **Orgs:** Natl Bar Assn, 1988-; Assn Bar City of New York, 1988-; Natl Assn Criminal Defense Lawyers, 1990-; Natl Action Network, board member, 1989-. **Honors/Awds:** Somerset Comm Action Program, Distinguish Legal Service, 1989; Natl Action Network, Martin Luther King Service Award, 1993. **Special Achievements:** Author, Minister Louis Farrakhan, Practice Press, 1986; Narrator, A More Perfect Democracy, Film Documentary, 1988. **Business Addr:** Partner, Torres, Martinez & Hardy, 11 Park Pl, Rm 916, New York, NY 10007-2801.

HARDY, MICHAEL LEANDER
Marketing manager. **Personal:** Born Feb 21, 1945, Petersburg, VA; married Jacqueline; children: Sheila Jacqueline, Michelle Lorraine. **Educ:** Columbia Univ New York City NY, BS 1966; Rollins Coll Winter Park FL, MCS 1973. **Career:** The Carborundum Co, mge maint servs & repairs pangborn 1979-; The Carburundum Co Pangborn Div, mgr market planning & control 1973-79; Martin-marietta Corp Orlando Div, prog planning analyst 1967-71; Martin-marietta Corp Orlando Div, asso engr 1966-67. **Orgs:** Bd mem Bethel Corp 1979-; mem Citizens Adv Com Wash Co Bd of Edn; bd mem Big Bros of Wash Co; past pres Orange Co FL Br NAACP 1971-73. **Business Addr:** Pangborn Blvd, Hagerstown, MD 21740.

HARDY, TIMOTHY W.
Attorney. **Personal:** Born Feb 7, 1952, Shreveport, LA; married Stacia Saizon Hardy, Oct 5, 1985; children: Nicole Saizon, Amanda Victoria. **Educ:** Southern University, BS, 1978; Southern University Law Ctr, JD, 1981. **Career:** LA Department of Justice, assistant attorney general, lands & natural resources div, environmental section, 1981-88; LA Department of Environmental Quality, assistant secretary, OSHW, 1988-90; LA Governor's Office executive assistant for environmental affairs, 1990-92; LA Department of Justice, director of public protection div, 1992-94; Lemle & Kelleher, partner, currently. **Orgs:** LA State Bar Association; American Heart Association, East Baton Rouge Div, president; The Nature Conservancy of LA, board of trustees, board member; Baton Rouge Chamber of Commerce, graduate, leadership class of 1992; Council for a Better LA, graduate, LA Leadership Class of 1994; Mid City Redevelopment Alliance, board of directors, vice pres; National Organization for the Professional Advancement of Black Chemists and Chemical Engineers; Phi Alpha Delta Law Fraternity. **Home Addr:** 3070 Yorktown Dr, Baton Rouge, LA 70808, (504)924-9945. **Business Addr:** Partner, Lemle & Kelleher, LLP, 301 Main St, 1 American Pl, Ste 1800, Baton Rouge, LA 70825, (504)387-5068.

HARDY, WALTER S. E.
Physician. **Personal:** Born Oct 9, 1920, Alcoa, TN; married Edna D; children: Cheryl. **Educ:** Johnson C Smith Univ, BS 1938; Meharry Univ, MD 1950. **Career:** Private practice, physician. **Orgs:** Mem NMA, AMA, AAFP; bd chmn Hillcrest Med & Nursing Inst; past pres Volunteer State Med Assoc; bd mem Home Vstg Nursing Assoc; vice pres Knoxville Ambulance Auth; bd chmn Knoxville Area Urban League; Squire Knoxville Cty Court; past pres Volunteer Bowling League; mem Better Bus Bureau Knoxville, C of C; mem Selective Svc, TN State Voters Council; bd mem Girls Club of Amer; comm man-at-large Knoxville United Way; dir Health Serv Knoxville Coll. **Honors/Awds:** Omega Man of the Year 1970. **Military Serv:** AUS warrant officer 1942-45. **Business Addr:** 2210 Vine Ave, Knoxville, TN 37915.

HARDY, WILLIE J.
Legislator. **Personal:** Born Jul 18, 1922, St Louis, MO; daughter of Willie White and James White; widowed; children: Charles, DeSales, Joan, Linda, Marinne, Diana, Lloyd. **Educ:** Atlantic Business School; George Washington Univ. **Career:** Council of DC, chwmn councilwoman; Dept of Environ Svcs, dep dir; Ofc of Mayor, dep dir; Sen Phillip Hart Toastmistress Intl Toastmistress Club, staff asst; Com on Housing & Econ Devel, chwmn. **Orgs:** Life mem Nat Council of Negro Women; mem PA Ave Devel Corp; adjunct prof Antioch Sch of Law; mem Com on the Judiciary; mem Comm on Finance & Revenue; mem Com on Finance & Revenue; chwman Comm Task Force for Safety of Children & Youth 1973; exec dir Metro Comm Aid Council 1967-71; exec dir Howard Univ Nghbrhd Council; instr Fed City Coll; partic CORE effort to deseg food establ; partic SCLC voters regis drive; coord DC residents attng Selma-to-montgomery March. **Honors/Awds:** Outst Woman of WA Phi Lambda Theta Sor 1967; Woman of Yr Afro-am News-

papers & Greyhound & Corp 1972; Comm Serv Award Metro Police Dept 1974; Kiwanis Award Kiwanis Intl 1976; Antioch Sch of Law Fdrs Award 1976. **Business Addr:** Dist Bldg, Washington, DC 20004.

HARDY-HILL, EDNA MAE
Psychologist. **Personal:** Born Feb 14, 1943, Thomasville, GA; daughter of Hagar Harris Hardy and Leroy Hardy; married Davis Vincent, Jun 22, 1974; children: Davis Vincent Jr (deceased), Michael A. **Educ:** Bennett Coll, AB 1965; Howard Univ, MS 1968. **Career:** National Inst of Mental Health, health scientist admnstr 1974-83, resch psycgst 1968-74, Behavioral and Applied Review Branch, chief, currently. **Orgs:** Treas Assoc of Black Psychologist 1983 Natl Conv; mem Peoples Congregational Church; Bennett Coll Alumnea Assoc. **Honors/Awds:** Hnr soc Beta Kappa Chi; Pi Gamma Mu; Psi Chi; Howard Univ Flwshp 1966-67; Bennett Coll Scholarship 1961-65; Outstanding Work Performance NIMH 1982, 1985, 1987, 1989-95, NIMH Dir Award for Significant Achievement 1989, Special Achievement Award, 1997; Bennett College, Award for Outstanding Accomplishments in Chosen Profession, 1993. **Business Addr:** Chief, Behavorial and Applied Review Branch, Natl Inst of Mental Health, 5600 Fishers Lane 9C26, Rockville, MD 20857.

HARDY-WOOLRIDGE, KAREN E.
Insurance company executive. **Personal:** Born Oct 29, 1951, Chicopee, MA; daughter of Janet Elizabeth Chaffin Lee and Humphrey Christopher Hardy; married Victor Woolridge, Jun 2, 1985; children: James, Matoaca, Kara Jean, Kendra. **Educ:** Springfield Tech Community College, Springfield, MA, AS, 1971; University of North Carolina, Elizabeth City, NC, BS, business administration, 1974; Western New England College, 1978. **Career:** Martin Insurance Agency, Springfield, MA, insurance sales, 1974-81; Regency Cove Hotel, Barbados, West Indies, general manager, 1981-83; Massachusetts Mutual Life Insurance Co., Springfield, MA, sales division consultant/recruiting manager, beginning 1983, associate director of IFM Sales, district manager, staff plans, 1991-. **Orgs:** Participant, Pro-Motion, 1989, 1991-; mentor, I Have a Dream Program; women's division coordinator, Seventh-day Adventist, 1991; professional development board chairperson, 1990, professional development board vice-chair, 1989-90, Massachusetts Mutual Life Insurance; parent advisor, SDA Community Youth/Young Adult Choir, 1989-; SDA Community Services, volunteer, 1990-. **Business Addr:** Associate Director of IFM Sales, District Manager, Staff Plans, Massachusetts Mutual Life Insurance Company, 1295 State St, Springfield, MA 01105.

HARE, JULIA REED
Journalist. **Personal:** Born Nov 7, 1942, Tulsa, OK; married Dr Nathan Hare. **Educ:** Langston Univ, BA 1964; Roosevelt Univ Chicago, MMEd 1966; DC Teachers Coll, certified elem educ 1967. **Career:** Chicago Public Schs, teacher 1966; DC Teachers Coll, supr student teachers 1967-68; Natl Comm Against Discrimination in Housing, pub relations dir 1969-72; Univ of San Francisco, instructor 1969-70; Golden W Broadcasters KSFO radio, dir comm affairs 1973-; The Black Think Tank, exec dir, currently. **Orgs:** Mem No CA Broadcasters Assn 1973-; hon bd Sickle Cell Anemia Devel Rsch Found 1976-; bd Afro-Amer Cultural & Hist Soc 1978-; bd of dirs Bay Area Black United Fund 1979-; publ "Black Male/Female Relationships" 1979-. **Honors/Awds:** Outstanding Educator of the Yr World Book Ency & Am Univ 1967; Abe Lincoln Awd for Outstanding Broadcaster of the Yr 1975; Cert of Appreciation Sickle CellAnemia Rsch & Educ 1976; Meritorious Comm Serv Awd CA NG 1979; Special Serv Awd CA Soc of CPA 1980. **Special Achievements:** The Hare Plan to Overhaul the Public Schools and Educate Every Black Man, Woman and Child, 1991. **Business Addr:** Executive Director, The Black Think Tank, 1801 Brush Street, Ste. 127, San Francisco, CA 94109.

HARE, LINDA PASKETT
Educational administrator. **Personal:** Born Jun 10, 1948, Nashville, TN; daughter of Juanita Hicks Paskett and Hulit Paskett (deceased); married Dr George C Hill; children: Nicole, Brian. **Educ:** Tennessee State Univ, BA (w/distinction) 1969; Indiana Univ, MS, 1974; Tennessee State Univ, EdD, 1984. **Career:** Gary IN Schools, English teacher 1969-80; Tennessee State Univ, adjunct English instructor 1985-88; Meharry Medical Coll, asst dir/corp & fdn relations 1983-84, special asst & deputy to the vice pres 1983-87, asst vice pres for institutional advancement, 1987-90, executive asst to the pres and corporate secretary, 1990-92, vice pres of institutional advancement, 1992-95; Middle Tennessee State Univ, vp for development and univ relations, 1995. **Orgs:** Consultant, Natl Baptist Publishing Bd, 1983-84; Tennessee Planning Comm of Amer Council on Educ, Natl Identification Program (ACE/NIP) 1986-; participant, Leadership Nashville, 1990-91; Cumberland Museums, bd mem; Council of Community Services, bd mem; mem, Council for the Advancement & Support of Education Commission on Philanthropy; Phi Kappa Phi, National Honor Society; Leadership Nashville Alum. **Honors/Awds:** Graduate Fellowship Tennessee State Univ 1980-81. **Business Addr:** Vice Pres for Development & University Relations, Middle Tennessee State University, 209 Cope Administration Bldg, Murfreesboro, TN 37132.

HARE, NATHAN
Psychologist, sociologist. **Personal:** Born Apr 9, 1933, Slick, OK; son of Tishia Lee Davis Hare Farmer (deceased) and Seddie Henry Hare (deceased); married Julia Reed, Dec 27, 1956. **Educ:** Langston U, AB 1954; Univ of Chicago, MA 1957; Univ of Chicago, PhD Sociology 1962; CA Sch of Professional Psychology, PhD Clinical Psychology 1975. **Career:** The Black Scholar The Black World Found, founding pub; Howard U, asst prof sociology 1964-67; Black Male-female Relationships, editor 1979-82; priv practice & clinical psychology 1977-; San Francisco State Coll Dept of Black Studies, chmn 1968-69; Instr 1961-63 & 1957-58; San Francisco Stat, lecturer part-time, 1984-88; private practice, psychology; The Black Think Tank, chairman of the board 1979-. **Orgs:** No Am Zone Second World Black & African Festival of Arts & Culture; Black Speakers Club. **Honors/Awds:** Co-editor Contemporary Black Thought 1973; co-editor Pan-Africanism 1974; Author of The Black Anglo Saxons, The Endangered Black Family 1984, Bringing the Black Boy to Manhood 1985 & various articles in mag & journals; Distinguished Alumni Award Langston Univ 1975; presidential citation Natl Assn of Blacks in Higher Education 1981; Natl Awd Natl Council for Black Studies 1983; Crisis in Black Sexual Politics 1989; Fire on Mount Zion, 1990; The Hare Plan: To Educated Every Black Man, Woman and Child, 1991; shared Marcus and Amy Garvey Award, Institute of Pan African Studies, 1990; United Negro College Fund Distinguished Scholar at Large, 1990. **Home Phone:** (415)474-1707. **Business Addr:** Chief Executive Officer, The Black Think Tank, 18001 Bush St, Ste 118, San Francisco, CA 94109, (415)929-0204.

HARELD, GAIL B.
Association executive. **Personal:** Born Apr 20, 1954, Providence, RI. **Educ:** College of Our Lady of the Elms, BA 1976; Springfield Coll, MA 1979. **Career:** Digital Equipment Corp, production skills instructor 1976-80; WMAS radio, news anchor; Burroughs Corp, manufacturing production skills instructor 1980-83, corp opers quality standards coord 1983; Burroughs World Headquarters, mgr after hours prog 1983-84, project mgr human resources 1984-85; Burroughs Corp, reg area human resource mgr; Unisys Corp, regional human resource mgr/organizational devel specialist 1985-87; Philadelphia Orchestra Assn, dir of human resources, 1989-. **Orgs:** Mem Providence Urban League 1976-87; mem Impact Assocs of Philadelphia 1981-82, Natl Black MBA Assn Detroit Chap 1984-87, ASPA Amer Soc for Personnel Admin 1987; personnel comm Morris County Chamber of Commerce 1985-87. **Honors/Awds:** Comm Serv Awd Impact Assocs of Philadelphia 1982; Burroughs Exemplary Action Awd 1986. **Business Addr:** Director, Human Resources, The Philadelphia Orchestra Association, 1420 Locust St, Philadelphia, PA 19102.

HAREWOOD, DORIAN
Actor, vocalist. **Personal:** Born Aug 6, 1950, Dayton, OH; married Nancy Harewood, Feb 14, 1979; children: Olivia Ruth, John Dorian. **Educ:** University of Cincinnati Conservatory of Music, BMus, voice and piano. **Career:** Actor, vocalist; Theater appearances include: "Brainchild," 1974; "Over Here!," 1974; "Miss Moffat," 1974; "Don't Call Back," 1975; "The Mighty Gents," 1978; "To Sir with Love," 1989; "Jesus Christ, Superstar," US tour; "Madam Lilly," 1993; film appearances include: Sparkle, 1976; Gray Lady Down, 1978; Looker, 1981; Against All Odds, 1984; The Falcon and the Snowman, 1985; Full Metal Jacket, 1987; Pacific Heights, 1991; Star Fire, 1992; television appearances include: "Foster and Laurie," 1975; "Strike Force," 1981-82; "Trauma Center," 1983; "Glitter," 1984-85; "The New Adventures of Jonny Quest," voice characterization, 1987; "Sky Commanders," voice characterization, 1987; "Roots: The Next Generations," 1979; "Amerika," 1987; "Hope Division," 1987; "We Are Vivian Dawn," 1989; "Murder,e Wrote," 1986; "The Jesse Owens Story," 1984; "Guilty of Innocence: The Lenell Geter Story," 1987; "Teenage Mutant Ninja Turtles," voice characterization, 'Shredder', 1990-; "The California Raisins," voice characterization, 1991; "I'll Fly Away," 1992; "The Trials of Rosie O'Neill," 1992;. **Orgs:** Actors' Equity Assn; Screen Actors Guild; American Federation of Television & Radio Artists. **Honors/Awds:** Theatre World Award, Don't Call Back, 1975; Image Award, nomination, Guilty of Innocence: The Lenell Geter Story. **Special Achievements:** Singer/songwriter, "Dorian Harewood: Love Will Stop Calling," album, Emeric Records, 1989; series creator, "Half 'n' Half," 1988.

HARGRAVE, BENJAMIN
Educational administrator. **Personal:** Born Dec 18, 1917, Wakefield, VA; son of Laura Blow Hargrave and Benjamin Hargrave; married Carolease Faulkner, Aug 31, 1943 (deceased). **Educ:** Springfield College, BS, 1941; San Francisco State University, MA, 1951. **Career:** Livingstone Coll, athletic dir 1941-42; Oakland Public Schools, teacher, principal 1941-68; California State Employment Serv, deputy dir 1969-74; self-employed, educ consultant 1974-. **Orgs:** Pres California Assn Secondary School Admin 1966-68; mem bd of dir Ind Educ Council of California 1963-76; mem Natl Council Upward Bound 1964-66; mem Natl Advisory Council Nrs Training 1965-67; mem bd of dir NAACP, Oakland Branch; mem bd of dir Alameda Co Mental Health Assn 1951-56; pres Men of Tomorrow 1966. **Honors/Awds:** Distinguished Alum Award, Springfield Coll 1971; Governors Award Vocational Educ California 1974; NAACP Freedom Fund Award 1988. **Military Serv:** US Army, staff sgt, 1942-46. **Home Addr:** 3468 Calandria Ave, Oakland, CA 94605.

HARGRAVE, CHARLES WILLIAM
Scientist (retired). **Personal:** Born May 12, 1929, Dandridge, TN; son of Electa Tulip Snapp Hargrave and Walter Clarence Hargrave; married Iona Lear Taylor. **Educ:** Johnson C Smith Univ, BS 1949; Washington Univ St Louis, MA 1952. **Career:** Dept of the Navy, physicist 1954-55; US Atomic Energy Commission, scientific analyst 1955-62; Natl Aeronautics and Space Admin, technical information 1962-89. **Orgs:** Advisory neighborhood commissioner DC Government 1979-84, 1991-96; pres First District Police Adv Cncl 1985-88; mem Mayor's Adv Comm on Budget and Resources; SW Neighborhood Assembly; Omega Psi Phi. **Honors/Awds:** Award of Merit JCSU Alumni Association 1979; Spaceship Earth NASA 1982, 1988; Alumni Award UNCF, Washington 1983. **Military Serv:** AUS 1952-54; USNR, 1955-89, retired; reserve unit co 1984-86. **Home Addr:** 600 Third St SW, Washington, DC 20024.

HARGRAVE, THOMAS BURKHARDT, JR.
Association executive. **Personal:** Born Oct 5, 1926, Washington, GA; married Meredith Higgins; children: Kenneth, Anna. **Educ:** Knoxville Coll, AB 1951; Springfield Coll, grad study. **Career:** James Welden Johnson Br YMCA FL, exec dir 1960-64; Pasadena YMCA, asst gen exec 1964-68; YMCA of LA, assoc gen exec 1968-71; YMCA of Metro Washington, pres 1973-. **Orgs:** Mem Rotary Club Intl; adv bd Studio Theatre; adv comm Tom Sawyer Training School; mem YMCA African Crisis Comm. **Honors/Awds:** Good Conduct USAF 1947; Cert of Civ Rights, FL NAACP 1964; author "Private Differences-General Good, A History of the YMCA of Metropolitan Washington," 1985. **Military Serv:** USAF sgt 1945-47. **Business Addr:** President, YMCA Metropolitan Washington, 1625 Massachusetts Ave, NW, Ste 700, Washington, DC 20036.

HARGRAVES, WILLIAM FREDERICK, II
Military pilot. **Personal:** Born Aug 18, 1932, Cincinnati, OH; son of Annie L Hargraves and William F Hargraves; married Maurine Collins; children: William III, Jock, Charles. **Educ:** Miami Univ, BS (Cum Laude) 1954, MA 1961. **Career:** USAF, rsch physicist 1961-65, aircraft commander 1965-70, air liaison ofcr 1970-71; Miami Univ, asst prof air sci 1971-74; Wright Patterson AFB, chief flight deck develop 1974-78; Pentagon Washington DC, deputy div chief 1978-82; Central State Univ, asst prof. **Orgs:** Founder Alpha Phi Alpha Miami Univ Chapt; leader/founder Pilgrim Baptist Men's Chorus; vice commander Veteran of Foreign Wars 1986; mem Phi Beta Kappa (first black in Miami chapt), Omicron Delta Kappa, Kappa Delta Pi, Pi Mu Epsilon; mem Sigma Pi Sigma, Phi Mu Alpha; charter mem Phi Kappa Phi. **Honors/Awds:** Rhodes Scholar candidate 1950; computer science advisor on North Central Evaluation Team and US Dept of Educ Washington DC; 6 publications "Magnetic Susceptability of Manganese Compounds," "The Effect of Shock Waves on various Plastic Nose Cone Materials"; Length, Mass, Time, & Motion in One Dimension (software program) 1986. **Military Serv:** USAF col 28 yrs; Air Force Commendation Medal w/two Oak Leaf Clusters, Flying Cross and Air Medal for Meritorious Achievement, Vietnam Serv Medal w/five Bronze Stars, Republic of Vietnam Commendation Medal, Natl Defense Service Medal. **Home Addr:** 123 W Walnut St, Oxford, OH 45056. **Business Addr:** Assistant Professor, Central State University, 210 Banneker Hall, Wilberforce, OH 45384.

HARGRETT, JAMES T., JR.
State senator. **Personal:** Born Jul 31, 1942, Tampa, FL; married Berlyn Chatard; children: Crystal Marie, James T, III. **Educ:** Morehouse Coll, AB 1964; Atlanta U, MBA 1965. **Career:** US Comptroller Currency, natl bank examiner, 1965-67; Aetna Life & Casualty Co, insurance underwriter, 1967-68; Leadership Devel Prog Tampa Urban League, dir, 1968-69; Community Fed Sav & Loan Assn, Tampa, FL, exec vice pres/manager, 1969-82; Florida State Representative, District 63, 1983-92; Florida state senator, 1992-. **Orgs:** Treasurer, Urban League 1971-75; cit adv com Hillsborough Co Sch Bd 1974-; Dem Exec Com 1974; member, Greater Tampa Chamber of Commerce; board of directors, United Way of Tampa; member, Florida Housing Adv Committee; member, Florida Sheriffs Assn; member, Tampa Bay Area Committee on Foreign Relations; member, Florida Council on Crime and Delinquincy. **Honors/Awds:** Omega Man of the Year, Omega Psi Phi Fraternity, 1971; Meritorious Community Service, Housing Urban League, 1971; Golden Sable Community Leadership Award, 1979; Martin Luther King Memorial Award, Tampa Organization of Black Affairs, 1986; Leadership Award, Florida Voter League, 1985; Appreciation Award, Florida Grape Growers Assn, 1984. **Business Addr:** Florida State Senator, District 21, PO Box 11025, Tampa, FL 33680.

HARGROVE, ANDREW
Engineer, educator. **Personal:** Born Apr 1, 1922, Richmond, VA; children: Andrea Marie, Larry. **Educ:** City Coll of NY, BEE 1966; NYU, MS 1968; PA State Univ, PhD 1975. **Career:**

New York City Bd of Educ, teacher 1960-62; New York City Transit Auth, elec engr 1962-68; PA State Univ, instructor 1972-74; Tuskegee Inst, prof 1979-83; Andrew Hargrove Consulting Engineer, proprietor 1986-; Hampton Univ, prof, 1983-87; Norfolk State University, professor, currently. **Orgs:** Committeeman NY Co 1966-70; registered prof engr NY, VA; mem Power Engrg Soc, Control Systems Soc, Inst of Elec & Electronic Engrs, Natl Soc of Prof Engrs, Amer Soc for Engrg Educ, Natl Tech Assn, Alpha Kappa Mu, Omega Psi Phi; mem Virginia Waste Mgmt Bd 1986-88. **Honors/Awds:** Mem Alpha Kappa Mu Honor Soc, Eta Kappa Nu Electrical Engineering Honor Soc; numerous books published. **Business Addr:** Professor, Norfolk State University, PO Box 2449, Norfolk, VA 23504.

HARGROVE, JOHN E.
Labor relations consultant. **Personal:** Born Dec 28, 1903, Texas. **Educ:** Wilberforce U, BS; Western Univ bus law & commerce 1922; KS state coll, grad work; u of CA, special work in labor. **Career:** Wells Fargo, labor rel consultant; tchr 5yrs; Fed Govt, labor rel advisor 1943; Unv of CA, special work in labor 1947; LA Co Grand Jury 1944 & 1971. **Orgs:** Pres SE Symp Assn; Our Authors Study Club; chmn bd dir Urban League; mem NAACP; Panhellenic; Comm Chest-United Way Campaign. **Honors/Awds:** Plaque Kappa Alpha Psi 1970; CA State Senate 1973; 34yr diamond feather United Way; Award of life membership for organizing Dining Car Employees on a major A-1 railroad Local Union No 465 AFL-CIO served as dist dir 12 yrs Pacific Coast Regional chmn of Joint Council 6 yrs; elec mem adv com LA City Unified Sch Dist Vol & Tutorial Prgms; mem Adv Com LA City Recreation Parks Dept Festival in Black; CA St Dir ofBr Assn for the Study of Afro-am Life & History; Cleveland OH Wilberforce Univ Natl Alumni Assn awarded 50 yr Gold Cert & Gold Green Pin Hon & given Cert for Meritorious Community Serv by LA Human Rel Commn 1977. **Business Addr:** 1200 Commonweatlh Ave, Fullerton, CA.

HARGROVE, JOHN R.
Judge. **Personal:** Born Oct 25, 1923, Atlantic City, NJ; married Shirley Ann Hayes; children: John R, Jr, Steven L, Janet Ruth, Lora Frances. **Educ:** Morgan State Coll, 1941-43; Army Spec Training Prog Engring, 1943-44; Howard U, BA 1946-47; Univ of MD Law Sch, LLB 1947-50. **Career:** Supreme Bench of Baltimore City, judge; Dist Ct of MD #1 Baltimore City, judge 1971-74; Munic Ct of Baltimore City, asso judge 1968-71; Howard & Hargrove, asso with law firm 1963-68; Peoples Ct Baltimore City, asso judge 1962-63; desig deputy US atty 1957-62; MD Dist, asst US atty 1955; gen prac 1950-55; MD Ct of Appeals, admitted to prac 1950. **Orgs:** Mem Baltimore City Bar Assn; Monumental City Bar Assn; MD State Bar Assn; Character Comm Ct of Appeals of MD; Nat Bar Assn; mem Adv Bd of Trustees Sheppard Pratt Hosp; bd of trustees Univ of MD Alumni Assn Internatl; Exec Com MD Judic Council; former chmn Character Comm Eighth Cir Ct of App; Adv Bd of Correc State of MD; Good Samaritan Hosp; Commis on Revision Crim Law & Proc; dele MD Const Conv; mem Comm on Judic; State ConstConv Commn; mem Comm on the Judic. **Military Serv:** AUS sgt 1943-46. **Home Addr:** 3524 Ellamont Rd, Baltimore, MD 21215.

HARGROVE, MILTON BEVERLY
District superintendent, clergyman. **Personal:** Born Oct 25, 1920, Birmingham, AL; son of Ruth Hargrove and Beverly Hargrove; married Blanche; children: Beverly III, Gayle, Ruth, William, John. **Educ:** Miles Coll, AB; Birmnghm AL; Gammon Theol Sem; MDiv Doctor Ministry, Drew Univ, Madison, NJ, DMin, 1982. **Career:** Galilee United Methodist Church, pastor; Trinity United Methodist Church, United Methodist Church, dist supt; E Meth Baltimore MD, pastor; Asbury Meth Hagerstown MD; Buena Vista Pitts PA; Simpson Meth Charleston WV; St Marks United Meth Montclair NJ; First Methodist United Methodist, Plainfield, NJ; United Methodist Church, Baltimore, MD, currently. **Orgs:** Mem Nu Beta Beta Chap of Omega Psi Phi Frat. **Honors/Awds:** John A Holmes Lodge #89 Free & Accep Masons Hon Cit Town of Montclair 1968. **Business Addr:** Clergyman, United Methodist Church, 730 Whitmore Ave, Baltimore, MD 21216.

HARGROVE, TRENT
Attorney. **Personal:** Born Aug 25, 1955, Harrisburg, PA; son of Odessa Daniels Hargrove and Willie Clarence Hargrove Sr; married Eugenia Russell Hargrove, Sep 8, 1984; children: Channing Leah, Tyler Trent. **Educ:** Bucknell Univ, Lewisburg PA, BA, 1977; Dickinson Law School, Carlisle PA, JD, 1980. **Career:** Office of Attorney General, Harrisburg PA, deputy atty, 1979-81; Pennsylvania Housing Finance Agency, Harrisburg PA, asst counsel, 1981-86; McNees Wallace & Nurick, assoc, 1987-90; Pennsylvania Department of Transportation, assistant counsel in charge of utilities, 1990-92; Office of Attorney General, chief deputy attorney general, Civil Rights Enforcement, 1992-. **Orgs:** Mem, Harrisburg Jaycees, 1984-, Dauphin County Bar Assn, 1986-; pres, Harrisburg Black Attorneys, 1986-87; bd mem, Volunteer Center, 1986-; external vice pres, Harrisburg Jaycees, 1986-87; mem exec comm, NAACP, 1987-; chmn mgmt comm, Volunteer Center, 1988-; bd mem, Harrisburg Sewer & Water Authority, 1988-; Harrisburg Authority, chairman, 1991-; Omega Psi Phi Fraternity, 1986-. **Home Addr:** 3018 Green St, Harrisburg, PA 17110.

HARKEY, MICHAEL ANTHONY (MIKE)
Professional baseball player. **Personal:** Born Oct 25, 1966, San Diego, CA. **Educ:** California State University, Fullerton. **Career:** Chicago Cubs, pitcher, 1988, 1990-94; Colorado Rockies, 1994-. **Honors/Awds:** Shares major league record for most putouts (3) by a pitcher in one inning, 1990; Sporting News, National League Rookie Pitcher of the Year, 1990. **Business Addr:** Professional Baseball Player, Colorado Rockies, 2001 Blake St, Denver, CO 80205-2000, (303)292-0200.

HARKINS, ROSEMARY KNIGHTON
Educational administrator. **Personal:** Born Aug 5, 1938, Amarillo, TX; daughter of Cloteal Knighton and Herbert Knighton; divorced. **Educ:** Amarillo Jr Coll, AA 1957; West TX State Univ, BS 1964; Univ of OK, MS 1971; Univ of OK Health Scis Ctr, PhD 1972; Central State Univ, BS 1976. **Career:** Veterans Admin Medical Center, hematology supvr 1968-70; Univ of OK Coll of Allied Health, asst prof 1972-77; School of Allied Health Professions Univ of OK, dir & assoc prof 1977-81; Univ of OK Coll of Allied Health, assoc dean & prof 1981-88; Howard Univ, Dean, College of Allied Health Sciences 1988-. **Orgs:** Consul Petroleum Training & Tech Serv Workman Inc 1978; consul Bd of Regents FL State Univ System 1983; consul Amer Physical Therapy Assn 1983; chmnbd dirs OK Minority Business Develop Center US Dept of Commerce 1982-88; vice chair bd of trustees OK Inst for Child Advocacy 1983-87; natl sec bd dirs Amer Soc of Allied Health Professions 1982-84; bd dirs mem Natl Adv Comm on Accreditation & Inst Eligibility 1981-83; mem, exec council, Natl Institute of Disability and Rehabilitation, US Dept of Education. **Honors/Awds:** Fellow Amer Soc of Allied Health Professions Washington DC 1984; Fellowship for Advanced Studies Ford Found 1971-72. **Military Serv:** US Army Reserve, colonel, 1981-91. **Business Addr:** Dean, College of Allied Health Sciences, Howard University, Washington, DC 20059.

HARKLESS-WEBB, MILDRED
Educator. **Personal:** Born Aug 17, 1935, Cedar Lane, TX; daughter of Cody Powell Harkless and Mayfield Harkless; married James E Webb, Jun 27, 1981. **Educ:** Prairie View A&M, BS 1957; San Francisco State Univ, MA 1976. **Career:** Webb's Pest Control, vice pres 1979-; Everett Middle School, teacher, currently. **Orgs:** Sponsor Scholarship Soc 1968-; mem NEA, CTA, ISBE, WBEA, CBEA, ABE 1970-; mem NAACP 1974-; staff rep ALC SFCTA 1976-; facilitator NBEA 1976-; sponsor Black Student Club 1983-; mem, Commonwealth Club of California, 1988-; co-chair, Self-Esteem/Student Performance Committee; San Francisco Business Chamber of Commerce Leadership Class, presenter, 1988. **Home Addr:** 35 Camellia Pl, Oakland, CA 94602. **Business Addr:** Teacher, Everett Middle School, 450 Church St, San Francisco, CA 94114.

HARKNESS, JERRY
Association executive. **Personal:** Born May 7, 1940, New York, NY; son of Lucille Harkness and Lindsay Harkness; married Sarah; children: Jerald, Julie Lyn, Brandon. **Educ:** Loyola Univ, Chicago, IL, BS, sociology, 1963. **Career:** Professional basketball player: New York Knicks, 1964, Indiana Pacers, 1968-69; United Way, campaign associate, 1969-; WTHR TV-13, weekend sports caster, 1969-81; Morning sports anchor WTLC Radio; Indiana Pacers, Indianapolis, IN, basketball analyst, 1983; Sports Channel, Chicago, IL, basketball analyst, 1988-; United Way of Central Indiana, director of community affairs, beginning, 1985; The Athlete's Foot, co-owner/manager, currently. **Orgs:** 100 Blackmen of Indianapolis, Inc, Executive board of directors, 1986-, exec director, 1997; member, Council of Black Executives, 1987-; board of directors, Police Athletic League of Indianapolis, 1986-. **Honors/Awds:** NCAA Silver Anniversary Basketball Team, 1988; 20 yr Volunteer Award, Indiana Black Expo, 1990; hit longest basketball 3-point shot in history, 1967; NCAA Champs, Loyola of Chicago, 1963; MVP, East West Allstar Game, 1963; Two time All-American; Boy Scouts This is your Life Award; Eastern Star Baptist Church. **Business Addr:** Co-owner/Manager, The Athlete's Foot, Circle Centre Mall, Indianapolis, IN 46208.

HARLAN, CARMEN
Broadcast journalist. **Personal:** Born Nov 4, 1953, Detroit, MI. **Educ:** University of Michigan. **Career:** WDIV-TV, Channel 4, Detroit, MI, news anchor, 1978-. **Honors/Awds:** Feted by National Coalition of 100 Black Women, Detroit, MI; selected as Detroit's top news anchor, Ladies Home Journal magazine, 1991. **Business Addr:** Anchorwoman, WDIV-TV, Channel 4, 550 W Lafayette, Detroit, MI 48226, (313)222-0444.

HARLAN, EMERY KING
Attorney. **Personal:** Born Jan 18, 1965, Gary, IN; son of Bertha Harlan and Wilbert Harlan. **Educ:** Siena Heights College, BA, 1986; University of Wisconsin Law School, JD, 1989. **Career:** US Court of Appeals for the Sixth Circuit, law clerk to the Honorable George Edwards; Ross & Hardies, labor & employment attorney, currently. **Orgs:** American Bar Association, vice chairman general practice section, Corporate Counsel Committee; Chicago Bar Association, minority counsel program steering committee; Democratic Leadership for the 21st Century, steering committee. **Honors/Awds:** University of Wisconsin Law School, Ray & Ethel Brown Scholarship, 1988. **Business Addr:** Attorney, Ross & Hardies, 150 N Michigan Ave, Suite 2500, Chicago, IL 60601-7567, (312)750-3617.

HARLESTON, BERNARD WARREN
Educational administrator. **Personal:** Born Jan 22, 1930, New York, NY; son of Anna Tobin H and Henry Mitchell Harleston; married Marie Ann Lombard; children: David Warren, Jeffrey Stuart. **Educ:** Howard Univ, BS 1951; Univ of Rochester, PhD 1955. **Career:** Univ of Rochester, instructor 1954-55, asst prof 1955-56, rsch assoc 1956; Lincoln Univ, provost & prof of psychology 1968-70, acting provost 1970; Tufts Univ, asst prof & prof of psychology 1956-68, 1970-80, prof psychology dean faculty arts & scis 1970-80, Moses Hunt prof psychology 1980-81; City Coll of the City Univ, pres, 1981-92. **Orgs:** Corp of MA Inst of Tech 1982-87; mem Visiting Comm to the Dept of Psychology & Social Rela at Harvard Univ 1982-; mem Bd of the Josiah Macy Jr Found 1984-; Mayor's Commn on Black New Yorkers of the City of New York 1986-, Mayor's Task Force Commn on the Homeless of the City of NY 1986-, Bd of the Afrian Amer Inst 1986-; adv cncl presidents to the Assoc of Governing Bds of Univs and Colls 1986-; Assn of Amer Coll Bd Member, 1982-86, chmn 1985-86; chmn, Mayor's Commn for Science and Technology of New York City 1984-87, bd mem, 1987-; co-chmn of the New York State Educ Department's Task Force on Children and Youth at Risk; Bd of the New York Hall of S cience, 1988-; mem, Advisory Comm to the New York Historical Society, 1988-;SSBd, Fund for NY Public Educ, 1988-; the Council on Foreign Rtions, 1989-. **Honors/Awds:** John H Franklin Awd from Tufts Univ African-Amer Cultural Ctr 1980; Psychologist of the Yr Awd from NY Soc of Clin Psychol 1983; Honorary Degrees Dr of Sci Univ of Rochester 1972, Dr of Laws Temple Univ 1982; New York Urban League's Frederick Douglass Awd 1986; Dr of Laws Hon Doctorate Lincoln Univ 1986; Distinguished Educator Award from the New York City Assn for Supervision and Curriculum Devel, 1988; recipient of invitation to participate in the Japan Foundation's Short-Term Visitors Program, 1988; Howard Univ Alumni Award for Distinguished Postgraduate Achievement in the Fields of Educ and Admin, 1989.

HARLESTON, ROBERT ALONZO
University administrator, educator. **Personal:** Born Jan 28, 1936, Hempstead, NY; son of Anna Elizabeth Tobin Harleston (deceased) and Henry M. Harleston Sr. (deceased); married Sheila C. Harleston; children: Robert, Bernice, Paul. **Educ:** Howard University, Washington, DC, BA, 1958; Michigan State University, East Lansing, MI, MS, 1965; Georgetown Law Center, Washington, DC, JD, 1984. **Career:** Criminal Justice Program, University of Maryland, Eastern Shore, director, currently. **Orgs:** Govenors Education Coordinating Committee on Correctional Institutions, 1997-; bd of dirs, Eastern Shore Red Cross, 1990-93; bd of dirs, Delmarva Boy Scouts, 1990-93; member, Rotary Club, 1990-93; member, Black Advisory Committee to the Episcopal Bishop, 1990-; member, Omega Psi Phi, 1953-; Interview Committee, Habitat for Humanity, 1995-. **Honors/Awds:** Maryland Classified Employees Association, Martin Luther King Jr Award, 1996. **Military Serv:** US Army, Brigadier General, 1959-89; numerous awards. **Home Addr:** 30420 Mallard Dr, Delmar, MD 21875.

HARLEY, DANIEL P., JR.
Government employee. **Personal:** Born Feb 16, 1929, Shelby, NC; married Lillian L Dent; children: Daniel, III. **Educ:** SC State Coll, BS 1954; Atlanta U, MSW 1956; Univ IL, 1957-58. **Career:** House, comm 1954-57; Kenwood Ellis Comm Center, 1957-60; Parkway Comm House, exec dir 1960-65; Neighborhood Youth Corps US Dept Labor Wash 1965-66; New York City BWTP, dep regional dir 1966-68; Bur Work Training Programs, regional dir 1968-70; Chicago, asso regional manpower adminstr 1970-72; Equal Employment Opportunity US Dept Labor, dir 1972-; Harrisburg PA, on loan to commonwealth of PA to head office of affirmative action 1976-78. **Orgs:** Mem Nat Assn Social Workers; Acad Certified Social Workers; NAACP; Chicago Urban League; Chicago Hearing Soc; Alpha Phi Alpha Frat; mem bd dir Chicago Hearing Soc Cosmopolitan C of C. **Honors/Awds:** Outstanding Citizen Award 1971; Certificate Performance Award US Dept Labor Manpower Adminstrn 1974. **Military Serv:** 1st lt 1946-51. **Business Addr:** Chicago, IL 60604.

HARLEY, LEGRAND
Association executive. **Personal:** Born Jan 19, 1956, Florence, SC; son of Willie Harley. **Educ:** Francis Marion College, Florence, SC, BS, political science, 1981. **Career:** Red Carpet Inn, Florence, SC, assistant manager, 1973-80; Florence County Community on Alcohol & Drugs, residential manager, 1981-84; South Carolina Dept of Youth Services, Columbia, SC, youth counselor, 1984-86; Lt Gov Mike Daniel, Columbia, SC, field coordinator, 1986-87; South Carolina Attorney General Office, Columbia, SC, administrative assistant, 1987-92; Merchants Assn of Florence, coordinator, 1993-95; Florence County Treasurer, asst, 1995-. **Orgs:** Pres, chairman, emeritus, South Carolina Young Democrats, Black Caucus, administrative board, lay leader, life member, Salem United Methodist Church; legal redress committee, leader, NAACP, 1982-; field representative, Florence Jaycees, 1980-82. **Honors/Awds:** Young Man of the Year, The Key Inc, 1980; Outstanding Young Men of America, US Jaycees, 1981; Young Democrats of Florence, Florence Young Democrats, 1982; Longest Serving Young Democrat in South Carolina, South Carolina Democratic Party, 1988; Outstanding & Most Loyal Young Democrat, South Carolina

Young Democrats, 1989. **Home Addr:** 209 Pearl Circle, Florence, SC 29501. **Business Addr:** Assistant, Florence County Treasurer, 180 N Irby St, City-County Complex Bldg, Florence, SC 29501.

HARLEY, PHILIP A.
Educator. **Personal:** Born in Philadelphia; married Ireleen I; children: Anthony, Antoinette, Richard, Michael, Bruce, Annette, Terri. **Educ:** Morgan State Coll, BA 1945; Temple U; Univ Cincinnati; Capital Univ Sch Theol; Garrett Theol Sem, MDiv 1956. **Career:** IL, IN, OH, SD, WI, pastor; Garrett Theol Seminary, assoc prof. **Orgs:** Chmn Regional Consultative Com Race; Mayors Com Human Relations; dist dir Research & Devel; ministries educ IN, SD; prog leadership devel Prog Council Northern IL Conf; v chmn Leadership Devel Com N Central Jurisdictron; regional vice pres Nat Com Black Churchmen; chmn Chicago Coordinating Com Black Churchmen; v chmn Serv Review Panel Comm Fund; Ch Federation Met Chicago; Chicago Conf Religion & Race; mem bd dir Welfare Council Met Chicago. **Military Serv:** USNR sp/x 1944-46. **Business Addr:** Garrett-Evangelical Seminary, Field Education Office, 2121 Sheridan Road, Evanston, IL 60201.

HARMON, CLARENCE
City official. **Educ:** Northeast Missouri State Univ, BS; Webster Univ, MPA, criminal justice and public administration. **Career:** St Louis Police Dept, various positions, commander of area I, 1988-90, Board of Police Commissioners, secretary, until 1991, chief of police, 1991-97; City of St Louis, mayor, 1997-. **Orgs:** International Association of Chiefs of Police; American Management Association; Webster University, board of trustees; St Louis Science Center, board of trustees; St Louis Symphony, board of directors; VP Fair Foundation, board of directors; Missouri Botanical Garden, board of directors; United Way of St. Louis, board of directors. **Honors/Awds:** Metropolitan Police Department, City of St Louis, four Letters of Commendation for outstanding performance of duty; Missouri Police Chiefs' Association, Police Chief of the Year, 1995; Donforth Foundation Fellow, John F. Kennedy School of Government, Howard University. **Special Achievements:** First African American chief of police in the St Louis Police Dept; developed Community Oriented Policing Service program as area commander at the St Louis Police Dept; implemented gun buy-back program as chief of the St Louis Police Dept, 1991. **Business Addr:** Mayor, City of St Louis, 1200 Market St, City Hall, Rm 200, St Louis, MO 63103.

HARMON, JAMES F., SR.
Business executive. **Personal:** Born Apr 18, 1932, Savannah, GA; married Clarissa V Poindexter; children: James F Jr, Valerie H Seay, Laurence E, Wendell E. **Educ:** NC A&T Coll, BS 1954; Troy State Univ, MS 1974; Air Univ, Sqd Officer School 1960-61. **Career:** Atlanta Marriott Hotels, personnel dir 1975-80; Marriott Hotels, reg dir of training 1980-82; Courtyard by Marriott Hotels, prop mgr 1983; Atlanta Perimeter Ctr Marriott, res mgr 1982-. **Orgs:** Mem Alpha Phi Alpha 1952-; pres Atlanta Falcon Club Inc 1983-; chmn Ed Comm of Natl Hosp Ed Mgr Assoc 1983. **Military Serv:** USAF lt col 1954-74; Command Pilot DFC, Air Medal, DSM, Vietnam Serv Medal. **Home Addr:** 3945 Somerled Trail, College Park, GA 30349. **Business Addr:** Manager, Marriott Hotel, 246 Perimeter Center Pkwy, Atlanta, GA 30346.

HARMON, JESSIE KATE. See PORTIS, KATTIE HARMON.

HARMON, JOHN H.
Attorney. **Personal:** Born Feb 10, 1942, Windsor, NC. **Educ:** BA 1963; Bach of Law 1965. **Career:** US Dept of Labor, solictor's off 1965-66; US House of Rep Com on Educ & Labor, asst coun 1966-67; Harmon & Raynor, owner 1967-. **Orgs:** Mem Fed Bar Assn, Craven Co Bar Assn, Nat Conf of Black Lawyers NC Academy of Trial Lawyers, Omega Psi Phi Frat; pres NC Assn of Black Lawyers; mem NAACP, SCLC, Black Prog Businessmen Inc; pres New Bern Chap NC Central Univ Alumni Assoc; pres Craven County Bar Assoc 1985-86. **Honors/Awds:** Merit Awd NC Cent Univ Sch of Law 1974. **Military Serv:** USAR e-5 1966-72. **Business Addr:** Owner, Harmon & Raynor, 1017 C Broad St, New Bern, NC 28560.

HARMON, M. LARRY
Industrial relations executive. **Personal:** Born Nov 15, 1944, Kansas City, MO; son of Vivian N Berry Harmon and E Morris Harmon; married Myrna L (Hestle); children: Robert T, M Nathan, Dana E. **Educ:** Rockhurst Coll, Kansas City MO, BA Industrial Relations, 1971; Univ of Massachusetts, Amherst MA, MBA, 1972. **Career:** Joseph Schlitz Brewing Co, Milwaukee WI, corporate employment mgr, 1978, Syracuse NY, industrial relations mgr, 1978-80; Anheuser-Busch Inc, Syracuse NY, industrial relations mgr, 1980-85, St Louis MO, sr exec asst, 1985-87, Baldwinsville NY, employee relations mgr, 1987-. **Orgs:** Mem, Amer Soc Personnel Admin, 1976-; Kappa Alpha Phi, 1982-; exec bd mem, Personnel Mgmt Council, 1987-; bd of dir, Onondaga County Uran League, 1987-. **Honors/Awds:** Black Achievers in Indus, YMCA of Greater New York, 1979; NAACP Image Award, Outstanding Men Achievers, 1989. **Military Serv:** US Navy, petty officer, 1962-66, Vietnam Serv Medal. **Business Addr:** Employee Relations Manager, Anheuser-Bush Inc, PO Box 200, Baldwinsville, NY 13027.

HARMON, SHERMAN ALLEN
Community relations representative (retired). **Personal:** Born Aug 6, 1916, Washington, IN; son of Rosa Lawhorn Harmon and Sherman Harmon; married; children (previous marriage): John Charles, Josephine Harmon Williams, Allen Sherman. **Educ:** Hampton Institute, BS, 1939; University of Pittsburgh, graduate work. **Career:** Centre Ave YMCA Pgh, prog exec, 1941-47; Moreland YMCA, Dallas TX, exec dir, 1947-49; Christian St YMCA, Philadelphia PA, prog dir, 1949-52; NC Mutual Life Co, Philadelphia PA, insurance counselor, 1952-54; Philadelphia United Way Fund, peer counselor, 1954-57; Redevelopment Auth of Phila, dir com rels, 1957-80. **Orgs:** Mem Metro Bd, mem Intl Comm of Natl Council, chair exec comm of Natl Youth Workers, YMCA; intl pres, Y's Men Intl, 1973-74; bd of Natl Council of YMCAs; NAACP; Urban League; mem Philadelphia Presbytery; chmn joint comm on merger of Faith & Second Presbyterian Churches into Germantown Comm Presbyterian Church; president, Phila Chapter Hampton Alumni Association, 1980-82. **Honors/Awds:** Man of the Year Y's Men of Philadelphia 1971; Family Man of the Year Natl Conf of Black Families 1980; 1st black intl dir for PA, 1st black intl serv coord, 1st black elected to Intl Exec Comm, 1st black vp; 1st black pres YMCA Men's Intl; World-Wide Service Club YMCAs of 60 Countries; Travels 200,000 miles visiting YMCAs in 35 countries. **Home Addr:** 134 W Upsal St, Philadelphia, PA 19119.

HARMON, WILLIAM WESLEY
Educator. **Personal:** Born May 26, 1941, Charlotte, NC; son of Evelyn M Norman; married Beverly J Pines; children: Hilary. **Educ:** Johnson C Smith Univ, BS 1968; Seton Hall Univ, MA 1978; Kansas State Univ, PhD 1984. **Career:** University Rsch Corp, consultant 1969-70; Univ of Medicine & Dentistry of NJ, dir student affairs 1970-80; The Wichita State Univ, asst dean 1980-85, dean 1985-90; vice pres, 1990-. **Orgs:** Consultant NC Public Health Adv Council 1968; pres Boys Club of Newark, NJ 1974; chairperson Council for Higher Educ Newark, NJ 1974-75; mem Health Professions Educ Adv Council NJ 1976-79; chairman Community Adv Bd Kean College NJ 1978-80; mem United States Jaycees 1980; mem Accreditation Team Amer Medical Assoc 1982-; pres Youth Development Service 1984. **Honors/Awds:** Mem Phi Delta Kappa 1981; mem Phi Kappa Phi 1982; Leadership Kansas KS Chamber of Commerce 1986; 20 articles in professional journals; 25 presentations at natl meetings. **Military Serv:** AUS E-4 3 yrs; Honorable Discharge 1962.

HARPER, ALPHONZA VEALVERT, III
Dentist. **Personal:** Born Feb 5, 1948, Alexander City, AL; son of Barbara B Harper and Alphonza V Harper; married Debra Sanders; children: Niaya A Harper. **Educ:** TN State Univ, BS 1969; Meharry Med Coll, DDS 1975. **Career:** Self-employed dentist, St Louis, MO, currently. **Orgs:** Mem Amer Dental Assoc, Natl Dental Assoc, Greater St Louis Dental Soc, Mound City Dental Soc 1975-, NAACP 1980-; vice pres Normandy Kiwanis Club 1979-. **Business Addr:** Dentist, 6830 Natural Bridge, St Louis, MO 63121.

HARPER, ALVIN CRAIG
Professional football player. **Personal:** Born Jul 6, 1968, Lake Wells, FL; married Jamise; children: Alexis. **Educ:** University of Tennessee, BA in criminal justice. **Career:** Dallas Cowboys, wide receiver, 1991-94; Tampa Bay Buccaneers, 1995-96; Washington Redskins, 1997; New Orleans Saints, 1997-. **Special Achievements:** Selected in the 1st round/12th pick overall in the 1991 NFL Draft; played in Super Bowl XXVII and XXVIII. **Business Addr:** Professional Football Player, New Orleans Saints, 5800 Airline Hwy, Metairie, LA 70003, (504)733-0255.

HARPER, ARCHIBALD LEONARD
Lawyer. **Personal:** Born Dec 11, 1912, Atlanta, GA; son of Theodore & Gertrude Harper; married Georgia F Harper, Dec 28, 1938; children: Conrad K, John V, Richard S. **Educ:** Morehouse College, AB, 1938; Wayne State Univ, 1940-42; Detroit College of Law, JD, 1950. **Career:** Works Project Administration, investigator; Wayne County Dept of Social Welfare, social worker; Wayne County Probate Court, Juvenile Court, referee; self employed, lawyer, currently. **Military Serv:** US Army Air Corp, sergeant, 1944-46.

HARPER, BERNICE CATHERINE
Government official. **Personal:** Born Feb 24, Covington, VA; widowed; children: Reginald. **Educ:** VA State Coll, BS 1945; Univ of So CA, MSW 1948; Harvard Univ, MSC 1959; Faith Grant College, LLD, 1994. **Career:** Childrens Hospital, social worker 1947-57; City of Hope Medical Ctr, dir social work 1960-74; Dept of HEW, chief nh branch 1970-72, dir div of ltc 1973-77, spec asst to the dir hsqb 1977-79, medical care advisor. **Orgs:** Mem Bd Intl Hospice Inst, Bd Intl Council of SW US Comm; mem steering comm NASW. **Honors/Awds:** Ida M Cannon Awd AHA 1972; PHS Superior Serv Awd 1977; Better Life Awd AHCA 1978; HCFA Admin Awd 1982; Univ of Southern California, Los Angeles, Distinguished Member of Los Amigos Award, 1993; Natl Hospice Organization, Person of the Year Award, 1993; Francine F Douglas Award for Outstanding Contributions to Women's Causes, 1993; Natl Assn of Social Workers Inc, Knee-Wittman Health/Mental Health Outstanding Achievement Award, 1990; Faith Grant Coll, LLD, 1994. **Business Addr:** Medical Care Advisor, Dept of Health & Human Serv, 200 Independence Ave SW, Washington, DC 20201.

HARPER, CONRAD KENNETH
Attorney. **Personal:** Born Dec 2, 1940, Detroit, MI; son of Georgia F Hall Harper and Archibald L Harper; married Marsha L Wilson; children: Warren, Adam. **Educ:** Howard U, BA 1962; Harvard Law Sch LLB 1965. **Career:** NAACP Legal Defense Fund, law clk 1965-66, stf lwyr 1966-70; Simpson Thacher & Bartlett, assoc 1971-74, partner 1974-93; US Department of State, legal advisor, 1993-96; Simpson Thacher & Bartlett, partner, 1996-. **Orgs:** Rutgers Law Schl lctr 1969-70; Yale Law Schl Lctr 1977-81; US Dept HEW consltnt 1977; NY Pub Lib Trustee 1978-93; NY City Bar, president, 1990-92; mem brd of editors AM Bar Assoc Jrnl 1980-86; Comm on Admissions and Grievances US Crt of Appeals (2nd Cir) 1983, Chrmn 1987-93; Brd of Dir, co-chair, Lawyers Comm for Civil Rights under Law, 1987-89; Vestryman St Barnabas Epis Chrch, Irvington NY 1982-85; Fellow Am Bar Fndtn; Fellow Am Coll of Trial Lawyers; mem Cncl on Foreign Rltns; chancellor, Epis Diocese of NY, 1987-92; Council of Amer Law Inst, 1985-; trustee, William Nelson Cromwell Foundation, 1990-; trustee, Metropolitan Museum of Art, 1996-; director, American Arbitration Assn, 1990-93 1997-; director, NY Life Insurance Co, 1992-93, 1996-; director, Public Service Enterprise Group, 1997-. **Honors/Awds:** Honorary LLD, City University of New York, 1990; Fellow, American Academy of Arts and Sciences; Honorary LLD, Vermont Law School, 1994; Howard University, Alumni Achievement Award, 1994; The Federal Bar Council, Whitney North Seymour Award, 1994; Bishops Cross, Episcopal Diocese of New York, 1992; Phi Beta Kappa, 1962. **Business Addr:** Partner, Simpson Thacher & Bartlett, 425 Lexington Ave, New York, NY 10017.

HARPER, CURTIS
Educator, research scientist. **Personal:** Born May 13, 1937, Auburn, AL. **Educ:** Tuskegee Inst, BS 1959; Tuskegee Instit, MS 1961; IA State U, MS 1965; Univ of MO, PhD 1969. **Career:** Univ of NC Sch of Med, assoc prof 1976-; Nat Inst of Envrnmtl Hlth Scs, sr staff flw 1972-76; Ept of Pharmclgy Univ of NC, instr 1971-72; Dept of Biochem Univ of NC, resrch assoc 1970-71; Dept of Biochem & Moleculr Biophysics Yale U, resch assoc 1969-70. **Orgs:** Mem, Am Chem Soc; Am Asn for Advmnt of Sci; Soc of Sigma Xi; Soc of Toxicology; Am Soc for Pharmacology & Experimental Therapeutics Human Relat Commin 1970-74; Drug Act Com 1971-73; Interch Counc Soc Act Com 1971-74; bd mem NC Civ Lib Union 1976-; bd mem Interch Counc Housing Author 1977-. **Military Serv:** USAR capt 1963-65. **Business Addr:** Research Assoc, Univ of North Carolina, School of Medicine, Dept of Pharmacology, Chapel Hill, NC 27514.

HARPER, DAVID B.
President. **Personal:** Born Dec 3, 1933, Indianapolis, IN; married Mae McGee; children: Vicki Clines, Sharon Chaney, Wanda Mosley, Lydia Restivo, Kathleen Bass, Carol, Kyra, David, Daniel, Ralph. **Educ:** Arizona State Univ, BS 1963; Golden Gate Univ, MBA 1968; Wayne Law School. **Career:** Bank of America NT & SA, beginning 1963; First Independence Natl Bank Detroit, pres/CEO 1969-76; Gateway Natl Bank, pres/CEO 1976-83; County Ford Inc, president 1983-88; David B Harper Management Inc, pres, 1988-; New Age Financial Inc, pres/CEO, 1989-93. **Orgs:** K-Mart Corp, bd of dirs, 1975-; Student Marketing Loan Assn, bd of dirs, 1973-; Detroit Edison, bd of dirs, 1975-83; Operation Food Search, bd of dirs; Cystic Fibrosis Found, bd of dirs; Central Inst for the Deaf, bd of dirs; St Louis Regional Medical Ctr Found, bd of dirs; VP Fair Found, bd of dirs; Confluence St Louis, bd of dirs. **Honors/Awds:** Hon Doctor of Laws degree, Eastern MI Univ, 1970; Univ of Missouri, Distinguished Volunteer Award, 1990. **Military Serv:** US Air Force, acct supv, 1954-58. **Business Addr:** Pres/CEO, New Age Financial, Inc, 3855 Lucas & Hunt Rd, Ste 223, St Louis, MO 63121.

HARPER, DEREK RICARDO
Professional basketball player. **Personal:** Born Oct 13, 1961, New York, NY; married Sheila; children: Darius, Danielle, Dana, Daria. **Educ:** Illinois, 1984. **Career:** Dallas Mavericks, guard, 1983-94; New York Knicks, 1994-96; Dallas Mavericks, 1996-97; Orlando Magic, 1997-. **Honors/Awds:** One of six NBA rookies to play in every game; second-team all-Am by AP as a jr; led the Big Ten in steals and assists as a soph & in steals as a jr; NBA All-Defensive Second Team, 1987, 1990. **Special Achievements:** NBA Draft, first round pick, #11, 1983; only the second player in NBA history to register 15,000 points, 6,000 assists, and 1,800 steals. **Business Addr:** Professional Basketball Player, Orlando Magic, 1 Magic Pl, Orlando, FL 32801, (407)649-3200.

HARPER, DWAYNE ANTHONY
Professional football player. **Personal:** Born Mar 29, 1966, Orangeburg, SC. **Educ:** South Carolina State College, graduated with a degree in marketing. **Career:** Seattle Seahawks, cornerback, 1988-94; San Diego Chargers, 1994-. **Orgs:**

NAACP. **Honors/Awds:** Sports Illustrated, All-NFL Team, 1991, 1995; Unsung Hero Award, 1995; MVP, 1995. **Business Addr:** Professional Football Player, San Diego Chargers, Qualcomm Stadium, 9449 Friars Rd, San Diego, CA 92108.

HARPER, EARL

Educator. **Personal:** Born Jul 7, 1929, Jackson, MS; married Clara Louise; children: Felicia, Denise, Julie, Earl, Andre Robinson. **Educ:** Grand Rapids Jr Coll, associate voc studies 1964; Western Michigan Univ, BS ind supervision 1968; Mississippi Tech 1970, MBA mgmt 1973, mgmt 1974; Texas Tech Univ, mgt 1974. **Career:** F E Seidman School of Business, chmn dept mgmt; Doehler-Jarvis, training dir, asst to plant mgr; Harper & Assoc Mgmt Consulting & Training, pres; Grand Valley State University, prof of mgt, 1971-. **Orgs:** Developed Grand Rapids, Michigan Model Cities Career & Acad Counseling Ctr 1971; developed Gen Acad Prog Grand Rapids & Muskegon Inner-City Coll Ed Prog for Grand Valley State Coll 1971; worked with comm to develop Higher Ed Prog Grand Rapids Model Cities 1972-73. **Special Achievements:** Publications: ''Management the Diversified Workforce: Current Efforts and Future Directions,'' Sam Advanced Management Journal, 1993; ''An Empirical Examination of the Relationship Between Strategy and Scanning,'' The Mid Atlantic Journal of Business, 1993; Numerous others. **Military Serv:** AUS corpl 1951-53. **Business Addr:** School of Business Administration, Grand Valley State University, 1 Campus Dr, Allendale, MI 49401.

HARPER, ELIZABETH

Health services management consultant. **Personal:** Born Jul 10, 1922, Cleveland, OH; married Kendrick Harper. **Educ:** Homer G Phillips School of Nursing, RN 1945; St John's Univ, BSN 1963; C W Post Coll, MPS 1975. **Career:** Homer G Phillips Hospital, staff nurse 1945-50; New York City Dept of Hospitals, staff nurse 1950-54, head nurse 1954-60, supervisor of nurses 1960-63; New York City Health & Hospital Corp, asst dir of nursing 1963-70, assoc dir of nursing 1970-72, dir of nursing 1972-81, nurse management consultant 1981-. **Orgs:** Mem Amer Nurses Assn 1968-; Licensed Nursing Home Adminis 1978-; mem Natl League for Nurses 1979-; state committeewoman 27th AD Queens Co 1982-; mem NY State Federation of Republican Women 1982-; mem 1984-, life mem 1991-, Republican Senatorial Inner Circle; mem Flushing Suburban Civic Assn; Flushing Council of Women's Organs Inc; Long Island Fed of Women's Clubs; Nassau County Fed of Republic Women; Natl Republican Congressional Comm; Judicial Dist Dir, 11th Judicial Dist, NY State Fed of Republican Women; Queens County Exec Comm 1982-; State Committeewoman 1982-. **Honors/Awds:** Numerous awards including Distinguished Serv Award 1972, Certificate of Serv 30 yrs 1980, Nurses Recognition Day Award 1981 New York City HHC Bird S Coler Hospital; City Council Citation City of New York 1981; Legislative Resolution Senate #1083 State of New York 1981; New York City HHC Bird S Coler Hospital Recognition Award 1981; Certificate of Recognition Natl Republican Congressional Comm 1984; Humanitarian Serv Award Queens Co Pract Nurses Assn 1981; Apprec and Dedication Award New York City HHC Assn of Nursing Dir 1981; Comm Adv Bd Recognition Award New York City HHC Bird S Coler Hospital 1981; Del Rep Pres Conv 1984; Certificate in Health Care Employee and Labor Rel from The Center to Promote Health Care Studies in cooperation with The Health CareManagement Group 1985; New York te Fed of Republican Women, President's Award, Honored 1986; Natl Republican Congressional Comm Certificate of Recognition 1985; Republican Party Presidential Achievement Award 1987; Delegate Republican Presidential Convention 1984 and 1988; guest of Vice Pres and Mrs. Dan Quayle at their home 1989 & 1990; photo session with President George Bush, 1991. **Business Addr:** Nurse Management Consultant, Ctr to Promo Hlth Care Studies, 14 Colvin Rd, Scarsdale, NY 10583.

HARPER, EUGENE, JR.

Educational administrator. **Personal:** Born Feb 1, 1943, Atlanta, GA; son of Sula Mae Harper and E Eugene Harper; married Maryetta, Sep 27, 1966; children: Angelia M Harper. **Educ:** Cameron State College, AA, 1966; Ohio State University, BS, 1971; Central Michigan University, MS, 1980. **Career:** Cols Recreation Department, district supervisor/director, 1967-72; Ohio State University, associate director of intramurals, 1972-88; Columbus Public Schools, director of athletics & student activities, 1988-. **Orgs:** Alpha Phi Alpha; Ohio Special Olympics, board of directors; Cols Parks & Recreation, board of directors and commission; Ohio State University National Youth Sports Program, consultant; Ohio Association for Health, Physical Education, Rec & Dance, chairperson; National Interscholastic Athletic Administrators Association; Ohio Interscholastic Athletic Administrators Association; Ohio High School Athletic Association; Alpha Phi Alpha, Alpha RHO Lambda Chapter. **Honors/Awds:** Ohio High School Athletic Association, Sportsmanship, Ethics & Integrity Awd, 1995-96. **Military Serv:** US Air Force, 1961-64. **Business Addr:** Director of Athletics & Student Activities, Columbus Public Schools, 270 E State St, Rm 301, Board of Education, Columbus, OH 43215, (614)365-5848.

HARPER, GERALDINE

Educator. **Personal:** Born Jan 27, 1933, Memphis, TN; daughter of Janie Lee Bolden Seay and James Edward Seay; married Charles N Harper, Mar 4, 1954; children: Dr Deborah Harper Brown, Elaine Harper Bell, Charles Terrence Harper. **Educ:** LeMoyne-Owen, Memphis TN, BS Education, 1955; Chicago State Univ, Chicago IL, MS Education, 1977. **Career:** Chicago Bd of Educ, Chicago IL, teacher, 1958-76, teacher-librarian, 1976-. **Orgs:** Chicago Teacher Librarians Assn, mem, 1980-, rooms comm chair, 1986-87, reservations sec, 1987-88, correspondence sec, 1988-; mem, Delta Sigma Theta Sorority; dir, Vacation Bible School, Lilydale First Baptist Church Chicago, 1983-; chair, Senior Citizens Comm, Top Ladies of Distinction Inc, Chicago Chapter, 1987-89. **Honors/Awds:** Laday of the Year, Top Ladies of Distinction Inc, Chicago Chapter, 1989.

HARPER, HARRY DANDRIDGE

Physician. **Personal:** Born Jul 15, 1934, Ft Madison, IA. **Educ:** Lincoln U; IA Wesleyan Coll; Grinnell Coll, BS; Howard Med Sch, MD 1963; Drake U; Univ of IA. **Career:** E%Xcalibur 9tl W Inc, pres; Sacred Heart Hosp Med Staff, pres 1971; Lee Co Med Soc vice pres 1971; Co Mental Hlth Ctr, dir 1971; IA State Penitentiary, sr cons; Mt Pleasant Mental Hlth Inst, cons; Lee Co Welfare Dept, inst; Planned Parenthood of SE IA; Headstary Mothers, recp; pvt prac psychiatry. **Orgs:** Mem Nat & Am Med Assns; Am & IA Psych Assn; Lee Co & IA Med Assn; Nat Assn of Interns & Resd IA Nat Guard; NAACP; Kappa Alpha Psi; Kiwanis Internat; YMCA; IA Commn for Blind; Keokuk Country Club; FM Country Club; C of C; Lee Co Crime Commn; IA Bd of Family Planning; past dir Boy Scouts of SE IA. **Honors/Awds:** Presented paper to Nat Med Assn Atlanta GA 1970; ''Comm Psychiatry'' paper presented to Assn of Med Suprs of Mental Hosp Houston TX; presented paper to World Fedn of Mental Hlth ''Family Planning in Mental Hosp'' 1970. **Military Serv:** Military serv IA NG comdr. **Business Addr:** 3766 Mill St, Reno, NV 89502.

HARPER, HILL

Actor. **Career:** Appeared in television shows and films including: ''Get on the Bus,'' ''Strange Days,'' ''Zooman,'' ''Steel,'' ''NYPD Blue,'' ''The Fresh Prince of Bel Air,'' and ''Married With Children.''. **Business Addr:** Actor, c/o Epstein, Wyckoff, Corsa, 280 S Beverly Dr, Ste 400, Beverly Hills, CA 90212, (310)278-7222.

HARPER, JOHN ROY, II (KWAME JAJA OBAYAMI)

Attorney. **Personal:** Born Sep 2, 1939, Greenwood, SC; son of John Roy Harper and Mary Frances Smith Harper; married Denise Adele Jefferson; children: Francesca Margo Denise Harper. **Educ:** Harvard Law School, 1959-60; Fisk Univ, AB, 1959; New York Univ, 1967; Univ of South Carolina Law School, JD, 1970. **Career:** Shell Oil Co Hqs, junior exec, 1964-67, law clerk, 1968; Mobil Oil Co Hqs, law clerk, 1969; NAACP Legal Defense & Education Fund, Inc, Earl Warren fellow, 1970-73, coop atty, 1973-; NAACP Special Contribution Fund, Inc, coop atty, 1976-; American Civil Liberties Union, coop atty, 1972-; Emergency Land Fund, coop atty, project coord, 1973-77. **Orgs:** Alpha Phi Alpha Fraternity, Inc, 1956-; United Citizens Party of SC, pres, chair & principal organizer, 1969-76; Blacks United for Action, Inc, founding chairman, 1968-76; Opportunities Industrialization Center (OIC) of SC, founding chairman, 1971-74; Prince Hall Grand Lodge of SC 32 degree Mason, Shriner, 1971-; SC Association of Black Elected Officials, founding pres, 1977-78; Black Caucus, Univ of SC Alumni Association, founding chairperson, 1980-82; Operation PUSH of SC, state coord, 1981-82; SC Conference, NAACP, general counsel, 1987-. **Honors/Awds:** Black Law Students Assn, USC Law School, Outstanding Barrister Award, 1997; NAACP, William Robert Ming Advocacy Award, 1991; SC Black Hall of Fame, Enshrinee, 1991; Univ of SC Alumni Assn, Outstanding Alumnus Award, 1981; SC Law Review, Business Manager, Editorial Board, 1968-70. **Military Serv:** US Army, E-5, 1961-64; Good Conduct Medal, 1964; Honorable Discharge, 1967. **Business Addr:** Chairman, John R Harper II, Attorney at Law, PA, 1545 Sumter St, Ste 209, Victory Savings Bank Bldg, PO Box 843, Columbia, SC 29202-0843, (803)771-4723.

HARPER, JOSEPH W., III

Educator. **Personal:** Born Jan 10, 1931, Charlotte, NC; married Mary A Turner; children: Delcia Marie, Lisa Yvette, Jonette Michelle. **Educ:** Johnson C Smith U, BS1955; A&T State U, MS 1963; A&T State U, NSF grants; Unive CA at Berkeley, cert molecular biol 1968; Western MI U; Univ NC at Charlotte. **Career:** E Mecklenburg Sr High School, asst prin 1974-; E Mecklenburg Adult Educ Center of Central Piedmont Comm Coll, dir, biology teacher 1969-73, teacher, coach 1955-74. **Orgs:** Mem NEA, NCEA; NC Prins Assn; adv bd Upward Bound Program Johnson C Smith U; past pres NC Southwestern Dist Ath Assn 1960-62, 1964-65; pastdir NC State Basketball Tourn Western Div AA Confs 1966-68; mem Model Cities Task Force; YMCA; Helping Hand Scholarship Adv Bd; Charlotte-MecklenburgRec Commn; Pan-Hellenic Coun; Omega Psi Phi. **Honors/Awds:** Dem Omega Man of Yr Award Pi Phi Chap 1974; sixth dist 1975; Bell & Howwel Schs Fellowship Award 1973; Most Understanding Tchr 2d Ward HS 1969; Outstand

ing Ldrshp Award Lincoln Co PTA 1967; outstandin serv plaque 1966; cert merit NC Sci Tchrs Symposium 1965; Coach of Yr NCHSAA Western Div football 1966; basketball 1967. **Military Serv:** AUS pfc 1952-54. **Business Addr:** Assistant Principal, East Mecklenburg High School, 6800 Monroe Rd, Charlotte, NC 28212.

HARPER, KENDRICK

Administrator. **Personal:** Born Sep 14, 1919, New York, NY; married Elizabeth Maxwell. **Career:** New York City Parks Recreation & Cultural Afrs, admin. **Orgs:** Life mem, 369th Vet Assn; life mem, VFW Proct Hobson Post 1896; mem, Black Republicans of NY State; exec mem, Queens County Rep Com Honoree Awds 1973; alternate delegate, Rep Pres Conv 1980; alternate delegate, Rep Pres Conv 1984; mem, US Senatorial Club 1985; mem 1985, life mem 1991-, Republican Senatorial Inner Circle; mem, Capitol Hill Club 1985; 27th AD Queens County, county comm chairman 1987; Flushing Suburban Civic Assoc of New York City 1987; Empire Club 1987. **Honors/Awds:** John S Snyder Meml Award, Robt A Taft Rep Club, 1983; Disting Serv Award, Queens Rep Co Comm, 1983; Rep Natl Comm, Campaign Victory Certificate, 1983; Robt A Taft Awd, 1976; Selec Serv Syst, Merit Serv Award & Medal, 1976; guest of Pres & Mrs Ford, 1976; City of New York Parks & Recreation, certificate of appreciation of 24 yrs of faithful service 1985; State of New York Legislative Resolution Senate No 940 by Senator Knorr 1986; guest of Vice President and Mrs. Dan Quayle at their home, 1989 & 1990; photo session with President George Bush, 1991. **Military Serv:** AUS 1939-45.

HARPER, LAYDELL WOOD

Marketing executive. **Personal:** daugHter of Felicia Wood and R Wood (deceased); divorced; children: Licia Lyn. **Educ:** Wayne State University, BA, 1980; Knight Ridder Institute, management, attended. **Career:** Detroit Free Press, downtown advertising manager, 1987-89; Detroit Newspaper Agency, features advertising general manager, 1989-90, co-op advertising manager, 1990-91, community affairs director, 1991-. **Orgs:** Berat Human Services, board member, 1992-; NAACP, marketing committee co-chair, 1992-; Science & Engineering, board of directors, 1991-93; United Negro College Fund, fashion fair co-chair, 1992; Project Pride Chamber, board of directors, 1992; BART, advisory board, 1991-92. **Honors/Awds:** City of Detroit, Testimonial Resolution, 1989; Friday Women's Club, Woman of the Year, 1988. **Business Addr:** Director, Community Affairs, Detroit Newspaper Agency, 615 W Lafayette, Detroit, MI 48214.

HARPER, MARY L.

Accountant. **Personal:** Born Feb 24, 1925, Emporia, KS; married Edward J. **Educ:** Lincoln Univ Jeff City MO; Emporia State Tchrs Coll Emporia KS; State Coll LA, LA. **Career:** Self Employ, accountant tax couns 1965-; LA Co Prob Dept Juvenile Reim Sect, invest 1960-63, girls coun; Cong Dist Dem Union, special asst. **Orgs:** Treas Dem Coal of Pomona Valley; Pol Action Chmn Pomona Valley NAACP bd pres NAACP So CA Area Conf 1971-73; treas NAACP So CA Area Conf 1966-71; commissioner City of Pomona; vice chmn Parks & Rec Commn; Pol Act Chmn NAACP So CA Area Conf 19 73-; bd dirs YMCA Outreach. **Honors/Awds:** Recip serv awd So Area Conf NAACP 1969, 71; elec Delegate Dem Chrtr Conf KC, MO 35th Cong Dist 1974 only blk cand in field of 12, one of two females.

HARPER, MARY STARKE

Association executive, research consultant (retired). **Personal:** Born Sep 6, 1919, Ft Mitchell, AL; widowed. **Educ:** PhD 1963; MS 1952; BS 1950; diploma RN 1941; credential competent in four professions, clinical pscychology, nursing, sociology, secondary edn. **Career:** Cntr for Minority Group Mental Health Progs, asst chief; Dept of HEW Nat Inst of Mental Health DHEW; positions in nursing, staff head nurse, supervisory, adminstrv, mgmt, cons, nurse edn, nurse adminstrn in Vets Adminstrn U of MN, instr; ULCA St Mary's Coll; dir nursing edn; Interdisciplinary Clinical Research, cons, research chief 1964-68; St Mary's Coll, instr sociology; Research consultant, currently. **Orgs:** Mem, bd dirs Nat League for Nursing; bd dirs Westchester Mental Health Assn; pres Mental Health Assn Peekskill Br Commnr Nursing Res 1969-74; chmn Adv Com to DC Mental Health Adminstrn 1972-; bd dirs DC Mental Health Assn; secretary, American Association for International Aging; publisher: 4 books in Geropsychology and Minority Aging; special advisor, Presidents Carter, Reagan, Bush, Clinton; dir, Policy Development & Research; White House Conference on Aging, 1981, 1995; scy, National Advisory Comm; Intl Assn on Aging. **Honors/Awds:** Tuskegee University, DSC, 1994; St Joseph College, LLD, 1995. **Home Addr:** 1362 Geranium St NW, Washington, DC 20012.

HARPER, MICHAEL STEVEN

Educator. **Personal:** Born Mar 18, 1938, Brooklyn, NY; son of Katherine Johnson Harper and Walter Warren Harper; married Shirley Ann; children: Roland Warren, Patrice Cuchulain, Rachel Maria. **Educ:** CA State Univ, BA, MA 1961-63; Univ of IA, MA 1963; Brown Univ, ad eundem 1972. **Career:** Harvard Univ, visiting prof 1974-77; Yale Univ, visiting prof 1976; Carleton Coll Northfield MN, benedict prof 1979; Univ of Cin cinnati, Elliston poet 1979; Brown Univ, prof of English 1970-, Israel J Kapstein professor of English, 1983-90; Distinguished Minority Professor, Univ of DE 1988; Distinguished Visiting Professor, Creative Writing, Macalester Coll, MN 1989. **Orgs:** Council mem MA Council Arts & Humanities 1977-80; judge Natl Book Awd Poetry 1978; Bicentennial poet Bicentennary Exchange, Britain/USA 1976; Amer spec ICA State Dept tour of Africa 1977; lecturer German Univ ICA tour of nine univ 1978 ed special issue of Carleton Miscellany 1980 on Ralph Ellison; bd mem Yaddo Artists Colony Saratoga Springs NY; ed bd TriQuarterly, the Georgia Review, Obsidian; ed Collected Poems of Sterling A Brown; publ Amer Journal by Robert Hayden 1978. **Honors/Awds:** Guggenheim Fellowship Poetry John Simon Guggenheim Found 1976; NEA Creative Writing Awd 1977; Melville-Cane Awd for Images of Kin New & Selected Poems Univ of IL Press 1978; Natl Humanities Distinguished Prof Colgate Univ 1985; books of poems, ''Dear John, Dear Coltrane'' 1970, ''History Is Your Own Heartbeat'' 1971, ''Song, I Want A Witness'' 1972, ''History As Apple Tree'' 1972, ''Debridement'' 1973, ''Nightmare Begins Responsibility'' 1975, ''Images of Kin'' 1977, ''Healing Song For The Inner Ear'' 1985, ''Chant of Saints'' 1979; Honorary Doctorate of Letters, Trinity College, CT 1987; Honorary Doctorate of Humane Letters, Coe College, 1990; First Poet Laureate, State of Rhode Island, 1988; Robert Hayden Memorial Poetry Award, UNCF, 1990; Phi Beta Kappa, visiting scholar, 1991. **Business Addr:** Professor, English Dept, Brown Univ, Providence, RI 02912.

HARPER, ROBERT LEE
Dentist. **Personal:** Born Oct 3, 1920, Longview, TX; married Eldora; children: Robert Jr, Beverly. **Educ:** Jarvis Christian Coll, 1939-42; Wiley Coll, BA 1945-48; Meharry Med Coll, DDS 1948-52. **Career:** Dentist pvt prac 1952-77; Jarvis Christian Coll, 1960-77. **Orgs:** Mem sec E TX Med Dental & Pharm Assn 24 yrs; pres Gulf State Dental Assn 1962; mem E TX Dist Dental Soc; TX Dental Assn; Am Dental Assn; Nat Dental Assn; Gulf State Dental Assn; Am Soc Dentistry Children; Am Acad Gen Dentistry; mem bd dir Logview C of C 1977; bd Parks & Rec Prgm 1969-75; Piney Woods Am Red Cross; chmn, adv bd Good Samaritan Nursing Home; bd mem Mental Hlth Assn Gregg Co; E TX Area Cncl BSA; past mem, bd Vocational Tech Training Longview Ind Sch Dist Hon; kkper of In mem Omega Psi Phi Frat; mem Kappa Sigma Pi Hon Dental Frat. **Honors/Awds:** Recpt Clinical of Dentistry 1952; Omega Man Yr 1967; candidate City Commr Longview 1967; recpt Silver Beaver Award BSA 1966. **Military Serv:** USN yeoman 1st class 1942-45. **Business Addr:** 1002 S Martin Luther King Blvd, Longview, TX 75602.

HARPER, RONALD
Professional basketball player. **Personal:** Born Jan 20, 1964, Dayton, OH. **Educ:** Miami Univ, Oxford, OH, 1982-86. **Career:** Cleveland Cavaliers, guard, 1986-90; Los Angeles Clippers, 1990-94; Chicago Bulls, 1994-. **Honors/Awds:** NBA All-Rookie Team, 1987. **Special Achievements:** NBA, Championship, 1996. **Business Addr:** Professional Basketball Player, Chicago Bulls, 1901 W Madison St, Chicago, IL 60612-2459, (312)455-4000.

HARPER, RONALD J.
Attorney. **Personal:** Born Dec 20, 1945, W Palm Beach; married Betty Vance; children: Ronald, Jr, Jennifer. **Educ:** Temple U, BA economics 1968; Temple Law Sch, JD 1971. **Career:** Haper & Paul, atty; OIC of Am Inc, atty; Comm Legal Serv Phila, atty 1971; NY Life Ins Co, salesman 1970; Metro Life Ins Co, salesman 1968. **Orgs:** Mem Nat Bar Assn; Philadelphia Bar Assn; Philadelphia Barristers Assn; Am Bar Assn; mem Bd of Mgrs Temple Univ 1974; Zion Bapt Ch; bd Community Legal Svcs. **Business Addr:** Attorney, 140 W Maplewood Ave, Philadelphia, PA 19144.

HARPER, RUTH B.
State official. **Personal:** Born Dec 24, 1927, Savannah; daughter of Sallie DeLoach and Rev Thomas DeLoach; married James Harper (deceased); children: Catherine, Deloris (deceased). **Educ:** Beregan Institute Philadelphia, grad; Flamingo Modeling Sch, grad; LaSalle Univ, graduate. **Career:** 196th Legislative Dist, state legislator 1977-91; Ruth Harper's Modeling & Charm Sch, owner/dir; Gratz HS, instr; Strawberry Mansion Jr HS, instr; Miss Ebony PA Schlrsp Pageant, producer. **Orgs:** Mem Nat Dem Committee; mem PA Council on the Arts; fdr pres N Cent Philadelphia Women's Pol Caucus; bd mem YMCA Columbia Br; bd mem ARC SE Chpt; pres Zion BC Ch Womens Serv Guild; life mem NAACP; Urban League; HOGA Civic League; bd mem Philadelphia Univ; board member, National Political Congress of Black Women; member, Continental Societies Inc; board of directors, Afro American Museum; life member, Natl Council of Negro Women. **Honors/Awds:** Recip citation of honor Philadelphia Tribune Newspaper 1963; NAACP Serv Award 1964; Bright Hope BC Ch Award 1965; Black Expo Award 1972; Cosmopolitan Club Award 1969; La-Mode Mannequins Inc Achvmt Award 1969; Freedom Award NAACP 1978; Women in Politics Cheynew State Univ 1978; service award YMCA 1979.

HARPER, SARA J.
Judge. **Personal:** Born Aug 10, 1926, Cleveland; daughter of Leila Smith Harper and James Weldon Harper. **Educ:** Western Reserve University, BS; Franklin Thomas Backus School of Law Western Reserve University, LLB. **Career:** 8th Appellate District, Cuyahoga, OH, judge, currently. **Orgs:** National Bar Assn, judicial council, historian. **Honors/Awds:** Ohio Court of Claims, Victims Award, 1990; Ohio Women's Hall of Fame, 1991; Western Reserve University Law School, Society of Benchers, 1992. **Military Serv:** US Marine Corps Reserve, military judge, Lt Col, retired 1986. **Business Addr:** Judge, 8th District Court of Appeals, Court House, 1 Lakeside, Rm 202, Cleveland, OH 44113-1085.

HARPER, SARAH ELIZABETH GRUBBS
Electro mechanical engineer. **Personal:** Born in Detroit, MI; married Arnell Harper. **Educ:** Lawrence Technological University, mech engrg; LA Harbor Coll, E/M engrg; Livingstone Coll. **Career:** Hughes Aircraft Co, sr assoc engr 1953-61; TRW Syst Grp, design engr 1967-69; Teledyne Sys Co, project design engr 1969-70; Rockwell Intl, mem tech staff 1970-77; consultant, currently; Electro mechanical engineer, Member of Technical Staff. **Orgs:** Mem Soc of Women Eng; mem Coll of Fellows; mem Alpha Kappa Alpha Sor; NAACP; mem Inst for the Advancement of Engrg; mem Engrg Adv Comm E LA Coll; mem LA Counc of Engrs & Scientists; California Representative, National Engineers and Professionals Association, 1975-77; member, National Conference on Women in Engineering, 1973; speaker, Engineering Advisory Committee for Colleges and High Schools, 1970-. **Honors/Awds:** Selected for inclusion in the Alpha Kappa Alpha Sor Heritage Series on ''Women in Sci & Engrg'' 1979; Grade of Fellow, Inst for the Advancement of Engrg 1977; Grade of Fellow, Society of Women Engineers, 1988. **Home Addr:** 4221 Don Jose Dr, Los Angeles, CA 90008.

HARPER, SHARI BELAFONTE. **See BELAFONTE, SHARI.**

HARPER, T. ERROL
Automobile dealership executive. **Personal:** Born Feb 12, 1947, Birmingham, AL; son of Callie O'Bryant Harper and Rev Theophilus E Harper; married Elaine Betz, Mar 23, 1975; children: Rena Nicole, Zachary Jordan. **Educ:** Morris Brown Coll, Atlanta GA, BA, 1970. **Career:** Ernst & Ernst, Philadelphia PA, auditor, 1970-73; Philadelphia '76 Inc, Philadelphia PA, controller, 1973-74; Dupont Co, Wilmington DE, staff accountant, 1974-76; Ford Motor Co, Dearborn MI, dealer trainee, 1977-78; Phillips Ford Inc, Conshohocken PA, business mgr, 1978-79; Harper Pontiac Inc, Upper Darby PA, pres, 1979-82; Heritage Lincoln-Mercury, Hackensack NJ, pres, 1983-. **Orgs:** Dir, Commerce & Indus Assn of New Jersey, 1985-, United Way of Bergen County, 1985-92; mem, Hackensack Lions Club, 1987-; dir, Black Ford & Lincoln-Mercury Dealer Assn, 1989-91. **Honors/Awds:** Hon Doctor of Humanities, Monrova College, Monrovia, Liberia, 1986. **Military Serv:** USMCR, Corporal, 1970-74. **Business Addr:** President, Heritage Lincoln-Mercury Sales Inc, PO Box 820399, Dallas, TX 75382-0399.

HARPER, TERRY
Professional baseball player (retired). **Personal:** Born Aug 19, 1955, Douglasville, GA. **Career:** Atlanta Braves, outfielder, 1980-86; Detroit Tigers, outfielder, 1987; Pittsburgh Pirates, outfielder, 1987. **Honors/Awds:** Braves Minor League Player of the Month for April & May 1982. **Business Addr:** Atlanta Braves, PO Box 4064, Atlanta, GA 30302.

HARPER, THELMA MARIE
State senator. **Personal:** Born Dec 2, 1940, Williamson County, TN; daughter of Clora Thomas Claybrooks and William Claybrooks; married Paul Wilson Harper, 1957; children: Dylan Wayne, Linda Gail. **Educ:** Tennessee State Univ, graduate, 1978. **Career:** Paul Harper's Convenience Markets, entrepreneur; financial analyst; city councilwoman; State of Tennessee, senator, currently. **Orgs:** Member, Davidson County Democratic Womens' Club; member, Cable Inc; member, National Hook-up of Black Women; member, Nashville Women's Political Caucus. **Honors/Awds:** First Black female ever elected to Tennessee's state senate. **Business Addr:** Senator, State of Tennessee, Legislative Plz, Ste 10A, Nashville, TN 37243.

HARPER, TOMMY
Baseball executive. **Personal:** Born Oct 14, 1940, Oak Grove, LA; son of Louetta Weir Harper and Ulysses Harper; married Bonnie Jean Williams Harper, Oct 6, 1962. **Career:** Cincinnati Reds, baseball player 1963-67; Cleveland Indians, baseball player 1968; Seattle Pilots, baseball player 1969; Milwaukee Brewers, baseball player 1970-71; Boston Red Sox, 1972-74, player; CA Angels, Oakland A's, 1975-76; Baltimore Orioles, 1976; Boston Red Sox, special asst to genl mgr; NY Yankees, minor league instructor, 1977-78; Boston Red Sox, public relations, minor league instructor, 1978-79, asst dir, marketing & promotions, 1980, major league coach, 1981-84, special asst to the general mger, 1985-86; Montreal Expos, minor league instructor, 1988-89, major league coach, 1990-. **Honors/Awds:** Seattle Post Intelligtencer, Man of the Year, 1969; Milwaukee Brewers, Most Valuable Player, 1970; Boston Red Sox, Most Valuable Player, 1973. **Business Addr:** Montreal Baseball Club Ltd, PO Box 500, Station M, Montreal, PQ, Canada H1V 3P2.

HARPER, WALTER EDWARD, JR.
Educator. **Personal:** Born Jul 10, 1950, Chicago, IL; son of Elizabeth Mercer Harper and Walter Edward Harper Sr. **Educ:** Loyola Univ, Chicago IL, AB History, 1972, MA Counseling Psychology, 1978; Inst for Psychoanalysis, Chicago IL, Certificate, Teacher Educ Program, 1979; Loyola Univ, Chicago IL, post-graduate studies, 1982-86. **Career:** Precious Brood Grammer School, Chicago IL, teacher, 1972-74; Loyola Univ, Chicago IL, admin, 1974-79; North Park Coll, Chicago IL, teacher, counselor, 1979-86; Brown Univ, Providence RI, asst dir financial aid, 1986-. **Orgs:** Bd mem, Eisenberg Chicago Boy & Girls Club, 1978, Loyola Univ, Upward Bound Program, 1978; C G Jung Center, 1980; bd mem, Friendship House/Chicago, 1981; Illinois Psychological Assn, 1982, Phi Delta Kappa, Loyola Univ Chapter, 1982, Assn of Black Admission and Financial Aid Admin in the Ivy League & Sister Schools, 1986, Eastern Assn of Financial Aid Admin; adv, NAACP Student Chapter, Brown Univ 1990; co-chairperson, Campus Ministry Affairs Committee, Brown Univ 1990; pres, Santore Society, Brown Univ 1990-91. **Honors/Awds:** Certificate of Merit, Chicago Youth Center, 1975; Most Eligible Bachelor/Promising Minority Professional, Ebony Magazine, 1976; Fellow, Soc for Values in Higher Educ, 1982; Workshop Leader, High School Summer Intern Program, Philadelphia Daily News, 1987; Workshop Leader, Atlanta Dream Jamboree, three day program for high school youth in Atlanta, 1988, 1989; Completed Management Development Program, Brown Univ, 1988. **Business Addr:** Anthropology Department, Brown University, PO Box 1921, Providence, RI 02912.

HARPER, WILLIAM THOMAS, III
Psychologist, educator. **Personal:** Born Sep 10, 1956, Newport News, VA; son of Queen V Harper and William T Harper Jr. **Educ:** Virginia State College, Petersburg, VA, BS, psychology, 1978, MEd, counseling, 1980; Hampton University, VA, advanced study, 1981-84; College of William and Mary, Williamsburg, VA, advanced study, 1986-87; Old Dominion University, PhD, education and psychology, 1991. **Career:** Hampton University, VA, director of student support services, 1980-88; US Army, Arlington, VA, psychologist and educator, 1986; Olde Hampton Business Education Center, VA, assistant professor, psychologist, vice pres of research, 1987-; Norfolk State University, VA, director of underclared students, 1989-; Old Dominion University, Norfolk, VA, assistant professor of counseling, 1990. **Orgs:** Kappa Alpha Psi Fraternity, undergraduate advisor, 1982-88, chairman of youth guide right, alumni chapter, 1987-89; Virginia Association of Black Psychologists, committee chairman, 1987-; Peninsula Literacy Council, counselor, 1982-88; Virginia Association of Administrator in Higher Education, committee chairman. **Honors/Awds:** International Platform Association, Board of Governors, 1990; College of William and Mary, Certificate of Recognition for the Fourth National Black Leadership Development Conference, 1990, 1991; Black Student Retention Conference Recognition, 1989, 1990; Black American Doctoral Research Award, 1991, 1992; YMCA, Armed Services Recognition, 1990; Boys Club of Greater Hampton, Roads Recognition, 1990; Christopher Newport College, Recognition for Achievement, 1985, 1986; Office of Human Affairs Achievement Award, 1990; Sarah Bonwell Hudgins Regional Center Volunteer Program Achievement Award, 1989, 1990; numerous others. **Home Addr:** 1042 44th St, Newport News, VA 23607.

HARPS, WILLIAM S.
Real estate executive. **Personal:** Born Jul 3, 1916, Philadelphia, PA; son of Blanche Hobbs Harps (deceased) and Richard Harps (deceased); married Justine McNeil Harps, Nov 14, 1942; children: Richard, Eunice. **Educ:** Howard U, BS 1943. **Career:** John R Pinkett Inc, first vice pres 1939-44; WA Bd of Realtors, chmn; Harps & Harps Inc Real Estate Appraisers & Counselors, pres 1984-. **Orgs:** Mem, intl pres Am Inst Real Estate Appraisers 1968-81; Soc Real Estate Appraisers; natl past pres Nat Soc Real Estate Appraisers; mem NY Real Estate Bd, WA Real Estate Brokers Assn, Lambda Alpha On Land Economics; bd dir Met Police Boys Club 1963- mem, bd trustees Fed City Council 1969-; vp, bd trustees Childrens Hosp 1969-; bd mem Tax Equalization & Review 1970-74; Mayors Economic Devel Comm 1970-74; DC Commn Judicial Disabilities & Tenure 1971-75; bd dirs Columbia Title Ins Co; Nat Bank WA 1971-86; Pepertual Fed Sav & Loan Assn 1971-87; pres WA Chapter #18 Amer Inst Real Estate Appraisers 1976; pres WA Bd of Realtors 1977; Investors 15 Inc; consult District Title Ins 1984-; mem Soc of Real Estate Counselors. **Honors/Awds:** Metro Womens Dem Club Awd 1971; Alumni Awd Howard Univ 1972; Jos Allard Awd Amer Inst Real Estate Appraisers 1974; Realtor of the Year 1980. **Home Addr:** 1736 Shepherd St NW, Washington, DC 20011. **Business Phone:** (202)682-2194.

HARRELL, ANDRE
Recording company executive. **Educ:** Lehman College, communications major, attended. **Career:** Uptown Entertainment, president, until 1995; Motown Records, pres, 1995-97. **Business Addr:** Former President, Motown Records, c/o Polygram Records, 825 8th Ave, New York, NY 10019.

HARRELL, CHARLES H.
Automobile dealership executive. **Career:** Harrell Chevrolet-Oldsmobile Inc, Flat Rock, MI, chief exec. **Orgs:** General Motors Minority Dealer Assn, pres, currently. **Business Addr:** Owner, Harrell Chevrolet-Oldsmobile Inc, 26900 Telegraph Rd, Flat Rock, MI 48134.

HARRELL, ERNEST JAMES
Military officer (retired), consultant. **Personal:** Born Oct 30, 1936, Selma, AL; son of Arrilla Moorer Harrell (deceased) and William Harrell (deceased); married Paola Boone Harrell, Jun 22, 1962; children: Ernest J II, Jolene. **Educ:** Tuskegee Institute, Tuskegee, AL, BS, 1960; Arizona State University, Tempe, AZ, MS, 1972. **Career:** US Army, various locations, general officer, commissioned officer, 1960-; Elt and Associates, consulting engineer, currently. **Orgs:** Regional vice pres, Society of American Military Engineers, 1986-91; dean of pledges, Omega Psi Phi Fraternity, 1958-60; vice chair, discipline committee, Arizona State University, 1967-70. **Honors/Awds:** Fellow, Society of American Military Engineers, 1988. **Military Serv:** US Army, Major General; Distinguished Service Medal, 1995; Legion of Merit, 1986, Bronze Star Medal, 1967, Meritorious Service Medal (3), 1971, 1979, 1982, Army Commendation Medal, 1970, Combat Infantryman Badge, Airborne Badge. **Business Addr:** Consulting Engineer, E H & Associates, 8051 N Como Dr, Tucson, AZ 85742, (520)575-7086.

HARRELL, H. STEVE
Automobile dealership owner. **Personal:** Born Apr 25, 1948; son of Lula Bell Thomas Harrell and James Harrell; divorced; children: Shemanthe E Smith, H Steve II. **Career:** Shelby Dodge, Memphis TN, pres, 1987-; H S Harrell Real Estate Invest, Atlanta, GA, pres, 1978-. **Orgs:** District chairman, Boy Scouts of America. **Business Addr:** Pres, Shelby Dodge Inc, 2691 Mt Moriah Rd, Memphis, TN 38115.

HARRELL, OSCAR W., II
Consultant. **Personal:** Born in Bristol, VA; son of Bernice W Harrell and Oscar Harrell Sr; married Dr. Sophia M Bailey; children: Oscar W III, Stafford B. **Educ:** Virginia Union Univ, BA 1957-60; Assumption Coll, Massachusetts, CAGS 1972-74; Brandeis Univ, PhD, 1994; research fellow Northeastern Univ, 1987-90. **Career:** Leonard Training School NC Bd of Corr, head counselor 1963-64; Gardner State Hospital, psych Soc Worker 1964-67; Rutland Heights Hosp, coord of rehab 1967-72; Mt Wachusett Comm Coll, faculty 1968; Fitchburg State Coll, asst dir of admiss, dir of minority affairs/AID 1974-81; Fitchburg State Coll, faculty 1976-80; Tufts Univ, dir of african amer center 1981-87; deputy asst comm, Massachusetts Department of Mental Retardation, 1987-90; consultant/educator, Assumption College, Institute for Social & Rehabilitation Service, 1996-. **Orgs:** Mem Alpha Phi Alpha Frat, Amer Psych Assoc 1976-78, Amer Personnel Guidance Assoc 1976-78, Amer Rehab Counseling Assoc 1976-78; mem & bd of dir MA Mental Health Assoc 1969-89, MA Halfway House Assoc; former pres MA Branch NAACP; sec & pres Soc Organized Against Racism 1982-; treas Greater Boston Interuniversity Cncl; vice pres MA Assoc for Mental Health; comm mem, Racial Justice Comm, Natl YWCA, currently; bd of dirs, Community Change Inc, Boston MA, currently; bd of ordained ministry, United Methodist Church, New England Conference. **Honors/Awds:** City rep Gardner Massachusetts Opportunity Council 1970-72; comm & chmn Sudbury Park & Recreation 1978-81; mem Governor's Advisory Comm to Correction 1980-82; Citation, Governor of Massachusetts, 1981; Citation, Massachusetts Senate 1987; Citation, Massachusetts House of Representatives 1987; performer (non-professional) in the play ''The Man Nobody Saw''; plaque, Outstanding Supporter of Education, Fitchburg Faculty, 1990; Plaque Appreciation as Director of the African American Center, Tufts Black Alumni. **Military Serv:** AUS E-5 1960-62. **Home Addr:** 15 Bent Brook Road, Sudbury, MA 01776.

HARRELL, ROBERT L.
Attorney. **Personal:** Born Aug 16, 1930, Ahoskie, NC; married Alice Fay Jamison; children: Anthony, Robert, Jr, Kyle, Kevin. **Educ:** NCCU, AB 1955; NCCU Law Sch, LLB 1958; NCCU Law Sch, JD 1970. **Career:** NY Co Bunlombe, asst pub defender 1973-; pvt prac 1965-73; Dailey & Harrell, partnership 1963-65; pvt prac 1960-63; Asso Coun & Legal Defense Fund Reorganized Hartford Co Cits Organ, atty 1961. **Orgs:** Chmn Asheville-Buncombe Co Cit Orgn 1965-70; mem Better Schs Com Buncombe 1965-69; delegate Nat Dem Conv 1972. **Military Serv:** AUS pfc 1951-53. **Business Addr:** PO Box 7154, Asheville, NC 28816.

HARRELL, WILLIAM EDWIN
City official. **Personal:** Born Mar 16, 1962, Norfolk, VA; son of Charity Nix Harrell and Adam Harrell Sr; married Johnna Carson Harrell, Nov 19, 1988; children: Charity Majette. **Educ:** Univ of VA, bachelors, urban & regional planning, 1984, masters, urban & regional planning, 1986, MPA, 1986. **Career:** City of Suffolk, Suffolk, VA, administrative analyst, 1986, sr administrative analyst, 1986-87, dir of mgmt services, 1987-90, dir of public utilities, 1990-. **Orgs:** Bd of dirs, Suffolk Chamber of Commerce, 1988-; fund distribution comm, United Way-Suffolk Div, 1988-90; vice pres, Great Bridge-Chesapeake Jaycees, 1989; Intl City Mgrs Assn, 1986-89; American Society for Public Admin, 1986-88; American Waterworks Association, vice chairman, Committee for Diversity; Conference of Minority Public Administrators; St John's AME Church, trustee. **Business Addr:** Director of Public Utilities, City of Suffolk, 446 Market Street, Suffolk, VA 23434.

HARRIGAN, RODNEY EMILE
Consultant. **Personal:** Born Jul 23, 1945, New York City, NY; married Elaine Mims; children: Pamela, Sherrice. **Educ:** Paine Coll, BS Math 1967; IBM System Rsch Inst, 1969; Howard Univ, MS Computer Sci 1975. **Career:** Royal Globe Ins Co, programmer 1968; Fed City Coll, assoc prof 1977; Howard Univ, assoc prof 1977; IBM, systems engr 1968-72, staff programmer 1972-75, proj mgr 1975-76, adv proj mgr 1976-77, systems engrg mgr 1977-79; Post Coll, instructor 1980-81; IBM, employee relations mgr 1979-81, spec proj mgr 1981-82, faculty loan prof 1982-92; NC A&T University, professor, computer science, currently. **Orgs:** Mem Assn for Computing Machinery; mem Data Processing Mgmt Assn; mem IEEE Computer Soc; mem Alpha Kappa Mu Honor Soc; mem Omega Psi Phi Frat. **Honors/Awds:** Alpha Kappa Mu Scholar of the Yr 1966; Honor Grad Awd 1967; Paine Coll Pres Awd 1967; IBM Golden Circle Awd 1975; IBM Symposium Awd 1972-74-75-76; IBM 100% Club Awd 1977-78 1981; Young Exec of Hartford Leadership Awd 1982; Operation Push Hartford Chap Awd 1981-82; NCA&J State Univ ACM Awd 1984. **Business Addr:** Professor of Computer Science, NC A&T State University, 1601 East Market St, Greensboro, NC 27411-0002.

HARRINGTON, DENISE MARION
Communication consultant. **Personal:** Born Apr 14, 1955, Washington, DC; daughter of Alma & Harold Greene; married Michael, Jan 14, 1989; children: Nia. **Career:** Harrington & Associates, co-owner, currently. **Orgs:** Boys & Girls Club of Portland, adv bd chair, 1992-. **Special Achievements:** Worked with Tiger Woods, Ken Griffey Jr, Vlade Divac, Michael Johnson, Mia Hann, Sheryl Snoopes, among others. **Business Addr:** President/Owner, Harrington & Associates, 3532 SE Oak, Portland, OR 97214, (503)236-5336.

HARRINGTON, ELAINE CAROLYN
Educator, organization executive. **Personal:** Born Aug 31, 1938, Philadelphia, PA. **Educ:** Tuskegee Inst, BS Elem Educ 1961; A&T State Univ, grad study 1962-64; Univ of CT Storrs, MA Supr Adm 1972. **Career:** JC Price School, teacher 1961-71; A&T State Univ, demonstration teacher 1965; Shiloh Baptist Church, dir cultural prog 1967; A&T State Univ, matls coord mus inst for jr high students 1968; Passaic Comm Coll, prof & acting dean of students 1972-80, prof acad founds 1980-87, professor, English department, 1988-. **Orgs:** Soloist Radio City Music Hall New York City 1958; mem/pres/secty NCEA & NJEA Educ Organs 1961-80; mem NEA 1961-80; mem/secty Zeta Phi Beta Sor Inc 1963-; mem Natl Alliance of Black Sch Educators 1973-; mem Amer Personnel & Guidance Assoc 1976-; mem YWCA; mem Christ Ch United Meth; former pres, Paterson Branch of NAACP; former elected mem, Paterson Brd of Education; chairperson, Regiona II, NAACP; mem, lay leader, Christ Church United Methodist, Paterson, NJ; Zeta Phi Beta Sorority, Inc; pres, NAACP, NJ State, currently. **Honors/Awds:** Outstanding Young Educator Awd Greensboro Public Schs NC 1968; Participant Leadership Seminar Guilford Co Schs NC 1969; Grad Scholarship Zeta Phi Beta Sor Inc 1971; 15 month Grad Fellowship EPDa Univ of CT 1971-72; NEH 1980 Seminar Fellowship Univ of Pgh 1980. **Business Addr:** Professor, English Department, Passaic Co Comm College, 1 College Blvd, Paterson, NJ 07505.

HARRINGTON, GERALD E.
Banking executive. **Personal:** Born 1945, Detroit, MI. **Educ:** Tennessee State Univ, 1967. **Career:** First Independence National Bank, senior vice pres/cashier, CEO, currently. **Orgs:** Member, American Institute of Banking; member, Bank Administration Institute; pres, GEH Enterprises Ltd. **Business Addr:** Chief Executive Officer, First Independence National Bank of Detroit, 44 Michigan Ave, Detroit, MI 48226.

HARRINGTON, OTHELLA
Professional basketball player. **Personal:** Born Jan 31, 1974. **Educ:** Georgetown. **Career:** Houston Rockets, 1997-. **Business Addr:** Professional Basketball Player, Houston Rockets, 10 Greenway Plaza, Houston, TX 77046, (713)627-0600.

HARRINGTON, PHILIP LEROY
Educator. **Personal:** Born Apr 27, 1946, Southern Pines, NC; son of Blanche McNeil Harrington and Neville W Harrington; married Chandra Salvi, Sep 15, 1968; children: Kafi Nakpangi, Kamala Nwena. **Educ:** North Carolina Central Univ, Durham NC, BS, 1968. **Career:** Roxbury Multi-Serv Center, Boston MA, educ program dir, 1972-74; Lena Park Community Devel Corp, Boston MA, program dir, 1974-76; Action for Boston Community Devel, Boston MA, admin, 1976-81; Dover-Sherborn Regional Schools, Dover MA, 1981-; Indeprep School, Boston MA, founder, dir, 1985-88; Freedom House, Boston MA, consultant, 1988-. **Orgs:** Educator, Massachusetts Dept of Educ, 1974-77; mem, Youth Motivation Task Force for Natl Alliance of Business, 1975-78; bd mem, Inner City Council for Children, 1976-80; dir, Boston Youth Devel Program, 1978-80; mem, Omega Psi Phi Frat, Iota Chi Chapter, 1982-; pres, founder, Parents of Black Students of Buckingham, Browne & Nichols, 1984-88; review comm, Massachusetts Arts Council, 1984-87; bd mem, Natl Alliance of Black School Educators, 1987-; vice pres, Black Educators Alliance of Massachusetts, 1988-. **Honors/Awds:** Performed in Black Nativity, produced by Natl Center of Afro-American Artists, Boston MA, 1984-89; Honoree, Museum of Afro-American History, Boston MA, 1988; Certificate of Recognition, Mayor of Boston, 1988. **Home Addr:** 27 Walden St, Cambridge, MA 02140.

HARRINGTON, ZELLA MASON
Director, nurse. **Personal:** Born Jan 29, 1940, St Louis, MO; married Melvyn A; children: Melvyn A, Jr, Kevin Mason. **Educ:** Jewish Hosp Sch of Nursing, diploma 1957-60; Webster Coll, BA1976; Webster Coll, MA 1977. **Career:** Nursing & Health Servs ARC, dir 1969-; Urban League of St Louis, health specialist 1968-69; Cardinal Ritter Inst, chief nurse trainer 1966-68; St LouisBd of Edn, practical nursing instr 1966; Vis Nurses Assn, sr staff nurse 1960-65; Nursery Found of St Louis, nurse consult 1963-65. **Orgs:** Mem, past pres, sec, treas, MO State Bd of Nursing 1974-; pres, vice pres Family Planning Council Inc Bd of Dirs 1976-77; faculty panel mem St Louis Univ Sch of Comm Med 1976-79; mem Health Adv Com Human Devel Corp 1977-; bd of dirs Maternal & Child Health Council Inc 1978-; comm consult Maternal & ChildHealth Council Inc 1979-; mem ANA 1961-80; mem Jack & Jill of Am Inc 1970-; mem Nat League for Nursing 1977-80. **Honors/Awds:** Assisted with pub ''Handbook for Home Health Aides'' Cardinal & Ritter Inst 1968; listed Outstanding Contributions of Blacks in Health Care Delta Sigma Theta Sorority 1977; George Washington Carver Award, Sigma Gamma Rho Sorority 1978. **Business Addr:** Nursing & Health Services, American Red Cross, 4050 Lindell Blvd, St Louis, MO 63108.

HARRIS, AL CARL
Professional football player. **Personal:** Born Dec 31, 1956, Bangor, ME; son of Gloria Smith Harris and Alfred C Harris Jr; married Margaret D'Orazio Harris, Apr 7, 1990. **Educ:** Arizona State, BS 1982. **Career:** Chicago Bears, linebacker 1979-88; Philadelphia Eagles, 1989-90. **Honors/Awds:** Has overcome injury problems and changing positions to become solid performer; started 8 games at DRE, 3 at LB in 1983; finished 8th on club in tackles (57) despite missing three games with turf toe; started 7 games at DRE in 1982 & last 11 games there in 1981. **Business Addr:** Professional Football Player, Philadelphia Eagles, 1989, Broad St & Pattison Ave, Veterans Stadium, Philadelphia, PA 19148.

HARRIS, ALONZO
Judge. **Personal:** Born Jul 20, 1961, Opelousas, LA; son of Aaron and Rosa B Harris; married Dawn W Harris, Dec 19, 1989; children: Ashley, Lanisha, Valenia, Alonzo Jr. **Educ:** Southern Univ, BS, 1983; Southern Univ Law Center, JD, 1986. **Career:** Harris and Harris Law Firm, attorney at law, 1983-87; 27th JDC St Landry Parish, district judge, 1993-. **Orgs:** Louisiana Judicial College, 1993-; Louisiana Bar Assn, 1987-; Amer Assoc Juvenile Judges, 1994-; Southwest Lawyers Assn, 1990-; Opelousas Rotary Club, 1994-. **Business Addr:** District Judge-27th Judicial District Court, State of Louisiana, PO Box 473, Opelousas, LA 70571, (318)948-0584.

HARRIS, ANTHONY
Utilities company executive. **Personal:** Born Jun 27, 1953, Chicago, IL; son of Roy & Alberta Harris; married Angela C Harris; children: Anthony, Alexander. **Educ:** Purdue University, BSME, 1975; Harvard Business School, MBA, 1979. **Career:** Standard Oil Co., Indiana, proj engineer & design engineer, 1975-79; Ford Motor Co., quality & production supervisor, 1979-81; Eastern Michigan University, visiting lecturer, 1980-81; Ford Aerospace & Communications, prog manager, 1981-86; Anaheim Lincoln Mercury, general manager, 1986-87; Sonoma Ford Lincoln Mercury, president/ceo, 1987-92; Pacific Gas & Electric Co., vice pres of sales & mktg, 1995-96, CEO Pacific Conservation Corp, 1995-, vice pres of business customer svc, 1996-. **Orgs:** National Society of Black Engineering, founder/AEB, 1975-; 100 Black Men of America, vice pres, 1990-92; Oakland Museum, board of directors, 1995-; OICW, board of directors, 1994-; Marcus Foster Foundation, board of directors, 1996-; Purdue University & Sonoma State College, president/advisory bd; American Society of Mechanical Engineers; Society of AUtomotive Engineers. **Honors/Awds:** NSBE, Founders Plaque, 1996; Black Employees Association, Eagle Awd, 1995; Purdue University, Tony Harris Scholarship, Annually. **Business Addr:** Vice Pres of Business Customer SVC, Pacific Gas & Electric, 123 Mission St, H28E, San Francisco, CA 94105, (415)973-3889.

HARRIS, ANTHONY
Professional football player. **Personal:** Born Jan 25, 1973. **Educ:** Auburn. **Career:** Miami Dolphins, linebacker, 1996-. **Business Addr:** Professional Football Player, Miami Dolphins, 2269 NW 199th St, Miami, FL 33056, (305)620-5000.

HARRIS, ARCHIE JEROME
Rehabilitation company executive. **Personal:** Born Dec 2, 1950, Atlanta, GA; son of Essie Lee Brown Harris and Richard E Harris Sr; children: Ajeenah K Harris. **Educ:** Morehouse Coll, BA 1972; Univ of GA, MEduc 1978. **Career:** Atlanta Public Sch System, sub teacher 1972-74; AP Jarrell Pre-Vocational Ctr, work adjustment inst 1974-75; Bobby Dodd Rehab & Industry Ctr, vocational eval 1975-77; Rehabilitation-Exposure Inc, pres 1983-; GA Dept of Human Resources Div of Rehab Serv, sr rehab counselor 1977-88; Rehabilitation-Exposure Inc, Atlanta, GA, pres, 1988-. **Orgs:** Mental Health Assoc of Metro Atlanta Inc 1983-; exec bd mem Statewide Minority Advocacy Group against Alcohol & Drug Abuse 1984-86; pres Atlanta Chap of the Assoc of Black Psychologists; pres, 1984-86, vice pres, 1990-, Atlanta Chapter of the Statewide Minority Advocacy Group for Alcohol & Drug Prevention, 1987-; bd mem, Mental Health Assn of Metropolitan Atlanta, 1989-; chairman, Multicultural Resource Center, Mental Health Assn, 1989-. **Honors/Awds:** Awards for Outstanding Serv & Dedication SMAGADAP 1983-86; Outstanding Young Men of Amer 1984-85; Outstanding Serv Awd Nigerian Student Council 1985; Bobby E Wright Community Serv Award, Assn of Black Psychologists, 1987; Mentor of the Year Award, Big Brothers/Big Sisters of Metropolitan Atlanta, 1988. **Home Addr:** 1948 Creekside Ct, Decatur, GA 30032. **Business Addr:** Pres & Project Dir, Rehabilitation-Exposure Inc, 1513 East Cloveland Ave Suite 105A, East Point, GA 30344.

HARRIS, ARTHUR LEONARD, III
Educator. **Personal:** Born Jul 12, 1949, Pittsburgh, PA; married Wendy; children: Arthur L IV, Wesley P. **Educ:** Comm Coll of Allegheny Co, AS 1971; Temple Univ, BA 1973; Univ of MA, MEd 1976, EdD 1986. **Career:** Univ of MA, grad asst 1973-74; Bd of Educ Springfield MA, classroom instructor 1974-82; Penn State Schuylkill Campus, program asst 1982-84; Penn State Hazleton Campus, dir continuing educ 1984-. **Orgs:** Bd mem Hazleton Leadership; past master Mt Nebo 118 Prince Hall Affiliated; mem Natl Univ Continuing Educ Assoc; mem Hazleton Area Chamber of Commerce; City Council, Pottsville PA, 1994-. **Home Addr:** 319 N Third St, Pottsville, PA 17901. **Business Addr:** Lecturer, Penn State Hazleton, Highacres-Acres, Div of Continuing Educ, Hazleton, PA 18201.

HARRIS, BARBARA ANN
Judge. **Personal:** Born Jul 18, 1951, Atlanta, GA; daughter of Rev & Mrs Thomas Harris Sr. **Educ:** Harvard Univ, AB (cum laude) 1973; Univ of MI Law Sch, attended 1976. **Career:** Justice Charles L Weltner, law clerk 1976-77; Northern Dist of GA, asst US atty 1977-82; Atlanta Municipal Court, assoc judge 1982-92, chief judge, 1992-. **Orgs:** Mem Eta Phi Beta 1980-; exec comm Leadership Atlanta 1987-88; mem State Bar of GA; bd mem Determine Fitness of Bar Applicants Supreme Court of GA; exec comm Gate City Bar Assoc 1985-87; founder GA Assoc of Black Women Attys; bd mem United Servicemen's Organization, Amer Bar Assn, Natl Conf of Special Court Judges; judicial council Natl Bar Assn; officer, Atlanta Womens Network; Drifters Inc, natl parliamentarian, 1990-; board member, Literary Volunteers; Georgia Supreme Ct, Commission on Race and Ethnic Bias, 1993-95, Commission on Equality, 1993-, Commission on Substance Abuse, 1995-. **Honors/Awds:** HO Smith Awd 1969; Jane L Mixer Awd Univ of MI 1976; Awd for Outstanding Public Serv One of GA's 50 Most Influential Black Women GA Coaltion of Black Women 1984; NAACP Awd 1985; Recognized as an Amicus Curiae of the Supreme Court of Georgia, 1995. **Business Addr:** Chief Judge, Atlanta Municipal Court, 170 Garnett St SW, Atlanta, GA 30335, (404)865-8102.

HARRIS, BARBARA CLEMENTE
Episcopal bishop. **Personal:** Born 1931. **Educ:** Urban Theology Unit, Sheffield, England, attended, 1979. **Career:** Sun Oil Co, public relations manager; ordained Episcopal priest, 1980; St Augustine of Hippo Episcopal Church, Norristown PA, priest-in-charge, 1980-84; Episcopal Church Publishing Co, exec dir, 1984-89; Massachusetts Diocese of the Episcopal Church, Boston MA, bishop, 1989-. **Honors/Awds:** Consecrated first female Episcopal Bishop, 1989. **Business Addr:** Bishop, Episcopal Diocese of Massachusetts, 138 Tremont, Boston, MA 02111.

HARRIS, BERNARD A., JR.
Astronaut, physician. **Personal:** Born Jun 26, 1956, Temple, TX; married Sandra Lewis; children: One. **Educ:** University of Houston, BS, 1978; Texas Tech University Health Science Center, MD, 1982; University of Texas Medical Branch, MS, 1996. **Career:** University of Texas Speech & Hearing Institute, research asst, 1975-78; Spectrum Emergency Care, private practice, 1983-85; South Texas Primary Care Group, private practice, 1985-86; San Jose Medical Group, private practice, 1986-87; NASA/Johnson Space Center, clinical scientist/flight surgeon, 1987-90, project manager, 1988-90, astronaut candidate, 1990-91, astronaut, 1991-; University of Texas School of Medicine, clinical professor, 1988-; Baylor College of Medicine, asst professor, 1989-; University of Texas School of Public Health, adjunct professor, 1989-; University of Texas Medical Branch, clinical associate professor, 1993-. **Orgs:** Texas Tech University, board of regents; American College of Physicians, fellow; American Society for Bone and Mineral Research; Association of Space Explorers; American Astronautical Society; Aerospace Medical Association; National Medical Association; Minnesota Medical Association; Texas Medical Association; Bexar County Medical Society; Boys and Girls Club of Houston, board of directors; Greater Houston Area Council on Physical Fitness and Sports, committee member; Manned Space Flight Education Foundation, board of directors. **Honors/Awds:** NASA Lyndon B Johnson Space Center, Group Achievement Award, 1993; NASA Space Flight Medal, 1993; National Technical Association, Physician of the Year, 1993, Achiever of the Year, 1993; Kappa Alpha Psi Fraternity, Achievement Award, 1993; NASA Outstanding Performance Rating, 1993; University of Houston Alumni Organization, Distinguished Alumnus, 1994; ARCS Foundation, Distinguished Scientist of the Year, 1994; Space Act Tech Brief Award, 1995; Honorary Docorate of Sci, Morehouse School of Medicine, 1996; Challenger Award, Ronald McNair Foundation, 1996; Award of Achievement, The Association of Black Cardiologist, 1996; numerous others. **Special Achievements:** First African-American to take a space walk, 1995; author and co-author of several scientific articles and papers. **Business Addr:** Astronaut, Physician, Spacehab, Inc, 1331 Gemini, Ste 340, Houston, TX 77058, (281)242-8737.

HARRIS, BERNARDO JAMAINE
Professional football player. **Personal:** Born Oct 15, 1971, Chapel Hill, NC; married Kellie; children: Bradley. **Educ:** North Carolina, attended. **Career:** Green Bay Packers, linebacker, 1995-. **Business Addr:** Professional Football Player, Green Bay Packers, 1265 Lombardi Ave, Green Bay, WI 54304, (414)494-2351.

HARRIS, BETTY WRIGHT
Chemist. **Personal:** Born Jul 29, 1940, Monroe, LA; daughter of Legertha Wright (deceased) and Henry Jake Wright; married Alloyd Harris Sr (divorced); children: Selita, Jeffrey, Alloyd. **Educ:** Southern Univ Baton Rouge, BS 1961; Atlanta Univ Atlanta, GA 1963; Univ of NM, PhD 1975. **Career:** Los Alamos Natl Lab, research chemist 1972-; Solar Turbines Inc, chief of chemical technology, 1982-84 (on leave from Los Alamos); CO Coll, chemistry teacher, 1974-75; MS Valley State Univ, math, physical science & chemistry teacher 1963; Southern Univ New Orleans, chemistry teacher 1964-72; Los Alamos Sci Lab, vis staff mem summers 1970-72; Intl Business Machines, vis staff mem summer 1969; Univ of OK, research asst summer 1966. **Orgs:** Mem Delta Sigma Theta Sorority 1959-; sec Central NM Section Am Chem Soc 1964-; mem Nat Consortium for Black Professional Devel 1975-; mem US Dept of Labor Women in Comm Serv 1978-; Sunday school, catechism teacher, Lutheran Ch Council; chmn, bd of dirs, Self-Help Inc; chmn, Mission Outreach Bd, sec, Multicultural Commn, Rocky Mountain Synod of the Evangelical Lutheran Church of Amer; mem, Women United for Youth, Albuquerque Public Schools; mem, outreach program, Los Alamos Natl Laboratory; mem, Planning Conf on the Status of Women in Sci, Washington DC (AAAS & NSF), 1977; natl mem NAACP 1975; mem Sigma Xi 1980-; mem Nat Tech Assn 1979-; Natl Assn of Parlimentarians, 1989-; legislative chmn & parlimentarian, Business & Professional Women, Los Alamos, 1987-. **Honors/Awds:** Area Gov of Yr Award, 1978, Able Toastmaster Award, 1979, Distinguished Toastmaster Award, 1980, Distinguished District, 1981, Toastmasters Hall of Fame; author of 6 articles published in professional journals & 8 internal reports for Los Alamos & Solar Turbines Inc; awarded patent in 1986; New Mexico Commission on the Status of Women, Trail Blazer Award, 1990. **Business Addr:** Research Chemist, Los Alamos Natl Laboratory, PO Box 1663, Mail Stop C920, Los Alamos, NM 87544.

HARRIS, BRYANT G.
Consulting engineer. **Personal:** Born Nov 5, 1916, Topeka, KS; son of Georgia Louise Harris and Carl Collins Harris; married Eugenia; children: Bryant II, Michael B. **Educ:** KS State Univ, BS 1939; IL Inst Tech, further studies course advanced testing methods; Small Bus Admin, courses business mgmt; Howard U, seminars intergroup relations; Cornell U, Wilhelm Weinberg seminars labor mgmt public interest; Amer Univ, course facilities mgmt; Control Data Corp, advanced tech course. **Career:** Natl Youth Admin, journeyman electrician 1939-42; Reliable Electric Co Local 134 AFL Chicago, 1939-40; Howard Univ, instr engrg defense training courses 1942-44; War Dept Field Inspections Office, elect engr 1943-45; KDI Corp, consult 1968-69; Howard Univ, asst to vice pres for admin 1969-84, retired asst to vice pres for business & fiscal affairs 1986; private practice, cons; JCH Assn Inc, part owner, sec/treas, 1989-; Harris Elect Co Inc, founder, pres 1946-; Washington DC, professional engineering board 1987-. **Orgs:** Am Inst Elec Electronic Engrs; Illuminating Engineering Soc; mem Nat Tech Assn DC Chpt; Assn DC Univ Phys Plant Mgrs; vice chmn Greater WA Business Cntr; bd advs Nat Alliance of Businessmen; Score; bd dir Better Business Bureau; pres, treas Bureau Rehabilitation; bd mem, pres DC Chamber of Commerce; bd dir Natl Business League; mem SE Neighbors; mem Public Interest Civic Assn; chmn DC Electrical Bd; bd mem Bureau of Rehabilitation; mem Natl Council of Engineering Examiners 1988-; mem Natl Society of Professional Engineers 1988-. **Honors/Awds:** Outstanding Contribution to Civic Betterment of Washington Comm; Outstanding Serv to District of Columbia Chamber of Commmerce; Business Perpetuation Awd Washington Area Contractors Assn; Outstanding Service on Behalf of the Engineering Profession, NHL Society of Professional Engineers 1988; Outstanding Service as Commissioner from MBOC, The Business Exchange Networks 1986; KSU College of Engineering, Distinguished Service Award, 1997; National Technical Award for Action to illuminate and promote the role of African Americans in Science and Tech, 1997. **Home Addr:** 3135 Westover Dr SE, Washington, DC 20020.

HARRIS, BURNELL
Educator, county court clerk. **Personal:** Born Oct 19, 1954, Fayette, MS; son of Louiza Harris and Levi Harris; married Dyann Bell; children: Tomika Tantrice, Tineciaa, Tiaura Tichelle. **Educ:** Alcorn State Univ, BA 1975, MS 1976. **Career:** West District Jr High School, instructor of history 1976-77; AJFC Comm Action Agency, instructor of adult ed 1977-78; Alcorn State Univ, instructor of history 1978-81; Grand Gulf Nuclear Station, bechtel security 1981-83; Jefferson County, circuit clerk 1984-. **Orgs:** Member Jefferson Co NAACP 1970-; member Phi Beta Sigma Fraternity 1976-; secretary Mountain Valley Lodge #6 1978-; member MS Circuit Clerks Assn 1983-; potentate Arabia Shrine Temple #29. **Honors/Awds:** Outstanding Leadership Award Governors Office of Job Development and Training 1978. **Business Addr:** Clerk Circuit Court, Jefferson County Circuit Court, PO Box 305, Fayette, MS 39069.

HARRIS, CALVIN D.
Educational administrator. **Personal:** Born Aug 27, 1941, Clearwater, FL; married Ruth H Owens; children: Randall, Cassandra, Eric. **Educ:** Univ of So FL, BA 1966; Northeast MO State Univ Kirksville, MA 1970; Nova Univ Ft Lauderdale, EdD 1975. **Career:** St Petersburg Jr Coll, dean, director of continuing educ, currently, provost, open campus, beginning 1979, dir spl prgm, 1975-79, dir student comm & serv, 1970-75; Pinellas Co School System, instructor, history, 1966-70. **Orgs:** State Employment & Training Council; Pinellas Co Coord Council; Pinellas Manpower Planning Consortium; State Of FL Standing Comm for Continuing Educ; chmn Pinellas Co Arts Council 1980; chmn Ponce de Leon Elementary Sch Adv Com; dep commissioner Clearwater Babe Ruth Baseball; delegate White House Conf on Families; guest columnist Evening Ind Newspaper; chmn Juvenile Welfare Bd; mem bd of dir Amer Red Cross, YMCA; mem adv bd 1st Union Bank; mem bd of dir Upper Pinellas Assn for Retarded Children, Employment & Devel Council. **Honors/Awds:** Past-Pres Award, Clearwater Amer Little League 1978; Certificate of Appreciation, Pinellas Co Sch Bd 1978; David Bilgore Memorial Award, Clearwater Kiwanis Club 1989. **Military Serv:** AUS sp/4th class 1960-63. **Business Addr:** Dean, Director of Continuing Education, St Petersburg Junior College, PO Box 1284, Tarpon Springs, FL 34688.

HARRIS, CARL GORDON
Educator. **Personal:** Born Jan 14, 1936, Fayette, MO; son of Frances Harris and Carl Harris, Sr. **Educ:** Philander Smith Coll, AB (Cum Laude) 1956; Univ of MO at Columbia, AM 1964; Vienna State Acad of Music, attended 1969; Univ of MO at Kansas City Conservatory of Music, DMusA 1972; Westminster Choir Coll, attended 1979. **Career:** Philander Smith Coll, choral dir asst prof of music 1959-68; VA State Univ, choral dir professor/chmn 1971-84; Norfolk State Univ, choral dir, prof/head, music dept, 1984-97; Bank Street Memorial Baptist Church, minister of music, 1991-; Hampton Univ, adjunct prof of music, 1997-. **Orgs:** Organist Centennial United Methodist Church 1968-71; organist/dir Gillfield Baptist Ch 1974-84; organist/dir Bank St Memorial Bapt Ch 1984-; bd dirs Choristers Guild Dallas TX 1981-87; dean Southside VA Chap Amer Guild of Organists 1984-85; adv panel VA Commn of the Arts 1980-84, 1992-; mem exec bd Tidewater Chap American Guild of Organists 1987-; VA State chmn Jazz and Show Choirs; mem Amer Choral Directors Assoc 1987-; music advisory panel, Southeastern Virginia Arts Assn, 1991-; National Association of Schools of Music Commission on Accreditation, 1992; Norfolk, Virginia Commission on the Arts and Humanities, 1992; Advisory Panel Virginia Youth Symphony, 1990; board of directors, I Sherman Greene Chorale, 1990. **Honors/Awds:** Disting Alumnus Awd Philander Smith Coll, 1975; Outstanding Alumnus Achievement Awd Conservatory of Music Univ of MO Kansas City 1982; AR Traveler Awd Gov Frank White State of AR 1982; published article on "Negro Spiritual" Choristers Guild Letters 1985; published article "Conversation with Undine Smith Moore," Black Perspective in Music 1985; Outstanding Teaching Award Norfolk State Univ, 1987; Author, The Future of Church Music, Proceedings of the National Asson of School of Music, 1994; Author, Guide My Feet, 1995; Reprint of "Conversation with Undine Smithmoore," in Source Readings In American Choral Music, 1996. **Home Addr:** 388 S Military Hwy, No A, Norfolk, VA 23502. **Business Addr:** Minister of Music, Bank St Memorial Baptist Church, 7036 Chesapeake Blvd, Norfolk, VA 23513, (757)857-0197.

HARRIS, CAROL R.
Sales manager. **Personal:** Born Jun 12, 1954, West Point, MS. **Educ:** Cornell Coll IA, BA 1976; Keller Graduate School of

Business, MBA 1978. **Career:** ADT Security Systems, sales manager, 1977-. **Orgs:** Co-chmn, Natl Convention NBMBAA, 1981; member, Natl Black MBA Assn, 1981-; treasurer 1986-89, vice pres 1991, Young Execs in Politics; co-chmn, Young Execs in Politics Awards Banquet, 1989. **Honors/Awds:** ADT Chicago Sales Representative of the Year, 1982, 1984, 1986; Youth Executive of the Year, Young Executives in Politics, 1986; ADT Career Development Program, valedictorian, 1992. **Business Addr:** Sales Manager, ADT Security Systems, 455 W Lake St, Elmhurst, IL 60126.

HARRIS, CAROLYN ANN
Systems analyst. **Personal:** Born Jun 1, 1953, Lynchburg, VA. **Educ:** Brown Univ, BA 1975; Rutgers Univ Graduate School of Mgmt, MBA 1984. **Career:** New Jersey Bell, computer programmer 1976-82; AT&T, mem programming staff 1982-. **Orgs:** Mem, Delta Sigma Theta Sorority Inc, 1976-; membership chair 1980-82, 1986-, recording sec, 1980-82 New Jersey Chap Black Data Processing Assoc; mem, AT&T Alliance of Black Employees, Crossroads Theater Guild & Benefit Commn; financial sec, Central Jersey Alumnae, Delta Sigma Theta Sorority, Inc, 1989-.

HARRIS, CASPA L., JR.
Association executive. **Personal:** Born May 20, 1928, Washington, DC. **Educ:** Amer Univ, BS 1958; Amer Univ Wash Coll of Law, JD 1967. **Career:** Peat Marwick Mitchell & Co, sr auditor 1958-62; Howard Univ, vice pres for bus & fiscal affairs, treas, comptroller 1965-87, chief internal auditor 1962-65, professor law sch 1967-87. **Orgs:** The Common Fund, board of directors; Connie Lee Insurance Co, board of directors, State of VA Debt Mgmt Commission; Presidential Commission on Historical Black Colleges & Universities; Columbian Harmony Soc; Natl Harmony Memorial Park; Supreme Court Bar; Amer, DC, VA Bar Assns; Amer Inst of CPA's; VA Soc of CPA's; The Academy of Mgmt; Financial Executives Inst; Natl Assn of Coll & Univ Bus Officers; mem of various other orgs; Fairfax Co Redevel & Housing Auth, commr, 1970-73; Natl Inst of Health, consult. **Honors/Awds:** Distinguished Alumni Award, The American University, School of Business Administration. **Business Addr:** President, Natl Assn of College & University Business Officers, 1 DuPont Circle NW, Washington, DC 20036.

HARRIS, CHARLES CORNELIUS
Purchasing and capital manager. **Personal:** Born Mar 2, 1951, Arkadelphia, AR; son of Lucy Lois Harris and Benjamin Franklin Harris; married Marva Lee Bradley (deceased); children: Charla Nicole. **Educ:** Stanford U, MCE 1974, BCE 1973. **Career:** Procter & Gamble Cincinnati, OH, Affrmtv Action spclst 1975-76, cost engr 1974-75, bldg design engr 1976-81, proj engr 1981-84, proj mgr 1984-91, program manager, 1991-94, purchasing manager, 1994-. **Orgs:** Adv Jr Achvmnt 1978-81; cnsltnt Cincinnati Mnrty Cntrctrs Asst Corp 1981; chm deacon bd Mt Zion Bapt Ch Woodlawn, OH 1983-96; mem Kappa Alpha Frat 1969-; Sun Sch tchr Mt Zion Bapt Ch Woodlawn, OH 1979-; Cincinnati NAACP, exec bd mem, 1994-96; Black Male Coalition, 1994-. **Honors/Awds:** EIT St of OH 1976; Schlrshp Stanford Univ 1968-73. **Home Addr:** 7337 Quail Run, West Chester, OH 45069. **Business Addr:** Purchasing Manager, Procter & Gamble, 5204 Spring Grove, Foodshop-2, Cincinnati, OH 45224.

HARRIS, CHARLES F.
Journalist director. **Personal:** Born Jan 3, 1934, Portsmouth, VA; married Sammie Jackson; children: Francis, Charles. **Educ:** VA State Coll, BA 1955; NY Univ Grad Sch, attended 1957-63. **Career:** Doubleday & Co Inc, rsch analyst to editor 1956-65; John Wiley & Sons Inc, vice pres gen mgr Portal Press 1965-67; Random House Inc, managing editor & sr editor 1967-71; Howard Univ Press, exec dir 1971-. **Orgs:** Mem Natl Press Club; mem bd dirs Reading is Fundamental; mem Assn of Amer Publishers; mem Assn of Intl Scholarly Publishers; mem Washington Area Book Pusblishers; adjunct prof of journalism Howard Univ; mem bd dirs Assn of Amer Univ Presses 1984; dir Laymen's Natl Bible Comm 1985. **Military Serv:** AUS 2nd lt 1956; Honorable Discharge. **Business Addr:** Executive Dir, Amistad Press, 22 Division Ave NE, Washington, DC 20019.

HARRIS, CHARLES SOMERVILLE
Sports educator. **Personal:** Born Aug 22, 1950, Richmond, VA; married Lenora Billings. **Educ:** Hampton Inst, BA/BS 1972; Univ of Michigan, MS 1973. **Career:** Hampton Inst, audio-vis specialist 1972-73; Newsweek, staff writer 1973; Univ of Michigan, asst athletic dir 1973-79; Univ of Pennsylvania, dir of athletics 1979-85; Arizona State Univ, dir of athletics, 1985-1996; Mid-Eastern Athletic Conference, commissioner, currently. **Orgs:** Mem Kappa Alpha Psi 1971-; mem Valley Big Brother 1985-; mem Valley of the Sun YMCA 1986-; mem Sigma Pi Phi 1987-; mem numerous natl collegiate athletic assoc comms. **Business Addr:** 102 N. Elm St., Suite 401, Greensboro, NC 27402.

HARRIS, CHARLES WESLEY
Educator. **Personal:** Born Sep 12, 1929, Auburn, AL; children: Neeka, Angela. **Educ:** Morehouse College BA 1949; Univ of PA, MA 1950; Univ of WI, PhD 1959; Harvard U, 1964; Univ of MI, 1966. **Career:** TX Coll, asst prof of political science 1950-53; Tuskegee Inst, asst prof political science 1954-56; Grambling State Univ, assoc prof of political science 1959-61; Coppin State Coll, assoc prof political science 1961-70; Howard Univ, associate dean, college of arts and sciences, prof of political science, currently. **Orgs:** Research assoc Xerox Corp 1968; div chf & sr spec Govt Div Cong Res Serv 1974-74; Alpha Phi Alpha Frat. **Honors/Awds:** James Fund Fellowship Univ of WI 1956-58; Ford Rsch Grant Ford Fnd 1969; Pi Gamma Mu Hon Soc Univ of PA Chap 1951; Alpha Kappa Mu Hon Soc; Brookings Institution, Visiting Scholar, 1987-88, 1995; Woodrow Wilson International Ctr for Scholars, Smithsonian Institution, Fellow, 1992-94. **Special Achievements:** Author: ''Congress & the Governance of the Nation's Capital'', Georgetown University Press, 1995; Perspectives of Political Power in the District of Columbia, National Institute of Public Management, 1981; ''Resolving the Legislative Veto Issue,'' Washington, DC, Natl Inst of Public Mgmt, 1979; ''Regional Councils of Government and the Central City,'' Detroit: Metropolitan Fund, 1970. **Military Serv:** AUS t-4 1947-48. **Business Addr:** Professor of Political Science, Howard University, 2400 6th St NW, Howard Univ, Washington, DC 20059.

HARRIS, CLIFTON L.
Construction/real estate contractor, mayor. **Personal:** Born Feb 3, 1938, Leland, MS; son of Gertrude Harris and Willie Harris; married Maxine Robinson; children: La'Clitterfer Charisse Harris. **Career:** Harris Construction Co, Arcola MS, owner, 29 years; C & M Realty Co, Arcola MS, owner, 9 years; Town of Arcola, Arcola MS, mayor, 1986-. **Orgs:** Mem, NAACP, 1969; Elk Lodge, 1984, Deercreek Natl Gas Dist, 1986-, Salvation Army, 1986; board member, American Red Cross, 1988-; treasurer, Mississippi Conference of Black Mayors, 1990; board member, NAACP. **Honors/Awds:** Certificate of Achievement, Delta Jr Coll, 1983-84; Certificate of Achievement, Howard Univ, 1988; Certificate of Accomplishment, Clark Atlanta University; Meritorious Service Award, NAACP. **Home Addr:** PO Box 383, Arcola, MS 38722.

HARRIS, COREY LAMONT
Professional football player. **Personal:** Born Oct 25, 1969, Indianapolis, IN; children: Lauren. **Educ:** Vanderbilt, BS in human resources. **Career:** Green Bay Packers, defensive back, 1992-94; Seattle Seahawks, 1995-96; Miami Dolphins, 1997-. **Business Addr:** Professional Football Player, Miami Dolphins, 2269 NW 199th St, Miami, FL 33056, (305)620-5000.

HARRIS, CORNELIA
Educator. **Personal:** Born Sep 30, 1963, Ennis, TX; daughter of Cleo Collins and Virgil L Collins, Sr; married Douglas E Harris, Jun 9, 1992. **Educ:** Texas Woman's Univ, B Social Work 1985; Alternative Certification Program, Dallas, TX, 1990-. **Career:** Federal Correctional Inst Seagoville TX, correctional intern 1984; TX Woman's Univ Police and Safety, student police aid 1985; Martin Luther King Jr Comm Ctr, social worker intern 1985; Big Brothers & Sisters of Metro Dallas, caseworker 1986-90; Dallas Independent School District, Dallas, TX, teacher, kindergarten, 1990-. **Orgs:** Mem Young Democrats TWU campus 1982-83; mem NAACP TWU Campus 1982-85; mem Alpha Omega Social Club TWU 1983-84; mem Delta Sigma Theta Sor Inc 1983-; mem Social Sciences Soc TWU Campus 1985; mem Natl Assn of Social Workers 1985-88, Natl Assn of Black Social Workers 1985-90. **Honors/Awds:** Natl Dean's List 1985-86; Outstanding Young Women of American, 1986.

HARRIS, CURTIS ALEXANDER
Investment banker. **Personal:** Born Jul 23, 1956, San Diego, CA. **Educ:** US Military Acad West Point, BS 1978; Wharton School at Univ of PA, MBA 1985. **Career:** Smith, Barney, Harris, Upham & Co, assoc public finance 1985-87; W R Lazard & Co, 1987-89; Kidder, Peabody & Co, asst vice pres 1989-. **Orgs:** Mem Alpha Phi Alpha 1980-, Black MBA Assoc 1985-, West Point Soc of NY 1985-, Natl Assoc of Securities Prof 1986-. **Military Serv:** USA capt 5 yrs; US Paratroopers Badge, Sr Instructor & Ordnance Corp 1978-83.

HARRIS, CYNTHIA JULIAN
Administrator. **Personal:** Born Oct 11, 1953, Burlington, NC. **Educ:** Univ of NC Chapel Hill, BA 1975; Univ of VA Charlottesville, MA 1977. **Career:** Employment Security Commission Greensboro NC, employment aide 1976; Project AID-SIR/ Richmond VA, rehab counselor 1977-78; North Carolina State Univ, dir of Upward Bound, sec of NCSU Black Faculty & Staff, 1986-87. **Orgs:** Workshop presenter SAEOPP Mobile AL 1985, NCCEOP Wrightsville NC 1986; sec exec bd NC-CEOP State Org 1985-87. **Honors/Awds:** Proposal Reader Dept of Educ Washington DC 1984. **Business Addr:** Dir, Upward Bound, NC State Univ, Box 7317, Raleigh, NC 27695.

HARRIS, DAISY
Disc jockey. **Personal:** Born Apr 22, 1931, Hattiesburg, MS; divorced; children: James, Jr, Anthony, Harold. **Educ:** Pearl River Jr Coll, Sec Cluster Course. **Career:** WDAM-TV, sec, receptionist 2 yrs; WORV Radio, dj, sec; CORE, sncc, complete ofc work. **Orgs:** NAACP; MFDP; civil rights work 1963-68; sec 5th dist Loyalist Dem Party; third class FCC Radio Lic; vol worker SCLC; chmn Voter Registrn. **Honors/Awds:** Most Popular Disc Jockey; award for work in Civil Rights; honored for work in comm serv 1973-74.

HARRIS, DAVID, JR.
Clergyman. **Personal:** Born Apr 12, 1931, Dallas, TX. **Educ:** Wiley Coll, BS 1957; Southwestern Seminary, BD 1967, MRE 1969; Teomer Sch of Religion, LLD 1981; Southwestern Seminary, MA 1983. **Career:** NAACP, advisor 1970-80; Suburban Tribune, publisher 1983-85; Second Corinthian Church, pastor 1970-. **Orgs:** Advisor Urban League 1980-85; pres Wiley Coll Alumni 1981-83; advisor Black Coll Alumni Assn 1984-85; mem Master Masons AF & AM. **Honors/Awds:** ''Jesse Jackson, Is He a Phony?'' the Suburban Tribune; ''The Jubilee Year'' Dallas Post Tribune 1984; ''The Story of Pacific Ave School in Dallas TX'' the Post Tribune 1983; ''What Happened to Booker T Washington Trophies?''; KY Col Honors; Hons from the City of Atlanta GA; Honors from the City of Detroit MI.

HARRIS, DAVID ELLSWORTH
Pilot (retired). **Personal:** Born Dec 22, 1934, Columbus, OH; son of Ruth A Estis Harris (deceased) and Wilbur R Harris (deceased); married Lynne Purdy Harris, Feb 26, 1989; children: Camian, Leslie. **Educ:** Ohio State Univ, BS 1957. **Career:** Amer Airlines, capt 1964-94. **Orgs:** Mem, former pres Organization of Black Airline Pilots; former mem NAI. **Honors/Awds:** Black Achievement in Indus Award, YMCA 1971. **Military Serv:** USAF cpt 1958-64. **Business Addr:** Captain, American Airlines, Logan Intl Airport East, Boston, MA 02128.

HARRIS, DAVID L.
Advertising executive. **Personal:** Born Apr 26, 1952, Washington, DC; son of Laura E Hart Harris and Reuben T Harris; married Sheila A Smith Harris, Aug 27, 1983; children: David Jr, Todd. **Educ:** Boston University, Boston, MA, BA, 1974; University of North Carolina at Chapel Hill, MBA, 1976. **Career:** Foote Cone & Belding, Chicago, IL, & New York, NY, account exec, 1976-79; Ketchum Advertising, Washington, DC, account supervisor, 1979-82; NY Ayer, New York, NY, vice pres, account supervisor, 1982-85; Ogilvy & Mather, Atlanta, GA, account supervisor, 1985-88; Lockhart & Pettus, New York, NY, senior vice pres, 1988-.

HARRIS, DERRICK
Professional football player. **Personal:** Born Aug 18, 1972, Willowridge, TX. **Educ:** Miami (Fla.). **Career:** St Louis Rams, running back, 1996-. **Business Addr:** Professional Football Player, St Louis Rams, One Rams Way, St Louis, MO 63045, (314)982-7267.

HARRIS, DEWITT O.
Postal service manager. **Personal:** Born Aug 10, 1944, Washington, DC; son of Corinne Banks Harris-Thomas and DeWitt Harris; married Brenda Bing Harris, Dec 31, 1968; children: Rhonda, Tanya. **Educ:** Johnson C Smith Univ, Charlotte, NC, BA, 1966; Southeastern University, Washington, DC, MBPA, 1979. **Career:** US Postal Service, Washington, DC, contact compliance examiner, 1968-76, manager, eeo complaints div, 1976-79, general manager affirmative action division, 1979-86, US Postal Service, Green Bay, WI, msc/manager postmaster, 1986-90; US Postal Service, Milwaukee, WI, dir city oper, 1988-90; US Postal Service, Dayton, OH, msc manager/postmaser, 1990-92. **Orgs:** Member, NAACP, 1966-. **Honors/Awds:** PCES Special Achievement Award, US Postal Service, 1988; Central Region Eagle Award, US Postal Service, 1988. **Military Serv:** US Army, E5, 1968-70, Bronze Star (2), Commendation Medal, Air Medal, Vietnam Cross of Gallantry, Purple Heart. **Business Addr:** District Manager, Customer Service and Sales, US Postal Service, 2970 Market St, Rm 306A, Philadelphia, PA 19104-9997.

HARRIS, DOLORES M.
Educational administrator (retired). **Personal:** Born Aug 5, 1930, Camden, NJ; daughter of Frances Gatewood Ellis and Roland H Ellis (deceased); children: Morris E Jr, Sheila D Rodman, Gregory M. **Educ:** Glassboro State Coll, BS 1959, MA 1966; Rutgers Univ, EdD 1983. **Career:** Glassboro Bd of Educ, tchr adminstr 1959-70; Camden Welfare Bd, supvr adult ed ctr 1968; SCOPE Glassboro Ctr, dir Headstart 1969-70; Natl ESL Training Inst Jersey City State Coll, assoc dir 1971; Glassboro State Coll, dir cont educ 1970-, acting vice pres for academic affairs 1989, dir of continuing educ 1990-91. **Orgs:** Bd dirs Adult Educ Assn of USA 1973-79; consul NJ Gov's Conf on Libraries & Info Serv 1979; examiner NY Civil Serv 1976-; chair of adv bd Women's Educ Equity Comm Network Project 1977-78 1980; bd dirs Glassboro State Coll Mgmt Inst 1975-; consul Temple Univ 1978-79; consul NY Model Cities Right to Read Natl Training Conf 1973-81; comm NJ Task Force on Thorough & Efficient Educ 1976-78; legislative comm Amer Assn for Adult & Continuing Educ 1982-; mem Gloucester Co Private Industry Cncl 1984-; 1st vice pres, 1984-88, pres, 1988-, Natl Assn of Colored Women's Clubs Inc 1984-; vice pres at large Northeastern Fedn of Colored Women's Clubs Inc 1983-;

·es vice pres other offices NJ State Fedn of Colored Women's lubs Inc 1972-80; pres South Jersey Chap of Links Inc 1984-; ·es vicepres otheffices Gloucester Co United Way 1968-; fndr nair of bd Glassboro Child Develop Ctr 1974-82; pres Glassoro State Coll Alumni Assn 1975-77; delegate Intl Women's r Natl Conf 1978; vice chair, 1983-86, chair, 1986-, Commn n Status of Women Gloucester Co NJ; Natl Council of Vomen, exec comm & educ chair. **Honors/Awds:** Disting Serv wd Assn for Adult Educ of NJ 1974; Disting Alumna Awd lassboro State Coll NJ 1971; fndr editor, Newsletter "For dults Only" Glassboro State Coll NJ 1970-74; editor, Newstter AEA/USA Commn on Status of Women Washington DC 973-75; Comm Serv Awd Holly Shores Girl Scouts NJ 1981; resident's Awd United Way of Gloucester Co Woodbury NJ 985; co-author "Black Studies Curriculumfor Corrections" arden State Sch Dist Trenton NJ 1975; Gloucester Cnty Busiess & Professional Women's Club, woman of the year awd 985; Holly Shores Girl Scouts, citizen of the year awd 1987; bony 100 MostInfluential Black Americans May, 1989, 1990; ose Award Delta Kappa Gamma, Alpha Zeta State 1989; Voman of the year Zeta Phi Beta, Gamma Nu Zeta 1989; Vomen of Achievement Award Douglas College aNJ State ederation of Women's Club 1991. **Home Addr:** RD1 Box 96, South Academy St, Glassboro, NJ 08028.

ARRIS, DON NAVARRO
iochemist. **Personal:** Born Jun 17, 1929, New York, NY; son f Margaret Vivian Berkley Harris and John Henry Harris; maried Regina B; children: Donna Harris-Wolfe, John Craig, Scott nthony. **Educ:** Lincoln Univ PA, AB 1951; Rutgers Univ, MS 959, PhD 1963. **Career:** Colgate Palmolive Research Ctr, sr ·s 1963-64; Rutgers Univ, asst research specialist 1964-65, ssoc prof 1975-77; Squibb Inst for Med Rsch, rsch fellow 965-; Temple University School of Medicine, assoc prof, curently. **Orgs:** Mem Amer Assoc Adv of Sci 1966-; mem, treas, d dir Frederick Douglass Liberation Library 1970-82; steering omm 1975-, sec 1986- Biochem Pharmacology Discussion roup of the NY Acad of Sci; mem Philadelphia Physiological oc 1978-, Amer Soc for Pharmacology and Exp Ther 1980-; onsultant US Army Sci Bd 1981-85; reviewer Natl Science 'oundation 1981-; advisory comm Biochem Section of NY cad of Sci 1983-; vstg lecturer Lincoln Univ PA 1983-; particant Natl Urban League Black Exec Prog; lecturer TX Southrn Univ 1984; editorial bd mem Journal of Enzyme Inhibition 985-; mem Sigma Xi, NY Acad of Sci, Amer Heart Assoc, mer Chem Soc, Theta Psi Lambda Chapter of Alpha Phi lpha, Mu Boule, Sigma Pi Phi; lecturer So Univ Baton Rouge A 1987. **Honors/Awds:** Author or co-author of 40 scientific apers, 40 scientific abstracts and 4 patents; Recipient of Harem YMCA Black Achievers Award 1984. **Military Serv:** AUS Medical Corp speclst 2 yrs. **Business Addr:** Research Fellow, ristol-Myers Squibb Pharmaceutical Research Institute, Dept f Cardiovascular Biochemistry, PO Box 4000, Princeton, NJ 8543-4000.

HARRIS, DONALD J.
Economist, educator. **Educ:** UCWI-London University, BA 961; University of California Berkeley, PhD 1966. **Career:** University of Illinois Champaign, asst professor 1965-67; University of Wisconsin Madison, associate professor 1968-71; Stanford University, professor 1972-. **Orgs:** Consultant to international agencies, private foundations and governments; researcher & lecturer at numerous universities & institutes in various countries including: Mexico, Holland, England, Brazil, taly, India, Africa, the Caribbean; bd editor, Journal of Economic Literature, 1979-84. **Honors/Awds:** Natl Research Council, Ford Found Fellowship 1984-85; numerous publications in professional journals & books; Fulbright Scholar, Brazil 1990, 1991, Mexico 1992. **Business Addr:** Professor, Dept of Economics, Stanford University, Stanford, CA 94305.

HARRIS, DOUGLAS ALLAN
Marketing executive. **Personal:** Born Feb 7, 1942, Burlington, NJ; son of Marvel Clark Harris and Milton Harris; married Myrna L Hendricks. **Educ:** Trenton State Coll, BA Educ 1964; Rutgers Univ Graduate School of Educ, MEd 1973; Fordham Univ Graduate School of Bus, MBA Mgmt & Mktg 1980. **Career:** NJ Bd of Educ, teacher 1964-69; Webster Div McGraw-Hill Book Co, dir of mktg serv 1969-76; RR Bowker, mgr Educ Admin book div 1976-79; Scott, Foresman & Co, marketing manager, 1980-86; American Dental Association, director of marketing, 1986-88; Silverman's Dental Supplies, marketing manager; Portfolio Associate Inc, project manager, currently. **Orgs:** Mem Council of Concerned Black Exec 1975-78, Amer Assn for Adult Continuing Ed 1980-; founding bd mem Literacy Volunteers of Chicago 1982-; vice pres bd Simek Mem Counseling Ctr 1983-; dir, Middle Atlantic Assn of Temporary Services 1989. **Honors/Awds:** Volunteer of the Year, North Shore Magazine 1985; Gold Award/Marketing Training, American Marketing Assn 1987; Ordained Baptist Deacon 1985. **Home Addr:** 10 Drummers Ln, Wayne, PA 19087. **Business Phone:** (215)627-3660.

HARRIS, EARL L.
State representative, entrepreneur. **Personal:** Born Nov 5, 1941, Kerrville, TN; son of Magnolia Hall Harris and Collins Harris; married Donna Jean Lara, 1969. **Educ:** Indiana University-Northwest, 1961-62; Purdue University, Calumet IN, 1966-67; Illinois Inst of Tech. **Career:** Inland Steel Company; Amer Maize Products Co, laboratory tester; Kentucky Liquors and Kentucky Snack Shop, owner, operator, currently; Indiana House of Representatives, legislator, 12th dist, 1982-. **Orgs:** NAACP; past pres, East Chicago Black Coalition, East Chicago Homeowners Assn; vice co-chm, Ways and Means Comm, Indiana House of Rep, currently. **Military Serv:** Naval Reserves, two years. **Business Addr:** Legislator, Indiana House of Representatives, State Capitol, Indianapolis, IN 46204.

HARRIS, EDDY LOUIS
Author. **Personal:** Born Jan 26, 1956, Indianapolis, IN; son of Georgia Louise Harris and Samuel Eddy Harris. **Educ:** Leland Stanford Jr University, BA, 1977. **Career:** Author of books: Mississippi Solo, 1988, Native Stranger, Simon & Schuster, 1992. **Honors/Awds:** A World of Difference, and American Motorcyclist Assn, MVP Award. **Special Achievements:** Author, South of Haunted Dreams, Simon and Schuster, 1993; Author, Still Life in Harlem, Henry Holt, 1996. **Home Addr:** 607 S Elliott Ave, Kirkwood, MO 63122.

HARRIS, EDWARD E.
Educator. **Personal:** Born Feb 27, 1933, Topeka, KS. **Educ:** Lincoln U, AB 1954; Univ IA, AM 1958, PhD 1963; WI U, post grad 1972. **Career:** IN Univ, Purdue Univ Indianapolis, assoc prof sociology 1968-; CA State Coll, asst prof 1965-68; Prairie View A&M Coll, TX, assoc prof 1963-64. **Orgs:** Mem Am & No Central Sociological Assns ed bd Coll Student Journal 1971-; contrib articles to professional jrnls. **Military Serv:** AUS 1965-56. **Business Addr:** Sociology Dept, IN Univ PurdueUniv, Indianapolis, IN 46208.

HARRIS, ELBERT L.
Educator (retired). **Personal:** Born Feb 16, 1913, Baltimore, MD; married Claudette Archer; children: Susan, Elbert Jr. **Educ:** West Chester State Coll, BS 1937; Howard Univ, MA 1939; Univ of MI, 1940; Oxford Univ, 1945; Univ of PA, PhD 1959. **Career:** St Paul Ind School, instructor 1940, acting dean 1941-42; Livingstone Coll, instructor 1946-59; Delaware State Coll, dept head language & literature 1959-60, dept head social science 1962-65; Cheyney State Coll, prof 1965-69; Swarthmore Coll, visiting lecturer 1968; Rutgers Univ, dir black studies and prof of history 1969-82, prof emeritus 1982; Northern Illinois University, Department of History, assistant professor, 1991-92. **Honors/Awds:** Livingstone College, Plaque; Rutgers, Award for Service to African-American Students, 1972; Academy of Human Service, 1974; two General Board of Education Grants; Danforth Fellowship. **Special Achievements:** Author: General Amemhals, Egyptian Warrior, Killers of the City, The Athenian, Sojourn in Persepolis, Private Undre Luneville of Harlem. **Military Serv:** US Army 1942-45.

HARRIS, ELIHU MASON
Legislator/attorney. **Personal:** Born Aug 15, 1947, Los Angeles, CA; son of Frances Harris and Elihu Harris, Sr.; married Kathy Neal. **Educ:** CA State at Hayward, BA 1968; Univ CA Berkeley, MA 1969; Univ of CA Davis,JD 1972. **Career:** Congresswoman Yvonne Burke, legislative asst 1974-75; Natl Bar Assn, exec dir 1975-77; Alexander Millner & McGee, partner 1979; State of CA, assemblyman.

HARRIS, EUGENE EDWARD
Personnel administrator. **Personal:** Born Feb 10, 1940, Pittsburgh, PA; married Marva Jo. **Educ:** PA State U, BA Labor Econ; Univ of Pittsburgh, MPA Public Admin 1969; Duquesne Univ Law Sch, JD 1980. **Career:** US Steel, mgr employment 1978-; asst mgr/mgr labor relations 1973-78, prog coord Gary Proj 1969, labor contract adminstr 1968, labor contract admnstr Clairton Works 1965, pers serv analyst 1964. **Orgs:** Chmn Gary Concentrated Employ Prgm 1969-73; chmn Gary Econ Devel Corp 1970-73; dir Gary Urban League 1970-72; treas Comm Partners Corp 1975-. **Honors/Awds:** Capt PA State Univ Basketball team 1962; hon mention, All-Am 1962. **Military Serv:** AUS sp4 1963-68. **Business Addr:** 600 Grant St, Pittsburgh, PA 15230.

HARRIS, FRAN
Professional basketball player. **Personal:** Born Mar 12, 1965. **Educ:** Texas, bachelor's and master's degrees in journalism. **Career:** Houston Comets, guard, 1997-. **Special Achievements:** Author: Dream Season; About My Sister's Business: The Black Woman's Road Map to Successful Entrepreneurship, 1996. **Business Addr:** Professional Basketball Player, Houston Comets, Two Greenway Plaza, Ste 400, Houston, TX 77046, (713)627-9622.

HARRIS, FRANCIS C.
Author, historian. **Personal:** Born Sep 25, 1957, Brooklyn, NY; son of Charles & Sammie Harris. **Educ:** Cambridge College, Masters of Education/MGMT, 1992. **Career:** Author: "Senior Researcher for A Hard Road," 1983-86; "To Glory: The History of the African," summer, 1987; "Arthur R Ashe, Jr, American Athlete," 1992-93; contributor to Paul Robeson: Artist & Citizen published by Rutgers Univ Press, 1998; wrote essay "Paul Robeson: An Athlete's Legacy;" author of "The Amistad Pictorial History of the African American Athlete Collegiate & Professional," 1998. **Business Addr:** Author/Historian, c/o Amistad Press Inc, 225 Lafayette St, Ste 806, New York, NY 10012, (212)965-8794.

HARRIS, FRANCO
Business executive, professional football player (retired). **Personal:** Born Mar 7, 1950, Fort Dix, NJ; son of Gina Parenti and Cad Harris; married Dana Dokmanovich; children: Franco Dokmanovich Harris. **Educ:** Penn State Univ, BS, 1972. **Career:** Pittsburgh Steelers, running back, 1972-83; Seattle Seahawks, running back, 1984; Franco's All Natural, pres; Park Sausages, owner, currently; Super Bakery Inc, owner, currently. **Honors/Awds:** Played in the AFC Championship Game, 1972, 1974, 1975, 1978, 1979; played in the Pro Bowl, 1972-78; NFL Rookie of the Year, 1972; won four Super Bowls with Pittsburgh Steelers; Penn State Univ, Distinguished Alumnus, 1982; Pro Football Hall of Fame, 1990. **Business Addr:** Owner, Super Bakery Inc, 201 McKnight Park Dr, Pittsburgh, PA 15237, (412)367-2518.

HARRIS, FRED
Publsiher, editor. **Personal:** Born Sep 27, Gary, IN; married. **Educ:** Indiana University; Columbia University. **Career:** Gary American Newspaper, editor, publisher; Vet in Politics, PR man; Amer Legion Post 498, comdr. **Orgs:** NAACP. **Honors/Awds:** Vet in Politics Award 1973; Am Legion Award 1972-75. **Military Serv:** US Army, private first class. **Business Addr:** Editor/Publisher, Gary American, 2268 Broadway, Gary, IN 46407.

HARRIS, FREEMAN COSMO
Publisher. **Personal:** Born Jul 14, 1935, Andrews, SC; married W Mae Harris; children: Audrey, Angela, Bontrice, Carla, Dane, Ronnie, Edwana, Alexandria, Melissa, Gabriel. **Educ:** Adjutant Gen Sch, Ft Ben Harrison, IN; RCA, NY; ATS, NY. **Career:** Denver Weekly News, publisher, K36CP TV, KAGM FM, currently; KBPI, sta mgr, commercial mgr, prgm dir, air personality; KFML Radio, air personality; KFSC Radio AE & AP; KDKO AM; WVOE Radio AE & AP; WYNN Radio AE & AP; WATP Radio AE & AP; Channel 4 Gospel Experience, host; Signal Sch of Broadcasting, instr; Denver Chronicle Newspapers, columnist, acct exec. **Orgs:** Mem Nat Newspaper Pub Assn; CO Press Assn; Advtsng Club of Denver; chmn bd & pres Dark Fire Publ House Inc; owner Tasta Printing Co; bd of dirs US Black C of C; pres emeritus Denver Black C of C; mem Black Media Inc; chmn E Neighborhood Anti-Crime Adv Counc. **Military Serv:** US Air Force, Airman 2nd Class. **Business Addr:** Publisher, Denver Weekly News, PO Box 5008, Denver, CO 80217-5008.

HARRIS, GARY LYNN
Educator. **Personal:** Born Jun 24, 1953, Denver, CO; son of Gladys Weeams and Norman Harris; married Jennifer Dean, May 19, 1984; children: Jamie Harris. **Educ:** Cornell Univ, Ithaca, NY, BSEE, 1975, MSEE, 1976, PhD in EE, 1980. **Career:** Natl Research & Resource Facility for Sumicron Structures, Ithaca, NY, asst, 1977-80; Naval Research Laboratory, Washington, DC, visiting scientist, 1981-82; Howard Univ, Washington, DC, assoc prof, 1980-; Lawrence Livermore Natl Laboratory, consultant 1984-. **Orgs:** Mem, Sigma Xi, Inst of Electrical & Electronic Engineers; chmn, IEEE Electron Devices, Washington Section, 1984-86; mem of selection comm, Black Engineer ofthe year, 1989. **Honors/Awds:** IBM Graduate Fellow, 1978-80; author of on the Origin of Periodic Surface Structure of Laser Annealed Semiconduct, 1978; Robert Earle Fellowship; 1980; author of SIMS Determinations on Ion Implanted Depth Distributions, 1980; author ofAn Experimental Study of Capless Annealing on Ion Implanted GaAs, 1983; author ofElectronic States of Polycrystalline GaAs & Their Effects on Phtovoltaic Cells, 1983; author of Geltering of Semi-Insulation Liquid Incapsulated GaAs for Direc t Ion Implanation, 1984. **Business Addr:** Materials Science Research Center, Howard Univ/Eng, L K Downing Hall, 2300 6th St, NW, Washington, DC 20059.

HARRIS, GERALDINE E.
Scientist. **Personal:** Born in Detroit, MI; divorced; children: Reginald, Karen. **Educ:** Wayne State Univ Med Tech, BS 1956; Wayne State Univ, MS Microbiology 1969, PhD Microbiology 1974. **Career:** Detroit General Hosp, med tech 1956-60; Parke Davis & Co, asst res microbiol 1961-66; Wayne St Univ Dept of Biol, rsch asst 1967-68; Wayne State Univ Coll of Med, tutor/advisor post baccal prog 1971-73; Drake Inst of Sci, consult 1971-73; Met Hosp Dt, microbiol 1975; Winston-Salem State Univ, asst prof microbiol 1975-77; Clinical Microbiology Group Health Assn Inc, chief; Allied Health Prog Devel Amer Assn State Colls & Univs Washington, assoc coord; Food & Drug Admin Center for Food Safety & Applied Nutrition, consumer safety officer 1980-. **Orgs:** Reg Amer Soc Clinical Pathology MT #28926 1956-; Amer Soc for Microbiol 1967-; Assn Univ Prof 1968-; Sigma Xi; Assn for Advance of Sci 1975-; consult Natl Caucus on Black Aged 1976; partic Educ Computers in Minority Inst 1977; mem Alpha Kappa Alpha Sor, Urban League, Orphan Found. **Honors/Awds:** NIH Pre-Doctoral Fellow 1968-71.

HARRIS, GIL W.
Educator. **Personal:** Born Dec 9, 1946, Lynchburg, VA; married Paula Bonita Gillespie; children: Deborah Nicole Gillespie-Harris, Paul Henry Gillespie-Harris. **Educ:** Natl Acad of Broadcasting, dipl radio &TV 1964-65; Winston-Salem Coll, AS 1969-71; Shaw Univ, BA 1977-80; NC A&T St Univ, MS 1981-82; Pacific Western Univ, PhD 1986. **Career:** WEAL/WQMG Radio Stations, oper dir 1972-79; Shaw Univ, dir of radio broadcasting 1979-81; Collegiate Telecommunications, system producer, sport dir 1981-84; SC St Coll, asst prof of broadcasting 1984-. **Orgs:** Mem Omega Psi Phi, Prince Hall Mason, NAACP. **Honors/Awds:** Citizen of the Week WGHP TV High Point NC 1977; Radio Announcer of the Year Dudley HS 1979; Outstanding Media Serv Triad Sickle Cell 1979; Outstanding Media Serv Mid-Eastern Athletic Conf 1983; Outstanding Media Serv Central Intercoll Athletic Assoc. **Military Serv:** USA sp5-e5 3 yrs; Army Commendation with "V" Device 1965-68. **Home Addr:** 416 Robinson St NE, Orangeburg, SC 29115.

HARRIS, GLADYS BAILEY
Administrative law judge. **Personal:** Born Mar 23, 1947, Boykins, VA; daughter of Dorothy R Ferguson Bailey and William L Bailey; married Stanley Christian Harris Sr, Aug 3, 1968; children: Stanley Jr, Chad Gregory, Adrienne Michelle. **Educ:** Virginia State Univ, Petersburg, VA, BS, biology, 1968; Univ of Richmond, Richmond, VA, JD, 1981. **Career:** School Board of the City of Richmond, Richmond, VA, general counsel, 1981-83; University of Richmond, Richmond, VA, adjunct professor, 1983-84, 1991-; Law Office of Gladys Bailey Harris, solo practicioner, Richmond, VA, 1983-86; Supreme Court of Virginia, Richmond, VA, hearing officer/administrative law judge, 1983-; Clute & Shilling, Richmond, VA, partner/attorney, 1986-87; Virginia Alcoholic Beverage Control Board, Richmond, VA, agency head/chairman of the board, 1987-90; Virginia Alliance for Minority Participation in Science & Engineering, VAMPSE, Richmond, VA, executive director, 1990-91; Law Office Of Gladys Bailey Harris, solopractitioner, Richmond, VA, 1990-92; Carpenter & Harris, Richmond, VA, partner, 1992-. **Orgs:** University of Richmond, Alumni bd mem, 1988-; board member, Local Community Colleges Board, 1991-; board member, Virginia Institute for Law and Citizenship Studies, 1988-; board member, Commonwealth Girl Scout Council of Virginia, 1988-; arbitrator, New York Stock Exchange, 1983-; commissioner, Circuit Court of the City of Richmond, 1991-; member, Virginia State Bar Committee on Professionalism, 1991-. **Honors/Awds:** Citizen of the Year, NAFEO/Virginia State University, 1990; SERWA Award, National Coalition of 100 Black Women, 1990; Distinguished Service Award, Richmond Area Program for Minorities in Engineering, 1988; Honorary Woodrow Wilson Fellow, Woodrow Wilson Foundation, 1968. **Home Addr:** 4210 Southaven Rd, Richmond, VA 23235-1029. **Business Addr:** Managing Partner, 321 Franklin St, Richmond, VA 23220.

HARRIS, GLEASON RAY
Chief estimator. **Personal:** Born Jun 19, 1952, Norfolk, VA; married Jacqueline Theresa; children: Devanae Nicole, Deondra Laneese. **Educ:** Attended, Univ of Louisville 1983; Louisville Voc/Tech Inst, A 1978. **Career:** Anderson & Assoc Architects, sr designer 1978-80; Kamex Construction, estimator/designer 1980-83; Tidewater Design Assocs, pres/designer 1984-86; Public Storage Inc, chief estimator 1986-. **Orgs:** Mem Amer Inst for Design & Drafting 1983, Louisville Minority Contractors Assoc 1984, KY State Highway Minority Contractors Assoc 1984; mem Louisville Urban League 1985. **Business Addr:** Chief Estimator, Public Storage Inc, 1230 S Capitol St SE, Washington, DC 20003-3523.

HARRIS, HARCOURT GLENTIES
Physician. **Personal:** Born Apr 16, 1928, New York, NY; married Charlotte L Hill; children: Harcourt Jr, Michael, Brian, Andrea. **Educ:** Fordham U, BS 1948; Howard U, MD 1952. **Career:** Physician, pvt pract 1960-; UAH, staff pos 2 yrs; Dearborn UAH, resdnt 3 yrs; Harlem Hosp, internship 2 yrs; Bd Certified Internist 1962; Highland Park Gen Hosp, chf of med, dir med educ 1973-76; Wayne State U, clin asst prof 1975-. **Orgs:** Life mem NAACP. **Military Serv:** AUS 1953-55. **Business Addr:** 15521 W Seven Mile Rd, Detroit, MI 48235-2927.

HARRIS, HASSEL B.
Clergyman, administrator. **Personal:** Born Jul 10, 1931, Garrard Cty, KY; son of Mr & Mrs William Harris Jr; married Elizabeth Ann Green; children: Dominico, Eric. **Educ:** Morehouse Coll, AB 1955; Simmons Bible Coll, DD 1972; Univ of MO, Grad Study 1966; Union Coll, attended. **Career:** Benedict Coll Columbia SC, dir mens personnel & publ rel 1955-58; Summer Work Camp Simsubry CT, dir 1955-58; St Paul Bapt Church, pastor 1960-70; Knox Cty OEO & Cumberland Valley OEO, personnel dir, acting dir 1965-70; Union Coll, 1st black staff mem dir fin aid 1969-73; Mt Moriah Ch, pastor 1970-; Cumberland River Comp Care Ctr (8 counties), occupational prog consult 1973-74, admin catchment b 1975-77; State Mental Health, mgr oper 1977-95; Gen Assoc of KY Baptists, moderator 1984-90. **Orgs:** Moderator London Dist Assoc 1962-84; chmn Cumberland River Mental Health-Mental Retardation Bd 1970-73; bd dir Knox Gen Hosp 1975-77; exec bd Gen Assoc 1962-; mem Human Relations Comm 1972. **Honors/Awds:** JJ Starks Awd Best Man of Affairs 1955; Commissioned KY Col 1968.

HARRIS, HELEN B.
Educator. **Personal:** Born Mar 6, 1925, High Point, NC; daughter of Hattie Whitaker Boulware and Willie Boulware; married Dr Wendell B Harris, Sep 4, 1951; children: Wendell B Jr, Charles B, Dr Hobart W. **Educ:** Bennett Coll, BA 1945; Univ of IA, MA 1952. **Career:** Prismatic Images Inc, exec producer. **Orgs:** Appointed by gov of state, mem St Neighborhood Educ Auth; bd mem Flint Public Schools; exec dir YWCA High Point NC 1945-48; program dir YWCA Des Moines 1948-51; sec Mayors Adv Comm; charter mem Flint Chap Delta Sigma Theta; mem Jack & Jill; pres League of Women Voters 1965; pres, bd of ed Flint 1973-74,75-76; life mem NAACP, Delta Sigma Theta, Urban League, ACLU; bd mem, NBD Genesee Bank 1980-89; trustee, Comm Found of Greater Flint 1986-89; pres, Flint Area Educ Found 1988-89; bd mem emeritus Questar School for Gifted 1987-89. **Honors/Awds:** 1st female black mem & 1st woman pres elected to Flint Bd of Ed; executive producer of film "Chameleon Street," Grand Prize winner, US Sun Dance Festival, 1990. **Business Addr:** Executive Producer, Prismatic Images Inc, 124 W Kearsley St, Flint, MI 48502.

HARRIS, HORATIO PRESTON
Dentist (retired), clergyman. **Personal:** Born Sep 25, 1925, Savannah, GA; son of Foustina Harris and Horatio Harris; married Barbara E Monroe; children: Gary P, Patricia L, Michael M, Dr Conrad W, Nancy E, Dr David M, Cathy C, Roxanne D, Robert H. **Educ:** Howard U, BS 1951, DDS 1956. **Career:** VA, Wash, IBM splst 1949; St Elizabeth Hosp, intern, oral surgery 1956-57; priv prac dentistry, Wash 1957-; Bur Dental Health, dental ofcr 1960-65; Howard U, instr 1966-67, asst prof 1967-71; minister 1973-82, Jehovah's Witness minister, 1982-. **Orgs:** Mem courtesy staff oral surgery, Freedman's Hosp; mem Am/Nat/DC Dental Assns; RT Freeman Soc; mem Omega Psi Phi. **Honors/Awds:** Honored UAU. **Military Serv:** USNR 1943-46.

HARRIS, HOWARD F.
Association executive. **Personal:** Born Apr 19, 1909, Monticello, AR; married Ozepher; children: Howard, Helen, Ozepher. **Educ:** Atlanta U, BA 1929. **Career:** Independent consult on pub housing; Housing Authority, City of Tampa, FL, exec dir ret 1977; field of pub housing 26 yrs; Monsanto Chem Co, nitric acid prod 6 yrs; Lincoln HS Bradenton, FL, science tchr 5 yrs; Booker Washington HS Tampa, tchr 4 yrs; Lee Co Training Sch Sanford, NC, science tchr 1 yr. **Orgs:** Past pres FL Housing & Redevel Ofcls; past mem Exec Council Southeastern Regional Council of Housing & Redevel Ofcls; mem White House Council on Aging1971; mem Omego Psi Phi 1926-; NAACP; bd dirs Big Bros; Tampa Chap Frontiers of Am Inc; N Tampa Optomist Club. **Honors/Awds:** Omega Cit of Yr 1969; award for excellence in adminstrn, Frontiers of Am 1968. **Business Addr:** 1514 Union St, Tampa, FL 33607.

HARRIS, J. ROBERT, II
Marketing consultant. **Personal:** Born Apr 1, 1944, Lake Charles, LA; son of Ruth E Boutte Harris and James Robert Harris; married Nathaleen Stephenson, Aug 28, 1965 (deceased); children: Evan Scott, April Ruth. **Educ:** Queens Coll, BA psychol 1966; City Univ of NY, MA soc 1969; Berlitz School Langs, postgrad 1974. **Career:** Equitable Life Ins Co, rsch analyst 1965-66; NBC, mktg rsch supvr 1966-69; Gen Foods Corp, grp mktg rsch mgr 1969-72; Pepsi Co Intl, assoc dir rsch 1972-74; Intern Mktg Res Pepsico Inc, plans, sup sur polls stud 130 count to provide info necessary for mktg co food & beverage products around world, assoc dir; JRH Markting Servs Inc, pres, currently. **Orgs:** Mem Amer Mktg Assn (one of org of groups Min Employee Prog which was inst in hir many blacks & other min mem into mktg res field); pres JRH Mktg Serv 1975-; dir rec lectr math & french proj Upward Bound 1966-67; mem European Soc for Opinion & Mkt Rsch; pres, bd dir Qualitative Rsch Consult Assn 1987-89; consult Volunteer Urban Consulting Group Inc; The Explorers Club, 1993-; NAACP; Omega Psi Phi. **Honors/Awds:** Recipient, Key of Success Mex City 1973; NY State Reg School 1961-65; David Sarnoff Fellow 1967; grant Howard Univ 1961-65; Franklin & Marsh Coll 1961-65; Roman Catholic. **Business Addr:** President, JRH Marketing Serv Inc, 29-27 41st Ave, Long Island City, NY 11103.

HARRIS, JACK
Radio station executive. **Personal:** Born Jul 8, Chicago, IL; son of Daisy Harris and King Edward Harris; married Janis A; children: Cindie M, Linda S, Jackie R, Esther, Charlene A, Trisha J, Jack II. **Educ:** Lincoln Univ, Govt 1959; Roosevelt Univ, 1964; Brown Inst of Broadcasting Engrs; 1970; Marquette University of Law 1972. **Career:** Former Chess recording artist; record producer and writer; Harris Family Publishing, pres; WCKX Radio Columbus/KBWH Radio Omaha, pres/gen mgr, currently; Communicator New Newspaper, president/publisher; Papa's One Stop Music, owner. **Orgs:** Mem NAACP; AQA FAT. **Honors/Awds:** Billboard Prog Dir & Announcer of Yr 1969; Citizen Awd for Outstanding Leadership 1983. **Military Serv:** USAF a2c 4 yrs. **Business Addr:** President/General Manager, WCKX/KBWH, 510 E Mound St, Columbus, OH 43215.

HARRIS, JACKIE BERNARD
Professional football player. **Personal:** Born Jan 4, 1968, Pine Bluff, AR; married Letrece; children: Jackie Jr. **Educ:** Northeast Louisiana, attended. **Career:** Green Bay Packer, tight end, 1990-93; Tampa Bay Buccaneers, 1994-. **Business Addr:** Professional Football Player, Tampa Bay Buccaneers, One Buccaneer Place, Tampa, FL 33607, (813)870-2700.

HARRIS, JAMES
Sports team manager. **Career:** Tampa Bay Buccaneers, West Coast scout, six years; New York Jets, asst general manager, currently. **Honors/Awds:** MVP, NFL Pro Bowl; leads the NFC in passing. **Special Achievements:** One of the first African American quarterbacks to start in the Natl Football League. **Business Addr:** Asst General Manager, New York Jets, 1000 Fulton Ave, Hempstead, NY 11550, (516)538-6600.

HARRIS, JAMES, III. **See JAM, JIMMY.**

HARRIS, JAMES A.
Association executive. **Personal:** Born Aug 25, 1926, Des Moines; married Jacquelyn; children: James, Jr, Jerald. **Educ:** Drake U, BA 1948, MFA 1955; Drake Div Coll, post grad work; OK A&M. **Career:** Nat Educ Assn, pres 1974-, vice pres 1973; Des Moines, art, human rel tchr 1954; Kansas City, elem tchr 1948; Langston U, tchr 1953-54. **Orgs:** Dir NEA; mem NEA Budget Com; mem Steering Com NEA Consti Conv; mem first ofcl delegation of Am Educators to Peoples Rep of China; spkr Nat Assem for Educ Research, Yamagata, Japan 1974; co-chmn with Dr Wise NEA Com on Am Revol - Bicen; served on many com of IA State Educ Assn, Des Moines Educ Assn; past dir Red Cross refugee shelter during Kansas City flood; bd mem Am Friends Serv Com; adminstr comm relations Forest Ave Baptist Ch; served on Mayor's task forces on educ & police-comm relations; NAEA Bd of Dirs liaison with Nat Assn of Art Edn; mem IA Assn of Art Educators; mem NAACP; Kappa Alpha Psi; dir Des Moines Chap Boys Clubs of Am. **Military Serv:** USAF pilot WwII. **Business Addr:** 1201 16 St NW, Washington, DC 20036.

HARRIS, JAMES ANDREW
Chemist (retired). **Personal:** Born Mar 26, 1932, Waco, TX; married Helen L; children: Cedric, Keith, Hilda, Kimberly, James. **Educ:** Huston-Tillotson Coll Austin, TX, BS 1953; CA State Univ Hayward, CA, MPA (pending thesis) 1975. **Career:** Tracer Lab Inc Richmond CA, radiochemist 1955-60; Lawrence Berkeley Lab, nuclear chemist Beta Spectroscopy Group 1960-66, nuclear chemist 1966-69, group leader/rsch chemist Heavy Isotope Prodn Group 1969-74, post doctoral recruiter Chem & Physics Div 1974-77, asst to div head, staff scientist Engrg & Tech Serv Div 1977-. **Orgs:** Mem Nat Soc of Black Chemists & Chem Engrs; bd mem Far WHS; mem PTA Pinole CA; member, Alpha Phi Alpha Fraternity, 1950-. **Honors/Awds:** Lectr at num univs & colls; Rsch Display at Oakland Museum & City Hall of Providence RI; DSc Degree Houston Tillotson Coll 1973; Cert of Merit Natl Urban League; Scientific Merit Awd City of Richmond; Outstanding Achievement Awd Marcus Foster Inst; Key to the City of Oakland, CA, 1988; Marcus A Foster Outstanding Alumnus, Oakland, CA, 1979. **Military Serv:** US Army, Sgt, 1953-55.

HARRIS, JAMES E.
Educational administrator. **Personal:** Born Sep 24, 1946, Castalia, NC; married Justine Perry; children: Kasheena, Jamillah. **Educ:** Montclair State Coll, BA 1968, MA 1970; Pub Serv Inst of NJ, 1974; Harvard U, summer 1974; NY U, 1973-. **Career:** Montclair State Coll, assoc dean 1986-, cross country coach 1975-, asst dean of students 1970-, counselor 1969-70; Bamberger's, Newark, asst to dir comm relations 1968; Montclair State Coll, res counselor Upward Bound Project summer 1966-67; Elko Lake Camp, NY, counselor 1965; Montclair State Coll, asst librarian 1964-67; Camp Weequahic, Lake Como, PA, porter 1964. **Orgs:** Consult Educ Testing Svc, Am Coll Testing Inc; Ctr for Opportunity & Personnel Efficiency, NJ; Nat Orientation Director's Assn; pres, Montclair State Coll Assn of Black Faculty & Adminstrv Staff; pres Educ Oportunity Fund Comm Adv Bd of Montclair State Coll; pres NJ Assn of Black Educators 1973-; mem No NJ Counselors Assn; Nat Assn of Personnel Adminstr; Am Personnel & Guidance Assn; Am Coll Personnel Assn; v-chmn NJ Amateur Athletic Union Women Track & Field Com; bd mgr NJ Assn of Amateur Athletic Union of Am; bd tsts Leaguers Inc; dir, coach, fdr Essex Co Athletic Club of Newark; Cross Country Coach at Montclair State Coll; mem Legislative Aide Com to Assemblyman Hawkins; N Ward Block Assn; cert mem NJ Track & Field Officials Assn;Amateur Athletic UnionOfficials; chmn NJ Black Issuesnvention Educ Task Force 1986-; pres NAACP Montclair Br 1983; mem Montclair Civil Rights Commiss1979-; chmn Presidents Council on Affirmative Action Univ of Med & Dentistry of NJ; mem Urban League of Essex County. **Honors/Awds:** Outstanding Black Educator Awd; Montclair State Coll Student Leadership Awd; Essex Co Volunteer Awd; Athlete of the Year Awd for Montclair St Coll. **Military Serv:** NJ NatlGuard cpt. **Business Addr:** Assoc Dean of Students, Montclair State College, Upper Montclair, NJ 07043.

HARRIS, JAMES G., JR.
Executive director. **Personal:** Born Oct 27, 1931, Cuthbert, GA; son of Eunice Mitchner Harris and James Harris Sr; married Roxie Lena Riggs; children: Peter C, Robin M. **Educ:** Hillyer Coll, Assoc Bus Admin 1956; Univ of Hartford, BS Bus Admin 1958. **Career:** State of CT, social worker 1958-59; EJ Korvette, acct payable supvr 1959-60; State of CT, social worker 1060-65; State Office of Economic Oppor, asst dir 1965-66; Gov John Dempsey, spec asst to gov 1966-70; Greater Hartford Comm Renewal Team, exec dir state civil rights coord 1970-82; CT Dept of Human Resources, commnr 1983-87; Data Institute Inc, consultant 1987-89; Bethol Center for Humane Services, consultant 1987-89. **Orgs:** Pres legislative chmn CT Assoc for Comm Action 1975-83; vice pres & panelist New England Comm Action Assoc 1977-80; mem Gov's Task Force on the Homeless 1983-; mem Adult Educ Study Commn 1984-; pres life mem Greater Hartford Branch NAACP 1962-64; chmn State Conf of NAACP chmn emeritus 1967-70; sec Alpha Phi Alpha 1964-66; mem Priorities Comm United Way 1984-; Gov's Designee Femia Distrib Comm 1984. **Honors/Awds:** Outstanding Serv Awd New England Chap of NAACP 1962; Charter Oak Leadership Awd Chamber of Commerce of Hartford 1964; Disting Serv Awd Phoenix Soc of Hartford 1979; Outstanding Serv New England CAP Dirs Assn 1981-83; Lifetime Achievement Awd Conn State NAACP Conf 1990; Hon DL, New Hampshire Coll, 1984. **Military Serv:** USAF sgt 4 yrs. **Home Addr:** 42 Tower Ave, Hartford, CT 06120.

HARRIS, JASPER WILLIAM
Educator/psychologist. **Personal:** Born Dec 10, 1935, Kansas City, MO; son of Mary P Harris and Jasper Harris; married Joann S Harper; children: Jasper Jr. **Educ:** Rockhurst Coll, BS Biology 1958; Univ of Missouri, MA 1961; Univ of Kansas, EdD 1971, PhD 1981. **Career:** Univ of Kansas research assoc 1969-77; Kansas City School Dist, teacher 1963-69, assoc supt 1977-86, superintendent 1986-, asst supervisor, 1988-91; Blue Springs School Districe, dir, 1992-. **Orgs:** Mem Phi Delta Kappa Frat, Alpha Phi Alpha Frat, Jr Chamber of Commerce, Rockhurst Coll Alumni Assoc, Univ of MO Alumni Assoc; vice chmn United Negro Coll Fund; mem adv bd & chmn educ and youth incentives comm Urban League; mem Science Teachers Assoc, Amer Educ Rsch Assoc, Amer Psychological Assoc, Univ of KS Alumni Assoc; life mem NAACP; mem Assoc for Supervision and Curriculum Develop, Personnel Rsch Forum; theta boule Sigma Pi Phi Frat; consultant Kaw Valley Medical Soc Health Careers Prog 1971-; participant in the Pres of the US Comm on Employment of the Handicapped White House Washington DC1980; selected reviewer for manuscripts submitted for publication in Exceptional Children 1984-85; apptd to MO State Dept Funding Comm Study Group by Commnr of Educ1985; apptd assoc editor Exceptal Children Journal 1985; bd of trustees, Park Coll, 1984-; Univ of Kansas, alumni bd mem. **Honors/Awds:** SPOKE Awd US Jaycees for Comm Svcs; Outstanding Young Man of Amer 1970; Outstanding Young Educator of Greater Kansas City Jr Chamber of Commerce; Life-time Teaching Certificate in Science for the State of MO; Life-time Administrative Secondary Certificate for the State of MO; Life-time Superintendent's Certificate; Special Educ Certification; apptd by the Office of the Sec of Educ Dept of Educ Washington DC to a review panel for identifying exemplary secondaryschools Washington DC 1985; numerous publications and book chapters. **Business Addr:** Director, Blue Springs School Dist, 1801 W Vesper, Blue Springs, MO 64015.

HARRIS, JAY TERRENCE
Media executive. **Personal:** Born Dec 3, 1948, Washington, DC; married Anna Christine; children: Taifa Akida, Jamarah Kai, Shala Marie. **Educ:** Lincoln Univ, BA 1970. **Career:** Wilmington News-Journal, general assignment reporter, 1970, urban affairs reporter, 1970-71, investigative reporter, 1971-73; Wilmington News-Journal Papers, special projects editor, 1974-75; Northwestern Univ, instructor of journalism/urban affairs, 1973-75, asst prof of journalism/urban affairs, 1975-82; Frank E Gannett Urban Journalism Ctr, asst dir, 1975-76, assoc dir, 1976-82; Northwestern Univ Medill Sch of Journalism, asst dean, 1977-82; Gannett News Svc, natl correspondent, 1982-84; Gannett Newspapers and USA Today, columnist, 1984-85; Philadelphia Daily News, exec editor, 1985-88; Knight-Ridder, vp of operations, 1988-94; San Jose Mercury News, chmn and publisher, currently. **Orgs:** bd mem: Joint Venture, Silicon Valley Network, the Bay Area Council; The American Ldshp Forum; Community Foundation of Santa Clara County; Tech Museum of Innovation; Santa Clara County Manufacturing Group; trustee, John S. and James L. Knight Foundation. **Honors/Awds:** Co-author of a series of articles on heroin trafficking in Wilmington DE that won Public Serv Awds from the Associated Press Managing Editors Assn and Greater PA Chapter of Sigma Delta Chi; Special Citation for Investigation of Minority Employment in Daily Newspapers Natl Urban Coalition, 1979; Par Excellence Awd for Distinguished Service in Journalism, Operation PUSH, 1984; Drum Major for Justice Awd Southern Christian Leadership Conf, 1985. **Business Addr:** Chairman and Publisher, San Jose Mercury News, 750 Ridder Park Drive, San Jose, CA 95190.

HARRIS, JEAN LOUISE
Mayor. **Personal:** Born Nov 24, 1931, Richmond, VA; daughter of Jean Pace Harris and Vernon J Harris; married Leslie J Ellis; children: Karin Denise, Cynthia Suzanne Ellis. **Educ:** VA Union U, BS 1951; Med Clg VA, MD 1955; Univ Richmond, DSC Hon 1981. **Career:** DC Dept Hlth, dir bur rsrcs dev 1967-69; Natl Med Assc Found, exec dir, 1969-73; Med Clg VA, prof fam prac 1973-78; VA Cabinet Post, sec of human rsrcs 1978-82; Control Data Corp, vice pres 1982-88; Ramsey Foundation St Paul MN, pres & C E0 1988-91; Univ of Minnesota Hospital and Clinics, senior associate dir, dir of medical a ffairs; City of Eden Prairie, mayor, 1994-. **Orgs:** Natl Acdmy Sci Inst of Med; Recominant DNA Cmn NIH; Pres Tsk Force Pvt Sec Initiatives 1981-82; bd trustees Univ Richmond 1982-; Links Inc 1973-90; VA State Bd Hlth 1982-84; v chn Pres Tsk Force Alcholism & Abuse; cncl mbr, Eden Prarie City Cncl, Rotary International 1987-; bd of dirs, St Paul United Way, 1991-94; bd of dirs, Minneapolis Girl Scout Cncl, 1991-; defense adv cncl, Women in the Service, 1986-89. **Honors/Awds:** Magnificent Seven VA Women's Pol Action Grp 1983; distngshd serv Natl Govr Assc 1981; nwsmkr of yr VA Press Women 1979; otstndg woman govt YWCA 1980; Top 100 Black Business & Prof Women, Dollars & Sense Magazine 1986; Recipient, First Annual SERWA Award Comm of 100 Black Women, Virginia Chapter, 1989. **Special Achievements:** Jean L Harris Scholarship established, Virginia Commenwealth Univ, 1993. **Home Addr:** 10860 Forestview Cir, Eden Prairie, MN 55347. **Business Addr:** Mayor, City of Eden Prairie, 8080 Mitchell, Eden Prairie, MN 55344.

HARRIS, JEANETTE G.
Business executive. **Personal:** Born Jul 18, 1934, Philadelphia, PA; divorced. **Educ:** Inst of Banking, 1959-70. **Career:** First PA Bank NA, banking ofcr, bank mgr; dept store bookkeeper, sales clerk. **Orgs:** Mem Urban League; bd dir YMCA; bd mem Philadelphia Parent Child Care Ctnr; mem & vis prof BEEP; mem Nat Assn of Black Women Inc; Philadelphia Black Bankers Assn; mem community orgn dealing with sr cit; past treas Ch Federal Credit Union; treas Merchants Assn Progress Plaza Shopping Ctnr. **Honors/Awds:** First black female bank mgr in Phila. **Business Addr:** Payroll Dept, Corestates Bank, PO Box 7618, Philadelphia, PA 19101.

HARRIS, JEROME C., JR.
City administrator. **Personal:** Born Dec 15, 1947, New York, NY; married Rosemarie Mcqueen; children: Rahsaan, Jamal. **Educ:** Rutgers Univ, BA Soc 1969, MS Urban Planning 1971. **Career:** Livingston Coll Rutgers, instr dept of community devel, asst to dean acad affairs 1969-73; Mayor's Policy & Devel Office Newark, dir urban inst 1973-74, urban devel coord 1974-75; Middlesex County Econ Opport Corp, dep exec dir mgmt & admin 1975-77; NJ Educ Opport Fund Dept of Higher Ed, asst dir, fiscal affairs 1977-78; Dept of Higher Ed, assoc dir budget & fiscal planning 1978-82; City of Plainfield, dir public works & urban devel 1982, dep city admin 1983, city admin 1983-. **Orgs:** Mem bd of dir Plainfield Econ Devel Corp; pres NJ Jaycees 1977; vice pres New Brunswick NAACP 1978-79; pres NJ Public Policy Rsch Inst 1979-84; chmn Middlesex Cty CETA Advisory 1979-83; 1st vice chmn NJ Black Issues Convention 1983-; mem Intl City Mgrs Assoc, Amer Soc of Public Admin, Conf of Minority Public Admin, Forum of Black Public Admin, NJ Municpal Mgrs Assoc. **Honors/Awds:** Serv Awd NJ Black United Fund 1984; Outstanding Black Ed NJ Assoc of Black Ed 1983. **Business Addr:** City Administrator, City of Plainfield, 515 Watchung Ave, Plainfield, NJ 07061.

HARRIS, JOHN CLIFTON
Physician. **Personal:** Born Jan 15, 1935, Greensboro, NC. **Educ:** NY Coll of Podiatric Med, Dr of Podiatric Med; Howard U, grad courses 1964-65; NC A&T, BS 1962. **Career:** Dr of Podiatric Med, self-empl; Addiction Rsrch & Treatment Corp, 1972-; Lyndon B Johnson Comm Health Cntr, staff podiatrist 1974-77; Towers Nursing Home, staff podiatrist 1970-71; 125th St Comm Med Grp, 1970-74. **Orgs:** Podiatry So of State of NY; Am Podiatry Assn; Acad of Podiatry; NY Co Podiatry Soc; bd dir Harlem Philharmonic Soc Inc; diplomate Nat Bd of Podiatry; NAACP; YMCA. **Military Serv:** USAF med serv spl, a/1c 1954-58. **Business Addr:** 470 Lenox Ave, New York, NY 10037.

HARRIS, JOHN EVERETT
Educator. **Personal:** Born May 31, 1930, New Haven, CT; married Emily Louise Brown; children: John E. **Educ:** Yale University, B 1953; Brown University, PhD, 1958. **Career:** Boston Univ, professor emeritus, 1991-, assoc prof of science 1970-91; MA Inst Tech, asst prof food toxicology 1965-70; Monsanto Rsch Corp, sr rsch chemist 1959-65; Yale Univ Medical School, rsch fellow 1957-59. **Orgs:** Mem Sigma Si; Am Chem Soc; Chem Soc, London; Am Assn for Advncmt of Sci; Am Acad of Sci; bd trustee SW Boston Comm Svcs; sci adv Cynthia Sickle Cell Anemia Fund Inc; past pres Stonybrook Civic Assn; mem Alpha Phi Alpha; NAACP; Urban League. **Honors/Awds:** Listed in Am Men of Sci & Ldrs of Am Sci; articles publ in Jour of Am Chem Soc Jour of Organic Chem Analytical Biochem & Biochem Abstracts publ in Meetings of Am Chem Soc. **Business Addr:** 871 Commonwealth Ave, Boston, MA 02215.

HARRIS, JOHN H.
Financial administrator. **Personal:** Born Jul 7, 1940, Wynne, AR; married Adele E Lee; children: Cheryl E, Angela M. **Educ:** So IL Univ, BS 1967; Southwestern Grad Sch of Banking 1973-74. **Career:** Gateway Natl Bank, vice pres, cashier 1967-74, exec vice pres 1975; Boatmens Natl Bank, operations officer 1976-77; School Dist of Univ City, dir of finance. **Orgs:** Mem Natl Bankers Assn 1967-, Amer Inst of Banking 1967-77, Bank Admin Inst 1968-73; adv Jr Achievement of MS Valley Inc 1967-77; dir treas St Louis Council Campfire Girls Inc 1972-73; former mem Phi Beta Lambda; mem Natl Assn of Black Accountants 1974-75; treas fund drive United Negro Coll Fund 1975; bd dir Inst of Black Studies 1977; mem NAACP, US Selective Serv Comm; dir treas Greely Comm Ctr Waring Sch PTA; dir King-Fanon Mental Health Ctr, Child Day Care Assoc; supervisory comm Educational Employees Credit Union; treas Block Unit #1144; dir Amer Cancer Soc. **Business Addr:** Assistant Superintendent, Sch Dist of University City, 8346 Delcrest, St Louis, MO 63124.

HARRIS, JOHN H.
Educator. **Personal:** Born Aug 12, 1940, Memphis, TN. **Educ:** LeMoyne Coll, BS 1962; Atlanta Univ, MS 1966; Memphis State University, PhD, 1990. **Career:** US Peace Corps, pc volunteer Accra Ghana 1962-64; LeMoyne-Owen Coll, instructor 1967-, mathematics/computer science department, chair, currently. **Orgs:** Mem Natl Assoc of Mathematicians 1986-87, Black Data Processing Assocs 1986-87, Amer Mathematical Soc 1987; member, Assn for Computing Machinery, 1990-91; Mathematical Association of America, 1996-97. **Honors/Awds:** UNCF Faculty Fellow 1978; IBM/UNCF Faculty Fellow, 1987-90. **Business Addr:** Prof of Math/Comp Sci, Department Chairman, LeMoyne-Owen College, 807 Walker Ave, Memphis, TN 38126, (901)774-9090.

HARRIS, JOHN J.
Business executive. **Personal:** Born Sep 18, 1951, Plymouth, NC; son of Jerome Harris. **Educ:** California State University, BA, 1972; University of California Los Angeles, MBA, 1974. **Career:** Carnation Company, vice president, general manager, currently.

HARRIS, JON
Professional football player. **Educ:** Virginia. **Career:** Philadelphia Eagles, 1997-. **Special Achievements:** NFL Draft, First round pick, #25, 1997. **Business Addr:** Profesional Football Player, Philadelphia Eagles, Broad St & Pattison Ave, Veterans Stadium, Philadelphia, PA 19148, (215)463-2500.

HARRIS, JOSEPH BENJAMIN
Company executive. **Personal:** Born Jun 8, 1920, Richmond, VA; son of Alice Burrell Harris and Joseph Brown Harris; married Pauline Elizabeth McKinney; children: Paula Jo, Joseph C, Joya R. **Educ:** VA Union U, BS 1949; Howard U, DDS 1953. **Career:** CA Howell & Co, pres 1967-72, chmn bd 1972-. **Orgs:** Am Dental Soc 1953-; MI Dntl Soc 1953-; Det Dntl Soc 1953-; Nat Dntl Soc 1955-; Am Dntl Fund 1980; Sigma Pi Phi 1970; Omega Psi Phi 1947-. **Honors/Awds:** Am Soc Dentistry for Children 1953; Detroit Howardite of the Year, Howard University Alumni Detroit 1991. **Military Serv:** AUS stf sgt 1943-46; Battle of Normandy; Good Conduct Medal; Vctry Medal World War II; Asiatic Pacific Theater with 1 Bronze Star 1944. **Home Addr:** 1190 W Boston Blvd, Detroit, MI 48202. **Business Addr:** Dir & Chmn of Board, CA Howell & Co, 2431 W Grand Blvd, Detroit, MI 48208.

HARRIS, JOSEPH ELLIOT, II
Automotive executive. **Personal:** Born Feb 21, 1945, Boston, MA; son of Muriel K Harris and Joseph E Harris; married Young-Ja Chung Harris, Jun 15, 1983; children: Joy Electra, Joseph E III. **Educ:** Howard University, BSEE, 1968; Rochester Institute of Technology, MBA, 1976; Northeastern University, Certificate of Advanced Studies, 1979. **Career:** Stromberg Carlson, electrical engineer, 1967-74; Xerox Corporation, sr mfg engineer, 1974-76; Ford Motor Co, buyer, 1976-78; Polaroid Corp, purchasing manager, 1978-91; Chrysler Corp, executive of special supplier relations, 1991-. **Orgs:** National Minority Supplier Development Council, board, 1992; National Association Purchasing Management, min bus dev group board, 1988-92; Try-Us, board, 1992; Michigan Minority Business Develop Council, board chairman, 1992; Oakland Boy Scout Council, board, 1992; Mattapan Community Health Center, board, 1989-91; Minority Enterprise Dev Week, vice chairman, 1988-91. **Honors/Awds:** Electronic Buyers News, Top Ten Purchasers, 1992; US Small Business Administration, small bus advocate of the year, 1989; Commonwealth of Mass, Min Bus Advocate of the Year, 1990; Buyer of the Year, New England Min Purchasing Council, 1988; Black Corp Pres of New England, Coordinator of the Year, 1988. **Special Achievements:** Microcomputer Technologies for Minority Sourcing, 1987; A Perfect Match, Minority Business News, 1992; Black Achievers, Boston MA, 1990. **Military Serv:** US Air Force, ROTC. **Business Addr:** Executive, Special Supplier Relations, Chrysler Corp, CIMS 484-01-20, 800 Chrysler Dr, East, Auburn Hills, MI 48326-2757, (313)252-6094.

HARRIS, JOSEPH JOHN, III
Educator, educational administrator. **Personal:** Born Oct 10, 1946, Altoona, PA; son of Ann M Hart Harris and Joseph John

Harris II; married Donna Ford Harris, Aug 24, 1988; children: Julie Renee, Khyle Lee. **Educ:** Highland Park College, AS, 1967; Wayne State University, BS, 1969; University of Michigan at Ann Arbor, MS, 1971, PhD, 1972. **Career:** Detroit Public Schools, teacher, assistant principal, 1968-73; Highland Park Public School, consulting project director, 1973; Pennsylvania State Univ, assistant professor, 1973-76; Indiana University, associate professor, 1976-83, professor, chair, center director, 1983-87; Cleveland State University, professor, dean, 1987-90; University of Kentucky, professor, dean, 1990-. **Orgs:** Editorial board, CSU Magazine, 1989-; board of trustees, Greater Cleveland Literacy Coalition, 1988-; advisory board, National Sorority of Phi Delta Kappa, 1988-; board of trustees, National Public Radio Affiliate-WCPNW, 1988-; board of directors, Marotta Montessori School/Cleveland, 1987-90; National Organization on Legal Problems in Education, board of directors, 1988-91; Lexington Arts and Cultural Center, board of directors; Holmes Group Ed Schools, E Lansing, board of directors. **Special Achievements:** Author: "Education, Society & the Brown Decision," Journal of Black Studies, 1982; "The Outlaw Generation," Educational Horizons, 1982; "Identifying Diamond in the Rough," The Gifted Child Today, 1990; "Public School-Univ Collaboration," Community Education Journal, 1989; "The Resurrection of Play in Gifted..," Journal for the Education of the Gifted, 1990; "The Elusive Definition of Creativity," The Journal of Creative Behavior, 1992; "Dissonance in the Education Ecology," Metropolitan Universities, 1991; "The American Achievement Ideology and Achievement Differentials Among Preadolescent Gifted and Nongifted African-American Males and Females," Journal of Negro Education, 1992. **Business Addr:** Professor and Dean, College of Education, University of Kentucky, 103 Dickey Hall, Lexington, KY 40506-0017.

HARRIS, JOSEPH PRESTON
Business executive. **Personal:** Born Apr 11, 1935, Rome, MS; married Otha L; children: Jacqui, Joe Jr. **Educ:** Chicago Tchrs Coll, BE 1956; John Marshall Law Sch, JD 1964. **Career:** Allstate Ins, reg vp; Allstate Ins, mgmt dev rotational 5 yrs; Allstate Ins, atty law div yrs; Allstate Ins, adjuster 2 yrs; Chicago Bd of Edn,tchr 1956-64. **Orgs:** Bd of dir Maywood Proviso State Bank 1973-76; mem IL & Chicago Bar Asnn 16 yrs; mem NAACP. **Business Addr:** 2431 W Grand Ave, Detroit, MI 48208.

HARRIS, JOSEPH R.
Educational administrator. **Personal:** Born Jan 29, 1937, Philadelphia, PA; son of Alice H Heiskell Harris and James T Harris; married Jean A Williams; children: Joseph R Jr, Keith A, Allison M. **Educ:** La Salle University, BA Govt 1954-58; Fordham U, MA Pol 1958-71; Hunter Clg CUNY, Urban Plng Course 1971; Fordham U, 1975-78. **Career:** US Peace Corps Cameroun W Africa, assoc dir 1964-66; NCCJ Natl Police Comm Relations, dir 1966-67; Manpower & Career Devel Agency NYC, spec asst cmsnr 1967-68; City Univ NY, dean, dir 1969-. **Orgs:** Cnsltnt/evaluator Bureau of Equal Ed State of PA 1980-; Mdl States Cmsn on Hghr Ed 1973-82; cnslnt USAID Ed Msn to Africa 1974; bd dir Natl CoaltnAdult Ed Orgn 1970; bd dir pres Friends Plainfield Lbry 1980-83; v chm bd dir NJ Edctnl Oprtnry Fund 1981-; bd dir NY Univ School of Continuing Educ; vice chairperson, board of trustees, Montclair State College, Upper Montclair, NJ. **Honors/Awds:** Vatterott Schor Vatterott Fdt St Louis MO Grad S 1958-60; otstndg yng man awrd Otstndg Am Fdt 1976; Ford Found Grant Ford Found 1981; Matsushita Found Grant 1987. **Military Serv:** AUSR spec ii 1962-68. **Business Addr:** Coordinator, City Univ of NY, Adult & Continuing Education Program Services, 535 E 80th St, Rm 403A, New York, NY 10021.

HARRIS, LARRY VORDELL, JR.
Sales executive. **Personal:** Born Jun 24, 1954, New York, NY; son of Marian Harris and Larry Harris, Sr (deceased); children: Karena, Dell. **Educ:** Drexel Univ, BS 1979, attended 1984-86; candidate for MBA, Finance. **Career:** Proctor & Schwartz, product specialist 1980-82; Exide Electronics, export sales mgr 1982-84; AMP Inc, sales engr 1984-l988; Senior Sales Engineering l989-; l988 District Performance Award Sales Performance, Industrial Division. **Orgs:** Mem Natl Black MBA Assoc, Prince Hall Masons of PA; co-founder Drexel Univ Black Alumni Assoc 1984; presiding partner Professional Investment Club of Philadelphia 1987-l989. **Honors/Awds:** l988 District Performance Award AMP Inc.l988. **Business Addr:** Senior Sales Engineer, P.O. Box 2216, Willingboro, NJ 08046.

HARRIS, LEE
Reporter. **Personal:** Born Dec 30, 1941, Bryan, TX; married Lois. **Educ:** CA State U, 1968. **Career:** Los Angeles Times, reporter; San Bernardino Sun Telegra, 1972-73; Riverside Press, 1968-72. **Military Serv:** AUS sp 4 1964-67. **Business Addr:** Times Mirror Sq, Los Angeles, CA 90053.

HARRIS, LEE ANDREW, II
Marketing manager. **Personal:** Born Mar 25, 1958, Akron, OH; married Karen D Swartz; children: Jason D. **Educ:** Heidelberg Coll, BS 1985. **Career:** Summit Co Sheriff's Dept, deputy sheriff 1981-83; Copy Data Systems Inc, opers mgr 1985-86, mktg rep 1986-87, mktg mgr 1987-. **Orgs:** Bd of dirs, Copy Data Systs Inc, 1987-; admin bd, Lincolnia United Methodist Church, 1987. **Honors/Awds:** Vice pres Black Student Union/Heidelberg 1984-85. **Home Addr:** 5701 121 Harwich Ct, Alexandria, VA 22311. **Business Addr:** Marketing Manager, Copy Data Systems Inc, 8474C Tyco Rd, Vienna, VA 22180.

HARRIS, LENNY (LEONARD ANTHONY)
Professional baseball player. **Personal:** Born Oct 28, 1964, Miami, FL. **Educ:** Miami-Dade Community College. **Career:** Cincinnati Reds, outfielder, 1988-89, 1994-; Los Angeles Dodgers, 1990-93. **Business Addr:** Professional Baseball Player, Cincinnati Reds, 100 Riverfront Stadium, Cincinnati, OH 45202, (513)421-4510.

HARRIS, LEODIS
Judge. **Personal:** Born Aug 11, 1934, Pensacola, FL; married Patsy Auzenne; children: Courtney, Monique, Darwin. **Educ:** Cleveland Coll Western Reserve U, 1952-57; Cleveland Marshall Law Sch, JD 1959-63. **Career:** Common Pleas Ct Juvenile Div, juvenile ct judge; pvt prac of law 1963-77. **Orgs:** Mem The Greater Cleveland Citizens League 1961-; mem Urban Affairs Com Cleveland Bar Assn 1975-77. **Honors/Awds:** Service award Cleveland Jr Women's Civic League 1978; Freedom Award Cleveland NAACP 1979; Man of the Yr Cleveland Negro Bos & Prof Women 1979; Silver Award OH Prince Hall Knights of Templar 1980; publ features Ebony, Nat Star, Nat Enquirer, Cleveland Plain Dealer Sun Mag; media appearances Today Show, Good Morning Am Show, British Broadcasting, Canadian Broadcasting Corp, numerous local TV & radio shows; speaks German & Russian. **Military Serv:** AUS spec 4th cl 1957-59. **Business Addr:** Common Pleas Court, 2163 East 22nd St, Cleveland, OH 44115.

HARRIS, LEON L.
Union official. **Personal:** Born in Nyack, NY; married Evelyn. **Educ:** Hampton Inst, 1948-50; RI Coll Edn, AA 1953-56; Harvard Univ, 1963. **Career:** ASFCME AFL-CIO, intl rep 1960-64; Providence, New England phys educ instr 1954-60; John Hope Settlement Providence, athletic instr 1950-53. **Orgs:** Dir Civil Rights Research Educ Retail Wholesale Dept Store Union & AFL-CIO CLC 1964-; natl life mem com NAACP; v chmn Manhood Found Inc; adv bd recruitment training program NY Black Trade Union Leadership Com; pres Greenwich Village NAACP 8 other chpts; former pres New Eng Golf Assn; natl vice pres United Golf Assn; Am Social Club; former chmn CORE Rochester; lectured several univ; mem A Philip Randolph Inst; Friends Nat Black Theater. **Honors/Awds:** Am Legion Honor Award Outstanding Athlete 1947; 16 Letterman; first black New Eng to sign with St Louis Cardinals 1952; Kansas City Monarchs.

HARRIS, LEONARD ANTHONY
Professional baseball player. **Personal:** Born Oct 28, 1966, Miami, FL; son of Rebecca Clark Harris and Arthur Harris; married Carnettia Evan Johnson, Feb 17, 1990. **Career:** Los Angeles Dodgers, infielder, 1989-. **Orgs:** Member, Optimist Club of Miami, 1990-91. **Business Addr:** Professional Baseball Player, Los Angeles Dodgers, 1000 Elysian Park Avenue, Los Angeles, CA 90012.

HARRIS, LESTER L.
Administration. **Personal:** marrIed; children: Michelle, Ernie, Leon, Lester. **Career:** Econ Oppty Cncl of Suffolk Inc, chmn. **Orgs:** Pres Deer Park NAACP 1973-74; vice pres Deer Park NAACP 1964-70; elected committeeman Babylon Dem Party; mem Suffolk Co Migrant Bd; mem Suffolk CoHansel & Gretal Inc; Deer Park Civic Assn; Negro Airman Intl Inc. **Honors/Awds:** Suffolk Co Humanitarian Award Suffolk Co Locality Mayor JF Goode & Ossie Davis 1973. **Business Addr:** 244 E Main St, Patchogue, NY 11772.

HARRIS, LORENZO W.
Physician. **Personal:** Born Jun 11, 1921, Spring Lake, NJ; married Mildred; children: Sharon Gail, Deborah Kay, Lorenzo III, Nancy Ren, Linda, Karen, Janet. **Educ:** Howard U, BS 1943; Howard Univ Med Sch, MD 1947; Homer G Phillips Hosp St Louis, internship & residency. **Career:** Asbury Park NJ, pvt prac of medicine; Jersey Shore Med Cntr, staff affiliation; City of Asbury Park, waterfronts management board. **Orgs:** Former mem Joint Com of Interprofl Rel of Monmouth Co Med Soc; Am Heart Assn; NJ Pub Health Assn; former med dir NJ State Assn; IEPOE of W; past pres Alpha Phi Alpha; former vice pres Monmouth Co Men's Club; former vchmn Asbury Park Council on Hum Rel; former exec com Shore Area Br NAACP; former lay reader & vestryman St Augustine's Episcopal Ch; former chmn Black Am of Monmouth Co; past vice pres of bd dir Monmouth Boys/Girls Club; former bd dir Westside Comm Coalition; past pres, Rosary Club of Asbury Park; lay reader, Trinity Episcopal Church. **Honors/Awds:** Apptd by Gov Richard Hughes to NJ Migrant Labor Bd 1962; elected delegate Dem Nat Conventions 1964, 1968; elected to city council Asbury Park 1973; Nat Conf of Christians & Jews Brotherhood Award 1974; Paul Harris Fellow Award, Rosary International; many awards from comm organizations. **Military Serv:** USAF capt 1952-54. **Business Addr:** 1033 Bangs Ave, Asbury Park, NJ 07712.

HARRIS, LORETTA K.
Librarian. **Personal:** Born Nov 20, 1935, Bryant, MS; daughter of Estella Kelley Parker (deceased); married James Joe Harris; children: Sheila Lynne Harris Ragin. **Educ:** S Illinois Univ, 1952-54; Kennedy-King Coll, certificate, 1971; City Coll of Chicago-Loop, diploma, 1974; Chicago State Univ, BA, 1983, MS, 1990. **Career:** Univ of Illinois Library, photographic tech 1957-59; S Illinois Univ Library, library clerk, 1959-63; John Crerar Library, order librarian, 1968-70; Univ of Illinois at Chicago, Library of Health Scis, library tech asst III, 1970-. **Orgs:** Council on Library/Media Tech Assts, mem chairperson, 1977-80, constitution chairperson, 1980-84, mem 1970-; mem Med Library Assn Midwest Chapter, 1976-; mem Health Science Librarians of Illinois, 1976-; mem Ontario Assn of Library Techs, 1977-; listed in Natl Deans List, 1982-83; mem Black women in the Middle West Project, 1984-, Amer Library Assoc, Standing Comm on Library Ed; mem Training of Library Supportive Staff Subcomm, 1979-81; mem Intl Federation of Library and Assn and Institutions Printing and Reproduction Committee IFLA annual meeting, 1985; mem Natl Council of Negro Women, 1986; Council on Library/Media Technical Assistants, Constitution chairperson, 1986-91, chairperson nominating committee, 1988; mem Illinois School Library Assn, 1990-; National Association of Negro Musicians, R Nathaniel Dett Branch, correspondence sec, 1993-; mem, Janice Watkins Award Comm. **Home Addr:** 8335 S Colfax Ave, Chicago, IL 60617. **Business Addr:** Library Technical Assistant, Univ of IL at Chicago, 801 S Morgan, Chicago, IL 60612.

HARRIS, LUCIOUS H., JR.
Professional basketball player. **Personal:** Born Dec 18, 1970, Los Angeles, CA. **Educ:** Long Beach State Univ. **Career:** Dallas Mavericks, guard, 1993-96; Philadelphia 76ers, 1996-97; New Jersey Nets, 1997-. **Business Addr:** Professional Basketball Player, New Jersey Nets, Brendan Byrne Arena, 405 Murray Hill Pkwy, East Rutherford, NJ 07073, (201)935-8888.

HARRIS, M. L.
Professional football player (retired), association executive. **Personal:** Born Jan 16, 1954, Columbus, OH; married Linda; children: Michael Lee II, Joshua. **Educ:** Univ of Tampa; Kansas State Univ. **Career:** Tight end: Hamilton Tiger-Cats (CFL), 1976-77; Toronto Argonauts (CFL), 1978-79; Cincinnati Bengals, 1980-85. **Orgs:** Founded ML Harris Outreach; Sports World Ministries.

HARRIS, MARCELITE J.
Military official. **Personal:** Born Jan 16, 1943, Houston, TX; daughter of Marcelite Elizabeth Terrell Jordan and Cecil Oneal; married Maurice Anthony Harris, Nov 29, 1980; children: Steven Eric, Tenecia Marcelite. **Educ:** Spelman College, Atlanta, GA, 1960-64; Squadon Officer School, Correspondence, Air Univ, Montgomery, AL, 1975; Central Michigan University, Washington, DC, 1976-78; Chapman College, Colorado Springs, CO, 1979-80; Air War Coll, Seminar, Air Univ, Montgomery, AL, 1982; University of Maryland, Okinawa, Japan, BS, 1984-86; Senior Officials in Natl Security, Harvard University, Boston, MA, 1989; CAPSTONE, Residence, Natl Defense Univ, Washington DC, 1990; Natl & Internal Senior Managers Course, Harvard Univ, Boston, MA, 1994. **Career:** Head Start, Houston, TX, teacher, 1964-65; US military, currently. **Orgs:** Member, Air Force Association, 1965-; member, Tuskegee Airmen, 1990-; member, Mississippi Gulf Coast Chamber of Commerce, 1987-90; member, Biloxi Rotary, 1989-90; member, Delta Sigma Theta, 1980-; mem, Bd of Dirs United Services Automobile Assn, 1993; Unite States Rep to the Women in NATO Comm, 1994. **Honors/Awds:** First African-American woman major general in the United States, 1995; first African-Amer woman brigadier general, USAF, 1990; Woman of the Year, New Orleans Chapter, Natl Sports Organization, 1989; Top 100 Afro-American Business & Professional Women, Dollars & Sense Magazine, 1989; White House Social Aide, Pres Carter, 1977-78; First Woman Aircraft maintenance officer, USAF, 1969; one of first two women cadet squadron commanders, USAF Academy, 1978; first woman Avionics and Field Maintenance Squadron Commander, Strategic Air Command, 1981-82; first woman dir of maintenance in the USAF, 1982; first woman deputy commander of maintenance in the USAF, 1986; has received numerous other civilian awards. **Military Serv:** US Air Force, Major General, 1995; Legion of Merit (twice); Bronze Star; Meritorious Service Medal (four times); Air Force Commendation Medal (twice); Distinguished Presidential Unit citation; Air Force Outstanding Unit Award (eight times), with Valor (one time-Vietnam War); Air Force Organizational Excellence Award, (twice); Vietnam Service Medal; Republic of Vietnam Gallantry Cross with Device; Republic of Vietnam Campaign Medal; Natl Defense Service Medal; Air Forces Overseas Long Tour Ribbon (twice); Air Force Overseas Short Tour Ribbon, others. **Business Addr:** HQ USAF/LGM, 1030 Air Force Pentagon, Washington, DC 20330-1030.

HARRIS, MARGARET R.
Pianist, conductor, composer, arranger. **Personal:** Born Sep 15, 1943, Chicago, IL; daughter of Clara L Harris and William D Harris. **Educ:** Juilliard Sch of Music, BS 1960-64, MS (summa cum laude) 1964-65. **Career:** Natl Endowment for Arts, cnsltnt 1971-74; Natl Opera Inst, cnsltnt 1971-76; Afilliate Artists Inc,

panelist 1972-82; Hillsborough Comm Clg, artist-in-residence; Bd of Educ NY, consultant; conductor, Chicago, St Louis, Grant Park, San Diego, Detroit, Winston-Salem, Minneapolis, American Symphonies; conductor, Los Angeles Philharmonic; guest soloist, Los Angeles Philharmonic, Zubin Mehta Conducting-M Harris Second Piano Concerto; University of West Florida, distinguished visiting professor, 1989-; City University of New York, Bronx Community College, adjunct professor, 1991-. **Orgs:** Judge Natl Assc of Negro Musicians 1980-; mem Mu Phi Epsilon Prof Music Sorority 1961-; Natl Assc Negro Musicians 1978-. **Honors/Awds:** Distnguished Alumni Prof Children's Sch 1971; Distinguished Musician Natl Assc Negro Musicians 1972; Outstanding Member Mu Phi Epsilon Music Sorority 1964; Dame Honour & Merit Knights of Malta Order of St John 1986. **Special Achievements:** Concert Tour of Germany, 1994; American Cultural Specialist for United States Information Agency, for the opera, "Porgy and Bess" in Russia, 1995. **Home Addr:** 165 W End Ave, #28N, New York, NY 10023.

HARRIS, MARION HOPKINS
Educator. **Personal:** Born Jul 27, 1938, Washington, DC; daughter of Georgia Greenleaf Hopkins and Dennis C Hopkins; divorced; children: Alan Edward MD. **Educ:** Univ of Pittsburgh, MUA 1981; USC, MPA 1985; Univ of Southern California, DPA 1985. **Career:** Westinghouse Corp Pittsburgh, housing consult 1970-71; Dept of Urban Renewal & Econ Devel Rochester NY, dir program planning; Fairfax Cty Redevel & Housing Auth, exec dir 1971-72; HUD Detroit Area Office, dep dir of housing 1973-75; US Gen Acct Office Wash DC, managing auditor 1975-79; Dept of Housing & Urban Devel Office of the Asst Sec, sr field officer for housing 1979-90, director of evaluation division, office of management & quality assurance, HUD, 1991-; Bowie State University, Graduate Program in Administrative Management, coordinator, professor; 1991-. **Orgs:** Pres, USC-WPAC Doctoral Assn, DC, 1979; exec bd mem, SW Neighborhood Assembly, DC, 1979; Black Women's Agenda 1980; chmn, Housing Comm DC League of Women Voters, 1980-82; Advisory Neighborhood Commissioner, 1986; Amer Acad of Social & Political Science, Amer Evaluation Assoc; chmn, Educ Comm Caribbean Amer Intercultural Org; ex-officio member, Bowie State University Foundation; mentor, Ron McNair Fellowships, 1991-; Sub cabinet, Citizens Advisory Board, Washington Suburban Sanitary Commission, 1989-; steering committee, Academic Leadership Institute, University of Maryland, 1993; co-chair, bd mem, Governor's Workforce Investment Bd, 1996-98; ASPA; Presenter, Academy of Business Admin. **Honors/Awds:** Carnegie-Mellon Fellow Univ of Pittsburgh 1970-71; Fellow Ford Found 1970-71; Outstanding Performance Award, HUD 1984, 1987; Secretary's Certificate of Achievement, 1988; Secretary's Group Award, 1990; Merit Award, 1990. **Home Addr:** 10947 Swansfield Rd, Columbia, MD 21044.

HARRIS, MARION REX
Business executive. **Personal:** Born Jun 30, 1934, Wayne County, NC; son of Virginia Harris and Eugene Harris; married Aronul Beauford Edwards; children: Amy, Angelique, Anjanette. **Educ:** LaSalle Ext Corres Law Sch, 1970; A&T State Univ, Hon Doc of Humanities 1983. **Career:** NC Dept of Trans, bd mem 1972-76; Off of Min Bus Enterprise Adv Bd, bd mem 1970-; Custom Molders Inc, bd of dirs 1976-83; Vanguard Investment Co, chief exec officer 1982-84; Rexon Coal Co, chmn of the bd 1981-; Intl & Domestic Develop Corp, chmn of the bd; A&H Cleaners Inc, proprietor/chairman of the board, 1965-; A&H Coin-Op Laundromat, proprietor/chairman of the board, 1970-. **Orgs:** Mem Fayetteville Area Chamber of Commerce 1965-; mem NC Coal Institute 1976-; dir Natl Business League 1980-; chmn Rexon Coal Co 1982-; dir Middle Atlantic Tech Ctr 1983-; bd of trustees St Augustine's Coll 1983-, A&T State Univ 1985-. **Honors/Awds:** Recognition in Black History Sears Roebuck Co 1969; Letter of Recognition/Excellence in Business US Dept of Commerce Off of Minority Business Enterprise 1972; Businessman of the Yr Natl Assn of Minority Certified Public Accountants 1982; "Driven" Business NC Magazine 1983; Horatio Alger Awd St Augustine's Coll 1983; Par Excellence Operation PUSH 1983. **Military Serv:** 82nd airborne E7 12 yrs; Silver Star; Good Conduct Medal; Army Accom. **Business Addr:** Chmn of the Board, Intl & Domestic Dev Corp, 4511 Bragg Blvd, Fayetteville, NC 28303.

HARRIS, MARJORIE ELIZABETH
Educational administrator. **Personal:** Born Dec 8, 1924, Indianapolis, IN; daughter of Violet T Harrison-Lewis and T Garfield Lewis; married Atty Richard Ray Harris, Nov 20, 1965; children: Frank L Gillespie, Grant G Gillespie, Gordon L Gillespie, Jason Ray Harris. **Educ:** West Virginia State Coll, Institute WV, BS, 1946; Univ of Michigan, Ann Arbor MI, MA, 1975, PhD, 1981. **Career:** Lewis Coll of Business, Detroit MI, faculty, 1946-60, admin asst, 1960-65, pres 1965-. **Orgs:** Bd of trustees, Lewis Coll of Business, 1950-; bd of commissioners, Detroit Public Library, 1970-86; regional dir, Gamma Phi Delta Sorority, 1989. **Honors/Awds:** Mayor's Award of Merit, Mayor City of Detroit, 1979; Spirit of Detroit, City of Detroit, 1979; 50 Most Influential Women in Detroit, Detroit Monthly Magazine, 1985; Excellence in Educ, Assn of Black Women in Higher Educ, 1986; Community Service, Detroit Urban League, 1988. **Business Addr:** President, Lewis College of Business, 17370 Meyers Rd, Detroit, MI 48221.

HARRIS, MARY LORRAINE
County official. **Personal:** Born Jan 18, 1954, Durham, NC; daughter of Mable Freeland Harris and Greenville E Harris (deceased). **Educ:** NC Central Univ, BA 1975; Univ of Miami, MS 1980. **Career:** Metro-Dade Transportation Admin, program analyst 2 1978-80, program analyst 3 1980-81, principal planner 1981-83, chief urban init unit 1983-84, asst to the exec dir 1984-88, asst to dep dir, 1988-90; Metro Dade Co, dept of human resources, administrator, 1990-. **Orgs:** Mem Natl Forum for Black Public Admins, Women's Transportation Seminar, Natl Assn for Female Executives, Amer Heart Assn of Greater Miami, NAACP; mem Conference of Minority Transit Officials and chair 1988-; chairperson, COMTO Mid-Year Conf; mem task force Inner City "Say No To Drugs"; mem Metro Dade County United Way Cabinet; Metro-Dade Office of Rehabilitative Services, Miami, FL, asst to dir, 1989; mem, Metro-Dade Women's Assn; member, Greater Miami Opera Guild, 1990-; board of directors, League of Women Voters, 1988-. **Honors/Awds:** Gold Awd United Way; Honored by Gov Bob Graham as Outstanding Black American in the State of Florida 1986. **Business Addr:** Assistant to Dir, Metro-Dade County Elderly Services Division, 111 NW 1st St, Suite 2210, Miami, FL 33128.

HARRIS, MARY STYLES
Scientist. **Personal:** Born Jun 26, 1949, Nashville, TN; daughter of Dr & Mrs George Styles; married Sidney E Harris. **Educ:** Lincoln Univ, BA Biology 1971; Cornell Univ, PhD Genetics 1975; Rutgers Med Sch, Post-Doctoral Study 1977. **Career:** Sickle Cell Found of GA, exec dir 1977-79; Morehouse Coll Sch of Med, asst prof 1978-; WGTV Channel 8 Univ of GA, scientist in residence 1979-80; Atlanta Univ, asst prof of biology 1980-81; GA Dept of Human Resources, dir genetic svcs; BioTechnical Communications, pres, currently. **Orgs:** Mem Public Health Assn 1977-; mem Amer Soc of Human Genetics 1977-; adj pub serv asst GA Bd of Regents Univ of GA 1979-80; comm adv bd Univ GA Pub TV Station WGTV 1980-83; mem Cong Black Caucus Health Brain Trust; mem Gov's Adv Council on Alcohol & Drug Abuse; mem GA Human Genetics Task Force. **Honors/Awds:** Gen Rsch Support Grant, Rutgers Med Sch 1975-77; Outstanding Young women of Amer 1977-78; Outstanding Working Woman of 1980 Glamour Mag 1979-80. **Business Addr:** 2058 North Mills Ave, Suite 214, Claremont, CA 91711.

HARRIS, MARYANN
Educational administrator. **Personal:** Born Jun 10, 1946, Moultrie, GA; married John W Harris; children: Paul, Justin. **Educ:** Knoxville Coll, BS 1969; Wayne State Univ, MA 1971; Nova Univ, EdD 1986; University of Akron, MA, 1992. **Career:** Case Western Reserve Univ, gerontology suprv 1972-74; Cuyahoga Comm Coll, gerontology consult 1975-80; City of Cleveland, gerontology consult 1980-81; Project Rainbow Assoc Inc, exec dir & founder 1980-; East Cleveland City Schools, bd mem; UAW- Ford Devel and Trainging Prog, reg coord. **Orgs:** Mem school bd East Cleveland City School Dist 1979-; gerontology consult Council of Econ Oppty of Greater Cleveland 1980-84; grants devel Cleveland Adult Training 1980-; pres & sr assoc Grantsmanship Rsch Council 1980-; exec comm mem Cuyahoga Cty Demo Party 1984; chmn youth comm NAACP 1985; 2nd vice pres Alpha Kappa Alpha 1985; Ohio Northeast Region Bd; Natl School Bds Assn Federal Relations Network, 1988-; Ohio Comm Educ Assn, pres. **Honors/Awds:** Gerontology Study Grant USA Admin on Aging 1969-71; Career Mother of the Year Cleveland Call & Post Newspaper 1984; Developing Intergenerational Comm Serv Prog Natl Alliance of Black School Ed 1984; Grandparents Riddles Proj Rainbow Assoc 1984; Women's Rights, Practices Policies Comm Serv Awd 1984; Ohio School Boards Assn, Award of Achievement, 1991-94. **Business Addr:** Bd Mem, East Cleveland City Schools, 15305 Terrace Rd, East Cleveland, OH 44112-2998.

HARRIS, MELVIN
Government official. **Personal:** Born Feb 9, 1953, Oxford, NC. **Educ:** NC Central Univ, BA 1975; The Amer Univ, MPA 1977; Natl Assn of Schools of Public Affairs and Public Admin, fellowship. **Career:** US Office of Personnel Mgmt, personnel mgmt specialist 1977; Amer Fed of State Co & Municipal Auth, rsch analyst 1977-78; Prince Georges Co MD, personnel/labor relations analyst 1978-79; Dist of Columbia Government, principal labor relations officer 1979-88; Howard University, director of labor/employees relations, 1988-92; City of Baltimore, labor commissioner, 1992-. **Orgs:** Pres Alpha Phi Omega NC Cntrl Univ 1973-75; Conf of Minority Pub Adm Amer Soc for Pub Adm 1978-; roundtable coord Natl Capitol Area Chap Amer Soc for Pub Adm 1980-83; chmn VA Voter Regis Educ Task Force 1984; co-fndr/treas Natl Young Prof Forum Amer Soc for Pub Adm 1981-83; bd of dir Natl Cncl of Assns for Policy Sci 1984-85; bd of dir Natl Capitol Area Chap Amer Soc for Pub Adm 1980-82 & 1984-85; Amer Univ Title IX Adv Comm 1984-; Alexandria Forum 1983-; co-chmn Young Prof Forum Natl Capitol Area Chap ASPA; camp dir Alex Young Dem 1982;Spnsr N VA Voter Reg Coalition 1983; Alex Dem Exec Comm 1983-84; pres Alex Young Dem 1983-84; exec vp VA Young Dem 1984-; chrmn VA Young Dem NVA Fundraiser 1985. **Honors/Awds:** Fellowship Natl Assn of Schools of Public Affairs and Public Admin Amer Univ 1975; Chap Service Awd Natl Capitol Area Chap Amer Soc for Public Admin 1983. **Special Achievements:** Author: New Directions in Personnel, 1976; Starting a County Program for Alcoholic Employees, 1977; co-author: The Supreme Ct and Pub Employment, 1976; Labor-Management Relations, 1977. **Business Addr:** Labor Commissioner, City of Baltimore, Office of the Labor Commissioner, 417 E Fayette St, Ste 1405, Baltimore, MD 21202.

HARRIS, MICHAEL NEELY
Cleric. **Personal:** Born Feb 5, 1947, Athens, GA; son of Mattie Neely Harris Samuels and William T Harris; married Sylvia Ann Jones, Nov 30, 1968; children: Crystal Michele, Michael Clayton. **Educ:** Morehouse College, BA, 1968; Eastern Baptist Theological Seminary, MDiv, 1975, DMin, 1984. **Career:** Philadelphia School District, research intern, 1968-69, administrative assistant; Office of Federal Evaluation, day-care program, 1969-71; First Baptist Church of Passtown, pastor, 1971-80; Emmanuel Baptist Church, pastor, 1980-89; Wheat Street Baptist Church, pastor, 1989-. **Orgs:** Wheat Street Charitable Foundation, chairman, 1989-; City of Atlanta, mayor's religious advisory board, 1992-; Sweet Auburn Area Improvement Association, director, 1992; Wheat Street Federal Credit Union, board member, 1989-; Morehouse School of Religion, trustee, 1991-; PNBC Home Mission Board, chairman, 1988-90; Roosevelt, New York Board of Education, board member, 1987-89. **Honors/Awds:** Morehouse College of Ministers Inductee, 1991; Eastern Baptist Seminary, Most Outstanding Preacher, 1975; Coatesville Club of Nat Negro and Business Professionals, Man of the Year, 1978; Queens County Nat Negro Business & Professional Women, Man of the Year, 1987. **Special Achievements:** Publication: "The He, Thee, Me Program: A Stewardship Plan to Undergird a Third World Missilogical Ministry in the Context of the Black Church in the United States of America," 1984. **Business Addr:** Pastor, Wheat Street Baptist Church, Christian Education Bldg, 18 William Holmes Borders Dr SW, Atlanta, GA 30312, (404)659-4328.

HARRIS, MICHAEL WESLEY
Educator, historian. **Personal:** Born Nov 9, 1945, Indianapolis, IN; son of Edwina N Bohannon and Harold I Harris; married Carrol Grier Harris (divorced 1982). **Educ:** Ball State University, Muncie, IN, 1963-66; Andrews University, Berrien Springs, MI, BA, 1967; Bowling Green State University, Bowling Green, OH, MM, 1968; Harvard University, Cambridge, MA, PhD, 1982. **Career:** Oakwood College, Huntsville, AL, instructor of music/German, 1968-71; University of Tenn-Knoxville, Knoxville, TN, asst prof of religious studies, 1982-87; Temple University, Philadelphia, PA, visiting asst prof of religious studies, 1987-88; Wesleyan University, Middletown, CT, associate professor of history, 1988-91; University of Iowa, professor, history and African-American world studies, currently. **Orgs:** Member, board of directors and co-chair of program committee, National Council of Black Studies, 1988-90; council member, American Society of Church History, 1990-93; member, American Historical Association, 1978-; member, American Studies Association, 1987-. **Honors/Awds:** Rockefeller Humanities Fellowship, Rockefeller Foundation, 1985-86; Research Fellowship, Smithsonian Institution, 1979-80; National Fellowships Fund Dissertation Fellowship, 1976-77; Board of Editors, History and Theory, 1990-92. **Special Achievements:** Author: The Rise of Gospel Blues: The Music of Thomas A Dorsey in the Urban Church, Oxford University Press, 1992. **Business Addr:** Professor, History and African-American World Studies, History Department, University of Iowa, 205 Schaeffer Hall, Iowa City, IA 52242, (319)335-2299.

HARRIS, MICHELE ROLES
Communications account executive. **Personal:** Born Jul 10, 1945, Berkeley, CA; daughter of Marguerite Barber Roles and Mahlon Roles; married Joseph Harris. **Educ:** Univ of San Francisco, BS 1978. **Career:** Ted Bates Advertising, assistant acct executive, 1979-82; Essence Magazine, acct executive, 1982-83; Johnson Publishing Co., acct executive, 1983-84; American Heritage Publishing, eastern sales manager, 1984-86; Gannett Co. Inc, acct executive, 1986-. **Orgs:** Asst account exec Ted Bates Adv 1977-82; account exec Essence 1982-83; The EDGES Group Inc, co-chair communications comm, 1986-. **Honors/Awds:** Gannett National Newspaper Sales Award, 1995. **Home Addr:** 4 Cedar Lane, Croton on Hudson, NY 10520. **Business Phone:** (212)715-5338.

HARRIS, NARVIE J.
Educator (retired). **Personal:** Born Dec 19, Wrightsville, GA; daughter of Anna Jordan and James E Jordan; married Joseph L Harris, Nov 19, 1945 (deceased); children: Daryll Harris Griffin. **Educ:** Clark Clg, AB 1939; Atlanta U, MED 1944; Tuskegee Inst; Univ GA; GA State U; TN State U; Wayne State Univ, Detroit Mich. **Career:** Decatur County GA, home economics & elementary teacher 1939-41; Henry County GA, home economics & elementary teacher 1941-42; Calhoun County GA, home economics teacher 1942-43; Albany State GA State Univ, teacher; Dekalb School System, instructor coord 1944-83. **Orgs:** Consultant, Morris Brown Clg & Atlanta U; supr, GA Assc Instctnl; sec-tres ASCD GA; Ch Sch Bells Awrd Pgm, GA Assn Edctrs; vice pres, Borders Courtesy Guild 1979-96; pres, GA Congress Clg PTA 1967-71, Royal Oaks Manor Clb 1961-96; bd of dirs, De Kalb Historical Soc 1981-96; Joseph B Whitehead Boys Club; pres, Decatur-Dekalb Retired Tchr Assn

1987; trustee, Wheat St Baptist Church, 1987-94, reelected, 1995-98, Church anniversary chair, 1990-92, Nonagevorian Awards sponsor, 1993; United Sisterhood Outreach Program, volunteer, Christmas program sponsor, 1992-. **Honors/Awds:** Bronze woman of yr Iota Pi Lambda Sorty 1965; Dynamic Delta Delta Sigma Theta Sorority Inc; Clark Clg Alumni Dynamic Edctr 1982; co authored History GA Congress Col PTA History 1970; co authored History Royal Oaks Manor Comm Clb 1979; Honorary Assoc Superintendent Dekalb Schls 1985; Clark Coll Distinguished Alumni Achievement Awd 1986; Ambassador from Georgia to Brazil 1974, England 1977, Africa 1972; Korea 1980; Cali Colombia 1981; also to Kyoto & Tokyo Japan; Moscow, Leningrad-Tibishi, 1989; Distinguished Alumni Atlanta Univ 1987; Plaque for Outstanding Service, Borders Courtesy Guild, 1993; Stylemaker of the Year Award, 1993; MLK Jr Center Volunteer Service Award, for Non-Violent Change, 1994; Plaque from Borders Courtesey Guild for Services Rendered, 1994, BJ Washington High School, Chairing 60th Reunion, 1934; Honored by Wheat St Bapt Church, 1995; Community Relations Council, Appointed by Mayor Maynard Jackson, 1993-94; Pres-elect of GA Retired Teachers Assn, 1994; Installed Pres of GRTA, 1995. **Home Addr:** 815 Woodmere Dr, NW, Atlanta, GA 30318.

HARRIS, NATHANIEL C., JR.
State official. **Personal:** Born Jan 1, 1941, Hackensack, NJ; son of Susan Satterwhite Harris and Nathaniel C Harris Sr; married Frazeal Larrymore, Feb 1, 1969; children: Courtney. **Educ:** Hampton Inst Hampton, BS 1964; Pace Univ NY, MBA 1979. **Career:** Aetna Life & Casualty, engrg account mgr 1966-68; Real Estate & Constr Div, dept head foreign collection/data processing 1968-71, acct officer 1971-73; Urban Affairs, staff officer 1973-75; RE Comm Devel, sr acct officer 1975-78; Citibank NA, asst vp, real estate-mktg/plnng 1979-80; Chase Manhattan Bank, vice pres real estate 1980-90; National Westminster Bank NJ, vice pres; Natwest New Jersey Community Development Corp, president, 1990-96; United National Bank, sr vice pres, 1996-. **Orgs:** Chmn fin comm, bd of dir Energy Task Force 1979-81; mem Omega Psi Phi, NAACP; bd of dir 1980-87, vice pres 1987- Neighborhood Housing Serv of NY City Inc pres bd of directors 1988-90; pres, Urban Bankers Coalition Inc New York City 1985-87; vice pres Natl Assoc of Urban Bankers 1986-87; pres, National Assoc of Urban Bankers 1987-88; pres, Neighborhood Housing Services of New York City Inc 1988-; board of trustees, Bloomfield College, 1991-96, vice chairman, 1994-96; trustee, Montclair, NJ Art Museum; trustee, Drumtwacket Foundation. **Honors/Awds:** Banker of the Year, Urban Bankers Coilition Inc, New York New York Inc 1989. **Military Serv:** AUS capt 1964-70; Vietnam Serv Medal; Vietnam Campaign Medal; Natl Defense Serv Medal. **Business Addr:** Senior Vice President, United National Bank, 1130 Rte 22 E, Bridgewater, NJ 08807, (908)429-2365.

HARRIS, NELSON A.
Architect. **Personal:** Born Jan 11, 1922, Youngstown; married Dorothy; children: Gayle Elizabeth, Nelson Jr. **Educ:** Univ IL, BA 1961. **Career:** 5th AUS Hdq, asst post eng 1956-60; Harris & Isensee, partner 1960-63; Nelson A Harris & Asso, principal 1963-; IL reg arch; IN; WI; MI; OH; PA. **Orgs:** Mem Am Inst Architects; Nat Org Minority & Architects; Guild Rel Archit;Consult City Chgo; mem NAACP; Urban League; Masons. **Honors/Awds:** Design award Guild Rel Architecture. **Military Serv:** AUS 1st sgt 1943-46. **Business Addr:** 9110 S Ashland Ave, Chicago, IL 60620.

HARRIS, NOAH ALAN, SR.
Physician. **Personal:** Born Apr 2, 1920, Baltimore, MD; married Dorothy W; children: Noah Jr, Merle. **Educ:** Howard U, BS 1942, MD 1945. **Career:** Physician. **Orgs:** Mem Monu Med Soc; Observ & Gyn Soc of MD; Chi Delta Mu Frat; mem Alpha Phi Alpha Frat. **Military Serv:** AUS capt 1953-55. **Business Addr:** 4200 Edmondson Ave, Baltimore, MD 21229.

HARRIS, NORMAN W., JR.
Physician. **Personal:** Born Sep 30, 1924, Washington, DC; married Helen; children: Karen, Patricia, Norman III, Charyl, Kathleen. **Educ:** Howard U, BS 1945, MD 1947; Harlem Hosp, intern; Provident Hosp, resd 1951; Freedmen's Hosp 1956. **Career:** Howard Univ Coll Med, urol 1956-; anat 1957-61; path 1947-48; Howard Univ Hosp, chf urol clin 1971-; exec com 1975-; PSRO, physic adv 1975-; amb care1975-. **Orgs:** Chm MCE Com 1975-78; chmn util rev Com 1977-; vd com 1976; mem Nat Cap Med Found 1975-; chmn Peer Review Commn NCMF 1978-80; staff mem Freedmen's Hosp 1956-75; Hadley Meml 1961-75; Cafritz Meml 1966-68; VA Hosp 1964-71; Howard Univ Hosp 1975-; mem WA Urol Soc; Med Soc DC; Medico-chir Soc; NMA; AMA; Dan Hale Will Med Club; Howard Univ Med Alumni; St Lukes PE Ch; mem Asso Photo Intern; What Good Are We Club; crucifer St Lukes Ch 1940-43; mem Alpha Phi Alpha Frat. **Honors/Awds:** Publ "Hematuria" "Comm Genito Urin Prob" "Genito-urin Compl of Sickle Cell Hemo" "Treat of Sickle Cell Dis Compl" "Prost & Thromboembol". **Military Serv:** AUS pfc 1943-46; USAF MC capt 1951-53. **Business Addr:** 1628 S St NW, Washington, DC 20009.

HARRIS, ONA C.
Organization executive. **Personal:** Born Jul 7, 1943, Detroit, MI; divorced; children: Michael. **Educ:** Wayne County Community College, AA; University of Detroit, BS, Health Care Administration; University of Detroit Mercy, MS Health Care Education & Health Care Administration, currently. **Career:** Carnegie Inst of Tech, medical asst, 1962-63; Blvd Gen Hosp, Southwest Detroit Hosp, sp chem tech, 1965-77; Quality Clinical Lab, Inc, suprv sp chem tech, 1977-86; Univ of Detroit, tech computer asst, 1986-89; Simon House, volunteer, 1989-90, asst dir, 1990-92, exec dir, 1992-. **Orgs:** AIDS Consortium, bd mem; Crains Nonprofit News, adv bd; Michigan Soc of Association Executives; Michigan Coalition Against Homelessness, bd mem; Michigan Prof Women's Network; Women's Economic Club; Natl Alliance to End Homelessness; Secular Franciscan Order, council mem, vice minister; Wayne County Neighborhood Leg Service, bd mem. **Honors/Awds:** Sec Franciscan Order, The Family Award, 1994; Messiah Baptist Church, Black Tribute, 1997; Crain's, Hon Mention, Crain's Best Managed Nonprofit, 1996; US Dept of Housing & Urban Dev, Drt of Excellence, 1997.

HARRIS, OSCAR L., JR.
Elected official. **Personal:** Born Jun 27, 1945, Chiefland, FL; son of Rosa Bell and Oscar L Harris Sr; married Alice Mae Wilson; children: Aurthur, Melissa, Lori, Corey. **Educ:** Univ of MA, MRP 1982. **Career:** Santa Fe Comm Coll, teacher 1975; Alchua Cty Schools, coach 1972-76; Archer Comm Progressive Org Inc, dir 1978-81; Archer Daycare Center, pres 1986-90; FL Assoc for Comm Action Inc, pres; Central FL Comm Action Agency Inc, executive director, currently. **Orgs:** Fellow Southeastern Leadership Devel Program Ford Found 1976-77; councilman City of Archer 1980; gubernatorial appointee North Central Regional Planning Council 1992-97; fellow Natl Rural/Urban Fellows Program 1981-82; mem Gainesville Chamber Leadership 1984, Natl Assoc of Black Public Admin 1984; mem Private Industry Council; vice pres Transportation Disadvantaged Commission; mem Vision 2000, Affordable Housing Coalition, Hunger Coalition; bd mem United Way. **Honors/Awds:** Grant Ford Found 1976, Natl Urban Fellows 1981; Housing Affordability Book Dept of Comm Affairs 1982; Ebony Award Gainesville Police Dept 1985; Alpha Phi Alpha Leadership and Achievement Award 1986; Oscar Harris Day in City of Gainesville Feb 4, 1986. **Home Addr:** PO Box 125, Archer, FL 32618. **Business Addr:** Executive Director, Central Florida Community Action Agency, 220 N Main St, Ste C, Gainesville, FL 32601.

HARRIS, PAUL CLINTON, SR.
Attorney. **Personal:** Born Mar 31, 1964, Charlottesville, VA; son of Pauline Jackson; married Monica L Harris, Oct 21, 1989; children: Paul Jr, Alexandra, Alanah Madison. **Educ:** Hampton Univ, BA, cum laude, 1986; George Washington Univ, JD, 1995. **Career:** US Army, 1986-90; Attorney, currently; VA House of Delegates, state rep, 1997-. **Orgs:** Charlottesville-Albemarle Children & Youth Comm; Albemarle Cty Republican, exec comm; Charlottesville-Albemarle Bar Assn; Charlottesville-Albemarle Chamber of Commerce, legislative action comm; Thomas Jefferson Inn of Court; Boys & Girls Club; DARE, honorary mem; Hampton Univ, pres of student body; Army ROTC Cadet Corps, commander. **Honors/Awds:** VA Military Inst Foundation, George C Marshall Leadership Award. **Special Achievements:** Won Republican primary with 72% of the vote, June 10, 1997; Won general election with 63% of the vote, November 4, 1997. **Military Serv:** US Army, 1986-90. **Business Addr:** State Rep, 58th Dist, Virginia House of Delegates, PO Box 406, Richmond, VA 23218, (804)698-1500.

HARRIS, PAUL E.
Chief executive. **Career:** Protective Industrial Insurance Co of Alabama Inc, Birmingham AL, chief executive. **Business Addr:** Protective Industrial Insurance Co, 237 Graymont Ave, Birmingham, AL 35204.

HARRIS, PEP (HERNANDO PETROCELLI)
Professional baseball player. **Personal:** Born Sep 23, 1972, Lancaster, SC. **Career:** Anaheim Angels, pitcher, 1996-. **Business Addr:** Professional Baseball Player, Anaheim Angels, PO Box 2000, Anaheim, CA 92803, (714)937-6700.

HARRIS, PERCY G.
Physician. **Personal:** Born Sep 4, 1927, Durant, MS; son of Norman Henry & Glendora (Roundtree Clark) Harris; married Evelyn Lileah Furgerson; children: 12. **Educ:** IA State Teachers Coll, 1947-49; Catholic Univ, 1951; American Univ, 1953; Howard Univ, BS 1953, MD 1957. **Career:** St Lukes Hospital, asst med dir, 1958-59, out patient clinic dir, 1959-61, audit and utilization review committee chairman, 1962-75, vp medical staff, 1973, secretary-treasure, 1974, pres-elect, 1975, pres, 1976; Linn County Medical Soc, parliamentarian, 1968-77, secretary-treasurer, 1977-78, vp, 1978-79; Linn County, deputy coroner, 1958-59, coroner, 1959-61, medical examiner, 1961-; Private practice physician, 1958-. **Orgs:** Iowa Foundation for Medical Care, 1977-; Mercy Hospital, Medical Liaison Committee; St Luke's Hosp, Public Relations Committee; Linn County Medical Society, Mass Immunization Measles, chairman, 1968; United Way, 1969-72, Nominating Executive Committee, 1972-76; Board of Oak Hill Engineering, 1973-75; Jane Boyd Community House, 1960-69, pres, 1967-69; Non-Profit Housing Corp, vp, 1973-; NAACP, life mem, Cedar Rapids Chapt, pres, 1964-66; Cedar Rapids Negro Civic Org, founder/pres, 1961-67; Cedar Rapids Community Cable, founder/pres, 1973-83; Cedar Rapids Cable Communications, vp, 1976-83; Iowa Bd of Regents, 1977-89; Community Mental Health Ctr of Linn County, 1974-82; Oakhill-Jackson Economic Development Corp, 1972-75; Cedar Rapids/Marion Human Relations Council, 1961-67; Mayor's Committee, Low Cost Housing, 1967; Non-Profit Housing Corp, 1969; Kirkwood Community Coll, Medical Advisory Committee, 1976-. **Honors/Awds:** NAACP, Community Service Award, 1979; Iowa Football Coaches Assn, 1980; B'nai B'rith, Community Bldg Award, 1982; Service to High School Athletics Award, 1982. **Special Achievements:** "Prime Guidelines to Good Health: Periodic Checkup," Cedar Rapids Gazette, Mar 14, 1979; "Room Rates Vary with Hospital Size, Cedar Rapids Under State Norm," Cedar Rapids Gazette, Jan 16, 1979; "Prescription Drug Price Methods Vary," Cedar Rapids Gazette, Nov 22, 1978; "Hospital Room Rate Breakdown in Cedar Rapids Bares Exceptional Deal," Cedar Rapids Gazette, Sept 27, 1978; numerous other articles. **Business Addr:** Physician, 119 & 3rd St NE, Cedar Rapids, IA 52401.

HARRIS, PETER J.
Editor/publisher. **Personal:** Born Apr 26, 1955, Washington, DC. **Educ:** Howard Univ, BA 1977. **Career:** Baltimore Afro-Amer, staff reporter/editor 1977-78, sports & culture columnist 1979-84; Genetic Dancers Magazine, editor/publisher. **Orgs:** Public relations consultant Council Independent Black Inst 1983-. **Business Addr:** 7102 Lockraven Rd, Temple Hills, MD 20748-5308.

HARRIS, RAY, SR.
Record company executive. **Personal:** Born Jun 30, 1947, New York, NY; divorced; children: Stacey Lynn, Ray Kwesi Jr. **Educ:** Bernard Beruch Clg, MBA, 1970. **Career:** Ted Bates Advertising Agency, media buyer, 1970-71; Atwood Richords Advertising Inc, account executive, 1971-74; RCA Records Inc, dir of r&b promotion, 1974-76, dir of r&r promotion & merchandising, 1976-78, div vp black music mrkt, 1978-80, div vp black music, 1980-82;Solar Records Inc, president; Harr-Ray Productions, president, 1985-87; Warner Bros Records, Black Music, vice pres of promotion, 1988-90, Black Music & Jazz, senior vp of marketing and promotion, 1991-. **Orgs:** Black Music Association, board of directors, 1979-84; Black United Fund, 1980-82; Living Legends Foundation, founder. **Honors/Awds:** Ray Harris Hall of Fame Delaware Valley Jobs Corp 1980; young black achvr awrd YMCA 1978; Black Entrmnt & Sports Law Assn, Special Recgntn Award, 1983, Hall of Fame, 1991; Billboard Magazine, National Promotions Person of the Year, 1988; Young Black Programmers Coalition, Award of Excellence, 1991; Southeast Music Conference, Chairman's Award, 1991; IMPACT Music Conference, Executive of the Year, 1990-93. **Business Addr:** Senior VP, Marketing and Promotion, Black Music, Warner Bros Records, 3300 Warner Blvd, Burbank, CA 91505.

HARRIS, RAYMONT LESHAWN
Professional football player. **Personal:** Born Dec 23, 1970, Lorain, OH; married Leslie; children: Shakia. **Educ:** Ohio State, attended. **Career:** Chicago Bears, running back, 1994-. **Business Addr:** Professional Football Player, Chicago Bears, 1000 Football Dr, Halas Hall at Conway Park, Lake Forest, IL 60045-4829, (847)295-6600.

HARRIS, REGGIE (REGINALD ALLEN)
Professional baseball player. **Personal:** Born Aug 12, 1968, Waynesboro, VA. **Career:** Oakland Athletics, pitcher, 1990-91; Boston Red Sox, 1996; Philadelphia Phillies, 1997-. **Business Addr:** Professional Baseball Player, Philadelphia Phillies, PO Box 7575, Philadelphia, PA 19101, (215)463-6000.

HARRIS, REX
Company executive. **Career:** International & Domestic Devt Corp, chairman, CEO, currently. **Business Addr:** Chairman, CEO, International and Domestic Development Corp., 4511 Bragg Blvd, Fayetteville, NC 28303, (919)864-5515.

HARRIS, RICHARD, JR.
Appraiser. **Personal:** Born Feb 26, 1923, Lima, OK; married Clarice V; children: Teresa K Hollid, Jay R, Marcia H, Rocklyn E. **Educ:** Milwaukee Sch of Engrg, electronic tech 1947-49. **Career:** US Post Office, letter carrier 1950-72; Homefinders Realty, real estate broker 1973-, appraiser 1975-. **Orgs:** Mem Natl Assn of Realtors 1973-; state chmn Equal Oppor KS Assn of Realtors 1978; sec vice pres pres Wichita Met Area Bd of Realtors 1978-80; mem S Central Economic Devel Bd 1973-74; mem KS Office of Minority Bus Enterprise 1975-77; mem Wichita Real Estate Adv Bd 1977-80; commr KS Real Estate Commn 1977-. **Honors/Awds:** Walter Morris Realtor of the Yr Awd 1982. **Military Serv:** AUS sgt 1943-45; Good Conduct Medal; Sharp Shooter Medal. **Business Addr:** Appraiser, Homefinders Realty, 1521 N Hillside, Wichita, KS 67214.

HARRIS, ROBERT ALLEN
Professor, conductor, composer. **Personal:** Born Jan 9, 1938, Detroit, MI; son of Ruina Marshall Harris and Major L Harris; married Mary L Pickens, Jun 8, 1963; children: Shari Michelle. **Educ:** Wayne State Univ, BS 1960, MA 1962; Michigan State Univ, PhD 1971. **Career:** Detroit Public Schools, teacher 1960-64; Wayne State Univ, asst prof 1964-70; MI State Univ, assoc prof, prof 1970-77; Northwestern Univ, Music Department, professor, 1977-. **Orgs:** Dir of music Trinity Church of the North Shore 1978-. **Honors/Awds:** Distinguished Alumni Award Wayne State Univ 1983; publ, Composer Boosey & Hawkes, Carl Fisher Inc, Mark Foster Publ, Heritage Music Press, Oxford Univ Press. **Business Addr:** Professor of Conducting, Northwestern Univ, School of Music, 711 Elgin Rd, Evanston, IL 60208.

HARRIS, ROBERT D.
Manager. **Personal:** Born Aug 31, 1941, Burnwell, WV; married Barbara. **Educ:** WV State Coll, BA 1966; Univ Akron Sch of Law, JD. **Career:** Firestone Tire & Rubber Co, indsl rel trainee 1966-67; Akron, indsl rel rep plant 1967-69; Fall River MA, mgr indsl rel 1969-71; Akron, mgr labor rel 1971-73; Akron, mgr indsl rel 1973-. **Orgs:** Mem Employers & Assn; exec com Summit Co; commr Civil Serv Comm Akron 1977; mem Am OH & Akron Bar Assns; adv bd YMCA; Nat Alliance of Businessmen's Youth Motivation Task Force; W Side Nghbrs; Alpha Phi Alpha frat; Akron Barristers Club; admitted to OH Bar 1976. **Honors/Awds:** Black Exec Exch Prog Nat Urban League; Ebony Success Story. **Military Serv:** AUS sgt E-5 1959-62. **Business Addr:** 1200 Firestone Pkwy, Akron, OH 44317.

HARRIS, ROBERT EUGENE PEYTON
Financial analyst. **Personal:** Born Sep 5, 1940, Washington, DC; son of Jane E Harris (deceased) and John F Harris; married Yvonne Ramey; children: Lisa, Johanna. **Educ:** Morehouse Coll, BA 1963; Long Island Univ, MBA 1981. **Career:** Equitable Life Assur Soc, exp exam; Bronx Community Coll Assn Inc, operations manager. **Orgs:** Mem 100 Black Men 1976; vice pres Battle Hill Civic Assn 1977; Illustrious Potentiat Elejmal Temple Shrine 1987; worshipful master Bright Hope Masonic Lodge 1981; mem Council of Concerned Black Exec New York City 1980; Assn of MBA Executives. **Military Serv:** USAR ltc 1964-89. **Home Addr:** 20 Jefferson Ave, White Plains, NY 10606. **Business Addr:** BCC Assoc Inc, W 181st & University Ave, Bronx, NY 10453.

HARRIS, ROBERT F.
Postal executive. **Personal:** Born May 15, 1941, Knight Station, FL; son of Gertrude Harris and James Harris; married; children: Roger, Lisa. **Educ:** Florida A&M Univ, BS, 1964. **Career:** Subcommittee on Governmental operations, US Senate, chief clerk, deputy staff dir; Bd Pub Instr of Polk Co, teacher & coach, 1966-72; Committee on Governmental Affairs, deputy director, beginning 1988; US Postal Service, vp of diversity development, 1994-. **Orgs:** Chmn bd dir Neighborhood Serv Cntr Inc of Lakeland; bd Cath Soc Serv of Central FL; mem Council of Concerned Citizens of Lakeland; Pi Gamma Mu. **Honors/Awds:** All Conf Track & Field; Cleve Abott Award for Track 1963; various track record awards. **Military Serv:** Airborne 1st lt 1964-66. **Business Addr:** Vice Pres, Diversity Development, US Postal Service, 475 L'Enfant Plaza SW, Washington, DC 20260-5600.

HARRIS, ROBERT L.
Utilities company executive. **Personal:** Born Mar 4, 1944, Arkadelphia, AR; son of Lucy Harris and Ben Harris; married Glenda Newell, MD; children: Anthony, Regina, Brittany, Phillip. **Educ:** Merritt Coll, AA 1963; San Francisco State Univ, BA 1965; Univ of CA School of Law Berkeley, JD 1972; Harvard Graduate School of Business, AMP, 1988. **Career:** Alameda Cty Probation Office, dep probation officer 1965-69; Pacific Gas & Electric Co, attny 1972, central division manager, 1989-93. **Orgs:** Natl Bar Assn, pres, 1979-80; admin mem, Blue Shield of CA 1979-92; chmn, Publ Law Sect, CA State Bar, 1980-81; Western Reg Pres, Kappa Alpha Psi, 1975-79; bd mem, San Francisco Lawyers Comm 1978-88; grand bd of dir, Kappa Alpha Psi 1980-88; pres, Wiley Manuel Law Found 1982-88; sec, Natl Bar Inst, 1982-87; lawyer fellowship, adv comm RH Smith Comm, Howard Univ School of Law, 1981-83; chmn, Legal Comm of Oakland Br NAACP, 1983-87; grand polemarch, Kappa Alpha Psi, 1991-95; bod, Port of Oakland, 1996-. **Honors/Awds:** NAACP Robert Ming Award; UNCF Frederick Patterson Award; National Bar Assn, C Francis Stratford Award. **Business Addr:** VP, Community Relations, Pacific Gas & Electric Co, PO Box 770000, Mail Code H28K, San Francisco, CA 94177, (415)973-3833.

HARRIS, ROBERT L., JR.
Educator. **Personal:** Born Apr 23, 1943, Chicago, IL; son of Ruby L Watkins Harris and Robert L Harris; married Anita B Campbell Harris, Nov 14, 1964; children: Lisa Marie, Leslie Susanne, Lauren Yvonne. **Educ:** Roosevelt University, Chicago, IL, BA, 1966, MA, 1968; Northwestern University, Evanston, IL, PhD, 1974. **Career:** St Rita Elementary Sch, Chicago, IL, 6th grade teacher, 1965-68; Miles College, Birmingham, AL, instructor, 1968-69; Univ of Illinois, Urbana, IL, asst prof, 1972-75; Cornell University, Ithaca, NY, director, 1986-91, assistant to associate professor, beginning 1975, associate professor, currently, special assistant to the provost, 1994. **Orgs:** President, Assn for the Study of Afro-Amer Life & Hist, 1991-92; chair/membership comm, American Historical Assn, 1989-94; chair/program comm, American Historical Assn, 1995; member/bd of directors, New York Council for the Humanitites, 1983-87; member/editorial bd, Journal of Negro History, 1978-96; member/editorial bd, Western Journal of Black Studies, 1990-; National Advisory Board, The Society for History Education, 1996-; General Editor, Twayne African American Histroy Series, 1990-. **Honors/Awds:** Teaching Afro-Amer History, American Historical Assn, 1992; Black Studies in the United States, The Ford Foundation, 1990; Rockefeller Humanities Fellow, SUNY at Buffalo, 1991-92; WEB DuBois Fellow, Harvard Univ, 1983-84; Ford Foundation Fellow, 1983-84; National Endowment for the Humanities Fellow, 1974-75. **Business Addr:** Assoc Prof, Africana Studies & Research Center, Cornell University, 310 Triphammer Rd, Ithaca, NY 14850.

HARRIS, ROBERT LEE
Professional football player. **Personal:** Born Jun 13, 1969, Riviera Beach, FL; married. **Educ:** Southern University, attended. **Career:** Minnesota Vikings, defensive tackle, 1992-94; New York Giants, 1995-. **Business Addr:** Professional Football Player, New York Giants, Giants Stadium, East Rutherford, NJ 07073, (201)935-8111.

HARRIS, ROSALIND JUANITA
Magazine publisher. **Personal:** Born Mar 19, 1950, Grand Rapids, MI; daughter of Ruth Boyd Smith and Doyle James; divorced; children: Lawrence, Donald. **Educ:** Davenport Coll of Business, 1969-70; Patricia Stevens Career Schools, 1972-73; UNO at Omaha, 1980-81; Metro State College, African Amer Leadership Institute, certificate, 1990-91. **Career:** Omaha National Bank, chartographer, 1975-77; Salt and Pepper Art Studios, owner/operator, 1977-80; Rees Printing Co, grapic artist, 1981; Colorado Homes and Lifestyles, production artist, 1981-82; DK Associates/Excel Svcs, Lowry AFB graphic artist, 1982-84; Production Plus/Spectrum Designs, owner/operator, 1984-; Urban Spectrum, publisher/art dir/owner, 1987-. **Orgs:** Colorado Black Chamber of Commerce, 1990-; Five Points Business Association, vice president/publicist, 1989-; Mothers and Daughters Inc, treasurer, 1989-; Rocky Mountain Women's Institute, dir, 1994-; Metro State College President's Community Advisory Council, 1994; Colorado Historical Society African American Advisory Council, 1994-95; Hiawatha Davis Campaign for Better Communities/Committee Chairs of Steering Com, 1995. **Honors/Awds:** YWCA, Women of Achievement Nominee, 1990; CBWPA-Co Black Women for Political Action, Business Award, 1991; CABJ-Co Assn of Black Journalist, Print Journalist of the Year, 1994; MLK Jr Humanitarian Award from Major Wellington E Webb, 1995; American Legion, Community Newspaper Media Award, 1995. **Business Addr:** Publisher/President, Urban Spectrum, 2721 Welton St, Denver, CO 80205, (303)292-6446.

HARRIS, RUTH COLES
Educational administrator (retired). **Personal:** Born Sep 26, 1928, Charlottesville, VA; daughter of Ruth Wyatt Coles and Bernard A Coles; married John Benjamin, Sep 2, 1950; children: John Benjamin Jr, Vita Michelle. **Educ:** VA State Univ, BS 1948; NY Univ Grad School of Bus Admin, MBA 1949; The Coll of William & Mary, EdD 1977. **Career:** VA Union Univ, instructor 1949-64, head of commerce dept 1956-59, assoc prof commerce dept 1964-69, prof, dir div of commerce 1969-73, dir Sydney Lewis School of Business Admin 1973-81; Sydney Lewis School of Bus Admin, mem mgmt team 1985-87, accounting department chair, beginning 1988. **Orgs:** Mem State Adv Council Community Serv Continuing Ed Prog 1977-80; bd of dir Amer Assembly of Collegiate Schools of bus 1976-79; mem adv bd Intercollegiate Case Clearing House 1976-79; mem Equal Oppty Comm AACSB 1975-76; bd of dirs Richmond Urban League 1979-84; agency eval comm United Way of Greater Richmond 1980-85; appointed 1983-85 by gov Robb to Interdepartmental Comm on Rate Setting for Children's Facilities; bd mem Richmond VA Chap Natl Coaltion of 100 Black Women; chairperson, Minority Doctoral Fellows Committee, American Institute of Certified Public Accountants, 1990-92; board of directors, VA Society of CPA's, 1995-1998. **Honors/Awds:** Co-author Principles of Accounting Pitman Publ Co 1959; 1st black woman to pass exam for CPA in VA 1962; Delver Woman's Club Award for Achievement in Business, 1963; Faculty Fellowship Awd United Negro Coll Fund 1976-77; Sears Roebuck Foundation Teacher of the Year Award, Virginia Union University, 1990; Outstanding Accounting Educator Award, Virginia Society of CPAs and American Institute of CPAs, 1991; Outstanding Faculty Award, Virginia State Council of Higher Education, 1992; Bell Ringer of Richmond, NAUW, 1992; Virginia Heroes, participant, 1991-94, 1996; Serwa Award, Virginia Commonwealth Chapter, Natl Coalition of 100 Black Women, 1989; Ebone Images Award, Northern VA Chapter, Natl Coalition of 100 Black Women, 1993; Nissan, HBCU Fellow, 1992; Tenneco Excellence in Teaching Award, 1995, VA Union Univ., Ditingushed Prof emeritus.

HARRIS, SARAH ELIZABETH
Human relations regional director. **Personal:** Born Dec 31, 1937, Newnan, GA; daughter of Sarah L Gates and Dan W Gates (deceased); married Kenneth Eugene; children: Kim Y Harris. **Educ:** Miami Univ, BS 1959, MEd 1967, PhD 1973. **Career:** Career Oppty Prog, univ coord 1970-73; FL School Desegregation Expert, consult 1971-77; General Electric Co, mgr supp serv 1973-75; Urban Rural Joint Task Force ESAA Proj, proj dir 1975-76; Sinclair Coll, consult 1976; Inst for Educ Leadership George Washington Univ, educ policy fellow 1977-78; Cleveland School Desegregation Exp, consult 1977; Citizens Council for OH Schools, staff assoc 1978-79; Dayton Urban League Inc, exec dir 1979-; Dayton Power & Light Co, dir community relations 1985; Dayton/Montgomery County Public Educ Fund, sr consult 1986; Montgomery County, treasurer 1987-91, commissioner, 1991-92; Natl Conf of Christians & Jews, regional dir, currently. **Orgs:** Member, Challenge 95 Network; member, Criminal Justice Committee; member, Dayton Women's Network; Self-Sufficiency Task Force; board of trustees, Wright State University; board of trustees, Sisters of Mercy Health Corporation; board of trustees, Parity 2000; Delta Sigma Theta, Inc; member, Corinthian Baptist Church. **Honors/Awds:** Children's Serv Awd; Jack & Jill of Am Dayton 1975; Outstanding Woman of the Year Iota Phi Lamba Dayton 1978; Salute to Career Women YWCA 1982; Outstanding Grad Awd Dayton Public Schools 1983; Top Ten Women 1983; Induction into the OH Women's Hall of Fame 1984; Martin Luther King Natl Holiday Celebration Meritorious Awd for Community Social Svcs; Miami Univ Bishop Alumni Medal, Outstanding Community Leader Awd Great Lakes Midwest Region of Blacks in Govt 1986; Dayton Champion Award, National Multiple Sclerosis Society, 1987; Mark of Excellence Award, National Forum of Black Public Administrators, 1991.

HARRIS, SEAN EUGENE
Professional football player. **Personal:** Born Feb 25, 1972, Tucson, AZ. **Educ:** Univ of Arizona, attended. **Career:** Chicago Bears, linebacker, 1995-. **Business Addr:** Professional Football Player, Chicago Bears, 1000 Football Dr, Halas Hall at Conway Park, Lake Forest, IL 60045-4829, (847)295-6600.

HARRIS, SIDNEY E.
Educator. **Personal:** Born Jul 21, 1949, Atlanta, GA; son of Marion Johnson and Nathaniel Harris; married Mary Styles Harris, Jun 26, 1971; children: Savaria B Harris. **Educ:** Morehouse College, Atlanta, GA, BA, 1971; Cornell University, Ithaca, NY, MA, 1975, Cornell University, Ithaca, NY, PhD, 1976. **Career:** Bell Telephone Laboratories, member of technical staff, 1973-78; Georgia State University, Atlanta, GA, associate professor, 1978-87; The Claremont Graduate School, Claremont, CA, professor and chairman, 1987-, Peter F Drucker Graduate Management Center, professor, dean, 1991-96; Property Secured Investment, Los Angeles, corp dir, 1994-95. **Orgs:** Associate editor, Office Knowledge Engineering, 1987-; officer, corporate director, Family Saving Bank, Los Angeles, CA, 1988-; associate editor, MIS Quarterly, 1989-92; member, editor advisory board, Business Forum, 1989-; vice chairman, Los Angeles County Productivity Commission, 1988-91; board of governors, Peter F Drucker Non-Profit Foundation, New York, 1991-; corporate director, The Service Master Company, Chicago, IL, 1995-; board of trustees, Menlo College, 1995-; corporate director, TransAmerica Investors, Los Angeles CA, 1995-; Beta Gamma Sigma, National Honor Society for Business Schools, 1994-. **Honors/Awds:** Cornell University Fellow, Cornell University, 1972-73; Bell Telephone Laboratories Fellow, Bell Telephone Laboratories, 1973-75; Sigma Xi, National Scientific Society, 1976-; Volunteer Service Award, National Computer Conference Committee, 1986; Dedicated Science Award, National Computer Conference Committee, 1988. **Business Addr:** Dean, College of Business Administration, Georgia State University, Atlanta, GA 30303.

HARRIS, STANLEY EUGENE
Banker. **Personal:** Born May 19, 1953, Columbus, OH; son of Julia Ann V Harris and Harvey J Harris Sr; married Gene C Thomas, Jun 25, 1977; children: Wade T. **Educ:** University of Notre Dame, BBA, 1975; Stonier Graduate School of Banking, ABA, 1997. **Career:** Banc Ohio National Bank, corporate banking management trainee, 1980-81, supervisor-credit research department, 1981-82, corporate banking representative 1982-84, assistant vice pres/manager credit research department, 1985-87, vice pres/manager community development, 1988-90; National City Corp., community reinvestment officer, 1991-92; National City Bank, Columbus, vice pres/manager public relations/min bus serv, 1992-94, vp, regional mgr, 1995-97, vp/mgr, gov accts, 1997-. **Orgs:** Columbus Urban League, first vice chr, 1992-94, chairman, 1994-95; Columbus Urban League, treasurer, 1986-91; Buckeye Boys Ranch, trustee, 1990-94; Ohio Development Finance Advisory Board, commissioner, 1986-94; I Know I Can, Inc, trustee, exec comm 1990-; Columbus Area Community Mental Health Center, treasurer, 1988-91; Ohio Student Loan Commission, commissioner, 1984-90; Columbus Foundation-Community Arts Fund, chairman, 1989-97; Mt Olivet Baptist Church, chair, trustee bd, 1993-. **Honors/Awds:** J C Penney Co, Golden Rule Award, 1984; Columbus Jaycees, 10 Outstanding Young Citizens, 1986; Columbus Area Leadership Program, graduate, 1986. **Business Phone:** (614)463-8658.

HARRIS, TEREA DONNELLE
Physician. **Personal:** Born Aug 5, 1956, St Louis, MO; daughter of Dixie Kay Gardner Harris and Dr. Samuel Elliott Harris. **Educ:** Fisk Univ, BA 1978; Meharry Medical Coll, MD 1982. **Career:** Henry Ford Hosp, resident 1983-86; Health Alliance Plan, staff physician 1986-88; Outer Drive Hospital, Lincoln Park MI, internist, 1988-91; Michigan Health Care Center, urgent care physician, 1991-92; Bi-County Hospital, internist, house physician, 1992-93; Henry Ford Hospital, fellow, Division of Infectious Diseases, 1993-95; Henry Ford Medical Center-Detroit Northwest, staff physician, 1995-. **Orgs:** Mem Natl Medical Assn, The Links Inc, Alpha Kappa Alpha Sor Inc, member, Outstanding Young Women of America; life member, Fisk Alumni Association; Meharry Alumni Association; board member, Homes for Black Children; Infectious Disease Society of America; American Society of Microbiology. **Home Addr:** 16260 Mayfair Dr. #101, Southfield, MI 48075, (248)483-4103.

HARRIS, THOMAS C.
Business executive. **Personal:** Born Mar 23, 1933, Paterson, NJ; married Betty M Kennedy; children: Thomas Jr, Michael, Elaine Jefferson, Brenda. **Educ:** Fairleigh Dickinson Univ, Teaneck NJ, BS Chemistry 1970; Columbia Univ NY, Cosmetic Science 1972; Fairleigh Dickinson Univ, Teaneck NJ, Surface Active Chemistry 1973. **Career:** Shulton Inc, chemist 1968; Revlon Inc, sr chemist 1974; American Cyanand Co, group leader research & devel 1977; Harris Chemical Co Inc, pres 1977-. **Orgs:** Bd dir Chamber of Commerce; Rotary Club Intl; bd trustee St Joseph's Medical Center; assoc minister Mission Church of God; natl correspondence secy Natl Mens Org; mem Cosmetic Chemistry Soc; Sales & Allied Chemistry Indus; advisor Youth for Christ. **Honors/Awds:** Gold Medal Atlantic Richfield Co Prime Sponsor of Olympic 1984; Excellence in Business US Olympics in LA. **Military Serv:** AUS Signal Corp sp 3/c 3 yrs; Natl Defense Serv Medal 1953-56. **Home Addr:** 602 14th Ave, Paterson, NJ 07504. **Business Addr:** President, Harris Chem Co Inc, 546 E 30th St, Paterson, NJ 07504.

HARRIS, THOMAS WATERS, JR.
Physician. **Personal:** Born Mar 12, 1915, Annapolis, MD; married Elsie. **Educ:** Morgan Coll, BS 1937; Howard Univ Med Sch, 1941. **Career:** Physician pvt prac; VA, med ofcr; Prov Hosp, chf dept radiol 1960-70; Nat Cancer Inst, flw radiol 1949-51. **Orgs:** Bd dir Dukeland Conval & Nurs Hm 1967—; med asso Vilge Med Cntr; Mediso Inc; mem Monu Med Soc; MD State Med Soc; Nat Med Soc; Balti City Med Soc; AMA; ACR; Kappa Alpha Psi; Chi Delta Mu Frat; YMCA; NAACP; Mediso Club; Liberterian Inc. **Honors/Awds:** Flwsp Nat Canc Inst 1949-51; achvmt awd VA 1974, 1977. **Military Serv:** AUS MC capt 1941-46. **Business Addr:** 4200 Edmondson Ave, Baltimore, MD 21229.

HARRIS, TOM W.
Playwright, librarian. **Personal:** Born Apr 30, 1930, New York, NY; son of Mary Harris and Melvin Harris. **Educ:** Howard Univ, BA 1957; UCLA, MA 1959; USC, MLS 1962. **Career:** LA Publ Library, librarian; Voice of Amer, writer 1953-55; Studio West Channel 22 LA, writer, dir; Inner City Cult Ctr LA, teacher 1968; Actors Studio, writer 1967-74; Pasadena Playhouse, playwright; LA Citizens Co, producer/dir. **Orgs:** Mem NAACP, Librarians Black Caucus; LA Black Playwrites; Dramatists Guild; Playwrites Co. **Honors/Awds:** Outstanding Contrib to Theatre in LA Citation LA City Council 1967; All CIAA, All Tournament Howard Univ 1956; Audrey Skirball-Kenis Foundation, Grant, for unplublished play project in library. **Special Achievements:** Playwright, author: 35 plays and short stories, 2 books of fiction; screenplays published: New American Plays, Vol III; musical: "Suds as Clothespins and Dreams," Pasadena Civic, 1990. **Military Serv:** US Army Ord Korea 1951-53.

HARRIS, TRICIA R.
Management executive. **Personal:** Born Feb 16, 1977, Weisbaden, Germany; daughter of Virginia Harris. **Career:** Intellectual Properties Management, file cler, scy, exec asst to chmn, 1995-96, licensing operations, mgr, 1996-97, dir, 1997-. **Business Addr:** Director, Licensing & Operations, Intellectual Properties Management (IPM), 1 Freedom Plz, 449 Auburn Ave, Atlanta, GA 30312.

HARRIS, TRUDIER
Educator, scholar. **Personal:** Born Feb 27, 1948, Mantua, AL; daughter of Unareed Burton Moore Harris and Terrell Harris Sr (deceased). **Educ:** Stillman Coll, Tuscaloosa AL, BA, 1969; Ohio State Univ, Columbus OH, MA, 1972, PhD, 1973. **Career:** The Coll of William and Mary, Williamsburg VA, asst prof, 1973-79; Univ of North Carolina, Chapel Hill NC, assoc prof, 1979-85, prof, 1985-88, J Carlyle Sitterson prof, 1988-; Univ of Arkansas, Little Rock AR, William Grant Cooper Visiting Distinguished, prof, 1987; Ohio State Univ, Columbus OH, visiting distinguished prof, 1988. **Orgs:** Mem, The Modern Language Assn of Amer, 1973-, Amer Folklore Soc, 1973-, Coll Language Assn, 1974-South Atlantic Modern Language Assn, 1980-, The Langston Hughes Soc, 1982-, Zeta Phi Beta Sorority Inc. **Honors/Awds:** NEH Fellowship for Coll Teachers, 1977-78; Carnegie Faculty Fellow, The Bunting Inst, 1981-83; Fellow, Natl Research Council/Ford Found, 1982-83; Creative Scholarship Award, Coll Language Assn, 1987; Teaching Award, South Atlantic Modern Language Assn, 1987; Rockefeller Fellowship, Bellagio, Italy, 1994; National Humanities Center Fellowship, 1996-97. **Special Achievements:** Author of: From Mammies To Militants: Domestics in Black American Literature, 1982; Exorcising Blackness: Historical and Literary Lynching And Burning Rituals, 1984; Black Women In The Fiction of James Baldwin, 1985; Fiction and folklore: The Novels of Toni Morrison, 1991; The Power of the Porch : The Storyteller's Craft in Zora Neale Hurston, Gloria Naylor, and Randall Kenan, 1996; editor of: Afro-American Writers Before The Harlem Renaissance, 1986; Afro-American Writers From The Harlem Renaissance To 1940, 1987; Afro-American Writers From 1940 To 1955, 1988; editor, Selected Works of Ida B Wells-Barnett, 1991; Afro-American Fiction Writers After 1955 in the dictionary of Literary Biography Series, 1984; Afro-American Writers After 1955: Dramatist and Prose Writers, 1985; Afro-American Poets After 1955, 1985; The Oxford Companion to Women's Writing in the United States, 1994; The Oxford Companion to African American Literature 1997; Call and Response The Riverside Anthology of the African American Literary Tradition, 1997; The Literature of the American South: A Norton Anthology, 1997; New Essays on Baldwin's Go Tell It On the Mountian, 1996. **Business Addr:** J Carlyle Sitterson Professor of English, University of North Carolina at Chapel Hill, CB# 3520 Greenlaw, Chapel Hill, NC 27599-3520.

HARRIS, VANDER E.
Educational administrator. **Personal:** Born Dec 27, 1932, Nashville, TN; married Janie Greenwood; children: Vander E Jr, Jason G. **Educ:** Fisk Univ, BS Math 1957; TN State Univ, Engineering Specialist, 1957-58; MIT, Facilities Mgmt 1973; Century Univ, MS Engineering 1979. **Career:** Ft Valley State Coll, supt of bldgs & grounds 1960-67; AL A&M Univ, coord of phys facility 1967-79; Fisk Univ, dir of phys plant 1969-76; Univ of TN Nashville, asst dir of phys plant 1976; Benedict Coll, dir of phys plant 1976-84; Fisk Univ, dir of phys plant, beginning 1984; Morgan State University, dir of physical plant, currently. **Orgs:** AME Church 1936; APPA 1960; NSPE 1969-; SC Soc of Engrs 1979-; Amer Inst Plant Engrs 1980-; adv bd, Who's Who 1983; bd of dir Crittenton Serv 1984. **Honors/ Awds:** Publ Utilities Systems NACUBO 1972; received Acad of Educ & Devel $10,000 Energy Awd 1980; appointed tech asst ISATIM UNCF Schools 1982; Cert Plant Engrs designation 1983; AIPE, fellow, 1990. **Military Serv:** Army Med Serv cpl 1953-55. **Business Addr:** Director, Physical Plant, Morgan State University, 1700 E Cold Spring, Baltimore, MD 21239.

HARRIS, VARNO ARNELLO
Correction officer. **Personal:** Born Aug 10, 1965, Cleveland, OH; son of Kathrine Harris and Howard Johnson; married Sarah-Jane Hill Harris, Jun 5, 1987; children: Michael Andrew Harris. **Educ:** Arizona State correspondance course, Oki, Japan, NADSAP, 1987. **Career:** US Marine Corps, Cherry Point, NC, admin clk, 1984-87; US Marine Corps, Oki, Japan, various positions, 1987-88; Cuyahoga County Sheriff's Department, Cleveland, OH, C/O, 1988-. **Orgs:** President, ZULU, Camp Kinser, Oki, Japan, 1987-88; president, Minority Association of Cuyahoga County Correction Officers, 1990-; Union Steward, UAW Local 1936, 1990-. **Military Serv:** USMC, L Cpl/E3, 1984-88; Rifle Marksman Badge, 1984-88; Meritorious Unit Commendation, 1988; Meritorious Promotion, 1986; Good Conduct Medal, 1987; Meritorious Mast, 1987; Sea Service Deployment Ribbon, 1988.

HARRIS, VERA D.
County official (retired). **Personal:** Born Nov 10, 1912, Palestine, TX; daughter of Estalla Pryor Dial and Caesar Albert Dial; married James A Harris, Sep 25, 1963 (deceased). **Educ:** Prairie View Coll, BS 1935; TX Co So U, MS 1950. **Career:** So Newsp Feat Dallas, home econ lectr 1935-37; TX Agr Extens, co extens agent 1937-73 (retired). **Orgs:** Mem sec Order East Stars 1945-46; mem Prairie View Alumni Assoc 1945-47; sec 1968-72, chmn const & bylaws 1969-70, chmn budget comm Gamma Sigma Chapt; pres 1945-47, sec 1972-77 Cambridge Village Civic Club; NRTA & AARP; pres Gardenia Garden Club; reprtr Optim 13 Soc Club 1970-72; life mem YWCA 1973; chmn Hlth Comm Houston Harris Co Ret Tchrs Assoc 1974; hist Home Econ in Homemaking 1974; Am Home Econ Assn; Prairie View Alumni Club; Sigma Gamma Rho Sorority; Epsilon Sigma Phi Frat; TX Home Econ Assn; Home Econ in Homemaking; Am Home Econ Assn; Houston Harris Co Ret Tchrs Assn; Clint Pk Unit Meth Ch; Nat Assn Exten Home Econs & Nat Assn Ret Fed Employ Sec; Houston Negro C of C; pres TX Negro Home Dem Agts Assn; mem Pine Crest Home Demo Club; pres Houston Harris Co Ret Tchrs; life mem, Gulfgate Chapter #941, YWCA, 1973-; mem, Grand Order of Court of Calauthe; vp, NARFE, National Assn of Retired Federal Employees. **Honors/Awds:** Certificate of Recognition TX Negro Home Demo Agts Assoc 1947; Prairie View & TX So Woman of the Week The Informer 1954; Cert of Awd Natl Assoc Fash & Access Design 1957; Distinguished Serv Awd TX Negro Home Demo Agts Assn 1962; Sigma of Yr Merit Awd 1973; "Palm Branch & Laurel Wreaths" Pal Negro Bus & Professional Wom Club 1976; 100 Plus Club The Prairie View Devel Fund 1976-78; Cooperative Extension Program, Prairie Vew A&M Univ 1986; Houston Harris County Retired Teachers Assn 1988; Gardenia Garden Club, Plaque, 40 year member, 1994; Certificate of Merit, Assn of Retired Black County Agents, 1991; Framed Memories, from Family & Friends, 1992; Sigma Gamma Rho, Dedicated Service, 1995; Prairie View A&M Univ, Coop Extension Prog, Cert of Appreciation, 1997. **Home Addr:** 5110 Trail Lake, Houston, TX 77045-4035.

HARRIS, VERNON JOSEPH
Manager (retired). **Personal:** Born May 18, 1926, Washington, DC; son of Beatrice V Robinson and Vernon J Harris Sr; married Georgetta Mae Ross; children: Elliott F, Cassandra Harris Lockwood, Georgette E H Lee , Wayne J, Verna J H Agen, Dolores A (deceased). **Educ:** Catholic University of American, BEE 1952. **Career:** General Elec AESD, mgr, sr engr, cons, project engr, design engr, jr engr 1952-88. **Orgs:** Past pres, past lt governor of the NY District of Kiwanis & mem Kiwanis Club of N Utica 1962-95; mem Coll Council SUNY Coll of Technology Utica 1968-84; mem Provost Post Amer Legion 1970-; past comdr Provost Post Amer Legion 1974-76; treas Central NY Chap Amer Heart assn 1975-80; treas NY State Affiliate Amer Heart Assn 1978-80; A Good Old Summer Time, Inc, Utica, NY, pres, 1995-97; bd mem & treasurer Cornell Cooperative Extension of Oneida County, 1991-97. **Honors/Awds:** Elfun Territorial Awd for Pub Serv Utica Elfun Soc Gen Elec AESD 1974-75; Elfun Man of Year Utica Chap Utica Elfun Soc Gen Elec AESD 1975; nominee Phillippe Awd for Pub Serv Gen Elec Co Fairfield CT 1977; Phillippe Awd winner for Pub Serv Gen Elec Co Fairfield CT 1978; private pilot's license 1990. **Military Serv:** Hon discharge 1946 from US Army Air Corp with rank of Sgt, was NCO in charge of base signal office with 387th ASG, Godman Fld KY, Freeman Fld IN, and Lockbourn Fld OH.

HARRIS, WALTER, JR.
University administrator. **Personal:** Born Jan 27, 1947, Suttles, AL; son of Arie L B Harris and Walter Harris Sr; married Henrietta Augustus Harris, Apr 17, 1976; children: Ayana Kristi, Askala Almaz. **Educ:** Knoxville College, Knoxville, TN, BS, 1968; Michigan State University, East Lansing, MI, MM, 1969, PhD, 1979; Harvard University, Cambridge, MA, diploma, 1990. **Career:** Knoxville College, Knoxville, TN, dir, choral activities, chair, music dept, dir, division arts and humanities; Arizona State University, Tempe, AZ, coord, undergraduate studies, music, asst dean, College of Fine Arts, acting dean, College of Fine Arts, associate dean, College of Fine Arts, interim asst vice pres academic affairs, vice provost, currently. **Orgs:** President, Arizona Alliance for Arts Education, 1991-93; member, board of trustees, Phoenix Boys Choir, 1990-; member, board of directors, Phoenix Symphony Orchestra, 1990-; member, International Council of Fine Arts Deans, 1985-; regional chairperson, American Choral Directors Assn, 1987-. **Honors/Awds:** Luce Fellow, Luce Foundation, 1977; NEH Fellow, 1974; Pi Kappa Lamda Honorary Fraternity, Michigan State University, 1968. **Home Addr:** 939 E Gemini Dr, Tempe, AZ 85283-3001. **Business Addr:** Vice Provost, Academic Affairs, Arizona State University, Office of the Senior VP and Provost, Administration 211, Tempe, AZ 85287-2803.

HARRIS, WALTER LEE
Professional football player. **Personal:** Born Aug 10, 1974, La Grange, GA. **Educ:** Mississippi State. **Career:** Chicago Bears, defensive back, 1996-. **Special Achievements:** NFL Draft, First round pick, #13, 1996. **Business Addr:** Professional Football Player, Chicago Bears, Halas Hall at Conway Park, 1000 Football Dr, Lake Forest, IL 60045-4829, (847)295-6600.

HARRIS, WESLEY L.
Educator, research engineer. **Personal:** Born Oct 29, 1941, Richmond, VA; son of Rosa M Minor Harris and William M Harris; married Sandra Butler Harris, Sep 21, 1985; children: Wesley Jr, Zelda, Kamali, Kalomo. **Educ:** University of Virginia, Charlottesville, VA, BS, aerospace engineering, 1964; Princeton University, Princeton, NJ, PhD, aerospace engineering, 1968. **Career:** Massachusetts Inst of Tech, Cambridge, MA, professor, aero engr, 1972-85; University of Connecticut, Storrs, CT, dean of engineering, 1985-90; University of Tennessee Space Inst, Tullahoma, TN, vice president, 1990-. **Orgs:** Member, American Helicopter Society, 1974-; member, American Institute of Aero & Astro, 1968-; member, American Physical Society, 1970-. **Honors/Awds:** Research, Sigma Xi, 1966; Scholarship, Tau Beta Pi, 1963; Teaching (MIT), Irwin Sizer Award, 1979; Research, AIAA, Fellow, 1992; Research, Connecticut Academy of Science & Engr, 1986.

HARRIS, WESLEY YOUNG, JR.
Clergyman. **Personal:** Born Jan 14, 1925, Medford, MA; son of Anna R Harris and Wesley Y Harris Sr; children: Wesley Y III, Wayne Preston. **Educ:** Wilberforce Univ OH, BS 1951; School of Social Work Boston Univ, 1961; SUNY Buffalo, MS 1964. **Career:** West Medford Comm Center MA, exec dir 1959-61; Comm Action for Youth Clevland OH, supvr couns serv 1964-66; Psy Dept Wilberforce Univ, dir counc & test, chmn 1965-66; OH Bureau of Vocational Rehabilitation, Columbus OH, supvr spec serv 1966-69; Montgomery Cty Opportunity Ind Center Dayton, exec dir, consultant 1969-70; Syra-

cuse Univ, lecturer, supvr 1969-71; State Univ Coll Potsdam NY, dir office of special programs 1971-75; State Univ Coll Brockport, dir ed opportunity center 1975-79; 1st Genesis Baptist Church, asst minister, min of christian educ 1980; Mon Co Dept of Social Servs, examiner 1981-. **Orgs:** Comm mem Natl Alliance of Bus Dayton 1969-70; mem Human Relations Council Dayton 1969-70; mem Alpha Phi Alpha 1948-, Amer Personnel & Guidance Assoc 1962-, Natl Rehab Assoc 1962-; chmn Natl Comm on Racism, Amer Rehab Couns Assoc 1972; mem Rotary Intl 1973-, Phi Delta Kappa 1974-; ed comm mem NAACP 1969-71, Madison HS Redesign Comm Rochester NY 1973-75; exec comm Greater Boston Settlement House Assoc 1959-71. **Honors/Awds:** Cert VRA Mgmt Trgn Manpower Devel Univ of OK 1967; Cert Workshop on Rehab of the Publ Offender Univ of Cinn 1968; Cert Human Relations Dept of State Personnel OH 1968; Cert Intergroup Relations Dept of State Personnel OH 1968. **Military Serv:** AUS capt 17 yrs; Good Conduct; Sharp Shooter; CBI Theater; Infantry Man's Badge; Asiatic Pacific; Korea Medals.

HARRIS, WILLA BING
Educator. **Personal:** Born Mar 12, 1945, Allendale, SC; daughter of Willa M Lofton Bing and Van Bing (deceased); married Dr Jake J Harris, Jun 3, 1972; children: KeVan Bing. **Educ:** Bennett Coll, BA 1966; Bloomsburg State Coll, MEd 1968; Univ of IL, EdD 1975. **Career:** White Haven State School & Hospital, classroom teacher, 1967-69; Albany State Coll, instructor, 1969; SC State Coll Orangeburg, asst prof & suprv of graduate practicum students, 1969-70; Univ of Illinois at Urbana-Champaign, Upward Bound, head counselor, 1971, asst to major advisor, 1971-73; Barber-Scotia Coll, asst prof of educ & psychology 1975-76; Alabama State Univ, Montgomery, coord, Central AL Regional Educ In-Serv Center, coord 1985-88, dir, Rural & Minority Special Educ Personnel Preparation, 1988, assoc prof & coord for special educ, 1976-, dir of emotional conflict, teacher preparation program, 1990-. **Orgs:** Consult Head Start 1977-80, 1984-85; lay delegate annual conf AL-West FL Conf United Meth Church 1980-90; bd of dir United Meth Children's Home Selma AL 1984-, ASU Credit Union 1984-87, Nellie Burge Comm Ctr 1985-; mem Amer Assoc on Mental Deficiency-Mental Retardation, AAUP, AL Consortium of Univ Dirs Spec Ed, Black Child Devel Inst, Council for Excep Children, Council for Children with Behavior Disorders, Div for Children with Commun Disorders, Div for Mental Retardation, Teacher Ed Div, IL Admin of Spec Ed, Kappa Delta Pi, Natl Assoc for Ed of Young Children, Natl Assoc for Retarded Citizens, Montgomery Cty Assoc for Retarded Citizens, Phi Delta Kappa, ASU Grad Faculty, AL State Univ Woman's Club, Montgomery Newcomers Club, Tot'n'Teens, Peter Crump Elem SchoolPTA State & Natl Chapt,tropolitan United Methodist Church, Adult II Sunday School Class, Committee Chmn Fund Raising Choir Robes, Organizer of United Meth Youth Fellow, Admin Bd; jurisdictional coordinator, Black Methodists for Southeastern Jurisdiction Church Renewal, 1989-; board member/finance chair, National Black Methodists for Church Renewal, 1989-; president/board of directors, United Methodist Children's Home, 1990-. **Honors/Awds:** USOE Fellow Univ of IL 1970-73; Ford Found Fellow Univ of IL 1972-73; Ed of Year AL Assoc Retarded Citizens 1982; Outstanding Educ, Montgomery County Assn for Retarded Citizens, 1982; Volunteer Services Award, Montgomery County Assn for Retarded Citizens, 1985; Distinguished Alumni Award, C V Bing High School, Allendale, SC, 1988. **Home Addr:** 2613 Whispering Pines Drive, Montgomery, AL 36116. **Business Addr:** Assoc Prof of Spec Educ, Alabama State Universiy, Box 288, Montgomery, AL 36101-0271, (334)293-4394.

HARRIS, WILLIAM ALLEN
Sociologist. **Personal:** Born Aug 3, 1937, Providence, RI; son of William A & Ruth Pell Harris; divorced; children: Rebecca Jackson, Kurt R, Trevor, Jimbo S. **Educ:** Univ of CA, Santa Barbara, BA, 1968; Yale Univ, MA, 1970; Stanford Univ, PhD, 1981. **Career:** Wesleyan Univ, asst prof, 1978-82; Univ of Virgin Is, research scientist, 1982-87; Clean Sites, research assoc, 1987-90; Univ of Iowa, visiting faculty, 1990-92; Boston Coll, asst prof, 1992-. **Orgs:** Amer Sociological Assn, 1977-; Assn of Black Sociologists, 1990-; Assn of Social & Behavioral Scientist, 1994-. **Honors/Awds:** Natl Fellowship Fund, Graduate Study, 1974-79; NDFL Fellowship, Japanese Language, 1969; NCEA Fellowship, Black Theatre, 1968; UCSB, Asian Studies, Top Graduate, 1968. **Special Achievements:** Author, Upward Mobility Among African Americans, 1996; Films of Spike Lee, 1995; Theory Construction, Sociological Theory, Vol 10, 1992; Theatrical Performances, CA & Virgin Islands, 1967-86; Best Asian Languages, Chinese & Japanese, 1957. **Military Serv:** US Air Force, E 3, 1957-60; Completed intensive course in Mandarin Chinese. **Business Addr:** Assistant Professor, Dept of Sociology, Boston College, 140 Commonwealth Ave, Chestnut Hill, MA 02167-3807, (617)552-4056.

HARRIS, WILLIAM ANTHONY
Curator, author, educator. **Personal:** Born Jan 25, 1941, Anniston, AL; son of Elizabeth Gay and Edwin; married Carole McDonald, Oct 7, 1966. **Educ:** Wayne State University, BA, 1971, MA, 1977. **Career:** JazzMobile, 1981-83; New Federal Theatre, 1983-85; Wayne State University, 1985-90; Center for Creative Studies, 1985-90; Museum of African-American History, curator, 1990-. **Orgs:** Detroit Council for the Arts, board member, 1987-. **Honors/Awds:** Theatre Communications, Metropolitan Life Collaboration Grant, 1991; Wayne State University, Art Achievement Award for Alumni, 1989; Rockefeller Foundation, Writer in Residence Grant, 1988; Martin Luther King, Jr, Rosa Parks Visiting Scholar Fellowship, 1987; State of Michigan, Paul Robeson Cultural Arts Award, 1985. **Special Achievements:** Publications: Robert Johnson: Trick the Devil, 1993; Stories About the Old Days, 1989; Every Goodbye Ain't Gone, 1989. **Military Serv:** US Army, sp4, 1966-68. **Business Addr:** Curator of Collections and Exhibitions, Museum of African American History, Detroit, 301 Frederick Douglass, Detroit, MI 48202, (313)833-9800.

HARRIS, WILLIAM H.
Educational administrator. **Personal:** Born Jul 22, 1944, Fitzgerald, GA; son of Sallie Harris and Robert Harris; married Wanda F Harris; children: Cynthia Maria, William James. **Educ:** Paine Coll, AB 1966; IN Univ, MA 1967, PhD 1973. **Career:** Paine Coll, instructor of history 1967-69; IN Univ, lecturer, professor of history 1972-82, dir cic minorities fellowships program 1977-82; Paine Coll, pres 1982-88; Texas Southern University, pres, 1988-94; Alabama State Univ, president, 1994-. **Orgs:** Augusta Chamber of Commerce/Augusta Rotary 1988, Leadership Augusta/Leadership GA 1982-84, Augusta Jr Achievement Bd of Dir 1984-88, ETS Bd of Trustees, 1984-90, UNCF Bd of Dir 1984-88, NAFEO Comm on Intercoll Athletics 1984-86, Lilly Endowment Inc Commiss on Lilly Open Fellowship 1984-87, Boy Scouts of America; bd of dir NAFEO 1985-88; GA Commission on the Bicentennial of the US Constitution, 1986-88; chair, Alabama Council of College and University Presidents, 1997-; Air Univ bd of Visitors, US Air Force, 1996-; bd of dir, Leadership Alabama, 1996-; bd of dir, Montgomery Area United Way, 1995-; bd of dir, Montgomery Metro YMCA, 1995-; bd of dir, Montgomery Chamber of Commerce, 1995-; bd of dir, City of Montgomery Industrial Development Board, 1995-; pres, Southwestern Athletic Conference (SWAC) Council of President, 1996-97. **Honors/Awds:** Susan O'Kell Memorial Awd IN Univ Bloomington 1971; IN Univ Distinguished Alumni Service Award, 1991; Paine College, Doctor of Laws, (Honoris Causa), 1991; Keeping the Faith Univ of IL Press 1977; Fulbright Fellow Univ of Hamburg 1978-79; The Harder We Run Oxford Univ Press 1982; Distinguished Son of Fitzgerald, Georgia Centennial Observance, 1996. **Business Addr:** President, Alabama State University, PO Box 271, Montgomery, AL 36101.

HARRIS, WILLIAM H., JR.
Attorney. **Personal:** Born Sep 8, 1942, New Orleans, LA; son of Victoria Fontenette Harris and William H Harris; married Cynthia; children: Alisa Carol, William H III. **Educ:** Xavier Univ, BA 1965; Howard Univ, JD 1968. **Career:** Greenstein Delorme & Luchs, PC, partner, 1989-. **Orgs:** Mem US Court of Appeals Wash DC; mem US Dist Ct; mem US Ct of Claims; mem NAACP; mem Am Dist of Colum & Nat Bar Assns; DC mayor's commiss on Rental Housing Production; mem Natl Assoc of Security Profls; Alpha Phi Alpha Fraternity. **Business Addr:** Partner, Greenstein Delorme & Luchs, PC, 1620 L Street NW, Suite 900, Washington, DC 20036-5605.

HARRIS, WILLIAM J.
Educator, author. **Personal:** Born Mar 12, 1942, Fairborn, OH; son of Camilla Hunter Harris and William Lee Harris; married Susan Kumin, Aug 25, 1968; children: Kate Elizabeth Harris. **Educ:** Central State Univ, Wilberforce OH, BA, 1968; Stanford Univ, Stanford, CA, MA, 1971, PhD, 1974. **Career:** Cornell Univ, Ithaca NY, asst prof, 1972-77; Epoch Magazine, poetry editor, 1972-77; Univ of California, Riverside CA, asst prof, 1977-78; State Univ of New York, Stony Brook NY, asst prof, 1978-85; Harvard Univ, Cambridge MA, mellon faculty fellow, 1982-83; State Univ of New York, Stony Brook NY, assoc prof, 1985-92; The Minnesota Review, poetry editor, 1988-92; The Norton Anthology of Afro-Amer Literature, advisory editor, 1988-; Pennsylvania State University, assoc prof, 1992-. **Orgs:** Mem, Modern Language Assn of Amer, 1971-. **Honors/Awds:** Cornell Univ Faculty Grant, 1974; SUNY Faculty Fellowships, 1980, 1982; Andrew W Mellon Fellowship in the Humanities, Harvard Univ, 1982, 1983; W E B Dubois Fellow, Harvard Univ, 1985; Outstanding Academic Book for The Poetry and Poetics of Amiri Baraka, Choice Magazine, 1986; author of: Hey Fella Would You Mind Holding This Piano a Moment, 1974; In My Own Dark Way, 1977; The Poetry and Poetics of Amiri Baraka: The Jazz Aesthetic, 1985; editor: The LeRoi Jones/Amiri Baraka Reader, Thunder's Mouth Press, 1991. **Home Addr:** 103 Cherry Ridge Rd, State College, PA 16803.

HARRIS, WILLIAM JOSEPH, II
Sculptor. **Personal:** Born Nov 19, 1949, Lansing, MI; son of William & Ella; children: Damon. **Educ:** UCLA. **Career:** Self-employed, sculptor, currently. **Orgs:** Decatur, GA Arts festival, co-chair, 1994-95; African American Parokaine Experience Museum, voluteer; Decatur-Dekalb Arts Alliance, board member. **Honors/Awds:** Works Catalogued Permanently in the African-American Design Archive at Smithsonian's Cooper-Hewitt Museum Dec Arts, 1994; Earl Pardon Memorial Invitational Award Exhibit, 1994; African Expressions, Spruill Center for the Arts, 1994. **Special Achievements:** Work of Art, which is traveling the US with the Uncommon Beauty in Common Objects, Exhibitions, sponsored by Lila Wallace Readers Digest Fund, National Afro-American Museum; Published 79th Annual Conference of the Association for the Study of Afro-American Life and History, 1994. **Business Addr:** Owner, Sculptured Creations, PO Box 752, Avondale Estates, GA 30002.

HARRIS, WILLIAM M.
Educational administrator. **Personal:** Born Jan 19, 1932, Middletown, OH; married Mary Buchanan; children: William, Walter, Adrienne. **Educ:** OH State, BS 1954; Univ ND, MS 1968. **Career:** Univ of MS Amherst, dir camp center 1977-; Rutgers Univ, dir camp center & stud act 1971-77; Rutgers Univ, asst dean of students 1969-71; Essex Co Coll, counselor 1968-69. **Orgs:** Mem Com on Minor Prog; Asso Coll Union Intern 1971-; help alien youth E Orange Bd Educ 1970-74; Vind Soc 1971-. **Military Serv:** USAF Reserves lt col. **Business Addr:** Campus Center, U of MA, Amherst, MA 01002.

HARRIS, WILLIAM MCKINLEY, SR.
Educator, consultant. **Personal:** Born Oct 29, 1941, Richmond, VA; son of Rosa Minor Harris; married Jessie Mathews; children: Rolisa Smith, Dana, Melissa. **Educ:** Howard U, BS Physics 1964; Univ Washington, MUP Urban Plng 1972, PhD Urban Plng 1974. **Career:** Cntr for Urban Studies Western Washington State Clg, dir 1973-74; Black Studies Dept Portland St U, chrmn 1974-76; Off Afro Am Afrs, dean 1976-81; Univ of Virginia, prof of city planning, 1987-; planning consultant, 1987-. **Orgs:** Charlottesville Planning Commission, 1981-; Charlottesville Bd of Zoning Appeals, 1991-; TJ United Way, bd of dirs, 1990-; American Inst of Certified Planners, 1978-; American Planning Assn, 1976-; NAACP, 1964-; People to People's Citizen Ambassador Program, 1993-; Development Training Inst, bd mem, 1988-. **Honors/Awds:** Danforth Assc Danforth Found VA 1980; outstanding serv Comm Dev Soc VA 1984; Citizen Ambassador Program, delegation leader to China, 1992, 1994; Monticello Community Action Agency, Teacher of the Year, 1990; Portland, Oregon Citizen of the Year, 1975. **Special Achievements:** Author of: ''Environmental Racism: A Challenge to Community Development,'' Journal of Black Studies, 1995; ''African American Economic Development in Baltimore,'' The Urban Design and Planning Magazine, 1993; ''Technology Education for Planners: A Century for African and People of African Descent,'' African Technology Forum, 1992; ''Professional Education of African Americans: A Challenge to Ethical Teaching,'' Business and Professional Ethics Journal, 1990; Black Community Development, 1976; Charlottesville Little League Basketball, coach, championships, 1982, 1988, 1992. **Military Serv:** USAF rotc cadet. **Business Addr:** Prof & Chair, Jackson State Univ, Dept Urban & Regional Planning, 3825 Ridgewood Rd, Box 23, Jackson, MS 39211.

HARRIS, WILLIAM R.
Clergyman. **Personal:** Born Jan 3, 1915, Concord, NC; married Doris Elaine Davis; children: Elaine Jeanne, Pauline, Marie. **Educ:** BS MDiv 1945. **Career:** Siloam Bapt Ch, minister. **Orgs:** 5 evang teams Africa 1969, 72, 77; dir audio vis educ & spl asst Sec For Miss Bd Nat Bapt Conv USA 1963-; sec Bapt Min & Conf Pittsburgh 1952-56; v moderator Allegheny Union Bapt Assn 1952-56; dean Rel W Theol Sem 1947-51; mem sec Mont Co Ment Hlth Cntr; bd Cent Mont Co Tech Sch;Allan Wood Steel Schol Com; dir Norris Area Sch Dist 11 yrs nonconsec term 11-77; United Fund. **Honors/Awds:** Gr Philad Fund; mem 1st black preach team S Africa Nat Bapt Conv USA 1975.

HARRIS, WINIFRED CLARKE
Educator. **Personal:** Born Sep 13, 1924, Norfolk, VA. **Educ:** Delaware State Coll, BS 1943; New York Univ, MA 1953; Univ of Delaware, graduate. **Career:** Booker T Washington Jr High School, chair english dept 1947-53; William Henry High School, chair english dept 1953-66; Delaware State Coll, chair dept ofenglish 1966-72; Delaware State Coll, dir federal relations and affirmative action, exec asst to president. **Orgs:** Exec comm Natl Consortium of Arts and Letters for Historically Black Colls & Univs 1974-; corporate rep Delaware State Coll Amer Assoc of Univ Women 1975-; mem Tri-State Commn on Educ 1984-; pres Dover Chap of The Links Inc 1986-; vice chair Delaware Humanities Forum; former chair Natl Sor of Phi Delta Kappa Inc; Phi Delta Kappa. **Honors/Awds:** Distinguished Comm Serv Awd Natl Sor of Phi Delta Kappa Eastern Region 1978; Woman of the Year in Educ Wilmington Chap of Natl Assoc of Univ Women 1983; publ ''Dialogue with a Teacher of Listeners, Readers, and Writers,'' DE State Dept of Public Instruction 1967. **Business Addr:** Exec Asst to the President, Delaware State College, 1200 North Dupont Hwy, Dover, DE 19901.

HARRIS, ZELEMA M.
Educational administrator. **Personal:** Born Jan 12, 1940, Newton County, TX; children: Narissa, Cynthia Bond, James (Jay) Harris. **Educ:** Prairie View A&M Coll, BS 1961; Univ of KS, MS 1972; Univ of KS, EdD 1976. **Career:** Metro Comm Coll, coord of eval 1976-78, dir of eval 1978-80, dir of dist serv 1980; Pioneer Comm Coll, pres 1980-87; pres Penn Valley Comm

Coll and Pioneer Campus 1987-90; Parkland College, president, 1990-. **Orgs:** Eval spec Office of Ed 1976; consult McMannis Assoc 1978-80; consult Natl Ctr for Voc Ed 1978-81; bd mem Black Econ Union 1981-85; Urban League of Greater Kansas City 1981-90; pres NAACP 1982-86; steering comm Mayor's Prayer Breakfast; Full Employment Council; Natl Conf of Christians & Jews; Downtown Minority Devel Corp; Public Bldg Auth; Quality Ed Coalition; former co-chair Kansas City's Jazz Commission; United Way of Champaign County; Champaign County Chamber of Commerce; Junior League of Champaign-Urbana, advisory board; Rotary Club of Champaign; Urban League of Champaign County. **Honors/Awds:** 60 Women of Achievement, Mid Continent Council of Girl Scouts 1983; Mary McLeod-Bethune, Alpha Phi Alpha 1983; Jefferson Awd, Channel 4 TV NBC 1984; 100 Most Influential Women, Globe Newspaper 1983, 1990; Recognition for Serv, Adv Committee on the House Select Comm on Children Youth & Females 1984; Recognition for Outstanding Participation the UNCF Lou Rawls Parade of Stars Fund-Raising TV spec 1983; One of the Most Powerful Women in KS City, KS Citian publ by C of C 1984; named gen chairman, Greater Kansas City, Missouri,United Negro College Fund Campaign, 1988; Panel of American Women, "One of 30 Women of Conscience," 1987; Gillis Center of Kansas City, MO, and the Kansas City Star Co., Kansas City Spirit Award, 1987; National Council of Christians and Jews, Protestant of the Year Citation Award, 1986; Dollars and Sense Magazine, One of Nations Most Influential Black Women, 1986; Publications: "Creating a Climate of Institutional Inclusiveness," President's Award Winner, 1992, Published in Community, Technical, and Junior College Times, Aug/Sept 1992; "Meeting the Growing Challenges of Ethnic Diversity," Community, Technical, and Junior College Times, Apr 1990; developed, "Vocational Evaluation Model," The Missouri Advisory Council on Vocational Education, 9th Annual Report, 1978. **Special Achievements:** Author, "Creating a Climate of Instituional Inclusiveness," Community, Technical, and Junior College Times, Aug/Sep 1992; "Meeting the Growing Challenges of Ethnic Diversity," Community, Technical, and Junior College Times, Apr 1990; developed, "Vocational Evaluation Model," The Missouri Advisory Council on Vocational Education, 9th Annual Report, 1978. **Business Addr:** President, Parkland College, 2400 W Bradley, Champaign, IL 61821-1899.

HARRIS-EBOHON, ALTHERIA THYRA

Educator, business executive. **Personal:** Born Jun 26, 1948, Miami, FL; daughter of Mary White-Harris and Andrew Harris; married John Ikpomwenosa Ebohon, Dec 25, 1987. **Educ:** Miami-Dade Community Coll, AA 1968; FL Atlantic Univ, BA 1970; Morgan State Univ, MS 1972; FL Atlantic Univ, EdS 1976; Nova Univ, EdD 1981; Post Doctoral Studies Barry Univ, Florida Intl Univ; Univ of Miami. **Career:** Dade County Public Schools, 28 years, educator; businesswoman 1988-. **Orgs:** 44 year mem New Mt Zion Missionary Baptist Church of Hialeah; mem Natl Educ Assoc 1970-; baptist training union directress New Mt Zion Missionary Baptist Church of Hialeah 1980-; bd mem Florida Baptist Conv, Inc 1986; life fellow Intl Biographical Assn, Cambridge, England, 1988-, Amer Biographical Inst 1988-. **Honors/Awds:** 1st place art display Miami-Dade Comm Coll Library Exhibit 1968; Awds Banquet Honoree by Senator Bob Graham, St Augustine, FL 1986. **Home Addr:** 475 NW 90th St, Miami, FL 33150. **Business Addr:** NIAM Inc of Florida, USA, 10150 NW 7th Ave, Miami, FL 33150, (305)759-8082.

HARRIS MCKENZIE, RUTH BATES

Government official (retired), human relations consultant, author. **Personal:** Born Aug 27, 1919, Washington, DC; daughter of Florence Phillips Carter and Harry B Delaney; married Alfred U McKenzie, Aug 25, 1987; children: Bernard Jr, Charles. **Educ:** FL A&M Univ, BS; New York Univ, MBA 1957. **Career:** District of Columbia Human Relations Commn, exec dir and equal employment opportunity officer DC 1960-69; Montgomery County MD Public Schools, dir human relations dept 1969-71; NASA, dept asst admin, public affairs, 1971-76; Dept of Interior Washington DC, human relations officer 1978-87 (retired); Ruth Bates Harris Associates, president, currently. **Orgs:** Founder/former pres, Cosmopolitan Business and Professional Women's Club; mem natl pr comm, bd mem Tuskegee Airmen Inc, East Coast Chapter; mem natl adv comm Federally Employed Women; Golden life mem Delta Sigma Theta Sor; life mem, Natl Council of Negro Women; Natl Advisory Committee; Amer Univ Women's Institute Advisory Commission. **Honors/Awds:** Keys to Cities of Cocoa Beach and Jacksonville FL 1980; recipient of over 100 awards including Omega Psi Phi Chapter Award; Sigma Gamma Rho Awd; Alpha Phi Alpha Chapter Award; Delta Sigma Theta Award; Hon Iota Phi Lambda; Women of Distinction Award, Andrews Air Force Base Chapter, Air Force Assn; Meritorious Service Award, Dept of the Interior, 1987; Pioneer Award, Tuskegee Airmen, 1989; Blacks in Sisterhood for Action, one of 12 Disting Black Women in the Nation 1986; one of Outstanding Women in Washington Area Washington Women Magazine; one of top 100 Black Business and Professional Women, Amer Dollars and Sense Magazine; author, Handbook for Careerists, Personal Power Words, and Trigger Words; autobiography, Harlem Princess: The The Story of Harry Delaney's Daughter, 1991;featured ihe Real Story of Integration of Astronaut Corps in NASA with foreword by Astronauts Alan Shepard and Guion Bluford.

HARRISON, A. B.

Physician. **Personal:** Born 1909, Portsmouth, VA. **Educ:** VA State Coll, BS; Meharry Med Coll, MD 1930. **Career:** South Hampton Meml Hosp, staff mem1945; Franklin VA, pvt pract 1936-; Provident Hosp, intern. **Orgs:** Mem Franklin VA City Cncl 1968-74; v mayor 1974-76; mayor 1976-. **Business Addr:** City Hall, Franklin, VA 23851.

HARRISON, ALGEA OTHELLA

Educator. **Personal:** Born Feb 14, 1936, Winona, WV; children: Denise, Don Jr. **Educ:** Bluefield State Coll, BS (Magna Cum Laude) Ed 1956; Univ of MI, MA Ed 1959, PhD Psych, Ed 1970. **Career:** Detroit Public School System, teacher; Inkster School System, Rsch Design, Urban Action Needs Analysis, Wayne County Headstart Program, MI Dept of Educ, consultant 1962-66; Highland Park School System, school diagnostician 1968-69; Oakland Univ, assoc prof, currently. **Orgs:** Mem Amer Psych Assoc, MI Psych Assoc, Assoc of Black Psych, Soc for Rsch in Child Devel, Assoc of Soc & Behavioral Sci; bd trustees New Detroit Inc, Roeper City & Cty Schools; mem Founders Soc, Your Heritage House A Black Museum, Natl Org for Women, Child Care Coord Council. **Honors/Awds:** Horace Rackham Predoctoral Fellow 1969-70; US Publ Health Grants, 1965-68; graduated second highest mem of class. **Business Addr:** Professor Psychology, Oakland Univ, Psychology Dept, Rochester, MI 48309.

HARRISON, BEVERLY E.

Attorney. **Personal:** Born Jun 17, 1948, Port Chester, NY. **Educ:** SUNY Oneonta, BA 1966-70; Univ of IL Coll of Law, JD 1970-73. **Career:** Counselor for Housing & Spec Equal Oppty Prog, grad asst 1970-73; SUNY Oneonta Legal & Affirm Action Affairs, asst to pres for employment 1974-81; SUNYS-tony Brook, spec asst to pres affirm action & equal employment 1981-83; Nassau Comm Coll, assoc vice pres personnel & labor relations 1983-. **Orgs:** Faculty adv Varsity Cheerleaders SUNY 1974-81; bd mem Amer Assoc of Univ Women 1978-79, bd mem Planned Parenthood of Otsego & Delaware Cty 1978-80; mem Amer Assoc for Affirm Action Nominating Comm 1979-80, Univ Faculty Senate Fair Employment Practices Comm 1979-81, State Univ Affirmative Action Council 1981-83; bd mem Amer Red Cross of Suffolk Cty 1981-83, Suffold Comm Devel Corp 1981-83; mem NY State Public Employer Labor Relations Assoc, Indust Relations Rsch Assoc, Metropolitan Black Bar Assoc, Committee of Minority Labor Lawyers, Natl Conf of Black Lawyers, Natl Assoc of Black Women Attny; bdmem Suffolk Cty Girl Scout Council; founder Assoc of Black Women in Higher Ed. **Honors/Awds:** Bell & Dragon Honor Soc; Leadership Soc; SUNY Oneonta; Public Serv Awd The 100 Black Men of Nassau/Suffolk Inc 1985. **Business Addr:** Assoc Vice Pres Persnl & Labor Rel, Nassau Community College, Stewart Ave, Garden City, NY 11530.

HARRISON, BOB

Professional football coach. **Personal:** Born Sep 9, 1941, Cleveland, OH; married Anna Marie Bradley; children: Lorraine Ellen, Barbara Annette. **Educ:** Kent State Univ, BS 1964, MEd 1969. **Career:** John Adams HS Cleveland, asst head football coach 1964-66, head football coach 1967-68; Kent State University, assoc admission director, asst football coach 1969-70; University of Iowa Iowa City, asst football coach 1971-73; Atlanta Falcons Professional Football Team, asst coach; Pittsburgh Steelers, asst coach, currently. **Orgs:** Offensive coord Cornell Univ Ithaca, NY 1974; asst football coach NC State Raleigh 1975-76; asst football coach Univ TN Knoxville 1977-82; mem NAACP1982-.

HARRISON, BOOKER DAVID (MULE BROTHER)

Mechanical engineer. **Personal:** Born Apr 23, 1908, Grant Parcolfax, LA; married Ernestine Carroll. **Educ:** So U, BS 1933; MI State ms 1947; tuskegee inst IN state u pra. **Career:** Carver Branch YMCA Fed Cred Un, treas mgr 1968-; Agr Exten Svc, aso co agt 1950-68, asso co agt 1933-50. **Orgs:** Pres Nat Negro Co Agts Assn 1957-58; pres So Univ Nat Alumni Fedn 1960-64; chmn fin com So Univ Bd of Suprs 1976-80; fin sec Evergreen Bapt Ch 1948-; basileus Omega Phi Psi Frat 1954-59; sec Shreveport Metro Plan Com 1978-. **Honors/Awds:** Agt of the yr Co Agt Assn 1955; plaque Compl of 30 yr serv US Dept of Agr 1966; cert of apprec of serv LA State Univ 1969; cert dist out servComm Lead of Am 1971; plaque out serv So Univ Alumni Fedn 1971-75; achieve awd Negro C of C 1976; various other awds YMCA & frat 1977-79.

HARRISON, BOYD G., JR.

Automobile dealership executive. **Personal:** Born Feb 23, 1949, Detroit, MI; son of Jessie Mae Trussel Harrison and Boyd G Harrison Sr; married Alfreda Rowell, Jul 19, 1969; children: Deonne, Devon. **Educ:** Detroit Coll of Business, Computer Science, 1972. **Career:** Ford Motor Co, Dearborn MI, inspector, 1968-72; Chevrolet Central Office, Warren MI, computer operations, 1972-85; Ford Motor Co Minority Dealer Training Program, Detroit MI, dealer candidate, 1985-86; West Covina Lincoln Mercury, W Covina CA, dealer, 1986-. **Orgs:** West Covina Chamber of Commerce, director, 1988-. **Honors/Awds:** America's Best & Brightest Young Business Professionals, Small Business Person of the Year. **Business Addr:** Dealer Principal, West Covina Lincoln Mercury Merkur, 2539 E Garvey, West Covina, CA 91791.

HARRISON, CAROL L.

Educator. **Personal:** Born Nov 15, 1946, Buffalo. **Educ:** English Psychology, BA 1968; PhD 1970. **Career:** Medailla Coll English Dept, instructor, asst prof, chmn 1970-73; Media-Communications Medaille Coll, acting dir, assoc prof 1974-; SUNY AB english educ colloquim 1972-; Am Assn Univ Prof 1968-; Modern Language Assn 1969-; Intl Plaform Assn 1972-74; Univ Buffalo Alumni Assn 1968-; Academic Com Buffalo Philharmonic 1971-73. **Orgs:** Vol work Buffalo Childrens Hosp 1972; Western NY Consortium English & Am Lit Prof 1974; Nomination Am Assn Univ Womens Educ Found. **Honors/Awds:** Outstanding Educators Am Award 1974. **Business Addr:** 18 Agassiz Circle, Buffalo, NY 14214.

HARRISON, CHARLES

Petroleum products distributor. **Career:** Crown Energy Inc, CEO, 1987-. **Special Achievements:** Company is ranked #85 on Black Enterprise's list of top 100 companies, 1994. **Business Addr:** CEO, Crown Energy Inc., 1130 E. 87th St., Chicago, IL 60619.

HARRISON, CHRIS

Professional football player. **Personal:** Born Feb 25, 1972. **Educ:** Virginia. **Career:** Detroit Lions, tackle, 1996-. **Business Addr:** Professional Football Player, Detroit Lions, 1200 Featherstone Rd, Pontiac, MI 48342, (248)335-4131.

HARRISON, DAPHNE DUVAL (DAPHNE D. COMEGYS)

Educator. **Personal:** Born Mar 14, 1932, Orlando, FL; daughter of Daphne Beatrice Alexander Williams and Alexander Chisholm Duval; married Daniel L Comegys Jr; children: Michael Alexander, Stephanie Dolores. **Educ:** Talladega Coll, BMus 1953; Northwestern Univ, MMus 1961; Univ of Miami FL, EdD 1971. **Career:** Marion & Broward Co FL, music tchr 1953-66; Broward Co FL, TV instr 1966-68; FL Atlantic Univ, asst prof educ 1969-70; Hallandale Middle Sch FL, dean of girls 1970-71; Benedict Coll, asso prof fine arts 1971-72; Univ of MD Baltimore County, assoc prof, chairperson, prof, Africana studies dept 1981-96, Center for the Study of Humanities, director, 1996-. **Orgs:** Proj dir, summer inst African & African Amer History culture & literature, 1984-85; proj dir Racism Intervention Develop Proj UMBC 1975-77; social planner New Town Harbison SC 1971-72; consult FL Sch Desegregation Consult Ctr 1965-70; ch music dir St Andrews Ch Hollywood FL 1960-70; bd mem CTD FL Educators Assn 1965-67; bd mem FL State Tchrs Assn 1963-65; mem Natl Assn of Negro Business & Professional Women, Alpha Kappa Alpha, Assn for the Study of Afro-Amer Life & Hist; Co-chair Black Family Committee of African American Empowerment Project; Commissioner of the Maryland Commission on African-American History & Culture; Sonneck Society; Intl Assn for Study of Popular Music. **Honors/Awds:** NEH Fellowship for University Professors, 1992-; NEH African Humanities Fellow UCLA 1979; Moton Ctr for Independent Studies Fellow Philadelphia 1976-77; So Fellowships Univ of Miami 1969-70; Theodore Presser Awd Talladega Coll 1951; Fulbright Fellow 1986; Outstanding Faculty of the Year, Black Student Union, UMBC 1988-89; Black Pearls: Blues Queens of the 1920's, Rutgers Univ Press 1988; Most Favorite Faculty Student Government Assn, UMBC 1989; The Classic Blues and Women Singers, Blackwell Press Guide to the Blues 1989. **Business Addr:** Director, Univ MD, Baltimore County, Center for the Study of Humanities, 5401 Wilkens Ave, Baltimore, MD 21228.

HARRISON, DELBERT EUGENE

Finance company executive. **Personal:** Born Aug 25, 1951, Flint, MI; son of Audrey and Eugene Harrison; married Mary Hill Harrison, Sep 4, 1982; children: Darren, Whitney, Danielle. **Educ:** Wilberforce University, Wilberforce, OH, BA, 1978. **Career:** Kemper Ins Co, Long Grove, IL, personnel assistant II, 1981-82; Allstate Ins Co, South Barrington, IL, division human resources mgr, 1982-86; Chemical Bank NY, Chicago, IL, vice pres, dir, human resources, 1987-88; Navistar Financial Corp, Rolling Meadows, IL, vice pres, human resources, 1988-. **Orgs:** Board of trustees, Latino Institute, 1986-90; advisory board member, Roosevelt Univ, Robin Campus, 1989-; Black Human Resources Network, secretary. **Home Addr:** 5727 Ring Ct, Hanover Park, IL 60103.

HARRISON, DON K., SR.

Educator. **Personal:** Born Apr 12, 1933, Nashville, NC; married Algeo O Hale; children: Denise, Don K. **Educ:** North Carolina Central Univ, BA 1953; Wayne State Univ, MA 1958; Univ of Michigan, PhD 1972; Licensed Psychologist. **Career:** Univ of Michigan Rehabilitation Rsch Inst, assoc prof and dir 1976; Univ of Michigan Rehabilitation Counseling Educ, assoc prof and dir 1975; Guidance and Counseling Program, Univ of Michigan, chmn 1974-77; Guidance and Counseling Program, Univ of Michigan, asst prof 1972-76; Vocational Rehabilitation, Wayne State Univ, adjunct asst prof 1972. **Orgs:** Dir PRIME Inc Detroi MI 1970-80; mem Am Psychol Assn; mem Personnel & Guidance Assn Rehab Couns Traineeship Rehab Srv Admin 1975. **Honors/Awds:** Outstanding Srv Awd MI Prsnl & Guid Assn 1976. **Military Serv:** AUS sgt 1953-55. **Business Addr:** Univ of Michigan Rehabilitation Research, 1360 School of Educ, Ann Arbor, MI 48109.

HARRISON, EMMA LOUISE
Educational administrator, educator, author. **Personal:** Born Apr 13, 1908, Mexia, TX; daughter of Lula Bell Glasco McDonald and Ulysess C McDonald; married Jesse Harrison, Oct 8, 1929. **Educ:** Houston-Tillotson, BA 1939; Univ of So CA, MS 1942, Doctorate 1944; Grad Study Tour, Scandinavian countries; Paul Quinn College, PhD, 1965; Baylor Univ, PhD, 1968. **Career:** City Schs of Waco, teacher/supervisor 1932-57; Summer School Los Angeles City Schs, teacher 1939-41; Paul Quinn Coll, prof/dean 1957-60; Huston-Tillotson, coll prof 1952-54, 1954-69; Baylor Univ, prof 1969-71; Waco Indep Sch Dist, trustee, 1976-89. **Orgs:** Trustee & church hostess St Luke AME Church Waco 1935; Alpha Kappa Alpha Sor former natl officer Chicago 1945; charter mem/org Doris Miller YMCA Waco 1947; charter mem/org Blue Triangle YWCA Waco 1950; bd mem Eco Opp Adv Corp 1965-83; bd of advisors KXXV 25 1980-; bd of adv mem Central TX Economic Devel District 1981-; bd of advisors Eco Opp Adv Corp 1984-; bd Legal Aid 1966-70; bd sec Centennial 1985-; mem/voter, League of Women Voters, 1975-; mem, Amer Cancer Soc, 1976-; Bell Ringer, Salvation Army Christman Cheer, yearly; charter org mem, NAACP, 1969-. **Honors/Awds:** Liberty Bell Awd Young Lawyers of Waco 1976; Liberty Bell Awd Young Lawyers of TX 1977; Yellow Rose of TX gov of TX 1978; pres Thos Jefferson KCEN-TV Corp Waco 1981; Disting Serv Award Alpha Kappa Alpha Sorority, Inc Chicago; honored in publication by Essai Seay; Black Women Role Models, 1986; Outstanding Woman of the Year, Delta Sigma Theta, 1986-87; Baylor Univ Founders Club as a Baylor Family Mem, Baylor Univ, 1989; Certificate of Appreciation, Amer Kidney Assn, 1989; author of 10 books; member, Governor's Capitol Councils. **Special Achievements:** Selected by President Bill Clinton as a Charter Member of The Americans for Change Presidential Task Force. **Home Addr:** 1405 McCloney St, Waco, TX 76704-1445.

HARRISON, ERNEST ALEXANDER
Educational administrator. **Personal:** Born Apr 10, 1937, Morganton, NC; son of Laura Mae Harrison and Mid Milton Harrison; married Karen Yvonne Perkins; children: Darius, Desiree. **Educ:** NC Centrl U, BA; NC Cntrl U, MA 1961; Univ of MI, PhD 1977. **Career:** Highland Park School District, asst superintendent, 1982-; Highland Park Comm Coll, exec asst to the pres & vice pres 1979, dir of personnel 1977-79, dir of evening sch 1975-77, dir Black Studies 1972-75, chief lbr negotiator 1976; Albany State Coll, prf History 1961-64; Univ of Rochester, consult Black History 1972; Detroit Pub Sch Systm, consult Black Hist 1974-76. **Orgs:** Mem Kappa Alpha Psi Frat; mem NAACP; mem MI Comm Coll Personnel Admin Assn; mem Natl Alliance of Black Sch Edctrs; mem N Central Assn of Jr Coll; mem Phi Delta Kappa; advisory bd, Grosse Pointe Academy. **Honors/Awds:** Merit Award United Negro Coll Fund. **Home Addr:** 19023 Muirland, Detroit, MI 48221. **Business Addr:** Assistant Superintendent, School District of the City of Highland Park, 20 Bartlett, Highland Park, MI 48203.

HARRISON, FAYE VENETIA
Anthropologist, educator. **Personal:** Born Nov 25, 1951, Norfolk, VA; daughter of Odelia B Harper Harrison and James Harrison (deceased); married William Louis Conwill, May 17, 1980; children: Giles, Mondlane, Justin. **Educ:** Brown University, BA, 1974; Stanford University, MA, 1977, PhD, 1982. **Career:** University of Louisville, assistant professor of anthropology, 1983-89; University of Tennessee-Knoxville, associate professor of anthropology, 1989-97; Univ of SC-Columbia, professor of anthropology, graduate dir of women's studies, 1997-. **Orgs:** Commission on the Anthropology of Women, International Union of Anthropological & Ethnological Sciences, co-chair, 1993-98; Association of Black Anthropologists, president, 1989-91, secretary, 1985-87, editor, 1984-85; American Anthropological Association, board of directors, 1990-91; Kentucky Rainbow Coalition, 1988-90; National Alliance Against Racist Political Repression; Democratic Socialists of America, 1990-; NAACP; Annual Review of Anthropology, editorial bd; Critique of Anthropology, editorial bd; Urban Anthropology, editorial bd; Identities, editorial bd; Womanist Theory & Research, editorial bd; University of Tennessee Press, editorial bd; East Tennessee Coalition to Abolish State Killing; Off of Justice, Peace, Integrity of Creation, Knoxville Roman Catholic Diocese, advisory bd; Black Faculty and Staff Assn, Univ of Tennessee-Knoxville, chair, 1995-97. **Honors/Awds:** Ford Foundation, Graduate Fellowship, 1976-78; US Department of Education, Fulbright-Hays Predoctoral Fellowships, 1978-79; Brown University, Samuel T Arnold Fellowship, 1974-75; Danforth Foundation, Compton Fellowship, 1981-82; Ford Foundation, Postdoctoral Fellowship, 1987-88; Phi Beta Kappa Certficate of Merit for Scholarly Achievement, 1993. **Special Achievements:** Editor & Contributor: ''WEB DuBois and Anthropology,'' special issue, Critique of Anthropology, 1992; editor and contributor: Decolonizing Anthropology, American Anthropological Association, 1991; editor and contributor: ''Black Folks in Cities Here and There: Changing Patterns of Domination & Response,'' special issue, Urban Anthropology and Cultural Systems in World Economic Development, 1988; ''Women in Jamaica's Urban Informal Economy,'' New West Indian Guide (reprinted in Third World Women and the Politics of Feminism, Indiana University Press), 1988 (1991); ''Jamaica and the International Drug Economy,'' TransAfrica Forum, 1990; performer: ''Three Women, One Struggle,'' Louisville, KY, International Women's Day Celebration Dayton, OH, 1989, Black Arts Festival, Summer 1990; author: Writing Against The Grain: Cultural Politics of Difference in Alice Walker's Fiction, Critique of Anthropology, 1993; Foreword, Comparative Perspectives on Slavery, 1993; ''The Persistent Power of Race in the Cultural and Political Economy of Racism,'' Annual Review of Anthropology, 1995; ''Give Me That Old Time Religion: The Genealogy and Cultural Politics of an Afro-Christian Celebration in Halifa County, NC,'' Religion in the South, 1995; co-editor, contributor, African American Pioneers in Anthropology, Univ of Illinois Press; contributed entries, ''The Blackwell Dictionary of Anthropology,'' 1998; ''The Gendered Politics and Violence of Structural Adjustment: A View from Jamaica;''in Situated Lives: Gender and Culture in Everyday Life, 1997. **Business Addr:** Professor of Anthropology, University of SC, 317 Hamilton Hall, Columbia, SC 29208, (803)777-4009.

HARRISON, HARRY PAUL
Educator (retired). **Personal:** Born Jan 10, 1923, Lawrenceville, VA; son of Eliza Harrison-Green and George E Harrison; married Teressa H; children: Vera, Zelma, Agatha. **Educ:** St Pauls Coll, BS 1952. **Career:** Greenville Co School System, teacher 1952-55; Bruns Co School System, teacher (retired) 1955-85; Bd of Supervisors, chmn. **Orgs:** Supt of Sunday School 1957-83; pres Brunswick Teachers Assoc 1968-69; pres Brunswick Ed Assoc 1970-71; chmn Poplar Mt Church's Bldg Comm 1977; chmn Brunswick Co Dem Comm 1978-90; treas Brunswick Co NAACP 1978-; dir Emergency Services Brunswick Co 1980-; chairman, Brunswick Co Social Services, 1989-90; vice chairman, Planning District #13, 1989-92; member, S S Community Services Board, 1990-. **Honors/Awds:** Back Bone NAACP 1976, 1980; Citizen of the Year Omega 1981; Outstanding Service, Bethany Baptist Assn, 1984-90. **Military Serv:** AUS corpl 1946-47; Army Occupation Medal; WWII Victory Medal. **Business Addr:** Chairman, Bd of Supervisors, Rt 2 Box 48, Lawrenceville, VA 23868.

HARRISON, HATTIE N.
Delegate. **Personal:** Born Feb 11, 1928, Lancaster, SC; married Robert; children: Robert, Philip. **Educ:** J C Smith; Community Educ Devel; Antioch Coll. **Career:** Dist 45, delegate; sr commn aide 1968-73; del sub-tchr 1962-73; mayors rep 1974; NH Sch Pub Reltns Assn, consult 1970; NH Aerospace Conv; Comm Sensitivity Training Comm Sch Div . **Orgs:** Fndr chmn Dunbar Comm & Cncl; mem Steering Com Univ MD; NAACP Comm Sch Wrkshp; fndr & spnsr Douglass Teen Club; ward ldr Mothers March 1950-60. **Honors/Awds:** Outstndng Ldrshp Awrd 1974; Wmn Yr Alpha Zeta 1974. **Business Addr:** MD State Delegate, MD General Assembly, 2503 E Preston St, Baltimore, MD 21213.

HARRISON, JAMES, JR.
Pharmacist. **Personal:** Born Oct 14, 1930, Pittsburg, PA; married Eunice Kea; children: Wanda, James III, Donna. **Educ:** BS 1954; Registered Pharmacist NJ 1956; Univ Freeman's Hosp, Intern 1 Yr. **Career:** Harrison Pharmacy Inc, pres; Berg Pharmacy, purchased 1971. **Orgs:** Sunday Schl Tchr; Boy Scout Ldr; mem adv bd Bloomfield HS; past pres & treas N Jersey Pharm; mem bd of dir Essex Co Pharm Soc. **Business Addr:** Harrison Pharmacy, 641 High St, Newark, NJ 07102.

HARRISON, JEANETTE LAVERNE
TV news reporter. **Personal:** Born Dec 4, 1948, Kyoto, Japan; married James Michael Sullivan; children: Katherine, James Brady. **Educ:** CO State Univ, BA (French) 1968; Univ of CA Berkeley, MJ 1973. **Career:** KPIX-TV San Francisco CA, TV news agent 1973-74; KTVU-TV Oakland CA, editor & apprentice 1973-74; KQED-TV San Francisco CA, reporter 1974-75; KGW-TV Portland OR, TV news reporter 1975-78; WTCN-TV Minneapolis MN, TV news reporter 1978-; KARE-TV, TV news reporter. **Orgs:** Mem Limited Thirty Black Prof Womens Orgn; Natl Hon Phi Sigma Iota 1970-; freelance jrnlst & wrtr. **Honors/Awds:** Comm serv Vet Frgn Wars Waite Park 1984; comm serv Gannet Corp MN 1984; missing chldrn Wrote & Prod 5 TV Series. **Business Addr:** TV News Reporter, KARE-TV, 441 Boone Ave, Minneapolis, MN 55427.

HARRISON, LISA DARLENE
Professional basketball player. **Personal:** Born Jan 2, 1971; daughter of Cobble Harrison and Larry and Darlene Koellner. **Educ:** Univ of Tennessee. **Career:** Columbus Quest, guard, 1996-. **Business Addr:** Professional Basketball Player, Columbus Quest, 7451 State Route 16, Dublin, OH 43016, (614)873-6555.

HARRISON, MARVIN DANIEL
Professional football player. **Personal:** Born Aug 25, 1972, Philadelphia, PA. **Educ:** Syracuse, bachelor's degree in retailing. **Career:** Indianapolis Colts, wide receiver, 1996-. **Special Achievements:** NFL Draft, First round pick, #19, 1996. **Business Addr:** Professional Football Player, Indianapolis Colts, PO Box 535000, Indianapolis, IN 46253, (317)297-2658.

HARRISON, MERNOY EDWARD, JR.
Educational administrator. **Personal:** Born Nov 15, 1947, Denver, CO; son of Doris L Thompson Jackson (deceased) and Mernoy E Harrison; married Frankie Gilliam Harrison, Jun 29, 1974; children: Dara T Harrison, Jelani T Harrison. **Educ:** Stanford University, Stanford, CA, BS, 1969; MBA, 1975; University of North Carolina, Chapel Hill, NC, PhD, 1988. **Career:** Ravenswood High School, East Palo, Alto, CA; Sequoia Union School District, Redwood City, CA, teacher, 1969-70; Kaiser Foundation, Los Angeles, CA, teacher,1970-72; San Mateo County, Redwood City, CA, analyst, 1973-74; Northern Carolina Central Univ, Durham, NC, Comptroller, 1974-81; California State Univ, Sacramento, CA, vice pres, 1981-97; Arizona State Univ, administrative svcs, vice provost, 1997-. **Orgs:** Treas, Sacramento-Yolo Camp Fire, 1982-86; vice pres, Western Assn of College and Univ Business Officers, 1989-90; pres, 1990-91; mem, bd of dir, Natl Assn of College and Univ Business Officers, 1988; chair, exec comm, California State Univ Business Officers Assn, 1983-85; Stanford University, board of trustees, 1992-97. **Honors/Awds:** National Achievement Scholar, 1965; Merrill Intern, 1974; Woodrow Wilson Fellow, 1974-76. **Business Addr:** Office of the Vice Provost, Administrative Services, Arizona State University, Main Campus, PO Box 872303, Tempe, AZ 85287-2303.

HARRISON, NANCY GANNAWAY
Dentist. **Personal:** Born Oct 20, 1929, Trinity, NC; married Robert; children: Renee, Susan. **Educ:** Shaw U, BS 1950; Howard U, DDS 1954; St Elizabeth Hosp Wash DC, intrnshp 1954-55. **Career:** Dentist, self-employed. **Orgs:** Mem Acad Gnrl Dntstry; Twin City Dntl Soc 1971; treas 1969; Old N State Dental Soc; NC Dntl & Soc; Am Dntl Assoc Urbn League Guild; Delta SigmaTheta Sor; sec Altrusa Ind; v pres bd dir YWCA 1973-75.

HARRISON, NOLAN
Professional football player. **Personal:** Born Jan 25, 1969, Chicago, IL. **Educ:** Indiana. **Career:** Oakland Raiders, defensive end, 1995-96; Pittsburgh Steelers, 1997-. **Business Addr:** Professional Football Player, Pittsburgh Steelers, Three Rivers Stadium, 300 Stadium Circle, Pittsburgh, PA 15212, (412)323-1200.

HARRISON, PAUL CARTER
Producer, director, writer, educator. **Personal:** Born Mar 1, 1936, New York, NY; son of Thelma Carter Harrison and Paul Harrison (deceased); married Wanda Malone, Aug 6, 1988; children: Fonteyn. **Educ:** New York Univ, 1952-55; Indiana Univ, BA, 1957; New School for Social Research, MA, 1962. **Career:** Howard Univ, asst prof of theatre arts, 1968-70; Kent State Univ, assoc prof of Afro-American literature, 1969; California State Univ, prof of theatre arts, 1970-72; Univ of Massachusetts at Amherst, prof of theatre arts and Afro-American studies, 1972-76; Choice Magazine, cultural consultant, 1973-83; Elan Magazine, contributing editor, theatre, 1981-83; Callaloo Magazine, contributing/advisory editor, 1985-88; The Evergreen College, curriculum/cultural diversity consultant, 1986; Columbia College, Theatre and Music Department, artistic producer, chairman, 1976-80, writer-in-residence, 1980-. **Orgs:** Theatre panel, Illinois Arts Council, 1976-79; exec comm, Natl Black Theatre Summit on Golden Pond. **Honors/Awds:** Obie Award, Best Play, ''The Great MacDaddy,'' 1974; Illinois Art Council, Grant, 1984; National Science Foundation, Fellowship, 1959-60; Rockefeller Foundation, Fellowship, 1985; Audelco Development Committee, Recognition Award, ''Tabernacle,'' 1981; Humanitas Prize, ''Leave 'Em Laughin''', 1981; NEA Playwrights Panel, 1992; Readers Digest Commission, Meet the Composer, 1992, 1995; NEA Playwrights Fellowship, 1995. **Special Achievements:** Director, plays: ''Junebug Graduates Tonight,'' 1969; ''Lady Day: A Musical Tragedy,'' 1972; ''My Sister, My Sister,'' 1981; ''The River Niger,'' 1987; producer, play: Black Recollections, 1972; conceptualized, directed: ''Ain't Supposed to Die a Natural Death,'' 1970; director: ''In an Upstate Motel,'' 1981; playwright, ''Tabernacle,'' 1981; ''Anchorman,'' 1988; ''The Death of Boogie Woogie,'' 1980; ''Goree Crossing,'' 1992; developer and producer, television film: playwright, ''Leave 'Em Laughin','' CBS-TV, 1981; playwright: ''The Experimental Leader,'' 1965; ''The Great MacDaddy,'' 1974; author: The Drama of Nommo, Grove Press, NY, 1973; In the Shawdow of the Great White Way, Thunder Mouth Press, 1989; Charles Stewart's Jazz File, 1985; screenwriter: Lord Shango, 1974; Youngblood, 1978; Gettin' to Know Me, 1980; editor: Kuntu Drama, anthology, Grove Press, NY, 1974; dir, ''Food for the GODS,'' 1994; editor: Totem Voices, Anthology, Grove Press; co-editor, Classic Plays from the Negro Ensemble Co, Univ of Pittsburgh Press, 1995; dir: ''Trial of One-Short Sighted Black Woman vs Safreeta Mae & Mammy Louise,'' 1997; editor, ''African American Review Special Issue on Black Theatre,'' winter, 1997. **Home Addr:** 360 E Randolph, Chicago, IL 60601. **Business Addr:** Writer-in-Residence, Department of Theatre and Music, Columbia College, 600 S Michigan Ave, Chicago, IL 60605.

HARRISON, PEARL LEWIS
Association administrator (retired). **Personal:** Born Jun 8, 1932, East Orange, NJ; married John Arnold Harrison; children: Lauren Deborah, Adrianne Carol. **Educ:** Juilliard School of

Music NY, Certificate 1952. **Career:** Pearl Lewis Harrison Piano Studio, dir 1953-83; Governor's Task Force to est the Suburban Essex Arts Cncl, mem 1978; City of East Orange, coord arts/culture 1979-80; City of East Orange, acting dir public relations 1986; City of East Orange, Dept of Arts and Cultural Affairs, director, 1986-90. **Orgs:** Mem New Jersey Music Educ Cncl 1960-77, Suburban Essex Arts Cncl 1978-82, Friends of NJ Opera 1982-, Essex Co Arts & Culture Planning Bd 1983-86; bd of trustees United Way of Essex & Hudson Co 1985-86; mem Black Composers Inc 1985-; mem NJ Motion Picture Commission 1986-; East Orange Arts & Cultural Inc, exec dir, 1986-88; East Orange Library Bd, 1986-90. **Honors/Awds:** White House Citation from Mrs Nancy Reagan for music/comm spirit 1983; Pride & Heritage Women of the Year Awd Int Year of Environ Concerns 1983; Resolution for Cultural Expertise Essex Co Bd 1983; State of New Jersey for Excellence Awd NJ State Senate 1983; Certificate of Appreciation for Comm Serv City of East Orange 1983; Founder of Annual Black Heritage Pioneer Family Awards, City of East Orange, 1986; United Nations Citation, 1989.

HARRISON, ROBERT WALKER, III
Educator. **Personal:** Born Oct 13, 1941, Natchez, MS; son of Charlotte Harrison and Robert Harrison; married Gayle Johnson; children: Robert, Seth. **Educ:** Tougaloo SC Coll, BS 1961; Northwestern Univ, MD 1966. **Career:** Vanderbilt Univ Sch of Medicine, instructor 1972-74, asst prof 1974-81, assoc prof 1981-85; Univ of AR for Medical Sci, prof 1985-. **Orgs:** Endocrine Society, Alpha Phi Alpha. **Military Serv:** USN lt comm 1968-70. **Business Addr:** Professor of Medicine, Rochester School of Medicine and Dentistry, PO Box 693, 601 Elmwood Ave, Rochester, NY 14642.

HARRISON, RODNEY SCOTT
Professional football player. **Personal:** Born Dec 15, 1972, Markham, IL. **Educ:** Western Illinois. **Career:** San Diego Chargers, defensive back, 1994-. **Honors/Awds:** San Diego Chargers, Defensive Player of the Year, 1996. **Business Addr:** Professional Football Player, San Diego Chargers, Qualcomm Stadium, 9449 Friars Rd, San Diego, CA 92108, (619)280-2111.

HARRISON, RONALD E.
Beverage company executive. **Personal:** Born Jan 11, 1936, New York, NY; son of Olive DeVaux Harrison and Edmund Harrison; married; children: Richard, David, Katherine. **Educ:** City Coll NY, BBA 1958; Boston Coll, Corp Comm Relations Prog 1986-87. **Career:** Pepsi Cola Metro Bottling Co NY, vp, area mgr; Pepsi-Cola Inc, Cincinnati dir special mkts 1966, control div Chicago dir training 1969, mgmt inst Phoenix dir training 1970, franchise devel NY dir 1972; area vice pres Pepsi Bottling Co 1975-79; no div vice pres Pepsi-Cola Co owned plants New England, Pgh, Milwaukee, vice pres 1979-81; Pepsi-Cola Inc, natl sales dir 1981-86; PepsiCo, vice pres of community relations, currently. **Orgs:** Nat Assn Mktng Devel; Sales Exec Club NY; bd trst NY Orphan Asylum Soc; bd Educ Spl Sch Dist Greenburgh; president, Business Policy Review Council; board member, Westchester Coalition; board member, New York State Job Training Partnership Council; member, American Marketing Assn; member, Executive Leadership Council; member, National Hispanic Corporate Council; member, Westchester Clubmen. **Business Addr:** Dir, Community Relations, PepsiCo, Anderson Hill Rd, Purchase, NY 10577.

HARRISON, ROSCOE CONKLIN, JR.
Public affairs director. **Personal:** Born Sep 20, 1944, Belton, TX; son of Roscoe Conklin Harrison Sr and Georgia Dell Moore Harrison; married Sandra K Smitha, Aug 27, 1966; children: Corinne Michelle. **Educ:** Temple Junior Coll, AA, 1962-64; Prairie View A & M Univ, BA, 1964-66; Univ of Mary Hardin Baylor, 1966-67. **Career:** KTEM Radio, announcer, 1960-64; Temple Daily Telegram, reporter, 1966-67; San Antonio Express News, reporter, 1967-68; Jet Mag, assoc editor, 1968-69; KCEN-TV, news bureau chief/reporter, 1970-76; Texas Attorney General John Hill, deputy press secretary, 1976-79; KCEN-TV, public affairs dir, 1979-93; Scott and White Memorial Hosp, assoc dir for special projects, currently. **Orgs:** Natl Assn of Health Services Executives, 1994-; American Soc for Health Care Marketing and Public Relations, 1994-; Temple Rotary Club, 1994-; Temple Cultural Activities Ctr, bd mem, 1991-; West Belton-Harris High Ex-Students Ass, pres, 1990-; Ebony Cultural Society, advisor, 1995; Tem-Bel Heart Assn, bd mem, 1994-; Temple Chamber of Commerce, 1994-. **Honors/Awds:** Texas Farmers Union, Broadcaster of the Year, 1993; Bell County Communications Professionals, Communicator of the Year, 1988; Texas Assn of Broadcasters, Distinguished Local Programming, 1977; Jefferson Awards Media Award, Outstanding Public Service, 1990. **Home Addr:** 3806 Wendy Oaks Dr, Temple, TX 76502. **Business Phone:** (817)724-1929.

HARRISON, SHIRLEY DINDY
Consumer packaged goods company executive. **Personal:** Born Apr 11, 1951, Syracuse, NY; daughter of Eve Uchal Harrison and Homer Leonard Harrison; divorced. **Educ:** Syracuse University, Syracuse, NY, BFA, 1973. **Career:** Artifacts Systems Ltd, Manchester, NH, graphic artist, 1973-74; PEACE, Inc, Syracuse, NY, director, community development, 1974-77; Miller Brewing Company, Milwaukee, WI, director, employee relations & compl, 1977-92; Philip Morris Companies, Inc, director of diversity management and development, 1992-96, vice pres, diversity management and development, 1997-. **Honors/Awds:** 100 Top Business & Prof Black Women, Dollar & Sense Mag, 1988; Community Service Award, Miller Brewing Company, 1986; 100 Best & Brightest Black Women in Corp America, Ebony Mag, 1990; Black Achiever, YMCA. **Business Addr:** VP, Diversity Management & Development, Philip Morris Companies, Inc, 120 Park Ave, 19th Fl, New York, NY 10017.

HARRISON, WENDELL RICHARD
Musician. **Personal:** Born Oct 1, 1942, Detroit, MI; son of Ossalee Lockett and Walter R Harrison. **Educ:** Highland Park Junior College; Detroit Institute of Arts Conservatory of Music. **Career:** Rebirth Inc, artistic director, 1978-; Musician, self employed, over 35 years. **Orgs:** National Jazz Service Organization, 1991-93. **Honors/Awds:** Arts Foundation of Michigan, Creative Artist Grant, 1992-97; National Endowment for the Arts, Fellowship Grant, 1978, 1992; Congressman John Conyers, Proclamation, 1992; Wayne County, Distinguished Service Award, 1985; Jazz Masters Award, Arts Midwest, 1993; Barbara Rose Collins, Proclamation; Detroit City Council, Distinguished Artist Award. **Special Achievements:** Live In Concert, compact disc, 1992; Forever Duke, compact disc, 1991; Fly By Night, compact disc, 1990; Be Boppers Method Book, educational publication, 1991; Compact Disc Release: 1993, "Something For Pops" featuring the Harold McKinney & Wendell Harrision Duet, 1995, "Rush & Hustle" featuring Wendell Harrison & the Clarinet Ensemble & James Carter; Battle of the Tenors with Eddie Harris & Wendell Harrison, ENSA Records.

HARRISON-JONES, LOIS
Educational administrator. **Career:** Dallas Public Schools, superintendent, until 1991; Boston Public Schools, superintendent, 1991-. **Special Achievements:** First African American superintendent of Boston Schools, 1991. **Business Addr:** Superintendent, Boston Public Schools, 26 Court St, Boston, MA 02108, (617)726-6250.

HARRIS-PINKELTON, NORMA
Educator, educational administrator. **Personal:** Born Oct 15, 1927, Philadelphia, PA; daughter of Olivia Gilbert Harris and Robert Reynolds Harris. **Educ:** Lincoln Sch of Nursing NY, nursing dip reg nurs 1950; Univ of Cincinnati, BSN 1963, MSN 1965, EdD 1976. **Career:** Jewish Hosp, psych unit gen staff spec duty 1962-65; Prep Employment Prog for Spec Youth, couns 1965-67; Univ of Cincinnati Coll of Nursing & Health, assoc prof psych nursing 1967-70; Univ of Cincinnati Inst for Rsch & Higher Ed, psychology of interracial relationships group leader 1971-73; Univ of Cincinnati & Coll of Nursing & Hlth, asst prof 1973-74; Cincinnati Health Dept, asst health comm, prof serv div 1980-81; Hampton Univ School of Nursing prof nursing, graduate program, dir gerontological nursing pract proj, and prof psychiatric mental health nursing; retired, 1993; Pinkelton Consults, owner, currently. **Orgs:** Mem Natl League for Nurses, Amer Nurses Assoc, United Black Fac Assoc Univ of Cincinnati, Council for Exept Children, Black Nurses Assoc; pres bd dir Winton Hills Med & Health Ctr 1979-81, Black Child Devel Inst; bd mem Cincinnati Ctr for Devel Disability; mem Mental Health & Mental Retard Children's Svcs; mental health adv Cathcment Area 3; mem Women's City Club Cincinnati; ind gr & family coun independent pract, 1975-81, 1985, 1991-; dir min nursing recruit Univ of Cincinnati 1978-80; dir ger nursing pract prog Hampton Univ 1981-83; facilitator Inst Rsch & Higher Ed Black-White Rel 1970-73; lay reader Christ Ed comm, choir St Cyprian's Epis Church, former, St Andrews Episcopal Church, Cin, Ohio; health serv comm Alpha Kappa Alpha 1977-81; Peninsula Mental Health Association, president, 1992-94, current chair; board mem, AIDS Hospice Development Circle; board member, Episcopal Diocese, 1991-; UASAP board member, consultant to educ program, 1992-95; NCGNP, research committee, chr, 1993-95; ESH, LHRC, assistant chair; ESH research committee mem, LWV Voter Service, chair. **Honors/Awds:** NDEA Fellow Univ of Cincinnati 1970-73; Sigma Theta Tau Natl Nursing Hon Soc 1973-. **Special Achievements:** "Mental Health" Osborne Carter Pinkelton & Richards, 1976-80; "People of Color", 1983; "Devel of African Amer Cur Content in Psych Mental Health Nursing", 1982. **Business Phone:** (757)247-3615.

HARROLD, AUSTIN LEROY
City official, clergyman. **Personal:** Born Jan 28, 1942, Omaha; son of Madeline Brown Harrold and Walter W Harrold; married Gussie; children: Sabrina Butler, Austin Harrold, Jr, Sophia Harrold. **Educ:** Lane Coll TN, BA Sociology 1964; Interden Theological Ctr & Phillips School of Theological Atlanta, MDiv 1968. **Career:** Barr's Chapel CME Church Paris TN, first appointment; St Mary CME Church, prev pastor; W Mitchell CME Church Atlanta, prev asst pastor; Lane Chapel CME Church, prev pastor; Turner Chapel CME Church Mt Clemens, formerly pastor; Calvary CME Church Jersey City, pastor; Phillips Mem CME Church, pastor; Russell CME Church, pastor; Mayor of Jersey City, exec sec 1981-85; US Dept of Commerce Bureau of the Census, community awareness specialist 1986-88; Interdenominational Christian Comm Church, pastor and founder 1985-; City of Jersey City, NJ, director water dept, 1989-. **Orgs:** Prev candidate for Dem Nomination to the Kansas House of Reps from 45th Dist; 1st vice pres Jersey City Branch NAACP; sec Interdenom Ministerial All of Jersey City Br NAACP; sec Interdenom Ministerial All of Jersey City & Vicinity; chpln Topeka Jaycees; co-chmn Employment Task Force coord com of Black comm; sec Interdenominational Ministerial Alliance of Topeka Vic; substitute teacher Mt Clemens HS; active in the nations war on poverty; central manger NE Macomb Act Center; mem bd dirs Macomb Co Child Guidance Clinic; mem Mt Clemens Minis Assn; pres Macomb Co Chapter NAACP; pres Christ Clemens Elem School PTA; WM Excelsior Lodge; past first vice pres Macomb Co Comm Human Relations Assn; dean Detroit Dist CME Church Leadership Training School; mem bd of pension MI-IN Annual Conf Third Epopal Dist of CME Church; sec MI dele to Natl Black Conv 1972; mem MI Dept Educ Vocational Rehabilitation Serv Vocational Rehabilitation; coun Mt Clemens DistOffice; chmn Mt Clemens Chapter Youth for Understanding; cand Mt Clemens City Comm; appointed to Macomb Co Office of Substance Abuse Advisory Council; bd mem Operation PUSH, 1975-; exec director, Concerned Clergy Jersey City, 1980-. **Honors/Awds:** Certificate of Merit Third Episcopals Dist of Christ Methodist Episcopal Church for work in Civil Rights movement 1960-62; selected to spend summer 1963 in Sierra Leone W Africa in Operation Crossroads Africa Project 1963; Dept of Sociology Award Dept of Religion & Philosophy Award; Effective Christ Leadership 1960-64; Outstanding Young Men of Amer Bd of Edns 1970, 1976. **Business Addr:** Pastor, Interdenominational Christian Community Church, 2 Oxford Ave, Jersey City, NJ 07304.

HARROLD, LAWRENCE A.
Production management. **Personal:** Born Apr 4, 1952, Belle Glade, FL; married Phyllis Lea; children: Lawrence Jr, Lamont, James. **Educ:** Hillsborough Comm Coll, AA 1975; San Francisco State Univ, BA 1977, MBA 1979. **Career:** Pacific Telephone, mktg office supervisor 1980-81; Westvaco Corp, production supervisor. **Orgs:** Mem Black MBA. **Military Serv:** USAF sgt 4 yrs. **Home Addr:** 2079 Brighton Dr, Pittsburg, CA 94565. **Business Addr:** Production Supervisor, Westvaco Corporation, 5650 Hollis, Emeryville, CA 94608.

HARRY, JACKEE. See JACKEE.

HART, BARBARA MCCOLLUM
Educator. **Personal:** Born Oct 14, 1937, Pittsburgh, PA; married Charles E; children: Brian Charles. **Educ:** Cheyney St Coll, BA 1966; Univ of Pittsburgh, MPA 1969; Univ of Pittsburgh, PhD 1986. **Career:** PA State Univ, asst prof 1970; PA House of Representatives, admin asst 1975-76; Model Cities, wlfr planner 1970; Hill House Assn, neighborhood devel specialist 1968-70; Urban League of Pittsburgh, dir rsch & planning 1966-68; Allegheny Co OEO, planning consultant 1970-74; Penn State-McKeesport, dir learning center. **Orgs:** Bd mem PARC 1970; bd mem PACE 1973; mem Pres Adv Com on Black Student Life PA St 1975; pres Pgh Alumnae 1978-80; Delta Sigma Theta Inc. **Honors/Awds:** Jessie Smith Noyes Flwshp 1967; Dean's List 1964-66; pres Honor Soc 1965; 1st Scholar of Yr 1964-65; Outst Srv Awd; Alpha Phi Sigma 1966; Master's Thesis Relocation implications for families in Carnegie, PA 1969; Doctoral Dissertation, A Description & Analysis of PA's Efforts to Equalize Educational Oppty 1986. **Business Addr:** Dir, Penn State University, University Dr, Mc Keesport, PA 15132.

HART, BRENDA G.
Educator. **Personal:** Born Jul 8, 1949, Williamstown, MA; daughter of Adalyne Monroe Hart and Thomas A. Hart; children: Patrick, Katheryn. **Educ:** Boston Univ, BA 1970; Univ of Louisville, MEd 1972. **Career:** Community Action Comm, manpower coord 1973; Univ of Louisville Coop Educ Office, asst dir 1973-77; Univ of Louisville General Engrg, asst dir 1977-81, dir 1981-94, dir, minority and women in engineering programs, 1994-. **Orgs:** Bd dirs Planned Parenthood 1980-86, INCOME 1980-94, Family & Children's Agency 1980-86; bd dirs Univ of Louisville Sch of Educ 1983-86; bd directors ElderServ/Senior House 1986-90; bd of dirs, Alumni Assn Univ of Louisville, 1993-; bd of dirs, National Assn of Minority Engineering Program Administrators, 1991-. **Honors/Awds:** Articles published in Journal of Non-White Concerns 1980, Measurement and Evaluation in Guidance 1981, Engrg Educ 1981, Applied Engrg Educ 1986; Initiated into Golden Key National Honor Society, honorary mem, 1990; received Outstanding Faculty Advisor Award, 1991; Natl Council of Negro Women, Bethune Service Award, 1996; Univ of Louisville, Office of Minority Services, 1996; Speed Scientific School Alumni Assn, Alumni Scholar for Service, 1996. **Business Addr:** Prof of Engrg Educ, University of Louisville, Speed Scientific School, Louisville, KY 40292, (502)852-0440.

HART, CHRISTOPHER ALVIN
Federal official, attorney. **Personal:** Born Jun 18, 1947, Denver, CO; son of Margaret Murlee Shaw Hart and Judson D Hart; divorced; children: Adam Christopher. **Educ:** Princeton Universi-

ty, BSE, 1969, MSE 1971; Harvard Law School, JD, 1973. **Career:** Peabody Rivlin & Lambert, assoc 1973-76; Air Transport Assoc, attorney 1976-77; US Dept of Transportation, deputy asst genl counsel 1977-79; Hart & Chavers, managing partner 1979-90; National Transportation Safety Board, member, 1990-93; Natl Hwy Traffic Safety Admin, deputy admin, 1993-95; Federal Aviation Administration, asst admin for system safety, 1995-. **Orgs:** Natl, Amer, Federal, Washington Bar Assns, 1973-; Princeton Engineering Adv & Resource Council, 1975-; dir/pres, Beckman Place Condo Assn, 1979-83; Federal Communications Bar Assn, 1981-; dir, WPFW-FM, 1983-; Lawyer Pilots Bar Assn, 1975-; Aircraft Owners & Pilots Assn, 1973-. **Honors/Awds:** "Antitrust Aspects of Deepwater Ports," Transportation Law Journal 1979; "State Action Antitrust Immunity for Airport Operators," Transportation Law Journal 1981. **Home Addr:** 1612 Crittanden St NW, Washington, DC 20011. **Business Addr:** Assistant Administrator, Federal Aviation Administration, 800 Independence Ave, SW, Rm 1016D, Washington, DC 20591.

HART, EDWARD E.
Physician. **Personal:** Born May 8, 1927; married Joycelyn Reed; children: Edward, Janet, Reed, Cynthia, Jonathan. **Educ:** Univ Toledo, BS 1946; Meharry Med Sch, MD 1949; Am Coll of Surgeons, FACS Fellow 1960. **Career:** Pvt Practice. **Military Serv:** USAF 1954-56. **Business Addr:** 1301 Tremonsburg, Ithaca, NY 14850.

HART, EMILY
Educator. **Personal:** Born Oct 29, 1940, St Joseph, LA; divorced; children: Tammylynn, Lynnella. **Educ:** So Univ Baton Rouge LA, BS Spch & Hrng 1966; Univ CA Los Angeles, Post Grad Wrk; Pepperdine Univ LA CA, MS Sch Mgmt & Admin 1974. **Career:** Compton Unified School Dist, teacher 1978-80, consultant 1975-78, teacher & speech therapist 1969-75; NV Countys, speech therapist 1968-69; Orleans Parish New Orleans, teacher 1978. **Orgs:** Vp Compton Comm Coll 1978; Los Angeles Co Trustee Assn 1977; pres Compton Comm Coll bd of trustees 1980; adv dir Univ of So CA Acad for Educ Mgmt 1978-79; mem CA Dem Prty Affrmtv Actn 1979-80; dir CA St Long Bch Math Engrng & Sci Achvmnt Bd; Accrdtatn Tm mem W Hills Coll. **Honors/Awds:** 1st black woman elected tro trustee compton Comm Coll 1975; 1st black woman elected Los Angeles Co Trustee Assn 1977; Love & Dvtn For Chldrn Awd, ParentAdv Cncl Compton 1972; Woman of Year Awd, Nat Cncl of Negro Women 1973; Outstndng Comm Serv Awd NAACP 1975. **Business Addr:** Compton Comm Coll Bd of Truste, 1111 E Artesia St, Compton, CA 90221.

HART, HAROLD RUDOFF
Business executive. **Personal:** Born May 6, 1926, Washington, DC. **Educ:** Cath Univ Washington DC; Univ Madrid Spain. **Career:** Martha Jackson W Gallery NY, vice pres dir. **Business Addr:** 1345 Shepherd St, Washington, DC 20017-2633.

HART, JACQUELINE D.
Educator/adminstrtor. **Personal:** Born in Gainesville, FL; daughter of Mrs Edna M Hart. **Educ:** Lane College, Jackson, TN, BS 1959; IN Univ, Bloomington, IN, 1965; Univ of FL Gainesville, FL, MEd 1970, EdS 1972, PhD 1985. **Career:** Alachua Public Schools, instructor 1967-70; Santa Fe Coll, instructor 1972-74; Univ of FL, dir/equal opp prog 1974-88; University of Florida, Gainesville, Florida, assistant vice president, 1988-. **Orgs:** Amer Assn of Affirmative Action, nominating committee; Delta Pi Epsilon; Kappa Delta Pi; League of Women Voters, former bd secty; City Commission on the Status of Women, legislative committee 1983-83; Delta Sigma Theta, Inc, former pres/life mem; Amer Cancer Soc Bd, 1984-; United Way of Alachua Cty, 1985-; Allocation Reviewer Committee; Institute of Black Culture Advisory Board, 1988; bd mem, United Nations Assn, Florida Division,1989. **Honors/Awds:** Leadership Gainesville VIII-City of Gainesville 1983; Leadership Achievement Awd Alpha Phi Alpha 1981; Administrative Leadership Awd City of Gainesville 1986; Distinguished Alumni Award, Natl Assn for Equal Opportunity in Higher Educ, 1989; Societas Docta, Inc 1988. **Home Addr:** 1236 SE 13th St, Gainesville, FL 32601. **Business Addr:** Assistant Vice President, University of Florida, Affirmative Action Office, 352 Tigert Hall, Gainesville, FL 32611.

HART, MILDRED
Librarian. **Personal:** Born Apr 24, Wadley, AL; daughter of Ella Mae Underwood Slaughter and Owen Slaughter; married Robert Lewis Hart, Aug 28; children: Monica Lynne. **Educ:** Cuyahoga Comm Coll; Notre Dame Coll, S. Euclid, OH; Ursline Coll, OH. **Career:** East Cleveland Public Library, East Cleveland, OH, branch manager, currently. **Orgs:** Board of the YWCA, North Central, East Cleveland, Ohio; board of the Cooperative Extension, Ohio State University; board of Cuyahoga Community College, Metro Alumni; 4-H Club advisor, Cooperative Extension, Ohio State University; St Marks Presbyterian Church; Educ Cuyahoga Comm Coll, Notre Dame Coll, Ursline Coll; East Cleveland Kiwanis Club; Berea Children's Home & Family Service; Northeast Ohio Neighborhood Health Services Inc; ST. Mark's Deacons Bd, moderator. **Home Phone:** (216)851-1067. **Business Addr:** Branch Manager, East Cleveland Public Library-North Branch, 1425 Hayden Ave, East Cleveland, OH 44112, (216)268-6284.

HART, NOEL A.
Fire marshal (retired). **Personal:** Born Dec 14, 1927, Jamaica, NY; son of Louise Mason Hart and Noel A Hart; married Patricia Spence Cuffee; children: Noel Jr, Alison, Ira, Jonathan. **Educ:** NYU, BA, 1954; Mt St Mary's, MBA, 1992; Emergency Management Institute, Emmitsburg, MD, education specialist, computers, administration, attended. **Career:** Exec Devel Program Natl Fire Acad, Emmitsburg MD, training instructor; Peoria Fire Dept, fire marshal 1977; NY City Fire Dept 1954-77; John Jay Coll, team leader, lecturer; Promotional & Career Training Program, prof; FEMA US Fire Admin, fire prevention specialist; Emergency Management Institute, Emmitsburg, MD, education specialist/group leader, 1987-. **Orgs:** Past pres Comus Scl Clb; mem trustee Port Chester Pub Library; bd dir Port Chester Carver Ctr; warden vestryman St Peters Episcopal Ch, Prince of Peace Episcopal Church; Diocese Cncl Episcopal Diocese Central PA; member, National Forum Black Public Administrators, 1988-; member, Chief Officers Resource Committee, 1986-; member, International Association of Black Professional Fire Fighters, 1969-. **Military Serv:** AUS pfc 1945-47.

HART, PHYLLIS D.
State official. **Personal:** Born Aug 8, 1942, Detroit, MI; daughter of Louise Boykin Ransom and James Davidson; married Raymond Hart (died 1987); children: Darlene Annette. **Career:** Ohio Dept of Natural Resources, EEO/contract compliance administrator, currently. **Orgs:** Member, Democratic National Committee. **Home Addr:** 1091 Ellsworth Ave., Columbus, OH 43206.

HART, RONALD O.
Elected official, educational administrator. **Personal:** Born Jun 9, 1942, Suffolk, VA; married Ethel D; children: Aprill Jenelle, Ryan O. **Educ:** NCA&T State Univ, BS Biol 1964; Hampton Inst, MS Biol 1968; Old Dominion Univ, Certification in Admin 1976. **Career:** John F Kennedy HS, 1964-76; Metropolitan Church Fed C Union, 1966-; Ruffner Jr HS, 1976-; Suffolk City Council, vice-mayor, Cypress rep. **Orgs:** Mem Omega Psi Phi Frat 1962-; mem & adv Stratford Terrace Civic League 1975-; mem Norfolk, VA, Natl Educ Assns 1976-; mem Odd Fellows Lodge 1978-; adv Cypress Comm League 1978-; member Metropolitan Baptist Church. **Honors/Awds:** Outstanding Educator Elks Lodge Suffolk VA 1975; Man of the Year Omega Psi Phi Frat Suffolk 1979. **Business Addr:** Vice Mayor Cypress Rep, Suffolk City Council, 129 County St, Suffolk, VA 23434.

HART, TONY
Correction counselor. **Personal:** Born Jul 27, 1954, Harlem, NY; married Judy Murphy; children: Tonya. **Educ:** SUNY, graduated (cum laude) 1978; SUNY New Paltz, M Humanistic Educ 1987. **Career:** Highland Educational Occupational Ctr for Juvenile Offenders, Orange County Jail, Marist Coll HEOP Program, counselor; Green Haven Correctional Facility, correction counselor; Marist Coll Humanities Dept, part-time coll instructor; Downstate Correctional Facility, Fishkill, NY, counselor, 1989-. **Orgs:** New York State Coalition for Criminal Justice; bd mem Coalition for Peoples Rights; Natl Rainbow Coalition; Newburgh Black History Comm. **Honors/Awds:** Special Academic Awd SUNY 1977; Outstanding Service Awd PreRelease Ctr Green Haven Correctional Facility 1986; Martin Luther King Jr Awd Newburgh Memorial Comm 1987; Black Humanitarian Awd Newburgh Free Academy 1987; Most Deserving Black Award, Newburgh Black History Comm, 1989.

HARTAWAY, THOMAS N., JR.
Church administrator. **Personal:** Born Mar 28, 1943, Lonoke County; married Arnice Slocum; children: Katina, Carla, Keith, Thomas III, Britt. **Educ:** Henderson St Tchrs Coll AR; Harding Coll, 1972-73; Inst of Pol Gov Batesville Coll, 1971-72. **Career:** Dixie Ch of Christ, pastor; Ch of Christ, st dir of chrstn edn; Carter Mondale Camp, st dep cam coord 1976; Hartaway Assoc Adv & Pub Rel, pres 1974-76; OKY Radio, gen sales mgr 1972-74; Ch of Christ, minister 1968-71; The AR Carrier Nwspr, publ 1975-76; The Black Cnsmr Dir, publ 1976-77. **Orgs:** Bd mem No Little Rock Dwntwn Dev Com; adv bd mem NLR Comm Dev Agy; bd mem Cntrl AR Chrstn Coll; bd mem consult HOPE Inc No Little Rock AR. **Honors/Awds:** Outst Yng Men of Am Awd 1976; best serv awd Pulaski Co Shrf Dept; outst ldrshp awd Conf of CME Chs. **Business Addr:** Director, Dixie Church of Christ, 916 H St, North Little Rock, AR 72114.

HARTH, RAYMOND EARL
Attorney. **Personal:** Born Feb 4, 1929, Chicago, IL; son of Helen M Harth and Daniel W Harth; married Fran Byrd; children: Cheryl, Raymond Jr, Douglass. **Educ:** Univ of Chicago Law Sch, JD 1952. **Career:** Attorney, self-employed. **Orgs:** Pres IL Conf of Brs NAACP 1962-65; chmn 1960-62, 66-69, hndled Num Civil Rghts Cases in State & Fed Cts 1960-72. **Military Serv:** ANG 1st lt 1948-64.

HARTMAN, HERMENE DEMARIS
Educator, publisher, writer. **Personal:** Born Sep 24, 1948, Chicago, IL; daughter of Mildred F Bowden Hartman and Herman D Hartman; married David M Wallace (divorced). **Educ:** Roosevelt Univ, BA 1970, MPh 1974, MA 1974; Univ of IL, MBA, 1994. **Career:** WBBM-TV-CBS, prof & asst mgr comm affairs 1974-75; Soul publ, columnist 1978-; The Hartman Group, pres 1978-80; City Coll of Chicago, prof 1980-83, dir of develop & comm 1983-88; vice chancellor of External Affairs 1988-89; Hartman Publishing, Chicago, IL, N'DIGO, publisher, editor, 1989-. **Orgs:** Mem Amer Acad of Poets 1979; adv comm on the Arts John F Kennedy Ctr 1979; adv bd Univ of IL Sch of Art & Design 1979; exhibit com Chicago Public Library Cultural Ctr 1979; exec com natl adv coun the John F Kennedy Ctr Wash DC 1980; producer of "Conversations with the Chancellor" Channel 20 Chicago; edited and compiled "A Lasting Impression, A Collection of Photographs of Dr Martin Luther King Jr". **Honors/Awds:** Chicago Emmy nomination for "Conversations with the Chancellor" TV show; Pioneer's Awd Natl Assn of Media Women Chicago Chap 1975; article pub, TV in Amer Culture, Crisis Mag 1978; "Great Beautiful Black Women" Johnson Products Co 1978; CEBA Awd PR Communications to Black Audiences 1979; The Quest of the Black Woman in the 80's US Black & The News 1980; Media Awds, Chicago Emmy Awd 1984-86; "Up and Coming Black Business & Professional Women" 1985; Silver Quill Awd 1985; Communicator of the Year 1986; Gold Quill Awd 1986; Paragon Awds 1986; Merit Awd 1986; Grand Gold Medals 1986; Communications Excellence to Black Audiences 1986; 2 Silver Awds 1985 & 1987; Gold Awd 1987. **Business Addr:** Publisher/Editor, N'DIGO, 401 N Wabash, Ste 534, Chicago, IL 60611.

HART-NIBBRIG, HAROLD C.
Attorney. **Personal:** Born Aug 16, 1938, Los Angeles, CA; married Deanna T McKenzie; children: Nand, Jaunice, Lauren. **Educ:** Political Sci, BA 1961, JD Law 1971. **Career:** Manning & Hart-Nibbrig, atty. **Orgs:** Vice pres LA Black Congress 1968; Western Ctr on Law & Pov 1968-71; Com Educ Devel & Referral Serv 1969-; Black Law Ctr Inc 1971-73; bd of dirs Amer Civil Liberties Union 1973-79; chmn bd Viewer Spon TV Found KVST-TV 1973-74; mem LA Co Bar Assn, LA Co Bar Assn Judiciary Comm; mem John M Langston Law Club. **Honors/Awds:** Order of Golden Bruin UCLA 1960; Martin Luther King Fellow Woodrow Wilson Fellow Found 1968; Serv Awd CA Jobs Agents Assn 1974; SCLC West Law & Justice Awd 1979; Image Awd NAACP 1980. **Military Serv:** AUS pfc 1961-64. **Business Addr:** Attorney, Manning & Hart Nibbrig, 4929 Wilshire Blvd, Ste 1020, Los Angeles, CA 90010.

HARTSFIELD, ARNETT L., JR.
Educator, attorney. **Personal:** Born Jun 14, 1918, Bellingham, WA; married Kathleen Bush; children: Maria Riddle, Paula Ellis, Charlean, Arnett, Barbara. **Educ:** Univ of So CA, BA Econ 1951; USC, LLB 1955. **Career:** CA State Univ Long Beach, assoc prof 1974, asst prof 1972-74; United Way, asst dir 1970-71; Comm Mediation Center, chief mediator 1967-69; Los Angeles Neighbrhood Legal Servs, exec dir 1965-67; CA Fair Employment, assoc counselor 1964-65; Private Practice, 1955-64; City of Los Angeles, fireman 1940-61. **Orgs:** Bd trustees S Bay Univ Coll of Law; pres Los Angeles City Cvl Serv Commn 1973-76; vice pres 1974-75. **Honors/Awds:** Man of Yr Comm Rltns Conf of So CA 1962; mem Cvl Serv Commn 1973, pres 1973-74, 75-76, vice pres 1974-75. **Military Serv:** 1st lt 369th infantry 1943-46. **Business Addr:** 7 & Bellflower, Long Beach, CA 90815.

HARTY, BELFORD DONALD, JR.
Restaurant franchisee. **Personal:** Born Nov 3, 1928, New York, NY; married Nell. **Educ:** Lincoln U, BA; Real Estate Inst; Post Coll. **Career:** Real Estate, sales, purch, syndication; Burger King Franchisee; Hotel Owner. **Orgs:** Gtr Harlem Real Estate Bd; mem 100 Black Men; Nat Assn of Real Estate Brkrs; PAC Com; state coord Realtists in NY. **Honors/Awds:** Several plaques Assn of RE Brkrs. **Military Serv:** AUS corpl 1952-54. **Business Addr:** 2370 Adam C Powell Award, New York, NY 10030.

HARTZOG, ERNEST E.
Educational administrator. **Personal:** Born Jan 8, 1928, York, PA; married Jeanne Leatrice Shorty; children: Daniel, Sharon. **Educ:** San Diego St U, BA 1955; San Diego St U, MA 1962; NY U, MA 1964; US Intl U, PhD 1969. **Career:** Portland Public Schools, asst supt comm relations staff devel 1972; Govt Studies System Philadelphia, program mgr 1970-72; Philadelphia Public Schools, rockefeller intern; Detroit Public Schools, 1969-70; Lincoln High School San Diego, prin 1967-69; San Diego High School, vice prin 1966-67; San Diego Public Schools, dir Neighborhood Youth Corps; San Diego Urban League, 1964-66; San Diego Public Schools, counselor 1961-63, teacher 1956-61. **Orgs:** Pres Nat Alliance of Black Sch Edctrs; mem Am Assn of Sch Admnstrs; mem Cnfdn of OR Sch Admnstrs; Alliance of Black Sch Edctr; OR Sch Actvts Assn; OR St Chmn; United Negro Coll Fund; screening com Martin Luther King Schlrshp Fund; mem NAACP; mem African Meth Epis Ch. **Honors/Awds:** Blue Key Nat Honor Soc. **Military Serv:** AUYS sgt 1946-49 1950-51. **Business Addr:** 501 N Dixon St, Portland, OR 97227.

HARVARD, BEVERLY BAILEY
Police chief. **Personal:** Born Dec 22, 1950, Macon, GA; married Jimmy Harvard; children: Christa. **Educ:** Morris Brown Coll, BA 1972; GA State Univ, MS 1980. **Career:** Atlanta Police Dept, police officer 1972-79; Atlanta Dept of Public Safety, affirmative action spec, 1979-80, dir of public info 1980-82; Atlanta Police Dept, dep chief of police 1982-94; police chief, 1994-. **Orgs:** Mem Leadership Altanta, bd of trustees; scy, Commission on Accreditation for Law Enforcement Ageencies; Police Executive Research Forums; Governor's Task Force on Police Stress, Natl Org of Black Law Enforcement Exec; mem exec committee, Intl Assoc of Chiefs of Police; Delta Sigma Theta Sor Inc 1979-; bd of dirs Georgia State Univ Alumni Assoc. **Honors/Awds:** Outstanding Atlantan 1983; Graduate Fed Bureau of Investigations Natl Acad 1983; Alumni of the Year Morris Brown Coll 1985; Woman of the Year, 1995; Graduate FBI National Executive Institute; 100 Most Influential Georgians; YWCA Woman of Year; SCLC Drum Major for Justice Award; Trumpet Award, 1998. **Business Addr:** Chief of Police, Atlanta Police Department, 675 Ponce de Leon Ave, Atlanta, GA 30388.

HARVELL, VALERIA GOMEZ
Librarian. **Personal:** Born Jun 27, 1958, Richmond, VA. **Educ:** VA State Coll, BS 1978; Pittsburgh Theol Seminary, MDiv 1983; Univ of Pittsburgh, MLS 1983. **Career:** Burr Oaks Regional Library System, chief librarian 1984-85; Newark Public Library, branch mgr 1985-86; Penn State Univ, head librarian 1986-. **Orgs:** Mem Amer Library Assoc, Amer Theol Library Assoc, PA Library Assoc, Black Librarian Caucus, Black Librarians Caucus. **Home Addr:** 900 E Pittsburgh St, Greensburg, PA 15601. **Business Addr:** Head Librarian, Penn State Univ/Fayette Campus, PO Box 519, Uniontown, PA 15401.

HARVEY, ANTONIO
Professional basketball player. **Personal:** Born Jul 9, 1970, Pascagoula, MS. **Educ:** Southern Ilinois Univ; Connors State Univ; Georgia Univ; Pfeiffer Univ. **Career:** CBA: Atlanta Eagles, 1993; NBA: Los Angeles Lakers, 1993-. **Business Addr:** Professional Basketball Player, Los Angeles Clippers, 3939 S. Figueroa St., Los Angeles, CA 90037, (213)748-8000.

HARVEY, CLARIE COLLINS
Company executive. **Personal:** Born Nov 27, 1916, Meridian, MS; daughter of Mary Rayford Collins and Malachi C Collins; married Martin L Harvey, Aug 1, 1943 (deceased). **Educ:** Spelman College, Atlanta GA, BA, 1937; Indiana College of Mortuary Science, Indianapolis IN, 1942; Columbia University, New York NY, MA, 1951; School of Metaphysics, Jackson MS, 1983-84. **Career:** Freelance bookkeeper, Jackson MS, 1937-39; Collins Funeral Home and Insurance Companies, Jackson MS, general mgr, 1940-70, president, 1970-; Unity Life Ins Co, chairman of board and chief executive officer, 1980-. **Orgs:** National Council of Negro Women; NAACP; Links Inc. **Honors/Awds:** First Woman of the Year, National Funeral Directors Association, 1955; outstanding alumni award, Spelman College, 1966; named outstanding citizen of City of Jackson MS, 1971; Top Hat Award, New Pittsburgh Courier, 1974; Clarie Collins Harvey Day in Mississippi declared by Governor William Waller, December 30, 1974; Churchwoman of the Year Award, Religious Heritage of America, Inc, 1974; International Upper Room Citation, 1976; named outstanding small business woman, central region, National Council of Small Business Management Development, 1976. **Business Addr:** President, Collins Funeral Home, Inc, 415 North Farish St, Jackson, MS 39202.

HARVEY, GERALD
Elected official. **Personal:** Born Feb 21, 1950, Macon, GA; married Cotilda Qanterman; children: Marcia, Gerald. **Educ:** Tuskegee Inst, BS Pol Sci 1972; GA Coll, MEd Behavior Disorder 1977. **Career:** GA Psycho-Educ Center, therapist 1973-85; City of Macon, councilman 1979-85. **Home Addr:** 1255 S Clarotina Rd, Apopka, FL 32703-7062.

HARVEY, HAROLD A.
Physician, educator. **Personal:** Born Oct 24, 1944; married Mary; children: 3. **Educ:** Univ W Indies, MB, BS 1969. **Career:** PA State Univ, assoc prof med; PA State Univ Milton S Hershey Med Ctr, assoc prof med, med oncologist, cancer research 1974-. **Orgs:** Amer Federation Clinical Research; Amer Soc of Clinical Oncology; Amer Assn for Cancer Research. **Honors/Awds:** Tufts New England Medical Center Hospital, resident fellow, 1970-74. **Business Addr:** Physician, Medical-Oncology Div, Pennsylvania State University College of Medicine, PO Box 850, Hershey, PA 17033.

HARVEY, JACQUELINE V.
Health educator. **Personal:** Born Jan 21, 1933, Gramercy, LA; daughter of Selena Robinson Pittman and Alexander B Pittman; married Herbert J Harvey; children: Cassondra Dominique, Gretchen Young, Herbert, Yolonda. **Educ:** Natl Voc Coll, Vocational Counseling 1951-53; So Univ New Orleans, Soc Mktg Cert 1968-69; Xavier Univ, Spec Training 1969-70; Loyola Univ, Adv Studies 1978; Southern Univ of New Orleans, New Orleans, LA; LA State Univ, Baton Rouge, LA, 1986-88, CPM candidate. **Career:** LA Family Planning Prog, New Orleans, dir comm services, family health counselor supr comm activity workers 1974-, sect supr family hlth cnslr 1970-74; Family Health Inc, team supr aux hlth wrkr 1968-69; LA Family Planning Prog New Orleans, aux hlth wrkr I 1967-68; Center for Health Training, state training mgr, 1982-; Louisiana Office of Public Health, Family Plng Prog, dir of community services, currently. **Orgs:** Consult Volunteer Mgmt 1967-; consult Outreach in Family Plng 1967-; pres Easton Community Schools Adv Council; mem Amer Public Health Assoc, NAACP; pres Minority Women for Progress; adv bd mem, Orleans Parish, Community School Program, 1970-; past chair, ad-hoc, ed comm, LA Public Health Assn, 1984-91; mem, Natl Family Planning & Reproductive Health Assn, 1989-. **Honors/Awds:** Recip Merit Award Family Health Found 1971; Comm Involvement Plaque Proj Enable 1967; Community Serv LA Black Women for Progress 1976; Outstanding Achievement Women in History NO LA 1976; Serv Awd Noteworthy Commun Leaders LA 1981; Merit Awd NO Human Relation 1982; Outstanding Service Award, Natl Assn of Neighborhoods, 1987; Service Award, Super Parent Support Network, 1989-90; Community Service Award, North of Neighborhood Devt, 1989-90. **Business Addr:** Dir of Community Services/State Training Manager, Louisiana Office of Public Health, Family Planning Program, 325 Loyola Ave, State Office Bldg, Room 610, New Orleans, LA 70112.

HARVEY, KENNETH RAY
Professional football player. **Personal:** Born May 6, 1965, Austin, TX; married Janice; children: Anthony, Marcus, Nathaniel (deceased). **Educ:** Laney College; Univ of California at Berkeley. **Career:** Phoenix Cardinals, linebacker, 1988-93; Washington Redskins, 1994-. **Honors/Awds:** Pro Bowl, 1994, 1995, 1996, 1997. **Business Phone:** (703)471-9100.

HARVEY, LINDA JOY
Radio broadcasting company executive. **Personal:** Born Jun 11, 1957, Detroit, MI; daughter of Royetta Lavern Phillips and Charles Edward Harvey; divorced; children: Rodgerick Keith Philson, Autumn Joy Philson. **Educ:** Spec's Howard School of Broadcasting Arts. **Career:** Booth Broadcasting Inc, promotions assistant, 1989-91; Mich Con Gas Co., boiler operator, 1975-; Fritz Broadcasting Inc, Mix 92.3 WMXD-FM, promotions director, on-air staff member, 1991-. **Orgs:** NAACP, lifetime member. **Business Addr:** Director, Promotions, Fritz Broadcasting, Inc, 15600 W 12 Mile Rd, Southfield, MI 48076, (313)569-8000.

HARVEY, LOUIS-CHARLES
Educator, theologian. **Personal:** Born May 5, 1945, Memphis, TN; son of Mary Jones Harvey and Willie Miles Harvey; children: Marcus Louis, Melanee Charles. **Educ:** LeMoyne-Owen Coll, BS 1967; Colgate Rochester Divinity School, MDiv 1971; Union Theological Seminary, MPhil 1977, PhD 1978. **Career:** Colgate Rochester-Divinity School, prof, 1974-78; Payne Theological Seminary, dean, 1978-79, pres, 1989-; United Theological Seminary, prof 1979-; Metropolitan AME Church, senior minister, 1996-. **Orgs:** Speaker, preacher, writer, workshop leader African Methodist Episcopal Church 1979-. **Honors/Awds:** Articles published Journal of Religious Thought 1983, 1987; Rsch grant Assn of Theological Schools 1984-85; pioneered study of Black Religion in Great Britain, 1985-86; biographer of William Crogman in Something More Than Human Cole, 1987. **Business Addr:** Senior Minister, Metropolitan AME Church, 1518 M St NW, Washington, DC 20005.

HARVEY, MAURICE REGINALD
Company executive. **Personal:** Born Sep 26, 1957, Atlanta, GA; son of Cardia B Harvey and Charle E Harvey; married Kimberly Kay, Mar 15, 1987. **Educ:** Georgia State; DeKalb; Atlanta Area Tech. **Career:** American Presedent Co, MIS director; Mentis, system programmer; Thacker, data processing manager; H J Russell & Co, computer programmer; Concept Technologies, president, currently. **Orgs:** Common Black Data Processor Assn. **Special Achievements:** Develop customs documentation system for international freight. **Business Phone:** (404)847-0999.

HARVEY, NORMA BAKER
Educator, business counselor. **Personal:** Born Nov 23, 1943, Martinsville, VA; daughter of Nannie Hobson Baker and John T Baker (deceased); married Dr William R Harvey; children: Kelly R, Christopher, Leslie D. **Educ:** VA State Univ, BS Elem Educ 1961-65; Fisk Univ, MA Educ Media 1976. **Career:** VA and AL, elem sch teacher 1965-68; State of MA Planning Office, admin asst 1968-70; Tuskegee Inst, rsch asst 1974-78; Hampton Univ, business counselor 1982-; Kelech Real Estate Corp, pres 1981-; Pepsi Bottling Company of Houghton Inc, secretary/treasurer 1985-. **Orgs:** Bd of dirs Amer Heart Assn 1981-83; panelist VA Comm for the Arts 1983-84; bd of dirs VA Symphony 1983-86; bd dirs United Way 1978-80; bd mem, Peninsula Council for the Arts 1978-80; mem, Planning & Research Committee for the United Way 1978-82; trustee, United Way 1985-87; board of trustees, Peninsula Fine Arts Center, 1990-; board of trustees, The Virginia Symphony, 1987-91; board of trustees, Virginia Museum of Natural History, 1990-91; board of trustees, The College of William & Mary, 1991-95; Peninsula Chapter of the Natl Conference of Christians & Jews, bd of trustees; Harbor Bank - Newport News, charter mem. **Honors/Awds:** Intl Progs at Tuskegee Behavioral Sci Rsch Tuskegee Inst 1976; Virginia Peninsula Chamber of Commerce Award for Minority Advocate Business Award, 1991; VA Peninsula Chamber of Commerce, Minority Bus Advocate Award, 1991; State of Virginia, Minority Advocates Business Award, 1992; State of VA, Minority Bus Advocate Award, 1992; VA Council on the Status of Women's Corp Achievement Award, 1993. **Business Addr:** Business Counselor, Hampton University, 55 E Tyler St, Hampton, VA 23668.

HARVEY, RAYMOND
Music director. **Personal:** Born Dec 9, 1950, New York, NY; son of Doris Walwin Harvey and Lee Harvey. **Educ:** Oberlin Coll, Oberlin, OH B Mus 1973, M Mus 1973; Yale Univ, New Haven CT, MMA 1978, DMA 1984. **Career:** Indianapolis Symphony, Exxon/arts endowment conductor 1980-83; Buffalo Philharmonic, assoc conductor 1983-86; Springfield Symphony Orchestra, music dir 1986-94; Fresno Philharmonic, music dir, 1993-. **Honors/Awds:** Engagements have incl, Detroit Symphony, New York Philharmonic, Buffalo Philharmonic, Indianapolis Symphony, Houston Symphony, Louisville Orchestra, Minnesota Orchestra, Atlanta Symphony, San Diego Symphony, St Louis Symphony, Utah Symphony; has conducted opera in US Canada and Italy. **Business Addr:** Music Director, Fresno Philharmonic Orchestra, 2610 W Shaw Ave, Fresno, CA 93711.

HARVEY, RICHARD CLEMONT, JR.
Professional football player. **Personal:** Born Sep 11, 1966, Pascagoula, MS; married Regina; children: Richard Jr, Tiffany. **Educ:** Tulane. **Career:** New England Patriots, linebacker, 1990-91; Buffalo Bills, 1992-93; Denver Broncos, 1994; New Orleans Saints, 1995-. **Business Addr:** Professional Football Player, New Orleans Saints, 5800 Airline Hwy, Metairie, LA 70003, (504)733-0255.

HARVEY, RICHARD R.
Savings and loans executive. **Career:** Tuskegee Federal Savings & Loan Assn, Tuskegee, AL, managing officer. **Business Addr:** Tuskegee Federal Savings and Loan Association, 301 North Elm St, Tuskegee, AL 36083.

HARVEY, STEVE
Comedian, actor. **Personal:** Born in West Virginia; divorced; children: twin daughters. **Career:** Stand up comedian; ABC-TV, "Me and the Boys," actor, currently. **Business Addr:** Actor, Me and the Boys, c/o ABC-TV, 77 W 66th St, New York, NY 10023, (212)456-1000.

HARVEY, WARDELLE G.
Clergyman. **Personal:** Born Jun 12, 1926, Booneville, IN; married Christine P Harvey; children: Marian Jeanette, Wardell, Monica Perirr, Dione. **Educ:** Tri-State Bapt Coll, 1957; Evansville Coll, 1958; Inter-Bapt Theol Sem, 1962, BTh, DD 1963, DCL 1970; Union Theological Seminary, DD, 1992. **Career:** Paducah Public Housing, commiss 1966-67; City of Paducah, city commiss 1968-75, mayor pro-tem 1970-72; Greater Harrison St Bapt Church Paducah, pastor; Cosmopolitan Mortuary, founder, owner; WG Harvey Manor, owner. **Orgs:** Mem Mayors Adv Bd 1964-66; vice pres KY Bapts Assoc 1964-66; past pres Bapt Ministers Alliance of Paducah Area 1965-67; auditor 1st Dist Assoc 1965; mem State Voca Ed Bd Chmn Comm Chest 1965; pres founder Non-Partisan League; mem Inter-Denominational Ministers Alliance, NAACP, Christ Ldrshp Conf KY Col, Duke of Paducah; RISE Committee, appointed chariman, 1995; NAACP Award, life member. **Honors/Awds:** Civic Beautification Awd; Optimist Club Blue Ribbon Awd; Voca Indust Ed Awd; Beta Omega Omega Chap of Alpha Kappa Alpha Pol Know-How; Outstanding Afro-American Man, 1995; NAACP Award, 1990. **Business Addr:** WG Harvey Manor, 1429 Reed Ave, Paducah, KY 42001.

HARVEY, WILLIAM JAMES, III
Cleric. **Personal:** Born Jun 18, 1912, Oklahoma City, OK; son of L Mae Johnston Harvey and Dr William J Harvey, Jr; married Betty JenkinsJean Nelson, Dec 25, 1983; children: William J, IV, Janice Faith, Edward, Jr. **Educ:** Fisk Univ, Nashville, TN, BA, 1935; Chicago Theological Seminary, M.Div, 1938. **Career:** Phila, pastor 1939-50; Okla City, pastor 1950-53; Pitts, pastor 1954-66; VA Union Univ, guest preacher 1946-48; Fisk Univ, guest preacher 1949; Cheyney State Teachers Coll, guest preacher 1949; Hampton Univ, guest preacher 1950; Prairie View State Coll, guest preacher 1951-52; OK State Univ, guest preacher 1953; Church History School Langston OK, prof of homiletics religion 1951-53; Pinn Memorial Baptist Church, Philadelphia, PA, pastor, 1939-50; Calvary Baptist Church, Oklahoma City, OK, pastor, 1950-54; Macedonia Baptist Church, Pittsburgh, PA, pastor, 1954-66. **Orgs:** Mem exec bd foreign mission bd Natl Baptist Convention 1949-50, exec sec 1961-; auditor PA Baptist Convention 1945-50; vice pres Philadelphia Baptist Ministers Conf 1950; pres Oklahoma City Ministers Alliance 1953; del const Convening Convention Natl Council Churches 1951; Natl Baptist Conv to World Baptist Alliance London England 1955; vice pres Pitts Baptist Ministers

Conf 1961; treasurer Allegheny Union Baptist Assn 1961-62; Ministers Conf 1961; preinvest editor World Bapt Alliance Rio de Janeiro Brazil 1959; mem Alpha Phi Alpha; Sigma Pi Phi; assoc editor Mission Herald 1950-54; bd of dir, Natl Baptist Convention USA, INC, 1961-; bd of dir, Bread for World, 1986-; bd of dir, Africa News, 1987-; bd of dir, Philadelphia Urban League, life mem, NAACP. **Honors/Awds:** Mason author of Baptist Fundamentals in an Emerging Age of Freedom 1958; various articles; Missionary Worker's Manual, 1963; Mission Educ for Tomorrow's Leaders, 1965; Sacrifice and Dedication, 1980; Editor-Mission Herald, 1961-; Bridges of Faith, 1989. **Business Addr:** Exec Sec St, Foreign Mission Bd, Natl Baptist Convention USA, Inc, 701 S 19th St, Philadelphia, PA 19146.

HARVEY, WILLIAM M.
Psychologist. **Personal:** Born Jan 25, 1933, Jackson, MS; son of Sarah McNeamer and William Harvey. **Educ:** Tougaloo Coll, BA 1954; Washington Univ, PhD 1966. **Career:** St Louis State Hosp, chief psychologist 1967-69; Washington Univ, lecturer in psychology 1966-72, adjunct prof; MS Enterprise Newspaper, editor; Narcotics Serv Council Inc, exec dir, currently. **Orgs:** Mem Natl Adv Council Natl Inst on Drug Abuse 1977-83; vice pres Natl Mental Health Assoc 1978-85. **Honors/Awds:** Fellow Menniger Foundation; US Public Health Rsch Fellow Washington Univ. **Business Addr:** Executive Director, Narcotics Service Council Inc, 2305 St Louis Ave, St Louis, MO 63106.

HARVEY, WILLIAM R.
Educational administrator. **Personal:** Born Jan 29, 1941, Brewton, AL; son of Mamie Claudis and Willie D C Harvey; married Norma Baker Harvey, Aug 13, 1966; children: Kelly Renee, William Christopher, Leslie Denise. **Educ:** Talladega Coll, BA 1961; Harvard Univ, EdD 1972. **Career:** Secondary school teacher 1965-66; Harvard Univ, admin coord Harvard Intensive Summer Studies Prog 1969, asst to dean for govt affairs 1969-70; Fisk Univ, admin asst to pres 1970-72; Tuskegee Inst, vice pres student affairs 1972-74, vice pres admin services 1974-78; Hampton Univ, pres 1978-; owner Pepsi Cola Bottling Co of Houghton, MI. **Orgs:** Bd of dirs Newport News S&L 1980; bd of visitors Univ of VA 1981; bd of dirs Natl Merit Scholarship Corp 1981; bd of dir Signet Banking Corp, 1989-; com member, President, Advisory Board, 1990-; com member, US Dept of Comm Min Econ Devel Council, 1990-; board of directors, American Council on Education, 1992; board of directors,Trigon Blue Cross Blue Shield, 1992; board of directors, Signet Bank Peninsula; bd of dirs, International Guaranty Insurance Co, 1990-; bd of trustees, Virginia Museum of Fine Arts, 1992; bd of trustees, Virginia Historical Society, 1992; American Council on Education's CMS on Government Relations; board of directors, Newport News Shipbuilding, Inc, 1996. **Honors/Awds:** Harvard Univ, Administrative Fellow, 1969; Woodrow Wilson Foundation, Martin L King Fellow, 1968-70, Woodrow Wilson Intern Fellowship, 1970-72; Virginia Cultural Laureate Award, 1992; Phi Delta Kappa, Harvard Chapter, Award, 1992; Honorary Degrees: Salisbury State Clg, LHD, 1983; Medaille Clg, PdD, 1987; Lemoyne-Owens Clg, LHD, 1988. **Military Serv:** US Army Natl Guard Reserve, lt col, 1981-. **Home Addr:** 612 Shore Rd, Hampton, VA 23669. **Business Addr:** President, Hampton Univ, Office of the President, Administration Bldg, Room 200, Hampton, VA 23668.

HARVEY-BYRD, PATRICIA LYNN
Journalist. **Personal:** Born Nov 13, 1954, Detroit, MI; married Prentiss Lewis Byrd; children: Michelle Renee. **Educ:** Attended, Mercy Coll of Detroit 1972-73, Univ of Detroit 1976-79, Saginaw Valley State Coll 1979-81. **Career:** WGPR TV & Radio Detroit, radio host 1976-77; WJBK TV Detroit, staff announcer 1977-79; WNEM TV Saginaw, anchor/reporter 1979-81; Cable News Network, anchor/corres 1981-85; WGN TV News Chicago, anchor/reporter 1985-. **Orgs:** Bd of governors Natl Acad of TV Arts & Scis 1986-; mem Chicago Assoc of Black Journalists 1986-; public serv work Girl Scouts of Amer 1987; board member, Governor's Task Force on Public-Private Child Care 1989; board member, Academic Development Institute 1988; Muscular Dystrophy Association 1988. **Honors/Awds:** Comm Serv Awd Buena Vista Township 1980; Chicago's Up & Coming Business & Professional Women 1986; IL Coalition Against Domestic Violence 1986; Emmy Award for AIDS Reporting National Academy of TV Arts & Sciences 1988; Peter Lisagore Award for Investigative Journalism into Pap Industry 1988; Journalist of the Year , National Association of Black Journalists 1988; Associated Press Award for Investigative Journalism Re: Pap Industry 1989; Illinois Broadcasters Association Award for Aids Reporting 1989; Blackbook's Business & Professional Award 1989. **Business Addr:** Anchorwoman, WGN News, 2501 W Bradley Place, Chicago, IL 60618.

HARVEY-SALAAM, DYANE MICHELLE
Dancer, teacher, choreographer, trainer. **Personal:** Born Nov 16, 1951, Schenectady, NY; daughter of Walter Franklin Harvey & Audrey Payne Harvey; married Abdel Rut Salaam, Jan 2, 1984; children: Khisekh Nekhekh-Naut. **Career:** NY Foundation for the Arts, artist in residence, 1982-97; Borough of Manhattan Comm Coll, adjunct prof, 1988-97; Lehman Coll, adjunct prof, 1989-97; City Ctr Educational Outreach, dance instr, 1993-97; Hofstra Univ, adjunct prof, 1996-97; Manhattan East Middle Sch, dance consultant, 1997-98; Forces of Nature Dance Theatre Co, founding mem, principal soloist, 1981-. **Orgs:** Actor's Equity, 1973; Screen Actor's Guild, 1977; Forces of Nature Dance Theatre, principal soloist, founding mem, 1982-; Troupe New York, advisory bd, mem, choreographer, 1997-. **Honors/Awds:** Audience Development Comm, Audelco, 1983; National Council of Arts Achievements, Monarch Merit Award, 1991; 2nd Black Theatre Conference, IRA Aldridge Award, 1995. **Special Achievements:** Choreographed "Herizon," 1987, 1996, 1997; "The Women of Plums," 1997; Oiga Mi Voz, 1997; "Ki-Ache Stories From the Belly," collaborated with Peggy Choy and Fred Ito, 1997; "Loves Fire," the Acting Co, evening of plays, 1998; Performed and toured with numerous dance companies. **Business Addr:** Principal Soloist, Forces of Nature Dance Theatre Co, c/o The Cathedral of St John the Divine, 1047 Amsterdam Ave, New York, NY 10025, (212)749-7720.

HARVIN, ALVIN
Reporter. **Personal:** Born Feb 20, 1937, NYC; married Norma Ellis; children: A Jamieson, Khary, Demetria. **Educ:** CCNY, BA 1967. **Career:** NY Post, sports reporter; NY Times, sports reporter. **Orgs:** Mem Baseball Writers Assn Am. **Business Addr:** Reporter, New York Times, 229 W 43 St, New York, NY 10036.

HARVIN, DURANT KEVIN, III
Cleric. **Personal:** Born Jul 5, 1966, Baltimore, MD; son of Rev Cynthia S Harvin and Durant Harvin Jr; married Lisa M Clark, Aug 4, 1990; children: Durant K Harvin IV, Dairia Kymber Harvin. **Educ:** Hampton University, BA, 1988; Colgate Rochester Divinity School, MDiv, 1991. **Career:** Hampton University, asst to the dean, 1987-88; Baber African Methodist Episcopal Church, student minister, 1988-91; Colgate Rochester Divinity School, minority recruiter, 1988-91; Bethel African Methodist Episcopal Church/Baltimore, executive assistant pastor, 1991-92; Richard Brown Church, senior pastor, 1992-. **Orgs:** Vice President, Interdenominational Ministerial Alliance, 1992-; Youngstown Commission for Social Justice, board of directors, 1992-; African Methodist Episcopal Ministerial Alliance, 1991-92; Forest Park Senior Center, board of directors, 1992-; National Association of Black Seminarians, national officer, 1989-91; National Association of Black Journalists, 1987-88. **Honors/Awds:** National Association of Black Seminarians, Distinguished Service, 1990, 1991; Colgate Rochester Divinity School, Distinguished Service, 1991. **Special Achievements:** Founder and Chief Facilitator, Operation GANG Youth Ministry, 1992; author, Journey From My Dungeon: Confessions of an African-American Child of Divorce, 1992. **Home Phone:** (216)744-5221.

HASAN, AQEEL KHATIB
Personnel administrator. **Personal:** Born Sep 10, 1955, Augusta, GA; married Venita Lejuene Merriweather; children: Aqeel. **Educ:** Augusta Area Tech Sch, diploma 1976-78. **Career:** Augusta News Review, columnist 1978-79; WRDW Radio, broadcaster 1978-80; Black Focus Magazine, columnist 1982; Richmond Co Bd of Educ, mem 1982-, pres 1983-84; Richmond Co Bd of Health, mem 1983-84; Employment Planning Consultants Inc, pres 1985. **Orgs:** Counselor Richmond Co Correction Inst 1876-80; minister American Muslim Mission 1977-80. **Honors/Awds:** Best athlete Augusta Area Tech School 1978; Citizen of the Year Omega Psi Phi Frat 1983; Citizen of the Year Augusta News Review 1983; Outstanding Young Man of America Jaycees Natl 1984. **Military Serv:** USMC lance corpl 2 yrs.

HASHIM, MUSTAFA
Political activist. **Personal:** Born Mar 18, 1935; married Hamida; children: Ishmail, Munira, Rasheeda. **Educ:** Islamic & African Inst of PA, 1962. **Career:** African-Amer Repatriation Assn Philadelphia, political activist, pres. **Orgs:** Goal of assn is to obtain land in Africa for the voluntary repatriation of African Americans who are the descendants of slaves, and to petition the US govt to cooperate with willing African states in programs to achieve this goal.

HASKINS, CLEM SMITH
University basketball coach. **Personal:** Born Aug 11, 1943, Campbellsville, KY; son of Lucy Smith Haskins and Columbus Haskins; married Yevette Penick Haskins, May 22, 1965; children: Clemette, Lori, Brent. **Educ:** Western Kentucky University, Bowling Green, KY, BS, 1967, MA, 1971. **Career:** Chicago Bulls, Chicago, IL, professional athlete, 1967-70; Phoenix Suns, Phoenix, AZ, professional athlete, 1970-74; Washington Bullets, Washingtin, DC, professional athlete, 1974-77; Western Kentucky Univ, Bowling Green, KY, director of continuing education center, 1977-78, assistant basketball coach, 1978-80, head basketball coach, 1980-86; University of Minnesota, Minneapolis, MN, head basketball coach, currently. **Orgs:** Member, National Assoc Basketball Coaches, 1977-; player representative, NBA Players' Assoc, 1971-73; member, Sherriff Boys and Girls Ranch, 1980-; mem Sigma Pi Phi, Omicron Boule, 1990. **Honors/Awds:** Kentucky High School Hall of Fame, 1988; First Team College All-American, NCAA, 1967; NBC Rookie Coach of the Year, 1980-81 (WKY); Ohio Valley Conference Coach of the Year, 1980-81; Kentucky Hall of Fame, 1990; Sunbelt Conference Coach of the Year, 1985-86; Assistant Coach of 1996 US Olympic Gold Medal Team, 1996; Western KY University, Distinguished Alumni, 1996; Western KY University, Hall of Fame. **Business Addr:** Coach, Men's Basketball, University of Minnesota, 516 15th Ave, SE, Bierman Bldg, Minneapolis, MN 55455.

HASKINS, CLEMETTE
College basketball coach. **Personal:** daugHter of Clem Haskins. **Career:** University of Dayton, women's basketball coach, 1994-. **Business Addr:** Women's Basketball Coach, University of Dayton, Athletics Dept., 300 College Pk., Dayton, OH 45469-1230, (513)229-4447.

HASKINS, JAMES S.
Author, educator. **Personal:** Born Sep 19, 1941, Demopolis, AL; son of Julia Brown Haskins and Henry Haskins. **Educ:** Georgetown University, BA, 1960; Alabama State University, BS, 1962; University of New Mexico, MA, 1963; New York Institute of Finance, certificate of Work of the Stock Exchange, 1965; attended New School for Social Research and City University of New York. **Career:** New York City Public Schools, teacher, 1966-68; New School for Social Research, part-time teacher, 1970-72; State University College, part-time teacher, 1970-72; Staten Island Community College, associate professor, 1970-76; Elisabeth Irwin High School, teacher, 1971-73; Weekend College, Indiana University/Purdue University, visiting lecturer, 1973-74; Manhattanville College, visiting lecturer, 1972-76; College of New Rochelle, visiting professor, 1977-; University of Florida, professor of English, 1977-; consultant to numerous educational and governmental groups and publishers, currently. **Orgs:** Authors Guild; National Book Critics Circle; member, Africa Roundtable, Phelps-Stokes Fund, 1987-; vice director southeast region, Commission on the Bicentennial of the Statue of Liberty, 1985-86; National Education Advisory Committee of the Commission on the Bicentennial of the Constitution, 1987-; New York Urban League; Phi Beta Kappa, Kappa Alpha Psi. **Honors/Awds:** Best Western Juvenile nonfiction book finalist, Western Writers of America, 1975; Coretta Scott King Award, 1977; Children's Book of the Year award, Child Study Association, 1979; Deems Taylor Award for writing in the field of music, ASCAP, 1979; thirty books selected as Notable Children's Books in the field of social science, Social Studies magazine; author of The Cotton Club, Random House, 1977; author of over forty-five biographies for children; author of numerous nonfiction books on social issues; Carter G Woodson Award, 1988, 1994, 1997; Washington Post/ Children's Book Guild Award, 1994. **Home Addr:** 325 West End Ave, 7D, New York, NY 10023. **Business Addr:** Department of English, University of Florida, 4326 Turlington, Gainesville, FL 32611.

HASKINS, JAMES W., JR.
Public relations representative. **Personal:** Born Dec 1, 1932, Sandusky, OH; married Janie L Moore; children: Lisa, Scott, Karen, Laura, Ronald, Sondra, Iona. **Educ:** Bowling Grn St U, BA 1959; Univ of PA, MSEd 1975, Doct Cand Educ Adm. **Career:** DuPont Invtn, editor 1971-, rsrch sci wrtr 1969-71; Chem & Engr & News, asst ed bur head 1966-69; US Atmc Enrgy Com, chem 1963-66; Cntrls RdtnInc, tech 1961-63; Prvdnc Hosp Sch Nrsng, sci instr 1962, bctrlgst-tech 1960-63; IUPAC Bk on Org Chem, editor; US Acad of Sci Host, mcrmlclr chem 1971. **Orgs:** Mem Am Chem Soc; AAAS; Nat Assn Sci Wrtrs Inc; Soc Tech Commnctn; Sigma Delta Chi; Intl Assn Bus Commnctrs; mem Blck Educ Forum; Urban League; NAACP; Alpha Phi Alpha; Wynfld Rsdnts Assn. **Honors/Awds:** Sci Wrtr Yr NY Voice 1972; Legion Hon; member Chpl 4 Chplns 1973; Phi Delta Kappa 1975. **Military Serv:** USMC sgt 1954-57. **Business Addr:** Pub Affairs Dept El, Du Pont de Nemours & Co Inc, Wilmington, DE 19898.

HASKINS, JOSEPH, JR.
Bank chief executive. **Personal:** marrIed; children: one son. **Educ:** Morgan State Univ, BA, Economics; New York Univ, MBA; Johns Hopkins Univ, Masters in Liberal Arts; Wharton School, Univ of Pennsylvania, banking certificate. **Career:** Chemical Bank, New York, loan officer; Midlantic Natl Bank, New Jersey; loan officer; Coppin State Coll, vice pres, business & finance; Prudential-Bache Securities, investment broker; Harbor Bank of Maryland, pres/CEO, 1987-. **Orgs:** Natl Banker's Assn; Amer Banker's Assn; The President's Roundtable; bd mem: Maryland Banking School, Academy of Finance, Better Business Bureau, Greater Baltimore Committee, Villa Julie Coll, Associated Black Charities, Maryland Industrial Devt Financing Authority. **Honors/Awds:** SBA Financial Advocate of the Year, 1989; Black Enterprise Magazine Top 20 Minority Owned Banks, 1990; Black Outstanding Marylander, 1991. **Business Addr:** Pres/CEO, Harbor Bank of Maryland, 25 W Fayette St, Baltimore, MD 21201.

HASKINS, MICHAEL KEVIN
Public relations consultant. **Personal:** Born Mar 30, 1950, Washington, DC; son of Frances Datcher Haskins and Thomas Haskins; married. **Educ:** Lincoln Univ, Oxford PA, BA Economics, 1972; LaSalle Univ, Philadelphia PA, MBA Finance,

1980. **Career:** Fidelity Bank, Philadelphia PA, asst mgr, 1972-76; First Pennsylvania Bank, Philadelphia PA, mktg specialist, 1976-77; Greater Philadelphia CDC, Philadelphia PA, sr project mgr, 1977-80; Emerson Electric, Hatfield PA, mktg analyst, 1980-82; Cooper Labs, Lang Horn PA, product mgr, 1982-83; First Pennsylvania Bank, Philadelphia PA, asst vice pres, 1983-89; Crawley Haskins & Rodgers Public Relations, Philadelphia PA, exec vice pres, 1989-. **Orgs:** Vice pres/sec, Greater Philadelphia Venture Capital, 1983-; dir, Pennsylvania Minority Business Devel Authority, 1988-91; pres, Richard Allen Museum Bd, 1989-91; Philadelphia Council for Community Advancement, bd of directors. **Honors/Awds:** Mother Bethel AME Bicentennial Award, 1987; Group Leader, Urban League of Philadelphia, 1988. **Business Addr:** Executive Vice President, Crawley, Haskins & Rodgers Public Relations, The Bourse, Independence Mall, Suite 584, Philadelphia, PA 19106.

HASKINS, MORICE LEE, JR.
Financial administrator. **Personal:** Born Jun 9, 1947, New Brunswick, NJ; son of Mary Toombs Haskins and Morice L Haskins, Sr; married Jane Segal; children: Rachel. **Educ:** Colgate University, BA, 1969; Hofstra University School of Law, JDL, 1978. **Career:** First TN Bank Corp, vice pres & trust officer, 1979-; NY State Educ Dept, Albany, exec sec, commn on educ oppor, 1974-75; NY State Educ Dept, asso in higher educ, 1971-75; State Univ of NY at Oswego, asso dean, dir full oppor prog1969-71; Colony S Settlement House Brooklyn, coor, soc studies curric, 1969. **Orgs:** Assn for Equality & Excellence in Educ, 1978-82; Natl Bar Assn, Memphis, 1979-; Amer Inst of Banking, Memphis, 1979-; Tau Kappa Epsilon; Mediator Memphis City Ct Dispute Prog, 1979-8l; vchmn, LaRose Sch Title I, Comm Adv Com, 1979-8l; Chicasaw Council, Boy Scouts of America, 1981-84; bd dir, Memphis Black Arts Alliance, 1982-86; loan comm, TN Valley Center for Minority Econ Dev, 1984-87; chmn, bd of dir, Dixie Homes Boys Club 1988-90; Shelby County Agricenter Commission, 1994-. **Business Addr:** Vice President/Trust Officer, First Tennessee Bank Natl Assn, P O Box 84, Memphis, TN 38101.

HASKINS, WILLIAM J.
Business management consultant. **Personal:** Born Oct 16, 1930, Binghamton, NY; son of Signora and William L; married Bessie White; children: Billy, Terri, Wendell. **Educ:** Syracuse Univ, BA 1952; Columbia Univ, MA 1953; NY Univ, cert adm 1954. **Career:** Boys Club of Amer, Milwaukee 1957-60, Richmond 1960-62; Natl Urban League, exec dir Eliz NJ 1962-64, mideastern reg 1964-66, deputy dir 1966-69; Natl Alliance of Businessmen, natl dir comm rel 1969-72; Arthur D Little, sr staff consult 1972; Eastern Reg Natl Urban League, dir; Human Resources Social Serv Natl Urban League, natl dir; Urban League Whitney M Young Jr Training Exec Develop and Continuing Educ Ctr, dir 1986; vice pres, National Urban League Programs, 1989-94. **Orgs:** Natl Council Urban League; exec mem NAACP; Pres Commn on Mental Health ; pub mem Pres' Strategy Council on Drug Abuse; bd mem Natl Cncl on Black Alcoholism; Alpha Phi Alpha Frat; chmn Human Environ Ctr Washington DC; 100 Black Men of New Jersey. **Honors/Awds:** Many athletic awds 1948-53; Athlete Yr 1951; Man of Yr 1970; Letterman of Distinction Syracuse Univ 1978; Pacesetters Awd Syracuse Univ Black Alumni 1979; 1982 inducted into NY State Athletic Hall of Fame. **Business Addr:** President, WJH Associates, 8306 Brookfield Rd, Richmond, VA 23227.

HASKINS, YVONNE B.
Attorney. **Personal:** Born Feb 23, 1938, Atlanta, GA; daughter of Rozlyn Douthard Blakeney and Joseph H Blakeney; married Harold J Haskins, Mar 15, 1969; children: Randall, Russell, Kristin. **Educ:** Spelman College, Atlanta, GA, 1954-56; Temple University, Philadelphia, PA, BS, Summa Cum Laude, 1968; Temple School of Law, Philadelphia, PA, JD, 1986. **Career:** University of Pennsylvania, Philadelphia, PA, security specialist, 1972-74; PA Commission on Crime & Delinquency, Philadelphia, PA, regional director, 1974-77; PA Board of Probation & Parole, Philadelphia, PA, regional director, 1977-86; Schnader, Harrison, Segal & Lewis, Philadelphia, PA, attorney, 1986-89; Ballard, Spahr, Andres & Ingersoll, Philadelphia, PA, attorney, 1989-. **Orgs:** President, Program for Female Offenders, Inc, 1987-; former president, Big Sisters of Philadelphia, 1980-88; board member, West Mt Airy Neighbors, Inc, 1989-. **Honors/Awds:** Appreciation Award of Black Pre-Law Society, Outstanding Service, Universityof Pennsylvania, 1988-89.

HASSELBACH, HARALD
Professional football player. **Personal:** Born Sep 22, 1967; married Aundrea; children: Terran. **Educ:** Univ of Washington. **Career:** Calgary Stampeders (CFL), 1990-94; Denver Broncos, 1994-. **Business Addr:** Professional Football Player, Denver Broncos, 13655 Broncos Pkwy, Englewood, CO 80112, (303)649-9000.

HASSELL, FRANCES M. See Obituaries section.

HASSELL, LEROY ROUNTREE, SR.
Justice. **Personal:** Born Aug 17, 1955, Norfolk, VA; son of Ruth Rountree Hassell and Joseph R Hassell Sr; married Linda Greene Hassell. **Educ:** Univ of VA, Charlottesville, VA, BA,

1977; Harvard Law School, Cambridge, MA, JD, 1980. **Career:** McGuire, Woods, Battle & Boothe, Richmond, VA, lawyer, 1980-89; Supreme Court of VA, Richmond, VA, justice, 1989-. **Orgs:** Advisory bd mem, Massey Cancer Ctr, 1989-; chmn, Richmond School Bd, 1985-89; dir, American Red Cross, 1985-89; dir, Carpenter Ctr for the Performing Arts, 1984-86; dir, Legal Aid, of Central VA, 1982-85; mem, ABA's Comm on Continuing Appellate Education, 1990-. **Honors/Awds:** Liberty Bell Award, American Bar Assn, 1990; Black Achievers Award, YMCA, 1985, 1986; Outstanding Young Citizen Award, Richmond Jaycees, 1987; Outstanding Young Virginian Award, Virginia Jaycees, 1987. **Business Addr:** Justice, Supreme Court of Virginia, 100 N 9th St, Richmond, VA 23219.

HASSON, NICOLE DENISE
Association executive. **Personal:** Born Sep 18, 1963, Chicago, IL; daughter of Beverly Hasson-Johnson and Willie Hasson. **Educ:** Western Illinois University, BA, 1985; Roosevelt University, MPA, 1991. **Career:** Western Illinois Affirmative Action Office, administrative assistant, 1985; National Opinion Research Co, assistant supervisor, 1986; Keck, Mahin & Cate, legal assistant, 1986; Horwitz, Horwitz & Associates, legal assistant, office manager, 1986-89; Alpha Kappa Alpha Sorority, Inc, office operations assistant director, 1989-. **Orgs:** NAACP, president, 1984-; Alpha Kappa Alpha, Inc, secretary, 1985-; Kiwanis International, 1991-; St Phillip Neri Woman's Board, publicity chairman, special events chairman, 1988-; Alpha Kappa Alpha Educational Foundation, 1988-; Top Ladies of Distinction, TTA advisor, program chair, beautification committee, 1991-; Friends of the Parks, 1991-. **Honors/Awds:** Women of Destiny, Woman of Destiny Protege Award, 1990; Friends of the Parks, Initiative Award, 1992; Alpha Kappa Alpha Educational Foundation, Alice Motts Scholarship, 1990; Alpha Phi Alpha, Miss Alpha Phi Alpha, 1983. **Home Addr:** 2015 E 67th St, Chicago, IL 60649, (312)288-5380. **Business Addr:** Office Operations Assistant Director, Alpha Kappa Alpha Sorority, Inc, 5656 S Stony Island Ave, Chicago, IL 60637, (312)684-1282.

HASTINGS, ALCEE LAMAR
Congressman. **Personal:** Born Sep 5, 1936, Altamonte Springs, FL; son of Mildred L Hastings and Julius C Hastings; divorced; children: Alcee II. **Educ:** Fisk U, BA 1958; Howard U; FL A&M Univ, JD 1963. **Career:** Allen and Hastings, Fort Lauderdale, FL, attorney, 1963-66, private law practice, 1966-77; Broward County, FL, circuit court judge, 1977-79; US District Court, judge, 1979-89; US House of Representatives, 1993-. **Orgs:** Broward County Bar Assn; Florida Bar Assn; American Bar Assn; National Bar Assn; American Trial Lawyers Assn; Broward County Trial Lawyers Assn; Broward County Criminal Defense Atty Assn; American Arbitration Assn; Broward County Classroom Teachers Assn; Broward County Council on Human Relations; State of Florida Education Commission; member, Task Force on Crime; board of directors, Urban League of Broward County; board of directors, Broward County Sickle Cell Anemia Foundation; member, Florida Voters League. **Honors/Awds:** Freedom Award, NAACP; Man of the Year, Kappa Alpha Psi, Orlando Chapter; NAACP Co Award, 1976; Humanitarian Award, Broward County Young Democrats, 1978; Citizen of the Year Award, Zeta Phi Beta, 1978; Sam Delevoe Human Rights Award, Comm Relations Bd of Broward County, 1978; Man of Year, Com Italian Amer Affairs 1979-80; Judge Alcee Hastings Day proclaimed by City of Daytona Beach in his honor Dec 14, 1980; Glades Festival of Afro Arts Awd, Zeta Phi Beta, 1981. **Business Addr:** State Representative, US House of Representatives, 1039 Longworth Bldg, Washington, DC 20515.

HASTINGS, ANDRE ORLANDO
Professional football player. **Personal:** Born Nov 7, 1970, Macon, GA. **Educ:** Georgia. **Career:** Pittsburgh Steelers, wide receiver, 1993-96; New Orleans Saints, 1997-. **Business Addr:** Professional Football Player, New Orleans Saints, 5800 Airline Hwy, Metairie, LA 70003, (504)733-0255.

HASTON, RAYMOND CURTISS, JR.
Dentist. **Personal:** Born Jul 24, 1945, Lexington, VA; married Diane Rawls; children: Lisa, Crystal, April, Tasha. **Educ:** Bluefield State, BS 1967; Howard Univ, DDS 1977. **Career:** Appomattox Public School Systems, teacher 1967-68; Milton Sumners HS, teacher 1969; DC Public School System, teacher 1969-73; Private Practice, dentist. **Orgs:** Mem Natl Dental Assoc 1987, Amer Dental Assoc 1987, General Acad of Dentistry 1987; mem Alpha Phi Alpha Frat, NAACP. **Honors/Awds:** Natl Science Foundation Scholarships 1971-72. **Home Addr:** 6425 Battle Rock Dr, Clifton, VA 22024.

HASTY, JAMES EDWARD
Professional football player. **Personal:** Born May 23, 1965, Seattle, WA. **Educ:** Washington State Univ, degree in communications. **Career:** New York Jets, defensive back, 1988-94; Kansas City Chiefs, 1995-. **Orgs:** Jessica Guzman Scholarship Foundation, founder. **Business Addr:** Professional Football Player, Kansas City Chiefs, One Arrowhead Dr, Kansas City, MO 64129, (816)924-9300.

HASTY, KEITH A.
Chief executive of packaging materials firm. **Career:** Best Foam Fabricators Inc, Chicago, IL, chief exec. **Business Addr:** Best Foam Fabricators Inc., 9633 S Cottage Grove Ave, Chicago, IL 60628.

HATCHER, ESTER L.
Educator (retired). **Personal:** Born Jan 2, 1933, College Grove, TN; daughter of Sadie K Hatcher and Marvin P Hatcher. **Educ:** TN State Univ, BS 1954; Univ of TN, MS 1970. **Career:** Univ of TN Knox Blount Anderson, extension agent 1954-65; Univ of TN Madison Cty, extension agent 1965-69; Univ of TN, asst prof, 1970-77, assoc prof 1977-84, prof 1984-90. **Orgs:** Mem Amer Home Econ Assoc 1965-; counselor Equal Employment Oppty Univ of TN 1973-90; mem Century Club Univ of TN 1975-; chmn nom comm TN Home Econ Assoc 1977; treas Home Demo Agents of TN 1978-80; mem Soc of Nutrition Ed 1978-; mem nominating committee, TN Home Economics Assn. **Honors/Awds:** Publ ''Teaching Nutrition to Youth'', ''SPIFFY Food Science'', ''Food & Nutrition Grades K-3'', ''Ideas for Visuals''; leader of publication's Food & Nutrition Section, 1978-90.

HATCHER, JEFFREY F.
Manager. **Personal:** Born in East Orange, NJ; son of Cordella Garnes and John Cornelius Hatcher; divorced; children: Troy. **Educ:** TN State Univ, attended 1965-69; The New School of Social Rsch, attended 1977-78. **Career:** Spot Time Ltd Natl TV Station Representatives, sales mgr 1979-82; MCA Television, account exec 1982-84; Channel Syndication Corp, marketing dir 1984-85; USA Network, regional mgr affiliate relations 1985-. **Orgs:** Mem Natl Acad of TV Arts & Scis, Intl Radio & TV Soc Inc, Natl Assoc of Minorities in Cable NY Chapter. **Business Addr:** Regional Mgr, Affiliate Relations, USA Network, Eastern Region, 1230 Avenue of the Americas, New York, NY 10020.

HATCHER, KENDRA DENISE
Advertising executive. **Personal:** Born Aug 18, 1971, Cincinnati, OH; daughter of Marshall & Artiemisia Hatcher. **Educ:** Ohio University, BS, 1993; Northwestern University, MS, 1994. **Career:** Leo Burnett USA, account planner, 1995-; Columbia Coll, part-time faculty, 1997-. **Orgs:** Zeta Phi Beta Sorority, mem, 1990-; Natl Pan Hellenic Council, Chicago Chap, vp, 1997-98; Abraham Lincoln Ctr, chair, 1997-98, Young Adult Bd, co-chair, 1996-97; Target Advertising Professionals, mem-at-large, 1996-; Advertising Educational Foundation Ambassador, 1997. **Special Achievements:** Wrote chapter intro in Business and Administrative Communication. **Home Addr:** 5143 S Kenwood, Unit 202, Chicago, IL 60615. **Business Addr:** Account Planner, Leo Burnett USA, 35 W Wacker Dr, Chicago, IL 60601-2311.

HATCHER, LILLIAN
Union representative. **Personal:** Born May 30, 1915, Greenville, AL; widowed; children: Carlene, John, Gloria. **Career:** UAW Intl Union, intl rep (1st Black woman appointed). **Orgs:** Commr vice chairperson Human Rights Comm; delegate MI Constl Conv 1961-62; vice chpsn 13th Congr Dist Chpsn Women's Com of the Bicent Commn 1976; Women's Comm bd mem NAACP Flight for Freedom Dinner 1977; precinct delegate 1948-; coalition Black Trade Unionists; Women's Economic Club of Detroit. **Honors/Awds:** Awd Intl Order of the Elks. **Business Addr:** International Representative, UAW Intl Union, 8000 E Jefferson Ave, Detroit, MI 48214.

HATCHER, LIZZIE R.
Attorney. **Personal:** Born Feb 8, 1954, Houston, TX; daughter of Azzie Wafer Parker and Fred Randall; married Sherman Hatcher, Feb 8, 1973; children: Charmonda, Marcus, Madeira. **Career:** Thomas M Burns, Ltd, Las Vegas, NV, attorney, law clerk, 1980-83; Lizzie R Hatcher, Las Vegas, NV, attorney, 1983-; Capital Murder Case Defense Panel, mem; Eighth Judicial District Court, paternity referee. **Orgs:** President, Las Vegas Chapter, NBA, 1985-87; member, Victory Missionary Baptist Church, 1986-; trustee, Victory Missionary Baptist Church, 1987-88; member, NAACP, Las Vegas Branch, 1988-; regional director, National Bar Association, 1990-. **Honors/Awds:** The Systematic Discriminatory Treatment of African-Americans in Capital Cases by the Criminal Justice System, Howard University Criminal Law Symposium, 1990. **Business Addr:** Attorney, 302 E Carson Ave, Suite 930, Las Vegas, NV 89101, (702)386-2988.

HATCHER, RICHARD GORDON
Consultant, lawyer, educator. **Personal:** Born Jul 10, 1933, Michigan City, IN; son of Catherine Hatcher and Carlton Hatcher; married Ruthellyn; children: Ragan, Rachelle, Renee. **Educ:** IN Univ, BS 1956; Valparaiso Univ, JD 1959. **Career:** Lake Co IN, deputy prosecuting atty 1961-63; City of Gary, city councilman 1963-67; mayor 1967-88; Hatcher and Associates, pres, 1988-; Valparaiso Univ, law prof, 1992-; Roosevelt University, Harold Washington Professor, political science, currently. **Orgs:** Dem Conf of Mayors 1977; instr IN Univ NW; many publs; chmn Human & Resources Devel 1974; mem Natl League of Cities; past pres, US Conf of Mayors; Natl Conf of

Black Mayors; Natl Black Polit Conv; former vice chair, Natl Dem Comm; Mikulski Commn report dem party policy; Natl Urban Coalition; natl chmn bd dir Operation PUSH; mem IN Exec Bd NAACP; mem Natl Dem Comm on Delegate Selection (co-author Com Report); founder Natl Black Caucus of Locally Elected Officials; Natl Black Caucus; IN State Dem Central Com; Assn Councils Arts; chair TransAfrica Inc; Jesse Jackson for Pres Campaign; pres Natl Civil Rights Museum and Hall of Fame; mem bd of dirs Marshall Univ Socof Yeager Scholars; fellow, Kennedy School of Govt, Harvard U; chair, African American Summit, 1989. **Honors/Awds:** Outstanding Achievement Civil Rights 10 Annual Ovington Awd; life mem & Leadership Awd NAACP; Man of Yr Harlem Lawyers Assn; Disting Serv Awd Capital Press Club; Disting Serv Awd Jaycees; Employment Benefactors Awd Intl Assn Personnel Employment Security; Serv Loyalty & Dedication Awd Black Students Union Prairie State Coll; Outstanding Cit Yr Awd United Viscounts IN; Inspired Leadership IN State Black Caucus; among 100 Most Influential Black Americans Ebony Magazine 1971; among 200 most outstanding young leaders of US, Time Magazine, 1974; Urban Leadership award, IN Assn of Cities and Towns, 1986; Natl League of Cities President's Award, 1987; Natl Black Caucus of Local Elected Officials Liberty Award, 1987; Honorary Doctorates, Coppin St College, DuquesneU, Fisk U, Valparaiso U, Clevnd St U. **Business Addr:** Law Professor, Valparaiso University, Valparaiso, IN 46383.

HATCHER, ROBERT
Automobile dealer. **Career:** Chicago Truck Center Inc, pres, currently. **Business Addr:** President, Chicago Truck Ctr Inc, 1015 W Pershing Rd, Chicago, IL 60609, (773)890-2400.

HATCHER, WILLIAM AUGUSTUS (BILLY)
Professional baseball player. **Personal:** Born Oct 4, 1960, Williams, AZ. **Educ:** Yavapai Community College. **Career:** Outfielder: Chicago Cubs, 1984-85, Houston Astros, 1986-89, Pittsburgh Pirates, 1980-90, Cincinnati Reds, 1990-92, Boston Red Sox, 1992-. **Business Addr:** Professional Baseball Player, Boston Red Sox, Fenway Park, 24 Yawkey Way, Boston, MA 02215, (617)267-9440.

HATCHETT, ELBERT
Attorney. **Personal:** Born Jan 24, 1936, Pontiac, MI; married Laurestine; children: 4. **Educ:** Central State Coll of OH, attended; Univ of MI, attended; FL A&M Univ, LLD. **Career:** Hatchett Brown Watermont & Campbell, attny 1969; Circle H Ranch Otter Lake MI, owner; Hatcett Dewalt Hatchel & Hall, sr parnter, attny. **Honors/Awds:** Num awds from local & state orgs for serv to community & outstanding contribs to the pursuit of human rights; Disting Alumni Awd FL A&M Univ. **Business Addr:** Trial Attorney, Sr Parnter, Hatchett, DeWalt, Hatchett, Hall, 485 Orchard Lake Ave, Pontiac, MI 48341.

HATCHETT, JOSEPH WOODROW
Judge. **Personal:** Born Sep 17, 1932, Clearwater, FL; son of Lula Hatchett and Arthur Hatchett; children: Cheryl Nadine Green, Brenda Audrey. **Educ:** FL A&M Univ, AB 1954; Howard Univ, JD 1959; Naval Justice Sch, Certificate 1973; NY Univ, Appellate Judge Course 1977; Amer Acad of Jud Educ, Appellate Judge Course 1978; Harvard Law Sch, Prog Instruction for Lawyers 1980, 1990. **Career:** Private Law Practice, Daytona Beach FL 1959-66; City of Daytona Beach, contract consul 1963-66; US Attorney, asst Jacksonville FL 1966; US Atty for the Middle Dist of FL, first asst 1967-71; Middle Dist of FL, US magistrate 1971-75; Supreme Court of FL, justice 1975-79; US Court of Appeals for the 5th Circuit, US circuit judge 1979-81; US Court of Appeals for the 11th Circuit, US circuit judge 1981-. **Orgs:** Mem FL Bar, Amer Bar Assn, Natl Bar Assn; bd dir Amer Judicature Soc; mem Jacksonville Bar Assn; mem DW Perkins Bar Assn; mem FL Chap of Natl Bar Assn; mem Phi Delta Phi Legal Frat, Phi Alpha Delta Legal Frat, Omega Psi Phi Frat. **Honors/Awds:** Stetson Law Sch Dr Laws 1980; FL Memorial Coll Honoris Causa Dr Laws 1976; Howard Univ Post Grad Achievement Awd 1977; High Risk Awd State Action Cncl1977; President's Citation Cook Co Bar Assn 1977; Most Outstanding Citizen Broward Co Natl Bar Assn 1976; Bicentennial Awd FL A&M Univ 1976; Comm SvcsAwd Edward Waters Coll 1976; An Accolate for Juristic Distinction Tampa Urban League 1975; Medallion for Human Relations Bethune Cookman 1975; Man of the YrAwd FL Jax Club 1974; first black person apptd to the highest court of a state since reconstruction; first black personelected to public office in a statewide election in the south; first black person to serve on a federal appellate court in the south; several publs including "Criminal Law Survey-1978" Univ of Miami Law Review; "1978 Devements in FL Law" 1979; "Pre-Trial Discovery in Criminal Cases" Fedl Judicial Ctr Library 1974. **Military Serv:** AUS 1st lt 1954-56; USMCR lt col 1977-. **Business Addr:** Judge, 11th Circuit Ct of Appeals, PO Box 10429, Tallahassee, FL 32302.

HATCHETT, PAUL ANDREW
Bank executive. **Personal:** Born May 27, 1925, Clearwater, FL; married Pearlie Young; children: Mrs Paulette Simms, Mrs Pamela Hunnicutt, Paul A II. **Educ:** Hampton Inst Hhmptn VA, BS 1951; FL A&M Univ Tlhs, MEd. **Career:** Clearwater Federal Savings & Loan, asst vice pres 1978-, personnel dir mktg 1972-78; Pinellas Co School System FL, teachar admin 1951-71. **Orgs:** Pres Clrwtr Kwns Club E 1974-; dir Clrwtr Slvtn Army 1973-76; chmn Pinellas Co Hsng Athrty 1974-; bd of trsts St Ptrsbrg Jr Coll 1978-; bd of trsts Med Cntr Hosp 1978-. **Honors/Awds:** Serv award St Ptrsbrg Jr Coll; serv award Pinellas Co Hsng Auth 1979. **Military Serv:** AUS 1st lt korean cnflct. **Business Addr:** PO Box 4608, Clearwater, FL 34618.

HATCHETT, WILLIAM F.
Personnel executive (retired). **Personal:** married Ora; children: Craig, Kimberley, Karen. **Educ:** Rutgers Univ, BS 1950; MA, school admin. **Career:** Verona Publ Schools, staff; Eastern PA League, pro basketball; McCoy Job Corps Ctr Sparta WI, set up & oper recreation & phys ed prog; RCA Corp, mgr 1966-68, employment admin & resources RCA Corp Staff, 1968-87; Performance Training Inc, vice pres beginning, 1987. **Orgs:** Consult & presentations Moods & Attitudes Black Man; past mem Lions Club; past dir Little League Prog; past bd of dir ARC; former commiss State NJ Publ Broadcasting Auth; adv council Econ Career Ed, State Bds Ed, Higher Ed; mem EDGES Group Inc; past mem Student Council, Crown & Scroll, Cap & Skull; chmn Natl Urban League, Whitney M Young Jr Training Center. **Honors/Awds:** Whitney M Young Jr Special Appreciation Award, National Urban League Inc, 1990; Key Women of America Inc, Special Achievement Award, York Manor, 1982; Rutgers University Football Hall of Fame, 1991, Basketball Hall of Fame, 1994; National Football Foundation & College Hall of Fame, Distinguished American Award, Essex county New Jersey Chapter, 1996; NJ Sports Writer Association, Hall of Fame. **Military Serv:** AUS 1st lt 1951-53. **Business Addr:** PO Box 1208, Spotsylvania, VA 22553.

HATHAWAY, ANTHONY, JR.
Clergyman. **Personal:** Born Apr 19, 1921, Edenton, NC; son of Liza Hathaway and Anthony Hathaway; married Etta Hankins Hathaway; children: Elizabeth, Teresa, Anthony, Roger, Edna, Gary. **Educ:** LUTC graduate; East Carolina Univ, currently. **Career:** North Carolina Mutual Life, agent, staff manager, 1955-85 (retired); Piney Grove AME Zion Church, Hawkins Chapel AME Zion Church, Union Grove AME Zion, Shiloh AME Zion Church, Porter's Chapel AME Zion Church, Poplar Run AME Zion Church, pastor, various years; Pleasant Grove AME Zion Chruch, pastor, currently. **Orgs:** Mem NAACP; Good Nghbrhd Cncl; PTA Nat Ins Assn; commissioner, Chowan County Planning Board; Chowan Hospital Chaplains; Albemarle Conference Budget Committee Member. **Honors/Awds:** Sales Manager of the Year, North Carolina Mutual Life, 1975, 1976, 1978, 1980, 1981. **Military Serv:** US Army, SSgt. **Business Addr:** PO Box 91, Edenton, NC 27932.

HATHAWAY, CYNTHIA GRAY
Judge. **Personal:** Born Jan 15, 1948, Detroit, MI; married Michael Hathaway. **Educ:** Wayne State Univ, BS; Univ of Detroit, MS, criminal justice; Detroit College of Law, JD. **Career:** Detroit Recorder's Court, Probation Department, probation officer; Law Offices of Cynthia Gray Hathaway, partner; Wayne County Circuit Court, court clerk; Detroit Recorder's Court, judge, currently. **Orgs:** Michigan Bar Assn; Detroit Bar Assn; American Bar Assn; Straker Bar Assn; Sports Lawyers Bar Assn. **Business Addr:** Judge, Recorder's Court, 1441 St. Antoine, Detroit, MI 48226, (313)224-2120.

HATHAWAY, MAGGIE MAE
County commissioner. **Personal:** Born Jul 1, 1925, Louisiana; divorced; children: Ondra Lewis. **Educ:** UCLA. **Career:** Studied golf under 4 prfls; LA Co, comm on alcoholism; Frederick Douglas Child Devel Cntr, soc wrkr 1967-. **Orgs:** Golf ed LA Sentinel News, 1st blck female golf ed; 1st blck female golfer to become mem Women's Pub Links; 1st blck female to become found of Bev Hills Hollywood NAACP; 1st blck female Commr on Alcoholism, 1st blck female golfer to organize a LA Co Youth Golf Found, donalted $30,000 by LA Co to train minority youth, Minority Asso Golfers, founded the "Image Awds" of Bev Hills NAACP, Image Awds raised $200,000 in past 5 yrs, placed by Comm on Alchlsm in Crts Div 80 to help place Minority Alcoholics in Clinics. **Business Addr:** Commission on Alcoholism, Los Angeles County, 313 N Figueroa, Los Angeles, CA 90012.

HATTER, HENRY
Engineer. **Personal:** Born May 21, 1935, Livingston, AL; son of Isabella McIntyre Hatter and Frank Hatter; married Barbara King Hatter, Apr 22, 1956; children: Marcus A, Kelly Mays, Henry II, DeAngelo Deloney. **Educ:** Sgnw Valley Coll, BS 1966; E U, MS Physics 1972. **Career:** Buick Mtr Div GMC, sr engr 1973-, chem engr 1965-69; GM, prod supv 1970-73, tech 1971. **Orgs:** Sec Gns Co Rep Pty 1972-76; alt del Nat Conv GOP 1976; Elctrl Coll 1976; 7th dist chmn GOP 1977, 1978; chmn Old Nwsbys Bck Mtr Div 1976; bd of dir Old Nwsbys; Gns Co Bcntnl Comm; Flint Riv Beautif Wrkshp; Clio Bcntnl Comm 1975; mem MI Trvl Commn 1979; vice pres Old Nwsbys of Gns Co 1979;rep GM Area Wide C of C; commissioner, Michigan Travel Commission, 1978-86; industrial member, Environmental Licensing Board, 1991-; trustee, Clio Board of Education, 1990-. **Honors/Awds:** MI Snt Cit G Rckwl 1974; nom Awrd of Exclnc GM 1977, 1979; Dstngshd Almns Awrd Sgnw Vly Coll 1978; Public Recognition, American Lung Assn; Public Recognition, Flint Childrens Museum; Public Recognition, Flint Pan Hellenic Club, 1991. **Home Addr:** 1238 E Farrand Rd, Clio, MI 48420.

HATTER, TERRY J., JR.
Judge. **Personal:** Born Mar 11, 1933, Chicago, IL; married Trudy; children: Susan, Allison, Terry, Scott. **Educ:** Wesleyan Univ, 1954; Univ of Chicago, Law School, 1960. **Career:** Office of Economic Opportunity, regional legal svcs director, San Francisco, 1967-70; Western Center on Law and Poverty, executive dir; Loyola Univ, professor, 1973-75; Office of the Mayor, executive assistant director of criminal justice planning, 1974-75; California Superior Court, judge, 1977-80; Federal District Court for the Central District of California, judge, 1980-. **Orgs:** Chair, Bd of Counsilors, University South CA, Law School; trustee, Mt St Mary's College; board member, Western Justice Ctr Foundation; bd of overseers, Rand Ct Justice Institute. **Business Addr:** Judge, U.S. District Court, US Courthouse, 312 N Spring St, Rm 175, Los Angeles, CA 90012, (213)894-5746.

HATTON, BARBARA R.
Educator. **Personal:** Born Jun 4, 1941, LaGrange, GA; divorced; children: Kera. **Educ:** BS 1962; MA 1966; MEA 1970; PhD 1976. **Career:** Tuskegee Inst, dean school of educ; Atlanta Public School System, teacher; Howard Univ, counselor; Federal City Coll Washington, asst dir, admin asst, dean student servs; Stanford Urban Rural Inst; assoc dir; Stanford Univ School of Educ, acting asst prof educ; Stanford Urban Coalition Task Force on Educ, 1974; Knoxville College, pres, currently. **Orgs:** Com Yearbook 1974-75; chprsn Ravenswood City Sch Dist bd trust; co-directed Iniative Imprvmnt Educ Governance 1973; East Palo Alto; vol comm activities; Alpha Kappa Alpha Sor; Psi Chi Honorary Soc in Psychology; Phi Delta Kappa Honorary Soc in Education. **Honors/Awds:** EPDA flw 1969-71; NDEA Flw 1965-66; Univ of Southern Cal, ROSE Award; SCLC, Drum Major for Justice Award; Howard Univ, Award for Distinguished Postgraduate Achievement. **Business Addr:** President, Knoxville College, 901 College St., Knoxville, TN 37921.

HAUGABOOK, TERRENCE RANDALL
Attorney. **Personal:** Born May 16, 1960, Detroit, MI; son of LaVerne Haugabook; children: Terrence Randall II. **Educ:** University of Michigan, BS, 1982; Detroit College of Law, JD, 1991. **Career:** UAW-Ford Legal Svcs Plan, staff attorney, 1991-94; Lewis, White & Clay, associate attorney, 1994-95; Wayne County Prosecutor's Office, assistant prosecuting attorney, 1995-. **Orgs:** Alpha Phi Alpha Fraternity Inc, 1979-; American Bar Association, 1991-; Michigan Bar Association, 1991-; Detroit Bar Association, 1994-; Wolverine Bar Association, 1991-; Life Directions Inc, adult mentor, 1993-. **Honors/Awds:** Lawyer's Cooperative Publishing, American Jurisprudence Book Awd in Professional Responsibility, 1991. **Business Addr:** Assistant Prosecuting Attorney, Wayne County Prosecutor's Office, 1441 St Antoine, Frank Murphy Hall of Justice, Rm 1231, Detroit, MI 48226-2381, (313)224-8368.

HAUGSTAD, MAY KATHERYN
Insurance company representative. **Personal:** Born Oct 18, 1937, Dallas, TX; married Paul Haugstad; children: Monika Moss, Veronica Moss, Karsten. **Educ:** So Univ, BS 1959; Yale Univ, MS 1960; Cath Univ, PhD 1971. **Career:** Howard Univ, rsch asst 1961-63, instructor 1963-66; Fed City Coll, asst prof 1968-69; Univ of NH, asst prof 1969-75, dept chmn 1972-73; Univ of Oslo, researcher 1977-86; Prudential Insurance and Financial Services, registered representative, 1987-. **Orgs:** Delta Sigma Theta Sor; Sigma Xi; LUTCF, life underwriting, trainer, council fellow. **Special Achievements:** Author, "The Effect of Photosynthetic Enhancement on Photorespiration in Sinapis Alba," Physiologia Plantarum 47, 19-24 1979; author, "Determination of Spectral Responses of Photorespiration in Sinapis Alba by CO2; Burst Effect of O2 & CO2 Compensation Concentrations," Photosynthetica 1980; author of several publications including: Effect of Abscisic Acid on CO2 Exchange in Lemna Gibba; Yield of Tomato & Maize in Response to Filiar & Root Appl of Triacontanol; Photoinhibition of Photosynthesis: Effect of Light & the Selective Excitation of the Photosystems on Recovery. **Business Addr:** LUTCF, The Prudential, 6805 Capital of Texas Hwy North, Ste 270, Austin, TX 78731.

HAUSER, CHARLIE BRADY
Educational administrator, legislator (retired). **Personal:** Born Oct 13, 1917, Yadkinville, NC; son of Callie V Hauser and Daniel M Hauser; married Lois Elizabeth Brown; children: Lois H Golding, Fay E Hauser-Price. **Educ:** Winston-Salem State Univ, BS 1936-40; Catholic Univ of Amer, 1941; Univ of PA, MS EdD 1946-47, 1950-51, 1956; TX Southern Univ, 1968. **Career:** 14th St Elementary School Winston Salem NC, teacher 1940-42; WV State Coll, instr 1947-50; Mary H Wright Elem School, principal 1951-55; Allen Univ, prof 1955-56; Winston-Salem State Univ, prof 1956-77, director of Teacher Educ 1968-76. **Orgs:** Bd mem Inter Municipal Coop Comm 1958-60; bd mem Dixie Classic Fair 1978-82; trustee Forsyth Tech Comm Coll 1977-93; former chmn bd Northwestern Reg ALANC; life mem, golden heritage, chmn NAACP; former chmn bd Patterson Ave Branch YMCA, former bd Mental Health Assn Forsyth

Cty; rep NC Gen Assembly 39th Dist 1983-84, 67th Dist 1985-86; life mem, NEA and Omega Psi Phi Fraternity; Forsyth Nursing Home Community Advisory Comm, Community Corrections Resources, Inc; board mem, Arts Council Winston-Salem, Forsyth County; Forsyth County Sr Democrats; YMCA Retired Men's Club; Bd American Heart Association, Winston-Salem; Prince's Feather Garden Club; Phi Delta Kappa Fraternity; Tanglewood Beautification Council. **Honors/Awds:** Cited by Bd of Governors of Univ NC 1977; Inducted Winston-Salem State Univ & CIAA/Sports Hall of Fame; Omega Man of the Year 1966 & 1984; plaques from various charitable, civic, educ and religious assns; awarded thirteen NAACP Million Dollar Club Medallions; named professor emeritus and awarded the degree of Doctor of Human Letters by Winston-Salem State University; Charles McLean-Sara Lee Corp, Comm Svc Awd; A Phillip Randolph Comm Svc Awd; The Kelly Alexander Sr. Humanitarian Awd; The Mental Health Bell Awd; YMCA, H E Staplefoote Awd; WSSU Alumni, Simon Green Atkins Distinguished Svc Awd; Northwestern Amer Lung Assn's, bd of dirs, honorary life mem. **Special Achievements:** Arrested in 1947 for refusing to move to the back seat of a Greyhound bus. **Military Serv:** AUS staff sgt; ETO Ribbon with 5 Battle Stars, Good Conduct Medal; 1942-45. **Home Addr:** 2072 K Court Ave, Winston-Salem, NC 27105.

HAVIS, JEFFREY OSCAR
Company executive. **Personal:** Born Dec 7, 1966, Chicago, IL; son of James & Thelma Havis; married Teterina Havis, Jul 16, 1993; children: Alexia Jade. **Educ:** Univ of IL at Champaign/Urbana, BS, mktg, 1990. **Career:** Northern Telecom, mktg intern, 1985-89; Otis Elevator, new equipment mgr, 1990-94; Rainbow Elevator Corp, gen mgr, 1994-; Executive Polishing, CEO, 1994-. **Orgs:** African Amer Elevator Professionals, pres, 1993-; Inroads Alumni Assn, 1990-; Minority Commerce Assn, 1988-90; Alpha Phi Alpha Fraternity, Inc, pres, 1987-. **Honors/Awds:** Dollar & Sense Magazine, Best & Brightest Business Professional, 1994. **Business Addr:** General Mgr, Rainbow Elevator Corp, 12620 Holiday Dr, Unit C, Chicago, IL 60658, (708)371-7700.

HAWES, BERNADINE TINNER
Computer company executive. **Personal:** Born Feb 16, 1950, Washington, DC; daughter of Geneva Childs Tinner and Bernard T Tinner; married William Hawes, Jul 23, 1971. **Educ:** Lincoln University, Lincoln Univ, PA, Phi Beta Kappa, BA, 1972; University of Pennsylvania, Philadelphia, PA, MA, 1980, ABD, 1980. **Career:** Lincoln University, Lincoln Univ, PA, research assistant, 1971-72; University City Science Center, Philadelphia, PA, director information systems, 1986-88, director research management, 1975-. **Orgs:** Chairperson, Black Alumni Society, 1990-91; member, United Way of SE Pennsylvania Fund Allocation, 1987-91; member, Women in Technology, 1986; board member, Philadelphia Doll Museum, 1988-91; board member, Application Development Center, 1987-91. **Business Addr:** Dir of Research Mgt, Univ City Science Ctr, 3624 Market St, Philadelphia, PA 19104.

HAWK, CHARLES N., JR.
Educator. **Personal:** Born Aug 10, 1931, Madison Hts, VA; married Amarylyiss Murphy; children: Charles Nathaniel III, Lloyd Spurgeon, Natalyn Nicole. **Educ:** Northwestern Univ School of Ed, BS 1953; Loyola Univ, MA 1966. **Career:** Chicago Public Schools, teacher 1953-56; Hoke Smith High Scool Atlanta, principal 1957-. **Orgs:** Mem Natl, Atlanta & GA Elem Prins Assoc, Natl Assoc Sec School Prins, NEA, Atlanta & GA Assoc Ed, Alpha Phi Alpha, Phi Delta Kappa, Mason,; bd mgrs YMCA; bd dirs Ralph C Robinson Boys Club, BSA. **Honors/Awds:** Outstanding Leadership Awd Boy Scouts Atlanta Reg 1969; Outstanding Leadership Awd YMCA 1974; Outstanding Leadership Awd Alpha Phi Alpha 1975. **Business Addr:** Principal, Hoke Smith High School, 535 Hill St SE, Atlanta, GA 30312.

HAWK, CHARLES NATHANIEL, III
Attorney, educational administrator. **Personal:** Born Oct 25, 1957, Atlanta, GA. **Educ:** Morehouse Coll, BA cum laude 1979; Georgetown Univ Law Center JD 1982. **Career:** Cooper & Weintraub PC, assoc 1982-83; Morehouse Coll, dir office of alumni affairs; Hawk Law Firm, attorney, currently. **Orgs:** Sec Deacon Bd Friendship Baptist Church 1978-; mem Council for Advancement and Support of Educ 1983-; chmn United Way Campaign Morehouse Coll 1983-; mem GA Bar Assn 1983-; of counsel Law Firm Cooper & Assoc 1983-; legal counsel Natl Black Alumni Hall of Fame 1983-; legal counsel Hank Aaron Found Inc 1984-; legal counsel Council of Natl Alumni Assoc Inc 1984-. **Honors/Awds:** Writer and dir of "Balls, Balloons, and Butterflies" presented 1981 Washington DC; artistic achievement Georgetown Univ Church Ensemble 1982; writer & dir "Black Gold" 1982 Washington DC; Serv Awd United Negro Coll Fund 1985. **Business Addr:** Attorney at Law, The Hawk Law Firm, 34 Peachtree St, Ste 1100, Atlanta, GA 30303, (404)681-1940.

HAWKINS, ANDRE
Educational administrator. **Personal:** Born Aug 1, 1953, Jacksonville, FL; son of Emma J Hawkins and Sylvester Hawkins; married Annette Campbell; children: Anika, Alicia, Antoinette. **Educ:** Univ of So CA, BA History 1971-75; FL Atlantic Univ, MEd Admin & Super, EdS Admin & Super 1976-85. **Career:** FL School for Boys, occupational counselor 1975-76, classroom teacher 1976-79; Indian River Comm Coll, academic counselor 1979, dir of educ 1979-82, dir of instructional serv 1982-86, asst dean of instruction 1986-. **Orgs:** Mem Univ of S CA Fla Atlantic Univ Alumni Assn 1976-; mem New Hope Lodge #450 1981-; mem Southern Regional Council on Black Amer Affairs 1981-; mem FL Adult Educ Assn 1981-; mem FL Adult & Comm Educ Assn 1982-; mem Amer Assn of Adult & Continuing Educ FACC 1982-; mem Ft Pierce Chamber of Comm St Luce Leadership I 1983-; pres 1986, chmn 1987 FL Assn of Comm Colls Indian River CC Chapt; bd of dirs St Lucie Co Learn to Read Literary Prog 1985-87; bd dirs FL Assn of Comm Colls 1987, St Lucie Co YMCA 1987; bd of dir, NY Mets Booster Club, 1987-; second vice pres, Florida Assn of Conn Colleges 1988, vice pres, 1989; bd of dir, Indian River Comm Mental Health Assn Inc 1989-; treasurer, Martin Luther King Jr Commemorative Comm,1989-. **Business Addr:** Asst Dean of Instruction, Indian River Community College, 3209 Virginia Ave, Fort Pierce, FL 34981.

HAWKINS, AUGUSTUS F.
Congressman (retired). **Personal:** Born Aug 31, 1907, Shreveport, LA; married Elsie. **Educ:** Univ of CA, AB economics 1931; attended grad classes Univ So CA Inst of Govt. **Career:** Elected to CA State Assembly 1934; US House of Reps 29th Dist of CA, congressman 1962-90. **Orgs:** In Congress, chmn House Educ & Labor Comm, chmn House Sub-comm Elementary, Secondary, and Vocational Ed, sponsored Economic Oppor Act, Vocational Educ Act, Equal Employment Oppor Sect of 1963 Civil Rights Act, sponsored the Humphrey-Hawkins Full Employment & Balanced Growth Act, Pregnancy Disability Act, Job Training Partnership Act, Youth Incentive Employment Act, Effective Schs Development in Educ Act; involved in many comm action progs including SE LA Improvement Action Council founder; Methodist; Mason. **Honors/Awds:** Author or co-author of more than 300 laws including one establishing CA low-cost housing prog, one which removed racial designations from all state documents.

HAWKINS, BENNY F., SR.
Dentist, periodontist, educator. **Personal:** Born Feb 27, 1931, Chattanooga, TN; son of Corinne Hawkins and Bennie Hawkins; married E Marie Harvey; children: Benny F Jr, Christopher Thomas, Rachel. **Educ:** Morehouse Coll, BS 1952; Meharry Med Coll, DDS 1958; Univ of IA, MS 1972, Certificate in Periodontics 1972. **Career:** USAF Dental Corps, lt col (retired) 1958-78; Univ of IA Coll of Dentistry, periodontics graduate, director, assoc prof periodontics 1978-93; Univ of IA, interim assoc provost, 1993-94, special advisor on minority affairs to provost & vp health sciences, 1995-. **Orgs:** Vestry Trinity Episcopal Church Iowa City 1980-83; bd dirs Iowa City Rotary Club 1982-84, 1991-93; 1998-2000; Human Rights Commission Iowa City 1983-86; vice pres Univ Dist Dental Soc 1984-85; pres Iowa Soc of Periodontology 1985-86; mem Amer Dental Assn, Amer Acad of Periodontology, Amer Assn of Dental Schools, Intl Assn for Dental Rsch; Omicron Kappa Upsilon Honorary Dental Fraternity, Iowa, president 1988-89; chairman, Organization of Post-Doctoral Periodontal Program Directors; president, Midwest Society of Periodontology 1992-93. **Honors/Awds:** Omicron Kappa Upsilon Hon Dental Frat Iowa 1980; Fellow Intl College of Dentists 1984; Distinguished Alumni of the Yr Awd (Meharry) Natl Assn for Equal Opportunity in Higher Educ 1986; American Coll of Dentists, Fellow. **Military Serv:** USAF Dental Corps lt col 1958-78; Air Force Commendation Medal 1976. **Business Addr:** Univ of Iowa, Coll of Dentistry Periodontics Dept, Iowa City, IA 52246, (319)335-7238.

HAWKINS, CALVIN D.
Attorney, clergyman. **Personal:** Born Jun 14, 1945, Brooklyn; son of Azalien Hawkins and Wallace Hawkins; married Lennie E James; children: Alia, Alex, Jason. **Educ:** Huntington Coll, AB 1967; Howard U, JD 1970; Wesley Theol Sem, MDiv 1974. **Career:** US Dept Just, atty 1971-74; Am U, asso chapl 1971-72; US Dept Just, comm rel splst 1971; Supreme Ct IN, admitted 1971; So Dist Ct IN, 1971; DC Ct Appeals, 1973; Dist Ct DC, 1973; Untd Ct Appeals DC, 1973; Supreme Ct USA 1974; Shropshire & Allen, Gary, IN, atty beginning 1974; attorney, currently. **Orgs:** Mem Am IN & Gary Bar Assns; DC Bar Unified; Thurgood Marshall Law Assn; ABA, Council on Urban State Local Govt Law Section; Huntington Coll, bd of trustees; Indiana Republican Platform Comm; Indiana Bd of Law Examiners; Indiana Bar Foundation; Bd of Legal Services of Northwest Indiana; First United Presbyterian Church of Gary, interim pastor; Lake County Bar Association; US Bankruptcy Ct, Northern Dist of Indiana, trustee. **Honors/Awds:** Nom Gov's Awd outstndg black coll student IN Civil Rights Comm 1965; social theol awd Martin Luther King Jr Hood Theol Sem 1971; Jonathan M Daniels Fellow Awd 1974; alumnus of yr awd Huntington Coll 1975; fellow awd Chicago Theol Sem 1976. **Business Addr:** Attorney, 4858 Broadway, PO Box M859, Gary, IN 46401.

HAWKINS, COURTNEY TYRONE, JR.
Professional football player. **Personal:** Born Dec 12, 1969, Flint, MI. **Educ:** Michigan State Univ. **Career:** Tampa Bay Buccaneers, wide receiver, 1992-96; Pittsburgh Steelers, 1997-. **Business Addr:** Professional Football Player, Pittsburgh Steelers, Three Rivers Stadium, 300 Stadium Circle, Pittsburgh, PA 15212, (412)323-1200.

HAWKINS, DORISULA WOOTEN
Educator. **Personal:** Born Nov 15, 1941, Mt Pleasant, TX; daughter of Artesia Ellis Wooten and Wilbur Wooten; married Howard Hawkins; children: Darrell, Derek. **Educ:** Jarvis Christian Coll, BS 1962; East TX State Univ, attended 1965; Prairie View A&M Univ, MS 1967; TX A&M Univ, attended 1970; Univ of Houston, EdD 1975. **Career:** Jarvis Coll, sec & asst public relations dir 1962-63; Roxton School Dist, instructor business 1963-66; Prairie View A&M Univ, assoc prof, 1966-96, head general business dept 1976-88; Jarvis christian Coll, dev officer, 1996-97, prof business administration, 1997-. **Orgs:** Adv bd Milady Publishing Co; exec bd mem TX Assn of Black Personnel in Higher Educ 1978-83; bd mem TX Bus Educ (TBEA) Assn 1978-83; pres Alpha Kappa Alpha 1982-85; chmn TX Business Thcr Educ Cncl 1985-87; mem Natl Bus Educ Assoc; mem Jarvis Christian Coll Bd of Trustees, 1986-88; pres Natl Alumni Assoc 1986-88. **Honors/Awds:** Dist Business Tchr of the Yr TBEA 1981; Disting Alumnus Jarvis Coll 1982; nominee State Tchr of Yr TBEA 1982; "Can Your Office Administration be Justified" TX Business Educator 1979; Disting Alumni Citation (NAFEO) 1986. **Business Addr:** Development Officer, Jarvis Christian College, PO Box Drawer G, Hawkins, TX 75765-0893.

HAWKINS, GENE
Educator. **Personal:** Born in Henderson, NC; son of Roxie Smith Hawkins and Argenia Hawkins Sr. **Educ:** Glassboro State, BS 1955; Temple Univ, MA 1969; Nova Univ, DEd 1976. **Career:** Dept Ford Twp Public Schools, math tchr 1955-64, chmn math dept/counselor 1957-67; Gloucester County Coll, dir financial aid 1968-74; The College Board, dir finan aid svcs. **Orgs:** Consultant ETS Upward Bound College Bd 1970-74; consultant Financial Aid Inst 1968-78; consultant HEW 1970-76; staff NJ Assn Coll & Univ Presidents 1982; treasurer Eastern Assn Financial Aid Adm 1973-75; mem Natl Councl Natl Assn Financial Aid Admin 1973-75; exec dir Glou County Economic Devel 1970-72; publicity dir NAACP 1963-66. **Honors/Awds:** Distinguished Alumni Award Glassboro State 1971; Black Student Unity Movement Award Glou County Coll 1970-71; Ten Yr Serv Award College Bd 1985; Distinguished Educator NJFOF Dir Assn 1979; Special Recognition NY Bd Educ 1982; Distinguished Service Award, New Jersey Student Financial Aid Administrators, 1989. **Military Serv:** USMC 1951-53. **Home Addr:** 3440 Market St, Ste 410, Philadelphia, PA 19104.

HAWKINS, HERSEY R., JR.
Professional basketball player. **Personal:** Born Sep 29, 1966, Chicago, IL. **Educ:** Bradley Univ, Peoria, IL, 1984-88. **Career:** Philadelphia 76ers, 1988-93; Charlotte Hornets, 1993-95; Seattle Supersonics, 1995-. **Honors/Awds:** NBA All-Rookie First Team, 1989. **Special Achievements:** NBA Draft, First round pick, #6, 1988. **Business Addr:** Professional Basketball Player, Seattle Supersonics, 190 Queen Anne Ave N, Seattle, WA 98109, (206)281-5850.

HAWKINS, HOWARD P.
Clergyman. **Personal:** Born Oct 19, 1900, Princeton, LA; married. **Educ:** Wshbrn Coll, BA 1931; Gmmn Theol Sem, BD 1934. **Career:** Christ Meth Epis Ch, ret mnstr; Ordnd Elder, 1931; Clrgymn, 45yrs itnrnt svc. **Orgs:** Pres Pasco WA Br NAACP 1962-66; mem Pasco Mnstrl Alli; Tri-Cities Mnstrl Alli; affil with Comm Actn & Com; Bntn-Frnkln Mtl Hlth Assn; Human Rights Com Srved on Ctzns AdvCom of Pasco Sch Dist No 1 1966-69; mem St Jms Chrstn Meth Epis Ch; mem AK-PCFC Conf of CME Ch; VFW. **Honors/Awds:** Mason Recip Am Thtr Mdl; 2 Brnz Bttl Strs; Vctry Mdl; Nat Def Mdl; Krn Serv Mdl; UN Serv Mdl; Armd Frcs Rsrv Mdl; helped to build 2 new chrs. **Military Serv:** AUS capt ret 1943-56; chpln.

HAWKINS, JAMES
Educational administrator (retired). **Personal:** Born Jul 2, 1939, Sunflower, MS; married Vivian D; children: Lisa, Linda. **Educ:** Western Michigan Univ, BS 1963; Wayne State Univ, MA 1967; Michigan State Univ, PhD 1972. **Career:** Pontiac Public School, teacher 1963-67, project dir 1967-68, principal 1968-72; Jackson MI Public School, asst supt 1973-75, deputy supt 1975-78; Benton Harbor Area School, supt 1978-84; Ypsilanti Public Schools, supt 1984-90; Assistant Supt Evanston, IL, 1990-91; Gary Community Schools, supt, 1991-97. **Orgs:** Mem Mayors Urban Entrp Com 1983-84, N Cntrl Regnl Lab 1984-85; State Prntshp Sch Rlthnshp Task Force 1984-85; Kappa Alpha Psi; Rotary Intl; NAACP; pres Mdl Cities Ed Assc 1984-85; mem Gamma Rho Boule 1986; bd of dirs United Way; Appointed by Governor to Governor's Commission in Community Service (Indiana), 1994. **Honors/Awds:** Otsdg com serv Benton Harbor Citizens Awrd 1983; man of yr Negro Bus & Prof Womens Clb 1977; guest aprnc Phil Donahue Show 1982; featured Articles People Mag Minimal Skills No Nonsense Ed 1982; Volunteer of the Year, Urban League of NW Indiana,

1992; Urban League of NW Indianam Outstanding Community Service Award, 1993-94; Mich State Univ, Outstanding K-12, Alumni Administrator of Year, 1994; Marcus Foster Outstanding Educator of the Year, NABSE, 1994. **Home Phone:** (219)938-6482. **Business Addr:** Superintendent of Schools, Gary Community School Corporation, 620 E 10th Place, Gary, IN 46402, (219)881-5400.

HAWKINS, JAMES C.
Corporate director (retired). **Personal:** Born Mar 26, 1932, Apalachicola, FL; son of Prudence Hawkins and Harold Hawkins; married Gloria M Edmonds; children: Brian, Cynthia. **Educ:** Univ of RI, BSME 1959; Northeastern Univ, MSEM 1971; MIT Sloane Sch 1977. **Career:** Rayethon Co & MIT Labs, sr engr 1966-68; Natl Radio Co, mgr of engrg 1968-70; consult 1971-77; Polaroid Corp, mgr 1973-77, sr mgr 1978-95, division mgr 1984, director 1989-95. **Orgs:** Int & ext consult various organs; past grand knight K of C; mem Actors Guild, ASME; CCD instructor; org & coach basketball team, tennis player, tutor, inst Karate; board of directors, Chamber of Commerce, Cambridge, MA, East Cambridge Savings Bank; trustee, Mount Auburn Hospital, Cambridge, MA; board of directors, YMCA. **Honors/Awds:** Scholarship LaSalle Acad; Cambridge Chamber of Commerce, chairman of the board, 1989-92. **Military Serv:** USAF 1951-55. **Business Addr:** Director of Technical Services, Polaroid Corp, 750 Main St-1C, Cambridge, MA 02139.

HAWKINS, JAMESETTA. See JAMES, ETTA.

HAWKINS, JOHN RUSSELL, III
Public affairs officer. **Personal:** Born Sep 7, 1949, Washington, DC; son of Mr & Mrs John Hawkins; married Michelle Mary Rector; children: John R IV, Mercedes Nicole. **Educ:** Howard Univ, BA 1971; Amer Univ, MPA 1976; Amer Univ Law Sch, JD 1979; Univ of London Law Faculty England, independent study. **Career:** Federal Trade Commn and US EEOC, personnel mgmt spec 1972-75; Pentagon Counterintelligence Forces US Army, admin ofcr 1975-77; Theoseus T Clayton Law Firm, law clerk 1979-80; US EEOC Public Affairs, asst dir for Public Affairs 1981-85; AUS Public Affairs, major 1986-. **Orgs:** Mem Phi Delta Phi Intl Law Frat 1978-; pres and chief counsel HRH Commercial Farms Inc of NC 1979-; cub scout leader Pack 442 1985-; treas St John the Baptist Home School Assoc 1986-; mem Kappa Alpha Psi. **Honors/Awds:** Sustained Superior Performance Federal Govt 1979-85; editorial writer for Washington Informer & Washington Afro 1985-86; Outstanding Young Men of Amer 1986. **Military Serv:** AUS major 10 yrs; Meritorious Service Medal, Army Commendation Medal, Army Achievement Medal. **Home Addr:** 2123 Apple Tree Lane, Silver Spring, MD 20904. **Business Addr:** Public Affairs Officer, Dept of the Army, Pentagon, Washington, DC 20310.

HAWKINS, LATROY
Professional baseball player. **Personal:** Born Dec 21, 1972, Gary, IN. **Career:** Minnesota Twins, pitcher, 1995-. **Business Addr:** Professional Baseball Player, Minnesota Twins, 501 Chicago Ave S, Minneapolis, MN 55415, (612)375-1366.

HAWKINS, LA-VAN
Restaurant executive. **Career:** La-Van Hawkins Inner City Foods, CEO, currently. **Special Achievements:** Company is ranked #93 on Black Enterprise's List of Top 100 Industrial/Service Companies, 1994. **Business Phone:** (404)816-7171.

HAWKINS, LAWRENCE C.
Educator, management consultant. **Personal:** Born Mar 20, 1919, Greenville, SC; son of Etta Hawkins and Wayman Hawkins; married Earline Thompson; children: Lawrence Charles Jr, Wendel Earl. **Educ:** Univ of Cincinnati, BA History 1941, BEd 1942, MEd 1951, EdD 1970; Univ of Cincinnati, AA (Hon) 1970, Wilmington College; Litt D, Cincinnati Technical College, attended. **Career:** Cert School Supt, elementary and secondary teacher 1945-52, school principal, dir 1952-67; Eastern MI Univ Ypsilanti, visiting asst prof 1955-60; Cincinnati Public Schools, asst supt 1967-69; Univ of Cincinnati, dean 1969-75, vice pres 1975-77, sr vice pres 1977-84; Omni-Man Inc, president, CEO 1981-; LCH Resources, pres, 1996-. **Orgs:** Bd of dir Wilimgton OH Coll 1980-90, Inroads/Cincinnati 1981; bd of dir Bethesda Hosp Deaconess Assn Cincinnati 1980-90; vice chmn Greater Cincinnati TV Ed Found WECT-TV 1983; co-chmn Cincinnati Area Natl Conf of Christians & Jews 1980-87; mem, Kappa Alpha Psi; bd of trustees Childrens Home 1978; adv bd on policy Cincinnati Council on World Affairs; mem, bd of directors, Mount St Joseph College 1989-93; trustee, vice chair, Student Loan Funding Corp, 1951-; mem, Cincinnati Assn, 1971-87; mem, Cincinnati Area Board Federal Reserve Bank, 1977-83; bd of dirs, Western-Southern Life Ins, 1990-. **Honors/Awds:** Awd of Merit Cincinnati Area United Appeal 1955, 1973; Certificate Presidents Council of Youth Opportunity 1968; City Cincinnati 1968; Charles P Taft Gumption Awd 1984; mem, Sigma Pi Phi, Kappa Delta Pi, Phi Delta Kappa; Cincinnati Area Natl Conference of Christians and Jews, Distinguished Service Award, 1988; Great Living Cincinnatian Award, Greater Cincinnati Chamber of Commerce 1989; Presidents Award, Public Relations Society of America, Cincinnati Chap, 1995. **Military Serv:** USAAF, lieutenant, Tuskegee Airman, 1942-45. **Business Addr:** President, LCH Resources, 3909 Reading Rd, Cincinnati, OH 45229, (513)861-4213.

HAWKINS, MARY L.
Educator, drug counselor. **Personal:** Born Mar 31, Columbus, GA; daughter of Eva Powell Hawkins-Robinson and Bruno Hawkins. **Educ:** Meharry Med Coll, Cert Dntl Hygn 1961; MI St U; Western MI U, BS 1976, MA 1979, SPADA, 1985; MI St Univ, rehabilitation cert candidate. **Career:** Benton Harbor Area Schools, Benton Harbor, MI, counselor/educator, currently; Link Crisis Intervention Center, St Joseph, MI, drug prevention educator, currently; Michigan Rehabiliation, Kalamazoo MI, substance abuse and vocational rehabilitation counselor, beginning 1988; Brass Foundation, Chicago, IL, project coordinator, 1986-87; Brrn Co Hlth Dept, sr dntl hygnst beg 1967; Priv Prac, dntl hygnst 1961-67. **Orgs:** Pres Nat Dntl Hygnst Assn 1973-75, pres elct 1971-73, vice pres 1970-71; mem Am Dntl Hygnst Assn 1961-; Business and Professional Women; Amer Assn of Univ Women; Natl Counselors Assn; Meharry Alumni Assn; spl consult Mnrty Affrs Com 1973-75; Tri-Co Hlth Plnrs Com 1970-75; mem NAACP 1963-; YWCA 1965-; Blossomland United Way, 1983-89; Operation PUSH, 1980—; Mrch of Dms 1970; member, EAP; member, MAADAC; member, NAADAC. **Honors/Awds:** Outstanding Dental Hygienist, Meharry's Alumni 1974; President's Award, Natl Dental Hygienists Assn, 1975. **Home Addr:** PO Box 320, St Joseph, MI 49085-0826.

HAWKINS, MICHAEL
Professional basketball player. **Personal:** Born Oct 28, 1972. **Educ:** Xavier (OH). **Career:** Boston Celtics, 1996-. **Business Addr:** Professional Basketball Player, Boston Celtics, 151 Merrimac St, 5th Fl, Boston, MA 02114, (617)523-6050.

HAWKINS, MURIEL A.
Educational administrator. **Personal:** Born Apr 22, 1946, Norfolk, VA; daughter of Frieda Robinson-Hawkins and George Hawkins; children: Jamal Scott. **Educ:** Univ of Health Scis Chicago Med Sch, BS 1974; The Citadel, MEd 1979; Loyola Univ of Chicago, PhD 1988. **Career:** Meharry Med Coll, radiographer/instructor 1967-70; Cook Co Hosp, clinical instructor 1970-76; Med Univ of SC/VA Med Ctr, instructor allied health 1976-79; Chicago State Univ, admin & asst prof 1980-. **Orgs:** Mem Phi Delta Kappa; mem Amer Soc Allied Health Prof; mem IL Soc Allied Health Prof; mem Amer Educ Rsch Assn; mem Midwest Rsch Assn; mem Assn of Supv & Curric Developers; mem Natl Soc of Allied Health; mem IL Comm on Black Concerns in Higher Educ; site visitor Joint Review Comm on Accreditation Radiography 1977-; recruitment specialist Clark Coll 1983; student affairs consultant/counseling Natl Coll of Educ 1984-88; enrollment mgt consult West Chester Univ 1985. **Honors/Awds:** Kellogg Fellow Amer Soc of Allied Health Professions 1983-84; "Role Modeling as a Strategy for the Retention of Minorities in Health Professions" presentation at annual ICBC meeting 1983 & Midwest Allied Health Symposium 1984 subsequently published in Journal of Ethnic Concerns; "Deaning in the Allied Health Professions," presentation at the ASAHP Annual Meeting Pittsburgh, PA 1986; ICEOP Fellow 1986-87; "Successful Coping Strategies for Black Graduate Students" Natl Conf of the AAHE Chicago, IL 1987; "Profile of An Allied Health Dean," Journal of Allied Health, 19:3, Summer 1990; Programs to Promote Minority Student Retention, paper, Annual Black Student Retention Conf, Las Vegas, 1991; "Mentorship and the Retention of First-Year College Students, paper, National Soc of Allied Health Mtgsh, DC, 1992; "Innovative Programs to Promote Student Persistence," paper, "Convention on College Composition of Communication, Cincinnati, 1992. **Home Addr:** 538 S Highland Ave, Oak Park, IL 60304. **Business Addr:** Dir, Academic Support Programs, Asst Prof, Radiological Sciences, Chicago State University, 9501 S King Dr, Chicago, IL 60628-1598.

HAWKINS, REGINALD A.
Dentist (retired), cleric. **Personal:** Born Nov 11, 1923, Beaufort, NC; son of Lorena Smith Hawkins and Charles Hawkins; married Anne Davidson Williams; children: Pauletta, Reginald Jr, Wayne, Lorena; married Catherine Elizabeth Richardson (divorced). **Educ:** Johnson C Smith Univ, BS 1948, BD 1956-85, MDiv 1973; Howard Univ, DDS 1948. **Career:** Private Practice Charlotte NC, dentist 1948-87; United Presbyterian Church, minister 1956-. **Orgs:** Chmn bd SE Reg Investment Corp; past pres Old N State Dental Soc, Charlotte Dental Soc; chmn Voter Reg Dr Mecklenburg Cty, Mecklenburg Org on Pol Affairs; guest lectr Princeton Univ 1966; fellow Royal Soc of Health 1973; mem Cncl on Admin Serv for United Presybterian Church USA; moderator/interim pastor of several churches in Catawba Presbytery; one of founders/mem Commn on Religion and Race of the United Presbyterian Church USA; NAACP; Kappa Alpha Psi; state pres, SCLC; Carolina Leg Black Caucus. **Honors/Awds:** Kappa Alpha Psi Awd 1960; Middle East Prov Outstanding Achievement Awd; Dentist of the Year 1962; Omega Citizen of the Year Alpha Kappa Alpha 1962; Johnson C Smith Univ, Hon Dr of Laws 1962; Scroll of Honor 1964; testified before US Sen Sub-Com on poverty 1965; Bruce W Klunder Meml Awd 1966; Alumni Awd Outstanding Achievement 1967; gubernat cand NC Dem pri 1968; Black Econ Devel Counc SBA 1968; Citation of Merit Old North St Dental Soc 1968; Awd Outstanding Civic Cont 1968; Dist Serv Awd Alpha Kappa Alpha Sor 1969; sued NC Dental Soc resulting in desegregation; sued NC Dept of Human Resources for reinstatement of medicaid benef its to adult dental patients & correction of other iniquities 1978; filed 1st civil rights suit against a YMCA which resulted in the admission of Negroes to all facilites; litigant in case challenging NC Pearsall Plan allowing state grants for students to private segregated schools; litigant against City of Charlotte challenging zoning laws, public discrimination & jobs; litigant against Charlotte-Mecklenburg School Bd for discrim; NC Black Legislative Caucus, Honor for Leadership in Politics and Civil Rights, 1996. **Military Serv:** US Army, dental corps, captain, 1951-53. **Business Addr:** Minister, United Presbyterian Church, 951 S Independence Blvd, Charlotte, NC 28208.

HAWKINS, STEVEN WAYNE
Attorney. **Personal:** Born Jul 10, 1962, Peekskill, NY; son of Ida Marie Boyd Hawkins and Peter Hawkins. **Educ:** Harvard Univ, BA, Economics, 1984; Univ of Zimbabwe, 1985-86; New York Univ, New York, NY, JD, 1988. **Career:** Honorable A Leon Higginbotham, Philadelphia, PA, law clerk, 1988-89; NAACP Legal Defense Fund, New York, NY, staff attorney, 1989-95; Natl Coalition to Abolish the Death Penalty, director, 1996-. **Orgs:** Bd of trustees, NY Univ, Ctr for Intl Studies, 1989-; comm mem, ABA Comm on Over-Representation of Minorities in the Criminal Justice System; mem, NY State Bar; mem, Bar of US Supreme Court. **Honors/Awds:** Skadden Fellow, Skadden, Arps, 1989-91; Ames Award, Harvard Univ, 1984; Rockefeller Fellow, Harvard Univ, Univ of Zimbabwe, 1985; American Jurisprudence Award, NY Univ Law School, 1987. **Business Addr:** Executive Director, NCADP, 1436 U St NW, Ste 104, Washington, DC 20009, (202)387-3890.

HAWKINS, THEODORE F. See Obituaries section.

HAWKINS, TRAMAINE
Gospel vocalist. **Personal:** marrIed Walter Hawkins (divorced); children: Jamie Hawkins, Trystan Hawkins; married Tommy Richardson; children: Demar Richardson. **Career:** Gospel vocalist. **Honors/Awds:** Dove Award for the traditional Black gospel album of the year, "Tramaine Hawkins Live!" 1991; Grammy Award. **Special Achievements:** Albums: "Tramaine Hawkins Live!"; "All My Best"; "O Happy Day," became the first of several of her gospel songs to cross over and become a hit on the country's pop music charts, 1969. **Business Addr:** Gospel Singer, c/o Sony Record, 1 Sony Dr., Park Ridge, NJ 07656, (201)930-1000.

HAWKINS, WALTER L.
Author, postal police, military official. **Personal:** Born Jan 17, 1949, Atlanta, GA; son of Walter & Helen Johnson Hawkins; married Carol H Hawkins, Jul 18, 1977; children: Winter L, Michael Donta, Whitney L. **Educ:** Atlanta Police Academy, 1971; Dekalb College, 1972; University of Georgia, 1977. **Career:** Atlanta Police Dept, police officer, 1971-72, detective, 1972-75; Fulton County Police, 1st Black sgt, 1975-82; Fulton County Sheriff Dept, sheriff, 1985-87; US Postal Inspection Service, postal police & chairman of Atlanta division's diversity committee, 1987-. **Orgs:** NAACP; NCOA; Millennial Lodge #537, MF&AM of W; Guiding Light Chapter #923; A-Plus. **Honors/Awds:** US Army Meritorious Service Medal, 1993, Commendation Medal, 1980, 1989; Fulton County Commissioners Proclamation "Walter Hawkins Day," 1994; City of Atlanta, Proclamation, "Walter Hawkins Day," 1994; US Postal Service Award, 1995. **Special Achievements:** Author: "African-American Biographies," 1992, 1994; author: "African-American Generals and Flag Officers," 1993. **Military Serv:** US Army, command sergeant major, 1968-70; USAR 1970-.

HAWKINS, WALTER LINCOLN. See Obituaries section.

HAWKINS, WILLIAM DOUGLAS
Business executive. **Personal:** Born May 14, 1946, Los Angeles, CA; son of Marian Parrish Hawkins and William D. Hawkins; married Floy Marie Barabino; children: William D, Yonnine, Kellie, Todd. **Educ:** Howard University, BA 1968. **Career:** US Congressman Samuel S Stratton, administrative assistant 1968-70; Security Pacific Natl Bank, commercial loan officer 1970-73; Natl Economic Management Association, sr vice president 1973-76; Korn Ferry Intl, managing associate 1976-84; The Hawkins Company, president 1984-. **Orgs:** Ed chair Black Businessmen's Assn of LA 1975; board of directors Boy Scouts of America, LA Council 1979-82; fundraiser LA Chapter United Negro College Fund 1984; member California Executive Recruiters Assn 1985; member NAACP; chairman Josephite Lay Advisory Bd 1988-92; bd of dir, LA Chapter American Red Cross, 1995-97; bd chair, College Bound, 1995-98; vp LA Archdiocese Catholic School Board, 1994-97. **Honors/Awds:** Award of Merit Boy Scouts of America 1977; Silver Beaver Boy Scouts of America 1989. **Business Addr:** President, The Hawkins Company, 5455 Wilshire Blvd., Ste 1406, Los Angeles, CA 90036.

HAWTHORNE, ANGEL L.
TV producer. **Personal:** Born May 31, 1959, Chicago, IL. **Educ:** Columbia Coll, BA 1981. **Career:** WLS-TV, desk asst 1980; ABC News, desk asst 1980-81, assignment editor 1981-85, field producer 1985-. **Business Addr:** Field Producer, ABC News, 190 N State St, Chicago, IL 60601.

HAWTHORNE, KENNETH L.
Business executive. **Personal:** Born in Mobile, AL; married Eugenia; children: Cecilia Hawthorne Patterson, Bruce, Bart. **Educ:** Pacific Western U, BBA; Univ of Pittsburgh, Tchng Cert. **Career:** New York City Dist Gulf Oil Corp, sales mgr 1971-73, mrktng mgr 1973-76; Gulf Trading & Transp Co (Gulf Oil Sub), vice pres 1976-81; Gulf Tire & Supply Co (Gulf Oil Sub), pres 1981-83; Gulf Oil Corp, mgr mgnt training dev; KLH & Associates, president, currently. **Orgs:** Mem Assoc Pet Inst 1978-84; mem Am Mgmt Asso 1978-; mem Am Soc for Training & Dev 1983-; bd mem Harlem YMCA Bd Mgr 1972-84; bd mem Houston NAACP Dinner Comm 1984; chm pub Houston UNCF Campaign 1984; Texas Southern University Business School, GRATUS, consultant; Hermann Hospital Society, advisory board; American Cancer Society, board. **Home Addr:** 2116 Embassy Dr, West Palm Beach, FL 33401.

HAWTHORNE, LUCIA SHELIA
Educator. **Personal:** Born May 6, Baltimore, MD; daughter of Daisy B Goins Hawthorne (deceased) and Edward W Hawthorne (deceased); divorced. **Educ:** Morgan State Univ, BS Lang Arts 1964; Washington State Univ, MAT Speech 1965; PA State Univ, PhD Speech Comm 1971. **Career:** Washington State Univ, teaching asst 1964-65; Morgan State Univ, instructor 1965-67; PA State Univ, teaching asst 1967-69; Morgan State, asst prof 1969-72, assoc prof 1972-75, assoc dean of humanities 1974-75, prof 1975-, chmn dept of speech comm & theatre 1972-75, 1984-87. **Orgs:** Chmn Commn on the Profession & Social Problems Speech Comm Assn 1972-75; mem Commn on Freedom of Speech Speech Comm Assn 1973-75; mem Bi-Lingual and Bi-Cultural Educ rep to TESOL for Speech Comm Assoc 1975-77; mem Speech Comm Assn, Eastern Comm Assn, MD Comm Assn, Assn of Comm Administrators; bd trustees Morgan Christian Ctr; life mem NAACP; Golden Heritage mem NAACP; Golden Life Member, Diamond Life Member, Delta Sigma Theta Sor Inc. **Honors/Awds:** Alpha Kappa Mu; Kappa Delta Pi; Lambda Iota Tau; Phi Alpha Theta; Promethean Kappa Tau; Alpha Psi Omega; Alpha Lambda Delta; Phi Eta Sigma; Danforth Assoc Danforth Found 1978-85; Academic Adminstrn Intern Amer Cncl on Educ 1974-75; Alumnus of the Year, Morgan State University, 1990-91; "Woman of The Year", Committee United to Save Sandtown, Inc, 1992. **Business Addr:** Professor, Morgan State University, Dept of Speech Communication, Baltimore, MD 21239.

HAYDEL, JAMES V., SR.
Life insurance chief executive. **Career:** Majestic Life Insurance Co Inc., New Orleans, LA, chief exec. **Business Addr:** Majestic Life Insurance Company Inc., 1833 Dryades St., New Orleans, LA 70113.

HAYDEN, AARON CHAUTEZZ
Professional football player. **Personal:** Born Apr 13, 1973, Detroit, MI. **Educ:** Tennessee, attended. **Career:** San Diego Chargers, running back, 1995-96; Green Bay Packers, 1997-. **Business Addr:** Professional Football Player, Green Bay Packers, 1265 Lombardi Ave, Green Bay, WI 54304, (414)494-2351.

HAYDEN, CARLA DIANE
Library administrator. **Personal:** Born Aug 10, 1952, Tallahassee, FL; daughter of Colleen Dowling Hayden and Bruce Kennard Hayden Jr; divorced. **Educ:** Roosevelt Univ, Chicago, IL, BA, 1973; Univ of Chicago, Chicago, IL, MA, 1977, PhD, 1987. **Career:** Chicago Public Library, Chicago, IL, children's librarian/library associate, 1973-79, young adult services coordinator, 1979-81; Museum of Science and Industry, Chicago, IL, library services coordinator, 1982-87; Univ of Pittsburgh, Pittsburgh, PA, assistant professor, 1987-91; Chicago Public Library, Chicago, IL, chief librarian/deputy commissioner, 1991-93; Enoch Pratt Free Library, director, 1993-. **Orgs:** Editor of newsletter, 1984-90, board member, 1990-93, Association for Library Services to Children, American Library Association; member, Black History Advisory Committee, Pennsylvania Historical and Museum Commission, 1988-91. **Honors/Awds:** Fred Hampton Humanitarian Award, 1980; Black & Hispanic Achievers Award, YMCA of Metro Chicago/Chicago Tribune, 1984; Kizzy Award, Revlon/Kizzy Scholarship Fund, 1991. **Business Addr:** Director, Enoch Pratt Free Library, 400 Cathedral St, Baltimore, MD 21201.

HAYDEN, FRANK
City official. **Personal:** Born in Quantico, VA. **Career:** City of Detroit, Department of Water and Sewage, contracts and grants manager, currently. **Orgs:** Wayne County Community Coll, District #3, trustee; American Water Works Association, mem; Public Affairs Council for AWWA, mem; Educational Task Force, mem; Michigan Minority Business Development Council, mem. **Honors/Awds:** MMBDC, Nominated for Coordinator of the Year. **Business Addr:** Contracts & Grants Manager, City of Detroit, Department of Water & Sewage, 735 Randolph, Detroit, MI 48226.

HAYDEN, JOHN CARLETON
Clergyman, educator. **Personal:** Born Dec 30, 1933, Bowling Green, KY; son of Gladys Gatewood Hayden and Otis Roosevelt Hayden; married Jacqueline Green; children: Jonathan Christopher Janani Hayden, Johanna Christina Jamila Hayden. **Educ:** Wayne State, BA 1955; Univ of Detroit, MA 1962; Coll of Emmanual & St Chad, LTh honors 1963; Howard U, PhD 1972; College of Emmanuel/St Chad, MDiv, 1991. **Career:** St Mary's School for Indian Girls, teacher, 1955; Detroit Public School, teacher, 1956-59; St Chad's Secondary School, instructor, 1962-64; Univ of Saskatchewan, Anglican chaplain, 1963-67, instructor in history, 1965-68; St George's Church, associate rector, 1968-71, 1973-82, 1986-87, Church of The Atonement, assistant, 1971-72; St Monica's Church, priest-in-charge, 1972-73; Howard Univ, asst professor of history, 1972-78, scholar in church history, 1978-79; Morgan State Univ, Department of History and Geography, chmn, 1979-86; Holy Comforter Church, rector, 1982-86; Frostburg State University, prof of history, 1986-87; Univ of the South School of Theology, associate dean, 1987-92; Episcopal Office for Black Ministries, consultant, 1992-94; St Michael and All Angels Church, priest-in-charge, 1992-94; Montgomery College, adjunct lecturer of history, 1992-94; Episcopal chaplain, lecturer in church history, Howard University, 1994-. **Orgs:** Ch Historical Soc; asso editor, "Episcopal Anglican History;" board of directors, 1975-85, Assn for Study of Afro-American Life & History; Am Historical Assn; Southern Historical Assn; Union of Black Episcopalians, Parliamentarian; pres, Saskatchewan Assn for Retarded Children, 1966-68; chmn youth conf, Saskatchewan Centennial Corp, 1964-67; Com for Community Improvement; pres, Black Episcopal Clergy, Washington Diocese, 1974-76; board of directors, Washington Urban League, 1980-87; board of directors, St Patrick's Episcopal Day School, 1981-87; secretary, board of trustees, St Mary's Episcopal Center, 1988-92; board of advisors, St Andrew's/Sewanee School, 1989-; Society for the Promotion of Christian Knowledge/USA Board, 1987-92; KANUGA Conference Center, program committee, 1989-93, diversity comm, board of advisors, 1996-; Evangelical Education Society, board of directors, 1992-; Washington Episcopal School, board of trustees, 1992-. **Honors/Awds:** Angus Dun Fellowship, 1973, 1974, 1978, 1989, 1995; Faculty Research Prog in the Social Sciences Award, 1973, 1974; Spencer Foundation Award, 1975; Am Philosophical Soc Award, 1976; Commn for Black Minsters, Grant, 1976-78; Bd For Theol Education, Fellowship, 1978-79; Robert R Moton Fellowship, 1978-79; Absalom Jones Award, 1987; Grambling University Award, Grambling State University, 1990; Kanuga Conference Center Award, 1991. **Business Addr:** Howard University, Episcopal/Anglican Ministry, PO Box 6, Washington, DC 20059.

HAYDEN, ROBERT C., JR.
Historian, author, educator. **Personal:** Born Aug 21, 1937, New Bedford, MA; son of Josephine Hughes Hayden and Robert C Hayden Sr; divorced; children: Dr Deborah Hayden-Hall, Kevin R Esq, Karen E. **Educ:** Boston Univ, Boston MA, BA, 1959, EdM, 1961; Harvard Univ, Cambridge MA, Certificate, 1966; Massachusetts Institute of Technology, Cambridge MA, Certificate, 1977. **Career:** Newton Public Schools, science teacher, 1961-65; Xerox Educ Division, science editor, 1966-69; Metropolitan Council for Educ Opportunity, Boston MA, exec dir, 1970-73; Educ Devel Center, Newton MA, project dir, 1973-80; Northeastern Univ, Boston MA, adjunct faculty, 1978-; Massachusetts Inst of Technology, Cambridge MA, dir, 1980-82; Boston Public Schools, Boston MA, exec asst to supt, dir project devel, 1982-86; Massachusetts Pre-Engineering Program, Boston MA, exec dir, 1987-91; Curry Coll, Milton MA, adjunct faculty, 1989-; University of Massachusetts, Boston, lecturer, 1993-; Art Inst of Boston, lecturer, 1994-; Schomburg Center for Research in Black Culture, scholar-in-residence, 1994-95; RCH Associates, president, currently. **Orgs:** Kappa Alpha Psi Frat, 1957; Natl Assn of Black School Educators, 1976-90; Black Educators Alliance of Massachusetts, 1980-92; secretary, Assn for Study of Afro-Amer Life and History, 1995-. **Honors/Awds:** Educ Press All-Amer Award, Educ Press Assoc of Amer, 1968; NAACP Serv Award, NAACP, 1973; Human Relations Award, Massachusetts Teachers Assn, 1979; Carter G Woodson Humanitarian Award, Omega Psi Phi, 1985; Martin Luther King Jr Award, Boston Public Schools, 1986; Humanitarian Serv Award, The Spiritual Assembly of the Baha'is of Boston, 1987. **Special Achievements:** Author: Eight African-American Scientists, 1970, Nine African-American Inventors, 1992; Eleven Black American Doctors, 1992; Boston's NAACP History 1910-1982, 1982; Faith, Culture and Leadership: A History of the Black Church in Boston, 1985; Singing For All People: Roland Hayes—A Biography, 1989; African-Americans in Boston: More Than 350 Years, 1991; African-Americans and Cape Verdean Americans in New Bedford, MA: A History of Achievement and Community, 1993; A Cultural Guide to African-American Heritage in New England, 1992; Multicultural Contributions to Science, 1996; Science & Technology: A Rich Heritage, 1997. **Business Addr:** President, RCH Associates, PO Box 5453, Boston, MA 02102.

HAYDEN, WILLIAM HUGHES
Investment banker. **Personal:** Born Apr 26, 1940, New Bedford, MA. **Educ:** Southeastern MA Univ, BS, BA 1962; New Eng Sch of Law, JSD 1967; New Sch for Social Rsch, cert 1968. **Career:** Atty Generals Office MA, 1963-67; US Dept of Treasury, 1966-67; Pres Comm on Civil Disorders, asst dir cong relations 1967-; NY State Urban Devel Corp, reg dir 1968-73; Grapetree Bay Hotels Co, gen partner 1973-75; E End Resources Corp, pres 1973-75; Metro Applied Rsch Ctr, sr fellow 1974-75; First Boston Corp, managing dir 1975-84; Bear Stearns & Co, managing dir, partner 1984-. **Orgs:** Former dir Wiltwyck Sch for Boys 1976-78; bd of dirs Urban Home Ownership Corp 1977; bd of dirs United Neighborhood Houses New York City 1977-; former dir First Women's Bank of NY 1979; trustee Citizen's Budget Comm City of NY 1981-; dir natl Assoc of Securities Profls.

HAYE, CLIFFORD S.
Attorney. **Personal:** Born Dec 20, 1942, New York; son of Sylvia Haye and Clifford Haye; married Jenelyn; children: Angela, Christopher. **Educ:** MI State Univ, NC Coll, BA 1966; Columbia Law Sch, JD 1972. **Career:** US Dept of Justice, trial attorney 1972-73; NY Stock Exchange, enforcement atty 1973-74; Teachers Ins Ann Assn, asst gen counsel, beginning 1974, senior counsel, currently. **Orgs:** Comm to elect Charles Evers Gov 1971; vol atty Comm Law Offices 1974-78; atty Indigent Panel Kings Co 1975-79; exec comm The Edges Group 1982-; bd mem Citizens Advocates for Justice 1983-. **Military Serv:** AUS 1st lt 1966-1969. **Business Addr:** Senior Counsel, TIAA-CREF, 730 3rd Ave, New York, NY 10017.

HAYES, ALBERTINE BRANNUM
Educator. **Personal:** Born Apr 3, Lake Providence, LA; married James T. **Educ:** So U, BS 1940; Univ of MI, MA 1952; George Peabody Coll for Tchr, specialist in edn; Univ of OK, EdD. **Career:** Caddo Parish Sch Bd, asst supt for comm affairs; Natchitoches Paris Sch LA, thcr; Lake Charles City Sch LA, tchr; Caddo Parish Sch LA, tchr; Booker T Washing HS Caddo Parish Sch, asst prin in charge of instr; Caddo Parish Sch, supr math sci edn; Centenary Coll LA, lecturer in edn; So Univ LA, prof of edn; NE State Univ LA, guest prof. **Orgs:** Vp Pride of Carroll Burial Ins Co Inc Lake Providence LA; vice pres Hayes Flower Shop Inc Shreveport LA; vice chmn United Way 1974; bd dir Intergrated Youth Svc; bd Dir United Way 1975; bd dir Shreveport Chap Am Red Cross. **Honors/Awds:** Zeta Woman of Yr 1965; Eucator of Yr. **Business Addr:** 1961 Midway, PO Box 37000, Shreveport, LA.

HAYES, ALVIN, JR.
Attorney. **Personal:** Born Apr 11, 1932, Cedar Rapids, IA; married Julia Wilburn; children: Alvin Douglas III, Robert Ellis. **Educ:** BA 1958; Univ of Bsd Law Sch, BLegal Languages 1961. **Career:** Agrico Chem Co, labor and EEO cnsl; WA State Hum Rights Commn, dir 1973-74; Priv Prac, law 1961-69; Woodbury Co, asst atty 1964-69. **Orgs:** Mem William Frank & Powell Consistory; Decatur Lodge #14; NAACP; Urban League; Share through Adoption; bd dir Alvin Douglas Hayes III Corp; mem Citizens Task Force; IA Bar Assn9; Sioux City Bar Assn; LS Dist Ct for No Dist fo IA; OK Bar Assn; Fed Dist Ct for the N Dist of OK. **Honors/Awds:** Award for outstanding performance in field of civil rights from Gov Robert D Ray 1973; award Outstanding Exec Dir of the IA Civil Rts Commin 1977. **Military Serv:** AUS sp3 1953-55. **Business Addr:** PO Box 3166, Tulsa, OK 74101.

HAYES, ANNAMARIE GILLESPIE
Educator. **Personal:** Born Sep 6, 1931, Flint; married Emery M; children: Colon, Marcus. **Educ:** MI St, BA, MA, MS, PhD. **Career:** Pontiac Public Schools, Inkster Public Schools, public school teacher; MI-OH Regional Lab, teacher trainer; MI State Univ, educ specialist; Univ WI Madison, rsch assoc; Coll of Educ Wayne State Univ, presently assoc prof. **Orgs:** Nat Assn Negro Bus & Professional Women; Nat Assn Black Fin Aid Adminstr; Nat All Black Educ; Am Educ Resrch Assn; Assn Study Negro Life & Hist; bd dir Intl Afro-Am Museum; Shrine Black Madonna Detroit; Councilwoman Erma Henderson Women's Concerns Conf. **Honors/Awds:** Woman of yr awd MI State Univ 1971; USAF Europe awd 1972; fellow resrch Williams Coll.

HAYES, CHARLES
Elected official. **Personal:** Born Oct 14, 1943, Catherine, AL; married Muriel. **Educ:** Selma Univ, Assoc 1971; Wallace Comm Coll, diploma 1973; Mobile Bus Coll, diploma 1970; Univ of S Alabama, further study 1983; Dale Carnegie, 1984. **Career:** 4th Judicial Circuit, spec investigator dist atty, indigent def comm; Wilcox Co, commissioner. **Orgs:** Mem Alberta Comm Health Clinic 1981-84; dir Alberta Comm Club 1983-85; mem Assn of Co Commissioners 1982-; deacon Salem Baptist Church 1982-; dir Alberta Comm Fire Dept 1984-; mem Wilcox Co Democratic Conf; mem AL Democratic Conf Black Caucus. **Honors/Awds:** Outstanding Leadership Awd Alberta Comm Club-Alberta AL 1984. **Military Serv:** AUS sgt E-5 1964-69; Code of Conduct Awd. **Home Addr:** Rt 1, Box 88, Catherine, AL 36728.

HAYES, CHARLES A. See Obituaries section.

HAYES, CHARLES LEONARD
Educator. **Personal:** Born Dec 16, 1921, Baton Rouge, LA; married Bette Harris; children: Charles Jerome, Jaime. **Educ:** Leland Coll, AB 1947; Loyola U, EdM 1949; Univ No CO,

EdD 1958. **Career:** Chicago, teacher 1948-49; NC A&T State Univ, instr 1949-52, asst prof 1952-56, prof 1958-61, chmn 1961-66; George Washington Univ, ace fellow 1966-67; US Office of Educ HEW, chief 1967-69; Albany State Coll, pres 1969-80; NC A&T State Univ, chmn beginning 1980, adjunct faculty, currently. **Orgs:** Am Assn of Univ Profs; Assn of Higher Edn; NEA; Phi Delta Kappa; Am Personnel & Guidance Assn; Am Coll Personnel Assn; Assn of Counselor Educators & Suprs; NC Psychol Assn; Kappa Delta Pi; bd dir Albany Urban League; Albany USO Council; exec bd Chehaw Council Boy Scouts of Am; Nat Conf of Christian& Jews; YMCA; Citizens Adb Com; mem Drug Action Council, Volunteers to the Courts. **Military Serv:** USN skd1c 1942-46. **Business Addr:** Adjunct Faculty Member, NC A&T State University, 1601 E Market St, Greensboro, NC 27411.

HAYES, CHARLIE (CHARLES DEWAYNE)
Professional baseball player. **Personal:** Born May 29, 1965, Hattiesburg, MS. **Educ:** Forrest County Agricultural. **Career:** San Francisco Giants, 1988-89; Philadelphia Phillies, third baseman, 1990-92; Colorado Rockies, professional baseball player, 1993-94; Philadelphia Phillies, 1995; Pittsburgh Pirates, 1996; New York Yankees, 1996-97; San Francisco Giants, 1998-. **Business Addr:** Professional Baseball Player, San Francisco Giants, 3 Com Park, San Francisco, CA 94124, (415)468-3700.

HAYES, CHRIS
Professional football player. **Personal:** Born May 7, 1972, San Bernardino, CA; children: Chris Jr. **Educ:** Washington State. **Career:** Green Bay Packers, defensive back, 1996; New York Jets, 1997-. **Business Addr:** Professional Football Player, New York Jets, 1000 Fulton Ave, Hempstead, NY 11550, (516)560-8100.

HAYES, CURTISS LEO
Educator/substitute teacher. **Personal:** Born Jan 10, 1931, Glasgow; married Opal Juanita Owens; children: Janice R Almond, Curtiss L Jr, Collin L. **Educ:** Morningside College, BA 1956; AZ State Univ, MA 1974; Dallas Theological Seminary, ThM 1980. **Career:** Secondary Public Schools, teacher 1956-75; Sudan Interior Mission, Christian educ coord 1980-84; Liberian Baptist Theol Seminary, theology instructor 1982-83; Dallas Bible College, missionary in residence 1984-85; Dallas Independent School Dist, substitute teacher. **Orgs:** Mem NAACP 1956; pres Desert Sands Teachers Assoc 1972; mem Stull Bill Steering Comm 1973; mem Natl Educ Assoc 1973; licensed minister Mt Zion Baptist Church 1980; instructor Monrovia Bible Inst 1982. **Honors/Awds:** College Orator Morningside College 1954; Diamond Key Awd Natl Forensic League 1972; Masters Rsch Project AZ State Univ 1974; Masters Thesis Dallas Theol Seminary 1980. **Military Serv:** AUS corpl 2 yrs; Honorable Discharge. **Business Addr:** Dallas Independent School Dist, 3807 Ross St, Dallas, TX 75204.

HAYES, EDWARD, JR.
Attorney. **Personal:** Born Jun 19, 1947, Long Branch, NJ; son of Bessie E Dickerson Hayes and Edward Hayes; married Alice Hall; children: Blair Hall, Kia Hall. **Educ:** Wesleyan Univ, BA 1969; Stanford Law Sch, JD 1972. **Career:** Commr Mary Gardner Jones FTC, clerk 1971; Citizens Communications Center, atty 1972-74; Hayes & White, partner atty 1974-84; Baker & Hostetler, partner atty 1984-92; US Department of Health and Human Service, counselor to the secretary; Hayes & Associates, founding partner. **Orgs:** Supreme Court Bar; DC Bar; bd mem National Capital YMCA; adv comm African Development Fund; bd mem Inst of Intl Trade & Devel; chmn, DC Chamber Intl Trade Comm. **Honors/Awds:** Articles publ Natl Bar Assn; Natl Assn of Broadcasters; Natl Assn of Black Owned Broadcasters; Cablelines Magazine. **Business Addr:** Counselor to the Secretary, Department of Health and Human Services, 1155 Connecticut Ave, NW, Washington, DC 20036, (202)429-6532.

HAYES, ELEANOR MAXINE
Television anchor/reporter. **Personal:** Born Feb 9, 1954, Cleveland, OH; daughter of Ruth Hayes and Jimmy Hayes. **Educ:** El Instituto Tecnologico de Monterrey, Monterrey, Mexico, 1971; Western Coll, Oxford, OH, 1972; Oberlin Coll, Oberlin, OH, Bachelors Degree, 1976. **Career:** WERE Radio, Cleveland, OH, anchor, reporter, 1976-79; WTOL-TV, Toledo, OH, investigative reporter; WTVF-TV, Nashville, TN, anchor; WISN-TV, Milwaukee, WI, co-anchor, 1983-87; WJW-TV 8, Cleveland, OH, co-anchor, 1987-. **Orgs:** Bd mem, American Sickle Cell Anemia Assn, 1989-. **Honors/Awds:** Emmy Award, Natl Assn of Television Arts & Sciences, 1990; Volunteer Achievement, United Black Fund of Greater Cleveland, 1991.

HAYES, ELVIN E., SR.
Business executive, professional basketball player (retired). **Personal:** Born Nov 17, 1945, Rayville, LA; married Erna; children: Elvin Jr, Erna Jr, Erica, Ethan. **Career:** San Diego Rockets, 1968-71, Houston Rockets, 1971-72, 1981-84, Baltimore Bullets, 1972-73, Capital Bullets, 1973-74, Washington Bullets, 1974-81; Greater Cleveland Ford-Mercury Inc, CEO, currently. **Honors/Awds:** All Star every year in the NBA; All Amer every year at Houston; Coll Player of the Yr 1968; only player in NBA history to have more than 1,000 rebounds every year; missed only six of 984 games in pro career; 4th all time minutes played (highest of active players); top active player in rebounds (5th all time); 7th all time scorer (one of 6 NBA players to score 20,000 pts & pull down 10,000 rebounds); 8th in NBA scoring 1979; 5th in rebounding; 5th in blocked shots. **Business Addr:** CEO, Greater Cleveland Ford-Mercury, Inc, PO Box 148, Cleveland, TX 77328-1148.

HAYES, FLOYD WINDOM, III
Educator. **Personal:** Born Nov 3, 1942, Gary, IN; son of Thelma Ruth Person Hayes and Charles Henry Hayes; married Charlene Moore; children: Tracy, Keisha, Ndidi, Kia-Lillian. **Educ:** Univ of Paris, Cert d'Etudes 1964; NC Central Univ, BA (Cum Laude) 1967; Univ of CA Los Angeles, MA (w/Distinction) 1969; Univ of MD, PhD 1985. **Career:** Univ of CA Los Angeles, instruction specialist 1969-70; Princeton Univ, lecturer dept of pol exec sec Afro-Amer studies 1970-71; Swarthmore Coll, vstg lecturer dept of history 1971; Univ of MD, asst coord Afro-Amer studies 1971-73, instructor 1971-77; Cornell Univ, instructor Africana studies 1977-78; Close Up Found, prog instructor 1979-80; Howard Univ, res asst, res fellow inst for the study of ed policy 1980-81, 1981-85; US Equal Employment Oppor Com, special asst to chmn 1985-86; San Diego State Univ, asst prof Africana studies 1986-. **Orgs:** Consultant Union Township Sch System 1971, Comm Educ Exchange Prog Columbia Univ 1972, MD State Dept of Educ 1973-75; mem Early Childhood Educ Subcomm FICE US Dept of Educ 1986. **Honors/Awds:** Outstanding Young Men of Amer 1977; Phi Delta Kappa Professional Educ Frat Howard Univ Chap 1982; "The Future, A Guide to Information Sources," World Future Soc 1977; "The African Presence in America Before Columbus," Black World July 1973; "Structures of Dominance and the Political Economy of Black Higher Education," Institute for the Study of Educational Policy Howard Univ 1981; "The Political Economy, Reaganomics, and Blacks," The Western Journal of Black Studies 1982; "Politics and Education in America's Multicultural Society," Journal of Ethnic Studies 1989; "Governmental Retreat and the Politics of African American Self-Reliant Development," Journal of Black Studies 1990. **Business Addr:** Asst Prof, San Diego State University, Dept of Africana Studies, San Diego, CA 92182.

HAYES, GRAHAM EDMONDSON
Attorney. **Personal:** Born Nov 2, 1929, Horton, KS; children: Sondra, Karen, Graham II, Alisa. **Educ:** Washburn U, AB 1956; Washburn U, JD 1957. **Career:** Sedgwick Co, dep dist atty 1958-62; KS Commn on Civil Rights, atty 1970-74; Wichita Commn on Civil Rights, examiner 1974; Wichita Commn on Civil Rights, atty 1975-; Private Practice, attorney at law. **Orgs:** Mem Supreme Ct of US; US Ct of Claimes; Tax Ct of US; US Dist Ct; Circuit Ct of US; Supreme Ct of KS; USAF Bd for Correction of Mil Records; St Bd of Law Examiners of KS; bd of dirs KS Trial Lawyers Assn; Am Trial Lawyers Assn; Nat Assn of Criminal Def Lawyers; past pres Urban League of Wichita; mem VFW Post 6888; Kappa Alpha Psi. **Honors/Awds:** Appt ExmnR 1976; KS State Bd for Admission of Attorneys 1979. **Military Serv:** USAF 1948-52. **Business Addr:** Attorney at Law, 2431 N Belmont St, Wichita, KS 67220-2830.

HAYES, ISAAC
Singer, songwriter, actor. **Personal:** Born Aug 20, 1942, Covington, TN; son of Eula and Isaac Hayes Sr; children: Veronica, Heather, Felicia, Ike III, four others. **Career:** As youth sang with various gospel & rythm & blues groups; played piano and saxophone in nightclubs; began writing songs with David Porter for Stax Records 1962; had pop and soul hits with songs by Burt Bacharach, Jimmy Webb; composer musical score film Shaft (1971); tv appearances: Rockford Files, A-Team; film appearances: I'm Gonna Git You Sucka; Escape From New York; Posse, 1993. **Honors/Awds:** Albums recorded include Black Moses (1971), Hot Buttered Soul (1969), Enterprise: His Greatest Hits, Hotbed (1978), Isaac Hayes Movement (1970), To Be Continued, Greatest Hit Singles (with Dionne Warwick), A Man and A Woman, U-Turn (1986), Don't Let Go (1979, gold album), Love Attack (1988), Branded; co-wrote Deja Vu, 1979, for Dionne Warwick; winner of numerous awards, including Oscar (Acad of Motion Picture Arts & Sci) 1972, Grammy.

HAYES, J. HAROLD, JR.
TV journalist. **Personal:** Born Apr 21, 1953, Pittsburgh, PA; son of Gladys Burrell Hayes and J Harold Hayes; married Iris Dennis Hayes, Jan 28, 1984; children: Kristin Heather, Lindsay Victoria. **Educ:** University of Pittsburgh, Pittsburgh, PA, BA, 1971-75. **Career:** WSIV-AM, Pekin, IL, announcer, 1976-77; WRAU-TV, Peoria, IL, weekend anchor/reporter, 1977-79; KDKA-TV, Pittsburgh, PA, reporter, 1979-. **Orgs:** Member, National Association of Black Journalists, 1987-; Trustee, Mt Ararat Baptist Church. **Business Addr:** News, KDKA-TV, 1 Gateway Center, Pittsburgh, PA 15222.

HAYES, JIM
Mayor. **Career:** City Council of Fairbanks, former councilman; State of Alaska, Consumer Protection Office, investigator, currently; City of Fairbanks, mayor, 1992-. **Special Achievements:** First African American to hold the post of Mayor in Alaska. **Business Phone:** (907)459-6881.

HAYES, JONATHAN MICHAEL
Professional football player. **Personal:** Born Aug 11, 1962, South Fayette, PA. **Educ:** Univ of Iowa, degree in criminology, 1986. **Career:** Kansas City Chiefs, tight end, 1985-. **Honors/Awds:** Considered one of the finest blocking tight ends in the NFL. **Business Addr:** Professional Football Player, Kansas City Chiefs, One Arrowhead Dr, Kansas City, MO 64129-1651.

HAYES, LEOLA G.
Educator. **Personal:** Born in Rocky Mount, NC; married Spurgeon S. **Educ:** BS; MA; MS prof diploma; PhD 1973. **Career:** William Paterson Coll of NJ, chmn Special Educ Dept, currently; Fair Lawn NJ, supervisor, spl educ 1957-64; Fair Lawn NJ, teacher of handicapped children; Blind Chicago, consultant 1954-57; Blind NY Inst for Blind, teacher 1953-54. **Orgs:** CEC; Vocational Rehab Soc; AAMD; NJEA; Drug Abuse Prog 1973-; Young People Counseling Session, Alpha Kappa Alpha Sorority. **Honors/Awds:** Recipient: Human Relations Award, Natl Bus & Professional Women; Nat Comm Ldrs Award; Hannah G Solomon Award; Ernest Melly Award. **Business Addr:** Professor of Special Education, William Paterson College, 300 Pompton Rd, Wayne, NJ 07470.

HAYES, MARION LEROY
Educator (retired). **Personal:** Born Dec 23, 1931, Jefferson Co, MS; son of Irene Rollins Hayes and Lindsey J Hayes; married Louise. **Educ:** Alcorn St Univ, BS 1961; South Univ, MEd 1971. **Career:** Hazelhurst Pub Sch, teacher 1961-66; Jefferson Co Sch, asst prin tchr 1966-75, supt of educ, (retired). **Orgs:** Mem Amer Assn of Sch Admin, Natl Educ Assn, MS Assn of Sch Supts, MS Assn of Educ, Jefferson Co Tchrs Assn; bd mem Copiah-Lincoln Jr Coll; planning bd chmn town of Fayette; bd of gov Educ Secur. **Honors/Awds:** Star Teacher MS Econ Coun 1970-72. **Military Serv:** USAF E-5 1950-54; US Army E-5 1956-60. **Home Addr:** PO Box 368, Fayette, MS 39069.

HAYES, MELVIN ANTHONY
Professional football player. **Personal:** Born Apr 28, 1973, New Orleans, LA. **Educ:** Mississippi State, attended. **Career:** New York Jets, guard, 1995-96; Tennessee Oilers, 1997-. **Business Addr:** Professional Football Player, Tennessee Oilers, c/o Baptist Sports Park, 7640 H 70-5, Nashville, TN 37221.

HAYES, MERCURY
Professional football player. **Personal:** Born Jan 1, 1973, Houston, TX. **Educ:** University of Michigan, bachelor's degree in communications. **Career:** New Orleans Saints, wide receiver, 1996-97; Atlanta Falcons, 1997-. **Business Addr:** Professional Football Player, Atlanta Falcons, Two Falcon Place, Suwanee, GA 30174, (404)945-1111.

HAYES, RICHARD C.
Educational administrator. **Personal:** Born Dec 13, 1938, Carbondale, IL; son of Eurma C Jones Hayes and William Richard Hayes Sr; married Joyce L Harris Hayes, Mar 19, 1961; children: Clinette Steele, Rachaelle Ruff, Richard. **Educ:** BA 1967; MA 1975. **Career:** So IL U, asst dir student development, asso u affirm action ofcr, internal compliance ofcr; Gov's Ofc Human Resources, dir; IL State Employment Svc, employment coord; SIU, acad adv gen studies; Carbondale, planning operator 1963-66. **Orgs:** Mem chmn Affirmative Action Officers Assn 1972-; consult AA/EEO; exec com Nat AAAO; past pres, Carbondale NAACP; Bethel AME Ch; past member, Tuscan Lodge #44 PHA; pres, Services for Seniors of Jackson County. **Military Serv:** USN 1956-58. **Business Addr:** Asst Director, Student Development, Southern Illinois University, Carbondale, Bldg T-40, Carbondale, IL 62901.

HAYES, ROLAND HARRIS
District court judge. **Personal:** Born Feb 4, 1931, Winston-Salem, NC; son of Juanita Hayes and John Hayes; married Barbara Spaulding; children: Roland Jr, John F, Reba J. **Educ:** Winston-Salem State Univ, BS 1952; NC Central Univ School of Law, JD 1971. **Career:** Wachovia Bank & Trust Co, asst cashier 1952-68; Legal Aid Soc of Forsyth Cty, staff atty 1971-72; Richard C Erwin Atty at Law, assoc atty 1972-74; General Practice, atty 1974-84; State of NC, Dist Court Judge, 1984-. **Orgs:** National Bar Association, 1985; mem Forsyth Cty Bar Assn 1971-, NC Bar Assn 1971-, Amer Bar Assn 1971-; mem NC Assn of Black Lawyers 1974-; mem Winston-Salem Bar Assn 1974-; Elder Cleveland Ave Christian Church; life mem NAACP; mem Omega Psi Phi Frat; mem Phi Alpha Delta Law Frat, mem Bachelor Benedict Club; NC Association of District Court Judges. **Honors/Awds:** Outstanding Civic Leaders of America, 1968; Cooperative Office Occupations Employer of the Year, 1980; Citizen of the Year, Omega Psi Phi Fraternity Inc, 1984; Man of the Year, Outstanding Achievement Award, Alpha Kappa Alpha Sorority Inc, 1986; Achievement Award, Winston-Salem Urban League, 1988; Distinguished Alumni Award, Natl Assn for Equal Opportunity in Higher Educ, 1990; Sara Lee Corp, Charles McLean Community Service Award, 1993; Achievement Award, Natl Women of Achievement, 1994. **Business Addr:** District Court Judge, State of NC, PO Box 20099, Winston-Salem, NC 27120-0099, (910)761-2478.

HAYES, VERTIS
Painter, sculptor, educator, lecturer. **Personal:** Born May 20, 1911, Atlanta, GA; son of Willa Hayes and Lather Hayes; married Florence Alexander; children: Vertis Jr, Gregory. **Educ:** Attended Natl Acad of Design, Florence Kane Sch of Art, Art Students League NY. **Career:** Fed Art Proj NYC, mural painter 1934-38; LeMoyne Coll TN, tchr chmn dept fine art 1938-49; Hayes Acad of Art, founder dir 1947-52; CA State Coll Immaculate Heart Coll, painter sculptor lecturer 1971-74. **Orgs:** Mem Painting & Sculpture Commn; mem Family Savs & Loan Assn, Home Savs & Loan Assn, Harrison-Ross ortuaries; 32 Degree Mason; past mem Harlem Artists Guild 1936-38; artists union. **Honors/Awds:** Carter Found Grant 1965; Founding Fellow Black Acad of Arts & Letters Inc 1969; Creative Comm Awd Art Inst of Boston 1971; Hon Degree Art Inst of Boston 1971.

HAYES-GILES, JOYCE V.
Gas company executive. **Personal:** Born in Jackson, MS; daughter of Myrtle Stigger Hayes and Isaac Hayes; married Ronald Giles; children: Kristen, Erica. **Educ:** Knoxville Coll, BA 1970; Univ of Detroit, MBA 1978; Wayne State Law Sch, JD 1985. **Career:** Chrysler Corp, salary admin analyst/supv 1971-76; Auto Club of MI, compensation adminr 1976-78; MichCon Gas Co, dir matl mgmt & other managerial positions, vice pres corporate resources, managing dir, currently. **Orgs:** Mem Natl Black MBA Assoc 1978-; exec comm & bd mem Amer Red Cross 1984; mem Detroit Bar Assoc 1985-, MI Bar Assoc 1986-; mem Natl Purchasing Assoc 1986-; chairperson personnel com vice pres of bd YWCA 1986-; life mem NAACP; mem Links Inc, Delta Sigma Theta Sor Inc; pres, Metropolitan YWCA 1988-89; Jack & Jill of America; board member, Detroit Urban League. **Honors/Awds:** Leadership Detroit Grad Chamber of Commerce 1982; Minority Achiever in Industry YWCA 1984; NAACP 100 Club Awd. **Business Addr:** Vice President, Corporate Resources, MichCon Gas Co, 500 Griswold, Detroit, MI 48226.

HAYES-JORDAN, MARGARET
Health services company executive. **Personal:** Born Jan 1, 1943; divorced; children: Fawn, Frederick. **Educ:** Georgetown University, Washington, DC, BSN, 1964; University of California-Berkeley, Berkeley, CA, MPH, 1972. **Career:** San Bernardino Community Hospital, San Bernardino, CA, staff nurse, 1964-65; Visiting Nurse Association of San Francisco, San Francisco, CA, public health nurse, 1966-67, private duty nurse, 1967-68; Comprehensive Child Care Project, Mt. Zion Hospital, San Francisco, CA, senior public health nurse, 1968-71; Lester Gorsline Associates, Terra Linda, CA, consultant, 1972; US Public Health Services, Region IX, Division of Resources Development, San Francisco, CA, deputy director, 1975-76, Health Planning and Facilities Branch, chief, 1976-78; San Francisco General Hospital and San Francisco Medical Center, San Francisco, CA, associate administrator of outpatient, community emergency services, 1978-90; Kaiser Foundation Health Plan, Oakland, CA, coordinator, licensing and accreditation, 1983, director, licensing, accreditation and quality assurance, 1983-84; Kaiser Foundation Health Plan of Georgia, Inc, Atlanta, GA, employee relations manager, 1984-86, health plan manager, 1984-86, associate regional manager, 1986; Kaiser Foundation Health Plan of Texas, Inc, Dallas, TX, vice president and regional manager, 1986-. **Orgs:** Executive board, American Public Health Assn; founding & past director, National Black Nurses Assn, Inc; past president & director, Bay Area Black Nurses Assn, Inc; founder & past director, Bay Area Black Consortium for Quality Health Care, Inc; Dallas Assembly; Dallas Citizens Council; advisory board, Dallas Women's Foundation; board of directors, Greater Dallas Community of Churches; board of directors, Texas State Board of Insurance High Risk Health Pool; school of nursing advisory council, University of Texas at Arlington; advisory board, Women's Center of Dallas. **Honors/Awds:** "The Interdisciplinary Health Team in Providing Nutrition Assessment," Nutrition Assessment, A Comprehensive Guide for Planning Intervention, 1984; Discovering the Issues: A First Step in Plan Development, December 1974; "Managed Competition Lets Employees Choose," Texas Hospitals, v. 44, n. 3, August 1988, p 17-18. **Business Addr:** Vice President and Regional Manager, Texas Region, Kaiser Permanente, 12720 Hillcrest, Suite 600, Dallas, TX 75230.

HAYGOOD, WIL
Journalist. **Personal:** Born Sep 19, 1954, Columbus, OH. **Educ:** Miami Univ, BA 1976. **Career:** The Columbus OH Call & Post, reporter 1977-78; Community Info & Referal, hotline operator 1978-79; Macy's Dept Store NYC, exec 1980-81; The Charleston Gazette, copy editor 1981-83; The Boston Globe, feature reporter. **Orgs:** Reporter The Pittsburgh Post Gazette 1984-85. **Honors/Awds:** Natl Headliner Awd Outstanding Feature Writing 1986; author of "Two on the River" Atlantic Monthly Press 1987. **Business Addr:** Feature Reporter, The Boston Globe, 135 Morrissey Blvd, Boston, MA 02107.

HAYLING, WILLIAM H.
Gynecologist, obstetrician. **Personal:** Born Dec 7, 1925, Trenton, NJ; son of Dr & Mrs William Hayling; married Carolyn Anne Mitchem; children: Pamela Hoffman, Patricia Price. **Educ:** Boston Univ, pre-med 1943-45; Howard Univ, MD 1949. **Career:** NJ Coll of Medicine/Dentistry, assoc prof ob/gyn 1960-80; King/Drew Medical Ctr, asst prof ob/gyn 1981-87, chief ambulatory ob/gyn 1981-. **Orgs:** Pres 100 Black Men of NJ 1975-78; bd Jersey City State Coll NJ 1975-80; pres Natl 100 Black Men of Amer Inc 1987; founder/pres 100 Black Men of LA Inc. **Honors/Awds:** Image Awd 100 Black Men of LA 1982; LA Sentinel Awd LA Sentinel Newspaper 1983; Presidential Awd Alpha Phi Alpha Frat 1984. **Military Serv:** US Army Medical Corps, capt, 1951-53; Bronze Star; Combat Medical Badge. **Business Addr:** Chief Ambulatory Ob/Gyn, King/Drew Medical Center, Dept of Ob/Gyn, 120-21 S Wilmington Ave, Los Angeles, CA 90059.

HAYMAN, WARREN C.
Educator. **Personal:** Born Oct 1, 1932, Baltimore, MD; married Jacqueline; children: Warren Jr, Guy, Julia. **Educ:** Coppin State Coll, BS 1961; Stanford U, MA 1967; Harvard U, EdD 1978. **Career:** Coppin State Coll, dean of edn; Ravenswood City Sch Dist, supt 1973-77; Ravenswood, asst supt 1971-73; Belle Haven, elem prin 1968-71; Baltimore City Schs, elem tchr 1961-66; Stanford Univ, faculty resident 1970-73; San Francisco State Univ, instr 1971-74; US Office of Educ, consult 1968-76. **Orgs:** Chmn bd dir Nairobi Coll 1970-76; chmn bd of dir Mid-Peninsula Urban Coalition 1973-75; reg dir of educ Phi Beta Sigma Frat Inc 1980. **Honors/Awds:** Circuluc schol honor soc Coppin State Coll 1961; elem math tchr fellow Nat Sci Found 1966; exper tchr flwshp US Ofc of Educ 1966; higher educ flwshp Rockfeller Found 1976-78; good conduct ribbon AUS 1955-57. **Military Serv:** AUS sp/2nd class 1955-57. **Business Addr:** Coppin State Coll, 2500 W North Ave, Baltimore, MD 21216.

HAYMON, ALAN
Concert promotion company executive. **Personal:** Born in Cleveland, OH. **Educ:** Harvard University, BA (w/honors), 1977, MBA (w/honors), 1980, studying ecomonics, currently. **Career:** A H Enterprises, founder, chairman, currently. **Special Achievements:** Most successful concert promoter of African-American music; entertainers include: MC Hammer, Eddie Murphy, Bobby Brown, Bell, Biv, DeVoe, New Edition, Patti La Belle, Frankie Beverly, numerous others. **Business Addr:** Chairman, AH Enterprises, PO Box 145, Newton Center, MA 02159, (617)332-9680.

HAYMORE, TYRONE
Government official. **Personal:** Born Mar 12, 1947, Chicago, IL; son of Mildred Ernestine Calhoun Haymore and T H Haymore. **Educ:** Thornton Jr Coll, AA 1969; Northeastern IL Univ, BA Ed 1986. **Career:** Chicago Transit Authority, rail clerk, 1968-; Village of Robbins, IL, village clerk, trustee, 1983-87, village clerk, 1989-. **Orgs:** Treas, 1981-87, president, 1987-, Robbins Historical Soc; dir Commiss on Youth Bremen Twp 1983; treas Black Elected Officials of IL 1984; mem IL Civil Air Patrole; mem, Municipal Clerks of Illinois, 1989-93. **Honors/Awds:** Christian Leadership Christ Crusader Church Robbins 1965; Music Scholarship to Summer Music Camp Eastern IL Univ 1965; Achievement Awd Mayor of Robbins for Ambulance Fund Drive 1984; Plaque for Outstanding Service as Treasurer, Black Elected Officials of Illinois, 1990; Robbins Recreation and Training Center, Plaque for Outstanding Historian in Robbins, 1992; Illinois Institute of Municipal Clerks, Municipal Clerk Certification, 1992; Certificate for Professionalism as a CMC, 1993. **Special Achievements:** Village of Robbins, 4 yr term, re-elected, clerk, 1993-; History Coloring Book entitled, Robbins, Illinois, co-author, 1994; Channel 14 Cable TV, 1st exec producer & dir, 1994-. **Home Addr:** 13557 Homan, PO Box 1561, Robbins, IL 60472. **Business Addr:** Village Clerk, Village of Robbins, Robbins Village Hall, 3327 W 137 St, Robbins, IL 60472.

HAYNES, ALPHONSO WORDEN
Educational administrator. **Personal:** Born in Brooklyn, NY; married Margaret S Alvarez; children: Thomas, Pia, Mia, Pilar, Alphonso III, Alejandro. **Educ:** Long Island U, BA 1965; Columbia U, MS 1967, MA 1974, EdD 1978. **Career:** New York City Dept of Welfare, admin & recreation 1953-67; Harlem Hospital Center, ped social worker 1967-69; Long Island Univ, dean of students 1969-79; Norfolk State Univ School of Social Work, assoc prof & program dir 1979-81; Old Dominion Univ, asst dean of student affairs. **Orgs:** Mem Natl Asso of Soc Wrkrs 1967-; mem Acdmy of Cert Soc Wrkrs 1969-; staff training consult Chesapeake Soc Serv 1979-80; bd mem Yng Adult & Campus Ministry 1983-; mem VA Asso of Stdnt Personnel Adm 1981-; mem Rsrch Focus in Black Ed 1980-; bd mem Columbia Univ Schl of Social Work Alumni Assoc. **Honors/ Awds:** Pi Gamma Mu Soc Sci Hnr Soc 1962; Karagheusian Mem Flwshp Columbia Univ 1965-67; outstndng edctr in Am. **Business Addr:** Asst Dean of Student Affairs, Old Dominion Univ, 1401 W 49 St, Multicultural Center, Norfolk, VA 23508.

HAYNES, BARBARA ASCHE
Educator, nurse. **Personal:** Born Jun 26, 1935, Rochester, PA; married Donald F Haynes. **Educ:** Chatham Coll, BSNE 1958; Univ of Pgh, MNE 1967, PhD 1984. **Career:** Allegheny Gen Hosp Sch of Nursing Pittsburgh, instr nursing 1959-67; Allegheny Comm Coll, asst prof nursing 1967-70, assoc prof/dept head 1970-74, dean of life sci/dir nursing prog 1974-79; Coll of DuPage, instr nursing 1979-80; Univ of IL Chicago Coll of Nursing, asst prof gen nursing/dir student serv 1981-. **Orgs:** Sec Univ of Pgh Sch of Nursing Alumnae Assn 1967-69; bd of dirs PA Nurses Assn 1973-77; chmn nominating comm Univ Pgh Sch of Nursing Alumnae Assn1974; bd of dirs United Mental Health of Allegheny Co1975-79; professional adv com NW Allegheny Home Care Prog 1976-79; v chmn conf grp on teaching PA Nurse's Assn 1977-79; comm on nursing educ PA Nurses Assn 1977-79; adv comm BSN Prog LaRoche Coll 1978-79; reg continuing educ adv comm Duquesne Univ Group 1978-79; pub "The Practical Nurse" & "Auto-Education" PA Nurse 1972; speaker "Multi-Media in Nursing Educ" Tchrs Coll Columbia Univ 1972; speaker "Coping with Change through Assessment & Evaluation" Natl League for Nursing-Council of Asso Degree Progs NY 1974; mem Sigma Theta Tau Alpha Lambda Chapt. **Business Addr:** Asst Prof of Gen Nursing, Univ of IL Coll of Nursing, 845 S Damen Ave, Chicago, IL 60680.

HAYNES, ELEANOR LOUISE
Business executive. **Personal:** Born in Warrenton, GA; widowed; children: SFC Jeffrey M Thomas. **Educ:** Fashion Inst, 1953; Sobleshon Inst 1972; Queensboro Comm Coll, Small Bus Mgmt 1978; Queens Coll, 1983-. **Career:** Garment Industry, fashion designer 1951-74; NY Voice, columnist 1968-; Good Serv & Group Travel, travel agency 1976-78; Coler Mem Hosp, dir public relations1978-, appointed liaison, adv bd 1987-. **Orgs:** Mem ViVants Soc & Civic Org 1969-; mem & officer Natl Assoc Negro Bus & Prof Women 1972-80; sec, treas Allied Fed Savings & Loan Assoc 1980-83; publ relations dir SE Queens Reg Dem Club 1980-; mem Natl Assoc Female Execs 1980-; mem Edges Group Inc 1980-; vice pres Council of PR Dir Health & Hosp Corp 1981-; 1st natl vice pres Natl Assoc Media Women 1981-; elected delegate Judicial Convention State of NY 1982-; mem Manhattan Chamber of Commerce 1983-, Jamaica Branch NAACP; elect pres Cncl PR Directors Health & Hospitals Corp City of NY 1985; judge Easter Boardwalk Parade Atlantic City NJ 1987. **Honors/Awds:** 30 awds & certs incl Excellence in-Serv Awd Natl Assoc Media Women 1983; Media Woman of the Year Long Island Chap Media Women 1983; Excellence in Journalism Awd SE Queens Dem Club 1982; Best Perf Awd Dunton Presbyterian Church 1981; Mother of the Year Awd from Assemblyman Guy R Brewer Queens Cty 1976. **Home Addr:** 23116 126th Ave, Jamaica, NY 11413.

HAYNES, EUGENE, JR.
Educator, composer. **Educ:** Juillard Sch of Music in NY, earned undergrad grad degrees in comp piano. **Career:** Lincoln U, prof; intl known as concert pianist; So IL Univ East St Louis Campus, prof of music & artist in residence 1979-; artist in residence at univ 1960-79; tchs advanced courses in piano improvisation music history; "The Wonderful World of Music" radio sta KSD St Louis, host classical music prog. **Honors/Awds:** Made New York City debut at Carnegie Hall 1958; since appeared there; appeared in every major city of Europe & Latin Am; featured on severalTV spls; orginal comps include String Quartet, Song Cycle, Symphony, Fantasy for Piano & Orchestra; awarded Maurice Loeb Prize for excellence in grad studies Juilliard Schl of Music in NY. **Business Addr:** State Community College, Dept of Humanities, 601 J R Thompson Blvd, East St Louis, IL 62201.

HAYNES, FARNESE N.
Attorney. **Personal:** Born Dec 25, 1960, Bluefield, WV; daughter of Melda & Jesse Haynes Sr. **Educ:** American University, BA, 1983; Howard University School of Law, JD, 1986. **Career:** Leftwich Moore & Douglas, staff attorney, 1987; US Department of Agriculture, staff attorney, 1987-93; UNCF, general counsel, 1993-. **Orgs:** Delta Sigma Theta Sorority, 1980-; DC Bar Association, 1988-; Maryland Bar Assn, 1989-; J Franklin Bourne Bar Assn, fundraising, 1990-92; Pennsylvania Bar Assn, inactive, 1986-93. **Honors/Awds:** Howard Law Journal, Editor in Chief, 1984-86; USDA, OCG, 1988; Commonwealth of VA, Notary Public, 1993; Managment Seminar for Senior Level Women. **Special Achievements:** Ineffective Assistance of Counsel, 28, HOWLJ191, 1985; Supreme Court of PA, 1986; District of Columbia Court of Appeals, 1988; Court of Appeals of Maryland, 1989; US District Court, District of Maryland, 1989; Supreme Ct of Virginia, 1995; US Supreme Ct, 1997. **Business Addr:** General Counsel, United Negro College Fund, 8260 Willow Oaks Corporate Drive, 4th Floor, Fairfax, VA 22031, (703)205-3400.

HAYNES, FRANK L., JR.
Attorney, executive. **Personal:** Born Aug 26, 1944, New York. **Educ:** Horace Mann Sch New York, 1962; Yale Coll, BA 1966; Yale Law Sch, LlB 1969. **Career:** Prudential Ins Co of Am; asst gen cns vice pres of law dept; Milbank, Tweed, Hadley & Mccloy, asso 1970-76; Western Cntr on Law & Proverty Univ of S CA Law Cntr LA, asso 1969-70; NAACP Legal Def & Educ Fund NY, legal intern summer 1968. **Orgs:** Admitted to bar 1971. **Honors/Awds:** Recip Fiske Stone Moot Ct Awd Yale Law Sch 1967.

HAYNES, GEORGE E., JR.
Educator (retired). **Personal:** Born Oct 23, 1920, Victoria, TX; married; children: George E III, Elizabeth (jemison). **Educ:**

Tuskegee Inst, BS 1942; NY ll, MA 1947. **Career:** Human Relations Dept Houston Ind Sch Dist, asst supt (retired); TX So U, vis prof; Kashmere Sr HS, prin 2 yrs; I M Terrell Jr High, prin 2 yrs; Kashmere Gardens Jr/Sr HS, asst prin; FL A&M Coll, summer vis prof 1955 & 1957; Tuskegee Inst AL, dept head 3 yrs; NY U, tchr. **Orgs:** Mem NEA Workshop "Deveoloping an Instructional Prog to Implement Cultural Pluralism"; mem Houston Council of Edn; TX Assn of Secondary Sch Prin; Houston Prin Assn; Nat Assn of Secondary Prins; pres Tuskegee Nat Alumni Assn; mem Phi Delta Kappa; Smithsonian Asso; mem Epsilon Pi Tau Honorary Industrial Frat; Alpha Phi Alpha Frat; Assn for Study of Afro-Am Life & History; Asso musicians of NY Local #802; mem NAACP; YMCA Century Club; Com of Religion &Race Unitedmeth Ch. **Military Serv:** Sgt 1943-46. **Home Addr:** 4702 Leffingwell St, Houston, TX 77026.

HAYNES, JAMES H.
Educational administrator. **Personal:** Born Nov 27, 1953, Pensacola, FL; son of Annie Sims and Jap Haynes. **Educ:** Pensacola Jr Coll, AA 1973; Morebouse Coll, BA 1975; Georgia State Univ, MEd 1977; Univ of IA, PhD 1979. **Career:** Atlanta Public Sch System, teacher 1975-77; Philadelphia Training Center, asst dir 1979-80; FL A&M Univ, dir of planning 1980-83; Morgan State Univ, dir of inst research 1983-84, vice pres of planning 1984, title III coord, 1988-. **Orgs:** Woodrow Wilson Nat'l Fellowship Foundation, 1980; Title III Prog Bowie State Coll, counsultant 1984-; Assoliation of Minority Hlth Profession Sch, consultant 1982; supervisor of admin for NTE, GMAT 1984-; Alpha Phi Alpha, Baltimore Morehouse Alumni Club, sec; NAACP; Morehouse Coll Nat'l Alumni Assoc; board of directors, Baltimore Employment Network. **Honors/Awds:** Honorary membership in Promethean Kappa Tau, Phi Delta Kappa, Phi Alpha Theta; Governor's Citation for services to youth in Baltimore community; Mayor's Citation for services to youth in Baltimore city. **Home Addr:** 3626 Greenmount Ave, Baltimore, MD 21218. **Business Addr:** Title III Coordinator, Morgan State University, Cold Spring Ln & Hillen Rd, Baltimore, MD 21239.

HAYNES, JOHN K.
Life insurance chief executive. **Career:** Superior Life Insurance Co, Baton Rouge, LA, chief exec. **Business Addr:** Superior Life Insurance Co., 7980 Scenic Hwy, Baton Rouge, LA 70807.

HAYNES, JOHN KERMIT
Educator. **Personal:** Born Oct 30, 1943, Monroe, LA; son of Grace Quanita Ross Haynes and John Kermit Haynes Sr; married Carolyn Ann Price, Aug 14, 1969. **Educ:** Morehouse Coll, BS 1964; Brown Univ, PhD 1970, Post Doctoral 1971; MA Inst of Tech, Post Doctoral 1973. **Career:** Brown Univ, teaching asst 1964-70; MIT, post doctoral & teaching asst 1971-73; Meharry Medical Coll, asst prof 1973-78; Morehouse Coll, prof & dir of health professions 1979-, chmn dept biology 1985-. **Orgs:** Mem Amer Assn for the Adv of Science; mem American Society for Cell Biol; mem American Chem Society; peer reviewer National Science Foundation; chmn bd dir Afro Arts Ctr 1970-72; mem bd dir Sickle Cell Found GA 1980-; mem bd trustees Morehouse Coll 1984-87; member, GRE Biochemistry, Cell and Molecular Biology Committee of Exam, 1989-92; Comm on Undergrad Sci Ed; Natl Res Council, 1994-; chairperson, Minor AFFs Comm; Am Soc Cell Biol, 1994-. **Honors/Awds:** David Packard Chair, Morehouse College, 1985-. **Business Addr:** David Packard Professor and Chairman Department of Biology, Morehouse College, 830 Westview Dr SW, Nabrit-Mapp-McBay Hall, Rm 134, Atlanta, GA 30314.

HAYNES, LEONARD L., JR.
Clergyman, educator. **Personal:** Born Mar 16, 1923, Austin, TX; son of Thelma Haynes and Leonard L Haynes Sr; married Leila Louise; children: Leonard III, Walter, Angeline, Leila. **Educ:** Huston Tillotson Meth Gammon Theol Sem, AB 1945; Boston Univ, ThD 1948. **Career:** Philander Smith Coll, dean 1948; Morristown Jr Coll, pres 1958; So Univ, prof 1960-; Wesley United Meth Church, minister 1960-. **Orgs:** Prchr Eng 1948, Orient 1972; chmn Human Relations Council 1967; lecturer Atlanta 1972; black task force LA Assn of Business & Indus; mem, exec comm LA Assoc of Business & Ind; ed The Black Comm within the United Methodist Church; dir OIC Baton Rouge LA; mem 33 Degree Mason; chairperson, Christians for Good Government 1989-90; mem, President George Bush Republican Task Force, 1989-. **Honors/Awds:** Meth Crusade Scholar 1947; Distinguished Alumnus Awd Boston Univ 1972; Outstanding Coll Teacher 1973; chmn bd Professional Psychotherapy 1977; JK Haynes Foundation Awd 1981; Natl Assn for Equal Oppor in Higher Educ Black Church Awd 1985; State of LA recognized 2/15/87 as LL Haynes Jr Day; Doctor of Humane Letters, Philander Smith College, 1990. **Special Achievements:** WBRTV Channel 19 News, commentary. **Business Addr:** Professor, Dept of Philosophy, Southern Univ, Baton Rouge, LA 70813.

HAYNES, LEONARD L., III
Government official. **Personal:** Born Jan 26, 1947, Boston, MA; son of Leila Davenport Haynes and Leonard L Haynes Jr; married Mary Sensley Haynes, Aug 10, 1968; children: Leonard IV, Eboni Michelle, Bakari Ali, Jabari, Kenyatta. **Educ:** Southern University, Baton Rouge, LA, BA, 1968; Carnegie-Mellon Univ, Pittsburgh, PA, MA, 1969; Ohio State University, Columbus, OH, PhD, 1975. **Career:** Institute for Services to Education, Washington, DC, dir, desegregation unit, 1976-79; National Assn State/Land Grant College, Washington, DC, director, public black colleges, 1979-82; Southern University System, Baton Rouge, LA, executive vice president, 1982-85, professor of history, 1985-88; Louisiana Depart of Education, Baton Rouge, LA, assistant superintendent, 1988-89; US Department of Education, Washington, DC, assistant secretary, 1989-91; adjunct faculty, The Brookings Institute, 1991-92; United States Information Agency, dir of academic programs, 1992-; senior consultant & national education goals panel, 1993; Univ of MD, visiting scholar, 1994; The American University, senior assistant to the president, 1994-. **Orgs:** Omega Psi Phi Fraternity, 1968-; Jack & Jill Inc, 1988. **Honors/Awds:** Honorary Doctor of Laws, Ohio State Univ, 1990; Honorary Doctor of Humane Letters, Tougaloo College, 1990; Honorary Doctor of Laws, University of St Thomas, 1990; Honorary Doctor of Laws, Alabama A&M Univ, 1990; Honorary Doctor of Laws, Stockton State College, 1991; Honorary Doctor of Public Administration, Bridgewater College, 1992. **Home Addr:** PO Box 1406, Ruston, LA 71273.

HAYNES, MICHAEL DAVID
Professional football player. **Personal:** Born Dec 24, 1965, New Orleans, LA; married Cookie Oubre. **Educ:** Northern Arizona. **Career:** Atlanta Falcons, wide receiver, 1988-93, 1997-; New Orleans Saints, 1994-96. **Business Addr:** Professional Football Player, Atlanta Falcons, Two Falcon Place, Suwanee, GA 30174, (404)945-1111.

HAYNES, MICHAEL E.
Government official, clergyman. **Personal:** Born May 9, 1927, Boston, MA. **Educ:** Berkshire Christian Coll; New Eng Shch Theo, ABM 1949; Shelton Coll. **Career:** Commonwealth MA State Parole Bd, mem; 12th Bapt Ch, sr minister 1965-; House Reps 7th Suffolk Dist, mem 1965-69; Norfolk House Crt, soc work staff 1957-64; Commonwealth MA Yth Serv Div, 1955-57; Robert Gould Shaw House, asst boys wrkr 1953-58; Breezy Meadows Camp, prgm dir 1951-62. **Orgs:** Chmn Metro Boston Settlement Assn 1965-67; bd dir New Eng Bapt Hosp; mem Citz Training Grp Boston Juv Ct; Cushing Acad; Gordon-Conwell Theo Sem ; Malone Coll; Boys' Club Boston; Roxbury Clubhouse; Mayor's Com Violence 1976; New Boston Com; City Boston Charitable Fund; chmn gov adv com State Chaplains; Ministeriail Alliance Grtr Boston. **Honors/Awds:** Recpt LLD Gordon Coll 1969; Dr Pub Serv Barington Coll 1971; DD Northeastern Univ 1978; publ "Christian-Secular Coop" Urban Mission 1974; "Five Minutes Before Midnight" Evang Missions 1968; Intervarsity Press Champion Urban Challenge 1979. **Business Addr:** 100 Cambridge St, Boston, MA 02202.

HAYNES, NEAL J.
Clergyman, educator. **Personal:** Born Aug 16, 1912, Eddyville, KY; married Ollie Hart; children: Marian. **Educ:** AB BTh MRE DD 1950. **Career:** St Louis & St Louis Co, elem tchr pub schs; Theology Wetern Bapt Bible Coll, instr; Western Bapt Bible Coll dean instrn; western bapt Bible CollSt Louis Center, dir; Antioch Dist Assn, mod; Missionary Bapt State Conv MO, exec sec; First Bapt Ch, pastor; Webster Groves Ministerial Alliance, pres 1960-61 & 1973. **Orgs:** Pres Gamma Tau Frat; mem Alpha Theta Zata Frat; mem In-Ter Faith Clergy 1970-74; chmn Audio-Visual Aid Dept Nat Bapt Conv USA Inc 1973-74; Mem Bapt Training Unoin Bd Nat Bapt Conv USA Inc; mem Preaching Team IV S Afrca 1975; chmn Ethics Com Bapt Pastor's Conf St Louis. **Honors/Awds:** Plaque Youth Dept Antioch Dist Assn 1972; outstanding membership award Antioch Dist Assn 1973. **Military Serv:** USAF first sgt 1943-46.

HAYNES, SUE BLOOD
Educational administrator, computer analyst/designer. **Personal:** Born Mar 21, 1939, Pine Bluff, AR; married Joe Willis; children: Rodney, Joe B. **Educ:** Seattle U, BA MA 1974; Unoin Grad Sch, PhD 1979; Bryn Mawr Coll, mgmt cert 1979. **Career:** S Seattle Comm Coll, dir spl prog 1974-; Seattle U, head couns 1972-74; IBO Data Processing Co Inc, exec officer owner 1969-76; The Boeing Co, systems analysts 1960-69, computer analyst, designer, 1989-. **Orgs:** Bd of dirs Educ Talent Search 1977-; bd of dir New Careers Found 1978-; editorial bd The Western Jour of Black Studies 1978-; mem Alpha Kappa Alpha Elta Epsilon Omega 1977-; vice pres bd of dir Counc on Black Am Affairs Western Region 1978-79; chairperson founder The Inner-City Health Careers Proj-jack & Jill of Am 1978-79. **Honors/Awds:** Community serv award Univ of Chicago 1974; pub sch vol award Seattle Pub Sch 1978; Martin Luther King Jr Meml Award Blanks Wooten Prodn 1980; dedication to black educ award Western Regional Counc on Black Am Affairs 1980; Fellowship Grant-Bryn Mawr Coll Puget Sound Minority Consortium 1980; Computer Design Award, Boeing Defense & Space Division, 1988. **Business Addr:** PO Box 4192, Renton, WA 98057.

HAYNES, ULRIC ST. CLAIR, JR.
Educational administrator. **Personal:** Born Jun 8, 1931, Brooklyn, NY; son of Ellaline Gay Haynes and Ulric S Haynes Sr; married Yolande Toussaint; children: Alexandra, Gregory. **Educ:** Amherst Coll, BA 1952; Yale Law Sch, LL B 1956; Harvard Business School Advanced Mgmt Prgm 1966. **Career:** US Dept of State, foreign serv officer 1963-64; Natl Security Council, stf 1964-1966; Mgmt Formation Inc, pres 1966-70; Spencer Stuart & Assn, sr vice pres 1970-72; Cummins Engine Co, vice pres mgmt devel 1972-75, vice pres Mid-East & Africa 1975-77; Am Embsy-Algeria, amb 1977-81; Cummins Engine Co, vice pres intl business planning 1981-83; Self-Employed, consultant 1984-85; SUNY Coll at Old Westbury, acting pres 1985-86; AFS Intl/Intercultural Programs, pres 1986-87; Drake Beam Morin, sr vice pres, 1988-91; Hofstra U Sch of Business, dean, 1991-96, executive dean for university international relations, 1996-. **Orgs:** Mem bd dir Amer Broadcasting Co 1981-84, Rohm & Haas Co 1981-84, Marine Midland Bank 1981-; mem sel comm Henry Luce Foundation Asian Scholars Program 1975-; mem Council on Foreign Rel 1968-; bd mem, Cncl of Amer Ambassadors; The Yale Club of NYC; honorary chrmn Indiana United Negro Coll Fund Drive, 1981; bd mem, Environmental Products Corp, 1993-; US Africa Airways, 1994-96; Hemmeter Enterprises, Inc, bd of dirs, 1994-96; Grand Palais Casino Inc, 1994-96; Pall Corp, 1994-. **Honors/Awds:** Martin Luther King Humanitarian Awd; Black Chrstn Caucus Riverside Church, New York City Martin Luther King Award; student bar assn; Howard Univ Law Schl; resolutions of commendation from IN State Senate & Assbly, CA State Senate, City of Detroit & LA; Alumni Award, Class of 1952; Amherst Coll, Afro-Amer Student Assn, Harvard Busn Schl; Liberty Bell Award IN Young Lawyers Assn; Freedom Award; IN Black Expo 1981; certified, US Dept of State; hon LLDs Indiana Univ, Alabama State Univ, Fisk Univ, John Jay College, Butler Univ. **Home Addr:** 19 Threepence Dr, Melville, NY 11747-3408. **Business Addr:** Executive Dean, Business Development Center, #123, Hofstra University, Hempstead, NY 11550.

HAYNES, WALTER WESLEY
Dentist (retired). **Personal:** Born Nov 16, 1919, St Matthews, SC; children: Saundra, Donald. **Educ:** Lincoln U, AB 1943; Howard Univ Coll Dentistry, DDS 1946. **Career:** 1st Presbyterian Ch of Hempstead, deacon 1962-67; Queens Gen and Tribro Hosp, 1960-65; Hempstead School, dentist 1962-93. **Orgs:** Pres Queens Clinical Soc 1961-62; Ethical Dent Soc 1975-77; mem ADA; NDA; 10th Dist Dental Soc; Beta Kappa Chi; Omega Psi Phi. **Honors/Awds:** Man of the Year Lincoln Univ 1967; Fellow of the Acad of Gen Dentistry 1984. **Military Serv:** AUS capt 1946-48.

HAYNES, WILLIAM J., JR.
Judge. **Personal:** Born Sep 5, 1949, Memphis, TN; son of Martyna Q McCullough and William J Haynes; married Carol Donaldson; children: Paz, Anthony, Maya. **Educ:** Coll of St Thomas, BA 1970; Vanderbilt School of Law, JD 1973. **Career:** TN State Atty Gen Office, asst atty general 1973-77; TN State Antitrust & Consumer Protection, dep atty general 1978-84, spec dep atty general for special litigation 1984; US District Court Middle District of TN, magistrate judge, 1984-. **Orgs:** Mem Amer Bar Assn 1978, 1985, 1988-91; vice chair, State Enforcement Comm, Antitrust Section; mem 1st vice pres Nashville Bar Assn, 1980-84; dist atty gen pro tem Shelby Cty Criminal Court 1980; mem Rotary Intl, 1980-90; mem bd of dir Cumberland Museum & Sci Ctr 1981-87; mem bd of professional responsibility TN Supreme Court 1982-84; mem bd of dir Napier Lobby Bar Assn 1983-84; chmn antitrust planning comm Natl Assn of Atty General 1984; mem, bd of advisors, Corporate Practice Series, Bureau of Natl Affairs, 1989,90; Lecturer-in-law Vanderbilt School of Law, 1987-94. **Honors/Awds:** Bennett Douglas Bell Awd Vanderbilt School of Law 1973; author, "State Antitrust Laws" published by the Bureau of National Affairs, 1988; Federal Exec Assn; Black History Month Award, 1990; Contributing Author, "The Legal Aspects of Selling & Buying," Shepard's McGraw Hill, 1991. **Business Addr:** US Magistrate Judge, US District Court, 649 US Courthouse, Nashville, TN 37203.

HAYNES, WILLIE C., III
Educational administrator, elected official. **Personal:** Born Nov 23, 1951, Opelousas, LA; son of Watkins Lillie Haynes and Willie C Haynes Jr; married Rebecca M Smith Haynes; children: Markisha A, Willie C IV. **Educ:** Southern Univ Baton Rouge, BS 1973, MAEduc 1976. **Career:** Clark Lodge #186, jr deacon 1975-88; Melville HS, asst principal 1982-88; St Landry Parish Police Jury, District 5 Juror, 1988-91. **Orgs:** Mem NAACP 1981-88; mem Governor's Council on Physical Fitness & Sports 1984-87; mem Acidiana Principal's Assn 1984-88; mem bd of dirs St Landry Parish Council on Aging 1985-88. **Business Addr:** Asst Principal & Sci Teacher, Melville High School, PO Box 466, Melville, LA 71353.

HAYNES, WORTH EDWARD
Educational administrator. **Personal:** Born Apr 20, 1942, Webb, MS; son of Annie Mae Haynes and Shellie Haynes (deceased); married Linden C Smith; children: Natasha C, Worth Edward. **Educ:** Alcorn State Univ Lorman MS, BS 1965; WI State Univ River Falls, MST 1971; IA State Univ Ames, PhD 1977. **Career:** Alcorn State Univ, youth camp dir 1964; Eva H Harris HS Brookhaven MS, tchr vocational agr 1964-69; Hinds Co AHS Utica, tchr vocational agr 1969-72; Utica Jr Coll, dir vocational tech educ 1972-74; IA State Univ Ames, instr agr

educ dept 1974-76, grad student adv 1976-77; Utica Jr Coll, dir vocational-tech educ 1977-; Governors Office of Job Develop & Trng, exec dir 1985-86; Div of Industrial Serv & Fed Prog, asst state dir 1986-; Office of Vocational Tech and Adult Education, Bureau of Business/Commerce and Technology, director, begin 1988; Mississippi Dept. of Education, Bureau of Vocational Community Development, director, currently. **Orgs:** Pres Utica Comm Devel Assoc 1978-80; pres Post Secondary Voc Dirs Assoc MS 1979; chmn Post Secondary State Evaluation Comm Voc Educ MS 1980; deacon, vice pres, laymen assoc, mem New Hope Bapt Church Jackson MS 1981-; sunday school teacher New Hope Church 1982-; president, Koahoama County Incubator, Clarksdale, MS, 1990-; state leader, State Baptist Association, 1990. **Honors/Awds:** Outstanding Tchr Awd MS Econ Devel Council Eva Harris High Sch Brookhaven MS 1967-69; Man of the Year Awd Alpha Phi Alpha Frat Natchez MS 1972; Achievement Awd Gamma Sigma Delta Honor Soc of Agr Ames IA 1976; Outstanding Contributions to Agr Educ IA Vocational Educ Assn Ames 1976; Outstanding Serv to Utica Jr Coll 1984; Outstanding Contribution to Economic Development, Gulf Coast Business Service Corp, 1986. **Business Addr:** Director Bureau of Voc. Community Development, Mississippi Dept. of Education, Box 771, 1105 Walter Sillers Bldg, Ste 1003, Jackson, MS 39205.

HAYRE, RUTH WRIGHT
Educator. **Personal:** Born in Atlanta, GA; daughter of Charlotte Crogman Wright and Richard R Wright Jr; married Talmadge B Hayre, Aug 26, 1937 (deceased); children: Sylvia E Hayre Harrison. **Educ:** Univ of PA, BS, MA, PhD 1948. **Career:** Wash DC/Phila, tchr 1942-52; Wm Penn HS Phila, PA, vice principal 1952-56, principal 1956-63; Philadelphia Sch Dist, dist supt 1963-75; Univ of PA Phila, adj prof 1976-79; Philadelphia Bd of Educ, mem, 1985-, president, 1990-92. **Orgs:** Mem Am Assn of Sch Admin, bd of trustees Citizens Commn on Public Educ Temple Univ Phila, PA 1968-80; bd of trustees Blue Cross of Greater Philadelphia 1978-89; mem, board of trustees Afro-American Historical Museum, 1980-. **Honors/Awds:** Distinguished Daughter of PA, 1960; Philadelphia (BOK) Award, 1976; Award of Distinction, Grad School of Educ Univ of PA 1977; Alumnae Award, Univ of PA; Honorary degrees: Temple Univ, LHD, l989; Univ of Pennsylvania, LLD, l989; LLD Medical College of PA, 1991; Natl PUSH Award Operation PUSH 1989; Philanthropist established fund to pay coll educ for 116 students 1988. **Home Addr:** 3900 Ford Rd, Philadelphia, PA 19131.

HAYSBERT, DENNIS
Actor. **Personal:** Born in San Mateo, CA; married Lynn Griffith; children: Charles, Katherine. **Educ:** American College of Dramatic Arts, Pasadena, CA; College of San Mateo. **Career:** Television appearances include: Lou Grant, Queen, Lonesome Dove, numerous others; film appearances include: Major League, Navy Seals, Love Field, Heat, Waiting to Exhale, Absolute Power, numerous others. **Orgs:** NETDAY. **Business Addr:** Actor, c/o Paradigm Talent Agency, 10100 Santa Monica Blvd, 25th Floor, Los Angeles, CA 90067, (213)277-4400.

HAYSBERT, RAYMOND VICTOR, SR.
Food company executive. **Personal:** Born Jan 19, 1920, Cincinnati, OH; son of Emma Haysbert and William D Haysbert; married Carol Evelyn Roberts; children: Raymond V Jr, Reginald, Nikita M, Brian R. **Educ:** University of Cincinnati, BSME, 1945; Wilberforce Univ, BS Math CL 1948; Central State Univ OH, BS Bus Admin CL 1949; Univ of MD, Dr Pub Serv 1984. **Career:** City of Cincinnati, boiler oper 1941-42; Central State Univ, instr 1947-52; Parks Sausage Co, genl mgr exec vice pres 1952-74, pres 1974-. **Orgs:** Dir Equitable Bancorp 1971-90; dir South Baltimore General Hosp 1973-84; dirC&P Telephone Co 1975-85; pres The Hub Orgn 1979-84; dir Richmond Dist Fed Reserve Bank 1984-; trustee Univ of MD Med System 1984-; dir Bell Atlantic Corp 1985-; mem, The President's Roundtable 1983-. **Honors/Awds:** Man of Yr Baltimore Marketing Assn 1971; Man of Yr Baltimore Business League 1968; Disting Citizens Square/Compass Club 1973; Irving Blum Awd United Way Central MD; Honorary Doctor Public Serv Univ of MD; Baltimore Business Hall of Fame, Junior Achievement Metropolitan Baltimore 1986; Business Executive of the Year, Baltimore Magazine, 1988. **Military Serv:** USAF; Civilian Aide to Sec of Army 6 yrs; various awds 1981-. **Business Addr:** President & CEO, Parks Sausage Co, 3330 Henry Parks Circle, Baltimore, MD 21215.

HAYWARD, ANN STEWART
Producer/director/writer. **Personal:** Born Aug 23, 1944, Philadelphia, PA. **Educ:** Simmons Coll, AB 1966; NY U, grad 1967-70; Am Film Inst Directing Workshop for Women 1977-78; Stanford U, professional jour fellow 1978-79. **Career:** Group Visionary Prodns Inc, writer reprtr prdcr 1980; KPIX TV Westinghouse Brdcstng Co, video prod 1979-80; ABC TV Network News Docum Div "Ams & All", prod dir writer 1976-78; ABC TV Network News Docum Div "Closeup", assoc prod 1973-77; ABC TV Network News, dir of research 1972-73. **Orgs:** Mem Dirs Guild of Am; mem Guild of Am.

HAYWARD, JACQUELINE C.
Journalist. **Personal:** Born Oct 23, 1944, East Orange, NJ; married Sidney G. **Educ:** Howard U, BA 1966. **Career:** WTOP TV 9, anchorwoman; WAGA TV 5, 1970-72; V Mayor's Ofc, asst to v mayor 1970; City of Miami, dir of Training 1969-70. **Orgs:** Delta Sigma Theta Sor; Nat Counc of Negro Women; Nat Bus & Professional Women; NAACP; Nat Assn of Social Workers. **Honors/Awds:** Women of the 70's Capitol Press Club; Outst Woman, Am Assn of Univ Women; woman of Achvmt, Nat Multiple Sclerosis Soc; publ Citizen of Yr Kiwanis Club, Toastmasters Club; Delta Sigma Theta. **Business Addr:** W-USA, 4001 Brandywine St NW, Washington, DC 20016.

HAYWARD, OLGA LORETTA HINES
Librarian. **Personal:** Born in Alexandria, LA; daughter of Lillie George Hines and Samuel James; married Samuel E Hayward Jr (deceased); children: Anne Elizabeth, Olga Patricia Hayward Ryer. **Educ:** Dillard Univ, AB 1941; Atlanta Univ, BS in LS 1944; Univ of Michigan, MA in LS 1959; Louisiana State Univ, MA History 1977; Louisiana State Univ, further study. **Career:** Marksville, LA, HS teacher 1941-42; Grambling Coll, head librarian 1944-46; New Orleans Public Library, librarian 1947-48; Southern Univ Baton Rouge, head of reference dept 1948-74, collection develop librarian 1984-86, head of reference dept 1986-88; head of Business and Social Sciences Collections ref dept. **Orgs:** Sec treas, vice pres, pres LA Chap Special Libraries Assn; mem Baton Rouge Cncl on Human Relations 1981-; banquet comm mem Baton Rouge Conf for Christians & Jews 1982-; vice chair 1985-86, chair 1986-87 LA Library Assoc Subject Specialists Sect; mem steering comm LA Comm for Develop of Libraries 1987-. **Honors/Awds:** Publications: "Annotated Bibliography of Works By and About Whitney M Young" Bulletin of Bibliography July/Aug 1974; "Spotlight on Special Libraries in LA" LA Library Assn Bulletin 41 Summer 1979; Subject Specialists Section, LA Library Assoc, Lucy B. Foote Award, 1990; LA So Miss Chapter, Special Libraries Assoc, Roll of Honor Award, 1995. **Home Addr:** 1632 Harding Blvd, Baton Rouge, LA 70807.

HAYWOOD, GAR ANTHONY
Writer. **Personal:** Born May 22, 1954, Hollywood, CA; son of Jack & Barbara Haywood; married Lynnette, Dec 5, 1981 (divorced); children: Courtney, Erin. **Career:** Bell Atlantic, field engineer, 1976; Novelist, writer, currently. **Orgs:** Mystery Writers of Amer, 1989; Private Eye Writers of Amer, 1988; American Crime Writers League, 1989. **Honors/Awds:** Private Eye Writers of America, Best First Private Eye Novel, 1988, "Fear of the Dark;" Private Eye Writers of America, Shamus Award, Best First Novel, 1988. **Home Addr:** 2296 W Earl Street, Los Angeles, CA 90039, (213)660-0040.

HAYWOOD, GEORGE WEAVER
Financial services co. director. **Personal:** Born Sep 30, 1952, Washington, DC; son of Marie Weaver Haywood and John Wilfred Haywood Jr; married Cheryl Lynn Jenkins, Mar 28, 1987; children: Allison Marie. **Educ:** Harvard College, AB, 1974, Harvard Law School, 1975-79. **Career:** Lehman Bros, associate, 1982-84, first vice pres, 1984-86, senior vp, 1986-88, exec vp, 1988-91, managing director, bond trader, 1991-. **Orgs:** Brooklyn Poly Prep School, board of trustees, 1992-.

HAYWOOD, HIRAM H., JR.
Clergyman. **Personal:** Born Jan 8, 1921, Key West, FL; married Charlean Peters; children: Hiram III, Yolanda, Yvonne. **Educ:** 2 yrs college. **Career:** US Naval Gun Factory Washington & Naval Ordnance Sta Indian Head MD, 32 yrs; Catholic Archdiocese Washington, permanent deacon, assigned to the Basilica of the National Shrine of the Immaculate Conception, The National Catholic Church, currently. **Orgs:** Knights of Columbus 4th deg. **Honors/Awds:** Fed Superior Accomplishment Awds 1960 1972. **Military Serv:** USAAF cadet & sgt 1943-46. **Business Addr:** Deacon, Basilica of the National Shrine of the Immaculate, Conception, Fourth St. and Michigan Ave., N.E., Washington, DC 20017-1566.

HAYWOOD, L. JULIAN
Physician, educator. **Personal:** Born in Reidsville, NC; son of Louise V Hayley Haywood and Thomas W Haywood Sr; married Virginia; children: Julian Anthony. **Educ:** Hampton Inst, BS 1948; Howard U, MD 1952, (Dist Alumni Award) 1982. **Career:** Univ of So CA, asst prof 1963-67; LAC/USC Med Ctr, dir, CCU 1966-; Univ of So CA, assoc prof 1967-76; Cmprhnsv Sickle Cell Ctr LAC/USC, dir 1972; Loma Linda U, clncl prof of med 1973-78; Univ of So CA, prof of med 1976-; LAC/USC Med Ctr, sr physician. **Orgs:** Pres Sickle Cell Disease Res Found 1978-89; past pres AHA/Greater Los Angeles Aff 1983; gvnrs comm Amer Coll of Phys 1981-; consltnt Martin Luther King Jr Hosp 1970-; flw Amer Coll of Cardiology 1968-, Amer Coll of Physcns 1964-, Amer Heart Assoc 1983-; cnsltnt CA State Dept of Health Hypertnsn Cntrl Prog, consultant, NHLBI; mem, Armed Forces Epidemiology Board, 1996-; various committees, HCT Div PHS. **Honors/Awds:** Certf of Merit City of Los Angeles 1982; Certf of recogntn Natl Med Assoc 1982; Newsmaker of the Year Nat Association of Medical Women 1982; dist Service Award AHA/GLAA 1984; Louis Russell Award, AHA 1988; Heart of Gold Award, AHA 1989; Distinguished Alumni, Howard University 1982; Award of Merit, American Heart Association 1991; over 400 scientific papers and abstracts; American College of Physicians, California Region 1, Laurente Award, 1997. **Military Serv:** USN lt 1954-56. **Business Addr:** Professor of Medicine, LAC/USC Medical Center, 1200 N State St Box 305, Los Angeles, CA 90033.

HAYWOOD, MARGARET A.
Judge. **Personal:** Born Oct 8, 1912, Knoxville, TN; daughter of Mayme F Austin and Jonathan William Austin; divorced; children: Geraldine H Hoffman. **Educ:** Robert H Terrell Law School, LLB, 1940. **Career:** General Practice, attorney, 1940-72; DC Council, member, 1967-72; Superior Court District of Columbia, assoc judge, 1972-82, senior judge, 1982-. **Orgs:** Natl Grand Basileus, Lambda Kappa Mu, 1948-52; moderator, United Church of Christ, 1973-75; DC Bar Assn; Washington Bar Assn; American Bar Assn; Women's Bar Assn; Bar Assn of the DC; Cosmopolitan Business & Professional Women's Club; People's Congregational United Church of Christ; Zonta Intl. **Honors/Awds:** Cited Lambda Kappa Mu, Outstanding Sorority of Year, 1947, 1968, 1972; NAACP Trophy, 1950; one of America's Outstanding Women, Natl Council of Negro Women, 1951; elected to Afro-American Newspaper Honor Roll, 1951; Sigma Delta Tau, Outstanding Professional Service, 1957; Natl Bar Assn Award, 1968; Woman of Year, Oldest Inhabitants, 1969; Woman Lawyer of Year, Women's Bar Assn, 1972; DC Women's Commission, Trophy, Hall of Fame Inductee; Washington Bar Assn, Charles Hamilton Medallion of Merit for Contribution to Jurisprudence, 1980; Honorary Degrees: Elmhurst College, humanics, 1974; Carleton College, DHL, 1975; Catawba College, DL, 1976; Doane College, DL, 1979; numerous other awards and honorary degrees. **Business Addr:** Senior Judge, Superior Court of the District of Columbia, 500 Indiana Ave NW, #5520, Washington, DC 20001.

HAYWOOD, NORCELL D.
Business executive, architect. **Personal:** Born Jan 23, 1935, Bastrop, TX; children: Natalie Dawn, Nan Deliah, David Norcell. **Educ:** Prairie View A&M Coll, 1954-55; Univ of TX, BA 1955-60. **Career:** Prarie View A&M Coll, instr schl of engineering 1960-61; planning dept 1961; Eugene Wukasch, architect eng TX 1961-63; O'Neil Ford & Assoc San Antonio, 1963-68; Norcell D Haywood & Asoc San Antonio, 1968-72; Haywood Jordan Mc Cowan Inc, pres 1972. **Orgs:** Mem Am Inst of Architects; TX Soc of Architects; San Antonio Chap Am Inst of Architects; Construction Specifications Inst; past pres 1971-73 Minority Architects Inc of TX & LA M Arch; Greater San Antonio C Of C; bd dir San Antonio BRC; life mem Alpha Phi Alpha; BBB of San Antonio Inc; bd of Prof FREE; bd dir Met YMCA; bd dir Mid Am Region YMCA; sec Nat Org of Min Architects; bd dir Healy Murphy Learning Cntr; Alamo Area Coun of Govt Regional Devel & Review Com; bd dir Nat Coun of YMCA; Univ of TX Schl of Architecture Dean's Coun; bd dir San Antonio Bus Resource Cntr; coach bd of dir San Antonio Symphony Soc; chmn Alamo City C of C. **Honors/Awds:** Recip Merit Award 2nd Bapt Ch San Antonio Am Inst of Architects Design Award Prog San Antonio Chap 1968; certificate of commendation Houston Municipal Art Commn 1973-74. **Business Addr:** 1802 S WW White Rd, PO Box 20378, San Antonio, TX 78220.

HAYWOOD, ROOSEVELT V., JR.
Business executive. **Personal:** Born Feb 6, 1929, Mount Bayou, MS; married Adel; children: 6. **Educ:** IN U. **Career:** Haywood Ins Agy, owner. **Orgs:** City Councilman at Large Gary; state chmn Fair Share Orgn; fndr pres United Cncl Midtown Bsnsmen; fndr pres Gary's Midtown Voters League; mem adv bdGary Urban League; vice pres Gary NAACP; co-foundr pres Gary Toastmasters; natl mem trustee Pilgrim Bapt Ch. **Business Addr:** 1983 Broadway, Gary, IN.

HAYWOOD, SPENCER
Professional basketball player (retired). **Personal:** Born Apr 22, 1949, Silver City, MS. **Career:** Denver Rockets, 1970, Seattle SuperSonics, 1971-75, New York Knicks, 1976-79, Los Angeles Lakers, 1980, Washington Bullets, 1982-83; European League (Italy), 1981-82. **Honors/Awds:** NBA All-Star Team 1972-75; has developed videotape to aid in the recovery of substance abusers; Denver, Rookie of the Year, Leading Scorer and Rebounder, MVP; All-Star Game MVP; Sonics, Four-Time First Team, All-Pro. **Business Addr:** c/o Public Relations Dept, New York Knicks, Four Pennsylvania Plaza, New York, NY 10001.

HAYWOOD, WILLIAM H.
Company executive. **Personal:** Born Nov 4, 1942, Raleigh, NC. **Educ:** St Augustines Coll, 1960; NC State at Raleigh, 1961; Univ of NC at Chapel Hill, 1964. **Career:** R & B Prod Phonogram Inc, vice pres 1977; Phonogram Inc, natl program mgr 1975-77; Bill Haywood Inc, pres 1973-75; DJ Prod, pres 1972-73; WOL Radio, DJ program dir 1967-72; WOOK Radio, program dir 1965-67; WLLE Inc, program dir 1962-65; Kirby Co, sales mgr 1960-62. **Orgs:** Dir, Washington Baltimore Chapter NATRA 1971; head Broadcast Commn BMA 1979.

HAYWOODE, M. DOUGLAS
Attorney, educator. **Personal:** Born Feb 24, 1938, Brooklyn; divorced; children: Alyssa, Arthur, Helene, Drake, Phillip, Edward. **Educ:** Brooklyn Coll, BA 1959; Brooklyn Law Schl, JD 1962; LLM 1967; New Sch Social Resrch, MA 1970; PhD Cand. **Career:** Private Practice Law, 1962; City of NY, prof Political Science 1969; New York City Branch NAACP, counsel 1962-64; Human Resources Admin NYC, assoc gen counsel 1972-74. **Orgs:** Mem New York City Bar Assn; Nat Conf Black Lawyers; Am Soc Intl Law; Intl African Centre; Enterprise 9 Investigation Agency, director. **Honors/Awds:** Governor personal Appointee, New York Housing Corp. **Business Addr:** 128 East 31st St, New York, NY 10016.

HAZEL, JANIS D.
Government and public relations executive. **Personal:** Born Jan 19, 1963, Detroit, MI; daughter of Charlie H and Gladys D Hazel. **Educ:** Univ of Michigan, BA political science, 1985; L'Institute de Touraine, Tours France, Intensive French Language Program, 1985. **Career:** Congressional Black Caucus Foundation Inc, intern, 1982; US Dept of Transportation, policy planning intern, 1983; Senator Donald W Riegle Jr, legislative aide, 1985-87; Building Owners and Mngs Assn International, legislative representative, 1987-89; Congressman John Conyers Jr, legislative director, 1989-91; Assn of America's Public TV Stations, mgr advocacy progs, 1991-. **Orgs:** Americn Society of Assn Execs, 1992-; Women in Govt Relations, 1994-; American Women in Radio and TV, 1991-; WPFW FM Radio, chairman advisory board, 1989-94; Pacifica Foundations, sec, board of dir, 1988-; Telecommunications Policy Roundtable, 1995; National Black Media Coalition, 1991-95; Alpha Kappa Alpha Sorority, 1982-; National Blk Programming Consortium, 1991-95. **Special Achievements:** Proficient in French; Exec producer, Congressional Black Caucus Foundation, Inc, legislative conference Jazz Issues Forum and Performance, 1989-94. **Business Addr:** Mgr, Advocacy Programs, Natl Affairs, Assn of America's Public TV Stations, 1350 Connecticut Ave., Ste. 200, Washington, DC 20036, (202)887-8413.

HAZELWOOD, HARRY, JR.
Judge. **Personal:** Born Oct 8, 1921, Newark; married Ruth Gainous; children: Harry, Stephen. **Educ:** Rutgers Univ, BA 1943; Cornell Law School, LLB 1945. **Career:** Atty, 1948; Co Prosecutor, asst 1956-58; City of Newark, municipal judge 1958-74; City Newark, chief judge 1970-74; Essex Co Ct, judge 1974-79; Essex Co, superior ct judge, currently. **Orgs:** Mem Am Essex Co NJ; Natl Bar Assn. **Business Addr:** Judge, 804 South 11th St, Newark, NJ 07108.

HAZZARD, TERRY LOUIS
Educational administrator. **Personal:** Born Jul 8, 1957, Mobile, AL; son of Ora D Sheffield Hazzard and Milton Hazzard; married Tanya Finkley Hazzard, Jun 27, 1981. **Educ:** AL A&M Univ, BS 1979; Univ of AL, MA 1980; The Florida State, EDS, 1991, Florida State University, EdD Degree 1996. **Career:** Univ of AL, financial aid peer counselor 1979-80, residence hall asst dir 1980, coord/coop educ 1980-81; Spring Hill College, counselor/upward bound 1981-85; Bishop State Community Coll, asst dean of students, 1985-, dean of students, 1990-91. **Orgs:** Alpha Phi Alpha Frat; Natl Assn of Student Personal Administrators; Choir Greater Mt Olive #2 Baptist Church; actor/entertainer Mobile Theatre Guild; vocalist Mobile Opera; AL Assoc for Guidance/Counseling; AL Assoc of Deans of Students; mem bd of dir Mobile (AL) Opera. **Honors/Awds:** Cum Laude AL A&M Univ 1979; broadway audition Detroit Music Hall 1979; Kappa Delta Pi Honor Soc Sch of Educ 1979-81; Honor Roll & Dean's List student 1978-79; vocalist, Miss USA Pagent, 1989; publications in the Eric System, ''Attitudes of White Students Attending Black Colleges and Universities,'' 1989, ''Affirmative Action and Women in Higher Education,'' 1989; Vocalist, Governor's Inauguration, Alabama; Publications: Sexual Harrassment: What's Good for the Goose is Good for the Gander; Eric System, 1989. **Special Achievements:** Publications: Is There a New Minority on the Coll Campus?, 1990; The Recruitment of White Students at Historically Black Colleges and Universities, 1989; Attitudes and perceptions of white students attending historically black colleges & universities, 1988. **Home Addr:** 6322 Hillcrest Oaks Dr, Mobile, AL 36693.

HAZZARD, WALTER R. (MAHDI ABDUL RAHMAN)
Sports administrator. **Personal:** Born Apr 15, 1942, Wilmington, DE; son of Alexina Sara Ayers Hazzard and Dr Walter R Hazzard Sr; married Jaleesa Patricia Shephard Hazzard; children: Yakub, Jalal, Khalil, Rasheed. **Educ:** UCLA, BS, 1964. **Career:** Los Angeles Lakers 1964-67; Seattle Super Sonics 1967-68; Atlanta Hawks 1968-71; Buffalo Braves 1971-73; Golden State Warriors 1972-73; UCLA, head basketball coach, 1984-88, staff associate to the vice-chancellor, 1989-; Los Angeles Sports Academy, pres and co-founder, currently. **Orgs:** X-NBA Players Association; Kappa Alpha Psi Frat; 100 Black Men of Los Angeles. **Honors/Awds:** Coach of 1985 Natl Invitation Tournament championship team; Selected charter member of UCLA Athletic Hall of Fame; Olympic Team Member, 1964; NCAA Player of the Year, 1964; NCAA Tournament Most Outstanding Player, 1964; Eighth-leading career scorer in UCLA history; Pacific Ten Conference Coach of the Year; Father of the Year; Athletes and Entertainers for Kids. **Business Phone:** (310)794-0536.

HEACOCK, DON ROLAND
Psychiatrist. **Personal:** Born Jun 2, 1928, Springfield, MA; son of Lucile LaCour Heacock and Roland T Heacock; married Celia Arce; children: Stephan, Roland, Maria. **Educ:** Colby Coll, BA 1949; Howard Univ Coll of Med, MD 1954. **Career:** Bronx Psychiat Ctr, dir adolescent Serv 1975-79; Mt Sinai Coll of Med, clinical asst prof in psychiatry; Knickerbocker Hosp, dept of psychiatry 1970-72. **Orgs:** Mem Am Psychiat Assn; NY Dist Br of APA; NY State Med Assn; Am Ortho Psychiat Assn; NY Cncl on Child Psychiatry; fellow Am Acad of Child Psychiatry. **Honors/Awds:** Diplomate Am Bd Psychiatry & Neurology 1962; diplomate Am Bd Child Psychiatry 1965; editor ''A Psycodynamic Approach to Adolescent Psychiatry'' 1980; author Black Slum Child Problem of Aggression 1977; num other papers; article, Suicidal Behavior in Black and Hispanic Adolescents, Psychiatric Annels, 1990. **Military Serv:** AUS capt 1956-58. **Business Addr:** 5 Kingswood Way, South Salem, NY 10590.

HEAD, DENA
Professional basketball player. **Personal:** Born Aug 16, 1970; daughter of James. **Educ:** Tennessee. **Career:** Ancona (Italy), guard, 1992-94; DKSK (Hungary), 1994-95; Mirande (France), 1996-97; Utah Starzz, 1997-. **Business Addr:** Professional Basketball Player, Utah Starzz, 301 West South Temple, Salt Lake City, UT 84101, (801)355-3865.

HEAD, EDITH
Elected official. **Personal:** Born Nov 16, 1927, Autaugaville, AL; married Toysie Lee Head; children: Alberta, Patricia A, Timothy L, Robert W. **Educ:** Wilkins Cosmetology Sch, graduated 1955; Market Training Inst, graduated 1968; Cuyahoga Comm Coll. **Career:** Clinic Inn Motel, desk clerk 1969-72; East Cleveland Public Library, front office aide 1972-74; Villa Angela School, media aide 1974-75; City of East Cleveland, commissioner 1978-; St James Luthern Church, Hunger Center, volunteer, Grand Parents Support Group, president, currently. **Orgs:** Pres Orinoco St Club 1968-82; pres Comm Action Team 1975; Cuyahoga Democratic Party 1975-; Natl League of Cities 1978-; OH Municipal League 1978-; pres The Comm for East Cleveland Black Women 1983-; Omega Baptist Church, correspondance secretary, senior usher board; Helen S Brown Senior Citizens Center, choir, sightseers club. **Honors/Awds:** Honorary Citizen City of Atlanta GA 1979; Special Recognition ECCJC E Cleveland 1980; Certificate of Appreciation City of E Cleveland 1984; Outstanding Work Citizens of E Cleveland 1982; St James Lutheran Church, Hunger Center, Volunteer of the Year. **Home Addr:** 13918 Northfield Ave, Cleveland, OH 44112-3204. **Business Addr:** President, The Grand Parents Support Group, St James Lutheran Church, 1424 Hayden Ave, East Cleveland, OH 44112.

HEAD, EVELYN HARRIS SHIELDS
Consultant. **Personal:** Born Jan 12, 1944, Memphis, TN; daughter of Alzie L Harris Fletcher and John L Fletcher; married Ernest A Head, 1980; children: Le'Sha' Renee. **Educ:** Mott Community College, associates degree, police administration, 1968; Eastern Michigan University, BSc, sociology and criminal justice, 1975; Ferris State University, BSc, business administration, personnel management, 1983; Columbia Pacific University, masters degree, business and public service, 1987, doctorate, business administration and management, 1987. **Career:** Flint Board of Education, Office of Staff Personnel Services; Eastern Michigan University, Office of Admissions, graduate assistant, 1975-76; University of Michigan, Office of Minority Affairs/School of Nursing, administrative assistant, 1977-80; Management Consultant Associates, president, 1983-86; Big Brothers/Big Sisters, public relations coordinator, 1984-85; Head and Associates, Inc, president, 1986-88, chief executive officer/business consultant, 1989-, chairman, 1991-. **Orgs:** Board of advisors, American Biographical Institute of Research, 1991; ambassador, Private Industry Council, 1988-93; member, Arlington Heights Chamber of Commerce, 1986-93; board of directors, League of Women Voters, 1986-93; vice president of public relations, Toastmasters International, 1987-91; organizational representative, Lake County Chamber of Commerce, 1983-86; member, Mecosta County Area Chamber of Commerce, 1983-86; board of directors, Business and Professional Women's Club, 1983-86; program planning consultant, Washtenaw County Black Nurses Association, 1977; faculty committee chair, Phi Gamma Nu Professional Business Sorority, 1981-86. **Honors/Awds:** Outstanding Financial Chair Recipient, Mecosta County Council for the Arts, 1986; Citation of Honor, Business and Professional Women's Club, 1984; Public Relations Award, Phi Gamma Nu Professional Business Sorority, 1983; Leadership of the Year Award, Administrative Management Sorority, 1982; Scholarship Achievement Award, Kappa Alpha Psi Fraternity, 1975; Outstanding Fundraising Award, Urban League, 1965; Outstanding Fundraising Achievement Award, Administrative Management Society, 1982; Outstanding Contribution Award, Wesley Methodist Foundation, 1983; Woman of the Year, 1991; Lifetime Achievement Academy nominee, 1992; Governing Bd of Editors, certificate of appreciation, 1992; One of Most Admired Men and Women representing Illinois, 1992-93. **Business Addr:** CEO, Chairman, Head and Associates, 944 Locust Dr, Ste 1A, Sleepy Hollow, IL 60118.

HEAD, HELAINE
Television director. **Personal:** Born Jan 17, Los Angeles. **Educ:** Univ San Francisco, BA 1968. **Career:** The American Conservatory Theatre, stage mgr, 3 yrs; Broadway productions include: Porgy and Bess, The Royal Family, Raisin', Ain't Supposed to Die a Natural Death, production stage manager; theatre productions include: Second Thoughts, The Yellow Pin, Orrin, The Effect of Gamma Rays on Man-in-the Moon Marigolds, director; televison credits include: ''The Family Business,'' ''Wiseguy,'' ''Tour of Duty,'' ''Annie McGuire,'' ''L.A. Law,'' ''Cagney and Lacey,'' ''St Elsewhere,'' ''Simple Justice,'' ''Law and Order,'' ''Sisters,'' ''Frank's Place,'' ''New York Undercover,'' ''SeaQuest,'' director; cable television credits include: ''Lena Horne: The Lady and Her Music,'' associate producer. **Honors/Awds:** Director's Guild Award, 1992.

HEAD, LAURA DEAN
Educator. **Personal:** Born Nov 3, 1948, Los Angeles, CA; daughter of Helaine Head and Marvin Head. **Educ:** San Francisco State Coll, BA 1971; Univ of MI, MA 1974, PhD 1978. **Career:** Univ of CA Riverside, 1973-76; Urban Inst for Human Develop, project dir 1978-80; Far West Lab for Educ Rsch & Develop, project dir 1980-81; San Francisco State Univ, prof black studies 1978-. **Orgs:** Chair of bd Marin City Multi-Serv Inst 1978-; chair Black Child Develop Inst 1978-81; Comm on School Crime CA State Dept of Educ 1981; bd of dir Oakland Men's Project 1988-; Committee to Organize the 20th Anniversary Commemoration of the 1968 San Francisco State University Student Strike 1988. **Honors/Awds:** Minority Fellowship Prog Amer Psych Assn 1976-77; Meritorious Promise Award San Francisco State Univ 1984. **Home Addr:** 3614 Randolph Ave, Oakland, CA 94602. **Business Addr:** Professor of Black Studies, San Francisco State Univ, 1600 Holloway Ave, San Francisco, CA 94132.

HEAD, RAYMOND, JR.
City official, business executive. **Personal:** Born Feb 23, 1921, Griffin, GA; son of Pauline Head and Raymond Head Sr; married Ceola Johnson; children: Cheryl Johnson, Raylanda Anderson, Raymond III. **Educ:** Tuskegee Inst, BS 1943. **Career:** Griffin Co, city commnr, 1971, mayor 1977, 1985, mayor pro tem, 1975, 1986, 1989; Cleanwell Cleaners, partnerand tailor, 1956—. **Orgs:** Mem treas steward Heck Chapel United Meth Ch 1948; comdr 1946-51 quartermaster 1951—, Vaughn-Blake VFW Post 8480; chrtr mem Morgan-Brown Am Legion Post 546; mem Spalding Improv League; Spalding Jr Achvmt; C of C GA Assoc of Retarded Children; Spalding Pike Upson Co Dept of Labor 1972; bd of Family & Children Serv 1970; del to Natl Dem Conv 1976; vol worker for Am Cancer Soc Inc Spalding Co Unit; Cert Lay Sprk United Meth Ch; chrmn Pastor Parish Rel Heck Chapel Red Oak Charge; mem Griffin Dist Commn on Bldg & Loc; United Meth N GA Conf Com on Ethnic Minority Local Ch; convener Griffin Spalding Co Commn Human Reltns; pres NAACP; bd dir Spalding & Convalescent Cntr; mem trustee bd N GA Meth Conf; mem Griffin Spalding Hosp Authority 1971;v chmn bd dir State McIntosh Trail Area Planning & 1 Commn 1975; appointed by GA Gov Carter to State Hosp Advisory Cncl 1972; GA Municipal Assn 6th Dist Dir 1974-75; Dem Natl Convention delegate; GMA Municipal Commission; Spalding Co Health Bd. **Honors/Awds:** Outstdng Community Serv Citizens of Spalding Co 1969; Dedicated Serv Laciso Club 1971; Outstdng Serv Awds 1st Black Elected Official Caballeros Dlub 1972; Civic Improv League 1976; Heck Chapel United Meth Ch 1977; 8 St Bapt Ch 1977; Bicentennial Awd Griffin Spalding Bicentennial Comm 1976 Awd for 30 yrs of dedicated Svc; Disting Serv Awd Mayor, Businessman, Religious Ldr, & Civic Ldr 1977; Ft Vlly St Coll 38th Ann Awd; Man of yr Awd; Griffin Spalding NNBPW Club 1977; proclamation by City of Griffin; Mayor Raymond Head Jr, lifetime mem Vauhn-Blake VFW Post 8480; citation, Locust Grove Masonic Lodge 543; Griffin Branch NAACP citation, 1977, Roy Wilkins Freedom Awd, 1985; Tuskegee U and Spalding County Athletic Halls of Fame, 1985;certificates of appreciation, American Heart Assn; Amer Len Post 546; General Griffin Chamber of Commerce award, 1989. **Military Serv:** AUS s sgt 1943-46. **Business Addr:** 118 N 8 St, Griffin, GA 30223.

HEAD, SAMUEL
City official. **Personal:** Born Nov 20, 1948, Tampa, FL; son of Grace Head (deceased); married Karen Grant Head, Oct 24, 1988; children: Samuel Sherman, Shaunda Denise, Jonathan Spencer. **Educ:** Florida A & M University, Tallahassee FL, BS, 1970; Valdosta State College, Valdosta GA, certificate in govt management, 1980; National University, MS, 1989; Golden Gate University, Las Vegas NV, MPA, 1992. **Career:** Atlanta Board of Education, Atlanta GA, educator, 1970-73; Harold A Dawson Real Estate Brokers, Atlanta GA, real estate executive, 1973-81; Federal Emergency Management Agency, Atlanta GA, management specialist, 1976-82; Cuban Refuge Operation, Key West FL, deputy federal coordinating officer, 1980; EG & G Inc, Las Vegas NV, assistant personnel security administrator, 1982-84; NV Economic Development Co, Las Vegas NV,

director of commercial revitalization, 1984-85; Clark County Manager's Office, Las Vegas NV, senior management analyst, 1985-92; City of Seaside, asst city mgr, 1992-. **Orgs:** International City Managers Association; American Society of Public Administrators; Conference of Minority Public Administrators; National Forum for Black Public Administrators; California League of Cities; National League of Cities; Florida A&M National Alumni Association; Monterey County Film Commission; chairman, State of Nevada Job Training Coordinating Council, 1988-90; chairman, Clark County Minority/Women Business Council, 1987-92; Toastmasters International; president, Uptown Kiwanis International Club, 1989-90; president, Las Vegas chapter, Alpha Phi Alpha Fraternity, 1983-87; Prince Hall Free and Accepted Masons. **Honors/Awds:** Meritorious Award, Uptown Kiwanis Club, 1988. **Business Addr:** Asst City Mgr, City of Seaside, 440 Harcourt Avenue, Seaside, CA 93955.

HEADLEY, SHARI
Actress. **Personal:** Born Jul 15, 1964, Queens, NY; married Christopher Martin; children: Kyler. **Career:** Actress; TV appearances: "All My Children," 1991-93; "Kojak: Ariana," 1989; "Gideon Oliver," 1989; "Kojak: None So Blind," 1990; "Walker, Texas Ranger," 1993; "Cosby," 1996; "413 Hope St.," 1997; Film roles: "Coming to America," 1988; "The Preacher's Wife," 1996; "A Woman Like That," 1997. **Honors/Awds:** Image Award nomination, 1998. **Business Addr:** Actress, J Michael Bloom Agency, 233 Park Ave S, 10th Flr, New York, NY 10003, (212)529-6500.

HEARD, BLANCHE DENISE
Information security administrator. **Personal:** Born Aug 9, 1951, Washington, DC; daughter of Marlene Coley and Albert M Winters Sr; married Emanuel F Heard Jr (deceased); children: Latricia Poole, Michael Poole, Mannikka Heard. **Educ:** Attended, Montgomery Co Jr Coll 1969, University Coll 1976; TN State Univ, 1972. **Career:** American Security Bank, supervisor 1974-75, sr edp auditor 1976-83; Savings Bank of Baltimore, sr edp auditor 1984-85; United States Fidelity & Guaranty, information interity admin 1985-88; US Fidelity & Guaranty, supvr, data security, 1988-93; Computer Based System Inc, currently. **Orgs:** Membership chair EDP Auditors Assoc 1980-81; intl sec EDPP Conference 1982; mem Data Processing Mgmt Assoc 1986, United Black Fund of Greater Baltimore 1986-87; mem, Black Data Processing Assn; Womens Aux, Baltimore Chapter of NAACP; Natl Assn of Female Executives. **Business Addr:** 2750 Prosperity Avenue, Suite 300, Fairfax, VA 22031.

HEARD, GEORGINA E.
Airline executive. **Personal:** Born Aug 8, 1952, Chicago, IL; daughter of George & Minnie Heard; married Paul Labonne; children: Marc Labonne. **Educ:** Bradley University, BS, 1974; DePaul University, MS, 1978; Institute of Family Therapy, 1979-80. **Career:** Comprehensive Care for Families, director, 1980-82; Inwood Community Mental Health Center, Washington Heights, unit chief, 1982-83; United Airlines, human resources staff manager, 1983-86, personnel administrator, 1986-88, benefits communication manager, 1988-93, human resources manager, 1993-. **Orgs:** Youth Guidance, director, 1993-; NAACP Fair Share Corp, Advisory Council, chairperson, 1993-; Annual Blackbook Music Awards, vice-chairperson, 1993; OIC National Technical Advisory Council, 1994-. **Honors/Awds:** United Airlines Human Resources Annual Award, 1991; Outstanding Young Woman of America, 1984. **Special Achievements:** In-School Consultation: School-based Community Mental Health, Educational Resources, 1981. **Business Phone:** (847)700-7289.

HEARD, HERMAN WILLIE, JR.
Professional football player. **Personal:** Born Nov 24, 1961, Denver, CO. **Educ:** Attended: Fort Lewis College, Univ of Southern Colorado. **Career:** Kansas City Chiefs, running back, 1984-. **Business Addr:** Professional Football Player, Kansas City Chiefs, One Arrowhead Dr, Kansas City, MO 64129-1651.

HEARD, LONEAR WINDHAM
Corporate executive. **Personal:** married James T. Heard, 1964 (died 1981); children: four daughters. **Educ:** Rust Coll, BA, 1964; Atlanta Univ, GA, MBA. **Career:** Rust Coll, sec to dir of public relations, sec to pres; Amer Natl Bank and Trust, statistical sec; James T. Heard Mgmt Corp, Cerritos, CA, co-mgr, became owner and pres; Rust Coll, vice pres of bd of trustees; Vermont Slauson, mem bd of dir. **Honors/Awds:** McDonald's Golden Arch Award, 1986. **Business Addr:** James T. Heard Management Corp., 17401 Woodruff Ave, Bellflower, CA 90706-6746.

HEARD, MARIAN L.
Organization executive. **Personal:** Born in Canton, GA; daughter of Indiana Billinglea and Ural Noble; married Winlow Heard, Aug 31, 1993; children: Gregory, Derek. **Educ:** University of Bridgeport, Junior College of Connecticut, AA, 1963; University of Massachusetts, Amherst, BA, 1976; Springfield College, MEd, 1978. **Career:** Inner-City Children's Center, executive director, 1972-74; Housatonic Community College, instructor, 1976-84; WICC Radio, Bridgeport, CT, radio show moderator, 1977-83; United Way, Eastern Fairfield County, CT, director, operations, 1981-88, associate executive director, 1988-89, president, chief executive officer, 1989-92, United Way, Massachusetts Bay, president, chief executive officer, 1992-. **Orgs:** Blue Cross and Blue Shield, MA, board member, 1992-; Fleet Bank of MA, NA, board member, 1992-; American Management Association; Executive Women's Group; National Business and Professional Women's Club; Non-Profit Management Group; Women in Philanthropy; Women in Radio and Television. **Honors/Awds:** Walter Memorial AME Zion Church, Youth Leadership Community Service Award, 1992; Big Sisters Association of Greater Boston, Women of Achievement Award, 1991; Cardinal Shehan Center, Golden Tee Award, 1990; Girl Scouts, Housatonic Council, Community Leadership Award, 1990; United Way of America, John H Garber Jr Minority Dev Award, 1988; honorary degrees from Providence College, Bridgewater State Univ, Fairfield Univ, Boston College, Northeastern Univ. **Special Achievements:** Contributor: Corp. Bylaws, 1990, Distribution Policy, 1988, Agency Allocation Procedures, 1980-88, United Way; Allocation/Distribution Policy, 1982; Agency Self-Support Policy, 1981. **Business Addr:** President, Chief Executive Officer, United Way of Massachusetts Bay, 245 Summer St Ste 1401, Boston, MA 02210-1121, (617)422-6600.

HEARD, NATHAN CLIFF
Author. **Personal:** Born Nov 7, 1936, Newark, NJ; son of Gladys Pruitt Heard and Nathan E. Heard; children: Melvin, Cliff, Natalie. **Career:** CA State Univ, Fresno, guest lecturer in creative writing, 1969-70; Rutgers Univ, New Brunswick, NJ, asst prof of English, 1970-72. **Orgs:** Mem, Natl Soc of Literature and the Arts. **Honors/Awds:** Author of Howard Street, Dial, 1968, To Reach a Dream, Dial, 1972, A Cold Fire Burning, Simon & Schuster, 1974, When Shadows Fall, Playboy Paperbacks, 1977, The House of Slammers, Macmillan, 1983. Author's awards from NJ Assn of Teachers of English, 1969, and Newark Coll of Engineering, 1973. **Business Addr:** Author, c/o Macmillan Publishers, Publicity Dept, 866 Third Ave, New York, NY 10022.

HEARN, ROSEMARY
Educational administrator. **Personal:** Born May 1, 1929, Indianapolis, IN; daughter of Mabel Lee Ward Hearn and Oscar Thomas Hearn. **Educ:** Howard University, BA 1951; Indiana University, MA 1958, PhD 1973. **Career:** Lincoln University, Jefferson City MO, english prof 1958-, dir of honors program 1968-72, executive dean/acad affairs 1983-85, spec asst to pres for acad affairs 1985-87, dean, College of Arts and Sciences 1989-, vp, Academic Affairs, 1997-. **Orgs:** Natl Assn of Teachers of English; College Language Assn; Delta Sigma Theta; Jefferson City United Way, secretary, board of directors 1983-; Missouri Community Betterment Awards Competition, judge 1983; Mo State Planning Committee, American Council on Education, Natl Identification Program, member 1983-; Planning Committee, Natl Association of State Land Grant Colleges and Universities, member 1985-; Mid-Missouri Associated Colleges & Universities, vice-chairperson executive committee mid-Missouri; mem Missouri Assn for Social Welfare; reviewer/consultant, Amer Assn of Univ Women; advisory panel, MO Council on Arts, 1987-; reviewer, Amer Library Assn; reviewer/consultant, US Dept of HEW, 1977-79; Commission, Urban Agenda, NASVLGC, 1992-; pres-elect, bd of dir, Council of Colleges of Arts and Sciences, 1997-. **Honors/Awds:** Outstanding teacher, Lincoln U, 1971; Development Proposals, Dept of HEW, district reader 1977-79; Phelps-Stokes (West Africa, 1975) NEH, grants received 1977-80; NEH, Division of Research Programs, proposal reviewer 1980-81; American Library Association, CHOICE, consultant-reviewer 1985-; Comm Serv Award, Jefferson City United Way, 1987. **Business Addr:** Dean of College of Arts and Sciences, Lincoln University, 820 Chestnut St, Jefferson City, MO 65101.

HEARNE, EARL
Government official. **Personal:** Born Aug 2, 1956, Calvert, TX; son of Ellen Foster Rosemond and Earlie Hearne; children: Timothy Earl, Tiffany Charisse. **Educ:** University of Texas, Austin, TX, BBA, finance, 1979; Texas A&M Corpus Christi, Corpus Christi, TX, MBA, management, 1982. **Career:** University of Texas, Austin, TX, clerk, typist I, 1976; Amoco Production Company, Corpus Christi, TX, administrative analyst, 1979-83; Corpus Christi ISD, Corpus Christi, TX, paraprofessional aide II, 1984-85; city of Corpus Christi, Corpus Christi, TX, management & budget analyst II, 1985-, associate auditor, 1992-; City of League City TX, internal audit dir, 1995; City of Houston TX, Municipal Court, administrative supervisor, 1996; Galveston County Treasurers Office, assistant county treasurer, 1996-. **Orgs:** Member: NAACP, 1987, Government Finance Officer's Assn, 1989-97, Texas Association of Assessing Officers, 1985-87, United Way Finance Advisory Committee, 1987-92, Nueces County Mental Health/Retardation Advisory Committee, 1988-90; coordinator, Leadership for Tomorrow, city of Corpus Christi, 1988-92. **Honors/Awds:** City of Corpus Christi, Incentive Award, budget reconciliations, 1988-89. **Special Achievements:** Author: Instructional Manual, City of Corpus Christi, 1989; 2nd edition, Instructional Procedural Manual - Budget, City of Corpus Christi, 1991. **Home Addr:** 2501 Gulf Freeway Unit 244, Dickinson, TX 77539-3241. **Business Addr:** Assistant County Treasurer, Galveston County Treasurer's Office, 601 Tremont, Ste 306, Galveston, TX 77550, (409)770-5388.

HEARNS, THOMAS
Professional boxer. **Personal:** Born Oct 18, 1958, Memphis, TN; children: Natasha, Thomas Charles K A. **Career:** Professional boxer. **Orgs:** Volunteer policeman Detroit Police Dept. **Honors/Awds:** Super Welterweight Champion; Amateur Boxer of the Yr Award 1977; Natl Golden Gloves 139 lb Champ 1977; Natl AAU 139 lb Champ 1977; Won WBA World Welterweight Championship 1980; Won WBC Super Welterweight Championship, 1982; Won WBC Middleweight Championship, 1987; Won IBF Lightweight Championship, 1991; has won 6 championships in five different weight classes; Fighter of the Yr "Ring Magazine" 1980; Fighter of the Yr Boxing Writers Assn 1980; Fighter of the Yr "Ring Magazine" 1985; defeated Earl Butler, cruiserweight, 1995.

HEARON, DENNIS JAMES
Computer company executive. **Personal:** Born May 18, 1941, New York, NY; son of Dorothy May Bowles Hearon and David Rossignole Hearon; married Diana Elaine Jackson Hearon, Apr 13, 1974; children: Elizabeth, Micheal. **Educ:** City Coll of NY, New York, NY, BE, mechanical eng, 1963; Brooklyn Polytechnic Institute, Brooklyn, NY, MS, industrial eng, 1967. **Career:** Grumman Aerospace, Bethpage, NY, engineer, 1963-67; IBM Corporation, Somers, NY, asst general mgr, 1967-. **Orgs:** Chair, Westchester Education Coalition, 1990-; bd mem, United Way of Westchester, 1983-84; steering comm, Westchester Academy, 1990-; mentor, Horizon Club, 1989-. **Honors/Awds:** Black Achievers Award, Chicago Urban League, 1979; Community Service Award, Horizon Club, Norwalk, CT Chamber of Commerce, 1990. **Business Addr:** Assistant General Manager, Business Support, IBM Corporation, PO Box 100, Route 100, Bldg #1 4N05, Somers, NY 10589.

HEARST, GARRISON
Professional football player. **Personal:** Born Jan 4, 1971, Lincolnton, GA. **Educ:** University of Georgia, attended. **Career:** Arizona Cardinals, running back, 1994-95; Cincinnati Bengals, 1996; San Francisco 49ers, 1997-. **Honors/Awds:** Victor Award, 1995. **Business Addr:** Professional Football Player, San Francisco 49ers, 4949 Centennial Blvd, Santa Clara, CA 95054, (415)562-4949.

HEATH, BERTHA CLARA
Humanitarian/historian. **Personal:** Born Jul 22, 1909, Middletown Township, NJ. **Educ:** Harlem Hosp Sch of Nursing, Diploma 1930; New York Univ, BS 1948; Columbia Univ, MA 1958. **Career:** New York Dept of Hospitals, clinician 1931-74; Clinton P and Mary E Heath Ctr, co-founder with Mon Co Park System NJ 1974-80. **Orgs:** Mem Harlem Hosp Alumni Assoc 1930-, NAACP 1930-, Natl Assoc of Grad Negro Nurses 1937-, Amer Red Cross 1940-, New York Public Library Assoc 1944-; lecturer Focus on Black History The Heath Family 1944-; mem Amer Assoc of Retired Persons 1974-, Monmouth Co Historical Soc 1975-, Middletown Township Historical Soc 1975-; charter mem Belford NJ Prayer Group 1979-; commissioner Middletown Human Rights Commn 1983-; mem Amer Assoc of Univ Women 1984-; mem Amer Library Assoc NIAB Club NJ 1987-; pres, trustee bd Clinton Chapel AME. **Honors/Awds:** Proclamation Human Rights Middletown Twp NJ 1986; Proclamation Afro Amer/Black History (Mayoral) Middletown Township NJ 1986; honorary mem Natl Police Officers Assoc of Amer NJ State Chap 1987-; saluted as a Black Historian and Humanitarian by The Asbury Park Press, Red Bank Register, Newark Star Ledger, Middletown Township Courier; Humanitarian Awd East Central Dist of the NJ State Fed of Colored Women's Clubs Inc 1987. **Home Addr:** 179 Harmony Rd, Middletown, NJ 07748. **Business Addr:** Founder, Clinton P & Mary E Heath Ctr, Tatum Park - Red Hill Rd, Middletown, NJ 07748.

HEATH, COMER, III
Educational administrator. **Personal:** Born Feb 22, 1935, Eastman, GA; married Lois J Burke. **Educ:** Wayne State Univ, BS 1962; Univ of MI, MA, couns & guidance, 1965; Wayne State Univ, EdD, 1961. **Career:** Wayne State Univ, guidance counselor 1968-75; City of Highland Park, sch comm coord 1975; Highland Park Comm Coll, dir admin/records 1976, vice pres for coll serv 1977, dean liberal arts & scis 1981, pres 1978-91; Hampton Middle School, guidance counselor, currently. **Orgs:** Kappa Alpha Psi Frat 1960-; Phi Delta Kappa 1962-; consult Interdisciplinary Approach to Counseling Wayne State Univ 1969; asst prof guidance/psychol St Clair Coll Windsor Canada 1971; consult Sch Liaison for Boy Scouts of Amer 1972; prof guidance couns Wayne State Univ European Prog Turkey/Germany 1972; Highland Park City Council 1984-. **Honors/Awds:** Humanitarian Awd Radio Station WJLB-Detroit 1968; "Where Do We Go From Here?" MI Chronicle 1975; Outstanding Achievement Awd Alumni Chapt/Highland Park Comm Coll 1978; African Puppets in Global Context El Instituto Mexicana Del Seguro El Departmento Del Distrito Fed 1979. **Military Serv:** US Army, spec/4, 1958-60. **Business Addr:** Guidance Counselor, Hampton Middle School, 3900 Pickford, Detroit, MI 48219.

HEATH, JAMES E.
Musician, educator. **Personal:** Born Oct 25, 1926, Philadelphia, PA; married Mona Brown; children: Mtume, Roslyn, Jeffrey. **Educ:** Theodore Presser School of Music, Studied Saxophone; Prof Rudolph Schramm, studied Orchestration. **Career:** Composer, over 80 compositions; played saxophone with Howard McGhee, Miles Davis, Dizzy Gillespie, Art Farmer, Clark & Terry & Own Bands; recorded 8 Albums; performed on 75 albums with other jazz greats; Aaron Copland School of Music, Queens Coll, New York City, prof 1987-. **Orgs:** Mem Jazz Repetory Co; mem Heath Bros Quartet, Jimmy Heath Quartet; advisor, Thelonious Monk Inst, 1090-; advisor, Louis Armstrong House, 1987-. **Honors/Awds:** Jazzmobile performed "The Afro-Amer Ste of Evolution" 1976; currently Teacher for Jazzmobile of New York City; instructor for Woodwinds, Housatonic Comm Coll Bridgeport; Jazz Pioneer Award BMI City Coll of New York 1985; Jimmy Heath Day in Wilmington NC 1985; Hon Doctor of Humane Letters Sojourner-Douglass Coll Baltimore MD 1986; Jazz Masters Award Afro-Amer Museum Philadelphia, PA; composed first symphonic work "Three Ears", 1988.

HEAVY D (DWIGHT MYERS)
Rap artist, actor, producer, business executive. **Personal:** Born in Jamaica, West Indies; son of Clifford and Eulahlee Myers. **Career:** Heavy D and the Boyz, rap singer; singles and albums include: Black Coffee and Nuttin But Love; album, "Waterbed Hev," 1997; Uptown Records, pres; Universal Music Group, senior vice pres, currently. **Orgs:** AFTRA, SAG, ASCAP. **Honors/Awds:** Soul Train Award; Two-Time Grammy Nominee (music). **Special Achievements:** Music career has earned three platinum records. **Business Addr:** MCA Records, 1755 Broadway, New York, NY 10019.

HEBERT, STANLEY PAUL
Attorney, business executive. **Personal:** Born Jun 18, 1922, Baton Rouge, LA; married Mary Lou Usher; children: 6. **Educ:** Univ of WI, PhB 1947; Marquette Univ Law School, JD 1950. **Career:** Bank of Amer, vice pres asst sec 1971-76, counsel; US EEOC, gen counsel 1969-71; US Govt Dept of Navy Office of Gen Counsel Washington DC, dep gen counsel 1963-69; State of WI & Pub Serv Commn of WI, commnr 1961-63; City of Milwaukee, City Atty's Offc, asst city atty 1958-61; atty private practice Milwaukee, 1956-58; atty private practice, Columbus GA, 1955-56; NC Coll Law School, assoc prof of law 1952-55; So Univ Law School, asst prof 1951-52; US Govt Office of Price Stabilization Milwaukee, investigator atty 1951; Wendell Rosen Black & Dean LLP, 1996; Gen Counsel, Port of Oakland, gen counsel, 1976-95. **Orgs:** CA Bar Assn; DC Bar Assn; US Supreme Court; US Ct of Appeals; GA Bar Assn; Fed Bar Assn; WI Bar Assn; formerly chmn Exec Comm Natl Catholic Comm Serv; vice pres mem Exec Comm & Bd Dir United Serv Orgns Inc; chmn Pastoral Commn's Comm on Role of Church in Changing Metro, Diocese of Washington DC; mem Bd Gov John Carroll Soc & Pastoral Commn, Archdiocese of Washington; mem Exec Comm WI Welfare Council; Exec Comm Intl Inst of Milwaukee; Exec Comm Madison Commn on Human Relations; exec comm Milwaukee & Madison Chapters of NAACP; mem bd trustees Voorhees Coll; adv bd CA State Univ Hayward; pres Natl Catholic Conf for Interracial Justice; Bay Area Urban League; chmn CA Atty Gen's Adv Commn on Comm Police Relation; regent, Holy Names College; mem bd Wiley Manuel Law Foundation; mem bd Marcus Foster Ed Institute; mem Sigma Pi Phi Frat, Alpha Gamma Boulé. **Honors/Awds:** Recip Pub Serv Award Delta Chi Lambda Chap Alpha Phi Alpha Frat Inc 1962. **Military Serv:** Served USAF WW II a/c; Capt USNR JAG Corp Ret. **Business Addr:** Wendel Rosen Black & Dean, LLP, 1111 Broadway, 24th Floor, Oakland, CA 94607.

HEBERT, ZENEBEWORK TESHOME
Business executive. **Personal:** Born Apr 1, 1942, Addis Ababa, Ethiopia; daughter of Aselefech Aderra and Teshome Shenqut; married Maurice Robert Hebert, Jan 28, 1968 (deceased); children: Teshome, Rachel. **Educ:** Univ of IL Coll of Pharmacy, BS 1967. **Career:** Michael Reese Hosp, pharmacist 1967-70; South Chicago Comm Hosp, pharmacist 1971-74; The Life Store, owner/mgr 1974-; Arthur Treacher Fish & Chips, owner/mgr 1978; Hebert & Moore Store for Men, owner/mgr; Hebert Montissore School, owner; Hebert Enterprises, president/ceo; Frusen Isladje Ice Cream, Chicago, IL, owner/president, 1987; Nino's Men's Clothing, Chicago, IL, vice president, 1987. **Orgs:** Mem Jack & Jill of Amer Inc, SNOB Inc; vice pres & mem 87th St & Stony Island Business Assoc. **Honors/Awds:** One of the Top 10 Black Business Women in Chicago; One of the Top 10 Best Dressed Women in Chicago. **Business Addr:** CEO, Herbert Enterprises, 1639 E 87th St, Chicago, IL 60617.

HECKER, BARRY
Professional basketball scout/coach. **Personal:** Born in Washington, DC; married Merle Hecker. **Educ:** Frostburg State College, graduate, attended; George Washington Univ, master's degree. **Career:** B S Leiden Basketball Club, Dutch Professional League, head coach, 1975-76; George Washington Univ, assistant coach; George Mason Univ, assistant coach; Westminster College, Salt Lake City, UT, head basketball coach, 1976-78; Bertka's Views National Scouting Service, scout; Cleveland Cavaliers, director of player acquisition, 1985-87; Los Angeles Clippers, director of scouting/assistant coach, 1987-. **Business Addr:** Director of Scouting/Assistant Coach, Los Angeles Clippers, 3939 S Figueroa St, Los Angeles Sports Arena, Los Angeles, CA 90037.

HEDGEPETH, CHESTER MELVIN, JR.
Educator, educational administrator, professor. **Personal:** Born Oct 28, 1937, Richmond, VA; son of Ethel Carter Hedgepeth & Chester Hedgepeth Sr (both deceased); married Thelma Washington, Aug 16, 1969; children: Chester III. **Educ:** Blackburn Coll, BA 1960; Wesleyan Univ, MA 1966; Harvard Univ, EdD 1977. **Career:** Maggie Walker HS, teacher 1960-65; Macalester Coll, instr in English 1968-71; VA Union Univ, instr English 1966-68, 1971-75; VA, Commonwealth Univ, coord of Afro-Amer studies 1978-; Univ of MD, dean arts & scis chmn English & languages 1983-95; African Language Project, principal investigator, 1992-98. **Orgs:** Mem Phi Delta Kappa Harvard Chap 1976-; mem Sigma Pi Phi (Gamma Theta); mem S Atlantic Modern Lang Assn 1978-; president, VA Humanities Conf 1982-83; author: Afro-American Perspectives in the Humanities, Collegiate Pub Co, 1980, Theories of Social Action in Black Literature, Peter Lang Pub, 1986, 20th Century African American Writers & Artists, ALA, 1991; senior editor, Maryland Review, 1986-96. **Honors/Awds:** Danforth Assoc Danforth Found 1980-86; Certificate of Merit, Goddard Space Flight Center, 1990; Distinguished Alumnus, Harvard University, 1986; Distinguished Alumnus, Blackburn College, 1992. **Home Addr:** 1008 Schumaker Woods Rd, Salisbury, MD 21801. **Business Addr:** Dept English & Languages, Univ of Maryland, Eastern Shore, Princess Anne, MD 21853.

HEDGEPETH, LEONARD
Bank chief executive. **Career:** United National Bank, Fayetteville, NC, chief exec. **Business Addr:** United National Bank, P. O. Box 1450, Fayetteville, NC 28302.

HEDGESPETH, GEORGE T., JR.
Financial administrator. **Personal:** Born Aug 9, 1949, Richmond, VA; married Portia Meade; children: George III, Sheldon. **Educ:** Lincoln Univ PA, BA 1971; Central MI, MA 1978. **Career:** Miami Dade Community Coll FL, dir of financial aid & vet affrs 1978; Moton Consortium Washington DC, asst dir 1977-78; Lincoln Univ PA, dir of financial aid 1974-77; Univ of Rochester NY, asst dir student activities 1972-74; Lincoln Univ PA, accountant 1971-72. **Orgs:** Comm mem on Need Analysis The Coll Bd; institutional rep Nat Assn of Student Financial Aid Administr; mem So Assn of Student Fin Aid Adminstrs; mem FL Assn of Student Financl Aid Adminstrs; mem Omega Psi Phi Frat. **Honors/Awds:** Outst young men in am Jaycees of Am 1978; scroll of hon for serv to stdnt Omega Psi Phi Frat Beta Chap 1977. **Business Addr:** VP for Business & Finance, Johnson C Smith University, 100 Beatties Ford Rd, Charlotte, NC 28216.

HEDGLEY, DAVID R.
Cleric (retired). **Personal:** Born Apr 22, 1907, Mobile, AL; son of Pauline Hedgley and Noah Hedgley; married Maybelle; children: David Jr, Christine. **Educ:** VA Union Univ, AB 1931; Univ Chicago, AM 1935; N Baptist Theological Sem, BD 1945; Shaw Univ, DD 1955; VA Union Univ, DD 1957. **Career:** FL A&M Univ, chaplain 1936-44; Evergreen Church, pastor 1940-44; 1st Baptist Church, pastor 1944-74; Pastor Emeritus, 1974; Rising Star Baptist Church, pastor 1953-74; retired 1975. **Orgs:** Ministers Conf Rowan Bapt Assn; State Baptist Convention; ordained to ministry Baptist Church; asst pastor Olivet Baptist Church 1931-36; mem Mayor's Goodwill Com 1962-65; Phi Beta Sigma; Mason; Lott Cary Foriegn Missions Convention; Natl Baptist Convention; NAACP; 32 Degree Mason has held many exec postions. **Honors/Awds:** Hon certificate Mayor 1972; hon Plaque Ministers 1969; plaque YMCA; hon pin Urban League 1965; minister yr NAACP 1972. **Business Addr:** 700 N Highland Ave, Winston-Salem, NC 27101.

HEDGLEY, DAVID RICE, JR.
Mathematician. **Personal:** Born Jan 21, 1937, Chicago, IL; son of Christine Kelly Hedgley (deceased) and Rev David R Hedgley, Sr; divorced; children: Angela Kay Garber, Andrea Kim. **Educ:** VA Union Univ, BS Biology 1958; MI State Univ, BS Math 1964; CA State Univ, MS Math 1970; Somerset Univ PH.D (computer science) Ilminister, England 1986-1988. **Career:** So Adhesive Corp, chemist 1958-59; Ashland Sch System, teacher 1961-65; Richmond Sch System, teacher 1965-66; NASA Dryden Flight Rsch Facility, mathematician 1966-. **Orgs:** Asst prof AU Coll 1975-78; consultant Manufacturing Tools Inc 1982-86; bd mem Local Black Adv Group 1984-87; consultant Univ of Washington 1984-. **Honors/Awds:** Superior Sustained Awd Recognition Awd, etc 1966-87; numerous scientific publications 1974-87; Best Paper of Year (Scientific) 1976; Natl Exceptional Engr Awd NASA 1983; Natl Julian Allen Awd NASA 1984; Natl Space Act Awd NASA 1984; Special Achievement NASA 1988; Tech Brief Award 1992; NASA Space Act Award, 1994. **Military Serv:** AUS E-4 2 yrs. **Home Addr:** PO Box 1674, Lancaster, CA 93539.

HEDGSPETH, ADRIENNE CASSANDRA
Journalist. **Personal:** Born Aug 29, 1959, Norfolk, VA; daughter of Beulah Hedgspeth Reid. **Educ:** Norfolk State University, Norfolk, VA, BA, 1977-81; Connecticut School of Broadcast, Farmington, CT, 1985. **Career:** Cincinnati Enquirer, Cincinnati, OH, reporter, summer, 1980; Shoreline Times, Inc, Guilford, CT, reporter, 1981-83; Norwich Bulletin, Norwich, CT, reporter, 1983-84; Register, New Haven, Ct, political columnist, 1989. **Orgs:** Member, NAACP, 1985; member, National Association of Black Journalists, 1989-. **Honors/Awds:** Media Award, Greater New Haven Section of National Council of Negro Women, Inc, 1990 Journalism Awards: 1st Place, Sigma Delta Chi, CT Chapter, 1989; National Dean's List, 1981. **Business Addr:** Political Reporter, Editorial Department, New Haven Register, 40 Sargent Dr, New Haven, CT 06511.

HEFLIN, JOHN F.
Educator. **Personal:** Born Apr 7, 1941, Sweetwater, TX; married Anita Blaz; children: Kyle, Jonathan. **Educ:** NM Highlands Univ, BA 1963; Stanford Univ, MA 1972, PhD 1977. **Career:** Portland State Univ, asst prof educ admin 1976-; OR Dept D, EEO program coord 1974-76; Stanford Univ, asst to dean 1971-74; Merced Union High School, Merced, CA, teacher/coach 1965-70; US Dept Interior Denver, CO, cartographer 1964-65. **Orgs:** Portland Urban League; OR Assembly for Black Affairs; OR Alliance of Black School Educators; CA Teachers Assn; OR Educators Assn; NEA; Natl Cnl Social Studies; Policy Student Orgn; Phi Delta Kapp; bd dir Mid-Peninsula Task Force Integrated Ed; Am Ed Research Assn; ed dir NAACP; Natl Alliance of Black School Educators; ntl chmn Rsrch Focus on Black Ed (Am Ed Research Assn); commissioner Portland Metro Human Realtions Committee; Assn for Supervision & Curriculm Dev. **Honors/Awds:** NW Association of Black Elected Officials; Foundation Leadrship Development Program fellow 1970-71. **Business Addr:** Assistant Professor, Educational Administration, Portland State University, PO Box 751, Portland, OR 97207.

HEFLIN, MARRION
Company executive. **Personal:** Born Aug 28, 1963, Akron, OH; son of Marion L Jackson and Lou J Jackson. **Educ:** Ohio University, BBA, 1985. **Career:** Huntington Bancshares Incorporated, vp, currently. **Orgs:** National Association of Black Accounts; American Institute of Certified Public Accountants; Ohio Society of Certified Public Accountants; College of Business Ohio University, past president, board of directors; On My Own, Inc, past board of trustees; Neighborhood House Inc, past board of trustees. **Honors/Awds:** Ohio University, Most Recent Graduate Award; Columbus Area Leadership Program. **Military Serv:** United States Army Reserves, cpt, 1982-; 10 Military Ribbons, Served in Operation Desert Storm. **Home Addr:** 3268 Long Cove Court, Pickerington, OH 43147, (614)575-1227. **Business Addr:** Vice President, Huntington Bancshares Inc, Hm122, PO Box 1558, Columbus, OH 43216, (614)480-6279.

HEFNER, JAMES A.
Educational administrator. **Personal:** Born Jun 20, 1941, Brevard, NC; married Edwina Long; children: Christopher, Jonathan, David. **Educ:** North Carolina A&T State Univ, BS 1961; Atlanta Univ, MA 1962; Univ of CO, PhD 1971. **Career:** Prairie View A&M College, teacher 1962-63; Benedict College, teacher 1963-64; FL A&M Univ, teacher 1964-65; Univ of CO, teacher 1965-67; Clark College, teacher 1967-71; Atlanta Univ, teacher 1973-74; Morehouse College, teacher 1974-82; Tuskegee Institute, provost 1982-84; Jackson State Univ, president 1984-91; Tennessee State Univ, pres, 1991-. **Orgs:** Consult Congrsmn Hawkins & Mitchell; United Negro Coll Fund; mem NAACP; Labor & Indstry Com; I-20 Coaltn; Atlanta Univ Ctr Fclty Forum; economic and business consultant to many organizations in the public and private sectors; consultant Congressional Black Caucus, Natl Institute of Public Management, the Dept of Transportation; mem Amer Economic Assn, Industrial Relations Rsch Assn, Natl Institute of Public Management. **Honors/Awds:** Hghst endwd chair Atlanta Univ Ctr; 1 grant train HS Grads & Drpts; author of more than 50 articles on economic research; authored or co-edited two books "Black Employment in Atlanta", "Public Policy for the Black Community, Strategies and Perspectives"; apptd by Gov Bill Allain as Mississippi's rep on the Southern Regional Educational Bd; Phi Beta Kappa; mbrshp MENSA; NAFEO Achievement Awd in Research. **Business Addr:** President, Tennessee State University, 3500 John A Merritt Blvd, Nashville, TN 37209-1561.

HEGAMIN, GEORGE
Professional football player. **Personal:** Born Feb 14, 1973. **Educ:** North Carolina State, attended. **Career:** Dallas Cowboys, tackle, 1994-. **Business Addr:** Professional Football Player, Dallas Cowboys, One Cowboys Pkwy, Irving, TX 75063, (214)556-9900.

HEGEMAN, CHARLES OXFORD
Surgeon. **Personal:** Born Jun 15, 1940, Detroit, MI; married Jessye Davis (divorced); children: Elisabeth, Veronica, Charles Jr, Edward; married Lyndia D Snead. **Educ:** Dartmouth Clg, AB 1962; Howard U, MD 1966. **Career:** Pvt Prac; West Adams Comm Hosp, attending surgeon 1973; Cedars of Lebanon Hosp,

1974; Queen of Angels Hosp, 1973; Kaiser Found Hosp, 1971; Charles R Drew & Postgrad Sch of Med, asst prof surg; Residency in Intergrated Surgical Residencies Univ of CA Irvine, surgical residencies 1971; LA Co Gen Hosp, intern 1967; Am Clg of Surgeons, fellow 1976; Good Samaritan Hosp; Centinella Hosp. **Orgs:** Society for Clinical Vascular Surgeons, 1975. **Honors/Awds:** American College of Surgeons, Fellow, 1976. **Military Serv:** AUS mjr 1971-73. **Business Addr:** 1818 S Western Ave, Los Angeles, CA 90006.

HEGGER, WILBER L.

Catholic ministries director. **Personal:** Born May 6, 1936, Lemoine, LA; son of Derotha Sam Hegger and Luke Hegger; married Marlene Mouton Hegger, Jun 4, 1960; children: Kevin Norbert. **Educ:** Grambling State Univ, Grambling, LA, BS, Math & Science, 1960; Univ of Southwestern LA, Lafayette, LA, post-baccalaueate, 1972-74; Diocese of Lafayette, Lafayette, LA, permanent diaconate formation program, currently. **Career:** Lafayette Parish School Bd, Lafayette, LA, math/science teacher, 1960-72; Univ Southwestern LA, Lafayette, LA, asst football coach, 1972-74; Prudential Insurance Co, Lafayette, LA, district agent, 1974-80; Chubby's Fantastic Cakes, Lafayette, LA, self-employed, 1980-; Diocese of Lafayette, Lafayette, LA, dir OBCM, 1989-. **Orgs:** Treas, Grambling Alumni Assn-Lafayette Ch, 1960-; chairperson, Ministers in Black Catholic Communities, 1988-90; jail minister, Diocese of Lafayette, 1986-. **Honors/Awds:** Bishop's Service Award, Diocese of Lafayette, 1989. **Home Addr:** 201 Becky Lane, Lafayette, LA 70508. **Business Addr:** Diocese of Lafayette, Office for Black Catholic Ministries, 129-A Immaculata Circle, Lafayette, LA 70501.

HEGMON, OLIVER LOUIS

Clergyman. **Personal:** Born Feb 28, 1907, Boling, TX; son of Martha Robin Hegmon and J.C. Hegmon; married Emma Louise Jones; children: Paul E, Beverly Ann. **Educ:** Conroe Normal & Indus Coll, BTh 1937; Union Bapt Theol Sem, Hon DD 1950; Union Bapt Sem Inc, Hon LLD 1953; Bishop Coll, BA 1970. **Career:** Antioch Missionary Bapt Ch, pastor; Truth Seekers Bible Sch (broadcast over sevrl radio & TV stations since 1936), pres; Var Pastorates, 1933-. **Orgs:** Vp Prgm Voters League of TX 1947-49; Mayor's Com on Human Relat 1949-51; pres Bapt Min Union 1951-56; pres McLennan Co Br NAACP 1955-59; vice pres bd dir Ft Worth Area Counc of Chs; life mem NAACP; bd mem United Fund 1970-71; Mayor's Com on Human Resources 1973-74; mem Nat Ch Pub Rel Com Bishop Coll 1973-74; vice pres Ft Worth Area Counc of Chs 1974-75. **Honors/Awds:** Recip ldr of yr award Doris Miller Br YWCA 1950; dist serv award TX State Conf of Br NAACP 1974; KNOK Radio Sta Award 1974. **Business Addr:** 1063 E Rosedale St, Fort Worth, TX 76104.

HEGWOOD, WILLIAM LEWIS

Biochemist (retired). **Personal:** Born Oct 5, 1918, San Antonio, TX; son of Mary Bivings Hegwood and William L Hegwood. **Educ:** Tuskegee Univ, BS 1939; New York Univ, MS 1947. **Career:** Biochemist; Artist. **Orgs:** Reserve Officer Assoc, mem; Retired Officers Assoc, mem; Kappa Alpha Psi 1942. **Honors/Awds:** Exhibited Metropolitan Museum, artist 1976. **Military Serv:** Army Chemical Corps, retired Lt Colonel AUS. **Home Addr:** 1901 Madison Ave #221, New York, NY 10035.

HEIDT, ELLEN SULLIVAN

Educator. **Personal:** Born Aug 27, Brunswick, GA; daughter of Lucille Baker Sullivan and Benjamin Sullivan; widowed; children: Arnold Joseph Heidt Jr, Benjamin Darwin Heidt. **Educ:** Savannah State Coll, Savannah GA, BS, 1946; Columbia Univ, New York NY, MA, 1950; Univ of Miami, Miami FL, IA, 1971; Florida Intl, Miami FL, 1986-88. **Career:** Dade County School Bd, Miami FL, teacher, 1956-; Miami Northwestern Sr High, dept chmn of English, 1967-70; Norland Sr High, dept chmn of English, 1970-74; Dade County School Bd, Miami FL, program coord, 1974-88. **Orgs:** University of Miami's Women's Guild, mem. **Honors/Awds:** Oustanding Serv in Educ, Alpha Kappa Alpha, 1978; Scroll of Friendship, City of Miami FL, 1980; Certificate of Appreciation, City of Miami FL, 1984; Natl Council of Negro Women, 1988; Plaques, Certificates for Years of Dedication, Miami Northwestern Sr High School; author of a proposal and initiator of successful program to improve students' SAT scores at Miami Northwestern Sr High School. **Home Addr:** 5621 NW 19th Ave, Miami, FL 33142.

HEIGHT, DOROTHY I.

Association executive (retired). **Personal:** Born Mar 24, 1912, Richmond, VA. **Educ:** NY Univ, MA; Attended, NY Sch of Social Work. **Career:** New York City Welfare Dept, caseworker 1934; Young Women's Christian Assn, dir Ctr for Racial Justice; Natl Council of Negro Women Inc, natl pres 1957-97. **Orgs:** Served on numerous commns bds including NY State Social Welfare Bd 1958-68; US Dept of Def Adv Com on Women 1952-55; ARC bd govs 1964-70; past pres Delta Sigma Theta Sor 1947-58; pres's comm for Employment of the Handicapped; mem ad hoc comm Public Welfare Dept Hlth Educ & Welfare; consult African Affairs to Sec State; mem women's comm Office Emergency Planning Pres's Comm on Status of Women; pres's comm for Equal Employment Oppor; bd dir CARE; Comm Rel Serv; bd govs ARC; natl bd YWCA; dir YMCA Ctr for Racial Justice; currently holds bd mem with 15 orgns. **Honors/Awds:** Written numerous articles; rec'd 14 awds including Disting Service Awd Natl Conf on Social Welfare 1971.

HEINEBACK, BARBARA TAYLOR

Hospital administrator. **Personal:** Born Dec 29, 1951, New York, NY; daughter of Robella Taylor and John Taylor; married; children: 1 son. **Educ:** Howard Univ, BA TV Comm 1971; Univ of Stockholm, Lang Arts 1975. **Career:** CBS TV, asst to prod "Face the Nation" 1969-71; Swedish Natl Radio Stockholm, free-lance journalist 1972-75; the White House, press asst to the first lady; Communications Satellite Corp (COMSAT), mgr pub relations 1976-87; Scripps Memorial Hospital, San Diego CA 1988-. **Orgs:** Special consultant public relations firms & Univ producer radio prog Sweden; dir Washington Urban League; dir Chamber of Commerce, Chula Vista CA; mem PRSA; Natl Assoc Health Developers, Natl Society Fund Raising Executives; Sunrise Bonita Rotary. **Honors/Awds:** Articles in Stockholm's major morning daily "Dagens Nyheter"; Plaques of Appreciation, President Carter, Pres Tolbert (Liberia); San Diego Arts Board; United Negro College Fund Steering Committee of San Diego. **Home Addr:** PO Box 8604, La Jolla, CA 92038-8604.

HEISKELL, MICHAEL PORTER

Attorney. **Personal:** Born Sep 11, 1951, Ft Worth, TX; married Gayle Regina Beverly; children: Marian Phenice, James Dewitt II. **Educ:** Baylor U, BA 1972; Baylor Law Sch, JD 1974. **Career:** Dawson Dawson Smith & Snodd, law clerk 1974-75; Galveston Co, asst dist atty 1975-80; Johnson Vaughn & Heiskell, atty; United States Atty, asst atty 1980-84; Johnson Vaughn & Heiskell, partner 1984-. **Orgs:** Del Phi Alpha Delta Law Frat Conv 1974; mem Galveston Co Bar Assn; vice pres sec Galveston Co Young Lawyers Assn 1977-78; Am Bar Assn 1976-77; TX St Bar Assn; TX Dist & Co Attys Assn; bd dir mem Gulf Coast Legal Found; Disaster Relief Com; TX Yng Lyrs Assn; Min Recruit Com Baylor Law Sch; pres Pi Sigma Alpha Baylor U; pres Agiza Funika Soc Serv Club Baylor U; pres elect Fort Worth Black Bar Assoc; vice pres Tarrant County Criminal Defense Lawyers Assoc; assoc dir TX Criminal Defense Lawyers Assoc. **Honors/Awds:** Mr Navarro Jr Coll Corsicana TX 1971; 1st black to grad from Baylor Law Sch; 1st black asst DA Galveston Co. **Business Addr:** Partner, Johnson, Vaughn & Heiskell, 600 Texas St, 2nd Fl, Fort Worth, TX 76102.

HELMS, DAVID ALONZO

Attorney. **Personal:** Born Jul 5, 1934, Evanston, IL; son of Edna J Peterson Helms and Hugh Judson Helms Sr; divorced; children: Donald Anthony, Cybil Estelle. **Educ:** Northwestern Univ Evanston, BS Bus Admin 1957; Boalt Hall Sch of Law, JD 1969; Attended, John F Kennedy Sch of Govt; Harvard Univ Cambridge 1985 Teaching Fellow. **Career:** Matson Navigation Co, mgr marketing rsch 1959-66; Paul Weiss Rifkind Wharton & Garrison, assoc atty 1969-73; State of CA, special asst to gov 1973-75; NAACP Natl Office & Western Regional Office, consul 1974-78; Bar Assn, exec sec civil rights 1974-79; David A Helms & Assocs, atty/consultant, 1974-; IL Inst of Tech Chicago Kent Coll of Law, asst dean & faculty 1979-81; Cases of Air Traffic Controller Terminations, 1981; Office of Regional Cnsl Fed Aviation Adminstrn, genl aviations attorney, 1982-84; Dr Hycel B Taylor Natl Pres Operation PUSH, legal counsel 1986. **Orgs:** Bd mem Public Advocates San Francisco 1973-76; bd mem KQED Channel 9 PBS San Francisco 1974-78; mem Natl Bar Assn 1973-; bd mem Family Focus Evanston 1983-; proj dir Chicago Volunteer Legal Serv Fndtn Chicago 1983-; consul NAACP Natl Ofc & Western Regional Ofc San Francisco New York City 1974-78; mem CA Assn of Black Lawyers 1975-79; mem Cook Co Bar Assn Chicago 1980-; mem Amer Bar Assn 1979-; mem Chicago Bar Assn 1979-; mem Urban League Chicago 1982-. **Honors/Awds:** One of Ten Outstanding Young Men Jr Chamber of Commerce San Francisco 1965-66, New York City 1970; Dean's Award Boalt Hall Sch of Law Univ of CA Berkeley 1969; Image Award NAACP Beverly Hills/Hollywood Branch 1974. **Military Serv:** USN aerographer's mate first class 1956-60; Disting Serv Medal Joint Task Force 7 Operation Redwing 1956. **Home Addr:** 1802 Hovland Ct, Evanston, IL 60201. **Business Addr:** Attorney/Real Estate Broker, David A Helms & Associates, 53 W Jackson Blvd, Suite 728, Chicago, IL 60605.

HEMBY, DOROTHY JEAN

Educational administrator. **Personal:** Born Aug 21, Greenville, NC. **Educ:** Essex Co Coll, AS Liberal Arts (Cum Laude) 1975; Montclair State Coll, Sociology & Social Studies (honor soc) 1975; Kean Coll of NJ, Student Personnel Serv (Summa Cum Laude) 1977. **Career:** Newark Bd of Educ, tchr 1974-76; Kean Coll of NJ, coll counselor 1976-77; Passaic Co Coll, coll counselor/admin 1978-. **Orgs:** Chairperson Passaic Co Coll Student Life 1983-84; mem NJ Black Issues Assoc 1984; comm mem NJ Assoc of Black Educators 1979-; chairperson HOPE Orgn 1978-82; mem NJ EOF Professional Assoc Inc 1978-; exec bd/secty Passaic Co Admin Assoc 1984-; counselor The Love of Jesus Ministry 1983-; advisor/consul Passaic Co Newman Christian Club 1983-; exec bd/treas Passaic County Coll Admin Assoc 1985-88; mem Amer Assoc for Counseling and Develop; chairperson, mission and goals middlestate committee, Passaic County Coll; bd mem Human Svcs Prog, Passaic Cty Comm Coll, co-chair Alcohol & Drug Awareness Comm, 1993-; NJ Higher Education Consortium. **Honors/Awds:** Graduate Scholarship NJ Personnel Guidance Assn 1976-77; Counselor of the Year Award, 1993; Excellence Awards, New Jersey Council of County Colleges, 1995. **Business Addr:** College Counselor/Admin, Passaic County College, College Blvd, Paterson, NJ 07509.

HEMMINGWAY, BEULAH S.

Educator. **Personal:** Born Mar 11, 1943, Clarksdale, MS; daughter of Pennie Ree Smith and Willie Smith Jr (deceased); married Theodore Hemmingway; children: Kofi Patrice, Julius Chaka. **Educ:** Coahoma Jr Coll, 1962; Alcorn State Univ, BS 1964; NC Central Univ, MA 1965; FL State Univ, PhD 1981. **Career:** Southern University, teacher, 1965-66; Voorhees College, teacher, 1966-67; Benedict College, teacher, 1967-72; Florida A&M University, associate professor, language & literature, beginning 1972, professor, currently. **Orgs:** Natl Council of Teachers of English; College Language Association; FL College, English Teachers, Undergrad Council for the College of Arts & Science 1982-; Role & Scope Committee 1976; Library Resource Comm 1977; Curriculum Comm for Lang & Lit; Southern Association of Colleges & Schools Editing Committee; Homecoming Committee 1983; chairperson Poetry Festival 1975-82; advisor Lambda Iota Tau 1975-82; search comm for vp academic affairs FL A&M Univ 1982; Coll Level Acad Skills Test Task Force; reader for scoring state-wide essays holistically; board of directors LeMoyne Art Foundation 1980-82; Mothers March of Dimes 1982-; vice pres Natl Council of Negro Women 1982-; Jack & Jill of America 1979-81; prog chairperson 112th anniv Bethel Baptist Church; Tallahassee Urban League; NAACP; panelist FL Division of Cultural Affairs 1986; American Popular Culture Assn 1988; Drifters Inc 1989. **Honors/Awds:** Florida A&M University, Teacher of the Year, 1987-88, Meritorious Service Award, 15-19 years, 1988; Teaching Incentive Award Program (TIP), Winner, 1993. **Special Achievements:** Author, publications include: "Critics Assessment of Faulkners Black Characters FL A&M Univ" 1978; "A Comparative Pilot Study by Sex & Race of the Use of Slang" Soc for Gen Syst Rsch 1978; "Abyss-Gwendolyn Brooks Women" FL A&M Univ Bulletin; read paper 45th Annual Convention of Coll Lang Assoc 1985 "Can Computer Managed Grammar Make a Difference That Makes a Difference?"; Author Chapter 4, "Through the Prism of Africanity: A Preliminary Investigation of Zora Neale Hurston's Mules and Men," presented paper at American Popular Culture Assn 1989; "Through the Prism of Africanity," Zora in Florida, 1991; seminar: "Black Women Writers," 1983; workshop: "Teaching English Composition," Bay County English Teachers, Panama City, Florida; numerous other publications. **Home Addr:** 545 Victory Garden Dr, Tallahassee, FL 32301. **Business Addr:** Professor, Language & Literature, Florida A&M University, Tallahassee, FL 32307.

HEMPHILL, FRANK

Educator. **Personal:** Born Nov 16, 1943, Cleveland; married Brenda; children: Tracie, Dawn, Frank John Parker, Jr. **Educ:** W KY U, BS 1968; Kent State U, MEd 1975. **Career:** Assoc Dean Students, Dir Acad Assts, 1975-; Tching Asst Biology, 1971-73; Shaw HS E Cleveland, biology teacher 1968-71. **Orgs:** Mem Minority Educ Serv Assn; vice pres Black Studie Consortium NE OH. **Honors/Awds:** Martha Jennings Fellowshp 1971; outst contrib award Alliance Black Consciousness Assn Hiram OH. **Business Addr:** Dean Students Ofc, Hiram Coll, Hiram, OH 44234.

HEMPHILL, MILEY MAE

Educator, cleric (retired). **Personal:** Born Jan 8, 1914, Gwinnett Co; married John R. **Educ:** Morris Brown Coll, AB 1950; Atlanta U, MA 1957; Coll of New Truth, DD, 1970. **Career:** Tchr Prin 23 Yrs; Gwinnett-Jackson Co & Winder City Sch, curriculum dir 9 Yrs; GA Dept of Edn, reading-English specialist 8 yrs; notary public, 1957-; West Hunter Street Baptist Church, associate minister, 1980-. **Orgs:** Life mem NEA; GEA; GTEA; ACS; pres Atlanta GA Jeanes Circiulum Dirs; dir Region IV Fine Arts; pres Royal Oaks Manor Comm Club; YMCA; Helen A Whiting Society, president, 1989-. **Honors/Awds:** Union Bapt Seminary, LLD, 1974, LHD, 1976; Bronze Woman of Yr in Educ 1966; Outstanding Personalities of the South, 1972. **Home Addr:** 896 Woodmere Drive, NW, Atlanta, GA 30318-6002.

HEMPHILL, PAUL W.

Director. **Personal:** marrIed Vernal. **Educ:** Wayne U, BA 1947. **Career:** Mayor's Ofc for Sr Citizens & Handicapped, dir field serv 1973-; Corrections & Yth Svc, dep dir 1970-73; Chicago Com on Urban Oppor, asst dir personnel 1968-70. **Orgs:** Mem Nat Counc of Soc Workers; mem Nat Assn for Comm Devel; Am Gerontological Soc; Am Soc for Pub Adm; Kappa Alpha Psi Frat. **Honors/Awds:** VIP award outst comm serv State of IL Lt Gov Ofc; award for outst serv to human family Chicago's "We Do Care" Com; award for outst training in comm resources HEW Region. **Military Serv:** USN. **Business Addr:** 330 S Wells, Chicago, IL 60606.

HEMPSTEAD, HESSLEY
Professional football player. **Personal:** Born Jan 29, 1972, Upland, CA. **Educ:** Kansas, attended. **Career:** Detroit Lions, guard, 1995-. **Business Addr:** Professional Football Player, Detroit Lions, 1200 Featherstone Rd, Pontiac, MI 48342, (248)335-4131.

HEMSLEY, SHERMAN
Actor, comedian. **Personal:** Born Feb 1, 1938, Philadelphia, PA. **Educ:** Attended, Philadelphia Acad Dramatic Arts; studied with Negro Ensemble Co NY, Lloyd Richards. **Career:** Actor, tv: All in the Family, 1973-75; The Jeffersons, 1975-85; Amen, 1986-; stage: Purlie, Broadway, 1970, played Gitlow; Don't Bother Me I Can't Cope; I'm Not Rappaport, 1987; The Odd Couple; Norman Is That You?, 1986; film: Alice in Wonderland, 1985; owner Love Is Inc (production company). **Orgs:** Mem AFTRA, Vinnette Carroll's Urban Arts Corps, Actors' Equity Assn, Screen Actors Guild. **Honors/Awds:** NAACP Image Awd 1976, 1987; Hollywood Fgn Press Assn award; Golden Globe award.

HENCE, MARIE J.
Violinist. **Personal:** Born Jul 2, 1936, Trenton, NJ. **Educ:** New Eng Conservatory Music, BM, MM 1958-60; Tanglewood, 1956-58; Yale Summer Sch Music & Art, 1960. **Career:** Musicians on Broadway, 1st female music contractor; Shubert Theatres, 1961-74.

HENDERSON, ALAN LYBROOKS
Professional basketball player. **Personal:** Born Dec 12, 1972, Indianapolis, IN. **Educ:** Indiana, bachelor's degree in biology. **Career:** Atlanta Hawks, forward, 1995-. **Special Achievements:** NBA, First Round Draft Pick, #16 Pick, 1995. **Business Addr:** Professional Basketball Player, Atlanta Hawks, One CNN Center, Ste 405, Atlanta, GA 30335, (404)827-3800.

HENDERSON, ANGELO B.
Journalist. **Personal:** Born Oct 14, 1962, Louisville, KY; son of Ruby M Henderson and Roger L Henderson; married Felecia Dixon Henderson, Oct 21, 1989. **Educ:** University of Kentucky, BA, journalism, 1985. **Career:** Walt Disney World, intern/attractions, 1982; WHAS-TV (CBS affiliate), reporting intern, 1983; The Wall Street Journal, Cleveland, OH, intern, 1984; Lexington Herald Leader, intern, 1984-85; Detroit Free Press, intern, 1985; St Petersburg Times, staff writer, 1985-86; The Courier-Journal, Louisville, KY, business reporter, 1986-89; Detroit News, business reporter/columist, 1989-93, city desk reporter, 1993-95; Wall Street Journal, staff reporter, 1995-. **Orgs:** Detroit Chapter of the National Association of Black Journalists, former president; Natl Assn of Black Journalists, parliamentarian, former natl and executive bd mem. **Honors/Awds:** Detroit Press Club Foundation, 1st Place, 1993; Unity Award for Excellence in Minority Reporting for Public Affairs/Social Issues, 1993; Natl Asson of Black Journalists Award, Outstanding Coverage of the Black Condition for a series of Business Stories, 1992; Best of Gannett Award for Business/Consumer Reporting, 1991. **Business Addr:** Deputy Bureau Chief, The Wall Street Journal, 500 Woodward Ave, Ste 1950, Detroit, MI 48226.

HENDERSON, AUSTRALIA TARVER
Educator. **Personal:** Born Feb 8, 1942, Ft Worth; married William. **Educ:** Univ IA, ABD 1975; OH U, MA 1965; Fisk U, BA 1964. **Career:** Univ IA, tchng resrch fellow 1971-74; FL A & M, instr 1968-71; Pontiac N HS, tchr 1966-69; MI Valley St Coll, instr 1965-66; AWAKE, tchr dir 1969; Prog Plan Proj Upward Bound, tchr 1968, 1971-72; FL A&M Univ Midwest Modern Lang Assn, present asst prof 1973-74; S Atlantic Mod Lang Assn, present; Coll Lang Assn present. **Orgs:** Organ staff Camp COCO Tallahassee 1970-71; retreat consult Race Rel FL Coll Campuses 1970. **Honors/Awds:** Four yr coll scholar Mary Gibbs Jones-Jesse H Jones Scholar 1960-64; fellow Nat Fellow Fund 1973-74.

HENDERSON, CARL L., JR.
Police officer. **Personal:** Born May 5, 1945, Pelahatchie, MS; son of Mary Sample Herderson (deceased) and Carl Henderson (deceased); married Eunice Henderson; children: Carl Dwaine, Gary Lee, Linette. **Educ:** Prentiss Junior College, Prentiss, MS, AS, 1966; University of New Haven, West Haven, CT, BS, 1976. **Career:** Hartford Board of Education, Hartford, CT, social worker, 1968-71; Hartford Police Dept, Hartford, CT, sergeant, supervisor, lieutenant, 1971-76, 1979-. **Orgs:** Pres, Hartford Guardians, 1988-92; member, Hartford Police Union, 1971-. **Honors/Awds:** Community Service Award, Hartford Guardians, Inc, 1980, 1987, 1995. **Military Serv:** US Army, Sergeant, 1976-79; Honorary Service Medal-Good Conduct, 1979. **Home Addr:** 90 E Burnham St, Bloomfield, CT 06002.

HENDERSON, CEDRIC
Professional basketball player. **Personal:** Born Mar 11, 1975. **Educ:** Memphis. **Career:** Cleveland Cavaliers, forward, 1997-. **Business Addr:** Professional Basketball Player, Cleveland Cavaliers, One Center Ct, Cleveland, OH 44115-4001, (216)659-9100.

HENDERSON, CHARLES
Engineer. **Personal:** Born Jul 30, 1937, Okolona, MS; married Janice Roberts; children: Eric, Marc. **Educ:** Northeastern U, BS 1960; UCLA, MS 1969, PhD 1973. **Career:** Aerospace Corp, dir data sys 1977-, sect mgr 1975-77, mem tech staff 1973-75; Aerojet Gen CA, engr spl 1970-73; N Am Rockwell CA, sr rsrch engr1968-70; Autonetics CA, rsrch engr 1960-68; DHE W, dev an automated human serv info sys; pub of sev tech papers on computer-aided med idagnosis; copenhagen Denmark, presented phD dissert at conf 1974. **Orgs:** Mem IEEE Biomed Engrng Soc; Eta Kappa Nu; mem PTA. **Military Serv:** AUS Signal Corps 2nd lt 1961-63. **Business Addr:** 2350 E El Segundo Blvd, El Segundo, CA 90245.

HENDERSON, CHERI KAYE
Association executive. **Personal:** Born Feb 3, 1947, Knoxville, TN; daughter of Marion Perry Henderson and James Noel Henderson. **Educ:** University of Tennessee at Knoxville, BS, 1974. **Career:** Knox County School System, instructor, 1974-76; Metropolitan Nashville Board of Education, instructor, adult basic education, 1976-78; Tennessee State Department of Economic & Community Development, assistant chief of procurement, 1976-78; Minority Business Opportunity Committee, executive director, 1978-79; Tennessee Minority Supplier Development Council, executive director, 1979-. **Orgs:** Citizens Bank Community Advisory Council; United Way of Middle Tennessee, board of directors; Nashville Business Incubation Center, board of directors; Northwest YMCA, board of managers; Leadership Nashville, alumnus; American Heart Association, board of directors; Third National Bank Economic Development External Council; Hugh O'Brien Youth Foundation; Matthew 25, Nashville Read. **Honors/Awds:** Minorities & Women In Business, Women Who Make A Difference, 1992, National Award of Excellence, 1990; Minority Business News USA, Women Who Mean Business, 1992; Davidson County Business & Professional Women, Woman of the Year, 1991; National Advisory Committee, Executive Director of the Year, 1983. **Special Achievements:** The Monthly, writer, The Tennessee Tribune, 1992; New Minority Business Resource Division for United Way, chair, 1991. **Business Addr:** Executive Director, Tennessee Minority Supplier Development Council, Inc, 220 Athens Way, Ste 105, Nashville, TN 37228, (615)259-4699.

HENDERSON, D. RUDOLPH
Attorney, federal official (retired). **Personal:** Born Jan 9, 1921, Cleveland, OH; son of Letha E Brooks and Disraeli R Henderson; married Irene Price. **Educ:** Case Western Reserve Univ, BA 1943, LLB 1954. **Career:** US Dept of State, dep asst legal adviser for consular affairs; Dept of State, staff asst to legal adviser 1977-96; Office of the Legal Adviser US Dept ofState, atty/advisor intl claims 1966-76; Pvt Practice Cleveland OH, atty 1954-66. **Orgs:** OH State Bar Assn 1954-.

HENDERSON, DAVID
Author/poet. **Personal:** Born in New York, NY. **Educ:** Bronx Comm Coll, 1960; Hunter Coll NY, 1961; New School for Social Rsch, 1962; East West Inst, 1964; Univ Without Walls Berkeley 1972. **Career:** SEEK prog City Coll of NY, lecturer 1967-69; CCNY, poet-in-resd 1969-70; Univ of CA Bekreley, lecturer 1970-72; full time author 1973-79; Umbra Publ, editor 1962-. **Orgs:** Vstg prof Univ of CA San Diego 1979-80, Manopa Inst CO 1981; consult Natl Endowment for the Arts 1967-68,80, Arts Commiss City of Berkeley 1975-77, Ed Dept City of Berkeley 1969; consult Berkeley Public School System 1968, NY Publ School Systems; mem Intl PEN 1972-, Afro-Amer Triad World Writers Union 1980-. **Honors/Awds:** Great Lakes New Writers Awd 1971; Felix of the Silent Forest poetry NY 1967; The Mayor of Harlem poetry NY 1970; The Low East poetry CA 1980; Voodoo Child biography NY 1979; Poetry in Permanent Archives Libr of Congress 1978. **Business Addr:** Editor, Umbra Publications, PO Box 4338 / Sather Gate, Berkeley, CA 94704.

HENDERSON, EDDIE L.
Engineer. **Personal:** Born Feb 25, 1932, Quincy, FL; son of Ruby Green Henderson and Ennis Henderson; married Velma Dean Hall; children: Tracy, Dionne. **Career:** Professional Fighter 1955-64; Freedmen's Hosp, 1961-67; Amer Broadcasting Co News Washington DC, NABET engr. **Orgs:** Mem Local 644 Intl Alliance Theatrical Stage Employees; Hillcrest Hts Bapt Ch. **Honors/Awds:** Amateur fighter Golden Gloves NY 1949-50; So Conf Air Force Japan 1953. **Military Serv:** USAF 1951-55. **Business Addr:** Engineer, ABC, 1717 DeSales St, Washington, DC 20036.

HENDERSON, ELMER W.
Government attorney. **Personal:** Born Jun 18, 1913, Baltimore; married Ethel; children: Lee, Stephanie, Jocelyn. **Educ:** Morgan State Coll, AB 1937; Univ of Chgo, AM 1939; Georgetown Univ Law Sch, JD 1952. **Career:** US Ho of Reps, sr couns of com on govt ops. **Orgs:** Mem bd dirs Supreme Life Ins Co of Am; former exec dir IL Commn on Condition of the Urban Colored Population; served as Chicago regional dir Pres Roosevelt's Fair Employment Prac Com 5 yrs; exec dir Am Counc on Human Rights 7 yrs. **Business Addr:** 1640 Upshur St NW, Washington, DC 20011.

HENDERSON, ERMA L.
Entrepreneur, city official (retired). **Personal:** Born Aug 20, 1917, Pensacola, FL; divorced; children: 2. **Educ:** Detroit Institute of Technology; Wayne County Community College; Univ of Michigan; Wayne State Univ, MA. **Career:** Detroit City Council, city councilwoman, 1972-90, president, 1977-90; City of Detroit, councilman Nicholas Hood, aide; Erma Henderson's Wholistic Health Foods, owner, currently. **Orgs:** Bd mem, Natl Council on Crime & Delinquancy; League of Women Voters; Natl Assn Soc Work Inc; Michigan Academy of Sci Arts & Letters; Assn of Black Soc Work WSU; mem Am for Dem Act Bd; mem Interfaith Act Coun; life mem NAACP; Natl Coun Negro Women; bd mem Black-Polish Conf; organizer Women's Conf of Concerns; bd chairwoman Michigan Coalition Against Redlining; co-founder, Black Research Foundation; Delta Sigma Theta Inc; Alpha Chapter, Gamma Phi Delta Sorority; past chwm Women in Municipal Govt; Natl Leag of Cities. **Honors/Awds:** Honorary member, Eta Phi Beta Sorority, Alpha Chapter; numerous awards for outstanding service to community; first black to win against a white opponent in a city-wide nonpartisan election; Honorary Doctor of Humane Letters, Shaw College. **Business Phone:** (313)861-7575.

HENDERSON, FRANK S., JR.
Government official. **Personal:** Born Oct 12, 1958, Oakley, KS; son of Meade A Jones Henderson and Frank S Henderson; married Lorraine M White Henderson, Mar 26, 1988; children: Ashley A. **Educ:** Barton County Comm College, Great Bend, KS, AA, 1981; Washburn University, Topeka, KS, BA, 1987. **Career:** Kansas Dept of Social & Rehabilition Services, Topeka, KS, mental health activity therapist, 1979-82, social service admin, 1982-85; Kansas Dept of Corr, topeka, KS, corrections specialist, 1985-87; Kansas Parole Bd, Topeka, KS, vice-chairman, 1988-89, member, 1987-88, chairman, 1989-90, past chairman, 1990-; Kansas Crime Victims Compensation Board, exec dir, 1995-. **Orgs:** Program chairman, Governor's Martin Luther King Commemoration, 1991; vice president, Mental Health Association of KS, 1988-90; member, NAACP, 1986; member, Topeka Sunset Optimist Club, 1989-; member, National Forum of Black Public Admin, 1990-; member, National Association of Blacks in Criminal Justice, 1989-; commissioner, Governor's Advisory Commission on Mental Health & Retardation Services, 1988-90; councilman, Kansas Criminal Justice Coord Council, 1989-90. **Honors/Awds:** Special Recognition Award, "Court-Appointed Special Advocate", Third Kansas Judicial District, 1987-89; Youngest Parole Board Chairman, 1989-90; Service Award, Sunset of Optimist Club, 1988. **Home Addr:** 2700 NE 46th, Topeka, KS 66617. **Business Phone:** (913)296-2359.

HENDERSON, FREDDYE SCARBOROUGH
Travel company executive (retired). **Personal:** Born Feb 18, 1917, Franklinton, LA; married Jacob R Henderson; children: Carol Tyson, Jacob Jr, Gaynelle Henderson-Bailey, Shirley Coleman. **Educ:** Southern Univ, BS 1937; NY Univ, MS 1950. **Career:** Spelman Coll, asst prof applied art 1950-61; Assn Negro Press Chicago, fashion editor 1951-56; WERD Radio, commentator 1953-56; Pittsburgh Courier, columnist 1961-63; Henderson Travel Service, pres 1961-92. **Orgs:** Board member, Atlanta Council of International Visitors, 1967-; board member, Martin Luther King Jr Ctr for Social Change, 1972-; mem Natl Bus & Professional Women's Clubs, League of Women Voters; mem adv bd Small Bus Devel Ctr; gov's appointee to White House Conf on Balanced Economic Growth; mem Women's C of C, Amer Soc of Travel Agents, Amer Assn of Univ Women; pres National Assn of Fashion & Accessory Designers; Links Inc; Zeta Phi Beta Sorority. **Honors/Awds:** World Mother of 1951, Atlanta Daily World; Special Achievement Award, Black Enterprise Magazine, 1975; Catalyst Award, Interracial Council Bus Oppor; designated Certified Travel Counselor; African Trophy Award; Rosenbluth Award, Amer Soc of Travel Agents; YWCA's Acad of Women Achievers; Candace Award in Bus, Coalition of 100 Black Women; Togo Govts Highest Civilian Award the Order of the Mono; Cote d'Ivoire Award. **Home Addr:** 1691 Simpson Rd NW, Atlanta, GA 30314.

HENDERSON, GEORGE
Educator. **Personal:** Born Jun 18, 1932, Hurtsboro, AL; son of Lula Mae Crawford Fisher and Kidd L Henderson; married Barbara Beard; children: George Jr, Michele, Lea Murr, Joy Zabel, Lisa, Dawn Johnson, Faith Mosley. **Educ:** Wayne State U, BA 1957, MA 1959, PhD 1965. **Career:** Church Youth Svc, soc caseworker 1957-59; Detroit Housing Commn, soc economist 1960-61; Detroit Urban League, com serv dir 1961-63; Detroit Mayors Youth Commn, pgm dir 1963-64; Detroit Pub Sch, asst supt 1965-67; Univ of OK, prof of human relations, currently. **Orgs:** Disting visiting prof USAF Acad 1980-81; consult US Dept of Def, US Dept of Justice, US Commn on Civil Rights, Social Sec Admin, Am Red Cross; mem Kappa Alpha Psi Frat; mem Am Sociological Assn; mem Assn of Black Sociologist; mem Assn for Supr & Curriculum Devel. **Honors/Awds:** Citation for Achievements in Human Relations, Oklahoma State Senate, 1978; Distinguished Community Serv Award, Urban League of Oklahoma City, 1981; Citation for Affirmative Action Activities in Higher Educ, Oklahoma House of Representatives, 1984; David Ross Boyd Distinguished Prof, Univ of Oklahoma, 1985; Civilian Commendation, Tinker AFB, Oklahoma, 1986; Outstanding Faculty Award, Univ of Oklahoma

Black People's Union, 1987; Outstanding Contributions, Osan Air Base, Korea, 1987; Trail Blazer Award, Oklahoma Alliance for Affirmative Action, 1988; Outstanding Teacher, Univ of Oklahoma Black Alumni Assn, 1988; Human Rights Award, Oklahoma Human Rights Commission, 1989; Oklahoma Black Public Administrators Excellence Award, 1990; Martin Luther King Jr Award, Univ of Oklahoma College of Health Black Student Assn, 1990; publications: ''Understanding Indigenous and Foreign Cultures'', 1989; ''Values in Health Care,'', 1991; ''Police Human Rel'' 1981; ''Transcultural Hlth Care'' 1981; ''Physician-Patient Communication'' 1981; ''The State of Black OK'' 1983; ''The Human Rights of Profsnl Helpers'' 1983; ''Psychosocial Aspects of Disability'' 1984; ''Mending Broken Children'' 1984; ''College Survival for Student Athletes,'' 1985; ''Intl Business & Cultures'' 1987; Regent's Distinguished Professor, University of Oklahoma, 1989; Distinguished Service Award, University of Oklahoma, 1992; American Association for Higher Education, Black Caucus Award for Educational Service, 1992; Cultural Diversity in the Workplace, 1994; Social Work Interventions, 1994; Migrant, Immigrants & Slaves, 1995; Human Relations Issues in Management, 1996. **Military Serv:** USAF a 2c 1953-55. **Home Addr:** 2616 Osborne Dr, Norman, OK 73069. **Business Addr:** Dean, College of Liberal Studies, Univ of OK, 1700 Asp Ave, Ste 226, Norman, OK 73072.

HENDERSON, GERALD (JEROME MCKINLEY)
Professional basketball player. **Personal:** Born Jan 16, 1956, Richmond, VA; married Marie Henderson; children: Jermaine. **Educ:** Virginia Commonwealth, attended. **Career:** Guard: Boston Celtics, 1979-84; Seattle SuperSonics, 1984-86; New York Knicks, 1987-88; Philadelphia 76ers, 1988-89; Detroit Pistons, 1989-91; Allstate Transportation Company, president, currently.

HENDERSON, GERALD EUGENE
Chief executive officer. **Personal:** Born Oct 6, 1928, Strongburg, NE; married Josephine W; children: Gerald M, Kaul B. **Educ:** NE Wesleyan U, BA 1957. **Career:** City of Lincoln Commn on Human Rights, exec dir 1968-; Lincoln Action Prgm, prgm dir 1967-68; Malone Comm Ctr, dep dir 1964-67; Fairmont Foods Co, salesman 1961-64. **Orgs:** Treas NE Chap Human Right Worker 1978; pres Family Serv Assn 1978; 1st vice pres Malone Comm Ctr 1980; pres Comm Action Lincoln Action Prgm 1969-80; bd mem Lincoln Salvation Army 1978-80. **Honors/Awds:** Recip NAACP Serv Award Lincoln Br 1964; JC Good Govt Award Lincoln JC's 1969; distngshd serv award United Nation Day 1976. **Business Addr:** Comm on Human Rights, 129 N 10th St, Lincoln, NE 68521.

HENDERSON, HENRY FAIRFAX, JR.
Electronics company executive. **Personal:** Born Mar 10, 1928, Paterson, NJ; son of Elizabeth Hammond Henderson and Henry F Henderson, Sr; married Ethel Miller Henderson, Dec 19, 1948; children: Kathleen Carter, Kenneth, David, Elizabeth. **Educ:** State Univ of NY Alfred, Cert, 1950; William Paterson Coll, Seton Hall Univ; New York Univ. **Career:** Howe Richardson Scale Co, engr 1950-67; HF Henderson Industries, founder (on part-time basis), 1954-67, pres/CEO (full-time), 1967-. **Orgs:** Commr Port Auth of NY & NJ; chmn Governor's Commission on Intnl Trade; dir NJ State Chamber of Commerce; mem World Trade Inst of the Port Authority of NY & NJ; advisory bd mem for curriculum at State Univ of NY Agricultural & Tech Inst; bd mem, the Partnership for NJ; bd of trustees, Stevens Inst of Tech; bd of dirs, General Public Utilities Corp; bd of trustees, Community Found of New Jersey; member, President's Commission on Executive Exchange; member, The Foundation of the New Jersey Alliance for Action; advisory committee member, Essex County Superior Court. **Honors/Awds:** Outstand Bus Achievement Award; NJ Black Chamber of Commerce; Edmond L Houston Foundation 1979; Most Outstand Minority Bus Award; Recog of Bus Achievement 1982 & Black Achievers Entrepreneur of the Yr 1982 Awards from Leaguers Inc; US Small Bus Admin Contractor of the Yr 1983; Outstand Achievement in Bus & Pub Serv Award; Urban League of Essex Co Award; Natl Assn of Negro Bus & Profesnl Womens Clubs Inc Award; Man of the Yr Award; Natl Conf of Christians & Jews Inc Brotherhood Award 1984; Man of the Yr 100 Black Men of NJ Inc; Company of the Yr Black Enterprise 1984; Distinguished Business Citizen of the Year from the NJ Business & Ind Assoc; received 28th annual Essex Awd for Outstanding Serv to Business, Industry & Humanity 1986; Natl Black MBAAssoc awd for outstanding contributions the business community & the Passaic Valley HS Distinguished Alumni Awd 1986; Berean Award, United Minority Business Brain Trust Inc, 1988; New Jersey Entrepreneur of the Year Finalist, Arthur Young & Co, 1988; Outstanding Service to Business and Humanity, Hudson County Urban League, 1989; Image Award, St James AME Church, 1990; Honorary Doctor of Laws, Kean College, 1987; Honorary Doctor of Engineering, Stevens Institute of Technology. **Home Addr:** 315 Rifle Camp Rd, West Paterson, NJ 07424. **Business Addr:** President/Chief Executive Officer, H F Henderson Industries, 45 Fairfield Pl, West Caldwell, NJ 07006.

HENDERSON, HERBERT H.
Attorney. **Personal:** married Maxine D McKissick; children: Cherly Lynne, Sherri Avis Willoughby, Gail Henderson-Staples, Leslie Jeanine, Michael Renaldo. **Educ:** WV State Coll, BS 1953; George Wash Univ Coll of Law, JD 1958. **Career:** Attorney, civil rights & general practice; Marshall Univ, part-time instructor in black history, 1967-80; Henderson & Henderson General Practice, Huntington, WV, sr partner, currently. **Orgs:** Mem Cabell Co Bar Assn; bd dir WV Trial Lawyers Assn; WV State Bar; Nat Bar Assn; Am Trial Lawyers Assn; Mountaineer Bar Assn; mem bd dir Region III Assn of Mental Hlth; chmn bd trustees Huntington Dist united Methodist Ch; state United Meth Ch Conf; pres Meth Men's Club; Ebenezer Meth Ch; mem Kappa Alpha Psi Frat; mem, bd of trustees, Morristown Coll; mgr & supvr, WV NAACP Jobs Program, 1978-; state pres WV NAACP, 1966-; mem, natl bd of dirs, NAACP, 1980-. **Honors/Awds:** W Robert Ming Award, NAACP Bd of Dirs; Justitia Officium Award, West Virginia Univ Coll of Law, 1989. **Military Serv:** US Army, 1946-49; US Army, Korean Conflict, artillery officer, 1953-55. **Business Addr:** 317 Ninth St, Huntington, WV 25711.

HENDERSON, HUGH C.
Government official. **Personal:** Born Dec 3, 1930, Poughkeepsie, NY; married Sandra V Bell; children: Hugh III, Denise. **Educ:** Kent Univ; Univ of Indiana; Univ of Illinois; Univ of Wisconsin. **Career:** State Dept of Employment Relat, sec 1979-; State of Wisconsin, indsl commr 1978-79; United Steel Workers of Amer, staff rep 1968-78; Valley Mold And Iron Co, maintenance electrician 1949-68. **Orgs:** Mem Intl Personnel Management Assn 1979-; mem bd of dir Milwaukee Urban League 1974-79; pres Milwaukee Frontier Club 1977-79; mem natl bd natl OIC 1978-; chmn of the bd Milwaukee Industrialization Center 1971-. **Honors/Awds:** Certificate of Appreciation OIC Bd of Dir 1978; Outstanding Community Effort Award Dane City State Employees Combined Campaign 1979; Enlightened Leadership, Dedicated Community Service Award Milwaukee Frontiers Club 1980. **Military Serv:** US Army, 1950-53; Combat Medal. **Business Addr:** Commissioner, State of Wisconsin, Labor & Ind Review Commission, PO Box 8126, Madison, WI 53708.

HENDERSON, I. D., JR.
Government official. **Personal:** Born Jul 23, 1929, Lufkin, TX; married Jerlean Eastland; children: Brenda Kay Heads, Lara Wayne Parker, Gwendolyn Joyce McKinley, Bruce Anthony. **Career:** Recinct #2 Angelina Co TX, county commr 1979-F Home Savings & Loans Assn, building supr 1972-79; Lufkin Foundry Inc, material control 1971-72. **Orgs:** Master mason Franfurt Germany 1962-65; master mason Mistletoe Lodge #31 Lawton OK 1966-77; master mason Southgate Lodge #42 Lufkin TX 1978-; deacon Mt Calvary Bapt Ch Lufkin TX; pres Angelina Co C of C 1979-. **Honors/Awds:** Recipient KSM w/1 Bronze SV Stara; NDSM; GMC w/5 Loops; Purple Heart AUS. **Military Serv:** AUS sfc-e-7 1951-70. **Business Addr:** Commissioner, Angelina County, PO Box 908, Lufkin, TX 75901.

HENDERSON, ISAIAH HILKIAH, JR.
Clergyman. **Personal:** Born Aug 16, Lexington, MS; married Ophelia; children: Georgia, Ruth. **Educ:** Am Bapt Theo Sem, BA MT DD HHD. **Career:** Friendship Bapt Ch, pastor minister; Pleasant Green Bapt Ch, minister pastor 1944. **Orgs:** Past moderator New Era Dist Assn; past pres Inter-denominational Ministers Alliance 1961; pres Missionary Bapt State Conv MO; pres Friendship Village; mem Human Rela Commn KS City; denom rep Metro Inter-Ch Agy; asst sec Nat Bapt Conv USA Inc; dir gen Nat Bapt Congress Christian Edn; partcpBapt World Alliance 1955, 70; mem Evang Crusade to Austrilia 1964; Bahama Isl 1965. **Honors/Awds:** Recpt Urban Design Award Munc Arts Commn KC 1972; award bd dir K C Bapt Comm Hosp 1972; outsdng achvmt award SN Vass 1975; spl citation Mayor KC Charles Wheeler & Jackson Co Legislators 1974. **Business Addr:** 2701 E 43, Kansas City, MO 64130.

HENDERSON, JACOB R.
Business executive (retired). **Personal:** Born Jun 27, 1911, Abbeville, SC; married Freddye Scarborough; children: Carole, Jacob Jr, Gaynelle, Shirley. **Educ:** SC State Coll, BS 1932; Atlanta Univ, MA 1934. **Career:** US Housing Auth, fiscal acctg clerk 1934-37, housing mgr 1941-63; W/EDA, economic devel rep; Henderson Travel Serv Inc, pres 1955-75, bd chmn 1976-94. **Orgs:** Pres emeritus Atlanta Urban League Bd Dir; bd mem Butler St YMCA; trustee 1st Congregational Ch; former regional vice pres Alpha Phi Alpha Frat for So Region; Thirty-third Degree Mason & Shriner; mem Sigma Pi Phi Frat; mem NAACP; radio moderator Butler State YMCA; Hungry Club Forum & one of its founders; mem Alpha Phi Alpha Frat; former Boy Scout Leader; mem exec comm Atlanta Univ Alumni Assn; mem City of Atlanta Charter Comm 1971-72. **Honors/Awds:** Atlanta's 200 ''City Shapers''; 25 Yr Serv Pin Bd Dir Urban League YMCA; Membership Campaign Awd; Urban League Equal Oppor Day Awd.

HENDERSON, JAMES H.
Educator, government official. **Personal:** Born Apr 20, 1937, Lexington, NC; son of Callie Spindell Henderson and Henry Henderson; married Joan E Woods; children: Tonya L, James H Jr, James, Jennifer, Janet, Jacqueline, Patricia. **Educ:** Community Coll of the Air Force, AAS Mgmt, AAS, Ed Methology 1978-81; Pikes Peak Comm College, AA General Studies 1978; Univ of Southern CO, BS 1979; Webster Univ, MA Mgmt 1982; Univ of Northern CO, MA Counseling 1983; Harvard Univ, Graduate School of Educ, Institute for the Management of Lifelong Education. **Career:** US Air Force, educ supt 1955-81; Ed Ctr Hurlburt Fld FL, educ counselor 1982-84; HQ Strategic Air Command, command educ counselor 1984-; USAF Civil Serv, HQ SAC/DPAE, assistant dir education services 1989; education specialist, currently. **Orgs:** Mem Recorder Kadesia Temple #135 1975-; mem Amer Assn for Adult Continuing Educ 1978-; mem Amer Numismatic Assn 1982-; mem Amer Assn for Counseling Development 1982-; midwest coord Military Educators/Counselors Assn 1983-; natl certified counselor Natl Bd of Certified Counselors 1984-. **Honors/Awds:** Counselor Guide (Military) 1984; Education Services Officer's Guide 1989. **Military Serv:** USAF Msgt 26 years; Good Conduct Medal; Commendation Medal; Meritorious Service Medal. **Business Addr:** Education Specialist, HQ ACC/DPPE, Air Combat Command, Hampton, VA 23665-2773.

HENDERSON, JAMES H. M.
Educator. **Personal:** Born Aug 10, 1917, Falls Church, VA; married Betty Francis; children: Ellen Wimbish, Dena Sewell, James F, Edwin B II. **Educ:** Howard Univ, Wash DC, BS 1939; Univ of WI Madison, MPh 1940, PhD 1943. **Career:** Univ of Chicago Toxicity Lab, rsrch asst 1943-45; Carver Research Fnd Tuskegee Inst, rsrch asso 1945-48/1950-68; CA Inst of Tech, resrch fellow 1948-50; Biology Dept Tuskegee Inst, prof & head 1957-68; Carver Resrch Fndtn Tuskegee Inst, dir 1968-75; MBRS Program Tuskegee Inst, prog dir 1973-87; Div of Natural Sci Tuskegee Inst, chm 1975-. **Orgs:** Nom comm Am Asso Adv of Sci Fellow; mem Am Soc of Plant Physgsts; mem Tissue Culture Asso; mem bd trustees Montreat-Anderson Coll 1973-78; bd mem Soc of the Sigma Xi 1982-85; mem bd of trustees Stillman Clg Tuscaloosa AL 1981-90. **Honors/Awds:** Alum Awd Howard Univ 1964 & 1975; eminent faculty awd Tuskegee Inst 1965, faculty Awd 1976 & 1980; UNCF Awd for Dist Schlrs 1982; Distinguished Serv Awd SS-ASPP 1984; Lamplighters Awd Beta Kappa Chi 1984; Golden Key Natl Honor Society, 1995. **Business Addr:** Chairman, Div of Natural Sci, Tuskegee University, Carver Research Laboratories, Tuskegee Institute, AL 36088.

HENDERSON, JAMES HENRY, SR.
Dentist. **Personal:** Born Jan 29, 1925, Henderson, NC; son of Sarah Evans Henderson and James Henderson; married Mabel J White, Jul 26, 1956; children: Eryn Janyce, Edith Janelle, James Henry Jr. **Educ:** Hampton Univ, BS 1948; Meharry Med Coll, DDS 1953; FRSH 1972; FAGD 1979; FADI 1986. **Career:** VA Hospital, intern 1955-56; LA State Dept Hospital, 1956-59; Private Practice, 1957-; Iberia Parish Hospital, Dauterive Hospital, Found Hospital, mem staff; NO Charity Hospital, visiting staff. **Orgs:** Mem Pelican Dental Assn; Chicago Dental Soc; Acad Gen Dentistry; Am Endodontic Soc; fellow of Royal Soc HealthEngland; mem LA Com Human Relations 1965-75; mem LA Dental Assn; mem Am Dental Assn; life mem NAACP; fellow Acad of Gen Dentistry; chmn Counc on Dental Health & Planning of LDA; consult HEW; House of Delegates LDA; founder pres Community Progress League 1960-63; mem House of Delegates NDA CH of Credentia; of NDA 1962-72, treas NAACP 1969-70,; dir/founder Bacmonila Ltd 1969-; bd LA Sugar Cane Festival; mem Beta Kappa Chi Sci Soc; life mem Alpha Phi Alpha; Shriner; Royal Vanders Social Club; trustee Mt Cal Bapt Ch; PTA; HS Booster Club; ESSACH Com New Iberia School Bd pres Pelican State Dental Assn 1974-75; reference com Natl Dental Assn 1973-; dirNatl Dental Assn Foundation mem Acadiana Dental Soc; trustee Natl Dental Assn; delegate Amer Dental Assn 1986-88; pres Natl Dental Assn 1989-; Iberia Parish Recreation & Playground Bd 1975-; consultant, Health and Human Serv 1989-; 33 degree Prince Hall Mason 1978-; Greater Iberia Chamber of Commerce, board of directors, 1990-92; American Dental Assn, life member; Natl Dental Assn, life member. **Honors/Awds:** Civic Achievement Awd Omega Psi Phi 1962; Awd of Merit LA Beauticians 1968; NAACP Talheimer Awd 1969, 70, 72; 5 NAACP Certificates of Merit; Alpha Phi Alpha Man of the Year Awd 1975-76; R B Jones Consistory #298 Outstanding Community Serv Awd; Notable Amer of Bicentennial Era; Merit Awd for Dedicated Service to Dentistry in LA Acadiana Dist Dental Soc; New Iberia Freshman High School Service Awd (10 years); Distinguished Service Award, Louisiana Recreation and Park Assn 1988; Distinguished Denist Award, Louisiana Dental Assn, 1991; Dental Fellow of Pierre Fouchard Academy; Fellow of American College of Dentistry, LA Distinguished Dentist Award, 1993. **Military Serv:** AUS sgt 1943-46; AUS Dental Corp 1952-55; US Army Reserve 1st lt 1955-59. **Home Addr:** 2718 Curtis Drive, New Iberia, LA 70560.

HENDERSON, JAMES J., SR.
Business executive (retired). **Personal:** Born Jan 22, 1908, Bristol, TN; son of Sallie Ann and William T; married Julia Mildred Hicks; children: Ann H B, James ''Biff'' Jr. **Educ:** Hampton Inst, BS 1932. **Career:** Bankers Fire Insurance Co Durham, NC, 1932, asst sec 1937, dir 1937; NC Mutual Life Inc Co, asst treasurer 1953-62, asst vice pres 1962-64, treasurer 1964, vice pres 1970-72, financial vice pres 1972-78, consultant

1978-1983. **Orgs:** Trustee Mechanics & Farmers Bank Durham; dir chmn & mem exec com Mutual Savings & Loan Assn 1979; Durham Homes Inc 1976-; mem bd Harrison Construction Co; mem exec com Durham Com Negro Affairs 1940-; chm Durham Civic Co 1950-58; vice chm Durham Housing Authority 1958-71, chm 1971-78; mem Citizen Adv Com Durham 1961-; bd of dirs Durham Chamber of Commerce 1979-80; former mem Gov Adv Com on Low Income Housing; trustee vice chm mem exec com Hampton Inst 1964-71, chm 1971-85; co-organizer Durham Business School 1949, pres 1949-52, bd dir 1949-57; bd dir John Avery Boys Club; pres chmn bd dir Daisy E Scarborough Nursery School; former vice pres dir exec com Durham Mem Nat Bus League; finci sec Natl Hampton Alumni Assn 1945-48; past pres Durham Chapter NC Conf; mem StJoseph's AME Church vice c sr bd trustees; founder, Durham Business & Professional Chain. **Honors/Awds:** Hamptonian of Year Award 1954; past grandkeeper records exchequer; past mem bd dirs exec com Kappa Alpha Psi Fraternity; mem Durham Alumni Chapter Keeper of Records 1933-58, Polemarch 1958-75; recipient Alumni award Hampton Inst 1967; Centennial Medallion 1968; first annual award City of Durham Human Relations Comm 1969; Outstanding Alumni Award Middle Eastern Province Kappa Alpha Psi 1971; civic award Durham Com on Negro Affairs 1972; Laurel Wreath Award highest award of Kappa Alpha Psi Fraternity 1974; New 5 million dollar 9 story high physical devel named ''J J Henderson Housing Center'' Housing Authority City of Durham 1979. **Home Addr:** 202 Pekoe Ave, Durham, NC 27707.

HENDERSON, JEROME VIRGIL
Professional football player. **Personal:** Born Aug 8, 1969, Statesville, NC; married Traci; children: Taylor Denise, Tyler Jerome. **Educ:** Clemson. **Career:** New England Patriots, defensive back, 1991-93, 1996; Buffalo Bills, 1994; Philadelphia Eagles, 1995; New York Jets, 1997-. **Business Addr:** Professional Football Player, New York Jets, 1000 Fulton Ave, Hempstead, NY 11550, (516)560-8100.

HENDERSON, JOHN L.
Educational administrator. **Personal:** Born Apr 10, 1932, Evergreen, AL; married Theresa Crittenden; children: Dana, Nina, John. **Educ:** Hampton Inst, BS 1955; Univ Cincinnati, M Ed 1967, Ed D 1976; Inst Afro-Am Studies Earlham Coll, 1971. **Career:** Wilberforce Univ, pres, currently; Univ of Cincinnati, dean student devel 1972-76; Univ Urban Affairs, dir; Xavier Univ Cincinnati, lecturer Psych Ed 1970-72; Raymond Walters Coll, instr Psychology Ed 1969-70; Univ Cincinnat, asst dean students 1968-69; Xavier Univ, research asst 1967-68; Univ Cincinnati, 1957-67; US Public Health Serv Cincinnati, research asst; Sinclair Comm Coll, Dayton OH, Amer Assn Higher Educ, vice pres for student services; Amer Coll Personnel Assn. **Orgs:** Mem Council on Black Am Affairs; bd of dirs Dayton Urban League 1977-; bd of Dirs Miami Valley Lung Assn 1978; bd of dirs Miami Valley Counc on Aging 1979; bd of dirs Miami Vlley Educ Oppor Ctr 1978; editorial bd Journal of Developmental and Remedial Educ 1980; Assn Non-White Concerns; Nat Assn Student Personnel Adminstrs; Phi Delta Kappa 1971; commr Cincinnati Human Relations Comm; Cincinnati Branch NAACP 1969; chmn Educ Com; Special Task Forceto Study Racial Isolation Cincinnati Pub Schs 1972-73; Cincinnati Manpower Planning Council 1971-72; bd trustees Cincinnati Sch Found 1973-75; appointed Chmn bd commrs Cincinnati Human Relations Comm; Developemental Educ Adv Com OH Bd Regents 3 yr term 1974; editorial bd NASPA Jour 1974. **Honors/Awds:** Hon chmn Cincinnati Black Expo 1971. **Military Serv:** AUS 1st lt 1955-57. **Business Addr:** President, Wilberforce University, 1055 N Bickett Road, Wilberforce, OH 45384-1091.

HENDERSON, JOYCE ANN
Educational administrator. **Personal:** Born Jan 12, 1947, Oklahoma City, OK; married William Gerald; children: Kevin G, Wm Kelly. **Educ:** Langston Univ Ok, BS 1969; Central State Univ Edmond OK MS 1973. **Career:** OK City School System Adult Educ, prin 1980-; Harvard Middle School OK City School System, asst prin 1978-80; Life Guthrie Job Corps Center, supvr basic educ & dept head of center 1976-78; Orchard Park Girls School Ok City School System, counselor 1974-76; Teacher Corps Univ of OK & OK City School System, teacher corps supvr 1972-74. **Orgs:** Bd mem Central State Univ Alumni Assn 1977-; sec & bd mem United Nations Assn OK City Chap 1977-; mem OK Educ Assn Prins Assn; 1978- sec OKC ChptAlpha Kappa Alpha Sor 1973-77; mem OKC Chap Jack & Jill of Am Inc 1975-; bd mem & v chairwoman OK Crime Comn 1978-; co-authored Tchr's Guide Black History OK OKC Sch Sys 1970. **Honors/Awds:** 2nd pl Midwestern Region Outstanding Soror Alpha Kappa Alpha Sor 1977. **Business Addr:** 715 N Walker, Oklahoma City, OK 73102.

HENDERSON, KEITH PERNELL
Professional football player. **Personal:** Born Aug 4, 1966, Carterville, GA. **Educ:** Univ of Georgia, attended. **Career:** Fullback: San Francisco 49ers, 1989-, Minnesota Vikings, 1992-. **Honors/Awds:** Played in NFC Championship Game, post-1989 and 1990 seasons. **Business Addr:** Professional Football Player, Minnesota Vikings, 9520 Viking Dr, Eden Prairie, MN 55344.

HENDERSON, LARRY W.
Human resources executive. **Personal:** Born Jan 12, 1954, Tallalah, LA; son of Annie Mae Henderson; married Victoria Stewart, Dec 28, 1985; children: Lawrence Elliott, Jazmin Nichole. **Educ:** Southern Univ, Baton Rouge, LA, BA, 1974; Iowa State Univ, Ames, IA, MS, 1977; Univ of MI, MBA, 1983. **Career:** Kaiser Aluminum & Chemical Corp, Oakland, CA, 1977-84; Pepsico Inc, zone personnel mgr, 1984-86; Henderson & Assoc, Chicago, IL, pres, founder, 1986-87; Baxter Healthcare Org, Deerfield, IL, vice pres, human resources, 1987-90; Tellabs Inc, Lisle, IL, vice pres, human resources, 1990-. **Orgs:** Bd of dirs, Joseph Holmes Dance Theater, 1990-; Human Resources Mgmt Assn of Chicago; Natl Electronic Assn; American Compensation Assn. **Honors/Awds:** Designed, implemented and communicated Human Resources systems to improve e mployee relations, involvement and ownership; awarded top corp safety award for excellence 2 of the last 3 yrs; developed & implemented comprehensive and innovative total compensation plans that include performance based short and long term rewards, and cost restraining benefit designs; in less that one yr, staffed 420 new mgmt positions for the start up of a new div; received a corp award for customer quality leadership, and led two Malcolm Baldrige Natl Quality submissions.

HENDERSON, LEMON
Auto dealership chief executive. **Career:** Broadway Ford Inc, Edmond, OK, chief exec; Quality Ford Sales Inc, Little Rock, AR, chief exec. **Business Addr:** Quality Ford Sales, Inc., 11200 W. Markham St., Little Rock, AR 72211.

HENDERSON, LENNEAL JOSEPH, JR.
Educator, consultant. **Personal:** Born Oct 27, 1946, New Orleans, LA; son of Marcelle Henderson and Lenneal Henderson; married Joyce E Colon, May 7, 1989; children: Lenneal C, Lenneal J III. **Educ:** Univ of CA Berkeley, AB (cum laude) 1968; Univ of CA, MA Political Science, Public Admin 1969; Univ of CA, PhD Political Science 1977. **Career:** San Jose State Univ Afro-Amer Studies, lecturer 1973-75; Shepard & Assoc, 1973-74; Morrison & Rowe, sr analyst 1974; Dukes Dukes & Assocs San Francisco, assoc consultant 1974-75; Howard Univ Washington, visiting prof Political Science 1975, prof school of business and public admin; Howard Univ 1979-87; Univ of TN Knoxville, head, prof of political science 1988-89; Federal Exec Inst, Charlottesville VA, prof 1989; Schaefer Center for Public Policy, Univ of Baltimore, sr fellow 1989-, distinguished professor of government/public administration, currently. **Orgs:** Mem, bd of dirs, acting pres Children & Youth Serv Agency; pres San Francisco African Amer History & Cult Soc; Campaign Human Devel; co-ed ''Journal on Political Repression''; affiliate Joint Center for Political Studies Washington 1971-; Conf of Minority Public Administrators 1972-; Amer Assn Univ Prof 1972-; educ bd The Black Scholar Mag; chmn Citizens Energy Advisory Comm Washington 1981-; Natl Rsch Council 1983-84; Ford Foundation Postdoctoral Fellow; Johns Hopkins School of Advanced Intl Studies Washington; visiting black scholar Fairfield Univ; bd of trustees Population Reference Bureau; bd of dirs Decision Demographics, Natl Civic League; bd of trustees, Chesapeake Bay Foundation, 1991-; board of governors, Citizen's Planning and Housing Association of Baltimore, 1990-. **Honors/Awds:** Outstanding Serv Award, San Francisco Afro-Amer History Soc 1975; Outstanding Educator Amer 1975; Distinguished Faculty Award, Howard Univ; Kellogg Natl Fellow 1984-87; author ''Black Political Life in the US'' 1972; Henry C Welcome Fellow, State of Maryland, 1989-92; Research Fellow, Rockefeller Foundation, 1981-83; Distinguished Chair in Teaching, University of Baltimore, 1992-93. **Home Addr:** 4530 Mustering Drum Way, Ellicott City, MD 21042-5949.

HENDERSON, LEROY W., JR.
Visual artist. **Personal:** Born May 27, 1936, Richmond, VA; married Helen Foy; children: Kerby, Keith. **Educ:** VA State Coll, BS 1959 Pratt, MS 1965f certificate educ broadcasting corp TV training sch 1971; Nat Acad TV Arts & Sci Film & TV Workshop, certificate 1973. **Career:** Free-lance photographer 1967-; Bedford-Lincoln Neighborhood Mus Brooklyn, art tchr 1968-70; Brooklyn Mus Educ Dept, art tchr 1968; New York City Sch System, art tchr 1962-66; Richmond Pub Sch System, art tchr 1959. **Orgs:** Bd mem Aunt Len's Doll & Toy Mus NY; mem Kappa Alpha Psi Frat Full Opportunities Com Acad of TV Arts & Sci 1970-73; Emergency Cultural Coalition 1968. **Honors/Awds:** Recipient certificate of excellence in design photography Mead Library of Ideas Mead Paper Co 1972; one show merit award photography Art Dir Club Inc & Copy Club of NY, 1974 Photo-Graphis Intl Annual Award of Outstanding Art & Photography; commendation for Heroic Performance from concerned parents & students of HS of Mus & Art New York City 1968. **Military Serv:** AUS sp/4 1959-61.

HENDERSON, LLOYD D.
Educational administrator. **Personal:** Born Jan 28, 1945, Monroe Co, AL; married Sarah A; children: Cheryl. **Educ:** AL State Univ, BS 1964; Univ of WY, MS 1971; Auburn Univ, grad study 1972. **Career:** Monroe Co Training Sch, coach head of math dept 1964-70; Monroe Co Monroeville AL, instr adult educ 1965; Univ of WY, instr physics 1971; Lurleen B Wallace State Jr Coll, instr math & physics 1971-74, dir div of student support & spec prog 1974-. **Orgs:** Mem AEA, NEA, SAEOPP; chmn trustee bd First Bethlehem Baptist Ch; mem Covington Co Civic Organ; mem Free & Accepted Masons of AL. **Honors/Awds:** Cert of Achievement FL A&M Univ 1970. **Business Addr:** Dir Div of Student Support, Lurleen B Wallace St Jr Coll, PO Box 1418, Andalusia, AL 36420.

HENDERSON, NANNETTE S.
Educator. **Personal:** Born Jun 9, 1946, Washington, DC; daughter of Edith Richardson Smith and Percival Carlton Smith; married Lyman Beecher Henderson, Nov 29, 1969; children: Kara Michelle, Kristi Bynn. **Educ:** Howard U, BS 1967, MS 1969; NC State U, PhD 1973. **Career:** Vance Granville Comm Coll, dir coll transfer prgm; NC State Univ Raleigh, asst prof plant pathology. **Orgs:** North Carolina Assn of Educators Amer Assn of Junior & Community Colleges; North Carolina Assn of Two-Year and Community College Biologists; treasurer, Science NC, 1990; member, National Science Teachers Organization, 1980-. **Honors/Awds:** Phi Kappa Phi Hon Soc; mem Beta Kappa Chi Hon Soc; creator of Live Animal Substitute, Ribbit 1980; Excellence in Teaching NC Dept of Community Colleges 1987; C.A.S.E. Teaching Award 1988; Tar Heel of the Week, News & Observer Newspaper 1988; O'Harris Award, National Science Teaxhers Assn, 1990. **Home Addr:** 516 W Ridgeway St, Warrenton, NC 27589. **Business Addr:** Chair, Science Dept, Vance Granville Community College, PO Box 917, Henderson, NC 27536.

HENDERSON, RAMONA ESTELLE. See PEARSON, RAMONA HENDERSON.

HENDERSON, REMOND
Government official. **Personal:** Born Sep 21, 1952, Los Angeles, CA; son of Ernestine Henderson and Riebert M. Henderson; married Joann Bukovich Henderson; children: Audra Elizabeth, Riebert Sterling. **Educ:** Central Washington State University, BA, accounting, 1974. **Career:** Ernst & Young, Los Angeles, CA, staff and senior accountant/auditor, 1974-77; Laventhol & Horwath, Los Angeles, CA, senior accountant/auditor, 1977-79; Kaufman & Broad Inc, Los Angeles, CA, internal auditor, 1979-81; Kaufman & Broad Inc, Irvine, CA, controller, 1981; Department of Community & Regional Affairs, internal auditor III, 1982-84; Department of Community & Regional Affairs, Juneau, AK, deputy director, division of administrative services, 1984, director, division of administrative services, 1984-. **Orgs:** President, Juneau Chapter of Blacks in Government, 1984-89; treasurer, Blacks in Government, Region X, 1986-88, Region V, pres, 1994-; member, Alaska Society of Certified Public Accountants; member, American Institute of Certified Public Accountants; co-founder, First Shiloh Missionary Baptist Church of Juneau; member, Juneau Rotary Club; emergency interim successor, Juneau Assembly Council; chair, Dr. Martin Luther King Jr. Commemorative Committee of Juneau, 1986-88; member, Juneau Arctic Winter Games Committee, 1990. **Honors/Awds:** Federal Employee of the Year, Citizens Selection Committee, 1988; Academic Scholarship, Washington Society of CPA's, 1972-74; President's Award, Blacks in Government, Region X, 1985, 1987, Special Achievement Award, 1990; Certificate of Appreciation, City and Borough of Juneau and The Business and Professional Women's Club of Juneau, 1986. **Business Addr:** Director, Div of Administrative Services, Dept of Community & Regional Affairs, State of Alaska, 150 3rd St, PO Box 112100, Juneau, AK 99811.

HENDERSON, RICKEY HENLEY
Professional baseball player. **Personal:** Born Dec 25, 1958, Chicago, IL. **Career:** Oakland Athletics, outfielder, 1979-84; New York Yankees, outfielder, 1985-89; Oakland Athletics, outfielder, 1989-93; Toronto Blue Jays, 1993-. **Honors/Awds:** Stole 130 bases in 1982 to shatter the single-season record of 118; Lou Brock, Maury Wills & Henderson are the only three major leaguers to have stolen more than 100 bases in a single season; Gold Glove Awd for his outstanding defensive play in the outfield; named outfielder on The Sporting News Amer League Silver Slugger team 1981, 1985; Sporting News Silver Shoe Awd 1982; Sporting News Golden Shoe Awd 1983; American League All-Star Team, 1980, 1982, 1983-88, 1990; American League Most Valuable Player, Baseball Writers' Assn of America, 1990. **Business Addr:** Professional Baseball Player, Toronto Blue Jays, 300 Bremner Blvd W, Ste 3200, Toronto, ON, Canada M5V 3B3.

HENDERSON, ROBBYE R.
Librarian. **Personal:** Born Nov 10, 1937, Morton, MS; daughter of Aljuria Myers Robinson (deceased) and Robert Allen Robinson (deceased); children: Robreka Aljuria. **Educ:** Tougaloo So Christian Coll, BA 1960; Atlanta Univ, MSLS 1968; So IL Univ, PhD 1976. **Career:** Patton Lane HS, head librarian 1960-66; Utica Jr Coll, head librarian 1966-67; MS Valley State Univ, acquisitions librarian 1968-69; MS Valley State Univ, dir of tech serv 1969-72, univ librarian 1972-. **Orgs:** Consult Office of Health Resources Oppor 1976-78; instr So IL Univ Carbondale 1976; consult MS Assn of Coll Council on Study Accreditation 1970; pres Progressive Faculty & Staff Women's Club 1978-80; owner/partner Itta Bena Nursey 1978; financial sec Alpha Kappa Omega 1979. **Honors/Awds:** Fellowship Li-

brary Admin Dev Prog 1973; Internship Mellon ACRL Prog 1974; Fellowship Developing Leaders in Developing Instns 1974-76; Fellowship cum laude 1976. **Business Addr:** Director of the Library, MS Valley State Univ, James Herbert White Library, Itta Bena, MS 38941.

HENDERSON, ROBERT DWIGHT
Computer company executive. **Personal:** Born Aug 16, 1942, McDonald, PA; son of Theresa & Preston Henderson; married Beatrice Ann, Apr 15, 1965; children: Robert Mark. **Educ:** University of Maryland, 1966. **Career:** NCR Crop: RIACT, assistant vice pres, Product Management, assistant vice pres, Enterprise Systems, assistant vice pres, Systems Integration, director, Business Operations, vice pres, general manager, currently. **Orgs:** ADAPSO, Systems Integration, board member, 1988-90; Blue Cross/Blue Shield, board of directors, 1980-82; United Way, North County, board of directors, 1995; NCR Country Club, board of directors, 1981-82. **Military Serv:** United States Air Force, ssgt, 1960-65. **Business Addr:** General Manager GSG Silicon Valley, NCR, 3350 West Bayshore Rd, Palo Alto, CA 94303, (650)849-1299.

HENDERSON, ROMEO CLANTON
Educator. **Personal:** Born Apr 23, 1915, Salisbury, NC; married Jestina Tutt; children: Gwynette, Patricia. **Educ:** Livingstone Coll AB 1936; Cornell Univ, MA 1938; PA State Univ, EdD 1950. **Career:** Swift Memorial Jr Coll Rogersville TN, instr dean 1939-43; SC State Coll Orangeburg, prof, chmn social sci, dean school of grad studies 1952-60; DE State Coll, prof educ, dean instrn. **Business Addr:** Professor Emeritus, Delaware State College, Dupont Highway, Dover, DE 19901.

HENDERSON, RONALD
Law enforcement official. **Career:** St Louis Police, Bureau of Patrol Support, dep chief, chief of police, currently. **Business Addr:** Chief of Police, City of St Louis, 1200 Clark Ave, St Louis, MO 63103.

HENDERSON, RUTH FAYNELLA
Educator, composer. **Personal:** Born Mar 16, Kansas City, MO; daughter of Ophelia Beatrice Henderson and Isaiah Hilkiah Henderson Jr. **Educ:** Bishop College, BS, elementary education, 1965; North Texas State University, MEd, early childhood, 1975; La Salle Univ, EdD, 1995. **Career:** Dallas Independent School District, early childhood educator; First Baptist Church of Hamilton Park, minister of music, 1969-89; Lighthouse Church of God in Christ, pianist, 1991-; Willow Grove Baptist Church, minister of music, 1992-. **Orgs:** Christians In Action, president; Christian Dating & Friendship Ministry, founder; Fruit Festival, producer, 1992. **Honors/Awds:** Asked to write theme song for Oprah Winfrey's television movie, "There Are No Children Here.". **Special Achievements:** Wrote and composed several songs on Florida Mass Choir album, Jeffrey LaValley New Jerusalem Choir album, James Cleveland Gospel Music Workshop albums, DFN Mass Choir album. **Home Addr:** 1811 Dancliff Dr, Dallas, TX 75224, (214)333-9559. **Business Phone:** (214)428-3866.

HENDERSON, STANLEY LEE
Educator (retired), musician. **Personal:** Born Oct 8, 1909, Albia, IA; son of Ola Johnson Henderson and Nicholas Henderson; widowed. **Educ:** Milwaukee State Tchrs Coll, BEd 1953; Univ of MI, MMus 1949; Univ of IA, PhD 1959. **Career:** Harris Teachers College, Department of Music, St Louis, MO, professor and chairman, 1960-76; Board of Education, St Louis, MO, teacher, 1936-60. **Honors/Awds:** Award Mo St Dept of Educ 25 yrs; Merit Serv 1965; Kappa Delta Pi Hon Soc; Outstanding Citizen Award, Mayor Cervantes St Louis, 1965; Muesher Medal for Outstanding Work in Instrumental Music, Music Dept, St Louis Pub Schls; Achievement and Distinguished Service Award, Clarence Hayden Music Guild, 1977; Outstanding Service, Board of Education, St Louis, MO, 1976; Outstanding Educational Training of Negro Youth, NANM, 1987. **Military Serv:** US Army, bandsman/medic TS-4, 1944-46.

HENDERSON, STEPHEN E. See Obituaries section.

HENDERSON, THELTON EUGENE
Federal judge. **Personal:** Born Nov 28, 1933, Shreveport, LA; son of Wanzie and Eugene M; children: Geoffrey A. **Educ:** Univ of California Berkeley, BA 1956, JD 1962. **Career:** US Dept Justice, atty 1962-63; FitzSimmons & Petris, assoc 1964-66; San Mateo County Legal Aid Society, directing atty 1966-69; Stanford Univ Law School, asst dean 1968-76; Rosen, Remcho & Henderson, partner 1977-80; Golden Gate Univ, assoc prof, School of Law, 1978-80; US Dist Court, 9th Circuit, CA, judge 1980-, chief judge, currently. **Orgs:** Natl Bar Assn; Charles Houston Law Assn. **Military Serv:** US Army, 1956-58. **Business Addr:** Chief Judge, 9th Circuit, US District Court, PO Box 36060, San Francisco, CA 94102.

HENDERSON, THERESA CRITTENDEN
Educator. **Personal:** Born Nov 11, 1937, Montgomery, AL; daughter of Willie L Crittenden and Jacob K Crittenden; married John L Henderson, Jun 28, 1969; children: Dana, Nina, Brent. **Educ:** University of Cincinnati, BS, education, fine arts, 1959, MEd, 1969. **Career:** Newark, New Jersey, public schools, teacher, jr high, 1959-60; New York City Public Schools, elem teacher, 1960-64; Cincinnati Public Schools, art teacher, 1964-83, assistant principal, 1983-84, principal, 1984-93, director, 1992-. **Orgs:** Alpha Kappa Alpha, 1957-; Delta Kappa Gamma, 1988-; Phi Delta Kappa, 1988-; The Links, Inc, chairman fundraising prog, vice pres, sec, 1972-; Woman's City Club, Urban Arts Committee, chairman, 1971-75; National Alliance of Black School Educators, 1988-; Cincinnati Contemporary Arts Center, president, 1980-84; Cincinnati Opera Board, 1991-; Playhouse in Park Board, publicity chr 50th anniversary. **Honors/Awds:** Cincinnati Technical College, Honorary Doctorate, 1992; Cincinnati Enquirer, Woman of the Year, 1989; National Conference of Christians & Jews, Brotherhood/Sisterhood Award, 1992; United States Department of Education, Excellence in Education Award, 1988, National Blue Ribbon Award, 1992. **Special Achievements:** Leadership Cincinnati, Class XIV, 1990-91; Discovery 70 Art Exhibit, National Art Exhibit, 1970; Cincinnati Art Museum Exhibit, local artists, 1960. **Business Addr:** Director of the Coalition of Innovative Schools, Cincinnati Public Schools, 3060 Durrell Ave E, Hoffman School, Cincinnati, OH 45207, (513)961-1724.

HENDERSON, VIRGINIA RUTH MCKINNEY
Psychologist (retired). **Personal:** Born Feb 19, 1932, Cleveland, OH; daughter of Ruth Berry McKinney and Dr Wade Hampton McKinney; married Perry A; children: Sheryl, Virginia, Perry Jr. **Educ:** Spelman Coll, AB Psych Bio 1953; Boston U, MA Psych 1955 Univ of NM, PhD 1974. **Career:** Mad Metro School Dist, school psychology 1976-; Univ of NM, psychology asst prof ped psychiatry, 1968-76; Seattle, school psychology 1967-68; Cleveland Metro General Hosp, psychologist 1963-65; Cleveland Guidance Center, psychologist 1957-59; Muscatatuck St School, dir nursery educ psychologist 1955-57; Madison School District, special asst to superintendent for equity & diversity, 1993-. **Orgs:** Am Psychol Assn 1965-90; Natl Assn of School Psychologist, 1977-; Am Assn on Mental Def 1964-; consultant Model Cities Day Care Center 1972-74; certified admin Brazelton Neonatal Behavior Assessment Scale; bd of dir All Faiths Receiving Home 1973-76; bd of trustees Mazano Day School 1974-76; bd dir TWCA 1977; First Baptist Church of Mad WI 1976-; bd of dirs Visiting Nurses Assn 1978-; bd of dirs Madison Urban League 1979-F mem Natl Assn of School Psychologist 1979-; pres, Women in Focus, 1987-; General Board, Amer Baptist Churches USA, 1983-92; bd of dir, Green Lake Conference Center, 1982-; Wayland Board, Univ Wisconsin, 1987-; chair, Minority Student Achievement Committee, Madison School District, 1988-; United Way Allocation Comm, 1987-91; African Amer Academy, pres, bd of dirs, 1992-; Mann Educ Opportunity Fund, co chair, 1991-; Dane County Economic Summit, 1991-93; Jr League of Madison Comm Advisory Bd, 1992-; Madison Civics Club, 1986-; Vantage Point, 1989-; Dist 4 Carl Perkins, Special Population, advisory comm for MATC, 1991-; Program Comm of Project Opportunity, 1989-. **Honors/Awds:** Grand Magna Cum Laude Spelman Coll 1953; Natl Certified School Psychologist, 1992; Distinguished Service Award, Madison School District, 1990; YWCA, Woman of Distinction, 1990; Omega Psi Phi Fraternity, Citizen of the Year, 1991; Madison Magazine's 50 Most Influential People, 1992, 1997; Tribute to Black Women, 1994; Mothers of Simpson Street, Woman of the Year Award, 1994. **Business Addr:** Madison Metropolitan Sch Dist, 545 W Dayton St, Madison, WI 53703.

HENDERSON, WADE
Organization executive. **Educ:** Howard Univ, bachelor's degree in sociology; Rutgers Univ School of Law, JD. **Career:** ACLU, legislative counsel, lobbyist; NAACP, bureau dir; Leadership Conference on Civil Rights, executive dir, currently.

HENDERSON, WILLIAM AVERY
Pilot, military officer. **Personal:** Born Jan 18, 1943, Ann Arbor, MI; son of William Henderson and Viola Henderson; married Francine, Jul 28, 1990; children: Nicole, Justin. **Educ:** Eastern Michigan University, BS in sociology and history, 1964. **Career:** General Motors Corp, pilot, 1974-93, chief pilot, 1993-; 127th Tactical Fighter Wing, assistant chief of the command post, chief of safety, 1977-90; Michigan Air National Guard Headquarters, plans officer, deputy director, 1990-93, brigadier general, 1993-95, major general, 1995-. **Orgs:** Kappa Alpha Psi, 1963-; Tuskegee Airmen, 1989-; National Guard Association of the US, 1977-; National Guard Association of Michigan, 1977-. **Special Achievements:** First African American brigadier general in the history of the Michigan Air National Guard; First African American to head General Motors' corporate fleet. **Military Serv:** US Marine Corps, 1964-74; Distinguished Flying Crosses (two), 1969, Air Medals (eight). **Business Addr:** Chief Pilot, General Motors Corporation, Detroit Metropolitan Airport, Bldg 530 E Service Drive, Romulus, MI 48174, (313)942-5620.

HENDERSON, WILLIAM TERRELLE
Professional football player. **Personal:** Born Feb 19, 1971, Chester, VA. **Educ:** North Carolina, attended. **Career:** Green Bay Packers, running back, 1995-. **Business Addr:** Professional Football Player, Green Bay Packers, 1265 Lombardi Ave, Green Bay, WI 54304, (414)494-2351.

HENDERSON-NOCHO, AUDREY J.
Activist. **Personal:** Born Aug 27, 1959, Sacramento, CA; daughter of Lillian Riccardo Henderson; married Kim Nocho (divorced 1988); children: Antiquia, Serenia, Asheley. **Educ:** Univ of ND, Grand Forks, ND, BA, BS, 1991. **Career:** USAFB NCO Club, Grand Forks, ND, cook, 1984-86; Univ of ND, Grand Forks, ND, student aid, EBT cultural ctr, 1986-89, mail sorter, 1989, student counselor, career service/job placement, 1990-. **Orgs:** Chairperson, ND Comm on Martin Luther King Jr Holiday, 1988; mem, ND Adv Comm to US Civil Rights Comm, 1991-93; mem, Mayors Human Needs Comm, 1990-; mem, Concerned Citizens Against Prejudice, 1990-; former chairperson, Multi-Ethnic Support Assn, Community Housing Resource Bd, 1987-89. **Honors/Awds:** Making of the King Holiday Award, 1991. **Home Addr:** 18 N Washington St, Grand Forks, ND 58203.

HENDON, LEA ALPHA
Human resources administrator. **Personal:** Born Mar 27, 1953, Hartford, CT; daughter of Willie Mae Wilcox Martin and Charles Martin. **Educ:** Boston Coll, Chesnut Hill MA, BA Education, 1975; Eastern New Mexico Univ, Portales NM, MA Psychology, 1979. **Career:** Boston Public Schools, Boston MA, teacher, 1975-77; Allstate Insurance Co, Farmington CT, office operations supvr, 1979-80; Aetna Insurance Co, Hartford CT, business systems analyst, 1980-83; Hartford Insurance Group, Hartford CT, office automation consultant, 1983-85; Aetna Life & Casualty, Hartford CT, recruiter, consultant, 1986-. **Orgs:** Advisory Bd, DP, Post Coll, 1987-88; mem, Amer Soc for Personnel Admin, 1988-; pres, Black Data Processing Assoc, Hartford Chapter, 1989-90; sec, ITC-Gavel, 1990-91; mem, Delta Sigma Theta Sorority.

HENDRICKS, BARBARA
Opera singer. **Personal:** Born Nov 20, 1948, Stephens, AR; daughter of Della Hendricks and M L Hendricks; children: 2. **Educ:** Univ of NE, BS; Juilliard School of Music NY, BMusic; Studied with Jennie Tourel. **Career:** Debut with San Francisco Spring Opera in Ormindo 1974; performed with maj opera co's in US, Europe incl Boston Opera, St Paul Opera, Santa Fe Opera, Deutsche Opera, Berlin, Aix-en-Provence Festival, Houston Opera, De Nederlandse Operastichting, Glyndebourne Festival Opera; recital & appearances with symphony orchs incl Boston Symphony Orch, NY Philharm, Los Angeles Philharm, Cleveland Symphony Orch, Philadelphia Orch, Chicago Symphony, Berlin Philharm, Vienna Philharm, London Symphony Orch, Orchestre de Paris, Orchestre National de France; appeared in film of La Boheme, 1988. **Honors/Awds:** Grand Prix dux Disque 1976; Commandeur des Arts et des Lettres given by French Govt 1986; has made over 50 recordings; Doctorat Honoris Causa, University of Louvain, 1990; Honorary Doctor of Music, Nebraska Wesleyan University, 1988; Honorary Member, The Institute of Humanitarian Law, 1990 in San Remo; Chevalier de la Legion d'Honneur, 1993; Special Advisor on interculturality to the Director General of UNESCO, 1994.

HENDRICKS, BARKLEY L.
Artist, educator. **Personal:** Born Apr 16, 1945, Philadelphia. **Educ:** Yale Univ Sch Art, BFA; MFA 1972; Bpa Acad Fine Arts, cert 1967. **Career:** CT Coll, artist, asst prof art 1972-, professor, currently; University of Saskatchewan, vis artist 1974; Glassboro State Coll, 1974; PA Acad Fine Arts, instr 1971, 72. **Honors/Awds:** People to People, Citizens Ambassador Fellowship, 1991 (PR China travel); Connecticut Commission on the Arts, Purchase Award, 1991; Artist Fellowship, Offset Lithography Institute, The Brandywine Workshop, Phila, Pa, 1987; Salute to the Arts Award, (Philadelphia, Pa) 1984; 43rd Annual Midyear Show, Butler Institute of American Art, Second Butler Medal, 1979; Connecticut Commission on the Arts, Individual Artist Award, 1979; American Academy of Arts and Letters, Childe Hassam Purchase Award, 1971 & 1977; Connecticut Artist Annual, Slater Memorial Museum, (first prize) 1976. **Special Achievements:** One Man Exhibitions include: Benjamin Mangel Gallery, Phila Pa, 1981 & 1993; Connecticut College, New London Conn, 1993, 1984, & 1973; Norwalk Community College, Norwalk Conn, 1993; Manchester Community College, Manchester Conn, 1992; Cape May County Art Gallery, Cape May, New Jersey, 1992; Housatonic Museum of Art, Bridgeport, Conn, 1988; Penna Academy of Fine Arts, Peale House Gallery, Phila Pa, 1985; Brattleboro Museum and Art Center, Brattleboro, VT, 1984; Walnut Street Theater, Phila Pa, 1983; and numerous others; Collections include: Chrysler Museum, Norfolk, Va; The Natl Afro-American Museum and Cultural Center, Wilberforce, Ohio; Connecticut Commission on the Arts Collection, Hartford Conn; Forbes Magazine Collection, New York, NY; University of Connecticut Law School, Hartford, Conn; Brandywine Offset Institute, Phila Pa; The Natl Center of Afro-American Artists, Inc, Boston, Mass; Philadelphia Museum of Art, Phila Pa; Pennsylvania Academy of the Fine Arts, Phila Pa; Uris Collection, New York, NY; and numerous others; Exhibitions Group Shows include: Laura Knott Gallery, Bradford College, Bradford, Mass, 1992, 1993; Connecticut College, New London, Conn, 1972-93; Benjamin Mangel Gallery, Phila Pa, 1981-93; Hera Art Gallery, Wakefield, RI, 1993; Philadelphia Art Alliance, Phila Pa, 1992, 1973, 1970, 1968; Central Connecticut State University, New Britain, Conn, 1992; Fine Arts Museum of Long Island, LI, NY, 1988; Black

American Art in Japan, Tokyo Japan, 1987; Erector Square Gallery, New Haven, Conn, 1986; and numerous others. **Business Addr:** Professor of Fine Arts, Connecticut College, New London, CT 06320.

HENDRICKS, BEATRICE E.
Attorney. **Personal:** Born Sep 18, St Thomas, Virgin Islands of the United States. **Educ:** Morgan State Coll, BS 1962; Howard Univ Law School, JD (Cum Laude) 1972. **Career:** William Morris Agency NY, jr acctn 1962-64; IRS, field agent 1964-69; Ford Motor Co, staff attny 1972-74; Acacia Mutual Life Ins, attny 1974-76; Acacia Mutual, asst counsel 1976-79; Dept of Housing & Comm Devel, asst corp counsel 1980-85; A&B Household Serv Inc, president, half-owner 1979-85, asst corp counsel, con affairs section, asst Corp Counsel, Special Lit Section, currently. **Orgs:** Former mem Natl Bar Assoc; Amer Bar Assoc; DC Bar Assoc; MI Bar Assn; Alpha Kappa Alpha Sor Inc; Inez W Tinsley Cultural Soc; Natl Assoc of Colored Women Clubs Inc; St Mary's Episcopal Church, junior warden, 1990; St Mary's Court, board of directors. **Business Addr:** Assistant Corp Counsel, Special Litigation Section, Enforcement Division, 441 E St NW, Washington, DC 20001.

HENDRICKS, CONSTANCE SMITH (CONSTANCE KASANDRA SMITH-HENDRICKS)
Educator. **Personal:** Born Aug 25, 1953, Selma, AL; daughter of Geneva Cornelia Glover Smith and Henry Daniel Smith Jr; divorced; children: Denisha Lunya. **Educ:** University of Alabama at Birmingham, BSN, 1974, MSN, 1981; University of Alabama at Tuscaloosa, graduate certificate, gerontology, 1987; Boston College, PhD, 1992. **Career:** Staff RN, 1975; University of Alabama at Birmingham, nursing associate faculty, 1975, instructor, 1981-82; Roosevelt Area Family Health Center, nurse practitioner, 1975-76; University Hospital, staff RN, 1976-78; Good Samaritan Hospital, director of nursing, 1982-83; Tuskegee University, assistant professor, 1983-85; John Andrew Hospital, nurse administrator, 1985-87; Auburn University, assistant professor, 1987-. **Orgs:** Chi Eta Phi Sorority, southeast regional director, 1985-; Association of Black Nurse Faculty, 1987-; Alabama State Nurses Association, member, 1975-, past board member; National Sorority of Phi Delta Kappa, 1988-; National League for Nursing, 1975-; Sigma Theta Tau International, 1985-, president elect, Theta Delta; Omicron Delta Kappa, 1981-; Greater St Mark Missionary Baptist Church, choir member, Bible instructor, 1986-. **Honors/Awds:** American Nurses Association, Ethnic/Minority Fellowhsip, 1990-92; Boston College, Graduate Minority Fellowship, 1989-92; Sigma Theta Tau, Nu chapter, Seed Reseacher Grant, 1992; Chi Eta Phi, Epsilon chapter, Crawford Randolph Scholarship, 1990; Myrtle Baptist Church, Academic Scholarship, 1990, 1992; Auburn University, Profession Improvement Leave, 1989-92, Research Grant in Aid, 1992. **Special Achievements:** Professionalism Showing, 1983; Sisterhood is Indeed Global, 1985; Understanding the Adolescent, 1985; Learning Orientations & Health Behaviors of African-American Early Adolescents in Rural Alabama, 1991; Choosing: An Essential Component of Becoming, 1992. **Home Addr:** 612 Kimberly Circle, Selma, AL 36701, (205)821-7344. **Business Addr:** Assistant Professor, Auburn University School of Nursing, 219 Miller Hall, Auburn, AL 36849-5418, (205)844-5665.

HENDRICKS, ELROD JEROME
Professional baseball coach. **Personal:** Born Dec 22, 1940, Charlotte Amalie, Virgin Islands of the United States; married Merle; children: Ryan, Ian. **Career:** Baltimore Orioles, 1968-72; Chicago Cubs, 1972; Baltimore Orioles, 1973-76; New York Yankees, 1976-77; Baltimore Orioles, 1978-79, coach, currently. **Honors/Awds:** Selected first "Man of the Year," Baltimore Chapter, National Conference of Christians & Jews; operated a two-week baseball camp for youngsters, three summers. **Business Addr:** Coach, Baltimore Orioles, Memorial Stadium, Baltimore, MD 21218-3646.

HENDRICKS, JON
Professional musician. **Personal:** Born Sep 16, 1921, Newark, OH; son of Willie Carrington Hendricks and Rev Alexander Brooks Hendricks; married Judith, Mar 26, 1959; children: Jon Jr, Michele, Eric, Colleen, Aria. **Educ:** Univ of Toledo, pre-law 1948-51. **Career:** Lambert, Hendricks & Ross, singer & songwriter 1960's; taught jazz at, Cal St, Sonoma, UC Berkeley, UCLA, Stanford; sang with and wrote for King Pleasure, Count Basie, Duke Ellington, Louis Armstrong, Dave Brubeck, Carmen McRae; Jon Hendricks & Co, singer & songwriter. **Orgs:** Appointed to bd of the Kennedy Center Honors Committee Washington, DC; Artistic Dir and Host of the Annual San Francisco Jazz Festival. **Honors/Awds:** Peabody Award and Emmy Award for Best Documentary of the Year for "Somewhere to Lay My Weary Head, The Story of the Dunbar Hotel" for KNXT; Voted Number One Jazz Singer in the World by London's Melody Maker 1968-69; 1981 Intl Critics Poll of Down Beat Magazine as the vocal group most deserving of wider recognition; Awarded Grammy for lyrics to the Manhattan Transfer's hit version of "Birdland"; created and performed on current Manhattan Transfer album "Vocalese" Playwrite,won 5 Grammy's; wrote produced directed & starred in hit show "Evolution of the Blues" which ran five years on broadway 1974-78; ran one year in Westwood Playhouse Los Angeles where nothing had ever run over six weeks; group Lambert Hendricks & Ross won 1st Grammy for Jazz Vocals. **Military Serv:** USA 1942-46 Cpl. **Home Addr:** Gateway Plaza 400, 375 Southend Ave, New York, NY 10280-1025.

HENDRICKS, LETA
Librarian. **Personal:** Born May 22, 1954, Galesburg, IL; daughter of Mary Martha Triplett Hendricks and Lee B Hendricks. **Educ:** Western IL Univ, BA (w/Honors) 1977; Atlanta Univ, MA 1979; Univ of Illinois, MS 1989. **Career:** Carl Sandburg Coll, instructor 1983; Galesburg Public Library, specl col lib 1980-89; Knox College, reference assistant 1986-89, instructor winter 1989; Ohio State University Libraries, minority library intern, 1989-91, head, Human Ecology Library, 1991-. **Orgs:** Member, NWSA 1982-; member, ALA, 1989-; member, ACRL, 1989-; member, Black Caucus of ALA, 1990-; member, Phi Kappa Phi, 1976. **Honors/Awds:** Foundation Scholar Western Il Univ 1976. **Home Addr:** 4783 Glaton Ct #B, Columbus, OH 43220.

HENDRICKS, MARVIN B.
Molecular biologist. **Personal:** Born Dec 4, 1951, Newnan, GA; son of Margaret Petty Hendricks and Jimmie Lee Hendricks; married Helen Porthia Talley, Dec 26, 1971; children: Bridget. **Educ:** Massachusetts Inst of Technology, Cambridge MA, BS, 1973; Johns Hopkins Univ, Baltimore MD, PhD, 1980. **Career:** Fred Hutchinson Cancer Research Center, Seattle WA, post-doctoral fellow, 1980-84; Integrated Genetics, Framingham MA, staff scientist, 1984-87, sr scientist, 1987-89; Repligen Corp, Cambridge, MA, research scientist, 1989-91; Cambridge NeuroScience Inc, Cambridge, group leader, 1991-95; Brigham & Women's Hospital, Boston, MA, research scientist, 1995-97; Millennium Pharmaceuticals, Inc, senior scientist, 1997-. **Orgs:** Mem, Amer Assn for Advancement of Science, 1976-, New York Academy of Science, 1984-; Amer Society of Mechanical Engineers, 1994-. **Honors/Awds:** MIT Scholarship, Massachusetts Inst of Technology, 1969; Valedictorian, Central High School, Newnan GA, 1969; 20 Articles in intl research journals, 1976-; co-author of articles in two books, 1980-; Post-doctoral Fellowship Awards, Amer Cancer Soc, 1980, Ann Fuller Fund (Yale Univ), 1980, Natl Inst of Health, 1980; featured in Ebony Magazine, 1988. **Home Addr:** 21 Perry H Henderson Dr, Framingham, MA 01701.

HENDRICKS, RICHARD D.
Business executive (Retired). **Personal:** Born May 26, 1937, Glen Cove, NY; son of Ruth Delamar Hendricks and William Richmans Hendricks; married Madelyn Williams, Jun 1960; children: Pamela, Jeannette, Natalie. **Educ:** Hofstra Univ, BBA 1960. **Career:** Abraham & Straus Dept Stores NY, dept mgr 1960-65; Johnson Pub Co, adv sales rep 1965-66; JC Penney Co, buyer; pres CEO Delamar Marketing International, 1997-. **Orgs:** Founder bd mem QNS Assoc Inc; founder pres LISA Prodns; spl lectr Black Exec Exchange Prog; lectr State Univ of NY; mem Urban League; trustee AME Zion Chi; treas 1963-64; Black Artist Assn; NAACP. **Honors/Awds:** Outstanding Achievement Awd, Intl Key Women of Amer 1974; Comm Serv Awd, Black Media Inc 1975. **Business Addr:** Buyer, JC Penney Co Inc, 14841 N Dallas Pkwy, Dallas, TX 75240-6760.

HENDRICKS, STEVEN AARON
Public relations manager. **Personal:** Born Feb 5, 1960, Kansas City, KS. **Educ:** Wichita State Univ, BA Journalism 1982. **Career:** Wichita Eagle-Beacon Newspaper, adv rep 1981; Pizza Hut Inc, comm asst 1982, operations mgr 1982-83; State of KS, aide to the governor. **Orgs:** Mem Withita State Univ Football Team 1978-82; mem WSU Advertising & PR Club 1980-82; mem Fellowship of Christian Athletes 1981-82; mem Adv & PR Club of Whichita 1981-82; mem Kappa Alpha Psi Frat 1982-; mem Black Democratic Caucus 1984-. **Honors/Awds:** Top Ad/PR Student WSU Adv & Public Relations Club 1980; Outstanding Student Stephan Adv Agency 1981; Student of the Year Adv & PR Club of Wichita 1981; Outstanding Young Man of America 1984. **Business Addr:** Aide to the Governor, State of KS, State Capitol-Gov's Office, Topeka, KS 66612.

HENDRIX, DEBORAH LYNNE
Association executive. **Personal:** Born Nov 30, 1961, Chicago, IL; daughter of Donna L. Radford Wright and Edward Wright, Jr.; married Charles W Hendrix, Apr 6, 1991; children: Catherine Elizabeth Hendrix. **Educ:** Howard Univ, Washington DC, BS, 1983; Roosevelt Univ, Chicago IL, paralegal certificate; Institute for Paralegal Trn, Chicago IL, certificate, 1984. **Career:** Winston & Strawn Law Firm, Chicago IL, corporate paralegal, 1984-85; Junior Achievement of Chicago IL, vice pres, ed serv, 1985-88; Junior Achievement of South Bend, IN, president, 1988-91; Junior Achievement Inc, director, training/seminars, 1991-94, vp of diversity, 1994-, vp of diversity and quality assurance, 1995-, vp of training, diversity and quality, 1996-, vp, training & culture change, 1997-. **Orgs:** NAFE, 1990-; Urban League of Colorado Springs; American Society of Training and Development, 1991-; After 5 Christian Business and Professional Women, 1992-; Workout Ltd, 1997; Goodwill Industry, 1998. **Honors/Awds:** Named most outstanding student, school of human ecology, Howard Univ, 1983. Chicago's Up & Coming Business & Professional Women, Dollars & Sense Magazine, 1988; Emerging Black Leaders, 1994; Outstanding Young Women of America, 1988. **Business Addr:** Vice Pres/Training & Culture Change, Junior Achievement, Inc, 1 Education Way, Colorado Springs, CO 80906, (719)540-6241.

HENDRIX, MARTHA RAYE
Educator, mayor. **Personal:** Born Aug 17, 1939, Mineral Springs, AR; daughter of Flossie Johnson Turner and Lewis Turner; married Clarence Hendrix Jr, Aug 5, 1963 (divorced); children: Marcia, Clarisse Renee', Christal Lynn. **Educ:** Shorter Coll, N Little Rock, AR, AA, 1959; Philander Smith, Little Rock, AR, BA, 1961; Henderson State Univ, Arkadelphia, AR, MA. **Career:** Howard County High School, Mineral Springs, AR, teacher, 1961-70; Saratoga School, Saratoga, AR, teacher, 1970-89; Town of Tollette, Tollette, AR, mayor, 1989-; Saratoga School District, Saratoga, AR, elementary pricipal, 1990-91. **Orgs:** Mem, Amer Educ Assn, 1961-89; Natl Educ Assn, 1961-89; Day Card Bd of Dir, 1975-80; EHC, 1985-89; Literacy Council, 1987-89; mem advisory bd, Municipal League, 1988-89; Hospital Advisory Bd. **Home Addr:** 301 Peach St, Tollette, AR 71851.

HENDRY, GLORIA
Actress, producer, singer, director, entrepreneur. **Personal:** Born Mar 3, Winterhaven, FL; daughter of Lottie Beatrice Sconions and George C Hendry. **Educ:** Essex Coll of Bus; LA City Coll; University of Phoenix. **Career:** Actress/films/TV including: Pumpkinhead II, South Bureau Homicide, Champion, Bare Knuckles, Savage Sisters, Hell Up In Harlem, Black Belt Jones, Live & Let Die, Slaughter's Big Rip-Off, Black Caesar, Appleman, For Love of Ivy, TV Blue Knight, CBS Flip Wilson Special, Love Amer Style, As the World Turns, producer Live Every Moment, W Indies Fest, Doin It variety show; Plays including Owl & the Pussycat, Raisin in The Sun, Medea, Stage Door, Lady Day at Emerson Bar and Grill, The Fantasticks, as well as several TV and Radio shows such as Morning Show with Julie Shaw, Hostess Radio NYC, completed over 200 commercials; Singing shows/revues/clubs and a few records. **Orgs:** Kwanza Foundation, exec dir Women in the Performing Arts Los Angeles; mem AEA/AFTRA, SAG; mem Greenwich CT NAACP. **Honors/Awds:** Hon Phi Beta Omega Frat Inc Rho Iota Chapt; Black Achiever in US Awd; Natl Assn of Tennis Awd; After Hours News Awd Newark; I Am Somebody Awd; Outstanding Celebrity Awd; Key to City Birmingham AL Mayor George G Seibels; Key to City Mayor Kenneth Gibson Newark NJ; Kathleen Brown Rice Tennis Awd; Buffalo Soldiers Awd 10th Calvary. **Business Addr:** 256 S Robertson Blvd, Ste 8103, Beverly Hills, CA 90211.

HENLEY, CARL R.
Business administrator. **Personal:** Born Jul 4, 1955, Los Angeles, CA. **Educ:** CA State Univ LA, BA Psychology 1977, MS Public Adminstr 1980; Whittier College School of Law, JD, 1991. **Career:** Universal Artists, asst to spl projects 1977-; Black Leadership Conf CSULA, adv 1977-; Backyard Prods, vice pres bd of dirs 1978-; LA United Sch Dist, couns asst 1979; Los Angeles Co, comm devel analyst asst 1979-; Universal Artists, assoc producer; NAACP Youth & Coll Div, reg dir 1980-82; HME Subsidiaries, vice pres 1982-. **Orgs:** Pres & cofounder LA NAACP Youth & Coll Div 1977-80; mem LA Cnty Dem Central Comm 1978-; exec bd mem S Central Planning Council of United Way of Amer 1979-80; del CA Dem State Party 1982-84. **Honors/Awds:** Hon Life Mem Award CSULA 1977; Hon Pres Emeritus LA NAACP Youth & Coll Div 1980; Comm Serv Resolution LA City Council 1980. **Business Addr:** Vice President, HME Subsidiaries, PO Box 67686, Los Angeles, CA 90067-0686.

HENLEY, VERNARD W.
Banking executive. **Personal:** Born Aug 11, 1929, Richmond, VA; son of Mary Crump Henley and Walter A Henley; married Pheriby Christine Gibson; children: Vernard W Jr, Wade G, Adrienne C. **Educ:** Virginia State Univ, BS 1951. **Career:** Mechanics & Farmers Bank Durham, NC, asst note teller 1951-52, cashier/head of personal loan dept 1954-58; Consolidated Bank & Trust Co, sec & cashier 1958-69, bd of dir 1961, vp/sec 1961; Unity State Bank Dayton, OH, chief exec ofcr 1969; Consolidated Bank & Trust Co, exec vice pres 1969-71, president, 1971-; chmn of bd, pres and trust officer 1983-84, chmn of bd, chief exec officer and trust officer 1984-. **Orgs:** Bd of trustees VA Museum of Fine Arts, 1983, exec exhibition & finance comm; bd of dir Richmond Renaissance, Inc, exec & finance comm; vice chmn Audit Comm City of Richmond 1983-88, chmn 1986-88; bd of trustees J Sargeant Reynolds Coll Found 1984; bd of trustees VA Union Univ 1984, exec & finance committees; lay mem, bd of directors Old Dominion Bar Assn, 1985; bd of trustees, Virginia Council on Economic Ed, 1985; bd of dirs, Virginia Bankers Assn, 1986-; bd of trustees, Univ Fund Virginia Commonwealth Univ, 1986; bd of trustees, Historic Richmond Found, 1986-; bd of dirs, Retail Merchants Assn of Greater Richmond, 1986-; Kiwanis Club of Richmond, 1978-; National Corp Comm of the United Negro Coll Fund, 1975-; bd of directors, Atlantic RuralExposition, 1976-; advisory bd, Arts Council Richmond, Inc, 1986-; advisory council, bd of trustees Salvation Army Boys Club 1970-; bd of directors, Virginia Region, Natl Conference of Christians & Jews; Richmond Advisory Council Small Business Admin 1989; bd of

dirs, Cities-in-School Foundation of Virginia 1989; bd of dirs, vice chmn, Virginia Housing Foundation, 1989; Virginia Bankers Assn, president, 1993-; board of directors, Owens & Minor Inc; Audit Committee, 1993; Comp & Benefits Committee, 1994. **Honors/Awds:** Order of Merit Boy Scouts of Am 1967; Man & Boy Awd Salvation Army Boys Club 1969; Citizenship Awd Astoria Beneficial Club 1976; Brotherhood Awd Richmond Chap Natl Conf of Christians & Jews 1979; Order & Citizenship Awd Indep Order of St Luke 1981; recipient of "The Quest for Success Award" for Black Entrepreneurs in America, sponsored by Miller Brewing Company and Philip Morris USA. **Special Achievements:** First African-American president of the Virginia Bankers Assn, 1993. **Military Serv:** AUS 1st lt 2 yrs; Bronze Star 1954. **Home Addr:** 1728 Hungary Rd, Richmond, VA 23228. **Business Addr:** Chief Executive Officer, Consolidated Bank & Trust Co, PO Box 26823, Richmond, VA 23261-6823.

HENRY, BRENT LEE
Attorney. **Personal:** Born Oct 9, 1947, Philadelphia, PA; son of Minnie Adams Henry and Wilbur Henry; married; children: Adam, A'isha. **Educ:** Princeton Univ, BA 1969; Yale Law Sch, JD 1973; Yale Univ, Master of Urban Studies 1973. **Career:** New Haven Housing Information Ctr, counsel 1973-74; Yale Univ, lecturer in Afro-Amer studies 1973-74; Jones Day Reavis & Pogue, atty 1974-78; NYCHuman Resources Adminstrn, dept admin 1978-79; Jones Day Reavis & Pogue, atty 1979-82; Greater Southeast Comm Hospital Found, dir of business and govt affairs 1982-84; Howard Univ School of Business Admin, adjunct prof, 1982-94; Medlantic Healthcare Group, vice pres/gen counsel 1985-. **Orgs:** Bd of trustees, Princeton Univ 1969-72; adv council Woodrow Wilson School of Pub & Intl Affairs Princeton Univ 1969-72; author "The Provision of Indigent Defense Servs in Greater Cleveland" Cleveland Found authored as staff mem of Concerned Citizens Commn on Criminal Justice 1975; ABA; NBA; Ohio Bar Assns; DC Bar Assn; board of directors, Natl Health Lawyers Assn, 1988-96, president, 1994-95; board of directors, Mental Health Law Project 1987-98; bd of dirs, Combined Health Appeal of the Natl Capital Area, 1989-93; Princeton University Alumni Council, executive committee, 1994-, vice chair, 1995-97; Public Welfare Foundation, board of directors, 1995-, chair, 1997-99. **Honors/Awds:** Frederick Abramson Award, DC Bar Association, 1996. **Business Addr:** Vice Pres/General Counsel, Medlantic Health Care Group, 100 Irving St, NW, Washington, DC 20010, (202)877-5953.

HENRY, CHARLES E.
Educator, consultant. **Personal:** Born Apr 14, 1935, Palestine, TX; son of Mrs Ophelia Spencer Henry and Rev E W Henry Sr; married Janice Normandyne OBrien; children: Melvin Wayne, Carolyn Janiece Henry Ross. **Educ:** Texas Coll Tyler, TX, BS 1956; Texas Tech Univ, MEd 1971, EdD 1974; Ericksonian psychotherapy and Psychoneuroimmunology, certified, 1980; Continous Improvement Facilitator and Facilitator Inst, certified, 1994; Univ of TX, Total Quality Management instructor, certified, 1995; Texas Tech Univ, Human Resources management, certified, 1996. **Career:** Lubbock Indp School Dist, sci inst 1956-72; Texas Tech Univ Project Upward Bound, cons/inst 1968-72; Texas Tech Univ HSC School of Med, coord/inst 1972-76; Henry Enterprises, educ cons/owner/manager; Wayland Baptist U, Adjunct Faculty, Educ. Admn./Supervision, 1997-98. **Orgs:** Mem Intl Platform Assn 1984-85; mem Amer Soc of Professional Cons; exec dir Mntl Health Assn Lubbock 1976-80, pres bd of dir 1972-76; vice pres Phi Delta Kappa Educ Fraternity 1975-76; life mem Alpha Phi Alpha Frat Inc 1980; mem NAACP; mem Texas Mental Health Counlrs Assn; Phi Delta Kappa, life mem 1986; Amer Assoc of Professional Hypnotherapists, mem; Diversity Comm chair Society for Human Resource Mgmt (SHRM), 1997-98; Education Foundation rep Theta Kappa Lambda Chap, Alpha Phi Alpha Fraternity, Lubbock, TX, 1993. **Honors/Awds:** Citation of Excell Texas Coll Tyler 1980; Community Serv Award Alpha Kappa Alpha Sor 1978; area 3-G coord Phi Delta Kappa Educ Fraternity 1977-78; Presidents Award Estacado HS PTA 1975-76; Phi Delta Kappa International, Service Key Award, 1996, Twenty-Five Yr. Membership Award, 1997. **Business Addr:** Educator & Management Consultant, Henry Enterprises, 2345 - 50th, Ste 104, Lubbock, TX 79412, (806)799-7322.

HENRY, CHARLES PATRICK
Educator. **Personal:** Born Aug 17, 1947, Newark, OH; son of Ruth Holbert Henry and Charles Henry; married Loretta Crenshaw Henry, Aug 23, 1968; children: Adia, Wesley, Laura. **Educ:** Denison University, Granville, OH, BA, 1969; University of Chicago, Chicago, IL, MA, 1971, PhD, 1974; Atlanta University, Atlanta, GA, post doctorate study (NEH), 1980-81. **Career:** Howard University, Washington, DC, asst prof, 1973-76; Denison University, Granville, OH, asst prof, dir, asst dean, 1976-80; University of California, Berkeley, CA, assoc prof, 1981-. **Orgs:** International exec committee 1989-, chair, board of directors 1986-88, Amnesty International USA; national secretary, National Council for Black Studies, 1981-83; congressional fellow, American Political Science Assn, 1972-73; National Council for Black Studies, president, 1992-. **Honors/Awds:** Co-author, The Chitlin' Controversy, University Press of America, 1978; editor, In Pursuit of Full Employment, Urban League Review, 1986; author, Culture and African American Politics, Indiana Press, 1990; author, Jesse Jackson, Black Scholar Press, 1991. **Business Addr:** Associate Professor, University of California, Berkeley, Afro-American Studies Department, 3335 Dwinelle Hall, Berkeley, CA 94720.

HENRY, DAVID WINSTON
Cleric. **Personal:** Born Dec 15, 1932, Willikies Antigua, West Indies; son of Greta Otto and William Henry; married Elda Joseph Henry, May 18, 1963 (died 1995); children: Maria, Michael; married Sonia Delores Spencer, Aug 6, 1995. **Educ:** El Seminario Episcopal Del Caribe, MA, 1966. **Career:** Anglican Diocese of the VI, priest, 1966-72; VI Govt, teacher, 1971-73, 1980-97, retired; Holy Cross Episcopal Church, vicar, 1987-91, rector, 1991-. **Orgs:** St Croix Christian Council, 1969-72.

HENRY, EGBERT WINSTON
Educator. **Personal:** Born Apr 28, 1931, New York, NY; married Barbara Jean. **Educ:** Queens Coll, BS 1953; Brooklyn Coll, MA 1959; City Univ of NY, PhD 1972. **Career:** Oakland Univ, prof 1974-; Herbert H Lehman Coll, prof 1969-74; Wayne State Univ, prof 1966-69; Marygrove Coll, prof 1973; NY State Maritime Coll prof 1973-74; Bronx Comm Coll, prof 1970-72. **Orgs:** Mem Soc of the Sigma Xi; Am Soc of Plant Physiolgst; Smithsonian Soc; Plant Growth Reg Wrkng Grp; MI Electron Microscopy Forum. **Honors/Awds:** Rsch Award Soc of the Sigma Xi 1971, 1974; Grant Herbert H Lehman Coll 1973; Oakland Univ Biomed Sci 1976; Oakland Univ Rsch Grant 1976; Oakland University Alumni Award for Outstanding Academic Advising, 1991. **Military Serv:** AUS 1953-56. **Business Addr:** Prof & Chairman, Biological Sciences Dept, Oakland University, Rochester, MI 48309.

HENRY, FOREST T., JR.
Educator. **Personal:** Born Jan 2, 1937, Houston; son of Belzora Butler Henry and Forest T Henry Sr; married Melba J Jennings; children: Felicia Denise, Forest III. **Educ:** Howard U, BS 1958; TX So U, M Ed 1971, adminstrv cert 1972. **Career:** Houston Independent School District, director of operations, 1989-, assistant superintendent of athletics and extracurricular activities, 1982-84; Phillis Wheatley Sr High School, Houston, TX, principal, 1984-89; Evan E Worthing Sr High Sch Houston, prin 1978-82; Carter G Woodson Jr HS Houston, prin 1974-78, asst prin 1971-74, teacher physical educ, head football coach & athletic dir 1968-70, golf coach 1960-70, asst football coach 1959-68, teacher 1959-68; F T Henry Income Tax & Real Estate Serv, 1958-. **Orgs:** Pres Greater Fifth Ward Citizens League 1972-; exec bd Bhouston Prin Assn 1972-; mem BSA; YMCA; TX Assn of Econdary Sch Prin; Nat Assn of Secondary Sch Prin; bd of dir N Side Sr Citizens Assn; Houston Assn of Supervison & Curriculum Develop; TX State Tchrs Assn; Alpha Phi Alpha. **Honors/Awds:** Worthing Scholarship; Nat Sci Summer Fellowship in Biology; Comm Serv Award Religious Heritage of Am. **Business Addr:** Director of Operations, Houston Independent School District, 228 McCarty, Building 22, Houston, TX 77029.

HENRY, HERMAN (SKEETER)
Professional basketball player. **Personal:** Born Dec 8, 1967, Dallas, TX. **Educ:** Midland Coll; Univ of Oklahoma. **Career:** CBA: Pensacola Tornados, 1990-91; Birmingham Bandits, 1991-92; NBA: Phoenix Suns, 1994-. **Business Addr:** Professional Basketball Player, Phoenix Suns, 201 E. Jefferson St., Phoenix, AZ 85004, (602)379-7900.

HENRY, I. PATRICIA
Business executive. **Personal:** Born Aug 20, 1947, Martinsville, VA; daughter of Ida Walker Pinnix; divorced; children: Hans, Tiffany. **Educ:** Bennett College, BS 1969. **Career:** General Electric Co, Inc, systems analyst 1970; Norfolk & Western Railway, systems analyst 1971; Ethyl Corporation, systems analyst 1972; EI DuPont de Nemours, staff assist to area head 1973-77; Miller Brewing Co, brewing manager 1992-95, plant mgr, 1995-. **Orgs:** Secretary Business and Professional Woman 1983; board of trustees Memorial Hospital; Master Brewers of America 1983; bd of directors Citizens Against Family Violence 1984-86; bd of trustees Carlisle School 1984-86. **Honors/Awds:** Natl Merit Finalist 1965; Summa Cum Laude Bennett College 1969; Kizzie Award Black Women Hall of Fame 1984; Top Black Achiever New York YMCA 1984. **Special Achievements:** First female to hold a led mgmt post in any major US brewery, 1995. **Business Addr:** Plant Manager, Miller Brewing Co, PO Box 3327, Eden, NC 27288.

HENRY, JAMES T., SR.
Retired educator. **Personal:** Born Sep 20, 1910, St Louis, MO; married Vivian Snell; children: 11. **Educ:** Univ of IL, BS 1933; IBIDMA, 1938; Ford Found Fellowship Univ of MI, 1966. **Career:** Central State Univ, retired prof of geography 1977; FL A&M, visiting prof of Geography 1950, 1952, 1955; Morgan State, visiting prof, Geography 1940; AL State, visiting prof, Geography, 1937, 1939; Danforth Fellowship Consortium Univ, 1960-70; Small Coll Consortiom Clark Univ Worcester, 1960; Univ WI Milwaukee, consultant 1968; Xenia United Nations Comm, gov chmn, 1968; Serv Acad Review Bd Airforce, 1968-69; City of Xenia, mayor 1969-72. **Orgs:** Life mem, Alpha Phi Alpha; 25 year certificate. **Honors/Awds:** Civic awards Alpha Phi Alpha; Omega Psi Phi; Phi Beta Sigma; Amer Legion; 2nd 51 Force Comm Aging; Third Degree KOFC; Alpha Phi Gamma Journalism; Phi Alpha Theta history; Pershing Rifles; Co-author numerous articles 1971-74; Prof Emeritus Earth Science CSU 1977; Affirmative Action Rev Spec Inertial Guidance Center Newark, 1st black elect to Xenia OH Cty Comm 1953, 1st ever to be re-elected to 6 consecutive 4 yr terms.

HENRY, JOHN WESLEY, JR.
Educational administrator (retired). **Personal:** Born Jun 3, 1929, Greensboro, NC; son of Carrie Lillian and John Wesley; children: Dawn Yolanda, John Wesley III, Pamela Michelle, Linda Leverne, Brenda Diane, Robin Karen. **Educ:** North Carolina A&T State University, BS, 1955; Chicago State University, MEd, 1965; VA Research Hospital, Chicago, certificate in personnel management, 1964; New York University, certification in vocational testing and evaluation, 1966; Chicago Cosmopolitan Free School, certificate in business management, 1964. **Career:** VA Hospital, Perry Point, MD, manual arts therapist, Phy Medicine & Rehab Service, 1955-58, acting chief, 1958-60; VA Research Hospital, Chicago, Vocational Testing & Evaluation, chief, 1960-70; Malcolm X Community College, City Colleges of Chicago, Tech & Occupational Education, dean, 1970-71, Academic Affairs, vice pres, 1971-73; Denmark SC Tech Education Center, associate director, 1973-77; Denmark Tech College, pres, 1977-85. **Orgs:** Bamberg County Industrial Development Commission, vice chairman, 1979; South East Regional Council on Black American Affairs, Amer Assn of Community & Junior Colleges, bd member, 1979-85; Chicago Westside Planning Commission, bd member, 1970-73; Phi Delta Kappa; Phi Theta Kappa, honorary life member; Phi Beta Lambda, honorary life member; Natl Council Resource Development; Natl Assn Tech Education; Council for the Advancement and Support of Education; Assn of Colleges and Universities; American Assn of Rehab Therapy; Natl Assn for Equal Opportunity in Higher Education; American Legion; Disabled American Veterans Assn; Assn for Supervision and Curriculum Development; Assn of American Colleges; Council for Occupational Education; Natl Commission for Cooperative Education; President's Roundtable; Natl Rehabilitation Assn. **Honors/Awds:** Southern Leadership Conference (SCLC), Award for Education Excellence; VA Research Hospital, Superior Performance Award. **Military Serv:** US Army, 1947-51. **Home Addr:** PO Box 25, Denmark, SC 29042.

HENRY, JOSEPH KING
Educational administrator, counselor, recruiter. **Personal:** Born Aug 2, 1948, St Louis, MO; son of Geraldine Henry and King Henry; married Diana Edwards. **Educ:** Lincoln Univ, BS Educ 1973; Boston Univ, MA 1974. **Career:** Humboldt Elem Sch St Louis, teacher 1972-73; Metro Council for Educational Oppor Inc, coord 1974-77; Univ of IA, Special Svcs, academic counselor 1985-86, grad outreach counselor 1986-87, graduate outreach coordinator 1987-, Graduate College, assistant to the dean, 1992, assistant to the dean for recruitment and minority affairs, currently. **Orgs:** Counselor Univ of Iowa Upward Bound Program 1980; pres Afro-American Studies Grad Student Assn 1982-83; instructor, grad teaching asst American Lives 1982; presented papers at the Midwest Modern Language Assn Conf 1982, 11th Annual Conference on South Asia 1982, Tenth Annual Conference on the Black Family, 1983; instructor, grad teaching asst Introduction to Afro-American Society; grad rsch asst The Univ of IA Office of Affirmative Action 1983-85; lecturer in history Cornell Coll Mt Vernon, IA 1985; The National Association of College Admissions Counselors Association and Conference, 1985; presented a paper on the Rev Dr Martin Luther King at the Annual Special Support Serv Honors Recognition Day Prog 1986; National Council of Black Studies, 1988; The Society for the Study of Multi-Ethnic Literature in the US, 1988; Organization of American Historians, 1988; Joint Center Political Studies Associate Program; Univ of Iowa Afric an American Council; St Louis Black Repertory Company, patron; Cote Brilliante Presbyterian Church; Unitarian Universalist Church; National Assn of Graduate A dmissions Professionals. **Honors/Awds:** Martin Luther King Fellowship to Boston Univ 1973; Phi Alpha Theta Intl Honor Soc in History 1974; "A Melus Interview, Ishmael Reed," The Journal of the Soc for the Study of the Multi-Ethnic Literature of the United States Vol II No 1 1984; Black Awds Honor Certificate of Recognition Univ of IA 1984; "Preliminary Afro-Amer Observations on Goan Literature," The Journal of Indian Writing in English V13 No 1 1985; "Public spiritual Humanistic Odyssey of Malcolm X," The Western Journal of Black Studies V 9, No 2 1985; "High-Tech, Higher Education, and Cultural Pluralism, A Systems Approach to New Prospects," The Journal of the Assoc for General and Liberal Studies V 15, No 3 1985; published articles in The Challenger and The Daily Iowa newspapers; selected asjudge for the 1992 Greek Finale the Black Greek Caucus; chaired the student paper session, "America in the Present-Cultural Influences of African-Americans in Politics, Music and Sports," for the annual CIC Fellows Conference hosted by University of Michigan (Ann Arbor), 1991; helped to organize and present a speaker at the first annual Survival Skills Conference sponsored by the Special Support Services program in 1991; selected to participate in the Pen Pal Partners program, sponsored by Special Support Services in cooperation with Grant Wood Elementary School, 1991, 1992;

Southern University in New Orleans, Letter of Recognition, 1994. **Special Achievements:** Interview with Ishmael Reed quoted in Mirrors, Conjurers and Priests: Defin ing African-Centered Literary Criticism by Joyce Ann Joyce, pp 269-72, 1994; qu oted in introduction of Race, Class, and the World System: The Sociology of Oli ver C Cox, 1987; author, "Recruiting Materials: Today and in the Future," Journ al of National Association of Graduate Admissions Professionals, v 5, n 4, pp 1 2, 20, June 1994. **Business Addr:** Assistant to the Dean for Recruitment & Minority Affairs, The Univ of Iowa, The Graduate College, 205 Gilmore Hall, Iowa City, IA 52242.

HENRY, JOSEPH LOUIS
Educator. **Personal:** Born May 2, 1924, New Orleans, LA; son of Mabel Valentine Mansion and Varice S Henry, Jr; married Dorothy Lilian Whittle (deceased) (died 1991); children: Leilani Smith, Joseph L Jr, Ronald, Joan Alison, Peter D; married Dr. Gracie Cua, Jan 5, 1995. **Educ:** Howard Univ, DDS 1946; Xavier Univ, BS 1948, ScD 1975; Univ of IL, MS 1949, PhD 1951; IL Coll of Optometry, DHL 1973; Harvard Univ, MA 1975. **Career:** Howard Univ, instructor to prof 1946-51, dir of clinics 1951-65, dean 1965-75, Harvard School of Dental Medicine, assoc dean/prof and chmn, oral diagnois and oral radiology, dean 1990. **Orgs:** Vp/fellow Amer Assoc for Advancement of Sci 1952 & 1972; pres Intl Assoc for Dental Res DC Section 1968; mem NIH Natl Adv Cncl on Hlth Professions 1968-72; pres Greater Washington Periodontal Soc 1970; commr US Commn on Educ Credit 1973-74; chmn Assoc of Black Fac & Admin Harvard Univ 1981-83; mem Inst of Medicine of the Natl Acad of Sciences 1981-; chmn bd of trustees IL Coll of Optometry 1982-86; Natl Res Cncl/Inst of Medicine Comm on an Aging Soc 1984-; mem Amer Optometric Assoc Cncl on Clinical Optometric Care 1984-; chmn Amer Assoc of Dental Schools Sect on Oral Diagnosis and Oral Medicine 1984-85; Academy of Oral Diagnosis, radiology and medicine, founding mem, chmn, Admin Bd-Council of Sections, Amer Assoc of Dental Schools, 1988; mem, Natl Advisory Council of the Health Professi 1990-94; Institute of Medicine's Committee, Future of Dental Educ. **Honors/Awds:** Awards from Urban League, NAACP, UNCF 1970; Distinguished Faculty Award Harvard Univ 1971; Dentist of the Yr Natl Dental Assn 1972; Dentist of the Year in DC 1973; DC Mayors Award for Serv to the City 1975; Natl Dental Assoc Presidential Awd 1976, 1978; Dean Emeritus Howard Univ Coll of Dentistry 1981; Distinguished Faculty Award Harvard School of Dental Medicine 1981; Natl Optometric Assoc Founder's Award 1985; Howard Univ Alumni Achievement Award 1986; Citation from Maryland Legislative House of Delegates for "Outstanding Contribution to Dentistry and Commitment to Excellence in Higher Education" 1986; Distinguished Faculty Award; Organization of Teachers of Oral Diagnosis & Service Award, American Assn of Dental Schools, 1995; over 100 articles published in journals in Dentistry, Dental Educ, Optometry & Health Sci 1948-. **Military Serv:** USAR 2nd Lt; 2515 Serv Unit pfc 1942-45; Good Conduct Medal 1944. **Business Addr:** Associate Dean & Prof Emeritus, Harvard School of Dental Med, 188 Longwood Ave, Boston, MA 02115.

HENRY, KARL H.
Attorney. **Personal:** Born Jan 21, 1936, Chicago, IL; son of Almeta Macintyre Henry and Karl H Henry; married Dolores Davis; children: Marc, Paula. **Educ:** Fisk U, Atnd; LA City Coll; Northwestern U; Southwestern Univ of Law LA, JD 1969; USC Law Shc Prac Aspects of Recording Indus, Post Grad. **Career:** Pvt Prac, atty 1970-; Juv Ct, referee 1975-76; Spartan Missile Proj McDonnel Douglas Corp, sr contracts negotiator 1969-70, sr Employee relations rep 1968-69; Green Power Found, mktng sales mgr 1968; Pabst Brewing Co, mchdsng salesman 1964-68; Sys Outlet Shoes, asst mgr 1962-63. **Orgs:** Mem LA Co Bar Assn; Am Bar Assn; Juvenile Cts Bar; Langston Law Club; LA Trial Lawyers Assn; past pres Englewood Youth Assn; mem Nat Police Assn; mem John F Kennedy Club; bd dirs Green Power Found; adv bd STEP Inc; bd dirs NAACP; pres Hollypark Homeowner Assn; dir Spec Prog PUSH. **Business Addr:** Attorney, 4050 Buckingham Rd, Los Angeles, CA 90008.

HENRY, KEVIN LERELL
Professional football player. **Personal:** Born Oct 23, 1968, Mound Bayou, MS. **Educ:** Mississippi State. **Career:** Pittsburgh Steelers, defensive end, 1993-. **Business Addr:** Professional Football Player, Pittsburgh Steelers, Three Rivers Stadium, 300 Stadium Circle, Pittsburgh, PA 15212, (412)323-1200.

HENRY, MARCELETT CAMPBELL
Educator (retired). **Personal:** Born Apr 16, 1928, Langston, OK; married Delbert V Jr; children: Jacqueline M, Sharon R, Delbert V III, Andrea D. **Educ:** Langston Univ, BS 1949; Univ of OK Norman, ME 1963; San Fran State Univ, ME Admin 1969; Walden Univ, PhD Admin 1973. **Career:** Anchorage Comm Coll AK Voc Homemaking Courses, tchr 1954-55; Anchorage Indep Sch Dist AK Lang Arts/Soc Stud, tchr 1956-59; Anchorage Comm Coll AK Adult Edn/Curriculum Devel, tchr/coord for summer tchrs wrkshps 1958-59; Anchorage Indep Sch Dist AK, tchr/homemaking 1960-65; Tamalpais Union HS Dist Mill Valley, CA, dept chmrn/tchr/dir of occupatnl training pgm 1966-74; CA State Dept of Edn, mgr summer sch/cons planning & devel/coord alternative edn/project mgr/cons secondary edn/state staff/liaison to co supts/dir 1974-96. **Orgs:** Real Estate Training 1959; curr spclst AK Dept of Educ 1964; mem Marin Co Home Ec 1966-68; Project FEAST City Coll San Fran 1968; consult Pace Ctr Sys Analysis Wrkshp Tamalpais HS Dist 1969; adv com/edn JC Penny Bay Area 1969-74; consult CA State Dept Voc Educ 1970; consult Marin Co Supt Offc Corte Madera, CA 1970; devel model curr "System Analysis" Tamalpais Union HS Dist 1970; state exec bd Delta Kappa Gamma Chi 1971; consult "Project Breakthrough" Tamalpais HS Dist 1972; CA State Dept 1973; review/eval panelist Right to Read Pgm HEW 1973; participant US Senate Select Com on Nutrition & Human Needs Wash, DC 1973; sub-com CA Attys Genl Consumer Educ 1975; rep State Supt of Pub Instr in Select of State Century III Leaders 1976-78; chmn/conf "Reform Thru Research" Phi Delta Kappa 1976; ch Phi Delta Kappa Dist II 1977, mem PDK Adv Bd; pres Sacramento Phi Delta Kappa 1977-78; cand Supt Co Off of Educ 1978; mem US Presidential Task Force 1981; pres, Assn for Multicultural Counseling and Development; pres, MC Henry Enterprises, 1997-98. **Honors/Awds:** Mother's Day Recog Awd for Outstand Contrib in Educ 1959; KBYR Radio Station Bouquet of the Day 1964; Delta Kappa Gamma Schlrshp 1966; Delta Kappa Gamma Chi State Mini Grant 1972; CA State Dept of Educ Research Grant 1972; Award of Merit CA Dept of Justice/Educ 1975; Award for Leadership in State Bicentennial Activ State Dept of Educ ARBC of CA 1976; Women of the Yr Delta Delta Zeta Cha Zeta Phi Beta San Fran 1976; Nat Sch Journlsm Award for Sch Publ Bicentennial Film Brochure 1977. **Home Addr:** PO Box 2256, Sacramento, CA 95812-2256.

HENRY, MILDRED M. DALTON
Educator. **Personal:** Born in Tamo, AR; children: Delano Hampton, Alvia Hampton Turner, Lawrence Hampton, Pamela Hampton Ross. **Educ:** AM&N College Pine Bluff, BS Music Ed 1971; Southern IL Univ Edwardsville, MS counselor ed 1976; Southern IL Univ Carbondale, PhD counselor ed 1983. **Career:** AM&N Coll, sec bus office 1949-51; St Paul Public Library, library asst 1956-58; AM&N Coll, lib asst/secty 1968-71; Pine Bluff School Dist, music teacher 1971-75; Southern IL Univ Edwardsville, library asst 1975; Watson Chapel School Dist, counselor 1976-77; Univ of AR at Pine Bluff, counselor 1978-80; Southern IL Univ at Carbondale, grad asst 1981; Carbondale Elem Sch Dist, teacher 1981-83; CA State Univ San Bernardino, asst prof 1983-. **Orgs:** Adv bd Creative Educators Inc Riverside 1983-; city commissioner Fontanta CA 1984-; exec bd Rialto/Fontana NAACP 1984-; pres Provisional Educ Services Inc 1984-; Amer Assn of Univ Profs; Natl Educ Assn; CA Faculty Assn; CA Teachers Assn; CA Assn of Counseling Develop; Assn of Teacher Educators; CA Black Faculty and Staff Assn; CA State Employees Assn, Inland Empire Peace Officers Assn; NAACP; Natl Council of Negro Women; steering comm San Bernardino Area Black Chamber of Commerce; San Bernardino Private Industry Council. **Honors/Awds:** Leadership Awards Atlanta Univ & UCLA 1978 & 1979; Citizen of Day Radio Station KOTN Pine Bluff 1980; Dean's Fellowship Southern IL Univ Carbondale 1980-81; Outstanding Scholastic Achievement Black Affairs Council SIUC 1981; publication "Setting Up a Responsive Guidance Program in a Middle School" The Guidance Clinic 1979. **Business Addr:** Assistant Professor of Education, California State Univ, 5500 University Pkwy, San Bernardino, CA 92407.

HENRY, ROBERT CLAYTON
Funeral director. **Personal:** Born Jul 16, 1923, Springfield, OH; married Betty Jean Scott; children: Robert C II, Alan Stefon, Lisa Jennifer. **Educ:** Cleveland Coll of Mortuary Sci, attended 1948-49; Wittenburg Univ, attended 1950-51. **Career:** City of Springfield, commr 1963-66, mayor 1966-68; Robert C Henry & Son Funeral Home, funeral director. **Honors/Awds:** LLD Central State Univ 1968. **Military Serv:** USAF t/sgt 1943-45; Pacific Theatre Bronze Star; Amer Theatre 1943-45. **Business Addr:** Funeral Dir, Robt C Henry & Son Funeral Hom, 527 S Center St, Springfield, OH 45506.

HENRY, SAMUEL DUDLEY
Educator. **Personal:** Born Oct 9, 1947, Washington, DC; son of Shendrine Boyce Henry and Rev Dudley Henry; married Ana Maria Meneses Henry, Dec 23, 1988. **Educ:** DC Teachers Coll, BS 1969; Columbia Univ, MA 1974, EdD 1978. **Career:** Binghamton, eng/soc studies teacher 1971-73; HMLI Columbia Univ Teachers Coll, rsch assoc 1975-77; Sch of Ed Univ MA Amherst, asst prof 1977-78; Race Desegregation Ctr for NY, NJ, VI & PR, dir 1978-81; San Jose State Univ, dir of Equal Opportunity & Affirmative Action; CSU Northridge, Northridge CA, School of Education, assoc dean (acting) 1988-; San Jose State Univ, San Jose CA, School of Social Sciences, assoc dean 1987-88, assistant vice pres for Student Affairs, 1989-92; Portland State University, executive director, Portland Educational Network, 1992-94; Urban Fellow and Associate Professor of Education, 1994-. **Orgs:** Exec bd Greenfield Secondary Sch Comm 1977-79; sponsor Harlem Ebonetts Girls Track Team 1980-81; exec bd Santa Clara Valley Urban League 1982-83; exec bd CAAAO,CA Assoc of Affirmative Action Off 1983-84; mem Prog Comm No CA Fair Employ Roundtable 1983-85; mem ASCD Assoc of Supr of Curr Ser 1984-85; mem bd of dirs Campus Christian Ministry 1984-85; San Jose Roundtable, chair-drug prevention task force. **Honors/Awds:** Outstanding Serv Awd Disabled Students SJSU 1982-83; Commendation Curr Study Comm East Side Union HS Dist 1984; AA in Higher Educ/2nd Annual Conf on Desegregation in Postsecondary 1984. **Military Serv:** ANG 1967-; AUSR 1972-. **Home Addr:** 1186 SW 12th Ct, Troutdale, OR 97060. **Business Addr:** Urban Fellow & Associate Professor of Education, Portland Educational Network, PO Box 751, Portland, OR 97207-0751.

HENRY, THOMAS
Educator. **Personal:** Born Nov 27, 1934, St Louis; married Gemalia Blockton. **Educ:** Lincoln Univ bs 1957; harris tchrs coll, atnd. **Career:** Turner Middle School St Louis, head art dept 1985; St Louis Co Transportation Commn by Co Supr Gene McNary, appointed; St Louis System, teacher 14 yrs; Free Lance 1 Yr, commercial artist 1962. **Orgs:** Bd dirs St Louis Co Grand Jury First Black Man to Head 1974-77; bd dirs Bicentennial for St Louis St Louis Co; chmn Distri Aunts & Uncles Give NeedyKids Shoes; resource dir Inner City YMCA; painted Portraits of Many Movie Stars & Celebs. **Honors/Awds:** Recip Cit of Week KATZ Radio; Honor Rehab Educ at Leavenworth KS; Honor Sigma Gamma Rho for Outstanding Artist in MO; Commissioned to Paint Portraits BillTriplett & Bill Contrell of Detroit Lions, Elston Howard of NY Yankees, Redd Fox, TV Star, Painting of Sammy Davis Jr Elvis Presley James Brown Ron Townsend of 5th Dimension. **Military Serv:** AUS pfc 1958-60. **Business Addr:** 2815 Pendleton Ave, St Louis, MO.

HENRY, WALTER LESTER, JR.
Physician, educator (retired). **Personal:** Born Nov 19, 1915, Philadelphia, PA; son of Vera Robinson Henry and Walter Lester Henry; married Ada Palmer. **Educ:** Temple Univ, AB 1936; Howard Univ Med Sch, MD 1941 (1st in class). **Career:** Howard Univ, asst & assoc prof 1953-63, chmn dept med 1962-73, prof med 1963-90; John B Johnson, prof of medicine, 1973-88. **Orgs:** Mem AMA, Natl Med Assn, Endocrine Soc, Assn Amer Physicians; certified in Endocrinology & Metabolism Amer Bd of Int Med; NAACP; Urban League; Sixth Presbyterian Church; Amer Bd Internal Med; regent Amer Coll Physicians (1st Black regent) 1974-; faculty trustee Howard Univ 1971-75; Amer Bd of Int Med, bd of governors, 1971-78; Amer College of Physicians, regent, 1974-80, laureate, 1993. **Honors/Awds:** American College of Physicians, Master (first black), 1987; American College of Physicians, Distinguished Teacher Awd, 1997. **Military Serv:** USMC maj WW II; US Army Bronze Star, cluster to Bronze Star 1942-44. **Home Addr:** 1780 Redwood Terrace NW, Washington, DC 20012.

HENRY, WARREN ELLIOTT
Educator. **Personal:** Born Feb 18, 1909, Evergreen, AL; married Jeanne Sally Pearlson; children: Eva Ruth. **Educ:** Tuskegee Inst, BS 1931; Atlanta Univ, MS 1937; Univ Chicago, PhD 1941. **Career:** Spelman & Morehouse Colleges, instr 1934-36; Tuakegee Inst, instr 1936-38, 1941-43; MA Inst Tech, staff member radiation lab 1943-46; Univ Chicago, instr 1946-47; Morehouse Coll, acting head dept physics 1947-48; Naval Rsch Lab Wash, super physicist 1948-60; Lockheed Missiles & Space Co, staff scientist srstaff engr 1960-69; Minority Participation in Physics, consult chmn com 1970-; Howard Univ, prof physics 1969-. **Orgs:** Fellow Amer Phys Soc; mem Amer Assn Physics Tchrs; Fedn Amer Scientists (chmn chap 1957-59); mem Inst Intl du Froid; Sci Rsch Soc Am (pres Naval Rsch Lab Br 1955); fellow AAAS; vice pres Palo Alto Fair Play Council 1968-69; presidential assoc Tuskegee Inst; grantee So Educ Found 1970-; mem Sigma Xi; author of articles & chapts in books. **Honors/Awds:** Honorary Doctorate, Lehigh Univ; Honorary LHD, Atlanta Univ; Carver Award, Natl Technical Achiever Award, Natl Technical Association, 1997. **Business Addr:** Howard University, PO Box 761, Washington, DC 20059.

HENRY, WILLIAM ARTHUR, II
Attorney. **Personal:** Born Feb 11, 1939, Canalou, MO; married Alice Faye Pierce; children: William III, Shawn. **Educ:** Lincoln U, BS 1962; Georgetown Univ Law Ctr, JD 1972. **Career:** Xerox Corp, patent atty; US Patent Ofc, patent exam 1966-72; IBM, rep 1964-66. **Orgs:** Mem DC Bar; DC Bar Assn; PA Bar; Am Bar Assn; Urban League; Nat Patent Law Assn; Rochester Patent Law Assn; Alpha Phi Alpha Frat. **Military Serv:** AUS 1/lt 1962-64. **Business Addr:** Counsel, Rochester Patent Opns, Xerox Corporation, Xerox Square, 20A, Rochester, NY 14644.

HENRY-FAIRHURST, ELLENAE L.
Company executive. **Personal:** Born Jan 6, 1943, Dayton, OH; daughter of Mr & Mrs Jack J Hart Sr; divorced. **Educ:** Miami Univ, BS, 1965; Univ of Detroit, MA, 1978. **Career:** Ford Motor Co, mgr, mktg research, 1968-86; Chrysler Corp, dealer candidate, 1986-88; Cumberland Chrysler-Plymouth, pres, general mgr, 1988-92; Huntsville Dodge Inc, pres, general mgr, 1992-. **Orgs:** Chrysler Minority Dealer Assn, secty/bd of dirs, 1989-; Dayton Contempory Dance Co, bd of dirs, 1993-; Sickle Cell Foundation, bd of dirs, 1989-. **Special Achievements:** Company is ranked #80 on Black Enterprise magazine's 1997 list of Top 100 Black businesses. **Business Addr:** President/General Mgr, Huntsville Dodge Inc, 6519 University Dr, PO Box 1528, Huntsville, AL 35807.

HENSLEY, WILLIE L.
Military official. **Career:** US Dept of Veterans Affairs, Ctr for Minority Veterans, head, 1995-. **Military Serv:** US Army, lt colonel, 22 yrs. **Business Addr:** Head, Ctr for Minority Veterans, US Dept of Veterans Affairs, 810 Vermont Ave, NW, Ste 700, Washington, DC 20420, (202)273-6708.

HENSON, CHARLES A.
Clergyman. **Personal:** Born Jan 5, 1915, Dallas, TX; married Helen M Hoxey; children: Helen Marie. **Educ:** Friends U, AB 1951; Union Bapt Sem, LlD; Prov Bapt Theol Sem, DD. **Career:** Zion Bapt Ch, pastor; CA State Congress of Christ End, pres; Martin Luther King Hosp, chpln. **Orgs:** Mem bd dirs LA Coun of Chs; past group leader World Bapt Youth Congress Beirut, Lebanon; chmn Adv Bd LA Sickle Cell Cntr; traveled extensively Europe, Asia, Africa, Holy Land 1955, 63, 68; mem CA Gen Adv Coun; served Preaching Mission Japan 1972. **Honors/Awds:** Commended outstanding serv to state of CA CA State Assembly 1967. **Business Addr:** 600 W Rosecrans Ave, Compton, CA 90220.

HENSON, DANIEL PHILLIP, III
Business executive. **Personal:** Born Apr 4, 1943, Baltimore, MD; son of Florence Newton Henson and Daniel P Henson, Jr; married Delaphine S; children: Darren P, Dana S. **Educ:** Morgan St Univ, BA 1966; Johns Hopkins Univ, 1968-70. **Career:** Baltimore City Pub Sch, tchr, 1966-67; Metropolitan Life Ins Co, assoc mgr, 1967-74; Dan Henson & Associates, president, 1973-77; Guardian Life Ins Co Am, gen agent, 1974-77; US Small Bus Adm, reg adm, 1977-79; Minority Business Dev Agency, dir 1979-81; Greater Baltimore Comm, dir, 1981-82; G & M Oil Co Inc, vice pres, 1982-84; Struever Bros Eccles & Rouse Inc, vice pres, 1984-. **Orgs:** Chairman of the Board, Devel Credit Fund, Inc 1982-; Grtr Baltimore Comm 1982-; board member, Baltimore Urban League 1982-88; board member, 1982-, chairman of the board, 1990-, Baltimore Sch for the Arts; chairman of the board, Investing In Baltimore, Inc; board member, Johns Hopkins Univ Inst of Policy Studies; board member, Home Builders Assn of of MD, 1981-82; board member, Federal Reserve Bank of Richmond, Baltimore Branch, 1991-; board member, Center for Ethics and Corporate Policy, 1989-. **Business Addr:** Vice President, Struever Brs Eccles/Rouse Inc, 519 N Charles St, Baltimore, MD 21201.

HENSON, DAVID BERNARD
Educational administrator. **Personal:** Born Mar 3, 1938, Orlando, FL; son of Mary A Nixon Henson (deceased) and Benjamin B Henson; married Earlene V Ovletrea Henson, Dec 23, 1962; children: Charles Dewayne, Mary P Henson Masi. **Educ:** Florida A&M Univ, Tallahassee, FL, BA, 1961; Tuskegee Institute, Tuskegee, AL, MS; University of Iowa, Iowa City, IA, PhD, 1972. **Career:** Howard University College of Medicine, Washington, DC, assst prof of biochemistry & interim chair of biochemistry, 1972-78; Yale University, New Haven, CT, dean of students, 1978-83; Florida Atlantic University, Boca Raton, FL, associate vice president/provost, 1983-86; Univ of Colorado at Boulder, Boulder, CO, associate vice chancellor, 1986-89; University of Colorado System, Boulder, CO, associate vice president for academic affairs, 1989-92; Alabama A&M University, Huntsville, AL, president, professor of chemistry, 1992-. **Orgs:** Member, Alpha Phi Alpha Fraternity Inc, 1957-; board of directors, Boys and Girls Clubs of America, Huntsville Chapter, 1992-; board of directors, National Association for Equal Opportunity in Higher Education, 1992-; board of directors, "I Have a Dream," Boulder Chapter, 1990-; Rotary International, Huntsville, 1991-; St John's AME Church, bd of stewards, 1992-; Huntsville Chamber of Commerce, bd of dirs; Alabama School of Math & Science, bd of dirs, 1992-. **Honors/Awds:** African Americans Who Make a Difference, Awarded by Urban Spectrum of Denver, 1988. **Business Addr:** President, Alabama A&M University, 108 Patton Hall, Normal, AL 35762.

HENSON, WILLIAM FRANCIS
Physician. **Personal:** Born May 21, 1933, Washington, DC; married Lucile Thornton; children: Rhonda Elaine Poole, David T, Russell Francis, Alan Everett. **Educ:** Lincoln Univ, AB 1955; Howard Univ Sch of Medicine, MD 1959. **Career:** VA Medical Ctr, staff physician 1963-64, section chief 1964-77, acting chief med 1977-78, chief medicine 1978-. **Orgs:** Mem Natl Medical Assoc 1964-, Medical Assoc of State of AL 1980-, Macon Co Medical Soc 1980-, AL State Medical Assoc 1982-; 33rd degree masonry, 1st lt commander, 2nd Lt commander Booker T Washington Consistory 1983-87, commander-in-chief 1987-89; high priest and prophet Mizraim Temple #119 1986-88. **Military Serv:** AUS Army Reserve Medical Corps major 15 yrs; Outstanding Officer 1207th US Hospital. **Business Addr:** Chief, Medical Services, VA Medical Ctr, Tuskegee, AL 36083.

HENSON, WILLIAM L.
Educator. **Personal:** Born Aug 7, 1934, Baltimore, MD; son of Mattie Ward Henson and Lawson Henson; married Audrey Mills Henson, Feb 2, 1957; children: Cheryl, Elizabeth, Kathleen. **Educ:** Maryland State College, BS, 1955; Penn State University, MA, 1957, PhD, 1967. **Career:** Commonwealth of Pennsylvania, Harrisburg, PA, egg law enforcer, 1957-59; USDA, Fredericksburg, PA, poultry inspector, 1959-63; Penn State University, University Park, PA, graduate research assistant, 1963-67, assistant to associate dean of agriculture, 1969-84, assistant to the dean of agriculture, 1984-; US Dept of Agriculture, University Park, PA, senior agricultural economist, 1967-84. **Orgs:** Minorities in Agriculture, Natural Resources, and Related Sciences, 1988-, president, 1991-92; member, American Agricultural Econ Assn, 1967-90; member, American Econ Assn, 1967-; member, Poultry Science Assn, 1967-90. **Honors/Awds:** Distinguished Alumni Hall of Fame, Maryland State College, 1986; Presidential Citation, National Assn for Equal Opportunity in Higher Education, 1987; Equal Opportunity Award, Penn State Univ, 1989; Equal Opportunity Award, Econ and Stat Service, USDA, 1980; Alumni Citizen Award, Black Greeks, Penn State Univ, 1988; Excellence in Advising Award, Penn State Univ, 1996. **Home Addr:** 125 Norle St, State College, PA 16801. **Business Addr:** Assistant to the Dean, Minority Affairs, College of Agriculture, Penn State University, 101 Agricultural Administration Building, University Park, PA 16802.

HERBERT, ADAM, JR.
Educational administrator. **Career:** Univ of North Florida, president; State Univ System, chancellor, currently. **Special Achievements:** First African American chancellor of Florida's ten public universities. **Business Addr:** Chancellor, State University System, 325 W Gaines St, Tallahassee, FL 32399, (850)487-1896.

HERBERT, BENNE S., JR.
Mediator. **Personal:** Born Sep 6, 1946, Bronx, NY; son of Marian C Boyde Herbert and Dr Benne S Herbert Sr (deceased); divorced; children: Ainah Reid. **Educ:** Ithaca Clg, BA 1969; Cornell U, Cert 1968-70; Hampton Inst, Cert 1970; Cleveland St, Cert 1984-85; Cleveland Marshall College of Law. **Career:** Ithaca Clg, asst dean of stdnts 1969-70; Am Arbitration Assn, dir 10-75; Arbitration & Mediation Serv, Inc, pres 1975-78, 1988-; Home Owners Warranty Corp, dir of cncltn 1978-80; Natl Acad Cncltrs, vice pr 1980-82; Travis & Staughn Cnsltnts Labor Rltns, vice pres 1982-84; Vstng Nurse Asso, vice pres 1984-88; FMHA, Ohio Region, chief mediator, 1989-. **Orgs:** Sr consult D A Browne Assn 1978-87; sr consult Herbert Grp Mgrs 1984-; mem Am Arbtrtn Assn 1985; pres Negotation Spclts Corp 1982-85; mem Black Prof Assn of Cleveland 1984-85; member, IRRA; member, ASTD; member, American Compensation Association; board of trustees, Eliza Bryant Center; member, National Bar Association, 1988-91. **Honors/Awds:** Ithaca College, Deans List, 1968-69; Outstanding Senior Award. **Special Achievements:** Author: How Settles Consumer Complaints, 1979; Preparing for Negotiation, 1984; Disputes Settlement in Chicago Housing, 1979; Arbitration of Minor Criminal Complaints, 1974.

HERBERT, DOUGLAS A.
Law enforcement official. **Educ:** Henrico County Sheriff's Office, Special Law Enforcement Academy. **Career:** Henrico County Sheriff's Office, jail security division, from corporal to sergeant, 1980-85, shift sergeant, 1985-87, lieutenant, 1987-88, captain, 1988-. **Special Achievements:** First African American captain with the Henrico County Sheriff's Office. **Business Addr:** Captain, Henrico County Sherriff's Office, PO Box 27032, Richmond, VA 23273, (804)672-4950.

HERBERT, JAMES BRUINEL. See Obituaries section.

HERBERT, JOHN TRAVIS, JR.
Attorney. **Personal:** Born Feb 17, 1943, Montclair, NJ; divorced; children: Stephanie, Travis, Suzanne. **Educ:** Seton Hall Law School, JD 1974. **Career:** Johnson & Johnson, atty, corp dir 1974-76, manager 1972-74; Allied Chem, corp staff 1969-72; Rugers Univ, adjunct prof 1973-; Central Jersey OIC, bd atty; Pitney Bowes, Stamford, CT, vice pres Corp Facilities & Admin 1983-. **Orgs:** Vol in Parole 1974-; chmn BALSA Seton Hall Law School 1973-74; coach Pop Warner Football 1975-77; organized Franklin Township Youth Athletic Assn 1976-77; mem Franklin Township Bd of Educ; Amer Bar Assn; Natl Bar Assn; New Jersey Bar Assn; Middlesex Co Bar Assn 1979-80; bd sec, gen counsel Rutgers Min Bus Co 1980; bd of Westchester Fairfield City Corp Councils Assoc 1985-; bd of mayors Transportation Management Round Table 1985-; corp liason, Natl Urban League of Stamford 1986-.

HERCULES, FRANK E. M. See Obituaries section.

HERD, JOHN E.
Educator. **Personal:** Born May 29, 1932, Colbert Co, AL; married Eleanor; children: Arnold, Garland. **Educ:** BS MS 1966, AA Cert 1976. **Career:** Russa Moton HS Tallassee, AL, instr; Cobb HS Anniston, AL, instr; Brutonville Jr HS AL, principal; Alexandria HS AL, principal; New Elam #1 Missi onary Baptist Church, pastor, currently. **Orgs:** Mem Alpha Phi Alpha; 1st Black pres of Calhoun Co Educ Assn 1972. **Military Serv:** USAF sgt 1/c 1951-55.

HEREFORD, SONNIE WELLINGTON, III
Physician. **Personal:** Born Jan 7, 1931, Huntsville, AL; son of Jannie Burwell Hereford and Sonnie Hereford; married Martha Ann Adams, Nov 1956; children: Sonnie IV, Kimela, Lee, Linda, Brenda, Martha. **Educ:** AL A&M U, BS 1955; Meharry Med Coll, MD 1955. **Career:** Calhoun Coll, prof of anatomy/physiology, 1996-; Oakwood Coll, campus phys 1957-73; AL A&M Univ, team physician 1962-, campus physician 1962-73, prof of histology 1960-68, prof of physiology 1960-68. **Orgs:** Chmn com for Desegregation of Huntsville, AL 1962-63; consult sickle cell anemia Delta Sigma Theta 1971-75; member, Omega Psi Phi; Boy Scouts and Girl Scouts, volunteer physician, 1956-93; Golden Gloves of Huntsville, volunteer physician, 1968-88. **Honors/Awds:** Distinguished Serv Award Voter Coord Com Huntsville, AL 1962; Distinguished Serv Award Oakwood Coll Huntsville, AL 1973; Meharry Medical College, Twenty-Five Year Service Award, 1980; Community Action Agency, Distinguished Service Award, 1980; Oakwood Church, Distinguished Service Award, 1980; Zeta Sorority, Distinguished Service Award, 1982; Madison County Midwives Assn, Distinguished Service Award, 1983; Alabama A&M University Athletic Department, Distinguished Service Award, 1985; Inducted into Huntsville, Alabama Hall of Fame, 1995. **Business Addr:** PO Box 2205, Huntsville, AL 35804-2205.

HERENTON, WILLIE W.
Mayor. **Personal:** Born Apr 23, 1940, Memphis, TN; married Ida Jones; children: Errol, Rodney, Andrea. **Educ:** LeMoyne-Owen Coll, BS 1963; Memphis State Univ, MA 1966; So IL Univ, PhD 1971. **Career:** Memphis City Sch System, elementary sch tchr 1963-67, elementary sch prin 1967-73; Rockefeller Found, fellow 1973-74; Memphis City Schs, dept supt 1974-78, supt of schs 1979-92; City of Memphis, mayor, 1992-. **Orgs:** Bd dir Natl Urban League; bd dir Natl Jr Achievement; mem Amer Assn of Sch Adminstr 1969-80; mem Natl Alliance of Black Educators 1974-; bd dirJr Achievement of Memphis 1979-; mem Natl Urban League Educ Adv Council 1978; bd dir United Way of Greatr Memphis 1979-. **Honors/Awds:** Raymond Foster Scholarship Awd So IL Univ 1970; Rockefeller Found Fellowship Rockefeller Found 1973; Alumnus of the Yr LeMoyne Owen Coll 1976; Named oneof Top 100 Sch Adminstrs in US & Can Exec Educator Journal 1980, 1984. **Business Addr:** Mayor, City of Memphis, 125 Mid-America Mall, Ste 200, Memphis, TN 38103.

HERMAN, ALEXIS M.
Government official. **Personal:** Born Jul 16, 1947, Mobile, AL. **Educ:** Xavier Univ, BA 1969. **Career:** Cath Soc Serv, soc worker 1969-72; Recruitment Training Prog, outreach worker, 1971-72; Black Women Empl Prog So Regional Cncl, dir 1972-74; Dept Labor Recruitment Training Prog, consult supr 1973-74; Women's Prog for Minority Women Empl Atlanta, natl dir 1974-77; Organization of Economic Cooperation and Development, White House representative; Natl Consumer Cooperative Bank, founding mem; Dept of Labor, Women's Bureau, dir 1977-81; president, A M Herman & Associates, CEO, 1981-; Democratic Natl Committee, deputy chair, chief of staff; 1992 Democratic Natl Convention Committee, CEO, 1991; Presidential Transition Office, deputy dir, until 1993; White House Office of Public Liaison, director, and asst to the President of the US, 1993-97, secretary of labor, 1997-. **Orgs:** Adams Natl Bank, bd mem; District of Columbia Economic Development Finance Corp, bd mem; Natl Council of Negro Women; Delta Sigma Theta Sorority Inc. **Honors/Awds:** Dorothy I Height Leadership Award; Central State Univ, honorary doctorate; Lesley Coll, honorary doctorate. **Business Addr:** Secretary of Labor, US Dept. of Labor, 200 Constitution Ave NW, Washington, DC 20210.

HERMAN, KATHLEEN VIRGIL
Communications administration. **Personal:** Born May 17, 1942, Buffalo, NY; children: Jonathan Mark. **Educ:** Goddard Coll, BA 1976; Boston Univ, MS Commun 1980. **Career:** Public Info Boston Edison, consult 1979; Minority Recruitment Big Sister Assoc, coord 1980; Council on Battered Women, comm educ dir 1980; Access Atlanta Inc, dir 1981; City of Atlanta, coord cable commun. **Orgs:** Mem Minorities in Cable, Natl Assoc of Telecom, Natl Fed of Local Programmers, Women in Cable; NAACP Media Comm, co-chair; American Women in Radio & TV. **Honors/Awds:** Publication, "Minority Participation in the Media", sub-committe on Telecom Consumer Protection & Finance of the Committee on Energy & Commerce, US House of Representatives, 98th Congress.

HERMANUZ, GHISLAINE
Educator. **Personal:** Born in Lausanne, Switzerland; daughter of Manotte Tavernier Hermanuz and Max Hermanuz; children: Dahoud Walker. **Educ:** ETH/Lausanne Switzerland, Arch Diploma 1967; Harvard Grad School of Design, 1968-69; Columbia Univ, MS Urban Planning 1971. **Career:** Candilis, Josic & Woods, architect 1964-65; Llewelyn-Davies & Weeks, architect 1967-68; Architects' Renewal Comm in Harlem, architect 1969-71; Urban Design Group City Planning Dept, urban designer 1972-73; Columbia Univ Grad Sch Architecture, prof of architecture; City Coll of New York, dir, City College Architectural Center; Hermanuz Ltd, principal, 1988-. **Orgs:** Landmarks

Harlem, board of directors; NGO Committee on Shelter and Community, board member. **Honors/Awds:** Fellowship Fulbright 1968, German Marshall Fund of the US 1979, Natl Endowment for the Arts 1982; Grant NY State Council on the Arts 1984, 1986, 1988; President's Fund for Excellence in Teaching, 1990; Municipal Art Society, IDEAS Competition, Urban Design Prize. **Business Addr:** Director City College Architectural Center, City Coll of New York, Convent Ave at 138th St, New York, NY 10031.

HERNANDEZ, AILEEN CLARKE

Business executive, urban consultant. **Personal:** Born May 23, 1926, Brooklyn, NY; daughter of Ethel Louise Hall Clarke and Charles Henry Clarke Sr; divorced. **Educ:** Howard U, BA (magna cum laude) 1947; Univ Oslo, postgrad (internat student exchange prog) 1947; NY U, 1950; Univ CA at LA; Univ of So CA; Intern Ladies Garment Workers Union, grad labor coll 1951; LA State Coll, MA 1961. **Career:** Intl Ladies Garment Workers Union LA, org asst educ dir 1951-59, dir pub relat & educ 1959-61; State Dept So Amer Countries, specialist in labor educ toured 1960; CA Fair Employ Prac Commn, asst chief 1962-65; US Equal Employment Commission, commissioner, 1965-66; San Francisco State Univ, lecturer/instructor in political sci 1968-69; Univ of CA Berkeley, instructor urban planning 1978, 1979; Hernandez & Associates San Francisco, owner/pres 1966-. **Orgs:** Western vice pres Nat Orgn Women 1967-70, pres 1970-71; co-found mem Black Women Organized for Act San Fran & Nat Hookup of Black Women chair; trust Urban Inst Wash, DC; bd mem MS Foundation for Women; bd dirs Natl Comm Against Discrimination in Housing 1969; Am Acad Politic & Soc Scis; Indus Relat Rsch Assn; American Civil Liberties Union; bd mem Foreign Policy Study Found Commn to Study US Policy towards S Africa; exec com Common Cause; steering exec com, co-chair, Natl Urban Coalition; president, bd of trustees Working Assets Money Fund; bd of overseers Inst for Civil Justice Rand Corp; advisor Natl Inst for Women of Color; treas Eleanor R Spikes Memorial Fund; advisory cmte, Program for Research on Immigration Policy, Rand & Urban Inst; bd mem, Death Penalty Focus; bd mem, Meiklejohn Civil Liberties Union; CA Comm on paign Financing; NAACP; Alpha Kappa Alpha; Bay Area Urban League; co-founder, Coalition for Economic Equity, vice chair, San Francisco 2000; commissioner, Bay Vision 2020; chair, CA Women's Agenda (CAWA); chair emerita, Citizen's Trust; Univ of CA, SF Foundation; bd Pesticide Edu Center; bd, Garden Project; bd, Meiklejoh Civil Liberties Inst; bd, Center for Women Policy Studies; bd, Citizen's Commission on Civil Rights. **Honors/Awds:** Named Woman of Yr Comm Relations Conf So CA 1961; recip Bay Area Alumni Club Disting Postgrad Achvmt Awd Howard Univ 1967; Charter Day Alumni Postgrad Achvmnt in Labor & Pub Serv Awd 1968; named one of 10 Most Distin Women Bay Area San Fran Examin 1968; Southern Vermont Coll Hon DHL 1979; Awd from Equal Rights Advocates 1981; Friends of the Commn on the Status of Women Awd 1984; SF League of Women Voters Awd "Ten Women Who Make a Difference" 1985; Parren J Mitchell Award, SF Black Chamber of Commerce, 1985; distinguished service award, Natl Urban Coalition, 1987; Earl Warren Civil Liberties Award, N California ACLU, 1989; Silver Spur Award, SF Planning & Urban Research Assn, 1995; WAVE award, Alumnae Resources, 1997. **Business Addr:** President/ Owner, Hernandez & Associates, 818 47th Ave, San Francisco, CA 94121.

HERNANDEZ, MARY N.

Librarian. **Personal:** Born Nov 21, 1940, Nashville, TN; daughter of Mary DeWees Hernandez (deceased) and Rafael Hernandez (deceased). **Educ:** Fisk University, Nashville, TN, BA, 1962; Tennessee State University, Nashville, TN, 1965-67, 1978-79, MS, 1985; Peabody at Vanderbilt, Nashville, TN, MLS, 1986. **Career:** Hubbard Hospital, Nashville, TN, asst admitting officer, 1979-80; Meharry Medical College, Nashville, TN, teaching asst, 1980-85; Volunteer St Com College, Gallatin, TN, instructor, 1986-88; Cheekwood Fine Arts Center, Nashville, TN, librarian, 1986-88; University of Tennessee at Chattanooga, Chattanooga, TN, asst prof, 1988-91, head, circulation services, 1989-91; University Library, University of Arizona, Tucson, assistant librarian, currently. **Orgs:** President, Art Libraries Society, TN-KY, 1989-90; president, Republican Women of Greater Chattanooga, 1990-91; member, ARLIS, NA Membership Committee, 1990-91, 1993-95; member, LoPresti Award, ARLIS, SE, 1990-91; member, Arts and Education Council, Southern Writers Conference, 1990-91; member, Black Caucus, American Library Assn, 1989-; president-elect, ARLIS, Arizona, 1993-94; board member, Tucson Jazz Society, 1992-; Council of Black Educators, Tucson. **Honors/Awds:** Dean's Award, Lupton Library of the University of Tennessee at Chattanooga, 1990; NEH Award, 1992-93. **Home Addr:** 3033 E 6th St, Apt F3, Tucson, AZ 85716-4811. **Business Addr:** Assistant Reference Librarian, University of Arizona, Tucson, AZ 85721.

HERNDON, CRAIG GARRIS

Photographer. **Personal:** Born Jan 23, 1947, Washington, DC; son of Lucy Frances Mills Herndon and Garris McClellan Herndon; married Valerie Ingrid Naylor, Aug 7, 1988; children: Stacey Arlene, Robert Eric, Marcus Vincent, Monica Amber, Maya Violet. **Educ:** Howard Univ, BA 1970. **Career:** Washington Post, photographer 1972-; Potomac Magazine, news aide 1968-72. **Orgs:** White House News Photographers Assn; Natl Assn of Black Journalists. **Honors/Awds:** National Assn of Black Journalists, Photographer of the Year, 1996. **Business Addr:** Photographer, The Washington Post, 1150 15th St NW, Washington, DC 20071.

HERNDON, GLORIA E.

Business executive. **Personal:** Born Aug 9, 1950, St Louis; married Brent Astaire. **Educ:** Johns Hopkins U, MA 1972; So IL U, BA 1970; Ahmadu Bello Univ, PhD 1978. **Career:** Amer Embassy London, financial economist; Ahmadu Bello Univ Nigeria, research 1978-79; Brooking Inst, research asst; Johns Hopkins, research asst; African-Amer Inst, prog asst; Dept State, escort interpreter; Carnegie Endowment Intl Peace Council Foreign Relations, research asst; Equitable Financial Services, insurance company executive 1984-. **Orgs:** Mem Accomplished Musician; Mu Phi Epsilon; Nat Economic Assn; Am Soc Intl Law; Nat Conf Black Political Scientist; Nat Council Negro Women; Nigerian-Am C of C; US Youth Council Research initial Black Caucus 1970-71; planner United Minority Arts Council. **Honors/Awds:** Distinguished Serv Award So IL Univ 1970; Nat Assn of Honor Students; Nat Negro Merit Semifinalist 1967; Magna Cum Laude Woodrow Wilson Fellow Finalist 1970; recip Rockefeller Found Fellow. **Business Addr:** Insurance Executive, Equitable Financial Services, 1803 Research Blvd, Rockville, MD 20850.

HERNDON, HAROLD THOMAS, SR.

Company executive. **Personal:** Born Oct 28, 1937, Lincolnton, NC; son of Elizabeth Herndon and John W Herndon Jr; married Catherine Thompson, Jun 30, 1962; children: Harold Jr, Dwayne, LaShawn, Colin. **Educ:** Bluefield State College, BS, 1959; University of Maryland, MS, 1980. **Career:** St Mary's Board of Education, music teacher, 1960-70, administrator, 1970-80; Compliance Corp., founder, president & CEO, 1980-. **Orgs:** National Contract Management Association, Chesapeake Bay Chapter, president, 1982-; Rotary International; St Mary's County Economic Development Commission; Society of Engineers and Scientists; Maryland 100; St Mary's Nursing Home, board member; St Mary's Vocational Technical Education Council; Tri-County Small Business Development Center, board member. **Honors/Awds:** St Mary's Human Relations Committee, Pathfinder Award, 1990; Minority Alliance, Outstanding Business Achievements, 1992; other awards from various organizations over the years. **Special Achievements:** Top 100 Black Businesses, Black Enterprise, 1991. **Business Addr:** President & CEO, Compliance Corp., 21617 Essex Dr S, Ste 34, Lexington Park, MD 20653, (301)863-8070.

HERNDON, JAMES

Attorney. **Personal:** Born May 14, 1925, Troy, AL; children: 2. **Educ:** Morehouse Coll, AB 1948; Howard U, LlB 1951. **Career:** Garry, Dreyfus, McTernan, Brotsky, Herndon & Pesonen; atty. **Orgs:** Pres San Francisco African Am Historical & Cultural Soc.

HERNDON, LANCE H. See Obituaries section.

HERNDON, LARRY LEE

Professional baseball player (retired), coach. **Personal:** Born Nov 3, 1953, Sunflower, MS; married Faye Hill; children: Latasha, Kamilah, Maya, Larry Darnell. **Educ:** Tennessee State Univ. **Career:** San Francisco Giants, outfielder, 1976-81; Detroit Tigers, outfielder, 1982-88, coach, currently. **Honors/Awds:** Willie Mac Award, San Francisco Giants, 1981; National League Rookie of the Year, Sporting News, 1976. **Business Addr:** Coach, Detroit Tigers Baseball Club, 2121 Trumbull, Detroit, MI 48216-1343.

HERNDON, PHILLIP GEORGE

Investment banker. **Personal:** Born Jul 3, 1951, Little Rock, AR; son of Georgia Mae Byrd Herndon and James Franklyn Herndon. **Educ:** Villanova Univ, PA, 2 years; Amer Legion Boy's State, 1968. **Career:** Pulaski Co, AR, surveyor; Just for Kicks Inc retail shoe store, owner 1973-74; KATV Little Rock, news reporter 1972; Black Rel Dir Youth Div Gov Winthrop Rockefeller's Re-Election Campaign, 1970; Pulaski Co, elected co-surveyor & 1st black elected official, 1972; Lt Governor Amer Legions Boys State, 1st Black elected 1968; Kip Walton Productions (TV/Motion Pictures), Hollywood, CA, production asst 1974-78; US Assoc Investment Bankers, Little Rock, AR, investment banker, 1985-87; Blinder, Robinson & Co, Denver, CO, asst manager Bond Department 1987-88; consultant, Colorado African/Caribbean Trade Office 1988-; consultant, Anisco Enterprises (import/export) 1988-; Manufacturing & Distributing International, sr vp, 1992-. **Orgs:** Dir of Community Relations GYST House, (fund raiser drug rehabilitation program); New Futures for Little Rock Youth, dir, volunteer services. **Honors/Awds:** Natl HS Track Champ Natl & state record holder high hurdles 1968; 1st Black inducted into Little Rock Central HS Hall of Fame 1969; recip over 200 full scholarship offers from coll & Univ nationwide 1969; Million Dollar Club, Blinder, Robinson & Company 1988.

HERNTON, CALVIN COOLIDGE

Educator. **Personal:** Born in Chatanooga, TN; children: Antone. **Educ:** Talladega Coll, BA Sociology 1954; Fisk Univ, MA Sociology 1956; Columbia Univ, Sociology 1961. **Career:** AL A&M University, sociology instructor, 1958-59; Edward Waters College, social science instructor, 1959-60; Southern University, sociology instructor, 1960-61; Central State Univ, poet in residence 1970; Oberlin Coll, black writer in residence 1970-72, prof black/creative studies 1973-; ABC Warner Bros TV, Burbank CA, technical consultant for "A Man Called Hawk," beginning 1988. **Orgs:** Writers Guild of America; Authors Guild/Authors League. **Honors/Awds:** The Coming of Chronos to the House of Nightsong, poetry, Interim Books 1963; Sex and Racism in America, Doubleday 1964; White Papers for White America, Doubleday 1966; Coming Together, Random House 1971; The Cannabis Experience, Peter Owen 1974; Scarecrow, Doubleday 1974; Medicine Man, Reed Cannon & Johnson 1977; The Sexual Mountain & Black Women Writers, Adventures in Sex, Literature & Real Life, Doubleday 1987. **Special Achievements:** Author of teleplay Beautiful Are the Stars, 1988. **Business Addr:** Professor of Black Studies, Oberlin College, Rice Hall, Oberlin, OH 44074.

HERRELL, ASTOR YEARY

Educational administrator. **Personal:** Born Feb 13, 1935, Fork Ridge, TN; son of Charity Herrell and Clarence Herrell; married Doris Vivian Smith; children: Patricia Faye. **Educ:** Berea Coll KY, BA 1957; Tuskegee Inst AL, MS Ed 1961; Wayne State Univ MI, PhD (inorg chem) 1973; Wayne State Univ, Science Faculty Fellow 1970-72. **Career:** St Augustine's Coll, instr 1961-63; Knoxville Coll, prof & chmn 1963-79; Winston-Salem State Univ, chmn physical sciences dept 1979-. **Orgs:** Chemist New Brunswick Lab NJ summers 1964-65; rsch chemist Sandia Lab NM summer 1975; consult Fisk UNCF Summer Inst summers 1977-83; mem Amer Chemical Soc 1969-; consult Winston-Salem/Forsyth County Schools 1983-85; bd of dir Forsyth County Environmental Affairs Board; Sigma Xi 1985-. **Honors/Awds:** Biography display Martin Luther King Libr DC 1984; several publns in natl and international science journals - last article publ in 1984. **Military Serv:** AUS Reserves Pfc served 6 yrs. **Business Addr:** Chairman, Physical Sci Dept, Winston-Salem State University, PO Box 13236, Winston-Salem, NC 27102.

HERRERA, CARL VICTOR

Professional basketball player. **Personal:** Born Dec 14, 1966, Trinidad and Tobago; married Monica; children: four. **Educ:** Jacksonville Junior Coll; Univ of Houston. **Career:** Real Madrid (Italy), forward, 1990-91; Houston Rockets, 1991-95; San Antonio Spurs, 1995-. **Special Achievements:** Venezuelan Olympic Team, 1992; NBA Championship Team, 1994-95. **Business Addr:** Professional Basketball Player, San Antonio Spurs, 600 E Market St, San Antonio, TX 78205, (210)554-7773.

HERRING, BERNARD DUANE

Educator. **Personal:** Born in Massillon, OH; son of Eva Herring and James Herring; married Odessa Appling; children: Kevin, Duane, Terez, Sean. **Educ:** Kent State U, BS (magna cum laude) 1952; Univ of Cinci Med Sch, MD 1956; LaSalle U, LLB 1963. **Career:** San Fran Gen Hosp, intern 1956-57; Brooklyn Vet Hosp, resident 1957-58; Crile Vet Hosp, resident 1958-59; Merritt Hosp, teaching 1966-84; Univ of CA Med Sch SF, asst clin prof of med. **Orgs:** Candidate CA Bar; bd cert Am Bd of Family Med; candidate Am Bd of Internal Med; Sabteca Music Co; Real Estate License CA; Am Soc of Internal Med; fellow Am Coll of Legal Med; Am Med Writers Assn; Am Diabetes Assn; mem Am Coll of Physician; Am Soc of Composers & Authors; Am Med Assn; Am Heart Assn; Pres Sunshine Vitamin Co; fellow Am Academy of Family Physicians 1983; mem Am Geriatric Society 1989; presiding overseer Watchtower Bible and Tract Society 1980-89. **Honors/Awds:** Cited by Phi Beta Kappa, staff Kent State Univ 1952; article "Kaposi Sarcoma in The Negro" 1963 Jama; Article "Hospital Priviledges" 1965 Cleveland Marshall Law Review; article "Pernicious Anemia and The American Negro" American Practitioner 1962; article "Hepatoma with Unusual Associations" J. National Medical Assn 1973; article "Cancer of Prostate in Blacks" J. Natl Medical Assn 1977; Listed Best Doctor in Am 1979; article, "Unravelling Pathophysiology of Male Pattern Baldness" 1985; Broker License Real Estate, 1991. **Special Achievements:** Board certified Geriatrics, 1994; Board certified Forensic Medicine, 1995. **Business Addr:** Assistant Clinical Professor, Univ of California Medical School, 400 29th St, Oakland, CA 94609.

HERRING, LARRY WINDELL

Dentist. **Personal:** Born Jul 8, 1946, Batesville, MS; married Rubbie P Herring; children: Cedric, La Canas Nicole, Yolanda. **Educ:** TN St U, BA 1967; Meharry Med Coll, DDS 1971. **Career:** Dentist, private practice, currently. **Orgs:** Mem Nat Den Assn; Am Den Assn; Pan-TN Den Assn; Tri-Lakes Study Club; Shelby Co Den Soc; mem NAACP; Omega Psi Phi; Masonic Lodge; W Camp MB Ch. **Military Serv:** USAF capt 1971-73. **Business Addr:** 114 Wood St, Batesville, MS 38606.

HERRING, LEONARD, JR.

Public relations executive. **Personal:** Born Oct 1, 1934, Valdosta, GA; son of Gussie Herring and Leonard Herring Sr; children: Leonard III, Lynne Rene. **Educ:** Univ of Cincinnati, BA 1960, BS 1964. **Career:** Colgate-Palmolive Co NYC/San Fran, mrktng staff asst 1963-64; Market-Cincinnati Bell Tele OH, accnts mgr staff asst 1964-66; Armco Steel Corp Middletown, OH, asst personnel 1966-67; Leonard Herring, Jr Pub Rel Ltd & Mgmnt, dir/pres ceo 1967-; Celebrity Tennis Tournament, Limited, pres, 1976-. **Orgs:** Life mem Kappa Alpha Psi 1960-; mem Univ of Cinci Aumni Assn 1964-; mem Am Tennis Professnl 1970-; mem Univ of Cinci 100 Disting Alumni 1970; mem US Tennis Writers Assn 1970-; mem Advertising Assn of Am 1972-; vice pres Pub Rel Soc of Amer 1972-76; vice pres US Lawn Tennis Assn 1975-76; mem Men of Achievement in the World 1976; bd mem United Way Los Angeles 1984-. **Honors/Awds:** Pub rel consult Movies, ''The Amityville Horror'', ''A Piece of the Action'', ''Part II Sounder'', ''Cross Creek''; confidante of the late Arthur Ashe; coached Cinci Chap of the Nat Jr Tennis Leagues Boys & Girls to 3 consecutive championships at US Tennis Open Forest Hills, NY 1972-74; tennis tournament producer: Aspen Celebrity Tennis Tournament, Aspen, CO; Tony Dorsett Celebrity Tennis Tournament, Dallas, TX; Carlos Palomino's Fiestas de Octubre Celebrity Tennis Tournament, Guadalajara, Mexico; Warren Moon Celebrity Tennis Tournament, Houston, TX; Oscar Robertson Celebrity Tennis Tournament, Cincinnati, OH; Fred Williamson Celebrity Tennis Tournament, Oakland, CA; Santa Monica Celebrity Tennis Classic, Malibu CA. **Military Serv:** US Army, lt; news coorespondent for the Stars & Stripes in Europe 1954-56. **Business Addr:** President, Celebrity Tennis Tournament, Limited, Le Montrose De Gran Luxe, 900 Hammond Street, Suite 434, West Hollywood, CA 90069.

HERRING, MARSHA K. CHURCH

Hospital administrator. **Personal:** Born Jun 23, 1958, Detroit, MI; daughter of Muriel & Rogers Church; married Cedric Herring, Jun 25, 1983; children: Christopher Earle, Kiara Nicole. **Educ:** University of MI-Ann Arbor, bachelors, general studies, 1980, masters, public policy, 1983. **Career:** US Senator Carl Levin, press asst, 1980-85; Humana Hospital Brazos Valley, dir of mktg, 1985-89; Greenleaf Hospital, dir of mktg, 1989-90; Christ Hospital, dir of mental health mktg, 1991-93; UIC Medical Center, dir of mktg, 1993-. **Orgs:** American Marketing Assn, 1980-85, 1993-; Alliance for Health Services Mktg, 1993-; South Suburban Chamber of Commerce, IL, 1992-, chair, health services committee, 1992-94; Crisis Center for So Suburbia, advisory bd member, 1992-93. **Honors/Awds:** Academy of Black Women in Health Professions, Recognition Award, 1994; Christ Hospital, Employee of the Month, Gold Star Award, 1993; HCA Greenleaf Hospital, Agape Award, 1990. **Business Addr:** Director of Medical Center Marketing, University of Illinois at Chicago Medical Center, 914 S Wood St, Rm 429 m/c 701, Chicago, IL 60612, (312)413-0026.

HERRING, WILLIAM F.

Cleaning company executive. **Personal:** Born Jul 28, 1932, Valdosta, GA; son of Viola Herring and Coy Herring; married Janet L; children: William Jr, Paul, Kristi. **Educ:** Wayne State U, BA 1961. **Career:** Buick Motor Div GM Corp, mgr dealer development 1979-, asst zone mgr 1977-79; Detroit Coca-Cola Bottling Co, dir of indsl relations 1973-75; Houdaille Industries, mgr indsl relations 1970-73. **Orgs:** Mem Detroit Police Comm Relations 1972; life mem NAACP 1976; mem Car & Truck Renting & Leasing Assn (CATRALA) 1977; member, National Advisory Council, NAACP, 1983-; board of directors, Urban League, 1985-88; member, United Negro College Fund, 1985-. **Honors/Awds:** Achievement Award United Fund 1972. **Military Serv:** AUS cpt 1952-54. **Business Addr:** Owner, WFH & Associates, 800 Savannah Ave, Canton, OH 44704.

HERRINGTON, PERRY LEE

Minority business consultant. **Personal:** Born Mar 26, 1951, Waynesboro, GA; son of Judy Herrington Miller and Theodore Miller; married Janet Bailey Herrington, Sep 27, 1980; children: Jeffrey Bailey, Tiese, Kara, Brittany. **Educ:** Univ of Chicago, Chicago, IL, certificate, Urban Studies, 1971; Coe Coll, Cedar Rapids, IA, BA, 1973; Lindenwood Coll, St Louis, MO, MBA, 1986. **Career:** Lynndale School, Augusta, GA, instructor of educables, 1973-74; Paine Coll, Augusta, GA, dir of recruitment & admissions, 1974-76; Yoorhees Coll, Denmark, SC, dir of institutional devt, 1976-78; American Can Co, St Louis, MO, labor relations assoc, 1978-87; CSRA Business League/Augusta Minority Business Devt Ctr, Augusta, GA, exec dir, 1987-. **Orgs:** Regional vice pres, Natl Business League, 1991-; bd dir/exec dir, CSRA Business League, 1987-; bd dir, GA Assn of Minority Entrepreneurs, 1991-; mem, GA Statewide Resource Network Initiative, 1990-; mem, NAACP, 1987-; bd dir, Augusta Mini Theatre, 1991-; bd dir/treas, Augusta Community Housing Resource Bd, 1987-. **Honors/Awds:** Regional MBDA Advocacy Award-Atlanta Regional Office, MBDA/US Dept of Commerce, 1990; Meritorious Service Award, Lucy C Laney High School Voc Ed Program, 1990; Sammy Davis Jr ''Yes I Can'' Award, St Louis Urban League/American Can Co, 1979, 1980; Meritorious Service Award (for institutional dev), Vorhees College, 1978; Directed a Consultant firm which has secured in excess of $80 million for its clients. **Business Addr:** Executive Director, CSRA Business League/Augusta Minority Business Development C, 1208 Laney-Walker Blvd, Augusta, GA 30901.

HERROD, JEFF SYLVESTER

Professional football player. **Personal:** Born Jul 29, 1966, Birmingham, AL; children: Marcus, Jeff Jr., Shauntel. **Educ:** Univ of Mississippi, attended. **Career:** Indianapolis Colts, linebacker, 1988-96; Philadelphia Eagles, 1997-. **Business Addr:** Professional Football Player, Philadelphia Eagles, 3501 S Broad St, Philadelphia, PA 19148, (215)463-2500.

HERRON, BRUCE WAYNE

Account executive. **Personal:** Born Apr 14, 1954, Victoria, TX; married Joyce LaDell Freeman; children: Monica Yvonne, Bruce Wayne Jr, Jordaya, Vance. **Educ:** Univ of New Mexico, Bachelors 1977. **Career:** Miami Dolphins, player 1977-78; Chicago Bears, player 1978-83; Accurate Air Express, owner 1982-83; Metro Media TV Channel 32, acct exec 1984; Chicago State Univ, dir of athletics; Waste Management Inc, acct exec, currently. **Orgs:** Dir Big Brothers/Big Sisters; volunteer Better Boys Found; hon chmn Sicle Cell Anemia 1982. **Honors/Awds:** Man of the Yr Big Brothers/Big Sisters; Byron Wizzer White Natl Football League Players Assn. **Business Addr:** Waste Management, Inc, 1500 N Hooper St, Chicago, IL 60622.

HERRON, CAROLIVIA

Educator, author. **Personal:** Born Jul 22, Washington, DC; daughter of Georgia C J Herron and Oscar S Herron. **Educ:** Eastern Baptist College, BA, English lit, 1969; Villanova University, MA, English, 1973; University of Pennsylvania, MA, comparative lit & creative writing, 1983, PhD, comparative lit & lit theory, 1985. **Career:** Harvard University, asst professor, African-American Studies and Comparative Literature, 1986-90; Mount Holyoke College, associate professor, English, 1990-92; Hebrew College, visiting scholar, 1994-95; Harvard University, visiting scholar, 1995. **Orgs:** Classical Association of New England, 1986-93. **Honors/Awds:** US Information Service, Fulbright Post-Doctoral Research Award, 1985; NEH, Visit to Collections Award, 1987; Radcliffe College, Bunting Institute Fellowship, 1988; Yale University, Beineke Library Fellowship, 1988; Folger Shakespeare Library, Post-Doctoral Research Award, 1989. **Special Achievements:** Author: Thereafter Johnnie, novel, 1991; Selected Works of Angelina Weld Grimke, 1991.

HERRON, CINDY

Actress, singer. **Personal:** marrIed Glenn Braggs; children: Donovan Andrew Braggs. **Career:** En Vogue, singer, albums include: Funky Divas, 1992; motion picture actress, Juice, 1992. **Special Achievements:** MTV Movie Awards, performed with En Vogue, 1992; Detroit International Auto Show, performed with En Vogue, 1990. **Business Phone:** (310)556-2727.

HERRON, VERNON M.

Consultant (retired). **Personal:** Born Oct 7, 1928, Charlotte; married; children: 3. **Educ:** Shaw Univ, AB, 1951; Johnson C Smith Univ, MDiv, 1958; Penn State Univ, MPA, 1978; Pittsburgh Theol Sem, Dmin, 1978. **Career:** Pub Programs, consult admin mgmt, beginning 1975; Am Bapt Ch Hdqrs, asst sec div soc ministries 1968-75; 2nd Bapt Ch Joliet, pastor 1962-68; Friendship BaptCh Pittsburgh, pastor 1955-62; 1st Bapt Dallas, pastor 1952-55; Hopewell Bapt, Jeannette, PA, pastor; Valley Forge, plng budget obj 1974, plng prgm obj 1973; Urban Training Ctr Chicago 1970; Valley Forge, strategic plng 1969-74; MI State U, conf plng 1968; Allentown State Hosp, clin psych 1959; Harrisburgh State Hosp, clin psych 1958; Shiloh Bapt Ch, S Philadelphia, asst to the minister; St Paul's Bapt Ch, W Chester PA, interim pastor, 1995. **Orgs:** Alpha Phi Alpha Frat; Prince Hall Mason.

HERVEY, BILLY T.

Aero space technologist. **Personal:** Born Apr 2, 1937, Naples, TX; married Olivia M Gray; children: Jewel, Marcus, Patrick. **Educ:** BS 1960. **Career:** Space Shuttle Pgm Ofc, currently assigned; Phys Schi Tech Mgr, served; Mission Control Ctr Houston on Greini & Apollo Flghts, nasa flight controller 1966-71; NASA/JOHNSON Space Center Houston; Kennedy Space Ctr Cape Kennedy, nasa & mehanical engr 1964-65; Gen Dynamics Corp Atlas F Missile Pgm Altus, OK,mech design engr test conductor; AUS Corps Engrs Ballistic Missle Ofc Altus, mech Engr 1960-62. **Orgs:** Mem Gulf Coast Soc; mem Trinity United Meth Ch; Prince Hall Free & Accepted Masonry; Douglas Burrell Consistory No 56; Ancient Accepted Scottist Rite; Ancient Egyptian Arabic Order Noble of Mystic Shrine N & S Am. **Honors/Awds:** Received group achvmnt awrd for support Gemini Missions; grp achvmnt flight operation awrd; Prsidential Medal of Freedom Awrd; participation on Apollo XiiiMission Operations Team; Johnson Spacecraft Ctr EEO Awrd. **Military Serv:** AUS 1962-64. **Business Addr:** Johnson Spacecraft Center, Houston, TX 77058.

HERZFELD, WILL LAWRENCE

Clergyman. **Personal:** Born Jun 9, 1937, Mobile, AL; married Thressa Mildred Alston (divorced); children: Martin, Katherine, Stephen. **Educ:** Attended, AL Lutheran Acad; Immanuel Luth Coll, AA 1957; Immanuel Luth Sem, MDiv 1961. **Career:** Christ Lutheran Church, pastor 1961; CA & NV Dist, urban minister 1966; Lutheran Council USA, regional mission exec 1968; Bethlehem Lutheran Church, pastor 1973-; Assn of Evangel Lutheran Church, vice pres 1976-, presiding bishop 1984. **Orgs:** Pres Tuscaloosa Chap SCLC 1963; vice pres Luth Human Relations Assn 1973-74; commr Alameda Cty Human Relations Commn 1977-78; vice pres Alamo Black Clergy 1973-; dir Natl Conf of Black Churchmen 1974-76; dir Black Theology Project. **Honors/Awds:** Outstanding Citizen Tuscaloosa Businessmen's League 1961-66; 3 Service to Youth Awds Barnes YMCA Tuscaloosa AL 1961-66; DD Ctr for Urban Black Studies 1975; Man of the Yr Mother's for Equal Educ 1976. **Business Addr:** Vice Pres, Association of Evangelistic Lutheran Churches, 959 12th St, Oakland, CA 94607.

HESTER, ARTHUR C.

Auto company executive. **Personal:** Born Mar 5, 1942, Columbus, MS; married Mae J Howard; children: Zina, Karen, Lisa, Arthur III. **Educ:** US Military Acad, BS 1965; Stanford U, MS 1970. **Career:** US Army, major; 11th Armored Cavalry Regiment Fulda West Germany, intelligence Officer; Admissions & Equal Admsn Oppr, asst dir; USMA & West Point, ofcr 1970-73; US Vietnam Germany, various command postions; General Motors, 1981-, plant mgr, Arlington, 1989-. **Orgs:** NAACP; Assn of US Army; Armor Assn; Blackhorse Assn; Master Mason; past mem, Assn of Black Business Students, NYU; trustee, Assn of Graduates USMA 1970-73; German-Am Cncl Fulda, W Germany 1973-; bd of dirs, Amer Youth Activities Fulda, West Germany 1974-. **Military Serv:** US Army, 1965-81; Recipient Silver Star, Bronze Star, Purple Heart; Meritorious Serv Medal; Vietnamese Cross of Gallantry with Silver Star; Nominee, Outstanding Junior Officer of the year, 1st Army, 1971. **Business Addr:** Plant Manager, General Motors Corp, 2525 E Abram St, Arlington, TX 76010.

HESTER, MELVYN FRANCIS

Organization executive. **Personal:** Born Dec 9, 1938, Kingston, Jamaica; son of Ditta White Hester and Glen Owen Hester; married Laura Pires Hester, Feb 17, 1990. **Educ:** Anderson University, Anderson, IN, BA (with honors), 1961; Indiana University, Bloomington, IN, MA, 1962; Columbia University, New York, NY, MSW, (with distinction), 1969; New York University, New York, NY, PhD (candidate), 1972-75. **Career:** Indiana University, Bloomington, IN, teaching asst, 1961-62; Keddy Brothers Construction, Massapequa, Long Island, NY, laborer, summers, 1958-61; Indiana University, Bloomington, IN, teaching assistant, 1961-62; Department of Social Services New York, NY, caseworker, case supervisor, 1963-72, director, administration, 1972-79; Human Resources Administration, New York, NY, executive deputy administrator, 1979-90; United Federation of Teachers, New York, NY, general manager, 1990-. **Orgs:** Mem, board of directors, National Forum for the Black Public Administrators, 1985-92; member, board of directors, National Forum for Black Public Administrators, 1985-; chairman, International Affairs Committee, One Hundred Black Men, 1987-; member, National Board of Directors, Caribbean Action Lobby, 1985-87; member, Benevolence Committee, Marble Collegiate Church, 1988-89; member, Church Growth Committee, Riverside Church, 1990; consultant, Long Term Planning Committee, Church of God (Anderson), 1983-; Church Growth Committee, Church Council, board of property and finance, trustee, Riverside Church. **Honors/Awds:** Distinguished Alumni Award, Anderson University, 1988; Fellow, Urban Academy for Management, New York City 1977-78; Teaching Assistant, Indiana University, 1962; Foreign Student Scholarship, Anderson University, 1957-61.

HEWETT, HOWARD

Vocalist. **Personal:** Born Oct 1, 1955, Akron, OH; married Nia Peeples (divorced); children: one son. **Career:** Member of vocal group Shalamar; solo artist, 1986-. **Special Achievements:** Album: ''Commit to Love,'' ''It's Time''. **Business Addr:** Vocalist, c/o Elektra Records, 75 Rockefeller Plaza, New York, NY 10019.

HEWING, PERNELL HAYES

Educator. **Personal:** Born May 13, 1933, St Matthews, SC; married Joe B; children: Rita, Johnny. **Educ:** Allen Univ, BS 1961; Temple Univ, MEd 1963; Univ WI, PhD 1974. **Career:** Palmetto Leader Newspaper, linotypist genl printer 1952-57; Allen Univ, supervisor dept printing 1958-61, instr 1961-62; Philadelphia Tribune, linotypist 1962-63; Allen Univ Columbia, asst prof business educ 1963-71; Palmetto Times Newspaper, woman's editor 1963-64; Palmetto Post Columbia SC, mgr editor 1970-71; Univ of WI Whitewater, prof business educ 1971-. **Orgs:** Delta Pi Epsilon Hon Bus Organization; Pi Lambda Theta Natl Honor & Professional Assn Women Educ 1972; Natl Bus Educ 1950; Amer Business Communications Assn; founder/dir Avant-Garde Cultural & Devel Orgn; Sigma Gamma Rho Sor Inc 1962; dev chpts Univ WI Madison 1973; WI Coord Council Women Higher Educ. **Honors/Awds:** Cofounder Palmetto Post weekly newspaper 1970. **Business Addr:** Professor of Business Education, Univ of Wisconsin, 800 W Main, Whitewater, WI 53190.

HEWITT, BASIL
Clergyman (retired). **Personal:** Born Jan 31, 1926, Colon, Panama; married May Shirley; children: Nidia, Gloria, Chris. **Educ:** KY So Coll, BA 1969; So Baptist Theol Sem, MDiv 1973. **Career:** Fifth St Baptist Church, asst pastor 1967-73; Emmanuel Baptist Church, pastor 1973-91. **Orgs:** Mem C of C; decty Laurel Clergy Assn 1974-75; exec comm Citizen's Adv Coun Pkwy. **Business Addr:** Pastor, Emmanuel Baptist Church, 11443 Laurel-Bowie Road, RR 2, Laurel, MD 20707.

HEWITT, JOHN H., JR.
Editor (retired). **Personal:** Born Aug 20, 1924, New York, NY; son of Agatha B Hewitt and John H Hewitt; married Vivian Davideson; children: John H III. **Educ:** Harvard Coll, 1941-43; NY Univ, BS 1948; NY Univ, MA 1949. **Career:** Instructor, Department of English, and co-chairman, Division of Humanities, Morehouse College, Atlanta, Georgia, 1948-52; reporter, New York Amsterdam News, 1952-56; administrative secretary, St. Philip's Church, New York, 1956-61; Medical Tribune, med writer 1961-72; Hosp Practice, sr edtr, mgng edtr 1972-75; Med Tribune, asso edtr 1975-80; Emerg Med, sr edtr 1980-82; Self-Employed 1982-86. **Orgs:** Mem Am Med Writer Assn 1965-89; mem Natl Assn of Sci Writers 1976-80; Trustee Manhattan Cntry Sch 1971-94; trustee, treas Schomburg Corp 1980-93; vestryman St Philip's Ch, 1952-56, 1982-91; United Hospital Fund's Municipal Hospital Visiting Committee, 1991-94. **Honors/Awds:** "The Sacking of St Philip's Church, NY" Hstrcl Mag of the Protestant Epscpl Ch, Vol XLVIV, No 1, 03/80; "New York's Black Episcopalians, In the Beginning, 1704-1722"; Afro-Americans in NY Life & History, Vol 3, No 1, Jan 1979; "The Search for Elizabeth Jennings, Heroine of a Sunday Afternoon in New York City"; New York History, Vol LX11, No 4, Oct 1990; A Black New York Newspaperman's Impressions of Boston, 1883; The Massachusetts Review, Vol XXXII, No 3, Fall, 1991; Mr Downing & His Oyster House, New York History, Vol 74, No 3, July 1993; An Enterprising Oysterman, Amer Visions, Vol 9, No 3 June/July, 1994; Unresting the Waters: The Fight Against Racism in New York's Episcopal Establishment, Afro-Americans in New York Life & History, Vol 18, No 1, Jan 1994; The Themes of Alvin C Hollingsworth, Black Art: An International Quarterly, Vol 2, No 1, Jan 1977; Shopping for Haitian Art, Black Enterprise, Apr, 1977; The Evolution of Luce Turnier, Black Art: An International Quarterly, Vol 3, No1, Jan 1978; Hale A Woodruff: Artist & Educator, School Arts, Vol 79, No 2, Oct 1979; No Other Island..The Art of Haiti, New Image Press, Pittsburgh, 1995; Remembering Hale Woodruff, the International Review of African American Art, Vol 13, No 4, Oct 1997; Peter Williams Jr: New York's First African American Episcopal Priest, In Press, 1998. **Home Addr:** 862 West End Ave, Apt 1, New York, NY 10025-4959.

HEWITT, RONALD JEROME
Business executive. **Personal:** Born Oct 31, 1932, Welch, WV; married Deanna Cowan; children: Ronald Jr, Kevin, Robert, Jonathan, Mkonto, Mwanaisha. **Educ:** Fisk U, BA 1955. **Career:** Detroit Housing Comm, supt of operations 1969, asst dir 1971, dir 1973; Comm & Econ Dev Detroit, exec dep dir 1974, dir 1974-79; Mayor Coleman A Young, exec asst 1979-; Department of Transportation, director, 1982-85; Detroit Planning Dept, dir, 1985-. **Orgs:** Downtown Dev Authority; Detroit Econ Dev Corp; Ford Cncl for Urban Econ Dev; CORD; SE MI Cncl of Govt; Detroit FinancialCenter Task Force; Museum of African-American History; Greater Detroit Economic Dev Group; brd of dir; Detroit Foreign Trade Zone; Detroit Economic Growth Corp; Detroit-Wayne Port Authority liaison; board member, Metropolitan Center for High Technology, 1985-; board member, Local Iniatives Support Corp, 1989-; Detroit Municipal Credit Union, board of directors. **Military Serv:** AUS 1956-58. **Business Addr:** Dir, Detroit Planning Dept, 2300 Cadillac Tower, Detroit, MI 48226.

HEWITT, VIVIAN DAVIDSON
Librarian, consultant (retired). **Personal:** Born Feb 17, New Castle, PA; daughter of Lela Luvada Mauney Davidson and Arthur Robert Davidson; married John H Hewitt Jr, Dec 26, 1949; children: John H III. **Educ:** Geneva Coll, BA 1943; Carnegie-Mellon, BS in LS 1944; Univ of Pittsburgh, Grad Stud 1947-48; Geneva Coll, LHD 1978. **Career:** Carnegie Lib of Pittsbgh, sr asst lib 1944-49; Atlanta Univ Sch Lib Sci, instructor/librarian 1949-52; Crowell-Collier Publishing Co, researcher asst to dir 1954-56; Rockefeller Found, librarian 1956-63; Katharine Gibbs Sch, dir lib info svcs 1984-86; Carnegie Endowment for International Peace NY 1963-83 (retired); Council on Foreign Relations 1987-88; Univ of Texas, Austin, faculty, Graduate School of Library & Information, 1985. **Orgs:** Librarian Carnegie Endowment for Intl Peace 1963-83; contributor to Professnl Journals; pres Spcl Libraries Assn 1978-79; exec com/sec of bd Graham-Windham Child Care & Adoption Agency 1969-87; exec com/sec Laymens Club The Cathedral of St John the Divine NY. **Honors/Awds:** Distinguished Alumni Award, Carnegie-Mellon Univ 1978; Distinguished Alumni Award, Univ of Pittsburgh 1978; Distinguished Serv, Black Caucus of Amer Lib Assn 1979; Hall of Fame Special Lib Assn 1984; Black Caucus of the American Library Association, BCALA Leadership in the Profession Award, 1993. **Home Addr:** 862 West End Ave, New York, NY 10025.

HEWLETT, ANTOINETTE PAYNE
Government official. **Personal:** Born in Martinsburg, WV; children: Adora. **Educ:** WV State Coll, BA; Columbia Univ, MA 1961. **Career:** Jefferson Co, teacher 1960; San Francisco Redevelop, relocation asst 1962-66; Oakland Redevelop, planner/reloc super 1967-76; City of Oakland, dir comm develop 1976-. **Orgs:** Mem Oakland Museum Assoc; mem Friends of Ethnic Art; mem Natl Forum for Black Public Admin; mem Amer Soc Public Admin; mem Natl Assoc Housing & Redevelopment Officials; mem Comm Club of CA; mem bd of directors Natl Comm Develop Assoc 1984-. **Business Addr:** Director, Community Development, City of Oakland, 1417 Clay St, Oakland, CA 94612.

HEWLETT, DIAL, JR.
Physician. **Personal:** Born Jul 26, 1948, Cleveland, OH; son of Lydia Hewlett and Dial Hewlett; married Janice M Chance; children: Kwasi, Tiffany, Whitney Joy, Brandon. **Educ:** Attended Univ of WI Madison; Univ of WI School of Med, MD 1976. **Career:** Harlem Hosp Center, internship & residency 1976-79; Harlem Hospital Center, chief med residency 1979-80; Montefiore Hospital & Albert Einstein Coll of Med, fellowship infectious diseases 1980-82; NY Med Coll, asst prof of med 1982-; Our Lady of Mercy Hospital, chief of infectious diseases. **Orgs:** Attending physician internal med, chief of infectious diseases Lincoln Med & Mental Health Center 1982-84; mem Amer Soc for Microbiology 1983-; ed bd Hospital Physicians Joyrnal 1984-; consult infectious diseases Our Lady of Mercy Hospital 1984-, Calvary Hospital for Terminally Ill 1985-; mem Infectious Diseases Soc of Amer 1986-; consult infectious diseases Lawrence Hospital 1987-; mem Manhattan Central Medical Society INMA. **Honors/Awds:** Co-captain Track Teach Univ of WI Big Ten Champions 1969-70; Diplomate Specialty Internal med Amer Bd of Internal Med 1980; Publs on, Tuberculosis & AIDS, Tropical Splenomegaly Syndrome, AIDS in Socially Disadvantages Groups, Chagas Disease in Diabetic Animals 1980-; Diplomate Subspecialty Infectious Diseases Amer Bd of Internal Med 1984. **Business Addr:** Chief of Infectious Diseases, Lincoln Medical & Mental Health Center, 234 East 149th St, Bronx, NY 10451.

HEWLETT, EVERETT AUGUSTUS, JR.
Attorney. **Personal:** Born Mar 27, 1943, Richmond, VA; married Clothilde. **Educ:** Dickinson Coll Carlisle PA, BA 1965; Golden Gate Univ Law Sch, JD 1975. **Career:** USAF, information spec 1965-69; Univ of CA Berkeley, writer-editor 1970-75; Bayview-Hunters Point Comm Defender San Francisco, staff atty 1976-80; Private Law Practice, attorney 1980-86; San Francisco Superior Court, court commissioner 1986-. **Orgs:** Bd dirs SF Neighborhood Legal Asst Found 1979-; bd dir SF Neighborhood Legal Asst Found 1979-; hearing officer SF Residl Rent Stabilization & Arbitration Bd 1980-82; bd dir CA Assn of Black Lawyers 1980-; vice pres Counseliers West 1980; pres William Hastie Bar Assn 1984; vice chmn SF Neighborhood Legal Asst Found 1984; parliamentarian Wm Hastie Bar Assn 1980-86; mem State Bar Comm on Legal Specialization 1982; mem CA State Bar Legal Serv Trust Fund Comm 1984-85. **Honors/Awds:** Editor of Best Newspaper in its class USAF Hamilton CA & Nakhon Phanom 1967 & 1968. **Military Serv:** USAF sgt 1965-69. **Business Addr:** Superior Court Judge, San Francisco Superior Court, 375 Woodside Dr, Youth Guidance Center, San Francisco, CA 94117.

HEYWARD, CRAIG WILLIAM
Professional football player. **Personal:** Born Sep 26, 1966, Passaic, NJ; married Charlotte; children: Craig Jr, Cameron, Cory. **Educ:** Univ of Pittsburgh, attended. **Career:** New Orleans Saints, fullback, 1988-92; Chicago Bears, 1993; Atlanta Falcons, 1994-96; St Louis Rams, 1997-. **Honors/Awds:** Running back, Sporting News College All-America Team, 1987; Ed Block Courage Award, 1993. **Business Addr:** Professional Football Player, St Louis Rams, One Rams Way, St Louis, MO 63045, (314)982-7267.

HEYWARD, ILENE PATRICIA
Telecommunications company executive. **Personal:** Born Apr 9, 1948, Plainfield, NJ; daughter of Bonlyn Pitts Nesbitt and William W Nesbitt Jr; divorced; children: Eric Eugene. **Educ:** Fairleigh Dickinson Univ, BS Chem/Math 1976; New York Univ, 1982-88 MS Chem; George Washington University, Project Management Masters Certificate, 1995. **Career:** AT&T Bell Labs, tech assoc 1976-77, sr tech assoc 1977-79, assoc mem of tech staff 1979-81, tech manager 1981-94, div mgr, 1994-97, general mgr, 1997-. **Orgs:** Advisory council, National Black United Fund, 1991-94; board member, Big Brothers Big Sisters Essex County, 1992-93; mem Amer Assoc for the Advancement of Science 1982-; conducts workshops pertaining to Black Women in the Corp Environment and Leadership Development, 1985-; Plainfield Teen Project, 1989-97; member, Alliance of Black Telecommunications Employees Inc, 1990-95; mem, Project Management Institute; bd, treasurer, Beacon School, 1997. **Honors/Awds:** Author and co-author, many articles in technical journals such as ACS and Journal of the Society of Plastic Engrs 1976-; author, chap in ACS Symposium Monograph Series 1985; featured in cover story of Black Enterprise 1985; Honored during Womens History Month by Bell Communications Rsch 1985; AT&T Architecture Award, 1992; African American Biography Hall of Fame, 1993. **Business Addr:** General Manager, AT&T VI, 211B Buccaneer Mall, St Thomas, Virgin Islands of the United States 00802, (340)776-6500.

HEYWARD, ISAAC
Radio station executive. **Personal:** Born Apr 30, 1935, Charleston, SC; son of Chrestina Capers Heyward and Rev St Julian Heyward (deceased); children: Regina Vermel Heyward (deceased), Bryant Isaac Heyward. **Educ:** Radio Broadcast Inst, New York NY, Certificate, 1967; Morris Coll, School of Religion, Orangeburg Extension, Certificate, 1975. **Career:** WHBI Radio, Newark NJ, program announcer, sales mgr, 1965-67; WRNW Radio, Mt Kisco NY, am announcer, dir, 1967-71; WQIZ Radio, St George SC, am announcer, sales mgr, 1971-85; WTGH Radio, Cayce SC, am announcer, sales mgr, general sales & station manager/president, currently. **Orgs:** Assoc ordained minister, St Paul Baptist Church, Orangeburg SC, 1971; Gospel Music Workshop of Amer (Announcers Guild), 1974; NAACP, South Carolina Brancy, 1974; Baptist Assn, Orangeburg SC, 1985; mem, Boy Scouts of Amer Council, 1986; pres, Go Gospel Radio Consultant, 1987. **Honors/Awds:** Second Runner-up DJ, Gospel of the Year, Lamb Records, 1978; Best Radio Gospel Program, Lee's Publication, 1979; Gospel Promotion, Gospel Workshop of Amer, 1982; Community Service, Amer Cancer Soc, 1982, 1983; Living Legacy, Natl Council of Negro Women, 1984; Boy Scouts of Amer Service, Boy Scouts of Amer, 1986; Honorary Doctor of Christian Ministry from the CE Graham Baptist Bible Seminary, 1996. **Military Serv:** US Army, Private, 1959. **Business Addr:** General Sales & Station Manager/President, Midland Communications, 1303 State St, PO Box 620, Cayce, SC 29033.

HEYWARD, JAMES OLIVER
Educator. **Personal:** Born Jul 17, 1930, Sumter, SC; son of Lue Heyward and Julian H Heyward Sr (deceased); married Willie Mae Thompson; children: James O Jr, Julian. **Educ:** South Carolina State Univ, BS 1953; Armed Forces Staff Coll, 1969; Shippensburg State University, MA 1972. **Career:** US Army, Deputy Cmdr Military Comm 1974-75; Cmdr TRADOC Field Element 1976-79 Alabama A&M Univ, prof of military science 1979-83, dir of admissions 1984-. **Orgs:** Amer Assn Collegiate Registrars & Adm Ofcrs, Equal Oppor Committee 1986-87, chair Equal Opportunity Committee, 1987-89; Phi Delta Kappa; chmn, Membership Comm, 1983-84, life mem, NAACP; Alpha Phi Alpha, Chapter Vice Pres 1984-87, pres, 1987-89, area dir, 1990-92; mem Human Relations Council Huntsville AL; Huntsville Citizens Police, quality council, chair, 1992-94; mem, Steward Bd, St John AME Church, 1985-. **Honors/Awds:** Mt Pisgah AME Church, Outstanding Son 1973; SC State Univ, ROTC Hall of Fame 1979; Alpha Phi Alpha Chapter, Man of the Year, 1989. **Military Serv:** US Army, Colonel 1953-83; Legion of Merit, Bronze Star, Joint Services Commendation, US Army Commendation Medal, Senior Parachutist Badge; Meritorious Serv Medal. **Home Addr:** 747 Bluewood Drive SE, Huntsville, AL 35802. **Business Addr:** Dir of Admissions, Alabama A&M University, PO Box 908, Normal, AL 35762.

HIATT, DANA SIMS
Educational administration. **Personal:** Born in Chickasha, OK; daughter of Muriel Crowell Sims and William Edward Sims; married James H Hiatt. **Educ:** Langston U, BA History (summa cum laude) 1968; Univ of KS Sch of Law, JD 1971. **Career:** Chicago IL, Oklahoma City OK, RH Smith Comm, law fellow 1971-73; City of Oklahoma, asst municipal atty 1974; Darrell, Bruce, Johnson & Sims Assoc, private practice law 1975-77; CO State Univ, title IX coord cncltn officer 1979-82, dir office of equal opportunity. **Orgs:** The Denver Chapter of Links Inc, Am Asso of Univ Women, Amer Assoc for Affrim Action, Higher Educ Affirm Action Dirs; public affairs chair, Junior League of Fort Collins, 1991-92. **Honors/Awds:** Outstndng Yng Woman Zeta Phi Beta Sor Okla City, OK 1975; R H Smith Law Fellowship. **Business Addr:** Dir Ofc of Eq Opptnty, Colorado State University, 314 Student Services Bldg, Fort Collins, CO 80523.

HIATT, DIETRAH
Journalist, school counselor. **Personal:** Born Sep 23, 1944, Washington, DC; married Robert Terry; children: Stephanie Gail, Benjamin Jesse. **Educ:** Howard U, BA 1965. **Career:** The Pierre Times, editorial columnist present; Sen George Mcgovern, comm rep; Nyoda Girl Scout Council, brownie ldr resource person 1976-77; Pierre Indian Learning Cntr, sch counselor; Pierre-Ft Pierre Head Start Prgm, vol tchrs asst 1973-74; Huron SD Daily Plainsman, reporter 1973-74; DC Dept of Pub Assistance, social serv rep caseworker 1968-70; US Peace Corps Vol Rep of Panama 1965-67. **Orgs:** Alpha Kappa Alpha; Am Assn of Univ Women 1972-74; treas Short Grass Arts Council 1974-75; membership chpn 1976; publicity chpn present; vice pres Nat Orgn for Women Central SD Chap 1975-; Dem Party precinct woman 1976-; chpn Hughes Co Dem Com; co-chpn Candidate Task Force SD Womens Caucus; mem Nat Abortion Rights Action League; mem State Professional Practices & Standards Commn of Dept of Educ & Cultural Affairs present. **Honors/Awds:** Choreographed & performed rev of dance & history for AAUW Cultural Study Group 1973; performed in modern & native Am dance recital for Arts Festival arts wrkshp

1973; nominated for Outstdng Young Woman of Am 1973, 77; candidate for Pierre Sch Bd 1976; candidate for SD State Senate 1978. **Business Addr:** 817 S Illinois Ave, #26, Mason City, IA 50401-5487.

HIBBERT, DOROTHY LASALLE
Educator. **Personal:** Born Sep 17, 1923, New York, NY; daughter of Lily Roper Hilbert and Arthur Hilbert, Sr. **Educ:** Hunter College, BA, 1945; Teachers College, Columbia University, MA, 1949; City College, Graduate Div, PD, 1983; Walden University, MN, doctorate, education, 1991. **Career:** Board of Education of New York City, PS 186 teacher 1947-59, HS 136 math teacher 1959-68, PS 146 & 36 asst principal 1969-79, PS 138 acting interim principal 1979-81, PS 93 asst principal 1981-85, PS 146 principal 1985-90; College of New Rochelle, instructor 1990. **Orgs:** Vice pres 1976-86, sec 1987, Intl League of Human Rights; planning participant, New York State Conf on Status of Women; sec, Amer Commn on Africa 1979-; asst examiner, Bd of Examiners 1982; conference chairperson, Bronx Reading Council 1985; mem, NAACP; mem, Assoc of Black Educators of NY 1986. **Honors/Awds:** Outstanding Educator, City Tabernacle Church 1980; Outstanding Principal of the Year, Morrisana Educ Council 1980; publications "The Role of the Nefers in Egyptian History," 1979, "Nubian Egypt and Egyptian Nubia," 1979, "Big Red Newspaper," Brooklyn NY. **Home Addr:** 90 Meucci Ave, Copiague, NY 11726.

HICKERSON, O. B. See SMITH, OTRIE.

HICKLIN, FANNIE
Educator (retired). **Personal:** Born in Talladega, AL; daughter of Willie Pulliam Frazier and Demus Frazier; divorced; children: Ariel Yvonne Ford. **Educ:** Talladega Coll, BA; Univ Michigan, MA; Univ of Wisconsin at Madison, PhD. **Career:** Magnolia Ave HS, Avery Inst, Burke HS, Tuskegee Inst, AL A&M Coll, Univ of Wisconsin at Madison, previous teaching experience; Univ of Wisconsin at Whitewater, assoc dean faculties 1974-88. **Orgs:** Bd of Visitors, University of Wisconsin-Whitewater bd of curators State Hist Soc of Wisconsin; Cen States Communication Assn; Speech Comm Assn; Alpha Kappa Alpha.

HICKMAN, ELNOR B. G.
Executive secretary. **Personal:** Born Jan 31, 1930, Jackson, MS; daughter of Lerone Sr and Alma Reed Bennett; married Caloway Hickman, Nov 19, 1983; children: Thelma B McDowell, Marshall L Bennett, Shirley L Bennett. **Educ:** Loop Junior College, AA, 1975. **Career:** Legal Assistance Foundation of Chicago, legal secretary, admin supvr, exec secretary, 1967-. **Orgs:** Professional Secretaries Intl, intl dir, Great Lakes Dist, 1988-90, intl sec, 1990-91, 2nd vp, 1991-92, 1st vp, 1992-93, pres-elect, 1993-94, intl pres, 1994-95. **Special Achievements:** First African American to hold the position of president of the Professional Secretaries Intl; Certified Professional Secretary Rating, 1977. **Business Addr:** Intl President, Professional Secretaries Intl, 343 S Dearborn St, Ste 700, Chicago, IL 60604, (312)341-1070.

HICKMAN, FREDERICK DOUGLASS
Network sportscaster. **Personal:** Born Oct 17, 1956, Springfield, IL; son of Louise Winifred Hickman (deceased) and George Henry Hickman (deceased); married Judith Tillman-Hickman, Feb 20, 1989. **Educ:** Coe College, 1974-77. **Career:** WFMB-FM Radio, newscaster, 1977-78; WICS-TV, sports director, 1978-80; CNN/Turner Broadcasting, sportscaster/commentator, 1980-84; WDIV-TV, sportscaster/commentator, 1984-86; CNN/Turner Broadcasting, sportscaster/commentator, 1986-; WALR-FM, sports director, 1992-. **Orgs:** Butkus Awards Voting Committee, 1991-. **Honors/Awds:** Ace Award Winner, 1989, 1996; Ace Award Nominee, 1988, 1989, 1990, 1991, 1992. **Business Addr:** Sportscaster, CNN/Turner Sports, One CNN Center, Atlanta, GA 30311, (404)878-1605.

HICKMAN, GARRISON M.
Educator. **Personal:** Born Jan 14, 1945, Washington, DC; married Cynthia Burrowes; children: Michael Barrington. **Educ:** VA Union U, BA 1967; Howard U, MDiv 1971. **Career:** Student Affairs & Affirmative Action Capital Univ & Abiding Saviour Lutheran Church, assoc dean present; Neighborhood Youth Corps Dept of Defense, teacher counselor 1967-68; Washington Concentrated Employment Program, 1968-70; DC City Govt, counselor 1971. **Orgs:** Mem Am Assn of Higher Edn; Nat pres Am Assn for Affirmative Action 1976-77; Nat chmn Conf on Inner City Ministries 1975-76; Nat Collegiate Honor Soc; coord com on Nat Crises Conf on Inner City Ministries; Coalition of Minority Profls in Am Lutheran Ch Colleges & Univ 1974-75; natl sec Conf on InnerCity Ministries 1973-74; OH reg chmn Coord Com on Nat Crisis 1973-75. **Business Addr:** 2199 E Main St, Columbus, OH 43209.

HICKMAN, JERRY A.
Administrator. **Personal:** Born Oct 3, 1946, Philadelphia, PA. **Educ:** Philadelphia Com Coll, AA 1971. **Career:** Parkview Hosp Phila, instr of inserv educ, asst supr of nursing 1973-76; nursing 1973-76; Philadelphia Coll of Osteo Medicine, operating room supr 1971-73, admin of primary health care ctr 1976-82. **Orgs:** Mem TREA Peoples Health Serv of W Philadelphia 1976-78; bd of dir W Philadelphia Com Mental Health Consortium 1976-82; bd dir Philadelphia C of C 1976-82; lay reader St Andrew St Monica Episcopal Ch 1976-; council mem Philadelphia Council Boy Scouts of Amer 1978-; bd mem, chair Consortium CA #4 Inc Comm Mental Health & Mental Retardation Progs 1979-82. **Military Serv:** USN 2/c petty officer (e-4) 1964-67. **Business Addr:** Dir of Nursing Services, Greenwich Home for Children, 2601 South 9th St, Philadelphia, PA 19148.

HICKMON, NED
Physician. **Personal:** Born Dec 5, 1934, Bishopville, SC; son of Nona Hickmon and James Hickmon; married Consuella Anderson; children: Ned Norman, David Wesley, Cheryl A. **Educ:** SC St Clg, BS 1955; Meharry Med Clg Nashville, TN, MD 1959. **Career:** Huron Rd Hosp Cleveland OH, intrn 1959-60; HG Phillips Hosp St Louis, MO, res ob/gyn 1960-62; G W Hubbard Hosp Meharry Med Clg Nashvl, chf resob/gyn 1962-63 us army hosp bremerhaven, germany, chief ob/gyn 1963-66; patterson army hosp ft monmouth, nJ, asst chf ob/gyn 1966-67; Private Prctc Hartford, CT, obstetrics & gyn 1968-. **Orgs:** Past dir, pres Comm Hlth Serv Hartford, CT 1972; mem Alpha Phi Alpha Frat Inc; member, Sigma Pi Phi Frat Inc. **Military Serv:** US Army Med Corps, Capt, 4 yrs. **Home Addr:** 21 Bloomfield Ave, Hartford, CT 06105.

HICKS, ARTHUR JAMES
Educator. **Personal:** Born Feb 26, 1938, Jackson, MS; son of Julia M Hicks and A. R. Hicks; married Pearlie Mae Little; children: Arnetta Renee, Roselyn Marie. **Educ:** Tougaloo Coll, BS 1960; Univ Illinois, PhD 1971; Missouri Botanical Gdns, NEA Postdoctoral Fellowship 1975-76; Natl Inst Health Extramural Assoc 1982; Inst of Educ Management, Harvard Univ 1989; Lilly Endowment Liberal Arts Workshop, Colorado College, 1992. **Career:** Grenada City School, biology & gen sci teacher chmn sci div 1960-64; Botany Dept Univ Illinois, grad stud 1965-71; Botany Dept Univ of Georgia, asst prof 1971-77; Natl Sci Foundation, vstg grants officer 1987; Biology Dept NC A&T, prof & chmn 1977-88; dean, Coll of Arts and Sciences 1988-. **Orgs:** Amer Inst of Biological Sci; Amer Soc of Plant Taxonomists; Assn of SE Biologists; Botanical Soc of Amer; North Carolina Acad of Sci; Intern Assn of Plant Taxonomists; Mississippi Academy of Sci; Sigma Xi; Torrey Botanical Club; past co-pres Gaines School PTA Athens 1973-74; bd of dir NE Girl Scouts of Amer 1977; bd of trustees Hill First Bapt Church Athens 1977; mem Swim Bd of Gov Athens Park & Rec Dist Athens 1977; mem Natural Areas Adv Com to North Carolina Dept of Natural Resources & Comm Devel 1978; adv bd Guilford Co NC Environmental Quality 1979-87; mem Alpha Phi Alpha; board of trustees, National Wildflower Research Center, 1991-93; Greensboro Beautiful and Greensboro Bog Garden, 1992-. **Honors/Awds:** Hon mem Beta Kappa Chi Sci Honor Soc 1960; sr bio award Tougaloo Coll 1960; NSF Summer Fellowship SIU Carbondale 1961; Univ Illinois Botany Fellowship Urbana 1968-69; So Fellowship Found Fund Fellow Univ Illinois Urbana 1969-71; NEA Fellowship Missouri Bot Gdn St Louis 1975-76; Faculty Award for Excellence in Science and Technology, White House Initiative on Historically Black Colleges and Universities, 1988; auth "Apomixis in Xanthium?" Watsonia 1975 "Plant Mounting Problem Overcome with the Use of Self-Adhesive Plastic Covering" Torreya 1976; co-auth, A Bibliography of Plant Collection & Herbarium Curation. **Business Addr:** Dean, NC A&T State Univ, College of Arts and Sciences, 312 N Dudley St Crosby Hall, Greensboro, NC 27411.

HICKS, CLAYTON NATHANIEL
Educational administrator, association executive, optometrist. **Personal:** Born May 2, 1943, Columbus, OH; son of Augusta Louvenia Hicks and Amos Nathaniel Hicks. **Educ:** OH State Univ, BS 1964, OD 1970. **Career:** OH Dept of Health, microbiologist 1965-70; OSU Coll of Optomertry, clinical instr 1970-; Driving Park Vision Ctr, optometrist 1970-; OH Dept of Human Svcs, optometric consult 1977-; Natl Optometric Assn, pres, meeting/conference planner 1984-; Annette 2 Cosmetiques, consultant, 1989-. **Orgs:** Pres Columbus Panhellenic Council 1975-80, Columbus Inner City Lions Club 1977-80, Neighborhood House Inc, Bd of Dir 1979-81, Martin Luther King Holiday Observance Comm 1981-83, Alpha Phi Alpha Frat 1981-83, Natl Optometric Assn 1983-85; Driving Park Mental Health Comm 1984; Nat'l Coalition of Black Meeting Planners 1984; consultant, Annette Cosmetiques, 1989-; executive director, Alpha Rho Lambda Educ Foundation 1989-. **Honors/Awds:** Outstanding Serv Awd Alpha Phi Alpha Frat 1981; Optometrist of the Year Natl Optometric Assn 1983; Citizen of the Week WCKX Radio 1986; Political Leadership Awd 29th Dist Citizens Caucus. **Business Addr:** Meeting Planner, Natl Optometric Assn, 1489 Livingston Ave, Columbus, OH 43205.

HICKS, DAISY C.
Educational administrator. **Personal:** Born Feb 13, 1919, Conyers, GA; daughter of Mattie Morse and Sherman Turner; married James Hicks, Sep 1941 (deceased); children: Norma Robinson, Schani Krug. **Educ:** Miner Teachers Coll Wash, DC, BS elem educ 1941; Queens Coll Flushing, NY, Professional Cert Guidance 1962; NY Univ, MA early childhood educ 1952; NYU/Queens Coll/City Coll, NY State Cert Dist Admin/School Admin 1982; NY Univ NY, candidate for doctoral degree 1979-85. **Career:** US Treasury, Washington DC, sales US Treasury Bonds 1941-45; Afro-Amer Newspaper, fashion editor 1945-49; Div Personnel Bureau of Educ Staffing, asst to the dir 1972-76; New York City Bd of Educ Div of Personnel, head Bureau of Special Recruitment 1976-81, administrator, dir, educational planner, 1989-91. **Orgs:** Pres NY Assn of Black Educators 1975-79; pres 402 W 153rd St Coop New York City 1983-85; exec dir Skills Review for Black Youth Seeking Scholarships for Higher Educ 1978-85; executive director, EPSS Consultative Service, 1990-; executive director, EPSS Consultative Service for School Systems and Agencies Serving Minority Youth, 1990-91. **Honors/Awds:** Woman of the Yr Zeta Phi Beta Sorority 1975; Comm Leader Award AKA Sorority (Bronx Chpt) 1985; Natl Educational Leadership Award NAACP 1981; Educator of the Year, New York Assn of Black Educators, 1989. **Home Addr:** 402 West 153rd St, New York, NY 10031. **Business Addr:** Director, Bureau of Specialized Recruitment, New York City Board of Education, 65 Court St, Rm 101-Level C, Brooklyn, NY 11201.

HICKS, D'ATRA
Singer. **Personal:** Born in Bronx, NY; daughter of Edna Hicks. **Career:** Actress, singer, several commercials, music videos, theatre appearances, currently. **Orgs:** AFTRA; SAG; ASCAP. **Honors/Awds:** Two Top 10 Records in Japan; toured extensively in Japan; NAACP Image Award Nominee, 1989; New York City Music Award Nominee, 1989.

HICKS, DELPHUS VAN, JR.
Law enforcement official. **Personal:** Born Feb 6, 1939, Ashland, MS; son of Gladys Woodson Hicks and Delphus Van Hicks Sr; married Frankie Marie Hamer Hicks, Jul 5, 1961; children: Early Hue, James Earl, Diane Lanell. **Educ:** TN Law Enforcement Acad, attended 1974; Donhue Barber College, Memphis, TN, master barber license, 1974. **Career:** Hardeman Co Sheriff Dept, sheriff 1978-; chief dep sheriff 1974, 1978; Hardemann Co, dep sheriff 1968-72; Reichold Chemical Inc, inspector, mixer, lead man, 1967-72; Leadman Reichhold Chem Inc, mixer/ insp 1967-72; Williams Candy Co, stockman 1961-62. **Orgs:** Vice president, Tennessee Sheriff's Association, 1978-; member, West Tennessee Criminal Investigation Association, 1980-; member, 25th Judicial District Drug Task Force, 1989-. **Honors/Awds:** First Black Chief Dep Sheriff Hardeman Co 1974; first Black sheriff in Tennessee, 1978; Outstanding Sheriff of the Year, Tennessee Sheriff Association, 1988-89; Tennessee Outstanding Achievements Award, Governor Lamar Alexander, 1981. **Military Serv:** US Army, E-5, 1962-67; Soldier of the Year, 1964; Good Conduct Medal, 1964. **Home Addr:** 503 E Jackson St, Bolivar, TN 38008. **Business Addr:** Sheriff, Hardeman County Sheriff Department, 315 E Market, Bolivar, TN 38008.

HICKS, DORIS ASKEW
Educational administrator (retired). **Personal:** Born May 24, 1926, Sulphur Springs, TX; married George P; children: Sherra Daunn. **Educ:** Butler Coll, AA 1946; Bishop Coll, BA 1948; Univ of TX, MLS 1959. **Career:** Rochester City Sch Dist Rochester NY, dir learning resources 1973-81; Rochester City Sch Dist Rochester, sch librarian 1969-73; Macedonia Sch Dist Texarkana, sch librarian 1962-69; Bowie Co Common & Independent Sch, multi sch librarian 1654-62; Naples Independent Sch Dist, tchr librarian 1952-54; Quitman Independent Sch Dist, tchr 1950-52. **Orgs:** Vp Sch Library Media Section, NY Library Assn; vice pres elect Sch Library Media Section, NY Library Assn; pres, unit V chmn Am Assn of Sch Librarian, ALA 1979-80; mem Mt Olivet Bapt Ch Scholarship Com 1976-; bd mem Hillside Children's Center 1977-81; chair fellowship com Rochester Chap of Zonta Int, 1979-80; Largo Comm Church, chairman, library committee, 1994-; Prince George's Maryland Chapter Links, Inc, vp, 1993-. **Honors/Awds:** NDEA grant Fed Govt Coe Coll IA 1964; NDEA grant Govt Syracuse Univ NY 1973; sch library & media program of year Am Assn of Sch Librarians 1975.

HICKS, DORIS MORRISON
Federal official. **Personal:** Born Jun 19, 1933, St Marys, GA; daughter of Renetta Jenkins Morrison and Eleazar Morrison; married Samuel Hicks, Sep 15, 1950; children: Barbara Caughman, Sheryl Stokes. **Educ:** Savannah State College, Savannah, GA, 1948-50, BS, 1954, certificate, 1959. **Career:** US Postal Service, Savannah, GA, distribution clerk, 1966-72, LSM operator, 1972-74, examination clerk, 1974-77, examination spec, 1977-79; training tech, 1974-79; US Postal Service, Ridgeland, SC, postmaster, 1979-. **Orgs:** Editor, MSC Newsletter, US Postal Service, 1975-86; member, Postal Life Advisory Board US Postal Service, 1980-82; chairperson, Women's Program, US Postal Service, 1979-83; member, Review & Selection Committee, US Postal Service, 1986-. **Honors/Awds:** Outstanding Achievement, Savannah Women's Program US Postal Service, 1986; Certificate & Award, Postal Life US Postal Service, 1981; Letter of Commendation, Southern Region, US Postal Service, 1976; Certificate & Award, Savannah Assn for Retarded Children, 1972, 1974; Letter of Commendation, Equal Employment Council US Postal Service, 1972. **Home Addr:**

510 W 45th St, Savannah, GA 31405. **Business Addr:** Postmaster, US Postal Service, 406 Main St, Federal Bldg, Ridgeland, SC 29936.

HICKS, EDITH A.
Elected government official, educational administrator. **Personal:** Born Sep 6, 1939, Barnwell, SC; married James Adams; children: Ronald, Curtis, Craig, Paul, Paula, Kevin. **Educ:** Antioch Coll, BA 1974, MA 1976. **Career:** Bd of Educ NYC, paraprof 1967-69; Morrisania Comm Corp, training sp 1969-70; Children Circle Day Care, day care dir 1970-75; Comm Sch Bd NYC, exec asst 1975-77; Bd of Educ NYC, asst principal. **Orgs:** Vice pres Comm Sch Bd of NYC; adjunct prof Touro Coll; instructor College of New Rochelle; female dist leader 78th Assembly Dist NYC; chairperson People's Development Corp, mem Comm Planning Bd #3. **Honors/Awds:** Sojourner Truth Black Women Business & Prof Group New York City Chapt; Woman of the Yr Morrisania Comm Council; Outstanding Comm Serv Bronx Unity Democratic Club. **Home Addr:** 575 E 168th St, Bronx, NY 10456.

HICKS, ELEANOR
Educational consultant, federal official. **Personal:** Born Feb 21, 1943, Columbus, GA; daughter of Annie Pearl Hicks and Carl Hicks. **Educ:** Univ of Cincinnati, BA (cum laude) 1965; Johns Hopkins Sch of Advanced Intl Studies (SAIS), MA Intl Relations 1967. **Career:** Univ of Cincinnati, Cincinnati, OH, advisor for international liaison, 1983-; Dept of State US Embassy Cairo, deputy polit sect, 1979-82; Dept of State Central Am Affairs, deputy 1976-78; Dept of State, policy analyst 1975-76; US consul to Monaco & in Nice Dept of State, 1972-75; Thailand Dept of State, desk officer 1970-72. **Orgs:** Bd mem, Women's Action Orgn Dept of State 1978; mem, Middle East Inst; mem, American Assembly, Columbia University (US Global Interests in the 1990s); mem, Alpha Kappa Alpha; mem, Phi Beta Kappa Univ of Cincinnati (UC) 1964-; director, Federal Reserve Branch, Cincinnati Branch, 1990-; board of trustees, Southwest Ohio Transportation Authority, 1984-; board treasurer, American Red Cross, 1987-89; marketing committee member, Cincinnati Convention Center and International Visitors Bureau. **Honors/Awds:** Honorific award Chevalier De Tastevin 1973; Civic Award in Intl Realm, Cavalieri Del Nouvo Europe (Italy) 1974; scholarship award named after her for outstanding arts & sci student (UC) Annual Eleanor Hicks Award 1974; Legendary Woman Award, St Vincent's, Birmingham AL, 1975; Leadership Cincinnati, 1988-; Golden Key National Honor Society, 1991-; Career Woman of Achievement, YWCA, 1985. **Business Addr:** Advisor for International Liaison, University of Cincinnati, 3158 Vine St (ML229), Cincinnati, OH 45221.

HICKS, H. BEECHER, JR.
Clergyman. **Personal:** Born Jun 17, 1944, Baton Rouge, LA; son of Eleanor Frazier Hicks and H. Beecher Hicks Sr; married Elizabeth Harrison; children: H Beecher III, Ivan Douglas, Kristin Elizabeth. **Educ:** Univ of AR Pine Bluff, BA 1964; Colgate Rochester, MDiv 1967, Dr of Ministry 1975; Richmond Virginia Seminary LLD honorary. **Career:** Second Baptist Church, intern pastorate 1965-68; Irondequoit United Church of Christ, minister to youth 1967-68; Mt Ararat Baptist Church, sr minister 1968-73; Antioch Baptist Church, minister 1973-77; Metro Baptist Church, senior minister 1977-; Colgate Rochester Divinity School and United Theological Seminary, adjunct professor. **Orgs:** Chmn Bd of Funeral Dirs 1985; vp, Eastern Reg Natl Black Pastors Conf; admin Natl Black Pastors Conf; bd Council for Court Excellence; asst sec Progressive Natl Baptist Convention, Co-chair American Baptist Ministers Council of D.C., pres Kerygma Assoc, A Religious Consulting Service; pres Martin Luther King Fellows, Inc; co-chair Ministers in Partnership (Pregnancy Prevention); board of trustees, United Theological Seminary, Dayton, OH. **Honors/Awds:** "Give Me This Mountain" Houston TX 1976; "Images of the Black Preacher, The Man Nobody Knows" Valley Forge PA 1977; "The Black Church as a Support System for Black Men on the Simon Syndrome" Howard Univ; Comm Leaders & Noteworthy Amers 1977; Gubernatorial Citation for Serv 1977; Martin Luther King Fellowship in Black Church Studies 1972-75; Preaching Through A Storm Zondervan Press 1987; author, Correspondence with a Cripple from Tarsus, Zondervan Press, 1990. **Business Addr:** Senior Minister, Metropolitan Baptist Church, 1225 R St NW, Washington, DC 20009.

HICKS, HENDERSON
Business executive (retired). **Personal:** Born Jul 11, 1930, Fairmont, WV; married Barbara; children: Alan H, Eric A. **Educ:** City Coll NY, BBA 1958. **Career:** Mark IV Travel Serv NYC, officer owner 1968-75; NY Met Trans Auth, dep asst contrlr 1968-92; Neighbrhd Bds HARYOU-ACT, coord contrlr 1965-68; NY State Atty Gen Office & NYS Housing & Fin Agy, auditor investigator 1962-65; NYC, catering mgr 1958-62; Gr NY Ballroom Assn, rep 1960-62. **Orgs:** City Coll Alum Assn; Nat Assn Black Accnt 1971-; NAACP; NY Urban League; dir 100 Black Men Inc; pres, Pathways for Youth (Boys Athletic League)New York City 1985-; trustee Metro Suburban Bus Authority, TWU Pension & Welfare Fund 1985-91; Comus Club, Brooklyn, NY, 1989-. **Military Serv:** US Army, adj gen corp 1951-53.

HICKS, HENRY BEECHER, SR.
Clergyman (retired). **Personal:** Born Sep 21, 1912, Uniontown, AL; married Eleanor Frazier; children: Sandra H Beecher Jr, William J. **Educ:** Leland Clg, BA; Oberlin Grad Sch of Theol, MDiv, 1944; Leland Clg, DD 1947; Central State U, DD 1963. **Career:** Mt Olivet Bapt Ch Columbus, sr Minister 1946-retirement; Hicks Travel Serv Inc,fdr 1966; Mt Olivet Credit Union, fdr 1960; Mt Olivet Bapt Ch, designer & construction supr; Bapt World Alliance, exec comm, retired. **Orgs:** Past pres La HS Principals Assc; chptr mem Omega Psi Phi; mem Natl Cncl Chs; pgm chmn Progressive Natl Bapt Con. **Honors/Awds:** Churchmanship awrd OH Bapt Gen Assc Inc; awrd in theology & soc welfare Omega Psi Phi; frontiers intrntl pres's citiation Columbus Chpt; man of yr Prince Halle Masons; awrd for distngshd ldrshp in ed Columbus Bd Ed.

HICKS, INGRID DIANN
Psychologist, educator, writer, consultant. **Personal:** Born Jun 17, 1958, Flint, MI; daughter of Barbara Mae Hicks and Walter Hicks. **Educ:** BA, psychology, 1980; MS, clinical psychology, 1982; PhD, clinical psychology, 1985. **Career:** University of Wisconsin, Medical School, assoc prof, 1985-91; Medical College of Wisconsin, private practice and consultant, 1991-. **Orgs:** American Psychological Association, 1985-; Wisconsin Psychology Association, 1985-; American Society of Clinical Hypnosis, 1985-; National Association of Black Psychologists, 1985-. **Honors/Awds:** YMCA, Black Achiever, 1990; Winston, Kool Achiever, 1991. **Special Achievements:** Author: For Black Women Only, The Complete Guide to a Successful Lifestyle Change -Health, Wealth, Love & Happiness, 1991; For Black Women Only (but don't forget about our men), play & book, 1995. **Home Addr:** 1003 E Lyon St, Milwaukee, WI 53202, (414)272-7555.

HICKS, JESSIE
Professional basketball player. **Personal:** Born Dec 2, 1971. **Educ:** Univ of Maryland, BA in criminal justice. **Career:** Juven Saski Baloia (Spain), 1993-94; Maryland Eastern Shore, asst coach, 1994-95; Bowie State Univ, asst coach, 1995-97; Utah Starzz, forward-center, 1997-. **Business Addr:** Professional Basketball Player, Utah Starzz, 301 West South Temple, Salt Lake City, UT 84101, (801)355-3865.

HICKS, LEON NATHANIEL
Educator. **Personal:** Born Dec 25, 1933, Deerfield, FL. **Educ:** KS State University, BS; Univ IA Stanford, MA post grad. **Career:** FL A&M Univ Concord; Lincoln Univ; Lehigh Univ; Webster University, art instructor, currently. **Orgs:** Coll Art Assn; Natl Conference Artists; Intl Platform Assn; Brandywine Graphic Workshop; Creatadrama Society; Kappa Alpha Psi; chmn bd exec & vice pres Hicks Etchprint Inc Philadelphia 1974. **Honors/Awds:** State rep Nat Conf Artists, MO, first prizes for prints, art work; Dictionary Intl Biography 1974; Black Artists Art publs 1969; American Negro Printmakers 1966; Directions Afro Am Art 1974; Engraving Am 1974; Albrecht Art Museum St Joseph. **Military Serv:** AUS 1953-56. **Business Addr:** Art Instructor, Webster University, 470 E Lockwood, St Louis, MO 63119.

HICKS, MARYELLEN
Judge. **Personal:** Born Mar 10, 1949, Odessa, TX; daughter of Kathleen Durham and Albert G. Whitlock; widowed; children: Erin Kathleen. **Educ:** TX Womans Univ, BA, Grad Work 1971; TX Tech Sch of Law, DJ 1974. **Career:** Bonner & Hicks, atty at law 1975-77; City of Ft Worth, mncpl ct jdg 1977-82; 231st Judicial Dist Ct, dist jdg 1983-85. **Orgs:** Fellow Natl Endwmnt for the Humanities 1980; con sec Natl Women Achvmnt 1985; State Bang TX; Natl Bar Assn; vice pres Natl Cncl of Negro Women; D Elta Sigma Theta Sor Jack & Jill Inc; former pres Font Work Black Bar Assoc; vice pres Sojourner Truth Cmty Theatre. **Honors/Awds:** Outstndng Black Wmn 1982; Outstndng Black Lawyer 1982; Female Newsmaker 1 Yr Press Club 1982; Citizen Awd Black Pilots of Amer 1986; Citizen of the Year SS Dillow Elem Schl 1987; Alumna Award Texas Woman's Univ 1989. **Business Addr:** Former Court of Appeals Judge, 231st Dist Court, 100 Weatherford, Fort Worth, TX 76102, (817)483-5630.

HICKS, MICHAEL
Professional football player. **Personal:** Born Feb 1, 1973. **Educ:** South Carolina State, attended. **Career:** Chicago Bears, running back, 1996-. **Business Addr:** Professional Football Player, Chicago Bears, 1000 Football Dr, Halas Hall at Conway Park, Lake Forest, IL 60045-4829, (847)295-6600.

HICKS, MICHAEL L.
Physician. **Personal:** Born Apr 8, 1960, Tuskegee Institute, AL; son of Lee Otis & Lillie R Hicks; married Rhonda M Hicks, Sep 14, 1991; children: Michael Leon II, Maya Michelle. **Educ:** Luther College, BA, 1981; University of Alabama at Birmingham, MD, 1986. **Career:** Henry Ford Hosp, gynecologic oncologist, 1992-. **Orgs:** National Medical Association; American Medical Association; Society of Surgical Oncologist; Society of Gynecologic Oncologist; American Society of Clinical Oncologist; American College of Obstetricians & Gynecologists. **Honors/Awds:** Roswell Park Cancer Institute, Fellow in Gynecologic Oncology, 1990-92. **Special Achievements:** Author of numerous medical articles.

HICKS, RAYMOND A.
Educational administrator. **Personal:** Born 1943?; married Georgia Hicks; children: Shannan, Michael, Jared. **Educ:** Louisiana Tech, master's degree; Illinois Univ at Carbondale, doctorate, higher education administration. **Career:** Grambling State Univ, pres, 1995-. **Business Addr:** President, Grambling State Univ, 100 Main St, PO Drawer 607, Grambling, LA 71245, (318)247-2000.

HICKS, RICHARD R.
Clergyman. **Personal:** Born Oct 20, 1931, Milford, DE; married Thelma Miller; children: Terri Lynn, Stephanie, Georgie Sue, Marjorie Louise. **Educ:** Hampton Inst, BS 1958; Crozer Theol Sem, MDiv 1964; VA Theol Sem; Univ MD; Howard U. **Career:** Williams VA, tchr 1958-59; Charlotte NC 1959-60; ferris Sch ofr Boys, counselor 1961-62; United Meth Chs, Townsend, DE, pastor 1961-63; Chestertown, MD1963-67; Princess Anne, MD 1967-70; Wesley Found Univ of MD Eastern Shore, dir 1967-70; Mt Joy United Meth Ch Wilm DE, pastor 1970-71; SE Reg Sec United Ministries in Higher Ed, 1971-74; Ministries to Blacks in Higher Edn, exec dir 1975-79; Howard Univ Wash DC, United Methodist chaplain 1977-80; Huntingtown Chg United meth Church, pastor 1980-85; Morgan State Univ Baltimore, instr religious studies 1985-; Morgan Christian Center, dir 1985-. **Orgs:** Bd dir Black Meth for Ch Renewal 1972-75; SE coord Nat Campus Min Assn; Minority-in-Serv Training & Scholarship Com 1976-76; Nat Conf Black Churchmen; past chmn Chestertown MD NAACP exec com; mem ACLU Cons, numerous papers & publs in field. **Military Serv:** AUS first lt 1952-55.

HICKS, SHERMAN G.
Clergyman. **Career:** Metropolitan Chicago Synod, bishop; First Trinity Lutheran Church, senior pastor, currently. **Orgs:** National AIDS Fund, bd of dirs; Bethphage Mission Inc; Community Family Life Svcs, bd of dirs; Lifeline, A Mental Retardation Partnership, bd of dirs; AIDS National Interfaith Network, bd of dirs. **Honors/Awds:** Wittenberg Univ, Alumni Citation, 1993. **Business Addr:** Reverend, First Trinity Lutheran Church, 309 E St NW, Washington, DC 20001.

HICKS, VERONICA ABENA
Laboratory manager. **Personal:** Born Feb 22, 1949, Awate, Ghana; daughter of Salone Atawa Dzeble, Kokroko and Stephen Kwani Kokroko; married Anthony M Hicks, Jun 6, 1980; children: Esi, Gloria, Tania. **Educ:** Univ of Ghana, Legon, BSc 1971, graduate diploma, 1972; Iowa State Univ, Ames, IA, MSc, 1976, PhD, 1980. **Career:** Ministry of Agriculture, Accra Ghana, nutrition consultant, 1976-77; ISU Dept Biochemistry & Biophys, Ames, IA, postdoctoral research fellow, 1980-81; Kellogg Company, Battle Creek, MI, nutritionist 1981-82, mgr nutrition research, 1982-84, dir nutrition, 1984-86, dir chemistry & physiology, 1986-. **Orgs:** Mem, Advisory Bd, Iowa State Coll of Consumer & Family Sciences, 1985-88; mem, Infant Health Advisory Bd, Calhoun County Dept of Health, 1983-. **Business Addr:** Dir, Chemisty & Physiology, Kellogg Co, Science & Technical Center, 235 Porter St, Battle Creek, MI 49017.

HICKS, WILLIAM H.
State official. **Personal:** Born Aug 27, 1925, Littleton, NC; married Margaret; children: Chiquita, Patricia, William, Linda. **Educ:** William Patterson Coll, BA. **Career:** State Co Housing, dir present; NJ State, assemblyman 1971-75. **Orgs:** Bd dir Paterson Boys Club; Damon House adv om equal opportunities ramapo coll; alderman patersons 4th ard 1966-71; mem am legion post 268. **Military Serv:** USN air corps 1943-46. **Business Addr:** State County, 317 Pennsylvania, Paterson, NJ 07503.

HICKS, WILLIAM JAMES
Physician. **Personal:** Born Jan 3, 1948, Columbus, OH; married; children: 3. **Educ:** Morehouse College, BS, 1970; University of Pittsburgh, School of Medicine, MD, 1974; University Health Center of Pittsburgh, Presbyterian-University Hospital, internship, 1974-75, residency, 1975-77; Ohio State University, Department of Hematology/Oncology, fellowship, 1977-79. **Career:** Grant Medical Center, Medical Oncology, associate director, 1979-, attending staff; Ohio State University, associate clinical professor of medicine, 1986-; Saint Anthony's Medical Center, attending staff. **Orgs:** Planned Parenthood of Central Ohio, board of trustees, 1989-95; State of Ohio Commission on Minority Health, 1987-; Natl Medical Assn, Columbus Chapter, 1979-, president, 1982-84; National Surgical Adjuvant Breast and Bowel Project, investigator, 1982-; Natl Black Leadership Initiative on Cancer Columbus Coalition, chmn, 1994-; Grant Medical Center, Internal Medicine Dept, chmn, 1989-91; State of Ohio Commission on Minority Health, vice chmn, 1993-; Ohio State University, assoc clinical prof of med, 1986-; Columbus Cancer Clinic, bd of dirs, 1982-86; American Society of Clinical Oncologists, 1986-; Columbus Chapter of the Natl Medical Assn, 1979-, pres, 1982-84; Franklin County Academy of Medicine, 1983-; Ohio State Medical Assn, 1986-; Sigma Pi Phi Fraternity, Inc, 1985-; Southwest Oncology Group, investigator, 1979-; Columbus Community Clinical Oncology Program, assoc principle investigator, 1983-, bd of trustees, 1983-, institutional review bd, 1983-; ECCO Family Health Center, consultant/hematology, 1979-; Grant Medical Center, assoc dir/medical oncology, 1979-; William J Hicks MD, private prac-

tice, 1979-; Alpha Phi Alpha Fraternity, Inc, 1968-. **Honors/Awds:** Alpha Kappa Alpha Sorority, Alpha Sigma Omega Chapter, Human Services Award, 1992; Columbus Monthly Magazine, One of Listed Top Doctors, 1992; Black Enterprise Magazine One of Listed Top Black Physicians, 1988; American Board of Medical Examiners, Diplomate, 1974; American Board of Internal Medicine, Diplomate, 1977; American Board of Medical Oncology, Diplomate, 1981; Alpha Rho Lambda Chapter of the Alpha Phi Alpha Fraternity, Alpha Excellence Award in Health Care, 1994; Minority Health Commission, Recipient Chairman's Award, 1994; Council of Black Students in Administration presents Professional Award for Outstanding Contributions to the Columbus Community-13th Annual Black Business Awards Banquet, 1989. **Special Achievements:** Author, publications include: ''Randomized Multicenter Trial of Cytosine Arabinoside with Mitoxantrone or Daunorubicin in Previously Untreated Adult Patients with Acute Nonlymphocytic Leukemia,'' Leukemia, Vol 4, No 3, p 177-183, 1990; ''Photodynamic Therapy for Cutaneous and Subcutaneous Malignant Neoplasms,'' Archives of Surgery, 124, p 211-216, 1989; numerous others. **Business Addr:** 340 E Town St, 8-300, Columbus, OH 43215-4622.

HICKS, WILLIAM L.

Professional engineer, general contractor. **Personal:** Born Jan 19, 1928, Yoakum, TX. **Educ:** Coll of Engr UC Berkeley, BS 1954. **Career:** Corps of Engrs LA, engr trainee; Daniel Mann Johnson & Mendenhall LA, design engr; Ralph M Parsons Co LA, design engr; Mackintosh & Mackintosh LA, civil engr; Hick Constrn Co, owner. **Orgs:** Mem Am Soc & Civil Engrs.

HICKS, WILLIE LEE (PRINCE DUROJAIYE)

Business executive. **Personal:** Born Jan 31, 1931, Bartow, GA; son of Lula Mae Brinson Hicks and Mike Hicks; married Doris Bowman Culley Hicks, Sep 10, 1952; children: Debra, Ajisafe, Kathy, Doris Jumoke. **Educ:** Baruch Sch of Bus & Pub Admin, BBA 1960; Heffley & Brown Sec Sch, attended 1955-56. **Career:** Durojaiye Assn, retailer distributor mfg 1968-73; African Investment Partnership Ltd, 1974; Durojaiye Trading & Commodity Corp, 1976-; United Mutual Life, 1975-; Mind Power, Inc, chairman, 1989-. **Orgs:** Sec Nile-Niger Corp 1957; pres Durojaiye Trading & Commodity Corp 1959-62; HKM Intl 1967; sec Natl Postal Alliance 1956; NAACP 1956; sec Angola Refugee Rescue Com; vice pres Soc of African Descendents; African-Amer Tchrs Assn; numerous other affiliations; vice president, United Peoples Movement. **Military Serv:** USAF A/1C 1951-55. **Business Addr:** Chairman, Mind Power Inc, 1223 Fulton St, Suite 4F, PO Box 254, Brooklyn, NY 11216.

HICKS-BARTLETT, SHARON THERESA

Social scientist. **Personal:** Born Nov 22, 1951, Chicago, IL; married David Charles Bartlett; children: Alani Rosa Hicks. **Educ:** Roosevelt Univ, BA 1976, MA 1981; Univ of Chicago, MA 1985. **Career:** IL Council on Cont Medical Educ, prog & activities sec 1975-78; Amherst Assoc, office mgr 1978-80; Univ of Chicago, convocation coord 1980-81; Univ of Chicago Urban Family Life Project, rsch asst 1985-. **Orgs:** Instructor Thornton Comm Coll 1982 & 1987; rsch asst Univ of Chicago 1983; freelance researcher Better Boys Foundation 1985; volunteer East Chicago Heights Comm Serv Ctr 1986-; literacy tutor (adults) Literacy Volunteers of Amer 1987-. **Honors/Awds:** Art & Science Scholar Awd Roosevelt Univ 1980-81; Title IX Fellowship for Grad Study Univ of Chicago 1981-85; Danforth-Compton Dissertation Awd Univ of Chicago 1986-87; Amer Sociological Soc Dissertation Awd Univ of Chicago 1986-87. **Home Addr:** 66 Water St, Park Forest, IL 60466. **Business Addr:** Research Asst/Doctoral Student, University of Chicago, Urban Family Life Project, 5811 So Kenwood Ave, Chicago, IL 60637.

HICKSON, EUGENE, SR.

Business executive. **Personal:** Born Jun 10, 1930, Arcadia, FL; married Verlene Deloris Stebbins; children: Eugene Jr, Vergena, Edward. **Educ:** Gubton-Jones College of Mortuary Sci, 1952. **Career:** Hickson Funeral Home;; owner; Arcadia FL, mayor. **Orgs:** 32 Degree Mason; Shriner; deacon Elizabeth Bapt Ch; chmn C of C; 2nd vice pres FA Martician Assc. **Honors/Awds:** FL Mortician Assoc Awd Sarasota Womens Clb 1971; FL Mortician Assoc 1972; FL Mortician Assn, 1975.

HICKSON, SHERMAN RUBEN

Dentist. **Personal:** Born Apr 3, 1950, Ridgeland, SC; son of Justine Odon Hickson and Glover M Hickson Jr (deceased); married Eavon Holloway; children: Sherman Jr (deceased), LaTonya, Thurston, Adrienne. **Educ:** SC State Coll, BS 1971; Meharry Medical Coll Sch of Dentistry, DDS 1975. **Career:** Private practice, general dentistry 1977-. **Orgs:** Mem SC Dental Assoc 1975-, Palmetto Medical Dental & Pharm Assoc 1976-87, Natl Dental Assoc 1976-87, Acad of General Dentistry 1978-87; mem Dickerson Lodge #314 Mason Prince Hall 1981-87, CC Johnson Consistory #136 1982-87, Cairo Temple #125 Shriners 1982-87, Orion Chap #135 Eastern Star 1986-87; 2nd degree black belt World Tae Kwon Do Assoc mem 1982-87; trustee, Friendship Baptist Church; life mem, NAACP; life mem, Omega Psi Phi Fraternity Inc; South Carolina Basketball and Football Officials Association; Mideastern Athletic College Football official. **Honors/Awds:** Meharry Medical College School of Dentistry, Dentsply Intl Merit Award. **Military Serv:** US Army, capt, 2 yrs; Letter of Commendation 1975-77. **Business Addr:** Dentist, 500 Richland Ave E, Aiken, SC 29801.

HICKSON, WILLIAM F., JR.

Dentist. **Personal:** Born Aug 27, 1936, Aiken, SC; son of Nina Hickson and William F Hickson Sr; married Charlestine Dawson (divorced); children: Nina R, William F, III, G G Oneal. **Educ:** SC State Clg, BS 1956; Meharry, DDS 1962. **Career:** General Dentist, pvt prac; WSSB Radio, South Carolina State College, radio host, 1985-. **Orgs:** Am Natl SC Palmetto Dental Assc; Cty dental dir OEO State; pres Palmetto Dental Assc; reg consult HEW Dist IV; mem Beta & Kappa Chi; Omega Psi Phi; past basileus Alpha Iota Boule; past sire Archon; Natl Bd Missions United Presbyterian Ch; mem NAACP; Fed Dental Cons. **Military Serv:** US Army capt 1963-65. **Business Addr:** Dentist, 109 Treadwell St, Orangeburg, SC 29115.

HIGGINBOTHAM, A. LEON, JR.

Judge (retired), educator. **Personal:** Born Feb 25, 1928, Trenton, NJ; divorced; children (previous marriage): Stephen, Karen, Kenneth, Nia. **Educ:** Purdue Univ, attended; Antioch Coll, BA 1949; Yale Law Schl, LLB 1952. **Career:** Harvard Univ, prof, 1993-; Paul, Weiss, Rifkind, Wharton, counsel, 1993-; US District Court and US Court of Appeals, 1964-93; Federal Trade Comm, commissioner, 1962-64; US Justice Dept, special hearing officer for conscientious objectors, 1960-62; PA Human Relations commission, commissioner, 1961-62; Norris, Green Harris & Higginbotham, partner, 1954-62; Philadelphia county, asst dist atty, 1953-54. **Honors/Awds:** Author, more than 100 published articles; author ''In the Matter of Color; Race and the American Legal Prcess,'' Oxford Univ Press 1978; over 80 honorary degrees; Presidential Medal of Freedom recipient. **Business Addr:** Professor, Harvard University, Cambridge, MA 02138.

HIGGINBOTHAM, EVE JULIET

Physician, educator. **Personal:** Born Nov 4, 1953, New Orleans, LA; daughter of Luther & Ruby Higginbotham; married Frank C Williams Jr, Jun 7, 1986. **Educ:** MIT, SB, 1975, SM, 1975; Harvard Medical School, MD, 1979. **Career:** Pacific Medical Center, intern, 1979-80; LSU Eye Center, resident, 1980-83; MA Eye & Ear Infirmary, fellow, 1983-85; Univ of Illinois, assistant professor, 1985-90; Univ of Michigan, assoc professor/assistant dean, 1990-. **Orgs:** American Academy of Ophthalmology, board of trustees, 1992-; Prevent Blindness America, board of directors, chair publication committee, 1990-; Women in Ophthalmology, board of directors, 1980-;, National Medical Assn; National Eye Health Education Program, Natl Eye Institute; Archives of Ophthalmology, editorial board, 1994-. **Honors/Awds:** Head Foundation, Fellowship, 1983; EB Durphy Fellowship, 1984; Knepp Award, 1984; Beem-Fisher Award, Chicago Ophthalmological Soc, 1985; PI/Clincial Center, AGIS & OHTS, National Eye Institute. **Special Achievements:** Glaucoma textbook including over 30 contributors; First female chair of a university-based Dept of Ophthalmology. **Business Addr:** Professor & Chair, Dept of Ophthalmology, University of Maryland Medical School, 22 South Greene St, Baltimore, MD 21201, (410)328-5929.

HIGGINBOTHAM, KENNETH DAY, SR.

Cleric. **Personal:** Born May 1, 1928, Worcester, MA; son of Olive Mary Elizabeth Bowman Higginbotham and Charles Washington Higginbotham Sr; married Ruth Kidd; children: Kenneth Jr, Maretta, Michael, Paul, Stephen, Keith, Andrea, Christopher. **Educ:** Trinity Coll, BA 1950; Berkeley Div Sch, MDiv 1954; Yale-Berkeley Div Sch, STD 1983. **Career:** St Philips Ch, rector 1957-68; Fisk Univ, Meharry Med Coll, TN State Univ, chaplain 1968-70; Fed City Coll, chaplain 1970-72; Episcopal Diocese of WA, asst to bishop 1971-79; Christ the Good Shepherd Ch LA, rector 1979-93; Diocese of Los Angeles, canon to the ordinary 1993-; All Saints By The Sea, Santa Barbara, CA, priest in charge, 1993; IBRU Ecumenical International Retreat Conference Ctr, Agbarha Otor, Nigeria, dir general, 1993-95; St Matthews, Pacific Palisades, CA, pastor assoc, currently. **Orgs:** Mem Franklin Co Welfare Bd 1965-68; chaplain Crenshaw Ctr Hosp; pres of bd Good Shepherd Ctr for Independent Living; chmn Diocese An Urban Caucus; mem Program Group on Christian Educ & Leadership Training for Diocese of LA; Union of Black Episcopalians; bd mem Encl of Chs Columbus OH; Green door; standingcom Diocese of So OH; chmn Commn on Black Ministries; mem Commn on Ministry; GOE reader; deputy General Convention 1985; public advisory dir Blue Cross of California 1989-90; chairman, Commission on Ministry, Los Angeles, 1991-; board member, North American Regional Committee, St George's College, Jerusalem, 1990-92. **Honors/Awds:** Pres MED USA Coll Sr Hon Soc; Fellow Bexley Hall Div Sch; Docotr of Sacred Theology, (STD), Berkeley, Yale Divinity School, New Haven, CN; Honorary Canon, St Paul's Cathedral, Los Angeles, CA; Honorary Canon, St Audrew's Cathedral, Warri, Nigeria.

HIGGINBOTHAM, PEYTON RANDOLPH

Physician. **Personal:** Born Aug 21, 1902, Lynchburg, VA; son of Ada V Wright Higginbotham and James L Higginbotham; married Miriam Gwendolyn Hughes, May 26, 1926; children: Lynn. **Educ:** Howard Univ Coll, BS Liberal Arts 1923; Howard Univ Sch Med, MD 1926; Freedman's Hosp, intern 1926-27. **Career:** WV State Bd Hlth, 1948-; Bluefield State Coll, college physician, 1932-91; Private Practice, physician. **Orgs:** Mem exec com So WV VA Reg Hlth Cncl; mem WV State Med Assn; AMA; WV Med Soc; NMA; staff mem St Luke's Hosp; assoc mem Beckley Appalachian Reg Appalachian Regional Hosp; mem Princeton Meml Comm Hosp; Mercer Co Planning Commn; bd dir Bluefield Comm Hosp; mem Alpha Phi Alpha Frat; Sigma Pi Phi; HM Club Am; Physician for Welfare Rev Bd Mercer Monroe & Summers Co; mem Scott St Bapt Ch; NAACP; past member, WV State Board; chairman of board, OH Health Services, 1978-91. **Honors/Awds:** Plaque Appalachian OH-9 Hlth Cncl; WV Med Soc; League for Serv; Freedman's Hosp; past pres plaque 50 yrs Continuous Serv; plaque Howard Univ Med Alumni Assn; plaque former interns & resd Freedmen's Hosp Med Res Capt; Honorary LLB Degree, Bluefield State College, 1980-. **Military Serv:** US Army, Capt, 1920-50.

HIGGINBOTHAM-BROOKS, RENEE

Attorney. **Personal:** Born Jan 3, 1952, Martinsville, VA; daughter of Charmion Higginbotham and Curtis Higginbotham; married Clarence Jackson Brooks, Jun 20, 1975; children: Leigh, Codie. **Educ:** Howard University, BA, 1974; Georgetown University Law Center, JD, 1977. **Career:** National Labor Relations Board, field attorney, 1977-79; U.S. Department of Health, Education & Welfare, civil rights attorney, 1979-87; private practice of law, 1987-; Texas Alcoholic Beverage Commission, chairman, currently. **Orgs:** Natl Bar Assn, 1979-; Links Inc, 1985-; Tarrant County Trial Lawyers Association, 1989-; State Bar of Texas, 1977-; Jack and Jill of America, 1990-; College of the State Bar of Texas, 1992. **Honors/Awds:** Dallas Black Chamber of Commerce, Quest for Success Award, 1992; Kappa Alpha Psi, Excellence in Law Award, 1992. **Special Achievements:** First African-American and first female member and chairman of the Texas Alcoholic Beverage Commission, 1991. **Business Addr:** Chairman, Texas Alcoholic Beverage Commission, Box 13217, Capital Sta, Austin, TX 78711, (512)465-4920.

HIGGINS, BENNETT EDWARD

Educator, mortician. **Personal:** Born May 5, 1931, Athens, AL; married Shirley Webb; children: Bennett Dion, Melessa Shawn. **Educ:** AL A&M U, BS 1953; Temple U;; Attended; Athens Clg, adv study. **Career:** Clements HS, Limestone Co Bd of Educ, teacher science 1957-; Peoples Funeral Home, mortician & funeral dir 1968-, owner founder 1965-; Atlanta Life Insurance Co, salesman 1953; Forniss Printing Co Birmingham, linotype operator 1953. **Orgs:** Pres Limestone Co NAACP 1978-; sec Limestone Dem Conf; chmn Boy Scout Troup No 154; mem Kappa Alpha Psi Frat. **Honors/Awds:** Recipient good conduct & rifle medals AUS 1954; orgnzr Local NAACP 1968; Keep Am Beautiful City of Athens 1977; achvmnt awrd Kappa Alpha Psi Frat 1978; outst serv awrd NAACP 1980. **Military Serv:** AUS corpl 1953-55. **Business Addr:** Clements High Sch, Athens, AL 35611.

HIGGINS, CHESTER A., SR.

Journalist, consultant. **Personal:** Born May 10, 1917, Chicago, IL; son of Josephine Carter and George Lee Higgins; married Maria Charlotte; children: Chester Jr, Janet, Pamela. **Educ:** Kentucky State College, Frankfort, KY, 1946-47; Louisville Municipal College, 1948-50. **Career:** Jet Magazine, associate editor/senior editor, 1959-72; Federal Communications Commission, special assistant to commissioner, 1972-77; Office of the Secretary of the Army, assistant chief of public affairs for media relations, 1977-81; NAACP, communications consultant, 1981-83, 1992-93; University of the District of Columbia, communications specialist, 1984-85; The National Urban Coalition, volunteer communications consultant, 1986; The National Caucus and Center on Black Aged Inc, director of communications, 1987-88; The National Newspaper Publishers Assn, news editor/assistant director, 1987-89; National Organization of Black Law Enforcement Officials, communications consultant and editor, 1990-. **Orgs:** Exec secretary, Natl Negro Labor Cncl Louisville Chap 1952; Capital Press Clb, Natl Press Clb; WA Press Clb; Natl & Broadcasting Club; NATAS; Natl Com of Black Lawyers; vice chmn Communications Com; Com for Commeration of Birthday of Dr Martin Luther King Jr; board member Project Build VOICE; NAACP. **Honors/Awds:** NAACP Labor Department, Keeper of the Flame Award, 1992; First Annual Black Heritage Series' Natl Black Excellance Awrd for Contrib to Black Experience Through the art of Communications, 1974; ''Committee for KY,'' Prize-Winning Essay, Over All, Clg Stdnts in KY 1946; Freedom Citation for Outst Serv in Behalf of the Emancipation Centennial Yr Commemoration, Detroit, 1963; Detroit Courier Nwspr Stf, Appreciation Awrd 1964; NPA First Place News Feature Awrd 1967; Keith L Ware Award, Judge in Journalism Competition, US Army, 1985; Judge, Black Press Hall of Fame, 1987, 1988. **Military Serv:** US Army, sgt WWII. **Business Addr:** Communications Consultant, 2139 Wyoming Ave NW, Washington, DC 20008-3915.

HIGGINS, CHESTER ARCHER, JR.

Photojournalist. **Personal:** Born Nov 6, 1946, Lexington, KY; son of Varidee Loretta Young Higgins Smith and Johnny Frank

Smith; divorced; children: Nataki, Chester III. **Educ:** Tuskegee Inst, BS 1970. **Career:** Exhibits NY & World-Wide Retrospective; USIA, sent to 65 countries 1975-76; NY Univ, instr 1975-78; NY Times, staff photographer 1975-. **Orgs:** Mem Natl Congress of Men, Intl Center of Photography, Pan Asian Repertory; represented by Photo Researchers. **Honors/Awds:** Works in Mus of Modern Art; Intl Ctr of Photography; Library of Congress; Vassar Coll; Tuskegee Inst Archive Ford Found Fellow 1972-74; Rockefeller Grant 1973; Natl Endowment of the Arts Grant 1973; African Disting Lectr 1975; United Nations Award; Am Graphic Design Award; Graphics Mag Award; Intl Ctr of Photog Grant; Art Dir Club of NY Award; Publishers Award, The New York Times. **Special Achievements:** Author: Black Woman, McCalls, 1970; Drums of Life, Doubleday, 1974; Some Time Ago, Doubleday, 1978; Feeling the Spirit: Searching the World for the People of Africa, Bantam Books, 1994. **Home Addr:** 57 S Portland Ave, Brooklyn, NY 11217-1301. **Business Addr:** Staff Photographer, The New York Times, 229 West 43rd St, New York, NY 10036.

HIGGINS, CLARENCE R., JR.
Pediatrician. **Personal:** Born Sep 13, 1927, E St Louis, IL; son of Louise Higgins and Clarence Higgins; married Edwina Gray; children: Rhonda, Adrienne, Stephen. **Educ:** Fisk Univ, 1948; Meharry Med Coll, 1953. **Career:** Homer Phillips Hospital St Louis, internship 1953-54, ped res 1954-56; Baylor Coll Med, res flwshp 1956-57, asst clinical prof peds; Peds Sec NMA, self-employed Ped, chmn 1973-; St Joseph Hospital, dir. **Orgs:** Alpha Phi Alpha Fraternity; Diplomat Amer Bd Peds; Fellow Amer Acad Peds. **Military Serv:** USAF 1957-59. **Business Addr:** 4315 Lockwood, Houston, TX 77026.

HIGGINS, CLEO SURRY
Educator. **Personal:** Born Aug 25, 1923, Memphis, TN; widowed; children: Kyle Everett, Sean Craig. **Educ:** LeMoyne Clg, BA 1944; Univ WI, MPh 1945, PhD 1973. **Career:** Bethune-Cookman Coll, acting acad dean 1976-; Div of Humanities Bethune-cookman Coll, chmn 1973-76; Div of Humanities, acting chmn 1970-73; Humanities St Johns & River Jr Coll, instructor 1964-70; Collier Blocker Jr Coll, dean students prsnl registrat instructor 1960-63; Central Acad HS, instructor reading 1958-60. **Orgs:** Chmn Div of Humanities Bethune-Cookman Clg 1948-56; vis prof WV State Clg 1948; chmn Bethune-cookman Clg 1946-48; instr Bethune-cookman Clg 1945-46;Fessenden Acad, instr 1943-44; mem Am Dialect Soc; mem Natl Cncl of Tchrs of Engl; mem Natl Cncl of Clg Pub Advsrs; mem Am Assc of Univ Women;mem Putnam Co Hist Soc; mem Emanuel United Meth Ch; chptr mem Daytona Br Chap of Links Inc 1956; fdr mem Beta Iota Sigma Sigma Gamma Rho Sor 1948; standing mem Vis Com of S Assc of Secondary Schs & Clgs 1948-56; organizer The Woemsn Serv league; spkr St Louis George Washington Day Observance 1959; natl pres Sigma Gamma Rho Sor 1962-63; asst chmn coordn team SACS Vis Team 1962; chmn planing grp Bilingualism in W Indies 1963; mem exec bd Putnam Co Chap Natl Found Marchof Dimes 1964; mem Bi-Racial Com Pum Co 1964-70; vol sec Putnam City Comm Action Pgm 1966; consult In-Serv Ed Meeting Putnam Co Sec Schs 1966; mem FL Citizens Com for Humanities 1972-73. **Honors/Awds:** Outst Educators in Am 1970; schlr in dept of engl Univ WI 1971; rec Charles Dana Faculty Schlrshp Univ NCF 1972-73; oratorical contest judge VFW Voice of Democracy Natl Pgm 1975; woman of yr Bethune-Cookman Clg 1975; panelist a Humanities Pgm for Disadvantaged 1976. **Business Addr:** Bethune Cookman Coll, 640 2nd Ave, Daytona Beach, FL 32114.

HIGGINS, ORA A.
Human resources administrator. **Personal:** Born Sep 24, 1919, Birmingham, AL; married William Higgins Sr; children: Murrell Duster, William, Jr. **Educ:** Northwestern Univ, BS 1946, MA 1955; Northwestern Univ Bus Law, grad work. **Career:** Spiegel Inc, asst personnel mgr 1946-; Ora Higgings Youth Foundation, founder, 1976, bd of dirs, currently. **Orgs:** Mem Chicago Comm on Human Relations Employment Com, State of IL Dept of Personnel Grievance Com; mem Natl Bus League, Chicago Guid & Personnel Assn Inc, Manpower Commn State of IL, Civil Serv Commn Oral Panel; adv bd Midwest Day Care Ctr; bd dir Rehab Workshop Assn; chmn DuSable HS Exemplary Project; sec bd dir Joint Negro Appeal; treas Jones Comm HS adv coun; Cosmopolitan C of C; chmn Youth Motivation Prog Chicago Assn of Commerce & Indus; gov bd, pres women's auxiliary, mem Tabernacle Comm Hosp & Health Ctr; mem Women's Div Natl Conf of Christians & Jews; natl chmn Women in Industry Federated Women's Clubs; faculty mem Dunbar Voc Evening Sch; chmn Awd Com Dunbar Voc HS adv council; Provident Hosp Women's Aux; personnel chmn Met YWCA; Corp Com Fund of Chicago;Personnel Mgmt Com Comm F; tech adv com Dawson Skill Ctr City Coll of Chicago; personnel mgmt Com Comm Fund; engineered Integration Prog for Loop dept stores 1950; Alpha Gamma Phi Sor; mem Greenview Comm Council. **Honors/Awds:** Awd from Chicago Assn of Commerce & Indus 1975; Awd Add Info Contrib to Bus World Cosmo Sec NCNW 1978; Merit Employ Awd Chic Assn of Commerce & Ind 1978; Woman of the Week WBEE Radio 1973; Assoc Orgn for Vocational Achievement 100th Yr Anniversary Emancipation Proclamation Merit Awd 1963; Chicago Daily Defender Round Table of Commerce 1961; Rosa Gregg Awd Bus & Indus of Natl Assn of Colored Women's Clubs Inc 1964; Alpha Gamma Phi Sor Outstanding Progressive Woman 1967; Disting Serv Awd Tuskegee Inst 1967. **Business Addr:** Founder, Ora Higgins Youth Foundation, 9424 S Parnell Ave, Chicago, IL 60620.

HIGGINS, RODERICK DWAYNE
Professional basketball player. **Personal:** Born Jan 31, 1960, Harvey, IL. **Educ:** Fresno State Univ, 1982. **Career:** Chicago Bulls, 1983-85, 1986, Seattle SuperSonics, 1986, San Antonio Spurs, 1986, New Jersey Nets, 1986, Golden State Warriors, 1987-92; Sacramento Kings, 1992-93; Cleveland Cavaliers, 1993-. **Business Addr:** Professional Basketball Player, Cleveland Cavaliers, Gund Arena, One Center Ct, Cleveland, OH 44115.

HIGGINS, SAMMIE L.
Clergyman, educator. **Personal:** Born May 11, 1923, Ft Worth; married Elizabeth; children: Pam, Don, Benita, Kim, Garry. **Educ:** Univ Denver, BS 1954; Western Theol Sem, BTh 1963; Merritt Clg, AA 1969; Univ UT San Fran State Clg. **Career:** Rev Higgins Has Been Very Active Politically in Various Rel Appts & in Tchg, meth clrgymn edctr. **Orgs:** Mem Variety of Assc & Coms; mem NAACP; Omega Psi Phi. **Honors/Awds:** Outst cit of Ogden 1964; outst Fin Ed Ofcr Poletechnic HS 1970; outst Faculty Mem & Tchr 1972.

HIGGINS, SEAN MARIELLE
Professional basketball player. **Personal:** Born Dec 30, 1968, Los Angeles, CA; son of Earle Higgins. **Educ:** Univ of Michigan, Ann Arbor, MI, 1987-90. **Career:** San Antonio Spurs, guard-forward, 1990-91; Orlando Magic, 1991-92; Los Angeles Lakers, 1992-93; Golden State Warriors, 1993-94; New Jersey Nets, 1994-95; Philadelphia 76ers, 1995-97; Portland Trailblazers, 1997-. **Business Addr:** Professional Basketball Player, Portland Trailblazers, 1 Center Court, Ste 200, Portland, OR 97227, (503)234-9291.

HIGGINS, STANN
Art director. **Personal:** Born May 16, 1952, Pittsburgh, PA. **Educ:** Columbia Coll of Communication Arts, BS, graphics/advt 1979; Art Inst of Chicago Jr Sch. **Career:** Jordan Tamraz Caruso Advt, art dir 1985, prod mgr 1979; Bentley Barnes & Lynn Advt, asst prod mgr 1978; Starstruk Prods, creative dir 1985; Raddim Intl Musicpaper, art dir, production mgr 1986. **Orgs:** Bd of dirs, chmn of graphics Yth Communications 1985. **Honors/Awds:** Work selected for, recip 2 hon mentions Art Inst of Chicago 1965; Dist Art Award Maywood Bd of Ed 1966; Cert of Apprec as Guest Speaker in Advertising Triton Coll 1981. **Business Addr:** Pres, StarStruck Productions, 8501 S Maryland, Chicago, IL 60619.

HIGGINSEN, VY
Producer, director. **Personal:** Born in New York, NY; daughter of Geraldine Higginsen and Reverend Higginsen; married Kenneth Wydro; children: Knoelle Wydro. **Educ:** Fashion Institute of Technology, New York, NY. **Career:** WBLS-FM, New York, NY, disc jockey; WRVR-FM, radio host; WWRL-AM, talk show host; NBC-TV, hostess of "Positively Black"; Unique N.Y. magazine, publisher; Supervision Inc, president/CEO, currently. **Special Achievements:** Director: "Mama I Want to Sing," the longest running off-Broadway African-American musical; first African-American female in advertising at Ebony Magazine; first African-American female radio personality in the prime-time New York radio market; first African-American female to produce another plawrights drama on Broadway; author: Mama I Want to Sing, based on the play; This Is My Song, a collection of gospel songs and spirituals for little children. **Business Addr:** President/CEO, Supervision, Inc, 26 W 71st Street, New York, NY 10023.

HIGGS, FREDERICK C.
Business executive. **Personal:** Born Jul 3, 1935, Nassau, Bahamas; married Beryl Vanderpool; children: Rory, Linda, Saundra. **Educ:** St John's Coll, 1947-51. **Career:** Lisaro Ent Ltd, pres 1973-; Charlotte St Prop, properties mgr 1971-73; Bahamas Airways, sta mgr 1965-70; New Providence Div of BGA. **Orgs:** Vice chmn, trnmnt dir, New Providence Div of BGA; first vice pres, Bahamas Confed of Amateur Sports; mem, Mental Health Assn Exec; mem, Scout Assn of Bahamas; sec, Amateur Boxing Assn of Bahamas. **Honors/Awds:** Intl Golf Tour Champion, Nairobi 1973.

HIGGS, MARY ANN SPICER
Educator. **Personal:** Born May 10, 1951, South Bend, IN; daughter of Willa B Thornton and Bobby Higgs Jr; married Jack Spicer IV, Dec 25, 1977; children: Jack V. **Educ:** North Texas State Univ, BA, psychology, 1973; Abilene Christian Univ, MPA, 1975; Drake University, MA, 1992. **Career:** Veterans Affairs Recruitment Office, Waco TX, Dallas TX, Lincoln NE, Knoxville IA, 1973-89; Herbert Senior High School, English instructor, 1992-; Communicator Newspaper, columnist, 1992-; Hoover High Drill Team, coach, 1994-, English Dept, chmn, 1997-. **Orgs:** Veteran's Administration, National Civil Rights Advisory Council, 1986-89, EEO Counselor trainer (Dist), Natl Trainer for Supervisor's EEO; national parliamentarian; Zeta Phi Beta Sorority, 1982-86, national vice pres, 1986-90, national director of leadership development, 1992-96; Hoover High Marketing Committee, co-chair, 1992; Performing Arts for Imani Players, Hoover High, director, 1992; SADD, Hoover High Branch, sponsor, 1992; American Institute of Parliamentarians, 1996-97; NAACP, Act So chair, 1995-97. **Honors/Awds:** Drake University, Women's Studies Graduate Student of the Year, 1992; North Texas State University, Yucca Beauty, 1971, Best Dressed, 1971, Student Senator, 1971-72; Drake University, Student Senate Committee, 1990-92, Director of Non-Traditional Graduate Students, 1991-92, Director of Multi-Cultural Theatre, 1991-92; Teacher of the Year, Nominee Hoover High. **Special Achievements:** Licensed Secondary Education Teacher, certified in English/Speech and Theatre, 1992. **Home Addr:** 6001 Creston Ave, #8, Des Moines, IA 50321-1219.

HIGH, CLAUDE, JR.
Employment corporation executive. **Personal:** Born Nov 5, 1944, Marshall, TX; son of Lolee Coursey and Claude High; married Nelda Nadine Spencer; children: Kino, Claude, III, Kimberli; married Renee Lea Watkins; children: Danielle, Marissa. **Educ:** University of Michigan, BA, 1974; Oakland University, MA, 1977. **Career:** Western Electric, installer, 1964-73; grocery store owner, 1973-74; Flint Board of Education, caseworker, 1974-75; Public Service Employment Agency, employment counselor, 1975, employment coordinator, 1975-76, executive director, 1976-81; Action Management Corporation, president/CEO, 1981-. **Orgs:** Burton Neighborhood House Service Board, secretary, 1980-84; Federal Emergency Management Agency, local board, 1991-; Metropolitan Chamber of Commerce, chairman, 1989-91, founder, 1986; Flint Chamber of Commerce, chairman, 1995-96, board member, 1987-97; Fair Bankng Coalition, 1990-97; General Motors/United Auto Workers Task Force, 1991-92; Insight Board of Directors, vice chair, 1995-; Chairs Personnel Committee, 1989-96; Sports Foundation Board, 1992; Genessee Food Bank, 1992-; Greater Flint Health Coalition, 1996-; chmn, Vines Menswear, Inc, 1996-; Genessee District Libraries Bd, 1996-; Axxon Computer Svcs, Inc, vice chmn, 1994-; Downtown Kiwanis, pres-elect; Flint Inner City Golf Club, pres, 1996. **Honors/Awds:** Warwick Hills Country Club, one of first two blacks invited to join, 1991; Detroit News Private 100, one of the fastest-growing companies in Michigan, 1990, 1991-92; State of Michigan, Outstanding Minority Entrepreneur, 1991; City of Burton, Certificate of Appreciation, 1986; Senate of Michigan, Resolution No 58, Honoring C High, 1991. **Special Achievements:** Author, Dialogue with Marijuana Users, 1980; First Black Chairman of Flint Chamber of Commerce, 1995. **Military Serv:** National Defense Cadet Corp, sgt, 1962. **Business Addr:** President/CEO, Action Management Corp., 915 S Grand Traverse, Flint, MI 48502, (810)234-2828.

HIGH, FREIDA
Artist, educator. **Personal:** Born Oct 21, 1946, Starkville, MS. **Educ:** Graceland Coll, AA 1966; No IL U, BS 1968; Univ WI, MA 1970, MFA 1971. **Career:** Univ WI, asst prof of art dept of Afro-Amer studies; artist-in-residence 1971; Contemporary African & Afro-Amer Art, rsch; Univ WI, dept studies various exhibitions 1970-; Trad African Art, major shows curator 1971, 72; Prints & Paintings Afro-Amer Art, curator 1972; WI Acad of Arts Letter Sci, one woman show latest reflections 1974; Studio Museum NY, 1976; KY State Univ, 1974. **Orgs:** Mem Nat Conf of Artists. **Honors/Awds:** WI Arts Bd Visual Arts Grant 1977; City Arts Grant Cultural Com Ofc of Mayor 1977. **Business Addr:** Univ of Wisconsin-Madison, Room 4223-Humanities, 455 N Park St, Madison, WI 53706.

HIGHSMITH, ALONZO WALTER
Professional football player. **Personal:** Born Feb 26, 1965, Bartow, FL; son of Walter Highsmith. **Educ:** Univ of Miami (FL), BS, business management, 1987. **Career:** Fullback: Houston Oilers, 1987-90, Dallas Cowboys, 1990-91, Tampa Bay Buccaneers, 1991-92; Kansas City Chiefs, 1993-. **Business Addr:** Professional Football Player, Kansas City Chiefs, 1 Arrowhead Dr, Kansas City, MO 64129.

HIGHSMITH, CARLTON L.
Package engineering company executive. **Personal:** chilDren: Alexis, Jennifer. **Educ:** University of Wisconsin, BA, 1973; University of Bridgeport, MBA, 1976; University of Connecticut, 1980; Duke University, 1992. **Career:** Rexham Corp., account manager, 1974-76; Amstar Corp., marketing manager, 1976-83; Specialized Packaging International Inc, president, chief executive officer, co-founder, 1983-. **Orgs:** American Marketing Association; American Management Association; Society of Plastic Engineers; Institute of Packaging Professionals; Paperboard Packaging Council; NAACP, life member; Urban League of Greater New Haven; New Haven Public Schools Advisory Board, cultural curriculum committee; Hamden Parks and Recreation Department, youth basketball coach. **Honors/Awds:** Black Enterprise Magazine, BE List 100, 1989-91; Canadian Packaging Association, Technical Merit Award, 1988; Gravure Technical Association of America, Gold Cylinder Award, 1989; Johnson & Johnson, Supplier of the Year, 1987. **Special Achievements:** Designer: Prevent Toothbrush carton, Johnson & Johnson; Bigelow Tea carton. **Business Addr:** President/CEO, Specialized Packaging Intl Inc, 3190 Whitney, Hamden, CT 06518.

HIGHTOWER, ANTHONY
Attorney, state representative, adjunct professor. **Personal:** Born in Atlanta, GA; son of Erie Beavers Hightower and John Vincent Hightower (deceased). **Educ:** Clark Coll, Atlanta GA, BA, 1983; Univ of Iowa, Iowa City IA, JD, 1986. **Career:** Self-employed, College Park GA, attorney, 1986-; Clark Coll, Atlanta GA, teacher, 1988-; City of College Park, College Park, GA, city councilman, 1986-90, mayor pro-tem, 1990; Clark Atlanta Univ, Atlanta, GA, adjunct prof, 1988-; State of GA, Atlanta, GA, state rep, 1991-. **Orgs:** Mem, NAACP, 1979-, Alpha Phi Alpha Frat, 1980-; bd mem, Clark Coll, 1982-83; natl bd mem, Alpha Phi Alpha Frat Inc, 1982-83; mem, State Bar of Georgia, 1986-, Natl Bar Assn, 1986-, Amer Bar Assn, 1986-, Natl League of Cities, 1986-, Natl Black Caucus of Local Elected Officials, 1986-, Georgia Municipal Assn, 1986-; bd mem, Fulton County Public Safety Training Center, 1989-. **Honors/Awds:** Selected for Membership, Alpha Kappa Mu Honor Soc, 1981, Pi Gamma Mu Intl Honor Soc, 1981; Participated and Completed Inaugural Class of South Fulton Leadership, 1987; Golden Rule Awards Panel, United Way/J C Penny, 1988; Appreciation Award, Metro Atlanta Private Indus Council, 1988; Political Service Award, Delta Sigma Theta Sorority Inc, 1988; Leadership Institute for Municipal Elected Officials, Univ of GA, 1989. **Home Addr:** 2210 Ross Ave, College Park, GA 30337.

HIGHTOWER, DENNIS FOWLER
Entertainment company executive (retired). **Personal:** Born Oct 28, 1941, Washington, DC; son of Virginia Fowler Hightower and Marvin William Hightower; married Denia Stukes; children: Dennis F Jr, Dawn D. **Educ:** Howard Univ, BS 1962; Harvard Business School, MBA 1974. **Career:** Xerox Corp Rsch & Engrg Group, mgr org plnng 1970-72; McKinsey & Co Inc, sr assoc & engagement mgr 1974-78; Gen Electric Lighting Bus Group, mgr oper plnng 1978-79; Gen Electric Mexico Lighting Affiliate, vice pres & gen mgr 1979-81; Mattel Inc, vice pres corp plnng 1981-84; Russell Reynolds Assoc Inc, exec dir 1984-86, managing dir and manager Los Angeles office 1986-87; The Walt Disney Company, pres, Europe/Middle East & Africa, 1987-95, Walt Disney Television & Telecommunications, pres, 1995-96; Harvard Bus Sch, Howard Univ, European Inst fo Bus Admin, guest lecturer, 1989-; international business consultant, currently. **Orgs:** Mem Kappa Alpha Psi 1960-, Harvard Club of NY City 1977-, Howard Univ Alumni Assoc 1978-, Bus Roundtable US Consulate Monterrey Mexico 1979-81; bd mem Monterrey Mexico Amer School Found 1979-81, Monterrey Mexico Chamber of Commerce 1980-81; board member/president, 1986-87, member, 1983-87, Harvard Bus School Assn of So CA; bd mem So CA Ctr for Nonprofit Mgmt 1984-87; mem steering comm Public/Private Partnership Prog DC Publ Sch System 1985-87; Harvard Bus Sch Alumni Council, 1986-89; mem Jonathan Club 1987-; member, Le Cercle Foch Paris, 1990-. **Honors/Awds:** COGME Fellow Harvard Business School 1972-74; Alumni Achievement Awd Howard Univ Alumni Assn So CA 1984; Disting Alumni Citation Natl Assn for Equal Opport in Higher Ed 1985; Howard Univ distinguished postgraduate achievement awd-business & admin service 1986; Top 25 Black Managers in Corporate America, Black Enterprise Magazine, 1988; Harvard Business School Alumni Achievement Award, 1992; The Edges Group Corporate Leadership Award, 1992. **Military Serv:** AUS maj 8 yrs; 2 Bronze Stars, 3 Air Medals, Joint Serv Commend Medal; 5 Army Commend Medals with "V", Purple Heart, Vietnam Honor Medal 1st Class; Ranger; Senior parachutist. **Business Phone:** (908)272-3150.

HIGHTOWER, EDWARD STEWART
Hypnotherapist. **Personal:** Born Feb 7, 1940, New York, NY; married Ola Cherry; children: Meredith, Allyson. **Educ:** Bloomfield Coll, BA 1964; Yeshiva U, MS 1971; DD, 1994. **Career:** Kings Co Hosp Ctr, exec asst, comm bd 1970-72, asso dir 1972-79; Gen Lrng Corp, reg mrkt dir 1969-70; Manpower Dev Training Prog, cnslng supr 1969; Williamsburg Adult Training Ctr, asst tchr in charge 1967-69; New England Life Insurance Co, insurance agent, 1979-81; Mutual of New York, sales mgr/agency supervisor, 1981-88; private practice, hypnotherapist, 1986-. **Orgs:** Bd of dir Commerce Labor Ind Corp of Kings 1973-80; pres Concerned Citizens for Ed of Gifted & Talented Children 1978-79; chmn City of NY Community Planning Bd #9 1979; pres Prospect Lefferts Gardens Neighborhd Assn 1979-80; asst commissioner, New York State Division of Housing, 1988-95; state committeeman, New York State Democratic Comm, 1981-86; district leader, 57th Assembly District, Kings County; bd of dirs, Vannguard Urban Improvement Assn, 1985-86; bd of mgrs, Bedford Stuyvesant YMCA; Natl Guild of Hypnotists; Alpha Phi Alpha Fraternity. **Honors/Awds:** Outstndng Young Men of Am 1970; Community Ldrs of Am 1972; Community Activist Award Nat Concl of Negro Women Flatbush Sec 1979; Outstndng Community Ldr Bedford Stuyvesant Jaycees 1980; National Guild Of Hypnotist, Member of the Year, 1989.

HIGHTOWER, HERMA J.
Federal government official. **Personal:** Born Jul 3, Mesa, AZ; daughter of Mae Kemp Harris and Oliver Harris; married Dr Claude George, Aug 3, 1984; children: Valerie, Kimberly. **Educ:** AZ State Univ, BA 1963, MA 1966, PhD 1977. **Career:** Roosevelt School Dist, classroom teacher 1963-70; AZ State Personnel Comm, training officer 1970-71; AZ Dept of Educ, educ program consultant 1971-74, dir ESEA Title I 1974-76, deputy assoc supt of schools 1976-78; Internal Revenue Servs, asst to dir 1978-79, asst dir 1980-81, asst district dir 1985-, district dir 1988-. **Orgs:** Adv bd AZ State Univ Model for Mobility of Women 1976; adhoc consultant Natl Inst of Educ, Natl Coaltion of Title I Parents, Lawyers Comm for Civil Rights Under Law 1976; Seattle Oppor Indus Ctr 1980-81; bd of dirs Seattle Urban League 1980-81; Bus Adm Tech Comm Seattle Jr Coll 1980-81; City of Phoenix Human Relations Comm 1977; bd of dirs Phoenix Urban League 1977-79; adhoc consultant Amer Educ Rsch Assn 1977; bd of dirs Phoenix Oppor Indus Ctr 1978-79; Senior Executive Assn 1980-; exec comm Resurgens Atlanta 1983-; bd of dirs YWCA 1985-; natl speaker on motivation/goalsetting; bd of dir United Way of Greater Des Moines 1988-; Rotary Club of Greater Des Moines 1988-;Nexus Breakfast Club; LINKS Inc; Delta Sigma Theta; board of directors, United Way of Central Maryland. **Honors/Awds:** First Black Female in the History of IRS to be Selected for its Executive Prog 1978; Distinguished Serv Award Natl Assn of Black Accountants 1982; Keynote speaker Governor's Salute to Black Women AZ 1986; Certificate of Merit, City of Atlanta 1988; First Black Female Director in History of IRS 1988; First Female Executive in nine-state region 1988; Partnership in Administration Award, Gen Serv Admin 1989; Outstanding Performance Rating 1990; Regional Commissioner's Leadership Award 1990; Distinguished Performance Rating 1991; Meritorious Presidential Rank Award; Coalition of 100 Black Women, Award Recipient, 1992; Outstanding Performance Rating, 1992. **Home Addr:** 3105 Edgewood Road, Ellicott City, MD 21043.

HIGHTOWER, J. HOWARD
Psychologist, educator. **Personal:** Born Feb 21; children: James Howard II, Tiffany Iwanonski, Terrance Remon, Mira Alyssa, Robert Dabon, Aarrun Cheree. **Educ:** Edward Waters Coll, BS 1969, LLD 1979; Michigan State Univ, MA 1971, PhD 1973; Nova Univ, Post-Doctoral Program in Clinical Psychoanalysis and Psychotherapy 1983-84; category I CME, American Psychiatric Assn, 1983-92, 1997-. **Career:** FL Div of Vocational Rehabilition, counselor 1970-71; MI State Univ Oseteopathic Medicine, clinical instructor in community medicine 1972-73; FL A&M Univ, grad psychology instructor 1975-76; Tri-County Community Health Bd Drug Abuse Treatment Program, chief psychologist, asst program dir 1971-74; Edward Waters Coll, chmn div of arts & sciences, psychology; FL Community College at Jacksonville, prof of psychology, sociology, and dactylology, currently; private practice, consulting psychologist; PPPAA, consultant to the Association for the Improvement of Minorities, 1993-. **Orgs:** Consulting clinical psychologist, Head Start Programs; chief clinical psychologist, dir of psychology, Youth Study Unit, Hope Haven Children's Hospital; psychology mentor, FL Community Coll at Jacksonville, 1985-; life member, NAACP; Dactylologist; "The Psychology Corner" series, The Jacksonville Advocate, and The Truth in Politics; National Council on Black American Affairs, charter member, 1990-; American Association for University Professors, 1990-; Republican Presidential Task Force, life member, 1987-. **Honors/Awds:** National Association of Negro Women, Special Award; National Association for Equal Opportunity in Higher Education, Distinguished Alumni Citation of the Year, 1986. **Special Achievements:** Author: Conflict Resolution, PPPAA, 1980-85, 1991 (1997-98 edition in process), Copley Publishing Group-MA, 1985, reprinted, 1991; Famanotophobia, in which a new type of phobia is isolated, NY Vintage Press Inc, 1987; received 3rd Dan degree Black Belt in Karate,"The Force of the Family," "UPICUDO", a mixture of Chinese Kenpo, Tae Kwon Do, Shotokon, and Goju, 1992-94; received first Dan Black Belt several years ago in "Hybrid-Snake-Mixed-Open Style"; designed/created, signs language laboratory for Florida Community College at Jacksonville, Downtown Campus: Multidimensional Sign Language Lab, 1992; "Creating Wholistic-Rapport for Enhancing Effective-Realistic Advisement," Edward Waters College Press, 1992; Consultant-Honorary Mem, AIM-IRS Assn for the Improvement of Minorities employed by the Internal Revenue Service; Natl "Motivational Speaker-Workshop Consultant;" Distinguished Faculty Award, 1995; Distinguished Professor; "Wholistic-Upicudo" training manual, 1995. **Military Serv:** USMC. **Business Addr:** Professor of Psychology, Sociology, and Dactylology, Florida Community College-Downtown, 101 W State St, Office A-2042, Jacksonville, FL 32202.

HIGHTOWER, MICHAEL
County official. **Personal:** Born in College Park, GA; son of Erie Hightower. **Educ:** Clark Coll Atlanta, BA Music 1979. **Career:** GA State Univ Atlanta, admin coord, asst to dir of physical plant oper 1979-; City Hall College Park, councilman, mayor pro-tem; Fulton County Commission, commissioner, currently. **Orgs:** mem Friendship Baptist Church 1965-, Eta Lambda Chap Alpha Phi Alpha 1979-, GA Municipal Assoc 1980-, Natl League of Cities 1980-; mem South Fulton Chamber of Commerce 1980-, Airport Intl Jaycees 1982-, mem bd of dir Jesse Draper Boy's Club 1983-; member, National Assn of Counties, pres currently; member, Fulton County Building Authority; member, Fulton County Water Resources Board; member, Grady Memorial Hospital Oversight Committee. **Honors/Awds:** Outstanding Serv to HS & Comm Atlanta Airport Rotary Club 1975; Man of the Year Award Alpha Phi Alpha 1979; Outstanding Young Men of Amer Award Amer Jaycees 1980, 1983; Disting Alumni Award from Men of Clark Coll 1980; Outstanding Young People of Atlanta Award 1980; Disting Comm Serv Award Woodward Acad 1981; Disting Comm Serv Award Friendship Baptist Church 1983; Awd of Appreciation Flipper Temple AME Church 1984; Professional Man of the Year, 1989. **Business Addr:** Commissioner, Attn: Joyce Larkin, Fulton County Commission, 141 Pryor St SW, 10th Floor, Atlanta, GA 30303.

HIGHTOWER, STEPHEN LAMAR
Business executive. **Personal:** Born Sep 21, 1956, Middletown, OH; son of Elsie Hightower and Yudell Hightower; married Brenda Ware Hightower, Oct 3, 1992; children: Quincy, Stephanie, Sabrina, Stephen Jr. **Educ:** Wright State University, 1978. **Career:** Prudential Environmental Technologies, Inc, president; Hi-Mark Corp., president; Hightowers Petroleum Co., president; Landmark Building Services, Inc, president, currently. **Orgs:** Black Male Coalition, 1992; SOS Committee, Inc, president, 1992; Minority Supplier Development Council, 1992; ABC Ohio Contractors, 1992; Junior Achievement, board of directors, 1992; United Missionary Baptist Church, 1992. **Honors/Awds:** Toastmaster International, 1986; State of Ohio, Top 100 Minority Business, 1981; Snyder Realtors, Salesman of the Year, 1979; Ceco Bldg, Largest Bldg Sold Midwest Region, 1989.

HIGHTOWER, WILLAR H., JR.
Company executive, engineer. **Personal:** Born Aug 8, 1943, Greenville, SC; married Josephine Holman; children: Willa J, Terri T. **Educ:** NC Coll at Durham, mathematics, 1964-65; SC State University, BS Math 1964. **Career:** US Army, battery commander 1965-67; USAR Defense Personnel Support Ctr, logistician 1981-89; WSRC, computer pgrmr 1967-79, buyer 1979-89, asst purchasing agent 1980-89. **Orgs:** Mem Augusta Area Purchasing Manag Assoc 80-, Amer Mgmnt Assoc 1980-, Reserve Officers Assoc 1968-; NAACP 1967-; brd of dir Aiken Chapter Am Red Cross1984-; city cnclmn City of Aiken, SC 1981-86; Aiken County Councilman 1986-. **Honors/Awds:** Presented Key to the City of Aiken 1986. **Military Serv:** US Army, LTC, 24 yrs; USAR 15 yr medal 1980; 81st ARCOM Cert of Achvmnt 1979. **Home Addr:** 682 Edrie St, Aiken, SC 29801, (803)648-3020. **Business Addr:** Lessons Learned Engineer, Westinghouse, Savannah River Company, Aiken, SC 29808, (803)952-7659.

HIGHTS, WILLIAM E.
Clergyman. **Personal:** Born in Cape Girardeau, MO; married; children: Dana Marie, Phyllis Ann. **Educ:** St Louis U; Wstrn Bapt Sem. **Career:** John Missionary Bapt Ch Sacramento, pastor 1962-; Third Bapt Ch San Francisco, asst to Dr FD Haynes 1959-62. **Orgs:** Moderator N Dist Bapt Assn; chmn Civic Com Sacramento Bapt Minister Conf; pres CA St Bapt Congress of Christian Ed; mem adv bd to supt of Sacramento Unified Sch Sys; pres Ch Srv Bureau of Sacramento; bd dirs Nat Bapt Conv USA Inc Off. **Business Addr:** 2130 4 St, Sacramento, CA 95818.

HILDEBRAND, RICHARD ALLEN
Clergyman. **Personal:** Born Feb 1, 1916, Winnsboro, SC; married Anna Beatrix Lewis; children: Camille Ylonne. **Educ:** Allen Univ, BA 1938; Payne Theol School, BD 1941; Boston Univ, STM 1948; Wilberforce Univ, DD 1953; Morris Brown Coll, LLD (hon) 1975. **Career:** African Meth Episcopal Church, ordained to ministry 1936, elected bishop 1972; Columbia & Sumter SC, pastor 1936-38; Jamestown & Akron OH, pastor 1938-45; Providence, pastor 1945-48; Bayshore NY, pastor 1948-49; Wilmington DE, pastor 1949-50; Bethel AME Church NYC, pastor 1950-65; Bridge St AME Church Brooklyn, pastor 1965-72; AME Church GA 6th Dist, presiding bishop 1972-76, 1st Dist Philadelphia 1976-. **Orgs:** Pres Manhattan Dirs Protestant Council 1956-60; chmn Chs for New Harlem Hosp New York City 1957-65; mem, pres New York City br 1962-64 NAACP; mem Alpha Phi Alpha, Masons;pres Atlanta N GA Conf AME Fed Credit Union 1972-76; chmn, bd dirs Morris Brown Coll, Turner Sem Interdenominational Theol Ctr 1972-76, Payne TheolSem 1976-; pres Council of Bishops AME Church 1977-.

HILDRETH, GLADYS JOHNSON
Educator, educational administrator. **Personal:** Born Oct 15, 1933, Columbia, MS; married Dr Eddie Hildreth Jr; children: Bertina, Dwayne, Kathleen, Karen. **Educ:** So Univ Baton Rouge LA, BS 1953; Univ of WI Madison, MS 1955; MI State Univ East Lansing, PhD 1973. **Career:** So Univ, assoc prof 1960-68; LA State Univ School of Human Ecology, prof family studies 1974-90; Texas Woman's Univ, Denton, TX, professor, 1990-. **Orgs:** Chmn jr div adv council LA State Univ 1979-80; state chmn aging serv LA Home Econ Assn 1978-80; consult Natl Assn for Ed of Young Children 1974-; Ctr for the Family Amer Home Econ Assn 1977-79; Delta Sigma Theta 1970-; mem Phi Upsilon Omicron So Univ Home Econ, Omicron Nu MI State Univ Human Ecology; National Council on Family Relations; Sect, TCFR; Texas Consortium On Geriatric Education. **Honors/Awds:** Grad School Fellowship MI State Univ Human Ecology 1970; Thelma Porter Fellowship MI State Univ

Human Ecology 1970; Recipient of the LA Home Econ Assn Disting District & State Serv Awd 1986; Nominated for Amer Council on Educ Fellow; Distinguished Faculty Fellowship Award, Louisiana State University; Distinguished Service Award, Southeast Council on Family Relations; Natl Council of Family Rel, Marie Peters Ethnic Minority Award. **Business Addr:** Professor, Family Sciences, Texas Woman's University, Denton, TX 76205, (940)898-2694.

HILL, ALFRED
Business executive (retired), realtor. **Personal:** Born Dec 25, 1925, Atlanta; son of Fannie M Hill and Alfred Hill; divorced; children: Alfred III, Gordon, Stanford. **Educ:** Howard U, BA 1952. **Career:** Newark Lamp Plant, empl specl; Equal Oppty & Urban Affairs & Hourly Skill Tng, Lighting Bus Grp, mgr; Euclid Lamp Plant Gen El Co, mgr empl & union rel 1985 (retired); Smythe, Cramer Co, Cleveland, OH, realtor, currently. **Orgs:** Mem Nat Urban Affairs Cncl 1972-; Corp Minority Panel; adv Lamp Bus Div Minority Panel; mem Hum Rels Cncl Cleveland; chmn United Torch-Affirm Act Com; Community Ldrshp Com; pres, bd mem Collinwood Community Srv Ctr; bd mem Karamu House Cleveland Area Cncl Hum Rels; mem Resrch & Dev Com Cleveland Urban League. **Honors/Awds:** Frontiersman Community Srv Award 1960. **Military Serv:** USAF, Captain, 1952-69. **Business Addr:** Realtor, Smythe, Cramer Co, 12435 Cedar Rd, Cleveland, OH 44106.

HILL, ANDREW WILLIAM
Pianist, composer. **Personal:** Born Jun 30, 1937, Chicago, IL; married Laverne Miller. **Career:** Organist, composer 1940-; recorded series of 10 released record LPS 1963-; records, "Point of Departure" 1964, "Judgement" 1964, "Black Fire" 1963; Roland Kirk Quartet, 1962; Lighthouse Grp, pianist 1962; Dianh Washington, accompanist 1954; compositions include, Symetry, Black Monday, Le Groits, Duplicity, Alfred, Reconciliation, Legacy, Promonition, Moon Child, Ghetto Lights, Violence, Hope, Illusion, Golden Spook 1970. **Orgs:** Bd dir, Fdr, Andrew Hill & Asso Inc 1966-. **Honors/Awds:** Nat Endowment Art Grantee 1971, 1974, 1976, 1979; Smithsonian Inst Prfmng Artist's Fellow 1972-76; NY St Cncl of the Arts Grantee 1974-75; Schlrshp New Coll of CA San Francisco 1979-80.

HILL, ANITA FAYE
Educator, attorney. **Personal:** Born 1956, Morris, OK; daughter of Erma Hill and Albert Hill. **Educ:** Oklahoma State University, psychology, BS (with honors), 1977; Yale University Law School. **Career:** Washington DC, law firm, 1980-81; US Dept of Education, asst to Clarence Thomas, 1981-82; US Equal Employment Opportunity Commission, special asst to Clarence Thomas, 1982-83; Oral Roberts University, law prof, beginning 1983; University of Oklahoma, College of Law, commercial law professor, 1986-96. **Orgs:** Antioch Baptist Church. **Honors/Awds:** Glamour Magazine, Woman of the Year, 1991. **Special Achievements:** Ms magazine, wrote article, "The Nature of the Beast," concerning sexual harassment, p 32, Jan-Feb 1992; speaker at conference on "Race, Gender and Power in America," Georgetown University Law School, Oct 1992; appeared on The Today Show, Oct 1992; speaker at conference at University of Pennsylvania, April 1992; kick off speaker at conference at Hunter College; appeared on 60 Minutes, Feb 1992; speaker at University of New Mexico; speaker at Rutgers University for women lawmakers' conference. **Business Addr:** Professor, College of Law, University of Oklahoma, 300 Timberdale Rd, Norman, OK 73019-0001, (405)325-4726.

HILL, ANITA JUNE
Company executive. **Personal:** Born Jul 25, 1946, Stuebenville, OH; daughter of Elmira Pratt Hill and Patrick Hill; divorced; children: Della Pulliam, Delbert Pulliam II, Todd Pulliam, Thomas Pulliam. **Educ:** Wayne State University, 1986-87. **Career:** Decal Holder Enterprises, president, 1987-. **Orgs:** High Museum of Art, docent, 1990-92; Market Place of Ideas for 1993 National Docent Symposium Steering Committee, co-chair, 1992-; March of Dimes, publicity committee for the 4th Annual Fashion Extravaganza co-chair; Georgia Minority Supplier Development Council, MBEIC Committee, 1991-92; Houston Business Council, 1991-92. **Honors/Awds:** Emmanuel Temple Churches, ministerial ordination, 1990; True Churches of the Apostolic Faith, national missionary chairperson, 1975-80. **Special Achievements:** Hooper Elementary School, Career Day speaker, 1991-92. **Business Phone:** (404)723-9532.

HILL, ANNETTE TILLMAN
Educator (retired). **Personal:** Born Nov 9, 1937, Copiah County, MS; daughter of Martha Coleman Tillman and Fayette Tillman; divorced; children: Gerri Lavonne Hill-Chance. **Educ:** Tougaloo Coll, BS 1956; Chicago State Univ, MS Educ 1971; attended, Jackson State Univ, Univ of MS. **Career:** Parrish High School, science/math teacher 1956-60; Chicago Public Schools, science teacher 1960-69; Wendell Phillips High School Chicago, counselor 1969-71; Jackson State Univ, counselor 1971-81; Hazlehurst High School, counselor, beginning 1982. **Orgs:** Mem MS Counselors Assn, Amer Assn of Counseling & Devel, Multicultural Assn Counseling & Devel, Hazlehurst Public Schools PTA; bd of dirs Central MS Chap Amer Red Cross 1978-81, 1985-88; adv commn mem Juvenile Justice State of MS 1981-89; chairperson Emergency Food & Shelter Adv Comm Copiah Co 1985-; vp Hazlehurst Branch NAACP. **Honors/Awds:** Certificate of Achievement Life Career Develop System 1976; Certificate of Appreciation Natl Foundation for Cancer Rsch 1982; Certificates of Appreciation for Healthfest Central MS Chap Amer Red Cross 1982, 1983; Natl Appreciation Awd Soc of Distinguished HS Students 1983. **Home Addr:** 321 N Massengill St, Hazlehurst, MS 39083.

HILL, ARTHUR BURIT
Transportation company executive (retired). **Personal:** Born Apr 2, 1922, New York, NY; son of Victoria Hill and Alton Hill; married Patricia Ruth Smith, Aug 5, 1956; children: Arthur Jr, Ernest, Victoria, Joanne. **Educ:** City Univ, NY, MPA 1973, BS 1966; City Univ NY MPA l973. **Career:** New York Police Dept, patrolman 1946, sgt 1956, lt 1960, capt 1964, deputy insp 1967, inspector 1969, asst chief 1971-73; United Parcel Serv, mgmt trainee 1973, vice pres public affairs 1975, vice pres 1973-92. **Orgs:** Life mem NAACP; dir Guy R Brewer Dem Club 1981-; Kappa Alpha Psi; Sigma Pi Phi-Alpha Sigma Boule; Guardsman; 32 degree Mason; New York City Municiple Water Finance Authority, director; North General Hospital in New York City, trustee; Apollo Theater Foundation, Harlem, New York, director. **Honors/Awds:** Comdtn Honor Legion, NYPD, 1950; lay reader NY Diocese Epsicopal Church, 1960-; William A Dawson Award Congressional Black Caucus, 1988; United Hospital Fund, Trustee of the Year Awd, 1993. **Military Serv:** AUS corpl 1942-46. **Home Addr:** 187-10 Ilion Ave, Jamaica, NY 11412.

HILL, AVERY
Optometrist. **Personal:** Born May 24, 1924, Evanston, IL; son of Julia Wesley Avery Hill and William Hill, Sr.; married Eleanor; children: Colette. **Educ:** IL Coll of Optometry, D Optometry 1948. **Career:** IL Visions Serv Inc Chicago, dir; staff mem Daniel Hale Williams Neighborhood Health Ctr 1972, Near N Childrens Ctr of Childrens Mem Hosp; Optometrist-consultant St. Mary of Nazareth Hosp Chicago. **Orgs:** Mem Optometric Assn, IL Optometric Assn, Central City Optometric Assn; mem Evanston Twp HS lay adv comm 1964-67, bd educ 1969-78, pres pro-temp 1972; Evanston Human Relations Commr 1968; steering comm Evanston N Suburban Urban League; bd of trustees Ebenezer Primm Towers; mem NAACP, Norshore Twelve Inc; trustee Garrett Theo Sem; family counseling serv of Evanston; bd of trustees Abbeville Assn of Evanston. **Honors/Awds:** NAACP Service to the Community Awd. **Military Serv:** USAF 1943-45; ETO Decoration Bronze Star with Oak Leaf Cluster. **Business Addr:** Optometrist, 5650 W Madison, Chicago, IL 60644.

HILL, BARBARA ANN
Educator. **Personal:** Born Mar 31, 1950, Brooklyn, NY; daughter of Delphine Chaplin Floyd and Robert Floyd; married Larry Hill; children: Vaughn, Kinshasa. **Educ:** Long Island Univ CW Post Ctr, BS 1974, MS 1984. **Career:** Howard T Herber Middle School, educator; parent involvement Coordinator, Tyrrell County Public Schools, Columbia NC, currently. **Orgs:** Mem NY State Public High Sch Athletic Assn 1976-92; founder, advisor Malverne Girls Varsity Club 1976-92; track chairperson Nassau Co HS Girls Track 1978-84; Nassau Girls Athletic Rep 1979-92; Black Educator Coalition of Malverne HS 1984-92; founder/advisor Carter G Woodson Black Studies Club 1984-92; sec Nassau Co Volleyball Coaches Assoc 1985-87; workshop coordinator Hempstead Pre-K Reading Workshop 1984-91; pres Ludlum PTA 1985-89; corresponding secretary, Nassau County High School Athletic Association, 1990-92; representative, Nassau County High School Athletic Council, 1987-92; treasurer, PTA, 1990-; Key Women of America Inc, 1986-92, vice pres, 1990-92; treasurer, Ludlum PTA, 1989-92; president, Alberta B Gray-Schultz Middle School PTA, 1991-92; Tyrell Elementary School Parents Planning Committee, 1992-93; Community Voices, 1992-; Emergency Food & Shelter Bd, chair, Church Road Emergency Food Closet, Food Pantry; Black History Club Program, Columbia HS & MS, founder, advisor; NC Breast Cancer Screening Program, secretary, Tyrrell County Lay Community Advisory Bd. **Honors/Awds:** Coach of the Year 1984, 5 time coach County Championship Track & Field Girls 1976-79, 1984; eight times Girls Track & Field Divisional & Conference Champions; Nassau County Class C Volleyball Champions, 1992; NY State Volleyball 1 Championship Sportsmanship Award, 1992; NC Governor's Volunteer Award for Children, 1994; Tobacco Belt Conference, Volleyball Coach of the Year, 1996; Tobacco Belt Conference Tournament, Volleyball Tournament Champions, 1996; Volleyball Coach of the Year, 1997. **Business Addr:** Parent Involvement Coordinator, Tyrrell County Public School, Elementary School Road, Box 157, Columbia, NC 27925.

HILL, BENNETT DAVID
Educator, clergyman. **Personal:** Born Sep 27, 1934, Baltimore, MD; son of Muriel Clarke Hill and David B Hill. **Educ:** Princeton Univ, AB 1956; Harvard Univ, AM 1958; Princeton Univ, PhD 1963. **Career:** University of Western Ontario, London CN, assistant professor, 1962-64; University of Illinois, Urbana, assistant and associate professor, 1964-78, dept of history, professor, 1975-81, chm, 1978-81; Benedictine Monk of St Anselm's Abbey, Washington District of Columbia, 1980-; University of Maryland, visiting professor, 1984-87; Roman Catholic priest ordained, 1985; Georgetown University visiting professor, 1987-. **Orgs:** Consltnt Natl Endowmnt for the Humanities 1978, Woodrow Wilson Natl Fdtn 1982; bd of dir American Benedictine Review; Princeton Club of Washington. **Honors/Awds:** Flw Amer Cncl of Learned Soc 1970-71. **Special Achievements:** Author, English Cistercian Monasteries and Their Patrons in the Twelfth Century, 1970; Church and State in the Middle Ages, 1970; co-author, A History of Western Society, 1979, 5th edition, 1990, A History of World Societies, 4th edition, 1991. **Home Addr:** 2252 Turk Rd, Doylestown, PA 18901.

HILL, BETTY J.
Manpower programs director. **Personal:** Born Aug 11, 1948; married. **Educ:** Los Angeles Harbor Jr Coll, AA 1970; California State Univ, BA 1973. **Career:** Compton Urban Corps, counselor 1973-74, chief counselor 1974-75; City of Compton Urban Corps, asst dir 1975-76, urban corps dir 1976-78; City of Compton, manpower program chief 1978-80, manpower programs dir 1980-. **Orgs:** Mem Employment Training Adv Comm, Natl Assoc for Female Execs, Veterans Comm, Compton NAACP, Prime Agent Council, Los Angeles Regional Coalition of Serv Providers, Human Resources Develop Comm, United Way Southeast Agenxcy Exec Comm, Natl Forum for Black Public Administrators, Young Men's Christian Assoc. **Business Addr:** Manpower Program Dir, City of Compton, 205 So Willowbrook Ave, Compton, CA 90220.

HILL, BILLY
Athletic trainer. **Personal:** Born Nov 10, 1947, Memphis, TN; son of Florence Nevilles and Dave Hill; married Emery Somerset (divorced 1981); children: Dale, Lesley, Brian, Enshane. **Educ:** Tennessee State University, 1965-68; The Ohio State University, BS, 1973. **Career:** The Ohio State University, head trainer, 1971-. **Orgs:** Upper Arlington Rotary Club, 1979-; Merry Makers Club Inc, 1979-; Omega Psi Phi, 1966-; Natl Athletic Trainers Assn, 1971-; district representative, Minority Trainers Assn, 1984-; president elect, Ohio Trainers Assn, 1990-92. **Honors/Awds:** Billy Hill Athletic Trainers Scholarship, Johnson & Johnson, 1990-; Trainer of Year Award (Collegiate), Ohio Trainers Association, 1988; Outstanding Staff Award, Black Greek Council, Ohio State Univ, 1990; Head Track Trainer, Olympic Games, Los Angeles, CA, 1984; Board of Directors, Martin Luther King Center, 1990-93; Presenter, Lecturer, National Trainers Convention, Indianapolis, 1990. **Military Serv:** US Army, spec 5, 1968-71; Medical Corpsman Achievement Award, Vietnam, 1968. **Home Addr:** 2500 Maplewood Dr, Columbus, OH 43231. **Business Addr:** Head Athletic Trainer, Ohio State University, 410 Woody Hayes Dr, Columbus, OH 43085.

HILL, BOBBY
County official. **Career:** Macomb County, board of commissioners, currently. **Business Addr:** Board of Commissioners, Dist 17, Macomb County, 2nd Floor, Court Bldg., Mount Clemens, MI 48043, (810)469-5125.

HILL, BRUCE EDWARD
Professional football player. **Personal:** Born Feb 29, 1964, Fort Dix, NJ. **Educ:** Arizona State Univ, attended. **Career:** Tampa Bay Buccaneers, wide receiver, 1987-. **Business Addr:** Professional Football Player, Tampa Bay Buccaneers, One Buccaneer Pl, Tampa, FL 33607-5797.

HILL, CALVIN
Businessman, consultant. **Personal:** Born Jan 2, 1947, Baltimore, MD; son of Elizabeth Hill and Henry Hill; married Janet McDonald; children: Grant. **Educ:** Yale U, BA 1969; SMU, Perkins School of Theology, 1969-71. **Career:** Dallas Cowboys, running back 1969-74; Hawaiians WFL, running back 1975; Washington Redskins, 1976-78; Cleveland Browns, 1978-81; Baltimore Orioles, bd of dirs. **Orgs:** Consultant NFL Cleveland Browns; Member, Yale Club of Washington, DC; exec board, Yale Development Board; Yale University Council, 1982-86; advisory board, Rand Corporation Drug Policy Research Center. **Honors/Awds:** NFL Champ Games 1970-71; Pro Bowl NFL All-Star Game 1969, 1972, 1973-74; named NFL Rookie of Yr 1969; Sporting News NFL Estrn Conf All-Star Team 1969; All NFL (Pro Football Writers Am) 1969, 1973; 1000 Yd Club 1972; Sporting News NFC All-Star 1973; mem Maryland Hall of Fame. **Business Addr:** Consultant, Dallas Cowboys, 1 Cowboys Pkwy, Irving, TX 75063.

HILL, CLARA GRANT
Educator. **Personal:** Born Oct 5, 1928, Hugo, OK. **Educ:** Philander Smith Coll, BA 1952; Memphis St U, MA. **Career:** Longview Elementary School, teacher 1985, chairperson, sixth grade teachers 1963-77; Memphis Educ Assn, faculty rep 1963-; Professional Growth Com, chairperson 1973-; acting prin 1972-77. **Orgs:** Com mem Curriculum Dev Elem Ed, apptd by St Commr of Ed 1977; mem Memphis Ed Assn; W TN Ed Assn; TN Ed Assn; mem Nat Ed Assn; mem, exec bd MEA 1973-76; chpsn, mbshp com MEA 1974-76; chpsn Status of Women in Ed MEA 1977; chpsn Screening Com Hiring Staff MEA 1977-78; chpsn Black Caucus MEA 1977; mem Credntls Com TEA 1976; mem Resltns Com TEA 1977; pres Dept of

Clsrm Tchrs TEA 1976-78; NAACP; exec bd mem, chpsn Xmas Seals 1975-76; basileus Sigma Gamma Rho Sor 1973-75; chpsn Outstnd Sigma Woman of Yr 1973-74; mem Mbrshp Com Reg & Nat Chpts of Sor; mem YWCA; pres Optimistic Chrtbl Soc Club 1969; mem Philander Smith Alum Assn; chpsn Constitution Com 1976; mem, pres Les Demonselles Brdg Club 1972; comm wkr Heart Fund; Cancer Fund; Birth Defects; tchr Sun Sch 1964-;pres Usher Bd 1972; dir Chrian Ed 1966-67; adv Jr Usher Bd 1970-; chpsn Birthmonth Flwshp 1973; mem Ada Cir of Missionary Soc; pres Dept of Clsrm Tchr TEA 1977. **Honors/Awds:** Five Outstndng Srv Awards MEA 1974-77; Ldrshp Training Award NEA 1976; 2 Comm Srv Awards, US Congressman Harold Ford TN 1976-77. **Business Addr:** 1085 Stafford Ave, Memphis, TN 38106.

HILL, CURTIS T., SR.
Insurance agent, educator. **Personal:** Born Jun 30, 1929, Vernon, OK; son of Virginia Hill and C L Hill; married; children: Sonya L, Curtis. **Educ:** BS 1950; Dental Tech 1953; Adviced Life Ins 1971. **Career:** State Farm Ins Co, agent; Jr HS, tchr. **Orgs:** Mem Natl Assc of Life Underwriters; vice pres Elkhart Co Life Underwriters; pres NAACP Chpt; pres Elkhart Urban League; bd dir Amer Cancer Soc; mem Natl Black Caucus of Sch Bd Mem; former life mem Chr of Elkhart NAACP; former bd mem Jaycees; former mem Elkhart Sch Bd. **Honors/Awds:** Rec Outst Historian Award IN Jaycees 1960; Award for Outst Contrib to Educ IN Sch Bd Assc 1974; mem Life Ins Millionaires Club 1972; first black candidate for Mayor of Elkhart. **Military Serv:** US Army Reserve, colonel (retired). **Business Addr:** Agent, State Farm Insurance Co, 2408 S Nappanee St, Elkhart, IN 46514.

HILL, CYNTHIA D.
Attorney. **Personal:** Born Feb 5, 1952, Bethesda, MD; daughter of Mamie L Landrum Hill (deceased) and Melvin Leroy Hill. **Educ:** Wellesley Coll, BA 1974; Georgetown Univ Law Ctr, JD 1977. **Career:** DC Office of Consumer Protection, law clerk to admin law judge 1977-78; League of Women Voters Educ Fund, staff atty litigation dept 1978-84, acting dir litigation dept 1984-85, dir of election serv and litigation 1985-90; District of Columbia Bar, asst executive dir for programs 1990-. **Orgs:** Mem Women's Div Natl Bar Assoc 1977-, Washington Bar Assoc 1978-, Women's Bar Assoc of the District of Columbia 1979-, Washington Council of Lawyers 1986-; bd of dirs, Metro Washington Planning and Housing Assn, 1980-89; Amer Society of Assn Execs, 1990-; Natl Assn of Bar Execs, 1990-; Assn for Continuing Legal Education, 1991-. **Honors/Awds:** Phi Beta Kappa. **Business Addr:** Assistant Executive Director for Programs, District of Columbia Bar, 1250 H St, NW, 6th Fl, Washington, DC 20005-5937.

HILL, DEBORAH
Personnel administrator. **Personal:** Born Oct 15, 1944, Long Beach, CA; daughter of Eva Hill and David Hill. **Educ:** CA State Coll Long Beach, BA 1967; Western State Univ Coll of Law, JD 1975. **Career:** Shell Oil Co, analyst 1968-76, sr emp rel analyst 1976-78, employee rel rep 1978-82, employee rel assoc 1982-85, service manager 1985-86, sr employee relations rep, beginning 1986, human resources mgr, currently. **Orgs:** Chmn personnel comm Alpha Kappa Alpha Sor Inc 1982-86; historian Intl Assn for Personnel Women 1983; Top Ladies of Distinction 1980-; trustee bd Wesley Chapel AME Church 1983-; Links, Inc 1986-; Leadership Long Beach, Class of 1990; bd of dir, NCCJ, 1990-; bd of dir, CRI, 1990-; bd of dirs, United Way, 1991-; trust fund commission mem, State Bar of CA, 1991; bd of dirs, Bouggess White Scholar ship Fund, 1990-91.

HILL, DEIRDRE HUGHES
Attorney. **Personal:** married. **Educ:** Loyola Law School, JD, 1985. **Career:** Los Angeles Police Commission, pres, 1993-96; Saltzburg, Ray & Bergman, attorney. **Business Addr:** Sr Associate Attorney, Saltzburg, Ray & Bergman, 10960 Wilshire, 10th Fl, Los Angeles, CA 90024.

HILL, DENNIS ODELL
Educator, college basketball coach. **Personal:** Born Nov 25, 1953, Kansas City, KS; son of Yvonne Marie Bennett and James Buster Hill; married Kathryn Kinnear Hill, Sep 4, 1982; children: Erica Nicole, Anthony Jerome. **Educ:** Southwest Missouri State Univ, Springfield, MO, BS, 1976. **Career:** Southwest Missouri State, Springfield, MO, asst basketball coach, 1978-89; Pittsburg State University, Pittsburg, KS, head basketball coach, 1989-. **Honors/Awds:** NAACP, Distinguished Community Service Award, NAACP-Springfield Branch, 1988. **Business Addr:** Men's Basketball Coach, Pittsburg State University, 1701 S Broadway, Pittsburg, KS 66762.

HILL, DIANNE
Educator. **Personal:** Born Mar 6, 1955, Newark, NJ; children: Tania Regina, Gary Robert. **Educ:** Caldwell Coll, BA Elem Educ 1977; Rutgers Univ, Certificate Early Childhood 1982; Jersey City State Coll, MA Spec Educ 1985. **Career:** Newark Bd of Educ, teacher 1976-77; Friendly Fuld Headstart Prog, teacher/policy comm mem 1977-80; Caldwell Coll, dir educ oppor fund prog 1980-. **Orgs:** Public relations officer NJ Educ Oppor Fund Professional Assoc 1982-86; mem policy council Friendly Fuld Headstart 1983-85; bd mem Irvington Comm Develop 1985-86, Women's Employment network; private sector rep Assoc of Independent Colls & Univs in NJ. **Honors/Awds:** Outstanding Black Women of the Year 1985; Outstanding Alumnae Awd Caldwell Coll BSCU & Faculty 1985. **Business Addr:** Dir, Educational Oppor Fund Prog, Ryerson Ave, Caldwell, NJ 07006.

HILL, E.C.
Professional basketball player. **Personal:** Born Jul 6, 1971. **Educ:** Northern Illinois Univ. **Career:** New England Blizzard, guard, 1996-. **Business Addr:** Professional Basketball Player, New England Blizzard, Hartford/Springfield Arena, 179 Allyn St, Ste 403, Hartford, CT 06103, (860)522-4667.

HILL, ELLYN ASKINS
Librarian (retired). **Personal:** Born Mar 13, 1907, Chicago, IL; daughter of Frances Askins and Samuel Askins; married Roosevelt T. **Educ:** Nrthwstrn U, 1925-26; Univ Chicago, 1927-28, 1936, 1940, 1955-56. **Career:** UFBL Bookstore, mgr 1975-80; Chicago Pub Lib, libn (ret) 1924-70 Johnson Pub Co, asst libn 1972. **Orgs:** Mem Local 1215 AFL-CIO; NAACP; Assn Study Afro-Am & Hist; Art Inst; ALA; Coretta Scott King Awards Com; Urban Leag exec bd YWCA; Friends of Chicago Pub Lib; life mem Universal Found for Better Living Inc; Christ Universal Temple; staff assn Chicago Pub Lib. **Honors/Awds:** Srv Award YWCA 1957-58; ofcl del ALA 1945, 1953, 1969; ofcl del Univ WI Lib Conf 1967. **Home Addr:** 11901 Ashland Ave, Chicago, IL 60643.

HILL, ERIC
Professional football player. **Personal:** Born Nov 14, 1966, Galveston, TX; children: Erica, Arielle. **Educ:** Louisiana State Univ, attended. **Career:** Phoenix Cardinals, linebacker, 1989-93; Arizona Cardinals, 1994-. **Business Addr:** Professional Football Player, Arizona Cardinals, 8701 S Hardy, Tempe, AZ 85284, (602)379-0101.

HILL, ERROL GASTON
Educator (retired). **Personal:** Born Aug 5, 1921; son of Lydia Caroline Gibson Hill and Thomas David Hill; married Grace Hope; children: Da'aga, Claudia, Melina, Aaron. **Educ:** Yale Coll, BA (Summa Cum Laude) 1962; Yale School of Drama, MFA 1962, DFA 1966; Royal Acad Dramatic Art, London, graduate diploma 1951; London Univ, Diploma in Drama 1951. **Career:** Author, director, playwright, theatre historian; US Engineers Trinidad, 1941-43; BBC London, announcer & actor 1951-52; Univ of WI, creative arts tutor 1953-58, 1962-65; Univ Ibadan Nigeria, tch fellow 1965-67; Richmond Coll, CUNY, assoc prof drama 1967-68; Dartmouth Coll, prof of drama and play director 1968-89. **Orgs:** Consult Natl Humanities Faculty 1971-80; Natl Assn Schools of Theatre; Amer Society for Theatre Research; Amer Theatre and Drama Society; Intl Federation for Theatre Research. **Honors/Awds:** Brit Coun Scholarship 1949-51; Rockefeller Found Fellow 1958-60; Theatre Guild Amer Fellow 1961-62; Gold Med Govt Trinidad & Tobago 1973; publs, Collections of Caribbean Plays 1958-79, The Trinidad Carnival 1972, The Theatre of Black Amers 1980, 1987, Shakespeare in Sable, A History of Black Shakespearean Actors 1984; Plays on Black Heroes 1989; Bertram Joseph Award for Shakespeare Studies 1985; Bernard Hewitt Award for Outstanding Research in Theatre History 1985; Guggenheim Fellowship 1985-86; Fulbright Fellowship 1988; Robert Lewis Medal for Lifetime Achievement in Theatre Research, 1996; National Endowment for the Humanities, Fellowship, 1997. **Home Addr:** 3 Haskins Rd, Hanover, NH 03755.

HILL, ESTHER P.
Art educator. **Personal:** Born Jun 7, 1922, Rocky Mount, NC; married Samuel W; children: Samesta Elaine. **Educ:** Columbia U, BS 1943, MA 1954; NY U, Matriculated in PhD 1962. **Career:** Univ NC Charlotte, asso prof art 1972-; Charlotte-Mecklenburg Schs, art tchr, asst supr, cons, prog asst 1951-72; professional exhibitor of prints, jewelry, paintings; S Ed Fund, text & earth paintings in Invitatinl Black Artists Exhibition 1985. **Orgs:** Chmn div higher ed, mem NC Art Ed Assn 1979-81; reg rep NAEA Com Minority Concerns 1978-81; life mem NEA; Am Assn Univ Women; Phi Delta Kappa; Alpha Kappa Alpha Sor; The Moles; 1st Bapt Ch; black adv bd WBT; natl pres Guys & Dolls Inc; bd trustees Mint Museum of Art. **Honors/Awds:** Srv Award Plaque Guys & Dolls 19698 1975; nominee Salute to Women Who Work 1969; Nc del S Arts Fed Conf Atlanta 1979; recip Doctoral Award NC Bd of Govs 1979-80; Afro-Am Cultural Ctr, Spirit Sq Honore for Contributions in Arts in the Comm, Gala Celebration 1981. **Business Addr:** President, Pinochle Bugs Social & Civic Club, 1624 Madison Avenue, Charlotte, NC 28216.

HILL, FANNIE E.
Association executive. **Personal:** Born in Americus, GA; widowed; children: Lt Col George F. **Educ:** BA 1927. **Career:** MS, GA, OK, educator 1927-47; YPD 12th Episcopal Dist AME Ch, AR, OK, dir 1947-67; RSVP Tulsa Metro Ministry, assoc dir 1985; OCOMS Bd of Regents, vice chmn, 1 year; Retired Senior Volunteer Program of Tulsa, associate director, coordinator, 26 years. **Orgs:** Dir Youth Cncl, 20 years; TMM City of Tulsa, 1971-97; Church Women United City of Tulsa, 1950-97; St of OK; YWCA, 15 years; life mem Woman's Missionary Soc AME Ch; Urban League, 10 years; NAACP, 10 years; Mayor's Cncl on Aging, 1992-97; Govs Status of Women, under 3 Governors; Zeta Phi Beta; Vernon AME Ch; pres Hands of Frndshp; pres Pastor's Wives Cncl Intrdnmntl, 10 years; Govs Commn on Status of Women; Natl Council of Negro Women; UMCA; bd Morton Health Ctr, 4 years. **Honors/Awds:** The Wife of the Yr 1971; 100% Attend Award, Connectnl Young Peoples Dept 1964; Mem of Yr, Vernon AME 1969; Humanitarian Award, Tulsa Yth 1973; Liberty Bell Award, Bar Assn 1974; Newsmaker Award, Women in Communicatns; Perfect Attendance Award, SS Tchr 1965-97; Violet Anderson Award for Finer Womanhood, Zeta Phi Beta 1975; Woman of Yr, NCCJ 1975; del Nat Dem Conv, Carter Div 1976; hostess at the Inaugural in Washington DC; apptd by Gov of State of OK as Ambassador of Goodwill; Tri County Council on Aging, City of Tulsa, 20 years, Charter Member Plaque, 1992; Historian of State Church Women, 1949-92, Honoree, 1996. **Business Addr:** Associate Director/Coordinator, Retired Senior Volunteer Program, 2121 S Columbia, Tulsa, OK 74114.

HILL, GEORGE C.
Educator. **Personal:** Born Feb 19, 1939, Moorestown, NJ. **Educ:** Rutgers U, BA 1961; Howard U, MS 1963; NY U, PhD 1967. **Career:** Univ Cambridge, England, NIH spl resrch fellow 1971-72; Squibb Inst Med Resrch, resrch invstgtr 1969-71; Univ KY Med Ctr, NIH post-doctoral fellow 1967-69; CO State Univ, assoc 1972-85; Meharry Medical College, dir, Div of Biomedical Sci, vice pres for Intl Programs, currently. **Orgs:** Mem AAAS; AIBS; Am Soc Protozoologists; Am Soc Parasitologists; Soc Biological Chem; Sigma Xi. **Honors/Awds:** NIH Res Career Dev Award 1974-79. **Business Addr:** Dir, Div of Biomedical Sci, VP, Intl Programs, Meharry Medical College, 1005 D B Todd Blvd, Nashville, TN 37208.

HILL, GEORGE CALVIN
Physician. **Personal:** Born Aug 29, 1925, Johnstown, PA; son of Mosetta Pollard and George C Hill; married Valentine Kay Johnson, Jun 12, 1959; children: Georgia Anne, Janet Marietta, Ellen Valentine. **Educ:** Univ Pittsburgh, PA, BS 1948; MS 1954; Meharry Medical Coll, Nashville, TN, MD 1954-58. **Career:** Harper Grace Staff, jr attend 1976; Hutzel Hospital, jr attend 1974; Brent Gen Hospital, sr attend 1972; Harper Hospital, 1971; Detroit Gen Hospital, 1971; Wayne St & Med School, asst lectr 1971; Private Practice, 1966-69; VA Hospital, staff surg 1966; Dearborn 1965-66; Saginaw Mi 1964-65; Am Bd Surg, diplo 1964; Dearborn VA Hospital, instr 1963-64; gen surg res 1959-63; Mercy Hospital, intrnshp 1958-59; self employed Detroit, MI, surgeon, 1966-87; Chrysler Corp, Detroit, MI, plant physician, 1983-91; Detroit Edison, dir of med staff, 1991-95; Ford Motor Co, plant physician, currently. **Orgs:** Am Coll of Surgeons; Am Trauma Soc; Intl Coll of Surgeons; Detroit Surg Assn; Detroit Surg Soc; diplomate Am Bd of Surg; Am Med Writers Assn; American Medical Assn; Wayne Co Med Soc; Natl Med Assn; Detroit Med Soc; Wolverine Med Soc Spkrs Bur; Am Cancer Soc; bd dirs United Health Org 1985-; chmn, Comm Occupational Health Safety, Wayne County Medical Society 1989-. **Honors/Awds:** Dr. Clarke McDermont Award 1962, 1963, Chi Delta Mu 1957. **Military Serv:** USN 1944-46; US Army Medical Corp, Active Reserve, col 1983-; Operation Desert Storm, 1990-91; retired 1995. **Business Addr:** Plant Physician, Ford Motor Corp, 26090 23 Mile Rd, Chesterfield, MI 48051.

HILL, GEORGE HIRAM
Business executive. **Personal:** Born Apr 13, 1940, Detroit, MI; married Alma Matney; children: Dylan Foster. **Educ:** Wayne State Univ, BA 1963, graduate work. **Career:** MI Bell Telephone Co, comm consultant employment supr/comm supvr 1963-68; Assist Negro Youth Campaign, exec dir 1967; Job Oppty Line WJBK-TV, host 1968-73; Chrysler Corp, labor rel supr/corp personnel staff 1968-71; Diversified Chemical Technologies Inc, pres, 1971-. **Orgs:** Treasurer, Greater Detroit Chamber of Commerce; bd of advisors, Univ of Detroit Business School; secretary, National Assn of Black Automotive Suppliers, 1990; board member, Michigan Minority Business Development Corp, 1976-91. **Honors/Awds:** Honored by Boy Scouts of Amer MI Dist 1973; Jr Achievement Award 1973; Citation Distinguished & Significant Contributions Wayne Co Comm Coll; Minority Businessman of the Year State of MI 1978; Outstanding Small Businessman of the Year State of MI 1979. **Business Addr:** President, Diversified Chemical Technologies, Inc, 15477 Woodrow Wilson, Detroit, MI 48238.

HILL, GILBERT
City official. **Personal:** Born 1932; married Delores Hooks. **Career:** Detroit Police Department, Detroit, MI, police officer commander, 1959-89; actor, Beverly Hills Cop, 1985; Detroit City Council, Detroit, MI, city councilmember, 1990-. **Honors/Awds:** Played Sgt Gilbert Todd in Beverly Hills Cop and Beverly Hills Cop II.

HILL, GRANT HENRY
Professional basketball player. **Personal:** Born Oct 5, 1972, Dallas, TX; son of Calvin and Janet Hill. **Educ:** Duke Universi-

ty. **Career:** Detroit Pistons, forward, 1994-. **Honors/Awds:** Co-rookie of the year with Jason Kidd, NBA, 1995; NBA All-Rookie First Team, 1995; NBA All-Star, 1995-98; All-NBA First Team, 1997; IBM Award, 1997; won a gold medal with the US Olympic Basketball Team, 1996; Henry Iba Award, Best Collegiate Defensive Player, 1992; Atlantic Coast Conference Player of the Year, 1992. **Special Achievements:** Selected #3 in the first round of the 1994 NBA Draft; first rookie to lead the fan balloting for the NBA All-Star Game, 1995. **Business Addr:** Professional Basketball Player, Detroit Pistons, 2 Championship Dr, Auburn Hills, MI 48326, (248)377-0100.

HILL, GREGORY LAMONTE
Professional football player. **Personal:** Born Feb 23, 1972, Dallas, TX. **Educ:** Texas A&M. **Career:** Kansas City Chiefs, running back, 1994-. **Orgs:** Greg Hill Time Charitable Foundation, founder. **Business Addr:** Professional Football Player, Kansas City Chiefs, One Arrowhead Dr, Kansas City, MO 64129, (816)924-9300.

HILL, HATTIE
Consultant. **Personal:** Born Jul 6, 1958, Marianna, AR; daughter of Carrie Flowers; married Terry, Nov 22, 1984. **Educ:** Arkansas State Univ, BA, education, 1977, MA, counseling, 1981. **Career:** TX Rehabilitation Commission, dir of training, rehabilitation counselor; Hattie Hill Enterprises, CEO. **Orgs:** Vision 100, co-founder; Dallas Women Together, 1989-; Natl Assn of Women Business Owners, 1992-; American Business Women's Assn, 1986-90; African American Women Entrepreneurs Inc, 1994-; Dallas Women's Convenant, 1993-; Leadership America, bd mem, 1993-; Trinity Med Ctr, exec bd mem, 1994-97; YWCA Dallas Women's Ctr, adv bd mem, 1994-. **Honors/Awds:** Today's Dallas Woman, Today's Dallas Woman of the Year, 1995; Dollars & Sense Magazine, Best & Brightest African American Business Woman, 1993, Hall of Fame, 1994; Dallas Business Journal, Forty Under Forty, 1994; Mirabella Magazine, Leading Women of the Future. **Special Achievements:** Articles: "Sensitivity Training: Do it Right!," Texas Banking, May 1994; "South Africa: The Good, The Bad & the Ugly," Sharing Ideas, Dec 1992; "Tip Off: Diversity," Dallas Business Journal; numerous other article and interviews; author: Women Who Carry Their Men; Smart Women, Smart Choices. **Business Addr:** CEO, Hattie Hill Enterprises, Inc, PO Box 802967, Dallas, TX 75380.

HILL, HENRY, JR.
Banking executive. **Personal:** Born Mar 19, 1935, Nashville, TN; married Mary E Hill; children: Michael E, Terrill E, Veronica E. **Educ:** Weaver Sch of Real Est, cert; Amer Inst of Banking, diploma 1981. **Career:** Citizens Svngs Bank & Trust Co, branch mgr/loan ofcr 1963-76, executive vice pres 1976-84, interim pres/CEO 1984, pres/CEO 1984-. **Orgs:** Bd dir Better Busn Bureau; bd dir Amer Inst Banking; bd dir Citizens Savings Bank & Trust Co; bd dir March of Dimes Birth Defectd Fd; chmn bd dir South St Comm Cntr; chmn trustees bd Progressive Bapt Ch; Man of the Year 1986; Natl Assoc of Negro Bus and Prof Women's Club, Inc 1986 Graduate of Leadership Nashville. **Honors/Awds:** Profiled Nashville Banner (newspaper) 1984; Profiled Nashville Tennessean (newspaper) 1984; Cert of Apprec South St Comm Center 1980. **Business Addr:** President & CEO, Citizens Bank, 1917 Heiman St, Nashville, TN 37208-2409.

HILL, JACQUELINE R.
Attorney. **Personal:** Born May 23, 1940, Topeka, KS; daughter of Noblesse Armenta Demoss Lansdowne and Boyd Alexander Hill (deceased); divorced; children: Dana Alesse Jamison. **Educ:** Univ of CA Berkeley, BA 1957-62; Univ of Southern CA, Teachers Credential 1965-66; Southwestern Univ School of Law, JD (cum laude) 1968-72; California State Univ, Long Beach, Certitificate in Calligraphy 1987-89. **Career:** Univ of CA Lawrence Radiation Lab, admin exec 1963-66; LA Unified School Dist, math teacher 1966-1973; LA Comm Coll Dist, evening instr 1972-75; Los Angeles County, deputy dist atty, 1973-; California State University-Long Beach, instructor, 1990-91. **Orgs:** CA State Bar; Amer Bar Association; CA State Adv Grp Juvenile Justice and Delinquency Prevention 1983-. **Honors/Awds:** Legal Book Awards Southwestern Univ School of Law 1969-72. **Business Addr:** Deputy District Attorney, Los Angeles County, 210 W Temple St, Los Angeles, CA 90012.

HILL, JAMES, JR.
Accountant. **Personal:** Born Aug 20, 1941, Baltimore, MD; married Sheree; children: James III, Brian. **Educ:** Central State Coll, BS 1964; Univ of Chicago, MBA 1967. **Career:** Union Carbon, cost accountant 1964-65; Alexander Grant & Co, auditor 1967-69; Chicago Economic Devel Corp, deputy dir 1968-70; Hill Taylor & Co, managing partner, 1972-. **Orgs:** Bd of dirs Chicago Commons Assoc 1970-; various comms Amer Inst of CPA's 1977-; state bd of accountancy State of IL 1980-; bd of dirs IL CPA Soc 1983-86, Provident Hosp 1983-86, treasurer, Better Government Assoc 1990-91; lifetime member, Kappa Alpha Psi Fraternity; member, Citizen Information Service; member, Economic Club of Chicago; member, Japan America Society; IL Inst of Tech, bd of trustees; Univ of Chicago Bus School, advisory comm. **Honors/Awds:** Certificate of Appreciation, National Association of Real Estate Brokers; Certificate of Merit, Central State University Alumni Association; Outstanding Professional Achievement, Central State University; Distinguished Service Award, Council for Community Service; Little Gold Oilcan Award, Chicago Economic Development Corporation; Certificate of Appreciation, Chicago State University. **Business Addr:** Managing Partner, Hill Taylor & Co., 116 S Michigan, 11th Fl, Chicago, IL 60603.

HILL, JAMES A., SR.
Minister, educator. **Personal:** Born Jun 10, 1934, Chicago, IL; son of Mrs Fannie M Whitney Hill and Mr Robert E Hill Sr; divorced; children: Carl J, Jewell Davis, Fannie M, James A Jr, Robert E. **Educ:** Chicago Baptist Coll, Sem Dept 1959; Blackstone School of Law, LLB 1962; Clarksville School of Theology, BD 1966, THD 1979; Amer Bible & Divinity Coll, ThM 1966; St John's Univ, BA 1974; Trinity Coll, MSSc 1976; Faith Evangelical Luthern Seminary, Tacoma WA, Doctor of Ministry 1989; Gradelupa College & Seminary, San Antonio TX, Doctor of Humanities 1988. **Career:** Wayne County EOE, dep dir 1967-69; Wayne County Probation Dept, probation officer 1969-72; Memphis Urban League, dep dir 1975-80; Methodist CME Church, minister 1950-. **Orgs:** Mem Gov's Comm on Human Rights, Fairbanks Human Relations Council; exec bd Fairbanks USO, United Fund Comm; chmn Boy Scouts of Amer; mem Fairbanks Ministerial Assoc, Anchorage Ministerial Assoc, The Amer Acad of Political & Soc Sci; asst state chaplain Elks State of MI Assoc; asst grand chaplain Elks Natl Assoc of the IBPOE of W; professional mem Adult Educ Assoc of USA; life mem AMVETS; mem The Amer Counselors Soc, Amer Ministerial Assoc, Natl Assoc of Social Workers Inc. **Honors/Awds:** Letters of Appreciation Govs Comm on Human Rights State of AK; Letters of Appreciation Fairbanks Human Relations Council; The NAACP State Level Svcs; Letters of Appreciation Univ of AK; Letters of Appreciation Mayor of the City of Fairbanks AK; First and only black mem of the clergy listed in the AK Literary Dir for the State of AK 1964; Plaques from the Eastern Star & Masonic Order; meritorious Serv Cert Masonic Order; Meritorious Serv Plaques Inkster Br of the US Jaycees 1967-68; Meritorious Serv Plaques Golden Gate Lodge, Sunset Temple, IBPOE of W; Certificate of Appreciation South Bend Urban league for Oustanding Community Leadership; Plaque Laymen Chapel CME Church for serv beyond the call of duty; Community Serv Awd The Hon Harold E Ford USCongressman 1977; Man of the Year, Chrisn Information & Service Center 1988, Outstanding Big Brother Award, Angelina County Juvenile Probation Serv 1988; Outstanding Family & Community Serv, The Hon Charles Wilson US Congressman 1988; Let's Study the Bible 1987; Evangelism for Today 1985. **Home Addr:** 3733 Juneau Street, P O Box 18616, Seattle, WA 98118. **Business Addr:** Minister, Curry Temple CME Church, 172 23rd Ave, Seattle, WA 98122.

HILL, JAMES A., JR.
Attorney general. **Personal:** Born Apr 23, 1947, Atlanta, GA; married CJ Van Pelt; children: Jennifer Joy. **Educ:** MI State Univ, BA 1969; IN Univ, MBA 1971, JD 1974. **Career:** OR Dept of Revenue, hearing ofcr; OR Dept Justice, asst atty gen, law clk; Judge Adv Gen Corp 1972; Bankers Trust Co 1970. **Orgs:** Mem OR State Bar Assc 1975-; mem Salem OR Chpt; NAACP; chrt mem OR Assembly for Black Affairs. **Honors/Awds:** Flwshp The Consortium Grad Study in Bus for Blacks IN Univ.

HILL, JAMES H.
Public relations executive. **Personal:** Born Aug 11, 1947, Toledo, OH; son of Cassie Hill and James Hill Sr; married Cynthia Carter, Mar 5, 1988; children: Jasmine Dianae. **Educ:** Ohio Univ, Athens OH, BS Journalism, 1969; Ohio Univ Graduate School, Athens OH, attended. **Career:** Owens-Corning Fiberglas, Toledo OH, merchandise supvr, 1970-75; WGTE-TV FM (PBS), Toledo OH, dir public information, 1975-77, producer/writer, 1977-80; S C Johnson, Racine WI, mgr operations, public relations, 1980-82; Sara Lee Corp, Chicago IL, dir of public relations and communications, 1982-86; Burrell Public Relations Inc, Chicago IL, pres/CEO, 1986-; Kaiser Foundation, Health Plan and Hospitals, vp of communications 1995-. **Orgs:** Bd mem, NAACP/Toledo, 1973-75; mem, PCC, 1983-, PRSA, 1983-; co-chairman/fundraising, UNCF/Chicago, 1983; bd mem, Children and Adolescent Forum, 1984-86, 1989-; mem, BPRSA, 1985-; membership comm, UNCF, 1985-; bd mem, Travelers & Immigrant Aid, 1989-; public relations advisory comm, Chicago Urban League, 1989-; Economic Club of Chicago, 1986-. **Honors/Awds:** Gold Trumpet, PCC, 1981; Silver Trumpet, PCC, 1981, 1986, 1989; CINE Golden Eagle, 1981; Gold Quil IABC, 1984; Silver Anvil (2), 1986. **Business Addr:** President/CEO, Burrell Public Relations Inc, 20 North Michigan Ave, Chicago, IL 60602.

HILL, JAMES L.
Association executive. **Personal:** Born Aug 21, 1928, Austin, TX; married Geraldine Holmes; children: Jacqueline (Howard). **Educ:** Huston-Tillotson Coll, BA Ed 1953; Univ of TX, MEd 1962. **Career:** TX St Bd of Ed, dir, Off of Urban Ed 1985; CTB/MCGRAW Hill, Manchester MO, eval splst 1973-74; Pt Arthur, dir, pupil prsnl 1968-73, dir testing 1964-68; Abilene, guidance cnslr 1959-64. **Orgs:** Mem NEA; TX St Tchr Assn; TX Prsnl & Guidance Assn; Am Prsnl & Guidance Assn; Phi Delta Kappa; past mem, bd dir Jefferson Co Ec Oppor Commn; mem TX Urban Adv Cncl; TX Urban Curriculum & Evaluation Cncls, Huston-Tillotson Coll. **Honors/Awds:** Spl Alumni Award 1972; chosen as one of 30 educators to tour Viet Nam with Bob Hope Troupe to present MEMO. **Military Serv:** USN 1948-53. **Business Addr:** TX Educ Agency, 201 e 11 St, Austin, TX 78701.

HILL, JAMES L.
Educational administrator. **Personal:** Born Oct 22, 1936, Bowling Green, OH; son of Flossie Mae Susan Hill and Joe L Hill; married Carolyn G Hill, Jun 8, 1963; children: Todd Derek, Candace Leah. **Educ:** Indiana State University, Terre Haute, IN, BS, physical education, 1965, MS, physical education, 1966; Central Michigan University, Mt Pleasant, MI, specialist educational administration, currently. **Career:** Arsenal Technical High School, Indianapolis, IN, teacher/coach, 1966-68; Shortridge High School, Indianapolis, IN, teacher/coach, 1968-70; Central Michigan University, Mt Pleasant, MI, instructor, 1970-74; Blue Lake Fine Arts Camp, Muskegon, MI, dir, summer counseling program, 1972-74; Central Michigan University, Mt Pleasant, MI, asst prof, 1974-75, acting dean of students, 1975-76, dean of students, 1976-79, vice pres, student affairs, 1979-. **Orgs:** Member 1975-, awards committee chair 1989-90, National Assn Student Personnel Administration; asst vice pres, NASPA Region IV-East, 1980-81; member 1977-, legislative committee 1980-82, Assn of College/University Housing Officers; member, American Council on Education, 1978-; member, Michigan Student Affairs Administration, 1976-; member, Phi Kappa Epsilon, 1966-. **Honors/Awds:** Distinguished Alumni, Indiana State University, 1989; Golden Key National Honorary Member, 1987, Mortar Board Honorary Member, 1983, Sigma Iota Epsilon Honorary Member, 1979, Central Michigan University; Indiana Wrestling Hall of Fame Inductee, Indiana High School Wrestling Coaches' Assn, 1974. **Military Serv:** US Navy, 1956-60; Honorable Discharge. **Home Addr:** 1841 W Pickard St, Mount Pleasant, MI 48858. **Business Addr:** Vice President for Student Affairs, Central Michigan University, 182 Warriner Hall, Mount Pleasant, MI 48858.

HILL, JAMES LEE
Educational administrator. **Personal:** Born Dec 10, 1941, Meigs, GA; son of Mr & Mrs Willie Lee Hill (deceased); married Flo J; children: Deron James, Toussaint LeMarc. **Educ:** Fort Valley St Coll, BS English 1959-63; Atlanta Univ, MA English 1963-68; Univ of Iowa, PhD American CIV 1971-76, 1978; Purdue Univ, post doctoral study 1981; John Carroll Univ, post doctoral study 1984. **Career:** Winder City Schs, instructor English 1964-65; Hancock Central High, chmn Eng dept 1965-68; Paine Coll, instructor English 1968-71; Benedict Coll, chmn Eng dept 1974-77; Albany State Coll, chmn Eng dept 1977-96, dean arts & sciences 1981-. **Orgs:** Consultant, Natl Rsch Project on Black Women 1979-81; sec Albany Urban League Bd 1979-81; chair, assoc, asst chair, Conf on Coll Comp & Comm 1980-83; chair, vice chair GA Endowment for Humanities 1981-83; mem Exec Comm NCTE 1982-83; pres Beta Nu Sigma Phi Beta Sigma Frat 1983-; chair Academic Comm on English-GA 1983-84; vice pres S Atlantic Assn of Dept of English 1984-85; bd dir Natl Fed State Humanities Councils 1984-87; mem Coll Section Comm Natl Council of Teachers of English 1985-89, chair, 1993-95; Professional Service: dir NEA Writer-in-Resd Prog ASC 1982-91; dir NEH Summer Humanities Inst ASC, 1983, 1984, 1989; Regional dir Southern Region Phi Beta Sigma; visiting scholar Natl Humanities Faculty; Georgia Desoto Commission; Georgia Christopher Columbus Commission; NCTE Summer Inst for Teachers of Literature, dir. **Honors/Awds:** NEH Fellow Atlanta Univ 1969; NEH Fellow Univ of IA 1971-74; Governor's Award in the Humanities, State of Georgia, 1987. **Special Achievements:** Publications: "Migration of Blacks to Iowa," "The Apprenticeship of Chester Himes," "The Antiheroic Hero in the Novels of Frank Yerby," A Sourcebook for Teachers of Georgia History; editor, Studies in African and African-American Culture; "Interview with Frank Garvin Yerby;" "Frany Yerby;" "The Foxes of Harrow;" "A Woman of Fancy.". **Home Addr:** 2408 Greenmount Dr, Albany, GA 31705. **Business Addr:** Dean of Arts & Sciences, Albany State College, 504 College Dr, Albany, GA 31705.

HILL, JAMES O.
City employee. **Personal:** Born Sep 5, 1937, Austin; married Eva Marie Mosby; children: Eva Marie, James O II, Dudley Joseph. **Educ:** Howard Univ, BA 1964; Nova Univ, MPA 1975. **Career:** City of Ft Lauderdale, asst city mgr, manpower analyst, admin asst 1971-; Boys Clubs of Broward Co FL, dir 1968-71; Boys Clubs of Newark, asst dir 1964-68. **Orgs:** Mem Intl City Mgrs Assc 1972-; Amer Soc of Pub Admin 1973-; ARC 1971-; Govs Crime Prevention Task Force 1971-; Elks 1970-; KC 1968; Seminole Hist Soc 1975; Ft Lauderdale Chamber of Comm 1971-. **Honors/Awds:** Educ achievement award USAF 1961; Youth Srv Award 1970; 3 Boys Club Srv Awards 1964-70. **Military Serv:** USAF a/1c 1958-62. **Business Addr:** PO Box 14250, Fort Lauderdale, FL 33301.

HILL, JEFFREY RONALD
Marketing manager. **Personal:** Born Nov 14, 1948, Philadelphia, PA. **Educ:** Cheyney State Clge, bS Sci 1972; Penn State

Univ PA, mrkt cert 1974. **Career:** Nabisco Inc, mrkt sales mgr; Hilltop Promotions Philadelphia, dir 1979-; Second Story/ Catacombs Disco Complex Phila, mgr 1978-79; 3rd Jazz Record Co & Retail Phila, mgr 1975-76; Philip Morris Tobacco Co NY, sales mgr 1972-75. **Orgs:** Mem Natl Hist Soc 1968-77; mem Black Music Assc; mem Amer Film Inst. **Honors/Awds:** Merit Achievement Award Amer Legion Philadelphia Post 1963. **Business Addr:** Navisco Inc, 201 Precision Dr, Horsham, PA 19044.

HILL, JESSE, JR.
Business executive (retired). **Personal:** Born in St. Louis, MO; son of Nancy Dennis Martin and Jesse Sr.; married Juanita Azira Gonzalez; children: Nancy, Azira. **Educ:** Univ MD, BS 1947; Lincoln Univ, BA; Univ of MI, M Bus Admin. **Career:** Atlanta Life Ins Co, actuary, vp/chief actuary, pres/CEO, 1949-95; Concessions Intl, pres, owner, 1979-. **Orgs:** Chmn campaign of Andrew Young 1972; campaign of Maynard Jackson; past chmn Natl Alliance of Businessmen; dir Marta; mem bd dir Delta Airlines; past chmn Atlanta Crime Commn; pres Enterprise Investments Inc; mem Amer Acad of Actuaries, Atlanta Actuarial Club, SE Actuarial Club; mem bd dir chmn Bldg Com of Martin Luther King Ctr for Social Change; mem bd dir Natl Urban Coalition Oppor Funding Inc; Natl Urban League; Voter Educ proj; bd Boy Scoutsof Amer, Bethune Cookman Coll, Provident Hospital; bd dirs Sperry Hutchinson Co, Communications Satellite Corp, Morse Shoe Co, Trust Co of GA, Knight Ridder Newspapers Inc, Natl Serv Industries Inc; Herndon Foundation, chm, retired. **Honors/Awds:** Received numerous honors & awds from civic & civil rights orgns; Annual Natl Urban League EOE Awd 1965; Most Disting Alumni Awd MO Lincoln Univ 1970; Abe Goldstein Awd Anti-Defamation League of B'nai B'rith 1973; Hon LLD Morris Brown Coll, Clark Coll 1972 1974; Chung-Ang Univ 1976; Univ of MI, 1994. **Military Serv:** Veteran Korean war. **Business Addr:** President/CEO, Atlanta Life Ins Co, PO Box 897, Atlanta, GA 30301.

HILL, JOHN C.
Education administrator. **Personal:** Born Jan 30, 1926, Terre Haute, IN; married Alyce Adams. **Educ:** IN State Teachers Coll, BS 1947, MS 1950; IN Univ, EdD 1965. **Career:** IN Schols, sci & math teacher 1947-50, hs principal 1950-56, supt of schools 1956-63; IN State Univ, prof ed admin 1965-, asst interim dean 1967-. **Orgs:** Exec dir IN Leg Study Comm 1963-65; consult Facility Plng to Architects/Schools 1965-; chmn CEFP I Great Lakes Reg 1969-72; ed bd Contemporary Ed 1972-, Black Amer Lit Forum 1969-, CEFP I Jrnl 1978-; mem Phi Delta Kappa 1954-, Phi Kappa Phi 1982-, IN Assoc of Public School Supts 1963-. **Honors/Awds:** Cert of Recognition Phi Delta Kappa 1979; Serv Citation Awd CEFP I 1972; Outstanding Educators of Amer OEA 1972,73,74,75,76; 1st Design Awd Progressive Architecture 1972. **Military Serv:** AAF sgt 1944-46; Air Medal, DFC, Good Conduct, Unit Service Citation 1945. **Business Addr:** Asst Dean Admin & Inst Serv, Indiana State Univ, School of Education, 1117 ISU, Terre Haute, IN 47809.

HILL, JOSEPH HAVORD
Attorney. **Personal:** Born Aug 19, 1940, Luverne, AL; son of Arneta Williams Hill and Huey Hill (deceased); married Jacqueline Bryant Andrews, Jun 30, 1963; children: Jason Joseph Kent Hill. **Educ:** Central State Univ, Wilberforce OH, BS, 1962; Akron Univ, Akron OH, JD, 1972. **Career:** Goodyear Tire and Rubber Co, Akron OH, chemist, 1965-69; Natl Labor Relations Bd, Cleveland OH, attorney, 1972-76; Montgomery Ward, Chicago IL, sr labor relations attorney, 1976-78; McDonald's Corp, Oak Brook IL, sr labor relations attorney, 1978-81, staff dir labor relations, 1981-83, dir of labor relations, 1983-95; AVP, labor relations, 1995-. **Orgs:** Life mem, Alpha Phi Alpha Frat, 1959-; bd of dir, Alpha Phi Alpha Homes Inc, Akron OH, 1972-76; pres, Alpha Phi Alpha Frat, Eta Tau Lambda, Akron OH, 1974-76; mem, NAACP, 1981, Urban League of Chicago, Amer Bar Assn, 1981-, Natl Bar Assn, 1984-; vice president, Theta Mu Lambda Chapter, Alpha Phi Alpha Fraternity, 1990-91. **Honors/Awds:** Akron Univ Law Review, 1971-72; President's Award, McDonald's Corp, 1981. **Military Serv:** US Army, Artillery (Field), captain, 1963-65. **Business Addr:** Assistant Vice Pres, Labor Relations, McDonald's Corp., Labor Relations Department 145, Jorie Blvd, Office Campus Bldg, Oak Brook, IL 60521.

HILL, JULIA H.
Educator (retired). **Personal:** Born Sep 28, Kansas City, MO; daughter of Ethel Williams Hicks and Arthur H Hicks; married Quincy T (deceased). **Educ:** Lincoln Univ, Jefferson City MO, BS (cum laude) 1943; Univ of Southern CA, LA, CA, Master's degree 1954; Nova Univ, Ft Lauderdale, FL, Doctorate of Educ 1982. **Career:** Kansas City, MO School Dist, elementary school teacher 1943-66, consultant/urban affairs 1966-67, coord Title I paraprofessional 1968-75, elementary school prin 1975-76; Pioneer Comm Coll, comm serv coord 1976-79, coord Northland Work and Training Unit 1980-81, evening coord Kansas City Skill Center 1982-85; Pioneer Comm Coll, coord of coll relations 1985-92. **Orgs:** Mem Kansas City, MO School Bd 1984-96; mem Kansas City Campus Ministers 1984-94; mem SW Bell Tele Adv Comm 1981-94; former pres Kansas City, MO NAACP Branch 1971-80; life mem chairperson Kansas City, MO NAACP Branch 1984-; life mem Alpha Kappa Alpha Sorority Beta Omega Chapter; life mem/golden heritage life mem NAACP. **Honors/Awds:** Dist Servs, Kansas City, MO Leon M Jordan Mem Award 1971; Citizen of the Year Omega Phi Psi Fraternity Kansas City, MO 1973; Ldrshp & Civil Rights, KS City, MO Baptist Ministers Union 1974; SCLC Black Woman on the Move in Civil Rights 1975; Othell G Whitlock Meml Award Comm Involvement 1976; Outstanding Serv Natl NAACP Civil Rights Award 1976; Afro-Amer Student Union Disting Comm Leadership 1977; Zeta Phi Beta Sor Outstanding Leadership; Greater Kansas City Business and Prof Women Sojourner Truth Award; Outstanding Civil Rights 1978; Outstanding Women of the Year Award; Beacon Light Seventh Day Adventist Church Outstanding Comm Serv 1979; Operation PUSH, Dr Martin Luther King Jr Awards; Girl Scouts of Amer Awd; Civil Rights Black Archives Award 1980-81; selectedfor list of 100 Most Infntial Blacks of Kansas City 1986-88; Harold L Holiday Sr Civil Rights Award NAACP 1988; Distinguished Service Award Lincoln University of Missouri National Alumni Assn 1990. **Home Addr:** 5100 Lawn Ave, Kansas City, MO 64130.

HILL, JULIUS W.
Physician. **Personal:** Born Jun 12, 1917, Atlanta, GA; married Luella Blaine; children: Sheila Lorraine. **Educ:** Johnson C Smith Univ, BA, 1933; Univ of IL, BS, MS, 1973; Meharry Medical College, MD, 1951; USC, orthopedic surgery, 1956. **Career:** Self-employed, physician, orthopedic surgeon, currently. **Orgs:** Past pres, Natl Med Assn, 1969-70; bd of dir, LA Co Hosp Cmsn, 1963-; Natl Med Fellowships Inc, 1970-; Charles R Drew Postgrad Med Sch, 1971-; Riverside Natl Bank, Houston; pres emeritus, Golden State Med Assn, 1960-72; pres, Natl Med Assn Fnd, 1974-; bd dir, Martin Luther King Hosp, LA; Amer Med Assn; CA State Med Assn; various assn clubs & committees; Phi Beta Kappa; Sigma Xi; Kappa Alpha Psi; Masons. **Honors/Awds:** Distinguished Serv Award, Natl Med Assn, 1970-71; outstanding service award, Charles R Drew Medical Society, LA. **Military Serv:** AUS, major, 1941-46.

HILL, KENNETH D.
Business executive. **Personal:** Born Jan 22, 1938, Bryn Mawr, PA; married C Irene Wigington; children: Kimberly Diane. **Educ:** Temple Univ, Assoc Arch Tech 1958; Univ of PA, Indust Mgmt 1972; Harvard Business School, PMD 1980. **Career:** Sun Co Inc, central sales training mgr 1969-71; Alliance Enterprise, pres 1971-73; Sun Co Inc, dist mgr 1973-75, proj mgr corp human resources 1975-76, div mgr mktg 1976-79, mgr corp citizenship 1979-84, vice pres publ affairs 1984-. **Orgs:** Chmn council of trustees Cheyney State Univ 1981; bd of trustees Comm Leadership Seminar 1983; pres Amer Assn of Blacks in Energy 1984-86; bd dir Private Industry Cncl 1984. **Honors/Awds:** Ebony Women's Awd for Comm Serv Womens Resource Network 1982; James McCoy Founder's Awd NAACP 1982; Centennial Awd for Advancement & Image Bldg Cheyney Univ 1983; Comm Serv Awd Urban League of Philadelphia 1983. **Military Serv:** AUS spec 4 1960-62; Good Conduct Medal, Soldier of the Month 1960-62. **Business Addr:** Vice Pres Public Affairs, Sun Refining & Marketing Co, 1801 Market St, Philadelphia, PA 19103.

HILL, KENNETH WADE
Professional baseball player. **Personal:** Born Dec 14, 1965, Lynn, MA. **Educ:** North Adams State. **Career:** St Louis Cardinals, pitcher, 1988-91; Montreal Expos, 1992-94; St Louis Cardinals, 1995; Cleveland Indians, 1995; Texas Rangers, 1996-97; Anaheim Angels, 1997-. **Business Addr:** Professional Baseball Player, Anaheim Angels, PO Box 2000, Anaheim, CA 92803, (714)937-6700.

HILL, LAURYN
Actress, singer, rapper. **Personal:** Born May 25, 1975, East Orange, NJ; children: Zion. **Career:** Actress, mem of The Fugees. Albums: Blunted on Reality, 1993, The Score, 1996; Acting (Movie): Sister Act II; Acting (TV): As the World Turns. **Business Addr:** Vocalist/Group, The Fugees, c/o Rufffhouse/ Columbia Records, 550 Madison Ave, New York, NY 10022, (212)833-8000.

HILL, LAWRENCE THORNE
Physician. **Personal:** Born Jan 15, 1947, Washington, DC; married Greta Dixon. **Educ:** Muhlenberg Coll, BS 1968; Howard Univ Coll of Medicine, MD 1972. **Career:** Georgetown Univ Rad Med, assoc dir 1976-84; Howard Univ, assoc prof radiation oncology 1976-; Washington County Hosp Rad Oncol, dir 1984-. **Orgs:** Bd dirs Amer Cancer Soc Washington County 1984-; chmn cancer comm and tumor bd, mem hospice comm, mem radiation safety comm Washington County Hosp;chmn Intl Cancer League; mem tumor bd Frederick Memorial Hosp; dir US Virgin Island Cancer Project; mem Intl Hospice Comm, Radiation Therapy Tech Howard Univ Coll of Allied Health; consultant Pan Amer Health Org. **Honors/Awds:** Junior Clinical Fellowship in Radiation Oncology Amer Cancer Soc 1977-80; AMA Physician Recognition Awd 1977,82,86; 11 publications including "Radiation Risks in Pregnancy," w/KL Mossman Obste and Gynecol 1982. **Business Addr:** Dir Radiation Oncology, Washington County Hospital, 251 East Antietam St, Hagerstown, MD 21740.

HILL, LEO
Business administrator. **Personal:** Born Mar 27, 1937, Columbus, TX; married Jacquelyne; children: Leo, Stacy. **Educ:** LA City Coll, 1955-58; LA State Coll, BA 1958-61; LA State Coll, Grad Work 1961-62; CA Tech, 1969; Pepperdine, 1970; Univ of CA, 1973; Univ of CA LA, Cert Ind Rel 1979, Cert Personnel Mgmt 1979; Inst of Cert Professional Mgrs, Cert Certified Mgr 1984. **Career:** RCA Serv Co, sr job devel admin; Hughes Aircraft Co, head eeo/affirm action prog 1977-81; Lockheed-CA Co, mgr equal oppor programs 1981-. **Orgs:** Dir comm prog Greater LA Community Action Agency; dir Program Monitoring, Neighborhood Youth Corps, Narcotics 1973; asst eeo 1972, dir personnel 1972 Economic & Youth Oppty Agency Gr LA; personell dir 1966-71, acting admin officer 1968-69 Neighborhood Adult Participation Proj Inc; rec dir Bethune Co Park; mem comm Florence-Firestone Coord Council & Case Conf; mem LA Area C of C Ed Comm, Men of Tomorrow, Hunters Elite Gun Club, Narcotics Task Force, Amer Soc Training & Devel; vice pres 1961, treas 1960 LA State Coll Inter-Frat Council; pres Kappa Psi Frat. **Honors/Awds:** All W State Conf 2 yrs; All S CA 2 yrs; Sam Berry Tournament Most Valuable Player; Broke-Tied 11 Records Jr Coll Career; CCAA 1st team 3 yrs; Leading Scorer NCAA Most Valuable; All Amer 2 yrs; CA State Univ Los Angeles Hall of Fame (Basketball) 1985. **Business Addr:** Manager Equal Oppor Programs, Lockheed-Calfornia Co, PO Box 551, Burbank, CA 91520.

HILL, MARION G.
Insurance company executive (retired). **Personal:** Born Oct 1, 1933, Rayville, LA; daughter of C S & Jessie Williams Gundy; divorced; children: Joseph M, Dwayne J, William D. **Career:** People's Progressive Insurance Co, pres, currently. **Orgs:** Rayville Community Civic Club, Inc; Rayville Rosenwald School Reunion.

HILL, MARVIN LEWIS
Printing executive. **Personal:** Born Aug 19, 1951, Indianapolis, IN; son of Luciele Campbell and Maurice Hill; married Deborah Jill Shaffer, Jun 10, 1989; children: Jessica Ashley, Alison Victoria. **Educ:** Indiana State University, 1971; Indiana University, criminal justice, 1974. **Career:** Marriott Corp., dist manager, 1974-78; Steak & Ale Restaurant, corporate trainer, 1978-79; MLH dba Sir Speedy, president, 1979-86; Shaffer-Hill, Express Press, president, 1986-. **Orgs:** Kiwanis International, dist chairman, young children #1, 1992, lt governor, I-I District, 1991; Village of Hoffman Estates, commissioner, 1991-94; Chamber of Commerce, Wheeling, president, 1983-85; Citizen Participation Organization, 1974. **Honors/Awds:** Kiwanis International, Distinguish Past Lt Governor, 1992; Village of Hoffman Estates, Outstanding Director, 1991. **Business Addr:** President, Express Press Inc, 2108 Stonington Ave, Hoffman Estates, IL 60195, (708)882-2234.

HILL, MARY ALICE
Association administrator. **Personal:** Born Sep 15, 1938, Marlow, GA; married Elton E Hill. **Educ:** NJ Coll of Commerce, Public Admin 1956; Univ Coll, Urban Studies 1972; Rutgers Univ, Certified Public Manager 1986; Natl Council of Negro Women, pres. **Career:** City of Newark, sr budget analyst 1972-83, mgmt info spec 1985, pres natl council of negro women. **Orgs:** Mem Amer Mgmt Assoc; mem Natl Assoc of Black Public Admin; pres Newark Sect Natl Council of Negro Women Inc; chmn US Selective Serv Bd #33; mem NJ State Univ of Med & Dentistry; bd pres Council on Affirm Action; chair Metropolitan BC Women's Day 1983; mem NJ Bethune Recognition Team Steering Comm 1985; officer Bethany 43, OES PHA Newark NJ; chair NJ Rainbow Coalition. **Honors/Awds:** Nomination Mayor's Comm Service Awd 1980; Rainbow Coalition Serv Awd 1984; chmn UMDNJ-PCAA 1987. **Home Addr:** 351 Seymour Ave, Newark, NJ 07112. **Business Addr:** President, Natl Council of Negro Women, PO Box 295, Newark, NJ 07102.

HILL, MERVIN E., JR.
Producer. **Personal:** Born Jul 12, 1947, St Louis. **Educ:** Grand Valley State Clge, BA; Wm James Clge; Allendale MI 1974. **Career:** WGVC-TV Allendale MI, asst to prod 1975-; Black Free Form Theatre Co Grand Rapids, actor, asst dir 1971-72; Living Arts Proj Grand Rapids Bd Educ, drama dir 1971-72; WOTV Grand Rapids, mgr 1973. **Honors/Awds:** Prod consult "Arbitration Mr Businessman"; assc prod ed "Portrait of African Journey"; author screenplay "The Neighborhood". **Business Addr:** WGVC TV 35, Allendale, MI 49401.

HILL, MICHAEL EDWARD
Editor. **Personal:** Born Nov 28, 1943, St Paul, MN. **Educ:** Coll St Thomas, BA 1965; Univ of Minnesota, M 1978. **Career:** Minneapolis Trib, reporter, asst city ed 1965-70; WA Post, copy ed, asst city ed, day sports ed, asst style ed, TV ed 1970-. **Orgs:** Mem Kappa Tau Alpha Univ Minnesota 1967. **Honors/Awds:** Recip coll scholarship Minneapolis-St Paul Baseball Writers Assn Amer 1965; Nieman flwshp Harvard Univ 1980-81. **Business Addr:** The Washington Post, 1150 15th St, NW, Washington, DC 20071.

HILL, OLIVER W.
Attorney. **Personal:** Born May 1, 1907, Richmond, VA; son of Olivia Lewis White-Hill and William Henry White II; married Beresenia Walker, Sep 5, 1934; children: Oliver W Jr. **Educ:** Howard Univ, AB 1931; Howard Univ Sch of Law, JD 1933. **Career:** Roanoke VA, lawyer 1934-36; Law Practice, 1939-61; FHA, asst to commr 1961-66; Hill Tucker & Marsh, attorney 1966-. **Orgs:** Mem City Council Richmond 1948-50; mem Pres Com on Gov Contracts 1951-54; founder 1942, Old Dominion Bar Assn; chmn Legal Com VA State Conf NAACP 1940-61; mem Richmond Dem Com 1955-61, 1966-74; bd mem leg com NAACP; mem Urban League; mem bd VA Reg Med Prog; mem NBA Richmond Bar Assn & Old Dominion Bar Assn; mem Omega Psi Phi, Sigma Pi Phi; numerous other civic orgs; mem VA State Bar Discipl Bd 1977-82; mem VA State Bar Judiciary Comm 1977-; former mem bd trustees St Paul's Coll; mem VA Bar Foundation 1985; pres Old Dominion Bar Assn Foundation 1985; fellow, Amer College of Trial Lawyers 1987-; mem, Omicrom Delta Kappa Honor Society 1989; mem, Commission onConstitution Rsion for Commonwealth of VA, 1968-69; trustee, George C Marshall Foundation 1989-94; bd of dirs, Evolutionary Change Inc, 1990-. **Honors/Awds:** Chicago Defender Merit Awd 1948; Howard Univ Alumni Awd 1950; co-recipient Russwurm Awd natl Publ Assn 1952; Omega Man of the Yr Omega Psi Phi 1957; VA State Conf Awd 1957, William Robert Ming Adv Awd 1980, NAACP; Lawyer of Yr NBA 1959; Democratic Party of Virginia Wm P Robinson Memorial Awd 1981; Brotherhood Citation Natl Conf of Christians & Jews 1982; Oliver W Hill Black Pre-Law Assn Univ of VA 1983; Richmond Amer Muslims Mission Ctr Pioneer Awd 1984; NAACP Legal Defense and Educational Fund, Inc The Simple Justice Awd 1986; Honorary Doctor of Laws: St Paul's Coll 1979, VA State Univ 1982, Virginia Union Univ 1988; The Judicial Council of National Bar Assn Awad 1979; The Charles H Houston Medallion of Merit, Washington Bar Assn 1976;Francis Ellis Rivers Award, NAACP Legal Defense anducational Fund 1976; Outstanding Contribution to the Legal System Award, Virginia Commission on Women and Minorities in the Legal System 1987; Hill-Tucker Public Service Award, Richmond Bar Association, 1989; Doctor of Humane Letters, VA Commonwealth Univ, 1992; Honorary Doctor of Laws, Univ of Richmond, 1994, T C Williams Law School, The Williams A Green Award for Prof Excellence, 1991; Strong Men & Women Excellence in Leadership Award Virginia Power, North Carolina Power, 1992; Apex Museum, Atlanta GA, Tribute to Oliver W Hill for contribution to Brown vs Bd of Education, 1992; Senate of VA, Senate Resolution No 84, Commending Oliver W Hill, 1992; VA State Bar, Lewis F Powell, Jr, Pro Bono Award, 1992; VA Education Assn, Friend of Educ Award, 1992; VA State Conference-NAACP, Branches Hall of Fame, 1992; Governor L Douglas Wilder's Commission on Campaign Finance Reform, Government Accountability and Ethics, member, 1992; Richmond Branch NAACP, Outstanding Service Award, 1992; Mid-Atlantic Region Alpha Kappa Alpha Sorority, Inc. Citizen of the Year Award, 1993; Amer Bar Assn, Standing Comm on Lawyers' Public Service, Responsibility 1993 Pro Bono Publico Award, 1993, Opportunities for Minorities in the Profession, The Justice Thurgood Marshall Award, 1993; Natl Bar Assn, Wiley A Branton Symposium Award, 1993; Black Law Student Assn, established at Univ of Richmond, T C Williams Law School, The Oliver W Hill, Sr, Lecture Series, 1993; Co-recipient, City of Richmond First Annual Distinguished Citizen, Hill-Powell Award, 1994; Urban League of Greater Richmond, Lifetime Achievement Award, 1994; Coll of William & Mary, Marshall Wythe School of Law, Medal of Merit, 1994; Amer Bar Assn, Section on Individual Rights & Responsibilities, The Justice Thurgood Marshall Award, 1994; Black Law Student Assn, established at Mrarhsll-Wythe School of Law, Coll of William & Mary, Oliver W Hill Scholarship Fund, 1994; City of Roanoke, Distinguished Citizen Citation Proclamation declaring Feb 14, 1995 as Oliver W Hill Sr, Day, 1995; VA State bar, Secion on Criminal Law Harry L Carrico Professionalism Award, 1995; The Honorable Judges of the Juvenile & Domestic Relations Court & Richmond City Council designated the new Courthouse the Oliver Hill Courts Bldg, 1996. **Military Serv:** AUS s/sgt 1943-45. **Home Addr:** 3108 Noble Ave, Richmond, VA 23222.

HILL, PATRICIA LIGGINS
Educator. **Personal:** Born Sep 18, 1942, Washington, DC; divorced; children: Sanya Patrice, Solomon Philip. **Educ:** Howard Univ Wash DC, BA cum laude 1965; Univ of San Francisco, MA English, 1970; Stanford Univ CA, PhD English/Amer Lit 1977. **Career:** Univ of San Francisco, prof of English, 1985-, assoc prof English 1979-84, dir ethnic studies 1977-, asst prof English 1977-79, English instructor 1971-77; Upper Midwest Tri-Racial Center, University of MN, resource consultant 1977-78; Urban Inst for Human Service Inc, research consultant 1976-80; Stanford University, teaching asst English 1974-77. **Orgs:** Bd dir Westside Mental Health Center 1971-78; SF Community College Bd 1972-78; CA Council of Black Educ 1973-. **Honors/Awds:** Recipient of fellowship, Natl Endowment for Humanities 1978; pub "The Dark/Black-Bad Light/White-Good Illusion in Joseph Conrad's 'Heart of Darkness' & 'Nigger of the Narcissus,'' Western Journal of Black Studies 1979; publications: Roots for a Third World Aesthetic Found in Black & Chicano Poetry, De Colores 1980; "The Violent Space, An Interpretation of the Function of the New Black Aesthetic in Etheridge Knight's Poetry,'' Black Amer Lit Forum 1980; General editor, "Call & Response: The Riverside Anthology of the African American Literary Tradition,'' Houghton Mifflin, 1997. **Business Addr:** Professor, English Department, University of San Francisco, 2130 Fulton St, San Francisco, CA 94117.

HILL, PAUL GORDON
Educator, counselor (retired). **Personal:** Born Mar 15, 1933, Gary, IN; son of Naomi Alexander Hill (deceased) and Daniel Hill Sr (deceased); married Cynthia Bryant Hill, Jun 24, 1989; children: Kenneth de Rouen-Hill. **Educ:** IN State Univ, PhD 1973; Kent State Univ, Adv cert 1965; TN A&I State Univ, MA 1965; IN State Univ, BA 1955. **Career:** Chicago Publ School, instr 1955-61, couns 1961-67, coord of guid in career devel prog 1967-68; IN State Univ, doctoral fellow 1968-70; Govs State Univ, dir stud serv & prof of human learning & devel 1970-73, disting univ prof of human learning & devel 1973-1989, retired, 1990. **Orgs:** Workshop IL Coll Personnel Assoc 1972; conflict resolution team Rich Twp Schl dist 1972-73; co-dir Non-Whites in NASPA 1975-76; mem Natl Assoc of St Personnel Admin 1974-77, Amer Personnel & Guid Assoc 1973-77, World Future Soc 1975, IL Assoc for Non-White Concern 1974-75, Amer Assoc for Higher Ed 1974-75; rsch task force handicapped Bur for Ed of Handicapped & Ed Testing Serv 1975; bd of dir Gavin Meml Found 1974-76; dir Proj Aquarius 1977-97; career devel workshop Amer Personnel & Guid Assoc Conf 1975; mem Amer Assn for Counseling and Devel. **Honors/Awds:** Blue Key Natl Scholastic Hon Soc; Pi Gamma Mu Hon Soc; Hulman 4.0 Average Scholarship Cert IN Univ; Kappa Delta Pi Hon Soc. **Special Achievements:** Author, "TAS/The Allegory of a Slave.". **Military Serv:** USN petty officer 1955-56. **Home Addr:** 22 Braeburn, Park Forest, IL 60466.

HILL, PEARL M.
Educational administrator. **Personal:** Born Apr 7, 1949, Portland, OR; children: Marla Dene. **Educ:** Univ of OR, BS Sociology 1971, MS Counseling/Psych 1973. **Career:** Univ of OR, academic coord 1970, counseling coord 1971, asst dir upward bound 1971, dir upward bound 1972-. **Orgs:** Sec Natl Council of Educ Oppor Assoc; mem Amer Personnel & Guidance Assn 1973-75; adv bd mem Univ of OR Financial Aid 1976-77; mem Northwest Assn of Special Progs 1977-80; mem Northwest Assn of Special Progs 1977-; founder Northwest Assn of Special Progs 1977; coord of First Annual Conf at PortLudlow 1977; mem Natl Coord Cncl of Educ Oppor Assns 1977-81; mem OR Alliance of Black Sch Educators 1978; mem Natl Alliance of Black Sch Educators1978; mem Urban League of Portland 1979; mem Natl Cncl of Educ Oppor Assns 1980-82; sec 1981; chair of adv bd Howard Univ Leadership Training 1981-82; founding mem Natl Cncl of Educ Oppor Assns Inc 1981; mem bd of trustees St mark's CME Church 1981; adv mem BOOST Educ Talent Srch Prog 1975-; mem NAACP 1978-; mem Delta Sigma ThetaSor 1982-. **Home Addr:** 2380 Riverview St, Eugene, OR 97403. **Business Addr:** Director-Upward Bound, 5204 Univ of Oregon, Eugene, OR 97403-5304.

HILL, RANDAL THRILL
Professional football player. **Personal:** Born Sep 21, 1969, Miami, FL. **Educ:** Miami (Fla.), BS in sociology. **Career:** Miami Dolphins, wide receiver, 1991, 1995-96; Arizona Cardinals, 1992-94; New Orleans Saints, 1997-. **Business Addr:** Professional Football Player, New Orleans Saints, 5800 Airline Hwy, Metairie, LA 70003, (504)733-0255.

HILL, RAY ALLEN
Educator. **Personal:** Born Sep 16, 1942, Houston, TX; son of Ann Stewart Hill and Cal Hill Jr (deceased). **Educ:** Howard Univ, Washington DC, BS 1964, MS 1965; Univ of California Berkley, PhD 1977. **Career:** Southern Univ, Baton Rouge LA, instructor 1965-66; Howard Univ, Washington DC, instructor botany 1966-75; Fisk Univ, Nashville TN, asst prof 1977-80; EPA, Washington DC, staff scientist 1978; NASA, Washington DC, staff scientist 1979; Univ of CA, San Francisco CA, visiting research assoc prof 1985; Lowell Coll Preparatory School, San Francisco CA, instructor 1986-; Purdue Univ, W Lafayette IN, visiting prof botany & plant pathology 1989, 1990, 1991; Alpha Distributors, owner, 1989-; Genentech, Inc, visiting scientist, 1992; DOE Fellow, staff scientist, 1993. **Orgs:** Mem Natl Inst of Science 1968-85, Amer Assn of Advanced Science 1972-85, Amer Soc Cell Biology 1972-85, Botanical Society of Amer 1972-85, Information Visitors Center 1975-, Alpha Phi Alpha Fraternity 1980-; bd mem Big Brothers of East Bay 1986-89. **Honors/Awds:** E E Worthing Fellow, E E Worthing Trust 1960-64; Faculty Fellow, Howard Univ 1972; Fellow, Ford Found 1975-77; Faculty Fellow, Natl Science Found 1975; NASA/ASEE Fellow, Stanford Univ 1983-84; published "Ultrastructure of Synergids of Gossypium hirsutum,'' 1977, and "Polarity Studies in Roots of Ipomea batatas In vitro,'' 1965; IISME Fellow, genentech, Inc, 1992, California Mentor Teacher, 1993-97; coach, 1st Place Science Bowl Team, Lowell College Preparatory, 1995-97; teacher advisor, Toshiba/NSTA ExploraVision Awards, 1st & 2nd Place, Lowell College Preparatory. **Home Addr:** PO Box 785, Cotati, CA 94931.

HILL, RAYMOND A.
Engineer. **Personal:** Born Jul 11, 1922, Savannah, GA; son of Stella Grant and Raymond Hill; married Lois Holmes; children: Lopez, Keith. **Educ:** A&T State Univ, BS 1950; George Washington Univ, advance study numerous certificates 1954-58. **Career:** Dept Agric Washington DC, cartographic aide 1951; BuShips DC, electronic engr 1951-58, sr engr 1958-59, supr electronic engr 1959-66; Naval Electronics System Command DC, 1966-70, electrons solid state devices unit head 1970-74; SEM Microelectronics & Mfg Tech, sect head, consult 1974-retired. **Honors/Awds:** Publs "Transistors Are They Reliable?" Military Electronics 1957; Military Transistor Specifications Bur Ships Journal 1957; "Radioactive Tubes" BuShips Journal 1957; "Radioactive Tubes Philco Tch" Rep Bulletin 1958; "Radioactive Tubes Danger" Military Electronics 1959; Spl Achievement Awd Tech Asst Electron Tubes by Def Supply Agency 1967; Spl Achievement Awd Tech Assistance DOD on Electron Tube Solid State Devices; DOD-AGED Awd 16 yrs professional svc; Lifetime Achievement in Engineering Administration, George Washington Univ, School of Engineering and Applied Science, 1997. **Military Serv:** AUS 1943-46.

HILL, REUBEN BENJAMIN
Attorney. **Personal:** Born Aug 1, 1938, Indianapolis, IN; son of Flossie M Hill and Joe L Hill; married Sheila; children: Philip, Martin, Nicholas. **Educ:** IN Univ, 1969; IN Univ Law Sch (cum laude), 1969-73. **Career:** IN State Police/Trooper, legal adv, 1964-74; Bingham Summers Welch & Spilman, assoc 1974-75; Marion Co, pros dep 1975-; Flanner House of Indianapolis, exec dir 1975-; Social Serv Agency, atty/exec dir; Butler Hahn Little & Hill, attorney. **Orgs:** Mem Indianapolis Lawyers Commn; bd dir IN Lawyers Commn; bd mem WYFI-20 Pub Broadcasting Svc; Childrens Museum; bd dir Metro Arts Council; Amer Bar Assn; Indianapolis Bar Assn; IN Bar Assn; Natl Bar Assn Adv Bd; Indianapolis Repertory Theatre; Kiwanis Club; Indianapolis Museum of Art Adv com; adv bd Indianapolis Urban League; Inner-City Y's Men Club; Indianapolis 500 Festival Bd Dir IN; IU Law Sch Min Enrollment Adv Com; Greater IN Progress Com; IN State Dept of Mental Health Bd Dir; Golden Glove Official IN; bd mem, Selective Service System; district appeal board, Alpha Eta Boule, Sigma Pi Phi Fraternity. **Honors/Awds:** Outstanding IN Citizen IN Black Bi-Centennial; WTLC Indianapolis Citizen of the Day; WTLC Man of the Year 1978. **Military Serv:** USAF 1957-61. **Business Phone:** (317)632-9411.

HILL, RICHARD NATHANIEL
Educational administrator. **Personal:** Born Nov 20, 1930, Port Chester, NY; son of Viola Stith Hill and Clarence J Hill; married Mayme Kathryn Hegwood; children: Richard H Jr, Lori S, Mark E. **Educ:** Chaminade Univ of Honolulu, MBA 1984; Univ of So CA, Ed D 1977; Chapman Coll, MA 1969; Univ of the Philippines, BA 1959. **Career:** Pacific Air Forces, educ admn 1970-72; Allan Hancock Coll, dir 1969-70; US Army Educ Ctr, NYAC & Fort Hamilton, acting educ services officer, 1985-; Chaminade Univ of Honolulu, acting asst dean, 1977-85, acting dean, 1974-77, dir, 1972-74. **Orgs:** Consultant Federally Emplyd Women 1983, Amer Assn for Adult & Cont Ed 1982, Waikiki Comm Cntr 1978; dir Univ of USC-HI Alumni 1979-; mem Wrld Affrs Forum of HI 1977-; pres Kiwanis Intrl Waikiki 1978-79. **Honors/Awds:** Outstanding Serv Awd Phi Delta Kappa, Univ of HA 1984; Certfct of Apprectn Federally Emplyd Women, Wash, DC 1983, Am Assn for Adult & Cont Ed, San Antonio, TX 1982; Dist Press Award Kiwanis International-CA, NV, HI Dist 1980; Certificate of Commendation, Alaska Adult Education Association, 1983; Outstanding Sustained Performance Award, Fort Hamilton, 1994; Certificate of Appreciation, Fort Hamilton, 1994. **Military Serv:** USAF ret ofcr, commendation medal 1969. **Business Addr:** Acting Education Services Officer, New York Area Command and Fort Hamilton, Brooklyn, NY 11252-5190.

HILL, ROBERT A.
Association executive. **Career:** Natl Assn of Minority Automobile Dealers, executive director, currently. **Business Addr:** Executive Director, National Association of Minority Automobile Dealers, 16000 W Nine Mile Rd, Southfield, MI 48075, (313)557-2500.

HILL, ROBERT BERNARD
Educational administrator. **Personal:** Born Sep 7, 1938, Brooklyn, NY; married; children: Bernard, Renee. **Educ:** City Coll of NY, BA 1961; Columbia Univ NYC, PhD 1969. **Career:** Bureau of Soc Sci Rsrch, vice pres sr rsrch assoc, 1981-86; Nat Urban League, Rsrch Dept, dep dir of rsrch 1969-72, director of research, 1972-81; Bureau of Applied Soc Rsrch Columbia Univ NY, rsrch asso 1964-69; Princeton Univ Fordham U, adj faculty 1969-73; Howard Univ Wash, DC, vis scholar soc dept sch of Human ecology 1975-77; Bur of the Census, chmn mem adv com on blck population, beginning 1974; Morgan State University, dir, urban reseach, currently. **Orgs:** Pres Wash, DC Sociological Soc 1975. **Special Achievements:** Author: "The Strengths of Black Families" Nat Urban League New York City 1971; "Informal Adoption Among Black Familie" NUL Rsrch Dept Wash, DC 1977; "Research on the African American Family,'' Auburn House, 1993; "The Strengths of African American Families: Twenty-five Years Later,'' 1997. **Business**

Addr: Dir, Urban Research, Morgan State University, Soldiers Armory, Room 204, Code Spring Lane & Hillen Road, Baltimore, MD 21239.

HILL, ROBERT J., JR.
Architectural engineer. **Personal:** Born Feb 23, 1943, Wilmington, NC; married Sheila G. **Educ:** A&T State Univ, BS 1971. **Career:** Norfolk Naval Shipyard, archit engr pub works. **Orgs:** Mem Soc Prof Naval Engr; Kappa Alpha Psi; YMCA; 35th St Karate Club; A&T Alumni Club. **Honors/Awds:** Letter Commendation Shipyard Comdr 1974. **Military Serv:** AUS 1962-65. **Business Addr:** c/o Becky Brown, Norfolk Naval Shipyard, Code 402, Portsmouth, VA 23709.

HILL, ROBERT K.
Business executive. **Personal:** Born May 12, 1917, San Antonio, TX; married Mildred. **Educ:** Univ of NE; Inst of Banking 1951-54. **Career:** Union Pacific RR, 1937-42; Epply Hotel Co, maitre d' 1942-46; self-employed 1946-50; Federal Reserve Bank 1950-54; Hill Enterprises, founder/mgr 1954-; Department of Justice, coordinator of weed and seed program, 1996. **Orgs:** Score counselor, Small Business Admin; sec/treas, NE Placement Assn; Insurance Underwriter; Notary Public; mem Omaha Real Estate Assn; bd dir Omaha Chamber of Commerce; Business Development Corp; United Comm Svc; Natl Conf Christians & Jews; Gene Epply Boys Club; Omaha Safety Coun; Legal Aid Soc; founder & dir Comm Bank of NE; Intl past pres, Frontiers Intl; Natl Federation of Independent Business; Central State Golf Assn (pres 5 yrs); past master Excelsior Lodge 2 Masonic Order; dir, Natl Bus League. **Business Phone:** (402)451-6652.

HILL, ROBERT LEWIS
Natural gas industry executive. **Personal:** Born Feb 23, 1934, Spartanburg, SC; son of Texanna Hardy Hill (deceased) and Modecai Hill (deceased); married Marcia Norcott Hill, Sep 28, 1957; children: Robin Lindsey, Lisa Beth. **Educ:** Southern Connecticut State University, New Haven, CT, BS, Education, 1960; Fairfield Univ, Fairfield, CT, 1965-67; Brandeis Univ, Waltham, MA, Certificate Human Resource Mgmt, 1980. **Career:** New Haven Board of Ed, New Haven, CT, teacher, 1963-65; Community Progress, Inc, New Haven, CT, counselor, trainer, 1965-67; Opportunities Indus Center, New Haven, CT, exec director, 1968-69; National League of Cities, Washington, DC, coord national urban fellows, 1969-71, natl director, vets prog, 1971-78, director, human resources & public safety, 1978-82; American Gas Assoc, Arlington, VA, vice pres cons, comm affairs; American Association of Blacks in Energy, executive director, consultant, currently. **Orgs:** Diaconate Bd, Peoples Congregational United Church of Christ, 1976-; Board of directors, Amer Assoc of Blacks in Energy, 1986-92; board of directors, Amer Assoc of Affirm Action 1, 1987-95; corp adv exec comm, National Forum for Black Public Admin, 1985-95; member, NAACP, 1982; member, National Urban League, 1985; member, Society of Consumer Affairs Professionals, 1987. **Honors/Awds:** Role Model Achievement Award, Fort Valley State College, 1989; Visiting Professor, Black Exec Exch Prog of Natl Urban League, 1988; Distinguished Supporter Award for Support of HBCU's, Dept of Interior, 1988; Outstanding Achievement Award, American Veterans Committee, 1974; Associate Fellow, Yale University, 1970. **Military Serv:** Air Force, Airman 1st Class, 1952-56; Good Conduct Award; Foreign Service Award. **Home Addr:** 12426 Herrington Manor Dr, Silver Spring, MD 20904.

HILL, ROSALIE A.
Educator. **Personal:** Born Dec 30, 1933, Philadelphia, PA; daughter of Anna Mae Elliott (deceased) and Joseph Behlin (deceased); children: Bernadette Hill Amos. **Educ:** FL A&M Univ, Tallahassee, FL, BSMEd, 1961; FL State Univ, Tallahassee, FL, PhD, 1985. **Career:** Florida A&M University, executive assistant to vice pres, currently; RA Hill & Assoc, educ consultant, Univ of S FL, dir, Equal Opportunity Affairs, FL State Univ, rsch assc; Leon Interfaith Child Care Inc, dir; staff dir; Taylor Co Adult Inst, basic educ teacher; FL A&M, counselor; Taylor Co Head Start Program, dir; Jerkins HS, music teacher. **Orgs:** Secr/vp/pres Taylor Co Educ Assc 1966-69; Taylor City Teachers Assn 1961; pres 1963-65; vice pres FL State Teachers Assc 1965; chairperson Dist III 1960-66; chairperson FL State Teachers Assn 1965-66; exec bd mem Dist Iii 1963-65; FL Educ Assn Small Co Prob Com 1967-69; chairperson Jerkins HS 1964-79; bd mem Taylor Co Sch Bd; PK Yonge Lab Sch; Leon City School Bd 1974-75; secr FL A&M Univ Alumni Assn 1974-76; Natl Assn 1974-; mem Amer Higher Educ Assn; Amer Assn of Affirmative Action Officers; Zeta Phi Beta Sor; Taylor Co Improvement Club Inc; Tri-Co Econ Cncl; Taylor Co Bi-racial Com; Region III Drug Abuse Com; Miss Black Amer Pageant; Amer Cancer Soc; Hillsborough Co Commn on Status of Women; special projects coord, Fl A&M Univ Natl Alumni Assn, 1985-;dist music dir, Tampa Conf AME Cches, 1985-; music dir, Bethel AME Church Tallahassee, Tampa Chapter of the NAACP and Greater Tampa urban League. **Honors/Awds:** Lewis State Scholarship 1952-56; Teacher of Year Jerkins HS 1960; Yearbook Dedication Jerkins HS 1960; Tampa Bay Most Influential Blacks, 1983; FL A&M Univ, Outstanding Alumni Hall of Fame, 1987; Martin Luther King Educ Award, Start Together on Progress, Inc, 1988; co-founder, FL Statewide Alumni Consortium of Historically Black Insts, 1985; founder, Conf on the Educ of Blacks, Tampa, 1982; served as role model for state, gave impetus to establishment of state activity. **Business Addr:** Executive Assistant-University Relations, Florida A&M University, 200 Lee Hall, Tallahassee, FL 32307.

HILL, RUFUS S.
Clergyman. **Personal:** Born Apr 8, 1923, Raymond, MS; son of Mary R Dixon Hill and Orville A Hill; married Ruth (divorced); children: Rufus, Thomasine, Beverly, Daphane. **Educ:** MS Indust Coll, AB 1951; MS State Univ, MA 1971. **Career:** Shannon MS, teacher 1951-55; Houston MS, teacher 1955-61; New Albany MS, teacher 1961-66; Clay Cty MS, teacher 1966-72; Christian Meth Episcopal Church, clergyman; Universal Life Ins, 1963-65; Union Fed Life Ins, 1965-66; Dixie Car Craft Cen, owner; 4-Way Pest Control Co, owner; Dixie Box Co, owner, 1991-. **Orgs:** Past chmn Union Co Comm Devel Council 1963-66; vice pres Clay Cty Comm Fed Credit Union 1971-74; mem MS Loyal Dem Party, Amer Legion Post #252 New Albany, FA Mason Lodge #171; founder of chap NAACP New Albany Devel Club, Union Co Life mem of Amvet; founder, director, Lee County Drug Dependency Rehabilitation Center Inc 1989-; Lee County NAACP, past president, 1994. **Military Serv:** US Army, corporal 1943-46; Campaign Medal, Good Conduct Medal; Bronze Star.

HILL, SAM
Building & construction contractor. **Personal:** Born Feb 22, 1918, Starkville, MS; married Martha Lue; children: Sammie Louis Moore, Julia McCarter, Butten, Hattie, Laura, Marilyn. **Educ:** US Army Inst of Educ, HS diploma 1947. **Career:** FHA Organization, contractor 1976-81; Loundes Co, carpenter 1954-88; Brown Ridge MB Church, asst minister 1978-; Lowndes Co, constable 1972-86. **Orgs:** Contractor for Future Home Admin 1976; minister Southern Baptist 1979; fireman Crawford MS 1978-82. **Honors/Awds:** Fireman's Awd Lowndes-Crawford 1978; Constable Awd Columbus MS. **Military Serv:** AUS sgt 10 yrs. **Business Addr:** NAACP, PO Box 91, Crawford, MS 39743.

HILL, SANDRA PATRICIA
Social worker. **Personal:** Born Nov 1, 1943, Peidmont, AL; daughter of Edith Palmore Hill and Theotis Hill. **Educ:** Berea Coll Berea, KY, BS (Home Ec) 1966; Southern Baptist Theo Seminary, MRE (Social Work) 1968; Univ of Michigan, MSW 1977; Cornell Univ, attending 1982-. **Career:** Harvard St Baptist Center, Alexandria, Virginia, assoc dir 1968-73; Harvard St Baptist Center, dir 1974-75; Home Mission Bd, S Baptist Convention, consultant 1977-1986, reserve status, 1987; Southern Baptist Theological Seminary, Louisville, KY, visiting prof, Social Work 1987-88; Empire State College, Ithaca, NY, mentor, community and human services, 1989-90; Displaced Homemakers Center, peer services/minority advocacy coordinator, 1989-. **Orgs:** Assn of Black Social Workers 1974-; Fold, Inc, Alexandria, VA 1970-75; sec/treasurer Southern Baptist Social Serv Assn, 1977-82; bd of dir, Reach Out Inc Atlanta, 1980; mem NAACP; Cornell Cooperative Extension of Tompkins County, vp Home Economics/Human Ecology Program Committee, strategic planning committee, 1991-; Task for Battered Women of Tompkins County, board of directors, vice chairperson, chairperson, strategic planning committee, 1992-; Black Women's Empowerment Group; Social Work Advisory Committee, Cornell Univ, chair, 1994-. **Business Addr:** Peer Services Coordinator, Displaced Homemakers Center, 315 N Tioga St, Ithaca, NY 14850.

HILL, SONNY. See HILL, WILLIAM RANDOLPH, JR.

HILL, SYLVIA IONE-BENNETT
Educator. **Personal:** Born Aug 15, 1940, Jacksonville, FL; daughter of Evelyn Harker Bennett and Paul Theodore Bennett, Sr.; children: Gloria Angela Davis. **Educ:** Howard U, BS 1963; Univ of OR, MS 1967, Ph D 1971. **Career:** UDC/Dept of Crimnl Justice, prof 1974-; Union for Exprmntng Coll & Univs, part-time core prof 1976-; Macalester Coll, asst prof 1972-74. **Orgs:** Sec gen Sixth Pan African Congress 1974; fndr and co-chrpsn Southern Africa Support Proj 1978-; founder/mem Strng Comm Free S Africa Movement 1984-; treasurer/bd TransAfrica Forum l984-; bd mem TransAfrica 1984-l990; bd mem New World Foundation l988-; associate director, USA tour for Nelson and Winnie Mandela, 1990. **Honors/Awds:** Nat'l Certfd Cnslr/Natl Brd for Certified cnslrs 1984-89. **Business Addr:** Professor of Criminal Justice, University District Of CO, 4200 Connecticut Ave NW, Washington, DC 20008, (202)274-5687.

HILL, TYRONE
Professional basketball player. **Personal:** Born Mar 17, 1968, Cincinnati, OH. **Educ:** Xavier Univ, bachelor's degree in communications arts. **Career:** Golden State Warriors, center-forward, 1990-93; Cleveland Cavaliers, 1993-97; Milwaukee Bucks, 1997-. **Business Addr:** Professional Basketball Player, Milwaukee Bucks, 1001 N Fourth St, Milwaukee, WI 53203, (414)227-0500.

HILL, VELMA MURPHY
Association executive. **Personal:** Born Oct 17, 1938, Chicago; married Norman Hill. **Educ:** No IL Univ Dekalb IL; Roosevelt Univ Chicago 1960; Harvard Univ, MEd 1969. **Career:** United Fedn Tchrs, asst to pres; New York City Training Inst, consult 1967-68; Amer Dem Action Washington, exec dir 1965-66; OEO summer recruit dir 1964-65; CORE, 1960-64. **Orgs:** Mem Labor Adv Com OEO 1970-71; Trade Union Com Histadrut Labor Seminar Israel 1969; Commn Status Women 1975. **Business Addr:** 260 Park Ave S, New York, NY 10010.

HILL, VONCIEL JONES
Municipal judge. **Personal:** Born Sep 23, 1948, Hattiesburg, MS; married Charles Edward Hill. **Educ:** Univ TX at Austin, BA 1969; Atlanta Univ, M Lib Sci 1971; Rice Univ, M Hist 1976; Univ TX at Austin, JD 1979; Southern Methodist University, Dallas, TX, masters of divinity, 1991. **Career:** Atlanta, GA Publ Schools, tchr 1969-70; Prairie View A&M Univ, asst circulations librarian 1971-72; TX Southern Univ, asst law librarian 1972-76; Public Utility Comm of TX, staff atty 1979-80; Dallas/Ft Worth Airport, asst city atty; St Luke Community United Methodist Church, Dallas, TX, asst pastor, 1985-; City of Dallas Municipal Court Judiciary, municipal court judge 1987-. **Orgs:** Chair/bd dir Methodism's Breadbasket 1983-85; committee chair Dallas Bar Assn 1985; sec JL Turner Legal Assn 1985; treas State Bar of TX Women & the Law Section. **Honors/Awds:** Univ Fellow, Rice Univ 1974-76; Ford Found Fellow, Atlanta Univ 1970-71. **Business Addr:** Municipal Court Judge, City of Dallas, 2014 Main St, Dallas, TX 75201.

HILL, WILLIAM BRADLEY, JR.
Attorney. **Personal:** Born Mar 3, 1952, Atlanta, GA; married Melba Gayle Wynn; children: Melba Kara. **Educ:** Wash & Lee Univ Lexington VA, BA 1974; Wash & Lee Univ Schl of Law Lexington, JD 1977. **Career:** State Law Dept Atlanta GA, asst atty gen 1977. **Orgs:** Mem State Bar of GA 1977; exec chmn Wash & Lee Univ Black Alumni Fnd 1980-. **Business Addr:** 185 Central Avenue, SW, Rm T8755, Atlanta, GA 30303.

HILL, WILLIAM RANDOLPH, JR. (SONNY HILL)
Union official (retired), sports editor. **Personal:** Born Jul 22, 1936, Philadelphia, PA; married Edith Hughes; children: K Brent. **Career:** CBS TV, editor 1977; Teamsters Local 169, sec, treasurer, bus agt & trust, 1960-93; Lancaster Red Roses Bsktbl Team, owner 1975; Eastern Basketball League, basketball player; WPEN Lct Sports & Humanitarian, analyst 1966-; Sonny Hill/John Chaney Basketball Camp, co-owner 1975-; WIP Sports Radio Talk Show, host, 1986-; WRIT Radio, Temple University Basketball, color analyst, 1993-; Philadelphia 76ers, executive advisor to president, 1996-; CoreStates Complex, executive advisor to president/CEO, 1995-. **Orgs:** Pres Charles Baker Meml Summer League 1960-; adv bd MacDonald's HS All Amer Team 1978-80; bd dir Big Brothers Assc Natl Comm opr PUSH; mem NAACP; Big Brothers; PUSH; pres, founder Sonny Hill Community Involvement League Inc, 1968-. **Honors/Awds:** Outst Com Srv Award Sports Mag 1970; human rights award Commin on Human Rel 1972; good nghbr award WDAS Radio 1973; Oxford Circle JC Award 1973; Man of Year award Fishtown 1973; Man of Year Nite Owl 1972-73; Tribune Charities 1976; Bsktbl Wkly Plyr Dev Award Toyota Motors 1977; Mutual Radio Broadcaster of NBA Championship 1980; Mellon Bank Good neighbor Awd 1985; John B Kelley Awd 1986; City of Hope Spirit of Life Awd; Whitney Young Leadership Award, Urban League of Philadelphia, 1990; Service Awd, Leon H Sullivan Charitable Golf Tournamet, Zion Community center, 1992; Educator's Roundtable Dr Wm H Gray Jr, Community Activist Awd, 1993. **Military Serv:** ANG 1959-65. **Home Addr:** 429 S 50th St, Philadelphia, PA 19143.

HILL, XACADENE AVERYLLIS
Physician. **Personal:** Born Aug 12, 1909, Yazoo City, MS; widowed; children: Walter Fox Jr. **Educ:** Univ of NE, AB 1933; Meharry Med Coll, MD 1937; Howard Univ, 1942. **Career:** St Louis Schools, school physician 1945-48; St Mary's Infirmary, instr venereal disease 1945-; St Marys Infirmary, instr 1946-52; Homer G Phillips Hosp,clinic physician, dir 1962-76; Private practice, semi-retired physician 1979-. **Orgs:** Mem St Louis Med Soc, MO State med Assoc, Mound City Med Forum, Natl Med Assoc, Amer Acad Family Physician, MO Acad Family Physician, Pan Med Assoc, Alpha Kappa Alpha 1929, NAACP; exec bd St Louis Acad Family Physician 1972-75; contribution memshp YWCA, Howard Univ 1942.

HILLARD, TERRY
Police official. **Personal:** marrIed Dorothy; children: 2. **Educ:** Chicago State Univ, BS, MS. **Career:** Chicago police dept, Area 2 deputy chief of patrol, until 1995, chief of detectives, 1995-98, superintendent, 1998-. **Orgs:** NOBLE; Chicago Westside Police Assn; FBI Natl Academy Associates; South Suburban Chiefs of Police Assn; Natl Commission on the Future of DNA Evidence; Domestic Violence Advocacy Coordinating Council; Illinois State Police Forensic Science Ctr at Chicago, advisory bd. **Honors/Awds:** Police Awards: Police Medal; Superintendent's Award of Valor; Police Blue Star Award; Carter Harrison/Lambert Tree Honorable Mention; Special Svc Award, Chicago Community Policing; Special Svc Award,

Democratic Natl Convention; 3 Department Commendations; Unit Meritorious Performance Award; Chicago Chamber of Commerce Award; 19 Honorable Mentions. **Special Achievements:** First African-American chief of detectives in Chicago. **Military Serv:** US Marine Corps, sgt, 1963-67; Presidential Unit Citation; Vietnam Svc Medal; Good Conduct Medal; Natl Defense Svc Medal; Republic of Vietnam Campaign Medal. **Business Addr:** Police Superintendent, Chicago Police Dept, 1121 S State St, Rm 501, Chicago, IL 60605, (312)747-5533.

HILLIARD, ALICIA VICTORIA
Broadcast journalist. **Personal:** Born Jan 4, 1949, Wadesboro, NC; daughter of Annie Louise Hilliard and George Allen. **Educ:** Morgan State University, BA, 1971; University of Wisconsin, Madison, Masters final exam incomplete, 1977-81. **Career:** Baltimore City Hospitals, nutrition asst/kitchen asst, 1970; State Attorney's Office, political science intern, 1970-71; Morgan State University, public relations asst, 1971-72; Housing Authority of Baltimore City, information asst, 1972-75; WMTV, reporter, producer, 1977-82; University of Wisconsin-Madison, teaching asst assoc, 1977-78; WISC TV, executive news producer, 1982-88; WHDH TV, news producer, 1988-. **Orgs:** Boston Association of Black Journalists, 1988-; National Association of Black Journalists, 1988-; Black Achievers/YWCA, mentor/volunteer, 1992-; Alpha Kappa Alpha Sorority, Inc, 1971-. **Honors/Awds:** Boston YWCA, Black Achiever, 1992; Veterans Benefits Clearinghouse Community Service Award, 1992; AFTRA-SAG, Special Chair Award, 1991; New England AFTRA-SAG, American Scene Award, 1991; National Association Black Journalists, Best Feature, 1991. **Special Achievements:** Gabriel Awards for coverage of Nelson Mandela visit to Boston, 1990; American Cancer Society, Sword of Hope Award, 1990; University of Missouri-Lincoln, Unity Award/Education, 1990, Unity Award/AIDS, 1990. **Business Addr:** Television News Producer, WHDH TV, New 7, 7 Bulfinch Pl, News Department, 3rd fl, Boston, MA 02114-2913, (617)725-0864.

HILLIARD, AMY S.
Marketing company executive. **Personal:** daugHter of Stratford & Gwendolyn Hilliard; children: Angelica, Nicholas Jones. **Educ:** Howard University; Harvard Business School, MBA. **Career:** Bloomingdale's, New York, buyer, four years; Gillette Inc, ten years, Boston, director of naricatics, Lustrasilk, marketing executive; Pillsbury Inc, Baked Goods Division, director of market development, until 1992; Burrell Communications Group, senior vp, director, Integrated Mktg Svcs, 1992-95; Hilliard-Jones Marketing Group, president/CEO, 1995-; DePaul University, adjunct professor. **Orgs:** Metropolitan Family Services, board of directors. **Honors/Awds:** Top 100 Businesswoman, Dollar & Sense, Business Executive of the Year, Delta Sigma Theta. **Business Addr:** President, Hilliard Group, Inc, 4823 S Kimbark Ave, Chicago, IL 60615, (773)924-9997.

HILLIARD, ASA GRANT, III
Educator. **Personal:** Born Aug 22, 1933, Galveston, TX; married Patsy Jo; children: Asa IV, Robi Nsenga Bailey, Patricia Nefertari, Hakim Sequenenre. **Educ:** Univ of Denver, BA Psych 1955, MA Counseling 1961, EdD Ed Psych 1963. **Career:** Denver Public Schools, teacher 1955-60; Univ of Denver, teaching fellow 1960-63; San Francisco State Univ, prof, dean of educ 1963-83; GA State Univ, disting prof of educ 1980-. **Orgs:** Dir of rsch Automated Serv Inc 1970-72; consult testing African History Child Devel; bd of dir Natl Black Child Devel Inst 1973-75, Amer Assn of Coll for Teacher Educ 1974-76; mem Natl Assn for the Ed of Young Children 1974-; bd of ethnic & minority affairs Amer Psych Assn 1982-84. **Honors/Awds:** Natl Defense Ed Act Fellow Univ of Denver 1960-63; Knight Commander of the Human Order of African Redemption 1972; Disting Leadership Awd Assn of TeacherEd 1983; Outstanding Scholarship Assoc of Black Psych 1984. **Military Serv:** Armored Infantry 1st lt 2 yrs. **Business Addr:** Professor of Education, Georgia State Univ, PO Box 243, Atlanta, GA 30303.

HILLIARD, DELORIES
Public administrator, court executive. **Personal:** Born in Texas; daughter of Ethel Wilson and Rufus Wilson Sr. **Educ:** Texas Woman's Univ, Denton TX, BS, MS, Univ Texas, Arlington TX, PhD candidate. **Career:** Dallas County MHMR, Dallas TX, quality assurance coord, clinical psychology specialist; City of Dallas, asst to dir (housing), court admin. **Business Addr:** Court Systems Administrator, City of Dallas, Dept of Court Services, 2014 Main St #100-B, Dallas, TX 75208.

HILLIARD, EARL FREDERICK
Congressman. **Personal:** Born Apr 9, 1942, Birmingham, AL; son of Iola Frazier Hilliard and William Hilliard; married Mary Franklin, Jun 9, 1966; children: Alesia, Earl Jr. **Educ:** Morehouse Coll, BA 1964; Atlanta Univ Sch of Business, MBA 1970; Howard Univ Sch of Law, JD 1967. **Career:** AL State U, asst to pres 1968-70; Pearson & Hilliard (Law Firm), partners 1972-73; Birmingham Legal Aid Soc, rgnl heber fellow 1970-72; State of AL state rep 1970-72, state senator 1980-92; US House of Representatives, congressman, 1992-. **Orgs:** Pres Amer Trust Life Ins Co 1977-90; pres Amer Trust Land Co 1980-; chmn AL Black Legsltv Caucus; life mem NAACP 1984, Natl Bar Assoc 1979, Morehouse Coll Natl Alumni Assoc 1983, Alpha Phi Alpha Frat Inc 1980; mem bd of Trustees Miles Law School l984-; mem bd of Trustees Tuskegee Univ l986-. **Honors/Awds:** Published The Legal Aspects of the Franchise Contract 1970; published How To Play Bid Whist 1984; father of the year Natl Orgnztn of Women 1981; outstanding ldrshp award Alpha Phi Alpha Frat, Inc 1980. **Business Addr:** Attorney, PO Box 11385, Birmingham, AL 35202.

HILLIARD, GENERAL K.
Cardiologist. **Personal:** Born Dec 12, 1940, Hempstead, TX; married Ida R McCree; children: Denise, Renee, Brian. **Educ:** Prairie View, BS 1960; Meharry Medical Coll, MD 1968. **Career:** Univ CA-Davis, int med 1972, cardiovas div 1974; AHA Alameda Cty Chapt, pres 1983-84; AHA Cal Affil, chmn elec prog comm; Peralta Hosp, dir cardiovas svcs. **Orgs:** Fellow Amer Coll of Cardiology 1976-87; bd of dir Assoc of Black Cardiol 1986. **Honors/Awds:** Mem Alpha Omega Alpha Honor Med Soc. **Military Serv:** AUS capt 1960-62.

HILLIARD, IKE
Professional football player. **Personal:** Born Apr 5, 1976. **Educ:** Florida. **Career:** New York Giants, wide receiver, 1997-. **Special Achievements:** NFL Draft, First round pick, #7, 1997. **Business Addr:** Professional Football Player, New York Giants, Giants Stadium, East Rutherford, NJ 07073, (201)935-8111.

HILLIARD, PATSY JO
City government official. **Career:** City of East Point Georgia, mayor, currently. **Orgs:** Atlanta Chapter of Links; Natl League of Cities Human Development Steering Comm; GMA Municipal Government & Administration Policy Comm, past chair; Atlanta Chapter, Delta Sigma Theta Sorority, Inc; GMA Unfunded Mundates Day, state chair; Georgia Municipal Assn, future cities task force. **Honors/Awds:** Graduate of the Regional Leadership Institute, 1994; Graduate, East Point Citizens Police Academy; Alpha Kappa Alpha, Public Service Award; US Conference of Mayors, Enhancing Comm Betterment Award, 1994; YWCA of Greater Atlanta, Salute to Women, Academy of Women Achievers, 1993; Trailblazers Award, Lyceum Div of Secondary Educ, Atlanta Public; Delta Sigma Theta Sorority, Inc, Torch Award; East Point Mayor & City Council Resolution for Service; Women for Morris Brown College, Government Award, 1993; Excellence in Government, NAHS; Omega Psi Phi Eta, Omega Chapter, Meritorious Award, 1993; Fulton County, Tony Comm, Certificate of Appreciation, 1995; Race Realtions Award, Resurgence Atlanta, 1994. Realtions Award, Resurgence Atlanta, 1994. **Special Achievements:** First African American and first female elected to the office of mayor in East Point. **Business Addr:** Mayor, City of East Point, 2777 East Point St, East Point, GA 30344, (404)765-1004.

HILLIARD, RANDY
Professional football player. **Personal:** Born Feb 6, 1967, Metairie, LA; married Lynette. **Educ:** Northwestern State-Louisiana. **Career:** Denver Broncos, defensive back, 1994-. **Business Addr:** Professional Football Player, Denver Broncos, 13655 Broncos Pkwy, Englewood, CO 80112, (303)649-9000.

HILLIARD, ROBERT LEE MOORE
Physician. **Personal:** Born Jan 1, 1931, San Antonio, TX; son of Robbie Moore Hilliard and Otho Earl Hilliard; married Mary Lou Moreno; children: Ronald, Bennie Karen Brown, Portia Denise Byas, Robert Jr, Rudyard, Robbie Lesley, Ruby Lucinda, Barbara Felix. **Educ:** Howard Univ, BS 1951; Univ of TX Medical Branch, MD 1956. **Career:** Natl Med Assn, trustee 1975-81, 1983-84; Natl Med Assn, pres 1982-83; TX Bank, dir 1975-88; Natl Medical Fellowships, dir 1982-; St Mary's Univ, trustee advisory bd 1983-90; TX State Bd of Med Examiners, mem 1984-91, pres, 1989-90; chairman, NMA Judicial Council, 1988-94; Women's Clinic of San Antonio, sr Ob/Gyn, currently. **Orgs:** Chmn San Antonio Housing Authority 1969-71; councilman San Antonio City Council 1971-73; commissioned as Honorary Admiral TX Navy State of TX 1978; comm San Antonio Fire & Police Civil Serv Comm 1978-80; Hon Div Surgeon 1st Calvary Div US Army 1983; vice chmn United Negro Coll Fund 1971-75; vice chmn City Water Bd San Antonio 1980-85; chmn City Water Bd 1986-88. **Honors/Awds:** Dedicated Serv 1973, Distinguished Leadership 1982 United Negro Coll Fund; Benefactor de la Communidad City of San Antonio 1981; Certificate of Appreciation State of TX House of Reps 1983; Achievement Award S Central Region AKA Sorority 1983; Distinguished Alumnus, University of Texas Medical Branch, 1991; Recipient, Howard University Distinguished Alumnus Awd, 1995;. **Military Serv:** USAF capt flight surgeon 1957-60. **Business Addr:** Womens Clinic of San Antonio, 710 Augusta, San Antonio, TX 78215.

HILLIARD, WILLIAM ALEXANDER
Clergyman. **Personal:** Born in Greenville, TX; married Edra Mae. **Educ:** Western Univ, AB; Shaeffer Theol Sem Western Univ, BD; Hood Theol Sem, DD. **Career:** African Meth Episcopal Zion Ch, bishop; ministerial pastorates in KS MO SC NC; AME Zion Ch, elected to Episcopacy; overseas mission work Zion Ch Ghana,Nigeria, Liberia, West Africa 1960; Zion Conf in GA OK KS MO CA WA OR, supr. **Orgs:** Chmn Div of Overseas Minis Natl Cnsl of Ch of Christ; trustee Livingstone Clge; mem Nom Comm of Degrees; chmn Land Use Comm; mem World Cnsl of Ch; natl Cnsl of Churches; NAACP; Urban League; Christian Com Cnsl of Detroit; Knight Great Band Liberia West Africa 1975; selected srv ldr Amer Relig Del to visit Taiwan China to survey & observe tech, ind educ dev of China. **Honors/Awds:** John Bryan Sm African Cen Mem Cit 12th Episcopal Dist AME Zion Ch; 1st AME Zion Rest Home Cit Laurinburg Dist Cen NC Conf; awards, Office of the Mayor, Mayor John H Reading; Office of Com Cnsl Mel Ravitz; 77th Legis of City of Detroit St of MI; OH House of Rep AL Concione; Father of Year MI Conf 1975; City of Los Angeles Thomas Ley Office. **Business Addr:** 690 Chicago Blvd, Detroit, MI 48202.

HILLIARD, WILLIAM ARTHUR
Journalist (retired). **Personal:** Born May 28, 1927, Chicago, IL; son of Ruth Little and Felix Henry Hilliard; divorced; children: Gregory Stephen, Linda Karen, Sandra Hilliard Gunder. **Educ:** Pacific University, BA, journalism, 1952. **Career:** Oregonian Publishing Co, 1952-94. **Orgs:** American Society of Newspaper Editors, pres, 1993-; Federal Reserve Bank of San Francisco, chairman, Portland Branch, board of directors, 1991, 1992, 1993; National Urban League, board of directors, 1973-78; National Conference of National Urban League, chairman, 1979-80; Alpha Phi Alpha Fraternity; National Association of Black Journalists; NAACP; Alpha Phi Alpha Fraternity, Freedom Forum First Amendment Center, advisory bd. **Honors/Awds:** Anti-Defamation League Torch of Liberty Award; University of Oregon Public Service Award; Amos E Voorhies Award (top newspaper award in Oregon), 1991; Pacific University, Honorary Law Degree; Urban League of Portland, Equal Opportunity Award; National Association of Black Journalists Presidential Award; Asian American Journalists Association Special Recognition Award; Native American Journalist Association Sculpture in Friendship Award; Oregon State University Distinguished Service Award; Western Oregon State College Distinguished Service Award. **Military Serv:** US Navy, Seaman 1st Class, 1945-46.

HILL-LUBIN, MILDRED ANDERSON
Educator. **Personal:** Born Mar 23, 1933, Russell County, AL; daughter of Mary Anderson and Luther Anderson; married Dr Maurice A Lubin; children: Walter H Hill, Robert T Hill. **Educ:** Paine Coll Augusta, GA, BA English Honors 1961; Western Reserve Cleveland, MA 1962; Indiana, 1964; Univ of Minnesota, 1965-66; Howard Univ & African-Amer Inst,1972; Univ of Illinois Urbana-Champaign, PhD English & African Studies 1974. **Career:** Paine Coll, instructor/asst prof 1962-65 & 1966-70; Hamline Univ, exchange prof 1965-66; Paine Coll, asst prof English/dir EPDA program 1970-72; Univ of IL, tchng asst/instructor 1972-74; Univ of Florida, assoc prof of English/dir English program for special admit students 1974-77, asst dean of graduate sch 1977-80, assoc prof of English & African Studies 1982-. **Orgs:** Proj assoc Council of Chief State School Officers Washington, DC 1981-82; consultant Amer Council on Educ 1981-; panel mem Adv Cncl Mellon Humanities Grant UNCF College Fund 1980-90; discipline comm in African Lit Fulbright Awards 1983-86; exec comm Coll Comp & Comm (CCCC) 1977-80; exec comm African Lit Assn 1983-89; pres Gainesville Chap of the Links 1985-87; pres FOCUS 1978-79; bd dir Gainesville/Alachua Co Center of Excell 1985-; Alpha Kappa Alpha Sor; pres, African Literature Assn 1987-88; dir, Gainesville-Jacmel Haiti Sister Cities Program, 1987-92; pres, The Visionaires, 1988-91; FL Humanities Council, bd of dirs, 1991-95; Santa Fe Community Coll District, bd of trustees, 1993-. **Honors/Awds:** Alpha Kappa Mu Honor Soc Paine Coll 1960; Travel-Study Grant to W Africa African-Amer Intl 19; Trainer of Teachers Fellowship Univ of Illinois 1973-74; coeditor of "Towards Defining the African Aesthetic" and articles in, "Southern Folklore Quarterly," "Coll Lang Assn Journal"; "Presence Africaine"; "Okike"; Leadership and Achievement Award, Nu Eta Lambda Chapter Alpha Phi Alpha Fraternity 1988; articles, "The Black Grandmother in Literature," in Ngambika, 1986; Gainesville Area Women of Distinction Award, 1992; Univ of FL, Teacher of the Year, 1994; Gainesville Comm on the Status of Women, Susan B Anthony Award, 1994. **Home Addr:** 6211 NW 23rd Lane, Gainesville, FL 32606. **Business Addr:** Assoc Prof, English & African Studies, University of Florida, Dept of English, 4008 TUR, Gainesville, FL 32611.

HILLMAN, GRACIA
Association executive. **Personal:** Born Sep 12, 1949, New Bedford, MA; daughter of Mary Grace Hillman and George Hillman; married Robert E Bates Jr; children: Hillman Martin. **Educ:** Univ of MA Boston, Coll of Public & Comm Svc, attended 1973-78. **Career:** MA Legislative Black Caucus, admin 1975-77; MA Dept of Correction, exec asst to commissioner 1977-79; MA Port Authority, public & govt affairs spec 1979;Joint Center for Political Studies, project dir 1979-82; Natl Coal on Black Voter Partic, exec dir 1982-87; Congressional Black Caucus Foundation, interim executive director, 1988; Dukakis for President Campaign, senior advisor for congressional affairs, 1988; Council on Foundations, executive consultant, 1989-90; League of Women Voters of the United States and League of Women Voters Education Fund, executive director,

1990-. **Orgs:** Mem Natl Political Congress of Black Women; sec United Front Homes Devel Corp New Bedford MA 1972-76; pres United Front Homes Day Care Center New Bedford-MA 1973-76; pres ONBOARD Community Action Prog New Bedford MA 1974-76; chairperson MA Govt Serv Career Prog 1977-78; v chairperson Center for Youth SvcsWashington DC 1985-; prog devel consult Congressional Black Caucus Found 1987. **Honors/Awds:** Appointed to MA Post Secondary Education (1202) Commission 1975. **Home Addr:** 3524 Texas Ave SE, Washington, DC 20020. **Business Addr:** Executive Director, League of Women Voters, 1730 M St, NW, Washington, DC 20036.

HILLS, JAMES BRICKY
Pharmacist. **Personal:** Born Oct 1, 1944, Opelousas, LA; married Beatrice M Hubbard. **Educ:** TX Southern Univ Coll of Pharmacy, BS 1971. **Career:** TSU School of Pharmacy Alumni, bd of dir 1978; Christian Coll of Amer, bd of dir 1985-86, vice chmn bd of regents 1985-86; La Porte Neighborhood Ctr, bd of dir 1986; La Porte Apothecary, owner; Lava Rock Apothecary, Pasadena, TX, owner, 1991-. **Orgs:** Bd of dir Harris Co Pharm Assoc 1982; career consultant North Forest ISD Health Prof 1984; chmn USAC, COGIC 1985; instructor Greater Emmanuel Bible Inst 1985; consultant Eastwood Health Clinic 1985; mem, by-law & constitution comm, 1986; chmn, House of Delegates, 1990-91, member, Texas Pharmaceutical Assn; member, NAACP; member, LaPorte Chamber of Commerce; vice president, LaPorte Neighborhood Center Inc, 1988-; president, Agape Investment Development Corp, 1990. **Honors/Awds:** Outstanding Educator of SS TX SC COGIC 1982; Outstanding Board Mem HCPA 1984; Outstanding Board Mem CCA 1986; Pharmacist of the Year, Harris County Pharm Assn, 1990; Daniel B Smith, Apha, 1994; Bowl of Hygeia, TPA, 1997. **Military Serv:** AUS E-5 2 yrs. **Business Addr:** Pharmacist, La Porte Apothecary, 410 E Fairmont Pkwy Ste B, La Porte, TX 77571.

HILLS, KENO
Professional football player. **Personal:** Born Jun 13, 1973, Tampa, FL. **Educ:** Southwestern Louisiana, attended. **Career:** New Orleans Saints, guard, 1996-. **Business Addr:** Professional Football Player, New Orleans Saints, 5800 Airline Hwy, Metairie, LA 70003, (504)733-0255.

HILLSMAN, GERALD C.
Association executive. **Personal:** Born Jul 7, 1926, Dayton, OH; married Julia. **Educ:** Marjorie Webster Jr Coll, AA 1975; Natl Inst Drug Progs, Cert 1975. **Career:** VA Hosp Brentwood CA, drug consult 1971-72; VA Hosp, drug consult 1972-73; USC Hosp, drug cons; Central City Bricks/Kick Proj, founder, prog dir 1970-. **Orgs:** Pres Partners for Progress; hon mem, bd dir W Coast Assoc of Puerto Rican Substance Abuse Workers Inc; adv bd mem Central City Substance Abuse Trng LA. **Honors/Awds:** Outstanding Comm Serv Awd Alliance Drug Ed & Prevention Tehachapi 1974; Outstanding Serv Young People San Bernardino 1974; Dynamic Leadership Awd Friends of Bricks 1974; Resolution CA State Assembly 1974; Congressional Medal of Merit Congressman Augustus F Hawkins 1976; num plaques. **Business Addr:** Program Dir, Central City Bricks/Kick Proj, 1925 S Trinity St, Los Angeles, CA 90011.

HILSON, ARTHUR LEE
Educational administrator, cleric. **Personal:** Born Apr 6, 1936, Cincinnati, OH; son of Bertha McAdoo Wilburn (deceased) and Shepard Hilson (deceased); married Florine McClary Hilson, Apr 3, 1982; children: Gabrielle, Antionette, David. **Educ:** Wheaton College, Springfield Christian Bible Seminary, Wheaton, IL, bachelor of theology; Andover Newton Theological Seminary, Newton Center, MA, MDiv; University of Massachusetts, Amherst, MA, MEd, 1974, EdD, 1979. **Career:** Human Resources Development Center, Newport, RI, human relations consultant, 1973; University of Massachusetts at Amherst, MA, administrative assistant to dean of graduate affairs, School of Education, 1973-75, department head, Veterans Assistance and Couseling Services, 1976-78, department head, University Placement Services, 1978-87, executive director, Public Safety, 1987-92; University of New Hampshire, faculty, american studies for student affairs, 1993-; New Hope Baptist Church, pastor, 1991-. **Orgs:** Member, Phi Delta Kappa; member, American Personnel Officers Assn; member, Eastern College Personnel Officers Assn; member, College Placement Council; member, NAACP; bd member, American Veterans Committee; chairman, Natl Assn of Minority Veterans Program Administrators; bd member, Natl Assn of Veterans Program Administrators; bd member, interim director, Veterans Outreach Center of Greenfield, MA; member, Intl Assn of Campus Law Enforcement Administrators; member, Intl Assn of Chiefs of Police; chairman, United Christian Foundation; charter president, Amherst NAACP; member, bd of dirs, Western Massachusetts Girl Scouts; member, bd of dirs, United Way of Hampshire County; School Bd, elected mem. **Honors/Awds:** Developed and faciliated over 100 workshops on human/race relations and multicultural communications; Kellogg Fellow, Kellogg Foundation, 1973-74. **Military Serv:** US Navy, CPO/Cmdr, 1954-73; Navy Achievement Medal. **Business Addr:** Pastor, New Hope Baptist Church, 263 Peverly Hill Rd, Portsmouth, NH 03801.

HILTON, STANLEY WILLIAM, JR.
Business executive. **Personal:** Born in Philadelphia, PA; son of Jennie Parsons Hilton Cooper and Stanley W Hilton, Sr; divorced; children: Richard H Hilton. **Educ:** Fisk Univ, BA 1959; Temple Univ, Grad Study 1959. **Career:** Mill Run Playhouse Niles IL, treas 1969-70; Shubert Theatre, co mgr "Hair" 1969-70; Orpheum Theatre San Francisco, mgr 1970-74; "My Fair Lady", "Jesus Christ Superstar", "No Place to be Somebody" San Francisco, co mgr; Park & Theatre Opers Art Park Lewiston NY, dir 1974; Evanston Theatre Co IL, bus mgr; Blackstone Theatre Chgo, mgr 1974-86; Emory & Company, owner, 1990-92; real estate and retail entrepreneur, currently; "Pope Joan," Chicago, general manager, 1996; "Hair," Chicago, general manager, 1996. **Orgs:** Coord ed & vocational couns Concentrated Employment Prog, Comm Coll Dist San Fran 1971-73; ofc mgr Cook Cty Dept of Publ Aid Chicago 1966-70; exec asst sec Bd of Pensions Meth Ch IL 1965-66; mem Assoc of Theatrical Press Agt & Mgr NY 1970-; reg soc worker IL 1966-; cert teacher & vocational couns CA 1971-. **Military Serv:** NGR 1960. **Home Addr:** 1540 N State Pkwy, Chicago, IL 60610.

HILTON, TANYA
Association executive. **Personal:** married Steven; children: Taylor, Justin. **Educ:** University of Minnesota, bachelor's degree, business; postgraduate study in England. **Career:** American Assn of University Women, Educational Foundation, director, currently. **Business Addr:** Director, Educational Foundation, American Association of University Women, 1111 16th St NW, Washington, DC 20036, (202)785-7700.

HINCH, ANDREW LEWIS, SR.
Government official. **Personal:** Born Sep 28, 1919, Mexico, MO; married Mary Ann; children: Andy Jr, Terry, Jaqueline, Henry, Shelia, Charles, Brenda, Lewis. **Educ:** Lincoln Univ Jefferson City MO, attd; Hampton Inst VA, attd 1944; IN Sch of Educ Indianapolis, attd; Joliet Jr Clge IL, attd. **Career:** Dist 5 City of Joliet, councilman; V W Detective Agcy, capt over investigators 1976-78; US Post Office, mail carrier. **Orgs:** Pres Natl Assc of Retired Fed Employees Local 655; mem Natl Assc of Letter Carriers; mem Joliet Chamber of Comm; past mem Metro Bd of Joliet YMCA; mem Briggs St YMCA Bd; mem Sr Citizen Bd; mem Drug Coordination & Info Cnsl; mem Comm Action Bd; pres Brooklyn Home Owners Assc; former scoutmaster; Bethelehem Luth Ch & Buffalo Post Amer Legion Troops; mem Amer Legion Post 1284. **Honors/Awds:** Beyond the Call of Duty Award US Post Office; 1st Black to hold Taxi-License Franchise City of Joliet; 1st Black to be elected to Joliet City Council 5th Dist. **Military Serv:** USN cm2 1943-68. **Business Addr:** City Of Joliet, 150 W Jefferson, Joliet, IL 60431.

HINDS, LENNOX S.
Attorney, educator. **Personal:** Born in Port of Spain, Trinidad and Tobago; son of Dolly Stevens Hinds (deceased) and Arthur Hinds; married Bessie; children: Brent, Yvette, Renee. **Educ:** City Coll, BS; Rutgers School of Law, JD 1972. **Career:** Natl Conf Of Black Lawyers, natl dir; Prisoner's Rights Organization Defense, dir 1971-72; Heritage Fnd, dir 1969-72; Citgo Corp, rsch sect chief 1964-69; Rutgers State Univ, prof of criminal law, chmn Administration of Justice Program, currently. **Orgs:** Permanent del UN Non-Govt Organization; Intl Assn of Democratic Lawyers; Intl Bd, Organization of Non-Govt Organizations; NJ Bar Assn; Committee on Courts & Criminal Procedure; Natl Minority Adv Commn for Criminal Justice; Natl Adv Council for Child Abuse; bd mem Society Mobilization Legal Project; past natl secretary Black-American Law Students Assn; past bd mem Law Students Civil Rights Research Council; State Bar of New York, New Jersey. **Honors/Awds:** J Skelly Wright Civil Rights Award; Assn of Black Law Students Community Service Award 1973; Distguished Alumnus Award Black Amer Law Students 1974; numerous publications. **Home Addr:** 42 Van Doren Ave, Somerset, NJ 08873. **Business Addr:** Chairman, Administration of Justice Program, Rutgers University, New Brunswick, NJ 08903.

HINE, DARLENE CLARK
Educator. **Personal:** Born Feb 7, 1947, Morley, MO; daughter of Lottie M Clark and Levester Clark; children: Robbie Davine. **Educ:** Roosevelt Univ of Chicago, BA 1968; Kent State Univ Kent OH, MA 1970, PhD 1975. **Career:** South Carolina State College, asst prof, 1972-74; Purdue Univ, asst prof, 1974-79, interim dir, Africana & Res Center, 1978-79, assoc prof 1979-81, vice provost, 1981-86, prof, 1986-87; Michigan State Univ, John A Hannah prof of history, 1987-. **Orgs:** Exec counc mem Assn for Study of Afro-Amer Life History 1979-81; editor Tru th, Newsletter of ABWH 1979-80; dir of publs Assn of Black Women Historians 19 79; member, Yale University Council's Committee on the Graduate School, 1988-93; member, board of directors, Consortium of Social Science Assns, 1987-91; nominating committee chair, American Historical Assn, 1988-89; executive council, Southern Historical Assn, 1990-93; Organization of American Histories, prog comm, 1998; Natl Academy for Critical Studies, exec comm, 1996-; Comm on Women, Southern Historical Assn, chair, 1996-98; Assn for the Study of African-American Life and History Carter G Woodson Scholar-in-Residence Comm, 1995; Assoc Editor, The Historian, 1995-. **Honors/Awds:** Author of: Black Victory, The Rise and Fall of the White Primary in Texas, 1979, Black Women in White: Social Conflict and Cooperation in the Nursing Profession 1890-1950, 1989; Otto Wirth Alumni Award for Outstanding Scholarship, Roosevelt University, 1988; Special Achievement Award, Kent University Alumni Assn, 1991; Outstanding Book Award, Gustavus Myers Center of Human Rights, 1990; Lauinia L Dock Book Award, American Assn for Nursing; Letitia Woods Brown Book Award, Assn of Black Women Historians, 1990; editorial board, Journal of Negro History, 1979-; Author: Speak Truth to Power: Black Professional Class in United States History, 1996, Hine Sight: Black Women and the Re-Construction of American History, 1994, Black Women in White: Racial Conflict and Cooperation inthe Nursing Profession 1890-1950, 1989, Black Victory The Rise and Fall of the White Primary in Texas, 1979, Zora Neal Hurston-Paul Robeson Award, The Natl Council for Black Studies, Inc, 1995, Letitia Woods Brown Memorial Anthology Prize, Assn of Black Women Historians, 1995, The Steffin Foundation, Inc, (for Black Women in America: An Historical Encyclopedia,) Editor, 1994, Outstanding Reference Source Award, Amer Library Assn, 1994; Coauthor, A Shining Thread of Hope: The History of Black Women in America, 1998. **Business Addr:** Professor, Hist Dept, Michigan State University, 301 Morrill Hall, East Lansing, MI 48824.

HINES, CARL R., SR.
Realtor. **Personal:** Born Mar 23, 1931, Louisville, KY; married Teresa Churchill; children: 4. **Educ:** Univ Louisville, BS; Louisville Sch Law. **Career:** Housing Opportunity Ctr, exec dir 1974; KY Gen Assembly Louisville, state rep 1985; Housing Opportunity Centers Inc, city dir, exec dir. **Orgs:** Mem Housing Task Force Louisville C of C; mem Mayor's Housing Task Force under Mayor Frank Burke; mem Nat Assn Comm Devel; bd dir State KY Housing Corp; mem Housing Com Louisville C of C 1985; couns Nat Center Housing Mgmt Wash; adv com Non-Profit Housing Center; v chmn Jefferson Co Bd Edn;mem Dist Lines Subcom Charter Com for Merger Louisville & Jefferson Co Schs; former mem bd Louisville NAACP, W Louisville Optimist Club; past chmn Shawnee Dist Boy Scouts Am; cur pres Just Men's Civic & Social Club; exec sec mem Louisville & Jefferson Co Comm Action Commn; v Chmn bd mgrs YMCA; Louisville Bd Educ 1968; re-elected 1968 & 1972; chmn Fifth Region KY Sch Bds Assn; gov's adv Cncl Edn; mem Fed Relations Network Nat Sch Bd Assn; dir Nat Caucus Black Sch Bd Mems & ChmnState KY. **Honors/Awds:** Various including Air Force Distinguished Flying Cross. **Military Serv:** USAF 3 yrs.

HINES, CHARLES A.
Military officer (retired), educational administrator. **Personal:** Born Sep 4, 1935, Washington, DC; son of Grace W Hines and Charles A Hines; married Veronica Lamb Hines, Aug 24, 1962; children: Tracy, Charles, Kelly, Christina, Michael, Nicholas, Timothy. **Educ:** Howard University, BS, physical education, 1962; Michigan State University, MS, police administration and public safety, 1970; US Army Command & Gen Staff College, master of military arts and sciences, 1971; Johns Hopkins University, PhD, sociology, 1983. **Career:** Univ of Maryland, Univ Coll, instructor/adjunct prof, 1971-; US Army, 1962-, dir of evaluation, War College, 1980-81, commander 14th military police brigade, 1983-85, dir officer personnel mgmt, 1985-87, dir of mgmt & budget, office of the deputy chief of staff for personnel, 1987-89, commanding general chemical and military police training ctrs, commanding general, Fort McClellan, AL, commandant, military police sch, beginning 1989; Smithsonian Inst, Protection and Health Services, dir, beginning 1992; Prairie View A & M Univ, pres, currently. **Orgs:** Alpha Phi Alpha Fraternity, Inc; FBI National Academy Associates; chr, Texas Military Strategic Planning Commission. **Honors/Awds:** Natl Boys and Girls Club Hall of Fame, inductee, 1992; Southern Christian Leadership Conf, Outstanding Black Man, 1994. **Military Serv:** US Army, enlisted, 1954-57; US Army, major general, 1962-92. **Business Addr:** President, Prairie View A & M Univ, Office of the Pres, PO Box 188, Prairie View A & M Univ, Prairie View, TX 77446.

HINES, GREGORY OLIVER
Actor, dancer. **Personal:** Born Feb 14, 1946, New York, NY; son of Alma Iola Lawless Hines and Maurice Robert Hines; married Pamela Koslow, Apr 12, 1981; children: Daria, Jessica Koslow, Zachary Evan. **Career:** Family tap dance act: Hines Kids, 1949-55; Hines Brothers 1955-63; Hines, Hines, & Dad, 1963-73; Severance, Jazz Rock Band, 1973-77; theater appearances include: Eubie!, 1978-79; Comin' Uptown, 1979-80; Sophisticated Ladies, 1980-81; Parade of Stars Playing the Palace, 1983; Night of 100 Stars II, 1985; Black Broadway; The Last Minstrel Show in New York; Jelly's Last Jam, 1992-93; film appearances include: Wolfen, 1981; History of the World Part I, 1981; Deal of the Century, 1983; Muppets Take Manhattan, 1984; The Cotton Club, 1984; White Nights, 1985; Running Scared, 1986; The Gregory Hines Show, 1997-. **Orgs:** Actors Equity Assn; Screen Actors Guild; American Federation of Television & Radio Artists. **Honors/Awds:** Three Tony Nominations 1979, 1980, 1981; Theater World Award, Eubie!, 1978-79; Tor Award; Dance Educators of America Award; co-host, 1984 Oscars; honoree, 1985 Dramatic Arts Award, achievements as stage/screen actor, contributions to The Cotton Club; Tony Award, best leading male in a musical, Jelly's Last Jam, 1992. **Business Addr:** Actor/Dancer, c/o Fran Saperstein Orga-

nization, 6310 San Vicente Blvd, #310, Los Angeles, CA 90048.

HINES, J. EDWARD, JR.
Attorney. **Personal:** Born Feb 26, 1908, Alexandria, LA; married Willie B Smith; children: Ethel Hines Battle, J E III, Zelda Ruth Turner. **Educ:** Parish of Rapiedes State of LA, asst dist atty 1972-; Alexandria, asst city atty 1971-72. **Career:** Mem LA State Bar; mem Alexandria Bar; pres Rapides Parish Voters League yrs; pres Alexandria Civ & Improvement Council 11 yrs; admin bd Newman United Meth Ch; mem Sch Bd Bi-Racial Com; appointed mem Bi-Racial Com of State of LA; alternate delegate To Dem Nat Conv 1968; mem Omega Psi Phi; 32 Deg Mason; Kisatchie-Delta Reg Planning & Dev Dist Inc; Cenla Health Planning Council. **Orgs:** Outstanding Citizen of the Comm 1965; Omega Man of the Yr Omega Psi Phi 1974. **Business Addr:** 1330 8 St, Alexandria, LA 71301.

HINES, JIMMIE
Automobile dealer. **Career:** Edmond Dodge Inc, chief executive officer, currently. **Special Achievements:** Company is #97 on Black Enterprise's list of 100 top auto dealers, 1994. **Business Addr:** CEO, Edmond Dodge Inc., 5535 Gatewood Dr, Sterling Heights, MI 48310-2227.

HINES, KINGSLEY B.
Attorney. **Personal:** Born Mar 27, 1944, Pasadena; married Anne; children: Tiffany, Garrett. **Educ:** USC, BA 1966; Loyola U, JD 1969. **Career:** So CA Edison Co, atty 1972-; Eng Sq Law Cntr LA 1970-71; Family Law Cntr, leg servs 1969-71. **Orgs:** Mem CA Bar Assn; LA Co Bar Assn; Langston Law Club. **Business Addr:** 2244 Walnut Grove Ave, Ste 341, Rosemead, CA 91770.

HINES, LAURA M.
Psychologist, educator. **Personal:** Born Oct 29, 1922, Covington, VA; divorced. **Educ:** Virginia State University, BA; New York University, MA; Fordham University, PhD. **Career:** Byrd S Coler Metro Hosp, psychologist 1960-65; Bd of Educ NYC, psychologist 1965-74, supervisor of psychologists 1974-79; Columbia Univ, consulting psychologist; Yeshiva Univ, professor emerita. **Orgs:** Fellow American Psychological Assn; Pres, school division, NYC Psychological Assn, 1983-84; bd of trustees, Lexington School for the Deaf, currently; American Psychological Assn; Natl Assn of School Psychologists. **Home Addr:** 156-20 Riverside Dr W, New York, NY 10032.

HINES, MORGAN B.
Dental surgeon. **Personal:** Born Aug 11, 1946, New York, NY; son of Emmie Hines and Edgar Hines; children: Morgan B Jr. **Educ:** Toledo Univ, attended 1964-68; Meharry Medical Coll, DDS 1973. **Career:** Hubbard Hosp, intern 1973-74; Maury Co Health Dept, dentist 1974-75; Meharry Medical Coll Dept of Oral Pathology, assoc prof 1975-76; Columbia TN, professional hypnosis practice 1976-; Private Practice Columbia TN, dentist 1974-. **Orgs:** Professional artist pen and ink, sculpture, oils, pencil; art showing at TN Arts League, TN Performing Arts Ctr, Columbia State Comm Coll, TN State Univ; chmn Maury County Fine Arts Exhibit 1983; piece in collection of art Mid State TN Regional Library 1985; mem TN Art League, Columbia Creative Arts Guild, Columbia Cof C; hospital staff Maury County Hosp; mem Amer Dental Assoc, Omega Psi Phi Frat Inc, TN Sheriff Org, TN Black Artist Assoc; bd of dirs Nashville Amateur Boxing Assoc, Maury Co Creative Art Guild, TN/AL/GA Amateur Boxing Hall of Fame. **Honors/Awds:** Coach of the Year Awd Spirit of Amer Tournament Decatur AL 1981; TN Special Deputy Sheriff; numerous art awds; numerous appreciation awds for dedication to youth and boxing; three articles Amateur Boxing Magazine 1980-82; poem published in "The World Book of Poetry" 1981. **Business Addr:** 418 West 6th St, Columbia, TN 38402.

HINES, RALPH HOWARD
Business executive. **Personal:** Born May 15, 1927, Chicago, IL. **Educ:** Univ of IL, BS 1949; Univ of Copenhagen, MA 1951; Univ of IL, PhD 1955. **Career:** USIA-US State Dept, cultural affairs officer 1955-60; AL State Univ, prof sociology 1960-63; Howard Univ, prof assoc sociology 1963-65; Meharry Med Coll, exec vice pres 1966-82, prof soc psychiatry 1965-. **Orgs:** Editor Journal Social & Behavioral Sci 1968-75; consult HEW Washington DC 1970-75 chmn bd Metro Transit Authority 1971-81; vice chmn bd TN Housing Devel Agency 1973-75; mem bd Comm Fed Savings Assn 1975-; pres Assn Social & Behavorial Sci 1975; mem Nashville Gas Co 1978; mem bd Comm Fed Savings Assn 1975-. **Honors/Awds:** Harold D West Awd Meharry Med Coll 1972; Fellow Amer Pub Health Assn Washington DC 1973; Doctor of Letters (LLD), Meharry Medical College 1976.

HINES, ROSETTA (THE ROSE)
Radio personality. **Career:** WJZZ, disc jockey, currently. **Special Achievements:** Celebrated 25 years in broadcasting, 1993. **Business Addr:** Disc Jockey, WJZZ, 2994 E Grand Blvd, Detroit, MI 48202, (313)871-0590.

HINES, WILEY EARL
Dentist. **Personal:** Born Apr 29, 1942, Greenville, NC; married Gloria D Moore; children: Wandria, Wiley, Derrick. **Educ:** Knoxville Coll, BS 1963; Meharry Med Coll, DDS 1971. **Career:** Oak Ridge Natl Labs, biologist 1963-65; Melpar, biologist 1965-67; St of NC, publ health dentist 1971-73; Howard Univ, asst clinical prof 1975; Private practice, dentist 1973-. **Orgs:** Mem Amer Dental Assn, Old N St Dental Assoc, E Med, Dental Pharm Soc, Alpha Phi Alpha, IBPOE, Prince Hall Mason; NC Dental Society; Fifth District Dental Society; Greenville Planning & Zoning Commission, 1981-86; Mental Health Assn; New East Bank of Greenville, bd of dirs, 1989-. **Military Serv:** USNR 1971-73. **Business Addr:** 608 E 10th St, Greenville, NC 27834.

HINES, WILLIAM E.
Family physician. **Personal:** Born Jun 16, 1958, St Louis, MO; son of Bessie M Hines. **Educ:** Northwestern University, Evanston, IL, BA, 1980; Univ of Missouri Columbia, Columbia, MO, MD, 1984; Ohio State University, Columbus, OH, MS, 1988. **Career:** Wayne State University, Detroit, MI, resident physician, 1984-87; Ohio State University, Columbus, OH, fellow/clinical instructor, 1987-88; Howard University, Washington, DC, assistant professor, 1989-90; Indiana University, Gary, IN, director-family practice & clinical assistant professor, 1990-92; Hines Family Care Center, president and chairman, currently. **Orgs:** Member, National Medical Association, 1985-; member, American Academy of Family Physicians, 1984-; professional board member, Student National Medical Assn Board of Directors, 1986-94; executive committee member, Student National Medical Assn Board of Directors, 1987-89, 1990-94; member, Professional Bd Member Emeotus, 1994; The Society of Teachers of Family Medicine, 1991-. **Honors/Awds:** National Medical Fellowship Award, National Medical Fellowship, 1980-81, 1981-82; Percy H Lee Award for Outstanding Alumni Achievement, Middlewestern Province, Kappa Alpha Psi Fraternity Inc, 1984, 1996; Recognition Award, Student National Assn, Region II, 1987; Black Student Leadership Award, Graduate Student, The Ohio State University, 1988; Grand Polemarch's Appreciation Certificate, Grand Chapter, Kappa Alpha Psi Fraternity Inc, 1988; Faculty Orientation Award, Society of Teachers of Family Medicine, 1991; Life Membership Student National Medical Assn, 1994. **Business Addr:** President and Chairman, Hines Family Care Center, Inc, 13300 New Halls Ferry Rd, Ste C, Florissant, MO 63033.

HINKLE, JACKSON HERBERT
Clergyman. **Personal:** Born Dec 17, 1943, Arkansas; children: Herby, Jack. **Educ:** Philander-Smith Coll, BA; Greenville Indus Coll, DD 1966; Northwestern U, grad sty. **Career:** Catherdral of Faith Inkster, MI, pastor cath hdqtrs 1975-; New Hebron Bapt Ch Little Rock, AR & St Bethel Bapt Ch Chgo, pastor; Stinson Cathedral Funeral Home, establ; Mobil Vido Tape Co, vp; Cath of Faith E Detroit, fdr pastor. **Orgs:** Fdr chmn Back to God Am Com; fdr pres Cathedral Christian Acad; fdr dir Nat Assn Black Soul Winning Chs 1974. **Honors/Awds:** Apprec cert Gov; outstdg serv awd New Bethel Bapt Ch 1973; author lectr evangelist. **Business Addr:** Founder, Pastor, Cathedral of Faith, 13925 Burt Rd, Detroit, MI 48223.

HINSON, ROY MANUS
Professional basketball player. **Personal:** Born May 2, 1961, Trenton, NJ. **Educ:** Rutgers Univ, New Brunswick, NJ, 1979-83. **Career:** Cleveland Cavaliers, 1983-86; Philadelphia 76ers, 1986-87; New Jersey Nets, 1987-92; Atlanta Hawks, 1992-. **Business Addr:** Professional Basketball Player, Atlanta Hawks, 1 CNN Center NW S Tower, Ste 405, Atlanta, GA 30335.

HINTON, ALFRED FONTAINE
Artist, educator. **Personal:** Born Nov 27, 1940, Columbus, GA; son of Johnnie Mae Sipp Hinton and Eddie H Hinton; married Ann Noel Pearlman, Aug 5, 1965; children: Adam, Melina, Elizabeth. **Educ:** Univ of IA, BA 1967; Univ of Cincinnati with honors, MFA 1970. **Career:** Toronto Argonauts, professional football player, 1963-67; Khadejha Primitive Prints Toronto, design consultant, 1967-68; Dickinson Coll, Carlisle, PA, instructor, 1969; Western Michigan Univ, asst prof of painting & drawing, 1970-77; Univ of Michigan School of Art, assoc prof in painting, 1977-82, prof of painting, 1982-. **Orgs:** Visual Arts Adv Panel MI Council for Arts 1973-; coordinator Visual Arts MI Academy of Science Arts & Letters 1972-74; exhibiting artist Gallery 7 Detroit 1970-; bd mem, Michigan Council for the Arts, 1980-84; exec bd mem, Concerned Citizen's for the Arts Michigan, 1983-86; panelist, Ongoing Michigan Artist Program, Detroit Inst of Arts, 1986-88; Master Panel Bd, Detroit Council for the Arts, 1987-. **Honors/Awds:** Research grant, Western Michigan Univ 1972-73; Flint Inst of Arts All MI Exhibition Purchase Award 1972; 16 one-person shows; 40 invitational & group exhibitions; All-Amer, co-captain, Most Valuable Player, Univ of IA Football Team 1961; Creative Artist Grant, Michigan Council for the Arts, 1985; State of Michigan Commission on Art in Public Places, 1986. **Business Addr:** Prof, School of Art, Univ of Michigan, 2055 Art & Architecture Bldg, Ann Arbor, MI 48109.

HINTON, CHRISTOPHER JEROME
Photographer, studio co-owner. **Personal:** Born Sep 23, 1952, Raleigh, NC; son of A M Hinton and J D Hinton. **Educ:** Winston-Salem State Univ, Winston-Salem NC, BA Music, 1975. **Career:** J D Hinton Studio, Raleigh NC, photographer, 1976-. **Orgs:** Phi Beta Sigma Frat, 1972-; Garner Road Family YMCA Back-A-Child Campaign; United Nero Coll Fund Campaign, 1989; NAACP Freedom Fund Banquet, annual. **Honors/Awds:** Phi Beta Sigma Frat Award; Business Award, Raleigh Alumnae Chapter Delta Sigma Theta; photography works featured in natl publications such as: Jet Publication, Black Radio Exclusive, Ohio Historical Soc. **Business Addr:** Co-owner, J D Hinton Studio, 515 South Blount St, Raleigh, NC 27601.

HINTON, GREGORY TYRONE
Attorney. **Personal:** Born Nov 22, 1949, Barrackville, WV; son of Amelia Hinton and Nathan Hinton; divorced; children: Gregory T II, Hamilton H, Carol Princess Jean. **Educ:** Fairmont State College, AB, 1978; West Virginia University, College of Law, JD, 1981; Kellogg Leadership Development Certification, 1995. **Career:** Thorofare Markets Inc, stock clerk/carry-out 1968-69; Hope Natl Gas Co, casual rouster 1970-71; Montana Power Co, elec clerk 1972-73; Gibbs & Hill, elec clerk 1973-75; N Central Opportunity Indus Ctr, exec dir 1975-78; Fairmont City Council, council member 1977-86, mayor 1983-85; WV Univ Coll of Law, consultant; attorney private practice; Fairmont St Coll, prof, 1989-. **Orgs:** Mem Montana Valley Assn of Health Ctrs Inc 1974-; deacon Good Hope Baptists Church 1974-; corp banking & business law & minority affairs comm WV State Bar 1984-86; vstg comm WV Univ Coll of Law 1984-87; adv bd WNPB-TV 1984-86; bd mem Fairmont Gen Hosp 1985-86; consul WV Univ Coll of Law 1985-; WV Adv Comm to US Commn on Civil Rights 1985-89; pres MT State Bar Assn 1986-88; ethics comm WV State Bar 1986-87; NAACP Legal Redress Comm. **Honors/Awds:** 1st black elected Mayor to a major city in WV 1983; Hon Mem Magnificent Souls 1983; Outstanding Young Man of Amer Jaycees 1979, 1984; WV Outstanding Black Atty Black Amer Law Student Assn Morgantown WV 1984; WV Outstanding Black Atty; Spec Award as Mayor from WV State Assn and PER-PDR Tri-State Conf ofCouncils IBPOEW PA-OH-WV 1984; Spec Award as Mayor from Dunbar HS class of 1947 1984; Honorary Mem Amer Soc for Nondestructive Testing Fairmont State Coll Sect 1984; Black Amer Law Student Assn Morgantown WV 1985; Outstanding WV Black Attorney; Wiliam A Boram Award, Teaching Excellence, 1996, 1997; Carnegie Foundation for the Advancement of Teaching, West VA Professor of the Year, 1997. **Home Addr:** 700 Locust Ave, Fairmont, WV 26554.

HINTON, HORTENSE BECK
College administrator. **Personal:** Born Apr 27, 1950, Charlottesville, VA; widowed; children: Shani O, Adisa A, Ajamu A. **Educ:** State Univ of NY, BA, psychology, 1971; Univ of DC MA, counseling, 1977; Univ of VA, Ed counselor Education, EdD, 1988. **Career:** Univ of District of Columbia, sr counselor/asst dir special serv program 1971-78; Univ of VA, assoc dean/director summer preparatory program office of afro-amer affairs 1978-88; Germanna Community College, director, Student Development Svcs, currently. **Orgs:** Mem Amer Assoc for Counseling & Develop, Natl Assoc Women's Deans & Counselors, Amer Assoc of Univ Women, Amer Assoc for Affirmative Action; clerk, trustee, youth advisor Free Union Baptist Church; Consultant, Alcohol and Other Drug Center, VA Commonwealth University. **Honors/Awds:** Community Serv Awd Culpepper Branch NAACP 1983; Martin L King Jr Faculty Awd Alpha Phi Alpha Inc Univ of VA 1986-87; Gubernatorial apptmt VA State Equal Employment Oppor Council 1986-94. **Home Addr:** 21325 Mt Pony Rd, Culpeper, VA 22701. **Business Addr:** Director, Student Devt Services, Germanna Community Coll, PO Box 339, Locust Grove, VA 22508.

HINTON, MILTON
Association executive. **Career:** Natl Assn for the Advancement of Colored People, Cincinnati Branch, president, currently. **Business Addr:** President, NAACP, Cincinnati Branch, 2500 Kemper Ln, Cincinnati, OH 45206, (513)281-1900.

HINTZEN, PERCY CLAUDE
Educator. **Personal:** Born Jan 26, 1947, Georgetown, Guyana; son of Vera Malfalda Khan Hintzen and Percival Coppin Hintzen; married Joan Alicia McIntosh; children: Ian, Shawn, Alicia, Candace. **Educ:** University of Guyana, Georgetown, Guyana, BS, 1975; Clark University, Worcester, MA, MA, 1976; Yale University, New Haven, CT, MA, 1977; MPhil, 1977, PhD, 1981. **Career:** Yale University, New Haven, CT, acting instructor, 1978-79; University of Guyana, Guyana, lecturer, 1977-78; University of California, Berkeley, CA, associate professor, 1979-; African Amer Studies, chairperson, 1994-; Peace & Conflict Studies, dir, 1994-. **Orgs:** Member, American Sociological Society, 1979-; member, Caribbean Studies Association, 1979; member, American Political Science Association, 1979-81. **Honors/Awds:** The Costs of Regime Survival, Cambridge University Press, 1989. **Business Addr:** Associate Professor, African-American Studies, University of California at Berkeley, 660 Barrows, Berkeley, CA 94720.

HIPKINS, CONRAD
Industrial company executive. **Career:** Automated Sciences Group Inc, chief executive officer, currently. **Special Achievements:** Company ranked #37 on Black Enterprise's List of Top Industrial/Service Companies, 1992. **Business Phone:** (301)587-8750.

HITCHCOCK, JIMMY DAVIS, JR.
Professional football player. **Personal:** Born Nov 9, 1971, Concord, NC. **Educ:** Univ of North Carolina, attended. **Career:** New England Patriots, defensive back, 1995-. **Business Addr:** Professional Football Player, New England Patriots, 60 Washington St, Foxboro Stadium, Foxboro, MA 02035, (508)543-7911.

HITE, NANCY URSULA
Producer, public relations assistant. **Personal:** Born Aug 1, 1956, White Plains, NY; daughter of Jesse and Forest Davis. **Educ:** Spelman Coll, BA 1978; Iona Coll, MS 1985. **Career:** WOVX-Radio Station, reporter 1978-79; Louis-Rowe Enterprises, public relations, exec sec to corp, 1979-; Potpourri WVOX Radio, producer, 1982-; Freelance journalist newspapers and magazines throughout the US, 1982-; Intl Photo News Service, mng ed; Conversation Rowe (radio show), producer; Natl Photo News Service, producer/managing editor 1985-. **Orgs:** Assoc editor New Rochelle Branch NAACP Newsletter 1985-86; Advisory New Rochelle NAACP Youth Council 1987; 3rd vice pres, New Rochelle NAACP; mem Alpha Kappa Alpha Sor; secretary, African American Guild of Performing Artists Inc; co-founder, African Heritage Educational Forum; co-founder, Ki Africa Taalimu Shule. **Honors/Awds:** Certificate The Publicity Club of New York 1981,82; Researcher "Break Dancing" pub by Shron Publication 1984; entertainment articles pub in "Right On" & "Class" Magazines Edri Communications; 1986 Outstanding Young Women of Amer. **Business Addr:** Exec Sec to the Corporation, Louis-Rowe Enterprises, 455 Main St Ste 99, New Rochelle, NY 10801.

HIXSON, JUDSON LEMOINE
Administrator. **Personal:** Born Jun 10, 1950, Chicago, IL. **Educ:** Univ of Chicago, BA 1972, MA Ed 1973, PhD candidate. **Career:** IL Bell Telephone, installer, repairman 1968-70; Univ of Chicago, counselor, instr pre-freshman prog 1970-72, dir pre-freshman prog 1970-72, rsch, therapist dept of psych 1974-76; Loyola Univ School of Social Work, instr 1976-79; Chicago Urban League, ed dir 1976-80; City Comm Detroit MI, asst to pres 1981; Chicago Public Schools Equal Educ Opportunity, coord for admin 1981-. **Orgs:** Pres, treas Henry Booth House Bd of Trustees 1975-; bd of dir IL Assoc for the Advancement of Blacks in Voc Ed 1977-80; pres Natl Council of Urban League Ed Specialists 1978-80; founder, Spirit Records 1979-; pres City-Wide Adv Comm Chicago Bd of Ed 1979-80; mem WSSD Radio 1980; pres, founder Four "M" Co Multi-Media Prod & Mgmt; consult Valpariaso & Northeastern IL Univ; bd of dir Girl Scouts of Chgo, Chicago United Ed Task Force, Hull House Assoc, IL Consultation on Ethnicity in Ed; consult US Congressional Black Caucus, Natl Urban League, IL Office of Ed, Human Resource Devel Columbia Coll School Dist in Seattle, Pittsburgh, New Orleans, San Diego, Dallas, Blue Island IL; consult Catholic Charities of Chgo. **Honors/Awds:** Howell Murray Alumni Awd for Achievement Univ of Chicago Alumni Assoc 1972; Comm Serv Awd Chicago Jr Assoc of Commerce & Ind 1978; Fifty Leaders of the Future Ebony Mag 1978; Ten Outstanding Young Citizens Chicago Jr Assoc of Commerce & Ind 1980; Outstanding Young Men of Amer 1980; Rsch Spec & Publ, testing,classroom mgmt, desegregation, student motivation, teacher/parent trng. **Business Addr:** Coordinator for Administration, Chicago Public Schools, Equal Ed Oppty, 1819 W Persking Rd 6 East, Chicago, IL 60609.

HOAGLAND, EVERETT H., III
Educator. **Personal:** Born Dec 18, 1942, Philadelphia, PA; divorced; children: Kamal, Nia, Ayan. **Educ:** Lincoln Univ PA, BA 1964; Brown Univ, MA 1973. **Career:** Philadelphia School System, English teacher 1964-67; Lincoln Univ, asst dir admissions 1967-69; Claremont Coll Black Studies, instr Afro-Amer poetry 1969-71; Brown Univ, univ fellow 1971-73; Southeastern MA Univ, assoc prof of English; University of Massachusetts at Dartmouth, prof of English, currently. **Orgs:** Member of Bahai Faith 1973-; clerk of corp/bd mem New Bedford Foster Grandparents Prog 1976-82; weekly columnist New Bedford Standard-Times 1979-82; contributing editor Amer Poetry Review 1984-; Wm Carney Acad New Bedford 1985; NAACP 1985. **Honors/Awds:** Univ Fellowship, Brown Univ 1971-73; Silvera Award for Creative Writing Lincoln Univ 1964; Gwendolyn Brooks Award for Fiction by Black World Mag 1974; Creative Artists Fellowship MA Arts & Humanities Competition 1975; NEH Fellowship 1984; fellowship from Artists Foundation Annual State Wide Poetry Competition 1986. **Business Addr:** Professor of English, University of Massachusetts, North Dartmouth, MA 02747.

HOARD, LEROY
Professional football player. **Personal:** Born May 5, 1968, New Orleans, LA. **Educ:** Univ of Michigan, education major. **Career:** Cleveland Browns, running back, 1990-95; Baltimore Ravens, 1996; Carolina Panthers, 1996; Minnesota Vikings, 1996-. **Honors/Awds:** Rose Bowl MVP award, 1989; Pro Bowl, 1994. **Business Addr:** Professional Football Player, Minnesota Vikings, 9520 Viking Dr, Eden Prairie, MN 55344, (612)828-6500.

HOBBS, ALMA COBB
Governmental official. **Personal:** Born Oct 16, 1949, Farmville, NC; daughter of Mr and Mrs Nathan R Cobb Sr; divorced; children: Steven L. **Educ:** North Carolina Central Univ, BS, 1970; North Carolina State Univ, masters, 1975, doctorate, 1981. **Career:** Windsor NC Extension Service, home ec & 4-h agent, 1970-73; Davidson Co Ext Service, 4-h agent, 1974-78; USDA (IPA), national program leader, 1988-89; Tennessee State Univ, adminstrator, 1981-90; USDA, asst deputy admin, 1990-94, deputy admin, 1994-. **Orgs:** Arlington Chapter of Links, treasurer 1993, 1992-; Hendersonville Links, vp 1990, 1982-92; Alpha Kappa Alpha Sorority; National Assn of Extension Agent 4-h Agents; Epsilon Sigma Phi; Phi Delta Kappa. **Honors/Awds:** Distingusihed Service Award, 1996; Outstanding Professional Achievements Award, 1996; African-American Achievers in Agriculture Award, 1996. **Special Achievements:** 25 educational publications, Tennessee State Univ, on a variety of issues related to textiles and clothing, 1982-88. **Business Addr:** Deputy Administrator, USDA, CSREES, AG Box 0925, Room 3444-S, 14th and Independence Ave, SW, Washington, DC 20250-0925.

HOBBS, DARYL RAY
Professional football player. **Personal:** Born May 23, 1968, Victoria, TX; married Tamiyka. **Educ:** Univ of Pacific. **Career:** Oakland Raiders, wide receiver, 1995-97; Seattle Seahawks, 1997-. **Business Addr:** Professional Football Player, Seattle Seahawks, 11220 NE 53rd St, Kirkland, WA 98033, (206)827-9777.

HOBBS, JOHN DANIEL
Educator, legislator. **Personal:** Born Oct 13, 1931, Washington, DC; married Mary A Saxon; children: Danielle A, John D Jr, Harold Krause, Karen Krause. **Educ:** Univ of Redlands CA, BA, MA 1962-69. **Career:** City of San Bernardino, councilman 1975-; Redlands Unified Sch Dist, tchr 1962-; Norton AFB CA, computer prog/syst analysis 1965-69; Past Polemarch San Bernardino Alumni Chap Southern CA Const Oppt Prog, educ consult & tutor 1968-75. **Orgs:** Kappa Alpha Psi 1967-69; mem Prince Hall Lodge #17 Masonic 1985; mem Govs Commn for Solar Energy 1985; mem Urban League NAACP NCMW 1985. **Honors/Awds:** Airman of the Month USAF 1954; Outstanding Achievement & Dedication to Serv NCMW SB Chpt/Westside Community Development SB/Operation Second Chance/Kappa Alpha Psi SB Chptr 1976-79. **Military Serv:** USAF s/sgt 1952-56. **Business Addr:** 300 North D St, San Bernardino, CA 92408.

HOBBS, JOSEPH
Physician, educator. **Personal:** Born Aug 5, 1948, Augusta, GA; married Janice Polk. **Educ:** Mercer Univ, BS 1970; Med College of GA, MD 1974. **Career:** Med College of GA, asst prof family med 1979-, instr family med 1978, chief resident 1977, family prac res 1976, med intern 1975. **Orgs:** Richmond Co Medical Society 1978; vice pres Stoney Med Dental Pharm Society 1979; team physician T W Josey High School. **Honors/Awds:** Recipient Commendation Family Practice Resident Medical College of GA 1978; Fellowship American Academy of Family Practice 1979. **Business Addr:** Assistant Professor, Family Medicine, Medical College of Georgia, 1120 15th St, Augusta, GA 30912.

HOBBS, MICHAEL ARTHUR
Reporter. **Personal:** Born Apr 25, 1947, Philadelphia, PA; son of Lois Stovall Hobbs and Sterling Hobbs. **Educ:** Cheyney State College, Cheyney, PA, 1966-68; Temple University, Philadelphia, PA, 1968-70. **Career:** Akron Beacon Journal, Akron, OH, reporter, 1970-75; Camden Courier-Post, Camden, NJ, reporter, 1980-87; Philadelphia Inquirer, Philadelphia, PA, reporter, 1980-87; Cleveland Plain Dealer, Cleveland, OH, urban affairs reporter, 1987-. **Orgs:** Member, National Association of Black Journalist, 1982-; member, NABJ, Cleveland Chapter, 1987-; member, Urban League, Cleveland Chapter, 1987-; Northeast Ohio Coalition for the Homeless, 1987-. **Honors/Awds:** First Place, Community Service, Cleveland Press Club, 1989; First Place, Community Service, Ohio AP, 1989.

HOBSON, CAROL J. See SMITH, CAROL J.

HOBSON, CEKIMBER (C. K)
Film producer, recording executive. **Personal:** Born Feb 20, 1938, Greensboro, AL; son of Lucy Hobson and Elijah Hobson. **Educ:** UCLA, BA; Ohio State University, Masters; Soundmasters Technical Institute, attended. **Career:** Star Globe Productions, chief executive officer, film producer, 1984-; Pirate Records, record producer, 1989-. **Orgs:** NAACP, currently; Black Screenwriters Association, currently; United Talent Alliance, founder, board member, 1987-. **Honors/Awds:** University of Hawaii, Honorary Doctorate, 1983; National Black Talent Association, Terrence Award, 1989; Cinematographers International, Carol Ludd Award, 1991; Senatorial Medal of Freedom, 1994. **Special Achievements:** Founder, United Talent Alliance, objective to train and employ minorities in all aspects of the film industry, 1987. **Military Serv:** US Army, sgt, 1955-58. **Business Addr:** President/CEO, Star Globe Productions, 1901 Ave of the Stars, Ste 1800, Los Angeles, CA 90067, (310)553-5541.

HOBSON, CHARLES BLAGROVE
Television executive. **Personal:** Born Jun 23, 1936, Brooklyn, NY; son of Cordelia Victoria Hobson and Charles Samuel Hobson; married Maren Stange, Jun 24, 1990; children: Hallie, Clara. **Educ:** Brooklyn College, 1955-60; Emory University, 1974-76. **Career:** ABC-TV, New York, NY, producer, 1967-71; WETA-TV, Washington, DC, television producer, 1967-89; Vassar College, Poughkeepsie, NY, instructor, 1969-71; Clark College, Atlanta, GA, director of mass communications, 1971-76; Visamondo Productions, Montreal, Canada, writer, 1988; Jamaica Broadcasting Corporation, consultant, 1988; WNET-TV, New York, NY, director of market planning, 1989-. **Orgs:** Consultant Natl Endowment for the Arts 1976-87, NEH; bd mem Amer the Beautiful Fund 1977-87; exec producer The Africans, From Jumpstreet, Global Links; mem Writer's Guild of Amer, African Studies Assn; consultant, Greycom International; consultant, National Black Arts Festival; bd mem, America The Beautiful Fund; Natl Black Programming Consortium, pres, bd of dirs; Museum of Modern art, educ sub-committee. **Honors/Awds:** Capital Press Club Awd 1968; Emmy Awd NATAS 1968; Governor's Awd Natl Acad Arts & Sci 1976; WC Hardy Awd 1981; Natl Black Prog Consortium Awd 1985; Ohio State Award 1987; One of the Leading TV Producers, Millimeter Magazine; The Japan Prize, 1987; Golden Eagle Award, CINE, 1987; Ohio State Award for Excellence in Educational Programming, 1988; Fulbright Scholar, The University of Munich Amerika Institute, 1996-97; Fulbright Scholar in Munich, Germany, 1996-97. **Military Serv:** US Army, pfc, 1962-63. **Home Addr:** 293 State St, Brooklyn, NY 11201.

HOBSON, DONALD LEWIS
Judge (retired). **Personal:** Born Jan 11, 1935, Detroit, MI; son of Theresa Lewis Hobson and Oscar Collins Hobson; divorced; children: Donna Lynne. **Educ:** Attended, OH State Univ; Eastern MI Univ, BSc History; MI State Univ, MA; Detroit Coll of Law, JD; Post Graduate Work, Univ of MI, Wayne State Univ Law School, Hampton Inst, US Naval Academy, US Naval Justice School, Natl Judicial College; Howard College, Wayne Community College. **Career:** Detroit Public Sch System, social science teacher 1957-64; Detroit Bd of Educ Job Upgrading Prog, coord; US Dept of Justice Washington; Goodman Eden Millender Goodman & Bedrosian Detroit, assoc partner; Common Pleas Ct for the City of Detroit, judge; Recorders Ct of Detroit, judge (retired). **Orgs:** Arbit panelist mem Detroit Regional Adv Cncl Amer Arbitration Assn; natl exec bd & adv bd Detroit Chap Natl Lawyers Guild; exec bd Amer Trial Lawyers Assn; Natl Bd Cncl on Legal Educ Oppors; hearing referee MI Civil Rights Comm; sec Income Tax Review Bd City of Detroit; MI Supreme Court's Spec Comm on Landlord-Tenant Problems; Natl Bd Natl Bar Assn; State Bar of MI Rep Assembly; counsel State Bar Grievance Bd; Wolverine Bar Assn treas vice pres pres & bd of dirs; Natl Assn for Equal Oppor in Higher Educ; Omega Psi Phi Fraternity; Phi Kappa Delta Fraternity. **Honors/Awds:** Eastern MI Univ Alumni Honors Awd 1974; Hon Doctor of Humane Letters by Shaw Coll Detroit 1977; Hon Doctor of Laws Degree & Hon Doctor of Divinity Degree; Black Lawyers, Law Practice and Bar Associations; 1844-1970: A Michigan History, 1987, The Wayne Law Review vol 33, No 5. **Military Serv:** USNR commander. **Home Addr:** 2136 Bryanston Crescent, Detroit, MI 48207.

HOBSON, MELLODY L.
Marketing executive. **Personal:** Born Apr 3, 1969, Chicago, IL; daughter of Dorothy Ashley. **Educ:** Princeton Univ, Woodrow Wilson School of Intl Relations & Public Policy, BA, 1987-91. **Career:** Ariel Capital Management Inc, senior vp & dir of marketing, currently. **Orgs:** Princeton Club of Chicago, secretary, 1991-; Civic Federation of Chicago, director; Chicago Public Library Brd, director; Chicago Architecture Foundation, trustee. **Honors/Awds:** Ebony Magazine, Leader of the Future, 1993. **Business Addr:** Senior Vice President & Director of Marketing, Ariel Capital Management Inc, 307 N Michigan Ave, Ste 500, Chicago, IL 60601, (312)726-0140.

HOBSON, ROBERT R.
Government official. **Personal:** Born Oct 20, 1930, Memphis, TN; children: Mafara, Alicia. **Educ:** Tennessee State Univ, BA Government 1952; Howard Univ, 1956-57; Johns Hopkins Univ, 1958-59. **Career:** President's Committee on Equal Employment/Office of Fed Contract Compliance, senior compliance advisor 1963-71; Natl Urban Coalition, asst to the President 1971-73; Office of Federal Contract Compliance, assoc dir 1973-82; White House, senior staff member. **Honors/Awds:** OFCCP Labor Department awards, 2 Merit Awards 1967 & 1969, Distinguished Service Career 1974, Special Achievement 1975-79, Commendation Excellent Service 1976. **Business Addr:** Senior Staff Member, The White House, Washington, DC 20500.

HOBSON, WILLIAM D.
Business executive. **Personal:** Born Apr 2, 1908, Martinsville, VA; married Virgia B; children: William D Jr. **Educ:** Piedmont Christian Inst, attended; Knoxville Coll. **Career:** Standard Garments, production supervisor 1933-43; Hobson's Esso Station, previously owner; W End Laudromat; City of Martinsville, councilman 1968-72; vice mayor 1974-76; Martinsville, mayor 1976-80. **Orgs:** Mem bd dirs, chairman of the board, Imperial Bldg & Loan Assn; mem Central Bus Dist Commn Martinsville VA; mem Trans & Safety Commn Martinsville VA; bd trustee Fayette St Christian Ch; bd dirs Martinsville-Henry County C of C; MARC Workshop; commn mem W Piedmont Planning Dist; chmn Enviroment Com; personnel com Virginia Municipal League; Martinsville-Henry County Voters Registration League; mem Martinsville Men's Round Table Club Office; board secretary Martinsville Electorial; board Martinsville Equalization. **Honors/Awds:** Distinguished Service Award, Men's Round Table Club. **Business Addr:** 1013 W Fayette St, Martinsville, VA 24112.

HOBSON-SIMMONS, JOYCE ANN. See SIMMONS, JOYCE HOBSON.

HODGE, CHARLES MASON
Educational administrator. **Personal:** Born Jun 25, 1938, Seguin, TX; son of Goldie M Campbell and Clifford D Hodge; married Elizabeth Howze; children: Gwendolyn, Clinton. **Educ:** Univ of AR at Pine Bluff, BA 1960; N TX State Univ, MEd 1969, EdD 1976. **Career:** Terrell HS Ft Worth, high sch teacher 1964-69; Jarvis Christian Coll, instr social studies educ 1969-73; AR Desegregation Ctr for Public Schs, assoc dir 1973-74; AR Dept of Higher Educ, coord for human resources 1974-76; Univ of Central AR, assoc prof teacher educ 1976-80; AR Dept of Higher Educ, asst dir rsch & planning 1980; Univ Central AR, asst vice pres acad affairs 1980-83, dean college of educ 1983-89; Lamar Univ, Beaumont TX, dean of college of education, 1989-. **Orgs:** Robert Morris College, member board of trustees, Philadelphia, 1992-; Texas Commerce Bank-Beaumont, member, board of directors, 1991; mem Sch Deseg Monitoring Team US Dist Ct, 1980; Unit Accreditation Bd of Nat'l Council for the Accred for Teacher Ed, mem 1986-; AR State Council for Econ Ed, mem 1987-89; Editorial Bd- Teacher Education & Practice Journal; member, American Association of Colleges for Teacher Education. **Honors/Awds:** Ford Fellow Ford Found 1971; Gubernatorial Appt AR Gov's Task Force on Mgmt 1979; AR Teacher Educ Certification Evaluation Comm 1984. **Business Addr:** Dean, College of Education, Western Michigan University, W Michigan Ave, Kalamazoo, MI 49008.

HODGE, CYNTHIA ELOIS
Dentist. **Personal:** Born Feb 23, 1947, Troop, TX; daughter of Doris Lydia Spencer and Robert Spencer; divorced; children: Delwyn Ray Madkins. **Educ:** Univ of Denver, Pre-dental 1973-75; Univ of OR Health Sciences Center School of Dentistry, DMD 1979; Univ of NC at Chapel Hill, Certificate 1985. **Career:** Dentistry for Children, assoc dentist 1979-82; Post Graduate Training Univ of NC, 1982-85; Meharry Medical Coll, chairperson dept of hospital dentistry 1985-90; Meharry Medical Coll, School of Dentistry, Nashville, TN, dir, general practice residency program, 1985-90; Solo Private Practice, general dentistry, 1990-; Univ of North Carolina, MPH, 1994. **Orgs:** Dental consultant Multnomah County Health Dept Portland OR 1979-81; dental consultant Health Advisory Bd, Albina Ministerial Alliance, Headstart Program 1980-82; dental coordinator regional Natl Dental Assn 1981-82; Headstart Program; Infectious Disease Control Comm, TN Dental Assn, I987-; Health & Educational Facilities Board of Metropolitan Davidson County, 1990-; chairperson, Committee on Minority Affairs; executive board, Nashville Cares Inc; American Cancer Society Professional Educational Committee; board of advisors, Natchez College, Natchez, Mississippi; Institute on Health Care for the Poor & Underserved, Meharry Medical College; member, National Dental Association, 1979-; member, American Dental Association, 1979-; member, American Association of Women Dentists, 1990-; National Dental Assn, 1979-; Academy of General Dentistry, 1994-; American Assn of Public Health Dentistry, 1994-. **Honors/Awds:** Certificate of Recognition Washington Monroe High School; Awd for Participation in Dental Field Experiences Washington Monroe HS Portland OR 1981; valuable contribution to the ''Scientific Session,'' Natl Dental Assn 1988; publisher and pres of Nashville Pride, Inc (weekly newspaper,) 1988; Assistant Secretary for Health Certificate of Commendation, James Mason, Assistant Secretary for Health-USA, 1989; Awd for Scientific Presentation, Natl Dental Assn, 1991, 1992. **Business Addr:** Dentist, Comprehensive Family Dentistry, 1915 Charlotte Ave, Ste 210, Nashville, TN 37203.

HODGE, DEREK M.
Government official. **Personal:** Born Oct 5, 1941, Frederiksted, VI; son of Enid Hodge and Rexford Hodge; divorced; children: Marisol, Jonathan. **Educ:** Michigan State Univ, BA 1963; Georgetown Univ Law Center, JD 1971. **Career:** Law Firm of Hodge Sheen & Finch, partner 1972; Private Practice, attorney 1978-84; USVI Legislature, senate president, 1984-86; Virgin Islands Government Comms Rules, Trade, Tourism & Economic Development, Conservation Recreation & Cultural Affairs, member, 1984-86; Govt of the Virgin Islands, lt governor 1986-. **Orgs:** Pres VI Partners for Health 1980-81; chmn, bd of dirs St Dunstan's Episcopal School 1983-84; titular head Democratic Party of the VI 1983-86; pres VI Bar Assoc 1984-86; mem VI Govt Comms Rules, Trade Tourism & Economic Devel, Conservation Recreation & Cultural Affairs 1984-86. **Honors/Awds:** Appreciation plaque 4-H Club of VI 1984; Certificate of Merit Small Business Devel Center 1986; Recognition plaque Lutheran Social Serv of VI 1986; Proclamation Fulton Co GA 1987; Certificate of Membership Joint Center for Political Studies Assoc Program 1987. **Military Serv:** AUS 1967; Army Natl Guard captain, staff judge advocate 1979-83. **Business Addr:** Lieutenant Governor, US Virgin Islands, 18 Kongens Gade, Charlotte Amalie, St Thomas, Virgin Islands of the United States 00802.

HODGE, DONALD JEROME
Professional basketball player. **Personal:** Born Feb 25, 1969, Washington, DC. **Educ:** Temple. **Career:** Dallas Mavericks, center, 1991-. **Business Addr:** Professional Basketball Player, Dallas Mavericks, Reunion Arena, 777 Sports St, Dallas, TX 75207, (214)988-0117.

HODGE, ERNEST M.
Automobile dealer. **Career:** Heritage Cadillac Inc, CEO, currently. **Special Achievements:** Company is ranked #49 on Black Enterprise's list ot Top 100 Auto Dealers, 1994. **Business Addr:** CEO, Heritage Cadillac Inc, 5550 Frontage Rd, Forest Park, GA 30050.

HODGE, MARGUERITE V.
Social worker. **Personal:** Born May 21, 1920, Avondale, PA; married Dee; children: Dee. **Educ:** Howard U, BA 1943; Univ of Chicago 1947. **Career:** Lung Assn, regional dir 1970-; Placement Student, field instr 1974; Information & Referral Serv, supr 1968-70; UCLA, field instr 1969-70; Prof & Vol Serv, supr 1965-68; UCLA, field instr 1966-67; Agency Co Ord 1960-64; Field Rep 1953-60; Municipal TB Santorium, med social worker 1949-51; Provident Hosp, med social worker 1947-48; Provident Hosp, psychiatric social worker 1948-49; Provident Hosp, med social worker 1944-46. **Orgs:** Mem Nat Conf of Social Welfare; Nat Assn of Social Workers; licentiate mem Royal Acad of Health; consult S Central Area Welfare Planning Coun; adv comLA Urban League Health & Welfare Com Headstart; SEARCH Bd USC Sch of Med; serv & rehab com Am Cancer Soc CA Div Cervical Cancer Screening Sub-com; Prog Planning Com So CA Pub Health Assn; LA Co Inter-agy Coun on Smoking & Health; Mayor's Adv Coun for Handicapped 1974; adv com Area IX Regional Med Prog; bd dir CA Assn for Mental Health 1973; discussion leader Alcholism Conf Welfare Plng Coun 1962; discussion leader Conf on Home Care Welfare Plng Coun & City of Hope 1962; registration chmn Pacific SW Regional Inst NASW 1966; panel participant for TB Assn; Numerous Other Com; mem Westminster Presb Ch; Alpha Kappa AlphaSor. **Honors/Awds:** Recipient Spl Recognition Award Bd Dir Lung Assn 20 yrs Serv 1974; Spl Award King-Drew Sickle Cell Cntr 1974; Spl Recognition Award S Central Area Plng Coun 1973; Spl Award Kedren Comm Mental Health Cntr; Comm Serv Award El Santo Nino Comm Devel Proj of Cath Welfare Bur 1972; Volunteer Serv AwardPatton State Hosp 1965-66. **Business Addr:** 1670 Beverly Blvd, Los Angeles, CA 90026.

HODGE, NORRIS
Broker, appraiser. **Personal:** Born Apr 3, 1927, Kingsville, TX; married Ruby Faye; children: Brenda, Theodora, Myrna. **Educ:** BBA MS 1962-64. **Career:** TX Southern Univ, asst prof; Friends Univ Wichita KS, asst prof. **Orgs:** Mem Am Economic Assn. **Honors/Awds:** So Economic Assn Recipient Ford Foundation Fellowship; Western Econ Assn; General Electric Fellowship Univ of Chicago. **Business Addr:** Hodge & Co, Realtors, 13027 Hiram Clarke, Houston, TX 77045.

HODGE, W. J.
Bible college president. **Career:** Simmons Univ Bible Coll, Louisville, KY, pres/chancellor. **Business Addr:** Simmons University Bible College, Louisville, KY 40210.

HODGE, WILLIAM ANTHONY
Extention specialist. **Personal:** Born Apr 26, 1962, Tuskegee Institute, AL; son of Lula Pearl McNair Hodge and Johnie Albert Hodge; married Audrey Maria Hicks Hodge, Dec 16, 1989. **Educ:** Tuskegee University, Tuskegee Inst, AL, BS, 1985; Auburn University, Auburn University, AL, MS, 1989. **Career:** Purdue Univ Dept of Agronomy, W Lafayette, IN, res asst, 1983; Walt Disney World, Epcot Ctr, Orlando, Fl, agricultural intern, 1983-84; Tuskegee University Schl of Ag, Tuskegee, AL, teaching asst, 1984-85; Oak Ridge Natl Labs, Oak Ridge, TN, research Asst, 1985; Auburn University, Auburn, AL, graduate res asst, 1986-89; Tuskegee University, Tuskegee, AL, soil scientist/water quality tech 1989-, extension specialist/water quality cooperative extension program, 1991-; Carter Funeral Home, manager, funeral director, 1992-. **Orgs:** Worshipful master, Prince Hall Masonic Lodge #17, 1990-; member, Alabama Agricultural & Forestry Leaders, 1989-; member, Alabama Farmers Federation, 1990-; member, Gamma Sigma Delta, 1987; member, American Society of Agronomy, 1983-; member, Negro Airmen International, 1988-; AL Funeral Directors Association, 1995-; AL Soil & Water Conservation Society. **Honors/Awds:** Outstanding Agronomy Student, American Society of Agronomy, 1985; Membership, Alpha Kappa Mu, Natl Honarary, 1985. **Home Addr:** PO Box 167, Union Springs, AL 36089. **Business Addr:** Extension Specialist-Water Quality: Cooperative Extension Prog, Tuskegee University, 209 Morrison/Mayberry Bldg, Tuskegee Institute, AL 36088.

HODGES, CAROLYN RICHARDSON
Educator. **Personal:** Born Nov 25, 1947, Roebling, NJ; daughter of Mary Catherine Richardson and Luther Kendrick; married John Oliver Hodges, Apr 8, 1972; children: Daniel Oliver. **Educ:** Beaver College, BA, 1969; University of Chicago, MA, 1971, PhD, 1974. **Career:** Central YMCA Community College, instructor of German, 1970-72; Kennedy-King Jr College, assistant professor of humanities, 1975-82; Univ of Tennessee, Knoxville, assistant professor of German, 1982-88, associate professor of German, 1988-. **Orgs:** Secretary/treasurer, Southern Comparative Literature Assn, 1990-; vice-president, Tennessee American Assn of Teachers of German, 1987-89; board member, Tennessee Foreign Language Teacher Assn, 1989-92; editorial reviewer, Soundings an Interdisciplinary Journal, 1985-91; member, Tennessee Collaborative Council on Foreign Language, 1986-. **Honors/Awds:** Chancellor's Citation for Extraordinary Service, Univ of Tennessee, 1987; Merrill Research Award, College of Education, Univ of Tennessee-Knoxville, 1990, 1992; Outstanding Advising, College of Liberal Arts, 1991; Dissertation Year Award, Ford Foundation, 1973-74; Trustee Fellowship, Univ of Chicago, 1969-73; Faculty Travel Award, Univ of Tennessee, 1983. **Home Addr:** 4815 Skyline Dr, Knoxville, TN 37914. **Business Addr:** Associate Professor of German, University of Tennessee, Knoxville, 701 McClung Tower, Knoxville, TN 37996-0470.

HODGES, CLARENCE EUGENE
Business executive. **Personal:** Born Oct 1, 1939, Princeton, NC; married Yvonne Mitchell; children: Clarence Jr, Courtney, Cassandra, Cathleen. **Educ:** Hamilton Inst, adv certificate 1966; Yale Univ, Urban Studies fellow 1973; Univ of Iowa, BA 1975; Occidental Coll, MA 1976, PhD Political Sci, Public Admin 1987. **Career:** St Louis Concentrated Employment Program, exec dir 1969-73; Dept of Human Resources City of Indianapolis, dir 1974-76; US Senator Richard Lugar, sr staff asst 1977-81; US Dept HHS, comm 1981-83; US Dept of State, deputy asst sec; Hodges & Associates, president, 1989-; African Continental Enterprises, Washington, DC, president, 1990-; Hodges & Associates, 1989-; Christian Record Services International, president, 1991-. **Orgs:** Chmn St Louis CORE 1967-69; vice pres St Louis Co NAACP 1968-69; pres/chair Indianapolis CAAP 1980-81; pres Profs Diversified Inc 1980-85; mem bd of trustees Oakwood Coll 1982-85; bd trustees Washington Inst for Contemp Issues; bd of trustees, Jarvis Coll; chairman, Youth Development Foundation, 1987-; executive committee member, Columbia Union, 1986-. **Honors/Awds:** CE Hodges School named for by Chicago Soc for Children; Fellowship Natl Urban Fellows 1973-74; Man of Year Natl Assn of Business & Prof Women 1976; Intl Manof Achievement 1977; Brotherhood Award 100 Black Men 1984; Doctor of Laws 1986; Achievers Award, Oklahoma Community Services, 1989; Public Service Award, Martin Luther King Holiday Commission, 1989; Outstanding Public Service Award, US State Dept, 1989; Achieves Award, Oklahoma Community Services, 1989. **Military Serv:** USAF 4 yrs. **Business Addr:** President, Christian Record Services International, 4444 S 52nd St, Lincoln, NE 68516.

HODGES, CRAIG ANTHONY
College basketball coach, former professional basketball player. **Personal:** Born Jun 27, 1960, Park Forest, IL; children (previous marriage): Jibril, Jamaal; married Allison D Jordan, 1996. **Educ:** Long Beach St Univ, 1978-82. **Career:** Guard: San Diego Clippers (franchise moved to Los Angeles in 1984), 1982-84, Milwaukee Bucks, 1984-88, Phoenix Suns, 1988, Chicago Bulls, 1988-92; Chicago State University, men's basketball coach, currently. **Orgs:** Operation Unite, president; Save The Youth; Three Point Inc, president. **Honors/Awds:** Named to Basketball Digest's Second Team All-Rookie squad in 1982-83.

HODGES, DALE
Professional basketball player. **Personal:** Born Jan 21, 1968, Trenton, NJ. **Educ:** St. Joseph's. **Career:** New England Blizzard, forward, 1997-. **Honors/Awds:** St Joseph's Hall of Fame, 1996. **Business Addr:** Professional Basketball Player, New England Blizzard, 179 Allyn St, Ste 403, Hartford, CT 06103, (860)522-4667.

HODGES, DAVID JULIAN
Educator, anthropologist. **Personal:** Born Jan 11, 1944, Atlanta, GA. **Educ:** NY U, PhD 1971, MA 1969; Morris Brown Coll Magna Cum Laude, BA 1966; Sophia Univ Tokyo, Spl Grad Study 1967; Columbia Univ 1965-66; Emory Univ GA 1965; Harvard U, Post Grad Study 1973. **Career:** Hunter Coll, prof Anthropology 1985; Heritage Musem NY, curator 1971-73;

Cornerstone for Change Inc, pres founder 1974-; Amer Anthrop Assn; Amer Assn Advancement of Science; Soc Applied Anthropology; Natl Soc Study Educ; Amer Assn Univ Prof Educ Action Specialist NY Comm Devel Agency 1969-71; Nassau Comm Coll Garden City, instr 1970; Voorhees Tech Inst NY, part time instr 1969-70; New York City Youth Bd, sr st club worker 1965-69. **Orgs:** Mem adv bd YMCA 1970-; PGM Serv Com YMCA Greater NY. **Honors/Awds:** NY Univ Founder's Day Award 1973; Phi Delta Kappa Hon Soc; Alpha Kappa Delta Hon Soc; Alpha Kappa Mu Hon Soc; Woodrow Wilson Fellowship 1965; So Educ Found Fellowship 1965; Doctoral Fellowship So Fellowships Fund 1969-71. **Military Serv:** AUS 1966-68. **Business Addr:** President, Cornerstone for Change, Inc, 695 Park Ave, New York, NY 10021.

HODGES, HELENE
Association executive. **Personal:** Born Apr 27, 1949, Schwabach, Germany; daughter of Eugenie Ann Hellwig Hodges and Joseph J. Hodges. **Educ:** Finch College, New York, NY, Bachelor's degree, 1971; St. John's University, Jamaica, NY, Master's degree, 1975, professional diploma, 1979, Doctorate, 1985. **Career:** Virgin Islands Dept of Education, Virgin Islands, teacher, 1970-71; New York Board of Education, New York, NY, teacher/school director, 1971-86; Association for Supervision and Curriculum Development, Alexandria, VA, director of research and information, 1986-93, dir of collaborative ventures, 1993-. **Orgs:** Education commission member, Martin Luther King Jr. Federal Holiday Commission, 1986-; steering committee member, NAEP, 1990; selection committee member, CSSO, National Teacher of the Year Program, 1991-; Phi Delta Kappa; member, National Alliance of Black School Educators. **Honors/Awds:** Distinguished Achievement, Educational Press Association, 1988; Award for Excellence in Educational Journalism. **Business Addr:** Director, Collaborative Ventures, Assn for Supervision and Curriculum Development, 1250 N Pitt St, Alexandria, VA 22314.

HODGES, JOHN O.
Educator. **Personal:** Born Jan 26, 1944, Greenwood, MS; son of Samantha Wilson Hodges and Tommy James Hodges; married Carolyn R Richardson Hodges, Apr 8, 1972; children: Daniel. **Educ:** University of Nantes, France, certificate, 1966-67; Morehouse College, Atlanta, GA, BA, 1968; Atlanta University, Atlanta, GA, MA, 1971; University of Chicago, Chicago, IL, MA, 1972, PhD, 1980. **Career:** Morehouse College, Atlanta, GA, director of language laboratory, 1969-70; Barat College, Lake Forest, IL, director of Afro-American studies, 1972-75, assistant professor of English, 1972-75; University of Chicago, Chicago, IL, assistant dean of university students, 1980-82; University of Tennessee, Knoxville, TN, associate professor, 1988-, acting head of department rel studies, 1989-90. **Orgs:** Member, American Academy of Religion, 1982-; member, Modern Language Association, 1981-; member, College Language Association, 1982-; member, South Atlantic Modern Language Assn, 1983; annual dinner committee, Urban League, Langston Hughes Society, 1984-. **Honors/Awds:** Merrill Overseas Fellow, Morehouse, 1966-67; Rockefeller Fellow, Rockefeller Foundation, 1970-71; Ford Fellow, Ford Foundation, 1976-78; NEH Fellow, National Endowment for Humanities, 1984. **Home Addr:** 4815 Skyline Dr, Knoxville, TN 37914. **Business Addr:** Associate Professor, Religious Studies, Department of Religions, University of Tennessee, 501 McClung Tower, Knoxville, TN 37914.

HODGES, LILLIAN BERNICE
Owner. **Personal:** Born Apr 2, 1939, Rosebud Island Mar, AR; married Alzetl Joe Nathan; children: Lillian L. **Educ:** Shorter Jr Coll, N Little Rock, AR, attended 1957-58; TX Women Univ Denton TX, attended 1965. **Career:** 19 countries of NAACP, liaison officer 1985; Local 282, United Furniture Workers of Am, rep 1977-80; Mr Tax of Am, mgr 1968-74; Univ of AR, nutritionist 1967; E Central Economical Corp, outreach person 1965-66. **Orgs:** Dir L R Jackson Girls Club of Am; Beautiful Zion Bapt Ch, sunday sch tchr 1976-80; Demo Women of Critt Co, vp; Critt Co Improvement Assn, ex-sec; NAACP Critt Co, pres 1972-78; State NAACP, vice pres 1973-75; Bd of METOG for Youth Services, bd mem 1973-75; Coalition for Better Broadcast, vice chmn 1968-71. **Honors/Awds:** Outstanding Religious Work Non-Denominational Council 1979; Outstanding Serv Award NAACP Local 1976; Outstanding Award for Minority Bus Minority Bus Development 1975; Outstanding Participation Univ S Census Bus 1970. **Business Addr:** President, Hodges & Sons, West Memphis, AR 72301.

HODGES, MELVIN SANCHO
Attorney. **Personal:** Born Jan 1, 1940, Columbia, SC; son of Aubrey Hodges and Hilliard Hodges Jr; married Ugertha Birdsong; children: Melvin II. **Educ:** Morehouse Coll, 1957-60; UC Santa Barbara, BA 1965; UC Berkeley, JD 1969. **Career:** IBM Corp, atty 1969-72; Hastings Law Coll, prof 1972-73; St of CA, dpty atty gen 1976-78; Chevron USA Inc, atty 1978-93. **Orgs:** Asst treasurer Amer Assn Blacks in Energy 1984-86; mem California Bar Assn; mem San Francisco Bar Assn; mem Charles Houston Bar Assn; fin com Bay Area Black United Fund 1982-84; board of trustees, UCSB Foundation, 1991-. **Honors/Awds:** Outstanding Legal Serv San Francisco Bar Asso 1983-84, 1994-97; outstanding legal Serv California Bar Assn 1983-84; Distinguished Alumni Award, Univ of California, Santa Barbara, 1990. **Home Addr:** 705 Grizzly Peak Blvd, Berkeley, CA 94708.

HODGES, PATRICIA ANN
Telephone company executive. **Personal:** Born Mar 24, 1954, Indianapolis, IN; daughter of Betty Brooks and Jeremiah McKeage. **Career:** Indiana School for the Deaf, residential asst, 1977-79; Indiana Vocational College, interpreter for deaf, 1979-83; Indiana National Guard, file clerk, 1983-85; Specialized Interpreter Service, pres, 1993-. **Orgs:** Indiana Register Chapter of Interpreters, currently; Black Deaf Advocate, currently; Indianapolis Resource Center for Independent, currently. **Honors/Awds:** Woman of the Rainbow Award, 1991; 100 Coalition of Black Women, 1992 Breakthrough Woman Award; State of Indiana, Distinguished Service Award, 1990; Ernest & Young Service, Nominated Entrepreneur of the Year, 1991. **Military Serv:** US Air Force Reserve, sgt, 1982-86. **Business Addr:** President, Specialized Interpreter Service, PO Box 88814, Indianapolis, IN 46208, (317)328-1584.

HODGES, VIRGIL HALL
Association executive (retired). **Personal:** Born Dec 6, 1936, Atlanta, GA; son of Dr. Ruth Hall Hodges and Virgil W Hodges; married Verna McNeil; children: Virgil Arthur III, Ruth-Ercile. **Educ:** Morris Brown Coll, BA 1958; New York Univ, MA 1959, 6th Year Certificate 1961. **Career:** Philander Smith College, asst prof, 1959-61; New York City Youth Board, area administrator, 1961-67; Coney Island Family Center, exec dir 1967-69; New York State Narcotic Control Comm, factly dir 1969-76; New York State Dept of Labor, Dir CETA Div 1977-81, Dpty Comm 1981-91; New York State, Martin Luther King Jr Commission and Institute for Nonviolence, executive director, 1991-95. **Orgs:** Bd of dir Labor Branch NAACP; bd of advisors MLK Jr Center for Nonviolent Soc Change; pres Minority Organizers for Voter Educ & Registration. **Honors/Awds:** Man of the Year Award Coney Island Comm 1968; Alumni Award Morris Brown Coll 1978; Public Serv Award New York State NAACP 1982; Humanitarian Award New York Martin Luther King Jr Support Group 1983; New York Alumni Award Morris Brown Coll 1987; Disting Serv Award of New York State Black & Puerto Rican Caucus 1987; Disting Serv Labor Branch NAACP 1987; Potoker Award of The New York State Brotherhood Comm 1988. **Home Addr:** 9 Compass Ct, Albany, NY 12205.

HODGSON-BROOKS, GLORIA J.
Psychotherapist, visual artist. **Personal:** Born Nov 28, 1942, Hartford, CT; daughter of Marion S Jackson Gill and Charles O Gill; married Peter C Brooks. **Educ:** Bennett Coll, BA 1965; Smith Coll Sch of Social Work, MSW 1979; Hartford Family Institute, Gestalt-Body Centered Psychotherapy 1976-83; Natl Assn of Social Workers certificates, 1982; state of CT cert in Social Work, 1987; Amer Bd of Examiners in Clinical Social Wrk certified dipl, 1988; studied visual arts at several colleges and seminars. **Career:** Child & Family Serv Inc, social worker 1974-77; Inter-Agency Svcs, social worker 1974-77; Hartford Family Inst, intern 1976-78; Private Practice, psychotherapist 1976-78; Child & Family Serv Inc, clinical social worker 1979-80; Dr Isaiah Clark Family & Youth Clinic, dir 1980-81; Hartford Family Inst, associate 1978-85; Private Practice, psychotherapist 1978-85; Psychotherapy & Counseling Assocs, psychotherapist/partner 1985-; Brooks & Brooks Ltd, Hartford CT, president, 1985—; Solitude Visual Arts Studio, Hartford CT, partner, 1989-. **Orgs:** Mem Natl Assoc of Black Social Workers 1972-, NAARPR 1977-85, Natl Assoc of Social Workers 1977-; counseling minority students Trinity Coll 1982-85; staff training Directions Unlimited 1984-85; mem CT Caucus of Black Women for Political Action 1984-86; assoc mem PRO Disabled Entrepreneur 1985-86; workshop leader on goal setting PRO Disabled Entrepreneur Goal Setting Workshops 1985-86; staff training communication Sandler Sales Inst 1986; administrative consultant CT Ctr for Human Growth & Develop 1986; mem Farmington Valley Arts Ctr 1986-; adv bd IAM Cares 1986-; Intl Sculpture Center; Amer Craft Council; Amer Craft Museum; charter mem, Natl Museum of Women in the Arts; Natl Trust for Historical Preservation. **Honors/Awds:** Program & Function Mem Commn to Study the Consolidation of Children's Serv mandate of the 1974 Session of the CT General Assembly 1974; published "An Exploratory Study of the Diagnostic Process in Gestalt Therapy," Smith College Library 1975; Social Worker for Justice Awd Smith Coll Sch for Social Work 1979; award for starting Dr Issiah Clark Family & Youth Clinic, 1988; art exhibits: Intl Biographical Centre, 1989, ECKANKAR Creative Art Festival, 1987, 1988, New England Hardweavers, 1987. **Business Addr:** President, Brooks & Brooks Ltd, 17 Litchfield St, Hartford, CT 06112.

HOFF, NATHANIEL HAWTHORNE
Educator. **Personal:** Born Jan 10, 1929, Baltimore, MD; son of Cora Lee Byrd Hoff and Benjamin F Hoff; children: Victoria Forbes, Annette, Yvette Boschulte, Nathaniel Jr, Ronald, Yvonne Bell, Christopher, Kevin. **Educ:** Morgan State Coll, BS (Magna Cum Laude) Biology/Sci Educ 1950; Johns Hopkins Univ, MEd Educ (Cum Laude) 1959; Post Grad Work, Morgan State Coll 1959, Cornell Univ 1962, Butler Univ 1964, Hampton Inst 1966, Western MD Coll 1973. **Career:** Anne Arundel Co Public Sch System, genl sci tchr 1952-54; Baltimore City Public Sch System, biology tchr 1954-67; MD State Tchrs Assn, field serv rep 1967-68, assoc in field serv 1968-; Public Sch Tchrs Assn, dir of field serv 1962-73, exec uniserv dir 1973-79; Prince George's Co Education Assn, MSTA Uniserv dir 1979-84; Baltimore City Tchr Assn, MSTA uniserv dir 1984-; MD State Tchrs Assn, assoc in field svcs. **Orgs:** Founding mem Kappa Phi Lambda Chap Alpha Phi Alpha Frat 1975-; mem Natl Staff Orgn 1979-; MSU bd liaison Morgan State Univ Found 1977-79; sec bd of regents Morgan State Univ 1975-80; assn evaluator of Norfolk Educ Assn Natl Education Assn 1970 1972; pres Grace AME Keglers 1980-; life mem MD StateTchrs Assn 1983; mem Professional Staff Assn 1983; life mem Delta Lambda Chap Alpha Phi Alpha Frat 1986-; mem Mayor's Task Force on Educ 1968-70; bd dirs MD Congress of Parents & Tchrs Assn 1973-74; mem NAACP, Urban League 1986-89; life mem Natl Alpha Phi Alpha Frat 1986-. **Honors/Awds:** Author of awd winning poems "War & Peace and the Negro" 1950; author of over 300 poems; Hon Scholarship Awd Morgan State Coll 1970-71; Resourcefulness Plaque Minority Affairs Comm Prince George's County Educ Assn 1982; plaque for Outstanding & Dedicated Serv to Minority Educators Black Caucus MD State Tchrs Assn 1982; Serv Awd Minority Affairs Comm Prince George's Co Educators Assn 1983; Certificate of Appreciation Prince George's Co Educators Assn 1983; inducted into Athletic Hall of Fame Morgan State Univ 1985. **Military Serv:** Armored Infantry acting sgt s-3 operations 1951-53; Amer Spirit of Honor Medal 1951. **Home Addr:** 10529 Morning Wind Ln, Columbia, MD 21044. **Business Addr:** Associate in Field Service, Maryland State Teachers Assoc, 344 N Charles St, Baltimore, MD 21201.

HOFFLER, RICHARD WINFRED, JR.
Physician. **Personal:** Born Jun 22, 1944, Lynchburg, VA; son of Julia Wilson and Richard Winfred Hoffler Sr; married Sylvia C; children: Edward, Erika. **Educ:** Hampton Inst, BA 1966; Meharry Med Coll, MD 1970. **Career:** Youngstown Hosp, intern 1970, resd 1971-74; Private practice, physician 1974-90; Staff Physician, Ambulatory Care VAMC, Hampton, VA, 1990-; Tidewater Disability Determination Services, state agency medical consultant, 1974-80, chief medical consultant, 1980-90. **Orgs:** Mem AMA, Norfolk Acad of Med, Norfolk Med Soc, Nat'l Med Assoc, state agency med consultant 1974-; Tidewater Disability Determination Services, chief medical consultant 1980-; Sentera Hospitals, consulting staff. **Honors/Awds:** Scholarship Student Hampton Inst 1963-64. **Business Addr:** Physician, R W Hoffler, Jr, MDPC, PO Box 898, Norfolk, VA 23501.

HOFFMAN, JOSEPH IRVINE, JR.
Physician. **Personal:** Born Apr 14, 1939, Charleston, SC; married Pamela Louise Hayling; children: Katherine, Kristen, Kara. **Educ:** Harvard Coll, AB 1960; Howard Univ, MD 1964. **Career:** Lenox Hill Hosp, internship 1964-66; Hosp for Special Surgery NY, orthopedic resd 1968-71; Joseph Hoffman MD, PC, pres. **Orgs:** Mem natl Med Assoc, AMA; pres Atlanta Med Assoc; mem NAACP, Urban League, Atlanta C of C, Omega Psi Phi; cert Amer Bd of Orthopedic Surgery 1973; fellow Amer Rheumatism Assoc 1972, Acad of Orthopedic Surgery 1977; pres, 100 Black Men of Atlanta. **Military Serv:** USN 1966-68. **Business Addr:** President, Joseph Hoffman MD, PC, 2945 Stone Hogan Rd, Atlanta, GA 30331.

HOGAN, BEVERLY WADE
Former government official, college administrator. **Personal:** Born Jul 5, 1951, Crystal Springs, MS; daughter of Mae Ether Easley Wade and W D Wade Sr; married Marvin Hogan, Jun 11, 1971; children: Maurice DeShay, Marcellus Wade. **Educ:** Tougaloo College, Tougaloo, MS, BA, 1973; Jackson State University, Jackson, MS, MPPA, 1990. **Career:** Mental Health Center, Jackson, MS, mental health therapist, 1973-74; Hinds County Mental Health Association, Jackson, MS, executive director, 1974-80; Mississippi Mental Health Association, Jackson, MS, executive director, 1980-83; Governor's Office of Federal/State Programs, Jackson, MS, executive director, 1984-87; Mississippi Workers' Compensation Commission, Jackson, MS, commissioner, begin 1987; Tougaloo College, Health and Wellness Center, dir, currently. **Orgs:** Chairperson, Jackson State University School of Business Advisory Council, 1988-; chairperson, Mississippi Campaign for the UNCF Telethon, 1987, 1988; public relations chairperson, Mississippi Children's Home Society, 1990-91; chairperson, National Child Support Implementation Project, 1986; southern regional director, Council of State Planning Agencies, 1985. **Honors/Awds:** Administrator of the Year, Mississippi Chapter, American Society of Public Administrators, 1986; Toll Fellowship, Council of State Governments, 1987; Woman of the Year, Business & Professional Women, 1989; Mississippi Now Distinction, University of Mississippi, 1987; Distinguished Leadership, Citizens of Crossroads, 1984. **Business Addr:** Director, Health & Wellness Ctr, Tougaloo College, Tougaloo, MS 39174, (601)957-7115.

HOGAN, CAROLYN ANN
City government official. **Personal:** Born Jul 13, 1944, New Orleans, LA; daughter of Yolanda Getridge Hogan Mosley and Elijah Hogan, Sr (deceased). **Educ:** Dillard Univ, BA 1966; Fisk Univ, MA 1969; Southern Illinois Univ, 1973-74. **Career:**

Dillard Univ, instructor 1969-73; Southern Univ New Orleans LA Instructor 1973-75; Orleans Parish Sch Bd, psychologist 1974-75; City of New Orleans, evaluation specialist 1976-79; Natl Opinion Rsch Ctr, opinion rscher 1980-82; Natl Testing Svcs, opinion rscher 1981; Transit Mgmt of Southeast LA, benefits specialist 1985-86, workers compensation rep 1986-. **Orgs:** Consultant Albert Wicker School's Special Educ Class Orleans Parish Sch Bd 1978; Gestalt Inst Psychodrama 1978-79; panelist on WDSU-TV Spectrum 50 entitled "A Salute to Women" 1979; Touro Infirmary and LSU Medical Ctr Psychiatry Seminar 1979; mem New Orleans Neighborhood Police Anti-Crime Council 1983-86; StressManagement Workshop Career Track Seminars 1985; scholarship comm Crescent City Chap of Conference of Minorities in Transportation 1986-87. **Honors/Awds:** APA ABPSI Natl Sci Foundation Vstg Scientist in Psychology 1971; US Public Health Serv Traineeship in Psychology So IL Univ 1973-74; researcher for President's Civil Adv Commn; publication "A Black Woman's Struggles in Racial Integration," and "In Defense of Brown," in integrated education in 1980,84 Horace Mann Bond Ctr for Equal Educ; Miss United Negro College Fund; Women's Inner Circle of Achievement Award, 1990, World Decoration of Excellence Award, 1989, American Biographical Institute.

HOGAN, EDWIN B.
Government affairs consultant. **Personal:** Born Sep 2, 1940, Cleveland, OH; son of Helen Marie Brock Hogan and Lonnie N Hogan; married Letitia G Jackson, Jul 26, 1988; children: Edwina R, Bryan C Jackson. **Career:** The Success Group, Inc, director of multicultural affairs, currently. **Orgs:** Ballet Met, vice chairman, 1990-; Maryhaven, vice chairman, 1991-; Columbus NAACP, executive committee, 1989-; Community Connections, 1992-. **Honors/Awds:** Ballet Met, Distinguished Service Award, 1992; Columbus School Board, Golden Ruler Award, 1992; City of Cleveland, "Edwin B Hogan Day", 1990; Ohio Attorney General, Certificate of Recognition, 1992. **Special Achievements:** DePaul University School of Law Review, 1974; Boston Globe Review, 1976; Toronto Contrast Newspaper, 1973-79. **Military Serv:** US Air Force, A2K, 1957-60. **Business Addr:** Director, Multicultural Affairs, The Success Group, Inc, 10 W Broad St, One Columbus Building, Ste 1360, Columbus, OH 43209, (614)221-0971.

HOGAN, FANNIE BURRELL
Librarian. **Personal:** Born Apr 6, New Orleans, LA; daughter of Lorenza Nicholas Burrell and Alexander Burrell, Sr.; children: Erica Whipple Jones, Maria Monique Renwick. **Educ:** Dillard Univ, BA 1945; Atlanta Univ, MSLS 1950; Atlanta Univ, MA Eng 78; Atlanta Univ, Natl Deans List 1982; Ed D 1985 (Educational Administration and Supervision). **Career:** Gilbert Acad New Orleans LA, Teacher 1942-45; Claflin Coll SC, head Librn 1950-54; Clark Coll Atlanta GA, head Librarian 1954-81; The Atlanta Univ Center Robert W Woodruff Library, head of Bibliographic Instruction, beginning 1981; Asst in the Government Documents Dept, Atlanta Univ Center Robert W Woodruff Library and Computer Literature Search Librarian for the Administration, Faculty, and Students of Atlanta Univ; Head of Curriculum Material and Editor of the Library's Official Newsletter "The Diversified Hexagon" 1987-. **Orgs:** Head librarian wrote Proposal for Library Orientation for Clark Coll Funded by NEH 1975-80; specially funded Program by the Lilly Endowment Inc for Clark Coll tchr of Bibliographic instruction 1984-86; Amer Library Assn mem; GA Library Assn mem; Alpha Kappa Alpha Sorority mem; Phi Delta Kappa Educational Fraternity mem of Research Comm and Newsletter Comm. **Honors/Awds:** Study tour to Poland Clark Coll and the Untd Meth Bd of Ed 1973; schlrshp for doctoral study Untd Meth Bd of ed 1981; schlrshp Dept of Ed Atlanta Univ 1982; Poem "All Ages Can Learn" published in the 1989 Anthology of Southern Poetry. **Home Addr:** 1981 Valley Ridge Dr S W, Atlanta, GA 30331. **Business Addr:** Head of Curriculum Materials, AUC Robert W Woodruff Libr, 111 James P Brawley Dr, S W, Atlanta, GA 30331.

HOGAN, JAMES CARROLL, JR.
Biologist. **Personal:** Born Jan 3, 1939, Milledgeville, GA; son of Leanna Johnson Hogan and James C Hogan, Sr; married Izola Stinson, Nov 29, 1959; children: Pamela Renita Robertson, Gregory Karl, Jeffrey Darryl. **Educ:** Albany State Coll, BS 1961; Atlanta Univ, MS 1968; Brown Univ, PhD 1972. **Career:** Hancock Co Bd of Educ, teacher/science dept chmn 1961-66; Atlanta Public Schools, science teacher 1967-68; Atlanta Univ, instructor 1967; Yale Univ, rsch assoc 1973-76; Howard Univ, asst prof dept of anatomy 1976-78; Howard Univ, asst prof graduate school 1976-78; Univ of CT, assoc prof health science 1979-82; UCONN Health Ctr, assoc prof & univ dir 1982-87; Connecticut Dept of Health Services, Hartford, CT, chief, clinical chem & hematology, 1990-. **Orgs:** Founder and chmn Rhode Island Comm on Sickle Cell Disease 1970-72; founder UCONN Health Sci Cluster Program's Parents Auxilary 1979; vice pres CT's Black Health Professionals Network 1982-86; Omega Psi Phi Fraternity Inc; bd advisors The Sickle Cell Assoc of CT Inc; Urban League, Atlanta Univ Honor Soc, Sigma Xi; AAAS, Amer Soc for Cell Biology, Natl Assoc of Medical Minority Educators Inc; mem New York Academy of Sciences, Alpha Eta Soc; asst clinical prof, Univ of Hartford, W Hartford, CT, 1988-; founder & pres, N Haven (CT) Assn of Black Citizens, 1988-; North Haven Community Service Commission, 1990; advisory board, Greater New Haven State Technical College, 1989-; founder, pres, CT Chapter National Technical Assn, 1988-; board of directors, A Better Chance Inc; board of directors Hartford Alliance for Science & Mathematics; life mem, chair, Education Committee, New Haven Chapter, NAACP; First African American elected to North Haven CT, bd of ed, 1993-; board of directors, Connecticut Public Health Assoc, 1995; board of directors, Natl Technical Assn, 1993-. **Honors/Awds:** Post-doctoral Fellowship Yale Univ 1972-73; Macy Scholar Marine Biological Lab Woods Hole MA 1978-80; Rsch Foundation Grant Univ of CT 1979-80; Post-doctoral Fellow Ford Foundation 1980-81; Yale University Visiting Faculty Fellow; Pres Natl Assoc Medical Minority Educators 1985-86; Ci Omicron Chapter, Omega Man of the Year Award, 1992; Certified Clinical Laboratory Director, State of CT, 1993. **Special Achievements:** Twenty publications including "An Ultrastructural Analysis of Cytoplasmic Makers in Germ Cells of Oryzias Laptipes," J Ultrastruct Res 62, 237-250; "Regeneration of the Caudal Fin in Killfishes (Oryzias laptipes and Fundulus heteroclitus)" J Cell Biol 91(2), pt 2, p110a, numerous presentations. **Home Addr:** 51 Pool Rd, PO Box 146, North Haven, CT 06473. **Business Addr:** State of Connecticut, Dept of Health Serv, Bureau of Laboratories, 10 Clinton St, Hartford, CT 06106, (860)509-8540.

HOGAN, WILLIAM E., II
Comuter company executive. **Personal:** Born Sep 30, 1942, Montgomery, AL; son of D S Hogan and William E Hogan; married Shadra Hogan, Sep 4, 1965; children: Shalaun, William E III. **Educ:** Oklahoma State University, Stillwater, OK, BS, 1965; Southern Methodist University, Dallas, TX, MS, 1969; Oklahoma State University, Stillwater, OK, PhD, 1973. **Career:** University of KS, Lawrence, KS, associate executive vice chancellor, 1978-84; AMIC, Lawrence, KS, president, 1982-84; Honeywell Inc, Minneapolis, MN, vice president, technology & business development, 1984-86, vice president, staff executive to president, 1986, vice president, corps TQS, 1987-88; vice president, IIO, 1988-. **Orgs:** Chair, Research Advisory Board, Greater Minnesota Corporation, 1989-90; chair, Historically Black Research University Foundation Board, 1990; chair, Minnesota High Technology Council, 1989-90. **Honors/Awds:** Outstanding Black Engineer of America, Companies & All Historically Black Colleges, 1989; International Business Fellow, Industry and College, 1989; Plaques for Outstanding Contribution to Minority Programs, University of Kansas Students, 1977, 1979; Outstanding Young Men in America, Chamber of Commerce, 1977; Service on White House Task Force on Education, President of USA, 1989. **Business Addr:** Vice President, Honeywell Inc, Inertial Instruments Operations, 2600 Ridgway Parkway, MN17-1639, Minneapolis, MN 55413.

HOGANS, WILLIAM ROBERTSON, III
Dentist/military. **Personal:** Born May 18, 1945, Bristol, VA; son of Alma G McDowell Hogans and William R Hogans, Jr.; married Grace Valdine Blaylock; children: William IV, Adrienne, Elliott, Bryon, Michael. **Educ:** Knoxville Coll, BS 1967; Meharry Medical Coll, DDS 1976; US Army Command and General Staff Coll Ft Leavenworth KS, Graduate 1986; advanced education program in prosthodontics, Walter Reed Army Medical Center, Washington DC, graduate 1990. **Career:** US Army Dental Corps, prosthodontist, currently. **Orgs:** Mem Amer Dental Assoc 1976-; vice pres 1977-78, pres 1978-79 Phi Beta Sigma Frat Inc; vice pres Meadow Village Elem PTA 1977-78; vice pres San Antonio TX Region II PTA 1978-79; mem Assoc of Military Surgeons 1982-, Rock's Military Social Club 1983-; fellow American College of Prosthodontists. **Honors/Awds:** Acad of Dental Radiology Awd for Outstanding Achievement Meharry Medical Coll 1976; Outstanding Young Men of Amer US Jaycees 1979; selected as US Army Dental Corps Representative to the Postgraduate Course in Fixed Prosthodontic at Canadian Forces Dental Serv Sch in Borden Ontario, Canada 1987; American Board of Prosthodontists, diplomate. **Military Serv:** AUS, col, 16 yrs; Air Force Outstanding Unit Citation 1977; Air Force Commendation medal w/1 Oak Leaf Cluster 1979, Expert Field Medical Badge 1983, US Army Commendation Medal 1983, US Army Achievement Medal 1983, Overseas Serv Ribbon 1983; Meritorious Service Medal 1988.

HOGGES, RALPH
Educational administrator. **Personal:** Born Aug 3, 1947, Allentown, GA; married Lilia N Pardo; children: Genithia L; Alicia I. **Educ:** Tuskegee Isnt Tuskegee, AL, BS 1971; Tuskegee Inst Tuskegee, AL, MEd 1972; Nova Univ Ft Lauderdale, EdD 1977. **Career:** FL Intl Univ Miami, assoc dean of student affairs 1978-; The Center for Minority Rsch Inc Miami, exec dir 1979-; FL Intl Univ Miami, admin asst to the dean 1974-78, coordinator of coll work-study program 1973-74, prsnl tech 1972-73. **Orgs:** Bd trusee Am Interdenominational Univ 1978-; bd dir The Ctr for Minority Rsrch Inc 1979-; mem Kappa Delta Pi 1971-; mem FL Clg Stdnt Afrs Assc 1978-; mem Phi Delta Kappa 1978-. **Honors/Awds:** Outst serv in ed Phi Beta Sigma Frat Miami 1978. **Business Addr:** Tamiami Trail Campus, Miami, FL 33199.

HOGU, BARBARA J. JONES
Artist, educator. **Personal:** Born Apr 17, 1938, Chicago, IL; married Jean-Claude Hogu; children: Kuumba. **Educ:** Howard Univ, BA 1959; Chicago Art Inst, BFA; Illinois Inst of Technology, MS; Governor State Univ, humanities studies, 1992-95. **Career:** Chicago Post Office, clerk 1961-64; Robt Paige Designs, designer 1968-69; lecturer 1968; Chicago Public High Schools, Art Inst high schs, 1964-70; Malcolm X Coll, asst prof, associate professor, currently. **Orgs:** Mem Bd Southside Comm Center 1971-; staff artist Third World Press 1973-; vice pres Natl Conf of Artists 1973-; lecturer Art History School of the Art Inst 1974-79; African Commune of Black Relevant Artists; Union Black Artists; innumerable group shows, one woman shows & exhibitions. **Honors/Awds:** Art History Honor Art Inst of Chicago 1962; Scholarship Art Inst of Chicago 1962-64; 1st Print Award Black Aesthetics "69" Serv Award; Natl Conf of Artist for 1972, 1974; Malcolm X Umoja Award 1973. **Home Addr:** PO Box 49425, Chicago, IL 60649. **Business Addr:** Associate Professor, Malcolm X College, Communications & Fine Arts, 1900 W Van Buren, Chicago, IL 60612, (312)850-7334.

HOGUE, LESLIE DENISE
Editor. **Personal:** Born Sep 1, 1966, Detroit, MI; daughter of Dennis O & Katherine F Green; married Earlonzo Hogue, Sep 26, 1997; children: Earlonzo Jr. **Educ:** Wayne State University, BA, 1992. **Career:** Surreal Magazine, editor, publisher, 1992-95; Computer Training & Support Corp, editor, 1995-96; Health Care Weekly Review, editor, 1996-. **Orgs:** Olive Tree Foundation, treas, 1997-; Institute for Health Improvement in Southeast Michigan, comm mem, 1997.

HOLBERT, JOANNE
Educator, elected official. **Personal:** Born in Washington, DC; daughter of Dr & Mrs Lelond Holbert. **Educ:** Peabody Teachers College, MA, 1968; Indiana Univ-Bloomington, EdD, 1975. **Career:** Wayne State Univ, College of Ed, assistant dean, 1977-; Oakland County, county commissioner, 1995-98; City of Pontiac, deputy mayor, 1986-89; Oakland Univ, assistant professor, 1975-77. **Orgs:** Alpha Kappa Alpha, 1965-; Oakland County Chapter, Links Inc, 1988-; NAACP, 1985-; Pontiac Urban League, 1992-. **Honors/Awds:** Women's Survival Center, Wonder Woman, 1990; YMCA Pontiac, Outstanding Women, 1991. **Business Addr:** Assistant Dean, Wayne State University, College of Education, Detroit, MI 48202, (313)577-1721.

HOLBERT, RAYMOND
Educator. **Personal:** Born Feb 24, 1945, Berkeley, CA; son of Carolyn Bernice Gary and James Albert Holbert; married Susan Demersseman, May 26, 1989; children: Onika Valentine, Lauren Dakota, Brian Jaymes. **Educ:** Laney Coll, AA 1964; Univ of CA, AB 1972, MA 1974, MFA 1975. **Career:** San Fran Comm Coll, prof art. **Orgs:** Mem Artists Books Advocate, Natl Conf of Artists. **Honors/Awds:** Exhibits at: San Francisco Art Museum 1972, Oakland Art Museum 1973, Berkeley 1974, Baylor Univ Waco TX 1975, Studio Museum Harlem NY 1977, Studio Museum Harlem NY 1979, Howard Univ Washington DC 1980, Helen Euphrat Gallery CA 1982, Brockman Gallery LA 1982, Grand Oak Gallery 1983; LA Mus of African Amer Art Printmakers 1984, CA Museum of African Amer Art 1986, San Francisco Art Commiss Gallery 1987; City Art Gallery, San Francisco. **Business Addr:** 1879 San Juan Ave, Berkeley, CA 94703.

HOLDEN, AARON CHARLES
Property master. **Personal:** Born Oct 27, 1942, Chicago, IL; son of Elizabeth Jones Holden and Cleveland Holden; married Willa Anderson Holden; children: Cynthia Denise, Aaron Charles. **Educ:** Washburne Trade School, Chicago, IL, chef, 1962-64; Olive Harvey, Chicago, IL, certificate, food sanitation, 1973-74. **Career:** National Broadcasting Co., Chicago, IL, lighting technician, 1970-78; AA Props International, Chicago, IL, property master, 1978-. **Orgs:** Member, NAACP, 1975-; member, Chicago Urban League, 1980-; member, Actor's Guild, 1980-; member, The Community Film Workshop, 1980-; member, Dusable Museum, 1982-. **Honors/Awds:** National AAU Runner Up, National AAU, 1960; Championship, CYO-Boxing, 1957-60; America's Best and Brightest Young Business and Professional Men, Dollars and Sense Magazine, 1989. **Business Addr:** Prop Master, AA Props International, Inc, PO Box 495B, Chicago, IL 60649.

HOLDEN, KIP. See HOLDEN, MELVIN LEE.

HOLDEN, MELVIN LEE (KIP HOLDEN)
State official. **Personal:** Born Aug 12, 1952, New Orleans, LA; son of Rosa Rogers Holden (deceased) and Curtis Holden; married Lois Stevenson Holden; children: Melvin II, Angela, Monique, Myron, Brian Michael. **Educ:** Louisiana State Univ, BA, journalism; Southern Univ, MA, journalism; Southern Univ School of Law, JD. **Career:** WXOK-Radio, news director; WWL-Radio, New Orleans, LA, reporter; WBRZ-TV, reporter; US Census Bureau, public relations specialist; Baton Rouge City Police, public information officer; Louisiana Department of Labor, Worker's Compensation Div, law clerk;

District 2, councilman, 1984-88; District 63, state representative, public relations specialist/attorney, currently. **Orgs:** Member, Xi Nu Lamba Chapter, Alpha Phi Alpha; member, Louisiana Bar Association; member, American Bar Association; member, National Bar Association; member, Greater Baton Rouge Airport Commission. **Honors/Awds:** Best Bets Award, Center for Policy Alternatives, Washington, DC; numerous community awards; Brown Pelican Award as one of the top environmental legislators of Louisiana. **Home Addr:** 234 Rivercrest, Baton Rouge, LA 70807. **Business Addr:** State Representative, State of Louisiana, 2013 Central Rd, Baton Rouge, LA 70807.

HOLDEN, MICHELLE Y.
Television news reporter. **Personal:** Born Mar 31, 1954, Toledo, OH; daughter of Ammie Edmond and Richard Holden; divorced; children: Richard. **Educ:** University of Toledo, Toledo, OH, 1972-75. **Career:** WDHO-TV, Toledo, OH, reporter, 1976; WBNS-TV, Columbus, OH, noon anchor, 1978-82, WHAS-TV, Louisville, KY, noon anchor, 1982-85; WEWS-TV, Cleveland, OH, weekend anchor, 1985-88; WBBM-TV, Chicago, IL, TV news reporter, 1988-90; KTTV-TV, Los Angeles, CA, TV news reporter, 1990; Encore Cable Host ''Trade Secrets,'' 1992; KCAL-TV, Los Angeles, CA, freelance reporter, 1993; Special Correspondent Conus Satellite Network for the OJ Simpson Trial, 1994. **Orgs:** Member, National Association of Black Journalists, 1982-; Alpha Kappa Alpha Sorority; First Baptist Church, Jeffersontown, KY. **Honors/Awds:** Female Broadcaster of the Year, National Association of Career Women, 1987; Ohio General Assembly Commendation, 1982; Greater Cleveland Enterprising Women, 1987; Fred Hampton Communications Award, 1989; Emmy Nomination News Reporting, 1991; Emmy Nomination News Writing, 1992. **Special Achievements:** Movie and Television Appearances: Speechless, Picket Fences, Knots Landing, MTV Dead at 21, Stranger by Night, Seaquest, The Positively True Adventures of the Alledged Texas Cheerleader Murdering Mom. **Business Addr:** Reporter, KTTV-TV, 5746 W Sunset Blvd, Los Angeles, CA 90028-8502.

HOLDEN, NATE
Government official. **Career:** City of Los Angeles, councilman, currently. **Business Addr:** City Councilman, Attn: Rachel Heller, City of Los Angeles, 200 N Spring St, Los Angeles, CA 90012, (213)485-3323.

HOLDER, ERIC H., JR.
Attorney. **Personal:** Born Jan 21, 1951, New York, NY; son of Eric Holder and Miriam R Yearwood Holder. **Educ:** Columbia Coll, BA, 1973, JD, 1976. **Career:** US Dept of Justice, Pub Integrity Sect, trial attorney, 1976-88; Superior Ct, Washington, assoc judge, beginning 1988-93; US Attorney for the District of Columbia, 1993-97; deputy attorney general, 1997-. **Special Achievements:** First African American to hold post of US attorney in Washington, DC. **Business Addr:** Deputy Attorney General, Department of Justice, Rm 4111, Washington, DC 20530.

HOLDER, GEOFFREY
Dancer, choreographer, actor, artist. **Personal:** Born Aug 1, 1930, Port-of-Spain, Trinidad and Tobago; son of Louise De Frense and Arthur Holder; married Carmen deLavallade, 1953. **Educ:** Queens Royal College, native dances in West Indies, 1948. **Career:** Roscoe Holder's Dance O Trinidad, stage debut, company member, 1942; formed own dance troupe, 1950, toured Puerto Rico and Caribbean, 1953, US debut, 1953, Broadway debut, 1954; Metropolitan Opera, solo dancer 1956-57; Kaufmann Auditorium, dancer, twice yearly, 1956-60; dramatic debut, Waiting for Godot, 1975; Show Boat, solo dancer, 1957; concerts with Geoffrey Holder Dance Co, 1956-60; appeared at: Festival of Two Worlds, Italy, 1958; Festividad, Ballet Hispanico, 1979; Brouhaha, choreographer 1960; Mhil Daiim, 1964; I Got a Song, 1974; Josephine Baker's Review, dancer, 1964; choreographer/costume designer, Three Songs for One; costume designer, The Twelve Gates, 1964; director/costume designer, The Wiz, 1975; director/costume designer/choreographer, Timbuktu, 1978; film appearances lude: All Night Long, 1961; Doctor Dolittle, 1967; Krakatoa East of Java, 1969; Everything You Ever Wanted to Know About Sex But Were Afraid to Ask, 1972; Live and Let Die, 1973; Swashbuckler, 1976; Annie, 1982; Boomerang, 1992; author: Black Gods, Green Islands, 1957; Geoffrey Holder's Cookbook, 1974; articles in Playbill; television appearances include: numerous television commercials; Stage Your Number, 1953; Aladdin, 1958; The Bottle Imp, 1958; the Tonight Show, 1975; Good Morning, America, 1976; Straight Talk, 1976; The Gold Bug, 1980; Your New Day, 1981; Alice in Wonderland, 1983; Hour Magazine, 1984; John Grin's Christmas, 1986; Ghost of a Chance, 1987. **Orgs:** American Federation of Television & Radio Artists; Actors' Equity Assn; AGMA; AGVA. **Honors/Awds:** Paintings exhibited at numerous galleries throught out the US and West Indies; recorded albums of West Indian songs and stories; Guggenheim Fellow, painting, 1957; Drama Desk Award, The Wiz, 1975; Tony Awards, Best Director of a Musical, Best Costumes, The Wiz, 1975; recipient, United Caribbean Youth Award, 1962; recipient, Monarch Award, Natl Council of Culture & Art, 1982; Clio Awards, commericals for television, 1970, 1971; Harold Jackman Memorial Award, 1982. **Business Addr:** Dancer/Choreographer, Donald Buchwald Associates, 10 E 44th St, New York, NY 10017.

HOLDER, IDALIA
Personnel administrator. **Personal:** Born Mar 19, 1947; divorced; children: Aisha Margaret. **Educ:** Northeastern University, BS (cum laude) 1973. **Career:** Harvard Univ Sch of Business Admin, admin asst 1971-73; The Carnegie Foundation for the Advancement of Teaching, admin asst 1976-78; Carnegie Corp of New York, personnel asst 1974-76, personnel administrator 1976-78, personnel dir 1978-83, asst corporate sec & dir of personnel 1983-86, dir of personnel and administrative services, currently. **Orgs:** New York Personnel Mgmt Assn; Assn of Black Foundation Execs; American Society for Personnel Admin; Women in Human Resources Mgmt; Intl Assn for Personnel Women; treas, New York Affiliate Natl Black Child Develop Inst; Administrative Mgmt Society. **Honors/Awds:** Sigma Epsilon Rho, 1973. **Business Addr:** Director of Personnel & Administrative Services, Carnegie Corp of New York, 437 Madison Ave, New York, NY 10022.

HOLDER, REUBEN D.
Government official, management consultant. **Personal:** Born Mar 21, 1923, New York, NY; son of Orneata Holder and Richard Holder; married Iris A Lumsby, Apr 3, 1948; children: Gregory Stewart Holder. **Educ:** City Coll of New York; Queens Coll City Univ of New York Urban Affairs, BA; Exec Seminar Center Kings Point New York; Fed Exec Inst Charlottesville Virginia. **Career:** New York Post Office, asst employment officer 1968; New York Reg US Post Office, reg manpower dev specialist 1969; US Civil Serv & Commn, fed reg equal employment opportunity rep 1971; US Govt Office of Personnel Management, chief reg staffing div 1973-; self employed, cons, lecturer 1971-; Holder Management Systems Inc, management cons, lecturer; chmn of bd dirs, UHURV Joint Development Corp 1988-; area rep, New York City Planning Bd #12, 1989-. **Orgs:** Mem 100 Black Men 1976-; life mem, Past pres Queens Dist, past chmn natl bd of dir 369th Vet Assc 1978; pres Black Fed Exec 1980; bd of dir Queens Br NY Urban League 1986-87; board of directors, Urban Renewal Committee of South Jamaica; board of directors, Neighborhood Based Coalition; chmn, Land Use Committee, NYC Community Planning Bd #12. **Honors/Awds:** Alpha Sigma Lambda, Upsilon Chap NY; Deans List Queens College. **Military Serv:** AUS sgt 1942-46; Bronze Star w/ 6 Battle Stars. **Home Addr:** 177-53 Leslie Rd, Jamaica, NY 11434.

HOLLAND, DARIUS
Professional football player. **Personal:** Born Nov 10, 1973, Petersburg, VA. **Educ:** Univ of Colorado, attended. **Career:** Green Bay Packers, defensive tackle, 1995-. **Business Addr:** Professional Football Player, Green Bay Packers, 1265 Lombardi Ave, Green Bay, WI 54304, (414)494-2351.

HOLLAND, DORREEN ANTOINETTE
Educator. **Personal:** Born Jul 29, 1968, Charlottesville, VA; daughter of Mr and Mrs Earl M Holland. **Educ:** Virginia Union Univ, BS, May 6, 1990. **Career:** Locust Grove Elementary, 5th grade teacher, 1990-93; Northside Christian School, 1-4 gr teacher, summer school; Charlottesville School System, project yes teacher, 5-6th grade, 1993-94; Fluvanna County School System, chapter 1 resource teacher, 1994-. **Orgs:** NAACP member, freedom funder organizer, 1993-; Amer Heart Assn, 1993-; Senior Class, sec, 1986-96; Bible Study, art teacher, 1993-; Youth organizer for church, 1993-. **Honors/Awds:** Lettie Pate, 1987; Alpha Kappa Mu, 1986. **Special Achievements:** NAACP, Senior Queen, 1994. **Home Addr:** Route 1, Box 259, Palmyra, VA 22963.

HOLLAND, ETHEL M.
Nurse. **Personal:** Born Oct 31, 1946, Washington, DC; married Reginald D Johnson. **Educ:** Immaculate Conception Acad, Washington, DC, HSD 1964; Mt Mrty Coll Ynktn SD, BS 1968; Nursing Catholic Univ of Amer Washington DC, MS 1974. **Career:** Childrens Hosp Natl Med Ctr, Washington, DC, serv dir, Acute Care, 1974-; DC General Hospital, clinical nurse, Dept of Pediatrics, 1970-73; 91st E Vac Hospital Vietnam, asst head nurse, 1969-70; Walter Reed Army Hospital, Washington, DC, staff nurse, 1968-69. **Orgs:** Vice pres, Registered Nurse Examination Bd 1979-88; Black Nurses Assn of Greater Metro Area 1978-; mem District of Columbia Nurses Assn 1968-88; charter mem Ethnic Nurses for Adv of Health Care Among Minorities 1978-80; vol Ancst Neighborhood Clinic, Washington, DC 1974; Sigma Theta Tau Kappa Chapter Washington DC 1974. **Honors/Awds:** Inducted into Natl Hon Soc for Nurses; Army Cmndtn Medal Mrtrs Serv Vietnam 1970; papers presented Nurse Care of Pts who Fail to Thrive 1979; Patterns of Elimination, 1976; Nursng Care of Patients with Sickle Cell Anemia, 1975. **Military Serv:** AUS 1st lt. **Business Addr:** Dir, Children's Hospital Natl Med Center, 3 Orange Nursing Service, 111 Michigan Ave NW, Washington, DC 20010.

HOLLAND, J. ARCHIBALD
Educator, marketing consultant, author. **Personal:** Born in Wilmington, DE; son of Helen Holland Stanley and Archibald Holland Sr. **Educ:** Lincoln Univ, Lincoln Univ PA, AB; Columbia Univ, New York NY, 3 years' graduate school. **Career:** Amer Mgmt Assn, New York NY, advertising promotion writer, 1960-63; Holt, Rinehart & Winston, New York NY, copywriter-editor, 1963-65; Grolier Educ Corp, New York NY, asst advertising dir, 1966-69; Grey Advertising Agency, New York NY, writer in residence, 1979-83; George G Garmus Assoc, New York NY, public relations assoc, 1983-85; Panamericana Co, New York NY, pres, 1985-89; New York City High Schools, part-time teacher, college lecturer, 1989-; The New School for Social Research, New York, NY, humanities professor, 1994-. **Orgs:** Direct Mktg Assn, 1963-69; Natl Writers Union, 1988-; NY Assn of Black Journalists, 1997-. **Honors/Awds:** New York Area Speech Champion, Intl Toastmasters, 1971; speech presentations: Eulogy for a Dying City, 1971, The Harlem Renaissance, 1988-89, The Legacy of Langston Hughes, 1988-89; author of ''Freedom to Kill,'' magazine article read in Congress by Senator Edward Kennedy, 1974; author of ''The Case for Calling Blacks Black,'' magazine article; author of novel, The Chinese Pagoda. **Military Serv:** US Army. **Home Addr:** 5008 Broadway #3B, New York, NY 10034.

HOLLAND, LAURENCE H.
Analytical chemist. **Personal:** Born Nov 8, 1926, Tampa, FL; son of Hazel Symonette Holland and Albert Holland Sr; married Rose Withers. **Educ:** Central State Univ, BS; Studies NY Univ Rutgers Univ & City Univ of NY, Grad. **Career:** Lederle Lab Amer Chem Soc, analytical chem; Amer Soc Quality Control. **Orgs:** Mem Legisltaive Penal Com; mem bd dir ROCAC; past pres life mem NAACP; exec bd Lederle Fed Credit Union; trustee, St Charles AME Zion Church; Alpha Phi Alpha. **Military Serv:** USN 1945. **Home Addr:** 434 Western Hwy, Orangeburg, NY 10962. **Business Addr:** Analytical Chemist, Lederle Laboratories, Bld 130, Room 401 C, Pearl River, NY 10965.

HOLLAND, LOYS MARIE
Public health administrator. **Personal:** Born Jun 9, 1950, Camp, MS; daughter of James & Ora Lee Flagg; married. **Educ:** Loop City College, Harold Washington, AA, 1971; National College of Education, BA, 1974. **Career:** Chicago Dept of Public Hth, clerical supervisor, 1975-95, public hth admin, 1995-; Robert Taylor Initative, dir, 1996-97. **Orgs:** CARDE, advisory bd, 1995-; Holman Hth Ctr, advisory bd, 1995-; Christ the King Lutheran School PTA, 1993-; Grand Blvd Foundation, 1995-. **Honors/Awds:** Boys Scouts of America, Outstanding Leadership & Community Services Award, 1997. **Business Addr:** Public Health Administrator, Chicago Department of Public Health, 4410 S State St, Chicago, IL 60609.

HOLLAND, MAJOR LEONARD
Architect, educator. **Personal:** Born Mar 8, 1941, Tuskegee, AL; son of Emily L Holland and Soloman M Holland (deceased); married Sceiva, Dec 28, 1966; children: Mark, Michael, John. **Educ:** Howard University, BArch, 1964. **Career:** US Army, corp of engineerss, 1964-66; Fry & Welch Architects, 1966-69; Tuskegee University, associate professor, 1969-; Major Holland Architect & Associates PC, vice pres, 1972-. **Orgs:** Alabama Architectural Foundation, president, 1991-; American Institute of Architects, fellow, chapter officer, 1969-; National Organization of Minority Architects, regional director, 1971-; Optimist International, youth activities chairman/mem, 1977-; Kappa Alpha Psi, chapter president, vice pres, 1967-; Design Alabama, board mem, 1991-; Greenwood Baptist Church, Deacon, 1978-; Boy Scouts of America, district program chairman, board mem, 1967-. **Honors/Awds:** American Institute of Architects, fellow, 1992; Boy Scouts of America, Silver Beaver Award, 1991; Department of Architecture, Tuskegee University, Faculty of the Year, 1978-81. **Special Achievements:** Kappa Alpha Psi Regional Achievement Award, 1983; Architectural Design Award for Tuskegee Municipal Complex, 1986; Businessman of the Year, 1978. **Military Serv:** US Army, corps of engineers, 1st lt, 1964-66; Commendation Award, 1965. **Business Addr:** President, Major L Holland, Architect & Associates, PC, 111 South Main St, PO Box 547, Tuskegee, AL 36083, (205)727-4079.

HOLLAND, ROBERT, JR.
Company executive. **Personal:** Born 1940, Albion, MI; son of Robert Sr; married Barbara Jean; children: Robert III, Kheri, Jaclyn. **Educ:** Union Coll, BS, mechanical engineering, 1962; Bernard Baruch Coll, MBA, 1969. **Career:** Mobil Corp, engineer, 1962-68; McKinsey & Co, associate/partner, 1968-91; City Marketing Inc, chairman, 1984-87; Gilreath Manufacturing, senior vp/chairman, 1987-91; Rokher-J Consulting Firm and Holding Company, chairman, beginning 1981; Ben & Jerry's Homemade Inc, pres/CEO, until 1996; WorkPlace Integraters, owner, 1997.

HOLLAND, ROBIN W.
Educator. **Personal:** Born May 23, 1953, Columbus, OH; daughter of Elizabeth W Jackson and Robert R Jackson; married Ralph V Holland Jr, Jun 20, 1987. **Educ:** Ohio State Univ, BS 1974, MA 1975. **Career:** Columbus Public Schools, reading

teacher 1975-76, gifted/talented teacher 1977-80, classroom teacher 1976-86, consulting teacher 1986-89, reading recovery/early literacy teacher, 1990-. **Orgs:** Mem Natl Educ Assn 1975-, Assn of Supervision and Curriculum Develop 1986-; chairperson-Educ Comm Central OH Club/Natl Assn of Negro Business & Professional Women 1984-87; mem St Philips Episcopal Church; member, International Reading Assn, National Council of Teachers of English. **Honors/Awds:** Martha Holden Jennings Scholar, Martha Holden Jennings Foundation, 1990-91. **Business Addr:** Windsor Academy, Columbus Public Schools, 1219 E 12th St, Columbus, OH 43211.

HOLLAND, SPENCER H.
Educator, psychologist. **Personal:** Born Sep 11, 1939, Suffern, NY. **Educ:** Glassboro State Coll, AB, 1965; Columbia Univ, AM, 1968, PhD, 1976. **Career:** Burnet Jr HS, teacher 1965-67; Essex Co Coll, asst prof 1968-73, chmn psychology dept 1970-73; Harlem Interfaith Counseling Serv, prev mental health teacher 1974-75; Child Abuse & Neglect Proj Div of Pupil Personnel Serv Washington DC Public Schools, coord 1976-90; Morgan State Univ, Ctr for Educatin African-American Males, dir, 1990-. **Orgs:** American Psychological Assn; Assn of Black Psychologists 1972-. **Honors/Awds:** Natl Fellowship Fund Fellow, 1973-76. **Military Serv:** USAF 1957-60.

HOLLAND, WALLACE E. See Obituaries section.

HOLLAND, WILLIAM MEREDITH
Attorney, judge. **Personal:** Born in Live Oak, FL; son of Annie Holland and Isaac Holland; children: William M, Jr, Maurice, Gian, Gaelim, Shakira. **Educ:** FL A&M Univ, AB 1947; Boston Univ Law Sch, JD 1951. **Career:** Atty; civil rights advocate; pres with Law Firm of Holland & Smith; municipal judge l973-l977. **Orgs:** Mem Legal Def NAACP; Amer Bar Assn Comm on Indiv Rights & Responsibilities; Amer Civil Liberties Union. **Honors/Awds:** NAACP Achievement Award; Amer Bicentennial Resource Inst; Phi Beta Sigma Achiev Award; Omega Psi Phi Man of the Year; Optimist Achiev Award; Phi Delta Kappa Award; Zeta Phi Beta Award. **Military Serv:** AUS Corpl 1943-46. **Business Addr:** Attorney, 131 US Highway One, PO Box 12365, Lake Park, FL 33403.

HOLLAND-CALBERT, MARY ANN
Registered nurse. **Personal:** Born Jul 12, 1941, New York, NY; daughter of Doris Wiles Vance and James Kirkland; married Clarence E Calbert, May 23, 1987; children: Toussaint Michael Holland. **Educ:** Washington Technical Inst, AAS, 1976; Univ of District of Columbia, BSN, 1987-. **Career:** St Elizabeth Hospital, Washington DC, psychiatric nurse coord, 1970-88; Greater Southeast Community Hospital, Washington DC, psychiatric nurse, 1988-. **Orgs:** Mem, Natl Council of Negro Women, 1976-; Chi Eta Phi Sorority Inc, mem 1976-, exec sec 1983-88; mem, Top Ladies of Distinction, 1986-; St Mark Presbyterian Church.

HOLLAND-CORN, KEDRA
Professional basketball player. **Personal:** Born Jul 31, 1972. **Educ:** Univ of Georgia. **Career:** San Jose Lasers, guard, 1997-. **Business Addr:** Professional Basketball Player, San Jose Lasers, 1530 Parkmoor Ave, Ste A, San Jose, CA 95128, (408)271-1500.

HOLLAR, MILTON CONOVER
Physician. **Personal:** Born May 6, 1930, Newark, NJ; son of Ruth L and Hector R; married; children: Michael C, Melia C, Marc C, Milton C. **Educ:** New York Univ, BA 1955, MA 1957; Howard Univ Coll Medicine, MD 1962; New York Psychoanalytic Inst, Graduated 1975. **Career:** Yeshiva Univ Albert Einstein Coll of Medicine, asst clinical prof psy; Bronx Psy Center, faculty mem 1976-; New Rochelle Guidance Center Lincoln Ave Clinic, med dir 1966-88. **Orgs:** Half-Way House Ex-offenders; mem New Rochelle CAA; mem Natl Med Assc; Amer Psychiatric Assc; Amer Psychoanalytic Assc; New York Pscyhoanalytic Soc Diplomate; Amer Bd of Psychiatry & Neurology; pres New York Metro Black Psychiatrists of Amer; mem Comm Social Responsibility Amer Psy Assoc; mem New York County Med Soc public health Comm on Minorities; mem Physicians Adv Comm Visting Nurse Serv Westchester. **Honors/Awds:** Published "Minority Students Psychological Notes for the 1980's" Journal Natl Assn of Student Pers Admin; co-chmn & coord, Apsychoanalya workshops "Impact of AIDS", 1988-. **Military Serv:** AUS maj 1951-53. **Business Addr:** General Counsel/Asst Sec, Rutgers Community Health Plan, 57 US Highway #1, New Brunswick, NJ 08901.

HOLLEY, JAMES W., III
Dental surgeon, city official. **Personal:** Born Nov 24, 1926, Portsmouth, VA; married Mary W; children: James IV, Robin. **Educ:** West Virginia State Coll, BS 1949; Howard Univ, DDS 1955. **Career:** Maryview Hospital/Portsmouth General Hospital, dental staff; Mayor, City of Portsmouth, 1984-87, 1996-. **Orgs:** Norfolk Comm Virginia State Dental Assn; Virginia Tidewater Den Soc; Old Dominion Den Soc; Natl Dental Assn; Amer Den Assn; Pierre Fauchard Acad; Portsmouth Den Soc; Chicago Den Soc; Cen Civic Forum; United Civic League; Miller Day Nursery; Gosport Dist Boy Scouts of Amer; Tidewater Council Boy Scouts of Amer; YMCA; United Fund; Portsmouth C of C; Citizens Planning Assn; Mayor Committee Year 2005; NAACP, life mem; Intl Group Clinics, founder & chmn; Ntl Guardsman, past pres, secretary; Portsmouth Sports Club, past pres; NH Negro Golf Assoc, past pres, founder; Chi Delta Mu, mem; Omega Psi Phi, life mem & past basileus; Fellowship Christian Church, founder, church council, past chmn, Church Assembly, past moderator; Retired Officers Assoc, 1996. **Honors/Awds:** Portsmouth Teachers, School Bell Award, 1960; Boy Scouts of Amer, Achievement Award, 1962; Natl Den Assn, Pres Award, 1963; Omega, Man of Year, 1963; Boy Scouts of Amer, Silver Beaver Award, 1963; Old Dominion Den Soc, Dentist of Year 1968; Old Dominion Soc, Pres Award, 1969; numerous other honors & awards; Honorary Doctor of Laws, W VA State Coll, 1996; Delta Sigma Theta Sorority, 1993; Norfolk State Univ, bd of visitors, 1993; Ntl Dentist of the Year, 1984; Omega Psi Phi Fraternity, Citizen of the Year, 1984; Howard Univ Dental Award, 1975; Minority Police Officers Assoc of Portsmouth, VA, hon mem, 1997; Hampton Rds Chapt of the Conf of Minority Public Admin, 1996. **Military Serv:** WW II. **Business Addr:** 446 Effingham St, Portsmouth, VA 23704.

HOLLEY, JIM
Pastor, author. **Personal:** Born Dec 5, 1943, Philadelphia, PA; son of Effie Mae King Holley and Charles James Holley Sr; married Phyllis Dean Holley (divorced 1982); children: Tiffani Dionne. **Educ:** Wayne State University, Detroit MI, PhD, Higher Education; University of Chicago, Chicago, IL, Master of Divinity. **Career:** Little Rock Baptist Church, Detroit, MI, pastor, 1972-; Cognos Adverting, Detroit, president, CEO, 1988-; Ashland Theological Seminary, dean. **Business Addr:** Pastor, Little Rock Baptist Rock, 9000 Woodward Ave, Detroit, MI 48202.

HOLLEY, SANDRA CAVANAUGH
Speech/language pathologist, educator. **Personal:** Born Mar 30, 1943, Washington, DC; daughter of Rebecca Arthur Cavanaugh and Clyde Howard Cavanaugh; children: David Marshall. **Educ:** George Washington University, AB 1965, AM 1966; Univ of CT, PhD 1979. **Career:** Southern CT State Univ, speech/language pathologist, prof 1970-; Rehab Center of Eastern Fairfield Co, speech pathologist 1966-70. **Orgs:** Chmn Humane Commission City of New Haven 1977-86; bd of dir American Natl Red Cross S Central Chap 1978-84; exec bd CT Speech & Hearing Assn 1971-83; bd dir New Haven Visiting Nurse Assn 1977-79; vice pres for adminstration, Amer Speech-Language-Hearing Assn 1983-85; mem bd of dir The Foote School Association 1985-89; pres American Speech-Language-Hearing Assn 1988. **Honors/Awds:** Danforth fellow Southern CT State College 1973-80; Leadership in Communications Award Howard Univ 1987; Honorary Doctor of Public Service degree George Washington Univ 1989; Fellow, American Speech-Language-Hearing Association, 1980; SCSU, Multicultural Founders Award, 1994; National Coalition of 100 Black Women, Milestone Award, 1994; Distinguished Alumna Award, Dept. of Speech & Hearing, George Washington Univ, 1997. **Business Addr:** Professor and Chairperson, Communication Disorders, Southern Connecticut State University, 501 Crescent St, New Haven, CT 06515.

HOLLEY, SHARON YVONNE
Librarian. **Personal:** Born Aug 15, 1949, Gainesville, FL; daughter of Rebecca Bryant Jordan and Johnnie Jordan; married Kenneth Holley, Aug 7, 1976; children: Nzinga, Asantewa, Makeda. **Educ:** Santa Fe Community College, Gainesville, FL, AA, 1968; Florida Atlantic University, Boca Raton, FL, BA, 1970; Wayne State University, Detroit, MI, MSLS, 1972. **Career:** Buffalo & Erie County Public Library, Buffalo, NY, librarian, 1972-. **Orgs:** Board member, pres, Afro-American Historical Association of Niagara Frontier, 1977-; member, Black Caucus-American Library Association, 1990-; former secretary, board member, National Association of Black Storytellers, 1986-; former board member, African-American Librarians of Western New York, 1990-; committee co-chair, Kwanzaa Committee of Buffalo, 1980-. **Honors/Awds:** Community Service, National Assn of Business and Professional Women, 1989; Black Family & Heritage, Alpha Kappa Alpha, Xi Epsilon Omega Chapter, 1989; Black History/Library Science, Empire State Federation of Womens' Clubs, 1988; Leadership as President, Afro-American Historical Assn of Niagara Frontier, 1985; Certificate of Merit, Buffalo & Erie County Public Library, 1984; Zeta Phi Beta Sorority Inc, Kappa Upsilon Zeta Chap, Woman of the Year, 1997. **Home Addr:** 31 St Paul Mall, Buffalo, NY 14209. **Business Phone:** (716)858-7194.

HOLLEY, VANCE MAITLAND
Business executive. **Personal:** Born Mar 18, 1941, Charleston, WV; son of Velda Holley and Orie Edwards; married Virginia Hilliard, Dec 28, 1983; children: Kathy Brown, Terri Love, Jackie Hilliard, Ronald Parker, Donald Parker. **Educ:** California Polytechnic University, Pomona, CA, BS, social science, 1972. **Career:** City of San Bernardino, youth activities counselor, 1971-72; Redevelopment Agency, City San Bernardino, administrative asst, 1972-73; Health Service Education Activity, health coord project dir, 1974-75; Lockheed Aircraft Service Co., human resource specialist, 1975-80, manager of EEO, 1980-86, corporate director, work force diversity and compliance programs, 1986-. **Orgs:** Minority Emp Journal, board of advisors, 1989-; LA Project W/Industry, vice chairman, 1986-; Aerospace Corp Comp Cnsl, founder, 1990-; National Black Business Roundtable, board of directors, 1992-; board of directors, BG Aero Structure; Patriots Publication, bd of dirs; Lockhead Leadership Fund, vice pres. **Honors/Awds:** Young People for Young People, Hall of Distinction Award, 1991. **Military Serv:** US Air Force, airman 1st class, 1961-64. **Business Addr:** Corporate Director, Work Force Diversity and Compliance Programs, Lockheed Corporation, 4500 Park Granada Blvd, Lockheed Corp, CA 91399, (818)876-2426.

HOLLIDAY, ALFONSO DAVID
Physician. **Personal:** Born Jun 10, 1931, Gary, IN; married Iris; children: Kathy, Alfonso III, Tony, Leroy, Ronnie, Dawn. **Educ:** IN Univ, BA 1952; IN Univ Sch Med, MD 1955; Univ of Chicago, MBA Health Administration, 1979. **Career:** Self-employed, physician/surgeon 1960-75; Family Nurse Practitioner Program, co-dir 1975-82; Med Ctr Gary, exec dir 1975-80; IN Univ NW, adj asst prof of nursing 1978-82; Group Health of NW IN Inc, pres 1979-80; Holliday Health Care PC, pres 1980-; Lake Co Jail Crown Point IN, med dir 1982-92; Gary Police Dept Gary IN, police surgeon 1982-87. **Orgs:** Diplomat Amer Bd Surgery 1964; flw Amer Coll Surgeons 1964; Amer Med Assn; IN State Med Assn; Natl Med Assn; Hoosier State Med Assn; Lake Co Med Soc; Amer Coll of Physician Executives 1984; accreditation surveyor for the Accreditation Assn for Ambulatory Health Care Inc 1979-; fellow, Amer Coll of Physician Executives 1984. **Honors/Awds:** Awd for Activities in field Human Rights NAACP 1976; IN Univ Don's Awd 1976; Disting Serv Midwest Assn of Com Health Ctrs Inc 1979; Natl HMO Management Fellow Georgetown Univ Sch of Medicine 1980; Natl HOM Management, Fellow, 1980-81. **Special Achievements:** American Society of Addiction Medicine, certified, 1990. **Military Serv:** USAF capt 1960-62. **Business Addr:** President, Holliday Health Care, PC, 8410 Maple Ave, Gary, IN 46403.

HOLLIDAY, BILLIE. See HOLLIDAY-HAYES, WILHELMINA EVELYN.

HOLLIDAY, COREY LAMONT
Professional football player. **Personal:** Born Jan 31, 1971, Richmond, VA. **Educ:** Univ of North Carolina, bachelor's degree in business administration, masters degree in athletic administration, 1997. **Career:** Pittsburgh Steelers, wide receiver, 1995-. **Business Addr:** Professional Football Player, Pittsburgh Steelers, Three Rivers Stadium, 300 Stadium Circle, Pittsburgh, PA 15212, (412)323-1200.

HOLLIDAY, FRANCES B.
Educator. **Personal:** Born in Chicago, IL; married Oliver M Holliday; children: David E Brown. **Educ:** DePaul Univ, BA 1949, MA 1962; Union Grad Sch, PhD 1977. **Career:** Chicago Public Schs, teacher 1950-68; Headstart Chicago, exec dir 1965-66; Loyola Univ, teacher 1969-70; Urban Teacher Educ Univ IL, instructor 1970-71; Title III Program in Early Childhood Dev Dist 65, dir 1971-74; NEU, instructor 1971-74; Title VII Emer Sch Aid Act Dist 65, director; Ctr for New Schools, pres & chmn of bd; Chicago Educ Corps, dir volunteer serv unit. **Orgs:** Mem Natl Alliance Black Sch Educators, Black Child Dev Inst; mem bd Assn Black Child Advocates; editorial adv bd mem Journal of Negro Educ; columnist author in field. **Business Addr:** Dir, Chicago Education Corps, 1819 W Pershing Rd, Chicago, IL 60609.

HOLLIDAY, JENNIFER (JENNIFER-YVETTE)
Singer, actress. **Personal:** Born Oct 19, 1960, Houston, TX; daughter of Jennie Thomas Holliday and Omie Lee Holliday; married Bishop Andre Woods. **Career:** Stage performances include: Your Arms Too Short to Box with God, 1979-80; Dreamgirls, 1981; Sing, Mahalia, Sing, 1985; television appearances include: Saturday Night Live, 1982; The Love Boat, 1986; In Performance at the White House, 1988; record albums: Dreamgirls, 1981; Feel My Soul, 1983; Say You Love Me, 1985. **Honors/Awds:** Grammy Award, Dreamgirls, 1981; Tony Award, Dreamgirls, 1981; Antoinette Perry Award, Best Actress in a Musical, 1982; Drama Desk Award, Best Actress in a Musical, 1982; Grammy Award, Best R&B Performance-Female, "And I'm Telling You I'm Not Going," 1983; Image Award, NAACP, 1983; Grammy Award, Best Inspirational Performance-Female, "Come Sunday," 1986; Texas Southern University, Distinguished Alumni Award.

HOLLIDAY, PRINCE E.
Health insurance executive. **Personal:** Born Sep 29, 1935, Chambers County, AL; married Marcia E Cypress; children: Eric, Morgan. **Educ:** Attended, Clark Coll Atlanta 1954-55; Univ of Detroit, AB 1975. **Career:** Blue Cross and Blue Shield of MI, mgr phy & prov serv 1968-74, asst vice pres gov mktg 1974-75, assoc dir cust affairs 1975-78, exec asst ext affairs 1978-83, dir civic affairs 1983-85, vice pres comm affairs 1985-; Metro Staff Temporaries/Prince Holliday Enterprises, president, currently. **Orgs:** Pres Metro Detroit Youth Founda-

tion; bd of dirs Police Athletic League; chmn bd of dirs Northside Family YMCA 1986-87; vice chmn Intl Freedom Festival 1986-87; mem Greater Detroit Chamber of Commerce; apptd by mayor Detroit Private Industry Cncl; pres Blue Cross and Blue Shield of MI Employee's Five Year Club 1986-87; sec Blue Cross and Blue Shield of MI HAP/PAC 1986-87; dist dir Public Relations MI District of Kiwanis 1986-87; exec comm Clark Coll C Eric Lincoln Lectureship; mem Detroit Kiwanis Club #1; golden heritage life mem NAACP; life mem Kappa Alpha Psi Frat; mem Booker T Washington Business Assoc; lt gov MI Dist of Kiwanis 1987-88; mem bd of dirs Junior Achievement Southeastern MI; mem bd of dirs Intl Inst of Detroit; mem bd of trustees Boys & Girls Clubs of Detroit. **Honors/Awds:** Spirit of Detroit Award Detroit City Cncl 1984; Testimonial Resolution Detroit City Council 1986; Metro Detroit YMCA Minority Achiever in Industry Award YMCA Metro Detroit 1986; lay mem MI Assoc of Osteopathic Physicians and Surgeons. **Military Serv:** USN usntn 1955-56; Honorable Discharge. **Business Addr:** President, Metro Staff Temporaries/Prince Holliday Enterprises, Inc, 28500 Southfield Rd, Lathrup Village, MI 48076.

HOLLIDAY-HAYES, WILHELMINA EVELYN (BILLIE HOLLIDAY)
Government official. **Personal:** Born Sep 10, Jacksonville, FL; daughter of Leah Ervin Holliday and John Holliday; married John (Jackie) Hayes, Aug 25, 1970; children: Stepson: John W II. **Educ:** New York University, BS; Columbia School of Social Work, graduate studies; New School for Social Research, MA, human resources; Institute for Mediation & Conflict Resolution, certified mediator. **Career:** Mt Vernon Police Dept, deputy police commissioner, 1994-95, commissioner, 1995-96; NYC Police Dept, dep commissioner for community affairs, 1984-94; Bd of Parole, NY State, commissioner, 1976-84; Vera Inst of Justice & Pretrial Service Agency, borough dir, 1974-76; NYC Police Dept, asst dir, exec dir, 1968-74; NYC Office of Probation, court reporting officer, 1961-68; NYC Dept of Socisl Services, caseworker, 1956-61. **Orgs:** Vice pres, bd dir, Wiltwyck School for Boys; chpn, bd dir, Wiltwyck Brooklyn Div; bd dir, Exodus House; consult, Equal Opp & Womans Career Mags; flw orgnzr, Harlem Improvement Project; hon pres, Friends of Northside Center for Child Development, 1974-; Delta Simga Theta; pres, Black Resources and Issues Now (BRAIN); Mid Manhattan NAACP; advisor, Greater NY Councils of Boy Scouts of Amer and Law Enforcement Explorer Scouts; consultant, Key Women of America; Manhattan Urban League; Women in Criminal Justice. **Honors/Awds:** Govt and community service award, Natl Council of Negro Women, 1989; America's Top 100 Black Women, 1985; Humanitarian Award, New York Chapter of Continental Soc Inc, 1985; Sojourner Truth Loyalty Award, Coalition of Black Trade Unionists, 1986; Achievement Award, Federation of Negro Civil Associates of New York, 1986. **Business Addr:** Deputy Police Commissioner, Mount Vernon Police Dept, Roosevelt Sq North, Mount Vernon, NY 10550.

HOLLIER, DWIGHT LEON
Professional football player. **Personal:** Born Apr 21, 1969, Hampton, VA; married Chandra, Mar 22, 1997; children: Deandre. **Educ:** Univ of North Carolina, BS in speech communications and psychology. **Career:** Miami Dolphins, linebacker, 1992-. **Business Addr:** Professional Football Player, Miami Dolphins, 2269 NW 199th St, Miami, FL 33056, (305)620-5000.

HOLLIMAN, ARGIE N.
Entrepreneur. **Personal:** Born Jun 8, 1957, Grand Rapids, MI; daughter of Mattie M Holliman and John Holliman; children: Stephine Bryant, Stephen Bryant, Shawn Bryant. **Educ:** Grand Valley State University, 1975-79; Columbia School of Broadcasting, BA, communications, 1982. **Career:** WEHB Radio, host/producer, 1980-82; WKWM Radio, news director, 1982-87; Sarah Allen Family Neighborhood Center, tutorial services director, 1987-88; South East End Neighborhood Association, crime prevention director, 1988-92; YWCA, volunteer services counseling center coordinator, 1990-; Creative Communications Centre, president, currently. **Orgs:** Coailition for Representative Government; Chamber of Commerce, co-chair public relations minority affairs, 1991-92; YWCA, co-chair, Racism Task Force, 1992-; PTA, chair public relations, 1988-89; Governor's Task Force on Youth Initiatives, chair, 1988-89; Grand Rapids Cable Access Center, chair, 1992-. **Special Achievements:** Actress, Community Mental Health Theatre Troupe, 1992-; co-founder, Oakdale Human Resource Center, 1990-; host/producer, "It's Time to Talk," 1990-; Co-founder, Burton St Church of Christ, 1989. **Business Addr:** President, Creative Communications Centre, 6475 28th St SE, Ste 126, Grand Rapids, MI 49506, (616)245-6197.

HOLLIMAN, DAVID L.
Company executive. **Personal:** Born Sep 13, 1929, Denver, CO; son of Dorothy Taylor Holliman and Ernest W Holliman Jr (deceased); married Mildred Helms Holliman, Dec 23, 1973; children: Rhoda, Lisa, Michael. **Educ:** Regis College, Denver, CO, BA, economics, 1990. **Career:** Continental Air Lines, Denver, CO, passenger ser-operations, 1966-86 (retired); United Maintenance, Inc, president, 1972-89; Primalon International Enterprise Ltd, CEO, 1989-; Queen City Services, courier service consultant, currently. **Orgs:** Mayor's Board of Appeals; Mayor's Black Advisory Commission; Colorado Black Roundtable; Colorado Centennial Ethnic Minority Council Bi-Centennial Commission; advisory group, Colorado Public Service Company; past president, PTA, Barrett Elementary School; Campbell Chapel AME Church, past trustee, steward bd, 1942-. **Honors/Awds:** Joseph E Seagram Vanguard Award; Past Grand Master Traveling Black and Gold Card/Pin, Colorado and Jurisdiction; Honorary Past Grand Master, Illinois, Arkansas, Tennessee and province of Ontario, Texas Jurisdiction; Man of the Year, Knights Templar, 1985; Honorary Captain, Syrian Temple No 49, Arabic Foot Patrol; Legion of Honor, Charter Member, 1974; Honorary Lieutenant, Denver Police Department; Past Imperial Potentate, Ancient Egyptian Arabic Order of Noble Majestic Shrine and its jurisdiction (PHA), 1988-90; Hall of Fame, Ira c Meadows, Knights Templar, 1985; Grand Inspector General, 330 United Supreme, Council, NJ, PHA, 1973, 1988. **Military Serv:** US Coast Guard, Petty Officer 1st Class, 1948-58; graduate of USCG Petty Officer School, Groton, CT; US Navy Firefighting School, Oakland, CA; Honorary Captain, Denver Police Dept; Ebony Magazine, One of 100 Most Influential People, 1989. **Home Addr:** PO Box 6844, Denver, CO 80206-0844.

HOLLIN, KENNETH RONALD
Educational administrator. **Personal:** Born Nov 6, 1948, Yuma, AZ; son of Cleo E Cook Hollin and James T Hollin; married Tammy Moore (divorced 1985); children: Cheyenne, Kenya, James, Antonio. **Educ:** Arizona Western College, Yuma, AZ, AA, 1968; Arizona State University, Tempe, AZ, BA, Secondary Education, 1973. **Career:** Phoenix Job Corps Center, Phoenix, AZ, counselor, 1973-75; Phoenix Opportunities Industrialization Center, Phoenix, AZ, counselor, 1975-80; Educational Opportunity Center, Phoenix, AZ, counselor, 1978-80; Abbey Rents, Phoenix, AZ, truck driver, 1980-82; Educational Opportunity Center, Phoenix, AZ, counselor, 1982-84; Arizona State University, Tempe, AZ, assistant director/school relations, 1984-. **Orgs:** Vice president, Arizona Multicultural Student Services Association, 1987-89; president, Citizen's Advisory Council, Phoenix Elementary School District #1, 1989-90; president, Garfield School PTO, 1987-90; chairman, Chapter I Parent Council, Phoenix Elementary School District #1, 1987-89; planning committee member, Statewide Parent Involvement Conference, Arizona Department of Education, 1988-89. **Honors/Awds:** Arizona State University, Affirmative Action Award, 1991. **Business Addr:** Assistant Director/School Relations, Arizona State University, Undergraduate Admissions, PO Box 870112, Tempe, AZ 85287-0112, (602)965-3040.

HOLLINGSWORTH, ALFRED DELANO
Business executive. **Personal:** Born Oct 26, 1942, Jackson, MS; married Hattie. **Educ:** Univ of CA, BS; Univ of WA, MA. **Career:** Crown Zellarbach, jr exec sales dept 1965-67; Fiberboard Corp, sales mgr 1967-68; Sheet Plant Corp, pres 1968-; Squat Corp, pres, owner 1970-. **Orgs:** Bd of dir Black Bus Assn; LAC of C Chmn "Hot Seat" prog; Rotary Club; founder Christian Bus Ministries, Youth for Bus Prog. **Honors/Awds:** Black Businessman of Month Nat Assn Mkt Devel; awds US Dept Commerce. **Business Addr:** President, Squat Corporation, 23441 Goldensprings Dr, Diamond Bar, CA 91765.

HOLLINGSWORTH, JOHN ALEXANDER
Educator (retired). **Personal:** Born Sep 25, 1925, Owego, NY; son of Florence Eve Haley Hollingsworth (deceased) and John Alexander Hollingsworth Sr (deceased); married Dr Winifred Stoelting; children: 5. **Educ:** NC A&T St Univ, BS Agriculture 1950; NC Central Univ, MS Biology 1960; Cornell Univ, Academic Yr 1962-63; NC A&T St Univ, MS Adult Educ 1985. **Career:** Fayetteville City Schools, science tchr 1959-68, science & math coordinator 1968-83; NC A&T St Univ, grad student 1983-85, staff develop intern; consultant, writer, beginning 1985. **Orgs:** Pres Fayetteville City Unit NCTA 1968-70; pres Fayetteville City Unit NCAE 1970-71; st Pres NC Sci Tchrs Asso 1971-73; mem Fayetteville Airport Com 1973-79; grad stdnt intern Major Int In Stress Mgmt & Prvn TV Hlth Care 1983-85; mem NEA, NCAE; life mem NEA-R; American Vision Foundation, Black World Foundation, National Museum of the American Indian; Ecology Action/Common Ground; NC Retired School Personnel; National Retired Teacher Association; National Caucus & Ctr for Black Aging; Association for the Study of African-American Life & History; National Association of Black Veterans; A&T Alumni Association; NC Retired Governmental Employees Association; NC Science Teachers Association. **Honors/Awds:** Writer/Dir ESAA Pilot Proj In Math 1974-80. **Military Serv:** US Army, captain 1943-46 1949-57; Served in Germany, Korea, and Hawaii. **Home Addr:** 61 Otalco Dr, Cherokee Village, AR 72529-6407.

HOLLINGSWORTH, PERLESTA A.
Attorney. **Personal:** Born Apr 12, 1936, Little Rock, AR; son of Eartha Mae Frampton Morris (deceased) and Perlesta G Hollingsworth; married Ada Louise Shine; children: Terri, Tracy, Perlesta, Jr, Maxie. **Educ:** Talladega Clg, AB 1958; Univ AR Law Sch, JD 1969. **Career:** Legal Extradition Ofcr of AR City Cncl, prosecuting atty 1971-; Little Rock City Bd, 1973-76, asst mayor 1975-76; Arkansas Supreme Court, assoc justice 1983-85; Hollingsworth Law Firm P A, attorney. **Orgs:** Mem Urban League, NAACP, Alpha Phi Alpha, Natl Bar Assc, Am Bar Assc, Sigma Pi Phi Frat. **Honors/Awds:** Omega Citizen of the Year 1975. **Military Serv:** AUS 1958-60. **Business Addr:** Attorney, Hollingsworth Law Firm P A, 415 Main St, Main Place Bldg, Little Rock, AR 72201.

HOLLINQUEST, LAMONT
Professional football player. **Personal:** Born Oct 24, 1970, Lynwood, CA. **Educ:** USC. **Career:** Washington Redskins, linebacker, 1993-94; Green Bay Packers, 1996-. **Business Addr:** Professional Football Player, Green Bay Packers, 1265 Lombardi Ave, Green Bay, WI 54304, (414)494-2351.

HOLLINS, HUE
Professional sports official. **Career:** NBA, referee, currently. **Business Addr:** NBA Official, National Basketball Association, 645 5th Ave, 15th Fl, New York, NY 10022-5986.

HOLLINS, JOSEPH EDWARD
Educational administrator. **Personal:** Born Dec 14, 1927, Baton Rouge, LA; married Louise T; children: Reginald, Larry, Patrice, Stephanie. **Educ:** Leland Coll, BS 1952; NM Styland Univ, 1957; Southern Univ, ME 1969. **Career:** Thomas A Levy, 1950-60; Upper Marengauin, principal 1960-. **Orgs:** Alderman Town Of Maringouin 1970-. **Home Addr:** P O Box 156, Maringouin, LA 70757.

HOLLINS, LEROY
Employee services company executive. **Personal:** Born Jul 1, 1945, Texarkana, TX; son of Willie Pearl Purifoy Hollins (deceased) and Robert Hollins (deceased); married Viola Anderson Hollins, Sep 21, 1968; children: LeTasha Renea, Shawn Ashley. **Educ:** Bishop Coll, Dallas, TX, Bachelors, 1970; Texas A & M, Dallas, TX, Masters, 1975. **Career:** Texas Instruments, Dallas, TX, Emp Svc & Recn Admin, 1970-79; Martin Marietta Astronautics Group, Denver, CO, mgr, employee svcs, 1979-. **Orgs:** Mem, Natl Employee Svcs & Recreation Assn Education & Research Foundation, 1990-91; mem, Natl Employee Svcs & Recreation Assn, 1970-, past pres; past pres , co-fndr, Denver Area Employee Svcs and Recn Assn, 1981-; deputy comm, Amateur Softball Assn, CO Assn of Rec Athletics; CO Parks & Recreation Assn. **Honors/Awds:** Jefferson Cup, Martin Marietta Corp, 1982; Operational Performance Awards, Martin Marietta Astonautics Group, 1981, 1982, 1990; Publications Award, Natl Employee Services & Recreation Assn. **Business Addr:** Manager, Employee Services, Martin Marietta Astronautics Group, PO Box 179, Denver, CO 80201.

HOLLIS, MARY LEE
Business owner, real estate broker. **Personal:** Born May 15, 1942, Miller, GA; married Albert H Hollis; children: Naomi M, Pat Ann. **Educ:** Sacramento City & State College, attended; real estate school, certificate of completion. **Career:** Self-employed, real estate firm, owner/director/broker, currently. **Orgs:** Advisory bd, Sacramento Bd of Realtors; Sacramento Assn for Artists; Sacramento Assn for Children; Trinity Church Choir. **Business Addr:** PO Box 221092, Sacramento, CA 95822.

HOLLIS, MELDON S., JR.
Attorney. **Personal:** Born Apr 22, 1945, Charleston, SC; son of Marie Hollis and Meldon Hollis; married Teresa K Harris (divorced); children: Meldon A. **Educ:** Univ of MD, BA 1971, MA 1974; Harvard Univ, JD 1977, MPA 1986. **Career:** US Dept of HEW, special asst to assist sec for educ 1977-79; Univ S Dept of Ed, dir of White House initiative on black coll and univ 1979-80; TX Southern Univ, vice pres for univ devel 1980-82; Harvard Univ, admin asst office of pres 1982-85; Northeastern Univ African-American Studies, lecturer 1982-86; Semmes, Bowen & Semmes, attorney; Chicken George Franchises, Inc, president; Meldon S Hollis & Associates, attorney/entrepreneur, currently; Radio Talk Show Host (WEAA), 1988-. **Orgs:** Dist of Columbia Veterans Assoc, exec dir 1970-74; MD Black Coalition for Higher Ed, vice chairman 1972-74; Friends of the Nat'l Zoo, bd of trustees 1979-80; exec comm Black Faculty and Admin Harvard Univ 1983-85; MA Bay Comm Coll, bd of trustees 1985-87; exec dir Harvard Law Sch Black Alumni Org 1985-87; mem Washington DC and MA Bar Assns; Baltimore City Bd of School Commissioners, president, 1988-89; Bd of School Commissioners; Baltimore Urban League, bd of dirs, 1991-, chairman of bd, 1994-. **Military Serv:** AUS, 1964-70; US Military Acad 1965-68. **Business Addr:** Attorney/Entrepreneur, 201 N Charles St, Ste 720, Baltimore, MD 21201.

HOLLOMAN, JOHN L. S., JR.
Health services administrator. **Personal:** Born Nov 22, 1919, Washington, DC; son of Rosa Victoria Jones Holloman and John L S Holloman; married Charlote Wesley; children: Charlotte, Ellen, Laura, Karin, Paul. **Educ:** Virginia Union Univ, BS (cum laude) 1940; Univ of Michigan Med, MD 1943; Virginia Union Univ, DSc 1983. **Career:** Private Practice New York City, 1947-; Health Insurance Plan of New York, vice pres 1972-74; New York City Health Hospital Corp, pres 1974-77;

Univ of North Carolina Public Health, Visting prof 1977-78; US Congress Ways & Means Comm, professional staff 1979-80; Medical Officer USFDA, regional 1980-85; W F Ryan Health Center, medical dir; St Lukes/Roosevelt Hospital, assistant attending physician, 1990-. **Orgs:** Pres bd of trustee Virginia Union Univ 1962-83; life mem NAACP, Sigma Pi, Natl Guardsmen, Alpha Phi Alpha; Amer Society of Internal Medicine; vice pres African Fund 1968-92; trustee, State University of New York, 1968-; pres, National Medical Assn 1966-67; national chmn, Physicians Forum 1965-66; National Academy of Social Insurance, 1992. **Honors/Awds:** Haven Emerson Award New York Public Health Assn 1970; mem Inst of Med Natl acad of Science 1972; Ernst P Boas Award Social Med 1975; Frederick Douglass Award New York Urban League 1976. **Military Serv:** AUS med corp captain 1944-46. **Home Addr:** 27-40 Ericsson St, East Elmhurst, NY 11369. **Business Addr:** Medical Dir, W F Ryan Hlth Ctr, 2160 Madison Ave, New York, NY 10037.

HOLLOMAN, THADDEUS BAILEY

Banking executive. **Personal:** Born Jun 30, 1955, Newport News, VA; son of Elsie Holloman and Paul Holloman; married Renee D Brown; children: Thaddeus Jr, Kelsey. **Educ:** Howard Univ, BBA 1977; Old Dominion Univ, Graduate Courses Public Administration 1982-83; Univ of VA, VA Bankers Assn, School of Bank Management, 1992. **Career:** Peat Marwick Mitchell & Co, auditor 1977-79; Student Loan Marketing Assoc, accountant 1979; Hampton Univ, accountant 1979-81; City of Newport News VA, auditor 1981-85; Community Federal Savings and Loan, 1985-90; Consolidated Bank, 1990-. **Orgs:** Bd of trustees of the C Waldo Scott Ctr for HOPE, 1993-; Newport News Educ Foundation, 1993-; 100 Black Men of America, Inc, 1992-; Newport News School Bd, 1992-; Phi Beta Sigma Fraternity, Inc, 1991-; charter mem, of the citizens review bd, Subsidized Housing, 1991-92; Virginia Bankers Assn, 1990; mem NAACP Newport News VA 1983-; mem Newport News Political Action Comm 1984-; treasurer Peninsula Habitat for Humanity 1985-; member/chairman, Board of Zoning Appeals, City of Newport News, VA, 1986-; member, Beta Gamma Sigma Business Honor Society, 1977-. **Business Addr:** Consolidated Bank & Trust, 101 N Armistead Ave, Hampton, VA 23669.

HOLLON, HERBERT HOLSTEIN

Personnel administrator. **Personal:** Born Aug 17, 1936, New York City, NY; married Margaret Catherine Zeitz; children: Herbert Holstein II, Christopher James. **Educ:** Morgan St Coll, BA Sociology 1955-59. **Career:** Los Angeles Cnty, dpty prbtn offcr 1961-66; Thomas J Lipton Inc, sls territory rep 1967-69, manpwr devel asst 1969-71; E R Squibb & Sons Inc, affrmtv actn mgr 1971-73; Cheseborough-Pond's Inc, mgr rcrtmn & mgmt devel 1973-75, dir equal opprtnty affrs 1975-79, dir prsnl admin 1979-. **Orgs:** Chrtr mem The Edges Group Inc 1969-; mem Xavier Univ of LA Cluster 1971-; mem past bd of dir Emp Mgmt Assoc 1973-; coach Juvenile Ftbl, Bsbl & Bsktbl 1977-; chrtr mem Julius Thomas Scty NUL 1979-; chrmn of bd Waterbury OIC 1982-; chmn of the bd Grtr Waterbury Area Prvt Indus Council 1985-.

HOLLOWAY, ALBERT CURTIS

Educator. **Personal:** Born Apr 22, 1931, Oxford, MS; son of Fred E Holloway; married Mary D Laing; children: Christopher Bondy. **Educ:** Oberlin Sch Commerce, asso deg 1957; Ashland Coll, BS 1961; OH State U, MSW 1967. **Career:** Mohican Youth Camp OH, supt 1966-68, lectr & couns; Ashland Coll, asst vis prof 1968-69; Scioto Vill, OH, dir clinical & chf soc wrkr 1968-70; MI State Univ, assoc prof 1970-; Lansing MI Comm Coll, assoc prof, visiting & part time. **Orgs:** Mem Nat Assn Soc Wrkrs; Acad Cert Soc Wrkers; Nat Coun Crime & Delinq; Am Pol & Soc Scientists; Coun Soc Wk Edn; Am Correctional Assn NASW; adv bd OH Correct Ct Servs; Community Services & Referral Center, Lansing, MI, mem of bd; Housing & Community Development Comm, City of East Lansing, MI; member, Black Social Workers Assn; member, Michigan Black Studies Assn; oral review board member, Michigan State Police; board member, Alliance for Childrens Mental Health. **Military Serv:** USAF s/sgt 1950-54. **Business Addr:** Associate Professor, School of Social Work, Michigan State University, 254 Baker Hall, East Lansing, MI 48824.

HOLLOWAY, ARDITH E.

Newspaper advertising account executive. **Personal:** Born Oct 9, 1958, Youngstown, OH; daughter of J Faye Matthews and James E Matthews (deceased); married Kenneth, Aug 28, 1982; children: Steffany, Autumn. **Educ:** Ohio State University, BA, speech communication, 1981. **Career:** Gulf Oil, vital source speaker, 1980-82; Metro Page of Columbus, sales representative, 1982-84, relief district manager, circulation department, 1984-85; Neighbor News, account executive, 1985-88; The Columbus Dispatch, account executive, retail advertising, 1988-. **Orgs:** United Way Speakers League; Columbus Urban League, resource development committee; Dublin Black Parent Association, equity committee co-chair; Faith Mission, volunteer; Columbus Metropolitan Club; Dahlberg Learning Center, board member; YMCA Black Achievers, board member. **Special Achievements:** As an account executive for The Columbus Dispatch, implemented several new special newspaper supplements: Think Before You Drink, Black History Month, Library Special Section, St Anthony Special Section, Argo & Lehne Gift Guide, AmeriFlora Events Pages, Expo Souvenirs, Buckeye Gymnastics, Discover Downtown, Huntington Center, Mt Vernon Plaza, and Kroger Employment; top salesperson for numerous special sections: Prom Time, Holiday Idea Guide, Dining Guide, Senior Lifestyles, In Time of Need, and Back to School. **Business Addr:** Account Executive, Columbus Dispatch, 34 S 3rd St, 5300 Crosswind, Columbus, OH 43215, (614)461-8819.

HOLLOWAY, DOUGLAS V.

Cable television executive. **Personal:** Born Jul 3, 1954, Pittsburgh, PA; son of Hattie Keys and Arnold Holloway; married L Susan Branche, Jun 10, 1990. **Educ:** Northeastern University; Emerson College, BS, 1976; Columbia University Graduate School of Business, MBA, 1978. **Career:** General Foods, assistant product manager, 1978-79; CBS TV Network, financial analyst, 1979-81; CBS Cable, sales rep, 1981-82; TV Cable Week, Time Inc, manager, national account, 1982-83; U.S.A. Network, director, national accounts, 1983-85, vice pres, affiliate relations, 1985-87, senior vp, affiliate relations, 1987-. **Orgs:** National Association of Minorities in Cable, board member, immediate past president, 1992-93, board member, president, 1990-92, board member, vice pres, 1988-90; Cable TV Administration and Marketing, board member, 1992-; Uptown Investment Associates, president, 1986-. **Honors/Awds:** NAMIC, Affiliate Relations Award, 1990; Crain New York Business Magazine, 40 Under 40 Professional Leadership, 1989. **Special Achievements:** Journal of Marketing, 1978.

HOLLOWAY, ERNEST LEON

Educational administrator. **Personal:** Born Sep 12, 1930, Boley, OK; married Lula M Reed; children: Ernest L Jr, Reginald, Norman. **Educ:** Langston Univ, BS 1952; OK State Univ, MS 1955; Univ of OK, EdD 1970. **Career:** Boley HS, sci teacher, principal 1955-62; Langston Univ, asst registrar, registrar, dean of student affairs, prof, vice pres for admin, acting pres, pres 1963-. **Orgs:** Nat Assn Sch Personnel Adminstrn, OK Coll Personnel Assn, pres 1975, OK Personnel Guidance Assn, Phi Delta Kappa, Imperial Council Shrines NW Consistory 33 Degree, educ found Alpha Phi Alpha Frat Inc; dir, Federal Reserve Bank of Kansas City, Oklahoma City Branch, 1990-; chmn bd of trustees, Logan Hospital and Medical Center; mem, Literacy Initiatives Commission, State of OK. **Honors/Awds:** "100 Most Influential Friends" Black Journ 1977; Distinguished Educator Award; Public Service Award; Martin Luther King Humanitarian Award. **Business Addr:** President, Langston University, PO Box 907, Langston, OK 73050.

HOLLOWAY, ERNESTINE

Educator. **Personal:** Born May 23, 1930, Clyde, MS. **Educ:** Tougaloo Clg, BS; NY U, MA; MI State U, NDEA. **Career:** Tougaloo Clg, dean stdnts 1965-, asst dean 1963-65, sect pres 1953-63; Coleman HS, tchr 1952-53. **Orgs:** Mem Natl Assc Stdnt Prsnl Admn 1976-78; mem Edtrl bd NASPA Jour 1972-75; mem Reg III Adv & Bd 1978; corp del Am Assc Univ Women; mem Vis ComSoc Assc Clg & Sch; mem Yth Task Grp Hinds Co Assc Mental Hlth; undergrad pgm adv Alpha Kappa Alpha Sor 1974-78, southeastern reg dir 1970-74; bd dir Opera S 1975-76; chtr mem Opera S Guild 1976-; mem Resr Com Jackson Mun Separate Sch Dist; Clg Com Natl Assc Women Deans & Cnslrs; consult Workshops & Conf Stdnt Prsnl Serv; mem Phi Delta Kappa Frat; MS Persnl Guid Assc; so Clg Prsnl Assc; mem Am Miss Assc; United Ch Christ for Study NY Univ Natl Def Ed. **Honors/Awds:** Awrd MI State U; alumnus yr Tougaloo Clg 1971; MS Black Women Natl Assc Colored Women's Clb 1976.

HOLLOWAY, HARRIS M.

Acquisitions analyst, funeral director, clergyman. **Personal:** Born Jan 26, 1949, Aiken, SC. **Educ:** Livingston Clg, BS 1966-71; Hood Theol Sem, 1970-71; Am Acad-McAllister Inst of Funeral Serv, PMS 1974. **Career:** Gen Motors Accept Corp, field rep, 1974-84, credit rep, 1984-93, customer relations supervisor, 1993-94, acquisitions analyst, 1994-; Pure Light Baptist Church, Newark, NJ, pastor; Perry Funeral Home, funeral dir; Carnie P Bragg Funeral Homes Inc, funeral dir 1972-78; NJ Dept of Labor Industry, emplymnt interviewer 1971-73. **Orgs:** Mem Garden State Funeral Dirs 1977; tres Tchr Corp Comm Cncl of Peterson 1979; mem Paterson Jaycees 1975-76; mem Rotary Clg of Paterson 1977-78; master mason Mt Zion Lodge No 50 (PHA). **Honors/Awds:** Named best lighting technician/best stage mgr/best Set Designer/most coop thespian Livingston Clg 1966-71. **Business Addr:** Perry Funeral Home, 34 Mercer St, Newark, NJ 07103.

HOLLOWAY, HERMAN M., SR.

State senator. **Personal:** Born Feb 4, 1922, Wilmington, DE; son of Hennie Hawk Holloway and William Holloway; married Ethel; children: Marlene, Sandra, Herman, John, Mercedes. **Educ:** Hampton Inst; DE State Coll, LLD 1969. **Career:** Deleware State Senate, senator, 1964-. **Orgs:** Became first black to serve on Joint Finance Comm in Gen Assembly; played active role in passage of DE Pub Accommodations Act; introduced legislation for correctional reforms training prgms for welfare recips in state; building inspector Wilmington Savs Fund Soc. **Honors/Awds:** Recip Outstanding Cit Award Alpha Phi Alpha Frat 1972; Distingshd Serv Awrd Wilmington Br NAACP 1972. **Business Addr:** 2008 Washington St, Wilmington, DE 19802.

HOLLOWAY, HILIARY H.

Banking executive, attorney. **Personal:** Born Mar 7, 1928, Durham, NC; son of Zelma S Holloway and J Sim Holloway; married Beatrice Gwen Larkin; children: Hiliary Jr, Janis L. **Educ:** NC Central Univ, BS Business Admin 1949; Temple Univ, EdM Business 1956; Temple Univ School of Law, JD Law 1964. **Career:** St Augustines Coll, business manager 1950-53; Kappa Alpha Psi Frat, exec dir 1953-65; Private Practice of Law, atty 1965-68; Fed Res Bank of Phila; asst counsel 1968-72, vice pres & gen counsel 1972-82, sr vice pres & gen counsel 1982-89; New Atlantic Bank, chairman/CEO, 1989-93; Marshall, Dennehey, Warner, Coleman & Goggin, partner, 1990-. **Orgs:** Grand Polemarch, Kappa Alpha Psi Frat 1976-79; bd of trustees NC Cntrl Univ 1977-85; bd of dir Philadelphia Museum of Art 1978-; Urban Bankers Assn; Amer Inst of Banking; Natl Bar Assn; Fed, Phila, Am, & PA Bar Assn; director, Mellon/PSFS Bank; chair PICA, Financial Oversight Authority for the City of Philadelphia, 1993-95; pres National Interfraternity Conference, 1996. **Honors/Awds:** Comm Serv Awrd Chapel of the Four Chaplains 1977; Martin L King Award Educators Round Table 1977; Laurel Wreath Award Kappa Alpha Psi Frat 1983; North Carolina Central University, Distinguished Alumni Award, 1986. **Special Achievements:** First Black president of the National Interfraternity Conference. **Home Addr:** 3900 Ford Road, Park Plaza #14-0, Philadelphia, PA 19131. **Business Addr:** 1845 Walnut Street, Philadelphia, PA 19103.

HOLLOWAY, J. MILLS

University executive (retired). **Personal:** Born Nov 17, 1924, Durham Co, NC; married Doris Moore; children: Jay, Ivan. **Educ:** NC Coll at Durham, BSC 1950. **Career:** St Augustine Coll, vice pres financial aff beginning 1970, business mgr 1957-70; J C Smith Univ, bus mgr 1952-57; Voorhees Coll, accountant 1951-52. **Orgs:** Mem Natl Assn Coll & Business Officers; Southern Assn Coll & Univ & Business Officers; Natl Assn Aux Enterprises; Kappa Alpha Psi; Coll & Univ Pers Assn; Natl Assc Financial Planners; Natl Assc Ed Buyers; mem NAACP; camp treas NC Sen Cand; tres St Augustine Coll Chpl; tres Wake Credit Union. **Honors/Awds:** Man of yr Kappa Alpha Psi 1972; evaluation team Southern Assc Coll 1973-74; consultant Title IX Higher Ed Act 1973. **Military Serv:** AUS sgt 1943-46.

HOLLOWAY, JERRY

Educator. **Personal:** Born May 14, 1941, Chicago, IL; married Mary Bowie. **Educ:** Parson Coll, BA 1959-63; Univ NV, M 1968-71. **Career:** Matt Kelly Elem Sch Las Vegas, tchr 1963-66; Las Vegas, coord rec prog elem stdnts 1965-66; coord summer work exprnc prog 1966; Washoe Co Sch Dist Reno, asstd in plcng & sprvsng disadvntgd stdnts in work experience prog 1966; Traner Jr HS Reno, tchr 1966-67, tchr, admin asst to prin, v prin 1968-69, dean of stdnts 1969-71; Traner Rec Prog City Reno Rec Dept, asst dir 1970-71; Washoe Co Sch Dist Reno, intergroup splst 1971-72, sch admin, curriculum coord. **Orgs:** Mem Reno-Sparks Br NAACP; chrtr mem past chmn Black Coalition Fair Housing Law Com; past chmn Human Rels Com NV State Educ Assn; past chmn, past com mem Cub Scouts Div BSA Las Vegas; sec treas Econ Oppor Bd Washoe Co; vchmn CETA Manpower Adv Plng Cncl; mem bd dir YMCA; chr retired sr ctzns vol prgm; commn Equal Rights Citizens. **Business Addr:** 425 E Ninth, Reno, NV 89502.

HOLLOWAY, JOAQUIN MILLER, JR.

Educational administrator. **Personal:** Born Dec 28, 1937, Mobile, AL; son of Ariel Williams Holloway and Joaquin M Holloway Sr; married Malvina Murray, Jun 5, 1960; children: Monica, Joaquin III, Josef. **Educ:** Talladega Coll, AB 1957; IN Univ, MS 1958, EdS 1960; Univ of AL, PhD 1976. **Career:** TX S Univ, instr 1958-61; Central HS, instr 1961-65; Mobile Co Pub Sch System, media splst 1965-69; Univ of S AL, prof of business 1969-, sr librarian & head of the instructional media ctr. **Orgs:** Consult Intl Paper Co 1977-80; consult Necott Devel Co 1978; consult Middle States Assn of Coll & Schs 1978; bd mem YMCA Dearborn Br 1975-86; bd mem Cine-Tel Commn 1976-; cncl mem AL State Cncl on the Arts 1979—; vice pres Culture in Black & White 1969-; host "Holloway House" progressive jazz program, WKRG AM-WKRG FM Radio 1969-79; mem Assn for Educ Comm & Tech, Minorities in Media, Omega Psi Phi Frat, Phi Delta Kappa, Omicron Delta Kappa; licensed lay reader in the Episcopal Ch; co-host of local UNCF Telethon 1983, 1984, 1988. **Honors/Awds:** Fifth Place Awd (photography) Allied Arts Council Competition 1974; Second Place Awd (photography) First Annual Fort Conde Arts Festival 1979; 3 First Place Awds Photog Mobile Soc of Model Eng 20th SER Conv 1980; one-man photog shows, including: Percy Whiting Gall, 1985, Tel Fair Peet Gall, Auburn U, 1986, Tacon Station Gall, 1986; George Washington Carver Mus, Tuskegee U, 1987, Fine Arts Mus of the South, 1987, Hay Center Art Gall, Stillman Coll, 1988, Isabel Comer Mus of Art, 1989; The John L LeFlore Civic Award, 1990; Gladys M Cooper Fine Arts Award, 1991. **Business Addr:** Prof, Sr Librarian, Head, Instructional Media Center, University of South Alabama, Library Building, Mobile, AL 36688.

HOLLOWAY, NATHANIEL OVERTON, JR.
Dentist. **Personal:** Born Jan 30, 1926, Holly Grove, AR; son of Mr & Mrs Nathaniel Holloway Sr; married Dorothy Gladys; children: Jacqueline, Nathaniel III, Rhoda. **Educ:** TN State Univ, BS 1949; Meharry Med Coll, DDS 1953. **Career:** Private Practice, dentist. **Orgs:** Past pres Ypsilanti Business & Professional League/Washtenaw Dist Dental Soc; mem, Wolverine Dental Soc, MI State Dental Soc, ADA Dental Soc Chmn, Deacon bd & Trust bd, Plymouth Congregational Ch; past gen chmn, NAACP Freedom Fund Dinner; past pres Detroit Duffers Golf Assn; mem Alpha Phi Alpha, Beta Kappa Chi. **Military Serv:** USN 1944. **Business Addr:** 401 S Hamilton St, Ypsilanti, MI 48197.

HOLLOWELL, DONALD L.
Attorney. **Personal:** Born Dec 19, 1917, Wichita, KS; married Louise Thornton. **Educ:** Lane College, AB; Loyola University Law Sch, JD. **Career:** Private practice, attorney, 1952-; USEEOC, reg dir 1966-76, reg atty, 1976-85; Arrington & Hollowell PC, attorney, partner, currently. **Orgs:** Bd trustees Spelman Coll; trustee Phillips Sch Theol; trustee Interdenom Theol Cntr; trustee Collins Chapel Hosp; Am, Natl & Atlanta Bar Assns; Gate City Bar Assn; State Bar GA; NAACP; Kappa Alpha Psi; Phi Alpha Delta; Sigma Pi Phi; Nat Alumni Council United Negro Coll Fund. **Honors/Awds:** Lawyer of Year, LDF, NAACP, 1965; Civil Rghts Awrd, Council Human Rel, 1966; Civil Liberties Award, ACLU, 1967; Equal Opportunity Day Award, Atlanta Urban League, 1969; Unsung Hero Awrd, NAACP, SE Reg, 1973; Charles Houston Alumni Award, Harvard Law Sch, 1974; Nestor Award, Georgia Legal History Foundation; Tradition of Excellence Award, State Bar of Georgia; Honorary Degrees: Clark College, LLD; ITC, LHD, Atlanta University, LLD; num other awards & citations. **Military Serv:** US Army, capt, 1935-46. **Business Addr:** Attorney, Arrington & Hollowell, PC, One-Ninety-One Peachtree Tower, 191 Peachtree St NE, Ste 3550, Atlanta, GA 30303-1735, (404)658-9900.

HOLLOWELL, JOHNNY LAVERAL
Military officer. **Personal:** Born Sep 13, 1951, New Orleans, LA; married Angie D; children: Chandler A, Ivory D, Alexandria B. **Educ:** Utica Jr Coll, AA 1971; Alcorn A&M Univ, attended 1971-72; Columbia Coll, BA 1980; Univ of Phoenix, pursuing MBA. **Career:** US Coast Guard, Marine Safety Office, commanding officer, currently. **Orgs:** Mem Big Brothers of Amer 1982-84; life mem Natl Naval Officers Assoc 1982-; life mem Omega Psi Phi Frat; Role Models Unlimited, 1990-91. **Honors/Awds:** Omega Man of the Year, 1992, Rho Nu Chapter. **Military Serv:** USCG, CDR; 2 Commendation Medals, 3 Achievement Medals, Letter of Commendation, Meritorious Team Commendation, Good Conduct Award. **Business Addr:** Commanding Officer, Coast Guard Marine Safety Office, 200 Jefferson Ave, Ste 1301, Memphis, TN 38103.

HOLLOWELL, KENNETH LAWRENCE
Labor union official. **Personal:** Born Mar 5, 1945, Detroit, MI; son of Rachel A Kimble Hollowell and Herman JDJ Hollowell, Sr; married Patricia J; children: Terrance L, Rhonda L. **Educ:** Wayne County Comm Coll, AA 1979. **Career:** Cook Paint & Varnish Co, rsch tech 1967-71; Teamsters Local Union No 247, business rep 1971-80, trustee and business rep 1980-82, recording sec and business rep 1982-85, vice pres and business rep 1985-87, pres and business rep 1987-88, secretary & treasurer/principal officer, 1988-. **Orgs:** Deputy imperial potentate Intl Shriners 1975-83; commissioner Civic Ctr City of Detroit 1976-94; first vice pres MI Assoc Masonic Grand Lodges 1979-; grand master Ralph Bunche Grand Lodge Intl Masons 1979-81; bd of dirs United Way of MI 1980-86, Metro Agency for Retarded Citizens 1981-94, Economic Alliance of MI 1982-; adv comm Ctr for Volunteerism UCS 1981-87; deputy supreme grand master Intl Masons 1983-86; supreme grand master Intl F&AM Masons 1986-89; trustee, Michigan Teamsters Joint Council No 43, 1989-95; recording sec, Michigan Teamsters Joint Council No 43, 1995; life member, NAACP, 1989-; executive bd member, Metro Detroit AFL-CIO, 1988-; member, Metro Detroit Convention & Visitors Bureau, 1986-, vice chairman, 1994; reserve officer, Detroit Police Reserves, 1970-94; bd member, Michigan Coalition of Black Trade Unionists, 1980-; bd member, Metro Detroit Chapter, A Phillip Randolph Insute, 1988-; Commissioner Detroit Police Department, 1994-; member, Industrial Relations Research Assn, 1981-; bd of dir, Metropolitan Realty Corp, 1992-; bd of dir, Robert Holmes Teamsters Retiree Housing Corp, 1990; bd of dir, Teamsters Credit Union of Wayne & Oakland Counties, MI, 1989-; bd of dir, MI Chapter International Assn of Exhibition Managers, 1987-93; bd member, Teamsters National Black Caucus, 1976-; vice chair, 1994-. **Honors/Awds:** Goodwill Ambassador Award, Minority Womens Network, 1987; Walter Campbell Community Services Award, Michigan United Labor Community Services School, 1977; Community Services Award, United Way for Southeastern Michigan, 1990; MI Assn of Masonic Grand Lodge Comm Services Award, 1994; Nelson Jack Edwards Award, (MI CETU), Apr 1994. **Military Serv:** USMC, sgt, 1963-67; Good Conduct Medal, Natl Defense Medal, Vietnam Service Medal, Vietnam Campaign. **Business Addr:** Secretary-Treasurer, Principal Officer, Teamsters Union Local #247, 2741 Trumbull Ave, Detroit, MI 48216.

HOLLOWELL, MELVIN L.
Urological surgeon. **Personal:** Born Nov 24, 1930, Detroit, MI; married Sylvia Regina Ports; children: Regina, Dana, Melvin Jr, Danielle, Christopher, Courtney, Sylvia. **Educ:** Wayne State Univ, BS 1953; Meharry Medical Coll, MD 1959. **Career:** MI Branch Amer Urological Assoc, pres 1976-77; Hutzel Hosp, vice chmn dept of urology 1980-87; Harper Grace Hosp Detroit, medical bd 1983-85, exec comm 1983-85; Southeast MI Surgical Soc, pres 1983-84; North Central Sect Amer Urological Assoc, exec comm 1984-86; Samaritan Health Ctr Sisters of Mercy, exec comm 1985-87, chmn dept of surgery 1985-. **Orgs:** Clinical asst prof, Dept of Urology Wayne State Univ Coll of Medicine; life mem NAACP; mem Kappa Alpha Psi Frat; mem GESU Catholic Church. **Honors/Awds:** Fellow Amer Coll of Surgeons; Amer Coll of Medical Directors Physician Executives; Royal Coll of Medicine; Amer Bd of Urology. **Military Serv:** AUS Medical Corp capt 1958-62; US Army Commendation Awd/Medal 1961. **Business Addr:** Urological Surgeon/Pres, Adult Pediatric Urology Assocs, 20905 Greenfield Rd, Southfield, MI 48075.

HOLLY, ELLA LOUISE
Management consultant. **Personal:** Born Aug 22, 1949, Philadelphia, PA. **Educ:** Mills Coll of Educ, BS 1971; Teachers Coll Columbia Univ, MA 1973; Case Western Reserve Univ, PhD 1986. **Career:** New York City Bd of Educ, teacher 1972-76; Natl Educ Assoc, educ specialist 1976-79; Cuyahoga Co Welfare Dept, dir career advancement prog 1980; Yale School of Organization and Mgmt, prof of organizational behavior 1986-. **Orgs:** Natl fellow Inst of Educational Leadership 1979-80; external mgmt consultant in public and private sector 1981-86; mem Assoc of Black Sociologists, Academyof Mgmt, Gestalt Inst, Natl Assoc of Women Studies, Amer Sociological Assoc. **Honors/Awds:** Innovating Programming Amer Public Welfare Assoc 1980; Outstanding Work in Educ and Social Services Cuyahoga Comm Coll 1980; Outstanding Young Women of the Year Greater Cleveland Urban League 1981; Amer Sociological Minority Fellowship 1983-86. **Business Addr:** Prof Organizational Behavior, Yale School of Org/Mgmt, 135 Prospect St, New Haven, CT 06520.

HOLMAN, ALVIN T.
Planning administrative manager. **Personal:** Born Jul 21, 1948, Wash, DC; married Karen. **Educ:** L A Harbor Coll, AA 1969; Univ WA, AB 1970; MI St U, M Urb-Plng 1972. **Career:** S CA Rapid Trans Dist, plng proj mgr; UHURU Inc, proj dir; City of Seattle, comm plng cnslt; Office Econ & Oppor Seattle, reg res cnslt; St of MI, urban plnr/comm plng spclst; Cunningham/Short/Berryman & Assoc, sr plng cnslt. **Orgs:** Mem Am Inst of Plnrs; Am Soc Plng Officials; Am Soc Plng Consltς Natl Assn Hsng & Rehab Offcls; Natl Assn Plnrs; Natl Assn Min Cnslts Urbans. **Business Addr:** Gardner & Holman Consulting, 3761 Stocker St, Ste 103, Los Angeles, CA 90008.

HOLMAN, BENJAMIN F.
Author, journalist, educator. **Personal:** Born Dec 18, 1930, Columbia, SC; son of Benjamin and Joanna Holman. **Educ:** Lincoln U, 1950; Univ KS, BS 1952; Univ Chgo, 1956. **Career:** Chicago Daily News, reporter 1952-62; WBBM-TV, commentator reprtr 1962-63; CBS News, edtr rprtr 1963-65; US Dept Justice, asst dir media rel div comm rel serv 1965-68; NBC News, prod rprtr 1968-69; Dept Justice, dir comm rel serv 1969-77; Univ of MD, prof of jour 1978-. **Orgs:** Adv com Urban Dev MI State U; IL Counc for Freedom of Rsdnce; bd mem Friendship Hse; mem Beatrice Caffrey Youth Serv & Ada S Mckinley House; Indepen Voters of IL; Jr Achvmnt Co; mem Ralph Bunche Prog United Nations Assn US of Am; Wash Urban League; Natl Adv Counc Nat Ctr for Dispurte Settlement Am Arbitration Assn; Assn for Educ Journ; MD-DE-DC Press Assn. **Honors/Awds:** Author: Sports & Mass Commun 1979; The Sports Commun Explosion 1981; The Symbiotic Adversaries 1981. **Military Serv:** AUS 1952-54; AUS reserve 1st lt 1955-65. **Business Addr:** Professor, School of Journalism, University of Maryland, Journalism Building, Room 4121, College Park, MD 20742.

HOLMAN, DORIS ANN
Retired educator. **Personal:** Born Feb 14, 1924, Wetumpka, AL; daughter of Mattie Banks Westbrooks and Willie G Westbrooks; divorced; children: DeWayne, Douglas, Desiree, Glenn. **Educ:** AL State Univ, BS 1944; Univ San Francisco, MA 1979. **Career:** Detroit City Schools; Compton Unified School Dist, teacher. **Orgs:** Mem NEA; Phi Delta Kappa Beta Phi; Natl Assn Univ Women; rep CA Teachers Assn St Council 1960-62; bd dir ATEB Corp; chmn Neg Council Compton Unified School Dist 1971-73; pres Compton Educ Assn 1971-74; bd dir Compton YMCA 1970-; regional dir Natl Tots & Teens 1972-; Neighborhood chmn GS of A; bd dir BS of A; bd dir Christian Day School Comm Lutheran Church; mem Intl Toastmistress Club; pres Women of the Church Comm Lutheran Church 1977, 1992-94; treasurer So Bay Conf Amer Lutheran Church Women 1977; sec Compton Educ Assn 1976-77; mem Compton School Dist Compens Educ Adv Council School Advisory Council; bd of dir Mid Cities Schools Credit Union 1988-91, pres, 1993; elect to bd for College and Univ Serv of the Amer Lutheran Church 1982-88; worthy matron, Gethsemane Chapter Order of Eastern Star, 1994. **Honors/Awds:** Pro Achievement Award Enterprise Teachers Assn 1968; Who Award CA Teacher Assn 1970; Teacher in Political Award Theological Bass Mem 1972; National Sorority of Phi Delta Kappa, Soror of the Year, 1994; Alabama State University Alumni Association, Los Angeles Chapter, Alumnus of the Year, 1989.

HOLMAN, FOREST H.
Executive assistant. **Personal:** Born Apr 2, 1942, Birmingham; married; children: Karriem Malik. **Educ:** Tuskegee Inst, BS 1965; MI State U, MA 1971, PhD 1974. **Career:** MI Consol Gas Co Detroit, mgr envrnmntl plng 1978-; Wayne St U, adj prof of Pol sci 1974-80; Shaw Coll of Detroit, adj prof of philos & soc inst 1974-78; City Chicago, tchr; Chicago Vice & Lords St Acad Inst, 1968; OIC, instr 1967-68; State Mi, senate rsrchr 1970-72; Tuskegee Inst , dir Frshmn studies & asst prof 1972-73; City Detroit, exec asst mayor; MI State U, asst prof Race & Urban Studies 1974-75. **Orgs:** Cvons Dept of Black Studies Eastern MI U; cons-cnslr Highland Park Dept of Human Resources Highland Park MI; couns MI Dept Human Resources 1974-45; mem Assn Study Negro Life & History; Assn Social & Bhvrl Sci; mem Alpha Phi Omega & Kappa Alpha Psi Frat; guest panelist Summer Bus Inst Wayne State U; panelist Neighborhood Legal Svc. **Honors/Awds:** Certificate Recognition Jacob A Citrin Meml Seminar & Gov Conf Unemployment. **Business Addr:** Mayors Office City Detroit, Detroit, MI.

HOLMAN, KARRIEM MALIK
Association executive. **Personal:** Born Apr 13, 1969, Chicago, IL; son of Forest & Beverly Holman. **Educ:** Howard Univ, BA, 1992. **Career:** MI Youth Corp, supervisor, 1988; Rep John Conyers, D-MI, legislative intern, 1989; Alliance for Justice, staff assistant, 1992-93; Gov Ann Richards Re-election Campaign, field coordinator, 1994; National Black Business Council, executive/legislative assn, 1994-. **Orgs:** Summit 1993 Health Care Coalition, legislative consultant, 1994; Participation 2000 PAC, mem alumni, 1994. **Special Achievements:** Participation 2000 PAC: selected from competitive pool of applicants to work on re-election of Gov Ann Richards; One of 5 African-Americans young people to work on a major gubernatorial campaign. **Business Addr:** Legislative Associate, Natl Black Business Council Inc, 1100 Wayne Ave, Ste 850, Silver Spring, MD 20910.

HOLMAN, KWAME KENT ALLAN
Journalist. **Personal:** Born Jul 4, 1953, New Haven, CT; son of M Carl Holman; married Miriam Rudder Holman, Feb 13, 1992; children: Kevin Alton, Donovan Joseph. **Educ:** Howard Univ, BS, 1977; Northwestern Univ, MSJ, 1981. **Career:** District of Columbia Govt, acting press sec to the mayor, 1980; Natl Summit Conference on Black Economic Devel, public relations consultant, 1980; Childrens Defense Fund, communication asst, 1980; WTOC-TV (Savannah, GA), reporter, talk show host, 1982-83; Macneil-Lehrer Newshour, producer/correspondent, 1983-93, congressional correspondent, 1993-. **Orgs:** Natl Assn of Black Journalists, occasional speaker, currently; Partners in Journalism, occasional editor, 1990-; Natl Press Club, occasional panelist, 1994-; Journalists Round Table (C-Span), occasional panelist, 1993-. **Honors/Awds:** George Polk Award for Natl Television Reporting, 1984; Natl News and Documentary Emmy, 1985; Joan Shorenstein Barone Award, 1994; Local News and Documentary Emmy, 1991. **Special Achievements:** Consulting Writer, ''AIDS and Race''-''The AIDS Quarterly: Fall 1989 with Peter Jennings'' (PBS), 1989. **Business Addr:** Congressional Correspondent, Macneil-Lehrer Newshour, 3620 S 27th St., Arlington, VA 22206, (703)998-2861.

HOLMES, ALVIN ADOLF
State official. **Personal:** Born Oct 26, 1939, Montgomery, AL; son of Willie Ann Holmes and John H Holmes; married Judy Holmes (divorced 1970); children: Veronica Holmes. **Educ:** Alabama State University, Montgomery, AL, BS, 1962, MEd, 1972, MA, 1979; Selma University, Selma, AL, LLD, 1982. **Career:** Alabama State University, Montgomery, AL, asst prof of history; State of Alabama, Montgomery, AL, state rep, currently. **Orgs:** Member, exec committee, Democratic Party of Alabama; member, NAACP; member, board of directors, SCLC. **Military Serv:** US Army, Sp-4, 1962-65; Good Conduct Medal. **Business Addr:** State Representative, State of Alabama, District 78, PO Box 6064, Montgomery, AL 36106.

HOLMES, ARTHUR, JR.
High-tech company executive. **Personal:** Born May 12, 1931, Decatur, AL; son of Arthur Jr and Grace L Holmes; married Wilma King Holmes; children: Deborah H Cook, Rick Fairley-Brown, Sharon H Key, Sharon Fairley-Nickerson. **Educ:** Hampton University, BS, chemistry, 1952; Kent State University, MBA, 1967. **Career:** Automated Sciences Group Inc, vp logistics, 1987-90, executive vp & coo, 1990, president & ceo, 1990-. **Orgs:** Omega Psi Phi Fraternity, 1952-; NAACP, Montgomery County Maryland, chairman, Education Committee, 1993-95; Retired Military Officers Association, president, 1994-; Maryland National Capital Park & Planning Commission, commissioner, 1994-. **Honors/Awds:** Omega Psi Phi Fraternity, Mu Nu Chapter, Businessman of the Year, 1993. **Military Serv:** US Army Material Command, director for readiness, 1980-82; US Army, deputy of the inspector general, 1982-83;

US Army for Logistics, asst deputy chief of staff, 1983-84; US Army, US Army Tank-Automotive Command, commanding general, 1984-87; Distinguished Service Medal, Legion of Merit, Bronze Star. **Home Addr:** 17104 Blossom View Drive, Olney, MD 20832. **Business Addr:** President & CEO, Automated Sciences Group Inc., 1010 Wayne Ave., Suite 700, Silver Spring, MD 20910.

HOLMES, BARBARA J.
Educator, communication specialist. **Personal:** Born Jun 26, 1934, Chicago, IL; daughter of Helyne Wilhaite and Wyess Wilhaite; married Laurence H Holmes; children: Carole, Helyne, Sheryl, Laurence. **Educ:** Talladega Coll, attended 1951-53; Univ CO, BA 1973, MA 1974, PhD 1978. **Career:** Natl Assessment of Educ Progress, writer 1977-83; State Educ Policy Seminary Prog co-sponsored by Educ Commn of the States & the Inst for Educ Leadership, natl coord; Former Director of Policy Studies, ECS; other educ prof organs, presentations; Consultant on Recruitment & Retention of Minority Teachers. Expertise in Teacher Education, Work Force Literacy, currently. **Orgs:** Mem Delta Sigma Theta Public Serv Sor; mem bd of dirs Whitney M Young Jr Memorial Foundation 1974-84; fellow Educ Policy Fellowship Prog 1982-83. **Honors/Awds:** Phi Beta Kappa Hon Soc 1974; Acad Fellowships Whitney M Young 1973-74; published over 20 articles and reports.

HOLMES, BRADLEY PAUL
Government official. **Personal:** Born Sep 14, 1953, Boston, MA; son of Sadako Ruth Sato Holmes and Melvin Felix Holmes. **Educ:** Dartmouth College, BA, 1975; Georgetown Univ Law Center, JD, 1978. **Career:** Windels, Marx, Davies, & Ives, assoc attorney, 1978-79; US District Court, law clerk to Judge Mary Johnson Lowe, 1979-81; Skadden, Arps, Slate, Meagher, & Flom, assoc attorney, 1981-84; Federal Communications Commission, legal advisor to commissioner, 1984-86, chief, policy & rules, Mass Media Bureau, 1986-89; US Dept of State, Bureau of Intl Communications & Information Policy, coordinator & director, 1989-.

HOLMES, CARL
Attorney (retired). **Personal:** Born Dec 13, 1925, New York, NY; son of Kathleen Holmes and Thomas Holmes; married Dolores Fennell, Aug 5, 1957; children: Deborah, Beverly. **Educ:** New York City Coll, BS 1950; Brooklyn Law Sch, 1953, JD 1967. **Career:** NYC, litigation atty 22 yrs; NY State Govt, 11 yrs; Rutledge Holmes & Willis, pvt pract; State of New York, assoc attorney, retired 1987. **Orgs:** Past vice pres District 28 Sch Bd Queens; rsrch Brown vs Bd Educ 1953; mem NAACP; ACLU; Macon B Allen Black Bar Assn. **Military Serv:** USNR 1944-46; storekeeper 3/class. **Home Addr:** 116-47 167th St, Jamaica, NY 11434-1721.

HOLMES, CARL
Business executive. **Personal:** Born Jan 6, 1929, Oklahoma City, OK; married Marvella; children: Carla D. **Educ:** Drake Univ, MBA 1951; LA State Univ, Fire Dept attended; Southern Methodist Univ, Fire Dept Admin attended; Univ of MD Fire Dept Staff & Command School, attended; Motivational Mgmt Schools, attended; OK Univ Equal Oppty Seminars, attended. **Career:** OK City Fire Dept, fire chief (retired) 1951-81; Carl Holmes & Assoc, dir 1980-. **Orgs:** Consult City of Ft Worth 1979, City of Atlanta 1980, City of San Francisco 1982, natl Fire Acad, WA DC Fire Dept; mem 26 affiliations incl Natl Fire Protection Assoc, Intl Assoc Fire Instr; assoc mem Natl Assoc of Black Mfgrs; fire serv training instr OK State Univ; cty chmn OK Lung Assoc; tech adv Training Mag; guest lecturer at 8 univ's incl Univ of MD, AZ, MI, AR; instr motivational mgmt for Phycol Chem Corp, Amer Airlines, TX Light & Power Inc, OK Natural Gas Inc, Continental Oil Inc, TX Instrument Inc. **Honors/Awds:** 7 publ incl Admin Problems of a Fire Dept, Auto Extrication for Rescue, Equal Employment Oppty Commiss Approach to Fire Dept Employment, The Fire Serv of the Future; Designed & implemented many progs incl a system which promoted 26 chief level positions in Atlanta GA, consult by Cty Admin for Tech Asst Orlando FL; implemented a Fire Station Location Prog & Eval System of the current status of its dept Minnetonka MN; rewrote entire entry level employment system Little Rock AR.

HOLMES, CARLTON
Marketing executive. **Personal:** Born Apr 1, 1951, New York, NY; married Dr Thelma Dye; children: Kyle, Arianna. **Educ:** Cornell Univ, BA 1973; Columbia Univ Grad Sch of Business, MBA 1975. **Career:** Lever Bros NYC, asst prod mgr 1975-77; Johnson & Johnson, product director 1977-82; Drake Bakeries, product mgr 1982-83; Block Drug Co Jersey City, director, new business development, 1983-89. **Orgs:** Mem Cornell Black Alumni Assn, Natl Black MBA Assn. **Honors/Awds:** NYS Regents Scholar 1968; Natl Achievement Scholar 1968; cofounder Cornell Black Alumni Assn 1976. **Home Addr:** 175 West 87th St #14H, New York, NY 10024.

HOLMES, CLAYTON ANTWAN
Professional football player. **Personal:** Born Aug 23, 1969, Florence, SC; children: Dominique, Colton Jackson, Kenya Briana. **Educ:** Carson-Newman. **Career:** Dallas Cowboys, defensive back, 1992, 1994-95; Miami Dolphins, 1997-. **Business Addr:** Professional Football Player, Miami Dolphins, 2269 NW 199th St, Miami, FL 33056, (305)620-5000.

HOLMES, CLOYD JAMES
Labor union official. **Personal:** Born Nov 23, 1939, Houston, TX; son of Charlene Cooper and Haywood Holmes; married Madelyn Holmes Lopaz, Sep 20, 1986; children: Reginald B, Patrice, Cloyd J Jr, Anthony, E'vett, Chakka, Charlene, Cloyd J II, Conchita Nickles, Antoinette M. **Career:** Ramada Inn, fry cook, 1960-63; Howard Johnson Hotel, fry cook, 1964-66; C W Post College, Automatique Food Service, chef, shop stewart, 1966-70; USEU Local 377, Long Island City, NY, business representative, 1970-71, financial secretary, treasurer, 1971-72, president, 1972-. **Orgs:** Intl Foundation of Employee Benefit Plan, 1970-; exec bd mem, vice pres, Retail Wholesale & Dept Store Union, 1978; former sec, treasurer, The Negro Labor Comm; exec vice pres, Huntington Boy's Club; former vice pres, NAACP, Greenwich Village Branch, mem, Huntington Branch; A Philip Randolph Institute, 1986, Coalition of Black Trade Unionists; American Cancer Society, Queen's Branch. **Honors/Awds:** Greenwich Village NAACP Branch, 1980; The Trade Union Women of African Heritage, 1981; NAACP Man of the Year, 1983; Negro Labor Comm Man of the Year, 1984; Amer Cancer Soc Greater Jamaica Unit for Notable Serv in the Crusade to Conquer Cancer Award, 1984. **Business Addr:** Labor Union President & Intl Vice President, United Service Employee's Union Local 377 RWDSU, AFL-CIO, 29-27-41st Ave #1006, Long Island City, NY 11101.

HOLMES, DARICK
Professional football player. **Personal:** Born Jul 1, 1971. **Educ:** Portland State. **Career:** Buffalo Bills, running back, 1995-. **Business Addr:** Professional Football Player, Buffalo Bills, One Bills Dr, Orchard Park, NY 14127, (716)648-1800.

HOLMES, DOROTHY E.
Psychologist, psychoanalyst. **Personal:** Born Mar 9, 1943, Chicago, IL; daughter of Queen McGee Evans Pryor and Major Moten Evans; married Raymond L M Holmes, Jun 29, 1985. **Educ:** Univ of IL, BS 1963; So IL U, MA Psych 1966, PhD Clinical Psych 1968. **Career:** Dept of Psych Howard Univ Hosp, associate prof; pvt prac; Dept of Psych Univ of MD, asst prof 1970-73; Univ of Rochester, instr & postdoctoral fellow 1968-70. **Orgs:** Nat Inst of Mntl Hlth; fellow Am Psych Assn; Sigma Xi; mem Amer Psychoanalytic Assn; District of Columbia Psychological Assn; Baltimore-Washington Institute and Society for Psychoanalysis; bd of dir Natl Register for Health Service Providers in Psychology, 1988-; bd of dir Professional Examination Service, 1987-. **Honors/Awds:** Publ 1 book & 7 sci articles and 3 book reviews. **Business Addr:** Dir, Clinical Psych Intrnshp, Howard University Hospital, Dept of Psychiatry, 2041 Georgia Ave NW, Washington, DC 20060.

HOLMES, E. SELEAN (EMMA)
Museum administrator. **Personal:** Born Jul 15, 1954, Cincinnati, OH; daughter of Harriet J Holmes and Bert L Holmes Sr. **Educ:** Knoxville College, 1972-73; University of Cincinnati, BA, 1979, MA studies, 1981-83; Yale University, program in African languages, 1983. **Career:** Traveler's Aid International Institute, foreign language coordinator, 1985; National Afro-American Museum & Cultural Center, curator, 1985-89; Smith College, director, Mwangi cultural center, 1989-90; YWCA, director of development & pr, 1990-91; Arts Consortium/African-American Museum, associate director, 1991-; Cincinnati Historical Society, museum center director of African American programs, 1992-96; cultural consultant, 1996-. **Orgs:** University of Cincinnati Friends of Women's Studies, past vice pres, 1991-93; YWCA, 1990-93; African Commentary Magazine, midwest representative, 1990; Massachusetts Association of Women Deans & Administrators, 1989-90; African Studies Association, 1986-; Cincinnati Art Museum, 1991-92; African-American Museums Association, treasurer, 1986-; USIA, International Visitors Center, 1993. **Honors/Awds:** Exhibited and sold artwork throughout the 1970s; extensive travel throughout the USA, Africa, Canada, Bermuda, Italy, 1975-96; Yale University, fellowship, program in African languages, 1983; The Alliance of Ohio Community Arts Agencies, grant for professional development, 1988; Philo T Farnsworth Video Award, 1993; Ohio Crime Prevention Association, Certificate of Appreciation, 1994; Applause Magazine Imagemaker Honoree, 1995; recognized by the Newspaper Assn of America for compiling the Cincinnati Enquirer Black History Month Teacher's Guide, 1996. **Home Addr:** PO Box 37727, Cincinnati, OH 45222.

HOLMES, EARL
Professional football player. **Personal:** Born Apr 28, 1973, Tallahassee, FL. **Educ:** Florida A&M. **Career:** Pittsburgh Steelers, linebacker, 1996-. **Business Addr:** Professional Football Player, Pittsburgh Steelers, Three Rivers Stadium, 300 Stadium Circle, Pittsburgh, PA 15212, (412)323-1200.

HOLMES, EVERLENA M.
Educational administrator. **Personal:** Born Feb 15, 1934, Eufaula, AL; daughter of Carrie B Howell McDonald and Oscar L McDonald; divorced; children: Rufus James Holmes, Parvin Warnell Holmes Porsche, Gregory Warren Holmes. **Educ:** KY State Univ, BS 1957; US Public Health Serv Sch for Med Record Administrators, RRA 1960; Baylor Coll of Medicine and Univ of Houston, MEd 1974; VA Polytechnic Inst & State Univ, EdD 1981; Harvard Univ, Institute of Educ Mgmt, Post Doctorate, 1987. **Career:** Central Oregon Comm Coll, dir med record tech prog 1971-73; Eastern KY Univ, chair dept of health record science 1975-79; TN State Univ, asst dean of allied health 1982-84; The George Washington Univ, dir med record admin 1984-85; Hunter Coll/Sch of Health Scis, dean, 1985-96; East Stroudsburg Univ, School of Health Sciences and Human Performance, dean, 1996-. **Orgs:** Mem, NAACP, Life mem; Asian American Higher Education Council, CUNY, 1990-96; commission on Dental Accreditation Public Member, 1984-90; mem Congressional Black Caucus Health Brain & Educ Brain Trust 1978-; bd dirs, Natl Soc of Allied Health 1982-; mem Commission on Dental Accreditation Appeals Board, 1990-94; American Public Health Association, mem; Board of Directors, Public Health Association, New York City; mem Caribbean Women's Health Association, Inc. 1992-96; National Council of Negro Women, Life mem; Phi Delta Kappa; Life mem; Phi Kappa Phi National Honor Society, Life mem; bd of dirs, Phelps-Stokes Fund, 1989-; Middle State Evaluator, 1990-; board of directors, Brookdale Center, Aging Geriatric Education Center, 1987-96; CORPA Committee on Recognition, 1995-97; board of directors, Convenant House, 1990-; Western Assn of Schools & Colleges, evaluator, 1995; Nat'l Commission on Allied Health, mem, 1994-95. **Honors/Awds:** Noyes Fellowship 1973-74; Duiguid Fellowship 1980-81; article "Two-Plus-Two Concept in the Preparation of Health Record Practitioners," Medical Record News; article, "Operating Ratios & Inst Characteristics Affecting the Responsiveness of Black Colls & Univs to Professional Allied Health Progs" Rsch in Post Secondary Educ; book "Allied Health Issues Related to Selected Minorities, A Bibliographic Reference"; Outstanding Achievement Award 1987; Minority Leadership Forum, ALE; 39th Forum of ACE/NIP Office of Women in Higher Educ; President's Medal, Hunter College, 1996. **Home Phone:** (717)676-0617. **Business Addr:** Dean, East Stroudsburg University, School of Health Sciences and Human Performance, 200 Prospect Street, East Stroudsburg, PA 18301-2999, (717)422-3425.

HOLMES, GARY MAYO
Business executive. **Personal:** Born Feb 3, 1943, Atlanta, GA; married Margie Cannon; children: Candace Nicole. **Educ:** Morris Brown Coll, BA 1969; Emory Univ Law Sch, 1970; GA State Univ, Atlanta Univ, further study. **Career:** Atlanta Legal Aid Soc, investigator 1968-69; Office of Economic Oppor, law intern 1970; General Learning Corp, VISTA trainer 1970-72, sr VISTA trainer 1972-73; Housing Auth of City of Atlanta, district mgr 1974-77, asst dir of housing mgmt 1977-78; State of GA Dept of Defense, training officer 1973-74; Cityof Atlanta, dir bureau of housing & physical develop 1978-85; Office of Econ Development, chief 1985-. **Orgs:** Designed & implemented first municipal tri-party participation prog in nation; reorganized Bureau of Housing & Physical Develop; developed innovative public/private partnership with sev lenders; negotiated largest single FNMA rehab loan in history of FNMA; spearheaded the implemen of a natl demonstration prog bythe Natl Assn of Real Estate Brokers Develop Co; chmn of bd Atlanta Jr Gold Adv Comm 1983-84; mem Natl Assoc of Housing & Redevelop Off 1978-; prog chmn Extra Point Club, Inc 1979-; mem Amer Soc for Public Admin 1982-; mem Conf of Minority Public Adminis 1982-; comm chmn Atlanta Alumni ChaptKappa Alpha Psi Frat Inc; mem Natl Housing Rehab Assn; mem US Comm on Civil Rights GA State Adv Comm; mem Amer Mgmt Assn; mem Natl Comm Develop Assn; mem US Conf of Mayors;mem Natl League of ies; mem Natl Leased Housing Assn; mem McDaniel Glen Falcons Youth Football; mem NAACP; mem chmn Northside Atlanta Jaycees; vol coord United Way; mem comm Young Men's Christian Assn; mem Forum for Black Publ Administrators 1983. **Honors/Awds:** Cited in Natl Assn of Housing & Redevelop Officials "Journal of Housing" 1981; cited in "Mortgage Banking" magazine 1982; cited in Bureau of Natl Affairs "Housing and Develop Reporter" 1983; recipient of three HUD Natl Merit Awds for Comm Develop Partnerships 1983; Outstanding Young Public Servant of the Yr Jaycees 1977-78; numerous civic and public serv awards. **Military Serv:** USAF airman 3rd class 2 yrs. **Home Addr:** 3330 Cascade Rd, SW, Atlanta, GA 30311. **Business Addr:** Office of Economic Development, 650 Omni Int South, Atlanta, GA 30335.

HOLMES, HENRY SIDNEY, III
Attorney. **Personal:** Born Apr 10, 1944, New York, NY; son of Annie Holmes and Henry Sidney Holmes Jr; married Albertha C Middleton; children: Monique Elizabeth. **Educ:** Columbia Univ, BA 1976; Hofstra Univ Sch of Law, JD 1979. **Career:** Lever Bros Co, acct mgr 1969-72; Black Life Discount Stores, owner 1970-76; Mudge Rose Guthrie Alexander & Ferdon, partner, currently. **Orgs:** Mem Amer Bar Assn 1979-; mem NY Bar Assn 1979-; mem 100 Black Men Inc 1983-; bd of dirs Natl Assn of Securities Professionals 1985-91. **Military Serv:** AUS finance corps spec 5th class 1966-68.

HOLMES, HERBERT
Physician. **Personal:** Born Sep 17, 1932, New York, NY; son of Kathleen Holmes and Thomas Holmes; married Carol (di-

vorced); children: Gerald, Christophe, Kathleen. **Educ:** Royal Coll of Surgeons Dublin Ireland, MD 1958. **Career:** United Hospitals of Newark, attending surgeon; Beth Israel Hosp, assoc attending surgeon; Univ of Med & Dentristry of NJ, clinical assoc prof. **Orgs:** Mem NJ State Med Soc, NJ Acad of Med, NJ St Soc of NMA, Essex Co Med Soc, NJ Soc of Ob-Gyn, NJ St Med Soc; bd of trustees Univ of Med & Dentistry of NJ 1972-; 100 Black Men of NJ; Royal Soc of Health; Amer Coll of Ob-Gyn; UMDNJ. **Business Addr:** 2130 Millburn Ave, Maplewood, NJ 07040.

HOLMES, JAMES ARTHUR, JR.
Minister, historian, chaplain. **Personal:** Born May 27, 1954, Charleston, SC; son of Maranda Phillips Holmes and James Arthur Holmes Sr. **Educ:** Allen University, Columbia, SC, BA, 1976; Interdenominational Theological Center, Atlanta, GA, M Div, 1982; Boston University, Boston, MA, STM, 1988-89, 1989-. **Career:** Shady Grove AMEC, Blythewood, SC, pastor, 1974-75; Rock Hill AMEC, Columbia, SC, pastor, 1975-76; Lagree AMEC, Sumter, SC, pastor, 1976-77; AME Church of SC, Columbia, SC, historical consultant, 1987-88; Charleston County Substance Abuse Commission, Charleston, SC, community resource person, 1990-. **Orgs:** Member: Reserve Officers' Association, 1986-, South Carolina Historical Society, 1985-. **Honors/Awds:** Annual AME Fellowship, International African Methodist Episcopal Church, 1989-91; Bishop Fredrick C James Fellowship, Bishop F C James, 1989; Doctor of Theology Fellowship, Boston University, 1989-91; author, The Thirty Bishops of South Carolina, 1987; "The Priority of Emanuel AME Church: The Longest Continuous AME Church in the South," AME Review, 1987; contributor, five chapters, African Methodism in South Carolina: A Bicentennial Focus, 1987; various others. **Military Serv:** US Army, captain (chaplain), 1977-86; US Army Reserves, captain (chaplain), 1986-; received Meritorious Service Ribbon, 1986, received Army Achievement Medal, 1985, received Army Service Ribbon, 1983. **Home Addr:** Two Court St, Charleston, SC 29403.

HOLMES, JAMES FRANKLIN
Federal official. **Personal:** Born Nov 1, 1945, Leesburg, GA; son of Rosa Johnson and Benjamin Holmes; married Elaine Durham, Aug 6, 1976; children: Marcel J Holmes. **Educ:** Albany State College, Albany, GA, BA, 1967. **Career:** US Cen Sub Bureau, Detroit, MI, survey statistician, 1968-73; US Census Bureau, Detroit, MI, program coordinator, 1973-79; US Census Bureau, Kansas City, MD, assistant reg director, 1979-82; US Census Bureau, Los Angeles, CA, assistant reg director, 1982-83; US Census Bureau, Philadelphia, PA, regional director, 1983-85; US Census Bureau, Atlanta, GA, regional director, 1985-. **Orgs:** Vice president, South Cobb Improvement Assn, 1988-; member, Atlanta Economics Club, 1986-; member, Southern Demographic Assn, 1988-; member, Atlanta chapter Amer Statistical Assn, 1990-; vice president, Mableton Tigers Youth Baseball Assn, 1988-; member, US Census Bureau Strategic Planning Committee, 1987-89. **Honors/Awds:** US Department of Commerce Bronze Medal Award, US Census Bureau, 1985; US Department of Commerce Silver Medal Award, US Department of Commerce, 1989-. **Military Serv:** US Army Reserve, Sergeant 1st Class, 1970-76. **Business Addr:** Regional Director, Atlanta Regional Office, US Census Bureau, 1365 Peach Tree St, NE, Suite 625, Atlanta, GA 30309.

HOLMES, JERRY
Professional football player. **Personal:** Born Dec 22, 1957, Newport News, VA. **Educ:** Chowan Junior College, attended; Univ of West Virginia, received in personnel mgmt. **Career:** New York Jets, 1980-83, 1986-87; Pittsburgh Maulers (USFL), 1984; New Jersey Generals (USFL), 1985; Detroit Lions, 1988-89; Green Bay Packers, cornerback; West Virginia, asst football coach, currently. **Honors/Awds:** Sporting News USFL All-Star Team, 1984, 1985; played in AFC Championship Game, post-1982 season; Hampton Univ, Black College National Champs, 1992, 1993.

HOLMES, KENNY
Professional football player. **Personal:** Born Oct 24, 1973. **Educ:** Miami. **Career:** Tennessee Oilers, defensive end, 1997-. **Special Achievements:** NFL Draft, First round pick, #18, 1997. **Business Addr:** Professional Football Player, Tennessee Oilers, c/o Baptist Sports Park, 7640 H 70-5, Nashville, TN 37221, (888)313-8326.

HOLMES, LARRY
Professional boxer. **Personal:** Born Nov 3, 1949, Cuthbert, GA; married Diane; children: Misty, Lisa, Belinda, Kandy and Larry Jr. **Career:** Worker at various businesses including: car washes, rock quarries, rug mills, foundries, construction company, janitorial services at hotel, training center; Muhammad Ali, sparring partner; Round 1 Bar & Disco, owner; sportswear store, owner; professional boxer, retired. **Honors/Awds:** Won World Boxing Council from Ken Norton 1978; resigned title to become champion of Intl Boxing Fed, 1984; undefeated record, 45 professional fights, 31 won by knockouts; One of Ten Outstanding Men in America, Junior Chamber of Commerce. **Business Addr:** Mr. Larry Holmes, Larry Holmes Enterprises, Inc., 91 Larry Holmes Drive, Easton, PA 18042.

HOLMES, LEO S.
City manager. **Personal:** Born Aug 19, 1919, Philadelphia, PA; married Mildred Evans; children: Artelia H. **Educ:** Cheyney State Coll, BA; Univ of PA & Temple U, addl study. **Career:** City of Chester, prsnl mgr, councilmn; Frederick Douglass Jr HS, math tchr & home sch vstr. **Orgs:** USPO Negro Rep Council of Delaware Co; Negro Rep State Council; DE Co Rep Exec Com; chmn DE Co Manpower Adv CounAm Leg Chester Br; bd dir YMCA; past pres Cheyney Alumni Assn; John A Watts Lodge #224 IBPOE; United Supreme Council AASR of FM PHA 33 deg. **Military Serv:** USAC 1942-45. **Business Addr:** City of Chester Municipal Bldg, 5 Welsh Sts, Chester, PA.

HOLMES, LESTER
Professional football player. **Personal:** Born Sep 27, 1969, Tylertown, MS. **Educ:** Jackson State Univ. **Career:** Philadelphia Eagles, guard, 1993-96; Oakland Raiders, 1997-. **Business Addr:** Professional Football Player, Oakland Raiders, 1220 Harbor Bay Pkwy, Alameda, CA 94502, (510)615-1875.

HOLMES, LITDELL MELVIN, JR.
Parks director. **Personal:** Born Jun 15, 1944, Crisfield, MD; son of Magdalene Collins and Litdell M Holmes Sr; married Elsie Hayward Holmes, Nov 20, 1971; children: Faye, Faith, Ivory. **Educ:** North Carolina A & T University, Greensboro, NC, 1962-63; George Washington University, Washington, DC, BA, 1968. **Career:** George Washington Univ, Washington, DC, night housekeeping sup, 1963-71; City of Wilmington, Wilmington, DE, parks supervisor, 1971-74; New Castle County, Wilmington, DE, parks supervisor, 1974-80, superintendent of parks, 1980-83; City of St Petersburg, St Petersburg, FL, parks director, 1983-. **Orgs:** Board of directors, Florida Turfgrass Association, 1989-91; board member, Community Alliance, 1989-91; youth committee chairman, Community Alliance, 1990-91; board of regents, National Recreation/Parks Assn Maintenance School, 1990-92; membership chairman, Florida Recreation/Parks State Association, 1990-92; president, National Forum/Black Public Administrators/Tampa Bay Chapter, 1991-92. **Honors/Awds:** County Achievement Award, Natl Assn of Counties, 1980; Executive Award, University of Georgia, 1984; Leadership St Petersburg, St Petersburg Chamber of Commerce, 1988; Leadership Tampa Bay, Tampa Bay Chamber of Commerce, 1990; Leadership Florida, State of Florida Chamber of Commerce, 1991. **Business Addr:** Parks Director, City of St Petersburg, Leisure Services, Parks Div, 1450 16th St, N, St Petersburg, FL 33704-4212.

HOLMES, LORENE B.
Educator. **Personal:** Born Jul 27, 1937, Mineola, TX; daughter of Jessie M Barnes (deceased) and William H Barnes (deceased); married Charles M Holmes Sr (deceased); children: Charles Jr, James Henry, Jessyca Yvette. **Educ:** Jarvis Christian Coll, BS 1959; Univ North Texas, M Bus Ed 1966, EdD 1970. **Career:** Jarvis Christian Coll, chairperson soc & behav sc div of eight coll prog 1971-75, chairperson business admin dir int progs 1975-78, chairperson div of social sci & business 1978-81, chairperson div of bus admin 1981-96, executive assistant to the president for external relations, 1996-. **Orgs:** Mem National Business Educ Assn 1964-; mem Texas Business Educ Assn 1972-; treasurer Hawkins Alumnae Chapter of Delta Sigma Theta Sorority 1983-; proposal reader United States Dept of Educ 1986, 1989; bd mem Hawkins Helping Hands 1987-; staff director Presidential Search Committee Jarvis Christian Coll 1987-88; mem bd of dir Greater Hawkins Chamber of Commerce 1987-; bd mem/sec Hawkins Public Library Board 1988-. **Honors/Awds:** Top Lady of the Yr Top Ladies of Distinction Inc 1982, 1985; Woman of the Yr Hawkins C of C 1982; Certificates of Honor E TX Chap of Links Inc Longview & Tyler TX 1980 1984; publs (approx 15) Professional Journals 1969-84; Certificate of Appreciation Amer Business Women's Assn, Lake Country Charter Chapter 1984; T A Abbott Faculty Excellence in Teaching Award 1988; Texas Business Education Assn, Business Teacher of the Year 1988; Certificate of Appreciation, Shawnee State Univ 1988; Certificate of Appreciation The Univ of North Texas Executive on Campus Program 1989; 6 chapters in yearbooks, 16 articles published, editorial reviewer for 2 textbooks; Profiles of East Texas, KLTV, 1991; honored by KLTV Channel 7 as one of eight East Texan "Profiles of East Texans—We're Proud of You," 19 filmed for Lou Rawls' Parade of Stars UNCF Telethon, Jarvis Christian College, 1992. **Home Addr:** PO Drawer 858, Hawkins, TX 75765. **Business Addr:** Executive Assistant to the President for External Relations, Jarvis Christian College, PO Drawer G, Hwy 80, Hawkins, TX 75765.

HOLMES, LOUYCO W.
Educator (retired). **Personal:** Born Apr 24, 1924, Washington, DC; son of Naomi Holmes and Louyco Holmes; married Carleen Watts; children: Richard L. **Educ:** Howard Univ, 1941-43; Rutgers Coll Pharmacy, BS 1946-50; NJ Coll of Med & Dentistry, DMD 1962-67. **Career:** Holmes Pharmacy, owner 1954-63; Gen Dental Practice, dentist 1967-; NJ Dental Sch, dental ed, Prof of Clinical Operative Dentistry 1967-89. **Orgs:** Mem 1956-63, pres 1958-59 NJ Pharm Assoc; vp/pres elect Commonwealth Dental Assn 1977-79, pres 1979-; chmn Budget Com 1977; Chi Delta Mu Frat; Nat Dental Assn; mem House of Dels 1974-77; chmn Credentials Com 1975; bd of trustees RL Garner Trust & Fund. **Honors/Awds:** Fellow of the Acad of Gen Dentistry 1982-. **Military Serv:** AUS sgt 1943-46.

HOLMES, MARY BROWN
Labor, industrial relations manager. **Personal:** Born Oct 20, 1950, Charleston, SC; daughter of Vernell P Brown and Rufus Brown; married William Holmes; children: Hosea L Banks, Joya N. **Educ:** Johnson C Smith Univ, BA 1971; Webster Coll, MA 1976. **Career:** Sea Island Comp Health, med social worker 1974-79; Trident Tech Coll, instructor 1980-82; Telamon Corp, deputy dir; South Carolina Dept of Corrections, admin judge, 1987-. **Orgs:** Elder St Paul Presby Church; mem Sea Island Comp Health 1973-74; mem Ocean Queen OES 1975; treas Charleston EOC Comm 1980; chair Natl Black Social Worker Org 1974-; mem SC School Bd Assn 1975-; chairperson St Paul Sch Bd 1975-. **Honors/Awds:** Notary of SC 1976-86; Outstanding Young Women of America 1978. **Home Addr:** PO Box 237, Hollywood, SC 29449. **Business Addr:** Administrative Judge, South Carolina Dept of Corrections, Lieber Correctional Institution, P O Box 208, Ridgeville, SC 29472.

HOLMES, PRIEST ANTHONY
Professional football player. **Personal:** Born Oct 7, 1973, Ft Smith, AR. **Educ:** Univ of Texas, attended. **Career:** Baltimore Ravens, running back, 1997-. **Business Addr:** Professional Football Player, Baltimore Ravens, 11001 Owings Mills Blvd, Owings Mills, MD 21117, (410)654-6200.

HOLMES, RICHARD BERNARD
Bank officer. **Personal:** Born Apr 4, 1951, Chicago, IL; son of Florence M Holmes and Robert B Holmes; married Marion Turner, Jul 2, 1977; children: Reginald B. **Educ:** Chicago City College, 1968-70; DePaul University, 1973-75; University of Phoenix, BSBA, 1989. **Career:** First National Bank of Chicago, senior tax accountant, 1972-79; Valley National Bank, trust tax administrator, 1979-82; The Arizona Bank, mgr, trust tax unit, 1982-85; Security Pacific Bank, employee benefit trust administration, 1985-89, systems conversion project consultant, 1989-90; Bank of America, mgr, employee benefit accounting, 1990-92, senior trust officer, 1992-. **Orgs:** National Association of Urban Bankers, president, 1996-97, vice pres finance, 1991-92, Western Region, vice pres, 1989-90; United Negro College Fund, accounting director San Diego, 1992-, accounting director Phoenix, 1988-90; Arizona Association of Urban Bankers, president, 1988-89; San Diego Urban Bankers, president, 1993-94. **Honors/Awds:** Man of the Year, Southern California Conference of the African Methodist Episcopal Church, 1996. **Military Serv:** US Army, sgt, 1971-72; Bronze Star, Vietnam Service Medal, 1972. **Home Addr:** 12765 Kestrel St, San Diego, CA 92129, (619)484-3243.

HOLMES, ROBERT A.
Educational Administrator, state representative. **Personal:** Born Jul 13, 1943, Shepherdstown, WV; son of Priscilla L Holmes and Clarence A Holmes; divorced; children: Donna Lee Vaughn, Darlene Marie Boyce, Robert A Jr. **Educ:** Shepherd Coll 1964; Columbia Univ, MA 1966, PhD 1969. **Career:** Harvard-Yale-Columbia Summer Studies Program, director, 1968-69; Southern University, associate professor, 1969-70; CUNY, Bernard Baruch College, director of SEEK 1970-71; Atlanta University, professor, 1971-; Georgia House of Representatives, state rep, 1975-; Governmental Affairs Committee, chairman; Southern Center for Studies in Public Policy, director, 1989-. **Orgs:** Joint Center for Political Studies, adjunct fellow, 1982-; National Conference of Black Political Scientists, president, 1973-74; Association of Social and Behavioral Scientists, president, 1976-77; YMCA Southwest Atlanta, chairman, board of directors, 1976-78; Research Atlanta, chairman, board of directors, 1978-79; Adams Park Residents Association, president, 1972-73; chair, board of trustees, 1992-; South Fulton Running Partners, president. **Honors/Awds:** Atlanta Jaycees, Outstanding Young Man of the Year, 1975; American Association of Adult Educators, Outstanding Legislator's Award, 1978; Shepherd College, Alumnus of the Year, 1978; Georgia Municipal Association, Legislative Service Award, 1989; Metropolitan Atlanta YMCA, Layperson of the Year Award, 1989; Clark-Atlanta University, Amoco Foundation Outstanding Professor Award; Fannie Lou Hamer Community Service Award. **Special Achievements:** Author/co-author: 18 monographs and books; 50 articles. **Business Addr:** Director, Southern Center for Studies in Public Policy, Clark-Atlanta University, 223 James P Brawley Dr, Atlanta, GA 30314.

HOLMES, ROBERT C.
Commissioner, attorney. **Personal:** Born Mar 20, 1945, Elizabeth, NJ; divorced; children: 1. **Educ:** Cornell U, AB 1967; Harvard Law Sch, JD 1971. **Career:** Roxbury, cir asso 1969-71; St of NJ, atty 1971; Newark Housing Devel & Rehab Corp Newark, exec dir 1971-74; NJ St Dep Comm Affairs, asst commr atty present. **Orgs:** NJ Bar Assn; Nat Bar Assn; Am Soc for Pub Adm; Garden St Bar Assn; NAHRO. **Honors/Awds:** Nat hon soc Cornell U; Deans List; 4 yr Teagle Found Scholar; Sr Men's Hon Soc MA NG. **Business Addr:** Wilentz, Goldman, Spitzer, 90 Woodbridge Center Dr, Woodbridge, NJ 07095.

HOLMES, ROBERT ERNEST
Attorney. **Personal:** Born Jul 24, 1943, NYC. **Educ:** NY U, BA 1966; NY Univ Sch of Law, JD 1969; Manhattan Sch Of Music & Univ of So CA, addl study. **Career:** Paul Weiss Rifkind

Wharton & Garrison, summer assoc 1968, part time atty 1968-69, assoc atty 1969-71; WA Sq Coll of Arts & Sci, guest lectr 1969-70, adj instr Amer Lit 1970-71; NY School of Continuing Educ, adj instr Black Amer 1969-70; Motown Record Corp, sr counsel 1971, legal counsel 1971; Columbia Pictures Music Group, sr vp, gen mgr, pres Columbia Pictures Music Publ Div. **Orgs:** Bd dir Pacific Psychotherapy Asso CA; bd dir NAACP; bd dir Constl Rights Found CA; bd dir Black Music Assoc; past pres Black Entertainment & Sports Lawyers' Assoc. **Honors/Awds:** Dean's List Temple Univ & NY Univ Sch of Law; Univ Schlrshp NY U, NY State Schlrshp NY U; Leopold Schepp Fnd Schlrshp NY U; various debate & pub spkng awrds; Am Jurisprudence Prize in Copyright; Military History Award Temple Univ 1963; recipient Fulbright-Dougherty Travel Grant 1967; Samuel Rubin SchlrshpCarnegie Fnd Schlrshp; author of numerous publs. **Business Addr:** Sr VP, Gen Manager, Pres, Columbia Pictures Music Publ, Columbia Plaza East, Room 231, Burbank, CA 91505.

HOLMES, ROBERT KATHRONE, JR.
Company executive. **Personal:** Born Sep 5, 1952, Louisville, KY; son of Cecile E Thompson Holmes and Robert K Holmes Sr; married Stephanie A Kennedy, Nov 20, 1982; children: Robert K III, Tomika C, Justin C. **Educ:** McKendree College, Lebanon, IL, business administration, 1988. **Career:** Kentucky Fried Chicken, Louisville, KY, mgr facilities, 1979-88; Brown-Forman Corp, Louisville, KY, vice pres, corp services, 1988-. **Orgs:** Past president, International Facility Management Assn, 1985-; member, National Assn for Corp Real Estate Executives, 1988-; member, International Society of Facility Executives, 1989-; Professional Certification: Certified Commercial Investment Member (CCIM). **Honors/Awds:** KFC-Adult Black Achiever, YMCA Black Achiever Program, 1988; Corp Team Work Award, Brown-Forman Corp, 1990; Kentucky Colonel; Leadership Louisville Class, 1989. **Business Addr:** Vice President, Corp Services, Brown-Forman Corporation, 850 Dixie Hwy, Louisville, KY 40210.

HOLMES, ROBERT L., JR.
Composer. **Personal:** Born Mar 29, 1934, Greenville, MS; married Lois E Mason; children: Ronda Lang, Reba Lynn. **Educ:** TN State U, BS 1956, MA 1970. **Career:** Pub mgr composer, arranger 1961; Moss Rose Pub, 1963; Tuneville Mus, 1964; Nashboro Record Co, artist repertoire dir 1967; Night Train, dir & arranger 1965; Multimedia Div Univ of CA, consult 1973; TV Peace Corps, composer producer radio 1971-73. **Orgs:** Many adv panels. **Honors/Awds:** Many schlrshps & grants. **Military Serv:** AUS 6th army band. **Business Addr:** Thompson House, Fisk Univ, Nashville, TN.

HOLMES, WENDELL P., JR.
Mortician. **Personal:** Born Feb 10, 1922, Brunswick, GA; married Vivian Altamese Broome; children: Wendell P Holmes III, Carolyn Holmes Nesmith. **Educ:** Hampton Inst, Pres of Class BS 1943; Eckels Coll of Mortuary Science, Pres of class Mortuary Science 1947. **Career:** Duval County Sch Bd, chmn 1980-84; Holmes & West Funrl Hm PA, pres 1956-86; pres, Wendell P Holmes, funeral director, 1986-. **Orgs:** Duval Cnty Schl Bd 1969-92; Century Natl Bank 1976-85; chrmn bd of trustees Bethune Cookman Coll; chrmn Hampton University Bd of Trustees; founding sire archon, Gamma Beta Boule, Sigma Pi Phi Fraternity; chairman, Hampton University Board of Directors; life mem, Alpha Phi Alpha Fraternity. **Honors/Awds:** Honorary Dr of Laws Degree Bethune-Cookman 1982; Small Bsnsnmn of the Yr Jacksonville Area-Chamber of Comm; Meritorious Srvc in Area of Human Rel Alpha Phi Alpha Frat; Silver Bell Award for Significant Contrib to Educ Duval Cnty Clsrm Tchrs Assn; Annual Brotherhood Award, National Conference of Christians & Jews, 1985. **Military Serv:** US Army, 1st lt, GMC, 3 1/2 yrs. **Home Addr:** 4022 Gillislee Dr, Jacksonville, FL 32209. **Business Addr:** Funeral Dir, 2719 W Edgewood Ave, Jacksonville, FL 32209.

HOLMES, WILLIAM
Systems programmer. **Personal:** Born Aug 19, 1940, Allendale, SC; married Diane T; children: Renada Irene, Eva Regina. **Educ:** VoorHees Coll, BS Math (summa cum laude) 1973. **Career:** USAF, legal specialist 1961-69; DuPont, sr engr. **Orgs:** Sec SC Conf of Black Mayors; mem NAACP; coach Little League Baseball; mayor (elected) City of Allendale 1976-88; mem Allendale County Industrial Development Bd. **Honors/Awds:** Alpha Chi Hon Soc Beta Chap VoorHees Coll 1972. **Military Serv:** USAF staff sgt 1961-69; Commendation Medal. **Business Addr:** Engineer, Dupont Savannah River Plant, Bldg 707-C Room 355, Aiken, SC 29801.

HOLMES, WILLIAM B.
Probation officer. **Personal:** Born Jan 31, 1937, Trenton, NJ; married Helen Vereen; children: Mark Wm, Allen C. **Educ:** VA Union U, BA 1959; Rutgers U, Grad Study. **Career:** E Dist of PA, US prbtn ofcr 1975-; State of NJ, parole ofcr 1966-75; Fed Job Corp, grp ldr 1966; State of NJ Div of Mntl Retardation, soc wrkr 1963-66; Mercer Co Welfare Bd, soc case wrkr 1962-63; Dept of Pub Welfare, soc case worker 1961-62; Fed Probation Ofcrs Assn, tchr 1960-61. **Orgs:** Past pres, vice pres Bd of Educ Lawrence Twnshp 1969-; bd dir Lawrence YMCA 1968-; mem past chmn Mercer Co Comm Coll EOF 1972-; exec bd NAACP Trenton; life mem past polemarch Kappa Alpha Psi Frat 1970-71. **Honors/Awds:** Pioneer Awrd for Achvmt, polemarch awrd Kappa Alpha Psi Frat; serv awrd BSA; cert of recog Lawrence Twnshp Recreation Commn; cert of recog Lawrence Twnshp Non-Profit Hsng; Achvmt Award for Disting Serv Kappa Alpha Frat; Achvmt Awrd NAACP; Recog Award for Outst serv Lawrence Twnshp. **Military Serv:** AUSR e-5 1960-66. **Business Addr:** 601 Market St, Philadelphia, PA 19106.

HOLMES, WILLIE A.
Sales associate. **Personal:** Born Jul 25, 1928, Warwick, VA; married Addie Smith; children: Audrey, Yolanda, Wendell. **Educ:** Quinn Coll, BS 1961. **Career:** Equit Life, dist sls mgr 1970-, asst dist mgr 1969, agent 1968-69; Litton Med Prod, slsmn 1955-68. **Orgs:** Mem Natl Assn Life Undrwrtrs 1968-; Career Sales Club 1974-; apptd mem CT Devel Auth 1976; Grtr N Haven Bus & Prof Assn; vice pres Bus Vent Inc; dir Urbn Leag NAACP; mem Alpha Phi Alpha 1957; Quinn Coll Alum Assn; Imm Bapt Ch. **Honors/Awds:** Prof First & only black mem apptd to CT Devel Auth; Man of Yr Alph Phi Alpha 1965; Awards NCA. **Military Serv:** AUS stf sgt 1952-54. **Business Addr:** 25 Science Pk, New Haven, CT 06511.

HOLMES, WILMA K.
Educator. **Personal:** Born Apr 25, 1933, Washington, DC; daughter of Edith T King and Elton F King; married Arthur Holmes Jr, Feb 19, 1983; children: Ricki Fairley Brown, Sharon Fairley Nickerson. **Educ:** DC Teachers College, Washington DC, BA, 1956; Stanford Univ, Palo Alto, CA, MA, 1970. **Career:** Montgomery County Public Schools, supervisor of instruction, 1987-92, director of human relations, 1970-84, human relations training coord 1970-71, language arts teacher specialist 1969-70, teacher, 1964-70; Vario School System, teacher 1960-69; Flower Valley Elementary School, elem principal, 1992-. **Orgs:** Nat Alliance of Black Sch Educators; Am Assn of Sch Adminstr; mem, Montgomery County Alumni Chap, Delta Sigma Theta Sor; Phi Delta Kappa Sor; Pi Lambda Theta Hon Eductrs Sor; Nat Urban Leag; Nat Counc of Negro Women; Takoma Park-silver Spring Comm Found; past bd dir YMCA; past bd mem Nat Girl Scouts; Nat Assn of Human Rights Workers; Elem Prin Assn Led Discussion on Human Relat Training for Eductrs at Nat Conf of Christians & Jews 1977; Exec Report in The Advertiser 1976; member, National Assn of Elementary Principals. **Honors/Awds:** "Back to Basics & Multiculturalism are not Mutually Exclusive" NEA Human Rights Conf; "Creative Solutions to Staff Reduction" AASA; woman of year Montgomery Co 1979; Design & Implemented Multiethnic Convention for Educators & Cnsltnt-Sexism; Presented Paper on Making Integration Work at AASA Conf 1976; NAACP, Montgomery County Branch. **Home Addr:** 17104 Blossom View Dr, Olney, MD 20832. **Business Addr:** Principal, Flower Valley Elem School, 4615 Sunflower Dr, Rockville, MD 20853.

HOLMES, ZAN W., JR.
Educator. **Personal:** Born Feb 1, 1935, San Angelo, TX; married Dorothy Burse. **Educ:** Huston-Tillotson Coll, BA 1956; Southern Methodist Univ, BD, 1959, STM, 1968. **Career:** Hamilton Park UMC, pastor, 1958-68; Texas state representative, 1968-72; Dallas Central District, North Texas Conference, 1968-74; Intern Program, Southern Methodist Univ, assoc dir, 1974-78; St Luke Community United Methodist Church, senior pastor, 1974-; Perkins School of Theology, Southern Methodist Univ, assoc prof of preaching, 1978-. **Orgs:** Judicial Council of the United Methodist Church; Bd of Regents of the University of Texas System, regent; Greater Dallas Community of Churches, past pres, bd of dirs; Comerica Bank, bd of dirs; State Fair of Texas, bd of dirs; Dallas Foundation, bd of dirs; Society for the Study of Black Religion; Black Methodist for Church Renewal; NAACP; Alpha Phi Alpha Fraternity; Legistlative Committee of the Texas Constitutional Revision Commission, chair, 1974; Tri-Ethnic Committee, chair, 1971; Dallas Pastor's Assn, pres, 1963. **Honors/Awds:** Jr Black Academy of Arts and Letters, Living Legend Award, 1991; Huston-Tillotson Coll, Humanitarian Award, 1991; Linz Jewelers & Dallas Morning News, Linz Award, 1991; Dallas Peace Ctr, Peace Maker Award, 1990; Dillard Univ, honorary doctors of laws, 1993; Huston-Tillotson Coll, honorary doctors of divinity, 1970. **Special Achievements:** First African American to hold the position of president of Dallas Pastor's Assn, 1963; author of chapter entitled "Black and United Methodist," in Our Time Under God is Now, Abingdon Press, 1993; author of Encountering Jesus, Abingdon Press, 1992; narrator: "Disciple" Bible Study Video, Cokesbury/Graded Press Video, 1987/1992; advisory committee for publications entitled Songs of Zion, Abingdon Press, 1981; Come Sunday-The Liturgy of Zion, Companion to SZO-Abingdon Press, 1990. **Business Addr:** Pastor, St Luke Community UM Church, 5710 E RL Thornton Freeway, Dallas, TX 75223.

HOLSENDOLPH, ERNEST
Reporter. **Personal:** Born Oct 31, 1935, Quitman, GA; son of Ethel Holsendolph and Wallace Holsendolpf; married Linda Shelby Holensdolph, Jan 8, 1972; children: Nora, Joseph. **Educ:** Columbia Coll, BA 1958. **Career:** Cleveland Press, reporter 1961-65; E Ohio Gas Co, editor 1965-67; Washington Star, reporter 1967-69; Fortune Magazine, assoc editor 1969-71; NY Times, reporter 1972-83; Plain Dealer, Cleveland, OH, business editor, 1983-89; Atlanta Journal Constitution, city editor, 1989-91, business columnist, 1991-. **Orgs:** Mem bd dirs Alumni Assn Columbia Coll. **Military Serv:** AUS. **Business Addr:** Business Columnist, Atlanta Journal Constitution, 72 Marietta St, Atlanta, GA 30302.

HOLSEY, BERNARD
Professional football player. **Personal:** Born Dec 10, 1973. **Educ:** Duke, attended. **Career:** New York Giants, defensive end, 1996-. **Business Addr:** Professional Football Player, New York Giants, Giants Stadium, East Rutherford, NJ 07073, (201)935-8111.

HOLSEY, LILLA G.
Educator. **Personal:** Born Aug 26, 1941, San Mateo, FL; children: Linita "Reesie". **Educ:** Hampton Institute, BS 1963; FL State University, MS 1971, PhD 1974. **Career:** East Carolina Univ, assoc prof home economics 1974-; FL State Univ, graduate rsch asst 1971, 1973; Gainesville High School, home economics teacher 1970-72; Lincoln High School, 1964-70. **Orgs:** Natl & Amer Home Econ Assns; Amer & Vocational Assn; NC Consumer Assn; Bethel AME Church; bd trustees Alpha Kappa Alpha; Kappa Delta Pi & Omicron Nu Honor Society; Phi Kappa Delta. **Honors/Awds:** Ford Foundation felllowship 1973-74; Danforth associate 1977; charter mem Putnam Co Educ Hall of Fame Palatha FL. **Business Addr:** Associate Professor, East Carolina University, School of Education, 1000 E Fifth St, Greenville, NC 27858.

HOLSEY, STEVE
Newspaper executive. **Career:** Michigan Chronicle, entertainment editor, columnist, beginning 1969, deputy editor and administrative advisor to the executive editor, currently. **Special Achievements:** Holsey's column entitled "Reflections," is the longest running entertainment column in the history of the Chronicle. **Business Addr:** Entertainment Editor, Columnist, Michigan Chronicle, 479 Ledyard, Detroit, MI 48201, (313)963-5522.

HOLSEY, WILLIAM FLEMING, JR.
Surgeon (retired). **Personal:** Born Apr 18, 1923, New York, NY; son of Lurine M Holsey and William F Holsey Sr; married Joyce Chambers; children: Denise, Dorine, William III. **Educ:** NY City Coll, BS 1943; Howard Univ, MD 1946. **Career:** St Mary's Hospital, chief of surgery, 1976-77; Private practice, surgeon, currently. **Orgs:** mem Tucson Metropolitan Energy Commn 1983-86; bd of dir Pima County Medical Soc; vice pres St Mary's Hosp Tucson; member, Arizona Board of Medical Examiners. **Honors/Awds:** Fellow Amer College of Surgeons; Certified, American Board of Surgery. **Military Serv:** USAF capt 1952-54. **Home Addr:** 6501 N Camino Arturo, Tucson, AZ 85718.

HOLT, ALINE G.
Administrative manager. **Personal:** Born Apr 2, 1942, Dallas, TX; married Richard Holt (deceased). **Educ:** LA City College, attended 1942. **Career:** City of LA, property mgmt dir 1962-72; Crenshaw Neighbors Inc LA, exec dir 1972-74; LA City Council Councilwoman Pat Russell's 6th Dist, comm serv aging specialist; LA City Comm Develop Dept, rent stabilization div 1979-84; retired. **Orgs:** Pres 1981-82, treas/secty 1978-81,past pres 1973-89, Los Angeles County Commission on Aging; mem PTA; pres Life Mem LA 1950-69; Girl Scouts of Amer & Boy Scouts of Amer leader & den mother 1958-60;1st vice pres & parlimentarian Crenshaw C of C Women's Div 1973-74; budget com spec United Way Western Region LA 1975; pres bd dir Crenshaw Consortium LA 1973-74; pres Les Bienfaisontes Charity & Social Club 1970-89; elected Women's Assn Rsch & Educ Assn mem 1974-75; mem Natl Caucus on the Black Aged Inc 1976-77; Natl Assn Bus & Professional Women of Amer 1975; Toastmasters of America, Los Angeles Chapter 1988-89. **Honors/Awds:** CA Legislature Assembly Concurrent Resolution; Women's Recognition & Equality Day in CA to Aline Holt 1973; Woman of Yr for Outstanding Serv to Crenshaw Comm Crenshaw Chamber of Commerce 1974.

HOLT, DELORIS LENETTE
Educator, author. **Personal:** Born in East Chicago, IN; daughter of Pearl Adams and Willis Adams; married Chester A Holt. **Educ:** Ball State Univ, BSEd 1956; UCLA Pepperdine Univ, credential 1969; Univ of San Francisco, MSEd 1978. **Career:** LA City Schs, parent involvement coordinator; Cleveland Public Schools, teacher; LA City Schs, advisor proj Follow Through; LA Unified Sch Dist, tchr, author, currently. **Orgs:** Alpha Kappa Alpha; established Kinderpress, 1991. **Honors/Awds:** Author bks published by Ward Ritchie Press 1971, Childrens Press 1973, LA Unified School Dist 1987; Merit Awd CA Assn Tchrs of Eng 1973; published Black Hist Playing Card Deck US Games Systems Inc 1978; Resolution of Commndtn LA City Cncl 1972; Early Childhood Education Instructional Guides for Teachers Kinderpress, 1991. **Business Addr:** Teacher/Author, Los Angeles Unified Sch Dist, 419 W 98th St, Los Angeles, CA 90003.

HOLT, DONALD H.
Business executive. **Personal:** Born Jan 22, 1941, Cleveland, OH; married Dianne Williford. **Educ:** J Carroll U, BS, BA 1964; Case Wstrn Res U, MBA 1971; Univ Akron, JD 1976. **Career:** Prmr Indus Corp, asst vice pres for corp prsnl admin; E OH Gas Co, asst to pres 1969-, spec asst to pres 1968-69, cst anlyst 1967-68. **Orgs:** Tst Urban Leag of Grtr Clvlnd; City Club of Clvlnd; Untd Way Serv; Rtry Club of Clvlnd; Blcks in Mgmt; NAACP; Alpha Phi Alpha; Nat Urban Afrs Cncl; OH St Bar Assn. **Honors/Awds:** Ldrshp Clvlnd Class of 1979-80; Alpha Kappa Psi Men of Achie 1977; 10 Outst Yng Men Jcs 1973. **Military Serv:** AUS 1st lt. **Business Addr:** 23512 Cedar Rd, Beachwood, OH 44122.

HOLT, DOROTHY L.
Educator, administrator. **Personal:** Born Nov 11, 1930, Shreveport, LA; married James S Holt III; children: James IV, Jonathan Lamar, Roderick Lenard. **Educ:** Wiley Coll Marshall TX, BS 1962; LA Tech Univ Ruston MS, 1973; Nrthwstrn St Univ, 1973-75; E TX St Univ Commerce, TX, EdD 1978. **Career:** Caddo Parish Educ Sec Assoc, pres & fndr 1954-62; Caddo Teachers Assoc, sec 1973-74; League of Women Voters of Shreveport, treas 1979-82, 1st vice pres 1982-83; LA Distributive Educ Assoc, treas 1979-80, pres 1980-81; Central High Alumni Assoc, treas 1980-93; Natl Assoc Adv of Black Amer, sec & bd mem 1983-85; Caddo Assn Educators, 2nd vice pres 1984-85; LA Assoc of Dist Educ Teachers Awards Comm, chairperson 1984-85; Caddo Parish School System, coord. **Orgs:** Chrmn Alpha Kappa Alpha Sor Smnrs 1983-85; 2nd vice pres Caddo Assn of Eductrs 1984-85; mem Phi Delta Kappa, Kappa Delta Pi, Natl Assoc of DE Tchrs, Amer Voc Ed Assoc, LA Assoc of DE Tchrs NEA, YMCA, YWCA; brd of trustees MDEA/AV Dist Ed Professional Devel Awrd; chrmn Caddo Parish Textbook Comm for Dist Educ Teachers; planner & presenter CPSB Professional Improvement In-Service Pgm; pres Ave BC Jr Mission; mem Allendale Branch YWCA Bd of Mgnt, Caddo Parish Teachers Fed Union, Ed Comm Ave Bapt Church Fed Credit Union; pres, Allendale Branch YWCA 1988-91; Shreveport Regional Arts Council; 1st vice pres, Civic Club, 1993; pres, Sigma Rho Omego Chap, Alpha Kappa Alpha Sorority, Inc, 1997-98; bd of dirs, David Raines Med Ctr. **Honors/Awds:** Outstanding Leadership Awards Natl DE 1983: Ave BC Educational Award, 1984; Booker T Washington High School Student Council Award; Appreciation Award, Muscular Dystrophy, HS chmn; Educator of the Year, Finalist; Outstanding coordinator & Fellowship Award, Leadership Devel, USOE; LA Vocational Assn, Teacher of the Year Award; published articles Journal of Business Educ & Business Educ Forum Mags; DECA Award; Shreveport Times Educator of the Year Award 1986; Outstanding Leadership Award Huntington HS; Southern Assoc Accreditation Chrprsn 1987; Alpha Kappa Alpha Sorority Civic & Community Award, 1992; Zeta Phi Beta Sorority, Outstanding Civic & Community Woman of the Year Award, 1991; Afro-American History Month Award, 1993; Wiley College Distinguished Alumni Award, 1996; UNCFund Award, 1996. **Home Addr:** 306 Holcomb Dr, Shreveport, LA 71103.

HOLT, EDWIN J.
Educator. **Personal:** Born in Shreveport, LA; son of Sammie Lee Draper Holt and James S Holt; married Dr Essie W; children: Lisa Michele, Rachelle Justine. **Educ:** Central St Univ, BA 1958; IN Univ, MS 1962; Univ of AR, EdD 1971; Univ of TN, Postdoctoral Study 1977. **Career:** Caddo Parish Sch Bd, classroom tchr 1959-67, guidance cnslr 1967-68, sch asst prin 1968-71, sch prin 1971-74, instr dir 1974-80, asst Supt 1980-90; Louisiana State University, associate professor of psychology, 1990-. **Orgs:** Univ adj prof LSU-br Univ 1972, LA Tech Univ 1973-75, Northeast LA Univ 1973-75, Northeast LA Univ 1973, So Univ 1976-79, Grambling St Univ 1980-84; founder and co-chmn "H" Enterprises 1980-81; bd of dir Rutherford House 1980-84; dir of summer youth work study pgm Trinity Baptist Church 1980-; co-dir of Afro Am Hist Actvts Trinity Baptist Church 1980-; pres LA Alpha Phi Alpha Frat 1981-83; Shreveport Clean Comm Cmmn 1981-86; bd of mgmt Caddo Dist PTA; 1981-90; bd of dir Norwela Council BSA 1981-86; appeal bd mem Selective Serv System 1981-89; bd of dir Council of Aging 1982-84; bd dir, American Heart Association, 1991-; bd of mgmt Carver Br YMCA 1982-87; Shreveport Proj Sel Sufficiency Task Force 1984-87; prof mem NEA, LEA, CAE, Phi Delta Kappa, Caddo Jt Adm Org; board of directors-Youth Involvement Prog 1986-9. **Honors/Awds:** Southern Fellowship Fund Univ of AR 1970-71; NDEA Fellow State Coll of AR 1968; John Hay Fellow Williams Coll 1964; Caddo Parish Educ of Year 1966; Alpha Phi Alpha Fraternity Man of Year 1972. **Business Addr:** Associate Professor of Psychology, Louisiana State University, One University Place, Shreveport, LA 71115.

HOLT, ESSIE W.
Educator. **Personal:** Born in Sicily Island, LA; married Dr Edwin J Holt; children: Lisa Michelle, Rachelle Justine. **Educ:** Grambling St Univ, BS; Univ of Ar, MEd, Educ Spclst; Univ of TN, EdD. **Career:** LSU-Shreveport, Caddo Parish School Bd: classroom teacher, guidance counselor; psychologist elementary prin, elementary instructional supvr, assistant superintendent of curriculum and instruction, assistant to supt, currently. **Orgs:** Alpha Kappa Alpha Delta Lambda Omega Chapter NEA; LEA; CAE; NAESP; PTA; past bd of dir United Way, Rutherford House, Juvenile Justice Prog Caddo-Bossier Day Care Asso Volunteer Sicke Cell Anemia Dr, Arthritis & Heart Foundation Drives; YWCA, board of directors; Child Care Services Board. **Honors/Awds:** Zeta Phi Beta Educator Awd Leadership Shreveport Grad CAE Educator of Yr awd LA Gov Comm For Women life mbrshp PTA recipient; Women Who Have made a Difference Award, LA PTA Service Scroll. **Home Addr:** 208 Plano St, Shreveport, LA 71103. **Business Addr:** Caddo Parish School Board, 1961 Midway, Shreveport, LA 71130.

HOLT, FRED D.
Clergyman. **Personal:** Born Feb 7, 1931, Macon, GA; married Nancy Smith; children: Larry, Kenny, Tim, Tony, Clevetta Rogers. **Educ:** Hartnell Coll, AA Human Sv 1980; Chapaman Coll, BA Sociology 1982; Goldengate Univ, 1983. **Career:** Salinas City Council candidate 1979-83; Salinas City Affirm Active Action Bd chp 1980-82; Sal Rent Mediation Bd mem 1981-83; St James CME Church Steward Bd chm 1983; Salinas NAACP mbrshp chm 1983-85; Holts Record Co v pres; St James AME Church, preacher, 1991-. **Orgs:** Sr deacon Fremont Masonic Lodge No 13 1958-82; mem Salinas Chamber of Commerce 1972-83; owner M & H Restaurant 1973-76; pres Salinas NAACP 1974-75; owner Nadon Enterprize 1981-85; life member NAACP 1984; KRS Omega Psi Phi Omicron Nu 1984-85; Legal Redress Officer Salinas Branch, NAACP, 1995-. **Honors/Awds:** Thalheimer Awd Class I NAACP 1975-76; Man Of The Year Awd NAACP 1979; Achievement Awd NAACP 1984; Omicron-Nu Omega Psi Phi Man of the Year, 1990,95; Vice-Basileus, 1987, Basileus Omicron-Nu, 1994-95; St James CME Church, Lay Leader Award, 1997. **Military Serv:** AUS E-7 1st Sgt 26 yrs; 1951 Good Conduct Army Commendation; 1972 Meritorious Awd; 1973 Bronze Star; Served in Vietnam, 1968-69. **Home Addr:** 1433 Shawnee Wy, Salinas, CA 93906.

HOLT, GRACE S.
Educational administrator. **Personal:** Born Jun 28, 1922, Union, SC; divorced; children: Colette. **Educ:** Spelman Coll, BA (Summa Cum Laude) 1942; Univ of Chicago, Cert in Teaching 1952-53; Univ of Chicago, Reading & Language Arts 1955; Northeastern IL Univ,MA 1969. **Career:** Chicago Schools, teacher 1949-67; Chicago Bd of Educ Dept of Curriculum, lang devel corps consultant 1965-67; Woodlawn Exp Schools Proj Chicago, master teacher 1966-68; Univ of IL at Chicago NDEA Inst Adv Grammar, instr summer 1968; Center for Inner City Studies Chicago, instr 1968-69; Chicago Consortium of Coll & Univ Urban Teacher Corps, instr summer 1969; Univ of IL at Chicago, assoc prof speach com 1969; Ford Found, language research fellow 1970-72; Univ of IL at Chicago, Black Studies coordinator 1971, prof speech com 1973, prof Black Study 1974, dir Black Study 1974; New City Devel Corp, program developer 1981-82; Univ of IL at Chicago, acting dir Black Study 1983-. **Orgs:** Delegate White House Conf on Children 1970; ed bd The Jrnl of Afro-Amer Issues 1975-77; mem Constitutional Conf the Natl Cncl for Black Studies 1976-77; discussant Dialogue of Ctr for Study of Dem Inst Chicago 1976-78; ed adv First World 1976-81; chair Ed Task Force Ntl Cncl Negro Women 1977; mem PresAssemb on St Policy Rsch at Univ of IL 1978; consult Cmnwlth Ed Div of Ind Rel 1980-81; mem Reg I Adv Cncl for Frgn Lang & Intl Stds Il St Bd of Ed 1980-81; trustee Elam Manision 1980; scrng brd IL Humanities Cncl 1980-81; ethnic ldr panel Heritage News Serv 1981; Blk Wmns wrkshp Org of Amer Hist &Assoc of Blk Wmn Hist 1981-82; mem CCCC Com on advis of Lang Stmt for 1980's & 1990's NCTE 1982-83; mem Wmns Netwk for Wash-Chicago 1982-83; conv Coll Stdntfor Harold Washington 1983; fndg conv C Liaison & Neg Comm, bd of dir, wmns comm, 1992 Chicago World Fair 1983-84; edit adv bd TESOL Qtrly1983-; bd of dir K Dunham Retrospective 1983-; mem exec com, chrprsn, educ & rsch comm, Blk Womens History Purdue Univ 1984; mem mil acad adv comm First Cong Dist Chicago 1984. **Honors/Awds:** Fellowship in Linguistics Northeastern IL Univ 1966-68; Outstanding Ed of the Year 1972; Patron's Choice Awd IL Arts Week The Cultural Ctr Chicago Public Library 1980; Awd for Excellence Council for Coll Attendance Natl Scholarship Serv for Negro Students 1981; Outstanding Contribs to the Psychological Welfare of of Afro-Amer Awd Black Students Psych Assoc Chicago State Univ 1981; Summer Scholarship the Program in Black Amer Culture & Scholarship Smithsonian Inst 1983; Invited Scholar Conf in the Study & Teaching of Afro-Amer History Amer Assoc Purdue Univ 1983; Awd for Professional Contrib in Community Political Action Women's Task Force 1st Congressional Dist Chicago 1984. **Home Addr:** 1226 East Madison Park, Chicago, IL 60615. **Business Addr:** Prof Communications/Blk Stds, 1919 W Taylor, Chicago, IL 60612.

HOLT, JAMES STOKES, III
Educator. **Personal:** Born Sep 23, 1927, Shreveport, LA; son of Sammie Lee Draper Holt and James Holt; married Dr Dorothy L Thomas; children: James IV, Jonathan Lamar, Roderick Lenard. **Educ:** Central State Univ, BS 1949; LA State Univ, MEd 1956; Univ of AR, EdD 1973; Lincoln Graduate Center, San Antoine Texas, MSA (Master Senior Appraiser) 1989. **Career:** Caddo Parish Sch Bd, math bio chem inst 1950-66; State Dept of LA, council mem state drug abuse 1972-74; Graduate School S Univ, faculty mem, 1972-79; Southern Univ, div chmn 1972-79; HHH Real Estate Investments Co, pres 1981; MRA Natl Assn of Master Appraisers 1982-; SU CAI Rsch Program, participant 1984-85; Southern Univ, prof of biology, currently; Holt Real Estate Appraisal Co, Shreveport, owner 1987-; Ruben Real Estate Co, Shreveport, LA, salesman, 1989; LA Ins Commission, licensed salesman, 1991. **Orgs:** Alpha Phi Alpha Frat 1947-; Beta Kappa Chi Hon Soc 1948-; LEA life mem teacher organ 1955-; NEA life mem teacher organ 1960-; Supt Sunday School Ave Baptist Church 1969-92; 3rd Degree Mason AF & AM 1970-; sec Shreveport Metro Bd of Appeals 1975-; pres Lakeside Acres Civic Assn 1968-; mem YMCA, NAACP, LA Council on Human Rights; co-chmn Biology Scholarship Awd Comm 1992; mem 20 yr Celebration Steering Comm for SU-Shreveport; mem, LA Home Managers Assn 1987-; mem, Natl Organization of Black County Officials (NOBCO) 1988-; Mem Shreveport Black Chamber of Commerce 1988; EAC charter member, National Society of Environmental Consultants, 1995. **Honors/Awds:** Caddo Educ Assn, Educator of the Year, Shreveport Times, Award, 1962; FL State Univ Radiation Biology Award, 1963; Southern Fellowship in Higher Educ Award, Univ of AR, 1972-74; Louisiana Education Assn Fourth District Distinguished Achievement Award, 1974; recipient of Scout Leaders Regional Tr Cert & Scoutmasters key; Natl Science Fellowship Biology Student, TSU, 1958, Dillard Univ 1962; Phi Delta Kappa, University of Arkansas, 1971; University of Texas, Academic Year Grant, National Science Foundation, 1960. **Home Addr:** 306 Holcomb Drive, Shreveport, LA 71103.

HOLT, JOHN J.
Government official. **Personal:** Born May 7, 1931, Richmond, VA; son of Susie B Holt and Samuel L Holt; married Andrea; children: Gwen, Greg, John, Keth, Derek, Brandon. **Educ:** VA Union Univ, BS 1961. **Career:** USAF, communications specialist 1952-56; Univ of MD, lab scientist 1963-69, personnel mgr 1969-74; MD Port Admin, human resources mgr 1974-. **Orgs:** Pres IPMA 1980-81; vice pres MAAAO 1985-87; mem Johns Hopkins Univ Metro Planning & Rsch Comm 1982-; bd dir United Way of Central MD 1985-87; chmn alloc United Way Comm Serv 1985; mem Venture Grant Comm (UWCS) 1984-; pres MAAAO 1987-89; sr arbitrator Natl Panel of Consumer Arbitrators 1988-. **Honors/Awds:** Governor's Citation for Outstanding Serv Balt, MD 1981; Furture Business Leaders of Amer Balt 1979; Dr Richard H Hunt Scholarship Award Comm Serv MD Assn Affirmative Action Ofcrs 1981; Citizen Citation Mayor of Baltimore 1989; Community Service Award Governor State of Maryland, 1989. **Military Serv:** USAF Sgt served 4 yrs; Natl Defense Serv Medal; Good Conduct Medal. **Business Addr:** Manager, Human Resources, Maryland Port Administration, 2510 Broening Hwy, Maritime Center, Point Breeze, Baltimore, MD 21224.

HOLT, KENNETH CHARLES
Educational administrator. **Personal:** Born Feb 9, 1948, Pine Bluff, AR; son of Velma Lovell Holt and Curtis Holt Sr; married Helen N Reed Holt, Aug 1972; children: Byron Kieth, Derrick Vaughn, Briana Dashon. **Educ:** Univ of Arkansas, Pine Bluff, AR, BS, 1970; Univ of Wisconsin, Milwaukee, WI, MS, 1978; superintendent program, 1988-. **Career:** Milwaukee Public Schools, Milwaukee, WI, teacher, 1970-80, asst principal, 1980-88, principal, 1988-. **Orgs:** Chairperson, WI Dept of Public Instruction-Program Review Panel for AIDS Education Programs, 1989-; co-chairperson, African American Male Youth Task Force-Milwaukee Public Schools, 1989-; exec comm, WI Black Historical Society, 1989-91; mem, Education for Employment Council for Milwaukee Public Schools, 1988-; mem, Natl Assn Secondary School Principals, 1989-; National Middle School Association, 1991-. **Honors/Awds:** Distinguished Man of Milwaukee for 1989, Top Ladies of Distinction Inc, 1989; selected to participate in the 1990 WI Admn Leadership Acad, 1989; featured in Ebony, Essence, Black Enterprise and Wall Street Journal, 1990; featured in Newsweek, School and College, Dollars and Cents, Jet, Association for Supervision & Curriculum Development-UPDATE, New York Times, Education Week, Executive Educator and New Republic; Milwaukee Times Weekly Newspaper, WITI TV6 and Warner Cable Company, Black Excellence Award Winner in Education, 1992. **Special Achievements:** Publications: Letter to the editor, The Washington Post, Feb 15, 1991; counterpart to Kenneth B Clark's opposition to the African-American Immersion schools, The Philadelphia Daily News, Mar 22, 1991; "An Island of Hope: Milwaukee's African-American Immersion Schools," The Journal of Negro Education, Fall 1991; "Milwaukee's Radical Answer to Multicultural Education," School Safety, Fall 1991; "A Rationale for Creating African-American Immersion Schools," Educational Leadership, Dec 1991/Jan 1992. **Business Addr:** Principal, Francis Parkman Middle School, 3620 North 18th St, Milwaukee, WI 53206.

HOLT, LEO E.
Judge. **Personal:** Born Jul 2, 1927, Chicago, IL; married Dorothy Considine; children: Pamela, Paula. **Educ:** John Marshall Law Sch, LLB 1959; Pvt Pract, law 1959. **Career:** Mem Cook Co Bar Assn; mem Kappa Alpha Psi Frat; Circuit Court of Cook County, judge, currently. **Honors/Awds:** Kappa Alpha Psi Achievement Awd 1971; Richard Westbrook Awd Cook County Bar Assn 1975; Robert R Ming Awd Cook County Bar Assn 1981; Oper PUSH Community Serv Awd 1981; South Subur-

ban Leadership Council Community Serv Awd 1985. **Military Serv:** USAF corpl 1945-47.

HOLT, LEROY
Professional football player. **Personal:** Born Feb 7, 1967. **Educ:** Univ of Southern California, history degree, 1990. **Career:** Miami Dolphins, fullback, 1990-. **Honors/Awds:** First team All-America, first team All-Pac 10, senior year; first team All-Pac 10, honorable mention All-America, junior year; honorable mention All-Pac 10, sophomore year. **Business Addr:** Professional Football Player, Miami Dolphins, 2269 NW 199th St, Miami, FL 33056-2600.

HOLT, MAUDE R.
Health services administrator. **Personal:** Born Aug 3, 1949, Thomaston, AL; daughter of Naomi Holt Levert and Henry J Holt; divorced; children: Andre, DeNeal Madry. **Educ:** AL A&M Univ, BS 1976; Univ of Miami, MBA/HA 1983. **Career:** Rochester Telephone, acct clerk 1972-76; Allstate Insurance, supervisor 1976-77; Jackson Memorial Hosp, asst administrator 1978-86; Metro-Dade, administrator; Alcohol & Drug Abuse Services Administration, administrator, state director, currently. **Orgs:** Mem Delta Sigma Theta Sor, Eta Phi Beta Sor, NAACP, Urban League, Coalition for the Homeless, Black Public Administrators, Natl Assoc of Counties Business& Professional Women, Amer Business Women, FL Voters League; pres Greater Miami Chap AL A&M Univ Metro-Action Plan. **Home Addr:** 100 Michigan Ave NE, A41, Washington, DC 20017.

HOLT, MIKEL
Editor. **Personal:** Born Mar 12, 1952, Milwaukee, WI. **Educ:** Univ of WI Milwaukee. **Career:** Sunday Insight, WTMJ-TV, panelist, 1994-; Milwaukee Comm Journ, edit 1976-; Milwaukee Star Times, mng edtr 1975-76, sports edtr photo journ 1974-75; Milwaukee Sentinel, intern 1968-69; Seabreeze Mag, Milwaukee edtr; DJ WCLG, asst prgm dir; Naval AP & Group Vietnam, hist writer 1971-72; Comnine Great Lakes IL, media rel ofcr 1972-73; Stringer Jet Mag, 1971-72. **Orgs:** Founder, Wisconsin Black Media Association; board director, Harambee Community School; past mem NAACP Youth Coun; past cochmn Black Awareness Study Group; Milwaukee Black Photo-Journ; WI Black Press; TUJU; vice pres Assn for Stud of Afro-Am Life & Hist; founder, Black Research Organization. **Honors/Awds:** Two-time winner Best Column Award NNPA; Braggs & Brooks Sports Serv Awrd 1974; Letter of apprc for brdcstng 1972; Community Service Award NNPA; Senate Award State of Wisconsin; Black Achvmt Awd 1976; Commnty Serv Awd UWM 1977; Comm Serv Awrd Black Stud Union 1977; Messner Impact Award, 1993; Men Who Dare Award, 1994; A Phillip Randolph Award, Recipient, 1994; NNPA Award for Best Feature Story, Mayoral Citation, 1996. **Military Serv:** US Navy, Petty officer second class, 1969-73. **Business Addr:** 3612 N King Dr, Milwaukee, WI 53212.

HOLT, VEITYA EILEENE (VICKYE)
Portfolio analyst. **Personal:** Born Jun 16, 1962, Indianapolis, IN; daughter of Janice Mai Thomas Ross and Mack Ross, Jr; married Charles Holt Jr, Sep 17, 1988; children: Jescika Nekole Holt. **Educ:** Univ of WI-Whitewater, BBA 1983, MBA 1985. **Career:** Univ WI-Whitewater Alumni Center, supervisor/telemarketing 1983, minority business program graduate asst 1983-85; Mazur-Zachow, interviewing telemarketer 1985; Cardinal Industries Inc, documents controller 1986-87. **Orgs:** Mem Alpha Kappa Alpha Service Sorority 1981-, Natl Assn of Black Accountants 1983-85; treas Univ WI Whitewater Choir 1983-85; mem St Mark AME Celestial Choir 1985, Natl Assn of Black MBA's 1986-. **Honors/Awds:** Black History Month Achievement Award; Silver Scroll Honor Society; Graduate Assistantship Univ WI-Whitewater 1982-83.

HOLTON, MICHAEL DAVID
Professional basketball player. **Personal:** Born Aug 4, 1961, Seattle, WA. **Educ:** UCLA, 1980-84. **Career:** Phoenix Suns, 1984-86, Chicago Bulls, 1986, Portland Trail Blazers, 1987-88, Charlotte Hornets, 1989-90.

HOLTON, PRISCILLA BROWNE
Educator, consultant. **Personal:** Born Dec 31, 1921, Hartford, CT; daughter of Lucille Ford Browne and Edward Ashton Browne; married John Lyle Holton, Dec 24, 1944; children: Mary Frances Dickerson, John K, Leslie Lucille Mumenthaler. **Educ:** St Joseph Coll for Women, BS 1946; Antioch Univ, MEd 1971. **Career:** Green Tree School, principal 1969-74; Antioch Univ, dir of special educ dept 1974-77, MEd prog administrator 1977-80; City of Philadelphia, coord of head start 1980-83; Self-employed, consultant; Holy Cross Day Care, interim director, 1989-90. **Orgs:** mem, chairperson Foster Grandparents, 1980-85; pres, Children's Village Adv Bd, 1980-85; exec bd mem, Council for Labor & Indus 1983-87; mem Delta Sigma Theta Sor, Youth Svcs, PA Acad of Fine Arts, Afro-Amer Museum, Smithsonian Inst, League of Women Voters, Natl Assoc for the Educ of Young Children; consultant Temple Univ, Community Coll, Beaver Coll, Wharton Settlement, Delaware Valley Assoc for Nursery/Kindergarden Teachers, Penn State, YWCA, Parent Child Ctr, Head Start, Mill Creek Day Care Ctr; TV appearances for toy manufacturer. **Honors/Awds:** Award for work done w/Children with Learning Disabilities VIP Serv Club 1980; Recognition of Comm Serv Chapel of Four Chaplains 1980; Disting Alumni AwdSt Joseph Coll 1983; Certificate of Appreciation Better Boys Found, 1986; publications Tips to ,Parents (weekly) Hartford Chronicle CT; co-authored Teachers Manual for Green Tree School. **Home Addr:** 428 East Montana St, Philadelphia, PA 19119.

HOLYFIELD, EVANDER
Professional boxer. **Personal:** Born in Atmore, AL; son of Annie Holyfield; married Paulette Bowen Holyfield, 1985 (divorced 1991); children: Evander Jr, Ashley, Ewin, Evette, Eden; married Dr. Janice Itson, Oct 4, 1996. **Career:** Professional boxer, currently; Evander Holyfield Buick/Subaru, Atlanta, GA, partner, currently. **Honors/Awds:** Bronze Medal, Los Angeles Olympic Games, 1984; Heavyweight Boxing World Champion.

HOMER, RONALD A.
Banker. **Personal:** Born Mar 1, 1947, Brooklyn, NY; son of Lena Taylor Homer and Allan V Homer; married Cheryl Bell Homer; children: Ronald Scott, Brian C. **Educ:** Univ of Notre Dame, BA 1968; Univ of Rochester, MBA 1971. **Career:** Action Inc, center dir 1968-69; Marine Midland Bank NY, asst vice pres 1970-79; Freedom Natl Bank of NY, exec vice pres & COO 1979-83; Boston Bank of Commerce, chairman & CEO 1983-. **Orgs:** Member, board of directors, New England Telephone Co, 1985-; treasurer, Massachusetts Industrial Finance Agency, 1985-93; president, National Bankers Association, 1983-84; Nellie Mae Inc, 1985-; Cambridge College, chairman, 1989-; Boston Foundation, 1990-; Greater Boston YMCA, 1990-; Wedgewood Capital Corp, 1992-; United Way of Mass Bay, vice chairman, 1992-; New York Telephone, bd of dirs, 1995-. **Honors/Awds:** Fellowship Consortium for Grad Study in Bus Univ of Rochester 1969-71; Honorary Doctor of Humane Letters, University of Massachusetts, 1988; Presidential Award, National Bankers Association, 1984; Professional Achievement Award, Boston Urban Bankers Association, 1986; Minority Business Award, Massachusetts Black Legislative Caucus, 1987.

HONABLUE, RICHARD RIDDICK
Physician. **Personal:** Born Apr 1, 1948, Staten Island, NY; children: Richard III, Xavier, Michael. **Educ:** Long Island Univ, AA 1968; Wagner Coll Grymes Hill, BS 1970; Meharry Med Coll, MD 1974. **Career:** Pildes Opticians NY, optical dispenser 1968-70; CBS Radio News, editors desk asst 1969; United Negro Coll Fund Pre-Med Prog Fisk Univ, tutor 1971; Dede Wallace Comm Mental Health Serv, consult 1976; Medical Exam Ctr, med dir 1977; Duke Univ Dept of Family Prac, asst clinical prof 1981-87; Family Health Care Ltd, owner, physician. **Orgs:** Pres Resident's Assn of Meharyy 1976; asst clinical prof George Wash Univ School of Allied Health Sci 1979; diplomate Amer Bd of Family Practice 1980;med examiner Comm of VA; Lord Chamberlain Soc; Tidewater TV Adv Comm; mem Tau Kappa Epsilon, AMA, AAFP, VAFP; chmn Reg II NMA 1984-85; pres Williamsburg Men's Club 1984; mem AMSUS, Natl naval Officers Assn, Frontiers Intl; fellow AAFP; life mem NAACP. **Honors/Awds:** Eagle Scout Awd 1966; Order of the Arrow. **Military Serv:** US Army Reserves capt med corps 1975-77; USNR Commander. **Business Addr:** Owner, Family Health Care, Ltd, 110 Cary St, Williamsburg, VA 23185.

HONEYCUTT, ANDREW E.
Educator. **Personal:** Born Jan 28, 1942, Homboldt, KS; son of Thelma Honeycutt and Ed Lee Honeycutt; married Pamela Hatchett, Jun 4, 1977; children: Michael, Andrea, Andrew Jr, Aaron. **Educ:** Ottawa University, BA, 1964; Boston University, MBA, 1970; Harvard University, DBA, 1975. **Career:** Florida A&M University, Florida Region II Housing Center, codirector, 1974-75, Management Sciences Division, chairman, 1974-77; Texas Southern University, Center for International Dev, associate director, 1979-81, interim department head, 1979-80; National Center for Housing Management District of Columbia, coordinator of organ development, 1983-1989, vice pres for strategic planning, 1990-91; Savannah State College, school of business, dean, 1991. **Orgs:** Savannah Regional Minority Purchasing Council, chairman, 1991-92; First Union Bank, board of directors, 1991-92; United Way, board of directors, 1991-92; Savannah Economic Development Authority, board of directors, 1991-92; HOSPICE Savannah, board of directors, 1991-92; Small Business Assistance Corp., board of directors, 1991-92; West Broad YMCA, board of directors, 1991-92; Private Industry Council, board of directors, 1991-92. **Honors/Awds:** Big Brother Association, MA, Big Brother Award, 1975; Small Business Institute, MS, Small Business Leardership Award, 1979; CAYA Fellowship, TX, Black Youth Role Model Award, 1983; National Center for Housing Management, DC, Fellow Award, 1987. **Special Achievements:** Author, "Foreign Direct Investment Strategies," Detroit Business Journal, 1988; "The Quality Improvement Process: Learning from Japan," Proceedings, 1989; "International Marketing Myopia: A Proposed Cure," International Management, 1989; "Management by Relationship - A Management Strategy for the 21st Century," 1990; "Competing with Global Quality Control," Journal of Business Strategies, 1990. **Military Serv:** US Army Military Intelligence, 1st lt, 1965-68, Airborne, 1966. **Business Addr:** Dean, School of Business, Savannah State College, Howard Jordan Business Building, PO Box 20359, Savannah, GA 31404, (912)356-2335.

HONEYCUTT, JERALD
Professional basketball player. **Personal:** Born Oct 20, 1974. **Educ:** Tulane. **Career:** Milwaukee Bucks, forward-guard, 1997-. **Business Addr:** Professional Basketball Player, Milwaukee Bucks, 1001 N Fourth St, Milwaukee, WI 53203, (414)227-0500.

HONORE, STEPHAN LEROY
Attorney. **Personal:** Born May 14, 1938, Urbana, OH; son of Lalu May Dolby Honore and Albert R Honore; married Flor; children: Francis, Andrew, Stephanie. **Educ:** Capital Univ, BS 1960; Univ of Toledo, JD 1974. **Career:** Peace Corps Columbia, Dominican Rep, 1961-66; US State Dept AID, 1966-68; Trans Century Corp, 1968-69; Model Cities Prog Toledo, 1970-71; Peace Corps Dominican Rep, 1978-81; Thurgood Marshall School of Law, law prof 1974-84 (leave of absence 1978-81); self-employed Houston, TX, attorney at law, import/export business, real estate, 1984-; Telecommunications, 1994-. **Orgs:** Student body pres Capital Univ 1960-69; presiding justice, student honor ct Univ of Toledo Coll of Law 1973-74; law reveiw, casenote editor Univ of Toledo Law 1973-74; bd of dir Immigration Counselling Ctr 1976-78; mem State Bar of TX, Natl Bar Assn, Houston Bar Assn, Amer Immigration Lawyers Assn; pres 1984-86, mem Parochial Sch Bd 1983-88; mem, bd of educ, Galueston-Houston Catholic Diocese, 1988-94, pres of bd, 1992-94. **Honors/Awds:** Articles on criminal & labor law publ in Univ of Toledo Law Review 1973-74. **Home Addr:** 4131 Levonshire, Houston, TX 77025. **Business Phone:** (713)664-3208.

HOOD, CHARLES MCKINLEY, JR.
Government official. **Personal:** Born Aug 9, 1936, Richmond, VA; son of Ethel Saunders Hood and Charles M Hood Sr; married Marion Overton Hood, May 28, 1960; children: Charles III, Brian M, Cheryl E. **Educ:** Hampton Institute, BS, 1959; University of Richmond; University of Oklahoma, MA, 1974. **Career:** US Army, 1960-; US Army War College, faculty member, 1983-84; US Army Europe, Herzogenaurach, Germany, commander, 1984-86; US Army Forces Command, Atlanta, GA, Chief Warplans, 1986-87; U.S. Forces Command, Atlanta, GA, deputy J5, 1987-88; U.S. Second Army, Atlanta, GA, chief of operations, 1988-90; U.S. Virgin Islands, St Thomas, VI, adjutant general, 1990-. **Orgs:** Alpha Phi Alpha, 1973-; Association of US Army, 1960-; Alumni Association War College, 1983-; Adjutants General Association, 1990-; National Guard Association, 1990-. **Honors/Awds:** National Black Heritage Observance Council, Inc, Humanitarian Service Award, 1992. **Military Serv:** US Army, major general, 1990-; Legion of Merit (3), Bronze Star (3), Meritorious Service Medal (3). **Business Addr:** Adjutant General, Virgin Islands National Guard, Rural Route 2, Box 9925, Mannings Bay Kingshill, St Croix, Virgin Islands of the United States 00851.

HOOD, DENISE PAGE
Judge. **Personal:** Born Feb 21, 1952; married Nicholas Hood III; children: two. **Educ:** Columbia University Law School. **Career:** City of Detroit, city attorney; Recorder's Court, judge; Wayne County Circuit Court, judge, 1992-94; Eastern District of Michigan, federal district judge, 1994-. **Orgs:** Detroit Bar Assn, member, 15 years, board of directors, 1983-, president, 1993; Assn of Black Judges of Michigan, president, 1991-92; Executive Council of the United Church of Christ, chairperson, 1991-93. **Special Achievements:** First African American woman elected president of the Detroit Bar Assn, 1993. **Business Addr:** Federal District Judge, Eastern District of Michigan, 235 Theodore Levin US Courthouse, 231 W Lafayette, Detroit, MI 48226, (313)226-3000.

HOOD, HAROLD
Judge. **Personal:** Born Jan 14, 1931, Hamtramck, MI; son of Lenore Elizabeth Hand Hood and W Sylvester Hood Sr; married Lottie Vivian Barnes Jones; children: Harold Keith, Kenneth Loren, Kevin Joseph, Karen Teresa. **Educ:** Univ of MI, BA (Phi Eta Sigma Scholastic Honorary) 1952; Wayne State Univ, JD (Bronze Key and Gold Key for Legal Scholarship) 1959 (Dist Alumni Awd) 1984. **Career:** Hood, Rice and Charity, atty 1959-61; City of Detroit, asst corp cnsl 1961-69; E Dist of MI, chief asst US atty 1969-73; Common Plea Ct of Detroit, judge 1973-77; Recorders Court of Detroit, judge 1977-78; 3rd Judicial Circuit of MI, judge 1978-82; MI Court of Appeals, judge 1982-. **Orgs:** Member Amer Bar Assn, State of MI Bar Assn, Detroit Bar Assn, director Amer Judicature Soc, Natl Bar Assn, Judicial Cncl of NBA, Assn of Black Judges Of MI Founder; trustee/vice chmn Kirwood General Hosp 1974-79; bd Mbr/pres Old Newsboys-Goodfellows 1974-; member Detroit Renaissance Lions 1975-; bd mem NCA/DD Greater Detroit Area 1976-; bd mem/chairman Natl Council on Alcoholism 1979-; Natl Judicial Coll, faculty 1980-82; adj prof Central MI Univ 1982-; Michigan Judicial Institute, faculty 1983-; Michigan Judicial Tenure Comm, commissioner 1986-94, chairman, 1988-90; chairman Michigan Supreme Court Committee on Standard Civil Jury Instructions 1987-; Old Newsboys-

Goodfellows, president 1987-88; chmn, Michigan Supreme Court Task Force on Race/Ethnic Issues in Courts, 1987-; chairman, Supremeurt Committee on Standard Civil Jury Instructions, 1987; director, Thomas M Cooley Law School, 1988-; president, Old Newsboys Goodfellows, 1988-89; commissioner, Office of Substance Abuse Services, State of MI, 1987-92; member, Golden Heritage Life; NAACP; trustee, Hartford Memorial Baptist Church; trustee, Michigan State Bar Foundation, 1992-; trustee, American INNS of Court Foundation, 1992-; member, Natl Advisory Council on Alcohol Abuse and Alcoholism. **Honors/Awds:** Ted Owens Awd Detroit Alumni Kappa Alpha Psi 1971; Fed Exec Bd Serv Awd 1972; Northern Province Achvmnt Awd Kappa Alpha Psi 1972; City of Inkster Merit Awd City of Inkster, MI 1976; Wayne St Univ Law Sch, Distinguished Alumni, 1984; Wayne State Univ, Distinguished Alumni Award, 1985; "Executive Alcoholism-A Special Problem," Labor-Management Journal, 1988; Michigan Corrections Commission, Judicial Servant Award, 1989; Augustus D Straker Distinguished Jurist Award, 1989; State Bar of Michigan Champion of Justice Award, 1990; Michigan Women's Hall of Fame, Phillip A Hart Award, 1991; Order of The Coif, WSU Law School, 1992; Washtenaw County Bar, Martin Luther King Award, 1992. **Military Serv:** USASC 1st lt 1952-54; Army Commendation Medal, Korean Serv Medal, Far East Service Medal 1954. **Business Addr:** Judge, MI Court of Appeals, 900 First Federal Bldg, Detroit, MI 48226.

HOOD, MORRIS, JR.
State representative. **Personal:** Born Jun 5, 1934, Detroit, MI; married Beverly; children: Denise, Morris III. **Educ:** Wayne State U. **Career:** Michigan House of Representatives, state representative, 1970-. **Orgs:** Member, Michigan Democratic Black Caucus; Economic Club of Detroit; Trade Union Leadership Council; Urban Alliance; Detroit Urban League; Friends of Belle Isle; Greater Lansing Democratic Business and Professional Assn; life member, NAACP. **Business Addr:** State Representative, Michigan House of Representatives, 8872 Cloverlawn, Detroit, MI 48204.

HOOD, NICHOLAS
Councilman (retired), minister. **Personal:** Born Jun 21, 1923, Terre Haute, IN; married Elizabeth Flemister; children: Nicholas III, Emory, Stephen, Sarah Cyprian. **Educ:** Purdue U, BS 1945; N Central Coll, BA 1946; Yale U, MA 1949; Olivet Coll, hon DD 1966; Divinity Sch Univ of Chgo, hon LittD, LLD 1966; N Central Coll, hon DD 1966. **Career:** City of Detroit, city councilman (retired); Plymouth Ch, sr minister; Dixwell Cong Ch, asst mnstr; Central Congressional Church, minister; Cong'l Chs of the US, vice mod; Non-Profit Hsg Ctr, pres; Fed Natl Mortg Assn Fndr Cyprian Ctr, adv com. **Orgs:** Bd mem Ministers Life & Cas Ins Co; mem bd trustees Hutzel Hosp; mem Indsl Hsg Study Tour Europe 1971; US rep World Conf on Non-Profit Hsg 1972. **Honors/Awds:** Outst mem 1949 class Yale Divinity Sch 1974; Amistad Award outstndng serv to Am 1977. **Business Addr:** Retired Councilman, Detroit City Council, 2 Woodward Ave, Rm 1340, Detroit, MI 48226-3413.

HOOD, RAYMOND W.
Legislator. **Personal:** Born Jan 1, 1936, Detroit; married Helen; children: Raymond, Jr, Roger. **Educ:** Fullerton Jr Coll. **Career:** MI House of Reps, asst floor ldr, rep 7th Dist, elected 1964. **Orgs:** Chmn Pub Hlth Com; mem Elections Com; Conservation & Recreation Com; Educ Com. **Honors/Awds:** One of the youngest Black legislators elected in House; reelected 1966, 1968, 1970, 1972, 1974, 1976, 1978. **Business Addr:** Dir, Dept Licensing & Regulations, PO Box 30018, Lansing, MI 48909.

HOOKER, DOUGLAS RANDOLF
Business executive. **Personal:** Born Mar 31, 1954, Moultrie, GA; son of Odessa R Walker Hooker and H Randolph Hooker; married Patrise M Perkins, Feb 17, 1979; children: Douglas Patrick Hooker, Randi Michelle Hooker. **Educ:** Georgia Inst of Technology, Atlanta GA, BS Mechanical Engineering, 1978, MS, Technology & Science, 1985; Emory Univ, Atlanta GA, MBA, 1987. **Career:** Georgia Power Company, Atlanta, GA, asst section supervisor, 1979-85; Bio-Lab Inc, Decatur, GA, dir of mktg svcs, 1990-; The Randof Group, CEO, currently. **Orgs:** Vice president, National Society of Black Engineers-Alumni Extension, 1991-; vice president, Georgia Tech Minority Alumni Committee, 1982-85. **Honors/Awds:** Woodruff Scholar, Emory University, 1985-87; Miller-Patillo Honoree, Patilloc Foundation, 1990. **Business Addr:** CEO, The Randof Group, 335 Glenhurst Ln, Atlanta, GA 30331.

HOOKER, ERIC H.
Clergyman. **Personal:** Born in Waco, TX; married Lois Nelson. **Educ:** Houston-Tillotson Coll, AB 1951; VA Union Univ, BD MDiv 1953; Prairie View Univ, MA 1979. **Career:** New Mt Zion Baptist Church, pastor 1970-82; Bishop Coll, dean of men 1970-79; 11th Congressional Dist, congressional aide 1979-85; McLennan Comm Coll, trustee; Second Baptist Church, pastor 1982-. **Orgs:** Mem Amer Assn Higher Educ 1985; 2nd vice pres Kiwanis Club 1985; pres Conference of Christians and Jews 1985; trustee bd McLennan Co Comm Coll 1982-. **Business Addr:** Pastor, Second Baptist Church, 1205 M L Cooper Dr, Waco, TX 76706.

HOOKER, JOHN LEE
Blues singer and guitarist. **Personal:** Born Aug 22, 1917, Clarksdale, MS; son of Minnie and William Hooker; married Martella (divorced); children: Robert, John Jr, Zakiya, Diane. **Educ:** Studied under Will Moore. **Career:** Blues musician and singer; signed with Modern Records, 1948; first single, Boogie Chillen, 1948; other hit songs include: Boom Boom, Crawling Kingsnake, I'm In the Mood; She's Long She's Tall; I LIke to See You Walk; Take Me As I Am; Seven Days and Seven Nights; numerous other songs and recordings; albums include: Folklore of John Lee Hooke, 1962; This Is Hip, 1980; Black Rhythm and Blues, 1984; The Healer, 1989; Film soundtrack contributions: Mister Brown, 1972; Hot Spot, 1990; American Heart, 1994; Heaven's Prisoners, 1996; Stealing Beauty, 1996; Rich Man's Wife, 1996; Film Appearances: Roots of American Music: Country & Urban Music, 1971; The Blues Brothers, 1980; Concert/Fesitval: Rolling Stones, Steel Wheels Tour, 1989; Nelson Mandela Rally, Oakland California, 1990; Bridge School Benefit in Mountain View California with Neil Young & Don Henley, 1991; and numerous others. **Honors/Awds:** Best Blues Album Award, Jazz and Pop Mag, 1968-69; Blues Hall of Fame Award, Ebony Mag, 1975; Folk Heritage Award, Smithsonian Institute, 1983; Madison Sq Garden Tribute to John Lee Hooker, 1990; inductee Rock & Roll Hall of Fame, 1991; Inductee, Rock Walk, Los Angeles, 1995; San Francisco Blues Festival Tribute to John Lee Hooker, 1995; Photograph on Tanzanian Government Postage Stamp, 1995; Blues Foundation Lifetime Achievement Award, 1996; Grammy Award, 1990, 1996; Grammy nominations, 1961, 1974, 1987, 1991, 1992, 1994; W C Handy Awards, 1986, Three in 1989, 1990, 1993, 1996. **Business Addr:** c/o The Rosebud Agency, PO Box 170429, San Francisco, CA 94117.

HOOKER, ODESSA WALKER
Assistant principal. **Personal:** Born Sep 21, 1930, Moultrie, GA; divorced; children: Douglas R, Melanie Ann, David A, Margaret P, Darrell W. **Educ:** Paine Coll, BA 1951; Atlanta Univ, Certification 1951; Univ of Cincinnati, MEd 1967. **Career:** Barnesville HS, english teacher 1951-53; Whittemore HS, english teacher 1954-55; Cincinnati Public Schools, elem teacher 1961-83, elem asst principal 1983-. **Orgs:** Co-choir dir and organist 1955-, bible class teacher 1977-, Peoples Tabernacle Bapt Church; volunteer organist Chapel Serv Bethesda Oak Hosp 1983-. **Honors/Awds:** 1st Black Pres Delta Psi Delta Kappa Gamma Intl Cincinnati OH 1986-88. **Home Addr:** 3906 Wess Park Dr, Cincinnati, OH 45217.

HOOKS, BENJAMIN LAWSON
Educator, attorney, clergyman. **Personal:** Born Jan 31, 1925, Memphis, TN; son of Bessie White Hooks and Robert B Hooks Sr; married Frances Dancy, Mar 21, 1951; children: Patricia Gray. **Educ:** LeMoyne College, attended, 1941-43; Howard University, attended, 1943-44; DePaul University, JD, 1948. **Career:** Attorney, 1949-65, 1968-72; Mutual Federal Savings & Loan Assn, co-founder, vice pres, director, chairman, 1955-69; Middle Baptist Church, pastor, 1956-72; asst public defender, 1961-64; Greater New Mt Moriah Baptist Church, pastor, 1964-; Shelby County Criminal Court, judge, 1965-68; Federal Communications Commission, 1972-78; NAACP, executive director, 1977-93; Chapman Co, senior vice pres, 1993; Fisk Univ, prof of social justice, 1993-. **Orgs:** Natl Bar Assn, judicial council; American Bar Assn; Tenessee Bar Assn; bd trustee, LeMoyne-Owen College; bd dir, Southern Christian Leadership Conference, 1968-72; grand chancellor, Knights Pythias; bd trustee, Hampton Institute; Natl Civil Rights Museum, bd member. **Honors/Awds:** Howard University, honorary LLD, 1975; Wilberforce University, honorary LLD, 1976; Central State University, honorary DHL, 1974, honorary LLD, 1976; Masons, Man of the Year Award, 1964, Gold Medal Achievement Award, 1972; Optimist Club of America Award, 1966; Lincoln League Award, 1965; Tennessee Regional Baptist Convention Award; Spingarn Award, NAACP, 1986; producer/host, Conversations in Black & White; co-producer, Forty Percent Speaks; panelist, What Is Your Faith?. **Military Serv:** US Army, staff sergeant, 1943-46. **Business Addr:** Prof, Social Justice, Fisk University, 1000 17th Ave N, Nashville, TN 37208-3051.

HOOKS, FRANCES DANCY
Educator. **Personal:** Born Feb 23, 1927, Memphis, TN; daughter of Georgia Graves Dancy and Andrew Dancy; married Benjamin Lawson; children: Patricia Louise, Gray. **Educ:** Fisk Univ, BS 1949; TN State Univ, MS 1968. **Career:** Shelby Co Schools of TN, teacher 1949-51; Memphis City Schools, teacher 1951-59, counselor-admin hs 1959-73; Memphis City Schools, counselor-pregnant girls 1976-77; NAACP; vol sect apptmt. **Orgs:** Dir Youth Activities Mt Monah Bapt Ch 1973-75; dir Youth Activities Middle Bapt Ch 1973-75; organizer People Power Project 1968; pres/co-founder Riverview KS Comm & Day Care Ctr 1969-73; president, Memphis Chapter, Links Inc, 1968. **Honors/Awds:** Outstanding Serv to Comm Memphia Vol Placement Prog TN 1973; Youth Chap Scholarship Fund Richmond VA NAACP 1979; Membership Awd Boston NAACP 1980; Hon Chairperson Awd KY State NAACP 1980. **Home Addr:** 6701 Park Heights, Baltimore, MD 21215.

HOOKS, JAMES BYRON, JR.
Educator (retired). **Personal:** Born Sep 23, 1933, Birmingham, AL; son of Bessie Ardis Hooks and James Byron Hooks Sr; married Marcell Elizabeth; children: Angelique L, James Byron III, Kimberly M, Jamal B, Joffrey B, Keisha M. **Educ:** IN Univ, BS 1955; Roosevelt Univ, MA 1969; Northwestern Univ, PhD 1975. **Career:** J M Harlan High, asst principal 1969-75; Skiles Middle Sch, principal 1975; Haven Middle Sch, principal 1976; Whitney Young, teacher/dean 1980-92; Hooks and Company Real Estate Investments, owner, 1989-; "Ritual Without Reality," and "Thread The Needle," cable TV producer. **Orgs:** Exec dir Talent, Inc 1971-; bd of dir Sullivan House Local Serv Syst 1984-89. **Military Serv:** USN airman 1st 1955-57. **Business Addr:** 6901 S Oglesby Ave, Ste 11C, Chicago, IL 60649.

HOOKS, MICHAEL ANTHONY
Government official, real estate appraiser. **Personal:** Born Oct 13, 1950, Memphis, TN; married Janet Dean Perry; children: Michael, Jr, Kristian Nichole. **Educ:** Lane College, Jackson, TN, 1968-69; Memphis State Univ, 1969. **Career:** Shelby County Assessor's Office, deputy tax assessor 1972-77; Gilliam Communications, Inc, account exec; State Technical Institute, lecturer/instructor; Michael Hooks & Assoc, president; Memphis, Tenn, city councilman. **Orgs:** Delegate Tenn Constitutional Conv 1977; councilman Memphis, TN 1979-; member NAACP; member PUSH, Inc; member of Knights of Pythion, Commitment Memphis, Omega Psi Phi Fraternity, Prince Hall Masonic Lodge, Memphis Downtown Photographic Society, Inc. **Honors/Awds:** Tenn Assn of Assessing Officers; Intl Assn of Assessing Officers; Society of Real Estate Appraisers; Natl Assoc of Real Estate Brokers; Memphis Board of Realtors. **Home Addr:** 2143 South Parkway East, Memphis, TN 38114. **Business Addr:** City Councilman, Dist 4, 993 South Cooper, Memphis, TN 38104.

HOOKS, MOSE YVONNE BROOKS
Educator. **Personal:** Born in Jackson, TN. **Educ:** Fisk Univ Nashville, BA 1960; Columbia Univ NY, MA 1963; Univ of TN Knoxville, EdD 1973. **Career:** Div of Career Studies Shelby State Community Coll, dean, 1979-, Allied Health Sciences Division, currently; Memphis City School System, instructional researcher 1973-76, modern & foreign language chtr 1960-70; Arts & Letters LeMoyne Owen College Memphis, part time prof; Arts & Letters Memphis St Univ, part time prof. **Orgs:** Bd mem Memphis TN Council of Govt 1976-80; natl bd US China Peoples Friendship Assn 1978-; Links Inc, Shelby County Chap 1979-; National and Regional Officer, 1984-. **Honors/Awds:** American Council on Educ Fellow in Acad Administration, Am Council on Educ Washington DC 1978-79; Citizen Diplomat US China Peoples Friendship Assn 1976-80; Citizens Diplomat, May International Festival, Memphis, TN, 1976-. **Business Addr:** Prof, Allied Health, Shelby State Community College, PO Box 40568, Memphis, TN 38174.

HOOPER, GERALD F.
Educator. **Personal:** Born Nov 19, 1923, Chicago; married Ann Marie Cooper; children: Gerald, Jr, Theresa, Ernest, Gwendolyn Joyce. **Educ:** PA St U, EdD 1953; Univ WI, MA 1953. **Career:** Chicago Post Office, clerk 1948; Xavier Univ, instructor 1948-50; Central CT State, asst prof 1966; FL A&M Univ, assoc prof 1953-. **Orgs:** Mem Nat Art Educ Assn; Lemoyne Art Found; Tallahassee Arts Council. **Honors/Awds:** Tchr yr 1958; purchase prize & hon mention, water colour Atlanta Univ 1956-69. **Military Serv:** S/sgt 1943-45; t/5 1950-51. **Business Addr:** Art Dept Vsl Arts & Humnts FL, Box 132, Tallahassee, FL 32307.

HOOPER, MICHELE J.
Corporate executive. **Personal:** Born Jul 16, 1951, Uniontown, PA; daughter of Beatrice Eley Hooper and Percy Hooper; married Lemuel Seabrook III, Sep 4, 1976. **Educ:** Univ of Pennsylvania, Philadelphia, PA, BA, 1973; Univ of Chicago, Chicago, IL, MBA, 1973-75; State of Illinois, CPA, 1981. **Career:** Baxter Corp, Chicago, IL, parenterals div, 1976-83, various finance positions, dir, coverage & reimbursement, 1983-85, vice pres, corporate planning, 1985-88; Baxter Corp Canada, pres, beginning 1988; Intl Business Group, Caremark Intl Inc, pres, currently. **Orgs:** Chmn bd of Baxter Credit Union Directors, 1981-88; mem, bd of dir, 1985-89, bd chmn, 1988, Joseph Holmes Dance Theatre; mem, The Economic Club of Chicago, 1986-; mem, bd of dir, Lake Forest Graduate School of Mgmt, 1987-88, mem, bd, Medical Devices Canada, 1988-; mem, Young President's Org, 1989-; mem, Comm of 200, 1989-. **Business Addr:** Pres, Intl Business Group, Caremark Intl Inc, 2215 Sanders Rd, Northbrook, IL 60062.

HOOVER, FELIX A.
Journalist. **Personal:** Born Jul 17, 1949, Columbus, OH; son of Felicia L O'Neal Hoover and Alfred B Hoover. **Educ:** Ohio State University, Columbus OH, BA, 1970; MA, 1976. **Career:** WLWC-TV, Columbus, OH, reporter/photographer/writer; Franklin County Public Defender, Columbus, OH, investigator; Columbus Recreation & Parks Dept, Columbus, OH, arts admn/grant writer; The Call & Post, Columbus, OH, sports editor, ad rep, deputy general mgr; The Omaha Star, Omaha, NE, advertising rep; The Columbus Dispatch, Columbus, OH, reporter, currently. **Orgs:** Treas, Columbus Assn of Black Journalists,

1988-90. **Honors/Awds:** Best Series, 3rd Place, Associated Press Society of Ohio, 1989. **Business Addr:** Journalist, The Columbus Dispatch, 34 S Third St, Columbus, OH 43215.

HOOVER, JESSE
Government official. **Personal:** Born Sep 6, 1918, Tamo, AR; daughter of Magonila Martin and William Hoover; married Dorothy Franks (died 1990). **Educ:** Wayne St U, 1952. **Career:** US Postal Serv, personnel action & records supr 1946-77; Detroit Postal Employees Cr Un, VP 1946-77, 1st black bd dir; City of Detroit, Detroit, MI, admin assistant to Councilman Hood, 1978-90. **Orgs:** Mem NAACP; Freedom Fund; The Moors Inc; 1st Nighters; Sagicornians; bd deacons & trustees Plymouth Cong Ch. **Honors/Awds:** Recd the US Postal Serv Bicentennial Awd 1976; Cert of Appreciation from MAACP 1976; co-chmn Annual Easter Teas; Mens Club; Pilot Club Cert Merit, Mens Club 1968; Cert Appreciation Easter Tea. **Military Serv:** AUS staff sgt 1941-45.

HOOVER, THERESSA
Church official (retired). **Personal:** Born Sep 7, 1925, Fayetteville, AR; daughter of Rissie Hoover (deceased) and James Hoover (deceased). **Educ:** Philander Smith Coll, BBA 1946; NY Univ, MA 1962. **Career:** Little Rock Meth Council, assoc dir 1946-48; Woman's Div of Christian Svc, field worker 1948-58; Dept of Christian Soc Relations, sec 1958-65; Sect of Prog & Educ for Christian Mission, asst gen sec 1965-68; Women's Div Bd of Global Ministries United Meth Ch, assoc gen sec 1968-90. **Orgs:** Bd trustees Paine Coll 1963-76; del World Council of Ch Assemblies Sweden 1968, Nairobi 1975, Vancouver 1983; bd mem Ch Women United 1968; Bossey Ecumenical Inst 1969-75; mem Nat Council of Ch 1969-72; Comm on Ch Participation in Devel 1970; bd trustees United Theol Sem; mem Nat Bd YWCA; bd curators Stephens Coll; mem exec com Nat Council of Negro Women; mem Central Comm World Council of Churches 1983-90. **Honors/Awds:** Doctorate of Humane Letters, Bennett College, 1990. **Home Addr:** 2240 East Oaks Drive, Fayetteville, AR 72703.

HOPE, JULIUS CAESAR
Clergyman, political and civil rights activist. **Personal:** Born Sep 6, 1932, Mobile, AL; son of Zeola King Hope and Rev Robert Hope; married Louise Portis, May 21, 1959; children: Rev Julius Escous, Tonya Louise. **Educ:** Alabama State College, Montgomery AL, BS, 1958; Interdenominational Theology Center, MST, 1961. **Career:** Zion Baptist Church, Brunswick GA, pastor, 1961-70; First Baptist Church, Macon GA, pastor, 1970-78; New Grace Missionary Baptist Church, Highland Park MI, pastor, 1979—; Political Action Chair, Brunswick GA branch NAACP, 1961-78; GA State Conference of NAACP Branches, president, 1967-78; NAACP Natl Office, New York NY, natl director of religious affairs, 1978—; NAACP Midwest Region III, regional director, 1988—. **Orgs:** Life member, NAACP; member, President's Commission on Civil Rights, 1977-81; member of board of directors, Project Smile, 1974-76; president, GA State Church School and Baptist Training Union Congress, 1974-78; director, Neighborhod Youth Corps, Coastal Ara of GA, 1967-78; Alpha Phi Alpha. **Honors/Awds:** Rev Julius C Hope Day, Brunswick GA, 1970, 1987; citation from city of Glen Cove, NY, 1978; special tribute for community service from State of MI, 1982; Outstanding Service Award, Council of Natl Alumni Assn, 1983; honorary degree, Birmingham Baptist Bible College, 1984; given key to Youngstown, OH, 1988; given proclamation from US Senator Howard Metzenbaum, 1988; Outstanding Service Award, Ohio Tri-County NAACP, 1989. **Military Serv:** US Air Force, airman first class. **Business Addr:** New Grace Missionary Baptist Church, 25 Ford Ave, Highland Park, MI 48203.

HOPE, MARIE H.
Educator (retired). **Personal:** Born Mar 6, 1927, Detroit, MI; daughter of Elvine P Holley and Leander C Holley; divorced; children: John Jerry Saunders Jr. **Educ:** Bennett College, BA, elementary education, 1948; Ohio State University, MA, elementary education, 1954. **Career:** Tazewell County VA School Board, elementary teacher, 1951-54; Cols Public Schools, substitute elementary schools, 1954-55, elementary teacher, Milo Elem Prek-K-1, 1955-73, Chapter I reading teacher, John XVIII Catholic School, 1973-75, parent oordinator Chapter I Elem School, 1975-87; Life Care Alliance, part time substitute senior dining center coordinator, 1987-94. **Orgs:** Alpha Kappa Alpha Sorority Inc, Alpha Sigma Omega, 1992; Aesthetics Social Club, president, 1992; Hilltop United Methodist Church, Ruth Circle UM Women, president, 1992; Cols South District United Methodist Church, associate lay member, 1992; United Methodist Church, lay speaker South District & West Ohio Conference, 1992. **Honors/Awds:** Greater Hilltop Community Development & Westside Messenger, Women of Character Award, 1992; Ohio House of Representatives, 1992 Women of Character Special Recognition Proclamation, 1992; Sojourner Truth Award, 1994; Voices of Black Women Award, 1996. **Special Achievements:** Writer, producer, performer, director, Harriet Tubman: A Moment in History, one-act play, 1992. **Home Addr:** 4419 Belcher Ct, Columbus, OH 43224, (614)268-5615.

HOPE, RICHARD OLIVER
Educator/sociologist. **Personal:** Born Apr 1, 1939, Atlanta, GA; married Alice Anderson; children: Leah, Richard Jr. **Educ:** Morehouse Coll, BA 1961; Syracuse Univ, MA 1964, PhD 1969. **Career:** Metro Applied Rsch Center, rsch assoc 1960-72; Brooklyn Coll, asst prof of Sociology 1968-72; Dept of Defense, dir of rsch 1972-74; Morgan State Univ, chmn & prof 1974-82; Indiana Univ at Indianapolis, chmn and prof dept of Sociology; MA Inst of Technology, exec dir, 1988-. **Orgs:** Assoc editor Journal of Inter-cultural Relations 1976-; visiting lecturer Univ of West Indies Mona Jamaica 1977; mem bd dirs Moton Foundation 1978-; mem bd dir Urban League, Flanner House of Indianapolis 1982-; mem Corporation Visiting Committee MIT 1982-. **Honors/Awds:** Rsch Fellow Goddard Space Flight Center 1976-78; publications "Racial Strife in the US Military," Praeger Publishing 1979; "Black Leadership," Black Organizations Univ Press 1980. **Military Serv:** Civilian GS-15 1970-74. **Business Addr:** Exec Dir, Quality Educ for Minority Project, 1818 N Street NW, Washington, DC 20036.

HOPKINS, ALBERT E., SR.
Pharmacist. **Personal:** Born Apr 3, 1928, Houston, TX; married Joetta Carothers; children: Albert E Jr. **Educ:** Xavier University, BS, pharmacy, 1949. **Career:** Marshall Pharmacy, chief pharmacist; US Army, Fort Bliss, chief pharmacist; Hopkins Prescription Pharmacy Inc, president/owner/manager, currently. **Orgs:** YMCA; Xavier Univ Alumni; Court Volunteers; Acres Home Civic Club; bd dir Who Cares; Texas Pharmaceutical Association; Harris County Pharmaceutical Association, currently, vice pres, 1973-74; Houston Pharmaceutical Association, currently, president, 1958-69, 1969-71; National Pharmaceutical Association, currently, prescription pharmacy pres, 1974-75; National Board of Pharmacy; NAACP. **Honors/Awds:** Mayor of Houston proclaimed Albert Hopkins Day 1973; Civic Awd, Prog Missionary Bapt Ch 1974. **Business Addr:** President/Owner/Manager, Hopkins Prescription Pharmacy, Inc., 7808 W Montgomery Rd, PO Box 38260, Houston, TX 77088.

HOPKINS, BARRY L.
Clergyman. **Personal:** Born Feb 15, 1943, Stamford, CT; married Elberta Fennell; children: 1. **Educ:** VA Union Univ, BA 1968, MDiv 1971; Lancaster Theol Sem, DMin; Pastoral Training Inst, grad. **Career:** 6th Mt Zion Bapt Church, pastor 1967-70; Urban League, consult 1968-69; Jackson Ward Proj So Bapt Conv, consult 1968-70; PA Found of Pastoral Counseling Inc, pastoral psychotherapist; Sts Mem Bapt Church, pastor; W Philadelphia Pastoral couns cntr, dir; Dimension Comm Affairs Prgm, host of On Target. **Orgs:** Africa comm Natl Comm Black Churchmen 1970-71; mem exec comm div Overseas Ministries Natl Council Churchs 1971-; vice pres Church World Serv Dept Comm 1971-; comm World Mission & Evangelism World Council Church 1971-; consult Prog to Combat Racism 1971; us rep Ecumenical Sharing of Personnel Comm 1971-; sec Africa & Spec Svc, bd Intl Ministries; mem Amer Baptist Churchs; mem gen bd Amer Bapt Church USA Valley Forge PA; mem bd Philadelphia Bept Assoc; mem bd Natl Ministries Amer Bapt Church USA; mem Amer Assoc of Pastoral Counselors, elected rep gen bd Amer Baptist Churches USA. **Honors/Awds:** Community Awd Jaycees 1958; Outstanding Man of the Year US C of C 1972; Business & Professional Women's Club, Comm Serv Awd 1980; The Chapel of 4 Chaplains Awd 1983; dir, Building Better Famalies Inc, a family homeless shelter, 1989.

HOPKINS, BRADLEY D.
Professional football player. **Personal:** Born Sep 5, 1970, Columbia, SC; married Kellie, Mar 9, 1995. **Educ:** Univ of Illinois, BS in speech communications. **Career:** Houston Oilers, tackle, 1993-96; Tennessee Oilers, 1997-. **Honors/Awds:** Voted First-Team, All-Rookie by Pro Football Weekly, Football Digest, and College and Pro Football Weekly, 1993. **Business Addr:** Professional Football Player, Tennessee Oilers, c/o Baptist Sports Park, 7640 H 70-5, Nashville, TN 37221.

HOPKINS, CHARMAINE L.
Insurance underwriter. **Personal:** Born Mar 14, 1946, Danville, VA; children: Cecily Hopkins Gray. **Educ:** Indiana Univ, BS Educ 1968. **Career:** Indiana Univ, day care specialist 1970-73; Prudential Insurance, various positions 1973-80; United Presidential Ins, chief underwriter 1980-87. **Orgs:** Supervisor Marion County Crisis/Suicide Intervention; business consultant, Project Business-Junior Achievement 1989; first vice pres, Council 6 International Training in Communication, 1989.

HOPKINS, DIANNE MCAFEE
Educator. **Personal:** Born Dec 30, 1944, Houston, TX; daughter of Valda Lois Baker McAfee and DeWitt Talmadge McAfee; married Dale William Hopkins, Jul 7, 1982; children: Scott McAfee. **Educ:** Fisk University, Nashville, TN, BA, 1966; Atlanta University, Atlanta, GA, MSLS, 1967; Western Michigan University, Kalamazoo, MI, EdS, 1973; University of Wisconsin-Madison, Madison, WI, PhD, 1981. **Career:** Houston Independent School District, Houston, TX, librarian, 1967-71; Dept of Education, Michigan, Lansing, MI, school librarian consultant, 1972-73; West Bloomfield Schools, West Bloomfield, MI, high school librarian, 1973-74; University of Michigan, Ann Arbor, MI, school librarian consultant, 1974-77; Wisconsin Dept of Public Instr, Madison, dir, school librarians, 1977-87; University of Wisconsin-Madison, professor, 1987-92, associate prof, 1992-. **Orgs:** Executive committee, educators of school library media specialists, 1988-91, member, editorial board, school library media quarterly, 1988-91, chair, AASL White House conference, 1986-92, American Assn of School Librarians; member, ALA presidents White House conference task force, American Library Assn, 1990-92; chair, local arrangement committee ALISE national conference, Assn of Library and Information Science Education, 1990-91; ALA Intellectual Freedom Comm, 1991-; AASL Vision Comm for New Natl Guidelines, 1995-. **Honors/Awds:** Recipient, US Dept of Education Grant, 1989; Beta Phi Mu International Library Fraternity, 1967; Phi Delta Kappa, 1980; Exceptional Performance Award, Wisconsin Dept of Public Instr, 1982; Winner, ALISE Research Award, 1992; Winner, Distinguished Service Award, American Association of School Librarians; Co-principal Investigator, Natl Library Power Evaluation, Dewitt Wallace-Readers Digest Fund, 1994-. **Business Addr:** Associate Prof, School of Library & Info Studies, University of Wisconsin-Madison, 600 N Park St, 4251 Helen C White Hall, Madison, WI 53706, (608)263-2900.

HOPKINS, DONALD RAY
Attorney, government official. **Personal:** Born Nov 14, 1936, Tulsa, OK; son of Carolyn McGlory Hopkins and Stacey E Hopkins; divorced; children: Yvonne Ann-Marie. **Educ:** University of Kansas, BA 1958; Yale University, MA 1959; University of California Berkeley, JD 1965; Harvard Law School, LLM (cum laude) 1969. **Career:** Univ of California Berkeley, teaching asst 1960-63, asst dean of students 1965-67, asst exec v chancellor 1967-68; NAACP Legal Defense Fund Inc, staff attorney 1969-70; Pacific Cons, exec vice pres 1970-71; Eighth California Cong Dist, dist admins 1971-; attorney in Private Practice 1981-. **Orgs:** Estate tax examiner US Treasury Dept 1965; coll teacher Univ of California Laney Coll 1966-68; Acad of Polit Sci; Arbitration Assn Bd of Arbitrators; bd dir ACLU, No California 1969-71; bd dir Univ of California Alumni Assn 1976-79; bd dir African Film Soc; bd dir Travelers Aid Soc; Kansas/Yale/Harvard/ Univ of California Alumni Assn; California State, Natl, American, Federal, Alameda Cty Bar Assns; bd dir Chas Houston Bar Assn; Amer Trial Lawyers Assn; Natl Conference of Black Lawyers; Natl Lawyers Guild; California Assn of Black Lawyers; bd dir Volunteer on Parole. **Honors/Awds:** Various achievement awds; contrib auth "Politics & Change in Berkeley" Nathan & Scott 1979; contrib author to several periodicals; Woodrow Wilson Fellow; Phi Beta Kappa; Pi Sigma Alpha. **Business Addr:** District Administrator, 8th CA Cong Dist, 201-13th St Ste 105, Oakland, CA 94612.

HOPKINS, DONALD ROSWELL
Physician. **Personal:** Born Sep 25, 1941, Miami, FL; son of J Leonard & Iva Major Hopkins; married Ernestine, Jun 24, 1967. **Educ:** Morehouse College, BS, 1962; University Chicago Medical School, MD, 1966; Harvard School of Public Health, MPH, 1970. **Career:** San Francisco Genl Hosp, intern, 1966-67; CDC, various positions, 1967-74; Harvard School of Public Health, assistant professor, 1974-77; Centers for Disease Control, assistant director, international health, 1978-84, deputy director, 1984-87; Carter Ctr/Global 2000, sr consultant, 1987-. **Orgs:** American Society of Tropical Medicine & Hygiene, 1965; Institute of Medicine, 1987. **Honors/Awds:** US Public Health Svcs, Distinguished Svcs Medal, 1986; Morehouse College, Honorary Doctorate, 1988; Emory University, Honorary Doctorate, 1994; MacArthur Foundation, Fellow, 1995. **Special Achievements:** Directed: "Smallpox Eradication Program," Sierra Leone, 1967-69; Directed: "Guinea Worm Eradication Initiative at CDC," 1980-87; Author: "Princes & Peasants: Smallpox in History," 1983; "At Carter Center," 1987. **Business Phone:** (404)266-2420.

HOPKINS, EDNA J.
Educator. **Personal:** Born Sep 29, 1924, Weathrfrd, TX; married Fritizer; children: Jr, Stephen. **Educ:** TX Coll, BA 1952; Columbia U, mA. **Career:** Compton Unified School Dist, Task Force PIRAMID, coord 1974; Enterprise School Dist, Task Force Early Chldhd Ed 1970, Task Force New Ling Program, supvr teacher Educ Workshops 1965-67, teacher 1958; LA County Schools, teacher 1955; Diboll TX Abilene TX. **Orgs:** Chrpsn PR&R Comm Ed Assn 1965-68; mem CA Tchr Assn; Nat Ed Assn; Compton Ed Assn; Int Assn Chldhd Ed; Delta Sigma Theta Nat vP for Nat Cncl Negro Wmn Inc 1970-; mem White Hse Conf onf Food, Hunger & Nutrtn 1969-; mem Bd Advs Am Yth Actn Org Inc 1974-; Nat Corp Bd, "Womn in CommServ Inc" 1968-; chrprsn Grtr LA WIGS Bd 1970-; Dir Chrstn Ed LA Dist Chrstn Meth Epis Ch; Dir Chrstn Ed Philllip Tem CME Ch 1970; sec/chmn Chld Care & Dev Ser Inc; mem Int Assn Vol Eds; bd dir Womn Coal Com Comm Actn 1970-73; bd dir Teen Age & Mthrs, Harriet Tubman Sch 1970-74; bd dir LA Cncl of Chs 1970-72; Educ Adv Comm PUSH. **Honors/Awds:** Apple Grammy Tchr of Yr 1968; awd Womn in 1972; Woman of Yr Chrstn Meth Epis Ch/Wmns Miss Soc 1972.

HOPKINS, ESTHER ARVILLA
Attorney. **Personal:** Born Sep 18, 1926, Stamford, CT; married T Ewell Hopkins; children: Susan, Thomas Jr. **Educ:** Boston

Univ, AB 1947; Howard Univ, MS 1949; Yale Univ, MS 1962, PhD 1967; Suffolk Univ, JD 1976. **Career:** VA State Coll, faculty 1949-52; New England Inst Med Rsch, biophysicist 1955-59; Amer Cyanamid Cor, rsch chem 1959-61; Polaroid Corp, scientist 1967-73, patent atty 1973-78, sr project admins 1979-. **Orgs:** Bd of govs Assn of Yale Alumni; chair Yale Medal Comm; natl bd YMCA of USA; pres-elect Genl Alumni Assn Boston Univ; finance comm Town of FraminghamMA; corp mem Cambridge Family YMCA; hon mem Boston Univ Women's Grad Club; bd of dir past pres Framingham Reg YMCA; chmn bd of assessors trustee 1st Parish; mem Alpha Kappa Alpha Sor; Soc for Promoting Theo Educ; past dean Stamfort Chap Amer Guild of Organists; natl scholar Natl Assn Coll Women 1963; disting alumni Boston Univ Coll of Liberal Arts 1975; Phi Beta Kappa; Sigma Xi; Sigma Pi Sigma; Beta Kappa Chi; Scientific Rsch Soc of Amer. **Honors/Awds:** Woman of the Yr Regional Family YMCA Framingham 1984; Boston Univ carlet Key; First Parish Awd 1977; Women of Achievement MA Fedn of Bus or Professional Women'sClub 1979; Woman of the Yr Framingham Bus & Professional Women's Club 1979; training grant USPHS 1962-66. **Business Addr:** Senior Project Adminis, Polaroid Corp, 38 Henry St, Cambridge, MA 02139.

HOPKINS, GAYLE P.
Assistant athletic director. **Personal:** Born Nov 7, 1941, Tulsa, OK; son of Sophia Jackson Hopkins and Elbert Hopkins; married Patricia Cartwright Hopkins, Jul 22, 1967; children: Alissa, Christopher. **Educ:** University of Arizon, Tucson, AZ, BA, 1965; San Francisco State, San Francisco, CA, MA, 1972; Claremont Graduate School, Claremont, CA, PhD, 1978. **Career:** San Francisco State, San Francisco, CA, physical ed coach, 1969-75; Claremont-McKenna, Claremont, CA, associate professor, 1975-83; Dept of Agriculture, Washington, DC, Northern region director, 1979-80; University of Arizona, Tucson, AZ, asst athletic director, associate athletic director, currently. **Orgs:** EEOC, Dept of Agriculture, Washington, DC, 1980; president, member, Natl Assn of Athletic Advisors Academics, 1983-; president, University of Arizona Black Alumni, 1987-; chairman, Black Studies, Tucson Unified School Dist. **Honors/Awds:** Olympic Team Track & Field, Tokyo, Japan, 1964; Hall of Fame, Drake University, University of Arizona, 1967; Coach of Year, San Francisco State University, 1974; Rule Committee, NCAA, 1975; Lyndon Johnson Congressional Fellowship, 1978. **Business Addr:** Associate Director of Athletics, University of Arizona, McKale Ctr, Rm 126, Tucson, AZ 85721.

HOPKINS, JOHN DAVID
Educator, radiologist. **Personal:** Born Mar 6, 1933, Trenton, NJ; son of Edith Harvey Hopkins and John P Hopkins Sr; married Lillian L Henry; children: John III, Kay, Lisa. **Educ:** Lincoln University, AB, 1954; Meharry Medical College, MD, 1958; OH State University, residency, 1963; Vanderbilt University, Fellowship, 1970. **Career:** Meharry Medical College, assoc prof, 1963-75, dir, 1970-75; Tuskegee VA Hosp, consult, 1965-68; Riverside Hosp, dir, 1972-75; VA Hosp, chief radiology, 1973-75; Norfolk Comm Hosp, radiologist, 1975-, pres of staff, 1983-85, chief radiologist; Lake Taylor Hospital, consultant radiologist, 1985-. **Orgs:** Amer College of Radiology; fellow, Amer Coll of Nuclear Physicians; Soc of Nuclear Medicine; adv bd, Comm Mental Health Ctr; Aeolian Club; Clinical Serv Com, East VA School of Med; bd dir, United Givers Fund; bd of trustees, Eastern VA Medical School; Natl Medical Assn; Amer Medical Assn; commissioner, Norfolk Public Health Dept, 1983-. **Honors/Awds:** Guest lecturer; 8 publications; Alpha Omega, Hon Med Soc; Sigma Pi Phi; examiner, Amer Board of Radiology, 1983-; case report, "Adrenal Tumors," Journal of Computed Tomography, 1988. **Military Serv:** AUS, lt col, 1968-70. **Business Addr:** Chief Radiologist, Norfolk Community Hospital, Norfolk, VA 23504.

HOPKINS, LEROY TAFT, JR.
Educator. **Personal:** Born Aug 19, 1942, Lancaster, PA; son of Mary E Hopkins and Leroy T Hopkins. **Educ:** Millersville St Coll, BA 1966; Harvard U, PhD 1974. **Career:** Millersville State Coll, asst prof of German 1979-; Urban League of Lancaster Co Inc, acting exec dir 1979, asso dir 1976-79; Hedwig-Heyle-Schule (W Germany), instr English 1974-76; NE Univ, instructor German 1971-72. **Orgs:** Adv Com on Black History PA Hist & Mus Commn 1979-; com person City of Lancasters Overall Econ Devel Prog; Bd Mem Lancastger Co Library/ Lancaster Neighborhood Hlth Ctr 1977-; chmn PA Delegation to White House Conf on Libraries 1978-79; 1st vice pres, Lancaster Historical Society, 1989-; mem, Pennsylvania Humanities Council, 1988-. **Honors/Awds:** Received Travelling Fellowship Harvard Univ 1969-70; Study/Visit Grant for EResearch, German Academic Exchange Service, 1989; Member of Honor Society, Phi Kappa Phi, 1991. **Business Addr:** Professor, Dept of Foreign Languages, Millersville University, Millersville, PA 17551.

HOPKINS, PEREA M.
Meeting planner. **Personal:** Born Apr 13, 1931, Marshall, TX; daughter of Margaret Perea McCane and Charles A McCane; married Milton M Hopkins Jr, EdD; children: Christina Elizabeth. **Educ:** Seton Hill College, BA, mathematics, 1953. **Career:** Ballistic Rsch Lab, Aberdeen Proving Ground MD, mathematician 1954-60; Spacetrack System Div LG Hanscom Field MA, mathematician 1960-68; Dynatrend Inc Woburn MA, staff accountant 1972-81; IOCS Inc, fin asst 1981-83; Heritage Meetings & Incentives Inc, acctg mgr 1983-; Krikorian Miller Associates, Bedford MA, operations mgr 1987-93; ECNE, meeting planner. **Orgs:** Mem Amer Assoc of Univ Women 1953-, Amer Math Assoc 1953-68, League of Women Voters of Bedford 1969-; chmn of human resources League of Women Voters of Bedford 1970-76; bd of dir Boston Childrens Svc; pres of bd of dir Roxbury Childrens Serv 1973-79; charter mem Middlesex County Chapter of Links Inc 1976-; pres, Middlesex County Chapter of Links 1976-77; corr sec Middlesex County Chapter of Links 1978-80; membership chairperson, Middlesex County Chapter of Links 1986-88, recording sec 1988-90; membership chmn, AAUW (Bedford-Lexington Branch) 1986-88; AKA Sorority/Rho Epsilon Omega Chapter; AAUW, Bedford Branch, vice pres, 1994-96; Alpha Kappa Alpha Sorority, Inc/Rho Epsilon Omega, treasurer, 1994-96. **Home Addr:** 8 Hilltop Dr, Bedford, MA 01730.

HOPKINS, TELMA
Actress, vocalist. **Personal:** Born Oct 28, 1948, Louisville, KY. **Career:** Tony Orlando and Dawn, singer; Isaac Hayes, backup singer; appeared in film, Future Cop, 1985; television appearances include: Love Boat, 1979, Bosom Buddies, 1980, Dance Fever, 1981, Fantasy Island, Gimme A Break, 1983-87, Circus of the Stars, 1985, Family Matters, 1989-, numerous others. **Business Addr:** Actress, "Family Matters", c/o ABC Productions, 2020 Ave of the Stars, 5th Floor, Los Angeles, CA 90067, (310)557-7777.

HOPKINS, THOMAS FRANKLIN
Researcher, educator, teacher (retired). **Personal:** Born in Culpepper, VA; son of Dorothy L Atkins Hopkins-Brown (deceased) and Thomas Hopkins (deceased); children: Winifred Louise, Thomas M, Charles M, Michael, Arthur G. **Educ:** Calvin Coolidge Coll Boston MA, BS 1955; MI St U, MS 1961; Boston Univ, PhD 1970. **Career:** Worcester Foundation for Experimental Biology, research asst, 1949-60, scientist, 1960-70; Univ of Connecticut, associate professor of biology, 1970-75; Univ of Maryland Eastern Shore, Dept of Natural Science chairman, 1975-86, professor of biology, 1986-94. **Orgs:** Mem, American Physiological Society 1970-; National Science Teachers Association. **Honors/Awds:** Published many journal articles. **Military Serv:** US Marine Corps, Cpl, 1943-46. **Home Addr:** 1602 Camden Ave, Salisbury, MD 21801, (410)742-5067.

HOPKINS, VASHTI EDYTHE JOHNSON
Educator (retired). **Personal:** Born Aug 22, 1924, Virginia; daughter of Matilda Ann Robinson Johnson and Louis Tenner Johnson; married Haywood Hopkins Sr; children: Haywood Jr, Yvonne Andrews, Sharon. **Educ:** Virginia Seminary & Coll, BS 1963; St Paul's Coll, BS Elem Educ 1967; Univ of Virginia, MEd 1969; Southwestern Univ, PhD Educ 1984. **Career:** Amherst City Public Schools, teacher 1963-67; Lynchburg Public Schools, teacher 1967-74; Sandusky Middle School, teacher 1974-82; Virginia Seminary & Coll, prof of English, 1991-97. **Orgs:** Dep organizer Order of Eastern Star PHA 1967-91; Eastern Theological Center; mem Zeta Chap Zeta Phi Beta Sor; life mem NEA, VEA, LEA, Univ of Virginia Alumni Assoc, Century Club St Paul's Coll; mem Daughter of Isis, Golden Circle Past LL Ruler; past pres Episcopal Church Women, pres Amity Soc, Bridgette Soc; mem Natl Sor of Phi Delta Kappa Inc Alpha Tau Chapter Lynchburg Virginia Chapter; Phi Delta Kappa Fraternity, past vice pres of membership; past pres, Lynchburg Retired Teachers, 1989-90; pres, District F Retired Teachers, 1990-92. **Honors/Awds:** Poetry published in Century Magazine 1960; Achievement Award Order of Eastern Star Chapter 40 1984; Outstanding Achievement Grand Chapter of Virginia OESPHA 1984; Golden Poet Award, World of Poetry 1989-96; poems published in 1989, 1992; Golden Treasury of Great Poems. **Home Addr:** Rt 5, Box 630, Lynchburg, VA 24501.

HOPKINS, WES
Professional football player. **Personal:** Born Sep 26, 1961, Birmingham, AL. **Educ:** Southern Methodist Univ, attended. **Career:** Philadelphia Eagles, free safety, 1983-. **Honors/Awds:** Played in 1983 Hula Bowl; named Most Valuable Defensive Player, Cotton Bowl; selected first team All-Pro by Newspaper Enterprises Assn; first team All-NFC, Pro Football Weekly; named Defensive Player of the Week, Sports Illustrated; Conference Defensive Player of the Week, NFL; named NFC Defensive Player of the Month; first team all-pro, AP, Newspaper Enterprise Assn; Pro Football Writers of Amer, The Sporting News, Sports Illustrated, NFL Films; second team, College and Pro Football Newsweekly; first team All-NFC, UPI and Football News; Eagles Defensive MVP; played in Pro Bowl, 1985. **Business Addr:** Philadelphia Eagles, Philadelphia Veterans Stadium, Broad St & Pattison Ave, Philadelphia, PA 19148.

HOPKINS, WILLIAM A.
Appointed official. **Personal:** Born May 27, 1943, Americus, GA; married Desi Page; children: Ellen, Ryan, Christopher, Leslee. **Educ:** Albany State Coll, BA 1968; GA State Univ, MPA 1984. **Career:** St Regis Paper Co, asst indust relations 1967-69; Sentry Ins, dist mgr 1969-72; Insurance Multi Line, territory mgr 1972-77; Piedmont Ins Agency, pres 1977-82. **Orgs:** Vp Atlanta Alumni KAY 1976-78; pres Albany State Alumni 1980-82; bd mem Morris Brown Coll. **Honors/Awds:** Outstanding Young Men of Amer Indust Relations St Regis 1969-72; Lt Col State of GA Governor Staff 1982. **Military Serv:** AUS capt 1962-66. **Business Addr:** Spcl Asst to the Commr of DOAS, Stof GA Dir Small Bus Affairs, 200 Piedmont Ave #1416, Atlanta, GA 30334.

HOPPER, CORNELIUS LENARD
Educational administrator. **Personal:** Born Aug 30, 1934, Hartshorne, OK; son of Hazel Pugh Hopper and Claude Hopper; married Barbara M Johnson; children: Adriane, Brian, Michael. **Educ:** OH Univ Athens, OH, AB 1956; Univ of Cincinnati Coll of Med, MD 1960. **Career:** Univ of WI Neurology, instructor 1967-68, asst prof 1968-71; Tuskegee Inst, med dir 1971-74; Univ of AL School of Med, asst clin prof 1971-79; Univ of CA, special asst for health affairs 1979-83; Univ of CA, vice pres for health affairs 1983-. **Orgs:** Consultant to Office of Special Programs Bureau of Health Manpower Educ NIH 1972-79; consult Amer Public Health Assn Div of Intl Health Program 1974-; pres AL State Med Assn 1974-79; assoc mem Amer Acad Neurology Natl Med Assn; mem Amer Assn for Advancement of Sci; mem Assn of Academic Health Centers; mem Golden State Med Assn; mem DHEW Natl Advisory Council on Professional Standards Review Org (PSRO) 1974-78; mem Natl Adv Comm to the Robert Wood Johnson Found Comm Hosp-Med Staff Sponsored Primary Care Group Practice Program 1974-82; mem VA Med Sch Asst Review Comm 1975-76; mem Natl Adv Comm to the Robert Wood Johnson Found Nurse Faculty Fellowships Program 1976-82; mem CA Health Manpower Policy Comm 1981-; mem Epilepsy Found of Amer, Natl Info and Resource Center Advisory Comm 1982-; vice pres, California Assn of HMOs Foundation, 1994-. **Honors/Awds:** Special Research Fellow in Demyelinating Diseases Natl Inst of Neurological Disease and Blindness 1967-68; Alumnus of the Year OH Univ 1985; Medal of Merit OH Univ 1985; publications including, PSRO, A Current Status Report Proceedings of Sixth Annual Conf on the Southern Region Conf on the Humanities and Public Policy May, 1976; The Health Care Delivery System, A Rural Perspective Contact '72 - Proceedings of the Governor's Health manpower Conference 174, 1972; with CG Matthews and CS Cleeland, Symptom Instability and Thermoregulation in Multiple Sclerosis Neurology 22, 142, 1972; with CS Cleeland and CG Matthews, MMPI Profiles in Exacerbation and Remission of Multiple Sclerosis Psychological Reports 27, 343, 1970. **Military Serv:** USN Battalion Surgeon 4th Marines served 2 yrs. **Home Addr:** l4201 Skyline Blvd, Oakland, CA 94619-3625. **Business Addr:** Vice President for Health Affairs, University of California System, 300 Lakeside Dr, 18th Fl, Oakland, CA 94612-3550.

HOPPES, ALICE FAYE
Community activist. **Personal:** Born May 20, 1939, Tucumcari, NM; daughter of Bessie Mae Gamble Kent and Harold Kent; married Willard Paul Hoppes, Aug 24, 1968; children: LaDonna Hall Gamble, Toia Hall Hezekiah, Deidra Hall Faulkner, Linda Gail Hoppes. **Educ:** Eastern New Mexico Univ, Portales NM, 1963-65. **Career:** Mountain Bell, Albuquerque NM, operator, 1970-74, accounts clerk, 1974-80, order writer, 1980-82; US West Communications, Albuquerque NM, maintenance admin, 1982-90. **Orgs:** Treasurer, Amer Business Women, 1981-82; chairperson, Black Child Devel Inc, 1983-84; nominee, State of New Mexico, State Representative Dist 24, 1985-86; ward chair, Ward 24B Democratic Party, 1985-87; vice pres, Natl Council of Negro Women, 1985-86; treasurer, Democratic Women of Bernalillo County, 1985-86; vice pres, Democratic Council, New Mexico, 1985-89; mem, Albuquerque City Minority & Women's Task Force, 1985-; pres, NAACP, Albuquerque Branch, 1984-96; pres, Nia Foundation, 1994-96; pres, Ujima Foundation, 1996-. **Honors/Awds:** Outstanding Community Serv, Mountain Bell Fund, 1986; Unsung Heroine, NAACP, 1986; Certificate of Appreciation, Outstanding Volunteer, Governor Toney Anaya, State of New Mexico, 1986; Certificate of Nomination, State of New Mexico, State Representative Dist 13, 1986; Outstanding Community Srv, Winnie Mandella Award, 1987; Certificate of Appreciation, Secretary of State, Rebecca Vigil-Giron, 1987; Toastmaster Intl Award, Toastmaster Intl, 1987; Omega Citizen of the Year, Omega Psi Phi Frat, 1987; Editor's Choice Awd, Outstanding Achievement in Poetry, The National Library of Poetry, 1996; Liberty Bell Awd, Law Day USA, 1995. **Home Addr:** 13113 Pinehurst Ave NE, Albuquerque, NM 87111-3049.

HOPPS, JOHN, JR.
Educational administrator. **Personal:** Born Jun 22, 1938, Dallas, TX; son of John (deceased) & Ethel; married June Gary Hopps, Apr 23, 1965; children: Jessica, Matthew. **Educ:** Morehouse College, BS, chemistry/math, 1958; MIT, MS, chemistry, 1961; Brandeis University, PhD, physics, 1971. **Career:** Nashua Corp, research scientist, 1964-67; Sanders Assoc, Inc, mgr laboratory for optical svcs, 1967-71; Ohio State Univ, Dept of Physics, asst prof, 1971-1977; Massachusetts Institute of Technology, research affiliate, 1977-1995; Charles Stark Draper Lab, chief, photonics technology, 1977-1995; Natl Sci Foundation, dir, div of materials research, 1992-95; Morehouse Coll, provost/sr vp of Acad Affairs, 1996-. **Orgs:** Natl Res Coun, natl

materials advisory bd; Oak Ridge Assoc Universities, bd of dirs; Amer Assn for the Advancement of Sci; Amer Physical Society; Amer Society for Metals; Carver Fund, advisory bd; Materials Research Society; Biosphere 2 Center, Columbia Univ, academic programs advvisory bd. **Honors/Awds:** Phi Beta Kappa; Ford Foundation Early Admissions Scholar, MC, 1954; Beta Kappa Chi, 1957; Morehouse College, Cum Laude Graduate, 1958; Golden Key Honor Society, 1996. **Special Achievements:** "Electromagnetic and Particle Scattering in Collisional Plasmas," 1976; "Direct Variational Approach to the Calculation of Dynamic Structure Functions," 1976; "MIT Reactor Fault, Tolerant Systems Demonstration," 1985; "Safety Parameter Display Systems: A High Information Reliability Design Concept," 1982; "New Perspectives on Materials Research Education in the US," 1994. **Business Phone:** (404)215-2647.

HOPSON, HAROLD THEODORE, II (SONNY)
Business executive. **Personal:** Born Jan 24, 1937, Abington, PA; children: Ronald, Lynette, Regina, Lisa-Shelia, Harold III, Kelley Lynette Washington, Ashley Lorraine Stanley, Ronald John II. **Educ:** Philadelphia Wireless Sch, 3 post grad courses, 3rd class Radio Telephone Operators License 1965. **Career:** Harold Randolph & Harvey Schmidt, div Ins Investigator, 1958-65; Philadelphia Tribune, writer/reporter, 1965-66; Pepsi Generation Come Alive Radio Personality, 1965-66; Radio station WHAT-AM Philadelphia, communicator & radio personality, 1965-71, 1980-86; Scene Philadelphia & Tribune, entertainment critic & reviewer 1966-67; Sonny Hopson's Celebrity Lounge, proprietor, 1969-73; WDAS AM-FM Radio Station, asst to president, 1978; WHTH-FM Radio, owner, 1986-; Steven M Kramer, Attorney at Law, Phila, NY, NJ, LA, special asst, 1977-97. **Orgs:** Pres, founder, new chairman, Concerned Communicators, 1971-; NAACP, 1957-; SCLC, 1965-; organizer, People United to Save Humanity, 1971-; Jazz at Home Club, 1968-; Natl Assn of Radio & TV Announcers, 1965-; cofounder, Natl Black Media Coalition. **Honors/Awds:** Special Serv Awd YMCA 1968; BSA Cit Awd 1967; Inter Urban Leag Awd of Phila 1967; Disc Jockey of Yr Awd 1969; Mayor of Phila Youth 1970; Sickle Cell Anemia Research Awd 1966; Jazz at Home Club of Am Achvmnt Awd 1971; mention in Books The Sound of Philadelphia & The Greatest Muhammad Ali; The Sonny Hopson Stories, Philadelphia Tribune; Life Mag, stories with Richie Allen; Sepia, stories with Major Coxsum and Sonny Wall, 1973; newspapers, Philadelphia Tribune, 1968, Philadelphia Enquirer, Philadelphia Daily News. **Military Serv:** USAF 1954-57. **Business Addr:** 4936 Wynnefield Ave, Philadelphia, PA 19131.

HOPSON, MELVIN CLARENCE
Development administrator. **Personal:** Born Jun 29, 1937, Sawyersville, AL; son of Irene Hopson and Lovell Hopson Sr; divorced; children: Steven, Wayne, Myra. **Educ:** Roosevelt Univ, BA English 1966. **Career:** Montgomery Ward, store Mgr 1968, dir EEO 1969-80; McDonalds Corp, assistant vp, diversity development, 1994-. **Orgs:** Bd mem Chicago Urban League 1971; pres Chicago Urban Affairs Council 1983; bd mem Chicago NAACP 1984; polemarch Kappa Alpha Psi; board of dirs, YMCA, 1985-; officer, Rat Pac Inc, 1980-. **Honors/Awds:** Man of year Chicago Urban League 1980; view from the top EEO Today Article 1980; Urban League. **Military Serv:** USAF sgt 1957-61. **Business Addr:** Assistant Vice-President, Diversity Development, McDonalds Corp, Kroc Dr, Hinsdale, IL 60523.

HORAD, SEWELL D., SR.
Educator. **Personal:** Born Jan 26, 1922, Washington, DC; married Ella Garnett; children: Sewell D, Jr, Denise H. **Educ:** Howard U, BS 1942; George Washington U, MA 1973. **Career:** Washington DC Public Schools, admin officer Special Educ present, teacher Mathematics, sci physically handicapped children 1958-72. **Orgs:** Prtcptd in summer sch, night sch prog 13 Yrs; instrumental in developing new techniques for tchng handicapped chldrn, some have been copyrighted; real estate salesman family owned bus 1946-; mem Mason; vice pres "What Good Are We" Club, oldest Black Clubs in DC; "Pro-duffers" Golf Club of DC; author "Fraction Computer", math book designed to solve fractional problems without finding least common denominator; invented an inf retrieval system. **Military Serv:** AUS capt 1942-46. **Business Addr:** 5511 Illinois Ave NW, Washington, DC 20011.

HORD, FREDERICK LEE (MZEE LASANA OKPARA)
Educator, author. **Personal:** Born Nov 7, 1941, Kokomo, IN; son of Jessie Tyler Hord and Noel E Hord; divorced; children: Teresa D Hord-Owens, F Mark, Laurel E. **Educ:** IN State Univ, BS 1963, MS 1965; Union Grad Sch, PhD 1987. **Career:** Wabash Coll, prof of black studies 1972-76; IN Univ, guest lecturer black studies 1976; Frostburg State Univ, asst dir minority affairs 1980-84; Howard Univ, prof of Afro-Amer studies 1984-87; W Virginia Univ, director for Center for Black Culture, 1987-88; Knox College, director of black studies, 1988-. **Orgs:** Performer/lecturer PANFRE 1981-; consulting editor Nightsun; regional consultant NAMSE; consultant on black studies Aframeric Enterprises; Association for Black Culture Centers, founder; pres, Natl Assn for Black Culture Centers. **Honors/Awds:** Governor's Awd for being the Outstanding Black Male Scholar in Indiana Colls & Univs 1963; poems and articles in major black journals such as Illinois Issues, Words Work, Black Books Bulletin, The Western Journal of Black Studies, Black American Literature Forum, Obsidian II; featured poet in Fall 1982 issue of The Western Journal of Black Studies; book of essays "Reconstruction Memory," Third World Press 1991; book of poems "Life Sentences: Freeing Black Relationships;" Third World Press, 1995; co-editor: "I Am Because We Are: Readings in Black Philosophy," 1995; book of poems "After-(h)ours," Third World Press 1974; lead article, West Virginia Law Review on Black Culture Centers, Summer 1989. **Special Achievements:** Editor of first book on Black Culture Centers: "Black Culture Centers: Inside Out," poem in 25th anniversary issue of Essence. **Business Addr:** Director of Black Studies, Knox College, Box 13, Galesburg, IL 61401.

HORD, NOEL EDWARD
Company executive. **Personal:** Born Jul 10, 1946, Kokomo, IN; son of Jessie Mae Tyler Hord and Noel Ernest Hord; married Cora Eileen Ritchie Hord, Jul 10, 1966 (deceased); children: Michelle Denise, Noel Daniel. **Educ:** Indiana State Univ, Terre Haute, IN, 1967. **Career:** Wohl Shoe Co, Clayton, MO, various responsibilities, 1967-84; Nine West Group, vp of operations, 1984-86, svp/gen mgr, 1986-87; Enzol Angiolini Div, pres, 1988-91, group pres, 1991-93; US Shoe Corp, Footwear Group, pres/CEO, 1993-. **Orgs:** Urban League's Natl Black Executive Exchange Program; Concerned Black Man of Action for Youth in Danbury, CT, co-founder; Hord Foundation, Danbury, CT, co-founder. **Honors/Awds:** James C Taylor Personal Award, Outstanding Work in Human Resources & Career Development, 1980; Footwear News Man of the Year, 1994. **Business Addr:** US Shoe Corporation, 1 Eastwood Drive, Cincinnati, OH 45227.

HORN, JOSEPH
Professional football player. **Personal:** Born Jan 16, 1972, Tupelo, MS; married Lacreshia; children: Jhia, Joseph. **Educ:** Itawamba Community College. **Career:** Kansas City Chiefs, wide receiver, 1996-. **Business Addr:** Professional Football Player, Kansas City Chiefs, One Arrowhead Dr, Kansas City, MO 64129, (816)924-9300.

HORN, LAWRENCE CHARLES
Educator. **Personal:** Born Jul 7, 1938, Abilene, TX; son of Isabella Wheeler Rhodes and Alonzo Horn; married Lee Ester Cross, Mar 6, 1971; children: Kenya La Dawn. **Educ:** TN St A&I Univ, 1956-57; Langston Univ, BMusEd 1957-61; Abilene Christian Univ, 1962; Univ of OK, MMED 1971. **Career:** AUS, infantry & bandman 1962-64; Woodson H S Abilene Pub Sch, Teacher 1964-65; Ms Valley St Univ, teacher 1965-. **Orgs:** Life mem Kappa Kappa Psi Hnry Band Frat 1959-; stdnt advsr Music Educators Natl Conf 1965-; mem AAUP 1965-; past pres coll div Ms Music Educ Assn 1982-83; sec Phi Delta Kappa 1982-; bd of dir Sch Of Religious Studies 1982-; basileus Omega Psi Phi Frat Inc 1983-90; instructor, Mid-Delta Band, MVSU 1986, 1989, 1990; MVSU Honor Band 1987; adv Alpha Kappa Mu Hon Soc 1985-; pres LS Rogers Elem School PTA 1988-89; Collegiate Division Sponsor, Mississippi Music Educators Assn 1988-; chairman, honor's committee, Mississippi Valley State University, 1989-91. **Honors/Awds:** Service Lyceum Com MVSU Lyceum Com 1980; Omega man of yr Beta Rho Chap Omega Psi Phi Frat 1982; soloist Messiah MVSU Concert Choir 1983 & 84; Service Award Phi Delta Kappa Utica Chapter 1988; MVSU Teacher of Year Miss Legislature 1989; Service Award, Omega Psi Phi Fraternity, Beta Rho Chapter, 1990. **Military Serv:** AUS pfc 2 yrs; sharp shooter 1962-64.

HORNBUCKLE, NAPOLEON
Electronics company executive. **Personal:** Born Feb 16, 1942, Birmingham, AL; son of Louisa Coleman Hornbuckle and Lee E Hornbuckle; married Dorothy Jeanne Hornbuckle, Sep 4, 1964; children: Scott, Vance. **Educ:** Tennessee State University, Nashville, TN, BA, electronics engineering, 1964. **Career:** Motorola Inc, Scottsdale, AZ, development engineer manager, comm division, 1965-, project engineer manager, comm division, project leader manager, comm division, marketing development manager, comm division, vice president/director, comm division, Motorola Inc, Chandler, AZ, vice president/general manager, SED, 1990-. **Orgs:** Member, Armed Forces Communications Assoc, 1976-, Electronics Industry Assoc, 1976-, National Security Industrial Assoc, 1984-, NAACP, 1987-, Omega Psi Phi Fraternity, 1964, Boule 1988-. **Honors/Awds:** Black Engineer of the Year, US Black Engineer Magazine, 1990; Mobil Corp, Council of Engineering Deans of the Historically Black Colleges and Universities, 1990.

HORNBURGER, JANE M.
Educator. **Personal:** Born Aug 26, 1928, Fayetteville, NC; daughter of Ella Carter Melvin and Roy D Melvin; married Aug 19, 1950 (divorced). **Educ:** Fayetteville State University, BS, 1948; New York University, MA, 1950, EdD, 1970. **Career:** Kinston, North Carolina Public Schools, teacher, grades 7-8, 1948-53; Wilmington, Delaware Public Schools, teacher, grades 2-9, 1954-66, supervisor reading/language arts, 1966-69, director teacher training, 1969-72, Boston University, assistant professor, 1972-77; Brooklyn College CUNY, associate professor, 1978-. **Orgs:** International Reading Association, board mem, 1987-90, chairperson, headquarters comm, 1989-90, chairperson, policy guidelines comm, 1981-83; National Council of Teachers of English, comm mem commctng research, 1989-92, classroom practices comm, 1978-81, 1985-88, editoral board, 1981-84; New York State Reading Association, chairman literacy advocate award, 1990-; Bronx Reading Council, president IRA honor council, 1987-89. **Honors/Awds:** International Reading Association, Leader in Literature, 1991; National Council of Teachers of English, Named to Talent File, 1989; New York State Reading Association, Regional Award in Reading Education, 1989; New York University Board of Trustees, Founder's Day Award, 1971; American Association University Women, Woman of the Year, 1968. **Special Achievements:** Author: African Countries and Cultures: A Concise Illustrated Dictionary, 1981; Focus: Teaching English Language Arts, 1981; "Deep Are the Roots: Busing in Boston," Journal of Negro Education, 1976; Teaching Multicultural Children, 1976; So You Have an Aide: A Guide for Teachers in the Use of Classroom Aides, 1968.

HORNE, AARON
College administrator. **Personal:** Born Dec 3, 1940, Chipley, FL; son of Laura & Albert Horne; married Myrtle Horne; children: Ericka, Michelle, Aaron Jr. **Educ:** Tennessee State Univ, BS, 1968; Roosevelt Univ, MM, 1972; Univ of Iowa, MFA, 1973, doctorate of musical arts, 1976; Univ of New Hampshire Institute for Enrollment, mgmt diploma, 1990; Harvard Univ, Graduate School of Education, diploma, 1993. **Career:** Floria A & M Univ, assistant professor, 1968-72; Univ of Iowa, lecturer, 1973-76; Texas Southern Univ, associate professor, 1976-77; Northwestern Univ, senior lecturer, 1982-89; Northeastern Illinois Univ, professor & dir of jazz studies, 1977-89; Bd of Governors Univs, asst vice chancellor for academic affairs, 1990-. **Orgs:** Duke Ellington Society, bd member, 1988-; American Assn for Higher Education, 1989-; Music Educators National Conference, 1977-; International Assn for Jazz Educators, exec bd, 1982-83, 1970-; Black Music Caucus, 1989-; Illinois Committee on Black Concerns in Higher Education, 1989-; National Assn of College Wind & Percussion Instructors, 1972-. **Honors/Awds:** Music Educators National Conference, Certificate of Excellence, 1984; Northeastern Illinois Univ, Presidential Merit Award, 1982; National Endowment of the Arts, Artist in Residence Grant/Award, 1982; National Assn of Jazz Educators, Outstanding Service to Jazz, 1981; Lublin Jazz Festival, Honored Participant, 1980. **Special Achievements:** Brass Music of Black Composers, Greenwood Press, 1995; Keyboard Music of Black Composers, Greenwood Press, 1992; String Music of Black Composers, Greenwood Press, 1991; Woodwind Music of Black Composers, Greenwood Press, 1990; Music Educators National Conference, Featured Artist, 1978. **Military Serv:** US Army, spec-4, 1958-61. **Business Addr:** Assistant Vice Chancellor for Academic & Student Affairs, Bd of Governors Universities, Chancellor's Office, 700 East Adams St, Ste 200, Springfield, IL 62701-1601.

HORNE, DEBORAH JEAN
Television journalist. **Personal:** Born Jul 26, 1953, Newport News, VA; daughter of Daisy Mae Pellman Horne and Willie Edward Horne. **Educ:** Hampton University, Hampton, VA, BA, 1975; Ohio State University, Columbus, OH, MA, 1976. **Career:** Providennce Journal, Providence, RI, general assignment reporter, 1976-81; WPRI-TV, East Providence, RI, chief reporter, 1981-. **Orgs:** Architectural preservation, board member, Elmwood Foundation, 1989-; board member, Big Sister Assn of RI, 1986-90; former pres, Delta Sigma Theta, Inc, 1974-; board member, Volunteer League of Rhode Island, 1981-82; volunteer, Shelter for Battered Women, 1983-86. **Honors/Awds:** Massachusetts Associated Press Highest Award, "A Question of Rape," special TV program, 1985; 1st place, features, "Chatham Houses: Washed Away," New England United Press International, 1989; 1st place, continuing coverage, "Ocean Dumping," lead reporter, 1989, 2nd place, spot news, "Coventry Chemical Fire," 1989, Massachusetts Associated Press Broadcasters Award. **Business Addr:** Chief Reporter, News, WPRI-TV, 25 Catamore Blvd, East Providence, RI 02914-1203.

HORNE, EDWIN CLAY
Dentist. **Personal:** Born Feb 16, 1924, Greensboro, NC; son of Annie Slade Horne (deceased) and Ellis Clay Horne (deceased); married Gene Ann Polk-Horne MD, Aug 23, 1952; children: Carol Anne Horne-Penn, Edwin Christian Horne. **Educ:** NC A&T State Univ, BS 1947; School of Dentistry Univ of PA, DDS 1952. **Career:** Harlem Hospital, assoc attending dentist 1954-95; Upper Harlem Comprehensive Care Ctr, attending dentist, attending dental supervisor 1985-89; Private Practice, dentist; North Central Bronx-Montefiore Hosp Affiliation, clinical assoc supervisor 1973-, adj prof of clinical dentistry for Columbia Univ Sch of Dental and Oral Surgery, 1980-; Univ of Pennsylvania, School of Dental Medicine, adjunct professor, 1994-. **Orgs:** Fellow, Am Coll of Dentists; Mem First District Dental Soc of New York; mem Omega Psi Phi Frat 1945-, Sigma Pi Phi Frat 1967-; mem Reveille Club of New York 1971-; mem Lions Intl Englewood NJ 1978-; corp mem, 1980-, brd 3rd vice pres, 1988-89, Schomburg Corp, Schomburg Ctr for Rsch in Black Culture; sire archon North East Region Sigma Pi Phi Frat 1987-88; mem North Carolina A&T State Univ

Alumni; mem bd of dirs Univ of PA-Metro New Jersey Alumni Assoc 1987; exec bd, U of PA Dental School Alumni Soc, 1989-90; comm mem visual aids Annual November Dental Convention New York City past 10 yrs. **Honors/Awds:** Man of the Year Awd Kappa Omicron Chap Omega Psi Phi Frat 1970; honored for 40 yrs Meritorious Membership Omega Psi Phi Frat August 1986 Washington DC. **Military Serv:** AUS. **Home Addr:** 374 Miller Ave, Englewood, NJ 07631.

HORNE, GENE-ANN P. See POLK, GENE-ANN.

HORNE, GERALD CHARLES
Professor. **Personal:** Born Jan 3, 1949, St Louis, MO; son of Jerry Horne and Flora Horne; married Savenda, May 25, 1994. **Educ:** Princeton Univ, BA, 1970; Univ California-Berkeley, JD, 1973; Columbia Univ , PhD, 1982. **Career:** Affirmative Action Coord Center, dir counsel 1979-82; Sarah Lawrence Coll, prof, 1982-88; Natl Conf of Black Lawyers, exec dir, 1985-86; Local 1199 Health and Hospital Workers Union AFL-CIO, special counsel, 1986-88; Univ of California, Santa Barbara, prof; Univ of North Carolina, prof, currently. **Orgs:** Natl Lawyers Guild, Intl Committee, chair, 1988-92; Natl Conf of Black Lawyers, Intl Committee, chair, 1982-85; Pears and Freedom Party, chair, 1991-92; American Federation of Teachers, Local 2274, sec/treas, 1976-78. **Honors/Awds:** Natl Conf of Black Lawyers, Hope Stevens Award, 1983; Univ of California, Santa Barbara, Getman Service to Students Award, 1990; Council on Intl Exchange of Scholars, Fullbright Scholar/Univ of Zimbabwe, 1995; Univ of Virginia, Carter G Woodson Fellow, 1991-92; City Univ of NY, Belle Zeller Visiting Prof, 1993-94. **Special Achievements:** Publications include: Black Liberation/Red Scare: Ben Davis and the Communist Party, London: Associates Univ Presses, 1994; Reversing Discrimination: The Case for Affirmative Action, Intl Publishers, 1992; Thinking and Re-thinking US History, Council on Intl Books for Children, 1989; Communist Front? Civil Rights Congress, London: Associates Univ Presses, 1988; Black and Red: W E B DuBois and the Afro-American Response to the Cold War, 1944-63, State Univ of NY Press, 1986.

HORNE, JUNE C.
Buyer. **Personal:** Born Sep 6, 1953, New York, NY; daughter of Ceceill Sledge Smith and Samuel Smith; married Frank Horne, Mar 30, 1972. **Educ:** Lab Inst of Merchandising, BS 1971. **Career:** Saks Fifth Ave, exec trainee 1971-72, asst buyer swimwear/sportswear 1976-78, buyer swimwear 1977-79, buyer designer sportswear 1978-82; Saks Garden City Branch, 1st black female store gen mgr 1982-84; Saks Fifth Ave, assoc div merch mgr designer sportswear 1985-92; dir of designer sportswear 1986-, sr buyer designer sportswear and RTW, 1992-. **Orgs:** Mem YMCA of Greater NY Black Achievers, Black Retail Action Group; Fashion Outreach. **Honors/Awds:** Black Achievers in Industry Awd YMCA of Greater NY 1979; Interviewed for NY Times Article ''A Buyer's View of the Busy World of Fashion'' 1980; Buyer Achievement Awd Black Retail Action Group 1982. **Business Addr:** Senior Buyer, Saks Fifth Avenue, 12 East 49th Street, New York, NY 10024.

HORNE, JUNE MERIDETH
Psychiatric technician (retired). **Personal:** Born Feb 23, 1936, Chicago, IL; daughter of Elizabeth Neal-Browder and William Browder; married Brazell Horne, Oct 6, 1954 (deceased); children: Brazell Rodney. **Educ:** Kennedy King Jr Coll, attended 1974-75. **Career:** Veterans Administration, psychiatric tech 1964-94. **Orgs:** Pres Browder and Watts Inc 1985; International Biographical Center, International Order of Merit, 1990; Women's Inner Circle of Achievement, American Biographical Institute, 1990; International Parliament for Safety and Peace, 1991, 1992. **Honors/Awds:** Emergency Escape Apparatus (invention) US Patent 4-498-557, 1985; Knighthood, 1991, Lofsensic Ursinius Order, Foundation Ethiopia Netherland; Knighthood, 1992, Order Souberain Et Militaire De La Milice Du Saint Sepuulcre of Confederation of Chivalry, Australia.

HORNE, LENA
Vocalist, dancer, actress. **Personal:** Born Jun 30, 1917, Brooklyn, NY; daughter of Lena Calhoun Horne and Edwin F Horne; married Louis J Jones (divorced); children: Gail, Teddy (deceased). **Career:** Theater appearances include: ''Dance with Your Gods,'' 1934; ''Jamaica,'' 1957; ''Tony Bennett and Lena Horne Sing,'' 1974; ''Lena Horne: The Lady and Her Music,'' 1981, toured major US cities, 1982; ''Nine O'Clock Revue,'' US and Canada, 1961; film appearances include: Duke Is the Tops, 1938; Cabin in the Sky, 1943; Stormy Weather, 1943; Broadway Rhythm, 1944; Till the Clouds Roll By, 1946; Death of a Gunfighter, 1969; The Wiz, 1978; television appearances include: ''Music '55,'' 1955; ''The Perry Como Show,'' 1959; ''Here's to the Ladies,'' 1960; ''Bell Telephone Hour,'' 1964; ''The Cosby Show''; ''Sanford and Son''; ''The Ed Sullivan Show''; ''The Tonight Show''; ''The Lena Horne Show,'' 1959; ''The Frank Sinatra Timex Show,'' 1960; ''The Milton Berle Special,'' 1962; ''Lena in Concert,'' 1969; ''Harry and Lena,'' 197''Keep US Beautiful,'' 1973; related career: Cotton Club, chorus member, singer, 1933; Noble Sissle's Orchestra, appeared with, 1935-36; Charlie Barnet Band, appeared with, 1940-41; writings include: In Person, autobiography, 1950; co-author, Lena, autobiography, 1965; recordings include: Birth of the Blues, 1940; Moanin' Low, 1940; Little Girl Blue, 1942; A Date with Fletcher Henderson, 1944; Till the Clouds Roll By, 1946; Words and Music, 1948; At the Waldorf, 1958; Sands, 1961; Like Latin, 1963; On the Blue Side, 1962; Lena Horne Sings Your Requests, 1963; Lena Goes Latin, 1963; Classics in Blue; Porgy and Bess; The Lady Is a Tramp; First Lady; The One and Only; Standing Room Only; Stormy Weather; We'll Be Together Again, Blue Note Records, 1994. **Orgs:** Actors' Equity Assn; Screen Actors Guild; American Federation of Television & Radio Artists; American Guild of Musical Artists; American Guild of Variety Artists; NAACP; Natl Council on Negro Women. **Honors/Awds:** Page One Award, New York Newspaper Guild; Black Filmmakers Hall of Fame; Handel Medallion, Highest Cultural Award; Drama Desk Award, Best Actress in a Musical; Third Annual Young Audiences Arts Award; Ebony's Lifetime Achievement Award; New York Drama Critics Poll Award, Best Performance by Female Lead in Musical, ''Jamaica,'' 1958, Circle Award, ''Lena Horne: The Lady and her Music''; Special Citation, Antoinette Perry Special Award, 1981; Spingarn Award, NAACP, 1983; Kennedy Center Honors Award, Lifetime Contribution to Arts, 1984; Paul Robeson Award, Actors' Equity Assn, 1985; Pied Piper Award, American Assn of Composers, Authors & Publishers, 1987; two Grammy Awards; Honorary Degrees: Howard University, Spelman College. **Business Addr:** Entertainer, c/o Edward White & Cot, 21700 Oxnard St, Ste 400, Woodland Hills, CA 91367.

HORNE, MARVIN L. R., JR.
Project manager. **Personal:** Born Mar 5, 1936, Richmond, VA; married Vernell Bell; children: Marvin III, Tracy R, Carl E, Kelly M. **Educ:** VA State Coll, BS Physics 1957; Howard Univ graduate school Physics, 1959-60; Univ of Rochester, MBA 1975. **Career:** US Naval Weapons Lab, math/physicist 1960-61; Gen Elec Co, physicist 1961-63; US Naval Weapons Lab, math/physicist 1963-65; Eastman Kodak Co, engrg mgr 1965-. **Orgs:** Mem Amer Inst of Aero & Astronautics 1963-67; mem Tech Marketing Soc of Amer 1978-; mem Sigma Pi Sigma 1954-57; mem Kappa Mu Epsilon 1954-57; mem Alpha Phi Alpha Frat 1954-; mem Beta Gamma Sigma 1975-; chmn Rochester City Planning commn 1977-82. **Military Serv:** AUS 1st lt 1957-59; Letter of Commendation. **Business Addr:** Engineering Manager, Eastman Kodak Co, 901 Elmgrove Rd, Rochester, NY 14650.

HORNE, SEMMION N.
Business executive. **Personal:** chilDren: Raymond N. **Educ:** Dorchester Academy; Spring Garden Inst. **Career:** Horne & Howard Const Co, line mechanic 23 yrs; Somerset Hls & Co Natl Bank, Pres Adv Bd. **Orgs:** NAACP pres; mem Rent Leveling Bd; Community Church of God. **Honors/Awds:** Awarded Life Mem Wise Owl Club.

HORNE, WESTRY GROVER
Educational administrator (retired). **Personal:** Born Feb 20, 1913, Rocky Mount, NC; son of Florida Horne and Westry Horne; married Dorothy Bailey; children: DeLois Jacqueline Brown, Dorothy Judith Hamblin. **Educ:** Clark Coll Atlanta, BS 1938; NY Univ, MA 1948; Univ of PA Phila, MS 1956. **Career:** Jasper Co Training Sch Monticello GA, prin 1938-39; Warren Co Training Sch Wise NC, asst prin & librarian 1939-40; Natl Youth Admin Prog A&T Coll Greensboro NC, prof & dir 1940-41; Natl Youth Admin for NC, dir 1941-43; USO Camp Edwards Hyannis MA, dir 1943-44; USO Prog Camp Kilmer, dir 1944-50; Harlem YMCA NY, gen prog sec 1950-58; Woodbridge Township Schs NJ, supv elem ed 1958-63; NJ State Dept of Ed, dir elem educ & coord of migrant educ 1963-67; Ofc for Civil Rights US Dept of HEW, dir ed div 1967-77; Fair Housing & Equal Oppor US Dept of Housing & Urban Devel, dir contract compliance 1977-78; Ofc Fed Contract Compliance Progs US Dept of Labor Newark, area dir, beginning 1978. **Orgs:** Mem Edges Group Inc; mem Amer Library Assn; charter mem Natl Assn of Social Workers; mem Amer Educ Assn; mem NEA; state pres Frontiers Intl Serv Clubs; chmn NC Council on Employment Oppors; pres USO Staff Conf Camp Kilmer NJ; chmn Natl Youth Admin Adv Council for NC; organizer vol groups from So NJ & New York City for couns & Hostesses for servicemen stationed & passing through Camp Kilmer NJ; mem Assn of Sec Intl YMCA; mem Masonic Order F & AM; mem Frontiers Intl Serv Clubs; mem NJ Duplicate Bridge Club; mem Amer Tennis Assn; mem Natl Rec Assn; mem Alpha Phi Alpha Frat; pres Coll Student Cncl;pres Coll Chap YMCA; pres Coll Dramatic Club; pres Alpha Phi Alpha Frat; vice chmn Watchung Area Council BSA; mem United Comm Fund Plainfield Area; bd dirs Plainfield ArеaYMCA; chmn adult prog & bership com Plainfield Area YMCA; supr Little Theatre Group Harlem; dir City & Statewide Tennis Activities. **Honors/Awds:** Outstanding Educator of Amer Awd NEA 1967; Outstanding Comm Serv Awd Frontiers Intl Serv Clubs 1975; named Westry G Horne Day City of Plainfield NJ 1980; Feb 28 1980 Westry G Horne Day Gen Assembly of NJ 1980.

HORNE-MCGEE, PATRICIA J.
Educational administrator. **Personal:** Born Dec 23, 1946, Ypsilanti, MI; daughter of Louise Hardwick Horne and Lacy Horne Sr; married Columbus McGee, Aug 4, 1979. **Educ:** MI State Univ, BA 1968; Univ of MI, MSW 1971; Eastern MI Univ, MA 1973; UCLA Management Fellow, 1993. **Career:** MI State Dept of Social Svcs, caseworker 1968-69; Ann Arbor Model Cities, social coord 1970-72; Washtenaw Co Comm Coordinated Child Care, exec dir 1971-74; Ferris State Univ, asst prof 1974-79; Mercy Coll of Detroit, assoc prof/program dir social work dept 1979-88; Wayne County Intermediate School District, assoc dir, 1987-94; Wayne State Univ, adjunct prof, 1988-; Washtenaw Community Coll, Ann Arbor, MI, adjunct prof, 1989-; Wayne County Regional Education Service Agency, director, 1994-. **Orgs:** Sec Huron Valley Assoc of Black Social Workers 1971-; Head Start, consultant Wayne Co, Washtenaw Co, Region V, Empire Design, CSR, 1980; planning commissioner City of Ypsilanti 1982-; bd mem, 1983-, 2nd Vice Pres, 1988-94, Huron Valley Girl Scouts; pres Ann Arbor Delta Sigma Theta 1985-87; mem Natl Assoc of Social Workers; mem Zoning Bd of Appeals City of Ypsilanti; vice pres, Michigan Council, Delta Sigma Theta Sorority. **Home Addr:** 925 Frederick St, Ypsilanti, MI 48197.

HORNSBY, ALTON, JR.
Educator, editor. **Personal:** Born Sep 3, 1940, Atlanta; married Anne R; children: Alton III, Angela. **Educ:** Morehouse Coll, BA, history, 1961; Univ of TX, MA, history, 1962, PhD, history, 1969. **Career:** Tuskegee Inst, instructor of history, 1962-65; independent editor, 1975-; Morehouse College, Department of History, assistant professor, acting chairman, 1968-71, associate professor, 1971-74, chairman, 1971-74, professor, 1974-, Fuller E Calloway professor of history, 1989-. **Orgs:** Assn for the Study of Afro-American Life & History, exec committee, 1977-; Assn of Soc & Behavioral Scientists, president, 1984-85, program committee chair, 1984; So Historical Assn, international committee, 1988-, exec committee, 1989-; State Committee on the Life & History of Black Georgians, chairman, 1968-; So Conference on Afro-American Studies, president, 1983-86, advsy committee, 1979-; editorial boards: The Atlanta Historical Journal, Plantation Societies in the Americas, Western Journal of Black Studies, Dictionary of Georgia Biography; Conference of Editors of Historical Journals; National Council for Black Studies; Organization of American Historians; Georgia Association of Historians. **Honors/Awds:** Woodrow Wilson Fellowship, 1961-62; So Educ Foundation Fellowship, 1966-68; Alpha Phi Alpha, Morehouse Coll, Teacher of the Year, 1971-72; WEB DuBois Award, 1989; United Negro College Fund, Distinguished Scholar, 1982-83, Humanities Fellow, 1981; Rockefeller Humanities Fellowship, 1977-78; Danforth Foundation Associate, 1978-81; Phi Alpha Theta; Phi Beta Kappa; WEB DuBois Award, 1989; Fuller E Callaway Professor of History, 1989; Atlanta Regional Federal Employers Award, 1989; Georgia Association of Historians, Distinguished Service Award, 1990; APEX Museum, Distinguished Historian Award, 1993. **Special Achievements:** Editor: The Dictionary of 20th Century Black Leaders, 1985; The John and Lugenia Burns Hope Papers, 1975-84; The Journal of Negro History, 1976-; author, works include: In the Cage: Eyewitness Accounts of the Freed Negro in Southern Society 1987-1929, 1971; The Black Almanac, 4th rev edition, 1977; The Negro in Revolutionary Georgia, 1972; Chronology of African-American History, 1991; Milestones in 20th-Century African-American History, 1993; articles and reviews in: Journal of Negro History; Journal of American History; Alabama Historical Review; and numerous others; lecturer: Ohio State Univ; Martin Luther King Jr Historic District; Paine College; Jackson State Univ; numerous others; consultant: So Assn of Colleges and Secondary Schools; National Endowment for the Humanities; Georgia Endowment for the Humanities; National Research Council; ''Black Public Education in Atlanta, Georgia: From Segregation to Segregation,'' Journal of Negro History, 1991. **Business Addr:** Chairman, Department of History, Morehouse College, Box 20, Atlanta, GA 30314.

HORNSBY, B. KAY
Mortician. **Personal:** Born Dec 9, 1906, Wolf City, TX; widowed. **Educ:** Bishop Coll Marshall TX, NA 1928; Hampton sch of Embalming Dallas, cert of proficiency 1930; Worsham Coll of Mortuary Sci Chicago, BS 1935. **Career:** Fleming Fraternal Beaumont TX, mortician 1930-35; Thomas Funeral Home Hearn TX, mortician 1935-39; Thomas & Brooks Funeral Home Temple TX, mortician 1939-46; Hornsby Funeral Home Temple TX, mortician/owner/mgr 1946-79; Hornsby & Murcherson Funeral Home, mortician/owner/mgr 1979-. **Orgs:** Pres Natl Council of Negro Women 1949-53; mem comm relations com NAACP Temple Br 1939-; sec Epsilon Nu Delta Mortuary Chap Zeta 1945-; mem Ch Women of Temple 1950-. **Honors/Awds:** Woman of the Yr Awd Independent Funeral Dir Assn of TX 1962; Dr T E Dixon Humanitarian Awd Temple NAACP 1977; David Henderson Jr Awd Temple Youth Council of NAACP 1977; 50 yrs Dedicated Serv Awd TX Funeral Dir Assn 1980. **Business Addr:** Manager, Hornsby & Murcherson Funeral H, 201 S 8th St, Temple, TX 76501.

HORNSBY, WALTER SPURGEON, III
Business executive. **Personal:** Born Sep 6, 1941, Augusta, GA; married Clara J; children: Walter IV, Wendell. **Educ:** Morehouse Coll, BA 1957-61; Univ MI, grad sch 1963. **Career:** The Pilgrim Health & Life Ins Co, exec vp actuary, 1975-76, exec vice pres, beginning 1976, chief executive, currently; Nat Ins Assn, actuary dir, beginning 1971; St Josephs Hosp, dir, begin-

ning 1977. **Orgs:** Mem Augusta Port Authority 1975-; 1st Vp United Way of Richmond & Columbia Co & N Augusta 1978, pres 1979; vice pres prog GA Carolina Council BSA 1979; sec The Sportsmans Boat Club Inc; 2nd vice pres treas chmn United Way 1974-; chmn trustee bd Antioch Bapt Ch 1975-; vchmn Augusta/Richmond Co Data Processing Com 1976-. **Military Serv:** AUS sp-5 1966-68.

HORRY, ROBERT KEITH
Professional basketball player. **Personal:** Born Aug 25, 1970, Andalusia, AL; son of Robert Horry Sr. and Lelia Horry. **Educ:** Alabama. **Career:** Houston Rockets, forward, 1992-96; Los Angeles Lakers, 1996-. **Honors/Awds:** NBA All-Rookie Second Team, 1993. **Special Achievements:** NBA Draft, First round pick, #11, 1992; NBA, Championship, 1994, 1995. **Business Addr:** Professional Basketball Player, Los Angeles Lakers, PO Box 10, Inglewood, CA 90306, (213)419-3100.

HORSFORD, ANNA MARIA
Actress, producer. **Personal:** Born 1949, New York, NY; daughter of Lillian Agatha Richardson Horsford and Victor A Horsford. **Educ:** Inter-American Univ of Puerto Rico, Puerto Rico, 1966-67. **Career:** Actress. Stage appearances: Coriolanus, 1965; In the Well of the House, 1972; Perfection in Black, 1973; Les Femmes Noires, 1974; Sweet Talk, 1975; For Colored Girls Who Have Considered Suicide/When the Rainbow Is Enuf, 1978; Peep, 1981; television appearances: The Guiding Light, 1979; Bill, 1981; Benny's Place, 1982; A Doctor's Story, 1984; Nobody's Child; Amen, 1986-91; Rhythm & Blues, 1992-; films include: An Almost Perfect Affair, 1978; Times Square, 1979; Love Child, 1981; Crackers, 1982. **Orgs:** Variety Club of America; pres, Black Women in Theatre, 1983-84; mem, Sc reen Actors Guild, American Federation of Television and Radio Artists, Actor's Equity. **Honors/Awds:** Best Comedy Actress, Brooklyn Links, 1963; Outstanding Leadership Award, NAACP, 1973.

HORTON, CARL E., SR.
Marketing executive. **Personal:** Born Apr 11, 1944, Philadelphia, PA; son of Dorothy L Horton and W S Horton; married Phyllis Sims Horton, Apr 1, 1969; children: Meredith, Carl Jr. **Educ:** Morgan State College, BA, 1967; University of Penn, Wharton Graduate Division, MBA, 1972. **Career:** General Foods Corp, asst prod mgr, 1972-73; Xerox Corp, sr marketing consultant, 1973-76; Heublein Inc, prod mgr, 1976-80; Jos E Seagram, sr prod mgr, 1980-86, group mktg director, 1986-87, vice pres group mktg director, 1987-92, director business dev, 1992-94, vp of marketing, Absolut Vodka, 1994-. **Orgs:** Life Insurance Co of New York, board of directors, 1990-; Guardsmen Connecticut Chapter, 1990-; Kappa Alpha Psi Fraternity, Stamford Alumni, Morgan State College, 1965-; CEBA Awards, advisory board, 1989-. **Honors/Awds:** Dollars & Sense Magazine, Blackbook Awards, 1990; NYC YMCA, Black Achievers Award, 1985. **Military Serv:** US Army, sp5, 1967-69. **Business Addr:** VP of Marketing, Absolut Vodka, House of Seagram, 800 Third Ave, New York, NY 10022, (212)572-7973.

HORTON, CARRELL PETERSON
Educator. **Personal:** Born Nov 28, 1928, Daytona Beach, FL; daughter of Mildred Adams Peterson and Preston S. Peterson; divorced; children: Richard. **Educ:** Fisk Univ, BA 1949; Cornell Univ, MA 1950; Univ of Chicago, PhD 1972. **Career:** Fisk Univ, instr/res asso 1950-55; Meharry Med Coll, stat anal 1955-66; Fisk Univ, prof & adm 1966-, dir div of soc sci, dean of academic affairs, 1996. **Orgs:** Bd of dir Rochelle Training Ctr 1968-84; consult Health Services Research 1977-80; bd of dir Wesley Foundation 1977; consult National Science Foundation 1979; cons National Research Council 1979; bd of dir Samaritan Pastoral Counseling Ctr 1983; mem, Bd of Higher Educ & Campus Ministry, UM Church, 1983-86. **Honors/Awds:** Urban league awd Jacksonville, FL 1949; grad Assistantship Cornell Univ 1949-50; faculty fellowships Ford Found IBM 1969-71; Article in Prof Journals. **Business Addr:** Director, Fisk University, Divison of Social Science, Nashville, TN 37208-3051.

HORTON, CLARENCE PENNINGTON
Physician (retired). **Personal:** Born Aug 29, 1910, Rome, GA; married Helen Annis Phillips; children: Clarence Jr, Chandler, Gregory, Lisa. **Educ:** Bluefield St Tchrs Coll, BS; Meharry Med Sch, MD 1937. **Career:** Alton Meml Hosp, surg med staff; St Anthonys Hosp, St Josephs Hosp, head emgcy staff 1974-77. **Orgs:** Mem Gtr Alton C of C, Madison Co 708 Bd; Alpha Phi Alpha; 33 Degree Mason; fellow Asso Intl Coll of Surgeons. **Honors/Awds:** Daniel Bowles Awd, Alpha Phi Alpha 1975; Int'l Coll of Surgeons, Full Fellow, 1978.

HORTON, DOLLIE BEA DIXON
Company executive. **Personal:** Born Apr 19, 1942, Fort Valley, GA; daughter of Lillian Byrd Dixon and Hezzie Dixon; married Cornelious Horton Jr, Nov 3, 1963; children: Alre Giovanni, Roderick Cornelious. **Educ:** Fort Valley State Coll, Fort Valley, GA, BS, 1964, MS, 1974; Atlanta Univ, certificate, French, 1966; USAF, certificate, 1974; Univ of MI, Ann Arbor, MI, certificate, 1975; Thomason Real Estate School, certificate, 1978; Phelps-Stokes, Washington, DC, certificate, 1978; Amer Assn of Community & Junior Colleges, Kiawah Island, SC, certificate, 1982; Georgia Insurance Pre-license School, certificate, 1988. **Career:** Pearl Stephens High School, Warner Robins, GA, teacher, 1964-67; Fort Valley State Coll, admin asst, 1967-74; HA Hunt High School, Fort Valley, GA, teacher, Spanish, 1968-69; Peach County Board of Educ, Fort Valley, GA, adult educ teacher, 1969-71; Fort Valley State College, asst dir of devt & placement, 1974-76, acting dir of coll & community relations, 1976-77, dir of coll & community relations, 1977-80; Warner Robins Air Logistics Center, Robins Air Force Base, GA, personnel staffing specialist, 1980-82; Valmedia Inc, owner, 1982. **Orgs:** Board of dirs, Peach County/Fort Valley Chamber of Commerce; Intl Toastmistress Clubs of America; vice pres, Georgia Coalition of Black Women; Georgia Assn of Broadcasters; Natl Assn of Broadcasters; Fort Valley State Coll Committee/Chamber of Commerce; Middle Georgia Minority Media Assn; Vogue Socialite Club; numerous others. **Honors/Awds:** Black Georgian of the Year in Business, 1983; Radio Station Owner of the Year, 1983; Broadcaster of the Year, Black College Radio. **Business Addr:** Owner, DUI School of Fort Valley, 110 S Camellia Blvd, Fort Valley, GA 31030, (912)825-8920.

HORTON, EARLE C.
Attorney. **Personal:** Born Mar 9, 1943, Tampa, FL; son of Helen Belton Horton and Earle Horton; children: Brett, Earle III. **Educ:** Fisk U, BA 1964; Cleveland St U, JD 1968. **Career:** Thunder Bay Communications, pres; Graves Haley Horton, atty, currently. **Orgs:** Mem 1st Black Law Firm in OH; spl counsel to Atty Gen OH; mem Am Bar Assn; OH St Bar Assn; Cleveland Bar Assn; John Harlan Law Club; Cleveland Fisk Univ Club; mem NAACP, Urban League, Norman Minor Bar Assoc. **Honors/Awds:** Recipient Meritorious Serv Awd, Cleveland Bar Assn 1971; Dist Serv Awd, John Harlan Law Club 1973.

HORTON, JOANN
Educational administrator. **Personal:** Born in Lenoir, NC. **Educ:** Appalachian State Univ, bachelor's and master's degree, French; Ohio State Univ, PhD, higher education administration. **Career:** Olive-Harvey Coll, curriculum coordinator, academic vice pres, provost; Tennessee Dept of General Services, asst commissioner; Iowa Community College System, state administrator; Texas Southern Univ, pres, 1993-95; American Council on Education, sr fellow, 1995-. **Honors/Awds:** Appalachian State University, Distinguished Alumnus; Texas Legislature, Commendation from House Chamber, 1995. **Special Achievements:** First female president of Texas Southern Univ. **Business Addr:** Senior Fellow, American Council on Education, 1 DuPont Circle, Washington, DC 20036.

HORTON, LARKIN, JR.
Business executive. **Personal:** Born Feb 18, 1939, Lenoir, NC; married Patricia Richardson; children: Larkin III, Gregory Derwin. **Educ:** Catawba Valley Tech Inst, Assoc Elect 1960; General Electric Control School, Master Controls 1961; Cleaver-Brooks Pressure Vessels, Cert Pressure Vessels 1961; Caldwell Comm Coll, Cert Powder Activated Tools 1972. **Career:** East Finley Auto Laundry, owner, 1972-; City of Lenoir, councilman at large, 1983-; Horton's Electric Co, owner/contractor, currently; professional photographer, currently; Electrical Consultant and Safety Specialist, ANSI, NIOSHA, & UL, instructor. **Orgs:** Trustee St Paul AME Church 1978-; bd of dir Natl Cancer Soc 1983-; mem Caldwell Friends Inc 1984-85; mem Gov Crime Prevention Comm; inspector, International Assn of Electrical Inspectors, 1980-; board member, National Cancer Society, 1983. **Honors/Awds:** Value Analysis Awd Burlington Ind 1980, 1981, 1982; Man of the Year The American Legion 1984; Lenoir Police Explorer Post 246, Appreciation Plaque, 1990; North Carolina Black Elected Municipal Official Committee, Plaque, 1991; North Carolina Textile Association, first Volunteer Service Award, 1986; City of Lenoir, Lenoir City Council, Key to the City, Resolution of Appreciation, 1991; Dr Martin Luther King Jr Award, 1991; City of Lenoir, Larkin Horton Jr Day Proclamation, Feb 23, 1992. **Home Addr:** 445 Arlington Circle NW, PO Box 242, Lenoir, NC 28645. **Business Addr:** Electrical Contractor, Horton's Electric Co, 445 Arlington Circle NW, PO Box 242, Lenoir, NC 28645.

HORTON, LARNIE G.
State employee. **Personal:** marrIed Katrena B; children: Larnie Glenn, Jr, Langston Garvey. **Educ:** Morris Brown Coll, AB; Univ NC-chapel Hill, completed degree & lang requirements for Masters Prog; Duke U, MDiv (Hon Dr); Nat Theo Sem & Coll. **Career:** Saxapaw, NC, pastor of ch 1960-64; Emanuel AME Ch, Durham, pastor 1964-66; Kittrell Coll NC, academic dean 1961-62, pres 1966-73; Gov for Minority Affairs, spl asst 1973-. **Orgs:** Mem bd trustees Vance Co Tech Inst 1968; mem bd dir Nat Lab for Higher Educ 1970; mem bd dir Soul City Found 1968; consult Am Assn of Jr Coll 1970-72; mem NAACP; Merchants Assn of Chapel Hill; Alpha Phi Alpha Frat; C of C of Henderson NC. **Honors/Awds:** Grad Cum Laude, Morris Brown Coll; Woodrow Wilson & Rockefeller Fellow; voted 1970 Civic Achievement Awd, Morris Brown Coll Nat Alumni Assn; presented Nat Alumni Assn Awd Stillman Coll 1970. **Business Addr:** Gov Ofc Admin Bldg, 116 W Jones St, Raleigh, NC 27611.

HORTON, LEMUEL LEONARD
Employee relations manager. **Personal:** Born Jun 29, 1936, Fort Valley, GA; married Yvonne Felton; children: Lorna Y Hill. **Educ:** Fort Valley State Coll, BS 1963. **Career:** Civil Service Robins AFB GA, warehouseman 1958-65; State of GA, comm serv consultant 1965-68; Ft Valley State Coll, dir student union 1968-71; The Research GP, assoc 1971-73; New York Life, field underwriter 1973; Gold Kist Inc, mgr employee relations 1973-. **Orgs:** Pres 1980-81, mem Resurgens, Intl Assoc of Quality Circles, IRRA, bd mem GA Chap Epilepsy Foundation; pres TAPS Epilepsy Foundation. **Honors/Awds:** Presidential Citation Natl Assoc for Equal Oppor in Higher Educ 1983. **Military Serv:** AUS sp2 3 yrs; AUS Reserve command sgt major 40 yrs; Army Achievement Medal 1982, Army Commendation Medal 1983, Meritorious Serv Medal 1986. **Business Addr:** Manager, Employee Relations, Gold Kist Inc, PO Box 2210, Atlanta, GA 30301.

HORTON, ODELL
Federal judge. **Personal:** Born May 13, 1929, Bolivar, TN; son of Rosa Horton and Odell Horton; married Evie L Randolph, Sep 13, 1953; children: Odell Jr, Christopher. **Educ:** Morehouse Coll, AB 1951; Howard Univ Law Sch, JD 1956. **Career:** Private law practice, 1957-62; Western District of Tennessee, asst US attorney, 1962-67; City of Memphis, Division of Hospital and Health Services, director, 1968; Shelby County Criminal Court, judge, 1969-70; LeMoyne-Owen College, pres, 1970-74; US Bankruptcy, judge, 1974-80; US District Court, judge, 1980-. **Orgs:** Member, American Council on Education; member, Assn of American Colleges & Univ; member, American Bar Assn. **Honors/Awds:** Disting Alumni Awd Howard Univ; 1970 Bill of Rights Awd; LM Graves Meml Health Awd 1969; Honorary LLD: Morehouse College, Mississippi Industrial College, 1969; numerous other awds; credited with creating a progressive pre-trial program for indigent persons charged with criminal violations. **Business Addr:** Judge, US Federal Court, Tennessee Western District, Federal Bldg, Memphis, TN 38103.

HORTON, RAYMOND ANTHONY
Professional football player, business owner. **Personal:** Born Apr 12, 1960, Tacoma, WA; married Leslie; children: Taylor. **Educ:** Univ of Washington, BA, sociology, 1983. **Career:** Cincinnati Bengals, cornerback, nickel back, safety, 1983-88; Dallas Cowboys, safety, 1989-; Long Shots (driving range), Seattle, WA, owner, currently. **Honors/Awds:** Post-season play, 1988: AFC Championship Game, NFL Championship Game; Ray of Hope food drive, Dallas, TX, organizer. **Business Addr:** Professional Football Player, Dallas Cowboys, One Cowboys Pkwy, Irving, TX 75063-4999.

HORTON, STELLA JEAN
Educator, educational administrator, business executive. **Personal:** Born Aug 16, 1944, Durham, NC; children: Braheim Knight. **Educ:** St Augustine's Coll, attended 1962-64; A&T State Univ, BS (magna cum laude) 1966; Rutgers The State Univ, MEd 1972, EdD 1986. **Career:** Orange Co Bd of Educ, teacher 1966-69; Rutgers The State Univ, assoc prof 1970-76; Alternative Sch Camden Bd of Educ, teacher/principal 1976-80; Juvenile Resource Ctr Inc, adm/exec dir 1980-. **Orgs:** Consul NJ Dept of Educ 1980-84; mem Urban League Camden Co 1981-83; Camden City Bd of Educ vice pres 1983-84, mem 1980-; mem 5th Legilsative Dist NJSch Bds 1983-. **Honors/Awds:** Serv to Young People Juvenile Resource Ctr Inc 1979; Comm Serv NJ Assn of Black Social Workers 1982. **Home Addr:** 1412 Van Hook St, Camden, NJ 08104. **Business Addr:** Executive Dir, Juvenile Resource Ctr Inc, 315 Cooper St, Camden, NJ 08102.

HORTON, WILLIE WATTISON
Professional baseball player (retired), sales rep. **Personal:** Born Oct 18, 1942, Arno, VA; married Gloria; children: Darryl I, Al, Darryl II, Gil, Terri Lyn, April, Pam. **Career:** Outfielder: Detroit Tigers, 1963-77, Texas Rangers, 1977, Cleveland Indians, 1978, Oakland Athletics, 1978, Toronto Blue Jays, 1978, Seattle Mariners, 1978-80; Ort Tool & Die Corp, sales rep, 1994-. **Honors/Awds:** American League All-Star Team, 1965, 1968, 1970, 1973; Most Valuable Player, Seattle Mariners, 1979; American League Comeback Player of the Year, Sporting News, 1979; hit 3 home runs in one game 1970, 1977; led AL designated hitters in strikeouts (114) 1977; 1st Mariner to drive in 100 runs in a season, 1979; Afro-American Sports Hall of Fame, 1992. **Business Addr:** Sales Representative, Ort Tool & Die Corp, 6555 S Dixie Hwy, Erie, MI 48133.

HOSKINS CLARK, TEMPY M.
Educator. **Personal:** Born Oct 25, 1938, Hazen, AK; married Wilber L Hoskins; children: Jamele, Monroe, Brian McKissic. **Educ:** Philander Smith Clge, BA 1963; Western MI Univ, MA 1971. **Career:** Grand Rapids Bd of Educ, elementary prin; McKinley Upper Grade Center Chicago IL, vocal music teacher; S Middle School Grand Rapids MI, vocal music teacher, chmn. **Orgs:** Minister of mus True Light Bapt Ch Grand Rapids; bd dir Blue Lake Fine Arts Camp; pres Negro Bus & Prof Club Inc; mem Delta Sigma Theta Sor; pres of local chap Delta Sigma Theta; travel abroad summer 1972 with hs students to Belgium Holland England & France. **Business Addr:** 50 Antoine SW, Grand Rapids, MI 49507.

HOSTEN, ADRIAN
Physician, educator. **Personal:** Born in Grenada, WI; married Claire C; children: Karen, Lester. **Educ:** Atlantic Union Coll, BA 1958; Howard Univ, MD 1962. **Career:** Howard Univ, chief nephrology div 1967-87, assoc prof 1972-82, prof 1982-, chairman department of medicine, 1988-; Med Intensive Care Unit Howard Univ Hospital, dir 1968-75; Bates Memorial HS, principal 1954-55, instructor 1966-68, asst prof 1968-72. **Orgs:** Natl Med Assn 1968-; Amer Soc of Nephrology 1971-; Intl Soc of Nephrology 1973-; FACP. **Business Addr:** Professor, Howard Univ College of Medicine, 520 W St NW, Washington, DC 20001.

HOSTON, GERMAINE A.
Educator. **Personal:** Born Jul 27, 1954, Fort Dix, NJ; daughter of Veretta Louise Harris Hoston and Walter Lee Hoston; married Ian James MacAuslan, May 30, 1987. **Educ:** Princeton University, Princeton, NJ, AB, 1975; Harvard University, Cambridge, MA, MA, 1978, PhD, 1981. **Career:** Princeton University, Princeton, NJ, research assistant, 1973-75; Harvard University, Cambridge, MA, teaching assistant, 1977-78; The Johns Hopkins University, Baltimore, MD, assistant professor, 1980-86; Maison Des Sciences De L'Homme, EHESS, Paris, France, visiting prof, 1986; Osaka City University, Osaka, Japan, visiting prof, 1990; The Johns Hopkins University, Baltimore, MD, associate professor, 1986-92; University of California, San Diego, professor, 1992-. **Orgs:** Center for Democratization and Economic Development, 1993-; Asia Society, member board of trustees, 1994-; Member, board of directors, Institute for East-West Security Studies, 1990-; member, board of trustees, Virginia Theological Seminary, 1988-; chair, Crossroads Programs board, Episcopal Diocese of Maryland, 1988-92; co-chair, Companion Relationship Committee, Episcopal Diocese of Maryland, 1987-92; member, Council on Foreign Relations, 1990-; council, candidate/elect, American Political Science Association, 1992-94; Northeast Asia Council; Association for Asian Studies, 1992-95, vice-chair, 1993-94. **Honors/Awds:** Marxism and the Crisis of Development in Prewar Japan, Princeton University, 1986; Rockefeller Foundation International Relations Fellowship, 1985-88; Fellowship for Independent Study and Research, National Endowment for the Humanities, 1984; Post Doctoral Grants for International Research, Social Science Research Council, 1984; International Fellowship, International Federation of University Women, 1982-83; The State, Identity, and the National Question in China and Japan, Princeton University Press, 1994. **Business Addr:** Professor, University of California, San Diego, Department of Political Science, 0521, 9500 Gilman Dr, La Jolla, CA 92093-0521, (619)534-3548.

HOTCHKISS, WESLEY AKIN
Educator, clergyman (retired). **Personal:** Born Jan 26, 1919, Spooner, WI; son of Fay W Hotchkiss and Codie L Hotchkiss; married Mary Ellen Fink; children: Tannia. **Educ:** Northland Coll, BA 1944, ThD 1958; Univ Chicago, MS 1948, PhD 1950; Yankton Coll, DD 1956. **Career:** Chicago Theol Sem, rsch assoc 1947-49; Greater Cinn Council Chs, rsch dir 1949-50; City Coll NY, lectr in geography 1960-; United Ch Bd, rsch dir 1950-55, sec 1955-58, gen sec for higher educ 1958-82 (retired). **Orgs:** Mem spl seminar higher educ Columbia 1962-; AAAS; Amer Sociol Assn; Religious Rsch Assn; former trustee Ripon Coll; Fisk Univ; Dillard Univ; Talladega Coll; Tougaloo Coll; Northland Coll; Huston-Tillotson Coll; Le Moyne-Owen Coll; Ripon Coll; Prescott Coll; Hawaii LOA Coll; trustee Affiliate Artists Inc; fellow Assn Amer Geographers. **Honors/Awds:** Pacific Univ, LLD, 1965; Illinois College, LitD, 1979; Talladega College, LHD, 1982; Northland College, LLD, 1958; Ripon College, LHD, 1982; Hawaii Loa College, LitD, 1983; Tougaloo College, LLD, 1984. **Military Serv:** AUS chaplain 1945-47.

HOUSE, JAMES E.
Consultant. **Personal:** Born Oct 6, Goldsboro, NC; son of Cleo Peoples House and Edward A House. **Educ:** Howard Univ, BS Mech Engrg 1963. **Career:** McDonnell Douglas Corp St Louis, test & structural engr 1963-67; Fairchild Hiller Corp, stress analyst 1967-68; The Boeing Co Seattle, rsch engr 1968-72; WIPCO Inc St Croix, vice pres treas 1972-77; Natl Assoc of Minority CPA Firms, Govt of DC, Jones & Artis Co Wash DC, consult 1981-86; JBH Associates, consultant 1986-87; The Eckenberge Group, Washington, DC, pres, 1987-. **Orgs:** Pres Student Govt School of Engrg & Arch Howard Univ 1962; chmn MD Frederick Douglas Scholarship Fund 1984-; mem VA Black Republican Council 1984-; mem VI C of C Econ Devel Comm, VI Businessmens Assoc, Minority Bus Devel Org, St Croix Howard Univ Alumni Assoc, Alpha Phi Omega; sec Republican Central Comm Prince Georges Cty MD 1982-84; chmn Black Republican Council Prince Georges Cty MD 1984-85; co-chmn Reagan-Bush 1984 Comm Prince Georges Cty MD 1984; chmn Maryland Black Republican Council 1985-87; 2nd vice chmn Maryland State Republican Party 1986-90; board member National Council of 100 1986-; director, OSDBU/USDA. **Honors/Awds:** Civil Rights Student Leader 1959-62; Touring Debater Intl AFSC Peace Caravan 1960; Serv Awd Alpha Phi Omega 1961; Disting Military Student Awd 1962; The News Amer Baltimore 1974; Mem of the Year Awd Natl Assoc of Black Mfgrs Inc 1975; Achievement Awd Estate Profit Civic Assoc of VI 1978; Achievement Awd Natl Assn of Minority CPA Firms Wash DC 1978; Achievement Awd MD Minority Contractors Assn 1986,87; Republican of the Year 1987; elected delegate, White House Conference on Small Business, 1986; Bush delegate, Maryland Republican National Convention 1988; Special Assistant to Governor of Virginia, 1994-96.

HOUSE, MICHAEL A.
Advertising company executive. **Personal:** Born Jul 13, 1941, Louisville, KY; son of Jamesetta & William T Hodges; children (previous marriage): Robert, Margoit, William; married Doris J. House. **Educ:** Howard Univ, 1965; Baruch Coll CUNY, MBA, 1974. **Career:** Amalgamated Pub Inc, pres, currently. **Orgs:** National Assn of Market Developers (NAMD), natl pres; 100 Black Men of New Jersey. **Military Serv:** US Army, 1st lt, 1965-67. **Business Addr:** President, Amalgamated Publishers Inc, 45 W 45th St, Ste 201, New York, NY 10036, (212)869-5220.

HOUSE, MILLARD L.
Educator. **Personal:** Born Jan 28, 1944, Langston, OK; married Anna Shumate; children: Milton, Signee, Millard, II. **Educ:** Langston Univ, BA 1966; Northeastern State Clge, MA 1971. **Career:** Dept Human Rel Tulsa Pub Sch, dir 1970-; Gilcrease Jr HS, soc sci instr 1966-70. **Orgs:** Mem NEA OK Educ Assc; Tulsa Assc Curriculum Supvrs & Dir; Tulsa Pub Sch Affirmative Action Com; Urban League; NAACP; Langston Univ Alumni Assc; YMCA; Kappa Alpha Psi; Phi Delta Kappa; Royal Housa Club; St John's Bapt Ch; Mayor's Commn Comm Relations. **Honors/Awds:** Outst Young Men Amer Award US Jaycees 1973; Kappa of Yr Award Kappa Alpha Psi 1974-75; publ. **Business Addr:** 3027 S New Haven, Tulsa, OK 74145.

HOUSE, N. GERRY
Educational administrator. **Career:** Memphis City Schools, superintendent, currently. **Orgs:** American Assn of Sch Admin; Phi Delta Kappa; Natl Assn of Black Sch Educators. **Honors/Awds:** Phi Delta Kappa Leadership Award; Martin Luther King Achievement Award; Communicator of the Year, Memphis Chapter of the Public Relations Society. **Business Addr:** Superintendent, Memphis City Schools, 2597 Avery Ave, Room 214, Memphis, TN 38112, (901)325-5300.

HOUSTON, AGNES WOOD
State official (retired). **Personal:** Born Jun 14, 1920, Westville, IL; daughter of Hattie Wood and Junius Wood; divorced. **Educ:** YMCA Bus Sch, 1940; Inst Bus Technique, 1960; courses sponsored by Civil Srv Commn 1967; courses at Univ IL & So IL Univ 1969; Lincoln Land Comm Clge; Sangamon State Univ. **Career:** State of Illinois, Dept of Revenue, Springfield, IL, EEO dir, 1943-85 (retired). **Orgs:** Pres NAACP; mem Govt Tech Staff on Youth; PTA; Sch Survey Com; Springfield & Sangamon Comm Action Prog; Springfield Fluoridation Com; pres Women's Intl League for Peace & Freedom 1978-80; mem IL Commn on Children 1980; YWCA; League of Women Voters; Assc Media Women. **Honors/Awds:** Gold Cert NAACP; Frontiers Intl Comm Srv Award; PTA Cert Excel Prog Planning 1958; Comm Srv Award Urban League 1977; Webster Plaque NAACP 1978; First Woman of Springfield IL Award Springfield Women's Political Caucus 1979; cert NAACP Natl Conv; chrmn Springfield Fair Housing Bd. **Home Addr:** 2301 E Laurel St, Springfield, IL 62703.

HOUSTON, ALICE V.
Educator. **Personal:** Born Dec 6, Baton Rouge, LA. **Educ:** So Univ, BA 1953; LA State Univ, MEd 1956; Univ TX, PhD 1974; Additional Study, Atlanta Univ, Kent State Univ, Western Reserve Univ; Univ of WA, attended; Univ of VA, attended; OK City Univ, attended. **Career:** Various teaching positions 1953-68; S Greenville Elem Sch Baton Rouge, prin 1968-69; Beechwood Elem Sch E Baton Rouge Parish Sch Bd, prin 1969-75; E Baton Rouge Parish Sch, supr of rsch & prog evaluation 1976-77, supr of evaluation of state & fed progs 1976; OK City Pub Schs, dir of curriculum serv dept 1977-82; Seattle Public Schools, asst supt 1982-91; Human Resources Recruitment and Development, director, 1991-. **Orgs:** Mem Assn Supvrn & Curric Dev; exec council ASCD 1979-81; mem of exec bd Natl Alliance Black Sch Educators 1975-79; mem Phi Delta Kappa, Kappa DeltaPi, NAACP, Zeta Phi Beta; bd of dirs, United Way of King County; trustee, The College Board. **Honors/Awds:** Awd plaque Girl Scouts 1964; serv United Meth Mission 1969; NDEA Grant 1965; Awd plaque Zeta Phi Zeta 1970; Awd Doctoral Fellowship to the Univ TX 1972-73; reception Hon Relig & Civic Act Hughes UMC, Zeta Phi Beta & Beechwood Elem Sch 1974; elected to Southern Univ Chap of Phi Delta Kappa 1975; Natl Alliance of Black School Educators Recognition for Outstanding Serv 1974-77,77-79; Outstanding Princ of Yr 1975; Outstanding Contributions in the Area of Educ 1977; Omega Psi Phi Recognition as Citizen of the Year 1981; Phi Beta Sigma, Alpha Phi Alpha, Benefit Guild; Awd for Knowledge & Understanding of the Art of Black Amers & Commitment to the Educ of All Students OK City OK Black Liberated Arts CenterInc 1982; nom President-Elect of Assoc for Supv & Curriculum Development 1984; present w the Benefit Guild Assoc Martin Luther King Jr Awd for providing Excellence in Educ 1985; received Awd of Merit for Community Serv Alpha Phi Alpha 1986. **Special Achievements:** Seattle Public Schools Middle College High School, high school dropout retrieval program housed at Seattle Central Comm Coll, founder, 1990. **Business Addr:** Assistant Superintendent, Seattle Public Schools, 815 4th Ave N, Mail Stop AA191, Seattle, WA 98109-1116.

HOUSTON, ALLAN WADE
Professional basketball player. **Personal:** Born Apr 4, 1971, Louisville, KY; son of Wade Houston; married. **Educ:** Tennessee, BA in African American Studies. **Career:** Detroit Pistons, guard, 1993-96; New York Knicks, 1996-. **Special Achievements:** NBA Draft, first round, eleventh pick, 1993. **Business Addr:** Professional Basketball Player, New York Knicks, 2 Pennsylvania Plaza, New York, NY 10121, (212)465-5867.

HOUSTON, BOBBY
Professional football player. **Personal:** Born Oct 26, 1967, Washington, DC. **Educ:** North Carolina State. **Career:** Green Bay Packers, linebacker, 1990; New York Jets, 1991-96; Kansas City Chiefs, 1997; San Diego Chargers, 1997-. **Business Addr:** Professional Football Player, San Diego Chargers, Qualcomm Stadium, 9449 Friars Rd, San Diego, CA 92108, (619)280-2111.

HOUSTON, CISSY (EMILY DRINKARD)
Gospel singer. **Personal:** marrIed John Houston; children: Whitney, Gary. **Career:** Drinkard Singers, family gospel group; Sweet Inspirations, singer, 1968; albums include: Sweet Inspiration and What the World Needs Now is Love; worked with: Atlantic Records, Muscle Shoals, and New York; backup work for: Elvis Presley, Aretha Franklin, David Bowie, Dionne Warwick, Wilson Pickett, numerous others; night club singer, currently; New Hope Baptist Church, Radio Choir, director, currently. **Honors/Awds:** Medal for Distinguished Humanitarian Leadership, University of Medicine & Dentistry of New Jersey, 1992. **Special Achievements:** Mother and aunt of singers Whitney Houston and Dionne Warwick; autobiographical documentary, "Sweet Inspiration," PBS-TV, 1988. **Business Addr:** Singer, c/o Whitney Houston, Arista Records, 6 W 57th St, New York, NY 10019.

HOUSTON, CORINNE P.
Food company executive (retired). **Personal:** Born Mar 24, 1922, Birmingham; daughter of Henrietta Perry and William Perry; married Olin Houston; children: Avis, David. **Educ:** 2 Year coll; 3 years business coll. **Career:** Head cashier 15 yrs; first black female asst mgr; first black store mgr; first female for large supermarket chain in country; Personnel & Public Relations Specialist Allied Supermarkets Inc Sec Gotham Hotel, retired. **Orgs:** Mem NAACP; chmn Drug Educ Comm; mem All Saints Episcopal Ch; former mem St Cyprians Episcopal Ch; first female Sr Warden; mem Urban League Guild; Sister Hood; member, Cite' d' E'troit chapter, Top Ladies of Distinction; exec board member, NAACP. **Honors/Awds:** Certf Merit Natl Black White Consumer Club 1974; Cited MI Chronicle; Top 10 Black Women City Detroit; Testimonial Resolution City Detroit Hnrng Corinne Houston Day W Grand Blvd named Corinne Houston Blvd one week; Resolution State MI.

HOUSTON, DAVID R.
Educational administration. **Personal:** Born Sep 1, 1936, Tyler, TX; son of Rev W B Houston; married Lillian Scott. **Educ:** TX Coll Tyler, BA 1957; North TX State Univ Denton, MA Music Ed 1964, EdD 1969; Univ of Houston TX, Post Doctorate 1972. **Career:** San Angelo TX Public Schools, teacher/band dir 1957-64; TX Coll Tyler, instructor of music/band dir 1964-67, prof of educ and chmn div of educ, dir ofteacher educ 1969-73; Ft Worth TX Public Schools, elem teacher 1968-69; Prairie View A&M Univ, adjunct prof of ed 1974-; Wiley Coll, vice pres acad affairs, admin asst to the pres 1973-88, exec vice pres 1988-. **Orgs:** Mem Natl Educ Assoc, Phi Delta Kappa, TX State Teachers Assoc, Assoc of Higher Educ, Amer Assoc of Colls for Teacher Educ, Southern Conf of Deans of Faculties and Academic Vice Presidents; life mem NAACP; mem YMCA, Boy Scouts of Amer; consultant Jamaica Hotel School Univ of the West Indies Kingston Jamaica 1979; pastor Smith Temple Church of God in Christ Jones Valley Comm Church of God in Christ Tyler TX; officer Mineola Dist Church of God in Christ; mem East TX Ministerial Alliance Church of God in Christ, Interdenominational Ministerial Alliance; state sunday sch superintendent TX Northeast Church of God in Christ. **Honors/Awds:** Ford Grant Found Ford Found 1964; Outstanding Achievement Awd Alpha Phi Alpha Frat 1978; 3 publications.

HOUSTON, IVAN J.
Insurance company executive. **Personal:** Born Jun 15, 1925, Los Angeles, CA; son of Doris Talbot Young and Norman O Houston; married Philippa Jones; children: Pamela, Kathi, Ivan A. **Educ:** Univ of CA Berkeley, BS 1948; Univ of Manitoba, actuarial science; Life Office Mgmt Inst, fellow; Amer Coll of Life Underwriters, charter life underwriter. **Career:** Actuary, 1948; Actuarial & Policyowners Serv Div, supr 1950, admin asst in charge 1952, asst sec actuarial 1954, actuary 1956, bd dir exec com mem 1959, vice pres actuary 1966; Golden State Mutual Life Ins Co, president/chief executive officer, 1970,

chairman of the board/CEO, 1980-90, chairman of the board, 1991-. **Orgs:** Assoc mem Conf of Actuaries in Pub Practice; mem Amer Acad of Actuaries; Amer Soc of Pension Actuaries; Intl Actuarial Assn; past pres Los Angeles Actuarial Club; mem Kappa Alpha Psi Frat; Sigma Pi Phi Frat; past mem bd of Regents Loyola Marymount Univ; corporate bd mem United Way of Los Angeles Inc; past mem bd dir CA C of C; past chmn of bd dir Los Angeles Urban League; past mem bd dir Pacific Indemnity Co; former chmn of bd dir M&M Assn; former mem bd dir Los Angeles C of C; former chmn of bd Life Ofc Mgmt Assn 1979-80; bd dir First Interstate Bank of CA, Pacific Thesis Group; former mem of bd, Kaiser Alum & Chem Corp, Family Savings and Loan; Commissioner of Los Angeles Human Relations Commission. **Honors/Awds:** First African-American elected to bd dir Amer Life Ins Assn. **Military Serv:** US Army, sgt maj. 1943-45; Purple Heart; Bronze Star; Combat Infantryman's Badge. **Business Addr:** Chairman of the Board, Golden State Mutual Life Ins, 1999 W Adams Blvd, Los Angeles, CA 90018.

HOUSTON, JOHNNY L.
Educator, administrator, mathematician, computer specialist. **Personal:** Born Nov 19, 1941, Sandersville, GA; son of Catherine Houston Vinson and Bobby Lee Houston; married Virginia Lawrence; children: Mave Lawrence, Kaiulani Michelle. **Educ:** Morehouse Coll, BA, 1964; Atlanta Univ, MS, 1966; Universite de Strasbourg, France, 1966-67; Univ of Georgia, 1969; Purdue Univ, PhD, 1974. **Career:** Atlanta Univ, chmn math & comp science, 1975-81; Fort Valley State Coll, coord of computer science, 1981-83, Callaway prof of computer science, 1983-84; Elizabeth City State Univ, vice chancellor for academic affairs, 1984-88, senior research professor of mathematics/computer science, 1988-. **Orgs:** American Math Society; Assn of Computing Machinery; Math Assn of America; Natl Assn of Mathematicians; dir, Black Cultural Center, Purdue Univ, 1972-73; exec sec, Natl Assn of Mathematicians, 1975-89; visiting scientist, Natl Center for Atom Research, 1976; co-dir, Natl Conf Math & Physical Science, Boulder, CO, 1979; pres & chmn of the bd, Intl Trade & Development Corp, 1979-86; visiting scientist, Lawrence Livermore Natl Lab, 1979, 1983; consultant Math/Comp Science Spec NIH-MARC Review Comm, 1982-86; visiting scientist, NASA Langley Research Center, 1989. **Honors/Awds:** Merril Scholar Univ de Strasbourg France 1966-67; Distinguished Service Award; invited speaker Purdue Univ 1980; invited speaker XI Intl Symposium on Math Programming Bonn Germany 1982; selected for Statewide Computer Science Review Team Bd of Regents Commonwealth of MA 1986; invited Keynote Speaker 43rd Annual Mtg NIS/Beta Kappa Chi 1986. **Home Addr:** 602 West Main St, Elizabeth City, NC 27909. **Business Addr:** Dept of Math and Computer Science, Elizabeth City State Univ, Parkview Dr, Elizabeth City, NC 27909.

HOUSTON, KENNETH RAY
Professional football player (retired). **Personal:** Born Nov 12, 1944, Lufkin, TX; married Gustie Marie Rice. **Educ:** Prairie View A&M, BSM, guidance counseling, 1967. **Career:** Defensive back: Houston Oilers, 1967-72; Washington Redskins, 1973-80. **Honors/Awds:** AFL Champ Game, 1967; holds NFL record for touchdowns on interceptions (9), Houston, 1967-71; named to All-AFC team, 1971; named All-Pro or All-NFC 7 straight years, 1973-79; Byron Whizzer White Award for Humanitarian Service, NFL Players Assn, 1980; played in AFC All-Star Game, 1968, 1969; played in Pro Bowl, 1970-76; inducted into Pro Football Hall of Fame, 1986. **Business Addr:** c/o Pro Football Hall of Fame, 2121 Harrison Ave NW, Canton, OH 44708.

HOUSTON, LILLIAN S.
Educator. **Personal:** Born Oct 24, 1946, Tyler, TX; married David Houston. **Educ:** TX Clge, BA 1966; E TX State Univ, studies; Stephen F Austin State Univ, studies; Prairie View A&M, studies; N TX State Univ, studies in Aging; E TX State Univ, MS Sociology 1975. **Career:** Nursing Home Admin Wiley Coll, instructor, program dir. **Orgs:** Sec Tyler ISD; Library & NTSU Denton; Library TX Clge Tyler; Library Tyler ISD Soloist, Original Gospel Templetts Recording Grp Concert Artist; implemented& directing vol training prog Wiley Clge Campus Marshall TX; TX Nrsg Home Assc; mem Natl Caucus on the Black Aged; mem Amer Assc of Retired Persons; mem Cole Hill CME Ch Tyler TX mem Local CYF Christian Youth Flwshp; dir Cole Hill CME Ch; mem bd of dir Tyler City Library Tyler TX mem AmerClge of Nrsg. **Business Addr:** Wiley Coll, Marshall, TX.

HOUSTON, MARSH S.
Consultant, coordinator. **Personal:** Born Mar 4, 1918, Cornersville, TN. **Educ:** TN State Univ, attd; Drake Univ, grad wk. **Career:** Des Moines Public Schools, consultant; New Horizons Project, asst coord; Model Cities, coord; Des Moines Public School, educ progs, teacher, math. **Orgs:** Vp Des Moines Educ Assc 1972-73; chmn 1973-74; Human Rel Com Aptd Des Moines Civil Serv Commn 1974 first black aptd to position; mem Omega Psi Phi Frat; Fndr Mu Omicron Chap in Des Moines. **Military Serv:** AUS e-7. **Business Addr:** 1214 E 15 St, Amos Hiatt Jr HS, Des Moines, IA.

HOUSTON, SEAWADON LEE
Banking executive. **Personal:** Born Aug 29, 1942, Liberty, MO; son of Thelma Merical and Samuel Houston; married Carole L Floyd, Jun 1976; children: Brenda, Toni, George, Michael. **Educ:** Golden Gate Univ, BA Business; Univ of WA, Banking School; Stanford Sloan Program, Graduate. **Career:** US Air Force, sgt 1960-65; Wells Fargo Bank, trainee 1965-66, several mgmt positions 1966-84, senior vice president 1984-90, executive vice president 1990-. **Orgs:** Bay Area Urban Bankers Assn; Consumer Bankers Assn, board member; Golden Gate University, trustee board member; Natl Assn of Urban Bankers, advisory bd; Stanford Sloan, advisory bd. **Military Serv:** USAF sgt 5 yrs; Far East Airman of the Year 1963. **Business Addr:** Executive Vice President, Wells Fargo Bank, 201 Third Street, San Francisco, CA 94103.

HOUSTON, W. EUGENE
Clergyman. **Personal:** Born Jul 1, 1920, Hot Springs, AR; married Doris A Cobbs; children: Bjorn, Cheryl Hunter. **Educ:** Johnson C Smith Univ, AB summa cum laude 1941, MDiv magna cum laude 1944, DD 1961; Columbia, phD 1952; Chicago, STD 1959; Mansfield Clge Oxford Univ, Cert 1971. **Career:** Eastern Area Rep Bd Pensions United Presby Ch USA, asst sec; St James Presby Ch NYC, interim pastor 1977; Westminster Presb Ch Cedar Manor Jamaica NY, pastor 198-75; Stated Clerk-Synod NE United Presb Ch, 1974-75; Rendall Mem Presb Ch Manhattan, pastor 1944-68; Dept Sanitation NY, chpln 1960-; NY Hosp Welfare Island & Elmhurst Queens, chpln 1950-60. **Orgs:** Exec dir Commn Religion & Race Presbytery of New York City 1963-65; dir Athletic Publ JC Smith 1942-44; Moderator-Synod NY 1962-63; v moderator Presbytery NY 1960-62; chmn Div Pastoral Care Queens Fed Chs 1969-74; pres Interdemoninational Ministers Meetings Greater NY 1970-74; pres Presb Council & W 1656-58; Polemarch NY Alumni Chap Kappa Alpha Psi 1958-60; pres General Alumni Assc Johnson C Smith Univ 1954-58; Kappa Alpha Psi; Alpha Kappa Mu; Delta Phi Delta; Chi Alpha; Assc Amer Protestant Hosp Chplns; Natl Presb Health & Welfare Assc; Insts Religion & Mental Health. **Honors/Awds:** Publ poet composer & arranger music; bass-baritone recitalist; contrb many articles varied publ Who's Who Harlem 1950; Amer & Amer Clge & Univ Students 1940; Kappa Alpha Psi Grand Chap Individual Meritorious Achievement Award; Charter Trustee Eisenhower Coll. **Business Addr:** 475 Riverside Dr, New York, NY 10027.

HOUSTON, WADE
Basketball coach. **Career:** Univ of Tennessee, Knoxville, TN, basketball coach, currently. **Business Addr:** Basketball Coach, University of Tennessee at Knoxville, Knoxville, TN 37916.

HOUSTON, WHITNEY
Singer, actress. **Personal:** Born Aug 9, 1963, Newark, NJ; daughter of Emily Houston and John Houston; married Bobby Brown, Jul 18, 1992; children: Bobbi Kristina Houston Brown. **Career:** Singer: Debut album, Whitney Houston, 1985; Second Album, Whitney, 1987; Third Album, I'm Your Baby Tonight, 1990; Bodyguard Soundtrack, 1992; The Bodyguard, actress, 1992; Waiting to Exhale, actress, 1995; The Preacher's Wife, actress, soundtrack vocalist, 1996; Cinderella, actress, 1997. **Orgs:** Whitney Houston Foundation for Children, founder. **Honors/Awds:** Key to the City of Newark; Several American Music Awards, Grammy Awards, Awarded Top Female Pop Vocalist; Multi-platinum debut album ''Whitney Houston'', sold over 9 million copies; MTV's Best Female Video Award, 1986; UNCF honoree, 1990; Stars Salute to Whitney for her support of Black Colleges, 1990; Appeared on the magazine covers of: Ebony, Essence, Jet, Glamour, Vogue, Cosmopolitan, and Seventeen; Pinnacle Award. **Business Addr:** Singer, c/o Arista Records, 6 W 57th St, New York, NY 10019.

HOUSTON, WILLIAM DEBOISE
Educational administration. **Personal:** Born Mar 10, 1940, Quincy, FL; son of Ada Houston and Albert Houston; married Elizabeth Shorter; children: William Carril, Kendra, Karli, Kylean. **Educ:** SC State Coll, BSEd 1963; NC A&T Univ, MEd 1972; Lehigh Univ, Admin Cert 1975. **Career:** Easton Area School dist, teacher 1964-74; Shawnee Intermediate School, asst principal 1975-. **Orgs:** Vp Easton City Council; chairperson Easton Econ Devel, Police Fire & Health Bd City of Easton; co-host Channel 39 Black Exposure TV Show; mem PA State Ed Assoc, Amer Assoc for Health Phys Ed & Recreation, Women's League of Voters, NAACP Exec Bd; bd mem Easton Boys Club, Private Indust Council; pres Pride & Joy Ed Nursery Inc, South Side Civic Assoc; bd of trustees Union AME Church; pres Easton City Council. **Honors/Awds:** Certificate of Appreciation NAACP 1967, 1982; Rainbow Festival Awd Bahai 1981; First Black Councilman City of Easton PA Certificate NAACP; First Black City Council Pres City of Easton; pres Easton City Council 1985-87, 1988-90. **Home Addr:** 201 Reese St, Easton, PA 18042.

HOUZE, JENEICE CARMEL WONG
Educator. **Personal:** Born Mar 26, New Orleans, LA; married Harold Emmanuel Houze; children: Harold Emanuel Jr, Miles Peter. **Educ:** Xavier Univ of LA, BA 1959; Univ of San Francisco, MA 1980, Admin Credential 1980; California State Univ, LDS Credential. **Career:** Chicago Sch Dist, teacher 1959-65; Torrance Unified Sch Dist, teacher 1965-, mentor teacher, 1991-. **Orgs:** Mem, sec 1983-93 Xavier Univ of LA Alumni 1965-, CA Teachers Assoc 1966-, Natl Educ Assoc 1966-, Torrance Teachers Assoc 1966-, Parent Teachers Assoc 1966-; Science Leadership, team member, 1993-; attended Dist Sci Workshop on Science Framework 1982-83; coord Career Awareness Prog Lincoln School 1982-84; staff develop clinical teaching Rowland Heights CA 1983-84; project writing team mem Lincoln Elem Sch 1983-84; Olympic Field Day chairperson, budgeting asst, coord ECT Musical Holiday Presentation 1983-84; facilitator Workshops Lincoln Elem Sch 1983-87; curriculum writer Gifted and Talented Prog Lincoln Elem Sch 1983-86; mem Univ of St Francis Alumni 1986-87; mem CA Assoc Gifted 1987; Language Arts Steering Committee, 1995-; Rdg Task Force, site mentor & lead teacher, 1995-97. **Honors/Awds:** Honorary Service Chairperson PTA Assoc 1983-84; Honorary Serv Awd Torrance PTA 1986-87; Recipient US Educators to Japan, 1992. **Business Addr:** Elementary Mentor Teacher, Torrance Unified School District, 2335 Plaza del Amo, Torrance, CA 90504.

HOVELL, LARRY L.
Automobile dealership executive. **Career:** Bay City Chrysler-Plymouth, Inc, CEO, currently. **Special Achievements:** Co. is ranked #91 on Black Enterprise magazine's list of top 100 auto dealers, 1992, #92, 1997. **Business Addr:** Chief Executive Officer, Bay City Chrysler-Plymouth Inc, 225 South Military Ave, Green Bay, WI 54303, (414)494-4040.

HOWARD, AGNES MARIE
Educator, business executive. **Personal:** Born Mar 5, 1924, Texarkana, AR; daughter of Booker T & Lizzie Williams; married Lowry P Howard, Jun 23, 1949; children: Lowri Howard-McGowan, Harriette Howard-Lee. **Educ:** Univ of Arkansas, Pine Bluff, AB, 1944; Univ of Wisconsin, EdM, 1950; Univ of California, EdD, 1991. **Career:** Texarkana Arkansas School Dist, English teacher/basketball coach, 1944-45; Hooks School Dist, English teacher/basketball coach, 1945-48; Liberty Eylau School Dist, teacher, 1953-83; Twin City Day Care Center Inc, CEO, 1985-. **Orgs:** Arkansas Early Childhood Commission, 1994-; Supreme Second Anti-Basileus National Sorority of Phi Delta Kappa Inc, 1993-; Arkansas Advocates for Children, 1985-; Miller County, SCAN Advisory Council, 1993-; Texas Education Political Action Committee, 1974-; Texarkana Child Watch, 1990-; Count me in Year 2000, 1990-. **Honors/Awds:** College Hill Baptist Church, Mother of the Year, 1969; Teacher of the Year, Liberty Eylau School Dist, 1971; City Federation of Clubs, Woman of the Year, 1974; Texarkana Alumnae, Delta Sigma Theta, Outstanding Delta, 1974; City Federation of Clubs, Woman of the Year, 1989. **Special Achievements:** Oklahoma Hall of Fame, 1989; A suggested plan for the administration of a public relations program; in the Twin City Day Care Center Inc, Texarkana, AR, 1991.

HOWARD, AUBREY J.
Business executive. **Personal:** Born Mar 23, 1945, Memphis, TN; married Patricia Claxton; children: Adrian K. **Educ:** Southwestern at Memphis, BA 1972. **Career:** Belz Enterprises, proj dir new hotels & commercial devel 1986-; Belz/Curits Outdoor Oper, mgr of real estate oper 1985-; TESCO Devel, dir of devel 1983-85; Doyen Assn Inc, pres 1977-83; Beale St Nat Historic Found, exec dir 1975; Intergovernmental Coord Dept Shelby Cty Govt, assoc dir for resrch 1974; Project on the Aging, asst asst dir 1973; Preventive Med Cntr, acting dir 1972; Mental Health Services, deputy dir, 1992. **Orgs:** Fellow Natl Endowment for the Humanities, 1977; chmn Midtown Memphis Mental Health Ctr, 1980-82; pres Ballet S Inc, 1980-82; Mason, NAACP; bd mem Memphis Oral School for the Deaf, 1985; Memphis Crisis Stabilization Center, 1985; State of TN Dept of Mental Health & Mental Retardation, 1986-94. **Business Addr:** Project Manager, Belz Enterprises, 5118 Park Ave, Memphis, TN 38117.

HOWARD, BILLIE JEAN
Educator, nurse. **Personal:** Born Jul 31, 1950, Chicago, IL. **Educ:** Univ of IL Chicago, BSN 1973; Loyola Univ, MSN 1976. **Career:** Univ of IL Hosp, staff nurse 1973-76; Univ of IL Coll of Nursing, instr 1976-77; Michael Reese Hosp, clinical spec 1977-78; Univ of IL Coll of Nursing, asst prof 1978-81; Chicago State Univ, asst prof nursing until 1987; Chicago Board of Education, school nurse, teacher, 1987. **Orgs:** Suprv Univ of Chicago Hosp 1981-83; assoc dir of nursing Provident Med Ctr 1983-84; asst prof nursing Chicago State Univ 1984-; Illinois School Health Association; past mem: Sigma Theta Tau, March of Dimes Perinatal Nursing Adv Council. **Home Addr:** 338 S Harper Ave, Glenwood, IL 60425-2056. **Business Addr:** Teacher, Nurse, Chicago Board of Education, Harlan High School, 9652 S Michigan, Chicago, IL 60628.

HOWARD, BRIAN
Professional basketball player. **Personal:** Born Oct 19, 1967, Winston-Salem, NC. **Educ:** North Carolina. **Career:** Dallas Mavericks, forward, 1992-. **Business Addr:** Professional Basketball Player, Dallas Mavericks, Reunion Arena, 777 Sports St, Dallas, TX 75207, (214)988-0117.

HOWARD, CALVIN JOHNSON
Law enforcement officer (retired). **Personal:** Born Oct 17, 1947, Miami, FL; son of Mary Magdalene Johnson Ferguson and Norman Howard; divorced; children: Tara Evette, Calvin Deon, Arlethia Michelle, LaTonya Linnell, Cortenay DeMaun, LaToya Linnett, Troy Everett, Jabari Deon, Christian Jerrod Jameel. **Educ:** Tarrant County Jr Coll, Hurst TX, AA Law Enforcement; Univ of Texas, Arlington TX; Abilene Christian Univ, Garland TX, BS Criminal Justice. **Career:** Dade County Seriff's Office, Miami FL, deputy Sheriff, 1969-70; Tarrant County Sheriff's Office, Ft Worth TX, deputy Sheriff, 1970-72; Dallas Police Dept, Dallas TX, police officer, beginning 1972, retired senior corporal, 1993. **Orgs:** Founder, Texas Peace Officers Assn, Dallas Chapter, 1975-77, 1st state vice pres, 1977-82; vice chmn, Southern Region, Natl Black Police Assn, 1980-84, chmn, 1984-92, natl chmn, 1988-90; NAACP, Congressional Task Force, Dallas Chapter, 1987; Inspiring Body of Christ, Dallas, TX, 1992; Dallas & Grand Prairie Texas NAACP, 1989. **Honors/Awds:** Appreciation Award, Texas Peace Officers Assn, Dallas Chapter, 1986; Leadership Award, Southern Region NBPA, 1987; Dallas Community Relations Comm, 1988; Outstanding Law Enforcement Officer Award, Greater Dallas; Community Relations Commission, Renault Robinson Natl Award, NBPA, 1988. **Military Serv:** US Army, SFC, SA US Army Intelligence; , US Air Force, SSG, 1965-71; TX Army Natl Guard, Airborne Medic; Ret US Army 1994. **Home Addr:** 721 Pinoak Dr, Grand Prairie, TX 75051.

HOWARD, DALTON J., JR.
Attorney. **Personal:** Born in Vicksburg, MS; married Marian Hill. **Educ:** Parsons Clge, BS 1964; Howard Univ Schl Law, JD 1974. **Career:** Nghbrhd Legal Serv Prog, managing atty 1975-; Wash Tech Inst, instr 1974-75; law student 1971-74; Mutual of NY, field underwriter 1968-69; Gary Schl Cty, tchr 1968-69. **Orgs:** Vp dir Movin' on Inc 1974-; Natl Bar Assc; Amer Bar Assc; Assc of Trial Lawyers of Amer; mem DC Bar Assc Sigma Delta Tau Legal Frat. **Honors/Awds:** AUS Bandsman 1969-71. **Business Addr:** Law Office of Howard Dalton, 1429 Good Hope Rd SE, Washington, DC 20002.

HOWARD, DESMOND KEVIN
Professional football player. **Personal:** Born May 15, 1970, Cleveland, OH; son of Hattie V Howard Dawkins Shockley and James D Howard. **Educ:** University of Michigan, Ann Arbor, BA, communications, 1992. **Career:** Washington Redskins, professional football player, 1992-95; Jacksonville Jaguars, 1995-96; Green Bay Packers, 1996-97; Oakland Raiders, 1997-. **Orgs:** 100 Black Men, 1992; Habari Gani, employee, 1992; National Consortium for Academics and Sports and the NCAA Foundation, chairman, 1992; Beale Harden Beale Inc, Peer Facilitator, program advisor, 1990; Special Olympics, spokesperson, 1992. **Honors/Awds:** Downtown Atheletic Club, Heisman Award, 1991; Walter Camp Foundation, Player of the Year, 1991; Maxwell Award, Offensive Player of the Year, 1991; ABC Sports, NCAA Offensive Player of the Year, 1991; MVP, Super Bowl XXXI, 1997. **Business Addr:** Professional Football Player, Oakland Raiders, 1220 Harbor Bay Pky, Alameda, CA 94502, (510)615-1875.

HOWARD, DONALD R.
Engineer. **Personal:** Born Oct 13, 1928, Wightman, VA; married Virdie M Hubbard; children: Jada Marni, Donald, Jr. **Educ:** BS 1959. **Career:** IITRI 1956-64; Mobil Oil Corp 1964-68; Principal Chem Engr Commonwealth Edison Co 1968. **Orgs:** Mem AICHE; mem ACS; Prof Black Chemists & Chem Engrs; mem Carter Temple CME Ch. **Military Serv:** USMC 1951-53. **Business Addr:** 72 W Adams, Chicago, IL 60603.

HOWARD, EDWARD T., III
Retail company executive. **Personal:** Born Jun 21, 1942, Beckley, WV; son of Lettie Gains Howard and Edward T Howard Jr; married LaRue Saunders Howard, Apr 5, 1961; children: GiAnna Watkins, Edward T IV. **Educ:** Marshall University, Huntington, WV, BA, psychology, 1965. **Career:** J C Penney, Huntington, WV, management trainee, 1965; J C Penney, Dayton, OH, store manager, 1980-83; J C Penney, Pittsburgh, PA, regional merchandise manager, 1983-86; J C Penney, Nashua, NH, district manager, 1986-89; J C Penney, Dallas, TX, director of geographic merchandising, 1989-90, vice president & director of investor relations, 1990-96; JcPenney Co, Southwestern Reg, Buena Park, CA, pres; West Region, Buena Park, CA, pres, currently. **Orgs:** Member, National Retail Assn; National Urban Leauge; NAACP; board of directors, Marshall University's Executive Committee of the Society of Yeager Scholars; California State University at Fullerton President's University, advisory bd. **Business Addr:** President, West Region, J C Penney Company Inc, 6131 Orangethorpe Ave, Buena Park, CA 90620.

HOWARD, ELIZABETH FITZGERALD
Educator, librarian. **Personal:** Born Dec 28, 1927, Baltimore, MD; daughter of Bertha McKinley James Fitzgerald and John Mac Farland Fitzgerald; married Lawrence C Howard; children: Jane Howard-Martin, Susan C, Laura L. **Educ:** Radcliffe Coll Harvard Univ, AB 1948; Univ of Pittsburgh, MLS 1971, PhD 1977. **Career:** Boston Public Libr, childrens Librarian 1952-56; Episcopal Diocese of Pittsburgh, resource librn 1972-74; Pittsburgh Theol Sem, ref Librn 1974-77; Univ of Pittsburgh, visiting lecturer 1976-78; W VA Univ, asst prof 1978-85, on leave sr librarian Univ of Maiduguri Nigeria 1981-82, assoc prof 1985-89, professor, 1989-93, professor emerita, 1993-. **Orgs:** Dir Radcliffe Alumnae Asso 1969-72; mem Brd of Trustees Ellis Sch Pittsburgh 1970-75; trustee Magee Womens Hosp 1980-94; Episcopal Diocese of Pittsburgh Cathedral Chapter 1984-86; Pittsburgh Chap of LINKS Inc; mem Amer Library Assoc, Children's Literature Assoc, Soc of Children's Book Writers; bd mem, QED Communications 1987-94; bd mem, Beginning With Books 1987-93. **Honors/Awds:** Library science honor soc Beta i Mu; candidate for bd of dirs Harvard Alumni Assoc 1987. **Special Achievements:** Author Articles in Professional Journals; author professional nonfiction, America as Story, 1988; author children's books, Train to Lulu's House, Chita's Christmas Tree, 1989, Aunt Flossie's Hats, 1991; Mac and Marie and the Train Toss Surprise, 1993; Papa Tells Chita a Story, 1995; What's in Aunt Mary's Room?, 1996; America as Story (2nd edition, with Rosemary Coffey), 1997. **Home Addr:** 919 College Ave, Pittsburgh, PA 15232.

HOWARD, ELLEN D.
Association executive. **Personal:** Born Apr 8, 1929, Baltimore, MD; daughter of Louise Tignor Dolvey and Lucious Norman Dolvey; divorced; children: Harold H, Jr, Larry K. **Educ:** Morgan State Coll, BS 1951; Johns Hopkins Univ, MA 1968. **Career:** Educ Talent Search US Office of Educ, exec dir; MD Educa Opportunity Center, exec dir. **Orgs:** Mem bd trustees Coll Entrance Exam Bd; DE DC MD Assc of Financial Aid Admin; 4th Dist Dem Org of Baltimore City; Natl Assc of Student Financial Aid Admin; Natl Council for Negro Women; MD Personnel & Guidance Assc; Natl Educ Assc; YWCA; NAACP; Baltimore Public School Teachers Assn; mem Delta Sigma Theta Inc; Baltimore Continental Soc for Underprivileged Children Inc; Town & Country Set; Baltimore Chap Moles Inc; Etc Ltd; Girl Scouts of Central MD Nominating Council; Natl volunteer planning progs in Mgmt & Audits for Girl Scouts of USA; mem Phi Delta Gamma, Gamma Chap Natl Hon Frat for Grad Women; Phi Lambda Theta Chi Chapter Natl Honor & Prof Assc of Women in Educ; Enon Baptist Church; mem Girl Scouts Central MD; mem MD Personnel and Guidance Association; memBaltimore Urban League and gue of Women Voters; mem Public S ool Administrators and Supervisors Association. **Honors/Awds:** Author ''Financial Aid for Higher Educ''; recip Certificate of Appreciation Amer Biog Inst 1975; Comm Serv Certificate 1974; Certificate of Achievement Morgan Coll ROTC 1974; Amer Legion Award; Intl Women's Yr Award; Outstanding Woman in Youth Devel Baltimore Alumni Chap of Delta Sigma Theta Inc; recip various awards & citations; Induction into the MECEO Hall of Fame as a founder; Mid-Eastern Association of Educational Opportunity Program Personel; MD State Award for Outstanding Services. **Business Addr:** Executive Director, Maryland Educational Opportunity Center, 2700 Gwynns Falls Parkway, Baltimore, MD 21216.

HOWARD, GEORGE. See Obituaries section.

HOWARD, GEORGE, JR.
Attorney. **Personal:** Born May 13, 1924, Pine Bluff, AR; married Vivan Smith; children: Etoria, George III, Risie, Renee, Vivian Alycia. **Educ:** Univ AR, BS, JD 1954; Morris-Booker Coll, LLD 1976. **Career:** Supreme Ct of AR, judge 1976-, apptd by Gov Pryor spc assoc justice; Eastern & Western Dists of AR, dist judge 1980-. **Orgs:** Comm on Professional Conduct; chmn AR State Claims Commn; pres Jeff Co Bar Assn; legal redress comm State Conf NAACP; past chmn AR Adv Com US Civil Rights Commn; mem Alpha Phi Alpha Frat; MW Prince Hall Grand Lodge; F & AM AR; past pres State Conf Branches NAACP Pine Bluff Br. **Honors/Awds:** Honoree in AR Sesquicentennial Celebration. **Military Serv:** USN seabees. **Business Addr:** US Dist Judge, Eastern & Western Dists of AR, 329 1/2 Main St, Pine Bluff, AR 71601.

HOWARD, GLEN
Brewing company executive. **Personal:** Born Sep 12, 1942, Detroit, MI; son of Rebecca Hall Howard (deceased) and Green Howard (deceased); married Sheila Perkins Howard, Feb 8, 1964 (divorced 1981); children: Sheryce, Glen Jr. **Educ:** Wayne County Community College, 1972-73. **Career:** A&P Tea Company, assistant manager, 1960-67; Detroit Edison, meter reader, 1967-68; The Drackett Company, sales representative, 1968-70; United Beverage Company, area manager, 1970-76; Great Lakes Beverage Company, area manager, 1976-85; Coors Brewing Company, community relations field manager, 1986-. **Orgs:** Life member, NAACP, 1973-; board of directors, Food Industry Council, Detroit Chamber of Commerce, 1989-; advisory council member, Detroit Chapter, Southern Christian Leadership Conference, 1990-. **Honors/Awds:** Detroit Fire Department, Community Service Award; City of Detroit, Recreation Department, Meritorious Service Award, Tuskegee Airmen Inc, Detroit Chapter, Appreciation Award. **Business Addr:** Community Relations Field Manager, Coors Brewing Company, 8420 W Bryn Mawr Ave, Ste 420, Chicago, IL 60631-3495.

HOWARD, GLEN
Clergyman. **Personal:** Born May 20, 1956, Oakland, CA; married Marian Byrd. **Educ:** LA Tech Univ, BS Psychology 1980; Gammon Theological Seminary, MDiv 1984. **Career:** Marc Paul Inc, mgmt 1976-79; Xerox Corp, sales/marketing 1980-81; United Methodist Church Iowa Conf, pastor 1984-. **Orgs:** Sec Ankeny Ministerial Assn 1985. **Business Addr:** Pastor, United Methodist Church, 206 SW Walnut, Ankeny, IA 50021.

HOWARD, GWENDOLYN JULIUS
Educator. **Personal:** Born Nov 15, 1932, Brooklyn; divorced; children: Calvin, Lisa C. **Educ:** Bethune Cookman Coll, BS 1956; Univ of No CO, MS 1974; Univ of No CO, EdD 1976. **Career:** Sunlight Beauty Acad-Kingston Jam Cri Deliq Task Force Mod Cities, assoc 1968-70; SE Reg NANB&PW Clubs, gov 1970-73; Gala Travel Inc Miami, co-owner; Dade Co Public Sch, school liaison juvenile justice support prog. **Orgs:** Mem Sigma Gamma Rho 1967-; pres Epsilon Chap Gamma Phi Delta 1978-81; pres Sigma Gamma Rho Gamma Delta Sigma Chap 1980-82; pres Miami Chap Top Ladiesof Distinction Inc 1983-87; YWCA NW exec bd 2 yrs; adv council Miami Dade Comm Coll 1984. **Honors/Awds:** Appreciation Awd Excellence Civic & Soc Club 1971; Natl Assn of Bus & Professional Women's Club 1971; Achvmt Awds Sigma Gamma Rho 1976, MAB & P's Women Clubs 1976, Gamma Phi Delta Sor 1976; nominee FL Women Hall of Fame 1984; Greater Miami Outstanding Influential Blacks 1984; Top Lady of the Year 1985-86. **Business Addr:** School Liaison, Educ Spec, Dade Co Public Sch, Juvenile Justice Support Prog, 3300 NW 27th Ave, Miami, FL 33142.

HOWARD, HENRY L.
Business executive. **Personal:** Born Jun 18, 1930, Augusta, GA; married Arnestine Chishom; children: Vincent, Karlton, Zachary, Henry DeWayne, Vertiz, Valerie, Jerrilynn. **Career:** Howard's Upholstery, owner; Supreme Fashion-Dot Inc, owner. **Orgs:** Pres CSRA Business League; mem BBB; D & B; Chamber of Comm; mem NFIB; chmn trustee bd Green Grove Bapt Ch; mem Optimist Club. **Honors/Awds:** Businessman of the Year 1971, 1973; Citizen of the Year Award 1970. **Business Addr:** 2047 Milledgeville Rd, Augusta, GA.

HOWARD, HOWELL J., JR.
Psychiatrist. **Personal:** Born Mar 26, 1938, Washington, DC; son of Consuelo Jones Howard and Howell J Howard Sr; divorced. **Educ:** Boston Univ Coll of Liberal Arts, AB 1959; Howard Univ Coll of Med, MD 1965. **Career:** Howard Univ, psychiatrist; Washington DC, private practice of psychiatrist 1970-73; Freedman's Hosp Howard Univ, res tng; Office of Forensic Psychiatry Dept Human & Resources Washington, staff psychiatrist. **Orgs:** Mem Med Soc of DC; Amer Med Assn; Natl Med Assn; Washington Psychiatric Soc; Amer Psychiatric Assn; Kappa Alpha Psi Frat. **Military Serv:** AUS med corps 1966-69.

HOWARD, JANICE LYNN
Company Executive. **Personal:** Born Dec 11, 1958, Magnolia, MS; daughter of Joe and Ruth Robertson; divorced; children: Kerrington Lavern. **Educ:** University of Southern, BS, journalism, 1980; Barry University theology. **Career:** John S & James L Knight Foundation, journalism prog assistant, 1990-; WPLG, TV-10, sales assistant, 1990; The Miami Herald, circulation manager, 1989; Washington Post, journalist, office manager, circulation, 1981. **Orgs:** Miami Mega-City Special Olympics, board of directors, 1995-; James K Batten Black Executive Forum, board, 1995. **Honors/Awds:** James K Batten Black Executive, Miami Black Executive, 1995. **Business Addr:** Journalism Program Assistant, John S & James L Knight Foundation, 2 S Biscayne Blvd, 1 Biscayne Tower, Miami, FL 33131, (305)908-2624.

HOWARD, JOHN ROBERT
Educator, attorney. **Personal:** Born Jan 24, 1933, Boston, MA; married Mary Doris Adams; children: Leigh Humphrey. **Educ:** Brandeis Univ, BA 1955; NY Univ, MA 1961; Stanford Univ, PhD 1965; J Du Pace Univ 1985. **Career:** Univ of OR, asst prof 1965-68; Rutgers Univ, assoc prof 1969-71; State Univ of NY, dean & prof 1971-80, State Univ of NY, prof of sociology 1971-; atty in private practice 1986-. **Orgs:** Bd mem United Way of Westchester 1976-78; bd of advs Inst for Urban Design 1978-; vice pres Soc for the Study of Social Problems 1978-79; bd mem Street Theater Inc 1978-80; bd Friends of the Nueberger Museum 1982-85. **Honors/Awds:** Publ Lifestyles in the Black, WW Norton 1969; The Cutting Edge, J B Lippincott Publ 1974; Urban Black Politics, Annals of the Am Acad 1978; various articles. **Business Addr:** Professor of Sociology, State Univ of NY, Lincoln Ave, Purchase, NY 10577.

HOWARD, JOSEPH CLEMENS
Federal judge. **Personal:** Born Dec 9, 1922, Des Moines, IA; married Gwendolyn Mae London, Dec 1954; children: 1 son. **Educ:** University of Iowa, BA, 1950; University of Washington Law School, 1951; Drake University, LLB, 1955, MA, 1957, JD, 1968; Washington & Lee University; Northwestern University Law School; University of Nevada. **Career:** Supreme Bench of Baltimore, probation officer, 1958-60, associate

judge, 1968-79; Howard & Hargrove Law Firm, attorney, 1960-64; City of Baltimore, assistant state's attorney, 1964-67, chief of trial section, 1966-67, assistant city solicitor, 1967-68; visiting professor/lecturer; US District Court of Maryland, district judge 1979-91, senior district judge, 1991-. **Orgs:** Drake University Law School Board of Counselors, 1970-73; Judicial CNL of Natl Bar Assn, chairman, 1973-74; Antioch Law School Board of Governors, 1976-79; Task Force to Examine Criminal Justice System in China, 1977; World Association of Judges, 1978-; All National & Local Bar Associations; Baltimore Urban Coalition; NAACP, life member; Mayor's Task Force on Community Relations; US Commission on Civil Rights; Maryland Jud Conference Executive Committee, chairman, 1977-78; Mayor's Task Force on Juvenile Delinquency, chairman; Citizens Planning and Housing Association, board of governors; National Bar FND, Legal Aid Bureau, board of directors; ABA; Phi Alpha Delta. **Honors/Awds:** First African-American admitted to Phi Alpha Delta Legal Frat, 1952; first African-American elected to City-Wide Office Supreme Bench of Baltimore City, 1968; Outstanding Service in State's Attorney's Office Chief of Trial Section, 1968; Bicentenial Judicial Award, Black American Law Students Association, 1976; Man of Year, NAT Association of Business & Professional Women's Clubs, 1979; first African-American appointed to US District Court for District of Maryland, 1979; Special Judicial Service Award, Herbert M Frisby Hist Society, 1980; Morgan State College, Honorary Degree, 1972. **Military Serv:** US Army, 1st lt, 1944-47; Commendation from Brigadier Gen Trudo, Philippine Command, 1945. **Business Addr:** Senior District Judge, US District Court, 101 W Lombard, Ste 340, Baltimore, MD 21201.

HOWARD, JOSEPH H.
Hospital administrator, dentist (retired). **Personal:** Born Jul 17, 1912, Chicago, IL; son of Eve Shumpert Howard (deceased) and Joseph H. Howard, Sr. (deceased); married Tommye Berry (deceased); children: Brock, Viki. **Educ:** Fisk Univ, AB 1935; Univ IL, DDS 1946; USC, MPH 1969. **Career:** Evanston Comm Hosp, dir dental serv 1948-50; City of Los Angeles, pub health dent 1966-70; LA Model City Dental Prog, coord 1969-70; Harbor Gen Hosp, dir comm dentistry 1970-73; UCLA, asst prof dentistry 1971-; Long Beach Genl Hosp, dental dir 1973-. **Orgs:** Inst chem Roosevelt HS; dental consult Suntown Palos Verdes Conv Hosp 1973; mem La Federation Dentaire Internationale; Amer Dental Assn; So CA Dental Soc; So CA Pub Health Assn; Amer Assn Pub Health Dentists; Western Soc of Periodontology; natl Dental Assn; Angel City Dental Assn; Amer Soc for Preventive Dentistry; Boys Work Sect YMCA 1936-37; mem LA Natl Library Week Com 1967; mem Dist Att Adv Council 1967; mem Mayor's Comm Adv Com 1967; Adv Bd Mahar House 1971; participant at lectures seminars & table clinics; author of numerous publications. **Honors/Awds:** Drums in the Americas Oak pub 1967; Gifts From ILE IFE Black History Museum Phil PA 1982; Drums 1982. **Military Serv:** USAF capt 1950-52. **Home Addr:** 1728 Victoria Ave, Los Angeles, CA 90019.

HOWARD, JULES JOSEPH, JR.
Human resources executive. **Personal:** Born Aug 24, 1943, New Orleans, LA; son of Ophelia Howard and Jules J Howard Sr; divorced; children: Gwendolyn. **Educ:** California State University, BA, business administration, 1975, MBA, 1977. **Career:** City of Carson, executive assistant, 1973-1979; Computer Careers Corporation, manager, 1979-1981; Great 400 Group International, executive director, 1981-. **Orgs:** Carson Lions Club, vice pres; Kappa Alpha Psi Fraternity; Carson Branch NAACP; California Institute for Employment Counseling; California Association of Personnel Consultants. **Business Addr:** Executive Director, Great 400 Group International, 500 E Carson St, Ste 105, Carson, CA 90745, (213)775-8729.

HOWARD, JUWAN ANTONIO
Professional basketball player. **Personal:** Born Feb 7, 1973, Chicago, IL. **Educ:** Univ of Michigan, graduated April 29, 1995. **Career:** Washington Wizards, forward, 1994-. **Orgs:** Serves as the NBA's National Spokesman for Reading is Fundemental. **Honors/Awds:** NBA All-Star, 1996. **Special Achievements:** Member of the Fab Five, Univ of MI, 1991-94. **Business Addr:** Professional Basketball Player, Washington Wizards, MCI Center, 601 F St NW, Washington, DC 20071, (301)622-3865.

HOWARD, KEITH L.
Optometrist. **Personal:** Born Feb 27, 1940, Buffalo, NY; son of Annie C Howard and Robert B Howard Sr; married Patricia; children: Jennifer, Kristopher. **Educ:** AA, BS, OD 1966. **Career:** Optical Corp, partner 1968; pvt prac 1969; Melnick, Howard, Grzankowski Opt, prof corp formed 1974; Southern Tier Optometric Center, vice pres, partner 1979-. **Orgs:** Natl & Amer Optometric Assn; Natl Eye Research Fnd Optometric Extension Prog dir Olean YMCA; Olean Comm Chest; EGO Health Studios Inc; bd mem, State Board of Optometry, 1985-89, 1989-93; bd mem and Region I director, Natl Optometric Assn 1988-89. **Honors/Awds:** Olean YMCA Man of Year 1970; one of two black optometrists in NY State. **Business Addr:** 168 N Union St, Olean, NY 14760.

HOWARD, LAWRENCE CABOT
Educator. **Personal:** Born Apr 16, 1925, Des Moines, IA; son of Louisa Maude Lewis Howard and Charles Preston Howard; married Elizabeth Fitzgerald; children: Jane, Susan, Laura. **Educ:** Drake Univ, BA 1949; Wayne State Univ, MA 1950; Harvard Univ, PhD 1956. **Career:** Hofstra Univ, instr asst prof 1956-58; Brandeis Univ, asst prof 1958-63; Peace Corps, Philippines, assoc dir 1961-63; Ctr on Innovation NY St Dept of Educ, assoc dir 1964; Univ of WI, dir human rel inst 1964-67; Danforth Found, vice pres 1967-69; Univ of Pittsburgh, dean, Graduate School of Public and International Affairs, 1969-73, prof 1973-94, professor emeritus, 1994-; Chatham College, distinguished visiting prof, 1995-; Government of the Bahamas, management consultant 1986-94. **Orgs:** Consult US Ofc Educ State Dept Bur Extnl Rsch; mem rsch & adv bd Com on Econ Devel; mem Natl Adv Comm Tchr Corps 1967-69; mem Pgh World Affrs Counc 1969-; Pgh Hist & Landmarks Found; mem exec council Natl Assn Sch Pub Affrs Adm 1971-73; Amer Soc Pub Admin 1972-; trustee Ch Soc for Coll Work, Drake Univ, St Augustine Coll, Seabury-Western Theol Sem, Epis Diocese of Pgh; Harvard Grad Soc for Advcmt of Study & Rsch; Deputy to Epis Diocesan Conv. **Honors/Awds:** Man of the Yr Alpha Phi Alpha 1949; Disting Alumnus Awd Drake Univ 1971; contrib articles to professional jours; natl pres of COMPA 1979-80; co-author "Public Adminstrn, Balancing Power & Accountability"; Fullbright Professor Univ of Maiduguri Nigeria 1981-82; mem Phi Beta Kappa; author, US Involvement in Africa South of the Sahara before 1960 (1988). **Military Serv:** US Army, 1943-45. **Home Addr:** 919 College Ave, Pittsburgh, PA 15232.

HOWARD, LEON
Educator. **Career:** AL State Univ, pres 1984-. **Business Addr:** President, Alabama State University, 915 S Jackson St, Montgomery, AL 36195.

HOWARD, LEON W., JR.
Business executive. **Personal:** Born May 3, 1935, Pittsburgh, PA. **Educ:** Univ of Pgh, attended 1974-; PA State Univ, attended 1968; licensed as broker 1971. **Career:** Robt C Golden, real estate 1956-57; Surety Underwriters Inc, vice pres 1970-73; Nationwide Ins Co, agency agreement 1972-. **Orgs:** Past chmn Labor & Indus Com Pgh NAACP 1974; past pres Pgh Branch NAACP 1975; past pres COPP; past vice pres PABU; past bd of dir Profit Making Prog for Black Catholic Ministries & Laymen's Council; exec bd mem Pgh Chap NAACP; exec bd mem Homewood-Brushton YMCA; commr City of Pgh Dept of City Planning; mem natl Assn of Sec Dealers; mem Pgh Life Underwriters Assn Inc; mem Natl Assn of Life Underwriters; mem Ins Club of Pgh Inc. **Honors/Awds:** Awd for Outstanding Contribution to the Struggle for Human Rights Western PA Black Polit Assembly. **Military Serv:** AUS paratrooper. **Business Addr:** Ins Broker/Agent, Nationwide Insurance Co, 564 Forbes Ave Ste 801, Pittsburgh, PA 15219.

HOWARD, LESLIE CARL
Public administrator. **Personal:** Born Jun 18, 1950, Aberdeen, MD; son of Ethel B Danley and Willis C Danley; married Corrine Felder; children: Kevin, Keith, Kenneth. **Educ:** Howard Univ, BA, 1980; Community College of Baltimore, AA, 1971, certificate electronics, 1982; Baruch Coll CUNY, MPA, 1984; Johns Hopkins Univ, certificate, 1989-90; University of Baltimore, School of Law, JD, 1996-97. **Career:** MD Dept of Human Resources, caseworker II 1975-77; Mayor of Baltimore, spec asst 1979-82; Neighborhood Housing Serv of Baltimore, prog dir 1982-83; Mayor of Detroit, spec asst 1983-84; Neighborhood Housing Serv of Baltimore, neighborhood coord asst dir, neighborhood dir 1985-87; City of Baltimore Development Corp, development director, 1988-96; Eubie Blake National Jazz Institute & Cultural Ctr, executive director, 1996-. **Orgs:** President, Alliance of Rosemont Community Organization, Inc, 1987-91; founding president, Maryland Low-Income Housing Coalition, 1989-91; steering committee member, Baltimore-Neighborhood Resource Center, 1990-92. **Honors/Awds:** Summer Scholarship Peabody Preparatory Sch 1967; Certificates Comm Serv RHATA Inc Calverton Jr High 1980, 1982; Natl Urban Fellowship Class of 1983-84; Concert Productions Hugh Masakela Leon Thomas et al 1970-; Lionel Hampton, 1998; mem Phi Alpha Theta Intl Honor Soc in History; Governor's Certificate of Appreciation; Wilson Park Community Serv Awd; Governor's Certificate, Community Service Award, 1989-90. **Home Addr:** 2322 Harlem Ave, Baltimore, MD 21216. **Business Addr:** Executive Director, Eubie Blake National Jazz Institute & Cultural Ctr., The Brokerage, 34 Market Pl, Ste 323, Baltimore, MD 21202, (410)625-3113.

HOWARD, LILLIE PEARL
Educator, educational administrator. **Personal:** Born Oct 4, 1949, Gadsden, AL; daughter of Zola Mae Howard and Walter Moody; married Willie D Kendricks (divorced 1986); children: Kimberly Denise Kendricks, Benjamin Richard Kendricks. **Educ:** Univ of South Alabama, Mobile, Al, BA, 1971; Univ of New Mexico, Albuquerque, NM, MA, 1972, PhD, 1975; Harvard University, Cambridge, MA, Grad of Institute for Educational Management, 1988. **Career:** Wright State Univ, Dayton, OH, associate prof of English, 1980-85, assistant dean, coll liberal arts, 1982-83, associate dean coll liberal arts, 1983-87, professor of English, 1985-, assistant vice pres for academic affairs, 1987-88, associate vice pres for academic affairs, 1988-94; Undergraduate Educ & Academic Affairs, assoc provost, 1994-. **Orgs:** Member, Modern Languages Association; member, American Association of Higher Education; member, Ohio Board of Regents Committee on the Enhancement of Undergrad education; member, Ohio Board of Regents Commission on Articulation and transfer; member, The National Association of Women Deans, Administrators, and Counselors; member, The National Association of Academic Affairs Administrators. **Honors/Awds:** Woodrow Wilson Finalist, 1971; Ford Foundation Fellow, 1971-75; Grant Recipient, National Endowment for the Humanities, 1987-90; Grant Recipient, Ohio Board of Regents, 1990. **Business Addr:** Associate Provost, Undergraduate Education & Academic Affairs, Professor of English, Wright State Univ, 105E Allyn Hall, Dayton, OH 45435.

HOWARD, LINWOOD E.
Banker. **Personal:** Born Mar 12, 1954, Roanake Rapids, NC; son of Norma and Alexander M; married Denise Laws; children: Marcellus, Jeniene. **Educ:** Livingstone College, BS, 1976; UNC-Chapel Hill, advancement, 1984. **Career:** First Union National Bank, branch mgr, 1976-86, consumer banking branch mgr/vice pres, 1986-93; Crestar Bank, market mgr, senior vice pres, 1993-. **Orgs:** Greenville Chamber of Commerce, board mem, 1992-; Greenville Area Council, board mem, 1992-; United Neighborhood Economic Development Corp, director, 1991-; Downtown Norfolk Council; Norfolk State Univ School of Business, bd of dirs. **Business Addr:** Senior Vice Pres, Crestar Bank, PO Box 2600, Norfolk, VA 23501-2600.

HOWARD, LYTIA RAMANI
Educator. **Personal:** Born May 6, 1950, Atlanta, GA; daughter of Gwendolyn Howard and G LaMarr Howard. **Educ:** Spelman College, BA 1971; Univ of Tennessee, MACT 1973; Atlanta Univ, MA 1978, EdD 1979; Interdenominational Theological Ctr, MRE 1984. **Career:** Spelman Coll, instructor, asst prof 1973-83, asst dean academic 1983-85; GA Inst of Tech, dir of special programs 1985-, asst dean for minority and special programs 1990-. **Orgs:** Mem Alpha Kappa Delta Sociological Honor Soc, Mid-South Sociological Assn, Natl Assn for Women Deans Administrators and Counselors, Southern Christian Leadership Council, Phi Delta Kappa, Amer Soc for Engrg Educ; bd mem Natl Consortium for Grad Degrees for Minorities in Engrg Inc 1985-86; mem Natl Action Council for Minorities in Engrg, Natl Assn of Minority Engrg Program Administrators, United Assn of Christian Counselors; chairperson bd of dirs Hinsley Day Care Ctr 1986; bd of trustees New Hope Church of God in Christ 1986; intl pres, The Sunshine Band, Church of God in Christ, Inc 1986-. **Honors/Awds:** Certificates Assoc of Colleges and Univs for International-Intercultural Affairs 1976; Alpha Kappa Delta Sociological Honor Soc; Central GA Scholarship Fund; Phi Delta Kappa; Proclamation City of Atlanta for Leadership in Community 1982; plaques Spelman Coll, New Hope Church, YWCA of Greater Atlanta, Central GA recognition; Proclamation, City of Detroit 1987; Plaque, Natl Assn of Business Women of America 1988; Proclamations: City of E St Louis, MO, 1992, City of Memphis, 1992, City of Daytona Beach, 1991. **Home Addr:** 371 Lynnhaven Dr SW, Atlanta, GA 30310. **Business Addr:** Assistant Dean for Minority and Special Programs, Georgia Inst of Technology, Coll of Engineering-0360, Atlanta, GA 30332.

HOWARD, M. W., JR.
Clergyman, educational administrator. **Personal:** Born Mar 3, 1946, Americus, GA; son of Laura Turner Howard and Moses William Howard, Sr; married Barbara Jean Wright; children: Matthew Weldon, Adam Turner, Maisha Wright. **Educ:** Morehouse Coll, BA 1968; Princeton Theological Seminary, MDiv 1972. **Career:** Reformed Church in AME, exec dir of the Black Council, 1972-92; president, New York Theological Seminary, 1992-. **Orgs:** Ordained minister Amer Baptist Chs 1974; moderator Program to Combat Racism of the World Council of Churches 1976-78; pres Natl Council of Churches 1979-81; bd of trustees Natl Urban League 1981-88; bd of trustees Independent Sector 1981-86; trustee Childrens Defense Fund 1981-86; pres Amer Comm on Africa; provided X-mas services to US Hostages in Iran in 1979; Chaired Ecumenical delegation which accompanied the Rev Jesse Jackson to obtain release of Lt Robt Goodman in Damascus, Syria; Human Rights Advisory Group of the World Council of Churches, unitil 1989; chair religious comm, Welcome Nelson Mandela to New York, 1990; mem, Council on Foreign Relations, 1997-; mem, Exec Comm of the Assn of Theological Schools, 1994-2000. **Honors/Awds:** Honorary Dr of Divinity Degree Miles Coll and Central Coll 1979-80; citations Mayors of Philadelphia, PA and Americus, GA 1981-84; distinguished alumnus award Princeton Sem 1982; Honorary Dr of Humane Letters Morehouse Coll 1984; Citations from the NJ ST Assembly; The City of Waterloo, Iowa; The Township of Lawrence, NJ; The Touissant Loverture Freedom Award by NY's Haitian Community; Chaired the Seminar against bank loans to South Africa in Zurich, Switzerland in 1982; The Measure of A Man Award, New York NAACP, 1993. **Business Addr:** President, New York Theological Seminary, 5 W 29th St, New York, NY 10001.

HOWARD, MAMIE R.
Educational administrator. **Personal:** Born Nov 24, 1946, Pascagoula, MS; daughter of Mr & Mrs E Howard. **Educ:** Pensacola Jr Coll, AS 1971; USA, BS 1976; UAB, MS 1979; Univ of AL, PhD 1988. **Career:** DW McMillan Hosp, gen duty rn 1967-71, suprv 1971-76; Jefferson Davis Jr Coll, instr 1976-78; Pensacola Jr Coll, dept chair allied health ed, 1978-90; CS Mott Community College, Flint, MI, dean, school of health and human sciences, 1990-. **Orgs:** Mem Amer Nurses Assn 1971-, USA Alumni Assn; consult Escambia Sickle Cell Disease Found 1979-82; mem UAB Alumni Assn 1979-, Committee for Allied Health Ed 1981-, AAWCGC 1982-; bd of dir FL Lung Assn 1983-90; chief exec officer State Mgmt Ltd 1985-86; dir at large Lung Assn 1986-90; mem Alpha Kappa Alpha; chairman PRIDE Committee of the Amer Lung Assn, 1989-90; Amer Lung Assn Board, Genesse County, MI, 1991-. **Honors/Awds:** Honor Award Kappa Delta Pi Grad Honor Soc 1981-; Selected as a Leader of the 80's FIPSE 1982; honored by the governor as an Outstanding Black American 1988; Leadership Award, Pensacola Chamber of Commerce, 1990; Outstanding Educator, Alpha Kappa Alpha Sor, 1990. **Business Addr:** Dean, C S Mott Community College, School of Health & Human Sciences, 1401 E Court St, CM 2313, Flint, MI 48502.

HOWARD, MILTON L.
Architect, association executive. **Personal:** Born Sep 3, 1927, Hurtsboro, AL; married Dolores Allen; children: Mark, James. **Educ:** KY State Clge; Univ of IL. **Career:** Milton Lewis Howard Assc Architects, architect & owner, currently. **Orgs:** Mem AIA; Natl Council Archit Registration Bds; Guild for Religious Arch Mem Arch Adv Panel GSA Region 1; Bldg Bd of Appeals City of Hartford; vice pres Hartford Comm Capital Corp. **Military Serv:** AUS 1950-52. **Business Addr:** 129 Weston St, Hartford, CT 06103.

HOWARD, NORMAN LEROY
Administrator. **Personal:** Born May 22, 1930, New York, NY; married Barbara; children: Karen, Dale, Steven. **Career:** Consolidated Edison Co of NY Inc, equal emplmt oppor coord; Inst Mediation & Conflict Resol, consult 1972-73; NYCPD, retired detective 1952-72; New York City Dept of Parks, playground dir 1948-51. **Orgs:** Mem 100 Black Men Inc; Boys of Yesteryear; 369th Vet Assc; K of C St Patricks Council; retired Guardians NYCPD; Intl Black Police Assc; Welterweight boxing champion amatuer New York City Dept of Parks 1943-44; Middleweight Champion Amatuer Met AAU 1945. **Honors/Awds:** Combat Cross for Bravery NYCPD 1955; 15 awards for Bravery & Excellent Police Work NYCPD; 1st black detective assigned to 40th squad Bronx 1954. **Military Serv:** AUS pvt el 1950-52; Good Conduct Medal. **Business Addr:** 4 Irving Pl, New York, NY 10003.

HOWARD, OSBIE L., JR.
Business executive. **Personal:** Born Feb 9, 1943, Memphis, TN; son of Bertha S Howard and Osbie L Howard Sr (deceased); married Rose O Ollie; children: John, Kendra, Nathan. **Educ:** Memphis State Univ, BBA 1967; Washington Univ, MBA 1971. **Career:** United American of Tennessee, Inc, senior vice pres and exec dir, 1995-; Secured Capital Developers, partner, 1988-91; City of Memphis, Treasury Div, treasurer and dir; TN Valley Center for Minority Economic Devel, exec vice pres 1979-88; Shelby Cty Gvt, asst chief adminstn officer 1978-79; Banks Findley White & Co CPA's, tax mgr 1974-78; Memphis Bus Resource Center, financial & specialist 1972-74; Exxon Co, financial analyst 1971-72; TN State Bd of Accountancy, CPA 1973. **Orgs:** Treasurer & co-founder New Memphis Development Corp, 1976; bd of dir, JK Lewis Center for Senior Citizens 1978-; graduate Business School Fellowship consortium for Graduate Study in Mgmt 1969; treasurer, Industrial Development Corp of Memphis and Shelby County, 1980-91. **Honors/Awds:** Washington Univ School of Business, Business Minority Council, Alumni Entrepreneur Award, 1991. **Home Addr:** 2093 Jamie Dr, Memphis, TN 38116. **Business Addr:** Senior Vice President, United American of Tennessee, Inc, 1991 Corporate Ave, Memphis, TN 38132.

HOWARD, PAUL LAWRENCE, JR.
Attorney. **Personal:** Born Sep 22, 1951, Waynesboro, GA; son of Gussie P Howard and Paul L Howard Sr; married Petrina M Moody, Jun 2, 1990; children: Jamila. **Educ:** Morehouse College, AB, 1972; Emory University School of Law, JD, 1976. **Career:** City of Atlanta, municipal court, deputy solicitor; Fulton County, district attorney's office, assistant district attorney; Thomas, Kennedy, Sampson & Patterson, associate; Fulton County, state court, solicitor, district attorney, currently. **Orgs:** Gate City Bar, bench & bar committee; National Bar Association; Atlanta Bar Association; Georgia Bar Association; Georgia Solicitors Association; NAACP; Urban League. **Honors/Awds:** Morehouse College, Achievement in Law, 1992; Providence Baptist Church Law, 1992; Georgia Association of Black Women Attorneys, 1992. **Special Achievements:** First African American district attorney in Georgia. **Military Serv:** Georgia National Guard, e-2, 1972-78. **Business Addr:** District Attorney, Fulton County, 136 Pryor St SW, Rm 301, Atlanta, GA 30303, (404)730-4979.

HOWARD, RAY F.
Government official. **Personal:** Born Oct 5, 1945, Troy, AL; son of Maudie L Bennett Howard (deceased) and Arthur Howard (deceased); married Sharon G Harvey Howard; children: Leslie R, Joy R. **Educ:** Cleveland State Univ, Cleveland, OH, BBA, 1970; Case Western Reserve Univ School of Management, Cleveland, OH, MBA candidate, 1970-72. **Career:** Bausch & Lomb & UCO, Rochester, NY, manager, planning and products, customer service, 1973-81; CIBA Vision Care, Atlanta, GA, national customer service manager, 1981-85; GMD, Dunwoody, GA, product marketing director, 1985-87; Project Marketing Group, Atlanta, GA, president, 1987-89; US Treasury Dept, IRS Division, San Jose, CA, assistant district director, 1989-. **Orgs:** Member, Senior Executives Assn, 1989-; member, Sales & Marketing Executives Club, 1983-89; member, American Society for Training and Development, 1987-89; member, American Management Assn, 1975-81; member, Product Development and Management Assn. **Honors/Awds:** Sales/Marketing Awards, Bausch & Lomb and CIBA Vision, 1976-85; Achievement Award, United Way, 1989; Excellence Award, Atlanta District, IRS, 1990. **Military Serv:** US Air Force, A3C, 1964. **Business Addr:** Assistant District Director, IRS Division of US Treasury, 55 S Market, Ste 900, San Jose, CA 95113.

HOWARD, RAYMOND MONROE, SR.
Clergyman. **Personal:** Born Sep 13, 1921, Many, LA; married Dorothy Mae Matthews; children: Raymond Jr, Sylvia Dean Norman, Sandra Laray Stuart, Shirley Ann Shields, Ralph Edgar, Sherry Marie Brown. **Educ:** Skyline Coll San Bruno CA, AA 1972; San Francisco Theol Sem, M Div 1974. **Career:** Paradise Missionary Bapt Ch, pastor 1955-; Prog Educ & Dist Congress of Christian Edn, pres 1970; Prog Educ Dist Assn, sec of finance 1963. **Orgs:** Pres organizer Daly City Community for Childrens Serv 1976-77; bus mgr CA State Bapt Convention Inc 1980; candidate Daly City Councilman 1972; pres organizer Black Churchmens Assn 1972; pres organizer Ingleside Churches Assn 1973; Combat Eurpoe/Africa Campaign. **Military Serv:** AUS mst sgt 1943-45. **Business Addr:** 2595 San Jose Ave, San Francisco, CA 94112.

HOWARD, ROBERT BERRY, JR.
City official (retired). **Personal:** Born Mar 29, 1916, Barnesville, GA; son of Annie C Collins Howard and Robert B Howard Sr; married Irene W Battle; children: Jean Margaret Holland. **Educ:** Buffalo Collegiate Center. **Career:** Buffalo Artistic Upholstering Co, receiving clerk 1936-37; Semet Solvay Co, utility man 1937-43; Buffalo Fire Dept, lieutenant 1943-51, capt 1951-60, fire commissioner, retired fire commissioner. **Orgs:** Field rep Natl Fire Protection Assn 1973-76; bd dir many civic orgns 1968-73; Fire Adv Bd NY State 1972-73; sec Metro Comm Intl Fire Chiefs Assn 1970-73. **Honors/Awds:** Man of the Yr Greater Niagara Frontier Adv Club 1970; Man of the Yr Jewish War Veterans Post 1969; chmn Brotherhood Week Natl Conf Christians and Jews 1968; chmn Cleanup Week Buffalo Chamber of Commerce 1969. **Home Addr:** 258 Sunrise Blvd, Amherst, NY 14221.

HOWARD, SAMUEL H.
Holding company executive. **Personal:** Born May 8, 1939, Marietta, OK; son of Nellie Gaines Howard and Houston Howard; married Karan A; children: Anica, Samuel. **Educ:** OK State Univ, BS 1961; Stanford Univ, MA 1963. **Career:** White House, spec asst fellow 1966-67; Howard Univ, dir 1967-68; HEW, consult to sec 1967-69; TAW Intl Leasing Corp, vice pres fin, sec, treas, 1968-72; Phoenix Comm Group Inc, founder, pres 1972-; Meharry Med Coll, vice pres fin 1973-77; Hosp Affiliates Intl Inc, vice pres 1977-81; Hospital Corp of Amer, vp, treas 1981-85; sr vice pres of public affairs Hospital Corp of America 1985-1988; Phoenix Holdings, chairman 1989-. **Orgs:** Mem Phi Kappa Phi, Blue Key, Beta Gamma Sigma, Delta Sigma Pi, Alpha Phi Alpha, Human Rels Council, Cordell Hall Council, Lariats, Sigma Epsilon Sigma, Fed of Amer Hosp, Fin Exec Inst, Board Nashville Branch of NAACP; UT School of Business Advisory Board; TSU Presidents Advisor Board, St Thomas Hospital Board of Councelors; Cchairman Nashville Convention Cntr Commission, Amer Hospital Assoc, dir of Nashville Chamber of Commerce; dir Corporate Child Care; dir Genesis Health Ventures. **Honors/Awds:** Oklahoma State University Business Hall of Fame; director, O'Charley's Inc; trustee, Fisk University. **Business Addr:** Chairman, Phoenix Healthcare Corp., 3801 W End Ave, Nashville, TN 37203.

HOWARD, SHIRLEY M.
Educator. **Personal:** Born Dec 15, 1935, Chicago, IL; married Johnnie Howard; children: Patrice, Paula, Christopher. **Educ:** Cook County School of Nursing, diploma 1960; DePaul Univ, BSN 1969, MS 1972. **Career:** Governors State Univ, prof Health Sci & Health Sci Instrctnl Prog Coord; Village Nursing Srv, co-owner; nursing admin, instr, publ health nurse. **Orgs:** Mem Natl League Nursing; Assc Rehab Nurses; Deans & Dirs Coun Baccalaureate & Higher Degree Progs; consult Robbins Human Resource Ctr; aux Independent Peoples Party; PTA; bd Family Health Ctr; adv Bd Kennedy-King Clge Nursing Alumni; bd Comprehensive Comm Health Planning & Dev Coun; Mini-grant ResearchProjs Gov's State Univ 1972-75. **Honors/Awds:** Certf of Merit Youth Motivation Com & Chicago Merit Employment Com 1971-72; author & proj dir HEW proj nursing educ & research. **Business Addr:** Governors State Univ, Park Forest, IL 60466.

HOWARD, STEPHEN
Professional basketball player. **Personal:** Born Jul 15, 1970. **Educ:** DePaul. **Career:** Utah Jazz, forward, 1992-96; San Antonio Spurs, 1996-97; Seattle Supersonics, 1997-. **Business Addr:** Professional Basketball Player, Seattle Supersonics, PO Box 900911, Seattle, WA 98109, (206)281-5850.

HOWARD, SUSAN E.
Writer. **Personal:** Born Apr 9, 1961, Fort Wayne, IN; daughter of Ferdie A Webster Howard and John Howard Sr. **Educ:** Syracuse University, Syracuse, NY, BS, 1983. **Career:** Frost Illustrated, Fort Wayne, IN, intern, 1978; Journal-Gazette, Fort Wayne, IN, intern, 1978-79; Daily Orange (campus paper), Syracuse, NY, editorial editor, 1982; Courier-Journal, Louisville, KY, intern, 1982; Atlanta Journal-Constitution, Atlanta, GA, sports writer, magazine writer, 1983-88; Newsday, Melville, NY, news reporter, feature writer, 1988-. **Orgs:** Member, NABJ, 1983-; member, National Black Women's Health Project, 1988-. **Honors/Awds:** NABJ, first place in sports reporting, 1986; Atlanta Association of Black Journalists, first place sports reporting, 1986; Front Page Award with Irene Virag & Edna Negron, feature reporting, 1989; Newsday Publisher's Award, for news project on segregation on Long Island, 1990. **Home Addr:** 4 Lawrence Hill Rd, Huntington, NY 11743-3114. **Business Addr:** Entertainment & Cultural Writer, Features Dept, Newsday, 235 Pinelawn Rd, Melville, NY 11747-4250.

HOWARD, TANYA MILLICENT
Computer systems engineer. **Personal:** Born May 4, 1968, Chapel Hill, NC; daughter of Sadie Ann Graves Howard and Charlie Edward Howard. **Educ:** Howard University, Washington, DC, bachelor of science in engineering, 1991. **Career:** Close-Up Foundation, Alexandria, VA, transportation clerk, 1989-; Department of Defense, Washington, DC, technical clerk, 1989-; Martin Marietta, Air Traffic Systems, systems engineer, 1991-. **Orgs:** Region II secretary, National Society of Black Engineers, 1990-91; chairperson, Institute of Electrical & Electronics Engineers, 1990-91; committee chair, Springfield Baptist Church, 1990-91; news editor, Howard Engineer Magazine, 1989-91; secretary, Howard University School of Engineering, 1989-90; Toastmasters, Inc, 1991-92; National Association of Female Executives, 1991-92. **Honors/Awds:** Academic Award, National Society of Black Engineers, 1990. **Home Addr:** 4613 Sargent Rd, Washington, DC 20017.

HOWARD, TY
Professional football player. **Personal:** Born Nov 30, 1973. **Educ:** Ohio State. **Career:** Arizona Cardinals, defensive back, 1997-. **Business Addr:** Professional Football Player, Arizona Cardinals, 8701 S Hardy, Tempe, AZ 85284, (602)379-0101.

HOWARD, VERA GOUKE
Educator. **Personal:** Born in Brooklyn; married. **Educ:** Baruch Clge, BBA 1958; NY Univ, MA 1969. **Career:** NY Inst Technology, counselor 1971-; NY City Bd of Educ 1963-71; Brooklyn Coll, adjunct instructor; Manpower Devel Training, teacher; Brooklyn Coll, prog lecturer; Social Worker Investigator New York City Dept Welfare. **Orgs:** Mem New York City Personnel Guidance Assc; Black Alliance Educators; Long Island Assc Black Cnslrs; vol cnslr. **Business Addr:** 1303 Park Pl, Brooklyn, NY 11213.

HOWARD, VIVIAN GORDON
Educator. **Personal:** Born Apr 22, 1923, Warsaw, VA; married Dr Roscoe C Howard (deceased); children: Linda G, Roscoe C Jr, Roderick W. **Educ:** VA State Univ, BS 1946, MS Elem Educ 1960, MS 1966, EdD Math Ed 1969; Hermenet of San Francisco, certified coach mgmt 1984; Action Technology, certified guide 1985. **Career:** Natl Institutes of Health, extramural associate 1981; Longwood College, visiting prof of math 1983-84; VA Tech, visiting prof of math 1984-85; VA State Univ, prof of math 1969-; Howard Enterprises, founder w/daughter; VA State Univ & VA Tech Univ, exchange prof to promote integration in higher educ, currently. **Orgs:** Consultant Natl Inst of Educ 1974-76; dir Secondary Prog for Gifted in Math Sci & English for DC Schools, Mediax Corp of CT 1976; math consultant DC Schools; assisted in organization of math labs in Anacostia schools 1975-77; workshop leader on Natl Level-Metric System & Math Labs; VA coordinator & natl bd Natl Coalition of 100 Black Women, establishing 6 chapters 1983-; VA coordinator Adolescent Pregnancy Child Watch of Children's Defense Fund 1984-. **Honors/Awds:** Human Relations Award in Educ, Minority Caucus of the VA Educ Assn of NEA 1984; Outstanding Political Service Award, Womens Vote Project Atlanta 1984; Distinguished Teacher, School of Natural Sciences VSU 1979; charter pres Kappa Delta Pi Honor Soc VSU; DuPont Fellow and 1st black grad student assigned to teach in the classroom, Univ VA; Metric Educ Plan for VA, Richmond Dept of Educ, Commonwealth of VA 1977; "Innovative Metric Educ Prog at VSU" presented in Miami & Denver and published in gvt documents; Bronz Award, Intl Film Festival for "Roads to Mathematics through Physical Education Art Music

and Educ'' Industrial Arts VSU Prog, commissioned by the US Office of Educ Dept of Health Educ & Welfare 1972. **Business Addr:** Prof of Mathematics, Virginia State Univ, Petersburg, VA 23803.

HOWARD BECKHAM, RUTH WINIFRED. See Obituaries section.

HOWE, RUTH-ARLENE W.
Educator. **Personal:** Born Nov 21, 1933, Scotch Plains, NJ; daughter of Grace-Louise Randolph Wood (deceased) and Curtis Alexander Wood (deceased); married Theodore Holmes Howe, Jun 29, 1957; children: Marian, Curtis, Helen, Edgar. **Educ:** Wellesley Coll, BA 1955; Simmons Coll Sch of Social Work, SM 1957; Boston Coll Law School JD 1974. **Career:** Cleveland OH Catholic Youth Serv Bureau, casewkr 1957-61; Tufts Delta Health Ctr Mound Bayou MS, housing devel consultant 1969-70; Simmons Coll Sch of Social Work, instr soc pol 1970-78; Law & Child Dev Project DHEW/ACYF Funded B C Law Sch, asst dir 1977-79; Boston Coll Law Sch, asst prof of law 1977-81, assoc prof of law with tenure, 1981-97, prof, 1998-. **Orgs:** Bd mem Boston League of Women Voters 1963-68; clerk Grimes-King Found for the Elderly Inc 1972-; guardian ad litem MA Family and Probate Court 1979-; ABA Tech to NCCUSL Uniform Adoption and Marital Property Acts 1980-83; reviewer CWLA Journal-Child Welfare 1984-91; mem MA Gov St Com on Child Support Enforcement 1985; mem MA Adv Comm on Child Support Guidelines 1986-; mem MA Gov/MBA Commn on the Legal Needs of Children 1986-87; NCCUSL Uniform Putative and Unknown Fathers Act Reporter 1986-88; member, editorial board, Family Advocate, ABA section of Family Law, 1989-95; mem, Massachusetts Supreme Judicial Court Commission to Study Racial & Ethnic Bias in the Courts, 1990-94; US State Department, Study Group on Intercountry Adoption, 1991-. **Honors/Awds:** Wellesley scholar Wellesley Coll 1955; Nat'l Inst of Mental Health Fellowship 1956-57; Co-authored, Katz McGrath Child Neglect Laws in Am ABA Press 1976; cited for contribution to legal ed MA Black Lawyers Asso 1983; Honored by MA Black Legislative Caucus 1988; Honored by Museum of Afro-American History as one of Sojourner's Daughters; Boston African American Women Who Make A Difference, an exhibition of portraits by photographer Lou Jones, 1991; Mary Ingram Ram Bunting Inst Radcliffe Coll, Hermon Dunlap Smith Fellow in Law & Social/Public Policy, 1994-95; Honored by Boston College Law School Alumni Association, 1996. **Business Addr:** Professor of Law, Boston Coll Law Sch, 885 Centre St, Newton Center, MA 02159.

HOWELL, AMAZIAH, III
Petroleum company executive. **Personal:** Born Oct 12, 1948, Goldsboro, NC; son of Theresa Reid Howell and Amaziah Howell Jr; married Jessica McCoy, Jul 8, 1978; children: Joy Elizabeth, Aimee Denise. **Educ:** Johnson C Smith Univ Charlotte NC, attended 1966-68; NY Inst of Credit, attended 1970; Amos Tuck Sch of Business, Dartmouth U, Minority Business Exec Program. **Career:** Howell Petroleum Products, Inc, Brooklyn NY, president, 1985—; Las Energy Corp, Roosevelt NY, vice pres, 1981-85; Assn of Minority Enterprises of NY Inc, exec dir 1976-77, 1979-81; Wallace & Wallace Fuel Oil Co, marketing mgr 1978-79; Ofc of US Senator James L Buckley, special assistant 1973-76; Manufacturers Hanover Trust Co, credit investigator 1968-72. **Orgs:** American Assn of Blacks in Energy; Brooklyn Chamber of Commerce; Brooklyn Sports Foundation, exec bd; Commission on Students of African Descent New York City Board of Education; Committee for Economic Development; District 13 Community School Board Business Advisory Council; Downtown Brooklyn Community Advisory Board and Oversight Committee, chairman; Environmental Action Coalition; Halsey Street Block Assn, vice president; Helen Keller Services for the Blind; Latimer-Woods Economic Development Corp; Long Island University Executive Advisory Council; Metropolitan Transit Authority (MTA) Advisory Council; New York/New Jersey Minority Purchasing Council; Public School 282, vp/PTA, chmn/Curriculum Comm, Planning Committee; US Courthouse Foley Square Advisory Committee; Cornerstone Baptist Church. **Honors/Awds:** Mayor Rudolph W Giuliani, New York City Business Advocate Award, 1994; New York Urban League, Building Brick Award, 1994; Environmental Action Coalition, Green Star Award, 1992; New York/New Jersey Minority Purchasing Council, Minority Supplier of the Year Award, 1989 & 1990; New York Chamber of Commerce & Industry, Small Businessman of the Year, 1990; Merrill Lynch, Ernst & Young & Inc Magazine, regional winner of the Entrepreneur of the Year, 1990; Natl Minority Supplier Development Council Inc, Supplier of the Year Regional Award Winner, 1990; Brooklyn Chamber of Commerce, Robert F Kennedy Memorial Award to Minority Business, 1989; Natl Minority Business Council, Outstanding Minority Business, 1987; United States Jaycees, JCI Senator, 1981. **Business Addr:** President/CEO, Howell Petroleum Products, Inc, Brooklyn Navy Yard, Building #292, Brooklyn, NY 11205.

HOWELL, CHESTER THOMAS
Company executive (Retired). **Personal:** Born Mar 23, 1937, Tarentum, PA; son of Jessie Leona Sharp Howell and Hunter Lee Howell; married Loretta J Lewis Howell, Jan 18, 1964; children: Tracey Lynn, Jennifer Lynne, Hunter Lee II. **Educ:** Allegheny Technical Institute, 1965-68; Third District African Methodist Episcopal Theological Institute, 1990-94. **Career:** Veterans Administration Hospital, nursing assistant, 1961-68; Atlantic Design Corporation, electrical engineer, 1968-72; Xerox Corporation, Pittsburgh, PA, district business manager, 1972-96, chief financial officer. **Orgs:** Past president, Metropolitan Area Minority Employees of Xerox, 1979; deacon, East End Baptist Tabernacle, Bridgeport, CT, 1981-88, Central Baptist, Syracuse, NY, 1988-90; past master, Free and Accepted Masons, Prince Hall, 1970-79; Human Rights Commission, Harrison Twshp School District; Habitat for Humanities, Family Nurture Committee; Editorial Review Board, Valley Daily News Dispatch. **Honors/Awds:** Black Achievers Award, YMCA, 1980; ordained African Methodist Episcopal minister, local deacon, Bethel AMEC, 1992; Ordained local elder Bethel AMEC., Tarentum, Pa 15084, 1996. **Military Serv:** US Air Force, Airman 1st Class, 1955-59. **Business Addr:** CFO, Xerox Corp., 750 Holiday Dr, Bldg 9, Pittsburgh, PA 15220.

HOWELL, GERALD T.
Insurance executive. **Personal:** Born Sep 18, 1914, Columbia, TN; married Vera; children: Lynn Marie, Marian Rachelle. **Educ:** TN State U, BS cum laude 1936. **Career:** Universal Life Insurance Company, Memphis, TN, agent & other offices, 1941-61, agency director, 1961-66, director of agencies, 1967, vice president/director of agencies, 1968-79, senior vice president/director of field operations, 1980-85, first vice president/secretary/CEO, 1986-89, president/CEO, 1990-. **Orgs:** Mem Nat Ins Assn; NAACP; Emmanuel Epis Ch Alpha Phi & Alpha; Mason; Shriner. **Honors/Awds:** Sportsmen's club spl serv award Nat Ins Assn 1974; blount award exceptional performance Nat Ins Assn 1974. **Military Serv:** AUS ETO 1st sgt 1942-45. **Business Addr:** President/CEO, Universal Life Ins Co, 480 Linden St, PO Box 241, Memphis, TN 38101.

HOWELL, MALQUEEN
Educator. **Personal:** Born Apr 3, 1949, Calhoun Co, SC. **Educ:** BA 1971, MA 1972. **Career:** Benedict Coll, English instructor. **Orgs:** Founding pres Calhoun Co Jr Improvement League 1966; mem NAACP; adv panel State Human Affairs Commn; Study & Preservation Black Hist; Art & Folklore Simons-Mann Coll 1973; voter educ proj & Heart Fund Campaign; United Way; Mt Carmel Bapt Ch Citation Conf Computing Minorit Instns. **Honors/Awds:** Alpha Kappa Alpha; cert MI Sch Med Div Addiction Scis 1974; cert Proj Assist Action Prog 1968. **Business Addr:** Benedict College, Harden & Blanding Streets, Columbia, SC.

HOWELL, RACHEL
Emergency medical technical specialist. **Personal:** Born May 28, 1961, Detroit, MI; daughter of Carmen Perry Howell and L C Howell; children: Bruce Howell, Ariana Howell. **Educ:** Franklin, basic EMT, 1986-87; Detroit EMS Traing Academy, EMT-S, 1990. **Career:** East Jefferson Market, Detroit, MI, cashier/lottery, 1980-84; Barnes and Noble (WCCC), Detroit, MI, cashier/clerk, 1984-87; Detroit Fire Dept, Detroit, MI, EMT, 1987-. **Honors/Awds:** Life Saver of the Year, Detroit East Medical Control, 1990-91; Life Saver of the Year, 100 Club, 1990-91. **Business Addr:** Emergency Medical Tech Specialist, EMS Division, Detroit Fire Department, 900 Merrill Plaisance, Detroit, MI 48203.

HOWELL, ROBERT J., JR.
Business executive. **Personal:** Born Feb 24, 1935, New York, NY; married Elestine. **Educ:** New Sch, MA; NY U, PhD cand. **Career:** Human Resources Adminstrn, Personnel Adminstrn; Div of Emply dep dir 1972-74; Professional Recruitment & Replacement, chief 1968-72, spl asst dir personnel 1967-68; Cornell Grad Sch & Indsl Labor Rel, consult 1970-71; NY State Civil Serv Commn for Professional Cands Internal Pub Personnel Assn, oral examiner. **Orgs:** 100 Black Men. **Military Serv:** Sp 4 1958-60. **Business Addr:** 271 Church St, New York, NY.

HOWELL, SHARON MARIE
Church official. **Personal:** Born Dec 6, 1950, Minneapolis, MN; daughter of Juanita Olivia Marino Howell and Tyler Jackson Howell, Jr. **Educ:** Xavier University of Louisiana, New Orleans, LA, BS, 1972; University of St. Thomas, St. Paul, MN, MA, 1985; St. Paul Seminary, St. Paul, MN, post graduate study, 1984-86; Midwest Canon Law Society Institute, Mundelein, IL, 1985. **Career:** Academy of Natural Sciences of Philadelphia, Avondale, PA, research assistant, 1972-74; 3M Company, St. Paul, MN, analytical chemist, 1974-76; Control Data Corp, Bloomington, MN, chemist, 1976-78; Minneapolis Institute of Art, assistant coordinator of exhibitions, 1978-79; Minnesota State Department of Agriculture, St. Paul, MN, analytical chemist, 1979-80; Home of the Good Shepherd, St. Paul, MN youth worker, 1980-83; Church of St. Leonard of Port Maurice, pastoral minister, 1983-84; University of St. Thomas, St. Paul, MN, director of multicultural & student services, director of diversity initiatives, currently; Archdiocese of St. Paul and Minneapolis, St. Paul, MN, intern, 1984-86, liaison for Black Catholic Concerns, 1986-; executive secretary, Archdiocesan Commission of Black Catholics, 1986-. **Orgs:** Board of directors, Catholic Charities, 1990-95; board of directors, Greater Minneapolis Council of Churches, 1989-91; Minnesota Interfaith Council on Affordable Housing, 1988-90; Leadership St. Paul, 1989-90; Association of Pastoral Ministers, 1984-; member, 1985-87, vice chair, 1986-87, Coalition of Ministerial Associations; associate member, Canon Law Society of America, 1984-; Commission on Evangelization, 1983-86; member, 1985-89, chair, 1987-89, Commission on Ministry; member, Sisters of St Joseph, Carondelet, St Paul Province; bd of trustees, College of St Catherine, St Paul, 1994. **Business Addr:** Director, Diversity Initiatives, University of St Thomas, 2115 Summit Ave Mail 4002, St Paul, MN 55105.

HOWELL, WILLIAM B.
Clergyman. **Personal:** Born Feb 19, 1932, High Point, NC. **Educ:** Winston Salem State Coll, BS 1965; La Salle Univ Corr Sch Chicago, LLB; ITC Gammon Theol Sem M Div, 1970; Brantridge Forest Coll England, hon DD 1972; Daniel Payne Coll, DD 1975. **Career:** High Point NC, law enforcement officer 1953-62; So Pines Pub Sch NC tchr, 1965-67; NC TN GA Conf, Pastorates; Turner Theol Sem Extension Prog, tchr of Theology 1973; ML Harris United Meth Ch, Minister. **Orgs:** Pres Columbus GA chap Operation PUSH; pres Columbus Phenix City Ministerial Alliance; mem NAACP; mem bd dir YMCA 1973-74; mem Gammon Sem Alumni Assn; ordained decon & elder United Meth Ch; past vice-chmnbd of missions S GA Conf 1972; vice chmn Ministry of S GA Conf 1972; mem commn on Religion & Race of S GA Conf Chpln of WK; GA State Senate 1972. **Honors/Awds:** Humanitarian Award Am Red Cross 1974; scholarship award bd of United Meth Ch1967; Ada Stovall Award for Academic Achievement 1970; Dr Martin & Luther King Award for Distinguished Serv 1974.

HOWELL, WILLIE R.
Police chief, private investigator (retired). **Personal:** Born May 27, 1926, Chicago, IL; married Evelyn; children: Barbara Ann Petty, William Roy, Gail Snoddy. **Educ:** FBI Grand Valley Coll, basic police tng. **Career:** Howell's Investigate Services, private investigator, currently; Muskegon Hts, chief of police 1976-89, comdr of operations 1975, capt 1968, det Lt 1967, Det 1963; Nat Orgn Black Law Enforcement Execs, policeman 1954. **Orgs:** Internal Assn & Chiefs of Police; mem Frat Order of Police; mem Comm Orgn Black Businessmen; mem Urban League; mem NAACP; coord Boy Scout Troop 277 Explorer Post 17;mem Muskegon Hts Lions Club; United Appeal Bd of Finance 1968-71; mem Gtr Harvest Bapt H; Sunday Sch tchr 1969-73. **Honors/Awds:** Police Officer of Year Muskegon Exchange Club 1966; Liberty Bell Award State Bar of MI 1967; Reverence for Law Award Mukegon Hts Eagles 1969; citation Blockade Com 1969; NWRO outstdng leadership award 1975; Jonathan Walker Award, Local Chapter of Urban League, 1986. **Military Serv:** USAF 1944-47. **Business Addr:** Private Investigator, Howell's Investigative Services, 707 E Lincoln, Muskegon Heights, MI 49444.

HOWZE, DOROTHY J.
Educator. **Personal:** Born Nov 24, 1923, Detroit, MI; married Manuel; children: Karen, Gloria. **Educ:** Wayne State Univ, BS; Univ of MI, MS 1966. **Career:** Detroit Public Library, clerk 1947-49; Detroit Bd of Educ, teacher; Detroit Public Schools at Cerveny & Winship Middle School, specialist, currently. **Orgs:** Mem, Intl Reading Assn; Wayne Alumni Assn; Met Reading Assn; MI Reading Assn & Curricuium Devel task force NEC Proj; Human Relations Com; coordinator Summer Head Start Prog Black Catholics Action; sec bd dir Black Secretarial; sec Nat Black Lay Cath Caucus; MI Black Lay Cath Caucus; 1 salute Black Wmn; Black Secretariat 1972; Alpha Kappa Alpha Alpha Rho Omega Chap Detroit MI; mem Beta Sigma Phi Fellowship; mem MI Assn of Middle Sch Educators; coun pres religious educ coor Holy Ghost Cath Ch; bd of dir Inter-Parish Sharing; del Archdiocese Pastoral Assembly; bd of mgmt for vol & mem of memshp com Downtown Br YWCA. **Business Addr:** Educational Specialist, 15055 Dexter, Detroit, MI 48238.

HOWZE, JOSEPH LAWSON
Clergyman. **Personal:** Born Aug 30, 1923, Daphne, AL. **Educ:** AL State Jr Coll; AL State Univ, BS 1948; St Bonaventure Univ, grad 1959; Phillips College, business management degree 1980. **Career:** Ordained priest Roman Catholic Ch 1959; pastor churches in, Charlotte, Southern Pines, Durham, Sanford, Asheville (all in NC) 1959-72; Natchez-Jackson, MS, aux bishop 1973-77; Biloxi, MS, bishop 1977-. **Orgs:** Trustee Xavier Univ New Orleans; mem MS Health Care Commn; mem admistrv bd NCCB/USCC; mem educ comm USCC; mem Social Devel and World Peace Comm; liaison com to natl Office of Black Catholics NCCB; bd dirs Biloxi Reg Med Cntr; Democrat; mem KC Knights of St Peter Claver; mem NCCB/USCC Vocation Comm. **Honors/Awds:** Became one of few Black bishops in history of Catholic Church in US; 1st Bishop of the New Diocese of Biloxi MS 1977; 1st Black Catholic bishop to head a Catholic Diocese in the USA since 1900; honorary degrees: University of Portland, 1974; Sacred Heart College, 1977; St Bonaventure University, 1977; Manhattan College, 1979; Bible Crusade College, 1987. **Business Addr:** Bishop, Catholic Diocese Biloxi, PO Box 1189, Biloxi, MS 39533.

HOWZE, KAREN AILEEN
Attorney, consultant. **Personal:** Born Dec 8, 1950, Detroit, MI; daughter of Dorothy June Smith Howze and Manuel Howze; children: Charlene, Karie, Lucinda. **Educ:** Univ of S California, BA 1972 (cum laude); Hastings Coll of Law, JD 1977. **Career:** Detroit Free Press, reporter 1971; San Francisco Chronicle, reporter 1972-78; Newsday, Long Island, asst editor 1978-79; Gannett Newspapers, Rochester NY, asst managing editor/ Sunday features editor 1979-80; USA Today, founding editor 1981, managing editor/systems 1982-86, managing editor/ international edition 1986-88; Gannett Co Inc, Corporate News Systems, editor 1988-90; management consultant, 1990-; Howze and Associates, Karen Aileen Howze, PC, attorney 1990-; Howard Univ School of Communications, lecturer, 1990-92; Adoption Support Institute, president/founder 1990-; American University School of Communication, professor 1991-94. **Orgs:** Mem Nat Assn of Black Journal; past mem Sigma Delta Chi; past mem Women in Commun; mem Alameda Co Comm Hlth Adv Bd; guest lectu local comm coll; mem, Amer Society of Newspaper Editors; vice-chair, Minority Opportunities Comm, Amer Newspaper Publisher's Assn; board of directors, North American CNL on Adoptable Children; board of directors MAAT Institute; board of directors Chelsea School; chairperson Mayor's Committee on Placement of Children in Family Homes; District of Columbia Bar Association & State of Maryland Bar Association, licensed to practice law in District of Columbia and Maryland. **Honors/Awds:** Business Woman of the Year, Spellman Alumni, Washington DC 1986; Senior Editor, And Still We Rise, interviews with 50 Black Americans by Barbara Reynolds 1987. **Special Achievements:** Making Differences Work: Cultural Context in Abuse and Neglect Practice for Judges and Attorneys, 1996. **Business Addr:** PO Box 1127, Silver Spring, MD 20910, (301)291-2290.

HOYE, WALTER B.
College administrator (retired). **Personal:** Born May 19, 1930, Lena, MS; son of Lou Bertha Stewart Hoye and William H Hoye Sr; married Vida M Pickens Hoye, Aug 28, 1954; children: Walter B II, JoAnn M. **Educ:** Wayne St Univ, BA 1954; UCSD Ext, Mngt Cert 1973. **Career:** MI Chronicle Nwspr, sprts ed/columnst 1964-68; San Diego Chargers Ftbl Clb, asst dir pblc rltns 1968-76; NFL media rltns/Super Bowl 1972-75; SD Urban League/Nghbrhd House Assn, pblc info off 1976; Educcultural Complex, dir support system; supervisor 1988-91. **Orgs:** 1st vice pres San Diego Urban League 1972-75; pgm review pnlst United Way/CHAD of San Diego Cnty 1972-74; brd of dirs Red Cross of San Diego Cnty 1975-77; nominator Outstndng Young Men/Women of Amer 1976-85; brd of dirs Pblc Access TV 1977-79; treas San Diego Career Guidance Assn 1981-82; Advisory Bd KPBS TV 15 1983-84; mem Int Assn of Auditorium Managers 1978, 1990-91; mem Rocky Mountain Assn of Student Financial Aid Administrators 1988. **Honors/ Awds:** Citizen of Month Cnty of San Diego 1979; Certificate of Recognition, California Legislative Assembly 1989. **Home Addr:** 6959 Ridge Manor Ave, San Diego, CA 92120-3146.

HOYLE, CLASSIE
Educator. **Personal:** Born Mar 26, 1936, Annapolis, MD; daughter of Truma Lawson Elliott and Nathaniel Daniel Gillis; married Daniel C Hoyle, Aug 21, 1955; children: Dennis James, Lynne Valarie Jones. **Educ:** Morgan State Univ, BS 1958, MS 1968; Univ IA, PhD 1977. **Career:** Lab scientist, 1958-59; sci tchr, 1960-68; Morgan State Univ, sci tchr 1968-73; grad tching asst, 1974-76; Cooperative Educ, coord 1976-77; Career Serv Placement Ctr, asst dir 1977-78; Univ of IA, dir affirmative action 1978-82; Clarke Coll, vice pres for academic affrs 1982-85; Univ of Iowa, Iowa City, IA, asst to the dean, 1985-90; NIH/ NIGMS, Bethesda, MD, health scientist admin, 1990-. **Orgs:** Admin asst Mt Lebanon Bapt Ch 1970-73; sec treas Fed Credit Union 1970-73; sec Morgan State Univ 1972-73; mem Natl Sci Tchrs Assn, Assn for the Educ of Tchrs of Sci, Natl Assn for Biology Tchrs; den mother Cub Scouts 1968, 1974; chairperson courtesy comm Morgan State Univ 1969-72; So Fellowship Fund 1975-76; Higher Educ Title III Grant 1973-75; Natl Sci Fellowships 1965-68; Senatorial Scholarship 1954-58; pres Phi Delta Kappa 1980; IA pres Amer Council on Educ Natl Identification Prog 1979-81; Kappa Delta Pi 1958; Beta Kappa Chi 1957; Alpha Kappa Mu 1957. **Home Addr:** 2089 Forest Dr, Annapolis, MD 21401. **Business Addr:** Health Scientist Administrator, National Institutes of Health, Natl Institute of General Medical Science, 5333 Westbard Ave, WW-NIGMS-Rm 950, Bethesda, MD 20892.

HOYT, KENNETH M.
Judge. **Career:** Federal judge, currently.

HOYT, THOMAS L., JR.
Educator. **Personal:** Born Mar 14, 1941, Fayette, AL; married Ocie Harriet Oden; children: Doria, Thomas III. **Educ:** Evansville Coll and Lane Coll, BA 1962; Interdenominational Theological Center, MDiv 1965; Union Theological Seminary, STM 1967; Duke Univ, PhD 1975. **Career:** Jefferson Park Methodist, assoc pastor 1965-67; St Joseph CME, pastor 1967-70; Fawcett Memorial, pastor 1970-72; Interdenominational Theological Center, professor 1972-78; Howard Univ, professor 1978-80; Hartford Seminary, professor 1980-. **Orgs:** Society of Biblical Literature; American Academy of Religion; Society for the study of Black Religion; Theology Commission of Consultation onChurch Union; CT Bible Society, board of directors; Christian Methodist Church; Alpha Phi Alpha; NAACP; Faith and Order Commission of Natl Council and World Council of Churches; Institute for Ecumenical and Cultural Research, board of directors. **Honors/Awds:** Rockefeller Doctoral Fellowship; Assn of Theological Schools Fellowship; worked on Joint Committee, which published an Inclusive Lectionary (year A,B,C,)1983-85; Natl Assn for Equal Opportunity in Higher Education, award; Bilateral Dialogue between Methodist/Roman Catholic Churches, participant; African Methodist Episcopal Zion/Christian Methodist Episcopal Unity Committee. **Home Addr:** 80 Girard Ave, Hartford, CT 06105. **Business Addr:** Professor, Hartford Seminary, 77 Sherman St, Hartford, CT 06105.

HOYTE, ARTHUR HAMILTON
Educator. **Personal:** Born Mar 22, 1938, Boston, MA; married Stephanie Hebron; children: Jacques. **Educ:** Harvard Coll, BA 1960; Columbia Univ Coll of Phys & Surgs, MD 1964; SF Gen Hosp, intern 1965; Presb Hosp, resident 1968. **Career:** Georgetown Medical Center, asst prof 1971-; Office of Economic Opportunity, med officer 1970-71; East Palo Alto Neighborhood Health Center, 1969-70; Kaiser Found Hospital, 1968-70. **Orgs:** Consultant Health Care Serv 1971-; mem Presidential Task Force 1976; Med Cos of DC 1972-; Med Chrgcl Soc of DC 1974-; DC United Way; Coalition of Health Advs 1975-; Boys Club of WA 1975-; pres DC Sci Fair Assn 1976-77. **Honors/Awds:** Civ Serv Awards WA Region Med Prog 1975; Mid Atlantic Regional Student Natl Med Assn 1975; US Senate Testimony on Ambulatory Health Serv in DC 1976. **Military Serv:** AUSR 1969-74. **Business Addr:** Georgetown University, Dept Community & Family Med, 3900 Reservoir Road, Washington, DC 20007.

HOYTE, JAMES STERLING
Attorney, educational administrator. **Personal:** Born Apr 21, 1944, Boston, MA; son of Patti Ridley Hoyte and Oscar H Hoyte; married Norma Dinnall, Dec 12, 1964; children: Keith Sterling, Kirsten Dinnall. **Educ:** Harvard Univ, AB, 1965, Law School, JD, 1968, Graduate School of Business, MA, PMD certificate, 1971, Kennedy School of Govt, 1986. **Career:** Arthur D Little Inc, sr staff, 1969-74, 1979-82; Massachusetts Sec of State, Boston MA, deputy sec, 1975-76; Massachusetts Port Authority, secretary-treasurer, dir of admin, 1976-79; Commonwealth of Massachusetts, cabinet sec, sec of Environmental Affairs, 1983-88; Coate, Hall & Stewart, partner, 1989-91; Massachusetts Horticultural Society, interim executive director, consultant, 1991-92; Harvard University, associate vice pres, assistant to the president, 1992-. **Orgs:** Amer Bar Assn, 1971-; sec, Massachusetts Black Lawyers Assn, 1976-78; bd of dir, Opportunities Indusrialization Center of Greater Boston, 1976-83; Natl Bar Assn, 1978-, Long Range Planning Comm, United Way of Massachusetts Bay, 1978; bd of dir, Roxbury Multi Serv Center, 1979-87; chmn, bd of trustees, Environment Comm, Boston Harbor Assn, 1989-; exec comm, bd of dir, 1,000 Friends of Massachusetts, 1989-; bd of trustees, Univ Hospital, 1989. **Honors/Awds:** Ten Outstanding Young Leaders, Greater Boston Jaycees, 1967; Black Achiever Award, Greater Boston YMCA, 1978; Alpha Man of the Year, Epsilon Gamma Lambda Chapter of Alpha Phi Alpha Frat, 1984; Governor Francis Sargent Award, Boston Harbor Assn, 1986; Frederick Douglass Award, Greater Boston YMCA, 1987.

HOYTE, LENON HOLDER (AUNT LEN)
Curator, teacher. **Personal:** Born Jul 4, 1905, New York, NY; daughter of Rose Best Holder and Moses E Holder; married Lewis P Hoyte, Sep 28, 1938 (deceased). **Educ:** NY Teachers Training Schl, attended 1930; City Coll of NY, BS 1937; Columbia Univ, CRMD degree in education. **Career:** NY City Public Schs, art tchr 1930-70; Aunt Len's Doll & Toy Museum, New York NY, founder, dir and pres, 1966—. **Orgs:** Lay advisory bd Harlem Hosp; 1st Basileus Phi Delta Kappa Sor 1953; Beta Epsilon 1955; pres & sec Hamilton Terrace Block Assoc 1973; writes column "Our Museum" Doll News. **Honors/ Awds:** Name on Bronze plaque St Phillips Epis Ch; Harlem YWCA award, 1962; Awds in Black 1972; Service Awd United Fedn of Doll Clubs Inc; Black History Before Your Eyes Westchester Urban League 1980; Brooklyn Tchr Humanitarian Awd 1983; Special Achievement Awd Harlem Week 1982; Building Brick Award, New York Urban League, 1985; Ethnic New Yorker Award, Mayor of City of New York, 1986; Educator of the Year award, City College of NY, 1988; Proclamation award, office of the council president, 1988. **Home Addr:** 6 Hamilton Terr, New York, NY 10031.

HRABOWSKI, FREEMAN ALPHONSA, III
Educator. **Personal:** Born Aug 13, 1950, Birmingham, AL; son of Maggie Hrabowski and Freeman Hrabowski; married Jacqueline Coleman; children: Eric. **Educ:** Hampton Inst, BA 1970; Univ of IL, MA 1971, PhD 1975. **Career:** Univ of IL at Urbana-Champaign, math instr 1972-73, admin intern 1973-74, asst dean 1974-76; AL A&M Univ Normal, assoc dean 1976-77; Coppin State Coll Baltimore, dean arts & scis div 1977-81, vice pres academic affairs 1981-87; Univ of MD, Baltimore County, vice provost, 1987-90, executive vice president, 1990-92, interim pres, 1992-93; Univ of Maryland, Catonville, pres, 1993-. **Orgs:** Alpha Phi Alpha; Hampton Inst, sr class pres, 1969-70; bd of trustees, Baltimore City Life Museums; Florence Crittenton Services Inc, advisory council; Peabody Institute, Johns Hopkins Univ; evaluator, Middle States Assn of Coll and Schools; Baltimore Equitable Society; Unity of MD Medical Systems; bd mem: Amer Coun on Educ, Baltimore Gas & Electric Co, Baltimore Comm Foundation, Ctr Stage, Greater Baltimore Comm, Joint Ctr for Political & Economic Development, McCormick & Co, Mercantile Safe Deposit & Trust Co, Merrick & France Foundation, Suburban Maryland High-Technology Coun. **Honors/Awds:** Scholarship for Study Abroad Amer Univ Cairo Egypt 1968-69; Phi Delta Kappa, Univ of IL at Urbana-Champaign 1971; Outstanding Alumni Awd, Hampton Univ, Baltimore Chapter; Outstanding Community Service Award, Tuskegee Univ. **Business Addr:** President, University of Maryland-Baltimore County, 1000 Hilltop Circle, Baltimore, MD 21201.

HUBBARD, AMOS B.
Educator. **Personal:** Born May 11, 1930, Dora, AL; son of Rev & Mrs A B Hubbard; married Irene Windham; children: Melicent Concetta. **Educ:** AL State Univ, BS 1955; IN Univ, MS 1960; Univ of TN; Univ of AL, Tuscaloosa; Michigan State University; University of Tulsa, OK. **Career:** Carver HS Union Springs AL, teacher & coach 1955-58; Riverside HS Northport AL, teacher 1958-68; Coll Ed Ach Prog Stillman Coll, dir 1968-72, dir ed devel prog 1972-74, athl dir 1972-79, dir spec serv prog 1976-, coord instr, tch learning 1975-, dir spec progs 1977-87, Stillman Coll, dean of students 1988-. **Orgs:** Mem Tuscaloosa Alumni, Kappa Alpha Psi; mem Brown Mem Presbyterian Church, Kappa Delta Pi 1973, Phi Delta Kappa 1973; coord Stillman Coll Danforth Proj 1973-75; mem comm of mgmt Barnes Br YMCA 1965-68; mem Tuscaloosa Civic Ctr Commiss 1971, Family Counseling Serv 1974; Kiwanis of Tuscaloosa, Mental Health Board; Narashino City Sister City Commission; Tuscaloosa County Community Housing Resources Board Inc. **Honors/Awds:** Cert of Achievement Awd Ed Improvement Proj of So Assoc of Coll & School 1973; Distinguished Serv Awd United Fund of Tuscaloosa Cty 1973. **Military Serv:** AUS corpl 1951-53. **Business Addr:** Dean of Students, Stillman College, PO Drawer 1430, Tuscaloosa, AL 35403.

HUBBARD, ARNETTE RHINEHART
Attorney. **Personal:** Born Jan 11, Stephens, AR. **Educ:** John Marshall Law Sch, JD 1969; So IL U, BS. **Career:** Chicago Board of Election Commissioners, Chicago, IL, commissioner, 1989-; Chicago Cable Commission, Chicago, IL, commissioner, 1985-89; Pvt law practice 1972-; Lawyers Com for Civil Rights Under Law, staff atty 1970-72. **Orgs:** Natl Bar Assn, 1975-; NAACP; 1st female pres, Cook Co Bar Assn; president, Association of Election Commission Officials of Illinois; Election Authority Advisory Committee, State Board of Elections of the State of Illinois; executive board, Illinois Association of County Officials; executive committee, International Association of Clerks, Recorders, Election Officials and Treasurers; bd of dirs, Alpha Kappa Alpha Sorority; Southern Illinois Univ Alumni Assn, pres, 1994-; The Chicago Network; Women's Bar Association of Illinois. **Honors/Awds:** First female president of the National Bar Association, 1981-82; Committee on Character and Fitness of the Supreme Court of Illinois. **Business Addr:** Attorney, Arnette R Hubbard & Associates, 134 N LaSalle St, Chicago, IL 60602.

HUBBARD, BRUCE ALAN
Attorney. **Personal:** Born Feb 7, 1948, Chattanooga, TN; son of Ruth Spratling Hubbard (deceased) and Robert McKinley Hubbard; married Constance Arrington, Jul 23, 1988; children: Read Spratling-Tate Hubbard, Ruth Arrington Hubbard, Caroline Benning Hubbard. **Educ:** Rutgers, AB 1969; Harvard Law, JD 1972. **Career:** Hale & Dorr, assoc 1972-73; US Dept HUD, atty/advisor 1973-75; The Continental Group, sr atty 1975-80; Northville Ind Corp, gen counsel 1980-83; Davis Polk & Warpwell, assc 1983-85; private practice, 1985-; Bruce A Hubbard, PC, currently. **Orgs:** Trustee Rheedlen Found 1976-85; House of Delegates NYS Bar Assoc 1978-81; Police Commissioner Stamford CT 1986-90; Nat'l Assn of Securities Professionals; Comm on African Affairs, Assn of the Bar of the City of NY 1994-; Rutgers Fund; HBLSA; Harvard Law Fund; trustee, King & Low-Heywood Thomas School 1985-91; trustee, Community Service Society of New York, 1988-; Board of Managers, Episcopal Mission Society of New York, 1992-; Board of Directors, Metropolitan Black Bar Association of New York, 1990-93; National Bar Association; board of overseers, Rutgers University Foundation, 1993-; associate trustee, Chi Psi Fraternity; Educational trust, 1992-; American Bar Assn; NY State Bar Association. **Honors/Awds:** Op-Ed NY Times 1978; Class of 1931 Award, Rutgers Alumni Assn 1979; Loyal Sons of Rutgers Coll, Cap & Skull 1986. **Military Serv:** USAR 1st lt 1969-75; MA Military Academy 1971.

HUBBARD, CALVIN L.
Educator (retired), artist. **Personal:** Born Jul 23, 1940, Dallas, TX; son of Mildred Criner Hubbard and Ressie Hubbard; married Evelyn McAfee Hubbard, Dec 21, 1968; children: Katrina, Tyletha, Yuressa. **Educ:** Aspen School of Contemporary Art, Aspen, CO, 1963; Texas Southern University, Houston, TX, BAE, 1966; Rochester Institute of Technology, Rochester, NY,

MST, 1971. **Career:** Houston Independent School Dist, teacher, 1969-70; City School District, Rochester, NY, teacher, 1970-96; Summer Workshop for Children, Turtle Pottery Studio, director, 1987-. **Orgs:** Coordinator of Art Show, Nazareth College, 1986-87; member, board of directors, Woodward Health Center, 1988; Junior Warden, Eureka Lodge #36, 1990-91; Worshipful Master, Eureka Lodge #36, 1995-96. **Honors/Awds:** Outstanding Leader in Secondary Education, 1976; Published in Black Art in Houston, Texas Southern Univ, 1977; Recipient Martin Luther King Cultural Art Award, Colgate Divinity School, 1984; Recognition Outstanding Teacher, University of Rochester, NY, 1986-; Dewitt Clinton Award, 1998. **Military Serv:** US Army, Sgt, 1966-69; Vietnam Service Award, Army Craft Contest, 1969. **Business Addr:** Owner, Turtle Pottery Studio & Gallery, 594 Brown St, Rochester, NY 14611.

HUBBARD, DARRELL
Company executive. **Personal:** Born Nov 14, 1966, Elizabeth, NJ; son of Christine Cox Hubbard and Ralph Hubbard. **Educ:** Wayne Comm College, Goldsboro, NC, AAS, 1984; NS Wesleyan College, Rocky Mtn, NC, BS, 1986; BA, 1988; NC State University, Raleigh, NC, MS, 1988. **Career:** Wayne Comm College, Goldsboro, NC, data processing instructor, 1984; NC State Univ, Raleigh, NC, teaching asst, 1985-86; Northern Telecom Inc, RTP, NC, sys app engr, 1985-86; Bell Northern Research, RTP, NC, protocol design staff, 1987-88; AT&T Bell Laboratories, Holmdel, NJ, computer engr, 1988-91; Network of Winners Inc, Woodbridge, NJ, pres, 1989-. **Honors/Awds:** Ebony Magazine, "30 Leaders of the Future," 1989; Magna Cum Laude, NC Wesleyan College, 1986; Computer System Lab Research Assistantship, NC State Univ, 1987; "Deterministic Execution Testing of FSM-Based Protocols," AT&T Technical Journal, 1990.

HUBBARD, HYLAN T., III
Insurance company executive. **Personal:** Born Jan 26, 1947, Lynchburg, VA; son of Florine Morris Hubbard and Hylan Thomas Hubbard Jr; married Christine Richardson Hubbard, Feb 11, 1967; children: Hylan T IV, Carmen D. **Educ:** Bowdoin Coll, Brunswick ME, AB, 1969; CPCU Designation. **Career:** Aetna Life & Casualty, Hartford CT, instructor/admin, 1974-75, Buffalo NY, mktg mgr, 1975-78, Hartford CT, regional dir, 1978-80, Harrisburg PA, gen mgr, 1980-82, Washington DC, gen agent, 1982, gen mgr, 1982-85, Hartford CT, vice pres field operations, 1985-90; Distribution System Management, Personal Auto & Homeowners, vice pres, 1991-92; Agency Development, vice pres, 1992-. **Orgs:** Univ of Washington, DC, bd of counselors, bd chair, 1985; Greater Hartford YMCA Board; Natl Urban Coalition Board; Clark Atlanta Univ Board; ACORD Board; Kappa Alpha Psi Foundation Board. **Honors/Awds:** America's Best & Brightest Young Business & Professional Men, Dollars & Sense Mag, 1987. **Business Addr:** Vice President, Agency Development, Aetna Life & Casualty, 151 Farmington Ave, TS3A, Hartford, CT 06156.

HUBBARD, JAMES MADISON, JR.
Dentist. **Personal:** Born in Durham, NC; married Gloria Carter; children: Linda Rose, James III, Phillip. **Educ:** NC Central U, BS 1945; Howard U, DDS 1949; UCLA; MPH 1974. **Career:** Jersey City Med Cntr, intern 1949-50; Durham, pvt prac 1950-62; Lincoln Hosp Durham, chief attending in oral surgery. **Orgs:** Pres of W Manchester Med Dental Cntr LA; staff mem Hollywood Presb Hosp Hollywood CA; bd dir & dental dir CompreCare Health Plan; bd mem, chmn 2nd Bapt Ch Credit Union; life mem NAACP; 32nd degree Mason & Shriner; Kappa Alpha Psi Frat. **Honors/Awds:** Recipient of Alexander Hunter Dental Soc Award 1963; CA Dental Coll's Award for Achievement 1973. **Military Serv:** AUS Dental Corps capt 1955-57. **Business Addr:** 600 W Manchester Ave, Los Angeles, CA.

HUBBARD, JEAN P.
Educator. **Personal:** Born Mar 5, 1917, Bedford, VA; married Portia. **Educ:** Wilberforce U, BS 1941; OH State U, MA 1945; Dayton Art Inst Univ of CA, further study; Tulane U. **Career:** TN State Univ, assoc prof 1947-50; Art Dept Central State Coll, chmn 1950-55; Southern Univ, instructor 1955-64; Dept of Fine Arts Southern Univ, chmn 1964-. **Orgs:** Mem Am Assn of Unive Prof; Coll Art Assn of Am Paintings in permanent collection at Carver Museum Tuskegee AL; commn Mural So Univ New Orleans; Blacksof LA & their contiribution to Culture of State of LA. **Business Addr:** PO Box 10403, Southern Univ, Baton Rouge, LA 70813.

HUBBARD, JOSEPHINE BRODIE
Social services executive. **Personal:** Born May 11, 1938, Tampa, FL; married Ronald C Hubbard; children: Ronald Charles, Valerie Alicia. **Educ:** Fl A&M Univ, BS with honors 1958; Univ of South Fl, MA with honors 1968. **Career:** Howard W Blake H S, teacher 1958-63; Chicopee H S, teacher 1965-66; NB Young Jr H S, guid counselor 1968-69; Univ of South FL, proj upward bound counselor coord 1969-71, spec serv dir and acad adv; Wright State Univ, acad adv 1973; Edwards Air Force Base, sub teacher 1974-75, guidance counselor 1978-80; Dept of the Army West Germany, guidance counselor 1978-80, collateral duty assignment, ed services officer 1980-81; Nellis Air Force Base, guidance counselor 1981-83; Family Support Center, chief of programs 1983-87, asst educ serv officer 1987-. **Orgs:** Family Support Ctr, rep; Directors of Volunteers in Agencies Org, mem 1983-; Southern NV Chap Federally Employed Women Inc 1983-; mem Federal Women's Program Interagency Council 1983-; scholarship chairperson Nellis Noncommissioned Officers Wives' Club 1985. **Honors/Awds:** Sustained Superior Performance Awd Family Support Ctr Chief of Programs 1985; Tactical Air Command Certificate of Recognition for Special Achievement 1985; Notable Achievement Awd Dept of the Air Force 1985; Sustained Superior Performance Awd Family Support Ctr Chief of Progs 1986; Sustained Superior Performance Award as director of Family Support Center, 1990-92. **Business Addr:** Director, Family Support Center, 56 MSSQ/MSF, Mac Dill AFB, FL 33608-5000.

HUBBARD, LAWRENCE RAY
Interior designer. **Personal:** Born Oct 23, 1965, Pittsburgh, PA; son of Sylvia Hubbard; children: John Perez, Hassan Perez. **Educ:** NYU, BA, BS, 1986. **Career:** Detroit Police Officer, 1987-94; Viggiano Interiors, president/owner, 1988-. **Orgs:** Optimist Club; ASID. **Special Achievements:** Appearances & articles: Detroit News; Detroit Free Press; WDIV-TV; Michigan Chronicle. **Business Phone:** (313)396-1991.

HUBBARD, MARILYN FRENCH
Entrepreneur, business executive. **Personal:** Born Oct 19, 1946, Lansing, MI; daughter of Mabel Brown French and Lester French (deceased); divorced; children: Paul Anthony Hubbard. **Educ:** Ferris State Coll, Big Rapids, MI, Assoc of Arts, 1969; Univ of Detroit, Detroit, MI, Bachelor of Business Admin, 1974; Univ Assoc, LaJolla, CA, Certificate Human Resources Mgmt, 1978-79; Chrysler Corp, Troy, MI, Certificate Minority Dealer Devel Program, 1986-89. **Career:** Wayne County Comon Pleas Court, official ct reporter, 1969-76; Marilyn Hubbard Seminars, Detroit, MI, pres, 1976-; Natl Assn of Black Women Entrepreneur, Inc, founder & natl pres, 1978-; adjunct prof, several coll & univ, 1978-; Chrysler Corp, Troy, MI, dealer candidate, 1986-89; Detroit Guide, SuccessSource, assoc regional editor; Marilyn Hubbard Seminars Inc, president, currently. **Orgs:** Bd of dir, Detroit Economic Growth Corp, 1980-, Advisory bd, 1984-88; Minority & Women's Task Force, 1984-; bd of dir, Natl Coalition of Black Meeting Planners, 1985-87; chmn, Governor's Entrepreneurial & Small Business Commn; US Small Business Admin, Small Business Devel Center. **Honors/Awds:** Natl 1980 Minority-Owned Business Advocate of the Year; Amer Top 100 Black Business & Prof Women, 1985; US Small Business Admin; Dollars & Sense Magazine; One of the first women to participate in Chrysler's Minority Dealer Devel Program; Success Story - Working Woman Magazine. **Business Addr:** President, Marilyn Hubbard Seminars Inc, PO Box 1375, Detroit, MI 48231.

HUBBARD, PAUL LEONARD
City official. **Personal:** Born Oct 31, 1942, Cincinnati, OH; son of Sylvia Hubbard and Paul Hubbard; married Georgia; children: Paul Anthony, Melissa (stepdaughter). **Educ:** Ohio U, BS Bus Ed 1961-65; Wayne State Univ-Detroit, MI, MSW 1969-71; IBM Exec Mgmt Training, Cert 1980; AMA Exec Training for Presidents, Cert 1982. **Career:** Stowe Adult Ed, instructor 1965; Detroit Public Sch, teacher 1965-71; Wayne County CC, consultant 1971-74; Downriver Family Neighborhood Service, associate dir 1971-74; New Detroit, Inc, sr vp, vice pres DHT transportation 1979-89, president, 1989-93; City of Toledo, dir of neighborhoods & housing, 1993-. **Orgs:** MI Bell Consumer Adv Group, mem (chmn 1984-89) 1980-; Metro Youth Prog, Inc, chmn 1983-87; Natl Assoc of Black Social Workers, natl vice pres 1982-86; US Selective Service Board, mem 1985-87; Internatl Exchange Bd of Directors, mem 1985-; MI Supreme Ct Subcommittee, chmn 1986-; pres Detroit Chap Natl Assoc Black Social Workers; Council of Political Education; bd of dir, Goodwill Industries of Greater Detroit; board of directors, Grand Valley University; board of directors, Marygrove College; board of directors, Southwest Hospital, board of directors, Channel 56; Federal Home Loan bank, bd. **Honors/Awds:** Outstanding service award, Det chap, Natl Assn of Black Social Workers, 1975; Lafayette Allen Sr Distinguished Service Award, 1979; Detroit City Council Testimonial Resolution for Community Services 1980; Wayne St U chap NABSW alumni of the year award, 1981; Gentlemen of Wall St Service Award 1984; American Cancer Soc service award, 1985; Black Enterprise Magazine service award, 1987; Natl Welfare Rights service award, 1988. **Business Addr:** Director, Neighborhoods, Housing & Economic Dev, City of Toledo, Department of Neighborhoods, Ste 1800, Toledo, OH 43604.

HUBBARD, PHIL
Professional basketball player. **Personal:** Born Dec 13, 1956, Canton, OH; married Dr Jackie Williams. **Educ:** Michigan. **Career:** Detroit Pistons, 1979-82, Cleveland Cavaliers, 1982-89. **Orgs:** Mem US teams that won Gold Medals at the 1976 Olympics in Montreal and The 1977 World Games; active in num local charitable causes; served as Cavs' rep and as Honorary Coach for the OH Special Olympics, 2 yr; nom for 1984 Walter Kennedy Awrd, a citizenship awrd given annually to an NBA player for his charitable & civic contributions. **Honors/Awds:** Emerged as a team leader & one of the best sixth men in the NBA; was only Cavalier to play in all 82 regular season games 1982-83.

HUBBARD, REGINALD T.
Automobile dealership executive. **Career:** Metrolina Dodge Inc, chief executive officer, currently. **Business Addr:** Chief Executive Officer, Metrolina Dodge Inc, 8525 South Blvd, Charlotte, NC 28217.

HUBBARD, STANLEY, SR.
Labor representative. **Personal:** Born Oct 29, 1940, San Marcos, TX; son of Virginia Algeray Byars Hubbard and Raymond William Hubbard; married Dorothy Irene Brice Hubbard, Aug 28, 1965; children: Kimberly M, Stanley Jr, Thaddaeus B, Horace B (deceased), Raymond W II, Duane C. **Educ:** San Antonio Community College, San Antonio, TX, AA, Middle Mgmt, 1974-79; Antioch University of Ohio, BA, labor studies, 1995. **Career:** Various electrical contractors, San Antonio, TX, apprentice, journeyman, 1963-73; San Antonio Building Trades, San Antonio, TX, program recruiter, 1973-79; AFL-CIO, Washington, DC, building trades program coordinator, 1979-81; IBEW, Washington, DC, international rep, 1981-. **Orgs:** Member, Greater Washington, DC branch, APRI, 1983-; board member, Clinton Boys & Girls Club, 1985-89; exec board member, IBEW Local #60, 1969-73; board member, Texas State PTA, 1976-79; president, Surratts/Clinton Democratic Club, 1989, 1992; Safety Equipment Institute, board of directors, general member. **Honors/Awds:** Wall Street Journal Award, San Antonio Community College, WSJ, 1976; Texas Life Membership, Texas State PTA, 1977. **Military Serv:** US Army, Specialist 4, 1959-62. **Business Addr:** International Representative, Construction & Maintenance, IBEW, 1125 15th St NW, Washington, DC 20005.

HUBBARD, TRENT (TRENIDAD AVIEL)
Professional baseball player. **Personal:** Born May 11, 1966, Chicago, IL. **Educ:** Southern (La.). **Career:** Colorado Rockies, outfielder, 1994-96; San Francisco Giants, 1996; Cleveland Indians, 1997; Los Angeles Dodgers, 1998-. **Business Addr:** Professional Baseball Player, Los Angeles Dodgers, 1000 Elysian Park Ave, Los Angeles, CA 90012, (213)224-1530.

HUBBARD, WALTER T.
Consultant. **Personal:** Born Oct 19, 1924, New Orleans, LA; son of Augustine Medina and Walter Hubbard; married Frances Washington; children: Walter, Donna, Colette, Anthony. **Educ:** Seattle U, bus course. **Career:** Local 17 AFL CIO Seattle, bus rep 1964-65; Project CARITAS, exec dir 1965-70; WA State Human Rights Com, contract compliance specialist 1970-; Am Arbitration Assn, Seattle center rep 1973-; Bangasser & Assoc, Business Planning, consultant; Washington State Board Prison Terms & Paroles, mem 1977-86; executive director, National Office for Black Catholics 1988-; Midtown Commons Community Development Corp, exec dir, 1994-. **Orgs:** Sec Model Capital Corp 1972-; bd mem Ecumenical Metro Ministry Seattle 1972-; bd mem Black Arts W Theatre Seattle 1975; pres Nat Office Black Cath 1972; Nat Cath Conf Interracial Justice 1968-73; chairperson Seattle Model Citizens Adv Council 1972-75; Civil Serv Commr King Co 1972-; pres Cntrl Area Civil Rights Com Seattle 1972; task force team mem No Ireland 1972; chairperson Black Higher Educ Seminar 1973; Wingspread; Johnson Found NCCIJ; mem Bd ofPrison Terms & Paroles WA 1977; mem bd of trustees Mattes Ricci Coll Seattle Univ & Seattle Preparatory Sch; mem Bd of Regents Seattle Univ 1974; mem Ecumenical group to White House Conf on Urban Policy 1978; Am del mem Elevation Archbishop Wash DC of Cardinal Wm Baum & 20 other cardinals around the world inRome by Pope Paul VI; del to Worlonf on Sov Jewry Brussel Belgium; participant in White House visit of Pope Paul II 1979; chair, Casey Family Program Foster Parents Services Seattle 1986-. **Honors/Awds:** Dist serv award Nat Cath Conf Inbteracial Justice 1973; citizen participation Award Seattle Model City Program 1974; Nat Office Commendation Serv 1973; Nat Office Black Cath UJIMA Award Nat Black Conv Cath New Orleans 1973; awarded Man in the St annual recognition Baltimore Black Cath Lay Caucus Our Lady of Charity Ch Brooklyn NY. **Military Serv:** AUS staff sgt 1943-45. **Business Addr:** 715 35th Ave, Seattle, WA 98122.

HUBERT-WHITTEN, JANET
Actress. **Personal:** marrIed James; children: Elijah Issac. **Educ:** Juilliard School; Loyola University, accounting. **Career:** Alvin Ailey dance company; television credits include: "One Life to Live"; "All My Children"; "Fresh Prince of Bel Air;" stage credits include: Sophisticated Ladies; Cats, Broadway. **Special Achievements:** Won scholarship to Juilliard School. **Business Addr:** Actress, c/o Michael Slessinger, 8730 Sunset Blvd, Ste 220, Los Angeles, CA 90069, (310)657-7113.

HUCKABY, HENRY LAFAYETTE
Physician. **Personal:** Born Jul 26, 1934, Crockett, TX; married Audria Mae Rain (divorced 1989); children: Seneca Kay, Arthur Craig, Sophia Katherine. **Educ:** Prairie View A&M Univ, BS 1956; Meharry Med Coll, MD 1965. **Career:** Houston Indepen Sch, sch tchr 1959-61; Harlem Hosp NYC, internship-surg 1965-66, residency-gen surg 1966-70; Columbia-Presbyterian Hosp, residency plastic surgery 1970-72; Baylor Coll of Medicine, clinical instructor plastic surgery 1973-77; attending plastic surgeon 1974-87; Private Practice, plastic & reconstructive surgery 1974-87, hand surgery, cosmetic surgery, critical

wound surgery, burn surgery 1974-87, micro-vascular surgery 1982-. **Orgs:** Mem Houston Medical Forum, Natl Medical Assn. **Military Serv:** AUS 1st lt 1956-58. **Business Addr:** Plastic Surgeon, PO Box 13687, 2619 Holman, Houston, TX 77219.

HUCKABY, HILRY, III
Judge. **Personal:** Born Jun 27, 1944, Shreveport, LA; married Pearl Aaron; children: Kimberly, Hilry IV, Kylaa G. **Educ:** Southern Univ, BA, 1966, JD, 1969. **Career:** Equal Employment Opportunity Cmsn, 1969-72; Huckaby & Piper, atty 1972-76; Huckaby & Associate, partner 1976-92; Fifth Circuit Court of Appeals, US District Court EW & Middle District, all other LA Courts, licensed to practise; NAACP Legal Defense & Educ Fund of NYC, cooperating atty; First District Court of Louisiana, judge, currently. **Orgs:** Shreveport Bar Assn; Natl Bar Assn; NAACP, Shreveport Chapter; Omega Psi Phi; YMCA, GW Carver Brch; Cooper Rd Community Civic Club Inc; bd of dirs, Community Orgztn for Drug Abuse & Control; 33rd degree Mason; bd of dirs, ACLU; Blacks United for Lasting Leadership; Galilee Baptist Church. **Honors/Awds:** Elected to Shreveport City Cncl, 1978-90, elected Chmn, 1979; elected Caddo District Judge, 1992. **Business Addr:** Judge, First District Court of Louisiana, 501 Texas St, Rm 620, Shreveport, LA 71101-5434.

HUCKABY, MALCOLM
Professional basketball player. **Personal:** Born Apr 7, 1972. **Educ:** Boston College. **Career:** Miami Heat, guard, 1997-. **Business Addr:** Professional Basketball Player, Miami Heat, 721 NW 1st Ave, Miami Arena, Miami, FL 33136, (305)577-4328.

HUDGEONS, LOUISE TAYLOR
Educational administrator. **Personal:** Born May 31, 1931, Canton, OH; married Denton Russell. **Educ:** Rsvlt Univ Chgo, BS 1952; Univ of Chgo, AM 1958; IN Univ Blmgtn, EdD 1974; Govs St Univ Pk Frst S IL, MBA 1977. **Career:** Central State Univ, dean School of Business Admin; Eastern NM Univ Coll of Business, dean 1978-; Chicago State Univ, asst prof, assoc prof, chmn, asst dean, acting dean 1969-78; State of IL, supvr Business Office Educ 1967-69; Chicago Public Schools, teacher 1955-67; MI Blvd Garden Apts, acct 1952-55. **Orgs:** Consult VA Plytchnc Inst 1966; consult IL St Univ 1971; consult Cntrl Sys Rsrch 1973; consult US Ofc of Educ 1975; consult Min Bus Opp Commn 1976-78; consJwl Osco Co 1977-78; consult Govs St Univ 1978; N Cntrl Assn Evltng Teams 1968-74; chmn Coll & Univ Div IL Bus Educ Assn 1970; chmn Evltn Supt Pub Schs IL 1972. **Honors/Awds:** Co-author Your Career in Mrktng Mcgrw Hill 1976; flwshp Am & Asmbly of Clgt Schs of Bus 1978; num spkng engag; svrl artcls pub. **Business Addr:** Central State University, Dean School of Business Admin, Wilberforce, OH 45384.

HUDLIN, REGINALD ALAN
Writer, film producer, director. **Personal:** Born Dec 15, 1961, Centerville, IL; son of Helen Cason Hudlin and Warrington W Hudlin. **Educ:** Harvard University, BA (cum laude), 1983. **Career:** Illinois State Arts Council, artist-in-residence, 1984-85; Ogilvy and Mather Advertising Agency, NY, 1986; University of Wisconsin-Milwaukee, visiting lecturer, film, 1985-86; Hudlin Bros Inc, NY, 1986-; director, writer, House Party, 1990; director, Boomerang, 1992; executive producer, writer, Bebe's Kids, 1992. **Honors/Awds:** Best Film Award, Black Cinema Society, 1984; Lillian Award, Delta Sigma Theta Sorority, 1990; Filmmakers Trophy, US Film Festival, 1990; Key to the City of Newark, 1990; Grantee, Production of the Year, Black Filmmaker Foundation, 1983, 1985, 1986; Fellow, National Endowment of the Arts, 1985; Black Filmmakers Hall of Fame, 1990; Nancy Susan Reynolds Award, Center for Population Options; Clarence Muse Award, 1991; Starlight Award, Black American Cinema Society, 1993. **Special Achievements:** Film work includes, director: Boomerang, 1992; director, writer: House Party, 1990; executive producer, writer: BeBe's Kids, 1992. **Business Addr:** Producer/Filmmaker, Hudlin Bros Inc, Tribeca Film Center, 375 Greenwich St, 6th Flr, New York, NY 10013.

HUDLIN, RICHARD A.
Educator. **Personal:** Born Apr 24, 1934, Clayton, MO; son of Myrtle Johnson Hudlin and Edward Warrington Hudlin Sr; married Wildemar Brown (divorced 1974); children: Richard Alphonso Jr. **Educ:** Princeton University, Princeton, NJ, 1951-54; University of the Philippines, Quezon City, Rep of Philippines, BA, 1958; Roosevelt University, Chicago, IL, MA, 1976; Atlanta University, Atlanta, GA, PhD, 1984. **Career:** Self-employed consultant, 1978-; Black Film Festival, Atlanta, GA, dir, 1980-81; Voter Education Project, Inc, Atlanta, GA, dir of research, 1980-83; New York Public Library, New York, NY, sr lib assoc, 1984-88; New York University, New York, NY, dir, 1988-90; State University of New York, Yonkers, NY, asst dean, 1991-. **Orgs:** Bd member, Bedford-Stuyvesant Vol Ambulance Corps, 1990-; board member, Black Press Institute, 1978-; chairman, Sci & Tech Program Admin Assn, 1988-90; academic committee co-chair, NYU Black Faculty & Admin Assn, 1988-90; member, American Mensa Society, 1985-. **Honors/Awds:** Educator, New York State Education Dept, 1988, 1990; Educator, New York City Board of Education, 1989; Educator, Mayor, City of New York, 1989; Educator, President, Borough of Manhattan, 1989; author or co-author of thirty-four publications, 1979-. **Military Serv:** US Air Force, A/1C, 1955-58.

HUDLIN, WARRINGTON
Film producer. **Educ:** Yale Univ, BA (cum Laude) Yale Scholar of the House 1974. **Career:** Black Filmmaker Found, co-founder/pres 1978—. **Orgs:** Bd of dirs Independent Feature Project 1979-; co-treas Independent Feature Project 1984-. **Honors/Awds:** Prod/dir Black at Yale, documentary film, 1974; prod/dir, St Corner Stories, feature film, 1977; prod/dir Capoeira of Brazil, documentary film, 1980; prod/dir, Color, tv drama, 1983; Clarence Muse Award, 1991. **Business Addr:** President, Black Filmmaker Foundation, 375 Greenwich Street, New York, NY 10013-2338.

HUDSON, ANTHONY WEBSTER
Personnel administrator (retired). **Personal:** Born Mar 23, 1937, Durham, NC; son of Adele Nixon Hudson and Emanuel Hudson; married Glenda; children: April Lynn, Verna Lea. **Educ:** Rutgers Univ, BA 1959; Columbia Univ, 1960-62; Wesley Seminary, American University, pursuing MDiv, 1995-. **Career:** Civil Service Comm, pers spec't 1962-70, dir prsnl 1970-74, dir eeo 1974-77; Defense Logistics Agcy, prsnl dir 1977-92; United Church of Christ, chaplain and pastor, 1995-. **Orgs:** Chair Prsnl Admin Comm US Dept Agric Grad Schl 1969-87; chair/mem Merit Brd MD/Nat'l Cap Park & Plng Comm 1974-86; pres/board of directors, WAEPA 1978-86; chair/mem, Montgomery County Merit System Protection Board, 1988-94. **Honors/Awds:** William A Jump Award for Excellence in Public Admin 1969; Defense Logistics Agency, exceptional civilian service award 1986. **Military Serv:** US Army, Capt, active duty, 1959-60, reserve duty, 1960-69. **Home Addr:** 7309 Pinehurst Pkwy, Chevy Chase, MD 20815-3140.

HUDSON, CHARLES LYNN
Professional baseball player (retired). **Personal:** Born Mar 16, 1959, Ennis, TX; married Nikki. **Educ:** Prairie View A&M Univ, BA, 1981. **Career:** Philadelphia Phillies, pitcher 1983-86; New York Yankees, pitcher, 1987-88; Detroit Tigers, pitcher, 1989. **Honors/Awds:** Allowed 3 earned runs or less in 24 of 30 starts; Named Pitcher of the Year 1982; Led league in ERA, wins & shutouts 1982; First rookie to hurl a complete game in NLCS history; named to Baseball Digest Rookie team 1983. **Home Addr:** 2124 Heather Glen, Dallas, TX 75232.

HUDSON, CHERYL WILLIS
Publisher, art director. **Personal:** Born Apr 7, 1948, Portsmouth, VA; daughter of Lillian Watson Willis and Hayes Elijah Willis III; married Wade Hudson, Jun 24, 1972; children: Katura J, Stephan J. **Educ:** Oberlin College, BA (cum laude), 1970; Ratcliffe College Publishing Procedures Course, 1970; Northeastern University, graphic arts management courses, 1971-72; Various courses at The Art Students League in NY; Parsons School of Design, 1973-76. **Career:** Houghton Mifflin Co, art editor, sr art editor, 1970-73; Macmillan Publishing Co, designer, design manager, 1973-78; Arete Publishing Co, assistant art director, 1978-82; freelance designer, special projects, 1979, 1985-88; Paperwing Press/Angel Entertainment, art director, freelance design consultant, 1982-87; Just Us Books, publisher, art director, 1988-. **Orgs:** Natl Assn of Black Book Publishers Multicultural Publishers Exchange, board of directors, 1990-92; Black Women in Publishing, 1990-92; Society of Children's Book Writers & Illustrators, 1989-. **Honors/Awds:** Publishers Marketing Association Award, publishing, 1991. **Special Achievements:** Author, Selection In The Multicolored Mirror: Cultural Substance in Literature for Children and Young Adults, 1991; Multiculturalism in Children's Books, 1990; Afro-Bets ABC Book, 1987; Afro-Bets 123 Book, 1988; Good Morning, Baby, 1992; Good Night, Baby, 1992; co-author, Bright Eyes, Brown Skin, 1990; Kwanzaa Sticker Activity Book, Scholastic Inc/Just Us Books, 1994; Articles have appeared in Edited by Violet Harris, Teaching Multicultural Literature in Grades K-8; "Creating Good Books for Children," A Black Publishers Perspective; Speaks Frequently on Topics Related to Creative Publishing of Books for Children, Focusing on African American Themes. **Business Phone:** (201)676-4345.

HUDSON, CHRISTOPHER RESHERD
Professional football player. **Personal:** Born Oct 6, 1971, Houston, TX. **Educ:** Univ of Colorado, bachelors degree in business, 1995. **Career:** Jacksonville Jaguars, defensive back, 1995-. **Honors/Awds:** Jim Thorpe Award, 1994. **Business Addr:** Professional Football Player, Jacksonville Jaguars, One Stadium Place, Jacksonville, FL 32202, (904)633-6000.

HUDSON, DIANNE ATKINSON
Television producer. **Career:** The Oprah Winfrey Show, supervising senior producer, executive producer, currently. **Business Addr:** Executive Producer, "Oprah", Harpo Productions, 110 N. Carpenter St., Chicago, IL 60607-2101, (312)633-0808.

HUDSON, DON R.
Editor. **Personal:** Born Sep 9, 1962, Shreveport, LA; son of Gladies Hudson and David Hudson Sr; married Miriam Caston Hudson, Dec 29, 1984. **Educ:** Northwestern State University, 1979-80; Northeast Louisiana University, BA, broadcast journalism, 1981-83. **Career:** Monroe News-Star, sports writer; Jackson Clarion-Ledger, sports writer; Monroe News-Star, sports editor; Atlanta Journal-Constitution, asst sports editor, Arkansas Gazette, sports editor; Orlando Sentinel, Sunday sports editor, currently. **Orgs:** National Association of Black Journalists; Associated Press Sports Editors; Orlando Black Achievers Program. **Honors/Awds:** Orlando YMCA, The Orlando Sentinel's Black Achiever, 1991-92. **Home Addr:** 121 Windy Hill Rd, Jackson, TN 38305. **Business Addr:** Sunday Sports Editor, Orlando Sentinel, 633 N Orange Ave, Orlando, FL 32802, (407)420-5327.

HUDSON, ELBERT T.
Savings and loan chief executive. **Career:** Broadway Savings and Loan Assoc, Los Angeles, CA, chief exec. **Business Addr:** Broadway Federal Savings and Loan Assn, 4501 South Broadway, Los Angeles, CA 90037.

HUDSON, ERNIE
Actor. **Personal:** Born Dec 17, Benton Harbor, MI; son of Maggie; married Jeannie Moore (divorced 1975); children: Ernest Jr, Rocky; children: Andrew, Ross. **Educ:** Wayne State University, graduated; University of Minnesota; Yale University School of Drama. **Career:** Various positions before acting including: janitor; Chrysler Corp, machine operator; MI Bell, customer rep; TV appearances include: Highcliffe Manor; The Last Precinct, 1986; Broken Badges, 1990; Angel Street, 1992; Roots: The Next Generations; White Mama; Love on the Run; Wild Palms, "Everything Must Go," 1993; guest appearances on various shows; film appearances include: Leadbelly, 1976; The Main Event, 1979; The Octagon, 1980; The Jazz Singer, 1980; Penitentiary II, 1982; Going Berserk, 1983; Two of a Kind, 1983; Joy of Sex, 1984; Ghostbusters, 1984; Weeds, 1986; Leviathan, 1989; Trapper County War, 1989; Ghostbusters II, 1989; The Hand That Rocks the Cradle, 1992; Sugar Hill, 1993; No Escape, 1993; The Cowboy Way, 1994; Airheads, 1994; The Crow, 1994; Congo, 1995; Clover, USA Network, 1997. **Military Serv:** US Marine Corps.

HUDSON, FREDERICK BERNARD
Business executive, television producer. **Personal:** Born Oct 29, 1947, Chicago, IL; son of Nellie Parham Hudson and Joseph T Hudson. **Educ:** Wayne State Univ, BA 1969; Yale Law Sch, attended 1970-71; New School for Social Rsch, MA 1975. **Career:** Elon Mickels & Assocs, planning dir 1978-79; Detroit City Council, staff analyst 1979-80; Southern IL Univ, visiting asst prof and coord 1980-81; Frederick Douglass Creative Arts Ctr, dir of public relations 1981-82; Centaur Consultants, pres; faculty mem, City Univ of NY, 1975-76, Coll of New Rochelle, 1986-87, Amer Business Inst, 1986-89; producer of television movies, "Things We Take" and "The Undercover Man". **Orgs:** Mem Assn of Independent Video & Filmmakers; mem Amer Planning Assn; mem Amer Mgmt Assn; comm consultant AT&T 1974; comm consultant Coro Found 1980; comm consultant Reality House 1982; instructor, District Council 37, 1989-. **Honors/Awds:** Poems short stories published in Freedomways, NY Quarterly; Citation of Merit State of MO Annual Poetry Contest 1980; New Writers Citation PEN 1984. **Business Addr:** President, Centaur Consultants, 142 W 72nd St, Suite 2A, New York, NY 10023.

HUDSON, FREDERICK DOUGLASS
Entrepreneur. **Personal:** Born Mar 13, 1928, Miami, FL. **Educ:** Univ of CA Berkeley, BA 1964; Univ of CA Berkeley Grad Sch. **Career:** Frederick Douglass Creative Arts Center, pres/artistic dir 1971-; Paramount Pictures, screen writer 1973-74; World Edn, writer 1972-73; Physics Library Univ of CA Berkeley, supr 1964-70; NY State Council on the Arts, film panel 1977-80, Special Arts Services Panel, 1984-87; Kennedy Center for the Performing Arts, Black commr; TV & Radio Station WNYC, bd of advisors; NY University Dramatic Writing Faculty. **Orgs:** Writer Guild of Am E; Dramatists Guild; Writers Guild of Am E Found, adv bd; National Endowment for the Arts, expansion arts theatre panel, 1991-, consultant, 1991-; Poet's House, board of directors. **Honors/Awds:** Leadership award Exxon Comm 1974; Andelco Award 1979. **Special Achievements:** The Educ of Sonny Carson, produced by Paramount Pictures, 1974; The Legend of Deadwood Dick, produced, 1978, New Heritage Theatre and Lincoln Center for the Performing Arts; Chanowski Productions, Amsterdam, Holland, writer, 1983-84; Blue Horse Productions, The Hague, Holland, writer, 1987. **Military Serv:** USAF tech sgt 1950-54. **Business Addr:** 270 West 96th St, New York, NY 10025.

HUDSON, HERMAN C.
Educator. **Personal:** Born Feb 16, 1923; married. **Educ:** Univ MI, BA1945; Univ MI, MA 1946; Univ MI, PhD 1961. **Career:** IN U, prof 1978; Afro-Am Affairs, dean 1970-; Dept of AfroAm Studies IN U, chmn 1970-72; Dept of Applied Linguistics IN U, chmn 1969-70; IN U, asso prof 1968-69; Univ MI, ind reading 1967-68; TC Columbia Univ English Prgm in Afghanistan, asst prof, dir 1961-67; VA State Coll, consult 1960;

NC Coll, asst prof 1959-60; Univ Puerto Rico, asst prof 1957-59; Univ MI, tchng fellow 1953-57; FL A&M U, instr 1946-51. **Honors/Awds:** Publs; "The Black Studies Prgm Strategy & Structure" 1971; "From Paragraph to Theme" 1972; "From Paragraph to Essay" 1975; "How To Make It In Coll" 1977; "The Black Composer Speaks" 1978.

HUDSON, JAMES BLAINE, III
Educator. **Personal:** Born Sep 8, 1949, Louisville, KY; son of Lillian Williamson Hudson and James Blaine Hudson II; married Bonetta M Hines-Hudson; children: Maya F, Travis M, Kenwyn K. **Educ:** Univ of Louisville, BS 1974, MEd 1975; Univ of Kentucky, EdD 1981. **Career:** School of Educ Univ of Louisville, admin coord 1974-75; West Louisville Educ Program Univ of Louisville, admin coord 1975-77, asst dir 1977-80, dir 1980-82; Univ of Louisville, assoc dir; Univ of Louisville Preparatory Division, associate director, 1982-92; assistant professor, Pan-African Studies, University of Louisville, 1992-. **Orgs:** Mem APGA, KPGA, ACPA 1976-; MENSA 1984-. **Honors/Awds:** Nat'l Merit Schlr 1967; Haggin Fellowshp Univ of K 1977-78; Black Faculty/Staff Mem of the yr Univ of L 1982. **Home Addr:** 4255 North Western Pkwy, Louisville, KY 40212-2930. **Business Addr:** Assistant Professor, Pan-African Studies, Preparatory Division, University of Louisville, Louisville, KY 40208.

HUDSON, JEROME WILLIAM
Educator. **Personal:** Born May 9, 1953, Washington, DC. **Educ:** Univ of MD, BA 1975; George Washington Univ, Grad Certificate 1980; Amer Inst of Hypnotherapy, PhD 1986. **Career:** YMCA, asst physical dir 1977-78; Wesley Early Childhood Ctr, dir 1978-79; Shore Up Inc, dir training & employment 1979-; Romejoy Inc, Salisbury, MD, chief executive officer, 1986-. **Orgs:** Adjunct faculty mem Salisbury State Coll 1978-80; governor's state adv cncl Office of Children & Youth 1978-; state adv comm mem Office Children & Youth 1980-; selection comm mem Foster Care Review Bd 1980-; lecturer universities and colls 1980-; bd of dir Heart Assoc 1980-81; vice pres Wicomico Cnty Council of Social Serv 1980-81; bd of dir Democratic Club Wicomico Cnty; Dance Instructor Salisbury City Hall Museum and Wicomico Cnty Recreation & Parks; Governors Task Force on Violence and Extremism; planning coord Lower Shore Career Day Prog; lec Afro-American History Week Phi Delta Kappa 1982; bd of dir Maryland Public Broadcasting-Chemical People Adv Bd; bd of dirs March of Dimes 1983, YMCA 1984-; mem Salisbury Chap Jaycees 1986-; Shore Up Inc, director of training & employment, 1979-87; Foster Care Review Bd, selection comm mem, 1980-87; YWCA, 1984-90; Rural Opportunity for Minority Enterprise Scholarship, founder, 1990-. **Honors/Awds:** Key to the City of Salisbury 1978; Outstanding Young Men of Amer US Jaycees 1981; Employee of the Year Shore Up Inc 1981; Producer Children & Youth Conf Governor of MD 1981; Enthusiastic Awd MD State Dept of Educ 1985-86. **Home Addr:** PO Box 3066, Salisbury, MD 21802.

HUDSON, JOHN D.
Corrections official. **Personal:** Born May 16, 1927, Atlanta, GA; married Delores Harris; children: Renee, Tony. **Educ:** Clark Coll, AB 1949; John Marshall Univ, JD 1968; Univ of LA, Police Admin 1969; Univ of GA, Cert Publ Admin 1972; GA State Univ, Publ Admin 1974. **Career:** Atlanta Police Dept, detective, vice squad, burglary squad, school detective, detective sgt 1967, internal security dist suprv detective lt 1968, commanding officer prostitution squad, internal security, commander of task force, crime prevention bureau, spec recruiting officer, training officer aide to police committee, police capt; Bureau Correctional Svcs, dir 1971-. **Orgs:** Bd mem Natl Assn Black in Criminal Justice, Amer Correctional Assn, Natl Org of Black Law Enforcement Exec; past pres Omega Chap Y's Mens Club, Douglas HS PTA; chmn bd of dir, YMCA Northwest Branch. **Honors/Awds:** Outstanding Achievement in Law Enforcement Eta Sigma Chap 1973; Clark Coll Man of the Year 1974; Leadership Atlanta 1974-75; Frontiers Intl External Awd 1976. **Home Addr:** 1159 Mobile St NW, Atlanta, GA 30314. **Business Addr:** Dir, Bureau of Corrections, 236 Peachtree St SW, Atlanta, GA 30335.

HUDSON, KEITH
Business executive. **Personal:** Born Mar 4, 1954, St Louis, MO; married Janeice Fay Gipson. **Educ:** O'Fallon Tech Sch Electronics, 1974. **Career:** Ted's One Stop Inc, vice pres Sales & mdse 1978-; Ted's One Stop, salesman 1975-78; Hudson Embassy, store mgr 1972-75; Metro Advt, acount exec 1977; Platinum Plus Records & Tapes, pres 1979. **Orgs:** Regular mem Dem Orgn 1973; mem Black Music Assn 1977. **Honors/Awds:** Gold record sales over 500,000 on Evelyn "Champaign" King's single "Shame" RCA Records & Tapes 1977; platinum LP Michael Jackson's "Off the Wall" album 1980. **Business Addr:** Ted's One Stop Inc, 3814 Page Blvd, St Louis, MO 63113.

HUDSON, LESTER DARNELL
Attorney. **Personal:** Born Mar 4, 1949, Detroit, MI; married Vivian Ann Johnson. **Educ:** Fisk U, BA 1971; Boston Coll, Law Degree; Law Sch Brighton MA, 1974. **Career:** Bell & Hudson, atty & sr partner; Boston Coll, legal internlegal asst 1973-74; City of Boston Law Dept, intern 1972-73; Boston Legal & Asst Proj, legal intern 1972. **Orgs:** Mem Detroit Bar Assn; mem NBA; mem ABA Young Lawyers sect; Urban Leag; PUSH Detroit; mem NAACP Crime Task Force com. **Honors/Awds:** Awd for Ldshp & Schlrshp Scott Paper Co Found 1971; Martin Luther King Awd for Ldrshp & Comm Invlmnt 1974. **Business Addr:** Bell & Hudson, 840 Buhl Bldg, Detroit, MI 48226.

HUDSON, MERRY C.
Government official. **Personal:** Born Dec 25, 1943, Baltimore, MD; married Robert L Hudson; children: Alicia; Stephen. **Educ:** Howard Univ, BA 1965, JD 1968; George Washington Univ, LLM 1972. **Career:** Equal Employment Opportunity Comm, supervisory attorney 1971-72; Univ of Maryland, affirmative action off 1975-76; Private Practice of Law, 1976-78; State of MD Comm on Human Relations, hearing examiner 1978-. **Orgs:** Univ of MD, eeo consultant 1976; Nat'l Assoc of Admin Law Judges, mem; Nat'l Bar Assoc, mem; DC Links, Inc, treasurer 1985-; Alpha Kappa Alpha, mem. **Honors/Awds:** Howard Univ, academic scholarships 1961-68; State of MD Personnel Dept, cert of appreciation 1980; Nat'l Judicial Coll, citation for distinquished service, faculty advisor 1982, Nat'l Assoc for Equal Opp, distinguished Alumni awd 1986. **Home Addr:** 1216 Edgevale Rd, Silver Spring, MD 20910.

HUDSON, PAUL C.
Bank executive, entrepreneur. **Career:** Broadway Federal Savings & Loan, chief executive officer, currently. **Special Achievements:** Company ranked #13 on Black Enterprise Top Financial Companies List, 1992.

HUDSON, ROBERT L.
Educator, physician. **Personal:** Born Oct 30, 1939, Mobile, AL; son of Claudia M Jackson Hudson Graham and Robert L Hudson (deceased); married Merry Brock; children: Alicia, Stephen. **Educ:** Lincoln Univ, BA 1962; Howard Univ, MD 1966. **Career:** Howard Univ Ctr for Sickle Cell Disease, physician coord 1971-72; Howard Univ, asst prof 1971-75; Howard Univ Ctr for Sickle Cell Disease, dep dir 1972-75; private practice, physician, currently. **Orgs:** Attending staff Howard Univ Hosp; Children's Hosp; Natl Med Ctr; Columbia Hosp for Women; DC Genl Hosp; mem bd dir Capital Head Start 1971-75; medcons Capital Headstart 1971-76; Med Soc of DC; Amer Acad of Pediatrics; Medico Chirurgical Soc of DC; Amer Heart Assn. **Business Addr:** Drs Crawford & Hudson, PC, 2600 Naylor Rd SE, Washington, DC 20020.

HUDSON, ROY DAVAGE
Educational administrator. **Personal:** Born Jun 30, 1930, Chattanooga, TN; son of Everence Wilkerson Hudson and James Roy Hudson; married Constance Joan Taylor, Aug 31, 1956; children: Hollye Hudson Goler, David K Hudson. **Educ:** Livingstone Coll, BS 1955; Univ of MI, MS 1957, PhD 1962; Lehigh Univ, LLD 1974; Princeton Univ, LLD 1975. **Career:** Univ of MI Med School, prof 1961-66; Brown Univ Med School, prof 1966-70; Brown Univ Graduate School, assoc dean, 1966-69; Hampton Univ, pres 1970-76; Warner Lambert, Parke-Davis, vice pres, pharmaceutical research 1977-79; The Upjohn Co, pharmaceutical research, dir central nervous syst rsch, 1981-87, Pharmaceutical Research and Development Europe; Upjohn Co, vice pres pharmaceutical research and devel, 1987-90, corporate vice president for public relations, 1990-92; Livingstone College, interim president, 1995-1996; Guidance Clinic, Kalamozoo, MI, executive director/CEO. **Orgs:** Bd dir Parke-Davis Co 1974-76; bd dir Chesapeake and Potomac Telephone Co 1972-76; bd dir United Virginia Bankshares 1971-76; chmn VA State Comm for Selection Rhodes Scholars 1973; bd dir Peninsula Chamber of Commerce 1970-76; bd dir Amer Council on Educ 1973-76; board of trustees, National Medical Fellowship, 1990; board of directors, Comerica Bank, 1990; advisory bd, Kalamazoo Math and Science Center, 1990. **Honors/Awds:** Danforth Fellow Danforth Foundation 1955-62; Outstanding Civilian Serv Award US Army 1972; Scholarship Award Omega Psi Phi Fraternity 1954-55; Distinguished Alumni Medallion Livingstone Coll 1969; Award of Merit for Continuous Service to Humanity, Omega Psi Phi Fraternity, 1974; Award for Exemplary Leadership Omega Psi Phi Fraternity, 1978; M L King/C Chavez/R Parks visiting prof, Univ of MI, 1989. **Military Serv:** USAF Staff Sgt 1948-52. **Home Addr:** 7057 Oak Highlands Dr, Kalamazoo, MI 49009.

HUDSON, STERLING HENRY, III
Educator. **Personal:** Born Jul 6, 1950, Hot Springs, VA; son of Mr & Mrs Sterling H Hudson Jr; married Cheryl White; children: Tara L. **Educ:** Hampton Univ, BA (w/Honors) 1973, MA 1979. **Career:** Hampton Univ, admissions counselor 1973-77, asst to dean of admissions 1977-78, asst dean of admissions 1978-82; Elizabeth City State Univ, dir of admissions/recruitment 1982-83; Morehouse Coll, dir of admissions 1983-93, assistant vice president for academic affairs/director of admissions, dean of freshmen, 1991-96, vice provost for admissions & enrollment management, 1996-. **Orgs:** Mem Natl Assoc of Coll Admissions Counselors 1973-, Amer Assoc of Coll Deans Registrars Adm Ofcrs 1973-, Kappa Delta Pi 1979-, Atlanta Urban League 1984-; rep Univ Ctr of GA 1984-86; council coll level serv Coll Bd 1985-88. **Honors/Awds:** Most Outstanding Grad Brother Iota Phi Theta 1980; writer Fin Aid for Minorities in Medicine, ed asst Fin Aid for Minorities in Medicine (series) Garrett Park Press 1980; Fleischman Foundation UNCF Study Grant 1986. **Business Addr:** Vice Provost for Admissions & Enrollment Management, Morehouse College, 830 Westview Dr, SW, Atlanta, GA 30314, (404)215-2712.

HUDSON, THEODORE R.
Educator (retired), author, consultant. **Personal:** Born in Washington, DC; married Geneva Bess; children: Eric, Vicki. **Educ:** Miner Teachers Coll, BS; NY Univ, MA; Howard Univ, MA, PhD. **Career:** Univ of DC, prof of English 1964-77; Amer Univ, adj prof of lit 1968-69, 1991; Howard Univ, grad prof English 1977-91, consultant, 1991-. **Orgs:** VP & Newsletter Editor, Duke Ellington Soc; past pres Highland Beach Cit Assoc. **Honors/Awds:** Most Disting Lit Scholarship Awd Coll Lang Assoc 1974; From LeRoi Jones to Amiri Baraka, The Literary Works Duke Univ Press 1973; num art in periodicals and books.

HUDSON, WILLIAM THOMAS
Federal official. **Personal:** Born Dec 14, 1929, Chicago, IL; son of Mary Hudson and Cornelius Hudson. **Educ:** Northwestern Univ, BS 1953; Univ of Chgo, MA 1954; Harvard Univ, MPA 1982. **Career:** Bur Retirement & Survivors Ins Balt, claims authorizer 1963-64; Hders Retirement & Survivors Ins, employee devel ofcr; Comm on EEO WA, detailed to pres; Ret & Survivors Ins, spec asst for EEO to dir 1964-65; Ofc Sec Dept HEW WA, dep EEO Officer 1966-67; Ofc Sec Dept Transp WA, cons, prgm mgr internal EEO prog, Natl Urban league Conv, resource 1967-70; Office Civil Rights USCG WA, chief 1970-83; US Dept of Transportation, dept dir of civil rights 1983-. **Orgs:** Member, Senior Executive Assn; member, Phi Delta Kappa, member, Hon Soc for Men in Ed. **Honors/Awds:** Silver Medal for Meritorious Achievement 1974. **Military Serv:** AUS 1954-56. **Business Addr:** Dept Dir Civil Rights, US Dept of Transportation, 400 7th St SW, Washington, DC 20590.

HUDSON, WINSON
Educator. **Personal:** widoWed. **Educ:** Comm Educ Extension Mary Holmes Coll. **Career:** Leake Co Chapter NAACP, pres 1961-74; Leake Co Head Start, social serv specialist. **Orgs:** Mem MS Council on Human Relations; MS Assn for Health Care for the Poor; bd mem ACLU; chmn Dem Party Leake Co. **Honors/Awds:** Recipient Many Awards for Outstanding Leadership in Civil Rights Movement.

HUDSON-WEEMS, CLENORA FRANCES
Educator. **Personal:** Born Jul 23, 1945, Oxford, MS; daughter of Mary Cohran Pearson and Matthew Pearson; married Dr Robert E Weems, Jr; children: Sharifa Zakiya. **Educ:** LeMoyne Coll, BA, 1967; L'Universite de Dijon, France, Certificate, 1969; Atlanta University, MA, 1971; University of Iowa, PhD, 1988. **Career:** Delaware State College, assistant professor, 1972-73; Southern Univ in New Orleans, asst prof of English 1976-77; Deleware State College, director of black studies, asst prof of English, 1980-85; Banneker Honors College, associate professor, 1988-90; University of Missouri-Columbia, associate professor, 1990-. **Orgs:** Western Jrnl for Black Studies, WA State Univ, ed bd mem; Coll Lang Assn, 1970-; Assn for Study of African-American Life and History, 1992-; African Heritage Studies Assn, 1985-. **Honors/Awds:** Natl Endowment for the Humanities, 1981; Committee on Institution Cooperation, 1983; Ford Fellowships, 1986-88; Honorary Outstanding Black Delawarean, 1986; Key to the City, Memphis, 1994; Alpha Kappa Alpha, Black Woman of the Year, 1994; Proclamation, State of Tennessee House of Representatives, 1994; Proclamation, Missouri Legislative Black Caucus, 1994; Resolution, Memphis City Council, 1994; Western Journal of Black Studies, Scholarly Achievement and Leadership Award, 1995. **Special Achievements:** Author: Emmett Till: The Sacrificial Lamb of the Civil Rights Movement 1994; Africana Womanism: Reclaiming Ourselves, 1993, "Africana Womanism: An Historical, Global Perspective for Women of African Descent" in Call and Response: African-American Literacy Tradition, 1997; "Self-Naming and Self-Defining: A Reclamation;" Sisterhood, Feminism and Power, 1997; Soul Mates, a novel, 1998; "Toni Morrison's World of Topsy-Turveydom: A Methodological Explication of New Black Literary Criticism," Western Journal for Black Studies, 1986; "The Tripartite Plight of African-American Women in Their Eyes Were Watching God and The Color Purple," Journal of Black Studies, 1989; "Cultural and Agenda Conflicts in Academia: Critical Issues for Africana Women's Studies," Western Journal of Black Studies, 1989; "Claude McKay: Black Protest in Western Traditional Form," Western Journal of Black Studies, 1992; "From Malcolm Little to El Hajj Malik El Shabazz: Malcolm's Evolving Attitude toward Africana Women," Western Journal of Black Studies, 1993; Co-author: Twayne US Authors Series, Toni Morrison, 1990; Interview with American Audio Prose Library, Inc, 1995; "Africana Womanism: An African Centered Paradigm in an African Centered Discipline," Western Journal of Black Studies, 1997; "Resurrecting Emmett Till," Journal of Black Studies, 1998; "20th Century African American Literature," An Historiographical & Bibliographical Guide to the African American Experience, Greenwood Publishers. **Business Addr:** Professor, Department of English, University of Missouri-Columbia, 107 Tate Hall, Columbia, MO 65211.

HUDSPETH, GREGORY CHARLES, SR.
Educator. **Personal:** Born Oct 1, 1947, San Antonio, TX; son of Louise Menefee Hudspeth and Charles Hudspeth; married Dollie Rivers Hudspeth, Dec 26, 1970; children: Gregory Jr, Brandon. **Educ:** Huston-Tillotson College, Austin, TX, BA, 1970; St Mary's University, San Antonio, TX, MA, 1975. **Career:** Northside Independent School District, San Antonio, TX, teacher/coach, 1971-78; St Philip's College, San Antonio, TX, associate professor, 1978-. **Orgs:** Deacon, Mt Zion First Baptist Church, 1987-; precinct chairman, Democratic Party, 1980-; life-member, Alpha Phi Alpha Fraternity Inc, 1968-; president, Faculty Senate, 1983-86, 1988-; trustee, Target 90/ Goals for San Antonio, 1985-89; vice-president, Huston-Tillotson College Alumni Assn/San Antonio, 1990-. **Honors/Awds:** Trail blazer, Texas Publishers Association, 1991; Black Americans in Political Science, American Political Science Association, 1988; San Antonian of the Day, WDAI Radio, 1970. **Home Addr:** 9302 Fallworth, San Antonio, TX 78250. **Business Addr:** Associate Professor, St Philip's College, Social Sciences Dept, 1801 Martin Luther King Dr, San Antonio, TX 78203.

HUESTON, OLIVER DAVID
Psychiatrist. **Personal:** Born Oct 23, 1941, NYC; divorced; children: Michael, David. **Educ:** Hunter Coll, BA 1963; Meharry Med Coll, MD 1968; Josiah Macy Fellow 1971-72; Columbia U, Attending Pediatrician 1971-72. **Career:** Harlem Hosp, chief Resident Pediatrics 1970-71; Harlem Hosp, gen psychiatric resident 1972-74, fellow child Psychiatry 1974-75; Columbia Univ Coll of Physicians & Surgeons, attending pediatrician 1971-72; Self Employed 1985. **Orgs:** Mem Pediatrician Flower 5 Ave Hosp Martin L King Evening Clinic 1971; clinical physician NY State Drug Abuse Control Com; dir Ambulatory Drug Unit #13 Harlem Hops; mem St Albans Martyr Episcopal Ch; Josiah Macy Fellow 1971-72. **Honors/Awds:** USAFR 1968-71. **Business Addr:** Oliver D Hueston MD, 843 Barbara Drive, Teaneck, NJ 07666.

HUFF, JANICE WAGES
Meteorologist. **Personal:** Born Sep 1, 1960, New York, NY; daughter of Dorothy L Wages; married Kenneth E Huff, Dec 3, 1983. **Educ:** The Florida State University, Tallahassee FL, BS, Meteorology, 1978-82. **Career:** National Service, Columbia, SC, weather trainee, 1978-80; WCTV-TV, Tallahassee, FL, weather intern, 1982; WTVC-TV, Chattanooga, TN, meteorologist, 1982-83; WRBL-TV, Columbus, GA, meteorologist, 1983-87; KSDK-TV, St Louis, MO, meteorologist, 1987-90; KRON-TV, San Francisco, CA, meteorologist, 1990-. **Orgs:** Member, American Meteorological Society, 1981-; member, National Association of Black Journalists, 1986-; member, Alpha Kappa Alpha Sorority, 1986-. **Honors/Awds:** Weathercasting, Seal of Approval, American Meteorological Soc, 1985; TV Emmy/Best Weathercaster, National Assn of Television Arts & Sciences, 1988. **Business Addr:** Meteorologist, News, KRON-TV (Ch 4), 1001 Van Ness Ave, San Francisco, CA 94109.

HUFF, LEON ALEXANDER
Producer, composer. **Personal:** Born Apr 8, 1942, Camden, NJ; married Stephanie Ann Saunders; children: Debbie, Detira, Leon II, Bilail, Inga, Erika. **Career:** With Kenneth Gamble, formed Excel Records, 1966, and Philadelphia Records, 1971; songwriter and producer of songs for Archie Bell and the Drells, Dusty Springfield, Wilson Pickett, Jerry Butler, The Intruders, Lou Rawls, The Jacksons, The O'Jays, Teddy Pendergrass, Harold Melvin and the Blue notes, The Three Degrees, The MFSB Orchestra, Billy Paul, The Jones Girls, Patti Labelle. **Honors/Awds:** Recipient Key to City of Camden; Record World Producer-Writer of Decade Award; Best Rhythm & Blues Producers Award, National Assn of TV & Recording Artists, 1968-69; numerous Grammy nominations and awards; The Number 1 Song Publishing Award; The Number 1 Record Company Award. **Special Achievements:** Over 300 gold and platinum singles and albums; formed Mighty Three Publishing Company; formed Philadelphia International Records. **Business Addr:** Record Producer, Composer, 309 S Broad St, Philadelphia, PA 19107.

HUFF, LOUIS ANDREW
Educator & business consultant. **Personal:** Born Jan 1, 1949, New Haven, CT; married Suzanne Elaine Cooke; children: Elaine Kai. **Educ:** Howard Univ, BA Economics Bus Finance 1971, MA Economics 1974, PhD Economics 1981. **Career:** Fed Reserve Bd, economist 1971-74; Lincoln Univ, asst prof 1977-80; CBC Rsch Inst, pres 1980-82; Univ of New Haven, asst prof 1980-82; 1st Buffalo Corp, economist/stockbroker 1983-; PA State Univ, asst prof of economics. **Orgs:** Bd mem CBC Inc 1982-; mem Western Economic Soc 1983-; economic consultant RIE Ltd 1983-; host & producer Economist Corner 1984-; chairperson housing NAACP Reading Chap 1984-; mem Atlantic Economic Soc 1984-. **Honors/Awds:** Rsch Study Awd Economics Natl Chap of Eastern States 1979; Outstanding Young Man in America Natl 1981; article published Atlantic Economic Journal 1985; Presented papers at num natl econ confs incl Montreal Canada 1983, Rome Italy 1985. **Business Addr:** Asst Prof Economics, PA State Univ, RD #5 Box 2150, Reading, PA 19608.

HUFF, LULA LUNSFORD
Company executive. **Personal:** Born Jul 5, 1949, Columbus, GA; daughter of Sally Bryant Lunsford and Walter T Lunsford; married Charles E Huff Jr, Jun 11, 1972; children: Tamara Nicole. **Educ:** Howard University, Washington, DC, BA, 1971; Atlanta University, Atlanta, GA, MBA, 1973; State of Georgia, CPA, 1978. **Career:** Ernst & Young, CPA Firm, Columbus, GA, accountant/auditor, 1973-76; Troy State University, Phenix City, AL, instructor, accounting dept, 1979-89, chairman, 1980-87, director of personnel mgmt graduate program, 1984-85; Consolidated Gov of Columbus, Columbus, GA, chief internal auditor, 1976-84; Pratt & Whitney, UTC, Columbus, GA, senior financial/cost analyst, 1984-85, financial supervisor, 1985-89, controller, 1989-96; Muscogee County Tax Commissioner, GA, 1997-. **Orgs:** YMCA, GA Society of CPAs; Urban League; PUSH; NAACP; Howard University Alumni Association; Natl Council of Negro Women; Jack & Jill of America Inc; Links Inc; Delta Sigma Theta Sorority Inc; board member, Girl Scouts; American Institute of CPA's; Leadership Columbus, GA; Uptown Columbus; Dale Carnegie; St Anne Catholic Church. **Honors/Awds:** Business Woman of the Year Award, Iota Phi Lambda Sorority Inc, 1979; Distinguished Black Citizen Award, WOKS Radio, 1978; Black Excellence Award, Natl Assn of Negro Business & Prof Women's Clubs Inc, 1977; Outstanding Service Award, St Benedict Catholic Church, 1971-76; Professional Woman of the Year Award, Iota Phi Lambda Sorority Inc, 1977; Achievement Award, Links Inc, 1976; Delta Mu Delta Natl Business Honor Soc Outstanding Woman of the Year, Ledger Enquirer Newspaper, 1976; Certificate of Merit for Excellent Community Leadership and Contribution to Good Government, Congressman Jack T Brinkley, 1976; Outstanding Achievement and Service Award, First African Baptist Church, 1975.

HUFF, WILLIAM
Business executive. **Personal:** Born Apr 10, 1920, Manchester, GA; married Beatrice; children: Ronald, Cherie Fae, Brian. **Educ:** Youngstown U, AB 1951; Univ of Pittsburgh, MSW 1969; OH State Univ Mgmt Devel Prog, Certificate 1968; Training Course Mattatuck Coll CT, Certificate of Housing Tech Training Course. **Career:** Plymouth Urban Cntr Louisville, exec dir 1973-; Pearl St Neighborhood House, exec dir 1970-73; Youngstown Area Comm Action Coun, asso dir 1965-70. **Orgs:** Fin chmn Commun Action Agency; mem CAC; Asso Neighborhood Cntr Hagstrom House US Military Reservation 1951-57; mem NAACP; Boys Wrk Com YMCA OH; Welf Rights Organz OH; past pres Prof Grp Wkrs OH; Stud Loan Com CT; Mod Cities Adv on Recreation; adv Teen Parent Club; co-chmn State Blk Polit Assemb KY; Black Social Workers of Louisville; Equal Justice Information Cntr Bd Louisville; LEAP Bd of Louisville Urban Leage; THETA Omega Chap of Omega PsiPhi; Russell Area Coun; adv com to WLKY TV of Louisville; Mayor's Human Relat Com OH. **Honors/Awds:** Recipient Award by Freedom Inc as A Native Son Youngstown OH 1971; Certificate of Housing Technician Course 1969; Certificate from OH State Univ Mgmt Devel Prog 1968; Hon KY Col. **Military Serv:** USAF 1944-45. **Business Addr:** 1626 W Chestnut, Louisville, KY 40203.

HUFFMAN, RUFUS C.
Association executive. **Personal:** Born Feb 5, 1927, Bullock Co, AL; married Callie Iola Harris; children: Rufus, Jr, Henry. **Educ:** AL State U, BS 1952, MEd 1966; NY U, Further Study. **Career:** Tchr Prin Coach; Russell Co Bd Edn, prin 1947-49; Augusta Co Bd Educ Prattville AL 1951-53. **Orgs:** Bullock Co Bd Educ Union Springs AL 1953-56; Randolph Co Bd Educ Cuthbert GA 1956-63; coord treas mgr Seasha Fed Credit Union Tuskegee Inst AL 1968-70; co-founder SE Self-Help Assn; organizer treas mgr SEASHA Fed Credit Union; consult OEO Comprehensive Health Program & Ford Found Leadership Devel Program; so educ field dir NAACP Spl Contrib Fund Inc 1985; pres Bullock Co Tchrs Assn; pres Bullock Co Athletic Assn; pres Union Springs NAACP 1966-70; chmn Bullock Co Coordntg Com 1966-70; chmn Bullock Co Recreational Bd 1973; life mem NAACP; v pres Bullock Co Improvement Orgn; mem bd dir So Poverty Law Center; Leadership Devel Program Selection Com; Union Springs Adv Com City Council; Great Books Western World Salesman; Distrib Success Motivation Inst. **Honors/Awds:** Tchr of Yr Bullock Co 1963-64; Joshua A Smith Award Outstanding Leadership Educ Human Devel in S; Certificate Honor NAACP Club 100. **Business Addr:** PO Drawer 190, Tuskegee Institute, AL 36088.

HUGER, JAMES E.
Business executive (retired). **Personal:** Born in Tampa, FL; married Phannye Brinson; children: James Ermine, Jr, Thomas Albert, II, John Leland. **Educ:** Graduated, Bethune Cookman Coll, West Virginia State Coll, Univ of MI. **Career:** Bethune-Cookman Coll, business mgr, admin asst to pres, assoc treasurer; Alpha Phi Alpha Frat Inc, genl secty; City of Daytona Beach FL, dir of community development, until 1994. **Orgs:** Life mem Alpha Phi Alpha Frat, NAACP; Elks; Masons; American Legion; Assn for the Study of Negro Life and History; Sigma Pi Phi Frat; The Civic League, Civitan, Shrine; bd of dirs: FL Health Care, FL League of Cities Intergovernmental Relations Comm, pres, bd of dirs, Stewart Treatment Ctr, SERC/ NAHRO's Comm and Redevelop Comm, The United Methodist Church, Volusia Governmental Employees Credit Union; pres bd of dirs Rape Crisis Ctr of Volusia Co Inc; chmn United Nations Comm 1985, Dr Martin L King Birthday Commemoration Comm; pres Volusia County Assn of Retarded Citizens; bd of dirs State Mental Health Assn; The Review Panel, Developing Institutions HEW Washington DC; State Commn on Aging; FL Bar Grievance Comm; Southern Growth Policy Bd; Rotary International; Commission on the Future of the South; minority enterprise development comm, Dept of Commerce; Governor's Martin Luther King Commission, May 1992; King Center for Community Development, advisory committee member, 1992-94, secretary, 1992; Metro Board of the Greater Daytona Beach YMCA, 1992-93; Bethune-Cookman College Southern College Alumni Assn, pres, 1992-93; National Community Development Association, president, 1992-93. **Honors/Awds:** Charles W Green Award for Outstanding Serv to Humanity; Man of the Year Alpha Phi Alpha Frat; Bethune Cookman Coll Awd Administrator of the Year, Medallion for Outstanding Contribution to Local Govt; Awd of Achievement NAACP; Humanitarian Awd NAACP; Equality Day Awd Natl Org for Women; Awd of Thank You, Disting Serv Awd, 1986, FL Assn of Retarded Citizens and Volusia Assoc of Retarded Citizens; Disting Serv Awd United Nations 1985; Certificates of Appreciation Halifax Hosp Med Ctr 1985, Links Inc 1985, Stewart Memorial United Methodist Ch 1986; Ray Sims Awd Outstanding Contribution in the Fight Against Heart Disease 1986; Dedication of Jimmy Huger Circle Assoc of Retarded Citizens Volusia Co 1986; Plaque of Appreciation Mary McLeod Bethune Ctr 1986; Awd of Appreciation Rape Crisis Ctr of VolusCo 1986; US Dept of Housing and Urban Development, Region IV, Award of Special Recognition, May 1993; Assn of Retarded Citizens, Volusia County, Inc, Certificate of Appreciation, May 1993; American Heart Assn, Bronze Service Award, June 1993, Volunteer R & R Chairman, Certificate of Appreciation, June 1993; Florida Alcohol and Drug Abuse Assn, Volunteer of the Year, 1993; The City of Miami Beach, Citizen of the Day, Oct 28, 1993; The King Center, Atlanta GA, Award of Excellence, Nov 18, 1993; Advisory Committee for the Center of Community Development, Award of Appreciation, Nov 18, 1993; Volusia County Council, James E Huger Day, Dec 14, 1993; Civic League of Halifax Area, Inc, J Saxton Lloyd Distinguished Service Award, January 22, 1994; Living Legacy Certificate of Recognition, National Caucus & Center of Black Aged, 1992; Volunteer of the Year, Florida Alchol & Drub Abuse Association, 1993. **Special Achievements:** Dedicated James Ethuger Living Learning Center, Bethune-Cookman College, 1990; Dedicated James E Huger Adolesence Complex, Stewart Marchman Center, 1994. **Military Serv:** US Marine Corps sgt major 4 yrs.

HUGGINS, CLARENCE L.
Physician. **Personal:** Born Apr 25, 1926, Birmingham, AL; son of Lucille Huggins and Clarence Huggins; married Carolyn King; children: Patricia, Clarence III, Daphne. **Educ:** Morgan St Coll, BS 1950; Meharry Med Coll, MD 1958; Huron Rd Hosp Cleveland, Intrn 1959, Srgcl Res 1959-63. **Career:** Cleveland Transit Sys, med dir 1969-72; Cleveland Acad of Med, bd of dir 1974-76; Medic-Screen Hlth Ctrs, pres 1974-84; Shaker Med Ctr Hosp, chf of surgery 1982-84; Private Practice, gen srgn; Metrohealth Hospital for Women, chief of surgery, 1989-; City of East Cleveland, OH, director of health, 1990. **Orgs:** Pres med stf Forest City Hosp Cleveland 1970-73; pres bd trustees Hough-Norwood Fam Hlth Ctr 1974-78; dir First Bank Natl Assn 1974-85; mem adv bd Robert Wood Johnson Found Natl Hlth Srvcs Prgm 1977-83; dir Ohio Motorist Assn AAA 1979-85; member, Seventy Second American Assembly, Columbia University, 1986. **Honors/Awds:** Diplomate Am Bd of Surgery 1964; fellow Am Coll of Surgeons 1966; pres Cleveland Med Assn 1970-72; co-founder Buckeye Hlth Pln HMO 1974-78. **Military Serv:** AUS 1st Lt Airborne Infntry 1944-46, 1951-52. **Business Addr:** General Surgeon, Private Practice, 13944 Euclid Ave 102, Cleveland, OH 44112.

HUGGINS, DAVID W.
Company executive. **Career:** RMS Technologies Inc, CEO, currently. **Special Achievements:** Company is ranked #5 on Black Enterprise's list of Top 100 Industrial Service Companies, 1994.

HUGGINS, HAZEL RENFROE
Business executive. **Personal:** Born Jun 18, 1908, Chicago; divorced. **Educ:** Chicago Normal Coll, Tchrs Cert; Univ Chicago, PhB 1933; Sorbonne-Paris Art History 1949-50; Painting Academie Julian Paris 1950; IL Inst Tech, MS Art Educ 1956; Northwestern U, Interior Design 1959-60. **Career:** Chicago Pub Schs, art instr 1927-70; YMCA Summer Camp Felsenthal Social Center, arts & crafts instr 1946-48; Moseley Sch Socially Maladjusted, headed art dept 1956-66; Initial Phase Nat Tchr Corps Program, selected by fed govt as master tchr 1966-67; Chicago Pub Schs, appointed supr art 1967; Emerita, art consult 1970; Renfroe Research, pres. **Orgs:** Mem Art Textbook Selection Com Chicago Bd Edn; mem City Wide Com Selected to Revamp Tchr Training Program DePaul Univ 1959; demonstrator teaching techniques Lectr on African & Afro-Am Art & Discussion Panelist for Spl Educ & Correctional Programs IL Art Educ Western Arts Univ IL Natl Conf Artists; judge Model Cities Buckingham Fountain Art Competition 1974; judge Regl Div Nat Scholastic Arts Competition 1970-75; judge Intl Stock Show Art Contest 1975; mem N Central Assn 1975; founding mem S Side Comm Art Center Educ Chmn 1939; charter mem

exec bd Metro Council Nat Council Negro Women; Served 3 Terms As presLambda Chap Delta Sigma Theta Sor 1938-41; Earned Womens' Defense Corps Army Uniform by Completing 100 Hrs Vol Serv WW II; Took Spl Training & Taught Gas-Mask& Messenger Courses to Adu During WW II; Organized 250 mem Career Women for LBJ Directed Activities During 1964 Campaign; adv Com Contemporary African Art Exhibit Field Museum 1974; bd dir Creative Children's Arts Winnetka 1985; Bravo Chap Lyric Opera Guild. **Honors/Awds:** Awarded HS Certificate Art Through Competitive Examination 1958; Selected to Organize Personnel & Direct Sales of Stamps Bonds During WW II Cited by TreasuryDept for Raising Unexpectedly Huge Amount Money; Awarded Delta Sigma Theta's Nat Scholarship 1949; Appointed by Gov Shapiro to IL Commn for Observance United Nations 25th Anniversary. **Special Achievements:** Honorary Appointment Business Women to the Research Board of Advisors of American Biographical Institute.

HUGGINS, HOSIAH, JR.
Management consultant. **Personal:** Born Aug 17, 1950, Chicago, IL. **Educ:** Univ of Akron, BA 1974; Newport Univ, MPA 1988. **Career:** Amalgamated Stationers, vice pres sales 1974-80; Xerox Corp, mktg exec 1980-83; Insight & Attitudes Inc, pres. **Orgs:** Bd of dirs Urban League of Cleveland 1978-80, YMCA 1979-85; natl pres Natl Assoc of Mgmt Consultants 1985-; assoc mem Institute of Mgmt Consult 1987. **Honors/Awds:** Outstanding Scholastic Phi Beta Sigma 1974; Outstanding Young Man of Amer 1982; Man of the Year Bel-Aire Civic Club 1983; "1983 Most Interesting People" Cleveland Magazine.

HUGGINS, LINDA JOHNSON
Telecommunications company executive. **Personal:** Born Nov 15, 1950, Oklahoma City, OK; daughter of Wallace C Johnson (deceased) and Wanda Fleming Johnson; married Howard Huggins III, Jun 10, 1972; children: Andrea Yvette, Valerie Diane. **Educ:** Langston Univ, Langston, OK, BS, mathematics education, 1972; Webster Univ, St Louis, MO, MA, business administration/management, 1977. **Career:** Southwestern Bell Telephone Co, Kansas City, MO, engineer, 1972-75; Southwestern Bell Telephone Co, St Louis, MO, area manager, 1976-; Licensed Real Estate Agent, 1981-. **Orgs:** President, St Louis Chapter, 1980-, national board member, 1984-92; Langston University National Alumni Association; publicity chair, 1990-91, member, 1969-, Alpha Kappa Alpha Sorority; member, NAACP, 1988-; member, St Louis Real Estate Board, 1981-; member, Missouri Real Estate Assn, 1981-; member, YWCA, 1988-; Greater Mt Carmel Bapt Church, Inspirational Choir, St Louis, MO; St Louis Metro Community Relations Team for SWBT. **Honors/Awds:** Distinguished Alumni, National Association for Equal Opportunity, 1988. **Home Addr:** 610 Brookstone Dr, Florissant, MO 63033.

HUGGINS-WILLIAMS, NEDRA
Educator. **Educ:** Fisk Univ, graduate; Univ of Utah, doctorate. **Career:** National Defense Univ, prof, currently. **Special Achievements:** First African American faculty member of the National Defense University.

HUGHES, ALBERT
Film writer/director. **Career:** Film director, currently. **Special Achievements:** Films (co-directed with brother Allen) include: Menace II Society, Dead Presidents. **Business Phone:** (310)550-4000.

HUGHES, ALLEN
Film writer/director. **Career:** Film director, currently. **Special Achievements:** Films (co-directed with brother Albert) include: Menace II Society, Dead Presidents. **Business Addr:** Film Director, ICM, c/o Jeff Robinov, 8942 Wilshire Blvd, Beverly Hills, CA 90211, (310)550-4000.

HUGHES, BERNICE ANN
Educator. **Personal:** Born Apr 10, 1959, Medina, TN; daughter of Rena L Hughes. **Educ:** Middle Tennessee State University, BSW, 1982, MA, 1990-91. **Career:** Middle Tennessee State University, physical plant supervisor, 1982-88, housing area coordinator, 1988-92, housing associate director, personnel and devt, 1992-. **Orgs:** Alpha Kappa Alpha, member of numerous membership chairperson committees, 1992-; Tennessee Association of College and University Housing Officers, executive board, 1988-92. **Business Addr:** Associate Director, Housing for Personnel & Development, Middle Tennessee State University, Main St, Murfreesboro, TN 37132, (615)898-5119.

HUGHES, CARL D.
Clergyman, educator. **Personal:** Born in Indianapolis; married Louise. **Educ:** WV State Coll Inst, BS 1942; Wharton Sch of Finance Univ of PA, MA 1943; Christian Theol Sem, BD 1957; Christian Theol Sem, MA 1958; Centrl Bapt Theol Semin of IN, DD 1975; Christian Theol Sem, MDiv 1972; IN Univ Sch of Law Wayne State Univ & Univ of Detroit, Post Grad Studies. **Career:** Mt Zion Bapt Ch Indianapolis, ministers asst 1952; Second Bapt Ch Lafayette 1952-56; St John Missionary Bapt Ch 1956-60; Christian Educ Met Bapt ChDetroit, dir 1960-61; Bethel Bapt Ch East Detroit, pastor 1961; Hughes Enterprise Inc, vice pres treas; Detroit Christian Training Cntr, former dean; Bus Educ Detroit Pub Sch, former tchr; Ch Bldr & Bus Educ Detroit Pub Sch, dept hd; Calvary Dist Assn Detroit, former instr; Wolverine State Conv SS & BTU Cong MI, former instr; Nat Bapt SS & BTU Congress, former instr; Central Bible Sem, former instr. **Orgs:** Membership com YMCA; membership Com NAACP; former mem Grand Bd Dir Kappa Alpha Psi Nat Coll Frat; Mason; budget com Nat Negro Bus League; treas StEmma Military Acad Parent Assn of Detroit; chmn bd of trustees Todd-Phillips Children Home of the Wolverine State Missionary Bapt Conv Inc; chmn of Finance Pastors' Div of the Nat Bapt Congress of Christian Edn. **Honors/Awds:** Received First John L Webb Award Nat Bapt Conv 1948; Author "The Ch Orgnzd For A Meaning Ministry" & "Financing the Local Ch Property". **Business Addr:** Bethel Baptist Church East, 5715-33 Holcomb, Detroit, MI 48213.

HUGHES, CATHERINE LIGGINS
Radio broadcasting company executive. **Personal:** Born Apr 22, 1947, Omaha, NE; daughter of Helen E Jones-Woods and William A Woods; children: Alfred Charles Liggins, III. **Educ:** Creighton Univ, Omaha, NE, 1966-69; Univ of NE, Omaha, NE, 1969-71; Harvard Univ, Cambridge, MA, 1975. **Career:** Harvard Univ, Washington, DC, lecturer, 1971-73; WHUR-FM, Washington, DC, sales mgr, 1973-75, gen mgr, 1975-78; WYCB-AM, Washington, DC, gen mgr, 1978; WOL-AM, Washington, DC, gen mgr, 1980-89; WMMJ-FM, Washington, DC, gen mgr, 1986-89; Radio one, chair, currently. **Orgs:** Bd mem, United Black Fund, 1978-88; bd mem, DC Boys/Girls Club, 1983-86; chmn, Community Comm Corp, 1985-87; Washington Post Recall Comm, 1987. **Honors/Awds:** Woman of the Year, Washington Woman, 1987; 1988 People's Champion Award, Natl Black Media Coalition, 1988; 1988 Kool Achiever, Communications, 1988; Woman of the Year, Women at Work of the Natl Capital Area, 1989; The Cathy Hughes TV Show, 1989. **Business Addr:** Chair, Radio One, 6437 14th St, Washington, DC 20012.

HUGHES, DANIEL WEBSTER. See Obituaries section.

HUGHES, DONNA LUNDIN
Public relations executive. **Personal:** Born Nov 25, 1949, Chicago, IL; daughter of Estella Walker Lundin Madden and Donald Lundin; married Michael Dean Hughes, Sep 3, 1972; children: Lyn, Natalie, Melissa. **Educ:** Iowa Wesleyan College, BA, 1971. **Career:** South Cook County Girl Scout Council, field executive, 1971-72; Seal of Ohio Girl Scout Council, field executive, 1972-76, director of communications, 1976-84, field supervisor, 1984-86, public relations director, 1986-90, assistant director, resource development & services, public relations director, currently. **Orgs:** Alpha Kappa Alpha, various positions, 1969-83; Public Relations Society of America, 1990-; Jack and Jill of America, children's activity coordinator, vice pres, 1989-; National Coalition of 100 Black Women, 1991-92. **Home Addr:** 5649 Dorsey Dr, Columbus, OH 43235, (614)459-0333.

HUGHES, ESSIE MEADE
Educator (retired). **Personal:** Born Dec 28, 1908, Baltimore, MD; daughter of Mary Anderson Hughes and Marshall Hughes. **Educ:** Morgan State Univ, AB 1929; Univ of PA, MS 1942; NY Univ, Doctoral 1956-61; VA Seminary & Coll, Doctor of Humane Letters 1987. **Career:** Baltimore School System, teacher of Latin 1929-34, sr high school latin teacher 1934-52, French teacher, 1935-41, Spanish teacher, 1942-52, coord & supervisor 1952-59, special asst 1959-61, Douglass High School, assistant principal, 1961-64, Western HS Baltimore MD, asst principal, 1964-71; 1st appointed black admin; Baltimore MD Educ Syst, retired school admin. **Orgs:** World traveler Canada, Africa, Europe, Middle East, Far East, South Amer, West Indies 1940-; adult educ teacher Baltimore School System 1945-52; mem NEA 1950-, Phi Delta Kappa Theta Lambda Pi 1960-; bd mem Baltimore Regional Red Cross 1969-79; mem MD Retired Teachers Assoc 1971-, AARP 1972-; educ consultant, Consumer Product Safety Commission 1973-78. **Honors/Awds:** Planning & Executing City-Wide Educ Expo 1970; Awarded the Fannie Randall Humanitarian Honor 1973; Public Spirit Awd Heritage Church 1979; Outstanding Teacher Frederick Douglass High School 1981; Disting Awd Natl Assoc for Equal Oppor 1984; Educational Excellence Fund for Educ Excellence 1986; received Doctor of Humane Letters degree VA Sem & Coll 1987; selected as Maker of Negro History by the Iota Phi Lambda Sor; Presidential Citation, National Assn for Equal Opportunity in Higher Education, 1984; Distinguished Alumna Award, Fund for Educational Excellence, 1986; Distinguished Mother Surrogate Award, Sharon Baptist Church of Baltimore, 1990. **Home Addr:** 1108 Harlem Ave, Baltimore, MD 21217-2430.

HUGHES, GEORGE MELVIN
Educator. **Personal:** Born Aug 26, 1938, Charlotte, TN; married Evelyn Benson; children: Vickie L, George M Jr. **Educ:** TN State Univ, BS 1961, MEd 1963; Univ of WI-Milwaukee, Post Grad studies 1967-68; Cardinal Stritch Coll, Post Grad studies 1983; Indiana Univ, Post Grad studies 1986. **Career:** Lafollette Elem School, teacher 1963-68; Parkman Middle School, asst principal 1968-71; Garfield Elem School, asst principal 1971-74; Lee Elem School, principal 1974-. **Orgs:** Bd dir Carter Child Develop Ctr 1981, Girl Scouts of Amer 1987, Phi Delta Kappa Milwaukee Chap 1987; panelist US Dept of Educ Ctr for Systems & Prog Develop Inc 1987; consultant Indianapolis Sch System 1987, Muscogee County Sch Dist Columbus GA 1987; life mem NAACP; consult Southwest Educ Devel Lab TX. **Honors/Awds:** Special Recognition Lee School Parent-Teacher Org 1983; Special Visit US Educ Sec William J Bennett 1986; apptd to Property Tax Review Bd in Mequon 1986-; invited to the White House Rose Garden by the President to a reception for the release of a book entitled "What Works, Educating Disadvantaged Children"; received a Natl Recognition by the US Dept of Education as part of the RISE (Rising to Individual Scholastic Excellence) effective school prog in Milwaukee Public Schools. **Military Serv:** Air Force ROTC 2 yrs TN State Univ.

HUGHES, GEORGE VINCENT
Automobile dealer. **Personal:** Born Apr 8, 1930, New York, NY; son of Marion Hughes and Lewis Hughes; children: Deirdre, Vincent. **Educ:** College of City of New York, MBA, 1954. **Career:** George Hughes Chevrolet, president, currently. **Honors/Awds:** Alpha Phi Alpha, 1950-. **Military Serv:** US Army, 82nd Airborne Infantry, captain, 3 yrs. **Business Addr:** President, George Hughes Chevrolet, US Route 9, Freehold, NJ 07728.

HUGHES, HARVEY L.
Attorney. **Personal:** Born May 7, 1909, Port DePosit, MD; married Ethel C. **Educ:** Univ of Pittsburgh Terrell Law Sch, LLB 1944. **Career:** Harris & Hughes Law Firm, partner; N Capitol Corp, gen counsel; Accredited to Present Claims in Ofc of VA 1955. **Orgs:** Mem Wash Bar Assn 1946; DC Bar 1972; Nat Bar Assn 1954; mem Legal Frat Sigm Delta Tau 1946; mem Alpha Phi Alpha Frat Fairmount Heights Civic Club; counselor St Martin's Boys Club 1972. **Business Addr:** 1840 North Capitol St, Washington, DC 20002.

HUGHES, HOLLIS EUGENE, JR.
Business executive. **Personal:** Born Mar 14, 1943, Tulsa, OK; son of Suzan Marie Brummell Hughes and Hollis Eugene Hughes Sr; married Lavera Ruth Knight, Aug 26. **Educ:** Ball State Univ, BS Soc Sci 1965, MA Sociology 1968. **Career:** S Bend Comm Sch Corp, tchr & coach 1965-69; Model Cities Prog/City of S Bend, exec dir 1969-74; Housing Assistance Office Inc, pres/dir 1974-. **Orgs:** Mem Amer Planning Assn 1975; mem, Natl Assn of Housing & Redevelopment Officials, 1978-; mem Amer Mgmt Assn 1979-89; mem Alpha Phi Alpha Frat Inc 1966-; mem Alpha Phi Omega Serv Frat 1967-; mem pres elect Ball State Univ Alumni Council 1974-; former pres/bd mem Family & Children Ctr 1978-79; former trustee S Bend Comm Sch Corp/Pub Library; vice pres S Bend Com Sch Corp/Pub Library 1978-; vice pres S Bend Com Sch Corp 1980-81; life mem NAACP; pres S Bend Comm Sch Corp 1981-82; pres South Bend Public Library Bd of Trustees 1984-85; mem IN Adv Comm to the US Commn on Civil Rights; former mem bd trustees Art Ctr Inc S Bend; trustee for Memorial Hospital; bd of trustees for Memorial Hospital Found, 1987-90; bd mem Youth Services Bureau; bd mem Community Education Round Tabledir, S Bend-Mishka Chamber of Commerce, 1987-; dir, Project Future of St Joseph County, 1987-; trustee, Ball State Univ, 1989-; member, Ball State Univ Black Alumni Assn, 1989-; vice president, Visions in Progress, 1986-; board of directors, St Joseph County Minority Business Development Council, 1991. **Honors/Awds:** Outstanding Citizen of IN Awd IN Civil Rights Commn 1976; George Awd for Outstanding Comm Serv Mishawaka Enterprise Record 1977; Distinguished Black Alumni, Ball State University Alumni Association, 1989; Benny Award, Ball State University Alumni Association, 1988. **Business Addr:** President, Housing Assistance Office Inc, 1047 Lincoln Way W, PO Box 1558, South Bend, IN 46634.

HUGHES, ISAAC SUNNY
Mathematician. **Personal:** Born Jun 29, 1944, Zachary, LA; married Anna Ceaser; children: Timothy, Troy, Jessica. **Educ:** Grambling Univ, BA 1962-66; Univ of North Carolina, Public Admin 1971-74. **Career:** King George VA, co super 1984-87; Naval Surface Weapons Ctr, mathematician 1967-; Co School Board 1989-90, 1993-95. **Orgs:** Worshipful Master KG Masonic Lodge #314 1978; cub master Boy Scouts of Amer 1978-81; mem Bd of Zoning Appeals KG 1981; mem Wetland Bd KG 1982; tie breaker Bd of Supervisors KG 1983; bd of trustee-chair Antioch Baptist Church KG; Worthy Patron Guiding Star Chapter #216; Fredericksburg Consistory #346; Magnus Temple #3; United Supreme Council, 33rd Degree Masons, Asst District Deputy Grand Master. **Honors/Awds:** Dept of Navy, Outstanding Performance 1974, High Quality Performance 1978, Special Achievement 1983, Superior Performance 1984; Sec of the Yr Prince Hall Masons of VA 1984; Distinguished Community Service, 1989; Superior Performance, 1990; Superior Performance, 1991; Superior Performance 1992; Superior Performance, 1993; Superior Performance, 1994. **Home Addr:** 10325 Oak Tree Drive, King George, VA 22485. **Business Addr:** Supervisor Mathematician, Naval Surface Weapons Center, PO Box 666, Dahlgren, VA 22448.

HUGHES, JIMMY FRANKLIN, SR.
Law enforcement official. **Personal:** Born Apr 10, 1952, Tuscaloosa, AL; son of Maryann Stanley Hughes and Lee Marvin Hughes; married Juanita Price, May 29; children: Trina Woodberry, Jimmy Jr, Jared. **Educ:** Youngstown State Univ, AS, 1989, BS, 1992, MPA, 1997; Northwestern Univ, Academy for Police Staff and Commander SPSC-22, 1986; Ohio Peace Officers Training Academy, police instructors certification, 1985; additional education/training in law enforcement. **Career:** Youngstown Police Dept, patrol officer, 1977-81, detective/sgt, 1981-87, lt, 1987-95, captain, 1995-. **Orgs:** Mid-American Teakwon Do Association; Natl Black Police Assn; past pres, Black Knights Police Assn; Mahoning County Drug and Alcohol Addiction Board; Mahoning County United Way Distribution Committee; Youngstown Urban League; Youngstown NAACP; assoc mem, Buckeye Elks Lodge #73 IBPOE. **Honors/Awds:** Gold Medals, Ohio Police Olympics; Meritorious Service Award, Youngstown Police Dept; Buckeye Elk Youth Athletic Awards; Community Service Award, Black Knights Police Assn; Commendation of Professionalism, Youngstown Police Dept; numerous Departmental Commendations and Community Recognition Awards. **Special Achievements:** First African-American condidate in the city's history for the rank of Captain, the Police Departments' highest rank. **Home Addr:** 3239 Oak St, Youngstown, OH 44505. **Business Phone:** (330)742-8900.

HUGHES, JOHNNIE LEE
Miner (retired). **Personal:** Born Nov 18, 1924, Coalwood, WV; son of Florine Westbrooke and George Hughes; married Sarah Etta Gibson; children: Leonard C Jones, Jacqueline Lee Jones, Moseley. **Career:** Osage West Virginia, mayor 1959-61, 1968-70; Ofc of Amer Asian Free Labor Inst Washington DC to Turkey, instr of mine safety 1979; Consolidated Coal Co, mine worker, until 1995. **Orgs:** Pres UMWA 2122 1978-80; mem Mine Com/Safety Com 15 yrs; mem Coal Miners Political Action Comm 4 yrs. **Honors/Awds:** 1st Black chief of police Monongalia Co WV; 1st Black mayor State of WV; Miner to Mayor publ Ebony Edition 1972; consult to Turkey Publ Miner's Jour 1980. **Military Serv:** USMC, Cpl, 1942-46. **Business Addr:** Consolidated Coal Co, Morgantown, WV 26505.

HUGHES, JOYCE A.
Educator, attorney. **Personal:** Born Feb 7, 1940, Gadsden, AL; daughter of Bessie Cunningham Hughes and Solomon Hughes Sr. **Educ:** Carleton Coll Northfield MN (magna cum laude), BA 1961; Univ Madrid Spain 1961-62; Univ MN Law Sch (cum laude), JD 1965. **Career:** Northwestern Univ School of Law, prof, 1979-, assoc prof, 1975-79; Chicago Transit Authority, general counsel, 1984-88; Continental Illinois Bank, attorney, 1982-84; Univ MN Law Sch, assoc prof 1971-75; Peterson & Holtze Minneapolis, consult 1971-74; Auerbach Corp Philadelphia, consult 1970-71; LeFevere Lefler Hamilton & Peterson Minneapolis, atty 1967-71; Judge Earl R Larson Minneapolis, law clk 1965-67. **Orgs:** Mem, Amer Bar Assn, Natl Bar Assn, Illinois Bar Assn, Cook County Bar Assn; dir, Chicago Bd of Educ, 1980-82; dir, Federal Home Loan Bank of Chicago, 1980-84; dir, First Plymouth Bank, 1971-82; trustee, Natl Urban League, 1972-78; trustee, Carleton Coll, 1969-94. **Honors/Awds:** Phi Beta Kappa, 1961; Fulbright Scholarship 1961-62; John Hay Whitney Fellowship 1962-63; Achievement Award Carleton College Alumni 1969; 100 Top Business & Professional Women, Dollars & Sense Magazine, 1986; Superior Public Service Award, Cook County Bar Assn, 1987. **Business Addr:** Prof, Northwestern Univ School of Law, 357 E Chicago Ave, Chicago, IL 60611.

HUGHES, LEONARD S., JR.
Judge. **Personal:** Born Jul 3, 1926, Kansas City, MO; married Mamie F Currie; children: Leonard, III, Kevin, Stefan, Shawn, Amy. **Educ:** AB LLB 1952; Washburn U, MJ 1952. **Career:** State MO, magistrate judge. **Military Serv:** USN WW II. **Business Addr:** Municipal Court, 2519 Tracy St, Kansas City, MO 64108.

HUGHES, MAMIE F.
City official. **Personal:** Born May 3, 1929, Jacksonville, FL; married Judge Leonard; children: Leonard, III, Kevin, Stefan, Patrick, Amy. **Educ:** Fisk U, BA; Univ MO 1950-51. **Career:** Kansas City, tchr 1951-52, 1957-62; Greenville, tchr 1954-56; Fed Agency Reg Dir for Action 1985; Head Start, vol 1968-69; St Joseph Cath Sch, vol tchr 1962-63; Carver Neighborhood Center, mem adv commn 1985. **Orgs:** Cath Interracial Council 1959-63; former bd mem, HPEED 1965-66; foundling com Vol Serv Bur; bd mem United Campaign Vol 1964-68; vol Martin Luther King Jr HS; Greater KS Coordinating Com Intl Women's Yr; Jackson Co Child Welfare Adv Com; Panel Am Women; 1st v chmn Mid-Am Regional Council BdGovs; chmn Commn Aging; chairperson Fed Exec Bd; past chmn Health & Welfare Com; mem KC MO Fair Housing Commn; vol parent 1965-66; foster Parent 1966-67; St Joseph Sch PTA; pres Greater KC Minority Women's Coalition Human Rights; recording sec Greater KC Hearing & Speech Center; bd mem Truman MedCenter; Parker Sq Housing Corp; Lincoln Black Archives; KC Crime Commn; YMCA Urban Svcs; Manpower Adv Mem Nat Council Negro Women; NAACP; Jack & Jill Am Inc; Greater KC Links Inc Serv UrbanYouth De LaSalle Eduenter; Beautiful Activists Vol Serv Woolf Bros & Germaine Monteil. **Honors/Awds:** Comm Serv Award; Serv Award NAACP Freedom Fund Dinner Com. **Business Addr:** Jackson Co Courthouse, 415 E 12 St, Kansas City, MO 64106.

HUGHES, MARK
Professional basketball player. **Personal:** Born Oct 5, 1966. **Educ:** Michigan State. **Career:** Toronto Raptors, 1996-. **Business Addr:** Professional Basketball Player, Toronto Raptors, 150 York St, Ste 110, Toronto, ON, Canada M5H 3S5, (416)214-2255.

HUGHES, ROBERT DANAN
Professional football player. **Personal:** Born Dec 11, 1970, Bayonne, NJ; married Tifanni; children: Jessica, Taurin Isaiah. **Educ:** Univ of Iowa, degree in communications. **Career:** Kansas City Chiefs, wide receiver, 1993-. **Business Addr:** Professional Football Player, Kansas City Chiefs, One Arrowhead Dr, Kansas City, MO 64129, (816)924-9300.

HUGHES, TYRONE CHRISTOPHER
Professional football player. **Personal:** Born Jan 14, 1970, New Orleans, LA. **Educ:** Univ of Nebraska, bachelor's degree in consumer science. **Career:** New Orleans Saints, running back, 1993-96; Chicago Bears, 1997-. **Honors/Awds:** Pro Bowl, 1993. **Business Addr:** Professional Football Player, Chicago Bears, 1000 Football Dr, Halas Hall at Conway Park, Lake Forest, IL 60045-4829, (847)295-6600.

HUGHES, VINCENT
State representative. **Personal:** Born Oct 26, 1956, Philadelphia, PA. **Career:** State of Pennsylvania, state representative, currently. **Orgs:** PA Legislative Black Caucus, chairman; Subcommitte on Health of the Health & Welfare Committee, chairman; State Government and Labor Relations Committees; PA Higher Education Assistance Agency, board of directors; State Government's Eastern Regional Conference Committee on Health & Human Services, council; Democratic Study Group, founding member; Philadelphia Commercial Development Corp., board member; Philadelphia Welfare Pride & Blacks Educating Blacks About Sexual Health Issues; Children First, cofounder. **Business Addr:** State Representative, South Office Bldg, Room 308, Harrisburg, PA 17120.

HULETT, ROSEMARY D.
Educational administrator. **Personal:** Born Sep 17, 1954, Chicago, IL; married Melvin D Hulett. **Educ:** Chicago State Univ, BSEd 1975; MSEd 1980. **Career:** Archdiocese of Chicago Cath Sch Bd, head teacher 1975-77, headstart dir 1977-78; Chicago Bd of Educ, Special Educ teacher 1978-80; Chicago State Univ, dir of alumni affairs 1980-. **Orgs:** Mem River Oaks Coop Towne House Mem Comm; mem River Oaks Coop Towne House Finance Comm; mem Natl Assoc for the Educ of Young Children 1975-77; mem Council for Exceptional Educ 1978-79; exec secty/treas Chicago State Univ Alumni Assn 1980-; chmn CASE V Career Advancement for Women and Minorities Comm 1985-88; bd mem Case V Bd of Dir 1987-89. **Honors/Awds:** Teacher of the Year Award Natl Assoc for the Educ of Young Children 1976; Special Educ Teaching Certificate Chicago Bd of Educ 1979; Certificate of Recognition for Alumni Admin Council for the Advancement of Secondary Educ 1980; Outstanding Young Professional Award Chicago Coalition of Urban Professional 1986. **Business Addr:** Dir of Alumni Affairs, Chicago State University, 95th St at King Dr, Chicago, IL 60628.

HULL, AKASHA (GLORIA T)
Educator, writer. **Personal:** Born in Shreveport, LA; daughter of Mrs Jimmie Thompson; children: Adrian L Prentice. **Educ:** Southern University, BA (summa cum laude), 1966; Purdue University, MA, 1968, PhD, 1972. **Career:** Univ of Delaware, prof of English 1972-88; University of California, Santa Cruz, professor, women studies 1988-. **Orgs:** Co-project dir, Black Women's Studies project 1982-84; Mellon Scholar, Wellesley Ctr for Rsch on Women 1983; Fulbright Senior Lectureship, Univ of the West Indies-Jamaica 1984-86; commission co-chair, Modern Language Assn; Natl Women's Studies Assn; advisor/consultant, Black American Literature Forum, Feminist Studies. **Honors/Awds:** Fellowship, Rockefeller Foundation 1979-80; Outstanding Woman of Color, Natl Institute of Women of Color 1982; Ford Foundation, Postdoctoral Fellowship 1987-88; AAUW Fellowship 1990; Books: All the Women are White, All the Blacks are Men, but Some of Us are Brave, Black Women's Studies 1982; Give Us Each Day, the Diary of Alice Dunbar-Nelson 1984; Color, Sex, and Poetry: Three Women Writers of the Harlem Renaissance 1987; Healing Heart: Poems 1973-1988, 1989; Works of Alice Dunbar-Nelson, 3 vols, 1988. **Business Addr:** Professor, University of California, Kresge College, Santa Cruz, CA 95064.

HULL, BERNARD S.
Research mechanical engineer (retired). **Personal:** Born Aug 1, 1929, Wetipquin, MD; married Marion Hayes; children: Karla L, Bernard S II. **Educ:** Howard U, BS 1951; Univ MD, grad credits mech engr. **Career:** Tamarach Triangle Civic Assoc, exec bd; White Oak Fed Credit Union, vice pres 1972-77; Naval Mat Command, Wash DC, corp planning div hdqrs 1985; Naval Surf Weapons Ctr, White Oaks MD, coll rela rep; Naval Surf Weapons Ctr, Silver Spring MD, research mech engr adv planning staff, until 1987. **Orgs:** Life mem NAACP. **Honors/Awds:** Distinguished Able Toastmaster Award 1974. **Military Serv:** AUS e-5. **Business Addr:** Research Engineer, Naval Surface Weapon Center, White Oak, Silver Spring, MD 20904.

HULL, ELLIS L., SR.
Contractor, (retired) cleric. **Personal:** Born Jun 4, 1928, Steele, MO; married Ollie Mae Hull (died 1992); children: Ellis, Jr, Leroy, Carmella, Juan, Shango, Veta Lacey; married Pamela J Hull. **Educ:** Andrews Univ Theology. **Career:** Anning & Johnson, 1952-64; H & H Constrn, 1964-; The Shoe Hull, owner; Williams & Hull Bonding Co, owner; Liberty Theatre, owner; Shango's Galley, owner; Pilgrim Rest Baptist Church, associate minister; Mt Zion Baptist Church, pastor, 1984-. **Orgs:** Pres Benton Harbor-Benton Township Minority Contractors Assn; Urban Renewal Bd; Benton Harbor Schs Adv Bd; Deferred Prosecution Adv Bd; Berrien Co Rept Party Exec Bd; Bd to reelect Gov Milliken; NAACP; co-chmn Benton Harbor-Benton Township Adv Bd. **Honors/Awds:** Contractor of Yr 1973. **Military Serv:** USN stm.

HULL, EVERSON WARREN
Government official. **Personal:** Born Oct 14, 1943, Nevis; married Melverlynn Surilina Spears; children: Randolph E, Cecilia A. **Educ:** Howard Univ, BA 1970, PhD 1977; Univ of MD, MA 1974. **Career:** Federal Natl Mort Assoc, economist 1973-76; The Amer Petroleum Inst, sr economist 1976-78; TRW Inc, sr economist 1978-79; Congressional Rsch Svcs, head money/banking quantitative economics 1979-83; US Dept of Labor, deputy asst sec for policy 1983-. **Business Addr:** Deputy Asst Sec for Policy, US Dept of Labor, 200 Constitution Ave NW, Washington, DC 20210.

HULL, GEORGE, JR.
Educator. **Personal:** Born Sep 30, 1922, Indianola, MS; married Jewell; children: George Ronald, Sharon Elaine. **Educ:** Alcorn A&M Coll, BS 1945; TN State Univ, MS 1949; OH State Univ, PhD 1957. **Career:** TN State Univ, chmn lower div of biology, coordinator grad studies research, natural science 1949-64; Grambling College, prof & head of dept of biological science 1964-66; Fisk Univ, prof & chmn dept of biology/dir div natural science & math 1966-. **Orgs:** Regional dir Natl Inst of Sci 1973-74; regional vice pres Beta Kappa Chi 1975; pres Fisk-Meharry-TN State Sigma Xi Club 1960-61; Sigma Xi; Frontiers Intl; Nashville Club pres 1973-75. **Military Serv:** USN 1944-46. **Business Addr:** Chairman, Dept of Biology, Fisk University, Dept of Biology, Nashville, TN 37203.

HUMES, EMANUEL I., SR.
Business executive. **Personal:** Born Jan 12, 1928, Miami; married Lillie. **Career:** Menelek Construction Co Inc, chmn bd dir; Bethlehem Steel Corp, sub-foreman 1950-70; Niagra Frontier Housing Development, field supt; BAW Construction Co; supt & coordntr; Urban Systems Housing Co, mgr; Church of God of Prophecy, minister 1950-70; E I Humes Cleaning & Janitorial Serv 1971-; Manlil Mgmt Corp 1973-; Humall Enterprises; E I Humes Construction 1971-; Ch of God of Prophecy, SS sput 1974. **Orgs:** Mem Greater Jefferson Businessmen's Assn; life mem NAACP. **Honors/Awds:** Recipient achievement award Black Enterprise Mag; Top 100 1974; Natl Defense Service Medal. **Military Serv:** AUS medical corp corpl 1953-55. **Business Addr:** 302 Kensington Ave, Buffalo, NY.

HUMPHREY, BOBBY
Professional football player. **Personal:** Born Oct 11, 1966, Birmingham, AL. **Educ:** Univ of Alabama, attended. **Career:** Running back: Denver Broncos, 1989-92, Miami Dolphins, 1992-. **Honors/Awds:** Running back, Sporting News College All-America Team, 1987; post-season play: AFC Championship Game, NFL Championship Game, 1989, Pro Bowl, 1990. **Business Addr:** Professional Football Player, Miami Dolphins, 2269 NW 199th St, Miami, FL 33056.

HUMPHREY, HOWARD JOHN
Engineer. **Personal:** Born Nov 5, 1940; son of Easton Humphrey; married Bernadette Barker; children: Hayden, Lynette. **Educ:** NYU, BE 1969; Univ of MI, Am Elec Pwr Spons Mgmt Training Prgm 1976. **Career:** Am Elec Pwr Serv Corp, group mgr civil engineering div 1988-, mgr materials handling div 1983-88, section head in materials handling div, asst section head, sr engr, engr, assoc engr, engr tech 1967-; Cl Frd Power Plant Solid Waste Disposal, specialist. **Orgs:** Reg Professional Engr NJ, OH & WV; Am Soc of Civ Engr. **Honors/Awds:** 1st Black Dept Head Amer Elec Power Serv Corp. **Business Addr:** Group Mgr, Civil Engineering Div, American Electric Power Serv, One Riverside Plaza, Columbus, OH 43216.

HUMPHREY, JAMES PHILIP
Elected official, public relations manager (retired). **Personal:** Born Jun 1, 1921, Sidney, OH; married Louise Strickland Lloyd; children: Rebecca Breaston, Patricia Sheffield, Mary

Weston, Janice Gaudy, James L, Helen Richard, James (deceased), Robert, Curtis, Debra Lloyd, Sheila, Cynthi. **Educ:** Morris Brown Coll, 1939-42; Cental States Coll of Physiatrics, DM. **Career:** Sidney Machine Tool Co, blueprint-dark room tech 1950-57, matl control mgr 1958-78, purchasing mgr 1979-84; Amos Press Inc, community relations dir 1984-. **Orgs:** Mayor-councilman City of Sidney 1975-; pres emeritus, Lima Dist Church School & BTU Inst; adv bd Upper Valley Joint Vocational School of Practical Nursing; mem Sidney-Shelby Cty Chamber of Commerce, Kiwanis Club; chmn NAACP; mem Natl Conf of Black Mayors, Kappa Alpha Psi; mayor-councilman City of Signey 1975; deacon Mt Vernon Baptist Church; vp, Ohio Tri-County NAACP; past recording secretary, Western Union District Baptist Assn, chair, Scholarhip Committee; past treasurer, Mechanicsburg District Missionary Inst; past chair, Salvation Army Advisory Bd; life mem, NAACP; Ohio State NAACP, chair for Afro American History; past pres, Sunset Kiwanis Club; Shelby County Corrections Planning Bd, Shelby County JTPA; Sidney Habitat for Humanity; Sidney Civil Service & Compensation Comm; Kappa Alpha Psi Fraternity; appointed by Governor Celeste, Trustee Bd of Ohio Veterans' Home in Sandusky; mem, Governor's Bd for Socially Disadvantaged Black Males. **Honors/Awds:** Outstanding Serv NAACP OH Conf of Branches 1982; Cert of Apprec Southern Christian Leadership Conf 1984, Spec Olympics Prog 1984; Soft Cover for Booklet Martin Luther King Gallery Exhibits; Establishment of 6 Annual James P Humphrey Scholarships for Black Achievers; Black Mayor of the Year Award for Ohio, 1984; Sidney's Black Achiever of the Year Award, 1987; Certificate of Appreciation, City Council & Staff of Sidney, 1991. **Military Serv:** AUS Med Corps sgt tech 3 1/2 yrs; Philippine Liberation Ribbon w/1 Bronze Star, Asiatic Pacific Theater Ribbon w/2 Bronze Serv Stars, Meritor Unit Awd. **Home Addr:** 1806 Cheryl Pl, Sidney, OH 45365.

HUMPHREY, KATHRYN BRITT
Educator (retired). **Personal:** Born Jan 24, 1923, Champaign, IL; widowed. **Educ:** Parkland Jr College, social studies; University of Illinois at Urbana, social and medical studies. **Career:** Champaign Park District, Physical Education in Public Schools at Recess, youth director, 1941-44; domestic service worker, 1941-53; University of Illinois, College of Veterinary Medicine, natural science lab asst, Microscopic Anatomy, histological technician, 1955-87. **Orgs:** Gamma Upsilon Psi, Scholarship Promotion, co-founder, 1973-; University of Illinois, YWCA; Natl Council of Negro Women; Carver Park Improvement Assn; University of Illinois Employee Credit Union, vice chairman, 1976-; Champaign-Urbana Mass Transit Board, 1990-; City of Champaign Township Board, 1986-90; Champaign Community Schools, District 4, board member, 1970-76; Black Caucus of School Board Members, central region, 1970-76; Urban League or Champaign County; Occupational Industrialization Council; Veterinary Medicine College, University of Illinois, affirmative action committee; Mt Olive Baptist Church, Missionary Dept, president, Board of Christian Education, Baptist General State Convention, Women's Auxiliary, past vice pres, Central District Assn of Illinois, past president. **Honors/Awds:** Recip Srv Award, Urban Leag, 5 Yr Pin; Srv Award, Young People's Dept of Cntrl Dist Assn; Srv Award, Bapt Gen St Conv of IL Young People's Dept 25 Yrs.

HUMPHREY, MARGO
Educator, artist, author. **Personal:** Born 1942, Oakland, CA; daughter of Dorothy Reed Humphrey and James Dudley Humphrey; married Thais Valentine Nysus (divorced). **Educ:** Merritt City College, 1960-63; California State-Hayward, Hayward, CA, 1963-68; California College of Arts and Crafts, 1973; Stanford Univ, Palo Alto, CA, 1974; University of California-Santa Cruz, attended. **Career:** Golden State Mutual Life Insurance Co, purchase 1968; Stanford Univ, teaching asst, 1972-74; Univ of California at Santa Cruz, asst prof of art, 1985; Univ of Texas at San Antonio, visiting associate, 1987; Margaret Trowell School of Fine Art, Kampala, Uganda, 1987; Univ of Benin, Benin, Nigeria, artistic specialist, 1987; Yaba Tec Institute, Nigeria, artistic specialist; Art Institute of Chicago, visiting associate, 1988-89; Univ of Maryland, asst prof, currently. **Orgs:** Member, NAACP; member, United Negro College Fund, 1990-91. **Honors/Awds:** "Eight" The Institute of Contemporary Art of the Virginia Museum Richmond 1980; The 1970's prints & drawings of Afro-Americans, Mus of the Center of Afro-Am Artists Inc, Boston 1980; Post Doctoral Fellowship, Ford Foundation, 1980-81; Tiffany Fellowship, 1988; first American to open the American Section, National Gallery of Art, Lagos, Nigeria; State Honor Proclamation, Mayor Henry Cisneros; Marcus Foster Award for Teaching Excellence, 1986; Commission, Oakland Ballet Co, design costume and stage sets, 1990; numerous others. **Business Addr:** Assistant Professor of Printmaking, Art Dept, University of Maryland, 1M324 Art/Sociology Bldg, College Park, MD 20742-1311.

HUMPHREY, MARIAN J.
Bank executive. **Career:** Medical Center State Bank, Oklahoma City, OK, chief exec. **Business Addr:** Chief Executive, Medical Center State Bank, 1300 North Lottie, Oklahoma City, OK 73117.

HUMPHREY, MARION ANDREW
Judge, clergyman. **Personal:** Born Nov 2, 1949, Pine Bluff, AR; son of Doris L Pendleton; married Vernita Gloria Thomas, Dec 27, 1986; children: Marion Andrew Jr. **Educ:** Princeton University, BA, 1972; Harvard Divinity School, MDiv, 1978; University of Arkansas Law School, JD, 1979. **Career:** State of Arkansas, assistant attorney general, 1981, circuit court judge, 1993-; self-employed, law practice, 1982-86, 1987-89; Allison Memorial Presbyterian Church, pastor, 1984-; City of Little Rock, assistant city attorney, 1986, municipal judge, 1989-92. **Orgs:** Arkansas Children's Hospital, board, 1992-; Lyon College, board; Little Rock Rotary Club, 1991-; NAACP, life time; Natl Bar Assn, judicial council, 1989-; Princeton Alumni Association of Arkansas. **Business Addr:** Judge, Circuit Court, Sixth Judicial District, Pulaski County Courthouse, Rm 420, 401 W Markham, Little Rock, AR 72201, (501)340-8590.

HUMPHREY, ROBERT CHARLES
Professional football player. **Personal:** Born Aug 23, 1961, Lubbock, TX. **Educ:** New Mexico State Univ, received degree in social work. **Career:** New York Jets, 1984-90; Los Angeles Rams, cornerback, kick returner, 1990-91; San Diego Chargers, defensive back, 1991. **Honors/Awds:** Kick returner, Sporting News NFL All-Star Team, 1984. **Business Addr:** Professional Football Player, San Diego Chargers, Jack Murphy Stadium, 9449 Friars Rd, San Diego, CA 92108.

HUMPHREY, SONNIE
Events coordinator. **Educ:** Hunter Coll, New York NY, BA, 1976. **Career:** Jackie Robinson Foundation, 1991-96. **Orgs:** Bd mem, YGB Leadership Training, 1971-; reporter, Hunter Coll News, 1974-76; coord, Luncheon/Fashion Event, 1980-89; award coord, Natl Coalition of 100 Black Women Candace Awards, 1982-89; talent coord, Motown Returns to Apollo; mem, UNCF Auxiliary Comm, 1984-; vice pres, New York Coalition of 100 Black Women, 1986-; pres, Zeta Delta Phi Sorority, 1987-; special events coord, UNCF Michael Jackson Benefit, 1988; volunteer, New York Host Committee of Grammys, 1991; presenter, Black History Makers Award, 1991; New York Women's Agenda, 1993-. **Honors/Awds:** Outstanding Service, Zeta Delta Phi Sorority, 1974, 1977 1986; Service To Youth Award, Kennedy Community Center, 1975, 1978; poems, "Black Women," 1977, "Young, Gifted and Black," 1980; Arts Bulletin Editor, 1981; Outstanding Young Women, 1982; Achievement Award, New York Coalition of 100 Black Women, 1984; Community Service, Joseph P Kennedy Community Center, 1985; Souvenir Journal Editor, 1985-88; Sorority Manual, 1988; Editor-Newsletter, Zeta Delta Phi Sorority, current; CBS-TV Advisory Committee For Black History Month Moments, 1995-. **Home Addr:** 3531 Bronxwood Ave, Bronx, NY 10469.

HUMPHRIES, CHARLES, JR.
Obstetrics/gynecology. **Personal:** Born Apr 14, 1943, Dawson, GA; married Monica Tulio; children: Charlie Christopher. **Educ:** Fisk Univ, BA 1966; Meharry Medical Coll, MD 1972. **Career:** Charlie Humphries Jr MD PC, president. **Orgs:** Mem Omega Psi Phi Frat, Dougherty Co Medical Soc, GA State Medical Assoc, Medical Assoc of GA; asst treas GA State Affiliate of Univ of IL 1972-73; alternate delegate to MAG Legislation Seesion; mem Southwest GA Black Hlth Care Providers. **Military Serv:** USN lcdr 1976-78. **Business Addr:** President, Charlie Humphries Jr MD PC, 802 N Jefferson St, Albany, GA 31701.

HUMPHRIES, FREDERICK S.
University president. **Personal:** Born Dec 26, 1935, Apalachicola, FL; son of Minnie Henry Humphries and Thornton Humphries, Sr; married Antoinette McTurner, Aug 20, 1960; children: Frederick S, Jr, Robin Tanya, Laurence Anthony. **Educ:** Florida A & M University, Tallahassee FL, BS (magna cum laude), 1957; University of Pittsburgh, Pittsburgh PA, PhD, 1964. **Career:** Private tutor of science and mathematics, 1959-64; Florida A & M University, Tallahassee FL, associate professor, 1964-66, University of Minnesota, assistant professor of chemistry, 1966-67; Florida A & M University, professor of chemistry, 1968-74, program director of thirteen-college curriculum program, 1967-68; Institute for Services to Education, Washington DC, program director of summer conference and thirteen-college curriculum program, 1968-74, three-universities graduate program in humanities, 1970-74, innovative institutional research consortium, 1972-73, study of science capability of black colleges, 1972-74, interdisciplinary program, 1973-74, and two-universities graduate program in science, 1973-74; Tennessee State University, Nashville TN, president, 1974-85; Florida A & M University, president, 1985-; consultant to numerous educational, social, and scientific organizations and commissions. **Orgs:** American Assn of Higher Education; American Assn for Advance of Science; American Assn of University Professors; American Chemical Society; American Assn of Minority Research Universities; NAACP; board of directors, American Cancer Society; board of directors, Barnett Bank; board of directors, Pride; board of directors, YMCA, 1987; MIT Visiting committee, 1982; Joint Committee on Agricultural Development, 1982; chairman, Advisory Committee of the Office of the Advancement of Public Negro College, 1982; secretary, American Council on Education, 1978; International Platform Association; National Merit Scholarship Corp; Natl Assn of State Universities & Land Grant Colleges, chairman; Walmart Corp, bd of dirs; Brinker International, bd of dirs; appointed by Pres Bill Clinton, White House advisory committee on Historically Black Colleges & Universities. **Honors/Awds:** Frederick S Humphries Day, City of Indianapolis, 1975; Outstanding Citizen of the Year Award, Nashville chapter Omega Psi Phi, 1976; certificate of appreciation, Governor of TN, 1982; certificate of appreciation, Dept of Health and Human Services, 1983; leadership grant, Prudential Life Insurance Co Foundation, 1988; Centennial Medallion, Florida A & M University; University Bicentennial Medal of Distinction and distinguished alumnus award, University of Pittsburgh; numerous service awards from civic and university groups. **Military Serv:** US Army Security Agency, officer, 1957-59. **Business Addr:** Office of the President, Florida A & M University, Lee Hall, Ste 401, Tallahassee, FL 32307.

HUMPHRIES, JAMES NATHAN
Attorney-at-law. **Personal:** Born Feb 15, 1958, Detroit, MI; son of Mary Jane Humphries and Andrew John Humphries; married Diane D Rogers, Dec 14, 1985; children: Charneise N Newton, Keyontay S, Kalon J, Kailea T. **Educ:** University of Michigan, BGS, 1980, JD, 1984. **Career:** Michigan State University, Cooperative Extension Program, 4H youth agent, 1984-87; Detroit City Council Research Division, analyst, 1987-89; City of Dearborn, Legal Department, assistant corporation counsel, 1989-95; Detroit Bd of Educ, attorney, 1995-. **Orgs:** Michigan Bar Association, 1986-; Wolverine Bar Association, 1986-; Detroit Bar Association, 1986-; Detroit Officials Association; Henderson School LSCO. **Home Addr:** 11137 Balfour, Detroit, MI 48224, (313)839-2132. **Business Phone:** (313)494-1114.

HUMPHRIES, JAY (JOHN)
Professional basketball player. **Personal:** Born Oct 17, 1962, Los Angeles, CA; married Carla Blair. **Educ:** Colorado, 1980-84. **Career:** Phoenix Suns, 1984-88, Milwaukee Bucks, 1988-92; Utah Jazz, 1992-. **Honors/Awds:** Big Eight All-Conf Team; Honorable Mention All-Am & Big Eight All-Defensive Team; Big Eight's All-Freshman team.

HUMPHRIES, PAULA G.
Judge. **Career:** State of Michigan, asst state attorney, 1979-84; Michigan Senator minority counsel, 1984-87; 36th District Court, court magistrate, judge, currently. **Military Serv:** Operation Desert Storm, veteran, 1991; Judge Advocate General Branch, major. **Business Addr:** Judge, 36th District Court, 421 Madison, Detroit, MI 48226, (313)965-8622.

HUNIGAN, EARL
Church administrator. **Personal:** Born Jul 29, 1929, Omaha, NE; married Lazell Phillips; children: Kirk, Kris. **Educ:** Univ MI, BBA 1952. **Career:** Civil Serv Comm, invstgtr 1956-60, prsnl splst 1962-63; USAF, mgmt analyst 1960-62; FAA, pers splst 1963-68; USCG, deputy director of civil personnel, 1968-69; Dept Transp, spl asst, asst sec admin 1969-71; S Region FAA, exec ofcr 1971-73; Food & Nutrution Serv USDA, dep admin for mgmt 1973-78; Smithsonian Inst, dir of prsnl training 1985; E&L Assoc, mgmt cons; Ebenezer AME Church, Ft Wash, MD, administrator, 1990-. **Orgs:** Alpha Phi Alpha; NAACP; Urban Leag; Phalanx; Am Soc Pub Admin. **Honors/Awds:** Sustained Superior Perf 1957-58, 1961, 1971; Quality Step Increase 1968; Spec Act 1963-73; Distngshd Military Instr Award 1969-71. **Military Serv:** AUS, colonel, retired. **Business Addr:** Ebenezer AME Church, 7707 Allentown Rd, Fort Washington, MD 20744.

HUNN, DOROTHY FEGAN
Nursing administrator (retired). **Personal:** Born Sep 1, 1928, Chandler, OK; daughter of Willie Fegan and John Fegan; married Myron Vernon Hunn Sr DDS; children: Myron Vernon BA, Jonathan Scott MD, William Bruce DDS. **Educ:** Memorial Hosp School of Nursing, RN 1952; Compton Comm Coll, AA 1969; CSU Dominguez Hills, BA 1976; Pepperdine Univ, MPA 1977; CSU Long Beach, PhN 1984, post-grad 1982-84. **Career:** Health Services Administration; Professor of Nursing and RCFE Administrator. **Orgs:** Mem Alpha Kappa Alpha Sor, Phi Delta Kappa Sor, Natl Assn of Univ Women; Auxillary to the Angel City Dental Soc, JUGS; The Links, Inc; First United Methodist Church. **Home Addr:** 820 Clemmer Dr, Compton, CA 90221. **Business Phone:** (562)989-1818.

HUNN, MYRON VERNON
Dentist. **Personal:** Born Aug 9, 1926, Sequndo, CO; married Dorothy Louise; children: Myron Jr, Jonathan, William. **Educ:** LA State Coll, BA 1954; Howard Univ, DDS 1958. **Career:** Private Practice, dentist. **Orgs:** Mem Natl Dental Assn, Amer Dental Assn; bd dirs YMCA 1970-73; personnel bd City of Compton 1967-70; mem Comm Redev Agency; Compton Optimist Club 1967-; pres trustee bd United Meth Ch 1970-73; C of C 1964-71. **Military Serv:** AUS 1951-54. **Business Addr:** 1315 N Bullis Rd #4, Compton, CA 90221.

HUNT, BARBARA ANN
Educator. **Personal:** Born in Aberdeen, MS; divorced. **Educ:** Bennett Coll Greensboro NC, BA 1948-52; Syracuse U, MSLS 1952-54; MS Univ for Women, MA 1969-73; Univ of IL, CAS 1971-73; Northwestern University, PhD, 1988. **Career:** MS Univ for Women, dir curr lab 1977-79; AL A&M Univ Huntsville, asst prof 1974-77; AL A&M University, acting dean, 1975-76; Bennett Coll Greensboro, head librn 1967-73; Dist 65 Evanston IL, librn cataloger 1961-66; Morgan State Coll, Baltimore MD, asst librn 1955-57; Rust Coll Holly Springs MS, head librn, assoc prof 1954-55; S Assn of Coll & Schools, consult 1968; Alabama State University, director of communications, 1983-85; University of Mississippi, African-American Novel Project, co-director, director, 1988-91; Knoxville College, Division of Arts & Humanities, acting head, 1993. **Orgs:** Mem bd of dir Wesley Found MS Univ for Women 1979-; mem bd of trustees Millsaps Coll Jackson MS 1979-; coord Wesley Found St James Meth 1979-; cert lay asso United Meth Ch; cochrprsn Local United Negro Coll Fund 1978. **Honors/Awds:** Cerf Lib Admin Dev Prog Univ of MD Coll Pk; University Fellowship, Northwestern University; Janet Green Flwshp, Nrthwstrn Univ 1980; Minority Flwshp St of MS 1979-81; Ford Found & Flwshp 1970-73; Minority Grant Univ of IL 1972; cadetship Syracuse Univ NY 1952-54. **Business Addr:** Acting Head, Division of Arts and Humanities, Knoxville College, Knoxville, TN 37921.

HUNT, BETTY SYBLE
Elected official. **Personal:** Born Mar 13, 1919, Forest, MS; married IP Hunt; children: Irvin D, Vera H Jennings, Garland H, Vernon. **Educ:** Scott Co Training Sch, diploma 1935; Jackson State Univ, BS 1964; Univ of MS, Reading 1969; MS College, Communication 1979. **Career:** Jackson State Bookstore, asst Mgr 1950-65; Canton Public Schools, teacher 1968-73; Packard Elec, assembler 1973-85; Hinds Co MS, election commissioner. **Orgs:** Founder JSU Campus Ministry for Methodist Students 1957; chairperson United Givers Fund 1968-69; mem Election Comm Assoc of MS 1980; mem 100 Black Women Coalition 1982; delegate Co Democratic Convention 1984; reelected Hinds Co Election Commissioner 1984; pres Women for Progress of MS Inc 1983-85; pres MS Chap Natl Coalition 100 Black Women. **Honors/Awds:** Certificate March of Dimes 1968; community excellence General Motors 1974; awd pin United Methodist Women 1984; certificate Three Quarter Way House 1984. **Home Addr:** 11517 Evelake Ct, North Potomac, MD 20878-2592.

HUNT, CHARLES AMOES
Librarian. **Personal:** Born Jan 21, 1950, Montclair, NJ; son of Juliet Adele Carter Bey and William Henry Hunt. **Educ:** MTI Business College, Newark, NJ, computer prog, 1968; Doane College, Crete, NE, BA, 1973; Doane College, Omaha, NE, teaching certificate, 1973; Syracuse Univ, Syracuse, NY, MSLS, 1975; University of the Pacific, Stockton CA. **Career:** The Chicago Public Library, Chicago, IL, branch librarian, 1975-78; Atlantic Richfield Co, Los Angeles, CA, technical librarian, 1978-79; California State Univ-Fullerton, Fullerton, CA, reference librarian, 1979; Kiddy College English School, Mishima City, Japan, English instructor, 1979-81; Stockton-San Joaquin County Public Library, Stockton, CA, adult services librarian, 1981-94, supervising librarian, 1991-. **Orgs:** Guest reviewer, Reference Books Bulletin Editorial Board, American Library Assn, 1975-79; reviewer, Booklist magazine, American Library Assn, 1976-79; member, Yelland Memorial Scholarship for Minority Students Committee, California Library Assn, 1987-88; member, Black Caucus of American Library Assn, 1975-78, 1981-; Community Information Section, Public Library Association of American Library Association, vice pres/president-elect, 1990-91, president, 1991-92; chair, CIS Nominating Com, 1993, 1994. **Honors/Awds:** Graduate fellowship, Syracuse Univ, 1974-75; Junior Semester Abroad Program, Doane College, 1972; Undergraduate Scholarship, Turrell Fund, East Orange, NJ, 1969-73; Gold Award for Best Newsletter, Manteca Kiwanis, 1988; Stockton, San Joaquin, United Way Recertification Team, 1994, 1995. **Special Achievements:** ''Role of the Public Manager in a Changing Environment,'' 1996. **Business Addr:** Branch Manager, Stockton-San Joaquin County Public Library, 2324 Pock Ln, Stockton, CA 95205.

HUNT, DARROLD VICTOR
Conductor. **Personal:** Born Jun 29, 1941, New Bedford, MA; son of Vera Watkins Hunt and Edward Hunt. **Educ:** New Bedford, Inst of Technology, New Bedford, MA, 1959-63; Juilliard School, New York, NY, BS, 1969, MS, 1970. **Career:** SUNY Purchase, Mt Vernon, NY, instructor, 1968-70; Brooklyn College, New York, NY, asst professor, 1970-73; Baltimore Symphony, Baltimore, MD, apprentice/asst conductor, 1973-77; Brooklyn College, New York, NY, associate professor/conductor, 1977-79; Urban Philharmonic Society, Washington, DC, founder/music director, 1970-. **Orgs:** Board, funding committee, DC Humanities Council, 1985-; board, minority outreach comm, Epilepsy Foundation of America, 1988-; music committee, DC Commission on the Arts & The Humanities, 1988-89. **Business Addr:** Founder/Music Director, Urban Philharmonic Society Inc, 410 8th St, NW, Suite 306, Washington, DC 20004.

HUNT, EDWARD
Company executive. **Career:** Stop Shop and Save, CEO, full owner (4 stores), co-owner (2 stores), 1976-; E & S Markets, president, currently. **Special Achievements:** Company is #9 on the Black Enterprise list of top industrial companies, 1992. **Business Addr:** President, E & S Markets Inc, 4514 Edmondson Ave, Baltimore, MD 21229, (410)233-7152.

HUNT, EUGENE
Banker. **Personal:** Born Jul 19, 1948, Augusta, GA; son of Mabel Williams Hunt and Alfred Hunt, Sr; divorced; children: Brian Eugene. **Educ:** Augusta Coll, BBA 1971; Augusta Coll, post-baccalaureate study 1978-79. **Career:** Citizen & So Natl Bank, now Nations Bank, mgr 1975, dir 1976, asst banking officer 1977, banking officer & branch mgr 1980-; asst vice pres in charge of Govt Banking Div, 1984. **Orgs:** Treasurer, Good Shepherd Baptist Church Inc, 1971-; sec, Central Savannah River Area Business League, 1976; pres, Central Savannah River Area Business League, 1979; mem, tech advisory bd Opportunity Indus Center, 1977-80; bd of dirs, Augusta Sickle Cell Center, 1977; loan exec, Natl Alliance of Businessmen, 1979-80; mem, Governor's Educ Review Commn, 1983-84; past chairman, Georgia Dept of Technical & Adult Educ, 1985-. **Honors/Awds:** Serv Award Natl Alliance of Businessmen 1977; Serv Award Good Shepherd Baptist Church Inc 1978; Appreciation Award Central Savannah River Area Youth Employment Opportunity Inc 1979; Businessman of the Year, Augusta Black Historical Soc, 1983; Businessman of the Year, Augusta Chapter Delta Sigma Theata, 1984. **Business Addr:** Asst Vice Pres, Nations Bank, PO Box 912, Augusta, GA 30903.

HUNT, ISAAC COSBY, JR.
Educational administrator, attorney. **Personal:** Born Aug 1, 1937, Danville, VA; married Elizabeth Raucnell; children: Isaac III. **Educ:** Fisk Univ, BA 1957; Univ of VA Law Schl, LLB 1962. **Career:** Securities & Exchange Comm, sttaf atty 1962-67; Natl Adv Comm on Civil Disordrs, fld team leader 1967-68; RAND Corp, rsch sttaf 1968-71; Catholic Univ of Amer, asst prof of Law 1971-77; Jones Day Renvis of Pogue, assoc 1977-79; Dept of Army, principal deputy general counsel 1979-81; Antioch School of Law, dean; US Securities and Exchange Commission, commissioner, currently. **Orgs:** Visiting lectr Bryn Mawr Coll 1970-77; co-chair Dist of Columbia Consmr Goods Bd 1974-76; bd of Govnrs Scty of Am Law Tchrs 1976-79; troop comm mem Boy Scouts of Am Trp 52 1982-; bd of trust 1985-, chair 1987- Sasha Bruce Youthwork Inc. **Honors/Awds:** Moderator Aspen Inst for Humanstc Stds 1973; Outstndng Civilian Serv Awrd Dept of the Army 1981. **Business Addr:** Commissioner, US Securities and Exchange, 450 Fifth St, NW, Washington, DC 20549.

HUNT, JAMES, JR.
Business executive. **Personal:** Born Oct 7, 1944, Hancock Co, GA; married. **Educ:** BS 1968. **Career:** Baldwin Co Bd of Educ, teacher 1968-70; E Cntrl Com Opportunity, deputy dir, vice pres 1985. **Orgs:** Chmn Hancock Bd Ed; acting dir Ogeechees Lakeview Mgmt Co Inc; mem Hancock Co Chap Black Elected Officials; Dem Club. **Honors/Awds:** Alumni Award, Kappa Alpha Psi 1971. **Business Addr:** Central Adminstrn Bldg, Mayfield, GA.

HUNT, JEFFREY C.
City Official. **Personal:** Born Oct 30, 1968, Detroit, MI; son of Anne Ruth Hunt-Ellis & Clyde Cleveland. **Educ:** Howard University, BA, 1991. **Career:** US House of Representatives, legislative asst, 1991; New World Technology Inc, chmn & CEO, 1995-. **Orgs:** Detroit Democratic Club, 1996-; Tomorrow's Leadership Today, PAC, chmn, founder, 1996-; Amer Heart Assn, bd mem, 1995-; United Way Comm Svcs, hth allocation comm mem, 1995; Million Man March Assn, 1995-; Ambitious Students Involved in Comm Svc, founder, 1987-; Mt Pavan Price Hall Affiliated, master mason, 1992-. **Honors/Awds:** Lyndon Baines Johnson Foundation, Presidential Fellowship, 1991. **Special Achievements:** Conducted Excel Leadership Prog, 1994; MI Political Leadership Prog, 1995; Greater Detroit Chamber of Commerce, Leadership Detroit, 1996. **Business Addr:** Staff Analyst, Detroit City Council, Research & Analysis Division, 9243 Broadstreet, Detroit, MI 48228.

HUNT, MAURICE
Educator. **Personal:** Born Dec 16, 1943, Birmingham, AL; son of Ora Lee Lawson Hunt and Percy Benjamin Hunt Sr; married Mary Elizabeth Sain, Aug 6, 1966; children: Michael Phillip. **Educ:** Kentucky State Coll, BS 1967; Iowa Univ, 1970-71; Drake Univ, MSE 1975. **Career:** Good Shepard H S, coach 1965-66; Glen Park Ambridge Elem Schools, instructor 1967-69, Tolleston H S, instructor/coach 1967-69; Grinnell Coll, instructor/coach 1969-77; Central State Univ, asst prof/coach 1977-79; Morehouse Coll, instructor/coach 1979-. **Orgs:** Mem Grinnell, IA Youth Comm 1969-71, Amer Football Coaches Assn 1970-; past mem Wrestling Fed 1970-73; mem Iowa Lions Club 1972-77; past mem Drake Relays Comm 1973-77; mem Iowa Human Rights Comm 1976-77; rater NAIA 1978; Sheridan Black Coll Pollster. **Honors/Awds:** Coach of Year Atlanta Daily World Newspaper, Atlanta Constitution Journal, SIAC, 100 Percent Wrng Clb 1979, Atlanta Extra Point Clb 1980-83, 1987-88; Athletics Hall of Fame, Kentucky State University, 1991; Phyllis Wheatley Award, Women's Federated Clubs, 1991; Honorary Undergraduate, Morehouse College, 1985. **Home Addr:** 4463 John Wesley Dr, Decatur, GA 30035. **Business Addr:** Physical Education Instructor, Morehouse College, 830 Westview Dr, Atlanta, GA 30314.

HUNT, O'NEAL
Judge. **Personal:** Born Jun 27, 1914, Palestine, TX; married Elnora Dorsey; children: Herbert, Jimmy, Norris, Amanda, Alice. **Educ:** TX A&M Univ, Farm Welding 1964, Pasture 1966; Southwest TX State Univ, 1983-84;, Justice of Peace Training 1984-85. **Career:** Green Bay Comm Ctr, pres 1967-82; Anderson Cty Courthouse, justice of peace. **Orgs:** Pres Cty Bldg Prog Comm 1962-66. **Honors/Awds:** Diamond Pin in Appreciation Awd Byrd-Frost Serv 1952; Statistician-Cert of Appt The Palestine Dist 1962; Cert of Recog East TX Leadership Forum 1975, And Cty Voters Comm 1975; Notary Public Comm 1982; Family of the Year Negro Bus & Professional Womens Club Inc 1982. **Business Addr:** Justice Of The Peace, Anderson County Court House, Precinct 2 Place 1, Palestine, TX 75801.

HUNT, PORTIA L.
Counseling psychologist, educator, consultant. **Personal:** Born Feb 12, 1947, East St Louis, IL; daughter of Ethel Hunt and Luches Hunt. **Educ:** Southern IL Univ Edwardsville, BS 1971, MS 1972; Indiana State Univ Terre Haute IN, PhD 1975. **Career:** State Comm Coll, counselor 1971-73; Portia Hunt & Assocs, psychologist 1979-; Eclipse Mgmt Consultant Group, pres 1986-; Temple Univ, prof 1975-. **Orgs:** Natl program chair Assoc of Black Psychologists 1979; advisory bd pres Eastern Coll Cushing Counseling Act 101 1980-86; bd mem Church World Inst Temple Univ 1980-86; Philadelphia Desegration School Dist; Survivors of the Move Bombing in Philadelphia & W Philadelphia Consortium Mental Health Center, consultant, 1985-86; bd mem ABRAXAS Foundation 1985-; former pres Delaware Valley Assoc Black Psychologists 1976-. **Honors/Awds:** Professional Affairs Serv Award Delaware Valley Assoc of Black Psych 1983; Psychology Award Serv to Black Comm Alliance of Black Social Worker 1985; Psychology Award Delaware Valley Assoc of Black Psychologists 1986; Kathryn Sisson Phillips Fellowship Scholar 1974; Women to Watch Award, Business Journal of Philadelphia, 1995. **Business Addr:** Professor of Counseling Psych, Temple University, 267 Weiss Hall, Philadelphia, PA 19122.

HUNT, RICHARD HOWARD
Sculptor. **Personal:** Born Sep 12, 1935, Chgo; divorced. **Educ:** Art Inst of Chgo, bA 1957; Belli Bar, Studied Sculpture; Univ of Chgo, Undergrad Std 1953-55. **Career:** Advant-Grade Sculptures, sculptor, creator; Sch of the Art Inst of Chgo, tchr 1961; Univ of IL Chgo, dept arch & art 1962; vis prof, vis artist at 7 schs including Yale U, Purdueu 1965, Nrthwstrn Univ 1968. **Orgs:** Perm coll of art, Mus in Chgo, Cleveland, Houston, NY, Buffalo, Milwaukee, Israel; work was exhibited in Artists of Chicago & Vicinity Exhbtn 1955-56; 62nd, 63rd, 64th Am Exhib of Art Inst of Chgo; Carnegie Intrnat Exhib in Pitts 1958; Mus of Mod New York City 1959; one-man Exhib in NYC, Chgo;participated in exhib Ten Negro Artists from US; First World Fest of Negro Arts, Dakar, Senegal 1966. **Honors/Awds:** Recip 6 Major Awards & Flwshps. **Business Addr:** 1017 W Lill St, Chicago, IL 60614.

HUNT, RONALD JOSEPH
Educational administrator. **Personal:** Born Dec 19, 1951, Uniontown, PA; married Karen Elaine Hill; children: Lynnette, Angela. **Educ:** Slippery Rock St Coll, BS Health, Phys Ed 1973, MEd Admin & Curriculum 1975. **Career:** Slippery Rock St Coll, asst dir admsns 1979-, temp instr of phys ed 1979, acting coord spec srv 1974, grad asst 1973, asst ftbl coach 1973-77, asst bsktbl coach 1978-79. **Orgs:** Bd of dir Connie Hawkins Bsktbl Incorp 1978-80; bd of dir W Side Comm Act Ctr 1979-80; bd of dir Lawrence County Cncl of Comm Ctrs 1979-80. **Honors/Awds:** Outstndng Athl in Am 1973; Outstndng Man in Comm, Jaycees 1979.

HUNT, SAMUEL D.
Senior relocation specialist. **Personal:** Born May 21, 1933, Fresno, CA; married Ruby; children: Terry, Lanetta, Stanley, Steven, Brian. **Educ:** 4 C's Coll, 1956; Fresno City Coll, Working Toward Degree in Public Admin. **Career:** Fresno Redevelopment Agency, senior relocation specialist, past west. **Orgs:** Reg dir Phi Beta Sigma Frat Inc; chrmn Fresno's Model Cities Ed Task Force; pres Epsilon Delta Sigma Chap, Phi Beta Sigma Frat Inc; pres 20th Cent Golf Club; pub rel chrmn Western St Golf Assn; mem King Soloman Lodge; Mt Sinai Consistory; prince hall aff spec rep Nat Urban Coal Conf 1973; paretn rep Fresno City Schs Atlanta. **Honors/Awds:** Winner ''Tray Award'' Ach in Ed & Cit Part. **Military Serv:** USAF 1951-55. **Business Addr:** Ste 200, T W Patterson Bldg, Fresno, CA 93728.

HUNTER, BRIAN LEE
Professional baseball player. **Personal:** Born Mar 5, 1971, Portland, OR. **Career:** Houston Astros, outfielder, 1994-96; Detroit Tigers, 1997-. **Business Addr:** Professional Baseball Player, Detroit Tigers, 2121 Trumbull St, Detroit, MI 48216, (313)962-4000.

HUNTER, BRIAN RONALD
Professional baseball player. **Personal:** Born Mar 4, 1968, El Toro, CA. **Educ:** Cerritos College. **Career:** Atlanta Braves, 1991-94; Pittsburgh Pirates, 1994-. **Business Addr:** Professional Baseball Player, Pittsburgh Pirates, PO Box 7000, Pittsburgh, PA 15212, (412)353-5000.

HUNTER, CECELIA CORBIN
Government official. **Personal:** Born Jul 8, 1945, Jersey City, NJ; daughter of Margaret Nelson Corbin and Leander M Corbin; divorced; children: Alicia Stacey. **Educ:** Harvard Univ, John F. Kennedy School of Govt, MPA, 1982. **Career:** Atlanta Off of Mayor Maynard Jackson, dir fed relations, 1974-81; ICMA Retirement Corp, manager, eastern region, 1982-1990; Atlanta Off of Mayor Maynard Jackson, chief of staff, 1990-91, dir olympic coordination, 1991-94; 1996 Atlanta Paralympic Games, vp, operations and services, 1994-. **Orgs:** 100 Black Women of Metro Atlanta, charter member, 1987; Atlanta Area Council of Campfire Girls, board member, 1976-1980; West End Neighborhood Development Corp, 1980-; ICMA Retirement Corp, asst sec - bd of directors, 1983-88; Catalyst Magazine, trustee, 1989-; Atlanta Business League, bd of directors, 1991-; Zoo Atlanta, bd of directors, 1991-; Atlanta Committee for the Olympic Games (ACOG), bd of directors, chair eeo committee, 1991-94. **Honors/Awds:** Word Processing, Spring Cover Story, 1975; Atlanta Constitution-Intown Extra, "Atlanta's Complete Count Committee," 1980; Dollars and Sense Magazine, Tribute to African-American Business and Professional Women, 1990; OIC Champion, 1994; Atlanta's Top 100 Black Women of Influence. **Business Addr:** VP, Operations & Services, 1996 Atlanta Paralympic Games, 1201 W Peachtree St, NE, Ste 2500, Atlanta, GA 30309-3448.

HUNTER, CECIL THOMAS
Educator. **Personal:** Born Feb 5, 1925, Greenup, KY; married Gloria James; children: Mildred C, Charlene James, Rosalind H Levy, Roderick, Gloria. **Educ:** Washington Jr Coll; FL A&M Univ. **Career:** Brownsville Middle School, teacher of math. **Orgs:** Past chmn Catholic Soc Svcs; chmn Governmental Center Auth; chmn Escambia Co Health Facilities Auth; comm mem bd dir Sacred Heart Found; mem Saenger Mgmt bd dir; mem Finance Comm & Gen Govt Comm City Council; past mem Hospice - Northwest FL Area Agency on Aging; St Anthony's Catholic Ch; Knights of Columbus; Jack & Jill of Amer; Kappa Alpha Psi Frat; Prefect in Third Order of St Francis Secular Franciscans; mem NAACP. **Honors/Awds:** Diocesan Medal of Honor; recip of Secular Franciscan Peace Award. **Military Serv:** Veteran of WWII. **Business Addr:** Teacher of Math, Brownsville Middle School, 3100 West Strong St, Pensacola, FL 32501.

HUNTER, CHARLES A.
Cleric, educator. **Personal:** Born May 7, 1926, Longview, TX; son of Ivernia Charlott Hunter and Wallace Alvin Hunter; married Annie Alexander; children: Alpha A, Rhonda A, Rhasell D, Byron C, Rosalyn A. **Educ:** Bishop Coll, BA 1947; Howard Univ, BD 1950; Philadelphia Divinity School, MTh, 1954, ThD 1958; Univ of North TX, MS, 1971. **Career:** Bishop Coll, professor of sociology 1961-72; Hope Presbyterian Church, Dallas, pastor 1962-68; Dallas Independent Schl Dist, sociological rsrch 1969-72, 1974-75; St Luke Presbyterian Church, Dallas, assoc pastor 1969-80; Univ of TX at Arlington, assoc prof 1972-73; Bishop Coll, professor sociology 1975-88; Dallas County Community of Churches, dir church and community 1989-. **Orgs:** Dir United Cmps Christian Fllwshp 1959-61; coord Amigos 1968-; bd mem Greater Dallas Housing Opportunity Ctr 1969-, Dallas Theater Ctr 1974-83, Red Cross Dallas 1975-81; Grace Presbytery, moderator 1985; bd mem, Trinity River Authority, 1983-89; mem Dallas Citizens/Police Relations Board, 1981-88; moderator, Synod of the Sun, 1991-93. **Honors/Awds:** Trail Blazer Award Business & Professional Women 1966; Outstanding Alumni Bishop Coll Alumni Assn 1966; Fair Housing Awrd Greater Dallas Housing Opporunity Ctr 1972; Vol Awrd First Lady's Volunteer TX 1980. **Home Addr:** 2329 Southwood Dr, Dallas, TX 75224.

HUNTER, CLARENCE HENRY
Public relations manager. **Personal:** Born Nov 1, 1925, Raleigh, NC; son of Katie L. Hunter and Wade H. Hunter; married Mary Ransom; children: Karen, Beverly, Katherine, Andrew. **Educ:** NY Univ, BS 1950. **Career:** Jrnl & Guide Norfolk VA, reporter, bureau mgr 1950-53; Ebony Mag Chicago IL, assoc editor 1953-55; Post-Tribune Gary IN, reporter 1955-62; WA Evening Star WADC, reporter 1962-65; US Commiss on Civil Rights WA DC, dir info 1965-69; WA Journalism Ctr WA DC, assoc dir 1969-71; Howard Univ, dir univ rel & publ 1971-73; General Motors Public Relations, staff assistant, 1973-78, Rochester Products Div, dir of communications and public relations, 1978-88, AC Rochester Division, manager of public affairs and communication, 1988-. **Orgs:** Public Relations Society of America; Austin Steward Professional Society; United Way of Greater Rochester; Martin Luther King Jr Festival Commission; GM Civic Involvement Program. **Honors/Awds:** Howard Coles Community Award, Association of Black Communicators, Rochester Chapter, 1984; Distinguished Achievement Award, Black Business Association of Greater Rochester, 1991; Kathryn B Terrell Award for Distinguished Volunteer Service, Urban League of Rochester, 1991. **Military Serv:** US Marine Corps, Sgt 1944-46. **Business Addr:** Manager of Public Affairs and Communications, AC Rochester Division, General Motors Corp, PO Box 92700, Rochester, NY 14692.

HUNTER, DALE RODNEY
Lobbyist. **Personal:** Born Oct 15, 1955, Los Angeles, CA; son of Rose Tyler and George Hunter; married Carolyn Veal, Nov 21, 1992. **Educ:** University of Northern Colorado, BA, journalism, 1978. **Career:** Los Angeles Sentinel Newspaper, staff writer, 1980-81; Asst to the Pres of Los Angeles City Council, 1982-83; Irvin Hampton Company, vice pres, 1983-89; Metropolitan Water District, lobbyist, 1989-. **Orgs:** Institute of Government Advocates, 1993; American Assn of Blacks in Energy; Collective Enterprise Group, board mem, 1989-. **Honors/Awds:** California State Senate, Certificate of Recognition, 1991; California State Assembly, Resolution of Achievement, 1992; Coro Foundation, Certificate of Completion, 1983.

HUNTER, DAVID
Educator, pastor. **Personal:** Born Aug 3, 1941, Enterprise, MS; son of Laura Hunter and Sandy Hunter (deceased); married Mary Williams; children: David Cornell, Christopher Dante. **Educ:** Alcorn State Univ, BS 1964; Cleveland State Univ, MEd 1974; Central Bible Coll, BA 1976; Trinity Theological Seminary, Newburgh, IN, doctoral candidate, currently. **Career:** E Cleveland Schools, teacher 1969-82; Bright Star Bapt Church, pastor 1972-. **Orgs:** Life mem Alpha Phi Alpha 1965-; mem Oper PUSH, NAACP; E Cleveland Board of Education, pres, 1988-89, 1991, mem; East Ministerial Alliance, president, 1994-95. **Honors/Awds:** Acad Scholarship Alcorn State 1962. **Business Addr:** 13028 Shaw Ave, Cleveland, OH 44108.

HUNTER, DAVID LEE
Educational administrator. **Personal:** Born Sep 10, 1933, Charlotte, NC; son of Mrs Annie L Boulware; married Margaret Plair; children: Karen Leslie, Jocelyn Jeanine. **Educ:** Johnson C Smith Univ, BS 1951; Atlanta Univ, MS 1964; Nova Univ, EdD 1979. **Career:** Carver College & Mecklenburg College, instructor of math 1957-63; Central Piedmont Community College, instructor of math 1963-71, coordinator college transfer prog 1971-73, dir of personnel 1973-75, vice pres, dean, general studies, beginning 1975, dean of arts and sciences, currently. **Orgs:** Amer Soc for Public Administration 1974-; North Carolina Assn of Community Colleges Instructional Admin 1975-; rep for CPCC League for Innovation in the Community College 1979-; financial sec bd trustees Little Rock AME Zion Church 1973; bd dir Charlotte Rehab Homes Inc 1978; bd dir ARC 1979; bd of dirs, Southern Regional Council on Black American Affairs; North Carolina SRCBAA. **Military Serv:** AUS corpl 1953-55. **Business Addr:** Dean of Arts and Sciences, Central Piedmont Community College, 1201 Elizabeth Ave, Charlotte, NC 28204.

HUNTER, DEANNA LORRAINE
Educational administrator. **Personal:** Born Dec 16, 1946, New York, NY; daughter of Hazel Glenn Williams and Harry Williams; children: Kimberly G. **Educ:** Hofstra Univ, BA English 1971, MS Counseling 1977; CAS Educational Administration 1990. **Career:** SUNY Farmingdale, career counselor 1979-80; Hofstra Univ, financial aid counselor 1980-82, asst dean of students 1982-85, school of law asst dean 1985-87, assistant dean University Advisement 1987-88, director CSTEP 1988-, STEP 1991-. **Orgs:** Lola T Martin Scholarship Assn, mem 1976-83; Dorothy K Robin Nursery School, mem/officer 1978-83; Hofstra Univ Alumni Senate, vice pres 1979-, Counselor Education Alumni Assn, founding mem/past pres 1979-, Minority Women's Task Force, mem/officer; Human Connections Inst, human relations consultant 1984-, Hofstra University Black/Hispanic Alumni, Sec. **Honors/Awds:** Lola T Martin Scholarship Assn, community service award 1979; Hofstra Univ Alumni Senate, "Senator of the Year" 1985. **Military Serv:** US Army Reserves, SSG 1975-83. **Home Addr:** 45 Hamilton Rd, Hempstead, NY 11550. **Business Addr:** Director, CSTEP & STEP, Hofstra University, 103 Mason Hall, Hempstead, NY 11550.

HUNTER, EDWINA EARLE
Educator. **Personal:** Born Dec 29, 1943, Caswell County, NC; daughter of Bessie Catherine Brown Palmer and Edgar Earl Palmer; married James Weldon Hunter Sr, Jul 2, 1966; children: James W Jr, Anika Z, Isaac Earl. **Educ:** Spelman Coll, BA 1964; Smith Coll, MAT 1966. **Career:** Vint Hill Farms Station, post chapel choir dir 1967-68; El Paso Comm Coll, instructor music 1975-76; Prince George's County Schools, music teacher 1969-72, director of vocal music 1979-. **Orgs:** Mem NAACP; pres, 1986-90, sec Columbia Chap NAASC 1984-; MSTA Greater Laurel Music Teachers Assn NEA, MENC, MMENC; Suzuki Assn; pres Columbia Chapter Natl Alumnae Assn of Spelman College 1987-; secretary-treasurer, NE Region, National Alumnae Association of Spelman College, 1992-. **Honors/Awds:** Recording "Children's Songs for Games from Africa," Folkways FCS 77855 1979; Distinguished Alumni Award NAFEO 1989; NEH Seminar Fellow, National Endowment of the Humanities, 1990. **Home Addr:** 10721 Graeloch Rd, Laurel, MD 20723. **Business Addr:** Director of Vocal Music, Prince George's County Schs, 13200 Larchdale Road, Laurel, MD 20708.

HUNTER, ELZA HARRIS
Educator. **Personal:** Born Jul 14, 1908, Little Rock; married Melva W Pryor. **Educ:** Langston U, BS; Univ of AR, MS; Atlanta U, NC St, Addl Study; Durham A&M Coll; Univ of OK; Shorter Coll, LLD 1957. **Career:** Shorter Coll Little Rock, acad dean 1973-77; Alumni Rel & Outreach, dir 1977-; N Little Rock Sch, dir instructnl srv & adult ed 1971-73; Jr HS, dir 1970-72; Jones HS, prin 1942-70, tchr 1935-42. **Orgs:** Mem N Little Rock Admin Assn; Nat Ed Assn; AR Ed Assn; Nat Assn of Secondary Sch Prin; Nat Assn for Pub Cont Adult Ed; bd trustees Shorter Coll; st mbrshp sec AR Sch Admin Assn; pres Urban Leag of Little Rock 1970-74; chmn N Little Rock Lib Commn; treas Urban Leag 1977-; bd of mgmt AW Young YMCA; met bd YMCA; pres Appollo Terr Housing Proj; Omega Psi Phi; sec Shorter Coll Grdns Housing Proj; IBP of Elks, Prince Hall Mason, 33 deg; Shriner Mohammed Temple #34; chmn, bd trustee Steward Bd, Miles Chapel CME. **Honors/Awds:** Has received various awards including Man of Yr, Omega Psi Phi 9th Dist 1971; Family of Yr, Urban Leag Little Rock 1971. **Business Addr:** Shorter Coll, 604 Locust St, North Little Rock, AR.

HUNTER, FREDERICK DOUGLAS
Attorney. **Personal:** Born Jan 30, 1940, Pittsburgh, PA; son of Elizabeth Hunter and Charlie Hunter; married Rosie M Kirkland; children: Frederick D, Deborah R. **Educ:** Univ of Pittsburgh, BS 1961, PhD 1967; Univ of Maryland, JD 1974. **Career:** The Lubrizol Corp, chief patent counsel, associate general counsel; EI Dupont De Nemours & Co, corporate counsel 1972-89; W R Grace & Co, sr rsch chem 1967-72. **Orgs:** Amer Bar Assn; Delaware Bar Assn; District of Columbia Bar Assn; AOA Fraternity; AIPLA. **Honors/Awds:** Publ 5 papers various sci jour. **Business Addr:** Chief Patent Counsel, The Lubrizol Corporation, 29400 Lakeland Blvd, Wickliffe, OH 44092-2298.

HUNTER, GERTRUDE T.
Physician, administrator. **Personal:** Born Mar 23, 1926, Boston; married Charles. **Educ:** Boston U, BA 1945; Howard U, MA 1946; Howard Univ Coll Med, MD 1950; Harvard Univ Grad Sch Bus Admin, PHMS 1972. **Career:** Pub Hlth Srv HEW, reg hlth adminstr 1973-; Boston, dep reg hlth dir 1971-72; Nat Ofc OEO & Head Start, sr ped 1965-71; Head Start, dir hlth srvs 1961-71. **Orgs:** Mem Am Acad Peds; Howard Univ Med Alumni Assn; Nat Med Assn; bd dirs Am Assn Sex Eductors & Cnslrs; Nat Family Guidance & Cnslng Srv; bd dirs Nat Cncl Black Child Dev; adv cncl Am Acad Med Dirs; Urban Leag; com to Improve Status of Women; Jack & Jill; NAACP; bd dirs People's Cong Ch; MA Heart Assn; bd dirs Boston Pub Housing Tenants Policy Cncl. **Honors/Awds:** Num med publ; Beta Kappa Chi Hon Soc; Kappa Pi Hon Med Soc; Nat Contrbns Hlth Care NAACP 1973; Award Met Boston Consumer Hlth Cncl. **Business Addr:** Howard Univ Coll of Medicine, Dept of Comm Hlth & Fmly Prac, Room 2400, Washington, DC 20059.

HUNTER, HOWARD JACQUE, JR.
State representative. **Personal:** Born Dec 16, 1946, Washington, DC; son of Madge Watford Hunter and Howard J Hunter, Sr; married Vivian Flythe; children: Howard III, Chyla Toye. **Educ:** NC Central Univ, BS 1971. **Career:** Hobson R Reynolds Elks Natl Shrine, mgr 1973-74; Hunter's Funeral Home Murfreesboro, owner 1974-; Hertford Co, commissioner, chmn of the bd, 1978-88; NC State Representative 5th District, currently. **Orgs:** Trustee First Baptist Church Murfreesboro 1974-; scoutmaster Troup 123 BSA 1976-; past mem Gov Crime Commission 1980; life mem Kappa Alpha Psi; NC Legislative Black Caucus, chairman; Gov Task Force on Welfare Reform; Gov Commission on a Competitative NC; NC Technological Dev Authority, bd of dirs; NC Rural Eco Dev Ctr, bd of dirs. **Honors/Awds:** Distinguished Serv Award Amer Jaycees 1980; Citizen of the Year NC Human Relations Comm 1981; NC Mental Health Assn, Legislator of the Year, 1993; NC Siera Club, Legislator of the Year, 1994. **Home Addr:** PO Box 418, Conway, NC 27820. **Business Addr:** State Representative, Northampton County, PO Box 506, Murfreesboro, NC 27855.

HUNTER, IRBY B.
Dentist. **Personal:** Born Jul 12, 1940, Longview, TX; married Staphalene Johnson; children: Constance A, Irby B. **Educ:** TX Coll Tyler, BS Chem 1961; Tuskegee Inst AL, MS Chem 1963; Univ TX Houston, DDS 1968. **Career:** Irby B Hunter DDS Inc Dallas, dentist gen 1971-; Dr WA Hembry Dallas, dentist gen 1968-70; Atlantic & Richfield Houston, chem (water) 1964-68; Houston ISD, tchr ad ed 1965-68. **Orgs:** Mem Am Dental Assn 1965-; pres MC Cooper Dental Soc Dallas 1974-78; pres Golf St Dental Assn of TX 1978-; mem of Steering Com, Small Sch Task Force Dallas ISD 1979-; mem of bd Comm Hlth Ctrs of Dallas Inc 1979-; Sir Orchun, Sigma Pi Phi Frat Dallas 1979. **Honors/Awds:** Spec Alumni Award TX Coll Tyler TX 1980. **Business Addr:** 2826 E Illinois, Dallas, TX 75216.

HUNTER, JAMES MACKIELL
Attorney, corporate officer. **Personal:** Born Feb 7, 1946, Macon County, GA; son of Odessa Hunter and Elton Hunter; married Lorraine Dunlap; children: Adrienne, Michelle, Hillary. **Educ:** Ft Valley State, BS, 1968; Howard University, JD, 1973; Harvard University, Practice Institute for Lawyers, 1991. **Career:** US Equal Employment Oppty Comm, trial attny 1973-

76, suprv trial atty 1976-78; M James Hunter & Assoc, principal partner 1978-81; M&M Products Co, Vice Pres and General Counsel (legal & human resources), 1981-90; Hunt, Richardson, Garner, Todd & Cadenhead, partner, 1990-93; Schnader, Harrison, Segal and Lewis, partner, 1993-. **Orgs:** Bd mem Atlanta Judicial Commiss 1978-, Grady Hosp Bd of Visitors 1983-, Clayton Jr Coll 1984-; Atlanta Jr College Board 1986; 100 Black Men of Atlanta, Inc; Leadership Atlanta, general counsel, member, 1988-93. **Honors/Awds:** Knox Awd Ft Valley State 1968; Omega Psi Phi Award, 1968; Outstanding Atlantans 1978; Outstanding Georgians 1984. **Military Serv:** US Army Reserves, 1968-74. **Business Addr:** Partner, Schnader, Harrison, Segal & Lewis, 215 Peachtree Center Ave, Atlanta, GA 30303, (404)215-8100.

HUNTER, JAMES NATHANIEL, II
Cleric. **Personal:** Born Aug 16, 1943, Glasgow, VA; son of Helen Louise Strawbridge Hunter and James N Hunter Sr; married Sharron Joy Condon, Jul 22, 1972. **Educ:** St Paul's College, BA, 1966; Bexley Hall, BD, 1969; State University of New York at Geneseo, MA, 1970. **Career:** School District of Rochester, teacher, 1970-72; U.S. Department of Interior, principal, counselor, teacher, 1972-83; Alaska Department of Adult Corrections, employment counselor, 1983-85; Fairbanks Resource Agency, supervisor, homeliving specialist, 1985-88; St Jude's Episcopal Church, vicar, 1988-, Jubilee Center, executive director, 1992-. **Orgs:** Kiwanis Club of North Pole, secretary, past president, 1989-; Breadline, Inc, secretary, 1985-; Union of Black Episcopalians, 1988-; Tanana Conference of Churches, 1985-; Commission on Ministry-Episcopal, secretary, 1990-; Tanana Interior Deanery, dean, 1990-; Alaska Interfaith Impact, chair, 1988-; Food Bank of Fairbanks, consultant. **Honors/Awds:** Martin Luther King, Jr Committee, Community Leader, 1988; Breadline, Inc, Outstanding Board Member, 1989; Fairbanks Resource Agency, Memorial Award for Outstanding Leadership, 1988; Bexley Hall, Rossister Fellowships, 1988, 1991; Domestic & Foreign Ministry, award to study in Israel, 1990; Citizen of the Year, North Pole Chamber of Commerce, 1996; Elected to North Pole City Council, 1994; Vice Mayor, 1996; Facilitator, Center for Healing of Racism. **Business Addr:** Vicar, Executive Director, Jubilee Center, St Jude's Episcopal Church, Box 55458, North Pole, AK 99705, (907)488-9329.

HUNTER, JERRY L.
Attorney. **Personal:** Born Sep 1, 1942, Mt Holly, NC; son of Annie B Hunter and Samuel Hunter. **Educ:** NC, BS; A&T State U, 1964; Howard Univ Schl of Law, JD 1967. **Career:** Roundtree Knox Hunter & Parker, Partner Law firm. **Orgs:** Mem US Supreme Court Bar; US Dist Court (MD & DC); US Court of Appeals & DC Court of Appeals; mem Natl Bar Assn; Am Bar Assn; DC Bar Assn; Assn of Plaintiffs Trail Atty; Sigma Delta Tau Legal Frat Alpha Kappa Mu Honor Soc; Kappa Pi Intl Honorary Art Soc. **Honors/Awds:** Co-authored article ''Current Racial Legal Developments'' 12 How-L J 299, Spring 1966 No 2; received Am Jurisprudence Award for Academic Achievement in Legal Methods & History. **Business Addr:** Partner, Roundtree, Knox, Hunter & Parker, 1822 11th St NW, Washington, DC 20001.

HUNTER, JOHN DAVIDSON
Insurance consultant. **Personal:** Born in Alabama; married Lucile Chandler; children: Louise, John D Jr, Joshua, Phillip, Jackie Owens. **Educ:** Graduate of Opelika HS, Selma Univ; extra corres courses in Business. **Career:** Protective Industrial Ins Co, rep 1962-81; Pilgrim Health Life Ins Co, rep 1981-. **Orgs:** Mem Tabernacle Baptist Church 1941-; mem NAACP 1950-; mem Dallas Cty Voters League 1975-; former mem The Selma City Council 1976-84; mem President's Democratic Club of AL 1977-85; mem Selma Black Leadership Council 1979-85; mem of exec comm Southwest AL Sickle Cell Anemia Assoc 1984-85; minister of the Rocky Branch Baptist Church 14 yrs. **Honors/Awds:** Received twenty prof achiev awds and four comm service awds. **Home Addr:** 1818 Martin Luther King St, Selma, AL 36701.

HUNTER, JOHN W.
County official (retired). **Personal:** Born Apr 18, 1934, Union, MS; son of Estella Hunter and Frank Hunter; married Rose-Mary White, Jul 3, 1956; children: Eric, Shawn. **Educ:** CS Mott Comm Jr Coll, Business Arts 1969. **Career:** 7th Dist Congressional Black Caucus Political Action Comm #659, chmn; Genesee County Bd of Health, bd of dir; Genesee County Bd of Commission, county commission 1974-86; Genesee County Road Commission, commissioner. **Orgs:** Bd of dir Natl Assoc of Ctys Welfare & Soc Serv Comm, Genesee Mem Hospital 1975-84, Model Cities Econ Devel Corp; chairperson Genesee County Human Serv Comm; precinct delegate, former delegate State Democratic Convention; mem Urban League, NAACP, Elks Vehicle City Lodge 1036. **Honors/Awds:** Leadership Award Black Business & Professional Womens Org 1978; Ambulatory Wing at Genesee mem Hospital in Flint MI was named The John W Hunter Wing 1984; The 1st black to be named to road commission, 5th black to serve in the State of MI as road commissioner; Frederick Douglass Award Natl Assn of Black Business & Professional Women Org 1987; A Philip Randolph Civic Right Award, 1989; National Media Women's Award, 1991.

HUNTER, KRISTIN (KRISTIN HUNTER-LATTANY)
Educator, writer. **Personal:** Born Sep 12, 1937, Philadelphia, PA; daughter of Mabel Manigault Eggleston and George L Eggleston; married Joseph Hunter (divorced 1962). **Educ:** University of Pennsylvania, BS, 1951. **Career:** Emory Univ, writer in residence, 1979; Univ of Pennsylvania, Dept of English, lecturer, 1972-79, adjunct assoc prof, 1980-83, senior lecturer, 1983-. **Orgs:** PEN, National Council of Teachers of English. **Honors/Awds:** Books: God Bless the Child, 1964; The Landlord, 1966; The Soul Brothers and Sister Lou, 1968; Boss Cat, 1971; The Pool Table War, 1972; Guests in the Promised Land, 1973; The Survivors, 1975; The Lakestown Rebellion, 1978; Lou in the Limelight, 1981; numerous articles, poems, reviews and short stories; New Jersey State Council on the Arts Prose Fellowship, 1981-82, 1985-86; Univ of Pennsylvania, Course Development Grant, 1983-84, Curriculum Development Grant, 1989-90; numerous others. **Business Addr:** Senior Lecturer, University of Pennsylvania, Department of English, 318 Bennett Hall, Philadelphia, PA 19104-6273.

HUNTER, LINDSEY BENSON, JR.
Professional basketball player. **Personal:** Born Dec 3, 1970, Utica, MS; married Ivy; children: one. **Educ:** Jackson State Univ. **Career:** Detroit Pistons, guard, 1993-. **Honors/Awds:** NBA All-Rookie Second Team, 1994. **Special Achievements:** NBA Draft, first round, tenth pick, 1993. **Business Addr:** Professional Basketball Player, Detroit Pistons, 2 Championship Dr, Auburn Hills, MI 48326, (248)377-0100.

HUNTER, LLOYD THOMAS
Physician. **Personal:** Born Feb 6, 1936, Des Moines, IA; married Janice; children: Cynthia, Laura, Elizabeth. **Educ:** Univ NE, AB 1957, MD 1962. **Career:** Univ So CA Univ CA Los Angeles, Asso Prof. **Orgs:** Diplomate Am Bd of Pediatrics; fellos Am Acad of Pediatrics; past pres LA Pediatric Soc; mem Charles R Drew Med Soc; AMA; Nat Med & Assn; Golden State Med Assn; CA Med Assn; LA Pediatric Soc; Kappa Alpha Psi Frat; life mem NAACP; Los Angeles Urban League; Alpha Omega Alpha Med Hon Soc. **Honors/Awds:** Merit award Army commendation medal; 1962; Univ NE Regents Schlrshp 1961-62. **Military Serv:** AUS med corps capt 1963-65. **Business Addr:** 3719 S La Brea Ave, Los Angeles, CA 90016.

HUNTER, NORMAN L.
Graphic artist. **Personal:** Born Aug 28, 1932, Eutaw, AL; married Claudia M; children: Kim Derek, Marc Cedric. **Educ:** Detroit Soc of Arts & Crafts; Art Inst of Chgo. **Career:** Jet & Black Stars mags, art dir; Supreme Beauty Products JPC Book Div; artist-designer; Ebony, designer of Books; Ebony Pictoral History of Black Am designed highly successful 3-vol set books 1972; Jet, Ebony, Black Stars, photographer; Johnson Library at Univ of Tex, photograph taken was accepted of Pres Lyndon B Johnson & Chicago Mayor Richard J Daley; Jet, page layouts & cover designs; Fashion Fair Cosmetics, artist, designer; Johnson Publ Co, art dir 1955-. **Honors/Awds:** Merit Awd for Best Typography Nat Newspaper Pub Assn's 1972; book design CEBA Award ''Dubois A Pictorial Biography''; Printers Industry Awd; book design BillCosby In Words & Pictures. **Military Serv:** AUS. **Business Addr:** Art Dir, Johnson Publishing Co, 820 S Michigan Ave, Chicago, IL 60605.

HUNTER, OLIVER CLIFFORD, JR.
Medical doctor. **Personal:** Born Feb 20, 1935, Kilgore, TX; married Shirley; children: Oliver, III, Stephen, Stephanie, Sherri. **Educ:** TX So U, BS 1956; Univ TX Med Sch, MD 1963. **Career:** Harris Co TX pvt practice 1967; Baylor Coll, instr 1967-73. **Orgs:** Mem Harris Co Med Soc; TX & Nat Med Assn; TX & Am Soc Intl Med; Houston Med Forum; life mem Kappa Alpha Psi; Univ of TX Med Br Alumni Assn 1974; TX So Univ Alumni 1975; Trinity Meth Ch; mem MacGregory Pk Civic Club; Big Bro; Cal Farley's Boy's Ranch; Nat Jewish Hosp; diplomate Am Bd Intl Med1970; Nat Bd Med Examiners 1964. **Honors/Awds:** Outstanding Alumnus TX Coll 1974. **Military Serv:** AUS pfc 1963. **Business Addr:** 2000 Crawford #830, Houston, TX 77002.

HUNTER, PATRICK J.
Educator. **Personal:** Born Oct 29, 1929, Elberton, GA; married Mildred R Powell; children: Patrick J Jr, Kim M Brown, Michael A, Jeffrey M. **Educ:** Univ of Bridgeport CT, BA 1958, MS 1959; NY Univ, PhD candidate. **Career:** CT Dept of Social Services, caseworker 1960-62; Birdgeport Inter-Group Council CT, exec dir 1963-66; Community on Training & Employment Stamford CT, exec dir 1966-68; Housatonic Community College, dept chmn 1975-81, prof of psychology, currently. **Orgs:** Rotary Intl Bridgeport CT 1963-66; planning council United Way Greater Bridgeport; board member SW CT Mental Health; pres Southwest Regional Mental Health Bd 1986-87; CT State Mental Health Bd 1987; Greater Bridgeport Catchment Area Council; Greater Bridgeport Regional Mental Health Adv Bd; vice pres Mental Health Social Club Greater Bridgeport Area. **Honors/Awds:** Citizen of Year, Col Charles Young Post 1963; Achievement Award, Radio Station WICC 1963; Outstanding Educator 1972. **Military Serv:** AUS corpl 1952-54; Korean Medal. **Business Addr:** Professor, Chair, Psychology Department, Housatonic Community College, 510 Barnum Ave, Bridgeport, CT 06608.

HUNTER, RICHARD C.
Educational administrator. **Personal:** Born May 4, 1939, Omaha, NE. **Educ:** Univ CA, DEd; San Francisco State Coll, MA; Univ Omaha, BA. **Career:** Berkeley, CA, teacher, asst principal, principal; Richmond, VA, Public Schools, superintendent; Dayton, OH, superintendent; Tokyo, Japan, teacher; Richmond, CA, prin; Seattle, asst dep supvr; Richmond, VA, Bd, assoc supvr; Valentine Mus Dominion Natl Bank; Richmond Chamber of Commerce; St Paul Coll; Univ of North Carolina at Chapel Hill, prof of educational admin; Baltimore City Public Schools, Baltimore, MD, superintendent, currently. **Orgs:** Kiwanis; Kappa Alpha Psi; Phi Delta Kappa. **Honors/Awds:** Good Government Awd, Richmond 1st Club; Honorary Doctorate, Univ of Richmond. **Business Addr:** Superintendent, Baltimore City Public Schools, 200 E North Ave, Baltimore, MD 21202.

HUNTER, ROBERT J.
Association executive. **Personal:** Born Aug 31, 1934, Clarksburg, WV; son of Marie Elizabeth Jackson-Hunter and Robert Joseph Hunter, Sr; children: Robert Edward, Dawn Marie, Robin Denise, Michael Randall. **Educ:** Philadelphia Police Acad, 1963; Univ of PA, Philadelphia Bar Assoc Prog 1966-67; Philadelphia Govt Training Inst Mgmt, 1966-67, Temple Univ Bus Admin, State Cert Bus Administrator 1976. **Career:** Hunters Employ Agency, owner-operator 1958-62; Philadelphia Police Officer, retired; McChatter Talk Mag, founder, editor-publisher 1976; Senate of PA, admin asst 1971-76; Found for Juvenile Decency, exec dir 1980-; Bulletin of the United Supreme Council, editor. **Orgs:** Frat Order of Police Philadelphia #5; founder, dir Committed & Concerned Citizens Council Inc; life mem Volunteers in Aid to Sickle Cell Anemia; past chmn Troop 702 & past chaplain Troop 604 BSA; founder, past pres Mens Brotherhood of St John AME Church; past potentate Shriner, Pyramid Temple #1; exec dir Natl Grand Assembly of Squirrels; Public Information Director United Supreme Council, 33 degree Masons 1989-; Masonic Lodge No 55, past master. **Honors/Awds:** 1 Bravery Awd, 8 Meritorious & Commendatory Citations Philadelphia Police Dept & FBI 1964-69; Disting Serv Awd Scottish Rite 32 & 33 Degree Mason; Meritorious Awd Star in the E Masonic Lodge; Comm Serv Awd PA Grand Lodge of Mason; Mason of the Year 1971; Matl Shriner Awd for Youth Concern & Involvement 1972; Masonic Publ Rel Awd State of PA 1973; PA Senate Candidate 1974; PA House of Rep Candidate 1980; Received Keys to Cities of Houston 1971, Detroit 1973, Newport 1974, Boston 1970; Chapel of Four Chaplains Legion of Honor Awd 1971; Natl Publ Rel & Publicity & Promo Dir Awd, The Imperial Council Shriners 1978-79; WPVI-TV Public Service Awd 1987; Liberty Bell, Mayor, City of Philadelphia PA 1989; Scottish Rite Mason of the Year, Pennsylvania, 1989. **Business Addr:** Executive Dir, Foundation for Juvenile Decency, 827 S 58th St, Philadelphia, PA 19143.

HUNTER, TEOLA P.
Government official. **Personal:** Born Feb 5, 1933, Detroit, MI; daughter of Olivia Johnson; married James Wendell Hunter, Jan 26, 1967; children: Denise Ciccel, Jeffrey, Anthony. **Educ:** University of Detroit, BS, 1958; Wayne State University, MEd, 1971. **Career:** Detroit Public School System, teacher, 1958-72; Buttons and Bows Nurseries and Preparatory Schools, founder, owner, operator, 1971-85; Michigan House of Representatives, member, 1981-82; Pro Tempore, elected speaker, 1989; Wayne County, Health Community Service, deputy director, 1992-93, county clerk, 1993- . **Orgs:** Women's Equity Action League, vice pres; Pi Lamda Theta; Links, Greater Wayne County Chapter; Downriver Community, board of directors; Diversified Youth Services, board of directors; Delta Sigma Theta Sorority; Citizen's Advisory Committee for Wayne County Youth; Children's Aid Society, board member; Aurora, bd of trustees; Omni Care, quality assurance committee, board member; Amer Heat Assn, bd mem; Detroit Urban League, bd of dirs; Michigan Health Care Corp, bd of trustees; NAACP, life mem; Resource Endowment Aiding Children Together with Love, (REACT with Love), founder. **Honors/Awds:** Path Finders Award, Black Students of Oakland University, 1982; Citizen of the Year Award, Detroit Medical Society, 1985; Outstanding Citizen Award, Gentleman of Wall Street, 1985; Black Legislature in Honor of Black History Month, Blue Cross/Blue Shield, 1986; Award of Merit for Outstanding Achievement/ Leadership Development and Community Relations, Core City Neighborhoodcs, Inc, City of Detroit, 1986. **Special Achievements:** First female speaker pro tempore in Michigan; first African American female to be Wayne County Clerk. **Business Addr:** Clerk, County of Wayne, 211 City County Bldg, Detroit, MI 48226.

HUNTER, TONY WAYNE
Professional football player (retired). **Personal:** Born May 22, 1960, Cincinnati, OH. **Educ:** Univ of Notre Dame, BS, economics, 1984. **Career:** Tight end: Buffalo Bills, 1983-84; Los Angeles Rams, 1985-86. **Honors/Awds:** Named to All-Rookie teams, UPI & Pro Football Weekly; won 4 letters for Notre Dame; two-time Playboy All-American, NEA All-American as a senior; selected for the ABC/NCAA college football tour, 1981; consensus All-American; OH Player of the Year, senior year.

UNTER, TRACEY JOEL
brarian. **Personal:** Born Jan 20, 1966, Philadelphia, PA; son ' Osalee Barbara Jenkins and William Hayes; married Kathen Jean Butler, Jul 26, 1992; children: Tracey Joel, Jalaal qil. **Educ:** Lincoln University, BS, philosophy, 1987; Univerty of Pittsburgh, School of Library and Information Science, LS, 1989. **Career:** Macmillian Publisihing Company, sumer intern, 1985; Balch Institute for Ethnic Studies, research/ atalog asst, 1986; University of Pittsburgh, SLIS, library asst,)88, resident asst, 1988; Free Library of Philadelphia, chilen's librarian, 1989-92; Lincoln University, special collecons librarian, 1992; American Library Association, ALA mirity fellow, 1992-. **Orgs:** American Library Association,)90-; Black Caucus American Library Association, 1989-; oncerned Black Men, Inc., National Delegate, 1987-; Pennsylania Citizens for Better Libraries, board member, 1992-; Linln University Alumni Association, vice pres, 1992-93; Iayor's Advisory Committee on Homeless, chairman, 1990-; ree and Accepted Masons, PHA, Hiram #5 Philadelphia,)91-; Groove Phi Groove, 1985-. **Honors/Awds:** International ederation of Library Associate, US Voting Delegate, 1991; 'hite House Conference on Libraries, Honorary Delegate,)91; Philadelphia Mayor's Office, Community Service ward, 1990; Univ of Pittsburgh, State Library Scholarship,)88-89; Lincoln University, W Fales Prize in Philosophy,)87. **Special Achievements:** Storytelling, Chicago Public Lirary, 1993; Lecture, Shepherd Coll, 1992; Lecture, Villanova niversity, 1992; lecture/publication, PA Black Conference on igher Education, 1992; Storytelling, Free Library of Philadelhia, 1991; workshop/lecture, Sixth Annual Virginia Hamilton onference, 1990. **Home Addr:** 2333 N Woodstock St, Philaelphia, PA 19132, (215)223-9666. **Business Addr:** ALA Mirity Fellow, American Library Association, 50 E Huron St, hicago, IL 60611, (312)280-5020.

IUNTER, WILLIAM ANDREW
ducator. **Personal:** Born Sep 6, 1913, N Little Rock, AR; son f Jessie D Hunter and W J C Hunter; married Alma Rose Buress. **Educ:** Dunbar Jr Coll, Little Rock, AR, AA 1933; Wilberrce Univ Wilberforce, OH, BS 1936; Iowa St Univ, Ames, IA, IS 1948, PhD 1952. **Career:** Dunbar Hgh School, Little Rock, R, instrctr Math & Science 1936-42; Tuskegee Inst AL, prof f Educ 1950-57, dean school of Educ 1957-73; AACTE, Vashington, DC, dir of multicltrl rsch project 1973-74; Iowa St niv, dir of rsrch inst for studies in educ 1974-79; Coll of Educ owa St Univ, prof of Educ 1979-83, prof emeritus of Educ, 983-. **Orgs:** Mem Kappa Alpha Psi Frat 1936-; pres Amer ssn of Coll for Tchr Educ 1973-74; Natl Tchr Exam Adv Bd ducational Testing Service 1973-78; consultant IA Dept of ublic Instruction on Human Relations 1975; life mem Tuskeee AL Civic Assn, Natl Educ Assn; mem Phi Delta Kappa, appa Delta Pi; Phi Kappa Phi; chmn, Commission on Chrisan Unity & Interreligious Concerns, North Georgia Confernce of the United Methodist Church, 1995-. **Honors/Awds:** or Outstanding Service to the Teaching Profession Tuskegee 972; Alumni Distinguishd Achievement Award Iowa State niv 1973; Lagomarchino Lauerate Award Coll of Educ Iowa t; author-editor, Multicultural Education Through Competeny-Based Teacher Educ, 1974; coauthor with Liem Nguyen: ducational Systems in Southeast Asia in Comparison with hose in the United States, 1979. **Military Serv:** US Army, ssgt, 942-46; Good Conduct Am, N African, European Theater. **Iome Addr:** 2202 Country Club Ct, Augusta, GA 30904.

IUNTER, WILLIAM L. See Obituaries section.

IUNTER-GAULT, CHARLAYNE
ournalist. **Personal:** married Ronald Gault; children: 2. **Educ:** Jniv of Georgia, graduate. **Career:** The New Yorker, reporter; 'he New York Times, reporter; The MacNeil/Lehrer Jewshour, reporter, natl affairs correspondent, 1978-97. **Honrs/Awds:** Awds include Emmys, journalism awds; 1986 George Foster Peabody Awd for Excellence in Broadcast Jouralism; reported on Apartheid, 1985. **Business Addr:** Correpondent, c/o National Public Radio, 635 Massachusetts Ave W, Washington, DC 20001.

IUNTER-LATTANY, KRISTIN EGGLESTON
Author, educator. **Personal:** Born Sep 12, 1931, Philadelphia, 'A; daughter of Mabel M Eggleston and George L Eggleston; narried John I Lattany Sr. **Educ:** Univ of PA, BS Ed 1951. **Career:** Pittsburgh Courier, columnist & feature writer 1946-52; avenson Bur of Advertising, copywriter 1952-59; Wermen & Schorr Philadelphia, advertising copywriter 1961-62; Univ of 'A Sch of Soc Work, research asst 1962; City of Philadelphia, nfo officer 1963-65; freelance writer, novels, journalism, fiction 1963-; Univ of PA, sr lecturer English 1972-. **Orgs:** Dir Walt Whitman Poetry Ctr 1977-79; mem Alpha Kappa Alpha, Modern Lang Assoc, PEN, Natl Council of Teachers of English, Authors Guild, NAACP; chair, fiction bd, Shooting Star Review, Pittsburgh PA 1989-. **Honors/Awds:** Books, "God Bless he Child" 1964; "The Landlord" 1966; "The Soul Brothers and Sister Lou" 1968; "Boss Cat" 1971; "Guests in the Promsed Land" 1973; "The Survivors" 1975; "The Lakestown Rebellion" 1978; "Lou in the Limelight" 1981; television, "Minority of One" CBS TV 1965; Fund for the Republic TV Documentary prize1955; John Hay Whitney Oppty Fellowship 1959-60; Philadelphia Athenaeum Literary Awd 1964; Bread Loaf Writers Conf Fellowship 1965; Council on Interracial Books for Children Prize 1968; Sigma Delta Chi Best Mag Reporting Awd 1969; Univ of WI Childrens Book Conf Cheshire Cat Seal 1970; Silver Slate-Pencil & Dolle Mina Awds The Netherlands 1973; Chicago Tribune Book World Prize 1973; Christopher Awd 1974; Natl Book Awd Nom 1974; Drexel Univ Childrens Lit Award 1981; NJ StateCcil on the Arts Prose Fellowship 1981-82, 1985-86. **Business Addr:** Senior Lecturer, University of Pennsylvania, 119 Bennett Hall, English Department, Philadelphia, PA 19104-6273.

HUNTLEY, LYNN JONES
Attorney. **Personal:** Born in Fort Lee, VA; daughter of Mary Ellen Jones and Lawrence N Jones. **Educ:** Attended Fisk Univ 1963-65; Barnard Coll, AB Sociology 1967; Columbia Univ School of Law, JD 1970. **Career:** Bernard Baruch Coll, teaching asst 1969-70; Judge Motley US Dist Ct NY, law clerk 1970-71; NAACP Legal Defense & Educ Fund Inc, asst counsel 1971-73; New York City Comm on Human Rights, general counsel 1973-75; NAACP Legal Defense Fund Inc, asst counsel 1975-78; Civil Rights Div US Dept of Justice, chief special litigation section 1978-81; Civil Rights Div US Dept of Justice, deputy asst atty general 1981-82; The Ford Foundation, program officer 1982-87; deputy director in charge human rights and social justice program 1987-91; Rights & Social Justice Program, dir, 1991-. **Orgs:** Mem Natl Bar Assn; admitted to Bar for US Dist Ct for So Dist of NY; US States Ct of Appeals for 2nd & 5th circuits; mem NY State Bar; former chair Fed Women's Program Advisory Comm at US Dept of Justice; former mem Black Affairs Program Advisory Comm; former mem bd of dirs Sheltering Arms Children's Svc; mem NAACP; former columnist Essence Magazine; former mem NY State Sentencing Guidelines Comm; former sec Black Amer Law Students Assn; former mem Columbia Law Review; former bd mem The Legal Aid Soc; mem, NYS Govenors Advisory Committee on Black Affairs; Barnard Coll, bd of trustees. **Honors/Awds:** First Black Woman on Columbia Law Review; Speciall Commendation Award at the US Dept of Justice; Sr Exec Serv Outstanding Performance Award & bonus at the US Dept of Justice; Outstanding Performance rating at the Ford Found. **Business Addr:** Dir, Rights & Social Justice Program, The Ford Foundation, 320 E 43rd St, New York, NY 10017.

HUNTLEY, RICHARD FRANK
Educator. **Personal:** Born Jan 25, 1926, Masury, OH; married Edith Marie Robinson; children: Dean, Lynn, Geoffrey, Steven, Donna Jean. **Educ:** Youngstown State U, BA; Univ Akron, MA. **Career:** City Youngstown, chief draftsman 1964-65; Youngstown Planning Comm, research asst 1966-70, asso planner 1970-71; Youngstown Demonstration Agency, sr planner1971; Youngstown State U, instr 1971-72; Youngstown Vindicator, dir comm relations 1972-74; Youngstown State U, instr 1974-. **Orgs:** Chmn bd Buckeye Elks Youth Devel Ctr; bd mem Mental Health & Mental Retardation; Soc for Blind; Buckeye Review Publ Co; mem Mahoning County Selective Serv Bd; Vet Foreign Wars; Elks Lodge #73; Masons F & Am; Am; Soc Planning Officials; Mayors Citizen Adv Com; dirs McGuffey Comm Ctr Bd; NAACP. **Military Serv:** AUS 1944-45; USAF 1945-48. **Business Addr:** 1098 Genessee Dr, Youngstown, OH 44511.

HURD, DAVID JAMES, JR.
Educator, musician. **Personal:** Born Jan 27, 1950, Brooklyn, NY. **Educ:** Juilliard School, attended 1959-67; Oberlin Coll, BMus 1967-71; Univ of NC Chapel Hill, attended 1972. **Career:** Trinity Parish, asst organist 1971-72; Duke Univ , asst dir choral activities, asst chapel organist 1972-73; Church of the Intercession NYC, organist & music dir 1973-79; Yale Inst of Sacred Music visiting lecturer 1982-83; commissions from various institutions, organizations & persons; composer; General Theological Seminary, prof of church music, organist 1979-; The Manhattan School of Music organ faculty 1984-; All Saints Church music director 1985-. **Orgs:** vice chairman The Standing Commission on Church Music (Episcopal) 1976-85; concert organist Phillip Trucken Brod Artist Rep 1977-; New York City Chap American Guild of Organists 1966-; Theta Chap Pi Kappa Lambda 1971-; aristic adv committee Boys Choir of Harlem 1978-; Assn of Anglican Musicians 1979-; Liturgical Committee Episcopal Diocese of NY 1982. **Honors/Awds:** First Prize in Organ Playing Intl Congress of Organists 1977; First Prize in Organ Improvisation Intl Congress of Organists Philadelphia 1977; organ recitalist AGO Biennial Natl Convention Minneapolis 1980; diploma in improvision Stichting Intl Orgelconcours Goud The Netherlands 1981; organ recitalist AGO Biennial Natl Conv 1986. **Business Addr:** Professor of Church Music, General Theological Seminary, 175 9th Ave, New York, NY 10011.

HURD, JAMES L. P.
Musician, educator. **Personal:** Born Aug 2, 1945, Bonham, TX. **Educ:** Washburn U, Mus B(hon), 1967; Am Conservatory of Music, MusM, 1968; Univ of So CA, MusD, 1973. **Career:** Calvary Bapt Ch Topeka, KS, organist dir 1962-69; Cultural Arts Div Topeka Recreation Comm, head of music 1965-67; Protestant Chapel KS Boys Sch Topeka, organist choir dir 1964-67, 1968-69; Lawndale Presb Ch Chgo, choir dir 1967-68; Blessed Sacrament Cath Ch Chicago, IL, organist 1967-68; Ward AME Ch LA, CA, organist dir 1969-73; Orgn & Mgmt Analyst State Hwy, Commn KS, 1969-70; El Camino Clg, organ instr, prof of music 1971-; First Presb Ch Inglewood, organist, dir of music, 1973-96; Long Beach City Clg, organ instr 1973; CA State Univ-Dominguez Hills, CA State Univ Long Beach, organ prof, currently; St Andrews Presb Ch of Redondo Beach CA, organist, dir of music, currently. **Orgs:** Mem Am Guild of Organists; Kappa Alpha Psi; Phi Mu Alpha; Adjuicator Music Tchrs Assc of CA. **Honors/Awds:** Listed in US Jaycees Outstanding Young Men of Amer 1980; Visiting Scholar, Position in Music, UCLA, 1988; City of Los Angeles Mayor's Certificate of Appreciation, Music Contributions to the Community. **Special Achievements:** Numerous Organ concerts throughout KS, IL, CA, and Austria. **Business Addr:** Professor of Music, El Camino College, 16007 Crenshaw Blvd, Torrance, CA 90506, (310)660-3701.

HURD, JOSEPH KINDALL, JR.
Surgeon. **Personal:** Born Feb 12, 1938, Hoisington, KS; son of Mildred Mae Ramsey Hurd and Joseph Kindall Hurd Sr; married Jean Elizabeth Challenger Hurd, Jun 20, 1964; children: Joseph Kindall III, Jason Hansen. **Educ:** Harvard Coll, AB (magna cum), 1960; Harvard Med Sch, MD, 1964. **Career:** Harvard Med School, clinical instr of surgery, 1972-; Lahey Clinic Found, gynecologist, 1972-, chm, dept of gynecology, 1988-; chairman, Council of Department Chairmen, 1991-; Tufts Medical School, asst clinical prof, ob/gyn, 1996-. **Orgs:** Treas 1979-84, pres 1986-87 Obstetrical Soc of Boston; pres New England Med Soc 1980; bd dir Freedom House Inc, Crispus Attucks Day Care Ctr, Roxbury Med Dntl Grp; adv comm, exec comm, vice-chairman, chairman, MA Section Amer Coll of Ob/Gyn, 1993-96; Amer Fertility Soc, Charles River Med Soc, AMA, NMA; councilor MA Med Soc; Amer Uro-Gynecologic Soc, Amer Assn Gynecologic Laporoscopy; Alpha Chap, Phi Beta Kappa; Iota Chi Chap, Omega Psi Phi; Beta Beta Boule, Sigma Pi Phi Fraternity; bd of governors, bd of trustees, Lahey Clinic 1977-91; finance & executive comm, Lahey Clinic 1987-90; councillor, 1990-93, dir, 1990-93, Harvard Medical Alumni Assn. **Honors/Awds:** Spencer B Lewis Award, Coleus Soc, Harvard Medical Sch, 1990. **Military Serv:** US Army, major, 1970-72; Army commendation medal, 1972. **Home Addr:** 18 Emerson Rd, Wellesley, MA 02181-3419. **Business Addr:** Chmn, Dept of Gynecology, Lahey Clinic Medical Ctr, 41 Mall Rd, Burlington, MA 01805.

HURD, WILLIAM CHARLES
Physician, ophthalmologist. **Personal:** Born May 17, 1947, Memphis, TN; son of Doris Hurd and Leon Hurd (deceased); married Rhynette Northcross; children: Bill Jr, Ryan. **Educ:** Univ of Notre Dame, BS 1969; MIT, MS 1972; Meharry Medical Coll, MD 1980. **Career:** General Electric Corp, systems engr 1969-70; TN State Univ, asst prof 1972-76; Univ of TN, intern 1980-81, resident physician 1982-85; Memphis Health Ctr, medical consultant 1981; Memphis Emergency Specialists, consulting physician 1982-84; Methodist Hospital, staff physician 1985-; Private Practice, physician. **Orgs:** Bd dirs Visiting Nurse Assoc 1985-. **Honors/Awds:** Former All American Track Athlete at Nortre Dame 1697-69; Notre Dame Univ Athlete of the Year 1968; former World Record Holder at 300 yd Dash Indoors 1968-72; Rhodes Scholar Semi Finalist 1969; Prof Musician & Winner at serveral Natl Jazz Festival Competition; Hold US Patent on a Medical Instrument; NCAA, Silver Anniversary Award, 1994. **Special Achievements:** Semi Annual Medical Mission trips to Mexico, Brazil, Senegal, and Africa. **Business Addr:** Physician/Opthalmologist, 1211 Union Ave, Ste 495, Memphis, TN 38104.

HURDLE, HORTENSE O. MCNEIL
Educational administrator (retired). **Personal:** Born May 20, 1925, Marlin, TX; daughter of Annie Mae Williams McNeil-Wade and Leroy McNeil; married Clarence Hurdle, Jan 15, 1949; children: Clarence II, Gaile Evonne. **Educ:** Prairie View U, BS 1947; Sacto State U, MA 1973; Sacramento State U, MS 1974. **Career:** Federal Govt, employee 1947-57; elementary teacher vice pres 1957-64; Compensatory Educ, dir 1964-68; Del Paso & Heights School Dist, elementary school prin, 1968-86 (retired). **Orgs:** Co-founder, Concerned Citizens of Greater Sacramento, 1976; mem Sacto Iota Phi Lambda Sor; CA Adminstr Assc CTA; Ed Young Child; Natl Alliance Black Edctrs; Sacto Black Edctrs; Wmn Div Dem Wmn; NAACP; mem Phi Beta Delta Frat; XI Field Chpt; Negro Cncl Wmn; Les Belles Artes Club, 1985-90; trustee, chairman of the board, Shiloh Baptist Church; assistant regional director, FWR Iota Phi Lambda Sorority, 1989-93. **Honors/Awds:** Distinguished Community Service Award, Sacramento Chamber of Commerce, 1967; B'nai B'rith Outst Awrd Serv 1966; resolution 53 Assembly Dist & Progessive 12 1970; outst soror of the Far Western Reg of Iota Phi Lambda Sorority 1980; Outstanding Service Award, Western Region, National Alliance of Black School Educators, 1991; Outstanding Service Award, Beta Tau Chap of Iota Phi Lambda, 1989. **Home Addr:** 1370 40th Ave, Sacramento, CA 95822.

HURLEY, JAMES EDWARD, JR.
Attorney. **Personal:** Born May 2, 1952, Cincinnati, OH; son of Myrtle Hurley and James E Hurley Sr; married Dawne Mann,

Oct 1, 1977; children: Morgan L. **Educ:** Morehouse College, Atlanta, GA, BA, 1974; St Xavier Graduate School of Business, Cincinnati, OH, MBA, 1978; Rutgers School of Law, Newark, NJ, JD, 1981. **Career:** Mobil Oil Corp, New York, NY, negotiator, multi-national oil and gas acquisitions, 1981-85; United States Dept of Justice, Office of the United States Trustee, southern district, New York, NY, counsel to the US trustee, 1983-86; Sherman, Citron & Karasik PC, New York, NY, bankruptcy atty, 1986; Rattet & Liebman, New York, NY, bankruptcy atty, 1987-90; Minter & Gay, New York, NY, bankruptcy and commercial litigation atty, 1990-. **Orgs:** Member, 100 Black Men, Inc, New York, 1989-; member, Bankruptcy Bar, New York, 1987-; chairperson, bankruptcy committee, Metropolitan Black Bar Assn, 1985-; member, Assn of the Bar of the City of New York, 1986-; member, Morehouse College Alumni Assn, 1986-; board member, Northern Manhattan Perinatal Group, 1989-. **Honors/Awds:** Phi Beta Kappa, Morehouse College, 1979; Attorney of the Year, Westchester Minority Chamber of Commerce, 1989.

HURSEY, JAMES SAMUEL
Educator (retired). **Personal:** Born May 9, 1931, Bridgeton, NJ; married Joyce Langston Washington; children: Joni Hursey-Young, Jennifer Elizabeth. **Educ:** Glassboro State Coll, BS; VA State Coll, 1955. **Career:** Bridgeton Housing Authority, commiss 1958-84; Bridgeton City Council, councilman 1982-85; Bd of Dir Child Devel Ctr, mem 1984-94; Bridgeton School System, teacher, until 1994; Cumberland Co Utilities Auth, 1985-1990. **Orgs:** Mem NAACP, Natl Black Caucus, NJ Assoc Black Elected Officials; sec Hur-Ed Inc; chmn of bd Cedar Hill Mem Park 1980; past mem bd dir YMCA. **Military Serv:** USN 1955-58. **Home Addr:** 31 Burt St, Bridgeton, NJ 08302.

HURST, BEVERLY J.
Association executive. **Personal:** Born Jan 16, 1933, Oberlin, OH; married Dr Charles G Hurst Jr; children: Chaverly Kikanza. **Educ:** Howard Univ, BA 1963, MA 1968. **Career:** Genl Acctg Office Washington, sec 1951-56; Crile VA Hosp, med sec 1956-61; Howard Univ, admin asst 1963-64, rsch asst 1964-67; DC Dept of Pub Health, rsch & training specialist 1967-68; New Careers Proj TRD, remedial educ supr 1968-69; Model Cities Tchr Aide Proj Kennedy-King Coll, coord 1969-70; IL Inst for Social Policy, eval analyst 1970-71; Chicago Urban League, rsch dir 1972-76; Comm Serv Admin, prog analyst 1980-82; US Railroad Retirement Bd,equal employment specialist 1982-84; US Corps of Engrs, equal employment oppor mgr 1984-. **Orgs:** Author of various articles papers & reports for professional journals; consult Youth Group Homes Proj DC Dept of Pub Welfare; comm splst Washington Concentrated Employment Proj United Planning Orgn; rsch consult Georgetown Univ Inst for Urban Serv Aides; AL Nellum & Assoc; consult to various other firms & assns; mem Amer Sociol Assn; Amer Acad of Polit & Social Sci. **Business Addr:** EEO Manager, US Corps of Engineers, 4500 S Michigan Ave, Chicago, IL 60653.

HURST, CLEVELAND, III
Educator, counselor, educational consultant. **Personal:** Born Sep 13, 1939, Montgomery, AL; son of Polly A Jackson Hurst and Cleveland Hurst Jr; married Jurlene Parker, Mar 25, 1978; children: Lonnie, Cleveland IV. **Educ:** Wayne State Univ, BS 1961, MA 1971. **Career:** Univ of Michigan, administrator, 1962-64; bowling instructor, 1969-; Oakland University, Rochester, MI, university administration, 1971-87; Detroit Board of Education, Detroit, MI, department head, 1987-; Calhoun Enterprise Inc, Montgomery, AL, consultant, 1989-. **Orgs:** Reg basketball ofcl; mem Amer & Michigan Prsnl & Guid Assc; Univ Michigan Clb Gr Detroit; Natl Assc Vet Program & Admnstr; Detroit School Assc; Detroit Math Club; exec bd & rec sec Cntr Educ Returning Vets; pres bd of dirs, Virginia Park Comm Investment Assoc, Inc (2.1 mill assets); sec bd of dirs, Wayne State Univ Black Medical Assoc Schlarship Fund; board of directors, Wayne State Univ Black Medical Assn; president, Virginia Park Community Investment Assn. **Business Addr:** Consultant, Calhoun Enterprise Inc, 19785 West 12 Mile Rd, Ste 628, Southfield, MI 48076.

HURST, ROBERT
Musician. **Career:** "The Tonight Show," musician, currently. **Business Addr:** Jazz Musician, "The Tonight Show", NBC-TV, c/o Jill Trenhurst, 3000 W Alameda Ave, Burbank, CA 91523, (818)222-0120.

HURST, RODNEY LAWRENCE
City councilman. **Personal:** Born Mar 2, 1944, Jacksonville, FL; married Ann; children: Rodney II, Todd. **Educ:** FL Jr Clg; Edward Waters Clg. **Career:** Self Employed, ins slsm 1975-; City of Jacksonville, proj dir 1973-75; Greater Jacksonville Ec Opportunity, proj dir 1971-73. **Orgs:** Co-host "Feedback" WJCT-TV 1969-71; ins & underwriter Prudential 1965-69; mem Welfare & Soc Serv Plcy Steering Com; mem of the Natl Assc of Co; mem Jacksonville Cncl on Cit Invlm; mem City Cncl Fin & Rules Com; mem Cable TV Com; chmn Agr & Rec Com; mem NAACP; mem Urban Lea; bd mem Boy's Clb; advsr Ribault Sr HS; mem Consortium to Aid Neglected & Abused Children. **Honors/Awds:** Man of yr Jacksonville Clb 1960; Flwshp grnt Corp for Pub Brdcstg 1969-70. **Military Serv:** USAF a/2c 1961-65. **Business Addr:** 220 East Bay St City Hall, Jacksonville, FL 32202.

HURT, JAMES E.
Business executive. **Personal:** Born Sep 29, 1928, Chicago; married Suellen Gleason. **Educ:** Am Inst Banking, Cert; Chicago State U, Presently Attending. **Career:** Drexel Natl Bank, vp, teller bkkpr field rep asst vice pres 1958-75; Inner-City Dev Corp, chmn bd. **Orgs:** Mem chmn adv bd Chicago Economic Devel Corp; bd Small & Bus Investment Corp; bd S End Jr C of C; Am Inst Banking; bd Untied Negro Clg Fund; Bus & Professional Men's Clb; adv bd Malcolm X Clg; adv bd Whitney Young Sch Bus; Urban Legue; YWCA. **Honors/Awds:** One of 10 outst young men Chicago; awrd US Smal Bus Admn; cert Merit Chicago Pub Schs 1967; Color Inc; Century Clb YMCA; outst serv awrd WBEE Radio; comm serv awrd 1971. **Business Addr:** Drexel Nat Bank, 3401 S Dr ML King Jr Dr, Chicago, IL 60616.

HURT, PATRICIA
Attorney. **Career:** Essex County, deputy administrator, prosecutor, currently. **Special Achievements:** First African American and first woman to serve as prosecutor in Essex County. **Business Addr:** Prosecutor, Essex County Prosecutor's Office, New Courts Bldg, 50 W Market St, Newark, NJ 07102, (973)621-4750.

HURTE, LEROY E.
Symphony conductor. **Personal:** Born May 2, 1915, Muskogee, OK; son of Dora Grayson Hurte and Charles Hurte; married Hazel. **Educ:** Los Angeles City Clg; Juilliard Sch of Music; Tanglewood Music Workshop; Fresno State Clg; Victor Valley College. **Career:** Symphony Orch Inglewood Philharmonic Assc, condr; Angel City Symphony Orch, fdr-condr; Los Angeles Comm Symphony; guest condr; CA Jr Sympnony; Kings Co & Symphony; Fresno Philharmonic; Hanford Choral Soc, choral condr Tamarind Ave SDA Ch. **Orgs:** Rotary Club, president, 1985-86; National Association of Negro Musicians. **Honors/Awds:** Achvmnt award Natl Assn of Media Women Inc 1973-74; commendation City of LA; commendation for Conducting Co of LA; Proclamation honoring Inglewood Symphony Orch, Inglewood, CA, 1985; Los Angeles Philharmonic Orchestra, Guest Conductor; Rotary Club, Paul Harris Fellow; Phi Theta Kappa. **Special Achievements:** Editor, publisher, Lyric Magazine, author of 3 books. **Business Addr:** Symphony Conductor, PO Box 1945, Apple Valley, CA 92307.

HUSKEY, BUTCH (ROBERT LEON)
Professional baseball player. **Personal:** Born Nov 10, 1971, Andarko, OK. **Career:** New York Mets, infielder, 1993, 1995-. **Business Addr:** Professional Baseball Player, New York Mets, 126th St and Roosevelt Ave, Shea Stadium, Flushing, NY 11368, (718)507-6307.

HUSSEIN, CARLESSIA AMANDA
Health services administrator. **Personal:** Born Sep 1, 1936, Baltimore, MD; daughter of Amanda Minor and Nathan Minor; children: Monica. **Educ:** Freedmen's Hosp School of Nursing, RN degree 1957; Univ of CA, San Francisco, BS Nursing 1966, MS Nursing 1967; Univ of CA, Berkeley, Dr of Public Health 1977. **Career:** Univ of CA-School of Public Health, associate dean 1971-73; Univ of CA-Epidemiology Dept, research dir 1974-77; Santa Clara County Health Planning Agency, executive dir 1977-80; LA County Health Planning Agency, executive dir 1980-83; LA County Fire Department, deputy health dir 1983-84; State Health Planning & Development Agency, dir 1984-88, deputy commissioner of public health, 1988-; District of Columbia Government, deputy commissioner of public health, 1989-91, chief, health planning & policy development, 1991-. **Orgs:** National Black Nurses Association; NAACP; cofounder Bay Area Black Nurses Assn 1969; consultant Rural Health Project-Ecuador 1973; member CA Governor's Task Force on Cost Containment 1982; chair-planning committee Children's Home Society 1982-84; technical advisor LA Voluntary Health Planning Council 1983-83; founder LA County Black Female Manager's Assn 1984; mem Amer Health Planning Assn 1985; mem, John Hopkins Child Survival International Health Board of Directors. **Honors/Awds:** Outstanding service Board of Supervisors-Santa Clara County 1980; recognition Board of Supervisors-Los Angeles 1984. **Business Addr:** Chief, Health Planning & Policy Development, Commission of Public Health, DC Government, 1660 L Street NW 11th floor, Washington, DC 20036.

HUTCHERSON, BERNICE B. R.
Educator. **Personal:** Born Apr 14, 1925, Newton, KS; married Hubert W; children: Pamela Dineen, Karla Michelle. **Educ:** Lanston Univ, BA 1950; Chicago Teachers Coll, 1952; Univ of KS, MSW 1969; Univ of Chicago, 1973. **Career:** Wichita State Univ, asst pross of soc work 1973; social worker 1954-72; Chicago, tchr 1950-54. **Orgs:** Pres KS co Social Workers Assn; Wichita Area Comm Action Program Inc; KS Conf on Social Welfare; mem Sedgwick Co; KS Mental Health Assn Boards; Sr Citizens Board; Nat Conf on Social Welfare; Am Pub Welfare Assn; Am Assn of Univ prof; charter mem Wichita OIC Board; mem Acadeny of Certified Social Workers; Suicide Prevention Service Counselor; past pres Youth Dept Calvary Baptist Church; Wichita Alumnea Delta Sigma Theta Inc; Matron KF Valley #97 OES; mem Nat Council of Negro Women; NAACP; professional adv com Family Planning Whichita Health Dept; KS Office of Minority Business Enterprises; bd educ #259 Professional Speakers Bureau. **Honors/Awds:** Phi Kappa Phi; Honorary Citation & Wichita Comm Planning Council. **Business Addr:** Box 25, Wichita, KS 67208.

HUTCHINS, FRANCIS L., JR.
Physician, educator. **Personal:** Born Jul 8, 1943, Ridley Park, PA; son of Mercedes Hutchins and Francis L. Hutchins; married Sandra; children: Keisha, Francis L. **Educ:** Duquesne University, BS 1965; Howard U, MD 1969; Lankenau Hosp, intern 1969-70; Ob-Gyn, resident 1970-73. **Career:** Temple University Hospital, Dept of Obstetrics & Gynecology, asst professor & dir of Family Planning, 1975-77; Thomas Jefferson University, Dept of Obstetrics & Gynecology, asst professor, 1977-81; Lankenau Hospital, Dept of Obstetrics & Gynecology, dir of research & education and dir of family planning, 1977-81; Commonwealth of Pennsylvania, Dept of Health, consultant in obstetrics, gynecology, and family planning for adolescents, 1980; Hahnemann University, Dept of Obstetrics & Gynecology, asst professor, 1981-84, director of family planning, director of ambulatory affairs and community medicine, 1981-84, director of Maternal/Infant Care Project, director, Division of Obstetrics, 1983-84, Department of Obstetrics, acting chairman, 1984, associate professor of clinical obstetrics and gynecology, 1984-85, clinical associate president, 1985; Booth Maternity Center, medical director, 1985; Plan Parenthood of Pennsylvania, medical director, 1985; City of Philadelphia, Department of Maternal and Child Health, medical director, 1985; Thomas Jefferson Medical College, clinical associate professor of ob-gyn, 1991; The Graduate Hospital, director of gynecology and women's services, 1992; private practice, currently. **Orgs:** Natl Medical Assn, 1973-; Obstetric Soc of Philadelphia, 1973-; American College of Obstetricians/Gynecologists, fellow, 1976; American Soc for Colposcopy and Colpamicroscopy, 1977-; Philadelphia College of Surgeons, 1978-; American Fertility Soc, 1989-; American Assn of Gynecologic Laparoscopists, 1987-; Marriage Council of Philadelphia, board of directors, 1991; Family Planning Council of SE Pennsylvania, board of directors, 1992. **Honors/Awds:** Author: "Developments in Contraceptive Prescribing Family Planning," Philadelphia Medicine, April 1979; "Outcome of Teenage Pregnancies," Medical Aspects of Human Sexuality, January 1980; "Adolescent Pregnancy Among Black Philadelphia," Urban League of Philadelphia, February 1981; "Uterine Fibroids Current Concepts and Management," The Female Patient, Oct 1990; "Myomectomy after Selective Preoperative Treatment with a Gonadotropin-Releasing Hormone Analog," The Journal of Reproductive Medicine, vol 37, number 8, Aug 1992; producer of video tape, Diabetes and Pregnancy, Clinical Issues in Female Patient, series 127, tape 12703, 1983; contributing editor: Federation Licensing Examination, McGraw-Hill, 1986; Pre-Test Foreign Medical Graduate Examination In Medical Science, McGraw-Hill, 1987. **Military Serv:** US Navy, Lt Cmdr, 1973-75. **Business Addr:** Physician, 1 Bala Ave, Ste 120, City Line & Bala Avenues, Bala Cynwyd, PA 19004.

HUTCHINS, JAN DARWIN
Businessman. **Personal:** Born Feb 11, 1949, Danville, IL; married Teri A Hope. **Educ:** Yale Coll, BA 1971. **Career:** KRON-TV, sports dir; KPIX-TV Westinghouse, sports, anchor/reposter 1974-80; WIIC-TV Cox Broadcasting, sports reporter 1972-74; AT&T Long Lines, sales supr 1971-72; SF Giants Baseball, pr dir, 1993-94; Golf Pro Intl, dir of communications, currently. **Orgs:** Mem Health & Wisdom. **Honors/Awds:** Los Gatos Town Council.

HUTCHINS, JOSHUA I., JR.
Clergyman. **Personal:** Born Apr 6, 1937, Huntingtown, MD; son of Lillian Victoria Brown and Joshua James Hutchins; married Gloria Walker Hutchins, Jun 30, 1962; children: Patricia, Tina, Joshua III. **Educ:** St Paul's College, Lawrenceville, VA, BS, 1958; ITC, Atlanta, GA, Master of Divinity, 1962; New York Theological Seminary, New York, NY, Doctor of Ministry, 1981. **Career:** Trinity UM Church, pastor, 1962-64; Lutherville-Greenspring Charge, pastor, 1964-67; Douglas UM Church, Washington, DC, pastor, 1967-73; Asbury UM Church, Annapolis, MD, pastor, 1973-79; Baltimore Annual Conference, district superintendent, 1979-84; Asbury UM Church, Washington, DC, pastor, 1984-. **Orgs:** Mem, Alpha Phi Alpha Fraternity, 1956-; bd of dir, Sibley Hospital, 1979-84; bd of governors, Wesley Seminary, 19775-85; life mem, NAACP; mem, Urban League, 1968-81; founder, OIC, 1975-79. **Honors/Awds:** Man of the Year, Governor-State of Maryland, 1978; Outstanding Participation, NAACP; Numerous Church Awards. **Business Addr:** Pastor, Asbury United Methodist Church, 926 11th St, NW, Washington, DC 20001-4488.

HUTCHINS, LAWRENCE G., SR.
Association executive. **Personal:** Born Sep 13, 1931, Danville, VA; son of Alfrezia Mimms Hutchins (deceased) and James E Hutchins Sr (deceased); married Rebbie Jacobs Hutchins, Jun 14, 1952; children: Karen H Watts, Lawrence Jr, Gary, Gerald. **Educ:** VA State Coll, Petersburg, VA, 1954-56; VCU, Richmond, VA, 1972-74. **Career:** Natl Assn of Letter Carriers, exec vice pres #496, 1962-69; pres of Richmond Branch #496, 1969-78; pres of VA State Assn, 1970-78; asst natl business agent, 1978-82; natl business agent, 1982-87; vice pres, 1987-. **Orgs:**

Pres, Richmond Branch A Philip Randolph Institute; chmn of constitution comm, Crusade for Voters, Richmond; co-fndr, Black Metro Little League, Richmond; trustee, Second Baptist Church, South Richmond; advisory bd, United Way; co-chair, Richmond Chapter MDA. **Military Serv:** Army, cpl, 1952-54. **Business Addr:** Vice President, National Association of Letter Carriers, AFL-CIO, 100 Indiana Ave, NW, Washington, DC 20001.

HUTCHINSON, CARELL, JR.
Physician, surgeon. **Personal:** Born Sep 21, 1930, Chicago, IL; son of Cleverless Woods Hutchinson and Carell Hutchinson Sr; married Gayle Goss Hutchinson, Jun 25, 1981; children: Carell III, Collette Tinu, Chauara Tayo, Chaka Toure, Jonathan Carell. **Educ:** Roosevelt U, BS 1958; Howard Univ Coll of Med, MD 1964. **Career:** Self-employed orthopaedic surgeon, 1969-79; Stateville Penitentiary, Joliet, IL, physician specialist, 1979-81; Tinley Park Mental Health Center, physician, 1981-85; Illinois Department of Mental Health, medical staff president, 1985-. **Orgs:** Chmn Polit Action Com Cook Co Phys Assn; Ins Mediation Com Chicago Med Soc; mem Peer Review Com Chicago Med Soc; IL St Adv Com on Pub Aid; 3yr appointment as alternate couns at large of Counc of Chicago Med Soc; chmn Med Com; mem Nat Bd of Dir John Howard Assn (Prison reform grp); orthopaedic consult Children's Hosp; member, Illinois Alcohol and Drug Dependency Association. **Honors/Awds:** Outstndg Young Dem of Yr 1959; first prize winner Orthopaedic Resrch Paper Competition 1968; Honorary Doctor of Metaphysical Law, Alpha and Omega School of Christian-Spiritual Education, 1979.

HUTCHINSON, CHESTER R.
Business executive. **Personal:** Born Mar 6, 1950, Birmingham, AL; married Lorraine Green; children: Treasure Genea, Reginald Chester. **Educ:** Univ of Santa Clara, BS Bus 1972. **Career:** Univ of Santa Clara, asst dir housing 1971-72; Kelloggs Sales Co, territorial mgr 1972-74; Fairchild Camera & Instr, employee relations spec 1974-76; Crocker Natl Bank, employment mgr 1976-78; Paul Masson Vineyards, mgr labor relations recruitment & safety 1978-81, asst dir of human resources 1981-83; Joseph E Seagram & Sons Inc, dir human resources. **Orgs:** Pres Vintner Employers Assoc 1978-85; vice pres Winery Employers Assoc 1980-84; trustee CA Winery Workers Pension Plan Trust 1980-85; bd of trustees RFK Farm Workers Med Plan 1980-85, Juan De La Cruz Farm Workers Pension Plan 1980-85.

HUTCHINSON, EARL OFARI
Author. **Personal:** Born Oct 8, 1945, Chicago, IL; son of Nina and Earl Hutchinson; married Barbara, Mar 5, 1988; children: Sikivu, Fanon. **Educ:** California State Univ, Los Angeles, BA, 1969, Dominguez Hills, MA, 1990; Pacific Western Univ, PhD, 1992. **Career:** Author, currently. **Orgs:** The Writers Guild. **Honors/Awds:** The Gustavus Myers Award; For the Assassination of the ___, Outstanding Book Award, 1995; Natl Black Journalist Award, Excellence for a Published Commentary, 1st Place; Blacks and Reds: Race and Class Confilct 1919-1990, 1995; Betrayed: History of Presidential Failure to Protect Black Lives, 1996; Beyond OJ: Race, Sex, and Class Lessons for America, 1996; The Crisis in Black and Black, 1998. **Special Achievements:** The Myth of Black Capitalism, 1970; The Mugging of Black America, 1990; Black Fatherhood I, 1992, vol II, 1993; The Assassination of the Black Male Image, 1994. **Business Addr:** Author/Jouralist, Middle Passage Press, 5517 Secrest Dr., Los Angeles, CA 90043.

HUTCHINSON, GEORGE
Educational administrator. **Personal:** Born Dec 19, 1938, Albuquerque, NM; son of Leona Hutchinson and John Hutchinson; married Gwen Pierce. **Educ:** California State Univ Los Angeles, BS 1969, MS 1971; United States International Univ, PhD 1977; National University, San Diego, California, Post Doctoral Law 1988. **Career:** California State Univ, assoc dean educ support serv 1986-; San Diego State Univ, asst prof dept of recreation 1973-79, asst dean 1974-77 assoc dean 1978-81 college of professional studies and fine arts, assoc prof dept of recreation 1979-, dir student outreach serv dir 1981-. **Orgs:** Mem Advisory Council for Minority Officer Recruiting US Navy 1977-; mem at large Industry Educ Council Greater San Diego 1980-; mem Phi Kappa Phi; mem bd dirs Amer Cancer Society 1984-; mem Athletic Adv Comm 1985-; mem Senate Comm Minority; mem CA Academic Partnership Program 1985-; mem Naval Reserve Officers Assn, Navy League of the US; member, San Diego Chapter, Urban League; member, State Bar of California, 1988-; president, Boy Scouts of America Explorers Division, 1988-. **Honors/Awds:** Honorary Mem US Navy ROTC Selection Bd Chief of Naval Opers Washington DC 1979-82; Distinguished Alumna San Diego Comm Leadership Develop 1980; Honorary Member Phi Kappa Phi San Diego State Univ 1980-86; 11 publications including "Trends Affecting Black Recreators in the Professional Society," California Parks and Recreation Society Magazine 1981; Role of Higher Educ in Educational Reform of Adolescents 1988; Meeting the Challenge of Technology 1988; Letter of Commendation, Mayor, City of San Diego, 1989; Proclamation, Board of Supervisors, 1990; Resolution, Assemblyman Chacon 75th District, 1990; San Diego Urban League, Letter of Commendation, 1991; National Black Child Dev Inc, Certificate of Appreciation, 1992; San Diego Housing Commission, Proclamation, 1992. **Military Serv:** USN captain 21 yrs; Letter of Commendation for Outstanding Serv to the Navy/Marine Selection Bd 1979-91; Meritorious Serv Medal 1980; Letter of Commendation,1981; Gold Star for Excellence in Recruiting 1981; Gold Wreath Awd for Excellence in Recruiting 1982-92; Navy Achievement, 1989; 2nd Meritorious Service Medal, 1990; 37th Gold Wreath for Excellence in Recruiting, 1990. **Business Addr:** Director, Student Outreach Serv, San Diego State Univ, Student Outreach Serv, San Diego, CA 92182-0777.

HUTCHINSON, JAMES J., JR.
Business executive. **Personal:** Born Sep 22, 1947, Chicago; divorced; children: Kelley, Jimmy. **Educ:** Dartmouth Coll, AB 1969; Amos Tuck Sch of Bus Adminstrn, MBA 1971. **Career:** First Natl Bank of Chicago, copr loan officer 1971-74; South Side Bank, exec vice pres 1974-80; Inter-Urban Broadcasting Co, vice pres 1977-81; Inter-Urban Broadcasting of New Orleans Partnership, exec vp, gen partner 1980-86; Inter-Urban Broadcasting Co, pres 1984-; Inter-Urban Rental Systems, pres 1985-; Savannah Cardinals Baseball Club, sec 1986-; Inter-Urban Broadcasting Group, pres 1986-. **Orgs:** Adv bd mem New Orleans Reg Vo-Tech Inst 1982-; commiss New Orleans Exhibitions Hall Auth 1986-; chmn Urban League of Greater New Orleans 1986-; exec comm mem Chambers Small Bus Council 1984; radio vice pres Greater New Orleans Broadcasters Assoc 1984-85; mem YMCA of Greater New Orleans, United Way, Metropolitan Area Comm, LA Childrens Museum, Private Industry Council, Greater NO Tourist & Convention Commission, Mayor Morials Superbowl Task Force, AP Tureaud Comm, Mayor Morials Bus Devel Council, Bus Task Force on Educ. **Honors/Awds:** Outstanding Achievement Awd Citizens Cultural Found 1978; one of the Ten Outstanding Black Businessmen in Chicago Awd 1979; Blackbook Urban League of Greater New Orleans Disting Serv Awd 1981; Metropolitan Area Comm Leadership Forum 1983; one of the Ten Best Dressed Men in New Orleans Men of Fashion. **Business Addr:** President, Inter-Urban Broadcasting Group, PO Box 19066, New Orleans, LA 70179.

HUTCHINSON, JEROME
Association executive. **Personal:** Born Jul 23, 1926, Louisville, KY; married Eleanor; children: Jerome, Jr, Seretha R. **Educ:** Univ of Louisville, AB 1951; Sch of Bus Adminstrn & Seminars on Small Bus Adminstrn, grad. **Career:** Jerome Hutchinson & Asso Inc, pres 1971-; Jonah Enterprises Inc Louisville, vP 1970-71; Econ Devel & Now Inc Louisville , exec dir 1969-70; Small Bus Adminstrn, mgmt splst 1966-69; Falls City Brewing Co, sales & pub rel rep 1956-66; Admiral Finace Co, credit investigator 1954-55. **Orgs:** Bd mem Louisville OIC 1970-72; bd mem & chmn Finance Com River Reg Mental Health Corp 1974-75; chmn bd dir Plymouth Urban Cntr 1974-; bd mem IMBE Washington 1969-70; chmn bd dir Continental Nat Bank of KY 1973-75. **Honors/Awds:** Ambassador of Goodwill Citation City of Louisville 1974; Citizen of Day Award WLOU Radio 1973; SBA Regional Mgmt Award 1968. **Military Serv:** USN 3rd class petty officer World War II. **Business Addr:** President, 4307 Elliott Ave, Suite 5, Louisville, KY 40211.

HUTCHINSON, LOUISE DANIEL
Historian. **Personal:** Born Jun 3, 1928, Ridge, MD; married Ellsworth W Hutchinson Jr; children: Ronald, David, Donna, Dana, Victoria. **Educ:** Miner Teacher Coll, Prairie View A&M, Howard Univ, 1952; Amer History & Afro-Amer Studies, Grad Hrs in Sociol. **Career:** Natl Portrait Gall SI, rsch of harmon collection 1971, ed rsch spec 1972-73; Natl Capitol Parks E Washington, ed rsch spec 1973-74; Anacostia Museum Smithsonian Inst, historial, dir of rsch 1974-. **Orgs:** Bd mem SE Neighbor House 1968-70; bd of dir WA Urban League 1968-70; mem bd SE Unit Amer Cancer Soc 1969-; chmn supt Council on Arts in Ed DC Publ School 1972-74; mem Natl Assoc of Negro Bus & Professional Women's Club Inc 1973-; ex comm, bd DC Citizens for Better Publ Ed 1974-76; mem Frederick Douglass Mem & Hist Assoc 1974-, Douglass ad hoc comm Natl Capitol Parks E; plng comm for bicent Smithsonian Inst. **Honors/Awds:** Author "The Anacostia Story, 1608-1930" 1977, "Out of Africa, From Kingdoms to Colonization", Smithsonian Press 1979, "Anna J Cooper, A Voice from the South" Smithsonian Press 1981; Exhibit Black Women, Achievements Against the Odds Smithsonian Traveling Exhib Svc. **Business Addr:** Historian, Dir of Rsch, Smithsonian Inst, ANM Rsch Dept, 1901 Fort Pl SE, Washington, DC 20020.

HUTCHISON, HARRY GREENE, IV
Law professor. **Personal:** Born Apr 12, 1948, Detroit, MI; son of Mary Robinson Hutchison and Harry Hutchison. **Educ:** Wayne State University, Detroit, MI, BA, 1969, MA, 1975; University of Michigan, Ann Arbor, MI, MBA, 1977; Wayne State University, Detroit, MI, JD, 1986. **Career:** Detroit Edison, Detroit, MI, business analyst, 1970-74; Ford Motor Co, Troy, MI, financial analyst, 1977-80; Lawrence Technological University, Southfield, MI, professor, 1981-89; University of Detroit, Detroit, MI, law professor, 1989-. **Orgs:** Senior policy analyst, Mackinac Center, 1987-; board of advisors, Heartland Institute, 1990-. **Business Addr:** Professor, University of Detroit, School of Law, 651 E Jefferson, Detroit, MI 48226.

HUTCHISON, PEYTON S.
Educational administrator. **Personal:** Born Mar 24, 1925, Detroit, MI; son of Gladys Palace Smith and Harry Greene Hutchison; married Betty L Sweeney PhD; children: Peyton Jr, Allison Leigh, Jonathan Alan. **Educ:** Wayne State Univ, BS Ed 1950, MEd 1955; Northern IL Univ 1969; MI State Univ, PhD 1975. **Career:** Detroit Public Schools, assistant principal 1964-65, admin asst 1966-73; City Coll of Chicago, suprv dir 1973-75; Chicago Urban Skills Inst, vice pres 1974-75; Chicago Urban Skills Inst,pres, 1975-84; Roosevelt Univ, part time faculty 1984-; City Coll of Chicago, exec dean; Hutchison Assoc (consulting business) currently. **Orgs:** Teacher Detroit Public Schools 1950-54; dir Green Pastures Camp Detroit Urban League 1959-65; asst principal Detroit Public School 1964-65; matl devel suprv Detroit Public Schools 1965-67; sr level rsch assoc MI State Univ 1968-69; chmn bd of dir Classic Chorales Inc 1983-; chmn Coll Univ Unit Amer Assoc of Adult Cont Ed 1983-; trustee Knoxville Coll 1984-; mem Alpha Phi Alpha; division director, Amer Association for Adult/Continuing Education. **Honors/Awds:** Pres Phi Delta Kappa Wayne State Univ 1963; Mott Doctoral Fellowship Charles Stewart Mott Found 1968; Carl Sandburg Awd Friends of Chicago Public Libr 1984; Comm Serv Awd Univ of Chicago Intl Kiwanis 1985. **Military Serv:** AUS sgt 1944-46. **Home Addr:** 688 Old Elm Rd, Lake Forest, IL 60045. **Business Addr:** Executive Dean, City Colleges Of Chicago, Richard J Daley College, 7500 S Pulaski Rd, Chicago, IL 60652.

HUTSON, JEAN BLACKWELL. **See Obituaries section.**

HUTT, MONROE L.
Business executive (retired). **Personal:** Born Mar 16, 1920, Evanston, IL; married LeJeune H; children: Monroe L Jr. **Educ:** IL Inst of Tech, attended 1942; Chicago Sch of Real Estate, attended 1948; Roosevelt Univ Sch of Music & Tchr Training Prog, attended 1965. **Career:** US Vet Admin Chicago, adjudicator 1946-50; Gen Auto Prod Inc, plant supr 1950-63; AUS Army Corp (civ), maint supr 1963-65; Midway Tech Inst Chicago, 1965-68; Brunswick Corp Chicago, job dev 1968-69; Quinco Mfg Corp, pres chmn bd, until 1987. **Orgs:** Pres's Coun Fellow Amer Inst of Mgmt; bd dir Chicago Minority Purchasing Council; mem IL Mfgrs Assn; mem Chicago S C of C; mem Amer Soc of Metals; mem VFW. **Honors/Awds:** Nom "Small Bus Subcontractor of Yr" by SBA 1971; Supplier Performance Awd Chevrolet 1971-72; Top Rung Citation Chicago Oppor Indsl Ctr 1970; "Min Bus Achievement Awd" 1970; Top 100 Black Businesses 1973. **Military Serv:** USN signalman 1942-46. **Home Addr:** 12605 S Edbrooke, Chicago, IL 60628.

HUTTON, DAVID LAVON
Educator (retired). **Personal:** Born in Kansas City, MO. **Educ:** CMSU, BS 1963; Hall of Recognition, 1963; UMKC, MA 1974. **Career:** Paseo HS, teacher 1965-79; Lincoln Acad N, teacher 1981-91; JA Rogers Academy, curriculum coordinator, 1991-95. **Orgs:** Mem AFT 1965-; bd of dirs, Ray Cnty Sesquicentennial Comm 1970-71; trustee, Bethel AME Chrch 1979-92, Voices of Bethel AME Church, president, 1994-95; mem NAACP 1983-; mem Building and Expansion of Bethel AME Church 1983-; National Council of African-American Men; Bethel AME Church, senior adult council pres; Million Man March, 1995; tax-aide counselor, AARP; ambassador, Alvin Ailey Dance Troupe, 1996; volunteer docent, Bruce Watkins Cultural Center, 1997. **Honors/Awds:** Hall of Recognition CMSU 1963; Outstanding Secondary Educator, 1975. **Military Serv:** AUS sp/4 3 yr; medal of good conduct 1956-59.

HUTTON, GERALD L.
Educator, consultant. **Personal:** Born in Pittsburg, KS; married Marjorie. **Career:** Lincoln & HP Study Schs Springfield Mo, tchr; Springfield Pub Schls, pub infor rep; St Louis Northwest HS, athletic dir & bus educ instr; pub television-utilization consult St Louis Educ TV Comm Commr Zoning Park Bd; officer Ancient Egyptian Arabic Order Nobles Mystic Shrine of North & South Am. **Orgs:** Mem Am Guild of Variety Artists; mem Anerucah Fedn of TV & Radio Artists; mem Am Equity Assn; mem Royal Vagabonds St Louis Mens Civic Club; mem St Louis Area Bus Tchrs Assn; mem Kiwanis Club; mem NAACP St Louis Br; hon past potentate PHA Shriners; mem United Supreme Council PHA So Jurisdiction 33rd deg Soloist World Series Games St Louis 1967, 1968; life mem Kappa Alpha Psi. **Honors/Awds:** Contrib Author "High Sch & Coll Typewriting" Textbooks; Festival Appreciation Award Sigma Gamma Rho Sorority Inc/Zeta Sigma chap Afro-am Arts.

HUTTON, MARILYN ADELE
Attorney. **Personal:** Born Jul 21, 1950, Cincinnati, OH. **Educ:** Fisk Univ, BA 1972; Harvard Law School, JD 1975; Hague Acad of Intl Law, Certificate 1983. **Career:** US Senator Lloyd M Bentsen, legislative aide 1975-76; The Procter & Gamble Co, corporate counsel 1976-81; Cincinnati Queen City Bowling Senate, corp sec 1980-82; NAACP, legislative cncl 1986-87; Natl Educ Assoc, atty human & civil rights spec; Arlington County, VA, Human Rights Commission, 1992-; Virginia State Coal and Energy Commission, 1994-. **Orgs:** legal adv comm Natl Bowling Assoc 1978-80; mem Intl Bar Assoc, Amer Soc of Intl Law, Amer & Federal Bar Assocs, District of Columbia

Bar Assoc, Amer Assoc of Art Museums, Corcoran Gallery of Art; mem US Court of Military Appeals, US Court of Appeals for the Federal Circuit, US Court of Appeals for the District of Columbia Circuit, District of Columbia Courts of Appeals. **Honors/Awds:** Author American Soc of Intl Law 1986, annual meeting report 1987. **Business Addr:** Attorney Human & Civil Rights, Natl Educ Assoc, 1201 16th St, Washington, DC 20036.

HUTTON, RONALD I.
Dentist. **Personal:** Born Jul 23, 1949, High Point, NC; son of Mr. & Mrs. Joseph E Hutton. **Educ:** Hampton Inst, BA 1971; Howard Univ Coll Dentistry, DDS 1975; Kambrough Army Hosp, General Practice Residency, 1975-76. **Career:** Winston-Salem Dental Care Plan Inc, dentist; Army Dental Corp, dentist 1975-78. **Orgs:** Mem bd trustees Promiseland Nurseries Inc; mem Assn of Mil Surgeons of US; Old North State Dental & Soc; NC 2nd Dist DentalSoc; Am & Nat Dental Assns; member, Academy of General Dentistry; Zoning Bd of Adjustments, Town of Lewisville; bd of trustees, Big Brothers-Big Sisters; bd of trustees, Montessori School of Winston-Salem, NC; exec bd, Old Hickory Boy Scout Council. **Honors/Awds:** Organized soc fellowship Campus of Hampton Inst 1969; Mastership, Academy of General Dentistry. **Military Serv:** Army dentist, 1975-78; US Army Reserves, colonel. **Business Addr:** Winston-Salem Dental Care Plan, 201 Charlois Blvd, Winston-Salem, NC 27103.

HUYGHUE, MICHAEL
Professional football administrator. **Career:** World League of American Football; Detroit Lions, general counsel, vice president of administration, 1993-94; Jacksonville Jaguars, sr vice pres of football operations, currently. **Business Addr:** Senior VP, Football Operations, Jacksonville Jaguars, 1 Stadium Place, Jacksonville, FL 32202, (904)633-6000.

HYATT, HERMAN WILBERT, SR.
Physician, cleric. **Personal:** Born Feb 19, 1926, South Pittsburg, TN; son of Wilma Hyatt and Robert Hyatt; married Elizabeth; children: Monique, Monica, Hamilton, Richard, Robert, Herman Jr. **Educ:** TN A&I State Univ, BS 1949; Meharry Med Coll, MD 1956; Lincoln Univ Law Sch, JD 1972; San Jose Bible College, San Jose, CA, BA, 1986. **Career:** Kern Gen Hosp, res ped 1957-59, chf ped dept 1963; AME Church, dist dir youth cong 1964-75; St James African Meth, pastor 1967-77; No CA Conf AME Church, admin asst to presiding elder; Mt Hermon African Methodist Episcopal Church, founder/pastor; private practice, pediatrician, currently. **Orgs:** Chmn dept ped San Jose Hosp 1971-72, Alexian Brothers Hosp 1973-74; ordained itinerant elder Bishop H Thomas Primm 1966; life mem NAACP; mem Advisory; mem Parents Helping Parents; vice pres Interdenominational Ministers Alliance 1987-; California Conference, African Methodist Episcopal Church, board of examiners, currently. **Honors/Awds:** Alpha Kappa Mu Natl Honor Soc 1948; "Poems from a Mountain" 1980-81; special recognition Award Santa Clara Human Rights Commission 1988; Resolution from the CA Assembly 1989; Resolution from the House of Representatives 1989; Commendation, city of San Jose 1989-90; Special Award Urban League 1988; Monrovia Coll, Honorary Doctor of Humanities 1987; San Jose City Coll, Honorary Assn in Art 1988; published book, A Cry for Help, 1991; received Valley of Hearts Award, parents Helping Parents, 1992; Man of the Year, San Jose, California citizen's Group, 1989; Wrote, directed and produced 3-act play for the Young People's Department of the California Conference of the African Methodist Episcopal Church, 1992. **Military Serv:** AUS sgt 1946. **Business Addr:** Physician, Minister, 12 S 14th St, San Jose, CA 95112.

HYDE, DEBORAH
Neurosurgeon. **Career:** Private practice, currently. **Orgs:** Beacon of Hope Mississippi Scholarship Foundation, Inc, found, 1991-. **Special Achievements:** One of four African-American female neurosurgeons in US. **Business Addr:** Neurosurgeon, 7230 Medical Center Dr, Ste 300, Canoga Park, CA 91307, (818)716-7003.

HYDE, MAXINE DEBORRAH
Physician, neurosurgeon. **Personal:** Born Jan 18, 1949, Laurel, MS; daughter of Ann McDonald and Sellus Hyde. **Educ:** Tougaloo Coll, BS Biology (cum laude) 1966-70; Cleveland State Univ, MS Biology 1971-73; Case Western Reserve Univ, MD 1973-77; Univ Hosps, internship 1977-78, neurosurgery residency 1978-82. **Career:** Univ Hosps, internship general surgery 1977-78, residency neurosurgery 1978-82; Guthrie Clinic, neurosurgical staff 1982-87; Canoga Park CA, private practice neurosurgery, 1987-. **Orgs:** Congress of Neurological Surgeons; Alpha Omega Alpha Med Honors Society; California Neurosurgical Society; American Association of Neurological Surgeons. **Honors/Awds:** Alpha Omega Alpha Honorary Med Soc 1977; featured story Ebony 1983; featured in first edition of Medica 1983; featured in First Register of Yearly Article on Young Professional Esquire 1984; featured story American Medical News 1984; received Doctor of Humane Letters from Tongaloo College, Tongaloo, Miss. **Special Achievements:** Publications: "5-Hydroxytryptophan decarboxylase and monoamine oxidase in the maturing mouse eye" 1973; "The Maturation of 5-hydroxytryptophan decarboxylase in regions of the mouse brain" 1973; "The maturation of indoleamine metabolism in the lateral eye of the mouse" 1974; "The maturation of monoamine oxidase and 5-hydroxyindole acetic acid in regions of the mouse brain" 1974; "Re-expansion of previously collapsed ventricles" 1982. **Business Addr:** Neurosurgeon, 7230 Medical Center Drive #300, Canoga Park, CA 91307.

HYDE, WILLIAM R.
Surgeon, educator. **Personal:** Born Nov 9, 1923, St Paul, MN; son of Marie T Hyde and William M Hyde; married Opal Brown; children: William R Jr, David J, Drew S. **Educ:** Howard Univ, BS (cum laude) 1944, MD 1947. **Career:** Harlem Hosp, internship; Freedmen's Hosp, residency; Columbia Univ, 1949-50; Harlem Hosp, 1952-53; Howard Univ, asst prof of surgery; VA Hosp Washington, DC Gen Hosp, Children's Hosp, Providence Hosp, sr attending surgeon; Howard Univ Coll of Med, surgeon; Washington Hospital Center, sr attending surgeon. **Orgs:** Mem DC Med Soc; NMA Fellow; Amer Coll of Surgeons 1958; diplomate Amer Bd of Surgery 1953; diplomate Natl Bd of Med Examiners; Washington Acad of Surgery 1974; Alpha Phi Alpha Frat; Southeastern Surgical Assn. **Honors/Awds:** Beta Kappa Chi, Kappa Pi Hon Soc. **Military Serv:** AUS med corps capt 1953-55. **Business Addr:** Physician, 3326 Georgia Ave NW, Washington, DC 20010.

HYLER, LORA LEE
Communications manager. **Personal:** Born Oct 4, 1959, Racine, WI; daughter of Leona McGee Hyler and Haward Hyler. **Educ:** University of Wisconsin-Milwaukee, Milwaukee, WI, BA, Mass Communications, 1981. **Career:** WISN Radio, an ABC Affiliate, Milwaukee, WI, news reporter, 1980-84; Wisconsin Natural Gas Co, Racine, WI, communications writer, 1984-88; Journal Communications, Milwaukee, WI, communications mgr, 1988-91; Wisconsin Electric Power Co., Milwaukee, public information representative, 1991-. **Orgs:** Member, Public Relations Society of America, 1990-; member, Wisconsin Black Media Association, 1988-.

HYLTON, ANDREA LAMARR
Librarian. **Personal:** Born Dec 12, 1965, Martinsville, VA; daughter of Gloria Mae Hodge Hylton and Vallie Walker Hylton. **Educ:** James Madison University, Harrisonburg, VA, BS, 1988; North Carolina Central University, Durham, NC, MLS, 1990. **Career:** Blue Ridge Regional Library, Martinsville, VA, library assistant, 1987; Spotsylvania County School Board, Spotsylvania, VA, librarian, 1988-89; North Carolina Central University, Durham, NC, graduate assistant, 1989-90; Family Healh International, Research Triangle Park, NC, intern, 1990-;. **Orgs:** President, NCCU Student Chapter of the American Library Assn, 1989-90; treasurer, NCCU Student Chapter of the Special Libraries Assn, 1989-90; member, Virginia Educational Media Association, 1986-90; member, NCCU School of Library and Information Sciences Curriculum Committee, 1990; student staff member, American Library Association, National Conference, 1990. **Honors/Awds:** Special Talent Award, North Carolina Central University, 1989; Jenkins-Moore Scholarship, School of Library & Information Sciences, NCCU, 1990.

HYLTON, KENNETH N.
Attorney. **Personal:** Born Jul 7, 1929, Roanoke, VA; son of Rev and Mrs S W Hylton; married Ethel Washington; children: Kenneth N Jr, Keith Norman, Kevin Nathaniel. **Educ:** Talladega Coll, BA; Wayne State U, MA; Boston Univ Sch of Law, JD. **Career:** Bailer, Lee, Long, Brown & Cain, partner, 1957-62; Wayne Co, MI, public administrator, beginning 1963; Swainson, Dingell, Hylton & Zemmol, partner, 1962-67; Civil Rights Commission State of MI, referee, 1962-67; NAACP Housing Corp, of counsel; Dingell, Hylton & Zemmol, partner, 1967-77; Kenneth N Hylton & Assocs, 1977-80; Hylton & Hylton PC, senior partner, 1980-. **Orgs:** Eastern & Western Federal Dist Court Bar of MI; 6th Circuit US Ct of Appeals Bar; Supreme Ct of the US Bar; VA State Bar; MI State Bar; Detroit Bar Assn; Wolvernine Bar Assn; American Bar Assn; Natl Lawyers Guild; American Judicature Soc; Workmen's Compensation Section and Condemnation Committee; American Trial Lawyers Assn; State Bar Grievance Bd, State of MI, former chairman; Alpha Phi Alpha Fraternity; NAACP; Westlawn Cemetery Assn of Detroit, Inc, pres and chairman of the bd of dirs; Natl Housing Conference, Inc, Wash DC, bd of dirs; Omnibank, Detroit, MI, sec of the bd and gen counsel. **Military Serv:** US Army first lt 1953-56. **Business Addr:** Legal Counsel/Investor, OmniBanc Corp, 10474 W Jefferson, River Rouge, MI 48218, (313)843-8850.

HYLTON, TAFT H.
Program analyst. **Personal:** Born Jun 22, 1936, Washington, DC; divorced. **Educ:** BS 1959; Washington Conservatory Music; Washington Inst Music. **Career:** Dept of Human Serv DC Govt, chief/Payments Br; Ofc Budget & Mgmt Sys DC Govt, budget & accounting analyst; choral conductor; tcht private piano; Voices of Expression Choral Ensemble, fndr dir. **Orgs:** Mem Am Choral Dir Assn; dir of sr choir New Bethel Bapt Ch; mem dir Anthem Choir Allen AME Ch; mem Cosmopolitan Choral Ensemble; Am Light OperaCo; Negro Oratorio Soc; 12th St Christian Ch; Univ Soc Piano Tchrs. **Honors/Awds:** Work Performance Award; Pub Health Serv NIH 1963; Eligible Bachelor featured Ebony Mag 1974.

HYMAN, EARLE
Actor. **Personal:** Born Oct 11, 1926, Rocky Mount, NC; son of Maria Lilly Hyman and Zachariah Hyman. **Educ:** Studied with Eva Le Gallienne at the Amer Theatre Wing; studied with Robert Lewis at the Actors Studio. **Career:** NY State Amer Negro Theatre, performer 1943; TV, performer 1953; Films, performer 1954; The Bamboo Prison, The Possession of Joel Delaney, performed 1972; House Party Playhouse, various roles 1974; The Green Pastures, played Adam Hezdrel; Huckleberry Finn, played Jim; played title-role of Othello in Norwegian; US tour and Carnegie Recital Hall 1963; The Cosby Show, played Russell Huxtable. **Orgs:** Reader for Amer Found for the Blind; recorded Alex Haley's Roots 1977. **Honors/Awds:** Show Bus Awd Othello 1953; Seagram Vanguard Awd 1955; Theatre World Awd 1956; GRY Awd for "Emporor Jones," Norwegian, Oslo, Norway, 1965.

HYMAN, MARK J.
Historian, author, publisher. **Personal:** Born Apr 25, 1916, Rocky Mount, NC; son of Eliza Vick Hyman and Joshua Hyman; married Mable V Hyman, Sep 19, 1947 (deceased); children: Beverley, Linda. **Educ:** Howard University; New York University, BA, MA; Temple University, PhD. **Career:** The Way Publishing Co, chairman, currently; Mark Hyman Associates, Inc, president, currently. **Orgs:** Philadelphia Urban League, chairman; Howard University Alumni Club of Philadelphia, chairman; Philadelphia Press Club, chairman; Edythe Ingraham History Club, chairman; Omega Psi Phi Fraternity, Inc, National Public Relations, director; Philadelphia American Cancer Society, vice pres; Afro-American Historical & Cultural Museum, Philadelphia, co-founder and board member. **Honors/Awds:** Bethune Cookman University, Mary McLeod Bethune Medallion; Philadelphia Tribune Front Page Award; Associated Press Broadcast Award; Afro American Historical Museum Award; Pennsylvania State Legislature Award. **Special Achievements:** Author, Blacks Before America, vol I, II, III, 1979; author, Blacks Who Died for Jesus, A History Book, 1983; author, Black Shogun of Japan, 1986; The America That Killed King, 1991. **Military Serv:** US Army, 2nd lt, 1940-43. **Business Addr:** Chairman, The Way Publishing Co, President Mark Hyman Associates, Inc, 5070 Parkside Ave, Ste 1122, Philadelphia, PA 19131.

HYMES, JESSE
Business executive. **Personal:** Born Feb 13, 1939, St Joseph, LA; married Addie B; children: Kenneth, Tracey, Trina. **Educ:** Univ Chicago, MBA 1972; Purdue Univ, AAS 1970. **Career:** Appaisers by KATT, residential real estate appraiser, currently; Joseph Schlitz Brewing Co, plant controller, asst controller 1975; control system adminstr 1975; plant accountant 1974; financial analyst 1972; Meade Elec Co, draftsman estimator 1969. **Orgs:** Bd dir Urban Arts 1976; pres PTA 1977; mem adv dom Boy Scouts of Am 1977; art council 1975-76; jr advisor Achievement 1975-76; NAACP. **Honors/Awds:** Urban League Black Achiever Award NY YMCA 1977; cogme fellowship grant 1972. **Military Serv:** AUS sp 4 1962-65. **Business Addr:** 4791 Schlitz Ave, Winston-Salem, NC 27107.

HYMES, WILLIAM HENRY
Federal official (retired). **Personal:** Born Feb 2, 1921, Sumter, SC; son of Susan Prince Hymes and George Hymes; married Edna Williams Hymes, Nov 19, 1949; children: William Jr, Darren. **Educ:** Penn State Univ, University Park, PA, BS, 1949. **Career:** US Navy Dept, Washington, DC, oceanographer, 1951-56; Johns Hopkins Univ, Operations Research Office, Silver Spring, MD, operations analyst, 1956-61; US Navy Dept, Washington, DC, scientific staff, 1961-76; Library of Congress, Washington, DC, physical scientist, 1976-82. **Orgs:** Member, Marine Technologic Society; member, American Geophysical Union, 1950-70; member, American Meteorological Society, 1949-70; secretary, Scientific Research Society of America, 1964-70; Tuskegee Airmen Inc, 1994-. **Honors/Awds:** Various Navy Dept performance awards, 1974-76. **Military Serv:** US Army Air Corps, Second Lt., 1942-46; awarded aircraft pilot rating, 1945; World War II Medal, 1946. **Home Addr:** 515 Cannon Rd, Silver Spring, MD 20904-3319.

HYNSON, CARROLL HENRY, JR.
State official. **Personal:** Born Dec 28, 1936, Washington, DC; son of Carroll and Adel; children: Michelle Hynson Green, Lejuene Tarra, Marcus Carroll, Brandee Carol. **Educ:** Penn State Univ, 3 yrs Sociology & Political Science 1955-59; Amer Univ, summer course/Sociology; Morgan State Univ, BA 1960. **Career:** Sonderling Broadcasting Co, chief announcer/acting prog dir 1965-75; Hynson's Real Estate, office mgr 1975-76; Ceda Corp, public affairs specialist 1976-77; Provident Hosp Inc, asst vice pres for devel & pub relations 1978-80; Balt/Wash Intl Airport, dir office of trade dev 1980-84; MD State Lottery Agency, dep dir sales 1984-88; dep Director Public Affairs 1984-. **Orgs:** Vice pres Scholarship for Scholars Comm 1984; bd of dir Epilepsy Found of MD 1982-; adv bd Baltimore Convention Bureau 1982-; Kappa Alpha Psi Fraternity. **Honors/Awds:** Life mem Phi Beta Pi Commerce Frat 1973; vice chmn Anne Arundel Co/Annap Bicentennial Comm; host/producer It Ain't Necessarily So-CBS 1976; host/producer The C Thing WRC-TV and Back to School Special Washington WHG-TV. **Home Addr:** 1205 Asquith Pines Pl, Arnold, MD 21012. **Business**

Addr: Deputy Dir Public Affairs, Maryland State Lottery Agency, Plaza Office Center Ste 204, 6776 Reisterstown Rd, Baltimore, MD 21215.

HYSAW, GUILLERMO LARK

Auto company executive. **Personal:** Born Dec 19, 1948, Bakersfield, CA; son of Guillermo & Georgia Hysaw; married Kimberly, Nov 7, 1987; children: S Jamal, Immari A, Megan Ashley. **Educ:** Oakland University, BA, 1972; Claremont Graduate School, MA, 1991, MBA, 1993, AMBA, 1996. **Career:** Lexus, sr market rep admin, 1987-88, venture capital planning mgr, 1988-89, natl advertising mgr, 1989-91, natl bus development mgr, 1991-92, natl mktg development mgr, 1992-93; Toyota, natl fleet mktg operations mgr, 1993-97, corp mgr of used vehicle dept, 1997-. **Orgs:** 100 Black Men of Los Angeles, Inc, vp; Natl Black MBA Assn of Los Angeles, vp; NAACP, Natl Comm, appointed by Julian Bond, life mem; Alpha Phi Alpha Frat, Natl External Fundraiser; Compton Comm Coll Foundation, bd of dirs, pres; Drew Medical Hospital, bd of dirs; 100 Black Men of America, Inc, natl co-chair of mktg, Natl Economic Development, strategic planning mem. **Honors/Awds:** General Motors Inst Bd of Regents, Executive Mgmt, 1990; Peter F Drucker Graduate Mgmt Award, 1990; Black Enterprise Magazine, Corporate Profile Awd, 1991; African Male Achievers Network, Corporate Role Model Awd, 1992, 1993, 1994. **Special Achievements:** Sports Illustrated Magazine, cover, 1969; Black Enterprise, corp profile article, 1991; Jet Magazine, corp profile article, 1997; over 200 Black Newspapers, corp profile article, 1997; Sphinx Magazine, corp profile article, cover, 1998. **Business Addr:** Corporate Manager, Used Vehicle Department, Toyota Motor Sales, USA, Inc, 19001 S Western Ave, Mail Drop A309, Torrance, CA 90509, (310)618-4521.

HYTCHE, WILLIAM P.

Educational administrator. **Personal:** Born Nov 28, 1927, Porter, OK; married Deloris Juanita Cole; children: Pamelia, Jaqueta, William Jr. **Educ:** Langston Univ, BS 1950; OK State Univ, MS 1958, EdD 1967. **Career:** Attucks Jr/Sr HS, tchr 1952-55; Ponca City Sr HS, tchr 1955-60; MD State Coll, asst prof 1960-66; Univ of MD, dept head assoc prof & dean of student affairs 1968-73, acting chmn 1973-74, chmn of liberal studies 1974-75, acting chancellor 1975-76, chancellor, beginning 1976, president, 1988-97, pres emeritus, currently. **Orgs:** Past pres Co-op Orgn Planning; mem bd dir Princess Anne Area C of C; mem Phi Sigma Soc; Alpha Phi Alpha; Holy Royal Arch Mason; Free & Accepted Mason; mem bd dir Natl Assoc for Equal Oppty in Higher Educ 1976-, Mid-Delmarva YMCA 1980-82; mem joint comm Agr R&D; mem bd dir InterFuture; mem Agribusiness Promotion Council 1985-; mem exec comm Natl Assoc of State Univs & Land-Grant Colls 1985-; American Council on Education, board member; President's Advisory Board on Historically Black Colleges and Universities; Secretary of the Interior's Advisory Board on Historically Black Colleges and Universities, chairman; Council of 1890 Presidents/Chancellors, chairman; USDA/1890 Task Force, co-chair; National Aquarium, advisory bd; Dept of Energy, Historically Black Colleges and Universities, task group; Federal Aviation Administration, Airway Science Task Force; Peninsula Regional Medical Ctr, bd of trustees; Del-Mar-Va, advisory council; Phi Delta Kappa; Phi Kappa Phi. **Honors/Awds:** Acad of Arts & Sci Fellow OK State Univ 1978; Listed in NAFEO Disting Alumni of the Year Brochure 1980; Oklahoma State University Alumni Association, Hall of Fame Inductee, 1993; Thurgood Marshall Educational Achievement Award, 1992; Tuskegee Univ, George Washington Carver Public Service Hall of Fame, 1994; honorary degrees: Fisk Univ, Washington Coll, Univ of MD Eastern Shore, Tuskegee Univ. **Special Achievements:** Author: Information Technology and the 1890 Land-Grant Colleges and Universities, Journal of Agricultural & Food Information, 1993; book chapt in A Century of Service, Land-Grant Colleges and Universities, 1890-1990, 1992; article, Historically Black Institutions Forge Linkages with African Nations; and others. **Military Serv:** US Army 1950-52. **Business Addr:** President emeritus, University of Maryland, E Shore, Princess Anne, MD 21853.

HYTER, MICHEAL C.

Business executive. **Personal:** Born Jan 2, 1957, Huntsville, AL; son of Betty L Hyter and Leroy Hyter Sr; married Dana Greer Hyter, Aug 22, 1981; children: Ashlei, Mike Jr, Donovan. **Educ:** Michigan State University, BS, 1978. **Career:** Hudson's, personnel manager, 1980-83; Mervyn's, manager, college relations, 1983-84; Dayton Hudson's Department Store, co. manager executive placement, 1989-87, co. director executive recruit, placement, 1987-89, store manager, West Lansing, 1989-90, store manager, Westland, 1990-91, director, human resources, 1991-93, co. vice pres, public affairs, currently. **Orgs:** Detroit Urban League, board member, 1992-; Efficacy Detroit, board member, 1992-; Henry Ford Hospital Health Systems, board member, 1990-; Metro Detroit Youth Foundation, 1990-; Madonna College, advisory council, 1987-89; Turning Point Inc, 1987-89. **Business Addr:** Vice Pres, Public Affairs & Corporate Communications, Dayton-Hudson's-Field's Department Stores, 700 Nicollet Mall, Minneapolis, MN 55441, (612)375-2836.

I

IBEKWE, LAWRENCE ANENE

Educator, educational administrator. **Personal:** Born Apr 17, 1952, Onitsha, Nigeria; son of Marcelina Ibekwe Ozumba and Eusebius Ibekwe; married Theresa Ibekwe Nwabunie, Mar 23, 1989; children: Lynn, Lawren, Lawrence Jr. **Educ:** Marshall Univ, Huntington, WV, 1979; Philander Smith Coll, Little Rock, AR, BA, business administration, 1980-81; Univ of AR, Fayetteville, MS, mgmt, 1982-83. **Career:** State School Board, Holy Rosary Teacher's Coll, Nigeria, library asst, 1975-78; Arkansas Commemorative Comm, Old State House, security officer, 1983-84; Philander Smith Coll, instructor, 1984-91; Shorter Coll, associate professor, 1984-, academic dean, 1988-90, Department of Business & Applied Science, head, 1987-88, 1991-; Arkansas Department of Heritage, management project analysis, 1992-93. **Orgs:** Advisor, Phi Beta Lambda, Philander Smith Coll, 1986-; advisor, Arkansas Assn of Nigerian Students, 1986-88; treasurer, Elite Social Club, 1987-; Knight of Columbus (3rd degree) 1987-; treasurer, Nigerian Professionals in Arkansas, 1991-92; campus coordinator (liaison person), Federal Funded International Studies Program, 1990-93; board of advisors, Little Rock Job Corp Program, 1989-91. **Honors/Awds:** Philander Smith College, Dean's List, 1980-81, PBL Business Club, Award of Recognition for Advising, 1986-89; Outstanding Young Men of America, Jaycees, 1981; several Outstanding Leadership and Performance Awards; Arkansas Association of Nigerians, Supervisory Council, chairman, 1986; Constitution Review, advisor, 1987, chairman, 1986, 1989, 1992; Man of the Year Award, 1991. **Home Addr:** PO Box 164431, Little Rock, AR 72216.

IBELEMA, MINABERE

Educator. **Personal:** Born Dec 9, 1954, Bonny, Rivers State, Nigeria; son of Violet Eredappa Jumbo and Ebenezer Tamunoibelema Jumbo; married Ibifiri Ibelema, Jan 8, 1994; children: Danielle Boma. **Educ:** Wilberforce University, Wilberforce, OH, BA, 1979; Ohio State University, Columbus, OH, MA, 1980, PhD, 1984. **Career:** Central State University, Wilberforce, OH, associate professor, 1984-91; Eastern Illinois University, Charleston, IL, associate professor, 1991-. **Orgs:** NAACP member, association for Education in Journalism and Mass Communication, 1987-; member, Central States Communication Association, 1987-; member, Popular Culture Association, 1986-; corresponding secretary, American Association of University Professors, Central State University Chapter, 1990-. **Honors/Awds:** Author, Tribes and Prejudice: Coverage of the Nigerian Civil War, chapter in Africa's Media Image, 1991; author, Identity Crisis: The African Connection in African-American Sitcom Characters, chapter in Sexual Politics and Popular Culture, 1990; Honorable Mention, Munger Africana Library, African Thesis Competition, California Institute of Technology, 1982. **Business Addr:** Associate Professor, Dept of Journalism, Eastern Illinois University, Buzzard Bldg, Charleston, IL 61920.

IBRAHIM, ABDULLAH (DOLLAR BRAND)

Pianist, composer. **Personal:** Born Oct 9, 1934, Cape Town; married Sathima; children: Tsakwe, Tsidi. **Educ:** Univ of Cape Town, attended. **Career:** Marimba Mus Ctr & Ekapa Records, dir; AS-Shams Rec Co; Karate, instr Cape Town S Africa; Composer, Liberation Opera, Kalahari 1978; pianist, composer. **Honors/Awds:** Rockefeller Grant 1968; Natl Endowment for the Arts; Talent Deserving Wider Recog Downbeat Mag 1975; Silver Awd 1973; Grand Prix Awd 1973. **Business Addr:** 222 W 23rd St, Hotel Chelsea #314, New York, NY 10011.

ICE, ANNE-MARE

Pediatrician. **Personal:** Born Mar 16, 1945, Detroit, MI; daughter of Garnet Terry Ice and Lois Tabor Ice. **Educ:** Fisk Univ, BA Chem 1966; Howard Univ Coll of Med, MD 1970; Milwaukee Children's Hosp, Internship residency pediatrics 1970-73; Madonna Univ, MSBA, 1996. **Career:** Private Practice, pediatrician 1973-. **Orgs:** Natl Med Assoc; Links, Inc; Delta Sigma Theta, Inc. **Business Addr:** 15521 W Seven Mile Rd, Detroit, MI 48235.

ICE CUBE (O'SHEA JACKSON)

Rapper, actor. **Personal:** Born 1969, South Los Angeles, CA; son of Doris Jackson and Hosea Jackson; married Kim; children: one. **Educ:** Phoenix Institute of Technology, 1988. **Career:** NWA, member, until 1990; solo music career, albums include: AmeriKKKa's Most Wanted, debut album, 1990; Death Certificate, 1991; The Predator, 1993; film appearances include: Boyz N the Hood, actor, 1992; Trespass, actor, 1993; Higher Learning, 1994; Friday, 1995; The Glass Shield, 1995; Street Knowledge Productions, president, 1990-. **Special Achievements:** Premiere magazine, guest movie reviewer, Straight Out of Brooklyn, 1991; The Predator entered Billboard's pop and black charts at Number 1, 1993. **Business Phone:** (213)778-6095.

ICE-T (TRACEY MORROW)

Actor, rap artist. **Personal:** Born 1958, Newark, NJ; married Darlene. **Career:** Rapper, recordings include: "The Coldest Rap," 1982; Rhyme Pays, 1987; Power, 1988; Colors motion picture soundtrack, 1988; The Iceberg/Freedom of Speech . . . Just Watch What You Say, 1989; New Jack City motion picture soundtrack, "New Jack Hustler," 1991; O G-Original Gangster, 1991; Body Count, 1992; Home Invasion, 1993; actor, films include: Breakin', 1984; New Jack City, 1991, Ricochet, 1992; Trespass, 1993; Surviving The Game, 1994; Johnny Mnemonic, 1995; TV appearance, New York Undercover, 1995, 1996; Players, 1997-. **Special Achievements:** Lollapalooza, performer, 1991.

IDEWU, OLAWALE OLUSOJI

Physician. **Personal:** Born Mar 14, Abeokuta Ogun, Nigeria; son of George B & Rali Idewu; married Linda Idewu, Sep 24, 1994; children: Ayodele, Olanrewaju. **Educ:** Blackburn College, BA, 1959; Freiburg University, West Germany, MD, 1966. **Career:** Ear, Nose & Throat Health Ctr, physician/owner, currently. **Orgs:** American Medical Association; Iowa Medical Society; American Academy of Otolaryngology, fellow; American College of Surgeons, fellow; International College of Surgeons, fellow; American Academy of Otolaryngol, Allergy; Rotary Club International, Harris, fellow. **Honors/Awds:** Nigerian-American Forum, Distinguished Person, 1990. **Special Achievements:** Scholarship to study Medicine, Heidelberg University, 1960; Nigerian Folk Tales. **Military Serv:** Air Force reserve, major, 1985-91.

IFALASE, OLUSEGEN (ERLIN BAIN)

Clinical psychologist. **Personal:** Born Sep 25, 1949, Nassau, Bahamas; son of Jennie Bain and Clifford Bain; children: Akilah-Halima, Kwasi Rashidi, Jamila Rashida. **Educ:** Univ of Miami, BA 1980, PhD 1986. **Career:** Center for Child Develop, psychologist 1979-82; Miami Mental Health Ctr, dir of substance abuse 1982-84; Dept of Youth and Family Develop, clinical psychologist 1985-92; Ujima Assocs Inc, exec dir 1986-. **Orgs:** Mem Mental Health Assn of Dade Co 1982-, Chiumba Imani African Dance Co 1983-, Natl Black Alcoholism Council 1984-; pres South FL Assoc of Black Psychologists 1986-; consultant Informed Families 1986, Switchboard of Miami 1986; mem Kuumba Artists Assoc 1986; consultant Family Health Ctr of Miami 1987. **Honors/Awds:** Natl Minority Fellowship Grant 1978-83; Community Serv Award Welfare Mothers of Dade 1982; Appreciation Award Dade Co Sch Bd 1986 and Inner City Task Force 1986.

IGHNER, BENARD T.

Musician. **Personal:** Born Jan 18, 1945, Houston, TX. **Career:** Almo Publ Co, staff son writer; Dizzy Gillespie & Lalo Schifrin, worked with both; singer; musician; arranger. **Military Serv:** AUS pfc 162-65. **Business Addr:** c/o Alamo Music Corp, 1416 N La Brea, Los Angeles, CA.

IGINLA, JAROME

Professional hockey player. **Personal:** Born Jul 1, 1977, Alberta. **Career:** Dallas Stars, 1995; Calgary Flames, 1995-. **Honors/Awds:** Canadian National Junior Baseball Team, All-Star Catcher Honors, 1992; George Parsons Trophy, 1995; Four Broncos Memorial Trophy, 1996; Canadian HL All-Star First Team, 1996; WHL All-Star First Team, 1996. **Business Addr:** Professional Hockey Player, Calgary Flames, Canadian Airlines Saddledome, PO Box 1540, Sta M, Calgary, AB, Canada T2P 3B9.

IGLEHART, LLOYD D.

Attorney. **Personal:** Born Apr 20, 1938, Dallas, TX; son of Helen Waggoner Iglehart and Lloyd Iglehart; married Vivian, Jun 20, 1964; children: Lloyd III, Stanley, Llauryn, Robyn. **Educ:** Lincoln Univ of MO, BS 1961; Howard Univ, JD 1969; Columbia Univ, MPH 1976. **Career:** Met Life Ins Co, atty 1969-73; RCA Consumer Electronics, atty 1973-74; University of Maryland Hospital, Baltimore, MD, administrator, 1976-80; Private Practice, attorney 1983-. **Orgs:** Mem Natl Health Lawyers Assoc, Natl Conf Black Lawyers, ABA, Amer Civil Liberties Union, Natl Bar Assoc, Washington Bar Assoc, PA Supreme Court, Supreme Court of TX, DC Court of Appeals, US Supreme Court, Phi Alpha Delta Law Frat, Alpha Phi Alpha Frat Inc. **Military Serv:** AUS 1961-63. **Business Addr:** Attorney, 5405 Twin Knobbs, Suite 4, Columbia, MD 21045, (301)596-1800.

IKE, REVEREND. See EIKERENKOETTER, FREDERICK J., II.

IKE, ALICE DENISE

Attorney. **Personal:** Born Mar 25, 1955, Washington, DC; daughter of Allyre Owens Ike and William Howard Ike Jr. **Educ:** University of Maryland, Baltimore County, BA, 1977, School of Law, JD, 1981. **Career:** Morgan State Univ, part-time instructor, 1984, 1985; Legal Services Institute, legal intern, 1980-81; Legal Aid of Maryland Inc, staff attorney, 1981-82; City of Baltimore, Office of the State's Attorney, assistant states attorney, 1983-85; Univ of Maryland, Baltimore County, part-time instructor, 1990-; Department of Health and Mental Hygiene, Office of the Attorney General, assistant attorney general, 1985-. **Orgs:** DC Bar Assn, 1982-; State of Maryland Bar

Assn, 1981-; Alliance of Black Women Attorneys, 1982-; Foster Care Review Bd of Baltimore City, chairperson of the bd, 1986-. **Business Addr:** Assistant Attorney General, Office of the Attorney General, Department of Health and Mental Hygiene, 300 W Preston St, Ste 302, Baltimore, MD 21201, (410)225-1868.

IMHOTEP, AKBAR
Performing artist. **Personal:** Born Dec 22, 1951, Perry, GA; son of Carrie L Ridley and Robert Hart; children: Akilah, Garvey, Sara-Maat. **Educ:** Georgia Tech, 1974-77; Paine College, BA. **Career:** Proposition Theatre, actor, 1977-79; Ctr for Puppetry Arts, puppeteer, 1979-86; Wren's Nest, storyteller in residence, 1986-; self-employed storyteller/puppeteer, 1986-. **Orgs:** Kawanda/Kwanzaa Network, founder/exec dir, 1993-94; Metro-Atlanta Kwanzaa Assn, chairman, 1986-92; Assn of Black Storytellers, 1991-; Puppeteers of America, 1986-; Omega Psi Phi, 1971-; NAACP, 1989-; Nation of Islam, 1975-78. **Honors/Awds:** Metro-Atlanta Kwanzaa Assn, Mzee Olutunji Award, 1992; WACP, Kwumba Award, 1990. **Special Achievements:** Performances throughout the southeastern US, 1989-; performances in three consecutive NBAF, 1988, 1990, 1992; performances in Jazz and Heritage Festival, 1994; published three volumes of poetry, 1982, 1988, 1994. **Business Addr:** Storyteller/Actor/Poet, The Arts Machine, PO Box 11386, Atlanta, GA 30310, (404)688-3376.

INCE, HAROLD S.
Dentist. **Personal:** Born Jan 7, 1930, Brooklyn; married Mary Ann Jackson; children: Nancy, Harold Jr. **Educ:** BS 1951; DDS 1956. **Career:** Self-employed, dentist health dept New Haven CT. **Orgs:** Mem ADA; CT Dental Assn; New Haven Dental Assn; adv bd First New Haven Nat Bank; mem Urban League; trustee Bias Stanley Fund; Alpha Phi Alpha. **Military Serv:** USAF capt 1956-58. **Business Addr:** PO Box 3021, New Haven, CT 06515.

INGRAM, EARL GIRARDEAU
Educator. **Personal:** Born Apr 18, 1936, Savannah, GA; married Carol L; children: Cheryl, Earl Jr, Keith, Kevin. **Educ:** IN U, MS; Savannah State Coll, BS. **Career:** US Dept of Edn, dir EEO 1971-; sr personnel staffing officer 1970-71; Youth Training Center, dir 1968-69; Svannah, tchr counselor. **Orgs:** NAACP. **Honors/Awds:** 2 spec awards for EEO significant number of African-Americans recruited for Dept of Edn. **Business Addr:** Vice President & University Equity Officer, George Mason University, Mason Hall, Room 105, MSN 2C2, Fairfax, VA 22030-4444.

INGRAM, EDITH J.
Judge. **Personal:** Born Jan 16, 1942, Sparta, GA; married Roy L Grant. **Educ:** Ft Valley State Coll, BS Elem Ed 1963. **Career:** Moore Elem Sch Griffin GA, tchr 1963-67; Hancock Central Elem Sparta GA, tchr 1967-68; Hancock Co, elected probate judge 1968-. **Orgs:** Mem State Natl & Intl Assoc of Probate Judges 1969; mem Voter Registration Assoc of GA 1972; comm chairwoman GA Coalition of Black Women 1980-, Hancock Co Womens Club 1964-, Macedonia Bapt Church Choir 1951-. **Honors/Awds:** Cert of Merit Booker T Washington 1973; NAACP Achievement Awd 1969; Fulton County's Outstanding Citizen's 1978; Atlanta Br NAACP Outstanding Courage in Southern Polit Arena 1979. **Business Addr:** Judge, Probate Court, Courthouse Sq, Sparta, GA 31087.

INGRAM, GAREY
Professional baseball player. **Personal:** Born Jul 25, 1970, Columbus, GA. **Career:** Los Angeles Dodgers, outfielder, 1994-95, 1997-. **Business Addr:** Professional Baseball Player, Los Angeles Dodgers, 1000 Elysian Park Ave, Los Angeles, CA 90012, (213)224-1530.

INGRAM, GREGORY LAMONT
Art advocate. **Personal:** Born Apr 10, 1961, Greensboro, NC; son of Bradley & Mary L Ingram. **Educ:** NYC Dept of Cultural Affairs, Artist's Certificate, 1985; Graduate citizens Comm, 1997. **Career:** New York City Housing Assn, artist consultant, 1993-; Harmony Visions Gallery, dir, 1994; GLI Graphics & Consultants, pres, currently. **Orgs:** Rush Philanthropic Arts Foundation, consultant, 1994-97; New York City Greenthumb Projects, Brooklyn, NY; Comm Board 5 Brooklyn NY, volunteer, 1996-97; St Paul Comm Ch, mem, 1997; Americorps, Black Ch Educ, mem, 1997; Brooklyn Parks, volunteer, 1997. **Special Achievements:** Kids-in-Biz Expo, 1994; Individual Exhibitions: Newspaper Collages, Spring Creek Branch Library, NYC, New Lots Branch Library, NYC; Group Exhibitions: The Grambling Show, Public Image Gallery, NYC, 1986; Democracy, Store Front Gallery, NYC, 1986; Group Show, Profile Gallery, NYC, 1984; Group Show, Brooklyn Terminal Show, NYC, 1983; Group Show, Fun Gallery, 1983; numerous grants and residencies; Commissions: Painted Playgrounds Boulevard Housing, NYC, 1984; Judge and Poster Design for "We Care About NY," NYC, 1986; NYC Greenthumb Projects, 1995-97; Mural, "East NY History," 1997; Mural, "Collaboration with PSBK," 1997.

INGRAM, JAMES
Musician, songwriter. **Personal:** Born Feb 16, Akron, OH. **Career:** Musician, songwriter, currently. **Honors/Awds:** Albums: Into The Night, 1983, It's Real, 1989, The Power of Great Music, 1991; Singles: Just Once, 1981, One Hundred Ways, 1981, Baby, Come to Me, 1982, How Do You Keep the Music Playing, 1983, Yah Mo B There, 1983, There's No Easy Way, 1984, What About Me, 1984; first artist in the history of pop music to win a Grammy Award without having released his own album. **Business Addr:** Musician, c/o Warner Bros, 3300 Warner Blvd, Burbank, CA 91510.

INGRAM, KEVIN
Business executive. **Personal:** Born in Philadelphia, PA. **Educ:** Massachusetts Institute of Technology, BChE, 1980; Stanford University, Western Electric Research Scholar in Engineering; Stanford University Graduate School of Business. **Career:** Lehman Brothers, associate; Goldman Sachs & Co, vice president, 1988-. **Special Achievements:** Listed as one of 25 "Hottest Blacks on Wall Street," Black Enterprise, 1992. **Business Phone:** (212)902-1000.

INGRAM, LAVERNE DOROTHY
Physician. **Personal:** Born Mar 1, 1955, Lawrenceville, VA; daughter of Lydia House Ingram and James Ingram; married Robert Dean. **Educ:** VA Union Univ, Richmond, VA, BS (cum laude), Biology, 1973-77; Harvard Univ, Cambridge, MA, 1975; Eastern VA Medical School, Norfolk, VA, MD, 1978-81; VA Commonwealth Univ, Richmond, VA, 1978. **Career:** Medical Coll of VA, Richmond, VA, lab asst, 1972-73, laboratory specialist, 1973-78; Howard Univ Hospital, Washington, DC, medical intern, 1981-82, radiology resident, 1982-85; US Navy, Norfolk, VA, head, radiology dept, 1985-87; US Navy, Portsmouth, VA, staff radiologist 1987-90; University of Texas Health Science Center, Houston, TX, staff radiologist, 1990-. **Orgs:** Vice pres, Natl Naval Officers Assn, 1985-86; mem, Soc Aid to Sickle Cell Anemia; Big Brother Big Sister, 1986-. **Honors/Awds:** Mem of the Year, Natl Naval Officers Assn Tidewater Chapter, 1988; Distinguished Serv Award, Natl Naval Officers Assn, Natl Award, 1988. **Military Serv:** US Navy, lt commander, 1985-90, US Navy Reserve, commander, 1992-; Navy Commendation, 1987; Certificate of Appreciation, 1988, 1989; Navy Achievement Award, 1990. **Home Addr:** 8219 Pine Thistle Lane, Spring, TX 77379. **Business Addr:** Asst Professor, Radiology, LBJ General Hospital, 5656 Kelley St, Houston, TX 77026.

INGRAM, PHILLIP M.
Computer company executive. **Personal:** Born Nov 14, 1945, Detroit, MI; son of Marion Martin Lewis and Henry Ingram; divorced; children: Marc J Ingram. **Educ:** Wayne State Univ, Detroit, MI, BFA, industrial design, 1971, MBA, 1978. **Career:** Gen Motors Engineering Staff, Warren, MI, project engr, 1964-78; Amer Motors Corp, Detroit, MI, principal engr, 1978-79; Systemation Corp, Detroit, MI, pres, 1979-80; Detroit Inst of Technology, Detroit, MI, assoc prof, 1980-81; Gen Automation, Detroit, MI, dist sales mgr, 1980-82; The Computer Group, Inc, Walled Lake, MI, pres, 1982-. **Orgs:** Mem, Engineering Society of Detroit, 1975. **Honors/Awds:** Reviewer, Natl Science Found Cause Grant Programs, 1980.

INGRAM, ROBERT B.
Mayor, educator. **Personal:** Born Aug 5, 1936, Miami, FL; son of Arimentha Ingram and Harold Ingram; married Delores Newsome Ingram, Jun 25, 1961; children: Tirzah Chezarena, Tamara Cheri. **Educ:** Florida International Univ, Miami, FL, BS, 1974, MS, 1975; Union Exp College & Univ, Cincinnati, OH, PhD, 1978. **Career:** City of Miami Police, Miami, FL, police officer, 1959-80; City of Opa-Locka Police, Opa-Locka, FL, chief of police, 1980-85; City of South Miami, South Miami, FL, city manager, 1985-86; Miami Dade Community College, Miami, FL, director of federal grant, 1986-89; City of Opa-Locka, Opa-Locka, FL, mayor, 1986-; Florida Memorial College, Opa-Locka, FL, professor, chairman, division of extension and continuing education, 1989-; Allen Chapel AME Church, pastor, 1994-. **Orgs:** Founder/president, NOBLE, Florida Chapter, 1981-83; founder/president, Lock Town Mental Health Center, 1978-80; founder/president, National Assn of Blacks in Criminal Justice; secretary, Dade County Mental Health, 1970-72; president, Center for Family & Child Enrichment, 1968-70; president, National Conference of Black Mayors, board, 1994-95. **Honors/Awds:** Pyramid of Success, National Forum of Black Public Administrators, 1987; NCTI/CIP Outstanding Contributions, Dade County Public Schools, 1988; Outstanding Service, NAREB, National Assn of Realtors, 1989; Distinguished Service, National Assn of Negro Business & Professional Women, 1990; Distinguished Service, Sisters of Opa-Locka, 1991; Theodore R Gibson Distinguished Service Award, 1992; author, "I Am an African Methodist Episcopal Elder," 1990. **Military Serv:** Military US Army, Sp4, 1956-59; Good Conduct & Expert Marksman. **Business Addr:** Professor, Chairman Extension and Continuing Educ, Florida Memorial College, 15200 NW 42nd Ave, Lehman Building, PO Box 133, Opa Locka, FL 33054.

INGRAM, STEPHEN
Professional football player. **Personal:** Born May 8, 1971, Seat Pleasant, MD; married Robyn. **Educ:** Univ of Maryland, BS in criminal justice. **Career:** Tampa Bay Buccaneers, tackle, 1995-. **Business Addr:** Professional Football Player, Tampa Bay Buccaneers, One Buccaneer Place, Tampa, FL 33607, (813)870-2700.

INGRAM, VALERIE J.
Broadcast journalist, producer. **Personal:** Born Dec 5, 1959, Chicago, IL; daughter of Bettie J Rushing Ingram and Archie R Ingram. **Educ:** Loyola University, Chicago, IL, 1990; Columbia College, Chicago, Il, BA, radio, writing, 1979. **Career:** WUSN Radio US99, Chicago, IL, senior sales assistant, 1984-85; CBS Radio Network, Chicago, IL, office manager, 1985-87; WBBM-AM Radio, Chicago, IL, associate producer, 1987-. **Orgs:** Member, radio ad hoc committee, International Lutheran Layman's League, 1990-; member, National Association of Black Journalists, 1990-; member, Lutheran Women's Missionary League, 1989-; secretary, Minority Employees Association, CBS Inc, 1985-90; Leader, Gospel Choir, 1989-, youth group officer, St Paul Lutheran Church Austin, 1986-88; Sunday school teacher, HS, 1988-90. **Honors/Awds:** Outstanding Volunteer, Aid Association for Lutherans Branch #385, 1989. **Business Addr:** Associate Producer, WBBM-AM Radio, CBS Inc, 630 N McClurg Ct, Chicago, IL 60611.

INGRAM, WILLIAM B.
Consultant. **Personal:** Born May 5, 1935, Lillesville, NC; married Dora Rebecca Plowden (deceased); children: Katrina, Eric, Elaine. **Educ:** Lincoln Univ, BA 1961; Univ of Southern CA, M Public Admin, 1977. **Career:** Co-owner, D'Lora's Boys Home, 1968-73; LA Co Museum, chief museum opers 1970-73; Riverside City Coll, training consultant 1977-; B&D Financial Servs, owner, 1980-; Orange Co Probation, training consultant 1981-; Supervising Deputy Probations Officer, 1961-87 (retired); Teacher, Moreno Valley School, 1984-. **Orgs:** Pres CA Coalition Black Bd members 1982; vice pres CA School bd Assn 1979-; pres Natl Caucus Black Bd members 1982-84; dir Perris Valley Martin Luther King Found 1983-85; mem CA Correction, Probation & Parole Comm 1984-85; pres-elect Riverside Co School Bd Assn 1985-86; bd of dirs Coalition CA Black Bd members; commr Riverside County Juvenile Justice; Pres, California School Bd Assn, 1989; vice president, National School Board Assn. **Honors/Awds:** Comm Serv Award Los Angeles Bd of Supvrs, 1980; Outstanding Bd Mem, Natl School Bd Assn, 1983; Proclamation Riverside Bd of Supvrs, Black supporter/Achievement 1984. **Military Serv:** AUS corpl 1953-56. **Home Addr:** Box 1289, Perris, CA 92572.

INGRAM, WINIFRED
Clinical psychologist. **Personal:** Born Dec 15, 1913, Seattle, WA; daughter of Ione Jeanette Clark Williams and LeRoy Robert Ingram. **Educ:** Univ of WA, BA 1937, MA 1938; Northwestern Univ, PhD 1951. **Career:** Neuropsychiatric Inst Ann Arbor, MI, psychologist 1950-56; Univ of MI Summer Sch Educ, lecturer 1953-55; Univ of MI Sch of Med Dept Psychiatry, instr 1954-56; Hawthorn Center for Children, dir dept clinical psych 1956-72; The Evergreen State Coll, faculty mem 1972-81, faculty mem Emerita 1981-. **Orgs:** Cons, Delta Home for Girls Detroit 1963-66, Port Huron Area School Dist 1966-68, Ypsilanti Early Educ Proj 1968-70, Adv Comm on Training in Clinical Psych 1967-72; mem Amer Assn for Advancement of Sci; mem Amer Psychol Assn; Delta Sigma Theta Sor; bd dir Ann Arbor Family Serv 1964-70; bd dir Ann Arbor Black Theatre 1969-71; Comm Committee for Coord of Child Care & Devel 1968-69. **Honors/Awds:** Community Scholarship 1933-34; US Public Health Serv Fellowship in Clin Psych Northwestern Univ 1948-50; Fellow of the Mary Ingraham Bunting Inst of Radcliffe Coll 1971; Alpha Kappa Delta Natl Soc Honor Soc 1936; Sigma Xi Natl Sci Honor Soc 1948. **Business Addr:** Mem of Faculty Emerita, Evergreen State College, Olympia, WA 98505.

INGRUM, ADRIENNE G.
Publishing consultant. **Personal:** Born Mar 21, 1954, St Louis, MO; daughter of Leontine Yvonne Pulliam Ingrum and Clister Jack Ingrum; married Arn Reginald Ashwood, May 24, 1977 (divorced 1996). **Educ:** Georgetown Univ, Washington, DC, BS, intl economics. **Career:** Harvard Univ, Boston, MA, staff asst, 1977-79; Grosset & Dunlap, New York, NY, assoc editor, 1980-82; Putnam Berkley Group, New York, NY, vice pres, exec editor, 1982-90; Waldenbooks, Stamford, CT, publisher, vice pres, Longmeadow Press, 1990-94; Crown Publishers, vp, dir of trade paperback publishing, 1994-96. **Orgs:** Women's Media Group; Go On Girl! Book Club. **Home Addr:** 43 St Nicholas Place, New York, NY 10031, (212)283-6466.

INNIS, ROY EMILE ALFREDO
Association executive. **Personal:** Born Jun 6, 1934, St Croix, VI; son of Georgianna Thomas Innis and Alexander Innis; married Doris Funnye; children: Roy (deceased), Alexander (deceased), Cedric, Patricia, Corinne, Kwame, Niger, Kimathi. **Educ:** City Coll of NY, 1952-56. **Career:** Harlem Commonwealth Council, dir 1967-68; Congress of Racial Equality, assoc dir 1968, natl dir 1968-81, natl chrmn 1981-. **Orgs:** Rsch chemist Vick Chemical Co 1958-63, Montefiore Hospital 1963-67; mem bd New York Urban Coalition, Haryou Act, Harlem Commonwealth Council. **Honors/Awds:** Research Fellow Metropolitan Applied Rsch Center New York City 1967. **Military Serv:** AUS sgt 2 Yrs. **Business Addr:** Natl Chairman, Congress of Racial Equality, 30 Cooper Sq, New York, NY 10003.

INNISS, CHARLES EVANS
Utility executive. **Personal:** Born Jun 13, 1935, New York, NY; son of Edna I Clarke Inniss and Sidney F Inniss; married Marjorie E Thomas Inniss, Feb 14, 1989. **Educ:** New York University, New York, NY, BS, economics, 1968, MPA, 1980. **Career:** Dun & Bradstreet, Inc, New York, NY, asst manager, 1962-69; Bedford Stuyvesant Restoration Corp, Brooklyn, NY, dir of area development, 1969-73; City of New York, NY, administrator of Brooklyn model cities, 1973-78; Brooklyn Public Library, Brooklyn, NY, public information dir, 1978-79; Brooklyn Union Gas, Brooklyn, NY, vice president, 1979-. **Orgs:** Vice chair, Bedford Stuyvesant Restoration Corporation, 1983-; past president, Brooklyn Children's Museum, 1983-; vice chair, Marcus Garvey Nursing Home, 1986-; past chair, Black Officers Association, 1980-; chair, Studio Museum in Harlem, 1980-; City University of New York, trustee, 1992-. **Honors/Awds:** Many awards for community service. **Military Serv:** New York Army National Guard, Capt, 1963-86. **Business Addr:** Vice President, Brooklyn Union Gas, One Metrotech Center, Brooklyn, NY 11201.

INYAMAH, NATHANIEL GINIKANWA N.
Educator. **Personal:** Born Jan 21, 1934, Mbaise, Nigeria; married Catherine; children: Christian, Caroline, Grace, Deborah, Hope, Samuel. **Educ:** Univ Nigeria, Diploma Tehol 1958; STM NW Seminary MN, BD MDiv 1969; Temple, MA 1973f Temple, PhD 1976;1971. **Career:** Nigeria, tchr 1951-53; Nigeria HS, 1954-55; Holy Trinity & Lutheran Nigeria, pastor 1959-66; LCA, asst & supply pastor; Camden NJ, teacher; positions in Nigeria Traditional Priest Earth Goddess; Trinity Lutheran Church, pastor & founder. **Orgs:** Bd dir & vice pres Lutheran Ch; pres Ezinihitte Cultural Union; vice pres Owerri Divisional Union; Owerri Provincial Union; WHO; exec mem Eastern Nigeria Soc Welfare Soc; youth prog dir; Utheran Commn Soc Equality Justice; Educ Com Minority Group; African Studies Assn. **Honors/Awds:** Crowned chief Okonko Igbo Soc US Lutheran Missionary At Large 1967-71; Aid Assn Lutheran Ins Scholarship 1967; NW Students Assn Scholarship 1968; Lutheran Wmn Missionary & League Scholarship 1969; Elmer O & Ida Preston Educ Trust Award 1969-71; Temple Univ Gradh Sch Award 1972, 73. **Business Addr:** PO Box 9786, Philadelphia, PA 19140.

IONE, CAROLE (IONE)
Author, psychotherapist, director, playwright, inter faith minister. **Personal:** Born May 28, 1937, Washington, DC; daughter of Hylan Garnet Lewis and Mrs Leighla Whipper; divorced; children: Alessandro, Santiago, Antonio. **Educ:** Bennington College, 1959; Helix Training Program in Psychotherapy and the Healing Arts, 1987; Chinese Healing Arts Center, Qi Gong Therapist, 1991; Natl Guild of Hypnotists, Advanced Clinical Hypnotherapist, 1994. **Career:** Renaissance Poets Series, cofounder, 1960s; Renaissance House, Inc, artistic dir, 1960s; Dream, Journal and Notebook wkshops, instructor, 1980-; Essence Magazine, contributing editor, 1980-82; Manhatten Theatre Club, director, writers in performance, 1980-82; Women's Mysteries, dir, 1987-; Live Letters, artistic dir, 1974-; Pauline Oliveros Foundation, vp, co-artistic dir, 1987-. **Orgs:** The Author's Guild, Inc, 1991-; Poets and Writers, Inc, 1979-; Natl Writers Union, 1988-; The Intl Womens Writing Guild, 1988-. **Honors/Awds:** South Carolina Comm for the Humanities, for A Diary of Reconstruction, 1985; Rockefeller Foundation and Natl Endowment for the Arts, for Njinga, The Queen-King, a play w/music and pageantry, 1987-91; New York State Council on the Arts and Poets and Writers, Inc, for Live Letters Presentation 1979-; Fellowships to the Macdowell Colony, Yaddo, Edward; Albee Foundation, The Writers Room. **Special Achievements:** Scripts: Njinga the Queen-King; A Diary of Reconstruction; Mirage, A Friend; New York City, Evidence; Script devel for Rizzoli Productions, NYC; Publications: Pride of Family, 4 generations of Amer Women of Color, Summit Books, 1991, Avon Books, 1992; The Coffee Table Lover, The Country Press, 1973; Unsealed Lips, Capra Press, 1990; Piramada Negra, The Country Press, 1973, Live Letters, Press, 1991; Contemporary Literary Criticism, 1989; Fiction, Reviews and Articles in: The Village Voice, New Dawn, Oui, Ms American Film Ambassador, Working Women; Oggi; Vogue; Christian Science; Monitor; Essence; Arcadie; Revue Literature; Readings and Presentations: Skidmore College, New School for Social Research, Teachers and Writers Collaborative, City College of New York, Columbia Green Comm Coll, Seattle Douglass-The Truth Library, The College of Charleston, Avery Institute, The New York Public Library, The Actors Institute, Manhattan Theatre Club, Natl Public Radio, CBS Nightwatch, The Open Center, SUNY, New Paltz, Omega Institute, Esalen Institute, New York Geneological Society, Shomburg Center, NY Public Library and Others. **Business Addr:** Co-Artistic Dir, Artistic Director, Live Letters, a literary program, Pauline Oliveros Foundation, PO Box 1956, Kingston, NY 12401, (914)338-5984.

IRBY, GALVEN
Government official (retired). **Personal:** Born Sep 29, 1921, Laurens, SC; son of Grace L Irby and Henry D Irby; married Delores Virginia Odden, Dec 17, 1957; children: Barbara J, Grace M, Kelley R Garrett, Vickie L Strickland, Sandra M Garrett, Galven C, Craig R. **Educ:** Youngstown Univ, 1946-48; Howard Univ, LLB, 1952. **Career:** Republic Iron and Steel Mills/Fabrication, 1940-49; US Postal Service, part time postal clerk, 1950-63; State of Oregon, Department of Employment Security, claims supervisor, 1954-63; Veterans Administration, legal disability rating specialist, 1972-86. **Orgs:** Pacific Lutheran Univ, bd of controls, 1988-, bd of regents, 1969-88, executive bd of bd of regents, 1983-88; Concordia College, Bd of Controls, advisor, 1973-75; Amer Lutheran, Department of Admission, executive/national bds, 1978-79, North Pacific District, Portland Conference, secretary-treasurer, 1965-67; Alpha Phi Alpha Fraternity, life mem; Pacific Lutheran Univ, bd of controls, 1988-94; Alpha Phi Alpha/NAACP School Mentoring Project, mem, 1989-; numerous others. **Honors/Awds:** US Veterans Administration, Public Service Award, 1969, Superior Performance Award, 1975, Public Appreciation Award for Community Service, 1975; Disabled Amer Veterans, National Commanders Award, 1982. **Military Serv:** US Army, sgt, 1942-45: 31 months of Overseas duty; Bronze Star; Good Conduct Award. **Home Addr:** 14343 NE Alton St, Portland, OR 97230.

IRBY, MARY
Automotive executive. **Personal:** Born Oct 19, 1944, Columbus, MS; daughter of Robert & Lettie B Swopes; divorced; children: Cassandra Delk, Robert Smallwood, Joseph Smallwood. **Educ:** Bowling Green State Univ, BLS, 1989; Central Michigan Univ, attended. **Career:** General Motors Corp, senior staff assistant, communications, 1968-. **Orgs:** Girl Scouts of the USA, second vice pres, 1987-89; Leadership Saginaw Alumni, bd member, 1994-; Reuben Daniels Foundation, bd member, 1994-; Big Brothers/Big Sisters, bd member, 1994-; Public Relations Society of America- White Pines Chapter, 1994-; Saginaw Comm Foundation, Distribution Committe, 1995; Alpha Kappa Alpha Sorority. **Business Addr:** Senior Staff Assistant, General Motors Corp, Metal Fabricating Division, 5607 New King St, Mail Code 483-622-316, Troy, MI 48098-2666, (810)696-2054.

IRELAND, LYNDA
Entrepreneur, business leader. **Personal:** Born Jan 2, 1950, Bronx, NY; daughter of Margaret McNair Johnson and Carwee Johnson; divorced; children: Francisco Marc & Maya Danielle Ireland. **Career:** African-Amer Inst, New York, NY, program dir, 1971-76; Hofstra Univ, Hempstead, NY, admin, 1979-84; Panache Professional Systems Inc, Hempstead, NY, CEO pres, 1979-84. **Orgs:** Bd mem, African Amer Hertiage Assn, 1981-85; bd mem, Minority Women's Task Force, NYS, N O W, 1985; delegate, White House Conf on Small Business, 1985-86; pres, Assn of Minority Enterprises of NYS, Inc, 1986-; bd mem, NYS Governor's Advisory Bd on Small Business, 1987-; Advisory Bd, Business Center, F.I.T., 1989. **Honors/Awds:** Outstanding Achievement, AMENY, 1985; Leadership Citation, Nassau County, 1987; Citation, Mayor of NY, 1987; Leadership Award, Women on the Job, 1988; Leadership Citation, Town of Hempstead, 1988; Mothers at Work, Role Model of the Year Award (lst recipient), Morningside Community Day Care Centers; advisor to upcoming book by Prentice Hall on minority vendor programs of ethical corps (Fortune 500); Public speaker on Minority Business Devel.

IRELAND, RODERICK LOUIS
State Supreme Court justice. **Personal:** Born Dec 3, 1944, Springfield, MA; divorced; children: Helen Elizabeth, Michael Alexander. **Educ:** Lincoln U, BA 1966; Columbia Law Sch, JD 1969; Harvard Law, LLM 1975. **Career:** Boston Juvenile Ct, judge 1977-90; Bd of Appeal on Motor Vehicle Policies & Bonds, chmn of bd 1977; Sec of Adminstrn & Finance MA, counsel 1975-77; Harvard Law Sch, teaching fellow 1975; Roxbury Defenders Com, dir 1971-74, Massachusetts Appeals Court, judge, begin 1990; MA Supreme Court, justice, currently; Northeastern University School of Law, faculty, currently, College of Criminal Justice, faculty, currently. **Orgs:** Bd of dirs Columbia Law Sch Alumni Assn; mem MA Bar Assn; mem Boston Bar Assn; mem ABA; mem MA Black Lawyers Assn; mem NY Bar Assn Bd Dirs Proj Aim; bd dirs First Inc; bd dirs Roxbury YMCA; bd dirs MA Minority Council on Alcoholism; mem Omega Psi Phi; mem Lincoln Alumni. **Honors/Awds:** Recip 10 Outstndg yng ldrs of Boston award Boston Jaycees 1979; 10 outstndg men of Am award US Jaycees 1980. **Special Achievements:** First African American justice On Massachusetts Supreme Court. **Business Addr:** Justice, Massachusetts Supreme Court, 1500 New Courthouse, Boston, MA 02108.

IRMAGEAN
Artist. **Personal:** Born Apr 9, 1947, Detroit, MI; daughter of Mamie Lee Sago Curry (deceased) and Theodore Curry; divorced; children: Sundjata T Kone. **Educ:** Wayne St Univ Monteith Coll, 1965-66; Grove Str Coll, AA 1974; CA Coll of Arts & Crafts, BFA 1976. **Career:** Isabelle Percy West Gallery CA Coll of Arts & Crafts Oakland, exhibit 1979; NY Carlsberg Glyptotek Museum Copenhagen Denmark, rep 1980; Los Medanos Coll Pittsburg, CA, exhibit artist 1980; Berkeley Art Center CA, exhibit 1981; Galerie Franz Mehring Berlin, Germany, exhibit 1981; SF Museum of Modern Art, exhibit 1981; Center for the Visual Arts Oakland CA, exhibit 1985; Spanish Speaking Citizens Found, Oakland, CA, guest art instructor, 1989; E Oakland Youth Devel Center, Oakland, CA, mural instructor, 1989; City Sites, CA Coll of Arts & Crafts, artist mentor, 1989; Berkeley Art Center, exhibitor, 1988; San Francisco State Univ, exhibitor, 1989; Koncepts Cultural Gallery, Oakland, CA, art instructor, 1989; Ebony Museum, Oakland, CA, exhibitor coord, 1989-90; Hatley Martin Gallery, San Fcisco, CA, exhibit, 1990; Capp Street Gallery, San Francisco, CA, public art installation, 1991. **Orgs:** Juror Vida Gallery SF, CA 1981; coord of US participation 11 Bienal del Grabado De Am Maracaibo, Venezuela 1982; juror, Festival at the lake, Craft/Art Market, Oakland, CA, 1989; Berkeley Juneteenth Association, Inc, board of directors, publicity chairperson, art drr, 1992; Art and Creative Writing Youth Competition Program, Golden State Life Insurance, juror. **Honors/Awds:** Amer Artist Today in Black & White Vol 11 1980 author Dr H L Williams; exhibit Dept De Bellas Artes Guadaljara, Mexico 1982; exhibit Brockman Gallery Prod LA, CA 1982; Hon mem Sigma Gamma Rho Sor 1986; Daniel Mendelowitz "A Guide to Drawing" 3rd ed Holt Rinehart and Winston 1982, 4th ed revised by Duane Wakeham 1988; Outstanding Women of the Twentieth Century, Sigma Gamma Rho Sorority, 1986; Certificiate of Appreciation, St Augustine's Church, 1988; feature, The Aurora, 1987, Sigma Gamma Rho Sorority, 1987; The CA Art Review, 2nd edition Amer Reference, Inc, 1988; Amer artist, 2nd edition, References, 1989; 1st Place, Best of Show, Ebony Museum, Expo 89-90, 1990; Black Scholar, vol 20, no 3 & 4, Black World Foundation (cover), 1990; Feature, Eugene White's Kujionia Magazine, 1990. **Special Achievements:** Selected publications: Anthology of Contemporary African-American Women Artists, 1992, A Guide to Drawing, 1993, Poetry: An American Heritage, 1993; Smell This 2, UC Berkeley, 1991; exhibitions: Prague, Czechoslovakia, Art of Ecology: Recycling the Collective Spirit, 1991, Richmond Art Center, Looking Out Looking In, 1992, Bomani Gallery, 1992; Curator, Ebony Museum, 1994-95; Voices of the Dream; African American Women Speak, Venice Johnson, Chronicle Books. **Business Addr:** Artist, PO Box 5602, Berkeley, CA 94705.

IRONS, EDWARD D.
Educational administrator. **Educ:** Harvard University, graduated. **Career:** Atlanta University Center, Altanta, GA, professor; City of Washington, DC, Office of Banking and Financial Institutions, superintendent; Clark-Atlanta University School of Business Administration, dean, currently. **Business Addr:** Dean, Clark-Atlanta University School of Business Administration, Wright Hall, James P. Brawley at Fair St, Atlanta, GA 30314.

IRONS, PAULETTE
State senator. **Personal:** Born Jun 19, 1953; married Alvin L. **Educ:** Loyola Univ, BBA; Tulane Univ, JD. **Career:** System engineer, 1976-83; constuction estimator, 1984-92; small business consultant, 1992; LA State, Dist 95, rep, 1993-95; LA State. Dist 4, 1995-.

IRONS, SANDRA JEAN
Educator. **Personal:** Born Jul 17, 1940, Middlesboro, KY; daughter of Rosa Green Carr (deceased) and Roy Carr (deceased); married Lethenius Irons (divorced 1978). **Educ:** Kentucky State University, Frankford, KY, BS, 1960; Purdue University, West Lafayette, MAT, 1965; Indiana University, Gary, IN, MS30. **Career:** State of Ohio Dept Public Welfare, Dayton, OH, caseworker, 1960-61; Gary Community School Corp, Gary, IN, teacher, 1961-71; Gary Teachers Union, Gary, IN, president, 1971-. **Orgs:** Vice president, American Federation of Teachers, 1974-; vice pres/defense, Indiana Federation of Teachers, 1971-; first vice president, NW Indiana Federation of Labor, 1987; treasurer, NW Indiana Council of Teachers Unions, 1984; co-director, Christian Education - New Revelation Baptist Church, 1979-; president, Mental Health Associaion in Lake Co, 1984-88. **Honors/Awds:** Fellowship, National Science Foundation, 1961-65; Gary Commission on the Status of Women, 1973-75. **Business Addr:** President, Gary Teachers Union, Local #4, AFT, 1301 Virginia St, Gary, IN 46407.

IRVIN, BYRON EDWARD
Professional basketball player. **Personal:** Born Dec 2, 1966, LaGrange, IL. **Educ:** Univ of Arkansas, Fayetteville, AR, 1984-86; Univ of Missouri, Columbia, MO, 1987-89. **Career:** Portland Trail Blazers, 1989-90; Washington Bullets, 1990-. **Business Addr:** Professional Basketball Player, Washington Wizards, One Harry S Truman Dr, Capital Centre, Landover, MD 20785-4798.

IRVIN, CHARLES LESLIE
Attorney. **Personal:** Born Mar 2, 1935, Corpus Christi, TX; son of Louise Irvin and Joseph Irvin; married Shirley Jean Smith; children: Kimberley Antoinette, Jonathan Charles. **Educ:** TX Southern Univ, BA 1964, LLB 1964; Cornell Univ, Exec Devel Course 1984; Wharton Sch of Business, Financial Course 1985. **Career:** US Dept of Labor Kansas City, MO, attorney 1964-67; US Dept of Labor Chicago, attorney 1967-73; Texaco Inc, senior attorney; division attorney Midland, Texas 1988-89; attorney Denver, Colorado 1989-90, regional counsel, beginning 1990; managing attorney, administration, White Plains, NY. **Orgs:** Mem TX & Colorado Bars Assn 1964-; US Supreme Ct; 9th & 5th Cir Ct of Appeals, TX Bar Foundation. **Military Serv:** AUS Sgt E-5 1955-58. **Home Addr:** 6156 Andershire Dr, Conroe, TX 77304-1480. **Business Addr:** Attorney, Private Practice, 314 Cochran, Conroe, TX 77301, (409)441-1555.

IRVIN, KEN
Professional football player. **Personal:** Born Jul 11, 1972, Lindale, GA. **Educ:** Memphis. **Career:** Buffalo Bills, defensive back, 1995-. **Business Addr:** Professional Football Player, Buffalo Bills, One Bills Dr, Orchard Park, NY 14127, (716)648-1800.

IRVIN, MICHAEL JEROME
Professional football player. **Personal:** Born Mar 5, 1966, Fort Lauderdale, FL; married Sandi; children: Myesha, Chelsea, Michael. **Educ:** Univ of Miami, BA, business management, 1988. **Career:** Dallas Cowboys, wide receiver, 1988-. **Honors/Awds:** NFL Alumni, Wide Receiver of the Year, 1991; Pro Bowl, 1991, 1992, 1993, 1994, 1995. **Business Addr:** Professional Football Player, Dallas Cowboys, 1 Cowboys Parkway, Irving, TX 75063, (214)556-9900.

IRVIN, MILTON M.
Business executive. **Personal:** Born in East Orange, NJ. **Educ:** US Merchant Marine Academy; University of Pennsylvania, Wharton School of Business and Finance. **Career:** Chase Manhattan Bank, lending officer; Salomon Brothers Inc, trader, 1977, vice president, 1979, director, senior manager, 1992-; Paine Webber, managing dir, 1988-90. **Special Achievements:** Listed as one of 25 ''Hottest Blacks on Wall Street,'' Black Enterprise, 1992. **Business Addr:** Director, Salomon Brothers Inc, 7 World Trade Center, New York, NY 10048-0000, (212)783-7000.

IRVIN, MONFORD MERRILL (MONTE)
Business executive (retired). **Personal:** Born Feb 25, 1919, Columbia, AL; married Dee; children: Pamela Irvin Fields, Patti Irvin Gordon. **Educ:** Lincoln Univ Chester PA, attended 2 yrs. **Career:** Cuban Winter League, professional baseball player; NY Giants, professional baseball player 1949-55; Chicago Cubs, professional baseball player 1956; Office of the Baseball Commiss, spec asst to the commiss; Diversified Capital Corp, vp. **Honors/Awds:** Elected to Baseball Hall of Fame 1973. **Military Serv:** Buck sgt 1313 GS Engineers - ETO, 1943-45. **Home Addr:** 11 Douglas Ct S, Homosassa, FL 34446.

IRVIN, REGINA LYNETTE
State government official. **Personal:** Born Sep 13, 1963, Columbia, MS; daughter of Carolyn J Barnes Irvin and Eugene Irvin. **Educ:** Alcorn State University, BA, 1985; Thurgood Marshall School of Law, JD, 1988. **Career:** Magistrate Karen K Brown, law clerk, 1988; Department of Navy, Naval Sea System Command, attorney, 1988-89; Attorneys S Ralph Martin Jr & Benjamin W Spaulding Jr, law clerk, 1989; Attorney Raymond Register, law clerk, 1989-90; Secret & Associates, law clerk, 1989-90; Department of Veterans Affairs, claims examiner, 1991; Mississippi Department of Human Services, child support enforcement officer, 1992-93; Mississippi Dept of Human Services, administrative hearings officer, 1993-. **Orgs:** Alpha Kappa Alpha Sorority Inc, basileus, anti basileus, grammateus, 1983-84; Political Science Society, secretary, 1983-84; Social Science Society, president, 1984-85; American Bar Assn, general mbr, 1985-88; Phi Alpha Delta Law Fraternity Intl, vice pres, 1985-88; Natl Bar Assn, Black Law Students Assn, vice pres, 1985-88; State Bar of Texas, Students Division, general mbr, 1985-88; Thurgood Marshall Law Review, staff mbr, 1985-88. **Honors/Awds:** Barrister's Wives, Scholastic Scholarship, 1986-87; BCI, Outstanding Leadership Award, 1989; TMSLR, Book Review Editor, 1987-88; Natl Dean's List, 1988-89. **Special Achievements:** Author: case comment, Thurgood Marshall Law Review, vol 12, num 1, p 271, Fall 1986. **Home Addr:** 1212 Maxwell St, Columbia, MS 39429, (601)736-4336.

IRVINE, CAROLYN LENETTE
Educator. **Personal:** Born Mar 7, 1947, Quincy, FL; daughter of Jessie M Jones McCloud and Robert L Green; married Freeman R Irvine Jr, Nov 28, 1977; children: Fredreka R, Freeman R III. **Educ:** Florida A&M University, Tallahassee, FL, BS, 1970; University of Florida, Gainesville, FL, MS, 1975; Florida State University, Tallahassee, FL, PhD, 1989. **Career:** Shanks High School, Quincy, FL, speech & English teacher, 1976-77; Florida A&M University, Tallahassee, FL, speech teacher, 1975-76, 1983-, English teacher, 1978-83. **Orgs:** Member, Jack and Jill of America, Inc, 1988-90; member, Associations of Teachers of America, 1989-90; member, Florida Speech Communication Association, 1984-91; member, Phi Delta Kappa, 1984-91; various others. **Honors/Awds:** ''A Speech Recipe,'' The SGS Communicator, the School of General Studies, Florida A&M University, vol. 10, number 3, December 1990; ''An Analysis of Speech,'' The SGS Communicator, the School of General Studies, Florida A&M University, vol. 8, number 4, December 1989; ''Cooperative Education: Its Role and Scope in Vocational Education,'' ERIC Clearinghouse on Adult Career and Vocational Education, Research in Education, 1985; ''Love,'' poem, in Anthology of Best Love Poetry, 1980; Certificate of Appreciation, Miracle Temple Daycare Center. **Home Addr:** 618 Brookridge Dr, Tallahassee, FL 32304.

IRVINE, FREEMAN RAYMOND, JR.
Educator. **Personal:** Born Sep 12, 1931, Madison, FL; married Carolyn Lenett Green; children: Rodney, Charlton, Pamela, Fredreka, Freeman III. **Educ:** FL A&M Univ, BS 1958; OK State Univ, cert 1960; Oak Ridge Associated Univs, cert 1966; Univ of TN, MS 1968, EdD 1972. **Career:** FL A&M Univ, electronics teacher, 1958-61, electronics and math teacher, 1964-67, assoc prof of industrial engineering, beginning 1969, chairman of industrial arts and vocational educ dept, 1976-82, faculty senior, 1978-81, prof of industrial arts, currently; Dillard Comp High School, Ft Lauderdale, FL, electronics teacher, 1961-63; Univ of TN, research assoc, 1967-69; FL State Univ, research assoc, 1974-75. **Orgs:** Publication Committee FL Industrial Arts Assn 1970-73; test coord NOCTI 1980-. **Honors/Awds:** Community Service Award, Sounds of Faith Radio Program, 1979-80; ''A Simplification of Parallel Resistance Calculation,'' School Shop Magazine, 1982; Teaching Vocational Educ to Handicaps, 1985. **Military Serv:** AUS staff sgt 3 yrs. **Home Addr:** 618 Brookridge Dr, Tallahassee, FL 32304. **Business Addr:** Associate Prof, Industrial Arts, Florida A&M University, Tallahassee, FL 32310.

IRVING, CLARENCE LARRY, JR.
Attorney. **Personal:** Born Jul 7, 1955, Brooklyn, NY. **Educ:** Northwestern Univ, BA 1972-76; Stanford Univ Law School, JD 1976-79. **Career:** Kirkland E Ellis, summer assoc 1977; Breed Abbott & Morgan, summer assoc 1978; Hogan & Hartson, assoc 1979-83; US Rep Mickey Leland, legislative dir & counsel 1983-87; US House of Representatives Subcomm on Telecomm & Finance, sr counsel 1987-. **Orgs:** Precinct captain Washington DC Democratic Party 1983-84; mem Natl Bar Assn 1980-; mem Natl Conf of Black Lawyers Comm Task Force 1983-; mem Variety Club of Greater Washington 1985-; chair House of Representatives Fair Employment Practices Committee 1985-87; Board of Visitors, Stanford Law School; board member, House of Representatives Child Care Center; co-chair, Amer Bar Assoc, Electronic Media Division, Committee on Communications Law. **Honors/Awds:** Pres Stanford Law School Class of 1979; Outstanding Young Man of America Jaycees 1979. **Business Addr:** Senior Counsel, US House of Representatives, Subcomm on Telecomm & Finance, Room 316 House Annex #2, Washington, DC 20515.

IRVING, HENRY E., II
Educational administrator. **Personal:** Born Apr 21, 1937, Paterson, NJ; married Jocelyn Miller; children: Vian, Farrah, Herman III, Christopher. **Educ:** Rutgers Univ, BA 1968; Seton Hall Univ, MA 1975; Princeton Univ, Prof Cert 1976. **Career:** Ayerst Labs, Inc, asst cr mgr 1968-71; Passonc County Community Coll, dean of students 1971-76; Catholic Diocese of Paterson, dir youth programs 1976-81. **Orgs:** Mem Mayors Council on Yth 1967-74, YMCA 1971-78; pres NJ Council Coll Deans & Stdnts 1974-75; mem Bd of Dirs Acts-Vim 1985; Efwc Diocese of Newark. **Honors/Awds:** Citizenshp Awrd Lions Club Paterson 1971. **Home Addr:** 360 9th Ave, Paterson, NJ 07514.

IRVING, LARRY
Government official. **Personal:** Born Jul 7, 1955, Brooklyn, NY; married Leslie Wiley, 1987. **Educ:** Northwestern Univ, BA, 1976; Stanford Univ Law School, JD, 1979. **Career:** Hogan and Hartson, attorney, 1979-83; Congressman Mickey Leland, legislative director and counsel, 1983-87; House Fair Employment Practices Commission, staff chair, 1985-87; Subcommittee for Telecommunications and Finance of the House Committee on Energy and Commerce, senior counsel, 1987-92; National Telecommunications and Information Administration, asst secretary of commerce/director, 1993-. **Orgs:** American Bar Assn; National Conference of Black Lawyers; District of Columbia Bar Assn; Stanford Law School Board of Visitors.

IRVING, OPHELIA MCALPIN
Librarian. **Personal:** Born Apr 4, 1929, Gadsden, AL; daughter of Lamae Prater McAlpin and Jerry McAlpin; married Charles G Jr; children: Cyretha C. **Educ:** Clarks Coll, AB 1951; Atlanta Univ, 1952; Syracuse Univ, MLS 1958, 1973; Drexel Inst of Tech, 1966; NC Central Univ, 1982. **Career:** Center High School Waycross, GA, librarian 1951-54; Spencer Jr High School Columbus, GA, librarian 1954-55; St Augustine's Coll Raleigh, NC, librarian 1955-68; NC State Library Raleigh, NC, asst chief info ser section 1968-91, Shaw University Raleigh, NC, resource librarian p/t, 1992-. **Orgs:** Alpha Kappa Alpha Sor 1954-; NC Library Assn 1955-; Jack & Jill of Amer Inc 1961-73; Amer Library Assn 1963-; YWCA 1965-; NC On Line Users Group 1982-; Microcomputer Users Group NC 1983-; Top Ladies of Distinction; member, Continental Societies Inc, 1990; member, Links Inc, 1991. **Honors/Awds:** Faculty Fellowship St Augustine Coll Raleigh, NC 1964; NC Road Builders' Award, 1991; Order of the Long Leaf Pine Award, 1991; appointed to the NC State Library Commission, 1992; BCALA Distinguished Award, 1992; NCLA Life Membership Award, 1997.

IRVING, TERRY DUANE
Professional football player. **Personal:** Born Jul 3, 1971, Galveston, TX; married Frankie; children: Breana. **Educ:** McNeese State, bachelor's degree in electrical engineering. **Career:** Arizona Cardinals, linebacker, 1994-. **Business Addr:** Professional Football Player, Arizona Cardinals, 8701 S Hardy, Tempe, AZ 85284, (602)379-0101.

IRVING-GIBBS, FANNYE
Administrator (retired). **Personal:** Born Sep 3, 1914, Prince George County, VA; daughter of Paul Rufus & Elizabeth Irving; widowed; children: Elizabeth Diaz-Holmes, Charlene Bouldes, Ruth I Bouldes. **Educ:** Univ of Albuquerque, AA, 1981; Univ of New Mexico, BA, 1988, MA, 1990. **Career:** NYC, Social Services, clerk, 1951-57, Transit Authority, clerk, 1957-65, Housing Authority, senior teller, 1965-79; Rio Rancho, New Mexico, municipal court clerk, 1980-84; Mount Calvary Baptist Church, dir of christian educ, 1994-96; American History, Inc, founder/project mgr, currently. **Orgs:** Girls Scouts of Amer, asst leader, leader, neighborhood chair, 1954-84; Civitans Chapter, sec, youth coord, pres, 1979-84; New Mexico Cancer Society, campaign chair, 1980; NAACP Chapter, sec, trea, 1935-93; AARP Local, housing coord, 1990-92; Albuquerque Convention & Visitors Bureau, greeter, 1992-94; Women United for Youth Tutoring and Mentoring Program, charter mem, 1986-96. **Honors/Awds:** Sr Foundation of New Mexico, Sr Hall of Fame, 1991; Natl Society of Black Engineers, Community Leadership, 1992; Albuquerque Jefferson, Community Service, 1992; Black Amer Heritage Fund, Lifetime Award, 1993; St Joseph Healthcare System & FHP, New Mexico, Sr Community Award, 1994; Univ of New Mexico, African-American Graduating Students and Student Services Appreciation, 1995; New Mexico Conference of Aging, 1995; Univ or New Mexico Alumni Assn, 100th Anniv 100 Alumni Faces, 1997; Fannye Irving-Gibbs Award, Univ of New Mexico Student Services, 1997. **Special Achievements:** College of Educ, Outstanding Student, 1990; The Tuskegee Story Paper; Status of African American Sr, Citizens in New Mexico Paper. **Home Addr:** 10316 Leymon Ct, NW, Albuquerque, NM 87114.

IRVIS, K. LEROY
State representative. **Personal:** Born Dec 27, 1919, Saugerties, NY; married Cathyrn L Edwards; children: Reginald, Sherri. **Educ:** NY State Tchrs Coll, AB (summa cum laude); Univ of NY, MA; Univ of Pittsburgh Law Sch, LLB; Univ of Pittsburgh Law Sch, JD. **Career:** Pittsburgh Urban League Magazine, editor, author; Baltimore school teacher; Pittsburgh Courier, newscaster; Asst DA 1957-63; Minority Caucus, chmn 1963-64; Majority Caucus, chmn 1965-66; Minority Whip, 1967-68, 73-74; Majority Ldr, 1969-72, 1975-77; Speaker 1977-78; elected mem Democratic Natl Comm 1982; Dem Natl Convention, del 1968-84 (every four years); Minority Leader 1979, Speaker, 1983-88; Pennsylvania House of Representatives, 1958-. **Orgs:** Mem, bd dirs Post-Gazette Dapper Dan Club; WQED-Pub TV; United Black Front; PA Council for Arts; Bidwell Cultural & Training Cntr; (TEAM) Training Employment & Manpower; Community Action of Pittsburgh; Urban League; Alumni Assn State Univ of NY at Albany; mem bd trustees Univ Pittsburgh; mem Univ Pittsburgh Med Sch Adv Com; St Hwy & Bridge Auth; St Pub Sch Bldg Auth; PA Higher Educ Facilities Auth; Neighborhood Assistance Adv Bd; trustee PA Southwest Assn; treas Joint State Govt Commn; Phi Beta Kappa; Phi Delta Phi; Order of Coif; Practice law in Fed Dist & Commonwealth Cts; hon chmn Pub Defender Assn; sculpter, painter, writer. **Honors/Awds:** Hon Dr of Laws Lincoln Univ 1979, Hon Dr of Laws St Univ of NY at Albany 1986; Man of the Year Awd B'Nai B'rith Anti Defamation League 1987. **Home Addr:** 205 Tennyson Ave, Pittsburgh, PA 15213.

ISAAC, BRIAN WAYNE
Employment administrator. **Educ:** NY Univ, BA 1976, M Public Admin 1984. **Career:** Long Island Lighting Co, training & educ coord 1977-79, EEO admin 1979-84, employment serv admin 1984-. **Orgs:** Pres Manhattan Spokesman Club 1977-78; mem The Edges Group Inc 1982-. **Home Addr:** 326 E 92nd St, Brooklyn, NY 11212. **Business Addr:** Employment Serv Admin, Long Island Lighting Co, 175 E Old Country Rd, Hicksville, NY 11801.

ISAAC, EARLEAN
Judge. **Personal:** Born Feb 11, 1950, Forkland, AL; daughter of Mary Virginia Smith Williams and Robert Percy Williams; married Johnny L Isaac, Apr 24, 1971; children: Johnny L Jr, Jamaine L, Janetha L. **Career:** Judge of Probate, Eutaw, AL, license clerk, 1971-75, chief clerk, 75-89, judge, 1989-. **Honors/Awds:** First Black Woman Probate Judge in Alabama, St Paul United Methodist Church, 1988; Citizen of the Year Award, Kappa Alpha Psi Fraternity, 1989. **Business Addr:** Judge, Probate Court, PO Box 790, Eutaw, AL 35462.

ISAAC, EPHRAIM
Educator, philologist, historian, scholar. **Personal:** Born May 29, 1936, Nedjio, Ethiopia; son of Ruth and Yishaq; married Dr Sherry Rosen; children: Devorah Esther, Raphael Samuel, Yael Ruth. **Educ:** Concordia Coll, BA 1958; Harvard Univ Div School, BD 1963; Harvard Univ, PhD 1969. **Career:** Harvard Univ, instr 1968-69, lecturer 1969-71, assoc prof 1971-77; Hebrew Univ, visiting prof 1977-79; Inst for Advanced Study Princeton, fellow 1979-80; Princeton Theol Sem/Hunter Coll, visiting prof 1980-81; Bard Coll, visiting prof 1981-83; Lehigh

Univ, visiting prof of religion Princeton Univ, visiting prof, 1983-85; Institute of Semitic Studies, dir 1985. **Orgs:** Dir general Natl Literacy Campaign of Ethiopia 1966-72; bd mem Amer Assn for Ethiopian Jews 1973-; pres Ethiopian Student Assn in North Amer 1959-62; vice chmn Ethiopian Famine Relief Comm 1984-; bd mem African Studies Heritage Assoc 1969-73; chmn Comm for Ethiopian Literacy 1963-68; treas Harvard Graduate Student Assoc 1962-65; chorale dir Harvard Graduate Chorale 1962-64. **Honors/Awds:** Second Prize Ethiopian HS Matric Award 1954; Ethiopian Natl Prize for literacy (Humanity) 1967; Outstanding Educators of Amer 1972; Fellow Endowment for the Humanities 1979; NEH Rsch Grant 1976-77; Harvard Univ Faculty Fund Rsch Grants; Concordia Coll Scholarships 1956-58; Univ Coll of Addis Ababa Fellowship 1954-56; author of Ethiopic book of Enoch, Doubleday, 1983, a history of religions in Africa (Oxford, forthcoming.). **Business Addr:** Director, Inst of Semitic Studies, 9 Grover Ave, Princeton, NJ 08540-3601.

ISAAC, EUGENE LEONARD
Educator. **Personal:** Born Aug 15, 1915, Natchez, MS; son of Isabella Isaac and Samuel Isaac; married Ardelma G Brown; children: Genette Leonardo, Doris Gene. **Educ:** Alcorn A&M Coll, BS 1940; IA State Coll, MS 1950; Emporia State Univ, educ splst 1965; Southern Illnois University. **Career:** Vocational Training Oak Park HS Laurel, teacher 1940-43, 1946-49; Utica Inst, counselor 1950-51; Savannah State Coll, head carpentry & woodworking dept 1951-58; MS Valley State Coll, chmn tech educ div 1958-75; Tech Edn, asso prof 1975-80, prof indust tech 1980-. **Orgs:** Administrative board chairman, United Methodist Church, currently; policy comm Tech Educ Dept Amer Vocational Assn 1977-79; Vocational Assn 1979-80; consult tech educ, Industrial Arts in Elem School; MS Teachers Assn; Amer Magnolia State Vocational Assn; Amer Council on Industrial Arts Teacher Education; Amer Legion; Phi Delta Kappa; lifetime trustee, Millsaps College; vice pres, Leflore County 4-H Club, currently; The Mississippi Conference, council on ministries, 1988, committee of district coordinators of church and society, 1989, episcopony committee of laymen, 1989, committee of equitable salaries, lay persons, 1989, church and society subcommittee, 1991, church and society committee, Grenada Greenwood District, 1991; council committee, Boys Club of Leflone County, 1986-; equalizing delegate, United Methodist Church, Mississippi Conference, 1985-88, 1991-94. **Honors/Awds:** Meritorious serv Award Utica field chap Phi Delta Kappa 1965; recipient serv to Youth Award YMCA Savannah 1958; Meritorious Serv Award MS Valley State Coll YMCA 1967; Man of the Year Award, Utica Chapter, Phi Delta Kappa 1978; Plaque Comm Coll, Leadership Award, Kansas state Teachers Coll, 1965; Teacher of the Year Award, Div of Tech Education, Mississippi Valley State Univ, 1980; Plaque, Outstanding Christian Service, Wesley United Methodist Church, 1982; Plaque for Outstanding & Dedicated Service, Sunday School - Perfect Attendance - Wesley United Methodist Church, 1993; Plaque Generous Devotion of Time and Talents, Outstanding Christian Servanthood, 1994; A Special Mission Recognition, The Women's Division, General Bd of Global Ministries; The United Methodist Church, 1994. **Military Serv:** US Army, Sergeant, 1943-45.

ISAAC, JOSEPH WILLIAM ALEXANDER
Physician. **Personal:** Born Dec 24, 1935; son of Agatha Henry Isaac and Timothy Isaac; married Gertrude Harris; children: Charles, Zoe, Joseph A. **Educ:** City Coll NYC, BS 1967; Howard U, MD 1971. **Career:** Freedmen's Hosp Wash DC, med intern 1971-72; Howard Univ Wash DC, resident Ob/Gyn 1972-76; Norfolk Health Dept, family planning phys 1976-77; Portsmouth Gen Hosp, chmn dept of Ob/Gyn 1985-88; Norfolk & Portsmouth VA, private practice Ob/Gyn 1977-; Norflk Comm Hosp, chairman department Ob-Gyn, 1991-; Portsmouth Gen Hosp, president of med staff, 1993-. **Orgs:** Mem AMA 1975-; mem Norfolk Med Soc 1976-; mem Norfolk Acad of Med 1977; mem Portsmouth Chamber of Commerce 1978-; mem Med Adv Com of Tidewater March of Dimes 1979-; diplomate Am Bd of Ob/Gyn 1978 fellow Am Coll of Ob/Gyn 1979; vice pres 1986-90, pres 1990-92, Old Dom Med Soc; pres Norfolk Med Soc 1985-87. **Military Serv:** US Army sgt 1959-62. **Business Addr:** Physician, 549 E Brambleton Ave, Norfolk, VA 23510.

ISAAC, TELESFORO ALEXANDER
Cleric. **Personal:** Born Jan 5, 1929, San Pedro Macoris, Dominican Republic; son of Violet Francis and Simon Issac; married Juana Maria Rosa-Zorrilla, Aug 30, 1961; children: Juan Alexander, Marcos Alexander, Miriam Elizabeth. **Educ:** Instituto Vazquez, 1948-50; Seminary of Haiti, 1954-58; Universidad de Santo Domingo, 1966-69; Seminario Episcopal del Caribe, MDiv, 1971. **Career:** Morey Hardware Store, Porvenir Sugar Mill, clerk, 1950-54; San Gabriel Episcopal Church, vicar, 1958-61; Jesus Nazarene Episcopal Church, vicar, 1961-65; San Andres Episcopal Church, vicar, 1965-69; San Esteban Episcopal Church, vicar, 1971-72; Diocese of Dominican Republic, diocesan bishop, 1972-91; Diocese of Southwest Florida, assistant bishop, 1991-. **Orgs:** Center Rehabilitation, Handicapped, president, board, 1985-91; Center Theological School, founder, president, board, 1975-91; Association for Human Rights, chairman, board, 1991; Caribbean Episcopal Seminary, chairman, board, 1975-76; Church World Service, board trustees, 1966-91; San Gabriel & Jesus Nazarene Schools, founder, principal, 1959-62; Dominican-American Language Institute, co-founder, 1964-; San Marcos & San Andres High Schools, founder, principal, 1966-70. **Honors/Awds:** City of San Pedro de Macoris, Distinguished Citizen, 1983; City University Los Angeles, Doctor of Divinity, 1977. **Special Achievements:** La Labor Educativa de la Iglesia Episcopal Dominicana, 1971. **Business Addr:** Assistant Bishop, Episcopal Diocese of Southwest Florida, 201 4th St N, St Petersburg, FL 33701, (813)823-2737.

ISAAC, YVONNE RENEE
Health care executive. **Personal:** Born Apr 13, 1948, Cleveland, OH; daughter of Venice Leona Hallom Isaac and Leon Warren Isaac; married Harold Erian Rhynie, Dec 30, 1983. **Educ:** Sarah Lawrence Coll, BA 1970; Rensselear Polytechnic Inst, MS 1972; Ploytechnic Inst of NY, MS 1976. **Career:** Ehren Krantz Grp, architectural planner; Perkins & Will NYC, proj mgr 1978-; Mobil Oil Corp NYC, sr analyst 1976-78; Perkins & Will SPA/ REDCO Inc NYC & Chgo, sr assoc 1972-76; Gen Elec Co Phila, rsrch analyst 1971-72; Pratt Inst Brooklyn, vis assoc prof 1977; Columbia Univ, vis assoc prof 1978-79; Metropolitan Transportation Authority NY, NY, assistant director 1985-86; New York City Health & Hospitals Corp, group director 1986-. **Orgs:** Bd of dir, Black Woman Collaborative 1975-; bd of dir Operation Open Cty 1977-; treas 1979-, board member 1991-, Sarah Lawrence Coll Black Alumni Assn. **Honors/Awds:** Fellow to pursue doctoral studies Urban Mass Trans Adminstrn. **Business Addr:** Project Executive, Harlem Ambulatory Care Bldg Project, New York City Health & Hospitals Corp, Harlem Hospital Center - Old Nurses' Residence, 4th Fl, 506 Lenox Ave, New York, NY 10037.

ISAACS, DORIS C.
Computer company executive. **Personal:** Born Jul 2, 1939, Columbus, OH; daughter of Lois Cox Boyce and Dr. John D White, Jr; married Thomas E Stallworth Jr, Nov 3, 1987; children: Kelly Carroll Michaels, Thomas E Stallworth, III, Kaleb Winslow Stallworth. **Educ:** Kent State Univ, Kent, OH, BS Educ, 1956-59. **Career:** IBM Corp, Syst Engr-Dir, Educ Operations, 1966-. **Orgs:** Mem, Advisory Bd Cobb County YWCA, 1986-89. **Honors/Awds:** Systems Eng Symposium, IBM, 1969, 1971-72; 100% Club, IBM, 1980-81; Systems Eng Mgr of the Year, IBM, 1975. **Home Addr:** 3685 Peachtree Rd, #8, Atlanta, GA 30319.

ISAACS, PATRICIA
Company executive. **Personal:** Born May 6, 1949, Georgetown, Guyana; daughter of Violet Isaacs; married Morty Greene; children: Krystal Louise. **Educ:** Dist of Columbia Teachers Coll; South Eastern Univ; Penn State. **Career:** McDonalds Corp, Michigan Region, dir of operations, 1975-91, regional vice pres, 1991-96, Jamaica's first McDonald's restaurant, managing dir,1996-. **Orgs:** Detroit Chamber of Commerce; bd mem, Homes for Black Children. **Business Addr:** Regional Vice Pres, SE Michigan, McDonalds Corp, 200 Town Center, Suite 700, Southfield, MI 48075.

ISAACS, STEPHEN D.
Aviation safety inspector. **Personal:** Born Feb 22, 1944, Boston, MA; children: Athelia, Stephanie. **Educ:** Howard Univ, B Mech Eng 1969, MBA 1973. **Career:** Office of Mgmt & Budget, Operations Rsrch Analyst 1973-76; US Nuclear Reg Comm, program analyst 1976-77; US Nuclear Reg Commn, FOIA officer 1977-86; Federal Aviation Adminis, aviation safety inspector 1986-. **Orgs:** Am Soc of Mech Engs 1973-; Am Soc of Access Profls 1980-86; acct exec Intrnl Monetary Founding Group, Inc 1984-86; bd of dirs Special Air Serv, Inc 1983-85; Washington Society of Engineers, 1985-. **Military Serv:** USCG E-4 intelligence specialist 1969-71. **Home Addr:** 1907 - 2nd St NW, Washington, DC 20001. **Business Addr:** Aviation Safety Inspector, Federal Aviation Administration, Flight Standards Service, 800 Independence Ave SW, Washington, DC 20590.

ISAACS-LOWE, ARLENE ELIZABETH
Portfolio manager. **Personal:** Born Oct 17, 1959, Kingston, Jamaica; daughter of Barbara C Davis Isaacs and Lawrence G Isaacs; married Walter J Lowe IV, Jul 26, 1986; children: Walter J V. **Educ:** Howard University, Washington, DC, BBA, 1981; Fordham University, New York, NY, MBA, 1990. **Career:** VSE Corp, Alexandria, VA, staff accountant, 1981-84; West World Holding Inc, New York, NY, senior accountant, 1984-87, accounting mgr, 1987-; Metropolitan Life, New York, NY, financial analyst, 1987-88, manager, 1988-89, controller, 1989-92, portfolio manager, 1992-. **Orgs:** Member-BEEP, National Urban League, 1988-; member, National Black MBA, 1990-; member, National Association Black Accountants, 1989-; board member, Rheedlen Foundation, 1991-. **Honors/Awds:** 100 Most Promising Black Women in Corporate America, Ebony Magazine, 1991; Beta Gamma Sigma Honor Society, Fordham Univ, 1990; America's Best & Brightest, Dollars & Sense Magazine, 1991.

ISAACS MCCOY, LESLIE ELLEN
Television producer, writer. **Personal:** Born Jun 24, 1962, Cambridge, MA; daughter of Joyce L Spears and Walter L Isaacs; married Herb McCoy, May 18, 1991. **Educ:** Spelman College, dual degree, English, Spanish literature, 1985. **Career:** Turner Broadcasting Systems, Inc, production assistant, 1987-85, public service coordinator, 1989-87, public service producer, writer, 1992-89; McCoy Productions, president, 1992-93; Film and Video, ACOG, manager, currently. **Orgs:** National Academy of Television Arts & Sciences, 1986-; Atlanta Association of Media Women, 1991-; National Academy of Cable Programming, 1987-; Atlanta Association of Black Journalists, public relations committee, 1990-; Moving in the Spirit, board member, 1989-; Safe Kids Coalition, past media advisor, 1992-89; League of United Latin American Citizens, SE Seaboard, past media advisor, Georgia state director, 1988-86. **Honors/Awds:** National Academy of Television Arts & Sciences, Southern Regional Emmy, 1991, 1992; The World Institute of Communications for Black Audiences, CEBA Award of Excellence, 1990, 1992; Dollars & Sense Magazine, Best & Brightest Young Professional Woman, 1992; Association of Media Women, tv production, feature, M Agnes Jones Elementary, 1992. **Business Addr:** Manager, Film and Video, ACOG, PO Box 1996, Atlanta, GA 30301-1996.

ISADORE, HAROLD W.
Attorney, librarian. **Personal:** Born in Alexandria, LA. **Educ:** Southern Univ, BS 1967; Southern Univ Schl of Law, JD 1970; SUNY at Buffalo Law Schl, Cert 1978. **Career:** US Dept of Labor Office of the Solicitor, atty 1970-73; Baton Rouge Legal Aid Scty, atty 1973-74; Public Defender of Baton Rouge, atty 1974-75; Southern Univ School of Law, assoc law libririan 1975-. **Orgs:** Mem Am Bar Assn, Natl Bar Assn, Delta Theta Phi Law Frat, Am Assn of Law Libraries, Kappa Alpha Psi Frat, Inc. **Honors/Awds:** Serv awrd Stdnt Bar Assoc, SU Law Schl 1970; Hypotext on Security Devices Southern Univ Pblshr 1979; Hypotext on Civil Procedure Vols 1 and 11 S Univ Pblshr 1980-81; Humanitarian Award, Louis A Martinet Legal Society; Southern Univ Law Center, Staff Award, 1980-81, 1985-87, 1990-94. **Business Addr:** Assoc Law Librarian, Southern Univ Law Schl, Baton Rouge Campus, Baton Rouge, LA 70813.

ISBELL, JAMES S.
Business executive. **Personal:** Born Sep 13, 1918, Pittsburgh; married Ann B McLeary. **Educ:** Northwester Sch Commerce; DePaul Sch Commerce. **Career:** Jackson Mut Life Ins Co, 1937; agency dir 1951-55; Chicago Met Mut Assur Co, sp rep 1956; asst agency dir 1957; adminstrv asst agency dir 1963; 2nd vice pres & adminstrv asst agency dir 1966f vice pres & adminstrv asst Agency dir 1967f vp-asso agency dir 1969; vp-agy dir 1970-. **Orgs:** Past chmn Agency Sect Nat Ins Assn; chmn Life Underwriters Hon Soc NIA; mem & past pres bd dir Chicago Ins Assn; chmn LUHS Nat Ins Assn;fndr Chicago chap Life Underwriters Hon Soc dist com; mem past chmn Oakland Dist Chicago Area Counc BSA; past bd mem RR Donnelly Boys Club; mem NAACP; Urban League. **Honors/Awds:** The Olive H Crosthwait Award CIA 1970; Nat Ins Serv Award 1971. **Military Serv:** AUS lt-col. **Business Addr:** 4455 Dr Martin Luther King Jr, Chicago, IL 60653.

ISHMAN, SYBIL R.
Educator. **Personal:** Born Jul 25, 1946, Durham, NC; married Reginald E Ishman. **Educ:** Univ of NC (Greensboro), BA 1968; NC Central Univ, MA 1971; Univ of NC (Chapel Hill), PhD 1980. **Career:** NC Central Univ, grad asst 1969-71, instr 1970-72; NC State Univ, assist prof 1980-. **Orgs:** Mem Am Assn Univ Women; Modern Lang Assn; Natl Counc of Tchrs of English; mem TESOL; Natl Smart Set Durham Chpt. **Business Addr:** Assistant Professor, NC State Univ, 281 Tompkins Hall, Raleigh, NC 27695.

ISIBOR, EDWARD IROGUEHI
Engineer, educator. **Personal:** Born Jun 9, 1940, Benin City, Nigeria; married Edwina Williams; children: Ekinadose, Emwanta. **Educ:** Howard U, BSc 1965; MIT, MSc 1967; Purdue U, PhD 1970. **Career:** School of Engineering & Tech TN State Univ, dean 1975-; Civil Engineering FL Intl Univ, assoc prof & head urban systems prog 1973-75; NOACA Cleveland, transportation engr 1972; Afro-Am Cultural Center Cleveland State Univ, dir 1970-71; Purdue Univ, research asst 1967-69; MIT, research asst 1965-67. **Orgs:** Mem Am Soc Enrg Edn; Transportation Research Bd Washington, DC; OH Soc Professional Engrs; C of C Reg engr OH. **Honors/Awds:** Sigma Xi hon soc 1970; Tau Beta Pi hon Soc 1964. **Business Addr:** Ofc of Dean Sch of Engineering & T, TN State Univ, Nashville, TN 37203.

ISLER, MARSHALL A., III
Company executive, businessman, real estate developer, consultant. **Personal:** Born Jan 9, 1939, Kinston, NC; son of Louise Douglas Isler (deceased) and Marshall A Isler, Jr; married Verna Harmon Bradford, Jun 14, 1996; children: Valerie L, Bryan C. **Educ:** Howard Univ, BSEE 1962; George Washington Univ, MEA 1971; Harvard Univ, PMD 1977. **Career:** Johns Hopkins Univ Applied Physics Lab, space sys officer 1967; Naval Air Sys Command, satellite proj engr 1971; Natl Bureau of Standards Law Enforcement Standards, security syst prog mgr 1973; Sen John Tunney, sci adv 1974; Natl Bureau Standards Dept Commerce Center Consult Prod Tech, dep dir 1978; Parametric Inc, pres; Isler Assoc, pres. **Orgs:** Mem How-

ard Univ Alumni Assoc, Omega Psi Phi Frat, SBF Credit Union; assoc Urban Land Institute; mem Durham Business and Professional Chain; mem Durham Chamber of Commerce; mem Natl Home Builders Assoc; mem Mayor's Downtown Redevelopment Comm Durham; pres Abiding Savior Lutheran Church Durham, NC 1989-91; vice pres Business & Prof Chain Durham, NC 1989-90; Bd of Dir Dispute Settlement Center Durham, NC 1989-90; member Human Relations Committee, Durham NC Chamber of Commerce 1990-91; member, Churches for Action, Durham, NC, 1990-. **Honors/Awds:** Congressional Fellowship 1973-74. **Military Serv:** USN Lt 1962-67; USNR Comdr 1967-.

ISMAIL, QADRY RAHMADAN
Professional football player. **Personal:** Born Nov 8, 1970, Newark, NJ; married Holly; children: Qalea. **Educ:** Syracuse. **Career:** Minnesota Vikings, wide receiver, 1993-96; Miami Dolphins, 1997-. **Business Addr:** Professional Football Player, Miami Dolphins, 2269 NW 199th St, Miami, FL 33056, (305)620-5000.

ISMAIL, RAGHIB RAMADIAN (ROCKET)
Professional football player. **Personal:** Born Nov 18, 1969, Newark, NJ; son of Fatma Ismail and Ibrahim Ismail; married Melani; children: Noe. **Educ:** University of Notre Dame, attended. **Career:** Toronto Argonauts (CFL), running back, 1991-93; Oakland Raiders, 1993-95; Carolina Panthers, wide receiver, 1996-. **Honors/Awds:** NCAA Indoor Championships, sprint runner. **Business Addr:** Professional Football Player, Carolina Panthers, 800 Mint St, Ericsson Stadium, Charlotte, NC 28202, (704)358-7000.

ISMIAL, SALAAM IBN
Association president. **Personal:** Born in Jersey City, NJ. **Educ:** Robert Walsh School of Business, 1978-79; Kean Coll of NJ, 1980-82; Union Cty Coll, 1983. **Career:** Elizabeth Youth Council, pres 1982-84; Union Cty Coll, vice pres 1983; NAACP, youth pres 1984; EYC After School Prog Rec Dept, coord 1984-85; Elizabeth Youth Council, pres; Salaam Ismial Communications, owner. **Orgs:** Youth leader Local Chap CORE 1973; chmn Kean Coll Black Student Union 1982; pres Elizabeth Youth Council 1982-85; mem Black Issue Convention, SouthernChristian Leadership 1984, Progressive Rainbow Alliance of NJ 1985; president, United Youth Council Inc; coordinator, Union of African Student Organizations, College Organization Statewide; bd, Urban League of Essex County Pediatrics Aid Foster Care, 1989. **Honors/Awds:** Medal of Honor Elizabeth Boys Scouts 1972; Outstanding Serv Kean Black Student Union 1982; Community Serv Elizabeth Youth Council 1983; Life Time Membership NAACP 1984. **Business Addr:** President, Elizabeth Youth Council, 455 Monroe Ave, Elizabeth, NJ 07201.

ISOM, EDDIE
Hotel industry executive. **Educ:** Livingstone Coll. **Career:** Marriott Corp, food and beverage dir; Howard Univ Hotel, gen mgr, currently. **Business Addr:** General Mgr, Howard University Hotel, 2225 Georgia Ave, Washington, DC 20001, (202)462-5400.

ISRAEL, MAE H.
Journalist. **Personal:** Born Apr 8, 1953, Robeson County, NC; daughter of Mae C Israel and Samuel L Israel. **Educ:** University of North Carolina, Chapel Hill, BA, journalism, 1975. **Career:** Greensboro Daily News, reporter, 1975-80; Charlotte Observer, reporter, assignment editor, 1980-89; Washington Post, assignment editor, 1989-. **Orgs:** Natl Assn of Black Journalists, 1978-; Washington Area Association of Black Journalists, 1989-; Delta Sigma Theta; Charlotte Area Assn of Black Journalists, 1985-89, president; Women in Communications, 1977-79; Southeastern Black Press Institute, 1977-79. **Honors/Awds:** North Carolina Press Assn, Press Award, Feature Writing, 1977; Landmark Communications, Excellence in Writing, 1978; Black Media Assn, News Writing, Feature Writing, 1985, 1986. **Business Addr:** Assistant Virginia Editor, Washington Post, 1150 15th St, NW, Washington, DC 20071, (202)334-4210.

ISRAEL, STEVEN DOUGLAS
Professional football player. **Personal:** Born Mar 16, 1969, Lawnside, NJ; married Lorae; children: Averi Lorae, Ashley Shardae. **Educ:** Univ of Pittsburgh, bachelor's degree in economics. **Career:** San Francisco 49ers, defensive back, 1995-96; New England Patriots, 1997-. **Business Addr:** Professional Football Player, New England Patriots, 60 Washington St, Foxboro Stadium, Foxboro, MA 02035, (508)543-7911.

ITA, LAWRENCE EYO
Educator. **Personal:** Born Dec 1, 1939, Calabar, Nigeria; married Autumn Dean; children: Eyo, Ekanem. **Educ:** Univ of MI, PhD 1970; London U, BSC 1962. **Career:** Univ of NV, assoc prof 1978; Bureau of Asso Serv, dir 1974-77; Commonwealth Asso, engineering consultant 1970-72. **Orgs:** Mem Am Soc of Engineering Educ 1974-; mem Am Soc of Heat Refrig & Air-Cond Ewngrs 1976-; mem Intl Soc of Solar Energy 1975-. **Honors/Awds:** Publs Jour of Chem & Engineering Data 1974-76. **Business Addr:** 4505 Maryland, Las Vegas, NV 89154.

IVERSON, ALLEN
Professional basketball player. **Personal:** Born Jun 7, 1975, Hampton, VA. **Educ:** Georgetown Univ. **Career:** Philadelphia 76ers, guard, 1996-. **Honors/Awds:** NBA All Rookie Team, 1997; Schick Rookie of the Year Award, 1997. **Special Achievements:** NBA Draft, First round pick, #1, 1996; first rookie in history to score 40 points or more in four consecutive games; NBA Player of the Week, 1997. **Business Addr:** Professional Basketball Player, Philadelphia 76ers, 1 Corestates Complex, Philadelphia, PA 19148, (215)339-7676.

IVERY, EDDIE LEE
Professional football player (retired). **Personal:** Born Jul 30, 1957, McDuffie, GA; married Anna; children: Tauvia Edana, Eddie Lee Jr. **Educ:** Georgia Tech, Indus Mgmt. **Career:** Green Bay Packers, running back, 1979-86. **Honors/Awds:** 609 carries, 3,517 rushing yards, Georgia Tech; All-Time NCAA Single Game Rushing Record, senior year; team captain and rep football squad Prestigious Tech Athletic Bd.

IVERY, JAMES A.
Federal government official. **Personal:** Born Jan 5, 1950, Zebulon, NC; son of Dorothy Ivery and Eugene Copeland; divorced; children: Jacinda D Ivery, Toshiba Ivery. **Educ:** Fayetteville State Univ, Fayetteville, NC, BS, 1972; Bucknell Univ, Lewisburg, PA, MPA, 1982. **Career:** Wake County Public Schools, Raleigh, NC, instructor/coach, 1972-74; Internal Revenue Service, Raleigh, NC, revenue officer, 1974-76; US Dept of Health & Human Services, Washington, DC, policy analyst, 1976-. **Orgs:** Life mem, Alpha Phi Alpha Fraternity, 1977-; mem, Natl Forum for Black Public Administrators, 1986-; mem, Mt Zion Baptist Church, Arlington, VA, 1986-. **Honors/Awds:** Outstanding Young Men of America, 1985; short story, Essense Magazine, "Say Brother Column," 1986; Distinguished Black College Graduate, Natl Assn for Equal Opportunity in Higher Education, 1988. **Business Addr:** Special Asst to the Deputy Under Secretary, US Dept of Health & Human Services, 200 Independence Ave, SW, Rm 630F, Washington, DC 20201.

IVEY, ARTIS. See COOLIO.

IVEY, HORACE SPENCER
Educator. **Personal:** Born Nov 13, 1931, DeLand, FL; married Barbara Edwards; children: Lawrence, Derek, Chandra, Allegra, Elliot. **Educ:** Smith Coll Sch for Soc Wrk; Syracuse U, 1962; Univ CT, MSW 1956f Univ Bridgeport, BA 1954. **Career:** SUNY Upstate Medical Center, assoc prof; State Univ Hospital, 1965, supvr 1961-62, social worker 1956-61, caseworker 1958-60. **Orgs:** Nat Assn of Social Workers; Acad of Certified Soc Workers; Med Social Work Sec; Unltd Prgm; Healther Serv Com Council on Aging; Am Hosp Assn Council on Volunteers; Syracuse Univ Rehab Council; num other affiliations. **Special Achievements:** Publications: "Factors in Selection of Patients for Home Chemo-Therapy," 1956; "Hospital Abortion Program Implication for Social Work Planning & Serv Delivery," 1971; numerous others. **Business Addr:** Upstate Med Ctr, 750 E Adams St, Syracuse, NY 13210.

IVEY, MARK, III
Physician, pharmacist. **Personal:** Born Apr 15, 1935, Ocala, FL; son of Mazie Ivey and Mark Ivey; married Evelyn Jacqueline Brown, Jun 5, 1958; children: Mark IV, Marlon, Michael. **Educ:** FL A&M Univ, BS Pharmacy 1958; Meharry Med Coll, MD 1973; Akron Gen Med Ctr, Ob-Gyn residency 1978. **Career:** Summit Co Health Dept Akron, dep health officer 1973-78; Akron City Health Dept, dep health officer 1974-78; Delta Comm Hosp & Clinic Mound Bayou MS, Ob-Gyn dir 1975; Planned Parenthood of Summit Co, consultant 1976-78; Planned Parenthood of Central FL, med dir 1978-94; Private Practice, physician & pharmacist. **Orgs:** Consult Intl Corr Soc of Ob-Gyn 1978-; bd dirs BSA Gulf Ridge Council FL 1978-80; co-dir United Negro Coll Fund Polk Co FL 1980; consultant, Polk County Chapter, FAMU Alumni Association. **Honors/Awds:** Lehn & Fink Award Outstanding Sr Pharm of FL A&M Univ 1958; First Black Resident in Dept of Ob-Gyn Akron Gen Med Ctr 1973; First Black Chief Gynecological Serv of Lakeland Regional Medical Ctr Lakeland FL 1985; Margaret Sanger Award, Planned Parenthood of Central Fla, 1989. **Business Addr:** Pharmacist-Physician, 505 Martin Luther King Ave Suite #2, Lakeland, FL 33805.

IVEY, REBECCA
Librarian. **Personal:** Born Jun 18, 1965, Union Springs, AL; daughter of Lillie Harris Ivey and Willie Frank Ivey. **Educ:** Alabama State University, Montgomery, AL, BA, 1988; Clark-Atlanta University, Atlanta, GA, MSLS, 1990. **Career:** Atlanta-Fulton Public Library, Atlanta, GA, library asst I, 1988-89, library principal assoc, 1989-90, childrens librarian, 1990-; Robert W Woodruff Library, Atlanta, GA, reference asst, 1990; DeKalb County Public Library, Atlanta, GA, childrens librarian, 1990. **Orgs:** Member, Zeta Phi Beta Sorority Inc, 1986-; member, American Library Assn, 1989-; member, Black Caucus of American Library Assn, 1989-. **Home Addr:** 6442 Abercorn St, Union City, GA 30291. **Business Addr:** Librarian, Atlanta-Fulton Public Library, 1 Margaret Mitchell Sq, Atlanta, GA 30303.

IVEY YARN, BARBARA LYNNE
Physician. **Personal:** Born in Knoxville, TN; daughter of Boyd S Ivey (deceased) and Geraldine Celestine Harris Ivey. **Educ:** Knoxville College, BS, 1963; Univ of Tennessee, 1962-63; Univ of Minnesota, MPH, 1969; Meharry Medical College, MD, 1973; Howard Univ Hospital, internship, 1974; Emory Univ Affiliated Hospitals, anesthesiology residency, 1975-77; Univ of Louisville, anesthesiology fellowship, 1982-83. **Career:** Knoxville City School, science teacher, 1963-64; Oak Ridge National Laboratory, research asst, 1964-67; Minnesota Head Start Program, public health educator and consultant, 1968; Univ of Minnesota Community Public Health Care Center, student health advisor, 1968-69; Public Health and Safety Administration, 1969; Greely School District Community Health Center, instructor/public health advisor, 1969; Matthew Walker Health Care Center, 1972-73; Munich Military Hospital, physician, 1974-75; Grady Memorial Hospital, anesthesiologist, 1975-78; US Public Health Services, senior surgeon, regional medical consultant; Dept of Health and Human Services, 1978-82; Cuban-Haitian Refugee Camp, chief medical officer, 1981-82; Humana Hospital, Dept of Anesthesiology and Dept of Respiratory Therapy, chair and division head, 1982-91; Atlanta Outpatient/Peachtree-Dunwoody Center, anesthesiologist, 1991-. **Orgs:** Beta Kappa Chi National Scientific Honor Society, 1962-; German-American Women's Group, 1974-75; American Embassy Women's Assn, secretary, 1974-75; Munich Military Catholic Wives Assn, director of family affairs, 1975; American Medical Assn; National Medical Assn; Georgia Medical Assn; NAACP, life member; Trinity Catholic Church; Atlanta Symphony Orchestra League, board of directors; Fortissimo Group; Heritage High School Parents Assn; YWCA; YMCA; American Heart Assn; Alpha Kappa Alpha Sorority; Knoxville College National Alumni Assn; The Links, Buckhead Cascade City Chapter, 1985-; Knoxville College, board of directors, 1991-; Fayette County Bank, co-founder, 1990. **Honors/Awds:** Alpha Kappa Alpha Sorority, Academic Scholarship Award, 1959-63; Public Health Scholarship Award, 1968-69; Jesse Smith Noyes Obstetrics and Gynecology Fellowship, 1969-72; Sloan Foundation, Medical Scholarship Award, 1969-73; Univ of Louisville, Fellowship in Anesthesiology, 1982-83; Public Health Service, Citation and Commendation Medal for Distinguished Service, 1978-82; United States Public Health Service, Special Assignment Ribbon Award, 1979; Habitat for Humanity, Knoxville Chapter, Plaque, 1992; Knoxville College, Distinguished Alumnus Award, 1993. **Home Addr:** 111 Stonington Dr, Peachtree City, GA 30269.

IVORY, CAROLYN KAY
Physician. **Personal:** Born Feb 21, 1944, Birmingham, AL. **Educ:** Berea Coll, BA 1965f Meharry Med Coll, MD 1971. **Career:** Jefferson Co Hlth Dept, hlth med ofcr 1973-; Chidlren's Hosp, resd pediatrics 1972-73; Univ KS 1972-73; Univ KS, 1972-73; Meharry Med Coll, intern 1971-72. **Orgs:** Mem Nat Med Assn; Am Acad Pediatrics; Jefferson Co Pediatric Assn. **Business Addr:** 1700 Ave E, Birmingham, AL 35218.

IVY, JAMES E.
Police official (retired). **Personal:** Born Sep 13, 1937, Memphis, TN; son of Mary Wells Coleman and John Ivy; married Sally Gibbs Ivy, Jan 23, 1980; children: Jacqueline, Pamela, Gwendolyn, Bridgette. **Educ:** Memphis State University; University of North Florida; National Executive Institute, National FBI Academy. **Career:** Memphis Police Department, Memphis, TN, police officer, 1963-73, lieutenant, 1973-79, captain, 1979-81, inspector, 1981-83, chief inspector, 1983-84, deputy chief, 1984-88, director, 1988-95. **Orgs:** International Associations of Chiefs of Police; Memphis Metropolitan Association of Chiefs of Police; National Executive Institute Alumni Association. **Honors/Awds:** Outstanding Achievement, Governor Ned McWherter, 1988; Dedicated Community Service, Moolah Temple #54; Dedicated Community Service, Breath of Life SD A Church, 1990; Outstanding Religious Service, Gospel Temple Baptist Church, 1991.

IZELL, BOOKER T.
Newspaper executive. **Personal:** Born Feb 14, 1940, Auburn, AL; son of Mr & Mrs Davis WalKer; married Birdie M Carpenter Izell, May 1, 1962; children: Gwendolyn R. **Educ:** Wright State University, accounting, 1968-70. **Career:** Dayton Newspaper, circulation manager, 1965-78; Springfield Newspaper, circulation director, 1978-84; Atlanta Journal/Const, single copy manager, 1984-87; COX Enterprises Inc, manager of human resources development, 1987-93; Atlanta Journal/Const, vice pres community affairs/diversity, 1993. **Orgs:** NAACP, 1975; National Association of Black Journalists, 1986; Atlanta Business Forum, board member, 1991; Atlanta Art & Business, board member, 1992; Atlanta Chamber of Commerce, 1992; Southern Circulation Manager Association, 1992-95; Alliance Theatre of Arts, board member, 1993; Regional Leadership Foundation, 1993; Newspaper Association of America, 1994; Clayton State University, trustee, 1996. **Honors/Awds:** Dayton Newspaper, Glenn L Cox Awd, 1975; Ohio President Awd, 1983. **Military Serv:** US Marines, cpl, 1958-61. **Business Addr:** Vice Pres, Community Affairs & Workforce Diversity, Atlanta Journal/Constitution, 72 Marietta St, NW, Atlanta, GA 30303, (404)526-5091.

J

JACKEE (JACKEE HARRY)
Actress. **Personal:** Born in Winston-Salem, NC; daughter of Flossie Perry and Warren Perry; divorced. **Educ:** Long Island Univ, Brooklyn Ctr, BA. **Career:** Television actress, Royal Family, Jackee, 227, Another World, The Women of Brewster Place, Sister, Sister; Broadway productions of "Eubie!," "The Wiz," and "One More Time." Films: Ladybugs; Former teacher at Brooklyn Tech High School. **Honors/Awds:** Emmy Award, Natl Acad of Television Arts and Sciences, 1987, for outstanding performance by a supporting actress.

JACKET, BARBARA JEAN
Educator, athletic director. **Personal:** Born Dec 26, 1935, Port Arthur, TX; daughter of Eva Mae Getwood-Pickney and Raymond Jacket. **Educ:** Tuskegee Institute, BS, 1958; Prairie View A&M University, MS, 1968; University of Houston, advanced studies, 1976. **Career:** Van Buren High School, physical education teacher; Lincoln High School, physical education teacher; Prairie View A&M University, professor of physical education, director of athletics, currently. **Orgs:** The National Collegiate Athletic Association; National Association of Intercollegiate Athletics. **Honors/Awds:** Olympic Committee, Head Coach 1992 Women's Olympic Track & Field Team, 1992; The Athletic Congress, Joe Robercher Award, 1992, The President's TAC Award, 1992; Gov Ann Richards, Yellow Rose of Texas Award (2), 1992; Texas Black Women's Conference, induction into the Texas Black Women's Hall of Fame, 1992; Tuskegee Athletic Hall of Fame, 1987; Cross Country Southwestern Athletic Conference, Coach of the Year, 1987; Indoor Southwestern Athletic Conference, Coach of ther Year, 1987; NAIA Indoor and Outdoor National Championship, Coach of the Year, 1987; US World Championships, head coach, 1986; Southwestern Athletic Conference Hall of Fame; NAIA Hall of Fame; Prairie View A&M University Hall of Fame. **Business Addr:** Professor of Physical Education, Director of Athletics, Prairie View A&M University, Hilliard Hall, Rm 5, PO Box 097, Prairie View, TX 77446, (409)857-4156.

JACKS, ULYSSES
Attorney. **Personal:** Born Jan 15, 1937, Coatesville, PA; son of Mable Jacks and Fred Douglas Jacks; married Esterlene A Gibson; children: Marcus U, Eric D. **Educ:** VA Union Univ, BS 1959; LaSalle Coll, accounting 1964-67; Howard Univ Law Sch, JD (Cum Laude) 1970. **Career:** Philadelphia Pub Schools, tchr 1964-67; Equal Empl Opp Commn, decision writer 1969-70; Howard Law Sch, admin asst univ counsel; Csaplar & Bok, assoc 1970-77; MA Highway Dept, deputy chief counsel 1977-. **Orgs:** Mem MA Black Lawyers; mem MA Bar Assn; mem Amer Bar Assn; dir, Opportunities Industrial Centers of Greater Boston, 1982-88; dir, Codman Square Housing Corporation, 1988-90; dir, The Commonwealth Co-operative Bank, 1991-. **Honors/Awds:** Development Editor Howard Univ Law Journal 1968-69; Tchng Fellow Howard Univ Law School 1969-70. **Military Serv:** US Army, sgt, 1960-62. **Business Addr:** Deputy Chief Counsel, Massachusetts Highway Dept, 10 Park Plaza, Boston, MA 02116.

JACKSON, ACY LEE
Educational administrator, consultant, entrepreneur. **Personal:** Born Sep 14, 1937, W Bainbridge, GA; children: Tsekani Allette. **Educ:** Westminster Coll N Wilmington PA, BA 1958; Univ of Pittsburgh, MEd 1964; Columbia Univ NYC, MA 1970. **Career:** CTI HS Sialkot W Pakistan, English teacher, coach 1958-61; Armaghan English Lang Inst Teheran Iran, dir 1970-72; Coll of Wooster, instructor-at-large 1972-78, assoc dean of students, dir of career planning & placement 1972-78; Colgate University, dir of career planning center , 1978-93, asst dean for supportive services, 1983-85, associate dean of students, 1985-93, co-director of office of intercultural resources, 1993-95; Acy L Jackson & Associates, owner, 1995-; Polo Ralph Lauren, Hecht's, polo specialist, 1996-. **Orgs:** Cons, guest lecturer Coll Placement Serv Bethlehem PA 1974-; consult US Office of Ed 1976-; cons, mem disting faculty Amer Mgmt Assoc 1978-; mem Coll Placement Council 1972-, Eastern Coll Pers Officers 1978-, Midwest Coll Placement Assoc 1972-78. **Honors/ Awds:** Author "The Conversation Class/Engl Teaching Forum Vol III" 1969; book reviewer Jrnl of Coll Placement 1972-78; author/poet "Black Forum", "The Poet", "Thistle" 1974-79; Colgate University, Administrative Development Award, 1985; Council for the Advancement and Support of Education, Silver Medal Award for Alumni Service to Colgate University, 1987. **Special Achievements:** Author, "Career Counseling for Minority Persons," Career Development in the 1980s: Theory and Practice, 1981; author, How to Prepare Your Curriculum Vitae, 1992, 2nd ed 1996.

JACKSON, ADA JEAN WORK
Educator (retired), consultant. **Personal:** Born Nov 16, 1935, Nashville, TN; daughter of Josephine Wilson Work and Lucuis Work Jr. (deceased); children: Andrea Eva Fitzpatrick Collins. **Educ:** TN State Univ, BS 1959, ME 1965; George Peabody Coll for Teachers, EdS guidance & counseling 1975; Vanderbilt Univ, PhD Educ Admin 1981. **Career:** Metro Public School, reading specialist 1964-76, careers spec 1976-77, guidance counselor 1977-79, asst principal 1979-83, coordinator of student referrals 1983-85, admin Comprehensive High School 1985-95, principal; J's Service Concept, owner, currently. **Orgs:** Mem Alpha Delta Omega, Alpha Kappa Alpha 1957-, MNEA, TEA, NEA 1959-, Phi Delta Kappa 1972-, Natl Assoc of Secondary School Principal 1978-; natl pres Natl Pan-Hellenic Council Inc 1985-89. **Honors/Awds:** Woman of the Year Gordon United Methodist Women's Honoree 1964; Natl Leader of Amer Award Natl Assoc of Equal Oppty in Higher Ed 1980; Soror of the Year Alpha Kappa Alpha 1987; Woman of the Year Natl Business & Prof Womens Org 1987; Professional Woman of the Year Natl Assn of Negro Business and Professional Women 1987; Distinguished Service Award Tennessee Black Caucus of State Legislators 1988. **Business Addr:** Owner, J's Service Concept, 6616 Valley Dr, Brentwood, TN 37027.

JACKSON, AGNES MORELAND
Educator. **Personal:** Born Dec 2, 1930, Pine Bluff, AR; married Harold A Jackson Jr; children: Barbara R Arnwine, Lucretia D Peebles. **Educ:** Univ Redlands, BA, cum laude, 1952; Univ of WA, MA, 1953; Columbia Univ, PhD, 1960. **Career:** Spelman College, instructor 1953-55; College of Basic Studies, Liberal Arts, Boston Univ, instructor, asst prof 1959-63; CA State Univ LA, asst & assoc prof 1963-69; Pitzer College, The Intercollegiate Dept of Black Studies, English prof 1969-. **Orgs:** Society for Values in Higher Educ Central Committee 1971-74; bd of dirs 1985-88, Modern Lang Assn; AAUP; Amer Assn of Univ Women; Danforth Assn Prog 1971-; adv counc & panels/ symposia at various English & other professional society meetings; bd of trustees 1981-85, 1985-89, pres 1983-84 Pomona Unified School District; nominating committee 1981-84, 1987-90 bd of dir 1984-86, 1988 Spanish Trails Girl Scout Council; Phi Beta Kappa Univ of Redlands 1982-. **Honors/Awds:** United Church of Christ Danforth Grad Fellowship 1952-59; So Fellowships Fund Award 1955; Society for Values in Higher Ed Cross-Disciplinary Post-Doctoral Fellowship; Distinguished Service Award Univ of the Redlands Alumni Assn 1973. **Business Addr:** Professor of English, Pitzer College, Claremont, CA 91711.

JACKSON, ALFRED THOMAS
Personnel administrator. **Personal:** Born May 30, 1937, Issue, MD; married Clarice Cecelia Brooks; children: Michael, Karen, Damien. **Educ:** Fisk U, BS 1964. **Career:** Employee Devel & Counseling 1980; dir of training NBC 1979-80; dir/orgn Devel NBC Bny 1978; mgr/orgn Devel NBC NY 1976; adminstr training & devel NBC NY 1976; Adminstr Training & devel 1975; Grand Union Co Elmwood Park NJ, mgr training & devel 1974-75f Grand Union Co Elmwood Park NJ Personnel Adminstr 1969-74; Grand Union Co 1965-69. **Orgs:** Pres Better Human Relations Council Bloomfield NJ 1973-78f chmn eof Com Adv Bd Bloomfield Coll 1973-77; bd of trustees Bloomfield Coll NJ, 1977-78. **Honors/Awds:** Received Oustanding Trainee of the Cycle AUS 1960; Black Achievers Award Harlem Ymca NY 1971. **Military Serv:** Aus E-2 1960. **Business Addr:** NBC, 30 Rockefeller Plaza Rm 1616, New York, NY 10020.

JACKSON, ALPHONSE, JR.
State official. **Personal:** Born Nov 27, 1927, Shreveport, LA; married Ruby H McClure; children: Lydia, Angela. **Educ:** So Univ, BA 1944; NY Univ, MA. **Career:** LEA, pres, 1965-70, past vice pres; teacher; NEA, state dir; state of LA, state representative, dist 2, 1972-. **Orgs:** Mem Natl Dept Elem Prin; Shreveport Bicent Comm; LA House of Reps, Health and Welfare Committee, currently. **Military Serv:** Military service during WWII.

JACKSON, ALTERMAN
Educator. **Personal:** Born Feb 28, 1948, Bronx, NY. **Educ:** Lincoln Univ, BA 1970; Millersville State Coll, ME 1973. **Career:** City of Lancaster, personnel asst 1970-71; School Dist of Lancaster, dir 1971-72; Millersville Univ, asst dir, counselor 1972-76; Lancaster Rec Commiss,; suprv 1974-76; Hahnemann Univ School of Med, dir, admissions 1976-. **Orgs:** Pres 307-Acad Fellowship 1968-69; mem Lancaster City Cty Human Rel Commiss 1971; comm mem King-Clemente Mem Scholarship Fund Trinity Luth Church 1972-77; reg rep PA State Ed Assoc 1972-77, PA Black Conf on Higher Ed 1973-76, NE Med Schools 1976-77; bd of dir Natl Assoc of Med Minority Ed 1976-77; reg rep Assoc Amer Med Coll 1977; past master Omega Psi Phi. **Honors/Awds:** Dean's List Lincoln Univ 1968-69; Outstanding Young Men in Amer 1976.

JACKSON, ALVIN B., JR.
City official. **Personal:** Born Mar 21, 1961, Miami, FL; son of Gussye M Bartley Jackson; married Dorothea U. Jackson, Mar 12, 1983; children: Alvin Bernard III, Carla, Desarae, Doreen, Kavell, Nicola, Sharonette, Tiffini. **Educ:** Univ of MD, College Park MD, BS, 1982. **Career:** Urban Resources Consultant, Washington DC, admin aide, 1979-81; Birch & Davis Assn, Silver Spring MD, government conference coordinator, 1982-83; Ft Lauderdale Coll, Miami FL, dir of admin, 1984; Real Estate Data Inc, Miami FL, county coordinator, 1985-88; Opa-Locka Commercial Devel Corp, Opa-Locka FL, commercial revitalization specialist, 1988; Town of Eatonville FL, town administrator, 1988-90; City of Eustis, director of human services, 1990-93; Economic Development Commission of Mid-Florida, Lake County coordinator, 1993-96; Deputy County Manager, Lake County Board of County Commissioner, 1996-. **Orgs:** Pastor, The Church of the Kingdom of God, 1984-97; mem, Amer Society for Public Administration, 1985; sec, The King of Clubs of Greater Miami, 1987-88; chairman, Day Care Committee, 1987-88, area pres, Dade County PTA/PTSA; mem, FL State Committee on Africa Amer History, 1988; mem, FL League of Cities Black Elected, 1988; mem, Preserve Eatonville Community Inc, 1988-; mem, Zora Neale Hurston Ad Hoc, 1988-90; state chairman, Progress Inc; council mem, FL State Historic Preservation Council, 1988-94; Bd of dir, The Center for Drug Free Living, 1989-91; board of directors, Lake Sumter Mental Health & Hospital, 1990-93; member, Golden Triangle Kiwanis, vice president, Lake County Urban Network; HRS Health & Human Service Local Board; Florida Department of Education Technical Committee on Marketing Education; bd of dirs, Florida Waterman Hospital Foundation, 1994-96; bd of regents, Leadership Lake, 1994-95. **Honors/Awds:** City Manager, Mayor's Award, 1991; Wall of Fame, Eustis High School, 1992; Apple From the Teachers Award, 1989; Washington Day Parade Marshall, 1995; Orlando Sentinel/Lake County League of Cities, Community Service Award, 1995; Community Service Award for Business Development, 1995; Black Achiever of Central Florida Award, 1997. **Home Addr:** PO Box 124, Eustis, FL 32727-0124. **Business Addr:** Lake County Board of County Commissioners, County Manager's Office, PO Box 7800, Tavares, FL 32778, (904)343-9449.

JACKSON, ANDREW
Educator sociologist. **Personal:** Born Feb 2, 1945, Montgomery, AL; married Dr Hazel Ogilvie; children: Yasmine Nefertiti. **Educ:** Yale Univ, Study Prog 1966; Univ of Nairobi Kenya, Ed 1969-70; Univ of CA, MA Ed, Psych 1970, MA 1972, PhD Soc 1974. **Career:** Desegregation Inst Emergency School Aid Act, consult 1977; Fisk Univ, adj prof 1978-; US Dept of Labor, hbc faculty fellow 1980; Natl Assoc for Equal Oppty in Higher Ed, consult 1981; TN State Univ, prof of soc 1973-. **Orgs:** Pres Assoc of Social & Behavioral Scientists Inc 1983-84; mem Ed Bd Jrnl of Soc & Behavioral Sci 1984-; chairperson, bd of dir Sankofa Dance Theatre1984-; mem Amer Soc Assoc, Amer Acad of Political & Soc Sci, Southern Soc Assoc, Amer Assoc of Univ Prof, Kappa Alpha Psi, Islamic Ctr Inc; life mem Assn of Social and Behavioral Scientists Inc. **Honors/Awds:** Delegate Crisis of Black Family Summit NAACP 1984; Article "Illuminating the Path to Community Self-Reliance" Journal of Soc & Behavioral Sci 1984; Textbook Sci of Soc, 1985; article "Apartheid, the Great Debate and Martin Luther King Jr" The AME Church Review Jan-March 1985. **Business Addr:** Professor of Sociology, Tennessee State University, 3500 John A Merritt Blvd, Nashville, TN 37203.

JACKSON, ANDREW PRESTON
Library director. **Personal:** Born Jan 28, 1947, Brooklyn, NY; son of Bessie Lindsay Jackson and Walter L Jackson Sr. **Educ:** York College, Jamaica, NY, BS, 1983-90; City Univ of NY, Queens, BS, bus admin, 1990; MLS Queens Coll, Flushing, NY, 1993-96; City Univ of NY, Queens MLS, Library Science; Public Librarians Prof Certificate, Univ of the State of NY, 1996. **Career:** New York City Agency for Child Development, New York, NY, coordinator of personnel services, 1971-76; Robinson Chevrolet, Novato, CA, customer relations mgr, 1976-78; Langston Hughes Community Library and Cultural Center, Corona, NY, executive director, 1980-. **Orgs:** Elmhurst Hospital Ctr, bd mem, 1983-; NAACP; ALA; Black Caucus, NY; York College, comm advisory council; Public Library Assn of the ALA. **Honors/Awds:** Minority Management Association, NY Telephone/NYNEX, Community Service Award, 1992; Baisley Park Club, National Association of Negro Business and Professional Women's Clubs, Inc, Man of the Year, 1991; York College (CUNY), Dean's List, 1990; East Elmhurst/Corona Civic Association, Community Service Award, 1989; Queens Federation of Churches, Outstanding Leadership in Queens Award, 1988; East Elmhurst Track Club, Community Service Award, 1986; North Shore Club, National Association of Negro Business and Professional Women's Clubs, Ombudsman Award, 1982; NY State Governor, African Americans of Distinction Award, 1994; Natl Assn of Equal Opportunity, Higher Educ, Distinguished Graduate Award, 1994; LAMA, certificate of Honor; Fulfilling the Dream Awd, WCBS-TV, 1996; Distinguished Alumni Awd, York Coll Alumni, Inc, 1996; Scroll of Honor, 4W Circle Arts and Enterprise, Inc. 1996; National Council of Negro Women, Inc, North Shore Chap, Community Service Award, 1997. **Military Serv:** US Air Force, E-5, 1964-68; Bronze Star, 1967. **Home Addr:** 105-18 29th Avenue, East Elmhurst, NY 11369.

JACKSON, ANNA MAE
Educator. **Personal:** Born Apr 10, 1934, Wetumpka, AL; daughter of Alice M Mitchell and Moses E Mitchell; children: Stevan, Sean. **Educ:** Bowling Green State Univ, BA 1959; Univ of Denver, MA 1960; CO State Univ, PhD 1967. **Career:** State Home and Training Schl Lapeer MI, staff psych 1960-61; State Home and Training Schl Wheatridge CO, chief psych 1962-68; Univ CO Health Sciences Ctr, assc prof psych 1968-. **Orgs:** Consult US Homes Inc 1975-78; visiting lecturer Afro-Amer

Studies Dept 1971-73; aqdv bd mem Schl of Comm and Human Srvs 1980-; pres Denver Rocky Mountain Chptr Assc of Black Psych; NAACP Park Hill Branch 1982-83; Denver Urban League. **Honors/Awds:** Educ Ach CO Black Women for Political Action 1983; Woman of the Year Regina's Soc and Civic Club 1977; contrb to Minority Educ CO Schl of Medicine 1978; Woman of Ach Denver Alumnae Chptr Delta Sigma Theta Sor 1976; Founders Award Assn of Black Psychologists 1987; Distinguished Chapter Service Award Denver-Rocky Mountain Chapter Assn of Black Psychologists 1987. **Business Addr:** Assc Prof of Psychiatry, Univ of CO Health Sciences, 4200 E 9th Ave C258, Denver, CO 80262.

JACKSON, ART EUGENE, SR.
Business executive. **Personal:** Born Jan 14, 1941, St Louis, MO; married Nodie Elnora Scales; children: Andrea Annette, Art Eugene Jr. **Educ:** Lincoln Univ, attended. **Career:** McDonnell Douglas, stock keeper 1966-69; Freeman Shoe Co, mgr, sales 1969-85; Mc Donnell Douglas-Tool & Parts Control Specialist. **Orgs:** Mem NAACP 1953; cub scout leader Boys Scout of Amer 1972; pres City of Northwoods 1974; treas/park bd City of Northwoods 1982; alderman City of Northwoods 1983-; treas Normandy Baseball League. **Honors/Awds:** DECA Trainer St Louis Public School 1980-81. **Military Serv:** USAF aic 4 yrs; Good Conduct, Sharp Shooting 1959-64. **Home Addr:** 4308 Oakridge, Northwoods, MO 63121.

JACKSON, ARTHUR D., JR.
Judge. **Personal:** Born Oct 31, 1942; married Suellen Kay Shea; children: Christopher Daniel, Kyle Joseph, Courtney Kathleen. **Educ:** OH No Univ, BS B Music Educ 1964, JD 1968. **Career:** City of Dayton Dept of Law, negotiator & asst city atty 1968-70; Jackson & Austin, atty at law 1969-71; City of Dayton, asst city prosecutor 1970-71; Dept of Justice So Dist of OH, asst US atty 1971-74; Dayton/Mont Co Crim Justice Ctr, legal spec/instr 1974-75; Skilken & Jackson, atty at law 1975-77; Dayton Municipal Ct, judge. **Orgs:** Deputy dir Pub Defender Assn 1975-76; instr Sinclair Comm Coll 1975-; adj prof of law Univ of Dayton Coll of Law 1977-; choir dir Epworth Meth Ch 1964-67; hearing officer OH Civil Rights Commn 1975-76; exec comm Mont Co Emergency Serv Cncl; Dayton Performing Arts Fund Bd; pres Dayton Ballet Co Bd. **Honors/Awds:** Outstanding Actor-Musical Dayton Co 1980; State Certified EMT Paramedic 1981 & 1984. **Business Addr:** 2812 161st Ave SE, Bellevue, WA 98008-5611.

JACKSON, ARTHUR JAMES
Educator. **Personal:** Born Jan 11, 1943, Union Springs, AL; married Beverly Fennoy; children: Monica D. **Educ:** Wayne State Univ, BS 1972, Sch of medicine MS 1976, PhD 1979. **Career:** Wayne State Univ, grad asst 1 1974-76, grad asst 2 1976-79; Meharry Medical Coll, asst prof of anatomy 1979-. **Honors/Awds:** Black Medical Assoc Awd for Excellence in Teaching WSU; Pre-Alumni Council Awd for Excellence in Teaching Meharry Med Coll 1980; Kaiser-Permanente Awd for Excellence in Teaching Meharry Medical Coll 1980. **Business Addr:** Asst Prof of Anatomy, Meharry Medical College, 1005 DB Todd Blvd, Nashville, TN 37208.

JACKSON, ARTHUR ROSZELL
Educational administrator. **Personal:** Born Aug 16, 1949, Fort Dix, NJ; son of Elouise Fussell Jackson and Arthur Jackson; married Celeste Budd, Jun 25, 1983; children: Kyle Arthur, Tamara Sheree. **Educ:** State Univ of NY, BA 1971, MA 1977; Univ of MA, Amherst, MA, EdD, l988. **Career:** Educ Opportunity Program, State Univ of NY, academic counselor 1971-72; State Univ of NY Binghamton, asst dir of student financial aide 1972-77; Financial Aid Serv Univ of MA, assoc dir 1977-82; Financial Aid Serv Univ of MA Amherst, dir, 1982-90; Eastern Connecticut State Univ, assoc dean of student affairs, currently. **Orgs:** Vice Chairman New England Coll Bd 1984-86; liaison/consultant Natl Consortium for Educ Access 1985-87; vice pres Eastern Assoc Student Financial Aid Administrators 1986; polemarch/pres Hartford Alumni Chap Kappa Alpha Psi 1986-87; bd of dir, MA Higher Educ Assistance Corp, l988-. **Honors/Awds:** Speaker Natl Assoc of Student Personnel Administrators 1995, Natl Conf on Black Retention 1986, College Bd Natl Forum 1986; pres, Eastern Assn of Student Financial Aid Admin, l989; Educational Resource Inst, chairman, 1994-96; Natl Assn of Students Personnel Admini, Conn state dir, 1993-95; President Clinton Post Secondary Education Transition Task Force, mem, 1992-93; Network on Equity and Excellence Award, National Assn of Student Personnel Admini, 1992. **Business Addr:** Assoc Dean, Student Affairs, Eastern Connecticut State Univ, 83 Windham St, Willimantic, CT 06226, (203)456-5282.

JACKSON, AUBREY N.
Dentist. **Personal:** Born Feb 11, 1926, Lynchburg, VA; married Laura Thompson; children: Aubrey, Kelly, Carl. **Educ:** Bluefield State Coll, BS 1949; Howard U, post-grad 1950; Meharry Med Coll, DDS 1954. **Career:** Dental Clinic Salem, pvt practice of dentistry & dir of dental clinic. **Orgs:** Mem NDA; Am Dental Assn; past pres WV Med Soc; WV State Dental Soc; pres Mercer-Mcdowell Dental Soc; Mcdowell Co Hlth Council; Chas Payne Dental Study Club; Bluefield Study Club; chmn Exec Comm NAACP; pol council Council of Southern Mountains; treas Alpha Zeta Lambda Chap Alpha Phi Alpha; treas Upsilon Boule Sigma Pi Phi. **Military Serv:** USN PhM 3rd cl 1944-46. **Business Addr:** Box 671, Keystone, WV 24852.

JACKSON, AUDREY NABORS
Business executive, librarian (retired). **Personal:** Born Jul 10, 1926, New Orleans, LA; daughter of Beluah Carney Nabors and Raymond Nabors Sr; married Freddie Jackson Sr, Jul 26, 1946 (deceased); children: Claudia J Fisher, Beverly J Franklin, Freddie Jr (deceased), Sharyll Muri Curley-Etuk, Antria Curley Wilson, Zefron Curley. **Educ:** Southern Univ Laboratory Sch Baton Rouge LA; Southern Univ & A&M College Baton Rouge LA, BA 1951, MEd 1966; Chicago Teachers College, 1959; Louisiana State Univ, various years, 1954-73. **Career:** JS Dawson HS, librarian 1951-54; Southdown HS, librarian 1954-55; Chaneyville HS Zachary LA, librarian 1955-81; Louisiana Legislative Bureau, sec 1979, 1980; Clerk of Court's Office, abstractor, 1982; Louisiana Senate Docket, legislative session 1982, 1983, 1984; census taker, 1990; Nabors Bid Tabulation Service, pres/owner, 1981-. **Orgs:** Greater Philadelphia Baptist Church usher; Delta Sigma Theta Sor Inc, golden life mem, treas 1971-75, 1979-; YWCA Author Comm; Southern Univ Alumni Fed, life mem; Women in Mainstream, charter mem; LA Womens Pol Caucus fin chair 1984-85, treas 1985; Baton Rouge Womens Pol Caucus 1st vice chair 1984-85, treas 1985-; Friends Intl, treas 1982-; LA Retired Tchrs Assn; LA Democratic Fin Cncl; Natl Retired Teachers Assn; Mayor Presidents Comm on Needs of Women 1982-85; exec bd of LLA sch librarian 1977-79; Human Resource & Development Corp., secretary, 1978-80; LA Association of Educators, library department, president, 1967-69, 1977-78; Rural Prog Adv Bd, treasurer, 1973, vice pres, 1973-74; National Education Association; LA Women in Politics, treasurer, 1986-; Baton Rouge Women's Politics, treasurer, 1986-; Southern University Alumni Federation, life mem; AARP; American Library Assn, life mem; American Assn of School Librarians; Centroplex, advisory committee, 1991-; Baton Rouge City Court, volunteer; Doug Williams Foundation, board of directors, 1988-; Louisiana Democratic State Central Committee, District 64, elected unopposed, 1992-96; Sixth Congressional District of Louisiana, sec, treasurer, 1993-; City-Parish Planning & Zoning Commission, 1994-99. **Business Addr:** President, Owner, Nabor's Bid Tabulation Serv, 23990 Reames Rd, Zachary, LA 70791.

JACKSON, AVA NICOLA
Attorney. **Personal:** Born Nov 10, 1957, Preston, MS; daughter of Alma Jackson and Enos Jackson; married Charles G Woodall, Nov 13, 1981; children: Raphael Kenzell Jackson Woodall, Amanda Nicola Jackson Woodall. **Educ:** Univ of MS, BS, social work and public administration, 1979, School of Law, JD, 1981. **Career:** Morris & Jackson, associate attorney, 1981-82; North Mississippi Rural Legal Service, managing attorney, 1983-90, executive director, 1990-. **Orgs:** Magnolia Bar Assn, 1981-; Mississippi Bar Assn, 1981-; Zeta Phi Beta Sorority, president, 1985-. **Honors/Awds:** NAACP, Kemper County Branch, Service Award, 1986; Zeta Phi Beta, Zeta of the Year, 1993; Mississippi Bar Assn, Legal Services Laywer of the Year, 1992; NMRLS, Leadership Award, 1991. **Home Addr:** Rte 2, Box 545A, Oxford, MS 38655.

JACKSON, BENITA MARIE
Physician. **Personal:** Born Aug 14, 1956, Englewood, NJ; daughter of Gloria Jackson and Benjamin Jackson. **Educ:** Mount Holyoke Coll, AB, 1978; Howard Univ, Coll of Medicine, MD, 1982; Emory Univ, MPH, 1989. **Career:** resident, Public Health, Preventive Medicine, Morehouse School of Med, 1987-89; group health assoc, staff physician dept internal medicine. **Orgs:** mem, Natl Med Assn, Amer Coll of Physicians, Amer Soc of Microbiology; volunteer physician, Catholic Archdiocese of Greater Washington Area/Immaculate Conception Church; Amer Public Health Assn. **Honors/Awds:** 1974 Natl Achievement Scholarship Finalist for Outstanding Negro Students.

JACKSON, BERNARD H.
Attorney, judge (retired). **Educ:** CCNY, BA; Brooklyn Law Sch, JD; NY Law Sch, grad work. **Career:** White and Case, of counsel, 1990-; New York State Supreme Court, justice, 1987-90; Bronx Criminal Ct, judge; Police Dept, legal staff; US Atty, asst; Dyett Alexander Dinkins, atty; OEO NE Region, area coord; Civilian Complaint Rev Bd NY, exec dir; Pete Rozells Nat Ftbl Leag, asst to commr; Gov of NY, spl asst; Urban Crisis in Am WEVD Radio, host; Endispute, vice president, senior judicial officer, currently. **Orgs:** Mem bd dir Settlement Hsng Fund; S Bronx Overall Econ Dev Corp; 100 Black Men; Police Athletic Leag NY; Nat Multiple Sclerosis Soc NY; Urban Leag; Mayor John Lindsay's Com Cty Marshals; Ctzns Union NYC; founding mem Nghbrhd Legal Serv Prgm; NAACP; Assn of Bronx Comm Orgns; Taft Yth & Adult Ctr; guest lectr John Jay Coll New Sch for Soc Rsrch Bernard M Baruch Coll; host The NY Urban Leag Presents WBLS-FM; mediator Cntr for Mediation & Conflict Resolution; arbitrator 1st Judicial Dept NY Bar; US Supreme Ct; US Customs Ct; Fed Circuit Dist Cts; Am Bar Assn; Fed Bar Counc; Bronx Co Bar Assn; Harlem Lawyers Assn. **Honors/Awds:** South Bronx Overall Development Corporation's Community Service Award, 1992-; ASPIRA, Outstanding Achievement Award, 1991.

JACKSON, BEVERLY ANNE
Business executive, television director. **Personal:** Born Nov 29, 1947, Philadelphia, PA; daughter of Alice M McConico Jackson (deceased) and Frank E Jackson Sr; children: Michelle Marie. **Educ:** Penn State Univ, BA, speech, broadcasting, 1969; Chas Morris Price Sch of Advertising & Journalism, advertising certificate, 1972. **Career:** School District of Philadelphia, substitute teacher, 1969-70; US Cencus Bureau, administrative clerk, 1970-71; RCA Service Co., special projects instructor, 1971-72; KATZ-TV Television, advertising sales, sales assistant, 1972; KYW-TV, Westinghouse Broadcasting Co., production assistant, 1972-74, associate producer, 1974-76, director, 1976-91; "The Joan Rivers Show," director, 1991-; "Gossip, Gossip, Gossip with Joan Rivers," director, 1992-; VerVe Graphix & Video, president, owner, currently. **Orgs:** Directors Guild of Am; American Women in Radio & TV; Delta Sigma Theta; volunteer Big Sister, Big Sisters of Philadelphia 1980; Intl TV Assn; Natl Academy of TV Arts and Sciences; Society of Motion Picture and TV Engineers; Intl Brotherhood of Electrical Workers; Natl Black Media Coalition; Natl Assn of Female Executives; Cherry Hill Minority Civic Assn. **Honors/Awds:** Natl Academy of Television Arts & Sciences, Philadelphia Chapter, Most Outstanding Television Talk Program, Series Emmy, for "Time Out," Beverly A Jackson, director, 1987-88. **Special Achievements:** First African-American female director hired by KYW-TV; believed to be the first African-American woman to direct a television program in the history of Philadelphia broadcast television. **Business Addr:** Director, The Joan Rivers Show, CBS Broadcast Center, 555 W 57th St, New York, NY 10019.

JACKSON, BEVERLY JOYCE
Television news producer. **Personal:** Born May 17, 1955, Detroit, MI; daughter of Laura Grogan Jackson and Samuel Jackson. **Educ:** University of Michigan, Ann Arbor, MI, BA, 1977. **Career:** WTOL-TV, Toledo, OH, news reporter, 1977-79; WGBH-TV, Boston, MA, news reporter, 1982-83; WCVB-TV, Boston, MA, producer, 1983-85; CBS News, New York, NY, producer, 1985-88; ABC News, New York, NY, producer, World News Tonight, 1988-93; NBC News, sr producer, currently. **Orgs:** Natl Assn of Black Journalists; Delta Sigma Theta Sorority Inc; Natl Association of Black Journalists, vp, 1984-85; Columbia Univ, adjunct professor. **Honors/Awds:** United Press International Award, 1984; Black Achievers Award, United Press International, 1985; Gabriel Award, National Catholic Association for Broadcasters & Communications, 1990; Judge's Award, World Hunger Media Awards, 1990, CINE Golden Eagle Award, 1992; George Washington Medal of Honor, 1992; Gabriel Award, 1992; Gold Hugo-Chicago International Film Festival, 1993. **Business Addr:** Senior Producer, NBC News, 30 Rockefeller Plaza, New York, NY 10112.

JACKSON, BLYDEN
Educator. **Personal:** Born Oct 12, 1910, Paducah, KY; son of Julie Jackson and George W Jackson; married Dr Roberta Hodges. **Educ:** Wilberforce Univ, AB 1930; Univ MI, AM 1938, PhD (Rosenwald Fellow 1947-49) 1952. **Career:** Public Schs Louisville, tchr English 1934-45; Fisk Univ, asst then assoc prof 1945-54; Southern Univ, prof English head dept 1954-62, dean grad sch 1962-69; Univ NC, prof English 1969-81, assoc graduate dean 1973-76, spl asst to graduate dean, 1976-81, prof English emeritus. **Orgs:** Mem Coll Lang Assn pres 1957-59; mem Natl Cncl Tchrs English, disting lectr 1970-71, chmn coll sect 1971-73, trustee rsch found 1975-; vice pres 1954-56, pres 1956-58 Coll Lang Assn; mem Speech Assn Amer; mem NC Tchrs English; mem Alpha Phi Alpha. **Honors/Awds:** Author "The Waiting Years"; co-author "Black Poetry in America"; assoc editor CLA Bull; adv editor So Lit Journal; contrib articles to professional jours; Honorary Degree, Wilberforce Univ, 1978; Doctor of Humane Letters, Univ of Louisville, 1977; Honorary Degree, Univ of North Carolina at Chapel Hill, 1985; Honorary Degree, Univ of Kentucky, 1990; author of "The Long Beginning, Vol. 1," A History of Afro-American Literature. **Business Addr:** Professor Emeritus of English, University of NC Chapel Hill, Chapel Hill, NC 27514.

JACKSON, BO (VINCENT EDWARD)
Professional baseball player (retired). **Personal:** Born Nov 30, 1962, Bessemer, AL; married Linda Jackson; children: Garrett, Nicholas, Morgan. **Educ:** Auburn Univ, undergraduate degree from Sch of Human Sci, 1996. **Career:** Kansas City Royals, 1986-90; Los Angeles Raiders, 1987-90; Chicago White Sox, 1991-94; California Angels, 1994-95. **Honors/Awds:** American League All-Star Team, 1989; Heisman Trophy Winner, Auburn Univ, 1985; Jim Thorpe Legacy Award, 1992. **Business Addr:** Retired Professional Baseball Player, California Angels, PO Box 2000, Anaheim, CA 92803.

JACKSON, BOBBY
Professional basketball player. **Personal:** Born Mar 13, 1973. **Educ:** Univ of Minnesota. **Career:** Denver Nuggets, guard, 1997-. **Business Addr:** Professional Basketball Player, Denver Nuggets, 1635 Clay St, Denver, CO 80204, (303)893-6700.

JACKSON, BOBBY L.
City official. **Personal:** Born Feb 19, 1945, Fayetteville, NC; married Gwendolyn; children: Martin, Marquisha. **Educ:** Essex

Coll of Bus, sr accountant; St Peter College, acctg. **Career:** Hudson Co Operation PUSH, chmn bd 1978-81; Jersey City Certified Develop Corp, bd mem 1981-; Jersey City Democratic Organ, chmn; Commissioner Ins, comm; City of Jersey City, city council pres. **Orgs:** Campaign mgr for Jesse Jackson NJ; staff mem Ken Gibson for Governor. **Honors/Awds:** Andrew Young Black Achievement Awd Lambda Omega Sor; Jesse Jackson Awd SC Chap Operation PUSH; Chap 1 Central Parent Council; Male of the Year CETA Inc Jersey City. **Home Addr:** 232 Wegman Parkway, Jersey City, NJ 07305. **Business Addr:** President City Council, City of Jersey City, 280 Grove St, Jersey City, NJ 07302.

JACKSON, BRENDA
Business executive. **Personal:** Born Oct 27, 1950, Aberdeen, MD; daughter of Henry Taylor (deceased) and Annie Marie (Ellison) Jackson. **Educ:** Prairie View A & M Univ, BS, 1972. **Career:** Dallas Power and Light Co, home service advisor, 1973-78, supr consumer services, 1978-81, community programs mgr, beginning 1981, vice pres of customer service, currently. **Orgs:** Tom Paukins Campaign for Congress, volunteer, 1978; Dallas County chpt Am Heart Assn, bd of dir; Bishop Coll, Museum of Afro-American Life and Culture, bd of visitors, 1979-; Dallas Black C of C; Am Home Econs Assn; TX Home Econs Assn; North TX Home Economist in Bus Am Assn; Blacks in Energy. **Honors/Awds:** American Heart Assn, Award of Merit, 1978. **Special Achievements:** Author (with Charlene Clark): The Children's Help Your Heart Cookbook, 1978. **Business Addr:** Vice President of Customer Service, Texas Utilities Co, PO Box 10001, Dallas, TX 75310, (214)812-6588.

JACKSON, BURNETT LAMAR, JR.
Dentist. **Personal:** Born Jan 31, 1928, Athens, GA; married Dorian Sara Gant; children: Burnett Lamar, Stephen Mouzon. **Educ:** KY State Coll, BS 1950; Meharry Med Coll, DDS 1960. **Career:** Dentistry Tuskegee, AL, pvt prac 1961-68, Philadelphia 1969-; John A Andrew Hosp Tuskegee Inst, chief dental serv 1961-68; Temple Univ & Philadelphia, pub health dentist 1968-70; W Nice Town-Fioga Nghbrhd Hlth Ctr, chief dental serv 1970-. **Orgs:** Mem A&M & Philadelphia Co Dental Assn, Jackson sec 1969-70, New Era 1972; AL Dental Soc; John A Andrew Clinic Soc Sec1965-68; Acad Gen Dentistry; mem Com for a Greater Tuskegee, AL 1966-68; Macon Co Action Com 1965-68; contrib articles to professional jours. **Military Serv:** AUS 1951-52. **Business Addr:** 3450 N 17 St, Philadelphia, PA 19140.

JACKSON, C. BERNARD
Composer. **Personal:** Born Nov 4, 1927, Brooklyn, NY. **Educ:** UCLA, BA, MA; Brooklyn Coll. **Career:** Dept of Dance UCLA, staff mem 1957-61; Alvin Ailey Dance Co S Amer Tour, musical dir 1963; Graduate Concerts Dept of Dance UCLA, musical dir 1964; Neuropsychiatric Inst Mental Health Programs, musician/resource consultant 1965; Dept of Dance UCLA, lectr 1966-67; Inner City Cultural Ctr LA, exec dir 1966-; Dept of Ethnic Studies USC LA, sr lecture 1967-; Inner City Inst for Performing & Visual Arts LA, founding dir 1967; composer; CCNY Theatre Dept, chair 1981-; Inner City Cultural Ctr, artistic dir, currently. **Orgs:** Bd mem CA Theatre Council; advisory bd Natl Arts Awards; arts advisory panel Univ of CA LA; arts advisory panel Amer Bicentennial Commn; arts advisory panel pres Commn on Mental Health; adv bd mem Radion Station KUSC; dance advisory panel Natl Endowment for the Arts; opera/musical theater panel Natl Endowment for the Arts, CA Arts Council Multi-Cultural Advisory Panel. **Honors/Awds:** Unity Award LA 1960; OBIE Award Best Musical for "Fly Blackbird" 1961-62; Resolution of Special Commendation LA City Council 1969; Resolution of Special Commendation LA City Council 1978; 3rd Annual Theatre Awards Dramalogue writing & direction for "Iago" 1980; Award for Outstanding Achievement in the Area of Play Writing for play "Iago" LA Weekly Magazine; CITIES Comm Serv Awd for musical "What Is to Be Done?" 1986; NAACP-TrailBlazer Award, Frances E Williams Lifetime Achievement Award. **Special Achievements:** Musical compostions include: Invisible Kingdom; Scudorama; Montage; Chameleon and the Lady; Two of Me; Arena; Blood of the Lamb; theatrical scores: Fly Blackbird; Earthquake; The Second Earthquake; The Nutcraker Triology; Lemur; numerous others. **Business Addr:** Executive Director, Inner City Cultural Center, 1308 So New Hampshire Ave, Los Angeles, CA 90006, (213)962-2102.

JACKSON, CALVIN BERNARD
Professional football player. **Personal:** Born Oct 28, 1972, Miami, FL; children: Kalyn, Carami, Calvin Jr. **Educ:** Auburn. **Career:** Miami Dolphins, defensive back, 1994-. **Business Addr:** Professional Football Player, Miami Dolphins, 2269 NW 199th St, Miami, FL 33056, (305)620-5000.

JACKSON, CARLOS
Law enforcement official. **Career:** Denver Sheriff's Dept, captain, major, currently. **Special Achievements:** Highest ranking African American in the Denver Sheriff's Dept; first African American major in the Denver Sheriff's Dept.

JACKSON, CAROL E.
Judge. **Educ:** Wellesley College, BA, 1973; Univ of Michigan, JD, 1976. **Career:** Thompson & Mitchell, attorney, 1976-83; Mallinckrodt Inc, counsel, 1983-85; US District Court, Eastern District MO, magistrate, 1986-92, district judge, 1992-; Washington Univ, adjunct prof of law, 1989-92. **Orgs:** St Louis Art Museum, trustee, 1987-91; National Assn of Women's Judges; Federal Magistrate Judges Assn; Missouri Bar; St Louis County Bar Assn; Metro St Louis; Mound City Bar Assn; Lawyers Assn of St Louis.

JACKSON, CHARLES E., SR.
Banker, financial officer (retired). **Personal:** Born Mar 18, 1938, Detroit, MI; son of Mary Elizabeth Jackson-King and Fred Dewitt Jackson Sr; married Maxine W Jackson; children: Melinda C, Charles E Jr, Summer M, David SW. **Educ:** Highland Park Jr College. **Career:** Veterans Administration Hospital, bio lab technician, 1959-66; Scott Paper Company, lab technician, 1966-67; MI Dept of Corrections, boys supervisor 1967-69; Security Insurance Group, inspector-safety engr 1969-70; Hartford Ins Group Detroit, underwriting coordinator 1970; MI Dept of Corrections, corrections specialist 1970-73; First Federal of Michigan, FSA, mortgage servicing officer-supervisor, asst vice pres, 1973-94. **Orgs:** Mem Natl Soc of Medical Rsch, Natl Assoc for Lab Animal Sci MI Chapt; mem Natl Assoc of Urban Bankers 1982, Urban Bankers Forum Inc 1982; pres Chap 19 MSEA Michigan State Employees; Rackham Symphony Choir; National Society for Medical Research; National Association for Lab Animal Science; Detroiters at Heart; Friends of Belle Isle. **Business Addr:** PO Box 38837, Detroit, MI 48238-0837.

JACKSON, CHARLES ELLIS
Municipal government administrator. **Personal:** Born Jan 30, 1930, Tampa, FL; son of Clara Yeoman Jackson and Ellis "Jim" Jackson; married Nellie Grace Smith, Dec 6, 1953; children: Donovan Renee, Ronald Eric. **Educ:** Clark Coll Atlanta, attended; Alaska Meth U, BS; AK Meth U, additional Studies. **Career:** AK Methodist Univ, assoc dean of students 1972-; Clinical Chem, chief 1955-70; AK Students Higher Educ Program, counselor 1970-72; Prov & Anchorage Comm Hospital, consultant 1955-70; Matunuska Maid Dairy, bacteriologist; AK Native Serv Hospital, med technologist; Valley Hospital; Elmendorf AFB AK Hospital, chief clinical chem; Alaska Methodist University, associate dean of students; Alaska Pipe Line Co, personnel director; Municipality of Anchorage, personnel administrator, sanitation supervisor, currently. **Orgs:** Mem Nat Assn of Student Personnel Adminstr; Am Assn of Clinical Chemists; AK Soc of Med Technologists; Pacific Assn of Coll Deans & Admssns Officers; AK State Assn of Guidance Counselors; past pres Anchorage Rotary Club; past pres Anchorage Toastmasters Club; bd mem City of Anchorage Human Relations Commn; bd dir Lions Internat; mem Omega Psi Phi Frat; World Affairs Council; Am Cancer Soc; pres Elem & Secondary Sch PTA; bd dir Kings Lake Mus Camp; house chmn Anchorage Symphony; investigator Elmendorf AFB EED Commn; vestryman St Marys Episcopal Ch; chmn of Worship & Parish Life Com; scoutmaster; cub scouts & BSA. **Honors/Awds:** Recipient Elks Oratorial Scholarship; Grand Union Pallsbearers Lodge Scholarship 1948; best dressed man 1974. **Military Serv:** USAF aviation cadet 1952-55, lab officer 1953-55. **Business Addr:** Supervisor of Sanitation Inspection, Municipality of Anchorage, 825 L St, Anchorage, AK 99519.

JACKSON, CHARLES N., II
Association executive. **Personal:** Born Mar 16, 1931, Richmond, VA; son of Thelma Manning and Miles M Jackson; married Marlene Mills; children: Renata, Andrea, Charles III. **Educ:** VA Union U, BS 1958; Temple U, Post Grad 1976; MS Southeastern U, Post Grad 1976. **Career:** The Nat Urban Coalition, vice pres adminstrn & finan; Agcy Intl Devl, sr auditor chf accnt; IRS Intell Div, spec agt; Phila, auditor & trea vol tech; Soc of American Foresters, Bethesda, MD, dir, finance & administration, 1991-. **Orgs:** Asst bd mem Wash Hosp Natl Assn Accts; natl Soc of Pub Accts Am Acctg Assn; Am Mgmt Assn Accredited; Accreditation Counc Acctg. **Military Serv:** USAF 1951-55. **Business Addr:** Director of Finance and Administration, Society of American Foresters, 5400 Grosvenor Ln, Bethesda, MD 20814.

JACKSON, CHARLES RICHARD, JR.
Professional sports executive. **Personal:** Born Jun 18, 1929, Yonkers, NY; married Mary Alice Crockett; children: Steven, Marc. **Educ:** Lincoln Univ, 1948-50; Adelphi Univ, BA 1953; Baruch Sch, MPA 1959. **Career:** Yonkers Police Dept, det 1952-67; Westchester Co Sheriff Dept, chf criminal investigator 1968-72; 3 State Narcotic Strike Force, comdr 1970-72; Con Edison Urban Afrs, asst to vice pres 1973; City Mgr, asst 1974-75; Natl Football League, asst dir of sec 1975-. **Orgs:** US Gov Presidential Task Force on Drug Abuse 1973; consult Polaroid Corp 1973-74; consult Boston PD 1973; Urban Afrs Task Force 1966; lectr Univ of OK 1973; Coll of Mainland 1973-75; Intl Narcotic Enformt Ofcrs Assn; Intl Assn of Chfs of Police; FBINA; NYPD Hon Legion; life mem Natl Sheriff Assn; NY State Assn of Chfs of Pol; Amer Soc for Indsl Security; pres Intl Narcotic Enforcement Ofcrs Assn 1977. **Honors/Awds:** Dept Awds & Cit for Distinguished Police Serv, 1952-73; New York City Det Educ Assn, 1968; one of 10 Outstanding Police Officers in US W Grand Jurors Awd, 1971; Humanitarian Awd Portchester Citizens Anti-Poverty Assn Inc, 1975; Gold Medal Award, 1992; Distinguished American, National Football Foundation & Hall of Fame, Oct 1992. **Special Achievements:** Author: "Coop with Police," 1968; "The Impact of Drugs on the Sport of Football," 1976. **Military Serv:** US Army, sp/4, 1954-55. **Business Addr:** Asst Dir of Sec, Natl Football League, 410 Park Ave, New York, NY 10022.

JACKSON, CHRIS. See ABDUL-RAUF, MAHMOUD.

JACKSON, CLARENCE A.
Automobile dealer. **Career:** Royal Dodge Inc, chief executive officer, currently. **Special Achievements:** Company listed #88 on Black Enterprise's list of top 100 auto dealers, 1994. **Business Addr:** CEO, Royal Dodge Inc, 555 Mantua Ave, Ste 45, Woodbury, NJ 08096, (609)848-5008.

JACKSON, CLARENCE H.
Educator, attorney, business executive. **Personal:** Born Aug 27, 1924, Pittsburg, TX; married Phyllis M Halliday; children: Anthony Lawrence, Phillip Michael. **Educ:** Prairie View A&M Coll, BS 1948; TX So Univ Sch Of Law, LLB. **Career:** Private Practice, attorney; tchr & instr 25 yrs; Oakland Small Bus Devel Cntr CA, proj dir; Pilgrim Life Ins Co, exec asst to pres; VA, asst toagy officer; Estate & Gift Tax U5 Treas Dept, examiner; San Joaquin Delta Community Coll Stockton CA, part-time instructor; Peral Peralta Coll Dist CA,presently Small Bus Mgmt Cons. **Orgs:** Mem CA Comm Coll; Am Mgmt Assn; former mem sch bd St Elizabeth Parish Oakland; editor & publisher of The Black Bus Newsletter; Black Bus Review; other black bus publs. **Military Serv:** USNR 1943-46; AUSR 1948-54.

JACKSON, CLAUDE
Chief executive officer. **Personal:** Born Sep 8, 1942, Aliceville, AL; married Drucilla Russ; children: Mikisha. **Educ:** AL A&M Univ, BS 1972; Tuskegee Inst, attended; Los Angeles State, attended; Air Route Traffic Control Biloxi MS, attended. **Career:** Guy James Construction Co, civil engr 1972; Greene Cty Bd of Educ, chair math dept & teacher 1979; Sumter County Bd of Educ, attendance suprv 1983, public info officer 1984; Sumter County Bd of Commiss, chmn. **Orgs:** Trustee AL Assoc of Cty Commisss State Ins Bd 1983-; chmn Sumter Cty Bd of Commiss 1983-87; mem of the exec comm, bd of dir TN-Tombigbee WaterwayDevel Council; exec comm TN-Tombigbee Reg Commiss; ex-officio Cty Health Bd. **Honors/Awds:** Designed 1st phase of Gainesville Lock to Corps Engrs Sepc; Program Participant Awd for the 56th Annual Convention of the Assoc of Cty Commiss of AL. **Military Serv:** USAF E-4; Airman of the Month Awd. **Business Addr:** Chairman, Sumter Co Bd of Commissioners, PO Box 70, Livingston, AL 35470.

JACKSON, CORNELIA PINKNEY
Educator (retired). **Personal:** Born in Marietta, GA; daughter of Louise Williams Pinkney-Hemphill and Cleveland Pinkney; married Ernest Jr, Aug 7, 1950; children: Andrea, Glenn. **Educ:** Clark Coll, 1948; Wayne State U, MA; MI State U; CT State Coll. **Career:** Pontiac School Dist, resource teacher 1963-87 (retired); elementary, 1955-63, 1948-50. **Orgs:** Pres Pontiac Educ Assn 1965-66; bd dir MI Educ Assn & NEA present; mem NEA Com & Prgm & Budget; charter member, Theta Lambda Omega of AKA; dev NEA Conv 1967-; World Confedn Orgn Tchg Professions 1973, 1977. **Honors/Awds:** Scholarship Clark College 1944; NDEA grant So CT State Coll 1966; Hilda Maehling Flwsp 1968; honoree Connie Jackson award 3rd World Ednr MI. **Home Addr:** 1249 C Kirts Blvd, Troy, MI 48084.

JACKSON, CURTIS M.
Educational administrator. **Personal:** Born Nov 15, 1938, Roselle, NJ; son of Nellie Jackson and Albert Jackson; married Lillian Brenda; children: Stacey, Scott. **Educ:** Newark State Coll, BA 1960; Seton Hall U, MA 1964; Fordham U, EdD 1976. **Career:** Elementary School, tchr 1960-64; Plainfield Jr High School, guidance counselor 1964-65; Upward Bound, counseling supvr 1964-66; Plainfield Sr High School, counselor 1967-68; Montclair State Coll, asst dir students 1968-69; Montclair State Coll, assoc dir 1969-78; Montclair State Coll, director intracollegiate academic programs, 1978-96; Montclair State Univ, Student Development Campus life, exec asst vp, 1997-. **Orgs:** Mem New Jersey PGA; APGA; mem Omega Phi Frat; Jr C of C; Black Coalition; consultant Exxon Research Corp 1968-72; member, Phi Delta Kappa; member, Alpha Sigma Chi. **Honors/Awds:** Omega Psi Phi Fraternity, Man of the Year, 1978. **Business Addr:** Montclair State College, Upper Montclair, NJ 07043.

JACKSON, DAMIAN JACQUES
Professional baseball player. **Personal:** Born Aug 16, 1973, Los Angeles, CA. **Educ:** Laney Junior College. **Career:** Cleveland Indians, infielder, 1996-97; Cincinnati Reds, 1997-. **Business Addr:** Professional Baseball Player, Cincinnati Reds, 100 Riverfront Stadium, Cincinnati, OH 45202, (513)421-4510.

JACKSON, DARNELL
State official. **Personal:** Born Feb 2, 1955, Saginaw, MI; son of Annie L Jackson and Roosevelt Jackson; married Yvonne K Givens, Jul 29, 1978; children: Brandon D, Elliott S. **Educ:** Wayne State Univ, BA, 1977, School of Law, JD, 1981; Kalamazoo Valley Community College, AS, law enforcement, 1993. **Career:** Wayne State Univ, Free Legal Aid Clinic, student attorney, 1979-81; Allan & Jackson PC, attorney at law, 1983-85; City of Saginaw, Attorneys Office, attorney at law, 1985-86; County of Saginaw, Prosecutors Office, assistant prosecutor, 1986-89, deputy chief assistant, 1990-93; Braun Kendrick et al, attorney at law, 1989-90; City of Saginaw Police Dept, deputy chief of police, 1993-96; Delta College-University Center MI, criminal justice instructor, 1990-96; State of MI, dir, Office of Drug Control Policy, 1996-; Motivational speaker, 1983-. **Orgs:** State of MI, Drug Education Advisory Comm, chair, 1996-; Partnership For A Drug-Free MI Steering Comm, co-chair, 1997-; State of MI, African American Male Health Initiative Steering Comm, co-chair, 1997-; Southeast MI High Intensity Drug Trafficking Area, HIDTA, executive comm, 1997-; State of MI, Dare Advisory Bd, 1996-; MI Youth Gang and Violence Task Force, 1997-; Westchester Village/Essex Manor, board of directors, 1994-96; United Way of Saginaw Cty, board of directors, 1996-; Saginaw Cty Child Abuse and Neglect Council, board of directors, 1994-96; Saginaw Valley State Univ, Multicultural Advisory Comm, 1991-96; Mr Rogers Say No to Drugs Prog, board of directors, 1991-95. **Honors/Awds:** FBI/Saginaw Cty Gang Crime Task Force, Award for Professional Excellence, 1995; MI State Legislature, Frederick Douglass Award for Community Service, 1991; Saginaw Police Department, Special Operations Unit, Award for Effort in War on Drugs, 1989; MI State Legislature, Special Tribute for Community Service, 1985; Wayne State Univ, Free Legal Aid Clinic, Community Service Award, 1980, 1981. **Business Addr:** Director, Office of Drug Control Policy, Michigan National Tower, Ste 1200, Lansing, MI 48913, (517)373-4700.

JACKSON, DARRELL DUANE
Attorney. **Personal:** Born Aug 7, 1965, Cleveland, OH; son of Mary D Jackson and William L Jackson Sr; divorced. **Educ:** The College of William and Mary, BA, 1987; George Mason University School of Law, JD, 1990. **Career:** Jay B Myerson Esquire, law clerk, 1988-89; Krooth & Altman, summer associate, 1989; Honorable Leonie M Brinkema, judicial law clerk, 1990-91; Honorable Marcus D Williams, judicial law clerk, 1991-92; Fairfax County Public Schools, substitute teacher, 1985-92; County of Fairfax, assistant county attorney, 1992-. **Orgs:** Virginia State Bar, 1991-; Fairfax County Bar, 1993-; Northern Virginia Black Attorneys Association, treasurer, 1992-; Chantilly High Pyramid Minority Student Achievement Committee; Marymount University Paralegal Advisory Committee, 1993-. **Special Achievements:** Author, The Sunset of Affirmative Action?: The City of Richmond vs JA Cronson Co, 1990; speeches: "Survival in Law School," 1990; "Judicial Clerkship," 1992. **Business Addr:** Assistant County Attorney, Office of the County Attorney, County of Fairfax, 12000 Government Center Pkwy, Ste 549, Fairfax, VA 22035-0064, (703)324-2421.

JACKSON, DAVID SAMUEL
Military official. **Personal:** Born Aug 29, 1940, Baltimore, MD; son of Leondora Brooks and Howard Jackson; married Judith Jeffries Jackson, Apr 24, 1965; children: David, Teresa, Kevin. **Educ:** US Military Academy, West Point, NY, BS, 1963; University of Michigan, Ann Arbor, MI, MS, nuclear science, 1976. **Career:** US Army, West Point, NY, professor of physics, 1970-73; US Army, Frankfurt, FRG, operations officer, 1973-76; US Army, Fort Ord, CA, battalion commander, 1977-79; US Army, Pentagon, Washington, DC, executive asst office of sec dev, 1983-86, division chief army space division, 1986-87; US Army, Adelphi Lab Ctr, Adelphi, MD, director space tech/research, 1987-. **Orgs:** Advancement chairman, Scout Troop 1519 Boy Scouts of America, 1981-83; chairman, Student Recognition Showcase Northern VA Pan Hellenic Council, 1988-90; stering committee, St Lawrence Catholic Church Pentecost 200, 1990-. **Honors/Awds:** Lieutenant of the Year, Ft Devens, MA, 1966; Regional Finalist White House Fellow, White House Fellowship Program, 1983; Author, "Hypermodernization", Resource Management Journal, 1981. **Military Serv:** US Army, colonel, 1963-; Defense Superior Service Medal, Legion of Merit, Bronze Star Medal, Meritorious Service Medal. **Business Addr:** Director, Army Space Technology and Research Office, 5321 Riggs Road, Gaithersburg, MD 20882.

JACKSON, DEBORAH BYARD CAMPBELL
Association executive. **Personal:** Born Oct 23, 1947, Bluefield, WV; married. **Educ:** Bluefield State Coll, BA 1968; Union Grad Sch, PhD; Human Resource Development, 1978. **Career:** Minority Involvement Prog, Natl Educ Assn, coord; Ctr Human Relations, professional asst; Assn Fed Credit Union, First African-American pres; CT Education Assn, first African-American exec dir. **Orgs:** Delta Sigma Theta; Natl Council Negro Women; Natl Educ Assn; NAACP.

JACKSON, DENISE
Business owner. **Personal:** Born Dec 10, 1953, Bellevue, NE; daughter of Evelyn E and Dennis E Jackson; children: Divonica M Harrell. **Educ:** Chicago State University, BA, 1976. **Career:** Federal Reserve Bank of Chicago, 1977; Community Equity Corp of Nebraska, 1978-80; Omaha National Bank, 1980-83; The Merchants National Bank, assistant vice pres, 1983-85; InterFirst Bank, asst vice pres, 1985-87; First American Bankshares, Inc, assistant vice pres, 1987-88; Omaha Small Business Network, Inc, assistant director, 1988-89; Jackson's Package Liquor, owner, currently. **Special Achievements:** First black bank officer, Merchants National Bank of Topeka, 1983; two newspaper articles during employment, 1983-84. **Business Addr:** 3159 Myrtle Ave., Omaha, NE 68131-1464, (402)457-4622.

JACKSON, DENNIS LEE
Educator. **Personal:** Born Feb 18, 1937, Pachuta, MS; married Annie Earl Anderson; children: Donna, Danna, DeAnna, Dennis II. **Educ:** Alcorn A&M Coll, BS 1959; Univ of Miami, MEd 1969, EdD 1977. **Career:** Oakley Training School, teacher 1959-64; Utica High School, teacher 1964-65, principal 1965-68; Orange County Public Schools, sr admin, 1971-. **Orgs:** Mem NAACP 1960-; mem AERA 1968-; mem FL Assoc Sch Admin 1971-; mem Leadership Orlando 1980-; supporter Urban League 1980-. **Honors/Awds:** 4-H Club Scholarship 1955; NDEA Fellow Univ of Miami 1968. **Military Serv:** AUS Spc-4 Army Reserve 10 yrs. **Business Addr:** Senior Administrator, Orange County Public Schools, 434 N Tampa Ave, Orlando, FL 32805.

JACKSON, DERRICK ZANE
Journalist. **Personal:** Born Jul 31, 1955, Milwaukee, WI; son of Doris Jackson and Samuel T Jackson; married Michelle D Holmes, Aug 16, 1980; children: Marjani Lisa Jackson, Omar Holmes, Tano Holmes. **Educ:** University of Wisconsin, Milwaukee, WI, BA, Mass Communication, 1976. **Career:** Milwaukee Courier, Milwaukee, WI, reporter, 1970-72; Milwaukee Journal, Milwaukee Journal, Milwaukee, WI, sportswriter, 1972-76; Kansas City Star, Kansas City, MO, sportswriter, 1976-78; Newsday, Melville, NY, sportswriter, New York city reporter, 1978-85, New England bureau chief, 1985-88; Boston Globe, Boston, MA, columnist, 1988-. **Orgs:** Member, National Assn of Black Journalists, 1977-; member, Boston Assn of Black Journalists, 1985-. **Honors/Awds:** Second Place, Commentary, Natl Assn of Black Journalists, 1990; Best New Columnist, Boston Magazine, 1989; First Place, Meyer Berger Award for New York City Reporting, Columbia University, 1986; First Place, Newsday Annual Award, Deadline News, 1985; First Place, Newsday Annual Award, Sportswriting, 1984. **Business Addr:** Columnist, Boston Globe, 135 Morrissey Blvd, Boston, MA 02107.

JACKSON, DONALD J.
Television programming executive. **Personal:** Born Sep 18, 1943, Chicago, IL; son of Lillian Peachy Jackson (deceased) and John W Jackson; married Rosemary; children: Rhonda, Dana. **Educ:** Northwest U, BS Speech 1965. **Career:** Cent Cty Marktg Inc, pres; WVON-RADIO, sales mgr 1967-70; WBEE-RAD, acct exec 1966-67; RH Donnelly, salesman 1965-66; Central City Productions, founder, pres, 1984-; Stone Fox Inc, pres, currently. **Orgs:** Pres of Inner-Cty Merch Group 1976; mem bd of Merchg Exec Club 1975; mem Chic Forum 1974; bd Mem NW Univ "N" Men's Club 1974; mem Oper PUSH; mem Chic Urban Leag; mem AMA; mem Chic Symphony Soc; mem Art Inst of Chic; member, Chicago United; member, Chicago Economic Club; member, National Association of Television Programming Executives; member, NAACP. **Honors/Awds:** Blackbook's Ten Outstand Black Bus People 1976; comm serv award IL Nurs Assn & Natl Med Assn 1975; Chic Jaycees award 1974; Sickle Cell Anemia Award, 1972. **Military Serv:** USN Lt JG 1972. **Business Addr:** President, Central City Productions, 223 W Erie, Suite 7NW, Chicago, IL 60610.

JACKSON, DOROTHEA E.
Educator (retired). **Personal:** Born Jul 18, Brooklyn, NY; daughter of Sarah Morton Flounoy and Dandridge L Flounoy; married Harvey C Jackson (deceased); children: Harvey B. **Educ:** Hampton University, Hampton, VA, BS; Wayne State University, Detroit, MI, MA, 1958, special, international curr doctoral work compl; Swansea University, Wales-British Isles, United Kingdom, USA, Canada, ambassadorship. **Career:** YWCA Columbus, active dir 1943-47; YWCA, Detroit, MI, youth & camp dir, 1947-49; Detroit Board of Education, Detroit, MI, elementary school teacher, 1951-56, teacher, exceptional children, 1957-67, reading coord, curr admin, 1967-69; Wayne State University Grad School, Detroit, MI, teacher trainer, 1969-71 (retired). **Orgs:** Mem NEA (ICEC) 12 years; Detroit Fed of Tchrs 18 years; Detroit Metro Rdng Coun; MI Reading Conf; ASAAH 20 years; pres Guild 1973-76; MI Assn for Emotionally Disturbed Children; Detroit Friends of the Library; ACLD; NCNW; MI State Conv of State Organizers; Kappa Frat Silhouette Aux; Prov Coord 1970-76; board member, Detroit Urban League, 1978-80; central reg coord, Natl Council of Urban League Guild, 1980-84; pres, Detroit Alumni Chapter, Delta Sigma Theta, Inc, 1961-63; pres, Natl Council of University Women, 1990-; pres, Oakman Blvd Community Block Club Assn, 1990-. **Honors/Awds:** Winner Nat Adams Prize Debate Medal; IMRID Award of Merit Peabody Reading Proj; human rel schlrshp Natl Coun of Christians & Jews 1959; Outstanding vol serv award Delta Home for Girls; Outstanding Vol Serv Award Urban League; Detroit Pub Sch Vol Serv Award; Kennedy camping Prog; First State Convenor, National Council of Negro Women; founder, member, Friends of African Art; quarter of a century member, National Urban League, 1950-91; Outstanding Service Award, State Senate of Michigan. **Home Addr:** 2445 Oakman Blvd, Detroit, MI 48238.

JACKSON, DOROTHY R.
Attorney. **Personal:** Born Apr 25, Brooklyn, NY; daughter of Willamina Belton Jackson and Ollie Jackson (deceased); married William W Ellis, PhD; children: Samantha Dorian Smith. **Educ:** Lincoln University, BA, 1971; Seton Hall University Law School, JD, 1978; Jackson State University, certificate, 1990; Harvard University, John F Kennedy School of Government, SMG, 1989. **Career:** New York City Board of Education, teacher of English, 1971-84, educational administrator, 1984-85; Vincent L Johnson ESQ, law assistant, 1985-86; Congressman Edolphus Towns, chief of staff, 1986-89; Samdor Enterprises LTD, president, chief executive officer, 1989-91; Congresswoman Barbara-Rose Collins, chief of staff, 1991-92; US House of Reps, Speaker Thomas S Foley, special counsel, beginning 1992; Congresswoman Eddie Bernice Johnson, chief of staff; legislative counsel to congressman Donald M Payne, currently. **Orgs:** Bridge Street AME Church Legal Society, president, 1987-88; ;New York Urban League, Brooklyn Branch, president, 1986-88; Alpha Kappa Alpha Sorority Inc, by-laws committee, legislative representative; Stuyvesant Heights Lions Club; Kings County Hospital Development Project, advisory board; Young Techocrats Inc, board of directors; Women's Campaign Network; National Association of Negro Business and Professional Women's Clubs. **Honors/Awds:** Concerned Women of Brooklyn, Woman on the Move Award, 1988; Mid-Brooklyn Civic Assn, Public Affairs Award, 1989; National Black Police Assn, Civil Rights Award, 1990; Harvard University John F Kennedy School of Government, Fellow, 1989. **Special Achievements:** Elected delegate: Judicial, 1985-87; New York State United Teachers; United Federation of Teachers. **Business Addr:** Legislative Counsel, Congressman Donald M Payne, 2244 Rayburn, House Office Bldg, Washington, DC 20515.

JACKSON, DUANE MYRON
Zoo curator, educator. **Personal:** Born Jan 6, 1948, Chicago, IL; son of Rev A P & Harriet Jackson; married Fleda M Jackson, May 18, 1974; children: Kimya, Kari. **Educ:** Morehouse College, BA, 1974; Univ of Illinois, MA, 1976, PhD, 1984. **Career:** Clark College, assistant professor, 1981-87; Morehouse Math/Science Upward Bound Prog, curr coord, 1991-; Morehouse College, assoc prof, Dept of Psychology, 1987-; Zoo Atlanta, curator of insects/research scientist, 1988-. **Orgs:** National Conference on Undergrad Research, bd of governors, 1993-; Council on Undergrad Research, councillor, 1994-; Animal Behavior Society, 1977-; American Assn of Zoo & Aquariums, 1992-; Intl Soc for Behavioral Ecology, 1994-. **Honors/Awds:** National Science Foundation, Research Experience for Undergrads, 1994; Smithsonian Institute, Short Term Visitor Fellowship, 1993; Ford Foundation, National Fellowship Award, 1979-80; Univ of Illinois, Graduate Fellowship, 1974; Morehouse College, Paul Mussen Award in Psychology, 1974. **Special Achievements:** Animal Activity and Presence of Docent Inteaction: Visitor Behavior at Zoo Atlanta, Visitor Behavior, 1994; Motivations that Drive Prejudice and Discrimination: Is the Scientific Community Really Objective?, J R & Adams, A Multicultural Prism: Voices from the Field, 1994; numerous other publications. **Military Serv:** US Army, Army Security Agency, sgt, 1967-71; Armay Commendation Medal, Vietnam, 1969. **Business Addr:** Curator of Insects/Research Scientist, Zoo Atlanta, 800 Cherokee Avenue, SE, Atlanta, GA 30315, (404)624-5866.

JACKSON, DWAYNE ADRIAN
Insurance company executive. **Personal:** Born Aug 3, 1955, New York, NY; son of Ina Stockton and George Jackson; married Cheryl Jackson, Sep 20, 1984; children: David, Courtney. **Educ:** Westfield State College, BA, 1977. **Career:** Crawford and Co Insurance Adjusters, adjuster, 1977-79; Massachusetts Mutual, second vice president, 1979-. **Orgs:** American Society of CLU/CHFC, chartered life underwriter,1990-; Junior Achievement, board of directors, 1993-; Dunbar Community Center, board of directors, 1993-; NAACP, Springfield chapter, board of directors, 1993-; Goodwill Industries, board of directors, 1994-; Visiting Nurses Association, board of directors, 1995-; pres of board of directors, Dunbar Community Center, 1996. **Business Phone:** (413)744-3580.

JACKSON, EARL, JR.
Microbiologist (retired). **Personal:** Born Sep 4, 1938, Paris, KY; son of Margaret Elizabeth Cummins Jackson and Earl Jackson Sr. **Educ:** KY State Univ, BS 1960; Attended, Univ of CT, Northeastern Univ, Univ of Paris; Northeastern Univ Boston MA, MS 1986. **Career:** Hydra Power Corp, chemical analyst 1964-68; Massachusetts General Hosp, sr rsch analyst dept of anesthesia 1968-81, microbiologist dept of medicine 1981-

95. **Orgs:** Mem Amer Soc for Microbiology, Amer Assoc for the Advancement of Science, KY State Univ Alumni Assoc; member, Northeast Assn for Clinical Microbiology & Infectious Disease; member, Amer Assn of Clinical Chemistry; member, New York Academy of Sciences. **Honors/Awds:** Outstanding and Distinguished Community Leaders and Noteworthy Amers Citation 1977; NAFEO Disting Alumni of the Yr Citation 1986; special articles published ''Hemoglobin-O2 Affinity Regulation, 43(4), 632-642'' 1977 Journal of Applied Physiology, ''Measurement of Levels of Aminoglycosides and Vancomycin in Serum'' May 1984 pp 707-709 Journal of Clinical Microbiology. **Home Addr:** 501 Fenwick Drive, San Antonio, TX 78239.

JACKSON, EARL C.
Educator. **Personal:** Born Aug 17, 1933, Alexandria, LA; son of Ethel Jackson and Walter Jackson; married Beverly A. **Educ:** BS Mech Eng 1955; MS Math 1973; MS Educ Admin 1975; NY State, professional license; PhD Mathematical Physics. **Career:** Wyandanch Meml HS, zero-gravity test teacher; Cockpit Lunar Module, lead engr secondary structure; Grumman Aerospace Corp, design engr; Boeing & Co, design engr; Elastic Syst Design, owner; Telephonics Corp, asst to chief engr; Sedco Systems Inc, mgr of engrg analysis sect, currently. **Orgs:** Chmn Math Dept Sgt. **Military Serv:** 3 yrs military svc; 3rd Armored Div Germany sgt. **Business Addr:** Manager Engineering Analysis Sect, Sedco Systems, Inc, 65 Marcus Dr, Melville, NY 11747.

JACKSON, EARL J.
Clergyman. **Personal:** Born Mar 11, 1943, Chattanooga, TN; son of Mrs Kathryn C Jackson and Mr James C Jackson (deceased); married Ms Barbara Faye Anderson; children: Earl Darelwin, Roderick Lamar. **Educ:** TN A&I State Univ, 1962-65; Am Baptist Theological Seminary, 1964-66; The Detroit Baptist Sem, ThG, BTh, DD 1969; The Emmanuel Bible Coll, BA, MDiv, MRE 1978. **Career:** KY Dept Human Resources, sr employment interviewer 1970-; New Bethel Baptist Ch, radio ministry 1969-. **Orgs:** Bowling Green Warren Co Chap NAACP; IAPES Employment Serv Organ; Bowling Green Alumni Kappa Alpha Psi Frat Bowling Green Noon Kiwanis Club; Bowling Green Warren Co Jaycees 1971-73; bd of dir Bowling Green War Memorial Boy's Club 1979-; asst chmn of bd Bowling Green Human Rights Commn 1976-79; bd of dirs, Bowling Green Noon Kiwanis Club; worshipful master the House of Solomon Ancient and Accepted Scottish Rite Masons of the World #769 1981-90. **Business Addr:** Radio Minister & Pastor, New Bethel Baptist, 801 Church St, Bowling Green, KY 42101.

JACKSON, EARLINE
Education administrator. **Personal:** Born Mar 26, 1943, Columbia, SC; children: Tanyl Lea, Tamara P Newsome. **Educ:** Molloy Coll, BA Psych/Soc 1982. **Career:** Cornell Univ FDC Pilot Prog, exec bd mem educ planning/assessment 1974-77; LI Minority Alliance Inc, educ/remedial serv prog coord 1978-82; ABWA Pandora Chapt, chairperson educ comm 1983; Molloy Coll, assoc dir HEOP. **Orgs:** Founder/exec dir FDC Assoc of Nassau Co Inc 1972-79; exec bd mem/Nassau Co Rep Licensed FDC Assoc of NYS Inc 1973-78; bd mem Daycare Council of Nassau Co Inc 1974-78; bd mem Comm Adv Bd Roosevelt NY 1976-78; Nassau Co Rep Cornell Univ FDC Prog Planning Comm 1978; chairperson emerita FDC Assn of Nassau Co Inc 1979. **Honors/Awds:** Meritorious Serv & Achievement FDC Assn of Nassau Co Inc 1978. **Business Addr:** Assoc Dir, St Thomas Aquinas Program, Molloy Coll, 1000 Hempstead Ave, Rockville Centre, NY 11570.

JACKSON, EDGAR NEWTON, JR.
Educator. **Personal:** Born Apr 20, 1959, Washington, DC; son of Joan F J Clement and Edgar Newton Jackson Sr. **Educ:** Univ of the DC, Washington, DC, BS, 1987; Grambling State Univ, Grambling, LA, MS, 1989; Howard Univ, Washington, DC, post graduate studies, 1989-90; Univ of New Mexico, Albuquerque, NM, PhD, 1995. **Career:** Warner Theatre, Washington, DC, box office mgr, 1979-81; Howard Univ, Washington, DC, aquatic mgr, 1981-, instructor, 1989-; Univ of the DC, Washington, DC, adjunct instructor, 1987-88; Grambling State Univ, Grambling, LA, instructor, 1988-89; University of New Mexico, Albuquerque, NM, teaching asst, 1990-91, athletic dept intern, 1991; Howard University, assistant professor, head swim coach, currently. **Orgs:** Member, Amer Alliance of Health, Physical Edn, Recreation and Dance, 1983-; member, Coun for Natl Cooperation in Aquatics, 1984-; chair, Aquatic Safety Comm, Amer Red Cross, 1985-; member, Natl Recreation and Park Assn, 1985-; member, Natl Org for Athletic Devel, 1987-; member, N Amer Soc for the Sociology of Sport, 1987-; life member, Omega Psi Phi; life member, NAACP, Grambling State Univ Alumni Assn, and Univ of the DC Alumni Assn; member, Kappa Delta Pi; life member, Washington Urban League; member, Phi Delta Kappa. **Honors/Awds:** Certif of apprec, Amer Red Cross, 1984; Intl and Multicultural Award, Univ of the DC, 1987. **Home Addr:** 6635 Harlan Pl NW, Washington, DC 20012-2138.

JACKSON, EDWARD R.
Educator. **Personal:** Born May 24, 1942, New Iberia, LA; son of Leona Strauss Jackson and Oliver Jackson; married Nedra Clem Jackson, Dec 19, 1975; children: Chris, Corey, Robert, Edward II, Camy. **Educ:** University of Southwestern Louisiana, Lafayette, LA, BA, 1963; Marquette University, Milwaukee, WI, MA, 1965; University of Iowa, Iowa City, IA, PhD, 1968. **Career:** Southern University, Baton Rouge, LA, assistant professor of political science, 1968-70; Fisk University, Nashville, TN, associate professor of political science, 1970-76; Howard University, Washington, DC, associate professor of political science, 1976-79; South Carolina State College, Orangeburg, SC, chair, dept of political science, 1979-86, vice provost academic affairs, 1986-. **Honors/Awds:** Honorable Mention, Woodrow Wilson Fellowship, 1963; Faculty Intern, National Science Foundation, 1967-68.

JACKSON, ELIJAH (ZEKE)
Company executive. **Personal:** Born Feb 9, 1947. **Career:** Navcom Systems Inc, president, CEO, currently. **Orgs:** Institute of Navigation; LORAN Working Group; Wildgoose Association. **Honors/Awds:** NAACP Award; Business Achievement Award; Christian Churches Award. **Special Achievements:** Co. ranked #61 on the Black Enterprise list of top 100 industrial companies, 1992. **Business Addr:** President, CEO, NAVCOM, 9815 Godwin Drive, Manassas, VA 22111.

JACKSON, ELLEN SWEPSON
Administrator. **Personal:** Born Oct 29, 1935, Boston, MA; married Hugh L; children: Ronica, Darryl, Sheryl, Troy, Stephanie. **Educ:** State Tchrs Coll, BS 1954; Harvard Kennedy Sch of Gov't (Inst of Politics Research Fellow MIT) Dept of Urban Studies & Planng, teaching fellow 1970; Harvard Univ Grad Sch of Edn, EDM 1971. **Career:** Operation Exodus, founder/dir 1965-69; Black Women's Commnty Devel Found Inc, natl dir 1969-70; Title IV HEW, contract compliance/project dir 1964, 1971-74; Freedom Hse Inst on Schst Edn, dir 1974-78; Northeastern U, dean/dir affirmative action. **Orgs:** Dir Patriot Bancorp 1982-; trustee John F Kennedy Library Found 1983-; trustee Boston Children's Hosp 1982-; chmn Mass Governor's Commnty Devel Coord Cncl 1984; dir Lena Park Cmmnty Devel Cntr 1983-; mem New England Minority Women Admin 1982-; mem Am Assn for Affirmative Action 1978-. **Honors/Awds:** Ellen S Jackson Children's Cntr Mission Hill Public Hsng 1983; Woman of Courage Black Women's Oral History Project Schesinger Lib Found 1984; hon degree dr of humanities Northeastern Univ 1976; hon degree dr of humane letters Univ of MA 1984. **Business Addr:** Dean/Dir Affirmative Act, Northeastern Univ, 360 Huntington Ave, Rm 175 RI, Boston, MA 02115.

JACKSON, ELMER CARTER, JR.
Attorney. **Personal:** Born Oct 22, 1912, Kansas City, KS; married Lucile Victoria Wright. **Educ:** Univ KS, BA 1933, BL 1935; Univ KS Sch of Law, Disting Alumnus Citation 1974. **Career:** Atty, pvt prac 1935-; State of KS, asst atty gen 1936-38; City Atty KS, asst 1939; Wyandotte Co Legal Aid Soc, gen counc 1963-68. **Orgs:** Exec dir Nat Bar Found 1968-72; pres Nat Bar Assn 1959-61; mem KS Bd of Regents 1970-; intl atty dir pub rel Frontiers Intl 1976-; chmn Legal Redress Com KS Br NAACP 1975-; commr Pub Housing Auth KS 1965-66; chmn KS Cty Zoning Appeal Bd 1953-65; trustee 1st AME Ch 1975-. **Honors/Awds:** C Francis Stradford Award Nat Bar Assn 1965; 33rd Degree Mason US Supreme Counc No Jurisdiction; award Prince Hall Grand Lodge of KS outst & meritorious Serv 1970. **Business Addr:** Jackson Law Office, 1314 N 5th St, Kansas City, KS 66101.

JACKSON, EMIL A.
Business executive. **Personal:** Born Feb 2, 1911, Natchez, MS; married Mildred Mayo Mcgrew. **Educ:** Univ Buffalo, 1948-50; Bryant & Stratton Bus Inst, 1952-54. **Career:** State Of NY Equal Employ Opp, retired field rep 1970; Majority Leader, gen clerk & aide 1968-70; engrossing clk 1967-68; New York Sen, sgt-at-arms 1966-67; Nelson & Rockefeller Minority Campaign, cmmttmn 1962; Nixon Minority Campaign, 1960; Emil Jackson Real Estate & Ins Agency Buffalo, ownr 1946-70; NY Central RR Dining Car Dept, waiter-in-charge 1929-43. **Orgs:** Past vice pres NAACP Buffalo; past exec bd mem Buffalo Urban League; past exec bd mem Buffalo Bd Realtors; past pres YMCA Bus & Prof Men Mens Club; vice pres Am Negro Labor Council; Civil Serv Empl Assn; Civil Serv Educ & Recreation Assn; Legis Counsel. **Honors/Awds:** Received for meritorious service Presidential Citation; business award Phi Beta Sigma 1950; Iota Phi Lambda 1952; cert of merit NAACP 1958; polit sem cert Buffalo C of C 1960; serv award Buffalo Urban League 1962; merit & service Award YMCA Bus & Prof Mens Club 1964. **Military Serv:** US Army, s/sgt 1943-46.

JACKSON, EMORY NAPOLEON (SIPPY)
Association executive, consultant. **Personal:** Born Oct 29, 1937, Magnolia, MS; son of Juanita Gordon Jackson and Aaron Napoleon Jackson; married Adrea Perry; children: Lisa A, Charles L. **Educ:** Newark State Coll, MA Counselling; Morehouse Coll, BA 1961; Adler Inst of Psychotherapy, 1974. **Career:** We Care About NY Inc pres 1986-; City of NY Dept Sanitation Deputy Commissioner 1983-86; DOE New York City Human Resources Admin, deputy commr 1980-; Urban League of Eastern MS, pres 1977-80; US Dept of Housing Urban Develop, spec & asst to sec 1976-77; Economic Devel Natl Urban League, deputy dir; Off Manpower Dev & Training Natl Urban Leag, natl dir; New York Urban League, comm org 1967; United Nations Intl Sch, tchr 1962; Natl Med Assn, cons; Intl Assn Official Human Rights Agencies, cons. **Orgs:** Vice pres US Team Handball Fed & Olypic Com Chmn Community Housing Resources Bd Boston; bd of dir Boston Private Ind; bd of dir Boston Metro Nab Natl Urban League Fellow; Natl Urban League 1969. **Honors/Awds:** Highest scorer in team handball North Amer 1965-70; outstanding achievement Boston City Council Resolution 1980; Community Serv Boy Scouts-Brooklyn District 1987, 88 & 89; Community Serv Girl Scout Council of Greater NY 1988. **Home Addr:** 1333 President St, Brooklyn, NY 11213.

JACKSON, ERIC SCOTT (SPIKE)
Educator, coach, educational administrator. **Personal:** Born Jan 26, 1964, Ann Arbor, MI; son of Geraldine Jackson and Lionel Jackson. **Educ:** Eastern Michigan University, BS, history, 1987; University of Cincinnati, Masters Program, counseling; Eastern Michigan University, Masters Program, history. **Career:** Ypsilanti High School, freshman coach, football, 1985-86; University of Cincinnati, graduate asst, football, 1987-89; Cornell University, freshman coach, football, 1989-91; ALma College, head track coach, asst football coach, 1991; Las Vegas Aces, professional spring football league, asst football coach, 1992; Alma College, defensive coordinator, pe supervisor, currently. **Orgs:** Black Coaches Association, network committee, 1992; American Football Coaches Association, 1991-; The Athletic Congress, track, 1991-. **Honors/Awds:** Arts & Science Undergraduate Symposium, Eastern Michigan University, 1987; Head Graduate Assistant Football, University of Cincinnati, 1988; Prep Player of the Week, Eastern Michigan University, football, 1982. **Home Phone:** (517)463-1359. **Business Addr:** Assistant Coach, PE Supervisor, Alma College, PE Center, Alma, MI 48801.

JACKSON, ESTHER COOPER
Editor. **Personal:** Born Aug 21, 1917, Arlington, VA; daughter of Esther Irving Cooper and George Posea Cooper; married James Edward Jackson, May 7, 1941; children: Harriet Jackson Scarupa, Kathryn Jackson Seeman. **Educ:** Oberlin Coll, AB 1938; Fisk Univ, MA 1940. **Career:** Southern Negro Youth Congress, exec sec 1940-50; Natl Urban League, educ dir1952-54; Natl Bd Girls Scouts of Amer, social worker 1954-; Freedomways Magazine, editor. **Orgs:** Managing editor Freedomways Magazine 1961-; PTA. **Honors/Awds:** Rosenwald Fellow 1940-41; Rabinowitz Fund Grant 1962-63; William L Patterson Foundation Award 1978; Natl Alliance of Third World Journalists 1981; Harlem School of the Arts Award 1987; Lifetime Achievement Award New York Assn of Black Journalists 1989. **Business Addr:** Editor, Freedomways Magazine, P O Box 1356, New York, NY 10276.

JACKSON, EUGENE D.
Business executive. **Personal:** Born Sep 5, 1943, Waukomis, OK; son of Queen Esther Royal and Joseph Gordon; married Phyllis; children: Stephanie, Bradley, Kimberly, Aisha, Bakari, Shasha. **Educ:** Univ of Missouri, Rolla, BS 1967; Columbia Univ, MS 1971. **Career:** Colgate Palmolive NYC, industrial engr 1967-68; Black Econ Union NYC, prod, proj engr 1968-69; Interracial Council for Bus Oppty NYC, dir maj indust prog 1969-71; Unity Broadcasting Network, pres; World African Network, chairman; Queens Inner-Unity Cable Systems, vice chairman. **Orgs:** Howard Univ Intl Sponsors Council; Alpha Phi Alpha Fraternity, Lincoln University, PA, board of directors; NACME, board of directors.

JACKSON, EUGENE L.
Business executive. **Personal:** Born Feb 14, 1939, Beckley, WV. **Educ:** Amer Inst Banking San Francisco, attended 1969-70; San Francisco City Coll, attended 1976-77. **Career:** Chem AH Thomas Co Phila, expediter 1956-58; Wells Fargo Bank, l/c negot 1968, asst operations ofcr, operations ofcr 1977, asst vice pres 1977-78, vice pres 1978-. **Orgs:** Planning bd mem Western Council Intl Banking 1978-70. **Business Addr:** Vice President, Wells Fargo Bank NA, 475 Sansome St 18th Fl, San Francisco, CA 94144.

JACKSON, FELIX W.
Physician. **Personal:** Born Sep 6, 1920, Woodville, MS. **Educ:** IL Coll Optometry. **Career:** Am Sch, self instr optomoligist; Strip Founders Inc, purchasing agent; US Post Office, carrier; FW Jackson Enterprises, owner. **Orgs:** Pres NAACP 1965-67; bd exec vice pres Forsyth Century Art 1964-68; v Chmn Model Cities Bd 1968-70; co-chm Human Rel & Comm Forsyth Cent Art 1960-68; mem Winston Salem Redevel Commn 1974-. **Honors/Awds:** Rep All Am City Event 1965; first black opth state NC; spl hon Orgn largest Pub Affairs Winston Salem; Lawrence Joel Day So Regional Concl for representing 5,000 in month. **Military Serv:** AUS. **Business Addr:** 533 N Liberty St, Winston-Salem, NC 27101.

JACKSON, FRANK DONALD
Business administrator. **Personal:** Born Jul 25, 1951, Luling, TX; son of Willie Louise Smith-Jackson and Robbie Jackson Sr; children: Tracy, Ayanna. **Educ:** Prairie View A&M Univ,

BA, geography 1973. **Career:** USS Long Beach CGN9, division off 1973-76; USS Coral Sea CU43, division off 1976-77; Naval Beach Group Det Mar 1-79, officer in charge 1979, 1st lt beachmaster unit II 1977-79; NROTC Prairie View, navigation/oper officer 1979-82; USN Reserves, lt comd; Mobile Mine Assembly Group Det 1310, comdg officer; The Prairie View Messenger, editor/pub; The Prairie View Vol Fire Fighter Assoc, pres; Prairie View A&M Univ, Memorial Student Center, dir 1982-87; dir of Auxiliary Services 1987-; Craft of Opportunity 2215 Galveston Texas, Commanding Officer, 1988-. **Orgs:** Prince Hall Mason 1970; Alpha Phi Alpha 1971; Gamma Theta Upsilon 1972; Phi Alpha Theta 1983; Natl Naval Officers Assn 1985; city councilman City of Prairie View 1982-92; County Commissioner-Waller County, 1991-96, reelected, 1996-; Chamber Commerce; Waller Cnty Historical Commission and Society, 1989-. **Honors/Awds:** Man of the Year, Memorial Student Center Adv Bd 1985; publisher Prairie View Messenger 1984-; Staff Member of The Year, Prairie View A&M Univ 1988-89; honorary degree, Prairie View A&M Univ, 1988-89. **Military Serv:** US Navy Reserves, commander, 1973-; 2 Navy Achievement Medal, Navy Commendation Medal 1989. **Business Addr:** Special Assistant To The President for Governmental Affairs, Prairie View A&M Univ, PO Box 475, Prairie View, TX 77446.

JACKSON, FRANKLIN D. B.
Business executive/federal official. **Personal:** Born Mar 21, 1934, Cypress, AL; son of Mary Jackson and J H Jackson; divorced; children: Franklin K, Debra R, Sabrina F, Delilah E, Jacquelyn R. **Educ:** Univ of N CO Greeley, BS Bus Adminstrn 1976; Univ Of N CO, M Public Admin 1977; Webster Coll St Louis, M of Health and Hospital Admin 1979. **Career:** Jackson's Enter Ltd, pres owner 1980; HUD, fair housing & EO spec 1978-; EEOC, employment opportunity specialist 1976-78. **Orgs:** Publicity chmn Univ of CO at Manuel 1972; bd of dir Occupational Industrialization Ctr 1977-; band leader Happy Jacks Combo And Dance Band; historian Kappa Alpha Psi Frat 1975-; mem Am Soc for Public Admin 1976-; research chmn Police Comm Denver 1977-78. **Honors/Awds:** Award for academic achievement Fitzsimons Army Med Ctr 1976; certificate of appreciation Optimist Intl of NE Denver 1978; outstndng serv awd Denver Alumni Chap Kappa Alpha Psi 1978; Univ S leadership award Am Conf on leadership 1978; bronze stars meritorious svc; medal various other serv medals AUS; medal of Gallantry with palm. **Military Serv:** AUS 1st sgt paratroopers. **Home Addr:** 9931 E Ohio Ave, Denver, CO 80231. **Business Addr:** PO Box 7096, Denver, CO 80207.

JACKSON, FRED H., JR.
Pilot (retired). **Personal:** Born Mar 12, 1933, Bridgeton, NJ; son of Hortence P Steward Jackson and Fred H Jackson, Sr; married Linda Lee Brokaski Jackson, Oct 5, 1991; children: Pamela, Antionette, Cheri, Fred, II, Courtney Page, Heather Schulte, Holly Schulte, Lisa Pullan. **Career:** Eastern Air Lines, pilot 1967-91. **Orgs:** Mem Negro Airman Intl; asst scout master Troop 254 1969-74; mem Black Airline Pilot's Assn; mem NJ Bd Real Estate Slsmn. **Military Serv:** USAF major 1953-67; Combat Crew Medal; NJ Air Natl Guard 1967-73; Natl Defense Svc Medal; Good Conduct Medal, Flight Instructor. **Home Addr:** 5 Deland Park B, Fairport, NY 14450.

JACKSON, FRED JAMES, SR.
Author, poet, educator. **Personal:** Born Jun 11, 1950, High Point, NC; son of Mary Jane Walker; divorced; children: Marrian Ann, Fred James Jr, Patrice M. **Educ:** Shreveport College, degree, 1977; University of Maryland, attended; Armed Forces Institute, certificate; University of San Diego, attending. **Career:** McClellan Air Force Base Logistic Ctr, procurement mgr, 1979-87; The Drug Intervention Network Inc, exec dir, 1987-92; US Dept of Agriculture, procurement officer, 1992-94; Grant Joint Union School District English teacher, dept chair, 1994-96; Black Rose Enterprise-Publishing, pres, CEO, 1986-; Sacramento Unified School District/Hiram Johnson High, lead teacher, computer education/business, 1995-. **Orgs:** Natl Edu Assn, 1994-; California Teachers Assn, 1994-; Natl Assn of Black School Educators, 1995-; City of Sacramento, Mayors Drug Gang Task Force, 1987-93; American Assn for the Advancement of Science, Black Church Project, 1992-95; State of California, peer counseling, leadership coord, 1996-, tobacco drug and alcohol program coord, 1996-. **Honors/Awds:** State of California Assembly, Certificate of Recognition, 1996, Senate Certificate of Recognition, 1996, Youth Authority Certificate of Appreciation, 1979; Association of African American Women, Certificate of Appreciation, 1988. **Special Achievements:** The Balcony, poem, 1994; They Call Me Names, book of poetry, pulitzer nomination, 1994; Lightning, Master of the Blues, fiction, pulitzer nomination, 1994; Passion In Black, poetry, pulitzer nomination, 1992. **Military Serv:** US Army, 1967-75 USAR, 1975-87; Four honorable discharges, the Viet Nam Cross of Gallantry, 1969; two presidential citations; and many more. **Business Addr:** Black Rose Enterprise - Publishing, PO Box 5283, Sacramento, CA 95817, (916)422-7730.

JACKSON, FREDDIE
Singer, composer. **Personal:** Born 1958. **Career:** Nightclub performer; back-up vocalist/cameo soloist with Melba Moore, 1984; Mystic Merlin (funk group), singer; solo recording artist and performer, beginning 1985, composer (with Paul Laurence), currently. **Honors/Awds:** Albums include: Rock Me Tonight, 1985; Just Like the First Time (platinum), 1987; Don't Let Love Slip Away, 1988; Time For Love, 1992; Private Party; American Black Gold Award for Outstanding Male Artist, 1986; Appeared in the film King of New York. **Business Addr:** Singer, c/o Capitol Records Inc, 1750 N Vine St, Hollywood, CA 90028.

JACKSON, FREDERICK
Business executive. **Personal:** Born Dec 29, 1928, Washington, DC; married Emily E Smith; children: Noell, Hillary. **Educ:** Howard U, BArch 1971. **Career:** Jackson & Tull Chartered Engr, pres 1974-; Ewell W Finley PC, vice pres 1970-74; Scrop S Nersesian Engr, chief eng 1965-70. **Orgs:** Mem Am Consulting Engrs Com 1974-; vice pres eastern region Nat Assn of Black Consulting Engrs 1976-77; pres Nat Assn of Black Consulting Engrs 1979-80;dist gov Intl 'y' Mens Clubs 1968-72; regional dir Intl 'y' Mens Clubs 1974-76. **Honors/Awds:** Man of the year YMCA 12th St 'y' Men's Club 1970. **Business Addr:** 2321 Wisconsin Ave NW, Washington, DC 20007.

JACKSON, FREDERICK LEON
Educator. **Personal:** Born Aug 15, 1934, Albany, NY; married Mildred Helen Hagood; children: Leon K, Anthony W. **Educ:** Oregon State Univ, BS 1976; Portland State Univ, MS 1977. **Career:** Portland Public Schools, handicapped teacher 1976-81, sixth grade teacher 1981-84, integration coord 1984-86, student transfer coord 1986-. **Orgs:** Dir Portland Assoc of Teachers 1978-86; KRS 1983-85, basileaus 1985-86 Omega Psi Phi; chair minority project Oregon Educ Assoc 1984-85; mem Oregon Alliance Black Sch Ed 1985-87. **Honors/Awds:** Leadership Awd for Service Oregon Educ Assoc 1982; Leadership Awd Minority Oregon Educ Assoc 1984; Man of the Year Omega Psi Phi Zeta Nu 1986,87. **Military Serv:** USAF E-6 tech sgt 1952-72; Outstanding Unit Awd. **Home Addr:** 2804 NE 25th, Portland, OR 97212.

JACKSON, GAIL P.
Public relations executive. **Personal:** Born Oct 29, 1960, Boston, MA; daughter of Edna Langston-Jackson and Tommie Jackson. **Educ:** Grahm Junior Coll, Boston, MA, AS, broadcast journalism, 1979; Suffolk Univ, Boston, MA, 1979-83; Harvard Univ, Cambridge, MA, advanced journalism courses, 1985-. **Career:** WCAS Radio, Cambridge, MA. public affairs rep, 1982-84; Boston Cable Co, consultant; City Auditor's Office, Boston, MA, admin aide, 1984-85; Massachusetts Dept of Public Health, media relations mgr, 1985-87; Boston Redevelopment Authority, community relations specialist, 1987-88; Wang Labs, Lowell, MA, public relations consultant, 1988-. **Orgs:** Mem, Natl Assn of Female Executives, 1988-; mem, Public Relations Society of America, 1989; mem, Boston Black Media Coalition, 1983-. **Honors/Awds:** President's Award, Grahm Junior College, 1979; Secretary's Award, 1979, Treasurer's Award, 1978, Ebony Awareness.

JACKSON, GARNET NELSON
Educator, author, columnist, poet. **Personal:** Born May 27, 1944, New Orleans, LA; daughter of Carrie Brent Sherman; married Anthony Jackson, Jan 2, 1970 (divorced); children: Damon. **Educ:** Dillard Univ, BA, 1968; Eastern MI Univ, 1970-72. **Career:** Flint Bd of Educ, teacher, 1968-; Self Employed, publisher, author, 1989-90; The Flint Editorial, columnist, 1989-90; The Flint Journal, columnist, 1990-94; Modern Curriculum Press, Simon & Schuster, author, pioneer of Beginning Biographies Concept, 1990-94. **Orgs:** NAACP, 1987-; Sylvester Broome Book Club, 1990-; The Greater Flint Optimist Club, 1993-; International Reading Association, 1996; American Library Association, 1996. **Honors/Awds:** Rejoti Publishing, Honorable Mention for Outstanding Poetry, 1987; NAACP, The Harambee Medal, 1991, The Dorothy Duke Evans Educator of the Year, 1991; Mt Zion Church, Award for Children's Literature, 1991; City of Flint, Office of the Mayor, Proclamation of Outstanding Citizenship, 1992; State of MI Gov Engler, Letter of Commendation, 1992; State of MI, The Christa McAuliffe Special Tribute Award, 1992; US Congress, Congressional Record, Proclamation of Outstanding Citizenship, 1992, Certificate of Special Recognition, US Senator, Don Reigle, 1992; Civil Park School, Special Tribute Award, 1992; Zeta Phi Beta Sorority, The Zeta Phi Beta Finer Womanhood Hall of Fame, 1993; NAACP, Educator of the Year Awd, 1991. **Special Achievements:** Wrote and published 5 books, 1989-90; Invited, contracted to make presentations on radio, tv and to various civic, religious, educational organizations, schools, universities, 1989-; authored 13 books, Beginning Biographies, 1990-94; Ebony Magazine, From the Bookshelf, Oct 1991; Essence Magazine, p 118, Feb 1995. **Home Addr:** 6168 Eastknoll Dr, Grand Blanc, MI 48439.

JACKSON, GARY MONROE
Attorney. **Personal:** Born Nov 10, 1945, Denver, CO; son of Nancelia Elizabeth Jackson and Floyd M Jackson Jr; married Regina Lee Jackson, Sep 30, 1986; children: Michael Mascotti, Tara Mascotti. **Educ:** University of Redlands, 1963-64; University of Colorado, BA, 1967, School of Law, JD, 1970. **Career:** Denver District Attorney's Office; chief trial deputy, 1970-74; US Attorney's Office, assistant US attorney, 1974-76; DiManna, Eklund, Ciancio & Jackson, partner, 1976-82; DiManna & Jackson, partner, 1982-. **Orgs:** Sam Cary Bar Association, founder, past president, Colorado Trial Lawyers Association, board of directors, 1980-; Denver Bar Association, board of trustees, 1980-81; Committee on Conduct, chair, 1982-86. **Honors/Awds:** US Department of Justice, Special Commendation, 1976. **Business Addr:** Attorney, DiManna & Jackson, 1741 High St, Denver, CO 80218, (303)320-4848.

JACKSON, GEORGE
Record company executive, entertainment industry executive. **Personal:** married. **Educ:** Harvard. **Career:** Paramount Television; Universal Pictures; Griot Entertainment Group, head; The Jackson-McHenry Company, co-founder; Elephant Walk Entertainment, co-founder, currently; Motown Records, pres/CEO, 1997-. **Special Achievements:** Produced films including: Krush Groove; Disorderlies; New Jack City; House Party 2 and 3; Jason's Lyric; The Walking Dead; A Thin Line Between Love and Hate. **Business Addr:** President/CEO, Motown Records, 825 8th Ave, New York, NY 10019, (212)333-8000.

JACKSON, GEORGE K.
Policeman. **Personal:** Born Mar 8, 1919, Detroit, MI; married Dorothy W. **Educ:** Morehouse Coll, BA 1941. **Career:** Detroit Police Dept, div commr 1973-; inspector 1971-73; lt 1970-71; sgt 1966-70; detective 1954-66; patrolman 1947-54. **Orgs:** Mem SE MI Chfs of Police Assn; mem Alpha Phi Alpha. **Honors/Awds:** 27 meritorious citations Detroit Police Dept. **Military Serv:** AUS capt 1941-46. **Business Addr:** C/O Fred Murphy, Exec Secy, Pension Bureau, 510 City County Bldg, Detroit, MI 48226.

JACKSON, GEORGINA
Communications company manager. **Personal:** Born Sep 30, 1957, Elizabeth, NJ; daughter of Rosalie Street Jackson and Charles Winfred Jackson. **Educ:** Upsala College, East Orange, NJ, BA (magna cum laude), 1980; New York University, New York, NY, MBA, 1992. **Career:** AT&T, New York, NY, supervisor, 1980-83, mgr, 1983-90; AT&T, Basking Ridge, NJ, district mgr, 1990-. **Orgs:** Founder, pres, Upward Connections, 1987-; lecturer, visiting prof, Foundation for Teaching Entrepreneurship to Disadvantaged, 1990; visiting prof, Youth Black Exchange Program, 1985-86; elected pres, Alpha Kappa Psi, National Business Fraternity, 1978-. **Honors/Awds:** Tau Beta Kappa Honor Society, Upsala College Charter Member, 1980. **Business Addr:** District Manager, Consumer Communications Services, AT&T, 131 Morristown Rd, Rm A2170, Basking Ridge, NJ 07920.

JACKSON, GERALD E.
Security company executive. **Personal:** Born Apr 13, 1949, Chicago, IL; son of Hazel Jackson and Bruce Jackson; married Denorsia Jackson, Oct 31, 1974; children: Gerald Jr, Gavin, Syreeta. **Educ:** Olive Harvey Coll, 1972; Roosevelt Univ, BBA, 1975. **Career:** Licensed private investigator; certified real estate broker; Chicago Police Dept, Chicago, IL, police officer; GEJ Security, CEO, pres, 1982-. **Orgs:** Mem, Chatham Business Assn, 1989; bd mem, Rosenblum Boys & Girls Club, 1989; mem, Chicago Assn of Commerce & Industry, 1986; mem, Natl Org of Black Law Enforcement Executives. **Honors/Awds:** Recipient Meritorious Service Award, United Negro College Fund, 1987; Pioneering Spirit Award, Rosenblum Boys & Girls Club, 1989; Entrepreneur of the Year Award (Finalist), Stein & Co, 1988, 1990.

JACKSON, GERALD MILTON
Attorney. **Personal:** Born Jan 8, 1943, Cleveland; son of Mary L Jackson and Albert Jackson; married Patricia A Mullins; children: Alisa, Carmen, Jason A. **Educ:** Kent State U, BA 1967; Univ Of CO Sch of Law, post grad legal training 1968; Case Western Reserve Univ Sch of Law, JD 1971. **Career:** Jackson & Jackson, partner, currently; Alexander Jackson & Buchman, atty partner in law firm; Lawyers for Housing ABA & Cleveland Bar, asst dir 1972-75; Reginald Heber Smith Comm Lwyr Fellow, 1971-73; OH General Assembly, legislative advocate 1971-72; E Cleveland, asst to law dir 1971; EEO Commn US Govt, case analysis 1970; Cleveland Trust Co, accnt 1969; Minority Students Enrichment & Scholarship Prog Univ of CO, dir 1968; Cuyahoga Co Dept of Welfare, cswrkr 1967-68; Cuyahoga Co Juv Detention Home, supr 1965. **Orgs:** V chmn Cleveland Chap Nat Conf of Black Lawyers 1974-75; mem NBA; vice pres John M Harlan Law Club Inc 1975-76; dist rep OH Assn Of Blk Attys 1974-75; mem ABA; Bar Assn of Gr Cleveland; Cleveland Lawyers Assn; mem NAACP; Citizens Leag of Cleveland; Legal Aid Soc; City of Cleveland. **Honors/Awds:** Recipient MLK & Award Baccus Law Sch 1970-71; organizer chm Black Am Law Students Assn Case Western Univ Sch of Law 1970-71; co-designer BALSA Emblem 1971; cert of apprec Bar Assn of Gr Cleveland 1973-75. **Business Addr:** Attorney, Jackson and Jackson, 3673 Lee Rd, Shaker Heights, OH 44120-5108.

JACKSON, GILES B.
Judge (retired). **Personal:** Born Mar 1, 1924, Richmond, VA; son of Bessie A Jackson and Roscoe C Jackson; married Mary Ever Jackson, 1964; children: Mignon Carter, Yvette Town-

send, Yvonne Jackson. **Educ:** Virginia State University, BA, 1948; Southwestern University, JD, 1953; University of Southern California, 1968; University of California at Berkeley, Judicial College, 1977. **Career:** Private practice, attorney, 1954-66; Los Angeles County Superior Court, comm, judge pro tem, 1966-77; Los Angeles Judicial District, judge, 1977-86. **Orgs:** Los Angeles County Bar Association; NAACP, life member; DAV, life member. **Military Serv:** US Marine Corps, NCO, 1943-46. **Home Addr:** 5625 Cambridge Way, #303, Culver City, CA 90230.

JACKSON, GOVERNOR EUGENE, JR.
Financial administrator. **Personal:** Born May 5, 1951, Linden, TX; married Linda Kay Sueing; children: Governor Eugene III. **Educ:** E TX State U, BS 1973; N TX State U, MEd 1978. **Career:** TX Woman's Univ, dir of financial aid 1976-; DeVry Inst of Tech, assoc dean of students 1973-76; E TX State Univ Sam Rayburn Memorial Student Center, bldg serv supr 1969-73. **Orgs:** Mem Nat Assn of Student Fin Aid Adminstr 1973-80; mem SW Assn of Student Fin Aid Admin 1973-80; mem nominating co TX Student Finan Aid Adminstrs 1979; mem adminstrv counc TX Woman's Univ 1977-80; mem Voter Registration Com Dallas, 1978-80; mem Adminstrv bd St Luke Mehtodist Ch 1978-80. **Honors/Awds:** Ldrshp award E TX State U, 1969-70, 1970-71; outst yng man of am Jaycees 1979. **Business Addr:** Texas Woman's University, PO Box 22628 TWU Station, Denton, TX 76204.

JACKSON, GRANDVEL ANDREW
Educator (retired). **Personal:** Born Jul 17, 1910, Taylor, TX; married Cora Mary. **Educ:** Huston-Tillotson Coll, AB 1936; San Francisco St Coll, MA 1955; Univ Of CA at Berkeley, postgrad 1951. **Career:** Human Rights Commn, coordinator 1964-; City & County of San Francisco, sr recreation dir 1946-64; Permanente Metals Corp, Richmond CA, pers cnsl 1943-44; Booker T Washington School Wichita Falls, teacher 1941-43; Wichita Falls, educ supr teacher public school 1937-44. **Orgs:** Commr Travelers Aid Soc 1968; bd mem BSA 1970; mem Arena Coun 1973; bd mem Allensworth Hist Adv Comm Proj 1969; commr Bay Area Soc Plan Coun 1959-63; bd mem UN of San Francisco 1970-; org & consult OMI Comm Proj in San Francisco; consult Richmond dist comm proj; consult Haight Ashbury Comm Proj; bd dir treas Sickle Cell Anemia Dis Found 1973; bd pres 1959-60; pres No Area Conf of Brs 1973; exec Com NAACP San Fran Br 25 yrs; Alpha Phi Alpha. **Honors/Awds:** Rec San Franciscan Foun Awd 1968. **Military Serv:** USNR 1944-46.

JACKSON, GRANT DWIGHT
Professional baseball coach. **Personal:** Born Sep 28, 1942, Fostoria, OH; married Millie; children: Debbie, Yolanda, Grant III. **Educ:** Bowling Green State Univ, Bowling Green, OH, attended. **Career:** Philadelphia Phillies, pitcher 1965-66; San Diego Padres, pitcher 1966; Philadelphia Phillies, pitcher 1967-70; Baltimore Orioles, pitcher 1971-76; NY Yankees, pitcher 1976; Pittsburgh Pirates, pitcher 1977-81; Montreal Expos pitcher 1981; Kansas City Royals, pitcher 1982; Pittsburgh Pirates, pitcher 1982; Pittsburgh Pirates, pitching coach, beginning, 1983; Cincinnati Reds, bullpen pitching coach, 1994-95; Coaching AAA Indianapolis Indians, Cincinnati Reds, 1996-97. **Honors/Awds:** National League All-Star Team, 1969; Winning pitcher of the last game of the World Series, World Series Champs, Pittsburgh Pirates, 1979. **Special Achievements:** Have capacity for Public Relations, advanced scouting, and Minor League Coordinating; Speak Spanish fluently. **Home Addr:** 212 Mesa Circle, Upper Saint Clair, PA 15241.

JACKSON, GREG ALLEN
Professional football player. **Personal:** Born Aug 20, 1966, Hialeah, FL. **Educ:** Louisiana State. **Career:** New York Giants, defensive back, 1989-93; Philadelphia Eagles, 1994-95; New Orleans Saints, 1996; San Diego Chargers, 1997-. **Business Addr:** Professional Football Player, San Diego Chargers, Qualcomm Stadium, 9449 Friars Rd, San Diego, CA 92108, (619)280-2111.

JACKSON, GREGORY
Automobile dealer. **Personal:** Born Jul 12, 1957, Detroit, MI; son of Roy & Doris; married Jackie B, Aug 6, 1982; children: Anika S, Gregory J. **Educ:** Morris Brown Coll, BS, accounting; Atlanta Univ, Graduate School of Bus, MBA, finance/mktg. **Career:** Arthur Andersen & Co, senior accountant, 1980-82; Stroh Brewery Co, controller, 1982-84; Kastleton Co, pres, 1984-91; Prestige Auto Group, pres, currently. **Orgs:** National Automobile Dealers Assn; Michigan Auto Dealers Assn; National Assn of Minority Auto Dealers; General Motors Minority Dealers Assn; NAACP; Kappa Alpha Psi Fraternity. **Business Addr:** President, Prestige Auto Group, G-7401 Clio Rd, PO Box 189, Mount Morris, MI 48458, (810)686-2310.

JACKSON, HAL
Broadcasting industry specialist. **Personal:** Born Nov 3, 1915, Charleston; married; children (previous marriage): Hal Jackson, Jewell McCabe, Jane Harley. **Educ:** Troy Conf Acad VT; Howard Univ. **Career:** WBLS, grp chmn; Inner City Broadcasting Corp, vp, group chairman; WLIB-AM, WBLS-FM Radio NYC, owners; Hal Jackson Prod, pres & exec; "Hal Jackson's Talented Teens Int" TalentPrgm, spon; Wash Afro-Am Newspapers, sports ed; ABC Radio Network, 1st black man on network radio reg sched prog; many other radio stations in MD, DC, NY, & NJ. **Orgs:** Leading pioneer in radio &TV inds estab many firsts as black man in this field; partic host natl telvsed cerebral Palsy Telethon; color comment for home games of NY Nets ABA Bsktbl Team; narra inter for natl synd radio spots for HEW to recruit yng peo for med & soc serv careers; NY Local & Nat Bd AFTRA; num other progs on radio & TV for various fund rais & civic causes. **Honors/Awds:** Man of yr award Beverly Hills Chap NAACP; "Image Awards" recep of 1st pres award for brdcstng; award for work among youth Pres JF Kennedy; disc Jockey of yr Fair Play Com based on comm & charitable endeavors; National Association of Broadcasters, Hall of Fame, 1991; Honored for 50 years of broadcasting by the House of Representatives; "Radio Living Legend Award," 1992; William Bethany Award, 1991; Coalition of 100 Black Women, Candace Award, 1991; Inducted in the "Radio Hall of Fame," 1995; Honored at Smithsonian Inst in Washington, DC, "Pioneering Achievements in Black Radio," 1997. **Business Addr:** Group Chairman, Inner City Broadcasting Corp, WBLS, 3 Park Ave, 40th floor, New York, NY 10016.

JACKSON, HAROLD BARON, JR.
Attorney. **Personal:** Born Dec 28, 1939, Washington, DC; son of Julia and Harold; divorced; children: Julie, Tiffany, Jaime. **Educ:** Marquette U, BA 1964; Marquette Univ Law Sch, Juris Doc 1967. **Career:** Milwaukee Cnty, 1st asst dist atty 1968; Milwaukee Bd of Sch Dir, pres 1970-72; Jackson & Clark Attys at Law, partner 1970-73; Marquette Univ Law Sch, prof of law 1972-73; circuit court judge; Senior Counsel Milwaukee Metropolitan Sewerage District 1986. **Orgs:** Mem Exec Bd of Milwaukee Jr Bar Assn 1970; chmn Criminal Law Section Milwaukee Bar Assn 1972; pres bd of dir Sojourner Truth House; chmn bd of dir Benedict Cntr for Criminal Justice; mem bd of dir Athletes for Youth. **Honors/Awds:** Outstand Jurist awarded by Friends in Law 1982; Man of the Yr Milwaukee Theological Inst 1978; winner of Am Jurisprudence Awards in Constitutional Law, Criminal Law & Jurisprudence. **Home Addr:** 1756 N Hi Mount Blvd, Milwaukee, WI 53208.

JACKSON, HAROLD JEROME
Journalist. **Personal:** Born Aug 14, 1953, Birmingham, AL; son of Janye Lee Wilson Jackson and Lewis Jackson; married Denise Estell Pledger Jackson, Apr 30, 1977; children: Annette Michelle, Dennis Jerome. **Educ:** Baker University, Baldwin, KS, BA, 1975. **Career:** Birmingham Post-Herald, Birmingham, AL, reporter, 1975-80; United Press Intl, Birmingham, AL, reporter, 1980-83, state news editor, 1983-85; Philadelphia Inquirer, Philadelphia, PA, asst national editor, 1985-87; The Birmingham News, Birmingham, AL, editorial board, 1987-94; The Baltimore Sun, staff writer, Baltimore, MD, 1994-. **Orgs:** President, Birmingham Assn of Black Journalists, 1988-91; member, Westminster Presbyterian Church, 1964-. **Honors/Awds:** Hector Award, Writing, Troy State University, 1990; APA Award, Writing, Alabama Press Assn, 1990; Green Eyeshade, Writing, Society of Professional Journalists, 1989; Merit Award, Writing, UPI, 1987; Achievement Award, Writing, Associated Press, 1978; Pulitzer Prize, Writing, Columbia University, 1991; National Association of Black Journalists, Journalist of the Year, 1991; Baker University, Alumnus of the Year, 1992; Birmingham Emancipation Association, Citizenship Award, 1993; Freedom Forum Professor of Journalism, Visiting, Univ of Alabama, Tuscaloosa. **Business Addr:** The Baltimore Sun, 501 N Calvert St, Baltimore, MD 21278.

JACKSON, HAROLD LEONARD, JR.
Financial analyst. **Personal:** Born Sep 26, 1955, Columbia, SC; son of Orion Virginia Meaders Jackson and Harold L Jackson, Sr; married Deborah Ann Knox Jackson, Feb 12, 1983; children: Matthew G, Jennifer E. **Educ:** Texas A & M University, College Station, TX, BBA, Finance, 1977. **Career:** Dresser Atlas, Houston, TX, office supervisor, 1977-83; Macy's, Houston, TX, assoc, 1984; Continental Airlines, Houston, TX, rev accounting supervisor, 1984-85; City of Houston, Houston, TX, fin analyst, 1985-. **Orgs:** Mem, Govt Finance Officers Assn, 1988-; mem, Natl Forum Black Public Admin, 1987-88. **Business Addr:** Financial Analyst II, Finance & Administration, City of Houston, 901 Bagby, Houston, TX 77251.

JACKSON, HENRY RALPH
Clergyman. **Personal:** Born Aug 22, 1915, Birmingham, AL; married Cheri J Harrell; children: Zita J. **Educ:** Daniel Payne Coll, BA; Jackson Theol Sem, BD; Wilberforce U, LlD; Monrovia Coll; Daniel Payne Coll; Campbell Coll, DD; Allen U, HHD. **Career:** N Memphis Dist AME Ch, presiding elder; Minimum Salary Dept AME Ch, fdr dir 16 yrs; AME Ch, pastor 25 yrs. **Orgs:** Fdr pres Brotherhood of AME Ch 8 yrs; mem gen bd AME Ch 8 yrs; del, gen conf AME Ch 1944-80; pres Christian Brotherhd Homes Inc 10 yrs, co-chmn Com on the Move for Equality; 32nd Degree Mason; mem State Dem Exec Com; hon mem State Co, Municipal Employees AFL-CIO; founding father Memphis Goodwill Boys Club. **Honors/Awds:** Life mem NAACP Meritorious Serv Awards Brotherhd AME Ch; Goodwill Boys Club; Mallory Knights Charitable Orgn; Memphis Welfare Rights Orgn; JUGS Inc; Co-Ettes Inc Congressman Harold Ford; Man of Yr, IBPOE; Citizens Award, Local 1733, AFSCME; Outstdng TN Award Gov Ray Blanton. **Business Addr:** 280 Hernando St, Memphis, TN 38126.

JACKSON, HERMOINE PRESTINE
Psychologist. **Personal:** Born Mar 11, 1945, Wilmington, DE; daughter of Ella B Roane Jackson and Herman P Jackson, Sr. **Educ:** Elizabethtown Coll, BA 1967; OH State Univ, MA 1979, PhD 1991. **Career:** Wilmington Public Schools, teacher 1967-68; Philadelphia Public School System, teacher 1968-74; Central MI Univ, instr 1979-81; State of NY West Seneca Devel Ctr, psych 1981-90; NY State Division for Youth, Buffalo Residential Center,psychologist, 1990-94; VA State Dept of Juvenile Justice, 1994-. **Orgs:** Amer Psych Assoc; Amer Assoc on Mental Retardation; Coalition of 100 Black Women. **Honors/Awds:** Outstanding Instr Centrl MI Univ 1981. **Business Addr:** Psychologist, Virginia Dept of Juvenile Justice, Bon Air Juvenile Correction Center, Richmond, VA 23235, (804)323-2574.

JACKSON, HIRAM
Company executive. **Career:** DMC Technologies, chairman/CEO, currently. **Orgs:** ACCESS, founder; NAACP, Detroit Branch, exec bd mem, Freedom Fund Dinner, chair. **Business Addr:** CEO, DMC Technologies, 220 W Congress St, Detroit, MI 48226, (313)964-4404.

JACKSON, HORACE
Association executive. **Personal:** Born Feb 19, 1935, Opelika, AL; son of Emma Lee Jackson and Howard Taft Jackson; divorced; children: David, Michael, Karen M Stewart. **Educ:** Tennessee A&I State Univ, BS, 1957; Washington Univ, MA Ed, 1969; Washington Univ, PhD, 1976. **Career:** Chattanooga Public Schools, cirriculum resource teacher, 1957-63; Rutgers Coll, lecturer, 1973-74; VA Polytechnic Institute, asst professor, 1974-75; East St Louis Center, coordinator of academic programs, 1976-77; St Louis Public Schools, divisional asst, 1978-83; Chattanooga Area Urban League, dir of programs, 1989-; Patners for Economic Progress, manager-minority Business Development; MIKA Information Svcs, pres, currently. **Orgs:** Mem, Kappa Alpha Psi, 1954-; mem, Kappa Delta Pi, 1970-; member, Phi Delta Kappa, 1970-. **Home Addr:** 5240 Polk St, Chattanooga, TN 37410.

JACKSON, ISAIAH ALLEN
Symphony conductor. **Personal:** Born Jan 22, 1945, Richmond, VA; son of Alma Alverta Norris and Isaiah Allen; married Helen Caroline Tuntland; children: Benjamin, Katharine, Caroline. **Educ:** Harvard Univ, BA (Cum Laude) 1966; Stanford Univ, MA 1967; Juilliard School, MS 1969, DMA 1973. **Career:** Juilliard String Ensemble NYC, founder/conductor 1970-71; Amer Symphony Orch, asst conductor 1970-71; Baltimore Symphony Orch, asst conductor 1971-73; Rochester Philharmonic Orchestra, assoc conductor 1973-87; Flint Symphony Orchestra MI, music dir/conductor 1982-87; Dayton Philharmonic Orchestra, music dir 1987-95; Royal Ballet London England, principal conductor 1986; music dir, 1987-90; Queensland Symphony Orchestra, Australia, principal guest conductor, 1993-95; Youngstown (OH) Symphony, music dir, 1996-. **Orgs:** Guest conductor San Francisco Symphony 1984; Toronto Symphony 1984, 1990; guest conductor Boston Pops 1983, 1990-94; guest conductor NY Philharmonic 1978; mem bd dir Ralph Bunche Scholarship Fund 1974-; mem music panel NY State Council on the Arts 1978; guest conductor Berlin Symphony 1989-95; BBC Concert Orchestra, 1987; Royal Liverpool Phil, 1995; Orchestre de la Suisse Romande, 1985, 1988; Dallas Symphony, 1993; Detroit Symphony Orchestra, 1983, 1985; Cleveland Orchestra, 1983-84, 1986-87, 1989-92; Houston Symphony, 1995; numerous recordings for Koch, Australian Broadcasting Corp. **Honors/Awds:** First Governor's Awards for the Arts Commonwealth of VA Richmond 1979; Signet Soc Medal For The Arts, Harvard U, 1991. **Business Addr:** c/o United Arts, 3906 Sunbeam Dr, Los Angeles, CA 90065.

JACKSON, JACQUELYNE JOHNSON
Educator. **Personal:** Born Feb 24, 1932, Winston-Salem, NC; divorced; children: Viola Elizabeth. **Educ:** Univ of WI, BS 1953, MS 1955; The OH State Univ, PhD 1960; Postdoctorals, Univ of CO Boulder 1961, Duke Univ 1966-68, Univ of NC Chapel Hill 1977-78. **Career:** Southern Univ Baton Rouge, asst/assoc prof 1959-62; Jackson State Coll, prof 1962-64; Howard Univ, asst prof 1964-66; St Augustine's Coll, visiting prof 1969-; Howard Univ, prof 1978-85; Duke Univ, instr-assoc prof of medical sociology 1966-. **Orgs:** American Society on Aging; former mem bd dir Carver Research Found of Tuskegee Univ 1970-87; life mem Tuskegee, AL Civic Assn 1959-; dir Natl Cncl on Black Aging 1975-; mem Amer Sociological Assn; mem Southern Sociological Soc; mem Gerontological Soc of Amer; Board of Directors, Natl Council on Aging; former president Association of Social & Behavioral Scientists; former chairperson Caucus of Black Sociologists; Ctr on Immigration Studies, 1997-. **Honors/Awds:** John Hay Whitney Fellow 1957-59; NSF Fellow 1957-; NIH Fellow 1966-68 & 1977-78; received number of awards from American Psychiatric Association, OSU, AAHA, ABS. **Special Achievements:** Author: "These Rights They Seek," 1962; "Minorities & Aging," 1980; approximately 100 chapters in books and articles since 1962. **Home Addr:** PO Box 51022, Durham, NC 27717-1022.

JACKSON, JAMES CONROY
Clergyman (retired). **Personal:** Born May 9, 1913, Scranton, PA; son of Ella Glascoe and James; married Daisy L Ledgister; children: Patricia Ann Cokley. **Educ:** Cheyney State Coll, BS Educ 1938; Philadelphia Divinity Sch, MDiv 1949; Univ of South, MST 1973. **Career:** St Philip's Epis Ch Dallas, vicar 1949-56; St Philip's Epis Ch Little Rock, AR, vicar 1956-62; Voorhees Coll, chaplain 1962-80; St Barnabus Epis Ch, priest-in-charge 1982-90. **Orgs:** Asst prof Voorhees Coll 1980; dean of coll work Diocese of SC 1978-80; bd mem Tri-County Comm Alcohol & Drug Abuse 1973-80; officer/bd mem Bamberg County mental Health 1974-80; exec bd Mental Health Assoc in SC 1982-89; chmn bd Urban League 1960-62. **Honors/Awds:** President Award Voorhees Coll 1979; NAACP Cited 1954; Big Brothers Dallas 1956; Parent Teachers Assn Little Rock, AR 1962; Rel Educ of Negro in SC prior to 1850 1965. **Military Serv:** AUS Corpl 1942-45. **Home Addr:** 4606 Sylvan Dr, Columbia, SC 29206.

JACKSON, JAMES E., SR.
Insurance company executive. **Personal:** Born Feb 4, 1943, Roberta, GA; son of J B Wornum & Dollie C Jackson-Wornum (both deceased); divorced; children: James Jr, Nsombi, Jawara, Brandon, Barenda. **Career:** Allstate Insurance Co., agency owner, 1971-; Dunhill Staffing Systems, CEO of Oakland/Macomb franchise, 1996-. **Orgs:** NAACP, 1978; Optimist Club of Detroit, 1991. **Honors/Awds:** Allstate Ins, Michigan Sales Leader, Auto Ins, Territory 3, 1995, FLPI Production, Territory 3, 1995, Life Ins, Territory, 3, 1995, Personal Property, Territory 3, 1995, Motor Club Membership, 1995. **Special Achievements:** Motivational speaker for agent seminars; Largest Allstate Agency in Michigan & Indiana Region; First minority CEO/owner of a Dunhill Staffing Systems Franchise. **Military Serv:** US Army, sgt, 1962-65. **Home Addr:** 5730 Roundhill Rd, Birmingham, MI 48009, (810)540-2951. **Business Addr:** Senior Account Agent, Allstate Insurance Co., 17051 W 10 Mile Rd, Southfield, MI 48075, (810)443-0000.

JACKSON, JAMES GARFIELD
Law enforcement official. **Personal:** Born Oct 24, 1933, Columbus, OH; son of Sarah Jackson and George Jackson; married Mary Jackson; children: James II, Jason. **Educ:** FBI Academy; Northwestern University; FBI National Executive Institute; Harvard University's John F Kennedy School of Government. **Career:** Columbus Division of Police, officer, 1958-67, sergeant, 1967-71, lieutenant, 1971-74, captain, 1974-77, deputy chief, 1977-90, chief, 1990-. **Orgs:** Major City Chiefs Association; International Association of Chiefs of Police; Ohio Association of Chiefs of Police; National of Black Law Enforcement Executives. **Special Achievements:** First Black police chief in the Columbus Division of Police; the only person in the Columbus Division of Police to place first on three written promotional examinations for sergeant, captain, and deputy chief; testimony for minorities and females helped bring about a federal court finding from which 75% of current black and female officers have benefited through employment, assignment, promotion, back pay, or a combination thereof. **Military Serv:** US Marine Corps, sergeant, 1951-54. **Business Addr:** Chief of Police, Columbus Division of Police, 120 Marconi Blvd, Columbus, OH 43215, (614)645-4600.

JACKSON, JAMES H.
Business executive. **Personal:** Born Apr 24, 1939, Waterloo, IA; married Janet L Norman; children: Denise Rene, Jacqueline Lee, Stephanie Ann, Christine Lynn. **Educ:** Univ of Northern IA, BA 1961; Univ of Detroit, 1968; NYU, 1974. **Career:** CIGNA Corp, sr vp; CT Gen Life Ins Co, second vice pres 1977-; Citibank NYC, vice pres 1973-77; ITT Corp NYC, exec 1971-73; Pepsi Cola Co, vice pres 1965-74; IAHo of Reps, former mem; N Milwaukee State Bank, bd of dir 1977-; Hartford Hosp CT, corporator 1978-; Children's Mus Hartford, bd of tsts 1979-. **Orgs:** Mem & former ofcr NAACP 1961-; mem Counc of Concerned Black Exec 1971-; sec Operation PUSH Hartford Chap 1979-; Black Achievers Harlem YMCA 1970; mem Zeta Boule Chap Sigma Pi Phi Frat 1977-. **Honors/Awds:** Univ of Northern Iowa, Hall of Fame.

JACKSON, JAMES HOLMEN
Construction executive. **Personal:** Born Oct 5, 1949, Newark, NJ; married Lynda P Valrie; children: Lamarr. **Educ:** Compu-Train, Computer Operator 1970; ICBO Rutgers Univ, Business Mgmt 1974; Bloomfield Coll, BA 1979. **Career:** Moldcast Lighting Div, asst mgr qc 1972-79; Condor Intl Corp, treas 1979-80; Internal Revenue Svcs, revenue officer 1980-83; Jacmin, Inc, pres 1982-. **Orgs:** Treas Citizens Improvement League 1979-82; pres Montgomery Ave Block Assoc Irv NJ 1979-83; chmn of the bd Sugar Bear Productions 1985-; bd of dirs People's Comm Corp 1986-, Budget Construction Co 1986-; consultant JS Minor Corp 1986-; chmn Tenant Assoc of 111 So Harrison East Orange NJ 1987-. **Honors/Awds:** Editorials Irvington Herald Newspaper 1979-82. **Military Serv:** AUS spec 4 military policeman 1 1/2; Honorable Discharge 1972. **Business Addr:** Owner/President, Jacmin, Inc, 210 Pinehurst Ave, Scotch Plains, NJ 07076.

JACKSON, JAMES SIDNEY
Educator. **Personal:** Born Jul 30, 1944, Detroit, MI; son of Johnnie Mae Wilson Taylor and Pete James Jackson; married Toni C Antonucci; children: Ariana Marie, Kendra Rose. **Educ:** MI State U, BS Psychology 1966; Univ of Toledo, MA Psychology 1970; Wayne State U, PhD Social Psychology 1972. **Career:** Lucas Co Family Ct Toledo, OH, probation cnslr 1967-68; Univ of MI Ann Arbor, asst prof 1971-76, asso prof 1976-85, prof 1986-; associate dean of Rackham Graduate School, 1988-92, faculty associate, Institute of Gerontology, 1988-, professor health behavior and health education, School of Public Health, 1990-. **Orgs:** Faculty assoc Inst for Social Research 1971-85; chair Social Psychology Training Prog Univ of MI 1980-86; faculty asso Ctr for Afro-Am & African Studies 1982-; chmn Nat Assn of Black Psych 1972-73; chmn Assn for the Adv of Psych 1978-80; mem bd of dir Public Comm on Mental Hlth 1978-83; mem comm on the status of black Amers Natl Rsch Council 1985-; rsch scientist Inst for Social Rsch 1986-; mem bd of trustees Assn for the Adv of Psychology 1986-; postdoctoral rsch fellow Groupe D'Etudes et Recherches Sur La Science Ecole Des Hautes En Science Sociale, Paris France; Chairman, Minority Task Force, Gerontological Society of American, 1989; National Advisory Mental Health Council, NIMH, 1989-. **Honors/Awds:** Early Carrer Contrib to Psych in Pub Interest Am Psych Assn 1983; Dist Fac Ach Award Univ of MI 1975-76; Urban Studies Fellow Wayne St Univ 1969-70; Sr Postdoctoral Fellowship Ford Foundation 1986-87; The Black American Elderly: Research on Physical and Psychosocial Health 1988; Daniel Katz Collegiate Professor of Psychology, 1994-95; Daniel Katz Distinguished Univ Professor of Psychology, 1995; Robert W Kleemier Award, Outstanding Research in Aging, 1994; Hill Distinguished Visiting Prof, Univ of Minnesota, 1995. **Business Addr:** Prof of Psychology, Univ of Michigan, 5118 Institute for Social Research, Ann Arbor, MI 48106.

JACKSON, JAMES TALMADGE
Dentist, educator. **Personal:** Born Nov 23, 1921, Freeman, VA; married Louise; children: June, James Jr, Jane. **Educ:** BS; DDS; FACP; FACD; FICD. **Career:** Howard U, asso dean clinical affairs; Georgetown U, prof; WA VA Hosp Central Dental Lab, chf. **Orgs:** Diplomate Am Bd Prosthodontists; flw Intl Coll & Prosthodontics; Intra-Theatre prosthodontic consult USAF bases. **Military Serv:** AUS lt col 25 yrs. **Business Addr:** 600 W St NW, Washington, DC 20001.

JACKSON, JANET
Vocalist, actress. **Personal:** Born May 16, 1966, Gary, IN; daughter of Katherine Jackson and Joseph Jackson; married James DeBarge (annulled 1985). **Career:** First appeared with her 8 brothers and sisters on TV specials at age 9, 1975; Cast as Penny on CBS "Good Times"; appeared on TV's "Different Strokes"; joined cast of Fame, 1984; singer, 1984-; actress, Poetic Justice, 1993. **Honors/Awds:** Albums include: Dream Street; Janet Jackson; Control (singles off album include Control, Nasty, What Have You Done for Me Lately, Let's Wait a While, Funny How Time Flies), 1986; Rhythm Nation 1814 (singles off album include Miss You Much, Livin' in a World, Someday Is Tonight), 1989; janet., 1993; two platinum albums; 1986/1996: Design of a Decade; The Velvet Rope, 1997. **Business Addr:** c/o A&M Records, 1416 N La Brea, Los Angeles, CA 90028.

JACKSON, JANET E.
Judge. **Educ:** Wittenberg University, BA, 1975; The National Law Center, George Washington University, JD, 1978. **Career:** Ohio Attorney General's Office, assistant attorney general, 1978-80, assistant chief of the civil rights section, 1980-82, chief of the crime victims compensation section, 1982, chief of workers' compensation section, 1983-87; Sindell, Sindell & Rubenstein, attorney, 1982-83; Franklin County Municipal Court, administrative and presiding judge, 1992, judge, 1987-97; Columbus City Attorney, 1997-. **Orgs:** Columbus Bar Association; National Conference of Black Lawyers; Women Lawyers of Franklin County; Ohio State Bar Association; Action for Children, board of directors; Wittenberg University, board of trustees; Columbus Mortar Board Alumni Club. **Honors/Awds:** National Conference of Black Lawyers, Distinguished Barrister Award, 1988; Franklin County Democratic Women, Outstanding Accomplishments Award, 1988; Metropolitan Democratic Women's Club, Community Service Award, 1989; Franklin County Mental Health Board, Warren Jennings Award, 1989; Columbus Education Association, Dr Martin Luther King Jr Humanitarian Award, 1991; YWCA, Women of Achievement Award, 1992; Columbus Association for the Education of Young Children, Citizen's Award, 1993; Pi Lambda Theta, Citations Award, 1993; National Conference of Black Lawyers and the Robert B Elliot Law Club, John Mercer Langston Award, 1994; numerous others. **Special Achievements:** The Blue Chip Profile, 1992. **Business Addr:** Columbus City Attorney, City Hall, 90 W Broad St, Rm 200, Columbus, OH 43215, (614)645-7385.

JACKSON, JANINE MICHELE
Journalist. **Personal:** Born Jan 30, 1965, Wilmington, DE; daughter of Wagner and Arva Marshall Jackson. **Educ:** Sarah Lawrence Coll, BA, 1985; New School for Social Research, MA, 1992. **Career:** FAIR, research director, 1992-; Labor at the Crossroads, host, 1994-. **Orgs:** Labor at the Crossroads, 1994-. **Honors/Awds:** Metro NY Labor Press Council, "Communicator of the Year," 1996. **Business Addr:** Research Director, Fairness & Accuracy In Reporting, 130 W. 25th St., New York, NY 10001, (212)633-6700.

JACKSON, JAREN
Professional basketball player. **Personal:** Born Oct 27, 1967, New Orleans, LA. **Educ:** Georgetown. **Career:** New Jersey Nets, guard, 1989-90; Wichita Falls Texans (CBA), 1990-91; Dayton Wings (WBL), 1991; La Crosse Catbirds (CBA), 1991-92; Golden State Warriors, 1992; Los Angeles Clippers, 1992-93; La Crosse Catbirds (CBA), 1993-94; Portland Trailblazers, 1993-94; Philadelphia 76ers, 1994-95; Pittsburgh Piranhas (CBA), 1995; Fort Wayne Fury (CBA), 1995-96; Houston Rockets, 1996; Washington Wizards, 1996-97; San Antonio Spurs, 1997-. **Business Addr:** Professional Basketball Player, San Antonio Spurs, 600 E Market St, San Antonio, TX 78205, (210)554-7773.

JACKSON, JERMAINE LAJUANE
Singer, television producer. **Personal:** Born Sep 11, 1954, Gary, IN; son of Katherine Jackson and Joseph Jackson; married Hazel Gordy (divorced); children: Jermaine II, Autumn; children: Jamie, Jeremy, Jordan. **Career:** Member of the Jackson 5, albums include: Diana Ross Presents the Jackson Five, ABC, Third Album, Goin' Back to Indiana, Greatest Hits of the Jackson 5, Get It Together, Dancing Machine, Moving Violation, 1969-76; member of the Jacksons, albums include: Victory, 2300 Jackson Street, 1984-92; solo artist, albums include: Jermaine, 1972; My Name is Jermaine, 1976; Feel the Fire, 1977; Frontiers, 1978; Jermaine, 1980; Let's Get Serious, 1980; I Like Your Style, 1981; Precious Moments, 1986; The Jacksons: An American Dream, mini series, co-producer, 1992. **Special Achievements:** Gold Album, My Name is Jermaine, 1976; Platinum Album, Victory, 1984.

JACKSON, JESSE L., JR.
Congressman. **Personal:** Born Mar 11, 1965; married Sandra. **Educ:** North Carolina A & T State Univ, BS, 1987; Chicago Theological Seminary, MA, 1990; Univ of Illinois Law School, JD, 1993. **Career:** National Rainbow Coalition, national outreach field director; US House of Representatives, congressman, 1995-. **Orgs:** President, "Keep Hope Alive" Political Action Committee; Democratic National Committee; Operation PUSH, vice president-at-large. **Honors/Awds:** Ebony Magazine, "50 Leaders of the Future". **Special Achievements:** Youngest appointed member of Democratic National Committee. **Business Addr:** Congressman, US House of Representatives, 312 Cannon House Office Bldg, Washington, DC 20515-1302, (202)225-0773.

JACKSON, JESSE LOUIS
Clergyman, civic leader. **Personal:** Born Oct 8, 1941, Greenville, SC; son of Helen Jackson and Charles Jackson; married Jacqueline Lavinia Brown Jackson; children: Santita, Jesse Louis, Jonathan, Luther, Yusef DuBois, Jacqueline Lavinia. **Educ:** Univ of IL, 1959-60; A&T Coll NC, BA Soc 1964; Chicago Theol Seminary, postgrad, DD (hon). **Career:** Greenville, SC Civil Rights Movement, leader 1960; directed a service of Statewide TV Prog 1962; Operation PUSH, natl pres 1972-83; Greensboro, NC Civil Rights Movement, mem 1963; NC Intercoll Councl on Human Rights, pres; Gov Stanford's Office, liaison officer; Congr of Racial Equality, field rep for southeastern region 1965; ordained to minister Bapt Church 1968; The Natl Rainbow Coalition, pres, 1984-; Appointed by President Clinton as the Special Envoy to Africa, 1997. **Orgs:** Assoc min Fellowship Missionary Bapt Ch; natl dir SCLC Operation Breadbasket by appointment of Dr Martin Luther King Jr 1967; natl dir Coordinating Council Comm Organizations 1966-71; Active Black Coalition for United Com Action; founder Operation PUSH Inc. **Honors/Awds:** Greensboro Citizen of the Year 1964 Windsor Comm Rec Center; Chicago Club Frontier's Intl Man of the Year 1968; Natl Med Assn Presidential Award 1969; Humanitarian Father of the Year Natl Father's Day Comm 1971; Presidential Award Natl Med Assn; author "Straight From The Heart," Fortress Press Philadelphia PA 1987.

JACKSON, JIM (JAMES ARTHUR)
Professional basketball player. **Personal:** Born Oct 14, 1970, Toledo, OH. **Educ:** Ohio State Univ. **Career:** Dallas Mavericks, guard, 1992-96; New Jersey Nets, 1996-97; Philadelphia 76ers, 1997-98; Golden State Warriors, 1998-. **Special Achievements:** NBA Draft, First round pick, #4, 1992. **Business Addr:** Professional Basketball Player, Golden State Warriors, 1001 Broadway, Oakland, CA 94607, (510)986-2200.

JACKSON, JOHN
Mayor. **Personal:** Born Jan 17, 1948, Hayneville, AL; married Katie Welch; children: Nina S, Kevin John. **Educ:** Tuskegee Inst, Cert in Quality Control 1964-66; Univ of MI, Insurance Executive 1967-69. **Career:** Ford Motor Co, final inspector 1969-72; Life Ins of GA, ins exec 1973-79; City of White Hall, mayor 1980-. **Orgs:** Chmn of bd Sellers Memorial Christian Church; Student Non-violent Coord Comm. **Business Addr:** Mayor, City of Whitehall, Rt 1 Box 191-B, Hayneville, AL 36040.

JACKSON, JOHN
Professional football player. **Personal:** Born Jan 4, 1965, Camp Kwe, Japan; married Joan; children: Josh, Jordan. **Educ:** Eastern Kentucky, degree in police administration, 1991. **Career:** Pittsburgh Steelers, tackle, 1988-. **Honors/Awds:** Pro Bowl alternate, 1994, 1996. **Business Addr:** Professional Football Player, Pittsburgh Steelers, Three Rivers Stadium, 300 Stadium Circle, Pittsburgh, PA 15212, (412)323-1200.

JACKSON, JOHN, III
Landscape architect. **Personal:** Born Aug 14, 1961, New York, NY; son of John & Lucille Jackson Jr; married Cathey J Jackson, Jul 3, 1983; children: John Jackson IV. **Educ:** Mississippi State University, bachelor of landscape architecture, 1983. **Career:** Pickering Firm, landscape architect, 1983-87; Toles Associates, director of landscape architecture, land planning/COO, 1987-90; Jackson Person & Associates Inc, President/CEO, 1991-. **Orgs:** American Society of Landscape Architects, 1986-, committee chairman, 1991-; Council of Federal Procurement for Architects & Engineers, vice chairman, 1995-; American Planning Association, 1984-. **Honors/Awds:** Tennessee American, Planning Award of Excellence, 1992; US Small Business Administration, West Tennessee Small Business Award, 1993; Memphis Business Journal, Small Business Award, 1994; US Small Business Administration, Tennessee Small Business of the Year, 1995; National Minority Supplier Development Council, Supplier of the Year Award, 1996. **Business Addr:** President, CEO, Jackson Person & Associates, Inc, 66 Monroe Ave, Ste 104, Memphis, TN 38103, (901)526-8386.

JACKSON, JOHN H.
Civil engineer. **Personal:** Born Jun 8, 1943, Boonville, MO; son of Elnora Smith Campbell and Louis R Jackson; married Mae Jones Jackson. **Educ:** Univ of MO, BS Civil Engrg 1968; Univ of Houston, MBA Finance 1975. **Career:** Dow Chemical, design engr 1968-72, project engr 1974-83; J F Pritchard & Co, design engr 1972-74; City of Miami, asst to dir public works. **Orgs:** Mem Amer Soc of Public Admin 1983-; mem Natl Forum for Black Public Admin 1984-. **Business Addr:** Asst Dir Public Works, City of Miami, 275 NW 2nd St, Miami, FL 33128.

JACKSON, JOHNNY, JR.
Legislator. **Personal:** Born Sep 19, 1943, New Orleans; married Ara Jean; children: Kenyatta Shabazz. **Educ:** So U, BA 1965; Univ of New Orleans, 1965-66. **Career:** Dist 101, state rep 1973-77; Desire Comm Ctr, exec dir 1963-73; Social Welfare Plng Counc, comm orgn 1965-68; Sears Gentilly, porter 1961-65; Logan Cab Co, dispatcher 1958-61. **Orgs:** Mem LA Legislature elected Gov's Food Stamps Adv Com 1977; House Com on Ways & Means 1977; mem Joint Com on Legis Counc 1977; Municipal & Prochial Gov't Com 1972-77; Hlth & Welfare Com of the House 1972-77; Joint Com on Hlth & Welfare 1972-77; subcom Career & Secondary Educ 1972-77; House Com on Edn1972-77; subcom on Hlth & Mental Disorders 1972-77; joint com on Spec Educ 1972-76; specl com on Students Concerns 1974-76; Gov's Com of Ad Valorem Taxes 1975; Gov's Com St Revenue Sharing 1974; Gov's Blue Ribbon Com on So Univ Crisis 1972; former bd mem NO Sickle Cell Anemia Found; bd mem Gtr NO Assn of Retarded Citizens; mem New Orleans Comm Sch 1973-77; Desire Credit Uniont 1975-77; pres OSEI Day Care 1975-77; New Orleans Jazz & Heritage Found; St RochComm Improvement Assn; Natl Black Spo Found; Desire Comm Housing Corp Affiliated; Desire Area Comm Counc Affiliated; Desire/FL Sr Citizens Prgm; Boy Scouts of Am; Urban League; NAACP; Free Southern Theatre; Desire Comm Ctr. **Business Addr:** State Rep & Dist, 101 3413 Press St, New Orleans, LA.

JACKSON, JOSEPH T.
Mechanical engineer. **Personal:** Born Oct 30, 1916, Atlanta, GA; married Legretta. **Educ:** Atlanta U. **Career:** Operating Engineers, master mechanic 1953-; Negro Am Labor Council (Westchester Chpt), chmn 1950-56; NY State NAACP Labor & Industry, chmn 1960-64; chmn of the bd Westchester/Putnam Affirmative Action Program 1972. **Orgs:** JF Kennedy Meml Award, Labor 1965; Civic Award New Rochelle Human Rights Commn 1978; Humanitarian Award Black Dem of Westchester 1978; Civic Westchester Affirmative Action Program 1978. **Business Addr:** 61 Mitchell Pl, White Plains, NY 10601.

JACKSON, JULIUS HAMILTON
Scientist, educator. **Personal:** Born Jan 6, 1944, Kansas City, MO; son of Julia Esther Jones Jackson and Virgil Lawrence Jackson Sr; married Patricia Ann Herring Jackson, Dec 22, 1979; children: Rahsaan Hamil, Sajida Lazelle, Ajani Josef. **Educ:** University of Kansas, Lawrence, KS, AB, 1966, PhD, 1969; Purdue University, W Lafayette, IN, postdoctoral, 1969-72. **Career:** Purdue University, W Lafayette, IN, postdoctoral research assoc, 1969-72; Meharry Medical College, Nashville, TN, asst prof of microbiology, 1972-76, assoc prof, chairman of microbiology, 1981-85, assoc prof, dir, hybridoma res support facility, 1985-87; Michigan State University, East Lansing, MI, assoc prof of microbiology, 1987-. **Honors/Awds:** Member, American Society for Microbiology; member, American Society of Biological Chemists, 1982-; chairman, Committee on Equal Opportunities for Minority Groups, American Society for Biochemistry and Molecular Biology, until 1992. **Business Addr:** Professor, Michigan State Univ, Dept of Microbiology, 267 Giltner Hall, East Lansing, MI 48824.

JACKSON, KAREN DENISE
Engineer. **Personal:** Born Jan 14, 1947, Chicago, IL; daughter of Kathryn Crawford and William Jesse Crawford; married Raymond Jackson, Apr 24, 1971; children: Cheo Oronde Diallobe, Ahkil Asaad Diallobe. **Educ:** Elmira College, BS, math & chem, 1976; Michigan State University, BSEE, 1984. **Career:** General Motors, foreman, 1977-82; Motorola, software engineer, 1984-. **Orgs:** Arizona Council of Black Engineers & Scientists, vice pres computer camp chairman, 1986-; Word-Wizards Toast Masters, charter secretary-treasurer, 1987-. **Honors/Awds:** US Black Engineer Magazine, Black Engineer of the Year for Community Service, 1992; The Career Communications Group; ACBES, High Five Award, 1991. **Special Achievements:** ACBES Summer Computer Camp, Chairman, 1989-92; first Black history radio program in Corning NY, 1974; created KomputerEd Tools, 1996; co-founder of business group for black women, Strictly Business. **Business Addr:** Software Engineer, Motorola Government Electronics Group, 8201 E McDowell Rd, Hayden Bldg, Scottsdale, AZ 85257-3893, (602)441-1197.

JACKSON, KARL DON
Publishing executive. **Personal:** Born Apr 18, 1947, Baltimore, MD; son of Frances Jane Jenkins and Donald Harris Jackson; married Gloria Bagley, Nov 16, 1968; children: Karlyn Irene, Karl Daniel. **Educ:** Baruch College, New York NY, 1968-74. **Career:** N W Ayer & Son, New York NY, account mgr, 1972-76; Black Enterprise Magazine, New York NY, advertising mgr, 1979-81; Amalgamated Publishers, Inc, New York NY, gen sales mgr, 1983-. **Honors/Awds:** Silver Anvil, PRSA, 1970. **Military Serv:** US Army, sergeant, 1966-68. **Home Addr:** 1771 Topping Ave, Bronx, NY 10457.

JACKSON, KEITH HUNTER
Educator. **Personal:** Born Sep 24, 1953, Columbus, OH; married Violet Smallhorne; children: Kamilah, Akil. **Educ:** Morehouse Coll, BS 1976; Georgia Tech, BSEE 1976; Stanford Univ, MS physics 1979, PhD 1982. **Career:** Hewlett Packard Labs, mem tech staff 1981-83; Howard Univ, asst prof 1983-. **Orgs:** Mem Amer Phys Soc, Optical Soc of Amer, Natl Soc of Black Physicists.

JACKSON, KEITH JEROME
Professional football player. **Personal:** Born Apr 19, 1965, Little Rock, AR. **Educ:** Oklahoma University, BS, communications, 1988. **Career:** Philadelphia Eagles, tight end, 1988-92; free agent, Miami Dolphins, tight end, 1992-. **Honors/Awds:** Sporting News, Rookie of the Year, 1988; played in Pro-Bowl, 1988-90. **Business Addr:** Professional Football Player, Miami Dolphins, 2269 NW 199th St, Miami, FL 33056.

JACKSON, KEITH M.
Executive. **Personal:** Born Nov 22, 1948, Springfield, IL. **Educ:** Dartmouth Coll, AB 1971; Columbia Univ, MS 1975. **Career:** Sahara Energy Corp, pres, Trans Urban East Orgn Inc NYC, consult econ dev & mkt analysis 1971-73; Rep Charles B Rangel US House Reps Wash, legis asst 1973-74; Congressional Black Caucus Inc, exec dir.

JACKSON, KENNELL A., JR.
Educator, historian. **Personal:** Born Mar 19, 1941, Farmville, VA. **Educ:** Hampton Inst VA, BA; King's Coll Cambridge Univ England; UCLA, PhD. **Career:** Stanford Univ Dept of History, asst prof 1969-78, assoc prof, 1979-;. **Honors/Awds:** Woodrow Wilson Scholar 1962; John Hay Whitney Scholar Univ Ghana 1963; Fulbright Scholar, Cambridge Univ, 1964-65; Foreign Areas Fellow, Kenya, 1965-68; Lloyd W Dinkelspiel Serv Undergrad Educ, Stanford Univ, 1972; Fellow, Society for the Humanities, Cornell Univ, 1997-98; Univ Fellow, Stanford Univ; Allan V Cox Award, Fostering Undergrad Research; chair, African-American Studies, 1980-89. **Special Achievements:** Publications: "America is Me: The Most Asked and Least Understood Questions About Black American History," Harper Collins. **Business Addr:** Dept History, Stanford Univ, Palo Alto, CA 94305.

JACKSON, KENYA LOVE
Entertainment company executive. **Personal:** Born Nov 25, 1963, Flushing, NY; daughter of Gladys Maria Knight and James G Newman II. **Educ:** Univ of San Diego, BA, 1986. **Career:** Cedar Sinai Hospital, Los Angeles CA, lab research technician, 1982-84; Jeremiah's Steak House, Dallas TX, asst manager, head cashier, 1984-85; Marquee Entertainment, Los Angeles CA, asst executive vice pres, 1986-87; Shakeji Inc, Las Vegas NV, executive administrator, 1987-; Kenya's Gourmet Bakery, Las Vegas NV, owner, 1994-. **Orgs:** Sec/treas, Newman Management Inc, 1987-; corporate dir KNS Production Inc 1987-; corporate director Knight Hair Care Inc 1988-; sec treas Ms G Inc 1988-; president, Kenya's Kitchen Inc, 1993. **Business Addr:** Executive Administrator, Shakeji Inc, 2801 Yorkshire Ave, Henderson, NV 89014.

JACKSON, KEVIN
Olympic athlete, coach. **Career:** US Olympic Athlete, freestyle wrestler, 1992; wrestling coach, currently. **Honors/Awds:** Olympic Games, Barcelona, Spain, Gold Medalist, 1992; World Champion, 1991, Pan Am Games, Champ, 1991, 1995. **Business Addr:** Gold Medalist, 1992 Games, c/o US Olympic Training Center, 1 Olympic Plaza, Colorado Springs, CO 80909, (719)578-4500.

JACKSON, KEVIN L.
Mktg manager. **Personal:** Born Mar 23, 1956, Washington, DC; son of Thomas & Dorothy Jackson; married Michelle, Jun 19, 1993; children: Bruce, Kevin Nolan. **Educ:** Lehigh University, BS, 1978. **Career:** NCR Corp, account mgr, 1978-82; Honeywell Federal Systems, account mgr, 1982-87; Honeywell Inc, mkt dev mgr, 1987-90; Alliant Techsystems, mgr, AF Programs, 1990-. **Orgs:** AFA-DW Steele Chap, vp, 1995-; Sports Enhancements, Inc, bd mem, 1997-. **Honors/Awds:** Alliant Great Performer Award, 1994; Honeywell Top Performer Award, 1989, Pacesetter Award for Sales Excellence, 1983, 1985, 1986; NCR Century Point Club, 1979, 1980, 1981. **Business Addr:** manager, Air Force Programs, Alliant Techsystems Inc, 1911 N Ft Myer Dr, Ste 800, Arlington, VA 22202.

JACKSON, LARRON DEONNE
Accountant, professional football player (retired). **Personal:** Born Aug 26, 1949, St Louis, MO; divorced; children: Laresa, Temple, Larron Jr. **Educ:** Missouri Univ, BS, 1971. **Career:** Professional football player: Denver Broncos, 1971-74; Atlanta Falcons, 1975-76; Monsanto Chemicals, management trainee, 1970; Touch-Ross, junior and senior staff accountant, 1972-74; Jackson and Montgomery Tax and Accounting Services, 1975; Jackson and Associates Financial Services, accountant, 1975-. **Honors/Awds:** Outstanding College Athlete of America, 1971; NFL All-Pro Rookie team, 1971; hon bd mem, Mathew-Dickey's Boy's Club, 1971.

JACKSON, LARRY EUGENE
Engineer. **Personal:** Born Feb 18, 1943, Chicago, IL; married Roberta O Staples; children: Crystal, Robyn, Larry Jr. **Educ:** Purdue U, BSME 1967. **Career:** Kaiser Eng Inc, proj eng 1977; Inland Stl Co, sr engr 1967-75. **Orgs:** Mem Amer Inst of Stl Engr Mem, Lake Area Untd Way Budgt Comm; Racing Chrmn, IN Ski Coun; pres bd of dir Gary & Bldg. **Honors/Awds:** Auth; mem Alpha Phi Alpha; mem Front Intl Gary Chap Art Pub AISE 1970. **Business Addr:** 35 E Wacker Dr, Chicago, IL 60601.

JACKSON, LATOYA
Entertainer. **Personal:** Born 1956, Gary, IN; daughter of Katherine Jackson and Joseph Jackson; married Jack Gordon, 1989. **Career:** Singer, dancer, currently; appearances include: Moulin Rouge, Paris, France, 1992; Las Vegas; New York; various countries in Euurope; albums include: You're Gonna Get Rocked, 1988; Imagination, 1986. **Special Achievements:** LaToya: Growing Up in the Jackson Family, autobiography, coauthor with Patricia Romanowski, Dutton, 1991; Geraldo, guest appearance; posed for Playboy magazine, 1989; Bob Hope's Easter Vacation in the Bahamas, tv special, participant, 1989; worked with Nancy Reagan's Just-Say-No Anti Drug campaign, 1987. **Business Phone:** (212)832-4849.

JACKSON, LEE ARTHUR
Government official. **Personal:** Born Apr 14, 1950, Lynch, KY; son of Marie Stokes Jackson and Sylmon James Jackson; married Carolyn Bates Jackson, Jun 3, 1978; children: Michelle Tarese. **Educ:** University of Kentucky, BA, 1973; Governmental Service Center Kentucky State University, Management Certificate (CPM), 1990. **Career:** Department for Employment Services, field office manager, 1975-. **Orgs:** Alpha Phi Alpha, district director, 1972; St Luke Lodge #123, 1972; Kentucky Association of State Employees/FPE, president, 1990; American Federation of Teachers/Federation of Public Employees, vice-chairman, 1992; Community Action Council Brothers Policy Board, chairman; Kentucky American Water Co Consumer Advisory Council. **Home Addr:** 3632 A Bold Bidder Drive, Lexington, KY 40517-3547. **Business Addr:** Field Office Manager, Department for Employment Services, 300 S Upper St, Lexington, KY 40508-2510, (606)246-2000.

JACKSON, LENWOOD A.
Judge. **Personal:** Born Jan 11, 1944, Concord, GA. **Educ:** Morris Brown Coll, BA 1966; Emory Univ Sch of Law, JD 1969; Univ of MI; Harvard Univ Cambridge, MA. **Career:** City Court of Atlanta, judge, 1992-; Patterson, Parks & Franklin, atty; Latimer Haddon & Stanfield, asso atty 1971-72; Nat Labor Relations Bd LA, atty; GA Gen Assembly, intern 1969; City of Atlanta Planning Dept, intern 1967; OEO Reg Coun, law clerk 1968; Johnson & Jordan, law clerk 1968-69; Emory Neighborhood Law Ofc, legal asst 1969. **Orgs:** Am Bar Assn; Nat Bar Assn; GA Bar Assn; Atlanta Bar Assn; Gate City Bar Asn; Nat Orgn on Legal Problems of Edn; Phi Delta Phi Legal Frat; Alpha Phi Alpha Frat; exec com Nat Coun of Sch Attys; Butler St YMCA. **Military Serv:** US Army res s/sgt 1969-. **Business Addr:** Judge, City Court of Atlanta, 104 Trinity Ave, Atlanta, GA 30335.

JACKSON, LEO EDWIN
Educator, elected government official (retired). **Personal:** Born Dec 30, 1925, Springfield, MA; son of Ethel Williams and Andrew J Jackson; married Barbara Lockwood; children: Reginald, Lionel T, Margo E. **Educ:** Tuskegee Inst Tuskegee AL, 1944-45; Mitchell Coll New London, Bus Admin 1970-72. **Career:** Gen Dynamics Corp, engrg aid 1958-68, sugg analyst 1968-70, shipyard plcmt rep 1970-71, coord on job training 1971-76, sr instr 1976-80; Inst for Cert of Engrg Techs, sr engr tech; City of New London CT, mayor 1980-91. **Orgs:** Bd of ed 1st Black Elected City of New London 1975-77; mem Electric Boat Mgmt Assoc, Biracial Comm of the Metal Trades Council; sec, treas Re-devel Agency; advsy capa Southeastern Reg Voctl Tech School; leading knight Victory Ldg of Elks IBPOE of W 1970-. **Military Serv:** AAC avia cadet 1944-46.

JACKSON, LEROY ANTHONY, JR.
Physician. **Personal:** Born May 11, 1935, Shreveport, LA; married Ruth Ann. **Educ:** Howard U, MD 1960. **Career:** Jackson Obstetrical PC, physician 1965-; Freedman's Hosp, intern 1960-61, resid training 1961-62; DC Gen Hosp, 1962-63; Freedmen's Hosp, 1963-65; Bur of Maternal & Child Hlth DC Hlth Serv Adminstrn, chief div of maternal hlth 1968-71; Maternity & Infant Child Proj, dir 1969-71; Shaw Comm Hlth Ctr NMA, dir 1971-73; Freedmen's Hosp, attending staff; Washington Hosp Ctr & Columbia Hosp for Women, courtest staff; Morris Cafritz Meml Hosp, active staff; Howard Univ Coll of Med Dept of Ob & Gyn, clinical instr part-time. **Orgs:** Certified by Am Bd of Ob & Gyn 1968; consNat Med Assn Found Inc 1970; Am Cancer Soc Uterine Site Com; DC Hlth & Welfare Counc Hlth Needs & Resources sub-com on Abortions; chmn Mayor's Task Force on Food Nutrition & Hlth; panel mem White House Conf on Food Nutrition & Hlth DC sub-panel & chmn; mem DC Med Soc; Medico-Chirurgical Soc; Washington Gyn Soc; Am Med Assn; Nat Med Assn; DC Pub Hlth Assn; mem Alpha Phi Alpha Frat; Alpha Kappa Mu Sci Frat; Chi Delta Mu Frat; charter mem Alpha Phi Omega Frat. **Honors/Awds:** Fellow Am Coll of Ob & Gyn; fellow Am Fertility Soc; author publs to professional jours. **Military Serv:** AUS Reserve maj. **Business Addr:** 4660 Martin L King Ave SW, Washington, DC.

JACKSON, LESLIE ELAINE. **See SOUTH, LESLIE ELAINE.**

JACKSON, LILLIAN
Association executive. **Personal:** Born in Montgomery, AL. **Educ:** Troy State University, AA; Alabama State University, BA, MA. **Career:** NAACP, Metro Montgomery Branch, director; Alabama State NAACP, president, currently.

JACKSON, LUKE
Dentist. **Personal:** Born Sep 17, 1919, Recovery, GA; married Shirley Ann Lead; children: Charles L, Wayne D, Shirlee Barnetta, Shirlene Elizabeth, Luke Jr. **Educ:** GA State Coll, BS 1942; Atlanta Univ, attended 1945-46; Meharry Med Coll, DDS 1951. **Career:** Meharry Med Coll, instr prosthetic dentistry 1951-53; Private Practice, dentist Chatanooga 1953-. **Orgs:** Bd orgnzr Peoples Bank of Chattanooga 1974-; diplomate Natl Bd Dental Examiners (pres 1957-59); Pan-TN Dental Assn; pres George W Hubbard Dental Soc 1953-; chmn Bus Div Chattanooga Council for Comm Action 1963-68; mem bi-racial Mayor's Comm 1963; Bapt (trustee 1955 coord bldg council 1970-71); mem bd mgmt Henry Br YMCA 1965-70. **Military Serv:** USNR WW II. **Business Addr:** 752 E 9 St, Chattanooga, TN 37403.

JACKSON, LURLINE BRADLEY
Medical supplies company executive. **Personal:** Born Aug 12, Dallas, TX; daughter of Alice Young (deceased) and Henry Bradley (deceased). **Educ:** North Texas State University, 1956-57; El Centro Jr College, 1969-74; Richland College, 1977-78; Respiratory Therapy School, 1980; Tarrant County Jr College, nursing home administration, 1983. **Career:** Presbyterian Hospital of Dallas, supervisor of respiratory therapy; Caring Medical Supply Co, founder, owner, president, CEO, currently. **Orgs:** Washington-Lincoln Alumni Association of Dallas, national vp, 1990-92; NAACP, Dallas Chapter; Natl Council of Negro Women, Inc, vp; National Caucus and Center on Black Aged; Altzheimer, Dallas Chapter, speaker. **Honors/Awds:** Welcome House Inc, Natl Council of Negro Women Inc, Oak Cliff Section, 1983; Iota Phi Lambda, Psi Chap, 1968; Dallas Metro Club of Natl Assn of Negro Business & Professional Women, 1989; Washington-Lincoln Alumni Assn of Dallas, 1989; Founders Award, She-Roes & He-Roes, 1990. **Business Addr:** President, Caring Medical Supply Co, 4301 Colonial Ave, Dallas, TX 75215, (214)421-0852.

JACKSON, LUTHER PORTER, JR.
Educator (retired). **Personal:** Born Mar 7, 1925, Chicago, IL; son of Johnnella Frazer Jackson and Luther P Jackson; married Nettie Lee; children: Luther P III, Lee Frazer (deceased). **Educ:** VA State Univ, BA 1949; Columbia Univ Grad Sch of Journalism, MS 1951; Rutgers Univ Ford Found Fellow, 1962-63; Columbia Univ Russell Sage Fellow, 1967-68. **Career:** NJ Record, 1949; NJ Herald News, 1949-50; Balti Afro-Amer, 1950; Chicago City News Bureau, 1951; The Newark News, 1951-58; The Washington Post, reporter 1959-63; IBM News, Corp Headquarters Edition, editor 1963-65; Communicating Research on The Urban Poor, cross-tell dir 1965-67; NAACP, assoc dir public relations/assoc editor of Crisis 1968; Columbia Univ Grad Sch of Journalism, prof of journalism; Professor Emeritus, 1991. **Orgs:** Exec bd Assn for Study of Afro-Am Life & Hist 1964-74; pres NY Branch ASAALH 1964-65; mem Omega Psi Phi Frat; NY Chapter, Natl Assn of Black Journalists. **Honors/Awds:** Research fellow Nat Endowment for The Humanities, subj "Black Towns in The US" 1974-75; visiting prof NC Agr & Tech Univ 1981-82; visiting Prof, NC Central Univ, 1988-89; Excellence in Teaching Award, 1991. **Military Serv:** USMC sgt 1943-46. **Home Addr:** 6 S Poe St, Hartsdale, NY 10530.

JACKSON, MABEL I.
Business executive. **Personal:** Born Oct 16, 1907, Leesville, LA; married Leonidas Jackson; children: Mary (coleman), Lucy (King), Leonidas Jr, William, Arnetta (Bartlow), Victor. **Educ:** Univ Cal Ext Ctr Berkeley. **Career:** Lee's Auto Detail Ctr, secbookkeeper. **Orgs:** Mem East Bay Business & Pro Women's Club; Business & Pro Women's Town Council; Cal & Serv Alliance Bd; Dem Bd Berkeley; charter mem organizer Rainbow Sign Berkeley Nat com ch Nat Council Negro Women; mem Federated Women's Club; exec bd YWCA, Berkeley; mem Eastern Star; exec bd Berkeley PTA; mem Beth Eden Bapt Ch Woman of Yr, East Bay Area. **Honors/Awds:** Outstanding community service awards Alpha Kappa Alpha Sor; YWCA; Nat Council Negro Women; Federated Women; Beth Eden Bapt Ch; Zeta Phi Beta Sor. **Business Addr:** 3901 Telegraph Ave, Oakland, CA 94609.

JACKSON, MANNIE L.
Corporate executive. **Personal:** Born May 4, 1939, Illmo, MO; married Cathy; children: two. **Educ:** Univ of Illinois, bachelor's degree; Univ of Detroit, master's degree, marketing and economics. **Career:** General Motors, until 1968; Honeywell Inc, various positions, beginning 1968, Communication Services Div, vp/gen mgr, 1981-87, Corporate Marketing, vp, currently; Harlem Globetrotters Intl Inc, chairman/CEO, currently. **Orgs:** Exec Leadership Council, founding mem/pres. **Honors/Awds:** Black Enterprise Magazine, recognzied as one of America's "40 Most Powerful Black Executives," 1988, 1993. **Business Addr:** Chairperson/Owner, Harlem Globetrotters International, 400 E Van Buren Street, Ste 300, Phoenix, AZ 85004.

JACKSON, MARK A.
Professional basketball player. **Personal:** Born Apr 1, 1965, Brooklyn, NY; married Desiree; children: Mark II, Heavyn. **Educ:** St John's Univ, Jamaica, NY, 1983-87. **Career:** New York Knicks, guard, 1987-92, Los Angeles Clippers, 1992-94; Indiana Pacers, 1994-; Player's Wear International, co-owner. **Honors/Awds:** NBA Rookie of the Year, 1988; NBA All-Rookie Team, 1988; NBA All-Star, 1989 . **Business Addr:** Professional Basketball Player, Indiana Pacers, 300 W Market St, Indianapolis, IN 46204, (317)263-2100.

JACKSON, MARVIN ALEXANDER
Educator, physician. **Personal:** Born Oct 28, 1927, Dawson, GA; son of Ruby L Mitchell Jackson and Sherman T Jackson; married Aeolian Loretta Mayo; children: Leigh, Brooke. **Educ:** Morehouse Coll, BS 1947; Meharry Med Coll, MD 1951; Univ MI, MI 1956. **Career:** Univ of MI, instructor 1955-56, asst prof 1957-60, assoc prof 1960-68, prof 1968-; consult path NIH 1968-; Natl Naval Medical Center, toxicology unit 1964-71; Armed Forces Inst of Path 1971; VA Hospital 1960-71; Hosp for Joint Dis, NY, resident 1956-57; Univ of MI, resident 1953-56; US Naval Hospital, physician 1952-53; US Naval Hospital, intern 1951-52. **Orgs:** AAAS; Am Assn of Anatomists; Assn of Path Chmn; Am Assn of Path; Am Soc of Clinical Oncology; Am Assn of Univ Profs; Coll of Am Path; Intl Acad of Path; member, Alpha Omega Alpha Honor Medical Soc. **Honors/Awds:** Amer Bd of Pathology, 1957; Natl Science Fnd Sr Postdoctoral Fellow, Univ Glasgow and Strangeways Research Lab, Cambridge, UK, 1967-68; guest investigator, NIH, Bethesda, MD, 1982. **Military Serv:** USNR Lt 1951-56. **Business Addr:** Prof, Dept of Pathology, College of Medicine, Howard Univ, 520 W St, NW, Washington, DC 20059.

JACKSON, MARY
Purchasing consultant. **Personal:** Born Jan 7, 1932, Lumpkin, GA; daughter of Ida B Robinson Beauford and Adie Beauford, Jr; married Arthur L Jackson, Jul 2, 1965; children: Richard L George III, Cynthia A George. **Educ:** Albany State Coll, Albany GA, BEd, 1953; Anchorage Alaska Community Coll, ABus, 1980, BS, 1997. **Career:** Sheraton Hotel, Washington DC, payroll supervisor, 1963-66; Westover AFB MA, procurement clerk, 1966-68; Edwards AFB CA, procurement clerk, 1968-71; Elmendorf ABF AK, purchasing agent, 1971-75; Automotive Parts, Anchorage AK, purchasing agent, 1975-78; Alaska Village Electric, Anchorage AK, purchasing manager, 1978-95; EMJ Travel, 1996-. **Orgs:** Past state pres, Alaska State Federation BPW/USA, 1983-84; past illustrious commandress, Daughter of Isis, 1980-81; past dir, Intl Affairs Purchasing Management, 1983-84; grand worthy matron, Prince Hall GC Order Eastern Star, 1987-90; educational advisor, Anchorage Community Coll, 1977-79; committee mem, Kimo News Advisory Council on Programming, 1978-80; State Grand Loyal Lady Ruler, Order Golden Circle, 1982-89; past sec, Soroptimist Intl, 1984-; past chairman, Job Service Executive Committee, 1985-; past chairman, Anchorage Community Block Grant Development (HUD), 1986-95; Links, Alaska Chapter, strategic long range cmte, chairperson, 1992. **Honors/Awds:** Delta Sigma Theta Sorority, 1952; Alpha Delta Zeta, Phi Theta Kappa Honor Society, 1978; Outstanding Service Award, purchasing management, 1983-84; Woman of the Year, Natl Business Women, 1984; Outstanding Achievement in Leadership, Prince Hall Masons F&AM, 1988; Community Service Award, Alaska Black Caucus, 1988; Community Service Award, Zeta Phi Beta Sorority, 1989; Imperial Deputy of the Desert, Isiserettes, 1988-; Alaska Village Electric, Employee of the Quarter, 1992; Outstanding Accomplishment in Business, North to the Future Business and Professional Women's Club, 1992; Outstanding Service Award in Public Relations, Imperial Court, Daughters of Isis, 1990; Outstanding Letters of Recognition for Community Service, Governor of Alaska, US Senator Stevens of Alaska, US Senator Murkowski of Alaska, Alaska State Representative Bettye Davis, retired Alaska State Senator Stergulewski; Mayor of Anchorage, Alaska Tony Knowles, A Tribute Day, Outstanding Comm Service, 1995. **Home Addr:** 8539 Crosspointe Ct, Antelope, CA 95843.

JACKSON, MATTIE J.
Labor official. **Personal:** Born Oct 3, 1921, Livingston, TX; widowed; children: Gail Lavarra. **Educ:** Attended, Johnson Business Coll, Healds Business Coll; San Francisco State Univ, Certificate of Completion Awd. **Career:** Koret of CA, garment worker/shop steward 1947-67; ILGWU, business agent 1967-70, intl vice pres. **Orgs:** Commnr SF Bd of Appeals 1967-; mem NAACP, Adv Bd SF Comm Coll, Social Concerns Commn Jones UM Church; exec bd SF Labor Council; exec bd Natl Negro Council of Women. **Honors/Awds:** Salute to Women of Labor Awd Senate Indust 1983; Certificate of Appreciation USO 1984; Apri Salute to Labor A Philip Randolph Inst 1987. **Business Addr:** Intl Vice President, ILGW Union, 660 Howard St, San Francisco, CA 94105.

JACKSON, MAYNARD HOLBROOK
Mayor (retired). **Personal:** Born Mar 23, 1938, Dallas, TX; married Valarie; children: Elizabeth, Brooke, Maynard III, Valerie Amanda, Alexandra. **Educ:** Morehouse Coll, BA 1956; NC Central State Sch Law, JD 1959. **Career:** City of Atlanta, mayor, until 1993; Jackson Patterson Parks & Franklin, founder, past partner; Neighborhood Law Office, Emory Comm Legal Serv Ctr, mgn atty; US NLRB, gen atty; Jackson Securities Inc, pres, currently. **Honors/Awds:** Youngest person to hold Atlanta's highest office; youngest mayor of major US city; Greatest Public Service performed, 35 yrs or under, 1974; 200 Young Leaders of America, Time Magazine, 1975; 100 Most Influential Black Americans, Ebony Magazine, 1976. **Special Achievements:** Instrumental in bringing 1996 Olympic Games to the city of Atlanta; Company is ranked #5 on Black Enterprise magazine's 1997 list of Top 100 Black businesses. **Business Addr:** CEO, Jackson Securities Inc, 100 Peachtree St NW, Atlanta, GA 30303-1906.

JACKSON, MICHAEL
Entertainer. **Personal:** Born Aug 29, 1958, Gary, IN; son of Katherine Jackson and Joseph Jackson; married Lisa Marie Presley-Jackson, May 26, 1994 (divorced 1995); married Debbie Rowe, Nov 1996; children: Prince Michael Jackson Jr, Paris Michael Katherine Jackson. **Career:** Lead singer, Jackson Five, the Jacksons, solo artist; recorded numerous single records & albums including: Got to be There, Rocking Robin, I Wanna Be Where You Are, Ben, With a Child's Heart, We're Almost There, Victory; career as solo artist includes the hits: Beat It, Billie Jean, Bad, The Man in the Mirror, Smooth Criminal; appeared on various televison programs including: The Ed Sullivan Show, Hollywood Palace, The Andy Williams Show, Goin' Back to Indiana, the Jacksons own special; appeared in film The Wiz, 1978; narrated ET, The Extra Terrestrial storybook, 1982; leader of Jacksons US Victory tour, 1984; Albums: Off the Wall, Thriller, Bad, Dangerous, HIStory-Past, Present And Future-Book 1, 1995, Blood on the Dancefloor, 1997. **Honors/Awds:** Male Vocalist of the Year, 1971; Jacksons ranked top in single-record sales, in album sales for new artists, 1970; group featured in animated cartoons on TV series, 1971; Gold & Platinum record awards; performed, Queen Elizabeth's Silver Jubilee, 1977; biggest selling solo album, Thriller, won 8 Grammy Awards, Album & Record of the Year, won over 140 Gold & Platinum Awards in 28 countries & 6 continents; 1985 recipient, ABAA Music Award for efforts to aid African famine victims, for conceiving and giving leadership to "USA for Africa," producing the album and video, We Are the World; autobiography, Moonwalk, 1989; listed in Guinness Book of World Records, winner most awards ever (7) at American Music Awards, 1984. **Special Achievements:** Founder, Heal the World Foundation, 1992; Toured Africa, 1992; Appearances at the Super Bowl, 1993; Interviewed by Oprah Winfrey, February 10, 1993, first interview as an adult-viewed by numerous countries; Appearance at President Clinton's Inauguration Ceremonies, 1993; Record setting contract with Sony Music, 1991.

JACKSON, MICHAEL DWAYNE (MICHAEL JACKSON DYSON)
Professional football player. **Personal:** Born Apr 12, 1969, Tangipahoa, LA; children: Latoie, Michael, Malik. **Educ:** Southern Mississippi, attended. **Career:** Cleveland Browns, wide receiver, 1991-95; Baltimore Ravens, 1996-. **Business Addr:** Professional Football Player, Baltimore Ravens, 11001 Owings Mills Blvd, Owings Mills, MD 21117, (410)654-6200.

JACKSON, MICHAEL RAY
Professional baseball player. **Personal:** Born Dec 22, 1964, Houston, TX. **Educ:** Hill Junior College, attended. **Career:** Philadelphia Phillies, pitcher, 1986-87; Seattle Mariners, 1988-91, 1996; San Francisco Giants, 1992-94; Cincinnati Reds, 1995; Cleveland Indians, 1997-. **Business Addr:** Professional Baseball Player, Cleveland Indians, 2401 Ontario, Cleveland, OH 44115, (216)420-4200.

JACKSON, MICHAEL W.
Judge. **Personal:** Born 1964?. **Educ:** Centre Coll, bachelor's degree; Florida State Coll of Law, law degree. **Career:** Alabama Fourth Judicial Circuit, asst district attorney; Selma Municipal Court, municipal judge, currently. **Orgs:** State Democratic Executive Committee. **Business Addr:** Municipal Judge, Selma Municipal Court, 1300 Alabama Ave, Selma, AL 36703, (334)872-8844.

JACKSON, MILTON
Musician, composer. **Personal:** Born Jan 1, 1923, Detroit, MI; son of Lillie Beaty and Manley Jackson; married Sandra Kaye Whittington Jackson, Jan 18, 1959; children: Chyrise Montelei Jackson. **Educ:** MI State Univ School of Jazz 1957. **Career:** Dizzie Gillespie NYC, musician 1945-; played piano & vibraphone with Woody Herman Band 1949-50, Howard McGhee, Tadd Dameron, Thelonieus Monk 1950-52; Modern Jazz Quartet 1953-; School of Jazz Lenox, MA, faculty mem 1957; Town Hall Concert New York City 1958; European Tour 1957-58; appearances with Avery Fisher Hall/Newport Jazz Festival/ Village Vanguard 1975; Milt Jackson Quartet, currently. **Honors/Awds:** Numerous recordings including, Jacksonville Opus de Jazz, Plenty Plenty, Soul Ballads in Blues, New Sounds in Modern Music, Modern Jazz Quartet, Bags & Flute, Bags & Trane, Jazz N'Samba, Milt Jackson Quintet Feelings, Live at the Museum of Modern Art; Numerous Downbeat Mag Awards 1955-59; Recip New Star Award Esquire Mag 1947; Encycl of Jazz Poll as "Greatest Ever" 1956; Metronome Poll Winner 1956-60; Playboy All-Stars Award 1959-60; Honorary Doctorate of Music, Berklee College of Music, 1989. **Military Serv:** US Air Force.

JACKSON, MURRAY EARL
Educator. **Personal:** Born Dec 21, 1926, Philadelphia, PA; married Dauris Smart; children: Linda, David. **Educ:** Wayne State U, MA 1954; Wayne State U, BA 1949. **Career:** Univ of MI, assoc prof Higher Edu, acting dir 1972-73; MI House of Representatives, comon colls & US, cons; N Cent Consult Examiner; Upward Bound Program Wayne State Univ, consultant adv; Detroit Council of Arts, 1975; Wayne County Community Coll, pres 1970-71, acting press 1969-70, exec dir 1969, exec sec 1968-69; Wayne State Univ, 1950-70; Urban Affairs, asst dean of students 1969-70, asst to vice pres; Coll Liberal Arts, exec asst 1955-64; Higher Educ Opportunity Com, coord dir 1963; Humanities, instructor 1958-60; Univ of MI, coord special projects 1965; Highland Park Jr Coll, instructor 1957-58. **Orgs:** Chmn Div 4 Sch of Educ 1972-74; mem Council of Univ & Colls Mid-am Assn of Equal Oppty Prgm Pers; chmn Black Faculty Sch of Edn; mem The Univ Evaluation Com; mem Career Planning & Placement Policy Com; mem Bd in Control of Intercoll Athl; mem Trio Prgm HEW Region 5; mem Cncl on Black Am Affr; mem Higher Educ Oppty Com Bd of dirs, 1st dist Dem Party MI 1965-69; Dem Party Educ Com; Citizens Adv Com to Det Pub Schs; Nat Bd for Theol Edn, Episcopal Ch 1971-73; pres Am Lung Assn of SE MI 1974-76; bd dir Nghbrhd Serv Orgn; bd dir Big Bro & Sister; The Detroit Council for Youth Serv Inc; Metro Detroit Citizens Devel Authority; Mayors Com for Rehab of Narcotic Addists; MI Episcopal Sch of Theology; mem NAACP; Polit Reform for Mayor, City of Detroit; Sr Citizen CommnCity of Detroit; v chmn Urballiance; chmn Detroit Council of Arts; adv Proj 350 Wayne State Univ Hon HHD Shaw U; Mackenzie Honor Soc Wayne State U; commendation by House of Reps State of MI. **Honors/Awds:** Awards in Learning; Elder W Diggs Award Kappa Alpha Psi; the Murray Jackson Serv Award Wayne Co Comm Coll; Citizen of Yr Award Unity Lodge 1975; Wayne CoComm Coll Founds Award Alumni Assn 1973; Disting Serv Award City of Detroit 1976. **Business Addr:** Assoc Prof of Education, The University of Michigan, Ctr for Higher Education, 2007 School of Education Bldg, Ann Arbor, MI 48109.

JACKSON, NATHANIEL G.
Educator. **Personal:** Born Sep 14, 1942, Elkins, WV; son of Carrie Brown Jackson and William Edgar Jackson; married Francis Lewis. **Educ:** Purdue U, BA 1964; Univ of OK, MA 1966; Emory U, MEd 1970. **Career:** Elkins YMCA, dir; Job Corps, training staff, tchr, coach, secondary edn; Higher Ed, adminstr, professional cons; Alderson Broaddus Coll Real Estate broker, dir of financial aid. **Orgs:** Midwest Assn of Financial Aid Adm past pres, State Assn for Retarded Cit; trustee Shiloh Bapt Ch; mem Rotary; A & Fm; United Fund Bd; Sr Cit Bd; Master Mason Mt Zion Lodge #14. **Honors/Awds:** Jaycee's Man of Yr 1969.

JACKSON, NORLISHIA A.
Editor. **Personal:** Born Oct 20, 1942, Washington, DC. **Educ:** Howard Univ, BS 1964; Catholic Univ of Amer, MA 1966; Fed City Coll, advanced study. **Career:** Washington Urban League, dir information 1969-71; Natl Business League, dir information 1972-73; Natl Consumer Information Center, dir information & publications 1973-74; Delta Sigma Theta Publications, editor 1969-; YWCA Home for Girls, dir 1976. **Orgs:** Mem Am Personnel & Guidane Assn; Capitol Press Club; Assn of Univ Women; mem YWCA, NCNW, Urban League. **Honors/Awds:** Alumni Achievement Award 1971; Outstanding Serv Award HUU Ctr 1968; Women of the Yr Award Big Sisters of Am Inc 1980. **Business Addr:** 636 E Capitol St NE, Washington, DC 20003.

JACKSON, NORMAN A.
Association director. **Personal:** Born Nov 16, 1932, NYC, NY; married Nellie; children: Deborah, Norma, Leona. **Educ:** BS, MA, PhD 1972. **Career:** FL Commn on Human Relations Commn, exec dir; Coll Entrance Examination Bd So Regional Office Atlanta, asst dir 1972-74; Minority Affairs FL State U, dir 1970-72; Student Comm Serv St Petersburg Jr Coll, dir 1965-70; St Petersburg, FL, chmn dept physical educ & athletic dir 1959-65; Univ AR, instr; Res Devel FL Jr Coll, asst dir. **Orgs:** Pres So Assn Black Adminstr 1973-74; cons, lecturer & writer FL Equal Access; mem Nat Council Measurement Edn; Phi Delta Kappa; Nat Assn Fin Asst Minority Students; Nat Alliance Black Sch Educator; AACJC; Am Pers & Guidance Assn; FL Assn Comm Coll; FL Assn Fin Aid Adminstrs; So Assn Financial Aid Adminstrs; FL Educ Research Assn; Nat Vocational Guidance Assn. **Honors/Awds:** Basketball Coach Yr 1964; fellowships, Kellogg, NDEA, Seeing Eye Corp; grants, UOES, So Educ Found. **Military Serv:** AUS 1 lt. **Business Addr:** Florida Junior College, 21 W Church St, Jacksonville, FL 32202.

JACKSON, OCIE
Business executive. **Personal:** Born 1904, Texas; widowed; children: Warren, Owen, Arthur Lee, Felix. **Educ:** Hampton Inst, attended. **Career:** Jackson Brothers Ranch, Ocie Jackson & Properties, owner. **Orgs:** Regent Lamar Univ Beaumont TX; dir Golden State Mutual Life Ins Co CA. **Honors/Awds:** One of the wealthiest black men in the US.

JACKSON, OLIVER L.
Artist, educator. **Personal:** Born Jun 23, 1935, St Louis, MO; son of Oliver Lee & Mae Nell Jackson. **Educ:** Illinois Wesleyan University, Bloomington, IL, BFA, 1958; University of Iowa, Iowa City, IA, MFA, 1963. **Career:** St Louis Comm Coll, St Louis, MO, art instr, 1964-67; Washington Univ, St Louis, MO, art instr, 1967-69; Southern IL Univ, E St Louis IL, instr, 1967-69; Oberlin Coll, Oberlin OH, Afro American Studies, assoc prof, 1969-70; California State Univ, Sacramento, prof of art, 1971-. **Honors/Awds:** Natl Endowment for the Arts, Awd in Painting, 1980; Nettie Marie Jones Fellowship in the Visual Arts, 1984; Art Matters, Inc, New York, NY, Artist Grant, 1988; Fleishhacker Foundation, Eureka Fellowship in Painting, 1993. **Special Achievements:** Exhibitions: Seattle Art Museum, 1982, Univ Art Museum/MATRIX, Berkeley CA, 1983, St Louis Art Museum, 1990, Crocker Art Museum, Sacramento CA, 1977, 1984, 1993, Newport Harbor Art Museum, Newport Beach CA, New California Art, 1993, all were solo exhibitions. **Business Addr:** Artist, c/o Anne Kohs & Associates, 115 Stonegate Rd, Portola Valley, CA 94028, (650)851-1933.

JACKSON, OSCAR JEROME
Physician. **Personal:** Born Dec 17, 1929, Fairfield, AL; son of Lillian Jackson and William Jackson; divorced. **Educ:** Howard U, BS; Howard U, MD. **Career:** Gen Surgical, internship & residency; private practice, surgery 1963. **Orgs:** Mem Am Bd Surgery 1963; Fellow Am Coll Surgery 1967; clin instr surgery Univ of CA; attending surgeon Mt Zion Hosp; dir John Hale Med Plan; chmn United Health Alliance; pres Business & Professional Assn; pres John Hale med soc; mem Omega Phi Psi Frat. **Honors/Awds:** Professional Chemistry Prize Howard U. **Military Serv:** Busaf capt 1956-59. **Business Addr:** 1352 Haight St, San Francisco, CA 94117.

JACKSON, PAMELA J.
City official. **Personal:** Born Jun 9, 1967, Louisville, KY; daughter of Donna W Jackson and Philip M Jackson. **Educ:** University of Pennsylvania, BA, economics, 1988; Wayne State University, MA, economics, 1993. **Career:** University of Pennsylvania Tutoring Center, counselor, advisor, 1985-88; Pryor, Govan, & Counts, investment banking associate, 1986-87; In The Black, Business to Business Publication, sales manager, 1987-88; City of Detroit, assistant to the Mayor, 1988-. **Orgs:** Wayne State University-City of Detroit Consortium, steering committee co-chair, 1991-; Coleman A Young Foundation, scholarship committee coordinator, recipient liaison, 1992-; 1990 Census Complete Count Committee, public relations sub-committee coordinator, fundraising sub-committee coordinator, 1990-91; Amandla Mandela Detroit Committee, logistics-operations coordinator, 1990. **Honors/Awds:** Honored by univ president for sucessful completion of BA, economics, in 3 years, 1988; elected as Precinct Delegate in Detroit, 1992. **Special Achievements:** Two Showings: abstract artistic paintings, 1990-91; photographic work of urban America honored as emotionally moving and technically well done. **Business Addr:** Assistant to the Mayor, City of Detroit, Mayor's Office, 1126 City County Bldg, Detroit, MI 48226, (313)224-3164.

JACKSON, PAUL L.
Educator, dentist. **Personal:** Born Aug 1, 1907, Wilson, NC; son of Annie H Jackson and Joseph S Jackson; married Margaret Tramel, Nov 17, 1990. **Educ:** Livingstone Coll Salisbury, NC, BS 1930; Univ PA, MS 1933; Temple Univ Sch Dentistry, DDS 1943. **Career:** Temple Univ Comprehensive Health Servs Prog, chief, professional servs 1969-; Temple Univ School Dentisitry, instr 1966-69; Private Practice, dentistry 1947-69; Stephen Smith Home Aged, consult 1947-69; Mouth Hygiene Assn, clinical dentist 1947; Howard Univ, asst prof operative dentistry 1947. **Orgs:** Life mem, Am & PA (house del) Dental Assns; Acad Gen Dentistry; Am Assn Dental Anesthesiologists; Philadelphia Co Dental Soc; Am Assn Geriatric Dentists; chmn bd dir Stephen Smith Towers; life mem, American Dental Association; life member, New Era Dental Society. **Honors/Awds:** NAACP; Fellowship Commn; Franklin Inst; Smithsonian Inst; British Dict 1967; Fellow Royal Soc Health 1969; Fellow Acad Gen Dent 1969. **Military Serv:** AUS dental corps maj 1943-46; Bronze Star.

JACKSON, PAZEL
Banking executive. **Personal:** Born Feb 21, 1932, Brooklyn, NY; son of Adalite Jackson and Pazel Jackson; children: Karen, Pazel, Peter, Allyson. **Educ:** City Coll of NY, BCE 1954, MCE 1959; Columbia Univ, MS Bus Admin 1972. **Career:** NYC, civil engr 1956-62; Worlds Fair Corp NYC, chief of design 1962-66; New York City Dept of Publ Works, dep gen mgr 1966-67; New York City Dept Bldgs, asst commiss 1967-69; Bowery Savings Bank NYC, sr vice pres 1969-86; Chemical Bank of NY, sr vice pres 1986-95; Chase Manhattan Bank, sr vice pres, 1996-. **Orgs:** Dir Natl Ho Partnership Corp NY State Urban Devel Corp, New York City Ho Devel Corp, Battery Park City Auth, Bedford Stuyvesant Restoration Corp; bd dir Com Serv Soc, Citizens Housing & Plnng Council; mem NY Professional Engrs Soc, ASCE, NY Bldg Congress, City Coll Alumni Assoc Lambda Alpha, Columbia Univ Alumni. **Honors/Awds:** Man of the Year Brooklyn Civic Assoc 1967; Spec Awd for Bldg Design Paragon Fed Credit Union 1968. **Military Serv:** AUS lt 1954-56. **Business Addr:** Senior Vice President, Chase Manhattan Bank, 380 Madison Ave, New York, NY 10017.

JACKSON, PRINCE ALBERT, JR.
Educator. **Personal:** Born Mar 17, 1925, Savannah, GA; married Marilyn Stuggles; children: Prince Albert, III, Rodney Mark, Julia Lucia, Anthony Brian, Philip Andrews. **Educ:** Savannah State Coll, BS 1949; NY U, MS 1950; Univ KS, Post Grad 1961-62; Harvard, NSF Fellow 1962-63; Boston Coll, PhD 1966. **Career:** William James HS Statesboro, tchr sci math 1950-55; Savannah State Coll, faculty 1955-, asso prof, math physics 1966-71; Savannah State College, Savannah, GA pres l97l-78. **Orgs:** Chmn Natural Sci Div Dir Institutional Self Study 1967-71, pres 1971-78; prof Sch of Sci & Tech; athl dir St Pius X HS Savannah 1955-64; teaching fellowvis instr Boston Coll 1964-66; consult sci math vice pres Bd Pub Educ Savannah & Chatham Co 1971; mem Educ Com US Cath Conf 1971-; mem So Regl Educ Bd 1971; mem Chatham-Savannah Charter Study Com; United Way Bd of Dir; TACTICS Nat Policy Bd; St Jude Guild; adv bd March of Dimes; adv com Nat Assessment of Educ Progress; Am Assn of State Colls & U's; Nat Assn for Equal Educ Oppty; Nat Sci Found Panel; mem exec com So Regl Educ Bd 1973-74; Am Assn Univ Profs; NEA; GA Tchrs Educ Assn; Nat Sci Tchrs Assn; Nat Counc Tchrs Math; Am Educ Rsrch Assn; Nat Counc on Measurement in Edn; Nat Inst Sci Bd mgrs W Broad St YMCASavannah 1962; v chmn St PiX Educ Counc Savannah 1967-; mem NAACP Savannah 1968-; adv Comm Devel Corp1969; bd dirs GA Heart Assn; Goodwill Inds; ARC; BSA; trustee GA Econ Counc. **Honors/Awds:** Recip outst ldrshp serv award Savannah State Coll Nat Alumni Assn 1967; liberty bell award Savannah Bar Assn 1973; Benedictine Medal of Excellence 1974; man of yr Alpha Phi Alpha 1960 & 67; outst educator award Nat Black Pub Assn 1975; S Region Man of Yr the Frogs Inc 1967. **Military Serv:** USNR 1942-46.

JACKSON, RANDOLPH
Justice. **Personal:** Born Oct 10, 1943, Brooklyn, NY; son of Rathenia McCollum Jackson and James Titler; children: two. **Educ:** NY U, BA 1965; Brooklyn Law Sch, JD 1969. **Career:** Mudge Rose Guthrie & Alexander, asso atty 1969-70; Private Practice of Law, 1971-81; New York City Family Court, hearing examiner 1981; Civil Court, Housing Part, judge 1981-87; Civil Court, judge 1987-88; Supreme Court Brooklyn NY, justice 1988-. **Orgs:** Life mem Nat Bar Assn 1971-; mem Brooklyn Bar Assn 1971-; mem Crown Hgts Lions Club 1980-; Sigma Pi Phi. **Honors/Awds:** Book, "How to Get a Fair Trial By Jury" 1978. **Business Addr:** Justice, Supreme Court, Kings County, 360 Adams St, Brooklyn, NY 11201, (718)643-2116.

JACKSON, RAYMOND DEWAYNE
Professional football player. **Personal:** Born Feb 17, 1973, Denver, CO. **Educ:** Colorado State. **Career:** Buffalo Bills, defensive back, 1996-. **Business Addr:** Professional Football Player, Buffalo Bills, One Bills Dr, Orchard Park, NY 14127, (716)648-1800.

JACKSON, RAYMOND T.
Educator. **Personal:** Born Dec 11, 1933, Providence, RI; son of Beulah B Jackson and Raymond T Jackson; married Inez Austin; children: Andrea C. **Educ:** New England Conservatory of Music, BMus (summa cum laude) 1955; Am Conservatory of Music Fontainebleau, France, Diploma 1960; Juilliard Sch of Music, DMA 1973, MS 1959, BS 1957. **Career:** Univ of RI, asst prof of music 1968-75; Mannes Coll of Music NY, instructor 1970-77; Concordia Coll Bronxville, NY, asst prof of music 1970-77; Howard U, prof of piano, 1977, chmn piano div and applied music studies, 1986-88; chmn Department of Music, 1989-92. **Orgs:** Concert pianist US, Europe, S Am 1951; lecture/recitalist "The Piano Music of Black Composers" Adjudicator Coll & Univ Piano Master Classes 1963; organist/choir dir Congdon St Baptist Ch Providence RI 1948-57; organist/choir dir Trinity Lutheran Ch Tenafly, NJ 1957-60; organist/choir dir Trinity Lutheran Ch Bogota, NJ 1961-72; organist 2nd Ch of Christ Scientist NY 1972-77; organist 1st Ch of Christ Scientist Chevy Chase, MD 1978; substitute organist, The First Church of Christ Scientist, Boston, MA, 1993; piano recording artist Performance Records Black Artist Series 1982; pres Raymond Jackson Music Forum; Baldwin Piano Roster of Disting Performing Artists. **Honors/Awds:** Prizewinner Intl Piano Competition Rio De Janeiro 1965; prizewinner Marguerite Long Intl Piano Compet Paris 1965; prizewinner Jugg Inc NY Town Hall Debut Award 1959; prizewinner Nat Assn of Negro Musicians 1957; fellowship Ford Found 1971-73; fellowship Roothbert Fund 1971-73; fellowship John Hay Whitney Found 1965; fellowship Eliza & George Howard Found 1960, 1963; elected into RI Heritage Hall of Fame 1966; hon mem Chopin Club Providence, RI 1966; George W Chadwick Medal New Eng Conservatory of Music Boston 1955, grad 1st in class (summa cum laude) Black Am Music 2nd Ed (Roach); The Music of Black Am 2nd Ed (Southern); Blacks in Classical Music (Abdul); Black Americana by Richard Long (1986), p.129. **Home Addr:** 1732 Overlook Dr, Silver Spring, MD 20903. **Business Addr:** Professor of Piano, Howard Univ, College of Fine Arts, Washington, DC 20059.

JACKSON, REGGIE MARTINEZ
Sports administrator, professional baseball player (retired). **Personal:** Born May 18, 1946, Wyncote, PA. **Educ:** AZ State Univ. **Career:** Kansas City Athletics, outfielder, 1967; Oakland Athletics, outfielder, 1968-75; Baltimore Orioles, outfielder, 1976; New York Yankees, outfielder, 1977-81; California Angels, outfielder 1982-86; Oakland Athletics, outfielder, 1987, hitting coach, part-time, beginning 1991; New York Yankees, special advisor to general partner, 1993-. **Orgs:** Former natl chmn Amyotrophic Lateral Sclerosis; Mr October Foundation for Kids, pres. **Honors/Awds:** AL MVP 1973; led AL in RBI's & HR's in 1973 AL 1971-74; set major league World Series record for consecutive HR's in a game 1977; holds Amer League record for consecutive seasons of 100 or more strikeouts (12 seasons); hit a homer in each of 12 Amer League parks 1975; 10 game World Series hitting streak; 9 Series home runs; 19th player ever to hit 20 or more homers 11 straight seasons; led Amer League in homers since 1974; Hon Big Brother of the Yr Big Brothers & Sisters Prog 1984; American League All-Star Team, 1971-75, 1977, 1978, 1980-82, 1986; Baseball Hall of Fame, 1992. **Business Addr:** Director of New Business Development, Viking Components, 30200 Avenida de las Banderas, Rancho Santa Margarita, CA 92688.

JACKSON, REGINALD LEO
Educator (retired), business executive. **Personal:** Born Jan 10, 1945, Springfield, MA. **Educ:** Yale Univ School of Art & Architecture, BFA, MFA 1970; SUNY Stony Brook, MSW 1977; Union Institute Cincinnati OH, PhD Commun, Visual Anthrop 1979. **Career:** Yale Univ School of Art and Architecture, instr 1970; Quinnipiac Coll, asst prof, filmmaking 1972; Biomedical Comm, asst media prod, dir 1972-74; Simmons College, tenured prof photocommun, prof commun 1974-95; founder/pres, Olaleye Communications, Inc, 1986-; The Photography Collective of Community Change, coord, 1995-97. **Orgs:** Consult NY State HEOP Higher Ed Oppty Prog 1975; mem Poetry Lives Series McDougal Littel & Co 1976, African Herit Inst Simmons Review Photo/Essay-Ghana Simmons Coll 1976; co-chmn of legis Comm METCO-MA Council for Ed Oppty 1977-; consult English HS 1977-; consult Charles E Mackey Middle School Photo 1979-; mem Natl Conf of Artists; Community Change Inc, president, 1992-93; FATE, 1989; Heightened Black Awareness, founding member, 1973; Massachusetts Association. **Honors/Awds:** Rsch Grants Simmons Coll 1975, 1977, 1980; Artist in Residence AAMARP Northeastern Univ Boston 1978-; MA Arts & Humanities Grant 1979; James D Parks Spec Awd Natl Conf of Artists 1979; Comm Fellowship MIT 1980; Fellowship Ford Found 1980-81; Ford Found Post Doctorate Fellowship MIT 1980; Smithsonian Rsch Fellowship Museum of Natural History 1981; John Anson Kitteridge Ed Fund Ella Lymon Cabot Trust 1982. **Business Addr:** President, Olaleye Communications Inc, 71 Windsor St, Boston, MA 02120, (617)445-3303.

JACKSON, RENARD I.
Educational administration. **Personal:** Born May 29, 1946, Chicago, IL; married Katherine Ann Fraizer. **Educ:** Kennedy-King Coll, AA 1970; Northern IL Univ, BS Ed 1973, MS Ed 1977, EdD. **Career:** Abraham Lincoln Center, asst program dir 1968-70; Northern IL Univ, dir upward bound 1973-77; Elgin HS, asst principal 1977-80; IL Youth Center St Charles, dir of ed. **Orgs:** Pres Creative Cons; steering comm Council Mgr Govt; vice chmn Bd of Trustees Elgin Comm Coll; chmn Elgin Planning Commiss; mem Rotay Intl. **Honors/Awds:** Past mem Elgin YMCA Coop Bd 1977-84; MWPM Marquette-Joliet Consistary #104; bd of dir Elgin United Way; active mem IL Assoc for Adv of Black Voc Ed. **Business Addr:** Dir of Education, Illinois Youth Center, PO Box 122, St Charles, IL 60174.

JACKSON, RICARDO
Judge. **Career:** Philadelphia Common Pleas Court, judge, currently. **Business Addr:** Judge, Common Pleas Court, 692 City Hall, Philadelphia, PA 19107, (215)686-7932.

JACKSON, RICHARD E., JR.
City official. **Personal:** Born Jul 18, 1945, Peekskill, NY; married Ruth Sokolinsky; children: Tara, Alice, Abigail, William. **Educ:** Univ of Bridgeport, BA Mathematics 1968. **Career:** Peekskill City Schools, math teacher 1968-; United Way of Westchester, board of directors 1969; Peekskill Field Library, board of directors 1974; Westchester County Republican Comm, county committeeman 1975; Peekskill City Republica; Comm, vice chairman 1976; Peekskill Housing Auth, board member 1982; City of Peekskill, councilman 1979-84, mayor, 1984-91, deputy mayor, beginning 1993; New York State Commissioner of Motor Vehicles, 1995-. **Orgs:** Dir Neighborhood Youth Corps Comm Action Program 1968; education comm NAACP 1981-83; deputy mayor City of Peekskill 1982-84; Westchester County Board of Ethics, 1984; Peekskill Idustrial Development Corporation, chairman, 1985-91; pres, Region I, Amer Assn of Motor Vehicles Administrators, (AAMVA), 1997; chmn, advisory bd, Government Technology Conference, 1997; mem, NY State Auto-Theft & Insurance Fraud Bd, 1997. **Honors/Awds:** National Science Foundation Award. **Business Addr:** New York State Commissioner of Motor Vehicles.

JACKSON, RICHARD H.
Engineering executive. **Personal:** Born Oct 17, 1933, Detroit; married Arlena; children: Deirdre, Gordon, Rhonda. **Educ:** Univ of MO; Univ of Wichita, Walton Sch of Commerce, postgrad 1971. **Career:** Nat Energy Corp IL, vice pres Ops 1975-; Gits Bros Mfg Co Chigo, vice pres engring; Boeing Corp, designed alternate landing gear sys & thrust reverser fail-safe sys for Boeing 747; disigned numerous components for various other air craft & space vehicles; Beech Aircraft, first black engr; Nat Aeronautics & Space Adminstrn Dept of Defense, cons, experiment team for Gemini space flights 5 through 12. **Business Addr:** 1846 S Kilbourn Ave, Chicago, IL 60623.

JACKSON, RICKEY ANDERSON
Professional football player (retired). **Personal:** Born Mar 20, 1958, Pahokee, FL; married Norma; children: Rickeyah. **Educ:** Univ of Pittsburgh, attended. **Career:** New Orleans Saints, linebacker, 1981-89. **Honors/Awds:** Played in Senior Bowl; was Defensive MVP in East-West Shrine Game; ABC Player of the Game vs Penn State, 1980; led NFC linebackers in sacks (12) for two consective seasons; led team in 1981 with eight sacks; played in Pro Bowl, 1983-86 seasons.

JACKSON, ROBERT, JR.
Reporter, columnist. **Personal:** Born Jan 15, 1936, Chicago, IL; son of Lucille Jackson and Robert Jackson; married; children: Dawn, Robert III, Randall. **Educ:** CO State Coll, BA 1957; Northwestern Univ, Columbia Coll, Additional Study. **Career:** Intl News Svc, reporter 1958; Chicago Am Chicago Today, reporter 1958-69; WBEE Radio Chicago, reporter 1964; Chicago Bulletin, editor-writer 1965; Chicago Urban League, writer-producer 1966; CCUO, dir publ info 1969-70; Argonne Natl Lab, dir publ info 1970-73; Provident Hosp & Training School, dir publ rel; Reg Alcoholism Info Prog Natl Council on Alcoholism, field dir 1975-; Rocky Mountain News, reporter. **Orgs:** Chicago Newspaper Reporters Assn 1965; Sigma Delta Chi 1965; mem United Black Journalist 1968; Council for Advancement of Sci Writing 1971; Atomic Industrial Form 1971; publ rel Soc of Amer 1971; bd dir S Shore YMCA 1972; Hosp Publ Rel Soc 1974. **Honors/Awds:** Nom for Assn Press Award 1965; nom for Pulitzer Prize 1963, l988; Urban League of Metropolitan Denver, Community Service Award; The NAACP's Community Service Award; Black Student Alliance at Metro State College, The Malcolm X Award; Coors, Distinguished Citizen Award; United Negro College Fund, Public Service Award; Five Points Business Assn, Award; The Hispanics of Colorado, Distinguished Service Award; The Colorado Assn of Blacks in Journalism, Outstanding Journalist in Print Award, 1993; Awards from the American Legion, The Denver District Attorney's Office, and several Denver area Schools. **Business Addr:** Reporter, Rocky Mountain News, 400 W Colfax Ave, Denver, CO 80204, (303)892-5399.

JACKSON, ROBERT ANDREW
Advertising executive. **Personal:** Born May 16, 1959, Reedville, VA; son of Lucy Jackson and Robert Albert Jackson; married Felicia Lynn Willis Jackson, Sep 1, 1985; children: Robert Andrew II. **Educ:** Florida A&M University, Tallahassee, FL, BS, 1981, MBA, 1983. **Career:** Leo Burnett Advertising, Chicago, IL, 1983-85; Bozell Advertising, Chicago, IL, 1985; Burrell Advertising, Inc, Chicago, IL, vice pres, client service director, 1986-. **Orgs:** Alpha Phi Alpha; FAMU Alumni Assn; Targeted Advertising Professional. **Business Addr:** Vice President, Client Service Director, Burrell Advertising, 20 N Michigan Ave, Ste 300, Chicago, IL 60602.

JACKSON, ROBERT E.
Association executive. **Personal:** Born Feb 10, 1937, Reading, PA; married Carol A Norman; children: Robert E, Jr, Jeannine, Monique, Gregory. **Career:** Food Serv Albright Coll, dir; Schuylkill Valley Restaurant Assn, pres 1974-76. **Orgs:** 2nd vice pres PA Assn Blind; pres Berks Co Assn Blind; bd dirs Camp Conrad Weiser; mem NACUFS. **Military Serv:** AUSR E-5 1955-62.

JACKSON, RONALD G., SR.
Policy analyst. **Personal:** Born Sep 7, 1952, New Orleans, LA; married Brenda J Bellamy; children: Ronald Jr, Tiffany, Joseph. **Educ:** Jackson State Univ, BA 1974; Howard Univ, MSW 1975; Antioch School of Law, JD 1985. **Career:** Sen Thad Cochran, staff asst 1974-77; So MS Legal Svcs, paralegal 1977; MS Gulf Coast Jr Coll, instructor 1978; Harrison Co Head Start Prog, project dir 1978-79; Univ of So MS, asst prof 1979-83; Natl Urban League, policy analyst; US Catholic Conference, policy advisor; Natl Assn of Social Workers, NASW, government relations assoc/lobbyist. **Orgs:** Public relations officer Forrest Co NAACP 1979-84; Omega Psi Phi Inc 1981-; Midtown Montessori School 1985-; St Ann's Infant & Maternity Home board member, 1989-; Covenant House, Washington DC, bd mem; Policy Comm Catholic, bd mem; Charities, Washington DC, bd mem. **Special Achievements:** First African-American staff assistant for Senator Thad Cochran, 1974-77. **Home Addr:** 5100 Barto Ave, Camp Springs, MD 20746. **Business Addr:** Executive Director, DC Catholic Conference, PO Box 29260, Washington, DC 20017, (202)853-5342.

JACKSON, RONALD LEE
Educator. **Personal:** Born Jul 13, 1943, Kansas City, MO; married Hattie Robinson; children: Taj, Yasmira. **Educ:** Harris Jr Coll, AA 1963; Washington U, AB 1965; So ILU, addtl study 1974-76. **Career:** IL State Univ, admissions couns 1969-70; Washington U, asst dir of admissions 1970-73, asst dean 1973-; Higher Educ Coord Counc, adm Com 1970-73; StLouis Com on Africa, 1975-76; US Senator John Danforth, asst. **Orgs:** Contr to founding of Counc on Black Affairs IL State Univ 1969-70; mem Leadership St Louis 1983; bd mem New City School 1984-86; mem Urban League Educ Comm 1984-; chmn United Way Comm Wide Youth Panel 1986-87; bd mem Cardinal Ritter Coll Prep HS 1987-; vice pres Westlake Scholarship Commn. **Honors/Awds:** CORD Fellow 1973; Leadership St Louis 1982-83; Minority Business Advocate Eastern MO 1986. **Military Serv:** AUS 1st lt 1966-69. **Business Addr:** Assistant, US Senator John C Danforth, 815 Olive Room 228, St Louis, MO 63101.

JACKSON, ROY JOSEPH, JR.
Photochemist. **Personal:** Born Feb 8, 1944, Cotton Port, LA. **Educ:** Southern Univ, Baton Rouge, LA, BS, 1965, MS, 1969; Univ of California, San Diego, PhD, chemistry, 1975. **Career:** Dow Chemical Co, research chemist, 1968; Southern Univ, instructor, 1969-70, grad assistant, 1967-69; Univ of California, teaching assistant, 1970-75; Shell Developing Co, research chemist, 1975-. **Orgs:** American Chem Society; Kappa Delta Pi; Alpha Phi Alpha; Black Action Committee. **Honors/Awds:** Numerous contributions to the study of photochemistry. **Military Serv:** AUS capt 1965-67, Bronze Star Medal. **Business Addr:** Senior Research Chemist, Shell Development Co, Westhollow Rsrch Cntr, Hwy 6 S, Houston, TX 77077.

JACKSON, ROY LEE
Professional baseball player (retired). **Personal:** Born May 1, 1954, Opelika, AL; married Mary. **Educ:** Tuskegee Institute, Tuskegee, AL, attended. **Career:** Pitcher: New York Mets, 1977-80, Toronto Blue Jays, 1981-84, San Diego Padres, 1985, Minnesota Twins, 1986. **Honors/Awds:** Voted MVP in baseball Tuskegee Inst 1974 & 1975; named to Appalachian All-Star Team.

JACKSON, RUDOLPH ELLSWORTH
Physician, educator. **Personal:** Born May 31, 1935, Richmond, VA; son of Jennie Jackson and Samuel Jackson; married Janice Diane Ayer; children: Kimberley R, Kelley J, Rudolph E Jr, Alison D Ligon. **Educ:** Morehouse Coll, BS 1957; Meharry Med Coll, MD 1961. **Career:** St Jude Childrens Rsch Hosp, asst mem in hematology 1969-72; Natl Heart Lung & Blood Inst, chief sickle cell disease branch 1972-77; Howard Univ Sch of Medicine, assoc prof dept of pediatrics 1977-79; Meharry Medical Coll, chmn dept of pediatrics 1979-83; Morehouse School of Medicine, act chr dept of pediatrics 1984-90; Association of

Minority Health Professions Schools AIDS Research Consortium, 1989-. **Orgs:** American Medical Assn; Natl Medical Assn; Amer Soc of Hematology, DHHS Secretary's Advisory Comm on lead, sickle cell disease & arthritis; Adv Ctme to Sec DHEW sickle cell disease 1971-72; Natl Advisory Council Natl Inst Arthritis Diabetes Digestive Kidney Diseases NIH DHEW 1979-83; Adv Ctme to Sec DHEW lead poisoning 1984; Pediatric Task Force, Ageny for Health Care Policy Research, 1991-; Advisory Committee on Immunization Practices, Center for Disease Control, DHHS, 1991-; Committee on Community Health Services, America Academy of Pediatrics, 1991-; Pediatric Task Force, Amer Academy of Medicine, 1992-; Assn of Med School Pediatric Dept Chmn Inc, 1980; Sigma Xi Scientific Soc, Howard Univ, 1978-; Alpha Omega Alpha Med Soc, Meharry Med Coll, 1980-. **Military Serv:** USN lt cmdr 5 1/2 yrs. **Home Addr:** 893 Woodmere Dr NW, Atlanta, GA 30318. **Business Addr:** Professor of Pediatrics, Morehouse School of Medicine, 720 Westview Dr SW, Atlanta, GA 30310.

JACKSON, RUSSELL A.
Educator. **Personal:** Born Feb 26, 1934, Philadelphia; married Elois; children: Cheryll Renne, Charles Russell. **Educ:** Cheyney State Coll, BA 1956; Temple U, MA 1962; Temple U, EdD 1970. **Career:** Philadelphia Schs, tchr prin; Chester PA, asst supt; E Orange NJ, supt 1968-72; Roosevelt Sch Dist #66, presently supt schs. **Orgs:** Mem Am Assn Sch Administr; Ariz Sch Admin Inc; Phi Delta Kappa Frat; pres Nat Alliance Black Sch Educ 1970-72; pres Greater Phoenix Supr Assn 1974-75; exec com Ariz Found for Blind. **Military Serv:** USN 1958.

JACKSON, RUSTY
Brewing company executive. **Personal:** Born Jan 25, Greenville, SC; daughter of Georgia Jackson and James Russell Jackson. **Career:** Trans World Airlines, New York, NY, flight attendant; IBM Corporation, Columbia, SC, marketing support representative; Lanier Business Products, Atlanta, GA, marketing support manager; Lexitron Corporation, Washington, DC, territory manager; Washington Convention Center, Washington, DC, special assistant to the general manager, 1981-84; Coors Brewing Company, Washington, DC, CR regional manager, 1984-. **Orgs:** Board member, National Kidney Foundation, 1988-91; board member, Leukemia Society, 1990-91; board member, DC Chamber of Commerce, 1990-95; board member, Metro Washington YMCA, 1990-92; board member, Washington Women League; board chairman, United Negro College Fund; commissions advisory board, Ladies Professional Golf Assn. **Honors/Awds:** Dollars & Sense African American Business & Professional Women, 1989; DC NAACP Presidents Award, 1985; Public Service Award, National Association of Black Co. Officials, 1988; Distinguished Golf Award, National Negro Golf Association, 1987. **Business Phone:** (301)333-0003.

JACKSON, RUTH MOORE
Library administrator. **Personal:** Born Sep 27, 1938, Potecasi, NC; daughter of Ruth Estelle Futrell Moore and Jesse Thomas Moore Sr; married Roderick Earle Jackson, Aug 14, 1965; children: Eric Roderick. **Educ:** Hampton Institute, Hampton, VA, BS, business, 1960; Atlanta University, Atlanta, GA, MSLS, 1965; Indiana University, Bloomington, IN, PhD, 1976. **Career:** Virginia State Univ, Petersburg, VA, librarian, 1965-69; Indiana Univ, Bloomington, IN, teaching fellow/visiting lecturer; Virginia State Univ, Petersburg, VA, associate professor, 1976-84; Univ of North Florida, Jacksonville, FL, assistant director of libraries, 1984-88; West Virginia University, Morgantown, WV, dean, university libraries, 1988-. **Orgs:** Member, American Library Association, 1976-; member, Association of College and Research Libraries, 1984-; member, West Virginia Library Association, 1991-; member, American Management Association, 1976-84; chair, West Virginia Higher Education Library Resources Advisory Council, 1988-; chair, West Virginia Academic Library Director's Group, 1989-; chair, West Virginia Academic Library Consortium, 1991-; Coalition for Networked Information, 1990-; West Virginia Legislative Committee, 1994-; Addison-Wesley Higher Education, technology board, 1996-. **Honors/Awds:** US Office of Education Fellow, US Office of Education, 1969-71; Competitive Research Award, Indiana Univ, 1973; Southern Fellowship Foundation Fellow, SFF, 1973-74; National Faculty Minorities Research Fellow, 1979-80; Outstanding Alumni Award, Hampton Institute, 1980; Distinguished West Virginian Award, 1992; Non-Italian Woman of the Year, 1992. **Business Addr:** Dean of University Libraries, West Virginia University, Wise Library, PO Box 6069, Morgantown, WV 26506-6069.

JACKSON, SAMUEL L.
Actor. **Personal:** Born 1949?, Chattanooga, TN; married LaTanya Richardson; children: Zoe. **Educ:** Morehouse College, dramatic arts. **Career:** Stage productions: A Soldiers Play, 1981; The Piano Lesson, 1987; Sally/Prince, 1989; The District Line, 1990; Two Trains Running, 1990; Home; Fences, Seattle Repertory Theater; Distant Fires, Coast Playhouse, 1993. Films: Together for Days; Ragtime, 1981; Raw, 1987; School Daze, 1988; Sea of Love, 1989; Do the Right Thing, 1989; Mo' Better Blues, 1990; Def by Temptation, 1990; Goodfellas, 1991; Jungle Fever, 1991; Jumpin' at the Boneyard, 1992; White Sands, 1992; Patriot Games, 1992; True Romance, 1993; Menace II Society, 1993; National Lampoon's Loaded Weapon I, 1993; Amos & Andrew, 1993; Jurassic Park, 1993; Against the Wall, 1994; Assault at West Point, 1994; The Court Martial of Johnson Whittaker, 1994; Fresh, 1994; Pulp Fiction, 1994; Kiss of Death, 1995; Die Hard With A Vengeance, 1995; A Time to Kill, 1996; The Long Kiss Goodnight, 1997; Eve's Bayou, 1997; 187, 1997; Jackie Brown, 1998; The Negotiator, 1998. **Orgs:** Just Us Theater Co, cofounder; Negro Ensemble Co. **Honors/Awds:** Cannes Film Festival, Best Supporting Actor, Jungle Fever, 1991; New York Film Critics Award for Jungle Fever, 1991; nominated for Academy Award, Best Supporting Actor, Pulp Fiction, 1995. **Business Addr:** Actor, c/o Intl Creative Mgmt, 8942 Wilshire Blvd, Beverly Hills, CA 90211.

JACKSON, SAMUEL S., JR.
Educator. **Personal:** Born Nov 8, 1934, Natchez, MS; married Margaret Atkins; children: Sharon, Orlando, Sheila, Samuel, III. **Educ:** Alcorn State University, BS, agricultural education and general science; An tioch College, MS, education administration. **Career:** Lincoln Attendance Center, high school teacher, school principal, 1957-66, 1967-68; Wilberforce University, associate director of cooperative education, 1 968-70, dean of students, 1970-78; Central State University, associate dean of students, 1978-83, vice pres for student affairs, 1983-96, special asst to the pres, 1995-96. **Orgs:** Phi Delta Kappa; American Personal Guidance Assn; National Assn of Student Personnel Administrators; American College Union Assn; National College Housing Assn; Admission and Financial State and National Organization; Ohio Student Pe rsonnel Association; Omega Psi Phi Fraternity; NAACP. **Honors/Awds:** National Science Foundation Scholarship, 1966-67; Wilberforce University, S GA Awards, 1980-85; Omega Psi Phi Fraternity, Man of the Year; Alcorn State Uni versity, Hall of Honors, 1995. **Military Serv:** AUS spl serv 1955-57. **Business Addr:** Wilberforce Univ, Wilberforce, OH 45384.

JACKSON, SANDRA STEVENS
Government official. **Personal:** married Jesse Jackson, Jr. **Career:** US Information Agency, Public Diplomacy program, sr coordinator, currently. **Business Addr:** Senior Coordinator, US Information Agency, Public Diplomacy Program, 301 Fourth St, SW, Washington, DC 20547, (202)619-6340.

JACKSON, SEATON J.
Medical doctor. **Personal:** Born Jun 13, 1914, Terrell, TX; married Kathryn Williams; children: Elaine J. **Educ:** Bishop Coll, BS 1936; Meharry Med Coll, MD 1941. **Career:** Provident Hosp Chicago, intern; Homer Phillips Hosp St Louis, residency; Army Med Field Serv Sch Carlyle PA; Jackson Clnic Hosp, owner & staff mem. **Orgs:** Mem NMA; AMA; staff mem Terrell Comm Hosp; mem Renassance Civic Club; Kappa Alpha Psi Frat. **Honors/Awds:** Serv award 1967; Bishop Coll Cit Award 1966; Beauticians Sor Chap Award 1968; 22 Marechal Niel Club Comm Serv Award 1971; Comm Award 1976. **Military Serv:** Medical Corp ret maj. **Business Addr:** Jackson Clinic Hospital, 612 S Rockwell, Terrell, TX.

JACKSON, SHIRLEY ANN
Government official. **Personal:** Born Aug 5, 1946, Washington, DC. **Educ:** Massachusetts Institute of Technology, SB, 1968, PhD, physics, 1973. **Career:** Fermi National Accelerator Laboratory, resident associate theoretical physicist, 1973-76; European Organization for Nuclear Research, visiting science associate, 1974-75; Bell Telephone Laboratories, technological staff, 1976-92; Rutgers Univ, prof of physics, currently; Nuclear Regulatory Commission, chair, 1995-. **Orgs:** American Physicists Society; AAAS; New York Academy of Science; Sigma Xi; National Institute of Science; Committee for Educating & Employing Women Scientists & Engineers; MIT Corp, board of trustees, 1975-85; Lincoln University, 1980-; National Academy of Science, 1981-82. **Honors/Awds:** Ford Foundation, Advanced Study Fellowship, 1971-73, Grant, 1974-75; Martin Marietta Corp, Fellowship, 1972-73; First African American female to receive PhD from MIT, and the first in the nation to get a doctoral degree in physics. **Business Addr:** Chair, Nuclear Regulatory Commission, 11555 Rockville Pike, Rockville, MD 20852.

JACKSON, STANLEY LEON
Professional basketball player. **Personal:** Born Oct 10, 1970, Tuskegee, AL. **Educ:** Univ of Alabama, Birmingham. **Career:** Minnesota Timberwolves, 1993-. **Business Addr:** Professional Basketball Player, Minnesota Timberwolves, 600 First Ave. N., Minneapolis, MN 55403, (612)337-3865.

JACKSON, STEVEN WAYNE
Professional football player. **Personal:** Born Apr 8, 1969, Houston, TX. **Educ:** Purdue Univ, attended. **Career:** Houston Oilers, defensive back, 1991-96; Tennessee Oilers, 1997-. **Business Addr:** Professional Football Player, Tennessee Oilers, c/o Baptist Sports Park, 7640 H 70-5, Nashville, TN 37221.

JACKSON, STUART WAYNE (STU)
Sports administrator, head coach. **Personal:** Born Dec 11, 1955, Reading, PA; son of Pauline Virginia Artist Jackson and Harold Russell Jackson; married Dr. Janet Elizabeth Taylor Jackson; children: Lauren, Taylor, Erin, Yanna. **Educ:** Univ of Oregon, Eugene, OR, 1973-76; Seattle Univ, Seattle, WA, BA, business management, 1978. **Career:** IBM, Los Angeles, CA, Mict Rep DPD, 1978-81; Univ of oregon, Eugene, OR, assistant coach, 1981-83; Washington Stte Univ, Pullman, WA, asist coach, 1983-85; Providence College, Providence, RI, assistnt coach, 1985-87; New York Knicks, New York, NY, assistant coach, 1987-89, head coach, 1989-90; Natl Basketball Assn, NY, dir of basketball operations, beginning 1991; Univ of Wisconsin, head basketball coach, 1993-94; Vancouver Grizzlies, pres & GM, 1994-, head coach, 1997-. **Orgs:** Natl Assn Basketball Coaches, 1981-87; National Basketball Assn Coaches, 1987-90. **Honors/Awds:** Father of Year, National Father of Year Committee, 1990. **Business Addr:** President/General Manager, Vancouver Grizzlies, 800 Griffiths Way, Vancouver, BC, Canada V6B 6G1, (604)899-7511.

JACKSON, SUZANNE FITZALLEN
Artist. **Personal:** Born Jan 30, 1944, St Louis, MO; daughter of Roy Derrick and Ann Marie (Butler) Jackson; divorced; children: Rafiki C D Smith-Mhunzi. **Educ:** SF State Univ, BFA, 1966; Otis Art Inst, studied with Charles White and Noel Quinn, 1968; Yale Univ, School of Drama, MFAD, 1990. **Career:** Painter, poet, 1960-; Freelance scenic and costume designer, 1986-94; St Mary's College of Maryland, scenographer, asst prof, 1994-96; Savannah College of Art & Design, professor of painting, 1996-. **Orgs:** Cave Canem African American Poets, 1996-; United Scenic Artists, Local 829, 1990-; Costume Society of America, 1990-. **Honors/Awds:** Intl Latham Foundation for a Humane Society and Kindness to animals, Scholarships, 1961; Grand Prize, Eyes and Ears Foundation, Intl Year of the Child Billboard Competition; Nomination for the First Natl Award in the Visual Arts, 1981; Idyllwild School of Music and the Arts, associates Fellowships for Etching/Bookmarking and Dance, 1982-84; Natl Museum of Women in the Arts, charter artists, registry, 1987; several others. **Special Achievements:** Numerous solo and group museum exhibitions, 1960-; numerous others. **Home Phone:** (912)233-8177. **Business Addr:** Professor of Painting, Savannah College of Art and Design, PO Box 3146, Savannah, GA 31402, (912)238-2487.

JACKSON, TAMMY
Professional basketball player. **Personal:** Born Dec 3, 1962. **Educ:** Florida, bachelor's degree in recreation. **Career:** Houston Comets, forward-center, 1997; Washington Mystics, 1998-. **Honors/Awds:** US Olympic Basketball Team, Bronze Medal, 1992. **Business Addr:** Professional Basketball Player, Washington Mystics, MCI Center, 601 F St NW, Washington, DC 20071, (301)622-3865.

JACKSON, THELMA CONLEY
Educator. **Personal:** Born Oct 2, 1934, Huntsville, AL; daughter of Jonas Conley and Alberta Conley; divorced; children: Kathleen Ann, Keith Elliott. **Educ:** Spalding Coll, BS Nursing 1956; Spalding Univ, MA 1972; Spalding Univ, MSN, 1989. **Career:** St Joseph Infirmary, staff nurse 1956-58; Evangelical & Reformed Deaconess Hosp, staff nurse & head nurse/instructor 1958-65; St Joseph Infirmary Sch of Nursing, instructor 1965-67; Sts Mary and Elizabeth Sch of Nursing, instructor 1967-69; Spalding Coll, asst instructor 1969-72; Jefferson Comm Coll, prof 1972-. **Orgs:** Mem Alpha Kappa Alpha Sor 1972-79, Amer Nurses Assoc 1972-, KY Nurses Assoc; volunteer spkr Amer Cancer Soc 1972-; member, Kentucky Black Nurses Association 1986-. **Business Addr:** Professor of Nursing, Jefferson Comm Coll/Dwntn Cmps, 109 East Broadway, Louisville, KY 40202.

JACKSON, TIA
Professional basketball player. **Personal:** Born Apr 21, 1972. **Educ:** Univ of Iowa, BA in media studies and film, 1995. **Career:** Phoenix Mercury, guard-forward, 1997-. **Business Addr:** Professional Basketball Player, Phoenix Mercury, 201 E Jefferson St, Phoenix, AZ 85004, (602)252-9622.

JACKSON, TOM
Professional athlete. **Personal:** Born Apr 4, 1951, Cleveland, OH. **Educ:** Louisville U, Bus. **Career:** Denver Broncos, linebacker 1973-86. **Honors/Awds:** Named by teammates as Broncos' most inspirational player for 3 seasons 1983; 3 appearances in Pro Bowl 1977, 1978 & 1979; All-Pro 2 times 1977, 1978; named Denver's defensive most valuable player in 1974, 1976 & 1977; MO Vlly Conf Player of the Yr 1970, 1972; Am Bowl; Blue-Gray Game. **Business Addr:** Broadcaster, ESPN Inc, 935 Middle St, ESPN Plaza, Bristol, CT 06010-7454.

JACKSON, TOMI L.
Association executive. **Personal:** Born Nov 28, 1923, Dallas, TX; daughter of Ida Stephens and Thomas Stephens; children: Joanne Ragan, Linda Marlane Craft. **Educ:** Wayne State U, BA 1940. **Career:** Channel 2 (TV), 1950; Channel 7 (TV), 1965; Det Water & Sewerage Dept, 1979; Tomi Jackson & Assoc, public rel. **Orgs:** Area VP Amer Women in Radio & TV; bd

mem Women's Advertising Club of Detroit; bd mem United Foundation; mem, Travelers Aid Society. **Honors/Awds:** Demmy Award United Found 1981. **Business Addr:** Public Relations, Tomi Jackson & Assoc, 17300 Pontchartrain Dr, Detroit, MI 48203.

JACKSON, TOMMY L.
Law enforcement. **Personal:** Born Apr 19, 1914, Livingston, AL; married Fonnie Mae Bolden; children: Shirley. **Career:** Sumter County Corlation, constable. **Orgs:** AL Democratic Conference 1985. **Home Addr:** Route 1 Box 60-A, Livingston, AL 35470.

JACKSON, TYOKA
Professional football player. **Personal:** Born Nov 22, 1971. **Educ:** Penn State, attended. **Career:** Miami Dolphins, defensive end, 1994; Tampa Bay Buccaneers, 1995-. **Business Addr:** Professional Football Player, Tampa Bay Buccaneers, One Buccaneer Place, Tampa, FL 33607, (813)870-2700.

JACKSON, VERA RUTH
Educator, photographer. **Personal:** Born Jul 21, 1912, Wichita, KS; daughter of Della Johnson Ruth and Otis Garland Ruth; married Vernon Danforth Jackson, Aug 12, 1931 (deceased); children: Kerry Otis (deceased), Kendall Roger. **Educ:** Univ of CA-Los Angeles, BA 1952, MA 1954; graduate courses, USC, UC-Irvine, UC-Riverside, UCLA in Educ and Art; doctoral candidate, USC, 1956. **Career:** CA Eagle (newspaper), staff photog, 1945-50; Los Angeles Unified School District, Los Angeles, CA, elementary school teacher, 1951-76, inservice demonstration, training and reading and resource teacher, 1970-76; Freelance, magazine articles; exhibits sculptor and photog, UCLA Gallery, Museum Science & Industry, Riverside Art Museum, Black Gallery Los Angeles, Public TV Channel 56 and Cable KDOC, LA Cinque Gallery New York and others 1948-87; Historical Enterprises, co-editor, educator, photographer, 1980-. **Orgs:** Publicist Urban League Guild; overview Black Women Artists as Social Critics, Black Gallery Faces of Africa; mem, press representative, LA County Art Museum, Riverside Art Museum; exhib in Farnsworth Gallery; mem Urban League, NAACP, Poverty Law, CA Retired Teachers Assoc; mem Women in Photography, Friends of Photography, Pacific Coast Writers Group, Municipal Art Gallery; mem CA Museum of Afro-Amer Art & Culture in LA, Black Women's Forum. **Honors/Awds:** Photographs ''A Portrait in Black'' Dorothy Dandridge by Earle Mills published by Holloway House 1970; articles published in art, photographic magazines and newspapers; one of the pioneer photographers in Jeanne Moutoussay-Ashe's book ''Viewfinders, Black Women Photographers,'' 1986; twenty letters to LA Times on subject of combatting racism; contributor to museums, galleries, magazines, including CA Afro-American Museum, Black Angelenos, Travel and Art magazine, and Design magazine. **Business Addr:** Educator/Photographer, Historical Enterprises Photo Images of '40s, 1004 Railroad St, Corona, CA 91720.

JACKSON, W. SHERMAN
Educator. **Personal:** Born May 21, 1939, Crowley, LA; married Frances P McIntyre; children: Sherlyn, Sherrese, W Sherman II. **Educ:** So Univ, AB 1962; NC Central Univ, MA 1962-63; OH State Univ, PhD 1969. **Career:** Alcorn Coll Lorman MS, instr 1963-64; Central State Univ, instr 1966-68; Univ of Lagos Nigeria, sr fulbright lecturer 1972-73; Amer Constitutionalism Miami Univ, prof 1969-. **Orgs:** History ed NIP Mag 1969-71; assoc ed NIP Mag 1971-75; ed consult Pentagon Ed Testing Svc; pres, founder Assoc for Acad Advancement 1969-; pres OxfordNAACP 1979-; consult NEH. **Business Addr:** Associate Professor, Amer Constitutionalism, Miami Univ, 241 Irvin, Oxford, OH 45056.

JACKSON, WALTER K.
Clergyman. **Personal:** Born Mar 28, 1914, Boley, OK; son of Adelaide and Eddie; married Eula Lee Wilhite; children: Waltine. **Educ:** Bishop Coll, AB 1937; OK Sch of Rel, BTh 1947; Morris Booker Mem Coll, DD 1955; OK Sch of Rel, DD 1964; Union Theol Sem, 1960-66. **Career:** St John Mission Bapt Ch, minister 44 yrs. **Orgs:** Mem bd of trust Bishop Coll Dallas, TX; mem bd dir Med Cent State Bank; Gov Com on Rehab of State of OK; Coalition of Civic Ldrshp of OK City; bd dir Progressive Bapt Nat Conv; bd dir OK Mission Bapt State Conv. **Honors/Awds:** Viola P Cutler Award Urban Leag of OK Cty OK 1970; Dr of Humane Letters, Virginia Seminary, Lynchburg, VA. **Business Addr:** 5700 N Kelley, Oklahoma City, OK 73111.

JACKSON, WARREN GARRISON
Company executive. **Personal:** Born in Yonkers, NY; son of Ethel R. Garrison Jackson and Charles R. Jackson; married Christena V, Sep 7, 1952; children: Tenley Ann, W Garrison, Terrance V. **Educ:** Manhattan College, Riverdale, NY, BS, 1952. **Career:** The New York Times, New York, NY, circulation manager; New York Amsterdam News, New York, NY, circulation director; Circulation Experti, Hartsdale, NY, president and CEO, currently. **Orgs:** Vice chairperson, Jackie Robinson Foundation, 1989-; trustee, White Plains Hospital, 1990-; trustee, Jackie Joyner Kersee Foundation, 1989-. **Honors/Awds:** Business Award, New York Chapter, LINKS, 1991; Outstanding Achievement, Omega Phi Si, 1988; OIC Achievement, OIC of America, New England Region, 1986. **Business Addr:** President and CEO, Circulation Experti Ltd, 280 N Central Ave Suite 210, Hartsdale, NY 10530.

JACKSON, WAVERLY
Professional football player. **Personal:** Born Dec 19, 1972. **Educ:** Virginia Tech. **Career:** Carolina Panthers, defensive tackle, 1997-. **Business Addr:** Professional Football Player, Carolina Panthers, 800 Mint St, Ericsson Stadium, Charlotte, NC 28202, (704)358-7000.

JACKSON, WILEY, JR.
Cleric. **Personal:** Born Jan 16, 1953, Atlanta, GA; son of Mr and Mrs Wiley Jackson Sr; married Mary Ann, Mar 20, 1993; children: Wiley Jackson III. **Educ:** South Georgia Coll; Dekalb Central Coll, AD; Beulah Heights Bible Coll, BA. **Career:** Frito-Lay, Inc, 1971-81; Gospel Tabernacle, pastor/founder, 1982-. **Orgs:** National Religious Broadcasters; Churches Uniting In Global Mission; Fellowship of Inner City Word of Faith Churches; Pentecostal Fellowship of North America; Morehouse Coll, board of preachers. **Honors/Awds:** Upscale Magazine, Top 50 Ministers. **Business Addr:** CEO, Gospel Tabernacle, 277 Clifton Street, Atlanta, GA 30316, (404)370-3800.

JACKSON, WILLIAM ALVIN (W. ALVIN)
Automotive company executive. **Personal:** Born Sep 20, 1950, Chicago, IL; son of Elnora & James Jackson; married Rita F Jackson, Jul 13, 1991; children: Richard A, Alyssa B, Danielle L. **Educ:** Loyola Univ, BSBA, 1975. **Career:** L-M Division of Ford Motor Company, zone mgr, 1975-79; Volkswagen of America, Inc, district sales mgr, 1979-82, advertising productions superior, 1982-84; shows & exhibits mgr, 1984-87; Jones Transfer Co, vp, sales & marketing, 1987-89; Chrysler International Corp, merchandising mgr, 1989-93, France & Spain, regional sales & mktg mgr, 1993-96, international fleet sales manager, 1996-. **Orgs:** Detroit Big Brother Program, mentor, 1990-93; Tia Nedd Organ Donor Foundation, board of directors, mem. **Honors/Awds:** Alpha Phi Alpha, Ambassador's Award, 1966; US Department of Commerce, Export Assistance Ctr, Cert of Recognition. **Special Achievements:** Proficient in French. **Home Addr:** 3283 Springbrook Ct, West Bloomfield, MI 48324-3252.

JACKSON, WILLIAM E.
Educator. **Personal:** Born Dec 1, 1936, Creedmoor, NC; married Janet. **Educ:** NC Central U, BA 1958; NY U, MA 1961; Univ PA, PhD 1972. **Career:** Yale Univ, asst prof German; Univ PA, instructor 1967-70; City Coll NY, 1961-64. **Orgs:** Mem Am Assn Tchrs German; NC Central Alumni. **Honors/Awds:** Scholarship Marburg, Germany 1958-59; publs in ''Neophilologus'' ''Colloquia Germanica'' & ''Germanica Studies in Honor of Otto Springer''; pub book ''Reinmar's Women'' Amsterdambenjamins 1980. **Business Addr:** Yale University, Dept of Germnic Languages, New Haven, CT 06520.

JACKSON, WILLIAM ED
Beverage company executive (retired), trucking company executive. **Personal:** Born Aug 6, 1932, Mason, TN; son of Mabel E Harris Jackson and Willie B Jackson; married Toria Catherine Hubbard Jackson, Oct 30, 1951; children: William E Jr, Michael A, Michelle D. **Educ:** Wilson Junior College, Chicago, IL, 1950-51, 1958-59; Univ of Illinois, Chicago, Chicago, IL, CBA, certificate, 1989-90. **Career:** Illinois State Police, Crestwood, IL, trooper, 1957-63; IBEW Local #1031, Chicago, IL, business agent, 1963-66; Schieffelin & Somerset Co, Chicago, IL, various position, 1968-94, vp, sr vp, central region mgr, 1981-94; WEJAC Inc Trucking, pres, currently. **Orgs:** Member, St Xavier College, Chicago, International Bus Advisory Council, 1989-91; mem, Link Unlimited, Chicago, 1987-; mem, North Carolina Central Univ Bd of Visitors, 1986-; chairman, Sky Ranch Foundation, Chicago Branch, 1981; Natl Assn of Sickle Cell Disease; QBG Foundation; IL Racing Bd Comm, appointed, 1995-. **Honors/Awds:** Black Achievers of Industry Award, New York City YMCA, 1973; Sky Ranch Foundation Man of Year, New York City, 1981; Inner City Liquor Assn Industry Award, 1982; Blackbook National Business & Professional Award, New York City, 1982; Clark College Alumni Assn, Outstanding Citizen Award, 1990. **Military Serv:** Army, Sgt, 1952-54; Soldier of Year, 1953.

JACKSON, WILLIE BERNARD, JR.
Professional football player. **Personal:** Born Aug 16, 1971, Gainesville, FL; children: Sir. **Educ:** Univ of Florida, bachelor's degree in telecommunications, 1993. **Career:** Jacksonville Jaguars, wide receiver, 1995-. **Business Addr:** Professional Football Player, Jacksonville Jaguars, One Stadium Place, Jacksonville, FL 32202, (904)633-6000.

JACKSON, WILLIS RANDELL, II
Educator, athletic director, coach. **Personal:** Born Sep 11, 1945, Memphis, TN; son of Louise Hallbert Johnson and Willis Randell Jackson; married Patricia F Crisp Jackson, Jan 21, 1991; children: Ericka, Hasani, Jamila. **Educ:** Rochester Jr Coll, certificate 1965; ND State Univ, BS 1967; SIU Edwardsville, MS & Admin Cert 1980. **Career:** Rochester Lourdes HS, head wrestling coach 1967-68; Soldan HS, head wrestling coach 1969-71; Lincoln Sr HS, head wrestling coach, 1971-74, athletic director, 1973-74; E St Louis Sr HS, head wrestling coach, 1974-84, athletic director, 1974-1981; Hughes Quinn Jr HS, teacher, head girls track coach, 1985-89; Hughes Quinn Rock Jr HS, teacher, currently, head girls track coach, 1989-91; Dr Jack's Sports Ltd, CEO, currently. **Orgs:** Mem IL Wrestling Coaches & Officials Assoc 1974-, NWCOA Wrestling Coaches & Officials Assoc 1974-, Natl Basketball Coaches Assoc 1985-, Natl Athletic Directors Assoc 1974-; pres, Grandmaster Athletic Assn; Southern Cross #112 Prince Hall Mason 1975-. **Honors/Awds:** IL State Athletic Dir of the Year Dist 15 1977,78; Coach of Year Wrestling East St Louis Journal 1975, ICBAA 1981. **Business Addr:** Teacher, Hughes Quinn Rock Jr High School, 9th & Ohio Ave, East St Louis, IL 62201.

JACKSON, WILMA LITTLEJOHN. **See DEMILLE, DARCY.**

JACKSON, YVONNE RUTH
Human resources executive. **Personal:** Born Jun 30, 1949, Los Angeles, CA; daughter of Giles B Jackson & Gwendolyn Battle; married Frederick Jackson Jr, Mar 24, 1989; children: Cortney, Douglass. **Educ:** Spelman College, BA, 1970; Harvard University School of Business, PMD, 1985. **Career:** Sears Roebuck & Co, assistant department manager/department manager, 1970-71, assistant buyer/assistant retail sales manager, 1972-77, personnel manager, 1977-79; Avon Products, Inc, executive recruiter emp relations manager/director of hr, 1979-85, director manufacturing, redeployment/ director hr international, 1985-87, vice pres international/vice pres human resources, 1987-93; Burger King Corp, senior vp worldwide human resources, 1993-. **Orgs:** Spelman College, board of trustees, 1996-; Spelman Corporate Women's Roundtable, chair, 1994-; Women's Foodservice Forum, board member, 1995; Catalyst, advisory board member, 1993-; Inroads of South Florida, board member, 1996-. **Honors/Awds:** YMCA, Black Achiever, 1986; YMCA of Greater NY, Y's Woman Achiever, 1992; Spelman College Alumnae Association, Business Achievement Awd, 1993. **Business Addr:** Senior VP, Human Resources, Burger King Corp., 17777 Old Cutler Rd, 5-S, Miami, FL 33157, (305)378-3111.

JACKSON-FOY, LUCY MAYE
Educator (retired). **Personal:** Born Sep 28, 1919, Texas; daughter of Louise Jackson and L J Jackson; married Joseph Daniel Foy, Dec 11, 1954. **Educ:** Attended, A&T Coll, OH State, Prairie View Coll, TX Woman's Univ; N TX State Coll, MS; Further study, KS State Tchrs Coll; KS Univ; KS Central MO State Univ, Univ MO. **Career:** Veteran Admin, employed 1946-50; A&T Coll, 1950-54; Hamilton Park HS, 1954-62; KC MO Sch Dist, vocational coord 1963-84 (retired). **Orgs:** Mem Natl Rehab Assn; Council for Exceptional Children; MO State Tchrs Assn; Disabled Amer Veterans; Natl Council Tchrs Math; NAACP; Natl Council Negro Women; mem Eta Phi Beta Sor; natl sec Eta Phi Beta 1968-74; sec KC Assn for Mentally Retarded Children past exec bd dirs; past mem Comm for Davis Brickle Report; Special Educ Adv Com; mem Community Serv for Greater KC; co-fndr Shelly Sch for Mentally Retarded; volunteer Adult Basic Education Program; Health Care AARP Bd of Kansas City; pres of Washington-Lincoln H.S. Club l987-88; Women's Chamber of Commerce of Kansas City, MO; St Andrew United Methodist Church. **Honors/Awds:** Outstanding Sec Educ of Amer 1974-75; Certificate from National WLAA l987-88. **Military Serv:** WAC 1942-45; Good Conduct Medal. **Home Addr:** 1414 E 28 St, Kansas City, MO 64109-1214.

JACKSON-GILLISON, HELEN L.
Attorney at law. **Personal:** Born Jul 9, 1944, Colliers, WV; daughter of George W Sr and Helen L Jackson (both deceased); married Edward L Gillison Sr; children: Edward L II. **Educ:** West Liberty State Coll, BS (with honors), 1977; West VA Univ Coll of Law, JD, 1981. **Career:** Helen L Jackson-Gillison Law Offices, attorney at law, 1981-. **Orgs:** WV State Bar; WV Trial Lawyers Assn; Mountain State Bar Assn; Hancock Count y Bar Assn; American Bar Assn; Natl Bar Assn; Amer Trial Lawyers Assn; Weirton Business & professional Women's Club; numerous others. **Honors/Awds:** BALSA, WV Coll of Law, Black Attorney of the Year Award, 1986. **Special Achievements:** First African-American female to began her own private law practice in Weirton, WV; First African-American female to serve on the Audit & Budget Committee and the Unlawful Practice of Law Committee, WV State Bar; First African-American appointed to the WV North Comm Coll Bd of Trustees; numerous other firsts for an African-American; Invited to visit Japan with US Attorney General, Edwin Meese, III, 1988; Invited to visit the People's Republic of China with People to People Legal Deleg, 1987; Invited by the People to People Intl Citizen Ambassador Program to visit the Soviet Union with Women in Law Delegation, 1987. **Business Addr:** Attorney at law, Helen L Jackson-Gillison Law Offices, 3139 West St, Weirton, WV 26062, (304)748-7116.

JACKSON-LEE, SHEILA
Congresswoman. **Personal:** Born Jan 12, 1950. **Educ:** Yale Univ, BA, 1972; Univ of Virginia, JD, 1975. **Career:** Attorney; Houston City Council, 1990-94; US House of Representatives, congresswoman, 1995-. **Business Addr:** Congresswoman, US House of Representatives, 1520 Longworth House Office Bldg, Washington, DC 20515-4318.

JACKSON-RANSOM, BUNNIE (BURNELLA JACKSON RANSOM)
Business executive. **Personal:** Born Nov 16, 1940, Louisburg, NC; daughter of Elizabeth Day Hayes and Burnal James Hayes; divorced; children: Elizabeth Jackson, Brooke Jackson, Maynard Jackson III, Rae Yvonne Ransom. **Educ:** NC Coll, BS 1961; NC Cent U, MS 1969. **Career:** Bennett Coll, inst 1962-63; EOA Inc, dir planning 1965-70; BJT Inc Self-employed, pres 1979-83; GA State Univ, inst 1981-; First Class Inc, pres, CEO 1975-; Georgia State Univ, Atlanta, GA, part-time instructor, 1981-90; Atlanta Artists, Atlanta, GA, manager/vpres, 1983-89. **Orgs:** Mem Public Relations Soc Arenek; mem Natl Assn of Media Women; mem Natl Org of Women; various posts held, Delta Sigma Theta Sorority 1951-85; various posts held, Jack & Jill of Amer 1978-85; bd mem NWGA Girl Scouts 1978; bd mem Atlanta Symp 1975; committee chair, 100 Black Women, 1988-; member, Assn of Black Journalists, 1990-; member, Links, Inc, 1990-; member, board of directors, Atlanta Chapter, NAACP, 1989-; Pres, Natl Coalition of 100 Black Women, Atlanta Chapter; Georgia Human Relations Commission. **Honors/Awds:** Special Award, Bronze Jubilee 1984; Community Relations PR Award, National Media Women, 1990. **Business Addr:** President, First Class, Inc, PO Box 42297, Atlanta, GA 30311, (404)696-9999.

JACKSON ROBINSON, TRACY CAMILLE
Marketing professional. **Personal:** Born Jun 4, 1966, Detroit, MI. **Educ:** University of Michigan, Dearborn, BSE, 1987, Ann Arbor, MBA, 1990. **Career:** 3M Corporation, mfg engineer, 1987-88; Kraft Foods, brand assistant, 1990-91, associate brand mgr, 1991-92, proj mgr, 1993-94, brand mgr, 1994-97; Amtrak, mkgt dir, 1997-. **Orgs:** Alpha Kappa Alpha Sorority, committee member, 1984-; Girl Scouts of America, troup leader, 1991-95; Uhlich Children's Home, board member, 1994-; Natl Black MBA Assn, 1993-. **Business Addr:** Amtrak Marketing Director, 210 S Canal, Ste 526, Chicago, IL 60606.

JACKSON-SIRLS, MARY LOUISE
Educator, cleric. **Personal:** Born Apr 7, 1944, Longview, TX; daughter of Millie Louise Mason Jackson and John Albert Jackson; married Sammie L Sirls, Aug 21, 1971 (died 1973). **Educ:** Texas College, BA in English, 1966; University of Missouri, MA, 1971, Ed Spec, 1980. **Career:** Board of Education, Kansas City, KS, English teacher, 1975-. **Orgs:** Board member, Advisory City Wide Singles Ministry, 1989-; National Education Association; Local Council of English Teachers. **Honors/Awds:** St Peter CME Church, Superior Leadership as Women's Day Chairperson, 1975, Youth Department, Appreciation for Dedicated Services, 1984; Kansas-Missouri Conference Missionary Society, Appreciation of Services Rendered, 1981; Sumner HS Class of '70, Appreciation of Continued Efforts in the Educational Field, 1985; Friends of Yates Branch Inc, Woman of Distinction, 1987; Greater Kansas City Chamber of Commerce, The Kansas City Star Company and The Learning Exchange, The Excellence in Teaching Award, 1987; Kansas City Board of Education, Excellence in Teaching Award, 1987. numerous other letters and certificates of recognition and appreciation. **Special Achievements:** Presenter: "Multicultural Learning in the Classroom," Teacher Inservice Day, 1986; "Jayhawk Writing Project," Teacher Inservice Day, 1985; honoree: Mary Louise Jackson-Sirls Day, City of Kansas City, May 14, 1987; appeared in "Moody Monthly," The Christian Family Magazine, March 1986; worked with the Kansas Governor's Academy at KU, summer of 1996 in Lawrence Kansas. **Home Addr:** 634 N 62nd St, Kansas City, KS 66102.

JACKSON-TEAL, RITA F.
Educator. **Personal:** Born Apr 26, 1949, Memphis, TN; children: Rashel, JanEtte, Teal. **Educ:** TN State Univ, BS 1971; Univ of MI, MA 1973; Ed D Candidate, Memphis ST Univ 1989. **Career:** Argonne Lab Argonne IL, student trainee 1971; Rust Coll Holly Springs MS, math instr, tutor 1973-75; Lincoln Lab Lexington MA, vstg scientist 1974; LeMoyne-Owen Coll Memphis, math instr 1975-78, dir Spec Serv Upward Bound & Learning Resource Ctr. **Orgs:** Coord Dual-Degree Engrg Prog 1977-80; chairperson Greek Letter Comm 1978-80; mem Cult & Ath Comm Rust Coll; mem Freshman Comm, Orientation Comm, Acad Standing Comm, Acad Task Force Cluster for Coop Ed Delta Sigma Theta; mem Delta Sigma Theta, Alpha Kappa Mu, Beta Kappa Chi, Kappa Delta Pi; vice pres TN Assoc of Spec Prog 1983-85; chairperson Delta Sigma Theta Scholarship Comm 1984-85; reg chairperson Southeastern Assoc for Ed Oppty Prog Personnel SAEOPPAnnual Conf 1985; pres TN Assn of Spec Prog 1985-87; chmn SAEOPP Scholarhsip Com 1986-87; chmn SAEOPP Constitution Com 1985-87; secy SAEOPP 1987. **Business Addr:** Dir Spec Services/Upward Bnd, LeMoyne-Owen College, 807 Walker Ave, Memphis, TN 38126.

JACKSON-THOMPSON, MARIE O.
Judge. **Personal:** Born Aug 14, 1947, Pittsburgh, PA; daughter of Nettie Marie Wall and Warren Joseph Oliver; married Henry Quentin Thompson Jr; children: Tony, Vincent, Alphonso, Joshua. **Educ:** Mt Holyoke Coll, BA 1969; Harvard Law Sch, JD 1972. **Career:** Cambridge and Somerville Legal Svcs, general trial work 1972-74; Tufts Univ, vstg lecturer 1973-74; MA Commn Against Discrimination, staff dir 1974-76; Exec Office of Admin & Finance, admin justice 1976-77, general counsel 1977-80; District Court Dept of the Trial Court Cambridge Div, justice 1980-. **Orgs:** Bd & Regional Director Natl Assn of Women Judges 1981-84; mem Natl Council of Juvenile and Family Court Judges 1981-89; bd of dirs Adolescent Consultation Svcs, 1996; Greater Boston Youth Symphony Orchestra 1985-87; Natl Conf of Christians and Jews 1985-87; mem Natl Assoc of Negro and Professional Women Inc, MA Juvenile Justice Adv Comm 1983-84; Alpha Kappa Alpha Sor Psi Omega Chapt; Middlesex Co Dist Attorney's Child Sexual Abuse Task Force 1985-86, Dist Court Standards Comm for Care & Protection and CHINS cases, 1990; mem Governor's Task Force Correction Alternatives 1985-86, Foster Care 1986-87; bd Judge Baker Guidance Center 1987-94. **Honors/Awds:** Outstanding Young Leader Boston Jaycees 1981; Leadership Massachusetts Black Lawyers 1981; "Use and Abuse of Certain Records in Custody Proceedings", Massachusetts Flaschner Judicial Institute 1984; "And They Do Not Live Happily Ever After: A Look at the Real Story of Family Violence", Mt Holyoke Quarterly 1986; Sojourner Truth Award, Natl Assn of Negro Business & Professional Women 1986; Community Justice Awd MA Justice Resource Inst 1985; Achievement Awd Cambridge YWCA 1985; numerous leadership achievement and serv awds; Sesquicentennial Alumnae Award Mt Holyoke Alumnae Assn 1988; Notre Dame College, Honorary PhD. **Business Addr:** Presiding Justice, Woburn Division, 30 Pleasant Street, Woburn, MA 01801.

JACOB, JOHN EDWARD
Company executive. **Personal:** Born Dec 16, 1934, Trout, LA; son of Claudia Sadler Jacob and Emory Jacob; married Barbara May Singleton, Mar 28, 1959; children: Sheryl Rene. **Educ:** Howard Univ, BA 1957, MSW 1963. **Career:** US Post office, parcel post sorting mach oper 1958-60; Baltimore City Dept of Public Welfare, caseworker 1960-63, child welfare casework suprv 1963-65; Washington Urban League, dir ed & youth incentives 1965-66, branch office dir 1966-67, assoc exec dir for admin 1967-68, acting exec dir 1968-70, spec lecturer 1968-69; Howard Univ School of Social Work, spec lecturer 1968-69; Washington Urban League, dir soc work field work student unit 1968-70; Eastern Reg Natl Urban League, dir comm org training 1970-; San Diego Urban League, exec dir 1970-75; Washington Urban League, pres 1975-79; Natl Urban League, exec vice pres 1979-81, pres & CEO, 1982-94; Anheuser-Busch Cos Inc, exec vp, 1994-. **Orgs:** Life mem Kappa Alpha Psi 1954; mem Natl Assoc of Social Workers 1961-; consult Natl Council of Negro Women 1967-69, Natl Urban League 1968-69; Howard Univ chmn bd of trustees 1971-78, chm 1988-; consult Timely Investment Club 1972-75; mem Judicial Nominating Com DC 1976-79; dir Local Initiatives Support Corp 1980-; mem natl Advertisement Review Bd 1980-83; mem adv comm NY Hosp 1980-83; dir A Better Chance 1980-83; dir NY Found 1982-85; corp dir NY Telephone Co 1983-; dir Natl Conf of Christians & Jews 1983-88; mem Rockefeller Univ Council 1983-88; Chairman Emeritus Board of trustees Howard Univ; Anheuser-Busch Companies, corp dir; New York Telephone Co, corp dir, 1983; corp dir Continental Corp 1985-; corp dir Coca Cola Enterprises Inc 1986-; dir Natl Westminster Bancorp 1990-. **Honors/Awds:** Whitney M Young Awd Washington Urban League Inc 1979; Special Citation Atlanta Club Howard Univ Alumni Assoc 1980; Attny Hudson L Lavell Soc Action Awd Phi Beta Sigma 1982; Exemplary Serv Awd Alumni Club of Long Island Howard Univ 1983; Achievement Awd Zeta Phi Beta 1984, Cleveland Alumni Chap Kappa Alpha Psi 1984; Alumni Achievement Awd Alpha Psi Atlanta Club Howard Univ 1984; Natl Kappaman Achievement Durham Alumni Chapter Kappa 1984; Blackbook's Bus & Professional Awd Dollars & Sense Mag 1985; Achievement Awd Peoria Alumni Chap Kappa Alpha Psi 1985; Forrester B Washington Awd Atlanta Univ School of Social Work 1986; Presidential Scroll St Augustine's Coll 1987; recipient of the United Way of America's National Professional Leadership Award 1989. **Military Serv:** US Army Reserve capt 1957-65; Airborne Parachutist Badge 1958. **Home Addr:** 14 Barnaby Ln, Hartsdale, NY 10530. **Business Addr:** Executive Vice President, Anheuser-Busch Cos Inc, 1 Busch Place, St Louis, MO 63118.

JACOB, WILLIS HARVEY
Educator, scientist. **Personal:** Born Jun 4, 1943, Lake Charles, LA; son of Alzetta Guillory Jacob and Willis Jacob. **Educ:** So U, BS 1965; Univ KS, PhD 1971. **Career:** Southern Univ, asst prof 1970-71; Baylor Univ, asst prof 1975-76, assoc prof 1976-77; Acad of Hlth Scis, chief basic sci br 1971-77; Dept of Clinical Investigation Madigan Army Med Ctr, physiologist 1978-83; US Army Medical Rsch and Develop Command, product mgr 1983-85; US Army Medical Matl Develop Activity, physiologist, pharmaceutical systems project mgmt 1985-88; Academy of Health Sciences, chief, anatomy & physiology branch, 1988-. **Orgs:** Mem Am Inst Biol Scis, Assn of Military Surgeons of the US, NY Acad of Sci, Phi Lambda Upsilon, Soc of Sigma Xi, Alpha Phi Alpha Frat, NAACP, Southern Univ Alumni Federation, Univ of KS Alumni Assoc. **Honors/Awds:** NDEA Title IV Fellowship 1970. **Military Serv:** US Army, Lieutenant Colonel, 1971-91; Army Commendation Medal, 1977, 1998, Meritorious Service Medal, 1983, Army Achievement Medal, 1987, National Defense Service Medal, 1971, 1991.

JACOBS, DANIEL WESLEY, SR.
Cleric, educator. **Personal:** Born Aug 26, 1933, Aragon, GA; son of Fannie Lou Cosby Jacobs Pannell (deceased) and Daniel Lott Jacobs (deceased); married Mary Louise Jenkins Jacobs, Jun 4, 1955; children: Daniel Jr, Reginald Eugene, Dana Michelle. **Educ:** Morris Brown College, BA, 1951-55; Turner Theological Seminary, MDiv, 1959-62; Emory University, PhD candidate, 1965-67; Columbia Theological Seminary, 1987-. **Career:** East Atlanta District, AME Church, presiding elder, 1971-72; Allen Temple, AME Church, pastor, 1972-77; St James AME Church, pastor, 1977-80; Steward Chapel AME Church, pastor, 1980-82; St Mark AME Church, pastor, 1982-85; Turner Theological Seminary, dean, 1985-. **Orgs:** President, deans council, Interdenominational Theological Center; president, Columbus Phenix City Ministers Alliance, 1978-80; housing commission chairman, Atlanta NAACP, 1973-77; secretary elect, Christian Counsel of Metropolitan Atlanta, 1977; president, Atlanta AME Ministers Union, 1970. **Honors/Awds:** Doctor of Divinity Degree, Faith College, 1984; Doctor of Divinity Degree, Payne Theological Seminary, 1986; Excellence in Leadership, Columbus Phenix City Ministers Alliance, 1979; Distinguished Alumnus, Turner Theological Seminary, 1986; Excellence in Theological Education, Turner Student Fellowship, 1987. **Home Addr:** 440 Dartmouth Dr SW, Atlanta, GA 30331.

JACOBS, ENNIS LEON, JR.
Attorney. **Personal:** Born Jan 19, 1954, Tampa, FL; son of Vetta and Ennis Sr; married Ruth, Aug 15, 1976; children: Bron, Jasmine. **Educ:** Florida A & M Univ, Magna Cum Laude, BS, technology, 1976; Florida State Univ Coll of Law, JD, 1986. **Career:** Eastman Kodak Co, systems analyst, 1976-80; RCA Corp, systems representatives, 1980-82; Florida Public Service Commission, staff attorney, 1986-89; Florida Attorney General, staff attorney, 1989-91; Florida Senate, staff attorney, 1991-93; Florida Legislative House, staff attorney, 1993-. **Orgs:** Tallahassee Habitat for Humanity, pres of board; National Bar Assn; Amer Bar Assn; Leon County Guardian Ad Litem. **Special Achievements:** Author, "State Regulation of Information Services," Barrister, ABA Young Lawyers Division, Spring 1991. **Home Phone:** (904)421-0119. **Business Phone:** (904)488-1489.

JACOBS, GREGORY ALEXANDER
Attorney, clergyman. **Personal:** Born Mar 10, 1952, Bilwaskarma, Nicaragua; son of Solomon N & Lynette G Jacobs; married Beverly C Jacobs, Sep 30, 1978; children: Charlotte Elizabeth, Stephanie Nicole. **Educ:** Princeton University, AB, 1974; Columbia Univ School of Law, JD, 1977; Bexley Hall Divinity School, MDiv, 1995. **Career:** Thompson, Hine & Flory, partner; St Philip's Episcopal Church, vicar, currently. **Orgs:** United Negro College Fund Foundations, chair, 1991-95; Society Bank, area bd of dirs, 1990-95; Diocese of Ohio, Episcopal, trustee, 1989-94; African-American Archives Auxiliary, bd of dirs, 1990-95; Minority Contractors Assistance Program, bd of dirs, 1985-97; Black Episcopal Seminarians, convenor, 1 yr, 1991-95; Diocesan Council, 1996-99. **Home Addr:** 3330 Elsmere Road, Shaker Heights, OH 44120, (216)991-5176. **Business Phone:** (330)535-7295.

JACOBS, HAZEL A.
Legislative policy analyst. **Personal:** Born Sep 25, 1948, Blakely, GA; daughter of Pearlia Jewell Allen and Leamon Allen; married Claude Jacobs, Jul 24, 1970. **Educ:** GA State Univ, BS, 1982, MPA, 1986. **Career:** City of Atlanta GA, admin asst, 1970-71, 1973-74, office mgr, 1974-78, legislative policy analyst, 1978-; Atlanta Charter Commission, admin asst, 1971-73. **Orgs:** Amer Assn of Public Admin, 1984-; Natl Assn of Professional Women, 1985-; Natl Forum for Black Public Admin, 1985-.

JACOBS, LARRY BEN
Chemical engineer. **Personal:** Born Dec 15, 1959, Arlington, GA; son of Mattie C Jackson Jacobs and Tommy L Jacobs; married Carolyn Laverne Malone, Nov 24, 1984; children: Matthew, Leah, Christopher. **Educ:** Tuskegee Inst, Certificate 1980, BSChE 1984. **Career:** International Paper Co, co-op engr 1980; Procter & Gamble, co-op engr 1982; Weyerhaeuser Co, professional intern 1984-86; Hercules Inc, process engr 1986-88; General Electric Co Burkville AL production engineer 1988-91; Hoechst Celanese Corp, Salisbury, NC, development engineer, 1991-; Charlotte, NC, business reengineer, 1992-96, activity base cost coord, 1996-97; Amoco Chemicals, sr chemical engineer, 1997-. **Orgs:** Mem AIChE 1980-86; assoc mem Tech Assoc of Pulp & Paper Industry 1980-86; steward/choir president Turner Chapel AME Church 1984-86; educ chmn Columbus MS Coalition of Black Organizations 1985-86; correspondent The Jackson Advocate 1986; toastmaster Toastmaster's Intl 1986-; math tutor Asbury UM Church 1987; secretary,

Tuskegee University Engineering Alumni Assn, 1988-; Soldiers Memorial AMEZ Church Steward 1991-; Salisbury, NC school advisory chairman, 1992-93; Rowan Co, NC Red Cross, bd of dirs, 1994-; City of Salisbury, advisory bd, 1994-; Leadership Roman, vp, 1997; Decatur Mission AMEZ Church, pastor, 1997-. **Honors/Awds:** "Down Route 82" Manuscript "The Jackson Advocate" 1986; Best Speaker/Best Evaluator RAAP Toastmasters Club 1986-87; North Carolina Governor's Volunteer Award, 1992. **Military Serv:** USAF Reserves, airman 1st class, 3 yrs; Armed Forces Comm & Electronics Assoc Citation, Certificate of Merit. **Home Addr:** 811 Longbow Dr. SW, Decatur, AL 35603.

JACOBS, NORMA MORRIS
Educator. **Personal:** Born May 3, 1949, Jackson, MS; daughter of Healon D Jefferson Williams and Hubert Turner Williams; married Billy George Jacobs, Jun 30, 1990; children: Thomas D Morris, Stacey R Morris. **Educ:** Univ of Texas, Austin, TX, BA, 1971; Louisiana State, Baton Rouge, LA, Post Bac, 1978-79; Univ of Houston, Houston, TX, MBA, 1985; Texas A&M Univ, College Station, TX, PhD, 1989. **Career:** Arthur Young & Co, Houston, TX, auditor, 1979-81; SCI Inc, Houston, TX, acct supv, 1981-82; Univ of Houston, Houston, TX, acct supervisor, 1982-84; Texas A&M Univ, College Station, TX, research asst, 1984-87; Penn State Univ, State College, PA, asst prof, 1987-. **Orgs:** Faculty Advisor, National Association of Black Accts, 1987-; member, American Acct Association, 1987-; member, American Institute of CPAs, 1986-; member, NAACP, 1985-. **Honors/Awds:** Outstanding Doctoral Student, Earnst & Young Foundation, 1987; CPA Certification, American Institute of CPA's, 1985. **Business Addr:** Assistant Professor, Accounting, Penn State University, 233 Beam Business Administration Bldg, State College, PA 16803.

JACOBS, PATRICIA DIANNE
Business executive. **Personal:** Born Jan 27, 1950, Camden, AR; daughter of Helen M Tate Jacobs and Felix H Jacobs; divorced; children: Branden Kemiah, Brittne Katelyn-Helen, Bradley Kareem-Felix. **Educ:** Lincoln Univ, BA 1970; Harvard Law School, JD 1973. **Career:** Lincoln Univ, asst dir finan aid 1970; Exxon Corp, legal assoc 1973-75; US Senate Sm Business Comm, asst min counsel 1975-77; Amer Assoc of MESBICS Inc, pres 1977-83; K-Com Micrographics Inc, pres. **Orgs:** Asst prof John Jay Coll of Criminal Justice 1974-75; dir Wider Opportunities for Women 1983-; dir/trustee Lincoln Univ 1983-; dir Cooperative Assist Fund 1983-. **Honors/Awds:** Regional Atty Advocate for Small Business DC Small Business Admin 1982; Lincoln Alumni Award Lincoln Univ 1981; Under 30 Achievement Award Black Enterprise 1978; Alumni Achievement Award Lincoln Univ 1990; Woman Owned Business Enterprise Award US Dept of Transportation 1987.

JACOBS, SYLVIA MARIE
Educator. **Personal:** Born Oct 27, 1946, Mansfield, OH; daughter of Murval Aletha Cansler Jacobs Porch and Love Jacobs; married Levell Exum, Jun 20, 1980; children: Levell Rickie Exum, Sylvia Agnes Jacobs Exum. **Educ:** Wayne State Univ, Detroit MI, BS, 1969, MBA 1972; Howard Univ, Washington DC, PhD, 1975. **Career:** McKerrow Elementary School, Detroit MI, teacher, 1969-72; Federal City Coll, Washington DC, visiting lecturer, 1973; Univ of AR, Pine Bluff AR, asst prof, 1975-76; North Carolina Central Univ, Durham NC, assoc prof, 1976-82, professor 1982-92, dept chair, 1992-; Univ of North Carolina, Chapel Hill, visiting prof, 1982; Univ of Florida, Gainesville, NEH seminar leader, 1988. **Orgs:** Mem, Delta Sigma Theta, 1968-; executive council, mem, Assn for the Study of Afro-Amer Life and History, 1995-98; co-convener, Southeastern Regional Seminar in African Studies, 1983-87; natl dir, Assn of Black Women Historians, 1984-88, co-publications dir, 1995-97; mem, Natl Council of Negro Women Inc, 1985-; mem, Southern Poverty Law Center, 1985-; mem, Committee on the Status of Minority Historians and Minority History, Organization of Amer Historians, 1987-90; mem, Organization of American Historians; mem, NAACP 1987-; mem, Amer Historical Assn; mem, African Studies Assn, 1976-. **Honors/Awds:** Letitia Brown Memorial Publication Prize, Assn of Black Women Historians, 1984, 1992; Fellowship for Coll Teachers, Natl Endowment for the Humanities, 1984-85; Distinguished Achievement Award, Howard Univ Alumni Club, 1985; Fellowship for Minority-Group Scholars, Rockefeller Foundation, 1987-88. **Special Achievements:** Editor, works include: Black Americans and the Missionary Movement in Africa, 1982; 36 articles, 1975-93; 8 book reviews, 1975-88; author: The African Nexus: Black American Perspectives on the European Partitioning of Africa, 1981. **Home Addr:** 4109 Cobscook Dr, Durham, NC 27707, (919)493-1024. **Business Addr:** Professor, North Carolina Central University, Department of History, Durham, NC 27707, (919)560-6271.

JACOBS, THOMAS LINWOOD
Government official. **Personal:** Born Feb 27, 1933, New York, NY; married Marcella Gilbert; children: Lauren. **Educ:** St Joseph's Coll & Sem, BS 1961; NYU, MSW, 1969; Amer Mgmt Assn; Mgmt Certificate, 1979. **Career:** Fordham Univ, adj prof, 1973-74; Office of Borough Pres Manhattan, deputy, 1974-77; John Jay Coll of Criminal Justice, adj assoc prof 1980-; NY City Dept of Probation, 1st Black commissioner. **Orgs:** Bd of dir One Hundred Black Men 1977-, Brooklyn Childrens Museum 1982-; bd of dir Catholic Inter-racial council New York City 1980-; former chmn Boys Choir of harlem 1981-83. **Honors/Awds:** Achievement Awd NY Fed of Negro Civil Serv Org 1983; Comm Outreach Awd Manhattan Cable TV 1984; Hon Dep Fire Chief New York City Fire Dept 1984; Dep Grand Marshal 17th Annual ML King Jr Parade, New York City 369th Vet Assoc 1984. **Business Addr:** Commissioner, NY City Dept of Probation, 115 Leonard St, Room 2 E l, New York, NY 10013.

JACOBS, TIM
Professional football player. **Personal:** Born Apr 5, 1970, Washington, DC; married Valerie, Jun 29, 1997; children: Taylor Arden. **Educ:** Delaware. **Career:** Miami Dolphins, defensive back, currently. **Business Addr:** Professional Football Player, Miami Dolphins, 2269 NW 199th St, Miami, FL 33056, (305)620-5000.

JACQUES, CORNELL
Business executive. **Personal:** Born Jul 12, 1949, Detroit, MI; son of Hazel J Jacques and Hernando Jacques; married Elaine Tribble, Aug 31, 1974; children: Monique S. **Educ:** Journeyman Air Traffic Controller, 1979; Mercer University, BBA, 1980. **Career:** Federal Aviation Administration, Journeyman Air Traffic Controller, 1974-81; Central Vending Co., route supervisor, 1983-85; Lockheed IMS, resident parking consultant, 1985-86; City of Detroit, parking commission coordinator, 1986-88; Lockheed Martin IMS, consulting, assistant vice pres, 1989-91, municipal services vice pres, 1991-. **Orgs:** International Parking Institute, 1985-; National Forum for Black Public Administrators, 1992-; Kappa Alpha Psi Fraternity, 1968-. **Honors/Awds:** Federal Aviation Administration, Special Achievement Award, 1980. **Military Serv:** US Air Force, sgt, 1969-73. **Business Addr:** Vice Pres, Lockheed Martin IMS, 1999 Broadway, Ste 2700, Denver, CO 80202, (303)295-2860.

JACQUET, JEAN BAPTISTE ILLINOIS (ILLINOIS)
Musician, band director. **Personal:** Born Oct 31, 1922, Broussard, LA; son of Maggie Trahan and Gilbert Jacquet; married Barbara Potts; children: Michael Lane, Pamela Baptiste. **Educ:** Percy H McDavid at Phillis Wheatley HS Houston TX, music training 1939. **Career:** Family orchestra led by father Gilbert until 1937; Milt Larking Band, 1938-39; Lionel Hampton Band, 1940-42; Cab Calloway Band, 1943; Stormey Weather 20th Century Fox, performer 1943; featured in jazz film classic "Jammin' The Blues," Warner Bros 1944; original mem of Jazz at the Philharmonic which created the historic 1944 concert recording "Philharmonic Blues Part II"; Count Basie Band, 1946; led All-Star Band 1947-65; led Trio with Jo Jones & Milt Buckner 1970's; formed Quintet with Slam Stewart 1980-82; Harvard Univ, teacher jazz music 1982-; Tufts Univ, UC San Diego, Univ of ID, Crane Coll, Clark Coll/Howard University seminars; formed present 16 piece Big Band 1983-. **Orgs:** Created the immortal solo on the classic recording Flying Home with the Lionel Hampton Band; compositions incl, Bottoms Up, You Left Me All Alone, Robbins Nest, Black Velvet, Port of Rico, For Europeans Only, Blues for New Orleans, The King. **Honors/Awds:** First Jazz Bassonist in the World; All Mem of Fam in Band; A Salute to Illinois Jacquet at Carnegie Hall Kool Jazz Festival; Commendation of Excellence Broadcast Music Inc; Cert of Apprec Smithsonian Inst; has recorded on all major record labels; most recent new release, "Jacquet's Got It", Illinois Jacquet and His Big Band, Atlantic Records.

JACQUET, NATE
Professional football player. **Personal:** Born Sep 2, 1975. **Educ:** San Diego State. **Career:** Indianapolis Colts, wide receiver, 1997-. **Business Addr:** Professional Football Player, Indianapolis Colts, PO Box 535000, Indianapolis, IN 46253, (317)297-2658.

JAGGERS, GEORGE HENRY, JR.
Educational administrator. **Personal:** Born Feb 27, 1926, Dallas, NC; married Ida Hayes; children: George Henry III. **Educ:** NC A&T State Univ, BS 1951, MS 1975; UNC Chapel Hill, cert 1978. **Career:** Pender Co NC, teacher 1951-59; Gaston Co Pleasant Ridge School, teacher 1959-66; Gaston Co Carr School, teacher (1st black) 1966-70; Gaston Co Ashley Jr HS, asst prin 1970-75; Gaston Co Hunter Huss HS, asst prin 1975-82; Gastonia Central Elementary School, principal 1982-. **Orgs:** Mem NCAE Prin Div; mem NEA; lt Gaston Co Police Aux; mayor pro tem (1st black) Town of Dallas NC 1978-80; alderman Town of Dallas NC 1980-82; governing body So Piedmont Health Systems Agency Inc 1980-83. **Honors/Awds:** Outstanding Officer Gaston Co Police 1971 & 1977; Omega Man of the Yr Omega Psi Phi Frat Inc 1972; Human Relations Awd NC Assn of Educators Gaston Co 1980; Serv Awd ARC 1980; Serv Awd Dallas Police Dept 1980. **Military Serv:** USN AOM 2/c 1944-46; Good Conduct Medal 1946. **Business Addr:** Principal, Gastonia Central Elem School, 100 E Second Ave, Gastonia, NC 28052.

JAGNANDAN, WILFRED LILPERSAUD
Pastor. **Personal:** Born Apr 19, 1920, Guyana; married Helen Mahadai Samaroo; children: Neville, Nora, Norris, Edward, Leonard. **Educ:** Guyana, diploma in Theology; USA, BTh; Toronto, BA; Toronto, MA MS U, MEd 1973; London, DD; Cambridge, BSc, JD 1979. **Career:** Univ Hosp Augusta, asso chapl 1976-; Trinity Presb Ch MS, pastor 6 yrs; Guyana Presb Ch, pastor 24 yrs; Presbytery in Guyana, moderator twice; clerk of presbytery 1 yr; Commr of Oaths to Affidavits, Justice of the Peace 8 yrs; Christ Presbyterian Church, pastor. **Orgs:** Chmn League of Friends; chmn Improv of Port Mourant Hosp; chmn Tchr Parent Assn of Belvedere Govt Sch; chmn Adult Educ at Port Mourant Com Cntr; chmn Corentyne Minister's Assn; mem bd of Govr's Berbiee HS; 5 yrs Pastor at Trinity USA; chapl at Mary Holmes Coll 2 yrs mem bd Tombigbee Coun on human rel; mem head start bd; mem minister's frat in w point MS; ldr of Christian Student Assn; mem GA Presbytery 1975-; chrprsn ecumenical rel GA Presbytery of the UP USA Ch 1977-78; mem citzs adv com Title IV Richmond Co Bd of Educ Augusta 1980-81; vol math tchr Lucy Laney HS Augusta present; volunteer 1980-83, chmn feeding prog 1981-84 Help Line. **Honors/Awds:** Rec plaque from Prairie Opport Inc 1974; cert from Personal of S 1972; Cert of Achiev of Educ Cambridge England 1974; recognition & appreciation Univ Hosp 1976,77,78-83; Chaplain of the Year for Faithfull & Loyal Serv Certs 1985,86. **Business Addr:** Pastor, Christ Presbyterian Church, Augusta, GA 30901.

JAM, JIMMY (JAMES HARRIS, III)
Record producer, songwriter, record company executive. **Personal:** Born Jun 6, 1959, Minneapolis, MN; married Lisa Padilla, Jun 1994; children: Tyler James. **Career:** Flyte Tyme Productions Inc, producer & songwriter, currently; Chm and A&R, Perspective Records with MCA's Universal Records, currently. **Honors/Awds:** With Terry Lewis has produced the following albums and groups: On the Rise, 1983; Just the Way You Like It, 1984 (The SOS Band); Fragile, 1984, High Priority, 1985 (Cherrelle); Alexander O'Neal, 1985 (Alexander O'Neal); Tender Love, 1985 (Force M.D.'s); Control, 1986, Rhythm Nation 1814, 1989, janet., 1993, The Velvet Rope, 1997 (Janet Jackson); Grammy Award for Producer of the Year, 1986; produced own label artists including: Sounds Of Blackness, Mint Condition, Lo-Key, Raja-Nee, Ann Nesby. **Business Addr:** Flyte Tyme Productions, Inc., 4100 W 76th Street, Edina, MN 55435.

JAMAL, AHMAD
Jazz musician, pianist. **Personal:** Born Jul 2, 1930, Pittsburgh, PA; divorced; children: Sumayah. **Career:** George Hudson Orch touring in 1940's, jazz pianist; Four Strings, player 1950; The Caldwells, toured as accompanist 1951; formed own trio 1951; recording contract, Okeh Records, Cadet Records; performer at, Jazz Alley Downtown Seattle, George's Chicago, Joe Segal's Jazz Showcase, Voyager West St Louis, Ethyl's Place, Fairmont Hotels, Cricket Theater in Hennepin Center for the Arts, Apollo Theatre Town Hall, Rainbow Grill (Waldorf Astoria), The Embers, Village Gate, the Iridium, The Village Vanguard; Atlantic Records, released "Digital Works", "Rossiter Rd", "Live at the Montreal Jazz Festival"; performing at the Umbria Jazz Fesitval in Italy, also in Finland, Blues Alley in Georgetown, The Blackhawk, Yoshi's in San Francisco/Oakland; "Crystal"; performed 2 years with Philip Morris Tour around the world: Berne Jazz Festival 1989, Pittsburgh, 1990, 1996. **Honors/Awds:** NEA, American Jazz Masters Award, 1994; Yale University, Duke Ellington Fel low, 1994; Djangod 'Or Award, 1996. **Special Achievements:** Only artist to have an LP in the album top ten of nat charts for 108 consecutive weeks But Not For Me; other albums incl, "All of You," "Jamal Plays Jamal," "At The Penthouse," "Extension," "The Awakening," "Freelight," "Naked City Theme," "One," "Digital Works," "Crystal," "Pittsburgh," "Chicago Revisited," "Live in Paris '92," "Ahmad's Blues," "Poinciana;" Telarc Recording Artist, "I Remember Duke, Hoagy & Strayhorn," 1995, "Chicago Revisited," 1994; Birdology Distributed by Polygram, "Live In Paris," 1994; "The Essence, Part 1," 1996; "The Essence, Part 2," 1997. **Business Addr:** Musician, Ellora Management, PO Box 295, Ashley Falls, MA 01222.

JAMERSON, JEROME DONNELL
Educator. **Personal:** Born Nov 2, 1950, Memphis, TN; son of Rosalee Butler Jamerson and J D Jamerson; divorced; children: Jenielle Denise, Kendra Deon. **Educ:** TN State Univ, BS 1973, MS 1972; Memphis State Univ, Nova Univ, EdD (pending). **Career:** Shelby State Comm Coll, instr of history 1973-78, asst prof of history 1979-80, assoc prof of history 1980-. **Orgs:** Past chmn Hollywood Day Care Center 1977; Life Mem, Omega Psi Phi Fraternity; Organizer, Council on Black Amer Affairs 1980; mem AAUP 1985, TN State Employees Assn 1985; co-chairperson Shelby State Professors Assn 1985; pres, Royal Gentlemens Social Club 1985; mem Greater St Luke MBC Church, Assn Study of Negro Life & History, Friends of Brooks Art Gallery, NAACP, Amer Assn of Univ Profs, Amer Assn of Community & Jr Colls, Assn of the Study of Afro-Amer Life & History, Org of Amer Historians, TN Assn of Community Action & Child Devel. **Honors/Awds:** Outstanding Young Man of the Year Jaycees 1978; Master's Thesis Dr Arthur Melvin Townsend & the Natl Baptist Convention Inc; Certificate of Appreciation Memphis Shelby County Headstart & Telephone Pioneers of Amer; Certificate of Award Outstanding Volunteer Serv to the Headstart Program 1983; Hon Mem Congressional Staff of Harold Ford; Phi Theta Kappa Award for

being 4.0 Instructor. **Business Addr:** Associate Professor, Shelby State Community College, Dept of Social Sciences, Memphis, TN 38104.

JAMERSON, JOHN WILLIAM, JR.
Dentist (retired). **Personal:** Born Sep 22, 1910, Savannah, GA; son of Julia Aline Belcher Jamerson and John WIlliam Jamerson; married Dorothy Louise Breaux, Sep 28, 1940; children: Dorothy Anders MD, Kathleen O'Quinn, Patricia Manson, John W III DDS. **Educ:** Lincoln Univ PA, AB 1933; Meharry Med Coll Sch of Dentistry, DDS 1941. **Career:** Private Practice, general dentistry. **Orgs:** Pres Chatham Dental Soc 1971-; life Mem NDA, ADA, Omega Psi Phi Frat, Mu Phi Chapt; NAACP; life mem GA Dental Assn; life mem SE Dist Dental Soc; life mem Lincoln Univ Alumni Assoc; mem Historic Review Bd, Savannah GA, 1986-89. **Honors/Awds:** Fellow Acad of General Dentistry 1983; fellow Acad of Dentistry Intl 1984; Annual Freedom Fund Honoree NAACP Savannah GA Branch 1986. **Military Serv:** USAF capt 1951-52. **Home Addr:** 601 Herb River Dr, Savannah, GA 31406-3216.

JAMES, ADVERGUS DELL, JR.
Educational administrator. **Personal:** Born Sep 24, 1944, Garden City, KS; son of Helen Lee James and Advergus D James Sr; married Anna Flave Glenn; children: Anthony David, Adam Glen. **Educ:** Langston Univ, BS 1966; OK State Univ, MS 1969. **Career:** Langston Univ, asst registrar 1966-69, dir admission & record 1969-70; Prairie View A&M Univ, dir 1970-85, dir admissions & financial aid 1986-88, dir, financial aid, 1988-. **Orgs:** Consultant State Student Financial Assistance Training 1979-80; pres TX Assn of Student Financial Aid Administrators 1981-82; mem Natl Council of Student Financial Aid Admin 1985-86; mem TX Guaranteed Student Loan Advisory Bd 1984-86; mem bd dirs Depelcin Center 1986; life mem Alpha Phi Alpha Fraternity; charter mem Prairie View Optimist Club; member, advisory board, Outstanding Rural Scholars, 1990-; advisory comm, bd of dirs, Greater East Texas Higher Educ Authority, 1995-; bd or dirs, The Texas Assn of Student Financial Aid Administrators. **Honors/Awds:** Distinguished Alumni, NAFEO, 1991. **Home Addr:** 7611 Hertfordshire Dr, Spring, TX 77379.

JAMES, ALEXANDER, JR.
Business executive. **Personal:** Born Nov 2, 1933, Branchville, SC; married Dorothy Jones; children: Audrey D, Gregory A, Kevin ES. **Educ:** City Coll NY, BEE 1961; NYU Grad Engrng, MSEE 1963; NYU Grad Business Admin, MBA 1986. **Career:** Bell Tele Lab, engr 1961-68; Market Monitor Data Inc, oper mgr 1968-69; EF Shelley & Co Mgmt Cons, sr vice pres 1969-75; Citibank NA, vice pres 1975-82; Group 88 Incorp, sr vp. **Orgs:** Mem Inst of Elec & Electronics Engr 1961-; mem Am Mgmt Assn 1975-; bd of dir Group 88 Inc Consult 1982-; bd of dir Urban Home Ownership Corp 1982-; chmn trustees Pilgrim Baptist Church 1978-; commnr Middletown Twp Human Rights Comm 1976-80; mem Natl Black MBA Assoc 1984. **Honors/Awds:** Hon chmn Monmouth Co Collition Comm 1980; Commnty Achievemnt Award Natl Assn of Negro Business & Professional Women's Clubs 1978; elected mem Eta Kappa Nu Elec Engr Hon Soc 1960; elected mem Tau Beta Pi Engr Hon Soc 1960. **Military Serv:** AUS splist 2nd cl 1953-55. **Home Addr:** 11 Sir Paul Ct, Middletown, NJ 07748-3542. **Business Addr:** Senior Vice President, Group 88 Incorp, One Penn Plaza, Floor 29, New York, NY 10119.

JAMES, ALLIX BLEDSOE
Educational administrator. **Personal:** Born Dec 17, 1922, Marshall, TX; son of Tannie E James and Samuel Horace James Sr (deceased); married Susie B Nickens; children: Alvan Bosworth, Portia V White. **Educ:** VA Union Univ, AB 1944, MDiv 1946; Union Theol Seminary, ThM 1949, ThD 1957. **Career:** Third Union Baptist Church, former minister; Mount Zion Baptist Church, former minister; Union Zion Baptist Church, former minister; Virginia Union Univ, instr Biblical studies 1947-50, dean of students 1950-56, dean of sch of theology 1956-70, vice pres 1960-70, pres 1970-79, pres emeritus, 1979-85, chancellor, 1985-. **Orgs:** National Conference of Christians and Jews Inc, board of directors, national executive board; Richmond Gold Bowl Sponsors, co-founder, president, board of directors; National Council for America's First Freedom, board of directors; Black History Museum and Cultural Center of Virginia Inc, president, board of trustees; Richmond Tommorrow, education task force, chairman; Leadership Roundtable, founder, chairman, board of directors; Virginia Electric and Power Co., board of directors; Consolidated Bank and Trust Co., board of directors; American Council of Life Insurance, university advisory council; Beekne Investment Co. Inc, board of directors; Alpha Phi Alpha Fraternity Inc; Sigma Pi Phi Fraternity Inc, Alpha Beta Boule; Moore Street Baptist Church, board of trustees. **Honors/Awds:** Alpha Phi Alpha, Beta Gamma Lambda Chapter, Outstanding Achievement Award, 1981; Richmond First Club, Good Government Award, 1985; Metropolitan Business League, MF Manuel Community Service Award, 1991; Fullwood Foods Inc, Exemplary Vision Award, 1992; International Ministers' Wives Association, The Shirley A Hart Award for Global Humanitarian Service, 1992; Honorary Degrees: University of Richmond, LLD, 1971; St Paul's College, DD, 1981. The University Chapel was named in his honor, The Alex B. James Chapel, 1992. **Special Achievements:** First African-American to serve as president of Virginia State Board of Education; Association of Theological Schools in the US; National Conference of Christians and Jews, Virginia Region; first African-American chairman, Richmond Planning Commission; Board of trustees, Virginia Union University named the restored University Chapel in Coburn Hall, The Allix B James Chapel, 1992; guest of the Government of Republic of Taiwan to explore possiblities for educational cooperation, 1976; conferences with European theological educators from Germany, Switzerland, Italy, France, and England, 1969; study of higher education in USSR, 1973; contributing editor, The Continuing Quest; author: Calling a Pastor in a Baptist Church; numerous articles, local and national publications and professional journals. **Home Addr:** 2956 Hathaway Rd, #302, Richmond, VA 23225. **Business Addr:** Chancellor, Virginia Union University, 1500 N Lombardy St, Richmond, VA 23220.

JAMES, ARMINTA SUSAN
Educator (retired). **Personal:** Born May 1, 1924, Erie, PA; daughter of Alice Bowers Martin and Leonard Martin; married Walter R Jr, Jun 30, 1951. **Educ:** Fisk Univ, BA 1946; Roosevelt Univ, MA in Educ Admin 1965. **Career:** Erie Co TB Assn, health educ worker 1946-48; Chicago Welfare Dept, child placement worker 1948-52; N Chicago School Dist 64, teacher 1955-65, elementary principal 1965-1986. **Orgs:** Sec/treasurer, IL Principals Assn, 1965-; Natl Assn of Elementary School Principals, 1965-; Natl Alliance of Black School Educators, 1977-; life mem, past pres, Alpha Kappa Alpha Sorority Lake Co Chapter, 1944-; former bd mem, Lake Co Urban League; ASCD; NAACP; vestry mem, Christ Episcopal Church; vestry & Christian educ coordinator, St Timothy's Church, Aiea Hawaii; Amer Assn of Univ Women; Hawaii Chapter, Links, Inc, 1988-; board of directors, St Timothy's Child Care Center. **Honors/Awds:** Educator of the Year, North Shore 12, 1975; Outstanding Woman of Lake County, Urban League, 1977; Outstanding Achievement Award, Omega Psi Phi Fraternity, 1978; Those Who Excell in Educ, Illinois State Bd of Educ, 1978; Outstanding Achievement in Educ, Waukegan YWCA, 1981. **Home Addr:** 95-201 Kahiku Place, Mililani, HI 96789.

JAMES, BETTY HARRIS
Educator. **Personal:** Born Jun 21, 1932, Gadsden, AL; daughter of Mary Etta Wacasey Harris and William Harris; married Joseph E James (deceased); children: Cecilia Denise James Joyce, Tyrone Michael, Tyshaun Michele. **Educ:** Univ of Pittsburgh, BS Educ, MEd (Magna Cum Laude) 1971, PhD 1974; Marshall Univ, MA 1976. **Career:** WV State Coll, prof of educ 1974-84, special asst to pres 1981-84; Livingstone Coll, assoc vice pres academic affairs 1984-86; Appalachia Educ Lab, dir regional liaison ctr 1986-. **Orgs:** Pres Charleston Branch NAACP 1979-81; mem Comm Council Job Corps 1979-; consultant WV Human Rights Commn 1980-; mem Phi Lambda Theta Hon Soc, Kappa Delta Phi. **Honors/Awds:** Danforth Assoc 1976; Faculty Meritorious Serv WV State Coll 1977; Meritorious Serv Livingstone Coll Student Govt 1985. **Home Addr:** PO Box 6194, Charleston, WV 25362. **Business Addr:** Director, Appalachia Educational Laboratory, 1031 Quarrier St, Atlas Bldg, Charleston, WV 25301.

JAMES, BETTY NOWLIN
Administrator. **Personal:** Born Feb 16, 1936, Athens, GA; married Lewis Francis James; children: Beth Marie Morris, Dewey Douglas Morris III. **Educ:** Fisk University, BA1956; Univ of Houston, MEd 1969, EdD 1975. **Career:** Houston Ind School District, teacher and music specialist 1958-71, federal programs asst 1972-74, assoc dir research/evaluation 1975-76; Univ of Houston-Downtown, coord instr planning/evaluation 1976-80, dir of inst research 1980-83, dir of inst serv 1983-. **Orgs:** Phi Delta Kappa Rschng Frat 1976-; allocations review panel United Way 1983-; worksite coord Tenneci Inc Cities in Schools Pro 1984; top black achiever awd committee Human Enrichment of Life Prog 1985-;Black Achiever Selection Committee Chair-Riverside, Gen Hosp 1986; Executive Boards Houston YWCA/UNCF, Patterson Awards Committee UNCF. **Honors/Awds:** Intellectual Dev Fund grantee Univ of Houston-Downtown 1982; Top Worksite Awd Tenneco, Inc 1984; Outstanding Woman of Univ Houston-Downtown Houston YWCA Bd 1985; HELP Outstanding Blk Achiever Awd Human Enrichment of Life 1985; Marquis Who's Who of Amer Women 1985. **Home Addr:** 3301 Oakdale, Houston, TX 77004. **Business Addr:** Dir of Inst Services, Univ of Houston-Downtown, One Main St, Houston, TX 77002.

JAMES, CARLOS ADRIAN
Marketing manager. **Personal:** Born Jun 1, 1946, Oyster Bay LI, NY; married Claudette Brown; children: Todd, Terrence, Carlos Jr. **Educ:** Canton Coll State Univ of NY at Canton, AAS 1967; LI Univ Brooklyn NY, BS 1970. **Career:** The Coca-Cola Co, mgr spl mkts planning 1979-; Atlanta Bus League, mgr 1978-79; Avon Prod Inc, budget Admn/div sales mgr 1972-78; NBC, budget adminstr 1970-72. **Orgs:** Mem Nat Assn of Market Developers 1980; mem Soc for Advancement of Mgmt; vice pres Zeta Alpha Phi; mem Urban League. **Business Addr:** Coca Cola Co, 610 North Ave, Atlanta, GA 30301.

JAMES, CARRIE HOUSER
Nurse educator. **Personal:** Born Nov 6, 1949, Orangeburg, SC; daughter of Lula Bell Riley Houser and Alfred Houser Sr (deceased); children: Gabrielle DeAnna, Claudia Michelle, Louis "Max". **Educ:** Univ of SC, Columbia, SC, BSN, 1971; Catholic Univ of America, Washington, DC, MSN, 1974; SC State Coll, Orangeburg, SC, 1989-90; Univ of SC, Columbia, SC, 1990-. **Career:** Children's Hosp Natl Med Ctr, Washington, DC, clinical specialist, 1974-76; Univ of SC-Coll of Nursing, Columbia, SC, instructor, 1976-78; Richland Memorial Hospital, Columbia, SC, dir of nursing, children's hospital, 1977-84; SC State Univ, Orangeburg, SC, asst prof, 1984-; The Regional Medical Ctr, Orangeburg, SC, relief staff nurse-pt, 1988-; Edisto Health District, Orangeburg, SC, consultant, child birth educator, 1989-. **Orgs:** Pres, SC Nurses Assn, 1990-94; treas, SC Nurses Foundation, 1988-93; sec, Orangeburg County, Ambulance Comm, 1987-98; mem, Congress of Economics, American Nurses Assn, 1990-94; mem, Maternal, Infant, Child Health Council for SC, 1990-94; recorder, SACS steering comm, SC State Coll, 1988-90; chair, Constituent Assembly, ANA, 1994-96; The Prioneer Nurse, 1995, by the Tri County Black Nurses Assn. **Honors/Awds:** Excellence in Education, Edisto, District Nurses Assn, 1989; Five Year Service Pin, Richland Memorial Hospital, 1982. **Home Addr:** 462 Meadowlark, NE, Orangeburg, SC 29115. **Business Addr:** Asst Prof, Nursing/Dept Advisor, South Carolina State Univ, Dept of Nursing, 300 College St, NE, PO Box 7158, Orangeburg, SC 29117.

JAMES, CHARLES ALEXANDER
Ambassador (retired). **Personal:** Born Jun 6, 1922, Washington, DC; married L Jane Woodley; children: Donald, Dennis, Peter, Karen. **Educ:** Middlebury Coll, BA 1949; Yale Law Sch, LLB 1952. **Career:** Niger, ambassador 1976-79; African Affairs, dep asst sec 1974-76; office of Near E Aff USAID, dir 1974-; Peace Corps, dir 1966-67; dep dir 1964-66; asst atty gen 1961-64; Pvt Pract, law 1954-61; Nathaniel S Colley, atty 1952-54. **Orgs:** Mem bd dir pres Family Serv Agency Stockton CA 1956-64; NAACP; Com of 100 Stockton; Stockton Redev Agy. **Honors/Awds:** LLD hon Middlebury Coll 1977. **Military Serv:** USN petty ofcr 1943-46.

JAMES, CHARLES FORD
Business executive. **Personal:** Born Dec 21, 1935, Rochester, NY; married Jean Hunter; children: Catherine, Deborah. **Educ:** Cornell U, BA 1957; Howard Univ Sch of Law, 1962-64; NY Univ Sch of Law, Dr of Jurisprudence 1966. **Career:** NY Tele, mgr 1964-. **Orgs:** Mem Nat Defense Exec Reserve 1966-; pres Millburn-Short Hills First Aid Squad 1985; mem Nat Ski Patrol Shawnee Mtn, PA; former mem Bd of Dir Urban League of Essex Co NJ 1966-74. **Military Serv:** AUS capt 1957-62. **Home Addr:** 151 Mohawk Rd, Short Hills, NJ 07078. **Business Addr:** District Manager, NY Telephone, 1095 Avenue of the Americas, New York, NY 10036.

JAMES, CHARLES H., III
Food distribution company executive. **Personal:** son Of Lucia and Charles H James II; married Jeralyn; children: C H James IV, Nelson. **Educ:** Morehouse College, undergraduate degree; Wharton Business School, MBA. **Career:** Continental Illinois National Bank and Trust Co, banking associate; C H James & Co, beginning 1985, president, 1987-88, CEO, 1988-. **Orgs:** Commerce Bank, board of directors; West Virginia Economic Development Authority, treasurer; University of Charleston, board of trustees; Charleston Area Medical Center, board of directors. **Honors/Awds:** US Dept of Agriculture, Minority Contractor of the Year Award, 1988, 1989, 1990; Small Business Administration, Mid-Atlantic Region Minority Small Businessman of the Year, 1990; US Dept of Commerce, Minority Supplier Distributor Firm of the Year, 1988; Black Enterprise magazine, Co. of the Year, 1992. **Special Achievements:** Company is #72 on the Black Enterprise list of top 100 industrial/service companies, 1992. **Business Addr:** CEO, C H James & Co, 601 50th St, Charleston, WV 25304, (304)925-4331.

JAMES, CHARLES HOWELL, II
Business executive. **Personal:** Born Nov 22, 1930, Charleston; married Lucia Jeanette Bacote; children: Sheila, Stephanie, Charles III, Sarah. **Educ:** Univ of Pennsylvania Wharton Sch of Finance & Commerce, BS 1953; WV State Coll, attended. **Career:** James Produce Co, salesman 1956-60; James Produce Co, sec treas 1961-63; James Produce Co, sec treas & gen mgr 1963-67; James Produce Co, pres & gen mgr 1967-72; C H James & Co, pres chmn 1972-91; The James Corp., chairman, chief executive officer, 1981-; West Virginia State College, special advisor to the president, 1992-, vice pres for administration, 1994. **Orgs:** Mem bd dir Charleston C of C; dist adv coun Small Business Adminstrn 1971-89; chmn Charleston C of C FFA Ham Bacon & Egg Show; mem US C of C; Asso WV Assn of Retail Grocers; vice pres Mountain State Busienssmen's Assn of WV 1974-75; commr & sec of bd Kanawha Intl Airport Auth 1969-79; bd trustees United Fund of Kanawha Valley 1967-75; bd dir Buckskin Coun BSA 1970-73; Rotary Club Charleston 1970-; chmn Mayor's Com on Interstate Understructure of Charleston 1973; bd dir Industrial adv coun OIC's of Am 1972-; bd dir Charston Progress Assn for Economic Devel; pres Alpha Iota Lambda Chap 1974-76; life mem Alpha Phi Alpha Frat; Sire Archon 1974 Upsilon Boule Sigma Pi Phi Frat; life mem

NAACP; bd trustees First Bapt Ch. **Honors/Awds:** Honorary soc Beta Gamma Sigma; top 100 businessmen Black Enterprise Magazine, 1974-90; Central WV Airport Authority award for outstanding contribution to the air transportation system of WV, 1969-79; US SBA Minority Small Business Person of the Year, WV District & Philadelphia Region, 1984; Future Farmers of America Honorary Farmer, 1975; Charleston Business and Professional Men's Club Businessman of the year, 1983; OIC Corporate Support award, 1984; Kanawha County WV Famous Person award, 1988; Alpha Phi Alpha Midwestern Region Business Leadership award, 1989; WV State College Presidential award, 1990. **Military Serv:** USAF capt 1953-56. **Business Addr:** Chairman, The James Corporation, Lock Box 10170 Station C, Charleston, WV 25357.

JAMES, CHARLES L.
Educator. **Personal:** Born Apr 12, 1934, Poughkeepsie, NY; married Rose Jane Fisher; children: Sheilah Ellen, Terri Lynn. **Educ:** SUNY New Paltz, BS 1961; SUNY Albany, MA 1969. **Career:** Swarthmore Coll Swarthmore PA, assoc prof 1973-, prof, 1983; SUNY Oneonta NY; asst prof & assoc prof 1969-73; Dutchess Comm Coll Pughkeepsie NY, instructor in English 1967-69; Spackenkill School Poughkeepsie NY, elementary teacher English 1961-67. **Orgs:** Mem Am Assn of Univ Prof; Modern Lang Assn; Coll Lang Assn. **Honors/Awds:** Monograph "The Black Writer in Am" Albany SUNY 1969; "From the Roots: Short Stories by Black Americans," Dodd Mead & Co in 1970, Harper and Row, 1975; post grad fellowship Yale Univ Danforth Found 1971-72; summer seminar Nat Endowment for the Humanities 1978; Natl Endowment for Humanities, Summer Research Grant, 1990, Fellowship for Coll Teachers, 1996-97; The George Becker Faculty Fellowship, 1992-93; The Eugene M Lang Faculty Fellowship, 1984-85; Visiting Assoc, Clare Hall Coll, Cambridge Univ, England, 1981; Sarah Lawrence Lightfoot, Prof of English Lit, 1997. **Military Serv:** AUS sgt 1955-57. **Business Addr:** Dept of English Lit, Swarthmore Coll, Swarthmore, PA 19081.

JAMES, CHARLES LESLIE
Insurance company executive. **Personal:** Born Sep 23, 1939, Montecello, AR; son of Mamie James; married Elaine James, Apr 19, 1966. **Educ:** American College of Life Underwriters, CLU, 1969; Sacramento City College, AA, 1970; San Francisco State University, BS, 1981. **Career:** Golden State Mutual, vice pres, 1961-. **Orgs:** Life Underwriters Association of Los Angeles, 1981-; Society of Fellow of Lime Management, 1981-; Society of Chartered Life Underwriters, 1989; Black Agenda, first vice pres, 1989; YMCA Los Angeles, board member, 1989; Hugh O'Brian Youth Foundation, advisory bd, 1990; Los Angeles County Sheriff Foundation, board member, 1989, 1993. **Honors/Awds:** County of Los Angeles Certificate of Appreciation, 1990; John C Fremont High School, Hall of Fame, 1993; Los Angeles County Sheriff's Department, Appreciation & Recognition, 1992. **Home Addr:** 3652 Kensley Dr, Inglewood, CA 90305, (310)677-4017. **Business Addr:** Vice Pres, Golden State Mutual Life Insurance Company, 1999 W Adams Blvd, Los Angeles, CA 90018, (213)731-1131.

JAMES, CHERYL (SALT)
Rap artist. **Educ:** Queensborough Community College. **Career:** Sears Roebuck and Co, telephone customer-service representative, until 1985; member of the group Salt-N-Pepa, 1985-; albums include: Hot, Cool & Vicious, 1986; A Salt with a Deadly Pepa, 1989; Blacks' Magic, 1990; A Blitz of Salt-N-Pepa, 1991; Juice, 1992; For Our Children: The Concert, contributor, 1993; singles include: "Push It," "Tramp". **Honors/Awds:** "Push It," gold single, 1988; A Salt with a Deadly Pepa, gold, 1988; Hot, Cool & Vicious, platinum, 1988; National Academy of Recording Arts and Sciences, Grammy Award nomination, rap category, 1989. **Special Achievements:** Recorded song for soundtrack of film Colors.

JAMES, CLARENCE L., JR.
Business executive. **Personal:** Born Oct 13, 1933, Los Angeles, CA; son of Marguerite James and Clarence James; married Patricia Douglas; children: Clarence III, Craig. **Educ:** John Muir Coll, AA 1952; OH State Univ, BS 1956; Cleveland State Univ, JD 1962; Case Western Reserve Univ, graduate program in public management science certificate 1968. **Career:** Cleveland Legal Aid Soc, civil dir 1964-68; City of Cleveland, Dir of Law/Dep Mayor 1968-71; James Moore & Douglas, attorney-at-law 1971-77; State of OH, atty general 1972-77; US Copyright Royality Tribunal, chmn/comm 1977-81; The Keefe Co, pres/chief operating officer. **Orgs:** Pres Law School Alumni Assoc 1970-71; mem bd of overseers Cleveland Marshall Coll of Law 1970-77; lst vice pres Legal Aid Soc of Cleveland 1972-73; memBd of Trustee Cleveland Bar Assoc 1972-75; dep state coord CA Carter/Mondale Pres Campaign 1976; state coord NJ DeRose for Governor campaign 1977. **Honors/Awds:** Uniform Consumer Credit Code Georgetown Law Journal 1969; 1969 Chamber of Commerce Awd for one of Ten Outstanding Men; holder in Dug Course the Business Lawyer 1971; report of committee on Housing NIMLO Municipal Law Review 1972. **Business Addr:** President/Chief Operating Officer, The Keefe Company, 444 North Capitol St, Washington, DC 20001.

JAMES, DANIEL, III
Military officer. **Personal:** son Of Daniel "Chappie" James Jr.; married Dana. **Career:** Airline pilot, Commander Adjutant General Texas National Guard; Texas Air National Guard. **Business Addr:** Adjutant General, c/o HQ Texas National Guard, 2210 W 35th St, Bldg 8, Austin, TX 78763.

JAMES, DARRYL FARRAR
Cleric. **Personal:** Born Jul 3, 1954, Bridgeport, CT; son of Laurayne Farrar James and Anthony Francis James Sr. **Educ:** Howard University, BA, 1976; Interdominational Theological Center, post graduate, 1976-77; Yale Divinity School, MDiv, 1977-79. **Career:** Trinity Cathedral, lay assistant to dean, 1979-81; St Matthew's & St Joseph's, assistant priest, 1981-85; Messiah-St Bartholomew Episcopal Church, rector, 1985-. **Orgs:** Project Equality Inc, national board member, 1989-; Chicago Board of Education, compliance committee chairman, 1991-; African-American Male Commission, 1991-; Aids Task Force, 1991-; Commission on Ministry, 1988-91; Howard University Alumni, Chicago Chapter, past president, 1990; Cathedral Shelter, 1986-90; Urban Strategy Commission, 1989; Interfaith Council for the Homeless, 1979; Kappa Alpha Psi, Chicago Alumni Chapter. **Honors/Awds:** Chicago Board of Education, 4 year appointment, 1990; Yale Divinity School, Scholarship, 1977; Alpha Kappa Alpha Monarch Awardee in Religion, 1994; Kappa Alpha Psi, Chicago Alumni Achievement Award in Religion. **Special Achievements:** Cultural Youth Exchange, 1992; Study Tour of South Africa, 1992; Study Tour of Kenya, Africa, 1979; Union of Black Episcopalians Conference Dean, 1992-93. **Business Addr:** The Reverend, Messiah-St Bartholomew Episcopal Church, 8255 S Dante Ave, Chicago, IL 60619, (312)721-3232.

JAMES, DAVA PAULETTE
Educational administrator. **Personal:** Born Jul 16, Sharon, PA. **Educ:** Westminster Coll, BA 1974; Hampton Inst, MA 1978; IA State Univ, PhD summer 1985. **Career:** Hampton Inst, grad asst women's div 1976-78; Slippery Rock State Coll, asst dir admissions 1978-79; Youngstown State Univ, academic advisor 1980-85. **Orgs:** Mem Natl Academic Advising Assoc; former 1st vice pres Natl Assoc of Negro Business & Prof Women's Clubs Ohio Valley Club; former bd mem Mercer Co NAACP; mem Urban League. **Honors/Awds:** Listed in 1982 edition of Outstanding Young Women of Amer; certificate & trophy Meritorious Volunteer United Negro College Fund Youngstown Area Campaign 1982-85. **Business Addr:** ACA Advisor Schl of Education, Youngstown State University, 410 Wick, Youngstown, OH 44555.

JAMES, DAVID PHILLIP
Educator. **Personal:** Born Sep 2, 1940, Greenville, NC; son of Lula Forbes James and John Oscar James; married Janie Russell; children: Lauren Nicole, Joi Melissa. **Educ:** Elizabeth City State Univ, NC, BS, 1962; Georgetown Univ, Washington, DC, MA, 1971; Nova Univ, Fort Lauderdale, FL, EdD 1978. **Career:** Pitt Co NC, teacher/coach, 1962-63; Clarke Co VA, social sci teacher/coach, 1963-67; Washington, DC Public Schools, Social Science teacher/coach, 1967-71; Prince George's Community Coll, educ admin, 1971-, dean of educational development and extension centers & special programs, currently. **Orgs:** Part-time consultant, self-employed, 1978-; Student Retention; mem, Natl Council Community Serv & Continued Educ, 1973-; mem, Adult Educ Assn, 1978-; mem, Amer Assn for Higher Educ, 1982. **Honors/Awds:** Outstanding Teacher of the Year, Washington, DC Public Schools, 1971; Phi Alpha Theta Intl Award, History, Georgetown Univ, 1971; 1st Black Assoc Dean, Prince George's Community Coll, 1979; Honored Graduate, Elizabeth City State Coll, NC, 1962; Honored as the Outstanding Admin, Prince George Community Coll, 1988; Honorable Mention Recipient, Maryland Assn for Higher Educ as Outstanding Educator, 1989; Named Project Dir of the Black & Minority Student Retention Programs, Prince George's Community Coll, 1988; Authored, "Black Issues in Higher Education," 1988, "Increasing the Retention Rates of Black & Minority Students Through Mentoring & Tutorial Services at Prince George's Community College," 1989. **Home Addr:** 6238 Satan Wood Dr, Columbia, MD 21044. **Business Addr:** Dean, Prince George's Community Coll, 301 Largo Rd, Largo, MD 20772.

JAMES, DION
Professional baseball player (retired). **Personal:** Born Nov 9, 1962, Philadelphia, PA. **Career:** Milwaukee Brewers, outfielder 1983-85; Atlanta Braves, outfielder, 1987-89; Cleveland Indians, 1989-90. **Honors/Awds:** Named The Brewers Rookie of the Yr 1984.

JAMES, DOROTHY MARIE
Certified financial planner. **Personal:** Born Aug 19, 1936, Snow Lake, AR; daughter of Annie Gardner and Morris Gardner; married Lee Andrew James (divorced); children: Michelle Veronica, Rodney Michael. **Educ:** TN A&I State Univ Nashville, BS 1959; San Francisco Law School, JD 1974; College for Financial Planning Denver Colorado CFP 1987; CLU Program, currently. **Career:** Legal secretary, 1959-74; Private Practice, atty 1974-83; Operational Sentinel, lectr 1975-77; Lawyers Club of San Francisco, lecturer 1978; IDS/American Express, financial planner 1983-; The Phoenix Co Atlanta GA CFP Registered Representative 1988. **Orgs:** Bd dirs YWCA of San Francisco 1975-77; bd dirs San Francisco Council of Churches 1979-; bd dirs EOC of San Francisco 1980-; trustee Connectional bd of Personel Services CME Church 1986; bd of dir Societas Docta Inc 1987-. **Honors/Awds:** Scholarship Lawyers Wives of San Francisco 1973; Mother of the Yr Knights of Honor Civic & Social Club 1976; nominee (professionl category) Black Enterprise 1978; Woman of the Yr (Oakland Dist) Christian Methodist Episcopal Church 1980; Lay Person of the Yr Christian Methodist Episcopal Church 1980; Pi Omega Pi Hon Soc TN A&I State Univ. **Home Addr:** 1690 Sierra Dr, Marietta, GA 30062. **Business Addr:** Dorothy James JD CFP, The Phoenix Company, 1050 Crown Pointe Pkwy, Suite 600, Atlanta, GA 30338.

JAMES, ELRIDGE M.
Educator. **Personal:** Born Mar 23, 1942, Eunice, LA; married Betty Lea Stewart; children: Rona La Ne, Heath Elridge Floront. **Educ:** Grambling State U, BS 1966; Wayne State U, MEd 1969; MI State U, PhD 1973. **Career:** NE LA Univ, mem grad faculty, asst prof sec & coun educ 1975-76; Quachia Parish Bd of Educ, asst prof & clinical prof 1974-; Grambling State Univ, assoc prof 1973-74; MI State Univ, graduate asst 1972; Great Lakes Steel Corp, indus instructor 1969-70; Ecorse HS, teacher 1968-70; CJ Miller Elementary School; Great Lakes Steel Corp, dir educ 1968-70; Ford Motor Co, supvr 1966-68. **Orgs:** LA Indsl Arts Assn; Am Vocat Assn; LA Assn Pub Sch Adult Edn; So Assn for Counselor Educ & Supervision; LA State Reading Council; Assn Supr & Curriculum Devel; mem Phi Delta Kappa; Scottish Rite Mason King Solomon's Lodge; Omega Psi Phi. **Honors/Awds:** Wrote several articles & books for Grambling Coll; dean's list of outstanding grads MI State U. **Military Serv:** USN 1960-62. **Business Addr:** NE LA Univ Sec Coun Educ, Monroe, LA 71202.

JAMES, ETTA (JAMESETTA HAWKINS)
Recording artist. **Personal:** Born Jan 25, 1938, Los Angeles, CA; daughter of Dorothy Leatherwood Hawkins; married Artis Dee Mills, May 20, 1969; children: Donto James, Sametto James. **Career:** Singer, 1943-; Johnny Otis, Los Angeles, CA, bandleader, 1954; Bihari Brothers, Los Angeles, CA, record company, 1954; Leonard Chess, Los Angeles, CA, record comp, 1960; Warner Brothers, Los Angeles, CA, record comp, 1978; Fantasy Record, Los Angeles, CA, record comp, 1985; Island Record, Los Angeles, CA, record comp, 1988. **Honors/Awds:** Lifetime Achievement, Rigby & Blues Assn, 1989; Living Legends Award, KJLH, 1989; Image Award, NAACP, 1990; W C Handy Award, 1989; Blue Society Hall of Fame, 1991; Inducted to Rock & Roll Hall of Fame, 1993; 5th Handy Blues Awards, 1993, 1994; Soul of American Music Award, 1992; 8 Gramy Nominations, Beyond War Award, Best Song, 1984; Grammy, Best Jazz Vocal, 1995. **Special Achievements:** Sang Opening Ceremony of 1984 Olympics, Saints Go Marching In. **Business Addr:** Etta James Enterprise, 16409 Sally Ln, Riverside, CA 92504.

JAMES, FELIX
Educator, cleric. **Personal:** Born Nov 17, 1937, Hurtsboro, AL; son of Blanche Clark James and Leroy James Sr; married Florence Bernard, Aug 7, 1985. **Educ:** Fort Valley State Coll, Fort Valley, GA, BS, 1962; Howard Univ, Washington, DC, MA, 1967; Ohio State Univ, Columbus, PhD, 1972; New Orleans Baptist Theological Seminary, New Orleans, Masters of Arts in Christian Education, 1991. **Career:** Columbia Public Schools, Columbia, SC, instructor of social studies, 1962-64; Howard Univ, Washington, DC, reserve book librarian, 1965-67; Tuskegee Inst, Tuskegee, AL, instructor of history, 1967-70; Southern IL Univ, Carbondale, asst prof of history, 1972-74; Southern Univ in New Orleans, chairman of history dept, 1974-75, prof of history, 1979-; Salvation Baptist Church, pastor and moderator; Mt Zion Miss Bapt, assoc, currently. **Orgs:** Assn for the Study of Afro-Amer Life and History, state direc, 1973-, co-chair of program comm, 1979-80, member of exec bd; member, New Orleans Martin Luther King Steering Comm, 1977-; member, faculty coun, Southern Univ in New Orleans, 1980-85; vice-chair of arrangement comm, ASBS Annual Meeting in New Orleans, 1983; member of exec bd, Louisiana Historical Assn, 1984-86; member of advisory bd, Annual City-Wide Black Heritage Celebration, 1985-; commr, New Orleans Bicentennial Comm, 1987-91; consultant, Ethnic Minorities Cultural Center, Univ of N Iowa, 1988; senior warden, DeGruy Lodge, Prince Hall Free and Accepted Masons, 1989; member, bd of direcs, S Christian Leadership Conf, 1983-; worshipful master, DeGruy Lodge No 7, Prince Hall Free & Accepted Masons, 1991-; Illustrious Comman of Kadosh, Eureka Consistory, No 7-Masons. **Honors/Awds:** Author of The American Addition: History of a Black Community, Univ Press of Amer, 1978; contributor to Dict of Amer Negro Biography, 1982, Dict of Louisiana Biography, 1986, Black Leadership in the 20th Century, 1989, Edn of the Black Adult in the US, 1989, and Twentieth Century Black Leaders, 1989. **Business Addr:** Prof, Dept of History, Southern Univ in New Orleans, 6400 Press Dr, New Orleans, LA 70126.

JAMES, FRANK SAMUEL, III
Attorney. **Personal:** Born Aug 10, 1945, Mobile, AL; son of Mr and Mrs Frank S James, Jr; married Jothany Dianne Williams; children: David RF, Jothany Michelle, Julia Dianne. **Educ:** Campbell Coll, BS 1973; Univ of AL, JD 1978; US Army War College, graduate, 1990. **Career:** Fed Judge Virgil Pittman, law clerk 1978-80; US Dept of Justice, asst us atty 1980-86; Univ of AL School of Law, prof, asst dean 1986-90; Berkowitz, Lefkovits, Isom and Kushner, partner, 1990-. **Orgs:** Mem Amer Bar Assoc 1978-, AL State Bar 1978-, Birmingham Bar Assoc 1980-; bd of mgmt Downtown YMCA of Birmingham 1984-86; mem of council Synod of the Mid South 1985-86; moderator, mem of council Birmingham Presbytery 1986; pres of bd 1988-90, chmn of bd, 1991-, Alabama Capital Representation Resource Center 1991-; director, Columbia Theological Seminary, 1991-; trustee, Farrah Law Society, 1990-; trustee, The Presbytery of Sheppards and Lapsley, 1990-. **Honors/Awds:** Author Contingent Fees in Domestic Relations Actions 3 Jrnl of the Legal Prof 209 1978; elected to bench and bar Legal Hon Soc 1978; author with Charles W. Gamble, Perspectives on the Evidence Law of Alabama: A Decade of Evolution 1977-87, 40 Alabama Law Review 95, 1988; author, ''Protecting Final Judgments: A Critical Overview of Provisional Injunctive Relief in Alabama,'' 20 Cumberland Law Review 227, 1990; Distinguished Alumnus, Campbell University, 1987. **Military Serv:** US Army Reserve, Colonel, 1965-; Bronze Star, Air Medal, Purple Heart, Army Commendation Medal, Meritorious Service Medal, Army Achievement Medal, Combat Infantryman's Badge, US Army Infantry Officer Candidate Hall of Fame, 1991. **Business Addr:** Attorney, Berkowitz, Lefkovits, Isom & Kushner, 2505 Cobblestone Way, Birmingham, AL 35226, (205)942-4035.

JAMES, FREDERICK C.
Bishop. **Personal:** Born Apr 7, 1922, Prosperity, SC; married Theressa Gregg. **Educ:** Allen Univ, BA 1943; Howard Univ, MDiv 1947. **Career:** AME Episcopal Church, ordained to ministry; Friendship AME Church Irmo SC, pastor 1945; Meml AME Church Columbia SC, bishop 1946; Wayman AME Church Winnsboro SC, bishop 1947-50; Chappelle Meml AME Church Columbia SC, bishop 1950-53; Mt Pisgah AME Church Sumter SC, bishop 1953-72; AME Church Dallas, bishop 1972-. **Orgs:** Bd dir Greater Little Rock Urban League; chmn bd Shorter Coll; founder Mt Pisgah Apts, Sumter, James Centre, maseru, Lesotho, Mem Nat Interfaith Com Fund for Open Soc Dem Clubs; mem Odd Fellows, Masons, Shriners; dean Dickerson Theol Sem 1949-53; pres Sumter br NAACP 1959-72; mem World Conf Church &Soc Geneva 1966; chmn Wateree Community Actions Agency 1969-72; bishop in Botswana, Lesotho, Swaziland, Mozambique, South Africa, Namibia 1972-76; presiding bishop AR, OK 1976-; chmn Commnission on Missions AME Church 1976-; mem Natl Council Church Christ USA 1979-; hon consul-gen representing Lesotho in AR & OK 1979-; del World Meth Council Honolulu 1981; sec AME Council of Bishops 1981. **Business Addr:** Bishop, African Meth Episcopal Church, 604 Locust St, North Little Rock, AR 72114.

JAMES, FREDERICK JOHN
Attorney. **Personal:** Born Sep 1, 1938, Chicago, IL; son of Frances Harris James and John Henry James; married Barbara L Penny; children: Frederick J, Edward A. **Educ:** Univ of Chicago 1955-58; San Francisco State Coll, BA 1968; UC Berkeley Grad Sch Bus, MBA 1972; UC Berkeley Boalt Hall Sch of Law, JD 1973. **Career:** California State Univ, lecturer 1976; Law Offices of Frederick J James, atty 1974-; Law Offices of Hiawatha Roberts, law clerk, atty 1972-74; Del Monte Corp, mgmt trainee 1966-68; Wells Fargo Bank, field auditor 1964-66. **Orgs:** Treas Black MBA Asso Berkeley CA 1973; research asst Center for Real Estate & Urban Economics 1970; bd mem Men of Tomorrow 1977; mem Charles Houston Bar Assn; Nat Bar Assn; ABA; ATLA; CTLA; bd, mem/legal counsel: No CA Black C of C and Oakland Alameda County Black Chamber of Commerce, 1978-; bd of Commissioners Oakland Housing Authority 1983-89; pres Alameda County Democratic Lawyers 1986. **Honors/Awds:** Academic scholarship Univ of Chicago 1955-58; Certificate of Recognition for Legal Services to poor Charles Houston Bar Assn 1979; Certificate of Appreciation for Writing Judicare Grant Proposal 1979. **Military Serv:** AUS e-4 1962-64. **Business Addr:** Attorney, Law Offices of Frederick James, 1624 Franklin St, Suite 1000-1002, Oakland, CA 94612-2824.

JAMES, GILLETTE ORIEL
Cleric. **Personal:** Born May 5, 1935; son of Ethlyn James and Samuel James; married Rosa Vernita Ferguson; children: Jennifer. **Educ:** God's Bible Sch & Coll Cincinnati, AB 1959; Univ of San Francisco, BA 1968; American Bapt Seminary of the West, MDiv 1970, DMin 1976. **Career:** Christian Union Church West Indies, pastor 1959-60; US Army, chaplain's asst 1961-62; Western Union, telephone recorder 1962-65; Grace Bapt Church San Francisco, organizer/pastor 1963-69; Beth Eden Bapt Church Oakland CA, minister of Christian educ 1970-71, senior pastor 1971-. **Orgs:** Dean Baptist Ministers Union of Oakland 1971-85; pres bd of dirs Social Serv Bureau of Oakland 1976-79; vice pres Northern CA Credit Union 1976-79; pres Black Amer Baptists Northern CA 1977-84; vice pres Black Amer Baptists USA 1985-90; exec sec CA State Baptist Convention 1985-86; vice pres Baptist Ministers Union of Oakland 1986-; chairman, Community Earthquake Disaster Committee, 1989-91; member, Mayor's Earthquake Relief Fund, 1989-91; Black America Baptist USA, president, 1991-; Executive Comm, Western Commission on the Ministry, 1992-; Amer Baptist Seminary of the West, trustee, 1992-. **Honors/Awds:** Caliborne Hill Awd for Acad Excellence Amer Bapt Seminary of the West 1970; Outstanding Immigrant Awd Intl Inst of East Bay 1977; Disting Serv Bapt Ministers Union of Oakland 1985; 4th annual Black Clergy Award, Bayview Multipurpose Senior Services. **Military Serv:** US Army cpl 1961-62; Good Conduct Medal 1961, Rifle Marksman Medal 1962. **Home Addr:** 2400 Havenscourt Blvd, Oakland, CA 94605. **Business Addr:** Senior Pastor, Beth Eden Baptist Church, Senior Pastor, Beth Eden Baptist Church, 10th & Magnolia, Oakland, CA 94607.

JAMES, GREGORY CREED
Educator. **Personal:** Born Feb 29, 1956, Chicago, IL; son of Dorothy Baker Minor and Silas James. **Educ:** Southern IL Univ, BA 1977, MS 1983; Roosevelt Univ, Paralegal Degree 1981. **Career:** Goldblatt's Dept Store, oper supt 1977-79; CNA Ins Co, supvr 1979-81; Southern IL Univ, counselor 1981-83; Harrisburg Area Comm Coll, instructor/counselor 1983-85; West Chester Univ, asst dir financial aid 1985-86; asst prof of counseling, Community Coll of Philadelphia, 1986-; Lehman Coll, Bronx, NY, assoc prof of counseling, 1990-. **Orgs:** Consultant Southern IL Univ Office of Financial Aid 1982-83, Amer Assoc for Counseling & Devel 1983; consultant PA Assn of Minority Students 1984; bd of dir mem Amer Big Brothers/Big Sisters 1984, Amer Coll Personnel Assoc, Phi Delta Kappa Hon 1984; presenter Natl Assoc of Financial Admin 1985, PA Assn of Student Financial Aid Admin 1985; volunteer, Big Brother/Big Sister, 1988; mem, Alpha Phi Alpha Fraternity, 1988; mem, NY Metropolitan Assn of Developmental Educators, 1990. **Honors/Awds:** Publications include The Survival of Black Colleges and Financing Your Coll Educ With Private Monies. **Business Addr:** Associate Professor, Lehman College, Bedford Park Blvd, Bronx, NY 10468.

JAMES, HAMICE R., JR.
Clergyman, educator. **Personal:** Born Apr 19, 1929, La Grange, TX; married Carolyn. **Educ:** St Mary's U, BBA 1961; St Mary's U, MA 1971. **Career:** Employment Counselor, state employment comm 1964-69; City Water Utility Co, dir human relations 1969-73; St Phillips Coll, instructor 1973-; Emmanuel Baptist Church, pastor 1971-. **Orgs:** Mem following San Antonio Economic & Business Assn; Personnel & Management Assn; TX Jr Coll Tchrs Assn; pres bd dir Am Cancer Society. **Honors/Awds:** Hon business Fraternity; hon Economic Frat. **Military Serv:** AUS sgar 1947-56. **Business Addr:** St Philips Coll, 2111 Nevada St, San Antonio, TX.

JAMES, HAWTHORNE
Actor, author. **Personal:** Born in Chicago, IL; son of A M Alene Hawthorne and Robert L Hawthorne. **Educ:** University of Notre Dame, BA, 1974; University of Michigan, MA, 1975. **Career:** Actor, currently; experience includes: Othello, 1990; The Color Purple; The Doors, 1991; The Five Heartbeats, 1991; The Fresh Prince of Bel-Air, 1992; The Water Engine, 1992; The Habitation of Dragons, 1992; I'm Gonna Get You Sucka; Speed, 1994; Seven, 1995; Heaven's Prisoners, 1996; Sparks, 1997; author, Necromancer. **Honors/Awds:** Two Los Angeles Drama-Logue Awards, 1982, 1989; Los Angeles Weekly Award, 1987; Two Nominations, NAACP Theatre Awards, 1984-89, Nomination, Best Writer, 1989. **Special Achievements:** Scholarship, The London Shakespeare Academy; winner, Ted Lange Ira Aldridge Acting Competition. **Business Addr:** Actor, Author, c/o Selected Artists Agency, 3900 W Alameda Ave, Ste 1700, Burbank, CA 91505-4316, (818)752-2721.

JAMES, HENRY CHARLES
Professional basketball player. **Personal:** Born Jul 29, 1965, Centreville, AL; married Carmen; children: Carmen, Helena. **Educ:** St. Mary's (TX), bachelor's degree in computer science. **Career:** Played in Spain, forward, 1988-89; Wichita Falls Texans (CBA); 1988-94; Cleveland Cavaliers, 1990-91; Scavolini Pesaro (Italy), 1992-93; Sacramento Kings, 1993; Utah Jazz, 1993; Los Angeles Clippers, 1993-94; Sioux Falls Skyforce (CBA), 1994-96; Houston Rockets, 1996; Atlanta Hawks, 1996-97; Cleveland Cavaliers, 1997-. **Honors/Awds:** CBA Playoffs, MVP, 1996; CBA, All-League first team, 1994; CBA, All-League second team, 1993, 1996. **Special Achievements:** CBA, Championship, 1996. **Business Addr:** Professional Basketball Player, Cleveland Cavaliers, One Center Ct, Cleveland, OH 44115-4001, (216)659-9100.

JAMES, HERBERT I.
Scientist/personnel manager. **Personal:** Born Mar 30, 1933, St Thomas; married Christine M Stolz; children: Herbert Jr, Robyn. **Educ:** Hampton Inst, BS; Clark Univ, MA, PhD; DB Hill Train Cs, insurance broker; DB Hill Train Cs, investment broker; LaSalle Ext Univ, bus mgmt. **Career:** DB Hill & Co, br mgr; DB Hill & Assoc, br mgr; Clark Univ, tchr asst; St Thomas HS, tchr; Exp Coll of the VI, tchr; Hampton Inst, tchr;ESB Inc, res sci 1965-76; Xerox Corp, scientist 1976-80; personnel manager l980-. **Orgs:** Mem Electrochem Soc, Amer Assn for Adv of Sci, Instrument Soc of Amer, Beta Kappa Chi, Alpha Kappa Mu, NY Acad of Sci; pub sci works in various journ; presentations given at various mtgs of sci soc & presented sci papers at various coll; guest spkr & vocal at various mtgs; Episcopal Diocese of PA num comm and groups; exec bd Bucks Co Boy Scouts; bd dir Freedom Valley Coun Girl Scouts; NAACP Fellowship Clark Univ; scholarship Hampton Inst. **Honors/Awds:** VI Pub Aff Awd 1965; JFK Library Minority Awd, pres of the US Commendation Award. **Business Addr:** Manager of Personnel, Xerox Research Centre of Canada, 2660 Speakman Drive, Mississauga, ON, Canada L5K 2L1.

JAMES, HERMAN DELANO
Educational administrator. **Personal:** Born Feb 25, 1943, St Thomas, Virgin Islands of the United States; son of Frances Smith James and Henry James; married Marie Gray; children: Renee, Sybil, Sidney. **Educ:** Tuskegee Inst, BS 1965; St Johns Univ, MA 1967; Univ of Pgh, PhD 1972. **Career:** Univ of Pgh, asst prof 1971-72; Univ of MA, asst prof 1972-78, assoc provost 1975-76, asst chancellor 1976-78; CA State Univ, vice provost 1978-82; Rowan College of New Jersey, vice pres 1982-84, pres 1984-. **Orgs:** Mem Cherry Hill Minority Civic Assoc 1982-84; bd mem NJ Educ Computer Network 1983-; chair-colleges Gloucester Co United Way 1985; bd of dirs, American Association of State Colleges & Universities; bd of trustees, Middle States Assn; vice chair, Presidents Council, 1996; bd of dirs, South Jersey Industries; bd of dirs, NJ State Chamber of Commerce; honorary trustee, NJ Symphony Orchestra; American Council on Education's Commission on Leadership Dev; Labor/Higher Education Forum, American Council on Education (ACE); adv comm, Amer Assn of State Colleges & Universities (AASCU), Ctr for Educational Opportunity & Achievement; Committie on Excellence in Teaching of the American Assn of State Colleges & Universities; Camden Education Alliance; bd of dirs, Council for Aid to Education; bd of trustees, NJ Futures; Martin Luther King Commission. **Honors/Awds:** Fellowship Natl Inst of Health 1968-71; Young Black Achiever Boston YMCA 1977; Outstanding Educator Williamstown Civic Assoc 1984; Eileen Tosney Award, Amer Assn of Univerity Administrators, 1994; Honorary Doctor of Laws, Tuskegee Univ, 1996. **Business Addr:** President, Rowan University, Glassboro, NJ 08028.

JAMES, JOHN
Trucking company executive, business administrator. **Career:** O J Transport, owner, CEO, currently; Motor City Intermodal Express, president, currently. **Business Addr:** CEO, Owner, OJ Transport, 4005 W Fort St, Detroit, MI 48209, (313)841-0070.

JAMES, JOYCE L.
Advertising & public relations company executive. **Personal:** Born Mar 5, 1950, Saginaw, MI; daughter of Pearline Walker Wililams and Andrew J Williams, Sr; divorced; children: Tanya L Donahue-Jackson. **Educ:** Delta Coll, Univ Center MI, AA, 1981. **Career:** WWWS Radio, Saginaw MI, station manager, 1977-80; producer of ''One-Up'' shows, 1977-80; WUCM TV, Saginaw MI, producer and volunteer program coord, ''Day by Day,'' 1978-82; Pride Inc, Saginaw MI, activity dir, 1980-82; YWCA, Saginaw MI, asst dir, 1982; Delta Coll, Univ Center MI, counseling specialist, 1983-87; Inland Area OIC, Riverside CA, specail projects dir, 1987-89. **Orgs:** Life mem, Opportunities Industrialization Center, 1978; chairperson, Intl Year of Child for City of Saginaw, 1979; public relations media consultant, committee to elect Dr Lawrence Crawford, 1981; mem, Assn of Junior League, 1982-; public relations media consultant, committee to elect Mildred Mason, 1983; mem, Junior League of Riverside, 1988-. **Honors/Awds:** 1st Black Female Radio Station Manager in Midwest Market, 1977; Community Service Recognition Award, Zeta Omega Zeta Saginaw Chapter, Zeta Phi Beta Sorority, 1979; Community Service Award, Saginaw County Sickle Cell Anenia Council, 1981; Outstanding Community Service Award, City of Saginaw International Friendship Games, 1982; columnist, Model City Newspaper, Saginaw MI.

JAMES, JUANITA T.
Publishing company executive. **Personal:** Born Oct 1, 1952, Brooklyn, NY; daughter of Nora Corlette James and Compton Carew; married Dudley Norman Williams Jr, Apr 9, 1988; children: Dudley Norman III. **Educ:** Princeton Univ, AB 1974; Columbia Univ Grad Sch of Business, MBA 1982. **Career:** Time Life Books Inc, editorial rsch 1976-78, editorial admin 1978-81; Time Inc, financial analyst 1981-83; Time Life Books Inc, vice pres human resources, 1983-86; Time Life Libraries Inc, pres/CEO, 1987-90; Book of the Month Club, Inc, vice pres, dir of specialty clubs, 1990-92, senior vp, editorial, 1992-. **Orgs:** Mem Natl Black MBA Assoc 1982-, Natl Urban League 1982-; bd mem The Green Door 1984-88; trustee Princeton Univ 1984-; mem Natl Coalition of 100 Black Women 1986-; Rouse Co., director, 1988-; Black Women In Publishing; The Women's Media Group. **Honors/Awds:** Black Achievers in Industry Awd Harlem YMCA 1979; Andrew Heiskell Awd for Comm Serv Time Inc 1982; Alumni Service Award, Assn of Black Princeton Alumni, 1988; Achievement Award, Greater New York chapter, Links, Inc, 1988; Hall of Fame Award, National Assn of Negro Business and Professional Womens Clubs, 1990; Corporate Women's Network, Achievement Award,

1994. **Business Addr:** Senior VP & Editorial, Book-of-the-Month Club, Inc, 1271 Ave of Americas, New York, NY 10020.

JAMES, KAY C.
State official. **Personal:** Born Jun 1, 1949, Portsmouth, VA; married Charles. **Educ:** Hampton Institute, Hampton, VA, BS, 1971. **Career:** NRLC, Washington DC, dir of public affairs, White House Task Force on the Black Family, 1986-88; Natl Comm on Children, commissioner, beginning 1987; 1985; US Dept HHS, Washington, DC, assistant secretary for public affairs, 1989; One to One, Washington, DC, exec vice president, beginning 1990, sr vice president & CEO, beginning 1991; White House Off of Natl Drug Control Policy, assoc dir, 1991; Commonwealth of Virginia, secretary of health & human resource, 1993-; Family Research Council, sr vice pres, beginning 1993. **Orgs:** Board member, National Commission on Children, 1988; National Right to Life Committee, director of publications, 1985. **Special Achievements:** Publishes, Never Forget. **Business Addr:** Secretary of Health & Human Resource, Commonwealth of Virginia, PO Box 1475, Richmond, VA 23212.

JAMES, KEVIN PORTER
Professional sports administrator. **Personal:** Born Aug 2, 1964, Wichita, KS; son of Alice Jean Porter and James Porter Jr. **Educ:** Dodge City Community College, AA, general studies, communications technology, 1984; University of Arizona, BA, radio/television, public relations, 1988. **Career:** University of Arizona, Luke Olson, men's basketball manager, 1984-88; VIP Event Management Services, assistant manager, southwest region, 1988-90; Orlando Magic, Brian C Wiliams, manager, 1991-; Fred L Slaughter, NBA scout, recruiter, 1992-. **Business Addr:** 1616 14th St, #D-1, Denver, CO 80202-1340, (303)256-0020.

JAMES, LUTHER
Educator, writer, director. **Personal:** Born Aug 8, 1928, New York, NY; son of Alice James and Joseph James; married Marguerite James (divorced); children: Robin, Julian; married Thelma James. **Educ:** Dramatic Workshop of the New Sch for Social Research, graduate 1951. **Career:** New York, director & teacher, 1956-64; Luther James Theatre Workshop, New York, NY, teacher, 1958-68; Arena Productions, MGM, Culver City, CA, asst to supervising producer, 1965-66; CBS-TV, Los Angeles, CA, executive producer, 1966-68; WGBH-TV, Boston, MA, producer "On Being Black," 1968-70; Negro Ensemble Co, NY, instructor, 1968-69; Los Angeles, CA, TV writer and director, 1970-75; Portland State Univ, California State University-Los Angeles & California State University-Northridge, teacher of drama, 1971-73; University of California San Diego Dept of Theatre, associate professor, 1975-; Oregon Shakespeare Fest, director of plays, 1980-. **Orgs:** Member, Directors Guild of America; member, Writers Guild of America; theatre editor, Crisis Magazine, 1986-; member, Actors Studio, 1960-75. **Honors/Awds:** John Hay Whitney Fellow study in England, France, Germany, Russia, 1959-60; Ford Found Fellow, study of Broadway theatre, 1962; study of Brazilian Performance Art, 1984; study of film technique Russia, Hungary, Czechoslovakia, 1986; study of performance in Jamaica, Barbados, Trinidad, 1987; study/seminar with Brazilian actors and directors, 1987; theatre development in Zimbabwe, 1988; study of performance in Cuba, 1989. **Special Achievements:** Television programming and production, Uganda Television, consultant, 1991. **Business Addr:** Professor, Dept of Theatre, University of California San Diego, 9500 Gilman Rd, La Jolla, CA 92093.

JAMES, MARQUITA L.
Educator. **Personal:** Born Nov 9, 1932, Philadelphia. **Educ:** Wilberforce Univ Wilberforce OH, BA 1955; Seton Ahll Univ S Orange NJ, MA 1966; Candidacy NY U, PhD 1974. **Career:** Nassau Comm Coll Garden City, Long Island NY, assoc prof History 1969-; Wyandanch Schools, Wydandanch NY, chmn 1964-68; Freeport NY, Afro-Amer History curr coor 1968-69. **Orgs:** Hist & ldr crea of estab of Afro-Am Hist Soc in Freeport & Long Island NY; activist leader in successful fight to deseg sch buses & discrim prac inFreeport Schls 1968-69; mem Assn Univ Prof Assn Afro-Am Edn; Am Hist Assn; Afro-Am Black Heritage Assn; Cong of Racial Equal; Coun on Interracial Books for Child; Alpha Kappa Alpha Sor; Nat Black Feminist Org; pres Nassau-Suffolk Br Assn for Study of Afro-Am Life & Hist. **Honors/Awds:** Listed among black edrs in Black Hist Museum Hempstead LI NY; natl def educ award Tchrs Coll Columbia Univ NY UL,; inst intl educ award Univ of Ghana Legon W Africa 1969; m l kingr jr grad fellow award NY Univ 1968-71. **Business Addr:** History Dept Nassau Community, Garden City, NY 11530.

JAMES, NAOMI ELLEN
Educator, nurse (retired), city official. **Personal:** Born Jan 14, 1927, Inkster, MI; married Samuel M James Sr; children: Saundra Parsons, Marcia Allen, Samuel Jr, Carolyn L Miles. **Educ:** Wayne County Community College, AAS, nursing, 1979; Wayne State Univ, BSN, 1983. **Career:** Wayne Cty Gen Hosp, attendant, 1947-70, hosp attend super I, 1970-77; Hutzel Hosp, staff nurse 1980-83; Visiting Nurse Assn, public health nurse, registered nurse, 1983-86; Inkster City Council, member, elected for four-year term, 1991, mayor pro tem, 1995. **Orgs:** St Clements Episcopal Church, Diocese of Michigan, trustee; Blessed Mothers Guild, 1980-, past president, past sr warden, vestry member; Gamma Phi Delta Sor, 1981-; Inkster School Bd, past president, secretary, 1981-91; Inkster YWCA of Western Wayne, board of directors; Eloise Credit Union, chairperson credit comm; Inkster Teen Health Center, advisory board; Delta Sigma Theta Sorority Inc; Inkster Housing Commission Task Force; Friends of Western Ctr Comm Advisory Council; Gamma Phi Delta Sorority, past pres. **Honors/Awds:** Woman Worth Watching, Inkster Ledger Star 1983; Outstanding Volunteer, City of Inkster 1983; Oustanding Women of the Year, Delta Sigma Theta Sor 1984; Sharon Seventh Day Adventist Church, Historical Treatise in Recognition of Academic Achievement and Contribution to the Community, 1992; YWCA, Woman of Achievement Honoree, 1994. **Home Addr:** 3051 Williams, Inkster, MI 48141.

JAMES, OLIVE C. R.
University library director. **Personal:** Born Dec 4, 1929, New York, NY; daughter of Edith E Brown Roach and Audley C Roach; married Edmond Austin James (divorced 1965); children: Alan E, Karen Straughn, Jeffrey A, Christopher E. **Educ:** City College of New York, New York, NY, BS, (magna cum laude), 1950, graduate work, 1950-52; Rutgers University, MLS, 1965, New York University, graduate work, 1973-76. **Career:** Queens College, CUNY, New York, NY, reference librarian and Department head, 1966-76; Stanford University, Stanford, CA, library Department chief, 1976-80; Library of Congress, Washington DC, Division chief, 1980-87; Yale University, New Haven, CT, consultant, 1985-86; San Francisco State University, San Francisco, CA, Library Director, 1987-. **Orgs:** Associate College and Resource Libraries, Executive board,University libraries section, pro gram and language planning Committee, Executive Committee of bibliographic instruction section;Friends of San Francisco Public Library, board, 1988-; Ocean Beach Homeowners Association, President, 1991-; Stanford University Librarians Assembly, President, 1979-80. **Honors/Awds:** Council of Research Libraries, UCLA Senior Fellow, 1987; Association of Research Libraries, Fellowship with Consultants Program, 1982; United States Department of Education, University of Maryland, Fellowship with Library Administration Development Program, 1973; Department of Education, France, Assistante de Langue Anglais, 1952-53; Member of four National Honor Societies: French, Spanish, Education, Librarianship. **Business Addr:** University Librarian, San Francisco State University, 1630 Holloway, San Francisco, CA 94132.

JAMES, PEGGI C.
Association executive. **Personal:** Born Dec 4, 1940, Dothan, AL; divorced; children: Rose, Roddy, Rolaunda. **Educ:** AL State U, BS 1967. **Career:** Human Resource Devel Corp, exec dir; Grimsley HS Ashford AL, teacher, 1967-69. **Orgs:** Mem AL Assn Comm Action Agys; NEA; Les Vingts Socialietes Club; Dothan Asn Women's Clubs; NAACP; bd dirs Civic Cntr Opera House. **Honors/Awds:** 4-yr scholarship AL Assn Women's Clubs 1957; HC Trenholm acad award 1958; Dothan woman of year 1974; AL woman achievement 1974. **Business Addr:** Executive Dir, Human Resource Dev Corp, 108 Main St, Enterprise, AL 36330.

JAMES, RICHARD L.
Educator. **Personal:** Born Jul 31, 1926, Asheville, NC; married Velma A Kinsey. **Educ:** Hampton Inst VA, BS 1949; Univ MI, MMus 1951; Univ MD, EdD 1968. **Career:** School of Educ Morgan State Univ, dean 1975-; Morgan State Univ Baltimore, assoc dean teacher educ 1973-75; Amer Assn Colleges Teacher Educ, assoc dir 1968-73; Prince George's County, teacher 1958-67. **Orgs:** Mem communications com Assn Tchr Educators; Assn Higher Edn; Multicultural Educ Com AACTE; Omega Psi Phi. **Honors/Awds:** Author educ publs. **Military Serv:** AUS 1945-46. **Business Addr:** Dept of Educ, Morgan State Univ, Baltimore, MD.

JAMES, ROBERT D.
Educational administrator. **Personal:** Born Aug 24, 1950, New Rochelle, NY; son of Shirley Clark and Everett Lanier James; married Cheryl D Holley; children: Angela Laura, Anika Laren, Jamaal Malik. **Educ:** SUNY at Brockport, BS 1972, MS 1975; SUNY at Albany, pursuing EdD, currently. **Career:** Baden St Settlement Counseling Ctr, asst dir 1973-74; SUNY at Brockport, counselor 1974-77; Educ Oppor Pgm, dir 1977-79; SUNY Brockport, EOC, exec dir 1979-87; SUNY Office of Special Programs, acting senior assoc 1987-91; Public Employment Relations Bd, mediator/fact finder 1985-; NYS Martin Luther King, Jr Institute for Non Violence, interim director, 1991; SUNY Central Office, associate vice chancellor office of special programs, 1991-. **Orgs:** Consult, Ctr for Urban Ethnic Affairs 1975-77; consult, Univ of Rochester Court Mntl Hlth Team 1974-79; mediator/fact finder, NYS Pub Employment Rel Bd 1985-; bd mem, YMCA of Rochester 1979-85; bd mem, Urban League of Rochester 1984-88; bd mem, Catholic Youth Organ 1979-87; bd mem, Legal Aid Society 1984-86; bd mem Am Diabetes Assn 1984-86; Singer Lakes Occ Ed Ctr, bd of governors; president, Tri-State Consortium of Opportunity Programs, 1988-. **Honors/Awds:** Outstanding Alumni Award; Outstanding Service Award, SUNY at Brockport 1988; Arthur A Schomburg Distinguished Service Award, Assn for Equality & Excellence in Educ, Inc 1989; Distinguished Service Award, SUNY 1990; Distinguished Service Award, Tri State Censortium, 1991. **Business Addr:** Associate Vice Chancellor, Office of Special Programs, State University of New York, SUNY Plaza, #N-506, Albany, NY 12246.

JAMES, ROBERT EARL
Bank executive. **Personal:** Born Nov 21, 1946, Hattiesburg, MS; son of Mr and Mrs Jimmie James, Sr; married Shirley B; children: Robert II, Anne, Rachelle. **Educ:** Morris Brown Coll, BA 1964-68; Harvard Univ, MBA 1968-70. **Career:** Armco Steel Corp Middletown, OH, accounting trainee 1967; C & S Natl Bank Atlanta, GA, mgmt trainee 1969; Savannah Tribune Savannah, GA, publisher; Carver State Bank Savannah, GA, pres, 1971-. **Orgs:** Gen partner Atlantic Investors; trustee mem Morris Brown Coll; mem White House Conf on Small Business; dir GA Telecommunications Commn; chairman of the bd, National Bankers Assn, 1990-92. **Honors/Awds:** Intl Bus Fellows 1983. **Business Addr:** President, Carver State Bank, 701 W Broad St, Savannah, GA 31498.

JAMES, RONALD
Telecommunications company executive. **Personal:** Born Dec 3, 1950; married Renee James; children: Joshua, Jordan. **Educ:** Doane Coll, Crete, NE, BBA, 1971; Creighton Univ, Omaha, NE, 1977. **Career:** US West Communications, Minneapolis, MN, vice pres, 1985-, regional vp, eastern region, currently. **Orgs:** The St Paul Companies, dir; Automotive Industries Holding Inc, dir; co-chair, Action for Children Comm, 1991-; United Way of Minneapolis; Ceridan Corp, director; Great Hall Investment Funds Inc, dir. **Honors/Awds:** Doane College, Oustanding Young Alumni, 1982, Honor D Award, Hall of Fame, 1988. **Business Addr:** Vice President, Minnesota Public Policy, US West Communications, 150 S 5th St, Suite 3300, Minneapolis, MN 55402.

JAMES, RONALD J.
Attorney. **Personal:** Born Apr 8, 1937, Centerville, IA; son of Jennie M Smith James and Raymond B James; married Patricia O'Donnell; children: Catlin, Kelly, Shannon, Ronald Jr, Kevin. **Educ:** Univ of MO, AB 1959; Am Univ Wash Coll of Law, JD 1966; So IL U, MA 1972. **Career:** EEO Commn, regional att 1972-75; Waterloo IA Commn on Human Rights, exec dir 1967; Waterloo IA, asst Co atty 1967-69; OEO, spl asst to dir 1970-71; spl atty to con to pres 1971-72; Congressman James Bromwell, staff asst 1963-64; US Dept of Labor, admin wage & hour div 1975-77; Squire Sanders & Dempsey, partner 1977-. **Orgs:** Mem ABA; NBA; IA Bar Assn; Supreme Court Bar; mem Urban League; Ohio Bar Assn. **Honors/Awds:** Nat speech honorary Delta Sigma Rho. **Military Serv:** AUS 1st lt 1960-63; USAR capt. **Business Addr:** Partner, Squire, Sanders & Dempsey, 4900 Key Tower, 127 Public Square, Cleveland, OH 44114.

JAMES, SHARPE
Mayor. **Personal:** Born Feb 20, 1936, Jacksonville, FL; married Mary Mattison; children: John, Elliott, Kevin. **Educ:** Montclair State College, graduate (with honors); Springfield College, Masters; Washington State University, Columbia University, Rutgers University, graduate study. **Career:** Newark Public Schools, seven years, teacher; Essex County College, professor, 18 years; City of Newark, NJ, councilmember, 1970-86, mayor, 1986-. **Orgs:** Founder, Little City Hall Inc; charter member and past president, Organization of Negro Educators; executive, Scholarship Assistance Guidance Assn; bd member, National League of Cities; member, US Conference of Mayors; member, executive committee, Newark Collaboration Group. **Honors/Awds:** Honorary Doctorate of Laws, Montclair State College, 1988; Montclair State College Distinguished Alumni Award; New Jersey State Tennis Association champion; Newark Senior Tennis Champion; City Livability Award, 1991; City & State, Most Valuable Public Official Award, 1992. **Military Serv:** US Army. **Business Addr:** Mayor, City of Newark, 920 Broadway St, Rm 200, Newark, NJ 07102.

JAMES, SHERRI GWENDOLYN
Attorney. **Personal:** Born Jun 25, Columbus, GA; daughter of Zelma James & Johnny James. **Educ:** Georgetown University, BA, 1984; University of GA Law School, JD, 1988. **Career:** District Attorney's Office, asst dist attorney, 1991-. **Orgs:** American Bar Association; National Bar Association; GA Association of Black Women Attorney's. **Business Addr:** Assistant District Attorney, District Attorney's Office, Judicial Circuit, PO Box 1827, Albany, GA 31707, (912)432-8177.

JAMES, SIDNEY J.
Educational administrator. **Personal:** Born Jun 25, 1935, Columbia, MS; married Margie Pope; children: Kenja. **Educ:** Alcorn State Univ, BS Health & Phys Educ 1958; Univ of So MS, MS Coll Counseling 1972, Specialist's Ed Admin 1981; Marquette Univ, Certificate Management Training Inst 1980. **Career:** Prentiss Normal & Indus Inst, coach & teacher 1960-67, dean of students 1967-73, dir of special progs 1973-81, pres 1981-. **Orgs:** Mem Adv Bd First Federal Savings & Loan 1984; Phi Delta Kappa 1980-; vice pres City Planning Comm Colum-

bia MS 1981-; mem MS State Job Training Coordinating Council 1983-; mem Shriner 33 Mason. **Honors/Awds:** Coach of the Year Southern Intercollegiate Congress Co 1965; Outstanding Service Awd SAEOPP 1981; Disting Service Awd Phi Delta Kappa 1983. **Military Serv:** US Army, specialist E4 2 yrs. **Home Addr:** 1200 Maxwell St, Columbia, MS 39429.

JAMES, STEPHEN ELISHA
Government administrator. **Personal:** Born May 19, 1942, Montgomery, AL; son of Hazel Todd James and Elisha James; married Janie James, Apr 5, 1964 (divorced 1989); children: Lydia Yvonne Boseman, Stephen Christopher James. **Educ:** Case Western Reserve, Cleveland, OH, BA, 1970, MSLS, 1971; University of Wisconsin, Madison, WI, PhD, 1983. **Career:** Cleveland Public Library, Cleveland, OH, librarian, 1969-73; Atlanta University, Atlanta, GA, professor, 1976-87; Public Libraries of Saginaw, Saginaw, MI, assistant director, 1987-90; Library of Michigan, Lansing, MI, division director, 1990-. **Orgs:** Accreditation committee member, American Library Association, 1990-92; intellectual freedom committee member, Michigan Library Association, 1988-92; member, Kappa Delta Lambda chapter, Alpha Phi Alpha, 1991-. **Honors/Awds:** Beta-Phi-Mu, American Library Association, 1984. **Military Serv:** US Navy, E-4, 1962-66. **Business Addr:** Director of Statewide Library Programs, Library of Michigan, 717 W Allegan, Lansing, MI 48909.

JAMES, TIMOTHY ARCEE
Convention sales manager. **Personal:** Born Mar 21, 1962, Rochester, NY; son of Harriet Jones and Arcee James Jr. **Educ:** Florida A&M University, Tallahassee, FL, BS, 1986. **Career:** McCarthy's Business Institute, Rochester, NY, computer teacher,1986-90; Greater Rochester Visitors Association, Rochester, NY, convention account executive, 1990-. **Orgs:** National Coalition of Black Meeting Planners, 1990; National Coalition of Title One, Chapter One Parents, 1990. **Honors/Awds:** Daughters of America Citizenship Award (Medal), 1973. **Business Addr:** Convention Sales Manager, Greater Rochester Visitors Association, 126 Andrews St, Rochester, NY 14604.

JAMES, TONI-LESLIE
Costume designer. **Personal:** Born Jun 11, 1957, McKeesport, PA; daughter of Alice B James and Leslie Burrell James; married David Higham, Feb 28, 1981; children: Cosima B. **Educ:** Ohio State University, BFA, 1979. **Career:** Theatre Arts, costume designer, currently. **Orgs:** United Scenic Artists Local 829; Sokka Gakki International. **Honors/Awds:** American Theatre Wine Award, 1992, Tony Nomination, 1992; Drama Desk, Drama Desk Nominations, 1991, 1992; Drama-Logue, Drama-Logue Award, 1991; Audelio Awards, Audelio Award Nominations, 1990, 1991.

JAMES, TORY
Professional football player. **Personal:** Born May 18, 1973, New Orleans, LA. **Educ:** Louisiana State. **Career:** Denver Broncos, defensive back, 1996-. **Business Addr:** Professional Football Player, Denver Broncos, 13655 Broncos Pkwy, Englewood, CO 80112, (303)649-9000.

JAMES, TROY LEE
State legislator (retired). **Personal:** Born Apr 18, 1924, Texarkana, TX; son of Anniebell Mack James and Samuel James; married Betty Winslow James, Dec 18, 1946; children: Laura M James-Smith. **Educ:** Fenn Coll, attnd; Bethany Coll; Western Reserve Coll. **Career:** 12th Dist Cuyahoga Co; Ohio House of Representatives, legislator, 1967 until retirement. **Orgs:** Bd mem Margie Homes for Mentally Retarded; Eliza Bryant Home for Aged; dem exec com bd of OH State Legislators Soc; chmn Com on Aging; pres 5th WardDem Club; chmn Economic Develop Comm; mem NCSL Comm Economic Develop; executive committee, Black Elected Democrats of Ohio; mem, Citizen's League; member, Consumer Protection Agency; member, Western Reserve Psychiatric Agency; member, Cleveland Assn for Children with Learning Disabilities. **Honors/Awds:** Legislator of the Year, Ohio House of Representatives; Outstanding Legislation to the Youth of Ohio, Ohio Educational Assn; Outstanding Legislation for Community Work, The Champs, Inc; Special Recognition for Community and Civic Work, Cleveland Business League; ENA Award for Outstanding Services to Youth, National Assn of Career Women; Special Appreciation, National Society of Social Workers. **Military Serv:** AUS 1943-46. **Business Addr:** State Representative, State House, Columbus, OH 43215.

JAMES, WILLIAM
Educator. **Personal:** Born May 10, 1945, Augusta, GA; son of Harriet Martin James and Hinton James; married Maria Dawson (deceased); children: Kevyn, William. **Educ:** Morehouse Coll, BA 1967; Howard U, JD 1972; Alanta U, MSLS 1973. **Career:** Federal City Coll, lectr 1972; Fed Trade Comm, law clerk, 1972; Atlanta Univ, grad asst 1972-73; Univ of TN, asst prof & asst librarian 1973-77; Univ of KY, asst prof of law/law librarian; assoc prof of law/law librarian Univ of KY 1977-82; prof of law/law lib l982-88; Villanova Univ, prof of law/dir of law library, 1988-95, associate dean for information svcs & professor of law, 1995-. **Orgs:** AALL; AALS; LSAC. **Military Serv:** AUS e-5 1969-71. **Business Addr:** Associate Dean for Information Svcs/Professor of Law, Villanova University, School of Law, Villanova, PA 19085, (610)519-7023.

JAMES, WILLIAM M.
Church official. **Personal:** Born Jun 4, 1916, Meadville, MS; son of Rosa Ann James and Warren James; married Juanita; children: Edward. **Educ:** Mt Beulah Coll, AA; Butler U, BS, B of Sacred Lit; Drew U, BD MA; Univ of Chgo, Drew Univ, grad courses. **Career:** Multi Ethnic Ctr for Ministry of the Northeastern Jurisdiction of the United Methodist Church, dir; Metro Comm United Methodist Ch NY, sr minister; Trinity United Meth Ch Bronx, formerly pastor; ordained deacon 1938; elder 1940; Drew Univ, dir. **Orgs:** Mem officer Natl Bd Of Educ of Methodist Church; organizer founder Ministerial Interfaith Assn which administers Halem Coll Assist Prog; Harlem Interfaith Harlem Counseling Assn; Found of Harlem; former pres New York City Br NAACP; chmn of bd Harlem Urban Develop Coop; founder, Young People's Foundation.

JAMISON, BIRDIE HAIRSTON
Judge. **Personal:** Born Jul 1, 1957, Martinsville, VA; daughter of Ida Dalton Hairston and Irvin Spencer Hairston Sr; married Calvin D Jamison Sr, Aug 14, 1982; children: Calvin D Jamison Jr. **Educ:** Coll of William & Mary, Williamsburg, VA, BBA, 1979; Marshall-Wythe School of Law, Coll of William & Mary, Williamsburg, VA, JD, 1982. **Career:** George W Harris, Jr & Assoc, Roanoke, VA, associate attorney, 1982-84; Roanoke Commonwealth Attorny, Roanoke, VA, asst commonwealth attorney, 1984-88; VA Polytechnic Institute, Blacksburg, VA, adjunct instructor, 1983-88; VA Attorney General, Richmond, VA, asst attorney general, 1988-90; Richmond Commonwealth Attorney, Richmond, VA, deputy commonwealth attorney, 1990-91; General District Court, Richmond, VA, judge, currently. **Orgs:** Corresponding sec, Girlfriends, Inc, 1984-; mem, Jack & Jill, Inc, 1990-; mem, Delta Sigma Theta, Inc, 1978-; mem, Old Dominion Bar Assn, 1982-; pres, Roanoke Chapter Old Dominion Bar Assn, 1985-87; bd mem, Big Brother/Big Sister, 1990-; bd mem, Garfield Memorial Fund, 1990-. **Honors/Awds:** SERWA Award - Coalition of 200 Black Women, 1992; Virginia Heroes Award, 1992. **Business Addr:** Judge, General District Court, 800 East Marshall, Richmond, VA 23219-1998.

JAMISON, GEORGE R., JR.
Professional football player. **Personal:** Born Sep 30, 1962, Bridgeton, NJ; married Arnella. **Educ:** Cincinnati, attended; University of Detroit, bachelor's degree in human resources development, 1990. **Career:** Philadelphia Stars (USFL), linebacker, 1984; Baltimore Stars (USFL), 1985; Detroit Lions, 1986-93, 1997-; Kansas City Chiefs, 1994-96. **Business Addr:** Professional Football Player, Detroit Lions, 1200 Featherstone Rd, Pontiac, MI 48342, (248)335-4131.

JAMISON, JUDITH
Dance theater executive. **Personal:** Born May 10, 1943, Philadelphia, PA; daughter of Tessie B Jamison (deceased) and John Jamison Sr. **Educ:** Studied dance with private teachers Marion Cuyjet, Nadia Chilkovsky, Joan Kerr, 1949-61; Fisk Univ, 1961-62; Univ of the Arts, Philadelphia, PA, 1963-64; Judimar Sch of The Dance. **Career:** Alvin Ailey Am Dance Theater, New York NY, principal, 1965-80; dancer/choreographer, 1980-89, artistic director, 1989-; guest appearances: American Ballet Theatre, Harkness Ballet, San Francisco Ballet, Dallas Ballet, Vienna State Opera, Munich State Opera, Hamburg State Opera; leading roles: Cry, Sophisticated Ladies, 1980; choreographer: Divining, 1984; Mefistofele, Judith Jamison: The Dancemaker; The Jamison Project, director, 1988-. **Orgs:** Bd member, Council of the Arts; participated Harper Festival Chicago 1965; participated Festival of Negro Arts Dakar Senegal 1966; participated Edinburgh Festival 1968. **Honors/Awds:** Dance Magazine Award, 1972; Key to City of New York, 1976; Distinguished Service Award, Harvard Univ, 1982; Distinguished Service Award, Mayor of New York City, 1982; Philadelphia Arts Alliance Award; The Franklin Mint Award; Candace Award, National Coalition of 100 Black Women; received honorary doctorates from the University of the Arts, Marymount Colleges, Middlebury College, Manhattanville College. **Special Achievements:** Dancing Spirit, co-author w/Howard Kaplan, 1993. **Business Addr:** Artistic Director, Alvin Ailey American Dance Theater, 211 W 61st St, 3rd Flr, New York, NY 10023.

JAMISON, LAFAYETTE
Marketing and sales consultant, educator. **Personal:** Born Oct 8, 1926, Cleveland, OH; son of Stella Jamison and Lafayette Jamison, Sr; married Elaine; children: Lynn, Dirk. **Educ:** Virginia Union Univ, BA 1952; John Carroll Univ, grad work. **Career:** Joseph Schlitz Brewing Co, present mgr, YMCA, Salvation Army; teacher, asst prin; VA Union U, dean of students; Urban League, dir; St Dept Hertz, consultant; HUD; Bureau of Mint. **Orgs:** Pres Allentown Boys Club 1968-73; So MD Basketball Officials 1969-74; Toastmasters Inc; Khayyam Man of Yr; Citation Boys Clubs of Am; Big Bros. **Honors/Awds:** Bask-Aerobics, designed for and dedicated to female athletes. **Military Serv:** USAF, cpl WW II. **Business Addr:** President, Et Al Ltd, PO Box 23883, Milwaukee, WI 53223.

JAMISON, LEILA DUNCAN
Operations assistant. **Personal:** Born Nov 6, 1932, Denmark, SC; divorced. **Educ:** Voorhees Jr Coll, Diploma 1953; SC State Coll, BS 1955; Am Univ Washington DC, MPA 1979. **Career:** Voorhees Coll, assoc dir devel alumni affairs & public relations; business dept instructor 1966-77, alumni affairs sec 1967-70, alumni affairs 1970-72; Voorhees Coll, Denmark SC 1973-75; Howard Univ, operations asst Office of Vice Pres for Devel & Univ Relations; Special Economics Asst Program Office of Governor Div of Economic Devel & Transportation, program info coordinator; Office of the Gov Div of Rural Improvement, community consultant. **Orgs:** Mem Am Assn Univ Women; Voorhees Coll Alumni Assn; NAACP; Denmark Comm Rel Com-crowned Miss Alumni VCNAA 1961-62; Delta Sigma Theta. **Honors/Awds:** Alumni Achievement Award 1963; Outstanding Young Woman Am 1968; Alumni Serv Award 1974; Certificate Appreciation NAC of UNCF 1975; Comm Ldrs & Noteworthy Ams 1975-76; rec'd Plaque for Unselfish & Outst Serv Voorhees Coll Nat Alumni Assn 1976; rec'd Faculty Staff Serv Award for 15 Yrs Serv & Voorhees 1976.

JANGDHARRIE, WYCLIFFE K.
Educator, pastor, business executive. **Personal:** Born Dec 12, 1926; married Jewell; children: Rosalyn, Wycliffe II, Carolyn. **Educ:** Oakwood Coll Huntsville, BA 1950; Amer Bapt Theol Sem Nashville, BRE 1955; Temple Univ Tchr Coll Philadelphia & Columbia Univ Tchr Coll NY, post grad; Norfolk State Coll, MA 1978; Jameson Bible Institute, Hon DD. **Career:** Trinidad, evang 1950-51; Louis Spilman & Co London England, docket clk 1952-53; Washington Hill Conv Home, business mgr 1954-; School Dist of Philadelphia, tchr 1959-65; Neighborhood Youth Corps, coord 1965-66; Philadelphia School Dist, teacher 1966-68; City of Philadelphia, asst to city managing dir. **Orgs:** Mem pub relat com 1964 Philadelphia Assn Nursing & Convlesc Homes; mem NW Comm Ambulance Corps; pres DE Valley Assn Family Serv 1968; mem bd Counc Black Clergy; So Christ Leadership Conf; State Ad Hoc Com on Nursing & convlsc Homes; mem Gr Philadelphia C of C; NAACP vice pres N Philadelphia 1968-70; pres W Philadelphia 1971-; chmn Prison Ref Com & mem State Bd; vice chmn Health & Welfare Counc W Phila; sec Parkside YMCA; mem Bldg Task Force; mem Fin Com Reg YMCA; served numerous other civic & professional groups; participation in panel discussions lectrs media appearances natl & intl confs & convs; pres/pastor The Reformed Seventh Day Adventist Church; pres Philadelphia Chap of the Natl Council for Church and Social Action. **Honors/Awds:** Black Civic Awd Progress Plaze; Four Chaplains Leg Hon Awd 1964; Fellow of Amer Coll of Nursing Home Adminstrs 1970. **Business Addr:** Asst to City Mng Dir, City of Philadelphia, 11 FL City Hall Annex, Philadelphia, PA 19107.

JARMAN, PATRICIA MORSE
Boxing judge. **Career:** Nevada Office for Hospital Patients, administrator, currently; International boxing judge, 1984-. **Special Achievements:** First female and currently only African American professional boxing judge in Nevada. **Business Addr:** Administrator, Office for Hospital Patients, 1850 E. Saliara, Ste. 101, Las Vegas, NV 89158, (702)486-8255.

JARMON, JAMES HENRY, JR.
Educational administrator. **Personal:** Born Jan 9, 1942, Sheffield, AL; son of Mr and Mrs James Jarmon Sr; married Lillie Watson; children: Elisa Ann, Monica Yvette, James Henry III. **Educ:** Alabama State University, BS 1965; Troy State University, MS 1977. **Career:** DA Smith High School, teacher 1965-70; Mixon Elementary School, teacher 1970-77; DA Smith Jr High School, asst principal 1977-80; Flowers Elementary School, principal 1980-81; DA Smith Middle School, principal 1981-. **Orgs:** Member Alpha Phi Alpha 1963-; member OEA AEA NEA 1965-; member ACSAS 1977-; chairman Recreation Board City of Ozark 1978-; city councilman City of Ozark 1980-; mem, Natl Middle School Assn 1980-; board of directors RSVP 1981-; board of directors Parents Anonymous 1983-; board of directors Ozark Chamber of Commerce; utilities board, City of Ozark. **Honors/Awds:** Appreciation Award, Ozark Voters League, President 1979; Man of the Year Ozark Voters League 1980; Appreciation Award, Carroll High School Ozark 1983; member Phi Delta Kappa 1977-. **Home Addr:** 201 Don Ave, Ozark, AL 36360. **Business Addr:** Principal, DA Smith Middle School, 159 Enterprise Rd, Ozark, AL 36360.

JARREAU, AL (ALWYN LOPEZ JARREAU)
Singer, songwriter. **Personal:** Born Mar 12, 1940, Milwaukee, WI; son of Pearl Jarreau and Emile Jarreau; married Phyllis Hall (divorced); children: Ryan. **Educ:** Ripon Coll, BS psychology 1962; Univ IA, MS psychology 1964. **Career:** Singer/songwriter; Recordings include: We Got By, 1975; Glow, 1976; Look to the Rainbow, 1977; All Fly Home, 1978; This Time, 1980; Breaking Away, 1981; L is for Lover, 1986; Heart's Horizon, 1989; Al Jarreau, 1992. **Honors/Awds:** Grammy Awd Best Pop Vocal 1981; number one jazz vocalist for Cashbox 1976; Italian Music Critics Awd Best Fgn Vocalist 1977; winner Readers' Poll Down Beat Mag 1977-79; Grammy Awd Best Jazz Vocalist 1978-79; has won a total of four Grammys.

JARRETT, GERALD I., JR.
Attorney, educator. **Personal:** Born Jul 18, 1947, Newark, NJ; son of Nelson & Zelma Jarrett; married Karen Jordan-Jarrett, Aug 3, 1985; children: Laini, Gerald Jr, Brandon, Michael. **Educ:** Western New Mexico University; Youngstown State

University, BA, 1971; Seton Hall School of Law, JD, 1974. **Career:** State of NJ Labor Department, hearings officer, 1977-79; State of NJ administrative law judge, 1979-81; Private Practice, attorney, 1981-85; NJ Assembly Majority Leader Office, legal assistant, 1985-86; NJ Public Defender Office, public defender, 1986-97; Essex County College, adjunct professor, 1996; St Augustine College, assistant professor, 1997-. **Orgs:** Garden State Bar Association, president, 1984-85, treasurer, 1983-84; National Bar Association, chairman of the administrative law section, 1979-81; Kappa Alpha Psi, 1968-; Essex Newark Legal Svc, board of directors & executive secretary, 1981-85. **Home Addr:** 30 Eastwood St, East Orange, NJ 07017, (201)678-8084.

JARRETT, HOBART SIDNEY
Educator (retired). **Personal:** Born Nov 1, 1915, Arlington, TX; son of Jo Pearl Nicholson Jarrett and Wilson Hendrix Jarrett; married Gladys Janet Wynne, Aug 20, 1939. **Educ:** Wiley Coll, BA 1936; Syracuse Univ, MA 1937; Harvard Univ, Grad Study 1939-41; Syracuse Univ, PhD 1953. **Career:** Langston Univ, instr, assoc prof, chmn of modern language dept, prof and dean of personnel 1937-49; Bennett Coll, prof and chmn humanities div 1949-61; Brooklyn Coll CUNY, associate prof English 1961-63; prof 1963-85; prof emeritus 1985-. **Orgs:** Pres Greensboro NC Citizens Assoc 1959-61; bd of dir Coll Lang Assoc, Coll Engl Assoc; pres greater NY Reg Coll Engl Assoc; life mem MLA; mem MHRA; Shakespeare Soc of Amer; Intl Shakespeare Assn; chmn Coll Sect Natl Council of Teachers of Eng 4 yrs; bd mem RR Moton Foundation 1984-; life mem NAACP, UNCF; One Hundred Black Men; Grand Boule Historian Sigma Pi Phi Fraternity 1987-95. **Honors/Awds:** Fellowship General Education Board Rockefeller Foundation 1939; 1st black scholar to receive rank of prof of eng Brooklyn Coll 1965; Outstanding Teacher Awd CUNY 1973; Presidential Medal for Excellence in Teaching Brooklyn Coll 1973; First CUNY professor to conduct live seminar cable tv 1973; Award for Excellent Alumnus New York City Chap UNCF 1973; Man of the Year Alpha Phi Alpha 1978; ed book rev dept "Boule Journal" Sigma Pi Phi Frat; Distinguished Alumni Awd Natl Assn for Equal Opportunity in Higher Educ 1987; commencement address Wiley Coll 1983 and 1987; Hon degree: Dr of Humanities Wiley Coll 1987; Special Tribute, Black Caucus, NCTE, 1989; recipient of numerous awds for scholarship & civic accomplishments; Stepping Stone to Freedom, Greensboro, 1990; Published numerous articles & reviews in learned jrnls. **Special Achievements:** Author, History of Sigma Pi Phi, First of the African-American Greek-Letter Fraternities, Volume II, 1995. **Home Addr:** 315 W 70th St, Apt 15 J, New York, NY 10023.

JARRETT, THOMAS D.
Educator (retired). **Personal:** Born Aug 30, 1912; son of Annie Sybil Jarrett and William R Jarrett; married Annabelle M Gunter; children: Paula Lynn. **Educ:** Knoxville Coll, AB 1933; Fisk Univ, AM 1937; Univ of Chicago, PhD 1947. **Career:** Central High School, Paris TN, instr 1933-37; Knoxville Coll, asst prof English 1937-40; Louisville Municipal Coll, assoc prof English 1941-43; Atlanta Univ, asst prof 1947-50, assoc prof 1950-55, prof English 1955-67, chmn dept of English 1957-67, acting dean school of arts & sci 1957-60, dean grad school of arts & sci 1960-67, chmn interim admin comm 1967-68, acting pres 1968, pres 1968-77; US Dept of State, consultant 1977-78. **Orgs:** Pres Natl Assn of Coll Deans & Registrars 1968-69; mem Commn on English Natl Council of Teachers of English 1968; chmn Natl Council of Teachers of English Nominating Comm 1962; chmn Res Comm Natl Council of Teachers of English 1951; book review poetry editor, Phylon, Atlanta Univ Journal of Race & Culture 1948-67; Comm on Ways & Means of Working With Public Natl Council of Teachers of English 1957-58; consultant Dept HEW 1966; appointed to adv comm for Natl Defense Language Devel Prog 1966-68; appointed to Georgia Sci & Tech Commn 1969; mem Natl Council of Teachers of English; Coll Language Assn; Assn of Amer Univ Professors; Conf of Deans of So Grad Schools; Council of Grad Schools in US. **Honors/Awds:** Gen Educ Bd Fellow 1939-40; Carnegie Grant for Rsch 1951-52; Distinguished Alumni Award, University of Chicago, 1980. **Special Achievements:** Numerous publications; first African American to preside at the National Convention of the National Council of Teachers of English, 1966; first African American to head the Rhodes Scholarship selection committee, 1974-76. **Home Addr:** 557 Fielding Ln SW, Atlanta, GA 30311.

JARRETT, VALERIE B.
Government official. **Personal:** Born Nov 14, 1956, Shiraz, Iran; daughter of Barbara Bowman and James Bowman; divorced; children: Laura. **Educ:** Stanford University, BA, psychology, 1978; University of Michigan Law School, JD, 1981. **Career:** Pope Ballard Shepard & Fowle Ltd, associate, corporate banking; Sonnenschein, Carlin, Nath & Rosenthal, Real Estate Department, associate; City of Chicago, Department of Law, deputy corp counsel for finance & development, Office of the Mayor, deputy chief of staff, Department of Planning, acting commissioner, Department of Planning & Development, commissioner, currently. **Orgs:** Lambda Alpha International; Center for International Business Education & Research; Southeast Chicago Commission, director; NAACP Legal Defense and Education-Chicago Fund, director; Local Initiatives Support Corp.; The Economic Club of Chicago; National Council for Urban Economic Development; Leadership Greater Chicago, director, 1988-89. **Honors/Awds:** Women's Business Development Center, Government Support Award, 1992. **Special Achievements:** Consolidated Department of Planning, Economic Development, and Urban Renewal, 1992; implemented a model program for the revitalization of three Chicago neighborhoods, 1992; created a business express unit to cut red tape to service Chicago businesses, 1992. **Business Addr:** Exec VP, The Habitat Co., 350 W Hubbard St, 5th Fl, Chicago, IL 60610, (312)527-7471.

JARRETT, VERNON D.
Journalist. **Personal:** Born Jun 19, 1921, Saulsbury, TN; married Fernetta; children: William, Thomas. **Educ:** Knoxville Coll, BA; Northwestern Univ, studied journalism; Univ of Kansas City, studied TV writing & producing; Univ of Chicago, urban sociology. **Career:** Chicago Tribune Newspaper, editorial page columnist, Tribune column appears 3 times weekly; radio/TV producer; moderator; "Black on Black," weekly show interviews with outstanding Black people; WJPC, radio show "The Vernon Jarrett Report.". **Orgs:** Natl Assn of Black Journalists, pres, 1977-79; bd of govs, Chicago Chapter Natl Acad of TV Arts & Sci; chmn of the bd, Dusable Museum of African-American History in Chicago; Sigma Delta Chi; visiting assoc prof of history; Northwestern Univ; teacher TV Course Amer History, City Coll of Chicago; NAACP, ACT-SO, founder, chairman. **Honors/Awds:** Nominated for Pulitzer Prize in journalism 1972-73; won numerous awards for his reporting.

JARVIS, CHARLENE DREW
Educational administrator. **Personal:** daugHter of Charles R Drew. **Educ:** Oberlin College, bachelor's degree; Howard Univ, master's degree; Univ of Maryland, doctorate degree. **Career:** Howard Univ, professor; Montgomery College, professor; Southeastern Univ, pres; District of Columbia City Council, councilwoman, 1979-. **Orgs:** Committee on Economic Development.

JASON, HENRY THOMAS
Law enforcement official (retired). **Personal:** Born Aug 22, 1921, Detroit, MI; son of Daisy Jason and William Jason; married Lillian; children: Mark Owens Jason. **Educ:** Wayne State U, Univ of MI; Henry Ford Comm Coll; Univ of MI. **Career:** Detroit Police Dept, retired dist commander 1947-74; City of Inkster, chief of police 1974-80 (retired). **Orgs:** Life mem NAACP; Detroit Police Lt & Sgts Assn; SE MI Assn of Chiefs of Police; Wayne Co Assn Chiefs of Police; mem Intl Assn Chiefs of Police IACP; Guardians MI Asso Black Law Enforcement Exec NOBLE; founding chmn Fabulous Floridians Social Club 1981; Palm Beach Paralyzed Vets Assn of Florida. **Honors/Awds:** Relations awd Cotillion Club Police Community 1966; Military Excellence Awd Detroit Police 1973. **Military Serv:** USAF 1942-46. **Home Addr:** 1064 Summerwood Circle, West Palm Beach, FL 33414.

JASON, JEANNE. **See WRIGHT, JEANNE JASON.**

JASPER, EDWARD VIDEL
Professional football player. **Personal:** Born Jan 18, 1973. **Educ:** Texas A&M, attended. **Career:** Philadelphia Eagles, defensive tackle, 1997-. **Business Addr:** Professional Football Player, Philadelphia Eagles, 3501 S Broad St, Philadelphia, PA 19148, (215)463-2500.

JASPER, LAWRENCE E.
Insurance company executive. **Personal:** Born Oct 25, 1946, Philadelphia; son of Geraldine and Lawrence Jasper (both deceased); married Diana Lundy; children: Laurette, Dawn. **Educ:** ICA; LUTC. **Career:** Pilgrim Life Ins Co, 1st asst to vice pres 1974, vp; Debit Agt, 1968-69; Supr 1969-71; Serv Asst Spectrum Arena, supr 1971-74; Pilgrim Life Insurance Co/ Pilgrim Mutual Insurance Co, vice president, currently. **Orgs:** NAACP; Young Great Soc; 19 St Bapt Ch Youth Dept; Interest in Bus Training of Black & Youth. **Honors/Awds:** Man of Year Pilgrim Life Ins 1970, 1972; 1st Black in mgmt Pilgrim Life; 1st man to rec Man of Year Award twice; youngest man & only black on bd of dir at Pilgrim Life. **Military Serv:** Sgt E-5 drill instr 1968. **Business Addr:** Vice President, Pilgrim Life Insurance Co/Pilgrim Mutual Insurance Co, 8049 Westchester Pike, Upper Darby, PA 19082.

JAVERY, MICHAEL
Corporate manager. **Personal:** Born Aug 16, 1953, Slidell, LA; son of George Javery Jr & Inez Gaddie Javery; married Peggy Veronica, Jul 2, 1994; children: Ryan Michael. **Educ:** West Hills College, BSEE, 1974. **Career:** US Navy, avionics officer, 1971-77, sr test engineer, 1984-88, chief test operations engineering, 1987-88, chief final assembly & test, 1988-89, chief TPS applications, 1988-89, sr staff engineer advanced mfg technology, 1989-91; Martin Marietta, mgr, TPS large structures, 1991-97, dir, manufacturing & test, 1997-. **Orgs:** YMCA, Dryades, Black achiever committee person, 1991-. **Honors/Awds:** MMC, Operational Performance Award, 1982; MCC-NASA, Astroaut Silver Snoopy, 1978; MMC, Mission Success Award, 1990; MMC, Space Shuttle Launch Honoree, 1982, 1992; Black Engineer, Outstanding Technical Contributions, 1992. **Military Serv:** US Navy, avionics officer, 1971-77; Good Conduct Medal, Vietnam Veteran. **Business Addr:** Director, Manufacturing & Test, Lockheed Martin Michoud Spaces Systems, PO Box 29304 (D3600), Building 102, New Orleans, LA 70189, (504)257-1530.

JAY, JAMES M.
Educator. **Personal:** Born Sep 12, 1927, Fitzgerald, GA; son of Lizzie W Jay and John B Jay; married Patsie Phelps; children: Mark E, Alicia D, Byron R. **Educ:** Paine Coll, AB 1950; OH State U, MSc 1953, PhD 1956. **Career:** OH State U, post doc fellow 1956-57; Southern U, asst prof to prof 1957-61; Wayne State U, asst prof to prof 1961-94, prof emeritus, 1994-; Univ of Nev, Las Vegas, adjunct prof, 1994-. **Orgs:** Member, National Advisory Committee for Microbiological Criteria for Foods, USDA, 1987-94; committee member, National Academy of Sciences, 1984-87; editorial board member, J Food Protection, 1981-97; panel member, Institute of Food Technology, 1991-95. **Honors/Awds:** Probus Award Wayne State Univ 1969; Dist Alumni Award Paine Coll 1969; Michigan Science Trailblazer Award, Detroit Science Center, 1987; Faculty Research Award, Sigma Xi Chapter, Wayne State University, 1988; Founders Award, Detroit Inter-Alumni Council of UNCF, 1986; Institute of Food Technologists, Fellow, 1996-. **Military Serv:** AUS sgt 1946-47. **Business Addr:** Adjunct Prof, Dept, Biol Sci, Univ Nevada Las Vegas, Las Vegas, NV 89154.

JAYCOX, MARY IRINE
Public relations executive. **Personal:** Born Aug 19, 1939, Camphill, AL; daughter of Betty Busby and Eddie B Knight; married James Curtis Jaycox; children: James Jr, Sharon, Mary, Thomas. **Educ:** Univ of Northern IA, BA 1984, MA 1986. **Career:** Har-lin Pre-School Erie PA, parent coord 1966-67; Sears Roebuck & Co, div mgr 1973-80; KBBG-FM Waterloo IA, talk show host 1981-84; Dubuque City of Festivals, promotions dir. **Orgs:** Freelance feature writer Waterloo Courier, Telegraph Herald Dubuque; housing analyst Comm Housing Resource Bd; YMCA mem & publicity comm Waterloo 1985-86; commissioner Cable Comm Teleprogramming. **Honors/Awds:** Poetry in Inner Weather library magazine 1983; Best Commercial Script 1984, Best Short Script Univ of Northern IA 1984. **Home Addr:** 1600 Shelby Dr, Dyersburg, TN 38024-3439. **Business Addr:** Public Information Coordinator, City of Dubuque, 13th & Central, Dubuque, IA 52001.

JAYNES, GERALD DAVID
Educator. **Personal:** Born Jan 30, 1947, Streator, IL; son of Lorraine Greenwood Jaynes and Homer Jaynes; children: Vechel, Hillary. **Educ:** Univ of IL-Urbana, BA (High Honors) 1971, MA 1974, PhD 1976; Yale Univ, MA 1984. **Career:** Univ of Pennsylvania, asst prof economics 1975-77; Yale Univ, asst prof of economics 1977-81, assoc prof economics 1981-84, prof economics 1984-; study dir Comm on the Status of Black Amers/Natl Rsch Council 1985-89; chair, African and Afro-American Studies, 1990-96. **Orgs:** Bd of economists Black Enterprise Magazine 1984-95. **Honors/Awds:** Adjunct Fellow Joint Ctr for Political Studies 1982-; book "Branches Without Roots, Genesis of the Black Working Class," Oxford Univ Press 1986; "A Common Destiny: Blacks and Amer Society" ed with R. Williams Jr, Natl Academy of Sciences Press 1989. **Military Serv:** AUS spl 5th class 3 yrs. **Business Addr:** Professor of Economics, Yale University, Dept of Economics, New Haven, CT 06520.

JEAN, KYMBERLY
Business owner. **Personal:** Born Dec 31, 1963, Chicago, IL; daughter of P Jean and H Jean. **Educ:** Los Angeles City College, AA, 1985. **Career:** Opposites Attract, president, founder, currently. **Orgs:** Toastmaster; Women's Referral Service; National Association of Women Business Owners; Black Women's Network. **Special Achievements:** Essence Magazine, 1993; Jet Magazine, 1992; The Oprah Winfrey Show, 1991; The Phil Donahue Show, 1992. **Business Addr:** President & Founder, Opposites Attract, 9016 Wilshire Blvd, Suite 701, Beverly Hills, CA 90211, (213)957-9797.

JEANBAPTISTE, CARL S.
Physician. **Personal:** Born Feb 15, 1930, Hinche, Haiti; divorced. **Educ:** Univ Haiti, 1951; Univ Haiti Med Schl, 1957; Meml Sloan-kettering Cancer Ctr, surg res 1966-68; Harlem Hosp Ctr, post-grad Training 1960-66; Surgery, Brooklyn Cumberland Med Ctr, asso atdng 1968-77; Brookdale & Brooklyn Jewish Hosp, asst atdng surgery 1970-77; St Univ NY, clinical instr. **Career:** Physician. **Orgs:** Provident Clinical Soc of Brooklyn; Kings Co Med Soc; NY St Med Assn; Nat Med Assn. **Honors/Awds:** Fellow Am Coll of Surgeons; diplomate Am Bd of Surgery; Brooklyn Surgical Soc Publ NY St Jour of Med 1972. **Business Addr:** 361 Eastern Parkway, Brooklyn, NY 11216.

JEFF, GLORIA JEAN
State transportation official. **Personal:** Born Apr 8, 1952, Detroit, MI; daughter of Harriette Virginia Davis Jeff and Doris Lee Jeff. **Educ:** University of Michigan, Ann Arbor, MI, BSE,

civil engineering, MSE, civil engineering, Masters of Urban Planning; Carnegie-Mellon University, Professional Program in Urban Transportation, certificate; Indiana Univ & Purdue Univ at Indianapolis/American Assn of State Highway Transportation Officials Management Institute, certificate; Michigan State Chamber of Commerce, Leadership Michigan. **Career:** Southeastern Michigan Transportation Authority, principal planner, program analyst, equipment engineer, 1976-81; Michigan Dept of Transportation, Multi-Regional Planning Div, Lansing, MI, div administrator, 1981-84, Urban Transportation Planning Div, div administrator, 1984-85, Bureau of Transportation Planning, assistant deputy dir, 1985-90, deputy dir, 1990-; University of Michigan, College of Architecture & Urban Planning, Ann Arbor, MI, adjunct professor, 1988-. **Orgs:** Member, Amer Planning Assn, Transportation Planning Div; member, bd of dirs, 1988-, vice pres, 1989-90, president, 1990, Amer Planning Assn, Michigan Chap; member, Michigan Soc of Planning Officials; member, Amer Institute of Certified Planners; member, board of directors, University of Michigan Alumni Assn; member, Women's Transportation Seminar; member, bd of dirs, Univ of Michigan College of Architecture & Urban Planning Alumni Soc; chair, Univ of Michigan College of Engineering, Minority Engineering Program, Office Celebration Committee, 1989-90; member, Transportation Res Bd, Statewide Multimodal Transportation Planning Committee;member, Delta Sigma Theta Sorority; vice chair, Intermodal Issues Committee, Amer Assn of State Highway & Transportation Officials, currently; vice chaiMississippi Valley Conference, Strategic Issues Committee, 1990-. **Honors/Awds:** Achievement Award, Michigan Chapter, Conference of Minority Transportation Officials, 1990; Distinguished Alumni Award, University of Michigan, 1991; Young Engineer of the Year, Detroit Chapter, National Society of Professional Engineers, 1979; Young Engineer of the Year, Detroit Chapter, Society of Women Engineers, 1979; SEMTA Board of Directors Resolution of Commendation Achievement Award, 1979; active with high school students pursuing scientific and engineering education. **Business Addr:** Deputy Director, Transportation Planning, Michigan Department of Transportation, 425 W Ottawa, 4th Fl, Lansing, MI 48909.

JEFFCOAT, JAMES WILSON, JR.
Professional football player. **Personal:** Born Apr 1, 1961, Long Branch, NJ; married Tammy; children: Jaren, Jackson, Jacqoline. **Educ:** Arizona State Univ, BA, communications, 1983; Univ of North Texas, MBA program, currently. **Career:** Dallas Cowboys, defensive end, 1983-. **Honors/Awds:** Dallas Cowboys' Man of the Year nominee, 1990; works with the Boys Clubs, Leukemia Society, Make-A-Wish Foundation, Sickle Cell Anemia Foundation (donates $100 for each of his sacks), and Special Olympics. **Business Addr:** Professional Football Player, Dallas Cowboys, One Cowboys Pkwy, Irving, TX 75063-4999.

JEFFERIES, CHARLOTTE S.
Educator. **Personal:** Born Mar 8, 1944, McKeesport, PA. **Educ:** Howard U, BS 1966; Rollins Coll, postgrad 1967; Duquesne Univ Sch of Law, JD 1980. **Career:** Seminole Co FL, teacher 1966-67; OIC of Erie, dir of couns 1967-70; Urban Coalition of RI, health planner 1970-71; Student Serv OIC of RI, dir 1971-72; Career Develop Brown Univ, assoc dir 1973-77; Neighborhood Legal Serv McKeesport, legal intern 1978-79; Office of US Attorney Dept of Justice, law clerk 1979-80; Honorable Donald E Ziegler Judge US Dist Ct Western Dist of PA, law clerk 1980-81; Horty Springer & Mattern PC, partner, 1981-. **Orgs:** Mem Delta Sigma Theta Inc; mem Amer Natl PA and Allegheny Bar Assocs; mem Homer S Brown Law Assoc, Soc of Hospital Attorneys; city councilperson Cityof Duquesne; mem YWCA of McKeesport; mem NAACP, Howard Univ Alumni Club; Allegheny County Air Pollution, advisory com, municipal advisory comm, mon valley commission; Natl Health Lawyers Assn. **Honors/Awds:** Apptmt law clerk Office of US Attorney 1979; appellate moot court bd Duquesne Univ 1979-80; Outstanding Student of the Year Black Amer Law Student Assoc Duquesne Univ Chap 1980; Richard Allen Awd Outstanding Civic contributions 1980; chmn Merit Selection Panel US Magistrates Western Dist of PA 1987, 1988. **Business Addr:** Attorney at Law, Horty Springer & Mattern PC, 4614 Fifth Ave, Pittsburgh, PA 15213.

JEFFERIES, GREG LAMONT
Professional football player. **Personal:** Born Oct 16, 1971, High Point, NC. **Educ:** Virginia. **Career:** Detroit Lions, defensive back, 1993-. **Business Addr:** Professional Football Player, Detroit Lions, 1200 Featherstone Rd, Pontiac, MI 48342, (248)335-4131.

JEFFERS, BEN L.
Government employee. **Personal:** Born Jun 18, 1944, Lake City, FL; married Salomia Lawson. **Educ:** MT State U; A&T U; McNeese State U. **Career:** LA Hlth & Human Rsrcs Admnstrn, dir Div Mgmt; LA Hlth & Human Resources Admnstr, dir; LA Commn on Human Rltns Rights & Rspnsblities, dir; Gov Edwin Edwards, cong aide; LA Democratic Party, chair, 1997-. **Orgs:** Chmn LA Coalition for Social Serv Program; state adv bd Comprehensive Hlth Planning; mem Dvlpmntl Disabilities Cncl; Nat Rehabltatn Assn; LA Rehab Assn; Am Soc for Train-

ing & Devel; Am Pub Welfare Assn; LA Hlth Assn mem Kiwanis Club of Lake Charles; Am Legion; Prince Hall Masons; past mem bd dir Advertising & Press Clubg of SW LA; past bd mem Foreman-reynaud Br YMCA; gen mgr Lake Charles Newsleader; former Exec asst to Pub of Newsleader Newspapers in LA & MS; editor Pub of Lake Charles Times; mem State Manpower Planning Cncl; mem NAACP. **Special Achievements:** First african American elected to chair Louisiana Democratic Party. **Military Serv:** USMC sgt 1963-67. **Business Addr:** Chairman, Louisiana Democratic Party, Baton Rouge, LA.

JEFFERS, CLIFTON R.
Attorney. **Personal:** Born Feb 8, 1934, Roxboro, NC; son of Clara Jeffers and Theron Jeffers; married Mary R Lloyd; children: Kwame. **Educ:** TN State Univ, AB (magna cum laude) 1956; Hastings Coll Law Univ CA, JD 1964. **Career:** State of CA, state deputy atty, 1964-69; US Dept HUD, reg admin, 1969-76; State of CA, chief asst state pub defender, 1976-84; James & Jeffers, sr partner, currently. **Orgs:** Mem Natl, CA, San Francisco Bar Assns; Charles Houston Bar Assn; bd of dir Bar Assn of SF 1984-; bd dirs Lawyers Club of San Francisco 1981-82; mem Amer Judicature Soc; pres SF NAACP 1966-69; bd dir Amer Civil Liberties Union of No CA 1969-73; SF Coun of Chs 1967-72; SF Econ Oppt Coun 1967-68; founding president William Hastie Lawyers Assn; bd dir Frederick Douglas Haynes Gardens; gen counsel 3rd Baptist Ch; bd dir CA Rural Legal Assistance Found; founding mem San Francisco Black Leadership Forum; trustee 3rd Bapt Ch; bd dir NAACP; bd of dir First District Appellate Project; co-founder, State Bar Standing Comm on Legal Services to Criminal Defendants; mem, CA Assn of Black Lawyers; co-founder and dir Third Baptist Gardens, Inc.; mem Afro-Amer Agenda Council. **Honors/Awds:** Outstanding Pres Awd NAACP 1967, 1969; Amer Jurisprudence Awd; US Dept HUD Equal Empl Oppt Awd; US Dept HUD Cert of Fair Housing Achvmt; NAACP Meritorious Serv Awds; guest lectr in Criminology Univ of CA Berkeley; Outstanding Performance Awd HUD; commendations San Francisco bd of supervisors; Certificate of Honor San Francisco bd of supervisors; guest lecturer Stanford Univ Law School; guest lecturer, Univ of Southern CA School of Law. **Military Serv:** USAF lt 1956-59. **Business Addr:** James & Jeffers, 870 Market St, Ste 1200, San Francisco, CA 94102.

JEFFERS, GRADY ROMMEL
Business executive. **Personal:** Born Jul 11, 1943, New York, NY; son of Alberta Jeffers and Robert Jeffers; married Maryann P; children: Anna, Debbie, Michael, Alberta. **Educ:** Bernard Baruch Coll; Manhattan Comm Coll, AA 1973. **Career:** Bankers Trust Co, asst vice pres commercial loan grp; Franklin Nat Bank, mgr 1969-74; Republic Natl Bank, vice pres, 1980-. **Orgs:** Mem 100 Black Men; Nat Bnkrs Assn mem Masons; Minority Bus & Devel; Nat Assn of Accountants; mem, Urban Bankers Coalition; sec, exec bd, Private Industry Council, 1989-. **Honors/Awds:** Nom Whitehouse Flwshp. **Military Serv:** USAF 1961-65. **Home Addr:** 762 Hartwell St, Teaneck, NJ 07666.

JEFFERS, JACK
Musician. **Personal:** Born Dec 10, 1928; son of Rose Elizabeth Bosfield (deceased) and George William Jeffers (deceased); married Cynthia Rogers Jeffers; children: Laura, Lee. **Educ:** Northeastern Univ, BS 1951; New York Univ Sch of Law, JD 1982. **Career:** State Univ of NY, prof emeritus of music. **Orgs:** Chmn 7 Arts Chap CORE 1964-66. **Military Serv:** AUS sp3 1956-58. **Home Addr:** 119 Manhattan Ave, New York, NY 10025.

JEFFERSON, ALPHINE WADE
Educator. **Personal:** Born Dec 31, 1950, Caroline County, VA; son of Ellie Mae Lewis Jefferson and Horace Douglas Jefferson; divorced. **Educ:** Univ of Chicago, AB 1973; Duke Univ, MA 1975, PhD 1979. **Career:** Duke Univ, Oral History Institute, instructor, 1974, Institute for Policy Science Research, assoc and coord of oral interviews, 1974, instructor in social science 1976; Northern IL Univ, instructor dept of history 1978-79, Center for Black Studies, faculty assoc, 1978-85, asst prof dept of history 1979-85; Southern Methodist Univ, vstg asst prof of history/interim dir of African-Amer Studies, 1984-85, asst prof history 1984-; College of Wooster, OH, assoc prof of History, 1984-. **Orgs:** Mem Amer Historical Assn, Assn for the Study of Afro-Amer Life and History, The Oral History Assn, The Org of Amer Historians, The Natl Cncl for Black Studies, The IL Cncl for Black Studies, The DuSable Museum of African Amer History; reader Natl Endowment for the Humanities 1980-; consultant Dwight Correctional Ctr Humanities Project 1980-81; reader The Newberry Library Inst Chicago 1984-; reader Scott Foresman and Co 1984-; mem adv bd Intl Journal of Oral History 1986-; mem bd of dir African Heritage Cultural Arts League 1986-; mem bd of dir The International Threatical Arts Society 1988-; mem bd of dir Huang International, Inc. 1988-; mem Dallas Independent School District, African-American Advisory Board 1988-. **Honors/Awds:** Alexander White Scholar The Univ of Chicago 1972-73; Fellow Duke Univ Oral History Prog 1973-76; Andrew W Mellon Postdoctoral Fellowship Harvard 1982-83; Natl Endowment for the Humanities Fellowship for Independent Rsch 1982-83; The Promise of World Peace Awd The Amer Baha'i Dallas TX 1986;

Most Popular Professor Awd Southern Methodist Univ Student Body 1986; first recipient The Margareta Deschner Teaching Awd Southern Methodist Univ Women's Studies Cncl 1986; Publications, chapters in books, articles, reviews and numerous papers presented at professional conferences. **Home Addr:** 135 W University Street, Wooster, OH 44691. **Business Addr:** Assoc Prof of History, The College of Wooster, Dept of History, Wooster, OH 44691.

JEFFERSON, ANDREA GREEN
Marketing and management consulting firm exec. **Personal:** Born Oct 9, 1946, New Orleans, LA; daughter of Herman and Bernice Johnson Green; married William Jefferson, Jun 13, 1970; children: Jamila, Jalila, Jelani, Nailah; Akilah. **Educ:** Southern Univ, BA, 1969; Rutgers Univ, MEd, 1970; Univ of New Orleans, EdD, 1979; Harvard Graduate School of Educational Mgt, 1989. **Career:** Southern Univ at New Orleans, dir of financial aid, 1980-81; New Orleans Public Schools, admin intern, 1982-83; supervisor of mathematics, 1983-84; instructional specialist, 1985-86, dir of instruction/staff development, 1986-87, dir of area I schools, 1987-88; Southern Univ at New Orleans, vice chancellor/student affairs, 1988-92; Grambling State Univ, coordinator/doctoral program, 1992-94. **Orgs:** Southern Univ, board of supvrs, 1995-; Congressional Black Caucus Found, board member, 1992-; Congressional Black Caucus Spouses, past chair/issue forum chair, 1992-95; Amistad Research Center, president of board, 1994-; Links New Orleans Chapter, past sec, fundraising chair, 1986-; National Council of Negro Women, past board chair/past board member, 1984-88; President's Council of Tulane Univ, 1991-; Louisiana State Univ Medical Center, Stanley S Scott Cancer Research Center, 1993; Women's National Democratic Club, 1991-. **Honors/Awds:** YWCA, Role Model, 1993. **Special Achievements:** Publication Board, Initiatives, scholarly journal of the National Assn of Women in Education, 1990-93; The College Student Affairs Journal, 1991-93; Ethnic Women Newsletters, editor, 1992-93; The Changing Faces of Aids, 1993; Congressional Black Caucus Spouses Publication. **Business Addr:** President, The A Group, Inc., 201 St Charles Ave, Ste 2526, New Orleans, LA 70170, (504)582-1212.

JEFFERSON, ANDREW L., JR.
Attorney. **Personal:** Born Aug 19, 1934, Dallas, TX; son of Bertha Jefferson and Andrew Jefferson; married Mary Brown; children: Andy, Martin. **Educ:** TX SU, BA 1956; Univ TX Sch Law, JD 1959. **Career:** Washington & Jefferson, Attys at Law, prtnr 1960-61; Bexar Co, asst-crim dist atty 1961-62; US Atty, Western Dist TX, chief asst 1962-67; Humble Oil & Ref Co, cnsl 1968-71; Domestic Rel #2, Harris Co, judge 1970-74; 208th Dist Ct, Harris Co, judge 1974-75; Jefferson Sherman & Mims, pvt Pract 1975-80; Jefferson & Mims, attorney, 1980-. **Orgs:** Mem, numerous offices, coms, Houston Bar Assn; mem, Houston Lwyrs Assn; mem, St Bar TX; mem, Am Bar Assn; mem, Fed, Nat Bar Assns; Alpha Phi Alpha Frat, Inc; Phi Alpha Delta Legal Frat, Tom Greener Chpt; NAACP; Pilgrim Cong United Ch Christ; Dwntwn Rotary Clb, Houston; TX Brkfst Clb; bd dirs, pres, Houston Cncl on Hum rel 1974-75; Houston Area Urban League; treas, 1st vp, Houston Legal Found 1973-74; Houston Bus Growth Corp; Gov's Drug Abuse Cncl; bd mgrs, YMCA S Cntrl Br; Navigation Bk; former chairman, Federal Reserve Bank of Dallas, Houston Branch; International Society of Barristers, 1996. **Honors/Awds:** Numerous guest spkr engagmnts; Nat Torch Liberty Award, Anti-Defamation League 1974; Forward Times Comm Serv Award 1975; Charles A George Comm Serv Award 1975; Nat Comm Serv Award, League United Latin Am Citizens 1975; Comm Serv Award, LaRaza 1974. **Military Serv:** AUS res capt. **Business Addr:** Attorney, Jefferson & Mims, 2100 Travis, Ste 707, Houston, TX 77002.

JEFFERSON, ARTHUR
Educational administrator. **Personal:** Born Dec 1, 1938, Alabama; children: Mark, Michael. **Educ:** Wayne State Univ, BS 1960, MA Pol Sci 1963, EdD 1973. **Career:** Detroit Public Schools, asst regional supt 1970-71, regional supt 1971-75, interim general supt 1975, general supt 1975-90; University of Michigan, distinguished visiting professor, 1990-95. **Orgs:** Mem Natl Polit Sci Hon Soc Pi Sigma Alpha; mem Natl & MI Councils Soc Studies; mem Assn for Supervision and Curr Devel; mem Amer/MI Assn of Sch Adminstr; mem Council for Basic Educ; mem Met Detroit Soc of Black Educ Adminstr; mem Natl Alliance of Black Sch Educators; mem Natl Review Panel on Study of Sch Desegregation; mem various other affiliations; bd of trustees Wayne State Univ Alumni Assn 1968-71; bd of gov Wayne State Univ Educ Alumni Assn 1968-71 1979-82; mem Amer Civil Lib Union, NAACP; bd of dir Council of Great City Sch; bd of trustees Detroit Econ Growth Corp; bd dir Detroit Educ TV Found; bd of adv Detroit Pre-Employment Training Ctr; bd dir Detroit Tchrs Credit Union; mem Econ Clubof Detroit; bd of dir United Found; mem 1 PTA Urban Adv Task Force; mem various other affiliations; chair, board of trustees, Museum of African History. **Business Addr:** General Superintendent Emeritus, Detroit Public Schools, 19445 Gloucester Drive, Detroit, MI 48205.

JEFFERSON, AUSTIN, JR.
Clergyman. **Personal:** Born in Aiken, SC; married Evelyn Griffin; children: Leonard A, Harry P, Evelyn L, Gene A. **Educ:** Temple School of Theology, 1953; Moody Bible Institute, attended; New Era Seminary, attended; Eastern Seminary, attended; Universal Bible Institute, Masters, Bible Study 1974. **Career:** Cleric, currently. **Orgs:** Bd of Foreign Missions; chairman, Bd St Home; Natl Baptist Convention; Methodist Christian Council; advisory bd, Eastern Seminary; vice pres, New England MS Convention 1971; Even Conference.

JEFFERSON, CLIFTON
Mayor, funeral director. **Personal:** Born Sep 10, 1928, Lynchburg, SC; son of Cassie McDonald Jefferson and John Jefferson; married Gwendolyn W Jefferson; children: Carolyn, Chrishinda, Lamont, Latisha Lenora. **Educ:** SC St Coll, BS 1946; Attended, Univ MD 1954; SC St Coll, MA 1968. **Career:** Fleming School, science teacher 1955-57; Mt Pleasant HS, asst prin 1957-77; Bishopville Middle School, principal, 1977-87; Lynchburg SC, mayor 1975-77, presently; Jefferson Funeral Home, owner. **Orgs:** Chmn admin bd Warren Chapel United Meth Sch; del SC Dem Conv; SC Morticians Assn; life mem NAACP; life mem Kappa Alpha Psi; United Meth Ch; Black Mayors of SC; NEA; SCEA; LCEA; SC Mun Assn. **Honors/Awds:** Natl Funeral Dir & Embalmer Assn Man of Yr SC Mortician Assn 1976; Achievement Awd Kappa Alpha Psi 1977; Dedicated Serv Awd Mt Pleasant HS 1977; first black mayor in Lynchburg, SC. **Business Addr:** Mayor, Jefferson Funeral Home, Lynchburg Town Hall, Lynchburg, SC 29080.

JEFFERSON, FREDRICK CARL, JR.
Educational administrator. **Personal:** Born Dec 30, 1934, New Orleans, LA; married June Greene; children: Crystal, Frederick, Christian. **Educ:** Hunter Coll NY, BS Music 1957, MA Music 1959, MA Guidance 1967; Univ of MA Amhurst, EdD 1981. **Career:** SUNY at Albany, prog assoc 1971-73; Univ of Rochester, dir educ oppor prog 1973-76, dir of minority student affairs & assoc dean of students 1976-85, asst to the pres, professor of education, director of institute of urban schools & education, currently. **Orgs:** Mem Action for a Better Comm 1976-, United Way 1978-; vice chmn bd of Dirs PRIS2M 1978-84; trainer Natl Training Labs 1978-; consultant New Perspectives Inc 1979-; mem William Warfield Scholarship Fund 1984-; mem bd of dirs Primary Mental Health Project 1985-; mem Austin Steward Professional Soc 1985-; mem Roundtable on Educ Change 1987-; mem Urban League of Rochester; asst prof Grad Sch of Educ & Human Develop at Univ of Rochester. **Honors/Awds:** Volunteer Serv Awds United Way 1978-86; ABC Serv Awd Action for a Better Comm 1979-86; PRIS2M 1983; Hispanic Leadership Awd 1985; publication "Creating a Multicultural Perspective" Assoc of Coll Unions Intl Bulletin 1986. **Business Addr:** Assistant to the President, University of Rochester, Administration 103, Rochester, NY 14627.

JEFFERSON, GARY SCOTT
Airline company executive. **Personal:** Born Nov 4, 1945, Pittsburgh, PA; son of Mr & Mrs Willard M Jefferson; married Beverly J Allen, Dec 30, 1967; children: Gary S, Kelly J. **Educ:** Indiana Univ of Pennsylvania, Indiana PA, BA, 1967. **Career:** United Airlines, vice president of the northeast region, currently. **Business Addr:** Vice Pres, Public Affairs, United Airlines, 455 N Cityfront Plz Dr, Ste 3100, Chicago, IL 60611.

JEFFERSON, GREG
Professional football player. **Personal:** Born Aug 31, 1971, Orlando, FL; married Twana. **Educ:** Central Florida, attended. **Career:** Philadelphia Eagles, defensive end, 1995-. **Business Addr:** Professional Football Player, Philadelphia Eagles, 3501 S Broad St, Philadelphia, PA 19148, (215)463-2500.

JEFFERSON, HILDA HUTCHINSON
Educator (retired), city government official. **Personal:** Born Jun 19, 1920, Charleston, SC; married James L Jefferson Jr; children: Marjorie, Leon, Charles, Herman, Edward, Jerome. **Educ:** Avery Normal Inst, Cert 1940; Tuskegee Inst, BS Home Econ 1944; Allen Univ, Advance Studies 1954; SC State Coll, Advance Studies 1955. **Career:** Stark Gen Hosp, asst dietician 1944-45; 6 Mile Jr HS, sci teacher 1945-46; Macedonia HS, home econ teacher 1946-47; Avery HS, dietician 1948-50; Baptist Hill HS, home econ teacher 1950-53; Lincoln HS, sci teacher 1955-58; Wallace HS, home econ teacher 1958-69; St Andrews Parish HS, home econ teacher 1969-82; Charleston SC, councilmember 1975-. **Orgs:** Mrm New Israel RE Church 1920-, NAACP 1950-, Charleston Cty Democratic Women 1976, Charlestons Art & History Comm 1976-, Natl League of Cities 1976-; chmn Traffic & Transp Comm 1980-; mem Charleston Area Comm Relations Comm 1980, SC Governors Comm on Hwy Safety 1980; mdm bd Carolina Art Assoc 1980, Charleston Museum 1980-, Trident United Way 1982-; mem Council of Governments 1983-; chmn Black Portrait Study Comm 1984-85; pres Gamma Zeta Chap Zeta Phi Beta 1984-86; sec Charleston Cty Municipal Assoc 1985-; porgy & bess adv comm Catfish Row Co Inc 1985-; adv council Charleston Area Sr Citizens Serv 1985-. **Honors/Awds:** Outstanding Contrib & Meritorious Serv as a Volunteer to the Community Charleston Fed of Womens & Girls Clubs 1972; Outstanding Serv & Dedication in the Fields of Ed 1976, Politics 1976, Serv 1979,84; 1st Black Woman City of Charleston selected Mayor Pro Tem 1976, 1984, 1992; Royal Light Awd Woman of the Year 1976; 1st Black Woman Home Econ of the Year for Charleston Cty & SC 1976; Recognized by Gamma Xi Omega Chap of Alpha Kappa Alpha 1977, Phi Beta Sigma, Omega Psi Phi; Contrib to Women Awd YWCA 1980; Safety Recognition of Dedicated & Outstanding Serv to the Citizens of SC-SC Governors Comm on Hwy 1982; Outstanding Serv to Community 1983. **Home Addr:** 11 Addison St, Charleston, SC 29403. **Business Addr:** Councilmember, District 4, 80 Broad St, Charleston, SC 29401.

JEFFERSON, HORACE LEE
Dentist. **Personal:** Born Oct 10, 1924, Detroit, MI; married Betty Lou Brown; children: Linda, Eric, Judith, Michael. **Educ:** Highland Park Jr Coll, 1946-48; Univ of MI Dental Schl, DDS 1953. **Career:** Dentist 1953; Herman Keifer City Hosp of Detroit, staff sr dentist, 1954-71; . **Orgs:** Mem Detroit Dist Dental Soc; MI Dental Assn; Am & Dental Assn 1953; pres Wolverine Dental Soc 1957; life mem Afro-am Museum of detroit 1975; life mem Alpha Phi Alpha Frat 1975; life mem NAACP 1979; Delta Dntl Plans of MI, corporate dir, 1977-83. **Honors/Awds:** Clinical Presentation at 15th Review Detroit Dist Dental Soc 1957; clinical presentations Wolverine Dental Soc 1971; forum Presentation Gamma Lambda Chap AOA 1973; Cancer Seminar Participation MI Cancer Found 1976. **Military Serv:** US Army, 1944-46; Meritorious Unit Award. **Business Addr:** 10040 Puritan, Detroit, MI 48238.

JEFFERSON, JAMES E.
City government. **Personal:** Born Jul 22, 1922, Redlands, CA; married Pearl. **Career:** Yuma City Council, mem 1973-. **Orgs:** Dir AZ Respiratory Disease Assoc 1971-75; ad hoc advisory comm AZ State Parks 1984. **Honors/Awds:** Man of the Year Yuma 1973; Disting Serv Yuma Area Housing Opportunity 1981, City of Yuma 1984. **Home Addr:** 200 S 10th Ave, Yuma, AZ 85364.

JEFFERSON, JOSEPH L.
Educator. **Personal:** Born Nov 8, 1940, Pensacola, FL; married Ida C Wedgeworth; children: Eric, Clynita, Steven. **Educ:** TX Southern Univ, BA, 1968, MA, 1971; OH State Univ, PhD, 1974. **Career:** Vocational Guidance Houston, counselor 1971; TX Southern Univ, admin asst to dean coll of arts & sciences dir inst; TX Southern Univ, assoc dir Office of Inst Research, prof College of Educ. **Orgs:** Mem Am Educ & Research Assn; Phi Delta Kappa; Assn for Inst Research; Am Counseling Assn; TX Counseling Assn; Kappa Alpha Psi Frat; Houston Jr Chamber of Commerce; Houston Lion's Club. **Honors/Awds:** Recip Grad Fellow TX So Univ 1970-71; Acad Year Inst Study Grant 1972-73 OH State U. **Military Serv:** AUS sp E5 1962-65. **Business Addr:** 3100 Cleburne, Houston, TX 77004.

JEFFERSON, JUNE L., JR.
Chaplain. **Personal:** Born Jun 25, 1924, Edgefield Co, SC; married Rosa L Lewis; children: Justin Lee, Jay Michael. **Educ:** Howard U, Wash DC, BS 1954, BD 1959, MDiv 1971. **Career:** Hopkins House Settlemnt, Alex VA, grp soc wrkr 1957-59; Children's Cntr, Laurel MD, cnslr 1963-64; Grater Corr Inst, PA, chpln 1964-65; US Postal Srv, Wash DC, pstl clrk 1947-52; security guard, salesman, cab drvr 1950-63; Zion Bapt Ch, Alexandria VA, asst pastor 1957-; DC Dept Corr DetentionSrv Bd, retired chpln 1985. **Orgs:** Mem, Am Protestant Chplns Corr Assn 1972-73; Luther Rice Coll 1970-73; Cptl Cab Coop Assn 1959-64; ch, Crime & Dlnqncy Cntrl Unit, Hlth & Wlfr Cncl, Wash 1971; pres, Potomac HS Athl Assn 1976-77; charter mem, YMCA; mem, Am Corr Assn 1967; mem, Silver Hill Dads Clb; SW Planning Cncl, Wash 1969-71; spec asst Capital Centre Kiwanis Club Landover MD. **Honors/Awds:** Cited, Recrtnl Dept, Wash 1970; chrmn, SW Recrtnl Cncl 1970-75; Academy Awareds Com, Wash 1974; grand prelate KP, Mason.

JEFFERSON, KAREN L.
Librarian. **Personal:** Born Oct 30, 1952, Eglin AFB, FL; daughter of Agnes McLean Jefferson and Henry S Jefferson. **Educ:** Howard University, Washington, DC, BA, 1974; Atlanta University, Atlanta, GA, MSLS, 1975. **Career:** Moorland-Spingarn Res Ctr, Howard University, Washington, DC, manuscript librarian, 1976-80, senior manuscript librarian, 1980-87, curator, 1987-93; Natl Endowment for the Humanities, Washington, DC, humanities admini, 1993-. **Orgs:** Co-editor, African American & Third World Archivist Roundtable Newsletter, 1987-93; board member, African-American Educational Archives Project, 1989-93; member, Black Caucus of ALA 1972-; member, Society of American Archivists, 1983-; Mid Atlantic Region Archives Conference, member, 1982-; Academy of Certified Archivists, member, 1989-. **Business Addr:** National Endowment for the Humanities, Div of Preservation & Access, 1100 Pennsylvania Ave, NW, Washington, DC 20506, (202)606-8570.

JEFFERSON, M. IVORY
Clergyman, attorney. **Personal:** Born Sep 10, 1924, Logan, WV; son of Mattie O. Wooten Jefferson and Ivory Pink Jefferson; married Reba N (deceased); children: Gwendolyn Allen, Sygna Blydenburgh. **Educ:** Attended, Univ of So CA, Univ of Manila; Emmanus Bible Sch, grad; Robert H Terrell Sch of Law, LLB LLD 1950. **Career:** Manpower Commn & Housing Div of Newport News Ofc of Human Affrs, consult in field of pastoral counseling; Sixth Mt Zion Baptist Temple, Hampton, VA, pastor, 1966-; Richmond Virginia Seminary, professor of systematic theology, 1990-. **Orgs:** Admitted to VA Bar 1951; admitted to US Supreme Ct Bar 1956; licensed & ordained in Gospel Ministry 1961 1963; moderator Tidewater Peninsula Bapt Assn; legal adv Progressive Natl Baptist Conv; mem validating Comm for the Fund of Renewal Amer Bapt Ch Inc; consult Office of Offender Aid & Restoration Newport News; chairman, Riverside Regional Medical Center Clergy Relations, 1990-; board member, Peninsula AIDS Foundation, 1988-; member, Peninsula Crime Line, 1988-; Peninsula Aids Foundation, chairman of bd, 1994-; Peninsula Crime Line, pres, 1995-. **Honors/Awds:** Authority in fields of pastoral counseling, taxation and domestic relations. **Military Serv:** US Army, T/3, 1943-46. **Home Addr:** 326 Duluth Ct, Hampton, VA 23666.

JEFFERSON, MARCIA D.
Librarian. **Personal:** Born Jan 2, 1935, Jamaica, West Indies; daughter of Marjorie Lewis Dyer (deceased) and Jacob A. Dyer (deceased); married Eugene Jefferson, Apr 2, 1966; children: Denise, Darryl. **Educ:** Brooklyn College, Brooklyn, NY, BA, 1957; Rutgers Univ School of Library Science, New Brunswick, NJ, MLS, 1959; SUNY-Stony Brook, Stony Brook, NY, MALS, 1987. **Career:** Brooklyn Public Library, Brooklyn, NY, page/librarian trainee, 1954-63; Bayshore/Brightwaters Public Library, Brightwaters, NY, reference librarian, 1963-66; Staff-Library/UST, Flushing, NY, New York World's Fair, summer 1965; Patchogue-Medford Schools, Patchogue, NY, school librarian, 1966-67; Bayshore/Brightwaters Public Library, reference librarian, 1969-; Suffolk Community College, Selden, NY, periodicals librarian, 1978-. **Orgs:** Board of trustees/elected member, Patchogue-Medford Lib., 1989-; member, Black Caucus/ALA, 1989-; member, SUNY-LA, 1988-; member, SCLA, 1978-; vice president, academic division of SCLA, DASL, 1990-. **Business Addr:** Professor of Library Services, Suffolk Community College, 533 College Rd, Selden, NY 11784.

JEFFERSON, MARGO
Journalist. **Personal:** Born in Chicago, IL; daughter of Ron and Irma Jefferson. **Educ:** Univ of Chicago Laboratory School; Brandeis Univ; Columbia Univ, journalism degree. **Career:** Columbia Univ, instructor; New York Univ, instructor; Vogue Magazine, editor; Newsweek Magazine, editor; New York Times, critic, 1993-. **Honors/Awds:** Pulitzer Prize, criticism, 1995. **Business Addr:** Critic, New York Times, 229 W 43rd St, New York, NY 10036, (212)556-1234.

JEFFERSON, OVERTON C.
Educator. **Personal:** Born in Port Arthur, TX; married Marjorie; children: Robert, Olida. **Educ:** Xavier U, New Orleans, AB 1949; NC Cntrl U, JD; NY Univ Sch Law, LLM. **Career:** Houston Legal Found, central office dir 1985; TX Southern Univ School of Law, asst prof 1953-58. **Military Serv:** AUS 1942-45. **Business Addr:** 609 Fannin Ave, Ste 1909, Houston, TX.

JEFFERSON, PATRICIA ANN
Appraiser. **Personal:** Born Nov 26, 1951, Richmond County. **Educ:** Augusta Coll, BBA 1973. **Career:** GA Power Co, customer serv rep 1969-73; Black Student Union Augusta Coll, sec & organizer 1971-73; Augusta/Richmond Co Human Relations Commn, admin asst to dir 1974-81; Augusta Focus Newspaper, genl mgr 1982-87; Pat Jefferson Realty/Appraisals, certified residential appraiser, 1987-. **Orgs:** Eta Theta Zeta Sorority, founder & dir Spiritualettes 1974-; Broker Pat Jefferson Realty; Certified Residential Appraiser, Jefferson Appraisal; mem, Spirit Creek Bapt Ch; board of directors, American Red Cross; board of directors, CSRA Business League; National Association of Real Estate Appraiser; Appraisal Institute, affiliate; GA Real Estate Appraisers Bd, bd mem; Operation Self Help, bd mem. **Business Addr:** Certified Residential Appraiser, Jefferson Appraisal, 1126 11th St, Augusta, GA 30901.

JEFFERSON, REGGIE (REGINALD JIROD)
Professional baseball player. **Personal:** Born Sep 25, 1968, Tallahassee, FL. **Career:** Cincinnati Reds, infielder, 1991; Cleveland Indians, 1991-94; Seattle Mariners, 1994; Boston Red Sox, 1995-. **Business Addr:** Professional Baseball Player, Boston Red Sox, Fenway Park, 24 Yawkey Way, Boston, MA 02215, (617)267-9440.

JEFFERSON, ROBERT R.
County official. **Personal:** Born Sep 21, 1932, Lexington, KY; married Katie E Scott; children: Robert Jr, Stanley. **Educ:** KY State Coll, BA, History, Political Sci, Biology, 1967, MA, Public Affairs, 1974. **Career:** Lexington-Fayette Urban County, councilmember, 1988-; US Bureau of Prisons, senior case mgr, 1974-83 (retired); US Public Health Hospital, various positions, 1957-74; IBM, assembler, 1959. **Orgs:** Committee organizer, Whitney Young Sickle Cell Center, 1973-74; acting exec dir, Urban Co Human Rights Commn, Lexington, 1974; mem, Omega Psi Phi; past dist rep & mem, Supreme-Council; mem, chmn, Human Rights Commn, 1969-83; Black & Williams

Comm Center; mem, Natl Conf on Christians & Jews; mem, LFUC Urban League, CORE, Bluegrass Black Business Assn, Agency Exec Forum; bd mem, Natl League of Cities, 1993-95; bd mem, KY League of Cities, 1990-. **Honors/Awds:** LFUCG Human Rights Commn Outstanding Serv Award, 1985; Micro-City Govt, Distinguished Service Award, 1985; Lima Dirve Seventh Day Adventist Church, Outstanding Serv Award, 1981; KY State Univ, Distinguished Serv Award, 1981; NCCJ, Brotherhood Award, 1979; Micro-City Univ, Honorary Doctorate Degree, 1975; Minority Affairs Comm Distinguished Services, 1973; Several Omega Psi Phi Fraternal Awards. **Military Serv:** USAF 1947-54; USAFR 1954-68. **Business Addr:** 200 E Main St, Lexington, KY 40507.

JEFFERSON, ROLAND SPRATLIN
Physician. **Personal:** Born May 16, 1939, Washington, DC; son of Devonia H Spratlin and Bernard S Jefferson; married Melanie L Moore; children: Roland Jr, Rodney Earl, Shannon Devonia, Royce Bernard. **Educ:** Univ of S CA, BA Anthropology 1961; Howard U, MD 1965. **Career:** Martin L King, Jr Hosp, asso prof 1972-75; Dept of Rehabilitation, consult 1972-78; Watts Hlth Found, staff psychiatrist 1973-80; Assn of Black Motion Picture & TV Producers, pres/founding mem 1980-81; Private Prac, physician. **Orgs:** Mem Writers Guild of Am W 1981; mem Nat Medical Assn 1969; bd of dir Am Sickle Cell Found 1973-76; bd of advisors Brockman Gallery 1976-78. **Honors/Awds:** Grassroots Award Sons of Watts 1977; Golden Quill Award Abffriham Found 1977; NAACP Image Award 13th Annual NAACP Image Awards 1980; 1st Place for Film Drama Black Filmmakers Hall of Fame 1980; author of 3 novels, The School on 103rd Street (1976), A Card for the Players (1978), 559 to Damascus (1985); Award of Merit by Black American Cinema Society 1989; Special Directors Award, 24th Annual NAACP Image Awards, 1992; Producer, Writer, Director of Feature Film ''Perfume'' 1989. **Military Serv:** USAF capt 1969-71. **Business Addr:** Physician, 3870 Crenshaw Blvd #215, Los Angeles, CA 90008.

JEFFERSON, SHAWN (VANCHI LASHAWN)
Professional football player. **Personal:** Born Feb 22, 1969, Jacksonville, FL. **Educ:** Central Florida, attended. **Career:** San Diego Chargers, wide receiver, 1991-95; New England Patriots, 1996-. **Business Addr:** Professional Football Player, New England Patriots, 60 Washington St, Foxboro Stadium, Foxboro, MA 02035, (508)543-7911.

JEFFERSON, WILLIAM J.
Congressman. **Personal:** Born Mar 14, 1947, Lake Providence, LA; son of Angeline Harris and Mose Jefferson; married Andrea Green Jefferson; children: Jamila Efuru, Jalila Eshe, Jelani, Nailah, Akilah. **Educ:** Southern University, Baton Rouge, LA, BA, English/political science, 1969; Harvard University, Cambridge, MA, JD, 1972; Georgetown Law Center, LLM, 1996. **Career:** US Court of Appeals, 5th Circuit, Judge Alvin B. Rubin, judicial clerk, 1972-73; US Senator J. Bennett Johnston, Washington, DC, legislative assistant, 1973-75; Jefferson, Bryan and Gray, New Orleans, LA, founding partner, 1976; Louisiana State Senate, Baton Rouge, LA, member, 1980-90; US House of Representatives, Washington, DC, member, 1990-. **Orgs:** Louisiana Bar Assn; Amer Bar Assn; Natl Bar Assn; DC Bar Assn. **Honors/Awds:** Legislator of the Year (twice), Alliance for Good Government; A.P. Tureaud Community Legal Services Award. **Military Serv:** US Army, Judge Advocate General, Capt, 1969. **Business Addr:** Member of Congress, US House of Representatives, 506 Cannon House Office Bldg, Washington, DC 20515.

JEFFERSON-FORD, CHARMAIN
Law enforcement official. **Personal:** Born Oct 2, 1963, Detroit, MI; daughter of Walter L Patton Jefferson and Hercules Jefferson; children: Krysten N Jefferson. **Educ:** Wayne State Univ, Detroit, MI, 1981-87. **Career:** Detroit Public Schools, Detroit, MI, clerk, 1978-81; Hudson's Dept Store, Detroit, MI, model, 1979-81; Grand Value Pharmacy, Detroit, MI, pharmacy tech, 1981-88; City of Southfield, Southfield, MI, police officer, 1988-. **Orgs:** Pres, Future Homemakers of America, 1980-81. **Honors/Awds:** First black female police officer in Southfield, MI. **Business Addr:** Police Officer, City of Southfield Police Dept, 26000 Evergreen Rd, Southfield, MI 48076.

JEFFERSON-MOSS, CAROLYN
Government official. **Personal:** Born Sep 20, 1945, Washington, DC; married Alfred Jeffrey Moss. **Educ:** Howard Univ, BA Pol Sci 1970, MA Pub Admin 1974. **Career:** Reps C Diggs & A Hawkins, congressional Black caucus legislative dir 1970-71; Exotech Systems Inc, sr asso/proj dir 1971-74; BLK Group Inc, sr asso/dir for survey rsch 1974-75; Mark Battle Asso Inc, sr asso dir of marketing/survey rsch div 1975-78; Dept of Commerce, dep to asst sec for congressional affairs 1978-. **Orgs:** Mem Alpha Kappa Alpha Inc 1968; mem Met Dem Women's Club 1974. **Honors/Awds:** Fellowship for Advanced Studies in Polit Sci Ford Found Joint Ctr for Polit Studies 1970-71. **Business Addr:** Deputy to Assistant Secretary, US Dept of Commerce, Congressional Affairs, 14th & Constitution Ave NW, Washington, DC 20230.

JEFFREY, CHARLES JAMES, JR.
Editor, clergyman. **Personal:** Born Oct 27, 1925, Tulsa, OK; married Louise Simmons. **Educ:** Amer Baptist Theological Seminary, Nashville, BTh 1948; Tulsa U, additional study. **Career:** Oklahoma Eagle Newspaper, editor 1985; Macedonia Baptist Church, pastor; Tulsa TV, commentator; minister, 1967; Gen Baptist Convention of Oklahoma, recording sec 1956-. **Orgs:** Mem, Enrolmnt & Com, Nat Bapt Conv of Am 1965; mem, Pub Rel Dept for Nat Conv; pres, Local NAACP; mem, Adv Bd, Okmulgee Pub Sch; Hum Rel Com, Okmulgee Sch for Retarded; bd for Comm Act Found; mem, bd OK Estrn Dev Corp; mem, Tulsa Press Clb. **Honors/Awds:** Recip, Cert of Appreaciation, US Jaycees 1972. **Military Serv:** USN 1943-45. **Business Addr:** PO Box 3667, Tulsa, OK 74106.

JEFFREY, RONNALD JAMES
Association executive, author, lecturer. **Personal:** Born Mar 11, 1949, Cheyenne, WY; son of Lillian Leola Carter Jeffrey and John Thomas Jeffrey; married Marilyn Mansell, Dec 10, 1978; children: Keeya, Kaylee. **Educ:** Chadron State Coll, BS in sociology and anthropology, 1972; Univ of Northern CO, MS in communications, 1976. **Career:** Laramie County Community College, instructor, 1980; Univ of Wyoming, instructor; Office of Youth Alternatives, director, 1971-. **Orgs:** Bd mem Juvenile Justice Adv Bd 1984-; bd mem Cheyenne Child Care Centers (NAACP) 1984; consultant 1975-; lecturer 1975-; dir Rocky Mountain Federal Bank 1988-89; pres Wy Assn of Marriage & Family Therapist 1986-88; American Association for Marriage and Family Therapy, clinical mem. **Honors/Awds:** Freedom Foundation, George Washington Honor Medal, 1977; Cheyenne Jaycees, Distinguished Service Award, 1978; American Institute of Public Service, Jefferson Award, 1980; Phi Delta Kappa Award for Service to Education, 1986. **Special Achievements:** Co-author: ''A Guide for the Family Therapist''. **Business Addr:** Dir, Office of Youth Alternatives, City of Cheyenne, 1328 Talbot Ct, Cheyenne, WY 82001, (307)637-6480.

JEFFREYS, JOHN H.
Management consultant. **Personal:** Born Mar 27, 1940, Youngsville, NC; married Constance Little; children: Gregory, Alvin. **Educ:** Shaw Univ, AB Soc 1962; Univ of GA, M Public Admin 1975; Univ of GA, ABD/DPA 1985. **Career:** Rowan Cty Salisbury NC Anti Poverty Prog, dir neighborhood serv ctr 1964-67; City of Hickory, dir human resources 1967-70;; US Adv Commiss for Intergovt Relations, 1st black intern 1969-70; Univ of GA, mgmt consult assoc. **Orgs:** 1st black elected commiss Clarke Cty Govt 1982; consult Intl Assoc City Mgrs 1983, Public Safety Personnel St Croix 1984, Amer Soc for Training & Dev 1984; parliamentarian GA Assoc of Black Elected Officials 1984; public safety & criminal justice comm Natl Assoc Counties; charter mem Natl Assoc Blacks in Criminal Justice. **Honors/Awds:** Man of the Year Phi Beta Sigma Delta Mu Sigma Chap 1977, 1981, 1983; 1st Black Clarke Cty GA Comm Elected 1982; Outstanding Mgmt Instr GA Clerks Assoc 1983. **Home Addr:** 140 Jones Dr, Athens, GA 30606. **Business Addr:** Management Consultant Assoc, Univ of Georgia, 1260 S Lumpkin St, Athens, GA 30602.

JEFFRIES, FRAN M.
Journalist. **Personal:** Born Jul 21, 1959, Yanceyville, NC; daughter of William & Elizabeth Jeffries; married Lawrence Muhammed, Jul 1, 1989. **Educ:** American Univ, BA, 1982; Indiana Univ, MA, 1984. **Career:** Post-Tribune, Gary Ind, reporter, 1984-87; The Courier-Journal, copy editor, reporter, asst city editor, neighborhoods editor, currently. **Orgs:** National Assn of Black Journalist; Society of Professional Journalists; Zenger-Miller management trainer. **Business Addr:** Neighborhoods Editor, The Courier-Journal, 525 W Broadway, Louisville, KY 40202, (502)582-4120.

JEFFRIES, FREDDIE L.
Government official. **Personal:** Born Apr 12, 1939, Gates, TN; son of Lora Jeffries (deceased) and Freddie R Jeffries; married Helen A Ginn, Jan 29, 1971; children: Elizabeth, Terri, Joyce, Lee. **Educ:** Tennessee State University, BSCE, 1961; University of Michigan, MSE, 1970; Industrial College of the Armed Forces, diploma, 1984; George Washington University, MPA, 1984. **Career:** United States Department of Commerce, Coast & Geodetic Survey, engineer, Environmental Science Service Administration, engineer, National Oceanic & Atmospheric Administration, Atlantic Marine Center, director. **Orgs:** American Congress on Surveying and Mapping; American Society of Photogrammetry, 1961-73; Society of American Military Engineers, director, 1970-. **Honors/Awds:** Tennessee State University, Distinguished Graduate Award, 1991. **Military Serv:** National Oceanic and Atmospheric Administration, Rear Adm, 1965-; Special Achievement Awards, 1986, 1987; Unit Citations, 1974, 1988; Karo Award, 1979; Order of St Barbara, 1977. **Business Addr:** Director, Atlantic Marine Center, Department of Commerce, National Oceanic and Atmospheric Administration, 439 W York St, Norfolk, VA 23510, (804)441-6776.

JEFFRIES, LEONARD
Educator. **Educ:** PhD. **Career:** New York State Commission on Education, Task Force on Deficiency Correction in Curriculum Regarding People of Color, former consultant, former member; City College of New York, Dept of African American Studies, chairman, until 1992, professor, currently. **Special Achievements:** Task Force's final report entitled, ''A Cirriculum of Inclusion''. **Business Addr:** Professor, Department of African-American Studies, City College of New York, 138th & Covant St, Rm 4150, New York, NY 10031, (212)794-5555.

JEFFRIES, ROSALIND R.
Educator, artist. **Personal:** Born Jun 24, 1936, New York, NY; daughter of Mary Gibson and Edmond Felix Robinson; married Dr Leonard Jeffries Jr, Nov 29, 1965. **Educ:** Hunter Coll, BA 1963; Columbia Univ, MA, 1968; Yale Univ, PhD, 1990. **Career:** Bishop's Bible College Church of God in Christ, New York, NY, assistant professor, 1991; Jersey City State College, Jersey City, assistant professor, currently; School of Visual Arts, New York, NY, senior teaching faculty, currently; City Univ NY, art hist, artist, prof 1972-; San Jose St Univ, asst prof 1969-72; Brooklyn Museum, lectr 1969; Group Seminars, Africa, co-ldr 1966-72; US Govt USIS, Abidjan, & Ivory Cst, W Africa, dir exhib 1965-66. **Orgs:** Lectr, univs, colls & comm cntrs-num one-woman art shows; cat writer, Museums; mem, Coll Arts Assn; CA St Art Historians; Nat Conf Artists; board of directors, Kem-Were Science Consortium, 1986-; director of art & culture, Association for the Study of African Classical Civilizations, 1986-; member, Blacklight Fellowship, Black Presence in the Bible, 1991-. **Honors/Awds:** Listed, Black Artists On Art; Afro-am Artist; Negro in Music & Art 1969; African Arts Mag, UCLA 1974; Enstooled as Queen Mother, Ashantehene Traditional Government of Ghana, 1988; Arts Achievement Award, President of Senegal, 1986. **Home Addr:** 96 Schoonmaker Rd, Teaneck, NJ 07666.

JELLERETTE DEJONGH, MONIQUE EVADNE
Author. **Personal:** Born Feb 26, 1959, Los Angeles, CA; daughter of Carole & Alphonso Jellerette; married Robert Charles deJongh, Jr, Apr 20, 1990; children: Dylan, Jordan. **Educ:** Boston University, School for the Arts, 1980-81. **Career:** NY Times Sunday Mag, asst art dir, 1986-87; Genigraphics, Inc, computer graphic artist, 1987; Thing of Beauty Productions, 1987-88; Times Sq Studios, art dir, 1987-91; MTV Graphics, electronic designer, 1993-94; Brownstone Underground, art dir, 1990-. **Orgs:** Brownstone Underground, original founder, art dir. **Special Achievements:** Whitney Houston & Disney, Touchstone, are making movie version of book, ''How To Marry A Black Man.''.

JEMISON, AJ D.
Retail executive. **Career:** Fairlane Town Center, general manager, currently. **Business Addr:** General Manager, Fairlane Town Center, 18900 Michigan Ave, Dearborn, MI 48126.

JEMISON, MAE C.
Former astronaut, physician, educator. **Personal:** Born Oct 17, 1956, Decatur, AL; daughter of Dorothy Green Jemison and Charlie Jemison. **Educ:** Stanford Univ CA, BChE, BA, African & African-American studies, 1977; Cornell Univ, MD, 1981. **Career:** Peace Corps West Africa, staff doctor; CIGNA Health Plans of CA in Glendale, general practitioner; NASA, astronaut, 1987-92; Dartmouth Coll, teaching fellowship, 1993-; The Jemison Group, founder, 1994-. **Orgs:** Board of directors, World Sickle Cell Foundation, 1990-92; advisory committee, American Express Geography Competition, 1989-; American Medical Assn; American Chemical Society; Americn Assn Advancement Science; Center for the Prevention of Childhood Malnutrition, Honorary Board Member. **Honors/Awds:** Essence Award, Essence Magazine, 1988; Gamma Sigma Gamma Woman of the Year, 1990; Honorary Board, Center to Prevent Childhood Malnutrition, 1988-; Honorary PhD, Lincoln Univ, 1991; Alpha Kappa Alpha, honorary member; numerous others. **Special Achievements:** First African American female to enter into space, September 12, 1992. **Business Addr:** Founder, The Jemison Group, PO Box 591455, Houston, TX 77259-1455.

JEMISON, THEODORE JUDSON
Clergyman. **Personal:** Born Aug 1, 1918, Selma, AL; married; children: Bettye Jane, Dianne Frances, Theodore Judson. **Educ:** AL St Coll, BS 1940; VA Union U, DM 1945, DD 1971; Natchez Coll, DD 1953. **Career:** Baptist Church, ordained minister; Mt Zion Baptist Church, Staunton, pastor, 1945-49; Mt Zion 1st Baptist Church, Baton Rouge, pastor 1949-; Natl Baptist Convention USA, pres, currently. **Orgs:** General secretary, Natl Baptist Convention USA Inc 1953; Natl Council of Churches in the US; LA Rights Commn; Baton Rouge Comm Rels Com; NAACP; pres, Frontiers Intl, Baton Rouge Chapter; Alpha Phi Alpha; Shriner; Mason. **Honors/Awds:** Citizen of the Year For Outstanding Contributions in civics, recreation, education, religion, City of Baton Rouge; Minister of the Year, Natl Beta Club, 1973; Distinguished Service Award, East Rouge Education Assn, 1973. **Business Addr:** 356 East Blvd, Baton Rouge, LA 70802.

JEMMOTT, HENSLEY B.
Company executive. **Personal:** Born Mar 14, 1947, New York, NY; son of Hensley Barton Jemmott and Alice Lucille Lee; married Lynn Hooper; children: Hensley, Dara. **Educ:** Syracuse U, BA 1968; Columbia U, MBA 1973. **Career:** Squibb Corp,

financial analyst 1973-78; Am Standard, sr financial anal 1978-79; Am Cyanamid Co (Am Far East Div), mgr planning 1979-81; Am Cyanamid Co (Lederle Intl Med), product mgr; Lederle Intl, Mgr Marketing Research, 1981-91; Wm Douglas McAdams, Inc, vice pres, 1991-93; Torre, Renta, Lazor, vp, 1993; The UniWorld Group, management supervisor, 1993-. **Orgs:** Bd of dir Am Lung Assn of NJ 1983-85; bd of dir Urban League of Manhattan 1977-79; Dir Amer Lung Assn of NJ 1984-87. **Business Addr:** Management Supervisor, The UniWorld Group, Inc, 100 Ave of the Americas, New York, NY 10013-1699.

JENIFER, FRANKLYN GREEN
Educational administrator. **Personal:** Born Mar 26, 1939, Washington, DC; son of Mary Green Jenifer and Joseph Jenifer; married Alfleda Jenifer; children: Brenda, Tracey, Ivan. **Educ:** Howard University, Washington, DC, BS, 1962, MS, 1965; University of Maryland, College Park, MD, PhD, 1970. **Career:** Livingston College, Rutgers Univ, New Brunswick, NJ, professor of biology, 1970-79, chairperson, biology dept, 1974-77; Rutgers University, Newark, NJ, assoc provost, 1977-79; N J Dept of Higher Ed, Trenton, NJ, vice chancellor, 1979-86; Massachusetts Bd of Regents of Higher Ed, Boston, MA, chancellor, 1986-90; Howard University, Washington, DC, president, 1990-94; Univ of Texas at Dallas, president, 1994-. **Orgs:** Board of Directors, Texaco Inc; board of directors, National Foundation for Biomedical Research; The Corp, Woods Hole Oceanographic Institute; board of directors, Golden Key National Honor Society; board of visitors, John F Kennedy School of Government, Harvard University; board of directors, United Way of Metropolitan Dallas, monitoring committee Louisiana Desegregation Settlement; board of trustees, University Research Association, Inc; Dallas Citizens Council. **Honors/Awds:** Honorary Doctor of Laws, Babson College, 1990; Honorary Doctor of Laws, Boston College, 1990; Honorary Doctor of Laws, Mount Holyoke College, 1990; Honorary Doctor of Humane Letters, Univ of Medicine & Dentistry of NJ, 1989; Honorary Doctor of Education, Wheelock College, 1990; Bowdoin College, Doctor of Science, 1992; University of Massachusetts at Amherst, Doctor of Laws, 1992; Kean College of New Jersey, Dotor of Humane Letters, 1992; Essex County Community College, Doctor of Scienc, 1992. **Business Addr:** President, Univ of Texas at Dallas, PO Box 830688, Richardson, TX 75083-0688.

JENKINS, ADAM, JR.
College business manager. **Personal:** Born Sep 9, 1942, N Carrollton, MS; married Margaree Gordon; children: Veronica, Randolph, Darryl. **Educ:** Alcorn A&M Coll, BS 1967; Univ of Omaha, 1968; MS State Univ, 1968-69; MS Coll, MBA 1975. **Career:** Utica Jr Coll, cashier 1967-68, bus mgr 1969-; Hinds Jr Coll, vice pres bus svcs. **Orgs:** Consult Natchez Jr Coll; mem MS Jr Coll Bus Mgrs Assoc, Natl Assoc Colls & Univs Bus Officers, NEA, MS Teachers Assoc, NAACP; sec treas Phi Beta Sigma 1971-72. **Business Addr:** Vice President Bus Services, Hinds Jr College, Raymond Campus, Raymond, MS 39154.

JENKINS, ADELBERT HOWARD
Educator. **Personal:** Born Dec 10, 1934, St Louis, MO; son of Helen Howard Jenkins (deceased) and Herbert Jenkins (deceased); married Betty Lanier; children: Christopher. **Educ:** Antioch Coll, BA 1957; Univ of MI, MA 1958, PhD 1963. **Career:** A Einstein Med Coll, post doctoral fellow 1962-64, asst instr, instr 1964-67; New York Univ Medical Center, asst prof 1967-71; New York Univ, New York, NY, assoc prof, 1971-, dir undergraduate studies psychology 1982-86, 1989-93. **Orgs:** Training consult Veterans' Admin Med Centers Bronx, Manhattan, Brooklyn; mem Amer Psychological Assn 1964-, fellow 1985-; fellow Soc for Personality Assessment 1974-; mem Natl Assn of Black Psychol 1968-. **Honors/Awds:** Scholar of the Yr Natl Assn of Black Psychologists 1983; Martin L King Jr Award NY Soc of Clin Psychologists 1984; author of book, "Psychol and African Americans, A Humanistic Approach" 1995; Golden Dozen Award, Excellence in Teaching, New York University, Faculty of Arts & Science, 1988; M L King, Jr-Rosa parks Visiting Prof, Psychology, University of Michigan, 1987. **Special Achievements:** NY State, psychologist, Dipl in CUM Psychol, ABPP. **Business Addr:** Psychol Clinic, New York University, 715 Broadway, New York, NY 10003.

JENKINS, ALTHEA H.
Librarian. **Personal:** Born Sep 11, Tallahassee, FL; daughter of Florence Brown Henry and Samuel Henry; children: James C II. **Educ:** FL A&M Univ, BSLS 1963; FL Atlantic Univ, LD Certificate 19-70; FL State Univ, MSLS 1972; Nova Univ, EdD 1977. **Career:** Indian River School Bd, school media specialist 1963-71; FL State Univ, graduate asst 1971-72; Miami-Dade Comm Coll, library dir 1972-80; Univ of S FL Sarasota, library dir 1980-91; American Library Assn, Chicago, IL, executive director ACRL, 1991-. **Orgs:** Mem Amer Library Assoc; American Association for Higher Education, 1997-2001; mem Assoc Coll & Rsch Libraries; pres FL Assoc Coll & Rsch Library 1983-85; mem Eckerd Coll Bd of Trustees 1984-; pres, FL Library Assn, 1988-89; Sarasota Chamber of Commerce, 1989; Sarasota County Historical Commn, 1988-; Sarasota County United Way Bd, 1987-; Sarasota County Community Found, 1988-; mem, Phi Delta Kappa, 1987-; 1st vice pres, Delta Kappa Gamma, 1986-; mem, Delta Sigma Theta, 1990-. **Honors/Awds:** "She Knows Where She is Going", Girls Clubs of America Award, 1989; Certificate of Appreciation Newtown Library Planning Bd 1981; Certificate of Appreciation Sarasota-Manatee Phi Delta Kappa 1984.

JENKINS, ANDREW
Director, affirmative action and liaison activities. **Personal:** Born Jul 20, 1936, Philadelphia, PA; son of Madeline Green-Jenkins and William Jenkins; married Patricia A Green Jenkins, Oct 25, 1958; children: Eric, Denise, Andrea, Andrew. **Educ:** Antioch Univ, BA Human Services 1982. **Career:** Mantva Comm Planners, pres 1967-85; City of Philadelphia Liaison Officer Anti-Poverty Agency 1971-79; City of Philadelphia Chairman Mayor's Citizen Advisory Committee 1977-79; Mt Vernon Manor Apts, pres 1978-85; Mantva Primary Health Ctr, pres 1984-85; First United Baptist Church Male Chorus, vice pres 1984-85; Mantva Comm Devel Corp, vice pres 1984-85; Philadelphia Redevel Authority, dir relocation & prop mgmt, exec dir, currently. **Orgs:** Pres Mantua Community Planners 1967-1979; Dir Univ of PA Commun Devel 1969-71; Community Organizer Univ of PA 1969-71; liaison officer Philadelphia Ant Pov Action Comm 1971-79; pres Mt Vernon Apartments 1978-; exec bd West Philadelphia Partnership Inc 1983-89; mem Amer Legion George J Cornish Post 1983-85, Natl Forum for Black Admin 1984-85; mem Mayor Wilson Goode's Labor Standard Bd 1985, Philadelphia Redevel Authority Labor-Mgmt Comm; real estate comm bd mem Martin Luther King Village Comm Assoc Inc; bd mem Stinger Square Corp. **Honors/Awds:** Man of the Year Philadelphia Jaycees 1971; Outstanding Young Amer, Natl Jaycees 1972; Good Leadership Citations Mayor Bill Green City Council & Gov Thornburgh 1982; Outstanding Leadership West Philadelphia C of C 1984; City Council Citations 1983, 1984; Congressman Bill Gray Awd 1982; Young Great Soc Awd 1985; Mantua Comm Leadership Awd 1985. **Military Serv:** US Air Force airman second class 4 yrs; Citation for Community Relation Basketball (in Italy), 1957. **Home Addr:** 3609 Spring Garden St, Philadelphia, PA 19104. **Business Addr:** Executive Director, Redevelopment Authority of the City of Philadelphia, 1234 Market St, 8th Fl, Philadelphia, PA 19107.

JENKINS, ANDREW JAMES
Senator. **Personal:** Born Jun 27, 1941, Brooklyn, NY; married Michelle Rios; children: Andrew Jr, Alexandra. **Educ:** Fordham Univ, Soc Sci 1969; Fordham Univ Law School, JD 1972. **Career:** CUNY Coll, adjunct prof; Jenkins Aings & Johnson Law Firm, atty; NY State Senate, senator. **Orgs:** Parliamentarian Guy R Brewer Dem Club; mem Knights of Pythias. **Honors/Awds:** Mem Natl Hon Soc.

JENKINS, AUGUSTUS G., JR.
Funeral director. **Personal:** Born Aug 24, 1943, New York, NY; son of W Louise Johnson Jenkins and Augustus G Jenkins, Sr; married Nellie Kirkland, Jul 12, 1970; children: Natalie, Ashley. **Educ:** Central State Univ, Wilberforce, OH, BS, 1965; Ohio State Univ, Columbus, OH, MS, 1966. **Career:** Jenkins Funeral Chapel, New York, NY, owner, 1970-; Black Tennis and Sports Found, New York, NY, founder and vice chair, 1977-; profl pilot flight instructor, 1985-. **Military Serv:** US Army Signal Corps, 1966-68. **Home Addr:** 144 Lake St, Englewood, NJ 07631.

JENKINS, BARBARA WILLIAMS
Librarian. **Personal:** Born Aug 17, 1934, Union, SC; daughter of Johncie Sartor Williams and Ernest N Williams; married Robert A Jenkins; children: Ronald, Pamela. **Educ:** Bennett Coll, BA; Univ IL, MSLS; Rutgers U, PhD. **Career:** Circulation libr; ref & documents libr; South Carolina State Coll, Whittaker Library, library dir & prof, dean, library & information services. **Orgs:** Mem SC Library Assn; SE Library Assn; Am Library Assn; Am Soc for Information Sci; Alpha Kappa Mu Hon Soc; Am Assn Univ & Profs Evaluator So Assn Coll & Schs; library consult instr; co-adj faculty Rutgers U; asso dir Inst for Libr in Corr Inst; mem NAACP; Delta Sigma Theta Inc S Atlantic Reg Dir 1968-70; mem Nat Com Constitution bylaws 1971-75; mem Links Inc; pres Orangeburg Chap 1975-77; consult WEEA Project "Contributions of Black Women to Am 1776-1977"; treas Blk Caucus of the Am Lib Assn 1976-78; adv com SC Museum Commin; contribtr/edtrl bd Publ SC Blks & Native Am 1977; vice area dir Southern Area The Links Inc 1979-83; mem Land Grant Library Directors' Assoc 1979-85; chmn ALA Black Caucus 1984-86; pres So Carolina Library Assoc 1986-87; bd of dirSOLINET Southeastern Library Netw l989-. **Honors/Awds:** John Cotton Dana Award; Design & Planning Award MF Whittaker Library; Boss of the Yr Awd Orangeburg Chap Professional Secretaries Assoc 1980; Service Awd 1890 Land Grant Library Directors' Assoc 1984; President's Award South Carolina Library Assn l987; Distinguished Service Award, SC State College, 1991. **Business Addr:** Dean, Library and Information Services, South Carolina State College, Whittaker Library, Orangeburg, SC 29117.

JENKINS, BILLY
Professional football player. **Personal:** Born Jul 8, 1974; children: Khalil. **Educ:** Howard University. **Career:** St Louis Rams, defensive back, 1997-. **Business Addr:** Professional Football Player, St Louis Rams, One Rams Way, St Louis, MO 63045, (314)982-7267.

JENKINS, BOBBY G.
Business executive. **Personal:** Born Sep 30, 1939, Detroit; married Clara Gibson. **Educ:** Wayne State Univ, BS 1966. **Career:** Ford Motor Co Lincoln-Mercury Div, gen field mr, mktg sales 1972-; Chicago, zone mgr 1969-71; Chicago, admin mgr, 1968-69. **Honors/Awds:** Top mktg student of yr Sales Mktg Execs Detroit 1967; Beta Gamma hon soc 1967. **Military Serv:** USN 1957-60. **Business Addr:** Ford Motor Co Marketing Sales, 2010 Webster Ste 360, Oakland, CA 94612.

JENKINS, CARL SCARBOROUGH
Physician. **Personal:** Born Jan 18, 1916, Wilberforce, OH; married Helen Mathis Jenkins; children: Carlen Jenkins Mandas. **Educ:** Wilberforce Univ, BS, Educ, 1937; Meharry Med School, MD, 1942. **Career:** Springview Center OH State Hosp for the Mentally Retarded, co-medical dir 1978-79; Wright State Medical Sch Prog on Pain, co-chmn 1979-80; Springfield Bdof Health, pres 1980-81; Inst for Advanced Rsch in Asian Sci & Med New York, prof of acupuncture 1982; Mercy Med Center, Springfield, OH, active staff, currently; Federal Aviation Agency, examiner, currently; Wright State Univ School of Medicine, assoc clinical prof, currently; Center for Chinese Med, prof, currently. **Orgs:** Chmn elect of the Exec Committee of Wright State Univ Acad of Med; full mem, Amer Academy of Med Acupuncture; full mem, Amer Soc of Bariatric Physicians; fellow, Amer Coll of Acupuncture & Chinese Med; mem, Wright State Acad of Med; mem, Springfield Board of Health; mem; Ohio State Med Assn; life mem, Amer Academy of Family Physicians; numerous others. **Honors/Awds:** Cert of Appreciation Wright State Univ Sch of Medicine; publications incl, "Transcutaneous Neural Stimulation" The Helping Hands Vol 20 1979; "How To Get Into Medical School" co-author John Nduaguba, PhD 1979; "TNS Relationship to Tryptophan Mechanism" 1982; "Indicator for Pain Rx" 1983, numerous other publications; Honorary Staff, Greene Memorial Hospital, Xenia, OH; Honorary Staff, Community Hospital, Springfield, OH. **Business Addr:** Physician, 2055 S Limestone St, Springfield, OH 45505.

JENKINS, CARLTON J.
Banker. **Career:** Founders National Bank of Los Angeles, chief executive officer, currently. **Special Achievements:** Company is ranked #14 on Black Enterprise's list of Top 100 financial companies, 1994. **Business Addr:** CEO, Founders National Bank, 4143 Crenshaw Blvd., Los Angeles, CA 90008, (213)290-4848.

JENKINS, CAROL ANN
News correspondent. **Personal:** Born Nov 30, 1944, Montgomery, AL; married Carlos Hines. **Educ:** Boston U, BS 1966f NY U, MA 1968. **Career:** WNBC-TV, news corr 1973-; ABC-TVREASONOR/SMITH Report Eyewitness News, corr 1972-73; "Straight Talk" WOR- TV, moderator 1971-72f News Report with Bill RyanWOR-TV, co-anchor reporter 1970-71. **Orgs:** Mem Membership Com AFTRA; Writers Guild of Am E; Nat Acad of Arts & Scis; Intl Radio & TV Soc; Am Women in Radio & TV; Nat Assn of Media Women. **Honors/Awds:** Recipient serv Award Harlem Prep Sch 1971; outstanding achievement Award Ophelia DeVore Sch 1972; outstanding achievement Award AL State Univ 1972; outstanding achievement Award Journalism Alpha Wives 1974. **Business Addr:** WNBC-TV, 30 Rockefeller Plaza, New York, NY 10020.

JENKINS, CHIP
Olympic athlete. **Career:** US Olympic Team, Men's Track and Field, 1992. **Honors/Awds:** Olymic Games, US Men's Track and Field 4 x 400 relay, relay member, Gold Medalist, 1992.

JENKINS, CLARA BARNES
Educator. **Personal:** Born in Franklinton, NC; daughter of Stella Griffin Barnes and Walter Barnes, Sr; divorced. **Educ:** Winston-Salem State Univ, BS Educ 1940; NC Central Univ, MA 1947; Univ of Pittsburgh, EdD 1965; NYU; Univ of NC Chapel Hill; NC Agric and State Univ. **Career:** Fayetteville State Univ, instr 1945-50; Shaw Univ, asst prof 1954-64; NC Agric and Techn State Univ, visit prof 1966-86; St Paul's Coll, prof 1964-. **Orgs:** Board of directors, Annual Giving Fund at the Univ of Pittsburgh 1976-; adv St Paul's Student VA Educ Assn, 1966-; Natl Educ Assn; founder and adv Sigma Lambda Chptr of Zeta Phi Beta Sor 1982; Amer Assn of Univ Profs; Natl Soc for Study of Edn; Amer Hist Assn; AAUW; Assn of Teacher Educators; VA Educ Assn; Doctoral Assn of Educators; Amer Academy of Polit and Soc Sci; AAAS; Amer Assn of Higher Edn; Acad of Political Sci; Amer Psychol Assn; The Marquis Biograph Libr Soc; The Intl Platform Assn; Phi Eta Kappa Scholastic Soc; Soc for Rsch in Child Devel; Jean Piaget Soc; Philos of Educ Soc; Soc of Professors of Edn; Kappa Delta Pi Honor Soc; Phi Delta Kappa; Zeta Phi Beta Sorority Inc; mem The History of Educ Soc, Amer Soc of Notaries. **Honors/Awds:** Citation First of Race to receive doctorate in Foundations of Education from Univ of Pgh; Plaque for Effective Class Instr NC Agr and Techn State Univ 1979; Dedicated and Humanistic Instr in Teaching NC Agr and Techn State Univ 1980; Outstanding Achievement Eastern Reg of Zeta Phi Beta Sor 1982; United Negro College Fund Faculty Fellow at University of Pittsburgh; grant recipient for doctoral study from American Baptist Convention, Valley Forge, PA; Human Serv Profls;

Teacher of the Year St. Paul's Coll 1988-89. **Home Addr:** 920 Bridges St, Henderson, NC 27536. **Business Addr:** Prof Education & Psychology, Saint Paul's College, 406 Windsor Avenue, Lawrenceville, VA 23868.

JENKINS, CYNTHIA
State legislator. **Personal:** Born Jul 21, 1924, Nashville, TN; daughter of Maynie Burnley and Stephen A Burnley; married Joseph D Jenkins Sr; children: Joseph D Jr. **Educ:** Univ of Louisville, BA History Political Science 1945; Pratt Institute, MLS Library Science 1966; Columbia Univ, Post Graduate. **Career:** Brooklyn Public Library, librarian 1960-62; Queens Borough Public Library, librarian 1962-82; New York Assembly, legislator. **Orgs:** Founder/chairperson Social Concern Comm of Springfield Gardens Inc 1969-82; Black Librarians 1970-75; founder/chairperson Social Concern Comm Develop Agency 1980-82; founder Caucus of Queens 1976-; mem of council Amer Library Assn governing body 1982-; founder/chairperson Social Concern Fed Credit Union 1984-. **Honors/Awds:** Community Service Awd Alpha Kappa Alpha Sor 1980; Distinguished Citizen Friends of Sr Citizens 1982; Political Leadership Awd Queens womens Political Caucus 1983; Outstanding Citizens Awd Omega Psi Phi Frat 1984; Alpha Kappa Alpha, Charter Membership; numerous others. **Home Addr:** 174-63 128 Ave, Jamaica, NY 11434.

JENKINS, DERON CHARLES
Professional football player. **Personal:** Born Nov 14, 1973, Saint Louis, MO; children: Syrus. **Educ:** Univ of Tennessee, degree in psychology. **Career:** Baltimore Ravens, defensive back, 1996-. **Business Addr:** Professional Football Player, Baltimore Ravens, 11001 Owings Mills Blvd, Owings Mills, MD 21117, (410)654-6200.

JENKINS, DREWIE GUTRIMEZ
Educational administrator (retired). **Personal:** Born Apr 1, 1915, Logan Co; son of Maggie Jenkins and John Jenkins; married Cornelia Watkins. **Educ:** West Virginia State Coll, BS 1948; West Virginia Univ, MS 1951; Bradley Univ, 1952-54. **Career:** Kanawha Co Bd Educ, retired consultant industrial arts; taught in various elem Jr & Sr HS; Industrial Arts Kanawha Co, supervisor. **Orgs:** Rep NEA; life mem AAIA; WV State Alumni Assn; Kanawha Co Alumni Assn; Kappa Alpha Psi Frat; Mayor's planning comm City of Charleston; Nat Educ Assn 1974; Am Ind Arts Assn; NASCD; WVASCD; WVEA; KCEA; AVA; Phi Delta Kappa; charter mem Ebony Black Golf Tournament of Huntington, WV; past pres, West VA Indsl Arts Assn; mem NDEA Title XI Inst for Advance Study of Indsl Arts 1968-69; Am Legion Post 57; minister of Communion of Catholic Ch; WVAVA Cath lecturer; past state department vice commander, 1986-87; life mem, AFA chaplain of State Dept of American Legion; Kappa Alpha Psi Fraternity; NAACP; American Ind Arts Assoc. **Honors/Awds:** West Virginia State College, Cit & Leadership Certificate, 1953, Hall of Fame Inductee, 1992. **Special Achievements:** First African-American tchr WV schl 1954; 1st African-American teacher of WV honored as teacher of the yr Am Ind Arts Assn 1965; first African-American supervisor ind arts Co & State; first African-American, men of volunteer Fire Dept Bd of Malden; Improvement Council of Malden; Boy Scout Ldrshp Certificate WVSC, first and only African-American member; com writing "Guide for Sch Adminstrs & Tchrs," Indsl Arts in Jr HS 1968. **Military Serv:** US Army, 1946-49; Pacific Combat Bravery. **Home Addr:** 3705 Malden Dr, Charleston, WV 25306.

JENKINS, EDMOND THOMAS
Educator (retired). **Personal:** Born Apr 4, 1930, Cleveland, OH; son of Amy Jenkins and James Jenkins. **Educ:** Howard Univ, BA 1953; Western Reserve Univ, MA 1956, MSSA 1966; Moreno Academy of Sociodrama Psychodrama and Group Psychotherapy, Certificate 1968. **Career:** TN A&I State Univ, instructor 1956-60; Garden Valley Neighborhood House, teen group worker acting dir 1960-64; Ionia State Hosp for Criminally Insane, clinical sw supervisor 1966-69; Case Western Reserve Univ, asst prof assoc prof 1969-92; assoc prof emeritus, 1992. **Orgs:** Certified mem Natl Assoc of Social Workers 1968-; life mem NAACP; member, Association for the Advancement of Social Work with Groups. **Honors/Awds:** Appreciation Awd St Andrews Episcopal Church 1980; Outstanding Prof Awd Assoc of Black Student Social Workers 1980; Teacher of the Year Alumni Assoc 1982; Licensed Ind Social Worker State of OH 1986. **Military Serv:** AUS corpl 2 yrs; Good Conduct Medal, Korean Serv Medal.

JENKINS, ELAINE B.
Consultant, business executive (retired). **Personal:** Born Apr 2, 1916, Butte, MT; daughter of Floy Smith Brown and Russell S Brown, Sr (deceased); married Howard Jenkins Jr, Jun 24, 1940; children: Judith E, Howard III, Larry. **Educ:** Denver Univ, BA; OH State Univ, MA. **Career:** Former teacher, integrating schools for the first time in Denver CO and Washington DC; public school administrator, first community coordinator in Washington DC; Black Educ Consulting Serv, founder, dir; One America Inc, pres/founder 1970-. **Orgs:** Mem Urban League 1967, United Givers Fund 1970; founder DC Alpha Wives; past pres Howard Univ Faculty Wives; natl co-chmn Delta Sigma Theta; delegate Natl Convention; natl vice pres Womens Black Political Caucus; chmn Ed Task Force; appt Nelson Comm; mem Citizens Adv Council on European Affairs; trustee DC Inst of Mental Health; mem Panel for HEW Fellows; mem City Council Adv Comm on Indus & Commercial Devel; chairperson Council of 100 Black Republicans; dir Found for the Preservation of the Two-Party System; mem Natl Social Action Commn, Delta Sigma Theta; pres appt Natl Adv Council of Voluntary Action; regional vice pres Assn of United States Army. **Honors/Awds:** Comm Appreciation Awd Tri-Schools of SW Washington DC 1970; appt by pres US Comm on Org of DC 1973; Eartha MM White Awd Natl Business League; Awarded Cosmopolitan BPW Club; appt by Pres Natl Adv Council on Educ of Disadvantaged Children 1974; Woman of the Year Awd Natl Business League Bd Delta Sigma Theta; sel by Sec of Def 45th Annual Joint Civil Orientation Conf; Honored by Dollars and Sense Magazine as Woman of the Year 1985; regional vice pres (first Black corporate vice pres), Assn of United States Army; Community Service Award, Univ of Denver, 1988; Lifetime Achievement Award, SBA. **Home Addr:** 3333 University Blvd, #1101, Kensington, MD 20895.

JENKINS, ELIZABETH AMETA
Educator. **Personal:** Born Mar 11, 1929, Brooklyn, NY; daughter of Ameta A Hackett-Hunte and Lionel A Hunte (deceased); divorced; children: Roland, Roderick, Howard, Rebecca, Leah. **Educ:** Molloy Coll, BA Soc Psy 1977; Hofstra U, MA Cnsl Ed Family Therapy 1985. **Career:** Nassau Co Dept of Social Svcs, social work aid 1965-68; Econ Oppor Cncl Roosevelt, NY, summer youth dir commnty organizer 1970-72; Alliance for Minority Group Leaders Inc, activities planner/parent coord 1972-77; Molloy Coll, cnslr. **Orgs:** Mem Assn for Equality & Excell in Educ 1979; mem LI Cncl of Stdnt Pers Admin 1981-; mem Assn of Black Women in Higher Educ 1977-; mem HEOP Professnl Organ LI Region 1978; mem Am Assn of Univ Women 1977; mem Am Bus Womens Assn 1984; pres Roosevelt Schlrshp Assn 1958-75; founding sec Nassau/Suffolk Hlth Sys Agency 1976-78; mem Nassau Co Task Force on the Status of Women 1977-79. **Honors/Awds:** Cert of Commendation Nassau Co Dept Hlth 1964; Dedicated Serv Alliance of Min Group Leaders Inc 1978; Ten Year Plaque for Dedicated Service, Molloy College, 1987; Ten Year Pin for Dedicated Service to Higher Education Opportunity Program Professional Organization, State Education Department HEOP, 1990. **Home Addr:** 50 Holloway St, Freeport, NY 11520. **Business Addr:** Counselor, Molloy Coll, 1000 Hempstead Ave, Rockville Centre, NY 11570.

JENKINS, ELLA LOUISE
Musician, singer, recording artist. **Personal:** Born Aug 6, 1924, St Louis, MO. **Educ:** Wilson Jr Coll, 1945-47; Roosevelt Coll, 1947-48; SF State Coll, 1949-51. **Career:** Free lance musician singer rec artist; conduted rhythm workshops & concerts around the US & other countries. **Orgs:** Mem Music Educ Nat Cofn; Intl Platform Assn; Am Soc of Composers. **Honors/Awds:** Num Awards. **Business Addr:** 1844 N Mohawk St, Chicago, IL 60614.

JENKINS, EMMANUEL LEE
Educational administrator. **Personal:** Born Aug 7, 1934, Greenville, NC; widowed; children: Darel, Gregory, Jerome, Tamara. **Educ:** Howard Univ, BA Pharmacy 1956; Long Island Univ, MS Educ 1974. **Career:** Rhodes Med, pharm 1956; Moore-Schley Cameron & Co, customers broker 1960-70; US Merchant Marine Acad, dir of admissions 1970-. **Orgs:** Ofcr Lakeview Educ Com 1968-73; rep Coll Bd 1973-; rep Natl Assn Coll Admissions Officers 1974-; mem Coll Bd Council 1982-83. **Honors/Awds:** Special Achievement Awd for Performance USMM Acad 1975; Special Achievement Awd 1983. **Military Serv:** USN cmdr served 23 yrs; Bronze Medal for Superior Fed Serv Maritime Admin 1978. **Business Addr:** Dir of Admissions, US Merchant Marine Acad, Kings Point, NY 11024.

JENKINS, FERGUSON
Pitching instructor, professional baseball player (retired). **Personal:** Born Dec 13, 1942, Ontario;married Maryanne (died 1991); children: two; married Lydia Jenkins, 1993. **Career:** Pitcher: Philadelphia Phillies, 1965-66, Chicago Cubs, 1966-73, Texas Rangers, 1974-75, Boston Red Sox, 1976-77, Texas Rangers, 1978-81, Chicago Cubs, 1982-83; Cincinnati Reds, pitching coach, 1992-93, roving pitching instructor, 1993-; Chicago Cubs, pitching coach. **Honors/Awds:** National League Cy Young Memorial Award, 1971; 20-game winner, six straight years; National League All-Star Team, 1967, 1971, 1972; elected to Baseball Hall of Fame, 1991; Canadian Athlete of the Year, 1967, 1968, 1971, 1974; Lou Marsh Trophy, 1971; Order of Canada, 1987. **Business Addr:** Pitching Coach, Chicago Cubs, 1060 W Addison St, Chicago, IL 60613, (312)404-2827.

JENKINS, FRANK SHOCKLEY
Author, poet, publisher. **Personal:** Born Apr 11, 1925, Seattle, WA; married Lynn Hamilton; children: Frank Alexander, Denise Shockley. **Career:** US Merchant marine, 1942-52; US Post Office, 1952-68; Time-DC Los Angeles, freight handler 1969-73; Hollywood, actor 1973-; Shockley Press, poet/publisher, currently. **Orgs:** Mem Screen Actors Guild; mem Teamsters 357; mem Screen Extras Guild, AFTRA. **Honors/Awds:** Publ, I Didn't Start Out To Be A Poet 1977, 1981; Black Mac Say 1981; works included in Emmy Awd Prog, 1982; Voices Of Our People, In Celebration Of Black Poetry, 1982; play "Last Man Out" LA 1975; play (poetic) "My World" coll 1979; publ "What It Is?" 1981; play "Nobody" LA, 1992. **Business Addr:** Publisher, Shockley Press, Box 36012, Los Angeles, CA 90036, (213)933-2393.

JENKINS, GAYLE EXPOSE
Nurse. **Personal:** Born Feb 12, 1927, Bogalusa, LA; married Monroe; children: Toni Harry, Don Expose, Willie E. **Educ:** Booker T Washington LPN School, LPN 1968. **Career:** Highland Park Hospital, LPN; Richards Beauty School, beautician 1950. **Orgs:** Sec Bogalusa Voter's League Civil Rights Group 1964-; mem Emergency School Aid Act 1975-77; dir Washington Parish Children's Council 1978; advisory bd Comm Devel Block Grant 1979-; school bd Bogalusa School Bd 1978-; mem Natl Caucus of black school bd mem 1979-; mem Natl Citizen Participation Council 1979-80; advisory bd Adolescent Pregnancy Program 1980-; mem LA Sch Bd Assn 1980-; mem Nursing Alumni Assn 1979-80. **Honors/Awds:** Ms Central, Central Memorial HS, 1946; Cert dep Gov Edwards LA 1973; Cert Dep Gov Treenla 1981. **Business Addr:** Bogalusa City Schools, 331 Cumberland St, Bogalusa, LA 70427.

JENKINS, GEORGE ARTHUR, JR.
Marketing executive. **Personal:** Born May 22, 1955, New York, NY; son of Margaret Dobson and George Dobson Sr; married Linda Ann Dawkins, Sep 17, 1983 (divorced 1990); children: Peter Anthony. **Educ:** Univ of Rochester, BA 1977; Univ of Chicago Grad Sch of Business, MBA 1979. **Career:** Xerox Corp, market analyst 1979-83; Natl Data Corp Rapidata Div, acct rep 1983-84; Mead Data Central Inc, mgr corporate markets, 1984-86; Real Estate Data Inc, dir electronic publishing 1986-87; Lotus Devel Corp, Prod Mgr, 1988-. **Orgs:** Mem Alpha Phi Alpha Frat 1977-; mem CARI Inc 1980-83, Dayton Chap Natl Black MBA Assoc 1984-86; mem Information Industry Assoc 1984-; Assoc MBA Executives, 1984-87. **Home Addr:** 67-R Cedar St, #2, Somerville, MA 02143. **Business Addr:** Marketing Manager, Lotus Development Corporation, 55 Cambridge Pkwy, Cambridge, MA 02142.

JENKINS, GEORGE E., III (GEORGE E. JORDAN)
Journalist. **Personal:** Born Jan 15, 1957, Chicago, IL; son of Wyndolyn H Jordan and George E Jenkins Jr; married Alicia A Lockett, Nov 25, 1989; children: Gwendolyn Faith. **Educ:** University of Minnesota, Associates degree, 1977, BS, 1979. **Career:** Boston Globe, intern, summer 1980; University of Minnesota Hospital, science writer; Minneapolis Tribune, reporter; Cleveland Plain Dealer, reporter; Miami News, political writer; New York Newsday, special writer, 1989-. **Orgs:** Natl Assn of Black Journalists, 1977-. **Honors/Awds:** Columbia University, Pulitizer Prize, Spot News, 1992; New York Society of Professional Journalists, Deadline Club Award, 1990; New York Newspaper Publishers Association, Local Reporting Excellence, 1990-91; Society of the Silurians, Spot News Reporting, 1992; NY Assn of Black Journalists, Investigative Reporting Award, 1990. **Special Achievements:** Natl Assn of Black Journalists, investigative reporting workshop, 1990-92; investigative reporters and editors computer-aided reporting workshop, 1993. **Business Addr:** Special Writer, New York Newsday, 2 Park Ave, 9th Fl, New York, NY 10016, (212)251-6800.

JENKINS, HARRY LANCASTER
Dental surgeon. **Personal:** Born Apr 22, 1932, Columbus, GA; married Janie R; children: Harry, Timothy, Anthony, Gary. **Educ:** Morehouse Coll, AB 1955; Meharry Med Coll, DDS 1962; Tuskegee VA Hosp, internship 1962-63. **Career:** Self-employed, dental surgeon; Maryview Hosp Portsmouth VA, staff; Portsmouth Gen Hosp; Norfolk Comm Hosp, staff mem. **Orgs:** Am Cancer Soc mem Truxton Lodge 199 F&M; mem Am Youth Orgn; Eureka Bus & Professional Club; adv bd VA State Civil Rights Commn. **Military Serv:** AUS corpl 1952. **Business Addr:** 3349 Portsmouth Blvd, Portsmouth, VA 23701.

JENKINS, HERMAN LEE
Educational administrator. **Personal:** Born May 7, 1940, Montgomery, AL; married Margaret Stephenson; children: Gloria, Herman Jr. **Educ:** Assoc of Amer Geography, scholar 1976; Clark Univ, BA 1974, PhD 1983. **Career:** Southern Christian Leadership Conf, comm organizer civil rights activist 1965-69; Clark Univ, dir of comm rel 1972; Amer Intl Coll, lecturer 1976; Queens Coll, exec asst to pres 1978-80; HL Jenkins Geographic Analysis Inc, pres & ceo 1978-; Self-employed, artist mapmaker 1961-; Queens Coll, asst vice pres. **Orgs:** Mem NAACP 1971-; mem 100 Black Men Inc 1978-; mem Assoc of Amer Geographers. **Honors/Awds:** Fellowship/president Metropolitan Applied Rsch Center 1967-68; Jonas Clark Scholar Clark Univ 1977. **Military Serv:** AUS pfc 3 yrs. **Home Addr:** 241-20 Northern Blvd, Douglaston, NY 11363. **Business Addr:** Asst Vice President, Queens College, 65-30 Kissena Blvd, Flushing, NY 11367.

JENKINS, JAMES
Professional football player. **Personal:** Born Aug 17, 1967, Staten Island, NY. **Educ:** Rutgers. **Career:** Washington Redskins, tight end, 1991-. **Business Addr:** Professional Football Player, Washington Redskins, 13832 Redskin Dr, Herndon, VA 22071, (703)471-9100.

JENKINS, JAMES E.
Clergyman. **Personal:** Born Jan 14, 1939, Patterson, GA; married Lodine Pollock; children: James, Nerville, Tonji, Calvin. **Educ:** Equiv BTh. **Career:** Seaboard Baptist Assn, asst dean & instr; Frndshp Miss Bapt Ch, #Minister-pstr; Seabd Bapt Assn Inc, fourth vice-moderator; Comm Devel Fund, 2nd vp; Haitian Refugee Info Cntr, founder exec dir. **Orgs:** Chmn Historical Commn Com Nat Bapt Conv USA Inc; mem Rotary Internat; appt to Gov Stop Crime Commn; org-chmn CRAC; mem Comm Rel Bd. **Honors/Awds:** Recip man of the yr 1971 Front of Am; citzn of the yr 1972 Sigma Alpha Chap Omega Psi Phi; Nathan Collier Award FL Mem Coll 1972; cert of recog 1972 Nat Sor of Phi Delta Kappa; outstdg Comm Serv 1973 Blk Professional Nrses Assn; Qual of Life Award Jonathan Paul Turner Mem Found 1974; Humanitarian Award AEAONMS Dau of Isi 1975. **Business Addr:** 740 NW 58 St, Miami, FL 33127.

JENKINS, JIMMY RAYMOND
Educational administrator. **Personal:** Born Mar 18, 1943, Selma, NC; married Faleese Moore; children: Lisa, Ginger, Jimmy Raymond Jr. **Educ:** Elizabeth City State Univ, BS 1965; Purdue Univ, MS, PhD 1969-72. **Career:** Elizabeth City State Univ, asst prof biol 1972, asst acad dean 1972, assoc prof biol 1973, vice chancellor acad affairs 1977, chancellor 1983-. **Orgs:** Mem NC Humanities Comm 1980, Governor's Oversight Comm, Natl Caucus for Black Aged, Elizabeth City Chap Kiwanis Intl, NC Bd of Sci & Tech, Amer Assoc of Higher Ed. **Honors/Awds:** Disting Alumni NAFEO; Outstanding Young Men in Amer; Boss of the Year Elizabeth City State Univ 1978. **Home Addr:** 1304 Parkview Dr, Elizabeth City, NC 27909. **Business Addr:** Chancellor, Elizabeth City State Univ, 1704 Weeksville Road, Elizabeth City, NC 27909.

JENKINS, JOHN
Mayor. **Career:** John Jenkins Academy of Personal Dev, owner, 1970-97; Bates Coll, dir of housing, 1986-88; Dirigo Corp, pres, 1988-97; City of Lewiston, ME, mayor, 1993-97; State Senator, ME, 1996-98; Multi-Cultural Development, UNVM dir, currently. **Honors/Awds:** Chamber of Commerce, Comm Service Awd; Maine Dev Foundation, Comm Leadership Awd; US Conference of Mayors, City Livability Awd. **Special Achievements:** World Martial Arts Champion, five times; World Martial Arts Hall of Fame, inductee. **Business Addr:** Mayor, City of Lewiston, PO Box 7205, Lewiston, ME 04243, (207)783-3413.

JENKINS, JOSEPH WALTER, JR.
Management consultant. **Personal:** Born Jan 28, 1941, East Orange, NJ; son of Annabelle Clarke Jenkins and Joseph Jenkins; married F Louise Diaz; children: Khalil, Medinah. **Educ:** TN State Univ, BBA, 1963; Farleigh Dickinson Univ, MBA, management, 1979. **Career:** General Motors, prod control coord 1963; Ford Motor Co, engrg analyst 1966; Travelers Ins Co, asst mgr persl admin 1968; Chubb Corp, eeo mgr 1974, asst vice pres of human resources; City of East Orange, bus administrator 1986-90; J W Jenkins and Co, pres 1990; Neward Board of Education, Pensions and Benefits Mgr, 1991-96. **Orgs:** Americans Sailing Association; pres Comm Day Nursery 1992; mem, Omega Psi Phi Fraternity Upsilon Phi Chapter, 1988-. **Honors/Awds:** Black Achievers Awd Harlem Branch YMCA 1976; Outstanding Service Optimist Club Orange/East Orange 1979; Outstanding Citizen Awd Eagle Flight of New Jersey, 1988. **Home Addr:** 7 Mountain Dr, West Orange, NJ 07052. **Business Addr:** President, J W Jenkins and Co, 7 Mountain Dr, West Orange, NJ 07052.

JENKINS, JULIUS
Educator. **Career:** Concordia College, Selma, AL, president/chancellor. **Business Addr:** President, Concordia College, 1801 Green Street, Selma, AL 36701.

JENKINS, KENNETH VINCENT
Educational administrator. **Personal:** Born in Elizabeth, NJ; son of Rebecca Meredith Williams Jenkins and Thomas Augustus Jenkins; divorced; children: 4. **Educ:** Columbia Coll NY, AB; Columbia Univ NY, AM; Columbia Univ, PhD candidate. **Career:** South Side High School, Rockville Centre NY, chmn English dept 1965-72; Nassau Community Coll, supvr adjunct faculty, prof English and Afro-Amer literature, chmn Afro-Amer studies dept 1974-. **Orgs:** Consultant in Eng, convener, chmn bd dir, Target Youth Centers Inc NY, 1973-75; Natl Bd Pacifica Found, mem 1973-80, chmn, pres 1976-80; chmn, Nassau County Youth Bd, 1979-; Phi Delta Kappa; Assn for the Study of Afro-Amer Life and History; Afro-Amer Inst NY; Mensa, 1968-70; Coun Black Amer Affairs; exec bd, NY African Studies Assn; African Heritage Studies Assn; mem, Governor's New York State Council on Youth, 1986-; advisory bd mem, Radio Station WBAI-FM NY, 1972-85; member, Schomburg Corp, 1989-; board member, Long Island Community Foundation, 1989-98; bd mem, New York State Youth Support Inc. **Honors/Awds:** Baker Award, Columbia Univ; community awards; author of essays, reviews "Last Day in Church"; Martin Luther King Jr Award, Nassau County, 1989. **Military Serv:** US Natl Guard. **Business Addr:** Professor, Chairperson, African-American Studies Department, Nassau Community College, Garden City, NY 11530.

JENKINS, LOUIS E.
Clinical psychologist. **Personal:** Born Dec 20, 1931, Staten Island, NY; married Althea L Jenkins; children: Le Toia M. **Educ:** Union Coll, BA 1954; Univ NE, MA 1959; Pepperdine U, MA Psychol 1970; PA State U, PhD Clinical Psy 1973. **Career:** Pepperdine Univ, assoc prof of psychology 1970-75; LA Union SDA Sch, tchr 1959-64; LA City Schools, teacher 1964-65, counselor 1965-66, school psychologist 1966-69; Dept of Psychology & Human Behavior, Martin Luther King Jr General Hospital LA, staff psychologist; CA Fam Study Cent Downey, CA, private practice. **Orgs:** NAACP; USC Comm Adv Bd; Am Psy Asso Comm Pilot; flight instr rating. **Military Serv:** AUS Med Corp sp3 1954-56.

JENKINS, LUTHER NEAL
Aerospace engineer. **Career:** NASA Langley Research Center, aerospace engineer, currently. **Orgs:** Omega Psi Phi Fraternity, Inc. **Honors/Awds:** Ebony, 50 Leaders of Tomorrow, November 1992. **Business Addr:** Aerospace Engineer, NASA Langley Research Center, Mail Stop 454, Hampton, VA 23681, (804)864-8026.

JENKINS, MARILYN JOYCE
Police officer. **Personal:** Born Jun 17, 1943, Detroit, MI; daughter of May Martin Mitchell and Madison Martin, Sr; married Virgil T Hollins, 1992; children: Simone Martin, Jamiil Brock Martin. **Educ:** Wayne County Community Coll, Detroit MI, currently enrolled. **Career:** City of Detroit MI, police officer, 1975-. **Orgs:** Founder/pres, 7 Mile Schaefer Youth Assn, 1978-87; presenter, Career Day, Newberry Elementary School, 1984; pres, Ladies on the Move, 1984-; treasurer, Southwest Aging Coalition, 1984-86; moderator, Educational Training Seminar, 1985; moderator, Gerontology Program Workshop, 1985; presenter, Courtis Elementary-Child Molestation Prevention Program, 1986; volunteer, Michigan Cancer Foundation, 1986-89; volunteer, March of Dimes, 1987-. **Honors/Awds:** Officer of the Year, Detroit Police Dept, 1978, 1985; Spirit of Detroit Award, Detroit City Council, 1985, 1988; Distinguished Service Award, Wayne County Executive, 1985; Top Cop Award, Detroit Chamber of Commerce, 1985; Police Community Service Award, Detroit Police Dept, 1985; Women Police of MI Certificate of Appreciation; Certificate of Appreciation, Mayor Coleman Young; Spirit of Detroit Award, First Mother & Daughter Police Officers (nationwide), 1989; Chairman of Women Police of MI for Region 18, 1991-93; March of Dimes Award, Volunteer, 1991; Certificate of Appreciation, Ennis House for Children, 1992; Police officer of Year Award from Detroit Chambers of Commerce. **Business Addr:** Police Officer, City of Detroit, 2110 Park, Detroit, MI 48226.

JENKINS, MELVIN
Professional football player. **Personal:** Born Mar 16, 1962, Jackson, MS. **Educ:** Cincinnati. **Career:** Canadian Football League, Calgary, 1984-86; Natl Football League, Seattle Seahawks, 1987-90, Detroit Lions, cornerback, 1991-93; Atlanta Falcons, 1993; Detroit Lions, 1993-94. **Honors/Awds:** Played in NFC championship game, 1991. **Business Phone:** (313)335-4131.

JENKINS, MELVIN E., JR.
Physician, educator. **Personal:** Born Jun 24, 1923, Kansas City, MO; son of Marguerite and Melvin; married Maria Parker; children: Janis, Carol, Lore, Ingrid, Colin. **Educ:** Univ of KS, AB 1944; Univ of KS Coll of Med, MD 1946; Freedman's Hosp, internship 1946-47, pediatric residency 1947-50; pediatric endocrinology Johns Hopkins Hospital 1963-65. **Career:** Freedman's Hosp, asst pediatrician 1950-59, assoc pediatrician 1959-69; Howard Univ Coll Med, clinical instr 1951-54, clinical asst prof 1954-55, asst prof 1957-59, assoc prof 1959-69; Univ of NE Med Ctr, pediatrician 1969-73, dir pediatric endocrine clinic 1969-73, prof vice chmn dept of pediatrics 1971-73; George Washington Univ, professorial lectr child health & devel 1973-; Hospital for Sick Children, attng staff 1973-91; Childrens Hosp Natl Med Ctr of DC, sr attng pediatrician 1973-; Freedmen's Hosp, chief pediatrician 1973-86; Johns Hopkins Univ, lectr dept of pediatrics 1974-; Howard Univ Coll of Med, prof chmn dept of pediatrics & child health 1973-86. **Orgs:** Policy adv com Ctr for Urban Affairs 1971-73; chmn Health Task Force; bd dirs Urban League of NE 1971-73; pres bd dirs Comprehensive Hlth Assn of Omaha Inc 1972-73; med dir Parent Ctr 1971-73; edtr in chief Pediatric Newsletter Natl Med Assn 1970-83; adv bd Human Growth Inc 1971; chmn med records com Freedmen's Hosp 1966, Howard Univ Hosp 1974-88; med sch rep Howard Univ Counc of Adm 1967, 1974; pres Freedmen's Hosp Med Dental Staff 1968-69; chmn ped sect Natl Med Assn 1966-69; consult Natl Inst of Health 1973-; campus rep Endocrine Soc 1974-80; subcom on growth hormone 1974-78; med adv com Nat Pituitary Agency 1975-78; med adv com Natl Found March of Dimes 1974-78; examiner Amer Bd of Pediatrics 1975-88, bd mem 1983-89; Natl Adv Rsch Resources Counc Natl Insts of Health 1974-78; Sigma Xi; Med Chirurgical of DC; Amer Assn for Advancement of Sci; Black Child Devel Inst Inc; Alpha Omega Alpha; Pediatric Surgery Comm Amer Bd of Surgery 1984. **Honors/Awds:** SAMA Golden Apple Awd 1963; Recog for Outstanding Contrib to Growth of Pediatric Sect Natl Med Assn 1966-69; Outstanding Achiev Awd So Christian Ldrshp Conf 1972; Outstanding Scholar-Teacher Awd Howard Univ 1984; Outstanding Contrib Citation City Council of DC 1984; Leadership in Medicine Award Univ of Kansas 1989; Melvin E Jenkins, Lectureship in Pediatrics, Howard University, 1995. **Business Addr:** Professor Emeritus, Dept of Pediatrics, Howard Univ, College of Medicine, Washington, DC 20059.

JENKINS, MELVIN L.
Attorney. **Personal:** Born Oct 15, 1947, Halifax, NC; son of Mr and Mrs S G Jenkins; married Wanda Holly; children: Shelley, Melvin Jr, Dawn, Holly Rae-Ann. **Educ:** NC A&T State Univ, BS 1969; Univ of KS School of Law, JD 1972. **Career:** Legal Aid Soc Kansas City, MO, staff atty 1972; US Dept of Housing & Urban Devel, staff atty 1972-73; US Commn on Civil Rights, regional atty 1973-79; US Commn on Civil Rights, acting staff dir, currently. **Orgs:** Bd of dir Joan Davis Special School 1984-; mem Natl Bar Assn; mem NE Bar Assn; mem Mayor's Human Rel Commn Kansas City, MO; mem Alpha Phi Omega Serv Frat; Omega Psi Phi Fraternity. **Honors/Awds:** Benton Fellowship Univ of KS Sch of Law; Smith Fellowship Legal Aid Soc; Civil Rights Award Blue Valley Lodge Masons. **Home Addr:** 8015 Sunset Cir, Grandview, MO 64030. **Business Addr:** Regional Dir, US Comm on Civil Rights, 400 State Ave, Ste 908, Kansas City, KS 66101.

JENKINS, MONICA
Human resources representative. **Personal:** Born Apr 7, 1961, San Francisco, CA; daughter of Marie Taylor Jenkins and James Jenkins. **Educ:** University of Santa Clara, Santa Clara, CA, BS, 1983. **Career:** First Nationwide Bank, San Francisco, CA, customer service rep, 1983-85, state sales trainer, 1985-90; Nordstrom, San Francisco, CA, sales assoc, 1989-90; Pacific Gas and Electric Co, San Francisco, CA, human resources assoc, 1989-90, human resoures rep, EEO/diversity unit, 1990-. **Orgs:** Member, CHOCS, 1990-; member, ACHRC, 1990-; member, BEA, 1990-. **Business Addr:** Human Resources Rep, EEO/Diversity Unit, Pacific Gas & Electric Co, 201 Mission St, Rm PISA, San Francisco, CA 94177.

JENKINS, OZELLA
Convention manager. **Personal:** Born Aug 13, 1945, Roanoke Rapids, NC. **Educ:** NC Central Univ, attended 1962-64; Howard Univ, attended 1964-65; Cornell Univ, attended 1974. **Career:** C&P Telephone Co, customer serv rep 1964-71; Pitts Motor Hotel, restaurant mgr 1964-72; Sheraton Washington Hotel, convention mgr 1972-. **Orgs:** Mem Natl Cncl of Negro Women 1962-; mem Natl Assoc of Catering Execs 1976-; mem Natl Coalition of Black Mtg Planners 1984-; business mgr Washington Chap JUGS Inc 1984-; vice pres Bonaire Homes Assoc 1985-. **Honors/Awds:** Certificate Daughters of the Amer Revolution 1979; Recognition of Excellence Successful Meeting Mag 1982,84,86; certificate/plaque Meeting Planners Intl 1984; plaque Natl Urban League 1985, US Marshal Service 1985, Metro Police Dept Washington DC 1985. **Business Addr:** Convention Manager, Sheraton Washington Hotel, 2660 Woodley Rd, NW, Washington, DC 20008.

JENKINS, ROBERT KENNETH, JR.
Attorney, business executive. **Personal:** Born Mar 11, 1947, Washington, DC; son of Bertha Thomas Jenkins and Robert Kenneth Jenkins Sr; divorced; children: Robert K Jenkins III. **Educ:** Howard Univ, BA 1970; George Washington Univ, JD 1974. **Career:** US Sec & Exch Comm, trial atty 1974-76; Direct Selling Assn, legisl counsel 1977; Natl YMCA, dep gen counsel real est operations 1978-80; Natl City Financial Serv Inc, pres, 1980-86; DC Dept of Housing & Community Development, asst dir, 1986-90; DC Local Development Corp, pres, CEO, 1990-93; DC Dept of Public & Assisted Housing, exec dir, 1993-. **Orgs:** Board member, YMCA of Silver Spring, MD, 1986-; Nations Bank Community Advisory Committee, 1990-; Sheridan School, board of trustees, 1991-93. **Business Addr:** Executive Director, DC Dept of Public & Assisted Housing, 1133 North Capitol Street NE, Washington, DC 20002.

JENKINS, ROGER J.
Association executive. **Personal:** Born Oct 26, 1939, Fort Pierce, FL; married Rose Oliver; children: Roger Jr, Courtney, Oren. **Educ:** Clark College, BA, 1962; Atlanta School of Social Work, MSW, 1964; University of Cincinnati, MCP, 1972, PhD, 1974. **Career:** Seven Hills Neighborhood Houses, exec dir, 1968-71; org dev consult for several major industrial org educ & rel systems; New Orleans Neighborhood Centers, group work, 1964-65. **Orgs:** Adv com Neighborhood Tech Inf Serv Am Soc Plann Offs; Am Sociological Assn; Am Soc of Plann Off; Nat Assn of Soc Work; Am Assn of Univ Prof; United Black Faculty, Univ of Cincinnati; Alpha Phi Alpha. **Honors/Awds:** Outstanding Young Man in America, 1972; spl cit, State of OH for Comm Serv; spl city, City of Cincinnati for Comm Dev. **Business Addr:** 701 Lincoln Park Dr, Cincinnati, OH 45203.

JENKINS, SHIRLEY LYMONS
Educator (retired). **Personal:** Born Aug 9, 1936, Pine Apple, AL; daughter of Mr & Mrs Hilliard Lymons; married Henry J Jenkins. **Educ:** Knoxville Coll, BS Educ 1958; Atlanta Univ, MA Educ 1969; Univ of AL, AA Educ 1974. **Career:** Boykin

High School AL, teacher 1959-62; Camden Academy AL, teacher 1962-68; Leeds Elementary School, AL, teacher 1968 (retired). **Orgs:** Southeastern regional dir Knoxville Coll Alumni Assn 1978-84; chairperson Teen-Life Birmingham Alumnae Delta Sigma Theta Sorority Inc 1983-85; chairperson Scholarship Natl Sor of Phi Delta Kappa Inc 1983-; pres Knoxville College Natl Alumni Assn Inc 1984-; mem bd trustees Knoxville Coll 1984-; mem Birmingham Alumnae Delta Sigma Theta Sorority Inc, Birmingham Chap Natl Sor Phi Delta Kappa Inc; mem Sixth Avenue Baptist Church Birmingham; Natl Council of Negro Women Inc; scholarship chairman, Phi Delta Kappa Sorority Inc, 1989-; deputy registrar, Jefferson County Alabama; secretary, board of trustees, Knoxville College. **Honors/Awds:** Outstanding Regional Dir Knoxville Coll Alumni 1978-84; President's Disting Serv Awds Knoxville Coll 1979, 1982; Hostess of Year Imperial Club Inc Debutante Ball 1983; Certificates Jefferson Co Bd of Health 1983-86; Certificate Outstanding Contribution Southern Region Delta Sigma Theta Sor 1984; Soror of the Month Phi Delta Kappa Sorority Inc 1985; Disting Alumna of the Year Citation Natl Assn for Equal Oppor in Higher Educ 1986; Citation Amer Federation of Teachers; life mem Knoxville College Natl Alumni Assn Inc; Soror of Year, Phi Delta Kappa Sorority Inc, 1989; Knoxville College Award, 1990; Golden Life Member, Delta Sigma Theta National Sorority Inc; Plaque, Knoxville College Football Team, 1992; Honarary Dr, Knoxville College, 1994; Plaque for Outstanding Services, Board of Trustees, 1996; Knoxville College, Student Plaque, 1997. **Home Addr:** 2692 20th St W, Birmingham, AL 35208.

JENKINS, TREZELLE SAMUEL
Professional football player. **Personal:** Born Mar 13, 1973, Chicago, IL. **Educ:** University of Michigan, bachelor's degree in political science, 1995. **Career:** Kansas City Chiefs, tackle, 1995-97; New Orleans Saints, 1997-. **Special Achievements:** Selected in the 1st round/31st overall pick in the 1995 NFL Draft. **Business Addr:** Professional Football Player, New Orleans Saints, 5800 Airline Hwy, Metairie, LA 70003, (504)733-0255.

JENKINS, VAN
Retired educatioinal administrator. **Personal:** Born Jan 23, 1911, Mobile, AL; son of Lillie Belle Jenkins and Van Jenkins; married Gloria M (Robinson). **Educ:** Wilberforce Univ, BS 1936; Univ Mich, MA 1969f Wayne State Univ; Detroit Inst Tech; George William Coll Chicago. **Career:** Govt serv 1940-46; NY Public Schools, teacher; Edward Waters Coll Jacksonville FL; Detroit YMCA, dir health & phys educ; Detroit Public Schs, teacher, coach, athletic dir, dept head asst prin, principal Northwestern High School, Detroit, MI. **Orgs:** Mem Brown Bombers Pro Football Team; Renaissance Pro Basketball Team; NAACP; Detroit Varisty Club; Frontiers Mens Club; MI Sportsmen Club; MI Coaches Assn; MI Assn Secondary Sch Prin; Petro-Detroit Assn Black Administrators; Phi Delta Kappa; Prince Happ Mason; Kappa Alpha Psi Frat Detroit Polemarch 1972-; mem Univ MI Alumni Club; Wilberforce Univ Alumni; Alumni Bd Trustee Wilferforce Univ. **Honors/Awds:** Football coach of year 1965; Teacher serv Award MI State Univ 1970; Distinguished Serv Award Wilberforce Univ 1971; Church Track & Field State of Mich 1970-72.

JENKINS, WOODIE R., JR.
Consultant. **Personal:** Born Jun 18, 1940, Washington, DC; son of Laura B Berry Washington and Rev. Woodie R. Jenkins, Sr. (deceased); married Ramona M Hernandez, Jun 21, 1968; children: Tammy Monique. **Educ:** Howard U, BS Physics 1964; NM St U, MS Mech/Industrial Engrg 1972. **Career:** Natl Range Operations, WSMR, NM, physicist 1964-70; Quality Assurance Office, WSMR, genl engr 1970-77; Quality Evaluation Div, WSMR, chief 1977-82; US Army Training and Doctrine Command's Systems Analysis Activity, WSMR, spl staff asst to tech dir 1980; Las Cruces, NM, city councillor 1980-85, mayor protem 1982-85; High Energy Laser Program Office, WSMR, assoc program mgr plans and opers 1982-84; High Energy Laser Systems Test Facility, White Sands Missile Range, chief test operations 1984-93; South Central Council of Governments Inc, transportation planner, 1993-96; Jenkins Consultant Service, CEO, 1996-. **Orgs:** US Army Tech Liaison Rep to the Amer Defense Preparedness Assn 1975-; Registered Professional Engr 1979-96; mem WSMR Speaker's Bureau 1979-82; Political Action Comm Dona Ana County NAACP Branch 1979-85; mem WSMR Commander's Committee on Hispanic and Black Employment 1980-85; mem Transportation Communications and Public Safety Policy Comm Natl League of Cities 1980-83; Deputy Activity Career Program Mgr for Engrs and Scientists at WSMR 1981-93; mem lecture circuit New Mexico Junior College 1986; vice chmn bd of dirs Southern New Mexico Human Development, Inc 1985-97; mem New Mexico Statewide Health Coordinating Council 1985-86; vice pres bd of directors, Las Cruces YMCA, 1988-89; chairman, Las Cruces Extra Territorial Zoning Commn, 1987-92; member, board of directors, White Sands Federal Credit Un, 1979-85. **Honors/Awds:** WSMR Commander's Awd 1983; published over 40 technical articles, papers, and presentations; 8 Performance Awds from the US Dept of Army; Certificate of Nobility New Mexico Secretary of State 1982; American Scientific Registry, American Governmental Registry, Intl Registry of Profiles, Natl Roster of Black Elected Officials; Certificate of Apreciation for Public Service, State of New Mexico, 1989; New Mexico Distinguished Public Service Award, State of New Mexico, 1990. **Home Addr:** 700 Turner Ave, Las Cruces, NM 88005, (505)524-1726. **Business Phone:** (505)524-1726.

JENKINS, YOLANDA L.
Educator. **Personal:** Born Dec 31, 1945, Chicago, IL; daughter of Dr & Mrs Charles Jenkins. **Educ:** Univ of WI, BA 1967; Boston Univ, MEd 1971; Univ of CA Berkeley, PhD 1982. **Career:** SRI Intl, field supervisor 1971-72; Urban Inst for Human Serv and Westside Community Mental Health Center, rsch assoc 1973-80; Univ of California-Berkeley Teacher Corps Prog, rsch assoc 1980-82; Atari Inst, mgr of prog evaluation & rsch, acting dir 1982-84; Apple Computer Inc, mgr of educ market analysis, dir community affairs 1984-89; IBM Corp, sr prog administrator 1989-. **Orgs:** Bd mem, Bay Area Black Child Advocacy Coalition, 1977-80; founder, Bay Area Black Women's Forum, 1978-79; consultant, San Francisco Foundation, 1980; fund-raising comm mem, Parent Infant Neighborhood Center, 1984; bd of dir, San Jose Children's Discovery Museum, 1986-87; bd of advisors, Women's Resource Center, Palo Alto CA, 1987; executive committee, vice pres, admin, Atlanta Women's Network, 1990-. **Honors/Awds:** Commendation Award, Coro Foundation San Francisco, 1973; Outstanding Young Women of Amer, 1980; Outstanding Contribution & Appreciation Award, Los Angeles Student Film Inst, 1983. **Business Addr:** Senior Program Administrator, IBM Corp, 4111 Northside Pkwy, Atlanta, GA 30309.

JENKINS-SCOTT, JACKIE
Health services administrator. **Personal:** Born Aug 18, 1949, Damascus, AR; married James M Scott; children: Amal James, Amber Dawn. **Educ:** Eastern MI Univ, BS 1971; Boston Univ School of Social Work, MSW 1973; Radcliffe Coll, Post Grad Rsch Prog 1975. **Career:** Commonwealth of MA Dept of Public Health, dir treatment serv reg mgr 1973-77; Roxbury Court Clinic, exec dir 1977-83; Dimock Community Health Ctr, pres 1983-. **Orgs:** Trustee Cousens Fund 1985-92; president Newton Chap of Jack & Jill of Amer 1985, Delta Sigma Theta; vice pres MA League of Health Ctrs 1987; sec Mass Public Health Assoc 1987-88, Consortium of Black Health Ctr Direct 1987; bd mem National Cooperative Bank. **Honors/Awds:** Outstanding Contribution of a Social Worker with Five Years or Less Experience Mass Chap of the Natl Assoc of Social Workers 1975; "Alcohol Abuse Among Black Women" Douglass Publ 1976; 1978 Lady of the Year Awd Project Understanding. **Home Addr:** 1063 Commonwealth Ave, Newton, MA 02159. **Business Addr:** President, Dimock Community Health Ctr, 55 Dimock St, Roxbury, MA 02119, (617)442-8800.

JENNINGS, BENNIE ALFRED
Executive director. **Personal:** Born Nov 21, 1933, Port Gibson, MS; married Mildred B Blackburn; children: Sharon, Marion, Brenda. **Educ:** Alcorn Univ, attended 1956-57; Grambling State Univ, BS Secondary Educ 1957-60. **Career:** Chesebrough-Pond's Inc, machine adjustor 1960-63; Gen Dynamics/Electric Boat Div, draftsman/apprentice trang admin 1963-70; OIC of New London Co Inc CT, exec dir 1970-. **Orgs:** Life mem NAACP; mem, Natl Council of Negro Women. **Honors/Awds:** Mgmt Devel Inst Awd GE Corp NY 1976; Gold Key Awd OIC of Am Philadelphia 1979; 10 Yr Serv Awd OIC of Am Philadelphia 1980; Dr M L King Jr Comm Serv Awd; Club Cosmos New London CT 1980. **Military Serv:** USAF A/3c 1951-55; Disting Serv Awd USAF 1951-55. **Business Addr:** Executive Dir, OIC of New London County Inc, 106 Truman St, New London, CT 06320.

JENNINGS, BERNARD WAYLON-HANDEL
Political activist, student. **Personal:** Born Jun 21, 1968, Bronx, NY; son of Louise Aiken Jennings and Allan Winston Jennings. **Educ:** Florida Memorial College, Miami, FL, bachelors of arts, 1991; Florida International Univ, certified course, Nov 1991; Florida A & M Univ, masters of applied social science in public adm, 1993. **Career:** City of North Miami Mayor's Economic Task Force, intern, fall 1987; State Representative Elaine Gordon, campaign coordinator, fall 1988, fall 1990; Florida Memorial College, intern to vp of student development, June 1990-Sept 1990, student govt assn pres, 1990-91; Metro-Dade County Commission, commission aide to commissioner Charles Dusseau, 1991-92; Florida A & M Univ, School of Graduate Studies Research & Continuing Ed, graduate asst to the dean of graduate studies, Jan 1992-Aug 1992; Florida A & M Univ, Campus Alcohol & Drug Resource Cent, dir, 1992-93; Gulf Atlantic Industrial Supply, Inc, June 1993-August 1993; Animation Concepts Inc, ceo/shareholder, 1993-; Florida Memorial College, Social Science Div, prof, 1994-; Metro-Dade County Commission, commission aide to chairman of thebd Arthur E Teele, Jr, Jan 1994-Aug 1994; Metro-Dade Transit Agency, transportation customer rep, 1994-. **Orgs:** Member, Student Government Assn, 1987-; president, Florida Memorial College Student Government Assn, 1990-; Computer Science Assn; Big Brother/Big Sister, Project Initiative; Kappa Alpha Psi Fraternity, Inc; Kiwanis Club; founder, president, United Students Against Drugs, 1987; member, Florida Memorial College Board of Trustees, 1990, 1991; NAACP; member, Citizens Crime Watch Community Committee; URGENT Inc, chair of advisory bd; Modern Free & Accepted Masons, Loyal Patterson No 373; Biscayne Gardens Civic Assn; Natl Student's Support Council for Africa, co-founder, natl coordinator, and parliamentarian. **Honors/Awds:** Police Explorer, North Miami Police Dept, North Miami, FL, 1986; awarded Key to the City, 1986; Acdemic Deans List, 1987; Award of Appreciation, United Students Against Drugs, 1987, Academic Award Certificate, 1988, Plaque, Appreciation for Efforts, Prospect 89, Academic Honor Roll, 1989, 1990, Florida Memorial College; Certificate of Academic Excellence, Alpha Phi Alpha Fraternity, Inc, Delta Psi Chapter, 1988; Certificate of Appreciation, TF-101 City of Miami, 1988; Volunteer of the Year in Dade County, Certification of Appreciation, Flagler Federal Directors of Volunteers in Agency's, 1988. **Special Achievements:** 2nd African/African-American Summit in Liberville, Gabon, Central Africa, natl coordinator, 1993; Culture Fest 92 in Cote d Ivorie, West Africa, seminar host & keynote speaker, 1992; First African/African-American Summit in Abidjan, Cote d' Ivorie, West Africa, natl delegate, 1991; campaign coordinator for numerous public officials. **Home Addr:** 14895 S River Dr, Miami, FL 33167.

JENNINGS, DEVOYD
Utility company executive. **Personal:** Born Sep 10, 1947, Los Angeles, CA; son of William & Margaret Jennings; married Gwendolyn Barbee, Jan 1, 1980; children: Shawn, Mark, Demeka. **Educ:** Texas Wesleyan Univ, majored in marketing, 1972. **Career:** Texas Utilities, staff assistant, 1973-77, customer rep, 1977-85, senior rep, 1985-. **Orgs:** Texas Assn A A Chambers, chairman, 1993-; Ft Worth Metro Bl Ch, chairman, 1986-93; US African Amer Chambers, vice chairman, 1993-; North Texas Commission, bd mem, 1992-; Ft Worth Chamber, bd mem, 1987-92; Ft Worth Minority Leaders, president, 1981-88; Ft Worth United Way, bd mem, 1987-93; Texas Wesleyan Univ, trustee, 1987-. **Honors/Awds:** Small Business Administration, Small Business Advocate of the Year, 1997; Arlington Texas NAACP, Malcolm X Award, 1994; Texas Leg Black Caucus, Merit, 1981; Human Relation Comm, Comm Serv, 1983; United Negro College Fund, Service, 1976; Tandy Corp, Mkt & Sales, 1968. **Special Achievements:** Executive Insights For Small Business, Input, 1993. **Business Addr:** Chairman, Texas Utilities, PO Box 970, Fort Worth, TX 76102, (817)215-6748.

JENNINGS, EVERETT JOSEPH
Engineer, consulting firm executive. **Personal:** Born Oct 9, 1938, Shelby, NC; son of Ardietha M C Jennings and Everett Jennings; children: Sharon B, Carl E. **Educ:** Catholic University, 1952; St Mary's University, BBA, 1959, BSIE, 1961; University of Iowa, 1963; University of Oklahoma, 1967. **Career:** San Antonio Fair, Inc, director, planning & scheduling, 1964; Meridian Engineering, project director, 1968; Branson Ultra Sonics, sr engineer, 1976; Evanbow Construction, dir construction mgmt, 1986; State of New Jersey, Department of Transportation, assistant commissioner, 1990; Tish, Inc, vp, operations, 1991; Jennings, Associates, Inc, president, currently. **Orgs:** Goodwill Industries of America, secretary, 1992; Newark Boys Chorus School, vp; SHARE, Inc, treasurer; Newark Improvement Program, treasurer; American Institute of Engineers, vp, 1965-68; American Association of Cost Engineers, president, 1985-88; Kiwanis International, lt governor, 1988-91; Habitat New Jersey, vp, 1990; Montclair Society of Engineers, pres; United Hospitals Medical Ctr Foundation, secretary; Metropolitan YMCA, board member. **Honors/Awds:** State of Rhode Island, Scholastic Honor Award, 1949; The Leaguers, Inc, Outstanding Leadership Award, 1986; Distinguished Men's Club, Medal of Honor for Education, 1990. **Special Achievements:** Orbital Path for Construction Projects, 1966. **Military Serv:** US Air Force, 1st lt, 1952-54. **Home Addr:** 44 S Munn Ave, East Orange, NJ 07018, (201)677-3989. **Business Addr:** President, Jennings & Associates, Inc, 333 Dodd St, East Orange, NJ 07017, (201)672-1562.

JENNINGS, LILLIAN PEGUES
Psychologist. **Personal:** Born May 24, Youngstown, OH; daughter of Jessie Pegues and Paul Pegues; children: Dan, Kim. **Educ:** Youngstown State Univ, BSEd 1954; Univ of Pittsburgh, MEd 1967, PhD 1971; Univ of MD, Post-Doctoral Study. **Career:** Warren Schools, teacher, 1954-57; Youngstown Schools, teacher/prog dir, 1957-66; ed consult 1966-67; Edinboro State Coll, coord of black studies, prof of ed & reading clinic 1968-71, affirm action officer 1972; Youngstown Publ School, head start prog dir, rsch staff assoc, multiple ed rsch teams; James Madison Univ College of Ed, assoc dean; HCA, clinical psychologist, prog supervisor, currently. **Orgs:** Mem Alpha Kappa Alpha, VA Assoc of School Psychol, Intl Reading Assoc; served on mayors comm of Human Resources Pittsburgh 1966-67; bd of dir Dr Barber's Ctr for Exceptional Children Erie; mem Phi Delta Kappa, Delta Kappa Gamma; chmn NCATE, Dept of Ed Accred Teams; mem Harrisonburg School Bd, VA Arts Commiss, Natl Alliance of Black School Ed; licensed Professional Counselor; vice chair Harrisonburg Sch Bd VA; Multiple Publications 1986,87; chaired multiple Accreditation teams; member, WIB. **Honors/Awds:** Res grants Ford Found, Erie Found, NSF; author of multiple publs & monographs.

JENNINGS, MARGARET ELAINE
Data processing consultant. **Personal:** Born May 22, 1943, Gadsden, AL; daughter of Izora Torbert Jones and Spencer

Small Jr; married Jarvis C Jennings (divorced 1987); children: Terrence A Hall, Regina Lynn Hall Clay, Jason D. **Educ:** Cuyahoga Community College, Cleveland, OH; Bowie State College, Bowie, MD, 1977; University of Southern California, Washington, DC, MPA, 1980. **Career:** Value Engineering Alexandria, VA, pgmr/analyst, 1975-77; Federal Reserve Bd, Washington, DC, data base admin, 1977-79; Booz Allen & Hamilton, Bethesda, MD, data base designer, 1979-86; Advanced Technology, Reston, VA, senior systems analyst, 1986-89; Perot Systems, Herndon, VA, senior systems analyst, 1989-90; Booz Allen & Hamilton, Bethesda, Md, senior systems analyst/asst program manager, 1990-. **Orgs:** Local Conf Coordinator 1984, fund raising 1985, public relations 1986, vice president 1986-87, president 1987-91, national executive director 1991-, Black Data Processing Associates. **Honors/Awds:** Conducted Work Related Seminars, 1987-90, Outstanding Leadership Award, 1988, 1990, Managed National Conference, 1991, Solicited and Acquired Corporate Sponsorship, Increased Chapter Membership, Black Data Processing Associates. **Home Addr:** 7110 Kurth Ln, Seabrook, MD 20706-2164.

JENNINGS, ROBERT RAY

Educator, educational administrator. **Personal:** Born Nov 15, 1950, Atlanta, GA; son of Mary Beeman Jennings and Forrest Jennings Sr. **Educ:** Univ of Ghana Legon West Africa, Charles Merrill Scholar 1971; Morehouse Coll, BA, Sociology, 1972; Atlanta Univ, MA, Educ Psych, 1974; GA State Univ Sch of Educ, Certificate in Gifted Educ 1975; Univ of GA, Certificate in Adult Basic Educ, 1978; Atlanta Univ, Educ Specialist in Interrelated Learning, 1979; Doctorate, Admin, 1982. **Career:** Atlanta Univ, asst to dir of public relations, 1973; Atlanta Public Sch, Hoffman reading coord 1973-76; Literacy Action Inc Atlanta, reading consultant 1974-75; Reading Learning Ctr Inc East Point, dir 1975-79; Atlanta Public Schs, tchr of the gifted 1976-79; Atlanta Univ, consultant dean's grant proj 1979-80; Atlanta Area Tech Sch, part-time prof 1979-84; Equal Employ Comm US Govt, equal oppor specialist 1979-82; Morris Brown Coll Atlanta, assoc prof 1982-84; US Equal Employment Oppor Commn, Atlanta Dist, official commn rep office of dir 1982-84, Washington, employee devel specialist 1984-85; asst vice pres, devel & placement, Atlanta Univ, 1985-88; Norfolk State Univ, vice pres of development, 1988-91; Albany State University, vp for institutional advancement, 1991-97; North Carolina Agricultural and Technical State University, vice chancellor for Development and University Relations and CEO for the Foundation, 1997-. **Orgs:** Pres, Atlanta Univ Natl Alumni Assn, 1979-81; mem, bd of dirs, Exodus Right-to-Read Program Adult Literacy Prog, 1980; bd of advisors, Volunteer Atlanta, 1980-84; parlimentarian Council for Exceptional Children Atlanta Area Chap 1980-81; bd of dirs, Parents Anonymous of GA, 1981-84; bd of trustees, Atlanta Univ 1981-85; founder and editor-in-chief Alumni Update of Leadership Atlanta 1982-; Self-Study Evaluation Comm, Morris Brown Coll, 1983-84; bd of dirs, Planned Parenthood, 1983-87; exec bd, Leadership Atlanta 1986-87; vice pres, Council for Advancement of Public Black Colleges & Universities, 1989-; NAACP Education Legal Advisory Board, chairman, 1987-; Leadership Albany, 1992-93; Southwest Georgia Comprehensive Health Institute, board of directors, 1992-; Community Relations Council and Turner Job Corp, Inc, Albany GA, mem board of directors, 1996-98; American Lung Assn, Albany Chap, mem board of directors, 1994-; West End Church of Christ, mem, 1988-; American Assn for Higher Educ, 1988-; American Biographical Inst, honorary mem, bd of advisors, 1987-; Council for the Advancement & Support of Education, 1984-; Phi Delta Kappa, 1982-. **Honors/Awds:** Outstanding Achievement Award, Economic Opportunity Atlanta 1972; Outstanding Serv Awd Atlanta Inquirer Newspaper 1972; Director's Award Frederick Douglass Tutorial Inst Morehouse Coll 1972; Outstanding Serv Award Student Natl Educ Assn, 1972; Awd of Excellence Student Mississippi Teacher's Assn, 1972; WSB TV & Radio Fellow 1975; Teacher of the Year Home Park School Atlanta 1976; Award of Excellence Wm Finch Sch PTA, 1976; Appreciation Award for Outstanding Leadership SM Inman Sch PTA 1976; Outstanding Chapter Mem of the Yr Atlanta Univ 1979; Best of Service Award Frank Lebby Stanton Sch Atlanta 1979; Alumnus of the Yr Atlanta Univ 1980; Special Serv Award, Council for Exceptional Children, Atlanta, 1981; Special Serv Award, Natl Bd of Dirs, Atlanta Univ Alumni, 1981; Phi Delta KappaPrssional Fraternity in Educ, 1982; cited by Atlanta Journal & Constitution Newspaper as one of Atlanta's Most Outstanding Volunteers, 1982; Outstanding Serv Award, United Way of Metro Atlanta, 1984; First Recipient Leadership Award in Educ, Delta Sigma Theta Sor, 1986; Outstanding Atlantan, 1986. **Home Addr:** 2005 King George Lane SW, Atlanta, GA 30331. **Business Addr:** Vice Chancellor, Development and University Relations, North Carolina A&T State University, Greensboro, NC 27411, (910)334-7654.

JENNINGS, SYLVESTA LEE

Banking executive. **Personal:** Born Jan 30, 1933, Halifax; son of Luella Freeman Jennings and Anthony Jennings; married Lillie Flippen, Jun 10, 1960; children: Mitchell. **Educ:** North Carolina A&T State Univ, Greensboro NC, BS, 1958; Univ of Virginia, School of Consumer Banking, Diploma, 1968; Rutgers Univ, Stonier Graduate School of Banking, Diploma, 1972. **Career:** First State Bank, Danville VA, pres, 1988-. **Orgs:** Danville Chamber of Commerce, 1989; Natl Bankers Assn, 1989; Prince Hall Masons of Virginia; Danville, VA School Bd; Southside VA Bus & Education Comm; Kappa Alpha Psi Fraternity Inc. **Honors/Awds:** Natl Assn for Equal Opportunity in Higher Educ Award, 1989; research selected for library at Rutgers Univ, Harvard Univ, and ABA, 1972. **Military Serv:** US Army, cpl, 1953-55. **Home Addr:** 121 Lovelace Drive, Danville, VA 24540.

JENSEN, MARCUS C.

Professional baseball player. **Personal:** Born Dec 14, 1972, Oakland, CA. **Career:** San Francisco Giants, catcher, 1996-97; Detroit Tigers, 1997-. **Business Addr:** Professional Baseball Player, Detroit Tigers, 2121 Trumbell Ave, Detroit, MI 48216, (313)962-4000.

JENSEN, RENALDO MARIO

Automobile company executive. **Personal:** Born Jun 29, 1934, New York, NY; son of Doris Davis Jensen and Octive Jensen; married Alicia Clark, Jan 26, 1959; children: Renaldo M, Malinda L. **Educ:** Howard Univ, Washington DC, BS Mech Engrg, 1958; Air Force Inst of Tech, Dayton OH, MS Aerospace Engrg, 1966; Purdue Univ, West Lafayette IN, PhD Aerospace Engrg, 1970. **Career:** US Air Force, officer, 1958-78; Ford Motor Co, Dearborn MI, advanced concepts aerodynamics, 1978-86, dir minority supplier devel, 1987-. **Orgs:** Mem, New Detroit, Inc, 1987-; mem, Greater Detroit Chamber of Commerce, 1987 -; bd of dir, Minority Business Dir, "Try Us," 1987-; bd of dir, Natl Minority Business Development Council, 1988-; bd of dirs Plum Hollow Country Club, 1995-; Amer Society for Mechanical Engineers; Amer Institute for Aeronautics and Astronautics; The Combustion Institute; Military Operations Research Society; mem, Alpha Phi Alpha Fraternity. **Honors/Awds:** Distinguished Service Award, Wisconsin Minority Purcchasing Council, 1988; Tau Beta Pi, Engineering Honor Society. **Military Serv:** US Air Force, Lt Col, 1958-78; Missile Combat Crew Award, 1970, Air Force Commendation Medal. **Home Addr:** 26510 Rose Hill Drive, Farmington Hills, MI 48334.

JERKINS, JERRY GAINES

Clergyman. **Personal:** Born in Loxley, AL; married Naomi Donald; children: Cntr, Gerald, Jennifer, Jacqueline. **Educ:** Austin Peay U, BS 1972; N TN Bible Inst, D Evang. **Career:** St John Bapt Ch Clarksville, TN, pastor 1967-; Haynes Chapel Bapt Ch, pastor. **Orgs:** Mem, Clarksville Ministerial Assn; ministerial rep, C of C; corres sec, Pastor's Conf Nat & Bapt Conv Am; PTA; bd, Children Cntr Hilldale Meth Ch; pres, Missionary Bapt St Conv; bd, United Givers Fund; adv bd, Montgomery Co Wlfr Dept; adv bd, Youth Challenge Cntr; pres, Dist Pastor's Conf; bd, Salvation Army; NAACP; gospel Progmr, Radio Sta WJZM. **Military Serv:** Mil serv sgt 14 yrs.

JEROME, JOSEPH D.

Cleric. **Personal:** Born Oct 17, 1951, Port-au-Prince, Haiti; son of Marie K Jerome and Thelamon Jerome. **Educ:** Suffolk County Community College, 1983; Long Island University CW Post, 1985; Seabury-Western Theological Seminary, M Div, 1991. **Career:** Family Consultation Services, 1984-86; Suffolk Child Development, 1985-87; US Legalization & Naturalization Services, 1987-89; St John's Episcopal Hospital; Interfaith Medical Center; Diocese of Long Island, Church of St Luke & St Matthew, priest, St. Philips Episcopal Church. **Orgs:** Union of Black Episcopalian, 1983-; Association of the Episcopal Black Clergy, 1989-; American Biblical Literature, 1991-; The Alban Institute, 1991-; Diocesan AIDS Commission, 1991-; NAACP, Long Island, 1991-; African People Organization, 1985-87; La Union Hispanica, 1983-87. **Home Addr:** 288 Lowell Ave, Islip Terrace, NY 11752.

JEROME, NORGE WINIFRED

Educator. **Personal:** Born Nov 3, 1930; daughter of Evelyn Mary Grant and McManus Israel Jerome. **Educ:** Howard Univ, BS (magna cum laude) 1960; Univ of Wisconsin, Madison, MS 1962, PhD 1967. **Career:** Kansas University Medical Center: dept of diet & nutrition, asst prof, 1967-69, dept of human ecology, aaso prof, 1969-72, dept of community hlth, asso prof, 1972-78, dept of preventive med, prof, 1978-95, community nutrition div, director, 1981-95; Nutritional Anthropology Communicator, ed, 1974-77; Ed Resources Ctrs, dir, 1974-77; Agency for International Development, Bureau for Science and Technology, office of nutrition, director, 1988-92; University of Kansas Medical Center, nutritionist, anthropologist, associate dean for minority affairs, School of Medicine, currently. **Orgs:** Academic advisor Children's Advert Review Unit 1974-88; media rep Bristol Myers Co 1981-82; research advisor Campbell Soup Co 1979-81; mem Mayor's Task Force on Food & Hunger 1983-88; founder/chmn Comm on Nutritional Anthropology 1978-79; bd mem Urban League of Greater Kansas City 1969-77; adv bd Jrnl of Nutr Plng 1977-84; mem World Food & Nutrition Study Natl Acad of Sci 1976; fellow Amer Anthro Assoc; fellow Soc of Appl Anthro; mem Soc of Med Anthro, Amer Publ Health Assocc, Amer Dietetic Assoc; Society of Behavioral Medicine; Society of Epidemologic Research; panelist White House Conf on Food Nutr & Health; mem US Assoc for the Club of Rome 1980-87; fellow Amer Coll of Nutrition, 1986-; president, Association for Women in Development, 1991-93; board of directors, Cooperative Development Fdation; board of trustees, University of Bridgeport; board of trustees, International Child Health Foundation; member, American Institute of Nutrition, 1978-; member, American Society of Clinical Nutrition, 1978-; bd of dir, Solar Cookers International 1992-, president, 1998-. **Honors/Awds:** Higuchi Research Achievemnt Award Univ of KS 1982; Citation for Service United Commnty Serv Kansas City, MO 1974; Matrix Award Women in Communications Inc 1976; Dairy Cncl Merit Award Greater Kansas City 1977, 1988; Spotlight Award, Women's Bureau, US Dept of Labor, 1990. **Home Addr:** 14402 W 68th St, Shawnee, KS 66216. **Business Addr:** Assoc Dean for Minority Affairs, U of KS Sch of Med, 3901 Rainbow Blvd, Kansas City, KS 66160-7304.

JERRARD, PAUL

Hockey coach. **Personal:** Born Apr 20, 1965. **Educ:** Lake Superior State Coll, BA, sports mgmt. **Career:** Kalamazoo Wings, player coach, 1992-. **Business Addr:** Player Coach, Kalmazoo Wings Hockey Team, 3620 Van Rick Dr, Kalamazoo, MI 49002.

JERVAY, MARION WHITE

Attorney. **Personal:** Born Mar 26, 1948, Mt Olive, NC; married. **Educ:** Univ of NC Wilmington, BA 1971; Nat Law Center, Geo Wash Univ Wash, DC,1973-74; Sch of Law Duke Univ Durham, NC, JD 1976. **Career:** Liggett Group Inc Durham, NC, corp atty 1977-; Hon Earl W Vaughn, NC Ct of Appeals Raleigh, rsrch asst 1976-77; Wade & Roger Smith Attys at Law Raleigh, rsrch asst 1975; Norfolk City Schs, tchr 1972-73; New Hanover Co Bd of Educ Wilmington, engl tchr 1972. **Orgs:** Mem NC State Bar; mem NC Bar Assn; mem Wake Co Bar Assn; mem NC Assn of Black Lawyers; mem ABA; mem Am Bus Women's Assn. **Business Addr:** Liggett Group Inc, 300 N Duke St, Durham, NC 27701-2047.

JERVAY, PAUL REGINALD, JR.

Newspaper executive. **Personal:** Born Oct 25, 1949, Atlanta, GA; son of Brenda Yancey Jervay (deceased) and Paul Reginald Jervay, Sr (deceased); married Evelyn Harrison Jervay, Jul 24, 1988; children: Jeneea, Adria, Shenay Dunston, Kelvin Dunston. **Educ:** NC Central Univ, Raleigh, NC, BS, 1971. **Career:** The Carolinian, Raleigh, NC, publisher, 1971-; Advantage Advertising, consultant; Carolina Call, publisher, currently. **Orgs:** Owner, treasurer, Nay-Kel Educ Ctr; bd chairperson, Triangle Opportunities Industrialization Center of Raleigh Inc. **Honors/Awds:** Service Award, St. Augustine's Coll, 1983.

JESSIE, WAYMON THOMAS

Educational administrator. **Personal:** Born Oct 10, 1945, Newark, NJ; son of Alyce Mildred Mead Jessie and Pirlon Thomas Jessie; married Vanessa; children: Jarret Thomas, Nassor Nuru. **Educ:** Essex Cty Coll, AS 1971; Rutgers Univ, BA 1974. **Career:** City of Newark, chief accountant 1975-76, chief of eval 1976-78; Comprehensive Empl & Training, dep dir 1978-81, dir 1981-82; City of Newark, asst to business admin; Assoc R. R. Brown & Co Inc Plainfield NJ 1986-; Newark Board of Education, affirmative action officer, currently; Minority Business Enterprises, affirmative action, dir, 1995-. **Orgs:** Mem Kenneth A Gibson Civic Assoc 1974-; real estate sales Dan Califri Inc 1980-; mem Natl Forum Black Public Admin 1982; charter mem Natl Black Child Development Inst 1982-; mem American Assn of Affimative Action Officers; licensed NJ State Realtor and Insurance Broker; deacon, Solid Rock Bapt Church, Irvington, NJ. **Honors/Awds:** Outstanding Young Man Amer Natl Jaycees 1976; Achievement Awd United Way 1979; Good Citizenship Kenneth Gibson Civic Assoc 1980; Comm Serv Awd Ralph Grant Civic Assoc 1981. **Military Serv:** AUS spec 4 1963-66. **Home Addr:** 650 S 19th St, Newark, NJ 07103. **Business Addr:** Affirmative Action Officer, Newark Board of Education, 2 Cedar St, Ste 702, Newark, NJ 07102.

JESSUP, GAYLE LOUISE (GAYLE JESSUP FRANKLIN)

Journalist, business executive. **Personal:** Born Jul 26, 1957, Washington, DC; daughter of Theresa W Jessup and Cedric B Jessup; married Charles L Franklin Jr, Aug 1, 1987; children: Charles Jessup Franklin. **Educ:** Howard University, BA, communications, 1978; Northwestern University, MSJ, broadcasting, 1982. **Career:** WTOC-TV, Savannah, GA, reporter, hostess, 1982-84; WGXA-TV, Macon, GA, anchor, reporter, 1984-86; WSB-TV, Atlanta, GA, assoc producer, 1986-87; WHMM-TV 32, Washington, DC, producer, hostess, 1987-; In-Focus Productions, president, 1991-. **Orgs:** Natl Assn of Black Journalists, 1990-; Montgomery County NAACP, 1989-; scholarship committee head, Doug Wiliams Foundation, 1989-91; mentor, Mentors Inc, 1989-; American Federation of Television & Radio Artists, 1988-. **Honors/Awds:** PBS Promotion and Advertising Award Nominee, PBS, 1988; Act-So Merit Award, Montgomery County NAACP, 1990; Georgia School Bell Award, Georgia State Board of Education, 1983; New York Times Scholarship, The New York Times Co, 1981; Gannett Journalism Scholarship, The Gannett Co, 1977. **Business Addr:** Producer/Hostess, Marketing Development, WHMM-TV 32, 2222 4th St NW, Washington, DC 20059.

JESSUP, MARSHA EDWINA
Educator. **Personal:** Born Nov 8, 1944, Washington, DC. **Educ:** Howard U, BS 1967; Univ MI, MS 1971; Cath U, 1973; Temple Univ, 1978. **Career:** Dept of Media Resources, chf med illus, dir; Nat Inst of Health, med illus 1972-74; US Dept of Agr Grad Sch, faculty mem 1971-74; Armed Forces Inst of Pathology, med illus 1972; Howard Univ Coll of Med, asst med illus 1968-69; Smithsonian Inst, free-lance sci illus 1967-68; UMDNJ Robert Wood Johnson Medical School, dept & adj assoc prof surgery dept, dir of media resources. **Orgs:** Vchmn, bd of gov 1984-86, mem accreditation comm 1984-87, chmn, bd of giv 1986-87 Assoc of Medical Illustrators; ne region bd of gov rep Assoc of Biomedical Communications Directors 1982-84. **Honors/Awds:** Cited Civic & Career Svc, Silver Spring MD Bus & Professional Womens Club 1973; US Civil Serv Task Force 1974. **Business Addr:** Dir of Media Resources, UMDNJ, Robert Wood Johnson Med Sch, 675 Hoes Lane, Piscataway, NJ 08854.

JETER, CLIFTON B., JR.
Theater executive. **Personal:** Born Feb 22, 1944, Martinsville, VA; son of Naomi Winston Jeter and Clifton B Jeter Sr; married Diane R Bates; children: Sheree, Amani, Aja. **Educ:** Howard U, BA 1967; Am U, MBA 1970; MD, CPA 1972; Harvard University, advanced management program, 1991. **Career:** Wolf & CO, CPA's, manager, 1975-77; John F Kennedy Center, controller, 1977-84, director of finance, 1985-91, chief financial officer, 1991-; Howard U, internal auditor 1974-75; Peoples Devel Corp, fin vice pres 1969-74; Peoples Involvement Corp, controller 1967-69. **Orgs:** Treas Quality Constrn Co 1974-77; Nat Inst for Tennis Devel 1975-77; Alpha Phi Alpha; Am Inst of CPA'S; MD Assn of CPA'S DC Inst of CPA'S; Nat Black MBA Assn; Nat Assn of Black Accts; Am Mgmt Assn; Assn of Practicing CPA'S; Harvard Club of Washington. **Business Addr:** Chief Financial Officer, John F Kennedy Center, Washington, DC 20566.

JETER, DELORES DEANN
Pharmacist. **Personal:** Born Mar 11, 1949, Union, SC. **Educ:** Univ SC Coll, Pharmacy 1973, Seeking PhD in Pharmacy Adminstrn. **Career:** Funderburks Drug, intern 1972; Moncrief Army Hosp, intern 1973; Richland Meml Hosp, clinical pharmacy 1973; Millers Pharmacy, reg pharmacist & mgr 1974. **Orgs:** Mem Am Pharmaceutical Assn; mem Palmetto & Med Dental Pharmaceutical Assn; mem Alcoholic & Drug Abuse Council; organist Calvary Bapt Ch. **Honors/Awds:** Cit day Columbia SC. **Business Addr:** 827 N Main St, Lancaster, SC.

JETER, DEREK
Professional baseball player. **Personal:** Born Jun 26, 1974, Pequannock, NJ. **Educ:** University of Michigan, attended. **Career:** New York Yankees, infielder, 1995-. **Business Addr:** Professional Baseball Player, New York Yankees, 161st St and River Ave, Yankee Stadium, Bronx, NY 10451, (718)293-4300.

JETER, JOSEPH C., JR.
TV engineer. **Personal:** Born Aug 16, 1961, Philadelphia, PA. **Educ:** Taylor Univ, BA Comm 1983, BS System Analysis/Political Sci 1983. **Career:** Taylor Univ, minority recruitment coord 1980-83, minority fund raising/planner 1982-83; Applied Energy Svcs, intern 1982; Bell of PA, asst mgr network engrg. **Orgs:** Vice pres Black Cultural Soc 1980-82; editorial writer Taylor Univ 1982-83; Pres Adv Comm Minority Recruitment Taylor Univ 1982-83; mem Student & Economic Leadership Forum 1982-83; seminar writer on career planning self-employed 1983-; minority recruitment writer and consultant self-employed 1983-; career planning writer and consultant self-employed 1983-. **Home Addr:** 115 E Washington Ln, Philadelphia, PA 19144.

JETER, JUANITA DOLORES (NIKKI JETER)
Journalist, public relations practitioner. **Personal:** Born Dec 20, 1946, Lackawanna, NY; daughter of Virginia L Easley Lowe and Samuel E Lowe Sr; divorced; children: Gavin Michael, Mario Stuart. **Educ:** University of DC, BA (summa cum laude), journalism, 1980, pursuing MA, human resourses development, 1992-. **Career:** DC Reading is Fundamental, assistant director, 1973-77; WPFW-FM, producer, broadcaster, host of a daily show, 1980-81; Positive Futures, Inc, consultant, communications specialist, 1980-81; National Public Radio, special assistant vice pres, 1981-88; WJLA-TV 7, staff manager, Seven on Your Side, 1984-85; Twenty-First Century Committee on African-American Males, writer, fund raiser, 1991; United Black Fund, Inc, director, public relations, 1991-. **Orgs:** Black Public Relations Society, charter member, special events committee, 1992; SGI-USA, chapter leader, 1975-92; VIP 1000, charter member, 1992. **Honors/Awds:** United Way of the National Capital Area, Community Service, 1989-90; United Black Fund, Inc, Community Service Award, 1989-90; Roger B Taney School, Honors Participant Program, 1992. **Special Achievements:** Articles in the Washington Informer Newspaper, freelance, 1991, by line, 1990. **Business Phone:** (202)783-9300.

JETER, SHEILA ANN
Writer, publisher. **Personal:** Born Mar 4, 1952, Indianapolis, IN; daughter of Helen L Jeter and Linzie E Jeter; married Lawrence E Johnson, Apr 20, 1980; children: Shelette Alexander. **Educ:** Indiana University-Purdue University of Indianapolis, 1971-73; Draughons Business Coll, 1982; Martin Univ, BA (magna cum laude), communications, 1991. **Career:** LS Ayres & Co, PBX operator, 1970-73; General Motors Corp, Deburr machine general, 1973-; Indianapolis Star, reporter, 1988; Twelve Gates Publications, writer/publisher, 1986-. **Orgs:** Vice president, Midtown Writers Assn, 1989-; founding president, Intl Black Writers, Indianapolis Chapter, 1988; board member, On the Road to Success, 1987. **Honors/Awds:** Outstanding Black Women of Indianapolis, NENW, 1990. **Special Achievements:** Author, Before It's Too Late, Twelve Gates Publications, 1986. **Home Addr:** 5169 E State St Apt 305C, Rockford, IL 61108-2354. **Business Addr:** Publisher, Twelve Gates Publications, PO Box 19869, Indianapolis, IN 46219.

JETER, THOMAS ELLIOTT
Dentist, educator. **Personal:** Born Jul 20, 1929, Washington, DC; married Tayloria. **Educ:** Howard Univ Coll Dentistry, DDS 1967; NY Univ Sch Dentistry, cert oral surgery 1969; Harlem Hosp, Resd; Cath Med Ctr, Oral Surg Flwsp. **Career:** Oral Surgeon, prac; Howard Univ Coll Dentistry, asst oral surg. **Orgs:** Dir Anxiety & Pain Control Prgm; co-chmn Fed & Pyramid Sect Am Heart Assn; chmn Emergency Treatment Com Howard Univ Atdg Oral Surgon; Howard U; Mary Immaclate Hosp; Howard Univ Educ Devel Com; St Johns; St Mar's Hosp; Howard Univ Hosp Credentials Com; local Coord Nat High Blood Pressure Educ Prgm Howard U; mem Nat Dental Assn; Robert T Freeman Dental Assn; Basic Life Support Emergency Cardiac Com Am Heart Assn/Nat Capitol Affilliate; mem Am Assn Hosp Dentists Sigma Xi; Montgomery Co MD. **Honors/Awds:** Am heart affl award Oral Surgery Outsdng Instr 1975; instr yr 1976; outsdng serv Am Heart Assn 1977; maj contrib ''Comp Control of Pain & Anxiety''; ''Plea to the Dental Prof & Hypertension Detection''; Jour Hosp Dental Prac; good conduct award. **Military Serv:** USN Hm2. **Business Addr:** 600 W St NW, Washington, DC 20059.

JETER, VELMA MARJORIE DREYFUS
Educator (retired). **Personal:** Born Jul 15, 1903, New Iberia, LA; daughter of Victoria Smith Dreyfus (deceased) and Jules Dreyfus (deceased); married Clell Edward Jeter, Aug 18, 1926 (deceased). **Educ:** Prairie View College, Prairie View, TX, AB 1932; Univ of New Mexico Albuquerque, Albuquerque, NM, 1935-36; Univ of CA Berkeley, Berkeley, CA, 1942, 1943-44; Texas Southern Univ, MA 1952; Lamar Univ, Beaumont, TX. **Career:** Port Arthur ISD, teacher, 1922-26, 1942-69; Roswell ISD, teacher 1932-42; Orange ISD, teacher, English & social studies 1921-32; TX Assoc of Teachers, pres 1961-62; Central Jurisdiction WSG, pres 1956-64; Natl Dental Aux, pres 1962; Grand Court Order of CA & Jurisdiction of TX, pres, bd of dir 1967-89; TX Employment Commission, 1983; retired educator. **Orgs:** Co-founder, Orange Childhood Devel Ctr 1972-, Thrift & Gift Shop for the Elderly 1975-; pres, NAACP 1980-; Golden Heritage mem; bd dir, Natl Fraternal Congress of America, 1986-89; TX Older Workers Task Force Commission; chmn exec bd, TX Assoc of Women & Girls Clubs; bd dir, Hughes School for Crippled Children; chmn, Area Agency on Aging, Southeast TX; bd dir/pres, House of Refuge: A Home for the Homeless; pres, Le Samedi Club, area director, Top Ladies of Distinction, Sr Citizens Assoc, Orange Comm Action Assoc, NCNW; Bishop's council, Salem United Methodist Church, 1964-68; chairman board, Church & Society Texas Conference, 1978-82; Texas Employment Committee, 1975; past basileus and other offices, Epsilon Theta Omega; silver star member, Alpha Kappa Alpha Sorority, 1950-91; partner, Habitat for Humanity, Americus, GA, 1986-91. **Honors/Awds:** Civil Rights Award NAACP 1950-87; TX Assoc of Teachers, Retired Teachers, TSTA, NEA 1960-87; columnist Forward Times 1962; Black Texans of Distinction 1970; Award of Distinction to Retired Educators, 1984; They Showed The Way Black Women of TX History 1987-; Sojourner Truth Award, Business and Professional Women; Woman of the Year, Zeta Phi Beta Sorority; TX Women of Courage Award; TX Democratic Party Sustaining Supporter Award; Governor's Award for Public Service; Black Women's Hall of Fame, 1986; RSVP program, 1973-91; many plaques, certificates, & trophies in areas of civic, civil rights, humanitarian, government, religion, politics, & education; Black Heritage Pioneers, Lamar College, Port Arthur, TX, 1990; Black Heritage Pioneers, Lamar College, Orange, TX & CME Church, Orange, TX991. **Home Addr:** 1202 N 3rd, Orange, TX 77630.

JETT, ARTHUR VICTOR, SR.
Business executive. **Personal:** Born Dec 16, 1906, Union Springs, AL; married Katie; children: Kay Baker, A. **Educ:** Morehouse Acad, grad 1928; Chicago Tech Sch. **Career:** Bankhead W Contractors & Devel Inc, pres; Atlanta Bd of Educ Estimating & Plan Reading, instr masonry trades 1948-51; Masonry Tredes & Utica Inst, instr 1932-34; Bricklayers Union Local #9 AFL, bus agt 1940-44; Masonary Trades, apprent com 1946-50; Dept of Labor, adv Com 1967-69; building contractor 1952-. **Orgs:** Past bd mem Atlanta Urban League 1944-74; mem YMCA; bd dir bd mem, past treas Atlanta Br NAACP; bd Nat Child Welfare Leag of Am; United Way; pres bd Gate City Day Nursery Assn; bd mem treas Consolidated Mortgage & Investment Co; mem Atlantic Chamber of Commerce; Nat Conf of Social Welfare; mem 1st Congregationsl Ch; UCC; v chmn Deacon Bd Morehouse Coll Alumni Assn. **Honors/Awds:** Good nghbr award Nat Conf of Christians & Jews 1972; life mem NAACP; plaque NAACP 1974. **Business Addr:** 825 Cascade Ave SW, Atlanta, GA 30311.

JETT, JAMES
Olympic athlete. **Career:** US Olympic Team, Men's Track and Field, team member, 1992. **Honors/Awds:** Olympic Games, US Men's Track and Field team, 4 x 400 relay, relay member, Gold Medalist, 1992. **Business Addr:** Gold Medalist, Men's Track & Field Team, c/o US Olympic Training Center, 1 Olympic Plaza, Colorado Springs, CO 80909, (719)578-4500.

JETT, JAMES
Professional football player. **Personal:** Born Dec 28, 1970, Charlestown, WV. **Educ:** West Virginia. **Career:** Oakland Raiders, wide receiver, 1994-. **Business Addr:** Professional Football Player, Oakland Raiders, 1220 Harbor Bay Pkwy, Alameda, CA 94502, (510)615-1875.

JEWELL, JERRY DONAL
Legislator, dentist. **Personal:** Born Sep 16, 1930, Chatfield, AR; married Ometa; children: Eldin, Avelinda, Sharon, Jerrod, Kason. **Educ:** AR AM&N Coll, grad; Meharry Med Coll School of Dentistry. **Career:** 3rd Dist AR, state sen first elected 1972; Pvt Prac Little Rock, dentistry. **Orgs:** Mem Am Dental Assn; Nat Dental Assn; pres All Inc; bd mem Eagle Life & Ins Co; life mem NACP; former pres St Conf of Br; pres Little Rock Br; Credential Comm 1972; Natl Dem Party Chrtr Comn Natl Dem Party 1973-75; mem Alpha Phi Alpha Vet Army Dental Corp. **Business Addr:** 721 E 21st St, Little Rock, AR 72206.

JEWELL, PAULA L.
Attorney. **Personal:** Born Aug 12, 1943, Indianapolis. **Educ:** Howard U, BA (cum laude) 1964; Columbia Univ Law Sch, JD 1968; Howard U. **Career:** Howard Univ, special asst to pres, asst gen counsel; HUD, Atty; HUD, special asst to gen asst sec; Comm Plan & Mgmt HUD, sec 1968-72; Nat Corp for Housing Partnerships Assoc Coun, 1972-73; Nat Urban Coal Prog Off for Housing & Urban Growth & Trans, 1973-74; NEA Dushane Fund, atty; Intl House NY, foreign student advisor; DC Board of Zoning Adjustment, bd mem. **Orgs:** Mem Experiment in Intl Living Sweden 1962, Sperry-Hutchinson Fellow Columbia; asst to city council comm DC Bar Assn 1974; vchmn Younger Lawyer in PublicServ ABA 1974; chairperson DC Minimum Wage Indust Safety Comm 1976-80; assoc editor Survey of Human Rights Law Columbia. **Honors/Awds:** Appt to US Commn on UNESCO ; served on Exec Com Nom Com & Chmn of Youth Com; Deans List Howard 1964; Liberal Arts Hon Prog.

JEWELL, TOMMY EDWARD, III
Judge. **Personal:** Born Jun 30, 1954, Tucson, AZ; son of Bobbie L Jewell and Tommie E Jewell Jr; married Angela Juzang Jewell, Apr 4, 1981; children: Taja Marie, Thomas IV. **Educ:** NM State U, BA 1976; Univ of NM, JD 1979. **Career:** Soc of Albuquerque Inc, staff atty legal aid 1979-; Rocky Mountain, regional dir; Black Am Law Students Assn 1977-79; Jewell, Jewell Kelly & Kitson, Albuquerque, NM, partner, 1981-84; State of New Mexico, Albuquerque, NM, metropolitan court judge, 1984-. **Orgs:** Mem Juvenile Justice Adv Com 1978-; com mem Gov Juvenile Code Task Force 1979-; member, Omega Psi Phi Fraternity Inc, 19874-; member, National Bar Association, 1980-. **Honors/Awds:** Dean's award Univ of NM Sch & of Law 1978-79; Reginald Heber Smith Fellow, Howard Univ Sch of Law 198-81; Outstanding Young New Mexican, New Mexico Jaycees, 1986.

JIGGETTS, DANNY MARCELLUS
Businessman/broadcaster. **Personal:** Born Mar 10, 1954, Brooklyn, NY; son of Hattie Campbell Jiggetts (deceased) and Floyd Jiggetts (deceased); married Karen; children: Lauren, Kristan. **Educ:** Harvard, BS; MBA; Northwestern U, attndg. **Career:** Chicago Bears; Nat 1st Bank of Chicago; Proctor & Gamble, sales rep; Bd of Urban Affairs of NY, field rep; USFL, NBC-WMAQ TV; CBS Sports; ABN/LaSalle Bank, asst vp; CBS sports/WBBM-TV Chicago, sports broadcaster; WSCR Radio, Fox-TV, WFLD, broadcaster, currently. **Orgs:** Mem Better Boys Found, Natl Hemophilia Found, Spec Olympics, Natl Sudden Infant Death Syndrome Found, Midwest Assoc for SickleCell Anemia, March of Dimes, Harvard Alumni Assoc. **Honors/Awds:** BPO Elks Youth Ldrshp Awd; Football 3 times All Ivy New England; Track 2 times All Ivy; Football All American 1976. **Business Addr:** WSCR Radio, Fox-TV, WFLD, 205 N Michigan Avenue, Chicago, IL 60601.

JOBE, SHIRLEY A.
Library director. **Personal:** Born Oct 10, 1946, San Bernadino, CA; daughter of Luejeannia Jobe and Fines Jobe; children: Robyn. **Educ:** Texarkana Coll, AA 1966; East TX State Univ, AB 1968; Simmons Coll, MSLS 1971. **Career:** John F Kenne-

dy Presidential Library, head librarian 1971-84; Boston Globe Newspaper Co, head librarian 1984-. **Orgs:** Vice pres, MA Black Librarians Network 1984-86; volunteer in Soup Kitchens to feed homeless; volunteer to visit incarcerated persons in MA prisons. **Honors/Awds:** Education Professional Develop Act Grant 1970; Black Achiever's Awd Boston 1987. **Home Addr:** 54 Mt Pleasant, Cambridge, MA 02140. **Business Addr:** Library Dir, The Boston Globe, 135 Morrissey Blvd, Boston, MA 02107.

JOELL, PAMELA S.
Organization executive. **Personal:** Born Feb 1, 1961, Greenwich, CT; daughter of Edith Marie Duncan Joell and Willis Harrison Joell; children: Amber Marie Joell,. **Educ:** Manhattanville Coll, BA 1982; Health Insurance Assoc of Amer, Certificate Group Ins 1986; St Louis Univ Metro College MBTI Certification 1988; Dun & Brdstreet Education Serv, Continuing Educ Unit. **Career:** NYS Bd of Educ, high school social studies teacher 1982-83; MONY Financial Svcs, group benefits special 1983-85; Equitable Life Assurance Soc, group contract analyst 1985-86; INROADS, manager 1986-, operations manager 1988-90, managing director, 1990-. **Orgs:** Genl meetings comm Minority Interchange 1985-86; mem Player's Guild Theater Performance Soc, NBN Comm Theatre Players; general mtgs mem NY Chap Minority Interchange 1987; leader Troop 309 Girl Scouts of Amer 1988-89. **Honors/Awds:** Merit Certificate Poetry World of Poetry Mag Jan 1988; Class of Leadership Greater Hartford, 1993; American Red Cross, board member, 1992-; Greater Hartford Chapter, advisory member; WPI Multicultural Program. **Special Achievements:** Poem published: East Harlem. **Business Addr:** Managing Director, Inroads/Greater Hartford, One State St, Suite 460, Hartford, CT 06101.

JOHN, ANTHONY
Financial company executive. **Personal:** Born Feb 19, 1950, New York, NY; son of Maggie Seriven John and Alfred S. John; married Elmira Cooper John; children: Genean Corrinda Jessica. **Educ:** Ohio State University, Columbus, OH, BS, computer science, 1977; Fairleigh Dickinson University, Paterson, NJ, MBA, 1981. **Career:** AT&T, Piscataway, NJ, computer programmer, 1978-80; self-employed computer programmer, 1981-90; Dow Jones, South Brunswick, NJ, systems project manager, 1990-. **Orgs:** President, South Jersey Black Data Processing Assn, 1987; president, North Jersey Chapter, Black Data Processing Assn, 1983-84; national treasurer, BDPA, 1982-84; member, Burlington County Concerned Black Men, 1989-; treasurer/board of trustees, Rossville AMEZ Church, 1989-. **Military Serv:** US Air Force, Staff Sergeant, 1971-78. **Home Addr:** 16 Crosswick Pl, Willingboro, NJ 08046.

JOHN, DAYMOND
Clothing company executive. **Career:** FUBU Clothing Co, designer/owner, currently. **Business Addr:** Designer/Owner, FUBU Clothing Co, 350 5th Ave, Ste 6617, Brooklyn, NY 11215, (212)564-2330.

JOHNICAN, MINERVA JANE
Company executive. **Personal:** Born Nov 16, 1939, Memphis, TN; daughter of Annie M Rounsoville Johnican and John Bruce Johnican, Sr. **Educ:** Central State Coll, 1956-57; TN State Univ, BS 1960; Memphis State Univ, Graduate Study, 1965. **Career:** Memphis City Schools, elementary sch teacher 1960-65, elem school librarian 1965-79; Shelby County Govt, county commissioner 1975-82; Memphis City Govt, city councilwoman at large 1983-87 (first only black to win an at-large seat); 1987 candidate for mayor (first serious black women to run for mayor in the south.). **Orgs:** Chmn pro-tem Shelby Co Bd of Comm 1976-77; pres Gazell Public Relations & Adv Co 1976-78; mem Natl Assoc of Counties Natl Bd 1978-81; past pres TN County Commission Assoc 1980-81; mem Alpha Kappa Alpha Sor 1958-; budget chmn Memphis City Council 1984; pres Alpha Termite & Pest Control Inc 1982-88, pres, Gazelle Broadcasting, Coy Inc; pres & owner of Commonwealth Consultants, Ltd. **Honors/Awds:** Distinguished History Makers Award Mallory Knights Org 1976; "A Salute to Minerva Johnican" Memphis Community Leaders 1977; Outstanding Women in Politics Alpha Kappa Alpha Sor 1978; Outstanding Leadership Award Coca Cola Co of Memphis 1979; Women of Achievement "COURAGE" Award Network Womens Org 1984; First Black to be elected to an At-Large Council the City of Memphis (received 40% of white votes cast); Person of Equality Award Memphis NOW Chapter; Citizen of the Yr Award Excelsior Grand Chapter of Order of the Eastern Star; 1986 NCCJ Govt Serv Award & TN Educ Assoc Humanitarian Award, 1986. **Home Addr:** 1265 Dunnavant St, Memphis, TN 38106. **Business Addr:** President, CEO, 631 Madison Ave, Memphis, TN 38103.

JOHNS, JACKIE C.
Dentist. **Personal:** Born Jul 14, 1953, Belle Glade, FL; son of Mattie M Johns and Gonte Johns. **Educ:** Texas Coll, BS (Cum Laude) 1976; Prairie View A&M Univ, MS 1976-77; College of Medicine and Dentistry of NJ, DMD 1981. **Career:** Dr AS Ford, dentist 1981-82; Dr CJ Beck, dentist 1981; Dr RL Levine, dentist 1982-83; US Veterans Admin Outpatient, dentist 1983-84; Dr Thomas Scholpler, dentist 1983-84; Self Employed (2 offices), dentist. **Orgs:** Mem Amer FL Dental Assocs, North East Regional Bd Palm Beach County Dental Assoc; mem The Acad of General Dentistry, Alpha Omega Frat; mem Westboro Business and Professional Women Org; Family & Comprehensive Dentistry, Boynton Bch, FL; Family & Comprehensive Dentistry, Belle Glade, FL; mem of the Intl Congress of Oral Implantologist; Family & Comprehensive Dentistry of W.P.B., of Fort Pierce FL. **Honors/Awds:** Nationally recognized in Journal of the Natl Dental Assoc for active participation in the 1978 Health Fair at NJ Dental School; Comm Serv Citations for work on voters registration drives; Pinacle Award by Being Single Magazine Chicago Ill, 1989; Professional Achievement Award, Black Achievement, Glades Alumnae Chapter, Delta Sigma Theta Sorority Inc, 1991. **Military Serv:** AUS Reserve capt. **Business Addr:** Dentist, 2600 N Australian Ave, Ste A, West Palm Beach, FL 33407.

JOHNS, MICHAEL EARL
Marketing consultant. **Personal:** Born Jan 14, 1945, Alexandria, VA; children: Michael E Jr. **Educ:** Howard Univ, BA, 1968; Wharton School of Finance, MBA 1972. **Career:** IBM Corp, systems engr 1968-71; Xerox Corp, financial mgr 1972-78; The Prism Corp, pres. **Orgs:** mem, Market Rsch Assn, 1980-, DC Chamber of Commerce 1984-.

JOHNS, SONJA MARIA
Surgeon. **Personal:** Born May 13, 1953, Washington, DC; daughter of Jannie Austin Johns and Ralph L E Johns; children: George Wheeler Jr, Ashante, Chiquita, Maria Wheeler. **Educ:** Howard Univ Coll of Liberal Arts, BS (summa cum laude) 1976; Howard Univ Coll of Medicine, MD 1978; Howard Univ Hosp Family Practice Residency, certificate of completion 1978-81; Aerospace Medicine Brooks AFB, San Antonio, TX, certificate, 1988-89. **Career:** Natl Health Plan Inc, physician-in-attendance 1981-82; Women's Medical Ctr, family practitioner 1983; District of Columbia Air Natl Guard, chief hospital serv 1983-; Warsaw Medical Ctr, family physician 1983-; 113th Medical Squadron, Andrews Air Force Base, MD, commander, 1991; Westmoreland Health Services, family practitioner, founder, owner. **Orgs:** Mem: Amer Acad of Family Physicians 1979-, Natl Medical Assoc 1980-, Amer Medical Assoc 1980-, NAACP 1980-, Assoc of Military Surgeons of the US 1983-, Northern Neck Medical Soc 1984-, vice president, Tapp Hospital, 1983-; co-founder, Black Business & Professional Coalition 1985-; bd mem, Richmond Co Comm Serv Assoc Inc 1985-; soloist soprano, Comm Chorus, Northern Neck Convention Choir, Northern Neck Choral Soc; advisor, 4-H Club Richmond Co; president, Tappahannock Kiwanis Club, 1990-. **Honors/Awds:** Chief Resident Dept of Comm Health & Family Practice 1980-81; Physician's Recognition Awd Amer Medical Assoc 1981-88. **Military Serv:** Air Natl Guard, Col, 1983-; Meritorious Service Medal, Air Force Commendation, Perfect Attendance, Air Force Longevity, National Defense, Outstanding Unit. **Business Addr:** Owner, Founder, Westmoreland Health Services, PO Box 1120, Warsaw, VA 22572-0640.

JOHNS, STEPHEN ARNOLD
Life insurance executive (retired). **Personal:** Born Aug 21, 1920, Chicago, IL; son of Bennie F Shannon Johns and Stephen A Johns; married Tanis Fortier, May 24, 1966; children: Brenda Johns Penney. **Educ:** Roosevelt Coll, BA 1947; FLMI Life Office Mgmt Assn, 1959; CLU Am Coll of Life Underwriters, 1964. **Career:** Senior vice pres & chief marketing officer 1980-83, retired 1985; Golden St Mutual Life Ins Co, vice pres agency dir 1974-80; asso agency dir 1970; asso agency dir 1964; asst agency off 1962; dir & Of agency educ & tn 1960; methods analyst 1957; Jackson Mutual Life of Chgo, 1942-47. **Orgs:** Mem bd dir Golden St Mutual Life Ins Co; Life Underwriters' Assn of LA LA NAACP; Urban League; Kappa Alpha Psi. **Military Serv:** AUS s/sgt 1943-46. **Home Addr:** 5221 Angeles Vista Blvd, Los Angeles, CA 90043.

JOHN-SANDY, RENE EMANUEL
Business executive. **Personal:** Born Jul 22, 1945; son of Miriam John (John-Hercules) and Sydney Oliver Sandy. **Educ:** St Benedicts Coll Trinidad, diploma 1959; NY Business Sch, diploma 1970; NY Univ, BSc 1972. **Career:** Cahners Publishing NY, cost control analyst 1971-73; McGraw Hill NY, magazine mfg 1973-77; Time-Life Inc NY, magazine mfg/paper control 1977-79; Class Magazine, publisher 1979-. **Orgs:** Dir Harlem Soccer Club 1974-83; bd of dirs Emmbel Import & Export Inc 1980-84. **Honors/Awds:** Awd for Excellence in Publishing Chap of the Trinidad & Tobago Alliance NY 1982; Honorary Image Award, Luster Products Inc-Chicago 1988. **Military Serv:** Intelligence unit British Army Trinidad & Tobago Regiment 5 yrs.

JOHNSON, ADDIE COLLINS
Educator. **Personal:** Born Feb 28, Evansville, IN; daughter of Willa Shamell Collins and Stewart Collins; married John Q Johnson; children: Parker Collins. **Educ:** Howard Univ, BS 1956; PBB Hospital, dietetic internship, RD 1957; Framingham State Coll, MEd 1968. **Career:** Boston Lying In Hospital, therapeutic dietitian 1957-61; Harvard School Public Health Rsch, dietitian 1963-64; Hour Glass Newspaper Kwajakin MI, editorial 1965-66; Foxborough Public School, teacher 1968-; Univ of MA Harbor Campus Dept of Nursing, nutritionist 1980-88; Bridgewater State Coll, asst professor, 1982-. **Orgs:** Finance chmn, bd of dirs MA Home Economic Assoc; mem Amer Dietetics Assoc, Society Nutritional Ed, Amer Home Economics Assoc, Circle Lets Inc, Delta Sigma Theta Sor, MA Teachers Assoc; mem Links Inc; past pres Boston Chap Links Inc; mem nominating comm Natl Links Inc 1978-79; mem American Assoc University Women (AAUS); membership chairperson, Delta Kappa Gamma, Iota Chapter, 1989-; National Science Foundation, Project Seed 1992. **Honors/Awds:** Presenter Northeast Regional Social Studies Conference 1984-85. **Business Addr:** Adjunct Asst Professor, Bridgewater State College, Dept HEP, Bridgewater, MA 02324.

JOHNSON, ADRIENNE
Professional basketball player. **Personal:** Born Feb 5, 1974. **Educ:** Ohio State, attended. **Career:** Cleveland Rockers, guard, 1997-. **Business Addr:** Professional Basketball Player, Cleveland Rockers, One Center Ct, Cleveland, OH 44115, (216)263-7625.

JOHNSON, ALBERT J.
Composer, musician. **Personal:** Born Dec 14, 1910, Dallas, TX; married Bernice Milbrey. **Educ:** New York Univ, studied with Prof Rudolf Schramm 1961. **Career:** Queens Coll, arranger, composer, musician, asst prof music; Constant Music Inc, pres; musician & arranger for Louis Armstrong, 1933, Benny Goodman, 1956-57, Dizzy Gillespie, Billy Eckstine, Sarah Vaughn, Count Basie; conducts workshops, concerts throughout the USA & Canada. **Orgs:** Mem NY Jazz Repertory Co; sec-treas JPJ Quartet; sec-treas Oliver Jackson & Budd Johnson's Inc. **Honors/Awds:** Smithsonian Inst award 1975; USO shows in the US & Europe.

JOHNSON, ALBERT JAMES
Golf starter. **Personal:** Born Aug 20, 1943, Phoenix, AZ; son of Eddie J Johnson and Albert Johnson; married Beverly (divorced); children: Kevin A Johnson. **Educ:** Univ of AZ, BS, mgmt, 1965. **Career:** Harlem Globletrotters, player 1965-67; Univ of AZ, asst coach 1968-72; Matthew Chevrolet & Orielly Chevrolet, Tucson, AZ, salesman, 1972-84; City of Tucson, Parks and Recreation, Starter II supervisor, currently. **Orgs:** Mem Active 20-30 Serv Club 1970-72; mem Randolph Mens Golf Club 1976-; mem Desert Trails Mens Club 1969-74; mem Univ of AZ & Alumni Club 1970-73; deacon & elder Trinity Presb Ch 1969-73; mem, Saguaro Mens Club, 1984-91. **Honors/Awds:** All Western Athletic Conference, Basketball, 1963, 1964, 1965; City of Tucson, Tom Price Memorial Golf Tournament Winner, 1990. **Business Addr:** Starter II Supervisor, Parks & Recreation, City of Tucson, 900 South Randolph Way, Tucson, AZ 85718.

JOHNSON, ALBERT LEE, SR.
Clergyman. **Personal:** Born Sep 12, 1923, Hugo, OK; married Eddie Mae; children: Carl, Dessie Mae, Annie Jewel, Bernard, Horace Lee, Iralles Laverne, Albert, Terease Monee, Yolanda Denise, Erick Oneal. **Educ:** Western Bapt Sem KC MO, attended; Western Baptist Bible Coll, D Humanities 1984; Guadalupe Coll Sequin TX, DD 1984. **Career:** Zion Grove Bapt Church KC MO, pastor. **Orgs:** Past pres Coun for United Action CUA; pres Cit for Ed Equality CEE; sec bd of dir Martin Luther King Jr Meml Hosp; 1st black pres Met Inner ChAgency; mem MICA; chmn bd of CUA Housing; past pres Bapt Ministers Union; past 1st vice pres Gen Bapt Conv of MO, KS, IA, NE & Co; mem Gen Bapt Conv MO, KS, NE; 1st vice moderator Sunshine Dist Assoc; co-admin Gen Bapt Nursing Home & Retirement Ctr; bd mem Black Political Org Freedom Inc; pres General Baptist Convention of MO, KS and NE 1980-85. **Business Addr:** Pastor, Zion Grove Bapt Church, 2801 Swope Pkwy, Kansas City, MO 64130.

JOHNSON, ALBERT WILLIAM, SR.
Automobile dealer. **Personal:** Born Feb 23, 1926, St Louis, MO; son of Anna Johnson and Oscar William Johnson; married Marion, Feb 2, 1952; children: Albert W Johnson Jr, Donald King Johnson, Anthony Johnson. **Educ:** Attended Lincoln Univ; Univ of IL, Champaign, IL, BS, 1942; Univ of Chicago, Chicago, IL, degree in hospital admin, 1955. **Career:** United Public Workers Union, former regional direc; Homer Phillips Hosp, St Louis, MO, former admitting supvr and asst to the admin and bus mgr; Al Johnson Cadillac-Saab-Avanti & Leasing Inc, Tinley Park, IL, pres, 1971-. **Orgs:** Member, citizens comm, Univ of IL; member, bd of direc, Better Business Bureau of Metro Chicago; vice pres, Variety Club of IL, Chicago chapter; bd member, Seaway Natl Bank; member, Execs Club of Chicago; member, Platformers Club; member, Metro club; member, Unicorn Club; life member, NAACP; member, Chicago United; sponsor, Chicago Berry-Johnson Business and Profl Person Recog Annual Award; founder, Messanger Found; founder, People United to Save Humanity Found; member, Orland Park Lions Club; hon member, Oaks Club; member, bd of direcs, Ingalls Memorial Hospital; pres, Pyramid Trotting Assn; member, Illinois Sports Facilities Authority, 1988-; chairman of the board, Variety Club Childrens Charities, 1987-; board member, Thresholds Psychiatric Rehab Center, 1990. **Honors/Awds:** Fellow, Chicago Defender Roundtable of Commerce; certif of excellence, Cosmopolitan Chamber of Commerce; Partner in Progress Award, Chicago Assn of Commerce and In-

dustry; Businessman's Award, Woodlawn Orgn; Black Excellence Award, Cultural Comm, PUSH; Top 100 Black Businessmen Award, Black Enterprise magazine; Man of the Year, Coalition for United Community Action; Humanitarian Award, Mayor Richard Hatcher, Gary, IN; certif of apprec, St Bernard's Hospital; certif of recog, Univ of Detroit; apprec award, CUS Natl Honor Soc; Black Businessman of the Year, Black Book NPSA; certif of merit, Adv Mgmt for Dealers, Oldsmobile; apprec award, Cosmopolitan Chamber of Commerce; certif of apprec, Chatham Business Assn; Time Magazine Quality Dealer Award, 1975; certifof apprec, General Motors CorpL Coun of Deliberation Award; Humanitarian of the Year Award, Coalition for United Community Action. **Business Addr:** President, Al Johnson Cadillac-Saab-Avanti & Leasing Inc, 8425 West 159th Street, Tinley Park, IL 60477.

JOHNSON, ALCEE LABRANCHE
Educator. **Personal:** Born Jul 22, 1905, Fernwood, MS; married Thelma Wethers (deceased); children: Al, Joyce J Bolden. **Educ:** Alcorn Coll, 1925; Fisk Univ, AB 1927; Columbia Univ, 1930-31, MA 1956; Univ of So CA, Further Study; Hon HHD Degrees, MS Bapt Sem 1972, Rust Coll 1974. **Career:** Prentiss Inst, instr 1927-30, dir of instruction 1931-36; Dept of Interior Washington DC Office of Educ Survey of Vocational Educ & Guidance, state supvr; Prentiss Inst, instr 1927-30, pres 1971-81, dir of instr 1973-, exec sec, bd of trustees 1981-. **Orgs:** Former pres 6th Dist Theacer Assoc, MS Teacher Assoc, MS Dist Teacher Assoc; mem Phelps-Stokes Fund Conf of Ed Leaders; life mem Amer Teacher Assoc, Natl Ed Assoc, MS Teacher Assoc; pres Prentiss Inst Jr Coll, MS Assoc of Developing Coll; chmn Western Div BSA; mem Alpha Phi Alpha, Phi Delta Kappa, 33rd Deg Mason, Voters League, NAACP, MS Reg Med Prog; past chmn bd 1st vice pres State Mutual Fed Savings & Loan, JDC Mutural Fed Credit Union; inst rep Heifer Proj Inc; only black pes So MS Plnng & Devel Dist Inc; mem MS Econ Council; ed comm, recorder, ed div White House Conf on Aging 1971; former vice pres Cty Council on Aging 1972; 1st black appt to the Probation & Parole Bd by Gov Wm Waller 1972. **Honors/Awds:** Silver Beaver Awd BSA; MS Man of the Year 1973; Greene Awd Alpha Phi Alpha So Reg 1973.

JOHNSON, ALEXANDER HAMILTON, JR.
Banking executive (retired). **Personal:** Born Oct 3, 1924, Greensboro, AL; son of Erma Johnson and Rev Alexander Johnson; married Delores Mitzie Russel; children: Alexander III. **Educ:** CA Pacific Univ, BA Public Admin 1978, MA Mgmt 1980. **Career:** Federal Aviation Admin, personnel staffing spec 1968-70, chief civil rights staff 1970-74; US Equal Empl Oppty Comm, compliance suprv 1974-81; The Arizona Bank, aa & equal em mgr, vp, retired 1992. **Orgs:** Pres Amer Fed of Govt Empl 1968; clerk of session Southminster Presbyterian Church 1980-84; chmn of bd Southminster Social Serv Agency 1981; pres Southwest Area Conf NAACP 1982-84; chmn Reg I NAACP 1984-85; keeper of records Phoenix Alumni Kappa Alpha Psi 1984-86; mem Sigma Pi Phi, Gamma Mu Boule 1988; mem Maricopa County Commission on Trial Court Appontments 1989. **Honors/Awds:** Outstanding Citizen Maricopa Cty NAACP 1978; Awd for Caring Phoenix City Human Serv Comm 1980. **Military Serv:** AUS corpl 1943-47.

JOHNSON, ALFRED
Company executive. **Personal:** Born Feb 12, 1952, Forest City, NC; son of Mae Pearl Johnson (deceased) and Leroy Johnson; married Barbara Aileen Carson Johnson, Aug 13, 1983; children: Jamaal, Tyreke, Megan. **Educ:** Livingstone College, BA, political science, 1974. **Career:** Harris Teetar Supermarket, mgr trainee, 1974; Isothermal Community College, 1974-81; Mobil Environmental Sanitation Services, co-owner/managing partner, 1981-. **Orgs:** New Bethal AME Zion, chairman of trustee board, 1978-; Rutherford Vocational Workshop, secretary/treasurer, 1989-90, vice pres, 1990-91, board member, 1983-92; Forest City Kiwanis Club, 1991-; Microenterprise Loan Review Board, 1989-; Red Cross, board of directors, 1984-; Regional Job Partnership Training Act Board, 1984-89; Hospice, board of directors, 1988-; Forest City Recreation Commission, 1976-81. **Honors/Awds:** The American Legion National Award for Hiring the Handicapped, 1987; State Award Volunteerism, 1989; Regional American Legion for Hiring the Handicapped, 1986.

JOHNSON, ALMETA ANN
Attorney. **Personal:** Born Mar 11, 1947, Rockingham, NC; daughter of V Louise Johnson Noel; divorced; children: Cesseli A Cooke, Harry E Cooke IV. **Educ:** OH State Univ, JD 1971; Johnson C Smith Univ, BA 1968. **Career:** Metzenbaum Gaines Finley & Stern, law clerk 1969-70; OH State Univ, rsch asst 1970-71; Benesch Friedlander Mendelson & Coplan, assoc atty 1971-75; City of Cleveland, chief police prosecutor, 1975-80; Private Practice, attorney; East Cleveland City Council, councilwoman, 1987-. **Orgs:** Chmn E Cleveland Citizens Adv Comm 1973-75, 1988-; chmn E Cleveland Charter Rev Commn 1976; bd mem sec treas OH Law Opportunity Fund; mem Amer Bar Assn, Bar Assn of Greater Cleveland, OH State Bar Assn, Black Women Lawyers Assn, Alpha Kappa Alpha; law dir Village of Woodmere 1983-86. **Honors/Awds:** Lett Civil Liberties Award OSU Coll of Laws 1971; 1 of 10 Most Influential Women in greater Cleveland The Plain Dealer 1975; NAACP Outstanding Young Citizen Cleveland Jaycees 1976. **Business Addr:** Attorney-at-Law, 13308 Euclid Ave, East Cleveland, OH 44112.

JOHNSON, ALVIN ROSCOE
Human resources executive. **Personal:** Born Oct 15, 1942, Alton, IL; son of Jennie C Keen and Cyrus L Johnson; married Thelma Marie Hart; children: Brent Alvin, Dirk Cyrus. **Educ:** Souther IL Univ Edwardsville, BS Bus Admin 1972, MBA 1982. **Career:** Olin Corp, mgr train & dev 1962-77, mgr personnel 1977-80; Babcock Industries Inc, senior vp human resources & administration, 1980-93; Yale New Haven Hospital, vp employee relations, 1993-. **Orgs:** Dir Amer Red Cross, Girl Scouts, Urban League, Acco Babcock Inc 1982-; treas & golden life mem NAACP, Alumni Assoc Ex Board of Directors; chair, deacons, Immanuel Baptist Church; mem Sigma Pi Phi; hr council Manufactures Alliance for Productivity Innovation, 1982-; life mem SIUE Alumni Assoc Ex Board of Directors 1975-77. **Military Serv:** AUS sgt E-5 1966-68. **Business Addr:** Senior Vice Pres Human Resources & Administration, Babcock Industries Inc, 425 Post Road, Fairfield, CT 06430.

JOHNSON, ANDRE
Professional football player. **Personal:** Born Aug 25, 1973, Southhampton, NY. **Educ:** Penn State. **Career:** Washington Redskins, tackle, 1996; Detroit Lions, 1997-. **Business Addr:** Professional Football Player, Detroit Lions, 1200 Featherstone Rd, Pontiac, MI 48342, (248)335-4131.

JOHNSON, ANDREW
Engineer. **Personal:** Born Jun 3, 1946, Gould, AR; son of Bertha Johnson and Andrew Johnson; married Helen L Fleming; children: Andrew Raphel, Heather Louise. **Educ:** Univ of AR at Pine Bluff, BS Chem 1968; Northeastern Univ, Certificate 1984. **Career:** IBM Corp, Endicott NY Eng/Mfg mgr 1976-80, Austin TX production control mgr 1980-82, Brooklyn NY functional mgr 1982-85, asst general mgr 1985-86, E Fishkill, NY, equipment engineering operations mgr, 1986-. **Orgs:** Baselius Omega Psi Phi Fraternity Inc Kappa Nu 1972; adv bd mem George Westinghouse HS 1984-86; Sunday school teacher 1984-, deacon 1987-, Pilgrim Baptist Church Nyack NY; chairman Economic Develop NAACP Spring Valley 1986, mem, Affirmative Action Comm, Rockland Children's Psychiatric Center, Rockland County, NY. **Honors/Awds:** Youth motivation table bd Natl Alliance of Business 1977-82; Presidential Citation NAFEO 1983. **Home Addr:** 2809 Aster Pass, Cedar Park, TX 78613-5350. **Business Addr:** Senior Engineer, International Business Machine, Z/56A Route 52, Hopewell Junction, NY 12533.

JOHNSON, ANDREW L., SR.
Attorney. **Personal:** Born Feb 5, 1905, Little Rock; married Henrietta Grinage; children: Kathryn Iona, Andrew L Jr. **Educ:** Central State Univ Wilberforce OH, BS 1930; Youngstown State Univ Law School, LLB 1934, JD 1969. **Career:** Mahoning Cty Youngstown OH, asst cty prosecutor 1937-41; Private practice, attny 1936-. **Orgs:** Mem US Dist Ct, No Dist of OH 1954; ct apptd hearing attny for mentally ill patients Woodside Receiving Hosp; mem Bd of Cty Visitors, OH State Bar Asoc 1936-, Amer Bar Assoc, Alpha Phi Alpha, NAACP; past treas, mem, bd of dir Org of Prot Men Youngstown; mem Mahoning Cty OH Dem Org; bdmn Woodwrth Gar Club; mem, bd of trust, attny, leg adv St Andrew AME Church 1923-. **Business Addr:** Attorney, 906 Metropolitan Tower Bldg, Youngstown, OH 44503.

JOHNSON, ANDREW L., JR.
Attorney. **Personal:** Born Oct 4, 1931, Youngstown, OH; married Joan Carol Phillips; children: Andrew III, Paul. **Educ:** Northwestern Univ, BS 1953; Cleveland State Univ Sch of Law, JD 1959. **Career:** Shaker Heights Municipal Ct, acting judge 1970-; Private Practice, atty 1960-; Real Estate, ownership, 1962-. **Orgs:** Pres Bar Assn of Greater Cleveland 1978-79; trustee Bar Assn of Greater Cleveland 1970-73; labor arbitrator Major Steel Companies of NE OH; host of TV prog KNOWLEDGE "Youth & the Law"; hearing examiner for OH Civil Rights Commn; chmn bd trustees Forest City Hosp Cleveland 1970-76; founding mem & first pres Cleveland Lawyers Assn Inc; mem Cleveland Council on Human Relations; former pres Home Owners Title Corp Cleveland; vice pres Northwestern Univ Alumni Club of Cleveland; life mem Alpha Phi Alpha Frat; charter mem, Judicial Council, Natl Bar Assn; charter mem, Eighth Judicial Conference; pres, bd of trustees, Forest City Hospital; managing partner, Tower Management Co, chairman, advisory comm; Forest City Hospital Foundation; life mem, NAACP; Natl Urban League; Sigma Pi Phi Frat. **Honors/Awds:** Merit Awd Northwestern Univ Coll of Arts & Sci 1979; Law Day Awd Cleveland Lawyers Assn 1969; Meritorious Serv Awd Cleveland Bar Assn 1970; Trust Shaker Lakes Regional Native Ctr 1977-; Alumnus of the Year Award, Northeastern Univ, College of Arts & Sci, 1979. **Military Serv:** AUS specialist 4th class 1953-55. **Business Addr:** Attorney, 33 Pub Sq, Ste 810, Cleveland, OH 44113.

JOHNSON, ANGEL PATRICIA
Educational administrator. **Personal:** Born Oct 8, 1942, Elbert, WV; daughter of Moncie Belcher and Cleo; married Milton W Johnson; children: Brian, Marc, Erik. **Educ:** Brooklyn Coll City Univ of NY, BA 1965; Rutgers Univ Grad Sch of Educ, MEd 1980; Rutgers Univ Grad Sch of Educ, EdD 1987. **Career:** Salvation Army Foster Home Svcs, social worker 1965-69; Georgian Court Coll, educ oppor fund asst dir 1977-78, upward bound project dir 1978-88; NJ Dept of Higher Education Trenton NJ Assistant Dir 1988-. **Orgs:** Vice pres Monmouth County Bus & Professional Women's Cncl 1977; bd dirs mem Assoc for Equality & Excellence in Educ 1981-82, 1984-89; mem Assoc of Black Educators 1983; bd of trustees mem Lakewood Prep School 1984-. **Honors/Awds:** Dedication to Success of Upward Bound Project Georgian Court Coll Comm Adv Bd 1981; Special Citation Assoc for Equality & Excellence in Educ 1982; Outstanding Upward Bound Dir Students Class of 1984. **Business Addr:** Assistant Director, New Jersey Deptartment of Higher Education, Office of College - School Collaboration, 20 W State Street, Trenton, NJ 08608.

JOHNSON, ANNE-MARIE
Actress. **Career:** Actress. **Honors/Awds:** Co-star of NBC's In the Heat of the Night; appeared in television movie Dream Date, 1989.

JOHNSON, ANTHONY
Professional basketball player. **Personal:** Born Oct 2, 1974. **Educ:** Charleston (SC), bachelor's degree in business administration. **Career:** Sacramento Kings, guard, 1997-. **Business Addr:** Professional Basketball Player, Sacramento Kings, One Sports Parkway, Sacramento, CA 95834, (916)928-6900.

JOHNSON, ANTHONY MICHAEL
Physicist. **Personal:** Born May 23, 1954, Brooklyn, NY; son of Helen Weaver Johnson and James W. Johnson; married Dr Adrienne Steplight, Jun 2, 1975; children: Kimberly, Justin, Brandon. **Educ:** Polytechnic Inst of NY, BS Physics Magna Cum Laude 1975; City Coll of the City Univ of NY, PhD Physics 1981. **Career:** AT&T Bell Laboratories, sr tech assoc 1974-77; doctoral can 1978-81; research in ultrafast optics & electronics; AT&T Bell Laboratories, mem tech staff 1981-, distinguished mem 1988-. **Orgs:** Mem Amer Physical Soc 1977-; mem Natl Soc of Black Physicists 1980-, tech prog co-char, 1989; mem Optical Soc of Amer 1982-; mem Inst of Elec & Electron Engrs 1982-; symposium organizer in "Ultrashort Pulses in Optical Fibers," 1985, vice-chmn on Tech Prog Com for "Ultrafast Optical Phenomena," 1985, symposium organizer in "Ultrashort Nonlinear Pulse Propagation in Optical Fibers," 1988, in Annual Mtg of Optical Society of Amer 1985; mem Amer Assoc for the Advance of Sci 1986-; mem tech council Optical Soc of Amer, chmn Tech Group on Ultrafast Optical Phenomena 1986-87; mem tech prog comm Annual Meeting of the Optical Soc of Amer 1986 (Seattle), 1987 (Rochester), 1988 (Santa Clara); mem tech prog comm Ultrafast Optics & Electronics for the Conf ofLasers & Electro-Optics 1986 (San Franco), 1987 (Baltimore); chmn Tech Prog Subcom Conference on Lasers and Electro-Optics (CLEO) 1988 (Anaheim), 1989 (Baltimore), tech prog co-chair, 1990 (Anaheim); mem R W Wood Prize Comm, Optical Soc of Am, 1989, chair, 1990; topical editor, Optics Letters, 1989-91; mem Optics News advisory comm, 1989-91; mem science and tech advisory board, Journal of the Natl Tech Assoc, 1989-. **Honors/Awds:** Undergraduate research award, Sigma Xi, 1975; Cooperative Research Fellowship, AT&T Bell Labs, 1975; chapters in books on laser usage, 1984, 1989; various patents in optics and electronics; guest editor, IEEE Journal of Quantum Electronics special issue, February 1988; AT&T Bell Labs Distinguished Technical Staff Award, 1988; Minds in Motion Award, Science Skills Center, Brooklyn, NY, 1989. **Business Addr:** Distinguished Member Technical Staff, AT&T Bell Laboratories, Room 4D-321, Crawfords Corber Rd, Holmdel, NJ 07733.

JOHNSON, ANTHONY SCOTT
Professional football player. **Personal:** Born Oct 25, 1967, Indianapolis, IN; married Shelly; children: Taylor, Kylie, Gabriel, Sierra. **Educ:** Notre Dame. **Career:** Indianapolis Colts, running back, 1990-93; New York Jets, 1994; Chicago Bears, 1995; Carolina Panthers, 1996-. **Honors/Awds:** Indianapolis Colts, Fan Club Player of the Year, 1992; Max Noble Award, 1992. **Business Addr:** Professional Football Player, Carolina Panthers, 800 Mint St, Ericsson Stadium, Charlotte, NC 28202, (704)358-7000.

JOHNSON, ARGIE K.
Educational administrator. **Career:** Biochemist; New York City Public Schools, 26 year veteran: teacher, principal, subdistrict superintendent, deputy chancellor for instruction; Chicago Public Schools, superintendent, currently. **Business Addr:** Superintendent, Chicago Public Schools, 1819 W Pershing Rd, Bldg 6 East, Chicago, IL 60619, (312)535-3700.

JOHNSON, ARTHUR E.
Company executive. **Educ:** Morehouse College. **Career:** IBM, executive assistant to chairman, vp, 1992, president and CEO of Federal Systems Co, currently. **Business Phone:** (301)493-1400.

JOHNSON, ARTHUR J.
Association executive, educational administrator (retired). **Career:** NAACP, Detroit Chapter, president, until 1992; Wayne State Univ, vp for univ relations, 1972-95. **Honors/Awds:** Articles: ''Stock Pickers Up Yonder; The Canadian Market: So Familiar, So Different,'' New York Times Magazine, June 12, 1988, ''Is Your City Ready for the Big Leagues,'' Nation's Cities Weekly, January 25, 1988, p. 6, ''The Pennsylvania Challenge,'' Maclean's, April 23, 1984, p. 26, ''Israel's Broken Coalition,'' Maclean's, April 2, 1984, ''A Barometer of Violence,'' Maclean's, March 5, 1984, ''The Collapse of a Nation,'' Maclean's, February 20, 1984; author, Breaking the Banks. **Business Addr:** Past President, Detroit Chapter, NAACP, 2990 E Grand Blvd, Detroit, MI 48202.

JOHNSON, ARTHUR L.
Teacher/government official. **Educ:** FL A&M Univ Tallahassee, BS Chem Math 1965; Pepperdine Univ, MS Admin 1974. **Career:** Inglewood CA School Dist, teacher, counselor; City of Gardena, Gardena planning comm. **Orgs:** Mem Amer Chem Soc 1969-71; mem Engrs Scientist Guild Lockheed Aircraft 1969-73; former mem Bicentennial Comm of Gardena 1976-77; mem Hollypark Homeowner Assn 1967-; chmn Dr Martin L King Jr Black Culture Comm of Gardena 1973-; dir S CA Planning Congress 1985. **Honors/Awds:** Teacher of the Yr Inglewood School Dist 1983; Seal of the City-City of Gardena 1983. **Military Serv:** AUS pvt 1st class 1944-45. **Home Addr:** 13116 Manhattan Pl, Gardena, CA 90249. **Business Addr:** Gardenia Planning Comm, City of Gardena, 1700 West 162nd St, Gardena, CA 90247.

JOHNSON, ARTHUR LYMAN
Educator. **Personal:** Born Aug 21, 1918, Hartford, CT; married Marie Love. **Educ:** Johnson C Smith U, BA 1941; Univ of Hartford, MEd 1952. **Career:** Hartford Neighborhood Ctrs, group worker 1946-47; AFL-CIO, bus agent 1947-49; State of CT Civil Rights Commn, supr & dir 1950-62; Hartford Human Rel Commn, exec dir 1964-79; WFSB-TV, producer & host 1971-77; Hartford Star & Inquirer, columnist/editor 1972-; Eastern CT State U, asso prof 1970-84, cons, currently. **Orgs:** Consult Commnty Renewal Team 1983-; pres Hartford Chap NAACP; mem Omega Psi Phi Carpe Diem Frat High Noon Greater Hartford Comm Cncl. **Honors/Awds:** Published, ''Beyond Ourselves''. **Military Serv:** USAF 1941-45. **Home Addr:** 78 Warren Ave, PO Box 2026, Vernon-Rockville, CT 06066.

JOHNSON, ARTHUR T.
Elected official. **Personal:** Born Oct 29, 1947, Earlington, KY; married Dorothy Radford; children: Belinda, Joy. **Educ:** Earlington HS, 1967; Austin Peay State Coll, 1967-68. **Career:** City of Earlington, councilman 1972-83, mayor 1984-. **Orgs:** Memshp Earlington Civic Club 1972-, memshp Earlington Volunteer Fire & Rescue Sqd 1967-; pres Earlington Jaycees 1982; bd dir Pennyrile Area Development Dist for Pennyrile Housing Corp; Junior Advisor rep Goodyear Tire and Rubber Co 1983-84. **Honors/Awds:** Citzen of the Year Hopkins Countains for Progress 1976; Hopkins Countians for Progress Man of the Yr 1985; Black Award Council Black Man of the Yr 1985. **Business Addr:** Mayor, City of Earlington, City Building, Earlington, KY 42410.

JOHNSON, AUDREYE EARLE
Educator. **Personal:** Born Aug 18, 1929, Memphis, TN; daughter of Mary Hairston Johnson (deceased) and Lyncha A Johnson Sr (deceased). **Educ:** Fisk Univ, Nashville, TN, BA, 1950; Univ of Chicago, MA, 1957; Univ of Denver, PhD, 1975. **Career:** Dept of Public Welfare, soc worker, 1950-54; Dept Public Welfare, Chattanooga, child welfare worker, 1955-56; Michael Reese Hospital-Med Center, social worker, 1957-67; MLK Neighborhood Center, Mt Sinai Hospital, dir, social serv, 1967-69; Meharry Med Coll, dir C & E, asst clinical prof, dept psychiatry, 1969-73; Univ of NC at Chapel Hill, School of Social Work, assoc prof 1975-. **Orgs:** Charter mem, Natl Assn Social Workers Acad Cert Soc Workers, 1955-; founder, 1968, secretary, 1974-76, vice pres, 1976-78, historian, 1974-; Natl Assn Black Social Workers, 1978-82; program chmn, Amer Public Health Assn Social Work Section, 1979-80; bd mem, Human Rights Comm Murdoch Center, 1976-86; bd mem, Mental Health Rsch & Devel Bd, Howard Univ, 1976; life mem, Assn Study Afro-Am Life & History, 1987; chairperson, Black Faculty/Staff Caucus at UNC-CH 1980-86; creator/director, Annual Black Experience Workshop UNC-CH 1980-; mem, former bd mem, Council on Social Work Educ & House of Delegates Rep to 1988; life mem, Assn of Black Women Historians, 1988; chairperson, Social Work Section of Amer Public Health Assn, 1986-87; life mem, NAACP, 1986; Natl Urban League; founder, Triangle Assn of Black Social Workers, 1975; CSWE, current member; life mem, National Council of Negro Women, 1991; faculty advisor, Alliance of Black Graduate and Professional Students, 1986-. **Honors/Awds:** Publications, ''The Black Experience, Social, Cultural and Economic Considerations,'' 1981; ''The Black Experience, Considerations for Health and Human Services,'' 1983; author of several published articles on Black contributions to social work and welfare; inducted into NC A&T Univ, Hall of Fame, 1988-; Honored by the Metrolina Chapter of the Natl Assn of Black Social Workers for ''Ten Years of the Black Experience Workshops'' at the Tenth Anniversary Celebration of the Black Experience Workshop, 1989; Certificate of Appreciation for Outstanding Service to the African-American Community In the Univ & Beyond, Black Faculty/Staff Caucus, Chapel Hill, 1990; Outstanding Achievement in Public Health Social Work Award, Social Work Section of the American Public Health Assn, 1990; NC State Assn of Black Social Workers names its scholarship fund the Audreye E Johnson Scholhip Fund, 1990; Inducted into Order of the Golden Fleece, the oldest and highest Honorary Soc on the campus of the Univ of NC at Chapel Hill, 1991; The Black Experience Workshops Collected Papers, Vols I, II, 1989; ''Catherine (Katy) Ferguson'' and ''Eartha Mary Magdalene'' in Black Women in the US; An Historical Encyclopedia, 1993; inducted as an initial honoree into ''A Consortium Honoring Women of Color in the Struggle,'' July 1991; selected to serve as a bicentennial speaker for the Univ of North Carolina-Chapel Hill, 1993; Certificate of Appreciation Plaque, James E Shepard Sertoma Club, 1993; Exceptional Volunteer Service Administration Award, American Red Cross, 1994; Certificate of Appreciation for Outstanding Service, UNC-CH Upward Bound Program, 1995; Award for Meritorious Service/Contribution to the African American Community, University of North Carolina at Chapel Hill, 1996; Alliance of Black Graduate and Prof Students, 10 Years of Dedicated Svc; Black Faculty and Staff Cancus, African American Comm of UNC-CH, Staff Counselor, 1996; 17th Annual Comm Academic Plaque, Martin Luther King Jr Award, 1998. **Special Achievements:** Publications: The National Association of Black Social Workers Inc: A History for the Future, 1988; article: ''Social Work,'' Jack Salzman, Daniel Lional, Smith and Cornel West, Encyclopedia of African-American Culture and History, New York Simon & Schuster Macmilliam, vol 5, pp 2516-2520, 1996. **Home Addr:** 4100 Five Oaks Dr, Townhouse #19, Durham, NC 27707. **Business Addr:** Assoc Professor Social Work, Univ of NC at Chapel Hill, 301 Pittsboro St, CB #3550, Chapel Hill, NC 27599-3550.

JOHNSON, AVERY
Professional basketball player. **Personal:** Born Mar 25, 1965, New Orleans, LA; married Cassandra; children: Christianne, Avery Jr. **Educ:** New Mexico Junior College, Hobbs, NM, 1983-84; Cameron Univ, Lawton, OK, 1984-85; Southern Univ, Baton Rouge, LA, 1986-88. **Career:** Seattle SuperSonics, guard, 1988-90; Denver Nuggets, 1990-91; Houston Rockets, 1991-92; Golden State Warriors, 1993-94; San Antonio Spurs, 1994-. **Honors/Awds:** Fannie Mae Foundation, Home Team Community Service Award. **Business Addr:** Professional Basketball Player, San Antonio Spurs, 600 E Market St, San Antonio, TX 78205, (210)554-7773.

JOHNSON, AYUBU. **See JOHNSON, BENJAMIN EARL.**

JOHNSON, B. A.
Government official. **Personal:** Born Mar 7, 1925, Swainsboro, GA; son of Mozella Johnson and George E Johnson; married Hattie T Thompson, Dec 27, 1957; children: Betty. **Educ:** Atlanta Coll of Mortuary Science, BS, 1946; Savannah State Coll, BA, 1950; Tuskegee Inst, MEd and MA, 1960; Georgia Southern Coll, SpEd, 1964. **Career:** Emanuel Co Bd of Edn, Swainsboro, GA, teacher, 1943-44, 1947-48, principal, 1974-81; Jefferson Co Bd of Edn, Louisville, GA, eacher, 1950-58; Screuen Co Bd of Edn, Sylvania, GA, asst principal, 1958-61; Laurens Co Bd of Edn, Dublin, GA, principal, 1981-94; Wadley, GA, mayor, 1981-94, 1997-. **Orgs:** Kappa Alpha Psi. **Honors/Awds:** Deacon of the Year, Piney Grove Baptist Church, 1976; Man of the Year, NAACP, 1977; Principal of the Year, 1981. **Military Serv:** US Navy, 1943-46. **Home Addr:** 135 Bedingfield St, PO Box 572, Wadley, GA 30477.

JOHNSON, BARBARA C.
Educator, elected official. **Personal:** Born Apr 11, 1931, New York, NY; married J David Johnson; children: Eleanore. **Educ:** NY Univ School of Educ, BS 1953; NY Univ School of SW, MSW 1957; Natl Inst Mental Health, Fellow 1970-71; Columbia Univ Sch of Social Work, advancedcert social welfare 1974. **Career:** Comm Serv Bureau, dir foster care 1961-67; Columbia Univ School of Soc Work, asst prof 1967-70; Africana Studies Dept Brooklyn Coll, deputy chairperson 1972-78; Bridge to Medicine Prog CCNY, instructor 1980-81; CONNECT-Child Abuse Prevention, dir 1981-83; Harlem Comm for Intl Visitors, dir 1983-. **Orgs:** Post office mem alumni Oper Crossroads Africa 1967-; membership chairperson Black Task Force Child Abuse 1982-; vice chairperson Comm Sch Bd Five Harlem 1982-; bd mem Alma John Workshop 1984-; bd of directors Natl Caucus Black Sch Bd Members 1984-. **Honors/Awds:** Comm Service Awds NABBPW Eastern Star 1968, 1982; Outstanding Teacher Brooklyn Coll Black Studies 1974-78; Intl Service 3rd World Trade Assn 1985; global contrivbutions AKA 1985. **Business Addr:** Dir, Harlem Comm for Intl Visitor, 230 W 137th St, New York, NY 10030.

JOHNSON, BEN (ROBERT)
Government official. **Career:** Office of Public Liaison, associate dir, special assistant to the president, 1996-. **Business Addr:** Deputy Assistant to the President, Deputy Director of Public Liaison, Office of Public Liaison, 1600 Pennsylvania Ave, NW, 121 OEOB, Washington, DC 20500, (202)456-2930.

JOHNSON, BEN D.
Insurance executive. **Career:** Winnfield Life Insurance Company, Natchitoches, LA, chief executive. **Business Addr:** Chief Executive, Winnfield Life Insurance Company, 315 North, Natchitoches, LA 71457.

JOHNSON, BEN E.
Coordinator. **Personal:** Born Jan 31, 1937, Ashley County, AR; married Marlene; children: Jan, Paula, Jay. **Educ:** Univ of WI Milwaukee, BS, 1975, Cert Pub Administration, 1987. **Career:** 6th Alderman Dist, alderman 1971-; Milwaukee Common Coun, pres; City of Milwaukee, city clerk; Milwaukee Area Technical College, small business coordinator, currently. **Orgs:** Black Caucus Natl League of Cities; 56th Dist vice pres WI League of Munic Exec Comm; joint congress state senate co supv & alderman; legis serv ctr Natl League of Cities Human Resources Comm; Milwaukee Area Manpower Council; Mil Urban Oserv; bd chmn Milwaukee Social Dev Commn 1974-; Milwaukee Econ Dev Comm; corp mem Milwaukee Urban League; bd dir CHPASW; adv com SE WI Reg Plan Commn; NAACP; bd of Greater Milwaukee Counc of Arts for Child; Milwaukee Rec Task Force; Sch Breakfast Coalition Bd; Milwaukee Pabst Theater Bd; Milwaukee Hear Soc Bd; Milwaukee Youth Serv Bureau Plan Com; Milwaukee House Task Force; adv bd Sickle Cell Anemia Found; adv bd Harambee Revit Proj; Milwaukee Repretory Theatre Bd; Milwaukee Perf Arts Ctr Bd; Milwaukee Caucus on Aging; MilwaukeeForum; N Side Bus Assn Fd mem; N Side Pol Action Ctr Found. **Honors/Awds:** Cent City Bus Fed Civic Awd 1975; Walnut Improvement Coun Civic Awd 1975; Friend of Arts Milwaukee Comm Journ; Comm Serv Awd First Bapt Ch; Communication Awd CC Rider; Comm Serv Awd Milwaukee Little League; Comm Serv Awd Upper Third St Merchants; Legis Awd Comm Pride Expo; Comm Serv Awd Youth Dev Ctr; Comm Serv Awd Milwaukee Theol Inst; Bicen Awd Central City; Recog & Appreciation Milwaukee Sch of Engr Scholarships from Univ of WI Milwaukee 1955. **Business Addr:** Small Business Coordinator, Milwaukee Area Technical College, Milwaukee Enterprise Center, 2821 N Fourth St, Milwaukee, WI 53212.

JOHNSON, BENJAMIN, JR.
Editor. **Personal:** Born Jul 9, 1950, Louisville, KY; son of Alyce Estelle Elzy Johnson and Benjamin Johnson Sr; married Mary Esther Bullard-Johnson, May 10, 1975; children: Jacquelyn Jameelah, Marilyn Majeedah. **Educ:** Lincoln University, Jefferson City, MO, BA, journalism, 1975; Wayne State University, Detroit, MI, 1983-84; University of Missouri, Columbia, MO, 1987-88. **Career:** Louisville Defender, Louisville, KY, reporter-photographer, 1970-71; Courier-Journal, Louisville, KY, reporter, asst city editor, 1974-78; Post-Tribune, Gary, IN, city editor, 1978-80; Detroit Free Press, Detroit, MI, asst to managing editor, 1980-85; University of Missouri Multicultural Management Program, Columbia, MO, executive director, 1986-87; Columbia Missourian, Columbia, MO, managing editor, 1987-90; St Peterburg Times, St Petersburg, FL, asst managing editor, 1990-; Who's What and Where Consulting Services, Inc, St Petersburg, FL, vice president, currently; managing editor, Multicultural Link, 1990-. **Orgs:** Pultizer Prize judge, Columbia University, 1991, 1992; founding president, Detroit Chapter, NABJ, 1980-82; board member 1979-80, member 1976-, National Association of Black Journalists; vice president, Society of Professional Journalists, Detroit, 1984-85; member, American Society of Newspaper Editors, 1987-92. **Honors/Awds:** Total Commitment Award, 1980, First Place, editorial writing, 1979, Unity Awards in Media; Brotherhood Award, National Conference of Christians and Jews, 1980; First Place, features photography, National Newspaper Publish Assn, 1974; Kentucky Derby, Best Thoroughbred Horse Handicapper in the Country, National Sportswriters Association, 1971. **Military Serv:** USMC, Cpl E4, 1968-70.

JOHNSON, BENJAMIN EARL (AYUBU JOHNSON)
Art director. **Personal:** Born Apr 23, 1943, Brooklyn, NY; children: Brian, Marilyn, Jerri, Nicole. **Educ:** Housatonic Comm Coll, AA art 1974; Univ of Bridgeport, BS art 1979. **Career:** ABDC Inc, project dir; CABHUA New Haven CT, pres 1976-77. **Orgs:** Bd of dirs Art Resources New Haven CT 1976; bd of dirs Channel 8 Affirmative & Action New Haven CT 1974; lectr/art Bapt Correctional Cntr 1974-78; coord/art Harambee Festival 1975; commr CT Commn on the Arts 1976-80; mem Thirdstream 1974-79; visiting lectr Hosuatonic Comm Coll 1976-79; visiting lectr/artist Sacred Heart Univ Individual Artist Garrant CT Commr of the Arts 1974. **Honors/Awds:** Best in show painting Barnum Festival 1976; 1st prize painting oils Barnum Festival 1977; 1st prize painting watercolor Barnum Festival 1979. **Military Serv:** US Air Force, E-4, 8 yrs.

JOHNSON, BENJAMIN WASHINGTON
Treasurer, army officer (retired). **Personal:** Born Jul 24, 1914, Hamilton, VA; son of Ellen Washington Johnson and Benjamin S Johnson; married Nannette Mack Palmer; children: Norbert Carl Benjamin. **Educ:** Columbia Univ NY, AB 1938; Univ of MD, MA 1964. **Career:** NJ State Man Training & Industrial Sch, instructor 1938-42; US Army, pvt to colonel 1942-69; Commonwealth of PA, bureau dir 1970-80; Capital Area Regional Solid Waste Authority, treas 1986-retirement. **Orgs:** Vice pres Urban League of Met Harrisburg 1978-84; vice pres

YMCA Bd of Dirs 1984-; pres Presbyterian Mens Council 1985; life mem NAACP; mem Urban League, VFW. **Honors/Awds:** Pennsylvania Sports Hall of Fame; Sigma Pi Phi; Alpha Phi Alpha; Two Yr Capt Track Team Columbia Univ; World Record Holder 60 Yds & 60 Meters. **Military Serv:** AUS col 27 yrs; US Legion of Merit, Distinguished Military Service Medal Korea, Army Commendation Medal, Several Campaign Medals 1942-69. **Home Addr:** 3301 North 3rd St, Harrisburg, PA 17110.

JOHNSON, BERNETTE JOSHUA
Justice. **Personal:** Born Jun 17, 1943, Donaldsonville, LA; daughter of Frank Joshua Jr & Olivia Wire Joshua; divorced; children: David Kirk, Rachael Denise. **Educ:** Spelman College, BA, 1964; Louisiana State University Law Center, JD, 1969. **Career:** US Department of Justice, summer intern, 1967; NAACP Legal Defense Fund, community organizer, 1964-66; New Orleans Legal Assistance Corp, attorney, 1969-73; self-employed, lawyer, 1973-77; AFNA National Education Foundation, dir, 1977-81; City of New Orleans, deputy city attorney, 1981-84; State of Louisiana, judge/justice, 1984-. **Orgs:** National Bar Association, chair-elect, judicial council, 1996-97; NBA, secretary, judicial council, 1992-96; Spelman College Alumnae Association, pres NO chapter, 1992-94; Zeta Phi Beta Sorority, financial secretary, 1992-94; Southern Christian Leadership Conf, pres, NO women, 1989-94; National Association Women Judges, district dir, 1992-94; YWCA, bd mem, 1992-94; NOLAC, bd pres, 1994-96. **Honors/Awds:** NAACP, Citizenship Award, 1996; Martinet Legal Society, 1995; NOLAC, Ernest N Morial Award, 1992; YWCA, Role Model Award, 1992. **Special Achievements:** Public Speaker; Community Organizer. **Business Addr:** Justice, Louisiana Supreme Ct, 301 Loyola Ave, New Orleans, LA 70112, (504)568-8062.

JOHNSON, BETTY JO
Educator. **Personal:** Born Aug 14, 1940, Rankin Cty, MS; daughter of Louise Hayes Johnson and Louis Johnson; divorced. **Educ:** Piney Woods School MS, AA (Highest Rank) 1960; Tougaloo Coll MS, BA 1964; Jackson State Univ MS, MEd 1971; Memphis State Univ Memphis, EdD 1976. **Career:** Jackson Publ School System MS, teacher 1964-67; Lawyers Com for Civil Rights Under Law Jackson MS, legal sec 1967-69; Cty Health Improvement Proj Univ of MS Medical Center, fiscal spec 1970; MS Dept of Public Welfare Title IV, planning & eval specialist 1972-73; Comm Ed Ext Jackson MS, curriculum spec Headstart 1972; Alcorn State Univ, visiting instructor 1973; Memphis State Univ, grad asst 1973-76; AR State Univ, assoc prof 1976-78; Shelby State Comm Coll, head dept of gen & early childhood educ, prof 1978-89; LeMoyne-Owen College, coordinator, professor, early childhood education 1989-96; Shelby State Community College, dept head of education, 1996-. **Orgs:** Kappa Delta Pi 1976-; Natl Association for the Ed of Young Children 1976; Phi Delta Kappa 1978-; Association for Childhood Ed; TN Association for Young Children; Memphis Urban League; Delta Sigma Theta; Memphis in May Ed Com; Memphis Association for Young Children; Tennessee Association for Supervision and Curriculum Development 1988-; bd of examiners, Tennessee Department of Education. **Honors/Awds:** Women of Color in the Struggle, A Consortium of Doctors, Atlanta, GA, 1991; Tennessee Outstanding Achievement Award, 1992. **Business Addr:** Head, Department of Education, Shelby State Community College, PO Box 40568, Memphis, TN 38174-0568, (901)544-5345.

JOHNSON, BEULAH C. See Obituaries section.

JOHNSON, BEVERLEY ERNESTINE
Government official. **Personal:** Born May 16, 1953, Chevenly, MD; daughter of Joanne Juanita Scott and Ernest Charles Lane; married Allen Johnson (divorced 1983); children: Allen II. **Educ:** University of Maryland, College Park, MD, BS, 1985. **Career:** Dept of Housing & Urban Development, Washington, DC, housing management officer, 1980-87; Boston Redevelopment Authority, Boston, MA, deputy director community/economic dev, 1987-. **Home Addr:** 25 Goodrich Road #2, Jamaica Plain, MA 02130.

JOHNSON, BEVERLY
Model, actress, singer. **Personal:** Born 1952, Buffalo, NY; married Billy Potter, 1971 (divorced 1973); children: Anansa. **Educ:** Northeastern University, pre-law, attended. **Career:** Glamour Mag, professional fashion model, 1971; Halston, runway model; National Airlines, television ad singer; appeared in numerous commercials; Vogue Mag, cover model, 1974, June 1975; Elle Mag, cover model; singer with Phil Anastasia; solo singer, album, Don't Lose the Feeling; film appearances include: Land of Negritude, 1975; Ashanti, 1979; National Lampoon's Loaded Weapon 1, 1992; Meteor Man, 1992; author, Guide to a Life of Beauty, Times Books, 1981; guest appearances on the Oprah Winfrey Show, Arsenio Hall Show; Revlon Cosmetics, professional model, currently; JC Penney Portrait Studio/Wilhelmina Modeling Agency promotional tour, natl young model search promoter, 1992. **Orgs:** Africare; Atlanta Black Educational Fund; AIDS Awareness Campaign. **Honors/Awds:** First Black cover model for numerous magazines including: Glamour, 1971, Vogue, August 1974, Elle.

JOHNSON, BILL WADE
Business executive. **Personal:** Born May 9, 1943, Idabel, OK; married Barbara. **Educ:** Central Oklahoma State Univ, BA 1965. **Career:** OIC Chicago IL, exec dir 1976-; OIC Pittsburgh PA, exec dir 1970-71; OIC Intl, field specialist 1970-71; Oklahoma City OIC, dir 1968-70; Night Training Oklahoma City OIC, supr 1965-68. **Orgs:** Chmn Frederick Douglass HA 1965-68; mem City of Chicago Manpower Planning Council; former convenor Region III OIC's of Amer; chmn bd dir Career Devel Inc; chmn bd Hill Dist Fed Credit Union 1975-76; mem bd dir Ozanam Strings; Kappa Alpha Psi Frat; Chicago Assembly; numerous other committees, boards and councils. **Business Addr:** 7 E 73rd St, Chicago, IL 60619.

JOHNSON, BOBBIE GENE
Elected government official, business executive. **Personal:** Born Jul 8, 1941, Bethpage, TN; son of Jim Carter Johnson; married Fenecia Wiggins, Jan 17, 1987; children: Sanjeanetta, Marty, Nichelle. **Educ:** TN State Univ, 1962. **Career:** City of Gallatin, planning comm 1968-78, indus bd 1982-; Mid-Cumberland Council, bd of dirs at large PIC 1982-; Co Court of Sumner Co, school comm 1982-; County Court, county comm; owner Mattie Lou's Flowers 1981-; pres Springfield Ford-Linc-Merc 1982-; pres Ford-Linc-Merc of Logan Co 1984-. **Orgs:** Mem NAACP; deacon First Baptist Church; patron OES; mem 32 Mason. **Honors/Awds:** Dollars & Sense 1989; Black Enterprise 1988.

JOHNSON, BOBBY JOJO
City official. **Personal:** Born Jan 11, 1947, Pine Hill, AL; married Estory Mason; children: James W, Jolanda, Joe. **Educ:** Booker T Washington Business College, diploma 1972. **Career:** Alabama Center for Higher Education, veteran counselor 1972-73; Wilcox County, commisioner 1981-95; Wilcox County Comm Camden, AL Comm Dist 5, chmn of County Comm 1989-95. **Orgs:** Life member Disabled American Veterans; political adviser Wilcox County Branch NAACP; president Wilcox County Dem Conf 1976; bd of dir Alabama New South Coalition 1989; chmn Political Action Comm Alabama New South Coalition 1989. **Honors/Awds:** Outstanding Young Men of America US Jaycees 1980; Lyndon B Johnson Political Freedom Award Alabama Dem Conference 1981; Hall of Fame, Zeta Eta Omega Chapter of Alpha Kappa Alpha Sorority, Inc, 1988. **Military Serv:** US Army, sp-4, 2 yrs; Purple Heart Vietnam Service Medal. **Home Addr:** PO Box 29, Pine Hill, AL 36769. **Business Addr:** Chairman, Wilcox County Commission, PO Box 488, Camden, AL 36726.

JOHNSON, BRENT E.
Educational administrator, consultant. **Personal:** Born Jan 17, 1947, Springfield, MA; son of Matilda Edmonds Johnson and Alvin Johnson; divorced; children: Jacye Arnee. **Educ:** Hampton Inst, BS 1968; West GA Coll, MA 1975-77; Atlanta Univ. **Career:** Presbyterian Church in US, personnel dir 1974-78; AMTAR Inc, vice pres 1977-80; Atlanta Univ, dir of admissions 1980-86; Consortium for Graduate Study in Management, St Louis, MO, director of marketing and recruiting, 1986-89; The Success Factor, Atlanta, GA, managing principal, 1989-; Clark Atlanta Univ, Atlanta, GA, asst dean & director of MBA program, 1991-. **Orgs:** Pres bd mem Northwest YMCA, 1975-78; consultant Grad Mgmt Adm Council 1984 ; mem Natl Hampton Alumni Assn 1972-; pres Atlanta Univ Staff Assembly 1981-84; chmn & founder Minority Admissions Recruitment Network 1981-86; chairman, Minority Affairs Advisory Committee, Graduate Management Admission Council, 1986-89. **Honors/Awds:** Contributor Black Collegian Magazine 1980-; Developed Destination MBA Program, National Black MBA Association, 1987; recognized for work with minorities in MBA programs, African-American MBA Assn, Univ of Chicago, 1990. **Military Serv:** USNG staff sgt 3 yrs. **Business Addr:** Asst Dean & Director of MBA Program, Clark Atlanta University, School of Business, J P Brawley Dr & Fair St, SW, Atlanta, GA 30314.

JOHNSON, BUCK (ALFONSO JR.)
Professional basketball player. **Personal:** Born Jan 3, 1964, Birmingham, AL. **Educ:** Univ of Alabama, University, AL, 1982-86. **Career:** Forward: Houston Rockets, 1986-92, Washington Bullets, 1992-. **Business Addr:** Professional Basketball Player, Washington Wizards, Capital Centre, 1 Harry S Truman Dr, Landover, MD 20785.

JOHNSON, C. CHRISTINE
Educational administrator. **Personal:** Born Jun 19, 1928, Jackson, MS; daughter of Cornelius Johnson and Simon Johnson; children: Edward Christian. **Educ:** Univ MD at Munich, MS 1960. **Career:** NY State Div Human Rights, field rep 1971; Hamilton Coll Clinton, NY, dir Higher Educ Opportunity Program 1972-. **Orgs:** Air Force Assn; Retired Officers Assn; past pres NY State Higher Educ Oppor Professional Orgn; NY state pres of Amer Assn of Non-White Concerns (now Amer Assn of Multi-Cultural Counseling & Development); NY State Health Sys Agency; Bd of Visitors of Central NY Psychiatric Cntr; NY State's only Forensic Psychiatric Center; Professional Bus Women's Assn; NAACP; Natl & NY State Assn Human Rights Workers; Opera Guild; rep Urban Renewal Prog Dayton, OH 1958; Joint Prot/Cath Choir; City Plann (Rome, NY C of C); Tri-State Mental Health Bd; pres Rome Day Care Ctr; Black Women in Higher Education; NY State Higher Education Opportunity Program/Professional Organization; Board of Visitors of Central NY Psychiatric Center, president; Frontiers International. **Honors/Awds:** NOW Unsung Heroine Spl Award of Honor for Achievement in Working with Young Coll Women 1978; nom Female Heroine of Yr Pac Air Force 1969 (10th of 250 candidates); Hamilton College Alumni Council Bell Ringer Award for Outstanding Achievement in Meritorious Service, 1991. **Military Serv:** USAF Maj 1950-70; Vietnam Hon Medal 1st Class; Outstanding Munitions Officer 1962; Recomm Viet People-To-People Prog Partic; Bronze Star; USAF Comm Medal. **Business Addr:** Dir Higher Education, Hamilton College, 198 College Hill Rd, Clinton, NY 13323.

JOHNSON, CAGE SAUL
Educator, scientist. **Personal:** Born Mar 31, 1941, New Orleans, LA; son of Esther Georgiana Saul Johnson and Cage Spooner Johnson; married Shirley; children: Stephanie, Michelle. **Educ:** Creighton Univ Coll of Med, MD 1965. **Career:** Univ So CA, instr in med 1971-74, asst prof med 1974-80, assoc prof medicine 1980-88, prof of medicine 1988-. **Orgs:** Chm Adv Comm Genetically Hndcpd Prsns Pgm, CA Dept Hlth Serv 1978-; vice-chm bd dir Sickle Cell Self-Help Asso Inc 1983-88; sec bd of directors, Sickle Cell Disease Research Foundation, 1986-94; sec, EE Just Society 1985-93, pres, 1993-95; review comm chmn, Nat Heart Lung and Blood Inst, 1989-91. **Honors/Awds:** Alpha Omega Alpha. **Military Serv:** AUS mjr 1967-69; Air Medal with "V". **Business Addr:** Professor of Medicine, University of Southern California, 2025 Zonal Avenue RMR 306, Los Angeles, CA 90033.

JOHNSON, CALIPH
Attorney, educator. **Personal:** Born Oct 3, 1938, St Joseph, LA; married Cheryl Helena Chapman. **Educ:** Univ of Maryland, BA 1964; San Jose State U, MA 1968; Univ of San Francisco Sch of Law, JD 1972; Georgtown Univ Law Ctr, LlM 1973. **Career:** Thurgood Marshall School of Law, Southwest Inst for Equal Employment, Thurgood Marshall School of Law TX Southern Univ, dir 1975-78; Office of Gen Counsel Equal Employment Opportunity Commn, appellate atty 1973-75; Inst for Public Interest Represent, atty 1972-73; Oakland Citizens Com for Urban Renewal, exec dir 1970-72; City of Oakland CA, admin analyst 1970-72; Univ of Miaduguri Nigeria, consultant 1978-80; Office of Lawyer Training Legal Serv Corp , advocacy trainer 1978-80; EEOC, hearing examiner 1979-80; Title VII Project Natl Bar Assn Bd of Dir Gulf Coast Legal Found, faculty. **Orgs:** Mem commn on law office exon Am Bar Assn; labor law sect Nat Bar Assn; civillitigation com Fed Bar Assn; civil procedure & clin sec assn of Am Law Sch; Grad Fellowship Inst for Pub Int Rep Georgetown Univ Law Ctr 1972-73; a response to crises of enforcing fair employment Houston Lawyer 1975; coursematerial on fair empl lit TX So Univ 1976; integrated clinical curr module TX So Univ & HEW 1978-80; teamsters v US Impact on Seniority Relief TX SoNBA Law Rev 1979. **Honors/Awds:** Book review Let Them Be Judges Howard Univ Law Jour 1980. **Military Serv:** USN lt 3yrs. **Business Addr:** 3201 Wheeler, Houston, TX 77004.

JOHNSON, CARL EARLD
Financial company executive. **Personal:** Born Dec 3, 1936, New York, NY; son of Gwendolyn Johnson and Francis Johnson; married Mozelle Baker, Jun 6, 1961; children: Brian A, Carla D. **Educ:** City University of New York, BS, 1958, MBA, 1963. **Career:** Western Electric, human resources associate, 1963-68; Mobil Oil Corp., human resources manager, 1968-86; Campbell Soup Co., acting director, government compliance, 1986-90; Philip Morris Companies, corporate manager, affirmative action, 1990-91; Summit Bank, vice pres, employee relations & compliance programs, 1991-. **Orgs:** National Urban Affairs Council-New Jersey, chair, employment committee, 1991-; The EDGES Group, 1990-; The Lions Club, 1992-; Society for Human Resources Management, 1976-; Medgar Evers College Curriculum Development Committee, 1974-76; Institute of Management Consultants, 1986-; Vice Pres's Task Force on Youth Motivation, 1969-75; Black Executive Exchange Program, visiting professor, 1970-; Hispanic Bankers Association of New Jersey, founder; New Jersey Urban Bankers Association, founder. **Special Achievements:** Shattering the Glass Ceiling, 1993; Employment Discrimination in the State of New Jersey (1980-1984), 1985; Employment Discrimination in New York (1980-1984), 1985; Employers Should Outline Job Terms and Conditions, 1985. **Military Serv:** US Army Reserve, captain, 1958-70. **Business Addr:** Vice Pres, Employee Relations & Compliance Programs, Summit Bank, 301 Carnegie Center, Princeton, NJ 08543.

JOHNSON, CARL ELLIOTT
Mechanical engineer. **Personal:** Born Oct 4, 1956, Houston, TX; married Mary Ann Jean; children: Patric, Cristina, Carren. **Educ:** Prairie View A&M Univ, BSME 1979. **Career:** Union Carbide, maintenance engr 1979-83; Monsanto Chemical Co, sr process engr 1984-85, process supervisor 1985-, utilities supervisor. **Orgs:** Corp solicitor United Way 1985-; youth basketball YMCA 1987; Speakers Bureau. **Business Addr:** Process Supervisor/Sr Engr, Monsanto Chemical Co, #1 Monsanto Rd, Nitro, WV 25143.

JOHNSON, CARL J.
Social worker. **Personal:** Born Aug 23, 1911, Houma, LA; son of Lenora McGuin Johnson and Spencer Johnson; married Narvella Moses Johnson, Mar 27, 1956; children: Carol Ann, Charlynne Diane. **Educ:** CA State Univ of LA, AA Mus, BA Sociology, BS Soc Sci, LLB. **Career:** Dance band leader & vocalist 1932-70; LA Cty, soc worker 1934-37; News Guardian Weekly, publ 1940-42; CA State Correctional School, group suprv 1940-43; LA Cty Juvenile Hall, boys couns 1947-48; LA Cty, dep marshal, lt ret 1949-69; CA Ofc of Econ Oppty, comm prog analyst 1969-71; City of LA, manpower analyst 1971-73; SW Comprehensive Med Corp, sr alcoholic couns 1973-76. **Orgs:** Real estate broker 1935-77; instr Rio Hondo Jr Coll 1967-68; instr Fremont Adult School 1962; US customs officer 1943; asst sgt-at-arms CA State Senate 1942; ins salesman Golden State Life Ins 1935; mem Douglass Life Ins 1940-41, 23rd Dist Comdr 1964-65, LA Cty Comdr 1971-71; vcomdr Dept of CA AmerLeg 1974-75; pres So CA Area Conf of NAACP 1962-64; treas Waller Lodge F&AM No 49 1941-44; vice pres LA Cty Young Rep 1938; state treas CA Young Rep 1946; chmn Rep Cty Central Comm 53rd Dist 1948; life mem Alpha Phi Alpha, NAACP, Amer Legion, LA Cty Sheriffs Relief Assoc; mem CA Vet Bd 1968-69, Egyptian Temple No 5, Platform Comm Rep State Central Comm; consult Amer Legion Natl Membership Comm. **Honors/Awds:** LA Cty Bd of Suprv Awd 1964; LA City Council Awd 1968; LA Human Rel Bur Awd 1968; LA Bd of Ed Awd 1964; LA Cty Marshal Awd 1968; Ventura Cty Marshal Awd 1968; CA Vet Bd Awd 1969. **Military Serv:** US Army, T-5, 1944-46. **Home Addr:** 976 E 55 St, Los Angeles, CA 90011.

JOHNSON, CARRIE CLEMENTS
Educator (retired), company executive. **Personal:** Born Jan 2, 1931, Atlanta, GA; daughter of Lucile Clements and Emanuel Clements; married Alfred James Johnson; children: Alfia Katherine. **Educ:** Morris Brown Coll, Atl, GA, BS 1951; Columbia Univ NY, MA 1954; State Univ of NY at Buffalo, EdD 1978. **Career:** Fulton Co Bd of Ed Atlanta, GA, high sch tchr 1951-61; Morris Brown Coll, Atlanta, GA, dir of career plng & plcmnt asst prof 1961-67; State Univ Coll at Buffalo, cnslr 1967-71, dir of cnslng serv 1971-83, assoc dir 1977-78, asst prof bsns stds 1983-85; dir of classified staff development Fulton Cty Schools 1986-88; Fulton County Board of Education, Atlanta, GA, exec dir, 1988-95; Johnson & Johnson, pres, currently. **Orgs:** HEW fellow US Govt Dept HEW 1979-81; Natl Urban League So Reg 1966-67; assoc dir VISTA Training; Am Prsnl & Guidance Asso 1967-; bd dir Buffalo Area Engineering Awrness for Minorities 1982; bd dir Child Dev Inst Buffalo 1983; schlrshp comm Buffalo Urban League 1984; vice pres Jack & Jill of America Inc 1974; Zeta Phi Beta; The Links Inc. **Honors/Awds:** Life Long Learning Awrd Alpha Kappa Alpha Sor Buffalo, NY 1984; Guide to Graduate Opportunities for Minorities 1971; selected HEW Fellow US Govt Dept Of HEW 1979; elected local, cnty, regnl Tchr of Yr 1959; Georgia Staff Development Council, Exemplary Award, 1990. **Home Addr:** 3965 Old Fairburn Rd SW, Atlanta, GA 30331.

JOHNSON, CARROLL JONES
Mayor, educational administrator. **Personal:** Born Mar 1, 1948, Blackville, SC; daughter of Louise Felder Jones and Rufus Jones; divorced; children: F Kelvin Johnson, Herman N Johnson, Wayne Johnson. **Educ:** Voorhees Coll, Denmark SC, BS, 1978; Univ of South Carolina. **Career:** Barnwell School Dist, Blackville SC, literacy coordinator, 1980-; mayor of Blackville SC. **Orgs:** Barnwell County Help Line, Barnwell County Community Improvement Board, NAACP. **Honors/Awds:** Community Service Award, Delta Sigma Theta, 1987; Public Service Award, Alpha Kappa Alpha, 1988; Citizen of the Year, Omega Psi Phi, 1989; Woman of the Year, Barnwell County Chamber of Commerce, 1989. **Home Addr:** PO Box 305, Blackville, SC 29817.

JOHNSON, CARROLL RANDOLPH, JR.
Music co. executive, cleric. **Personal:** Born Jun 13, 1951, Baltimore, MD; son of Delores Patricia Johnson and Carroll R Johnson Sr; married Muriel Minor Johnson, Aug 29, 1970; children: Duane, Sherry, Keith. **Educ:** Johns Hopkins University, BA, 1972. **Career:** C & P Telephone, bus ofc asst mgr, 1972-77; Praise Recording Co, president, 1977-79; Bell Atlantic, computer consultant, 1979-87; Evergreen Co., president, 1987-; Maximum Life Christian Church, pastor, currently; Zamar Music Group, president, currently. **Orgs:** Baltimore Council for Self-Esteem, chairman of the board, 1991-; Baltimore Cable Access Corp, board member, 1992; Mid-Atlantic Diocese-Bibleway Churches, executive secretary, 1991-. **Special Achievements:** Mayor's Citation, Outstanding Community Service, 1992; Maximum Life Songs, released gospel album, 1991. **Home Phone:** (410)298-1238. **Business Addr:** President, Zamar Music Group, 1928 Woodlawn Dr, Baltimore, MD 21207, (410)597-9925.

JOHNSON, CATO, II
Health company executive. **Personal:** Born Aug 26, 1947, Memphis, TN; son of Frankie Scales Johnson and Cato Johnson; married Georgette Alexander Johnson, May 12, 1976; children: Cato III. **Educ:** Memphis State University, BS, education, 1970, MS, education, 1971; Tennessee School of Banking, Vanderbilt University. **Career:** Memphis Urban/Memphis State University, manpower specialist, 1971-73; General Motors Acceptance Corporation, field representative, 1971-74; First Tennessee Bank, personnel assistant, 1974-75; First Tennessee National Corporation, affirmative action coordinator, 1975-78, personnel administrator and affirmative action coordinator, 1978-80, manager of personnel, 1980-81; Memphis State University, assistant to director, 1981-83; The Regional Medical Center, vice president of corporate affairs, 1983-85; Methodist Health Systems, senior vice president of corporate affairs, 1985-. **Orgs:** Board of directors, Tennessee Comprehensive Health Insurance Pool; Memphis Convention and Visitors Bureau; Kiwanis; Governor's Council on Health & Physical Fitness; Tennessee Human Services Advisory Council; Junior League of Memphis Board; president's council, LeMoyne-Owen College; bd of dirs, TN Comprehensive Health Ins Pool; advisory comm, Sr Citizen's Services; editorial bd, WPTY Channel 24; bd, Jr League of Memphis; pres council, LeMoyne-Owen Coll; mem, Arts in the Park, Memphis Arts Festival; co chair, Mayor WW Herenton Transition Team, parks & facitities comm; vice chair, bd of dirs, Memphis Area Chamber of Commerce; exec comm, Boy Scouts of America; Memphis Zoological Bd; Memphis & Shelby County Sports Authority Bd; Goals for Memphis Race Relations Comm; Mayor's Mud Island Task Force; mem, Memphis & Shelby County Med Society; pres, Univ of Memphis Natl Alumni Assn; Jim Rout, Shelby County Mayor-elect, transition team, Don Sundquist; Gov of TN, transition team. **Honors/Awds:** Appeared on numerous radio and T.V. talk shows. **Business Addr:** Senior Vice President, Corporate Affairs, Methodist Health Systems, 1211 Union Ave, Suite 700, Memphis, TN 38104.

JOHNSON, CHARLES
Educator (retired). **Personal:** Born Jul 28, 1927, Acmar, AL; married Carol Ann; children: Carla, Charles. **Educ:** Howard Univ, BS 1953, MD 1963; DC Gen Hosp, Internship in Med 1963-64. **Career:** Lincoln Hosp, private practice, 1967-70; Duke Univ Medical Center, Durham, NC, 1970-96, asst prof of medicine, 1970-74, assoc prof of medicine, 1974-95, prof of medicine, 1995-96, prof of medicine emeritus, 1996, special advisor to chancellor for health affairs, 1997-. **Orgs:** Mem Durham Acad of Med; mem bd of admiss Duke Univ of Coll of Med 1976-81; mem Kappa Alpha Psi 1950-, Amer Soc of Intl Med, Amer Coll of Physicians, Amer Diabetes Assoc; adv comm Minority Students NC; pres Old North State Medical Society, 1973-75; chmn Reg III NMA 1975-78; sec House of Delegates NMA 1975-77; vspeaker House of Delegates NMA 1977-79; speaker House of Delegates NMA 1980-81; dir NMA Africa Health Proj 1975-80; bd of trustees, NMA, 1982-1988, sec bd of trustees, 1984-86, chmn bd of trustees, 1986-88, pres-elect, 1989-90, pres, 1990-91; Doric Lodge 28, Durham Consistory 218, Shriner, Zafa Temple 176, 33rd Deg Mason, St Titus Epis Ch. **Honors/Awds:** Disting Kappaman Achievement Awd Durham Alumni Chap 1978; Elected Outstanding Physician of the Year 1980; Duke Univ, Medal for Distinguished and Meritorius Service, 1997. **Military Serv:** USAF s/sgt 1946-49, capt 1953-57, Jet Fighter Pilot. **Home Addr:** 1209 East Pointe Dr, Durham, NC 27712.

JOHNSON, CHARLES BERNARD
Sports journalist. **Personal:** Born Mar 9, 1954, Detroit, MI; son of Bessie Mae Gayden Johnson (deceased) and Ira B Johnson (deceased); married Tara Halsey Johnson, Jul 1, 1989; children: Janay, Julius. **Educ:** Michigan State University, East Lansing, MI, BA, journalism, 1975. **Career:** The Flint Journal, Flint, MI, sports columnist, 1975-88; USA Today, Washington, DC, sports writer, 1988-; Black Entertainment TV Sports Report, Washington, DC, panelist, 1988-. **Orgs:** Sports task force steering committee, Natl Assn Black Journalists, 1989-; president, NABJ-Mid Michigan Chapter, 1986-87. **Honors/Awds:** Honorary Inductee, Greater Flint Afro-American Hall of Fame, 1988; Man of the Year, Flint Golden Gloves, 1982; Honored for Community Service, National Assn of Media Women Inc, 1987, Central Flint Optimists, Club, 1985; In Appreciation for Effort, Greater Flint Wrestling Coaches Assn 1984. **Business Addr:** Sports Writer, USA Today, 1000 Wilson Blvd, Arlington, VA 22229, (703)276-5944.

JOHNSON, CHARLES E.
Administrator. **Personal:** Born Jul 1, 1946, Woodville, MS; married Bessie M Hudson; children: Vanessa Lashea, Adrianne Monique, Andrea Melita, Krystal Charlese. **Educ:** Alcorn State U, BS 1968; So U, MEd 1971. **Career:** Wilkinson Co School Dist, supt of Educ 1976-97; Amite Co School Dist, teacher 1974-75; Brookhaven School Dist, teacher 1972-73; Wilkinson Co School Dist, teacher 1969-71; Bay St Louis School Dist, teacher 1967-69. **Orgs:** NAACP; Mississippi Teachers Association; Mississippi Association of School Superintendents; Mississippi Cattlesmen Association; National Cattlesmen Association. **Honors/Awds:** Charles E Johnson Classroom Bldg Centreville MS 1980; Charles E Johnson, Administration Bldg, Woodville, MS, 1997. **Business Addr:** Principal, Iberville Parish School Bd, PO Box 1008, Plaquemine, LA 70765, (504)687-7066.

JOHNSON, CHARLES EDWARD
Industrial scientist. **Personal:** Born Feb 24, 1938, Dallas, NC; son of Ira G Johnson and Lydia D Johnson; married Gladys E Hawkins; children: Nikolas, Andre, Sean, Markus, Karari. **Educ:** Morgan State Univ, BS 1960; Univ of Cincinnati, PhD 1966. **Career:** Morgan State Univ, prof of biology 1973-74; Community Coll of Baltimore, lecturer 1974; The Union Cincinnati, adjunct prof 1980-81; Procter & Gamble Co, section head 1981-88; Clairol Inc, Stamford CT, mgr 1988-, manager, currently. **Orgs:** Mem AAAS 1980-83, Amer Soc for Microbiology; bd trustees West End Health Clinic 1980-82. **Honors/Awds:** NDEA Fellowship; Patent detergent composition containing protedytic enzymes elaborated by Thermactinomyces Vulgaris 15734, 1972. **Business Addr:** Director, Technical Support, Clairol Inc, 1 Blachley Rd, Stamford, CT 06902.

JOHNSON, CHARLES EDWARD, JR.
Professional baseball player. **Personal:** Born Jul 20, 1971, Ft Pierce, FL. **Educ:** Miami (Fla.). **Career:** Florida Marlins, catcher, 1994-. **Business Addr:** Professional Baseball Player, Florida Marlins, Pro Player Stadium, NW 199th St, Miami, FL 33169, (305)356-5848.

JOHNSON, CHARLES EVERETT
Professional football player. **Personal:** Born Jan 3, 1972, San Bernardino, CA; married Tanisha; children: Charles III. **Educ:** Univ of Colorado, degree in marketing. **Career:** Pittsburgh Steelers, wide receiver, 1994-. **Business Addr:** Professional Football Player, Pittsburgh Steelers, Three Rivers Stadium, 300 Stadium Circle, Pittsburgh, PA 15212, (412)323-1200.

JOHNSON, CHARLES H.
Educator. **Personal:** Born Mar 5, 1932, Conway, SC; married Vermelle J; children: Temple, Charles H Jr. **Educ:** SC State Coll, BS 1954; SC State Coll, MEd 1969; VA State Coll; Univ SC Columbia SC. **Career:** Claflin Coll Orangeburg SC, dean of students; educator & prin pub sch 1962-67; Claflin Coll, various advancing positions 1967-. **Orgs:** Mem SC Sutdent Personnel Assn; So Coll Personnel Assn; Nat Stud Pers Adminstrs; Nat Educ Assn; Professional Club Inc (life mem); bd dir Orangeburg Co Council on Aging; VFW; bd dir Orangeburg United Fund; bd trustees Trinity United Meth Ch; Omega Psi Phi; IBPO Elks of the World; life mem, SC State University Alumni; NAACP; Chaflin Coll, distinguished bd of visitors; life mem, PTA; bd of dirs, United Way; bd of dirs, Palmetto Lou Cty Health Systems; commission mem, Orangeburg Area Development Ctr. **Honors/Awds:** Cert of merit lifetime scholarships Peace Officers Training Svc; recipient various Naval Awards & Citations; Honorary Doctorate Aspen University, 1997. **Military Serv:** USN petty officer.

JOHNSON, CHARLES H.
Attorney. **Personal:** Born May 24, 1946, New Haven, CT; son of Helen Taylor Johnson and Charles H Johnson. **Educ:** Hotchkiss School, Lakeville, CT, 1964; Yale Univ, BA 1968; Yale Univ Law Sch, JD 1972. **Career:** Montgomery McCracken Walker & Rhoads, attorney private practice 1972-75; US Food & Drug Admin, asst chief counsel 1975-79; US Equal Employ Oppor Commn, supervisory trial atty 1978-79; CT Gen Life Ins Co, atty 1979-82; New England Mutual Life Ins Co, counsel & asst sec, 1982-93; attorney, private practice, 1993-; Whittier Law School, Los Angeles, CA, adjunct prof, 1995. **Orgs:** Mem Natl Bar Assn. **Honors/Awds:** Operations Crossroads Africa-Ethiopia 1964; Peace Corps Volunteer Senegal W Africa 1968-69. **Military Serv:** AUS Hon Discharge 1976. **Business Addr:** Attorney, PO Box 2803, Venice, CA 90294, (213)295-9920.

JOHNSON, CHARLES LEE
Dentist. **Personal:** Born Dec 18, 1941, Atlanta, GA; son of Ollie Lee Moore Johnson and Willie James Johnson; divorced; children: Nichole Denise, Charlena Natasha. **Educ:** Morris Brown Coll, BS 1964; Meharry Med Coll, 1964-65; Howard Univ, DDS, 1969; Univ of MD Provident Hospital, certificate of oral surgery internship, 1970; Walter Reed Hospital; Emory Univ; Medical Coll of GA; Intl Congress of Oral Implantology (Paris), post doctoral studies 1972. **Career:** Private practice, dentist; Metro-Atlanta Doctor's Clinic; Ben Massell Char Dental Clinic, staff 1972-; Atlanta Coll for Med & Dental Assistance, consult 1972-. **Orgs:** Am Endodontic Soc; Am Soc of Clinical Hypnosis; Jamaica Dental Soc; Am Dental Assn; GA Dental Assn; N Georgia Dental Soc, vice pres; Acad of Gen Dentistry; Morris Brown Coll Alumni Assn; American Cancer Soc; Atlanta C of C, life member; Phi Beta Sigma 1962; dean of Probates & Pledgees Chi Delta Mu 1966; vice-pres Local Chpt; Butler St YMCA 1972; exec bd dir, Atlanta Urban League; St Anthony Catholic Church; Academy of General Dentistry. **Honors/Awds:** Football scholarship Morris Town Coll 1960; Acad Scholarship GA Higher Educ Assn, 1964-69; President, Med Tech Class, Meharry Coll, 1964-65; Beta Beat Beta Scientific Honor Society, Honorary Member; N Georgia Dental Society, Vice Pres; Howard University, Chi Delta Mu, Vice Pres, 1966; Phi Beta Sigma, Dean of Pledgees and Probates, 1962;. **Business Addr:** Dentist, PC, Metro Atlanta Doctors Clinic, 649 Ashby St NW, Atlanta, GA 30318.

JOHNSON, CHARLES RICHARD
Educator, author, political cartoonist. **Personal:** Born Apr 23, 1948, Evanston, IL; son of Ruby Elizabeth Jackson Johnson and Benjamin Lee Johnson; married Joan New, Jun 1970; children: Malik, Elizabeth. **Educ:** Southern Illinois University, BA 1971, MA 1973; State University of New York at Stony Brook, 1973-76. **Career:** Chicago Tribune, cartoonist, reporter, 1969-70; St Louis Proud, art staff, 1971-72; Univ of Washington, asst prof, 1976-79, assoc prof, 1979-82, prof of English, 1982-; writer and cartoonist, currently; Seattle Review, fiction editor, 1978-. Writings include: Faith and the Good Thing, 1974; Oxherding Tale, 1982; Black Humor, 1970; Half-Past Nation Time, 1972; Charlie's Pad, 1970; Chrlie Smith and the Fritter Tree, 1978; Booker, 1983; The Sorcerer's Apprentice, 1986; Middle Passage, 1990; contributor to numerous anthologies and TV series. **Orgs:** Bd mem, former dir, Associated Writing Programs Awards Series in Short Fiction. **Honors/Awds:** Named journalism alumnus of the year by Southern Illinois Univ, 1981; Governors Award for Literature, State of Washington, 1983; Callaloo Creative Writing Award, 1983; Citation in Pushcart Prize's Outstanding Writers section, 1984; Writers Guild Award for best children's show, 1986; nomination for PEN/Faulkner Award, PEN American Center, 1987; Writer's Guild Award for Best Children's Show (Booker), 1984. **Business Addr:** Professor, Department of English, University of Washington, Seattle, WA 98105.

JOHNSON, CHARLES RONALD, SR.
Legislator & attorney. **Personal:** Born Feb 17, 1951, New York, NY; married Nancy Bradford; children: Jessica Ashley, Charles Ronald Jr. **Educ:** Dartmouth Coll, AB 1971; Univ of CA Berkeley, JD 1974. **Career:** 76th Asmbly Dist NY, assmblymn 1978-80; Atty, pvt prac 1976-78; Sen Minority Ldr NY, criminal justice analyist 1975-76; Bronx Co NY, asst dist atty 1974-75. **Orgs:** Pres DeWitt Clinton Alumni Assn 1979-80. **Honors/Awds:** Man of yr award New York City Housing Police Guardians Assn 1979; man of yr Bronx Lebanon Hosp Ctr; Comm Ldrshp Award 1980; legislator of yr Nat Urban Coalition 1980. **Business Addr:** 1188 Grand Concourse, Bronx, NY 10451.

JOHNSON, CHARLES V.
Judge. **Personal:** Born Jun 11, 1928, Malvern, AR; son of Laura Miller Johnson and Charlie Johnson; married Lazelle S; children: James W Brown, Tracy L, Terri Lynn. **Educ:** AR AM&N Coll Pine Bluff, BA 1954; Univ of WA School of Law Seattle, 1957. **Career:** Attorney, private practice, 1958-69; Municipal Court Seattle, judge, 1969-80, presiding judge 1971-72; State of WA King Cty Superior Court, judge 1981-; Presiding Judge King County Superior Court, 1989-93. **Orgs:** Mem bd of dir WA State Mag Assoc; charter mem Judicial Council Natl Bar Assoc; mem Seattle-King Cty Bch-Bar Liaison Com; mem Amer Jud Soc, Phi Alpha Delta; treas MCT Inc, Cent Area Com for Civil Rights 1963-70, 1st AME Church 1960-; chmn bd mgmt E Madison Branch 1964-69, bd dir Met Br 1964-, pres Metro Branch 1972-73 YMCA; pres Seattle Br NAACP 1959-63; pres NW Area Conf 1965-71; mem natl bd dir 1968-, chmn 1973-79 Natl Legal Comm; chmn Seattle Model Cities Adv Council 1968-72; mem Seattle Lawyers Com for Civil Rights 1968-69; mem Royal Esq Inc; Kiwanis; adv com US Comm on Civil Rights; pres Amer Judges Assoc 1981-82; natl pres Sigma Rho Hon Soc 1954-55; Board member Natl Center for State Courts 1985-90. **Honors/Awds:** Distinguished Citizens Awd Model Cities Seattle 1973; 1st Citizens Awd Seattle 1973; Man of the Year Awd Alpha Phi Alpha 1973; Distinguished Community Awd for United Way, YMCA Service to Youth Award, Benefit Guilds Martin Luther King Community Services Award; Links Human Rights Award; Award for Distinguished Service, Seattle-King County Bar Association 1991; Distinguished Service Award of the National Center for State Courts; Distinguished Alumnus, University of Washington School of Law 1992; Municipal League of King County, Distinguished Service Award, 1994; King County, Public Official of the Year Award, 1994; Washington State Bar Assn, Outstanding Judge Award, 1994. **Military Serv:** Univ S Army, Staff/Sgt, 1948-52. **Home Addr:** 415 Randolph Ave, Seattle, WA 98122.

JOHNSON, CHARLES W.
Educator, business executive. **Personal:** Born Jun 29, 1929, San Antonio; married Josie W Robinson; children: Patrice Y, Norrene E, Josie I. **Educ:** Fisk Univ Nashville, BA magna cu laude math 1951; MA Inst of Tech Cambridge, grad study math 1951-52; Univ MN Minneapolis, grad study mat 1959-62. **Career:** Honeywell Inc, 1956-; Sys Dev Cent, dir 1970-73; Bus Dev & Eng, dir 1973-76; Bus Dev & Eng, vice pres general mgr 1976-; Univ MN, asst prof elec eng1959-60; MN A&M Coll Las Cruces, part-time instr math 1968; MA Inst of Tech Cambridge. **Orgs:** Mem Transonic Aircraft Cont Proj 1952-54; mem Am Mgmt Assn; bd trust Carleton Coll Northfield MI 1970; natl bd trust Nat Urban League 1970-; chmn New Skills Bank Nat Urban League 1973; bd dir Met Med Cent Minnea 1971-73; bd of dirs Denver C of C 1978-; bd dir Ault Inc Minnea 1970-; adv bd NW Nat Bank N Am Off Minnea 1971-73; bd & dir J W Robinson & Sons Houston 1968-; MN state gen chmn Uni Negro Coll Fund 1972; chmn Urban Affairs Com Uni Fund of Minnea 1969; mem Prior Determination Com Uni Fund Minnea; has held many off in various org in the past. **Honors/Awds:** Has publ sev technical papers; distinguished serv awards 2 Minnea & St Paul Urban Leagues 1973; rockefeller fellow award 1951; distinguished serv award Un Fund Minnea Area 1969. **Military Serv:** AUS spec 2nd class 1954-56. **Business Addr:** Vice President, Honeywell Inc, Computers & Manufacturing, Honeywell Plaza MN12-5326, Minneapolis, MN 55408.

JOHNSON, CHARLES WILLIAM
Educational administrator. **Personal:** Born Jan 25, 1922, Ennis, TX; married Mattie Shavers; children: Charles Jr, Phillip Noel, Livette Suzanne. **Educ:** Prairie View A&M Univ, BS 1942; Univ of Southern CA, MS 1947; Meharry Medical Coll, MD 1953. **Career:** Rockefeller Inst for Medical Rsch, visiting investigator 1957-59; Meharry Medical Coll, instructor 1947-49, asst prof 1949-52, acting dept chmn/assoc prof 1953-59, dean school of grad studies 1967-81, vice pres for rsch 1978-81, vice pres and dean school of grad studies 1980-81, vice pres and interim dean school of medicine 1981-82, vice pres for academic affairs emeritus, 1989-. **Orgs:** Mem bd of dirs and chmn bd of governors Cumberland Heights Fdn; mem Amer Soc of Microbiologists, AAAS, Amer Acad of Allergy; mem and vice pres MidCumberland Council on Drug and Alcohol Abuse; mem Amer Assoc of Pathology, Amer Assoc of Clinical Immunology and Allergy, Assoc for Gerontology in Educ,Soc of Rsch Administrators; mem Society of Sigma Xi, Alpha Omega Alpha Hon Soc, Kappa Pi Honorary Soc. **Military Serv:** USCG signalman 1st class 3 yrs. **Business Addr:** Vice Pres for Academic Affairs, Emeritus, Meharry Medical College, 1005 D B Todd Blvd, Nashville, TN 37208.

JOHNSON, CHAS FLOYD
Producer, attorney. **Personal:** Born Feb 12, Camden, NJ; son of Bertha Seagers Johnson and Orange Maull Johnson; married Anne Burford Johnson, Jun 18, 1983; children: Kristin Suzanne. **Educ:** Univ of Delaware 1960-61; Howard Univ, BA 1962; Howard Univ Sch of Law, JD 1965. **Career:** Howard Berg Law Offices, attorney 1965; US Copyright Office, attorney 1967-70; Swedish Ministry of Justice Stockholm, Sweden, attorney 1970; Universal Television, prod coordinator, 1971-74, associate prod, 1974-76, producer, 1976-82, suprvsng prod 1982-, executive producer 1985-. **Orgs:** Screen Actors Guild of America; Producers Guild of America, board of directors; Writers Guild of America; National Academy of Television Arts & Sciences; American Film Institute; Omega Psi Phi; Caucus for Producers, Directors and Writers, 1990-; Crossroads Theatre Arts Academy, 1990; board of directors, Kwanza Foundation, 1985; board of directors, American Independent Video Filmmakers, 1985-90; vice chairman, The Media Forum, 1978-82; Assn of Black Motion Picture and Television Producers, 1980-82. **Honors/Awds:** Emmy Award, Rockford Files, Best TV Drama; Alumni Achvmnt Award Stony Brook Coll Prep, 1979; Outstanding Alumnus Howard Univ Alumni Club of So CA, 1982; Outstanding Alumnus Howard Univ, 1985; LA Area Emmy Award Winner for producing and performing in a KCET/PBS Special "Voices of Our People, A Celebration of Black Poetry" 1981; 3 Emmy Nominations for: Rockford Files, 1978-79, 1979-80, Magnum PI 1982-83, 1983-84; City of LA, Commendations, 1982, 1993; CA State Legislature, Commendation, 1982; CA State Senate, Commendation, 1982; Hawaii State Senate, Commendation, 1988; Hawaii House of Representatives, Commendation, 1988; City of Honolulu, Commendation, 1988. **Special Achievements:** Production credits include: "Rockford Files," producer, 1974-80; "Bret Maverick," producer, 1981-82; "Magnum PI," co-executive producer, 1982-88; "BL Stryker," co-executive producer, 1988-90; "Revealing Evidence," NBC Movie of the Week, executive producer, 1990; "Quantum Leap," co-executive producer, 1992; "Baa Baa Black Sheep," pilot, producer, 1975; "Hellinger's Law," pilot, producer, 1980-81; "Simon and Simon," pilot, producer, 1980; "Silver Fox," pilot, co-creator, executive producer, 1991; "Rockford Files" Movies for TV, 1994-; author: "The Origins of the Stockholm Protocol," US Copyright Society, 1970; co-author: Black Women in Television, 1990. **Military Serv:** US Army, ssgt, 1965-67; Army Commendation Medal, 1967. **Business Addr:** Executive Producer, Universal TV, The Rockford Files, Ren-Mar Studios, Bldg D, 846 North Cahuenga Blvd, Los Angeles, CA 90038.

JOHNSON, CHRISTINE
Administrator. **Personal:** Born Feb 1, 1946, Tyler, TX; children: Ralph Bessard, Roderic Bessard. **Educ:** CA State U, BA 1967f CA State U, MA 1972; Univ of CA Berkeley, doctorate in progress. **Career:** Coll of Alameda, dean student serv 1978-; Coll of Alameda, asst dean 1976-78; Contra Costa Coll, chairperson of counseling-instr 1974-76; Fresno State Univ, asst prof 1971-74; Fresno State Univ, coordinator live & learn center 1969-70; Fresno Co Economic Opportunity Comm, counselor job develop 1968-69. **Orgs:** Consult Regional Ofc of Health & Welfare Head Start San Francisco; CA State Univ Law Enforcement Training Prog; com on status of women Univ of CA Berkeley; mem Am Personnel & Guidance Assn; mem Am Assn of Univ Women; mem Council on Black Am Affaris. **Honors/Awds:** Summer inst fellow Bryn Mawr Summer Inst 1979; outstanding young women of am Fresno 1976; golden educator's award Fresno state Coll 1973; white house fellows finalist Commn on White House Fellows 1972. **Business Addr:** Coll of Alameda, 555 Atlantic Ave, Alameda, CA 94501.

JOHNSON, CLARISSA
Artist, entrepreneur. **Personal:** Born Nov 14, 1913, Detroit, MI; daughter of Bertha Bissell Cassey (deceased) and Alfred Cassey (deceased); married Alfred Johnson, Nov 25, 1960; children: Shirley Pembroke, Rodney Pearson, Laurence Pearson, Glenn Pearson, Charlotte Watson, Patricia Hall. **Career:** Clarissa's Creations, owner, 1978-. **Honors/Awds:** Recognition Award, Negro Business & Professional Womens Club, 1989; Wayne County Community Service Award, 1985; First Place Award, North Rosedale Park Festival of Arts, 1990. **Business Addr:** Owner, Clarissa's Creations, PO Box 47307, Oak Park, MI 48237.

JOHNSON, CLEVELAND, JR.
Communication company executive. **Personal:** Born Aug 17, 1934, Eufaula, AL; son of Arline Petty Johnson and Cleveland Johnson, Sr; married Joan B Maloney; children: Keith Michael, Genevieve Carolyn, Kelly Marie, Cleveland III. **Educ:** Tri State Univ IN, BS 1955; NY Univ, M Public Admin 1975; Attended, Adelphi Univ; NY Police Acad Police Science Program, graduate 1959. **Career:** Investors Planning Corp of Amer 1960-65; Islip Dept of Community Affairs, director 1965-70; Town of Islip Housing Authority, executive director, 1966-71, dir of personnel 1969-70, deputy town supervisor, 1969-71; County of Suffolk Riverhead NY, deputy county exec 1972-79; SUNY at Farmingdale, exec asst to the president 1979-81, vice pres, prof of business, 1981-89; Johnson Diversified Inc, president, 1969-; FCD Construction Corp, president, 1981-88; Allstate Life Insurance Co, director 1983-; Moran Equity Fund, director, 1990-95; bd of dirs, Dental World, Inc, 1985-87; US Department of Health and Human Services, regional director, 1990-93; Health Care Receivable Funding Corp, exec vp, 1995-97; JJED Home Healthcare Agency, partner, 1997-. **Orgs:** Chmn Credentials Comm Natl Black Rep Comm; chmn Economic Develop Comm Natl Black Rep Council; NY State Grand Lodge Education Com chmn; Southside Hosp Advisory Council; pres adv commn on Equal Opportunity State Univ of Farmingdale; pres adv council & assoc trustee Dowling Coll; pres emeritus Urban League of Long Island; Bay Shore Central Islip Branch NAACP; Academy of Political Sci, Columbia Univ;former vp, bd of trustees, Long Island Hlth & Hsptl Planning Cncl Inc; natl co-chrm, Natl Black Republican Cncl, 1988-90; founding president, New York State Black Republican Cncl, 1974-78; bd of dirs, WLIW-TV Channel 21, 1986-92; president, Central Islip Bd of Ed, 1972-80; Selective Service System, Local Bd 118, chairman, 1988-; Cornell Cooperative Extention, Suffolk County, vice pres, 1994; illustrious deputy-at-large, United Supreme Council, AASR, Prince Hall Affiliation, 1994-; chmn, Selective Service System, Local Board #2, 1996-97. **Honors/Awds:** 1968 Award for Comm Relations Natl Council of Negro Women; 1969 Civic Achievement Award NY State Grand Lodge Prince Hall Masons; 1969 Distinguished Alumni Award Tri State Univ; 1966 Public Serv Award Islip Spanish Amer Council; 1966 Comm Serv Award Carleton Park Civic Assn; Sovereign Grand Inspector General 33rd Degree AASR Prince Hall Affiliation 1974; 1984 Presidential Award for Comm Svcs; American Assn for Affirmantive Action, Region II, Distinguished Service Award, 1993; Distinguished Citizen Award, Washington Times Foundation, 1996. **Military Serv:** US Army, spc-4, 1957-59, Reserves, 1st sgt, 1959-66. **Business Phone:** (516)822-5050.

JOHNSON, CLINISSON ANTHONY
Judge. **Personal:** Born Nov 16, 1947, Memphis, TN; married Andrea Yvonne Morrow; children: Collin Anthony; Terrence GalonTiffany Gayle. **Educ:** Fisk Univ Nashville, BA history 1969; Univ of TN Law Sch Knoxville, JD 1972. **Career:** Memphis Municipal Ct Sys, city ct judge div IV 1976-; Shelby Co Pub Defenders Ofc Memphis, asst pub defender 1974-75; City Atty's Ofc Memphis, part-time pub defender 1972-74; Ratner Sugarmon Lucas & Salky Law Ofc Memphi, asso assy 1972-76. **Orgs:** Mem, TN Bar Assn 1972-; mem, Memphis & Shelby Co Bar Assn 1972-; mem, Nat Bar Assn 1972-; mem, NAACP 1985. **Business Addr:** City of Memphis Municipal Cour, 128 Adams Ave, Memphis, TN 38103.

JOHNSON, CLINTON LEE, SR.
Rehabilitation supervisor, city councilman, pastor. **Personal:** Born Mar 16, 1947, Mobile, AL; son of Clara Chapman Johnson and Alfred F Johnson; married Barbara Gibson Johnson, May 20, 1972; children: Ginnessa L, Ashley T, Clinton Jr. **Educ:** Alabama A&M University, Mobile, AL, BA, government, 1969; University of South Alabama, Mobile ALA, MA, (honors) rehab cons, 1973; Mobile College, Mobile, AL, BA, (honors) 1982. **Career:** Vocational Rehabilitation Service, Mobile, AL, supervisor, 1970-; Mobile City Council, Mobile, AL, vice president, 1985-; Shiloh Baptist Church, Mobile, AL, pastor, 1988-. **Orgs:** Member, Alpha Phi Alpha Fraternity, NAACP, Alabama League of Municipalities, chairman, Legislative Committee for Alabama Rehab Assoc, member, Boy Scouts of America. **Honors/Awds:** Service Award, Interdenominational Ministers Alliance, 1986; Service Award, Boys Club of America, 1987; Citizen of the Year, Palestine Temple #16, 1985; Citizen of the Year, Alpha Phi Alpha Fraternity, 1985. **Home Addr:** 1032 Dunaway Dr, Mobile, AL 36605.

JOHNSON, COLLIS, JR.
Dentist. **Personal:** Born Nov 17, 1946, Oklahoma; son of Ruby Johnson and Collis Johnson; married Marsha Michele Jones; children: Jonathan Ashley, Rachael Christine, Laura Michelle May. **Educ:** Langston Univ OK, BS 1969; Meharry Med Coll TN, DDS 1973; Martin Luther King General Hospital, general res 1974. **Career:** Denver, private general dentistry 1977-; Pilot City Health Center Minneapolis, general dentistry dept 1974-77. **Orgs:** Mem Am Dental Assn; Natl Dental Assn 1977-; asst treas Alpha Phi Alpha Inc; mem Denver Urban League; pres, Clarence T Holmes Dental Society, 1986; bd of dental examiners, State of CO, 1997-2001. **Honors/Awds:** Board of Directors, Concorde Cancer College. **Business Addr:** Dentist, 1756 Vine St, Denver, CO 80206.

JOHNSON, COSTELLO O.
Company executive. **Personal:** Born Feb 14, 1938, Chicago, IL; son of Dorothy and Adrian Johnson; married Eunita Flemings Johnson, Aug 26, 1967; children: Gina Perry, Pamela Eatman, Darin. **Educ:** Chicago Academy of Fine Arts, BA, 1962; Illinois Institute of Technology; Univ of Illinois. **Career:** Montgomery Wards, designer, space planner, 1968-68; Contract Interiors, designer, space planner, 1968-70; Desks, Inc, sales associate, 1970-73; Haworth/Chicago, president, 1973-79; Costello Johnson & Associates, president, 1979-89; Corporate Office Systems, Inc, ceo/president, 1989-. **Orgs:** Urban Gateways, board of dir; United Charities, board of dir; Jesse Owens Found, friends committee; Chicago Minority Business Development Council, exec board member; Marcy Newberry Association, co-chairman, fundraiser; Alpha Phi Fraternity. **Business Addr:** CEO, Corporate Office Systems Inc., 1333 N. Kingsbury, Ste 309, Chicago, IL 60622.

JOHNSON, CYNTHIA
Organization executive, community activist. **Personal:** Born Aug 19, 1958, Detroit, MI; daughter of Willie L & Beverly Johnson; married Hoskins (divorced); children: Wallace, Tyhecia, Henry. **Educ:** Wayne County Community College, AA, 1989; Walsh College, BBA, 1992. **Career:** Wayne County Neighborhood Legal Ctr, prog consultant, 1992-94; Inkster Schools, crisis intervention consultant, 1994-95; Wayne County Government, intern, 1994-95, victim's witness assistant, 1995; GOGIRLS, director, 1995-. **Business Addr:** Executive Director, Giving Our Girls Incentive (for) Real Life Situations (GOGIRLS), 29999 Pine St, Inkster, MI 48141, (313)467-6132.

JOHNSON, CYNTHIA L. M.
Lawyer. **Personal:** Born Mar 1, 1952, Detroit, MI; daughter of Frances E (deceased) & Robert Alexander Johnson; children: Alexandra, Lauren, Joshua. **Educ:** Univ of Michigan, BA, 1973; Master of Public Health, 1975; Detroit College of Law, JD (cum laude), 1984. **Career:** Detroit Med Foundation/ Michigan HMO Plans, Inc, deputy dir, 1975; New York City Health Hospital Corp, sr health analyst, 1976-77; United Autoworkers healthcare, consultant, 1977-83; Michigan Court of Appeals, judicial law clerk, 1983-89; Michigan Supreme Court, judicial law clerk, 1985-87; Clark Hill PLC, formerly known as Clark, Klein & Beaumont, PLC, partner, 1987-. **Orgs:** Michigan Bar Assn, 1984-; Wolverine Bar Assn, 1984-; NAACP; Delta Sigma Theta Sorority, 1990-; Lula Belle Stewart, bd of dirs, 1994-; Mercy Health Care Corp, finance committee, 1993-. **Business Addr:** Partner, Clark Hill, PLC, 500 Woodward Avenue, Ste. 3500, Detroit, MI 48226-3435, (313)965-8263.

JOHNSON, CYRUS EDWIN
Business executive. **Personal:** Born Feb 18, 1929, Alton, IL; son of Jennie Cornelia Keen Johnson (deceased) and Cyrus L Johnson; married Charlotte E Kenniebrew; children: Judie, Rene. **Educ:** Univ of IL, BS 1956, MA 1959; Harvard Business School, 1974. **Career:** Farmer 1946-50; Urbana Lincoln Hotel, asst mgr 1953-59; IL Bell Telephone Co, dist mgr 1959-72; Gen Mills Inc, vp; MGO Facilities & Svcs, dir. **Orgs:** Dir AULT Inc, Lifespan Inc; former trustee Gen Mills Found, Natl Minority Business Campaign; former dir Abbot-Northwestern Hospital; former deans adv council Purdue Univ, Business School, Harvard Business School Assoc; bd of dir W VA State College Foundation 1988-; Business Advisory Bethune-Cookman College Div of Business 1989-; national board of directors, Girl Scouts of the USA, 1990-. **Honors/Awds:** Amer Legion Scholarship Awd 1943; Portraits of Success Awd Purdue Univ, Old Masters 1975; Fellow Chicago Defender Roundtable of Commerce 1967. **Military Serv:** AUS 1950-52. **Business Addr:** Vice President and Dir, MGO Facilities & Serv, PO Box 1113, Minneapolis, MN 55440.

JOHNSON, DARRIUS
Professional football player. **Personal:** Born Sep 17, 1972, Terrell, TX. **Educ:** Univ of Oklahoma. **Career:** Denver Broncos, defensive back, 1996-. **Business Addr:** Professional Football Player, Denver Broncos, 13655 Broncos Pkwy, Englewood, CO 80112, (303)649-9000.

JOHNSON, DAVE
Professional basketball player. **Personal:** Born Nov 16, 1970, Morgan City, LA. **Educ:** Syracuse. **Career:** Portland Trail Blazers, guard/forward, 1992-. **Business Addr:** Professional Basketball Player, Portland Trailblazers, 1 N Center Court St, Ste 200, Portland, OR 97227-2103, (503)234-9291.

JOHNSON, DAVID, III
Company executive. **Personal:** Born Jun 16, 1943, Tallahassee, FL; son of Charlemae B Johnson and David Johnson Jr. **Educ:** Florida A&M University, BS, 1965. **Career:** IBM, staff programmer, 1968-80; AT&T Bell Laboratories, member technical staff, 1980-82; Johnson Comupter System Design, chief executive officer/president,1982-. **Military Serv:** US Army, 1st lt, 1966-68; Bronze Star. **Business Addr:** Chief Executive Officer/President, Johnson Computer System Design, PO Box 4580, Fort Lauderdale, FL 33338-4580, (305)763-4713.

JOHNSON, DAVID E.
Banker. **Personal:** Born Aug 4, 1960, Jackson, MS; son of Rev & Mrs Earnest Johnson; married Doris Martin-Johnson, Mar 11, 1989; children: D'Ebonie Marie. **Educ:** Jackson State University, BS (magna cum laude), 1982; American Inst of Banking, 1983-87; Hinds Comm Coll, AA, (summa cum laude) 1987; Louisiana State Univ School of Banking, 1992. **Career:** Deposit Guaranty National Bank, supply clerk, 1979-80, records clerk, 1980-82, management trainee, 1982-83, asst mgr/ account profitability analysis, 1983-84, credit analyst, 1985, asst vp/asst branch mgr, 1985-89, vp/branch mgr, 1989-93, vp & comm affairs officer, 1993-. **Orgs:** Zion Chapel Church of God in Christ, bd of trustees, 1989-, pres Youth Act Council, 1994-, Sunday school superintendent, 1987-, chair, Building Fund Committee, 1994-, choir pres & musician, 1972-, National Assn of Urban Bankers, Jackson Chapter, charter mem, treasurer, 1992-; Bethlehem Center, bd of dirs, 1994-; New Life for Women, bd of dirs, 1994-. **Honors/Awds:** YMCA, Professional Black Achiever of the Year, 1984; Jackson State Univ, Bus Management Academic Award, 1982, Pre's List Scholar, 1982, National Dean's List Scholar, 1981. **Business Addr:** VP & Corp Community Affairs Officer, Deposit Guaranty National Bank, 200 E Capitol St, 18th Fl, Deposit Guaranty Bank Building, Jackson, MS 39215-1200, (601)354-8237.

JOHNSON, DAVID FREEMAN
Biochemist. **Personal:** Born Jan 28, 1925, Nashville, TN; married Gloria D Tapscott, 1947; children: Toni Y, David G. **Educ:** Allegheny College, BS, 1947, DSc, 1972; Howard Univ, MS, 1949; Georgetown Univ, PhD, 1957. **Career:** Howard Univ, chemistry instructor, 1949-50; Freedmans Hospital, Washington, DC, res chemist, 1950-52, res chemist, 1952-71; USDA Graduate School, instructor,1958-60; Foundation for Advanced Education in Science, Inc., NIH, 1960-; National Institute of Arthritis & Metabolic Diseases, analytical chemistry lab, chief, 1971-. **Orgs:** AAAS; American Chem Society; Federation of American Socs & Exp Biol; American Phys Society. **Business Addr:** Chief, Lab of Analalytical Chemistry, Natl Inst of Health, NIH Bldg 8, Room B2A-17, Bethesda, MD 20892.

JOHNSON, DAVIS
Financial company executive. **Personal:** Born Feb 23, 1934, Detroit, MI; son of Hubert Johnson; married Alphia Bymun, Jun 21, 1958; children: Cheryl Rene Johnson. **Educ:** Wayne St U; Harvard U; MI St U; Investment Seminar; Notre Dame. **Career:** Investors Divrsfd Srv, Inc, div sales mgr 1972-, dist sales mgr 1969-72, sales rep 1966-69. **Orgs:** Mem, Nat Assn, Securities Dealers; mem, NAACP; Booker T Wash Bus Assn; Cotillion Clb; Big 10 Alumni Assn; Metro Cntrctrs; Jugs African Med Assn. **Military Serv:** AUS corpl 1952-54. **Business Addr:** CEO, Johnson's Financial Service Inc, 15565 Northland Dr, Suite 600 W, Southfield, MI 48075.

JOHNSON, DENNIS
Television company executive. **Career:** Showtime Entertainment Group, senior vice president of movies and series, West Coast, senior vice president, currently. **Special Achievements:** First African American to hold the position of senior vice president at Showtime Entertainment Group. **Business Addr:** Senior Vice President, Showtime Entertainment Group, 10 Universal City Plaza, 31st Floor, Universal City, CA 91608, (818)505-7700.

JOHNSON, DIANE
Educator, author (retired). **Personal:** Born May 17, 1929, Milwaukee, WI; married Theodore H Johnson. **Educ:** Univ WI, BS, PhD 1971. **Career:** Marquette Univ Med Sch, lab instr 1954-55; Inst for Enzyme Res, proj asst 1955-66; Univ WI Coll of Letters & Sci, asst dean 1968-78; WHA Radio Series "Educational Decision-making", panelist 1971-72; "The Undergraduate Student, A Case Study", panelist 1972-73; Univ of WI, asst dir of athletics 1978-. **Orgs:** Mem Amer Personnel & Guidance Assn; pres Natl Assn of Academic Advisors for Athletics 1982; WI Coll Personnel Assn; Natl Assn Women Deans Adminstrs & Couns; mem Alpha Kappa Alpha Sor; adminstr, counselor, vice pres 1973-75 WI Assn Women Deans; chmn WI Drug Quality Council 1976-69; several Univ WI coms srch screen coms; mem Madison Bd Zoning Appeals; chrpsn Coalition Minority Women of UW-Madison 1974-75; mem oral exam bds for state WI; NAACP; Oakwood Lutheran Homes, board of directors, 1991-. **Honors/Awds:** EB Fred Fellow 1964-71; Outstanding Serv Awd Delta Sigma Theta & Alpha Phi Alpha 1973-74; 1st Black valedictorian of non-black hs Milwaukee Lincoln 1946; Disting Serv Awd Wisconsin Alumni Assn 1981; University of Wisconsin Alumni Club, Distinguished University Achievement Award, 1988.

JOHNSON, DONN S.
Journalist. **Personal:** Born May 9, 1947, St Louis, MO; son of Ivory M Dodd Johnson (deceased) and Clyde E Johnson, Sr; married Earlene Beverly Breedlove, Jun 1, 1969; children: Lauren Beverly Johnson. **Educ:** St Louis Comm Coll Florissant Valley, AA 1976; Webster Coll, BA 1977. **Career:** KWK Radio St Louis, newsman/disc jockey 1970-72; WIL Radio St Louis, newsman/dir comm rel 1972-78; KTVI Channel 2 St Louis, anchor/reporter 1978-; St Louis American Newspaper, columnist. **Orgs:** Mem advisory bd Mass Communications Forest Park Comm Coll 1972-; mem Greater St Louis Black Journalists Assoc 1979-; mem St Louis Press Club 1980; vice pres St Louis Chapter, American Federation of Radio & TV Artists (AFTRA); board of directors St Louis Gateway Classic Foundation. **Honors/Awds:** Howard B Woods Memorial Award for Journalism Black Student Assoc Webster Coll 1977; Best News Story of the Year Award Greater St Louis Black Journalists Assoc 1978; Black Excellence in Journalism Award, Greater St Louis Black Journalism Assn, 1978, 1984, 1986, 1988-89; Unity Awards in Media, Lincoln Univ, 1985; Media Award, Gifted Assn of MO, 1987; Media Award of Excellence, Missouri Assn of Community and Junior College, 1990; Emmy (local), Academy of Television Arts and Sciences, 1989. **Military Serv:** AUS corpl 1966-67. **Business Addr:** Anchor/ Reporter, KTVI Channel 2, 5915 Berthold Ave, St Louis, MO 63110.

JOHNSON, DONNA ALLIGOOD
Banking executive. **Personal:** Born Oct 25, 1956, Detroit, MI; daughter of Cynthia Elvira Vincent Alligood and Douglas Lacy Alligood; married Curtis Charles Johnson, Jun 27, 1987. **Educ:** Tufts Univ, BS 1978. **Career:** BBDO, acct coord 1978-79, asst account exec 1980-82, account exec 1983-85, senior account exec 1985-88; Citicorp POS Information Services marketing mgr 1988-90, product mgr 1991. **Orgs:** Mem NAACP. **Business Addr:** Product Manager, Marketing, Citicorp POS Information Services, 750 Washington Blvd, Stamford, CT 06902.

JOHNSON, DORIS ELAYNE
Librarian, instructor. **Personal:** Born Jul 13, 1954, Orangeburg, SC; daughter of Angie Pearl Glover Johnson and Roscoe Johnson Sr; children: LaTroy Damon. **Educ:** South Carolina State College, Orangeburg, SC, 1976; Clark Atlanta University, Atlanta, GA, MSLS, 1990. **Career:** South Carolina State University, Orangeburg, SC, library technical assistant, 1982-89, librarian/reference & information specialist/instructor, 1991-. **Orgs:** Member, Atlanta Law Library Association, 1989-; member, South Carolina Library Association, 1991-; member, American Library Association, 1989-; Delta Sigma Theta Sorority. **Honors/Awds:** Minority Stipend, Atlanta Law Libraries Assn, 1990; Delta of Year, 1997. **Home Addr:** 901 Corona Dr, Apt 3D, Orangeburg, SC 29115. **Business Phone:** (803)536-7045.

JOHNSON, DOROTHY TURNER
Librarian, educator (retired). **Personal:** Born Jan 18, 1915, Dublin, GA; daughter of Eva Montgomery Turner and Thomas Turner; married Harold Martin Johnson (died 1977). **Educ:** Spelman College, Atlanta, GA, AB, 1938; University of Wisconsin, Madison, WI, BS, library science, 1949; Western Reserve University, Cleveland, OH, MS, library science. **Career:** Dade County Public Schools, Homestead, FL, teacher, 1934-36; Florida Normal and Industrial Institute, St Augustine, FL, librarian, 1939-41; Spelman College, Atlanta, GA, assistant librarian, 1941-42; Detroit Public Library, Detroit, MI, children's librarian, 1949-50; Cleveland Public Library, Cleveland, OH, head, classrooms division, 1950-65; Cuyahoga Community College, Cleveland, OH, head, library technology, 1965-80. **Orgs:** Member, American Library Association, 1956-80; member, Association of University Professors, 1975-80; member, Urban League Guild, 1975-; member, ACLU, 1965-; member, Alpha Kappa Alpha Sorority, 1947-. **Honors/Awds:** Fulbright Scholarship, US Office of Education, 1976. **Special Achievements:** Author, One Day, Mother/Un Dia, Madre, 1996. **Military Serv:** US Army (WAAC), PFC, 1942-45.

JOHNSON, DOUGLAS H.
Educator. **Personal:** Born May 1, 1943, Bolivia, NC; married Shirley L. **Educ:** Cheyney St Coll, Cheyne PA, BA 1969; Univ RI, Kingston, m comm planning 1971. **Career:** Univ of RI, asst prof Comm Planning; Wilmington Metro Area Plann Corr Council, Wilmington DE, sum intern 1970; Inst, comm planning 1974-; Comm Plann in CPAD, asst prof 1974-; State of RI, Providence, consultant to Office of Continuing Educ 1974. **Orgs:** Prin, vp, Comm Found 1973-; ed, Nat Assn of Planners, Nwsltr 1973-75; mem, Am Soc Plann Off; Nat Assn of Plann; Am Assn Univ Prof; mem, United Wrk-Study Fellow, US Dept of Hsg & Urban Dev 1969-71. **Honors/Awds:** Std Award, Am Inst of Plann 1971; recevied, Natl Flwshp Fund Award, Academic Yr for PhD studies at MIT 1976-77. **Business Addr:** Grad Curriculum Comm Planning, Kingston, RI 02881.

JOHNSON, EARL
Electronic engineer. **Personal:** Born Jun 25, 1943, Gilmer, TX; son of Ella Johnson and Lunnie Johnson; married Pamela G Huddleston Johnson, Nov 18, 1990; children: Marla A. **Educ:** Electronic Technical Institute, 1967-68; Mesa Jr College, 1975-

76. **Career:** Conic Corp, electronic assembly, 1967-68; Ryan Aeronical, electronic assembly, 1968-69; Ketema Aerospace & Electronics, jr engineer, 1969-90; John Sound Lab, president, owner, 1990-. **Military Serv:** US Army, sergeant, 1964-67. **Business Addr:** President/Owner, John Sound Lab, 9243 Fairlawn St, Santee, CA 92071, (619)258-8342.

JOHNSON, EARL E.
Educational administrator (retired). **Personal:** Born Sep 28, 1926, Atlantic City, NJ; son of Minnie Lee Fields Johnson and George Johnson; married Juanita Hairston; children: Brett, Jeffrey. **Educ:** WV State Coll, BS in Educ 1951; Galssboro State Coll, MA in Elem Adm 1964. **Career:** Penn Ave Sch Atlantic City, NJ, prin 1964-67; Mass Ave Sch, prin 1967; Atlantic City Pblc Sch, dir Title III 1967-68; Ind Ave Sch Atlantic City,NJ, prin 1968-84; Atlantic City, NJ Pblc Sch, adm asst/elem serv, asst supt elementary services, executive asst supt. **Orgs:** Chm schlrshp comm Miss Am Bd of Dir 1964-; former vice pres Atlantic Co Adm Assn 1964-; mem Kiwanis Clb of Atlantic City 1964-; mem former bas Upsilon Alpha Chptr Omega Psi Phi Frat; mem former pres Atlantic City Chptr NAACP; Atlantic City, Bd of Educ, 1995-98. **Honors/Awds:** Outstndng Blck Ed Blck Atlantic City Mag 1982; Outstndng Ed Ind Ave Sch Parent Adv Cncl 1978; Outstndng Ctzn 4h Clb ofv Atlantic Co 1973-75; Outstndng Ed Kenneth Hawkins Am Legion No 61 1974. **Military Serv:** US Fld Arty 2nd lt 1946; comm 1951.

JOHNSON, EARVIN, JR. (MAGIC JOHNSON)
Professional basketball player (retired), business executive. **Personal:** Born Aug 14, 1959, Lansing, MI; son of Christine and Earvin Sr; married Earleatha (Cookie) Johnson; children: Andre, Earvin III, Elisa. **Educ:** Michigan State University. **Career:** Magic Johnson Enterprises Inc, owner; performer, tv endorsements; LA Lakers, guard, 1980-92; Pepsi-Cola Co of Washington, co-chair, beginning 1991; Los Angeles Lakers, head coach, 1994, vp, guard, 1996. **Honors/Awds:** Tallest point guard, NBA history; World Class Athlete, MI State; 184 season scoring average; leads all NBA guards with 7 rebounds per game; NBA Player of the Week; 3 games, 89 pts/35 rebounds/34 assists, 1980; Schick Pivotal Player Award; top vote getter on Sporting News All NBA Team; autobiography, Magic, 1983; won 2 playoff MVP Awards; numerous NBA All Star teams; NBA MVP 1987, 1992; US Olympic Basketball Team, 1992; served as Honorary Parade Grand Marshal for Texas Southern Univ's 50th Anniversary Parade. **Business Addr:** Los Angeles Lakers, 3900 West Manchester Blvd, PO Box 10, Inglewood, CA 90306, (310)419-3100.

JOHNSON, ED F. See Obituaries section.

JOHNSON, EDDIE BERNICE
Congresswoman. **Personal:** Born Dec 3, 1935, Waco, TX; divorced; children: Dawrence Kirk Jr. **Educ:** St Mary's College of Notre Dame, nursing diploma, 1955; Texas Christian University, BS, nursing, 1967; Southern Methodist University, MS, public administration, 1976. **Career:** Texas House of Representatives, member, 1972-77; Department of H.E.& W., region VI director, 1977-79, executive assistant to director of primary health care, 1979-81; Sammons Enterprises Inc, assistant to president, 1981-87; Visiting Nurse Association, vp, governmental affairs, 1981-87; Texas State Senate, 1986-93; US House of Representatives, 1993-. **Orgs:** American Nurses Association, currently; Links Inc, Dallas chapter, currently; Dallas Black Chamber of Commerce, currently; NAACP, currently; Girlfriends Inc, currently; Alpha Kappa Alpha Sorority, currently; National Council of Negro Women, past president, currently; National Order of Women Legislators, past vp and secretary, currently. **Special Achievements:** Bishop College, LLD, 1979; Jarvis Christian College, LLD, 1979; Texas College, LLD, 1989; United Negro College Fund, Dallas, Scholar Award, 1992; NAACP, Juanita Craft Award in Politics, 1989; Democratic Deputy Whip, Secretary of Congressional Black Caucus. **Business Addr:** Congresswoman, US House of Representatives, Longworth HOB, Room 1123, Washington, DC 20515, (202)225-8885.

JOHNSON, EDDIE C.
Judge (retired), attorney. **Personal:** Born Jun 1, 1920, Chicago, IL; married Olivia; children: Edward, Ella. **Educ:** Roosevelt U, AB; John Marshall Law Sch, JD; Loyola U, attend. **Career:** Jones, Ware and Greaud, official counsel, currently; Circuit Ct, Cook Co IL, judge 1965-91; Pvt Pract, atty 1952-65; Ellis, Westbrook & Holman, Gillen and Owens, 1961-65; Gayles, Johnson, and Handy, 1957-61; Brooks, Rhett & Johnson, 1953-55. **Orgs:** Mem Cook Co & Nat Bar Asn, Judical Cncl of NBA. **Honors/Awds:** John Mouskell Law School, Distinguished Service and Alumnus Awards; The Push Foundation Award; Illinois Judicial Council, Meritorious Service Awards & Judicial Career Service Award. **Business Addr:** Official Counsel, Jones, Ware & Greaud, 180 N LaSalle St, Ste 3800, Chicago, IL 60601.

JOHNSON, EDMOND R.
Attorney. **Personal:** Born Jun 26, 1937, Plymouth, NC; married Thelma Crosby; children: Edrenna Renee, Erica Ronelle. **Educ:** NC Centrl U, BA 1959; Howard U, JD 1968. **Career:** Pvt pract law 1970-; DE Tech Comm Coll, tchr law clk 1968-69. **Orgs:** Mem NC Acad Trial Lawyers; NC State Bar; Nat & Am Bar Assns; NC Black Lawyers Assn; NAACP; Alpha Phi Alpha. **Business Addr:** 916 W 5th St, Charlotte, NC 28201.

JOHNSON, EDNA DECOURSEY
Educator (retired). **Personal:** Born Jun 1, 1922, Baltimore, MD; married Laurence Harry. **Educ:** Coppin St Clg, BS 1944; Rutgers U, Cert Group Dynamic Human Relations 1950, 56; Johns Hopkins U, Post Grad Work Consumer & Law 1954; Univ of WI, Cert Fin Money Mgmt 1966. **Career:** Baltimore City Public Schools, elementary teacher 1944-63; Baltimore Urban League, dir consult serv 1963-78; Comm Coll of Baltimore & other Comm Clgs, part-time instructor 1975-92; Northwest Baltimore Corp, exec dir 1979-82; MarylandFood Bank, prog dir 1979-82; Natl Assoc Negro Business & Professional Womens Clubs Inc, prog dir 1979-82. **Orgs:** Consumer adv American Egg Bd 1979-84; bd mem Consumers Union 1st Black Woman 1972-84; bd mem Natl Coalition for Consumer Ed 1982-86; mem Zeta Phi Beta Sor Coppin Alumni ; past pres Baltimore Club Mid Alantic ABWA 1970-73; past Governor Dist Natl Asso Negro Bus & Prof Womens Clubs, 1967-71, 1973-75; past Natl Corresp, 1971-73; Heritage United Church of Christ 1971-73. **Honors/Awds:** Natl Meritorious Sojourner Truth Balto Club Natl Asso Negro Business & Prof Womens Club Inc 1974; Lambda Kappa Mj 1972; The Pilomathians 1982; 100 Outstndng Women Delta Sigma Theta Sor. **Home Addr:** 3655 Wabash Ave, Baltimore, MD 21215.

JOHNSON, EDWARD, JR. (FAST EDDIE)
Professional athlete. **Personal:** Born Feb 24, 1955, Ocala, FL; married Diana Racisz. **Educ:** Auburn U, attnd 30 hrs personne mgmt. **Career:** Atlanta Hawks, professional basketball player present; Eddie Johnson Enter Inc, pres & found. **Orgs:** Mem Muscular Dystrophy; mem NAACP; mem UNCF. **Honors/Awds:** MVP 1979-80; 2nd All-Def 2 yrs. **Business Addr:** Professional Basketball Player, C/O Charlotte Hornets, 100 Hive Drive, Charlotte, NC 28217.

JOHNSON, EDWARD A.
Educator. **Personal:** Born Feb 25, 1940, New York, NY. **Educ:** City Coll of NY, BS 1968, PhD 1978. **Career:** NY Institute of Technology, physics instructor, 1986-; Pace University, physics instructor, 1988-; John Jay College, math adjunct lecturer, 1990-. **Orgs:** NAACP. **Business Addr:** Instructor, NY Institute of Technology, 1855 Broadway, New York, NY 10023.

JOHNSON, EDWARD ARNET
Professional basketball player. **Personal:** Born May 1, 1959, Chicago, IL; married Joy; children: Jade Alexis, Justin Edward. **Educ:** Illinois. **Career:** Kansas City Kings, forward/guard, 1981-85; Sacramento Kings, 1985-87; Phoenix Suns, 1987-91; Seattle SuperSonics, 1991-93; Charlotte Hornets, 1993-94; played in Greece, 1994-95; Indiana Pacers, 1995-96; Houston Rockets, 1996-. **Honors/Awds:** NBA Sixth Man Award, 1989. **Business Addr:** Professional Basketball Player, Houston Rockets, PO Box 272349, Houston, TX 77277, (713)627-0600.

JOHNSON, EDWARD ELEMUEL
Educator. **Personal:** Born in Crooked River, Jamaica; son of Mary Elizabeth Blake Johnson and Rev Edward E Johnson; married Beverley Jean Morris; children: Edward E, Lawrence P, Robin Jeannine, Nathan J, Cyril U. **Educ:** Howard Univ, BS 1947, MS 1948; Univ of CO, PhD 1952. **Career:** Southern Univ Baton Rouge LA, prof & assoc dean of univ 1955-72; LA State Univ Med Sch, clinical prof of psychiatry 1969-72; United Bd for Coll Development, dir 1972-74; Univ of Medicine & Dentistry of NJ Robt Wood Johnson Med Sch, prof of psychiatry 1974-. **Orgs:** Panelist Science Faculty Develop Natl Sci Foundation 1978-82; site visitor Natl Inst of Health 1978-; consultant Bell Laboratories Holmdel NJ 1982-85; bdof trustees Crossroads Theatre Co 1983-; bd of dirs PSI Assoc Inc 1984-. **Honors/Awds:** Fellow Amer Assoc for Advancement of Science; life mem The Soc of the Sigma Xi; memb Pi Gamma Mu Natl Social Science Honor Soc, Psi Chi Natl Psychology Honor Soc; over 50 scientific publications including book chapt; Beta Beta Beta Biological Honor Society, Thirty-third Degree Mason, Prince Hall Affiliation; member, Sigma Pi Phi Fraternity; member, Alpha Phi Alpha Fraternity. **Military Serv:** AUS 1st lt 1951-53. **Home Addr:** PO Box 597, East Brunswick, NJ 08816. **Business Addr:** Professor of Psychiatry, Robt Wood Johnson Medical Sch, Univ of Medicine & Dentistry of New Jersey, 675 Hoes Lane, Piscataway, NJ 08854, (908)235-4600.

JOHNSON, EDWARD M.
Business executive. **Personal:** Born Jan 15, 1943, Washington. **Educ:** BArch 1967; Master, City Planning 1970. **Career:** Edward M Johnson, & Associates, PC; Architects & Urban Planners, 1969-; JJ Lord Construction Co, pres. **Orgs:** Mem, American Inst of Architects; Design Review Panel DC; Department of Housing and Community Development. **Honors/Awds:** Recip, US Housing & Urban Dev Fellow; Doxiodus Fellow; Urban Transp Fellow. **Business Addr:** 3612 12th St, NE, Washington, DC 20017.

JOHNSON, ELAINE MCDOWELL
Federal government executive. **Personal:** Born Jun 28, 1942, Baltimore, MD; daughter of Lena Blue McDowell and McKinley McDowell; married Walter A Johnson, 1978 (divorced); children: Nathan Murphy Jr, Michael Murphy. **Educ:** Morgan State Univ, BA 1965; Univ of MD, MSW 1971, PhD, 1988. **Career:** State of MD, acting regional dir 1971-72; Natl Inst on Drug Abuse, public health advisor 1972-76, Div of Comm Assistance, deputy dir/dir 1976-82, Div of Prevention & Communications, dir 1982-85; ADAMHA, exec asst to admin 1985; Natl Inst on Drug Abuse, deputy dir 1985-88, dir, Office for Substance Abuse Prevention 1988-90; ADAMHA/SAMHSA, acting admini, 1990-92; Ctr for Substance Abuse Prevention, dir, 1992-. **Orgs:** Ordained officer Presbyterian Church 1981-84; natl dir drug abuse prevention prog Zeta Phi Beta Sor 1986-92; consultant US Information Agency, US State Dept; Links Inc. **Honors/Awds:** National Services to Youth Award, Links Inc, 1986; Natl Award for Outstanding Leadership in Improving Health Care in the Black Comm, Natl Medical Assn, 1988; Prevention Award for Defining and Advancing the Science of Prevention, Natl Drug Information Center of Families in Action, 1988; F Elwood Davis Award for Govt Official Responsive to the Needs of Youth, Boys and Girls Clubs, 1989; National Council on Alcoholism and Drug Dependence Inc; President's Meritorious Award for Outstanding Federal Leadership, 1991; National Federation of Parents, National Leadership Award, 1991; President's Distinguished Service Award, Outstanding Federal Leadership, 1993. **Special Achievements:** Author: ''Cocaine: The American Experience,'' The Cocaine Crisis, D Allen, ed, NY Plenum Press, 1987; ''The Impact of Drug Abuse on Women's Health,'' Public Health Reports, 1987; ''The Government's Response to Drug Abuse Problems Among Minority Populations,'' Journal of the Black Nurses Association; ''Preventing Alcohol Abuse: A Move Towards a National Agenda,'' Principles and Practices of Student Health, Foundations, Vol 1, H Wallace, et al, eds, Third Party Publishing Co., 1991. **Business Addr:** Director, Center for Substance Abuse Prevention, Rockwall 2 Bldg, 5600 Fishers Ln, Rockville, MD 20857.

JOHNSON, ELLIS BERNARD
Professional football player. **Personal:** Born Oct 30, 1973, Wildwood, FL; married Simone; children: Nichole, Ellis Bernard Jr. **Educ:** University of Florida. **Career:** Indianapolis Colts, defensive tackle, 1995-. **Special Achievements:** Selected in the 1st round/15th overall pick in the 1995 NFL Draft. **Business Addr:** Professional Football Player, Indianapolis Colts, PO Box 535000, Indianapolis, IN 46253, (317)297-2658.

JOHNSON, ELMORE W.
Business executive. **Personal:** Born Jul 12, 1944, Richmond, VA; son of Elmore Johnson Jr and Fannie Mae; married Lynne Saxon; children: Kendall, Elmore, Jr, Marc. **Educ:** VA Union U, BA; Temple U, adv studies. **Career:** Hartranft Comm Corp, exec dir 1973-, comm serv coord 1972-73; Neighborhood Renewal Prog, comm splst 1971-72; Philadelphia, Dept of Licenses & Insps, comm; US Dept of Housing & Urban Dev; Neighborhood Dev Prog, comm splst 1971; Century Metalcraft Corp, rep 1970-71; St Empl Commn, unempl intrvwr 1969-70; Hanover Inst for Boys, supr 1967. **Orgs:** Youth Services Coordinating Commission, St Christopher's Hospital for Children; North Philadelphia Partnership, North Philadelphia Regional Urban Design Assistance Team; BSA; Colorado Community Youth; Parent Child Care Center; Fairhill/Norris Tenant Council. **Honors/Awds:** Holy Cross Luth Ch; Chapel of Four Chaplains; Award, Martin Luther King Cntr; North Philadelphia Leadership Award; Youth Services Award. **Military Serv:** US Army, 1967-69; Pruntv Med Specialist. **Business Addr:** 2415-35 Germantown Ave, Philadelphia, PA 19133.

JOHNSON, ENID C.
Educator. **Personal:** Born Oct 15, 1931, Miami; divorced. **Educ:** Talladega Coll, AB 1953; Barry Coll, MS 1967. **Career:** Miami YWCA, adult prog dir; Chicago, grp wrkr; Dade Co Sch Sys, tch 1955, cnslr 1967, asst prin 1971, asst prin for guidance 1985. **Orgs:** Mem, NEA; mem, FEA; mem, Dade Co Adm Assn & Guidance Assn; mem, S FL Guidance Assn; mem, Am & Sch Cncl Assn; mem, Am Guidance & Prsnl Assn; mem, AAUW; mem, Hi Delta-Kappa; bd dir, Miami YWCA; bd dir, FL Conf United Ch of Christ; charter mem, Ch of Open Door; mem, UCC Fruits of the Sts; mem, Miami Inter Alumni Cncl, UNCf; mem, Sigma Gamma Rho Sor. **Honors/Awds:** Cert of Apprec, Sigma Gamma Rho Sor. **Business Addr:** 6750 SW 60th St S, Miami, FL 33143.

JOHNSON, ERIC G.
Business Executive. **Personal:** Born Mar 29, 1951, Chicago, IL; son of George Eillis & Joan Betty Johnson; married Pamela Johnson, Apr 8, 1979; children: Lecretia, Erin, Cara, John. **Educ:** Babson College, BAS, 1972; University of Chicago, MBA, 1977. **Career:** Proctor & Gamble, 1972-75; Johnson Products, pres, CEO, 1988-92; Baldwin Ice Cream Co, pres, CEO, 1992-; Baldwin Richardson Foods Co, pres, CEO, 1997-. **Orgs:** Young Presidents Org; Dr Martin Luther King Ctr, bd of dirs; Chicago State Univ, bd of dirs; Babson Coll, bd of trustees; Olympia Fields Country Club; Glenwood School for Boys, bd of trustees; Comm for Economic Dev; NAACP, bd of dirs. **Honors/Awds:** Boy Scouts of America, Leadership Awd; 100

Black Men of America, Annual Recognition Awd; Willi Wilson Foundation, Humanitarian Awd; Chicago State College; Honorary Doctor of Letters; Lincoln Memorial, Jobs, Peace, Freedom Awd. **Special Achievements:** Lifelink Celebrity Challenge; The Ideal Black Gold Trade Show. **Business Addr:** President/CEO, Baldwin Richardson Foods Co, 4440 W Lincoln Hwy, Ste 205, Matteson, IL 60443, (708)283-1820.

JOHNSON, ERMA CHANSLER
Educational administrator. **Personal:** Born Jun 6, 1942, Leggett, TX; married Lawrence Eugene Johnson; children: Thelma Ardenia. **Educ:** Prairie View A&M Univ, BS 1963; Bowling Green State Univ, MEd 1968. **Career:** Turner High School, teacher 1963-67; Bowling Green State Univ, grad asst 1967-68; Tarrant Cty Jr Coll Dist Ft Worth TX, assoc prof 1968-72, asst dir of personnel 1973-74, dir of personnel 1974-81, vice chancellor human resources. **Orgs:** Pres Fannie M Heath Cultural Club 1974-75, 1978-80; Ft Worth Amer Revolution Bicentennial Comm 1974-76; bd of dir 1974-78, treas 1977-78, Ft Worth-Tarrant Cty Supportive Outreach Svc; Task Force 100 1976; vice pres Ft Worth Minority Leaders & Citizens Council 1976-78; Ft Worth Public Transp Adv comm 1976-80;bd of dir Comm Devel Fund 1976-80; Ft Worth Girls Club 1976-81, pres 1979-81; Ft Worth Keep Amer Beautiful Task Force 1977-78; comm vice chairperson, bd of dir United Way of Metropolitan Tarrant Cty 1979; Ft Worth Central Bus Dist Planning Council 1979-81; seminar leader Coll & Univ Personnel Assoc 1980-; Ft Worth Citizens on the Move, 1983; Forum Ft Worth; sec Mt Rose Baptist Church; bd of dir Ft Worth Black Chamber of Comm; charter mem TarrantCty Black Historical & Genealogical Sovice pres Links Inc; sec bd of dir Mt Rose Child Care Ctr; chmn oper comm Dallas/Ft Worth Airport Bd; consult Coll& Univ US Civil Comm Serv 1972-; chmn Dallas/Ft Worth Intl Airport Bd 1987. **Honors/Awds:** Grad Asstship Bowling Green State Univ 1967-68; One Week Ed & Professional Devel Act Grant in Vocational Ed 1969, four week 1970; Nominated Outstanding TeacherTarrant Cty Jr Coll 1971; Listed in Outstanding Ed of Amer 1972, Outstanding Young Women in Amer 1975; Ft Worth Black Female Achiever of the Year 1977. **Home Addr:** 2362 Faett Court, Fort Worth, TX 76119. **Business Addr:** Vice Chancellor/Human Resrces, Tarrant County Junior College, 1500 Houston, Fort Worth, TX 76102.

JOHNSON, ERNEST KAYE, III
General surgeon. **Personal:** Born Feb 7, 1950, Ocala, FL; son of Delores Johnson and E K Johnson; married Clara Perry; children: Ernest IV, Clara Delores. **Educ:** Univ of FL, Pre-Med 1971; Meharry Medical Coll, MD 1975; Hubbard Hosp Meharry Medical Coll, General Surgery 1980. **Career:** Student Natl Medical Assoc, vice pres 1973-74; Meharry House Staff Assoc, vice pres 1975-76; Infinity III Inc, vice pres 1983-85. **Orgs:** Mem Matthew Walker Surgical Soc 1975-87, RF Boyd Medical Soc 1975-87, Nashville Acad of Medicine 1980-83, TN Medical Assoc 1980-83; mem Alpha Phi Alpha; mem Apollo Club 1990-91. **Honors/Awds:** Honorary mem US House of Representatives 1983; Honorary Deputy Sheriff Nashville Davidson Co 1984. **Business Addr:** 3803 Hydes Ferry Pike, Nashville, TN 37218.

JOHNSON, ERNEST L.
Banker, attorney. **Personal:** Born Aug 24, 1950, Ferriday, LA; son of Florence Johnson and Evans Johnson Sr; married Pamela Taylor, Oct 30, 1992; children: Emanuel, Louisa, Ernest II. **Educ:** Grambling State University, BS, 1973; Southern University School of Law, JD, 1976. **Career:** Johnson, Taylor & Thomas, sr partner, 1980-89; Southern University Law Center, professor; Life Savings Bank, chairman of the board, president, currently. **Orgs:** Louisiana NAACP, exec vp, 1991-; Louisiana State Bar Association, 1976-; Louis A Martinet Legal Society, 1986-; Project Invest in Black, board of directors; Church Point Ministries Feed a Family, board of directors. **Honors/Awds:** NAACP, National President Leadership Award, 1992; Louis A Martinet Legal Society, Leadership Award, 1991; JK Haynes Education Foundation, The Prestigious Seervice Award, 1990; Southern University Law Center, Earl Warren Fellowship, 1973-76; Scotlandville Jaycees, Scotlandville Man of the Year Award, 1990. **Special Achievements:** Lead counsel, Clark v Roemer, restructuring Louisiana judical system; general counsel, Louisiana state conference of NAACP, first vice pres, 1991; co-host, Legally Speaking Program. **Home Addr:** 12124 Sullivan Rd, Baton Rouge, LA 70818, (504)261-6469. **Business Phone:** (504)775-6133.

JOHNSON, ERVIN, JR.
Professional basketball player. **Personal:** Born Dec 21, 1967, New Orleans, LA. **Educ:** Univ of New Orleans, bachelor's degree in general studies, 1997. **Career:** Seattle SuperSonics, center, 1993-96; Denver Nuggets, 1996-97; Milwaukee Bucks, 1997-. **Special Achievements:** Was the commencement speaker at his graduation from the University of New Orleans, 1997. **Business Addr:** Professional Basketball Player, Milwaukee Bucks, 1001 N Fourth St, Bradley Center, Milwaukee, WI 53203, (414)227-0500.

JOHNSON, EUNICE WALKER
Publishing executive. **Personal:** Born in Selma, AL; married John H; children: John Harold, Linda. **Educ:** Talladega Coll, BA; Loyola U, MA; Univ of Chicago, cmpltd courses in studies of the great books; Northwestern U, postgrad; Ray Vogue Sch of Interior Decorating, Attend. **Career:** Johnson Pub Co, Inc, sec-treas. **Orgs:** Mem, Women's Bd of Art & Inst of Chicago; mem, Nat Found for the Fashion Ind; mem, bd dir, Talladega Coll, found by maternal grndfthr; bd dir, Woman's Div, United Negro Coll Fund; mem, Midwest Ballet; trustee, Harvard St George Sch, Chicago; dir, Adoptive Info Citizenry Com; dir, Women's Bd, Univ of Chicago; bd mem, Hyde Pk-Kenwood Women's Aux of IL; aid soc pres, Children's Hm. **Honors/Awds:** Named, by Pres Richard Nixon as a spl ambasador to accompany Mrs Nixon to Liberia for inauguration of country's new pres 1972; %Two models she selected forhaute couture-designer Emilio Pucci became first blacks to prtcpt in a showing of fashions at famed Pitti Palace, Florence, Italy 1964. **Business Addr:** 820 S & Michigan Ave, Chicago, IL 60605.

JOHNSON, EUNITA E.
Company executive. **Personal:** Born Jul 21, 1939, Chicago, IL; daughter of Ella Peters Flemings and Amos Flemings; married Costello Johnson, Aug 26, 1967; children: Gina Perry, Pamela Eatman, Darin. **Educ:** Wilson City College, 1957-59; National College of Education, 1974-77. **Career:** Corporate Office Systems, vice pres, 1989-; Costello Johnson & Associates, vice pres, 1979-89; Eucos Manufacturing, owner, 1970-74. **Orgs:** Docent Program, Harold Washington Library, chairman fundraising; Chicago Committee, Jessee Owens Foundation, committee chairperson; Chicago Regional Purchasing Council; North Shore Chapter Jack & Jill of America, chapter president, 1978-92; Dempster and Chicago Ave Merchants Association, president, 1971-74; Chicago Urban League, 1989-. **Honors/Awds:** Southside Community Center, Outstanding Business Women of the Year, 1988. **Business Addr:** VP, Corporate Office Systems Inc, 1333 N Kingsbury, Ste 309, Chicago, IL 60622, (312)440-9300.

JOHNSON, EVELYN F.
Judge. **Personal:** Born Mar 23, 1925, Chicago, IL; daughter of Ella Freeman and Henry Freeman; married Glenn T; children: Evelyn A, Glenn T. **Educ:** Univ of Chicago, BA 1946; John Marshall Law Sch, JD 1949, LLM 1950. **Career:** Pvt Prac, Chicago, atty 1950-73; St of IL, exec asst to sec 1973-; Cook County Circuit Court, judge. **Orgs:** Mem Cook Co Bar Assn; mem Am Bar Assn; mem Chicago Bar Assn; mem IL Bar Assn; mem Women's Bar Assn; mem World Peace Through Law; mem Conf of Conciliation Cts; mem YWCA; mem NAACP; mem Urban League; trustee Woodlawn African Meth Episcopal Ch 1960-. **Honors/Awds:** Cook Co Bar Assn Award 1973; Citation of Merit, John Marshall Law Sch 1973. **Business Addr:** Cook County Circuit Court, 2600 Daley Center, Chicago, IL 60602.

JOHNSON, EZRA RAY
Professional football player. **Personal:** Born Oct 2, 1955, Shreveport, LA; married Carmen. **Educ:** Morris Brown College, attended. **Career:** Defensive end: Green Bay Packers, 1977-87, Indianapolis Colts, 1988-90, Houston Oilers, 1990-. **Honors/Awds:** Ranked among NFC leaders with 14 1/2 quarterback sacks, 1983; led defense in strike-shortened season with 5 sacks, & shared tackle honors for defensive line, 1982; led defensive line in solo tackles with 53, 1990; Pro Bowl, 1978. **Business Addr:** Professional Football Player, Tennessee Oilers, c/o Baptist Sports Park, Nashville, TN 37221.

JOHNSON, F. J., JR.
Association executive (retired). **Personal:** Born Jan 30, 1930, Marshall, TX; son of Leedonia Johnson and Fury J Johnson; married May Joyce Wood; children: Teri, Valerie. **Educ:** Univ of Washington, BA; Univ of OR, additional study. **Career:** Nat Educ Assn; mgr, tchr rights div; NEA, former coordinator of minority involvement prog; Shoreline Sch Sys Seattle WA, former tchr, English department head. **Orgs:** Former Mem exec bd Greater Seattle; Coun of Tchr of English; past pres Shoreline Educ Assn 1964-65; edited SEA Scope Assn newspaper; participant in NCTE Conv; mem SEA Scope Adv Bd; chmn Right to Read Com; chmn Com on the Profession PSCTE; consult & speaker for Secondary Sch & Leadership Conf on Student Govt & Parliamentary Procedure; chmn bd Finance Mt Zion Bapt Ch; pres bd dir Mt Zion Bapt Ch Fed Credit Union; pres Beta Omicron Chpt; Phi Beta Sigma. **Honors/Awds:** Author of several publications; recipient John Hay Fellow Univ of OR 1964. **Business Addr:** 1201 16 St NW, Washington, DC 20036.

JOHNSON, F. RAYMOND
Business executive. **Personal:** Born May 10, 1920, Richmond, TX; married; children: Bernarde, Sheryl, Floyd. **Educ:** So CA Coll Bus, attended 1953. **Career:** Self-Employed, pub acctnt 1955-65; Oppor Indslzn Ctrs of Amer, job develop specialist 1965-68; S Cent Improv Action Counc, dep dir 1968-70; Usina Comm Devel Corp, exec dir 1970-74; Barker Mgmt Inc, gen mgr 1974-78; CA Housing Finance Agency, state housing consultant 1978; Hjima Housing Corp, dir 1978-83. **Orgs:** Chmn bd of dirs Hjima Comm develop Corp 1978-83; mem NAACP, Urban League, YMCA, Brotherhood Crusade. **Honors/Awds:** Cong Citation Asst of Minority Entrepreneurs Bus Devel LA Co. **Military Serv:** AUS s/sgt 1941-45.

JOHNSON, FRAN
Company executive. **Personal:** Born Jan 5, 1939, Chicago, IL; daughter of Ernestine Conway and Leon Covington; married; children: Humont Berry II, Derek C Berry, T David, Mark E, Maria L. **Educ:** Chicago State University, BS, 1973, MSed, 1975; University of Cincinnati, pursuing EdD, 1981-. **Career:** Chicago Board of Education, Michael Reese Hospital; Job Opportunity thru Better Skills, assistant director; Central YMCA College, director, secretarial training; Chicago State University, director, special training unit, 1973-77; Kennedy King College, professor, 1977-80; Greater Cincinnati Chamber of Commerce, director, YES Program, 1980-83; University of Cincinnati, 1981-; Elite Travel Services, president, chief executive officer, 1983-. **Orgs:** United Way, trustee, 1989-; Cincinnati Local Development Council, trustee, 1990-; Xonta International, 1992-; Greater Cincinnati Business Owners Board, 1992-; Inter American Travel Agency Society, 1983-; African Travel Association, 1977-; Private Industry Council, 1983-89; Withrow Local School Council Board, 1989-; NAACP. **Honors/Awds:** YWCA, Woman of the Year, 1992; YMCA, Black Achiever, 1992; US Small Business, Woman of Enterprise, 1991; President of United States of America, Summer Jobs Merit Award, 1984; Joseph E Seagrams associate managers, Outstanding Achievement, Business & Community Services, 1990. **Special Achievements:** African Appointment Book, 1990-95. **Business Addr:** President, CEO, Elite Travel Services, Inc, PO Box 3492, Cincinnati, OH 45201-3492, (513)861-8555.

JOHNSON, FRANK
Professional basketball player. **Personal:** Born Nov 23, 1958, Weirsdale, FL; married Amy. **Educ:** Wake Forest, BS 1981. **Career:** Washington Bullets, 1981-88, Houston Rockets, 1988-89; Phoenix Suns, 1992-. **Honors/Awds:** Career high with 15 assists; 1st round draft choice; Honorable Mention on 1982 All-Rookie Team; the top 10 NBA players in assists (4th) 1983; Honorable Mention All-Am by AP & UPI; selected to the All-ACC Team; named outstndng player in Aloha Classic.

JOHNSON, FRANK J., SR.
Publisher. **Personal:** Born Sep 1, 1939, Hope, AR; son of Jettie Irene Wingfield Johnson and Odell Johnson Sr; married Betty J Logan; children: Troy, Frank Jr. **Educ:** CA State Univ Fresno, BA Educ 1963. **Career:** Fresno Colony Sch Dist, teacher 1963-69; West Fresno Sch Dist, principal/counselor 1970-74, dist supt 1975-79; Grapevine Magazine, publisher/editor 1969-84; Who's Who of Black Millionaires Inc, CEO/publisher. **Orgs:** Mem Phi Beta Sigma Frat 1959-; mem West Coast Black Publishers Assn 1979-; exec dir, Non-Profit Housing Assn, (NOAH, Inc), 1995-. **Honors/Awds:** Author, Who's Who of Black Millionaires, 1984; first Black School Dist Supt in Central CA 1975-79; mem Civil Service Bd Fresno CA 1977-81; Alpha Phi Alpha Frat Outstanding Achievement Educ/Publ 1978; Outstanding Teacher West Fresno Sch Dist 1969, Admin 1977; Outstanding Educator, California Black School Board Association, 1989. **Military Serv:** AUS; Comm Serv Awd 1974. **Business Addr:** CEO/Publisher, Who's Who of Black Millionaires, PO Box 12092, Fresno, CA 93776.

JOHNSON, FRANK SCOTT
Marketing executive. **Personal:** Born Feb 22, 1956, Roanoke, VA; son of Roberta M Cooper Johnson and Paul E Johnson. **Educ:** Virginia State University, BS, business, 1979. **Career:** James McGraw, Inc, 1979-81; CCP Mfg Corp, 1982; MAGA Sales, Inc, 1983-86; MSI & Associates, chief executive officer, 1986-; International Sales and Svc Co, director sales and mktg, 1987-89. **Orgs:** Cons to small business; planning com, Virginia Business Opportunity Fair; Valley Home for Adults, board of directors, 1980; Virginia Regional Mnority Purchasing Council; Hampton Rds C of C; National Contract Mgmt Assn; Tidewater Regional Minority Purchasing Council; Virginia State University Alumni Assn; Omega Psi Phi. **Business Phone:** (804)583-6550.

JOHNSON, FRED D.
Educator. **Personal:** Born Mar 7, 1933, Fayetteville, TN; married Dorothy G; children: Fredna, Sheraldine. **Educ:** TN St U, BS; Memphis St U, MEd; Univ TN, EdD 1974. **Career:** Shelby Co Bd Ed, sci consult 1968-, supr, adult ed 1967-68; sci tchr 1954-67; Shelby Co Bd of Educ, asst supt for instr 1977-; McKenzie Group and LA Bd Regents, consultant, 1994-97. **Orgs:** Mem, bd, BSCS; com, Nat Conv Prog 1972; chmn, Area Conv 1974; bd mem-at-large, NSTA 1985; NEA 1985; ASCD 1985; AAAS 1985; NASS1985; KDP 1985; AASA 1985; Optimist 1985; NAACP 1985; bd dir NAACP; interim supt, Shelby Co Schools, 1997; pres, Natl Sci Teachers Assn, NSTA, 1997-98; prog off, Natl Sci Foundation, NSF, 1986-87. **Honors/Awds:** Outstndng Tchr Award, TN Acad Sci 1971; NAACP, District Service Award, 1983; NABSE, District Role Model, 1994. **Military Serv:** AUS e-5 1955-57. **Business Addr:** Asst Supt for Instr, Shelby Co Schools, 160 S Hollywood St, Memphis, TN 38112.

JOHNSON, FREDERICK DOUGLASS
Educator. **Personal:** Born Mar 28, 1946, Chattanooga, TN; married Jacqueline Faith Jones; children: Kyle. **Educ:** Oakwood Coll Huntsville AL, 1965-66; Union Coll Lincoln NE, 1966-68; NE Weslyan Univ, BA 1972; Univ of NE, MA 1980.

Career: Randolph School Lincoln NE, teacher 1972-75, team leader 1976-83; Belmont School Lincoln NE, asst principal curriculum coord 1983-86; asst principal, Park Elementary School Lincoln, NE. **Orgs:** Mem Phi Delta Kappa, Natl Ed Assoc, NE State Ed, Lincoln Ed Assoc Lincoln Public Schools Minority Connection, Guidance Study Comm, Personnel Recruitment Comm, Allan Chapel Seventh-Day-Adventist Church, Amer Legion, Kiwanis, Malone Community Ctr; bd mem Allan Chapel Church, Allon Chapel Church, Child GuidCtr of Lincoln; mem NE Weslyan Career Ctr. **Military Serv:** AUS E-5 1 1/2 yrs; Good Conduct Medal, Asian Serv Medal. **Home Addr:** PO Box 73, Hedgesville, WV 25427.

JOHNSON, FREDERICK E.
Engineer. **Personal:** Born Jun 24, 1941, Detroit, MI; son of Naomi H Johnson and Tommie L Johnson; married Sandra A; children: Frederick II, Seth. **Educ:** Wayne State Univ, BEE 1964; Syracuse Univ, MEE 1969. **Career:** IBM Endicott Lab, line printer test mgr, instrumentation & mech analysis, mgr of prod devel, engr mgr proj ofc, mgr RAS design, instructor/developer (retired); WUCI Radio Station, former president; FESAJ Enterprises, TQM Specialist, president; Binghamton University, Adjunct Inst. **Orgs:** Exec comm NY, PA Health Systems Agency; adv engr, tech asst, engr IBM; pres, bd dirs Broome Ct Urban League; pres Iota Theta Lambda Chap Alpha Phi Alpha 1977-79; treas bd of dir NY, PA Health Systems Agency; trustee Trinity AME Zion Church; publ chmn Broome Cty NAACP, Alpha Phi Alpha, Iota Theta Lambda, Buddy Camp Assoc 1970; chmn Minority Bus Adv Comm Broome Cty NY; mem, IEEE.

JOHNSON, G. R. HOVEY
Judge. **Personal:** Born Nov 13, 1930, Richmond, VA; married Joan C Crocker; children: Marjorie, Patricia, GR Hovey II. **Educ:** Prairie View A&M Coll, BS 1951; George Washington Univ, MS 1974; Georgetown Univ, JD 1977. **Career:** Private Practice of Law, attorney 1977-82; Office of Public Defender, criminal defense lawyer 1979-82; 7th Judicial Circuit of MD, circuit court judge. **Military Serv:** US Army, col 23 yrs; (2) LM, DFC, (3) BSM, (2) MSM, (6) AM, (2) JSCM, ARCOM. **Home Addr:** 16014 Audubon Lane, Bowie, MD 20716. **Business Addr:** Circuit Court Judge, 7th Judicial Circuit of MD, Court House, Upper Marlboro, MD 20772.

JOHNSON, GAGE
Physician. **Personal:** Born Aug 19, 1924, Belzoni, MS; children: Shara, Gage Jr. **Educ:** Tougaloo Coll, BA 1950; Howard U, MD 1955; Cleveland Metro Gen Hosp, resd ob-gyn 1960-64; Am Coll, flw, ob-gyn. **Career:** Outer Dr Hosp, chf ob-gyn; Self, physician. **Orgs:** Mem AMA; mem Nat Med Assn; Wayne Co Med Soc; Detroit Med Soc; sec Fort & St Med Clinic; life mem NAACP. **Honors/Awds:** Mem Alpha Phi Alpha Frat. **Military Serv:** USN seaman 1st class 1943-46. **Business Addr:** Physician, 29260 Franklin Rd, Southfield, MI 48034.

JOHNSON, GENEVA B.
Association executive. **Personal:** Born in Aiken County, SC; daughter of Lillie Mae Bolton and Pierce Bolton. **Educ:** Albright Coll, BS 1951; Case Western Reserve Univ, MSSA 1957. **Career:** YWCA Houston, program dir; Wernersville State Hosp in PA, psychiatric social worker; Children's Aid Soc, supervisory positions; United Way of Berk's Co, asst exec dir; United Way of DE, dir; United Way of Greater Rochester, assoc exec dir; United Way of America, sr vice pres; Family Serv Amer, pres, chief executive officer 1983-. **Orgs:** Consultant: Council of Jewish Federations; YWCA; Natl Fellowship Prog, WK Kellogg Foundation; Natl Urban League; Big Brothers/Big Sisters of Amer; NAACP; bd of dirs National Center for Learning Disabilities; board member: The Foundation Center; Indiana University-Center on Philanthropy; Case Western Reserve University, Mandel Center for Nonprofit Organizations; University of Wisconsin-Milwaukee; Medical College of Wisconsin; Salzburg Seminar; National Center for Nonprofit Boards; Wisconsin Energy Corp and Wisconsin Electric & Power Co; fellow, National Academy of Public Administration. **Honors/Awds:** One of twenty women selected to attend the Jerusalem Womens' Seminar held in Israel and Egypt; Hon Doctor of Humanities Albright Coll, 1983; Distinguished Serv Awd Case Western Reserve Univ, 1983; Awd for Outstanding Serv to Natl Urban League Movement; one of the Top 100 Black Business and Professional Women in Amer, Dollars & Sense Magazine, 1986; F Ritter and Hettie L Shumway Distinguished Serv Awd 1986-; elected NAPA. **Business Addr:** President, CEO, Family Service America, 11700 West Lake Park Drive, Park Place, Milwaukee, WI 53224.

JOHNSON, GEORGE, JR.
Fireman. **Personal:** Born Apr 15, 1934, Warrenton, GA; children: Inc. **Educ:** Inst of Tech; GA Tech; Schell Sch of Marking & Mgmt. **Career:** Richmond Co Fire Dept, various positions 1968-70; chief, 1970-. **Orgs:** E Augusta Action Comm; Augusta-Richmond Co Hum Rel Task Force; GA Assn for Black Elected Officials; Dem Party of GA; Eureka Grand Lodge; NAACP; CSRA. **Honors/Awds:** Involvement Council Award 1971-72; big bro cert appreciation GA Assn for Retarded Children Inc. **Military Serv:** AUS sgt 1951-64. **Home Addr:** 3712 Columbia Dr, Martinez, GA 30907.

JOHNSON, GEORGE ELLIS
Consultant. **Personal:** Born Jun 16, 1927, Richton, MS; son of Priscilla Johnson and Charles Johnson; married Joan B Johnson (divorced); children: Eric, John, George Jr, Joan Marie. **Career:** SB Fuller, employed during 1944; Johnson Products Co Inc, pres, CEO, 1954-89, consultant, 1989-. **Orgs:** Dir Independence Bank of Chicago; bd dir Commonwealth Edison Co; chmn of the bd Indecorp Inc; dir Amer Health & Beauty Aids Inst; pres George E Johnson Educ Fund, George E Johnson Found; mem Babson Coll; exec bd Boy Scouts of Amer; gov mem Chicago Orchestral Assoc; bd of trustees Chicago Sunday Evening Club; bd of dir Chicago Urban League, Dearborn Park Corp, Intl African C of C Inc; natl adv comm Interracial Council of Bus Oppty; vice pres JrAchievement of Chicago; bd dir Lyric Opera of Chicago; principal Chicago United; bd dir Econ Club of Chicago; mem The Commercial Club; sponsoring comm NAACP Legal Defense Fund; bd dir Natl Asthma Ctr, Northwestern Memorial Hosp, Operation PUSH, Protestant Found of Greater Chicago; bd of trustees Northwestern Univ; mem The-Hundred Club of Cook CountLeadership Greater Chicago; chmn, Indecorp. **Honors/Awds:** Abraham Lincoln Ctr Humanitarian Serv Awd 1972; D of Bus Admin Xavier Univ 1973; D of Humanities Clark Coll 1974; D of Commercial Sci The Coll of the Holy Cross 1975; DL Babson Coll 1976; DHL Chicago State Univ 1977; DL Fisk Univ 1977; DL Tuskegee Inst 1978; Amer Black Achievement Awd Ebony Mag 1978; DHL Lemoyne-Owen Coll 1979; Harvard Club of Chicago Public Serv Awd 1979; DL Lake Forest Coll 1979; Horatio Alger Awd 1980; Babson Medal 1983; Hall of Fame, JA Chicago Business, 1985; began own hair care company, Johnson Products Co Inc, which achieved listing on Amer Stock Exchange in 1971 as 1st black-owned company to be listed on a major stock exchange. **Home Addr:** 180 E Pearson, Chicago, IL 60611. **Business Addr:** Consultant, Johnson Products Co Inc, 8522 S Lafayette, Chicago, IL 60620.

JOHNSON, GEORGIA ANNA LEWIS
Physician (retired). **Personal:** Born Feb 1, 1930, Chicago, IL; daughter of Sarah Lewis Scoggins and Robert L. Lewis; children: Barbara, Ruth, Mary. **Educ:** West MI Univ, attended 1948-51; Univ of MI Med Sch, MD 1955. **Career:** Evanston IL, intern 1955-56; Ypsilanti St Hosp, phys 1960-65; Ingham Co Health Dept, phys 1967-69; Int Med Coll, asst prof 1969-75; MI State Univ, dir adoles serv 1973-; Olin Health Ctr, staff phys 1969-1987, retired. **Orgs:** Mem NAACP; AMA; MSMS; Ingham Co Med Soc; AKA sor; AEI Women's Med Frat; Kappa Rho Sigma Hon Sci Frat; MSU Black Women's Fac Assn; Black Fac & ADM Assn; Sickle Cell Anemia Found; bd of trust Capital Area Comp Health Plan Assn; chmn Adv Com Hlth Serv Agcy; bd of dir mem Comp Family Hlth Proj; hospitality commission, Michigan Publishers Assn, 1989-; member, Great Lakes Booksellers Assn, 1990-. **Honors/Awds:** Dean's list West MI Univ 1948; Scholarship Jessie Smith Noyes Sch 1951-55; dist alumna awd West MI Univ 1972; book ''Children's Poems'' 1958; article ''The Interview Workshp'' Jour Med Educ 1974; pub ''Self Instruct Unit Black Skin'' 1973; ''The Black Female Her Image & Choice of Med Care'' 1974; ''The Black Patient-A Catal of Abuses'' Med Dimension 1974; Persp on Afro-Amer Women 1975; publisher, ''Webster's Gold,'' 1990. **Special Achievements:** Publications: Towpath to Freedom, 1989; Webster's Gold, 1990; published by Georgia A Johnson Publishing Company, The Baby Who Knew Too Much, 1993; Black Med Graduates of the Univ of Michigan & Selected Black Michigan Physicians, 1995; Facts, Artifacts and Lies, or the Shackling of Women (comments on the socialization of women); Michigan Senior Olympian, track, 1996-97.

JOHNSON, GEORGIANNA
Labor union administrator. **Personal:** Born Dec 13, 1930, Asheville, NC; daughter of Amelia Starks Johnson and William Fisher Johnson; married Eugene W Smith, Jul 30, 1950; children: Eugenia Smith Sykes. **Educ:** Empire State, New York NY, 1976; Long Island Univ, New York NY, BA in Sociology, 1976; Hunter Coll, New York NY, Master in Sociology, currently attending. **Career:** New York State Employment Office, New York NY, claims examiner, 1950-63; Sherman Thursby, New York NY, insurance adjuster, 1963-68; Hospital for Joint Diseases, New York NY, case aide, 1968-79; Orthopaedic Institute, New York NY, social work asst, 1979-86; Drug, Hospital and Health Care Employees Union, Local 1199, New York NY, pres, 1986-. **Orgs:** Mem, Alpha Kappa Alpha Sorority, 1986-; mem, Black Trade Unionists, 1986-; mem, Coalition of Union Women, 1986-; mem, Natl Alliance Party, 1989-. **Honors/Awds:** Equality for Social Justice Award, Health PAC, 1987; Supportive Spirit Award, 37 Women Committee, 1987; Outstanding Achievement Award, NY Urban League, 1987; Service/Action Beyond Call of Duty Award, Central Brooklyn, 1988; Labor Recognition Award, NAACP, 1988.

JOHNSON, GERALDINE ROSS
Attorney. **Personal:** Born May 13, 1946, Moline, IL; married John T Johnson; children: Christine E, Glenda R, John T Jr. **Educ:** Augustana Coll, BA 1968; Univ of PA Sch of Social Work, MSW 1974; Univ of IA Coll of Law, JD 1982. **Career:** Linn Co IA Dept of Soc Svcs, caseworker 1968-69; Children's Serv City of St Louis, intake case worker 1969-70; Get Set Day Care, preschool tchr 1970-72;Franciscan Mental Health Ctr, social worker 1974-78; Davenport Civil Rights Commn, attorney 1984-86; City of Davenport Legal Dept, atty 1986-. **Orgs:** Mem Iowa State Bar Assoc, Scott Co Bar Assoc; mem Sounds of Peace Choral Group 1981-86; mem Davenport Civil Rights Commn 1982-84; bd of dirs Family Resources Inc 1982-; mem Delta Sigma Theta Public Serv Sor Inc 1984-; volunteer United Way 1986; guest speaker Upward Bound, Marycrest Sociology Dept, MeritEmployment Council, Blackhawk Coll Alpha Ctr; mem Tabernacle Baptist Church Moline IL; mem Pulpit Comm 1986. **Honors/Awds:** Survey of sex educ literature on file in the British Library by request 1984. **Business Addr:** Staff Attorney, City of Davenport, City Hall 226 W Fourth St, Davenport, IA 52801.

JOHNSON, GLENN T.
Judge. **Personal:** Born Jul 19, 1917, Washington, AR; son of Reola Thompson Johnson and Floyd Johnson; married Evelyn Freeman; children: Evelyn A, Glenn Jr. **Educ:** Wilberforce Univ Xenia, OH, BS 1941; John Marshall Law School of Chicago, JD 1949, LLM 1950; Natl Coll of State Trial Judges Reno, NV, 1971; Appellate Court Judges Seminar, NYU, 1974. **Career:** State of IL, asst atty general 1957-63; Metro Sanitary Dist of Greater Chicago, sr atty 1963-66; Circuit Court of Cook County, IL, judge 1966-73; Appellate Court of IL 1st Dist, justice 1973-. **Orgs:** Mem Bench & Bar Section Council IL Bar Assn 1983; fellow Am Acad of Matrimonial Lawyers 1972-; trustee John Marshall Law School of Chicago 1976-; fellow IL Bar Foundation 1984-; mem Judicial Council Natl Bar Assn 1970-; mem NAACP; mem Urban League; mem YMCA; mem Chicago Boys & Girls Club; mem Cook County Bar Assn, mem Chicago Bar Assn; mem The Original Forty Club of Chicago; member, Judicial Council of African Methodist Episcopal Church, 1976-; trustee, Woodlawn AME Church, 1960-; member, American Bar Assn; member, World Assn of Judges, 1973-. **Honors/Awds:** Citation of Merit John Marshall Sch of Law 1970; Judge of Yr Cook County Bar Assn 1973; Certificate of Appreciation IL State Bar Assn 1975-76; Outstanding Serv Natl Bar Assn 1970; Workpaper (Madrid, Spain) Sentencing Procedures in the US of Amer 1979; Workpaper (San Paulo, Brazil) Recent Trends in Family Law in the US 1981; Workpaper (Cairo, Egypt) The Legal Response To Child Snatching In US 1983. **Military Serv:** AUS chief warrant officer-3 1942-46; NG 1950-59; Reserve 1959-63. **Home Addr:** 6133 S Evans Ave, Chicago, IL 60637. **Business Addr:** Justice, Illinois Appellate Court, 3000 Richard J Daley Ctr, Chicago, IL 60602.

JOHNSON, GLORIA DEAN
Librarian. **Personal:** Born Jul 30, 1948, Morton, MS; daughter of Loucille Davis Johnson and Leroy Johnson; children: John Courtney, Anthony Wayne. **Educ:** MS Valley State Univ, BS English Educ 1970; Univ of MS, MLS 1974; MS State Univ, attended; Jackson State Univ, attended; Univ of Southern MS, Hattiesburg, MS, 1986, 1990. **Career:** Charleston Middle School, teacher/libr 1970-72; Morton Jr High School, teacher 1972-74; Meridian Jr Coll, circulation libr 1974-77; Allstate Ins Col, unit suprv 1977-78; East Central Jr Coll, asst librarian 1978-. **Orgs:** Mem MS Assoc of Ed, Natl Assoc of Ed; former mem MS Library Assoc; Alpha Kappa Alpha Sor Inc 1969-; mem, American Library Association, 1990-91. **Home Addr:** Star Rte Box 83, Morton, MS 39117.

JOHNSON, GOLDEN ELIZABETH
Attorney, educator. **Personal:** Born Mar 21, 1944, Newark, NJ. **Educ:** Douglass Coll, AB 1961-65; Rutgers Newark Sch of Law, JD 1968-71. **Career:** Hoffman La Roche Inc, gen atty 1977-; Rutgers Law Sch, prof 1976-; Newark Muncpl Ct, judge 1974-77; Hoffmann-La Roche Inc, atty 1974; Comm Leagl Action Wrkshp, proj dir 1972-74; State of NJ, dep atty & gen 1971-72; US Atty Ofc, intern 1970; W Kinney Jr HS, tchr 1969; Newark Legal Serv, intern 1969; Spec Rsrch Lab, microblgst 1965-68. **Orgs:** Mem NJ State Bar Assn; Essex Co Bar Assn; Garden State Bar Assn; present mem bd of Gov & exec comm Nat Bar Assn; past pres bd mem Women's Div Nat Bar Assn; bd of tst NJ State Opera; bd of tst & past chmn Newark-Essex Co Legal Serv & Joint Law Reform; bd of dir Ctrl Ward Girls Club; mem NJ Adv Bd US Commn on Civil Rights 1973-77; bd of dir Leaguers Inc; mem NJ Coll of Med & Denistry's Bd of Concerned Citzs 1972-75; NAACP; life mem Nat Cncl of Negro Women; chtr mem Assn of Black Women Lwyrs; mem liaison City of Newark for Essex Co Fed of Dem Women 1977; 100 Women for Integ in Govt; mem Rutgers Newark Sch of Law Alumni Assn. **Honors/Awds:** Comm serv awd Rutgers Law Sch 1972; comm serv awd Donald Tucker Civic Assn 1974; achvmt awd Essex Co Civic Assn 1975; black woman achvmt awd COM-BIN-NATION 1975; life mem Guild Legal Serv; awd Nat Cncl of Negro Women 1975; achvmt awd No Reg of Fedn of Colored Women's Club 1975; oust achvmt NJFedn of Colored Women's Club 1975; achvmt awd Delta Sigma Theta Inc 1975; comm serv awd Newark Title 1 Ctrl Parents Cncl 1975; achvmt awd Neward Sect Nat Cncl of Negro Women 1975; awd of excell Oper PUSH 1975; comm serv awd Roosevelt Homes Housing Proj 1975; achvmt awd Nat Assn of Negro Bus & Professional Women's Clubs 1975; comm serv awd Essex Co Legal Serv 1975; serv awd Newark Housing Cncl Comm 1976; disgshd serv awd Seton Hall Univ 1976; certof apprctnCtrl Ward Girls Club 1976; Oper PUSH Tidewa Women Achvmt Awd 1976; achvmt awd Dr Martin Luther King Jr Comm Ctr 1976; achiev awd Guyton-Callahan Post 152 1976; outsdng Woman of Yr NJ Jaycee-ETTES 1977; hon life mem

Zeta Alpha Iota 1977; Alumni Roster of Superior Merit E Side HS 1977;Outstdg Young Woman of Am 1975, 77; gen Couns to Young Dems of NJ. **Business Addr:** 555 Mount Prospect Ave, Newark, NJ 07104.

JOHNSON, GREGORY WAYNE

Educator. **Personal:** Born Dec 6, 1953, Washington, DC; son of Nita Jones and Sidney Johnson; married Brenda Hayes, Dec 31, 1977. **Educ:** Ohio State Univ, Columbus, BA Political Science, 1978. **Career:** Fellowship of Reconcilation, Nyack NY, director, 1987-89; Physicians for Social Responsibility, Washington DC, coordinator, 1989-. **Orgs:** Co-founder, Blacks Against Nukes, 1981-. **Honors/Awds:** Certificate of Merit, Ohio State, 1976; newsletter 1981-; fellowship of reconciliation magazine-reviews, 1987-89.

JOHNSON, HARLAN C.

Educator (retired). **Personal:** Born Jul 17, 1919, Eminence, KY; son of Elizabeth Helen Johnson and Joseph S Johnson. **Educ:** New York Univ, BS 1950, MA 1952; Attended, Univ of WY, Univ of PR, Univ of Mexico, Harvard Univ, John Jay Coll of Criminal Justice 1986-89; Fordham University, Lincoln Center, currently. **Career:** New York Univ, teacher Business Ed 2 yrs; Southern Univ Baton Rouge, teacher Business Ed 1 yr; New York City Bd of Educ, retired teacher; participant in the pre-release program of Rehabilitation, Green Haven Prison; Peer Drug Counselor with Community Services Committee NY City. **Orgs:** Mem NBEA, UFT, Riverside Prison Ministry 1984-; mem/volunteer Riverside Shelter 1985-; Alpha Phi Alpha. **Honors/Awds:** Humanitarian Service Plaque, Green Haven Prison, Stormville NY 1987. **Military Serv:** AUS staff sgt 1943-46; Asiatic-Pacific Theater w/2 Bronze Stars, Philippine Liberation w/1 Bronze Star, Good Conduct Medal, World War II Victory Medal.

JOHNSON, HAROLD R.

Educator, educational administrator (retired). **Personal:** Born Jan 9, 1926, Ontario;son of Catherine Johnson and Lee Johnson; married Marion; children: Robert Harold, Karen Elizabeth, Alan Douglas. **Educ:** Patterson Collegiate Inst, Windsor; Univ of Western Ontario, BA; Wayne State Univ, MSW. **Career:** Windsor Labor Commn for Human Rights & Intl Union of United Brewery Soft Drink & Distillery Workers of Amer, exec dir 1951-57; United Comm Serv of Met Detroit, planning consult 1957-61; Neighborhood Serv Orgn Detroit, assoc dir 1961-69; Office of Youth Serv State of MI, dir 1970; Univ of MI Senate Assembly, 1st black chmn; Univ of MI, dean, school of social work, 1981-93, special counsel to the pres, 1993-94, sec of Univ, 1994-95; Prof of Social Work, 1969-95; Prof of Health Behavior & Health Educ, 1976-95. **Orgs:** Consult Province of Alberta 1979 Univ of Regina 1978, Univ of Toronto 1978-84, Temple Univ 1978; consult MI Commn on Corrections 1972; US Dept of Justice 1972; Famiy Neighborhood Serv So Wayne Co 1972; City of Detroit-Charter Revision Commn 1971; Met Fund 1971; Center for Urban Studies Wayne State Univ 1969; Wayne Co Planning Commn 1968-69; Mayor's Devel Team Detroit 1967; pres Assn for Gerontology in Higher Educ 1979; past chmn Met Detroit Chap 1963-64; mem Natl Assn of Social Workers; fellow Gerontological Soc; mem Council on Social Work Edn; Acad of Certified Social Workers; Assn of Black Soc Workers; past chmn Blue Ribbon Cit Com Wayne Co Bd of Supvr; past vice pres chmn Prog Com Northeastern Wayne Co Child Guidance Clinic; past mem Detroit Public SchRsch Panel; past vice chmn MI common Criminal Justice; cmmr Amer Bar Assn, 1985-91, 1993-; consultant, Yeungnam Univ, Republic of Korea, 1984-; consultant, Univ of Iowa, 1987. **Honors/Awds:** Hon PhD, Yeungnam Univ Korea 1984; Alumni of the Year Award, Wayne State Univ, 1985; School of Social Work, dean emeritus, 1996; prof emeritus of social work, 1996; Health behavior & Health Educ, prof emeritus, 1996; author of numerous reports & papers. **Military Serv:** Royal Canadian Armoured Corps sgt. **Home Addr:** 3000 Glazier Way, Ann Arbor, MI 48105.

JOHNSON, HARRY A.

Educational administrator. **Personal:** Born Nov 22, 1920, Norfolk, VA; married Mae Coleman; children: Sharon Lynne, Jeffrey Alan. **Educ:** VA State Coll, BS 1942; Columbia Univ Tchr Coll, MA 1948, PhD 1952; Sorbonne Univ of Paris, post doctoral study 1958. **Career:** Visiting prof & consultancies at many colls & univs; VA State Coll, prof of educ dean summer sch. **Orgs:** Bd dir CINE Intl; bd dir Intl Journal of Instructional Media; adv bd Library & Educ Media Stanford Univ CA; bd dir Dept of Libr Sci & Educ Media NEA; mem Com Intl Pour Le Developpement Des Activities Educatives et Culturelles En Afrique Italy; mem Amer Assn of Univ Profs; Kappa Delta Pi Natl Hon Soc; Assn for Supervision & Curriculum Devel; Phi Delta Kappa Prof Educ Frat; VA Educ Assn; Natl Educ Assn; Kappa Alpha Psi Frat; Reserve Officers Assn. **Honors/Awds:** Fulbright Rsch Scholar at Paris 1958-59; Amer Men of Sci 1963; Natl Register of Prominent Amers 1973; Awd Outstanding Media Educator of Yr VAECT 1970; Leaders in Educ 1975; Association for Education, Communications and Technology, Distinguished Service Award, 1993; author of numerous publications. **Military Serv:** AUS WWII; AUS Reserve capt retired 1942-74. **Business Addr:** Prof Emeritus, Education, VA State University, Dept of Education, Petersburg, VA 23803.

JOHNSON, HARVEY

City official. **Personal:** Born in Vicksburg, MS; married Kathy Ezell; children: Harvey III, Sharla. **Career:** Jackson State Univ, professor; Mississippi Gaming Board, commissioner; City of Jackson MS, mayor, 1997-. **Special Achievements:** First African American mayor of Jackson, MS.

JOHNSON, HENDERSON A., III

Business executive (retired), educational administrator, dentist. **Personal:** Born Dec 19, 1929, Nashville, TN; son of Minerva Hatcher Johnson and Henderson A. Johnson; married Gwendolyn Gregory, Jun 14, 1952; children: Gregory Paul, Andrea Lynn, H Andrew IV. **Educ:** Fisk U, Hnrs, BS 1950; Springfield Coll, MA, MS 1951; Med Coll of VA, RPT 1952; Western Reserve Univ Sch of Dnstry, DDS 1959. **Career:** H Andrew Johnson DDS, Inc, president, 1959-89; Western Reserve Sch Dnstry, clin instr 1966-69; Highland View Hosp, staff 1985; Pvt Prct Dnstry, 1988; president, Management Office Design Inc 1982-86; dir Dental Prgm Enhancement Project Cuyahoga Comm Coll 1985-89; district director, Cuyahoga Comm College 1986-. **Orgs:** Chairman, 1971-84, chairman emeritus, 1991, Cuyahoga Comm College Foundation; dir Cleveland Pub Radio WCPN 1983-89; vice pres Ctr for Human Rels 1984-88; pres Shaker Hghts Pub Lbry 1978-83; vice pres Cleveland Public Radio WCPN 1986-89; Ohio Educational Broadcast Network Commn 1988-91, board of directors, 1992, vice chair, 1995-; Metro Health Hosp Foundation, consultant; Commission on Accreditation of the American Physical Therapy Association. **Honors/Awds:** Ctzn of Yr Omega Psi Phi Frat Cleveland 1974; Dstngshd Alumni Awrd Fisk Univ 1976; elected to the International Coll of Dentists 1986. **Military Serv:** USAF 1st Lt 1953-54. **Home Addr:** 16506 Fernway Rd, Shaker Heights, OH 44120.

JOHNSON, HENRY

Educator. **Personal:** Born Mar 15, 1937, Atlanta, GA; son of Dr & Mrs K M Johnson; children: Eric, Ian, Stephanie, Rhonda. **Educ:** Morehouse College, BA; Atlanta University, MSW; University of Michigan, post-grad fellowship, Menninger Foundation. **Career:** Ft Wayne State School, psychiatric social worker 1960-62; Menninger Clinic KS, trainee in post-grad psyciatric social work 1962-63; WJ Maxey Boys Training Sch MI, dir group care & counseling div 1964-70; Northville State Hosp Soc Serv Dept, conx group serv 1966-69; Opportunity School Of Educ Univ Of Michigan, assoc dir prog for educ 1970-72; Univ Of Michigan, vice pres student serv 1972-90, vice pres, community affairs, 1990-; Alumni Assoc, sr consultant, 1992-; Consultant-evaluator, North Central Assoc, 1984. **Orgs:** Trustee of Ann Arbor Sch Dist 1968-74; United Fund chmn Univ of MI 1973; mem trust adv bd for Charitable Trust; atty gen adv bd State of MI 1972; mem state bd of MI Assn for emotionally Disturbed Children; chairman, Washtenaw United Way; sire archon, Sigma Pi Phi Fraternity, 1986-88; regional vice pres, NASPA IV-E, 1976-78; Univ of MI, Alumni Assn, sr consultant, 1992-; North Central Assn, consultant evaluator, 1984. **Honors/Awds:** Recipient Huron Valley Social Worker of Yr 1973; Inst for Higher Education, Harvard, Certificate, 1984. **Business Addr:** Vice President of Student Serv, University of Michigan, 2012 Fleming Bldg, Ann Arbor, MI 48109.

JOHNSON, HENRY WADE

Production company executive. **Personal:** Born Jun 13, 1947, Boston, MA; son of Helen Wade Johnson and Henry Johnson; married Naja Griffin; children: Shavi Kharim Uhuru, Damani Kharim Ode. **Educ:** Harvard College, BA, 1970. **Career:** PBS-Boston, WGBH-TV, filmmaker, 1970-79; Blackside Inc, producer, developer, 1979; Rainbow Television Workshop, vice pres of production, 1979-84; television series production, 1985-89; Warner Bros Television, vice pres of film & tape production, currently. **Orgs:** African-American Entertainment Coalition; Westside Prep, bd of dirs; Black Filmmakers Foundation; Directors Guild of America; Assn of Producers and Associate Producers. **Honors/Awds:** NAACP, Sandra Eves Manly Team Player Award, 1993; Amer Society of Lighting Designers, Man of the Year, 1991. **Special Achievements:** Producer: ''Two of Hearts,'' 1979; ''The Children Shall Lead,'' 1979; ''Righteous Apples,'' ''The Young Landlords,'' ''The Grand Baby''; television series: ''Growing Pains,'' 1985-90; ''Just the Ten of US,'' 1987-90; developer/producer: ''Eyes on the Prize,'' 1979. **Home Phone:** (213)936-6306. **Business Addr:** VP, Film & Tape Production, Warner Bros Television, 4000 Warner Blvd, Bldg 14, Ste M, Burbank, CA 91522, (818)954-1102.

JOHNSON, HERMON M., SR.

Business executive, alderman. **Personal:** Born May 5, 1929, Gilbert, LA; son of Comay Anderson Johnson and Samuel Vanora Johnson; married Alfreta Thompson; children: Hermon, Jr, Cheryl Lynn, Darryl, Josef. **Educ:** SU, Baton Rouge, LA, BS 1955; MS Valley St Coll, Elem Tchr Cert 1959. **Career:** Magnolia Mutual Life Ins Co, ofc mgr 1955-59; Myrtle Hall Sch, tchr 1964-66; comm & action splst 1966-68; Tufts Delta Hlth Ctr, ec dev splst 1967-73; Comm Hlth Ed, dir 1973; Dept of Patient Hlth Srv & Resource Coord, dir 1973-; Paul Revere Life Ins Co, sales rep. **Orgs:** Vice-mayor, alderman Mound Bayou 1961; pres Mound Bayou Dev Corp 1961-63; dir Mound Bayou Credit Union 1960-71; asst ctr dir Delta Hlth Ctr, 1975-77; pres, Delta Housing Dev Corp; mem Am Legion Post 220; Mound Bayour Civic Club; Mound Bayou Conversation & Rec League; trustee Bethel AME Ch. **Honors/Awds:** Rookie of the Year Award, 1995; Achiever Award, 1986-87; Challenger Award, 1990; Life ANA Award, 1991. **Military Serv:** AUS corpl 1951-53. **Home Addr:** PO Box 262, Mound Bayou, MS 38762.

JOHNSON, HESTER

Automobile dealership executive. **Career:** Metro Lincoln-Mercury Inc, vp, general manager, currently. **Business Addr:** VP, General Manager, Metro Lincoln-Mercury Inc, 7301 South Blvd, Charlotte, NC 28273.

JOHNSON, HOWARD R.

Judge. **Personal:** Born Aug 20, 1942, Atlanta, GA. **Educ:** Morehouse Coll, BA 1970; Univ of Miami, JD 1973. **Career:** Private Practice, assoc lawyer 1973-75; City of Atlanta, public defender 1975-80, assoc judge 1980-82, chief judge 1982-. **Orgs:** Mem Gate City Bar Assoc 1973-, Atlanta Bar Assoc 1973-. **Honors/Awds:** 1st Public Defender City of Atlanta 1975; 1st Black Chief Judge City of Atlanta 1982. **Military Serv:** USAF airman 1st class 1962-66. **Business Addr:** Chief Judge Municipal Court, 175 Decatur St SE, Atlanta, GA 30303.

JOHNSON, I. S. LEEVY

Business executive. **Personal:** Born May 16, 1942, Richland County, SC; married Doris. **Educ:** Benedict Coll SC, BS 1965; Univ of SC, JD 1968; Univ of MN, Asso of Mortuary. **Career:** SC Gen Assembly, mem; Self, atty; Benedict Coll, former Instr; Funeral Dir, licensed embalmer. **Honors/Awds:** One of three black legisl in SC since Reconstruction. **Business Addr:** President, Johnson, Toal & Battiste, 1500 Hampton St #100, Columbia, SC 29201-2925.

JOHNSON, IOLA VIVIAN

Journalist. **Personal:** Born Oct 10, 1947, Texarkana, AR. **Educ:** Univ Of AZ, Pol Sci & Journalism 1971; Univ Of TX, M Pending. **Career:** WFAA TV Dallas, anchor reporter/talk show host 1973-; The Periscope Tucson, managing ed 1972-73; KVOA TV Tucson, reporter anchor/photographer 1971-73; AR Daily Wildcat Univ Of AL, staff writer 1971; Wash Post DC, summer intern 1969. **Orgs:** Mem Wigma Delta Chi 1968; mem Am Women in Radio & TV 1972-; mem Nat Assn Of Black Journalist 1977-; chmn pub com Dallas Chap of Links Inc 1973-; mem Am Quarter Horse Assn 1979; mem TX Palimino Horse Breeders Assn 1979. **Honors/Awds:** Best Anchor Person in Dallas Ft Worth Dallas Morning News Readers Poll 1980; Braniff 727 Nicknamed ''Iola''. **Business Addr:** WFAA TV, Communications Center, Dallas, TX 75202.

JOHNSON, IVORY

Educator. **Personal:** Born Jun 11, 1938, Oakland, MS; married. **Educ:** Harris Tchrs Coll St Louis, AA 1960; BA 1962; St Louis U, MEd 1969; PhD 1974. **Career:** Ferguson-Florissant Reorganized School Dist, Title I prog dir; Berkeley School Dist St Louis Co, elem sch prin 1969-; St Louis Univ, instructor 1973-; St Louis Bd of Educ, teacher 1962-69; Urban Rural Teacher Renewal Inst St Louis Public School System, consultant 1974. **Orgs:** Mem MO State Tchrs Assn; St Louis Suburban Principals Assn; MO Assn Elem Sch Prins; White House Conf Edn; Nat Assn Elem Sch Prins; Urban League; YMCA; MO PTA; bd dirs Metroplex; Kappa Alpha Psi NDEA Fellowship 1968. **Honors/Awds:** J Jerome Peters Professionalism Award Kappa Alpha Psi 1975.

JOHNSON, J. BERNARD

Entrepreneur. **Personal:** Born Oct 4, 1942, New Bern, NC; son of Clarestine Royal Johnson and Jethro Johnson (deceased); married Zandra Sue Troxler, Nov 1967; children: Zaundra Yolanda, Rhonda Pillar. **Educ:** North Carolina College at Durham, BS, business administration, 1964; University of Pennsylvania, Wharton School, MBA, 1973. **Career:** Stern's Department Store, buyer trainee, 1964-65; IBM Corp., regional administrator, 1965, 1967-71; Peat Marwick Mitchell, business consultant, 1971-73; Region F Health Planning Corp, assistant director, 1973-75; EF Hutton, stockbroker, 1975-77; Barclays American, financial analyst, 1977-79; YoRhon Packaging, CEO, 1979-. **Orgs:** First Baptist Church-West, chairman, board of directors, board of finance; City of Charlotte, budget advisory chairman; Charlotte Chamber of Commerce, small business advisory chairman; The Employers Association, board of directors; United Way, board of directors; Johnson C Smith University, business advisory, board of visitors; United Family Service Board, treasury, 2 years; Private Industry Council, board member; Charlotte/Mecklenburg Schools, chairman, Vocational Development Advisory Council. **Honors/Awds:** Central Piedmont Community College, Certificate of Appreciation, 1985; United Way Leadership Development, Participation Certificate, 1987; Charlotte Business League, Certificate of Appreciation, 1986; City of Charlotte, Certificate of Appreciation, 1985, 1987; United Family Services, Certificate of Appreciation, 1988; North Carolina Department of Public Instruction, Certificate of Appreciation, 1987. **Military Serv:** US Army, spc 4, 1965-67. **Business Addr:** President/CEO, YoRhon Packaging Co, 1721 Toal St, PO Box 32051, Charlotte, NC 28232, (704)376-0018.

JOHNSON, JACOB EDWARDS, III
Educator. **Personal:** Born Feb 21, 1922, Charleston, WV; son of Nena P Edwards Johnson and Jacob Ralph Johnson Jr; married Dalsie Quicke Pullen Johnson, Mar 6, 1944 (died 1979); children: D'Ana E, J Edwards IV. **Educ:** West Virginia State College, Institute, ES, 1928; North Carolina Central University, 1940; Kentucky State University, 1940-43; University of Wisconsin Law School, 1949; Howard University Law School, LLB, 1950, JD, 1968; National University Law School, 1952; George Washington University, 1956. **Career:** US Department of Justice, federal legal liaison, retired; District of Columbia Department of Justice, Corrections, and Parole Board, 35 years; professor of law and criminal justice, currently. **Orgs:** IBPO Elks, past grand exalted ruler(w/honors), legal liaison officer, 1984-91, W Grand Federal Census, officer, 1989-92, Elks Veterans, national service officer, 1984-91, Civil Liberties Department, Elks grand commissioner, 1992; life member, commander, 1983-84, American Legion Post 5, Washington, DC, 1983-84; life member, vice commander, 1989-91, Veterans of Foreign Wars Post 7456, Fairmount, MD, 1983-91; life member, service officer, 1983-91, Disabled American Veterans Post 7, Camp Springs, MD; life member, NAACP; life member, National Bar Association; numerous others. **Honors/Awds:** Kappa Alpha Psi, 50 Year Award, 1991; IBPO Elks, Past Grand Exalted Ruler, with Honors, 1984. **Military Serv:** US Army Air Force, 1st Sgt, 1942-46; WWII Victory Medal, Good Conduct Medal, Pacific Theatre Medal, American Theater, numerous others. **Home Addr:** 4548 Natahala Dr, Clinton, MD 20735-4313.

JOHNSON, JAMES, JR.
Baker, bakery supervisor (retired). **Personal:** Born Sep 25, 1933, Sandersville, GA; son of Lizzie Mae Morris Johnson (deceased) and James Johnson Sr; married Annie Bell Jenkins Johnson, Dec 31, 1956; children: James III, Kelvin, Darryl, Vincent, Yolanda, Terance. **Career:** New Modern Bakery, Detroit, MI, baker, supervisor, beginning 1954. **Orgs:** President, trustee, member, exec board, finance committee memeber, Local 78 Bakers Union, 1958-. **Military Serv:** US Army, Private 1st Class, 1955-57; Conduct Medal.

JOHNSON, JAMES A.
Government employee. **Personal:** Born in Eudora, AR; married Beulah Naomi Crosby; children: Jacquelyne Johnson Jackson, Jeanne Johnson Penn, Viola Elizabeth. **Educ:** NY U, BCS 1926; MCS 1931; further grad study. **Career:** Shaw U, prof 1929-30; Tuskegee Inst, dean sch business 1931-40; Tuskegee Inst, postmaster 1940-47; Veterans Hosp Tuskegee AL, chief educ therapy 1947-68. **Orgs:** #Mem Acad Political & Social Sci; Amer Accounting Assn; vice pres Nat Soc Accountants; 1st vice pres Amer Assn For Rehabilitation Therapy 1956-57, chmn natl membership com 1957-58, speaker Ho Delegates 1958-68; pres co-organizer Tuskegee Fed Credit Union 1957-; pres co-organizer Tuskegee Dev Corp 1970-; ch Trustee Bd Washington Chapel AME Ch; pres chmn bd dirs Washington Chapel Charitable Found Inc; pres chap 751 Nat Assn Retired Fed Employees; 33 deg Mason Shriner; life mem Tuskegee Civic Assn; mem NAACP; life mem Kappa Alpha Phsi Frat. **Honors/Awds:** Community Leader Amer Award 1969; Cert & Honor Ala State Conf NAACP 1971; Cert Merit Shrine Mizraim Temple No 119 1973; Father of Yr Washington Chapel AME Ch 1974. **Business Addr:** 310 Montgomery Rd, Tuskegee, AL 36083.

JOHNSON, JAMES EDWARD
Educational administrator (retired). **Personal:** Born Sep 1, 1931, Cuthbert, GA; married Mable Lumpkin; children: James Jr, Meryl, Joni. **Educ:** Morehouse Coll, BS 1956; Atlanta Univ, MA, Ed Adm 1971, EdD, Ed Adm 1980. **Career:** DeKalb Co Schools, teacher 1956-57; Atlanta Public Schools, teacher 1957-60; Herff Jones Co, mfr rep 1961-69; Atlanta Public Schools, coordinator of personnel 1969-71, prin 1971-73, dir of personnel 1973-74, dir of employee relations & personnel, beginning 1976, associate superintendent, until 1994. **Orgs:** Mem & del Natl Educ Assn Atlanta Tchr Assn & GA Assn of Educs 1956-; mem del Amer Assn of Sch Persnl Admins 1970-71; mem Assn of Educ Neg 1976-; consul GA Sch Bd Assn 1975; consul GA C of C 1976; consul MS Educ Serv Ctr 1976; consul GA Assn of Educ Leaders 1976; consul GA Assn of Educs 1976; consul Professional Assn of GA Educators 1977; mem bd of dir Grady Homes Boys Club 1965-; memshp worker YMCA 1961-; sec chmn Schlrshp Comm Alpha Phi Alpha Frat 1955-; committeeman Radcliffe Presby Ch 1956-; committeeman scoutmaster BSA 1957-; mem Ofcl Quarterback Club 1957-; mem Jr C of C 1962-64; mem Atlanta C of C 1963-64. **Honors/Awds:** Deans List Morehouse Coll; mem Beta Kappa Chi Sci Hon Soc; Top Salesman Awd Herff Jones Co; Dist Serv Awd Morehouse Coll; EPDA; Fellowship Doctoral Cand Atlanta Univ. **Military Serv:** USMC sgt 1951-54.

JOHNSON, JAMES H.
Labor union official (retired), cleric. **Personal:** Born Aug 5, 1932, Mohobe, MS; son of Leesie Sowell Johnson and Eugene G Johnson; married Carrie B Miller; children: Carrie Arlena, Michele Francine, Yolanda Clarice, Vivian Jamie. **Educ:** Wells HS Chgo, IL. **Career:** Kentile Flrs Inc Chgo, IL, prod wrkr 1956-69; URW Akron, OH, fld rep 1969-77, dist dir 1977-96; Cntrl Church of God, assoc pstr 1973-84, pstr 1984-87; pastor Johnson Memorial Church of God 1987-. **Orgs:** Orgnzr & 1st pres Bellwood Comm 1976-79; bd of dir & adv A Philip Randolph 1980-83; mem NAACP 1980; bd of dirs IPAC 1983-. **Military Serv:** USMC pfc 1952-55; Nat Defense Svc; Korean Serv Medal w/2 stars; UN Serv Medal; Korean PUC.

JOHNSON, JAMES KENNETH
Physician, surgeon. **Personal:** Born Oct 9, 1942, Detroit, MI; son of Frances C Brantley Johnson and William R Johnson; married Jean E Hayes, Jul 11, 1965; children: Kalyn J Johnson, Kendell J Johnson. **Educ:** Wayne State Univ, Detroit MI, BS, 1964; Meharry Medical Coll, Nashville TN, MD, 1969; Yale Univ, New Haven CT, 1973-76. **Career:** Strong & Johnson MD, PC, Detroit MI, physician, surgeon 1976-; Southwest Detroit Hospital, Detroit MI, medical director, vice pres of medical affairs, 1986-. **Orgs:** Pres, Detroit Medical Society, 1988-. **Honors/Awds:** Distinguished teacher, Department of Family Practice, Wayne State Univ Medical School 1983. **Military Serv:** US Army, major, 1971-73.

JOHNSON, JAMES R.
City official. **Personal:** Born Feb 19, 1934, Cory, MS; son of Rev and Mrs T J Johnson; married Lottie Johnson; children: Tamaria, Jay, Thomas, Jamel. **Educ:** Jackson State Univ, BS 1955, MS 1973. **Career:** MS Public School, teacher 1957-63; Bib Dist, pres; Jackson State Univ, resident counselor & dean of men, commissioner of camp sec 1963-68; Dynamic Photos & J & M Assoc Inc, partner 1968-75; Capital Studios Photos & Flowers, pres 1975-83; City of Jackson MS, proj dir sr aides prog 1983-; Mississippi State Department of Human Services, State Council on Aging, director, currently. **Orgs:** Jackson St Univ Sen Mens' Counselor & Dean of Men 1963-68; chairman of the board Nat Bus League Local 1971-; co-organizer MS State Bus Organ 1974; chmn Jackson St U's Dev Fund; chmn Seminole Dist BSA; chmn Finance Seminole Dist BSA; Hinds Co, St Ex Comm of MS Rep Party; chair, Metro Area Private Industry Council, 1990-91. **Honors/Awds:** Outstanding Black Mississippian 1972; Omega Psi Phi Soc Serv Award 1972; Jackson State Coll Alumnus of Year in Politics 1972; Outstanding Leadership Awd Natl Bus League 1975; Dedicated Serv to Jackson Public School 1982; Outstanding Support of MS Headstart Assn 1985. **Special Achievements:** First African-American member, Jackson, Mississippi, School Board, 1971. **Military Serv:** US Army MOS food serv 1955-57. **Home Addr:** 2841 Shrewsbury Ct, Jackson, MS 39209.

JOHNSON, JAMES S.
Physician. **Personal:** Born Feb 22, 1918, Stull, KS; married Grace C; children: James, Nelson, Thomas. **Educ:** Washburn Univ, BS, 1939; Howard Univ, MD, 1945. **Career:** Kansas City, MO, private practice, Ob/Gyn; Model Cities Health Center, Admin consultant; Univ MO, Kansas City Med Center, consulting Ob/Gyn; Menorah Med Center, teaching staff mem; St Joseph & Martin Luther King Memorial Hospitals, teaching staff mem; Lawrence Aviation, dir. **Orgs:** Mem Jackson Co & Kansas City Med Socs; Kansas City Gynecological Soc; YMCA; Sigma Pi Phi; Midwesterners Club; Heart of Am Golf Club; Negro Airman Internat; Paseo Bapt Ch State Champion MO Pan Med Soc. **Honors/Awds:** Father of the Year Award, YMCA, 1962. **Business Addr:** 4301 Cleveland, Kansas City, MO 64130.

JOHNSON, JAMES WALTER, JR.
Attorney. **Personal:** Born May 12, 1941, Washington, DC; married Eva M Murdock; children: Kimberely, Stephanie, Christopher. **Educ:** Howard Univ, BS 1963; George Washington Univ, MS 1969, JD 1971. **Career:** Lockheed Missile & Space Co, assoc engr 1963-64; US Patent Office, examiner 1965-66; Mitre Corp, staff 1968-71; Communication Satellite Corp, patent attny 1971-74; GE Co, div patent consult 1974-78; Intelsat, patent consult 1978-. **Orgs:** Mem DC Bar Assoc, PA Bar Assoc, Natl Bar Assoc, Amer Patent Lawyers Assoc; reg US Patent Attny; mem Kappa Alpha Psi. **Military Serv:** AUS capt 1966-68. **Business Addr:** Asst Legal Advisor, Intelsat, 490 L'Enfant Plaza SW, Room 7078, Washington, DC 20024.

JOHNSON, JARED MODELL
Company executive, educational administrator. **Personal:** Born Oct 31, 1960, Milwaukee, WI; son of Florence Ladon Johnson and Wilbert David Johnson. **Educ:** Milwaukee Area Technical College, 1979-80; University of Wisconsin, Milwaukee, 1980-84, currently. **Career:** Aspii Contracting and Development Corp., president, currently. **Orgs:** Milwaukee Public Schools, board of directors. **Home Addr:** 2337 N Weil St, Apt 2, Milwaukee, WI 53212, (414)562-3266.

JOHNSON, JAY (SUPER JAY)
Radio manager/announcer. **Personal:** Born Apr 2, 1947, Louisville, KY; married Arneda Moncure; children: Jason Troy, Tiffany Faye. **Educ:** Attended, Triton Coll, Coll of Professional Broadcasting Chicago. **Career:** WGRT Radio, announcer 1968-71; WVON Radio, announcer 1971-75; WBBM-TV, announcer 1974-75; WISH-TV, reporter/host 1978-85; WTLC-FM, program dir 1975-. **Orgs:** Pres Jay Johnson Enterprises; bd mem Amer Lung Assoc Indy Chapt; consultant Indiana Black Expo, Ctr for Leadership Develop; comm mem PAXI 10th Pan Amer Games 1986-87. **Honors/Awds:** Air Personality or Program Dir of the Year Billboard magazine 1974,80,82; Air Personality or Program Dir of the Year Black Radio Exclusive magazine 1977,78,79,85,86; Super Jay Johnson Day City of Indianapolis 1977; Outstanding Serv as Host UNCF 1978-85; Excellence Awd Operation PUSH 1981; Success Awd Black Woman Hall of Fame Foundation 1984. **Military Serv:** AUS 3 yrs.

JOHNSON, JEH VINCENT
Architect, lecturer. **Personal:** Born Jul 8, 1931, Nashville, TN; son of Marie Burgette Johnson and Charles Spurgeon Johnson; married Norma Edelin; children: Jeh Charles, Marguerite Marie. **Educ:** Columbia Coll, AB 1953; Columbia Univ, March 1958. **Career:** Paul R Williams, Architect, designer/draftsman 1956; Adams & Woodbridge Architects, designer 1958-62; Gindele & Johnson PC, architect pres 1962-80; LeGendre Johnson McNeil Architects, partner 1980-90; Jeh V Johnson, FAIA, architect 1990-. **Orgs:** Lecturer Vassar Coll 1964-; consultant Dutchess County Planning Bd 1984-; dir The Bank of the Hudson, 1977-; NY St Arch Registration Bd 1973-84; Am Inst of Arch 1963-; found mem Natl Org of Minority Arch 1972-; mem Sigma Pi Phi; dir Scenic Hudson, Inc, 1996-. **Honors/Awds:** Students Medal AIA, NY 1958; William Kinne Fellows Traveling Flwshp (Europe) 1959; elected to Fellowship Am Inst of Arch 1977; designed over 300 major projects & 4300 housing units 1963-97. **Military Serv:** AUS sgt 1953-55. **Business Addr:** 14 Edge Hill Rd, Wappingers Falls, NY 12590.

JOHNSON, JERRY CALVIN
Athletic director, coach, educator. **Personal:** Born Jun 20, 1920, Tulsa, OK; married Vaster M; children: Dr Jerry C Jr, Wandra Haywood, Oliver. **Educ:** Fayetteville State Univ, BS 1950; Columbia Univ, MA 1951. **Career:** Ridgeview HS, teacher, coach 1951-58; LeMoyne Owen Coll, athletic director/coach, professor of health, physical education, and recreation, 1959-. **Orgs:** Volunteer Amer Red Cross 1959-; consult Natl Youth Sports Prog 1972-82; bd of dir Memphis Shelby Cty Old Age 1975-80; adv council TN State Bd of Ed 1984-; vice pres Southern Intercollegiate Conf 1984-. **Honors/Awds:** Coach of the Year NCAA 100% Wrong Club 1975; State Legislature Proclamation State of TN 1976; Faculty Mem of the Year LeMoyne Owen Coll 1980; Recreation Award, Memphis Park Commission, 1985. **Business Addr:** Prof Health Phys Ed Rec, LeMoyne Owen Coll, 807 Walker Ave, Memphis, TN 38126.

JOHNSON, JERRY L.
Communications company executive. **Personal:** Born Dec 4, 1947, Freeport, IL; son of Katherine Moseley Johnson and Charles W. Johnson; married Raye Sandford Johnson, May 17, 1968; children: Jeri Lynne, Jonathan Wellesley. **Educ:** Northeast Missouri State University, Kirksville, MO, BS, education and psychology, 1969; Northern Illinois University, DeKalb, IL, MS, 1970; Western Illinois University, Macomb, IL, education specialist certificate; Massachusetts Institute of Technology, Cambridge, MA, MS, management, 1983. **Career:** Galesburg Public School District 205, Galesburg, IL, principal, 1972-76; NWB Telephone Co, Minneapolis, MN, management asst, 1976-81, district plant manager, 1981-82; NWB Information Technologies, Omaha, NE, CEO, 1984-85, president & CEO, 1985; US West, Inc, Denver, CO, vice pres-residence planning, 1986-87; US West Home & Personal Services, Phoenix, AZ, vice pres & general manager, 1987-90; US West Communications, Inc, Western Region, Network & Technology Services, Seattle, WA, vice president, 1990-92; Network & Technology Services, vice pres, 1993-. **Orgs:** Member, Intl Soc of Sloan Fellows; member, Visiting Committee, Sloan School of Management, Massachusetts Institute of Technology; member, Sigma Pi Phi Boule; member, Kappa Alpha Psi, member. **Honors/Awds:** ''One of Top 25 Most Powerful Black Executives in Corporate America,'' Black Enterprise Magazine, January, 1988. **Business Addr:** Vice President, Network and Technology Services, US West Communications, 1801 California, 52nd Fl, Denver, CO 80202.

JOHNSON, JESSE J.
Writer, military officer (retired). **Personal:** Born May 15, 1914, Hattiesburg, MS; married Elizabeth C. **Educ:** Tougaloo Coll, AB 1939; Amer Ext School of Law, LLB 1950; Hampton Inst, MA 1964. **Career:** US Army, lt col, 1942-62. **Honors/Awds:** Guest speaker colls & univ. **Special Achievements:** Wrote: Ebony Brass, Black Soldiers, Black Armed Forces Officers 1736-1971; 5 other books about African-American men & women in military servs in the US. **Military Serv:** US Army, retired lt col, 1942-62.

JOHNSON, JESSE J.
Psychological consultant. **Personal:** Born Jul 14, 1921, New Madrid, MO; married Annie E Robinson; children: Jesse, Walter, Beverly. **Educ:** Dillard U, BS 1946; Northwestern U, MS 1949; Northwestern U, PhD 1951; Center for Mental Health NYC, 4 yr Certificate in Psycoanalysis Post Grad 1967. **Career:** Jesse J & Johnson Asso, presently psychol cons; VA Tuskegee AL & Montrose, NY, supr Psychologist 1951-67; Briarcliff Coll, lecturer; State Univ of NY,asso prof; To Industry, cons; Graham Home for Children NY, cons; HEW, cons. **Orgs:**

Mem Am Psychol Assn; pres Assn of Black Psychologists; travel agency Jayjay Travel White Plains NY; chmn Corporate Concerns Com Operations PUSH; mem Council of Concerned Black Executives; mem Soc of Sigma Xi. **Military Serv:** Sgt 92 Infantry Div 1943-45. **Business Addr:** Jay Jay Travel, 149 Grand St, White Plains, NY 10601.

JOHNSON, JIMMIE
Professional football player. **Personal:** Born Oct 6, 1966, Augusta, GA. **Educ:** Howard Univ, bachelor's degree in consumer studies, 1989. **Career:** Washington Redskins, tight end, 1989-91; Detroit Lions, 1992-93; Kansas City Chiefs, 1994; Philadelphia Eagles, 1995-. **Business Addr:** Professional Football Player, Philadelphia Eagles, 3501 S Broad St, Philadelphia, PA 19148, (215)463-2500.

JOHNSON, JOAN B.
Company executive. **Personal:** Born 1929; married George E. Johnson (divorced 1989); children: Eric. **Career:** Johnson Products Co, Chicago, IL, with company since 1954, vice president, 1965-75, treasurer and director, 1975-89, chairman, 1989-. **Honors/Awds:** Johnson Products Company is ranked 24 on Black Enterprise's list of top 100 Black businesses. **Business Addr:** Chairman, Johnson Products Co, Inc, 8522 S Lafayette, Chicago, IL 60620.

JOHNSON, JOE
Author, poet, educator, journalist. **Personal:** Born Jan 18, 1940, New York, NY; son of Lillian Mae Young and Alonzo D Johnson Sr; married Harriet Nicole Luria, Aug 1, 1967; children: Jeremiah Joseph. **Educ:** Columbia Univ, BA, 1970; Columbia Univ Teachers Coll, MA, 1973; New School for Social Research, additional studies; Columbia Univ, grad fellow of art history and archaeology. **Career:** City Univ City College, teacher, 1970-71; Reed Cannon & Johnson Publishing, editor-publisher, 1973-77; Crisis Magazine, book editor; Ramapo Coll of NJ, assoc prof of literature, 1971-, co-chairperson of African-Amer Inst. **Orgs:** Chmn, Black Lit Panel NE Modern Language Assn, 1974. **Honors/Awds:** Published poetry book, At the Westend, 1976; published "Hot" Telephone Book, 1977; published Tight, Lee Lucas Press, 1978. **Home Addr:** 365 South End Ave, New York, NY 10280. **Business Addr:** Assoc Prof, Literature, Ramapo Coll of New Jersey, 803 Ramapo Valley Rd, Mahwah, NJ 07430-1680.

JOHNSON, JOHN
Organization executive. **Career:** Wayne County Neighborhood Legal Services, staff attorney, supervising attorney, deputy director; National Consumer Law Center, staff attorney; UAW Legal Service Plans, managing attorney; Legal Aid & Defender Assn, chief counsel; NAACP, Detroit Branch, executive director, currently. **Business Addr:** Executive Director, NAACP-Detroit Chapter, 2990 E Grand Blvd, Detroit, MI 48202.

JOHNSON, JOHN H.
Publishing company executive. **Personal:** Born Jan 19, 1918, Arkansas City, AR; son of Gertrude Johnson Williams; married Eunice; children: Linda Johnson Rice. **Educ:** Univ Chicago; Northwestern Univ. **Career:** Supreme Liberty Life Ins Co; WLOU Radio Sta, pres; Johnson Publ Co Chicago, IL, chief executive officer/publisher of Ebony, Jet and EM Magazines 1942-; Fashion Fair Cosmetics, Ebone Cosmetics, Supreme Beauty Products; American Black Achievement Awards TV Program. **Orgs:** Chmn Supreme Life Ins Co; dir, Dial Corp, Zenith Radio Corp, Chrysler Corp; trustee Art Inst Chicago; fellow Sigma Delta Chi; mem US Chamber of Commerce; dir Mag Pubs Assn. **Honors/Awds:** John Russwurm Award Natl Newspaper Pubs Assn 1966; Spingarn Medal NAACP 1966; Henry Johnson Fisher Award Magazine Pubs Assn 1971; Communicator of the Year Award Univ Chicago Alumni Assn 1974; Columbia Journalism Award 1974; accompanied US Vice Pres on goodwill tour to nine African countries 1975; named to Acad Disting Entrepreneurs Babson Coll 1979; Chicago Boys Club Chicagoan of the Year 1983; Natl Press Foundation Award 1986; Black Enterprise No. 1 Black Business Award 1986; Black Enterprise No. 1 Black Business Award; inducted into Black Press Hall of Fame 1987; inducted into The Publishing Hall of Fame Folio Educ Trust, Inc 1987; Salute to Greatness Award Martin Luther King Center for Nonviolent Social Change Harold H. Hines, Jr. Benefactors' Award, United Negro Coll Fund 1988, Equapportunity Award, Natl Urban League 1988; inducted into Illinois Business Hall of Fame, EXCELL Award, Intl Assn of Business Communicators, inducted into Natl Sales Hall of Fame, Natl Conf of Christians and JEWS (NCCJ), NCCJ Founders Award, Natl NCCJ Mass Media Award, Special NCCJ Bd Award; numerous honorary degrees, 1989; Inducted into the Chicago Journalism Hall of Fame, 1990; Distinguished Service Award, Harvard University Graduate School of Business Administration, 1991; Salute to the Media Award, Impact Publications; Africa's Future Award, United Nations Children's Fund, 1992; Booker T Washington Speaker's Award, Booker T Washington Business Association Heritage Award, Executive Leadership Council, 1992; The Dow Jones Entrepreneurial Excellence Award, Dow Jones and The Wall Street Journal, 1993; Inducted into the Entrepreneurship Hall of Fame, The University of Illinois at Chicato, 1993; The Monarch Award for Communications, Alpha Kappa Alpha Sorority, Inc, 1993; The First Annual Arkansas Black Hall of Fame, The Arkansas Regional Minority Suppliers Development Council, 1993; Communication Award, Center for Communication, Inc, 1995; Presidential Medal of Freedom, 1996; Corporate Pioneer Award, Business Policy Review Council, 1996; Lifetime Achievement Award, American Advertising Foundation, 1996; National Business Hall of Fame Award, National Junior Achievement, 1997. **Business Addr:** Publisher, Chairman, Chief Executive Officer, Johnson Publishing Co, Inc, 820 S Michigan Avenue, Chicago, IL 60605.

JOHNSON, JOHN J.
Association executive. **Personal:** divoRced; children: Gloria, Don, Kavin, Felita. **Educ:** Sojourner-Douglass Coll, BA. **Career:** Kentucky Inst for Community Devt, trainer, 1968-69; Southern Kentucky Economic Opportunity Council, dir of field operations & training, equal opportunity officer, 1969-70; Louisville-Jefferson County, Community Action Commission, supervisor, 1971-75; Louisville-Jefferson County, Human Relations Commission, assoc dir, 1975-77; Kentucky Commission on Human Rights, dir of community services, 1977-84; Community Action Agency, exec dir, 1984-86; NAACP, Voter Education Dept, natl dir, 1986-89, Labor Dept, natl dir, 1988-, Armed Services & Veteran Affairs Dept, natl dir, 1990-, exec asst to the exec dir, 1989-. **Orgs:** NAACP, Life & Golden Heritage Member, 1963-; Lampton Baptist Church; Natl Urban League, local chapter; A Philip Randolph Inst, natl bd of dirs; Natl Coalition of Black Voter Participation, natl bd of dirs; Martin Luther King Jr Federal Holiday Commission, alternate commissioner; Natl Committee of Pay Equity, bd of dirs; numerous other memberships, 1972-. **Honors/Awds:** US Dept of Defense Award, 1991; US Bureau of the Census, Natl Services Program Award, 1990; City of Franklin, KY, Ambassador of Goodwill Award, 1989; Kentucky Dept of Education, Golden Apple Leadership Award, 1987; Kentucky Conference of NAACP Branches, Award of Merit, 1986; NAACP, Natl Bd of Dirs, Award of Appreciation, 1986; Phi Beta Sigma Fraternity, Distinguished Service in Social Action Natl Award, 1985; Mae Street Kidd Auxiliary, Human Service Award, 1984; Whitney M Young Jr Award; numerous others. **Business Addr:** Exec Asst to the Exec Dir, NAACP, 4805 Mt Hope Dr, Baltimore, MD 21215-3297, (410)486-9104.

JOHNSON, JOHN THOMAS
Physician. **Personal:** Born Feb 8, 1942, St Louis, MO; married Geraldine Ross; children: Christine E, Glenda R, John T Jr. **Educ:** Parsons Coll, BS 1967; Philadelphia Coll of Osteopathic Medicine, DO 1974. **Career:** Davenport Medical Ctr, intern 1974-75, resident 19075-76; Private Practice, physician 1976-. **Orgs:** Mem Amer Osteopathic Assoc 1976-, Iowa Osteopathic Medicine Assoc 1976-, Scott County Medical Soc 1976-; bd of dirs Davenport Medical Ctr; volunteer physician Silver Gloves, Boy Scouts 1985. **Honors/Awds:** Awd & Roast Sepia Guild 1977; Certificate of Appreciation The Honor Comm 1982; Recognition Awd Christian Comm Serv 1982, Calvary SDA Church 1983; Certificate of Appreciation Senior Citizens 1985; Recognition Awd Davenport Medical Ctr 1986. **Military Serv:** AUS e4 1963-65. **Business Addr:** PO Box 2794, Davenport, IA 52809-2794.

JOHNSON, JOHN W.
Attorney, law professor. **Personal:** Born Nov 6, 1934, Summerfield, LA; children: John, Jr, Julian. **Educ:** Georgetown Univ Law Center, LlM 1964; Howard Univ Sch of Law, JD 1962; So Univ Baton Rouge, BA 1957. **Career:** AT & T, atty 1972; NY Law Sch, law prof 1978-; US Dept of Just Wash, trial lawy 1964-68; OH Bell Tel & Co Cleveland Corp ABA, lawy 1968-72. **Orgs:** Nat Bar Assn; NY Bar Assn; OH Bar Assn; DC Bar Assn; LA Bar Assn; World Peace thru Law; Adm to Prac before Supreme Ct of US Sigma Delta Tau Legal Frat Part in LA first "sit in" demonstrn 1960 case reviewed by US Sup Ct Garner V LA. **Military Serv:** Active military duty 1957-59. **Business Addr:** AT&T 195 Broadway, Ste #1117, New York, NY 10007.

JOHNSON, JOHNNIE L., JR.
Attorney. **Personal:** Born Nov 1, 1946, Nesbitt, MS; son of Beulah M Merriweather Johnson and Johnnie L Johnson II; married Bethiness Theodocia Walker, Jun 7, 1970; children: Johnnie L IV, Gregory Lloyd, Justice Millsaps, Ahmad Nakeill. **Educ:** Morris Brown Coll, BA 1967; OH Northern Univ, JD 1970. **Career:** Dept of Justice, asst us atty 1970-73; Equal Employment Oppty Commission, asst reg atty 1973-75, spec asst to comm 1975-78, dir trial team II 1978-81; EEOC, assistant Gen Counsel, 1981-83; director, Legal & Special Pol Div, 1983-84; Director Special Projects, 1984-85; sr trial attorney, 1985-. **Orgs:** Pres Morris Brown Coll Alumni Assoc 1985-92, mediator, DC Mediation Service 1989-; bd of directors, Ohio Northern Univ Law Alumni Assoc 1988-; pres, Mediterranean Villa Cluster Assn l986-; Mediator, Multi-Door Disput Resolution Center, 1990-; president, BF Jones Bar Association, 1970-73; president, Board of Directors, Memphis & Shelby City, Legal Services Assn 1972-74; first vice president, Memphis Chapter, Federal Bar Assn, 1972-74; lecturer, Ohio Northern University College of Law 16th Annual Law Review Symposium. **Honors/Awds:** Donnie Delaney Comm Defense Awd 1974; Outstanding Young Man of Amer 1979; participant in "Old Dominion 100 Mile Endurance Run" 1979, Empire State Run Up 1979, 1980, JFK 50 Miler 1980; Ohio Northern University, College of Law, 16th annual Law Review Symposium, lecturer. **Home Addr:** 11644 Mediterranean Court, Reston, VA 22090, (703)471-0848. **Business Addr:** Senior Trial Attorney, Equal Employment Opportunity Comm, 1801 L St, NW, Washington, DC 20507.

JOHNSON, JOHNNY B.
Educator (retired). **Personal:** Born Feb 17, 1920, Rison, AR; married Mildred Mazique; children: Johnny Jr, Mrs Patricia Berry, Revawn. **Educ:** Agricultural Mechanical & Normal Coll, BS 1948; MI State Univ, MS 1948, MA 1955; Univ of AR, EdD 1963. **Career:** AM&N Coll, dean of men 1949-61; Univ of AR-Pine Bluff, prof 1963-73, interim chancellor 1973-74, vice chancellor academic affairs 1974-76, prof acting chancellor vice chancellor 1976-86, provost/vice chancellor. **Orgs:** Mem AR Educ Assoc, Natl Educ Assoc, Amer Assoc of Higher Educ 1949-86; mem Kiwanis Intl 1975-86. **Honors/Awds:** Fellowship Southern Educ Foundation 1962; listed Outstanding Educators of Amer 1975; Outstanding Civilian Service Awd Army ROTC 1974. **Military Serv:** AUS tech sgt 1942-45; Bronze Star. **Home Addr:** #67 Watson Blvd, Pine Bluff, AR 71601.

JOHNSON, JON D.
State senator. **Personal:** Born Aug 17, 1948. **Educ:** Southern University, BS; Loyola University, MBA. **Career:** City of New Orleans, Mayor's Human Rights Comm, member, 1974-80; Louisiana State House of Representatives, state representative, 1980-85; Louisiana State Senate, state senator, 1985-; commodity broker; New Orleans Health Corp, chairman, currently. **Orgs:** National Assn of MBA Executives; Urban League of Greater New Orleans. **Business Addr:** State Senator, State Capitol, Baton Rouge, LA 70804.

JOHNSON, JONDELLE H.
Executive director. **Personal:** Born Mar 11, 1924, Charleston, SC; children: Carolyn, Jo Ann, Winfred, Edgar. **Educ:** Allen Univ Columbia, SC, AB 1945; Atlanta U, MA 1953; Emory Univ Atlanta. **Career:** Atlanta, GA Bd of Edn, tchr 1957-69; Dekalb Co GA Bd of Edn, tchr 1949-57; Cobb Co GA Bd of Edn, tchr 1946-47; Atlanta Inquirer Newspaper, soc editor 1961-67; Atlanta Inquirer Newspaper, mng editor 1966-67; Atlanta Voice Newspaper, soc editor 1967-74; Atlanta Voice Newspaper, news editor 1967-74; Bronze Am Mag, southeastern editor 1964-65; Atlanta Br NAACP, presently exec dir. **Orgs:** Mem Atlanta PTA Council; GA Educ Assn; NEA; GA PTA Congress; Atlanta Pub Sch Adv Council; Cit Trust Bank & Comm Adv Bd; WIGO Radio Adv Bd; Nat Bus & Professional Women's Club Mem Wheat St Bapt Ch; Met Assn for Blind Vol Com; Exec Bd NW Br YMCA; Maude Daniels Chap for Retarded; Atlanta Urban League Guild; Atlanta Theater Guild; Iota Phi Lambda Sorority; vote dep registrar; Exec com Fulton & Co Rep Party; exec bd Atlanta Br NAACP; State Pub Relations Dir F&AA York Masons & Eastern Stars; YMCA; Atlanta Urban League Coalition on Census; exec com Fifth Dist Rep; Lincoln-Douglass Rep Club;Met Rep Women's Club; Metro Atlanta Summit Leadership Congress; Heroines of Jericho; Eastern Star Order of Nat Compact; USA-FAA Masons; All Cit Registration Com; precinctchmn 108 House Dist; bd mem Nat Clie Council; Consult Educ In-serv Workshops for Tchrs; Washington High Comm Sch Adv Com; coordinator Tutorial Prog in Poverty Areas; YMCA Membership Drives. **Honors/Awds:** Recipient First Place Awards in Pub Serv Nat Newspaper Assn 1964, 65, 67; Woman of the Yr in Human & Relations Bronze Woman of the Yr Iota Phi Lambda Sorority 1967; Outstanding Educator's Award GA PTA Congress 1968; Fulton Co Rep Serv Awards 1969, 70, 73; Woman of Yr Award Metro Atlanta Summit Leadership Congress 1974; Citizenship Award Las Amigas Club 1968; YWCA-GAY Y Serv Club Award 1968; NAACP Leadership Award 1972; Fulton Co Rep Century Cluf Awards 1971-72; Dekalb Co Grad Scholarship for Outstanding Teaching summers 1952-53; Nat Continental Soc Bicentennial Distinguished Black Am Award 1975; YMCA Trophy for Leadership 1968; Nat Negro Women's Bus & Professional Leadership Award 1970; Freedom Award by Cit for Freedom 1971. **Business Addr:** 859 1/2 Hunter St NW, Atlanta, GA 30314.

JOHNSON, JOSCELYN ANDREA
Assistant account executive. **Personal:** Born Feb 27, 1966, Pontiac, MI; daughter of Jacqueline M Mullen Johnson and Kenneth R Johnson Jr. **Educ:** Univ of MI, Ann Arbor, MI, BA, political science & English, 1988. **Career:** Univ of MI, Ann Arbor, MI, writing skills asst, 1986-87, peer information counselor, 1988-89; AAA MI, Dearborn, MI, customer service rep, 1989-90; Hermanoff & Assoc, Farmington Hills, MI, asst acct exec, 1990-. **Orgs:** Mem, Public Relations Society of America, 1991-; mem, Delta Sigma Theta Soroity, Inc, 1986-. **Honors/Awds:** 376th Daily Pt of Light, US White House, 1991.

JOHNSON, JOSEPH
Professional football player. **Personal:** Born Jul 11, 1972. **Educ:** Louisville, attended. **Career:** New Orleans Saints, defensive end, 1994-. **Business Addr:** Professional Football Player, New Orleans Saints, 5800 Airline Hwy, Metairie, LA 70003, (504)733-0255.

JOHNSON, JOSEPH A.
Educator. **Personal:** Born Jun 9, 1925, Columbus, OH; married Olivia Scott. **Educ:** Allen U, BS; Columbia U, MBA; NY U, MA. **Career:** Allen Univ, Columbia SC, dir gen studies 1973-; Federal Projects Allen Univ, dir 1973-; Special Servs, dir 1970-73; asst prof Business 1968-70; business mgr 1950-56. **Orgs:** Mem Phi Delta Kappa; mem Province Polemarch; Kappa Alpha Psi; chmn Jacks of Columbia Jack & Jill; Bethel AME Ch. **Military Serv:** AUS 1943-45. **Business Addr:** Allen Univ, Columbia, SC 29204.

JOHNSON, JOSEPH B.
Educational administrator. **Personal:** Born Sep 16, 1934, New Orleans, LA; son of Lillie Mickens Johnson and Sidney T Johnson; married Lula Young; children: Yolanda Dixson, Joseph III, Juliete, Julie. **Educ:** Grambling State Univ, BS, 1957; Univ of CO, Boulder, MS, 1967, EdD, 1973; Harvard Univ, certificate, 1976. **Career:** Booker T Washington High School, Shreveport, teacher, 1962-63; Greenville Park High School, teacher, 1963-69; Univ of CO, Boulder, exec asst to the pres, 1975-77; Grambling State Univ, pres, 1977-91; Talladega College, pres, 1991-. **Orgs:** Mem, NAFEO, Amer Council on Educ, Amer Assn of Univ Admins; Officer, YMCA, 1977; mem, Kappa Alpha Psi Fraternity, AME Church; bd trustees, State Colls & Univs for the State of LA, chmn, Pres' Council, 1982-83; Southwestern Athletic Conf, chmn Pres's Council 1982-84; mem, Gov's Economic Devel Comm 1984, commission on coll SACS, 1985; chmn, LA delegation SACS, 1985; mem, Steering Comm for Historically Black Colleges; adv Office of Educational Rsch Improvement, US Dept of Educ, 1987; mem bd of advisors, Who's Who in South & Southwest; bd of dir, Univ of CO Alumni Assn, Boulder, 1989-92; Natl Collegiate Athletic Assn, Pres' Commn, 1989-93; Amer Assn of State Colleges & Universities' Comm on Humanities. **Honors/Awds:** Distinguished Serv to Educ Awd, Harris-Stowe State Coll, 1987; Honorary Doctors of Law, Western MI Univ, Jewish Natl Fund Tree of Life Award, 1985; Natl Alliance of Business Leadership Award, 1984; Distinguished Alumni Achievement Award, Univ of CO; Thurgood Marshall Educ Achievement Award, 1988; Assn of Social & Behavioral Scientists Inc, WEB Dubois Award, 1988; Honorary Doctor of Philosophy, Gandhigram Rural Univ, India, 1988. **Military Serv:** AUS Sgt 1958-62. **Business Addr:** President, Talladega College, 627 W Battle St, Talladega, AL 35160.

JOHNSON, JOSEPH DAVID
Business executive. **Personal:** Born Oct 26, 1945, Poplar Bluff, MO; son of Curley Johnson and Archie Johnson; married Julie Hamilton; children: Joy Laurice, Joelle Devon. **Educ:** Lincoln Univ, BS Education 1968, MS Educ Admin 1969. **Career:** General Mills Inc, comp per mgmt 1969-72; Dayton Hudson Corp, sr comp specialist 1972-73; Intl Multifoods Corp, div per mgr 1973-75; Xerox Corp, various per mgmt pos 1975-83; vice-pres human resources 1983-88; pres, CEO The Telein Group, Inc, 1988-. **Orgs:** Co-founder Exchange Inc Professional Assoc 1973-74; bd of dir Eltrex Indus 1982-83; life mem Alpha Phi Alpha Fraternity 1965-; pres Advisory Bd Eltrex Ind 1984-; mem Amer Comp Assn, Natl Assn of Corp Black Professionals, NAACP, SCLC, Urban League, PUSH, Lincoln Univ Alumni Assn; bd of advisors Univ of So CA Center for Org Effectiveness; bd dirs United States Academic Decathalon 1986-; mem Exec Exchange Program Natl Urban League; mem Exec Leadership Council. **Honors/Awds:** Community Serv Award Orange County Links 1985; Outstanding Alumni Achievement Award Lincoln Univ 1986-87; subject of case study on human resources at the Harvard Business School, 1985. **Military Serv:** AUS (military intelligence) 1st lt 1970-72; Distinguished Military Graduate Lincoln Univ ROTC Program 1968. **Business Addr:** President/CEO, The Telen Group, Inc, Katella Corporate Ctr, 4281 Katella Ctr, #109, Los Alamitos, CA 90720.

JOHNSON, JOSEPH EDWARD
Educator (retired). **Personal:** Born Aug 7, 1934, Wilmington, DE; son of Dorothy Dean Johnson and Joseph E Johnson, Sr. (deceased); married Ella B McAlister (deceased); children: Kevin. **Educ:** Central State Univ, BS 1957; Seton Hall Univ, MA 1965; Univ of MA, EdD 1976. **Career:** Burnett JHS, teacher 1959-66; Wilm Pub Sch, v prin 1966-68, prin 1968-71, dir of presonnel & employee rel 1971-75, asst supt 1975-77, supt 1977-78; New Castle Co Sch, dep supt instr 1978-81; Red Clay Consol Sch Dist, supt 1981-90. **Orgs:** Mem Amer Assn of Sch Admin; Phi Delta Kappa Educ Frat; Natl Alliance of Black Sch Educs; Kappa Alpha Psi Frat; Sigma Pi Phi Boule; past chairman mem bd of dir Delaware Div Amer Cancer Society 1987-98; mem bd of directors YMCA of Delaware 1980-98; mem bd of directors Boys Club of Delaware 1985-98; bd of dirs, Delaware Futures; bd of professional responsibility, Delaware State Supreme Court; Council on Corrections; bd of dirs, Historical Soc of Delaware. **Honors/Awds:** Rockefeller Fellowship; Sch Supt; Superintendent of Year, Delaware, Delaware Chief School Officers 1989. **Military Serv:** AUS 1st Lt 1957-59; AUS Reserve Capt 1959-66. **Home Addr:** 3113 N Van Buren St, Wilmington, DE 19802.

JOHNSON, JOSHUA
Communications specialist. **Personal:** Born Dec 30, 1949, Sumpter, SC; son of Marjorie Johnson and William Johnson; married Phyllis Graham; children: Terrence, Derrick. **Educ:** Eastman Kodak Co Rochester NY, Photog Courses 1976; Rochester Inst of Tech, 1975 & 77; Rutgers Univ Coll, BS Mgmt; NY Microscopical Soc, attended 1981. **Career:** NJ Med Sch & CMDNJ, asst med photographer 1968-70; NJ Dental School, principal biomed dental photographer 1970-; Univ of Medicine & Dentistry of NJ, biomedical photographer/mgr of photographic serv 1984-. **Orgs:** Active mem Biology Photographer Assn 1973-; mem NY Microscopical Soc; illustrator of dental textbooks for dentists & assts "Four Handed Dentistry For Dentists & Asst" 1974; 2nd Book Clinical Mgmt of Head Neck & TMJ Pain & Dysfunctions 1977; Artical "Clinical Cameraman" Biomed Communications Journal 1980; Lecturer Dentists &Cental Students on Intra Oral Photography; illustrator of Many Articles of Highly Recognized Natl & Intl Dental Jour; co-founder & First Black Dental Photographer of Educ Communications Cntr NJ Dental Sch; mem Amer Business Mgmt Assoc 1987-. **Business Addr:** Mgr Photographic Serv, Univ Med & Dentistry of NJ, 100 Bergen St, Newark, NJ 07103.

JOHNSON, JOY J.
City official, clergyperson (retired). **Personal:** Born Nov 2, 1921, Laurel Hill, NC; married Omega Foster. **Educ:** Shaw U, AB, LLD 1945 & 1972. **Career:** First Bapt Ch Fairmont NC, pastor; State Parole Commn, apptd beginning 1978; state legislator, 1972-78; Fairmont, NC, mayor. **Orgs:** Mem Fairmont City Cncl 1966-70; Robeson Co & Dem Exec Com 1968-71; So Region Pres Prog Natl Bapt Conv 1970-72; Pres Gen Bapt State Conv of NC Inc; life mem NAACP; Shriner; dir Town & Country Bank; mem Alpha Phi Alpha; Mason; Shaw Univ Theol Frat; NC Black Caucus; vice pres, pres Fairmont Human Relations Cncl; chmn House Com on Human Resources 1975-79. **Honors/Awds:** Author of "From Poverty to Power," "The Modern Day Prodigal"; recipient Fairmont Man of Yr Awrd 1971; State Bapt Dist Citizen Awrd 1972; State NAACP & Mason Awrd 1971; Shaw Univ Dist Awrd 1974; Robeson Co Human Relations Awrd 1972; Gen Bapt State Conv of NC Inc Statesman & Humanitarian Awrd 1975; first black mayor of Fairmont, NC.

JOHNSON, JOYCE COLLEEN
Government director. **Personal:** Born Oct 24, 1939, Terre Haute, IN; married Ronald E Johnson. **Educ:** IN State Univ, BS 1961. **Career:** US Dept of Housing & Urban Develop, equal oppor specialist 1973-78, multifamily housing rep 1978-83, dir fair housing and equal oppor 1983-91, housing consultant, real estate owned branch, 1991-. **Orgs:** Tutor Boy's Club 1968-71; education coord Intl Toastmistress 1980-83; botanical mgr Deco-Plants 1980-82; consultant American Cancer Soc 1982-; regional sec Alpha Pi Chi Sorority 1983-; housing advisor NAACP 1984-85. **Honors/Awds:** Scholarship Alpha Pi Chi Sor 1965; co-author of book Certificate of Achievement US Dept of Army 1966; Recognition of Community Involvement NAACP 1984; Certificate of Excellence Alpha Pi Chi Sor 1985. **Business Addr:** Dir, US Dept of Housing & Urban Dev, 151 North Delaware, Indianapolis, IN 46204.

JOHNSON, JULIA L.
Government official. **Personal:** Born Jan 18, 1963, Clermont, FL; daughter of Abraham and Gloria Johnson. **Educ:** Univ of Florida, BS, business admin, 1985, JD, 1988. **Career:** Maguire, Voorhis & Wells, associate, 1988-90; Dept of Commun Affairs, asst gen counsel, 1990-92, legis affairs dir, 1991-92; Florida Public Service Commission, chair, 1997-, commissioner, 1993-. **Orgs:** Natl Assn of Regulatory Utility Commissioners, communication's comm; Govs State Energy Advisory Council; State of Florida Women's Political Caucus; Leon County Govt Mgt Efficiency Council; Boys & Girls Club of the Big Bend, board of dir, chairman; Women Executives in State Government, board of directors; University of Florida National Black Alumni Association, board of directors; Women's Political Caucus; Tallahassee Women Lawyers; Tallahassee Barristers Association; National Bar Association; Tallahassee Urban League. **Honors/Awds:** Twelve Great Women Of Florida, 1994; America's Best & Brightest Business & Professional Men and Women 1994; Ebony Magazine's Young Leaders of the Future, 1993; University of Florida, Hall of Fame; Florida Blue Key; City of Gainesville, Human Relations Award. **Special Achievements:** "Consumer Bulletin" Column featured in 12 Florida African-American Newspapers. **Business Addr:** Chair, Florida Public Service Commission, 2540 Shumard Oak Blvd, Tallahassee, FL 32399-0854.

JOHNSON, JULIANA CORNISH
International managing director. **Personal:** Born Jun 26, 1957, Salisbury, MD; daughter of Julia Cornish and Jerome Cornish; married Douglas K Johnson, Feb 14, 1989. **Educ:** Cornell Univ, BA (w/Honors) 1978; Harvard Grad Sch of Business, MBA 1982. **Career:** Chase Manhattan Bank, intern 1978; Huntington Natl Bank, sr analyst 1979-80; The World Bank, intern 1980; American Telephone & Telegraph Co, mgr 1982-89. **Orgs:** Mem Harvard Alumni Assoc 1982-89, Harvard Grad Sch of Business Black Alumni Assoc 1982-89, Natl Black MBA Assoc 1983-89; sponsor Oakland Ensemble Theatre 1984-89; bd of dirs Bay Area Black United Fund 1985-89. **Honors/Awds:** Top 50 Fast Track Young Executives Business Week Magazine 1987; Woodford Memorial Public Speaking Awd. **Business Addr:** District Manager, International Marketing, Rm N594, 412 Mt Kemble Ave, Morristown, NJ 07960.

JOHNSON, JULIUS FRANK
Military officer. **Personal:** Born Feb 8, 1940, Fort Leavenworth, KS; son of Gladys Slayton Johnson and Louis Belfield Johnson; married Jay Dianne Westbrook, Aug 19, 1977; children: Julia Nichole Johnson. **Educ:** Lincoln University, BS, 1964, MEd, 1972; US Army Command and General Staff College, 1974; US Army War College, 1984. **Career:** Eighth US Army, Korea, rifle and reconnaissance platoon leader; Presidential Honor Guard, commander; 101st Airborne Division, Vietnam, co. commander; Military Assistance Command Vietnam, commander, special forces team; US Army Europe, commander, 2d battalion, 36th infantry, 3d armored division, commander, 3d brigade, 3d infantry, deputy commander, 1st armored division; Armed Forces Inaugural Committee, director of the joint staff; US Army First Region, US Army ROTC Cadet Command, commanding general, currently. **Orgs:** Kappa Alpha Psi Fraternity, 1963-; Boy Scouts of America, district chairman, 1990-. **Honors/Awds:** Edges Group, Excalibur Award, 1989; African-American Biography Hall of Fame, 1992; Lincoln University Hall of Fame, 1971; Leavenworth High School Hall of Fame, 1992. **Military Serv:** US Army, brigadier general, 1964-; Silver Star Medal, 1968, 1969; Defense Superior Service Medal, 1989; Bronze Star, 1967, 1971; Defense Meritorious Service Medal, 1990; Meritorious Service Medal, 1990; Air Medal, 1967; Vietnamese Cross of Gallantry, 1967; Vietnamese Service Medal, 1967, 1971; Army Commendation Medal, 1967; National Defense Serve Medal, 1967, 1991. **Business Phone:** (919)396-5301.

JOHNSON, JUSTIN MORRIS
Judge. **Personal:** Born Aug 19, 1933, Wilkinsburg, PA; son of Irene Olive Morris Johnson and Oliver Livingstone Johnson; married Florence Elizabeth Lester Johnson, Jun 25, 1960; children: William Oliver, Justin Llewellyn, Elizabeth Irene. **Educ:** Univ Chicago, AB, 1954, Law School, JD, 1962; attended Univ of VA, 1982-83. **Career:** Partner/sole proprietor, Johnson & Johnson, 1962-77; Board of Education, School District of Pittsburgh and Pittsburgh-Mt Oliver Intermediate Unit, assistant solicitor, 1964-70, solicitor and assistant secretary, 1970-78; Berkman Ruslander Pohl Lieber & Engel, partner, 1978-80; Superior Court of PA, judge, 1980-; adjunct professor, Duquesne Univ School of Law. **Orgs:** Active elder Bethesda Presbyterian Church; mem Natl Cong Bar Examiners 1969-83; mem, PA Bd Law Examiners 1969-89, vice chairman 1975-83, chairman 1983-89; bd of trustees Mercy Hospital 1976-93, Southside Hosp 1978-88, United Way of Allegheny Co 1979-90; Carnegie Mellon University, 1988-93, 1995-; Pittsburgh Theological Seminary, 1985-93; Princeton Theological Seminary, 1992-; Urban League of Pittsburgh; hearing comm PA Supreme Court Disciplinary Bd. **Honors/Awds:** Bond Medal, Univ Chicago, 1954; Dr Martin Luther King Jr Citizen's Medal, 1973; Top Hat Award, 1981, for distinguished judicial service; Homer S Brown Service Award, 1982; Man of the Year, Bethesda Presbyterian Church, 1983; President's Award, Pennsylvania Trial Lawyers Association, 1983; Award of Merit, Pittsburgh Young Adult Club, 1983; St Thomas More Award, 1985; Public Service Award, Pittsburgh chapter, ASPA, 1986. **Military Serv:** USAF aircraft comdr 1956-59, USAFR maj 1963-73. **Home Addr:** 4915 Bayard St, Pittsburgh, PA 15213, (412)683-7424. **Business Addr:** Judge, Superior Ct of Pennsylvania, 330 Grant St, Suite 2702 Grant Bldg, Pittsburgh, PA 15219, (412)565-3604.

JOHNSON, KELLEY ANTONIO
Professional football player (retired). **Personal:** Born Jun 3, 1962, Carlsbad, NM. **Educ:** Los Angeles Valley College; Univ of Colorado. **Career:** Wide receiver: Denver Gold (USFL), 1985; Ottawa Rough Riders (CFL), 1986; Indianapolis Colts, 1987; Detroit Lions, 1989.

JOHNSON, KENNETH LANCE
Professional baseball player. **Personal:** Born Jul 6, 1963, Cincinnati, OH; son of Phyllis Olivia Webster and Kenneth Robert Johnson; married Sharon Brown Johnson, Dec 14, 1985. **Educ:** Triton Jr College; University of South Alabama. **Career:** St Louis Cardinals, outfielder, 1984-87; Chicago White Sox, Chicago, IL, outfielder, 1988-93; Cincinnati Reds, 1993-. **Honors/Awds:** Triton Junior College, World Series, 1982, 1983; Univ of South Alabama, 3rd team All-American; Minor League Baseball, NY Penn League, Rookie of the Year, MVP, 1984; Florida State League, All-Star Team; Texas League, All Star Game, MVP, 1986; Amer Assn Rookie of the Year, MVP, 1987; Chicago White Sox Triple-A MVP, 1988, 1989; Pacific Coast League, All Star, 1989; St Louis Cardinals, attended the World Series, 1987; Chicago White Sox, Most Improved Player, 1990. **Business Phone:** (513)421-4510.

JOHNSON, KENNETH LAVON
Judge. **Personal:** Born Jul 26, 1937, Columbia, MS; son of Minnie O Johnson and Geylon Johnson; married Carolyn Elizabeth Dischert, Sep 5, 1970; children: Sara Elizabeth, Jennifer Lorraine. **Educ:** Southern Univ & A&M Coll, BA 1955-59; Howard Univ School of Law, B of Law 1960-62. **Career:** Judge Advocate Gen Corps, capt US Army 1962-66; US Dept of Justice, trial attny 1967-69; Baltimore Lawyers Comm for Civil Rights Under Law, exec dir 1969-70; private law practice, 1970-82; judge, currently. **Orgs:** Mem Natl Assoc for Advance-

ment of Colored People 1969-; prof Univ of Baltimore School of Law 1988-; prof Villa Julia College 1988-. **Honors/Awds:** Distinguished Comm Serv Baltimore Frontier Club 1974; MD 7th Congressional Dist Awd Congressman Parren J Mitchell 1981; Outstanding Comm Serv Vanguard Justice Soc 1982. **Military Serv:** Judge Advocate Gen Corps capt, 1962-66, chief Military Justice Section 1964-66; National Defense Military Medal, 1966. **Business Addr:** Judge Circuit Court, Circuit Court for Baltimore, 111 N Calvert St, Baltimore, MD 21202.

JOHNSON, KERRY GERARD (KERRY KRAFT)
Graphic artist, cartoonist. **Personal:** Born Sep 30, 1966, Nashville, TN; son of Dorothy Johnson; married Tawanda Williams Johnson; children: Deandria, Autumn. **Educ:** Ohio State University, 1986-89; Columbus College of Art and Design, BFA, 1989. **Career:** Ohio State University, cartoonist, 1988-89; Purpose Magazine cartoonist, 1991; This Week, graphic artist, 1990-92; North Hills News Record, graphic artist, 1992-; Kerry Kraft Studios, owner/operator, currently; Pittsburgh Post-Gazette, graphic journalist, 1994-, news page designer, currently; Knight-Ridder Tribune Graphics Network, editor, illustrator; Pittsburgh Tribune Review, deputy graphics editor. **Orgs:** Alpha Phi Alpha Fraternity, Inc, publicity director, 1988-89; Quill and Scroll Honor Society, 1984; Natl Assn of Black Journalists; Pittsburgh Black Media Federation; NAACP; Society of Newspaper Design; PA Publishers Assn, 1995; Natl Assn of Black Journalists, 1996. **Honors/Awds:** Urban Profile, Top 25 Under-Thirty Finalist, 1992; Communicator News, Citizen of the Week, 1991; The Black Greek Council Award, 1989; Columbus College of Art and Design, scholarship, 1988-89; Golden Quill Award, 1996; Pittsburgh Black Media Foundation Award, 1993-96. **Special Achievements:** Youth Page, Youth Purpose, 1992; Driving Park Library, Art Exhibition, 1991; North Hills News Record, Communicator News, various illustrations; Kerry Kards and Kerry Klothes, currently. **Home Addr:** D445 McKnight Circle, Pittsburgh, PA 15237, (412)367-0862.

JOHNSON, KEVIN MAURICE
Professional basketball player. **Personal:** Born Mar 4, 1966, Sacramento, CA. **Educ:** Univ of California, Berkeley, CA, 1983-87. **Career:** Cleveland Cavaliers, guard, 1987-88; Phoenix Suns, 1988-. **Honors/Awds:** All-NBA Second Team, 1989, 1990, 1991, 1994; NBA Most Improved Player, 1989; J Walter Kennedy Citizenship Award, 1991; NBA All-Star, 1990, 1991, 1994. **Business Addr:** Professional Basketball Player, Phoenix Suns, PO Box 515, Phoenix, AZ 85001, (602)379-7867.

JOHNSON, KEYSHAWN
Professional football player. **Personal:** Born Jul 22, 1972, Los Angeles, CA; children: Maia. **Educ:** Univ of Southern California. **Career:** New York Jets, wide receiver, 1996-. **Honors/Awds:** The Sporting News, First team All-American, 1995; First player selected in the NFL Draft, 1996. **Special Achievements:** Author, Just Give me the Damn Ball!: The Fast Times and Hard Knocks of an NFL Rookie, 1997. **Business Addr:** Professional Football Player, New York Jets, 1000 Fulton Ave., Hempstead, NY 11550, (516)560-8100.

JOHNSON, LANCE (KENNETH LANCE)
Professional baseball player. **Personal:** Born Jul 6, 1963, Cincinnati, OH. **Educ:** South Alabama. **Career:** St Louis Cardinals, outfielder, 1987; Chicago White Sox, 1988-95; New York Mets, 1996-97; Chicago Cubs, 1997-. **Business Addr:** Professional Baseball Player, Chicago Cubs, Wrigley Field, 1060 W Addison St, Chicago, IL 60613, (312)404-2827.

JOHNSON, LARRY DEMETRIC
Professional basketball player. **Personal:** Born Mar 14, 1969, Tyler, TX; married Celeste Wingfield, 1994; children: Larry Jr, Lance, Lasani. **Educ:** Odessa Junior College; UNLV, 1991. **Career:** Charlotte Hornets, forward, 1991-96; New York Knicks, 1996-. **Honors/Awds:** NBA Rookie of the Year, 1992; NBA All-Rookie first team, 1992; All-NBA second team, 1993. **Special Achievements:** NBA Draft, first round pick, #1, 1991. **Business Addr:** Professional Basketball Player, New York Knicks, 2 Pennsylvania Plaza, New York, NY 10121, (212)465-5867.

JOHNSON, LAWRENCE E., SR.
Attorney. **Personal:** Born Sep 22, 1948, Waco, TX; children: Daphne, Lawrence Jr, Demitria, LaShunia. **Educ:** Prairie View A&M Univ, BS Elect Engineering 1971; George Washington Univ, JD 1975. **Career:** Insurance salesman, 1969; IBM, design engineer 1970; General Electric Corp, sales engineer 1971-72, patent engineer 1972-76; Private Practice, attorney. **Orgs:** Pres of bd Legal Serv Corp 1983; pres bd Mitchell Funeral Home 1982-85; dir HOT Legal Serv 1981-85; sec, McLennan Community Coll Bd of Trustees. **Business Addr:** Attorney, 410 M Bank Tower, Waco, TX 76701.

JOHNSON, LECTOY TARLINGTON
Physician. **Personal:** Born Nov 28, 1931, Tyler, TX; married Helen Collier; children: Lectoy Tarlington, II, Lynelle Teresa. **Educ:** TX Coll Tyler, TX, BS Chemistry 1952; Howard Univ Coll of Med, MD 1956; Washington Univ St Louis, Anesthesiology 1960; Amer Bd Anesthesiology, Diplomate 1963-; Amer Coll of Anesthesiology, Fellow 1963-. **Career:** Riverside Gen Hosp Houston, chmn dept anesthesiology 1960-68; St Joseph Hosp Houston, chmn dept anesthesiology 1970-80; Univ TX Med Sch Houston, act chmn dept anesth 1973; St Joseph Hosp Houston, acad chf of anesth 1970-80; Private Practice, physician. **Orgs:** Mem, Harris Co Med Soc, TX Med Soc, Natl Med Soc, Intl Anesthesia Rsch Soc, Undersea Med Soc, Gulf Coast Anesthesia Soc, Houston Surgical Soc; chmn bd dir Assn Anesthes Houston 1970-80; bd dir Standard Sav & Loan Houston 1984-; med dir Ocean Corp Houston 1970-78; pres Gulf coast Anesth Soc Houston 1979-80; comm chmn Boy Scouts of Amer WL Davis Dist 1974-75; life mem Kappa Alpha Psi Frat. **Honors/Awds:** Cert of Excellence Gulf Coast Chapter of Inhalation Therapists; Outstanding Instr Award St Joseph Hosp Surgical Dept. **Business Addr:** PO Box 784, Houston, TX 77001-0784.

JOHNSON, LEMUEL A.
Educator. **Personal:** Born Dec 15, 1941, Nigeria; married; children: Yma, Yshelu. **Educ:** Oberlin Clg, BA 1965; PA St U, MA 1966; Univ of MI, PhD 1969. **Career:** Dept of English Univ of MI, prof; English Univ of Sierra Leone Fourah Bay Clol, lecturer 1970-72; Radio Forum, host 1970-71. **Orgs:** Sierra Leone Broad Serv Freetown; Pres African Lit Assc 1977-78. **Honors/Awds:** Recipient hopwood awds for Short Story & Essay Cont 1967-68; Bredvold Prize for Scholar Publ; citation for "The Devil, the Gargoyle & the Buffoon, The Negro as Metaphor in West Lit" 1971; Dept of Eng Univ of MI awd 1972; pub num poems & translations; Highlife for Caliban 1973, "Hand on the Navel" 1978. **Business Addr:** Professor, University of Michigan, Ann Arbor, MI 48109.

JOHNSON, LEON
University executive. **Personal:** Born Jul 14, 1930, Aiken, SC; married Janie L; children: Leon Jr, Lisa J. **Educ:** SC State Coll, BS 1955, MS 1959; MI State Univ MD State Coll, Univ MD. **Career:** Clemson Univ, asst count agent 1955-62; Univ of MD, extension agent Com & Resource Devel. **Orgs:** Mem MD Assn County Agricultural Agents; Teamwork Planning Com; charter founding mem Comm Dev Soc; Comm Resource Dev Task Force Com; SEMIS Work GroupCom; Task Force on Comm Dev Progs; govS com on Migratory Labor; pres Somerset County Comm Action Agency Inc; Tri-county Migrant Com Inc; 2nd vP Somerset County Civic AssnInc; mem Delmarva Adv Council Migrat Com; Princess Anne Area C of C; bd dirs Coston Recreation Council; mem Somerset County Civil Defense bd; comm orgn for Progress Inc; bd dirs Somerset County Head Start; mem for Propress Inc; mem Zion Hill Bapt Ch; Omega Psi Phi Frat; Epsilon Sigma Phi Frat; Delmarva Ecmenical Agency Rural Coalition; bd dir MD Chs United Board Recognitions Countys Head & Start Program; Migrant Programs; CommAction Agency. **Business Addr:** U Maryland Civi Ctr, Crisfield Ln, Princess Anne, MD 21853.

JOHNSON, LEON
Professional football player. **Personal:** Born Jul 13, 1974. **Educ:** North Carolina. **Career:** New York Jets, running back, 1997-. **Business Addr:** Professional Football Player, New York Jets, 1000 Fulton Ave, Hempstead, NY 11550, (516)560-8100.

JOHNSON, LEON F. (SARGE)
City official. **Personal:** Born May 19, 1926, Salem, NJ; son of Elsie and Elwood; married Margaret Ford, Feb 17, 1946 (deceased); children: Nancy Brown, Kathryn Watford. **Career:** Salem County Jail, corrections officer; Special Police, Salem City, 1955-60, police officer, 1962-88, retired as sergeant; Salem City, councilman, 1988-92; Salem City, mayor, 1991-. **Orgs:** Fraternal Order of Police, lifetime member; American Legion, Post #444; Mt Hope Methodist Church, Salem, lifetime member. **Honors/Awds:** Policeman of the Year, 1971-72; National Policeman of the Yer, 1968-69. **Special Achievements:** NAACP Award, 1992; Seven Day Adventist, 1992; Mt Picah Church Award, 1992. **Military Serv:** US Army, sergeant, 1945-46. **Home Addr:** 18 Davis Ave, Salem, NJ 08079, (609)935-2996. **Business Addr:** Mayor, City of Salem, 1 New Market St, Salem, NJ 08079, (609)935-4550.

JOHNSON, LEROY
College president. **Career:** Miles College, Birmingham, AL, pres/chancellor, currently. **Business Addr:** President, Miles College, Birmingham, AL 35208.

JOHNSON, LEROY REGINALD
Attorney. **Personal:** marrIed Cleopatra. **Educ:** BA 1949; MS 1951; LlB 1957. **Career:** Leroy Johnson Law, attorney offices; Atlanta Pub Sch System, instr 1950-54; Solicitor Generals Staff Fifth Judicial Dist Atlanta, crim investigator 1957-62; 38th Dist Fulton Co GA, elected state senator 1962. **Orgs:** Chm Senate & Judiciary Com vP Fourth Cir of Am Law Students Assn; mem exec Com Atlanta Negro Voters League; bd dir Atlanta Inquirer; bd dir Campfire Girls Inc; exec com Atlanta Com for Coop Action; pres GA Assn of Citizens Dem Clubs; mem GA Bar Assn; vP Gate City Bar Assn; mem bd dir YMCA; Phi Beta Sigm; 33 Deg Mason. **Honors/Awds:** Recipient Russwurn Award Nat Publ Assn 1962; Citizen of Year Award Omega Psi Phi 1963; Freedom Award MAACP 1963; Scottish Rite Mason of Year; Lovejoy Award IBPOEW 1963; apptd by Pres Johnson as Spec Ambassador to Independence Ceremonies in Zanzibar 1963. **Business Addr:** Executive Dir, Atlantic Fulton Co Stadium Aut, 521 Capital One SW, Atlanta, GA 30312.

JOHNSON, LEROY RONALD
Educator. **Personal:** Born Jan 25, 1944, Smithville, GA; son of Ozzie May Stamper Johnson and Charles A Johnson; married Martina Flintrop (divorced); children: Sean, Stephen, Sydney. **Educ:** Univ of Caen France, Licence-es Lettres Ancient & Medieval History 1966-69; The Sorbonne Univ of Paris, Maitrise-es Lettres Medieval History 1971; Univ of MI, PhD African History 1981. **Career:** Inst St Jean-Eudes France, dir & teacher 1969-70; Inst St Joseph Paris, dir & teacher 1970-72; MI State Univ, instructor 1973-77; Univ of FL, asst prof history 1977-78; Bryn Mawr Coll, lecturer African Hist; Towson State University, asst prof of history; Moorhead State University, assoc prof, dept of humanities, currently. **Orgs:** Reg officer French Fed of Basketball Coaches 1964-72; hon mem African Students Assoc France 1966-72, West Indian Students Assoc France 1966-72; lecturer Ctr for Afro-Amer & African Studies Univ of MI 1978-79; sr lecturer history Univ of Lagos Nigeria 1982-83; lecturer history Bryn Mawr Coll 1983-86. **Honors/Awds:** French govt scholarship Caen, Paris France 1967-68, 1971-72; Natl Defense Foreign Lang Fellowship MI State Univ 1972-73; Rackham Fellowship Univ of MI 1973-75.

JOHNSON, LESHON EUGENE
Professional football player. **Personal:** Born Jan 15, 1971, Tulsa, OK. **Educ:** Northeastern Oklahoma A&M; Northern Illinois, bachelor's degree in studio art. **Career:** Green Bay Packers, running back, 1994-95; Arizona Cardinals, 1995-. **Business Addr:** Professional Football Player, Arizona Cardinals, 8701 S Hardy, Tempe, AZ 85284, (602)379-0101.

JOHNSON, LILLIAN MANN
Educator, administrator. **Personal:** Born Dec 18, 1948, Springfield, MA; daughter of Ruth Freeman Mann & Donald Mann; married Thornton B Johnson, Jr, Jun 26, 1971; children: Joshua, Zachary. **Educ:** Central State University, BS, 1970; Central Michigan University, MSA, 1985. **Career:** JC Penney Co, merchandise presentation supervisor, 1980-83; Central Michigan University, prog coordinator, center rep, 1983-88; Wright State Univ, academic advisor, univ division, 1987-89, asst dir, career svcs, 1989, asst dir, Bolinga Ctr, 1989-92, dir Bolinga Ctr, 1992-. **Orgs:** American Assn of Univ Women, vp WSU Branch, 1996-; Alpha Kappa Alpha Sorority, pres, 1996-, corres scy, mem, 1994-96; Organization for Black Faculty & Staff, pres, 1996-97; Wright State Univ, vp, 1995-96; Dayton Art Institute Outreach, bd mem, 1993-; Phi Delta Kappa Fraternity, mem, 1985-88; NAACP; Dayton Urban League. **Honors/Awds:** Alpha Phi Alpha Fraternity, Alpha Woman of the Year, 1995. **Special Achievements:** One Woman Art Exhibit, Wright State Univ, 1996; Art Exhibit, Greene City Library, 1977. **Business Addr:** Director, Bolinga Cultural Resources Center, Wright State University, 3640 Colonel Glenn Hwy, E107 Student Union, Dayton, OH 45435, (937)775-5645.

JOHNSON, LINDA DIANNE
Optometrist. **Personal:** Born Feb 5, 1954, Richland, MS; daughter of Adam and Gertrude; married James Walter Carson Jr, Apr 28, 1984 (divorced 1988); children: James Walter III. **Educ:** Jackson State Univ, BS, 1974; Indiana Univ School of Optometry, OD, 1978. **Career:** Jackson Hinds Comprehensive Health Center, director of optometry, 1978-. **Orgs:** National Optometric Assn, pres, currently; Mississippi Optometric Assn; Southern Council of Optometrists; American Red Cross, Central Mississippi Chapter. **Honors/Awds:** Jackson State Univ National Alumni Assn, Outstanding Professional Achievement Award, 1980; Jackson State Univ, Hinds Alumni Chapter, Distinguished Service Award, 1982. **Special Achievements:** First African American female optometrist in the state of Mississippi. **Business Addr:** Director of Optometry, Jackson-Hinds Comprehensive Health Ctr, PO Box 3437, Jackson, MS 39207, (601)364-5106.

JOHNSON, LIVINGSTONE M.
Judge. **Personal:** Born Dec 27, 1927, Wilkinsburg, PA; married Leeburn; children: Lee Carol, Oliver Morris, II, Judith Lee, Livingstone James, Patricia Lee. **Educ:** Howard Univ Wasngtn DC, AB 1949; Univ MI Law Sch,JD 1957; Coll of St Judiciary, Grad Nat 1973. **Career:** Johnson & Johnson Law Firm, ptnr 1957-73; Cnty Solctr, asst 1962-73; Fifth Jud Dist PA, judge 1973-. **Orgs:** Mem Amer Bar Assn; Amer Bar Found; Amer Judicature Soc; PA Bar Assn; Allegheny County Bar Assn; bd gov 1967-74, Pub Ser Com 1965-; assn trial lwyres in crim; Crt Allegheny Cty Bar Assn; mem PA Conf of St Trail Jdgs; bd Dir St Peters Chld Dev Ctrs Inc; ARC; Boys Club Wstrn PA; Ile Elegba Inc; Bus & Job Dev Corp Comnty Relse Agcy; Azanan Strgs Inc; mem Grtr Ptsbrg Civ Lgue; BS of Amer; Omega Psi Phi; NAACP; Panel of Jdgs; past bd mdm NAACP 1962-68; Urbn Lgue 1963-68. **Honors/Awds:** Louis Caplan Hum Rel Award 1975; honors Dist Flyng Cross; commdtn Medal; oak leaf. **Military Serv:** USAF 1st ltn 1949-54. **Business Addr:** Judge, Ct of Common Pleas 5th Judicia, Pittsburgh, PA 15206.

JOHNSON, LLOYD A.
Government official. **Personal:** Born Aug 5, 1932, Boston, MA; married Constance Riley; children: Scott A, Alison E. **Educ:** Howard Univ, BA 1954; Aldephi Univ, MSS 1957; Georgetown Univ Law Ctr, JD 1984. **Career:** Worked with troubled ind & families under public & private auspices, 1954-66; Local Comm Corps, exec dir 1966-69; Comm Dev Agency, dir evalutation & rsch 1966-69; Urban Ctr of Columbia Univ, dir 1969-74; US House of Representatives, subcomm on postal opers & svcs, labor counsel subcomm on labor. **Orgs:** Mem Acad of Certified Social Workers; mem Natl Bar Assn; mem Natl Assn of Social Workers; consult lecturer at various colleges & univs; certified socialworker NY State; bd dir Amer Orthopsychiatric Assn; Natl Assn of Soc Workers; Acad of Cert Soc Works. **Honors/Awds:** Outstanding Alumni Awd nominee Howard Univ. **Home Addr:** 1121 Holton Lane, Takoma Park, MD 20912. **Business Addr:** Labor Counsel, Subcommittee on Labor, US House of Representatives, Washington, DC 20515.

JOHNSON, LONNIE
Professional football player. **Personal:** Born Feb 14, 1971, Miami, FL; married Ushanda; children: Tyrone. **Educ:** Florida State. **Career:** Buffalo Bills, tight end, 1994-. **Business Addr:** Professional Football Player, Buffalo Bills, One Bills Dr, Orchard Park, NY 14127, (716)648-1800.

JOHNSON, LONNIE L.
National director. **Personal:** Born Dec 23, 1932, Hickory, MS; children: Derian, Jocelyn, Andrea, Lonnie II. **Educ:** Roosevelt Univ Chicago, 1957 attended. **Career:** Chicago PO, 1962; began labor actities in 1963, shop steward, local vp, local pres; Mail Handlers Union , natl educ dir 1965; central reg reg, 1967; Postal Union, first black natl AFL-CIO pres 1969; Mail Handlers Union, first natl dir 1970; Johnson Consultant Co, labor consultant. **Orgs:** Mem NAACP; mem Urban League. **Honors/Awds:** Key to City of New Orleans 1970; Key to City of Kansas City 1975; honored by a host of affiliated labor locals. **Military Serv:** AUS corpl 1952-54. **Business Addr:** Labor Consultant, Johnson Consulting, 718 W Bittersweet Place, Chicago, IL 60613.

JOHNSON, LORNA KAREN
Administrator. **Personal:** Born Mar 12, 1958, Washington, DC; daughter of Evangeline Richardson Johnson and Malcolm Johnson. **Educ:** Adelphi Univ, BA 1980; Rutgers Univ School of Law, JD 1983; Rutgers Univ School of Regional & Policy Planning, MA. **Career:** Urban Tech Dept of City Planning, urban tech 1984-85; Pres, Urban League of Essex Co, 1983-. **Orgs:** Vice chmn, bd dir Jubilations Dance Co 1984-; mem, bd dir Big Brothers Big Sisters 1986-; vice chair, Woodson Foundation. **Honors/Awds:** New Jerseyan of the Year, Star Ledger Newspaper; NY Times, Academy of Women Achievers.

JOHNSON, LORRAINE JEFFERSON
Educator (retired). **Personal:** Born Dec 7, 1918, King George Cty, VA; daughter of Sadie Corey Jefferson (deceased) and Robert W Jefferson (deceased); married Samuel D Johnson (deceased); children: Samuel D Jr, Susanne J Watson, Stanley D. **Educ:** Howard Univ, BS 1940, MS 1942; Marquette Univ, Cert 1948; Univ of PA; Univ of California, Berkeley; Montgomery Jr Coll, 1968. **Career:** Howard Univ, lab instr 1943-47; Livingstone Coll, sci teacher 1943-47; Howard Univ, sci teacher 1950-53; Publ School Dist of Columbia, sci teacher 1954-80; Mayors Office, steering committee. **Orgs:** Life mem Alpha Kappa Alpha 1938-, pres, chmn nominating comm DC Chap 1972-75, chmn nominating comm North Atlantic Region 1982-85; mem of bd, chmn comm Hillcrest Childrens Ctr 1980-86; life mem Natl Council Negro Women; mem Amer Assoc Univ Women, DC Retired Teachers Assoc; bd of dir Phyllis Wheatley YWCA 1982-; bd mgrs Anthony Bowen YMCA 1984-; mem United Black Christians UCC; vice pres Women's Intl Religious Fellowship 1985-86; mem NRTA Howard Univ Alumni DC; asst treas Church Women United; moderator Lincoln Congregational Temple UCC; Ward 2 Repre DC State Comm 1988-91; pres Women's Intl Religious Fellowship 1987-89; treasurer Church Women United 1988-89; sec DC Retired Teachers Assn 1988-89; chair, legislative committee, DC Retired Teachers Assn, 1991-92; trustee, church, Lincoln Temp 1991-92. **Honors/Awds:** Outstanding Biology Teacher Awd DC School; Outstanding Teacher Awd Jr Citizens Corp 1981; 5 natl sci found grants 1948-68; community volunter AARP-DC 1989. **Home Addr:** 1010 S St NW, Washington, DC 20001.

JOHNSON, LORRETTA
Business executive. **Personal:** Born Oct 29, 1938, Baltimore, MD; married Leonard; children: Leonard Jr, Jeffrey, Kevin. **Educ:** Coppin State Univ Baltimore MD, BS 1976. **Career:** Baltimore Tchrs Union, pres paraprofessional chap 1978-; Baltimore Tchrs Union, paraprofessional chirperson 1970-76; Baltimore City Pub Schs, paraprofessional 1965-70; Am Fedn of Tchrs, vP 1978. **Orgs:** Exec bd Met AFL-CIO 1978; conS research of Better Schs 1980. **Honors/Awds:** Community Serv Award United Way campaigh 1976; Vol Serv Award MD State AFL-CIO COPE 1977; Meritous Achievemnt Award United Tchrs of New Orleans 1977; Meritous Achievement Award A Phillip Randolph Inst 1978. **Business Addr:** 2533 St Paul St, Baltimore, MD 21218.

JOHNSON, LOUIS W.
Episcopal priest. **Personal:** Born Sep 13, 1903, New Haven, CT; married Winonah. **Educ:** Howard U, AB 1933; Phil Div Sch, ThB 1936. **Career:** Chaplain Training Sch for Boys Warwidk NY, asst chaplain; St Phillips Indianapolis, vicar; St Marys Chester, Vicar; St Pauls No PA & Ascension W Chester;St Thomas Epis Minneapolis, rector; Parochial Schs, res lctr, bd edn; NAACP, pres & vP interdenoml; Minst ALL; TCOIC in Twin Cities, co-fndr. **Orgs:** Bd mem Minneapolis Cncl of Chs; bd Urban League; bd Travelers Aid Soc; ed edn, chrmn Negro Ch Fund. **Honors/Awds:** Ecumenical Soc Awards YMCA; Minstl Assn; Minneapls mayor; State Gov.

JOHNSON, LOUISE MASON
Educator (retired). **Personal:** Born Jun 20, 1917, Franklin, VA; married Tracy Owen Johnson. **Educ:** NC Coll Durham, 1936-37; Shaw Univ, BA Elem Educ 1960-63; Kittrell Coll, night course. **Career:** Dr SM Beckford, secretary 1941-59; Franklin Co Schools, teacher 1963-67; Vance Co Schools, teacher 1967-82. **Orgs:** Reporter/typist/sec of The Aster Garden Club over 40 yrs; mem of The Urban-Suburban Garden Club; deacon/pres Presbyterian Women-Cotton Meml Presbyterian Ch (mem 40 yrs); mem Retired Teachers Assn of NC; free-lance typist; typing teacher; donates time and knowledge of typing for churches and other organizations. **Honors/Awds:** Cert of Appreciation from church and former schools; Cert of Merit from Vance Co Schls Henderson, NC; Hon Lt Gov to and for the Great State of NC to uphold good govt (appointed by Jimmy Green); Cert from the NC Assn of Educators (Retirement Cert); Silver-brass Plates from Eaton-Johnson Student Body Vance Co Schools for Dedicated Svc. **Home Addr:** 715 Powell St, Henderson, NC 27536.

JOHNSON, LUCIEN LOVE
Physician. **Personal:** Born Dec 26, 1941, New Orleans, LA; children: Lucien III, Kimberly, Yewande. **Educ:** Purdue University, BS 1962; Howard University, MD 1966. **Career:** Physician, cardiologist, currently. **Orgs:** American Medical Assn; Natl Medical Assn; California Medical Assn. **Honors/Awds:** Has written and published two articles in medical journals. **Military Serv:** US Army, captain 1966-67. **Business Addr:** Cardiologist, Physician, 3756 Santa Rosalia Dr, Los Angeles, CA 90008.

JOHNSON, LUTHER MASON, JR.
Educational administrator. **Personal:** Born Nov 23, 1930, Brooklyn, NY; son of Constance Anglin Johnson and Luther Mason Johnson, Sr.; married Joan C Arrington; children: Lori H Luis, Luther III, Lance K. **Educ:** Pratt Inst, city & regional planning; New York City Comm Coll, AAS Construction Tech 1959; NY Univ, BS Indus Arts Educ 1966, MA Higher Educ Adm in 1970. **Career:** St Univ of NY Urban Ctr, coord of business affairs 1966-69, dir 1968-70; New York City Comm Coll, dean 1970-84; New York City Tech Coll, prof 1973-86, vice pres of admin 1984-86 (retired); Facilities Mgmt Consultant, pres, currently. **Orgs:** Trustee Episcopal Found for Educ 1976-; bd mem New York City Tech Coll Found 1980-; mem 100 Blk Men of NY 1978-; mem Am Soc of Cert Eng Tech 1972-; wrdn St Philips Episcopal Church Brooklyn 1975-; Chairman and Commissioner of the City University of New York Civil Service Commission, 1990. **Honors/Awds:** Distinguished Alumnus Award New York City Comm Coll 1983; Professor Emeritus conferred February 1, 1986. **Military Serv:** US Army, Signal Corps cprl 1951-53. **Home Addr:** 1404 Union St, Brooklyn, NY 11213. **Business Addr:** President, Facilities Mgmt Consultant, 1404 Union St, Brooklyn, NY 11213.

JOHNSON, LYMAN T. See Obituaries section.

JOHNSON, MAGIC. See JOHNSON, EARVIN, JR.

JOHNSON, MAL
Journalist, business executive. **Personal:** Born Jul 4, 1924, Philadelphia, PA; daughter of Johnnie Reeves Hooser (deceased) and Bishop Hooser (deceased); married Frank Johnson, Jan 4, 1959 (deceased). **Educ:** Temple Univ; Brookings Inst, Economics in Journalism. **Career:** Cox Broadcasting Corp, 1st female natl corr 1970; WKBS-TV; Coffee Break, host; Lets Talk About It; Dialing for Dollars Movie, 1966; traveled Africa served radio & TV coord consult 1974; produced documentaries Europe, Middle E, Israel; WAMU FM-TV, monthly guest reporter "Overseas Mission"; WA Workshops Congressional Sem, lectr communications; Mt Vernon Coll, guest lectr; Military Schools in England, Guam, teacher 1954-60; Cox Enterprises, dir community relations, 1973-92, sr correspondent, 1969-92; MediaLinx International, president, currently. **Orgs:** Bd dir Am Women in Radio & TV; ch of bd Am Women in Radio & TV Educ Found; past pres WA Chap Am Women in Radio & TV; chmn AWRT Study Tours; chmn AWRT Intl Broadcasters Prgm; mem US House of Reps US Senate Radio & TV Corr Asso; mem White House Corrs Assn; US Dept of State Corrs Assn; mem NAACP; Urban League; YWCA; bd chmn Natl Womens Conf Comm; chmn Intl Broadcast Study Tours to China Far East Europe Scandinavian Countries; commissioner UNESCO; bd of dir UNIFEM; executive committee of bd of directors, Women for Meaningful Summits, 1993-; board of directors, Communications Consortium, 1990-; first vice president, International Association of Women in Radio & TV, 1989-; board member, National Press Club Fdt; 1988-; Community Club Awards, national director, 1992-. **Honors/Awds:** USN Comm Serv Award 1969; USN Recruiting Serv Award 1970; 2000 Outst Women of the World Award 1970; Dist Serv Award Dayton OH 1972; commend part in Presidential visit to Austria USSR, Iran, & Poland 1972; Outst Female Decision Maker of Yr 1974; Black Journalist Hall of Fame, National Assn Black Journalists, 1990; Outstanding Leader, Norfolk State University, 1990; Woman of Achievement, American Women in Radio & TV, 1980; Natl Black Media Coalition, Women of Strength Award, 1994. **Home Addr:** 7237 Worsley Way, Alexandria, VA 22315. **Business Addr:** President, MediaLinx International, 2020 Pennsylvania Ave, NW, Suite 267, Washington, DC 20006.

JOHNSON, MARGIE N.
Educator, nurse (retired). **Personal:** Born Aug 21, 1938, Jacksonville, TX; daughter of Vivian Johnson and E J Johnson (deceased); divorced. **Educ:** Prairie View A&M University, RN/BS, 1960; Indiana University, MS, 1963; Texas Woman's University, PhD, 1977. **Career:** Jarvis Christian College, college nurse, 1960-61; UCLA, Neuropsychiatric Division, staff nurse, 1961-62; Fort Dodge College, instructor, 1962-64; Wayne State University, assistant professor, 1965-72; Department of Nursing, University Ibadan, Nigeria, deputy director, 1974-77; Texas Woman's University, associate processor, 1987-88; Tuskegee University School of Nursing & Allied Health, dean & professor, 1988-97. **Orgs:** Amer Assn of Colleges of Nursing; National League for Nursing, 1968-; American Nurses Association, past alt delegate for Texas, 1962-; Sigma Theta Tau, 1976-; National Black Nurses Association, 1982-; American Nurses Foundation, 1982-; Association of Black Nursing Faculty in Higher Education, 1988-; Phi Lambda Theta, 1978-88. **Honors/Awds:** Chi Eta Phi, National Honors Society for Black Nurses, 1990; Clemson University, Distinguished Scholar in Residence Nursing, 1985-86; National Institute Mental Health, Doctoral Fellowship, 1975-77. **Special Achievements:** Author, F Fredinger and others, "Health Promotion Belief-Health Values," 1991; with Arnold Nieswiadomy, "Chart Reading and Anxiety," Jour Nur Educ, 1989; with Beard, Psychosocial Stress and Blood Press, J Blk Ns Assoc, 1987; with others, Goad, Canada, "Attitudes Toward Nursing-Males," Jour Nrs Edu, 1984; with Morakinyo, "Role Perception and Role Enactment," Intl J Nurs Studies, 1983. **Home Addr:** Route 3, Box 617, Jacksonville, TX 75766, (903)589-8190.

JOHNSON, MARGUERITE M.
Educational administrator. **Personal:** Born Sep 23, 1948, Wilmington, DE; daughter of Elizabeth Milburn and Norris R Milburn (deceased); married George Stephen Johnson, Aug 1971; children: Stephanie M, Stephen M. **Educ:** Morgan State Univ, Baltimore, MD BA, 1966-70; Indiana Univ of PA, Indiana, PA, MA, 1976; Temple Univ, Philadelphia, PA EdD, 1987. **Career:** Delaware Technical & Comm Coll, Stanton-Wilmington Campuses, acting dir of continuing educ, dir of continuing edu, 1979; Delaware Technology & Comm Coll, Stanton Campus, asst dir of continuing educ 1975-79; Delaware Technical & Comm Coll, Stanton Campus, acting asst dir of continuing educ 1973-75; Delaware Technical & Comm Coll, Northern Branch, gen educ devel instructor/coordinator 1970-73, office of the pres, exec dean of instruction & student services, 1992-; Terry Campus, vp, campus dir, 1994-. **Orgs:** Amer Assn of Women in Comm Colleges; Amer Assn of Univ Women, Dover Chapter; Natl, NE Region, AACC the Rotary Downtown Club of Dover; DE Central Delaware Economic Development Council; Delaware Manufacturing Alliance, Zonta International of Wilmington Area. **Honors/Awds:** Distinguished Kellog Fellow, 1989-90; Assn of Black Women in Higher Education, Leadership Award, 1993; Natl Council on Black Amer Affairs, Northeast Region, Outstanding Service Award, 1991; Brandywine Professional Assn, Special Service Award, 1991; People To Watch, Delaware Today Magazine, 1995. **Business Addr:** Vice Pres/Campus Director, 1832 N DuPont Pkwy, Dover, DE 19901.

JOHNSON, MARIE ELIZABETH
Fashion company executive, fashion design educator. **Personal:** Born Jun 3, 1948, New York, NY; daughter of Emily L Johnson and Wilmer T Johnson; married Warren R Colbert; children: Warren Jr. **Educ:** West VA State Coll, 1966; Howard Univ, BA Ed 1970. **Career:** Washington DC Public Schools, teacher 1969-70; Bonwit Teller/Retail, assoc buyer 1970-74; The Gap Stores, mgr 1974-76; Pierre Cardin/Gallant, sales rep 1977-79; Laboratory Institute of Merchandising, instructor, 1977-87, 1991-; Lester Hayatt, vice pres 1980-82; Special Concepts, pres, instructor; 1982-85; Articolo Inc, pres, 1986-87 LW Assoc, Inc NYC pres 1988-; Parsons School of Design, instructor, 1989-; Fashion Institute of Technology, New York City, NY, instructor, 1991-. **Orgs:** Volunteer NY School for the Blind 1965-66; mem NY Urban League, NAACP; interm Consumer Distribution Committee NY Urban League 1969; college bd B Altman & Co 1969; mem The Fashion Group Garment Mfg Org 1978-; coll summer intern program volunteer Urban League 1989-89. **Honors/Awds:** Written articles US Mag, NY Daily News, NBC Dallas 1980, Black Enterprise 1981; Black Designer Awd L Hayatt 1980-81; Client of the Year Interacial Council Bus Opportunity 1983; guest appearance Fox Broad-

casting Network NYC 1985. **Business Addr:** President, LW Assoc, Inc, PO Box 391, New York, NY 10116.

JOHNSON, MARIE LOVE
Consultant. **Personal:** Born Dec 18, 1925, South Bend, IN; married Arthur. **Educ:** IN Univ, BS 1951; Univ of Hrtfrd, MEd 1953; Univ of CT, PhD 1978. **Career:** East Hartford Bd of Educ, spch path 1949-60, supr 1960-77; Shadybrook Lang &Learning Ctr, clin dir 1971-76, exec dir 1977-78; self-employed, consultant, currently. **Orgs:** Pres JGM Corp 1971-78; mem clin & cert bd Am Spch & Hrng Assn 1969-75; vice pres Am Spch & Hrng Assn 1977-78; pres CT Spch & Hrng Assn 1971-75; pres Hrtfrd Alumnae Chptr Delta Sigma Theta 1954-56; bd of fin Town of Vernon 1963-65; chmn bd of mgrs YMCA 1976-78. **Honors/Awds:** Comm serv Delta Sigma Theta 1966; fellow Am Spch & Hrng Assn 1972; honors CT Speech & Hearing Assn 1970; tribute luncheon CT Speech & Hearing Assn 1975 . **Home Addr:** 78 Warren Ave, P O Box 2026, Vernon-Rockville, CT 06066.

JOHNSON, MARION I.
Architect, business executive. **Personal:** Born Oct 16, 1915, Longview, TX; married Crozet; children: Francis M, Carol Ann. **Educ:** Prairie View A&M U, BS 1938; Univ of Md, 1959; Fed Exec Inst, 1972; Advanced Guided Missile Sch, 1960. **Career:** H & J Home Improvement Co, architect & pres; Div of Contracts US Atomic Energy Commn, asst dir 1971-74; Logistic US Atomic Engery Commn, dep asst dir 1969-71; AID US Dept of State, spl asst to the asso asst adminstr 1967-69; AID US Dept of State, asst to dir mgmt 1963-66; Air Defence Missile Battalion, commanding officer 1962; Nat Security Agy, dir mgmt & tech staff 1955-60; WV State Coll, asst prof of military sci & tactics 1951-53; Hurelco Land & Devel Corp, pres 1963-70. **Orgs:** Chmn bd Hurelco Land & Devel Corp 1971-; vP No VA Fair Housing Inc 1962-66; vice-chmn Urban League No VA Chap 1969-71; bd mem VA Council on Human Relations 1964-73; pres & alexandria VA Council on Human Relations 1970-73; chmn Minority Housing Com City of Alexandria 1966-73; mem spl com Planning& Zoning City of Alexandria 1965; mem planning adv commn City of Alexandria 1972-78; life mem NAACP. **Honors/Awds:** NAACP Award Nat Capital Area Nat Conf Christian & Jews 1974; City of Alexandria Award 1973; Comm Leader of Am Award 1969; VA State Council on Human Relations Award 1973; Bronze Stat Medal for Valor 1945; Oak Leaf Cluster to Bronze Star Medal for Maritious Serv 1954; Army Commendation Medal 1962. **Military Serv:** AUS lt col 1942-63.

JOHNSON, MARJORIE LYNN
Organization executive. **Personal:** Born Oct 26, 1961, Beloit, WI; married Dale B Johnson; children: Dale Austin. **Educ:** Spelman College, graduate; Long Island Univ, paralegal degree with distinction. **Career:** Stay-At-Home Mother Motherhood Network, founder/pres, 1994-. **Special Achievements:** publishes the MotherSpeak newsletter; author, ''So, You're a Stay-At-Home Mother,'' 1996. **Business Addr:** Founder, Stay-At-Home Mothers Network, 331 W 57th St, Ste 313, New York, NY 10019, (212)501-6479.

JOHNSON, MARK A.
Financial services executive. **Personal:** Born Aug 10, 1950, Washington, DC; son of Walter R & Charlotte M Johnson; married Vera-Marie, Jul 12, 1975; children: Maya, Marci. **Educ:** Bowie State Univ, BS, 1972; Univ of Maryland, MBA, 1979. **Career:** Suburban Trust Bank, employment mgr, 1972-75; Central Intelligence Agency, personnel officer, 1975-77; AT&T Long Lines, account supervisor, 1977-80; Sallie Mae, vp of business development, 1980-. **Orgs:** Kappa Alpha Psi Fraternity, Inc, 1970-; National Black MBA Assn, 1990-; Black Ski, DC, bd of dirs, 1984-; National Brotherhood of Skiers, 1984-; US Ski Assn, 1992-; US Ski Coaches Assn, 1992-; NAACP, 1994-; Kappa Alpha Psi Foundation of Maryland, bd of dirs, 1991-. **Honors/Awds:** Prince Georgians on Camera, Public Access CATV Inc, Distinguished Service, 1987; Kappa Alpha Psi, Humanitarian Award, 1984; Bowie State Univ, Athletic Hall of Fame, 1986. **Special Achievements:** Alpine Pre-Course, Level 1, Certified Ski Race Coach, 1994.

JOHNSON, MARLENE E.
City official. **Personal:** Born Jul 1, 1936, Milwaukee, WI; daughter of Elizabeth Leher Davis and Edward Jay Davis; married John Odom; children: Jan, Paula, Jay. **Educ:** Univ of WI Milwaukee, BS 1979. **Career:** Boston Store, saleswoman 1954-64; WXIX-TV Channel 18 Milwaukee,TV hostess 1962; Milwaukee Public Sch System, social improvement instr 1966-70; First WI Natl Bank, teller 1973-75; City of Milwaukee, alderman 1980-; City of Milwaukee, Milwaukee, WI, alderwoman, 1980-. **Orgs:** Bd of dirs Bookfellows-Friends of the Milwaukee Pub Lib 1976-80; bd dir Milwaukee Symphony Orches 1977-80; pres Women's Aux of the Milwaukee Courier 1975-76; div leader YWCA Leader Luncheon 1977; lifetime mem NAACP 1980; century mem Boy Scouts of Amer Milwaukee Banner E Div 1974-75; bd dir vice chmn MECCA, 1988-92; vice pres bd dir Milwaukee United Way, 1988; mem Milwaukee Redevelop Auth, 1980-92; mem bd dir Milwaukee Convention & Visitors Bureau; mem OIC-GM; mem Pabst Theater Bd of Dirs; mem Natl League of Cities Comm & Economic Develop Steering Comm; vice pres WI League of Municipalities 6th Senate Dist; chairwoman, 1980-92; Milwaukee Area Tecnical College Board, 1990-92; member, board of director, Private Industry Council, 1990-91; Commissioner of the Milwaukee Metropolitan Sewerage District 1994-95. **Honors/Awds:** Quota Buster Awd YMCA Milwaukee 1975; Women in Our Lives 1978; Milwaukee Women Today 1979; Mayoral Proclamation 1985; Milwaukee Realist Presidential Awd 1986; Award of Excellence in Community Service, CYD, 1990; Citation by the Senate State of Wisconsin, 1987; Gamma Phi Delta, Outstanding Public Service Award, 1992; Inducted into African-American Biographies Hall of Fame in Atlanta, GA, April 1994. **Business Addr:** Alderwoman, Common Council, 200 E Wells St Rm 205, Milwaukee, WI 53202.

JOHNSON, MARTIN LEROY
Educator. **Personal:** Born Dec 31, 1941, Westminster, SC; son of Beatrice Williams Johnson and James Courtney Johnson; married Jo Ann Clinkscales; children: Yolandra, Martin II. **Educ:** Morris Coll Sumter, SC, BS 1962; Univ of GA Athens, GA, MEd 1968, EdD 1971. **Career:** Anderson, SC, math tchr 1962-67; Univ of GA, grad asst 1967-71; Rutgers Univ New Brunswick, assist prof/math education 1971-72; Univ of MD-College Park, assist, assoc and full professor of education 1972-89. **Orgs:** Vice pres Rsrch Cncl for Diagnstc & Prscrptv Math 1978-80; pres MD Cncl Tchrs of Math 1985-86; consultant 1984-85, program dir 1985-86, 1987, Natl Science Found; chair, Research Advisory Committee, Natl Council of Teachers of Mathematics 1988-89; editorial bd member, Journal for Research in Mathematics Education, 1991-94, chair, 1993-94; president, Research Council for Diagnostic & Prescriptive Mathmematics, 1993-95. **Honors/Awds:** Fulbright Schlr Nigeria 1983-84; book - Guiding Each Child's Learning of Math - Char Merill 1983; articles- Journal for Research in Mathematics Education, The Arithmetic Teacher, and NCTM publications; Distinguished Minority Faculty Member, Univ of Maryland College Park 1985; Mathematics Educator of the Year, Maryland Council of Teachers of Mathematics, 1989. **Business Addr:** Professor/Chairperson, Dept of Curriculum & Instruction, Univ of Maryland, College of Education, College Park, MD 20742, (301)405-3145.

JOHNSON, MARY BEATRICE
Federal government official. **Personal:** Born Jul 25, 1952, Edwards, MS; daughter of E Lorean Marshall Johnson (deceased) and Robert J Johnson, Sr. **Educ:** Utica Jr Coll MS, AA Business Admin 1972; Alcorn State Univ Lorman NJ, BA Business Admin 1974; Univ of MN, MBA 1977; Alcorn State Univ, MS Agr Economics 1983. **Career:** Agriculture Dept Alcorn State, rsch asst 1982-83; Dept of Defense, contract negotiator 1984-. **Orgs:** Mem NAACP, Heroines of Jericho, Amer Fed of Govt Employees, Intl Training in Commun; Natl Council of Negro Women, 1988. **Honors/Awds:** Featured in April 1985 Ebony Magazine; appeared in Woman's World, Sunbelt & MS Farm Bureau Magazine; Natl Dean's List 1983; Presidents List 1982, 1983; Master's Thesis Topics Upward Mobility of Black Workers, ''The Rise of the Black Manager'' 1977, ''The Economic Impact of Bechtel Power Corp,'' 1983, Claiborne Cty MS, A Study of Change in Selected Factors 1973-83.

JOHNSON, MATTIEDNA
Nurse. **Personal:** Born Apr 7, 1918, Amite County, MS; daughter of Minnie Ramsey Johnson and Isaac Johnson; divorced; children: Bobby Lou, Robert Jr, Patricia E, Frances M Kelley. **Educ:** Jane Terrell Memorial Hospital School of Nursing, RN 1940; Northwest Institute of Medical Technology, MT 1943; Ashland Theological Seminary, MA Divinity 1987. **Career:** Greater Cleveland-Ohio State ANA, private duty nurse 1959-87; Home Nursing, Church Nursing, teacher 1960-. **Orgs:** Consecrated Diocanal Minister United Methodist Church 1986. **Honors/Awds:** Be Involved Nurse Award Greater Cleveland Nurses 1974; 50 Year Pin American Red Cross 1985; Pioneer Award NBNA 1986; Living Legacy Award NCCBA 1986; Merit Award presented by Congressman Oaker 1986; Searle Community Service Award, 1992; International Society for Hypertension among Blacks. **Special Achievements:** Placed in the Congressional Record October 23, 1990 by Congressman Louis Stokes; Developed the medication Terramycin, cure for Scarlet Fever ''The Miracle Drug of the Century;'' Author, Life's Story ''Tots Goes to Gbarnga,'' 1993-94; Honorary Degree Nomination, The University of the District of Columbia, Washington DC, 1995. **Home Addr:** 13606 Abell Ave, Cleveland, OH 44120.

JOHNSON, MELVIN CARLTON, III
Professional football player. **Personal:** Born Apr 15, 1972, Cincinnati, OH; children: Adonis. **Educ:** Univ of Kentucky, attended. **Career:** Tampa Bay Buccaneers, defensive back, 1995-. **Business Addr:** Professional Football Player, Tampa Bay Buccaneers, One Buccaneer Place, Tampa, FL 33607, (813)870-2700.

JOHNSON, MELVIN RUSSELL
Physician, military. **Personal:** Born Aug 26, 1946, Courtland, VA; married Joyce. **Educ:** Hampton Inst, BA 1968; Meharry Med Coll, MD 1972. **Career:** Wm Beaumont Army Med Ctr, staff pulmonologist, asst ch pulmonary disease 1980; Womack Army Hosp, chf dept med 1977-80, chf pulmonary disease 1976-77,staff intern 1976; Brooke Army Med Ctr, resd intern med 1972-73; Cape Fear Valley Hosp, asso staff internist 1975-77. **Orgs:** Mem Omega Psi Phi Frat 1971; Nat Assn Resd & Interns 1972; asso mem Am Coll Phys 1973; mem CA Whittier Med Soc 1973; Nat Med Assn 1974; AMA 1975; Med Lincensure GA 1973; TX 1974; NC 1975; VA 1977. **Honors/Awds:** Recpt Nat Defense Ribbon 1972; Flwshp Pulmonary Diseases Brooke AMC 1978-80. **Military Serv:** AUS mc lt col 1975-.

JOHNSON, MERTHA RUTH
Educator. **Personal:** Born in Jackson, MS; children: Victoria M. **Educ:** Jackson State Univ, BS 1956; Univ of San Francisco, MEd 1977, MPA 1983. **Career:** Chicago School System, educator 1960-66; East Chicago School System, educator 1967-70; Manpower Training Program, administrator/teacher 1966; OICW, administrator/teacher; San Mateo School Dist, educator 1970-81; Neighborhood Housing Servs, exec dir 1982-83; Atlanta School System, instructor, currently. **Orgs:** Parlimentarian Natl Council of Negro Women; mem Business & Professional Women's Club; mem Atlanta Federation of Teachers, NAACP, SCIC; consultant, Literacy Project Black Cacus, GA State Legislature; Atlanta's Ministry to International Students. **Honors/Awds:** Lecturer/consultant Multicultural Educ & Black History; author ''Black History Study Manual''; publication ''A Study of the Leadership Factors Involved in the Operation of a Successful Neighborhood Housing Program''; selected poetry; Oak Tree Award, Outstanding Teacher of the Year; National Endowment for the Humanities, Fellow, 1994; Eli Wallace Research, Fellow, 1993. **Special Achievements:** Workshop Coordinator for Zora Neale Hurston Exhibit; Consultant, SETCLAE, African-American Images Publications; participated in development of model curriculum for teaching Dr King's non-violent principles in schools; African-American Infusion Methodology; Great Books discussion leader; contributing writer: Color Magazine; Atlanta Voice. **Business Addr:** Instructor, Humanities Magnet, Atlanta School System, 45 Whitehouse Dr SW, Atlanta, GA 30314.

JOHNSON, MERVIL V.
Business executive. **Personal:** Born Dec 20, 1953, Fort Worth, TX. **Educ:** TCU, BA Spanish/French 1976; Universite de Nice France, business school 1976-77; TX Christian Univ, M Pub Admin 1982. **Career:** City of Fort Worth, admin asst 1978-79; City of Fort Worth-Library, spanish/french instructor 1980-83; North Central TX Council of Govts, reg clearinghousecoord 1980-84; ICMA Retirement Corp, service rep 1984-. **Orgs:** Chmn univ liaison Urban Mgt Assts of N TX 1982-84; chmn newsletter Conf of Minority Public Admin 1983-84; mem Phi Sigma Iota Soc of Languages 1975-; mem Intl City Mgt Assn 1981-; mem Amer Soc for Public Admin 1981-. **Honors/Awds:** ITT Fellow Intl Teleph & Teleg 1976-77; Clarence E Ridley Scholar TX City Mgt Assn 1980-81; ICMA scholarship Intl City Mgt Assn 1981; NCTCOG Urban Fellow N Central TX Council of Govts 1980-82. **Business Addr:** Service Representative, 5116 Libbey Ave, Fort Worth, TX 76107.

JOHNSON, MICHAEL
Automobile dealer. **Personal:** Born Sep 8, 1959, Detroit, MI; son of Ernestine Johnson and Eural Johnson; married Cheryl R Batchelor, Sep 29, 1990; children: Michael Byron. **Educ:** Wayne State University, BA, 1983; University of Detroit School of Law, JD, 1986. **Career:** Dreisbach Cadillac, service representative, 1977-87; UAW, staff attorney, 1987-89; General Motors, dealer candidate, trainee, 1989-90; Durand Chevrolet-Geo-Pontiac-Olds, Inc, president, currently. **Business Addr:** President, Durand Chevrolet-Geo-Pontiac-Olds, Inc, 9009 Lansing Rd, PO Box 198, Durand, MI 48429, (517)288-2657.

JOHNSON, MICHAEL
Olympic athlete. **Personal:** Born Sep 13, 1967, Oak Cliff, TX; son of Ruby Johnson and Paul Johnson Sr. **Educ:** Baylor University, BA, business, 1990. **Career:** US Olympic Team, track and field, 1992, 1996; High Mountain Outback Adventures, Lake Tahoe, owner, currently. **Honors/Awds:** Male Athlete of the Year, Track and Field News, 1990; first place 400 meters, Mobile 1 Invitational, 1991; Gold Medalist, World Track and Field Championships, Tokyo, 1991; first place 200 meters, Mobile IAAF Grand Prix, 1991; Olympic Games, Gold Medalist, 1992, Historic Double-Gold Medalist, 1996. **Special Achievements:** Broke own record for 200 meter, World Track and Field Championships, 1991. **Business Addr:** Olympic Athlete, Men's Track & Field Team, US Olympic Committee, 1750 E Boulder St, Colorado Springs, CO 80909, (719)632-5551.

JOHNSON, MICHAEL ANTHONY
Science educator. **Personal:** Born Jan 15, 1951, New York, NY; children: Dieynaba. **Educ:** New York City Tech Coll, AA 1971; City Coll of NY, Pre-Med 1973; Empire State Coll, BS Sci Educ 1985. **Career:** DMC Energy, consultant 1981-84; Energy Task Force, science writer 1982-83; New York City Tech Coll, rsch project 1983-84; Science Skills Ctr Inc, exec dir 1980-. **Orgs:** Pres Student Alumni Assoc Empire State Coll 1982-86; mem NY Acad of Scis, Amer Assoc for Advancement of Sciences. **Honors/Awds:** Positive Father of the Year Awd 1984; Outstanding Young Amers 1985; Clark Fellow in Science

& Math Educ Columbia Univ 1986-; Outstanding Achievements in Comm PHNC 1986; Professional Awd Natl Assoc Negro Bus & Professional Women 1987; Recognition Awd Women's League of Science & Medicine 1987. **Business Addr:** Executive Dir, Science Skills Center Inc, PO Box 883, Brooklyn, NY 11238.

JOHNSON, MICHAEL L.
Attorney. **Personal:** Born Aug 1, 1958, Bonn, Germany; son of Martinus & Barbara; married Andrea, Aug 22, 1980; children: Christopher, Carl, Alyse. **Educ:** Berklee College, bachelor, music education, 1979; Wayne State University, MEd, 1981; University of Michigan, Law School, JD, 1986. **Career:** Dickinson Wright, Law Firm, attorney associate, 1986-89; Ameritech, Advertising Services, attorney, 1989-91, Michigan, regulatory attorney, 1993-94, Telephone Industry Services, vp general counsel, 1994, Pay Phone Services, vp general counsel, 1994-. **Orgs:** American Bar Association, 1987-; Illnois State Bar, 1994-; Michigan State Bar, 1986-; Chicago Bar Association, 1995-; Detroit Bar Association, 1987-94; Wolverine Bar Association, 1987-93. **Business Addr:** VP, General Counsel, Ameritech, Pay Phone Services, Telephone Industry Services Unit, 225 West Randolph Street, #15C, Chicago, IL 60606, (312)220-8881.

JOHNSON, MICHELE
Sales representative. **Personal:** Born Aug 12, 1959, Brooklyn, NY. **Educ:** Boston Univ, BS 1981; Attending, Fordham Univ. **Career:** CBS Inc, clippings coord 1981-82, admin asst 1982-83, sr sales asst 1983-86; JP Martin Assoc Inc, exec asst 1986-87; Taylor Made Press, sales rep. **Orgs:** Mem CBS Black Employees Assoc 1981-86, Natl Assoc of Black MBA's 1986-, Assoc of MBA Execs 1986-, Advtg Club of NY 1986-; dir Union Bapt Church Youth Comm 1986-; volunteer Roosevelt Ctr for Comm Growth 1987-. **Home Addr:** 148 Elmwood Ave, Roosevelt, NY 11575.

JOHNSON, MILDRED H.
Educator. **Personal:** Born Jan 1, Cleveland, OH; daughter of Owena Bradshaw; married John B, Jan 29, 1949. **Educ:** West Virginia State College, BA; Wayne State University, MA; University of Detroit, MA. **Career:** Detroit Metropolitan Mutual Ins Co, office mgr, 1948-63; Detroit Public Schools, teacher, 1963-76, learning disability teacher, 1976-80, teacher consultant, 1980-89; Educational Guidance Tutoring Center, director, owner, 1986-. **Orgs:** Phi Delta Kappa Honors Fraternity; National Associate of Negro Business & Professional Women; Gamma Phi Delta Sorority; United Negro College Fund, Womens Division. **Honors/Awds:** Greater Rising Star, Grand Chapter, Urban Bible College; Order of Eastern Star, Detroit. **Home Addr:** 19167 Sorrento, Detroit, MI 48235, (313)342-8156. **Business Addr:** Owner/Director, Educational Guidance Tutoring Center Inc, 17500 W McNichols, Detroit, MI 48235, (313)535-7851.

JOHNSON, MILTON D.
Business executive. **Personal:** Born May 27, 1928, Sour Lake, TX; married Robbie Russell; children: Paula, Pamela. **Educ:** Paul Quinn Coll, BBA 1951. **Career:** Union Carbide Corp, employee rel asso 1964-; Victoria TX, tchr 1956-64. **Orgs:** Mem bd educ LaMarque IN Schs 1972-; chmn adv bd First State Bank Hitchcock TX; pres C of C 1974. **Military Serv:** AUS 1951-53. **Business Addr:** PO Box 471, Texas City, TX 77590.

JOHNSON, MINNIE REDMOND
Educator (retired). **Personal:** Born Feb 27, 1910, Clarksville, TN; daughter of Julia Thomas Redmond and Dr Robert L Redmond; married Dr E Milton Johnson, Dec 20, 1959 (deceased). **Educ:** Fisk Univ, BA, 1932; Atlanta Univ, BLS, 1944; Univ of Chicago, MA, 1945. **Career:** Memphis Public School teacher, 1933-37; Atlanta Univ School of Library Serv, instructor, 1945-46; Fisk Univ, asst Librarian 1946-49, 1950-52, acting librarian, 1949-50; Hampton Inst, head librarian, 1952-58; Chicago State Univ, head catalog dept, head of library office campus center, Reference Librarian; acting dir, 1958-73; Chicago State Univ, head of library, Crane branch, 1958-65, reference librarian, Main Library 1965-66, head librarian West Center 1966-69, cataloger Main Library 1970-72, head of catalog dept 1972-73, acting dir of libraries 1973-74. **Orgs:** Dir, Hampton Book Fair, Sponsored by Children's Book Council of NY; AAUW Hampton Public School & Hampton Inst Library, 1956-58; work through retired Sr Volunteer Program (Hull House affiliate) with Amer Public Works Assn & Blind Serv Assn, 1985-. **Honors/Awds:** Authored, "Standards for Coll Libraries", published in Coll & Rsch Libraries, 1959; Coll-Comm Book Fair, Publishers Weekly, 1956; Some Observations on Faculty/Library Relations, VA Librarian, 1958.

JOHNSON, MIRIAM B.
Businesswoman. **Personal:** Born in Washington, DC; married Norman B. **Educ:** Miner Tchrs Coll Wash DC; Brooklyn Coll, cum laude 1972. **Career:** Black Musicmakers Inc, exec dir; Husband's Law Office, office mgr. **Orgs:** Active comm worker for over 25 yrs; vol sec for Brooklyn Br NAACP; mem bd dir Brooklyn Assn for Mental Health; mem exec board of Brooklyn Nureau of Comm Serv for over 7 yrs; chrprsn Mental Health Com of Health Sys Agency Dist Bd; mem Urban Commn of Episcopal Diocese of Long Island; parliamentarian historian of Brooklyn Lawyers Wives; prog chairperson of Gr NY Links Inc; former mem Comm Relations Com of Central YWCA; exec board Stuyvesant Comm Cntr during era of gang wars in the 40's & 50's; gen chairman of City Wide Com of Looking Glass Ball a fund raising play ball for the construction & devel of Mac Donough St Comm Cntr in Bedford-Stuyvesant. **Honors/Awds:** Recepient for comm serv from Berean Bapt Ch 1950's & 1974; NY Amsterdam News; Mac Donough St Comm Cntr in 1963; awarded baccalaureate degree in Sociologycum laude. **Business Addr:** 79 Decatur St, Brooklyn, NY 11216.

JOHNSON, MITCHELL A.
Professor (retired), corporate financial executive. **Personal:** Born Mar 1, 1942, Chicago, IL; son of Marcella Johnson and Mitchell Johnson; divorced; children: Mitchell Matthew, Margo K. **Educ:** University of California Los Angeles, BA, 1965. **Career:** Washington Redskins, pro football player, 1972; Student Loan Marketing Association, senior vp, corporate financer, 1973-. **Orgs:** Washington Association of Money Managers, funding president, 1982-; Mentors Inc, board of directors, 1990-; Arena Stage, board of directors, 1987-. **Business Addr:** Senior Vice Pres, Corporate Finance, Student Loan Marketing Assn, 1050 Thomas Jefferson St NW, Washington, DC 20007.

JOHNSON, NATHANIEL J., SR.
Information resource management executive. **Personal:** Born Oct 1, 1940, Philadelphia, PA; son of Violet Beatrice Branch Johnson and Lucius James Johnson; married Fannie Mary Long Johnson. **Educ:** LaSalle University, Philadelphia, PA, BA, computer and information sciences, 1990; University of Texas at Austin, MBA, 1993. **Career:** The RCA Corp., New York, NY, senior systems specialist, 1968-70; Electronic Data Systems, New York, NY, systems engineer, 1970-72; The Hertz Corp., New York, NY, New York Data Center, manager, 1973-80; Amerada Hess Corp., Woodbridge, NJ, manager of computer services, 1980-83; SCT Resource Management Corp., Malvern, PA, executive director, computer services, 1983-87; Milwaukee County, Milwaukee, WI, manager of information management services division, 1987-88; School District of Philadelphia, programmer, 1967-68; Kirk Engineering Co., mathematics technician, 1965-67; Prairie View A&M University, executive director of information systems, 1990-. **Orgs:** Association of Computing Machinery, 1987-88; financial aide advisory committee member, Wayne County Community College, 1984-85; Society of Information Management, 1987-88; Government Management Information Systems, 1987-88; In Plant Management Association, 1987-88; Minorities in Computer Related Occupations, 1987-88; executive dir info systems, Prairie View A&M Univ, currently; MIS Curriculum Advisory Board, Marquette University, 1987-88; Texas Association of State Supported Computing and Communications, board of directors, 1992-.

JOHNSON, NIESA
Professional basketball player. **Personal:** Born Feb 7, 1973. **Educ:** Univ of Alabama. **Career:** Long Beach Stingrays, guard, 1996-98; Seattle Reign, 1998-. **Business Addr:** Professional Basketball Player, Seattle Reign, 400 Mercer St, Ste 408, Seattle, WA 98109, (206)285-5225.

JOHNSON, NORMA HOLLOWAY
Judge. **Personal:** Born in Lake Charles, LA; daughter of Beatrice Williams Holloway and Henry L Holloway; married Julius A Johnson. **Educ:** DC Teachers Coll, BS 1955; Georgetown Univ Law Ctr, JD 1962. **Career:** Dept of Justice, trial atty 1963-67; District of Col, asst corp counsel 1967-70; Superior Court of DC, judge 1970-80; US Dist Court for Dist of Col, district judge 1980-. **Orgs:** Fellow Amer Bar Fndn; dir Natl Assoc of Black Women Attorneys; mem Amer Judicature Soc; Natl, Amer, & Washington Bar Associations; Natl Assoc of Women Judges; dir, DC Street Law; director, Judiciary Leadership Development Committee. **Business Addr:** Chief Judge, US District Court for District of Columbia, 2315 US Courthouse, Washington, DC 20001.

JOHNSON, NORMAN B.
Attorney. **Personal:** Born in Lake Charles, LA; married Julius A. **Educ:** Georgetown Univ Law Ctr, JD 1962; DC Tchrs Coll, BS 1955. **Career:** Superior Ct of DC, judge 1970-; DC, asst corp counsel 1967-70; Dept of Justice, trial atty 1963-67. **Orgs:** Dir Am Judicature Soc; dir Nat Assn of Women Judges; Nat Assn of Black Women Attys; Nat Bar Assn; Wash Bar Assn; Am Bar Assn. **Business Addr:** 79 Decatur St, Brooklyn, NY 11216.

JOHNSON, NORMAN J.
Educator. **Personal:** Born Sep 8, 1919, Cape Girardeau, MO; married Helen Louise Watkins; children: Michael Oliver. **Educ:** KY State Univ, AB 1941; Univ MI, MA 1947, EdD 1959. **Career:** Lancaster Public Sch, tchr 1941-42; Xavier Univ, chmn dept health & physical educ 1948-49; Bluefield State Coll, 1950-56; Prairie View A&M Coll, 1956-63; Lincoln Univ, chmn dept phys educ & athletics 1963-. **Orgs:** Mem Amer & MO Assns Health Phys Educ & Recreation; exec coun Black Educ Coun Human Svcs; asst dist commr BSA; personnel com GSA; ARC; NAACP. **Honors/Awds:** Outstanding Leadership Awd Alpha Kappa Alpha; Merit Hon Awd BSA. **Military Serv:** AUS 1st lt 1942-46. **Business Addr:** Chmn Dept Phys Educ & Ath, Lincoln Univ, Jefferson City, MO 65101.

JOHNSON, NORRIS BROCK
Educator. **Personal:** Born Apr 29, 1942, Chicago, IL; divorced. **Educ:** MI State Univ, BA English 1965, MA English 1967; Univ of MI, MA Anthropology 1971, PhD Anthropology 1976. **Career:** Dept of Anthropology Univ of NC, asst prof 1980-85, assoc prof 1985-92; professor, 1992-. **Orgs:** Rsch in Japan and China on Zen Buddhist temple architecture and landscape gardens; faculty assoc Natl Humanities Faculty 1980-; fellow Amer Anthropological Assoc 1980-; mem Assoc of Black Anthropologists; bd mem Soc for Humanistic Anthropology. **Honors/Awds:** Spencer Foundation Grant, 1990, Fellow Landscape Architecture Dumbarton Oaks, Washington, DC; Fulbright Lecturer 1985-86 Univ of Tokyo and Waseda Univ Tokyo Japan. **Business Addr:** Professor, Department of Anthropology, University of North Carolina, Chapel Hill, NC 27599-3115, (919)962-2389.

JOHNSON, ONETTE E.
College president. **Career:** Prentiss Institute Junior College, Prentiss, MS, president/chancellor. **Business Addr:** Prentiss Institute Junior College, Prentiss, MS 39474.

JOHNSON, OTIS SAMUEL
Educational administrator. **Personal:** Born Mar 26, 1942, Savannah, GA; son of Lillian Brown Spencer and Otis Johnson; divorced. **Educ:** Armstrong State Coll, AA 1964; Univ of GA, AB 1967; Atlanta Univ, MSW 1969; Brandeis Univ, PhD 1980. **Career:** City of Savannah Model Cities Program, deputy director, 1969-71; Simmons College of Social Work, special instructor, 1975-76; Savannah State College, assistant professor, 1976-80, associate professor, 1981-87, professor, 1987-91, head department of social science, 1980-84, head department of social work, 1985-88, professor of social work and sociology, 1987-91; City of Savannah, alderman 1982-88; commissioner, Housing Authority of Savannah, 1989-; Chatham-Savannah Youth Futures Authority, executive director, 1988-. **Orgs:** Member, Acad of Certified Social Workers 1971-; secretary, Georgia Chapter, Natl Assn of Social Workers 1984-86; member, Assn for the Study of Afro-Amer Life & History, Central Baptist Church Trustees, Alpha Kappa Delta Sociological Honor Soc, Pi Gamma Mu Social Sci Honor Frat; board of directors, Natl Council of Community Mental Health Centers, 1988-91; American Legion; Black Community Crusade For Children, Childrens Defense Fund; National Community Building Network; board member, Mary Reynolds Babcock Foundation, 1996-. **Honors/Awds:** Social Worker of the Year SE GA Unit of NASW 1984; Social Worker of the Year, GA Chapter of NASW 1995. **Military Serv:** US Navy, 1959-62, received honorable discharge; Naval Reserve, 1962-65. **Business Addr:** Executive Director, Chatham-Savannah Youth Futures Authority, 316 E Bay, Savannah, GA 31401, (912)651-6810.

JOHNSON, PARKER COLLINS
Educational administrator. **Personal:** Born Oct 17, 1961, Boston, MA; son of Addie Collins Johnson and John Quincy Johnson III. **Educ:** Williams College, BA 1984; Harvard University, Cambridge, MA, EdM, 1990. **Career:** Fitchburg State Coll, asst dir of admissions 1984-85; Bentley Coll, asst dir of admissions 1985-87; Tufts Univ Medford MA, asst dir of admissions, 1987-89; Harvard Univ, Cambridge MA, graduate student, 1989-90; American Council on Education, Washington, DC, researcher, 1990; California State University, Northridge, CA, counselor, 1990-92; Gettysburg College, Cultural Advancement, dean, 1992-96; Assn of American Colleges and Universities, assoc director of curriculum, 1996-. **Orgs:** Mem Natl Assoc of College Admissions Counselors 1984-89; mem Greater Boston Interuniversity Counsil 1985-89; vice pres bd dirs Fitchburg Comm Action Ctr 1985; mem-at-large New England Consortium of Black Admissions Counselors 1985-89; volunteer Boston Youth at Risk 1986-89; external co-chair, on New England Consortium of Black Admissions Counselors Inc 1987-89; mem American Assn of Higher Education 1987-; bd mem Massachusetts Pre-Engineering Program 1988-90; mem Trans Africa Inc Boston Chapter 1987-90; YMCA; committee member, International Programs Committee, 1989-94. **Honors/Awds:** Outstanding Community Service Award, African Amer Center, Tufts Univ, 1989. **Home Addr:** PO Box 341439, Los Angeles, CA 90034. **Business Phone:** (213)740-2881.

JOHNSON, PATRICE DOREEN
Journalist. **Personal:** Born Jul 17, 1952, New York, NY; daughter of Irma Levy Johnson and Wilbourne Johnson. **Educ:** Barnard Coll, BA 1974; Columbia Univ Grad Sch of Journalism, MSJ 1976. **Career:** Dauntless Books, asst editor 1974-75; Encore Am & Worldwide News, assoc editor 1976-80; Newsweek Magazine, researcher/reporter 1981-96; Money Magazine, reporter 1997-. **Orgs:** Panelist Am's Black Forum TV show 1978-79; mem Natl Alliance of Third World Journalists 1980-85. **Home Addr:** 355 West 85 St, New York, NY 10024.

JOHNSON, PATRICIA ANITA
Educational administrator, director. **Personal:** Born Mar 17, 1944, Chicago, IL; children: David, Todd. **Educ:** Oberlin Coll, BA 1961; Graduate School for Comm Devel, Fellowship 1982-83; US Intl Univ, MFA Candidate 1985. **Career:** Brockman Gallery Productions, curator 1976-78; New Visions Gallery, owner 1978-82; Multicultural Arts Inst, curator 1982-83; San Diego Comm Coll Dist, cultural affairs coord 1982-85; South Dallas Cultural Center City Arts Prog, dir 1985-. **Orgs:** Exhibition consultant Multicultural Arts Inst 1981-83; grant recipient CA Arts Council 1983-85; mem Catfish Club of San Diego 1983-85; adv comm San Diego Arts Festival Bd 1985; bd mem City of San Diego Public Arts Adv Bd 1985; founder IN-ROADS an organ of Black Professional Singles 1985. **Honors/Awds:** Achievement in Fine Arts Awd City of Los Angeles 1978; Achievement in Fine Arts San Diego Black Achievement Awds 1985; Comm Serv Awd San Diego Chap NAACP1985. **Business Addr:** Dir, South Dallas Cultural Center, 1925 Elm St, City Arts Prog - Majestic Thea, Dallas, TX 75201.

JOHNSON, PATRICIA DUMAS
Educator & elected official. **Personal:** Born Aug 12, 1950, Memphis, TN; married Lloyd G Johnson; children: Lloyd Timothy; Lila Victoria. **Educ:** TN State Univ, BS Math 1973; Univ of IL Chicago, attending. **Career:** 3-M Co, indust engr 1973-78; Ford Motor Co, indust engr 1978-79; Sears Roebuck & Co, indust engr 1979-85; Bellwood School Dist #88, bd mem 1983-; Computerized Business Svcs, president. **Orgs:** Panelist Chicago Youth Motivation 1974-78; mem Delta Sigma Theta Sor 1979-; vice pres Parent Teachers Assoc 1981-83; Cosmopolitan C of C. **Honors/Awds:** Image Awd Fred Hampton Scholarship 1982; Editor School Dist 88 Newsletter 1982; mem Black Caucus Natl School Bd Assoc 1984; Outstanding Woman of Amer 1985. **Business Addr:** President, Computerized Business Services, Catfish Digby's West, 2135 S 17th Ave, Broadview, IL 60153.

JOHNSON, PATRICIA DUREN
Insurance company executive. **Personal:** Born Oct 22, 1943, Columbus, OH; daughter of Rosetta J Duren and James Duren; married Harold H Johnson Jr, Dec 25, 1965; children: Jill Johnson. **Educ:** Ohio State Univ, Columbus, BS Educ, 1965; Univ of Michigan, Ann Arbor, Grad School Mgmt, 1984. **Career:** Teacher in Long Beach CA, San Bernardino CA, Cincinnati OH, Thetford Village UK, 1966-72; ITT Hartford, Portland OR, sales rep, 1972-73; Blue Cross of CA, Woodland Hills CA, sr vice pres, 1975-, national marketing officer, currently. **Orgs:** Bd dir, Amer Cancer Society, 1988-94; mem, Amer Hosp Assn, 1976-; mem, Women in Health Admin, 1979-; mem, pres, Delta Sigma Theta Soroity (OSU), 1964-65. **Honors/Awds:** Author of ABC's of Medicare, 1976; author of How Kids Earn Money, 1978; Women of Achievement, YWCA, 1979; NAACP/LDEF Black Woman of Achievement, 1987; One of 10 Corp Black Women, Essence Magazine, 1989; One of 100 Best and Brightest Black Women in 1990, Ebony Magazine. **Business Addr:** Natl Marketing Officer, Blue Cross of California, PO Box 9078, Oxnard, CA 93031-9078.

JOHNSON, PATRICIA L.
Lawyer, educator. **Personal:** Born Jan 29, 1956, New York, NY; daughter of Mamie Johnson. **Educ:** John Jay Coll of Criminal Justice, BA 1977, MA 1979; Cornell Univ Sch of Law, prelaw prog 1978; Rutgers Sch of Law Newark, JD 1985; Office of Court Admin NY Frontline Leadership Certificate 1988. **Career:** Bureau of Alcohol Tobacco & Firearms, student aide 1977; US Rsch Svcs, branch mgr 1979-82; Bronx Family Court, notifications supervisor 1982-83; Bronx District Attorney's Office, legal asst 1983-85; Judicial Friends, law intern 1985; Bronx District Attorney's Office, asst dist atty 1985-86; Bronx Public Admin Office, assoc counsel 1986-88; Walter Kaitz Foundation Fellowship finalist 1989; John Jay Coll of Criminal Justice, New York, NY, adjunct prof, 1986; Bronx Surrogate's Court, Bronx, NY, deputy chief clerk, 1988-. **Orgs:** Mem Black Women Attorneys 1981-; mem Natl Bar Assoc 1983-; mem Phi Alpha Delta Law Frat Intl 1983-; mem Professional and Business Women 1985-, NAACP 1985-, Natl Women's Political Caucus 1985-, Black Entertainment and Sports Lawyers Assoc 1986-; recording sec Black Bar Assoc of Bronx County 1986-; corresponding sec/chair program bd Black Bar of Bronx 1987-89; exec dir & founder Black Entertainment & Sports Tribune 1989-; Big Sister, The Big Sisters, Inc, 1989; chairperson, Entertainment & Sports Law Comm for Metropolitan Black Bar Assn, 1989-; exec dir, Black Entertainment & Sports Tribune, 1989-. **Honors/Awds:** Outstanding Achievement w/Distinction Rutgers Women's Rights Reporter 1985; Assoc of Black Law Students Serv to Black Comm 1985; moderator Entertainment & Sports Law Forum Black Bar Assoc of Bronx Cty 1987; battling the motion picture assoc of Amer movie rating of "The White Girl" published in NY Law Journal 1988; Walter Kaitz Foundation Fellowship Finalist, 1989. **Home Addr:** GPO Box 813, Bronx, NY 10451-0813.

JOHNSON, PAUL EDWIN
Psychologist, cleric (retired). **Personal:** Born Dec 27, 1933, Buffalo, NY; son of Maggie J Johnson; married Shirley Ann Williams; children: Paula Rene, Darryl Edwin. **Educ:** Talladega Coll AL, AB (Psych) 1955; Harvard Univ, MA, MS (Psych) 1957; Hartford Semnry Fndtn, CT, Master-Dvnty 1958; Auburn Univ, MEd (Couns Psy) 1974, EdD (Counc Psy) 1980. **Career:** N Cngrgtnl Ch NYC, NY, asso mnstr 1958-62; US Army, chpln (ltc, ret) 1962-72; AL Dept MH & MR, cnsltnt III-MR div 1972-79, dir qlty assrnc-MR Div 1979-94; Pvt Pract, psychlgst & mnstr; 1st Cngrgtnl-Chrstn Ch Montgomery, AL, 1980-94. **Orgs:** Bd dir Montgomery Council on Aging 1982-84; chmn Lgsltv Strke Frc Am Mntl Hlth Cncl Assn 1983-84; pres AL Mntl Hlth Cnslrs Assn 1983-84; cnsltnt AL Dept of Pub Safety-Acad 1983-85; cnsltnt AL Cncl on Hghr Educ (HBC's) 1984-85; exec comm Montgomery Area United Way 1984-86; mem AL Bd of Examiners in Counseling 1986-90. **Honors/Awds:** Delta Phi Kappa, Alpha Phi Alpha. **Military Serv:** AUS chpln (ltc, ret) 21 yrs; Silver Star; Bronze Star (3); Meritorious Svc; Army Comm Med (3) 1962-72; Air Medal (3), Vietnamese Cross of Gallantry; Master Parachutist Badge. **Home Addr:** 118 Elm Dr, Montgomery, AL 36117.

JOHNSON, PAUL L.
News photographer. **Personal:** Born Oct 27, 1943, Savannah, GA; married Angelyne Russell; children: Monifa Ife, Ayeola Binta. **Educ:** Matriculated Savannah State Coll; Univ of Ghana; Univ So IL; Univ of FL. **Career:** Acad Black Culture as dir Savannah Model Cities Cult Ctr 1969-72; prof three free TV pub serv progs 1971-72; Acad of Black Culture Inc, co-founder; KTUL-TV, news photographer. **Orgs:** Bd dir Inner City Comm Ctr 1970-72; art instr local cap agency EOA 1970; slide lectures Savannah State Coll, pub schs & libraries; mem PUSH, ASALH & NAACP. **Honors/Awds:** Yr scholarship Omega Psi Phi 1961; One man show-paintings Savannah State Coll 1967; designed covers for Expression 1969 & Expression 1970; poems published Expression 1970; co-prod Black radio prog 1970-72; guest poet GA Poetry Soc 1971; one man show photo Savannah State Coll 1972; Outstanding Young Man of AmerAwd 1972. **Military Serv:** AUS spl 5 1967-68. **Business Addr:** KTUL-TV, PO Box 8, Tulsa, OK 74101.

JOHNSON, PAUL LAWRENCE
Judge (retired). **Personal:** Born Sep 23, 1931, Coatesville, PA; married Dorothy Elizabeth Flowers; children: Bruce Michael, Darryl Lawrence. **Educ:** St Paul's Coll, 1950-53. **Career:** Lukens Steel Co, shearman, 1957-63; estimator, 1963-70; Timestudy Tech, 1970-84; Coatesville City Council, pres 1980-85; Supreme Court of PA, district justice 1985-93. **Orgs:** Bd mem Credit Union Lukens 1972-; pres Trustees of Hutchinson Church 1972-; pres Lancaster Co Chap Credit Unions 1984-87; bd Coatesville Sr Citizens Ctr 1983-88, United Way 1987-90. **Honors/Awds:** Outstanding Comm Serv Award, J Frederic Wiese 1984. **Military Serv:** AUS corpl 1954-56. **Home Addr:** 514 Elm St, Coatesville, PA 19320.

JOHNSON, PEPPER
Professional football player. **Personal:** Born Jul 29, 1964, Detroit, MI; children: Dionte. **Educ:** Ohio State. **Career:** New York Giants, linebacker, 1986-92; Cleveland Browns, 1993-95; Detroit Lions, 1996; New York Jets, 1997-. **Honors/Awds:** Pro Bowl, 1990, 1994. **Business Addr:** Professional Football Player, New York Jets, 1000 Fulton Ave, Hempstead, NY 11550, (516)560-8100.

JOHNSON, PHYLLIS CAMPBELL
City official. **Personal:** Born Jul 21, 1954, Fort Worth, TX; daughter of Ann Miller Campbell and Mira G Campbell. **Educ:** Univ of Texas, Arlington TX, BA Communication, 1979, MA Urban Affairs, 1984. **Career:** Texas Instruments, Dallas TX, manufacturing supervisor, 1979-82; City of Fort Worth TX, human services coordinator, 1984-87, administrative asst, 1987-88, fiscal services administrator, 1988-. **Orgs:** Mem, Neighborhood Advisory Council, 1983-; mem, Urban Management Asst of North Texas, 1984-; mem, Texas Municipal League, 1985-; mem, Network for Executive Women, 1985-; sec, North Texas Conference of Minority Public Adminstrators, 1986-87; vice pres ntc, Natl Forum for Black Public Administrators, 1987-88; mem, Tarrant County League of Women Voters, 1987-88; mem, NAACP; mem, Fort Worth Metropolitan Black Chamber of Commerce; mem, Minority Leaders and Citizens Council. **Honors/Awds:** Kappa Delta Pi Honor Society, Univ of Texas at Arlington, 1979-; Urban Fellowship Recipient, North Central Texas Council of Governments, 1984; Notable Woman of Texas, Awards and Honor Society of America, 1984-85; Outstanding Young Women of America, OYWOA, 1986; Leadership Fort Worth Award, Fort Worth Chamber of Commerce, 1988. **Business Addr:** Fiscal Services Administrator, Park and Recreation, City of Fort Worth, 100 North University, Suite 239, Fort Worth, TX 76107.

JOHNSON, PHYLLIS MERCEDES
Business executive (retired). **Personal:** Born Apr 17, 1919, Hutchinson, KS; married James P Johnson; children: Beverly. **Educ:** Lincoln Univ, BS 1941; Washington Univ, MA 1965; So IL Univ, attended 1967-68. **Career:** Teacher home econ, 1942-46; MO Div of Empl Sec, dist mgr 1951-79. **Orgs:** Mem Alpha Kappa Alpha; past pres St Louis Personnel & Guid Assn; mem MO Personnel & Guid Assn; NAACP; Urban League; Intl Assn Personnel in Empl Sec; AAUW. **Honors/Awds:** Merit Awd St Louis Personnel & Guid Assn 1973.

JOHNSON, POMPIE LOUIS, JR.
Banking executive. **Personal:** Born Dec 19, 1926, Pocatello, ID; son of Nellie B Johnson and Pompie L Johnson, Sr; married Marylynn T Hughes; children: Tamara, Karen. **Educ:** ID St Univ, BA 1950; Boston Univ Sch of Law, JD 1952; Am Svngs & Loan Inst, Diploma 1967; Am Inst of Bnkng, Diploma 1971. **Career:** Boston MA, atty 1952-55; Mutual of Omaha Ins Co, sls & Clms 1956-60; Golden State Mutual Life Ins Co, plng spclst 1960-62; Safety Svngs & Loan Assn, vice pres-mgr 1963-66; Security Pacific Natl Bank, (1st blk mgr) vice pres-mgr 1967-72; CA Fed Svngs & Loan Assn, vice pres corp svngs 1973-. **Orgs:** Bd of dir Watts CA Econ Dev Comm 1973-76; bd of dir Inglewood CA Chmbr of Comm 1975-78; bd of dir Inglewood CA Mrchnts Assn 1975-78 ; bd of dir Gardena CA Econ Dev Comm 1983-; asst treas CA State Rep Cntrl Comm 1974-78; pres SW Los Angeles Rotry Clb 1979-80; Rotary International, District 5280, Governor's Representative, 1994-95; Rotary International, District 5280, Chairman of Club Service, 1995-96. **Honors/Awds:** Delegate/mem Perm Org Comm Rep Natl Conv 1972; delegate Rotry Intl Conv Rome, Italy 1979; Unsung Hero Awrd LA Sntnl Nwspr 1972; Rotarian of Yr Los Angeles Rtry 1982. **Military Serv:** USAF cprl 1945-46. **Business Addr:** Vice President, California Fed S & L Assn, PO Box 18934, Los Angeles, CA 90018.

JOHNSON, R. BENJAMIN
Government official. **Personal:** Born Jul 14, 1944, Marion, AR; son of Willie B Clay Johnson and Robert Lee Johnson; married Jacqueline Vassar Johnson, Dec 6, 1975; children: Nancy, Rahman, Endesha, Jua, Sekou. **Educ:** Attended, Indiana Univ, Antioch Coll, Tufts Univ, Prince George's Comm Coll Mgmt Inst. **Career:** WSBT TV, news reporter and host afternoon talk show; Action Inc, director of employment; Manpower Assistance Program, manpower specialist; Youth Advocacy Program, director, 1971-73; St Joseph County Credit Union, manager/treasurer, 1975-77; Credit Union Inst Natl Center for Urban Ethnic Affairs, director, 1977-79; The White House Office of Consumer Affairs, director of consumer programs/special asst to consumer advisor to the pres 1979-81; Natl Credit Union Admin, special asst to the chmn of the bd 1981-82; Black Resource Guide Inc, president, 1981-; Dept of Consumer & Regulatory Affairs Washington, administrator business regulation admin 1983-87, administrator housing & environmental regulation admin 1987-88; special asst to the mayor, 1988-89; Dept of Public and Assisted Housing, director, 1989-91; The White House Office of Public Liaison, deputy asst to pres, 1993-. **Orgs:** Chmn The South bend Black Voters Assn; vice pres Valley Chapter of Credit Unions; chmn St Joseph County CETA Advisory Bd; has held elected positions in 20 professional civic and social orgs; publisher, The Black Resource Guide. **Honors/Awds:** Distinguished Government Serv Award, 1987, 1990; Outstanding Professionals Award Business Exchange Network 1987; publications New Credit Union Mgmt Systems 1969, The Community Development Credit Union 1977, 1979 editions, The Black Resource Guide 1981-91 editions. **Military Serv:** US Army; Honorable Discharge. **Business Addr:** Deputy Director, Office of Public Liaison, The White House, 1600 Pennsylvania Ave, Washington, DC 20006, (202)456-2930.

JOHNSON, RALPH C.
Certified public accountant. **Personal:** Born Dec 4, 1941, Pittsburg, TX; married Nadine; children: Stacie. **Educ:** Oakwood Coll, BS 1964; Wichita State Univ, MS 1967. **Career:** Fox & Co Kansas City, staff accountant 1964-71; AL A&M Coll, assoc prof bus adminstr 1967-68; Ralph C Johnson & Co, founder 1971-. **Orgs:** Licensed CPA KS 1966, MO 1971; mem Amer Inst of CPA's. **Business Addr:** Founder, Ralph C Johnson Co, 106 W 11th St, #1630, Kansas City, KS 64105-1806.

JOHNSON, RANDALL MORRIS
Educational administrator. **Personal:** Born Nov 21, 1936, Chicago, IL; son of Dorothy Beard Johnson (deceased) and William Johnson (deceased); married Marva J Goldsmith; children: Terri A, Christopher L. **Educ:** Northern IL Univ, BS 1958, MS 1959; Univ of Chicago, PhD (TTT Fellow) 1975. **Career:** Northwestern Med Sch, lab tech 1958; Phillips HS, teacher 1959-69; Kennedy King Coll, prof biology 1969-76, chmn natl sci math dept 1970-76, dean of arts & sci. **Orgs:** Super MAT Grad Stud in Sci 1970-72; super Student Teach N IL Univ 1971-72; consul Sci Dist #22 Chicago Bd of Educ; dir Cosmopolitan Comm Chuch Choir 1970-85; bd mem Gospel Arts Workshop Inc 1979-85; mem Chicago Council Fine Arts 1983, 1984; dir Voices of Melody Inc 1980-82; mem Alpha Phi Omega 1955-; mem Phi Mu Alpha 1956-; bd of dir ECC Music Workshop of Chicago 1988-89; dir Kennedy-King Community Chorus 1985-; dir St John Church-Baptist 1988-; panelist Chicago Council of Fine Arts 1991-92; mem Assn for Supervision and Curriculum Development 1991. **Honors/Awds:** TTT Fellowship Univ of Chicago 1969; Guest Conductor Chicago Musician Assoc Messiah 1979; Outstanding Choir Dir Chicago Musicians Assoc 1979; Outstanding Educator Ora Higgins Foundation 1980; Hon mem Phi Theta Kappa Lambda Rho Chap 1983; Outstanding Achievement Awd Natl Assoc of Negro Musicians 1986; "Freedom Symphony"- a musical drama of the African American Experience 1986; Outstanding Achievement R N Dett Musicians Assoc 1989. **Home Addr:** 7342 S Euclid Ave, Chicago, IL 60649. **Business Addr:** Dean

of Arts & Sciences, Kennedy King College, 6800 S Wentworth Ave, Chicago, IL 60621.

JOHNSON, RAY

Business executive (retired). **Personal:** Born Dec 13, 1935, Port Gibson, MS; son of Norah Johnson; married Marcia Ann; children: Raymond Bradley, Fredrick Norman. **Career:** McDonald's Corporation, natl oper adv bd; McDonald's Restaurants, owner-operator of 10 stores; Ray Johnson Enterprises Inc, president & CEO. **Orgs:** AZ State Athletic Comm, chmn-commissioner 1981-83; Round-One Production, president 1983-86; AZ State Liquor Comm, chmn 1983-; City of Phoenix Civil Service Comm, commissioner 1986-; Chairman Regional Operator Advisory Board McDonald's Owner/Operator 1989; dept review bd, Phoenix Police Dept, 1990. **Honors/Awds:** Phoenix AZ Human Resource Businessman of the Year 1980; AZ & US Small Businessman of the Year 1984; Alcorn State University, Honorary doctorate. **Military Serv:** USAF 4 years. **Home Addr:** 7643 N 20th St, Phoenix, AZ 85020.

JOHNSON, RAYLEE TERRELL

Professional football player. **Personal:** Born Jun 1, 1970, Fordyce, AR; married Diann; children: Brooke, Brecena, Brandy, Bryce. **Educ:** Univ of Arkansas, majored in business education. **Career:** San Diego Chargers, defensive end, 1993-. **Business Addr:** Professional Football Player, San Diego Chargers, Qualcomm Stadium, 9449 Friars Rd, San Diego, CA 92108, (619)280-2111.

JOHNSON, RAYMOND L.

Police chief. **Personal:** Born Apr 20, 1936, Arkansas; son of Lucy Johnson and Grady Johnson; children: Ava. **Educ:** CA State Univ Sacramento, BA; State of CA, lifetime teaching credential. **Career:** Bakersfield CA, police dept; CA Highway Patrol, chief southern div; City of Inglewood Police Dept, chief of police; Office of Criminal Justice Planning, exec dir. **Orgs:** Pres Peace Officers Assn of Los Angeles County; mem CA Peace Officers Assoc, CA Police Chiefs, Inter-Agency Chief Officers, Intl Assoc of Police Chiefs, Los Angeles County Police Chiefs Assn, South Bay Police Chiefs, Amer Mgmt Assoc, Natl Org of Black Law Enforcement Exec, Los Angeles-Lusaka Zambia Sister City Comm, Senate Task Force on Child Abuse, Natl Criminal Justice Assoc, Assoc of Black Law Enforcement Exec, CA Dist Atty Assoc; bd dir Oscar Joel Bryant Assoc; dir Homer Garrott Scholarship Found; bd of advisors Los Angeles Child Passenger Safety Assoc; honorary bd mem Amer Cancer Society; Assn of Black Law Enforcement Executives; Amer Mgt Assn; Automobile Club of South CA, Traffic Safety Advisors Program; past mem Boy Scouts of Amer Task Force;past member of State Task Force on Ga and Drugs, CA Council on Criminal Justice; CA District Attorneys Assn; representative/accreditation task force CA Peace Officers Assn; CA Police Chiefs Assn Inc; Homer Garrott (retired judge) Scholarship Foundation, director; Independent Cities Assn of LA County; Inglewood Coalition on Alcohol and Drugs; Inter-Agency Chief Officers; Intl Assn of Police Chiefs mem of Narcotics and Dangerous Drugs Committee; Loved Ones of Homicide Victims, bd mem; LA Child Passenger Safety Assn bd mem; LA County Police Chiefs Assn; Natl Assn of Blacks in Criminal Justice; Natl Criminal Justice Assn; Natl Organization of Black Law Enforcement Executives chairman of Awards Committee 1989; Oscar Joel Bryant Assn bd of directors;Peace Officers Assn LA County past pres current bd mem, chairman Uniform Reporting Committee on Gangs; Police Foundation; Police Mgt Assn; Senate Task Force on Child Abuse past mem; South Bay Police Chiefs/Criminal Justice Admn Assn. **Honors/Awds:** Hon mem Special People Involved in Community Endeavors. **Military Serv:** USMC. **Business Addr:** Executive Director, Office of Criminal Justice Planning, 1130 K St, Ste 300, Sacramento, CA 95814.

JOHNSON, RAYMOND L., SR.

Banker. **Personal:** Born Jul 31, 1922, Providence, RI; son of Lelia Johnson and Jacob Johnson; married Evelyn Allen Johnson, Sep 30, 1950; children: Raymond L Jr, Marjorie, Robert A. **Educ:** Howard University, Washington, DC, BS, 1950; Rochester General Hospital, Rochester, NY, med tech, 1951; Howard Univ School of Law, Washington, DC, JD, 1956. **Career:** Mathew C Long, gen prac law; All Cts of CA, admtd to prac 1964; Grp Hlth Assn, asst lab supr 1953-56; Cedars of Lebanon Hosp, med tech; Mt Sinai Hosp, med tech; Univ Hosp, chf med tech 1957-61; Advanced Bio-Chem Lab, asst med lab supr; US Congressman Edward R Roybal, spl asst 1962-68; Charles R Drew Medical School, asst prof of law; UCLA Medical School, asst prof of law; County of Los Angeles, Los Angeles, CA, special counsel, beginning 1976; attorney, Los Angeles, CA. **Orgs:** Chmn Hosp Hlth & Welfare Com Westside br NAACP; mem Hlth Cncl & Med-Legal Consult Watts-U So CA; gen counsel W Adams Comm Hosp; apptd by State Bar of CA to State Bar of CA Com to confer with CA Med Assn; licensed lab tech; Nat Adv Hlth Cncl; med-legal Coins CA Bar; arbitrator Am Arbitration Asszn; mem Judge Pro Tem panel of LA Mun Ct; adminstr Small Bus Devel Ctrs; AMA; LA Trial Layers Assn; State Bar of CA Jucicial Com; Am Arbitration Assn; Fed Ofc of Econ Oppty; mem Law Ofc Mgmt Com LA Co Bar Assn; LA Town Club; Am Soc of Hosp Attys; California State Bar, 1964-; judge pro tem, Los Angeles Superior Court; pres, Howard Univ Law Alumni Assn. **Honors/Awds:** Dem cand US Congressman 1968; alumni award Howard Univ 1961; guest spkr Pres's Nat Adv Commn 1967; attended White House Civil Rights Conf 1966; del Am Bar Assn 1956; cand LA City Cncl; Outstanding Attorney Award, Los Angeles Sentinel, 1976; Howard University Outstanding Achievement Award; Watts Outstanding Achievement Award, 1966. **Military Serv:** USAF Air Force Cadet Pilot 1943-45. **Home Addr:** 4200 Don Mariano Dr, Los Angeles, CA 90008. **Business Addr:** Attorney, 316 W Second St, Ste 1204, Los Angeles, CA 90012.

JOHNSON, RAYMOND LEWIS

Educator. **Personal:** Born Jun 25, 1943, Alice, TX; married Claudette Willa Smith; children: Malcolm Patrice. **Educ:** Univ of TX (Phi Beta Kappa, Phi Kappa Phi), BA 1963; Rice Univ, PhD 1969. **Career:** Univ of MD, asst prof 1968-72, assoc prof 1972-80; Inst Mittag-Leffler, visiting mbr 1974-75; Howard Univ, prof 1976-78; McMaster Univ, visiting professor, 1983-84; Univ of MD, prof of math 1980-, chair 1991-96. **Orgs:** Edtrl comm Am Math Soc 1982-86; bd of governors, Institute for Mathematics and Its Applications, 1993-96; scientific advisory committee, Mathematical Sciences Research Institute, 1994-98; bd of dirs, Nastl Assn of Mathematicians, 1994-96; MIE advisory bd, Spelman Coll, 1994-. **Honors/Awds:** Distinguished Minority Faculty 1986. **Special Achievements:** Co-organizer, first Conference for African-American Research in the Mathematical Sciences, MSRJ, 1995; co-organizer, first Applied Mathematics and Minorities, Connections to Industry IMA, 1996-. **Home Addr:** 6916 Woodstream Ln, Seabrook, MD 20706. **Business Addr:** Professor of Mathematics, Univ of Maryland, Math Dept, College Park, MD 20742.

JOHNSON, REBECCA M.

Educator (retired). **Personal:** Born Jul 10, 1905, Springfield, MA; daughter of Harriet B Johnson and William D Johnson. **Educ:** Fisk Univ, BA 1927; Attended, Northwestern Univ 1934, Springfield Coll 1943; Columbia Univ, MA 1948. **Career:** Columbia SC Public School Dept, elem teacher 1927-35; Charleston SC Educ 24 Hr Camp for Unemployed, dir 1935; Columbia SC Public School Dept, jr high math teacher 1935-43; Springfield MA Public School Dept, jr high math teacher 1943-46, principal of 4 different elem schools 1947-75 (retired); Visiting Lecturer, Mount Holyoke College, Springfield College, American International College. **Orgs:** Life mem Springfield NAACP Bd 1960-89; bd of dirs Springfield Tech Comm Coll; bd mem Springfield Child Guidance Clinic Inc 1985-89; co-chair Scholarship and Educ Resource Network of Urban League 1985-89; mem Alpha Kappa Alpha Sor; mem Delta Kappa Gamma Hon Soc Women Educators; chmn scholarship comm St John's Congregational Church; mem Black-Jewish Dialogue Committee; mem John Brown Archives Committee, St John's Church. **Honors/Awds:** Woman of the Year Harambee Holiday 1975; Black History Awd in Field of Educ Trailblazers US Post Office 1987; Woman of the Year B'Nai Brith Springfield Chapt; Educ Awd for First Black Public School Principal Springfield; Human and Comm Serv Awd Springfield Muslim Mission; Dedicated Serv Awd as board mem Springfield Tech Comm Coll awarded by MA Bd of Regional Comm Colls; Award for Spirit and Dedication to Freedom 350 years of Black presence in MA, Museum of Afro-Amer History.

JOHNSON, RHODA E.

Educator. **Personal:** Born Nov 14, 1946, Bessemer, AL; daughter of Peacolia Dancy Barge and Foy Barge Sr; married Ruffer Johnson, Jun 7, 1968; children: Ryan, Robert. **Educ:** Tuskegee Institute, Tuskegee, AL, BS, 1968; University of Michigan, Ann Arbor, MI, AM, 1970; University of Alabama, Tuscaloosa, AL, PhD, 1980. **Career:** University of Michigan, Ann Arbor, MI, student research asst, 1969-70; Tuskegee Institute, Tuskegee, AL, instructor, 1970-77, asst prof, 1977-81, assoc prof, dir of MARC, 1982-85; University of Alabama, Tuscaloosa, AL, visiting prof, acting dir, 1985-86, assoc prof, chair, 1986-92; assoc prof, 1992-. **Orgs:** Member, steering committee, 21st Century Leadership Project, 1989-; bd member, National Voting Rights Museum, 1994-; bd member, National Review Bd, Alabama Historical Commission. **Honors/Awds:** Minority Access to Research Careers Grant, ADAMHA, 1982-85; Higher Education Component Grant, Southern Education Foundation, 1980-81; Poverty and Mental Health in the Rural South, CSRS/USDA, Carver Foundation, 1978-83; editor, Women's Studies in the South, Kendall/Hunt, 1991. **Business Addr:** Former Chair, Women's Studies, University of Alabama, Box 870272, 101 Manly, Tuscaloosa, AL 35487-0272, (205)348-9556.

JOHNSON, RICHARD HOWARD

Government official (retired). **Personal:** Born Jan 7, 1931, Jersey City, NJ; son of Della H Johnson and Richard S Johnson; married D Winona; children: Sandra Ellen Harris, Richard Nicholas. **Educ:** VA Union Univ, AB Sociol (Cum Laude) 1953; Boston Univ Sch of Social Work, MA 1955. **Career:** Camp Downingtown, dir 1953-55; US Army Hospital, chief psychiatric sw 1955-57; Hawthornden State Hosp, psychiatric social worker 1957-59; Cuyahoga Co Court of Common Pleas, marriage counselor 1959-65; Maternal and Child Health, coord neighborhood serv 1965-68; Hough Parent-Child Ctr, dir 1968-72; Parent & Child Ctrs Head Start Bureau OCD-DHEW, chief 1972-; Parent Involvement Branch HSB, ACYF, DHHS, chief social serv, 1975-91. **Orgs:** Mem Kappa Alpha Psi Frat; Boule-Sigma Pi Phi Frat; Natl 30-Yr Oldtimers; COSPICS; NAEYC; NASW; NCBCD. **Honors/Awds:** Departmental Awd for Chairing Task Force DHHS HSB 1986; Departmental Leadership Awd DHHS 1987; "Exploring Parenting" 1976, "Exploring Self-Sufficiency" 1982, "Looking at Life" 1986. **Military Serv:** AUS specialist 3rd class 2 yrs, 1955-57.

JOHNSON, RITA FALKENER

Interior designer. **Personal:** Born in Arlington, VA; married Waldo C Falkener. **Educ:** Academie Julien Paris, 1964-65; Grande Chaumi re Paris, 1964-67; Pratt Inst, BFA 1964. **Career:** Esq residential & commerical interior design; Essence Mag, home editor 1975-77. **Orgs:** Allied Bd Trade; mem Nat Home Fashions League Inc Professional showcase; YWCA Designers' Showhouse 1976; Designers' Showhouse 1977; YWCA Showhouse 1977. **Business Addr:** 50 Pierrepont St, Brooklyn, NY 11201.

JOHNSON, ROBERT

Health administrator. **Educ:** Univ of Michigan; Tennessee State Univ. **Career:** St Louis Regional Medical Center, president and CEO; Grady Memorial Hospital, Atlanta, GA, executive director; Fulton-DeKalb Hospital Authority, secretary, treasurer; Detroit Medical Center, executive vice president, COO, currently. **Business Addr:** Exec VP/COO, Detroit Medical Center, 4201 St. Antoine, Detroit, MI 48201, (313)745-6035.

JOHNSON, ROBERT

Government official. **Career:** White House Office of Public Liaison, dep asst to the President, dep dir for public liaison, currently. **Business Addr:** Special Asst to the President/Deputy Director for Public Liaison, White House Office of Public Liaison, 122 OEOB, Washington, DC 20502, (202)456-2930.

JOHNSON, ROBERT

Automobile dealer. **Personal:** Born Jul 15, 1937, Chicago, IL; son of Thelma Fisher Payne and Ben Charles Johnson; married Carolyn P Williams Johnson, Feb 4, 1984; children: Craig M, Laura L Barnett. **Educ:** Chicago Teachers College, Chicago, IL, 1960-65. **Career:** Allstate Insurance Co, Chicago, IL, agent, 1968-78; Bob Johnson Chevrolet Inc, Buffalo, NY, president, 1981-85; Bob Johnson Chevrolet, Rochester, NY, president, 1985-. **Orgs:** Vice chair, Urban League, 1986-91; member, General Motors Minority Dealer Assn, 1983-84; board member, United Way of Rochester, 1990-91; board member, National Urban League, 1996; board member, Rochester Chamber of Commerce, 1995-96; board member, St Josephs Villa, 1994-96; board member, Rochester Telephone Co, 1996; board member, New York Auto Dealers Assn, 1993-96; board member, Rochester Auto Dealers Assn, 1992-96; pres, Brockport Ford, Brockport, NY, 1996-. **Honors/Awds:** Community Fellow, SUNY College at Buffalo, 1985; Top 100 Dealers, Black Enterprise Magazine, 1986-95; Time Magazine Quality Dealer Award, NY, 1998. **Military Serv:** US Air Force, Airman 1st Class, 1954-58. **Business Addr:** President, Bob Johnson Chevrolet, Inc, 1110 Stone Rd, Rochester, NY 14616, (716)663-4040.

JOHNSON, ROBERT B.

Educator. **Personal:** Born Aug 19, 1928, Fair Bluff, NC; married Virginia J; children: Ronald Hal, Jacquelyn Foster. **Educ:** A&T State Univ, BS 1950, MS 1959. **Career:** HS Loris SC, sci tchr 1955-63; Coastal Jr Coll, chem instr 1959-61; Pleasant Grove Elem Sch Rains SC, prin 1963-67; Mullins Sch Dist SC, elem sch prin 1968-; Lower Marion County, superintendent. **Orgs:** Mem Mullins City Coun 1970-82; Pee Dee Reg Devel Coun; Human Resource Devel Coun. **Business Addr:** Superintendent, Lower Marion County, School Dist #3, Rains, SC 29589.

JOHNSON, ROBERT H.

Educator. **Personal:** Born Nov 24, 1938, NYC; divorced; children: Vietta. **Educ:** Smith U, BS 1960; LIU, MS 1964; St John's U, PhD 1970. **Career:** Pharma-Verona Chem Co, chemist 1961-62; Hum Affairs Res Center, consultant 1970-72; R H Clark & Assoc, partner 1974-; LIU, teacher 1964-75; Medgar Evers Coll of CUNY, teacher 1975-76, dean of students 1977-. **Orgs:** Mem Am Chem Soc; Am Assn for Advance Sci; NY Acad Sci; Nat Assn Black Chemists & Engr; mem, bd trustee Nat Black Sci Stds Org 1972-; Fed Drug Addict Prog. **Honors/Awds:** Outstndng Young Men of Am 1971; Outstndng Educators of Am 1973. **Business Addr:** The Brooklyn Cntr, Long Island Univ, Brooklyn, NY 11201.

JOHNSON, ROBERT JUNIUS

Company executive. **Personal:** Born Mar 19, 1929, Richton, MS; son of Priscilla Dean Johnson and Charles Davis Johnson; married Patricia Sutton Johnson, Jan 1, 1992; children: Robert II, Kemberly Nicole. **Career:** Johnson Products Co Inc, dir of distribution, currently. **Business Addr:** Director of Distribution, Johnson Products Co, 8522 S Lafayette Ave, Chicago, IL 60620-1398, (312)483-4100.

JOHNSON, ROBERT L.
Business executive. **Personal:** Born in Hickory, MS; married Sheila. **Educ:** Univ of IL, graduate; Princeton Univ, MA. **Career:** Corp for Public Broadcasting; Washington Urban League; Hon W E Fauntroy, Congr Delegate frm DC, press secty; Nat'l Cable TV Assn, vice pres govt rel 1976-79; Black Entertainment Television, founder, pres/CEO 1980-. **Orgs:** Black Entertainment TV; vice pres for govt affairs NCTA 1978-79, bd of dirs 1982-84; bd mem, Hilton Hotels Corp; Amer Film Inst; Advertising Council; bd mem, Board of Governors of the Natl Cable Academy; bd mem, Walter Kaitz Foundation; bd mem, Washington Metro Cable Club; bd mem, District Cablevision; bd mem US Airways; bd mem United Negro Coll Fund. **Honors/Awds:** Pres Awd NCTA 1982; Image Awd NAACP 1982; Pioneer Awd Capital Press Club 1984; Business of the Year Awd DC Chamber of Commerce 1985; Cablevision Magazine's 20/20 Vision Award, 1995; Communicator's Awd, Black Radio Exclusive; CEBA Awd, World Institute of Black Communications, Inc; Distinguished Alumni Awd, Princeton Univ; Turner Broadcasting Trumpet Awd, 1993; Executive Leadership Council Awd, 1992; Hall of Fame Award Broadcasting and Cable Magazine 1997; Grand Tam Award CTAM; Good Guys Award Natl Women's Political Caucus 1997. **Business Addr:** Founder/Chairman/CEO, Black Entertainment TV, 1900 W Pl, NE, Washington, DC 20018.

JOHNSON, ROBERT L.
Physician, educator. **Personal:** Born Aug 7, 1946, Spartanburg, SC; son of Clalice Brewton Johnson and Robert Johnson; married Maxine Gilchrist Johnson, Jun 24, 1972. **Educ:** Alfred University, BA, 1968; College of Medicine and Dentistry of New Jersey, MD, 1972. **Career:** Martland Hospital, pediatric intern, 1972-73, pediatric resident, 1973-74, dir of adolescent medicine, 1976-78; St Michael's Medical Ctr, dir of adolescent medicine-clinic, 1976-; Children's Hospital of New Jersey, dir of adolescent medicine, 1976-; New York Medical Sch, asst attending physician, 1976-84; Univ of Medicine & Dentistry of New Jersey, asst professor of clinical pediatrics, 1976-83, associate professor of clinical pediatrics, 1983-89, associate professor of clinical psychiatry, 1989-, professor of clinical pediatrics, 1989-; University Hospital, dir of adolescent medicine, 1978-; Prof of pediatrics, 1995-, New Jersey Med School, Adolescent Medicine- Pediatrics, Director, Currently. **Orgs:** Fellow, Amer Acad of Pediatrics, 1974-, Sect on Adolescent Health Care, 1974-, fellow, Amer Acad of Pediatrics, New Jersey Chap, 1974-; chp, Comm on Adolescence, 1983-; Soc for Adolescent Medicine, 1986-; chp, Comm on Sports Medicine & Accident Prevention, 1976-78; board member, Adolescent Health Ctr of the Door, 1977-, chm, 1982-; bd of trustees, Frost Valley YMCA, 1979-; bd of deacons, Union Baptist Church, 1978-, chm, 1987-; bd of trustees, Day Care Coordinating Council, 1980-81; vice pres for Health Affairs, Intl Ctr for Integrative Studies, 1980-; board of directors, Institutefor the Development of Youth Programs, 1983-; bd of trustees, Newark Boy's Clubs, 1984-; board of directors, Sex Information & Education Council of the US, 1988-; Carnegie Corp, Substance Abuse Advisory Comm, 1989-; New Jersey State Bd of Medical Examiners, 19, credentials committee chair, 1990-, treasurer, 1990-91, secretary, 1991-; AAP, Committee on Careers and Opportunities, chair, 1992, National Task Force on the Access of Minority Children to Health Care, chairman, 1991-; The Oregon Health Plan Board of Medical Examiners, advisory committee, 1992; Pediatrics in Review, editorial board, 1990-. **Honors/Awds:** Exceptional Merit Award, Univ of Medicine & Dentistry of New Jersey, Newark, NJ, 1982-83; Citizen of the Year Award, New Jersey Assn of Black Social Workers, Essex Chapter, 1988; New Jersey Pride Award in Health, 1989; Roe v Wade Anniversary Award, New Jersey Coalition for Abortion Rights, 1989; Community Service Award, Alpha Kappa Alpha Sorority, 1989; January 19, 1989 proclaimed Dr. Robert L Johnson Day, City of Newark, NJ; Outstanding Achievement Award, Centennial Comm of Orange, 1989; Recognition Award, Sunshine Club of Newark & Friends, 1990; New Jersey Perspectives Magazine, Outstanding Service in Health Awareness Award, 1992. **Special Achievements:** Author: "The Sexual Abuse of Boys," New York State Journal of Medicine, p 132, 1989; "Contraception for Adolescents," Female Patient, p 52-55, 1978; co-author: "Roundtable: The Adolescent Patient," Female Patient, p 57-63, 1977; "Problem Behaviors of Adolescence: A Clinical Perspective," American Journal of Family Therapy, p 72-75, 1985; "Sexual Victimization of Boys," Journal of Adolescent Health Care, p 372-376, 1985; "Replacing the Work of Pediatric Residents: Strategies and Issues," Pediatrics, p 1109-1110, 1990; "Depression in Inner City Adolescents Attending an Adolescent Medicine Clinic," Journal of Adolescent Health, p 316-318, 1991; "Acquired Immunodeficiency Syndrome: New Jersey High School Students Knowledge, Attitudes and Behaviors," AIDS Education and Prevention, p 21-30, 1991; "Sexual Behaviors African-American Male College Students and the Risk of HIV Infection," Journal of the Natl Medical Assn, 1992. **Business Addr:** Director of Adolescent Medicine-Pediatrics, University of Medicine and Dentistry of New Jersey, New Jersey Medical School, 185 S Orange Ave, Newark, NJ 07103-2757, (973)972-3277.

JOHNSON, ROBERT T.
District attorney. **Career:** New York City, Bronx, asst dist attorney, eight years, district attorney, 1989. **Honors/Awds:** First black to hold position of district attorney in New York state. **Business Addr:** Bronx District Attorney, 198 E 161st St, Bronx, NY 10451.

JOHNSON, RON
Professional football player. **Personal:** Born Sep 21, 1958, Monterey, CA. **Educ:** California State Univ at Long Beach, attended. **Career:** Hamilton Tiger-Cats (Canadian Football League), 1982-84; Portland Breakers (USFL), 1985; Philadelphia Eagles, wide receiver, 1985-. **Business Addr:** Professional Football Player, Philadelphia Eagles, Veterans Stadium, Broad St and Pattison Ave, Philadelphia, PA 19148.

JOHNSON, RONALD CORNELIUS
Public administrator. **Personal:** Born Oct 2, 1946, Amelia County, VA; married Bessie; children: Aisha. **Educ:** VA St Coll, BA 1969; Univ of Cincin, MA 1973; Xavier U, MEd 1977. **Career:** Ronson Mgmt Corp, pres; US Dept of HUD, specialist asst; Univ of DC, dir inst in comm & public serv; US Dept of Housing & Urban Dev, mgmt analyst; Model Cities Program, admin; The Jewish Hospital, 1st coord employee relations. **Orgs:** Pres Ronald C Johnson Asso Inc; bd dir Bushido Inc; srvs on natl panel Am Acad for Ed Dev; natl chmn Conf of Minor Pub Admin 1975-76; mem Nat Cncl Am Soc for Pub Adminstrn 1975-76; chmn Fairfax Cty Urban Leag; mem Rural Am Inc; Nat Assn Hous & Rehab Off; mem NAACP; mem Natl Com on Responsive Philantropy. **Honors/Awds:** ASPA Apprec Award; Jewish War Vet Award; Urban Leag Serv Award; Conf of Min Pub Admin Award; Danforth Fellow. **Military Serv:** AUSR 1st lt. **Business Addr:** 1331 H St NW, Washington, DC 20005.

JOHNSON, ROOSEVELT YOUNG
Educator. **Personal:** Born Jul 2, 1946, Spartanburg, SC; married Lina; children: David. **Educ:** Howard U, BS 1968; IN U, PhD 1972. **Career:** Howard Univ Coll of Medicine, asst prof 1975-; Pacific Lutheran Univ, 1973-75. **Orgs:** Mem Am Soc for Microbiologists; Soc Sigma Xi; pres Langley-mcCormick PTA 1977-. **Honors/Awds:** Postdoc flw Univ WA 1972-73; postdoc flwsp NIH 1972-73. **Business Addr:** Asst Prof Dept of Botany, Howard University, Washington, DC 20059.

JOHNSON, ROY EDWARD
Professional baseball player (retired). **Personal:** Born Jun 27, 1959, Parkin, AR. **Educ:** Tennessee State Univ, Nashville, TN, attended. **Career:** Montreal Expos, outfielder 1984-85. **Orgs:** Helped in building the Expos minor league complex at Lantana in the 1983-84 off-season. **Honors/Awds:** Played Winter League ball in Mexican League with Hermosillo, named Most Valuable Player; made the A-New York-Penn League All-Star squad in center field; captured Expos' minor league player of the month awards; named Southern League player of week; won the Am Assn batting title 1982 with 367 avg & figured in 135 runs in 102 games.

JOHNSON, ROY LEE
Brewing company executive. **Personal:** Born Jun 30, 1955, Charleston, MS; son of Viola Sayles Johnson and James Johnson; married Vicki Jo Williams, May 10, 1980. **Educ:** Fisk Univ, Nashville TN, BS, 1977; Michigan State Univ, E Lansing, MBA, 1990. **Career:** Ford Motor Co, Detroit MI, financial analyst, 1977-83; The Stroh Brewery, Detroit MI, mgr of financial planning, 1983-91, director of financial planning, 1991-. **Orgs:** National Black MBA Association; Michigan State University, Advanced Managment Program Club. **Home Addr:** 18820 Jeanette, Southfield, MI 48075. **Business Phone:** (313)446-2104.

JOHNSON, ROY STEVEN
Journalist. **Personal:** Born Mar 19, 1956, Tulsa, OK; son of Ida Mae Brooks Jenkins (deceased) and Roy Johnson (deceased); married Barbara Y Johnson; children: Edwyn Lawrence, Anna Brooks. **Educ:** Stanford University, Stanford, CA, BA, 1978. **Career:** Sports Illustrated, writer, reporter, 1978-81; The New York Times, sportswriter, 1981-87; Atlanta Journal-Constitution, columnist, 1987-89; Sports Illustrated, New York, NY, senior editor, 1989-94; Money Magazine, senior editor (special projects), 1994-. **Orgs:** Member, National Association of Black Journalists, 1985-; International Amateur Athletic Association; Arthur Ashe Athletic Assn, board of directors; Roy S Johnson Foundation, founder & president; Homeboy Golf Tournament, bd of dirs. **Honors/Awds:** Service Award, NY Association of Black Journalists, 1996; Communicator of The Year, National Black MBA Assoc (NY Chapter), 1997. **Special Achievements:** Author, with Earvin "Magic" Johnson, Magic's Touch, Addison-Wesley, 1990; author, w/Charles Barkley, Outrageous, Simon-Schuster, 1992. **Business Addr:** Editor-at-Large, Fortune, Time & Life Bldg, 1271 Avenue of the Americas, 16th Fl, New York, NY 10020.

JOHNSON, SAM
Automobile dealership executive. **Career:** Sam Johnson Lincoln-Mercury-Merkur Inc, Charlotte, NC, chief exec; Metro Lincoln-Mercury Inc, Charlotte, NC, chief exec; S & J Enterprises, Charlotte, NC, chief executive, currently; Universal Ford, Inc, Richmond, VA, chief exec; Metro Ford Sales Inc, Tupelo, MS, chief exec; Cross Creek Lincoln Mercury Subaru, Inc, Fayetteville, NC, chief exec. **Business Addr:** President, S&J Enterprises, 5201 E Independence Blvd, Charlotte, NC 28212.

JOHNSON, SAMUEL HARRISON
Business executive (retired). **Personal:** Born Aug 31, 1916, Bowling Green, KY; married Edith; children: Cynthia, Pamela. **Educ:** Lane Coll, 1935-37; IN U, AB 1955, MA 1957, MS 1959. **Career:** Natl Scholarship Serv & Fund for Negro Students, dir 1992; Natl Board, Mission of The Presbetary Church, USA, dir, educ counseling serv bd; Marion Co Juvenile Court, probation officer; IN Med School Cons, HEW Office of Educ, staff. **Orgs:** Minority Engr Ed Proj; A Better Chance; Macy Found; Inst for Serv to Ed; Nat Assn of Coll Admissions Cnslrs; Acad of Certified Soc Wrkrs; Am Personnel & Guidance Assn; Nat Assn of Soc Wrkrs; Nat Assn of Std Fin Aid Assistance; orgnr, Fndr Assn of Non-White Concerns; volunteer, Fulton Co Juvenile Ct. **Honors/Awds:** Publ "A Case for Structure" Am Jour of Orth; WB Dubois Award, Super 17 7BS, Volunteer Award.

JOHNSON, SARAH H.
Councilwoman. **Personal:** Born Mar 10, 1938, Charleston, SC; divorced. **Educ:** Clark Coll, 1956-57; Elkins Inst, Grad 1974. **Career:** Greenville MS, councilwoman 1985; Headstart, area dir 1971-74. **Orgs:** Sec Delta Min Nat Cncl Ch 1968-71; xec sec Star Inc 1967; sec Weddington Wlm Sch 1964-65; bd dir Black Meth for Ch & Renewal 1971-73; gen bd ch soc UMC 1972-76; fellow MS Inst Politics 1972; Gov's Compreh Hlth Planning Adv Cncl 1974-75; radio lic course, rec FCC 1st Class Radio-tele Oprtrs Lic. **Honors/Awds:** Elks Serene Lodge No 567, Civil Liberties Plaque; 1st black elected off of Greenville 1974; Tallahatchie Co Dev League, Silver Cup Outstndng Civic Achiev1974; Sunflower Co NAACP Plaque Outstndng Civic Achiev 1974; Elks Serene Lodge No 567, Civil Liberties Citation for Courageous Struggle Against Injustice 1973; Elite Civic & Soc Club Citation Outstndng Achiev Politics 1974; Queen City Lodge FM & AM, Woman Yr Award 1973; Woman Yr Award 1975, by the Utility Club Inc.

JOHNSON, SARAH YVONNE
Educational administrator. **Personal:** Born Aug 17, 1950, Los Angeles, CA; married Frank Johnson Sr; children: Frank Jr, Ingrid Yvette. **Educ:** Tuskegee Inst, BS 1972; Harvard Univ, EdM 1973. **Career:** PENN Cultural Ctr, assoc dir 1973-75; Beaufort Cty Bd of Ed, spec ed teacher 1975-76; Renaissance Wives Headstart Prog, ed dir 1976; Vacca Campus State School for Delinquent Youth, principal 1976-. **Orgs:** Mem AL Juvenile Justice Assoc 1979-, Harvard Club of Birmingham, Positive Maturity Adv Bd 1981-85. **Honors/Awds:** Outstanding Young Women of Amer Nomination 1975,83; Outstanding Serv Awd Miles Coll Comm Sports Prog 1981; Outstanding Serv Awd Positive Maturity Foster Grandparent Prog 1981; 1st Black Principal of Vacca Campus. **Business Addr:** Principal of Vacca Campus, Alabama Youth Services, 8950 Roebuck Blvd, Birmingham, AL 35206.

JOHNSON, SHANNON
Professional basketball player. **Personal:** Born Aug 18, 1974. **Educ:** Univ of South Carolina. **Career:** Columbus Quest, guard, 1996-. **Honors/Awds:** US Olympic Festival Basketball Team, Gold Medal, 1993; US Jones Cup Basketball Team, Bronze Medal, 1995, Gold Medal, 1996. **Business Addr:** Professional Basketball Player, Columbus Quest, 7451 State Route 16, Dublin, OH 43016, (614)873-6555.

JOHNSON, SHARON REED
Educational administrator. **Personal:** Born Aug 25, 1944, Wichita, KS; divorced; children: Michael. **Educ:** Northern IL Univ, BA sociol 1972; Roosevelt Univ, MA urban studies 1973; Univ of Manchester England, Cert Environ Design & Social Planning 1973. **Career:** Northeastern IL Planning Comm, intern 1972-73; West NY Bd of Ed, teacher 1974, coord gifted ed & asst principal; PS No 3, principal, currently; Gifted & Bilingual Educ, grants, affirmative action & special events, principal assigned to supt's office. **Orgs:** Fin sec St Nicholas Tennis Club 1983-84; pres Mayor's Council for Youth/Sr; commun rep North Hudson Headstart; asst affirm action officer West NY Bd of Ed; bd mem Hudson Cty Coords Gifted Ed; State Coord Gifted Ed, West NY Administrators Assn, St James Episcopal Church Vestry; Natl Assn of Elementary School Principals; Montclair Drifters. **Honors/Awds:** Northeastern Illinois Planning Comm, Tuition Grant, 1972-73. **Special Achievements:** First to institute Convocations for Gifted Students, West NY; coordinator: West NY Art Exposition; West NY Sci Fair; Principal of the first elementary school to be completely wired for the Internet in West NY. **Business Addr:** Principal, PS No 3, 5401 Polk St, West New York, NJ 07093.

JOHNSON, SHEILA MONROE
Librarian. **Personal:** Born Nov 27, 1957, Southern Pines, NC; daughter of Esther M Monroe; married Michael Leon Johnson, Feb 14, 1982; children: Jade Taylor Johnson. **Educ:** Winston-Salem State University, Winston-Salem, NC, BA, 1980; Uni-

versity of North Carolina, Greensboro, NC, MLS, 1987. **Career:** Carpenter Library Bowman Gray School of Medicine, Winston-Salem, NC, circulation supervisor, 1982-85; Forsyth County Public Library, Winston-Salem, NC, head, periodicals & documents, 1985-. **Orgs:** Member, American Library Association, 1988-; member, North Carolina Library Association, 1986-; newsletter co-editor, Remco of NCLA, 1986-; president, Alumni Assn of UNC, Greensboro Department of Library and Information Studies, 1989-90; member, New Members Roundtable of NCLA, 1986-. **Honors/Awds:** Minority Scholarship, Medical Library Assn, 1985; Young Careerist Award, New Members Roundtable of NCLA, 1989. **Business Addr:** Head, Periodicals & Documents, Business Science, Forsyth County Public Library, 660 W Fifth St, Winston-Salem, NC 27101.

JOHNSON, SHIRLEY
Librarian. **Personal:** Born Mar 9, Baltimore, MD; daughter of Virginia Williams Marshall and George Garland Marshall; married Edward D Johnson (divorced 1988); children: Melvin Jerome Davis Jr (deceased). **Educ:** University of Baltimore, MD, BA, 1986; University of Pittsburgh, PA, MLS, 1989. **Career:** Enoch Pratt Free Library, Baltimore, MD, 1969-; librarian, 1989-. **Orgs:** American Library Assn, 1988-; Maryland Library Assn, 1985-; University of Baltimore Alumni Assn, 1987-; Black Caucus of the American Library Assn, 1988-; University of Pittsburgh Alumni Assn, 1989-. **Honors/Awds:** Enoch Pratt Free Library, Esther J Piercy Award, 1994. **Business Addr:** Branch Manager, Dundalk Avenue Branch, Enoch Pratt Free Library, 912 Dundalk Avenue, Baltimore, MD 21224, (410)396-9074.

JOHNSON, STAFFORD QUINCY
Educator. **Personal:** Born Jan 2, 1948, Alameda, CA; son of Rosa Mae Johnson and Quincy; married Beverly Breaux Johnson; children: Jamaal, Rashaad. **Educ:** Laney Coll, AA 1968; Univ of CA-Berkeley, BS 1970; CA State Univ, MS 1980. **Career:** Univ of CA-Berkeley, counselor. **Orgs:** Co-founder Black Staff and Faculty Organization (BSFO) UCB 1979-; chair George P Scotlan Endowment Fund 1986-; chair Black Staff and Faculty Org 1987-; founder of BSFO Recognition Awards, Ceremony and BSFO Gospel Program 1988. **Honors/Awds:** Booklet "EOP Peer Counselor Program," Univ of CA-Berkeley 1980; articles "Achieving Success Through Self-Awareness," 1982, "Overcoming Academic Difficulty," African Perspectives 1985; recipient of BSFO Outstanding Staff Award 1988; Chancellor's Outstanding Staff Award, 1995. **Home Addr:** 141 Doncastee Drive, Vallejo, CA 94591.

JOHNSON, STEPHANIE ANNE
Educator. **Personal:** Born Aug 19, 1952, Harrisburg, PA; daughter of Virginia E Johnson & Dr Lawrence J Johnson (deceased). **Educ:** Emerson College, Boston, 1974; San Francisco State University, MA, 1994. **Career:** Model Maker-Noel Gregorian, San Francisco, apprentice, 1983-85; California State Univ, Monterey Bay, prof of visual & public arts, 1995-; Kunstforeningen, Copenhage, Denmark, 1996. **Orgs:** Intl Assn of Stagehands & Theatical Employees, IATSE, 1993-; Intl Assn of Lighting Designers, IALD; Headlands Ctr for the Arts, affiliate artist. **Honors/Awds:** National Endowment Fellowship, Design Arts, 1983. **Special Achievements:** Guest lecturer: UNIV of CA, Berkeley, Spelman Coll, Atlanta, San Fran State Univ, De Melkweg, Amsterdam; many solo & group exhibitions: The Richmond Art Ctr, CA; Historic Oakland Cemetery, GA; Falkisk Art Ctr, CA; Herbst Pavilion, CA. **Home Addr:** 2740 Mabel St, Berkeley, CA 94702.

JOHNSON, STEPHANYE
Business development consultant. **Personal:** Born Jul 27, 1959, Brooklyn, NY; daughter of Eartha L. Grant Johnson and Gene E. Johnson; children: Alexander, Kraig. **Educ:** Univ of PA Philadelphia, BA 1980; Univ of NC Chapel Hill, MBA 1984. **Career:** Univ of PA, admin asst 1976-80; Port Authority of NY & NJ, auditor 1980-82; The Pillsbury Co Green Giant Co, financial analyst 1984-86; The Pillsbury Co Burger King Corp, sr product analyst 1986-89; SJO Associates Inc, Miami, FL, managing director, 1989-; Urban Development Corp of Greater Miami, director of marketing, 1989-90; Kendall Square Associates, Inc, consultant, 1992-93; Ernst & Young, LLP-Sr compliance specialist, 1994. **Orgs:** Consultant small business Business Student Assoc 1982-84; volunteer Big Brothers/Big Sisters 1984-; girl scout leader Minneapolis Cncl 1984-86; dir Greater Minneapolis Big Bros/Big Sisters 1985-86; recruitment/membership comm co-chair Natl Black MBA Assoc 1985-86; mem Natl Assoc of Black Accountants 1986-; pres South Florida Chapter, Natl Black MBA Assn 1989-90. **Honors/Awds:** Consortium Fellowship Consortium Prog for Grad Study in Mgmt 1982-84; Service Awd Big Brothers/Big Sisters Minneapolis 1985; Family Christian Assn of America Black Achiever 1988. **Business Addr:** Managing director, SJO Associates Inc, 3600 South State Rd, #47, Miramar, FL 33023, (305)598-4902.

JOHNSON, STEPHEN L.
Finance company executive. **Personal:** Born Dec 14, 1944, Denver, CO; son of Mary Helen Bess; married; children: Chemaine D, Scott S, Matthew R. **Educ:** Univ of Denver, 1963-66; Univ of San Francisco 1978-80. **Career:** The Denver Post, reporter/editor 1968-72; Industrial Indemnity, asst mgr public relations 1972-74; Bank of America, sr public info ofcr 1975-79; First Interstate Bank, vice pres public relations 1979-83; First Nationwide Financial Corp, a subsidiary of Ford Motor Co vp/dir corp communications and appt 1st vice pres of subsidiory, 1987; appointed sr vice pres 1988. **Orgs:** Trustee CA Neighborhood Housing Found 1980-85; dir Dance Gallery of Los Angeles 1984-; dir Communications Bridge (Los Angeles) 1984-87 finance chair mayor's Committee on Housing the Homeless; mem, conf bd, Public Affair Executive Comm 1987-; Advisory Bd, San Jose State Univ 1987-; director, YMCA, San Francisco, 1990-. **Honors/Awds:** Directors Award for Public Service CA neighborhood Housing Foundation 1980; Honoree JFK School of Govt, Harvard Univ, for Housing Scholorships 1988. **Military Serv:** AUS Capt 1966-70; Bronze Star; Vietnam Serv Medals; Company Commander in Vietnam 1968.

JOHNSON, STERLING
Judge. **Personal:** Born May 14, 1934, Brooklyn, NY; married Barbara; children: Sterling III, Alicia Daniels, Jennifer. **Educ:** Brooklyn College, BA 1963; Brooklyn Law School, LLB 1966. **Career:** Southern Dist, asst US attorney 1967-70; Civil Complaint Review Bd, exec dir 1970-74; DEA, exec liason officer 1974-75; Special Narcotics Prosecutor's Office, special narcotics prosecutor beginning 1975-; US District Court, judge, currently. **Orgs:** Bd dir Police Athletic League 1975-; chmn Drug Adv Task Force Natl Adv Comm CDR USNR Annapolis 1975-. **Honors/Awds:** Distinguished Serv Award Assn of Voluntary Agencies on Narcotic Treatment 1977; Distinguished Black Amer Drug Enforcement Adminstrn 1979. **Military Serv:** USNR, captain. **Business Addr:** Judge, US District Court, 225 Cadman Plaza East, Brooklyn, NY 11201.

JOHNSON, T. J.
Automobile dealer. **Career:** Team Ford-Mercury, Inc, Tarboro, NC, dealership, owner, currently; Crossroads Ford-Mercury, Inc, Jesup, GA, dealership, owner, currently; Summerville Ford-Mercury, Inc, Summerville, SC, dealership, owner, currently. **Special Achievements:** Listed as #82 of 100 top auto dealers, Black Enterprise, 1992. **Business Addr:** Owner, Summerville Ford, 103 Old Trolley Rd, Summerville, SC 29485, (803)873-3550.

JOHNSON, TAMMY ADELE
Promoter, advertising assistant. **Personal:** Born Oct 26, 1965, Murfreesboro, TN; daughter of Mary J Johnson. **Educ:** Middle TN State Univ, Murfreesboro TN, BS, 1988. **Career:** Minority Newsletter, Murfreesboro TN, reporter, 1986; WSMV TV, Nashville TN, intern, 1987; Freelance Producer, Murfreesboro TN, 1988; WTVF TV, Nashville TN, videotape editor, 1988-89; WRCB TV, Chattanooga TN, promotion advertising asst, 1989-. **Orgs:** Chairperson, NAACP Natl Youth Work Committee, 1986-89; ex-officio, Bd of Dir NAACP; Agnes Jones/Jackson Scholarship Committee NAACP; Alpha Kappa Alpha Sorority. **Honors/Awds:** WW Law Award NAACP, 1987; Amer Business Women Scholarship, 1984-88; Chairperson of 1st Martin Luther King Jr March in Murfreesboro TN with nearly 2000 marchers, 1987.

JOHNSON, TAYLOR HERBERT
Cleric, administrator. **Personal:** Born Feb 17, 1933, Cleveland, OH; son of Elgenia Johnson; married Beverly King, Sep 8, 1962; children: Kimberly Rene, Taylor Herbert II. **Educ:** Voorhees Jr College, diploma, liberal arts, 1959; Pace University, BA, 1971; Interdenominational Theological Center, MDiv, 1973. **Career:** Trinity Cathedral, dean's assistant; St Augustine Church, vicar; St Philip Church, rector; Youngstown State University, campus minister; Youngstown Urban League, associate director; Grace Episcopal Church, assistant rector; Queens Hospital, pastoral care director, currently. **Orgs:** Omega Psi Phi Fraternity Inc, Nu Omicron Chapt, 1960-, Basileus, 1992-93; Union of Black Episcopalians, 1967-; Lions Club International, 1992-; St George Society, spiritual director, 1988-. **Honors/Awds:** Mahoning County Community Corrections, Service Award, 1983; Metropolitan Ecumenical Ministry, Service Award, 1976. **Military Serv:** US Marine Corps, cpl, 1950-54; UN Medal, Korean Service Medal, Military Serv Medal. **Business Addr:** Pastoral Care Director, 82-68 164th St, S/N 702, Jamaica, NY 11434, (718)833-2054.

JOHNSON, THEODORE, SR.
Military officer (retired). **Personal:** Born Aug 23, 1920, Ft Mitchell, AL; married Mattie E Butler; children: Theodore Jr, Winfred O, Frederick L, Larry E, Welton C, James C, Jeffrey M. **Educ:** Univ of MD, attended; Brookdale Comm Coll, Degree Comm Mental Health; Stockton State Coll Pomona NJ, BS 1978, MA 1982; Kean College of NJ, Union NJ MA Counseling 1982. **Career:** AUS Field Artillery Brigade Battery, 829 Tank Destroyer Batallion, shipped Southampton England, basic training 1941; Le-Harve France Siefried Line Germany, 1944; SW Pacific, 1945, stateside 1946-50, Korea 1950; German Occupation duty, 1952-55; AUS Signal Corp & R&D Lab, 1955-64; VA Blind Ctr Hines Hosp, rehab 1965; AUS, retired 1964. **Orgs:** Mem Red Bank Comm Ctr Inc, Title I Adv Comm & ADv Comm Proj Seed; past mem, exec comm, past vp, chmn Vet Affairs; pres Red Bank Branch NAACP; mem VFW #438, Disabled Vet Org Prince Hall Masonic Lodge, Oswitchee Lodge 785; exec dir & natl pres NAACP Achievement Awd 1973; European African Mediterranean & Europe Theatre, Asiatic Pacific Theater Oper Medal; Motion Picture Photography. **Honors/Awds:** Amer Theater Oper Medal; European African Mediterranean & Europe Theater; Asiatic Pacific Theater Oper Medal; Motion Picture Photography; Past Pres Awd in Appec of Untiring & Devoted Serv as pres for 6 Yrs The Greater Red Bank Br of NAACP 1980. **Home Addr:** 248 Leighton Ave, Red Bank, NJ 07701.

JOHNSON, THEODORE A.
Attorney. **Personal:** marrled Maureen Anette Foster; children: Christian. **Educ:** Sherwood Music Sch, AB 1970; Western St Univ Coll Law, LLB 1972. **Career:** Co of Orange, deputy dist atty; WSU, instr of law 1973-; Santa Ana Coll, instr 1975-77. **Orgs:** Sec Orange Co Sel Srv Bd 1972-; chmn bd Orange Co Fair Housing Cnsl 1974-; pres NAACP Orange Co CA Br 1973-; mem Am Bar Assn; CA Bar Assn; Orange Co Bar Assn; Nu Beta Epsilon Nat Law Frat. **Business Addr:** 700 Civic Ctr Dr, PO Box 808, Santa Ana, CA 92701.

JOHNSON, THEODORE L.
Educator. **Personal:** Born May 27, 1929, Sanford, FL; married Gwendolyn B; children: Jawando L, Angela Y Johnson. **Educ:** AZ State Coll Flagstaff, BS in Ed 1956; AZ State Univ Tempe, 1957; Bethune Cookman Coll, In-service; Northern AZ Univ, MAT in Engl 1969. **Career:** Crooms HS Sanford, FL, instr 1956-66; No AZ U, grad asst 1966-67; Cope Jr HS Redlands, CA, instr, 1967-69; No AZ U, instr 1969, dir, Upward Bound Prog 1971, asst prof of eng 1976-. **Orgs:** Natl Educ Assn 1956-; dir Upward Bound Pgm No AZ Univ 1970-71; coord Bilingual Pgm No AZ Univ 1973-78; Affrmtv Actn Coconino Co 1984-. Kappa Alpha Psi, 1959-. **Honors/Awds:** Blue Key Hnr Frat No AZ Univ 1955; artcle Black Author Black Life Kappa Jrnl; Outstndng Fclty Mem No AZ Univ 1984. **Home Addr:** 2 E Silver Spruce, Flagstaff, AZ 86001. **Business Addr:** Assistant Professor of English, Northern AZ University, C University Box 6032, Flagstaff, AZ 86011.

JOHNSON, THOMAS H.
Evangelist. **Personal:** Born Aug 5, 1932, Longview, TX; son of Gladys Johnson Morrison and Allen Groggs Sr; married Maggie L Stewart, Sep 27, 1958; children: Crystal Louise Johnson-Turner, Cathi Lynn Wilson. **Educ:** Southwestern Christian Coll Terrill TX, BA 1955. **Career:** Madison Ave Ch Christ, evangelist 1955-. **Orgs:** mem NAACP 1975-. **Honors/Awds:** Coord TV Spec "Cause for Christ" 1973; Christian Youths in Ac 1974; honored 25 yrs serv minister, & Madison Ave Ch of Christ Wichita 1980; Honored 32 year Madison Ave Church of Christ 1987; chmn Jamie Harris Livertransplant Fund 1987 (raise over $100,000 for 6 yr old girl by Aug 1987); Christian Question and Answer Panelist KWCH-Channel 12. **Business Addr:** Evangelist, Madison Ave Church of Christ, 1740 N Madison Ave, Wichita, KS 67214.

JOHNSON, TIFFANI
Professional basketball player. **Personal:** Born Dec 27, 1975. **Educ:** Univ of Tennessee. **Career:** San Jose Lasers, center, currently. **Business Addr:** Professional Basketball Player, San Jose Lasers, 1530 Parkmoor Ave, Ste A, San Jose, CA 95128, (408)271-1500.

JOHNSON, TIMOTHY JULIUS, JR.
Artist. **Personal:** Born Dec 30, 1935, Chester, SC; son of Lois Peay Johnson and Timothy J Johnson Sr; married Patricia B Hoye; children: Darryl Julius, Dianne Patrice. **Educ:** MI State Univ, attended 1954-56. **Career:** Visual Display Arts Chanute AFB IL, supervisor 1979-82; US Govt Air Force, illustrator, currently. **Orgs:** Leader/comm B mem Boy & Girl Scouts of Amer 1964-70; mem Alpha Phi Alpha 1955-; library bd mem Village of Rantoul IL 1979-82; mem The River Art Group 1983-84. **Honors/Awds:** 1st place in the Chanute Fine Arts Festival; 2nd place in paintings & 3rd place in sculptures in Urbana St Fair; 1st place and Best of Show in the Danville Fine Arts Festival; 1st and Best of Show in the Tech Exhibit Peoria; Best of Show 1982 Black Heritage week Chanute AFB. **Business Addr:** Visual Information Specialist, US Govt Air Force, HQ (AIA) Air Intelligency Agency, San Antonio, TX 78243-5000.

JOHNSON, TOBE
Educator. **Personal:** Born Sep 16, 1929, Birmingham, AL; son of Evelyn Johnson and Tobe Johnson; married Goldie Culpepper; children: Tobie, Cheryl. **Educ:** Morehouse BA 1954; Columbia Univ, PhD 1963. **Career:** Prairie View A&M, instr 1956-57; Prairie View, asst prof 1961-62; Univ Pittsburgh, visiting assoc prof 1956-66; Carleton Coll, prof 1968; Morehouse Coll, asst prof 1958-59, assoc prof 1962-66, prof 1967-. **Orgs:** Dir Urban Studies Program, Frmr Cncl; mem Am Political Sci Assn; mem Bd Examiners Educ Testing Ser, Grad Rcrd Exam Political Sci 1972-76; mem Am Soc Public Admin; mem Conf Minstry Pub Admin Bd, United Way of Atlanta; S Ed Found; Natl Assn Reg Cncls; Atlanta Reg Comm Hons, Phi Beta Kappa; mem Natl Academy of Public Administration 1981-. **Honors/Awds:** Awards, Columbia Univ Fellowship 1954-55; John Hay Whitney Fellowship 1959-60; Post-Doctoral Fellowship, Ealeton Inst of Politics & Natl Ctr Educ in politics faculty

fellow to Dem Pres Nom Conv 1954; Post-Doctoral Rsrch Flw, Ford Found 1968-69; United Negro College Fund Distinguished Fellow 1981-82. **Military Serv:** USAF s-sgt 1949-52. **Business Addr:** Professor, Morehouse College, Box 43, Atlanta, GA 30314.

JOHNSON, TOMMIE ULMER
Educator. **Personal:** Born Jun 23, 1925, Gary, IN; daughter of Mosell Sadler Ulmer and Abraham Ulmer; married Walter H Johnson, Mar 24, 1951 (deceased). **Educ:** Wayne State Univ, BS 1961, MEd 1964, EdD 1971. **Career:** City of Detroit, senior stenographer, 1948-59; Detroit Public Schools, teacher 1961-68; Wayne State Univ, asst prof 1971-76, assoc prof 1976-, assoc prof/asst provost 1985-. **Orgs:** Vstg prof Norfolk State Univ 1978; sponsor Delta Pi Epsilon Wayne State Univ Grad Chap 1980-; mem MI Occupational Teacher Educ Assoc 1982-; consultant to public agencies, foundations, and professional assocs; mem Alpha Kappa Alpha Sor; life mem NAACP; asst treas/trustee Second Baptist Church of Detroit; mem Amer Educ Rsch Assoc, Amer Vocational Assoc, MI Business Educ, Natl Business Educ Assoc, Women's Economic Club; vice president, Iota Phi Lambda, 1974-91; golden heritage member, NAACP. **Honors/Awds:** Ford Foundation Fellowship for Advanced Study 1971; publ "The Retail Community as a Classroom" Journal of Education for Business 1985; President's Bonus Award, Wayne State University, 1991-93; Inducted into the Detroit Western International High School Hall of Fame, 1993. **Home Addr:** 5655 Greenway, Detroit, MI 48204-2176.

JOHNSON, TRE
Professional football player. **Personal:** Born Aug 30, 1971, Manhattan, NY. **Educ:** Temple Univ, bachelor's degree in social administration, 1993, master's degree in social work. **Career:** Washington Redskins, guard, 1994-. **Honors/Awds:** Pro Bowl alternate, 1996. **Business Addr:** Professional Football Player, Washington Redskins, 13832 Redskin Dr, Herndon, VA 22071, (703)471-9100.

JOHNSON, TROY DWAN
Professional football player (retired). **Personal:** Born Oct 20, 1962, New Orleans, LA. **Educ:** Southeastern Louisiana Univ; Southern Univ. **Career:** Wide receiver: Denver Gold (USFL), 1985; St Louis Cardinals (later, Phoenix Cardinals), 1986-87; Pittsburgh Steelers, 1988; Detroit Lions, 1989.

JOHNSON, ULYSSES JOHANN, JR.
Educator (retired). **Personal:** Born Aug 11, 1929, Winter Haven, FL; married Thelma Mae Simmons; children: Marcus A, Melanie Aida. **Educ:** Fisk Univ, BS 1951; Univ of Denver, MS 1955; TN Tech Univ, EdS 1973. **Career:** Rochelle Jr-Sr HS, teacher/counselor/coach 1951-69; Polk Comm Coll, counselor 1969-1971; Polk Cmmty Coll, DSS Spec dir 1971-73, counseling dir 1973-86. **Orgs:** Past pres Central Fl Guidance Assn 1972-73; past master Samson Lodge 142 F & A M Masons 1980-84; charter mem FSC Chapter Phi Delta Kappa 1983-86. **Honors/Awds:** Keeper of records Kappa Alpha Psi 1980; clerk of voting Precinct 21-Polk Cty Voting Office 1976-86; Cameo Awd Winter Haven Little Theater 1986; Man of the Year Lakeland Alumni Chap 1985; Outstanding Boys St Chr Post 201 Amer Legion Dept FL 1984; SCABBA Adm of the Year AACJ Colleges 1986. **Military Serv:** AUS corporal 1952-54; Good Conduct Medal, French Cord of War 1953. **Home Phone:** (813)293-1966.

JOHNSON, VALRIE E.
Educator. **Personal:** Born in Newton, TX; widowed; children: Michael G. **Educ:** Tillotson Coll, BS, MEd; TX S U; Univ Houston, EdD, Admin & Supr. **Career:** HISD, tchr 1952-70, cons, hum rels 1970-73, curriculum coord, reading spclst 1973-75; Houston Comm Coll, part-time tchr 1972-77; Houston Ind Sch Dist, staff dev & Prog 1977-. **Orgs:** Mem Phi Delta Kappa Hon Soc; Houston Tchrs Assn; TX Classroom Tchrs Assn; TX St Tchrs Assn; Nat Ed Assn; mem Alpha Kappa Alpha Sor. **Honors/Awds:** Houston Jr C of C Award 1967; Houston Tillotson Alumni Award 1971; Hum Rels Award, Nat Ed Assn 1970.

JOHNSON, VANCE DOUGLAS
Building company executive. **Personal:** Born Sep 3, 1948, Richmond, VA; son of Wilnette Johnson and Alfred Johnson; married Margery Tibbetts, Aug 31, 1985; children: Courtney Janaye. **Educ:** Smithdeal-Massey Business College, certificate; DePaul University, BA, economics. **Career:** Sears Roebuck and Co, sr auditor/controller, 1972-86; Allstate Insurance Co, accounting division manager, 1986-91. **Orgs:** Institute of Internal Auditors, secretary, newsletter editor, treasurer, 1982-; EDPAA, 1988-90; ASTD, 1988-91. **Honors/Awds:** Institute of Internal Auditors, certified internal auditor, 1986; EDPAA, certified information systems auditor, 1988; Life Management Institute, fellow, 1990; Institute of Internal Auditors, International, Best Newsletter, 1985, Most Improved Newsletter, 1985. **Military Serv:** US Army, spec-4, 1980-81; Outstanding Soldier, Vietnam, 1980. **Business Phone:** (312)743-4440.

JOHNSON, VANCE EDWARD
Professional football player. **Personal:** Born Mar 13, 1963, Trenton, NJ. **Educ:** Arizona University. **Career:** Denver Broncos, wide receiver, 1985-.

JOHNSON, VANNETTE WILLIAM
Educational administrator. **Personal:** Born May 27, 1930, Little Rock, AR; son of Laura Delorius Miller Johnson (deceased) and Charlie Johnson (deceased); married Delois V Davis, Aug 8, 1959; children: Juliette Laureen Lewis, Alberta Lynnette Shelton, Melanie Annette Dumas, Leontyne Delois Howard. **Educ:** AK AM&N Coll, BS 1952; Univ of AR, MEd 1961; Univ of AR, DEd 1970. **Career:** Merrill HS, teacher/asst coach 1952-57; AR AM&N Coll, asst coach/instructor 1957-62, head football coach/AD 1962-74; Univ of AR Pine Bluff, athletic dir 1974-75, acting dept chair/athletic dir 1980-83, dept chair/athletic dir 1983-84, dept chair, prof 1984-. **Orgs:** Commiss AR Commiss on Human Relations 1977-81; justice of the peace Jefferson County 1977-; corp bd Jefferson Comprehensive Care Center 1981-; educ comm Pine Bluff Chamber of Commerce 1982-; commiss Pine Bluff Transportation Commission 1982-; long range planning Pine Bluff Chamber of Commerce 1985; NAACP; Pine Bluff/Jefferson County Clean & Beautiful Comm 1982-85, 1992-; Pine Bluff Convention Center Comm, finance comm 1977-; Literacy Council of Jefferson County, advisory board 1987; sec Jefferson County Democratic Central committee 1990-; pers Jefferson County Black Elected Officials Assn 1990-; finance committee chmn Jefferson County Quorum Court 1989-; Democratic State Committee, 1990-. **Honors/Awds:** Fellowship Southern Educ Found 1967-70; Pres Jefferson Cty Black Caucus 1978-; Vice Pres AR Black Caucus 1981-. **Home Addr:** 1905 Collegiate Dr, Pine Bluff, AR 71601. **Business Addr:** Professor, Univ of Arkansas, Health, Phys Ed Dept, North Univ Dr, Pine Bluff, AR 71601, (870)543-8678.

JOHNSON, VAUGHN ARZAH. See Obituaries section.

JOHNSON, VERDIA EARLINE
Company executive. **Personal:** Born Jul 14, 1950, Fort Worth, TX; married Everett N Johnson Jr. **Educ:** Howard Univ, BA 1972; New York Univ, MBA 1974. **Career:** Colgate Palmolive NY, asst product mgr 1974-77; Standard Brands NY, sr product mgr 1977-81; Nabisco Brands NJ, sr product mgr 1981-84; BCI Mktg Inc NY,dir of marketing 1984-85; Black Enterprise Magazine NY, advertising dir 1985-86; The JEM Group Inc, pres; Gannett Outdoor Co, vice pres, sales; Graham Gregory Bozell Inc, managing dir, currently. **Orgs:** Mem NAACP 1980-; Howard Univ Alumni Club; mem Advertising Women of NY. **Honors/Awds:** Dean's Scholarship Howard Univ 1970-72; Consortium Scholarship NY Univ 1972-74. **Home Addr:** 7002 Blvd East #8I, Guttenberg, NJ 07093.

JOHNSON, VERMELLE JAMISON
Association executive, educational administrator. **Personal:** Born Aug 2, 1933, Islandton, SC; married Charles Harry; children: Charles H Jr, Temple Odessa. **Educ:** SC St Coll, BS 1955, MEd 1969; Univ of SC, PhD 1976. **Career:** Claflin Coll, prof & chairperson dept of business admin 1985; SC State Coll, asst prof business educ 1969; Public Schools SC, teacher 1962-68; Federal Employee, 1957-62; AL State Coll, 1956-57; Univ of ND inst partic; Univ of RI; South Carolina State College, provost, director, currently. **Orgs:** Past st sec SC Bus Ed Assn; mem Alpha Kappa Mu Hon Soc; Delta Mu Delta Nat Bus Frat; Phi Delt Akappa Hon Soc; Iota Phi Lambda Bus Sor; Nat Bus Ed Assn; SC St Bus Ed Assn; Alpha Kappa Alpha Sor; Daughter Elk; IBPOE of W; Sunday school teacher Trinity United Meth Ch; Conference of Chief Academic Officers of the Southern States, pres, 1991-. **Honors/Awds:** Resrch and Analysis of Congruence Between Competencies, Requisite for Sec Sch Bus Ed Tchrs, & Prep Received in Tchr Ed Progs; author "A Look at Today's Increased Opptys for Adequately Prepared Bus Grad in SC, 1972, "Bus Educs Have A Tremendous Bill to Fill" 1970, "So You Think You're Ready to Teach" 1964, Bus Ed A Momentous Challenge in the 70s"; first minority female pres of Conf of Chief Academic Officers of the Southern States. **Business Addr:** Provost, Director, South Carolina State College, Orangeburg, SC 29117.

JOHNSON, VICKIE
Professional basketball player. **Personal:** Born Apr 15, 1972; daughter of Susie Johnson. **Educ:** Louisiana Tech, attended. **Career:** New York Liberty, forward, 1997-. **Honors/Awds:** Louisiana Player of the Year, 1996. **Business Addr:** Professional Basketball Player, New York Liberty, Two Penn Plaza, New York, NY 10121, (212)564-9622.

JOHNSON, VINCENT L.
Attorney. **Personal:** Born Aug 12, 1931, Brooklyn, NY; married Gertrude; children: Vincent Jr, Melissa. **Educ:** Brooklyn Coll, BA 1958; St John's Univ, LLB 1960, JD 1963. **Career:** Fields & Rosen, asst atty 1960-61; Kings Co, asst dist atty 1968; Laufer & Johnson, prtnr 1968-. **Orgs:** Mem Brooklyn Bar Assn; mem Phi Alpha Delta Law Frat; bd of dir 100 Black Men of NY 1970-90; past mem bd of dir NAACP 1956-75. **Honors/Awds:** Subject of Police Athl League Post Police Athl League 1964. **Military Serv:** USAF airmn 1st cls 1951-55. **Business Addr:** Attorney, 26 Court St, Ste 309, Brooklyn, NY 11242.

JOHNSON, VINNIE
Radio analyst, former professional basketball player. **Personal:** Born Sep 1, 1956, Brooklyn, NY. **Educ:** McLennan Community College, Waco, TX, 1975-77; Baylor Univ, Waco, TX, 1977-79. **Career:** Seattle SuperSonics, 1979-81; Detroit Pistons, player, 1982-91, radio analyst, currently; Pistons Packaging, pres, currently. **Honors/Awds:** Member of NBA championship teams, 1989, 1990. **Business Addr:** President, Pistons Packaging, 4015 Michigan Ave, Detroit, MI 48210.

JOHNSON, VIRGINIA ALMA FAIRFAX
Dancer. **Personal:** Born Jan 25, 1950, Washington, DC; daughter of Madeline Murray Johnson and James L Johnson. **Educ:** Attended New York Univ, 1968-69, 1978-; Fordham University, 1990-. **Career:** Guest artist Capitol Ballet, Chicago Opera Ballet, Washington Ballet, Baltimore Civic Youth Ballet, Stars of World Ballet in Australia, Detroit Symphony, Natl Symphony, Eugene Ballet; appeared in major film "A Piece of the Action"; TV includes Dance in Amer, Ancient Songs of Children, Night of 100 Stars; solo concert at Maymount Coll White House appearances for Pres Carter & Reagan; Blanche duBois in a Streetcar Named Desire for PBS Great Performances; Dance Theatre of Harlem, principal dancer 1969-; A Creole Giselle, NBC. **Honors/Awds:** Young Women Achievers 1985; hon mem Alpha Kappa Alpha Sor; Dance Magazine Award, 1991. **Business Addr:** Principal Dancer, Dance Theatre of Harlem, 466 W 152 St, New York, NY 10031.

JOHNSON, VITERIA COPELAND
Journalist. **Personal:** Born Apr 6, 1941, Evergreen, AL; daughter of Tessie Longmire Copeland and Robert Copeland; divorced; children: Doneria, Eric. **Educ:** Paine College, Augusta, GA, 1959-62; University of Wisconsin-Milwaukee, Milwaukee, WI, 1972-73. **Career:** Twin City Observer, Sun, Minneapolis-St Paul, MN, columnist, reporter, 1968-70; Minneapolis Tribune, Minneapolis, MN, reporter, 1969-71; Milwaukee Courier, Milwaukee, WI, reporter, 1972; Milwaukee Urban League, Milwaukee, WI, public relations coordinator, 1972; Cutler-Hammer, Inc, Milwaukee, WI, public relations writer, 1972-73; Inner City News, Mobile, AL, editorial asst, 1989-. **Orgs:** Chairperson, public relations, Young Republicans, 1969-70; public relations, National Council Negro Women, 1968-70; member, League of Women Voters, 1970; secretary, Woodcock School PTA, 1977-79; volunteer, UNCF, 1990-. **Business Addr:** Editorial Assistant, Inner City News, 212 S Dr Martin Luther King Dr, PO Box 1545, Prichard, AL 36610.

JOHNSON, WALDO EMERSON, JR.
Educator. **Personal:** Born Mar 13, 1955, Americus, GA; son of Addie Ben Johnson (deceased) and Waldo Emerson Johnson Sr. **Educ:** Mercer Univ, Macon, GA, AB 1977; Univ of MI Ann Arbor, MI, MSW 1979; School of Social Serv Admin, Univ of Chicago, PhD, 1993; University of Michigan, Ford Foundation Posdoctoral Fellowship, 1994-96. **Career:** GA Sw Coll Upward Bound, proj coord 1979-82; Washtenaw Cty Comm Mental Health Ctr, staff assoc 1978-79; New Detroit Inc, comm organizer 1978; Alpha Phi Alpha Frat Inc, asst exec secr for programs 1982-85, develop consult 1985-; Firman Community Services, Chicago, IL, director, youth & family svcs, 1987-90; Loyola Univ of Chicago, Chicago, IL, assistant professor, schl of social work, 1991-96, assistant professor, schl of social service administration, 1996-. **Orgs:** Chicago Chap of Black Social Workers; mem, Task Force on Effective Programs & Research, National Campaign to Prevent Tenn Pregnancy; mem, Working Group on Male Family Formation & Fertility, Federal Interagency Forum on Child & Family Statistics; secy bd of directors, Proj IMAGE 1985-; mem, Southside Branch, NAACP 1982-; founding mem, The Arts Forum of Urban Gateways, Chicago, 1985-; Illinois Chapter, National Assn of Social Workers, 1985-; Council on Social Work Education, 1985-. **Honors/Awds:** Doctoral Fellowship, Council On Social Work Education Washington, DC 1985-88; Dist Serv Awd Alpha Phi Alpha Frat Inc 1984; Grad Fellowship, Univ of MI, Ann Arbor, MI 1978-79; Dedicated Service Award, Child Life Network of American Red Cross, 1988; Graduate Fellowship, University of Chicago, 1985-; Graduate Fellowship, Illinois Council on Educational Opportunity Program, 1989-; Ford Foundation Postdoctoral Fellowship in Urban Poverty Research, 1994-96. **Business Addr:** Assistant Professor, School of Social Service Administration, University of Chicago, 969 E 60th St, Chicago, IL 60637, (773)834-0400.

JOHNSON, WALLACE DARNELL
Professional baseball player. **Personal:** Born Dec 25, 1956, Gary, IN; son of Myrtle Moody Johnson and Roy Johnson. **Educ:** Indiana State University, Terre Haute, IN, accounting, 1976-79. **Career:** Peat Marwick, Chicago, IL, staff accountant, 1983-84; Interstate Development & Supply Corporation, Indianapolis, IN, treasurer, 1985-88; Montreal Expos, Montreal, Quebec, baseball player, 1984-90; W D Johnson & Associates, president; Atlanta Braves, coach, 1995-. **Orgs:** Gamma Gent Alumni Association, 1977-; Main Street Gary, treasurer, 1991-. **Honors/Awds:** Indiana State University Athletic Hall of Fame, Indiana State University, 1985; Academic All-American, COSIDA, 1979; McMillan Award for Leadership, Indiana State University, 1979; Most Valuable Player, Florida State League, 1980; American Association All-Star Team, 1985; NCAA Post-Graduate Scholarship Recipient, 1979.

JOHNSON, WALTER J.
Educational administrator, counselor. **Personal:** Born Dec 31, 1957, Toledo, OH; son of Maggie Johnson and Thomas Johnson; married Elise Hood; children: David Walter. **Educ:** N Central Coll, BA Speech/Comm Theater 1980; Natl Coll of Educ, MS Mgmt Develop of Human Resources 1986. **Career:** Proctor & Gamble, sales rep/mgmt training 1980-83; N Central Coll, admin counselor/minority rep 1983-87, dir of athletic development, currently. **Orgs:** Consultant/adviser Minority Student Assoc N Central Coll; mem Harvey Chap Natl Jaycees; asst women's track coach Eisenhower HS 1982-83; mem IL Assoc of Mem Coll Admissions Counselors 1983-; mem, NCAA; mem, College Conference of IL & Wisconsin, Director Committee. **Honors/Awds:** HL Richards HS First Black Vice Pres Student Counsel 1975, First Black Vice Pres Sr Govt 1976; Outstanding Alumnus Award Black Student Assoc NCC 1983; established the North Central Coll Minority Scholarship Fund 1984; publication "The Plight of Black Students on a Predominately White Campus" NCC Chronicle; Outstanding Student Serv Award N Central Coll; Handy Order Top Sales Award Procter & Gamble Chicago Dist. **Home Addr:** 1609 Redpoll Ct, Naperville, IL 60565-2319. **Business Addr:** Dir of Athletic Development, North Central College, 30 N Brainard St, Naperville, IL 60566.

JOHNSON, WALTER LEE
Educator. **Personal:** Born May 23, 1918, Greensboro, NC; son of Rev Fonce Johnson; married Rita Doss Johnson; children: Jennifer Rose, Tommye L Johnson. **Educ:** NC AT&T State Univ, Greensboro NC, BS, 1942; Univ of IL, Urbana IL, MS Agronomy, 1947, PhD Agronomy, 1953. **Career:** Southern Univ, Baton Rouge LA, instructor 1947-50; Florida A&M Univ, Tallahassee FL, Dir Div Agricultural Sciences 1972-84, prof 1953-84. **Orgs:** Chairman Dept of Higher Educ, FL State Teachers Assn, 1955-64; Advisory Council, State Dept of Natural Resources, 1971-76; Natl Soil Conservation Committee, 1974; Southern Deans & Dir of Agriculture, 1972-84; Alpha Phi Alpha Fraternity. **Military Serv:** US Army, Battalion Sergeant Major, 1942-46. **Home Addr:** 609 Gore Avenue, Tallahassee, FL 32310.

JOHNSON, WALTER LOUIS, SR.
City official. **Personal:** Born Jan 2, 1949, Bastrop, LA; son of Dorothy Williams Bolden and Samuel Johnson; married Esther Robinson Johnson, Mar 30, 1973; children: Walter II, Erik. **Educ:** San Francisco City College, San Francisco, AA, 1969; St Mary's College, Moraga, CA, BA, 1984. **Career:** City of Oakland, Oakland, CA, director of retirement systems, 1972-. **Orgs:** Member, National Forum of Black Public Administrator, member, American Society of Public Administrator, member, National Conference of Public Employees' Retirement Systems, member, California Association of Public Retirement Systems. **Military Serv:** US Army, Sergeant 1st Class, 1977, Soldier of Year. **Home Addr:** 4108 Fairway Ave, Oakland, CA 94605. **Business Addr:** Director of Retirement Systems, Retirement Systems, City of Oakland, 475 14th St, Suite 1120, Oakland, CA 94612.

JOHNSON, WALTER THANIEL, JR.
Attorney at law. **Personal:** Born May 18, 1940, Greensboro, NC; son of Gertrude Alexander Johnson and Walter T Johnson, Sr; married Yvonne Jeffries, Apr 20, 1985; children: Walter III, Vernon K, Lisa Yvonne, Shannon Tamara. **Educ:** A&T State U, BS 1961; Duke Univ Sch of Law, JD 1964; Univ of North Carolina Chapel Hill Govt Executives Inst 1981; Univ of North Carolina Chapel Hill Justice Exec Program 1984. **Career:** Frye & Johnson, atty; Guilford Co Superior Ct, asst dist atty 1968-69; USAF, judge adv 1965-68; Law Office of Elreta Alexander, asso 1964-65; Redevel Com Greensboro, relocation adv 1962-63; Public Storage & Warehousing Inc, sec, exec com 1971-76; Barjo Inc, sec, exec com 1973-; Duke Univ Law Sch, adjunct prof of law 1975-; Barbee & Johnson partner 1987-88; Barbee Johnson & Glenn partner 1988-. **Orgs:** Mem Greensboro Bd Dirs of NC Nat Bank 1976-; vice pres planning for United Way of Greensboro 1969-71; mem, chmn, Greensboro Cty Bd of Educ 1970-; mem Bdof Govs NC Bar Assn 1975-; chmn NC Inmate Grievance Co Com 1975-; chmn bd trustee Univ NC 1974-; bd mem Eastern Music Festival 1972-76; chmn North Carolina Parole Comm 1981-85; Adjunct prof North Carolina Central School of Law 1985-87; vice chmn Greensboro Vision 1985-; bd mem Greensboro Economic Devel Council 1988-. **Honors/Awds:** Outstdng young men of NC NC Jaycees 1970; Freedom Guard Award NC Jaycees 1970-71; disting serv award Greensboro Jaycees 1970; Peacemaker Award Carolina Peacemaker Newspaper; vice pres Assn of Paroling Authorities 1982-85; Citizens Comm on Alternatives to Inceration 1981-83. **Military Serv:** USAF capt 1961-68. **Business Addr:** Partner, Barbee Johnson & Glenn, 102 N Elm Street, 804 Southeastern Bldg, Greensboro, NC 27401.

JOHNSON, WALTON RICHARD
Physician (retired). **Personal:** Born Aug 16, 1909, Bessemer, AL; son of Leona Johnson and John B Johnson; divorced; children: Walton Jr, Kristin D. **Educ:** Morehouse Coll, BS 1934; Howard Univ, MD 1949; Univ PA. **Career:** Life Ins, salesman; Multinat Mktg Corp, instructor, HS Dir; Med Practice, physician (retired). **Home Addr:** 4000 Gypsy Ln, Unit #316, Philadelphia, PA 19144.

JOHNSON, WARREN S.
Business executive. **Personal:** Born Apr 7, 1947, Philadelphia, PA; married Peggie A Parham; children: Warren S. **Educ:** Hampton Inst, BA Ec1969; Temple U, (grad sch) 1973-75. **Career:** Fischer & Porter Co, mgr compensation & benefits 1973-; PA Hosp, training spclst prsnl, generalist 1970-73; PA Bell & Tele, mgmt dev trainee 1969-70. **Orgs:** MemAm Compensation Assn 1976; exec at large Philadelphia Survey Grp 1976-; mem Am Soc Prsnl Admin 1977-; consult YMFT Wrkshp, Alliance of Bus. **Business Addr:** 125 E County Line Rd, Warminster, PA 18974.

JOHNSON, WAYNE ALAN
Consultant. **Personal:** Born May 22, 1961, Springfield, MA; son of Beverly May Riley Johnson and Karl Anthony Johnson Sr; married Terri Clara Colbert Johnson, Jun 1, 1991. **Educ:** George Washington Univ, BBA 1983; Univ of WI-Madison, MBA 1984; Georgetown Univ Washington, DC, JD credits. **Career:** Freedom Federal Savings, record dept mgr 1976-79; US House of Representatives Honorable Edw P Boland, staff asst 1980-83; IBM, marketing rep 1985-88, marketing programs mgr, 1989-90, marketing mgr, 1990-; consultant, 1992-. **Orgs:** Consultant/participant IBM Adopt-A-School 1985-86; mem Natl Black MBA Assoc 1986-88; mem NAACP 1989; mem Ebeneezer AME Church 1989-. **Honors/Awds:** College Scholarship Awd Emhart Corp 1979; MBA Fellowship Awd Consortium for Grad Study 1983; IBM 100% Club 1986, 1987, 1991. **Home Addr:** 2 Marigold Ct, Silver Spring, MD 20906. **Business Addr:** Consultant, IBM, 6705 Rockledge Drive, 7th Fl, Bethesda, MD 20817, (301)564-3833.

JOHNSON, WAYNE J.
Attorney. **Personal:** Born Mar 21, 1958, Oakland, CA; son of Juanita & Benjamin Francis Johnson; married Miriamne, Nov 18, 1980; children: Kisha M, Afiya Tanzania, Zuberi Ogbonna, Jelani Bakari. **Educ:** Univ of CA at Berkeley, AB, 1979; Univ of CA, San Francisco, Hastings Coll of the Law, JD, 1983. **Career:** Office of US Congressman Ronald V Dellums, adm aide, 1979-85; Office of Counsel for NAACP, San Francisco Region, assoc, 1985-; Law Office of Moore & Moore, of counsel, 1987-; Law Offices of Wayne Johnson, chief counsel, 1992-. **Orgs:** Exec Bd for Congressman Ronald V Dellums, 1984-; Alameda County Economic Development, Urban Revitalization Committee, advisory bd, 1993-. **Special Achievements:** Castlemont High School, asst wrestling coach, 1986-89; Oakland High School, head wrestling coach, 1989-92. **Business Addr:** Chief Counsel, Law Offices of Wayne Johnson, 440 Grand Ave, Ste 300, PO Box 30712, Oakland, CA 94604.

JOHNSON, WAYNE LEE
Teacher, business consultant. **Personal:** Born Oct 28, 1953, Hartford, CT; son of Betty Hawthorne Johnson and Hubert L Johnson (deceased); married Bertha J; children: Jamaal Trumaine, Marquis Jawaan, Brittnee Nicole. **Educ:** Grambling State Univ, BA 1975; Univ of Hartford Grad Sch of Business. **Career:** The Hartford Ins Group, work measurement analyst 1975-77, sr work meas analyst 1977-79, mgmt consultant 1979-86; Citytrust, vice pres 1986-89; Hartford Neighborhood Housing Services, executive director, 1990-91; Fox Middle School, teacher, 1991-. **Orgs:** Assn of Internal Mgmt Consultants 1981-; Toastmasters Intl Organization 1982-84; bd of dirs IMPACT 1985; Blue Hills Child Care Ctr Hartford 1986-; Hartford Proud and Beautiful, board of directors. **Honors/Awds:** Honor Grambling State Univ 1973; Dean List Grambling State Univ 1974,75; wrote article "Starting Up a New Internal Management Consulting Department" AIMC Forum 1988. **Home Addr:** 20 Donna Lane, Windsor, CT 06095.

JOHNSON, WAYNE WRIGHT, III
County government official. **Personal:** Born Oct 26, 1953, Galveston, TX. **Educ:** Univ of TX, BA 1976; S. TX Coll of Law, JD, 1980. **Career:** State of TX, Galveston County, asst attorney general, 1984-87, commissioner, 1989-; TX Dept of Labor & Stand, pers dir, EEO coordinator 1976-78; St Sen AR Schwartz, legis aide 1973-75; Galveston County, assistant criminal district attorney, 1981-84. **Orgs:** Mem Laborers' Intl Union of No Am 1972-; mem NAACP; mem Galveston Cnty Yg Dem; pres LaMarque HS student body 1972; pres TX AFL-CIO Youth Citizen Conf 1971; natl bd mem Am for Dem Action 1972-73; chmn Dem prec conv 1972, 1974, 1976; chmn cred comm Galveston Co Dem conv 1974. **Honors/Awds:** Galveston Cnty NAACP Outst Supp Awd 1976; del Dem Nat conv NY City 1976; alt-del Dem Nat conv Miami 1972; Jr Fellow, UT, 1974-76; Galveston Branch NAACP, NAACP Freedom Fund Award; Galveston County Observer News, Citizen of the Year; Galveston Coalition of Black Democrats, Distinguished Citizen Award, 1991. **Business Addr:** County Commissioner, Pct 3, Galveston County, 1301 FM 646, Dickinson, TX 77539.

JOHNSON, WENDELL L., JR.
Business executive. **Personal:** Born Dec 10, 1922, Lexington, KY; married Rose E Vaughn; children: Wendell III, Edith, Jeffrey, Brian. **Educ:** Hampton Inst, BA 1947; Atlanta Univ, MSW 1949. **Career:** Chicago Housing Auth, asst dep dir of mgmt, dep exec dir 1956-; Psychopathic Hosp, psy soc worker 1952-56; Cook Co Hosp, med soc worker 1951-52; Chicago Welfare Dept, caseworker 1949-51. **Orgs:** Past mem S Side Cent Comm Work 1965-66; Grand Blvd Oakwood Comm Coun 1965-66; 2nd Dist Police Workshop 1965-66; bd mem Cit Adv Com Jnt Yth Dev Com 1967-69; pres Neigh Inst Adv Com; mem Comm Adv Bd Cabrini-Green Unit Cook Co Dept of Pub Assistance 1967-70; bd mem N Area Bd, Chicago Youth Ctrs 1968-71; mem 8th Dist Police Wkshp 1967-76; mem Chicago Chap Natl Assn Housing & Redev Ofcls 1968-76; mem Boy Scouts of Am; mem NAACP; mem, trustee Lilydale First Bapt Ch; mem Roseland Hts Comm Assn; mem Hampton Inst Alumni; mem Atlanta Univ Alumni; 1st Tee Golf Club. **Honors/Awds:** Cert of Appreciation, Kiwanis Club of N Cent Chicago 1967; Superior Pub Serv Award, Chicago Assn of Commerce & Ind 1973; Great Guy Achvmt Award, WGRT-RADIO 1973; commend for ded to pub serv 1973; Cert of Appreciation, Chicago Youth Ctr 1976; award, appreciation of serv resid coun Cabrini-Green Homes 1966-76; Bronze Star; Purple Heart. **Military Serv:** AUS tech/sgt 1943-45. **Business Addr:** Region 3 Office, Chicago Housing Authority, 500 E 37th St, Chicago, IL 60653.

JOHNSON, WENDELL NORMAN, SR.
Military official, educational administrator. **Personal:** Born Dec 20, 1933, Boston, MA; son of Ida M. Johnson and Oscar A. Johnson; married Helen L. Underwood, Nov 15, 1958; children: Laura Lynn, Lois Underwood, Wendell Norman, Jr. **Educ:** New England Coll of Pharmacy, Boston, MA, BS, 1955; US Naval Postgrad School, Monterey, CA, certif, 1962; Natl War Coll, Washington, DC, certif, 1975; American Univ, Washington, DC, MA, 1976. **Career:** US Navy, USS Dahlgren, commanding officer, 1976-78, USS Jason, commanding officer, 1979-82, Destroyer Squadron 35, commodore, 1982-83, Pentagon, director of research and devel, 1983-84, Pentagon, director of planning and programming logistics, 1984-87, US Naval Base, Charlotte, SC, commander, 1987-89; Mine Warfare Command, commander, 1987-1988; Boston Univ, Boston, MA, vice pres/dean of students, 1989-. **Orgs:** Member, US Naval Inst, 1980-; member, Govs Roundtable on Literacy, 1988-; consultant, Coun on Edn, 1988; lecturer, Coun for Higher Edn, 1988-; board member, YMCA; board member, Charleston Chamber of Commerce; board member, United Way; Boston University Charter School, president. **Honors/Awds:** Proclamation, City Council of Jacksonville, FL, for civic accomp, 1972; Distinguished Leadership Award, Omega Phi Psi, 1988; Doctor of Letters, Coll of Charleston, 1989; Distinguished Leadership Award, YMCA SE region, 1989; Distinguished Service Award, Commonwealth of MA, 1989; North Eastern University, Outstanding Alumni Award, 1989. **Special Achievements:** Author: US Navy Minority Recruiting Guide, 1968; Communications Model for Integration of Blacks into the Navy, 1976. **Military Serv:** Legion of Merit, Meritorious Service Medal, Navy Commendation Medal, Navy Achievement Medal, Combat Action Ribbon, Order of Sikatuna (Phillippines). **Business Addr:** Vice President & Dean of Students, Boston University, 775 Commonwealth Ave, Boston, MA 02115.

JOHNSON, WENDY ROBIN
Buyer. **Personal:** Born Dec 26, 1956, New York; daughter of Dolores Elizabeth Dominguez Johnson and Clarence Woodson Johnson, Jr (deceased); married Keith Andrew Hill, Sep 12, 1992. **Educ:** Elizabeth Seton Coll, AAS Liberal Arts 1980; Marymount Manhattan Coll, BBA Finance 1983; Manhattan College Bronx NY MBA 1985-87. **Career:** RCA Records, buyer specialist 1976-83; PolyGram Records Inc, mgr of purchasing 1983-85; Kraft Foods Corp, assoc buyer 1985-86; buyer, 1987-95, sr buyer, 1995-. **Orgs:** Mem Delta Sigma Theta Sor Inc 1979-; troop leader Girl Scout Council of Greater NY 1983-; mem Natl Assoc of Female Execs 1984-; Founder We Buy 1988-; Asst Dean Learning Center Canaan Baptist Church 1988-; Instructor Junior Achievement Project Business 1989-. **Honors/Awds:** Recipiant of 1984 Outstanding Young Women of America 1984. **Special Achievements:** Co-founder Nuff Said!, 1992; Crossroads, 1993. **Business Addr:** Sr Buyer, Kraft Foods, 250 North Street, Suite E1-2, White Plains, NY 10625, (914)335-2927.

JOHNSON, WILBUR EUGENE
Attorney. **Personal:** Born Mar 1, 1954, Columbia, SC. **Educ:** Univ of SC Aiken; Augusta Coll GA, BA History 1976; Univ of SC Law Ctr, JD 1979. **Career:** Palmetto Legal Srv, staff atty 1979-; Richland Co Pub Def Agy, law clk 1977-79. **Orgs:** Mem SC Bar Assn; Urban League Guild; Kwanza Com 1979-. **Honors/Awds:** Outstndng Coll Athl of Am 1973-74; flwshp Earl Warren Legal Training Prog 1976-79. **Business Addr:** 35 E Calhoun St, Sumter, SC 29150.

JOHNSON, WILHELMINA LASHAUN
Financial administrator. **Personal:** Born Aug 13, 1950, Ft Worth, TX. **Educ:** Tarrant Cty Jr Coll, AA 1970; TX Christian Univ, BS 1983; Univ of TX Arlington 1987. **Career:** City of Ft Worth, admin intern 1979, admin asst 1979-83, admin analyst 1983-. **Orgs:** Mem Conf of Minorities Assoc 1979-, Urban Mgmt Assn of North TX 1979-, Amer Soc of Public Admin 1980, Intl City Mgmt Assoc, 1980-, Natl Forum of Black Public Admin 1984-. **Business Addr:** Admin Budget Analyst, City of Fort Worth, 1000 Throckmorton St, Fort Worth, TX 76104.

JOHNSON, WILLARD RAYMOND
Educator. **Personal:** Born Nov 22, 1935, St Louis, MO; son of Dorothy Neoma Stovall and Willard Johnson; married Vivian Robinson; children: Caryn L, Kimberly E. **Educ:** Pasadena City Coll, AA 1955; UCLA, BA 1957; Johns Hopkins School of Advanced Intl Studies, MA 1961; Harvard Univ, PhD 1965. **Career:** MIT, asst prof 1964-69, assoc prof 1969-73; Circle Incorporated Boston, exec dir and CEO, 1968-70; MIT, prof 1973-96, prof emeritus 1996. **Orgs:** Vice pres African Heritage Studies Assn 1978; mem Amer Political Sci Assn 1965-; mem Natl Econ Assn 1971-82; Natl Conf of Black Political Scientists 1971; mem US Natl Comm for UNESCO 1960-66; bd mem Boston New Urban League 1967-72; bd mem Natl Scholarship Fund for Negro Students 1958-59; mem New England Political Sci Assn 1966-69; mem Council on Foreign Relations 1973-97; mem Black Forum on Foreign Affairs 1976-78; mem Assn for Study of Afro-Amer Life & History 1968-72; bd mem Assn of Concerned African Scholars 1977; natl co-chr Assn of Concerned African Scholars 1983-89; bd mem World Univ Serv 1958-60; bd mem Interfaith Housing corp, 1970; chmn bd The Circle Complex (Roxbury) 1970-72; chmn Africa Policy Task Force McGovern for Pres Campaign 1972; mem Democratic Party Adv Council Foreign airs Study 1976; pres TransAfrica Inc Boston Chap 1981-90; bd mem TransAfrica Inc Natl 1977-95; dir Business Management for Economic Develop Rsch Project, 1973-95; dir Communications Component of African American Issues Ctr MIT Ctr for Intl Studies 1982-91. **Honors/Awds:** Ford Foundation Foreign Area Training Fellowships 1959, 1960, 1963, 1964; John Hay Whitney Found Oppt Fellowship 1961; Research Grant Center for Intl Studies MIT 1971; Research Grant Technology Adaptation Project MIT 1973-74; resident fellow Rockefeller Center at Belagio Italy 1987; Fulbright Fellowship to West Africa 1987; Boston YMCA Black Achievers Award, 1899; Boston Museum of African-American History Black Men of Vision Award, 1992; Fulbright Seminar in Indonesia, 1991. **Business Addr:** Professor Emeritus of Political Science, Massachusetts Institute of Technology (MIT), E53-367, Cambridge, MA 02139.

JOHNSON, WILLIAM
Bank executive. **Career:** OmniBanc Corp, chairman, currently. **Business Addr:** Chairman, Omni Bank Corp., 10474 W. Jefferson, River Rouge, MI 48218, (313)843-8850.

JOHNSON, WILLIAM A.
Educator (retired). **Personal:** Born Aug 21, 1917, Norfolk, VA; son of Blanch Reid Johnson (deceased) and Ozeas Johnson (deceased); married Louise Brown; children: William Jr, Dewitt. **Educ:** Bluefield State Coll, BS 1940; Columbia Univ, MA 1949; Attended, Univ of Strasburg France 1952, Boston Univ, Univ of VA, Old Dominion Univ, Hampton Institute. **Career:** Norfolk County, principal 7 schools 1941-60; Title IV Program Emer School Assist Prog, dir 1969-74; Head Start (5 yrs Summers), dir 1965-69; Intergroup Education, dir 1969-73; Chesapeake Public Schools, asst supt for general admin. **Orgs:** Mem AASA, VASA, ASCD; past pres Tidewater Supervisors Group; CEA; NEA; past vice pres Tidewater Reg Suprs; past chmn Two So Assn of Coll & Schs; bd dir Local Amer Cancer Soc; Mental Health Assn 1957-70; United Comm Fund 1973-; Hunton YMCA; Tidewater Health Foundation; SE Lung Assn; Kirk Cone Rehabilitation Ctr; mem NAACP; mem trustee bd Queen St Baptist Ch; Omega Psi Phi; Chesterfield Club; mem Comm Correction Resource Bd 1989-. **Honors/Awds:** Alpha Phi Alpha Humanitarian Awd 1974; Nat Sor Phi Delta Kappa Inc Awd 1969; Amer Cancer Soc Awd 1966; Omega Man of the Year Lambda Omega Chapter Omega Psi Phi 1988; Special Service Awd, United Way of South Hampton Roads 1991; Outstanding Service Tidewater Childcare Assn 1985. **Military Serv:** AUS CIC 1st lt 1942-45 & 1952-53; Bronze Star Medal Awd; 4 US Commendations; sev battle stars. **Business Addr:** 545 Fernwood Farms Road, Chesapeake, VA 23320.

JOHNSON, WILLIAM A., JR.
City official. **Personal:** Born Aug 22, 1942, Lynchburg, VA; son of Roberta Davis Johnson and William A Johnson, Sr; married Mary Ann Griffin (divorced); children: Kelley M, Kristin R, Wynde A. **Educ:** Howard Univ, BA, 1965, MA, 1967. **Career:** City of Rochester, NY, mayor, 1994-; Urban League Rochester, pres and CEO, 1972-93; Urban League Flint MI, dep exec dir 1971-72; Genesee Comm Coll Flint, instructor political science 1967-71; Natl Hwy Users Conf Washington, legislative analyst 1966-67; US Supreme Ct, student aide 1966. **Orgs:** Co-founder, Com for a More Rep Govt; organist New Bethel ME Ch 1975-91; co-founder Black Leadership Study Group; trustee Monroe Community Coll Rochester NY 1976-82; NY St Employment & Training Council 1977-83; v chmn 1978-79; chmn 1979-83; pres Urban League of Rochester Economic Devel Corp 1985-93; mediator Factfinder, NYS Public Employment Relations Bd 1985-93; Sigma Pi Phi Fraternity, Gamma Iota Boule 1987-, sire archon, 1994-96, grapter 1996-98; Board of Directors, Eltrex Industries, Inc. 1982-93; civil svc commissioner, City of Rochester, 1980-90; co-founder, Austin Steward Professional Society, 1985-90; chairperson, 1992-93, board of directors, vice chairperson, New Futures Initiative Inc, 1988-91; University of Rochester Graduate School of Education, trustees visiting committee, 1991-; member, New York State Board of Social Work, 1988-93. **Honors/Awds:** Fellowship Falk Found 1964-65; hon soc Pi Sigma Alpha 1967; Jefferson Award for Outstanding Public Service, Amer Inst for Public Service 1986; Vernon E. Jordon Jr. Fellowship, Natl Urban League 1986-87; Doctor of Humane Letters, KeuKa College, 1990; First African American mayor of Rochester, NY (elected November 1993). **Home Addr:** 999 Meigs St, Rochester, NY 14620, (716)461-5269. **Business Addr:** City Hall, Rm 307A, 30 Church St, Rochester, NY 14604, (716)428-7045.

JOHNSON, WILLIAM A., II
Business executive. **Personal:** Born Dec 31, 1952, Columbia, SC. **Educ:** CA State Univ LA, BS Civil Engrg 1975; Stanford Univ, MS Civil Engrg & Structural Engrg 1976, Degree of Engrg & Civil Engrg 1981; Harvard Univ Grad School, MBA 1986. **Career:** LA Cty Flood Control Dist, engrg aid 1973-75; Bechtel Inc San Francisco, civil/structural designer 1975-76; Pacific Soils Engrg Inc LA, civil/geotechnical engr 1976-77; Bechtel Inc San Fran, civil/structural engr 1978-79; Kercheval & Assoc Inc, 1980; WA Johnson & Associates, owner 1983. **Orgs:** Mem Amer Assoc of Univ Profs, ASCE, Amer Soc of Engrg Ed, CA Soc of Professional Engrs, Natl Soc of Black Engrs, NSPE, Structural Engrs Assoc of CA, Prestressed Concrete Inst, San Francisco Bldg Code Rev Comm-ASCE&SEAOC; vol asst ASCE; corr mem Comm on Minority Progs; mem Natl Rsch Council Common Minorities in Engrg, Minority Grad Engrg Ed Task Force, NAACP; vol chmn Summer Jobs Exposure Prog; mem San Fran Engrs Soc Comm on Manpower Trng, CA State Ofc of Emergency Svcs, Post Earthquake Inspection Prog Advocate, MInorities in Engrg; reg professional engr CA, KS, MO, NV; founding mem & 1st elected Natl Chairperson Emeritus; founding mem Black Grad Students Org Stanford Univ; tech rsch Area of Soil-Structure-Interaction Analysis; pres Harvard Business SchBlack Alumnae Assoc 1987-89; mem N Black MBA. **Honors/Awds:** Publ several articles in Natl Soc of Black Engrs Newsletters, papers in ASCE Civil Engrg Ed Conf 1979; workshop on Retention of Minority Undergrad Engrg Students sponsored by MIT & Natl Rsch Council; Leadership Awd NSBE as 1st Natl Chairperson Emeritus.

JOHNSON, WILLIAM ARTHUR (BILLY WHITE SHOES)
Professional football player (retired). **Personal:** Born Jan 27, 1952, Bouthwyn, PA; married Barbara; children: Marcia, Kendra, Jared. **Educ:** Widener College, attended. **Career:** Wide receiver: Houston Astros, 1974-80; Montreal Alouettes, 1981; Atlanta Falcons, 1982-87; Indianapolis Colts, 1988. **Honors/Awds:** NFL's Comeback Player of the Year, 1983; Falcon's Top Punt Returner of All-Time; led NFC in punt returns 1982; led NFL in punt returns, 1975, 1977; established NFL record for punt return yards (3123); tied NFL record for most touchdowns on combined returns in a season (4), 1975; played in Pro Bowl, 1975 (MVP), 1977, 1983.

JOHNSON, WILLIAM C.
Mortgage banker (retired). **Personal:** Born Jul 1, 1930, New York, NY; children: William C Jr, Anthony C (deceased), Anita C, Robert W. **Educ:** US Navy, 3 years college credits while serving. **Career:** First California Funding Inc, sr vice pres. **Orgs:** American Legion, Jackie Robinson Post 252. **Military Serv:** USN sr chief petty officer 30 yrs; Vietnam Service Medals, Good Conduct Medal, European Occupation Natl Defense. **Business Addr:** Senior Vice President, First California Funding Inc, 6820 La Tijera Blvd Ste E15, Los Angeles, CA 90045.

JOHNSON, WILLIAM E.
Clergyman. **Personal:** Born Apr 16, 1936, Centerville, AL; married Rosylyn E Pearson; children: Jamena, Lawrence, Jacquelyn, Louis, Janeen. **Educ:** Aram&N, BS 1958; CA Western U, BA 1968; Sch of Theol Claremont CA, RelD. **Career:** SE United Presb Ch, minister; St Andrews Presb Ch UPUSA; Hollypark UM Ch, Gardina CA, asso pastor 1968-72. **Orgs:** Conducted numerous training grps on Hum Rels-Race Rels for HS & Chs; mem NAACP; Urban League; pres SE San Diego Lion's Club 1974-75; polemarch KappaAlpha Psi Frat San Diego Alumni Chap 1974-75; mem CA St Dem Cntrl Com 1977; bd dir Heartland Hum Rels Assn; various Citizens Adv Coms; Beta Kappa Chi Hon Soc. **Honors/Awds:** Man of Distinction Award, Heartland Hum Rel Assn 1973. **Military Serv:** USMC 1958-67. **Business Addr:** 210 S Euclid Ave, San Diego, CA 92114.

JOHNSON, WILLIAM EDWARD
Professional football player. **Personal:** Born Dec 9, 1968, Chicago, IL. **Educ:** Michigan State. **Career:** St Louis Rams, defensive tackle, 1997-. **Business Addr:** Professional Football Player, St Louis Rams, One Rams Way, St Louis, MO 63045, (314)982-7267.

JOHNSON, WILLIAM HENRY. See Obituaries section.

JOHNSON, WILLIAM L.
Psychologist, psychoanalyst. **Personal:** Born May 23, 1932, NYC; son of Artimeza Ward and Richard Johnson; married Vera Peterkin; children: Toni Ann, Hillary Sloan. **Educ:** Inst Advanced Psychological Studies, Postdoctoral Diploma Psychoanalysis 1968; Adelphi Univ; Yeshiva Univ, PhD Clinical Psychology 1964; City Coll, MS 1957; New Sch Soc Resrch, MA 1955; Queens Coll, BA 1953. **Career:** Private Practice, psychoanalyst 1964-; Orange Co Mental Health Clinics, chief psychologist 1962-64; NY St Training School Boys, consult psychologist; US Peace Corps Ankara Turkey; Falkirk Hosp Central Valley NY; NYS Rehab Hosp, psychologist 1959-62; Kings Pk St Hosp, clin Psychologist 1959; USAF, Mitchel AFB, prsnl psychologist prsnl lab 1957. **Orgs:** Am Psychol Assn 1957-74; St Psychol Assn 1959-74; pres Orange Co Psychol Assn 1963-64; Assn Black Psychologist 1972-74; Adelphia Univ Postdoctoral Soc 1969-74. **Honors/Awds:** Alvin Johnson Prize Scholarship New Sch for Soc Rsch 1953. **Business Addr:** Psychologist-Psychoanalyst, 300 Mercer St, New York, NY 10003.

JOHNSON, WILLIAM PAUL, JR.
Computer consultant. **Personal:** Born Jul 17, 1963, Washington, DC; son of Elizabeth Ann Johnson and William Paul Johnson (deceased). **Educ:** Univ of Washington DC, Washington DC, BBA, (w/honors), 1988; Syracuse Univ, Syracuse, NY, attended, 1981-83; Howard University, Washington, DC, MEd, 1993. **Career:** Harry Diamond Labs (US DOD), Adelphi MD, computer specialist, 1981-87; US Treasury, Bureau of Engraving & Printing, Washington DC, computer specialist, 1987-89; Comp-U-Staff, Silver Springs MD, computer analyst/programmer, 1989-; McDonald-Bradley Inc, McLean, VA, senior programmer/analyst, 1989-94; Computer Info and Support Services, consultant, co-owner, 1987-91; Advanced Automation Technologies, Inc, sr consultant, 1994-. **Orgs:** Pres, Univ of Washington DC Data Processing Mgmt Assoc, 1986-87; educ chairperson, Black Data Processing Assoc, 1987-91; founder/pres, Univ of Washington DC Black Data Processing Assoc, 1987-88, coach, Natl High School Computer Competition Team (DC Chapter), 1988-95; chairperson, Univ of Washington DC Coll of Business Student Advisory Council, 1988; pres, Black Date Processing Assn, Washington DC Chapter, 1991-95. **Honors/Awds:** Syracuse Univ Academic Scholarship Award, 1981-83; Athletic Scholarship Offer for Swimming, Howard Univ, 1981; Marion S Barry Scholarship Award, Univ of Washington DC, 1987; Mem of the Year, Washington DC Chapter of Black Data Processing Assoc, 1988-91; Full Trustee Scholarship, Howard Univ School of Education, 1990-93; Natl member of the Year, Black Data Processing Assocs, 1991, numerous leadership awards, 1991-95. **Home Addr:** 849 Venable Pl, NW, Washington, DC 20012.

JOHNSON, WILLIAM RANDOLPH
Chemist. **Personal:** Born Jul 25, 1930, Oxford, NC; son of Marina Townes and William R Johnson Sr; married Wendolyn; children: Wendolyn, Pamela, William III. **Educ:** NC Central Univ, BS 1950; Univ of Notre Dame, MS 1952; Univ of PA, PhD 1958. **Career:** Philip Morris Rsch Ctr, senior scientist; W R Grace & Co, res chem 1961-63; FL A&M U, prof of chem 1958-61. **Honors/Awds:** Publ J Polymer Sci 1960; 9 US pat, publ Jour of Org Chem 1971; 3 publ Tobac Sci 1973; 2 publ Nature 1973; 3 publ Chem & Ind 1973, 1975, 1979. **Military Serv:** Army Chem Corps corpl 1953-55. **Business Addr:** Senior Scientist, PO Box 26583, Richmond, VA 23261.

JOHNSON, WILLIAM SMITH
Chemical company executive, clergyman. **Personal:** Born Apr 24, 1941, Salisbury, MD; son of Delcie Mae Markland and Alonzo Lester Johnson; married Jacqueline Andrea Dennis; children: William Jr, Andrea. **Educ:** University of Maryland, Eastern Shore, BS, 1963; Eastern Bible Inst, diploma, pastoral min, 1985; Salisbury State University, grad study; Howard University Divinity School, grad study; Capitol Bible Seminary, grad study. **Career:** Wicomico Co Bd of Education, teacher, 1963-64; US Govt, computer programmer, 1964-65; Detroit Lions, professional football player, 1965; Sussex Co Bd of Education, teacher, 1965-66; EI duPont De Nemours Co Inc, systems specialist, 1966-. Wallace Temple African Methodist Episcopal Zion Church, pastor, 1991-96; Mount Hope AME Zion Church, pastor, 1996-. **Orgs:** Adv bd mem Wicomico Co Housing Authority 1983-84; adv bd mem Wicomico Co Sch Rezoning Comm; mem NAACP; Prince Hall Mason; asst pastor St James AME Zion Church; life mem Salisbury High Assn. **Honors/Awds:** Univ of MD Eastern Shore Athletic Hall of Fame; Outstanding Service Awd for Church Serv Assistance; NAFEO Distinguished Alumni of Year 1983; Ordained Elder of AME Zion Church 1986. **Home Addr:** PO Box 1225, Salisbury, MD 21802. **Business Addr:** Systems Specialist, E I DuPont De Nemours Co Inc, 400 Woodland Rd, Seaford, DE 19973.

JOHNSON, WILLIAM T. M.
Educator. **Personal:** Born Oct 22, 1921, Philadelphia, PA; children: 2. **Educ:** VA St Coll, BS 1943; Univ of PA, MS 1947, PhD 1950. **Career:** D I DuPont de Nemours & Co, resrch chem 1949-63; Lincoln Univ, prof of chem 1963-; Univ PA School of Medicine, rsch assoc 1971-; PA Hospital, non-clinical investigator 1971-. **Orgs:** Pres United & Political Act Com of Chester Co 1968-; pres Hum Rels Cncl of W Chester PA 1963-65; bd dir W Chester Comm Ctr 1975-. **Honors/Awds:** Roon Award, Resrch First Pl 1961; Lindback Award for Distngshd Tchng 1965; John B Knecht Brthrhd Award 1965. **Military Serv:** AUS eto 1943-46. **Business Addr:** Chem Dept, Lincoln University, PA 19352.

JOHNSON, WILLIAM THEOLIOUS
Attorney. **Personal:** Born Dec 24, 1943, Columbus, OH; married Gloria Kindle;; children: Michael, Michelle. **Educ:** Capital Univ, AB 1968; Capital Univ, OH State Univ, JD 1972. **Career:** Dunbar Kienzle & Murphey Law Firm, atty 1972-75; Johnson & Ransier Co LPA, managing partner 1975-79; Private Practice, atty 1979-; KBLE OH Inc, pres 1979-. **Orgs:** Chmn Black Amer Law Student Assn; chmn Law Day; Phi Alpha Delta Law Frat; vice pres Student Bar Assn; natl chmn Elections Comm Amer Bar Assn Law Student Div; pres Franklin Co Legal Aid & Defender Soc; vice chmn Franklin Co Mental Health & Retardation Bd; bd mem spec cnsl Columbus Urban League; trustee Columbus Zoo; trustee OH Found for Independent Colls; natl chmn Minority Affairs Comm Natl Cable TV Assn; mem Legislative Comm NCTA; trustee Franklin Co Public Defender Comm; ruling elder Bethany Presbyterian Ch; mem Columbus, Amer, Natl Bar Assns; hearing officer OH Civil Rights Commn; hearing officer OH Dept of Educ; arbitrator United Steelworkers; Natl Cable TV Assn; OH Cable TV Assn; admitted to practice before, Supreme Ct of US, US Court of Appeals, US Dist Ct,US Tax Ct. **Honors/Awds:** Outstanding Young Man in Columbus Columbus Jr C of C 1972; Outstanding Comm Serv Awd Columbus Bar Assn 1978; Gold Key Awd; Lutheran Brotherhood Scholarship; Hugh H Huntington Awd; Amer Jurisprudence Book Awd; West Publishing Co Constitutional Law Book Awd; selected Ten Outstanding Young Men in Columbus; Columbus Bar Assn Comm Serv Awd. **Business Addr:** President, KBLE OH Inc, 1156 Alum Creek Dr, Columbus, OH 43209.

JOHNSON, WILLIE
City official (retired), musician, vocalist. **Personal:** Born May 26, 1925, Florence, SC; son of Evelener Richardson and Luther Johnson; married Fredericka Helen Gadsden; children: Franklin Lewis Johnson. **Educ:** Wayne State Univ, 1970; Cass Tech HS, cert of accomplish 1971; MI Career Inst, cert of grad 1974. **Career:** Wayne Co Gen Hosp, Wayne Co guard 1951-78; Wayne Co, deputy sheriff 1961-68; Kaufman & Broad Homes, super 1961-69; State of MI, asst chief fire & safety officer 1978-; Personal Accomplishment, songwriter 1955-; City of Inkster, city councilman, retired 1990; minister of music, gospel singer, 1992-. **Orgs:** Mem Inkster NAACP 1974-; mem Central Wayne Co Sanitation Auth 1975-77; mem Inkster Civil Defense Policy Bd 1975-; comm mem Nankin Transit Comm 1977-; mem Broadcast Music Inc 1984-; publ Wiljoe Music BMI 1984-; producer Inkster's New Sounds on "Inkster's New Sound" label 1984-; Nashville Songwriters Assoc International 1990; Broadcast Music Inc (BMI) 1984-; mem, Natl Black Caucus; bd mem, MI Assn of Govt Employees, 1991. **Honors/Awds:** Cert of appreciation Wayne Co Bd of Comm 1978; special tribute from State of MI Sen Plawecki & Rep Wm Keith 1978; won lawsuit as private citizen in state supreme ct to return money to citizens Home Owners' Org 1971-78; Disting Employee of the Yr Walter P Reuther Psych Hosp 1981; 1st Place Trophy at Sumpter Township Rodeo for compositions & vocalist 1988. **Military Serv:** USN seaman 1st class 1943-46; Asia/Pacific Campaign Medal; Good Conduct Medal; personal letter from secy of Navy; WWII Victory Medal. **Home Addr:** 4066 Durand Ct, Inkster, MI 48141.

JOHNSON, WILLIE F.
Commissioner. **Personal:** Born Sep 27, 1939, Jacksonville, FL; married Bernice Lowery; children: Thandeka. **Educ:** Allen U, BA 1961; Univ of PA, MSW 1970. **Career:** Commonwealth of PA Dept of Pub Wlfr, Sthestrn Reg, commr, ofc of yth serv 1974-; Yth Dev Ctr Philadelphia, exec dir 1972-74, cnslr 1961-64; Children's Hosp, soc serv dir 1970-72; Yth Dev Ctr S Philadelphia, cnslr 1966-67; Nat Biscuit Co, foreman 1965-66; SC Pub Sch, tchr 1961-64. **Orgs:** Mem Yth Serv Com for Philadelphia; Yth Serv Com for Philadelphia United Fund; adv bd of Minority Ed & Grp Training Labs; mem YMCA; Am Corr Assn; PA Assn of Parole Probtn & Corr. **Business Addr:** RM 1303 STATE OFC BLDG, 1400 Spring Garden St, Philadelphia, PA 19130.

JOHNSON, WYNEVA
Attorney. **Personal:** Born Oct 28, 1948, Greenwood, MS. **Educ:** Georgetown Univ Law Ctr, LLM 1977; Univ of PA, JD 1974; Wheaton Coll, BA 1971. **Career:** Howard Jenkins Fr Nat Labor Rel Bd, counsel to bd mem 1974-. **Orgs:** Admitted PA Bar 1974; admitted MS Bar 1976; exec bd Wheaton Coll Alumnae Assn; former chmn Com of Black Alumnae. **Honors/Awds:** Nom Outsdng Young Women of Am 1976. **Business Addr:** 1717 Pennsylvania Ave NW, Room 745 A, Washington, DC 20570.

JOHNSON-BLOUNT, THERESA
Librarian. **Personal:** Born Jan 11, 1952, Lafayette, LA; daughter of Rosella Veazie Johnson and Willie Johnson (deceased); married William Blount III, Mar 20, 1976; children: Tyaisha Alyce, Wilicia Ellen, Remus Allen. **Educ:** Southern University, Baton Rouge, LA, BS, marketing, 1973; Graduate School, Louisiana State University, Baton Rouge, LA, 1989; Texas Woman's University, Denton, TX, MLS, 1990. **Career:** Mid-County Dirt Pit, Port Arthur, TX, assistant manager, 1973-75; Wilson's Jewelers, Baton Rouge, LA, invoice clerk, 1976-77; US Coast Guard, Baton Rouge, LA, storekeeper, 1975-78; Woman's Hopsital Neonatology Unit, acquisitions librarian, consultant, 1985-; Tulane Medical Center Neonatology Unit, acquisitions librarian, consultant, 1985-; Louisiana State University, Troy H Middleton Library, library associate II, 1979-90, librarian, 1990-. **Orgs:** Library Staff Assn, 1980-; American Library Assn, 1988-; ALA Black Caucus, Government Round Table, 1990-; Special Libraries Assn, 1988-, bulletin editor, 1992-94; LSU, Intl Hospitality Foundation, host family, 1988-, Black Faculty and Black Staff Caucus, 1985-, Black Students Support Group, 1985-89; TWU, Mary Hufford Hall, RHA Representative, 1989-90; American Therapeutic Recreation Association, library consultant; LLA GODORT, elected vice chair, 1995-96, chair, 1996-97. **Honors/Awds:** Scholarship, Beta Phi Mu; academic scholarship, Texas Woman's University; Donna Jean Billington Scholarship; Graduate Assistant Award Library/LRC, Texas Woman's University; Certificate of Appreciation, Texas Woman's University and National Alumnae Association; Service Award, Louisiana State University; author, "Pull a String for Results: Strings Used as Therapeutic Activities," School Library Media Activities Monthly, June 1991; author, "Making Sausages: Old Fashioned Boudin," Southern Living, November 1983; author, Cooking from Bayou Courtableau, 1984; author, Lagniappe Cookbook, 1984; Outstanding Family Awd, Family Svc of Greater Baton Rouge; ASPECT Host Family, 1996-97. **Special Achievements:** Author of articles including "International Year of the Family: Libraries Can Be a Family Educational Affair," Documents to the People, 1994; "United Nations Depository Collection at Troy H Middleton Library," Louisiana Library Assn, LLA Bulletin, 1992; "Characteristics of Automoted Acquisitions Systems in Organizations Belonging to the Assn For Higher Education of North Texas," Texas Woman's Univ, ERIC, 1992; "A Selected List of Basic Health Science Reference Sources," American Therapeutic Recreation Assn, Newsletter, 1992; "Nutty Popcorn Balls," Southern Living, 1988; "Making Sausages: Old Fashioned Boudin," Southern Living, 1983; "Pull a String for Results: Strings Used as Therapeutic Activities," School Library Media Activities Monthly, 8(2), p 31-33, Oct 1991; "A Selected List of Basic Health Science Reference Sources," American Therapeutic Recreation Assn Newsletter, 8(1), p 8, Jan/Feb 1992; "Characteristics of Automated Acquisitions Systems in Organizations Belong to the Assn of Higher Education of . . . ," ERIC Clearinghouse, Syracuse University, 1992; Special Libraries Assn, LA/Southern Mississippi Chapter, bulletin editor; TWU, Booking Binding Workshop, organizer, 1990; Southern University Recreation Dept, banquet organizer, 1992. **Military Serv:** US Coast Guard, SK3, 1975-78. **Home Addr:** 8926 High Point Rd, Baton Rouge, LA 70810.

JOHNSON-BROWN, HAZEL WINFRED
Educator, nurse. **Personal:** Born Oct 10, 1927, West Chester, PA; daughter of Garnet Henley Johnson and Clarence L Johnson; married David B Brown. **Educ:** Harlem Hospital of Nursing, Diploma 1950; Villanova Univ, BS 1959; Columbia Univ Teacher's Coll, MS 1963; Catholic Univ, PhD 1978. **Career:** Letterman General Med Center, instructor, 1963-66; Valley Forge General, supvr, 1966-67; US Army, med rsch & devel command project dir, 1967-73; Univ of MD Sch of Nursing, dir, asst dean, 1976-78; US Army Hospital Seoul Korea, asst for nursing 1978-79; Georgetown Univ Sch of Nursing, asst prof 1983-84, adjunct prof 1985; George Mason Univ, prof, school of nursing, 1986-. **Orgs:** Amer Nurses Assn, 1957-; Sigma Theta Tau 1977-; Assn of US Army 1978-; lifetime mem, Nursing Educ Alumnae Assn Teacher's Coll Columbia Univ; honorary mem, Chi Eta Phi Alpha Chapter, Natl Black Nursing Sor, Delta Sigma Theta. **Honors/Awds:** Recognition Award Tuskegee Inst Sch of Nursing 1981; Henry O Flipper Award Military Law Section Natl Bar Assn, 1981; Distinguished Prof of Nursing & Military Sci, Prairie View A&M Univ, 1981; Bethune Tubman Truth Award Black Women Hall of Fame Found, 1981; Roy Wilkins Meritorious Serv Award, NAACP; Amer Black Achievement Award, Business & Professions Ebony Magazine 1983; Golden Heart Award, 1983; Black Nurse of Year Greater Washington Area Black Nurses Assn 1984; Natl Inst for Women of Color Award, 1984; National Coalition of 100 Black Women, Candace Award, 1984; Dollars and Sense Magazine, One of 100 Black Business & Professional Women, 1985. **Special Achievements:** Guest lecturer: Georgetown University; University of Maryland; George Mason University School of Nursing; national/local TV & radio interview participation, 1979-82; "Women's Issues and Professional Nursing," Night Watch, 1983; "The Different Drummer Series," African-American history month programming, PBS-TV, 1983-84. **Military Serv:** US Army Nurse Corps, brigadier gen, 28.5 yrs; First African-American woman General in history of Military Services; Evangeline C Bovard Army Nurse of the Yr Award 1964; Army Commendation Medal 1966, First Oak Leaf Cluster; Nurse of Yr Dr Anita Newcomb McGee Award Daughters of the Amer Revolution, 1971; Legion of Merit, 1973; Meritorious Serv Medal, 1979; Order of Military Med Merit, 1983; US Army ROTC Serv Award, 1983; Distinguished Serv Medal, 1983.

JOHNSON-CARSON, LINDA D.
Health administrator, optometrist. **Personal:** Born Feb 5, 1954, Richland, MS; daughter of Gertrude Johnson and Adam Johnson; divorced; children: James III. **Educ:** Jackson State Univ, BS 1974; Indiana State Univ School of Optometry, Doctor of Optometry 1978. **Career:** Jackson Hinds Comp Health Center, dept head, Optometry, 1978-. **Orgs:** Member, Mississippi Optometric Assn 1978-, asst to grad & undergrad comm, 1979-81, legis comm, 1989-, public relations co-chair, 1989-90, chmn, 1991-93, mem development & retention chair, 1993-; Southern Council of Optometrists 1974-; member & bd of dir Natl Optometric Assn 1974-, trustee at large, 1981-83, region III trustee, 1983-85, scy, 1989-93, vp, 1993-95, pres-elect, 1995-97, pres, 1997-99; bd of dir, central Mississippi chapter Amer Red Cross 1988-; exec bd, American Red Cross Central Mississippi Chapter, 1989-; mem American Optometric Assn, 1978-80, 1989-; mem, exec comm, AOA Comm Ctr, 1992-96; Amer Red Cross Central MS, chap chair volunteer svcs, 1988-91, 2nd vice chair, bd of dirs, 1991-93, vice chair, bd of dirs, 1993-95, chair, bd of dirs, 1995-97. **Honors/Awds:** First black female optometrist in MS 1978; Professional Achievement Jackson State Univ Natl Alumni Assn 1980; Distinguished Serv Jackson Hinds Alumni Chapter Jackson State Natl Alumni Assn 1982; honorary member, Beta Beta Beta Biological Honor Soc, Jackson State Univ, 1984; Certificate of Appreciation, Ms Optometric Assoc, 1990; Volunteer of the Month, American Red Cross Central Ms Chapter, 1990; Certificate of Appreciation, Jackson State Univ, Dean of Libraries, 1991; Optometrist of the Year, Natl Optometric Assn, 1993; American Red Cross, Central MS Chapter, J Tate Thigpen Awd, 1994; JC Penney Golden-Rule Award, Top 10 Finalist Award, 1997; You've Made a Difference Award, Community Working to Unite Youth Organization of Rawkin Cty, 1997; MS Commissioner, Volunteer Svc Commendation, 1996-97. **Business Addr:** Department Head of Optometry, Jackson Hinds Comp Health Center, 4433 Medgar Evers Blvd, Jackson, MS 39213.

JOHNSON COOK, SUZAN DENISE
Clergyman. **Personal:** Born Jan 28, 1957, New York, NY; daughter of Dorothy C Johnson and Wilbert T Johnson; married Ronald Cook, Oct 11, 1991; children: Samuel David. **Educ:** Emerson College, BS (cum laude), 1976; Columbia University Teachers College, MA, 1978; Union Theological Seminary, MDV, 1983; United Theological Seminary, Doctor of Ministry, 1990. **Career:** Mariners' Temple Baptist Church, senior pastor, 1983-; Multi Ethnic Center, executive director/founder, 1986-; New York City Police Department, chaplain, 1990-; Harvard University,Divinity School, visiting professor, 1991-. **Orgs:** New York Coalition 100 Black Women, vice pres, 1991-; American Baptist Churches, 1981-; Multi Ethnic Center, founder, 1986-. **Honors/Awds:** Essence Magazine, Essence Woman, 1983; YWCA Award, 1986; Young Achievers, NCNW, 1988. **Special Achievements:** Co-Author, Preaching In Two Voices, Judson: Valley Forge, 1992; Editor, Wise Women Bearing Gifts, Judson: Valley Forge, 1988. **Business Addr:** Pastor, Mariners' Temple Baptist Church, 3 Henry Street, New York, NY 10038, (212)233-0423.

JOHNSON-CROCKETT, MARY ALICE
Physician. **Personal:** Born May 6, 1937, Anderson, SC; daughter of Bernice McAlister Johnson and William P Johnson; married Edward D Crockett Jr (deceased); children: Edward D III, Alison V, Sharon P. **Educ:** Howard Univ Coll of Liberal Arts, BS 1958; Howard Univ Coll of Medicine, MD 1962. **Career:** Freedman Hospital, intern 1963; DC General Hospital, Veterans Admin, Howard Univ, resident internal medicine 1963-66; Walter Reed Army Medical Center, medical officer 1966-67; Veterans Admin Hospital Downey IL, staff physician 1967-69; Community Group Health Found Inc, staff physician & acting medical dir 1969-72; Home Care Serv Bureau, medical officer, medical dir 1972-; Hospice Care of DC, medical dir 1979-82; private practice, internal medicine & geriatrics. **Orgs:** Consultant Income Maintenance Admin 1971-86; employee, health physician Law Enforcement Agency Admin & Consumer Products Safety Commn 1975, 1976-77; member exec comm Potomac PTA 1976-81; track physician Bowie Race Track 1977-81; professional adv comm Hospice Care of DC 1983-, UpJohn 1985-; steering comm Sidwell Friends School 1984-85; parent Support Group Youth Choir Plymouth Congregation UCC; consultant Natl Health Serv 1972-82; pres, W Henry Greene Friends of Music Soc 1988-. **Honors/Awds:** Lucy Moten Fellowship Award for Foreign Travel Howard Univ 1957; Intern of the Year Howard Univ 1963; Hospice Award Hospice Care of DC 1983; Ronald C Newman Award Jackson-Newman Found Inc 1987. **Business Addr:** Medical Dir, Home Care Services Bureau, DC General Hospital, Box 38, Washington, DC 20003.

JOHNSON-CROSBY, DEBORAH A.
Business executive. **Personal:** Born Jan 15, 1951, Chicago; divorced; children: Malik Fanon. **Educ:** Univ WI, BA 1974. **Career:** Mt Sinai Hosp, staff worker bus office 1969; Northside Comm Credit Union, loan clerk, comm relations 1970-71; Concentrated Employment Program, staff worker; Operation Breadbasket, pub relations dir 1972-73; Milwaukee Times, rptr 1973-74; Milwaukee Star Times, managing editor 1974-75; Milwaukee Bus Fedn, dir; free-lance journalist; communications consultant. **Orgs:** Mem Black Media Alliance WI; Pub Relations Comm; information officer Black Comm Student Alliance 1972-73; Milwaukee Assn; mem bd dirs Peckham Jr HS1974. **Business Addr:** 3811 N 20 St, Milwaukee, WI 53206.

JOHNSON-HELTON, KAREN
College administrator. **Personal:** Born May 20, 1947, Cincinnati, OH; daughter of Ruth Lee Payne and James C Payne; married Malcolm Helton, Jun 29, 1995. **Educ:** Ohio University, Athens, OH, BA, 1969; Atlanta University, Atlanta, GA, MSW, 1976; University of Michigan, Ann Arbor, MI, 1978; Texas A & M University, 1992. **Career:** LeMoyne-Owen College, Memphis, TN, dir of planning, 1976-82; Mary Holmes College, West Point, MS, federal programs coord, 1982-86; Rust College, Holly Springs, MS, proposal writer, 1986-87; Wiley College, Marshall, TX, associate vice-president, 1987-88, assistant to president, 1988-. **Orgs:** Bd mem, Harrison county United Way, 1997-00; National Rep to UNCF; Zeta Phi Beta Sorority, 1992-96, Third Anti-Basileus, 1990-93; member, public relations committee, Zonta International, 1989-; steering committee member, Top Ladies of Distinction, 1989-; district commissioner, Cub Scouts of America, 1986-87; State of Texas Democratic Party, 1992-. **Honors/Awds:** Certificate of Outstanding Achievement, US Dept of Educ, 1996, 1997; Certificate of Professional Merit, US Dept of Educaton, 1986, 1987; Nominated to White House Fellows Program, 1984; Congressional Proclamation, Outstanding Services to Youth, Congressman Harold Ford, 1981; Carnegie Fellow, Carnegie Foundation/Atlanta University, 1975-76; 1992 nominee for '93 Class, Leadership Texas; nominee for Governor's Advisory Committee, 1991. **Business Addr:** Director of Sponsored Programs, Wiley College, Office of Sponsored Programs, 711 Wiley Ave, Room 103, Thirkield Hall, Marshall, TX 75670.

JOHNSON-ODIM, CHERYL
Educator. **Personal:** Born Apr 30, 1948, Youngstown, OH; daughter of Elayne Jeffries; married Carlton Odim; children: Chaka Malik, Rashid Jamil, Maya Ruth. **Educ:** Youngstown State Univ, BA (cum laude) 1972; Northwestern Univ, MA 1975, PhD 1978. **Career:** Loyola Univ of Chicago, dir Afro-Amer studies 1978-, asst prof 1978-80; Northwestern Univ, asst dir African studies 1980; Loyola Univ, Chicago, IL, assoc prof, currently. **Orgs:** Co-chairperson IL Council for Black Studies 1979-; co-chairperson for membership Assn of Black Women Historians 1979-; bd mem Chiaravalle Montessori Sch 1980; co-chair, elected to board of directors, 1992, Women's Caucus, African Studies Assn, 1988-; National Women's Studies Association Journal, appointed editorial board, 1992. **Honors/Awds:** Fulbright Hays Dissertation Year Fellow 1976; research affiliate Univ of Ibadan Nigeria 1976 co-editor "The Pan-Africanist" Northwestern Univ 1975; Monticello Fellow, 1990. **Business Addr:** 6525 N Sheridan Rd, Chicago, IL 60626.

JOHNSON-SCOTT, JERODENE PATRICE
Physician. **Personal:** Born Dec 15, 1952, Atlanta, GA; children: Lawrence Edward. **Educ:** Spelman Coll, BS 1974; Meharry Medical Coll, MD 1978. **Career:** Atlanta Urban League, director-medical specialist program, currently. **Orgs:** Mem Natl Assoc of Residents & Interns 1981-, Amer Medical Assoc 1983-; instructor Atlanta Urban League 1983-; vice pres Inner City Life Foundation 1984-;mem Natl Medical Assoc; mem Smithsonian Inst, Women's Health Network, Inner City Life Foundation. **Honors/Awds:** Articles published Cascade Chronicle newspaper.

JOHNSTON, ERNEST (ERNIE)
Journalist. **Personal:** Born Nov 25, 1938, Roanoke Rapids, NC; son of Bessie W Johnston (deceased) and Ernest Johnston Sr (deceased); divorced; children: Tanya White, Rhonda Cox. **Educ:** North Carolina A&T State University, BS, 1960; Columbia University, interracial reporting fellow, 1971-72. **Career:** Star-Ledger, reporter, 1964-68; New York Post, reporter, 1968-73; Long Island Press, reporter, 1973-75; Herald News, copy editor, 1975-77; New York Amsterdam News, managing editor, 1977-81; freelance writer, 1981-87; National Urban League, communications specialist, public relations & communications department, 1987-95; Crossroads Theatre, dir of public relations, 1996-97; LeJay Associates, pres, currently. **Orgs:** North Carolina A&T State University National Alumni Association, first natl vice pres, chairperson, public relations committee, former editor, A & T Today; North Carolina A&T State Alumni Association, northern New Jersey chapter, president, 1978-83; North Carolina A&T State Alumni Association, central, New Jersey shore chapter, president, 1990-93; New York Press Club, 2nd vice president, 1968-69; Men's Club, Elmwood Presbyterian Church, 1985-90; Pastor Nominating Committee, Bethel Presbyterian Church, co-chairperson; A&T Alumni Assn, regional dir, NE region, 1993-95; Breast Cancer Ctr of Harlem, mem, advisory bd. **Honors/Awds:** East Orange, New Jersey Chamber of Commerce, First Place Black & White Photo Award, 1985; Harlem YMCA, World Service Award, 1981; North Carolina A&T State Alumni Association, northern New Jersey chapter, Special Recognition Award, 1982; Caribbean American Designers & Models, Contribution to Mankind Award, 1980; Black Spectrum Theatre Co, Service Award, 1979; North Carolina A&T State Alumni Association, Alumni Achiever, 1991; NAFEO Award, 1995. **Special Achievements:** Managing editor, The Negro Almanac, a reference work on the African-Americans, 1981, 1990. **Military Serv:** US Army, Sp4, 1962-64. **Business Addr:** LeJay Associates, 4500 Bordentown Ave, Ste 1148, Sayreville, NJ 08872, (732)238-8230.

JOHNSTON, GLADYS STYLES
Educational administrator. **Personal:** Born Dec 23, 1942, St Petersburg, FL; daughter of Rosa Moses Styles and John Edward Styles; married Hubert Seward Johnston, Jul 30, 1966. **Educ:** Cheyney University, BS, social science, 1963; Temple University, MEd, educational administration, 1969; Cornell University, PhD, 1974. **Career:** Chester School District, Chester, PA, teacher, 1963-66; West Chester School District, PA, teacher, 1966-67, asst principal, 1968-69, director of summer school, 1969-71, principal, 1969-71; Chester County Board of Education, Chester, PA, director of Head Start, 1967-69; Cornell University, teaching asst, 1971-72, research asst, 1972-74; Rutgers University, Educational Administration & Supervision, asst professor, 1974-79, chairperson, 1979-83, assoc professor, 1979-83, chairperson, Dept of Management, 1983-85; College of William and Mary, Williamsburg, VA, visiting professor, 1982-83; Arizona State University, College of Education, Tempe, AZ, dean & professor, 1985-91; DePaul University, Chicago, IL, provost & academic vice president, 1991-. **Orgs:** Board of directors, Foundation for Senior Living, 1990-91; board of directors, KAET-TV, 1987-; board of directors, Education Law Center, 1979-86; advisory council to board of trustees, Cornell University, 1981-86; board of trustees, Middlesex General University Hospital, 1983-86; various positions, American Educational Research Assn; member, Assn for Supervision and Curriculum Development; member, American Assn of Colleges for Teacher Education; member, National Conference of Professors of Educational Administration. **Honors/Awds:** Outstanding Alumni, Temple University; Andrew D. White Fellowship, Cornell University; Phi Kappa Phi Honor Society; Alpha Phi Sigma National Honorary Scholastic Fraternity, Cheyney State College; author, "The Emerging Redefinition of Federal Educational Policy: Implications for Educational Excellence," Journal of Educational Evaluation and Policy Analysis; "The Carnegie Report: A Retrospective," Journal of Arizona School Board Association, Fall 1986; "Rule Administration and Hierarchical Influence of the Principal: A Study of Teacher Loyalty to the Principal," Educational Administrative Quarterly, Fall 1986; author, Research and Thought in Administration Theory: Developments in the Field of Educational Administration, 1986; numerous other books, articles, and reviews.

JOHNSTON, HENRY BRUCE
Administrator. **Personal:** Born Jul 4, 1927; married Cora Virginia Jackson; children: Geraldine, Mark, Lisa, Steven. **Educ:** St John's Univ Brooklyn, Attend; Univ Boston, natl grad; St Univ Farmingdale NY, AAS; St Univ Stoney Brook NY, MA, BS. **Career:** Suffolk Co Hum Rights Commn, exec dir 1985; St Univ Farmingdale, instr criminal justice; Suffolk Comm Coll, instr criminal justice; Police Acad Suffolk Co Police Dept, instr; Globe-Trotters Professional Bsktbl Org, former mem. **Orgs:** Bd of dir LI Sickle Cell Proj Nassau & Suffolk; bd dir Suffolk Rehab Ctr; bd of dir Suffolk Co Adv Bd Youth Srvs; bd of dir Diocesan Task Force for Poverty & Racism Nassau & Suffolk; adv bd of dir Crime Control Cncl Suffolk Co; bd of dir ed com NCCJ, Nassau & Suffolk; bd of dir Awards Com SCPD; bd of dir Boy Scouts of Am Suffolk Co; bd of dir Phi Beta Sigma Frat; bd of Dir Econ Opportunity Cncl Suffolk Co; bd of dir Urban League of LI Nassau & Suffolk Co; bd of dir Alcoholism Adv Commn Suffolk Co; mem NYCPD Youth Squad PAL Div; NAACP Nassau & Suffolk; Lions Club Hauppauge NY; bd of ed Grievance Com Hauppauge HS. **Honors/Awds:** Purple Heart, AUS; Am Def Srv Medal, AUS; European-African Middle E Srv Medal AUS; Asiatic Pacific Srv Medal, AUS; Hunting PAL Award 1958; Top Bsktbl Ofcl 1960-61, 1969; Police Youth Award, SCPD 1961-62; Medal for Bravery, SCPD 1964; Outstndng Bsktbl Ofcl 1966; Meritorious Srv, SCPD 1967; Masons RecognitionAward, King Tyre Lodge 1967; Professionalization Award, SCPD 1969; Man of Yr NANBPW 1974; Black Std Union, SU Farmingdale 1975. **Military Serv:** AUS 1st sgt 1942-45. **Business Addr:** Co Center, Veterans Hwy, Smithtown, NY 11787.

JOHNSTON, JULIA MAYO. **See MAYO, JULIA A.**

JOHNSTON, WALLACE O.
Engineering consultant (retired). **Personal:** Born Nov 8, 1929, New York, NY; son of Mary Smith Johnston and Wallace Johnston; children: Asao, Toshio, Paige, Leana, Glen. **Educ:** City Coll of NY, BSME 1963, Grad Mech Eng Study 1967; US Dept of Defense, Environ Eng 1968. **Career:** New York City Bd of Educ, eng 1959-68; Hannaham & Johnston, prtnr 1968-76; Wallace Johnston Engs, proprietor, chief engineer. **Orgs:** Bd of dir NY Assn Cnslt Engrs 1974-76; mem Nat Soc Professional Engr 1967-; mem FL Engineers Society, 1987-; tutorial dir Kappa Alpha Psi 1979; mem Natl Tech Assn 1982-; mem Math Assoc of Amer. **Honors/Awds:** Tech Paper Bldng Systems Dsgns New York City 1976; Hnrbl Mntn Lincoln Wldng Inst OH 1961; Dsgn Awrd BSA Prgrsv Arch 1971; Lcnsd Engr FL Bd ProfLcsng 1967; Design Awd, Rochester NY, Convention Ctr, 1993. **Special Achievements:** Library of Congress, Copyright, blinking lighted Kappa Alpha Psi Diamond. **Military Serv:** USAF airmn 1st cls 4 yrs; Good Cndct, Korean Theatre, Am Defense 1950-54. **Home Addr:** 11250 Riddle Dr, Spring Hill, FL 34609.

JOHNSTONE, LANCE
Professional football player. **Personal:** Born Jun 11, 1973, Philadelphia, PA. **Educ:** Temple Univ. **Career:** Oakland Raiders, defensive end, 1996-. **Business Addr:** Professional Football Player, Oakland Raiders, 1220 Harbor Bay Pkwy, Alameda, CA 94502, (510)615-1875.

JOINER, BURNETT
Educational administrator. **Personal:** Born Nov 10, 1941, Raymond, MS; son of Arcine Joiner and Burnett Joiner; married Inez Dixon; children: Michael, Christopher. **Educ:** Utica Jr Coll, AA 1962; Alcorn State Univ, BS 1964; Bradley Univ, MA 1968; Univ of SC, PhD 1975. **Career:** Oliver School Clarksdale, MS, principal 1968-71; York School Dist #1, asst supt of schls 1971-73; SC Coll Orangeburg, SC, asst prof 1974-75; Atlanta Univ Atlanta, GA, exec dir/assoc prof 1975-80; Grambling State Univ, exec academic dean and prof, 1984-91; LeMoyne-Owens College, pres, 1991-. **Orgs:** Mem Ouachita Valley Boy Scouts 1982-; charter mem Grambling Lion's Club 1983-; consultant US Dept Educ 1983-85; commr LA Learning Adv Commn 1984-85; commr LA Internship Commn 1984-85; mem Natl Inst of Education Study Group on Teacher Edn; chaired special comm in Coll of Educ Univ of SC on student advisement; past mem Curriculum Comm Sch of Educ at SC State Coll; mem Ruston-Lincoln C of C; vice chairperson Comm on Social Concerns Lewis Temple Church; conducted numerous workshops and seminars for more than 50 schools, agencies and community groups; mem of the bd of dir Teacher Ed Council for State Coll and Univ, American Assoc of Coll for Teacher Ed; mem of the Governor's Internship Commission and Learning Adv Commission. **Honors/Awds:** Publications, "The Teacher Corps Policy Board; Three Perspectives on Role and Function" 1979; "A Documentation Primer; Some Perspectives from the Field" 1979; "New Perspectives on Black Education History" Book Review for the Journal of Negro History in progress; "Identifying Needs and Prioritizing Goals Through Collaboration" 1978; "Education That Is Multicultural; A Process of Curriculum Development" 1979; "The Design, Implementation and Evaluation of a Pre-Service Prototype Competency-Based Teacher Education Model" 1975; "Maximizing Opportunities for Professional Improvement" 1983; Improving Teacher Education: A Conscious Choice, co-author. **Business Addr:** President, LeMoyne-Owen College, 807 Walker Ave, Memphis, TN 38126.

JOINER, CHARLES, JR.
Professional football player (retired). **Personal:** Born Oct 14, 1947, Many, LA; married Dianne; children: Jynayna, Kori. **Educ:** Grambling College, BS, business administration, 1969. **Career:** Wide receiver: Houston Oilers, 1969-72; Cincinnati Bengals, 1972-75; San Diego Chargers, 1976-85, assistant coach after retirement; Gulf Oil Co, management trainee, 1971. **Honors/Awds:** Four varsity letters Grambling; All Southwestern Athletic Conf, 1968; named All Pro & All AFC second team, AP and UPI, 1980; MVP and Most Inspirational Player, San Diego Chargers, 1983; established NFL record for most pass receptions (716); played in Pro Bowl, 1976, 1979, 1980; testimonial in Lake Charles on "Charlie Joiner Day," May 15, 1982 and Nov 20, 1986. **Business Addr:** Assistant Coach, San Diego Chargers, 9449 Friars Road, Jack Murphy Stadium, San Diego, CA 92108.

JOLIVET, LINDA CATHERINE
Librarian. **Personal:** Born Mar 5, 1950, New Orleans, LA; daughter of Nancy Evans Jolivet and Fred Douglas Jolivet; children: Shakira N Scott. **Educ:** University of Southwestern Louisiana, Lafayette, LA, BA, 1974; University of California, Berkeley, Berkeley, CA, MLIS, 1988; San Francisco State University, San Francisco, CA, currently. **Career:** Lafayette Parish School Board, Layfayette, LA, teacher, 1975-80; Oakland Post Newspaper Group, Oakland, CA, advertising asst, 1980-81; Berkeley Public Library, Berkeley, CA, library asst, 1982; University of California, Berkeley, Berkeley, CA, clerical asst, 1982-83, library asst, 1983-84; Oakland Public Library, Oakland, CA, library asst, 1984-86; East Bay Negro Historical Society Museum-Library, Oakland, CA, curator-librarian, 1986-87; Stanford University, Palo Alto, CA, asst librarian, 1989-90; College of Alameda, Alameda, CA, librarian, 1990-. **Orgs:** Secretary 1990, coordinator, scholarship committee 1991, California Librarians Black Caucus, Northern Chapter; program asst, National Black Child Development Institute, East Bay Area Affiliate, 1990-91; founder, dir, board member, Adesua Bea Learning Center and Educational Services, 1982; member, American Library Association, 1985-91; member, Northern California Center for the Study of Afro-American Life and Culture, 1991. **Honors/Awds:** Graduate Minority Fellowship, University of California-Berkeley, 1984-85; Graduate Equity Fellowship Award, San Francisco State University, 1990-91; author, Preparations of Librarians to Serve a Multicultural World, Women Library Workers Journal, 1988; author, African and African American Audiovisual Materials: A Selected Bibliography, Stanford University Libraries, 1990.

JOLLEY, SAMUEL DELANOR, JR.
Educational administrator. **Personal:** Born Feb 1, 1941, Fort Valley, GA; son of Samuel and Mary Jolley; married Jimmye Hambry, Dec 24, 1963; children: Terena J Washington, Samuel

D III. **Educ:** Fort Valley State College, BS (magna cum laude), 1962; Atlanta University, MS, 1965; Indiana University, EdD, 1974. **Career:** High school mathematics teacher; Fort Valley State College, instructor of mathematics, 1967-70, assistant professor of mathematics, 1970-75, associate professor of mathematics, 1975-82, chairman, Division of Education, 1983-85, dean of School of Arts & Sciences, 1985-93; Morris Brown College, president, 1993-. **Orgs:** Omega Psi Phi Fraternity, 1960-; Sigma Pi Phi Fraternity, 1991-; Alpha Kappa Mu Honor Society; Phi Delta Kappa Education Fraternity; Beta Kappa Chi Scientific Honor Society; Mathematical Association of America; Golden Key National Honor Society; NAACP; Atlanta Chamber of Commerce; Fort Valley State College National Alumni Association, life member; Atlanta University Center's Council of Presidents, board member; Atlanta Systemic Initiative Advisory Council, board member; Allen Temple AME Church, stewards bd, Comm on Finance; Atlanta Paralympics Organization Committee, board of directors, 1994-; Salvation Army, advisory board, 1995-; Atlanta University Center, board member, 1993-; University Center in Georgia, board member, 1993-; University Community Development Corp, board member, 1993-; American Council on Education, 1993-; 100 Black Men of Atlanta, 1995-;. **Honors/Awds:** Leadership Atlanta Georgia Informer, One of the Fifty Most Influential African American Males in Georgia, 1994, 1995; Omega Psi Phi Fraternity, Omega Man of the Year, 1985, 1993; honored by: NAACP; Fort Valley State Coll, Natl Alumn Assn. **Home Addr:** 4410 Park Center Dr, Atlanta, GA 30331. **Business Addr:** President, Morris Brown College, 643 Martin Luther King Jr Dr, NW, Atlanta, GA 30314-4193, (404)220-0100.

JOLLY, ELTON
Organization executive, educator. **Personal:** Born Oct 15, 1931, Claymont, DE; son of Ozella Jones Jolly and Elton Jolly; married Rowena Mozelle Anderson, Sep 22, 1956; children: Elton Brett, William David. **Educ:** Cheyney University, Cheyney, PA, BS, elementary education, 1954; Temple University, Philadelphia, PA, MS, educational administration, 1964. **Career:** Philadelphia Board of Education, Philadelphia, PA, teacher/administrator, 1954-65; Opportunities Industrialization Centers of America, Philadelphia, PA, executive vice chairman, 1965-. **Orgs:** Member, National Alliance of Business, 1984-; member, Black Leadership Forum, 1978-; member, NAACP, 1960-; founding chairman, National Youth Advocacy, 1980-; member, National Assessment Governing Board, 1987-90. **Honors/Awds:** Job Training Professional of the Year, NAB, 1988; James Duckrey Outstanding Alumni Award, Cheyney University, 1978; Secretary of Education Citation for Service, Office of Education, 1989; Secretary of Labor Special Service Award, Dept. of Labor, 1989; Achievement Award, NAACP, 1988. **Military Serv:** US Army, Sp 3, 1954-56; received Good Conduct Medal, Outstanding Leadership Award. **Home Addr:** 6001 Drexel Rd, Philadelphia, PA 19131.

JOLLY, MARVA LEE
Artist educator. **Personal:** Born Sep 11, 1937, Crenshaw, MS; daughter of Mattie Louise Williams Pitchford and Floyd Pitchford, Sr; divorced. **Educ:** Roosevelt Univ, BS 1961; Governors State Univ, MA 1974. **Career:** Univ of Chicago Lab Schools, teacher 1961-65; Chicago Youth Centers Head Start, teacher 1965, dir 1965-69; Chicago Commons Child Develop, program dir 1969-74; Chicago State Univ, prof of ceramics and practicing artist; Suburban Health Systems Agency, Chicago, IL, educator coord, 1977-82; Chicago Youth Centers, Chicago, IL, dir Headstart, 1967-77. **Orgs:** Pres Artisan 21 Gallery 1981-85; self-taught ceramic/sculptor artist 1981-; bd mem African Amer Artist Roundtable 1985-, Exhibitions Comm Chicago Cultural Ctr; volunteer Southside Comm Art Center; curator Saphire and Crystals Black Women's Art Exhibition 1987; curator Earthstones and Rainbow Colors Clay & Textile by Black Chicago Artists; founder Mud Peoples Black Women's Resources Sharing Workshop; bd of dir, Urban Traditions, 1984-; bd of dir, Chicago Cultural Center, 1986-; sponsor, Children's Intl, 1986-. **Honors/Awds:** Best of Category Black Creativity Museum of Science & Industry 1984; Top Ten Emerging Black Chicago Artists 1986-87; Invitational Exhibition Changing Perceptions Columbia Coll Gallery; American Visions Afro-Amer Art 1986; Columbia Motion Pictures "Date Night" 7 art works by Marva Jolly for this movie; art work exhibited and sold Esther Saks Gallery Chicago; Today's Chicago Woman (profile,) 1988; artist in Residence - Lakeside Group, 1988. **Home Addr:** 5326 Hyde Park Blvd, Chicago, IL 60615.

JOLLY, MARY B.
Educational administrator. **Personal:** Born Oct 23, 1940, New Orleans, LA; daughter of Audrey Leufroy Bouligny and Oliver Bouligny; married Herbert Nicholas Jolly; children: Helaina, Nyla, Chanelle. **Educ:** Loyola Univ, BS 1975; Univ of New Orleans, M 1982. **Career:** Jefferson Parish Sheriff's Office, personnel dir 1976-80; Loyola Univ, personnel dir 1980-88; New Orleans Public School System, personnel admin, 1988-. **Orgs:** Consultant Human Resources, EEO, Policies & Procedure 1980-; mem Coll and Univ Personnel Administration 1980-, LA Equal Oppor Assoc 1980-; exec bd mem Intl Information Assocs Personnel/Payroll System Users Group 1981-; regional conf program chair Amer Assoc for Affirmative Action 1986; pres of the bd Personnel Mgmt Assoc, New Orleans Metro Chap of Amer Soc of Personnel Administration 1986/87; mem Cross Keys Hon Serv Soc Loyola Univ; agency relationscomm United Way of Greater New Orleans. **Honors/Awds:** Outstanding Serv to Community Urban League of New Orleans 1984; Outstanding Contribution to the City of New Orleans recognized by the Mayor of New Orleans 1984. **Business Addr:** Personnel Administrator, New Orleans Public School System, 4100 Touro St, New Orleans, LA 70122.

JONAS, ERNESTO A.
Physician, educator. **Personal:** Born Nov 13, 1939, Panama, PA; son of Laura Maria Anderson de Jonas and Harold L. Jonas; married Mary E. Cullen, Jan 15, 1965; children: Jorge A. Jonas, Clarissa M. Jonas. **Educ:** Univ of Nueva Leon, Monterrey, Mexico, MD, 1966. **Career:** Nassau County Medical Ctr, E. Meadow, NY, chief, div of emergency medicine, 1973-76, direc, coronary care unit, 1976-79, chief, div of cardiology, 1979-, direc, cardiovascular training program, 1979-; SUNY at Stony Brook, asst prof of medicine, 1973-88, assoc prof of medicine, 1988-. **Orgs:** Fellow, Amer Coll of Physicians, 1977-; fellow, Amer Coll of Cardiology, 1981-; member, exec comm, Dept of Medicine, SUNY at Stony Brook; member, bd of directors, Amer Heart Assn, Nassau Chapter; member, Physician Edn Comm, Amer Heart Assn. **Honors/Awds:** Excellence in Teachin Award, SUNY at Stony Brook, 1980; Disting Serv Award, Assn of Black Cardiologists, 1987; author of articles in medical journals; Distinguished Leadership Award, Amer Heart Assn, 1992. **Business Addr:** Chief, Division of Cardiology, Nassau County Medical Center, 2201 Hempstead Turnpike, East Meadow, NY 11554.

JONES, AARON DELMAS, II
Professional football player. **Personal:** Born Dec 18, 1966, Orlando, FL. **Educ:** Eastern Kentucky Univ, attended. **Career:** Pittsburgh Steelers, defensive end, 1988-93; New England Patriots, 1993-. **Business Addr:** Professional Football Player, Miami Dolphins, 2269 NW 199th St, Miami, FL 33056.

JONES, ALBERT ALLEN
Clergyman. **Personal:** Born Apr 2, 1913, New Orleans; married Beaulah Mae Houston. **Educ:** Xavier U, PhB, AB 1952. **Career:** Pub Sch, tchr; Bapt Training Union Assn Ministers Alliance, tchr; Union Bapt Theol Sem LA, instr. **Orgs:** Asst dir Dept Christian Ed 1st Dist Missionary Bapt Assn; dir Bapt Training Union LA Bapt St Conv S & Region; mem bd trustees 1st Dist Missionary Bapt Assn; former pres, Mem Ponchartrain Pk Improvement Assn DD, conferred Inter-bapt Theol Ctr. **Military Serv:** World War II vet, sgt. **Business Addr:** Ephesian Bapt Ch, 4020 Melpomene Ave, New Orleans, LA 70125.

JONES, ALBERT J.
Educator (retired). **Personal:** Born Nov 25, 1928, Pittsburgh, PA; married Hattie E; children: Jeffrey L, Bertina M. **Educ:** MD St Coll, BS; Univ Pittsburgh, MEd. **Career:** Somerset HS, sci tchr 1954-56; Wm C Jason HS, physics tchr 1956-66; Seaford HS, physics tchr 1966-71; DE Tech Comm Coll, cnslr 1971-74; DE Tech Comm Coll, adult ed coord 1974-87; DE Tech Comm Coll-South, Georgetown DE, test coordinator 1988-94, counselor, 1971-94. **Orgs:** Omega Psi Phi 1948-; Am Assn Physics Tchr 1966-71; DE Coll Cnslrs Assn 1971-74; Sussex Co Cnslrs Assn 1971-74; DE Foster Child Rev Bd 1979-80; Laurel DE Town Cncl 1971-75; DE College Counseling Assn, 1971-94; Suffex County Counseling Assn, 1971-94; Delaware Counseling Personnel Assn, 1971-94; Sussex County Senior Services, Inc, board of directors, 1991-95; Laurel Senior Center, board of directors, 1996; Delaware Retired School Personnel Assn, 1995-96. **Honors/Awds:** Nat Sci Found Grants Morgan St Coll 1958, Howard U, 1962, SC St Coll 1964, Univ Detroit 1965; St Laurence Univ 1968; Cnslrs In-Srv 1971, Training Inst OK St U; Univ of DE in-serv training inst 1981-84; Athletic Hall of Fame Univ of Maryland Eastern Shore 1975. **Business Addr:** Retired College Counselor, DE Tech & Comm College, PO Box 610 Rt 18, Georgetown, DE 19947.

JONES, ALBERT L.
Educational consultant. **Personal:** Born Sep 7, 1945, Bremerton, WA; son of L C Jones; married Sandra Augustine Hailey, Jun 11, 1970; children: Albert L Jr, Maya Augustine. **Educ:** Central Washington State Univ, Ellenburg, WA, BA, 1967; Univ of Washington, Seattle, WA, MA, 1970, PhD, 1974, Post Doctorate, 1982. **Career:** Seattle Schools, Seattle, WA, principal, 1975-82, area dir, 1982-87; Wichita USD #259, Wichita, KS, assoc supt, 1987-88, deputy supt, 1988-89; Richmond Public Schools, Richmond, VA, div supt, 1989-; Invest Yourself, educational consultant, 1991-. **Orgs:** Bd of dir: Richmond Chamber of Commerce, 1990-; Richmond Renaissance, 1990-; State Library Bd, 1989-; Regional Cities in Schools, 1989-; Mathematics Science Ctr, 1989-. **Honors/Awds:** Master Teacher Trainer, Univ of WA, 1974; Most Outstanding Young Educator, Chamber of Commerce, 1979; NAACP Citizen Award, Wichita, KS, 1988. **Home Addr:** 7442 W Mercer Way, Mercer Island, WA 98040. **Business Addr:** Educational consultant, Invest Yourself, 8441 SE 68th Street, Suite 314, Mercer Island, WA 98040, (206)236-1217.

JONES, ALEXANDER R.
Public relations manager. **Personal:** Born Jan 21, 1952, Washington, DC. **Educ:** MA Inst of Tech, BS 1970-74. **Career:** Nat Commn on Law Enforcement & Soc Justice Ch of Scientology, asso dir 1985. **Orgs:** Exec dir Citizens' Com for Comm Involvement 1985; ed "Unequal Justice-Under The Law" 1979-80. **Honors/Awds:** Author, newspaper column, Law & Social Justice, 1980-. **Business Addr:** Ch of Scientology, 2125 S St NW, Washington, DC 20008.

JONES, ALFREDEAN
Educational administrator. **Personal:** Born Sep 30, 1940, Jonesville, SC; married Betty Jean Smith; children: Pamela, Shelia, Dean. **Educ:** SC State Coll, BS 1963; NC A&T State Univ, MS 1972; Lehigh Univ, Adm Cert 1975. **Career:** Chicago Cubs Minors, player 1963-67; NJ Correctional System, supervisor of recreation 1964-67; Easton Area School Dist, teacher 1967-75, administrator 1975-87. **Orgs:** Bd of dirs 1st vice pres Housing Authority 1976-; bd of dirs Educ Day Care Ctr, Children Home of Easton; 1st vice pres Easton Branch of NAACP. **Honors/Awds:** Certificates of Appreciation Graduating Class of 1984, Children Home of Easton 1985, Easton Branch of NAACP 1986. **Home Addr:** 155 Reese St, Easton, PA 18042. **Business Addr:** Assistant Principal, Easton Area School Dist, 25th & William Penn Hwy, Easton, PA 18042.

JONES, ALPHONZO JAMES
Physician. **Personal:** Born Nov 13, 1946, Idabel, OK; son of Ada Jones and B J Jones (deceased); married Dorothy Ann Henderson; children: Dorothy Annette, Veronica Adele, Rose. **Educ:** OK Baptist, BS (Cum Laude) 1968; Howard Univ, MD 1972. **Career:** US Navy, medical officer (achieved rank Lt Commdr, incl residency fam med) 1973-77; private practice Memphis, TN, physician 1977-82; St Paul Hospital Dallas TX, medical staff 1983-; CIGNA Healthplan of TX Dallas, staff physician 1983-. **Orgs:** Chf of staff Garland Center CIGNA Healthplan 1983-84; bd of governors Memphis Health Center Inc 1979-81; mem Amer Acad of Family Physicians, Natl Medical Assoc, CV Roman Medical Soc Dallas. **Honors/Awds:** Howard Univ Alumni Award for highest scholastic average over 4 yrs med sch; Alpha Omega Alpha Med Honor Soc 1971 induction; Physician of the Yr Bluff City Med Soc Memphis, TN 1981; Fellow Amer Acad of Fam Physicians 1978; certified, American Bd of Family Practice 1976, recertified 1982, 1989, 1994. **Military Serv:** USN Lt Cdr 1973-77. **Home Addr:** 1700 N Yale Blvd, Richardson, TX 75081.

JONES, AMMIA W.
Clergyman. **Personal:** Born Jan 31, 1910, Mesic, NC; married; children: four. **Career:** Town of Mesic, former commissioner, Clergyman, currently. **Orgs:** Past president, Mesic Branch, NAACP; fmr committee, Town of Mesic. **Home Addr:** Rt 1, Box 308, Bayboro, NC 28515.

JONES, ANDRUW RUDOLF
Professional baseball player. **Personal:** Born Apr 23, 1977. **Career:** Atlanta Braves, outfielder, 1996-. **Business Addr:** Professional Baseball Player, Atlanta Braves, 521 Capitol Ave SW, Atlanta, GA 30312, (404)522-7630.

JONES, ANN R.
Educator. **Personal:** Born Jul 5, 1921, New Castle, PA; married Paul L Jones; children: Connie E Rose. **Educ:** Livingstone Coll, BA 1944; Univ of Pittsburgh, MSW 1964, PhD 1978. **Career:** Irene Kaufmann Ctr, prog dir 1952-60; Anna Heldman Ctr, prog dir 1960-64; Action Housing, dir of training 1964-66; Community Action, dir of training 1966-70; Univ of Pittsburgh, prof. **Orgs:** Provost adv comm Womens Concerns; dir Soc Work Field Educ; nom comm Natl Council Soc Work; site visitor Natl Council Social Educ Work; mem adv comm Allegheny Children Youth Svcs; pres Hazelwood Neighborhood Council; mem bd dir Three Rivers Adoption Council. **Honors/Awds:** Post-Gazette Disting Woman 1969; Black Studies Univ of Pittsburgh Black Studies 1980; Disting Alumni Univ of Pittsburgh 1985; Task Force Recognition Cty Commissioners 1986. **Business Addr:** Professor, University of Pittsburgh, 2217 Cathedral of Learning, Pittsburgh, PA 15260.

JONES, ANNETTE MERRITT. See **MERRITT-CUMMINGS, ANNETTE.**

JONES, ANTHONY, JR.
City official (retired). **Personal:** Born Sep 21, 1933, New York, NY; son of Pearl Jones and Anthony Jones; married Arnoline Whitten; children: Leslie Ann. **Educ:** NY Univ, BS 1958, MS 1964. **Career:** Bd of Educ NYC, sci tchr 1959-69; Bedford Stuyvesant Restoration Corp, dir of emplymnt 1969-79; OIC of NY, div mgr 1979-81; So Bronx Dev Org Inc, proj dir 1981-87, dir of Emplymnt & Trng; NY City Police Dept, dir victim & volunteer serv beginning 1987. **Orgs:** Exec comm Manpower Plng Cncl New York City 1975-79; comm mem Mayors Comm on Adoption 1973-75; comm mem Alexander's Dept Store Affirmative Actn Comm 1973-75; mem Rotry Clb Bklyn, NY 1975-79; mem Kappa Alpa Psi New York Chptr 1956-65. **Honors/Awds:** Natl Sci Alfred Univ, NY 1964; Fndtn Univ of Puerto Rico 1966. **Home Addr:** 8611 Great Meadow Dr, Sarasota, FL 34238.

JONES, ANTHONY WARD
Business executive, music industry manager. **Personal:** Born Aug 15, 1947, Wilmington, NC; son of Mary Elizabeth Frasier and William Jones Sr; married Linda Gunn-Jones, Dec 27, 1988; children: Marilouise Elizabeth. **Educ:** Hampton University, BS, marketing, 1969; UCLA, MBA studies. **Career:** Munch-A-Million, vice pres, marketing, 1987-89; Surface Protection Industries, manager, corporate sales, 1989-91; Universal Paints and Coatings, president, currently. **Special Achievements:** Gold and platinum records: "Car Wash," MCA Records, 1977; "In Full Bloom," Warner Bros Records, "Strikes Again," Warner Bros Records. **Business Addr:** President, Universal Paints and Coatings, 2345 New Bern Ave., Raleigh, NC 27610.

JONES, ARNOLD PEARSON
Educational administrator (retired). **Personal:** Born in Chicago, IL; son of Arnold Jones and Tommie Jones; married Joan L; children: Victoria, Arnold, Douglas. **Educ:** Western MI Univ, BS 1950; DePaul Univ, MEd 1955; Univ of IL Urbana, PhD 1972. **Career:** Chicago Public Schools, teacher, school psychologist, principal 1965, asst supt of schools 1967-69; Malcolm X Coll, vice pres acad 1969-70; Northeastern IL Univ, prof psychology, spec asst to pres 1971-78; City Colleges of Chicago, exec vice chancellor human resources & labor relations, professor emeritus. **Orgs:** Comm Human Rights Commission 1981-83; bd of dirs ACLU; mem educ task force Chicago Urban League; life mem NAACP; mem educ core comm Chicago United; mem Alpha Phi Alpha; past natl pres Amer Bridge Assoc, Natl Assoc of Affirm Action; mem school bd nominating comm City of Chicago. **Honors/Awds:** Phi Beta Kappa. **Military Serv:** AUS capt 2 yrs. **Business Addr:** Executive Vice Chancellor, City Colleges of Chicago, 226 West Jackson, Chicago, IL 60601.

JONES, ARTHUR
Government official. **Career:** Executive Office of the President, Press Office, deputy press secretary, currently. **Business Phone:** (202)456-2580.

JONES, ASBURY PAUL
Clergyman. **Personal:** Born Sep 23, 1914, Lynchburg, VA; married Annie Marie Holt; children: Annette, Paul Jr, Anita, Marion. **Educ:** Conroe Normal Indsl Coll, BTh 1955, BD 1958; Linfield Coll, DD 1974. **Career:** Sacramento Br Conroe Coll, prof 1953-; New Hope Bapt Ch Sacramento CA, minister 1955-. **Orgs:** Dean of Christian Educ St John Dist BTU Sunday Sch Cong 1957-68; pres of cong St John Dist BTU Sunday Sch Cong 1968-77; first vice pres CA Baptist State Convention 1970-. **Honors/Awds:** First Black Chaplain appointed CA Senate 1973. **Military Serv:** AUS sgt t/4 3 yrs; Army Commendation Medal. **Business Addr:** Minister, New Hope Baptist Church, 3700 32nd St, Sacramento, CA 95820.

JONES, AUDREY BOSWELL
Attorney. **Personal:** Born in Dallas, TX; daughter of Alice Ellis Boswell and George Lawson Boswell; married Winfield Jones (deceased); children: Ronald. **Educ:** Univ of MN, Undergrad; TN St U, BS 1933; SW Law Sch, JD 1956; Univ of S CA, CA St, Grad Work. **Career:** Self-employed, atty at law 1958-; St of CA, welfare agt 1949-51; LA Dept Soc Srv, supvng soc wrkr 1937-52; LA Police Commn, hearing exam; Cal new car dealer board president. **Orgs:** Past pres, mem CA & New Motor Vehicle Bd 1969-; bd of dirs SE Symphony Assn, United Stroke Prog; Am Bar Assn; Langston Law Club; Black Women Lawyers; Wilshire Bar Assn; LA Co Bar Assn; arbtn panel LA Co Bar Assn; S CA Women Lawyers; mem Eastern Star; Heroine of Jericho; past Nat ofcr Alpha Kappa Alpha Sor; past pres LA Soc Wk Local AFL 1976; past ofcr Tiffany Guild Crippled Childrens Soc, Pres 12 Big Sisters; Oper of Faustine Home for Girls. **Honors/Awds:** Cert for Comm Srv, LA Hum Rel Comm; num awards & recognitions; Anheuser Busch Comm Service Award, Phillys Temple.

JONES, BARBARA ANN POSEY
Educator, educational administrator. **Personal:** Born Jun 23, 1943, Oklahoma City, OK; daughter of Alma Vertena Inglemon Posey and Weldon Burnett Posey; married Mack H Jones, Apr 1, 1964; children: Patric Lumumba, Tayari A, Bomani B. **Educ:** Univ of OK, AB 1963; Univ of IL, AM 1966; GA St U, PhD 1973. **Career:** TX Southern Univ, instructor, 1966-67; Atlanta Univ, instructor 1968-69; Clark College, prof, economics, 1971-87; Prairie View A&M Univ, head, dept of economics and finance, 1987-89, dean, college of business, 1989-. **Orgs:** Sec-treas Nat Econ Assn 1975-80; papers del at meetings of Nat Econ & Assn, Am Econ Assn, Nat Conf of Blk Pol Sci, Ind Rel Res Assn; Southern Business Administration Association, board of directors, 1992-; American Assembly of Collegiate Schools of Business, board of directors, 1994-97, Exec Committee, 1995-97, Implementation Committee of Accreditation Task Force, candidacy committee, 1992-94; bd of trst Clark Coll 1973-74, 1975-79; bd of directors, Nat Econ Assn, 1971-; bd of editorial adv, Review of Black Political Economy, 1975-; Am Econ Assn, 1983-. **Honors/Awds:** Srv in civil rights Russell Bull Award 1963; Outstnd Indep Std, Univ of OK 1963; Distinguished Professor, Delta Sigma Theta, 1981-83; Mortar Bd. **Home Addr:** 11630 Cypresswood Dr, Houston, TX 77070. **Business Addr:** Dean, Prairie View A&M University, College of Business, Po Box 638, Prairie View, TX 77446.

JONES, BEN F.
Educator. **Personal:** Born May 26, 1942, Paterson, NJ. **Educ:** William Paterson Coll, BA 1963; NY Univ, MA 1967; Pratt Inst, MFA. **Career:** Natl Conf of Art, pres 1978-80, vice pres 1981-84; Sulaimoan Dance Co, chmn of bd 1981-83; Jersey City State, prof of art. **Orgs:** Mem NJ Printmkng Cncl 1979-; mem World Printmkng Cncl 1980-; mem Natl Conf Artists; bd mem Friends of Music & Art in Hudson Co 1985; exhibited at many galleries and museums throughout the country; mem bd of advisors Woodson Foundation of NJ. **Honors/Awds:** Flwshp grant Natl Endowmnt for Arts 1974-75; flwshp grant NJ State Cncl the Arts 1977-78, 1983-84; 1st Pl & 2nd Pl in art comp Atlanta Life Ins 1982-83; Grant Jersey City State Coll 1982-83; Career Dev Awrd of Excel Passaic Cnty Coll Paterson, NJ 1984; Excellence in the Arts Delta Sigma Theta Sor 1985. **Business Addr:** Professor of Art & Artist, Jersey City State, Kennedy Blvd, Jersey City, NJ 07305.

JONES, BENJAMIN E.
Business executive. **Personal:** Born Sep 8, 1935, New York, NY; married Delcenia R; children: Leslie, Delcenia. **Educ:** Brooklyn Coll, BA 1971; Pace U, MBA 1974. **Career:** Capital Formation Inc Econ Devel Found NYC, pres 1971-; Interracial Council for Business Opportunity NYS, program dir 1971; Gen Precision Inc, sr contract admin/negotiator/signer 1966-71; ESX Div Paal Corp, accountant 1962-66; Radio Recepter Co, admin 1959-60; MBA Mgmt Consult Ins, Columbia Univ, dir 1973-. **Orgs:** Mem, Minority Business Opportunity Comm Fed Exec Bd, 1972-; bd of dir, Upper Park Ave Comm Assn Day Care Center, 1974-; mem, Amer Mgmt Assn; mem, Natl Business League; mem, Council Concerned Black Execs; mem, Natl Assn Black Mfrs; mem, Assn MBA Execs; mem, NAACP; mem, One Hundred Black Men Inc; mem, Uptown Chamber of Commerce; mem, NY Urban League; mem, Amer Assn MESBICS. **Military Serv:** USAF 1955-58. **Business Addr:** President, Minority Business Exchange, One Madison Ave, New York, NY 10010.

JONES, BERNARD H., SR.
Administrator. **Personal:** Born Feb 13, 1931, Pittsburgh, PA; married Geraldine C Johnson; children: Bernard H Jr, Hylene K, Cornell D. **Educ:** Knoxville College, BA 1957; Duquesne University, Mgmt Inst Program. **Career:** Pittsburgh's Commission of Human Relations, co-worker 1963-64; Urban Redevelopment Authority, Pittsburgh, dir community improvement 1964-68; Allegheny Conf on Community Devel, assistant dir 1968-; POISE Foundation, president and dir 1980-. **Orgs:** Urban Youth Action, Inc, founder and honorary chairman 1966; The Misters, Inc & The Misters Investment Assoc, founder and president 1967; UMP Investment Club, founder and managing partner 1973; Pittsburgh Rotory Club, member 1974-; Pittsburgh Business Resource Center, board of dir 1979-; POISE Foundation, founder, president and dir 1980; West Penn Motor Club AA, board of dir 1984-; NAACP, life member. **Honors/Awds:** Top Hat Award-New Pittsburgh Courier 1967; Natl Alliance of Business Award-NAB Washington, DC 1979; Pennsylvania NAACP State Award 1981; Man of The Year Award-Pittsburgh Gallat Ladies Club 1982. **Military Serv:** USM Private 1951. **Business Addr:** President, Poise Foundation, Allegheny Conference on Comm Devt, 423 Sixth Ave, #1000, Pittsburgh, PA 15219.

JONES, BERNIE
Journalist. **Personal:** Born Jun 21, 1952, Baltimore, MD; son of Sumoria Clacks Jones and Newbern L Jones; married Beverly Harvey (divorced 1985); children: Linsay Morgan. **Educ:** University of North Carolina, Chapel Hill, NC, AB, 1974. **Career:** Baltimore News American, asst news editor, 1980-81, night news editor, 1981-82; San Diego Union, San Diego, CA, assist news editor, 1982-85, politics editor, 1985-86, asst news editor, 1986-88, news editor, 1988-95; Opinion Pages, editor, 1995-. **Business Addr:** Editor Opinion Pages, San Diego Union-Tribune, 350 Cameno de la Reina, San Diego, CA 92108.

JONES, BERTHA DIGGS
Writer, lecturer. **Personal:** Born in Richland, GA; divorced; children: Betty Jean. **Educ:** Cen School of Business Buffalo, 1968; Columbia, personnel; POHS NY, 1967. **Career:** Diggs Assoc Urban Affairs Cons, pres; NYS Or Nation, first black sec of labor 1944-55; FEPC, consultant 1945; EEA-WDP, Supr. **Orgs:** Mem & adv com NYS Div Housing 1961-69; bus consult NYS Dept of Commerce 1970-71; sec State Labor Dept 1973-75; mem Pres Adv Counc Pace Univ NY 1966-77; mem adv council Corsi Labor/Mgmt Inst Pace Univ 1966-77; exec NYS dir Crispus Attucks Rep Lge 1938-55; statewide orgnr & exec dir State Bapt Congress 1956-69; consult to chmn Buffalo Housing Auth 1942; org first Jr Club Nat Assn Negro Bus & Professional Women NYS 1945; designed Nat Empl Pool 1946; memUrban League; NAACP; bd dir Brooklyn Chap Am Red Cross; Am Acad Polit & Soc Sci Ctr for Study of Presidency. **Honors/Awds:** Silver Cup Natl Rep Council 1948; Sojourner Truth Award 1964; Meritorious Serv Award State Amer Legion Unit; Serv Award Visiting Nurse Assn of Brooklyn 1967-69; cert of serv NYS Labor Dept 1975; Comm Serv Award, Woman of Year Philadelphia Church of Universal Brotherhood 1977; author Home & Family Seminars 1956; continuous publ newsletters 1935-77; natl hon mem Lambda Kappa Mu Sor.

JONES, BERTHA H.
Educator. **Personal:** Born Oct 30, 1918, Earle, AR; married Joseph R; children: Malcolm. **Educ:** Illinois State Univ, BE; Ball State Univ, MA; Northwestern Univ; Michigan Univ; Loyola Univ; Indiana Univ; Northwest and Purdue Univ. **Career:** Gary Public Schools Educational Talent Search, dir 1969-; speech teacher 1951-56; English tchr 1956-59; counselor 1959-69. **Orgs:** IN Proj Dir & Assoc chrm v chrm; IN Pers and Guidance Assoc; Am Pers and Guidance Assoc Dele from IN; adv bd for IN Univ Northwest Campus; spec serv Midwest Assoc Stu Fin Aid Admin; Upward Bound adv bd Metro Corps OEO Delegate Agcy bd dir; Delta Sigma Theta; YWCA Teen Comm bd dir; Van Buren Bapt Ch; Urban League Consumer Ed Task Force IN U. **Honors/Awds:** Award of serv to students 1974; IN Pers and Guidance Assoc Merit Award in Guidance 1973; elected Supreme 1st Anti-basileus of Nat Sorority of Phi Delta Kappa 1969, 1971; Pi Lambda Theta; Hnr Soc for Women in Ed 1961. **Business Addr:** 2131 Jackson St, Gary, IN 46407.

JONES, BETTY JEAN T.
Educator. **Personal:** Born Jul 14, 1943, Charleston, SC; daughter of Helen Grant Tolbert and Fred W. Tolbert; married Donald W. Jones, Nov 27, 1965; children: Tracey. **Educ:** Hampton Inst VA, BS 1965; Fairfield Univ CT, MA 1970; Univ of VA, EdD, 1990. **Career:** University of Virginia, Charlottesville, VA, clinical instructor, 1986-; Charlottesville HS VA, biology tchr VA 1974-86; Lane HS, tchr 1973-74; Charlottesville HS, tchr 1974-; Fairfield U, grad study 1968-69; Dolan Jr HS CT, sci tchr 1965-68; Charlottesville High School, Science Dept, chairperson, 1994-. **Orgs:** Mem Charlottesville Educ Assn bd dir 1974-; Am Assn of Univ Women 1970-; Nat Assn of Biology Tchr 1965-; VA Assn of Sci Tchr 1973-; Nat Educ Assn; participant Parent-Edn Conf Univ of VA; mem Alpha Kappa Mu; Beta Kappa Chi Nat Honor Soc; Delta Sigma Theta Sorority; treas Barret Day Care Center bd 1973-; American Assn for Higher Education, 1973-; American Assn for Higher Education Black Caucus, 1973-; Kappa Delta Pi; Friends Within; Junior League of Charlottesville; Family Service Bd of Charlottesville; Virginia Science Leadership Assn; Emergency Food Bank of Charlottesville, bd. **Honors/Awds:** Martin Luther King Fellow; Charlottesville Public Schools Outstanding Educator Award.

JONES, BILLY EMANUEL
Physician, city official. **Personal:** Born Jun 11, 1938, Dayton, OH; son of Callie Jones and Paul Jones; children: Alexander. **Educ:** Howard U, BS 1960; Meharry Med Coll, MD 1965; New York Medical College, residency in psychiatry 1966-69; New York University, Robert Wagner Graduate School of Public Service, MS, 1990. **Career:** Metropolitan Hospital CMHC, asst dir 1971-73; Coney Island Hosp Dept Psychiatry, assoc dir 1973-74; Fordham Hospital Dept Psychiatry, dir 1974-77; NYMC/Lincoln Hosp Dept of Psychiatry, dir 1977-90; New York City Department of Mental Health, Mental Retardation and Alcoholism Services, commissioner 1990-; NYMC/Lincoln Medical and Mental Health Center, Department of Psychiatry, 1977-88, medical director, 1988-90; NYC Health and Hospitals Corp., president, 1992-. **Orgs:** Pres Black Psychiatrists of Amer 1978-80; prof of Psych NY Med Coll 1985-90; fellow Amer Psychiatric Assn 1983-; diplomate Amer Bd of Psychiatry and-Neurology 1977-; mem New York City Comm Serv Bd 1980-90; mem NYS Alcohol Drug Abuse & Mental Health Block Grant Comm 1983-90; mem 100 Black Men. **Honors/Awds:** "Manic Depressive Illness Among Poor Urban Blacks" Amer Journ of Psych Vol 138#9 May, 1981; "Survey of Psychotherapy with Black Men" Amer Journ of Psych Vol 139 #9 Sept, 1982. **Military Serv:** AUS Major served 2 yrs 1969-71. **Business Addr:** Health Care Consultant, Private Practice of Psychiatry, 56 Hamilton Terrace, New York, NY 10031.

JONES, BOBBY
Educator. **Personal:** Born Feb 28, 1933, New York, NY; married Dolores; children: Lisa, Ivan. **Educ:** Morehouse Coll, AB 1953; Columbia U, MA 1957; Univ of GA, EdD 1973. **Career:** Mercer Univ, chmn educ dept 1972-; Upward Bound Mercer Univ, dir 1970-72; Bib Cty School System, curriculum dir 1968-70; Ballard-Hudson Sr High, teacher 1963-68; Mercer Univ, dir math workshop 1975-79. **Orgs:** Mem GAE.

JONES, BOBBY M.
Professional baseball player. **Personal:** Born Apr 11, 1972, Orange, NJ. **Career:** Colorado Rockies, pitcher, 1997-. **Business Addr:** Professional Baseball Player, Colorado Rockies, 1700 Broadway, Ste 2100, Denver, CO 80290, (303)292-0200.

JONES, BONNIE LOUISE
Attorney, judge. **Personal:** Born Feb 3, 1952, Philadelphia, PA; daughter of Thelma Mills Jones and William Smith Jones. **Educ:** Lincoln Univ, BA 1970; NC Central Univ School of Law, JD 1982. **Career:** VA Legal Aid Soc, law clerk 1982-83; Newport News Police Dept, permits examiner 1983-85; Hampton Roads Regional Acad of Criminal Justice, training/evaluation specialist 1985-86; Blayton Allen & Assocs, assoc attorney 1986-88; self-employed atty Hampton VA, 1988-; McDermott, Roe & Sons, 1992-96; College of William and Mary, School of Law, adj prof, 1994-97; Hampton Gen Dist Court, judge, 1996-. **Orgs:** Mem Phi Alpha Delta Law Fraternity 1982-; mem Big Brother/Big Sisters of Peninsula 1985; mem

Amer & VA Bar Assocs 1986; mem Assoc of Trial Attorneys of Amer; mem PA Bar Assn 1987-; Hampton Bar Assn 1988-92; council vice pres Intl Training in communication council II 1988-89; Commission in Chancery for the Hampton Circuit Courts; Girls, Inc of The Greater Peninsula, former president board of directors. **Honors/Awds:** Commendation for 5 city talent show from Committee for Educ of Gifted Students Hampton School System 1979; on-air attorney for WAVY Channel 10 Midday TV program 1990-96; series of lectures to Chinese lawyers, journalists, and economists at Hampton Univ on practicing law as a minority in Amer; on-air atty for WVEC Channel 13, midday, 1987-92. **Business Addr:** Hampton Gen Dist. Ct., P.O. Box 70, Hampton, VA 23669.

JONES, BOOKER TEE, SR.

Association executive. **Personal:** Born Jun 30, 1939, Mesic, NC; son of Mary Jones and Hezekiah Jones; married Loretta Johnson; children: Hilda Davis, Booker T Jr, Marietta, Coretta. **Educ:** LaSalle Ext Univ, AA, acct, 1959; Central Appraiser Soc, real estate appr designation 1971; Natl Center for Housing Mgmt, housing mgmt certificate 1981. **Career:** Kingsborough Realty Inc, real estate salesman 1963-67; One Stop Home Sales Co, owner, broker, appraiser 1967-74; Booker T Jones Real Estate Brokers, president, real estate broker, 1972-; Department of HUD, real estate appraiser, 1972-73; Costal Progress Inc, coordinator, admin 1977-80; Twin Rivers Opportunity Inc, housing dir 1980-85, exec dir 1985-. **Orgs:** President United Communities Assn Net Inc 1975-85; bd of dir, Craven County Fed Credit Union 1979-82; vice chmn of bd Pamlico County Bd of Ed 1980-85; chmn of bd of dir NC Section 8 Housing Assn Inc 1984-85, bd mem 1985-; Pamlico County Planning Board, appointee, 1991; Low Income Housing Task Force, New Bern, NC, appointee, 1991; Costal Community Development Corp., board of directors, chairman, 1991; NC Housing Finance Agency, bd of dirs, 1994-; Appointed by NC Governor to mem of NC Housing Finance Agency, board of directors, 1994. **Honors/Awds:** Outstanding Serv The United Way 1977; Leadership Training the Natl Citizen Participation Council Inc 1979; NC Governor's Appointment Pamlico Cty Transp Efficiency 1982; Exemplarary Serv NC Sect 8 Housing Assoc Inc 1984; appointed to local advisory committee, 1988-; advisory board, North Carolina Dept of HUD, 1988-; Twin Rivers Opportunities Inc, Outstanding Service Award, 1989-90, 15 Year Employment Longevity Honor, 1992; Congresswoman Eve Clayton, Congressman Mel Watts, and North Carolina Governor Jim Hunt, Distinguished Guest Honors, 1991. **Home Addr:** PO Box 68, Grantsboro, NC 28529.

JONES, BRENT M.

Photographer, educator, journalist. **Personal:** Born Feb 11, 1946, Chicago, IL; married Ingrid. **Educ:** Columbia Coll, BA 1969. **Career:** Chicago Art Inst, tchr 1976-; freelance photographer & writer; Black Associated Enterprises, chief photographer 1970-73; Columbia Coll, instr creative writing; 1969-70; one-man exhibitions; US Rep; 2nd World Black & African Festival of Arts & Culture; photos from FESTAC Ebony; Opportunity Industrialization Training Cntr, English instr & asst dir pub relations 1969-70. **Honors/Awds:** Management Mag contrib ed 1969-70; article Tribune Mag. **Business Addr:** 540 N Lake Shore Dr, Chicago, IL.

JONES, BRIAN KEITH

Professional football player. **Personal:** Born Jan 22, 1968, Iowa City, IA. **Educ:** Texas. **Career:** Indianapolis Colts, linebacker, 1991; New Orleans Saints, 1995-. **Business Addr:** Professional Football Player, New Orleans Saints, 5800 Airline Hwy, Metairie, LA 70003, (504)733-0255.

JONES, BUTLER ALFONSO

Educator, sociologist. **Personal:** Born Jul 22, 1916, Birmingham, AL; son of Nettie B Jones and Jackson C Jones; married Lillian E Webster, Dec 27, 1939 (died 1978). **Educ:** Morehouse Coll, AB 1937; Atlanta Univ, AM 1938; NYU, PhD 1955. **Career:** Atlanta Univ Lab Schools, teacher 1938-42; Talladega Coll, prof Social Science 1943-52; OH Wesleyan Univ Delaware, assoc prof sociology 1952-69; Cleveland State Univ, prof dept sociology 1969-, chmn 1969-76; Oberlin Coll, visiting prof 1962-63; Hamline Univ, 1966-67. **Orgs:** Mem Ohio Valley Social Soc; Soc for Applied Anthropology; Amer Soc Assn; Soc for Study Social Problems; Assn for Study of Negro Life & History; conducted extensive soc rsch on effectiveness of law in directing social change. **Honors/Awds:** Phi Beta Kappa; Alpha Kappa Delta (sociology).

JONES, CALDWELL

Professional basketball player. **Personal:** Born Aug 4, 1950, Mc Gehee, AR. **Educ:** Albany State Coll. **Career:** Philadephia 76ers, 1976-82, Houston Rockets, 1982-83, Chicago Bulls, 1984-85, Portland Trail Blazers, 1986-89, San Antonio Spurs, 1989-90. **Honors/Awds:** Set a new career high in free throw percentage hitting (837) from the line.

JONES, CALVIN BELL

Visual artist, painter. **Personal:** Born Jan 7, 1934, Chicago, IL; son of Kathryn Elizebeth Bell Jones and Melvin Jones; married Irene Tabron Jones, Dec 12, 1953 (divorced); children: Bryon Eugene Jones. **Educ:** Art Inst Univ of Chicago, BA drawing/paint/illus 1957. **Career:** AFAM Creative & art dir Hallmark Card Inc adv sals promo 1960-62; Gallery Studio & Cultural Cntr, co-dir 1970-75; Tuesday Publs (Sunday Supplement), illustrator 1970-75; Black Book Bulletin-Third World Press, creative & art dir 1971-73; Chicago Mural Project Group, master muralist 1976-80; Chicago Tribune Magazine, illustrator 1977-78; C Jones Inc, painter/illustrator, currently. **Orgs:** Painter/illust Coca Cola (famous Black Amer series) 1976; painter/artist Motorola (50th yrs); Natl Conf of Artist Coord of Regions 1983-85; mem Natl Conf of Artist 1970-80; visual artist/cons Ebony Talent Creative Arts Found 1977-80; US Rep/delegate Intl Arts & Cultural Festac 1977; Mural Commission Competition, The National Black Arts Festival, 1990; Beefeater Collection "Art of Good Taste" 1992. **Honors/Awds:** Builders Award Third World Press 1977; Natl Endowment (Mural Painting Grant) Natl Endowment of the Arts 1978-79; Aaron Douglas Muralist Award Natl Conf of Artist 1979 & 1983; Artist in Residence Univ of IL Urbana 1980; Achievement Award in the Arts Kappa Alpha Psi 1988; 24' X 125' Mural "Bright Moments-Memories of the Future" 1987; mural commission competition, The Natl Black Arts Festival, 1990; Beefeater Collection, Art of Good Taste, 1992.

JONES, CARL

Clothing company executive. **Personal:** Born in Tennessee. **Career:** Designers Screen Printing, founder, 1982-85; Surf Fetish, founder, 1985-90; Cross Colours Clothing, president, 1990-94, sold in 1994, founder moved into licensing. **Honors/Awds:** Co. is ranked #80 on Black Enterprise magazine's list of top 100 industrial/service companies.

JONES, CARL L.

Association executive. **Personal:** Born Jan 21, 1933, Elmore City, OK; married Leontine. **Educ:** Langston U, BS 1954; OK State U, grad study 1957; Washington U, 1967, 1970. **Career:** Langston U, accountant 1954-55, chief accountant, asst bus mgr 1956-61, dir pub relations 1961-66; IBM, adminstr Staff 1966-67; St Louis Human Devel Corp, asst comptroller 1967-73; Urban League St Louis, controller 1973-; Kingsway Merchants Assoc, exec dir 1981-86; St Louis Oppty Industrialization Ctr, exec dir 1987-. **Orgs:** Mem Nat Assn Black Accountants; Am Accounting Assn mem Union Memorial United Meth Ch; Omega Psi Phi Frat keeper of finance; Nat Budget Com 1973; Frontiers Club Internat; commr St Louis Area Council Boy Scouts Am; life mem NAACP. **Honors/Awds:** Award of Excellence St Louis Human Devel Corp 1969; Cert for Outstanding Alumni for Lincoln HS Chickasha OK. **Military Serv:** AUS reserves 1958-64.

JONES, CAROL JOYCE

Community activist. **Personal:** Born May 4, 1938, Detroit, MI; daughter of Victoria Shelton Thomas (deceased) and Leroy Thomas Sr; married Lindell Jones, Jul 31, 1965; children: Millicent Ann, Derik Lindell, LaRese, Milada Velice. **Career:** Blue Cross-Blue Shield, Detroit, MI, stenographer, 1956-59; Central Methodist Church, Detroit, MI, secretary, 1959-63; Zwerdling, Miller, Klimist & Maurer, Detroit, MI, legal secretary, 1963-66; Wayne State Univ, Detroit, MI, executive secretary, 1966-80; Edsel & Eleanor Ford House, Grosse Pte, MI, docent, 1983-; Detroit East CMHC, Detroit, MI, executive secretary, 1989-; Detroit East Committee MEntal Health Center, executive secretary, 1989-91; Highland Park Community College, executive secretary to the president, 1992. **Orgs:** President, Church Women United of Detroit, 1989-; member, CWU of Michigan, 1985-; member, board of directors, Southeastern Area of American Baptist Churches of Michigan, 1984-; member, board of directors, Christian Communications Council of Metro Detroit Churches, 1985-; Host "Open Doors", WDIV-TV, 1989-; Volunteer, Cottage Hospice of Grosse Pointe, 1983-.; mem at large, North American Baptist Women's Union, 1992-97; mem at large, Church Women United Common Council, 1992-96. **Honors/Awds:** Take Time to Care, Detroit Lions Club #1, 1991; National Coalition of 100 Black Women, Detroit Chapter Community Service Award, 1991; Valiant Woman Award, Church Women United of Detroit, 1993. **Home Addr:** 10470 E Outer Dr, Detroit, MI 48224.

JONES, CAROLINE ROBINSON

Advertising executive. **Personal:** Born Feb 15, 1942, Benton Harbor, MI; daughter of Mattie Robinson and Ernest Robinson; children: Anthony. **Educ:** Univ of MI, BA 1963. **Career:** Benton Harbor News Palladium, writer; J Walter Thompson, copywriter 1963-68; Zebra Assoc, vp, co-creat dir 1968-70; Kenyon & Eckhardt Advt, sr copywriter 1970-72; Black Creative Group, creative dir 1972-75; Batten Barton Durstine Osborn Advt, vice pres creat suprv 1975-77; Mingo-Jones Advertising Inc, exec vp, creative dir, 1977-87; Caroline Jones Inc, pres 1987-. **Orgs:** Bd mem, Women's Forum, Long Island University, Ad Council, NY City Partnership, The Smithsonian Ctr of Advertising History, NY State Banking; mem Advertising Women of New York, Committee of Zoo; lecturer Advertising & Mktg Cons; host "In the Black, Keys to Success," WOR-TV New York; Wall Street Journal "Creative Leaders" Campaign. **Honors/Awds:** 1st Black female vice pres of major advertising agency; 100 Outstanding Creative People in Amer 1976, 1997; Foremost Women in Commun 1971; Matrix Awd 1982; Clio Awds, CEBA Awards; Numerous Anny Awds; WPIX Film Awd; Intl Radio & TV Soc Awd; Ford Motor Co Creative; Publ "Living Legends in Black" Bicen Trib 1977; Advertising Copywriter Kiplinger Press 1977; Contrib ed, num advertising trade publ & Black mags; 100 Black Women Achievement Awd 1975; Links Inc of Westchester Awd 1975; Natl Assoc of Bus & Professional Women Awd 1975; Advertising Women of the Year, 1990; Ellis Island Medal of Honor, 1997. **Business Addr:** President/CEO, Caroline Jones Inc, 641 Lexington Ave, Fl 21, New York, NY 10022-4503, (212)754-9191.

JONES, CAROLYN

Professional basketball player. **Personal:** Born Jul 28, 1969. **Educ:** Auburn Univ. **Career:** New England Blizzard, guard, 1996-. **Business Addr:** Professional Basketball Player, New England Blizzard, 179 Allyn St, Ste 403, Hartford, CT 06103, (860)522-4667.

JONES, CAROLYN G.

Consultant. **Personal:** Born Aug 5, 1943, Chattanooga, TN; daughter of Paralee Johnson Goolsby and Clyde Goolsby; married Edward G Jones, Nov 26, 1980; children: Larketta, Harry Charles, Arthur, Edward Lee. **Educ:** Emory Univ of Atlanta, BS 1976. **Career:** Metro Hosp West, dir of med records 1972-74; Erlanger Alton Park Hlth Cntr, administ asst 1974-76; Chattanooga State Comm Coll, prog dir 1976-81; CJ Enterprises, Inc, pres. **Orgs:** Chrpers Ed Comm Chatta Area Med Rec Cncl 1984-85; chrpers Publ Rel CAMRC 1983-84; mem By-Laws Comm TMRA 1983-84; co-dir Nursing Guild Hawkinsville Bapt Ch 1984-85; mem Chatt Minority Busn Dev 1984; mem Chamber of Commerce; chair Political Actia Committee, National Coalition of 100 Black Women Chatt Chapter; Chatt Area Urban League; Chatt Leadership Grad; mem National Assn of Community Health Centers; mem Hawkinsville Missionary Baptist Church. **Honors/Awds:** Woman of the Year Glenwood Busn & Professional Women's Club 1982; Outstanding Achievement Off of Minority Busn Devel 1983; Service Busn Award Chatt Minority Busn Busn 1984; Entp of the Year 1985; House Resolution No 1 TN House of Representatives 1986; Business of the Year, Urban League 1987; Hamilton County Minority Small Business Person Award, Small Business Adm, 1990; Small Business Person of the Year, Chamber of Commerce, 1990; Chatt "Women of Distinction", 1997; ATHENA Award; Jane Cozby Henderson "Woman of Achievement"; Adm Award for Excellence 304-1063; Heroes of Public Housing; "Fifteen Women That Make A Difference;" Women in Business Advocate of the Year Award. **Home Addr:** 324 Willow Glen Rd., Chattanooga, TN 37421. **Business Addr:** President, CJ Enterprises, Inc, 7010 Lee Highway, Ste 214, Chattanooga, TN 37421.

JONES, CASEY C.

State representative, insurance company executive. **Personal:** Born Jun 15, 1915, Princeton, KY; son of Clarence Jones; married Lovell; children: Casey, Jr, Leverne, Clarence, Sarah, Bill, Marsha, Curtis, George, Marilyn. **Educ:** Graduate Knoxville Coll; attended Univ of Toledo. **Career:** Co Govt exp; Casey Jones Ins Agy, owner; Lucas Co, personnel dir 1966-68; Lucas Co Child Center, pupil personnel dir & dir Rec 1968-69; Lucas Co, sanitary engr insp 1949-66; IN YMCA, gen prog sec 1960-66; state representative, currently; State appointed chmn Local Government; Rules Comm, Finance Comm. **Orgs:** Mem Public Pers Assn Am; Nat Soc State Legislators; Nat Council State Govt; exec bd mem A Philip Randolph Inst; bd mem equal opport planning assn Sec Black Elected Democrats OH; grand lodge officer IBPOE W Elks; mem Nat bd of Gov Cncl of State Governments; bd mem Black Clearing House Elected Officials; trustee Model Cities bd mem Comm Health Planning Council Northwestern OH; hon mem OH Dental Soc; sec Black Elected Democrats of Ohio 1974-; chmn Central Coordinating Committee Lucas County; vice chmn Lucas County Democratic Party; chmn House of Representatives Local Govt Comm. **Honors/Awds:** Outstanding Legislator Award by OH Assn Public Sch Employees; OH youth comm Cert Outstanding Leadership; amateur & professional basketball & softball player; Hall of Fame Scott High School; Harlem Globe Player; Black Legislator of the Year Award; Legislator of the Year, Dental Society Education Dept. **Business Addr:** State Representative, 45th House District, 355 Pinewood Ave, Toledo, OH 43602.

JONES, CEDRIC

Professional football player. **Personal:** Born Apr 30, 1974, Houston, TX; son of Annette Jones. **Educ:** Univ of Oklahoma. **Career:** New York Giants, defensive end, 1996-. **Honors/Awds:** The Sporting News, All-America first team, 1995. **Business Addr:** Professional Football Player, New York Giants, Giants Stadium, East Rutherford, NJ 07073, (201)935-8111.

JONES, CEDRIC DECORRUS

Marketing executive. **Personal:** Born Jun 1, 1960, Norfolk, VA. **Educ:** Duke Univ, AB, history and political science, 1982. **Career:** New England Patriots, wide receiver, 1982-90; Independent Sports Radio Network, expert analyst, 1989-91; H B Hadley & Associates, financial consultant, 1992-93; NFL Properties Inc, manager of youth programs, 1993-94, senior manager of club marketing services, 1994-. **Orgs:** NFL Youth Development Task Force. **Honors/Awds:** Roxbury Comprehensive

Community Health Center, Man of the Year, 1987. **Special Achievements:** Member of 1985 AFC Championship team; played in Super Bowl XX against the Chicago Bears. **Business Addr:** Senior Mgr, Club Marketing, NFL Properties Inc, 410 Park Ave, New York, NY 10022.

JONES, CHARISSE MONSIO
Journalist. **Personal:** Born Sep 2, 1965, San Francisco, CA; daughter of Jean Stephanie Laing Jones and Charles Milton Jones. **Educ:** University of Southern California, Los Angeles, CA, BA (cum laude), 1987. **Career:** Wave Newspaper, Los Angeles, CA, intern, 1985; Los Angeles Herald Examiner, Los Angeles, CA, reporter, 1986-88; Los Angeles Times, Los Angeles, CA, reporter, 1989-93; New York Times, reporter, 1993-. **Orgs:** Board member, Black Journalists Association of Southern California, 1989-93; member, National Association of Black Journalists, 1986-; member, Golden Key Honor Society, 1984-; USC Mentor Program, 1990-93. **Honors/Awds:** Los Angeles Press Club Award, for riot coverage, 1992; Co-writer one of 10 stories to win 1993 Pulitzer Prize for riot coverage; finalist for Livingston Award, 1993. **Business Addr:** Reporter, New York Times, 229 W 43rd St, New York, NY 10036.

JONES, CHARLES
Professional basketball player. **Personal:** Born Apr 3, 1957, McGehee, AR. **Educ:** Albany State, 1979. **Career:** Played in CBA, 1979-80, 1982-85; played in Italy, 1981-82; Philadelphia 76ers, 1984; San Antonio Spurs, 1984; Chicago Bulls, 1984; Washington Bullets, 1985-93; Detroit Pistons, 1994; Houston Rockets, 1995-. **Honors/Awds:** All-Metro Conf second team; conf player of week twice. **Business Addr:** Professional Basketball Player, Houston Rockets, 10 Greenway Plaza, Houston, TX 77046, (713)627-0600.

JONES, CHARLES, JR.
Educator. **Personal:** Born May 12, 1946, Bronx, NY; son of Mae Jones and Charles Jones; married Linda Marie Coggshall. **Educ:** BS 1969; MS 1972; PhD candidate Columbia Univ. **Career:** Central CT State Univ, grad asst 1970-72, dir of educ opportunity program & asst basketball coach 1970-, dir educational support services; dir athletics, 1994-. **Orgs:** Mem Hartford Bd of Approved Umpires 1969; mem Kappa Delta Pi 1970; coord Annual Thanksgiving Food Drive for Deprived Families in New Britain Area 1970-; mem Natl Assoc of Basketball Coaches 1970-; mem CT State Employees Assoc 1970-; bd trustees Catholic Family Serv Assoc 1971-; CT Commn for Higher Educ Accrediting Team 1972; coord the making of film demonstrating aspects of educ opport program 1973; faculty adv Ebony Choral Ensemble 1974-75; bd trustees CT Yankee Girl Scouts; pres (basic) Black Admin Staff Instr at Central; field reader govt grants; Phi Delta Kappa Sect Conn Assoc Educ Oppors Prog; coord Minority Youth Business Conference; FAC advisor Junior Class, PEP dancers; vice pres Connecticut Assn Educ Opportunity Personnel; faculty advisor Senior Class,bd directors CCSU Alumni; pres, CT Assn Educ Opportunity Prog, 1991-92; NEAEOPP, tresurer, 1992. **Honors/Awds:** Co-host cable TV series ''Pioneers''; Minority Alumni Awd; Afro-Amer Organization Student Awd; Puerto Rican Union Recognition Awd; Harrison J Kaiser Alumni Service Award, Central Connecticut State Univ, 1989; Advisor of the Year, Central Connecticut State University, 1990-91; Distinguished Service Award, 1991-92; Originator, Endowed Scholarship Fund for Disadvantaged Students. **Business Addr:** Director Athletics, Central Connecticut State Univ, 1615 Stanley St, New Britain, CT 06050, (860)832-3038.

JONES, CHARLES A.
Educator. **Personal:** Born Sep 25, 1934, Brooklyn; married; children: David, Kevin, Michael, Jason. **Educ:** Coll Ozarks Clarksville AR, BA 1958; Fordham Univ NY, MSW 1964; Univ MI Ann Arbor, PhD 1977. **Career:** Univ TX, dir social work prog; Univ of MI, asst prof 1971-79; Antioch Coll, extramural assn 1970-71; Antioch Coll Yellow Springs OH, assoc dir 1969-71; Office of Economic Opportunity Chicago, reg admin 1969; Vista Chicago 1967-69; Office of Economic Opportunity Washington DC, program devel assoc 1966-69. **Orgs:** Vista Wash DC 1965-67; housing consult New York City Housing Authority 1965-66; NY Social Investigator 1958-60 Human Svcs; mem Acad Cert Social Workers; Nat Assn Comm Devel; chmn Continuing Ed Task Force; NABSW 1979; del NASW Del Asmbly Huron Valley 1979; mem Nat Conf Planning Com; NCSW 1979; mem NABSW/CSWE/AAUP/NACD/MLHS/AEA/USA/NASW/TABPHE. **Honors/Awds:** Finalist Danforth Fellow; various local community citations for communioty serv. **Military Serv:** AUS e-5 1955-56.

JONES, CHARLES D. (C. D)
State senator. **Personal:** Born Mar 25, 1950; married Carol Charles. **Educ:** Southern University, BA, JD; University of Illinois, MA; US Army Institute for Administration. **Career:** Asst dist attorney, 1976-79; State of Louisiana, state representative, dist 17, beginning 1980, state senator, dist 34, currently; attorney, currently. **Orgs:** Louisiana Bar Association; Northern Louisiana Legal Assistance Corp; Louisiana Sickle Cell Anemia Association, board of directors, currently. **Military Serv:** US Army Reserves, capt. **Business Addr:** Senator, State of Louisiana, PO Box 3043, Monroe, LA 71210, (318)325-2644.

JONES, CHARLIE
Professional football player. **Personal:** Born Dec 1, 1972, Hanford, CA. **Educ:** Fresno State, speech communications major. **Career:** San Diego Chargers, wide receiver, 1996-. **Business Addr:** Professional Football Player, San Diego Chargers, Qualcomm Stadium, 9449 Friars Rd, San Diego, CA 92108, (619)280-2111.

JONES, CHERYL ARLEEN
Television programmer. **Personal:** Born Sep 2, 1963, Portsmouth, VA; daughter of Donna R & Maxwell Jones. **Educ:** Virginia Polytechnic Institute & State Univ, BA, 1986. **Career:** Discovery Networks, mgr, daytime programming, 1986-91, sr account mgr, 1991-93; Discovery Pictures, sr account mgr, 1993-96; Discovery Channel Pictures, director program management, 1996-. **Orgs:** Natl Academy of Cable Programming, 1986-; Natl Academy of Televison Arts & Sciences, 1988-; International Documentary Assn, 1990-; Museum of Broadcasting, 1992-; Amer Women In Radio & Television, mem, prog, committee, 1991-92; Women in Cable, 1987-92; Big Sister of the Wash, Metropolitan Area, big sister, 1992-. **Business Addr:** Senior Account Mgr, Discovery Communications, Inc/Discovery Pictures, 7700 Wisconsin Ave, Bethesda, MD 20814, (301)986-1999.

JONES, CHESTER
Federal official, law enforcement executive (retired). **Personal:** Born Nov 10, 1925, Louisville, KY; son of Robert & Esther Jones (deceased); married Katherine C Jones, Jun 30, 1955; children: Kim Joan Wallace, Chestina K Jones. **Educ:** Bellarmine College, BS, 1982; University of Louisville, MS, 1984. **Career:** Louisville Sand & Gravel, truck owner/operator, 1946-48; US Postal Svc, mail clerk, 1946-71, postal manager, 1971-80; Jefferson County Sheriff's Office, 1982-94. **Orgs:** National Alliance of Postal Supervisors, 1971-; Fraternal Order of Police, 1982-; National Sheriff's Association, 1982-; Alpha Phi Sigma National Criminal Justice Honor Society, 1982-; Veterans of Foreign Wars, 1996-. **Honors/Awds:** National Honor Society, 1984. **Military Serv:** US Navy, Seaman 1-C, 1944-46; Victory Medal; American Area Camp Medal; Asiatic-Pacific Area Camp Medal. **Home Addr:** 500 Brook Stone Way, Louisville, KY 40202, (502)245-7014.

JONES, CHESTER RAY
Attorney. **Personal:** Born Nov 9, 1946, Jackson, MS; son of River Lee Clark Jones (deceased) and William Jones, Sr (deceased); married Queen Jackson; children: Jaala, Heddie Rabekah. **Educ:** Tougaloo Coll, BA Sociology 1968; MS Coll Sch of Law, JD 1978; Harvard Univ Grad Sch of Educ, Inst on Employment and Training Admin summer 1981. **Career:** Abbott House Irvington-on-Hudson NY, child care worker 1968; Republic of Philippines, peace corps volunteer 1968-70; Governor's Office of Job Devel & Training, equal employment opportunity 1978-85; MS State Dept of Public Welfare staff attorney 1988-89; MS State Dept of Human Services sr attorney 1989-. **Orgs:** Mem MS State Bar Assn 1979; mem Magnolia Bar Assn 1985-; mem Hinds County Bar Assn 1979; mem Amer Trial Lawyers Assn 1979; Alpha Phi Alpha Frat Inc 1965; mem natl Inst for Empl Equity 1982; mem Amer Legion (Post 214) 1984; mem The Natl Urban League 1984. **Honors/Awds:** Harvard Univ's Institute on Employment and Training Admin summer 1981. **Military Serv:** US Coast Guard, 3rd class petty ofcr, 4 yrs; Good Conduct Award 1974. **Home Addr:** 154 Wimbledon Court, Jackson, MS 39206. **Business Addr:** Attorney, State Department of Human Services, PO Box 738, Brandon, MS 39042.

JONES, CHRIS (CHRISTOPHER CARLOS)
Professional baseball player. **Personal:** Born Dec 16, 1965, Utica, NY. **Career:** Cincinnati Reds, outfielder, 1991; Houston Astros, 1992; Colorado Rockies, 1993-94; New York Mets, 1995-96; San Diego Padres, 1997; Arizona Diamondbacks, 1998-. **Business Addr:** Professional Baseball Player, Arizona Diamondbacks, BankOne Ballpark, 401 E Jefferson, Phoenix, AZ 85004.

JONES, CHRIS TODD
Professional football player. **Personal:** Born Aug 7, 1971, West Palm Beach, FL. **Educ:** Miami (Fla.), bachelor's degree in criminal justice. **Career:** Philadelphia Eagles, wide receiver, 1995-. **Business Addr:** Professional Football Player, Philadelphia Eagles, 3501 S Broad St, Philadelphia, PA 19148, (215)463-2500.

JONES, CHRISTINE MILLER
Educator, government official. **Personal:** daugHter of Christine M Jones; married Robert E Jones Sr; children: Robert E Jones Jr. **Educ:** Huston Tillotson Coll Austin, TX, BA 1953; Univ TX, grad study; George Washington Univ Wash, DC, grad study. **Career:** MD State Govt, state delegate 1982-; Prince George's Co Bd of Edn, public sch teacher 1966-. **Orgs:** Mem Natl Educ Assn 1966-; mem MD State Teacher's Assn 1966-; mem Prince George's Educators Assn 1966-; mem MD Legisl Caucuses 1982-; mem Prince George Mental Hlth Assn 1980; mem Natl Conf of Christians & Jews 1976-. **Honors/Awds:** Serv Award MD State Tchrs Assn 1984; Serv Award Prince George Coalition on Black Affairs 1983; Serv Award Links Inc 1983; Serv Award Delta Sigma Theta Sor 1982. **Business Addr:** Teacher, Prince George's Co Bd Educ, 4518 Beech Rd, Temple Hills, MD 20748.

JONES, CLARA STANTON
Librarian (retired). **Personal:** Born May 14, 1913, St Louis, MO; daughter of Etta James Stanton and Ralph Herbert Stanton; married Albert Dewitt Jones, Jun 25, 1938; children: Stanton, Vinetta, Kenneth. **Educ:** Spelman College, Atlanta, GA, AB, 1934; University of Michigan, Ann Arbor, MI, ABLS, 1938. **Career:** Dillard University, New Orleans, LA, reference librarian, 1938, 1942-44; Southern University, Baton Rouge, LA, cataloger, 1940-41; Detroit Public Library, Detroit, MI, reference, branch librarian, 1944-70, director, 1970-78; University of California, Berkeley, regents lecturer, 1979-80. **Orgs:** NAACP, 1940-; Women's League for Peace and Freedom, 1950-; ACLU, 1960-; United Nations Association, 1980-; National Council of Negro Women, 1980-. **Honors/Awds:** American Library Association, Lifetime Member Award, 1983; Honorary Doctor of Humane Letters: Shaw University, Detroit, MI; North Carolina Central University, Durham, NC; St Johns University, Jamaica, NY; Pratt Institute, Brooklyn, NY; Ball State University, Muncie, IN; Grand Valley State University, Allendale, MI; Wayne State University, Detroit, MI; Northern Michigan University, Marquette, MI; Spelman College, Atlanta, GA. **Home Addr:** 325 Vernon St, #404, Oakland, CA 94610.

JONES, CLARENCE
Professional football player. **Personal:** Born May 6, 1968, Brooklyn, NY; married Shari. **Educ:** University of Maryland, attended. **Career:** New York Giants, tackle, 1991-93; St Louis Rams, 1995; New Orleans Saints, 1996-. **Business Addr:** Professional Football Player, New Orleans Saints, 5800 Airline Hwy, Metairie, LA 70003, (504)733-0255.

JONES, CLARENCE J., JR.
City government official. **Personal:** Born Apr 17, 1933, Boston, MA; son of Elizabeth Middleton and Clarence J Jones; married Wanda Hale, Sep 3, 1983; children: Meta, Nadine, Mark, Michael, Melissa, Kenneth, Mark Duane. **Educ:** Winston-Salem State NC, BS 1955; Goddard Coll, MS. **Career:** City of Boston, youth worker, 1960-65; Boston Juvenile Ct, probation officer 1965-68; City of Boston, dir youth activities commission, 1968-72, dir human rights 1972-76, dep mayor 1976-81; Boston Redevelopment Authority, chmn, bd of dirs, 1989-. **Orgs:** President Winston-Salem State Alumni; 1st vice pres Winston-Salem State Univ 1984-; chmn trustees 12th Baptist Church; bd mem Girls & Boys Clubs; board of directors, Citizenship Training Groups, Boston Juvenile Court. **Honors/Awds:** Outstanding Citizen Afro-Amer Police 1980; Outstanding Alumnus Winston-Salem State Univ 1983; Martin Luther King Jr Drum Major for Peace 1986; numerous other awards. **Military Serv:** US Army, Pfc 1955-57; Good Conduct Medal 2 yrs. **Business Addr:** Chairman, Bd of Dir, Boston Redevelopment Authority, 1 City Hall Square, Boston, MA 02201.

JONES, CLIFTON PATRICK
Librarian. **Personal:** Born May 11, 1927, Chapel Hill, NC; married Clara Baldwin; children: Michael, James, Twana, Allison. **Educ:** Univ of NC, 1962-63; Brooklyn Inst, 1964-65; Durham Tech Coll, 1965-66. **Career:** Univ of NC, various positions to library asst past 27 yrs. **Orgs:** Suprv Durham Soil & Water Conservation 1972-; pres, bd mem Amer Arthritis Assoc 1973-, NC Hemophilia Found 1980-82, Amer Psoriasis Found. **Honors/Awds:** Colonel Honorable Order of Kentucky Colonels 1976-.

JONES, CLIFTON RALPH
Educator. **Personal:** Born Oct 2, 1910, Nanticoke, MD; married Susan Elizabeth Sutton; children: Jo Ann B. **Educ:** VA Union Univ Richmond, BA 1935; Univ of IA Iowa City, MA 1939, PhD 1943; Attended, London Sch of Economics London England 1952-53; Columbia University, New York, NY, postdoctoral study, summers, 1951, 1952. **Career:** Fisk Univ Nashville, res fellow/instr 1941-43; Florida A&M Univ Tallahassee, prof of sociology 1945-46; Morgan State Univ Baltimore, prof of sociology 1946-63; Amer Univ, visiting prof 1956, 1961, 1963, 1964; Bryn Mawr Coll, 1969-70; College of Liberal Arts Howard Univ, assoc dean 1975-85; Howard Univ Washington, prof of sociology 1963-. **Orgs:** Staff mem President's Commn on Rural Poverty 1966-67; consultant US Dept of Labor 1965-66; consultant & prog mgr Franklin Inst 1969-70; consultant US Dept of the Navy 1973-75, Tech Rep Div Philco Corp. **Honors/Awds:** GEB Research Fellow, Fisk Univ, General Educ Bd, 1940-41; Rosenwalk Fellow Univ of Iowa; Amer Sociological Assoc Visiting Scholar Delaware State Coll 1972; Outstanding Scholar Delta Tau Kappa Intl Social Science Honor Soc 1975; Alpha Man of the Year Delta Lambda Chap Alpha Phi Alpha 1981; Outstanding Serv Coll of Lib Arts Howard Univ 1983. **Military Serv:** AUS t/5 1943-45; Enlisted Men's Service Ribbon 1945. **Home Addr:** 1190 W Northern Pkwy #524, Baltimore, MD 21210. **Business Addr:** Professor of Sociology, Howard Univ, 2600 6th St NW, Washington, DC 20059.

JONES, CLOYZELLE KARRELLE
Educator. **Personal:** Born in Detroit, MI. **Educ:** Wayne St U, EdD 1970. **Career:** Univ of MI, full prof 1970-; Wayne State Univ, instructor 1969-70; Detroit Public Schools, teacher 1961-68. **Orgs:** Asso Dir, treas Boys' Clubs MI Assn 1961-65; bd mem Ethnic Hertg Found 1972-; mem Chancellor's Adv Univ of MI 1970-77; fdr 1st adv Assn Black Stds Univ of MI 1970-71; chrmn Univ of MI Policy Bd Adv 1971; chrmn Spec Proj Adv Com, Univ of MI 1973-75; mem Admissions Policy Com Univ of MI 1974-75; cons, tchrcoord Det Bd of Ed 1968-77; mem, exec com Interdisciplinary Studies Div Univ of MI; mem, exec com Div of Ed Univ of MI; mem Finan Aids Bd Univ of MI 1974-77; mem Gov Inst on Talented-Gifted 1979-; mem ed com New Detroit Inc; mem Wayne St Univ Coll of Ed Alumni Bd Gov; pres Nat Urban Ed Assn 1979-81; dir Urban & Reg Studies Univ MI; coord, Spcl Needs Grad Concentration Univ MI; mem MI Cncl for Arts; Nat Conf of Assoc Urban Ed 1977;symposium; bd mem Wayne Cnty4h 1972-; mem Asso Children w Learn Disab 1972-; Asso Tchr Ed 1972-; MI Asso for Supv of Std Tchrs 1972-; exec bd mem Asso Urban Ed 1972-76; chmn Task Force 1972-; Phi Delta Kappa. **Honors/Awds:** Nat Assn for Urban Ed Harvard Prize Book Award, (schlrshp); Miller HS Alumni Assn; listed in "Leaders in Am Ed", 70th Yrbk Nat Soc for Study of Ed1971; del address Nat Conf of Asso Urban Ed 1976-78; del 2 papers Ann Conf of Black Fam in Am Univ Louisville 1977-80. **Military Serv:** AUS 1961. **Business Addr:** 4901 Evergreen Rd, Dearborn, MI 48128.

JONES, CLYDE EUGENE
Attorney. **Personal:** Born Dec 5, 1954, Birmingham, AL; son of Bennie Jones and Clyde Jones; married Julia Norment; children: Jakarra Jenise, Jasmine Jekesha. **Educ:** Knoxville Coll, BA 1976; Univ of MS, Pre Law Cleo Fellow 1976; Samford Univ Cumberland School of Law, JD 1979. **Career:** Jefferson Cty Family Court, law clerk, baliff 1979-80; 10th Judicial Circuit AL, dep dist attny 1980; 5th Judicial Circuit AL, asst dist attny 1980-84; Penick, Williams & Jones, attny partner 1985-87; private practice 1987-. **Orgs:** Senator Jr Law Class Cumberland School of Law 1977-78; law clerk Shores & Larkin 1978; student prosecutor, law clerk Jefferson Cty DA Office 1978-79; pres Young Dem of Macon Cty 1981-84; mem AEAONMS 1984-, Shriner, Mizraim Temple #119 1984-; bd of dir Magic City Bar Assoc 1985-86; vice pres Magic City Bar Assoc 1987; Vestavia-Hoover Kiwanis Club, Magic City Jaycees, Alpha Phi Chapter, Omega Psi Phi Fraternity Inc; pres, 1990, bd of dir 1991, Magic City Bar Assn; deacon 6th Ave Baptist Church. **Honors/Awds:** Basileus Omega Psi Phi 1974-76; undergrad dist rep Omega Psi Phi 1975-76; undergrad vice pres Natl Pan Hellenic Council 1975-76; hon mem Attny Gen Staff State of AL 1979; Proclamation 12/16/84 Clyde E Jones Day Mayor Tuskegee AL 1984; Leadership Birmingham 1989 Class; Leadership Birmingham Alumni Assn 1990-; 101 Black Men of Birmingham 1990. **Business Addr:** Attorney, Pythian Temple Building, 310 18th St N, Suite 3006, Birmingham, AL 35203.

JONES, COBI N'GAI
Soccer player. **Career:** Olympic athlete, soccer player, 1992; Los Angeles Galaxy, professional soccer player, starting 1996; Brazilian First Division. **Orgs:** The World Cup Team, 1994; United States National Soccer Team, 1995. **Special Achievements:** World Cup Soccer Team against Brazil, starter player, 1994.

JONES, CORNELL
City councilman. **Personal:** Born Jan 6, 1923, Paris, TN; married Dorothy Lee Jones. **Educ:** W Kentucky Trade Sch 1949. **Career:** Merit Clothing Co 1964-74; Mayfield, KY, councilman 1973-76; Ingrosoll Rand-Centac Co, 1976-. **Orgs:** Mem Christian Ch 1947-; organiz NAACP 1962 (pres 3 years); Local 2523 IAMAW; chmn Amer Legion Post 136. **Military Serv:** US Army, 1943-45; Recipient 2 Battle Stars, Normandy Beachhead 1944 & Rhine River, Germany 1945.

JONES, CURLEY C.
Librarian. **Personal:** Born Feb 23, 1941, Rossville, TN; son of Susie Palmer Jones and Cleve Jones. **Educ:** Saints Jr Coll, AA 1965; Tougaloo Coll, BA 1969; St Univ NY Geneseo, MLS 1971; Univ of UT, MEd 1975; Univ of IL, CAS 1977. **Career:** Rochester City Sch Dist Roch, NY, tchr intrn 1969-70, sub tchr 1970-72; Univ of IL, grad stdnt 1976-77; Univ of UT Marriott Libraries, librarian. **Orgs:** Life mem Amer Library Assn 1972; Mtn Plns Lib Assn 1973; UT Hist Soc & ULA 1973; life mem NAACP 1984; Association for the Study of Negro Life and History, life member. **Honors/Awds:** Contbd Chicano Bib Univ of UT 1973; contbd to Blk Bib Univ of UT 1974; Compiler of Black Bib Univ of UT 1977; Editor of Supplement to Black Bib Univ of UT 1981. **Business Addr:** Reference Librarian, Univ of Utah, Salt Lake City, UT 84112.

JONES, DAMON
Professional football player. **Personal:** Born Sep 18, 1974. **Educ:** Southern Illinois, attended. **Career:** Jacksonville Jaguars, tight end, 1997-. **Business Addr:** Professional Football Player, Jacksonville Jaguars, One Stadium Place, Jacksonville, FL 32202, (904)633-6000.

JONES, DARYL L.
State senator. **Personal:** Born Aug 31, 1955. **Educ:** Air Force Academy, Colorado Springs, CO, BS, 1977; Univ of Miami School of Law, Miami, FL, JD, 1987. **Career:** US Air Force, phantom pilot, 1977-84; 11th Circuit US Court, Judge Peter T Fav, federal judicial clerk, 1987-88; Puerto Rico National Guard, pilot, 1988-89; Dade County Attorney's Office, aviation div, 1988-90; FL House of Representatives, 1990-92; FL Senate, senator, 1992-; Dept of Air Force, secretary designate, 1998-. **Special Achievements:** First African American civilian secretary of US Air Force. **Military Serv:** US Air Force, F-4, phantom pilot, 1977-84; Puerto Rico Air National Guard, A-7D corsair II pilot, 1988-89; US Air Force Reserves, 1989-. **Business Addr:** Senator/District 40, Florida Legislature, 9300 S Dadeland Blvd, Ste 401, Miami, FL 33156, (850)487-5127.

JONES, DAVID L.
Financial services company executive. **Personal:** Born Dec 30, 1950, Charles City, VA; son of Joseph H Sr and Vernell Jones; married Pauline R Jones, Aug 20, 1983; children: Eric Anthony, Christopher David. **Educ:** Williams Coll, BA, 1974; Univ of North Carolina School of Bus, 1985; Kellogg School of Bus, Northwestern Univ, 1987, 1996. **Career:** GMAC, credit manager, 1983-85, sales mgr, 1985, asst control branch mgr, 1985-87, bus devel mgr, 1987-88, control br mgr, 1988-90, asst mgr-plans, 1991-93, vp-plans, 1993-. **Orgs:** Highland Park Comm, High School, advisory board 1994-; Credit Research Center, advisory board, Purdue Univ, 1993-; Farmington Public Schools, diversity committee, 1996; Junior Achievement of SE Michigan, board of directors, 1996; American Heart Assn, Farmington Hill, MI, bd of dirs, 1997-. **Honors/Awds:** Concerned Black Men Assn, Outstanding Role Model, 1994. **Home Addr:** 29764 Harrow Drive, Farmington Hills, MI 48331. **Business Addr:** Vice President of Plans, General Motors Acceptance Corp, 482-1X2-224, 3044 W Grand Blvd, General Motors Building, Annex 224, Detroit, MI 48202, (313)556-3618.

JONES, DAVID R.
Business executive, attorney. **Personal:** Born Apr 30, 1948, Brooklyn, NY; son of Justice & Mrs Thomas R Jones; married Dr Valerie King; children: Russell, Vanessa. **Educ:** Wesleyan Univ, BA 1970; Yale Law School, JD 1974. **Career:** US Senator Robert Kennedy, senate intern 1967; Fed Dist Judge Constance Baker Motley, law clerk 1974-75; Cravath Swaine & Moore, litigation assoc 1975-79; NY City Mayor Koch, spec advisor 1979-83; NY City Youth Bureau, exec dir 1983-86; Community Service Society of NY, pres & CEO 1986-. **Orgs:** Trustee Wesleyan Univ 1984-96, emeritus, 1996-; pres Black Agency Executives of NY 1988-94; Carver Federal Savings and Loan Association, bd mem, 1989-95, chairman of the board, 1996-; dir Jobs for the Future 1990-; NY City Health & Hospital Corp, dir, 1993-; Primary Health Care Dev Corp, vice chair, 1993-95; Black Leadership Commission on AIDS, bd, 1993; John F Kennedy School of Government, advisory bd, 1994; Barnard-Columbia Center for Leadership on Urban Public Policy, advisory bd, 1994; NY Historical Society, trustee, 1994. **Honors/Awds:** Thomas J Watson Fellow Thomas J Watson Found 1970; Honorary MA Wesleyan Univ 1982. **Business Addr:** President & Chief Executive Officer, Community Service Soc of NY, 105 E 22nd St, New York, NY 10010.

JONES, DEACON. See JONES, GROVER WILLIAM, JR.

JONES, DEBORA ELAINE
Program analyst. **Personal:** Born Nov 27, 1959, Richmond, VA; daughter of Gwendolyn Camille Vaughn Jones and Vance Howard Jones Sr. **Educ:** Douglass College, Rutgers University, New Brunswick, NJ, BA, 1982; Seton Hall University, South Orange, NJ, MPA, 1984; Howard University, Washington, DC, PhD, 1992. **Career:** Department of Commerce/International Trade Administration, Washington, DC, 1984-85; District of Columbia, City Council, Washington, DC, research assistant, 1985; Executive Office of the Mayor, Washington, DC, program research assistant, 1985-86; District of Columbia Commission for Women, Washington, DC, executive administrator aide, 1987; Congressional Youth Leadership Council, Washington, DC, advisor, 1988; National Aeronautics and Space Administration, Johnson Space Center, program analyst, 1988-. **Orgs:** Coalition of 100 Black Women, 1992; National Association for Female E xecutives 1984-; Howard University Alumni Club of Northern Virginia, 1990-; past president, Pi Sigma Alpha Political Science Honor Society, 1988-89; American Society for Public Administration, 1984-87. **Honors/Awds:** NASA Exceptional Performance Award, 1992; Howard University Graduate Fellow, 1986-89; Seton Hall University Graduate Assistant, 1982-84; Emmet E Dorsey Competitive Scholarship, Howard University, 1988; Howard University Cooperative Education Student of the Year, Howard University Co-op Program, 1991; NASA Special Service Cash Award, 1992.

JONES, DELMOS J.
Educator. **Personal:** Born Jul 12, 1936, Alabama; children: Valen, Adrian. **Educ:** San Francisco State Coll, BA 1959; Univ of AZ, MA 1962; Cornell Univ, PhD 1967. **Career:** Univ of CO, asst prof 1967-70; CUNY, assoc prof, prof 1970-. **Orgs:** Fellow Am Anthropol Assn; fellow Soc for Applied Anthrop; program chmn 29th Annual Meeting of Soc for Applied Anthrop Boulder 1970; assoc ed Human Orgn 1970-73; mem program com 70th Annual Meeting of Am Anthrop Assn NY 1971; mem com on minorities in anthropology Am Anthrop Assn 1971-73; exec bd Soc for Applied Anthrop 1972-75; prelim review panel Foreign Area Fellowship Program of Social Sci Rsch Cncl & Am Cncl of Learned Soc 1972-73; co-chmnAnnual Meet of Soc for App Anthrop Amsterdam 1974; selection com Foreign Area Fellowship Program of Soc Sci Rsch Cncl 1974-75; mem Task Panel on Mental Health of Black Am; Pres Com on Mental Health 1977; mem Com on Ability Testing Natl Acad of Sci 1977-80; mem at large Cncl on Anthrop & Educ 1979-81; mem Soc Sci TrainingReview Com HEW PHS ADAMHA NI1977-78. **Honors/Awds:** Guest Editor Reviews in Anthropology Vol 4 No 5; SE Asian Program Fellowship Cornell Univ 1962-63; Foreign Area Fellowship Program 1964-66; SE Asian Program Fellowship Cornell Univ 1967; Fulbright Fellowship Thailand 1970-71; Participant in mumerous field rsch programs & grants 1964-82; Numerous publications, 1961-. **Business Addr:** Professor, CUNY Graduate Center, 33 W 42 St, New York, NY 10036.

JONES, DELORES
Utility company manager. **Personal:** Born Apr 4, 1954, Chicago, IL; daughter of Josephine Walls Jones and Rufus Jones. **Educ:** Kent State University, Kent, OH, BA, 1976; Ohio State University, MA, 1980. **Career:** Burns Public Relations, Cleveland, OH, communications specialist, 1976; Tribue Chronicle, Warren, OH, assistant editor, 1976-79; Ohio Edison Company, Akron, OH, senior information representative, 1980-97; Kent State University School of Journalism, part-time instructor, 1989; FirstEnergy Corp, Community Support, manager, currently. **Orgs:** Public Relations Society of America, Akron Area Chapter, 1981-, board of directors, 1983-89, secretary, 1987, president, 1988; Summit County Victim Assistance Program, board of trustees, 1990-, secretary, 1991, chairperson of public relations committee, 1993-; Western Reserve Girl Scout Council, board of directors, 1989-91; National Inventor's Hall of Fame, communicatons advisory board, 1989-91; Ohio Board of Regents Economic Education Security Act Panel, 1986-90; National Technology Students Assn Advisory Board, Ohio Chapter, chairman, public relations cmte, 1987-90; National Science Teachers Association, 1983-; Ohio Crime Prevention Association, 1989-; Fallsview Psychiatric Hospital, citizen's advisory board, 1991-96; Arthritis Foundation, communications council, 1984-86; Summit Education Partnership Foundation, corporate representatives committee, 1994-; USA Today Citizens, Advisory Board, 1995-; Miracle Tutoring and Learning Center, bd of dirs, 1993-94; Kent State University School of Journalism and Mass Communications, public relations sequence advisory bd, 1994-. **Business Addr:** Manager, Community Support, First Energy Corp., 76 S Main St, Akron, OH 44308, (216)384-5022.

JONES, DEVERGES BOOKER
Marketing manager. **Personal:** Born Mar 13, 1950, Brooklyn, NY; son of Elma DeVerges Jones and Booker T Jones; married Beverly Moss, Aug 29, 1981; children: Matthew DeVerges Jones. **Educ:** Morehouse College, Atlanta GA, BA 1972; Columbia Univ, 1970; Cornell Univ, Ithaca NY, MBA 1974. **Career:** General Foods Corp, White Plains NY, assoc product mgr 1967-78, product mgr 1978-79; Clairol, Inc, New York City, product group mgr 1979-81; Pepsi-Cola USA, Purchase NY, marketing mgr of new products/bottler devel 1981, natl business planning mgr 1982-83, mgr of packaging 1983-84; sr marketing mgr 1984-86; Uniworld Group Inc, New York City, account supervisor 1986-88, vice pres/mgmt supvr 1988-. **Orgs:** Mem Assn of MBA Executives.

JONES, DONALD W.
Business executive, educator. **Personal:** Born Dec 7, 1939, Trenton, NC; married Betty Jean Tolbert; children: Tracey La Verne. **Educ:** Hampton Inst VA, BS 1962; Fairfield Univ CT, MA 1969; OH U, PhD 1973. **Career:** Adv to Pres on Minority Affairs, asst to pres; Univ VA Charlottesville, asst prof 1972-; New Haven Redevel Agency, housing devel officer 1968-70; Norwalk Job Orientation Program, instructor 1967-68; Urban League of Westchester Co Inc, assoc dir in charge of economic devel & employment, training adv, field rep 1966; New York City Dept of Labor, labor-mgmt prac adj 1965-66. **Orgs:** Chmn Time & Pl Comm, Middle Atlantic Reg, Nat Hampton Alumni Assn; mod Panel Disc Nat Hampton Alumni Assn; part Invit Sem on Deseg in Pub HigherEd spons by Howard Univ Sch of Bus & Pub Admin; 1st vp, pres Nat Black Caucus; mem Speech Communication Assn; Intl Communication Assn S Assn of Black Admin Pers; Am Assn of High Ed; Nat Ed Assn of US; Intl Platform Assn; Lib Com OH Univ 1971-72; exec sec, Instnl Self-Study Proj Univ of VA 1972-; Comm Coll Adminstrv Com Univ of VA 1972-; Afro-Am Std Com Univ of VA 1972-; exec sec Presidential Adminstrv Com on Comm Coll Univ of VA 1972-74; chmn Presidential Adminstrv Com on Comm Coll Univ of VA 1974; Presidential Adminstrv Com Ed & Employ Oppor, Oblig & Rights Univ of VA 1975; past pres NC 4-H Clubs; NY Hampton Alumni Club;pres Interfrat Cncl 197 Unit Negro Coll Fund 1973; chmn Plan Com Univ of VA, VA Comm Coll Artic Conf 1974-; VAComm Coll Conf Univ of VA 1974; Nat Hamp Alumni Assn, Mid Atlantic Prog 1975-. **Honors/Awds:** Outst Srv to Univ in Area of Human Rel, Black Stds

of Univ of VA 1976; Awarded Queen Elizabeth of England Medal, Charlottesville Albermarle Bicent Commn 1976; United Negro Coll Fund Vol Ldrshp Award, United Negro Coll Fund 1977; UNCF Lapel Pin 1977; Thomas Jefferson Area United Way Award 1977; name put int timecapsule for srv as mem of Charlottesville Albemarle Bicent Comm, will Be opened during Tricennial Celeb July 4 2076.

JONES, DONNA L.
Music publisher. **Personal:** Born Apr 18, 1959, Detroit, MI; daughter of Carol & Fred Ross; married David Jones, Sep 16, 1990; children: Evyn. **Educ:** USC, Entrepreneur Program, 1993-94. **Career:** International Svcs, owner, 1980-82; Creative Entertainment, vp, 1982-88; Transition Music; owner, currently. **Orgs:** NARAS, 1982-; AIMP, 1996; NMPA, 1982. **Honors/Awds:** EMBOL-LA, Entrepreneur of the Year, 1996. **Special Achievements:** Hollywood Reporter; one of the Top 50 Most Powerful Women, 1996; Recognized by Black Enterprise as One of 17 Top Rising Stars in Entertainment, 1996; USC Business Enterprise Network; Certificate of Achievement. **Business Addr:** President/Founder, Transition Music Corp, 11328 Magnolia Blvd, Ste 100, North Hollywood, CA 91601-3705, (818)760-1001.

JONES, DONTA
Professional football player. **Personal:** Born Aug 27, 1972, Washington, DC. **Educ:** Univ of Nebraska, degree in accounting and business administration, 1994. **Career:** Pittsburgh Steelers, linebacker, 1995-. **Business Addr:** Professional Football Player, Pittsburgh Steelers, Three Rivers Stadium, 300 Stadium Circle, Pittsburgh, PA 15212, (412)323-1200.

JONES, DONTAE' ANTIJUAINE
Professional basketball player. **Personal:** Born Jun 2, 1975, Nashville, TN. **Educ:** Northeast Mississippi Comm College; Mississippi State. **Career:** New York Knicks, forward, 1996-97; Boston Celtics, 1997-. **Business Addr:** Professional Basketball Player, Boston Celtics, 151 Merrimac St, Boston, MA 02114, (617)523-3030.

JONES, DORINDA A.
Executive. **Personal:** Born May 27, 1926, Trenton, KY; married John M; children: Dawna Lynn, John, Jr. **Educ:** BA 1953; Wayne St U, MSW 1955. **Career:** Hum Resources Dept, exec asst to dir 1985; Mayor's Com, Hum Resources Dev Detroit, exec Dir 1971-73, dir office of prog plann-res & eval 1970; Wayne St Univ Sch Soc Work Detroit, asst prof 1969-70. **Orgs:** Dept hd Soc Serv for Head Start Detroit Pub Schs 1966-68; dir Oversees Proj, Nat Fed Settlements & Comm Ctrs New York City 1964-66; prog Supv, bd dir Gleiss Meml Ctr, Protest Comm Serv 1959-64; soc grp worker & supv Neighborhood Serv Org 1955-58; princ soc planning & dev consult City of Detroit; mem Nat Assn Soc Workers; Nat Assn Black Soc Workers, Acad Cert Soc Workers; Am Socl Pub Admin; Cncl Minority Pub Admin; mem Delta Sigma Theta Sor; Bethune Sect, Nat Cncl of Negro Woman. **Business Addr:** 801 City Co Bldg, Detroit, MI 48221.

JONES, DUANE L.
Business executive. **Personal:** Born Mar 11, 1937, Duquesne, PA. **Educ:** Univ Pittsburgh, BS 1959; Univ Oslo, Sorbonne U, Paris, adv study 1962-63; NY U, MA 1970. **Career:** Black Theatre Alliance, exec dir 1976-; Antioch Coll, Dept of Literature assoc prof 1971-76; NY Univ, Opportunities Program English program coordinator 1967-71; Harlem Prep, English dept 1965-67; Prince Edward Co Farmville VA, English dept 1965; TV Film Negro Ensemble Co Natl Black Theatre, actor; Opera Ebony Richard Allen Center, stage dir; Caribe Magazine, guest editor. **Orgs:** Mem New York City Mayor's Commn on Culture, Art 1979-81; mem Alpha Phi Alpha Actors Equity Negro Actors Guild; bd of dirs PRIDE on TV 1980. **Honors/Awds:** Phyllis Wheatley Schlrshp Univ of Pittsburgh 1955; PA St Schlrshp Univ of Pittsburgh 1955-59; Phelps-Stokes Flwshp, Lectr Univ of Niamey Niger 1975. **Business Addr:** 410 W 42nd St, New York, NY 10036.

JONES, EARL FREDERICK
Elected government official. **Personal:** Born Jul 20, 1949, Yanceyville, NC; married Adri-Anne Donnell. **Educ:** NC Central Univ, BA Pol Sci 1967-71; TX Southern Univ School of Law, JD 1973-76. **Career:** Greensboro Legal Aid Found, assoc attorney 1976-81; Offender Aid & Restoration, dir 1981-; City of Greensboro, councilmember. **Orgs:** Co-founder NC Black Caucus of Legal Serv Employees 1979; mem Guilford Co Assoc of Black Lawyers 1982-; bd mem Shiloh Baptist Church Housing Bd 1983-; exec bd mem NC Black Municipal Elected Officials Bd 1984. **Honors/Awds:** Comm Serv Awd NAACP Greensboro 1983; received appointment as Honorary Atty Gen to and for the State of NC 1983. **Business Addr:** Councilmember, City of Greensboro, 301 S Elm St Ste 210, Greensboro, NC 27402.

JONES, EDDIE CHARLES
Professional basketball player. **Personal:** Born Oct 20, 1971, Pompano Beach, FL. **Educ:** Temple University. **Career:** Los Angeles Lakers, forward-guard, 1994-. **Honors/Awds:** NBA All-Rookie First Team, 1995; NBA All-Star, 1997, 1998. **Business Addr:** Professional Basketball Player, Los Angeles Lakers, POB 10, Inglewood, CA 90306, (310)419-3100.

JONES, EDITH IRBY
Physician. **Personal:** Born Dec 23, 1927, Conway, AR; daughter of Mattie Irby and Robert Irby; married James Beauregard; children: Gary Ivan, Myra Jones Romain, Keith Irby. **Educ:** Knoxville College, BS, mchem/bio/physics; Northwestern University, clinical psychology, 1948; University of Arkansas School of Medicine; West Virginia College of Medicine, postgrad, 1965; Cook Co Graduate School, postgrad, 1966; Methodist Hospital, postgrad, self assessment course, internal med, 1974; Baylor College of Medicine, cont ed, pract therapeutics, 1977; University of Texas Medical Review, fundamentals of therapeutics, 1977; Hermann Hospital, cardiopulmonary course, 1978; American Heart Assn, adv cardiopul life support course, 1978. **Career:** University Hospital, intern 1952-53; general practice, AR, 1953-59; Baylor Affiliated Hospitals, resident, 1959-62; private practice, TX, 1962-; Baylor College, asst professor, clinical med; University of Texas, asst prof, clinical med; Riverside Hospital Medical Staff, exec comm, secy of staff; dir, Prospect Med Lab; advisory bd, Houston Council on Alcoholism; Comm for Revising Justice Code in Harris Co; secy, bd of dir, Mercy Hospital Comp Health Care Group; partner, Jones, Coleman & Whitfield. **Orgs:** Admin comm, Univ of TX School of Med; pres, Natl Med Assn; Houston Amer Revolution Bi-centennial Comm; pres, AR Med, Dental & Pharmaceutical Assn; chmn, Internal Med Comm, St Eliz Hosp; med adv, Selective Bd #60; bd of dir/chmn, Comm for Homemakers Serv Family Service Ctr; chmn, Delta Rsch & Educ Found; bd of dir, Houston Council on Human Relations; Comm on Hypertension, chmn, Scientific Council, bd of dir, Natl Med Assn; bd, Third Bank Control Grp; TX Health Assn; comm on Drug Abuse, Houston ISD; adv med bd, Visiting Nurses Assn; bd of dir, Sudan Corp; bd of dir, Afro Amer BookDistributors; med adv bd, Planned Parenthood of Houston; chmn, SW Volunteers Delta-one Amer; Questions & Answers in Health Care, KCOH Monthly Radio. **Honors/Awds:** Golden Anniversary Award, Zeta Phi Beta, 1970; Distinguished Service Award, Houston Section of Natl Council of Negro Women, 1972; service to promote the efficient administration of justice, American Judicature Society, 1973; Kato Models, Woman of Year, 1974, Lois Allen Humanitarian Award, 1975; certificate of recognition, contribution in field of medicine, Antioch Baptist Church, 1975;life mem, Natl Council of Negro Women; Houston League of Business & Prof Women Achievement Award, 1977; citation for volunteer service, Eta Phi Beta, 1978; Edith Irby Jones Day, State of Arkansas, 1979; President's Distinguished Service Award, Knoxville College Natl Alumni Assn, 1979; Exemplary Service to and Support of Profesor of Education, 1979. **Home Addr:** 3402 S Parkwood Dr, Houston, TX 77021. **Business Addr:** Physician, Internal Medicine, 2601 Prospect St, Houston, TX 77004.

JONES, EDWARD LEE (TOO TALL JONES)
Professional football player (retired). **Personal:** Born Feb 23, 1951, Jackson, TN. **Educ:** Tennessee State Univ, degree in health and physical education. **Career:** Dallas Cowboys, defensive lineman, 1974-78, 1980-89; Professional Boxer, 1979; guest appearance on TV's "Different Strokes"; Imperial Investors, partner. **Orgs:** Active in promoting Special Olympics. **Honors/Awds:** MVP 1982; All Pro 1981 NEA, 1982 by AP; played in Pro Bowl, 1981-83 seasons.

JONES, EDWARD LOUIS
Author, historian, educator. **Personal:** Born Jan 15, 1922, Georgetown, TX; son of Elizabeth Steen Jones and Henry H Jones; married Lynne Ann McGreevy, Oct 7, 1964; children: Christopher, Teresa; married Dorothy M Showers, Mar 1, 1952 (divorced 1963); children: Cynthia, Frances, Edward Lawrence. **Educ:** Univ of WA, BA (2) 1952, BA 1955; Univ of Gonzaga, JD 1967. **Career:** Hollywood Players Theatre, prod, dir 1956-58; Roycroft Leg Theatre, prod, dir 1958-59; WA State Dept of Publ Asst, soc worker 1958; Seattle Water Dept, cost acctg clerk 1960-61; State of WA, attny gen office 1963-66; Seattle Oppty Indust Ctr, suprv 1966-68; Univ of WA, asst dean a&s 1968-, lecturer. **Orgs:** Consult State Attny Gen Adv Comm on Crime, State Supr of Counseling; vice pres WA Comm on Consumer Interests, Natl Council on Crime & Delinquency; bd mem Natl Acad Adv & Assn; ed NACADA Jrnl; mem Natl Assn of Student Personnel Admin, The Amer Acad of Pol & Soc Sci, The Smithsonian Assn; historical advisor, Anheuser Busch. **Honors/Awds:** Moot Court Contest, First Place, 1953. **Special Achievements:** Author: Profiles in African Heritage, Black Zeus, 1972; Tutankhamon, King of Upper & Lower Egypt, 1978; Orator's Workbook, 1982; The Black Diaspora: Colonization of Colored People, 1989; co-author, Money Exchange Flashcards, Currency Converters, 1976; From Rulers of the World to Slavery, 1990; President Zachary Taylor and Senator Hamlin: Union or Death, 1991; Why Colored Americans Need an Abraham Lincoln in 1992; Forty Acres & a Mule: The Rape of Colored Americans, 1995. **Military Serv:** US Army, 2nd Lt, 1940-46. **Business Addr:** Lecturer (retired), American Ethnic Studies, Univ of Washington, 3931 Brooklyn Ave, NE, Ethnic Cultural Ctr, HH-05, Seattle, WA 98195.

JONES, EDWARD NORMAN
Government official, educator (retired). **Personal:** Born Jul 25, 1914, Hampton, VA; son of Alberta Jones and Edward Jones; married Agnes Verbena Phillips Jones, Dec 25, 1937. **Educ:** Hampton University, BS, 1936; Hampton Institute, MA, 1973. **Career:** Hampton Institute, Student Affairs, acting associate dean, 1974-84, dormitory director, 1972-74; Junior High School, Hampton VA, teacher, 1974-72; USPO, Hampton VA, supr, foreman of del, 1957-69, letter carrier, 1938-57; Rosenwald High School, Madisonville KY, teacher, 1936-38. **Orgs:** Bachelor Benedict Club, past president, secretary; Nat Assn of Letter Carriers, past branch pres; Natl Assn of Postal Supr, past branch pres ; VA St Assn of Letter Carriers, past chairman of the exec bd; Nat Ed Assn; VA Ed Assn; Hampton Ed Assn; First Baptist Church, past trustee 1987-90, Men's Club, past pres; Alpha Phi Alpha Fraternity Inc, Eastern Reg, Dist #7, Areas #7, #8, risk management coordinator, Tidewater N Virginia Assn of Chapters, asst dir, Delta Beta Lambda Chapter, past pres, District #7 Eastern Reg, past area dir, Virginia Assn of Chapters, Resolution and Recommendation Committee, chairman, 1988-, Resolution and Recommendation Committee, Eastern Reg, chairman, 1984-, Gen Convention, 1990-95; Kappa Delta Pi; ARC, past mem, bd of dirs. **Honors/Awds:** Alpha Phi Alpha, Delta Beta Lambda Chapter, Certificate of Merit, 1975; Alpha Man of the Year, 1985; Alpha Patriarch of the Year, 1989. **Military Serv:** US Army, corporal, 1943-46. **Home Addr:** 42 Bainbridge Ave, Hampton, VA 23663.

JONES, EFFIE HALL
Educational administrator (retired), consultant. **Personal:** Born Jan 13, 1928, Washington, DC; daughter of Mary Lou Washington Hall and William S Hall; married Edward William Jones Sr; children: Edward W Jr, Franz Emil, Kevin Dennis. **Educ:** Morgan State U, BS 1949; Cath U, MA 1966; George Washington U, EdD 1985. **Career:** Dist of Columbia Public Schools, teacher, counselor 1952-67, vice prin 1967-70; Montgomery Co Md Publuc Schools, vice prin, prin 1970-76; Amer Assn of School Admn, assoc exec dir 1976-91; educ consultant, currently. **Orgs:** Member, American Association of School Administrators; member, American Educational Research Association; member, Business and Professional Women's Clubs Inc; member, National Alliance of Black School Educators; member, National Council of Administrative Women in Education; member, National Urban League; member, Phi Delta Kappa. **Honors/Awds:** Women at the top film Dept of Ed Womens Equity 1980; hon by Mc Graw Hill Pblshr Otstndg & Cntrbtr To Women & Memories in Ed Admn 1985; speakg of people Ebony Mag 1982; Honorary Doctorate, New Mexico State University, 1989; Educational Leadership Award, Northeast Coalition of Education Leaders, Inc, 1988; Effie Jones Award, Florida Aware, 1990; American Association of School Admin Distinguish Service Award for Leadership, 1992.

JONES, ELAINE R.
Attorney. **Personal:** Born Mar 2, 1944, Norfolk, VA. **Educ:** Howard Univ, AB, 1965; Univ of VA, LLB, 1970. **Career:** NAACP Legal Defense & Educational Fund, pres, director-counsel, currently; attorney. **Orgs:** Natl Bar Assn; Old Dominion Bar Assn; VA Trial Lawyers Assn; Intl Federation of Women Lawyers. **Honors/Awds:** Panel of arbitration Amer Stock Exchange; Delta Sigma Theta Sor; Recognition Award, Black Am Law Students' Assn for Outstndng Legal Serv to the Comm 1974; Spl Achievement Award, Natl Assn of Black Women Attys 1975. **Special Achievements:** First female director-counsel of the NAACP Legal Defense and Educational Fund; First African-American female law student at the Univ of Virginia's law school. **Business Addr:** Director-Counsel, NAACP Legal Defense & Educational Fund, 1275 K St NW, Ste 301, Washington, DC 20005, (202)682-1300.

JONES, ELNETTA GRIFFIN
Educator. **Personal:** Born Jul 7, 1934, Mullins, SC; married Aaron Mullins Jones; children: Aaron Daryl. **Educ:** SC St Coll, BS 1957; Shippensburg State Coll, ME 1972; American Univ, DEd 1979. **Career:** Rosenwald High School, teacher 1957-59; AUS/Air Force, Educational Dev Cntr, Wiesbaden, Germany 1960-63; AUS Infantry Cntr, Ft Benning, GA, teacher 1964-66,1969-70;Shippensburg Univ, asst dir of Act 101 Program 1972-76, dir Act 101 Program 1976-78, asst vice president for acad affairs 1979-80, assoc dean ofspecial academic programs 1980-82, dean special academic programs 1982-. **Orgs:** Numerous consultantships; mem PA Assoc of Developmental Educators, The PA Black Conference on Higher Educ, Phi Delta Kappa, Natl Academic Advising Assoc, The Natl Political Congress of Black Women, The Shippensburg Civic Club, Delta Sigma Theta, Inc; Natl Assoc of Developmental Educators. **Honors/Awds:** Outstanding Humanist Awd Shippensburg Univ Black Alumni 1985; 5 publications including contributor to "Research in Higher Education," 1983, The Amer University Press Washington, DC. **Business Addr:** Dean Special Academic Programs, Shippensburg University, DHC #112, Shippensburg, PA 17257.

JONES, EMANUEL DAVIE
Automobile dealer. **Personal:** Born Apr 1, 1959, Atlanta, GA; son of Leroy & Ethlyn Jones; married Gloria Jones, Apr 6, 1990; children: Emanuel D, II, Elam D. **Educ:** Univ of Pennsyl-

vania, BSEE, 1981; Columbia Univ, MBA, 1986. **Career:** IBM, product eng, 1981-84; Arthur Anderson, consultant, 1986-88; Ford Motor Co, dealer candidate, 1988-92; Legacy Ford-Mercury Inc, president, 1992-. **Orgs:** Henry County Chamber of Commerce, dir, 1994-96; Henry County Rotary Club, dir, 1994; Henry County High School Scholarship Foundation, dir, 1994-; Leadership Henry, 1993-; United Way of Henry County, advisory bd, 1995-; Georgia Dept of Labor, advisory bd, 1994-; Shiloh Baptist Church, chairman,stewardship ministry, 1994-95. **Honors/Awds:** Henry County High School, Businessman of the Year, 1993; Henry County Police Dept, Businessman of the Year, 1993; Shiloh Baptist Church, Distinquished Service Award, 1994; Ford Motor Co, Top Profit Dealer, 1994; US Department of Commerce, Atlanta Regional Entrepreneur of the Year, 1996; Atlanta Minority Service Firm of the Year; Alonzo Crim High School, Businessman of the Year, 1996. **Military Serv:** US Army Corps of Engineers, captain, 1980-; Army Service Ribbon, Distinquished Service Award. **Business Addr:** President, Legacy Ford-Mercury Inc, 413 Industrial Blvd, PO Box 736, McDonough, GA 30253, (404)914-2800.

JONES, EMIL, JR.
State senator, senate minority leader. **Personal:** Born Oct 18, 1935, Chicago, IL; son of Marilla Mims Jones (deceased) and Emil Jones, Sr. (deceased); married Patricia; children: Debra Ann, Renee L, John M, Emil III. **Educ:** Roosevelt Univ, 1953-55; Loop College, AA (dean's list), 1971. **Career:** Licensed Sanitation Engineer; US Post Office; Democratic Organization 21st Ward Regular, precinct capt, 1962-70; Southern Dist Water Filtration Plant, mem exec bd orgn & chlorine engineer, 1964-67; Chicago City Council, sec to alderman, 1967-73; Democratic Organization 34th Ward Regular, precinct captain, 1971, executive secretary, 1971, public relations, 1972; Illinois House of Representatives, state representative, 1973-82; Illinois State Senate, state senator, 1982-. **Orgs:** Morgan Park Civic League. **Honors/Awds:** Friend of Education Award, Illinois State Board of Education; Illinois Delta Kapp Appreciation; Leadership Award, Coalition to Save Chicago Schools; Civil Rights Award, Illinois Department of Human Rights; Award for Assisting Disadvantaged Youth, Chicago Urban League. **Business Addr:** State Senator, Illinois State Senate, 309 A Capitol Building, Springfield, IL 62706.

JONES, EMMA PETTWAY
Educator. **Personal:** Born Jul 29, 1945, Boykin, AL; daughter of Allie Pettway and John B. Pettway; married J Jones (divorced); children: James, John, Tracy, Malik. **Educ:** Albertus Magnus Coll, 1978-80; NH Coll, Manchester, BS 1981, MBA 1985; CUNY Law School Queens, JD 1988. **Career:** New Haven Fed Credit Union, organizer/mgr 1979-81; EMA Assoc, pres 1980-86; Jones Turner & Wright, legal asst 1986-87; Williams & Wise, legal intern 1987; independent consultant. **Orgs:** Exec dir People Acting for Change New Haven CT; researcher Yale Univ Provost Dept; consultant, trainer Legal Assistance New Haven CT, Public Housing Prog Tenant Representative Council, NH Coll, Organizational Development Inst Cheyney State Coll, Fair Haven Mediation Prog; exec dir CT Afro-American Historical Society; chairperson Natl Econ Devel & Law Ctr; vice pres New Haven YWCA. **Honors/Awds:** Received numerous Certificates of Excellence & Outstanding Service Awards. **Home Addr:** 286 James St, New Haven, CT 06513.

JONES, ENOCH
Cleric. **Personal:** Born Aug 19, 1922, Biloxi, MS; children: Stephen, Enoch Lee, Janet. **Educ:** Am Bapt Sem, BTh, 1954; Fisk Univ, BA, 1956, MA, 1957; Scarrit Coll, additional study; Houston Tillotson Coll, hon doctorate degree. **Career:** Friendship Bapt Church, pastor, 1952-61; ABT Sem, teacher & dean of chapel, 3 yrs; 15th Ave Baptist Church, pastor. **Orgs:** Natl Bapt Convention USA Inc, 1956; TN BM&E Conv; trustee of ABT Sem; minister for prisoners at state prison; conducts joint worship serv with Woodmont Bapt Church/White Church; viewed yearly by 50,000 on TV; Beta Epsilon Hon Soc. **Honors/Awds:** Winner of Outstanding Sermon of Year Award, Natl Bapt Convention Inc; named for Leadership Nashville, 1977-78; hon dep sheriff of Davidson County, 1977; invited to Washington to partcipate in Inauguration of Pres Carter; judge, Best Sermon of the Year, Natl Bapt Pulpit of Natl Bapt Conv Inc; guest preacher, John B Falconer Lect & Monrovia Liberia, 1978; col aide de camp Gov Staff 1978; hon sgt-at-arms, TN St House of Reps; hon del, US House of Rep 1980; recipient of three battle stars for serv in Italy 92nd Inf Div 3yrs. **Business Addr:** 1203 9 Ave N, Nashville, TN 37208.

JONES, ERNEST
Business executive. **Personal:** Born Jul 20, 1923, Suffolk, VA; married Mary Ann Mckoy; children: Brenda, Ernest, Wanda, Cheryl, Marc. **Educ:** St Paul's Coll Lawrenceville VA. **Career:** Rite-way Cleaners & Tailors, owner 1956-; tailor 1947-56. **Orgs:** Mem St Luke's Epis Ch 1949-; mem bd dir Businessmen's Assn; Dixwell Comm House; Dixwell Plaza Merchants Assn; 32 Deg Past Master Prince Hall Masons;past pres Craftsmans Club; instr, tailoring Opportunities Industrialization Ctr New Haven CT; mem New Haven Black Elected Officials. **Military Serv:** AUS bandsman 1943-46. **Business Addr:** Rite-Way Cleaners & Tailors, 190 Dixwell Avenue, New Haven, CT 06511.

JONES, ERNEST EDWARD
Attorney, association executive. **Personal:** Born Nov 21, 1944, Savannah, GA; son of Luella Williams and Orlando Jones; married Denise Rae Scott, Feb 14, 1981; children: Jamal Jones, Kahlil Jones. **Educ:** Dickinson Coll, Carlisle PA, AB Economics, 1966; Temple Univ School of Law, Philadelphia PA, JD, 1972. **Career:** District Attorney's Office, Philadelphia PA, asst district atty, 1972-74; Temple Univ School of Law, Philadelphia PA, general counsel 1974-77; Community Legal Services, Philadelphia PA, deputy director 1977-79, executive dir, 1979-83; Greater Philadelphia Urban Affairs Coalition, executive dir, 1983-. **Orgs:** Corporate Dir, Corestates Financial Corp, 1987-; mem, Natl Bar Assn, 1988; mem, Philadelphia Bar Assn; chair, Philadelphia Housing Authority, 1991-92; Devereux Foundation, 1993-; Redevelopment Authority of Phil, 1991-; Thomas Jefferson Univ, 1989-. **Military Serv:** US Army, Korea, company commander, 1967-69. **Business Addr:** Executive Director, The Greater Philadelphia Urban Affairs Coalition, 1207 Chestnut St, 7th Fl, Philadelphia, PA 19107.

JONES, ERNEST LEE
Professional football player. **Personal:** Born Apr 1, 1971, Utica, NY; married Maria; children: Andrea, Deja. **Educ:** Oregon. **Career:** New Orleans Saints, defensive end, 1995; Denver Broncos, 1996-. **Business Addr:** Professional Football Player, Denver Broncos, 13655 Broncos Pkwy, Englewood, CO 80112, (303)649-9000.

JONES, ERVIN EDWARD
Medical technologist. **Personal:** Born Oct 4, 1938, Lake City, SC; married Pauline; children: Vincent, Yvette, Michael. **Educ:** Franklin Sch Sci & Arts, 1959; Montg Cnty Comm Coll; Morris Coll, 1957. **Career:** Philadelphia Coll of Osteo Med, med Tech 1973-; Norristown PA, coun bd 1974-. **Orgs:** Chmn Opport Coun 1968-69; Shmn Pub Safety PA Police & Dept 1974-; chmn negot comm Boro 1976-77; chmn Norristown House Comm 1977; 1st black chmn pub safety Boro 1974-; 2nd black elected coun Boro 1974-; past mem Norristown Advis Comm 1968-70; past mem Norristown Jaycees 1970-72; mem MT Zion AMC Ch. **Honors/Awds:** Won state supreme ct dec subpoena power of Boro Coun 1976; hon mem young Dem of Montg Cnty 1976. **Business Addr:** 1030 Walnut, Norristown, PA 19401.

JONES, ESTHER B.
Track & field athlete. **Personal:** Born Apr 7, 1969, Chicago, IL; daughter of Laura Jones and Virgil Jones; married. **Educ:** Louisiana State University. **Career:** US Olympic Team, track & field athlete, currently. **Orgs:** Alpha Phi Omega Service Fraternity; LSU Student Alumni Association; LSU Sociology Club. **Honors/Awds:** NCAA Track & Field Champion, 100m, 200m, 4x100m, 1990; 21-time All-American at LSU; Co-American Record Holder, 4x100m relay, Collegiate Woman; 4x200m Relay, Collegiate Woman; World University Games, Gold Medal, 4x100m Relay, 1990; Olympic Games, Gold Medal, 4x100m Relay, 1992; State of Los Angeles, Corbert Award 1990; inducted into the State of Wisconsin Hall of Fame for Athletes, 1992. **Special Achievements:** Poweraide Commercial with Deion Sanders. **Business Addr:** Athletic Representative, Nike, 1 Bowerman Dr, Beaverton, OR 97005.

JONES, EVA
Manager. **Personal:** Born Mar 15, 1931, Frenchman's Bayou, AR; married James A B; children: 6. **Educ:** CP Bus Coll, attended 1950. **Career:** Firestone Tire & Rubber Co, traffic mgr 1968-; Gen Tel, supr/traffic 1963-68. **Orgs:** Sch bd mem Dist 87th Bloomington IL 1971-79; pres sch bd & Bloomington 1977-78; city council Bloomington 1979-; pres Normal Champaing Chap of Links Inc 1979-81; mem Delta Nu Alpha 1979-; hairperson adv bd Sunnyside Neighborhood Center Bloomington IL; mem admission & priorities com United Way; mem Assn of Commerce & Industry of Mclean Co; mem Bloomington's Transportation Club; clerk Mt Pisgah Bapt Ch; mem NAACP; coordinator Minority Voters Coalition. **Business Addr:** 66 Veteran Pkwy, Bloomington, IL 61701.

JONES, FERDINAND TAYLOR, JR.
Psychologist, educator. **Personal:** Born May 15, 1932, New York, NY; son of Esther Lillian Harris Haggie Jones and Ferdinand Taylor Jones; married Myra Jean Rogers Jones, Nov 26, 1967; children: Joanne Esther Jones-Rizzi, Terrie Lynn. **Educ:** Drew U, AB 1953; Univ of Vienna, PhD 1959. **Career:** Riverside Hospital NY, staff psychologist 1959-62; Westchester County Community Mental Health Bd, chief psychologist 1962-67; Lincoln Hospital Mental Health Serv NY, training consultant 1967-69; Sarah Lawrence Coll Bronxville NY, psychology faculty 1968-72; Brown Univ, dir psychology serv, 1972-92, prof of psychology & lecturer psychiatry human behavior, 1972-97, prof of psychology emeritus, 1997-; Univ of Dar es Salaam, visiting prof, 1993-94. **Orgs:** Pres Westchester Cnty Psychol Assc 1967-69; bd dir Am Orthopsychiatric Assc 1984-87; Women & Infants Hosp, board of directors, 1983-89; mem Am Psychological Assn, Assc Black Psychologist, Am Assc Univ Profs Soc for Psych Study of Social Issues; scholar-in-residence Schomburg Center for Rsch in Black Culture 1987; president, American Orthopsychiatric Assn, 1989-90. **Honors/Awds:** Distinguished Service Award West Cnty Psychol Assn 1972; Charles H Nichols Awrd Brown Univ Afro Am Studies Dept 1980; Alumni Achievement Award in Science, Drew University, 1988; Elizabeth H. LeDuc Award for Teaching Excellence, Brown Univ, 1997. **Military Serv:** US Army sp3 1953-56. **Business Addr:** Prof of Psychology, Brown Univ, Box 1853, Providence, RI 02912.

JONES, FLORESTA DELORIS
Educator. **Personal:** Born Dec 14, 1950, Hopewell, VA. **Educ:** Barry Coll, BA (Magna Cum Laude) 1972; MI State Univ, MA 1975. **Career:** State Journal Lansing MI, Detroit Free Press, staff writer intern 1974; Richmond Afro-Amer, staff writer, reporter 1975-76; State Office of Min Bus Enterprise, prog info office, ed spec 1976-78; VA State Univ, adj faculty 1977-78; Georgian Court Coll, dir & adj faculty ed oppty fund prog 1978-82; Brookdale Comm Coll, writing team faculty 1982-. **Orgs:** Mem NJ Ed Oppty Fund Professional Assoc, AAUW, Women in Commun, Intl Comm Assoc, NAACP, Soc of Professional Jrnl, Assoc for Equality & Excellence in Ed, YWCA, Annual Womens Conf Comm, Goodwill Chorus of Petersburg VA. **Honors/Awds:** Scholarship Awd Natl Scholarship Serv & Fund for Negro Studies 1969; Sigma Tau Delta English Hon Frat Berry Coll 1970-72; Alpha Chi Beta of GA Coll Hon Berry Coll 1971-72; Grad Fellowships & Grad Assistantships MI State Univ 1972-74; Articles Publ in Detroit Free Press, Lansing State Jrnl, Richmond AFRO, US Info Agency & other newspapers. **Business Addr:** Writing Team Faculty, Brookdale Comm College, Applied Humanities Inst, Lincroft, NJ 07738.

JONES, FRANCIS
Association executive. **Career:** National Black McDonald's Operators Association, president, currently. **Business Phone:** (213)962-2806.

JONES, FRANK
Security guard, mayor, chief of police. **Personal:** Born Oct 25, 1950, Sellers, SC; son of Pearl Melton Jones and John Jones; married Sylvia G Jones, Apr 1974; children: Dennis, Tyrone, Deon Jones. **Educ:** Marion-Mullins Voc, Agriculture Mechanics, 1967-70; State of SC Law Enforcement, Basic Law Enforcement, 1974; Francis Marion Coll, Science and Law, 1976; SC Criminal Justice Academy, Columbia SC, First Line Supervisor, 1983-85, Traffic Radar Operator, 1987-88; Florence Darlington Tech, Jail Removal Initiative 1983. **Career:** Hargrove Groceries, Sellers SC, clerk; Latta Police Dept, Latta SC, policeman, 1971-73; Marion Police Dept, Marion SC, lt policeman, 1973-87; Jones Groceries, Marion SC, owner; Mcleod Hospital, Florence SC, security guard; Town of Sellers SC, mayor and chief policeman. **Orgs:** Adviser, Sellers Junior Policeman Department. **Honors/Awds:** Hazardous Material Training, Familiy Line System, 1981; Guest Relation Program, Mcleod Hospital, 1988; Outstanding Policeman of the Year, Marion Jaycees, 1977-88; Law Enforcement Torch Run, SC Law Enforcement, 1989; Outstanding Community Worker, Baptist Educ and Missonary, 1989. **Military Serv:** Coordinator Military Police, private. **Business Addr:** Mayor & Chief Policeman, Town of Sellers, Sellers Town Hall, PO Box 116, Sellers, SC 29592.

JONES, FRANK BENSON
Pilot, clergyman. **Personal:** Born Aug 21, 1938, Kansas City, MO; son of Frankie Helen Boyd Jones and Benson Jones; married Mary S McClendon; children: Eleanor, Angela, Gregory, Mia. **Educ:** California State Univ, Dominguez Hills, BA, 1995. **Career:** Jones Computer Systems, pres 1983-; United Air Lines, pilot 1966-; Pentecostal Temple, pastor, 1992-. **Orgs:** Editor Black Panther Newspaper 1969; dir Contra Costa County Emerg Food & Med Serv 1972-73; pres PPCP Fed Credit Union 1971-72; editor Richmond Crusader Newspaper 1973-75; sec/treas Comm Developers Inc 1973-76; ecumenical dir Church of Acts 1977-78; pastor Church of Acts 1977-83. **Military Serv:** USAF Cpt 1957-66; Air Medal with 8 Clusters; Air Force Commendation Medal. **Business Addr:** United Air Lines, PO Box 5505, Carson, CA 90749.

JONES, FRANKLIN D.
Educator. **Personal:** Born Dec 7, 1935, Oakland, MS; son of Mr & Mrs Robert Jones; married Allene; children: Cedric D, Tamekia L. **Educ:** Mississippi Industrial Coll, BS 1961; MS Univ, further studies 1970's; Delta State, further studies 1984. **Career:** Charleston Elementary, teacher 1961-80; Oakland Elementary, teacher 1980-; Town of Oakland, mayor. **Home Addr:** Route 1, Box 191, Oakland, MS 38948. **Business Addr:** Teacher, Oakland Elementary, Route 1, Box 191, Oakland, MS 38948.

JONES, FREDERICK DOUGLASS, JR.
Assistant city attorney. **Personal:** Born Oct 8, 1955, Albuquerque, NM; son of Ruth Carey Jones and Frederick Jones, Sr. **Educ:** Earlham Coll, Richmond IN, BA, 1980; University of New Mexico, Albuquerque NM, School of Law, JD, 1984. **Career:** State of New Mexico, Albuquerque NM, asst district attorney 1984-87; City of Albuquerque, NM, asst city attorney, 1987-. **Orgs:** Pres, New Mexico Black Laywers Assn, 1986-88; mem, NAACP, 1986-; mem, Natl Bar Assn, 1986-; bd of dir, New Futures Inc, 1988-. **Honors/Awds:** Honorarium, Amer Bd of Trial Advocates, 1984, NAACP, 1989; Pappy Seed Award, Univ of New Mexico School of Law 1984.

JONES, FREDRICK E.
Auto dealer. **Career:** Fred Jones Pontiac-GMC Truck, Inc, Brookfield, WI, chief executive officer, 1984-. **Orgs:** Canaan Baptist Church, chairman trustee board; NAACP, lifetime mem; Wisconsin Auto & Truck Dealers Association, officer. **Business Addr:** Fred Jones Pontiac-GMC Truck, Inc, 13000 Capital Dr, Brookfield, WI 53008.

JONES, FURMAN MADISON, JR.
Physician. **Personal:** Born Nov 1, 1927, New York, NY; married Ermajeanne; children: Phillip, Joi, Furman III. **Educ:** Tufts Univ, BS 1948; Meharry Medical Coll, MD 1953. **Career:** Private Practice, physician. **Orgs:** Mem Omega Psi Phi 1948-87, Natl Negro Golf Assoc 1969-; dir Home Health Serv Harlem Hosp 1976-94. **Military Serv:** AUS capt 3 yrs. **Business Addr:** 470 Lenox, New York, NY 10037.

JONES, G. DANIEL
Clergyman. **Personal:** Born in Norfolk, VA; son of Estelle Campbell Jones (deceased) and George Raymond Jones (deceased); married Geraldine S Saunders; children: Bryant Daniel. **Educ:** VA Union Univ, BS 1962; Andover Newton Theological School, MDiv 1966; Howard University's Divinity School, DMin 1978. **Career:** Ministry St John Baptist Church Woburn, MA, pastor 1965-67; Messiah Baptist Church Brockton, MA, pastor 1967-73; Zion Baptist Church Portsmouth, VA, pastor 1973-82; Grace Baptist Church of Germantown, Philadelphia, PA sr pastor 1982-; graduate adjunct, School of Theology, Virginia Union Univ 1979-82; undergraduate instructor Philosophy of Religion Norfolk State Univ, Norfolk, VA 1973-82. **Orgs:** 2nd Vice Pres Amer Bapt Churches of the South 1981-82; Hampton Inst Minister's Conf 1973-; mem general bd Amer Baptist Churches USA; bd mem, Lutheran Home at Germantown 1986-94; Executive Comm Bd, Lott Carey Baptist Foreign Mission Com; chair, the Centennial Committee; moderator Philadelphia Baptist Assn, 1996-98; Ministers Council, American Baptist Churches, 1988-, pres, 1998- 2002; first presidents, ministers council, AM Baptist Churches of the South, 1974-76; first president, Ministers Council, Philadelphia Baptist Assn, 1987-90. **Honors/Awds:** Human Relations Award Omega Psi Phi Frat Inc Portsmouth, VA 1979 & 1982; 1st Place Sermon Contest Amer Bapt Churches of PA and DE 1984; Key to City of Brockton, MA 1983; Citations from City of Portsmouth, VA and Sch Bd 1980 & 1982; Doctoral Thesis, ''Educational Ministries in the Black Baptist Churches of Norfolk and Portsmouth, VA''; ''Man of the Year'' Grace Baptist Church of Germantown 1989; The Jubilee Service Award, Philadelphia Fisk Alumni Club, 1988; Life mem, Omega Psi Phi Fraternity, Inc; The United Supreme Council, Prince Hall Masons, Northern, 1996; Citations from City of Philadelphia & House of Representatives, Commonwealth of Pennsylvania, 1996. **Business Addr:** Senior Pastor, Grace Baptist Church of Germantown, 25 W Johnson St, Philadelphia, PA 19144.

JONES, GARY
Theater director. **Personal:** Born Jun 29, 1942, Chicago, IL; son of Jessie Tolbert Jones and Leonard Jones. **Educ:** IL Inst of Tech Inst of Design, 1963-64. **Career:** Kungsholm Min Grand Opera of Chicago, scenic designer & principal puppeteer 1969-71; Blackstreet USA Puppet Theatre, dir, founder 1975-. **Orgs:** UNIMA-USA Union Internationale de la Marionnette, Puppeteers of America. **Honors/Awds:** Designed exec prods Porgy & Bess, Carmen, The King & I, My Fair Lady, Gypsy 1969-71; 5 week sold out engagement at the Smithsonian Inst Div of Performing Arts 1980, 1982; 3 month tour of Iceland, West Germany, Holland, Portugal 1984; The Brody Arts Foundation Fellowship Program Los Angeles 1987; Artist in Residence Fellowship, California Arts Council, 1989; Artist Fellowship, Los Angeles Dept of Cultural Affairs, 1990; Los Angeles Arts Recovery Grant, 1992; Disney KJLH Crystal Castle Award, Outstanding Achievement, 1997. **Business Addr:** Dir, Blackstreet USA Puppet Theatre, 4619 W Washington Blvd, Los Angeles, CA 90016.

JONES, GARY DEWAYNE
Professional football player. **Personal:** Born Nov 30, 1967, San Augustine, TX; married Tina Haskins, 1992. **Educ:** Texas A&M University. **Career:** Pittsburgh Steelers, safety, 1990-. **Business Phone:** (412)323-1200.

JONES, GAYL
Author, educator. **Personal:** Born Nov 23, 1949, Lexington, KY; daughter of Lucille Wilson Jones and Franklin Jones; married Bob Jones (died 1998). **Educ:** Connecticut College, BA, 1971; Brown Univ, MA, 1973, DA, 1975. **Career:** Univ of Michigan, Ann Arbor, MI, prof of English, 1975-83. **Honors/Awds:** Author of Corregidora, Random House, 1975, Chile Woman, 1975, Eva's Man, Random House, 1976, White Rat, Random House, 1977, Song for Anninho, Lotus Press, 1981, The Hermit-Woman, Lotus Press, 1983, Xarque and Other Poems, Lotus Press, 1985; The Healing, 1998. **Business Addr:** Gayl Jones, c/o Beacon Press, 25 Beacon St, Boston, MA 02108.

JONES, GAYNELLE GRIFFIN
Government official, attorney. **Personal:** Born Nov 20, 1948, Dallas, TX; daughter of Reverend and Mrs Marvin C Griffin; married Robert Allen Jones, Dec 26, 1986; children: one daughter, two stepsons. **Educ:** Emerson Coll, BA, 1969; Boston Coll Law School, JD, 1972. **Career:** Boston Legal Assistance Project, attorney, 1972-73; State Mutual Life Assurance Co, counsel, 1973-75; Boston Edison Co, counsel, 1975-79; Ouachita Parish District Attorney's Office, assistant district attorney, 1981-82; Jones, Jones, and Jones, partner, 1979-82; Harris County District Attorney's Office, assistant district attorney, 1982-89; Southern District of Texas, assistant US attorney, 1989-92; First Court of Appeals, justice, 1992; Vinson and Elkins LLP, attorney, 1993; Southern District of Texas, United States attorney, 1993-. **Orgs:** State Bar of Texas, grievance committee, continuing legal education, lecturer; National College of district Attorneys, faculty; Attorney General's Advocacy Institute; Houston Trial Lawyers Assn; Cate School, trustee; Wheeler Ave Baptist Church; NAACP; Houston Bar Assn, community affairs subcommittee. **Honors/Awds:** National Assn of Black Prosecutors, Pioneer Award, 1994; National Forum of Black Public Administrators, Star of Achievement Award, 1993; Women Who Did, Bessie Coleman Trail Blazer Award; American Bar Assn, Judge Edward R Finch Speech Award, 1995; Young African American Achievers, Super Achiever Award, 1995; International Assn of Credit Card Investigators, Prosecutor of the Year, 1991; Texas Advisory Council, Outstanding Arson Prosecution, 1989. **Business Addr:** US Attorney, US Attorney's Office, 910 Travis, Ste 1500, PO Box 61129, Houston, TX 77208-1129.

JONES, GEORGE H.
Educator. **Personal:** Born Feb 21, 1942, Muskogee, OK; son of Bernice Weaver Jones and George H Jones. **Educ:** Harvard Coll, BA 1963; Univ of CA Berkeley, PhD 1968. **Career:** University of MI, asso prof of bio 1975-, asst prof of Zoology 1971-75; Inst of Health Univ of Geneva, Switzerland 1968-71; prof of Biology Univ of MI 1986-89; Emory Univ, prof of biology, 1989, graduate dean, vp for research, 1989-95. **Orgs:** Mem NY Acad of Sci; American Society for Microbiol; American Society for Biochemistry and Molecular Biology. **Honors/Awds:** Helen Hay Whitney Found Postdoctoral Fellowship; Ford Foundation postdoctoral fellowship 1982; Univ Teaching Award Univ of MI 1989; over 40 publications in scientific journals; Goodrich C White Professorship, 1997. **Business Addr:** Department of Biology, Emory University, Atlanta, GA 30322.

JONES, GEORGE WILLIAMS
Urologist. **Personal:** Born Jul 13, 1931, Mobile, AL; son of Bernice Williams Jones and Joseph W Jones; married Edna Robinson Jones; children: Randall, Carleton, Janet, George B, Adria T. **Educ:** NC Coll, BS 1953; Howard Univ, MD 1960. **Career:** Freedman's Hospital, intern 1960-61, asst surgery resident 1961-62, asst resident urology 1962-64, chief resident urology 1964-65; Memorial Sloan Kettering, 1965-67, chief urology, 1967-80; Howard Univ Coll of Medicine, assoc prof of urology 1972-76, chairman of urology, 1972-88, prof of urology 1984-; Urologic Assocs, surgeon. **Orgs:** Bd of dirs Natl Kidney Foundation of Natl Capitol Area 1981-; bd mem DC Div, Amer Cancer Soc 1984-, pres and chairman of the bd, 1993-94; mem The Amer Assoc of Clinical Urologists, The Amer Coll of Surgeons, Assn for Acad Surgery, Amer Tissue Culture Assn, Soc of Univ Urologists, Assn of Amer Med Colls, Washington Urologic Assoc, Mid-Atlantic Section, Amer Urological Assn, The Soc of Surgical Oncology, Amer Med Assn, Amer Assn of Clinical Urologists, Amer Assn of Cancer Educ; chmn Bd of the Capital Area Health Plan; president, National Kidney Foundation, DC National Cap Area, 1991-92; vice president, American Cancer Society Inc, DC Division, 1991-93, pres, 1993-94; national chairman, Prostatic Cancer Task Force, American Cancer Society, 1990-; chair, American Cancer Task Force for Prostate Cancer for American College of Surgeons, 1993-; ACOG, chair. **Honors/Awds:** Charles R Drew Award, Most Worthy Scientific Contribution at the Natl Medical Assoc Convention Cincinnati, OH 1965; Thomas Jefferson Award, Fox Productions WTTG Channel 5 TV Washington, DC 1986; numerous presentation, lectures; 29 publications including contributing editor in ''American Cancer Society's Book on Cancer,'' the chapter Urinary Tract Cancer published by Double-Day 1986; ''Idiopathic Renal Arteriovenous Fistual, Spontaneous Closure,'' Urology Vol XXIX No 1 pp 86-89, 1987; fellow in urology/oncology, Memorial Sloan Kettering, 1965-67; American Board of Urology Award, Howard University Hospital, 1972. **Military Serv:** AUS specialist 1955; DC Natl Guard 1st lt Medical Corps 1961, capt Medical Corps 1962. **Business Addr:** Professor, Division of Urology, Howard University College of Medicine, 2041 Georgia Ave NW, Suite 4C02, Washington, DC 20060.

JONES, GERALD E.
City employee, educator. **Personal:** Born Nov 2, 1937, Chicago, IL; married Barbara; children: Gerald E, III. **Educ:** Loyola Univ, master's 1970; Illinois Teachers Coll, 1965-66; Malcolm X Coll, AA 1963-; Chicago State Coll, business educ degree 1963-65. **Career:** City Council 7th Ward, first black mem 1973; Behavioral Science Dept Trinton Coll, 1972-74; GE Jones & Assoc, pres 1967-71; Kennedy King Coll, instructor 1970-71; Malcolm X Coll, coordinator 1970; Malcolm X Community Coll, 1969-70; Chicago City Coll, teacher 1968; Chicago City Coll, director of business 1967-69; Chicago Bd of Educ, teacher 1965-67; Concerned Minority Businessmen, spokesman. **Orgs:** Mem Amer Business & Economics Soc Chicago; assoc sec Amer Mgmt Assn; Assn School Business Officials US & Canada; IL Retailing & Marketing Found; NAACP; Afro-Amer History Club; Operation PUSH; C of C; S Shore Community Center; YMCA; Kiwanis. **Military Serv:** AUS med specialist.

JONES, GERALD WINFIELD
Government official. **Personal:** Born Jun 27, 1931, Jetersville, VA; son of Daisy Peachy L Jones (deceased) and Emmett Jones, Jr; married Ann H; children: Crenshaw, Cassandra Coleman, Lessie, Eric. **Educ:** VA State Coll, AB 1952; Howard Univ, LLB 1960. **Career:** Dept of Justice, Civil Rights Division, atty, 1960-65, superervising atty chief voting sect, 1965-, acting deputy asst atty general, 1988-. **Orgs:** Mem bd dirs Melwood Hort Training Ctr, 1975-83; mem Natl Bar Assn; mem Govt Lawyers Sect Natl Bar Assn. **Honors/Awds:** Superior Performance Awd Dept of Justice 1964; Spec Commendation Awd Dept of Justice 1972; Atty Gen Disting Serv Awd 1973 1983; Atty Gen's Awd for Upward Mobility 1978; Sr Exec Serv Meritorious Awd 1982, 1985-89; Presidentiaql Rank Meritorious Exec Award, 1990. **Military Serv:** AUS 1st lt 1952-55. **Business Addr:** Acting Deputy Assistant Attorney General, Dept of Justice, PO Box 66128, Washington, DC 20035-6128.

JONES, GERALDINE J.
Educator. **Personal:** Born Jul 30, 1939, Seaford, DE; divorced; children: Monica. **Educ:** DE State Coll, BS 1961; Central MI, MA Business Admin 1977; Temple Univ, 1986; Doctoral Candidate, TGSA. **Career:** Division of Social Services, social worker 1962-64; Head Start Camden Summer, social worker 1965, dir 1971; Migrant Program Summer, home coord 1974; CapitalSchool District, visiting teacher, educator; public speaker, currently; soloist, currently; free-lance writer, currently; Parent Educator, 1990-; Parent Early Educ Ctr, currently. **Orgs:** NEA; DSEA; Assn Visiting Teachers; Capital Assn; Tri-Co Investment & Savings Assn; Intl Assn Pupil Personnel Workers; adv council, DE Adolescent Program, 1985-89; Delta Sigma Theta; Natl Council Negro Women; Whatcoat United Methodist Church; DE State Coll Alumni Assn; Kent Co Alumni Assn; vol tchr Black Studies DE Youth Servs, 1980-; asst treas, UM Women, Whatcoat UM Church Dover; Kent County Chap DE State Coll Alumni; treas, Wm C Jason Alumni; Delaware Assn of Certified Vstg Teachers; lay leader Whatcoat UM Church; Miss Alumni 1986-87; DE State Coll, consultant; Delaware Technical & Community College, Minority Recruitment Bd; Delaware State College, Natl Alumni Assn, immediate past pres; JH Wms Ensemble, Yesterday's Youth, Gospel ensemble; United Methodist Church, General Conference, delegate,1992, Penisula Delaware Conference, delegate, NE Jurisdictional Conference, delegate, 1992, Annual Conference, delegate, 1990-; UMW, Peninsula Delaware Conference, immediate past pres, 1990-; NE Jurisdiction, UM Church, Upper Atlanta Regional School, asst dean; Delta Sigma Theta, Sussex Co Alumni Assn, treasure; Whatcoat UM Church, Summer Day Camp, director. **Honors/Awds:** African-American scholarship fund John Wesley United Methodist Church; Presidential Citation, NAFEO, 1993; Barnabas Award, UMC, Pen-Del Conference, 1990; James R Webb; scholarships; poem pub IAPPW Jornal 1974; Sigma Iota Epsilon Central MI 1979; Youth Serv Awd Whatcoat United Methodist Church 1984; Alumnus of the Year, Delaware State Coll 1985; Certificate of Appreciation, NAACP Central Delaware Branch, 1985; Serv Awd, Peninsula Conf United Methodist Women; Sigma Iota Epsilon Honor Society, Central Michigan, 1978; African-American leaders in Delaware, 1994; Recipient of the Alberta Brown Award, UMC, Martin Luther King Celebration, Pen-Del Conference, 1993. **Special Achievements:** Capital Attendance Program, organizer, originator, program to encourage positive school attendance and drop out prevention; CPP, Community Partnership Program, Organizer & Originator, 1993. **Business Addr:** Educator, Capital School District, 945 Forest St, Dover, DE 19901.

JONES, GERI DUNCAN
Association management executive. **Personal:** Born Nov 28, 1958, Chicago, IL; daughter of Carrie Gates Duncan and Grandee Duncan; married Michael A Jones, Jan 13, 1979; children: Michael A II, Marlon G, Marcus E. **Educ:** Eastern Illinois Univ, Charleston, IL, BA, 1979; Keller Graduate School of Business Management, Chicago, IL, 1982. **Career:** Charles A Davis & Associates, Chicago, IL, account executive, 1979-83; Debbie's School of Beauty Culture, Chicago, IL, public relations director, 1983-84; American Health & Beauty Aids Inst, Chicago, IL, account executive, 1984-88, executive director, 1988-. **Orgs:** Board of directors, Heritage of Afro American Beauty Industry, 1988-; member, Chicago Society of Association Executives, 1985-; member, Zeta Phi Beta Sorority, 1976-; Amer Society of Assn Executives; nat advisory comm, Madame C J Walker Spirit Awds; advisory bd, Urban Call; The Trade Magazines for Unbran Retailers. **Honors/Awds:** Excellence Award, Universal College of Beauty, 1988; Outstanding Business and Professional African-American Women, Blackbook, 1990; Black Enterprise Magazine Top 25 Black Women of 1994. **Business Addr:** Executive Director, American Health and Beauty Aids Institute, 401 N Michigan, Chicago, IL 60611, (312)644-6610.

JONES, GLENN
Vocalist, songwriter. **Personal:** Born in Jacksonville, FL; married Genobia Jeter-Jones. **Career:** Albums include: Glenn Jones, 1987; All for You, 1990; Greatest Hits, 1992; Here I Go Again, 1992; singles include: "Call Me," "I've Been Searchin' (Nobody like You)," "Say Yeah," "In You.". **Special Achievements:** At age 16, signed a recording contract with the Rev James Cleveland. **Business Phone:** (212)307-1459.

JONES, GRACE
Actress, singer. **Personal:** Born Jun 12, 1954; children: one son. **Career:** Former model; actress, singer, and peformance artist, currently; Film appearance in Boomerang, 1992. **Honors/Awds:** Top model for fashion magazines Vogue and Elle, numerous appearances in Stern. Films include: Conan the Destroyer; Deadly Vengeance; Grace Jones-One Man Show; Grace Jones-State of Grace; Siesta; Straight to Hell; Vamp; A View to a Kill; albums include: Warm Leatherette; Fame; Portfolio; Living My Life; Nightclubbing; Inside Story.

JONES, GREGORY ALLAN
Insurance executive. **Personal:** Born Aug 15, 1955, New York, NY; son of Alline & Willie Jones; married Sharon, Aug 30, 1980; children: Kimberly, Gregory Jr. **Educ:** Lehman College, BA, 1977; Insurance Institute of America, ARM, 1989. **Career:** American International Group, underwriter, 1977-79; INA special risk, jr underwriter, 1979-82; Chubb & Son, sr underwriter, 1982-86; Albert G Ruben & Co., vice pres, 1986-90; Near North Brokerage, sr vice pres, 1990-95; USI/Max Behm, sr vice pres, 1995-. **Orgs:** American Filmmakers Institute, 1992-; Black Filmmakers Foundation, 1990-. **Honors/Awds:** Lehman College, Athlete of the Year, 1977. **Business Addr:** Senior VP, USI/Max Behm & Associates Inc, 14140 Ventura Blvd, 3rd Fl, Sherman Oaks, CA 91423, (818)971-5469.

JONES, GREGORY WAYNE
Insurance executive. **Personal:** Born Dec 29, 1948, Newark, OH; son of Gordon & Mildred Jones; married Helen, Feb 6, 1968; children: Brian, Derek. **Educ:** Franklin University, BA, 1974; Hood College, MA, 1981; University of Penn Wharton School, MBA, 1984. **Career:** State Farm, underwriter, 1969-75, personnel rep, 1975-81, division manager, 1981-85, executive assistant, 1985-88; deputy regional vice pres, 1988-93, regional vice pres, 1993-. **Orgs:** 100 Black Men of Sonoma County, president/founder, 1989-93; CA State University Northridge, board of trustees, 1993-; LA Jr Achievement, board of directors, 1993-; LA Chamber of Commerce, board of directors, 1995-; Wellness Community, board of trustees, 1994; 100 Black Men of LA, 1996-; LA Minority Dev Group, board of advisors, 1996-. **Honors/Awds:** Jr Achievement of America, Bronze Leadership Awd, 1996; Empowerment Achievement Awd, Corporate Innovator Awd, 1995; Dollars and Sense Magazine, Corporate Trailblazer Award. **Military Serv:** US Army, National Guard, sp4, 1968-73. **Business Addr:** Regional Vice Pres, State Farm Insurance Co., 31303 Agoura Rd, Westlake Village, CA 91363, (818)707-5001.

JONES, GROVER WILLIAM, JR. (DEACON JONES)
Professional athlete. **Personal:** Born Apr 18, 1934, White Plains, NY; married Tiki; children: Monica. **Educ:** Ithaca Coll, BS. **Career:** Chicago White Sox, player, scout, instr, minor league mgr 1955-75; Houston Astros, hitting coach 1976-82; NY Yankees, scout 1983; San Diego Padres, hitting coach 1984-87; Baltimore Orioles Minor League, hitting coach, advance scout, 1987-. **Honors/Awds:** Mem Westchester Co & Ithaca Coll Hall of Fame; 1st Black Man Recog Hall of Fame Cooperstown; Honored Nations Top Am Legion Player 1951; Silver Bat Award Winner 1956. **Military Serv:** Military 1957-58. **Business Addr:** Baltimore Orioles, Oriole Park At Camden Yards, 333 W Camden St, Baltimore, MD 21201.

JONES, GUS
Association executive. **Career:** Michigan Black Horsemen's Assn, president. **Business Addr:** President, Michigan Black Horsemen's Association, 29716 Briarbank, Southfield, MI 48034.

JONES, GWENDOLYN J.
Library worker. **Personal:** Born Oct 31, 1953, Holly Springs, MS; daughter of Mary E Johnson Smith and Willie Payton Smith; married Willie Frank Jones, Oct 30, 1971; children: Anthony Tyrone, Clarissa Danyell. **Educ:** Northwest Jr College, Senotobia, MS, AS, 1978; Rust College, Holly Springs, MS, BS, 1984. **Career:** Rust College, Holly Springs, MS, technical service asst, 1979-. **Orgs:** Jones Grove Missionary Baptist Church, announcer 1983-, president/pastor's aid 1985-. **Honors/Awds:** Certificate of Attendance, BTU Congress, 1988; Certificate of Appreciation, Rust College International Alumni Assn, 1986; Agency Parent of the Year Award, ICS Headstart Inc, 1979-80; Certificate of Appreciation, Jones Grove MB Church, 1987; Certificate of Appreciation, Holly Springs/ Marshall Co, Rust Club, 1992; Certificate given by Post Matron's Jurisdiction of MS, 1994. **Home Addr:** 123 Old Hwy 7 South, Holly Springs, MS 38635.

JONES, H. THOMAS, II
Utility company executive. **Personal:** Born Sep 28, 1944, Maxton, NC; son of Nannie Ruth Webb Jones and Henry Thomas Jones Sr; married Joyce McDougald Jones, Dec 30, 1965; children: Thomasia Elva. **Educ:** Amarillo Jr College, Amarillo, TX, 1964; Pembroke State University, Pembroke, NC, BS, accounting, 1972; Central Michigan University, Mount Pleasant, MI, MA, business, 1979. **Career:** Carolina Power & Light Co, Raleigh, NC, various positions, 1972-. **Orgs:** Board member, American Cancer Society, 1989-91; vice chairman, Columbus County Minority Business Council, 1989-90; chairman, Columbus County Youth Enrichment Council, 1990-91; board member, United Carolina Bank, 1990-91; board member, Columbus County Hospital, 1990-91; Rotary Club, 1988-91. **Honors/Awds:** Alpha Man of the Year, Alpha Phi Alpha Fraternity, 1982. **Military Serv:** USAF, Sgt, 1963-67. **Home Addr:** 314 Edgewood Cir, Whiteville, NC 28472.

JONES, HARDI LIDDELL
Federal government official. **Personal:** Born Nov 2, 1942, St Louis, MO; son of Jamesetta B Liddell Jones and Thomas H E Jones; married Yvonne A Thompson Jones, Nov 16, 1963; children: Miriam Yvette, Sandra Lynnette. **Educ:** St Paul's Coll, BS (Cum Laude) 1962; Attended, Univ of MD-College Park 1963, George Washington Univ 1965. **Career:** US Naval Oceanographic Office, physical oceanographer 1962-63; US Fish & Wildlife Svcs, physical oceanographer 1963-65; US Naval Oceanographic Office, physical oceanographer 1965-67; Underwater Systems Inc, oceanographer 1967-71; US Naval Oceanographic Office, equal opportunity officer 1971-74; Bureau of Reclamation US Dept of Interior, dir office of equal opportunity 1974-81; US Dept of Treasury IRS, asst to the commissioner 1981-89; IRS, Office of Chief Counsel, special assistant to associate, 1989-. **Orgs:** Pres Prince George's County Club Frontiers Intl 1980-82; chmn bd of dirs Combined Comms in Action Prince George's County MD 1981-; mem Sigma Pi Phi Frat Beta Mu Boule 1981-; chmn labor and industry comm Prince George's Co MD NAACP 1983-; chmn bd of trustees St Paul's Coll Lawrenceville VA 1985-88; life mem Kappa Alpha Psi Frat Inc; first vice pres Prince George's NAACP 1990-; pres Prince George's Country Club Frontiers Int, 1991-; Prince George's County Branch NAACP, president, 1991-; Beta Mu Boule, Sigma Pi Phi Fraternity, Sire Archon, 1993-. **Honors/Awds:** Citation Oceanographer of the Navy 1974; Community Serv Awd Combined Communities in Action 1981; Distinguished Alumnus St Paul's College 1985; Presidential Award Prince George's NAACP 1987; Meritorious Honor AIM-IRS, 1988. **Home Addr:** 10215 Buena Vista, Seabrook, MD 20706.

JONES, HARLEY M.
Educator. **Personal:** Born Jun 12, 1936, Brooklyn, NY. **Educ:** Brooklyn Coll, BA 1956; Yale Sch of Arch, MA 1960. **Career:** Environmental Design Piratt Inst Brooklyn, Full prof, chmn 1972-75; NY State Counc on the Arts, colnterior Desing Mag, juror comp held by 1975; Bedford Stuyvesant Restoration Corp, supr architect; Westerman & Miller, project designer; ARCH Architect's Research Com in Harlem Gowanusboerum Hill Asso, consult to; Edgar Rafel William Lescaze, designer; Archit Practice in NYC, Specializing in Comm oriented projects; Residential Projects, Churches and Non-profit Projects. **Orgs:** Bd mem Soc of Preservation of Weeksville & Bedford Stuyvesant History; mem Interior Design Educ Counc; board mem Studio Museum in Harlem; mem Nat Preservation Hotel. **Honors/Awds:** Project chosen for show of Am Students Abroad 1959; exhibited in "Black Architects" show NY AIA 1972; Mellon Grant, 1986.

JONES, HAROLD M.
Musician. **Personal:** Born Mar 25, 1934, Chicago, IL; son of Rosetta Jones and William Henry Jones; married Wanda J Hudson, Jul 10, 1953; children: Ernest Milton, Louis Eugene, Antar Patrice. **Educ:** Sherwood Music School, certificate; Juilliard Sch of Music, diploma 1959. **Career:** Flutist and educator, Metropolitan Music School, Tremont YMHA, Bronx House Music School, Merrywood Music Camp, Juilliard School of Music, Preparatory Division, Westchester School of Music, Manhattanville College, Manhattan School of Music, Preparatory Division, City University of New York, teacher; The Antara Ensemble, dir, conductor. **Orgs:** Board member, 1965-, president, 1976-79, New York Flute Club; member, National Flute Assn, 1979; member, American Federation of Musicians, Local 802. **Honors/Awds:** Solo performances: Symphony of the New World; Municipal Concerts Orchestra and the American Symphony Orchestra; The Conservatory Orchestra of Brooklyn College; Chamber Orchestra for the Black American Music Symposium; South Arkansas Symphony; The Philharmonic of Greensboro, NC; Jackson Symphony Orchestra; numerous recital, orchestra, ensemble, and theatrical appearances. Collaborated with the Audubon String Quartet, the Fresk String Quartet, pianist Leon Bates, and guitarist Peter Segal. Recordings include: Vivaldi Concerti, Max Goberman; Island in the Sun, Harry Belafonte; Trio for Flute, Oboe, Piano, Howard Swanson; Poem for Flute and Harp, N Mondello; Robeson; POV, John Lewis; Harold Jones; From Bach to Bazzini; Afternoon Fantasies; CD, Just As I Am; Let Us Break Bread Together, Leonarda Records, Key to the City of Jackson, Tennessee, 1991. **Home Addr:** 100 W 94 St, New York, NY 10025.

JONES, HELEN HAMPTON
Librarian. **Personal:** Born Jun 9, 1941, Portsmouth, VA; daughter of Helen Bowen Hampton and George Livingston Hampton Sr (deceased); married James W Jones Jr (divorced 1974); children: Ginger R, Jewell W. **Educ:** Livingstone College, Salisbury, NC, BS, 1962; Syracuse University, Syracuse, NY, MS, 1975. **Career:** Norfolk State University, Norfolk, VA, clerk-stenographer, typist, 1963-75, acting library dir, 1976, asst acquisitions librarian, 1976-79, acquisitions librarian, 1979-88, acting asst dir of personnel, 1989-90, collection mgmt librarian, 1988-91; Elizabeth City State Univ, acquisitions librarian, 1997-. **Orgs:** Chairman, Portsmouth Public School Board, 1982-86; charter appointee, Portsmouth Municipal Finance Committee, 1972-74, 1978-80; vice chair, Portsmouth Parking Authority, 1979-80; chairman, Portsmouth Pan Hellenic Council, 1966-67; member, Virginia Library Assn, SE Library Assn, American Library Assn, 1975-. **Honors/Awds:** Honorary Life Member, National PTA, Portsmouth PTA Council, 1986; Honorary Life Member, Virginia PTA, Douglass Park School, 1985; Most Valuable Employee, Virginia Governmental Employees Assn, 1986; Citizen of the Year, Eureka Club, Inc, 1984; Medallion Award, Brighton Rock AME Zion Church, 1984. **Home Addr:** 1006 Robinson Rd, Portsmouth, VA 23701.

JONES, HENRY
Professional football player. **Personal:** Born Dec 29, 1967, St Louis, MO. **Educ:** University of Illinois, bachelor's degree in psychology, 1990. **Career:** Buffalo Bills, defensive back, 1991-. **Honors/Awds:** Pro Bowl, 1992. **Business Addr:** Professional Football Player, Buffalo Bills, One Bills Dr, Orchard Park, NY 14127, (716)648-1800.

JONES, HERBERT C.
Physician. **Personal:** Born Aug 1, 1936, Demopolis, AL; son of Bettie Mae Young Jones and Tom Allen Jones, Jr; married Bessie Chapman Jones, Jun 13, 1958; children: Sandra Jo Jones, Nancy Gayle Jones, Herbert Chapman Jones, Lisa Carol Jones. **Educ:** Talladega Coll, Talladega AL, 1953-56; Indiana Univ, Bloomington IN, AB 1957, MD 1961; Univ of IL Medical Center, Chicago IL, Residency in Otolaryngology, 1965-68. **Career:** Self-employed surgeon, Atlanta GA, 1968-. **Orgs:** Otolaryngology Section, Natl Medical Assn, former chairman, 1969-; fellow, Amer Academy of Otolaryngology, 1969-; American College of Surgeons, 1972-; GA State Medical Assn; NAACP; American Board of Otolaryngology, director, 1994-; American Academy of Otolaryngology, director, 1993-. **Honors/Awds:** Alpha Omega Alpha Honor Society, 1961; Father of the Year in Medicine, Concerned Black Clergy of Atlanta, 1987; Outstanding Physician in Otolaryngology, Black Enterprise Magazine, 1988; Physician of the Year, Atlanta Medical Assn 1990. **Military Serv:** US Air Force, Captain, 1961-65. **Business Addr:** Physician, 285 Boulevard NE, Ste 415, Atlanta, GA 30312.

JONES, HORTENSE
Consultant. **Personal:** Born Jan 10, 1918, Franklin, VA; married Theodore T Jones; children: Theodore Jr, Theodora Blackmon, Lawrence. **Educ:** Hampton Inst, BS 1947; NYU, MA 1950. **Career:** Newport News, tchr 1936-41; Cadman Cntr, tchr 1948; Day Care Cntr, educ dir 1948-50; City Day Care Ctrs, dir 1950-56; tchr 1956-63; More Effective Schs, dir & asst dir 1964-72; Childhood Edn, asst dir 1963-64, 1972-75; Ctr for Sch Dev New York City Bd of Edn, dir 1975-83; La Guardia Comm Coll, CUNY, adjunct prof; consultant in early childhood/ elementary education. **Orgs:** Tech Inst Peach Corp 1966-72; adj instr Queens Coll, Medgar Evers Coll 1972-75; dir early childhood educ 1979-80; mem NJ Day Care Council; mem Detroit Tchrs Assn; conducted workshops in, Akron, OH; Gary, IN; Indianapolis, IN; Canton, OH; Glen Falls, NY; Rochester, NY; consult Migrant Educ Conf 1970-72; Child Care Worker Training Prog Rutgers Univ 1971-72; lectr for num organizations. **Honors/Awds:** Mother of the Year Que Ives 1968; Sojourner Truth Award Natl Negro Bus & Professional Women's Club 1968; Comm Serv Award Preschool 1974; Day Care Award, Newark, NJ, 1977. **Business Addr:** Newark Day Care Council & St Paul Christian Community School, 131 Livingston St, Brooklyn, NY 11201.

JONES, HOWARD JAMES
Educator. **Personal:** Born Jun 19, 1944, Benton, LA; son of Elnora Morris Jones and Woodrow Jones; married Joyce Kemp Jones, Dec 12, 1971; children: Jonora Kinshasa, Howard James III. **Educ:** Southern University, Baton Rouge, LA, BA, 1966; Howard University, Washington, DC, MA, 1968; Washington State University, Pullman, WA, PhD, 1975. **Career:** Grambling State University, Grambling, LA, instructor, 1967-70; Univ of South Mississippi, Hattiesburg, MS, assistant professor, 1974-76; Prairie View A&M Univ, Prairie View, TX, instructor, 1976-78; Texas Southern Univ, Houston, TX, assistant professor, 1978-82; Prairie View A&M Univ, Prairie View, TX, associate professor, 1985-. **Orgs:** Secretary/treasurer, Southern Conference on Afro-American Studies Inc, 1979-; 2nd vice president, Association of Caribbean Studies, 1989-. **Honors/Awds:** Graduate Studies Fellow, Southern Fellowships Fund, 1970-75; Academic Scholarship Holder, Louisiana Academic Sch, 1962-66. **Business Addr:** Secretary, Treasurer, SCAASI, PO Box 330163, Houston, TX 77233-0163.

JONES, I. GENE
Educational administrator. **Educ:** Jarvis Christian Coll, BA 1942; Ball State Univ, MA 1963; Univ of MI, PhD 1974. **Career:** Denver Public Schls, tchr and adm asst 1954-62; Ball State Univ, asst prof 1962-64; Central Comm Coll, instruct, Inglewood, CA, 1964-66; Unified School Dist, reading resource and curriculum devel spec 1966-68; Eastern MI Univ, asst prof of education 1969-73; GA State Univ, adjunct faculty 1975-78; Albany State College, asst dean-academic affairs 1973-78; St Paul's Coll, vice pres for academic affairs 1978-, provost, 1988. **Orgs:** Bd of directors YWCA Denver 1960-62; bd of directors United Way of Dougherty Cty 1975-78; team capt GA Heart Fund Assn 1977-78; mem New Mexico First. **Honors/Awds:** Amer Book Co textbooks published 1967; Exxon Fellow Amer Council of Educ Educl Leadership Devel 1975; Distinguished Alumni Award, Jarvis Christian College 1985; Presidential Citation, National Assn for Equal Opportunity in Higher Education 1986. **Home Addr:** 1601 Pennsylvania, NE, Winrock Villas H-10, Albuquerque, NM 87110.

JONES, IDA KILPATRICK. See WHITE, IDA MARGARET.

JONES, IDA M.
Educator, lawyer. **Personal:** Born Aug 18, 1953, Omaha, NE; daughter of Mary Cooper Jones and Jonathan Jones; married Harry Edward Williams (divorced 1980); children: Kenneth, Eugene, Kamali, Jamilla. **Educ:** Creighton Univ, Omaha, NE, BA, 1974; New York Univ, New York, NY, JD, 1977. **Career:** Legal Aid-Criminal Appeals, New York, NY, associate appellate counsel, 1977-79; Legal Aid Society, Omaha, NE, staff attorney, 1979-81; Univ of Nebraska, Omaha, Omaha, NE, assoc prof, 1981-87; California State Univ, Fresno, Fresno, CA, prof, 1987-. **Orgs:** Western Business Law Assn, 1st vp, 1988, pres, 1990; American Business Law Assn, mem, 1985-, officer, 1986; Nebraska Bar Assn, mem, 1982-; New York Bar, mem, 1978-; CA Bar Assn, mem, 1990-; Beta Gamma Sigma, mem, 1985-; Alpha Sigma Nu, mem, 1974-. **Honors/Awds:** Educational Innovation, Craig School of Business Award, 1990; Meritorious Performance, California State Univ, Fresno, 1988, 1990; Research Awards, California State Univ, Fresno, 1987-91; Research Awards, UNO, 1987; Verna Mae & Wayne A Brooks Professor of Business Law, first recipient, 1996-99. **Home Addr:** 5382 N Angus, Fresno, CA 93710. **Business Addr:** Professor, Finance/Business Law Dept, School of Business, California State Univ, Fresno, Cedar & Shaw Aves, Fresno, CA 93740-0007, (209)278-2151.

JONES, IDUS, JR.
Clergyman (retired). **Personal:** Born Apr 18, 1927, Philadelphia, PA; son of Rosa Lee Lowe (deceased) and Idus Jones; married Cora F Coleman; children: Carol A Burlark, Maria F Parker, George I, Michael R, Raymond G, Eugenia R Moten, Cheryl A Barber, Joette F, Harold D, Anna K Minor, Idus III, Charles. **Educ:** IN Univ PA, continuing educ Black studies 1970, BA Sociology Anthropology 1972; Pgh Theological Seminary, MDiv 1975; United Theological Seminary, Dayton, OH, Dr Min, 1991. **Career:** Cornerstone Baptist Church, minister 1958-60; Church of the Living God, minister 1960-70; Pleasant Hills Baptist Church, asst pastor 1970-72; John Wesley United Methodist Church, pastor 1973-74; Brushton United Methodist Church, pastor 1974-80; John Stewart United Meth Church, pastor 1980-81; Ebenezer United Methodist Church, pastor/chmn; Ebenezer Comm Outreach Bd, 1981-; Heart-Hand Housing, Phillipi, WV, director, 1988-89; Harry Hosier Memorial United Methodist Church, founding pastor, 1990-96; Marshal College of Grad Studies, adj prof; IN Univ of PA, Dept of Soc, visitation lecturer; Salem Industrial home for Youth, visitation chaplain. **Orgs:** Visitation minister at various Correctional Inst throughout Eastern PA and NJ area; super Ebenezer Comm Outreach Ctr Inc; mem Huntington Food Bank Inc; mem Tri-State Evangelistic Assn; mem NAACP; charter mem Psi Beta Beta Chap Omega Psi Phi Frat Inc; mem Kiwanis Club Intl; chairperson Emphasis Comm; mem Tri State Area Council No 672 Boy Scouts of Amer; mem Mt Moriah Lodge No 36 F&AM; consistory St Cyprian No 4 Sahara Temple No 2 AEAO NMS Inc; mem Gov's Commn on Crime Correction Delinquency Subcomm Juvenile; bd of dirs Salvation Army; bd ordained minister WV Dist; chaplain in charge Cabell County Jail WV; life member, NAACP, 1988; WV Children Connt; United Bank, bd dir; Beckley WV Kiwanis Club; American Legion Post #44. **Honors/Awds:** Minister of the Yr Awd Hand-in-Hand 1977; Scottish Rite Mason of the Yr Awd AASR F AM (PHA) 1978; Human Serv Awd Teen Challenge Western PA; Black Pastors Ministerial Comm Awd 1987; Munster Comm Service Award; Beckley Police Dept, Juvenile Section, Comm Service Award; WV Ed Assoc, Effie Mayhorn Brown Award. **Military Serv:** USN seaman 1st class 4 yrs; Amer Campaign Medal; Asiatic-Pacific Campaign Medal; Good Conduct Medal; WWII Victory Medal; Korean Medal; USCG Boatsw 13 yrs. **Home Addr:** Rt2, Box 71-J, Philippi, WV 26416.

JONES, INGRID SAUNDERS
Beverage company executive. **Personal:** Born Dec 27, 1945, Detroit, MI; daughter of Georgia Lyles Saunders and Homer L Saunders; divorced. **Educ:** Michigan State University, East Lansing, MI, BA, education, 1968; Eastern Michigan University, Ypsilanti, MI, MA, education, 1972. **Career:** Detroit Wayne County Child Care Coordinating Council, Detroit, MI, executive director, 1974-77; Atlanta Urban Fellow, Atlanta, GA, special assistant, Atlanta City Council, 1977-78; City of Atlanta, Atlanta, GA, legislative analyst for Atlanta City Council president, 1978-79, executive assistant to the mayor, 1979-81; Coca-Cola Company, Atlanta, GA, director Urban Affairs, 1987-88, assistant vice president Urban & Governmental affairs, 1988-92, vice pres, Corporate External Affairs, 1992-, chairperson, Coca-Cola Foundation, 1992-. **Orgs:** Bd of dirs: UNICE; Atlanta Neighborhood Devel Corp; Central Atlanta Progress, Congressional Black Caucus Foundation; Natl Minority Supplier Development Council; Exec Leadership Council Foundation; The Woodruff Arts Ctr; GA Dept of Industry, Trade and Tourism; Just Us Theater Co; United Way of Metro Atlanta; Metropolitan Community Foundation; Atlanta Empowerment Zone Corp; The Atlanta Business League; The Links; Delta Sigma Theta Sor; Society of Intl Business Fellows; Atlanta Women's Network; Intl Women's Forum; National Forum of Black Public Administrators. **Honors/Awds:** Fellowship Atlanta Urban Fellow, City of Atlanta, 1977-78; 100 Black Business & Professional Women Award, Dollar & Sense Magazine, 1978; 100 Black Female Corporate Executives, Ebony Magazine, 1990; Natl Equal Justice Award, NAACP, 1997; Women of Achievement Award, YWCA; Distinguished Comm Svc Award, Atlanta Urban League, 1996; DECA Award, Atlanta Bus Chronicle; Herbert H Wright Comm Svc Award, Natl Urban Legaue; Corp Pioneer Award, Bethune-DuboisFund; Hon Doctor of Humanities, MI State Univ; Hon Doctor of Humanities, Morris Brown Coll. **Business Addr:** Vice Pres, Corporate External Affairs, The Coca-Cola Co, PO Drawer 1734, Atlanta, GA 30301.

JONES, IRMA RENAE
Police officer. **Personal:** Born Feb 20, 1942, Uriah, AL; daughter of Lamb & Willie Virginia Harris; married Robert Lloyd Jones, Jan 7, 1980; children: Lisa White, Tiffany Dotson, Robin. **Educ:** Wayne County Comm College, AA, 1973; Wayne State Univ, BS, 1982; Eastern Michigan Univ, MLS, 1989. **Career:** New York Univ, clerk typist, 1960-64; Columbia Univ, clerk typist, 1965-68; Pacific Bell Telephone, operator, 1968; Bethlehem Steel, typist, 1968-71; WXYZ-TV, typist clerk, 1971-72; Detroit Partition Co, secretary, 1972-77; Detroit Police Dept, police officer, 1977-. **Orgs:** NAACP, 1991-; DPD Law Enforcement Explorers, advisor, 1988-; BUOY 13, bd member, 1988-; Children's Center Outpatient, advisory committee, 1991-93; Burton Detention Center, advisory committee, 1991-94. **Honors/Awds:** Detroit Police, Officer of the Year, 1994; Plymouth United Church of Christ, Community Services, 1994; Detroit Police Law Enforcement Explorers, Dedication to Exploring, 1994; Boy Scouts of America, Devoted & Untiring Work to Detroit Police Law Enforcement Explorer Post 1313, 1994. **Home Addr:** 5245 Avery, Detroit, MI 48208. **Business Addr:** Community Relations Officer, Detroit Police Dept, 13th Precinct, 4747 Woodward, Detroit, MI 48201.

JONES, ISAAC, JR.
Computer company executive (retired), consultant. **Personal:** Born Jun 19, 1933, Opelika, AL; son of Katie Chisolm Jones (deceased) and Isaac Jones Sr (deceased); married Zerelene E White. **Educ:** AL State Univ, BSEd, 1954; State Univ of NY, Binghamton, MS, mgmt, 1971. **Career:** IBM, Boulder, CO, mgr, 2nd level, 1980-81; IBM, Brooklyn, mgr, 3rd level, 1984; IBM Division Headquarters, sr business planner, 1984-1992; IZY Consultants Inc, president, currently. **Orgs:** National Black MBA Association, Inc.

JONES, JACQUELINE VALARIE
Journalist. **Personal:** Born Aug 7, 1954, Washington, DC; daughter of Alice Pope and Melvin C Jones; children: Tony. **Educ:** George Washington Univ, BA journalism, 1976; Cleveland State Univ, English, 1979-80. **Career:** Mutual Broadcasting/Mutual Black Network, tape ed, 1975-77; UPI, Atlanta, reporter, 1977-78; Cleveland Plain Dealer, reporter, 1978-80; Balt Eve Sun, reporter, 1980-81; Washington Star, reporter, 1981; Detroit Free Press, reporter, copy ed, 1981-84; Mpls Star Tribune, copy ed, 1984-87; NY Newsday, adm ed, night city ed, asst city ed, copy ed, 1987-92; Phila Daily News, city ed, 1992-. **Orgs:** Natl Assn of Black Journalists Parliamentarian, vp, print, 1989-95. **Business Addr:** Assistant City Editor, Washington Post, 1150 15th St. NW, Washington, DC 20071, (202)334-6000.

JONES, JAMES
Professional football player. **Career:** Detroit Lions, 1993-. **Business Phone:** (313)335-4131.

JONES, JAMES ALFIE
Professional football player. **Personal:** Born Feb 6, 1969, Davenport, IA. **Educ:** Northern Iowa, degree in science, 1992. **Career:** Cleveland Browns, defensive tackle, 1991-94; Denver Broncos, 1995; Baltimore Ravens, 1996-; Jones' Tire Service, co-owner. **Honors/Awds:** Cleveland Browns, Edge NFL Man of the Year, 1993; Cleveland Touchdown Club, Humanitarian Award, 1993. **Business Addr:** Professional Football Player, Baltimore Ravens, 11001 Owings Mills Blvd, Owings Mills, MD 21117, (410)654-6200.

JONES, JAMES B.
Automotobile dealer. **Career:** Macon Chrysler-Plymouth Inc, CEO, 1978-. **Special Achievements:** Company is ranked #20 on the Black Enterprise list of Top 100 auto dealers, 1994. **Business Addr:** CEO, Macon Chrysler-Plymouth Inc., 2110 Eisenhower Pkwy., Macon, GA 31206, (912)781-0760.

JONES, JAMES BENNETT
Government official. **Personal:** Born Jun 2, 1931, Wilson, AR; son of Marie Jones and Will Jones; married Mary Frances Bynum; children: Theresa, Gwendolyn. **Educ:** Lawrence Inst of Tech, BS 1963; Wayne State U, 1972. **Career:** Detroit Bldg Authority, gen mgr 1976-; Detroit Gen Hosp, dir of planning 1973-76; dir 1971-73; proj mgr 1968-71; sr asso 1965-68; Lawrence & of Tech, instr 1973-; Detroit Water & Sewer, architect l976-82; Saudi Arabia, senior construction mgr l982-85; Ford Motor Co architect/engineer l985-87; City of Milwaukee, asst supt l987-. **Orgs:** Bd dir, treas Friends of Econ Devel 1972-75; Am Inst of Architects; MI Soc of Architects; Nat Assn of Minority Architects; Nat Fire Prevension Assn; Fire Safety Adv Com MI Phi Beta Sigma; Optimist Internat; pres Kingsmen Soc Club 1966-76; NAACP; Urban Alliance; Am Mgrs Assn; Amer Public Works Assn; Natl Assn Housing Redevelopment Officials. **Honors/Awds:** Nat award Nat Urban League 1973; natl march of dimes 1974; career guidance award Detroit Housin Com 1972. **Military Serv:** AUS corpl 1951-53. **Home Addr:** 3220 North Sherman Blvd, Apt 2, Milwaukee, WI 53202. **Business Addr:** DPW/Bureau of Bridges, 841 N Broadway, Suite 3ll, Milwaukee, WI 53202.

JONES, JAMES C.
Business executive. **Personal:** Born Feb 14, 1913, Westmoreland Co, VA; married Gertrude Robb; children: Beverly, Collis, Sheila. **Educ:** Howard Univ; Catholic Univ. **Career:** James C Jones Builders Inc, pres 1947-; Construction Supr Cassell Contruction, 1943-47; Phelps Vocational Sch, tchr blueprint reading & woodworking 1938-43; Oliver B Cassell & Construction Co, construction supr 1936-38; Morrison Bros Construction Co, foreman 1935-36. **Orgs:** Mem bd of trustees Minority Contractors Assn of DC; historian Natl Tech Assn; mem Mayors Task Force NAACP; Urban League; past pres Holy Name Soc; past treas Archidiocesan Holy Name Union; past treas, vice pres & mem of bd dir Sierra Club of Washington; mem Archbishops Annual Comm on Appeal for Execs Gifts; Omega Psi Phi. **Honors/Awds:** Plaque for outstanding business leadership Washington Minority Contractors; plaque for outstanding serv Natl Tech Assn; past pres outstanding award from Holy Name Soc of St Anthony's Catholic Church. **Business Addr:** 5331 Georgia Ave NW, Washington, DC.

JONES, JAMES EARL
Actor. **Personal:** Born Jan 17, 1931, Tate County, MS; son of Ruth Williams Jones and Robert Earl Jones; married Julienne Marie Hendricks (divorced); married Cecilia Hart, Mar 15, 1982; children: Flynn Earl. **Educ:** Univ of MI, BA 1953; Amer Theatre Wing, diploma 1957. **Career:** Actor. Plays include: Romeo and Juliet; Wedding in Japan; Sunrise in Campobello; Much Ado About Nothing; The Sleep of Prisoners; The Birds; The Caine Mutiny; Velvet Gloves; The Tender Trap; Arsenic and Old Lace; The Desperate Hours; The Pretender; The Cool World; King Henry V; Measure for Measure; The Blacks; A Midsummer Nights Dream; The Apple; Moon on a Rainbow Shawl; Infidel Caesar; The Merchant of Venice; The Tempest; Toys in the Attic; PS 193; Macbeth; The Love Nest; The Last Minstrel; Othello; The Winter's Tale; Mr Johnson; Next Time I'll Sing to You; Bloodknot; King Lear; Of Mice and Men; Paul Robeson; Master Harold and The Boys; films include: Dr Strangelove; The Comedians; The Man; The River Niger; Swashbuckler; Bingo Long Traveling All-Stars and Motor Kings; Exorcist II, The Heretic; The Greatest; The Last Remake of Beau Geste; A Piece of the Action; Allan Quartermain and the Lost City of Gold; The Bushido Blade; Conan the Barbarian; Blood Tide; Gardens of Stone; Matewan; Conan the Barbarian; Coming to America; Field of Dreams; Three Fugitives; Into Thin Air; The Grand Tour; Scorchers; I Can't Lose; The Hunt for Red October; Sommersby; Excessive Force; Meteor Man; Patriot Games; Sneakers; Clear and Present Danger; Clean Slate; Sandlot; Confessions: Two Faces of Evil; Cry the Beloved Country; voice of King Mufasa in The Lion King; voice of Darth Vader in the Star Wars Trilogy; TV appearances include: The Defenders; East Side/West Side; Camera 3; Look Up and Give; The Cay; King Lear; Big Joe and Kansas; UFO Incident; Jesus of Nazarath; The Greatest Thing That Almost Happened; Guyana Tragedy, The Story of Jim Jones; Me & Mom; Paris; The Golden Movement, An Olympic Love Story; Sojourner; A Day Without Sunshine; Gabriel's Fire; Pros and Cons; Under One Roof; Homicide, 1997; What The Deaf Man Heard, 1997. **Orgs:** Screen Actors Guild, Actors' Equity Assn; American Federation of Television and Radio Artists; National Council of the Arts; Theatre Communications Group, board of directors. **Honors/Awds:** Recip, The Village Voice Off-Broadway Awards, 1962; Theatre World Award, 1962; Drama Desk Award, 1964, 1967, 1969, 1970; Obie Award, 1965; Tony Award for Best Actor, Great White Hope, 1969, Best Actor, Fences; Golden Gate Award, 1975; Golden Hugo Award, 1975; Gabriel Award, 1975; Grammy Award, 1976; Medal for Spoken Language, American Academy of Arts and Letters, 1981; inducted into Theatre Hall of Fame, 1985; Antoinette Perry

Award, 1987; Outer Critics Circle Award, 1987; Emmy Award, Soldier Boys, 1987; ACE Award, 1989; Emmy Award, Heatwave, 1990; Los Angeles Film Teachers, Jean Renoir Award, 1990; Bank of Delaware, Commonwealth Award for Distinguished Service in the Dramatic Arts, 1991; Emmy Award, Gabriel's Fire, 1991; NAACP, Hall of Fame Image Award, 1992; National Medal of the Arts, 1992. **Business Addr:** Actor, c/o Bauman & Hiller, 5750 Wilshire Blvd, PH 5, Los Angeles, CA 90036, (213)932-6026.

JONES, JAMES EDWARD, JR.
Educator. **Personal:** Born Jun 4, 1924, Little Rock, AR; son of Alice J. Truman; married Joan Cottrell Turner; children: Evan, Peter. **Educ:** Lincoln Univ, BA 1950; Univ IL Inst Labor and Indus Relations, MA 1951; University of Wisconsin School of Law, JD 1956. **Career:** US Wage Stabilization Board, industrial relations analyst, 1951-53; US Department of Labor, legislative attorney, 1956-63, counsel for labor relations, 1963-66; Office of Labor Management Policy Development, director, 1966-67; associate solicitor, Division of Labor Relations and Civil Rights, 1967-69; Univ WI-Madison, vistg prof law and indus relations 1969-70; Inst for Rsch on Poverty, assoc 1970-71; Inst Relations, Rsch Inst, dir 1971-73; Ctr for Equal Employment and Affirmative Action, Indus Relations Rsch Inst, dir 1974-; Univ WI, prof of law 1970-, Bascom prof law 1982-91; Nathan P Feinsinger Professor of Labor Law, 1991-93; Prof Emeritus, 1993-. **Orgs:** National Bar Assn; member, State Bar of Wisconsin; American Bar Assn, 1985-; public review board member, UAW, 1970; advisory committee, National Research Council National Academy of Sciences, 1971-73; Wisconsin Governor's Task Force on Comparable Worth, 1984-86; Madison School District Affirmative Action Advisory Committee, 1988-91; National Academy of Arbitrators, 1982-. **Honors/Awds:** Sec Labor Career Service Awd Dept Labor 1963; John Hay Whitney Fellow; contributor articles, chapters to professional publs; Smongeski Award, 1988; Alumni Achievement Award, Lincoln University, 1967; Order of the Coif, 1970; Phi Kappa Phi, 1987; Prof of the Year, UW Leo Students, 1986; Hilldale Award, Social Sci Div, 1991; Martin Luther King Humanitarian Award, City of Madison, WI, 1991; C Clyde Ferguson, Jr Memorial Award, American Assn of Law Schools Minority Group Section, 1993; Distinguished Service Awd, Wisconsin Law Alumni Association, 1995; Distinguished Alumni Awd, University of Illinois, 1996; Society of American Law, Teachers Achievement Award, 1998. **Military Serv:** US Navy, 1943-46. **Business Addr:** Professor of Law, Univeristy of Wisconsin, University Law School, Madison, WI 53706.

JONES, JAMES MCCOY
Educator. **Personal:** Born Apr 5, 1941, Detroit; son of Marcella Hayes-Jones and Arthur McCoy Jones; married Olaive Burrowes; children: Shelly, Itenash. **Educ:** Oberlin Coll, BA 1963; Temple U, MA 1967; Yale U, PhD 1970. **Career:** The Franklin Institute, Philadelphia, psychology research, 1964-66; Harvard Univ, assistant professor soc psychology, 1970-74; associate professor soc psychology, 1974-76; Education Development Center, Exploring Childhoood Project, senior scholar, 1973-74; Boston Office Lawrence Johnson & Assocs, dir 1974-76; National Institute for Adv Studies, staff dir, 1976-77; Amychol Association, Minority Fellowship Program, director, 1977; Univ of Delaware, professor of psychology, 1982-. **Orgs:** Exec dir Pub Int Am Psychol Assn, 1987-91; Assn of Black Psychologists; Soc for the Psychol Study of Study of Social Issues; educ consult Journal of Personality & Social Psychology; Journal of Clin Psy; Psychology Bulletin; NIMH Small Grant Review Com; assembly of Behavioral Sci 1973-77; adv bd WEB Dubois Research Inst; Comm Research Review Com Roxbury MA 1970-74. **Honors/Awds:** Glen Grey Mem Scholar Oberlin Coll 1959-63; Hon Sterling Fellow Yale Univ 1968-69; NIMH Predoctoral Fellow 1967-70; John Simon Guggenheim Fellow 1973-74. **Special Achievements:** Author: ''Prejudice and Racism''; ''The Black Experience''. **Business Addr:** Professor of Psychology, University of Delaware, Newark, DE 19716, (302)831-2271.

JONES, JAMES P.
Dentist. **Personal:** Born Mar 28, 1914, New York, NY; married Ada Celeste. **Educ:** Howard Univ Dental Coll, DDS 1941; New York U, BS chemistry. **Career:** Private Practice, dentist; Dept of Oral Surg Harlem Hosp, attending dentist 1946-; Dept of Dentistry Sydehham Hosp, attending dentist; Dept of Social Serv, investigator; Dept of Probation, probation officer. **Orgs:** Bd of dirs/delegate First District Dental Soc; bd mem New York City USO; bd chmn Amistad Housing Devel; asso dir Sydenham Hosp Model Cities Facilities. **Honors/Awds:** Fellow Am Coll of Dentist; fellow Intl Coll of Dentist; fellow New York Acad of Dentist; fellow Am Acad of Dentist Internatl. **Military Serv:** AUS major 1941-46. **Business Addr:** 219 W 138 St, New York, NY 10030.

JONES, JAMES R., III
Health care executive. **Personal:** Born Apr 1, 1944, Morristown, NJ; son of Elizabeth B Jones and James E Jones; married Janet Watkins-Jones, Feb 12, 1967; children: Jill, Jackie, Jimmy. **Educ:** University of Nebraska, undergraduate degree, secondary education/library science, 1966; Central Michigan University, graduate degree, management/personnel, 1979. **Career:** Professional Football Player, teacher, 1966-70; New York Jets Professional Football Club, assistant director of personnel, 1970-72; Jersey Central Power and Light Co., manager of employment, 1972-80; Gannett Co Inc, director, affirmative action and employee relations, 1980-84, vp, employee relations, 1984-91; John Hopkins University, vp for human resources, 1991-95; Franciscan Health Systems, vp of human resources, 1995-. **Orgs:** Kappa Alpha Phi; Executive Leadership Council, Black Human Resources Network; Edges; Society for Human Resources Management; Human Resources Roundtable, senior vp. **Home Phone:** (201)538-5783. **Business Addr:** VP, Human Resources, Franciscan Health Systems, 1 Mac Intyre Drive, Aston, PA 19014-7796, (610)358-9245.

JONES, JAMES V.
Automobile dealer. **Personal:** Born May 16, 1942, Jackson, NC; son of Viola M Brown-Jones and James Jones; divorced; children: James III. **Educ:** North Carolina Central Univ, Durham NC, law degree, 1976. **Career:** Ozone Ford, Ltd, Ozone Park NY, pres, 1987-.

JONES, JAMES WESLEY
Cleric. **Personal:** Born Oct 30, 1935, Lake Commerant, MS; married Annie Catherine Proctor; children: James Jr. **Educ:** Detroit Bible Coll, attended 1959-61; Am Bapt Sem, attended 1964-65. **Career:** Mt Moriah Bapt Cincinnati, pastor 1965-; New Liberty Bapt Detroit, asso minister 1959-65; Electronic Media Cincinnati, 1972; increased black employment; increased black on-air personalities; increased black oriented programming, all netword affiliated TV stations; created comm access to TV & radio through progson all stations; independently produced over 60 spls on 3 network affiliates 1973-; James Wesley Housing; operator creator of thousands of job opportunities; working on minority participation cable TV. **Orgs:** Mem World Bapt Alliance 1965-80; mem Bapt & Conv USA Inc 1965-80; chmn social action Missionary Bapt Dist Assn Cincinnati 1980-; pres/exec producer Black Cultural Prodn Inc 1971-80; chmn Coalition of Blacks Concerned for Justice & Equality Media 1971-80; bd mem So Leadership Conf 1973-;chmn Hunger Coalition; expanding free feeding progs to thousands; pres M M Devel Corp. **Honors/Awds:** Golden Mick Award WCIN Radio-wlw Radio Cincinnati 1975 & 1977; Giant Among Men Award Women In Communications 1976; Outstanding Contrib Media to Community WLW-TV 5 Cincinnati 1977; Contrib Histo Soc 1979. **Business Addr:** 1169 Simmons St, Cincinnati, OH 45215.

JONES, JENNIE Y.
Educator. **Personal:** Born May 26, 1921, Woodlawn, IL; widowed; children: Johnetta, Harry, Jerry, Danny. **Educ:** SIU Carbondale IL, BEd, BEd 1942; Univ IL, MA 1949. **Career:** Child Devel Lab SIU Carbondale , asst prof & dir; Head Start SIU, regional training ofcr 1970-74; prog dir 1973; Carbonate Sch Dist #95, tchr 1948-70. **Orgs:** Mem bd dirs IL assn for Educ of Young Children Children; Delta Kappa Gamma; adv com Training & Technical Assistancemodel Citied; bd dirs State Comm Coordinated Child Care; adv com Lincolnland Comm Coll. **Honors/Awds:** Hon advisory consult award Jackson Co Mental Halth Bd IL Assn Head Start Dirs 1975. **Business Addr:** Dept of Child & Family, 1168 SIU, Carbondale, IL 62901.

JONES, JENNIFER
Opera singer. **Personal:** Born in Wilmington, DE; children: 3. **Educ:** Curtis Institute of Music, BM, 1975. **Career:** Opera singer, currently; Houston Grand Opera, alto soloist, 1980; Montreal Symphony, soloist, 1980; New York Philharmonic, soloist, 1979; Israeli Philharmonic, soloist, 1976, 1980; Los Angeles Philharmonic, soloist, 1976, 1978, 1980; Philadelphia Orchestra, soloist 1973; Grant Martha Baird Rockefeller & Found Philadelphia Orchestra Competition, soloist 1973.

JONES, JESSE W.
College educator/administrator. **Personal:** Born Jan 16, 1931, Troup, TX; married LaBelle; children: Penola Washington, Tacora Ballums, Phelisha, Jesse Jr, David, Stephen, Lilla. **Educ:** TX Coll, BS 1954; Univ of UT, Advanced Work 1956; Highlands Univ, MS 1956; AZ State Univ, PhD 1963. **Career:** TX Coll, instructor of chem 1956-58; AZ State, rsch assoc 1958-63; TX Coll, chmn/prof 1963-68; Bishop Coll, chmn/prof 1968-. **Orgs:** Pres Bishop Coll Fed Credit Union 1969-85; vice chmn City of Dallas Bd of Adjustment 1977-82; pres Dallas Cty Democratic Progressive Voters League 1977-85; vice chmn Dallas Environ Health Commiss 1983-; mem Amer Chem Soc; fellow Amer Scientific Soc; sec Searcy's Youth Found; fellow Amer Inst of Chemists. **Honors/Awds:** Salutatorium EJ Scott High School 1950; Outstanding Citizenship Mu Gamma Chap Omega Psi Phi 1976; Silver Beaver Awd Boys Scouts of Amer 1983; Craft Awd in Politics Dalls Chap NAACP 1984; UNCF Disting Scholar 1986; TX Black Legislator's Citizenship Awd 1987.

JONES, JIMMIE DENE
Business consultant. **Personal:** Born Feb 26, 1939, Childress, TX; married Thelma Wilkerson; children: Vickie Harris, Jimmie D Jr, Amanda Lene Scott, Darryl Bryan. **Educ:** St Marys Coll, BS, BA 1973; George Washington Univ, MBA 1978; College of Financial Planning, Certificate 1984. **Career:** Law Engineering, personnel dir 1979-86; J&L Financial Svcs, owner 1986-; business consultant, 1982-. **Orgs:** Mem Northern VA Minority & Professional Business Assoc 1984; chmn, exec, LB Bailey Foundation for Youthful Entrepreneurs. **Honors/Awds:** Proclamation for Volunteer as Financial Counselor County Extension Office 1986. **Military Serv:** AUS cmd sgt major E9 22 yrs; Army Commendation Medal, Bronze Star. **Home Addr:** 14760 Independent Lane, Manassas, VA 22111.

JONES, JIMMIE SIMMS
Professional football player. **Personal:** Born Jan 9, 1966, Lakeland, FL; children: Jimmeria, Jimmie Jr. **Educ:** Miami (Fla.), attended. **Career:** Dallas Cowboys, defensive tackle, 1990-93; Los Angeles Rams, 1994; St Louis Rams, 1995-97; Philadelphia Eagles, 1997-. **Honors/Awds:** NFL, Extra Effort Award, 1995; St Louis Rams, True Value Hardware Man of the Year Award, 1995. **Business Addr:** Professional Football Player, Philadelphia Eagles, 3501 S Broad St, Philadelphia, PA 19148, (215)463-2500.

JONES, JOHN L.
Photocopy company executive. **Personal:** Born Jan 18, 1939, Delray Beach, FL; son of Willie Mac Jones and James Jones; married Betty Jones; children: Jonathan Vance Jones. **Educ:** Butler U, B Psych & Span 1960; Temple U, M Psych 1964; Boston U, EdD Human Rel 1970. **Career:** Project Follow Through, NTL-IABS, dir 1970-71; Mgmt Consultant firm, Vice Pres owner 1968-71;General Electric Co, Mgr personnel devl 1966-67; empl mgr 1966-67;General Foods, communications specialist 1965-66; Dept of Defense supply inventory mgr; Xerox Corp, mgr human resources planning, dir corporate affirmative action 1974-77; mgr corporate person devl 1972-77; mgr region training & orig 1971-72; Xerox of Canada, mgr mgmt & org dev 1975-77; Xerox Stamford, mgr corp human resources 1977-80; Xerox; personnel mgr 1880-81; Dir Corp Employer Resources 1987. **Orgs:** Chmn business policy review counsel; Chmn, natl consortium for educational access; audit committee, Boys choir of Harlem; executive comm, Program to increase minorities in business. **Honors/Awds:** Martin Luther King fellow, Boston Univ. **Business Addr:** Director/Personnel, Americas Operations, Xerox Corporation, PO Box 1600, Stamford, CT 06904.

JONES, JOHN P.
Educational administrator. **Personal:** Born Mar 1, 1915, Tyler, TX; married Nollie V; children: Rhoda, John. **Educ:** TX Coll, AB; Univ of Chicago, AM. **Career:** Jarvis Christian Coll Hawkins TX, head of english dept, chmn of humanities & Asst to pres 1962-72, pres 1972-76; Texas Coll, academic dean 1976-81, deandir of institutional advancement 1981-85, interim pres 1985-86, dean/dir of institutional advancement 1986-. **Orgs:** Dir, Institutional Self-Study TX Coll, 1982-84; Coordinator, Isatim Program, TX Coll 1982-87. **Honors/Awds:** Hon degrees LD Texas Coll 1972; Hum D, LLD Texas Christian Univ 1972. **Military Serv:** AUS staff sgt 1942-45. **Business Addr:** Dean of Inst Advancement, Texas College, 2404 N Grand Ave, Tyler, TX 75702.

JONES, JOHNNIE ANDERSON
Attorney. **Personal:** Born Nov 30, 1919, Laurel Hill, LA; son of Sarah Ann Coats Jones and Henry E Jones; married Sebell Elizabeth Chase (divorced); children: Johnnie Jr, Adair Darnell, Adal Dalcho, Ann Sarah Bythelda. **Educ:** Southern U, BS in Psychology 1949; Southern Univ Law Sch, JD in Law 1953. **Career:** Universal Life Ins Co, ins agcy 1947-48; US Post Office, ltr carrier 1948-50; Southern Univ Law Sch, law sch stdnt 1950-53; LA State Bar Assc, lwyr 1953-; Jones & Jones, sr lwyr. **Orgs:** Asst parish atty City Parish Govt 1969-72; state rep LA House of Rep 1972-76; sr lwyr Jones & Jones Atty at Law 1975-; mem Frontiers Clb Intnl 1962-, Alpha Phi Alpha Frat 1972-, NAACP 1936-. **Honors/Awds:** Cert of aprctn LB Johnson & HH Humphrey 1964; frontierman/yr Frontiers Clg Intrntl 1962; plaque Alpha Kappa Alpha Sorority 1972; most otsndng Mount Zion First Bapt Ch 1970. **Military Serv:** AUS warrant ofcr 1942-46; Good Conduct Medal 1942-46. **Business Addr:** Attorney, Jones & Jones Attorneys-at-Law, 263 Third Street, Ste 702, Baton Rouge, LA 70801-1703.

JONES, JONI LOU
City government official. **Personal:** Born Aug 24, 1932, Ellisville, MS; divorced; children: Andre, Stepfon, Valerie. **Educ:** Adelphia University, Natl Drug Institute, training course, 1972. **Career:** City Municipality of Ellisville, Ward III, alderman, currently. **Orgs:** Roosevelt Community Service Committee 1983-; temporary president, Natl Council of Negro Women 1984; NAACP. **Honors/Awds:** Courts of Common Pleas, Volunteers in Probation 1973; Notary Public, State of Mississippi Executive Dept 1982; Appreciation Award, Asst Cub Scout Program 1983. **Home Addr:** P O Box 736, Ellisville, MS 39437-0736.

JONES, JOSEPH
Educator. **Personal:** Born Jun 3, 1928, Albany, GA; son of Hattie Turner Jones and Joseph Jones; married Etta M; children: Jo-

setta I, Robyn M Thomas. **Educ:** Morris Brown Coll, BS 1950; Northwestern Univ, MSc 1952; OH State U, PhD 1960. **Career:** TX Southern Univ, dean of grad sch; Univ of Sci & Tech Ghana W Africa, Fulbright-Hays prof 1972-73; Acad Affairs St Augustine's Coll, vice pres 1969-72; St Augustine's Coll, acad dean 1966-69; St Augustine's Coll, head dept of biology 1952-57; Title III Proj St Augustine's Coll, coordinator; duties abroad in several countries; consultant on strategic planning and education. **Orgs:** Dir Natl Sci Found & Atomic Energy Commn Inst for Teacher of Sci; mem Visitation Teams to evaluate instr in various coll in southeastern states Danforth Asso; Fellow of OH Acad of Sci; mem Sigma Xi Sci Honor Soc; Alpha Mu Honor Soc; OH Acad of Sci; Am Soc of Parasitologists; Nat Sci Tchr Assn; Am Museum of Natural History; Alpha Phi Alpha Frat. **Honors/Awds:** International Educator's Award, 1993; Delaney Educator of the Year Award, 1981; Recipient Sr Fulbright-Hays Professorship, Ghana W Africa 1972; United Negro Coll Fund Fellowship 1959; Special Danforth Grad Fellowship 1958; BA awarded cum laude 1950. **Business Addr:** Professor of Biology, Texas Southern Univ, 3100 Cleburne St, Houston, TX 77004.

JONES, K. C.
Basketball coach. **Personal:** Born May 25, 1932, Taylor, TX; son of Eula Daniels Jones and K C Jones Sr; children: six. **Educ:** University of San Francisco, graduated. **Career:** Boston Celtics, professional basketball player, 1956-67, assistant coach, 1978-82, head coach, 1983-88, vice president for basketball operations, 1988-89; Hartford, professional basketball player, 1967-68; Brandeis Univ, Waltham MA, head coach, 1968-71; Los Angeles Lakers, assistant coach, 1971-72; San Diego Conquistadors, head coach, 1972-73; Capital Bullets, head coach 1973-75; Milwaukee Bucks, assistant coach, 1976-77; Seattle SuperSonics, head coach, 1989-92; New England Blizzard, ABL, head coach, 1997-. **Orgs:** Blizzard, coach. **Honors/Awds:** Won Olympic Gold Medal with the USA Basketball Team, 1956; earned eight championship rings as a player for the Celtics and two as their head coach; Inductee, Naismith Memorial Basketball Hall of Fame, 1989. **Military Serv:** 1956-58.

JONES, K. MAURICES
Writer. **Career:** Author, currently. **Special Achievements:** Author, Say It Loud; author, Spike Lee & The African American Filmmakers. **Home Addr:** 12111 Monica, Detroit, MI 48204, (313)491-0663.

JONES, KATHERINE ELIZABETH BUTLER
Educational consultant. **Personal:** Born Mar 19, 1936, New York, NY; daughter of Meme Elgitha Clark Butler (deceased) and Theodore Harold Butler (deceased); married Hubert Jones; children: Karen, Lauren, Harlan, Renee, Lisa, Hamilton, Cheryl, Tanya. **Educ:** Mt Holyoke Coll, BA 1957; Simmons Coll, MS 1967; Harvard Univ, EdD 1980. **Career:** Boston Public Schools, teacher 1958-59; Newton Public Schools, coord for ed prog 1966-76; Simmons Coll, instr 1967-69; School Systems Public & Independent MA, consult 1968-; Wheelock Coll, instr 1976; Cambridge Public Schools, supvr staff & prog 1977-81; self-employed as educ consultant, currently. **Orgs:** Bd dir METCO 1966-73; bd trustees Mt Holyoke Coll 1973-78; 1st black mem Newton School Comm 1978-85; minority affairs comm Natl Assoc of IN Schools 1984-89; bd Boston Childrens Serv 1985-; bd Family Serv Assn 1986-, vice chairperson 1989-91; Massachusetts Coalition for the Homeless 1989-95. **Honors/Awds:** Ed Excellence Scholarship to Student Black Citizens of Newton 1976; Serv to METCO City of Newton 1976; Contrib to Integrated Ed METCO Boston Staff 1976; Serv Above Self Newton Chamber of Commerce 1974; Doctoral Dissertation School Consolidation in Newton 1980; Citizens Who Make a Difference Contrib to Mental Health MA Assoc of Mental Health 1982; Tribute to 350 years of Black Presence in Massachusetts Honoree, Museum of Afro-American History 1988; Nominating Committee for Alumnae Trustees Mt Holyoke College, 1990-92; Schomberg Scholar in Black Culture New York Public Library, 1991-92; Award Black Alumnae Conference, Mt Holyoke College, 1994; Faculty Boston Univ, Afro-American Studies Program, 1993-95; Newton Citizen Recognition of Distinction, 1994; New England Pen Writers, Discovery Author Non-Fiction, 1996; Family History Exhibitor Museum of our National Heritage, Lexington, MA, 1995. **Home Addr:** 1087 Commonwealth Ave, Newton, MA 02159.

JONES, KELSEY A.
Educator. **Personal:** Born Jul 15, 1933, Holly Springs, MD; married Virginia Bethel Ford; children: Kelsey Jr, Cheryl Darlene Campbell, Eric Andre, Claude Anthony. **Educ:** MS Industrial Coll, AB (Summa Cum Laude) 1955; Garrett Theol Seminary NW Univ, MDiv 1959; Univ of MI Medical Center, clinical pastoral care and counseling, 1960; Wesley Medical Center, post graduate certificate, 1967; MS Industrial Coll, DD 1969; National Parole Institute, National Council of Crime and Deliquency-State Univ of NY-Albany, School of Criminal Justice-Inst on Man and Science, certificate, 1970; Geroge Mason Univ, cert, 1984. **Career:** Walls Meml Ch Chicago, pastor 1956; Lane Meml Ch Jackson, MS, pastor 1959-62; Cleaves Temple Omaha, NE, pastor 1962-65; St Matthew Ch Wichita, KS, pastor1965-70; Israel Metro Church, Wash, DC Min of Celebration & Human Resources, natl pulpit 1970-72; Fed City Coll (UDC Mt Vernon Campus), vis lectr in Black history 1973-75; INTER/MET, dir of Bacc & Liason consult 1973-77; Univ of DC Van Ness Campus, prof social sci 1972-77; UDC (Van Ness Campus), chmn dept soc/behavioral sci 1977-78; Dept Criminal Justice, prof 1978-79; The President of the US, special asst for Environmental Health, Occupational Safety & Instit Security 1984-86; Univ of DC Dept of Criminal Justice, asoc prof, 1978-82, chairman 1979-91, professor, 1982-94, justice prof emeritus, currently; KAJ Assocites, pres/CEO, currently. **Orgs:** Dean Leadership Educ ea of 3 confs of 3rd Episcopal Dist; sec KS/MO Annual Conf 1962-70; delegate Gen Conf of Christ Meth Epis Ch 1966; delegate Centennial Session Gen Conf 1970; sec NY/WA Ann Conf Vis Chpl Meth Pop Cook Cnty Jail 1956-58; aptd staff Recep-Diag Cntr MI Correct Commn 1961; mem Acad of Criminal Justice Scis, North Atlan Conf of Criminal Just Educators, Inst for Criminal Justice Ethics, Natl Criminal Justice Assn, NortheasternAssn of Criminal Justice Educators, Amer Soc for Indust Security, Natl Assn of Chiefs of Police, Amer Soc for Publ Admin, ASHE (Amer Assn for Higher Edn); chmn State Bd of Probation & Parole 1967; mem Phi Alpha Frat Mu Lamda Chap DC; 1st vice pres Wichita Urban League; bd dirs Bros Inc; mem LEAP com for deseg of pubschools in Wichita. **Honors/Awds:** Presidential Citation, Natl Assn for Equal Opportunities in Higher Edn; Alumnus of the Year; Disting Serv Award Howard Univ Univ Without Walls; Disting Serv Award Univ of DC Lorton Student Govt Assn for contribution to the Lorton Prison Project; Awarded certificate for wkshp on Crime Prevention for Colleges and Universities, Campus Crime Prevention Programs, 1985; nationally in demand as public speaker & lecturer; written & published many papers and articles. **Business Addr:** Professor & Chairman, Univ of DC Dept Criminal Just, 4200 Connecticut Ave NW, Washington, DC 20008.

JONES, KENNETH LEROY
Surgeon. **Personal:** Born May 6, Kinston, NC; children: Kathryn, Amber, Jonathan. **Educ:** Amherst Coll, BS 1973; Howard Univ Coll of Medicine, MD 1978. **Career:** US Public Health Serv Johns Hopkins Hosp, general surgery resident 1978-83; Advanced Industrial Medicine Inc, vice pres/medical dir; East Coast Health Org Inc, pres med dir.

JONES, LAFAYETTE GLENN
Marketing executive. **Personal:** Born Feb 17, 1944, Cincinnati, OH; married Wanda S Harriel; children: Kevin, Keith, Melanie, Glenn, Tara. **Educ:** Fisk U, BA 1965; Howard U, grad study 1965-66; Stanford U, cert Mktg Mgmt 1976. **Career:** American Health & Beauty Aids Institute, exec dir; Johnson Prod Co Chgo, vice pres mktg & sales 1979-; Hunt-Wesson Foods Div, Norton Simon Inc, mktg mgr Hunts Manwich & Tomato Paste 1974-79; Pillsbury Co, Refrig Foods Div, prod mgr Hungry Jack; Birds Eye Div, Gen Foods Corp, asso prod mgr Orange Plus 1970-72; Imperial Margs Food Div, Lever Bros Co, prod mdse asst Golden Glow 1969-70; Sta WOL, Sonderling Brdcst Co, dir mdse, pub rel 1967-69; Job Corps, ABT Asso, Westinghouse Learning Corp YMCA, dir prgm act 1965-67; Supreme Beauty Products, Chicago IL, vice pres & gen mgr, 1988-. **Orgs:** Bd dir hon Am Youth Fedn 1972-74; vp, bd of trst Mardan Educ Ctr; mem Nat Assn of Mkt Dev; Urban League. **Honors/Awds:** Author articles on mktg; Natl Business League's Frederick Douglas Patterson Award, 1987. **Business Addr:** Vice President & General Manager, Supreme Beauty Products, 820 S Michigan Ave, Chicago, IL 60605.

JONES, LARRY WAYNE
Aerospace/propulsion systems manager. **Personal:** Born Jul 8, 1950, Mt Pleasant, TX; son of Dorothy T Jones and Don G Jones; married Beverly Pope Jones, Mar 12, 1976; children: Martin, Thomas, Andrew. **Educ:** US Dept of Defense, Fort Belvoir, VA, defense systems management college, 1985; US Naval Academy, Annapolis, MD, BS, 1973. **Career:** Pratt & Whitney Div United Technologies Corp, manager, Engineering Planning Resources, 1979-. **Orgs:** United States Naval Academy Alumni Association. **Military Serv:** US Marine Corps, Lt Colonel, reserve, 1973; Received pilot wings US Navy, 1975. **Business Addr:** Manager, Engineering Planning & Resources, Pratt and Whitney, Government Engines & Space Propulsion, PO Box 109600, West Palm Beach, FL 33410-9600.

JONES, LAWRENCE N.
Educational administrator (retired). **Personal:** Born Apr 24, 1921, Moundsville, WV; son of Rosa L Jones and Eugene W Jones; married Mary Ellen Cooley; children: Lynn Walker Huntley, Rodney Bruce. **Educ:** WV State Coll, BS in Educ 1942; Univ of Chicago, MA in Hist 1948; Oberlin Grad Schl of Theology, BD 1956; Yale Univ Grad Schl, PhD in Religion 1957, 1961. **Career:** Fisk Univ, dean of chapel 1960-64; Union Theological Seminary NY, dean prof 1965-75; Howard Univ Divinity Schl, dean prof 1975-91, dean emeritus, 1991-. **Orgs:** Mem United Church Pod for World Ministries 1975-81; consult Lilly Endowment Inc, Congress of Natl Black Churches, Grad Theological Union 1983; chrmn Civil Rights Coord Comm Nashville 1962-64; pres Soc for Study of Black Religion 1974-77; secr Assc Theological Schls 1981-82; bd mem WHMM TV Public Advisory Board 1984-. **Honors/Awds:** Lucy Monroe Flwshp Oberlin Grad Schl 1956; Rosenwald Schlrshp Rosenwald Fund 1942; Rockefeller Doctoral Flwshp Rockefeller Brothers 1959-61; LLD, West Virginia State College 1965; DHL, Jewish Theological Seminary 1971; DD, Chicago Theological Seminary 1975; DD, Shaw University, 1986; DD, Episcopal Theological Seminary in Virginia, 1992. **Military Serv:** Quartermaster capt 1943, 1946, 1947, 1953. **Home Addr:** 1206 Devere Dr, Silver Spring, MD 20903.

JONES, LAWRENCE W.
Educator. **Personal:** Born Feb 6, 1942, Newport News, VA; married Lolita Diane Grey; children: Lawrence W Jr, Leonard W. **Educ:** Hampton Inst VA, 1960-64; Bowie State Tchr MD, BS in Educ 1965-67; Univ of MA Amherst, EdD 1970-73. **Career:** Bd of Educ NYC, tchr reading specialist 1977-; Univ of City of NY Medgar Evers Coll, asst prof educ 1974-77; Univ of MA Brooklyn COP Program, supvr student teaching 1971-73; Univ of MA, teaching asst 1970-73; Bd of Educ NYC, tchr 1967-73; Youth-in Action Neighborhood Youth Corp, remedial coordinator 1973; DeSign Team Sprinfield Ave Comm Sch Newark, consult educ 1978; Mayor Newark, spl asst educ program 1979-. **Orgs:** Mem Omega Psi Phi Frat 1972-; consult wedn program Day Care Centers Pvt Sch in New York City 1975-; mem One Hundered Black Men 1978-. **Honors/Awds:** Degree with high honors, Bowie State Tchr 1967; Innovation in Teaching Dissertation, Univ of MA 1973; publ Classroom Mgmt Ind of Instruction 1973-74; Comm Serv Awards, Brooklyn COP & Comm Life Center 1974-78; Measuring Children's Growth in Reading Expanding Reading Experience 1978.

JONES, LEANDER CORBIN
Educator. **Personal:** Born Jul 16, 1934, Vincent, AR; son of Una Bell Jones and L C Jones; married Lethonee Angela Hendricks; children: Angela Lynne, Leander Corbin. **Educ:** Univ of AR at Pine Bluff, AB 1956; Univ of IL, MS 1968; Union Graduate Institute, PhD 1973. **Career:** Chicago Public Schools, English teacher 1956-68; Peace Corps Volunteer, English teacher 1964-66; City Colls of Chicago, TV producer 1968-73; Meharry Medical Coll, media specialist 1973-75; Western Michigan Univ, assoc prof Black Amer studies, 1975-89, prof 1989-. **Orgs:** Mem Kappa Alpha Psi 1953-; mem exec comm DuSable Mus African Amer History 1970-; designer of programs in theatre andTV for hard-to-educate; pres TABS Ctr 1972-; mem AAUP 1973-; mem Natl Council of Black Studies 1977-, MI Council of Black Studies 1977-, Popular Culture Assoc 1978-; chmn Comm Against Apartheid 1977-; mem South African Solidarity Org 1978-; mem MI Org African Studies 1980-; commander Vets for Peace Kalamazoo 1980-; pres Black Theatre Group of the Kalamazoo Civic Players 1980-83; bd of dirs Kalamazoo Civic Players 1981-83, MI Commn on Crime and Delinquency 1981-83; pres Corbin 22 Ltd 1986; Lester Lake Corp, secretary of the bd, 1992. **Honors/Awds:** "Roof Over My Head" TV Series WDCN Nashville 1975; acted in and directed several plays Kalamazoo 1979-86; author "Africa Is for Reel," Kalamazoo 1983; exec producer & host for TV series "Fade to Black" 1986. **Military Serv:** AUS pfc 1956-58. **Home Addr:** 3721 S Westnedge Ave, Suite 222, Kalamazoo, MI 49008. **Business Addr:** Prof, Black Amer Studies, Western Michigan University, Kalamazoo, MI 49008.

JONES, LEELAND NEWTON, JR.
Educational administrator (retired). **Personal:** Born Jun 15, 1921, Buffalo, NY; son of Julia M Anthony Jones and Leeland N Jones, Sr; married Carlita Murphy, May 5, 1945; children: Dr Leeland Anthony Murphy Jones, Dr Johnaaron Murphy Jones, Carlita C M J Perkins. **Educ:** Univ of Buffalo, BA 1947; UB Law School 1948-5l. **Career:** Met Serv Accnt, owner; Erie County supervisor, 1948; Buffalo City, council 1950-54; pres, pro-tem City Council, 1953-54; NYS Com vs Discrimination, field rep 1957-60; Buffalo Urban League, assoc dir 1964-67; NYS Ed Dept Adult Ed, task force dir; Erie Comm Coll, asst vp; OJT Prgm JET Chamber of Commerce, dir. **Orgs:** Organizer & 1st Treas US Student Assn 1946; mem DAV, Amvets, Am Leg; 32nd Prince Hall Mason, Shrine; past pres Black Hist Found; pres trustee, University of Buffalo; board UB Alumni Association; intl pres, Intl Veterans Association; Chef de Gare pres 40/8 Veterans Assoc; AAA Western & Central NY, exec comm; Jesse Ketchum Scholars Awards Committee, board member; State and Local Americanism, chair; Congressman Nowak (Dem) and Quinn (Rep) Comm to select candidates to US Service Academies; Bethel AME Church, associate minister; Buffalo and Erie County Hist Soc, board. **Honors/Awds:** Alpha Kappa Boule-Sigma Pi Phi Fraternity, Man of the Year, Jr Chamber of Commerce; Civil Liberties Award IBPOE of W; National Elks Oratorical Scholarship Winner; City of Buffalo Man of the Year 1988; UB Football Scholarship 1940; Bison Head Honor Society 1942; UB Athletic Hall of Fame, 1990; Urban League, Family Life Award, 1994. **Military Serv:** US Army, lt, sig c. **Home Addr:** 89 E Depew Ave, Buffalo, NY 14214.

JONES, LEMUEL B.
Personnel assistant. **Personal:** Born Mar 3, 1929, Norway, SC; married Mary Jamison; children: Mark, Karla, Jarret, Eric Jamison. **Educ:** BS 1952. **Career:** EI DuPont Co, operator chemical 1952-65; Production & Quality Assurance, foreman 1965-72; EEO, personnel asst 1972-. **Orgs:** Pres chap NAACP; vice pres PTA; vice pres Sunday Sch Conv; mem Kappa Alpha Psi Frat

Inc. **Honors/Awds:** US Army Achievement Award. **Military Serv:** USN 1946-48; AUSR maj 1952-. **Business Addr:** E I du Pont Co, Savannah River Plant, Aiken, SC 29801.

JONES, LENOY
Professional football player. **Personal:** Born Sep 25, 1974, Marlin, TX. **Educ:** Texas Christian Univ, attended. **Career:** Houston Oilers, linebacker, 1996; Tennessee Oilers, 1997-. **Business Addr:** Professional Football Player, Tennessee Oilers, c/o Baptist Sports Park, 7640 H 70-5, Nashville, TN 37221.

JONES, LEON C.
Cleric. **Personal:** Born Apr 16, 1919, Laurel, MS; married Rubye L Brown; children: Kathryn. **Educ:** BA 1962; MSW 1968; American Baptist Seminary of the West, ThD, 1984. **Career:** Second Bapt Ch Everett WA, pastor 1960-69; State Dept Pub Assistance, social caseworker 1963-66; supr caseworkers & soc workers 1968-69; Wash Bapt Conv, area minister 1969-83; Seattle Pacific Coll, inst Black Am history & culture 1968-85; Bellevue Coll, 1969; Seattle Comm Coll, 1971; Seattle U, 1970-; Martin Luther King Jr Memorial Baptist Church, Renton, WA, pastor, 1978-; Seattle University, adjunct professor, Theology and Religion, 1985-. **Orgs:** SOIC 1967-68; mem Nat Acad Soc Workers 1970-; WA Assn Soc Workers 1973-; chmn; president Black United Clergy PAC NW 1973-90. **Military Serv:** USN cook 1st class 1938-46. **Business Addr:** 13611-SE 116th St, Renton, WA 98059.

JONES, LEONADE DIANE
Newspaper executive. **Personal:** Born Nov 27, 1947, Bethesda, MD; daughter of Landonia Madden Jones and Leon Adger Jones. **Educ:** Univ of Pittsburgh, PA, 1965-67; Simmons Coll, Boston MA, BA (with distinction), 1969; Stanford Law School & Graduate School of Business, JD, MBA, 1973. **Career:** Capital Research Co, Los Angeles CA, research analyst, 1973-75; The Washington Post Co, Washington DC, asst sec & asst treasurer, 1975-79; Post-Newsweek Stations, Washington DC, dir of financial services, 1979-84, vice pres business affairs, 1984-86; The Washington Post Co, asst treasurer, 1986-87, treasurer, 1987-. **Orgs:** Mem, California Bar 1973-; mem, DC Bar, 1979-; mem, Amer Women in Radio & TV, 1979-84; treasurer and mem bd of dir, Big Sisters of Washington Metro Area, 1984-85; pres, 1984-85, mem bd of dir, 1982-89, Washington District of Columbia - Baltimore, MD Chapter of Stanford Business School Alumni Assn; board of directors, Stanford Business School Alumni Association, 1985-88; bd of dir, DC Contemporary Dance Theatre, 1987-88; corp co-chair, Duke Ellington Fundraiser, mem of advisory council, Charlin Jazz Society 1988-92; mem, Natl Assn of Corp Treasurers, 1989-; advisory board member, WHMM-TV, Washington, DC, 1989-; member, The Edges Group, Inc, Metropolitan Washington DC Chapter, 1989-; advisory council member, Graduate School of Business, Stanford University, 1991-; board of directors, Washington Performing Arts Society, 1990-; board ofustees, American Institute for Managing Diversity, Inc, 1991-; Simmons College Corporation, 1992-. **Honors/Awds:** Honoree, Salute to African-American Business and Professional Women, Dollars & Sense Magazine, 1990; inductee into DC Women's Hall of Fame, 1992; National Coalition of 100 Black Women, Candace Award for Business, 1992. **Business Addr:** Treasurer, The Washington Post Co, 1150 15th Street, NW, Washington, DC 20071.

JONES, LEONARD WARREN
Attorney. **Personal:** Born Sep 20, 1965, Washington, DC; son of Lawrence & Lolita Jones. **Educ:** Norfolk State University, BS, 1988; College of Insurance, MBA, 1992; Thomas M Cooley Law School, JD, 1992. **Career:** Private practice, currently; NYC Department of Probation, asst general counsel. **Orgs:** Omega Psi Phi Fraternity, Inc; 100 Black Men Inc. **Military Serv:** US Army Reserves, 1st lt.

JONES, LEORA (SAM)
Athlete. **Personal:** Born Aug 11, 1960, Mt Olive, NC; daughter of Ruthie Mae Jones and Ernest Jones. **Educ:** Louisburg Junior College, associate degree, 1978-80; East Carolina University, attended, 1980-82. **Career:** Bayer Pharmaceuticals, Bayer-leverkusen, West Germany, marketing assistant; 1985-86; First Citizens Bank, phillipsburg machine operator, 1989-90, 1992-; Natl Olympic Team, Team Handball, asst coach, 1993-95. **Orgs:** Colorado Team Handball Association, vice pres, 1992-. **Honors/Awds:** US Team Handball Federation, USA Team Handball Player of the Year, 1984, 1986, 1988, 1991; City of Mt Olive, Sam Jones Day, 1984, 1988, 1992; USTHF, 3-time Olympian, 1984, 1988, 1992; James E Sullivan Award, Team Handball Athlete of the Year, 1991; Presidential Commendation, White House (special mention), 1992. **Special Achievements:** Guest speaker at NC Amateur Women's Sport Foundation, Feb 1993. **Home Addr:** 110 Elmore St, Mount Olive, NC 28365, (919)658-4081.

JONES, LEROI. **See BARAKA, IMAMU AMIRI.**

JONES, LESTER C.
Automobile dealer. **Career:** Pasadena Lincoln-Mercury Inc, CEO, currently. **Special Achievements:** Company is ranked #99 on Black Enterprise's list of Top 100 Auto Dealers, 1994. **Business Addr:** CEO, Pasadena Lincoln-Mercury Inc, PO Box 820399, Dallas, TX 75382-0399, (214)793-0645.

JONES, LEWIS ARNOLD, JR.
Physician, consultant. **Personal:** Born Sep 16, 1950, Detroit, MI; son of Lewis A Jones Sr & Berlene I Jones; married Pamela D Jones, Nov 14, 1992; children: Jennifer, Alicia, Lewis Alexander. **Educ:** Wayne State University, 1969-72; University of Michigan, Medical School, 1974-78, Medical Degree, 1978; Diagnostic Radiology Residency, Providence Hosp, 1978-82. **Career:** Tri-County Radiology PC, radiologist, 1983-84; Harper Hosp, radiologist, 1984, director of gastrointestinal radiology div, 1984; WSU School of Medicine, clinical instructor, 1985-92, assistant professor of radiology, 1992-97; Karmanos Cancer Institute, 1992; MI Department of Community Health, physician consultant, 1997-. **Orgs:** Radiological Society of North America, 1979-; American College of Radiology, 1989-; Association of University Radiologists, 1993-; American Medical Association, 1994-; Karmanos Cancer Institute, community advisory, community mem, 1994; NIH Women's Health Initiative, co-investigator, Detroit Clinical Ctr, 1996-97; American Cancer Society, board of directors, mem, Oakland Cty Michigan Div, 1988-. **Honors/Awds:** Providence Hosp, Outstanding Radiology Resident Awd, 1982; American Cancer Society, Volunteer Leadership Awd, 1988; American Cancer Society, Life Svc Awd, 1990; New Metropolitan Detroit Club of the National Association of Negro Business & Professional Women's Clubs Inc, Frederick Douglass Awd, 1996. **Special Achievements:** First winner of the Essence Magazine/Preferred Stock Cologne "What a Man Contest," 1995; Named co-chair of the "Year of the Women's Health" steering committee state of Michigan (Michigan Department of Community Health), 1996; "Partners for Life" a woman's health seminar, created and presented by Lewis A Jones, MD & Florine Mark, CEO, Weight Watchers International, 1996. **Business Addr:** Michigan Department Of Community Health, 3423 N Martin Luther King Jr Blvd, PO Box 30195, Lansing, MI 48909.

JONES, LISA PAYNE
Educational administrator. **Personal:** Born Dec 30, 1958, Camp Zama, Japan; daughter of Eleanor Towns Hamilton Payne and Dr. Charles Benjamin Payne, Jr; married Peter Lawson Jones, Oct 12, 1985; children: Ryan Charles, Leah Danielle. **Educ:** Eastern MI Univ, BBA 1980; business courses, Case Western Reserve Univ, 1982-85. **Career:** AmeriTrust Co NA, general analyst I 1980-82, II 1982-85, III 1985-86; Cuyahoga Metro Housing Authority, marketing mgr 1986-88, leasing/marketing mgr 1989, leasing/transfer mgr 1990-91, marketing coordinator, 1992-94. **Orgs:** Delta Sigma Theta Sor Inc 1978-; project business consultant, Junior Achievement 1982-83; Cleveland Branch, NAACP 1982-; chairperson, 1983, treas 1984-85, Operation Greater Cleveland: Big Vote, 1983-85; Urban League of Greater Cleveland, 1985-; Natl Black MBA Assn Inc, 1986; League of Women Voters, 1987; Amer Marketing Assn, 1987-89; trustee, Shaker Hts Alumni Assn, 1988-95; board member, Shaker Schools Foundation, 1990-94; second vice president, Shaker Hts PTO, 1995-96; PTO Strategic Planning Committee, Shaker Heights Alumni Association, executive director, 1995-. **Honors/Awds:** EMU Coll of Business Academic Achievement Awd 1978; Honors Awd Delta Sigma Theta Inc EMU 1979. **Home Addr:** 3532 Norwood Rd, Shaker Heights, OH 44122. **Business Addr:** Registar, Shaker Hts Bd of Education, 15600 Parkland Drive, Shaker Heights, OH 44120, (216)295-4324.

JONES, LLOYD O.
County treasurer. **Personal:** Born Aug 6, 1944, Charles City, VA; married Terri. **Educ:** Morehouse Coll, BA 1964; Univ of So CA, MBA 1971; Coll of William & Mary, JD 1975. **Career:** Eastman Kodak Co, accountant, cost engr 1964-65; Charles City Co, co treas; SEDFRE Inc, part-time cons. **Orgs:** First vice pres Local Br NAACP; adv, bd mem Colonial Bank Providence Forge VA; bd mem Charles City New Kent Comm Action Aby; mem Local PTA; Local Civic League. **Military Serv:** AUS payee disbursement specialist 1965-67. **Business Addr:** PO Box 38, Charles City, VA 23030.

JONES, LOIS MAILOU
Educator (retired), artist. **Personal:** Born Nov 3, 1905, Boston, MA; daughter of Caroline Dorinda Adams Jones and Thomas Vreeland Jones; married Louis Vergniaud Pierre-Noel, Aug 8, 1953 (deceased). **Educ:** Boston Museum Sch Fine Arts, diploma 1927; Designers Art Sch, 1928; Columbia Univ Summer School, 1931-33; Academie Julian, Cert 1938; Howard Univ, AB 1945; Academie de la Grande Chaumiere, Paris, Cert 1962. **Career:** Grace Ripley Studios, costume designer 1920-25; Palmer Mem Inst, art dept head 1928-30; free lance textile designer 1928-31; Assn Study Negro Life & Hist, illustrator 1930-53; Howard Univ, professor emerita design & watercolor painting, 1930-77. **Orgs:** Intl exhibits; 35, one person exhibits; paintings in many museums & colls incl Boston Mus of Fine Arts, Brooklyn Mus, Corcoran Gallery of Art, Phillips Collection Hirshhorn Mus, Atlanta Univ, Howard Univ, Natl Portrait Gallery, Natl Women's Museum of Art; Caribbean & Afro-Amer Women Artists-Budek Slide Inc 1983; film "50 Years of Painting Lois Mailou Jones," by Prof Abiyi Ford, Howard Univ Film Dir; mem, Alpha Kappa Alpha Sorority, 1930-; mem, Artists Equity, 1953-; mem, National Conf of Artists, 1972-; Milwaukee Art Museum; National Palace, Port-au-Prince, Haiti; Metropolitan Museum of Art, NYC; Studio Museum in Harlem. **Honors/Awds:** Diplome Honneur et Merite Haiti Govt; Robert Woods Bliss Oil Painting Landscape Award; 3 Howard Univ Research Grants: Comtemp African Art, Contemp Haitian Art & Afro-Amer Art; author "Peintures Lois Mailou Jones;" hon PhD CO State Christian Coll 1973; hon PhD Suffolk Univ 1981; Candice Award Met Mus 1982; Alumni Awd Howrard Univ; hon PhD, MA Coll of Art 1986; Women's Caucus for Art, Honor Awd for Outstanding Achievement in the Visual Arts Cooper Union 1986; hon PhD Howard University Humanities 1987; hon PhD, Atlanta College of Art, Fine Arts, 1989; oil painting "Chou-Fleur et Citrouille," Lila Acheson Wallace Wing, Amer Paintings, Metropolitan Museum of Art; Howard University Gallery of Art, Gallery No 3: The Lois Mailou Jones and James L Wells Gallery 1989; Fine Arts Faculty Award forExcellence in Thing, Howard Univ, 1975; "Les Fetiches," 1938, purchased by the National Museum of American Art for their private collection; "Africa," a Homage to Dr Martin Luther King Jr, purchased for the permanent collectioon of the National Museum of Women in The Arts; Findlay University, Honorary PhD, 1993; Degree Humane Letters, Tougaloo College, Miss, 1994; Concoran School of Art, Honorary PhD, 1996; Studio Museum on Harlem, NY, Award, 1996; Franz Bader Award, 1962; Luban Watercolor Award, first place, 1958. **Home Addr:** 4706 17 St NW, Washington, DC 20011.

JONES, LOREAN ELECTA
Government official. **Personal:** Born Jun 29, 1938, Arlington, TN; daughter of Alcorna Harris Matthews and Earnest Matthews; married Jimmie Jones, Oct 1, 1954 (deceased); children: Gale Carson, Dale J, Elna Brunetti, Ervin C, Denise Jimenez, Dennis R, Teresa Y, Terry O (deceased). **Educ:** Owen Coll, AA 1968; LeMoyne-Owen Coll, BA 1970; Memphis State Univ, MS 1977. **Career:** State of TN Dept of Mental Health, social worker 1970-75; State of TN Dept of Corrections, parole officer 1975-78; US Dist Cts Western Dist of TN, probation officer, 1978-84, fed drug treatment specialist, 1984-90, supervising probation officer, 1990-92, deputy chief probation officer, 1992-. **Orgs:** Comm mem, Black on Black Crime Task Force 1979-; Fed Probation Officers Assoc; PUSH, 1980; NAACP, life membership, 1980; apptd to bd of trustees, Gov of TN Arlington Devel Ctr 1972-73; sec, treas, Southeast Region Federal Probation Officers Assn 1983-85; historian, Natl Council of Negro Women 1983; TN Selective Service Local Bd 38; sec, LeMoyne Owen Alumni Assn; Amer Probation & Parole Assn; Amer Assn of Counseling & Develop; Natl Alliance of Business Youth Motivating Task Force 1982-83. **Honors/Awds:** Citizen of the Week Awd WLOK Radio Station 1978; Distinguished Leadership Awd Outstanding Serv to the Human Serv Profession 1987; National Certified Counselors Certificate. **Special Achievements:** First female probation/parole officer, WD/TN, 1978. **Business Addr:** Deputy Chief, US Probation & Parole Office, 167 Mid-America Mall, Rm 234, Memphis, TN 38106.

JONES, LOUIS CLAYTON
Attorney. **Personal:** Born Nov 13, 1935, Lawrenceburg, KY; married Barbara Ann Griffin. **Educ:** Howard Univ, BA (Summa Cum Laude) 1953-57; Univ de Bordeaux Fulbright 1957-58; Yale Law School, LLB 1958-61. **Career:** New School for Social Rsch, lecturer 1977; New York Law School, assoc prof 1976-78; SUNY, lecturer 1969-72; KY Comm on Human Rights, asst dir 1962-63; CBS News, asst to dir of bus affairs 1963-64; Louis Clayton Jones PC, attny. **Orgs:** Mem Phi Beta Kappa Howard Univ 1956; Natl Emergency Civil Liberties Comm, exec comm 1972; bd of dir Fund for New Priorities in Amer 1974-. **Honors/Awds:** Fulbright & John Hay Whitney Fellowships Univ de Bordeaux 1957-58. **Business Addr:** Attorney, Louis, Clayton, Jones PC, 75 Maple St, Brooklyn, NY 11225.

JONES, LUCIUS
Educator. **Personal:** Born Jun 16, 1918, Birmingham, AL; married Vivian D; children: Vivian Eilene. **Educ:** AL A&M, cert in Printing 1936; Lincoln U, BS1973; San Jose State, additional study 1973. **Career:** Flashlight Herald Knoxville, linotype operator 1937; Tulsa Art Printer Tulsa, shop foreman 1939-48; OK Eagle Tulsa; Modern Litho-Print Co Jefferson City MO,linotype operator 1973; Lincoln Univ, instr. **Orgs:** Mem Danforth Assoc 1963-; seminar leader Typographers Union 1972-74; mem Intl Graphic Arts Educ Assn; Am Vocational Assn; deacon & minister of music Second Bapt Ch Jefferson City; chmn Midwest Reg Selection Comm Danforth Assoc 1973; intl comm to nominate First Albert Schweitzer Prize 1975; dir Jefferson City Comm Male Chorus; mem NAACP; Omega Psi Frat Inc; United Investment Club; mem Jefferson City Industrial Development Commission. **Honors/Awds:** Lincoln Univ Bd of Curators Award for Serv 1973. **Business Addr:** Instructor, Lincoln Univ, PO Box 29, Jefferson City, MO 65101.

JONES, MABLE VENEIDA
Insurance company manager. **Personal:** Born Sep 20, 1950, Detroit, MI; daughter of Fannie Jones and James U Jones. **Educ:** Eastern Michigan University, BS, special education, 1972; Iowa State University, MS, guidance and counseling, 1973; Wayne State University, 1978; Western Michigan University, doctoral candidate, currently. **Career:** Wayne State University, Upward Bound, director, 1973-76; Ford Motor Co., industrial relations program administrator, 1976-80; AAA

Michigan, employee relations area manager, beginning 1980, employee services area manager, training & development area manager, executive loan, Detroit strategic planning project, crime task force, sales administration area manager, group services area manager, branch manager, currently. **Orgs:** Women's Economic Club; Neighborhood Services Organization, board of directors; Round Table of Christians and Jews, annual dinner committee; Afro-American Museum, membership committee; United Negro College Fund; Urban League, youth development board; Ennis, board of directors; NAACP, lifetime member. **Honors/Awds:** YWCA, Minority Achiever Award, 1985; AAA, Volunteer of the Year, 1986; March of Dimes, Miss Teamwalk, 1984; Upward Bound, Silver Anniversary Achievement, 1992; AAA, Outstanding Service Award, 1990-93; Wolverine Bar, Ossawa Sweet Award, 1994. **Home Addr:** 35479 Heritage Ln, Farmington, MI 48335, (313)471-5293. **Business Addr:** Sr. Consultant, AAA Michigan, 1 Auto Club Drive, Dearborn, MI 48126, (313)336-1000.

JONES, MARCUS
Professional football player. **Personal:** Born Aug 15, 1973, Jacksonville, FL. **Educ:** Univ of North Carolina, attended. **Career:** Tampa Bay Buccaneers, defensive tackle, 1996-. **Honors/Awds:** The Sporting News, All-America Second Team, 1995. **Business Addr:** Professional Football Player, Tampa Bay Buccaneers, 1 Buccaneer Pl, Tampa, FL 33607, (813)870-2700.

JONES, MARCUS EARL
Educator. **Personal:** Born Jan 7, 1943, Decatur, IL; son of Bernetta Mayweather Jones and George Jones; married Valerie Daniel; children: Anthony, Malik, Omar, Taisha, Samira, Malaika, Na'el, Amina, Jamia. **Educ:** Southern IL Univ Carbondale, BA Geog 1965; Chicago State Univ, MA Geog 1969; Univ of Ghana, Certificate 1968; Southern IL Univ, PhD Geog 1978. **Career:** Southern IL Univ Carbondale, ombudsman 1972-73; FL A&M Univ, asst prof geog 1973-76; Univ of So FL Tampa, vstg prof geog 1976-77; Morris Brown Coll, chair & prof geog 1978-85; Valdosta State Coll, prof of geog 1986-87; Chicago Public Schools, teacher, 1988-89; Claflin College, Orangeburg, SC, assoc professor, 1990-95. **Orgs:** Mem Assoc of Amer Geographers, member, Southeastern Assoc of Geographers, member, Assoc of Social and Behavioral Scientists Inc, member, African Studies Assoc; member, West African Research Association, 1991-92. **Honors/Awds:** Book "Black Migration in the United States with Emphasis on Selected Central Cities," Century Twenty One Publishing 1980; article "Black Counterstream Migration, New and Return Migrants to the South, 1965-78," Natl Council of Black Studies 1982; co-author, Lower Socio-Economic and Minority Households in Camden County, GA, Atlanta University, 1987; Fulbright-Hays Commission, grant to study in Egypt, 1994; Fulbright Research Scholar, American Univ in Cairo, 1995-96. **Home Addr:** 664 Stanley St, Orangeburg, SC 29115. **Business Addr:** Associate Professor, Department of History and Sociology, Claflin College, Orangeburg, SC 29115, (803)535-5367.

JONES, MARCUS EDMUND
Television journalist. **Personal:** Born Feb 12, 1960, Washington, DC; son of Lillie Brown and Clarance Jones; married Janice Lyons, May 28, 1983; children: Nathan Aaron Alexander. **Educ:** Boston University, Boston, MA, BS, 1982. **Career:** Daily Evening Item, Lynn, MA, columnist, 1976-78; Boston Globe, Boston, MA, correspondent, 1977-78; WILD-AM, Boston, MA, news anchor/reporter, 1977-82; WQTV, "Boston Live!," Boston, MA, producer/host, 1980-81; Satellite News Channel, Stamford, CT, news associate, 1982-83; WEZN-FM, Bridgeport, CT, news reporter, 1984; WUSA-TV, "Eyewitness News," Washington, DC, reporter trainee, 1984-85; WBZ-TV, "Ten O'Clock News," Boston, MA, news reporter, 1986-91, "The Group", videotape editor, 1991-92; WBZ-TV, "News 4," Boston, MA, freelance reporter, 1993; Lowell Cable TV, "News Ctr 6," Lowell, MA, news dir, 1992-94; Northeastern Univ, Boston, MA, journalism dept, lecturer, 1991-94; WFX, NC8; New England Cable News, Newton, MA, freelance reporter, 1994-95; WFXT "Fox 25 News at Ten," Dedham, MA, freelance reporter, 1995; Newschannel 8, Springfield, VA, Washington, DC reporter, 1995-96. **Orgs:** Member, National Association of Black Journalists, 1989-; BAJK, 1989-95; WABJ, 1995-; member, NAACP, 1970-82; mem, Boston Assn of Black Journalists, 1989-95; mem, Washington Assn of Black Journalists, 1995-. **Honors/Awds:** American Lung Association, 1990; Emmy Award nominee, two categories, feature and special reporting, Boston, New England Chapter National Academy of Television Arts and Sciences, 1990; Emmy Award nominee, one category, news event, Boston, NE Chapter, NATAS, 1991; American Lung Assn, Outstanding Anti-Smoking Report, 1990. **Home Addr:** 16177 Taconic Cir, Dumfries, VA 22026-1524.

JONES, MARILYN ELAINE
Government field representative. **Personal:** Born Dec 17, Waco, TX; children: Spencer. **Educ:** TX Woman's Univ, MA 1970, BS 1972, PhD 1978. **Career:** Early Childhood Educ TX Woman's Univ, consultant 1970-74; TX Woman's Univ, prof/lab instructor 1972-74; Paul Quinn Coll, counselor/placement dir 1974-83; Prairie View A&M Univ, instructor 1980-84; General Land Office State of TX, field rep. **Orgs:** Licensed by the TX State Bd of Examiners of Prof Counselors; mem Delta Sigma Theta Sor; mem NAACP; mem Natl Assoc for Young Children; mem APGA; mem TX Coalition of Black Democrats; mem Eastern Star; city councilmember first female elected 1980-84; vice pres Heart of TX Council of Govs 1982-84; mayor Pro-Tem Waco City Council 1983. **Honors/Awds:** Serv Awds Phi Delta Kappa Inc Gamma Upsilon Chapt, Citizens of Waco, Waco City Council, Heart TX Council of Governors; Quality of Life Awd NTSU/TWU Alumni1981; Women of the Yr Progressive Women of Wichita KS 1982. **Home Addr:** 1604 Harrison Ave, Waco, TX 76704.

JONES, MARK E.
Attorney. **Personal:** Born Oct 15, 1920, Indianapolis, IN; son of Pearl Campbell Jones and Mark E Jones, Sr; divorced; children: 4. **Educ:** Roosevelt Univ, AB 1948; Loyola Univ, JD 1950. **Career:** Jones Ware & Grenard, atty, partner; Chicago TV Commission, commissioner; Cook Co IL, Circuit Ct Judge 1963-80; atty pvt practice 1957-63; Cook Co, asst state atty 1951-57. **Orgs:** Founding mem, treas Judicial Council; mem Nat Bar Assn; Am Bar Assn; Cook Co Bar Assn; bd trustee Roosevelt Univ; bd dir Better Boys Found; life mem NAACP; pres bd dir Southside Community Art Center. **Honors/Awds:** Recipient 1st prize, Chicago Bar Assn Art Show for Painting 1965-66; 1st prize Englewood & Lake Meadows Art Fairs 1970, 1973. **Military Serv:** USN 1942-45. **Business Addr:** Attorney at Law, Jones Ware & Grenard, 180 N LaSalle St, Ste 801, Chicago, IL 60601.

JONES, MARSHA REGINA
Journalist. **Personal:** Born Jan 26, 1962, Brooklyn, NY; daughter of Iona Louisa Williams Jones and Eudolphin Jones; married Donald Collins; children: Hollis Danielle. **Educ:** Nazareth College, Advanced Placement Courses Spanish 1978-80; Purdue Univ, BA Journalism 1980-84. **Career:** Purdue Exponent Newspaper, reporter 1981-83; Purdue Reports Magazine, reporter 1983-84; Black Cultural Ctr Newspaper, reporter 1983-84; About Time Magazine, editorial asst/reporter 1984-88, assistant editor, 1988-89; Project KID, communications consult, 1988-90; SUNY Brockport, NY, marketing communications mgr, 1989-93; Rochester Business Magazine, Rochester, NY, contributing editor, 1989-93; Roc Live/After Dark, host/producer, 1991; Rochester Metro Challenger, contributing editor, columnist, 1991-; Rochester Museum & Science News, contributing editor, 1992; The Communicator, Rochester Assn of Black Communicators, editor, 1993; Hillside Children's Center, public relations coordinator, 1993-95; Scene Entertainment Weekly, contributing editor, 1995-97; Camp Good Days and Special Times, public relations director, 1995-96; Planned Parenthood, mktg communications coord, 1997-. **Orgs:** Mem Soc of Professional Journalists 1980-, National Association of Black Journalists, 1988-, East HS Ebony Culture Club; Black Scholars Mentor Program Urban League of Rochester NY Inc 1985-89; Black Scholars Alumni Comm Urban League of Rochester Inc 1985-89; mem Amer Red Cross Minority Screening Campaign Comm 1985-88; mem Village Gate Theater 1985-88; mem 1986, sec 1991, Rochester Assoc of Black Communicators; mem Rochester Purdue Alumni Assoc; board member, R Nelson Mandela Scholarship Fund, 1989-93; member, SUNY Brockport Faculty Senate, 1990-91; member, City Newspaper Editorial Advisory Board, 1990-93; member, vice pres, Montgomery Neighborhood Center Youth Advisory Board, 1990-93; member, Rochester Assn of Black Communicators Film Festival, 1991; Rochester Association of Black Communicators, president, 1992-94; Guyanese American Association, 1992; Action for A Better Community 20th Anniversary Gala Committee, 1990; United Negro College Fund Committee, 1992; Boys and Girls Club of Rochester, bd of dirs, 1994-, Bowl-a-thon Committee, 1993-95; RABC 9th Annual Ethnogenre Film Festival, chair, 1993; RABC 10th Annual Ethnogenre Film Festival, co-chair, 1994; Hillside's Working Together Team, 1993-95; Bill Klein's 13th Annual Academy Awards Committee, publicity chair, 1995-; Hillside Art Diversity Project, co-chair, 1995; Assn for Women in Communications; Public Relations Society of Amer; Monroe Council on Teenage Pregnancy. **Honors/Awds:** Black Scholar Award Urban League of Rochester NY Inc 1980; Purdue Reamer Honorary Soc Purdue Univ 1983 (first black student to be inducted in honor society, to hold office in honor society, to be elected to exec council); Howard G McCall Award Purdue Univ Black Cultural Ctr 1984; Grand Prix Award Purdue Univ 1984; Matrix Award nominee, Women in Communications, 1988; published A People's Pledge, 1989; University Photographer's Association of American's President's Award, 1991; SUNY Brockport's Black Male Support Group Award, 1992; Natl Leadership Council's Capitol Award, 1991. **Special Achievements:** "My Father's Child, My Mother's Daughter," Visions & Viewpoints: Voices of the Genesee Valley, 1993; "Friendship 1337," Visions & Viewpoints: Voices of the Genesee Valley, 1994. **Home Addr:** 211 Woodstock Rd, Rochester, NY 14609-7240.

JONES, MARTHA E.
Retired educator. **Personal:** Born Feb 14, 1926, Lumberton, NC; daughter of Rev & Mrs H C Jones. **Educ:** Winston-Salem State Univ, BS 1946; A&T Univ, M 1954; Attended, Ohio State Univ, NC Central Univ. **Career:** Wardell Chapel AME Zion Church, organist 1953-82; Cleveland Co Teachers Fed Credit Union, mgmt consultant. **Orgs:** Mem NEA, NCAE; life mem NAACP, Alumni Assoc Winston-Salem State Univ. **Honors/Awds:** Certificate of Appreciation Today's Ebonites Womens Club 1984; Community Civic Educ Work NAACP Cleveland Co Chap 1984; Plaque-Wardell Chapel AME Zion Church. **Home Addr:** 309 Wilson St, Shelby, NC 28150-4551.

JONES, MARVIN MAURICE
Professional football player. **Personal:** Born Jun 28, 1972, Miami, FL; children: Jada. **Educ:** Florida State. **Career:** New York Jets, linebacker, 1993-. **Honors/Awds:** Rotary-Lombardi Award, 1992; Dick Butkus Award, 1992. **Business Addr:** Professional Football Player, New York Jets, 1000 Fulton Ave, Hempstead, NY 11550, (516)560-8100.

JONES, MAVIS N.
Dentist. **Personal:** Born Mar 7, 1918, Canton, MS; married Bernard; children: Bernard C Jr, Thelma Shepherd. **Educ:** Meharry Med Coll, DDS 1948, RDH 1938. **Career:** MS State Bd Health, itinerant dental hygienist; Ft Jackson SC, dental hygienist; Meharry Med Coll, inst dental hygiene; Jackson Hinds Comp Health Cntr, dental surgeon, pvt pract. **Orgs:** Mem MS Am & Nat Dental Assns; MS Dental Soc; life mem NAACP; mem Business Women's League. **Honors/Awds:** WYCA Merit Award 1973; 1st female dentist; 1st & only black female dentist in MS. **Business Addr:** 1102 Woodrow Wilson, Jackson, MS 39213.

JONES, MAXINE
Vocalist, songwriter. **Personal:** Born in Paterson, NJ. **Career:** Member of the group En Vogue, 1988-; albums include: Born to Sing, 1990; Remix to Sing, 1991; Funky Divas, 1992; singles include: "Hold On," "Lies," "Free Your Mind," "This Is Your Life," "My Lovin' (You're Never Gonna Get It)," "Desire," "Yesterday.". **Honors/Awds:** Born to Sing, platinum, 1990; National Academy of Recording Arts and Sciences, Grammy nominations: rock duo or group, best short video, "Free Your Mind"; R&B duo or group, Funky Divas. **Special Achievements:** Cameo appearance in movie Aces. **Business Addr:** Singer, En Vogue, c/o David Lombard, Top Talent Management, 1680 N Vine St, Ste 1000, Los Angeles, CA 90028, (213)962-8016.

JONES, MEREDITH J.
Government official. **Personal:** Born Mar 24, 1948, Hartford, CT; daughter of Dr Cyril J & Rose Randolph Jones. **Educ:** Swarthmore College, BA, 1968; Yale Law School, JD, 1974. **Career:** Chickering & Gregory, partner, 1983-86; Bechtel Financing Services, Inc, senior counsel, 1986-93; Natl Oceanic & Atmospheric Administration, general counsel, 1993-94; Federal Communications Commission, Cable Services Bureau, chief, 1994-. **Orgs:** Assn of the Bar of the City of New York; Federal Communications Bar Assn; Natl Assn of Minorities in Cable. **Business Addr:** Chief, Cable Services Bureau, Federal Communications Commission, Federal Communications Commission, 1919 M Street, NW, Washington, DC 20554, (202)418-7200.

JONES, MERLAKIA
Professional basketball player. **Personal:** Born Jun 21, 1973. **Educ:** Florida, bachelor's degree in public recreation. **Career:** Cleveland Rockers, guard-forward, 1997-. **Business Addr:** Professional Basketball Player, Cleveland Rockers, One Center Ct, Cleveland, OH 44115, (216)263-7625.

JONES, MICHAEL ANDREA
Clergyman, psychologist. **Personal:** Born Aug 6, 1937, Atlanta, GA; married Linda; children: Gattie. **Educ:** GA State U, BA; Atlanta U, MA; Am U, ED. **Career:** Morris Brown Coll, dir; Mitchell Chapel, pastor. **Orgs:** AME Ch Atlanta Ass of Educators; GA Assn of Educators; GA Cncl Of Chs 1977-; So Christian Leadership Conf; United Youth Adult Conf; mem NAACP; So Christian Leadership 1959-; Atlanta Christian Cncl 1975-. **Business Addr:** Fayetteville Parish AME, PO Box 430, Fayetteville, GA 30214.

JONES, MICHAEL ANTHONY
Professional football player. **Personal:** Born Apr 15, 1969, Kansas City, MO; married Leslie; children: Taelor, Moriah, Ashley. **Educ:** Missouri. **Career:** Los Angeles Raiders, linebacker, 1991-94; Oakland Raiders, 1995-96; St Louis Rams, 1997-. **Business Addr:** Professional Football Player, St Louis Rams, One Rams Way, St Louis, MO 63045, (314)982-7267.

JONES, MICHAEL DAVID
Professional football player. **Personal:** Born Aug 25, 1969, Columbia, SC; married. **Educ:** North Carolina State, attended. **Career:** Phoenix Cardinals, defensive end, 1991-93; New England Patriots, 1994-. **Business Addr:** Professional Football Player, New England Patriots, 60 Washington St, Foxboro Stadium, Foxboro, MA 02035, (508)543-7911.

JONES, MICHELE WOODS
Educational administrator (retired), consultant. **Personal:** Born Oct 3, 1945, Los Angeles, CA; daughter of Mary Ellen Harris and David A Francis; married Reginald L Jones, Jan 3, 1988; children: Sjaun, Leasa. **Educ:** Phoenix College, AA, 1965; Univ of California, Berkeley, BA, history, 1969, grad study, history, 1969-70; California State Univ, Hayward, MS, educational psychology, 1979. **Career:** Univ of California, Berkeley, co-director, special summer project, 1968, Educational Opportunity Program, counselor, 1968-70, tutorial staff coordinator, 1970-72, counselor coordinator, 1972-73, Student Info Ctr, asst dir, 1973-77, Student Learning Ctr, asst dir, 1977-81, principal student affairs officer, 1981-83, dir of student activities and services, 1983-89, assistant to the vice chancellor and staff ombudsperson, 1989-91; Consultant: Newport News Sch District; City of Hampton Social Servs in Multicultural Communications & Problem Solving; Cobb & Henry Publishers, pres, currently. **Orgs:** Mem, past pres, sec, Alpha Kappa Alpha sorority, 1967-; campus liaison, Black Alumni Club, Univ of California, Berkeley, 1969-; bd of dirs, California Alumni Assn, Univ of California; Order of the Golden Bear, 1975-; Assn of Black Psychologists; Educational Resource Council, 1979-; advisory board, Ctr for the Study, Education & Advancement of Women, Univ of California, Berkeley; honorary member, Golden Key Natl Honor Society, 1985; honorary member, Delta Delta Delta sorority, 1986; Natl Assn of Student Personnel Admins; Natl Orientation Directors Assn; Soroptomist Intl; Univ & Coll Ombudsman Assn 1989-; bd of dirs, Natl Assn of Black Public School Admins, 1990-; Jack & Jill of America, Hampton Chapter, program dir. **Honors/Awds:** Outstanding Black Women of California, 1981-82; Recognition Award, African Students' Assn, Univ of California, Berkeley, 1982; Michelle Woods Scholarship established in her honor by Alpha Kappa Alpha sorority, Univ of California, Berkeley, 1983; Rosalie M Stern Award, California Alumni Assn, 1984; Citizen of the Year awd from Basileus-Epsilon Mu/Omega Psi Phi Fraternity, 1986; Black Alumnae of the Year, Black Alumni Club, Univ of California, Berkeley, 1987; Outstanding Service Award, Univ of California, Berkeley, 1988; Management & Professional Achievement Award, Univ of California, Berkeley, 1991; Univ of California, Berkeley, The Berkeley Citation, 1991. **Business Addr:** Pres, Cobb & Henry Publishers, Hampton, VA.

JONES, MICHELLE
Fundraising organization administrator. **Personal:** Born May 10, 1954, Columbus, OH; daughter of Ora Jones and Ralph Jones. **Educ:** Ohio State University, 1972-75; Columbus State Community College, 1981-83. **Career:** Columbus Public Schools, secretary, 1974-83; The United Way of Franklin County, secretary, 1983-85, communication coordinator, 1985-. **Orgs:** Women in Communications, Inc, 1985-87; Youth Advocate Services, 1988-91. **Business Addr:** Communications Coordinator, United Way of Franklin County, Inc, 360 S Third St, Columbus, OH 43215, (614)227-2784.

JONES, MILES JAMES
Pathologist. **Personal:** Born Nov 22, 1952, Abington, PA; son of Jessie Jones and James Jones; married Linda D Ableitner; children: Dominick, Jessica. **Educ:** Princeton Univ, attended 1970-73; Howard Univ Medical School, MD 1977; post grad work at Cleveland Clinic, 1977-78, Mayo Clinic, Mayo Graduate School of Medicine, 1978-82. **Career:** Armed Forces Inst of Pathology, pathologist 1982-84; Herring Hosp, pathologist & lab director 1985-; Temple Medical Reference Laboratories, pathologist, 1989-. **Orgs:** Mem editorial bd Minnesota Medicine 1980-87; med adv comm American Red Cross, St Louis Chapter; coroner's physician Alexander Co, Johnson Co, Polaski Co 1984-; Herrin Rotary 1985-; clinical asst prof of pathology So IL Univ Carbondale Medical Sch 1986-; mem IL State Medical Society, Williamson County Medical Socs; mem Intl Acad of Pathology, Intl Soc of Gynecologic Pathologists, AMA, Amer Acad Forensic Sciences; fellow Coll of Amer Pathologists, Amer Soc of Clinical Pathologists; alternate house of delegates Coll of Amer Pathologists; member, United States and Canadian Academy of Pathology; member, Williamson County Medical Society; member, Illinois Society of Pathologists. **Honors/Awds:** Natl Science Found fellowships 1968-70; Natl Sudden Infant Death fellowship, 1975; Stowell-Orbison Award for Pathologist in Training, US-Canadian Division, Intl Acad of Pathology, 1982; 5 publications including ''Verrucous Squamous Cell Carcinoma of the Vagina,'' w/LA Ballard and HS Levin, Cleveland Clinic Quarterly 48; 6 abstract presentations; 3 book reviews published.

JONES, MILTON H., JR.
Financial institution executive. **Personal:** Born Jul 25, 1952, Atlanta, GA; son of Helen E Jones and Milton H Jones Sr; married Shelia Pitts Jones; children: Milton C, Tiffany M. **Educ:** University of Notre Dame, BBA, acctg, 1974. **Career:** Peat, Marwick, Mitchell & Co, 1974-77; Citizens and Southern National Bank, 1977-91; NationsBank, executive vice pres, 1991-. **Orgs:** Leadership Atalanta, executive committee; Leadership Georgia, Class 1992; Techwood Park Inc, chairman; Metropolitan Atlanta YMCA; Southwest Atlanta YMCA, executive committee; Atlanta Urban Bankers Association; Salvation Army Boys & Girls Club, advisory council; Georgia Council on Child Abuse, advisory board of directors; Atlanta Econ Dev Corp, chairman, board of directors; Atlanta Local Dev Corp, board of directors. **Honors/Awds:** Atlanta Urban Bankers Association, Pioneer Award, 1992; NationsBank, Hero Award, 1992. **Business Addr:** President, Dealer Financial Services Group, Executive Vice President, NationsBank Corp, 600 Peachtree St NE, Atlanta Plaza, Atlanta, GA 30308, (404)607-6033.

JONES, NANCY REED
Educator, business executive. **Personal:** Born Jun 15, 1928, Bamberg County, SC; daughter of Josie Bell Reed and Aaron Reed; married Oct 1, 1950 (widowed); children: Pat Jernan Jones Hagood, Wendy. **Educ:** Temple University, 1956; Claflin College, BS, 1958; South Carolina State College, MS, 1961; University of South Carolina, 1962-64. **Career:** Bamberg County Board of Education, 1948-80; National Testing Service, part-time, 1977-78; Augusta, Georgia, Board of Education, 1979-89; Victoria Slipper Retail and Manufacturing Co, president/chief executive officer, 1985-. **Orgs:** Union Baptist Chruch; American Education Association; American Guidance Association; Bamberg Ehrhardt High School, director of guidance; Pastors Aid Club, president. **Honors/Awds:** Guidance Award, 1978; Teacher of the Year, 1983; Alpha Kappa Sorority Award, 1990; Delta Sigma Thada Award, 1991.

JONES, NAPOLEON A., JR.
Judge. **Personal:** Born Aug 25, 1940, Hodge, LA; children: Lena L. **Educ:** San Diego State Univ, BA 1962, MSW 1967; Univ of San Diego School of Law, JD 1971. **Career:** CA Rural Legal Asst Modesto, attny 1972-73; Defenders Inc of San Diego, attny 1973-75; Jones & Adler San Diego, attny 1975-77; San Diego Municipal Court, judge 1977-82; San Diego Superior Court, judge 1982-94; US District Court, judge, 1994-. **Orgs:** California Black Attorneys Association; Sigma Pi Phi Fraternity; Kappa Alpha Psi f=Fraternity; Natl Assoc of Women Judges; Natl Bar Assoc; past pres, Earl B Billiam Bar WASN; mentor, Nia UMOIA Valencia Park Elem School; bd of visitors, San Diego State University, School of Social Work; bd mem, Project Restore-Women's Drug Treatment Program; advisory bd, Friend to Friend; dir USD Law Alumni Association Bd, 1994-95; bd of dirs, San Diego City Coll Foundation; advisory bd mem, Family Literacy Foundation; bd mem, Community Partnership Committee. **Honors/Awds:** Reginald Heber Smith Fellowship 1971-73; Disting Alumni School of Social Work Merit; USD Law School & SDSU Coll of Human Svcs; Judge of the Year, California Association of Black Lawyers, 1993; Honorary Doctor of Laws, California Western School of Law, 1994; Judge of the Year Award, Louisiana Association, 1995; Deputy District Attorney's Association, Judicial Excellence Award, 1995; The State Bar of California and University of California, Certificate of Appreciation, 1996; numerous others. **Business Addr:** Judge, US District Court, South District of CA, US Courthouse, 940 Front St, Ste 2125, San Diego, CA 92101-8912, (619)557-2993.

JONES, NATHANIEL, SR.
Elected official. **Personal:** Born Oct 3, 1948, New Orleans, LA; married Brenda; children: Natalie, Nathaniel, Natash. **Educ:** Southern Univ, attended 1968-73. **Career:** King Triumph BC, member 1969; Southern Univ Recreation Club, vice president 1970-72; Prince Hall Masons, member 1973; Lutcher and Gramercy Jaycees, member 1984. **Orgs:** Member Rive Parishes Improvement League 1972; chairman Building & Planning Comm 1975 & 1981; board of directors LA Black Municipal Assn Caucus 1982 & 1983; member USWA 1973-; member LA Municipal Assn 1981-; member Natl League of Cities 1983; member Lutcher-Gramercy Jaycees 1984; dist coordinator Natl Black Caucus of LEO 1984-; member NAACP. **Honors/Awds:** Worked Summer Youth in Drug Program 1985. **Military Serv:** ROTC Southern Univ Baton Rouge, LA. **Business Addr:** Alderman, Town of Lutcher, Box 456, Lutcher, LA 70071.

JONES, NATHANIEL R.
Judge, attorney, administrator. **Personal:** Born May 13, 1926, Youngstown, OH. **Educ:** Youngstown Univ, BA 1951, LLB (Honorary) 1956. **Career:** NAACP, gen counsel 1969-79; Fair Employment Practices Comm City of Youngstown, exec dir 1966-69; Private practice, attny; US Attny No Dist of OH, former asst attny; US Court of Appeals 6th Circuit, judge. **Orgs:** Dep gen counsel Pres Comm on Civil Disorders 1967; co-chmn Civilian-Mil Task Force on Mil Justice 1972. **Honors/Awds:** Headed three-man team which investigated grievances of black servicemen in W Germany. **Business Addr:** Judge, US Court of Appeals 6th Crct, 432 US Post Office & Court House Bldg, Cincinnati, OH 45202.

JONES, NELLIE L.
Elected official, commissioner. **Personal:** Born Apr 11, 1933, Minter City, MS; children: James Jr, Sandra, Jerry, Michael, Audrey Jones Kenner, Jennifer Jones Witherspoon, McDaniels. **Educ:** MS Vocational Coll, 1955. **Career:** Metro Sanitary Dist of Greater Chicago, commissioner, currently. **Orgs:** Steering Police Comm Mayor's Task Force; beat rep pres of 2nd Ward Women; LAC Comm Aux Democratic Org. **Honors/Awds:** Affirmative Action 1978; Black Contractors United 1982; Robert Taylor Homes 4 Star Assn 1983; Outstanding Awd United Comm Action 1984. **Business Addr:** Commissioner, Metro Sanitary District, Cook County, 100 E Erie St, Chicago, IL 60611.

JONES, NETTIE PEARL
Educator, author, educational administrator. **Personal:** Born Jan 1, 1941, Arlington, GA; daughter of Delonia Mears Jones Whorton and Benjamin Jones; divorced; children: Lynne Cheryl Harris. **Educ:** Wayne State Univ, Detroit, MI, BS, Secondary Educ, 1963; Marygrove Coll, Detroit, MI, MEd, Reading, 1971; Fashion Inst of Technology, New York, NY, Advertising, Communications, 1973-76. **Career:** Detroit Bd of Educ, Detroit, MI, teacher of secondary social studies, English, reading, 1963-72; Royal George School, Greenfield Park, Quebec, teacher of secondary English, 1966-68; Martin Luther King School, New York, NY, teacher of reading, 1971-72; Wayne State Univ, Detroit, MI, lecturer, visiting writer, 1986-87; Chmn Wayne County Commr, Detroit, MI, writer, 1988; Wayne County Community Coll, Detroit, MI, teacher of devel reading, 1988; Michigan Technological Univ, Houghton, MI, asst prof, writer in residence, 1988-89, minority affairs asst to the vice pres, 1989-. **Orgs:** Detroit Women Writers, 1985; Amer Assn of Univ Prof, 1986; adjudicator, 1989 Michigan Governor's Artist Awards. **Honors/Awds:** University of Chicago Divinity School, Benjamin Mays Scholar, 1990-92; Yaddo Fellow Writer, 1985; one of the Most Promising Novelists, New York Times Book Review, March 17, 1985; Notable New Artist, Contemporary Literary Criticism Yearbook, 1985; Individual Artist, Michigan Council of the Arts Award, 1986; second runner-up, DH Lawrence Competition, 1987; Grant for Fiction, Natl Endowment of the Arts, 1989. **Special Achievements:** Author, works include: Fish Tales, 1984; Mischief Makers, 1989; ''When Crack Comes Home,'' non-fiction short story, Detroit Free Press Magazine, Feb 5, 1989; Detroit: Beauty in This Beast; Anita at the Battle of the Bush, Thomas on the Hill: Dark Town Strutters Ball; ''Abrilaharris Quest,'' a television script designed for Detroit Public Schools.

JONES, NINA F.
Educational administrator (retired). **Personal:** Born Jul 30, 1918, Madison, GA; daughter of Hallie Flemister and Sumner Flemister; married Dr William M Jones; children: William M Jr, Steven L. **Educ:** Central YMCA Clge, AB 1938; Chicago Tchrs Clge, MEd 1942; Loyola Univ Chicago, EdD 1975. **Career:** Chicago Public Schools, teacher 1942, prin 1965, dist supt 1969, asst supt personnel 1975, sec bd of examiners 1983-88. **Orgs:** Mem Alpha Kappa Alpha Sor 1940, Alpha Gamma Pi Sor 1967; Pi Lambda Theta. **Home Addr:** 9156 S Constance, Chicago, IL 60617.

JONES, NOLAN E.
Government official. **Personal:** Born Dec 11, 1944, Houston, TX; son of Hester Neal Ross and Ernest Jones. **Educ:** Texas Southern University, Houston, TX, BA, 1968; Swarthmore College, Swarthmore, PA, post baccalaureate, 1968-69; Washington University, St Louis, MO, MA, 1973; PhD, 1975. **Career:** The University of Michigan, Ann Arbor, MI, assistant professor, 1973-78; National Governors Association, Washington, DC, committee director, 1978-94, group director, 1995-. **Orgs:** Council member, American Political Science Association, 1990-92; secretary, National Conference of Black Political Scientist, 1976-78; secretary, Allen Adams Federal Credit Union, 1989-92. **Honors/Awds:** Woodrow Wilson Doctoral Dissertation Fellow, 1972-73; Graduate Fellow in Public Law, Edna F Gellhorn, 1970-72; 10th Year Award, National Governors, Association, 1989; The Order of the Palmetto, State of South Carolina, 1985; Honorary Tar Heel, State of North Carolina, 1989; Excellence in Emergency Management Award, Federal Emergency Management Agency, 1993; The Patrick Henry Award, National Guard Association of the United States, 1996. **Military Serv:** US Air Force, airman 2nd class, 1962-65. **Business Addr:** Director, Human Resources Group, 444 North Capitol St, Suite 267 NW, Washington, DC 20001.

JONES, OLIVER, JR.
Educator. **Personal:** Born Aug 6, 1947, Savannah, GA; son of Jannie Jenkins Jones and Oliver Jones; married Vernita Christian Jones, Sep 2, 1967; children: Olivia, Deidra. **Educ:** Savannah State College, Savannah, GA, BS, 1970; University of Illinois, Champaign, IL, MA, 1974, PhD, 1979. **Career:** Rust College, Holly Springs, MS, assistant professor, 1978-79; Florida A&M University, Tallahassee, FL, associate professor, 1979-, director center for public affairs, 1982-. **Orgs:** Council member, Conference of Minority Public Adm, 1985-89; council member, National Conference of Black Political Scientists, 1986-90; president-elect, National Conference of Black Political Scientists, 1990-91; chairman of board, Frenchtown Area Development Authority, 1986; council member, Tallahassee Informed Parents, 1990-92; member, NAACP; member, American Political Science Association, member, Association of Behavioral Sciences. **Honors/Awds:** Outstanding Public Servant, Florida Attorney General, 1990; Distinguished Service, COMPA, 1989; Public Service Award, Brinbridge Community College, 1989; Outstanding Leadership, NOBLE, Florida, 1989; Service Award, FAMU, 1991. **Military Serv:** Army, Specialist 4th Class, 1971-80. **Business Addr:** Dir, Center for Public Affairs, Florida A&M University, 412 Tucker Hall, Tallahassee, FL 32307.

JONES, OZRO T., JR.
Clergyman. **Personal:** son Of Bishop & Mrs Ozro T Jones; married Regina Shaw Jones; children: Stephen, Soren. **Educ:** Temple U, BS 1945; Temple U, MA 1946; Temple Univ Sch of Theol, STB; Temple U, STM 1953; Temple Univ Sch of Religion & Philosophy, STD 1962. **Career:** Holy Temple Ch of God in Christ, pastor; Commonwealth of PA Ch of God in Christ, juris bishop 1973-; Holy Temple Ch of God in Christ, asso pastor 1963; Meml Ch of God in Christ, pastor 1953; Ch of God in Christ to Liberia W Coast Africa, missionary 1949; Young People's Ch of Holy Temple, leader 1941. **Orgs:** Organized Tuesday Night Young People's Ch Svc; Sons of Gideon; Dau of Ruth; Young People's Choral of Holy Temple; Upper Room Fellowship; Pentecostal Student Youth Conf; Big Bros & Big Sisters Fellowship; bd mem Oppty Indsln Ctr Inc; mem Cncl of Christian Missionaries in Liberia; asso editor YPWW Quarterly Topics; co-editor The Christian View of Life; pres Intl Youth Congress Of Ch of God in Christ; began Christ Seeks You youth rallies; writer of 3 hymns. **Honors/Awds:** Church of God in Christ, Elevated to 2nd Assistant Presiding Bishop, 1997. **Business Addr:** Juridsictional Bishop, Commonwealth Of Pennsylvania, Church of God in Christ, 336 N 60th St, Philadelphia, PA 19139.

JONES, PATRICIA. **See SPEARS-JONES, PATRICIA KAY.**

JONES, PATRICIA YVONNE
City government official. **Personal:** Born Oct 22, 1956, Muskegon, MI; daughter of Juanita Henry Jones and Theo Jones; children: Dwayne. **Educ:** Muskegon Comm Coll, Practical Nursing diploma 1978, AS 1978; Grand Valley State College, currently. **Career:** Hackley Hosp & Medical Ctr, licensed prac nurse II 1978-; City of Muskegon Hts, councilwoman. **Orgs:** Mem MI Licensed Practical Nurse Assn 1978; mem NAACP 1981; bd mem Muskegon Comm Coll Adv Bd 1982; mem Harriet J Cole Order of Eastern Stars 1983; gen mem Natl Black Caucus Local Elected Official 1983; gen mem Muskegon Hts Bd of Commerce 1984; Vice Pres Muskegon Black Women Political Caucus; treasurer, 1990-, vice pres, 1992; Mich Women in Municipal Gov't pres beginning 1990, president elect 1993-; Muskegon County Black Womens Caucus; pres 2400 Reynolds Block Club 1990-; mem Muskegon Heights Economic Dev 1990-. **Honors/Awds:** Outstanding Citizen Achievement, Muskegon Heights High School Class of 1974, 1984, 1989; Outstanding Community Service, Muskegon County Black Womens Political Caucus, 1989; Outstanding Achievement, Census Bureau 1989; Certificate of Policy Drugs in Community Program, Michigan State Univ, 1990. **Business Addr:** Councilwoman, City of Muskegon Hts, 2724 Peck St, Muskegon Heights, MI 49444.

JONES, PATRICK P.
Association executive. **Personal:** Born Apr 8, 1928, Bulloch County, GA; son of Mittie Ann Russel Jones and Miles Albert Jones; children: Andre Jones. **Career:** Gen builder; farmer; lumber checker; crop reporter & landscaping; plant machine operator; Devel Unique Services Ourselves, chmn bd dir; Jones & Jones Homeground Improvement Serv; operator; Blending-Aires Singers, mgr. **Orgs:** Pres NAACP 1965-; mem PAC; Church Trustee Bd; mem Church Programing Comm; Group Song Leader; pres Assn for Progressive Educ & Political Action; chmn, Church Work Comm, Montgumery Branch NAACP; teacher, Oconnee Zion Asst Sunday & BTU Congress. **Honors/Awds:** Man of Yr Award; William M Boyd Award; Citizenship Award; NAACP Award for Branch Programming; Certificate for Voter Registration.

JONES, PEARL PULLINS
Association executive, court clerk (retired). **Personal:** Born Jun 29, 1915, Birmingham, AL; daughter of Willie Harris Pullins and Charles Pullins; married Thomas O Jones, Feb 13, 1936 (deceased); children: Constance Gilliard, Thomas O, III, Michael T Jones. **Educ:** NY Univ Sch of Mdse & Bus Mgmt, AA 1954. **Career:** Louis Harris & Assocs New York NY, natl field supr 1966-73; Louis Harris & Assocs NY, field interviewer 1963-66; New York City Health Dept Jamaica, sr clerk 1960-63; AUS, sr clerk; Ordinance Dept Raritan NJ, 1942-43; Alexander Dept Stores NYC, mgr price change dept 1939-42, 1945-48, 1951-55; Rio Rancho, NM, deputy court clerk, 1982-85. **Orgs:** Pres NAACP NW Mesa NM Branch; founder, pres Natl Key Women of Amer Queens Branch 1956-74; co-founder, pres NW Mesa NM NAACP 1978-80; first vice pres NM State Conf of Branch NAACP 1978-80; chaplain Amer Assn of Retired Persons Unit 78 Rio Rancho 1976-79; chaplian Disabled Amer Vet Aux 1976-78; first vice pres Lutheran Church Women All Saints Lutheran NM 1977-78; vice chairperson, Democratic County Org, Sandoval City, NM, 1985-89. **Honors/Awds:** Juez Comisionado Comm Award, Lt Gov Robert Ferguson NM 1978; Certificate of Appreciation Award, NM State Conf of Branch NAACP 1979; Certificate of Recognition Serv,Lt Gov Roberto Mongragon 1979; Colonial & Aide de Camp, Gov Bruce King 1979; Certificate of Appreciation, Shirley Hooper Sec of State 1980; NM Mesa NAACP Award: first pres 1979-81; state conf of NM NAACP; Outstanding Service Award, 1983-84; City of Rio Rancho, NM Municipal Ct 1982-85; Faithful Service Award.

JONES, PERCY ELWOOD
Physician. **Personal:** Born Jun 25, 1940, Richmond, VA; married Nora; children: Sabrina, Christopher. **Educ:** VA Union Univ, 1961; Meharry Med Coll, MD 1968. **Career:** Med Coll VA, pathology resd, pathology intern 1968-73; L Richardson Meml Hosp, chf staff, pathologist 1975-. **Orgs:** Pathologist Amer Soc Clinical Pathologists; mem Old N State Med Soc; Natl Med Assn; mem Kappa Alpha Psi Frat; Greensboro Med Soc; Guilford Co Med Soc; Hayes-Taylor YMCA; fellow of College of Amer Pathologists; fellow of Amer Soc of Clinical Pathologists; diplomate Amer Bd of Pathology; life mem NAACP. **Military Serv:** USAF Maj 1973-75.

JONES, PETER LAWSON
State representative, attorney, college instructor. **Personal:** Born Dec 23, 1952, Cleveland, OH; son of Margaret Diane Hoiston Jones and Charles Whitman Jones; married Lisa Payne Jones, Oct 12, 1985; children: Ryan Charles Jones, Leah Danielle Jones. **Educ:** Harvard Coll, BA 1975; Harvard Law School, JD 1980. **Career:** Hon Yvonne B Burke US House of Rep, pres & leg aide 1975-76; Carter-Mondale Pres Campaign, writer & spokesman 1976; Carter-Mondale Transition Planning Group, transition officer 1976-77; Office of Intergovt Relations & Congressional Affairs HUD, liaison officer 1977; Dyke Coll Cleveland OH, instructor 1980, 1983; Supreme Court of OH, law clerk 1982-83; attorney 1980-; Ohio Works Co, pres 1984-85; Shaker Heights, OH, councilman, 1984-91. **Orgs:** Mem board of trustees, Cuyahoga County Bar Assn 1990-; pres, board of trustees, Metropolitan Strategy Group; treasurer Harvard Law School Assn of Cleveland 1986-, co-general counsel, 1995-; mem Executive Comm Cuyahoga County Democratic Party 1986-; mem board of trustees, Court Community Service Agency; mem District 12 Council of Delegates, Ohio State Bar Assn; life mem Cleveland Branch NAACP; mem Mt Zion Congregational Church, UCC. **Honors/Awds:** Harvard Rhodes Scholarship Nom; Harvard John F Kennedy Inst of Politics Summer Fellowship; Harvard Natl Scholarship; Paul Revere Frothingham Scholarship; Currier House Sr Creativity Awd; Meritorious Achievement Awd US Dept of HUD 1977, PUSH-Excel Program 1981; graduate, Leadership Cleveland Program, 1985; The Eastside Coalition Comm Serv Awd 1986; Inductee, Shaker Heights Alumni Assn Hall of Fame 1987; Outstanding Young Clevelander Public Service Jaycees 1989; Black History Month Community Service Award, East Ohio Gas Co/WZAK-FM, 1992; Good Neighbor Certificate of Appreciation, United Area Citizens Agency, 1992; Democrat of the Year Award, Shaker Heights Democratic Club, 1996; "The Family Line" a full length play produced at Harvard Coll 1975, Ohio Univ, 1976; staged reading at the E Cleveland Community Theatre 1985. **Special Achievements:** First African-American nominated to run for lieutenant governor of the State of Ohio. **Home Addr:** 3532 Norwood Rd, Shaker Heights, OH 44122-4968, (216)561-8988. **Business Addr:** 77 S High St, Columbus, OH 43266-0603, (614)466-5441.

JONES, PHILLIP ERSKINE
Educator. **Personal:** Born Oct 26, 1940, Chicago, IL; son of Dorothy R Jones; married Jo Lavera Kennedy; children: Phyllis, Joel. **Educ:** Univ of IL, BS 1963; Univ of IA, MA 1967, PhD 1975. **Career:** Chicago Youth Ctrs, group work counselor 1963-64; Flint Comm Schs, secondary tchr phys ed 1967-68; Univ of IA, dir special support serv 1970-75, asstvice pres & dir affirmative action asst prof of counselor educ 1975-78, assoc dean of student serv & asst prof of counselor educ 1978-83, dean of student serv & asst prof of counselor educ 1983-89, associate vice president of academic affairs & dean of students, 1989-97, vice pres for student services and dean of students, 1997-. **Orgs:** Mem IA City Human Relations Comm 1972-74; chair IA City Human Relations Comm 1974-75; human relations training sessions IA City Fire Dept 1985; field reader for spec serv prog US Office of Educ 1980-87; human relations workshop Dept of Correction Serv Session 1981; re-entry workshop for tchrs IA City Sch Dist; consul redevelopment of training prog for educators in USOE; field reader for grad & professional oppor progs US Office of Educ 1978; consul HUD. **Honors/Awds:** Rep US Ethnic Professional Exchange Prog to W Germany; Sister Cities Intl; Carl Duisberg-Gesellschaft; and Instut fur Auslandsbeziehungen; numerous publications including "Special Educ & Socioeconomic Retardation" Journal for Spec Educators Vol 19 No 4 1983; Commentary "Student Decision Making, When and How"; College/Career Choice, Right Student Right Time Right Place; proceedings of the 1972 ACT Invitational Conf Iowa City. **Business Addr:** Vice President for Student Services, Univ of IA, Rm 114 Jessup Hall, Iowa City, IA 52242.

JONES, POPEYE (RONALD JEROME)
Professional basketball player. **Personal:** Born Jun 17, 1970, Dresden, TN; married Amy; children: Justin, Seth, Caleb. **Educ:** Murray State. **Career:** Dallas Mavericks, forward, 1993-96; Toronto Raptors, 1996-98; Boston Celtics, 1998-. **Business Addr:** Professional basketball player, Boston Celtics, 151 Merrimac St, Boston, MA 02114, (617)523-6050.

JONES, QUINCY DELIGHT, JR.
Producer, composer, arranger. **Personal:** Born Mar 14, 1933, Chicago, IL; son of Sarah J and Quincy Delight Sr; married Peggy Lipton, 1974; children: Quincy III, Martina-Lisa, Jolie, Kidada, Rashida, Kenya Julia Miambi Sarah. **Educ:** Berklee School of Music (Boston), grad; Seattle Univ, one term; Boston Conservatory. **Career:** Formed rock band at age 15 with friend Ray Charles, playing throughout the Seattle area; travelled with Lionel Hampton band to Europe at age 18; arranged, composed and produced for Billie Holliday, Dinah Washington, Count Basie, Duke Ellington, Sammy Davis Jr, Sarah Vaughn, Dizzy Gillespie, Frank Sinatra, Johnny Mathis, Lena Horne, George Benson, Brothers Johnson, Michael Jackson, Peggy Lee, Chaka Khan, others; music dir, 1961; first black vp Mercury Records, 1964; scored over 33 major motion pictures including: The Wiz, In Cold Blood, In the Heat of the Night, Blues for Trumpet and Koto; produced Michael Jackson's first solo album, Off the Wall; produced Michael Jackson's Thriller album; Qwest Records, owner, founder, 1981-; executive producer & wrote score for the movie, The Color Purple; Dept of State tour of Near East, Middle East, and South America, Dizzy Gillespie Orchestra, co-organizer, 1956; Barchlay Disques, Paris, music dir, 1956-60; independent composer, conductor, 1965-; works include: Brand New Bag, Sounds .. Stuff Like That (platinum), Walking in Space, This is How I Feel about Jazz, Back on the Block, producer, 1990; Vibe magazine, founder, 1993. **Honors/Awds:** Nominated for Oscar Awards for four film scores; received 20 Grammy Awards and over 50 Grammy nominations; 1979 production of Off the Wall sold over 8 million copies and at that time a record breaking four top-10 singles; album, The Dude received an unprecedented 12 Grammy nominations in 1981 and won 5 Grammy Awards; 8 Grammy nominations in 1983 (most by one person in a year); ABAA Music Award for efforts to aid African famine victims, and for conceiving and giving leadership to USA for Africa, producing the album, We Are the World; numerous others including honorary degrees from Loyola Univ and Seattle Univ. **Business Addr:** Founder, Qwest Records, 282 Fifth Ave, New York, NY 10001, (212)597-4862.

JONES, QUINCY DELIGHT, III
Music producer, songwriter. **Personal:** Born Dec 23, 1968, London, England; son of Ulla Anderson and Quincy D Jones Jr. **Career:** Music producer, writer; Q D III Sound Lab, owner, currently. **Special Achievements:** Producer, writer: 4 songs for LL Cool J's album, 1993, 5 songs for YoYo's album, 1993; scored music: "Fresh Prince of Bel-Aire," "Out All Night," NBC-TV, Menace II Society, Hughes Bros Productions, 1993. **Business Addr:** Owner, Q D III Soundlab, 3856 W Martin Luther King Jr Blvd, #109, Los Angeles, CA 90008, (213)291-7124.

JONES, RANDY KANE
Attorney. **Personal:** Born Oct 25, 1957, Jacksonville, NC; son of Julia Mae Saunders Jones and Henry Jones; children: Randy. **Educ:** Univ of NC, BA 1979, Sch of Law JD 1982. **Career:** Judge Advocate General's Corps, attorney 1983-86; asst United States attorney, 1987-. **Orgs:** Federal Bar Assn, 1984-, Amer Bar Assn, 1985-, Christian Fellowship Cong Church 1985, BE SLA 1986-; Parlimentarian Earl B Gilliam Bar Assn 1988-; mem of the bd California Assn of Black Lawyers 1989-92; Chairman Veterans Affairs NAACP San Diego Branch 1989-; National Bar Association, 1989-, regional director, 1991-93; Earl B Gilliam Bar Association, president, 1990-91, member of board, 1987-; San Diego County Crime Victims, board member, 1991-94; Leadership, Education, Awareness, Developmemt, graduate, 1991; NC State and California State Bar Association; San Diego County Bar Association; Urban League San Diego Chapter; Natl Bar Assn, vp, 1993-95; Voices for Children, board mem, 1993-; Natl Bar Assn, pres, 1996-. **Military Serv:** USN lt 3 yrs; Defense Counsel of Quarter 1983-86; USNR, CDR 1987-. **Business Addr:** Assistant, United States Attorney, 940 Front St 5-N-19, San Diego, CA 92189.

JONES, RAYMOND DEAN
Judge. **Personal:** Born Nov 30, 1945, Pueblo, CO; married Carolyn S; children: Latoya Bryant, Ruth Marie, Raymond Dean II. **Educ:** CO Coll, BA 1967; Harvard Law, JD 1971. **Career:** CO Supreme Court, clerk to chief justice, 1971-72; Holme Roberts & Owen, atty 1972-74; Met Denver Dist Atty Consumer Office Prosec of Consumer Defrauders,chief counsel 1974-77; Denver County Court, judge 1977-78; Denvery District Court, judge 1979-. **Orgs:** Mem bd dir New Dance Theatre Inc 1972-, CO State Bd of Law Exam 1973-; mem, vp, bd dir Denver Oppty Inc 1974-; mem St Bd CO Humanities Prog 1977, Gov Task Force Labor Legis 1976, Gov Task Force on Employ Agencies 1976; pres Sam Cary Bar Assoc; mem Denver Bar Assoc, CO Bar Assoc, Amer Bar Assoc, natl Bar Assoc; sec CO Dem Party; chmn CO Black Caucus 1973-74; del Dem natl Conv 1976; mem Amer Judges Assoc, CO Assoc of District Judges, Bar of State of CO, Fed Dist of CO, 10th Fed Circuit, US Supreme Court; faculty Natl Judicial Coll Reno NV; bd of trustees Colorado Coll Colorado Springs; mem Colorado Council on the Arts; numerous community bds. **Honors/Awds:** Marshal of the Class Harvard Univ Law School 1971; Barney Ford Comm Awd for Law & Justice 1977; listed in The Amer Bench 1977; author "A Search for Better Police Serv & An End to Police-Comm Tensions in Black Urban Neighborhoods & An Examination of Comm Control of Police" 1971; numerous community awds Denver and Colorado. **Business Addr:** 780 Steele St, Denver, CO 80206.

JONES, RAYMOND MORRIS
Engineer, educator (retired). **Personal:** Born Nov 29, 1922, St Louis, MO; son of Cassie B Jones and Raymond E Jones; married Frances; children: Michael, Byron, Sandra, Patricia. **Educ:** Howard Univ, BSCE 1947; Univ of MI, MSSE 1954. **Career:** Howard Univ, instr to prof 1947-84; RM Jones & Assoc, consultant 1965-; Howard Univ, retired prof civil engineering. **Orgs:** Mem NTA, ASCE, ASEE, APHA, NABCE, EABCE, AIDIS; former mem Reg III GSA Adv Panel, DC Bd of Appeals & Rev, Joint Conf Comm, World Wide, Water Resources,AID. **Military Serv:** USN seaman 1/c 1945-47.

JONES, REGGIE
Professional football player. **Personal:** Born May 5, 1971, Kansas City, KS. **Educ:** Louisiana State. **Career:** Carolina Panthers, 1995; Kansas City Chiefs, 1996-. **Business Addr:** Professional Football Player, Kansas City Chiefs, One Arrowhead Dr, Kansas City, MO 64129, (816)924-9300.

JONES, REGINALD L.
Educator. **Personal:** Born Jan 21, 1931, Clearwater, FL; son of Moses & Naomi Jones; married Michele Woods; children: Juliette, Angela, Cynthia, Sjaun, Leasa. **Educ:** Morehouse Coll, AB 1952; Wayne State Univ, MA 1954; OH State Univ, PhD 1959. **Career:** Miami Univ, asst prof 1959-63; Fisk Univ, assoc prof 1963-64; UCLA, asst prof 1964-66; OH State Univ, prof vice chmn dept of psychol 1966-69; Univ of CA Riverside, chmn & prof dept of educ 1969-72; Haile Selassie Univ Addis Adaba Ethiopia, prof & dir testing ctr 1972-74; Univ of CA Berkeley, prof 1973-75; Univ of CA Berkeley, chmn dept of afro-amer studies prof of educ 1975-78, 1985-87, faculty, asst to the vice chancellor, 1982-84, 1987-90; Hampton Univ, Dept of Psychology, chair and distinguished prof, 1991-94; Hampton Univ Center for Minority Special Education, dir, 1991-96. **Orgs:** Natl chmn Assn of Black Psychol 1971-72; fellow Amer Psychol Assn; mem Council for Exceptional Children; guest ed Journal of Black Psychology; assoc ed Amer Journal of Mental Deficiency; editor Mental Retardation 1979-83; 100 Black Men of the Virginia Peninsula; Alpha Alpha Chapter, Omega Psi Phi. **Honors/Awds:** Scholarship Award, Assn of Black Psychologists, 1979, 1986; J E Wallace Wallin Award, Council for Exceptional Children, 1983; Education Award, American Assn on Mental Retardation, 1988; Citation for Distinguished Achievement, OH State Univ, 1983; Berkeley Citation, Univ of CA, Berkeley, 1991. **Military Serv:** US Army med corps 1954-56. **Home Addr:** 1 Sutton Pl, Hampton, VA 23666.

JONES, RENA TALLEY
Educator. **Personal:** Born Aug 3, 1937, Pine Mountain, GA. **Educ:** Morris Brown Coll, BA 1960; Atlanta U, MS 1967; Wayne State U, PhD 1974. **Career:** Spelman Coll, asst prof of biology, chairperson 1973-; Wayne State Univ, graduate asst 1967-73; Fulton County Bd of Educ, instructor 1961-66; Lee County Bd of Educ, instructor 1960-61; Washington DC, partic, pre-med health careers advs & conf; Columbia MD; Pinehurts NC; Tulane Medical Coll; Univ of FL School of Med; Argonne Natl Lab on Air Pollution, course; Macy Summer Inst in Premed Educ, 1977; Chautauqua-type Prgram for Rnat Sci Found, reviewer Health Careers Office, dir. **Orgs:** Mem hlth careers com; adv Atlanta Univ Ctr Viol Hon Soc; mem Am Assn for Advcmt of Sci; Am Soc for Microbiol; GA Acad of Sci; asso mem Socof Sigma Xi; Beta Kappa Chi Nat Sci Hon Soc; sci fair judge, sec sch. **Honors/Awds:** Nat Sci Found Grant 1966-67; Spec Hlth Careers Opport Grant-dir; tchng Asstshp Wayne State Univ 1967-73; biol publ 1968-74. **Business Addr:** Associate Professor, Spellman College, 350 Spelman Lane SW, Atlanta, GA 30314.

JONES, RICHARD JULIUS
Association executive. **Personal:** Born Aug 27, 1945, Toledo, OH; son of Mary Jones and Arthur Jones; children: Bobby Clay, Desmond Cardell, Edwin Cotton, Lawrence Alexander, Edward Howard, Sandra Davis, Fred Hayes. **Educ:** Central State University, 1964-66; Toledo University, 1972-74; Upsala College, management, 1980; Bradley University, management, 1982. **Career:** Boys & Girls Club: Toledo, unit director, New York, guidance director, Newark, unit director, Peoria, executive director, America, national staff, Stockton, assistant executive director, currently. **Orgs:** Peoria Housing Authority, chairman of the board, 1980-90; United Way Executive Director Association, president, 1987; Optimist Club, president, 1987; Kiwanis Club, vice pres, 1985; Bradley University Chief Club, 1984; Rotary Club, 1989; Illinois Council on Aging, board member, 1985; Human Relation Committee, 1982-87. **Honors/Awds:** Omega Psi Phi, Citizen of the Year Award, 1987, 1988; Peoria Housing Authority, Commissioner of the Year, 1985, 1987, 1988; Peoria Christian Leadership Council, Citizen of the Year, 1988; Peoria InterCity Youth Council, Outstanding Community Leader, 1987; Peoria Community Action Agency, Outstanding Community Leader, 1987; Peoria School District, Community Leader Award, 1987; Boys & Girls Club of America, National Keystone Advisor, 1984; Boys & Girls Club of Newark, Staff Award Man/Boy, 1977; Boys & Girls Club of Toledo, Man of the Year, 1974; Boys & Girls Club of Peoria, Outstanding Staff Award, 1990. **Home Phone:** (209)478-3854. **Business Phone:** (209)466-1264.

JONES, RICHMOND ADDISON
Graphic designer. **Personal:** Born Jul 9, 1937, Chicago, IL; son of Mabel Betty Crouse and Silas Philip Jones; married Christine Ann Osada; children: Philip Frederick. **Educ:** Univ of IL, 1956-57; Amer Acad of Art, AA 1957-59; School of Visual Arts 1959-61. **Career:** Batten Barton Durstine & Osborn, asst/assoc art dir 1961-66; J Walter Thompson Co, art dir 1966-68; Jones James & Jameson Inc, pres 1968-69; Fuller Smith & Ross, art dir 1969-70; Richmond A Jones Graphics, owner/designer 1970-. **Orgs:** Mem Intl House Assoc 1959-62; dir/mem Sponsors for Ed Opportunities 1965-70; founder/vp/mem Group for Advertising Progress (Devel Minority Opportunities) 1966-70; dir/mem IL Epilepsy League 1972-74; dir/mem Soc of Typographic Arts 1972-; mem Amer Inst of Graphic Arts 1975-; mem Chicago Press Club 1980, Chicago Assoc of Commerce & Industry 1986. **Honors/Awds:** Highest Readership (2 awds) Design News 1966; Published Art Direction Mag 1968; Selected Top Creative Visual Talent Amer Showcase 1978-; winner of Max Awd for brochure produced for Underwriters Labs Inc from TCR Graphics 1985; judge for Typographers Intl Awd Prog 1985; judge for awards program Acad for HealthServ Mktg of Amer Mktg Assoc 1986. **Military Serv:** AUS Sergeant 1962-68; Marksmanship, Good Conduct Medal, Cert of Achievement 1963-64. **Home Addr:** 2530 W Eastwood Ave, Chicago, IL 60625.

JONES, ROBERT ALTON
Attorney. **Personal:** Born Jan 30, 1944, Houston, TX; son of Gloria C Jones and Robert J Jones; married Velma Chester Jones; children: Jessica Elizabeth. **Educ:** TX So U, BA, 1972; Thurgood Marshall School of Law, Houston, TX, JD. **Career:** Anderson Hodge Jones & Hoyt Inc, Houston, TX, stockholder & vice pres 1974-; Univ Houston, part-time professor; Teamster's Local 968, official 1969-73; Private Practice, atty, 1983-. **Orgs:** Mem Houston Lawyer's Assn; State Bar of TX; ABA; TX Crim Defense Lawyer's Assn; Bus & Professional Mens Orgn; Phi Alpha Delta; US Dist Ct, So & Eastern Dist of TX; participant Am Bar Assn Seminar of Criminal Defense Litigation; bd mem, The Ensemble Theatre. **Honors/Awds:** Recipient achvmnt awards from Student Govt & Student Bar Assn; Am Jurisprudence awards for Debtors & Creditors Rights & Oil & Gas.

JONES, ROBERT BERNARD, SR.
Musician, educator. **Personal:** Born Oct 2, 1956, Detroit, MI; son of Evelyn Jones & Jimmie Fletcher; married Bernice, Oct 11, 1986; children: Robert Bernard Jones II, Arnesia Nicole. **Educ:** Wayne State University, BA, 1979. **Career:** Wayne State University, student assistant, 1974-79; Detroit Public Schools, broadcast technician, 1979-86; WDET-FM, director, Detroit Radio Information Service, 1986-94, broadcast sales manager, 1994; Self-employed, blues musician, educator, 1994-. **Orgs:** Detroit Blues Society, founding member, 1986-; Detroit Radio Information Service, advisory board, 1994-; Friends School Music Festival, advisory board, 1993-; Wayne State University, affiliate faculty, Music Department. **Honors/Awds:** Detroit Monthly Magazine, Hall of Fame, 1990; Metro Times Magazine, Best Blues Instrumentalist, 1990, 1991. **Special Achievements:** Ann Arbor Folk Festival, Performer, 1992; Henry Ford Museum, "Roots of Rhythm," Program MC & Participant, 1994; Old Songs Festival, Albany NY, Performer, 1994; "The Blues Experience," 4-part Lecture/Performance, Monroe MI, Library System, 1994; Chicago Blues Festival, Performer, 1995. **Home Addr:** 16900 Strathmoor, Detroit, MI 48235, (313)838-0507.

JONES, ROBERT EARL
Clergyman. **Personal:** Born Feb 11, 1942, Franklinton, NC; married Karen; children: Darrell Amani. **Educ:** Houston-Tillotson Coll, BA 1965; Yale Univ, MDiv 1969, STM 1970; United Theological Seminary, DMin, 1994. **Career:** Coll Hill Comm Ch (UP), asst pastor, sr pastor, currently; Grand Ave United Ch of Christ, asst pastor 1974-77; New Haven Anti-Poverty Agy, dep dir 1974-75; Yale Div Sch, asst prof 1970-74; Fair Haven Parents Ministry, exec dir 1967-74; So CT State Coll, adjunct prof 1974-75; Quinnipiac Coll, sem instr 1968-69. **Orgs:** Adv bd CT Mental Health Center 1974-77; bd pres Black Coalition of New Haven 1970-75; vp, bd pres Natl Coalition for Econ Justice; consultant Natl Acad for Churches in transition 1970-75; Natl Alliance of Businessmen of New Haven 1970-72. **Honors/Awds:** Richard Allen Achievement Award 1970; Albert B Beebe Award 1970; Washington Times Foundation National Svc Awd, 1996. **Business Addr:** Senior Pastor, College Hill Community Church, 1547 Philadelphia Dr, Dayton, OH 45406.

JONES, ROBERT G.
Production company executive. **Personal:** Born Jul 4, 1936, Ft Worth, TX; son of Ruby Faye Jones and Ocie Jones (deceased). **Educ:** USC, 1953-58. **Career:** LA Herald Dispatch, entertainment editor 1957-68; Rogers & Cowan, acct exec 1968-70; Motown Records, publ mgr 1970-75, exec dir press & art rel 1975-87; MJJ Productions, vice pres, communications & media relations, 1987-. **Orgs:** Bd dir USO 1977-83, vice pres 1983-84; bd dir Hollywood C of C; chmn bd dir Beverly Hills NAACP 1971-83; pres Black Public Rel Soc of Southern CA 1985-87; president, Black Public Relations Society of America, 1988-89. **Honors/Awds:** Image Awards 1973-74 responsible for raising over $180,000 for br with those 2 award shows; Natl Black Showcases 1986; Par Excellence Awd in Oakland CA; Pioneer of Excellence NY 1989; Black Radio Exclusive, Soul Train, Jack the Rapper, Black Public Relations Society Special Awards of Achievement, 1989; NAACP, 25th Anniversary Image Awards, Sterling Award, 1993; Prame Award, National Association of Market Developers; Los Angeles Sentinel, Sentinel Men of the Year; Black Entertainment Television, prime-time television documentary, "Bob Jones Godfather Black Hollywood," produced by Belma Johnson; Greater Los Angeles African-American Chamber of Commerce, Fred Snowden Humanitarian Award, 1995; Hollywood Arts Council, Special Friend, 1996; Black Radio Excl Mag, Champion Honoree. **Business Addr:** Vice President, Communications & Media Relations, MJJ Productions, 9255 Sunset Blvd, Ste 1100, West Hollywood, CA 90069.

JONES, ROBERT LEE
Professional football player. **Personal:** Born Sep 27, 1969, Blackstone, VA; married Maneesha; children: Cayleb, Isiah. **Educ:** East Carolina, attended. **Career:** Dallas Cowboys, linebacker, 1992-95; St Louis Rams, 1996-. **Honors/Awds:** United Press International, NFC Defensive Rookie of the Year, 1992; USA Today, All-Pro, 1994; Won three Super Bowl rings with the Dallas Cowboys. **Business Addr:** Professional Football Player, St Louis Rams, One Rams Way, St Louis, MO 63045, (314)982-7267.

JONES, ROBERT WESLEY
Business executive. **Personal:** Born Jul 24, 1929, Boston, MA; son of Lillian Evans Jones and John Jones; children: Todd, Stacy, Austin. **Educ:** Howard Univ, 1950; NY Univ, BS 1956; NY Law Schl, Cert NY Bar 1960. **Career:** Pianta Dosi and Assc, vice pres 1966-1968; Ctiy of NY, deputy comm 1964-66; Burnett Constr Co, ex vice pres 1968-1970; Robert W Jones and Assc Inc, pres. **Orgs:** Pres Independent Fee Appraisers (NYC) 1984-, Citizens Housing and Planning Council 1974-; chrmn Tougaloo Clge Bd of Trustees 1980-; mem bd adv NY Univ Real Est Inst 1974-; exec comm Assc for Better NY 1975-; mem bd adv Federal Natl Mtg Assc 1985-; mem, Advisory Board, New School for Social Research (Milano Graduate School) 1993; mem Executive Committee 14th Street Local Development Committee, 1993; Chairman Emeritus, Tougaloo College, 1996; Senior Advisor, Columbia Partners Investment Management LLC, 1996; Director, Landon Butler Co., 1996. **Honors/Awds:** Articles on housing and planning 1970; Adj Prof NY Univ Real Est Planning 1972-; Doctor of Human Letters, 1996. **Military Serv:** USMC sgt 1950-53; Purple Heart 1952. **Business Addr:** President, Robert W Jones & Assc Inc, 2 Fifth Ave, Ph C, New York, NY 10011-8842.

JONES, RODERICK WAYNE
Professional football player. **Personal:** Born Jan 11, 1974. **Educ:** Univ of Kansas, bachelor's degree in human development/family living. **Career:** Cincinnati Bengals, tackle, 1996-. **Business Addr:** Professional Football Player, Cincinnati Bengals, One Bengals Dr, Cincinnati, OH 45202, (513)621-3550.

JONES, ROGER CARVER
Professional football player. **Personal:** Born Apr 22, 1969, Cleveland, OH; married Angela. **Educ:** Tennessee State. **Career:** Tampa Bay Buccaneers, defensive back, 1991-93; Cincinnati Bengals, 1994-96; Tennessee Oilers, 1997-. **Business Addr:** Professional Football Player, Tennessee Oilers, c/o Baptist Sports Park, 7640 H 70-5, Nashville, TN 37221.

JONES, RONALD LYMAN
Human resources executive. **Personal:** Born Mar 29, 1945, Dayton, OH; son of Cecile E Jones and Major E Jones; children: Dana L Bullock, David, Aubre. **Educ:** Central State University, Fisk University. **Career:** Battelle Memorial Institute, trainer, 1974-88, personnel mgr, BPMD, 1980-88; OCLC, mgr, employee rel & dev, 1988-91, mgr of human resources, 1991-93, dir of admin svcs, 1993-. **Orgs:** ASTD, president of Central Ohio Chapter; PACO; ASTD, Black Caucus. **Military Serv:** US Army, 1s lt, 1968-70; Bronze Star, Army Commendation Medal. **Business Addr:** Director of Administrative Services, OCLC, 6565 Frantz Rd, Dublin, OH 43017.

JONES, RONDELL TONY
Professional football player. **Personal:** Born May 7, 1971, Sunderland, MA. **Educ:** Univ of North Carolina, attended. **Career:** Denver Broncos, defensive back, 1993-96; Baltimore Ravens, 1997-. **Business Addr:** Professional Football Player, Baltimore Ravens, 11001 Owings Mills Blvd, Owings Mills, MD 21117, (410)654-6200.

JONES, ROSALYN EVELYN
Attorney. **Personal:** Born Apr 26, 1961, Frankfurt, Germany; daughter of Col & Mrs Harry T Jones. **Educ:** Harvard/Raddiffe Colleges, AB (magna cue laude), 1983; Oxford Univ, St John's College, 1983-84; Harvard Law School, JD, 1987. **Career:** Gibson, Dunn & Crutcher, attorney (corp & entertainment) 1987-89; Rosenfed, Meyer & Susman, attorney (entertainment),

1989-91; Manatt, Phelps & Phillips, partner, attorney (music), 1991-97; Rosalyn E Jones, attorney at law, 1997-. **Orgs:** Black Entertainment & Sports Lawyers Assn, bd of dirs; American Bar Assn, 1993-; California Bar, 1987-; District of Columbia Bar, 1988. **Honors/Awds:** Harvard Radcliffe Coll, Phi Beta Kappa; Oxford Univ, St John's Coll, Harvard Knox Fellow. **Business Addr:** Attorney, Rosalyn E Jones, Esq, 2040 Avenue of the Stars, Ste 400, Los Angeles, CA 90067, (310)286-9826.

JONES, ROSCOE T., JR.
Dentist. **Personal:** Born Jan 25, 1935, Washington, DC; married Marva A J; children: Nancy Ellen. **Educ:** Howard U, BS 1958; Howard U, DDS 1965. **Career:** Self-employed, dentist 1968-; Dental Clinic Ft Belvoir AUS Dental Corp, acting chief 1966. **Orgs:** Mem Robert T Freeman Dental Soc 1970; mem Acad of Gen Dentistry 1973-; treas Metro Dental Assoc Chartered 1978-; Sunday sch tchr All Souls UnitarianCh 1970-77. **Honors/Awds:** Outstanding Cadet, Howard U. **Military Serv:** AUS ROTC 1959; AUS cpt served 2 1/2 yrs. **Business Addr:** 1238 Monroe St NE, Washington, DC 20017.

JONES, ROY JUNIOS
Educator. **Personal:** Born Nov 15, 1925, Longview, TX; married Pauline Carol Finley; children: Roderick, Arlyss, Valerie. **Educ:** Morgan State Univ, BS, psychology, 1951; Howard Univ, MS, 1954; Am Univ, PhDsociology-psychology 1961. **Career:** Crownsville State Hospital, chief psychology servs, dir research 1961-62; Washington Action for Youth, dir training 1963-64; Howard Univ, mem faculty & admin 1964, asst clinical prof psychiatry 1967-69, prof urban studies 1969-77, dir Center Comm Studies 1967-72, urban studies program 1967-72, asst dean Graduate School 1967-71. **Orgs:** Chmn bd examiners psychol, Wash, 1972-78; mem Am Soc Training Devel, natl chmn professional standards, ethics com 1969; Am, Eastern, DC, MD Psychol Assns; AAAS; soc psychol pres Social Systems Intervention Inc, Wash, 1967-; bd chmn Soc Systems Devel Inst Inc 1980-; consult govt pub & pvt agys; mem DC adv com US Commn Civil Rights 1968-78; govt rev bd Mayor's Youth Oppor Serv 1969; bd overseers Dag Hammarskjold Coll, Columbia, MD 1967-71; bd dirs Wash Heart Assn 1969-72; chmn gov Bd council Univ Instr Urban Affairs 1970-76; dir Nat Assn Minority Group Urbanologists; Psi Chi; Alpha Kappa Mu; consult editor Jour of Professional Psychology 1969-76. **Military Serv:** Decorated Bronze Star Medal; AUS 1944-46. **Business Addr:** 3603 14 St NW, Washington, DC 20010.

JONES, RUTH BRASWELL
Business executive. **Personal:** Born Nov 24, 1914, Rocky Mount, NC; daughter of Arkanna Sanders Braswell and William Braswell; married Eddie J Jones (deceased). **Educ:** Brick Jr Clge, Salutatorian 1933; Elizabeth City State Clge, BS Educ 1938; A&T State Univ, MSc Educ (Hnr Stdnt) 1959. **Career:** Halifax Cty School, elementary teacher 1933-62; Rocky Mount City School, elementary teacher 1962-80; Hammocks Beach Corp, pres. **Orgs:** Pres NC Tchrs Assc 1968-70, NC Assc of Educ 1971-72; dir Natl Educ Assc 1975-80; parliamentarian Natl Educ Assc 1968-73, SW regional dir NEA classroom teachers 1972-76; NC Chptr Zeta Phi Beta Sor 1975-80, Gaylor Chptr Order of Eastern Star 1982-84; NEA-R advisory council; Rocky Mount Human Relations Council; pres Brown-Pearson Federated Clb; president, Hammocks Beach Corporation, 1968-91; president, Leisurettes, 1985-89. **Honors/Awds:** Terry Sanford Award for Ldrshp and Creativity in Educ 1972; NEA'S Trenholm Award for fostering intercultural understanding 1982; NC Distg Women's Award For Outstanding Educ 1984; article pub Blacks in Amer History from 1492 to the Present; Libby D Koontz Award, North Carolina Human Relations, 1990; Inclusive Leadership Award, NCAE, 1990; Outstanding Educator and Leader, Zeta Phi Beta Sorority, 1980. **Home Addr:** 509 Myrtle Ave, Rocky Mount, NC 27801.

JONES, SAM H., SR.
Business executive. **Personal:** Born Jun 29, 1938, Denver, CO; married Carolyn Ruth Spain; children: Marya, Sam, Michael. **Educ:** Regis Coll Denver, CO, BA sociology (cum laude) 1966; Univ of NM Sch of Law, JD 1969. **Career:** US Equal Employ Oppor Comm, regional atty; Univ of NM Sch of Law, dir title vii law clinic lectr in law 1975-76; US Equal Employ Oppor Commn, sr trial atty 1973-75; Boise Cascade Corp Diversified Mfg, compliance mgr 1971-73; Reginald Herber Smith Comm Lawyer Flwhp Prog Albuquerque Legal Aid Soc, atty 1970-71. **Orgs:** Prog dir CO Civil Rights Commn 1969-70; mem 10th Circuit Ct of Appeals 1969; mem State Bar of NM 1969-; mem Nat Bar Assn 1971-; mem US 5th Circuit 1978-. **Honors/Awds:** Margaret Keiper Daley Awd Univ of NM Sch of Law. **Military Serv:** USN petty ofcr 2 1957-62. **Business Addr:** President, Indianapolis Urban League, 850 N Meridian St, Indianapolis, IN 46204.

JONES, SAMUEL
Athletic director. **Personal:** Born Jun 24, 1933, Laurinburg, NC; son of Louise K Jones and Samuel Jones; married Gladys Chavis; children: Aubre, Phyllis, Michael, Terri, Ashley. **Educ:** North Carolina Coll, BS. **Career:** Boston Celtics, professional basketball player 1957-69; North Carolina Central Univ, head basktball coach; New Orleans Jazz Basketball Team, LA, asst coach; Fed City Coll, Washington, dir athletics 1969-77; Blue Ribbon Sports, NIKE Shoe Div, head of promotions; DC Public Schools, Washington, DC, athletic director, 1989-. **Orgs:** Mem Kappa Alpha Psi. **Honors/Awds:** North Carolina Hall of Fame, 1980; Naismith Hall of Fame, 1984; Black Athletes Hall of Fame, 1985; Nelms Hall of Fame; CIAA Hall of Fame, NCCU Athletic Hall of Fame. **Military Serv:** AUS.

JONES, SELWYN ALDRIDGE
Professional football player. **Personal:** Born May 13, 1970, Houston, TX. **Educ:** Colorado State. **Career:** New Orleans Saints, defensive back, 1994; Seattle Seahawks, 1995-96; Denver Broncos, 1997-.

JONES, SHALLEY A.
Banking executive. **Personal:** Born Sep 17, 1954, Moorehead, MS; daughter of Rosie Lee Matthews and Robert Lee Matthews; married Ernest Jones, Jun 17, 1977; children: Shantea K, Ernest J II. **Educ:** University of Miami, BA, 1975; Florida International University, MSM, 1983. **Career:** First Union National Bank, assistant vp, loan processing manager, 1976-84, assistant vp, regional manager, 1984-85; Chase Federal Bank, first vp, beginning 1985; SunBank Miami, NA, CRA & Consumer Compliance, vp, 1994-95; Fannie Mae, dir of community investment; Miami Dade Partnership Office, director, currently. **Orgs:** National Association of Urban Bankers, president, 1991-92; Miami-Dade Urban Bankers Association, president, 1987-89; Metro-Miami Action Plan, chairperson, 1991-94; Eastern Financial Credit Union, director, 1993-94; Alpha Kappa Alpha Sorority, Inc, 1974-; NAACP, Miami-Dade chapter, executive board, 1992-94; United Negro College Fund, advisory board member, 1991-93; National Black MBA Association, south Florida chapter, 1990-; Dade County Housing Finance Authority, life mem, board member, 1996-. **Honors/Awds:** American Banker Newspaper, Top 40 Banker Under 40, 1992; Dollars & Sense Magazine, America's Best & Brightest, 1991; Miami Dade Urban Bankers Association, Banker of the Year, 1992; City of Miami, Unsung Hero Award, 1992; South Florida Business Journal, Up & Comers Award/Banking, 1989. **Business Addr:** Director of Miami-Dade Partnership Office, Fannie Mae, 1000 Brickell Ave, Ste 600, Miami, FL 33131, (305)577-9940.

JONES, SHARON DIANA. See CHARIS, SISTER.

JONES, SHERMAN J.
Educational administrator. **Personal:** Born Jan 12, 1946, Newport News, VA; son of Sherman E and Leola Mae Jones; married J Janice, Dec 22, 1967; children: Kimberely, Sherman E. **Educ:** Williams College in Amer Studies, BA, 1968; Harvard Univ in Gen Mgt, Finance, and Organizational Behavior, MBA, 1970; Harvard Univ in Admin, Planning and Policy Analysis, EdD, 1978. **Career:** Cresap, McCormic & Padget Inc, mgt consultant, 1972-75; Academy for Educational Development Inc, mgt consultant, 1975-77; Fisk Univ, vp for admin, 1977-80, vp and acting dean of univ, 1980-82; Tuskegee Univ, exec vp and prof of mgt, 1982-91; Clark Atlanta Univ, provost/vp for academic affairs/prof of business admin, 1991-93; Southern Normal School, pres, headmaster, ceo, 1993-. **Orgs:** St Andrews Sewanee School, board of advisors, 1986-92, board of trustees, 1994-; YMCA, board of directors, 1994-; Harvard Alumni Assn, board of dir, 1991-93; Harvard Graduate School of Education, 1987-91, chairman, 1990-91; John A Andrew Community Hospital, mgt comm, 1982; The American Institute for Managing Diversity, Inc, advisory council, 1984-; Better Business Bureau of Nashville Middle Tennessee Inc, board of dir, 1978-82; Nashville Comm on Foreign Affairs. **Honors/Awds:** Selected Teaching Fellow in Education at Harvard Graduate School of Education for 1976-77; Appointed a Woodrow Wilson Admin Intern at Central State Univ in Ohio in 1970-71, served as assistant to the pres. **Special Achievements:** ''Difficult Times for Private Black Colleges,'' Change magazine, March 1984; ''Adapting Governance, Leadership Style and Mgt to a Changing Environment,'' in Black Colleges and Universities: Challenges for the Future, Antoine Garibaldi, editor, Praeger, 1984; Faculty Involvement in College and University Decision-Making, unpublished doctoral dissertation, 1978; Faculty Involvement in Coll and Univ Decision Making, in Managing Turbulence and Change, John D Millett, editor, Jossey-Bass, Autumn 1977. **Home Addr:** 1151 Briarcliff Pl NE, Atlanta, GA 30306. **Business Addr:** President/Headmaster, Southern Normal School, PO Box 408, Kirkland Rd, Brewton, AL 36427, (334)867-4831.

JONES, SHERMAN JARVIS
State representative. **Personal:** Born Feb 10, 1935, Winton, NC; son of Gladys Cherry Jones and Starky Jones; married Amelia Buchanan Jones, Dec 16, 1956; children: Sheila, Shelly, Shelton. **Educ:** Kansas City Community College, Kansas City, KS, 1974-75. **Career:** Kansas City Police Dept, Kansas City, detective/sergeant, 1965-88; Professional baseball player, 1953-65; State of Kansas, state senator, currently. **Orgs:** Member/chairman, Wyandotte County Park Board, 1984; vice pres/comm chairman, Optimist International, 1973; chairman, Legislative Black Caucus of Kansas. **Military Serv:** US Army, SP4, 1958-60. **Home Addr:** 3736 Weaver Dr, Kansas City, KS 66104.

JONES, SHIRLEY JOAN
Educational administrator. **Personal:** Born Nov 26, 1931, New York, NY; children: Susan, Sande Jr. **Educ:** NY Univ, BA 1954, MA 1956, MSW 1964; Columbia Univ, Doctorate of Soc Work 1977. **Career:** NY Univ Schl of Social Wrk, asst prof 1967-70; State Univ NY at Stony Brook, assc prof 1972-78; NY Univ Metro Studies, adj prof 1973-77; Univ of Southern MS, dean prof 1978-89; SUNYA, Sch of Soc Welfare, prof, currently. **Orgs:** Comm Commission of Child Support Enforcement 1985; bd dir Gov Office of Vol Citizen Participation 1985; bd dir Natl Alliance of Bus 1982-85; mem Natl Assc of Black Soc Wrkrs, Natl Assc of Social Wrkrs, Council on Social Work Educ, Intl Assc of Social Work; mem State Constitutional Change Comm 1986-87, Intl Comm of NASW; commr on accreditation Council on Social Work Educ; US Census Bureau, minority advisory committee, for year 2000 Census; Natl Head Start/Dept of Health & Human Services, expert panelist. **Honors/Awds:** Waldoff's Ach 1983; Soc Wrkr of the Year NABSW MS Chptr 1983; Distg Srv Award Gov Office of Vol Citizen Part 1983; Woman of the Year Hattiesbg City Businessmen's Club 1981; Dedicated Serv Awd NABSW Natl 1986; Certificate of Appreciation DHHS/OHDS/AFCYF 1986; Martin Luther King Award, SUNYA, 1993; City of Albany Award, Human Rights, 1994; Distinguished Professor, 1994; Elected Senator, SUNYA Central Univ, Senate, 1995; Elected Secretary of SUNYA Univ Senate, 1993, 1994. **Business Addr:** Distinguished Service Professor, Univ at Albany, State Univ of New York (SUNYA), School of Social Welfare, 135 Western Avenue, Albany, NY 12222.

JONES, SIDNEY ALEXANDER
Physician. **Personal:** Born Sep 25, 1934; son of Ann E Jones and Herbert A Jones; married Vuriley Maria Harris; children: Raquel, Erika. **Educ:** Univ W Indies, MB, BS 1963; Freedmens Hosp, intern 1964-65; Howard Univ Hosp, residency 1965-69. **Career:** Howard Univ, asst instr 1967, asst prof 1971, dir 1976; Parkside Neighborhood Health Clinic, chief 1969-71; DC General Hosp, med officer 1971-76, chairman Ob/Gyn. **Orgs:** Mem Am Fertility Soc; Am Coll Ob-Gyn; Royal Soc of Med; Intl Coll of Surgeons; DC Med Soc. **Honors/Awds:** Daniel Hale Williams Award 1966. **Business Addr:** Chairman Ob/Gyn, DC General Hospital, 19th & Massachusetts Ave SE, Washington, DC 20003.

JONES, SIDNEY EUGENE
Social services administrator. **Personal:** Born Jul 11, 1936, New York, NY; son of Harriett E Mason and Herman E Jones; married Yolande Goodison; children: Cydnie, Stephen. **Educ:** Columbia College, BA 1959; Columbia Univ Sch of Social Work, MS 1968. **Career:** New York City Dept of Social Svcs, field dir 1968-70; Mayor's Office NYC, dist mgr 1970-76; State Communities Aid Assoc, project dir 1976-78; Comm Serv Soc, administrator 1978-88; NYS council on the Arts, deputy director 1988-91; Episcopal Mission Society, deputy director, 1991-. **Orgs:** Mem Alpha Phi Alpha Frat 1956-; mem Mt Vernon Human Rights Commn 1982-84, Mt Vernon Youth Board 1984-86. Member National Association of Social Workers, cofounder, Association of Black Social Workers, 1967. **Honors/Awds:** Blanche Ittleson Awd Social Serv Career Ctr 1973. **Military Serv:** Army Natl Guard capt 1953-65. **Business Addr:** Deputy Director, The Episcopal Mission Society, 18 W 18th St, New York, NY 10011.

JONES, SONDRA MICHELLE
Educator. **Personal:** Born Sep 7, 1948, Norfolk, VA. **Educ:** Morgan State, BA 1970; Univ of PA Sch of Edn, grad work; Harvard Univ Grad Sch of Edn;Temple U, grad study Master's Cand 1977. **Career:** Buck Lane Memorial Community Day Care Center, Haverford, PA, dir 1976-; Devel Disabilities Day Care Center PA; educ dir comm coord teacher 1972-73; St Martin's Day Care Center Baltimore, teacher 1971-72; Health & Welfare Council of Baltimore, social work trainee 1968; STOP Program Norfolk, VA, rec counselor 1967; Health & Welfare Council, social work trainee 1966. **Orgs:** Mem Alliance of Blk Soc Workers; Ivy Club of Alpha Kappa Sor; Nat Assn for the Educ of Young Children; Phil Assn for Retarded Children; Child Welfare League of Am; Phil Coord Child Care Counc 4 C'S; Nat Counc of Blk Child Devel; Black Child Devel Inst. **Honors/Awds:** Particptd in Harvard Univ Early Childhood Educ Prog unde Schlrshp from Harvard U.

JONES, SPENCER
Clergyman. **Personal:** Born Mar 24, 1946, Poplar Bluff, MO; son of Evelina Jones and Frank Jones; married Kathy AE Drake; children: Daliz E, Trayon D, Shemen A, Melinet MB. **Educ:** Central Bible Coll, BA Religion 1972. **Career:** Southside Tabernacle, pastor, currently. **Orgs:** Alternate presbytery Assemblies of God; vice pres of Student Govt; mem Natl Inner-City Workers Conference; mem of the bd of Chicago Teen Challenge; mem of the Decade of Harvest Committee; speakers at the 1989 General Council; pres, Local School Council, 1988-; community rep, 1990-; block club pres, 1986-; Black Representative of the Assemblies of God; Beat Representative for the Chicago Police Dept. **Honors/Awds:** Article in The Pentecostal Evangel 1984, The Pentecostal Minister; Alumnus for CBC, 1990; Honor Society Sigma Beta Theta, 1972; Proclamation from the United States House of Representatives as an Out-

standing Citizen. **Military Serv:** AUS sp4, 1966-67. **Business Addr:** Pastor, Southside Tabernacle, 7724 S Racine, Chicago, IL 60620.

JONES, STANLEY BERNARD
Higher education administrator. **Personal:** Born Mar 18, 1961, Greenwwod, SC; son of Maggie P Jones and Herbert C Jones, Jr. **Educ:** Radford Univ, BS 1984, MS Educ 1987. **Career:** Radford Univ, asst dir of admissions, dir, special student services. **Orgs:** VA Admin Council on Black Concerns 1984-; Treasurer 1988-; EEO, mem 1985-; NAACP, mem 1985-; National Association of Student Personnel Administrators 1987-; Assoc of Handicapped Student Service Programs in Postsecondary Education 1987-; Omega Psi Phi Fraternity 1988-. **Honors/Awds:** Outstanding Young Man of American 1985; Outstanding Service Award Radford Univ Chapter NAACP 1988. **Business Addr:** Director, Special Student Services, Radford University, PO Box 5705, Radford, VA 24141-5705.

JONES, STEPHANIE TUBBS
Attorney. **Personal:** Born Sep 10, 1949, Cleveland, OH; daughter of Mary E Tubbs and Andrew E Tubbs; married Mervyn L Jones; children: Mervyn L II. **Educ:** Case Western Reserve Univ, BA 1971, Law Sch JD 1974. **Career:** Case Western Reserve Univ, Cleveland, OH, resident director, 1971-74, research instructor, part time instructor in Afro-American Studies program, 1974; Northeast Ohio Regional Sewer District, asst gen counsel 1974-76; Cuyahoga County Prosecutor's Office, asst co prosecutor 1976-79; Equal Employment Opportunities Commission, trial attorney 1979-81; Cleveland Municipal Ct, judge 1982-83; Common Pleas Court of Cuyahoga Co, judge 1983-91; Cuyahoga County, prosecuting attorney, 1991-. **Orgs:** Past trustee, Cleveland Hearing & Speech Ctr; past trustee, Legal Aid Soc of Cleveland, Bethany Baptist Church; past trustee, Regional Council on Alcoholism; trustee, Federation for Community Planning; mem, Greater Cleveland Alumnae chapter, Delta Sigma Theta Sorority Inc; mem, Cleveland Bar Assn; mem, Natl Bar Assn; mem, past treas, Norman S Minor Bar Assn; past pres, member, bd of trustees, Cleveland Public Library; trustee, Community Reentry Prog, Leadership, Cleveland 1983-84. **Honors/Awds:** Martin Luther King Jr Award recipient, Case Western Reserve Univ, Law School, 1974; Outstanding Young Woman of America, 1982; featured in Ebony magazine, 1983, 1984; Young Alumnus Award, Case Western Reserve Univ, 1984; Panhellenic Council Action Award, 1984; Urban League of Greater Cleveland award for volunteer service in law and justice, 1986; Woman of the Year award, Cleveland Chapter, Natl Association of Negro Business and Professional Women's Clubs, 1987; Outstanding Citizens Award, Minority Construction Coalition, 1987; Pacesetter Award, Directory of Greater Cleveland's Enterprising Women, 1987; Valued Alumnus Award, Collinwood High School, 1988; Centennial Citation, Flora Stone Mather College, Case Western Reserve Univ, 1988. **Business Addr:** Prosecuting Attorney, Cuyahoga Co, 1200 Ontario St, Justice Center, 8th Fl., Cleveland, OH 44113.

JONES, SUSAN SUTTON
Educational administrator. **Personal:** Born in Nanticoke, MD; daughter of Emma Evans Sutton and Douglas Judson Sutton; married Dr Clifton Ralph Jones; children: George Henry Miles Jr. **Educ:** Fisk Univ, BS 1946; Johns Hopkins Univ, Master of Educ 1965; Temple Univ, Doctor of Educ 1984. **Career:** Dept Publ Asst Philadelphia PA, caseworker 1946-49; Baltimore City Publ Schl, biology tchr 1949-63, guidance cnslr 1963-67, schl admin 1967-84; Edmondson Sr HS, principal 1975-84; Morgan State Univ, visiting prof 1986-. **Orgs:** Historian Baltimore Alumna Delta Sigma Theta; pres Baltimore Chptr Continental Soc 1983-; historian, pres, mem Alpha Wives 1983-85; pres Alpha Phi Alpha 1986; bd of dir Delta Foundation, Baltimore Alumnae; charter mem The Societas Docta, Inc Feb 1987; mem Foster Care Review Bd 1987-91; commr Department Social Services Commn Advisory 1988-91; vice pres Morgan State Univ National Assn of Parlimentarians 1990-91; volunteer Court Appointed Special Advocate for Children 1989-. **Honors/Awds:** Awardee Natl Science Fnd 1958; prin Ford Fnd High Schl Grant 1982-83; Publ Srv Award Miles W Connor Chptr VA Union Univ 1983; citation for excellence in maintaining discipline Phi Delta Kappa 1980; panelist MD Humanities Council 1984, Natl Assoc of Secondary Sch Admin 1984; Mayor's Citation for public service 1987; Founders Day Service Award Delta Sigma Theta 1987. **Home Addr:** 1190 W Northern Pkwy 524, Baltimore, MD 21210, (410)435-8986.

JONES, THEODORE
Educator, elected official (retired). **Personal:** Born Dec 23, 1923, Menifee, AR; married Laura Mattison; children: Linda Paxton, Theodore Jr. **Educ:** UAPB, BS 1949; attended UCA Conway, AR. **Career:** Pine St HS, principal 1966-70; Conway Jr HS, teacher. **Orgs:** Bd mem Falkner Cty Selective Serv 1975-78; pres AR Voc Teachers Assoc 1983-84; bd mem AR Vocational Assoc 1983-84; Notary Public. **Honors/Awds:** Cert of Appreciation for Service of Selective Serv Bd Mem by Pres Gerald Ford 1976; ALFDC Rural Economic Development Award, 1994. **Special Achievements:** Dedication of Theodore Jones Elementary School, 1994; first African American justice of the peace in Faulkner County Dist 11. **Military Serv:** AUS corpl 1944-46; Good Conduct Medal. **Home Addr:** 1258 Lincoln St, Conway, AR 72032.

JONES, THEODORE A.
Certified public accountant. **Personal:** Born in Pueblo, CO; married B Mae Howard; children: Janice, Lynn. **Educ:** Univ of IL, BS 1933, CPA 1940. **Career:** Jones Anderson & Co, partner 1940-; Nat Bd NAACP-SCF 1976-; Chicago Pk Dist, commr 1977-; King Tercq Mcdonalds Franchises, chmn; Chicago Burr Oak Cemetary Assn, sec treas & dir; Serv Federal Savings & Loan Assn, sec treas & dir; WJPC Radio, pres 1970-74; Dept of Revenue, State of IL, dir 1967-69; OEO, reg dir 1966-67; Supreme Life Ins Co, sr vp, gen mgr 1955-67. **Orgs:** Mem Am Inst of CPAs; IL Soc of CPAs; Nat Assn of Tax Adminstr; bd trustees Univ of IL; bd trustees Talladega Coll; bd mem Economic Club of Chicago; mem Chicago br NAACP; adv commn Cook Co Personnel; Chicago Commn on Human Relations; Cosmopolitan C of C; People United to Save Humanity; mem Chicago Yacht Club; Burnham Park Yacht Club; Royal Coterie of Snakes; The Forty Club; The Chicagoans; Beta Boule, Sigma Pi Phi. **Honors/Awds:** Recipient Thomas J Crowe Award, Cath Interracial Couns 1958; Beta Gamma Sigma, Scholastic Honors; NAACP Outstanding Serv Award 1971. **Business Addr:** 471 E 31st St, Chicago, IL 60616.

JONES, THEODORE CORNELIUS
Educator, dentist. **Personal:** Born Sep 29, 1941, Jackson, MS; married Clintoria Inge; children: Dana, Vann, Margo, Kristen, Karrin. **Educ:** Tougaloo Coll, BS 1962; Howard U, DDS 1966; Walter Reed, cert 1969; cert 1970; Tufts U, 1973. **Career:** Univ of MS School of Dentistry, asst prof 1974-; Private Practice, 1974-; Howard Univ, extramural practice 1975; Jackson Hindscompr Health Center, staff dentist 1972-73; MS private practice 1970-71. **Orgs:** Am Den Assn; Nat Den Assn; Am Assn of Orthodontists; MS Den Assn; MS Den Soc; Jackson-Tougaloo Alumni Club; pres Tufts Assn of Orthodon; AlphaPhi Alpha; Musica Sacra Singers; New Stage Theatre. **Military Serv:** USAF capt 1966-68. **Business Addr:** PO Box 9606, Jackson, MS 39206.

JONES, THERESA C.
Automobile dealer. **Career:** Northwestern Dodge Inc, owner, currently. **Business Addr:** Owner, Northwestern Dodge Inc, 10500 W 8 Mile Rd, Ferndale, MI 48220, (313)399-6700.

JONES, THERESA DIANE
Government administrator. **Personal:** Born Jun 7, 1953, Erie, PA; daughter of Mable R Jones and Parker P Jones. **Educ:** Edinboro State Coll, BA 1976. **Career:** Pinellas Oppor Council Inc, sr outreach worker 1976-77; Information & Referral, suicide intervention spec 1977; City of St Petersburg, relocation officer 1977-80, administrative serv officer 1980-86, MBE coord 1986-93; Tampa General Healthcare, MBE coord 1993-96; City of St. Petersburg, MBE coord 1996-. **Orgs:** Bd dirs Pinellas Oppor Council Inc 1984-89; bd govs St Petersburg Area Chamber of Commerce 1985; co-chair Community Alliance 1985; real estate assoc LouBrown Realty & Mortgage Inc 1985-88; sec Natl Forum Black Public Administrators, Tampa Bay Chap 1986-88. **Honors/Awds:** Graduate Presidential Classroom for Young Americans 1971; graduate Leadership St Petersburg 1984; Up & Comers Award, Price Waterhouse 1988. President's Award, Greater Florida Minority Development Council, 1989; Tampa/St. Petersburg Minority Business Development Center, in appreciation of enthusiastic support of minority-owned business, 1991. **Home Addr:** PO Box 3986, St Petersburg, FL 33731. **Business Addr:** Minority Bus Enterprise Coord, City of St Petersburg, PO Box 2842, St Petersburg, FL 33731.

JONES, THERESA MITCHELL
Business executive. **Personal:** Born May 12, 1917, Denison, TX; married Artis Jones; children: Leroy, Pat, Michael, Anthony. **Educ:** Compton Coll CA, AA 1951; Univ of Pacific, BS 1973. **Career:** LA County Bureau of Public Assistance, clerk-typist 1951-55; Beauty Salons, propr 3 1956-66; Real Estate, part-time salesman 1961-74; Elementary Sch, teacher 1971-74; City of Stockton Comm Devel Renewal Redevel Agency, relocation/real estate asst 1974-. **Orgs:** Mem Natl Beauty Culturist League 1959-66; dir SE Ctr 1968-70; dir WICS San Joaquin Co 1970-; assoc mem Stockton Real Estate Bd 1972-75; organizer dir Progressive Youth of Compton; supr Jr Ch. **Honors/Awds:** Woman of the Yr Awd LA Alpha Lambda Chap of Theta Nu Sigma Sor 1966; Awd UOP Comm Involvement Prog 1973. **Business Addr:** Relo/Real Estate Asst, Comm Devel Renewal Redevel Agency, City of Stockton, 742 E Charter Way, Stockton, CA 95206.

JONES, THOMAS L.
Attorney. **Personal:** Born Jan 12, 1941, Greenwood, MS; married Nettie Byrd; children: Martilla R, Nicole L, LaTanya Dionne, Thomas II. **Educ:** Tougaloo Coll, BS 1963; Howard Univ Law Sch, 1971. **Career:** Continental Tel Corp, asst vp, legal atty 1972-; Fed Hwy Adminstrn, Wash, spl asst chief counsel 1971-72; Neighborhood Consumer Info Ctr, Wash, prog dir 1970-71; Cook Co Circuit Ct, probation officer 1965-66; US Peace Corps, Philippines, 1963-64. **Orgs:** Mem Am, Nat, DC Bar Assns; Practicing Law Instr; Phi Alpha Delta; adv couns Fed City Coll Psychology Dept; mem Urban League. **Military Serv:** AUS sp/5 1966-68. **Business Addr:** Partner, McFadden, Evans & Sill, 2000 M St NW, Ste 260, Washington, DC 20036.

JONES, THOMAS RUSSELL
Retired judge, attorney, publishing executive. **Personal:** Born Aug 5, 1913, Brooklyn, NY; married Bertha; children: Margaret, David. **Educ:** St John's Univ, LLD; NYU, LLM (Intl Law). **Career:** General Practice, atty; Civil Ct NYC, judge; Supreme Ct State of NY, justice; The Children's Times Newsletter, pres, publisher. **Orgs:** Pres Supreme Ct Justices Assn NYC; mem NY State Constl Conv; mem NY State Assembly; founder/chmn Bedford Stuyvesant Restoration Corp 1966-72; founder Unity Democratic Club 1959-64. **Military Serv:** ETO mem Gen Ct Martial Bd 1st Lt. **Business Addr:** Attorney-At-Law, 160 Montague St, Brooklyn, NY 11201.

JONES, THOMAS W.
Financial services company executive. **Career:** Teachers Insurance and Annuity Association/College Retirement Equities Fund, president, currently. **Business Addr:** President, Teachers Insurance & Annuity Association/College Retirement Equities Fund, 730 Third Ave, New York, NY 10017, (212)490-9000.

JONES, TONY EDWARD
Professional football player. **Personal:** Born May 24, 1966, Royston, GA; married Kamilla Orr, Feb 14, 1992; children: Tony Jr. **Educ:** Western Carolina, BS in management, 1989. **Career:** Cleveland Browns, tackle, 1988-95; Baltimore Ravens, 1996; Denver Broncos, 1997-. **Business Addr:** Professional Football Player, Denver Broncos, 13655 Broncos Pkwy, Englewood, CO 80112, (303)649-9000.

JONES, TOO TALL. See **JONES, EDWARD LEE.**

JONES, VANN KINCKLE
Physician. **Personal:** Born Nov 20, 1940, Flushing, NY; son of Eunice Joyner Jones and Eugene Kinckle Jones Jr; married Judith; children: Karen, Glenn. **Educ:** Cornell U, BA 1962; Howard Univ Coll Med, MD 1966. **Career:** Brooklyn Hospital Center, asst attending physician; Private practice, 1972-; Interfaith Medical Center, dir med clinic 1974-88; Downstate Med Ctr, asso attdng physician, asst clinical prof med 1976-; Montfiore Hospital, Resd, 1968-70; Kings Co Hosp, Resd 1967-68; intern 1966-67. **Orgs:** Mem NY State Med Soc; Kings Co Med Soc; Am Coll Physicians; diplomate Am Bd Intl Med; mem Alpha Omega Alpha Hon Med Soc, 1966. **Honors/Awds:** Hon mention All Am Lacrosse, Cornell Univ 1962; Fellow, American College of Physicians. **Military Serv:** USAF maj 1970-72. **Business Addr:** 10 Plaza St, Brooklyn, NY 11238.

JONES, VELMA LOIS
Instructor. **Educ:** Lemoyne-Owen Coll, BA; Columbia Univ, MA; Memphis State Univ, MI State Univ, grad study. **Career:** Hyde Park Elem Sch Memphis, instr; LeMoyne Owen Coll, MI Coll & Memphis Univ, master tchr for student tchrs; Cypress Jr HS Memphis, instr math. **Orgs:** Memphis Educ Assn; exec bd Memphis Educ Assn; parliamentarian co-fdr mem chrpsn Memphis chap Natl Educ Assn Black Caucus; del TN Educ Assn Rep Assembly 1970-79; del Natl Educ Assn Rep Assembly 1971-79; past pres W TN Educ Assn; bd dirs TN Educ Assn; Natl Cncl of Tchrs of Math; TN Cncl of Teachers of Math; Memphis area Teachers of Math; NEA concerns Com; TN Educ Assn; vice pres Memphis Dist Laymen's Cncl CME Ch; sec Soc Rel Missionary Soc ofW TN Ann Conf CME Ch; asst sec W TN Ann Conf & chpsn of com on soc concerns; parliamentarian TN Conf of NAACP Branches; Women's Missionary Cncl of CME Ch; mem Compilation com to revise the Ch Discipline; mem Staff for Leadership Fellows Prog & Pre-Boule Workshop of Alpha Kappa Alpha Sor; pastS Eastern Regional Dir; chtrmem Memphis Chaptr Amer Inst ofrliamentarians; N Memphis Area Adv Cncl; Natl Cncl of Negro Women; mem TN State Educ Assn; v chrpsn Shelby Co Housing Auth; Am Inst of Parliamentarians; dir Christian Educ Trinity Christian Meth Epis Ch. **Honors/Awds:** First woman pres Memphis Br NAACP; Excellent Leadership & Outstanding Serv Awds Alpha Kappa Alpha 1966-70; Women of Yr 1974; Missionary of Yr 1975; Twenty Most Prominent Memphians 1975; Women Making History 1976; Brotherhood Awd 1977; Outstanding Woman in S Eastern Region; Women of Yr 1970; Comm Serv Awd 1958 1978; Certificate of Merit Awd NAACP 1972; numerous other civic awds; Outstanding Woman of the Yr Awd NAACP Women's Natl Conf 1980. **Business Addr:** Math Instructor, Cypress Jr High School, 2109 Howell, Memphis, TN 38108.

JONES, VERA MASSEY
Chief judge. **Personal:** Born 1943. **Educ:** Fisk University, BA, history, 1965; University of Detroit Law School, 1969. **Career:** University of Detroit Urban Law Program, clinic division, 1967, research division, 1968-69; private-practice attorney, 1969-70; Legal Aid and Defender Association of Detroit, deputy defender, 1970-73; Detroit Recorder's Court, Traffic and Ordinance Division, referee, 1973-79, judge, chief judge, currently. **Orgs:** National Association of Women Judges, secretary, 1982-83, founding member; Michigan Black Judges Association; NAACP, Women's Committee; Delta Sigma Theta; State Bar of Michigan, Judicial Conference. **Special Achievements:** Rated preferred and well-qualified, Civic Searchlight, 1990; rated outstanding, Detroit Bar Association, 1990. **Business Addr:** Presiding Judge, Criminal Division Wayne Circuit Ct, Frank Murphy Hall of Justice Bldg, 1441 St Antoine, Detroit, MI 48226, (313)224-2487.

JONES, VERNON A., JR.
Clergyman (retired). **Personal:** Born Sep 19, 1924, Brunswick Co, VA; son of Harriet Rhodes Simmons and Vernon A Jones; married Lillian Clark; children: Cecilia, Harriett, Vernelle. **Educ:** VA Union U, AB 1945; Bishop Payne Div Sch, BD 1948; VA Theol Sem, MDiv. **Career:** St Andrew's Episcopal Ch Tuskegee Inst, rector 1960-90; vicar 1957-60; St Stephen's Ch Petersburg VA, rector 1953-57. **Orgs:** Sec Coun Episcopal Diocese AL 1975-78; mem Diocesan Liturgical Comm 1973-; Dept Ministry Higher Educ 1957-67; Lions Club; bd dirs Tuskegee Fed Credit Union; chmn Model Cities Commn.

JONES, VICTOR TYRONE
Professional football player. **Personal:** Born Dec 5, 1967, Zachary, LA. **Educ:** Louisiana State University. **Career:** Houston Oilers, 1990-91; Denver Broncos, 1992; Pittsburgh Steelers, 1993; Detroit Lions, currently. **Business Addr:** Professional Football Player, Detroit Lions, 1200 Featherstone Rd., Pontiac, MI 48342, (810)335-4131.

JONES, VICTORIA C.
Television producer. **Personal:** Born Dec 30, 1947, Denver, CO; daughter of Marvin K Dillard & Pearl E Reagor; children: Lisa A Camille Jones. **Educ:** Western Univ, BA, BS, 1972; Harvard Univ, EDM, 1979. **Career:** WB2-TV, co creator "People Are Talking," 1979-80, creator "Coming Together," 1980-81, producer, 1980; WHDH-TV, producer, 1982-95, exec producer, 1995-, sr producer, 1995-. **Orgs:** Bunker Hill Community College, bd of visitors; National Museum of the American Indian, bd mem; National Association of Black Journalists, bd mem; Coalition of 100 Black Women, Boston Chap, cofounder; Boston Association of Black Journalists, past pres. **Honors/Awds:** New England Emmys, Emmy, 1977-96; Iris Award, 1984, 1989, 1990; Ohio State, Outstanding Award for Excellence, 1986; YWCA, Tribute to Excellence, 1990; National NAACP Special Image Award, 1983. **Special Achievements:** Special Projects: "Voices of Violence," award winning documentary, narrated by people affected by domestic violence, 1996; "Save Our Children..Save Our Neighborhood," year long campaign WHDH-TV, 1992; "Mandela's visit to Boston," 1990; "Journey of Courage," docu-drama, 1988; "Million Man March," documentary, 1995. **Business Addr:** Sr Producer/Programming, WHDH-TV/NBC, 7 Bulfinch Pl, Boston, MA 02114, (617)725-0828.

JONES, VICTORIA GENE
Public relations executive. **Personal:** Born Jan 30, 1948, Oakland, CA; daughter of Lottie Emelda Charbonnet and Eugene Leocadio Balugo; divorced; children: Brandon Wells. **Educ:** Pepperdine University, Malibu, CA, BS, business management, 1983. **Career:** Pacific Telephone, Oakland, CA, long distance operator, 1965-66; Pepsi Cola Bottling, Oakland, CA, goodwill ambassador, 1965-66; Southern California Gas Co, Los Angeles, CA, clerk typist, 1966-67, quality control clerk, 1967, public affairs reference center clerk, 1967-72, public affairs reference center work director, 1973-74, community relations representative, 1974-76, community services representative, 1976-79, professional employment administrator, 1979-80, public affairs representative, 1980-82, account executive, 1982-84, community involvement energy programs administrator, 1984-85, market services manager, 1985-88, state governmental affairs manager/lobbyist, 1988-. **Orgs:** President, Capitol Network, 1992-; member, Institute of Governmental Advocates, 1988-; Women in Advocacy, 1988-; California Elected Women's Association for Education and Research, 1988-; American Association of Blacks in Energy, 1988-; Sacramento Urban League, 1989-; Los Angeles Urban League, 1980-88. **Honors/Awds:** Black Woman of Achievement, NAACP Legal Defense and Education Fund, 1990; Mayor's Certificate of Appreciation for Community Involvement, City of Los Angeles, 1990; Certificate of Recognition, California State Assembly, 1990.

JONES, VIDA YVONNE
Educational administrator. **Personal:** Born Aug 30, 1946, Collinston, LA; daughter of Helen Taylor Jones and Willie L Jones; married Abdul LaBrie (divorced 1974); children: Ghania. **Educ:** San Francisco State University, San Francisco, CA, BA, 1969; University of California, Berkeley, CA, MA, city planning, 1972; University of California, San Francisco, CA, PhD, 1986. **Career:** Univ of California, San Francisco, CA, assistant planner, 1972-73, associate planner, 1973-75, senior planner, 1975-77, principal analyst, 1977-87, Institute for Health & Aging, assistant director, training & administration, 1987-. **Orgs:** Chair, board of directors, Bay Area Lupus Foundation, 1987-88; chair, Minority Outreach Committee, 1985-87; member, National Forum for Black Public Administrators; member, American Sociologist Association; member, American Planners Association. **Honors/Awds:** Curriculum Develpment Grant, Special Minority Aging, Academic Geriatrics Resource Prog, 1990; Lupus & Black Women, Black Women's Health Book: Speaking for Ourselves, 1990. **Home Addr:** 32726 Bass Lake St, Fremont, CA 94536.

JONES, VIOLA
Government official. **Personal:** Born Apr 27, 1933, Goodnight, OK; daughter of Jeanette Hardimon House and John W House; married Charles H Jones II, Feb 2, 1952; children: Charlesetta, Carolyn, Cynethia, Charles III. **Educ:** Langston University, Langston, OK, BS, 1973. **Career:** Langston University, Langston, OK, youth specialist community dev, 1972-82; City of Langston, Langston, OK, currently. **Orgs:** Missionary president, St Mark District, 1987-; mayor, City of Langston, 1987-; member, Business Professional Women, 1988-; member, Langston Beautiful Federated Club, 1972-; chairperson, Oklahoma Baptist State Missionary Presidents, Inc, 1981-. **Honors/Awds:** Most Outstanding Woman, Governor's Office, 1990; Most Outstanding Citizen, Oklahoma Baptist State Convention, 1990; Dedicated Services, Langston University, 1982; Water Systems Achievement Mgmt, Oklahoma Rural Water Association, 1988; Completing Hours for Municipal Officers, Oklahoma Municipal League, 1988. **Home Addr:** PO Box 506, Langston, OK 73050.

JONES, WALTER
Professional football player. **Personal:** Born Jan 19, 1974. **Educ:** Florida State. **Career:** Seattle Seahawks, 1997-. **Honors/Awds:** Rookie of the Month, October 1997. **Special Achievements:** NFL Draft, First round pick, #6, 1997. **Business Addr:** Professional Football Player, Seattle Seahawks, 11220 NE 53rd St, Kirkland, WA 98033, (206)827-9777.

JONES, WALTER L.
Editor. **Personal:** Born Nov 30, 1928, Bloomington, IL; married Cleo E Brooks; children: Walter, Jr, Stephen, Joy. **Educ:** Illinois State Univ; Tennessee A&I State Univ; Univ of Illinois. **Career:** The Milwaukee Courier Newspaper, editor, asst publisher; Milwaukee Star, editor 1964-71; Info Newspaper Gary, managing editor 1959-63. **Orgs:** Mem Milwaukee Advertising Club; Alpha Phi Alpha; Sigma Delta Chi; pres Northside & Businessmen's Assn; mem NAACP. **Honors/Awds:** Var awards for newspaper writings. **Military Serv:** USAF airman third class 193-55. **Business Addr:** Milwaukee Community Journal, 3612 N Green Bay, Milwaukee, WI 53212.

JONES, WILBERT
Food consultant, scientist. **Personal:** Born Mar 14, 1964, Clarksdale, MS; son of Thelma Jones. **Educ:** Loyola University of Chicago, BS, chemistry, 1984; Ecole DeGastronomie Francaise Ritz Escoffier, Paris France, 1990, 1992. **Career:** Kraft Foods, product dev mgr, 1985-93; Butterball Turkey Co, consultant, 1995; Kraft Foods, consultant, 1996-98; William Rainey Harper Coll, instructor, 1995-98; Sinai Med Ctr and Hospital, food consultant, 1997; LaChoy-Terr Yakis' Co, sr training mgr, consultant, 1997-98. **Orgs:** Union League Club of Chicago, 1995-; International Association of Culinary Professionals, 1996-; Toastmasters International, Chicago, 1995-. **Honors/Awds:** National Council of Negro Women, Purple Reflection Award, 1997; Kraft Foods, Technology Research Award, 1989, 1990. **Special Achievements:** The New Soul Food Cookbook, Birch Lane Press, 1996; The Healthy Soul Food Cookbook, Citadel Press, 1997; Mama's Tea Cakes: 101 Soul Food Desserts, Carol Publishing Group, 1998. **Business Addr:** President, Healthy Concepts, Inc, 1400 N Lake Shore Dr, Ste 4F, Chicago, IL 60610.

JONES, WILLIAM
Alderman. **Personal:** Born Sep 14, 1934, Youngstown, OH; married Eunice L Rogers; children: Lowell, Diane Marie, Sherri Lynne. **Educ:** Houston-Tillotson Coll, BA 1961; Trinity U, CT State Coll, grad study 1967-69; Univ MA. **Career:** City of New Haven, dir of organizational devel 1980-, city town clerk 1978-80, chmn Dem Tow 1976-78, alderman 1970-78, dir of com 1975-77; New Haven Health Care Inc, dir health educ & comm relations 1972-75; IBM Corp, sales rep 1965-67; Xerox Corp, 1969; Services Inc, pres 1968-72; S Central Comm Coll, lectr 1969-72. **Orgs:** Adv Tri-State Transp Comm 1971; vice-chmn New Haven Black Coalition 1972; fdr New Haven Black Arts Theatre 1967; vice-chmn bd New Haven Opportunities Industrialization Cntr 1967-69; mem CT Dem Central Comm 1968-70; mem Nat Urban League 1970; mem Alpha Fi Alpha; exec vice-chmn Caucus CT Dems 1967-71;Am Cancer Soc; Quinnipiac Council of Boy Scouts; Dixwell Neighborhood Corp; chmn New Haven Reg Com on Hypertension; cmmr COMMN on Higher Edn; pres New Haven Midget Football League; mem New Haven Human Serv Com; CT Assn of Local Legislators; Nat Black Caucus of Local Elected Officials; mem Urban Lealgue; NAACP. **Honors/Awds:** Recipient Man of the Yr Award, Human Relations Council 1970. **Military Serv:** USAF 1954-58. **Business Addr:** 200 Orange Hall of Records, New Haven, CT 06503.

JONES, WILLIAM A., JR.
Clergyman. **Personal:** Born Feb 24, 1934, Louisville, KY; married Natalie Barkley Brown; children: William III, Elsa, Lesley, Jennifer. **Educ:** Univ of KY, BA 1958; Crozer Theol Sem, BD 1961; Benedict Coll, SC, Hon DD 1969; Colgate Rochester-Bexley Hall-Crozer Theol Sem, PhD 1975. **Career:** 1st Baptist Church Phila, pastor 1959-62; Bethany Baptist Church Brooklyn, pastor 1962-. **Orgs:** Preacher at churches, conventions, conferences univs & colls in Amer, England, Israel, India, Australia, W Africa; pres Prog Nat Bapt Conv 1968-70; prof Black Ch Studies Colgate Rochester Bexley Hall Crozer 1972-76; preacher for NBC's "Art of Living" 1977; frequently featured Conf Echoes Family Radio Network; mem Martin Luther King Jr Fellow Inc; mem Genl Council Bapt World Alliance; trustee, vis prof, Colgate Rochester Div Sch; vis prof Princeton Theol Sem; coord Min's Com on Job Oppors for Brooklyn 1963-64; bd chmn Bedford Stuyvesant Youth in Action 1965-67; founder/chmn Greater NY SCLC Operation Breadbasket 1967-72; chmn Natl SCLC Operation Breadbasket 1972-73; vis prof Practical Tehol Union Theol Sem 1975-76; chmncombd Kings Co Hosp Ctr 1970-77; adj prof romiletics Wesley Tehol Semsh DC 1976-77. **Honors/Awds:** Editor Missions Outlook 1961-62; cited "Man in the News" NY Times; Man of the Yr Brooklyn Jaycees 1967; Outstanding Brooklynite NY Recorder Poll 1970; Ophelia Devore Achievement Awd 1970; Black Heritage Assn Awd 1971; Capital Formation Comm Leader Awd 1971; Comm Serv Awd Brooklyn Chap Phi Beta Sigma 1972; Frederick Douglass Awd NY Urban League 1972; Natl Assn of Health Serv Exec Awd 1975; Disting Serv Awd Colony Club First AME Zion Ch Brooklyn 1977; Freedom Awd Comm Mus of Brooklyn Inc 1978; listed in 100 Most Influential Black Amers Ebony Magazine 1979; co-author "The Black Ch Looks at the Bicentennial" PNB Pub House Elgin IL 1976; author "Freedom of Conscience, The Black Experience in Amer" Religious Libertyin the Crossfire of Creeds-Ecumenical Press Philadelphia 1978; author "God ine Ghetto" PNB Pub House Elgin IL 1979; 1 of America's 15 Outstanding Black Preachers Ebony Mag 1984; article contribs Bapt Progress-Black Monitor-Founds-Freeing The Spirit-The NY Recorder-The Amsterdam News; doctoral thesis The Gospel & the Ghetto. **Military Serv:** AUS 1st lt 1954-56. **Business Addr:** Pastor, Bethany Baptist Church, 460 Sumner Ave, Brooklyn, NY 11216.

JONES, WILLIAM ALLEN
Film company executive, attorney. **Personal:** Born Dec 13, 1941, Philadelphia, PA; son of Gloria T Jones and Roland E Jones; married Dorothea S Whitson; children: Darlene, Rebecca, Gloria, David. **Educ:** Temple Univ, BA (Magna Cum Laude) 1967; Harvard Business School, MBA 1972; Harvard Law School, JD 1972. **Career:** Walt Disney Prod, attny 1973-77, asst treas 1977-79, treas 1979-81; Wyman Bautzer Rothman Kuchel Silbert, attny 1981-83; MGM/UA Entertainment Co, vp, gen counsel corp & sec; United Artists Corp, sr. vp, corp gen counsel 1986-91; Metro Goldwyn-Mayer Inc, executive vice president, gen counsel & secretary, 1991-94, exec vp, Corporate Affairs, 1995-97, sr exec vp, 1997-. **Orgs:** Bus mgr Los Angeles Bar Jrnl 1974-76; mem Amer Bar Assoc 1974-, State Bar of CA 1974-, Los Angeles Cty Bar Assn 1974-; bd dir Harvard Bus School Assoc of So CA 1985-88; bd of trustees Marlborough School; board of governors, Institute for Corporate Counsel, 1991-94; board of directors, The Nostalgia Network Inc, 1990-94; Pathe Communications Corp, board of directors, 1991-92; Metro-Goldwyn-Mayer Inc., board of directors, 1991-92; Flintridge Preparatory School, board of trustees, 1993-96; Motown Picture Association of America, board of directors, 1995-; Santa Monica Chamber of Commerce, board of directors, 1996-. **Honors/Awds:** Pres Scholar Temple Univ 1967; mem History Honor Soc 1967, German Honor Soc 1967, Political Sci Hon Soc 1967. **Military Serv:** USAF airman 1st class 4 yrs. **Business Addr:** Executive Vice Pres, Corporate Affairs, Metro-Goldwyn-Mayer Inc., 2500 Broadway, Santa Monica, CA 90404.

JONES, WILLIAM BARNARD
Beverage company executive. **Personal:** Born Nov 20, 1957, St Louis, MO; son of Alice Narvelle Dunn; married Phyllis, Sep 7, 1985; children: Tanya Nichole, William Barnard II, Ryan Laroy Willard, Ciara Alice Hope. **Educ:** Washington University, St Louis, BA, 1980. **Career:** Anheuser-Busch, sr consultant, development, 1989-90, national budget administrator, 1990-92, executive asst to vp, 1992-93, national mgr, field sales, 1993-95, sales dir of MI, 1994-95, vp of region sales, 1995-. **Orgs:** Inroads, Inc, 1980-; 100 Black Men, 1997-; NFL Alumni Association, 1995-. **Honors/Awds:** Dollar & Sense Magazine, Corporate Trailblazer Award, 1997. **Business Addr:** Vice Pres, Region Sales, Anheuser-Busch, Inc, 30850 Telegraph Rd, Ste 200, Bingham Farms, MI 48025.

JONES, WILLIAM BOWDOIN
Diplomat, consultant, lecturer, lawyer. **Personal:** Born May 2, 1928, Los Angeles, CA; son of LaVelle Bowdoin Jones and William T Jones; married Joanne F Garland, Jun 27, 1953; children: Lisa Jamison, Dr Stephanie A Marioneaux, Walter C. **Educ:** Univ of CA-Los Angeles, AB 1949; Univ Southern CA, JD 1952. **Career:** Private Practice, attorney-at-law 1952-62; US Foreign Service Officer, diplomat 1962-84; US Dept of State, Washington, deputy assistant secretary of state, 1969-73; US Dept of State, Paris France, chief, US mission to UNESCO, 1973-77; US Dept State chairman US-Japan cultural conference, Hawaii, 1973; US Dept of State, ambassador to Haiti 1977-80; Hampton University, diplomat-in-residence, 1980-81; Univ of VA, ambassador in residence 1984-85; Woodrow Wilson Foundation, Princeton, NJ, fellow, 1986-87; US House of Rep Subcommittee on Western Affairs, staff dir, 1987; The International Business Law Firm, partner, 1988-91; Hampden Sydney College, Sydney, VA, bd of trustees, 1992-, adjunct professor, 1991; Pepperdine University, distinguished visiting professor, 1993. **Orgs:** Sigma Pi Phi-Boule; Kappa Alpha Psi; Washington Intl Club; CA Bar; District of Columbia, US Supreme Court; Bar of the US Court of Intl Trade 1988; bd of dirs,

American Association for the United Nations, National Capital Region, 1996-; US Council, United Nations University, 1997-; James Madison Society, Hampden-Sydney College, 1996-. **Honors/Awds:** Outstanding Public Serv CA Legislature 1972; Professional Achievement UCLA Alumni 1980; Merit Awd Alumni Univ So CA 1981; Key to City Los Angeles 1981. **Special Achievements:** First African American to be named chief of the US Mission to UNESCO, Paris. **Home Addr:** 4807 17th St NW, Washington, DC 20011, (202)722-1808.

JONES, WILLIAM C.
Obstetrician, gynecologist. **Personal:** Born Oct 22, 1933, Richmond, VA; married Evora Williams; children: Lisa, Mark, Lori, Michael, David, Lydia. **Educ:** VA State Coll, BS 1953; Howard U, 1957-59; Meharry Med Coll, MD 1963; Duke Univ Med Cntr, 1967-68. **Career:** Physician Ob/Gyn pvt practice Richmond, VA 1968-; Duke Univ & affiliated hosps, Durham, NC, fellow, Endocrinology 1967-68; Hubbard Hosp, Meharry Med Coll, residency & internship 1963-67. **Orgs:** Mem Am Coll Ob/Gyn; mem Richmond Acad of Medicine; mem Richmond Med Soc; Old Dominion Med Soc; cert Am Bd of Observ & Gyn; Kappa Alpha Psi Frat. **Military Serv:** AUS 1st lt 1954-56. **Business Addr:** 2809 N Ave, Richmond, VA 23222.

JONES, WILLIAM EDWARD
Educator. **Personal:** Born Jul 4, 1930, Indianapolis, IN; married Janet; children: Leslye. **Educ:** Butler U, BS 1956; IN U, MS 1960. **Career:** Broad Ripple HS, prin 1970-; IN State Univ, counselor, instructor, vice prin, dean 1964-68; Crispus Attucks HS, teacher 1957-61. **Orgs:** Consult HEW; Urban Sch Affairs, OH State U; Midwest Equal Oppt Cntr; Univ Psgh; Gen Asst Cntr; Desegregation Nat Assn; mem Secondary Sch Prin; Phi Delta Kappa; IN Secondary Sch Adminstr; adv cncl Danforth Found; elder Witherspoon United Presb Ch; mem Grtr Indianapolis Progress Com; Kappa Alp Psi; NAACP; Urban League flw Danforth Sch Adminstr 1975-76; John Hay flw Humanities 1964. **Military Serv:** USAF 1952-55. **Business Addr:** 1115 E Broad Ripple Ave, Indianapolis, IN 46220.

JONES, WILLIAM J.
Engineer. **Personal:** Born Mar 23, 1915, New York, NY; married Dorothy; children: 3. **Educ:** BS 1941; MS 1951. **Career:** US Army, chief test equipment & meas, Signal Corps Lab; Lincoln Lab, MA Inst Tech, staff mem; Harvard Univ, lecturer 1960-75; MA Inst Tech, sr staff engr 1975-. **Orgs:** Sr mem Inst Elec Engr Commr, Civil Rights & Human Relations 1965-70; trustee SE MA Univ 1971-; dir Garden City Bank. **Business Addr:** Sr Staff Engineer, Massachusetts Institute of Technology, Newton, MA 02160.

JONES, WILLIAM JENIPHER
Clergyman. **Personal:** Born Oct 27, 1912, Spring Hill, MD; son of Margret Sadie Jones and Richard Edward Jones; married Pauline Payne; children: William Edward, William David. **Educ:** Attended, Cordoza Business Sch 1929; TN Christian Univ, BDiv 1977; YMCA Local Comm Coll, BS Real Estate; Moraine Valley Comm Coll, real estate broker/appraiser; Biblical Studies, certificate; Univ of IL Commissioners Training Inst, 1985. **Career:** Chicago Transit Authority, station transportation clerk 1953-77; Village of Robbins, village trustee 1969-77; IL Police & Fire Commn Bd, commnr chaplain 1984; St John Comm Ch, pastor 1985-. **Orgs:** Gen ins broker Universal Ins Agency 1970; agent United Ins Co of Amer 1953; debit mgr Supreme Life Ins Co 1978; special deputy Pape Security Serv 1977; sec Village of Robbins Fire & Police Commnr 1983; village trustee Village of Robbins 1969-77; chaplain IL Fire & Police Commnrs Assn 1983-85; vice pres South Suburban Legal Aid Harvey IL 1970; chmn South Suburban Mayors Planning Group 1969-77; past comdr Robbins Memorial Post 1281 Amer Legion 1975; past master Alpha Omega Masonic Lodge #121 Robbins 1979; pres Concerned Citizen Party Robbins IL 1981. **Military Serv:** Quarter master staff sgt 1943-46; Good Conduct Medal; 3 Battle Stars; Medal of Honor. **Home Addr:** 3702 W 135th St, Robbins, IL 60472. **Business Addr:** Pastor, St John Community Church, 13430 South Harding Ave, Robbins, IL 60472.

JONES, WILLIAM LAWLESS
Editor. **Personal:** Born Oct 20, 1914, Frankfort, KY; son of Ada Anderson Jones and Paul W L Jones; married Helen Elizabeth Lewis; children: Paul W L II, Robert L, Terence L. **Educ:** Fisk Univ, BA 1938; Univ of MI, MA 1939; Univ of Cincinnati, MEd 1973. **Career:** AUS, various intell & admin pos 1941-66; Job Corps NJ, ed spec 1966-69; Univ of Cincinnati, coord min recruiting 1969-73, asst prof 1973-79; NIP (now NJEMA) Magazine, entertainment editor. **Orgs:** Writer jazz music columnist NIP Magazine 1969-; tchr history and appreciation of jazz Univ of Cincinnati 1973-75, 1991-95; TV News Commentator For NAACP Presents; secretary of bd trustees Greater Cincinnati Council Performing Arts 1991-97; writer and lecturer Jazz Prog of the Council. **Honors/Awds:** Writer 3-Hour Documentary Video Prod The Evolution of Black Music IN Cincinnati 1980-82; prepared curriculum Jazz Studies for the Union for Experimenting Clges and Univ in Cincinnati 1984; Greater Cincinnati Urban League's Heritage Award, 1994; Greater Cincinnati Jazz Society's Lifetime Achievement Award, 1997. **Military Serv:** AUS lt col; Bronze Star; Army Commendation Medal. **Home Addr:** 4500 Perth Ln, Cincinnati, OH 45229.

JONES, WILLIAM O.
Clergyman. **Personal:** Born Feb 16, Covington, TN; married Helen Crombie; children: 4. **Educ:** Moody Bible Inst; KY State, BS; Gammon Theol Sem, BD; Murry's Theol Sem, DD. **Career:** Chattanooga Bible Center, dean & dir; Home Mission Bd So Bapt Conv 1975-; pastorates TN, KY. **Orgs:** Asst sec Nat BYPU Bd 1947-54; editor Intermed Nat BYPU Qrtly; precinct chmn 12-5 Dist 8 yrs; chaplain CCC Camp 1935-37. **Honors/Awds:** AUS 1941-45. **Military Serv:** AUS 1941-45. **Business Addr:** 805 E 9 St, Chattanooga, TN.

JONES, WILLIAM W.
Educator. **Personal:** Born Apr 8, 1928, Pageton, WV; children: Valerie Jones Hairston, - 1968-74; bd. **Educ:** Mercer Co Barber Sch, Bluefield, WV, diploma 1947-48; Bluefield State Coll, BS building-constr 1954-58; WV U, MSW 1970-72. **Career:** Parkersburg Community Coll, asst prof 1978-, instr 1974-78; Hall Acres Child Care Cntr & Wood Co Juvenile Detention Cntr, Parkerburg, WV, dir 1974-78;Concord Coll, Athens, WV, instr 1974; WV Dept of Welfare Juvenile Delinquency Serv, soc worker/state coord 1972-74; Fed Reformatory for Women, Alderson, WV, consult 1971; WV Dept of Welfare, social worker 1962-70; gen contractor, building trades 1958-62; barber, Bluefield & Princeton WV 1953-68; Norfolk & Western Railway Co, mail handler 1949-62. **Orgs:** Mem Mercer Co Steering Com for the Est of Juvenile Facilaities 1972-74; mem Mercer Co Bd of educ Adv Council 1973-74; pres City Economic Oppor Office, Bluefield, WV 1966; pres HS Athletic Boosters Club 1967-69; bd of dir Mercer Co Oppor Workshop for Retarded Children 1968-74; bd of dir WV Div ofRehab Serv 1967-74; bd of dir Easter Seal So 1968-70; mem NAACP; mem Nat Assn of Social Workers; chmn educ com local branch NAACP, Parkersburg, WV; sec-treas WV Undergrad Social Work Educators Assn; lic minister Zion Bapt Ch Parkersburg, WV 1977-; mem & past dist chmn VFW; mem Civitan Club; mem Midtown Kiwanis Club; bd dir Commn on Race & Relgn; bd dir Logan Job Training & Info Cntr; exec bd Boy Scouts of Am; bd dir WV Assnon Crime & Delinquency; bd dir West-Central RegnlJuv Detention Cntr; youtir Zion Bapt Ch; co-founder of first 3 small group homes in WV, WV ChildCare Assn, 1976. **Honors/Awds:** Public Service Award, WV Dept of Welfare 1973; Recognition for Loyalty & Dedication, VFW, 1968-69; article pub in the Nat Juvenile Det Assn Newsletter, "Communication Skills Is A Two-Way Street"; attended numerous conferences & workshops; radio-tv appearance, In Regard to Juv Delinquency Activities; guest spkrnumerous organizations; counselor/advisor/volunteer worker many organizations & groups. **Military Serv:** AUS corpl 1951-52. **Business Addr:** Parkersburg Comm Coll, Rt 5 Box 167 A, Parkersburg, WV 26101.

JONES, WILLIE
State government official. **Personal:** Born Oct 16, 1932, Seaboard, NC; married Jacqueline J Gibbs Jones; children: Sharon von Hulsebus, Kurtis. **Educ:** Long Island Univ, BA 1964; Pace Univ MBA 1974. **Career:** New Jersey Highway Authority, director of human resources, 1988-. **Orgs:** HR Society for Human Resources Management; Mem Natl C of C; Natl Assn Mfrs; Natl Business League; Corp Urban Affairs Adv Comm; Public Affairs Coun; Natl Minority Purchasing Coun; Econ Devel Coun; mem numerous offices, committees, NE region; Natl Urban Affairs Coun; Natl Urban League; Golden Heritage life mem NAACP; Natl Urban Coalition; EDGES Group, Food Markets Inst; bd of adv Felician Coll; Artist Family Theater Proj; Natl Assn Marketing Devel; Military Acad Selection Comm; Toastmaster Intl; past mem, USAF Speakers Bureau; Gen "Hap" Arnold Air Soc; Ancient Free & Accepted Masons; New York City Ed Adv Eastern Dist. **Honors/Awds:** Red Hot Scouting Award; Natl Hon Soc Pi Gamma Mu; Merit Award, Black Media; Special Humanitarian Award, Supermarkets General Corp; Outstanding Achievements Award, Perth Amboy Branch, NAACP; First Affirmative Action Award, Congress of Racial Equality; Roy Wilkins Meritorious Service Award, New Jersey NAACP Urban Programs; Civil Rights Award, Hoboken Branch, NAACP. **Military Serv:** USAF ret 20 yrs. **Business Addr:** Director of Human Resources, New Jersey Highway Authority, Executive Offices, Woodbridge, NJ 07095.

JONES, WINTON DENNIS, JR.
Chemist. **Personal:** Born Jun 23, 1941, Terre Haute, IN; son of Katherine Sims Jones (deceased) and Winton Jones; married Sandra Murdock; children: Winton III, Kimberly L. **Educ:** Butler Univ, BS Pharm 1963, MS Pharm Chem 1966; Univ of KS, PhD Med Chem 1970. **Career:** Merrell Dow Rsch Inst, sr rsch chemist 1970-. **Orgs:** Mem Big Brothers of Hamilton County 1972-82; assoc advisor Boy Scouts of Amer #494 1973-; chairperson Forest Park Housing Comm 1976-78; congressional sci couns OH 1st Dist 1978-; treas Tech Sci Soc of Cincinnati 1979; bd of dir Amer Chem Soc 1979; charter mem Natl Org of Black Chemists & Chem Engrs Cincinnati Chapter. **Honors/Awds:** Fellowship Natl Inst of Health 1969-70; Citation City of Forest Park OH 1982; 19 publications, 29 patents, 5 presentations; Certificate of Appreciation, City of Forest Park, OH, 1982. **Home Addr:** 1464 Longacre Dr, Cincinnati, OH 45240. **Business Addr:** Senior Resident Chemist, Marion Merrell Dow Res Institute, 2110 E Galbraith Rd, Cincinnati, OH 45215.

JONES, WOODROW HAROLD
Educator. **Personal:** Born May 29, 1913, Wewoka, OK; married Lucille White; children: Ethel. **Educ:** Langston U, BS 1937; Columbia, MA 1947; Univ of OK, PhD 1954. **Career:** OK Public Schools, teacher 1939-46; Langston Univ, instructor Biology 1948-50; Fisk Univ, assoc prof 1953-56; Southern Univ, prof Biology 1956-60; Univ of Pacific, postdoctoral fellow 1960-61; NASA, rsch sci 1962-69; San Francisco State Coll, prof 1969-; NSF, postdoctoral Fellow 1960-61. **Orgs:** Mem Am Soc Limnology & Oceanography; AASS; Ecol Soc Am; mem Sigma Xi; NAACP; Urban League; Beta Beta Beta; Phi Sigma; Omega Psi Phi. **Business Addr:** 1600 Halloway, San Francisco, CA 94132.

JONES, YVONNE DE MARR
Educational administrator, civil rights leader. **Personal:** Born in Dayton, OH; divorced; children: Diane R-Singh, Bercenia, Shelley Smith. **Educ:** Hunter College, BA 1947, MA 1955. **Career:** Elmsford Public Schools, 1955-84; Westchester Community College. **Orgs:** Greenburgh Neighborhood Health Center Board; chair Westchester, Martin Luther King Jr Institute; St Francis Episcopal Church, ECW, pres; pres Westchester Association for the Study of Afro-American Life and History; past branch pres White Plains Greensburgh NAACP. **Honors/Awds:** Recognition, Assn Study, Afro-Amer Life & History 1976; 1976 Comm Merit Award Operation PUSH Westchester 1976; Achievement Award Westchester Co Club BPW 1978; Recogniton Westchester Black Women's Political Caucus 1984; Key Women of Westchester Award 1987; Natl Council of Negro Women, Westchester Section, Community Service Award, 1989; Woodburn Correctional, Appreciation Award, 1989; Sing-Sing Prison, Appreciation Award, 1990; National Association of Black Social Workers, Community Enhancement Award, 1991; Mercy College Westchester Comm College Awards, 1995. **Home Addr:** 118 N Evarts Ave, Elmsford, NY 10523.

JONES, YVONNE HARRIS
Business executive. **Personal:** Born Sep 15, West Palm Beach, FL; daughter of Mary G Lightfoot Thomas and Albert Thomas; married Alan C Jones, May 4, 1988. **Educ:** City Coll of NY, BA 1970; New School for Social Rsch, MA 1977. **Career:** NY Life Insurance Co, training asst 1970-72; Fed Reserve Bank of NY, sr training specialist 1972-76; Amer Stock Exchange, managing director, 1976-96; Yvonne Harris Jones Enterprises, president, currently. **Orgs:** Pres Zeta Delta Phi Graduate Chapter 1970-76; visiting prof Urban League Black Exec Exchange Program 1976; Coalition of 100 Black Women 1977-; mem advisory bd Murry Bergtraum HS 1979-; mem board of directors, HealthWatch Information Service; mem advisory bd NCNW Women's Center 1983-; mem SEC Sec Indus Comm on EEO 1981-, Society for Hum Res Mgt, 1976-; adv bd Career Oppor in Accounting Profession (COAP), 1991-; member, NY Club, NANBPWC, 1985-. **Honors/Awds:** Black Achievers in Indus Award, YMCA Harlem Branch 1979; contributed article to professional magazines, 1984; Corporate Achievement Award Negro Business & Professional Women's Clubs Inc 1985; Salute to Black Business & Professional Women, Dollars & Sense Magazine 1989; Mary McCloud Bethune Award, National Council of Negro Women, 1991. **Home Addr:** 29 Winthrop Dr, Cortlandt Manor, NY 10566. **Business Addr:** President/CEO, Yvonne Harris Jones Enterprises, PO Box 20, Mohegan Lake, NY 10547.

JONES, YVONNE VIVIAN
Educator. **Personal:** Born Jul 29, 1946, New York, NY; daughter of Irene Washington Jones and Ernest Jones; married Sylvester Singleton; children: Michael Kenneth. **Educ:** Amer Univ, BA 1971, PhD 1976. **Career:** Eugene & Agnes E Meyer Found, assoc dir 1971-74; Univ of Louisville, asst prof 1975-81, assoc prof anthropology 1981-, dept of Pan African Studies, chair, 1995-. **Orgs:** Pres of bd Planned Parenthood of Louisville Inc 1977-81; chair, Minority Group Mental Health Prog Review Comm Natl Inst of Mental Health 1979-82. **Honors/Awds:** Outstanding Scholarship Grad Level Amer Univ 1976; Outstanding Young Woman of Amer 1978. **Business Addr:** Associate Professor, Department of Pan African Studies, University of Louisville, KY, Louisville, KY 40292.

JONES, ZOIA L.
Educator (retired). **Personal:** Born Oct 2, 1926, Iota, LA; daughter of Elena Laws-Lemelle (deceased) and Joseph Lemelle (deceased); married Everette Jones, Sep 27, 1947; children: Zoia Sylvia Jones-Blake. **Educ:** Certificate, Special Educ, Prairie View A&M Univ, 1981; MEd, Guidance, TX Southern Univ, 1976; Certification in Elementary Education, 1963; BS, Home Econ, (cum laude), TX Southern Univ, 1960. **Career:** Evangeline Parish, Rougeau, LA, teacher, 1944-47; Texas Southern University, instructor, 1960-61; HISD, Houston, TX, teacher, 1961-90; Houston-Harris County Project, volunteer coordinator, 1967, Magnet School, administrative task team, 1975; Globe Advocate, past columnist; Houston Informer, past columnist; KCOH Radio Station, past moderator; Natl Council of Negro Women, Dorothy I Height Section, president, currently. **Orgs:** Past activities advisory comm VISTA; Houston Chamber of Commerce, membership committee; Women in Community Serv, 1968-70; NAACP; Black Art Center; Black

Art Museum; RGM Rose Mary Grand Chapter OES TX; United Negro College Fund; Delta Sigma Theta, Houston Metropolitan Alumnae Chapter, charter officer, golden life mem; May Week Comm; charter board member, Adopt Black Children Comm; Eta Phi Beta Sor Inc; Assn study Negro Life & History, life mem; past activities, Houston Teachers Assn; TX Classroom Teachers Assn; TX State Teachers Assn; NEA; All Nations Rescue Mission; McGregor Park Women, charter officer, president; past columist, Forward Times; TX Southern Univ, Natl Alumni Assn; Civil Court #3 Harris County, commissioner; New Pleasant Grove Baptist Church, Senior Mission II, pres, Sunday School, teacher, youth supervisor, Young Women's Auxiliary. **Honors/Awds:** Distinguished Serv Award, Houston Classroom Teachers Assn; Delta Sigma Theta Sor, state social action chairperson Southwest Region; supreme general, Grand Chapter OES of USA, past supreme grand matron; Letter of Commendation, President George Bush, 1990; Letter of Commendation, Sen Lloyd Bentsen, 1990; Letter of Commendation, Sen Phil Graham, 1990; Texas Senate and House of Representatives, Resolutions of Commendation, for 30 yrs of Service as an educator, 1990; Houston-Harris County Retired Teachers Assn, Distinguished Service Award, Humanitarian in Civil Rights, 1994; Texas State Teachers Assn, Houston Ed Assn, Human Relations Award for an Individual, 1994; Natl Council of Negro Women, Dorothy I Height Sect, first ''Hall of Fame'' inductee, 1994-95; Natl Council of Negro Women Coordinator, Tribute to Black Women Community Leaders, Leadership Breakfast, 1992-98; Eta Phi Beta Soroity Inc, Xi Chapter, Founders Day Speaker, 1994; Mt Lebanon Baptist Church, Women's Day Speaker, 1994; YWA, Distinguished Award, 1997. **Home Addr:** 3417 Charleston, Houston, TX 77021.

JONES-GRIMES, MABLE CHRISTINE
Educator, home economist. **Personal:** Born Dec 6, 1943, Malden, MO; daughter of Anna Mae Turner Jones and Albert Jones; married James Robert Grimes, Dec 21, 1969; children: Ori Brandon Jones Grimes. **Educ:** Univ of MO-Columbia, BS 1965, MS 1968, PhD 1976. **Career:** Univ of MO Coop Extension Svcs, home economist 1965-68; Delta Headstart Program, home economist 1968-69; Univ of MO 4-H Program, youth specialist & asst prof Human Dev & Family Studies 1969-. **Orgs:** Bd mem Planned Parenthood Inc 1985-; pres Kappa Chi Omega Chap of Alpha Kappa Alpha Sor Inc 1986-87; mem Chamber of Commerce, Women's Network 1986; mem Amer Home Economics Assn l965-; mem Natl Council of Family Relations l980-; pres, bd of directors, Planned Parenthood of Central MO l988-90; Faculty Advisor Delta Tau Chapter of Alpha Kappa Alpha Sorority l983-. **Honors/Awds:** Meritorious Serv Awd State 4-H Office 1983; Institute for Management of Life Long Learning Harvard Univ 1984; Fellow, Natl Inst In Adult & Continuing Educ, Univ of Georgia, l989-90; Univ of MO South African Faculty Exchange Program with Univ of Western Cape l989; Presentation & Article ''Race and Leadership Styles of Women'' 1988. **Special Achievements:** Consultant, trainer in cultural diversity & intercultural communications, 1990-93. **Business Addr:** Asst Prof Human Dev and Family Studies, Univ of Missouri-Columbia, 309 D University Hall, Columbia, MO 65211.

JONES-SMITH, JACQUELINE
Company executive. **Personal:** Born Nov 5, 1952, Bronx, NY. **Educ:** Swarthmore College, BA, 1974; Syracuse University, MLS, 1978; American University School of Law, JD, 1984. **Career:** MAXIMA Corporation, systems librarian/division manager, 1979-85; Montgomery County, assistant county attorney, 1985-87; Federal Election Comm, staff attorney, off of genl counsel, 1987-89; Consumer Product Safety Comm, chairman, 1989-95; MAXIMA Corp, exec vp/bd mem, 1995-96, pres, COO, bd mem, 1996-. **Orgs:** American Bar Association, National Bar Association, Maryland State Bar Association. **Business Addr:** President/COO, MAXIMA Corp, 4200 Parliament Pl, Lanham, MD 20706, (301)459-2000.

JONES-TRENT, BERNICE R.
Librarian. **Personal:** Born Apr 22, 1946, Michie, TN; daughter of Ellen Hodge Ray and E C Ray; married Julius Trent, Jun 16, 1984. **Educ:** Jackson State University, Jackson, MS, BA, cum laude, 1968; Rutgers University, New Brunswick, NJ, MLS, 1969; Rutgers Univ, SCILS, New Brunswick, NJ, PhD candidate, 1984-. **Career:** Newark Business Library, Newark, NJ, jr librarian, 1969-70; Rutgers-Dana Library, Newark, NJ, business librarian, 1970-82; Rutgers Univ Library School, New Brunswick, NJ, acting dir/prof dev studies, 1982-83; Rutgers Univ Library, New Brunswick, NJ, staff development librarian, 1983-84; Rutgers-Kilmer Library, New Brunswick, NY, public services librarian, 1984-85; Old Dominion Univ Library, Norfolk, VA, head of reference dept, 1985-87; Norfolk State Univ, Norfolk, VA, director of library, 1987-89; Montclair State College, Upper Montclair, NJ, director of library, 1989-. **Orgs:** Member, American Library Assn (ALA), 1975-; member, Assn of College and Research Libraries, 1975-; Member, Black Caucus of the ALA, 1974-; member, Library Administration & Management Assn, 1978; chair, Leadership Discussion Group and Women Admin Discussion Group, 1988-90; life member, Alpha Kappa Alpha Sorority Inc, 1965-; charter member, New Jersey Black Librarians Network, 1975-. **Honors/Awds:** Academic Scholarship, Jackson State Univ, 1964-68; Title II B Scholarship, Rutgers Univ, 1968-69; County Committee Woman, East Orange, NJ, 1984-85; Scholarship, Special Libraries Assn, 1968. **Home Addr:** 2217 Crossing Way, Wayne, NJ 07470. **Business Addr:** Director of Library Services, Sprague Library, Montclair State Univ, Upper Montclair, NJ 07043, (201)893-4301.

JONES-WILSON, FAUSTINE CLARISSE
Educator (retired). **Personal:** Born Dec 3, 1927, Little Rock, AR; daughter of Perrine Marie Childress Thomas and James Edward Thomas; married James T Jones, Jun 20, 1948 (divorced 1977); children: Yvonne Dianne Jones, Brian Vincent Jones; married Edwin L Wilson Sr, Jul 10, 1981. **Educ:** Dunbar Junior College, Diploma, 1946; University of Arkansas at Pine Bluff (formerly AM&N College), AB, 1948; University of Illinois, AM, 1951, EdD, 1967. **Career:** Gary Public Schools, teacher, 1955-62, librarian, 1964-67; University of Illinois, Urbana, teaching assistant, grad student, 1962-64, Chicago, College of Education, assistant professor, 1967-69; Federal City College, associate professor, adult education, 1970-71; Howard University, Department of Education, assistant professor, 1969-70, various positions, beginning 1971, professor; prof emerita, currently. **Orgs:** American Educational Studies Association, nominating committee, 1974-75, program committee, 1975-76, executive council, 1976-79, 1985-86, Butts lecture committee, 1978-79, president, 1984-85, nominating committee chair, 1981-82; John Dewey Society, executive board, 1976-79, 1988-90, nominating committee chair, 1992; Society of Professors of Education, executive board, 1981-87, nominating committee chair, 1979; Phi Delta Kappa, Howard University Chapter, president, 1986-87, executive committee, 1986-; National Council on Educating Black Children, East Coast Steering Committee, chair, 1986-88, 1990-92, board of directors, 1986-, third vp, 1992-94; Charlotte Hawkins Brown Historical Foundation Inc, advisory council; numerous others. **Honors/Awds:** National Dunbar Alumni Association, Detroit Chapter, Outstanding Alumna Award, 1973; National Black Press Association, Frederick Douglass Award, 1979; NAFEO/UAPB, Distinguished Alumna, 1984; Howard University, Distinguished Scholar/Teacher, 1985; Natl Bar Assn, Gertrude E Rush Award, 1990. **Special Achievements:** Author: The Changing Mood in America: Eroding Committment?, 1977; A Traditional Model of Educational Excellence: Dunbar High School of Little Rock, AR, 1981; ''The Black Family,'' African-American Almanac (formerly the Negro), 1983, 1989, 1993; ''External Crosscurrents and Internal Diversity: An Assessment of Black Progress 1960-1980,'' Daedalus, 1981; ''Why Not Public Schools,'' Journal of Negro Education, 1992; Editor in Chief Emerita, Journal of Negro Education; ''Alleviating the force of Poverty on urban poor Children,'' in Early Child Development & Care, 1992; co-editor Encyclopedia of African-American Education, Greenwood Press, 1996; Senior fellow, Phelps Stokes Fund, associate editor, Journal of Education for Students Placed at Risk, Johns Hopkins University/Howard University. **Home Phone:** (301)596-5328. **Business Addr:** Professor Emerita, School of Education, Howard University, 2400 Sixth St NW, Academic Support Bldg A, Washington, DC 20059-0001.

JORDAN, ABBIE H.
Educator. **Personal:** Born in Wilcox County, GA; daughter of Leah Jones Williams and Samuel Williams; married Dr J Wesley Jordan; children: W Kenneth. **Educ:** Albany State Coll, BS 1949; Atlanta Univ, MA 1953; Univ of GA, PhD, 1979. **Career:** Tuskegee Inst, instr; Atlanta Univ Complex, instr of reading; Jr HS Ben Hill Cty, principal; Veterans School, principal, instr; GA-SC Read Conf, org & dir; Savannah Morning News, ed-op columnist; Savannah State Coll Reading Inst, founder; US Office of Education (EPDA). **Orgs:** Consultant in reading for the Southeastern Area of the US; mem adv comm IRA Resol Comm 1974-; exec sec/treasurer Savannah Hospital Authority 1975-; mem adv comm GA Hist Found 1974-80, Telfair Art Acad 1975-80, Basic Ed & Reading 1977-78; mem, exec bd NAACP 1977-83; coord/founder of the Society of Doctors Inc 1986-; founder/director, The Consortium of Doctors, Ltd, 1989. **Honors/Awds:** Outstanding Teacher of the Year 1973; featured in Essence Mag 1976; Novelet ''Ms Lily'' 1977; authored numerous articles; featured in Atlanta Constitution Journal, June 1988; Jet, Sept 28, 1992, Oct 5, 1992. **Business Addr:** Founder/Director, The Consortium of Doctors Ltd, PO Box 20402, University System, Savannah, GA 31404.

JORDAN, ANDREW
Professional football player. **Personal:** Born Jun 21, 1972, Charlotte, NC. **Educ:** West Charlotte, attended. **Career:** Minnesota Vikings, tight end, 1994-97; Tampa Bay Buccaneers, 1997-. **Business Addr:** Professional Football Player, Tampa Bay Buccaneers, One Buccaneer Place, Tampa, FL 33607, (813)870-2700.

JORDAN, ANNE KNIGHT
Civic worker. **Personal:** Born Jul 8, Tampa, FL; married Dr Carl R Jordan; children: Dr Carmen A Jordan Cox, Dr Karen T, Harold K. **Educ:** Howard Univ, AB 1949, postgrad 1955; Savannah State Coll, attended 1957; Catholic Univ, attended 1958; Univ GA, continuing educ 1967-68; Armstrong State Coll, attended 1971-72. **Career:** Soc Sec Agency Baltimore, clerical 1941-42; Dept Pub Welfare Wash, staff foster care serv 1943; Dept of Anatomy & Pharmacology Howard Univ Wash, sec 1948-49; US Civil Serv Commn Investigations Wash, clerical 1953; Savannah, tchr spl educ 1956-57; Tots & Teens Savannah Chapt, 1965; Grasshoppers Socio-Civic Club 1973; Adopt-A-Family MS Delta Poverty Area, 1970; Jr Nat Med Assn, 1970; Happy Homemaker, editor 1970. **Orgs:** Pres Woman's Aux Natl Med Assn 1969-70; chmn adv bd 1970-71; pres Woman's Aux GA State Med Assn 1961-62; basileus Sigma Gamma Rho 1961-62; life mem, executive board member, NAACP; life mem, executive board member, March of Dimes; Natl Found Savannah Chap League of Women Voters; GA Council Human Relations; ex bd Speech & Hearing; delegate Natl Counc Cath Women 1964; White House Conf Health Nutrition & Food 1969; NAACP Natl Conv NY 1959, MN 1960; dir of SE region National Association of Black Military Women, 1996-98. **Honors/Awds:** Sigma of Yr Awd Sigma Gamma Rho 1962; Intl Platform Assn 1976; Historical Preservations of Amer 1976; cert State GA, Univ GA, GA Defense Dept teach Civil Defense Courses; certified season color analyst & fitness consultant 1984. **Military Serv:** US Army, WAC. **Home Addr:** 1627 Mills B Lane Ave, Savannah, GA 31405.

JORDAN, BETTYE DAVIS
Entrepreneur. **Personal:** Born Sep 14, 1946, Tampa, FL; daughter of Ethel Davis and Lee Davis; children: Lisa Darlene Walker, Christopher Charles White II. **Educ:** Univ of Tampa, BS Medical Tech 1968. **Career:** B Davis Enterprises, owner; Harambee Enterprises, president. **Orgs:** Bd mem FL Med Tech Assoc 1979-; exec bd mem 1980-86, vice pres 1986-, NAACP Tampa; bd mem Women's Survival Ctr 1981-83; vice pres Pride of Joy Enterprises 1982-85; mem Movie Guild 1984-86; mem Tampa Urban League 1987, Civic Review Bd 1987; bd mem College Hill Dev & Comm Cv Org 1987; vice pres NAACP 1989-91. **Honors/Awds:** Life mem NAACP; Medical Technologist Awd Univ Comm Hosp 1982; Natl Assoc for Female Exec Inc 1984. **Home Addr:** 1804 E 21st Ave, Tampa, FL 33605. **Business Addr:** President, Harambee Enterprises, 3525 N 22nd St, Tampa, FL 33605.

JORDAN, BRIAN O'NEIL
Professional baseball player. **Personal:** Born Mar 29, 1967, Baltimore, MD. **Educ:** Richmond University. **Career:** Atlanta Falcons, safety, 1989-91; St Louis Cardinals, outfielder, 1992-. **Business Addr:** Professional Baseball Player, St Louis Cardinals, Busch Memorial Stadium, 250 Stadium Plaza, St Louis, MO 63102, (314)421-3060.

JORDAN, CARL RANKIN
Physician. **Personal:** Born Jul 24, 1924, Savannah, GA; married Anne; children: Carmen, Karen, Harold. **Educ:** Howard Univ Coll of Arts, BS 1946; Howard Univ Coll Med, MD 1948. **Career:** Self-employed, physician; Charity Hosp, prgm training prgm, gen pelvic surgery, 1949-51, 1953-57; Freedman's Hosp, intern 1948-49; Harvard, postgrad surg edn; Mayo Clinic; Cook Co Grad Sch & Med; Univ Vienna; Emmory Univ; Univ Cinc; Univ MD; Johns Hopkins; Med Coll GA; Univ MS Med Ctr; Med Univ SC; Charity Hosp, chf surgery 1960-64. **Orgs:** Past pres Cath Laymen's League GA 1957-59; pres Howard Univ Alumni Club 1971-; past pres S Atlantic Med Soc 1956; GA State Med Assn 1959; chmn bd 1960; ofcr Nat Med Assn; organized & established Jordan Clinic 1979; mem, bd tst 1968-75; sec Exec Com 1972-74; chmn Time & Place Com 1973-75; life mem NAACP 1959; ofcr NAACP; chmn, treas 1959-60; regional vice pres Cath Holy Name Soc 1970-71; flw Am Soc Abdominal Surgeons 1961; Intl Acad Proctology 1975; diplomate Intl Bd Proctlogy 1976; mem AMA. **Honors/Awds:** Physician Reg Award 1976-79; Cert Apprt, Nat Med Assn 1976; Master Surgeon's Cert 1958; recertified Intl Bd of Proctology 1980; hon citz, Louisville KY 1974. **Military Serv:** AUS MC capt 1951-53.

JORDAN, CAROLYN D.
Investment banker, lawyer. **Personal:** Born Mar 7, 1941, Fort Worth, TX. **Educ:** Fisk U, BA 1963; Howard U, JD 1966. **Career:** Pryor, McClendon, Counts & Co Inc, Investment Bankers, senior vice president, 1992-; US Senate, Banking, Housing and Urban Affairs Committee, counsel, 1974-92; Herman A English, atty 1971-72; Compton CA, dep city atty 1970-71; Economic & Youth Opportunities Agency Los Angeles, prog mgmt splst 1969-70; VA Regional Ofc Los Angeles, veterans claims adjudicator 1968-69; Library of Congress, copyright examiner 1966-68. **Orgs:** Mem Links Inc, State Bar of CA; Los Angeles Co Bar Assn; Nat Bar Assn; Bar of the Dist of Columbia; Kappa Beta Pi Intl Legal Sorority; Intl Law Soc; Delta Sigma Theta Sorority; member, DC Board of Labor Relations, 1975-78. **Honors/Awds:** Award for Contributions to Small Business, National Assn of Black Manufacturers; Award for Community Service, Delta Sigma Theta Sorority; Award for Contributions to the Field of Law, National Bar Assn. **Business Addr:** Senior Vice President, Pryor, McClendon, Counts & Co Inc, 1350 I St NW, #530, Washington, DC 20005.

JORDAN, CAROLYNE LAMAR
Educational administrator, psychologist. **Personal:** Born in Augusta, GA; daughter of Serena James and Peter Lamar; married Lawrence M Jordan; children: Lara Gayle, Samuel Lamar. **Educ:** Fisk Univ, BA 1960; New England Univ, MMus 1970; Harvard Univ, EEd 1977. **Career:** Hamilton Central School, dir

of music 1962-67; Lexington Public Schools, supervisor of music 1967-70; Salem St Coll, prof of psychology & music 1971-83;Suffolk Univ, asst to the president 1983-88; LeMoyne-Owen College, vice-president academic affairs, 1988-90; Harvard University, visiting scholar, 1990-91; Assoc Dean for Grad Studies, Maryville Univ, 1992-93; Federal Express Corp, corporate trainer, 1993-; Human and Educational Resource Services, president, currently. **Orgs:** Board mem Friends Nat'l Center of Afro-American 1971-73; mem American Psychological Assoc 1977-; trustee Cambridge Friends School 1980-84; exec bd Natl Amer Friends Serv Comm 1983-; chairperson long range plng comm Suffolk Univ; renway consortium Retention Comm; pres Human Resources Cons; past pres Alpha Kappa Alpha Sorority; exec bd mem ACE/NIP 1985; exec bd Freedom House 1985; former bd mem Memphis Urban League; bd mem Family Service of Memphis; bd mem Memphis Symphony Orchestra; bd mem, Porter Leath Childrens Ctr, Memphis; bd mem, YWCA. **Honors/Awds:** Ford Found Grant Harvard Univ 1975-77; Radcliffe Grant to Grad Women 1975; Disting Serv Awd Salem St Coll 1980; Natl Endowment for the Humanities Harvard 1982; Outstanding Young Men of Jaycees 1982; Humanities Post Doct Grant Harvard Univ; Amer Council on Ed Forum Participant; presidential Fellow Smith Coll 1986-87; American Council on Ed; Leadership Memphis, 1990-91.

JORDAN, CASPER LEROY
Library consultant (retired). **Personal:** Born Mar 5, 1924, Cleveland, OH; son of Leola Lloyd Jordan and John Jordan. **Educ:** Case-Western Reserve Univ, AB 1947; Atlanta Univ, MS in LS 1951. **Career:** Wilberforce Univ, chief librarian 1951-61; Nioga Library Syst, asst dir 1961-68; Atlanta Univ, prof library serv 1968-79, univ librarian 1974-79; Atlanta-Fulton Pub Libr, acting dir 1986-87, deputy dir 1979-89; adjunct prof, Atlanta Univ 1979-89; consultant, DeKalb Public Library System 1990-91. **Orgs:** Active mem various professional organizations in OH, NY, GA; editor ''Free Lance'' 1950-80; contributor to professional journals; mem NAACP (br pres 1967-68, reg officer 1966-68); officer CORE 1963-66; Beta Phi Mu Hon Libr Sci Frat; book editor AME Church Review 1984-; African-Amer Family History Assoc 1976. **Honors/Awds:** Alumni Resident Lecturer Atlanta Univ Library School 1987; Outstanding Black Librarian, Black Caucus of Amer Library Assoc, 198l; Author of ''Bibliographical Guide to African American women Writers'' Greenwod Press 1991; ''The African Methodist and the African American Experience,'' AME Publishing House, 1991; co-author, Famous First Blacks, 1993; Co Editor, Notable Black American Women, II, 1995. **Home Addr:** 2041 Fairburn Rd, SW, Atlanta, GA 30331-4812.

JORDAN, CHARLES
Professional football player. **Personal:** Born Oct 9, 1969, Los Angeles, CA; married Kymberly; children: Lauren, Charles III. **Educ:** Long Beach City College. **Career:** Green Bay Packers, wide receiver, 1994-95; Miami Dolphins, 1996-. **Business Addr:** Professional Football Player, Miami Dolphins, 2269 NW 199th St, Miami, FL 33056, (305)620-5000.

JORDAN, CHARLES WESLEY
Clergyman. **Personal:** Born May 28, 1933, Dayton, OH; son of Naomi Azelia Harper and David Morris Jordan; married Margaret Crawford, Aug 2, 1959; children: Diana, Susan. **Educ:** Roosevelt Univ, BA 1956; Garrett-Evangelical Theological Seminary, MDiv 1960. **Career:** Woodlawn United Methodist Church, pastor 1960-66; Rockford IL Urban Ministries, dir 1966-71; Northern IL Conference Council, program staff 1971-82; Chicago Southern Dist, supt 1982-87; St Mark United Methodist Church; Chicago, IL; senior pastor l987-. **Orgs:** Chairperson UM Natl Strategy on New Church Develop 1980-84; bd of trustees Garrett-Evangelical Theol Seminary 1982-; life mem Kappa Alpha Psi Frat; dir, United Methodist General Council on Ministries, l980-88; Delegate, United Methodist General Conf l976, l980, l984, l988; religious affairs chair Chicago NAACP 1990-; bd mem Community Mental Health Council 1989-. **Honors/Awds:** Achievement Awd in Religion from the Chicago Alumni of Kappa Alpha Psi Frat 1986; Hall of Fame, Wendell Phillips High School l989. **Military Serv:** AUS pfc 1953-55. **Business Addr:** Sr Pastor, St Mark United Methodist Church, 8441 St Lawrence Ave, Chicago, IL 60619.

JORDAN, CLAUDIA J.
Judge. **Career:** Denver County Court, judge, currently. **Orgs:** Colorado Bar Assn; Sam Carey Bar Assn. **Honors/Awds:** Black Hall of Fame, Colorado. **Business Addr:** Judge, Denver County Court, 1437 Bannock St, City-County Bldg, Denver, CO 80202, (303)640-2054.

JORDAN, DARIN GODFREY
Professional football player. **Personal:** Born Dec 4, 1964, Boston, MA; married Andrea Hayes. **Educ:** Northeastern University, BA, speech communication, 1988. **Career:** Pittsburgh Steelers, 1988; free agent, Los Angeles Raiders, 1989-91; San Francisco 49ers, line backer, 1991-. **Business Phone:** (408)562-4949.

JORDAN, DAVID LEE
Educator. **Personal:** Born Apr 3, 1933, Greenwood, MS; son of Cleveland Jordan and Elizabeth Jordan; married Christine Bell; children: David Jr, Joyce Jordan Dugar, Donald, Darryl. **Educ:** MS Valley State U, BS 1959; Univ of WY, MS 1969. **Career:** Greenwood Voters League, pres 1965-; The Greenwood Pub Sch System, sci tchr 1970-; president, Greenwood City Council, 1985. **Orgs:** Mem Leflore Co Br of the NAACP 1960-; mem Leflore Co & Democratic Exec Com 1976-; mem Nat Democratic Platform Civil Rights Adv Com 1978; chmn MS ValleyState Univ Nat Alumni Assn Legislative Commn 1980; assisted blacks in getting elected to pub Office in Leflore Co govt 1970-; demanded that blacks be appointed to bds & commns 1970-. **Honors/Awds:** Gov Merit Award, Gov Office 1974; JH White Meml Award, MVSU Nat Slumni Assn 1977; Comm Serv Award, Omega Psi Phi Frat 1977-79; invited White House meet Pres Carter, White House Staff 1978-79; sued the city of Greenwood to change its government resulting in blacks being elected to the city council; sued the state of Mississippi to change the second congressional district resulting in a Black being elected to the US Congress. **Military Serv:** AUSR pfc 1960-62. **Business Addr:** City Hall, 106 E Scott St, Greenwood, MS 38930.

JORDAN, EDDIE
Professional basketball coach. **Educ:** Rutgers. **Career:** Sacramento Kings, head coach, 1996-. **Business Addr:** Head Coach, Sacramento Kings, One Sport Pkwy, Sacramento, CA 95834, (916)928-6900.

JORDAN, EDDIE J., JR.
Government official. **Personal:** Born Oct 6, 1952, Fort Campbell, KY; son of Eddie J Jordan Sr & Gladys McDaniel Jordan (deceased); married Charmaine E Age-Jordan, Jul 1974; children: Aisha Zakiya, Chad-Hassan Akil, Julian Khalid. **Educ:** Wesleyan Univ, Middletown, CT, BA, 1970-74; Rutgers Law School, Newark, NJ, JD, 1974-77. **Career:** Pepper, Hamilton & Scheetz, assoc; Southern Univ Law School, professor, 1981; US Attorney's Office, assist US attorney, 1984-87; Sessions & Fishman, assoc, 1987-90, partner, 1990-92; Bryan, Jupiter & Lewis, of counsel, 1992-94; US Dept of Justice, US attorney, 1994-. **Orgs:** Human Relations Commission, City of N Orleans, advisory comm human relations, 1993; LA State Bar Assn, bd of governors, 1984; Metropolitan Area Comm, bd of dirs, 1990-94; Planned Parenthood of LA, bd of dirs, 1989-94, vice pres, bd of dirs, 1991-93; St Thomas/Irish Channel Consortium, bd of dirs, 1990-94; NAACP, 1993-95. **Honors/Awds:** Louis A Martinet Legal Society, A P Tureaud Award, 1992. **Special Achievements:** In Search of the Meaning of RICO, LA State Bar Assn; Changing Carnival's old ways is a progressive step, The Times Picayune; Recent Dev in the Law Manual, LA State Bar Assn, 1985-96; Louisiana Appellate Practice Handbook, Lawyers Cooperative Publishing, contributing author. **Business Addr:** US Attorney, US Attorney's Office, Eastern District of Louisiana, 501 Magazine St, Hale Boggs Federal Bldg, Rm 210, New Orleans, LA 70130, (504)589-4321.

JORDAN, EDDIE JACK, SR.
Artist, educator. **Personal:** Born Jul 29, 1927, Wichita Falls, TX; son of Mr & Mrs. Oscar Williams (deseased); married Gladys McDaniel (died 1992); children: Eddie Jack, Jr, Gregory Keith, La Kara Jovarn. **Educ:** Langston Univ, BA 1948; IA Univ, MA 1949; State Univ of IA, MFA 1956; IN Univ, MS 1973, DEd 1975. **Career:** Claflin Univ, chmn dept of art 1950-Army; Allen Univ, chmn dept of art 1954-56; Langston Univ, chmn dept of art 1956-61; Southern Univ at NO, chmn dept of art 1961-. **Orgs:** Natl co chmn Comm for Devel of Art in Negro Colls 1962-; pres, adm bd Bethany United Ch 1968-80; mem comm Phi Delta Kappa Inc 1980-81; pres bd of dirs Natl Conf of Artists 1983-; sec treas New Orleans Ctr of Creative Arts 1983-; life mem NAACP; life mem Alpha Phi Frat Inc; life mem, National Conference of Artists. **Honors/Awds:** Rec'd 41 awds in local regional & natl competition; Sculpture Awd Rhode Island Natl, Philbrook Museum in OK, Walker ARt Ctr MN, Gibbs Art Museum SC, Carnegie Inst Pgh; 2 sculptures as a first of Blacks purchased for IN Museum 1974; Delta Phi Delta Natl Hon Art Frat; Dissertation ''Past Present and Future of NCA'' 1973; foreign exhibition Africa Germany Russia Caribbean, Africa 1973-77. **Military Serv:** AUS corpl S-3 draftsman 1951-52; Inf Btn; Formal Btn Salute & Citation. **Home Addr:** 5545 Congress Dr, New Orleans, LA 70126. **Business Addr:** Professor, Southern Univ of New Orleans, Art Dept, 6400 Press Dr, New Orleans, LA 70126.

JORDAN, EMMA COLEMAN
Educator, attorney. **Personal:** Born Nov 29, 1946, Berkeley, CA; daughter of Myrtle Coleman and Earl Coleman (deceased); children: Kristen Elena, Allison Elizabeth. **Educ:** CA State U, BA 1969; Howard U, JD 1973. **Career:** Stanford Law School, tching fellow 1973-74; Univ of Santa Clara, asst prof 1974-75; Georgetown Univ Law Center, prof; Univ of CA Sch of Law, acting prof 1975-80, prof 1980-. **Orgs:** Mem Nat Conf of Black Lawyers; Nat Bar Assn; Am Soc of Intl Law; pub mem CA State Bd of Dental & Exmnrs; Am Assn of Law Schs Sects on Commercial Law & Contracts, Minority Grps; mem Charles Houston Bar Assn; bd of dir CA Assn of Black Lawyers; pres Soc of Amer Law Teachers 1986-88; chr CA St Bar Financial Inst Comm; chr AALS Financial Inst & Consumer Fin Serv Sect; bd mem Consumer Action; adv comm Natl Consumer Union Northern CA; mem Amer Law Inst; executive committee, 1988-91, president-elect, 1991-92, president, 1992-93; Assoc of Amer Law Schools; special asst, Attorney General of the US, 1981. **Honors/Awds:** Co-editor with Anita F Hue, Race, Gender and Power in America, Oxford University Press, 1995; Publs litigation without representation; The Need for Intervention to Affirm Affirmative Action, Harvard Civil Liberties Civil Rights Law Rev 1979, ''After the Merger of Contribution & Indemnity, What are the Limits of Comparative Loss Allocation'' AR St Law Rev 1980; ''Problems & Prospects of Participation in Affirmative Action Litigation'' UC Davis Law Rev 1980; Limitations of the Intl Lega Mech Namibia 1972; Outstdng Acad Achvmt Award Phi Alpha Delta 1973; grad 1st in class Howard Law Sch 1973; articles: ''Ending the Floating Check Game,'' Hastings Law Review, 1986; ''Taking Voting Rights Seriously,'' Nebraska Law Review, 1986. **Business Addr:** Professor, School of Law, Georgetown University, 600 New Jersey Ave, Washington, DC 20001-2075.

JORDAN, FREDERICK E.
Civil engineer. **Personal:** Born Apr 27, 1937, Loveville, MD; son of Mr & Mrs Lewis E Jordan. **Educ:** Howard U, BSCE; Stanford Univ, MSCE. **Career:** FE Jordan Assoc, Inc, president, currently; Nat Counc of Minority Consul Engn, pres 1976-77; Bonelli, Young , Wong & Biggs, San & Fran, div civ-struct engr; Bechtel Corp San Fran & Charles T Main Consult Engrs, Boston, struct engr; Riverside Dept Pub Works Riverside CA, civ engr; LA Air Def Command, dir civ engr; Sandrestrom Air Force Base Greenland, asst chf engr pvt pract, 1968; West Assn Minority Consult Engr, pres 1974; Am Soc Civ Engr SF Sect, sec dir 1974-. **Orgs:** Mem Nat Soc Prof Engr; consult Engrs Assn US; Struct Engrs Assn CA; Soc Am Mil Engrs; fnd mem,past pres, chmn bd dir Engr Soc Com Manpower Training Inc; fnd mem 1st chmn No CA Counc Black Prof Engrs; past vice pres San Fran Forum Am Soc Civ Engrs; mem engr adv & bd CA State Univ San Fran; past mem San Fran Engr Counc; pres bd dir Bay Area Urban League Inc 1972-73; pres, San Francisco Black Chamber of Commerce, 1989-94; pres, CA Assn of Better Govt, 1990-91; councilman, San Francisco Private Industry Council; councilman California, Department of Transportation Business Council; Commissioner, San Francisco Parking and Traffic Commission; commissioner, California State Commission on the Status of the African-American Male, commissioner. **Honors/Awds:** Bay Area & State of CA outstanding civ engr in comm activity Am Soc Civ Eng 1967-68; distinguished alumni award Bay Area Howard Univ Alumni Club 1972; Distinguished Black in Sci & Engineering in US Oakland Mus Assn 1973; several Publs, 20 other awards; Governor's Award, Best Small Business Contractor in State of CA, 1993; Minority Service Firm, Five Western States, 1993; One of Ten Outstanding Businesses in the US, 1993. **Military Serv:** US Air Force, 1st Lt. **Business Addr:** President, FE Jordan Associates, Inc, 90 New Montgomery, Suite 610, San Francisco, CA 94105.

JORDAN, GEORGE E. **See JENKINS, GEORGE E., III.**

JORDAN, GEORGE LEE, JR.
Dentist. **Personal:** Born Nov 2, 1935, Norfolk Co, VA; married Marguerite W; children: George III, Bernard. **Educ:** Cen St U, BS 1957; Fisk U, MA 1963; Meharry Med Coll, DDS 1971. **Career:** Michigan State Univ, asst prof 1972-76; Meharry Med Coll, instr 1971-72; Phoenix, sci tchr 1964-67; WA DC, tchr 1963-64; Protsmouth VA, tchr 1958-62; Pontiac Sch Dist, consult 1974-77; Olin Health Ctr, dir 1975-76; Lakeside Health Ctr, dir 1972-75; Virginia Clinic, PC, dental director, 1977-1986; private practice, dentist, 1986-. **Orgs:** NAACP; Pontiac Area Urban League. **Honors/Awds:** Citation, Pontiac Schs 1977; outst citizen, Omega Psi Phi 1967; outst tchr Jaycees WA DC 1962. **Military Serv:** US Army, reserves, 2nd lt, 1957-58. **Business Addr:** CEO, George L Jordan Jr, DDS, LTD, 860 Greenbrier Cir, Ste 503, Chesapeake, VA 23320.

JORDAN, GEORGE WASHINGTON, JR.
Engineering executive. **Personal:** Born Mar 11, 1938, Chattanooga, TN; son of Omega Davis Jordan and George W Jordan Sr .; married Fredine Sims; children: George Washington III. **Educ:** Tuskegee Univ, BSEE 1961; GA Inst of Tech, MSIM 1978; Emory Univ, management inst 1976. **Career:** Boeing Co, engr 1961-65; Gen Elec Co, engr 1965-66; Lockheed-Georgia Co, engr/mgr 1966-. **Orgs:** United Way (VIP); Chmn/mem Atlanta Zoning Bd 1978-84; mem Natl Mgmt Assn 1966-; mem Merit Employees Assn 1975-; mem Assn of MBA Execs 1978-; mem Inst of Management Science 1978-; sr mem Amer Inst of Aero/Astro 1973-; life mem Alpha Phi Alpha Frat 1957-; mem NAACP 1985-; bd of deacons, council on Christian ed, youth leadership council, Sunday school teacher, royal ambassador counselor, fin comm, asst treas, chmn march bd, business manager, Christian Fellowship Baptist Church; member, American Management Associates, 1991; member, Smithsonian National Associates, 1991; bd of trustees, Shorter College. **Honors/Awds:** Natl Mem of Flt Sim Tech Comm AIAA 1984-; Dollars & Sense, Outstanding Business and Professional Award, 1991. **Home Addr:** 3609 Rolling Green Ridge SW, Atlanta, GA 30331. **Business Addr:** Engineering Dept Manager, Lockheed-Georgia Co, 86 So Cobb Dr SE, Marietta, GA 30063.

JORDAN, HAROLD WILLOUGHBY
Physician. **Personal:** Born May 24, 1937, Newnan, GA; son of Dorothy W. Jordan and Edward P. Jordan (deceased); married Geraldine Crawford; children: Harold II, Vincent, Karen, Kristie. **Educ:** Morehouse College, BS, 1958; Meharry Medical College, MD, 1962; G W Hubbard Hospital, rotating internship, 1963, medical residency, 1964; Vanderbilt University Hospital, psychiatric residency, 1967. **Career:** Meharry Medical College, Department of Psychiatry clinical instructor, 1965-67, instructor, acting director of outpatient department, 1967-68, assistant professor, director of psychiatric outpatient clinic, 1968-71, professor, chairman of dept of psychiatry, 1979-97; Vanderbilt Univerissity Hospital, courtesy staff member, 1967-, clinical instructor, 1968-72, clinical assistant professor, 1972-; Florence Crittendon Home, psychiatric consultant, 1967; State Divisional Vocational Rehabilitation, Intensive Treatment Center, psychiatric consultant, 1967-71; Fisk University Student Counseling Center, psychiatric consultant, 1969-71; Tennessee Department of Mental Health/Mental Retardation, assistant commissioner,1971-75, commissioner, 1975-79; Tennessee State University, psychiatricnsultant, 1984—; Cumberland Hall Hospital, attending physician, 1985—. **Orgs:** Member, NAACP, 1957, American Psychiatry Association, 1967, American Association of University Professors, 1967, R F Boyd Medical Society, 1968, National Medical Association, 1970, Black Psychiatrists of America, 1973, Tennessee Medical Associationn, 1975, Nashville Academy of Medicine, 1975, American Association of Chairmen of Psychiatry 1979, Alpha Omega Alpha Honorary Medical Society, 1980, Sigma Pi Phi. **Honors/Awds:** Certificate of Recognition, Nashville Chapter, Association of Black Psychologists, 1976; certificate of appreciation, Joseph P Kennedy Jr Foundation, 1976; certificate of recognition, Metro Atlanta Chapter of National Association of Human Rights Workers, 1976; awarded plaque, National Association of Black & Social Workers, 1977; plaque, Harriet Cohn Mental Health Center, 1979; plaque, Meharry Medical College Class of 1980; President's Award, Meharry Medical College, 1987. **Special Achievements:** Harold W Jordan Habilitation Center, dedicated in Nashville TN, 1987. **Military Serv:** US Army Reserve, captain, 1963-69; Tennessee Army National Guard, lieutenant colonel, 1974-81. **Business Addr:** Professor of Psychiatry, Meharry Medical College, 1005 D B Todd Blvd, Nashville, TN 37208.

JORDAN, J. PAUL
Business executive. **Personal:** Born in Duquesne, PA; son of William & Rebecca Jordan; divorced. **Educ:** University of Michigan, attended; University of Detroit, BS. **Career:** Jordan & Associates, CEO; Meadow Village Partnership, CEO; Ujama Development Co, CEO; Minority Chamber of Commerce, CEO. **Orgs:** Federal Reserve Bank, advisory bd; Federal Home Loan Bank, advisory bd; Greater Milwaukee Convention & Visitors Bureau, multicultural committee; National Black Chamber of Commerce; American Defense Preparedness Association, district dir; US Small Business Association, advisory bd. **Business Addr:** President, Milwaukee Minority Chamber of Commerce, 509 W Wisconsin Ave, Ste 606, Milwaukee, WI 53203, (414)226-4105.

JORDAN, J. ST. GIRARD
Attorney. **Personal:** Born Feb 29, 1944, Philadelphia, PA; son of Emma Jane and Henderson Jordan; married L Elaine Bullock; children: Daniel, Mark, Chonda, Kijsa. **Educ:** Temple Univ, ABS 1969, BS 1970; Univ of PA Law Sch, JD 1973. **Career:** SmithKline Corp, finan analyst 1967-69, sr mkt rsch analyst 1960-70; Black Book TV Prod, vice pres treas 1969-72; Norden Labs Lincoln & VPO Inc Omaha, corp officer; Goodis Greenfield Henry Shaiman & Levin, assoc 1973-74; SmithKline Corp, group general counsel 1974-, asst general counsel, asst secretary, 1986, asst sec 1987; gen counsel, director & sec Consumer Products Inc 1987; WKW Inc, counsel, 1990; consulting activities before Expert Committee on Drug Dependence, Geneva Switzerland; United Nations Council on Narcotic Drugs, Vienna Austria, 1989-92; Menley James Inc, counsel, currently. **Orgs:** Pres Barristers Assn of Philadelphia Inc 1976-77; Natl, Amer, PA, Phila, NJ,& Camden Co Bar Assns; legal com United Negro College Fund Dr 1977; vice chmn AHI Law Com Washington DC; pres Philadelphia Fed of Black Bus & Professional Orgs; NAACP; Mt Zion Baptist Church; United Fund/Way; Neighborhood Servs Comm adv bd Christian St YWCA; bd of dirs United Comm United Way Agency 1982-84; chmn AHI Law Comm 1982; exec comm Barristes Assn of Philadelphia 1986-87; Govt Affairs Comm Proprietry Assn; board, Camden County Girl Scouts, NJ 1991-92; Federal Judiciary Mediation Board, 1992-; Municipal Tax Bureau, official counsel, 1995-. **Honors/Awds:** Outstanding Student Award Temple Univ 1968; Tribune Outstanding Citizen Centennel Awd 1984. **Military Serv:** US Air Force, A/1C, 1962. **Business Addr:** Counsel, Menley James, Inc, Commonwealth Corporate Center, 100 Tournament Dr, Horsham, PA 19044.

JORDAN, JACQUELYN D.
Nurse, educator. **Personal:** Born Mar 3, 1948, Waterbury, CT; divorced; children: Ayanna Jordan, Derek Jordan. **Educ:** Adelphi Univ, PhD, nursing, 1995. **Career:** Mount Sinai Hospital, clinical nurse specialist, 1982-86; University of Connecticut, asst professor of nursing, 1985-86; Bristol Hospital, patient care mgr, 1986-88; Bridgeport Hospital, head nurse, neuro intensive care unit, 1988-1989; Western Connecticut State University, associate professor of nursing, currently. **Orgs:** Association Black Nursing Faculty in Higher Education, 1990-; Sigma Theta Tau, 1982-; National Black Nurses Assn, 1991; National Political Congress of Black Women, 1989; bd of dir, NH Political Congress of Black Women, 1997. **Honors/Awds:** US Air Force, Nurse Educator Award, 1991, 1992; Negro Business & Professional Women's Clubs, Professional Trailblazer's Award, 1984; Yale Univ Chapter, Sigma Theta Tau, Dissertation Award, 1994; Assn of Black Nursing Faculty, Dissertation Award, 1994. **Special Achievements:** Certified clinical nurse specialist, medical & surgical, 1991. **Military Serv:** US Army, Sp5, 1966-69. **Home Addr:** 71 Traverse St, Waterbury, CT 06704, (203)573-1679. **Business Phone:** (203)837-8560.

JORDAN, JOHN EDWARD
Dentist, business executive. **Personal:** Born Nov 17, 1930, Nashville, TN; son of Mary Richardson Jordan and John E Jordan; divorced; children: John E III. **Educ:** Lincoln University, PA, BA, 1952; Meharry Medical College, Dental School, DDS, 1957; Fisk University; Wayne State University; Lincoln University; post grad courses, University of Tennessee Dental School; University of Arkansas; Meharry Medical College School of Dentistry. **Career:** Jordan Copy Svc, owner, 1960-87; Shirts Unlimited Clothing Store, partner, 1972-79; dentist in private practice, 1958-. **Orgs:** VP, board of directors, Northeast Mental Health Ctr 1978-85; Middle Baptist Ch, laymen, president, 1985-95, trustee, 1983-89, superintendent, 1990-95, santuary choir, pres, 1992-95 trustee bd, vp, 1992-95, men's choir, 1980-1995; Memphis City Baptist Laymen, corresponding secretary, 1990-93, fin secretary, 1986-87; chmn dental health Shelby Co Dental Soc Pen TN Dental Assn 1965-89; participant dentist Memphis Health Fair 1984-89; chmn Memphis Shelby Co Headstart Policy Council 1985-87; chmn, contact rep Memphis Br Afro-American Historical Assn 1980-89; pres Hyde Park Hollywood Comm Develop Block Club 1992; bd of dir PMA; chmn Headstart Policy Council 1986-87; chmn Dental Health Month for Shelby City Dental Soc NDA; bd of dirs, President Hooks Dimick Day Care, 1989; Memphis Neighborhood Watch, 1990; Evergreen Optimist Club, vp, 1991-93; Hyde Park Neighborhood Coalition, pres, 1993-95; Lewis Ctr Senior Citizens, 1993-95; Austin St Neighborhood Watch, 1992-95; KAppa Alpha Psi, Germantown Alumni Chapter, 1992-95. **Honors/Awds:** Certificate of Achievement Middle Baptist Church 1984; Dental Health Week Achiev Awd ADA Shelby Co Dental Soc Pan TN Dental Assn 1983-84; Certificate Northeast Mental Health Ctr Bd Dirs 1984; Plaques from Shelby Cty Dental Soc for dedication to Dentistry for 28 yrs, North Memphis Tennis Club-Thanks 1986, NE CMTY Mental Health Cntr in appreciation for Outstanding Contributions 1978-85; Meharry Medical College Presidents Awd 1957-82; certificates from Douglass Optimist Club charter mem, Natl Childrens Dental Health Month 1985-87, Middle Baptist Church in appreciation 1984, Gov Lamar Alexander appreciation for helping senior citizens; Positive Mental Attitude Association Dr Martin Luther King Awd 1985; honorary mem Hyde Park Alumni Assoc 1983; Proclamation Stof TN Rep Larry Turner Pridedamp 1985; Plaque, Northeast Community Health Center, 1985; Outstanding Service Plaque, PMAA Board of Directors, 1991; US House of Representatives Proclamation, Congressman Harold Ford, 1982; Evergreen Optimist Club, Plaque and Certificates. **Business Addr:** Dentist, 2154 Chelsea Ave, Memphis, TN 38108.

JORDAN, JOHN WESLEY
Clergyman. **Personal:** Born Sep 10, 1941, Edenton, NC; son of Annie Louise Jordan Holley and Earl Holley; divorced; children: Johann Earle, Christian W.A. **Educ:** Elizabeth City State Univ, BS English 1963; Teachers Coll Columbia Univ, MA English 1964; A Phillip Randolph Inst, 2 courses 1973; Columbia Univ, advance study 1974; NC State Univ, 1 course 1976. **Career:** Savannah State Coll, instr in humanities 1964-66; Eliz City State Coll, instr in humanities 1965; Claflin College SC, instr in humanities 1966; Hampton Univ, instr in humanities 1966-67; New York City Bd of Education, English teacher 1967-74; HQ USAG Ft Bragg, NC, personnel actions spec 1975-77; Camp Casey, Korea, awards and decorations spec 1977-78; Ft Bragg, NC, ID card sgt NCOIC 1978-81; Ft Shafter, HI, NCOIC of personnel actions 1982-84; Fort Drum NY, personnel actions sgt 1984-86; personnel admin ctr supervisor HHC 1st Bn 7th FA 1986-88, supervisor Transition Center 1989-91; Watertown Correctional Facility, Watertown, NY, English teacher 1988; Watertown Urban Mission, Watertown, NY, director Operation Breakthrough 1988-89; Faith Fellowship Christian School, volunteer English teacher,1990-91; City of Refuge Christian Church, Great Bend, NY, pastor, 1988-. **Orgs:** Editor, Refuge Flame City of Refuge Christian Church of HI 1982-84; volunteer minister Watertown Correctional Facility Watertown, NY 1984-, Cape Vincent Correctional Facility 1988-; Gouverneur Correctional Facility, 1991-92; mem religious advisory bd Watertown Correctional Facility 1988-; volunteer lay religious leader Ft Drum Prayer/Bible Study/ Fellowship 1984-88; 1st vice pres 1985, pres 1986 Full Gospel Business Men's Fellowship Intl (Ft Drum/Charthage Chpt); mem Watertown/Jefferson County NAACP 1988-; chmn worship comm Ft Drum Gospel Svcs; speaker for FGBMFI; bd mem New Gate Prison Ministry; Faith Fellowship Christian School, bd of educ, 1990-95. 1990-. **Honors/Awds:** Bearer of Mace/Top Grad Class of 1963 Eliz City State Univ 1963; American Spirit Honor Award (Aug 1975) Ft Jackson, SC; Omega Psi Phi Fraternity Undergrad Scholarship 1962; Grad Scholarship 1963; academic graduate of Advance Non-Commissioned Officer Course class 1985-86 Administration Ft Ben Harrison IN; first Annual Freedom Fund Award, Watertown/Jefferson County NAACP, 1989; DaySpring Cards, USA Pastor of the Year, 1998. **Military Serv:** AUS, sgt 1st class, 1975-88; Army Commendation Medal (1st Oak Leaf Cluster); Army Achievement Medals; Certificates of Appreciation; Meritorious Service Medal, 1988. **Home Addr:** 32020 Wilton Rd, Carthage, NY 13619, (315)775-4953. **Business Phone:** (315)493-4329.

JORDAN, JOSEPHINE E. C.
Transportation agent. **Personal:** Born Dec 13, 1935, Philadelphia, PA; daughter of Josephine Connor and Clarence Connor; married Rev Harry A Jordan Sr (deceased). **Educ:** Allied Corporation, Business Certificate 1971. **Career:** Amtrak, reservation/information agent, currently. **Orgs:** Daughter of Isis 1983-, Heroines of Jericho 1983-; Past Worthy Matron, Hadassah Chap #91 OES 1985-87; mem Court of Cyrenes 1987-; Order of Golden Circle; Past Royal Perfect Matron of Faith and Fidelity, Ladies Circle of Perfection; Past District Deputy, Past District Lecturer, 4th OES Destrict. **Home Addr:** 2202 Airacobra St, Levittown, PA 19057.

JORDAN, JUNE M.
Educator, author. **Personal:** Born Jul 9, 1936, Harlem, NY; daughter of Mildred Maude Fisher Jordan and Granville Ivanhoe Jordan; divorced; children: Christopher D Meyer. **Educ:** Barnard Coll, attended 1953-57; Univ Chicago, attended 1955-56. **Career:** CCNY, asst prof 1968; Sarah Lawrence Coll, writing faculty 1968-71; Yale Univ, visiting lectr 1974-75; Loft Mentor Series Minneapolis, vstg mentor poet 1983; SUNY at Stony Brook, assoc prof of English 1978-82, dir The Poetry Ctr 1986-, dir the creative writing prog 1986-89; prof of english 1982-89; Univ of California, Berkeley, prof of Afro-American Studies and Women's Studies 1989-. **Orgs:** Bd dirs Poets & Writers 1979-87; exec bd PEN Amer Ctr 1980-84; exec bd Amer Writers Congress 1981-83; judge Lamont Prize Acad of Amer Poets 1981, 1982, 1983; judge The Massachusetts Cncl on the Arts Awds in Poetry 1984; bd dirs Center for Constitutional Rights 1984-97; mem Authors Guild Council 1986-91; bd of governors The NY Foundation of the Arts 1986-92; bd of dir The Nicaraguan Culture Alliance 1986-. **Honors/Awds:** Rockefeller Grant in Creative Writing 1969; Prix de Rome in Environmental Design 1970; CAPS Grant in Poetry 1978; NEA Fellowship in Poetry 1982; Fellowship Awd in Poetry NY Foundation for the Arts 1985; Massachusetts Cncl on the Arts Awd in Contemporary Arts 1985; 24 books published to date; poetry readings; keynote lectures, playwright, political columnist for The Progressive Magazine; lyricist & librettist for The New American Opera, I Was Looking At The Ceiling, and Then I Saw the Sky, music by John Adams; Lifetime Achievement Award, 14th Annual Celebration of Black Writing, 1998. **Special Achievements:** Postage Stamps for World Literacy: postal tribute to most influential African American writers & authors of the 20th century, June Jordan: Uganda ''Great Writers of the 20th Century'', 1997. **Business Addr:** Poet & Professor of African-American Studies, University of California-Berkeley, 660 Barrows Hall, #2572, Berkeley, CA 94720.

JORDAN, KENNETH ULYS
Educator. **Personal:** Born Apr 10, 1944, South Pittsburg, TN; divorced; children: Kenneth II, Michael. **Educ:** Univ of TN, BS 1966; Vanderbilt Law Sch, JD 1974. **Career:** corporate personnel specialist, General Foods Corp.; associate director, Fair Employment Practices, assistant dean of administration, Vanderbilt Law School; director, Vanderbilt University Opportunity Dev Ctr; Meharry Medical College, vice pres of administration and general counsel; US Dept of Justice; chief of staff, Justice Management Div; executive assistant, Governor of Tennessee; assistant adjutant general, Air, Military Dept of Tennessee; managing director, National Transportation Safety Board; executive director, National Committee for Employer Support of the Guard and Reserve. **Orgs:** board of directors, Family & Childrens Svcs; board of directors, Nashville Urban League; board of directors, University Club of Nashville; board of directors, United Way of Middle Tennessee; board of directors, Tennessee State Museum Foundation; vice president, Association of Black Faculty & Administrator at Vanderbilt; president, Vanderbilt University Credit Union; president, Association of Vanderbilt Black Alumni; president, Napier-Looby Bar Association; fellow, Nashville Bar Foundation; membership, Tuskegee Airmen, Inc, East Coast Chapter. **Honors/Awds:** US Law Week Award, Vanderbilt Univ Law Sch 1974. **Military Serv:** USAF capt 1966-70; retired Brigadier General, Tennessee Air National Guard. **Business Addr:** 1555 Wilson Boulevard, Ste 200, Arlington, VA 22209-2405.

JORDAN, LEROY A.
Administrator. **Personal:** Born Dec 27, 1941, Murphysboro, IL; married Johnetta Williams; children: Laura, Loralean, Jennifer. **Educ:** So IL Univ, BS Elem Educ 1964; Sangamon State Univ, MA Educ Admin 1972. **Career:** Hopkins Park Pembroke Township Sch, teacher 1964-65; Sch Dist 186 Springfield IL, tchr adult educ/prin 1965-69; State Bd of Educ Div of Vocation-

al Tech Educ, consult rsch & devel 1969-72; Sangamon State Univ, asst dir applied studies 1972-75, dir applied studies & experimental learning 1975-81, dean innovative & experimental studies 1982-85. **Orgs:** Mem IL Assn of Sch Bd 1976-; educ adv com Springfield Jr League 1978-80; corp bd of dir Meml Hosp Springfield Jr League 1978-80; corp bd of dir Meml Hosp Springfield IL 1979-84; pres bd of educ Springfield IL 1976-77, 1980-81; mem Natl Sch Bd Assn 1976-82; pres bd dir Statesmen Drum & Bugle Corps 1978-81; mem Natl Com Campaign for Human Devel Natl Cath Conf 1979-82. **Honors/Awds:** Outstanding Leadership Awd Black Caucus Sangamon State Univ 1979-80; Cert of Appreciation Bd of Control Springfield Area Voc Ctr 1979-80; Outstanding Citizen Springfield IL Urban League 1980. **Business Addr:** Dean, Innovat & Exp Studies, Sangamon State Univ, Sheppard Rd, Springfield, IL 62708.

JORDAN, MABEL B.
Educator (retired). **Personal:** Born Mar 17, 1912, Raleigh, NC; daughter of Sophia Hampton Bryant and Sarie Bryant; married Anthony Jordan. **Educ:** Shaw Univ, AB 1933; NC Central Univ, Grad Study. **Career:** Nash Cty, prin 1933-46; Middlesex Elem, principal 1946-56; South Nash, 8th Grade 1956-69; Middlesex, spec math 1969-75 (retired). **Orgs:** Pres Nash Co Tchr 1963-65; dept chrmn Intermediate Dept 1965-68; ACT Pub Chrmn ACT 1972-73, bldg rep 1970-74; pres Franklin Bd Union Women 1964-66, Raleigh Sect Negro Women 1973-77, South Park Comm Floral 1973-77. **Honors/Awds:** NC Resource Use NC Central Univ 1967; Tchr of the Year South Nash 1969, PTA Award 1969; NCNW Comm Srv Award Raleigh Sect of NCNW 1973, 1985.

JORDAN, MARILYN E.
Financial administrator. **Personal:** Born Aug 31, 1944, Yonkers, NY; married Limuary Alja Jordan Jr. **Educ:** Central State U, BS 1966; City Coll NY, MA, MA Advanced Cert grad hon 1974, 1972-74, 1976; Columbia U, doctoral candidate (pending) 1978-80. **Career:** New York City Bd of Edn, dir of finance; New York City Bd of Edn, acting prin 1976-77; New York City Bd of Edn, asst prin 1972-76; New York City Bd of Edn, tchr in charge 1970-72; New York City Bd of Edn, tchr 1967-70; IBM, programmer 1966-67. **Orgs:** Treas CCNY Black Alumni Assn 1980; mem Am Assn of Sch Admin 1980; mem Assn of Sch Bus Officials 1980; mem Nat Educ Assn 1980; publicity dir Teaneck & Englewood Vicinity Ass of Negro Bus & Professional Women Club 1980; mem NY Urban League 1980; mem NAACP 1980; mem Alpha Kappa Alpha Sorority1980. **Honors/Awds:** Grad Student Award, City Coll Grad Student Council 1971, 1972, 1974; Nat Tchng Award; Outstanding Tchr of Am 1972. **Business Addr:** 1377 Jerome Ave, Bronx, NY 10452.

JORDAN, MARJORIE W.
Multiservices coordinator. **Personal:** Born Jan 12, 1924, New Orleans; widowed; children: Cornelius, Emmett. **Educ:** Dillard U, BA magna cum laude 1944; Univ of Chgo; Univ of Cincinnati; Coll of Comm Serv Comm Health Adminstrn. **Career:** Cincinnati Health Dept, coordinator of health programs; Housing Opportunities Made Equal, dir. **Orgs:** Mem Nat Assn Black Soc Workers; mem OH Pub Health Assn; mem Professional Soc of Pub Health Workers of OH; mem Nat Conf on Soc Welfare; mem Bd Nat Non-Profit Housing Corp; bd mem, sec, exec com mem 7 Hills Neighborhood Houses Inc; exec com Easy Riders Inc; bd Urban League; ARC; Am Cancer Soc; co-chmn Consumer Affairs Commn of Fed; exec bd, chmn Consumer Forum; exec com Hosusing Opportunities Made Equal Inc; Unitarian Universalist Serv Com Bd (Nat); Womans City Club; Social Serv Assn; other ciic orgns. **Honors/Awds:** Recip Serv Award, Am Cancer Society 1972. **Business Addr:** 614 Provident Bank Bldg, 7 & Vine Sts, Cincinnati, OH 45202.

JORDAN, MICHAEL
Professional basketball player, entrepreneur. **Personal:** Born Feb 17, 1963, Brooklyn, NY; son of James Jordan (deceased) and Deloris Peoples Jordan; married Juanita Vanoy, Sep 2, 1989; children: Jeffrey Michael, Marcus James, Jasmine Mickael. **Educ:** Univ of North Carolina. **Career:** Chicago Bulls, guard, 1984-93, 1995-; Michael Jordan's: The Restaurant, owner, 1993-; Chicago White Sox, minor league player, 1994-95; Launched own line of athletic clothing, JORDAN Brand, a subdivision of NIKE, 1997. **Honors/Awds:** NBA Most Valuable Player, 1988, 1991, 1992, 1996; All-NBA First Team, 1987-93, 1996, 1997; NBA Defensive Player of the Year, 1988; NBA All-Defensive First Team, 1988-93, 1996, 1997; NBA Finals Most Valuable Player, 1991, 1992, 1993, 1996, 1997; NBA All-Star, 1985, 1987-93, 1996-98; NBA All-Star Most Valuable Player, 1988, 1996; NBA Rookie of the Year, 1985; won gold medals with the US Olympic Basketball Team, 1984, 1992; founded Michael Jordan Celebrity Golf Classic, to raise money for United Negro College Fund, 1989; Jim Thorpe Award, 1992; selected as one of the 50 Greatest Players in NBA History, 1996; Sporting News, 100 Most Powerful People In Sports, Number One, 1997. **Home Addr:** Owner, Michael Jordan's: The Restaurant, 500 N La Salle, Chicago, IL 60610, (312)644-3865. **Business Addr:** professional basketball player, Chicago Bulls, 1901 W Madison St, Chicago, IL 60612-2459, (312)455-4000.

JORDAN, MICHELLE DENISE
Attorney. **Personal:** Born Oct 29, 1954, Chicago, IL; daughter of Margaret O'Dood Jordan and John A Jordan; divorced. **Educ:** Loyola Univ, BA (magna cum laude) 1974; Univ of MI Law School, JD 1977. **Career:** States Attorney's Office of Cook County, attorney, 1977-82; private law practice, 1982-84; Illinois Attorney General's Office, 1984-90, chief of the environmental control division, 1988-90; Hopkins & Sutter Law Firm, partner, 1991-94; US EPA, deputy regional admin, Region five, currently. **Orgs:** Mem Chicago Bar Assn 1977-, Cook County Bar Assn 1977-, Natl Bar Assn 1980-, IL State Bar Assn 1978-, bd mem Loyola Univ Alumni Assn 1984-87; mem Prof Women's Auxiliary of Provident Hospital 1981-82; subcommittee co-chmn, Chicago Bar Assn, Young Bar Assn, 1986-87; mem, Child Witness Project, Task Force, 1987-88; mem, Hearing Div, Chicago Bar Assn, Judicial Evaluation Comm, 1987-88; investigator, investigations, Chicago Bar Assn, Judicial Evaluation Comm, 1986-87; member, Art Institute of Chicago, 1990; environmental law committee member, Chicago Bar Assn, 1989. **Honors/Awds:** Operation PUSH Womens Day Award 1978; America's Top 100 Business & Professional Woman, editorial bd Dollars & Sense Magazine, 1988; instructor, IL Attorney General's Training Program, 1988; instructor, Chicago Bar Association's Young Lawyers Intensive Trail Practice Program, 1986; Susan E. Olive National EEO Award, US EPA, 1996. **Business Addr:** Deputy Regional Admin, US EPA, 77 West Jackson, 19th Fl, Chicago, IL 60604.

JORDAN, MONTELL
Vocalist. **Personal:** Born in Los Angeles, CA. **Educ:** Pepperdine Univ, BS. **Career:** Part-time jobs, advertising; vocalist, Def Jam, 1995-, songs include: This Is How We Do It, Falling, I Like, What's On Tonight. **Special Achievements:** First Def Jam R&B artist to hit #1 on pop chart, This Is How We Do It, 1995. **Business Addr:** Vocalist, c/o Def Jam Recordings, Inc, Def Jam Music Group, 160 Varick St, New York, NY 10013, (212)229-5200.

JORDAN, ORCHID I.
Legislator. **Personal:** Born Aug 15, 1910, Clay Center, KS; married Leon M. **Educ:** Wilberforce Univ OH, grad. **Career:** MO 25th Dist, state rep 1970-; Pan Am World Airways Monrovia Livera, former travel agt, ofc mgr. **Orgs:** Co-founder Freedom Inc Kansas City. **Business Addr:** 2745 Garfield Ave, Kansas City, MO 64109.

JORDAN, PATRICIA
Educator. **Personal:** Born Sep 26, 1951, New York, NY; daughter of Clifford and Juanita James; married Jack M Jordan, Apr 1, 1992; children: Alexa Juanita. **Educ:** Vassar Coll, BA, 1972; City Coll, MS, 1976; Hofstra Univ, PhD, 1991. **Career:** Cross High School, math instructor, 1972; Lee High School, math instructor, 1972-73; Park East HS, math instructor, advisor, 1973-74; Martin Luther King Jr HS, math instructor and dean, 1974-76; Malverne HS, math instructor, 1976-80; Roslyn HS, math instructor, 1980-; State Univ of NY at Old Westbury, math instructor, 1988-. **Orgs:** Assn of Black Psychologist; Assn of Black Educators of NY; NAACP; NYC Dept of Juvenile Justice, advisory board member. **Honors/Awds:** Walt Disney Co, American Teacher Award for Mathematics, 1993; NY State Dept of Ed, NYS Teacher of the Year, 1993; Lakeview,NY-NAACP, Humanitarian Award, 1993. **Business Addr:** Math Instructor/Coord, Cultural Activities, Roslyn Public School District, Round Hill Road, Roslyn Heights, NY 11577, (516)625-6345.

JORDAN, PATRICIA CARTER
City official. **Personal:** Born Jan 23, 1946, Washington, DC; daughter of Olivette Glaude Carter and Nelver Sherman Carter; married Richard O Jordan Jr, Aug 21, 1965; children: Orisha Katrina Jordan. **Educ:** Howard Univ, Washington, DC, degree in sociology; Top 40 Mgmt Training Program, City of NY, graduate; Columbia Univ Graduate School of Arts and Sciences, graduate. **Career:** City of NY Housing Preservation and Devel/Office of Housing Management & Sales, admin mgr, currently; City of New York Board of Education, asst to deputy chancellor; City of New York High Div, management consultant; Communications Institute, New York, communication supervisor; Foundation for Change in Inter-Racial Books for Children, consultant/instructor; Public Education Assn, consultant; US Dept of Justice, Community Relations Service, community relations specialist and trainer; Hunter College Dept of Urban Affairs, research asst/adjunct lecturer; HARYOU-ACT Assoc, research associate; Columbia Univ Graduate School of Arts and Sciences, research/teaching asst. **Orgs:** Director of research and development, Black Citizens for a Fair Media, 1971-; chairperson, Upper Manhattan Mental Health Inc; board member, Foundation for Minority Interest in Media. **Honors/Awds:** Author, Youth in the Ghetto—A Study of the Consequences of Powerlessness and a Blueprint for Change, HARYOU-ACT, 1964. **Home Addr:** 50 W 97th St, #4R, New York, NY 10025.

JORDAN, PAUL SCOTT (RICKY)
Professional baseball player. **Personal:** Born May 26, 1965, Richmond, CA. **Career:** Philadelphia Phillies, infielder, 1988-94; California Angels, 1995; Seattle Mariners, 1996. **Orgs:** Diabetes Help; Kids Basketball Camp. **Honors/Awds:** Player of the Year, Phillies Organization, 1987; 31st National League Player to hit Homerun in First Major League At Bat. **Business Phone:** (215)463-6000.

JORDAN, RANDY LOMENT
Professional football player. **Personal:** Born Jun 6, 1970, Henderson, NC; married Romonda; children: Raven. **Educ:** Univ of North Carolina, bachelor's degree in speech and communications, 1993. **Career:** Jacksonville Jaguars, running back, 1995-. **Orgs:** Fellowship of Christian Athletes. **Business Addr:** Professional Football Player, Jacksonville Jaguars, One Stadium Place, Jacksonville, FL 32202, (904)633-6000.

JORDAN, REGGIE (REGINALD)
Professional basketball player. **Personal:** Born Jan 26, 1968, Chicago, IL. **Educ:** Southwestern; New Mexico State. **Career:** Grand Rapids Hoops (CBA), guard, 1991-93; Yakima Sun Kings (CBA), 1993-94; Los Angeles Lakers, 1994; Yakima Sun Kings, 1994-95; Sioux Falls Skyforce (CBA), 1995-96; Atlanta Hawks, 1996; Portland Trail Blazers, 1996; Minnesota Timberwolves, 1996-. **Honors/Awds:** CBA, All-League first team, 1996; CBA, All-Defensive team, 1993, 1996. **Special Achievements:** CBA, Championship, 1995, 1996. **Business Addr:** Professional Basketball Player, Minnesota Timberwolves, 600 1st Ave N, Minneapolis, MN 55403, (612)337-3865.

JORDAN, ROBERT
Concert pianist, educator. **Educ:** Eastman School, BM; Juilliard School, MS; studied under Cecile Genhart and Rosina Lhevinne. **Career:** Triad Presentations Inc, bd of directors, advisory council; Morgan State University, artist in residence, 1976-78; University of Delaware, artist in residence, 1979; Northern Michigan University, visiting Martin Luther King Professor, 1987; University of Michigan, Ann Arbor, visiting professor, 1991; SUNY, Fredonia, School of Music, professor of piano, 1980-. **Orgs:** Inaugurated Minority Scholarship Fund, University of Delaware, 1979. **Honors/Awds:** Recipient, four different awards, 1975; one of 13 pianists chosen nationally to commission a composition from an American composer & give world premiere at Kennedy Center, 1976; Fulbright Scholarship, Germany, 1965-67. **Special Achievements:** Appearances in recital and with orchestra on four continents; appeared as soloist with Prague Symphony, Bavarian Radio Orchestra, Buffalo Philharmonic, Baltimore Orchestra, Chattanooga Orchestra, Erie Chamber Orchestra; recitals in capial cities, including appearances at Avery Fisher Hall, Alice Tully Hall, Kennedy Center; Silver Jubilee concert celebrations in Suriname, South America, Paris, France, and USA; Orion Master Recordings; recent appearances at the Festival in Le Touquet.

JORDAN, ROBERT A.
Social worker. **Personal:** Born Dec 4, 1932, Atlanta; married Edna Fraley. **Educ:** Clark Coll, AB 1958; Atla U, MA 1969; Univ of GA, post grad 1972-73. **Career:** Atlanta Public School System, reading teacher 1972-, social worker 1972, teacher 1966-72; Fulton County School System, teacher 1961-66. **Orgs:** Bd Dir Atlanta Assn of Educ (past vp); mem GA Educ Assn; NEA; Professional Rights Comm, AAE mem, Educ Chmn, Forward GA Assembly; pres Jazz Disciples Club; mem State Dem Party; Phi Beta Sigma; bd of trustees Ebenezer Bapt Ch; articles written "Parent Input In Publ Schs" & "Why SAT Scores Are Low"; appeared on Radio (WRNG) & TV (ch 5, 2, 11, 30); co-host Jazz Radio Prog, Stat WYZE; collector of Jazz Records five thousand albums; interviewed for article "State of Jazz in Atlanta", Constitution Nwspaper; aauthor article "Profile of a VIP"; article "What's Wrong with Education". **Military Serv:** AUS pfc 1953-55. **Business Addr:** 1890 Bankhead Hwy, Atlanta, GA 30318.

JORDAN, ROBERT HOWARD, JR.
Broadcast journalist. **Personal:** Born Aug 31, 1943, Atlanta, GA; son of Millicent Dobbs Jordan and Robert H Jordan; married Sharon Lundy, Dec 20, 1970; children: Karen Millicent Jordan. **Educ:** Attended Morehouse Coll, Atlanta GA, and Fisk Univ, Nashville TN; Roosevelt Univ, Chicago IL, BA, 1975; Northeastern Ill Univ, MA, 1994. **Career:** WSM TV, Nashville TN, reporter/announcer, 1970-73; WGN TV, Chicago IL, reporter, 1973-78; CBS News, Chicago IL, reporter, 1978-80; WGN TV, anchor/reporter, 1980-. **Orgs:** Mem, Amer Federation of Radio & Television Artists, 1972-; mem, Chicago Assn of Black Journalists, 1983-; mem bd of dir, John G Shedd Aquarium, 1987-; mem bd of dir, Evanston Hospital, 1987-. **Honors/Awds:** Black Achievers of Industry, YMCA of Metropolitan Chicago, 1975; Appreciation Award, Chicago Dental Society, 1976; co-host, UNCF Telethon, 1981-; co-host, MS Telethon, 1983-; master of ceremony, Black and Hispanic Achievers Industry, 1985-89; Article/Scuba Diving, Chicago Tribune Newspaper, 1988. **Military Serv:** US Army, spc 4th class, outstanding trainee, company D, 9th BN USATCI, 1965-68. **Business Addr:** Anchor/Reporter, WGN-TV, 2501 Bradley Place, Chicago, IL 60618.

JORDAN, ROBERT L.
Cleric. **Personal:** Born May 20, 1906, Knoxville, TN; married Maisie Norman; children: Robert Lee Jr, Emma Goldie, Kenneth Samuel. **Educ:** Chapman Coll, AB 1936; Univ of MI, MA

1945; Bethany Coll, DD 1969. **Career:** West Challenger LA, bus mgr newspaper 1932; Young Men's Civic Assn, field rep 1933-35; E Side Comm Ctr LA, asst supt 1933-35; Committee of Friendly Relations LA, chmn 1934-36; City of LA, ordained minister 1936, asst minister 1935-36; United Christian Ch, pastor 1936-74. **Orgs:** Primary organizer Inter-Denom Ministers Alliance Detroit 1937; chmn Social Action Comm Natl Conv Christian Chs 1954-56; vice pres state conv ChristianChs MI 1959; mem Soc Serv Dept Detroit Council Chs 1960, bd dir 1968; bd dir Campas Christian Fellowship Wayne State Univ 1960-70; vice pres Natl Christian Missionary Conv 1954-56; pres Natl Christian Missionary Conv 1956-58; delegate 3 world conv Ch of Christ Scotland 1960, PuertoRico 1965, S Australia 1970; mem Inter-Denom Ministers All Detroit; mem Kappa Alpha Psi; pres W Side Pastors Alliance; exec bd Triangel Assoc; mem Grass Roots Orgn; pres Inter-Denom All Detroit 1970-72; mem MI State Fair Bd 1965-70; mem NAACP; mem Detroit Comm Relations Com Police Commn 1970-72; mem Mayors Ministers Adv Com 1972-74; memPlanned Parenthood MinisteAdv Com. **Honors/Awds:** Longevity Awd Disciple Ministers Detroit 1962; Biographies & Negro Preachers of Amer; auth "Two Races in One Fellowship" 1944; Colored Disciples in MI 1942; auth "Black Theology Exposed" 1983. **Home Addr:** 15710 Indiana, Detroit, MI 48238.

JORDAN, SANDRA D.
Educator. **Personal:** Born Dec 3, 1951, Philadelphia, PA; married Byron N Jordan, Jul 21, 1973; children: Nedra Catherine, Byron Neal, II. **Educ:** Wilberforce University, BS Ed, magna cum laude, 1973; University of Pittsburgh Law School, JD, 1979. **Career:** US Dept of Justice, asst US attorney, 1979-88; US Dept of Independent Counsel, Iran Contra, assoc counsel, 1988-91; University of Pittsburgh Law School, prof, 1989-. **Orgs:** Homer S Brown Law Association, 1979-; National Bar Association, 1979-; Disciplinary Bd, Supreme Court of PA, 1990-94; Pennsylvania Judicial Conduct Bd, vice chair, 1994-. **Honors/Awds:** US Attorney General Special Commendation, 1984; Allegheny County Bar Association, Exceptionally Qualified for Judiciary, 1992. **Special Achievements:** Published "Classified Information & Conflicts," Columbia Law Review vol 91, No 7, 1991. **Business Addr:** Professor, University of Pittsburgh, School of Law, 3900 Forbes Ave, Rm 529, Pittsburgh, PA 15260, (412)648-1988.

JORDAN, STANLEY
Jazz musician, composer. **Personal:** Born Jul 31, 1959, Chicago, IL. **Educ:** Princeton University, BA, music, 1981. **Career:** Jazz guitarist, composer. **Honors/Awds:** Has played with Dizzy Gillespie, Benny Carter, Quicy Jones, Michal Urbaniak, and Richie Cole. Albums include: Touch Sensitive, 1983; Magic Touch, 1985; One Night With Blue Note Preserved (with others); Hideaway (with Stanley Clarke), 1986; Standards, Volume 1, 1987; Blind Date (soundtrack, with others), 1987; Morning Desire (with Kenny Rogers); Artists Against Apartheid—Sun City (with others); RU Tuff Enough (with Rebee Jackson). Award from Reno Jazz Festival; two Grammy nominations. **Business Addr:** Jazz Musician, c/o EMI-Manhattan Records, 1750 N Vine St, Hollywood, CA 90028.

JORDAN, STEVE RUSSELL
Professional football player. **Personal:** Born Jan 10, 1961, Phoenix, AZ; married Anita. **Educ:** Brown Univ, BS, civil engineering, 1982. **Career:** Minnesota Vikings, tight end 1982-. **Honors/Awds:** Set Brown Univ record for most receiving yards in a game (188); played in Pro Bowl, 1986-89 seasons. **Business Addr:** Minnesota Vikings, 9520 Viking Dr, Eden Prairie, MN 55344-3825.

JORDAN, THOMAS ALTON
Forensic clinical social worker, historian, writer. **Personal:** Born Feb 12, 1932, Beaufort, NC; son of Lillian Rhodes Jordan and Edward Jordan; divorced; children: Lili A, Christopher T, Patrick. **Educ:** Morgan State College, BA, 1957; New York Univ-School of Social Work, MSW, 1971; Columbia Univ, doctoral studies, School of Ed Teachers College, 1973-74; Yale Univ, advanced certificate, Drug Dependancy Institute; New England School of Alcohol Studies, advanced certificate. **Career:** Baltimore Public Schools, teacher, 1958-60 New York City Human Resources, admin, caseworker to supvr, admin supvr, 1963-74; Graduate School, asst professor, Univ of Maryland School of Social Work, 1973-74; Providence American, columnist, 1982-94; Urban League of RI, consultant/human resources social worker, current; State of RI, clinical social worker (forensics), 1978-; Providence American, former columist; The Pepper Bird Magazine, director of promotion/columnist, currently. **Orgs:** Alpha Phi Alpha Fraternity; National Assn of Social Workers; Marathon Club of RI; historian, Beaufort-Queen St High School Committee; lector, St Johns Episcopal Cathedral; Bannister House, board of dir; RI Black Heritage Society; RI Black Media Coalition, past pres. **Honors/Awds:** New York City, paid annual educational leave, 1967-68 1970-71; Employee Longevity Award, State of RI, 1995; New England Institute of Alcohol Studies, scholarship, 1975; Yale Univ school of med, Drug Training Scholarship, 1976; APA, Poet of Merit Award, 1989. **Special Achievements:** Author, If A Pond Looks Like An Alligator Lives There, 1988; The Night They Raided Mission Hill (book), Waterwork Press; Co-author, Self Enucleation-Diagnosis and Treatment (medical); The Carousel in Central Park, poem, 1988; A Church Defines It's Self Concept, column, 1993; The Alligator Who Saved Christma, short story; History The Souls of Black Civil War Navy Veterans. **Military Serv:** US Infantry, Corporal Squad Leader, 1951-53; Sigmund Rhee Medal; Infantry Man's Combat Badge.

JORDAN, THURMAN
Accountant. **Personal:** Born Dec 2, 1938, Harrisburg, IL; son of Lutishia Jordan and Joseph Jordan; married Teiko Ann; children: Eric, Neal, Philip. **Educ:** Roosevelt U, BSBA 1966; Univ of Chicago, MBA 1982; IL, CPA 1972. **Career:** Meris Laboratories Inc, sr vp/cfo, 1995-97; Financial consultant, 1994-95; Chicago Osteopathic Health Systems, vice pres/CFO, 1989-94; Signode Corp, vice pres, controller 1976-88; Arthur Andersen & Co, audit mgr 1966-76. **Orgs:** Mem IL Soc CPA's Am Inst CPA's; Alumni Chicago Forum; former mem Chicago United; vice chmn Operation & Effectiveness Com; mem Agency Serv Com Comm Fund; bd mem United Way of Chicago, Evanston Art Center; bd mem Gould Academy. **Honors/Awds:** Black Achiever Award, YMCA, 1974. **Military Serv:** AUS PFC 1961; Outstanding Trainee Awd. **Home Addr:** 2743 Ridge Ave, Evanston, IL 60201.

JORDAN, VERNON E., JR.
Attorney. **Personal:** Born Aug 15, 1935, Atlanta, GA; married Ann Dibble Cook; children: Vickee, Antoinette Cook, Mercer Cook, Janice Cook. **Educ:** DePauw University, BA, 1957; Howard University Law School, JD, 1960; Harvard University, Institute of Politics, John F Kennedy School of Government, fellow, 1969. **Career:** Natl Urban League Inc, president; United Negro College Fund, executive director; Voter Education Project, Southern Regional Council, director; US Office of Economic Opportunity, atty, consultant; NAACP, GA field director; Georgia and Arkansas, private legal practice; Akin, Gump, Strauss, Hauer & Feld, LLP, senior partner, currently. **Orgs:** Director of various organizations, including: American Express Co, Bankers Trust Co, Bankers Trust New York Co, Calloway Golf Co, Dow Jones & Co Inc, Ford Foundation, J C Penney Co Inc, Revlon Group, Ryder System Inc, Sara Lee Corp, Union Carbide Corp, Xerox Corp; trustee of various organizations, including: DePauw University, Howard Univ, Joint Center for Political & Economic Studies, LBJ Foundation, Natl Academy Foundation; membership in: International Advisory Committee of Daimler-Benz, Alfalfa Club, American Academy of Arts & Sciences, Metropolitan Club, University Club; The Joint Center for Political and Economic Studies, bd of governors, 1998-. **Honors/Awds:** Honorary degrees from over 55 colleges and universities throughout the United States. **Special Achievements:** Federal appointments include: Council of the White House Conference, "To Fulfill These Rights," 1966; Natl Advisory Commission on Selective Service, 1966-67; American Revolution Di-Centennial Commission, 1972; Presidential Clemency Board, 1974; Advisory Council on Social Security, 1974; Secretary of State's Advisory Committee on South Africa, 1985; Points of Light Initiative Foundation, President's Advisory Committee, 1989. **Business Addr:** Senior Partner, Akin, Gump, Strauss, Hauer & Feld LLP, 1333 New Hampshire Ave NW, Suite 400, Washington, DC 20036, (202)887-4260.

JORDAN, VINCENT ANDRE
Architectural designer. **Personal:** Born Mar 14, 1965, Nashville, TN; son of Geraldine Crawford Jordan and Harold Willoughby Jordan. **Educ:** Yale University, New Haven, CT, BA, 1987; University of California, Berkeley, Berkeley, CA, Masters of Architecture, 1989. **Career:** Gresham, Smith & Partners, Nashville, TN, intern, 1985-86; Centerbrook Architects, Essex, CT, intern, 1988; Kohn Pederson Fox Associates, New York, NY, architectural designer, 1989-. **Honors/Awds:** Thirty Leaders of the Future, Ebony Magazine, 1989. **Business Addr:** Designer, Kohn Pedersen Fox Associates, PC, 111 W 57th St, New York, NY 10012.

JORDAN, WESLEY LEE
Educator. **Personal:** Born Jan 6, 1941, Petersburg, VA; married Alice Barber; children: Wesley. **Educ:** State Coll, BS 1963; Fordham U, MS 1965 columbia u, edd 1976. **Career:** Pace Univ, asst prof of math 1969-; Belmont Abbey Coll, 1964-67. **Orgs:** Mem Nat Counc of Tchrs of Math Math Assn of Am; Am Assn of Univ Profs Trustee, Shiloh Bapt Ch; J. **Honors/Awds:** 1st black & full-time faculty mem of So white coll, Belmont Abbey Coll 1964. **Business Addr:** 78 N Broadway, White Plains, NY 10603.

JORDAN, WILBERT CORNELIOUS
Physician. **Personal:** Born Sep 11, 1944, Wheatley, AR; son of Annie Mae Jordan and William Jordan. **Educ:** Harvard Coll, AB 1966; Case Western Reserve, MD 1971; UCLA, MPH 1978. **Career:** Center for Disease Control, epidemiologist 1973-76; US Public Health Svcs, lt commander 1973-78; Los Angeles County, area public health chief 1979-83; Drew Medical School, assoc prof 1979-87; King-Drew Medical Ctr, dir grad education; UCLA, asst prof, public health; Charles Drew Univesity of Medicine and Science, dir, AIDS Institute. **Orgs:** Life mem NAACP 1978-; sec of bd PSRO Area XXIII 1980-84; chmn of bd Minority AIDS Project LA Cty 1984-87; bd mem NAMME 1984-87; mem Coalition Against Black Exploitation 1985-87; chmn of bd Sallie Martin Foundation 1986-87; med dir Natl Convention of Gospel Choirs & Choruses Inc; mem Undersea Medical Soc; mem Amer Venereal Disease Assn, Assoc Amer Med Colls, Natl Med Assn; pres Inglewood Physicians Assoc; grad liaison Natl Assoc of Minority med Educators; chmn, Black Los Angeles AIDS Commission; editor, South Central AIDS Newsletter. **Honors/Awds:** Outstanding Physician of Year SNMA 1973; Recognition Awd NAMME 1984; also numerous articles; Recognition Award, NAMME, 1988; Recognition for Service, Warwick Foundation, 1990; Recognition for Service, Brotherland Crusade, 1991; Charles R Drew Medical Society, Physician of the Year, 1992; Los Angeles Sentinel Newspaper, Man of the Year, 1992; Tau Eta Psi Nursing Sorority, Special Humanitarian Award, 1992. **Business Addr:** Dir Graduate Education, King-Drew Medical Center, 12021 So Wilmington, Los Angeles, CA 90059.

JORDAN, WILLIAM ALFRED, III
Educator. **Personal:** Born Feb 1, 1934, Durham, NC; divorced; children: Vanessa Whitted, Alexander DuBois. **Educ:** Georgetown Univ, BS, 1955; Northwestern Univ, MA, 1960; Columbia Univ, MS, 1962. **Career:** Lecturer, currently; Assoc Negro Press, correspondent 1961-63; Zambia Star, Lusaka, Zambia, asst editor 1964-65; NY Times, fgn corr 1964-65; Wash Post, reporter 1965-66; Govtl Affairs Inst Washington, program officer 1966-67; Howard U, instr journalism 1966-67; Metro Applied Rsch Ctr, jr fellow 1968-69; Pratt Inst, asst prof social sci 1968-73; Nat Commis Critical Choices for Am Africa, consul 1974-76; Sonoma St U, assoc prof anthropology 1971-82; City Councilman City of Cotati CA, 1974-80; CA State Polytechne Univ, lecturer, 1982-96; School of Social Sciences, UC Irvine, lecturer, 1991-; Social Sciences Department, Santa Monica College, lecturer, 1995-. **Honors/Awds:** Martin Luther King Fellow NY Univ 1970-71; Ford Found Fellowship 1972-73; Kenya E Africa; chmn Faculty Council Pratt Inst 1971; Natl Endowment of the Humanities Museum of African Art Wash DC 1979. **Business Addr:** Lecturer, University of California, Irvine, School of Social Sciences, Irvine, CA 92697, (714)824-1640.

JORDAN-HARRIS, KATHERINE
Political activist. **Personal:** Born Oct 30, 1927, High Point, NC; daughter of Ruth Green Jordan and Anthony Leopold Jordan; married Ernest Micheaux (divorced 1956); children: Lydia Micheaux Marshall, Anne Micheaux Akwari. **Educ:** Morgan State University, Baltimore, MD, BA, 1954. **Career:** Monroe County Dept of Social Services, supervisor, 1975-85. **Orgs:** President, Rochester Committee for Justice in Southern Africa, 1990; board member, National Aliance Against Racism & Political Repression, 1987-; member, Judicial Process Committee, 1980-; member, NAACP, 1990; standing committee, Epis Diocese of Rochester, NY, 1983-86. **Home Addr:** 2323 Porter St NW, Washington, DC 20008-1204.

JOSEPH, ANITA DAVIS
Association executive. **Personal:** Born Nov 20, 1948, Steubenville, OH; daughter of Bertha Lee Ross Davis and Herman Dover Davis Sr; married Moses Franklin Joseph II, Jun 25, 1977; children: Moses Franklin II, LaNita Shera. **Educ:** Ohio University, BS, communications, graduate studies; Woodrow Wilson College of Law. **Career:** Butler Street YMCA, associate director, special projects, 1970-74; Atlanta Public Schools, teacher, 1974-77; American Humanics, Georgia State University, executive director, 1977-84; Big Brothers/Big Sisters Metropolitan Atlanta, executive director, 1984-91; YMCA of USA, director, financial development, 1991-. **Orgs:** YMCA World Alliance, executive committee in Geneva, Switzerland, 1982-85; National Society Fund Raising Executives, co-chair, cultural diversity; Ohio University Fund Raising, co-chair, fund raising committee; United Way Board of Directors, Atlanta, chair, agency assn; National Council Planned Giving Council; Fulton County Board of Education, planning committee; Rotary One, program committee; Mental Health Association of Atlanta, board of directors; Delta Sigma Theta, 1972-. **Honors/Awds:** NSFRE, Certified Fundraising Executive, 1986; West End Rotary, Distinguished Service Citation, 1991; Leadership Georgia, 1975; Leadership Atlanta, 1987; Outstanding Atlanta, Outstanding Atlantan, 1984. **Special Achievements:** Serves as keynote speaker for non-profit organization; consultant, training; motivational speaker; "Annual Giving," article; "Old Tradition Renewed," article. **Business Addr:** Director, Financial Development, YMCA of the USA, 101 N Wacker Dr, 14th Fl, Chicago, IL 60606, (312)269-0543.

JOSEPH, JAMES ALFRED
Chief executive officer. **Personal:** Born Mar 12, 1935, Opelousas, LA; married Doris Taylor; children: Jeffrey, Denise. **Educ:** Southern Univ, BA 1956; Yale Univ, BD, MA 1963; Southeastern Univ, LLD 1982; Univ of MD, DPS 1984. **Career:** Claremont Coll, chaplain and prof 1969-70; Irwin-Sweeney-Miller Fnd, exec dir 1970-72; Cummins Engine Co, vice pres 1972-77; US Dept of Interior, undersec 1977-81; Yale Divinity Sch, visiting prof 1981-82; Council on Foundations, pres. **Orgs:** Chmn US Comm on Northern Marianas 80-86; bd dir Cummins Engine Fnd 1981-87, Colonial Williamsburg 1981-87, Pitzer Coll 1972-77; mem Council on Foreign Rel 1981-85, The Hague Club 1983-87, Adv Com US Dept of State 1982-84, Bd of Visitors Duke Univ 1981-83; bd of dir Brooking Inst 1985-, Salz-

bert seminar 1985-; Atlantic Council 1985-, United Nations Assoc 1986-; mem adv comm Natl Academy of Sci 1982-83; bd dir Children Defense Fund 1983-, Africare 1982-. **Honors/Awds:** Public Serv Award, Yale Afro Amer Alumni 1976; Visiting Fellow Oxford Univ 1985; Business Person of the Year, Natl Assn of Concerned Business Students 1974; co-editor, Three Perspectives on Ethnicity 1972; chmn US Gov Del 1977, UN Conf in Kenya 1977. **Military Serv:** Med Serv Corps 1st lt 1956-58. **Business Addr:** President, Council on Foundations, 1828 L Street, NW, Washington, DC 20036.

JOSEPH, JENNIFER INEZ
Educational administrator. **Personal:** Born Mar 25, 1948, New Amsterdam, Guyana; daughter of Inez Gwendolyn Chung and Vincent Percival Chung; married Richard A Joseph, Jul 27, 1968; children: Mark Vincent, R Anthony, Robert Lionel. **Educ:** British Open University, BA, 1975; Harvard Graduate School of Education, MEd, 1984. **Career:** University of Ibadan, Nigeria, publications, administrative officer, 1976-79; Oxford University, England, clinical trial coordinator, 1979; Dartmouth College, assistant affirmative action officer, 1980-81, assistant to the director, career and employment services, 1981, director, intensive academic support program, assistant dean of freshmen, 1981-85, assistant director, admissions & financial aid, 1985-86, senior associate director, admissions and financial aid, 1986-89; Centers for Disease Control, Epidemiology Program Office, associate director, 1989-90; Morehouse College, executive assistant to the president, 1991-92, vp, policy and planning, 1992-. **Orgs:** Association of Black Admin & Financial Aid Officers of the Ivy League & Sister Schools, 1985-89, co-chair, 1987-88; Emory University/Pew Charitable Trusts Science & Math Program, consultant, advisory board member, 1989-90; Atlanta Youth Enrichment Program, advisory board member, 1991-; Saturday Youth Enrichment Program, Atlanta, GA, co-founder, coordinating committee chair, 1990-. **Honors/Awds:** Centers for Disease Control, Performance Award, 1990. **Special Achievements:** "CDC's Medical Detectives: At the Forefront of Public Health," Journal of the National Student Medical Association, 1991; Council of Freely Elected Heads of Government, International Observer Team, Guyana Elections, 1992; "At Home on Election Day," Atlanta Journal/Constitution, 1992. **Business Addr:** VP, Policy & Planning, Morehouse College, 830 Westview Dr SW, Gloster Hall, Ste 322, Atlanta, GA 30314, (404)215-2645.

JOSEPH, LLOYD LEROI
Motion picture soundman. **Personal:** Born Sep 18, 1934, Los Angeles, CA; son of Blondine Jackson and Al Lee Joseph; married Jeannette S Jones, Dec 18, 1981; children: Darnetta, D'Anna. **Career:** KIIX Channel 22, Los Angeles, CA, chief broadcast audio engineer, 1963; RPM Recording Studio, Los Angeles, CA, chief recording engineer, 1965-66; Genisco Technology Corp, Compton, CA, test engineer, 1967-69; CB Sound, Los Angeles, CA, recording engineer, 1969; KNXT/CBS News, Los Angeles, CA, newsreel soundman, 1969-77; Universal Studios, Universal City, CA, transfer and production recordist, 1977-. **Honors/Awds:** Emmy, Television, 1976; Features: Melvin and Howard, Psycho III, Best Little Whore House in Texas; Televison Series: Columbo, Magnum PI, Murder She Wrote, Simon and Simon; Documentaries: Blacks in the Media, Plight of the Jews in Russia. **Military Serv:** US Navy, US Army, E-5, 1950-57. **Home Addr:** 1920 Lake Ave, Ste 108, Altadena, CA 91001-3059.

JOSEPH, RAYMOND ALCIDE
Reporter. **Personal:** Born Aug 31, 1931, San Pedro de Maco, Dominican Republic. **Educ:** Univ of Chgo, MA 1964; Wheaton Coll, BA 1960; Moody Bible Inst, dipl 1957. **Career:** Wall St Journal, Div Dow Jones, staff reporter; "Haiti-Observateur," co-publ. **Orgs:** Found 1st printshop for WI Mission in Haiti 1950; ed, Creole Mmthly "Reyon & Lumie"; translated, edited, publ, New Testament in Creole for Am Bible Soc1960; sec gen of "Haitian Coalition" NY opposition to regime of Duvalier; organizer, daily pol broad cast to Haiti in French; edited "Le Combattant Haitien" in French & Eng. **Business Addr:** 22 Cortlandt St, New York, NY 10007.

JOSEPH-MCINTYRE, MARY
Director. **Personal:** Born Jan 12, 1942, Shreveport, LA; children: Jarrett. **Educ:** Contra Costa Jr Coll, 1962; Willis Coll of Bus, 1963; Univ CA, 1966; Univ of San Francisco, continuing education, business administration, 1983. **Career:** UC Berkeley, coord sec pool 1968-71, sec 1963-78; N Peralta Jr Coll, sec to pres 1971-72; UC Berkeley, pscy dept 1972-74; Oakland Met Enterprises, administrative asst 1975-76, exec dir 1976-79; Dukes, Dukes & Assoc, project administrator 1979-83; "Sweet Touch", owner 1984-; City of Oakland Youth Advisory Commission, staff liaision, 1989-91; City of Oakland, Office of Parks and Recreation, administrative services manager, 1989-; Alameda County Youth Services Forum Member, 1989-; Third Ace, Inc, board secretary, 1989-. **Orgs:** Nat Frat of Student & Tchrs 1958-60; NAACP 1961-65; League of Women Voters 1964-70; vol Kilimanjaro House 1968; Black Caucus 1968-69; Nat Contract & Mgmt Assn 1977-; Negro Women Bus & Professional Inc 1977-84. **Honors/Awds:** President, TAPS Prgm; membership Albany Youth Cncl, 1959-60; Alameda Co March of Dimes, Award, 1960; No CA Adoption Agency; Univ CA, Outstanding Merit Increase, 1968. **Home Addr:** 3922 Turnley Ave, Oakland, CA 94605.

JOSEY, E. J.
Educator. **Personal:** Born Jan 20, 1924, Norfolk, VA; son of Frances Bailey Josey and Willie Josey; married Dorothy Johnson (divorced); children: Amina. **Educ:** Howard Univ, AB 1949; Columbia Univ, MA 1950; State Univ of NY Albany, MSLS 1953; Shaw Univ, LHD 1973; Univ of Wisconsin-Milwaukee, DPS 1987; North Carolina Central Univ, HHD, 1989; Litt D Clark, Atlanta University, 1995. **Career:** Columbia Univ, desk asst 1950-52; NY Public Library Central Branch, tech asst grade 1 1952; NY State Libr, part-time asst 1952-53; Free Library of Philadelphia, librarian 1953-54; Savannah State Coll, instructor social science 1954-55; DE State Coll, librarian & asst prof 1955-59; Savannah State Coll, librarian & assoc prof 1959-66; NY State Educ Dept, assoc in acad & rsch libraries 1966-68, chief bureau of acad & rsch libraries 1968-76, chief bureau of specialist library serv 1976-86; University of Pittsburgh, prof school of info sciences, prof emeritus. **Orgs:** Pres Albany Branch Assn for Study of Afro-American Life & History; Amer Assn of Univ Prof; Amer Acad of Political & Social Sci; NY Library Assn; Freedom to Read Foundation, board of directors; American Library Association, president, 1984-85; executive director 1960-86, pres 1982-86, bd of trustees, 1969-86, chmn program comm, 1972-82, Albany Branch, NAACP; ed bd Dictionary of Amer Lib History; bd advisors Childrens Book Review Svc; American Civil Liberties Union, 1966-. **Honors/Awds:** ALA Black Caucus, Award for Distinguished Serv to Librarianship, 1979; NY Black Librarians Caucus, Award for Excellence, 1979; Distinguished Alumni Award for Contributions to Librarianship, School of Library & Info Science, SUNY, 1981; Distinguished Serv Award, Library Assn of City Univ, NY, 1982; Award for Distinguished Comm Leadership as Pres of Albany NAACP; DC Association of School Librarians Award, 1984; Africa Librarianship Award, Kenya Library Association, 1984; New York Library Association Award, 1985; President's Award, NAACP, 1986; Honorary Doctor of Humanities, North Carolina Central Univ, 1989; Equality Award, American Library Association, 1991; Demco Award for Distinguished Service to Librarianship, Black Caucus of ALA, 1994; Award for Distinguished Service to Librarianship, Penn Library Association, 1996. **Special Achievements:** Author of numerous publications. **Military Serv:** Military serv 1943-46. **Business Addr:** Professor Emeritus, Information Sciences, University of Pittsburgh, Pittsburgh, PA 15260.

JOSEY, LERONIA ARNETTA
Government official. **Personal:** Born in Norfolk, VA; children: Quenton C. **Educ:** Spelman Coll, BA 1965; Univ of Maryland Sch of Soik & Comm Planning, MSW 1973; Syracuse Univ Coll of Law, JD (cum laude) 1977; Maxwell Sch of Citizenship Public Affairs Syracuse Univ, MPA 1977. **Career:** US Dept of Housing & Urban Devel, Washington DC, atty 1977-81; Maryland Parole Commission, commr 1981-. **Orgs:** Pres Natl Assc Blck Women Atty 1983-; dir Echo House Found 1978-82, Med Eye Black Bd 1981-82, Luic Carroll Jackson Museum 1982-. **Honors/Awds:** 3rd hon grad Spelman Coll; law sch senate awd 1977; White House flwshp finlst 1977. **Home Addr:** 3700 Locheam Dr, Baltimore, MD 21207. **Business Addr:** Commissioner, MD Parole Commsn, Ste 601 1 Investment Pl, Towson, MD 21204.

JOURNEY, LULA MAE
Appointed official. **Personal:** Born May 8, 1934, Doddsville, MS; divorced; children: Larry, Callie Sanders, Linda, Ronnie, Marilyn Kirk, Blondina. **Educ:** Delta Indust Inst Bus School Doddsville MS, 1954; Market Training Inst Indianapolis IN, 1958; IN/Purdue Univ, 1979. **Career:** Center Twp Trustees Office, investigator of Marion Cty Home, asst supvr, supvr of investigators, asst chief supvr of oper 1965-. **Orgs:** Former pres Indianapolis Pre School 1972; bd of dir Citizens Neighborhood Coaltion 1976-; city-cty councilor 10th dist City-Cty Council 1976-; bd of dir Mapleton/Fall Creek Assoc 1977-; past chmn of mem comm Amer Bus Women Assoc 1981; state coord of municipal women in govt Natl League of Cities 1982-; minority leader dem caucus City-Cty Council 1985. **Honors/Awds:** Key to the City City-Cty Council 1976; Cert for Coop Beyond the Call of Duty Ctr Twp Trustees Office 1978; Cert of Appreciation Indianapolis Pre-school 1978; Two Certs for Suprv of the Month Ctr Twp Trustees Office 1979; Cert for Serv Rendered IN Assoc of Motorcycle Clubs 1983. **Home Addr:** 2020 N New Jersey St, Indianapolis, IN 46205.

JOWERS, JOHNNIE EDWARD, SR.
Association executive. **Personal:** Born Jul 1, 1931, Lynchburg, SC; son of Bernice Jowers (deceased) and Loro Jowers (deceased); married Paltine Horton Jowers, Sep 30, 1956; children: Johnnie E Jr, Deborah J. **Educ:** Johns Hopkins University, certificate, advanced studies, education, 1954; Shaw University, AB, 1957; North Carolina Central University, MS, 1958; New York University, certificate, organization & administration, 1965. **Career:** Edgecombe County Board of Education, secondary school teacher, 1958-59; The Salvation Army, physical director, 1959-60, program director, 1960-63, unit director, 1963-68; Baltimore City Schools, secondary school teacher, 1968-74; The Salvation Army, executive director, 1974-. **Orgs:** Frontiers International Inc, Baltimore club pres, 1979-80; Progressive First Baptist Church, trustee, 1975-; Shaw University Alumni Association, corresponding secretary, 1975-; Baltimore Frontiers Club, Chaplin, 1992-; United Way of Central Maryland Speaker's Bureau, 1978-94; Shaw University National Homecoming Banquet, chairman, 1990; Shaw University Capital Campaign, area co-chairman, 1991-. **Honors/Awds:** Shaw University, Student of the Year, 1953, inducted into Athletic Hall of Fame, 1984; The Salvation Army Boys Club, Man & Boy Award, 1973; The Salvation Army, Distinguished Service Award, 1984; Baltimore City Schools, Outstanding Teacher Award, 1970. **Special Achievements:** History of Intercollegiate Athletics at Shaw University, 1958; "Boosting Your Speeches," 1989; "Publicity: Everybody's Job," 1989. **Military Serv:** US Army, pfc, 1954-56; Expert Rifleman, Good Conduct Medal. **Home Addr:** 2800 E Coldspring Ln, Baltimore, MD 21214, (410)254-1557. **Business Phone:** (410)366-4997.

JOY, DANIEL WEBSTER
Judge. **Personal:** Born Apr 15, 1931, Middleton, NC; son of Mattie Griffith Joy and Andrew Joy; married Ruby M Collins; children: Darryl, Kathry. **Educ:** State Univ of NY at Albany, BA 1952; Brooklyn Law Sch, JD 1957. **Career:** Rent & Rehab Admin, chief counsel 1967-70, commr 1970-73; Housing Preservation & Devel Dept, commr 1973-83; Queens County Civil Court, judge 1984-85; Justice Supreme Court, 1985-. **Orgs:** Mem Assn of the Bar City of NY 1976-83; chairman bd of dir Edwin Gould Foundation 1980-; mem Queens County Bar Assn 1981-; mem Macon B Allen Black Bar Assn 1982-; mem Natl Bar Assn 1983-. **Honors/Awds:** Community Service Award, Lambda Kappa Mu Sorority, 1996. **Military Serv:** AUS pfc 1952-54.

JOY, JAMES BERNARD, JR.
Clergyman. **Personal:** Born Jan 16, 1937, Washington, DC. **Educ:** St Mary's Univ Balto MD, BA 1958; Gregorian Univ Rome Italy, STB (summa cum laude) 1962; Cath Univ Wash DC, MA 1970. **Career:** Holy Name Ch, asst pastor 1962-65; Holy Comforter Ch, asst pastor 1965-66; St Thomas More Ch, asst pastor 1966-1969; Sacred Heart Ch, asst pastor 1969-74; Holy Redeemer Ch, asst pastor 1974-76; St Gabriel's Ch, pastor 1976-85; Ft Sill OK, church pastor 1985-. **Orgs:** Bd dir Carroll Pblshg Co 1985-, Washington Cath Historical Soc 1978-; mem DC Citizens Traffic Bd 1965-70, chrmn 1968-70. **Military Serv:** AUSR maj 1969-; ASR 1975; CSR 1969; AUS 1985-. **Home Addr:** 26 Grant Cir N W, Washington, DC 20011. **Business Addr:** Pastor, St Gabriels Ch, Fort Sill, OK 73503.

JOYCE, DONALD FRANKLIN
Librarian, educator. **Personal:** Born Nov 4, 1938, Chicago, IL; son of Pearl Jackson and Raleigh W Joyce. **Educ:** Fisk Univ, BA 1957; Univ of IL, MS 1960; Univ of Chicago, PhD 1978. **Career:** Chicago Public Library, branch librarian 1960-69; Harsh Collection, Chicago Public Library, curator 1969-81; Downtown Library, Tenn State Univ, coordinator/assoc professor 1981-87; Dean of the Library & Professor; Austin Peay Stat Univ, currently. **Orgs:** Mem 2 committees Amer Librarians Asn 1970-; IL Librarians Assn; ALA Black Caucus; consultant Natl Endowment for the Humanities 1979-84; book reviewer Nashville Tennessean 1981-; College Land Assoc 1982-. **Honors/Awds:** CIC Doctoral Fellowship Univ of Chicago 1973-78; Gatekeepers of Black Culture, black-owned book publishing in the US, 1817-1981 (Greenwood Press 1983); Blacks in the Humanities, 1750-1984, A Selected Annotated Bibliography (Greenwood Press, 1986); Numerous articles in professional journals; Black Book Publishers in the United States, 1817-1990, (Greenwood Press, 1990); Distinguished Service Award, ALA Black Caucus, 1993. **Special Achievements:** Contributing editor, African-American Almanac; contributor, "The Oxford Companion to African American Literature," 1997; evaluator, National Endowment for the Humanities; consultant, Southern Assn of Coll and Schools. **Business Addr:** Felix G Woodward Library, Austin Peay State Univ, Clarksville, TN 37043, (615)648-7618.

JOYCE, ELLA (CHERRON HOYE)
Actress. **Personal:** daugHter of Bunnie Hoye; married Dan Martin. **Educ:** Eastern Michigan University; business college; Yale Repertory Theater, trained with Lloyd Richards. **Career:** Ford Motor Co, secretary; actress, theater experience includes: Don't Get God Started, Two Trains Running, Milestones in Drama, The First Breeze of Summer, Chapter, Ma Rainey's Black Bottom; film experience includes: Common Ground, Choices, Stop or My Mom Will Shoot; television experience includes: Search for Tomorrow, One Life to Live, Roc Live, 1991-. **Honors/Awds:** Audelco Best Dramatic Actress, for Black Theater Excellence; TOR Award for Best Dramatic Actress, in Off-Broadway category. **Business Phone:** (310)201-8800.

JOYNER, ARTHENIA LEE
Attorney. **Personal:** Born Feb 3, 1943, Lakeland, FL; married Delano S Stewart. **Educ:** FL A&M Univ, BS 1964, Coll of Law JD 1968. **Career:** Booker T Washington Jr HS, teacher, 1964-65; FL House of Reps, admin asst to Rep Jose Lang Kershaw, 1969; attorney at law, general practice, 1969-. **Orgs:** Hillsborough Comm Housing Resource Bd; Citizen Adv Comm Hillsborough Co Sch Bd; League of Women Voters; PUSH; Allen Temple AME Church; NAACP; Tampa Urban League; Tampa

Alumnae Chap Delta Sigma Theta Inc; bd mem Helding Hand Day Nursery 1978-84; bd mem Travelers Aid Soc Inc 1980-84; pres Bay Area Legal Serv 1983; life mem & held various positions in Natl Bar Assn; Amer, FL, Hillsborough Co Bar Assns; FL Assn of Women Lawyers; Natl Assn of Women Lawyers; George E Edgecomb Bar Assn; Hillsborough Co Assn of Women Lawyers; participant Lawyers Against Apartheid, 1985. **Honors/Awds:** First African-American female atty in Tampa; second female pres, Natl Bar Assn; Outstanding Leadership Award, FL Chapter, NBA, 1977; NBA Pres Award, Natl Bar Assn, 1982; Outstanding Leadership Award, Bay Area Legal Serv Inc, 1983; 100 Most Influential Blacks in America, Ebony Magazine, 1985. **Special Achievements:** Appointed by President Clinton to the US Delegation to the Asia and Pacific regional preparatory meeting for the Fourth World Conference on Women, Jakarta, Indonesia, 1994.

JOYNER, CLAUDE C.
Federal official. **Personal:** Born Nov 8, 1950, New Haven, CT; son of Minnie Joyner (deceased) and Claude Joyner (deceased); married Dolores Brandow Joyner, Nov 21, 1987. **Educ:** Maple Springs Baptist Bible College & Seminary, MRE, 1997; Central State Univ, BS 1974; Pepperdine Univ, MBA 1983. **Career:** Lincoln Natl Life Insurance Co, system designer 1974-76; First Interstate Bank, operations officer 1977-79; Aerospace Corp, programmer 1979-80; Transaction Tech Inc, systems analyst 1980-84; Electronic Data Systems, sr systems analyst 1984-85; Booz Allen & Hamilton, associate 1985-86; Contel ASC, sr system analyst 1986-87; Computer Based Systems Inc, staff analyst, database administrator, 1987-91; Joyner Design Ltd, CFO, 1990-; Crystal City, VA, sr database specialist, 1991-96; US Patent Trademark Office, computer scientist, 1996-. **Orgs:** Mem Deaf Pride Inc 1980-86; mem student outreach comm Natl Black MBA Assn 1984-87; educ chairperson Black Data Processing Assoc, DC Chapter, 1985-87; licensed minister, 1991-, assistant superintendent, 1992-94, Sunday school teacher 1986-94, Mt Sinai Baptist; staff volunteer, treasurer, Mt Sinai Outreach Center 1987-94; treasurer, Right Way Ministries Inc, 1992-96, chmn trustee bd, 1997-; Sunday school teacher, asst training union dir, 1995-, disciple training dir, 1994-, Kendall Baptist Church, 1994; Kendall Baptist Church, dir Benevolence Comm, 1997-. **Home Addr:** 2210 Dawn Lane, Temple Hills, MD 20748-4213.

JOYNER, GORDON L.
Attorney, county commissioner. **Personal:** Born Feb 11, 1950, Fort Valley, GA; son of Helen L Joyner and Henry W Joyner; children: Ashley, Shannon. **Educ:** Morehouse College, Atlanta, GA, BA (summa cum laude), 1972; Harvard Law School, Cambridge, MA, JD, 1975. **Career:** Kilpatrick & Cody Law Offices, Atlanta, GA, attorney, 1975-78; American Bar Assn, Washington, DC, assistant director, 1978-79; US Department of Housing and Urban Development, Washington, DC, legal counsel, dir of fair housing enforcement, 1979-82; Atlanta Municipal Court, Atlanta, GA, judge, 1985-87; Fulton County Board of Commissioners, commissioner, 1987-; self-employed attorney, currently. **Orgs:** Chairman, Fulton County Board of Elections, 1985-87; life member, NAACP; member, National Urban League; Alpha Phi Alpha Fraternity; secretary, Atlanta Harvard Club, 1983; member, Mayor's Task Force on Public Education; member, Southern Christian Leadership Conference. **Honors/Awds:** Phi Beta Kappa; Government Executive-In-Residence & Visiting Professor, Morehouse Coll, 1981-82; Official Guest of Israel & Germany Governments, 1989-90. **Business Addr:** Commissioner, Fulton County Government, 141 Pryor St, Suite 10023, 10th Flr, Atlanta, GA 30303, (404)730-8210.

JOYNER, IRVING L.
Attorney, educator. **Personal:** Born Dec 11, 1944, Brooklyn, NY; son of Dorothy Joyner and McLean Spaulding; divorced; children: Lauren, Kwame, Tuere. **Educ:** Long Island Univ, Brooklyn NY, BS, 1970; Rutgers Univ School of Law, Newark NJ, JD. **Career:** United Church of Christ Comm for Racial Justice, New York NY, dir of criminal justice, 1968-78; Currie & Joyner, Raleigh NC, attorney at law, 1978-80; Natl Prison Project of ACLU, Washington DC, staff attorney, 1980-81; Currie, Pugh & Joyner, Raleigh NC, attorney at law, 1981-85; NC Central Univ School of Law, Durham NC, assoc dean and prof of law, 1985-. **Orgs:** Mem/former pres, NC Assn of Black Lawyers, 1977-; mem, NC State Bar, 1977-; mem, Natl Bar Assn, 1977-; mem, NC Academy of Trial Lawyers, 1977-; Federal Bar Advisory Council, 1985-. **Honors/Awds:** Outstanding Contribution to Racial Justice, Assn of Black Law Students, 1977; Paul Robeson Award, Black Amer Law Student Assn, 1977; Professor of the Year, NCCU Student Bar Assn, 1985; Living Legacy Award OA Dupree Scholarship Foundation, 1987; Outstanding Contribution to Civil Rights, Wake Forest Black Law Student Assn 1987; author of The Black Lawyer in NC, article, 1988; Conflicts of Interest, article, 1988; Police Misconduct Litigation CLE manuscript and Law Review article, 1991; Preparation and Use of Requests for Jury Instructions, CLE manuscript, 1988; Criminal Procedure in NC, book, 1989; Supplements to Criminal Procedure in North Carolina, 1991-94; The Status of African-American Lawyers in North Carolina, article, 1992; President's Award by La-Grange, Frink Alumni and Friends Assn, 1991; Lawyers of the Year Award by North Carolina Assn of Black Lawyers, 1995; Outstanding Teacher's Awd, North Carolina Central University Law School Student Bar Association. **Business Addr:** Professor of Law, North Carolina Central University School of Law, 1512 S Alston Ave, Durham, NC 27707.

JOYNER, JOHN ERWIN
Medical doctor. **Personal:** Born Feb 7, 1935, Grambling, LA; son of Mary Rist Joyner and John E Joyner; married Joyce N Sterling; children: Sheryl, John III, Monica. **Educ:** Albion Coll, BS 1955; IN Univ Sch of Medicine, MD 1959, Straight Surg Internship/Neurosurgery Residency 1959-67. **Career:** Winona Mem Hosp, dept chmn of neurology & neurosurgery 1980-; IN Univ Sch of Medicine, assoc prof of neurosurgery 1983-; Winona Hosp Medical Staff & Exec Council, secty-treas 1985; RehabCare, med dir 1986-; Natl Med Assoc IN, pres-elect; Maxihealth, medical director; Meridian IPA, CEO. **Orgs:** Mem Fellow Amer Coll of Surgeons; mem Royal Soc of Med London England; mem Amer Assoc of Physicians & Surgeons; mem Neurosurgical Soc of IN; mem Indianapolis Urban League; mem IN Conservation Council; mem American Legion; chmn bd of dirs CT Scanner Assocs 1977-84; life mem NAACP 1979-; mem NIH Tech Merit Review Comm 1981, 1982; mem AMA Health Policy Agenda for the Amer People 1982, 1983, 1984; sec chmn of Regional Constituent Socs Natl Med Assoc 1983-1984, 1980-84; mem Congress of Neurological Surgeons 1967-; chmn of bd 100 Black Men of Indianapolis Inc 1984-87; chmn bd of dirs Meridan Scanner Assoc Inc 1984-89; mem IN State Health Coordinating Council 1985; mem, World Medical Assoc, The Soc of Prospective Medicine; patrons comm 10th Pan American GamesIndianapolis 1986-87; mem medical luation comm IN Univ Sch of Med; pres Natl Med Assn l987-88; Amer Medical Assn l967-; Marion County Medical Soc l967-; Amer Academy of Neurological & Ortho Surgeons l985-; past pres, Natl Medical Assn l988-89; Natl Black Health Conf Steering Comm l988-; Minority AIDS Advisory Comm l988-; Alpha Eta Sigma Pi Phi (Boule). **Honors/Awds:** Martin Luther King Freedom Awd SCLC Indianapolis 1972; Sickle Cell Anemia Found Awd 1973; Friend of Youth Awd YMCA Kokomo IN 1976; AMA Physician's Achievement Awd Natl Med Assoc 1980; AMA Physicians Recognition Awd Amer Med Assoc 1983; Dr of Humane Letters, Martin Center Coll; Distinguished Public Service Award for NMA, US Dept of Health & Human Serv; Scroll of Merit Natl Medical Assn; Benjamin Hooks Award, Gary in NAACP; Outstanding Serv Award, Scott United Methodist Church, Indianapolis. **Military Serv:** AUS med serv grp capt 1961-64. **Business Addr:** 3202 North Meridian, East Building Ste 201, Indianapolis, IN 46208.

JOYNER, LEMUEL MARTIN
Director. **Personal:** Born Jun 20, 1928, Nashville, TN; married Barbara; children: Lemuel Jr, John M, Christopher A, Dennis L, Victor P, Lonnie. **Educ:** Univ Notre Dame, BFA 1957, MFA 1969. **Career:** Mntl Hlth Ctr of St Joseph City Inc, art therapist 1985; Day Treatment Ctr, co-devel 1972-; Ofc of Inter-Cultural Dev, spl asst to pres 1970; St Mary's Coll Notre Dame, asst prof of art 1965-71; Liturgical Artist 1958-65. **Orgs:** Am Art Therapists Assn; S Bend Art Assn; S Bend St Acad; Nat Cncl of Artist; Alpha Phi Alpha. **Honors/Awds:** Excellence in Tchng Award, St Mary's Coll 1969; Outst Contrib to Std Life Award; Model Upward Bound Prog 1966; pringint in Black Dimensions In Am Art 1969. **Business Addr:** Center for Creative Orchestrtn, 18067 State Road 23, South Bend, IN 46637.

JOYNER, RUBIN E.
Educational administration. **Personal:** Born Dec 5, 1949, Trenton, NJ; married Phyllis A; children: Zanada, Ciarra. **Educ:** Rider Coll, BA 1970-73; Trenton State Coll, MEd 1975-77. **Career:** Ocean County Coll, dir educ opportunity fund 1986. **Orgs:** NJ Ed Opp Assoc, 1978; American Assoc Counseling Dept 1979; Soc for Special & Ethnic Studies 1979; Monmouth Coll, dir black student Union 1979-85; Acceleration Computer Sci Prog, co-founder 1983-85; Organization Black Unity, dir 1985; Access Prog, founder 1986; Student Leadership Ed Opp, co-chairperson1986. **Honors/Awds:** Monmouth Coll, appreciation awrd black student union 1984; Outstanding Young Men of the Year 1985. **Business Addr:** Director, Educ Oppy Fund, Ocean County College, College Drive, Toms River, NJ 08753.

JOYNER, SETH
Professional football player. **Personal:** Born Nov 18, 1964, Spring Valley, NY. **Educ:** Univ of Texas at El Paso, attended. **Career:** Philadelphia Eagles, linebacker, 1986-93; Arizona Cardinals, 1994-96; Green Bay Packers, 1997-. **Business Addr:** Professional Football Player, Green Bay Packers, 1265 Lombardi Ave, Green Bay, WI 54304, (414)494-2351.

JOYNER-KERSEE, JACKIE
Track and field athlete, professional basketball player. **Personal:** Born Mar 3, 1962, East St Louis, IL; daughter of Mary Joyner and Alfred Joyner; married Bob Kersee, Jan 11, 1986. **Educ:** University of California, Los Angeles, CA, BA. **Career:** Track and field athlete; Richmond Rage, professional basketball player, 1996-; Elite Sports Marketing, pres, currently. **Orgs:** Jackie Joyner-Kersee Community Foundation; UCLA Alumni Association; Athletic Congress Athletics Advisory Board; member, board of directors, St Louis Girl's Club; spokeswoman, State Games of America. **Honors/Awds:** James E Sullivan Award for Most Outstanding Amateur Athlete, 1986; Silver Medalist, Los Angeles Olympics, American record holder in heptathlon, 1984; American Outdoor record holder in long jump, 1985; UCLA Scholar Athlete, 1985; Broderick Cup for Collegiate Woman Athlete of the Year, 1986; Most Valuable Player, UCLA basketball and track and field, 1986; American Indoor Nationals champion, long jump, 1986; world record in heptathlon, Goodwill Games, Moscow, US Olympic Festival, 1986; Outstanding Athlete of the Goodwill Games, Soviet Life magazine, 1986; Olympia Award for Outstanding Athlete in Sports, Scholarship and Leadership, 1986; City of Hope Victor Award, 1986, 1987; Woman Athlete ofthe Year, Track & Field News, 1986, 1987; St Louis Athlete of the Year, 1986; Amateur Sportswoman ohe Year, 1986, 1987; Jesse Owens Memorial Award, 1986, 1987; tied world record in long jump, Pan American Games, Indianapolis, IN, 1987; Gold Medalist, heptathlon, Long Jump, World Championship, Rome, 1987; broke records in shot put, and heptathlon, US Olympic Trials, 1988; US record in 100m hurdle, 1988; Gold Medalist in long jump, Seoul Olympics, 1988; Essence Award winner, 1988; AAF's World Trophy recipient, 1989; Honorary Doctorate, Univer of Missouri, 1989; US Olympic Team, gold medal winner, 1992; Jackie Robinson Foundation, Robie Award, 1994.

JUDSON, HORACE AUGUSTUS
Educational administrator. **Personal:** Born Aug 7, 1941, Miami, FL; married Beatrice Gail; children: Tamara Renee, Sonya Anita, Sojourner Maria, Jessica Gail. **Educ:** Lincoln U, BA 1963; Cornell U, PhD 1970. **Career:** State Univ of New York College, Plattsburgh, pres/chancellor, 1994-; California State Univ, provost/vp, until 1994; Morgan State Univ, vice pres acad affairs 1974-79, prof 1974-86; Morgan State Coll, assoc dean 1973-74, assoc prof 1972-74, asst prof 1969-72; Bethune-Cookman Coll, asst prof 1969. **Orgs:** Mem, Am Chem Soc; Am Assoc Higher Ed; Omega Psi Phi; Rotary; Miner Inst Board; Am Assn of Univ Admin; Intl Assoc of Univ, Pres; Amer Assn of State Colleges and Universities; The Research Foundation of State Univ of New York, bd of dirs; Trudeau Inst, bd of trustees; Clinton Cty Area Development Corp, bd of dirs; Boy Scouts of America, Adirondack Council, advisory bd. **Honors/Awds:** Several articles in the Jour of Am Chem Soc 1970; rsrch, flwshp, Cornel Univ 1965-69; Doctor Science Honorary, Lincoln U, PA, 1994; Award for Professional Excellence, Nat Tech Assoc, 1984. **Military Serv:** AUS md civ aide to sec 1975. **Business Addr:** President, State University of New York, 101 Broad St, Plattsburgh, NY 12901-2601.

JUDSON, WILLIAM THADIUS
Professional football player. **Personal:** Born Mar 26, 1959, Detroit, MI. **Educ:** South Carolina State College, BS, business admin, 1981. **Career:** Miami Dolphins, 1982-89; Detroit Lions, cornerback, 1990-.

JULIAN, JOHN TYRONE
Educational administrator. **Personal:** Born Sep 3, 1947, Rayne, LA; married Evelyn West; children: Karen, Shellie. **Educ:** Grambling State Univ, BS 1969; LA State Univ, MEd 1975, EdS 1978. **Career:** Rayne HS, teacher 1969-70; USAF Sheppard AF Base Wichita Falls, med instructor 1970-73; Armstrong Elementary, teacher 1973-77; Ross Elementary, principal 1977-. **Orgs:** Acadia Parish Police Jury 1980-88; Natl Assn of Elementary Sch Principals 1985-; LA Assn of Principals 1985; LA Assn of Sch Executives 1985-; Knights of Peter Claver 1984-; Amer Legion Post 15 1992-; Acadia Admins Assn, pres 1985-. **Honors/Awds:** Merit Scholar Grambling State Univ 1966-69; Alpha Phi Alpha Frat Grambling State Univ 1967. **Military Serv:** US Air Force, sgt, 1970-73; Master Instructor Certificate. **Home Addr:** 103 Becky Drive, Atwood Akers, Crowley, LA 70526. **Business Addr:** Principal, Ross Elementary, 1809 West Hutchinson Ave, Crowley, LA 70526.

JULIAN, PERCY L., JR.
Attorney. **Personal:** Born Aug 31, 1940, Chicago, IL; son of Anna Johnson Julian and Percy Julian. **Educ:** Oberlin Coll, BA 1962; Univ WI, JD 1966. **Career:** Julian, Olson & Lasker, sr partner; Private Practice, attorney 1966-. **Orgs:** Coop atty & spl counsel NAACP-LDF, Amer Civil Liberties Union, Ctr Constl Rights; rep many civil rights groups; lectr Univ WI 1970-77, 1979-80; profl photographer 1960-66, 1978-; mem WI State Bar, Fed Bar Western Dist WI, Eastern Dist WI, So Dist IL, Cent Dist IL, 5th 7th 8th 9th & 11th Circuit Ct Appeals; US Ct Appeals; DC/US Supreme Ct; ABA, Dane Co Bar Assn; Natl Assn Criminal Defense Lawyers; Bar Assn 7th Fed Circuit; mem Amer Soc of Magazine Photographers; Natl Press Photographers Assn; Professional Photographers of Amer; chmn WI State Personnel Bd 1972-76; chmn WI State Com US Commn Civil Rights 1978-82; mem WI Council Criminal Justice 1972-80; Cit Study Com Judicial Orgn 1971-72; Employment Rel Study Commn 1975-77; NAACP; Amer Civil LibertiesUnion; state bd Amer Civil Liberties on 1969-74. **Honors/Awds:** Mem of the Yr Awd WI Civil Liberties Union 1972; many speaking & debate awds; Lawyer of the Year Award, Center for Public Representation, 1978; Wisconsin Law Alumni Assn, Univ of Wisconsin Law School, 1980; Fair Housing Advocate Award, Fair Housing Council of Dane Co, 1988. **Business Addr:** Attorney, 330 E Wilson St, Madison, WI 53701-2206.

JUNIOR, E. J., III (ESTER JAMES)
Professional football player. **Personal:** Born Dec 8, 1959, Salisburg, NC; married Jacquelyn; children: Adam. **Educ:** Univ of Alabama, degree in public relations. **Career:** Linebacker: St Louis Cardinals (later, Phoenix Cardinals), 1981-88; Miami Dolphins, 1989-. **Orgs:** Counselor (off-season), Hyland Medical Ctr; Matthews-Dickey Boys Club in St Louis. **Honors/Awds:** Voted to Alabama's Team of the Decade (1970's); named to the Strength Coaches All-American team; Outstanding Defensive Performer in 1981 Senior Bowl; named to several All-Rookie teams, 1981; played in Pro Bowl, 1984, 1985. **Business Addr:** Professional Football Player, Miami Dolphins, 1989, ATTN: PUBLIC RELATIONS DEPT, 2269 NW 199th St, Miami, FL 33056-2600.

JUNIOR, ESTER JAMES, JR.
Educational administrator. **Personal:** Born Feb 11, 1932, Claxton, GA; son of Mable R Myrick Junior and Ester J Junior Sr; married Eva G Westbrook Burton; children: Avis, EJ III, Keith, Lori M Burton, Lesli M Burton. **Educ:** Morehouse Coll, BA 1952; Atlanta Univ, MBA 1954. **Career:** Tuskegee Inst, intern for coll fiscal & bus mgmt 1954-55; Southern Univ, mgr of aux enterprises 1955-57; Jarvis Christian Coll, business mgr 1957-59; Livingston Coll, business mgr 1959-61; Albany State Coll, dir of business & finance 1961-68; Fisk Univ, asst vice pres for business & finance 1968-73; Meharry Medical Coll, dir of budget & purchasing 1973-76; Univ of AR, vice chancellor for fiscal affairs 1976-78; TN State Univ, vice pres for business affairs 1978-80; Meharry Medical Coll, asst vice pres for bus & finance 1980-82; Fort Valley State Coll, vice pres for business & finance 1982-87 Ft Valley State College, asst prof, 1987-. **Orgs:** Mem past basileus Omega Psi Phi Frat 1950-; mem accreditation comm Southern Assoc of Schools 1968-84; mem exec comm Middle TN Cncl of Boy Scouts 1973-80; mem Phi Delta Kappa 1976-; comm mem on porject review Southern Assoc of Colls 1978-79; mem Financial Exec Inst 1978-; mem dir Peach Co Chamber of Commerce 1982-; chmn Scholarship Comm Southern Assoc of Coll & Univ Business Officers 1982-83; mem Sigma Pi Phi Frat 1983-; mem bd of deacons Trinity Baptist Church 1986-; mem exec comm on business affairs Natl Assoc of State Univ & Land Grant Colls 1986-87. **Home Addr:** 103 Cochran Court, Byron, GA 31008. **Business Addr:** Vice Pres Business and Finance, Fort Valley State College, 1005 State College Drive, Fort Valley, GA 31030.

JUNIOR, SAMELLA E.
Educator, musician. **Personal:** Born Dec 15, 1931, Chattanooga, TN; married Ester James; children: Avis, E J. **Educ:** Spelman Coll, AB 1953; LA St U, m Music Ed 1957; George Peabody Coll, PhD 1977. **Career:** East HS, prin 1978; Whites Creek Comprehensive HS, asso prin; Pearl HS, Cumberland Jr HS, prin 1975-78; Joelton HS, asst prin 1974-75; Isaac Litton Jr HS, 1971-74; Highland Hts Jr HS, tchr 1969-71; Carver Jr HS, tchr dir, chmn 1963-68; E Baker HS & Elem Sch, tchr 1961-63; Livingstone Coll, prof 1959-60; Jarvis Christian Coll, 1957-59; Leland Coll, instr, dir 1956-57; HS, tchr 1953-57. **Orgs:** Choir dir, minist, Mt Zion Bapt Ch; First Bapt Ch; Disciples of Christ Ch; asst organist, First Bapt Ch; choir dir, minister of music, current pres, Spelman Clb; pres, vp, sec, com chmn, mem, Delta Sigma Theta Inc; treas, Nat Cncl of Negro Women; treas, Black Expo; sec, Albany St Coll Wives; com chmn, mem, NEA, MNEA, TEA, NASSP, TASSP, ASCD, ATE, Phi Delta Kappa, AAUW, Nashville Pin; pres-elect, Middle Region TEA; chmn, Metro Cncl of Tchr Ed; mem, Nat Flwshp of Ch Muscns; NAACP; vice-chmn bd, Operation PUSH. **Business Addr:** E Nashville Sr H S, Nashville, TN 37206.

JUPITER, CLYDE PETER
Nuclear science and engineering company executive. **Personal:** Born Oct 31, 1928, New Orleans, LA; married Pat (Schofield) Jupiter, Nov 27, 1987; children: Carol A Gariboldi, Lisa A Jupiter-Byles, Joan C, Deanne, Matthews, Mike Schank, Steve Schank, Chris Schank, Erika Schank. **Educ:** Xavier Univ New Orleans, BS Physics 1949; Univ of Notre Dame S Bend, MS Physics 1951. **Career:** Lawrence Radiation Laboratory, Livermore CA, 1956-64; Gen Atomic Co San Diego, staff sci 1964-69; EG&G Inc Santa Barbara, mgr radiation physics dept 1969-70; EG&G Inc Albuquerque, dir of applied sci 1970-71; EG&G Inc Las Vegas, mgr radiation & environmental sci dept 1971-75; US Nuclear Reg Commn, tech asst to dir of rsch 1975-78, program mgr waste mgmt 1978-82; US Nuclear Regulatory Comm, sr policy analyst office of policy eval 1982-86; Howard Univ Sch of Engineering, adjunct prof nuclear engineering program 1981-86; Jupiter Corporation president 1986-. **Orgs:** Mem Amer Nuclear Soc 1965-; bd dir Amer Nuclear Soc 1976-79, 1994-97; mem Alpha Phi Alpha Frat 1947-; mem NAACP; mem Health Physics Society; mem American Assn for the Advancement of Science. **Honors/Awds:** Teaching Fellowship Univ of Notre Dame S Bend IN 1949-50; elected to Grade of Fellow Amer Nuclear Soc 1980. **Military Serv:** AUS sp-3 1954-56. **Business Addr:** President, Jupiter Corporation, 2730 University Blvd W, Ste 900, Wheaton, MD 20902.

JUSTICE, DAVID CHRISTOPHER
Professional baseball player. **Personal:** Born Apr 14, 1966, Cincinnati, OH; married Halle Berry, Dec 31, 1992 (divorced 1996). **Educ:** Thomas More College, Crestview Hills, KY, attended. **Career:** Atlanta Braves, outfielder/infielder, 1989-97; Cleveland Indians, 1997-. **Honors/Awds:** National League Rookie of the Year, Baseball Writers' Association of America, 1990. **Business Addr:** Professional Baseball Player, Cleveland Indians, 2401 Ontario, Cleveland, OH 44115, (216)420-4200.

K

KADREE, MARGARET ANTONIA
Physician, educator. **Personal:** Born Jun 25, 1952, Tunapuna, West Indies; daughter of Ella and Fitzroy Vidale; married Adegboyega J Kadree, Apr 24, 1976; children: Temilade, Shijuade, Yewande, Hafsa. **Educ:** New York Univ, BA, 1976-79; State of New York at Buffalo School of Medicine, MD, 1979-83. **Career:** Morehouse School of Medicine, asst prof med, 1993-, chief infectious diseases, 1993-, dir of clin res prog, 1984-, dir of HIV prevention in youth, subproject of MSM zambian HIV prevention project, 1993-; Center for Disease Control, guest researcher, 1994-, dir, clinical research program, 1994-. **Orgs:** Food and Drug Admin, microbiologic devices comm, 1994-; Georgia State Task Force on AIDS, 1994-; American Lung Assn, education comm, 1994-; Atlanta Metropolitan TB Task Force, 1993-. **Honors/Awds:** State Univ of New York at Buffalo School of Med, Dean's Award, 1983; Upjohn Pharmaceutical Co, Outstanding Resident, 1986. **Special Achievements:** Author "How Safe is Safe Sex?" Ebony Magazine, July 1994; "Adolescents and HIV," New York City Cable, December 1992; "HIV and AIDS," Washington View Magazine, February 1992; "AIDS," Washington Post, health section, June 1991. **Business Addr:** Chief of Infectious Diseases, Asst Professor of Medicine, Morehouse School of Medicine, 720 Westview Dr., SW, Rm 1235, Atlanta, GA 30310, (404)752-1880.

KAFELE, BARUTI KWAME
Educator, author, motivational speaker. **Personal:** Born Oct 22, 1960, Orange, NJ; son of Delores C James and Norman G Hopkins; married Kimberley Broughton, Jun 3, 1989; children: Baruti H. **Educ:** Middlesex County College, AS, 1985; Kean College, BS, 1986. **Career:** New York City Board of Education, teacher, 1988-89; Baruti Publishing, owner, president, publisher, 1990-; East Orange Board of Education, teacher, 1992-. **Honors/Awds:** Phi Kappa Phi National Honor Society, 1986; Lambda Alpha Sigma Liberal Arts & Science Honor Society, 1986; Black Student Union Academic Achievement Award, 1986; UB and US Literary Achievement Awards, Best New Writer Male, 1991. **Special Achievements:** Author, A Black Parent's Handbook to Educating Your Children, 1991; author, Goal Setting: For Serious Minded Black Folks, 1991; author, A Black Student's Guide to Goal Setting, 1992; author, Goal Setting: A Black View, 1992. **Business Addr:** President, Baruti Publishing/Baruti Productions, PO Box 4088, Jersey City, NJ 07304, (201)433-9484.

KAIGLER, MARIE. See KAIGLER-REESE, MARIE MADELEINE.

KAIGLER-REESE, MARIE MADELEINE (MARIE KAIGLER)
Broadcaster, counselor. **Personal:** Born Jan 25, 1945. **Educ:** Fisk University, BA, 1965; Wayne State University, master's, 1969; Wayne State University, 1983. **Career:** Wayne County Juvenile Ct, caseworker aide, 1965-66; Michigan Employment Security Commission, employment counselor, 1966-67; Northern Systems Company, behavioral counselor, 1967-70; Detroit Board of Education, school community agent, 1970-78; Wayne County Community College, part-time instructor, 1969-82; WJLB, co-host and producer of People Want to Know, 1972-79; private practice, MORE, group individual instructor, seminar instructor, 1975-85; Wayne State University, College of Education, research asst, dean's office, 1985-86; WXYT, radio journalist, 1990-. **Orgs:** Exec bd chair, political awareness, Michigan Association of Counseling and Development, 1989-90; chair, education bd of dir, American Association of University Women, 1990; chair, membership exec bd, Republican Women's Forum, 1986-; chair, political awareness, Michigan Employment Counseling Assoc, 1987-. **Honors/Awds:** Michigan Citizen Newspaper articles: "The Single Homemaker," Oct 8-14, 1989, p. 6, "Aging Black Leadership," Sept 24-30, 1989, p. 6, "Being Black Is Not Enough," Sept 17-23, 1989, p. 6, "Why Republican?," Jul 30- Aug 5, 1989, p. 6, "The Black Agenda 1900-2000: Get Real!," Apr 9-15, 1989, p. 6; Certificate of Appreciation, Guest Lecturer, College of Nursing, Wayne State University, 1988; Most Inspiring Counselor, Oakland Community College, 1982; "Appreciation Service" commendation, President of the U S, Washington, DC, 1981; candidate, state representative, 1990; candidate, Wayne County Commissioner, 1990; various others. **Business Addr:** Radio Journalist Broadcaster, WXYT AM 1270, 15600 W 12 Mile Rd, PO Box 905, Southfield, MI 48037.

KAISER, ERNEST DANIEL
Librarian (retired). **Personal:** Born Dec 5, 1915, Petersburg, VA; son of Elnora B Ellis Kaiser and Ernest B Kaiser; married Mary G Orford, 1949 (deceased); children: Eric, Joan. **Educ:** CCNY, attended 1935-38. **Career:** Advisor, author 10 intro's for Arno Press series The Amer Negro, His History & Literature 145 vols; McGraw Hill Pub Co New York, R R Bowker Co New York, Chelsea House Publ, Univ Massachusetts Press Amherst, reviewer consultant editor; co-editor & contrib editor, The Negro Almanac 1971, 1976, 1983, 1989; 1993; Black Titan, WEB DuBois: An Anthology 1970; Paul Robeson, The Great Forerunner 1978, 2nd ed 1985; Encyclopedia of Black Amer, 1981; Freedomways Reader, 1977; editor; Science & Soc, contrib editor; Freedomways Magazine, co-fndr & assoc editor 1961-85; adviser, Gale reference series: Contemporary Black Biography; Schomburg Ct, admin assoc staff mem 1945-86 (retired). **Honors/Awds:** Author "In Defense of the People's Blk & White Hist & Cult, 1970; co-author "Harlem, A Hist of Broken Dreams, 1974; contributor William Styron's Nat Turner: Ten Black Writers Respond, 1968; Harlem: A Community in Transition, 1964; In Black America, 1968; The Year of Awakening, 1969; Twentieth Century Interpretations of Invisible Man, 1970; EJ Josey & Ann A Shockley Handbook of Black Librarianship, 1977, 1998; RW Logan & M R Winston Diction of Amer Negro Biography, 1982, 1998; numerous essays bk reviews introductions & bibl pub in many books, mags & newspapers; Plaque Kappa Sigma Chap Sigma Gamma Rho 1982; Humanitarian Awd Harlem School of the Arts 1985; Ernest D Kaiser Index to Black Resources named in 1985 at Schomburg Center; The Kaiser Index to Black Resources, 1948-86, 5 vols, 1992; has bibliographies of his work in Richard Newman's Black Access: A Bibliography of African American Bibliographies, 1984, and in Betty K Gubert and Richard Newman's Nine Decades of Scholarship: A Bibliography of the Writings 1892-1983 of the Staff of the Schomburg Center for Research in Black Culture, 1986; co-editor, forthcoming book on the Civil Rights Movement from "Freedomway" Magazine; A History of Black Legacy: New Yorker, African-Americans, 1997; completed Elton C Fox's bibliography in "250 years of African-American Art," 1981, Artist and Influence, vol 17, Hatch-Billops Collection, 1998. **Home Addr:** 31-37 95 St, East Elmhurst, NY 11369.

KAISER, JAMES GORDON
Service company executive. **Personal:** Born Feb 28, 1943, St Louis, MO; son of Jane Aileen Gordon and Samuel Arthur Kaiser; married Kathryn Juanita Mounday; children: Lauren Elizabeth. **Educ:** UCLA, BA, 1966; MIT, MS, 1973. **Career:** Corning Incorporated Corning NY, sales rep 1968-70, sales promotion specialist 1970-72, product line mgr 1973-75, business planning mgr 1975-76, general mgr sales & marketing 1976-79, mgr new business develop 1979-81, business mgr 1981-84, vice pres and general mgr 1984-86, senior vice president, beginning 1987; Enseco Inc, pres, CEO, 1992-94; Quanterra Inc, currently. **Orgs:** Sun Company, bd of dir, 1993-; The Stanley Works, bd of dirs; International Assn of Environmental Testing Labs, bd of dirs, 1994-; The Keystone Ctr, bd of trustees, 1993-; Wharton Spencer Stuart Dirs Instituite, bd of dir; Executive Leadership Council, founding mem, past pres, past bd mem. **Honors/Awds:** Houghton Award, Total Quality, Corning Inc, 1992; The Partner Development Award, Society of Black Professionals, 1991; Honorary Doctorate, Humane Letters, Florida A&M Univ, 1988; Blue Ribbon Giver's Award, Corning Hospital & Founders Pavilion, 1991. **Military Serv:** USNR jg 2 yrs; Navy Achievement Medal, Natl Defense Medal, 2 Bronze Stars Vietnam Svcs, Republic of Vietnam Campaign Medal. **Home Addr:** 111 Falcon Hills Dr, Highlands Ranch, CO 80126.

KAISER-DARK, PHYLLIS E.
Political appointee. **Career:** The White House, confidential assistant, currently. **Business Addr:** Confidential Assistant, Rm 350 Old Executive Office Bldg, 17th St & Pennsylvania Ave NW, Washington, DC 20503, (202)395-4852.

KALU, NDUKWE DIKE
Professional football player. **Personal:** Born Aug 3, 1975, Baltimore, MD. **Educ:** Rice Univ, attended. **Career:** Philadelphia Eagles, defensive end, 1997-. **Business Addr:** Professional Football Player, Philadelphia Eagles, 3501 S Broad St, Philadelphia, PA 19148, (215)463-2500.

KAMAU, MOSI (ANTHONY CHARLES GUNN WHITE)
Educator. **Personal:** Born May 5, 1955, Chicago, IL. **Educ:** Univ of Minnesota, BFA 1979; Florida State Univ, MFA 1983; Temple Univ, PhD candidate, African-Amer Studies, 1989-. **Career:** Tutle Contemporary Elem School, pottery instructor, 1977-78 Talbot Supply Co Inc, welder 1979-80; Florida State Univ, asst preparator 1980-81; Williams Foundry, foundryman 1981-82; St Pauls Coll, asst prof of art 1984-89. **Orgs:** Natl Council of Black Studies; African American Assn of Ghana; African Heritage Assn. **Honors/Awds:** Intl Exchange Scholarship from Univ of Minnesota to Univ of Ife Ile, Ife Nigeria 1976-77; Sculpture/$5000 Natl Endowment of the Arts, Visual Arts, Washington DC 1984-85. **Military Serv:** USN Reserve E-3 1984-90; grad with honors 1984. **Home Addr:** 1639 W Grange, Philadelphia, PA 19141.

KAMOCHE, JIDLAPH GITAU
Educator. **Personal:** Born Dec 1, 1942, Kabete, Kenya; married Charity Njambi; children: Nyakio, Kamoche Gitau. **Educ:** Amherst Col, BA 1967; Univ of MA, MA 1969; State Univ of NY at Buffalo, PhD 1977. **Career:** African & Afro-Amer Studies Univ of OK, asst prof of History dir 1977-; State Univ Coll Buffalo, asst prof History 1972-77; African & Afro-Amer, dir; State Univ Coll Buffalo, stud 1970-72. **Orgs:** Mem Several African & Afro-am Studies Orgns 1970-80; past vice pres Assn of Black Personnel Univ of OK 1978-79. **Honors/Awds:** Recipeint inst of intl Educ Fellowship NY 1968-69; author Afro-am Life & Hist 1977; author articles & book reviews in several scholarly journs 1977-;recipient coll of arts research fellowship Univ of OK 1979-80; author ''Umoja'' 1980. **Business Addr:** Associate Prof, Department of History, University of Oklahoma, 455 W Lindsey, Norman, OK 73019.

KANE, EUGENE A.
Columnist. **Personal:** Born May 15, 1956, Philadelphia, PA; son of Eugene & Hattie. **Educ:** Temple Univ, BA, 1980. **Career:** The Philadelphia Bulletin, reporter, 1980; The Milwaukee Journal, reporter, 1981-85, features writer, columnist, 1985-. **Orgs:** Natl Assn of Black Journalist, 1994; Wisconsin Black Media Assn, 1984-. **Honors/Awds:** John S Knight Fellowship, Stanford Univ, 1992-93; First Place Commentary, Amer Society of Sunday & Features Editors, 1989. **Business Addr:** Metro Columnist, The Milwaukee Journal-Sentinel, 333 W State St, Milwaukee, WI 53201, (414)223-5521.

KANE, JACQUELINE ANNE
Educator. **Personal:** Born Aug 27, 1946, New York, NY; daughter of Jacqueline Jones Kane and Philip Gough Kane. **Educ:** Morgan State Univ, AB 1968; State Univ New York Coll Oneonta MS, 1974; State Univ of New York at Albany, PhD, 1997. **Career:** New York City Dept of Soc Srvs, caseworker 1968-70; State Univ of New York Clge At Oneonta, coord of cnslng & acad adv 1970-75; State Univ of New York at Albany, adjunct instructor, 1984-88; New York State Educ Dept, dir resource ctr for higher educ, 1976-81, associate in higer education opportunity, 1976-. **Orgs:** Conf comm chair newsletter editor, bd mem Assc of Black Women in Higher Educ 1978-92; mem New York State Planning Comm Amer Council of Educ Natl Ident Proj 1980-92; pres 1983-85, 1997-, chmn fin comm 1985-87; Financial Secretary, 1987-90, Treasurer 1990-93, corresponding scy, 1995-97, Albany New York Alumnae Chptr Delta Sigma Theta Sor Inc 1983-; bd mem 1984-93, chmn youth serv comm 1986-90; Asst Secretary, 1990-92; Albany Area Chptr Amer Red Cross 1984-; President, Capital Chapter Assoc of Black Women in Higher Education 1989-92. **Honors/Awds:** Schrlshp award Delta Sigma Theta Sor Inc 1981; Hilda H Davis Award for Distinguished Leadership and Service by a Professional; SAGE, a scholarly journal of black women 1988; NOW, Wave Award, 1994; Albany Branch NAACP, African American Women of Distinction, 1996. **Business Addr:** Associate, Higher Educ Opportunity, New York State Education Dept, 1071 EBA, Albany, NY 12234.

KANI, KARL (CARL WILLIAMS)
Clothing designer. **Personal:** Born in Brooklyn, NY. **Career:** Cross Colours, 1991-94; Karl Kani Infinity, president and CEO, currently. **Business Addr:** President/CEO, Karl Kani Enterprises, c/o Cynthia Atabarry, 3801 Broadway, Los Angeles, CA 90037, (310)318-3100.

KAPPNER, AUGUSTA SOUZA
Educational administrator. **Personal:** Born Jun 25, 1944, New York, NY; daughter of Monica Fraser and Augusto Souza; married Thomas Kappner; children: Tania, Diana. **Educ:** Barnard College, New York, NY, AB, 1966; Hunter College, New York, NY, MSW, 1968; Columbia University, New York, NY, DSW, 1984. **Career:** State University of New York, School of Social Welfare, Stony Brook, NY, asst prof, 1973-74; LaGuardia Community College, Queens, NY, assoc prof, 1974-78, dean, cont education, 1978-84; City University of New York, New York, NY, univ dean, academic affairs, 1984-86; Borough of Manhattan Community College, New York, NY, president, 1986-. **Orgs:** Member, board of directors, National Council on Black American Affairs/AACJC; appointed by Governor Mario Cuomo to the New York State Child Care Commission; appointed by Mayor David Dinkins to the New York City Temporary Commission on Early Childhood and Child Caring Programs; vice chair, board of trustees, Marymount Manhattan College; chair, Marymount Manhattan College Presidential Search Committee; pres, chair, board of directors, Women's Center for Education and Career Advancement. **Honors/Awds:** Certificate of Achievement, The Comptroller of the City of New York, 1990; Community Service Award, Hawks International, Inc, 1990; The Harlem School of Arts Humanitarian Award, 1990; Columbia University Medal of Excellence, 1988; Barnard College Medal of Distinction, 1988; Hunter College Hall of Fame, 1987. **Business Addr:** President, Borough of Manhattan Community College, 199 Chambers St, Rm S750, New York, NY 10007.

KARANGU, DAVID
Automobile dealer. **Career:** Fairway Ford of Augusta Inc, CEO, currently. **Business Addr:** Owner/President, Fairway Ford of Augusta Inc., 4333 Washington Rd, Evans, GA 30809-9512, (706)854-9200.

KARPEH, ENID JUAH HILDEGARD
Attorney. **Personal:** Born Apr 4, 1957, Mainz; daughter of Marion Catherine White Cooper and Martin Sieh Karpeh, Jr. **Educ:** University of Pennsylvania, BA, international relations, 1979; New York University School of Law, New York, NY, JD, 1983. **Career:** O'Donnell and Schwartz, New York, NY, associate attorney, 1983-85; WNET, 13, New York, NY, associate general counsel, 1986-88; MTV Networks, Inc, New York, NY, counsel law and business affairs, 1988-90; CBS Broadcasting Inc, New York, NY, independent legal counsel, 1990; Arts and Entertainment Network, New York, NY, director, legal and business affairs, 1990-. **Orgs:** Bar Association of the City of New York, currently; Black Entertainment and Sports Lawyers Association, currently. **Business Addr:** Director, Legal and Business Affairs, Arts and Entertainment Network, 235 E 45th St, New York, NY 10017.

KASHIF, GHAYTH NUR (LONNIE KASHIF)
Editor, consultant, author, TV producer/director. **Personal:** Born Sep 9, 1933, Raeford, NC; son of Annie Mae Bethea Dale and Lonnie Smith (deceased); married Hafeeza N A; children: Alif-Ahmed, Rul-Aref, Shazada Latifa, Sadara Barrow. **Educ:** Keesler Comm Chenute USAF, Dip (Tech Mass Comm) 1953; Univ MD Grant Tech (CA), 1953; NY Schl of Writing, Dip 1955. **Career:** Muhammad Speaks Bilalian News, Wash Bur chief 1968-78; Bilalian News AM Journal, editor 1978-81; Intl Graphics Kashif News Svc, consult writer 1981-85; Internatl Inst of Islamic Thought, editor 1987; American Journal Muslim Social Scientists, consultant 1986-87; Journal Iqraa and Open Magazines and Metropolitan Magazines, exec editor 1982-84, 1985; TV director, producer, Islam in Focus, Warner Cable TV, Virginia; Masjidush-Shora, Washington, DC, imam, 1990-; American Muslim Council, Washington, DC, dir cong affairs, 1990-; Black Congressional Watch, editor, 1990-. **Orgs:** Pres chmn Bilalian News Inc 1978-81; dir secr treas Metro Magazine Inc 1982-83; dir Shaw Bus Inc 1985; consult Intl Graphics/IQraa Magazine 1981-1987; mem Natl Red Cross 1985, Capital Press Club 1985, Org 3rd World Journal NNPA 1987; rep Black Media Inc 1982-83; dir comm Majdush Shura; mem Internatl platform; comm Bilalian Economic Devel Corp 1985-87; dir, The Roundtable for strategic studies 1989. **Honors/Awds:** 1st Annual Freedom Jour Award Univ of DC 1979; Fred R Doug Award HU (Muhammad Speaks) 1977; Excel in Jour CM Fnd 1979; ''Sacred Journey'' author 1986; ''Questions, The Quranic Response''. **Military Serv:** USAF s/sgt; Distinguished Natl Defense Srvc Medal; Good Conduct Medal 1955. **Home Addr:** 3506 Varnum St, Brentwood, MD 20722.

KASHIF, LONNIE. See KASHIF, GHAYTH NUR.

KAUFMAN, MEL
Professional sports administrator. **Personal:** Born Feb 24, 1958, Los Angeles, CA. **Educ:** Cal Poly San Luis Opispo, attended. **Career:** Washington Redskins, outside linebacker, 1981-88, personnel scout, 1990-. **Honors/Awds:** Started in Super Bowl, 1983, 1984, 1988. **Business Addr:** Personnel Scout, Washington Redskins, 21300 Redskin Park Dr, Ashburn, VA 22011-6100, (703)478-8900.

KAUFMAN, NAPOLEON
Professional football player. **Personal:** Born Jun 7, 1973, Kansas City, MO. **Educ:** University of Washington. **Career:** Oakland Raiders, running back, 1995-. **Special Achievements:** Selected in the 1st round/18th overall pick in the 1995 NFL Draft. **Business Addr:** Professional Football Player, Oakland Raiders, 1220 Harbor Bay Pky, Alameda, CA 94502, (510)615-1875.

KAZADI, MUADIANVITA MATT
Professional football player. **Personal:** Born Dec 20, 1973. **Educ:** Tulsa, attended. **Career:** St Louis Rams, linebacker, 1997-. **Business Addr:** Professional Football Player, St Louis Rams, One Rams Way, St Louis, MO 63045, (314)982-7267.

KAZI, ABDUL-KHALIQ KUUMBA
Editor, writer, consultant. **Personal:** Born Dec 15, 1951, New Orleans, LA; son of Yvonne Gavion Ferrouillet and Wilbur F Ferrouillet; married Sandra Pierre; children: Zijazo, Ambata, Mandela, Ahmad. **Educ:** Tulane Univ, attended 1969-71; Univ of New Orleans, attended 1985-86; Stanford Univ, 1993. **Career:** Moret Press, printer 1971-80; Figaro Newspaper, production Associate 1980-81; Black Collegiate Serv Inc, copy editor 1981-83, assoc editor 1983-86, managing editor 1986-, production mgr 1989-; Worldwide Concepts Inc, editor, writer, 1992-; Times-Picayune Publishing Corp, editor, 1994-. **Orgs:** Founder/mem Black Runners Organization 1980-; mem National Assn of Black Journalists 1988-89; mem, Amer Muslim Council, 1992; mem, Council on Amer-Islamic Relations, 1994; mem, Holy Land Foundation, 1994. **Honors/Awds:** Unity Awd in Media Lincoln Univ of MO 1985, 1989-90; Keynote Speaker/Black History US Dept Agriculture 1986; keynote speaker, Black Students on White Campuses Conference, Georgia State Univ 1989; guest panelist, Print Journalism Seminar, Southern Univ at New Orleans 1989; keynote speaker, Alpha Phi Alpha-Cornell Univ. 1991-; Keynote Speaker, Univ of N Carolina-Wilmington, 1993; Speaker, African Holocaust Conference, Bowling Green State Univ, 1993. **Home Addr:** 22 Chatham Dr, New Orleans, LA 70122.

KEA, ARLEAS UPTON
Attorney. **Personal:** Born Mar 31, 1957, Weimar, TX; daughter of Henry & Lillie Mae Upton; married Howard E Kea, Apr 19, 1986; children: Chase, Arlyce Mallory. **Educ:** Univ of TX, BA, 1979; Univ of TX School of Law, JD, 1982. **Career:** US Dept of Labor, benefits review bd attorney, 1982-85; FDIC, sr attorney, Fidelity Bd Claims, 1985-89, counsel, Criminal Restitution, 1989-91, asst general counsel, 1994-96, ombudsman, 1996-. **Orgs:** US Supreme Court Bar, 1989-; State Bar of TX, 1983-; Natl Bar Assn, 1985-; Federal Bar Assn, 1985-87; Natl Conference of Black Lawyers, sec, 1982-88; Alpha Kappa Alpha Sorority; Lomas AME Zion Church, chairman bd of stewards, 1988-90; Tutor/Mentoring Prog, vice chair, 1992-. **Honors/Awds:** FDIC Special Achievement Award, 1987-89; Outstanding Woman of Lomax AME Zion Church, 1990. **Business Addr:** Ombudsman, Federal Deposit Insurance Corp, 550 17th St, NW, Room 4090, Washington, DC 20429, (202)942-3859.

KEANE, HORACE JAMES BASIL
Dentist. **Personal:** Born Mar 21, 1926, Boston, MA; married; children: Karen, Mark. **Educ:** Howard Univ, BS 1948; Howard Univ Coll of Dentistry, DDS 1952. **Career:** Howard Univ Coll of Dentistry, clin instr 1954-57; Jamaica WI, Govt Dental Officer 1957-59; private practice 1957-; first Jamaican Full Length Film, ''Harder They Come'' played role of ''Preacher''; many radio and TV appearances in Jamaica and Britain. **Orgs:** Pres, Jamaica Dental Assn, 1965-68; mem, Illinois, District of Columbia & Jamaica WI Dental Bds; rep, Dental Conf in England, 1968; rep, NDA Conv, 1970-72; dental adv, Minister of Health Re-Establishment Dental Aux School; mem, JDA; ADA; mem, Omega Asi Phi; Jamaica Labour Party; Calabar Old Boys Assn; Lions Club; Melbourne, Lucas, Kensington Cricket Clubs; toured UK as guest of British govt. **Honors/Awds:** Published various articles in Daily Gleaner; recipient, Order of Distinction, Jamaican Govt, 1978. **Military Serv:** USNR lt comm 1952-57.

KEARNEY, JESSE L.
Attorney. **Personal:** Born Jan 14, 1950, Gould, AR; son of Ethel Virginia Curry Kearney and Thomas James Kearney; married Sheryl Rene Rogers Kearney, Dec 21, 1977; children: Phillip James, Jessica Leigh. **Educ:** University of Arkansas, Fayetteville, AR, BA, political science, 1973; University of Arkansas School of Law, JD, 1976; National Judicial College, Reno, NV, Certificate, 1989. **Career:** Kearney Law Office, attorney, Magnolia, AR, 1976-77, Pine Bluff, AR, 1981-82; State of Arkansas, Office of Attorney General, Little Rock, AR, asst attorney general, 1977-79; State of Arkansas, Office of the Governor, Little Rock, AR, special asst to the Governor, 1979-81; Arkansas State Claims Commission, Little Rock, AR, commissioner, 1981; Cross, Kearney & McKissic, Pine Bluff, AR, attorney/partner, 1982-89, 1990-; State of Arkansas Judicial Dept, Pine Bluff, AR, ciruit/chancery court judge, 1989-90. **Orgs:** Member: W Harold Flowers Law Soc, 1977-, Jefferson County Bar Assn, 1981-, Arkansas Bar Assn, 1977-, Arkansas Trial Lawyers Assn, 1987-, Amer Bar Assn, 1977-, Amer Trial Lawyers Assn, 1984-. **Business Addr:** Attorney, Cross, Kearney and McKissic, 100 Pine St, Ste 13, PO Box 6606, Pine Bluff, AR 71611.

KEARSE, AMALYA LYLE
Judge. **Personal:** Born Jun 11, 1937, Vauxhall, NJ. **Educ:** Wellesley Coll, BA 1959; Univ Michigan Law Sch Ann Arbor, JD 1962. **Career:** Hughes Hubbard & Reed, assoc 1962-69; NY Univ Law Sch Washington Sq, adjunct lectr 1968-69; US Court of Appeals, circuit judge. **Orgs:** Exec com Lawyers Com for Civil Rights Under Law 1970-79; mem Amer Law Inst 1977-; fellow Amer Coll of Trial Lawyers 1979-; mem Pres's Comm for Selection of Judges 1977-78; bd dirs NAACP LD&E Fund 1977-79; bd dir Natl Urban League 1978-79. **Honors/Awds:** Cum Laude; Order of the Coif; Jason L Honigman Awd for Outstanding Contribution to Law Review Edit Bd. **Business Addr:** Circuit Judge, US Court of Appeals, Foley Square, Rm 801, New York, NY 10007.

KEARSE, BARBARA STONE
Government official. **Personal:** Born Apr 17, 1936, Washington, DC; daughter of Essie Jones Stone and Albert Stone; married David Kearse, Oct 1, 1960 (died 1985); children: Lori A, David A. **Educ:** Syracuse University, Syracuse, NY, BA, 1957, 1960-61. **Career:** Department of Air Force, Syracuse, NY, chief employee/labor relations, 1970-84; Department of Air Force, Washington, DC, personnel management, Spec, 1984-85, personnel management analyst, 1985-87; Defense Mapping Agency, Fairfax, VA, chief employee relations, 1987-90; Department of Navy, Arlington, VA, head employee relations, 1990-. **Orgs:** National Syntaktes, Lambda Kappa Mu Sorority Inc, 1989-; basileus, Lambda Kappa Mu Sorority Inc, Theta Chapter, 1988-; board of directors, YMCA, 1980-83; board of directors, Syracuse Girls Club, 1980-83; St Timothy's Church, senior warden, 1988-91. **Honors/Awds:** Woman of Achievement, Delta Sigma Theta Sorority Inc, 1981; Manager of the Year, Department of Air Force, 1982; Distinguished Service Key, Lambda Kappa Mu Sorority Inc, 1984. **Business Addr:** Discrimination Complaints Manager, OCPM HQ, Department of the Navy, 800 N Quincy St, Code 02A3, Arlington, VA 22203-1998.

KEARSE, GREGORY SASHI
Editor. **Personal:** Born Feb 13, 1949, Brooklyn, NY; divorced; children: Nina Monique. **Educ:** Howard U, BA English 1974, Communications Research, PhD candidate. **Career:** New York Times, internship, 1969; WABC-TV NY, news asst, writer, 1970-71; Etcetera Mag, assoc editor, 1971-72; Mutual Black Radio Network, news editor, writer, 1974-78; Howard Univ Press, editor, 1978-85, editorial consultant, 1985-88; Applications Systems, technical writer, 1989-. **Orgs:** St John's #12, Prince Hall Grand Lodge, Mt. Vernon Chapter #1 (Royal Arch Masons); National Rifle Association; Sigma Delta Chi Soc of Prof Journalists; Authors League & Authors Guild of America; American Association of University Presses; Washington Area Publ Association; Big Brothers of Greater Washington; AFTRA; Johnathon Davis Consistory #1 (Supreme Council of the 33rd Degree); Scottish Rite Research Society; The Phylaxis Society; Public Affairs Office. **Honors/Awds:** Writer's Digest Creative Writing Award, 1970; Public Svcs Award, Sec of Labor, 1977; Radio Commentary Award, 1976. **Special Achievements:** Ebony Mag; Encore; Modern Black Men Mag; Essence Mag; Washington African-American Newspaper Columnist; Chess Life; Karate Illustrated; The Continenet Newspaper, writer, book review editor; African Faces Mag, editor-in-chief; Campus Lifestyle Mag; New Directions; Chronicle of Higher Education; publications, Scottish Rite Journal, Phylaxsis Notes, Masonic Digest. **Business Addr:** Technical Writer, Howard University, Information Systems & Svcs, 2301 Georgia Ave, NW, Washington, DC 20059.

KEATON, WILLIAM T.
College president/chancellor. **Career:** Arkansas Baptist College, Little Rock AK, president/chancellor. **Business Addr:** Arkansas Baptist College, Little Rock, AR 72202.

KEBEDE, ASHENAFI AMDE (ASHENAFI AMADE-MARRIAM)
Educator. **Personal:** Born May 7, 1938, Addis Ababa, Ethiopia; son of Fantaye Nekere and Balanbaras Kebede; married Elleni Gebre Meskel, May 7, 1964 (divorced); children: Nina, Senait, Yared. **Educ:** University of Rochester, BA, 1962; Wesleyan University, MA, 1969, PhD, 1971. **Career:** US Peace Corps, counselor/teacher, summer 1962; Ethiopian Ministry of Education, director/teacher, 1962-68; Wesleyan University, instructor, 1968-71; Queens College, CUNY, assistant professor, 1971-75; Brandeis University, assistant professor, 1976-80; Florida State University, Center for African-American Culture, professor/director, 1980-. **Orgs:** Ethiopian National Music Committee, president, 1963-71; International Music Council, UNESCO, 1964-69; Society for Ethnomusicology, 1964-90; Florida Arts Council for African-American Affairs, executive director, 1982-90; Ethius, Inc, executive director, 1989-. **Honors/Awds:** Haile Selassie Foundation, Outstanding Young Ethiopian Scholar, 1958; UNESCO, UNESCO Expert to Sudan, 1979; Institute for International Education, Senior Fulbright Scholar to Israel, 1986-87. **Special Achievements:** Founded Ethiopia's Institute of Music, 1963; first African to conduct the Hungarian State Orchestra in Budapest, 1967; commissioned by UNESCO, wrote the syllabus for Sudan's Institute of Music, Dance and Drama, 1979; numerous books, monograms, articles and compositions in Black Perspectives in Music, Musical Quarterly, Ethnomusicology. **Business Addr:** Professor, Center for African-American Culture, Florida State University, 210 S Woodward Ave, B-105, Tallahassee, FL 32306, (904)644-3252.

KEE, MARSHA GOODWIN
Government official. **Personal:** Born Oct 3, 1942, Durham, NC; daughter of Margaret Catherine Kennedy Goodwin and Lewis Marshall Goodwin; divorced. **Educ:** Spelman Coll, Atlanta GA, BA, 1964; Atlanta Univ, Atlanta GA, MA, 1969. **Career:** NC Central Univ, Durham NC, instructor of sociology, 1966-72; NC State Univ, Raleigh NC, instructor of sociology, 1973-74; Durham Coll, Durham NC, counselor/director, 1974-80; NC Office of State Personnel, Raleigh NC, personnel analyst, 1980-89; County of Durham, NC, dir equal opportunity/affirmative action, 1989-. **Orgs:** Mem, Delta Sigma Theta Sorority Inc, 1967-; mem, Intl Personnel Mgmt Assn, 1985-; mem, NAACP, 1987-; mem, Nat Forum for Black Pub Admin, 1989-; mem, NC Minority Women's Business Enterprise, 1989-; Financial Secretary, NCCU Educational Advancement Foundation 1989-. **Honors/Awds:** Alpha Kappa Delta, Natl Sociological Honor Society, 1965; Outstanding Young Women in Amer, 1975; Outstanding Soloist, White Rock Baptist Church, 1985; Outstanding Soloist, St Joseph's AME Church Lay Organization, 1988, pastor's soloist, 1989.

KEELER, VERNES
Construction company executive. **Career:** V Keeler & Associates Inc, New Orleans LA, chief executive, 1971—. **Business Addr:** Chief Executive, V Keeler & Associates, Inc, PO Box 3424, New Orleans, LA 70177.

KEELS, JAMES DEWEY
Mayor (retired). **Personal:** Born Jan 12, 1930, Blackfork, OH; son of Hulda Howell Keels and G Dewey Keels; married Dorothy M Wilmore; children: James Dewey Jr, Tawana Lynn Simons. **Educ:** Univ of Cincinnati Ev Coll, attended 1971. **Career:** US Post Office, postal clk 1953-78; Village of Woodlawn, counc 1969-71, mayor 1972-79; US Post Office, supr del & collection 1979-80; Address Information Systems, mgr 1981-85, retired 1985. **Orgs:** Exec officer treas OH Mayors Assn; cr comm mem Cincinnati Postal Empl Cr Union 1969-; mem Hamilton Co Mun League 1972-79; mem Woodlawn Action Club; mem Valley YMCA Cincinnati; cmdr John R Fox #631 Amer Leg 1960-64; mem New Hope Baptist Church; mem Cincinnati Postal Empl Cr Union 1969-; past exec vice pres Natl All Fed Empl 1969-72; vice pres, 1989-93, 1995-96, president, 1994-, Gallia Economic Development Association; president, Emancipation Celebration Committee, 1989-94; finance chairman, Gross Branch YMCA, 1980-88. **Honors/Awds:** First black mayor Vill of Woodlawn 1972; first black chmn Post Office Cr Union 1974-75; KY Colonel Hon Or KY Col Commonw 1971; Award of Merit, Pride Magazine 1979; Outstanding Community Service, Gen Assembly Ohio Senate, 1979; first black elected officer treasure of Ohio Mayor Assn, 1978; Elected member of Govs of Ohio Exec Comm, The Ohio Rural Development Partnership, 1993. **Military Serv:** AUS corpl 1951-53. **Home Addr:** PO Box 179, Rio Grande, OH 45674.

KEELS, PAUL C.
Automobile dealer. **Career:** Kemper Dodge, Inc, Cincinnati OH, chief executive, 1988. **Business Addr:** Kemper Dodge, Inc, 1280 E Kemper Rd, Cincinnati, OH 45246.

KEEMER, EDGAR B.
Medical doctor. **Personal:** Born May 18, 1913, Washington, DC; children: 6. **Educ:** IN U, BS; Meharry Med Coll, MD 1936; Freedmens Hosp, residency 1937-38. **Career:** Detroit Inner City, gynecology 1939-. **Orgs:** Active militant civil rights struggle & Women's right abortion; forced USN accept black Drs 1943; mem Nat Assn Repeal Abortion Laws; Kappa & Alpha Psi; pres Surf Club; mem MI Pub Health Assn; Big Game Hunting Safaris Africa; med adv Clergy Counseling Problem Pregnancy; publ many articles Therapeutic Abortion Pub. **Honors/Awds:** Cit Yr 1974; Feminist Yr nomination Nat Assn Soc Workers 1974. **Business Addr:** 1111 David Whitney Bldg, Detroit, MI 48226.

KEENE, PAUL F., JR.
Painter, educator (retired). **Personal:** Born Aug 24, 1920, Philadelphia, PA; son of Paul F & Josephine B; married Laura M Keene, Dec 24, 1944; children: Paul-Jacques, Lydia B. **Educ:** Philadelphia School of Industrial Arts, 1939-41; Tyler School of FA, Philadelphia PA, BFA, BS Ed, 1947, MFA, 1948; Academie Julien, Paris France, certificate, 1948-52. **Career:** Tyler School Fart, instructor, 1947-48; Centre D'Art Haiti, director of courses, 1952-54; Phila College of Art, prof, 1954-68; Bucks County Comm Coll, prof, 1968-85. **Honors/Awds:** John Hag Whitney, Fellowship, 1952, 1954; Temple Alumni Award, 1967; Philadelphia College of Art, Alumni Award, 1972; Brandywine Workshop, Vandersee Award, 1990. **Special Achievements:** Art in America, new talent, 1954. **Military Serv:** Army Air Corp, signal corp, 2nd lt navigator, 1940-45.

KEENE, SHARON C.
Business executive. **Personal:** Born Feb 27, 1948, Philadelphia, PA. **Educ:** Morgan State Univ, BS 1970; Univ of PA, MLA 1976. **Career:** Natl Park Svc, chief planning & fed prog 1980-. **Business Addr:** Division Chief, Natl Park Service, 75 Spring St, Atlanta, GA 30303.

KEENON, UNA H. R.
Judge. **Personal:** Born Dec 30, 1933, Nashville, TN; daughter of Mary L Gowins-Harris and Charles L Harris; children: Gregory M Rhodes, Patrick Washington k Washington. **Educ:** Tennessee State University, BA, 1954; Cleveland State University, College of Law, JD (cum laude), 1975; Ashland Theological Seminary, currently. **Career:** Cuyahoga County Welfare Department, social worker, 1957-60; Cleveland Public Schools, teacher, 1960-75; Legal Aid Society, attorney, 1975-78; Johnson, Keenon & Blackmon Law Firm, partner, 1978-80; Cuyahoga County Public Defender, Juvenile Division, attorney-in-charge, 1980-83; UAW Legal Services Plan, managing attorney, 1983-86; East Cleveland Municipal Court, judge, 1986-. **Orgs:** NAACP, board member, 1992-; Hitchcock House, board member, 1992-; Community Guidance, board member, 1992-; YWCA, Northern Branch, board member, 1989-; mem AKA Sorority, 1952-; Black Women Political Action Committee, founding president, 1982-86, board member, 1986-; Natl Council of Negro Women, 1986-. **Honors/Awds:** East Cleveland Citizens for Sound Government, MLK Jr Altruism Award, 1993; Women in Community Service, Role Model for Women Award, 1992; East Cleveland Black Police Officers Association, Meritorious Service Award, 1988-89; St James Lutheran Church, Servant Award, 1990; East Ohio Gas Honor Award, 1992; Woman in Service Award, 1993; Hitchcock Ctr Award, 1993. **Home Addr:** 16148 Cleviden Rd, East Cleveland, OH 44112. **Business Addr:** Judge, East Cleveland Municipal Court, 14340 Euclid Ave, East Cleveland, OH 44112, (216)681-2213.

KEGLAR, SHELVY HAYWOOD
Psychologist, business executive. **Personal:** Born Dec 13, 1947, Charleston, MS; son of Minnie M Keglar Miller and John H Ratliff; married Robbia Steward, Mar 7, 1970; children: Shelvy Jr, Robalon, Skyler, Ronelle, Stanford. **Educ:** Kaskaskia Junior College, Centralia, IL, Associate Degree, 1966-68; Arkansas State Univ, Jonesboro, AR, BA, sociology, 1968-70, MA, rehabilitation counseling, 1974; Indiana Univ, Bloomington, IN, PhD, educational psychology, counseling psychology, 1979. **Career:** Hamilton Center, Terre Haute, IN, associate director, 1974-84; Atterbury Job Corps, Edinburgh, IN, psychologist, 1979-; Midwest Psychological Center Inc, Indianapolis, IN, president, 1984-. **Orgs:** Vice president, membership chair, 1988-89, president, 1986-87, National Black Child Development Institute, Indianapolis affiliate; president, Terre Haute Minority Business Association, 1983-84; president, Indiana Association of Black Psychologists, 1982-84; American Psychological Association; Association of Black Psychologists; Society of Clinical and Experimental Hypnosis; numerous others. **Honors/Awds:** Strong-Turner Alumni Club, Arkansas State Univ, Service Award, 1988; Indiana Association of Black Psychologists, Outstanding Service Award, 1984; Arkansas State Univ, Outstanding Alumnus, 1991; Centralia Sports Hall of Fame, 1991. **Special Achievements:** Author: "Workfare and the Black Family," Black Family, vol 6:2, 1986; "Alcohol and Drug Abusers in a Family Practice Resident's Ward," w/M Clarke, Alcohol and Research World, 4, 1980; numerous others. **Military Serv:** US Army, SP 4, 1971-73; received Post Commendation Award. **Business Addr:** President, Midwest Psychological Center, Inc, 3676 Washington Blvd, Indianapolis, IN 46205.

KEITH, DAMON JEROME
Federal judge (retired). **Personal:** Born Jul 4, 1922, Detroit, MI; son of Annie L Williams Keith and Perry A Keith; married Rachel Boone Keith, Oct 18, 1953; children: Cecile, Debbie, Gilda. **Educ:** West Virginia State College, AB, 1943; Howard University Law School, LLB, 1949; Wayne State University Law School, LLM, 1956. **Career:** Office of the Friend of the Court, City of Detroit, attorney, 1951-55; Wayne County Board of Supervisors, 1958-63; Keith, Conyers, Anderson, Brown & Wahls, Detroit, MI, senior partner 1964-67; Eastern District of Michigan, chief US judge, 1967-77; US Court of Appeals, 6th Circuit Court, Detroit, MI, judge beginning 1977. **Orgs:** Chmn MI Civil Rights Commn 1964-67; trustee Med Corp Detroit; trustee Interlochen Arts Acad; trustee Cranbrook Sch; mem Citizen's Adv Com Equal Educ Opportunity Detroit Bd Edn; vice pres United Negro Coll Fund Detroit; 1st vice pres emeritus Detroit Chap NAACP; mem com mgmt Detroit YMCA; Detroit Council Boy Scouts of America; Detroit Arts Commn; mem Amer (council sect legal educ and admission to bar) Bar Assn; mem Natl Bar Assn; mem MI Bar Assn; Detroit Bar Assn; Natl Lawyers Guild; Amer Judicature Soc; Alpha Phi Alpha; Detroit Cotillion; University of Notre Dame Law School, advisory council; University of Detroit Mercy, board of trustees; Detroit Symphony Orchestra, vice chairman; Leukemia Society of America Inc. **Honors/Awds:** Spingarn Medalist 1974; named 1 of 100 Most Influential Black Americans, Ebony Magazine, 1971, 1977; honorary degrees: Univ of Michigan, Howard Univ, Wayne State Univ, Michigan State Univ, New York Law School, Detroit College of Law, West Virginia State College, Univ of Detroit, Atlanta Univ, Ohio State Univ, Central Michigan Univ, Eastern Michigan Univ, Morehouse College, New York Law School, Hofstra Univ, DePaul Univ, Yale Univ, Western Michigan Univ, Tuskegee Univ, Lincoln Univ; Afro-Asian Institute Histadrut of Israel, Menorah Award, 1988; The Rotary Club of Lansing, Governor's Minuteman Award, 1991; The State Bar of Michigan, Champion of Justice Award, 1991; The National Bar Association, C Francis Stratford Award, 1992; The Progressive National Baptist Convention, Martin Luther King Jr Freedom Award, 1992; The Wolverine Bar Association, Thurgood Marshall Award, 1993; Howard University, Alumni Award for Distinguished Postgraduate Achievement, 1994; numerous others. **Special Achievements:** Publications: "We the People Have Lots to Celebrate," Detroit Free Press, Jan 29, 1987; "Ashmore: Hearts and Minds: The Anatomy of Racism from Roosevelt to Reagan," University of Michigan Law Review, vol 87, no 4, p 1040, 1983; "A Responsibility to Serve Black Community," Detroit Free Press, Nov 24, 1988; numerous others. **Business Addr:** Judge, US Court of Appeals, 231 W Lafayette St, Rm 240, Detroit, MI 48226, (313)226-6890.

KEITH, DORIS T.
Federal official (retired). **Personal:** Born May 28, 1924, Washington, DC; daughter of Viola M Taylor (deceased) and Rev Dr Julian A Taylor (deceased); married DeWitt Keith Jr (deceased); children: DeWitt Keith III. **Career:** DC Assn Women Highway Safety Leaders, Inc, pres 1982-; DC Govt, Washington DC, chmn Traffic Adjudication Appeals Bd. **Orgs:** Chmn DC Citizens Traffic Bd; past fin secy DC Fed of Civ Assn; mem Bus & Prof Assn of Far NE; NE Council Amer Cancer Soc; mem Holy Comforter - St Syprans; past mem DC Hlth & Welfare Council; co-founder 14th Prec Adv Council; past mem Commrs Youth Council; mem Hacker's Lic Review Bd; past pres River Terr Comm Org, River Terr PTA; mem Natl Captl Area Boy Scouts; past mem Automotive Consumer Action Panel; mem Traffic Adjud Appeals Bd 1979-; mem AAA Adv

Bd 1977-; bd trustees Amer Cancer Soc; mem Natl Assn Women Hwy Safety Leaders Inc 1982-; past mem DC bd of zoning St Luke's Church. **Honors/Awds:** Awd Woman of the Yr Dist Hlth & Welf Cncl 1966; Afro Woman of Yr 1952, 1966; Awds Cancer Soc, Heart Assn, Comm Chest, BSA; UCF Crime Council; D C Dept Public Works 1986; Citizens Traffic bd 1985; AAA Advisory bd 1987; mem Mayor's Advisory Council Alcohol, Drug Traffic 1985. **Home Addr:** 3453 Eads St, NE, Washington, DC 20019. **Business Addr:** President, DC Assn Women Highway Safety Leaders, 2000 14th St NW, Frank Reeves Bldg, 7th Fl, Washington, DC 20009.

KEITH, KAREN C.

Track & field coach. **Personal:** Born Apr 16, 1957, Boston, MA; daughter of Margaret Stokes Keith and Albert Keith. **Educ:** Florida State Univ, Tallahassee Fl, BS Educ, 1978; Boston Coll, Chestnut Hill MA, M Ed Admin/Supervision, 1989. **Career:** Beth Israel Hospital, Brookline MA, phlebotimist, 1978-83; US Youth Games Team, coach, 1980-81; Newton South High School, coach, 1981-83; Brown Jr High School, Newton MA science/pysical educ teacher, sports coach team leader, administrator, 1981-87; Boston College, head coach track & field, 1989. **Honors/Awds:** mem, New England Select Side Rugby Team, 1985-86; Division I Region I Coach of the Year, 1987; Brookline High School Hall of Fame Sagamore Award, 1988. **Business Addr:** Head Track & Field Coach, Boston College, Conte Forum, Chestnut Hill, MA 02167.

KEITH, LEROY

Former educational administrator. **Personal:** Born Feb 14, 1939, Chattanooga, TN; son of Lula Keith and Roy Keith; married Anita Halsey; children: Lori, Susan, Kelli, Kimberly. **Educ:** Morehouse Coll, BA 1961; Indiana Univ, MA 1968, PhD 1970. **Career:** Chattanooga Publ School, science teacher, 1961-66; Neighborhood Serv Program, Chattanooga TN, dir, 1966-68; Indiana Univ, Human Relations Comm, exec sctry, 1968-69, Bureau of Education Placement, administrative assistant, 1969-70; Dartmouth Coll, assistant professor of education, William Jewett Tucker Foundation Internship Program, director, 1970-71, assistant dean of the college, assistant professor of education, 1971-72, assoc dean/asst prof of educ & urban studies, 1972-73; Univ of MA System, assoc vice pres, 1973-75; MA Bd of Higher Ed, chancellor, 1975-78; Univ of the Dist of Columbia, exec vice pres, 1978-82; Univ of MD, vice pres for policy & planning, 1983-87; Morehouse Coll, Atlanta, GA, pres, 1987-94. **Orgs:** One to One Mentoring Partnership; bd, Savannah Business Group; The Foundation for Memorial Medical Ctr; Telfair Museum of Art; First City Club; Savannah Area Chamber of Commerce; mem, CEO Council of the Savannah Area Chamber of Commerce. **Honors/Awds:** Alvin & Peggy Brown Fellowship Aspen Inst for Humanistic Studies 1980; 100 Top Young Leaders in Amer Acad, Change Magazine & Amer Council on Educ 1978; Dist Alumni Serv Indiana Univ Bloomington 1977; Resolution for Outstanding Achievement Tennessee House of Representatives 1976; Honorary Doctor of Laws, Bowdoin College, 1990; Phi Beta Kappa; graduate school, University Fellowship; Dartmouth College, LLD, 1991. **Business Addr:** Chairman/CEO, Carson Products Co., PO Box 22309, Savannah, GA 31403.

KEITH, LUTHER

Newspaper executive. **Personal:** marrIed Jacqueline Hall-Keith; children: Erin. **Career:** Wayne State University, Journalism Institute for Minorities, founding director, 1985-87; The Detroit News, general assignment reporter, business editor, assistant managing editor, currently. **Honors/Awds:** Michigan Journalism Hall of Fame, 1995. **Special Achievements:** First African-American sportswriter for a major Detroit daily newspaper, 1973; first African-American reporter assigned to the state capital bureau in Lansing, 1979; first African-American newsroom editor at The Detroit News, 1982. **Business Addr:** Assistant Managing Editor, Detroit News, 615 W. Lafayette Blvd., Detroit, MI 48226, (313)222-6400.

KEITT, L. (LIZ ZIMMERMAN)

Adviser, purchasing agent. **Personal:** Born Nov 28, 1938, Calhoun County; married Joseph L; children: Vincent Lewis, Marvin. **Educ:** Claflin Coll, BS Phys Educ 1970; SC State Coll MEd Guidance 1974. **Career:** Claflin Coll, purchasing agt present; NAACP State of SC, adv 1975-; Student Govt Assn, adv 1975; Claflin Coll Gospel & Choir, adv 1974-78; Alpha Kappa Sor, adv 1973-; NAACP Claflin Coll, #Adv 1972-; Mt Carmel Bapt Ch Cameron SC, supt 1971-. **Orgs:** Chairperson Lower Savannah Grassroots Adv Com 1976-; sec Claflin Coll Nat Alumni Assn 1976-; sec Dem Women's Club 1977-79; coordinator Ward III Voters 1978; reg dir Miss Black Universe Pageant in Orangeburg Co 1979. **Honors/Awds:** Outstanding Comm Leader Bd of Dir (Newspaper) 1975; Outstanding NAACP Adv NAACP Ms 1976-77; Outstanding Serv NAACP Claflin Coll 1978; Adv Award NAACP Portland OR 1978; Outstanding Adv NAACP Charlotte NC 1980. **Business Addr:** Purchasing Agent, Claflin College, College Ave, NE, Orangeburg, SC 29115.

KELLAR, CHARLES LIONEL

Attorney (retired). **Personal:** Born Jun 11, 1909, Barbados, West Indies; son of Irene Smith and Charles Miller Austin; married Bettye Clarke, Aug 17, 1975; children: Degrey, Michael, Michael Charles. **Educ:** City College of New York, BS, 1932; City University of New York, MS, 1933; St Johns University Law School, LLB, 1941. **Career:** City of New York Borough, Brooklyn , Domestic Relations Court, 1935-38; Kings County Court, senior probation officer, 1939-43; US Draft Board 205, chairman, 1941-45; US Department of Justice, Elections Fraud Bureau, 1948-49; attorney. **Orgs:** Omega Psi Phi Fraternity; NAACP, life mem, Brooklyn, NY Branch, past president, Las Vegas Branch, past president; Natl Bar Assn, life mem. **Honors/Awds:** NAACP Equal Justice Award. **Special Achievements:** First African-American to pass Bar of Nevada, 1962; sued State Bar of Nevada and Supreme Court of Nevada for discrimination, 1963-65; admitted to practice law by Nevada Supreme Court Order, 1965; brought law suits and as a result desegregated the Nevada State Prison, Nevada casinos, and Public School of Clark County Nevada, and succeeded in writing law which after adoption resulted in creation of Nevada Equal Rights Commission.

KELLER, EDMOND JOSEPH

Educational administrator, educator. **Personal:** Born Aug 22, 1942, New Orleans, LA; married Genevieve Favorite; children: Vern A, Erika V. **Educ:** LA State Univ New Orleans, BA 1969; Univ of WI Madison, MA 1970, PhD 1974. **Career:** IN Univ Bloomington, asst-assoc prof 1974-83; Comm on Inst Cooperation, dir cic minority fellowships prog 1982-83; Univ of CA Santa Barbara, chmn black studies 1983-84, assoc prof 1983-87, assoc dean grad div, professor, 1987-90; UCLA, professor, political sci, director, African studies, 1990-. **Orgs:** Chmn Current Issues Comm African Studies Assn 1981-84; editor African Studies Assoc, A Jrnl of Africanist Opinion 1982-; editor, TransAfrica Forum, 1993; editor, Journal of African Policy Studies, 1992-; bd mem Oxfam Amer 1985; executive director, University of California President's Task Force on Black Student Eligibility, 1988-90; associate editor, Western Political Quarterly, 1984-91; vice president, 1990-91, pres, 1991-92, African Studies Assn; member, Council on Foreign Relations, 1990, Overseas Development Council. **Honors/Awds:** Dissertation Rsch Fellowship Ford Found 1972-73; African-Amer Scholars Council Post-Doctorate 1976-77; Post Doctorate Natl Fellowship Fund 1980-82; Ford Found Post Doctorate Ford Found 1981-82; Fellow, American Council on Education, 1987-88. **Military Serv:** AUS E-5 3 yrs. **Business Addr:** Professor of Political Science, Director, African Studies, University of California at Los Angeles, Bunche Hall 4286, Los Angeles, CA 90024-1472, (310)825-3686.

KELLER, MARY JEAN

Controller (retired). **Personal:** Born Nov 6, 1938, Mt Vernon, NY; daughter of Grace McNair Mizell and Raymond Mizell; married Thomas Keller, Dec 18, 1971; children: Ericka. **Educ:** New York Univ School Commerce, BS 1960; Columbia Univ, MS 1978. **Career:** Hoffbert & Oberfest, CPA's; Bedford Stuyvesant Restoration Corp, asst treas/dir fin; Foreign Policy Study Found, Inc, treasurer; Lisc, Inc controller. **Orgs:** Bd of Trustees, St Paul Christian School; SASA (Sisters Assisting South Africa); Mt Vernon Alumni Association.

KELLEY, DANIEL, JR.

Association executive. **Personal:** Born Nov 19, 1922, Muncie, IN; married Zelma M Fisk; children: Stephanie C, James E. **Educ:** Indiana U, 1964. **Career:** Ind Steel & Wire Co, electrician 1945-1968; United Steelworkers of Am, staff rep 1968-; Muncie City Councilman, pres & budget-finance com chmn 1967. **Orgs:** Mem bd dir United Fund 1967; adv council & mem Gateway Health Clinic 1970; citizen adv bd mem Ball State Univ IN Univ Medical Prog. **Military Serv:** AUS 1940-45. **Business Addr:** 206 1/2 E Willard St, Muncie, IN 47302.

KELLEY, DELORES G.

Educator, state official. **Personal:** Born May 1, 1936, Norfolk, VA; daughter of Helen Jefferson Goodwin and Stephen Goodwin; married Russell Victor Jr; children: Norma, Russell III, Brian. **Educ:** VA State Coll, BA Philos 1956; New York Univ, MA Educ 1958; Purdue Univ MA Comm (grad tchg fellow) 1972; Univ of MD, PhD, Am Studies 1977. **Career:** New York City Protestant Council, dir Christian Educ 1958-60; Plainview JHS, tchr of English 1965-66; Morgan State Univ, instr of English 1966-70; Purdue Univ, grad teaching fellow in speech 1971-72; Coppin State Coll, dept chmn lang lit & philos 1976-79, dean of lower div, 1979-89, prof, communications, 1990-; MD State Delegate (elected from 42nd district), 1991-94; MD State Senator, 10th District, 1995-. **Orgs:** Mem Alpha Kappa Alpha 1955-; vol host family Baltimore Council Intl Visitors 1976-; Roots Forum project grant MD Com on Humanities & Pub Policy 1977; mem evaluation team Hood Coll MD State Dept of Educ 1978; reviewer & panelist Natl Endowment for the Humanities 1979-80; chairperson adv council Gifted & Talented Educ Baltimore City Sch 1979-; bd mem Harbor Bank of MD 1982-; exec bd Baltimore Urban League; sec MD Dem Party 1986-90; pres, Black/Jewish Forum of Baltimore, 1990-92; chair, Baltimore Chapter, Natl Political Congress of Black Women, 1993-95; MD Commissioner on Criminal Sentencing Policy, 1996-98; bd, Institute Christian Jewish Studies, 1989-; pres-elect, Women Legislators of MD, 1997-98. **Honors/Awds:** PhD Thesis ''Rhetorical Analysis of 1884-1888 Controversy, Response of Presbyterian Church in US to Evolution'' 1977; Gov's apptmt State Com on Values Educ 1980; fellow Amer Council on Educ 1982-83; mem Baltimore Jewish Council Fact-Finding Mission to Israel 1987; Coppin Critical Reading Grant, National Endowment for the Humanities, 1988-89. **Business Addr:** 6660 Security Blvd, Ste 10, Baltimore, MD 21207.

KELLEY, JACK ALBERT

Museum curator, educator. **Personal:** Born Aug 23, 1920, Alberta;son of Fannie Cobbs Kelley and Frank A Kelley; married Rose Lee Conley, Apr 26, 1946; children: Jacqueline K Waters, Pamela K Lamar, Keith A Kelley, Elizabeth R Kelley. **Educ:** California State University, Fresno California, BA (physical educ) 1946. **Career:** Fresno City Police Department, sgt detective, FPO, 1949-71; Boys Group Sur; CA State Univ Fresno, coordinator law enforcement training proj, 1972-80; Fresno City Coll, curator, Fresno County African Amer Cultural Museum; African-American American Historical and Cultural Museum of the San Joaquin Valley, pres, currently. **Orgs:** Lifetime mem Varsity Ftball; trust Carter Meml AME Ch; YMCA mem; Gamma Xi Chap Phi Beta Sigma Frat; past pres Past Potentate Saphar Temple #117; past v chmn Model City Bd; mem Shriners; Black Educators of Fresno; pres African American Cultural and Historical Museum for the San Joaquin Valley, currently. **Honors/Awds:** All-City team in basketball, football, baseball; All-Valley Football Team 1941; CSUF 1942 All-Western Basketball; hon mention Little Am Football 1942; One of Fresno's Fabulous ''100'' Citizens, 1985; Community service Awards, City of Fresno 1971, Phi Beta Sigma Fraternity 1980, United Black Men 1988, NAACP 1989; African Methodist Episcopal Church, Northern Conf, 1994; Martin L King Jr Community Serv Award, 1995; KSEE 24 TV, Fresno, one of only five African-Americans to be honored, 1995. **Military Serv:** US Army tank corps, sergeant, 1942-44. **Home Addr:** 5295 E Tulare, Fresno, CA 93727.

KELLEY, ROBERT W.

State official. **Personal:** Born Nov 25, 1940, Nashville, TN; children: Robert, Jr, Lanedria, Christopher Shea. **Educ:** TN State U, BS 1963; Syracuse U, 1963; Foreign Serv Inst, 1966; US Intl Univ Steamboat Springs CO, 1970. **Career:** Nashville Urban League, asso dir 1969-70; Met Nashville Educ Assn, dir field serv 1970-72; Meharry Med Coll, prog ofcr, materials mgr hosp & hlth svc; S St Comm Ctr, dir; OIC Inc, 1978-80; TN State Univ, proj dir, instr Div of Cont Educ 1982-83; advertising specialist 1983-; TN Department of Human Svcs, caseworker, currently. **Orgs:** Mem Alpha Phi Alpha Frat 1960-; mem NAACP; Urban League; Psi Delta Kappa Educ Frat; Nat Educ Assn vice pres Civitan Intl NW Nasville 1974-75; Nashville Chap Nat Assn of Human Rights Workers Nat Bd 1974; mem Transformed Liberty Inc 1987. **Honors/Awds:** Honorary Sgt At Arms TN State Senate 1971; publ, writer, volunteer, summer issue Peace Corps Vol Mag 1971; publ Tenth Anniversary Issue US Peace Corps Magazine '' A Plan for Future Peace''; The Peace Corps, World Beyond War Awd, 1987. **Home Addr:** 2924 Glenmeade Dr, Nashville, TN 37216.

KELLEY, ROBERT WILLIAM

Cleric (retired), lecturer. **Personal:** Born Feb 26, 1913, Springfield, OH; son of Lucinda M Kelley (deceased) and William Kelley (deceased); married Mattiedna Johnson; children: Bobby Lou, Robert Jr, Patricia Jenkins, Frances Mark. **Educ:** Ohio Wesleyan University, 1938; Union Theological School, 1941. **Career:** Negro Methodist Episcopal Church, missionary, Gbarnga, Liberia, 1940s, United Methodist Church, 1964; Mt Pleasant UMC; Cory UMC; Strongsville UMC; St Paul UMC; Aldensgate UMC, pastor associate, pastor emeritus; member of church for 43 years until retirement. **Orgs:** NAACP; CORE; Interdenominational Ministerial Alliance; Ohio Wesleyan University, bd of trustees; United Methodist Church, bd of pensions; Knuth Center, prayerful chaplain; Omega Psi Phi, 1940-. **Business Addr:** Pastor Emeritus, Aldensgate United Methodist Church, 4038 Eastwood Ln, Warrensville Heights, OH 44128.

KELLEY, WILBOURNE ANDERSON, III

Government official. **Personal:** Born in Montgomery, AL; son of Carrie Lee Kelley and Wilbourne A. Kelley II; married Barbara Jean Anthony, Jun 29, 1980; children: Caron Yvonne Hawkins, Wilbourne A. Kelley IV, Krystal Arden Kelley. **Educ:** Wayne State University, Detroit, MI, 1952-53, 1954-55; University of Michigan, Ann Arbor, MI, 1953-54; US Military Academy, West Point, NY, BS, 1959; Iowa State University, Ames, IA, MS, 1964; US Army Management School, Fort Belvoir, VA, certificate, 1965; Harvard University, Cambridge, MA, certificate, 1967. **Career:** US Army Corps of Engineers, began as 2nd lieutenant, became major, 1959-70; Michigan Consolidated Gas Company, Detroit, MI, became vice president of gas operations, 1970-83; Charter County of Wayne, Detroit, MI, director of engineering and county highway engineer, 1985-86, assistant county executive in office of public services, 1987-. **Orgs:** Dir, Amer Soc for Personnel Administration, 1972-76; member of business advisory committee, Greater Opportunites Industrialization Center, 1972-75; member, New Detroit, Inc, 1972-75; dir, Greater Detroit Safety Council, 1972-75; member, Task Force 100, City of Detroit, 1973; member, Business Office Career Education Task Force, US Government,

1975; Major Gifts chm, Boy Scouts of America, Detroit Council Central Section, 1977-79; president of bd of dirs, 1986-88, Wayne County Easter Seal Soc; dir, Michigan Easter Seal Soc, 1980-88; chm of bd of trustees, Peoples Community Church, 1987-90; Sinai Hospital Board of Directors, 1992. **Honors/Awds:** Author, X-Ray Diffraction Analysis of Lateritic Soils, Iowa Academy of Sciences, 1964; author, Revision of Personnel Policies and Reorganization of the City of Detroit under the New City Charter, Office of the Mayor of Detroit, 1974; distinguished service award, Amer Soc for Personnel Administration, 1976; award of excellence, Boy Scout of Amer, Detroit, MI, 1977, 1978, 1979; Trail Blazer Award, Assn of Business Engineering & Science Students & Professionals, 1977; Minority Achiever in Industry award, YMCA, 1980; Volunteer of the Year Award, Wayne County Easter Seal Soc, 1981, 1988, & Michigan Easter Seal Soc, 1988. **Military Serv:** US Army, Corps of Engineers, 1959-70; Purple Heart, Air Medal, Army Commendation Medal, Bronze Star, Legion of Merit, Special Certificate of Achievement from Government of Liberia. **Home Addr:** 19140 Gloucester, Detroit, MI 48203. **Business Addr:** Assistant County Executive, Wayne County Office of Public Services, 415 Clifford Avenue, Detroit, MI 48226.

KELLEY, WILLIAM E. (BILL)
Association executive, account executive. **Personal:** Born Feb 15, 1939, Los Angeles, CA; son of Laura Mae Kelley and LeRoy Kelley Sr (deceased); married Joann Oliver, Sep 23, 1968; children: Darren LeRoy, Jason Wardell. **Educ:** Whittier College, BA, 1960; US Naval War College, 1972; George Washington University, MS, 1972. **Career:** International Committee of YMCA's, fellow, 1960-61; YMCA of Los Angeles, program director, 1961-62; Smith, Bucklin & Associates, account executive, 1990-; National Association of Corporate Treasurers, executive director, currently. **Orgs:** National Naval Officers Association, 1972-; Naval Order of the US, 1990; American Society of Association Executives, 1989-; The Retired Officers Association, 1990-; Disabled American Veterans, 1990-. **Honors/Awds:** Lancer Society of Whittier College, Alumni Achievement, 1989. **Military Serv:** US Navy, captain, 1962-90; Legion of Merit, Joint Service Medal, Vietnam Service. **Business Phone:** (202)857-1115.

KELLEY, WILLIAM MELVIN
Author. **Personal:** Born Nov 1, 1937, New York, NY; married Karen Isabelle Gibson; children: Jessica, Tikaiji. **Educ:** Harvard Univ, 1956-61. **Career:** Author: A Different Drummer 1962, Dancers on the Shore 1964, A Drop of Patience 1965, Dem 1967, Dunford Travels Everywhere 1970; articles, "If You're Woke You Dig It" New York Times Magazine, May 20, 1962; "The Ivy League Negro" Esquire, August 1963; "An American in Rome" Mademoiselle, March 1965; "On Racism, Exploitation, and the White Liberal" Negro Digest, January 1967; "On Africa in the United States" Negro Digest, May 1968; numerous anthologies; Dancers on the Shore, reissued by Howard Univ Press 1983. **Honors/Awds:** Dana Reed Literary Prize, Harvard Univ, 1960; Bread Loaf Scholar, 1962; John Jay Whitney Foundation Award, 1963; Rosenthal Foundation Award, National Institute of Arts and Letters, 1963; Black Academy of Arts & Letters Prize for Fiction, 1970. **Business Addr:** The Wisdom Shop, P O Box 2658, New York, NY 10027.

KELLMAN, DENIS ELLIOTT
Company executive. **Personal:** Born Jul 6, 1948, New York, NY. **Educ:** Yale Coll, BA 1970; Harvard Law Sch, JD 1975; Harvard Business Sch, MBA 1975. **Career:** Le Boeuf Lamb Leiby & Macrae, assoc attorney; Columbia Pictures Industries Inc, counsel; Bertelsmann Music Group, dir legal and business affairs. **Orgs:** Mem Intl Federation of Phonogram and Videogram Producers, British Phonograpic Industry, Black Music Assoc, Harvard Business Sch Black Alumni Assoc, Harvard Law Sch Black Alumni Assoc. **Business Addr:** Dir Legal & Business Affairs, Bertelsmann Music Group, One Bedford Ave, London WC1B 3DT, England.

KELLOGG, REGINALD J.
Cleric. **Personal:** Born Jul 2, 1933, Ann Arbor, MI. **Educ:** Assumptn Sem & Coll, BA 1961 Univ Laval PQ, MA 1965; Univ Bordeaux France, lic lit 1967. **Career:** Cent Cath High Sch Toledo OH, tchr 1961-65; Holy Trin Milwaukee, 1966; St Francis Coll Kitwe Zambia, tchr hd lang dept 1967-70; Cent Cath High & Ft Wayne IN, tchr, asst princ 1970-72; Bishop Luers High Sch Ft Wayne IN, tchr; Cath Ch Dioc of El Paso, priest, asso pastor; St Francis Basilica, Assis, Italy, tour director, English-speaking confessor, currently. **Orgs:** Secy Amer Assn Tchrs of Fr & Sp N IN Chptr 1970-72; mem Nat Blk Cath Clrgy Caucus 1970-93. **Business Addr:** Sacro Convento, Piazza Inferione di S Francesco, I-06082 Assisi Santario, (PG), Italy.

KELLY, CHRIS
Vocalist. **Personal:** son Of Donna. **Career:** With Chris Smith, member of the group Kriss Kross; album: Totally Krossed Out, 1992; singles include: "Jump," "Warm It Up.". **Special Achievements:** Has appeared on "Good Morning America," "The Arsenio Hall Show," "In Living Color," Sprite commercial. **Business Phone:** (212)833-8000.

KELLY, DAVID A.
Business executive. **Personal:** Born May 7, 1938, Chicago; married Sandra McKendrick; children: Denise, Michele, Renee, David. **Educ:** Roosevelt Univ Chicago, BS, BA 1960; CPA 1962; Loyola Univ Sch Law, JD 1967. **Career:** Arthur Andersen & Co Chicago, partner 1967-; IRS Chicago, agt 1960-67. **Orgs:** Mem, Natl Soc CPA's; Amer Inst CPA's; IL Soc CPA's; Chicago Bar Assn; Amer Mgmt Assn; treas, John Howard Assn 1975; trustee, IL Childrens's Home Aid Soc 1977; hearing bd Univ Civil Serv Sys IL 1974 Bd S Shore Commn; treas, Merit Employment Counselor; Assn Commerce & Industry; Loyola Univ Alumni Assn guest speaker, tax seminars; accounting consultant, Black Businessman's Seminar, Malcolm X Coll 1970. **Business Addr:** 69 W Washington, Chicago, IL 60602.

KELLY, EARL LEE
Educator. **Personal:** Born Mar 13, 1956, Prentiss, MS; children: Earl L Jr, Eric N, Adrianne C. **Educ:** Jackson State Univ, BS 1977, MS 1979; Meharry Medical Coll, MD 1983. **Career:** Jackson Area COGIC Youth, vice pres 1977-79; Martin Luther King Jr General Hospital, intern 1983-84, resident 1984-86; Meharry Medical Coll, instructor/fellow. **Orgs:** Mem Amer Medical Student Assoc 1980-86, Amer Acad of Family Physicians 1983-85; provider/supervisor Saturday Clinic Manchester Medical Group 1985-86. **Honors/Awds:** Water Pollution Control Tech IV MS Air and Water Pollution Central Commn 1979; Honor Student Biochem Meharry Med Coll 1980.

KELLY, ERNECE BEVERLY
Educator, journalist. **Personal:** Born Jan 6, 1937, Chicago, IL; daughter of Lovette Nathalia and William Ernest. **Educ:** University of Chicago, AB, 1958, MA, 1959; Northwestern University, PhD, 1972. **Career:** University of Wisconsin, assistant professor, 1978-81; Kingsborough Community College, associate professor, 1984-. **Orgs:** College Language Association, 1972-; National Council of Teachers of English, director, task force on racism & bias in teaching of English, 1970-80; Conference on College Composition and Communication, executive committee, 1971-74. **Honors/Awds:** Humanities Council of New York; Speakers in the Humanities, 1992-99; City University of New York, research grant, 1989; Schomburg Center for Research in Black Culture, scholar in residence, 1988; National Endowment on the Humanities, awarded summer seminar, 1978. **Special Achievements:** Film reviews, Crisis Magazine and New York area newspapers, 1991-; 138 Commonly Used Idioms, student booklet, 1989; Searching for America, National Council of Teachers of English, 1972; Points of Departure, John Wiley & Sons, 1972. **Home Addr:** PO Box 648, Elmhurst, NY 11373. **Business Phone:** (718)368-5000.

KELLY, FLORIDA L.
Educator. **Personal:** Born Oct 13, 1920, Chesterfield, SC; married George; children: Joyce Kelly Moore. **Educ:** Howard U, BA 1938-44; NY U, MA 1953-54; CW Post, 1974. **Career:** Bd of Educ NY City, reading specialist 1975-; Libr Bd of Educ of New York City, teacher 1962-75; Elementary Bd of Educ of New York City, teacher 1954-55. **Orgs:** Bd of dir porg chmn "Big Sisters"; Educ Action of Beta Omicron Chap 1970-; fund raising chmn Nat Sorority of Phi Delta Kappa 1970-; leadership com Black Trade Unionists AFL CIO 1970-; mem Jamaica Br NAACP; chap leader PS 160 Queens 1969-79; pres Social Serv Club Calvarty Bapt 1975-; mem Delta Sigma Theta Inc Queens Alumnae. **Honors/Awds:** Chap Leader Award United Fedn of Tchrs 1979; Article Pub Education Black Youth to Live in a Multi Racial Soc 1977; Article Pub "Bibliography of Black History-ednl Perspectives" 1975; Outstanding Serv Award Nat Sorority of Phi Delta Kappa Inc Beta Onicron Chap 1975; Community Serv Award & Negro Bus & Professional Women Jamaica Club 1968; Baisley Park Women's Business and Professional Award of The Sojourner Truth Award, 1984; Superintendent of the Calvary Baptist Church School, 1981-89; PS 160 Library named for Florida L Kelly of the Walter Francis Bishop Elementary School, 1990. **Business Addr:** Board of Educ, P S 160 109 59 Inwood St, Jamaica, NY 11435.

KELLY, IDA B.
Business owner. **Personal:** Born Jun 2, 1925, Yazoo, MS; children: seven. **Career:** Pizza Queen, Inc, Detroit, MI, owner, vice president, 15 years. **Honors/Awds:** Businesswoman of the Year, National Association of Business and Professional Women, 1988. **Business Addr:** Owner, Pizza Queen, Inc, Cobo Hall Conference Center, PO Box 1002, Detroit, MI 48231.

KELLY, JACK ARTHUR
Dentist. **Personal:** Born Oct 28, 1916, Covington, GA; son of Edna Mary Jeffries Kelly and Leonard O Kelly; married Marian Cameron, Dec 28, 1947; children: Carla, Gaines. **Educ:** Morehouse Coll, BS 1939; St Aquinas Junior Coll, Kalamazoo, MI, 1944; Western Michigan State, Grand Rapids, MI 1945; Meharry Medical Coll, DDS 1955. **Career:** Kelly's Cleaners, owner 1948-49; Atlanta Bd of Educ, Atlanta, GA, science/math teacher 1949-50; LO Kelly Jeweler, partner/mgr 1950-53; self-employed, dentist 1955-. **Orgs:** Chairman and vice pres NDA Bd of Trustees 1986; pres Natl Dental Assoc 1987; life mem Alpha Phi Alpha Chi & Lamda Chapt; mem Atlanta C of C; mem Amer and GA Dental Assocs, Northern Dist Dental Soc; pres North Georgia Dental Society 1980; mem Masonic Lodge, Prince Hall #112. **Honors/Awds:** Dentist of the Year N GA Dental Soc 1976; President's Awd NDA 1975; Serv Awd GA Dental Soc 1979, 1980; Serv Awd NDA 1979, 1982; Pedodontia Prize, class of 1955, Meharry Dental School; official photographer, Meharry Dental Sch, 1953-55; inventor, producer, marketer of product, Magic Seasoning. **Business Addr:** Dentist, 210 Auburn Ave, Ste 1, Atlanta, GA 30303.

KELLY, JAMES CLEMENT
Clergyman. **Personal:** Born Sep 29, 1928, Bethlehem, PA; married Loretta; children: Lynne, James Jr, Susan. **Educ:** VA Union U, BA 1964; VA Union Sch Rel, MDiv 1967. **Career:** Calvary Bapt Ch, Clergyman. **Orgs:** Mem at Large BSA; mem Queens Fedn Chs; Rotary Club Jamaica; mem Prog Nat Bapt NY; life mem NAACP; mem NY Mission Soc; vP Home Mission bd; PNBC; mem Admin bd of Am Bapt Chs of Metro NY pres Calvary Bapt Fed Credit Union. **Honors/Awds:** Recpt CIB Badge. **Business Addr:** 111 10 New York Blvd, Jamaica, NY 11433.

KELLY, JAMES JOHNSON
Military officer (retired). **Personal:** Born Mar 29, 1928, High Point, NC; son of Elsie Johnson Kelly and Nathan Kelly (deceased); married Sallie Mae Williams; children: Eva Mae Kelly-Jones, Thomas Edward, Cheryl Yvonne Kelly-Oliver. **Educ:** Univ of MD, 1957; Our Lady of the Lake Univ, BA 1971, MEd 1973. **Career:** USAF, opers ofcr, sqdrn comdr, remote air base comdr, sr pilot & expert weapons controller, instructor pilot, maj 1971 retired; city of San Antonio TX Planning Commissioner 1988-, vice chm, 1990-93. **Orgs:** Mem NAACP, So Poverty Law Ctr, Retired Officers Assoc, Disabled Amer Veterans, Community Workers Council of San Antonio, San Antonio Club of OLLU of San Antonio, Lackland AF Base Officers Club, Chap #5 DAV; lifetime mem TX Congress of PTA; mem Star of the West Masonic Lodge 24, New St Mark Missionary Bapt Church of San Antonio; 1st black cand for city council Dist 6 San Antonio TX 1977; 1st black budget officer Edgewood Urban-Rural Council 1977; former mem bd of trustees Our Lady of the Lake Univ; former pres OLLU Alumni Assoc; adv Brentwood Jr H PTA; chmn Brentwood Athletic Booster Club; mem St John Bosco PTC; treas John F Kennedy H Athletic Booster Assoc; pres Bethel Neighborhood Council 1986-91; pres Community Workers Council San Antonio TX 1987-91; Texas Democratic Party, 1992-; NAACP 1958-; SCLC, 1962-; mem, American Assoc of Retired Persons (AARP), 1986-. **Honors/Awds:** UN Serv Medal; Natl Def Medal; USAF Outstanding Unit Awd; USAF Good Conduct Medal w/3 OLC; ROKPUCE; WW II Occupation Medal Japan; Nominated for Third Annual Martin Luther King, Jr. Distinguished Achievement Award, Bexar County, SA, TX, 1989; Community Distinguished Service Award, 1994. **Military Serv:** USAF maj 1946-71; Legion of Merit; Meritorious Serv Medal; WW II Victory Medal; Korean Serv Medal; AUS Commendation Medal; USAF Commendation Medal w/2 OLC.

KELLY, JOHN PAUL, JR.
Banker. **Personal:** Born Mar 8, 1941, New Orleans, LA; son of Dorothy M Jones Kelly and John P Kelly, Sr (deceased); married Lethia A Robinson, Sep 19, 1981; children: John P III, Byron M Smith, Phillip L Smith, Kelli C Smith, Lauren E. **Educ:** Manhattan Coll, Bronx NY, BS, 1963; City Univ of NY, New York NY, MS, 1965. **Career:** Citicorp, New York NY, asst vice pres, 1970-74; Midwest Natl Bank, Indianapolis IN, pres, 1974-83; Natl Bankers Assn, Washington DC, pres; Unibind of Washington DC, managing partner, 1987-; MMB & Associates, Washington DC, partner, beginning 1988; Founder's Natl Bank of Los Angeles, CEO; Enterprise Federal Savings Bank, pres/ceo, currently. **Orgs:** Life mem, Kappa Alpha Psi, 1965-; bd mem, Indianapolis Chamber of Commerce, 1979-85; mem & state treasurer, Air Force Assn, 1979-81; bd mem, Citizens Gas & Coke Utility, 1980-85; bd mem & sec, Indianapolis Airport Authority, 1981-85; mem, Governor (IN) Fiscal Policy Advisory Council, 1981-85; chairman, Capital Fund Drive, 1982; bd mem, Natl Business League, 1987-; bd mem, Amer Society of Assn Executives, 1988-. **Honors/Awds:** Four-Year Academic Scholarship, Manhattan Coll, 1959; Dean's List, Manhattan Coll, 1963; Academic Scholarship, City Univ of NY, 1964; Top Performing Bank in US, Bank Admin Institute, 1981, 1982. **Military Serv:** US Air Force, captain, received US Air Commendation Award, 1963-70. **Business Phone:** (301)773-9720.

KELLY, JOHN RUSSELL
Government official. **Personal:** Born Nov 18, 1947, Utica, MS; son of Mr and Mrs John H Kelly; married Bernell Topp; children: Jon Felice, Kristi Bernell. **Educ:** Alcorn State Univ, BS 1970; Wayne State Univ, MEd 1972; Univ Southern MS, PhD 1979. **Career:** US Army, education specialist 1971-72; MS Cooperative Ext Svcs, youth develop specialist 1973-79; Sea Grant Adv Svcs, marine specialist 1979-83; US Navy Family Serv Ctr, dir. **Orgs:** Pres Resources Mgmt Inc 1981-; deputy dir Navy Family Serv Ctr 1983-90; pres governing bd Phillips Coll 1985-93; pres MS div Amer Cancer Soc 1986-88; general vice pres Alpha Phi Alpha Frat 1987-91; pres Harrison Co United Way 1987-89; pres J & B Printing, Inc DBA Print Shack 1987-93; vice chair, American Cancer Society National Bd of Directors, 1997-. **Honors/Awds:** Outstanding Young Man in Ameri-

ca, National Jaycees, 1979, 1982. **Military Serv:** AUS sgt 2 yrs. **Business Addr:** Dir, US Navy Family Service Ctr, Construction Battalion Ctr, Bldg 29, Gulfport, MS 39501.

KELLY, JOSEPH WINSTON
Professional football player. **Personal:** Born Dec 11, 1964, Sun Valley, CA; son of Joe Kelly Sr. **Educ:** Univ of Washington, received degree, 1986. **Career:** Cincinnati Bengals, linebacker, 1986-. **Honors/Awds:** Post-season play, 1988: AFC Championship Game, NFL Championship Game.

KELLY, LEONTINE T. C.
Bishop (retired). **Personal:** Born in Washington, DC; daughter of Ila M Turpeau and David D Turpeau; married Gloster Current (deceased); children: Angela, Gloster Jr; children: John David, Pamela. **Educ:** Attended West Virginia State Coll; Virginia Union Univ, graduated, 1960; Union Theological Seminary, Richmond, VA, MDiv, 1969. **Career:** Schoolteacher; Galilee United Methodist Church, Edwardsville, VA, pastor; Virginia Conf Council on Ministries, staff mem; Asbury United Methodist Church, Richmond, VA, pastor, 1976-83; United Methodist Church, Nashville, TN, mem of natl staff, 1983-84; California-Nevada Conf, San Francisco, CA, bishop, 1984-89 (retired). **Honors/Awds:** First black female bishop in a major religious denomination.

KELLY, MARION GREENUP
Organization executive. **Personal:** Born Nov 28, 1947, Baton Rouge; married Harlan H; children: Ingrid, Ian. **Educ:** H Sophie Newcomb Coll Tulane U, BA 1969; Tulane U, MEd 1970. **Career:** Mayors Ofc New Orleans, cit partic coord 1975-; Headstart, tchr 1970-71; Neighborhood Coord, asst exec dir 1971-73. **Orgs:** Mem Nat Assn Planners 1971-73; Am Soc & Planning Ofcls 1971-74; Honors Educ Soc 1970-73; Gr New Orleans Presch Assn 1970-74; Childrens Bur New Orleans 1973-74. **Honors/Awds:** Civic Orgn awards pub schs Baton Rouge 1963-64. **Business Addr:** City Hall BE10, New Orleans, LA 70112.

KELLY, MICHAEL RAYMOND
Professional baseball player. **Personal:** Born Jun 2, 1970, Los Angeles, CA. **Career:** Atlanta Braves, outfielder, 1994-95; Cincinnati Reds, 1996-97; Tampa Bay Devil Rays, 1998-. **Business Addr:** Professional Baseball Player, Tampa Bay Devil Rays, One Tropicana Dr, St Petersburg, FL 33705.

KELLY, R. (ROBERT)
Vocalist. **Personal:** Born in Chicago, IL; son of Joann (deceased). **Career:** Vocalist, songwriter, producer, dancer; USBL, Atlantic City Seagulls, basketball player, 1997. **Honors/Awds:** NAACP, Image Award, Outstanding Song, "I Believe I Can Fly," 1997; Grammy, Award for Best Male R&B Vocal Performance, Best Song Written for a Motion Picture or for Television, Best R&B Song, 1998. **Special Achievements:** Albums: Born into the '90s; 12 Play (double-platinum); Hot singles include: Sex Me (Parts 1 2); Bump N' Grind; Your Body's Callin. **Business Addr:** Vocalist, c/o Jive Records #(BCA), 137-139 W. 25th St., New York, NY 10001, (212)727-0016.

KELLY, SHARON PRATT
Mayor. **Personal:** Born Jan 30, 1944, Washington, DC; daughter of Mildred Petticord Pratt and Carlisle Edward Pratt; married Arrington Dixon (divorced); children: Aimee Dixon, Drew Dixon, Khrys Kelly. **Educ:** Howard Univ, BA, political science, 1965; Howard Univ Law School, JD 1968. **Career:** Joint Center for Political Studies, house counsel 1970-71; Pratt & Queen PC, assoc 1971-76; Antioch School of Law, prof 1972-76; Potomac Electric Power Co, assoc general counsel 1976-79, dir of consumer affairs 1979-83, vice pres of consumer affairs, 1983-86, vice pres of public policy, 1986-90; Washington, DC, mayor, 1990-. **Orgs:** Mem Amer Bar Assn, Unified Bar of the DC, DC Women's Bar Assn; natl committeewoman DC Dem State Comm; vice chair DC Law Revision Comm 1977-83; treas Democratic Natl Comm; member, National Women's Political Caucus; member, Links Club; member, Jack & Jill Club. **Honors/Awds:** Falk Fellow, Howard Univ 1962-65; article, "Software Statutes & State Decisions" Howard Univ Law Journal, Vol 13, 1967; Distinguished Service Award, Federation Women's Clubs, 1986; Presidential Award, NAACP, 1983; Distinguished Leadership Award, United Negro College Fund, 1985; first female African-American mayor of a major U S city, 1990. **Business Addr:** Mayor, Washington, DC, Washington, DC 20005.

KELLY, THOMAS, JR.
Financial administrator. **Personal:** Born Apr 2, 1951, Augusta, GA; married Geraldine; children: Thomas III, Tiffany Nicole. **Educ:** Augusta Coll Schof Bus, BBA 1973; Augusta Coll;; MBA 1978. **Career:** Med Coll of GA Talmadge Meml Hosp, asso hosp adminstr 1978-; Med Coll of GA Talmadge Meml Hosp, asst hosp adminstr 1976-78; Med Coll of GA Talmadge Meml Hosp, fiscal & affairs analyst 1975-76; Med Coll of GA Talmadge Meml Hosp, cost Accountant 1974-75; Med Coll of GA Talmadge Meml Hosp;; gen assountant 1973-74. **Orgs:** Mem Hosp Financial Mgmt Assn 1975-; chmn Internal Audit Com Health Center Credit 1977-79; loan exec United Way Agency 1978-79. **Business Addr:** Med Coll of GA Eugene, Talmade Meml Hosp 1120 15th St, Augusta, GA 30912.

KELLY, THOMAS MAURICE, III
Quality manager. **Personal:** Born May 26, 1950, Des Moines, IA; son of Jane A Kelly and Thomas M Kelly Jr; married Gwendolyn Faye Howard; children: Thomas IV, Patrick. **Educ:** Luther Coll, BA acctg 1968; Luther Coll, BA economics 1972. **Career:** John Deere Component Works, mgr, Cost Acctg & Auditing 1979; Deere & Company, 1980. **Orgs:** Past chrmn brd dir Jesse Cosby Neighborhood Ctr; mem, brd dir Jesse Cosby Neighborhood Ctr; brd of trustees mem YWCA; div ldr United Way Campaign 1982; campaign worker Jr Achvmnt 1982; pres Superv Club; allocation panel mem United Way Campaign 1984; mem brd dir Peoples Health Clinic; mem bd dir Waterloo Chmbr Comm; mem brd dir Amer Red Cross, Hawkeye Chptr; mem brd dir Black Hawk Cnty Economic Develop Ment Cncl; brd dir & mem Waterloo Seratoma Serv Club; mem Waterloo Optimist Serv Club; mem Natl Assoc of Accountants. **Honors/Awds:** CPA IA 1977.

KELSEY, GARY MATTHEW
Administrator/educator. **Personal:** Born Jun 30, 1954, Washington, DC. **Educ:** Allegheny College, BA 1976; Howard University, MEd 1987. **Career:** US Treasury Dept, student intern 1971-72; Alleghany College, asst dir of admin 1975-78; University of Pennsylvania, dir of minority rec 1978-83; Copper State College, assoc dean of students 1983-85; The College Board, assoc dir admissions and guidance services 1985-. **Honors/Awds:** William Bentley Prize-Allegheny College 1976; Outstanding Young Men of America 1981 and 1986; Natl Association of College Admissions Counselors; Natl Alliance of Black School Educators; Natl Scholorship Service Fund for Negro Students. **Business Addr:** Associate Dir, The College Board, 3440 Market St Ste 410, Philadelphia, PA 19104.

KELSEY, JOSEPHINE
Educational administrator. **Career:** Center for Creative Studies, pres, 1991-93. **Special Achievements:** As president of Center for Creative Studies, became first CEO of the corporation formed by the merger of the College of Art and Design and the Institute of Music and Dance.

KEMP, C. ROBERT
Business executive. **Personal:** Born May 26, 1934, Detroit, MI; son of Reda Kemp and Clemie Kemp; married Wilbertean Yvonne Bowser; children: Ronald Brown, Andrea Beaubien, Roderick Kemp, Jenine Hunter. **Educ:** Univ of Washington EEE Studies, 1962; Carnegie Fellowship, Cert 1968; Alexander Hamilton Inst, BA 1971; UCLA Exec Prog, Cert 1972; UCLA Grad Schl of Mgmt, MBA 1977; MIT Exec Prog, Cert 1984; Stanford Grad Bus Sch, Cert 1986. **Career:** TRW Systems Inc (Aerospace/Engr), mem tech staff 1963-69; Interracial Council for Bus Opportunity, vice pres 1969-73; Economic Resources Corp, pres and CEO 1973-78; Interagency Council for Minority Bus Enterprise US Dept of Commerce, exec dir sp asst to secr 1978-79; Opportunity Funding Corp, pres and CEO 1979. **Orgs:** Dir Safeway Stores Inc, Sovran/DC Natl Bank; chrmn, Syndicated Comm, Inc, Fulcrum Venture Capital Corp; dir Natl Urban Coalition; National Black United Fund. **Honors/Awds:** Flwshp Carnegie Inst 1968 Urban; Exec Ldrshp Outstanding Citizen City of Los Angeles; Outstanding Comm Srv State of CA; Recognition Articles Living Legends in Black Amer Black Enterprises. **Military Serv:** USAF airman 1st class 1953-57.

KEMP, EMMERLYNE JANE
Musician. **Personal:** Born May 6, 1935, Chicago, IL; daughter of Janie Lee Harris Kemp (deceased) and Robert Louis Kemp (deceased); divorced. **Educ:** New York University, music education, 1971; Monterey CA, MPC 1960; Berklee School of Music, Boston, MA, jazz subjects, summer 1965; Northwestern University, piano, 1952-54; private piano, with Egon Petri, 1955. **Career:** Beth Eden Bapt Church 1st Concert, 1942; Berkeley Little Theater, classical piano, 1950; played with jazz groups during military service 1956-59; theater show piano, 1958; appeared solo & with groups in HI, OR, NV, & AZ; Santa Clara Coll, concert with jazz group, 1961; first network television appearance, San Francisco, 1961; based in New York City 1965; Radio & TV commercial voice overs 1966; ASCAP writer; produced original songs for children, CBS-TV, 1968; created musical for children, Ballad of Box Brown, 1974; performed in and contributed lyrics and music for first Broadway company of Bubbling Brown Sugar, 1975-76; performed on more than 40 campuses in 20 states, 1966-77; European performaces, 1980-; other musical are: Tomorrow's Woman, Someone To Sing To, spring 1992. **Honors/Awds:** First place, National Talent Competition, Bapt Ushers Washington DC 1953; Second place, Golden State Chapter, NANM, 1954; SFCA, Natl Endowment for the Arts Grant, 1977; ASCAP awards. **Military Serv:** US Army, Sp4, 1956-59. **Home Addr:** 626 Riverside Dr, Apt 21J, New York, NY 10031.

KEMP, LEROY PERCY, JR.
Automobile dealer. **Personal:** Born Dec 24, 1956, Cleveland, OH; son of Jessie Bell Kemp and Leroy Percy Kemp Sr; married Linda Diane Isabell, Nov 16, 1991; children: Brandon Elliott, Jordan Lee, Mercedes Christina. **Educ:** University of Wisconsin-Madison, BBA, marketing, 1979, MBA, marketing, 1983. **Career:** Burrell Advertising, account executive, 1985-87; Clairol, Inc, associate, product manager, 1987-89; Ford Motor Co. Minority Dealer Training Program, 1989-91; Forest Lake Ford, president, owner, 1991-. **Orgs:** Ford Lincoln Mercury Minority Dealer Assn; Natl Assn of Minority Automobile Dealers; USA Wrestling Natl Governing Body. **Honors/Awds:** United States Olympic Team, freestyle wrestling, 1980; First American to become Three-time World Freestyle Wrestling Champion, 1978, 1979, 1982; at age 21, the youngest American to win world championships, 1978; National Wrestling Hall of Fame, inductee, 1989; George Martin Wisconsin Wrestling Hall of Fame, 1983; Pan American Games, Two-time Gold Medalist, 1979-84; Seven-time National Freestyle Wrestling Champion; two-time Ohio State High School Wrestling Champion, 1973-74. **Business Addr:** President, Forest Lake Ford, Inc, 231 19th St SW, Forest Lake, MN 55025, (612)464-4600.

KEMP, SHAWN T.
Professional basketball player. **Personal:** Born Nov 26, 1969, Elkhart, IN. **Educ:** Univ of Kentucky, Lexington, KY, 1988-89; Trinity Valley Community College, Athens, TX, 1988-89. **Career:** Seattle SuperSonics, forward, 1989-97; Cleveland Cavaliers, 1997-. **Honors/Awds:** NBA All-Star, 1998. **Business Addr:** Professional Basketball Player, Cleveland Cavaliers, One Center Ct, Cleveland, OH 44115-4001, (216)659-9100.

KENAN, RANDALL G.
Author. **Personal:** Born Mar 12, 1963, Brooklyn, NY. **Educ:** University of North Carolina, Chapel Hill, NC, BA, 1985. **Career:** Alfred A Knopf, New York, NY, editor, 1985-89; Sarah Lawrence College, Bronxville, NY, lecturer, 1989-; Vassar College, Poughkepsie, NY, lecturer, 1989-; Columbia University, New York, NY, lecturer, 1990-. **Honors/Awds:** New York Foundation of the Arts Grant, 1989; MacDowell Colony Fellowship, 1990; author: A Visitation of Spirits, Grove Press, 1989; Let the Dead Bury Their Dead, Harcourt, Brace, 1992. **Business Addr:** Lecturer, Writing, Sarah Lawrence College, Bronxville, NY 10708.

KENDALL, LETTIE M.
Educator, government official. **Personal:** Born May 2, 1930, Magnolia, AR; married Robert B; children: Yvonne, Sharon, Donald, Ronald. **Educ:** AR Bapt Coll, BS 1951; Bishop Coll 1951; TN State U; Austin Peay State U, MA 1974; Austin Peay State U, EdS 1979. **Career:** Woodruff County Sch Sys, tchr 1951-52; Clarksville & Mont City Sch 1961; Byrns L Darden Sch 1966; Moore Elem & Cohn Schs, prin 1977-; Clarksville Sch. **Orgs:** Mem Clarksville Mont City Educ Assn; past mem TEA, MTEA, NEA; Kappa Delta Pi; Dept Byrns L Darden Sch; Middle TN Council IRA; attended numerous workshops; mem Co Commrs Assn of TN; Adv Com EEO bd Ft Campbell KY; Sch Com of County Ct; NAACP; Clarksville Comm Devel Com; v chmn Recreational & Historical bd of the County Com; past dir St John Bapt Ch Sunday Sch.

KENDALL, MAE ARMSTER
Educator. **Personal:** Born Dec 22, 1934, Thomasville, GA; married Charles M; children: George C Armster, Earle A Armster, Trent Kendall, Kendrick Kendall. **Educ:** NY Univ, BS 1963; Bank State Coll of Ed NYC, MS 1968; Univ of GA Athens, Doctorate 1977. **Career:** NY Univ Rehabilitation Center Child Div, asst to supvr 1959-63; Thomasville City Schools, Thomasville GA, teacher 1963-68; Univ of GA, Atlanta Public Schools, instructor early childhood educ 1968-71; GA State Univ, Univ of GA, Early Childhood Educ Inst, dir 1970-73; US Office of Educ & Govt VI Head Start School System, consultant 1971-73; Univ of GA, Atlanta Public Schools, assoc dir, teacher corps 1971-73; Multicultural Inst Univ of NE, Prairie View Coll, consultant 1975-76; Governors Task Force, Office of the Governor, State of GA, consultant 1975-76; Atlanta Public Schools, dir cur, 1983-92; Univ of GA, Atlanta Teachers Corp, dir 1973-82; Clark Atlanta Univ, assoc prof, 1984-. **Orgs:** Pres GA Assoc on Young Children 1976-77; mem, com chmn Delta Sigma Theta Sor Atlanta Alumnae Chap 1977-; governing bd mem Natl Assoc Ed of Young Children 1979-83; adv bd ASCN 1984; mem NAACP, AAUP, Phi Delta Kappa, ACEI, GAYC; Ron McNair Foundation, bd mem. **Honors/Awds:** Ed Scholarships NY Univ & Bank St Coll 1960-63, 1967-68; NDEA Fellow Univ of GA 1965; Ford Found Leadership Fellow Ford Found 1967-68; Bronze Woman of the Year City of Atlanta 1976; Two citations Outstanding Ed Achievement Atlanta Const 1976-79; Medallion of Excellence, State of Georgia 1983. **Special Achievements:** Author: "Sisters! You Have Class? Then, Strut Your Sass," 1990.

KENDALL, MICHELLE KATRINA
Pharmacist, pharmacy supervisor. **Personal:** Born Aug 5, 1952, Detroit, MI; daughter of Evelyn Cayce and Louis A Cayce; married Jeffrey M Kendall, May 20, 1989; children: Christopher M. **Educ:** Wayne State University, BA, biology, 1983, BS, pharmacy, 1987. **Career:** Wayne State University, student research asst, 1972-84; Children's Hospital, pharmacy intern, 1984-87; Perry Drug Store Inc, pharmacy supervisor, 1987-. **Orgs:** Detroit Pharmacy Guild, currently; Lambda Kappa Sigma, 1986-; Crockett Vocational Center, advisory board, 1992-. **Home Addr:** 15724 Tuller, Detroit, MI 48238, (313)342-8084. **Business Addr:** Pharmacy Supervisor, Perry Drug Stores Inc, 5400 Perry Dr, Pontiac, MI 48340, (313)538-2780.

KENDALL, ROBERT, JR.
Attorney. **Personal:** Born Feb 11, 1947, Thomaston, GA; married Lolita Marie Toles; children: Yolanda Yvette, Robert III. **Educ:** Ft Valley State Coll, BS Educ 1969; TX So Univ Sch of Law, JD 1973. **Career:** US Dept of Justice, asst dir civil division. **Orgs:** Mem Phi Beta Sigma Frat 1968; mem Phi Alpha Delta Law Frat 1969. **Honors/Awds:** Spl Achievement Awds for Sustained Superior Performance of Duty US Dept of Justice Washington DC 1977, 1985, 1989, 1990 and 1992. **Military Serv:** AUS E-5 2 yrs; Bronze Star. **Business Addr:** Assistant Dir, US Dept of Justice, 10th & PA Ave NW, Washington, DC 20530.

KENDALL, SHIRLEY I.
Education administrator. **Personal:** Born Jun 26, 1954, Manhattan, NY; married Victor Parris; children: Victor Kendall. **Educ:** Morrisville Ag & Tech Coll, AA 1974; SUNY Oneonta, BS Early Secondary Ed 1976; SUNY State Ed Dept, Public School Teacher Cert 1981; SUNY Oneonta, MS Counseling 1984. **Career:** Ed Oppty Program SUNY Oneonta, counselor 1977-79, instr peer counseling 1977-79, admissions counselor 1979-80, asst dir 1980-82, asst to pres. **Orgs:** Mem Amer Assoc for Affirm Action 1982-85, Assoc of Black Women in Higher Ed 1984-85; vice pres bd of dir State Univ Coll at Oneonta Childrens Ctr 1984-85. **Honors/Awds:** Excellence in Academic Achievement SUNY Oneonta Ed Oppty Prog 1976; Serv to Third World Assoc Students Third World Assoc 1985.

KENDRICK, ARTIS G.
Cleric. **Personal:** Born May 11, 1914, Stamps, AR; married Jeanette Kendrick; children: Barbara Ann. **Educ:** Am Bapt Coll of the Bible Nashville, BTh 1965; Univ of AZ, AB 1956; Seter Bapt Cntrs Houston, DD 1976; Providence Theol Sem LA CA, DD. **Career:** Various locations, Pastor 1940-65; Pilgrim Bapt Ch, Pastor 1965-. **Orgs:** Mod Providence Dist Assn; assn exec Bapt Ministers Conf of LA; pres Paradise Bapt State Convention 1944-49 & 1957-63; chaplain State Legislature of AZ 1960-65; mem bd dir ARC 1960-62; pres AZ Narcotics Educ Assn 1959-60; moderator Providence Missionary Assn of Los Angeles; mem trst bd Am BaptColl of the Bible; mem corporate bd Natl Bapt Sunday Sch publ bd Organizer & leader in church construction in AZ. **Special Achievements:** California State Baptist Convention, First Vice President, 1988-92; been a pastor for 55 years. **Business Addr:** 950 E 45 St, Los Angeles, CA 90011.

KENDRICK, CAROL YVONNE
Attorney. **Personal:** Born Jan 29, 1952, New York, NY; daughter of Marguerite Holloway Kendrick and E Curtis Kendrick; married John A DeMicco, May 6, 1989. **Educ:** New York University, BA, 1974; New York University School of Law, JD, 1977; New York University School of Law, LLM-Corporations, 1991. **Career:** Office of the Bronx District Attorney, asst dist attorney, 1977-1981; New York Life Insurance Co, associate counsel, 1981-97, Ann Taylor, Asst gen counsel, 1997-. **Orgs:** Riverside Opera Ensemble, founder and board member, 1984-; Village Light Opera Group, producer, 1976-; Minority Interchange, speaker, 1983-84. **Honors/Awds:** Ebony Magazine, Best and Brightest Black Women in Corporate America, 1990. **Business Addr:** Assistant General Counsel, c/o Ann Taylor, 142 W 57th St, New York, NY 10019, (212)541-3230.

KENDRICK, CURTIS L.
Librarian. **Personal:** Born Jun 13, 1958, Queens, NY; son of Marguerite Sanford Holloway and Ercell Curtis Kendrick; married Mary Beth Souza Kendrick. **Educ:** Brown University, Providence, RI, BA, 1980; Simmons College, Boston, MA, MS, 1984; Emory University, Atlanta, GA, MBA, 1992. **Career:** Brown University, Providence, RI, library assoc specialist, 1981-83; Oberlin College, Oberlin, OH, asst to the dir of libraries, 1984-86; State University of New York, Stony Brook, NY, head, circulation dept, 1986-90; Information Consultant, Decatur, GA, ceo, 1990-92; Harvard University, assistant director of libraries, 1992-. **Orgs:** American Library Association, 1983-; Association of College & Research Libraries, 1985-; Library Administration and Management Association, 1990-; Library Information Technology Association, 1990-. **Honors/Awds:** Beta Phi Mu, National Honor Society, 1983; Faculty Travel Research Grant, SUNY at Stony Brook, 1989; Title II-B Fellowship, US Department of Education, 1983; Emory Scholar Fellowship, 1990-92; George Mew Organization and Management Award, 1992. **Special Achievements:** Author, The Competitive Advantage of Librarians, Managing Resource Sharing in the Electronic Age, 1996; author, The Design & Operation Off-site Storage in Support of Preservation Programs, Erice 96 Conservation and Restoration of Archive & Library Materials Conference, 1996; author, A User-Centered View of Document Delivery & Interlibrary Loan, Library Administration and Management, 1994; author, Performance Measures of Shelving Accuracy, Journal of Academic Librarianship, 1991; author, Minority Internship/Scholarship in Library and Information Sciences, College & Research Libraries News, 1990; author, Cavalry to the Rescue, College & Research Libraries News, 1989. **Business Addr:** Assistant Director, Harvard University Library, 1280 Massachusetts Ave, Ste 404, Cambridge, MA 02138.

KENDRICK, JOY A.
Lawyer. **Personal:** Born Sep 11, Burlington, NC; daughter of Sarah L Kendrick and Charles Kendrick. **Educ:** Univ of North Carolina at Chapel Hill, BA, 1977; State Univ of New York at Buffalo, JD, 1981; Indiana Univ, MBA, 1985. **Career:** Alamance Technical College, orientation librarian, 1977-78; Cora P Maloney College, academic coordinator, 1980-81; Neighborhood Legal Services Inc, staff attorney, 1981-83; law clerk, 1979-81; NCR Corporation, business intern, 1984; JA Kendrick Business Enterprises Inc, president, 1985-; Law Office of Joy Kendrick, managing counsel, 1985-. **Orgs:** Erie County Bar Association; New York State Bar Association; American Bar Association; Leadership Buffalo, 1988; Chamber of Commerce, board of directors, 1987-90; Buffalo Private Industry Council, board of directors, 1990-; Buffalo Business, contributing writer; Minority Business Council, bd of directors; Housing Assistant Center, bd of directors. **Business Addr:** Lawyer/Business Consultant, Law Office of Joy A Kendrick/JA Kendrick Business Enterprise, 107 Delaware Ave, Ste 327, Buffalo, NY 14202, (716)855-2251.

KENDRICK, L. JOHN, SR.
Paper co. executive. **Personal:** Born May 13, 1932, Monticello, KY; son of Marie Kendrick and Wesley Kendrick; divorced; children: L John Jr, Rozalind Denese Hopgood, Debra Jo Hopgood. **Career:** Kendrick Paper Stock Co, chief executive officer, 1954-. **Orgs:** Jefferson County Housing Authority, chairman, 1972-74; Just Mens Club, 1969-72; Jefferson County Chamber of Commerce, 1968-81; Jefferson County NAACP, 1968-92; Governors Club, 1990-; Corinthian Baptist Church, finance committee. **Honors/Awds:** State of Illinois, Governors Corp Recycling Award, 1989; Certificate of Recognition for Efforts in Recycling, 1988. **Military Serv:** US Air Force, 1951-54. **Business Addr:** Chief Executive Officer, Kendrick Paper Stock Co, 1000 Salem Rd, Mount Vernon, IL 62864, (618)242-4527.

KENDRICK, TOMMY L.
Educational administrator. **Personal:** Born May 29, 1923, Sycamore, GA; son of Salbe Kendrick and George Kendrick; married Geneva Bhanton; children: Deborah Elane, Welchel, Diane H, Denise. **Educ:** Fort Valley State Coll, BSA 1948; Tuskegee Inst MS Educ 1958, MAdm & Sup 1969. **Career:** Ft Baptist Church, supt Sunday School 1955-85, clerk 1961-85; Masonic Lodge, wishful master 1968-; elem school principal; School of Theology, Chatto Valley Bible Coll, Edison, GA, dean, 1989-93. **Orgs:** Worshipful master Prince Hall Masons 1950-85; mem Co Bd of Commission 1976-95; mem State Assn of Co Comm 1976-95; mem Order of Consery 32 Mason 1979-95; deputy grand master Prince Hall Masons 1987-95; mem GTA 1970-85; mem Natl Assoc of Educators 1970-85; mem Page Prof Org 1983-. **Honors/Awds:** Citation from 1st Bapt Church of Georgetown, 1992; Man of the Year, 1988. **Home Addr:** Route 2, Box 234, Georgetown, GA 31754.

KENLAW, JESSIE
College basketball coach. **Career:** University of Houston, women's basketball coach, currently. **Business Phone:** (713)221-8000.

KENNARD, PATRICIA A.
News anchor. **Personal:** Born Jun 26, 1949, Canton, OH; daughter of John Byrd (deceased) and Velva Whiting Williams; divorced; children: Maya Khalilah. **Educ:** Central State Univ, BS, 1972; Univ of Akron Sch of Grad Studies, 1975-76. **Career:** Harford Jr High School, lang arts teacher, 1972-73; Canton Urban League; educ specialist (counselor) 1973-79; WHBC, radio newscaster, 1976-79; Group One Media Group, television reporter, 1980-86; Summit Radio Group, DKM, Radio Group, Rubber City Radio Group, 1986-97. **Orgs:** Assn of Black Professional Business Women; NAACP; American Cancer Society, youth council advisor; Zeta Phi Beta Sorority, Inc; Natl Children's Miracle Network Telethon for Children's Hospital, local co-host; Mentoring Mothers; The House of the Lord; Boys and Girls Club of Summit County;. **Honors/Awds:** Black Media Award, 1982; Crystal Award, 1992. **Home Addr:** 493 Storer Avenue, Akron, OH 44320.

KENNARD, ROBERT ALEXANDER. See Obituaries section.

KENNARD, WILLIAM EARL
Government official. **Personal:** Born Jan 19, 1957, Los Angeles, CA; son of Helen & Robert A Kennard; married Deborah D Kennedy, Apr 9, 1984. **Educ:** Stanford Univ, BA, 1978; Yale Law School, JD, 1981. **Career:** Natl Assn of Broadcasters, fellowship, 1981-82, asst general counsel, 1983-84; Verner, Liipfert, Bernhard, McPherson & Hand, assoc, 1982-83, partner, 1984-93; Federal Communications Commission, general counsel, 1993-97, chairman, currently. **Business Addr:** Chairman, Federal Communications Commission, 1919 M St NW, Rm 614, Washington, DC 20554, (202)418-1000.

KENNEDY, ADRIENNE LITA
Playwright, lecturer. **Personal:** Born Sep 13, 1931, Pittsburgh, PA; daughter of Etta Haugabook Hawkins and Cornell Wallace; married Joseph C. Kennedy, May 15, 1953; children: Joseph Jr, Adam. **Educ:** Ohio State University, BA, 1952; Columbia University, graduate study. **Career:** Playwright; Yale University, lecturer, 1972-74; Princeton University, lecturer, 1977, professor, currently; Brown University, visiting associate professor, 1979-80. **Orgs:** Member, PEN. **Honors/Awds:** Plays include: Funnyhouse of a Negro, 1962; The Owl Answers, 1963; A Lesson in a Dead Language, 1964; The Lennon Play: In His Own Write (with John Lennon and Victor Spinetti), 1967; Sun: A Poem for Malcolm X Inspired by His Murder, 1968; Cities in Bezique, 1969; Boats, 1969; An Evening With Dead Essex, 1973; A Movie Star Has to Star in Black and White, 1976; A Lancashire Lad, 1980; Orestes and Electra, 1980; Black Children's Day, 1980; Solo Voyages, 1985; memoir, People Who Led to My Plays, 1987; contributor to books. Obie Award for Funnyhouse of A Negro, Village Voice, 1964; Guggenheim Memorial Fellowship, 1967; Rockefeller Grants, 1967-69, 1974, 1976; CBS Fellow, 1973; Stanley Award for Play Writing; others.

KENNEDY, ANNE GAMBLE
Educator, musician (retired). **Personal:** Born Sep 25, 1920, Charleston, WV; daughter of Nina Clinton Gamble and Henry F Gamble; married Matthew W Kennedy; children: Nina Gamble. **Educ:** Fisk Univ, AB (Cum Laude) 1941; Oberlin Coll, BM 1943; Juilliard School of Music, 1951; George Peabody Coll, 1970; private study with concert artist Ray Lev 1945-50. **Career:** Tuskegee Inst, instr 1943-45; Talladega Coll, assoc prof 1945-48; Concerts throughout US, Haiti, Jamaica, VI; concerts on coll campus; Fisk Jubilee Singers, accompanist 20 yrs, incl European Tour in 1956; many duo-piano recitals with Matthew Kennedy; Fisk Univ, assoc prof of piano 1950-81. **Orgs:** Mem Womans Adv Bd of the TN Performing Arts Found; music consult Nashville C of C; mem John W Work III Mem Found; mem Middle TN Music Teachers Assoc, Nashville Chap of Links, Nashville Fine Arts Club; music comm 1st Bapt Church Capitol Hill; mem Alpha Kappa Alpha. **Honors/Awds:** Cum Laude & Dept Honors from Fisk; Scholarship at Oberlin Conserv of Music.

KENNEDY, BRENDA PICOLA
Judge. **Personal:** Born in Mexia, TX; daughter of Lois Bertha Hobbs Kennedy and Jimmie Vernon Kennedy; divorced; children: Mallore Kennedy Caldwell, Pilar Elise Caldwell. **Educ:** University of Texas, Austin, BJ, 1977, School of Law, JD, 1981. **Career:** City of Austin, asst city attorney, 1981-82; Travis County, District Attorney's Office, asst district attorney, 1982-87, County Court-at-Law #7, judge, 1987-. **Orgs:** State Bar of Texas, 1981-; Travis County Bar Assn, 1982-; Autsin Black Lawyers Assn, 1981-; Links, 1992-; Delta Sigma Theta Sorority Inc, 1974-; Jack and Jill Inc, 1992-; Laguna Gloria Art Museum, board of directors, 1987-; Umlauf Sculpture Garden and Museum, board of directors, 1992-94; Leadership Texas Alumnae Assn, board of directors, 1990-94. **Honors/Awds:** Thurgood Marshall Legal Society, Virgil C Lott Alumni Award, 1993. **Business Addr:** Judge, County Court-at-Law #7, 1010 San Antonio, PO Box 1748, Rm 200, Austin, TX 78701, (512)473-9679.

KENNEDY, CAIN JAMES
Circuit court judge. **Personal:** Born Apr 2, 1937, Thomaston, AL; son of Carrie Kennedy (deceased) and Marcus Kennedy; married Brenda J; children: Celestine Carrie. **Educ:** Los Angeles Cty Coll, AA 1964; CA St U, BA 1966; George Washington U, JD 1971. **Career:** 13th Jud Circuit AL, circuit judge, currently; St of AL, st rep; Kennedy, Wilson & Davis Law Firm, partner. **Orgs:** Mem of, Mobile County Urban League, Governor's Commission on Crime 1979-80, Law Enforcement and Justice Leadership Mobile, Amer Friends Service Committee Southeast Region; bd of dir Penelope House of South Alabama 1981-82; bd of dir Sickle Cell Disease Assoc Inc Gulf Coast AL. **Military Serv:** US Navy Reserves, Judge Advocate General, Capt. **Business Addr:** Circuit Judge, 13th Judicial Circuit, Mobile Govt Plaza, Court Building, 205 Govt Street, Mobile, AL 36602.

KENNEDY, CALLAS FAYE
Educator. **Personal:** Born Oct 13, 1954, Lisman, AL. **Educ:** Sacramento City Coll, AA (w/honors) 1975; CA State Univ of Sacramento, BA 1978. **Career:** Sacramento County Headstart Programs, teacher/dir 1978-83; Children's Home Soc of CA, prog specialist 1983-84; Pacific Oaks Coll, instructor 1984; Yuba Comm Coll, instructor 1985; Child-Human Development specialist, currently. **Orgs:** Chairperson Natl Black Child Develop Inst 1978-; chairperson Sacramento Area Black Caucus Inc 1983-85; treas CA Child Passenger Safety Assn 1983-; consultant/speaker Child Develop Inc 1985, Marriage and Family Counselors Inc 1986; conference speaker Sacramento Valley Assn for Educ of Young Children; Sacramento Black Women's Network and Sacramento County Children,s Commission; Co-chairman, Coalition of Sacramento Women's Organizations. **Honors/Awds:** Lewis Lamtier Awd Pacific Bell 1984; Black Female Educator Black Educators for Action 1985; Human Rights Awds Sacramento City/Cty 1985-86; YWCA, Outstanding Women of the Year, 1990. **Home Addr:** 5930 Mclaren Ave, Sacramento, CA 95822.

KENNEDY, CORTEZ
Professional football player. **Personal:** Born Aug 23, 1968, Osceola, AR; children: Courtney. **Educ:** Northwest Mississippi Junior College; Univ of Miami, bachelor's degree in criminal justice. **Career:** Seattle Seahawks, defensive tackle, 1990-. **Honors/Awds:** First-team All-America choice, Sporting News, 1989; Marcus Nalley Trophy, 1992; NFL Players Assn, Defensive Lineman of the Year, 1992; NFL Defensive Player of the Year, 1992; Associated Pres, Defensive Player of the Year, 1993; Pro Bowl, 1991, 1992, 1993, 1994, 1995, 1996; Steve Largent Award, 1996. **Business Addr:** Professional Football Player, Seattle Seahawks, 11220 NE 53rd St, Kirkland, WA 98033, (206)827-9777.

KENNEDY, FLORYNCE
Attorney. **Personal:** Born Feb 11, 1916, St Louis, MO. **Educ:** Columbia U, BA 1948; LlD 1951. **Career:** Media Workshop & Comsumer Info Svc, lawyer, polit activist, dir; Feminist Party Co-author Abortin Rap Avortement Droit Des Femmes, fdr. **Honors/Awds:** Contrb articles to various publs. **Business Addr:** 699 Rhode Island St, San Francisco, CA 94107.

KENNEDY, FLOYD C.
Psychologist, educator. **Personal:** Born Jun 14, 1925, Wheeling, WV; married Geraldine C Broussard; children: Lisa Marie, Kevin Eugene. **Educ:** Howard U, BS 1950; CA State Coll, MA 1957. **Career:** USAF, personnel psychologist 1952-55; USAF, Personnel officer 1956; USAF, research & devel officer 1957-62; USAF, behavioral scientist 1963-70; Met State Coll, counseling & psychologiszt 1970-75; Counseling & Career Devel, asso dir; Met State Coll, asst prof psychology. **Orgs:** Mem Am Correctional Assn 1966-71; mem Am Personnel & Guidance Assn; Nat Council of Family Relations; volunteer probation counselor Denver Co Ct; mem Psi Chi Nat Psychol Honorary Soc 1951-52; Omega Psi Phi Frat. **Honors/Awds:** Recipient USAF Merit Serv Medal 1970. **Military Serv:** USAF major 1970. **Business Addr:** Met State Coll, 1006 11th St Ave, Denver, CO 80204.

KENNEDY, HENRY H., JR.
Judge. **Personal:** Born Feb 22, 1948, Columbia, SC; son of Rachel Spawn Kennedy and Henry H Kennedy; married Altomease Rucker, Sep 20, 1980; children: Morgan Rucker, Alexandra Rucker. **Educ:** Princeton Univ, AB, 1970; Harvard Law School, JD, 1973. **Career:** Jones Jay Reavis & Poque, 1973; US Attorney's Office, asst US attorney, 1973-76; US District Court, magistrate, 1976-79; Superior Court of DC, judge, 1979-97; United States Distric Court, 1997-. **Orgs:** Sigma Pi Phi; Washington Tennis Foundation; Board of Dirs, American Bar Assn, Standard Committee Barristers. **Honors/Awds:** Trial Lawyers Assn of Metropolitan Washington DC, H Carl Mooltrie Award, Judicial Exellence 1997; Founders Award, Princeton Univ Comm House, 1995. **Business Addr:** Judge, US Courthouse, 333 Constitution Ave, NW, Washington, DC 20001, (202)879-1202.

KENNEDY, HOWARD E.
Perfume designer. **Personal:** Born Nov 30, 1941, Fernandina Beach, FL; son of Cecil D Watson Kennedy Williams and Charles Emmanuel Kennedy; divorced. **Educ:** St Petersburg Jr Coll, St Petersburg FL, Assoc, 1962; NY Inst of Tech, New York NY, 1977-80. **Career:** Revlon, Bronx NY, apprentice perfumer, 1965-70; Pfizer Consumer Products, chief perfumer, 1970-87; Royal Essence Ltd, New York New York, pres, 1987-; H K Enterprises, Union City, NJ, pres, 1990-. **Orgs:** Pres, NAACP Youth Council, 1961-62; mem, Society of Cosmetics Chemists, 1970-; dir, Amer Society of Perfumers, 1975-; mem, Fragrance Foundation, 1988-; mem, Natl Business Council, 1988-; bd of directors and trustees, United Methodist Home; pres, Amer Soc of Perfumers, 1997-98. **Honors/Awds:** Outstanding Entrepreneur of the Year, Natl Black MBA Assn, 1989; Black Achievers in Industry, NY Chapter Greater YMCA, 1985; Outstanding Entrepreneur of the Year, Natl Black MBA Assn, 1989; Business Achievement Award, Black Retail Action Group, 1990; Sweet Earth Fragrances, 1971; Wild Musk & Musk for Men Fragrances, 1973; Complice Fragrance, 1979; Sophia Fragrance, 1982; Stetson Fragrance,Lady Stetson, 1986; Iron Fragrance, 1987; De Kuyper Peachtree Schnapps Flavor Scent, 1987; Grand Marnier Flavor Scent, 1988; Seagrams Extra Wine Cooler Flavor, 1988; Billy Dee Williams Fragrance, 1989; Undeniable for Women, 1990; Undeniable for Men, 1991; Seagram's Sun Frost Tea Wine Cooler, 1992; Kraft Foods' Country Kitchen Syrup Flavor, 1994; Southern Exposure Fragrance, Terry Ellis. **Military Serv:** US Army, pfc, 1962-65. **Business Addr:** President, H. K. Enterprises, Inc, 380 Mountain Rd, Ste 1814, Union City, NJ 07087.

KENNEDY, JAMES E.
Educator. **Personal:** Born Sep 30, 1933, Jackson, MS; son of Esther Shelwood and Tim Kennedy; divorced; children: Jia Lynette, Jason Edward. **Educ:** AL State U, BS 1954; IN U, MAT 1964. **Career:** Mobile Co Pub Sch, instr 1958-67; Mobile Co Public Sch, admin 1967-68; Univ of So AL, instr asst prof, prof of art 1968-78; University of South Alabama, chairman of art department, 1978-. **Orgs:** Mem The Coll Art Assn; mem Nat Conf of Artist; mem Kappa Alpha Psi; Adv Eta Nu Chap Univ So AL; mem culture in black & white mobile; bd mem Fine Arts Museum of the South; dir, curator Amer Ethnic Art Slide Library. **Honors/Awds:** Exhibitor in innumerable shows & recipient of 19 awards. **Military Serv:** USAF s/Sgt 1954-58. **Business Addr:** Professor of Art, Univ of Southern Alabama, 307 University Blvd, Mobile, AL 36688.

KENNEDY, JAMES E.
Pastor, auto company supervisor (retired). **Personal:** Born Jun 21, 1938, Weir, MS; son of Girtha Kennedy and Ethel Kennedy; married Thelma Brown, Sep 18, 1960; children: Sandra Kennedy, Sheri Kennedy, Stephon Kennedy. **Educ:** John Wesley Coll, Owosso MI, BA, 1976; Southern Seminary, Louisville KY, Graduate. **Career:** General Motors Corp, Flint MI, supervisor, 1956-87, retired; Mount Carmel Baptist Church, Flint MI, pastor, 1981-. **Orgs:** Bd of dir, Genesee Baptist Assn; family ministry consultant, Genesee Baptist Assn; family ministry consultant, Baptist State Convention of MI; Sunday School, SBC; bd chair, Genesee County Commission on Substance Abuse; Advisory Council GCCSA; national chairperson, Pro-Minority Action Coalition; GCCSA; board of directors, Urban League of Flint; chairman of the board, Urban Committee of Boy Scouts of America; Chaplain, Flint Police & Fire Department; past president, Interfaith Prevention Group, sponsor-Mr Rogers "Say No"; Big Brothers, Big Sisters. **Honors/Awds:** Frederick Douglas Award, Natl Assn of Business & Professional Women Inc, 1989. **Business Addr:** Pastor, Mount Carmel Baptist Church, 1610 W Pierson Rd, Flint, MI 48504.

KENNEDY, JAYNE. See KENNEDY-OVERTON, JAYNE.

KENNEDY, JIMMIE VERNON
Educational administrator. **Personal:** Born Oct 6, 1925, Mexia, TX; married Lois Betha Hobbs; children: Demetra James, Brenda Picola. **Educ:** Prairie View A&M Colld bs 1948; u of TX, med 1963. **Career:** Temple High School, vice prin 1975-80; Bon Hdm Jr High, asst prin 1971-75; Meridith Jr High Temple, prin 1969-71; Dunbas High School Temple, prin 1967-69; Dunbar High Sch Temple, asst prin 1964-67; Temple High, vocational agr teacher 1956-64; Cold Springs ISD, vocational agr teacher 1948-56. **Orgs:** Mem TX Assn of Secondary Sch Prin; mem Nat Educ Assn; mem TX State Tchrs Assn; bd of dirs Temple Fed Credit Unoin; chmn Bd Sr Citizens Inc; chmn Bd of Salisbury Day Care Center; chmn City Bd of Housing; mem Temple City Planning Commn. **Honors/Awds:** Recipient plaques & achievement awards from all Orgns Servec. **Business Addr:** Temple Independent Sch Dist, 415 N 31st, Temple, TX 76501.

KENNEDY, JOSEPH J., JR.
Educator (retired), violinist, arranger, composer. **Personal:** Born Nov 17, 1923, Pittsburgh, PA; son of Mr & Mrs Joseph J Kennedy Sr; married Thelma Marion Copeland; children: Joseph J III, Victoria Lynn. **Educ:** VA State Univ, BS 1953; Duquesne Univ, MMus 1960; Carnegie Mellon Univ, applied music. **Career:** Broadcast Music Inc, arranger/composer/violinist; VA Polytechnic Inst & State Univ, retired professor Emeritus of music, 1995. **Orgs:** Mem Amer Fed of Musicians, Music Educ Natl Conf, Phi Mu Alpha Sinfonia, Phi Delta Kappa; guest conductor Cleveland Summer Symphony 1965; Encyclopedia of Jazz in the Sixties & Seventies Leonard Feather Horizon Press New York City 1966, 1976; guest conductor All American Dir Orch Chi 1968; Black American Music, Past & Present Hildred Roach Crescendo Publishers Boston 1973; natl bd mem Amer Youth Sym & Chorus 1973; bd dir Richmond Symphony 1974; bd dir Rotary Club Richmond 1981; guest conductor Kentucky All State Orchestra Cincinnati OH 1982; guest soloist Natl Assn of Jazz Educators Columbus OH 1984; adv bd Richmond Jazz Soc; former chairman of strings, International Association of Jazz Educators, 1990. **Honors/Awds:** Jazz Composer-in-Residence, Roanoke Symphony, 1993-94; Proclamation, Richmond Jazz Society & City of Richmond, VA, Sept 10 1996. **Military Serv:** AUS WW II. **Home Addr:** 3201 Griffin Ave, Richmond, VA 23222.

KENNEDY, JOYCE S.
Educator. **Personal:** Born Jun 15, 1943, St Louis, MO; divorced. **Educ:** Harris Tchr Coll, AB 1965; St Louis U, MEd 1968; MI State U, PhD 1975. **Career:** Coll of Arts & Sciences Governors State Univ, occupational educ coordinator, prof 1975-; Meramec Jr Coll, counselor 1971-74; Forest Park Jr Coll, counselor 1969-71; St Louis Job Corps Center for Women, counselor 1968-69; Carver Elementary School, teacher 1966-68. **Orgs:** Mem Am Personnel and Guidance assn; mem IL Assn of Non-White Concerns; mem IL Guidance and Personnel Assn; keynote speaker Roseland Community Sch Graduation 1978; facilitator Career Awareness Workshop 1978; speaker Harvey Pub Library 1978; Urban Counseling Fellowship Nat Mental Health Inst MI State Univ 1972-74. **Honors/Awds:** Cert of Recognition for Outstanding Serv IL Guidance adn Personnel Assn 1977; Distinguished Prof Governors State Univ 1977; Outstanding Young Woman of Am Award 1978. **Business Addr:** College of Arts & Sciences, Governors State University, University Park, IL 60466.

KENNEDY, KAREL R.
Educator, health services administrator. **Personal:** Born May 6, 1946, Greeleyville, SC; son of Susie Kennedy and Ben Kennedy. **Educ:** Howard Univ, BS 1967, MD 1971. **Career:** Greater Harlem Nursing Home, medical director, currently; Mt Sinai College of Medicine, assistant clinical professor, currently. **Business Addr:** Internal Medicine, 1058 Hurger Dr, Georgetown, SC 29440.

KENNEDY, LINCOLN
Professional football player. **Personal:** Born Feb 12, 1971, York, PA; married; children: four. **Educ:** Univ of Washington. **Career:** Atlanta Falcons, tackle, 1993-95; Oakland Raiders, 1996-. **Business Addr:** Professional Football Player, Oakland Raiders, 1220 Harbor Bay Pkwy, Alameda, CA 94502, (510)615-1875.

KENNEDY, MARVIN JAMES
Corporate director. **Personal:** Born Apr 18, 1931, Ben Wheeler, TX; married Linzel Harmon; children: Wendolyn K Walker, Patrick A, Marva L, Angela M. **Educ:** Prairie View A&M U, BS 1952; Univ of TX San Antonio, MA 1975. **Career:** Bexar Co OIC, exec dir 1974-; HQ 5th Army Ft Sam Houston race rela officer 1972-73; HQ 5th Army Ft Sam Houston, chief readiness oper officer 1969-72; Army Rep of Vietnam, inspector gen adv dir 1968-69; Prairie View A&M Coll, ROTC prof 1966-69. **Orgs:** Mem exec dir Assn of OIC's 1975-; mem past vice pres San Antonio Personnell & Mgmt Assn 1976-; mem Am Soc of Training Devel 1979-; exec com mem United Negro Coll Fund 1976-; review com mem Metro Youth Orgn 1978-; fund review com United Way 1979-. **Honors/Awds:** Recipient of bronze star air & commendation medals AUS 1960-66; appreciation award San Antonio Personnel & Mgmt Assn 1978; comm serv award Nat Counc of Negro Women Inc 19790; outstanding performance award Kappa Alpha Psi 1979; Outstanding Performances Award, 1974-94. **Military Serv:** AUS maj served 21 yrs.

KENNEDY, MATTHEW W.
Educator, musician (retired). **Personal:** Born Mar 10, 1921, Americus, GA; son of Mary Dowdell Kennedy and Royal Clement Kennedy; married Anne Lucille Gamble; children: Nina Gamble Kennedy. **Educ:** Fisk Univ, AB 1946 (cum laude); Juilliard School of Music, MS 1950. **Career:** Fisk Univ, assoc prof 1947-48, 1954-84, acting dean music dept 1975-78; piano soloist natl & intl; Fisk Jubilee Singers, dir 1957-67, 1971-73, 1975-83, 1985-86 (retired). **Orgs:** Mem Music Teachers Natl Assn; mem Sigma Upsilon Pi; Omega Psi Phi; deacon Baptist; mem Nashville Fine Arts Club; First Baptist Church; Omega Psi Phi; TN Arts Comm 1968-82; bd mem John W Work Mem Found 1973-; program chmn Nashville Fine Arts Club 1967-69; bd mem Nashville Symphony Assn 1975-78. **Honors/Awds:** Gabriel Scholarship Fisk Univ; Sigma Upsilon Pi Honor Soc Fisk Univ 1946; United Negro Coll Fund IBM Faculty Fellowship 1969; Omega Man of Yr 1974; Distinguished Negro Georgians; Special Achievements solo recitals, Carnegie Hall recital; Natl Gallery of Art; Town Hall Philadelphia 1958-60; Spirituals published Abingdon Press Nashville 1974. **Military Serv:** AUS m/sgt 1943-46.

KENNEDY, NATHELYNE ARCHIE
Civil/structural engineer. **Personal:** Born Jun 1, 1938, Richards, TX; daughter of Ernestine Linten Archie and Nathaniel L Archie; married James D Kennedy, Dec 27, 1961; children: Tracey A, David J. **Educ:** Prairie View A&M Univ, BS Arch Engr 1959. **Career:** Alfred Benesch & Co, engr 1960-72; Bernard Johnson Inc, engr 1978-81; Nathelyne A Kennedy & Assoc Inc, pres, engr 1981-. **Orgs:** Mem Amer Soc of Civil Engrs, Natl Soc of Professional Engrs, TX Good Roads Transportation Assn; American Consulting Engineers Council; Society of American Military Engineers. **Business Addr:** President, Nathelyne A Kennedy & Assoc Inc, 6100 Hillcroft, Ste 710, Houston, TX 77081, (713)988-0145.

KENNEDY, SANDRA DENISE
State representative. **Personal:** Born Dec 25, 1957, Oklahoma City, OK; daughter of Doll Baby Alford Kennedy and Leland W Kennedy; children: Mahogany. **Educ:** Coursework at Phoenix Coll, Phoenix AZ, 1975; Maricopa Technical Coll, Phoenix AZ, 1975-86; South Mountain Comm Coll, Phoenix AZ, 1975-86; Mesa Comm Coll, Mesa AZ, 1975-86; Arizona State University, Tempe AZ, 1975-86. **Career:** State of Arizona, state representative. **Orgs:** Office aide, Natl Youth Corps, 1974-75; tutor, Valle del Sol City of Phoenix performer, Black Theatre Troupe, 1981; mem, Natl Assn for Executive Women, 1983-; volunteer, Valley Christian Center, 1983-1984; consultant, Kennedy & Associates, 1984-; bd mem, Arizona Cactus Pine Girls Scout Council, 1987-; ex-officio mem, Phoenix Community Alliance, 1987. **Honors/Awds:** Outstanding Young Woman of America, 1984.

KENNEDY, THEODORE REGINALD
Educator. **Personal:** Born Jan 4, 1936, Winter Haven, FL. **Educ:** Univ of WA Seattle, BA 1970; Princeton Univ NJ, MA 1972; Princeton Univ NJ, PhD 1974. **Career:** SUNY Stony Brook, assoc prof Antrhopology 1980-; SUNY Stony Brook,

asst prof anthropology 1974-80; The Boeing Co Seattle, employee 1961-69. **Orgs:** Consult Howard Univ Press 1980; mem adv group Nat Endowment for the Humanities 1980; mem NAACP 1967; mem Nat Hist Soc 1974-; mem Assn of Am Anthropologists 1970-. **Honors/Awds:** Recipient numerous fellowships & grants Afro-Am, Study Prof Univ of WA; Princeton U; Univ of PA; Ford Found; HEW; Research Found of NY 1969-75; numerous research experiences Seattle New York City Philadelphia NJ Spain So US W & E Coasts US Vigin Islands; ''Relations in a So Comm'' Oxford Press 1979; pub ''Black Argot asociolanguistic analysis of black lyfestyle through verbal & non-Verbal communication'' oxford u press; dissertation ''you gotta deal With It the relationship in the black domestic unit''; lectr u of WA u of CA stanstudents. **Military Serv:** AUS pfc 1959-60. **Business Addr:** St Univ of NY at Stony Brook, Anthropology Dept, Stony Brook, NY 11794.

KENNEDY, WILLIAM J., III
Business executive. **Personal:** Born Oct 24, 1922, Durham, NC; son of Margaret Spaulding Kennedy and William J Kennedy Jr; married Alice C Copeland; children: William J IV. **Educ:** VA State Coll, BS 1942; Univ of PA, MBA 1946; NY Univ, MBA Finance & Investments 1948; NY Univ, grad studies 1948-50; Stanford Univ, executive program 1971. **Career:** NC Mutual Life Ins Co, pres, ceo, chmn bd dirs. **Orgs:** Bd dir Investors Title Co Chapel Hill NC; bd dir The Quaker Oats Co Chicago; bd visitors NC Central Univ Durham NC; charter mem NC Soc of Financial Analysts; Conf Bd NY; bd dir and vice chair Mechanics & Farmers Bank; UNC Ventures Inc; NC Order of the Tar Heel One Hundred; bd visitors Duke Univ, The Fuqua School of Bus; bd dir NC 4-H Devel Fund Inc; bd dirs Mobil Corp NY; bd dir Jones Group Inc Charlotte; bd dir Pfizer Inc NY; chair, President Carter's Advisory Committee on Small and Minority Business Ownership, 1980-81; mem various other business, cultural and civic organizations. **Honors/Awds:** Selected by Ebony Magazine as on of the 100 most influential Black Americans, 1973—; annual award for professional achievement, Tribune Charities, 1974; annual achievement award, Black Enterprise magazine, 1975; Pathfinder Award, Opportunities Industrialization Centers of America, 1976; C C Spaulding Insurance Award, Natl Business League, 1976; Twenty First Century Foundation Achievement Award, 1977; VA State College Alumnus of the Year, 1977; inducted into National Minority Business Hall of Fame, 1977; NY Univ Grad School of Business Admin Alumni Association Achievement Award, 1980-81; 1985 Business and Professions Award Honoree for achievements as pres of NC Mutual Life Insurance Company, the largest Black-managed insurance company in the US;Ebony Magazine American Black Achievementard, 1985; honorary Doctor of Laws, NC Central Univ, 1986; J E Walker Humanitarian Award, Natl Business League, 1987. **Military Serv:** AUS lieutenant 1943-45. **Business Addr:** President/Chairman Board Dirs, NC Mutual Life Ins Co, 411 West Chapel Hill St, Durham, NC 27701.

KENNEDY, WILLIAM THOMAS, JR.
Clergyman, educator (retired). **Personal:** Born Mar 18, 1928, Washington, DC; son of Hattie T. Kennedy and William T. Kennedy Sr; children: Stephanie. **Educ:** Dist Columbia Tchrs, BS 1953; Wesley Theol/Drew Theol, STB/BD 1955-60; Wesley Theol, STM 1968. **Career:** Yale Divty Schl, assoc prof 1969-78; Wesley AME Zion Chrh Phila, pastor homeo/pratl theol 1971-83; Eastern Bpt Semy adj prof preaching 1978-85; Tioga United Methd Chrh, pastor 1983-85; Drew Theol Seminary, adj prof preaching 1985-; Grace UM Church, pastor retired 1995; Consortium for Theological Education, pro preaching 1989-; Arch St UM Church, associate minister, currently. **Orgs:** Prsdg elder Barbados Dist/AME Zion 1980-; prof socio/rel Eastern Coll 1977-79; prof soc Mattatuck Coll 1964-68; prest Waterbury Conn NAACP 1964-68; chrmn Waterbury Hmn Rel Comm 1964-68; town Comm Waterbury Conn 1964-70. **Honors/Awds:** Dr divty Livinstone Coll 1980; professional cassette Lyman Beecher Series Yale 1969; Hester Lectures, Golden Gate Theological Seminary, 1996. **Military Serv:** AUS pers admn tech 2. **Home Addr:** 2228 Georges Ln, Philadelphia, PA 19131.

KENNEDY, WILLIE B.
City & county official. **Personal:** Born Nov 5, 1923, Terrell, TX; daughter of Isa Bell Borders Williams and Abraham C Williams; married Joseph G Kennedy, Mar 1, 1954 (deceased); children: Paulette Marie Fobbs. **Educ:** San Francisco State Univ, BA 1975. **Career:** San Francisco Human Rights Commn, commissioner 1979-80; San Francisco Redevelopment Commn, commissioner 1980-81; Gamma Phi Delta Sorority Far Western Region, regional dir 1974-82; City & County San Francisco, supervisor. **Orgs:** Mem, Univ of CA Volunteer Aux 1978-90; mem Natl Assoc of Colored People 1979-; pres Methodist Federation of Social Concern 1979-; mem Natl Council of Negro Women Golden Gate Section 1981-; natl pres Gamma Phi Delta Sorority; bd of supvrs City and County of San Francisco 1981-; delegate Assn of Bay Area Govts 1981-; mem Natl Assn of Black Co Officials 1981-; mem Natl Forum of Black Public Admins 1982-; mem Natl Black Caucus of Local Elected Officials 1982-; mem North Coastal Co Supvrs Assn, 1984-; bd of dirs Co Supervisors Assn of CA 1986-; exec comm Co Supervisors Assn of CA 1986-; mem City Democratic Club of San Francisco, Chinese Amer Democratic Club, Democratic Women's Forum, CA Democratic Black Caucus; African American Agenda Council, chairperson, 1981-;mem California Council on Paerships, 1984-; mem Black Leadership Forum, 1981-. **Honors/Awds:** Woman of the Year TX Coll Alumni 1976, 1981, 1984; Distinguished Serv San Francisco Black Chamber of Commerce 1982; Comm Serv San Fran Business & Prof Women Inc 1982; Outstanding Serv Natl Council Negro Women Golden Gate Section 1983; Certificate of Merit SF Mayor's Summer Youth Prog 1983; Outstanding Contributions to Minority Business Develop US Dept Commerce 1984; Hon DL Urban Bible Coll School of Religious Studies Detroit MI. **Business Addr:** Supervisor, City & County San Francisco, 235 City Hall, San Francisco, CA 94102.

KENNEDY, YVONNE
State official, educational administrator. **Personal:** Born Jan 8, 1945, Mobile, AL. **Educ:** Bishop State Jr Coll, AA 1964; Alabama State Univ, BS 1966; Morgan State Coll, MA 1968; Columbia Univ, advanced study, summers of 1972 & 1973; Univ of AL, PhD, 1979. **Career:** Southern Assn of Colleges & Schools, assoc dir, cooperative prog educ improvement prog; Bishop State Community Coll, coord, higher educ achievement prog 1971-74, English instr 1968-71, pres, 1981-; Morgan State Coll, Baltimore, asst, English dept 1966-68; State of Alabama, state representative, dist 103, currently. **Orgs:** Mem, English & Verbal Skills Comm, Educ Testing Serv, Princeton NJ, 1972; mem, Human Relations Commn, Alabama Educ Assn, 1972; advisory committee mem, Southeastern Conf on English in 2-Year Coll, 1972-74; bd dir, YMCA 1973-; bd dir, Opportunities Industrialization Ctr, IOC, 1973-; mem, Women's Missionary Correctional Coun, Christian Methodist Episcopal Church; chm, Mobile County United Negro Coll Fund Campaign 1980; bd of trustees, Miles Coll, Birmingham; dir, Bd of Christian Educ; NAACP; mem bd of dirs, Amer Assn Higher Educ, Amer Assn Jr and Comm Colleges; Southern Region, Delta Sigma Theta Inc, pres, currently. **Honors/Awds:** Elected ''Miss Alabama State Univ,'' 1965; recipient of Outstanding Community Serv Award, Mobile AL, 1973; Queen of Mobile Area Mardi Gras Assn, 1973; awarded grad fellowship, Columbia Univ, NY, summers of 1972 & 1973; recipient of President's Award, Alabama State Univ, 1964 & 1966; honorary LHD, AL Interdenominational Seminary, 1986; Kermit Mathison Award, Univ of Montevallo, 1985. **Business Addr:** President, Bishop State Community College, 351 N Broad St, Mobile, AL 36690.

KENNEDY FRANKLIN, LINDA CHERYL
Journalist. **Personal:** Born Oct 7, 1950, Brooklyn, NY; daughter of Marjorie J Edwards and Adam C Falcon; married Lonnie Franklin, Sep 20, 1982; children: Kennedy M. **Educ:** Univ of NE, 1968-69; Macalester Coll, BA 1972. **Career:** KING-TV Seattle, news reporter, anchor 1976-; KGW AM Portland, news reporter, anchor 1974-76; WOW-AM Radio Omaha, news reporter 1973-74; KOWH-AM Radio Omaha, pub affairs mgr 1972-73; KOLN/KGIN-TV Lincoln, intern 1968; KMTV Omaha, news intern 1968. **Orgs:** Mem, AFTRA 1976-; mem NAACP 1980-91; local board member, 1988, national board member, 1991, American Federation of Television & Radio Artists; member, National Association of Black Journalists, 1989-. **Honors/Awds:** Recipient First Place Spot News Reporting Award, Sigma Delta Chi NW 1979, 1983, 1988, 1990; Washington Education Association, Best Special Documentary, 1990; Emmy Nomination, Outstanding Biographical Documentary, National Academy of Television Arts & Sciences, 1990. **Business Addr:** Reporter/Anchor, KING-TV, PO Box 24545, Seattle, WA 98124.

KENNEDY-OVERTON, JAYNE (JAYNE KENNEDY)
Actress, model, sportscaster, TV host. **Personal:** Born Oct 27, 1951, Washington, DC; married Bill Overton; children: Savannah Re. **Career:** Laugh-In, Dean Martin Show, Mysterious Island of Beautiful Women, Death Force, Big Time, Cover Girls, Wonder Woman, Police Story, Trapper John MD, Hollywood Squares, Dance Fever, actress; Greatest Sports Legend, 1st female host; CBS NFL Today, anchorwoman; Pan Am Games, AAU Indoor Track & Field Championship, features;Body & Soul, actress; Jayne Kennedy's Complete Exercise Prog Beginner thru Advanced, Love Your Body exercise albums; Radiorobics, syndicated radio prog host;Coca Cola, rep; Butterick's patterns, helped design line of exercise and active sportswear 1984; Jayne Kennedy Enterprises, owner, actress. **Orgs:** Finale speaker Great Amer Talk Festival 1982; public services The Lose-Natl Toll Free Number for finding lost children, Health Hotline Natl Cncl of Negro Women, Help to find our MIA's, Black Women Portrait of Dignity Black History Month, host summer program for children Communication Bridge. **Honors/Awds:** Emmy Award for coverage of 1982 Rose Bowl Parade; Belding Award 1985. **Business Addr:** Dan Pitragello, William Morris Agency, Inc, 151 El Camino Dr, Beverly Hills, CA 90212.

KENNEDY-SCOTT, PATRICIA
Hospital administrator. **Career:** Attorney; Michigan Health Center, chief operating officer, currently. **Special Achievements:** White House Health Care Task Force. **Business Addr:** Chief Operating Officer, Michigan Health Center, 2700 Martin Luther King, Jr Blvd, Detroit, MI 48208, (313)361-8000.

KENNEY, VIRGIL COOPER
Educator. **Personal:** Born Feb 23, 1926, Shreveport, LA; married Locellous. **Educ:** Grambling Coll, BS 1946; TX So U, MED 1961; Atlanta U, 1963; UCLA, 1968; TX A&M, 1969. **Career:** School of Educ TSU, asst prof; Spelman Coll, dorm dir 1963; Coddo Parish School, prin 1958-63; Alsalom Jones Jr HS, teacher 1949-54. **Orgs:** Dir testing TSU 1964; asst prof & educ 1971; asst prof educ coord of elementary student tchg prgm 1974; mem NAACP; Zeta Phi Beta Sor Inc; Am Personnel & Guidance Assn; TX Assn of Coll Tchrs; Am Psychol Assn. **Honors/Awds:** Recpt NDEA Flwsp 1959; Crounzellerbach Award.

KENNEY, WALTER T.
Mayor. **Personal:** Born Dec 3, 1930, Richmond, VA; son of Lois Moore Kenney and Jacob Kenney; married Maime Mallory, 1962; children: Wilma Battle, Walter T, Marvette Denise. **Educ:** Old Dominion College; Federal City College; West Virginia University. **Career:** US Postal Service, clerk, 1954-85; City of Richmond, VA, city councilmember, 1977-90, mayor, 1990-. **Orgs:** Natl vice president, American Postal Workers, AFL-CIO, 1970-80; life member, NAACP; Big Brothers of Richmond. **Honors/Awds:** Outstanding Leadership, Eastview Civic League, 1970; Certificate of Appreciation, Richmond Crusade for Voters, 1976; Outstanding Appreciation of Service, Black Awareness Assn, 1979. **Military Serv:** US Army, SSgt, 1948-52. **Business Addr:** Mayor, City of Richmond, 900 E Broad St, Richmond, VA 23219.

KENNISON, EDDIE JOSEPH, III
Professional football player. **Personal:** Born Jan 20, 1973, Lake Charles, LA. **Educ:** Louisiana State. **Career:** St Louis Rams, wide receiver, 1996-. **Honors/Awds:** St Louis Rams, Carroll Rosenbloom Memorial Award, 1996. **Special Achievements:** NFL Draft, First round pick, #18, 1996. **Business Addr:** Professional Football Player, St Louis Rams, One Rams Way, St Louis, MO 63045, (314)982-7267.

KENNON, DANIEL, JR.
Business executive (retired). **Personal:** Born Aug 1, 1910, Pensacola, FL; married Verna Herron; children: Rozmond, Dannetta. **Educ:** Talladega Coll, AB 1932. **Career:** Teacher, 1932-37; US Postal Svcs, 1937-67; Bradford's Funeral System, vice pres 1967-73; Bradford's Ind Ins Co, vice pres 1967-73; Bradford's Funeral System Inc, pres treas 1974-; Bradford's Ind Ins Co, pres treas 1974-. **Orgs:** Bd dir Urban League 1974; Fellowship House 1970-76; mem NAACP; YMCA; BSA; Metro AME Zion Ch; Omega Psi Phi Frat; B'Ham Housing Bd of Appeals; Downtown Action Com. **Honors/Awds:** C of C Disting Serv Awd Talladega Coll Alumni 1965; pres Talladega Coll Alumni Assn 1959-67; Herman H Long Awd United Negro Coll Fund 1976; Honorary LHD Talladega College, 1992; The National Black College Alumni Hall of Fame, 1992. **Business Addr:** President/Treasurer, Bradford's Industry Insurance Co, 24 N Tenth Ave N, Birmingham, AL 35204.

KENNON, ROZMOND H.
Physical therapist. **Personal:** Born Dec 12, 1935, Birmingham, AL; married Gloria Oliver; children: Shawn, Rozmond Jr. **Educ:** Talladega Coll, BA, 1956; Univ of CO, certificate, 1957. **Career:** St John's Hosp St Paul, asst chf physc thrpst 1957-58; Creighton Mem St Joseph's Hosp Omaha, Asst chf physc thrpst 1958-61; Sis Kenny Inst Minnea, asst chf & physc thrpst 1962; Sis Kenny Instr Minnea, chf physcl thrpy 1962-64; Mt Sinai Hosp Minnea, consltnt in physcl thrpy 1963-70; Rozmond H Kennon RPT Inc, 1964; Physician's Physical Therapy Serv, self-empl; Ebenezer Nurs Home Minnea, chf physcl thrpst; Texa-tonka Nurs Home, consltnt in physc thrpy; Cedar Pines Nurs Home; Villa Maria Nurs Home; all of Minnea; Midway Hospital, St. Paul. **Orgs:** Mem Amer Physcl Thrpy Assn; Amer Reg of Physc Thrpsts; mem Soc-ec Com; past chrmn Prof Prac Com; bd mem past secy MN Chap Amer Physcl Thrpy Assn; ptnr Physcl Thrpy ptnr RKR Assocts; past mem MN Long-Term Care Physcl Thrpy Int & Grp Intntl Cong Physcl Thrpy; mem bd dir Southdale YMCA; Edina Humn Rghts; Southside Medical Center, board member. **Honors/Awds:** Author various artls on phycl thrpy. **Business Addr:** 1518 East Lake St #206, Minneapolis, MN 55407.

KENNY, ALFREIDA B.
Attorney. **Personal:** Born Mar 12, 1950, Richmond, VA. **Educ:** Syracuse U, AB 1968-72; Columbia Univ Sch of Law, JD 1972-75. **Career:** Federal Reserve Bank of NY, staff atty 1975-76; Harper & Row Publ Inc, asst gen counsel 1976-80; Weil Gotshal & Manges, assoc 1980-84; Cooper & Kenny, partner 1984-. **Orgs:** Mem Phi Delta Phi Legal Frat 1973-; mem Nat Assn of Black Women Atty 1977-; mem Am Bar Assn 1977-; mem Assn of the Bar of the City of NY 1977-; pres Assn of Black Women Atty NY 1978-80; mem Com on Labor & Employ of the assn of the Bar of the City of NY; bd of dir Nat Bar Assn Women's Div 1980-82; treas 1975-80, mem bd of dirs 1975-, vice pres Alumni Assn Columbia Law Sch Class of 1975, 1980-85; vice pres Friends of Syracuse (Black Alumni Assn) 1979-80; admitted to the bar of Dist Ct for Southern Dist of NY, Dist Ct Eastern Dist for the Dist of NY, US Supreme Court 1981, Ct of Appeals for the 6th Circuit; mem Zeta Phi Beta Sor Inc 1980-; mem Paul Robeson Scholarship Comm Co-

lumbia Univ Sch of Law 1980-; Civil Court Comm of Assoc of Bar of the City of NY 1986-. **Honors/Awds:** Publications, ''The Voting Rights Act of 1965 & Minority Access to th Polit Process'' Columbia Human Rights Law Review Vol 6 No 1 1974; Charles Evans Hughes Fellowship Columbia Law Sch 1976; Outstanding Young Women of Am US Jaycees 1978; Professional Awd for Outstanding Serv Natl Assn of Negro Business & Professional Women's Club; Columbia Univ Chap Outstanding Alumnus Awd Black Law Students Assn.

KENT, DEBORAH STEWART
Automotive executive. **Personal:** Born Mar 10, 1953, St Louis, MO; daughter of Leodas & Earline Stewart; children: Jessica, Jordon, Wendell L Coleman Jr. **Educ:** Southern Illinois Univ, BA, 1975; Washington Univ, MA, 1977. **Career:** General Motors, 1977-87; Ford Motor Co, area mgr, 1987-92, asst plant mgr, 1992-94, plant mgr, 1994-96, quality dir, vehicle operations, 1996-. **Orgs:** Boy Scouts, executive bd, 1992-94; Governor's State Univ, bd of dirs, 1992-94.

KENT, MELVIN FLOYD
Supervisor. **Personal:** Born Oct 22, 1953, Panama City, FL; son of Viletta McIntyre Kent and Floyd M Kent, Jr; married Donna Dunklin Kent, Sep 22, 1990; children: Preston J, Shante D, Shanice L. **Educ:** Gulf Coast Community Coll, AA 1974; University of South FL, BA 1977. **Career:** Domestic Laundry and Cleaners, crew supervisor 1970-74; International Paper Co, shop keeper 1975; Sears Roebuck & Co, credit interviewer 1978; Bay County Juvenile Detention Ctr, detention supervisor beginning, 1978-; FL Dept of HRS, Foster Care Unit, children and families counselor, currently. **Orgs:** Vice pres/secty Xi Sigma Lambda Sphinx Club 1985; sec Xi Sigma Lambda Chap Alpha Phi Alpha 1986. **Home Addr:** 909 Bay Avenue, Panama City, FL 32401. **Business Addr:** Children & Families Counselor, Florida Dept of Children & Families, Foster Care Unit, 500 West 11th Street, Panama City, FL 32401.

KENYATTA, MARY
Educator. **Personal:** Born Aug 14, 1944, Greenville, SC; widowed; children: Malcolm Joseph Kenyatta, Asante Luana Kenyatta. **Educ:** Temple University, Philadelphia, PA, BA, 1980; Harvard Graduate School Education, Cambridge, MA, EdM, 1986. **Career:** United Presbyterian Church, USA, Wayne, PA, co-director, WIL Project, 1971-75; Williams College, Williamstown, MA, associate dean, 1981-88; New Jersey Dept Higher Education, Trenton, NJ, exec asst to vice chancellor, 1988-89; Millard Fillmore College, Buffalo, NY, associate dean, 1989-. **Orgs:** Chair, nominations committee, Association for Continuing Higher Education, 1990; vice president, Society Organized Against Racism, 1985-88. **Business Addr:** Associate Dean, Millard Fillmore College, State University of New York at Buffalo, 3435 Main St, 128 Parker Hall, Buffalo, NY 14214-3007.

KERNER, MARLON
Professional football player. **Personal:** Born Mar 18, 1973, Columbus, OH. **Educ:** Ohio State. **Career:** Buffalo Bills, defensive back, 1995-. **Business Addr:** Professional Football Player, Buffalo Bills, One Bills Dr, Orchard Park, NY 14127, (716)648-1800.

KERN-FOXWORTH, MARILYN L.
Educator. **Personal:** Born Mar 4, 1954, Kosciusko, MS; daughter of Manella LouBertha Dickens-Kern (deceased) and Jimmie Kern (deceased); married Gregory Lamar Foxworth, Jul 3, 1982; children: Lamar Foxworth II. **Educ:** Jackson State Univ, BS Speech 1974; FL State Univ, MS Mass Communications 1976; Univ of WI-Madison, PhD Mass Communications 1982. **Career:** FL State Univ, comm specialist 1974-76; General Telephone, personnel rep 1976-78; Univ of TN, asst prof 1980-87; Texas A&M Univ, assoc prof, 1987-. **Orgs:** Exec comm Assn for Educ in Journalism 1980-; mem Natl Council of Negro Women 1980-; mem Assn of Black Communicators 1980-; mem Natl Comm Assn 1982-; mem Intl Platform Assn 1982-; advisor Campus Practitioners 1982; mem Public Relations Soc of Amer 1982-; consultant/assoc editor Nashville Banner 1983; minister of educ Mt Calvary Baptist Church 1983; staff mem Graduate Teaching Seminary 1983-; adviser Public Relations Student Soc of Amer 1983-; mem Natl Fed of Press Women 1983-; mem Natl Assn of Media Women 1983-; mem Natl Fed of Exec Women 1983-; advisory comm Phillis Wheatley YWCA 1983-; mem Black Media Assn; Black Faculty & Staff Assn newsletter editor; regional corres Still Here. **Honors/Awds:** Valedictorian of graduate class 1974; Readers Digest travel grant 1979; 1st prize Alan Bussel Rsch Competition 1980; Leadership Award Assn of Black Comm 1980; Kizzy Award Black Women Hall of Fame Found 1981; PR Fellow Aloca Professional 1981; Amon Carter Evans Awd Scholar 1983; Women of Achievement Univ of TN 1983; Unity Awards in Media 2nd Place Lincoln Univ 1984; num publs & presentations incl, ''Helping Minorities, Student Organizations Can Fill Gaps in Minority Programs'' Journalism Editor 1982, ''Advertising More Than a Black Face'' Black Journalism Review 1981, ''A Challenge to Your Future GTE Automatic Electric'' 1977, ''All Minority Grads-Opportunity Is Knocking'' 1982; 1st & only black in the nation to receive a PhD in Mass communications with a concentration in advertising & public relations; Speciaward Recognition of Excellence PRSA Chap Knoxville TN 1985; author Alex Haley's bio for Dictionary of Literary Biography, Afro-American Writers After 1955 published 1985; PRSA, advisor of the year 1985; Poynter Institute Fellow, 1988; Amer Press Institute Fellow, 1988; Pathfinder Award, Public Relation Institute, 1988; Agnes Harris AAUW Postdoctoral Fellow, 1991-92. **Home Addr:** 3710 Stillmeadow Dr, Bryan, TX 77802-3913. **Business Addr:** Associate Professor, Dept of Journalism, Texas A&M University, 230 Reed McDonald Building, College Station, TX 77843-4111.

KERNISANT, LESLY
Obstetrician/gynecologist. **Personal:** Born Aug 15, 1949, Port-au-Prince, Haiti; son of Claire Albert and Rene Kernisant; married Danielle Duclos; children: Lesly Jr, Natalie. **Educ:** Howard Univ Liberal Arts, BS 1971; Howard Univ School of Medicine, MD 1975. **Career:** Harlem Hospital, exec chief resident in Ob/Gyn 1978-79; Natl Health Serv Corps, physician 1979-81; Mid-Brooklyn Health Assn, clinic dir 1981-86; Interfaith Hospital, clinical instructor 1980-; Brookdale Hospital, assoc attending 1981-; Central Medical Group of Brooklyn, Ob/Gyn partner 1983-89, chief of Ob/Gyn department, 1989-. **Orgs:** Exec comm mem Haitian Biomedical Foundation 1987, Central Medical Group 1987. **Honors/Awds:** Best Chief Resident Certificate Harlem Hosp Dept of Ob/Gyn 1979. **Business Addr:** Chief of OB/GYN Department, Central Med Group of Brooklyn, 345 Schermerhorn St, Brooklyn, NY 11217.

KERNODLE, OBRA SERVESTA, III
Attorney. **Personal:** Born Dec 11, 1947, Philadelphia, PA; son of Mary S Kernodle and Aubrey S Kernodle; divorced; children: Whytni, Raigan, Obra, IV. **Educ:** Temple Univ, BBA 1969; Columbia Univ Sch of Law, JD 1974. **Career:** IBM Corp, rep 1970-71; Sun Co, Inc, atty, 1974-75; US Department of Energy, appointed regional rep, region III, 1979-81; Philadelphia Black Date Processing Assn, counsel; Attorney at Law, private practice, 1981-. **Orgs:** Pres Black Amer Law Students Assn 1972-74; mem Philadelphia Urban Coalition Comm Task Force 1974-; NAACP 1974-; Barrister's Assn of Phil 1974-; AFNA 1975-; general counsel Philadelphia Urban League 1983-94. **Honors/Awds:** Charles Evans Hughes Fellow Columbia Univ School of Law 1972-74. **Military Serv:** US Army 1969-70. **Business Addr:** Attorney, 1425 Spruce St, Ste 200, Philadelphia, PA 19102.

KERR, HORTENSE R.
Music educator, pianist. **Personal:** Born Apr 3, 1926, Detroit, MI; daughter of Helen G Reid and Lorenzo E Reid; married Thomas H Kerr Jr (died 1988); children: Thomas H III, Judy E. **Educ:** School of Music The Univ Michigan, BMus 1947, MMus 1951; Catholic Univ of Amer, Washington, DC, Doctor of Musical Arts, 1996. **Career:** W Charlotte Sr High School Charlotte, NC, dir vocal music, 1951-70; Dept Perf Arts Charlotte-Mecklenburg Schools, asst to dir, 1970-73; Univ of North Carolina, Charlotte, assoc prof 1973-77; Howard Univ, Washington, DC, assoc prof 1977-. **Orgs:** President Natl Black Mus Caucus 1990-92, pres elect, 1988-90; bd mem, Garth Newel Mus Center, Hot Springs, VA, 1984-; Teacher Ed Association, 1992-94; pres elect, Natl Black Music Caucus, 1988-90; resch chmn, Dist of Columbia Mus Ed Assn, 1980-84; student mem chmn, Dist Columbia Mus Educators Assn, 1977-80; pres, North Carolina Mus Educ Assn, 1971-73; pres, North Carolina State Mus Teacher Assn, 1961-70. **Honors/Awds:** Mem Pi Kappa Lambda Honorary Music Fraternity, 1980-; mem Sigma Alpha Iota Intl Music Fraternity, 1983; Piano chamber music Perf, 1970-; Duo piano performances, 1980-;. **Business Addr:** Assoc Professor of Music, Howard Univ, 2400 Sixth St NW, Washington, DC 20059.

KERR, STANLEY MUNGER
Attorney. **Personal:** Born Sep 30, 1949, Des Moines, IA; son of Arlene Munger Kerr and Richard Dixon Kerr; married Myrna Hill, May 22, 1971; children: Mila, Tamara Aldridge. **Educ:** Christian College of the Southwest, 1967-69; Univ of Texas, 1970-71; Huston-Tillotson College, BA, 1975; Univ of Texas School of Law, JD, 1977. **Career:** Church of Christ, preacher, 1966-71; Austin Ind School Dist, bus driver and maintenance, 1972-78; Austin State School, relief supervisor for mentally retarded, 1970-78; Private Law Practice, 1977-87; Huston-Tillotson Coll, government dept head, 1978-81; City of Austin Texas, senior civil rights investigator, 1981-88; Travis County, Texas, Probate Court, mental health attorney, 1987-. **Orgs:** State Bar of Texas, 1977-; Austin Black Lawyers Association, 1978-; Democratic Party, precinct chair, state and county convention delegate, 1972-; St James Episcopal Church, senior warden, stewardship chair, 1971-; AFSCME Local 1624, exec vp, board member, 1983-; Austin Metropolitan Ministries, delegate, 1978-; Trinity Broadcasting Network, partner, 1987-. **Business Addr:** Mental Health Attorney, Travis County Probate Court, PO Box 1748, Austin, TX 78721, (512)473-9258.

KERR, WALTER L.
Attorney. **Personal:** Born Mar 26, 1928, Cleveland, OH; son of George H Kerr, Sr; married Ruby Cowan Kerr; children: Diane. **Educ:** Kent State Univ, BBA 1957; Cleveland Marshall Law School, JD 1962. **Career:** Yellow Cab Co, taxicab driver 1953-55; Postal Clerk, 1955-57; Internal Revenue Service Cleveland, agent 1957-83; Attorney at Law. **Orgs:** Admitted OH Bar 1963; mem Cleveland Bar Assn 1963, Cuyahoga Co Bar Assn 1963, OH Bar Assn 1963; mem John Harlan Law Club 1963; EEO counselor Cleveland Dist Internal Revenue Serv 1973-77; exec bd mem Chap 37 Natl Treas Emp Union 1974-83; assn exec E 147 St Club 1969-71; trustee Shiloh Baptist Church 1968-80; business mgr Shiloh Baptist Church Gospel Chor & Shiloh Male Church 1968-76; assn exec Shiloh Educ Bd 1971-72; chmn Supv Audit Comm Shiloh Credit Union 1973-86; assn exec The Metro Chorus 1974-89; pres Cleveland Chapter Amer Jr Bowling Cong 1974-78; trustee Forest City Hosp 1974-76. **Honors/Awds:** Fed Comm Serv Award Cleveland Program Exec Bd 1976; Cleveland Dist Equal Opportunity Program Commendation IRS 1976; Award Tax Inst Cleveland Public School System. **Military Serv:** AUS sgt 1st class 1947-53; Good Conduct Medal 1950. **Business Addr:** Attorney, 4500 Lee Rd, Rm 130, Cleveland, OH 44128, (216)587-0785.

KERSEY, B. FRANKLIN, IV
Attorney. **Personal:** Born Oct 28, 1942, Richmond, VA. **Educ:** TN State U, BS 1964; Howad Univ Sch of Law Washington, JD 1968; George Washington Univ Nat Law Cntr Washington, 1971. **Career:** Atty Gen Ofc, legal intern 1966; US Dept of Justice Washington; Congressman Robert NC Nix D PA, legislative analyst 1968; US Dept of Justice, admins of justice spec comm relations serv 1969-71; Match Institutiond sr legislative analyst 1971-72; Fed City Coll Washington, Washington lecturer 1973-; Commissioner Colston A Lewis EEO Comm Washington, spec asst 1973-. **Orgs:** Mem Nat Bar Assn; mem Am Civil Lebierties Unoin; mem Dist of Columbia Bar Assn; bd of dir Dist of Columbia ACLU bd of gov MD ACLU consultant to Nat Bar Found Wash; Urban Law Institute Wash; The Urban Institute Wash; Dist of Columbia Bd of Ed & Intensive Ed Devel Prog Univ of MD; regional dir Young Lawyers; sec Nt Bar Assn; mem NAACP; mem Nat Urban League; legal counsel TN State Alumni Assoc Washington; mem Nat Conf of Black Lawyers; Big Brother Nat Capitol Big Brothers Inc. **Honors/Awds:** Ford found fellowship Howard Univ Sch of Law Wash 1964-68; urban fellowship George Washington Univ Nat Law Cntr 1969-71; athletic scholarship TN State U; citation of apprecitation Univ of MD Intensive Ed Devel Prog 1972.

KERSEY, ELIZABETH T.
Administrator. **Personal:** Born Oct 30, 1956, Wadesboro, NC; married Marion W Kersey; children: Mario, Kinyotta, Fateana. **Educ:** Anson Tech Coll, AAS 1977. **Career:** Anson Tech Coll, secretary to dean of instruction 1977-. **Orgs:** Mem Professional Secretary Intl 1983-; chairperson Anson Cty Social Serv Adolescent Parenting Program 1984-; secretary Parent Teacher Org 1984-; pres Anson Tech Coll Alumni Assoc. **Honors/Awds:** Outstanding Woman Young Women of Amer 1983; Notary 1983; Employee of Quarter Anson Tech Coll 1983; Anson Cty's Sec of the Year 1985. **Home Addr:** Rt 1, Box 199, Polkton, NC 28135.

KERSEY, JEROME
Professional basketball player. **Personal:** Born Jun 26, 1962, Clarksville, VA. **Educ:** Longwood College, Farmville, VA, 1980-84. **Career:** Portland Trail Blazers, forward, 1984-95; Golden State Warriors, 1995-96; Los Angeles Lakers, 1996-97; Seattle Supersonics, 1997-. **Business Addr:** Professional Basketball Player, Seattle Supersonics, PO Box 900911, Seattle, WA 98109, (206)281-5850.

KEY, ADDIE J.
Health care administrator. **Personal:** Born Jan 1, 1933, Suffolk, VA; daughter of Bertha Walters Myrick and Woodrow Wilson Myrick; married Leon E Key, Nov 30, 1959; children: Angela N, Lynn E, Leon A, Leroy N, Leonard H, Larry M, Lennell W. **Educ:** Morgan State Coll, AB 1954; Univ of PA Sch of Social Work, 1958-59. **Career:** Baltimore Dept Soc Servs, caseworker 1956-59; Barrett Sch Girls & Montrose Sch Girls, soc wkr 1960-65; Baltimore Bd Election Suprs, registrar 1965-71;Anne Arundel Co Dept Soc Servs, day care soc wrkr 1971-80; Baltimore City Dept of Soc Servs, comm resources coord 1980-85; Anne Arundel County Executive's Drug and Alcohol Program, asst coord 1985-87; US Depart of Health and Human Servs, ADAMHA, Office for Substance Abuse Prevention (OSAP) Public Health Advisor 1987-. **Orgs:** Co-founder/dir Neighborhood Action Coalition for Substance Abuse Prevention 1982-; chmn East Baltimore Chem People Task Force 1983-; bd mem MD Federation of Parents for Drug Free Youth 1984-; bd of advisors Fed Reformatory Women 1970-78; pres Benj Banneker Elem Sch PTA 1975-77; pres Cecil Comm Sch Cncl 1970-71; adv bd Baltimore Urban League 1968-76; pres Metro Child Devel Council 1966-70; Rep State Central Com; del Constl Conv MD 1967-68; asst dir youth prog St Paul Bapt Ch 1961-63; coord E Baltimore Comm Info Ctr 1965-67. **Honors/Awds:** Mayor's Citation 1983; Outstanding Contribution in Community Substance Abuse Prevention, Coppin State Coll 1989. **Special Achievements:** Author: Substance Abuse Prevention Within Inner-City Communities, work in progress. **Business Addr:** Public Health Advisor, US Dept of Health & Human Servs, Alcohol, Drug Abuse & Mental, Office for Substance Abuse Prevention, 5600 Fishers Lane, Room 9A-40, Rockville, MD 20857.

KEY, JUNE ROE
Educator (retired), educational administrator. **Personal:** Born Jul 3, 1917, Paris, TX; daughter of Clareese Halbert Roe (deceased) and Napoleon B Roe (deceased); divorced. **Educ:** Wiley Coll, BA 1938; Reed Coll, 1945; OR State Univ, MA 1971; Grad Work, Univ of CA Berkeley 1951, NM Western Silver City NM 1962, Eastern NM Portales 1963, TX State Univ Houston 1964, Pacific Univ Forest Grove OR 1967; Oregon State Univ, Corvallis, OR, MA, 1973. **Career:** Lamar Cty TX School, educator 1938-40; Douglas HS Sherman TX, educ 1940-41; Lamar Cty HS, educator 1941-44; Pentagon Overseas Div of Educ Amer Schools, educ 1954-56; Roswell City Schools, educator 1949-67; Urban League of Portland OR, staff dir 1967-69; Tongue Pt Job Corps, counselor 1969; OR State Univ, teacher corps 1969-71, assoc dir supvr 1971-73; OR State Univ, asst prof 1974; Adams HS, vice principle 1973-79; Oregon State Univ, honorary prof 1974-75; Cleveland HS Portland, administrative vice principle 1979-80; Portland Public School, plant operations sec, civil service bd, 1982-; Freemont United Methodist Church, teacher, adult education classes, Black History, Native American, and Hispanic history. **Orgs:** Delta Sigma Theta, nominating committee, 1990-91, economic development committee; Freemont United Meth Church, co-chairperson, Black College Committee; Oregon State Univ, board of visitors; Paris Texas Club of Oregon, secretary; Historical Cemetery Association, vice pres, 1994; NAACP, mem, 1994-; Paris Jr College Multicultural Committee, mem, 1995; Paris Education Foundation, mem, 1996; Mt Zion United Methodist Church, Paris, TX, mem; The Greeks of Paris, 1996. **Honors/Awds:** Delta Sigma Theta Sorority, Woman of Excellence, 1992; chaired the search and purchase of real estate for Delta Sorority house; have written several articles for hometown newspapers, on Black History, Feb 1995. **Home Addr:** 410 6th St NE, Paris, TX 75460.

KEYES, ALAN L.
Talk show host, columnist, lecturer. **Personal:** Born Aug 7, 1950, New York, NY; married Jocelyn Marcel, 1981; children: Francis, Maya, Andrew. **Educ:** Harvard University, BA, 1972, PhD, 1979. **Career:** US Department of State, foreign service officer, 1978, consular officer, Bombay, India, 1979-80, desk officer, Zimbabwe, 1980-81, policy planning staff, 1981-83, US representative to United Nations Economic and Social Council, 1983-85, assistant secretary for international organization affairs, Washington, DC, 1985-88; candidate for US Senate from Maryland, 1988; Citizens Against Government Waste, Washington, DC, president; WCBM radio, Owings Mills, MD, "America's Wake-Up Call," host, currently. **Special Achievements:** Republican candidate for presidential race, 1996; Author, Masters of the Dream: The Strength and Betrayal of Black America. **Business Addr:** Host, America's Wake-Up Call, WCBM Radio, 68 Radio Plaza, Owings Mills, MD 21117, (410)356-3003.

KEYES, ANDREW JONATHAN, SR.
Engineer, government employee (retired). **Personal:** Born Oct 18, 1918, Newark, NJ; son of Mr & Mrs A Keyes; married Elizabeth Jackson; children: Debbie Angelos, Carlton; children: Gwendolyn, Andrew J Jr. **Educ:** Newark Coll of Engineering, Newark, NJ, BSME, 1957. **Career:** Mun Base Prof & Exp, proj mgr 1968-; Picatinny Arsenal, proj engr 1957-80; NY Naval Shipyd, draftsman 1942-57; Tracor Tech Inc, Picatinny Arsenal, Dover, NJ, computer consultant, 1980-. **Orgs:** Mem Am Def Pres Assn; former pres Roxbury Twshp bd of educ; mem, Tuskegee Airmen. **Military Serv:** US Army Air Force, sgt, 1942-44. **Home Addr:** 178 Eyland Ave, Succasunna, NJ 07876.

KEYMAH, CRYSTAL T'KEYAH (T'KEYAH CRYSTAL KEYMAH)
Actress, producer, writer. **Personal:** Born in Chicago, IL. **Educ:** Florida A&M University, BS, theater, 1984. **Career:** Chicago Public Schools, substitute teacher, 1984-89; Actress, performance experience includes: Christmas Carol, Goodman Theatre, 1987-89; Call To Action Touring Co, member, 1989; Love Letters, stage play, 1991; Some of My Best Friends, theatrical tour, 1991-, Five Heartbeats Live 1994; Quantum Leap, NBC-TV, guest artist, 1992; ROC-Live, HBO-TV, special guest, 1993; In Living Color, Fox-TV, cast member, 1990-94; The Commish, ABC-TV, guest star, 1994; John Larroquette Show, NBC-TV, guest star, 1994-95; On Our Own, ABC-TV, cast member, 1995; One Last Time, executive producer/actress, 1995; Cosby, actress, 1997-. **Orgs:** My Good Friend, celebrity partner, 1993-, honorary board member, 1994-; NAACP, 1991-; Institute for Black Parenting, active volunteer, 1991-; Delta Sigma Theta Sorority Inc, lifetime member, 1983-; Natl Council of Negro Women, lifetime member, 1992-; FAMU Alumni Association, 1985-; Citizens Committee for Juvenile Court, volunteer, 1987-88; Illinois Visually Handicapped Institute, volunteer, 1986-87. **Honors/Awds:** NAACP Theatre Award, Best Actress and Best Play for "Some of My Best Friends", 1994; Institute for Black Parenting, Amazing Love, 1993; Emmy Award, In Living Color, Fox-TV, 1990; Florida A&M UNV, T'Keyah Keymah Theatre Scholarship, 1990; Miss Black America Pageant, First Runner-Up, 1985; Miss Black Illinois, 1985. **Special Achievements:** Author: Some of My Best Friends, 1992; panelist, Women in the Arts, w/Rosalind Cash and Trazana Beverly, 1991; Playboy of the West Indies, US Premiere, International Theatre Festival, 1988. **Business Addr:** Owner, In Black World, PO Box 93425, Los Angeles, CA 90093, (213)878-5547.

KEYS, DORIS TURNER. See TURNER, DORIS.

KEYS, RANDOLPH
Professional basketball player. **Personal:** Born Apr 19, 1966, Collins, MS. **Educ:** Univ of Southern Mississippi, Hattiesburg, MS, 1984-88. **Career:** Cleveland Cavaliers, 1988-89; Charlotte Hornets, 1989-.

KEYSER, GEORGE F.
Engineer, educator (retired). **Personal:** Born Sep 27, 1932, Washington, DC. **Educ:** San Jose State Coll, BS 1965; Univ of MD, MS 1968; Washington Univ St Louis, DSc 1973. **Career:** US Army Ord Sch, philco field engr 1957-60; Philco W Dev Labs, tech writer 1960-65; Univ of MD, grad teaching asst 1966-68; McDonnell Astronautics St Louis, electronics design engr 1968-70; Washington Univ, asst prof 1973-74; Howard Univ, assoc prof elec engrg dept, retired, 1989; Natl Science Foundation, program director, Engineering directorate, 1992-93. **Orgs:** Mem Sigma Xi; Amer Asso Adv Sci; Inst Elect & Electronic Engrs; Amer Asso Artit Intl, Assoc for Computational Linguistics. **Honors/Awds:** Owens-Corning Fiberglas Scholarship 1965. **Military Serv:** USN, electronics tech 1st class 1953-57.

KHADAR, MOHAMED A.
Engineer. **Personal:** Born Dec 17, 1946, Jimmi Bagbo, Sierra Leone; son of Achaj Yusuf & Haja Memunah Khadar; married Barbara Khadar, Jan 11, 1974; children: Rasheeda, Memunah, Mounrah, Rajheed, Zahra. **Educ:** Cairo Polytecnical Institute, 1968; North VA Community College, AS, 1979; University of Maryland, BA, 1982. **Career:** Holy Cross Hosp, engineer, 1980-; Metropolitan Condos Bldg, engineer, 1990-. **Orgs:** Africa Cultural Ctr, director/founder, 1983. **Business Phone:** (301)871-1397.

KHAN, AKBAR. See ELLIS, ERNEST W.

KHAN, CHAKA
Singer. **Personal:** Born Mar 23, 1953, Chicago, IL; divorced; children: Milini, Damien. **Career:** Rufus, featured singer recorded num albums; Europe, tour; Japan, tour; SAm, tour; Solo artist, currently. **Honors/Awds:** Platinum album for Rufus featuring Chaka Khan; Intl Assn of African American Music, Diamond Award, 1992. **Special Achievements:** Album: The Woman I Am, 1992. **Business Addr:** Singer, c/o Raeven Productions, 11440 Chandler, Ste 200, North Hollywood, CA 91601.

KHAN, RICARDO M.
Artistic dir. **Personal:** Born Nov 4, 1951, Washington, DC; son of Mustapha & Jacqueline Khan; divorced. **Educ:** Rutgers Univ, Rutgers Coll, BA, 1973; Mason Gross School of the Arts, MFA, 1977. **Career:** Rutgers Univ, teacher, 1974-77; Various Prof Theaters & Films, actor, dir, 1977-; Crossroads Theatre Co, co-founder, artistic dir, CEO, 1978-. **Orgs:** Theatre Communications Group, pres of bd, 1994-; Black Leadership Conference, 1993-. **Honors/Awds:** Rutgers Univ, Hall of Distinguished Alumni, 1992; Middlesex & Camden Cty East, Visionary Leader Awd, 1992; City News Publishing Co, Chap of NAACP, NJ's 100 Most Influential, 1996; Rutgers Univ, Honorary Doctorate of Fine Arts, 1997; New Jersey Governor's Award, 1997. **Special Achievements:** Directed world premiere, "The Darker Face Of the Earth;" written by US Poet Laureate, Rita Dove; director: "The Amen Corner," "Harriet's Return," "Haarlem Nocturne," "Flyin' West," "Betsey Brown," "Black Eagles.". **Business Addr:** Artistic Director/Co-Founder, Crossroads Theatre Co., 7 Livingston Ave, New Brunswick, NJ 08901, (732)249-5581.

KHATIB, SYED MALIK
Educator. **Personal:** Born May 7, 1940, Trenton, NJ; children: Koren Clark, Adam Christopher. **Educ:** Trenton State Coll, BA 1962; UCLA, diploma African Studies 1962; MI State Univ, MA 1966, PhD 1968. **Career:** Stanford Univ, asst prof 1969-75; SF State Univ, assoc prof 1978-82; Princeton Univ, visiting lecturer 1984; Trenton State Prison MCC, instructor 1985; Rahway State Prison MCC, instructor 1985; Mercer Coll, adjunct assoc prof; SUNY at New Paltz, Department of African-American Studies, associate professor, chairman, 1985-88; Marist College, associate professor of communication, 1988-. **Orgs:** Mem editorial bd Assn of Black Psychologists 1970; consultant SRI 1970; SSRC 1971; HEW 1972; 10 publications in the areas of methodology philosophy & psychology. **Honors/Awds:** Dean's Honor List Trenton State Univ 1960; NDEA Fellow MI State Univ 1965-67; Postdoctoral Fellow Univ of PA 1968; Issue Editor Journal of Social Issues vol 29, 1973; mem editorial bd Journal of Black Psychology, 1974-76; recipient, Comm Serv Award Bay Area, 1975. **Military Serv:** Peace Corps Vol Nigeria 1962-64. **Home Addr:** 50 Dublin Rd, Pennington, NJ 08534.

KIAH, RUTH JOSEPHINE
Association executive, educator. **Personal:** Born Apr 16, 1927, Elkhart, IN; daughter of Cora Green Brown and Lexie Brown; married Thomas H Kiah Jr, Sep 18, 1980; children: Richelle Renee Dade. **Educ:** Wayne State University, Detroit, MI, BS, 1948, MEd, 1954, EdD, 1975. **Career:** Mercy College Reading Methods Course, instr, 1966-67, consultant, 1962-74, facilitator of change needs assessment trainer & problem analysis for school staff, 1974-83; Detroit Public Schools, Office of Adult Cont Educ, coordinator, 1967-72, dept of staff devel & tchr training, tchr corps coordinator, 1972-; teacher, Detroit Public Schools MGT Academy, on camera teacher reading, 1962-67, WTVS 56; administrative asst, 1968-84; Wayne State University, Detroit, MI, executive director of Detroit Center for Professional Growth and Develpopment, 1984-, adjunct associate professor, 1985-. **Orgs:** Mem Women's Economic Club, 1982; board of directors, membership chairperson, secretary, 1978-91, Friends International Institute; board of directors Michigan Coalition of Staff Development and School Improvement 1987-92; board of directors Effective Instruction Consortium 1987-91; mem Assn of Supervisors and Curriculum, 1980-; mem Phi Delta Kappa, Wayne State University Chapter 1985-; executive board, Michigan Coalition for Staff Development and School Improvement, 1984-; faculty advisory/member, Phi Lambda Theta, 1986-. **Honors/Awds:** Author of several books; award in recognition & of creativity pioneering spirit & serv to youth Womens Fellowship & Youth Ministry Plymouth United Ch of Christ Detroit 1971; Quarterly Publications Professional Development Programs with Thematic Inservice Modules 1984-; A Multi Faceted Approach to Staff Development and Its Relationship to Student Achievement 1975; Distinguished Contribution to Field Reading Instruction, Wayne County Reader Assn, 1988; Distinguished Alumna, Wayne State University, 1988; Outstanding Service Award, Friends International Institute, 1990. **Home Addr:** 2360 Oakman Blvd, Detroit, MI 48238.

KIDD, CHARLES C., SR.
Educational administrator. **Personal:** Born Aug 9, 1936, Washington, DC; son of Charles & Lorraine Kidd; married Mary A Kidd, Jun 12, 1959; children: Charles, Crayton, Chinyere, Cy, Change, Chekesha, Chaka. **Educ:** Case Inst of Technology, Civil Engineering, BS, 1958; State of Ohio, PE, 1963; University of Michigan, MS, Sanitary & Industrial Hygiene Engineering, 1964, MS, Radiological Health Physics, 1967, PhD, Environmental Health Sciences, 1970. **Career:** Olive-Harvey College, president, 1973-75; Chicago State University, vice pres for administrative affairs, 1975-76; engineering & educational consultant, 1976-77; South Shore National Bank, vice pres, 1977; Florida A&M University, dean/professor, 1977-92, associate vice pres/professor, 1993-96; York College CUNY, president, 1996-. **Orgs:** Alpha Phi Alpha Fraternity Inc; Health Physics Society; American Association of Blacks in Energy; Tallahassee Chap, 100 Black Men of America. **Honors/Awds:** US Department of Energy, HBCU Faculty Fellowship, 1994-96; Florida Marine Fisheries, Commission, 1994-97; US Department of Commerce, Marine Fisheries Advisory, 1995-99. **Special Achievements:** The Role of 1890 Land-Grant Institutions in Meeting Long Term National Agricultural Research Needs, Sub-committee on National Resources, Agricultural Research and Technology, Committee on Science and Technology, US House of Representatives, 1982; Research and Other Strategies for Energy Conservation within Agricultural Communities in Florida, Sub-committee on Energy Dev and Applications, Committee on Science and Technology, US House of Representatives, 1983; A Center for Environmental Technology Transfer: A Model for Minority Involvement, HBCU/MI Consortium Regional Environment Technology Transfer Forum, 1992; Report of the Florida Commission on Environmental Equity and Justice, Florida Department of Environmental Protection, Florida A&M University, 1995. **Military Serv:** US Air Force, captain, 1960-66. **Business Addr:** President, York College, 94-20 Guy R Brewer Blvd, No 2H02, Jamaica, NY 11451.

KIDD, FOSTER
Dentist. **Personal:** Born Feb 2, 1924, Lake Charles, LA; son of Louvenia Levy Kidd and Sylvester Kidd; married Pearl Coleman; children: Foster Jr, Cheryl, Jocelyn. **Educ:** Fisk U, BA 1949; Meharry Coll of Dentristy, DDS 1953. **Career:** Pvt Prac, dentist 1953. **Orgs:** Mem ADA; NDA; TX Dental Assn; Gulf State Dental Assn; Dallas Co Dental Soc; MC Cooper Dental Soc; TX State Bd of Dental Examiners 1973; Flw Acad ofGen dentistry 1973; vis clinical asso prof Pedodontics 1975-; pres GSDA 1966; bd dir Dallas Co Dental Soc 1973; pres elec TX State Bd Dental Examiners 1977; pres chmn bd Soc for Rsrch & Study of Negro in Dentistry 1969; v chmn Acad of Dentistry for Children of Nat Dental Assn 1968-77; vice pres TX Soc of Dentistry for Children 1977; charter mem YMCA 1969; life mem NAACP 1977; treas Concerned Voters Cncl 1977; mem, vice chair, bd of trustees New Hope Bapt Ch; mem Sigma Pi Phi; Omega Psi Phi Club; Rotary Internat. **Honors/Awds:** Recpt outsdng achvmt award in dentistry Com of 100 of Dallas Black C of C 1976; publ "Pediatric Dentistry Provided by TX Negro & Dentists" TX Dent Jour 1968; "Role of Dentist & Dental Assn in These Changing Times" NDA 1967; "Selection & Appointment of Black Dentists to State Bd of Dental Examiners" NDA 1976; "Profile of Negro in Am Dentistry" Howard Univ Press 1978; Am Thtr Campaign Medal; Asiatic Pacific Campaign Medal; 1 Bronze Star; Good Conduct Medal; Victory

Ribbon; 2 Overseas Serv Bars. **Military Serv:** AUS sgt 1943-45. **Business Addr:** 1420 Martin Luther King Blvd, PO Box 15763, Dallas, TX 75215.

KIDD, HERBERT, JR.
Association executive. **Personal:** married Grace Erby; children: 5. **Career:** Association executive, currently. **Orgs:** Pres, Bessemer Branch NAACP; Bristol Steel Corp; New Zion No 2 Choir; vice pres, Choir Union; Bessemer Voters League; Bessemer Civic League; Bessemer Progress Assn; Citizens Committee Bessemer; Candidate of Order of Elks. **Military Serv:** US Navy. **Business Addr:** PO Box 884, Bessemer, AL.

KIDD, JASON FREDRICK
Professional basketball player. **Personal:** Born Mar 23, 1973, San Francisco, CA. **Educ:** University of California. **Career:** Dallas Mavericks, 1994-97; Phoenix Suns, 1997-. **Honors/Awds:** NBA, Co-Rookie of the Year with Grant Hill, 1994-95. **Special Achievements:** Selected in the first round, second pick, of the NBA Draft, 1994. **Business Addr:** Professional Basketball Player, Phoenix Suns, PO Box 1369, Phoenix, AZ 85001, (602)266-5753.

KIDD, WARREN LYNN
Professional basketball player. **Personal:** Born Sep 9, 1970, Harpersville, AL. **Educ:** Middle Tennessee State. **Career:** Philadelphia 76ers, 1993-. **Business Addr:** Professional basketball player, Philadelphia 76ers, PO Box 25040, Philadelphia, PA 19147, (215)339-7600.

KIDD, WILLIE MAE. See ROBINSON, KITTY.

KILCREASE, IRVIN HUGH, JR.
Judge. **Personal:** Born Nov 21, 1931, Nashville, TN; son of Carrie E Kilcrease and Irvin H Kilcrease Sr; married Kathleen Lacy; children: Irvin Hugh III. **Educ:** Nashville School of Law, JD 1966; Tennessee State Univ, 3 3/4 yrs; Natl Judicial Coll, Certificate 1983. **Career:** US Vet Admin Reg Office, claims examiner 1966-68; Private practice of Law, attny 1968-72; City of Nashville; 1st asst public defender 1969-72; US Attny Office, asst attny 1972-80; TN Court of the Judiciary (the disciplinary court for TN Judges), presiding judge, 1989-91; State of Tennessee Judiciary Dept, chancery court judge, currently. **Orgs:** Dist commander Amer Legion Dept of Tennessee 1961-62; dir Nashville Chap of Urban League 1971-72; pres Fed Bar Assoc 1975-76; mem Phi Beta Sigma 1976-; pres Frontiers 1979; dir Nashville Bar Assoc 1982-85, Napier-Looby Assoc 1984-89. **Honors/Awds:** Fed Employee of the Year Fed Exec Assoc 1973; Vice Chmn Governors Commiss on Status of Women 1973; Grand Master Masonic Grand Lodge AF&AM Tennessee 1974-75; Presiding Judge Trial Judges of Nashville-Davidson Cty 1984-85. **Military Serv:** US Army corpl 1952-54; Good Conduct Medal. **Home Addr:** 945 Inverness Avenue, Nashville, TN 37204. **Business Addr:** Chancery Court Judge, State of TN Judiciary Dept, 402 Davidson County Courthouse, Nashville, TN 37201.

KILDARE, MICHEL WALTER ANDRE
Neurological surgeon. **Personal:** Born Jan 15, 1935, Tunis, Tunisia; son of Deay Andre Kildare and George Walter Kildare; married Paula S Calahan, Aug 23, 1983. **Educ:** Univ of MA, BS 1957; Meharry Medical Coll, MD 1961. **Career:** Minneapolis Hennepin General Hospital, intern 1961; Univ of IA-VA Med Center, general surgery resident 1966; New York Univ, resident neurological surgery 1969-74; Iowa Methodist Hospital, attending neurosurgeon 1977-84; Robert Packer Hospital, attending neurosurgeon 1984-85; United Communities Hosps, attending neurosurgeon. **Orgs:** Medical serv comm IA Medical Soc 1977-84; mem Amer Medical Assn 1976-, Iowa Midwest Neurosurgical Soc 1977-, Congress of Neurological Surgeons 1978-, Amer Assn of Neurological Surgeons 1983-, CA Assn of Neurological Surgeons 1987; American College of Surgeons 1989. **Honors/Awds:** Alpha Omega Alpha 1960; Certification Amer Bd of Surgery 1969; ''Annals of Neurology'' Journal of Neurosurgery 1980; Certification Amer Bd of Neurological Surgery 1982, Fellow, Amer Coll of Surgeons 1989. **Military Serv:** US Medical Corps capt general surgeon, 1966-68 Vietnam; National Service, Vietnam Valor-Clusters. **Business Addr:** Neurosurgeon, 710 Fourth Street Suite A, Marysville, CA 95901.

KILGORE, THOMAS, JR. See Obituaries section.

KILGORE, TWANNA DEBBIE
Model, former Ms Black America. **Personal:** Born 1954. **Career:** Immanuel Prod Inc, exec dir. **Honors/Awds:** Won Miss Black Washington DC 1976; Miss Black America 1976-77; as title holder traveled US & Europe; contracted with Avon as beauty consultant spokeswoman.

KILIMANJARO, JOHN MARSHALL
Educator (retired), business executive. **Personal:** Born Jun 6, 1930, Little Rock, AR; married Culey Mae Vick. **Educ:** Univ of AR, BA 1952; Univ of AR, MA Ed D 1965; NC A&T State U, attended. **Career:** Carolina Newspapers Inc, publisher, pres; NC A&T State Univ, prof speech & theatre beginning 1969; instructor English 1955-58, 1962-69; AR A M & N Coll, prof English 1959-61; State Univ of IA, teaching fellow 1958-59. **Orgs:** Exec dir Richard B Harrison Players 1969-; pres NC Balck Pubs Assn; board of directors Children's Home Soc Greensboro Arts Soc; mem, past president, NADSA ATA; former 2nd vice pres, NAACP; consult, Civil Rights; Comm Action Programs NC Fund; mem Guilford Co Young Dem; board of directors, NC Autism Society; Omega Psi Phi. **Honors/Awds:** Recipient O Henry award for artistic excellence Greensboro C of C 1973. **Military Serv:** USN 1949-50; USMC 1952-54.

KILLENS, TERRY DELEON
Professional football player. **Personal:** Born Mar 24, 1974, Cincinnati, OH. **Educ:** Penn State Univ. **Career:** Houston Oilers, linebacker, 1996; Tennessee Oilers, 1997-. **Business Addr:** Professional Football Player, Tennessee Oilers, c/o Baptist Sports Park, 7640 H 70-5, Nashville, TN 37221.

KILLINGSWORTH FINLEY, SANDRA JEAN
Diversity communications consultant. **Personal:** Born Aug 14, 1950, Chicago, IL; daughter of Lee Hunter Killingsworth and Cleve Killingsworth; married Eddie Franklin Finley, Aug 26, 1972; children: Bakari Khalid Ali. **Educ:** Loyola Univ, Chicago, IL, BA, 1972. **Career:** Chicago Bar Assn, Chicago, IL, director of public relations, 1977-79; Chicago Economic Development Corp, Chicago, IL, director of public relations, 1978-79; 5100 Communications, Chicago, IL, president, 1980-. **Orgs:** Past president, League of Black Women, 1987-89; board member, Chicago Youth Centers, 1990-; board member, Chicago Chapter, NAACP, 1989-; board member, Brass Foundation, 1989-. **Honors/Awds:** Entrepreneur of the Year, PUSH, 1988; National Council of Negro Women Award, 1986; Kizzy Award, Kizzy Scholarship Fund, 1979; Chicago's Up & Coming, Dollars & Sense Magazine, 1985; Meritorious Commission Citation, City of Chicago, 1985; Federal Womens Program, US Air Force, 1983; Public Programs Committee Field Museum of Natural History, 1992-; Public Programs Committee, Field Museum of Natural History, 1992-. **Business Phone:** (708)754-0825.

KILLION, THEO M.
Personnel executive. **Personal:** Born Apr 13, 1951, Montgomery, WV; son of Maggie Lewis Killion and Omega Killion; divorced; children: Aliya Killion, Niyama Killion. **Educ:** Tufts Univ, Medford MA, BA, 1973, MEd, 1975. **Career:** Concord Public Schools, Concord MA, teacher, 1973-75; Harvard Univ, Cambridge MA, asst dir Upward Bound, 1971-75; RH Macys, New York NY, vice pres executive personnel, beginning 1975, senior vp, currently. **Orgs:** Black Retail Action Group, 1975-; Simmons Coll Advisory Board, 1988-; For A Better Chance Inc, board of directors. **Honors/Awds:** Gold Pencil Award, Black Retail Action Group, 1982; Business Achievement Award, Black Retail Action Group, 1987.

KILPATRICK, CAROLYN CHEEKS
Congresswoman. **Personal:** Born Jun 25, 1945, Detroit, MI; daughter of Willa Cheeks and Marvel Cheeks; divorced; children: Kwame, Ayanna. **Educ:** Ferris State College, AS 1965; Western MI Univ, BS 1968; Univ of MI, MS 1977. **Career:** REA Express, sec 1962-63; Detroit Public Schools, teacher 1971-78; MI House of Representatives, state rep, 1978-96; US House of Representatives, congresswoman, 1996-. **Orgs:** Mem Brd Trustees New Detroit 1983; mem Brd Trustees Henry Ford Hosp 1984; mem Resource Committee Your Children Our Children (documentary) 1984; Natl Org 100 Black Women; Natl Order Women Legisl; vice chair Intl Affairs Comm of the Natl Black Caucus of State Legislators; chair, Michigan Legislative Black Caucus, 1983-84; Michigan House Appropriations Committee, Democratic chairperson of the House Transportation Budget Committee, 1993. **Honors/Awds:** Anthony Wayne Award for Leadership, Wayne State U; Distinguished Legislator Award, Univ of MI; Burton Abercrombie Award; appointed by Gov James Blanchard to represent MI in first African Trade Mission, 1984; Woman of the Year Award, Gentlemen of Wall Street, Inc; first African American woman to serve on the House Appropriations Committee. **Business Addr:** Congresswoman, US House of Representatives, 503 Cannon House Office Bldg, Washington, DC 20515-2215.

KILPATRICK, GEORGE ROOSEVELT
Physician. **Personal:** Born Dec 9, 1938, New Bern, NC; son of Priscilla Bryant Kilpatrick and George Kilpatrick Sr; married Lillian Farrington; children: Michaux, Gregory, La Tonya. **Career:** NC Textile Occupational Lung Dis Panel, physician; Private Practice, pulmonary diseases & internal med. **Orgs:** Mem Amer Thoracic Soc, Greensboro Med Soc, Natl Med Soc, Amer Med Assn, mem Amer Bd of Internal Med #43697 1973; licensure NC #18881 GA #12504. **Honors/Awds:** Triad Sickle Cell Anemia Foundation, Appreciation Award, 1991. **Military Serv:** US Army Medical Corps, colonel, 1970-95. **Business Addr:** 601 E Market St, Greensboro, NC 27401.

KILPATRICK, RICHARDO IVAN
Attorney. **Personal:** Born Feb 14, 1952, Lakeworth, FL; son of Winifred C Kilpatrick and George W Kilpatrick; married Carole Camp Kilpatrick, Aug 10, 1985. **Educ:** Harvard University, BA, 1973; University of Michigan Law School, JD, 1982. **Career:** Shermeta, Chimko & Kilpatrick PC, partner, currently. **Orgs:** American Bar Association, litigation committee; Federal Bar Association; Oakland County Bar Association, federal court committee; Association of Trial Lawyers of America; American Bankruptcy Institute, board of directors, various communitys; National Association of Bankruptcy Trustees, ethics committee; National Association of Chapter 13 Trustees, chairman, creditor's auxiliary; Harvard Club of Miami; University of Michigan Alumni Association; Consumer Bankruptcy Association, co-founder, past president. **Business Addr:** Partner, Shermeta, Chimko & Kilpatrick, P.C., 445 S Livernois, Ste 221, Rochester, MI 48308, (313)652-8200.

KILPATRICK, ROBERT PAUL
Government official. **Personal:** Born Feb 9, 1945, Newton, GA; son of Julia Ann Kilpatrick and Delander Kilpatrick; married Mary Williams-Kilpatrick, Aug 5, 1981; children: Reginald J Williams, Robert Paul II. **Educ:** Morehouse College, BA, 1967; Antoich School of Law, MA, 1984; Howard University School of Law, JD, 1987. **Career:** US Department of Education, administrative intern, 1968-71, program management specialist, 1971-74, equal employment opportunity specialist, 1974-80, complaints analysis and conciliation unit chief, 1980-84, special emphasis program manager, 1984-88, evaluation affirmative action and data analysis unit chief, 1988-. **Orgs:** Cub Scouts, assistant pack leader, 1991-92; Big Brothers of American, big brother, 1974-79; Blacks in Government, charter member, Department of Education. **Honors/Awds:** US Department of Health, Education and Welfare, Superior Service Group Award, 1971. **Special Achievements:** Apperance, Dept of Education, Health and Human Services nationwide Black history program, C-SPAN, Feb 20, 1992; one of the developers of Upward Mobility in the Federal Government, 1971. **Home Addr:** 4314 Bowen Rd SE, Washington, DC 20019, (202)583-7586. **Business Addr:** Chief, Evaluation, Affirmative Action & Data Analysis Unit, US Dept of Education, 400 Maryland Ave SW, Washington, DC 20202, (202)401-3560.

KILSON, MARTIN LUTHER, JR.
Educator. **Personal:** Born Feb 14, 1931, E Rutherford, NJ; son of Louisa Laws Kilson and Martin Luther Kilson Sr; married Marion Dusser de Barenne; children: Jennifer Greene, Peter Dusser de Barenne, Hannah Laws. **Educ:** Lincoln Univ, BA 1953 (valedictorian magna cum laude); Harvard Univ, MA Polit Sci 1958, PhD Polit Sci 1959. **Career:** Harvard Univ Dept Govt, tchng fellow 1957-59; Harvard Ctr for Intl Affairs, res fellow 1961-72; Harvard Univ, tutor govt 1962-67; Univ of Ghana, visiting prof 1964-65; Harvard Univ, asst prof of govt 1967-69; Ford Found, consultant 1973-74; Harvard Univ, prof of govt 1969-. **Orgs:** Res fellow Ford Found Foreign Area Training Prog 1959-61 W Africa; has authored many articles & books on Polit Devel Africa, Urban Politics, Intl Politics, Afro-Amer Politics, Ethnic Studies; mem NAACP; fellow Amer Acad of Arts & Sci; Founding fellow of Black Acad of Arts & Letters; bd dir Amer African Studies Assn 1967-69. **Honors/Awds:** Harvard Grad Fellowship 1953-55; John Hay Whitney Opp Fellowship 1955-56, 1958-59; Fellow Black Acad of Arts & Letters; Fellow Amer Acad of Arts & Sci; Fellow Guggenheim Found 1975-76; visiting scholar Un Chpts of Phi Beta Kappa 1974-75; consult Fulbright-Hayes Intl Exchange Prog 1972-; consult Ford Found 1972-73; Frank G Thomson Professorship in Gov't, Harvard Univ, 1987-. **Business Addr:** Professor of Government, Harvard Univ, Dept of Littauer Cntr, Cambridge, MA 02138.

KIMBER, LESLY H.
Business executive. **Personal:** Born Aug 13, 1934, Boonville, NC; married Pauline Johnson; children: Duane, Terri, Mark. **Educ:** Morehouse Coll Atlanta, bus admin major; George Washington U. **Career:** City of Fresnod council member; CA advocate newspaper, publsiher; central valley printing co inc, pres; fresno co pub defender's ofc, criminal investigator; CA State Univ Fresno, formerly taught, lectures throughout city and state. **Orgs:** Mem West Coast Publishers Assn; pres of bd of dir King of Kings Housing Corp; pres West Fresno Optimist Club; co-chmn KFSN-TV Minority Advisory Committee; vice pres Fresno Free Coll Found; mem and steward Carter Memorial African Methodist Ch; serves on ad committe Greater Fresno Area Plan; bd mem West Fresno Boys Club; mem King of Kings Community Cntr Bd; mem Centarl CA Criminal Justice Planning Bd; served on Fresno Co Reorganization Committee Kimber; throughhis paper has initiated action to promote justice & equality for the minority community of Fresno. **Business Addr:** City Hall Council Office, 2326 Fresno St, Fresno, CA 93721.

KIMBLE, BETTYE DORRIS
Educational administrator, musician, educator (retired). **Personal:** Born Jun 21, 1936, Tulsa, OK; daughter of Ethel Kimble and J C Kimble; divorced; children: Jay Charles, Cheleste Kimble-Botts. **Educ:** Tulsa Univ, BME 1959; Pepperdine Univ, MA 1979, MS 1980. **Career:** Sapulpa OK Bd of Educ, music instructor 1959-61; Hamlin KS School Dist, coordinator of Music

1961-62; Kansas City MO School Dist, music instructor 1963-67; Willowbrook Jr High, choral dir & vocal music educ 1967-79; Compton Unified School Dist, chairperson performing & visual arts, teacher/choral dir 1967-; Centennial HS instructor 1979-90, supervisor of visual & performing arts, 1991-93; Music Dir, Play Production, "Man Called Jesus;" Music Consultant, Play Production, "Been In The Storm So Long.". **Orgs:** Mem Phi Delta Kappa Pepperdine Chapter 1983-; scholarship chairperson (EHP) NA of NM 1983-; composer/music publisher for Broadcast Music Inc 1983-; lecturer and choral consultant 1984-; dist missionary dir Southern CA Conf 1985-; commissioned to write choral arrangement to "Inner City Blues" Rod McGrew Scholarship Inc; mem Performing Arts Council, NEA, MENC Educ, NARAS, NAS Recording; Amer Choral Dir Assn; Chairperson, Compton NAACP Act-So Project. **Honors/Awds:** Teacher of the Year Centennial Sr High School 1982; Honored for Music Serv City of Inglewood CA 1983; Commendation for Music Serv to Church & Comm County of Los Angeles; Musical Tribute for Contributions to Music Industry Kimble Comm Choir; founder/dir internationally known "Kimble Community Choir"; Religious Musical Called "Revelation"; Honorary LHD The London Institute for Applied Research 1992. **Home Addr:** 8013 Crenshaw Blvd, Inglewood, CA 90305.

KIMBLE, BO (GREG)
Professional basketball player. **Personal:** Born Apr 9, 1967, Philadelphia, PA. **Educ:** Univ of Southern California, Los Angeles, CA, 1985-86; Loyola Marymount Univ, Los Angeles, CA, 1987-90. **Career:** Los Angeles Clippers, guard, 1990-92, New York Knicks, 1992-93. **Honors/Awds:** 6th All-time Single Season (NCAA); Scoring leader, 35.3, NCAA, 1990. **Business Addr:** 1999 Ave of The Stars #2100, Los Angeles, CA 90067.

KIMBREW, JOSEPH D.
City government official. **Personal:** Born May 31, 1929, Indianapolis, IN; married Carolyn; children: Joseph D Jr, Tracey. **Career:** Indianapolis Fire Dept, mem 32 years, deputy chief of admin, 1985-87, appointed first black chief of fire dept 1987. **Orgs:** Bd of dirs Greater Indianapolis Federal Firefighters Credit Union 10 yrs; mem NAACP 1968-. **Honors/Awds:** Firefighter of the Year 1968; Overall Achievement Award Center for Leadership Develop 1987; mem Red Cross Hall of Fame; designated Distinguished Hoosier by Governor of IN. **Military Serv:** AUS corpl 2 yrs. **Business Addr:** Fire Chief, Indianapolis Fire Department, 555 N New Jersey, Indianapolis, IN 46204.

KIMBRO, DENNIS PAUL
Educator, author. **Personal:** Born Dec 29, 1950, Jersey City, NJ; son of Mary Kimbro and Donald Kimbro; married Patricia McCauley, Jan 14, 1972; children: Kelli, Kim, MacKenzie. **Educ:** Oklahoma University, BA, 1972; Northwestern University, PhD, 1984. **Career:** Smithkline Beckman Corp, sales and marketing, 1978-87; ABC Management Consultants, Inc, consultant, 1988-91; The Center for Entrepreneurship Clark Atlanta University School of Business and Administration, associate professor & director, 1992-96. **Honors/Awds:** Dale Carnegie, Personal Achievement Award, 1988; Dennis P Kimbro Day, City of Detroit, September 12, 1991; Dennis P Kimbro Day, City of Dayton, September 20, 1991; The United Negro College Fund, Parade of Stars, 1992; Texas Association of Black Personnel in Higher Education, Award of Excellence, 1992; City of Savannah Georgia, Keys to the City, 1992; Small Business Director's Association, 1992; City of Macon Georgia, Keys to the City, 1992; various others. **Special Achievements:** Author: Think and Grow Rich: A Black Choice, 1991; Daily Motivations for African-American Success, 1993; What Makes the Great Great: Strategies for Extraordinary Achievement, 1977; numerous others. **Home Addr:** 3806 Brandeis Court, Decatur, GA 30034, (770)981-8166.

KIMBROUGH, CHARLES EDWARD
Veterinarian, clergyman, real estate broker. **Personal:** Born Jun 24, 1927, Prospect, TN; son of Azie Smith Kimbrough (deceased) and Sterling Kimbrough (deceased); children: Adric L. **Educ:** TN State U, BS 1956; Tuskegee Inst, DVM 1960; So IL Coll Bible, cert 1965. **Career:** Sparta, area veterinarian 1960-69; Meat & Poultry Inspection Program, supr veterinary med officer 1969-75; New Hope Missionary Bapt Ch, pastor 1964-69; Mt Zion Missionary Bapt Ch, 1970-74; Bordeaux Realty Plus, broker, co-owner, currently. **Orgs:** Mem Middle TN Veterinary Med Assn; past pres Nashville Branch, NAACP; Phi Beta Sigma Frat; TN State Univ Alumni Assn; TN Voters Council; Phi Beta Sigma Eta Beta Chpt. **Honors/Awds:** Sigma Man of the Year, Phi Beta Sigma, Eta Beta Chapter, 1974; Citizen of the Year, Omega Psi Phi Fraternity, 1977. **Military Serv:** US Army, Sergeant, 1947-53; Purple Heart, Medical Combat Badge, Bronze Star. **Home Addr:** 3852 Augusta Dr, Nashville, TN 37207. **Business Phone:** (615)227-3898.

KIMBROUGH, DAVID. See Obituaries section.

KIMBROUGH, KENNETH R.
Government official. **Personal:** Born in Oklahoma; son of Irvin and Irene Kimbrough; married Juneanne Kimbrough; children: Karin. **Educ:** Oklahoma State Univ, BA, industrial engineering; Univ of Rochester, MBA, finance. **Career:** Intl Paper Company, 1980-87; Ameritech-IL Bell Telephone, general mgr for real estate svcs, 1987-93; General Svcs Admin, commissioner, public buildings, 1993-. **Orgs:** NACORE; Civil Research, Engineering Research Foundation; Leadership Greater Chicago, fellow. **Business Phone:** (202)501-1100.

KIMBROUGH, MARJORIE L.
Author, educator. **Personal:** Born Jul 11, 1937, Brookhaven, MS; daughter of Louise P Lindsay and William T Lindsay; married Walter L Kimbrough, Dec 20, 1964; children: Walter M, Wayne M. **Educ:** University of California, BA, 1959; Interdenominational Theological Center, MRE, 1965. **Career:** Lockheed Aircraft Corp, mathematical engineer, 1959-63; Burroughs Corp, programming languages consultant, 1963-66, systems representative, 1966-70; Advanced Systems, Inc, video technical instructor, 1970-72; Interdenominational Theological Center, instructor, 1972-73; Management Science America, sales training specialist, 1973-87; Clark Atlanta University, asst prof, 1987-. **Orgs:** Phi Beta Kappa, 1957-; Delta Sigma Theta, 1956-; Church Women United, lecturer, 1987-; Grady Hospital, volunteer, 1987-; United Methodist Clergy Spouses, vice pres, 1966-; Georgia Council for Arts, 1988-91; Cascade United Meth Church. **Honors/Awds:** Mirabella Magazine, Woman of the 90s Award, 1994; Bennett Coll, Phenomenal Woman Award, 1993; State of Georgia, 1991 Author of the Year, Non-Fiction, 1992; Clark Atlanta University, Faculty Excellence in Teaching, 1989, 1990, 1991; Ladies of Distinction, Trailblazer-Enhancing Role and Status of Women in Education, 1991; H Ross Research, Woman of the Year, 1987. **Special Achievements:** Everyday Miracles, Dimensions Press, 1997; "Thanksgiving & Praise," 365 Meditations for Mothers of Teens, Dimensions Press, 1996; She is Worthy, Abingdon Press, 1994; Beyond Limitations, Abingdon Press, 1993; "Meditations for January," 365 More Meditations for Women, 1992; Accept No Limitations, Abingdon Press, 1991; Matthew Video Presentations, Methodist Publication House, 1990; "Mark's Gospel," The Strong Son of God, 1992. **Home Addr:** 4340 Pompey Dr SW, Atlanta, GA 30331. **Business Phone:** (404)880-8234.

KIMBROUGH, ROBERT L.
Dentist. **Personal:** Born Aug 20, 1922, Birmingham, AL; married Luequster Murphy; children: Kernelia, Donna Lynn. **Educ:** Univ of IL Coll of Dentistry, DDS 1951. **Career:** Chicago, dentist pvt practice. **Orgs:** Program chmn Chicago Dental Soc 1975-76; pres Kenwood Hyde Park Dental Soc; vice pres Med Assn Chicago; fellow Acad of Gen Dentistry; treas Legis InterestCom IL Dentist; chrmn Peer Review Com IL St Dental Soc; dir Highland Community Bk Chicago; mem Am Dental Assn; Nat Dental Assn; Lincoln Dental Soc; IL State Dental Soc; Am Soc for Practice of Childrens Dentistry; pres Southside Comm Arts Center; past exec com Chicago Br; life mem NAACP; mem Urban League. **Honors/Awds:** 1st lt AUS Dental Corps 1951-53. **Military Serv:** 1st lt AUS Dental Corps 1951-53. **Business Addr:** 3233 King St, Chicago, IL 60616.

KIMBROUGH, TED D.
Educational administrator. **Personal:** Born in Chicago, IL. **Career:** Compton, CA School System, superintendent, 1982-89; Chicago Public School System, superintendent, 1990-. **Business Addr:** Superintendent, Chicago Public Schools, 1819 West Pershing Rd, Chicago, IL 60609.

KIMBROUGH, THOMAS J.
Educator (retired). **Personal:** Born Apr 24, 1934, Morristown, NJ; son of Gladys Kimbrough; married Eva Harden; children: Jerome Joseph. **Educ:** Wilberforce U, BS 1956; Xavier U, MEd 1969. **Career:** Sch for Creative & Performing Arts, teacher, currently; Student Servs Laurel Oaks Career Devel Ctr, supvr 1976-79; Educ OH Youth Comm, asst supt 1974-76; Princeton City Schools, asst prin 1972-73; Princeton Schools, advisor staff on race rel 1970-72; guid couns 1969-70; Middletown, OH, educator 1963-90 (retired). **Orgs:** Consultant, Nat Equal Educ Inst Hartford, CN; consultant, Equal Educ Office Ind; treas, Interracial Interaction Inc; pres, Funds for Legal Defense; chmn, Educ Com Middletown Coun for Human Dignity; exec comm, Middletown Br NAACP; chmn, Educ Comm NAACP; cofounder, Anti-Klan Network; chairman, political action committee, NAACP, 1991. **Military Serv:** AUS Sp3 1956-58. **Home Addr:** 6049 Todhunter Rd, Middletown, OH 45044.

KIMBROUGH-JOHNSON, DONNA L.
Utility copmany personnel director. **Personal:** Born Aug 26, 1948, Oklahoma City, OK; daughter of Irene Betty Jones and Irvin Roger Kimbrough; divorced; children: Dawn Marie, Jason Leigh. **Educ:** Univ of WA, BA (with distinction) 1977, MBA 1980; NFBPA-Executive Leadership Institute, 1983. **Career:** Dept of Public Welfare, Washington, DC, social service caseworker 1971-75; City of Seattle Water Dept, personnel specialist 1978-80; Seattle Public Schools, classification admin 1980-86; Pierce Transit, mgr of personnel 1986-89; City of Seattle Water Dept, mgr of human resources, 1989-94; Clover Park School District, dir of human resources, 1994-97; King County Solid Waste, asst dir, 1997-. **Orgs:** Delta Sigma Theta; Urban League of Metro Seattle Guild, pres, 1995-98; NFBPA Seattle; King Co Womens Political Caucus. **Honors/Awds:** Leadership Excellence Award, Seattle Water Dept, 1991; Advanced Management, Prog Grad, City of Seattle, 1991. **Home Addr:** 10233 66th Ave S, Seattle, WA 98178-2514. **Business Addr:** Assistant Director, King County Solid Waste, 600 Yesler Wy, Seattle, WA 98104, (206)296-4388.

KIMMONS, CARL EUGENE
Educator (retired). **Personal:** Born Apr 10, 1920, Hamilton, OH; son of Mary Vandoren Whitaker Kimmons and Posey Meadows Kimmons; married Thelma Jean Lewis; children: Karen Toni West, Larry Carlton, Kimberly Ann Kimmons-Gilbert. **Educ:** CT Coll, BA (magna cum laude) 1973; Univ CT, MA 1976; S CT State Univ, Sixth Year Certificate 1986. **Career:** USN, mess attendant third class 1940, master chief yeoman 1960, lt 1963; Bd of Educ Waterford CT, tchr 1973; Waterford HS, teacher, 1973-95. **Orgs:** Top secret control officer USN 1961-70; navy liason officer to bi-racial com City of New London CT 1965-66; private airplane pilot 1965-95; fitness leader YMCA New London CT 1978-89. **Honors/Awds:** WW II Victory Medal; Phillipine Liberation Ribbon; Submarine Combat Insignia w/5 Bronze Stars; enlisted Submarine Qualification Insignia; Navy Commendation Medal w/Combat Distinguished Device; Presidential Unit Citation; Navy Unit Commendation; Meritorious Unit Commendation; Good Conduct Medal w/1 Silver Star; Asiatic-Pacific Campaign medal w/1 Silver & 4 Bronze Stars; Amer Campaign Medal; Amer Defense Serv Medal w/Fleet Clasp; Navy Occupational Medal with Europe Clasp; Natl Defense Serv medal w/Bronze Star; first Black to become a commissioned officer from mess attendant rating. **Military Serv:** USN retired lt 1940-70. **Home Addr:** 982 Hartford Rd, Waterford, CT 06385.

KIMMONS, WILLIE JAMES
Educator, administrator. **Personal:** Born Apr 4, 1944, Hernando, MS; children: Tonia. **Educ:** Lincoln U, BS 1966; No IL U, MS 1970; No IL U, PhD 1974. **Career:** Downtown Campus Wayne Comm Coll, dean 1979-; St Francis Coll, dean 1977-79; Central State Univ, dir 1976-77; NC Central Univ, asst vice chancellor 1973-76; No IL Univ, instructor 1969-73; Sikeston HS, instructor 1966-67; Antioch Coll adjunct prof 1976-; Univ of Dayton Graduate School, lecturer 1976; Shaw Univ, adjunct prof 1974-76; Natl Lab for Higher Educ, consultant 1973-74. **Orgs:** Mem Cncl on Black Am Afrs; Nat Alliance of Black Educs; Kappa Alpha Psi Frat; Am Assn for Hghr Edn; Nat Univ Extensions Assn; Adult Educ Assn of USA; Soc of Ethnic & Spec Studies; Am Assn of Jr & Comm Coll; Phi Delta Kappa; Profnl Educ Frat; Am Persnl Guid Assn; NEA Athletic schlrsp 1962-66; tchng flshp 1969-70; Educ of Yr 1975-76; post doc flwshp Am Mgmt Assn 1975-76; publ Cont Educ for the Elderly OH Dominican Coll 1976; Black Adminstrs in Pub Comm & Coll Carlton Press Inc 1977. **Military Serv:** AUS 1st lt 1967-69. **Business Addr:** 1001 Fort St, Detroit, MI 48226.

KINCAID, JAMAICA
Writer. **Personal:** Born May 25, 1949, St John's, Antigua-Barbuda; daughter of Annie Richardson; married Allen Shawn; children: 2. **Career:** Bennington College, educator; writer; New Yorker, New York, NY, staff writer, 1976-; Harvard, educator. **Honors/Awds:** Writings include: At the Bottom of the River (short stories), 1983; Annie John, 1985; A Small Place, 1988; Lucy, 1991; The Autobiography of My Mother, 1996; frequent contributor to periodicals, including the New Yorker; Morton Dauween Awd, Amer Academy and Inst of Arts & Letters.

KINCHEN, ARIF S.
Actor, entertainer, writer. **Personal:** Born Feb 7, 1973, Las Angeles, CA. **Career:** Entertainment Partners, extra, 1990-96; Immortal Records, promoter, street mktg, 1993-94; Loud Records, Steven Rifkind Co, street mktg, video promotion, 1995-96; Big Ticket Television, actor, 1996; Ed Weinberger Co, MTM, actor, 1996-. **Orgs:** Zera Foundation, exec consultant, 1997-; Actors & Entertainers for Kids, volunteer, 1997-; Comics for Kids, 1997-. **Honors/Awds:** Various city & state awards. **Special Achievements:** Songs used on show "Sparks" on UPN and in "Roots III" episodes, 1997. **Business Addr:** CEO, Arif S Kinchen Inc, PO Box 351091, Los Angeles, CA 90035-9998, (310)287-8546.

KINCHEN, DENNIS RAY
Law enforcement official. **Personal:** Born Oct 11, 1946, Shreveport, LA; son of Heareace Kinchen and M B Kinchen; married Ruthie Douglas Kinchen, Oct 24, 1988; children: Darrick Ray. **Educ:** Bossier Community College, AS, 1990; Louisiana Tech, BS, 1992, pursuing MA, currently. **Career:** Shreveport Police Department, patrolman, 1969-78, corporal, 1978-80, sergeant, 1980-82, lieutenant, 1982-87, captain, 1987-. **Orgs:** Paradise Baptist Church; National Organization of Black Law Enforcement Executives; FBINA, Louisiana Chapter; Brothers & Sisters of the Shield, corresponding secretary; Woodlawns Mentor Program; Louisiana Tech Alumni Association; Bossier Parish Community College Alumni Association; Leadership Council; Chamber of Commerce. **Honors/Awds:** San Antonio Police Department, Certificate of Training, 1989; Shreveport Police Department, Departmental Unit Citation, 1991, 1992, Distinguished 20 Years Service Award, 1989, Police Training Academy, 40 Hour Retrainer, 1992; Project ACCEPT Program, Services Rendered Certificate, 1992; US Department of Justice,

Law Enforcement Certificate of Training, 1992; FBI Academy, Quantico, VA, Law Enforcement, 1978; various commendation certificates. **Special Achievements:** The Detectives National Magazine, 1974. **Military Serv:** US Navy, sgt, 1963-67; National Defense Service Medal, Vietnam Service Medal, Republic of Vietnam Campaign Medal. **Business Addr:** Captain, Shreveport Police Dept, 1234 Texas Ave, PO Drawer P, Shreveport, LA 71161-0040.

KINCHLOW, HARVEY BEN
Broadcast journalist. **Personal:** Born Dec 27, 1936, Uvalde, TX; son of Jewell Kinchlow and Harvey Kinchlow; married Vivian Jordon Kinchlow, Jan 16, 1959; children: Nigel, Levi, Sean. **Educ:** SW Texas Junior College, 1972; University of Virginia, Darden Graduate Business School, 1984. **Career:** Christian Farms, executive director; CBN, executive vp; Good Life Broadcasting Network, president; The Christian Broadcasting Network, co-host, 700 Club. **Honors/Awds:** SW Texas Junior College, Associate Award, 1972; Phi Theta Kappa, Outstanding Alumni, 1988. **Special Achievements:** Plain Bread; Making Noise and Going Home; You Don't Have To If You Don't Want To. **Military Serv:** US Air Force, staff sgt, 1955-68; American Legion Award of Merit, 1972. **Business Addr:** 1920 Centerville Turnpike, Ste 125, Virginia Beach, VA 23464, (757)523-8680.

KINDALL, LUTHER MARTIN
Educator. **Personal:** Born Nov 1, 1942, Nashville, TN; son of Lucy Moore Kindall and Bruce Kindall; married Dr Alpha J Simmons; children: Kimberly, Katrina. **Educ:** TN State Univ, BS 1967, MS 1968, EdD 1973. **Career:** TN State Univ, asst prof of psychology 1968-70; Brushy Mountain State Prison, instr of psychology 1972; Roane State Comm Coll, asst prof of psychology 1972-73; Kindall & Associates Consulting Co, president; Univ of TN, prof of educ psychology 1973-. **Orgs:** Chmn UT Commn for Blacks; asst prof NIMA Summer Inst UT-K Sch of Social Work 1979; state coord Project to Utilize Educ Talents 1968; pres TN Alliance of Black Voters 1979-; mem Omega Psi Phi Frat 1973-; unsuccessful candidate for gov of State of TN 1982; pres Comm Relations Council of Knoxville Job 1986; Commissioner Tennessee Human Rights Commission 1985-; pres Elk Development Co 1988-89. **Honors/Awds:** Alpha Kappa Mu Honor Soc 1966-; Phi Delta Kappa 1973; Outstanding Teacher of the Yr UT Panhellenic and Intrafraternity Councils 1978-79; various publ; Phi Kappa Phi 1978; Phi Lamda Theta 1985-. **Special Achievements:** Candidate, Democratic Primary for Governor of Tennessee, 1982. **Business Addr:** Prof of Educ Psychology, Univ of Tennessee, 108 CEB, Knoxville, TN 37916.

KINDER, RANDOLPH SAMUEL, JR.
Financial services executive. **Personal:** Born Dec 12, 1944, Chester, PA; son of Mildred White Ricks and Randolph Samuel Kinder; married Joan Logue, Dec 13, 1986; children: Lowell Henry, Catherine Henry, Christopher Henry, Randolph Samuel Kinder III. **Educ:** Howard Univ, Washington DC, BA, 1967; Univ of VA, Charlottesville VA, executive program, 1986. **Career:** Dept of Housing & Urban Devel, Washington DC, executive asst to secretary, 1977-79; Dept of Health & Human Services, Washington DC, chief of staff to secretary, 1979-81; The Equitable, New York, vice pres, 1981-82, Milford Conn, vice pres, 1982-84, New York, NY, vice pres, 1984-86, Secaucus NJ, sr vice pres, 1986-. **Orgs:** Bd of dir, The Coro Foundation, 1987-; bd of trustees, Lincoln Univ, 1988-; bd mem, NY City Health & Hospitals Corp, 1989-. **Honors/Awds:** Black Achievers in Industry, Harlem YMCA, 1982. **Business Addr:** Sr Vice Pres, Pension Financial Mgmt Group, The Equitable Financial Companies, 200 Plaza Drive, Secaucus, NJ 07094.

KINDLE, ARCHIE
Automobile dealer. **Career:** Plaza Ford Lincoln-Mercury Inc., owner, currently. **Business Addr:** CEO, Plaza Ford Lincoln-Mercury Inc., PO Box 1774, Lexington, NC 27292, 800-548-9717.

KING, ALBERT
Professional basketball player. **Personal:** Born Dec 17, 1959, Brooklyn, NY. **Educ:** Univ of MD, College Park, MD, attended. **Career:** NJ Nets, 1981-87, Philadelphia 76ers, 1988, San Antonio, 1989. **Honors/Awds:** Named to The Sporting News All-Amer First Team 1981.

KING, ANITA
Writer, editor, researcher. **Personal:** Born Feb 3, 1931, Detroit, MI. **Educ:** Univ Detroit, B Mus 1956. **Career:** Essence Mag, copy-editor 1969-71; Family Tree Black History Series, contributing editor/creator 1973-78; free-lance editor copy-editor proofreader writer/researcher 1972-. **Special Achievements:** Author, Quotations in Black, 1981; author, An Introduction to Candomble, 1987; Samba! And Other Afro-Brazilian Dance Expressions, 1989; Contemporary Quotations in Black, 1996. **Home Addr:** 10 E 138th St 8E, New York, NY 10037.

KING, ARTHUR THOMAS
Educator. **Personal:** Born Feb 10, 1938, Greensboro, AL; son of Elizabeth Williams King and Harvey James King; married Rosa Marie Bryant, Jun 24, 1962; children: Donald, Kevin. **Educ:** Tuskegee Univ, BS 1962; SD State Univ, MS 1971; Univ of CO, PhD 1977. **Career:** USAF Acad, asst prof of economics 1970-74; Air Force Inst of Tech, assoc prof of economics 1979-82; Baylor Univ, prof of economics 1982-, coord of minority affairs 1984-. **Orgs:** Pres bd dirs EOAC (community action prog) 1987-89; pres bd dirs Heart of Texas Goodwill 1986-88; president, Natl Economic Assn, Amer Econ Assoc; mem bd of dir Goodwill Industries of Amer, Inc. **Special Achievements:** Numerous articles published on economics 1978-. **Military Serv:** USAF lt col 20 yrs; 2 Air Force Commendation Medals; 2 Meritorious Serv Medals. **Business Addr:** Professor, Baylor University, Dept of Economics, PO Box 98003, Waco, TX 76798, (817)755-2263.

KING, B. B. (RILEY)
Blues singer, guitarist. **Personal:** Born Sep 16, 1925, Indianola, MS; son of Nora Ella Pully King and Albert King; divorced; children: 8. **Career:** Blues singer and guitarist. Albums include: Anthology of the Blues; Better Than Ever; Boss of the Blues; Doing My Thing; From the Beginning; Incredible Soul of B.B. King; The Jungle; Let Me Love You; Live, B.B. King Onstage; Original Sweet 16; Pure Soul; Turn On With B.B. King; Underground Blues; Live at the Regal, 1965; Electric B.B. King, 1969; Completely Well, 1970; Indianola Mississippi Seeds, 1970; Live and Well, 1970; Live in Cook County Jail, 1971; Back in the Alley, 1973; Guitar Player; Love Me Tender, 1982; Take It Home; Rhythm and Blues Christmas; Midnight Believer. Has toured extensively throughout the US and around the world; B B King's Blues Club, owner, 1991-. **Orgs:** Founding mem John F Kennedy Performing Arts Center 1971; cofounder, Foundation for the Advancement of Inmate Rehabilitation and Recreation. **Honors/Awds:** Golden Mike Award, National Association of Television and Radio Artists, 1969, 1974; Academie du Jazz Award (France), 1969; Grammy Award for Best Rhythm and Blues Vocal, Male, for The Thrill Is Gone, 1970, Grammy Award for Best Traditional Blues Recording for My Guitar Sings the Blues, 1986; Lifetime Achievement Award, National Academy of Recording Arts and Sciences, 1987; Humanitarian Award, B'nai B'rith Music and Performance Lodge of New York, 1973; Honorary Doctorate, Tongaloo College, 1973, Yale University, 1977; received numerous other awards during career; Univ of Mississippi, Natl Award of Distinction, 1992; Trumpet Awards, special honoree, 1997. **Military Serv:** US Army, 1943. **Business Addr:** c/o Sidney A Seidenberg, 1414 Avenue of the Americas, New York, NY 10019.

KING, BARBARA LEWIS
Cleric. **Personal:** Born Aug 26, 1930, Houston, TX; children: Michael Lewis. **Educ:** Texas Southern Univ, BA 1955; Atlanta Univ, MSW 1957, course work completed EdD; Univ of Metaphysics, DD 1978; Christian Church of Universal Philosophy, DD 1984. **Career:** South Chicago Comm Serv Assn, exec dir, 1966-68; Chicago City Coll Malcolm X Campus, dean, community relations, 1967-69; Atlanta Univ Sch of Social Work, instructor 1970-71; South Central comm Mental Health Ctr, dir 1971-73; Spelman Coll Atlanta, dean of students 1973-74; Barbara King School of Ministry, founder/president 1977-; Hillside Intl (Church), founder/minister 1971-; National/Intl speaker, preacher, teacher. **Orgs:** Rules committee Democratic Natl Committee 1984; board member Christian Council of Metro Atlanta; board treasurer Intl New Thought Alliance; captain & chaplain Fulton County Sheriff's Dept, Atlanta Sheriffs Services; Fulton County Development Authority Board; Atlanta Business League Board. **Honors/Awds:** Achievement in Religion (numerous awards) local, state, natl & intl organizations 1974-; author of six books, several monographs, sermons & messages on tape;television show hostess ''A New Thought, A New Life'' weekly half-hour program, aired regionally; Zeta of the Yr Award Zeta Phi Beta Sorority Inc; presented keys to cities of Roanoke, VA; Tuskegee, AL and Macon, GA. **Business Addr:** Minister & Chief Executive, Hillside Intl Truth Center, 2450 Cascade Rd Sw, Atlanta, GA 30311.

KING, BERNARD
Professional basketball player (retired). **Personal:** Born Dec 4, 1956, Brooklyn, NY; married Collette Caeser. **Educ:** Univ of TN. **Career:** NJ Nets, 1977-79, Utah Jazz, 1979-80, Golden State Warriors, 1980-82, NY Knickerbockers, 1982-85, 1987, Washington Bullets, 1988-93; New Jersey Nets, 1993. **Honors/Awds:** NBA Player of the Year Sporting News; Player of the Month for Feb; Player of the Week for Feb 6th; 1st time since 1967 that anyone in the NBA had scored 50 or more points in consecutive games on consecutive nights; Named to NBA All-Rookie Team 1978; 1st-ever winner of NBA Comeback Player of the Year Awd 1980-81 while with Warriors; All-Amer 1976; named 3 times to Southeast Conf All-Star team.

KING, BERNICE ALBERTINE
Attorney, author. **Personal:** daugHter of Coretta Scott King and Martin Luther King Jr. **Educ:** Spelman College, BS, psychology; Emory University, MDiv, JD, 1990. **Career:** City Attorney's Office, internship; Georgia Retardation Center, student chaplain; Georgia Baptist Hospital; attorney, currently; minister; Voice Communications Network, minister; Juvenile Court Judge, clerk, 1990-92; Greater Rising Star Baptist Church, asst pastor, currently. **Orgs:** King Center, bd of dirs; Nat'l Black MBA's. **Business Addr:** c/o MLK Ctr for Nonviolent Social Change, 449 Auburn Ave., Atlanta, GA 30312.

KING, BRETT
Television executive. **Educ:** Penn State, BFA. **Career:** WNYC-TV, production assistant, 1981-86; TV show Saturday Night Live, production coordinator, 1986-87, unit producer, 1987-90; Lost Planet Productions, music video/promo producer, 1990-91; Quincy Jones Entertainment, director of television development, 1991; Vibe magazine, exec consultant; Twentieth Century Fox Television, director of current programming, 1993-96; Paramount Television Group, vice pres of current programs, 1996-. **Business Addr:** Vice President of Current Programs, Paramount Network Television, 5555 Melrose, Hollywood, CA 90038, (213)956-5000.

KING, CALVIN E.
Educator (retired). **Personal:** Born Jun 5, 1928, Chicago, IL; son of Florence King and David King. **Educ:** Morehouse Coll, AB 1949; Atlanta Univ, MA 1950; Ohio State Univ, PhD 1959. **Career:** Tennessee State Univ, prof math & head dept physics & math 1958-88 (retired); Dept Math Fed Adv Teachers Coll Lagos Nigeria, spec math 1962-64. **Orgs:** Mem Mathematical Assn of America; Natl Council of & Teachers of Math; mem Beta Kappa Chi Hon Scientific Soc; mem Omega Psi Phi; mem Alpha Kappa Mu Natl Hon Soc. **Military Serv:** AUS corpl 1951-53; Counter Intelligence Corps.

KING, CECILIA D.
Government official. **Personal:** Born Sep 11, 1950, Detroit, MI; daughter of Barbara Abigail Means Byrd King and William Alfonzo King. **Educ:** University of Michigan, Ann Arbor, MI, BA, 1973; University of Pennsylvania, Wharton School, Philadelphia, PA, MBA, 1976. **Career:** Citicorp (subsidiaries), Oakland, CA, vice pres, 1976-84; Michael Prince & Associates, Los Angeles, CA, consultant, 1984-85; FHP, Inc, Fountain Valley, CA, financial planning mgr, 1985-86; Merrill Lynch & Co, New York, NY, sr financial analyst, 1986-88; Financial Services Corp, New York, NY, chief financial administrative officer, 1988-. **Orgs:** Member, Financial Womens Association, 1990. **Business Addr:** Chief Financial & Administrative Officer, Administration, Financial Services Corp, 110 William St, 3rd Floor, New York, NY 10038.

KING, CELES, III
Business executive. **Personal:** Born Sep 18, 1923, Chicago, IL; married Anita Givens; children: Tobi, Teri, Toni, Mike. **Educ:** Pacific Coast Univ CA, LLB 1951; Pepperdine U, MBA 1972; Laurence U, PhD 1977. **Career:** King Bail Bond Agy, bondsman 1951-; ins broker & real estate agt 1951-. **Orgs:** Chrm LA Col Bail Agents Assn Pres CA Bail Agents Assn 1979-80; CA State Chmn CORE, Congress of Racial Equality 1979-80; asst prof CA State Univ of LA Pan African Studies; Master of Bus Adminstrn; Pepperdine Univ Grad Sch Adminstr 1973-75; past pres LA City Human Relations Commn; past pres LA NAACP; exec dir LA Rumor Control & Info Cntr; co-founder LA Unifed Sch Bd Black Educ Commn 1969-; LA Brotherhood Crusade 1968; pres bd of trustees Laurence Univ Santa Barbara, CA 1975-; vice pres Natl Assn of Private Nontraditional Schls & Colls; Natl Assn of Black Military Officers, charter member. **Honors/Awds:** LA Langston Bar Assoc Outstanding Comm Serv Award 1965, 1973; CORE Award for Significant Contrib to Cause of Freedom & Human Dignity 1964; CA State Assembly Resolution Commending Credit to Comm & State 1965, 1970; LA NAACP Award for Outstanding Contrib to NAACP Movement 1963; Outstanding Bus Leadership LA Bus Assn 1965; Outstanding Comm Serv Award Com for Rep Govt 1965; LA Comm Achievement Award 1968; LA Martins Award 1970, 1973; Natl Assn of Black Military Officers, Military Achievement Award, 1990. **Military Serv:** USAF lt. **Business Addr:** King Bail Bond Agency, 1530 W King Blvd, Los Angeles, CA 90062.

KING, CEOLA
City official. **Personal:** Born Jun 10, 1927, Macon, MS; children: Terasa. **Career:** Town of Old Memphis, council mem. **Home Addr:** Rt 1 Box M 158C, Aliceville, AL 35442.

KING, CHARLES ABRAHAM
Attorney. **Personal:** Born Feb 27, 1924, New York, NY; son of Ruby Chaplin King and Charles Roy King; married Nellie Alexander; children: Alexandra, Victoria. **Educ:** NY Univ Sch of Bus, BS 1949; Fordham Univ Sch of Law, LLD 1952. **Career:** Deluxe Lab, sr acct 1951-59; King & Jones Esqs, 1960-63; Nat Bur of Casualty Underwriters, asst cnsl 1964-68; Ins Rating Bd, cnsl 1968-70; Ins Svc Ofc, cnsl 1970-72; Metro Property & Liability Ins Co, vice pres & genl counsel, 1973-88; Arnelle and Hastie, Esqs, of Counsel; Cooper, Liebonitz, Royster & Wright Esqs of Counsel, currently. **Orgs:** Chair Bd dir NY Motor Vehicle Accident Indemification Corp, 1985-88; chair Legal Committee, Alliance of American Insurers, 1986-88; trustee Barber-Scotia Coll; mem Amer Bar Assn, council member Tort and Insurance Practice Section, 1990-; NY State

Bar Assn; RI Bar Assn; Natl Bar Assn; Ind adv com Recodification for NY State Ins Law; Ins Com Amer Arbitration Assn; past mem Ind Adv Com implementation of state no-fault auto ins law; vis prof Natl Urban League's Black Exec Exchange Program. **Military Serv:** AUS 2nd lt 1943-46; USAR 2nd lt, 1946-50. **Home Addr:** 16 Midway Rd, White Plains, NY 10607-2109. **Business Addr:** Attorney, Cooper, Liebowitz, Royster & Wright, Esqs, Tarrytown Elmsford Corp. Ctr, 3 West Main St, Elmsford, NY 10523-2414.

KING, CHARLES E.
Educator. **Personal:** Born Oct 8, 1911, Waynesboro, GA; married Edythe Louise McInver, Jun 4, 1938. **Educ:** Paine Coll Augusta GA, BA 1937; Univ of MI Ann Arbor, MA 1940; Univ of Chicago, Chicago, PhD 1951. **Career:** NC Central Univ, prof emeritus/sociologist 1977-; St Augustine's Coll, visiting prof 1984-85; NC Central Univ, research constlt 1984-85. **Orgs:** Pres Hble Elders/Kiwanis Club 1984; dir Hnble Elders/Kiwanis Club 1981-85; vice pres Univ of Chicago Club/NC 1981-; Arbitrator Natl Consumer Arbitration Panel/Better Business Bureaus. **Home Addr:** 1008 Chalmers St, Durham, NC 27707. **Business Addr:** Prof Emeritus/Sociology, NC Central Univ, 1008 Chalmers St, Durham, NC 27707.

KING, CHARLES E.
Singer. **Personal:** Born Jul 6, 1920, Cleveland, OH; married Helen Grieb; children: Dolissa, Darla. **Educ:** Heidelberg Coll OH, 1938-39; Juilliard School of Music, NY, 1948. **Career:** Baritone singer/minister present; Karamu Theater Cleveland OH, mgr/actor/voice tchr 1950-53; The Charles King Choir NY, dir/founder 1948-50; Wings Over Jordan Choir on CBS, dir/singer 1941-48. **Orgs:** Pres Charles King Orgn 1971-; pres/owner King Worm Ranch 1975-79; pres/owner King Tree Nursery 1979-; songleader/speaker/leader CFO Internatl 1952-; minister/founder The Awareness Center 1965-; songleader-retreat dir Unity Sch of Practical Christianity 1968-; toured USA/Europe/Far East/ Australia/Jamaica/Trindad/Mexico/Tahiti/Fiji Island 1941-; singer appeared on all major concert stages of USA 1941-; invited by the Pentagon to entertain servicemen in Vietnam& Korea 1970-71; numerous recordings; actor/singer in Porgy & Bess/Showboat/The Medium/Kiss Me Kate/Lost in the Stars/ Mikado/Carmen Jones/The Maid in & Mistress. **Business Addr:** Reverend, The Awareness Center, Rt 3 Box 600, Walla Walla, WA 99362.

KING, CLARENCE MAURICE, JR.
Government executive (retired), association executive. **Personal:** Born Jul 25, 1934, Greenwood, MS; son of Eddie Mae King and C Maurice King; married Brenda J Mitchell; children: Mark, Michael, Jeffrey, Cierra, Lydia. **Educ:** Detroit Institute of Commerce, Accounting Certificate 1961; Wayne State Univ, BS 1974; Central MI Univ, MS 1981. **Career:** Internal Revenue Servcs, tax auditor 1961-65, group mgr 1965-68, branch and div chief 1968-76, asst dist dir 1976-81, district dir 1981-89; retired 1989; Langston University, Langston OK, asst professor accounting 1989-90, Wichita Minority Supplier Council of the Wichita Area Chamber of Commerce, Wichita, KS, executive director, 1990-92. **Orgs:** Alto saxophonist Jerry Childers Quartet; lecturer Wichita State Univ; archon Alpha Nu Boule Sigma Pi Phi 1986-; life mem NAACP; bd of directors Natl Business League; mem 32 degree Prince Hall Mason, IRS campus exec for Langston Univ & Wichita State Univ; mem Wichita Rotary; board of director, Goodwill Industries. **Honors/Awds:** Outstanding Comm Activity Sigma Gamma Rho 1986; Corporate Achiever Award, Urban League Guild of Wichita, 1988. **Military Serv:** AUS sgt E-5 5 yrs; Good Conduct Medal, European Occupation, Natl Defense and Marksman 1954-59. **Home Addr:** 6526 O'Neil, Wichita, KS 67212.

KING, COLBERT I.
Editorial writer. **Personal:** Born Sep 20, 1939, Washington, DC; son of Amelia Colbert King and Isaiah King (deceased); married Gwendolyn Stewart, Jul 3, 1961; children: Robert, Stephen, Allison. **Educ:** Howard Univ, BA 1961, grad studies. **Career:** The Washington Post, editorial writer, 1990-; Exec Vice Pres, 1981-90, Riggs Natl Bank; Exec Dir, World Bank, 1979-81; Treasury Dept, asst sec, legislative affairs, 1977; Govt Relations, Potomac Electric Power Co, dir 1976-77; Comm on DC, senator, staff dir 1972-76; Senator Mathias of MD, legislative dir 1975-; re-election & campaign aid 1974; VISTA, dir program & political analyst, 1970-71; HEW, special asst under sec, 1964-70; US Dept St Foreign Serv Attache, 1964-70. **Orgs:** Bd of dir, Africare, 1987-89; trustee, Arena Stage Theatre, 1986-88. **Honors/Awds:** HEW Fellowship Prog 1970-71; NAACP 1969; Distinguished Serv Award, US Sec of Treasury, 1980; lecturer, JFK Inst of Politics, Harvard Univ 1983; lecturer, Foreign Serv Inst 1982-86; Distinguished Graduate Award in Business, Bd of Trustees, Howard Univ, 1987. **Military Serv:** AUS 1 lt 1961-63. **Business Addr:** Editorial Writer, The Washington Post, Editorial Dept, 1150 15th St, NW, Washington, DC 20071.

KING, CORETTA SCOTT
Civil rights activist. **Personal:** Born Apr 27, 1927, Marion, AL; daughter of Bernice McMurry Scott and Obidiah Scott; married Martin L King Jr, Jun 18, 1953 (died 1968); children: Yolanda Denise, Martin Luther III, Dexter Scott, Bernice Albertine. **Educ:** Antioch Coll, AB, 1951; New England Conservatory of Music, Mus B, 1954, MusD, 1971. **Career:** Martin Luther King Jr Center for Nonviolent Social Change Inc, Atlanta, GA, pres/CEO, 1968-; Cable News Network, commentator 1980-; freelance journalist, currently. **Orgs:** Delegate to White House Conf on Children and Youth, 1960; sponsor, Comm for Sane Employment; mem, exec bd, Natl Health Insurance Comm; mem, bd of direc, S Christian Leadership Conf; mem, bd direc, Martin Luther King Jr Found, Grt Britain; trustee, Robt F Kennedy Meml Found; mem, Ebenezer Baptist Church; mem, Women's Intl League for Peace and Freedom; mem, NAACP; mem, bd of mgrs, United Church Women; mem, Alpha Kappa Alpha (hon); mem, Choir & guild adv, Baptist Club; Links; member, So Rural Action Project Inc; chairwoman, Commission on Economic Justice for Women. **Honors/Awds:** Outstanding Citizenship Award, Montgomery Improvement Assn, 1959; Merit Award, St Louis Argus, 1960; Disting Achievement Award, Natl Orgn of Colored Women's Clubs, 1962; Louise Waterman Wise Award, Amer Jewish Cong Women's Aux, 1963; Myrtle Wreath Award, Clevel Hadassah, 1965; Award for Excell in field of human relations, Soc Fam of May, 1968; Univ Love Award, Premio San Valentine Comm, 1968; Wateler Peace Prize, 1968; Dag Hammarskjold Award, 1969; Pacem in Terris Award, Intl Overseas Serv Found, 1969; Leadership for Freedom Award, Roosevelt Univ, 1971; Martin Luther King Meml Medal, Coll City of NY, 1971; Intl Viareggio Award, 1971; named Woman of the Year, Natl Assn Radio and TV Announc 1968; Ann Brotherhood Award, Natl Coun of Negro Women; delegate todisarmament conf, Geneva, Switzend. Honorary degrees: Boston Univ, Marymount Manhattan College, Brandeis Univ, Morehouse College, Wilburforce Univ, Univ of Bridgeport, Morgan State College, Bethune-Cookman College, Keuka College, Princeton Univ, Northeastern Univ, Bates College; author, My Life With Martin Luther King Jr, 1969; numerous periodical articles. **Special Achievements:** Interviewed for the Spike Lee film "4 Little Girls," 1997. **Business Addr:** Founder, Martin Luther King Jr Center, Nonviolent Social Change Inc, 449 Auburn Ave, NE, Atlanta, GA 30312.

KING, DELUTHA HAROLD
Physician. **Personal:** Born Jan 17, 1924, Weir, KS; married Lois; children: Michael, Ronald. **Educ:** Western Res, BS, 1962; Howard University, College of Medicine, 1956; Freedmen's Hosp, intern, 1956-57, resident, urology, 1957-61. **Career:** Physician, pvt prac, 1965-; VA Hosp, chf urology, 1961-65; VA Hosp, consult, 1966-72; SW Comm Hosp, chief of staff, 1979; Hughes Spalding Pavilion, staff & mem; GA Bapt Hosp; Crawford W Long Memorial Hosp; Physician & Surgeons Hosp; St Joseph's Infirmary; Atlanta W Hosp. **Orgs:** Amer Urol Assn; flw, Am Coll Surgeons; Atlanta Urol Soc; bd of trustees, Natl Med Assn, 1979-; GA State Med Assn; Med Assn GA; AMA; Metro-Atlanta Med Assn; bd of trustees, SW Comm Hosp, 1979-80; pres, Atlanta Hlth Care Found, 1973-; chmn bd, Metro Atlanta Hlth Plan; sec, co-fndr, chmn bd, Sickle Cell Found, GA; pres, board of trustees, Atlanta Med Assn, 1974; bd mem, Cancer Network, GA State Com; bd mem, chmn, Physicians Com, GA Partners, 1976; Kappa Alpha Psi; Gov Task Force, HSA Devel, 1975; pres, N Ctr GA, Hlth Systems Agency; bd mem, Metro-Atlanta Counsel on Alcohol & Drug Abuse; 2nd vice pres, Natl Assn Sickle Cell Disease; bd mem, pres-elect, GA State Med Assn; bd mem, Amer Cancer Soc; natl pres, Howard Univ Alumni Assn, 1978-80; apptd Nat Council on HlthPlanning & Development; p pres, Atlanta Club, Howard Univ Alumni Assn; Published article: "Hyperparathyroidism" Journal of the Medical Assn of GA, 1966. **Honors/Awds:** Outstanding achievement as Chief Resident in Urology, Assn of Former Interns & Residents, Freedmen's Hosp, 1961; special award for service, Atlanta Med Assn; Alpha Omega Alpha. **Military Serv:** AUS, tech, 1943-45. **Business Addr:** 2600 Martin Luther King Dr SW, Atlanta, GA 30311.

KING, DEXTER
Organization executive. **Personal:** Born 1961, Atlanta, GA; son of Dr. Martin Luther King Jr. (deceased) and Coretta Scott King. **Educ:** Morehouse College, attended, 1979-81. **Career:** Corrections officer, 1981-83; business consultant, music producer and music promoter, 1983-89; Martin Luther King Jr Center for Nonviolent Social Change, entertainment coordinator, 1988-89, pres, 1989, chairman and chief executive officer, 1995-.

KING, DON
Boxing promoter. **Personal:** Born Aug 20, 1931, Cleveland, OH; married Henrietta; children: Debbie King Lee, Carl, Eric. **Career:** Ernie Shavers, Larry Holmes, boxing mgr; George Foreman-Ken Norton, Ali-Foreman, Ali-Frazier, promoted prize fights; Don King Sports Entertainment Network, owner, pres; King Training Camp, owner; Don King Prod, president, chairman, and CEO, currently. **Orgs:** Supports United Negro Coll Fund; mem Oper Push, The Martin Luther King Center for Social Change, Trans-Africa, The Anti-Apartheid Assoc; bd mem President's Physical Fitness Council. **Honors/Awds:** Helped mastermind the Jacksons Victory Tour; Man of the Year Awd Natl Black Hall of Fame 1975; Urban Justice Awd Antioch School of Law 1976; Heritage Awd Edwin Gould Serv for Children 1976; Minority Businessman of the Year Gr WA Bus Ctr; Man of the Year NAACP; World Boxing Council Promoter of the Decade 1974-84; US Olympic Comm for Outstanding Support & Serv 1980; The Presidential Inaugural Comm George Herbert Walker Bush Awd 1981; Natl Black Caucus Awardee of theYear 1981; North Amer Boxing Fed Promoter of the Year 1983-84; Natl Police Athletic League for Unselfish dedication & generous contribs 1983; World Boxing Council Humanitarian Awd 1984; Black Entertainment & Sports Lawyers Assoc Merit Awd 1986; IN Black Expo Freedom Awd 1986; The Pigskin Club of WAOnly in Amer Can a Don King Hen Awd 1986; Dr Martin Luther King Jr Humanitarian Awd The Jamaica Amer Soc in Assoc with the US Info Serv 1987; Natl Youth Movement Crack Buster of the Year Awd 1986; Guantes Mag Promoter of the Year Awd; A True Champion of Humanitarian Causes IN State Branch NAACP 1987; East Chicago Chap IN Black Expo Martin Luther King Humanitarian Awd 1987; Minority Oppty for Racial Equality More Inc in Appreciation on Don King's Devotion to His Fellow Man 1987. **Business Addr:** Chairman, Chief Exec Officer, Don King Productions, Inc, 871 W. Oakland Park Blvd., Oakland Park, FL 33311.

KING, DONALD E.
Judge. **Personal:** Born Mar 24, 1934, Atlantic City, NJ; son of Edna King and James E. King; married; children: 1. **Educ:** Lafayette Coll, AB 1956; St John's Univ Law Sch, LlB 1960; St John's Univ Law Sch, JD 1964. **Career:** Zashin & King, partner 1962-70; City of Newark, asst corp counsel 1970-73, corp counsel 1973-74; Juvenile & Dom Rel Court, Essex County, NJ, judge 1974-80; Rutgers Inst for Cont Legal Educ Rutgers Law Sch, instructor; Superior Court of New Jersey, judge, 1980-. **Orgs:** Mem Pi Lambda Phi; PAD Legal Fraternity; Essex Co Bar Assoc; NJ Bar Assn; American Bar Assn; Nat Bar Assn; Urban League; NAACP Appointed to Essex Co Ethics Comm by NJ Supreme Ct; pres, Garden State Bar Assn. **Military Serv:** US Army, 1st lt.

KING, EARL B.
Association executive. **Personal:** Born Jan 5, 1953, Chicago, IL; son of Mildred R King & John Barksdale; married Darryl S King, Jun 7, 1991; children: Earl B King II. **Educ:** North Texas State Univ, BA, special ed, 1976. **Career:** NO DOPE EXPRESS FOUNDATION, pres & CEO, 1986-. **Orgs:** Continental Basketball League, 1977-78; Western Basketball Assn, 1979-80; European Basketball League, 1980; San Diego Clippers, 1982-83, 1978-79; NAACP, 1994-. **Honors/Awds:** Dollars & Sense, Business & Professional, 1994; NAACP, National Outstanding Comm Service, 1994; Black Heritage Expo, Humanitarian of the Year, 1994; Secretary of State, Outstanding Comm Service & State, 1993; DEA/Dept of Justice, Outstanding Contribution in Drug Law Enforcement. **Special Achievements:** First 4 year letterman in 22 years at North Texas State Univ, 1976. **Business Addr:** Pres/CEO, No Dope Express Foundation, 901 E 104th St, Chicago, IL 60628.

KING, EDGAR LEE
Hospital executive. **Personal:** Born in Shellman, GA; son of Bertha King and J B King; married Georgia Roberta Chester; children: Laura Smith, Edgar Jr. **Educ:** Northwestern Univ; Georgia State Coll; Univ of IL, CPA 1980. **Career:** Allier Rdo Corp, sr accountant 1958-61; Schwab Rehabilitation Hosp, business manager 1961-63, controller, 1963-73, assoc administrator, 1973-79; Hospital of Englewood, chief finance officer 1980-88. **Orgs:** American Institute of CPA's; Illinois Society of CPA's; Health Care Financial Management Assn; American Hospital Assn; IL Hospital Assn; Natl Assn of Hospital Serv Exec; Chicago Urban League. **Honors/Awds:** Delta Mu Delta, Beta Chap, Northwestern Univ.

KING, EMERY C.
Journalist. **Personal:** Born Mar 30, 1948, Gary, IN; son of Natalie Harridy King and Emery H King; married. **Educ:** Indiana Univ, Bloomington, IN, 1965-66; Purdue Univ, Hammond, IN, 1967-71. **Career:** WJOB-Radio, Hammond, IN, reporter, 1970-72; WWCA-Radio, Gary, IN, reporter, 1972-73; WBBM-Radio, Chicago, IL, reporter, 1973-76; WBBM-TV, Chicago, IL, reporter, 1976-80; NBC News, Washington, DC, correspondent, 1980-86; WDIV-TV, Detroit, MI, anchor/reporter, 1986-. **Orgs:** Member, board of directors, Society of Yeager Scholars, Marshall Univ, 1986-91; member, board of directors, Detroit Symphony Orchestra; member, National Assn of Television Arts and Sciences. **Honors/Awds:** Emmy Award, National Assn of Television Arts and Sciences, 1977, 1979; 1st Place, Monte Carlo International Film Festival Award for NBC White Paper Documentary, "America Black and White," 1982. **Business Addr:** Anchor/Reporter, WDIV-TV, 550 W Lafayette Blvd, Detroit, MI 48231.

KING, FREDERICK L., JR.
Gaming official. **Personal:** Born Nov 16, 1957, Washington, DC; married Teresa, Aug 18, 1979; children: Ryan, Erin. **Educ:** Central State University, BS, 1980. **Career:** Pepsi Cola USA, regional sales manager, 1987-90; Drackett Products Co, business development manager, 1990-92; Philip Morris USA, trade mktg director, 1992-94, sales director, 1994; M&M Mars/Kal Kan, regional manager, 1994-96; DC Lottery & Charitable Games Control Board, executive director, 1996-. **Orgs:** Multi State Lottery, board member, mem devt committee; National Association of State & Prov Lotteries, co-chair steering com-

mittee, mktg committee; CSU Business Advisory Council, board member; FOCUS, founder; Kappa Alpha Psi Fraternity, Inc, polemarch Cincinnati Alumni, 1999. **Honors/Awds:** United Negro College Fund, Volunteer Awd, 1989. **Military Serv:** US Army, capt, 1980-94; ARCOM, 1983. **Business Addr:** Executive Director/CEO, DC Lottery & Charitable Games Control Board, 2101 Martin Luther King Jr Ave, SE, Washington, DC 20020, (202)645-8010.

KING, GAYLE
Talk show host, news anchor. **Personal:** Born in Chattanooga, TN; divorced; children: William, Kirby. **Educ:** Univ of Maryland, BA, psychology. **Career:** Worked in local television in Baltimore and Washington, DC; WDAF-TV, Kansas City, weekend anchor; WFSB-TV, Hartford, CT, even anchor, 1981-; ''Cover To Cover,'' co-host, 1992; The Gayle King Show, host, 1997-98. **Honors/Awds:** Local Emmys, nominated for six, won three. **Business Addr:** Talk Show Hostess, The Gayle King Show, 10 Constitution Plaza, Hartford, CT 06103-1810.

KING, GEORGE W., JR.
Financial consultant. **Personal:** Born Nov 22, 1936, Huntington, NY; son of Flossie King and George W King; married Paula Brittan, Jan 19, 1972; children: Cynthia Ann, Emily Jeanne, George W III. **Educ:** Maryland State College, UMES, BS, 1958. **Career:** Merrill Lynch, Pierce, Fenner & Smith, account executive; Thomson McKinnon Sec Inc, branch manager, vp; Advest Inc, vp; Ferris Baker Watts Inc, vp, investments, currently. **Orgs:** Baltimore Bond Club; International Society of Retirement Planners; Chesapeake Planned Giving Council; CPA Club, executive director; Women's Institute for Financial Education, founder. **Honors/Awds:** New York Stock Exchange, COMA Award, 1986. **Military Serv:** US Navy, senior lt, 1959-64. **Business Addr:** VP, Investments, Ferris Baker Watts Inc, 100 Light St, 8th Fl, Baltimore, MD 21202, (410)659-4633.

KING, GWENDOLYN STEWART
Public utility exec. **Personal:** Born in East Orange, NJ; married Colbert I King; children: Robert, Stephen, Allison. **Educ:** Howard Univ, BA (cum laude) 1962; George Washington Univ, 1972-74. **Career:** US Dept of HEW, 1971-76; US Dept of HUD, dir div of consumer complaints 1976-78; US Sen John Heinz, sr legislative asst 1978-79; Commonwealth of PA, Director, Washington Office, 1979-86; The White House, deputy assistant to the President 1986-88; US Dept of Health & Human Services, Social Security Admin, commissioner, 1989-92; PECO Energy Company, senior vp, currently. **Orgs:** Board member Martin-Marietta Corp, 1992; Board member Monsanto Co, 1993. **Honors/Awds:** Annual Achievement Award, Xi Omega Chapter of Alpha Kappa Alpha, 1990; Ebony Black Achievement Award, 1992; Drum Major for Justice Award, SCLC, 1989. **Business Addr:** Senior VP, Corporate and Public Affairs, PECO Energy Co., 2301 Market St, Philadelphia, PA 19101.

KING, HODGE
Educator. **Personal:** Born Nov 10, 1914, Dooly County, GA; married Hattie F Burson. **Educ:** Morris Brown Coll, AB 1940; New York U, MA 1952; New York U, 1959; cert 1959. **Career:** Turner Co Jr High, principal 1970-80; Uereka High Sch, prin 1946-70; Turner Cty Bd of Edn, tchr 1940-41. **Orgs:** Regional dir GA Tchr & Educ Assn 1949-54; dist exec sec GA Interscholastic Assn 1949-64; pres GA Interscholastic Assn 1968-70; vice pres Morris Brown Coll Nat Alumni southeastern reg 1977- Shriner Mason 1957-; stewart-trustee Emmery Chapel AME Ch 1959-; pres Alpha Phi Alpha Frat Gamma Omricrom Chap 1960-62. **Honors/Awds:** Meritorius serv award Am Cancer Soc 1967; meritorius serv award GA Interscholastic Assn 1970; meritorius serv award Boy Scout of Am 1974; meritorius serv award Morris Brown Coll Nat Alumni Assn 1979. **Military Serv:** AUS msgt 1941-45. **Business Addr:** Turner City Jr High, Ashburn, GA 31714.

KING, HOWARD O.
Federal official. **Personal:** Born Aug 24, 1925, Pensacola, FL; son of Lula King and Willie King; married Lillie Marie Pollard; children: Howard O, Jeanne K Carr, William C. **Educ:** Florida A&M Univ, BS 1956; Fed Exec Inst 1979. **Career:** Office of Civil Rights, FAA, Washington DC, dep dir 1972-; FAA, Atlanta, regional civil rights officer 1970-72; US Forest Serv Atlanta, regional intergroup relations specialist 1967-70; Dept of Defense, Atlanta, contract compliance officer 1965-67; Naval Air Sta Pensacola, various titles 1941-65; Washington Adult Sch Pensacola, adult educ 1957-65; HO King Sales & Serv Pensacola, proprietor 1958-65. **Orgs:** Bd of dirs, MDTA Pensacola, 1963-65; sec, Bi-Racial Comm Pensacola, 1963-65; officer, Ebenezer Baptist Church, Atlanta, 1985-. **Honors/Awds:** Good Conduct Medal, USN, 1945; award, SNEAD, 1956; citizenship award, NAACP, 1965; citizenship plaque, City of Pensacola, 1965; certificate of achievement, Dept of Transportation, FAA, 1972; outstanding achievement award, Natl Black Coalition of FAA Employees, 1978; Scouters, Key & Silver Beavers Awards, 1992; The Livingston Ivy Award, For Making a Difference, Pensacola FL, 1994. **Military Serv:** USN petty officer 1st class 40 months.

KING, HULAS H.
Manufacturing consulting executive. **Personal:** Born Oct 9, 1946, East St Louis, IL; son of Willie Mae Patton King and Robert King (deceased); married Linda Bolton King, Dec 25, 1966; children: Gail, LaTasha. **Educ:** Southern Illinois University, Edwardsville, IL, BS, data processing, 1972, MBA, marketing, 1974, MS, international relations, 1975, MS, mgmt science & systems, 1978; University of Missouri, Columbia, MO, MS, industrial engineering, 1982. **Career:** United States of America, Collinsville, IL, bagger, 1964-65; Dow Chemical Company, scalper helper, 1965; Ford Motor Company, Hazelwood, MO, body shop work, 1966; McDonnell Aircraft Company, St Louis, MO, manufacturing engineering positions, 1966-89; McDonnell Douglas Systems Integration Co, St Louis MO, project director, Team Columbus, 1989-91; EDS-Unigraphics, St Louis, MO, director, Industry Marketing Team, 1992, director, Industry Operations Team, 1993-. **Orgs:** Chairman, Business Advisory Council, Southern Illinois Univ, 1989; board member, Junior Engineering Technology Society, 1985-; regional coordinator, Numerical Control Society, 1980-; board of directors, Greater St Louis Health Systems Agency, 1977-81; advisory council, Lewis & Clark Community College, 1988-; program evalutor, Accreditation Board of Engineering Technology, 1980-; technical vice pres, Association for Integrated Manufacturing-Tech, 1986-89; chairman, Professional Business Leadership Council, 1992-; advisory board, Child Assistance Program, 1982-. **Honors/Awds:** Charter Inductee to African-American Biographics Hall of Fame for Outstanding Contributions in Engineering, 1994; Engineer of the Year, 1989; St Louis Gateway Engineer's 1989; Salute to Excellence Award-Science, St Louis American, 1989; Distinguished Alumni Award, Southern Illinois University, 1989; Citizen of the Year Award, OMEGA's, 1978; Beta Gamma Sigma Scholastic Award, Southern Illinois University, 1979. **Military Serv:** US Army, Spc sgt; Army Accommodation Medal, Vietnam Service Award. **Business Addr:** Director, Industry Operations Team, EDS-Unigraphics, 13736 Riverport Dr, Maryland Heights, MO 63043.

KING, JAMES, JR.
Science and engineering manager. **Personal:** Born Apr 23, 1933, Columbus, GA; son of Lucille Jameson Williams (deceased) and James King (deceased); married Jean H King, Mar 23, 1966 (divorced 1986); children: Jennifer King Schlickbernd, Jeffrey King. **Educ:** Morehouse Coll, Atlanta GA, BS, 1953; CA Institute of Technology, Pasadena CA, MS, 1955, PhD, 1958. **Career:** Jet Propulsion Laboratory, manager, Pasadena CA, 1969-74; NASA, Washington DC, space shuttle environmental effects, 1974-75, dir upper atmospheric research office, 1975-76; Jet Propulsion Lab, Pasadena CA, program manager for atmospheric sciences, 1976-81, technical manager for Space Science and Applications, 1981-84; Morehouse College, Atlanta, GA, chemistry professor, 1984-86; Jet Propulsion Lab, technical manager, 1986-88, deputy asst lab dir, Technical Div, 1988-93, asst lab dir, 1993-94; Director for Engineering and Science, 1995-. **Orgs:** Mem, Sigma Xi, 1958-; mem, Amer Physical Society, 1960-; mem, Amer Chemical Society, 1960-; bd of dir, Pasadena Child Guidance Clinic, 1969-72, 1980-86; mem, LA Air Pollution Control, 1971-74; mem, Caltech YMCA Bd of Dir, 1972-74; mem, Amer Assn for the Advancement of Science, 1976-; dir, Caltech Alumni Assn, 1977-80; mem, Amer Geophysical Union, 1977-80; chairman, Pasadena Community Devel Committee, 1982-83; mem, Pasadena Planning Commission, 1989-93. **Honors/Awds:** Fellowship, Danforth Foundation, 1953; Scholarship, General Educ Board, 1953; Certificate of Merit, Natl Council of Negro Women, 1968; nominee for the US Jaycee's Distinguished Service Award, 1966; Phi Beta Kappa, 1975; author of 13 articles in professional journals. **Business Addr:** Director for Engineering and Science Div, Jet Propulsion Laboratory, 4800 Oak Grove Dr, Bldg 180, Rm 500, Pasadena, CA 91109.

KING, JEANNE FAITH
Marriage, family, child counselor. **Personal:** Born Sep 20, 1934, Philadelphia, PA; daughter of Minnie H Hines King and Julian Frederick King; divorced; children: Heather O Bond Bryant. **Educ:** Antioch Coll LA, BA 1977, MA Clinical Psychology 1987. **Career:** Performing Arts Soc of LA,TV producer 1969-70; Watts Media Ctr, pr instr 1972-74; WTTW-Chicago Pub TV, TV production 1975; Self Employed, free lance comm/pr 1976-78; Central City Comm Mental Health Ctr, dir of pub relations 1978;Jeanne King Enterprises, consultant firm 1984-; Valley Cable LA, producer cable TV show ''Jazz 'n U'' 1984; Local Jazz Clubs, free lance entertainment specialist 1984; Julia Ann singer Ctr in Family Stress Prog, intern 1985-86, intern family therapy prog 1986-87; Rosa Parks Sexual Assault Crisis Center LA, counselor 1987-; Play It Safe with SASA, consult & trainer for focus consult teaching 1987; Marriage Family Child Counselor, intern; In the Beginning Corp, pres 1978-; consultant for New Horizons; MFCC private practice, 1988-. **Orgs:** Exec dir Performing Arts Soc of LA 1973-74; cons, contrib Black Art, An Intl Quarterly 1976-79; mem Black Womens Forum 1978-80; bd dir Ureaus Quarterly Magazine 1978-80; mem LA, Salvador Sister Cities Com 1978-80; mem California Assn of Marriage, Family, Child Therapists, 1987-; mem bd of dirs Centinela Child Guidance Clinic 1988-89. **Honors/Awds:** Public Serv Awd; Watts Summer Festival Awd 1969; Comm Contribution Head Start Awd 1970; Outstanding Serv Awd Compton Comm ARts Acad 1971; Outstanding Serv Awd Natl Conf of Artists Awd 1975; Day of the Drum Festival Mistress of Ceremonies 1984 Watts Tower Art Ctr LA CA; co-editor ''Day of the Drum Festival Book''; Marla Gibbs Comm Award, 1987. **Home Addr:** 5811 Bowcroft Street, #1, Los Angeles, CA 90016.

KING, JIMMY
Professional basketball player. **Educ:** University of Michigan. **Career:** Toronto Raptors, professional basketball player, 1995-. **Special Achievements:** NBA, Second Round Draft Pick, #35 Pick, 1995; Former member of the University of Michigan's Fab 5 team. **Business Addr:** Professional Basketball Player, Toronto Raptors, 20 Bay St., Ste. 1702, Toronto, ON, Canada M5J 2N8, (416)214-2255.

KING, JOHN G.
Inventor. **Personal:** Born Feb 24, 1925, Parkdale, AR; son of Beadie L King and Love M King; married Ruth Cunningham King, May 1949 (divorced); children: Sandra Nelson, Janice Hannah, John E; married Deborah Mables, Oct 22, 1994. **Educ:** Chicago City College, IIT, industrial elec, 1947-49; Coyne Trade School, tv service/refrigeration, 60 weeks. **Career:** King Reserach Lab, Inc, owner, currently. **Orgs:** American Legion, 1953-92; AARP. **Special Achievements:** Inventor, Early Warning Sonic Transducer, US Patented, 1972; 2nd Patent, 1966. **Military Serv:** US Army, Combat Engineers, private, 1944-46. **Home Addr:** PO Box 700, Maywood, IL 60153. **Business Addr:** Owner, King Research Lab, Inc, 150 S 12th Ave, PO Box 700, Rear, Maywood, IL 60153-0700, (708)344-7877.

KING, JOHN L.
Human resources executive. **Personal:** Born Apr 29, 1952, Detroit, MI; son of Lillie Mae Hannah King and Johnnie L King. **Educ:** Oakland Univ, Rochester MI, BA Human Resources, 1975. **Career:** County of Oakland, Pontiac MI, employment coordinator, 1972-78; Visiting Nurses Assn, Detroit MI, sr personnel representative, 1978-80; Rehabilitation Institute, Detroit MI, dir human resources, 1980-88; The Detroit Medical Center, Detroit MI, compensation admin, 1988-89, manager equal employment plan, 1989-92, director equal employment planning, 1992-. **Orgs:** Mem, NAACP, 1980-; mem, Michigan Devel Disabilities Council, 1983-; mem, Mayor's Handicapper Advisory Council, 1987-; treasurer, SW Detroit Community Mental Health Services Group, 1987-; mem, Natl Assn for the Advancement of Blacks in Health, 1988-; program devel chairperson, Healthcare Personnel Admin Assn of SE Michigan, 1988-90; special projects chairperson, 1989-90, pres elect 1990-91, president, Healthcare Personnel Admin Assn of SE Michigan, 1991-92. **Honors/Awds:** Testimonial Resolution, Detroit City Council, 1983, State of Michigan Senate, 1984. **Business Addr:** Director, Equal Employment Planning, The Detroit Medical Center, 4201 St Antoine, 9C/UHC, Detroit, MI 48201.

KING, JOHN Q. TAYLOR, SR.
Educational administrator. **Personal:** Born Sep 25, 1921, Memphis, TN; son of Alice Taylor King Johnson (deceased) and John Quill Taylor (deceased); married Dr Marcet Alice Hines, Jun 28, 1942 (died 1995); children: John Q Jr, Clinton Allen, Marjon King Christopher, Stuart Hines. **Educ:** Fisk Univ, BA 1941; Landig Coll of Mortuary Sci, Diploma 1942; Huston-Tillotson Coll, BS 1947; DePaul Univ, MS 1950; Univ of TX at Austin, PhD 1957. **Career:** US Army, pvt to capt 1942-46; King Funeral Home, Austin TX, mortician, 1946-55; Kings-Tears Mortuary Inc, funeral dir & embalmer (part-time) 1955-, pres, 1984-; Huston-Tillotson Coll, instr, 1947-52, asst prof, 1952-54, prof of math, 1954-88, dean 1960-65, pres 1965-88, chancellor 1987-88, chancellor and pres emeritus, 1988-, director and chair, Center for the Advancement of Science, Engineering and Technology, 1985-. **Orgs:** General secretary, Natl Protestant Brotherhood, 1966-80; pres, Union Welfare and Burial Assn, 1941-85; senior vice pres, Amer Underwriters Life Insur Co, 1986-89; Dir TX Comm Bank-Austin; trust Austin Coll Sherman TX; pres King-Tears Mortuary Inc; life mem NAACP & Natl Urban League; Phi Beta Kappa; Alpha Phi Alpha Frat; Sigma Pi Phi Frat; Phi Delta Kappa; Philosophical Soc of TX; mem Austin Greater E Kiwanis Club 1966-88; mem, past chmn Austin Civil Serv Comm; founder Union Natl Bank; church lay leader, United Methodist Church; director, secretary, Foundation for Insurance Regulatory Studies. **Honors/Awds:** Southwestern U, LLD, 1970; St Edward's U, LLD, 1976; Austin Coll, LHD, 1978, Fisk U, 1980; DSc, Huston-Tillotson Coll, 1988; Alumni Awds Huston-Tillotson Coll & Fisk Univ; Roy Wilkins Meritorious Award NAACP; Disting Serv Awd TX Lutheran Coll; Arthur B DeWitty Awd Austin Branch NAACP; Martin Luther King Humanitarian Awd; Frederick D Patterson Award, Alpha Phi Alpha; Minority Advocate of the Year, Austin Chamber of Commerce; Military/Education Award, San Antonio League, Natl Assn of Business & Professional Women's Clubs; Brotherhood Award, Natl Conf of Christians & Jews; co-author: math texts; co-author, Stories of Twenty-Three Famous Negro Americans, Steck-Vaughan, 1967, Famous Black Americans, Steck-Vaughan, 1975; Booklet on Life of Mrs Mary McLeod Bethune; Distinguished Alumnus Award, Students' Assn, Univ of Texas-Austin,1990; Meritorious Achievement in Education Award, Natl Sorority, Phi Delta Kappa, 1991; Philanthrophist

of the Year, Austin Chapter, National Society of Fundraisers, 1991; Man of the Year Award, Independent Funeral Dirs of Texas, Inc, 1994; George Washington Honor Medal, Freedoms Foundation at Valley Forge, 1994; appointed by Texas Gov George W Bush to Texas Funeral Svc Commission, 6-year term, also to chair Commission's Budget & Finance Committee, 1997. **Military Serv:** US Army, maj gen, (WWII, 1942-46; USAR 1946-83); TX State Guard lt gen 1985; received many combat & other military ribbons, decorations & awards. **Home Addr:** 2400 Givens Ave, Austin, TX 78722-2105. **Business Addr:** Director and Chair, Center for the Advancement of Science, Eng, & Tech, Huston-Tillotson College, 900 Chicon St, Austin, TX 78702-2793.

KING, JOHN THOMAS
Emergency medical service administrator (retired). **Personal:** Born Dec 9, 1935, Detroit, MI; son of Frances Berry King and John King; married Joan Ardis King, Mar 18, 1955; children: Victoria D King, John K King, Pamela A King. **Educ:** Wayne State University, Detroit, MI. **Career:** Detroit Police Dept, Detroit, MI, police cadet, 1954-57; Detroit Fire Dept, Detroit, MI, firefighter, 1957-72, lieutenant, 1972-77, fire marshal, 1977, asst to fire commissioner, 1978-87, chief administrator, 1987-93. **Orgs:** Board member, CYO, 1973-; committee member, New Detroit, 1974-; pres, member, Phoenix Black Firefighters, 1970-80; pres, Toastmasters, 1976-78; alternate, Detroit Police & Fire Pension, 1986-. **Business Addr:** Retired Chief Administrator, EMS, Detroit Fire Department, 900 Merrill Plaisance, Detroit, MI 48203.

KING, JOSEPH PRATHER
Child psychiatrist. **Personal:** Born Jul 15, 1927, Cuthbert, GA; son of Mae Belle Prather King and William King Sr. **Educ:** Univ of Chicago, 1943-46; IN Univ, BS, Pre-Med 1946-48; IN Univ, MD 1947-51; City Hosp, Cleveland, OH, Rotating Internship, 1951-52; Hines VA Hosp, Chgo, IL, Psychiatry Res 1952-53; Manhattan VA Hosp, NYC, Psychiatry Residency 1955-57; Northside Cntr for Child Devel, Child Psychiatry 1957-61. **Career:** IN State Dept of Mental Health, assoc dir Child Mental Health Div 1972-74; IN Med Schl, clinical asst prof Psychiatry 1972-82; Midtown Mental Health Methadon Clinic, assoc med dir 1974-85; Buchanan Counseling Cntr of Methodist Hosp, consultant 1976-85; Westinghouse Head Start, mental health consultant 1979-80; Quinco CMHC, consultant 1983-84; S Central Mental Health Cntrs, child psychiatrist 1983-84; Indiana State Sch for the Deaf, consultant 1985-86; Mood Swing Clinic, psychiatrist currently; Humana Hospital Adolescent Psych Ward, child psychiatrist 1989-90; Foster Care Agency, consultant, 1992-. **Orgs:** Mem NY Cnty Med Soc 1956-, Amer Med Assn 1956-, IN State Med Assn, 1972-, Amer Psychiatric Assn 1956-; chmn Harlem Neighborhood Assn, Mental Health Comm 1959-66, bd mem 1965-72; New York City Council on Child Psychiatry 1962-72; vice chmn Courts Comm 1962-63; mem Comm on Integration 1965-66; Interracial Group Therapists Workshop 1965-66; mem Aesculapian Med Soc 1973-; mem Black Psychiatrists of Amer 1974-; bd mem Marion County Guidance Clinic 1976-78, vice pres 1978-79; bd mem IN Council Family Relations 1977-79; mem Mental Health Delivery Sys Comm IN Univ Schl of Soc Work 1978-79; mem advisory comm Central IN Health Sys Agency 1979-80; mem Marion Cnty Med Soc 1972-, IN Psychiatric Soc 1972-; consultant Diagnostic Prescriptive Learning Cntr of Purdue Univ, 1982-83. **Honors/Awds:** Papers; "Traps in Comm Psychiatry" 1968, "Identity Changes in the Amer Negro" 1969, "Issues in the Devel of Comm Mental Health Serv in the Inner City" 1970, "Therapeutic Comm in Ghetto Facilities" 1970, "Recovery, Inc" 1970, "Changing Attitudes Towards Homosexuals" 1972, "Audiovisual Alternatives , A Way Around the Reading Problem" 1973. **Business Addr:** Psychiatrist, Mood Swing Clinic, 740 East 52nd St, Ste #6, Indianapolis, IN 46205.

KING, JOSEPHINE
Insurance company executive. **Career:** Chicago Metropolitan Assurance Co, CEO, currently. **Special Achievements:** Company is ranked #5 on the Black Enterprise list of top Insurance Companies, 1994. **Business Phone:** (312)285-3030.

KING, JULIAN F.
Attorney. **Personal:** Born May 20, 1931, Philadelphia, PA; married Shirley A Mackey; children: Andrea Victoria. **Educ:** Lincoln Univ PA, BA (cum laude) 1953; Temple Univ Schl Of Law, DL 1956. **Career:** Office of Philadelphia Dist Atty, assistant dist attorney 1963-66; PA Const Conv, delegate 1967-68; Commonwealth of PA, judge, Court of Common Pleas, 1971-88; attorney, currently. **Orgs:** Former chairman Brd of Dir Blue Cross of Greater PA 1981-86; lectur in law Temple Univ Schl of Law 1985-86; Sigma Pi Phi Fraty; Kappa Alpha Psi Fraty; brd of mgrs Christian St YMCA; Lecturer, criminal justice, Commun Coll of Philadelphia, 1980-81. **Honors/Awds:** Man of yr S Philadelphia Brch of NAACP 1973; govr citation Serv to Commonwlth 1973; Recog Awd United Auto Workers Fair Govt Pract 1981; Black Aerospace Workers Awd 1983. **Military Serv:** US Army, sergeant, 1956-58. **Business Addr:** Attorney, 1300 Robinson Bldg, 42 S 15th St, Philadelphia, PA 19102, (215)568-8040.

KING, LAWRENCE C.
Business executive. **Personal:** Born in Washington, DC; married Beulah; children: Larry, Craig. **Educ:** Howard Univ, BA 1951. **Career:** Gen Foods Corp NY, regional sales mgr; Gen Foods Corp, former assoc market research mgr, dist sales mgr & sales devel mgr. **Orgs:** Mem Urban League; Kappa Alpha Psi. **Business Addr:** 250 North St, White Plains, NY 10605.

KING, LAWRENCE PATRICK
Public works executive. **Personal:** Born Feb 3, 1940, Detroit, MI; son of Vivian and Samuel; married Deborah Barrett, Dec 15, 1990; children: Dereck Jackson, Alexandria King. **Educ:** University of Detroit, 1962; Cleveland State University, BSME, 1974; University of Dayton, 1979; University of Michigan, 1990. **Career:** General Electric, sr market development engineer, 1977-79, manager, marketing services, 1979-80; Babcock-Wilcox, marketing specialist, 1980-81, sr marketing specialist, 1981-93. **Orgs:** Air Waste Management Association; National Technical Association, past president, 1986-87; American Association of Blacks in Energy; National Invention Center, trustee. **Honors/Awds:** National Technical Association, Samuel Cuereniers Distinguished Service Award, 1985. **Special Achievements:** Challenges Associated with Increased Coal Consumption, 1992; Incineration in the Management of Hazardous Wastes, 1986. **Home Addr:** 1460 Commonwealth Dr, Akron, OH 44313-5714, (216)867-4879. **Business Addr:** Assistant Director of Administration, Dept Environmental Svcs, Summit County, 25 N Main St, Akron, OH 44308, (216)643-2406.

KING, LEWIS HENRY
Consultant. **Personal:** Born in Birmingham, AL; son of Lilly Bell Taylor King and Tony J King; married Annie M Caster King, Sep 9, 1951; children: Debra, Cynthia, Lewis Jr, Marlon. **Educ:** Miles College, Birmingham, AL; Lawson Community College, Birmingham, AL; Samford University, Birmingham, AL, BS, 1978. **Career:** US Postal Service, Birmingham, AL, postman, 1951-81. **Orgs:** Board member, emeritus, National Coalition Title I, Chapter I Parents, Meeting Planners International; American Society of Association Executives; Religious Conference Management Association; National Coalition of Black Meeting Planners; board of directors, Birmingham Jefferson Civic Center Authority. **Military Serv:** US Army, Technician 4th Grade, 1944-46; Good Conduct, Expert Rifleman, 1944. **Home Phone:** (205)322-3219. **Business Addr:** President, United Management Enterprises, 648 Center Way, SW, Birmingham, AL 35211, (205)322-3219.

KING, LEWIS M.
Scientist, professor. **Personal:** Born Oct 5, 1942, Trinidad; son of Gladys King and Henry King; children: Eric. **Educ:** Howard Univ, BS 1967; UCLA, MA 1968; UCLA, PhD 1971. **Career:** UCLA, psychology lecturer 1967-71; Martin Luther King Jr Hosp, chief psychologist 1971-73; Drew Med Sch, dir research 1972-74; Drew Med Sch, prof psychiatry 1972-74; Dir Fanon Res & Devel Center, Drew Med Sch; Drew Medical School, Dean. **Orgs:** Bd dir Behavior Res & Dev 1970-74; chmn Comm Res Review Com LA 1972-74; dir Trinidad Drama Guild 1960-63. **Honors/Awds:** Howard Univ Scholarship 1964-67; outstanding contribution to student life Howard Univ 1966; Dean's honor role 1964-67; UN Institute of Intl Educ Fellowship 1965-67; Physcics Honor Soc Howard Univ 1965; Distinguished Teaching Award UCLA 1969-70; first black PhD in Psychology from UCLA. **Business Addr:** Charles R Drew, University of Medicine, 1621 E 120th St, Los Angeles, CA 90059.

KING, LLOYD
Educator. **Personal:** Born Sep 13, 1936, Zinnerman, LA; married Ann Adkins; children: Vicki, Eric. **Educ:** Grambling State Univ, BS 1960; LA Tech Univ, MS 1971; LA Tech Univ, post grad study 1975. **Career:** Pinecrest HS, teacher vice pres coach 1961-68; Winnfield Sr HS, tchr 1968-75; Winnfield Middle School, teacher 1985-. **Orgs:** Past pres Winn Educ Assn; adv com Title I prog Winn Parish; mem Natl Educ Assn; mem LA Tech Alumni Assn; dir Indoor Recreation for Blacks; past program dir Local Radio Prog Hobdy's Soul Sauce; past publicity dir Math Dept LA Educ Assn; mem Natl Aerospace Educ Assn; past pres Grambling Alumni Assn; mem Winn Parish Voters League; counselor Job Training Participation Act Summer Youth. **Honors/Awds:** Winn Educ Assn Teacher of the Yr 1971; cited for Outstanding Serv to Educ & Comm 1972 Winn Educ Assn; nominee for Tchr of Yr 1973, 74, 75; Honorary Sec of State 1974; cited for Outstanding Serv Winn Parish Voters League 1975; Outstanding Serv Citation LA Educ Assn 1976; Voters League Teacher of the Year 1985. **Military Serv:** Sgt 1960-62 reserves 5yrs.

KING, MARCELLUS, JR.
Marketing executive. **Personal:** Born Jun 14, 1943, Tampa, FL; married Romaine C Ruffin; children: Marcellus III. **Educ:** Hampton Inst VA, BS (dean's list) 1965; Rutgers Univ NJ, MBA 1976; The Am Coll, CLU 1978. **Career:** Prudential Investments, associate mgr group pension, 1970-71, mgr group pensions, 1971-74, dir group pension servs 1974-85, director of mktg, 1985-95, vice pres of mktg, 1995-. **Orgs:** Guest speaker Minority Interchange 1978-80; pres Omega Phi Epsilon 1961; mem allocations com United Way of Morris Co NJ 1975-80; vice pres Urban League of Essex Co NJ 1976-80. **Honors/Awds:** Medic of the Year Award AUS 1971; designation CLU The Am Coll 1978; exec mgmt prog Prudential Ins Co 1980, registered representative, 1987. **Military Serv:** AUS sp 6th class 1966-72. **Business Addr:** 751 Broad St, Newark, NJ 07102.

KING, MARTIN LUTHER, III
Government official. **Personal:** Born in Montgomery, AL; son of Martin Luther King, Jr (deceased) and Coretta Scott King. **Educ:** Morehouse Coll, BA, political science and history. **Career:** Fulton County Georgia, commissioner, 1986-93; Southern Christian Leadership Conference (SCLC), 1998-. **Business Addr:** President, Southern Christian Leadership Conference, 334 Auburn Ave NE, Atlanta, GA 30303.

KING, MARY BOOKER
Educator. **Personal:** Born Jul 14, 1937, Quitman, GA; married Grady J; children: Felicia, Adriene, Karon. **Educ:** Morris Brown Coll, BA 1959; Atlanta U, MA 1961; Nova U, Ed D 1975. **Career:** Miami Dade Comm Coll, prof of language arts 1975-; Miami Dade Comm Coll, dept chmn of reading 1973-75; Miami Dade Comm Coll, assoc prof of English 1970-72, prof of English, 1979-97. **Orgs:** Commr Dade Co Com on the Status of Women 1978-80; consult Devel of Coll Programs in Reading & Writing; chairperson Women Involved in Comm Affairs 1979-80; mem Educ Task Force Com 1979-80. **Honors/Awds:** Outstanding Young Women of Am 1971; comm leadership award Kappa Theta Delta 1972. **Business Addr:** Miami Dade Comm Coll, 300 N E 2nd Ave, Miami, FL 33132.

KING, MATTIE M.
Association executive (retired). **Personal:** Born Sep 4, 1919, Savannah, GA; daughter of Hattie Livingston and Lemuel Latimer; married Robert Vincent King, Jan 21, 1938; children: Arlene King Robinson, Robert V King III, Carole Y King, Derek Richard King. **Educ:** Brooklyn Coll, BA 1974. **Career:** Bedford Stuyvesant Comm Legal Serv Corp, adminstr; fiscal ofcr 1970-71; adminstrv Sec 1968-70; Fleary Gibson & Thompson, exec sec 1956-68; William H Staves & Judge Lewis S Flagg Jr, legal sec; Port Embarkation, purchasing clk 1949-50; Mail & Records, supr 1947-49; asst supr 1946-47; Spl Mail & Records Div, supr; USAF, Special Mail and Records 1943-45. **Orgs:** Mem bd of dirs Bedford-Stuyvesant Restoration Corp; 2nd vice pres Brooklyn Br NAACP; mem Bedford-Stuyvesant Restoration Constrn Corp & RDC Commercial Ctr Inc; Comm Plng Bd #3 Borough of Brooklyn NYC; mem Concord Bapt Ch; Sisterhood Concord Ch; Unity Dem Club 55 AD; Com Elect John F Kennedy. **Honors/Awds:** Distinguished serv award OES; Grand Ct Daug Sphinx Serv award; award Rebecca Chap 23 OES; leading cit award Brooklyn Recorder; supreme grand financial sec Nat Order Eastern Star; 11 yr serv award Com Action for Legal Serv Inc 1968-79; 10 Yrs Serv Bd of Dir Award Bedford-Stuyvesant Restoration Corp 1967-77; Freedom Fund Award, Brooklyn Branch NAACP 1981; Family of the Year, Bedford Temple Salvation Army 1990.

KING, ORA STERLING
Educational administrator. **Personal:** Born Oct 15, 1931, Delta, AL; daughter of Mary Sterling and William Sterling; married; children: Sherri. **Educ:** Spelman Coll, BA 1954; Atlanta Univ, MA 1969; Univ of Maryland, PhD, 1982. **Career:** Atlanta Public Schools, teacher/instructional coord 1954-72; Federal City Coll, reading dept chair 1975-78; Univ of the District of Columbia, asst prof of educ 1978-81; Coppin State Coll, prof & dept chair of C&I, 1981-88, dean Division of Education, 1988-90, dean, Division of Education and Graduate Studies, 1990-91, professor of education, coord of Masters of Arts in teaching, 1991-. **Orgs:** 1st vice pres Natl Alumnae Assn of Spelman Coll 1982-86; mem editorial adv bd Innovative Learning Strategies Intl Reading Assn 1985-86; pres Natl Alumnae Assn of Spelman Coll 1986-88; mem Alpha Kappa Alpha Iota Lambda Chap; president Columbia Chapter NAASC 1990-95. **Honors/Awds:** Mem editorial adv bd Reading World Coll Reading Assn 1982-84; mem US Delegation to the People's Republic of China US China Scientific Exchange 1985; twenty articles published in educational journals 1979-92; published textbook Reading & Study Skills for the Urban College Student, Kendall/Hunt Publ 1984, 1988, 2nd ed; received NAFEO Distinguished Alumni Award, 1988; Fulbright Scholarship Recipient, Monrovia, Liberia, 1988. **Home Addr:** 9537 Kilamanjaro Road, Columbia, MD 21045-3942. **Business Addr:** Professor of Education, Coppin State College, 2500 W North Ave, Baltimore, MD 21216, (410)383-5655.

KING, PATRICIA ANN
Educator. **Personal:** Born Jun 12, 1942, Norfolk, VA; daughter of Grayce King and Addison King; married Roger Wilkins, 1981; children: Elizabeth Wilkins. **Educ:** Wheaton Coll, BA 1963; Harvard Law School, JD 1969. **Career:** Dept of State, budget analyst 1964-66; Equal Employment Opportunity Commn, special asst to chmn 1969-71; Dept of Health Educ & Welfare, dept dir office of civil rights 1971-73; Civil Div Dept of Justice, dep asst atty general 1980-81; Georgetown Univ, assoc prof of law 1974-88; Georgetown Univ, Law Center, prof of law, 1988-. **Orgs:** Natl Commn for Protection of Human Subjects 1974-78; sr rsch scholar Kennedy Inst of Ethics 1977-;

fellow Hastings Inst NY 1977-; Recombinant DNA Adv Com 1979-82; pres Commn for the Study of Ethical Problems in Med & Rsch 1980-81; chmn Redevelopment Land Agency DC 1976-79; US Circuit Judge Nominating Com 1977-79; board, Russell Sage Foundation 1981-91; Amer Law Institute 1988-; National Academy of Sciences, Institute of Medicine; bd, Women's Legal Defense Fund, 1987-; bd of trustees, Wheaton Coll, 1989-. **Honors/Awds:** Honorary LLD, Wheaton College 1992; Distinguished Serv Award HEW 1973; Secretary's Special Citation HEW 1973; John Hay Whitney Fellowship John Hay Whitney Found 1968; "The Juridicial Status of the Fetus" MI Law Review 1647, 1979; co-author "Law Science and Medicine" 1984. **Business Addr:** Professor of Law, Georgetown Univ, 600 New Jersey Ave NW, Washington, DC 20001.

KING, PATRICIA E.
Attorney. **Personal:** Born Jan 16, 1943, Chester, SC. **Educ:** John C Smith Univ Charlotte, NC, BS 1965; NC Central U, JD; Durham, NC, honor in Constitutional Law & Pleadings. **Career:** Bell & King, atty; Jenkin Perry Pride, researcher 1969-70; Pearson Malone Johnson & Dejermon, researcher 1967-69; Chester, SC, sch tchr 1965-66; Funeral, Directress & Atty. **Orgs:** Mem NC Bar Assn; Black Lawyers Assn; Am Bar Assn; NC Bar Found; NC State Bar Assn. **Honors/Awds:** OIC Award 1972. **Business Addr:** Attorney at Law, 623 East Trade St, Charlotte, NC 28202.

KING, REATHA CLARK
Association executive. **Personal:** Born Apr 11, 1938, Pavo, GA; married Dr N Judge King Jr, 1961; children: N Judge III, Scott Clark. **Educ:** Clark College, BS, 1958; Univ of Chicago, MS, 1960, PhD, chemistry, 1963; Columbia Univ, MBA, 1977. **Career:** Natural Bureau of Standards, research chemist, 1963-68; York College, New York, assistant professor of chemistry, 1968-70, associate professor of chemistry & associate dean of natural science & math division, 1970-74, chemistry professor & associate dean of academic affairs; Metropolitan State University, St Paul, MN, pres, beginning 1977; General Mills Foundation, pres/exec dir, currently. **Orgs:** AAAS; American Chemistry Society; National Organization of Professional Advancement of Black Chemists and Chemical Engineers; Sigma Xi; Exxon Corp, bd of dirs. **Honors/Awds:** YMCA of St Paul, MN, Educational Leadership Award, 1984; CIBA-GEIGY Corporation, Execeptional Black Scientist Award, 1984; Boy Scouts of America, Indianhead Council, Spurgeon Award for Community Work, 1985; National Bureau of Standards,Outstanding Publication Award; Empire State College of SUNY, Honorary Doctorate, 1985. **Business Addr:** President/Exec Dir, General Mills Foundation, PO Box 1113, Minneapolis, MN 55440.

KING, REGINA
Actress. **Personal:** Born 1971?. **Career:** The Artists Group Ltd, Talent and Literary Agency, actress, currently. **Special Achievements:** Film credits include: Friday; Higher Learning, 1994, Poetic Justice, Boyz N The Hood, A Thin Line Between Love and Hate, 1996, Jerry Maguire, 1996, How Stella Got Her Groove Back, 1998, Mighty Joe Young, 1998, Enemy of the State, 1998; Television credits include: "Living Single," New York Undercover," Northern Exposure," "227," "Silver Spoons," "Frankly Female," "Ira Joe Fisher;" Theatre credits include: Wicked Ways; Seymour and Shirley; 227; A Rainy Afternoon; This Family; The Weirdo. **Business Addr:** Actress, Friday, c/o The Artists Group Ltd, Talent and Literary Agency, 10100 Santa Monica Blvd, Ste 2490, Los Angeles, CA 90067-4115, (310)552-1100.

KING, REGINALD F.
Engineer. **Personal:** Born Mar 11, 1935, Powellton, WV; son of Marie Fairfax King and Isaiah King; married Grace V Tipper; children: Reginald T, Thaxton E. **Educ:** Youngstown State Univ, BE 1961; San Jose State Univ, grad study. **Career:** Reynolds Electronics, co-owner dir engr 1968-70; NASA, rsch engr 1961-. **Orgs:** Mem IEEE; NAACP, KAY Frat; publs in field; ISA. **Honors/Awds:** NASA Tech Brief Awd; Patent in Field; Registered Professional Engineer-Electrical Engineering, State of California 1975; Registered Professional Engineer-Control System, State of California, 1978. **Military Serv:** USAF 1954-58. **Business Addr:** Research Engineer, NASA Ames Res Center, N213-4, Moffett Field, CA 94035.

KING, RICHARD DEVOID
Psychiatrist. **Personal:** Born Nov 19, 1946, New Orleans, LA; children: Khent. **Educ:** Whittier Coll, BA 1968; Univ CA San Francisco Med Ctr, MD 1968; Univ So CA Med Ctr, intern 1973; Univ CA Med Ctr, resd 1976. **Career:** Fanon Mental Hlth Rsrch & Devel Ctr, develmt schlr 1976-; San Francisco, psychotherapy rsrch 1974-; Goddard Coll, faculty adv 1975-76; Univ CA, asst tchr 1970; Nghbrhd Yth Cor, educ aide 1969; lab tech 1968; factory wrkr 1967; Lose Angeles, tchr aide 1965; UCLA, lab asst 1964; Palm Springs, lectr 1977; School of Ethnic Studies Dept of Black Studies SF State U, lectr 19780; Aquman Spiritual Ctr, prin 1976-77. **Orgs:** Pres Black Psychiatrists of No CA 1978-80; pres Black Psychiatrists of CA 1980; mem Am Coll of Surgery; Fanon Adv Cncl; Atlanta Med Assn; Nat MedAssn; Assn of Black Psychologist 1977; lectr Martin Luther King Hosp 1977; Black Hlth Ldrsp Conf 1977; Pan-Am Conf 1977; mem Nat of Islam 1969-71; Black Psychiatrist of Am 1975-; Am Psychiat Assn 1975-; mem Nat Inst of Mental Hlth Ctr Devel Prgm 1973-; US Pub Hlth Serv. **Honors/Awds:** Bibliographymelannin 1977; Pineal Gland Rev 1977; Uracus 1977-79. **Military Serv:** Lt com 1973-78. **Business Addr:** c/o Dr. Thelissa Harris, Black Psychiatrists of America, 664 Prospect Ave, Hartford, CT 06105.

KING, RICHARD L.
Entrepreneur. **Personal:** Born Oct 17, 1942, Flint, MI; son of Johnnie E & Richard L King. **Educ:** Roosevelt University, BSBA, 1966; Harvard Business School, 1972. **Career:** Richard King Sr Realtors, manager, Property Management Dept, 1962-66; Chicago Board of Education, administrative assistant to the assistant superintendent of schools, 1966-70; City of Flint, administrator, Economic Development Division, 1972-94; Shape of Future Habitats To Come, president, 1994-. **Orgs:** National Black MBA Assn; National Association of Homebuilders; Flint Community Development Corporation, 1982-94. **Honors/Awds:** Michigan Municipal League, First-Place, Annual Achievement Competition for the City of Flint, Genesee County Urban Investment Plan, 1994. **Business Addr:** President, Shape of Future Habitats To Come, Inc., PO Box 3283, Flint, MI 48502-0283, (810)233-7483.

KING, ROBERT SAMUEL
Educational administrator. **Personal:** Born Oct 16, 1921, Philadelphia, PA; married Rosalie Ernestine Ilivier; children: Gwendolyn Susan, Nancy Gail. **Educ:** WV State Coll, 1943-44; Univ of PA, AB (Physics) 1956; Temple U, grad 1959. **Career:** Philadelphia Coll of Pharmacy & Sci, dir of planning, affirmative action officer 1975-80, dir student affairs 1974-75; Naval Air Engineering Ceter Philadelphia, supr mechanical engineer 1961-74, physicist 1956-61; Veterans Admin, insurance underwriter 1950-55. **Orgs:** Mem bd of dirs Magee Meml Hosp 1975-80; mem bd of dirs Berean Savings Assn 1978-80; chmn west sub area cuncil Health Systems Agency Southeast PA 1979-80; mem bd of dirs West Philadelphia Corp 1964-80; mem bd of dirs Univ City Sci Center 1970-80; bd of trustees Comm Coll of Philadelphia 1972-80. **Honors/Awds:** ETO Central Phinel & Asia-pac Award AUS; Quality of Life Award W Philadelphia Corp 1965; winner area dist speech contests Toastmasters Intl 1972-73; panelist, presenter reg annual conf, Assn Comm Coll Trustees 1978-80; article "Identifying Urban Community Coll Needs" ACCT Trustee Quarterly 1978-79. **Military Serv:** AUS tech sgt 1943-46. **Business Addr:** Phil Coll of Pharm & Sci, 43rd St & Kingsessing Mall, Philadelphia, PA 19104.

KING, ROSALYN CAIN
Pharmacist, health services administrator. **Personal:** Born Sep 10, 1938, New York, NY; daughter of Ethel C Davis and Samuel Cain; married Dr Sterling King Jr; children: Kristin, Aaron. **Educ:** Duquesne Univ, BS 1962; Univ of CA-Los Angeles, MPH 1972; Univ of Southern CA, PharmD 1976. **Career:** Howard University, guest lecturer, 1977-; SECON Inc, vice pres 1977-80; Agency for International Development, Charles R Drew Univ of Medicine and Science, public health advisor/pharmacy & expert consultant 1980-85, assoc dir office of intl health 1985-86, dir office of intl health 1986-87, Department of Family Medicine, instructor, 1984-87, associate professor, 1987, International Health Institute, director, 1987-; Florida A&M University, College of Pharmacy and Pharmaceutical Sciences, adjunct associate professor, 1985-; Xavier University, College of Pharmacy, adjunct associate professor, 1987-. **Orgs:** Chairperson, Ambulatory Care Comm, Amer Public Health Assn, 1979-; mem, Amer Public Health Assn, Amer Pharmaceutical Assn, Natl Pharmaceutical Foundation; deaconess, Mt Calvary Baptist Church, Rockville MD. **Honors/Awds:** Elected to Rho Chi Natl Pharmaceutical Honor Soc 1961; The Hildrus A Poindexter Award Black Caucus of Health Workers 1976; Certificate of Appreciation presented by Sec of USDHEW 1978; Distinguished Serv Award Natl Pharmaceutical Foundation 1982; Community Service Award, National Assn of Black Hospital Pharmacists, 1986. **Business Addr:** Director, Minority Health Prof, 20 Executive Park Dr NE #2021, Atlanta, GA 30329-2206.

KING, RUBY E.
Consultant. **Personal:** Born Mar 3, 1931; married; children: Cynthia, Paul, Gayle, Carol. **Educ:** W Mich U, MA 1968; Mich U, BA 1963. **Career:** Natl Education Assn, asst exec director, public affairs; Minority Affairs Div MI Educ Assn, consultant 1971-; Mich U, educator 1968-71; Mich Univ Campus Sch, supv 1967; elementary sch educator 1961-67. **Orgs:** Mem, bd dir ASCD 1971-74; mem MEA Prof Staff Assn; mem Lansing Urban League; mem Gen Educ Adv Com; mem State Advisory Bd Migrant Education 1971; mem Governor's Task Force Improving Education 1970; group leader NEA Urban Educ Conf 1969; chrmn Personnel Com Grand Rapids YWCA 1971; mem Mayor's Adv Bd on Housing 1971; mem Bd Dir Grand Rapids Legal Aid Soc 1971; bd dir YWCA 1970-71; chmn Educ Com Grand Rapids Model Cities Prog 1969-71. **Honors/Awds:** Nom Teacher of Yr Grand Rapids 1965.

KING, RUBY RYAN
Educator. **Personal:** Born Jan 26, 1934, Oktaha, OK; married Clifford King; children: Diane, Gerald, LaDonna. **Educ:** BS 1957; MS 1975; OK St U, fthr study 1975. **Career:** Home Economics Coop Extention Program, area program agent 1976-; Langston Univ, Family Living Specialist Cooperative Extention Serv 1972-; Morningside Hospital LA, supvr 1961-63; OK Medical Center, supvr 1957-60. **Orgs:** Chmn Parafessional Training Conf Langston Univ 1973-74; Sec Ext Homemakers Group Kingfisher, OK 1971-72; prog chmn Western Dist Bapt Convention 1968; mem Am Home Econ Assn; Okla Home Econ Assn (Sec 1974-75); Am Assn of Univ Women; Nat Counc on Family Relations; Phi Delta Kappa; Phi Upsilon Omicron; Langston Univ Alumni Assn Inspector, Election Bd Kingfisher, OK 1971; mem Young Mens Christian Assn; mem NAACP; mem Intl Fed for Home Econ; mem Kingfisher Lioness Club; mem Alpha Kappa Alpha Sor Inc (Beta Omicron Omega Chpt); mem Am Home Econ Assn World Food Supply Comm Home Mgmt Sec 1975-. **Business Addr:** Box 970, Langston, OK 73050.

KING, RUTH J. See PRATT, RUTH JONES.

KING, SHAKA C.
Company executive, clothing designer. **Personal:** Born Mar 16, 1959, Miami, FL; son of Evelyn and Willie King Jr. **Educ:** Pratt Institute, BFA, 1978-82. **Career:** Shaka King Menswear, ceo, currently. **Orgs:** Black Fashion Collective (BFC), founder, 1994-; Fashion Outreach (FO), 1994-; Black Alumni of Pratt (BAP), 1992-. **Honors/Awds:** TFA, Playboy New Talent Award, Absolut Sublaztion Showcase. **Special Achievements:** Cothing worn in magazines including: NY times, YSB, New Word; SKM customers include: Spike Lee, Boys II Men, Will Downing, Branford Marsalis, Lou Gossett Jr, Erika Alexander, TC Carson, Malik Sealy, Blair Underwood, Jada Pinkett, Malik Yoba, Tommy Ford, Chris Webber and Alonzo Mourning; launched mail order catalog, 1997. **Business Addr:** Designer, Shaka King Menswear, 207 St James Pl, Ste 3L, Brooklyn, NY 11238, (718)638-2933.

KING, SHAWN
Professional football player. **Personal:** Born Jun 24, 1972, West Monroe, LA; children: Charity. **Educ:** Louisiana State; Northeast Louisiana. **Career:** Carolina Panthers, defensive end, 1995-. **Business Addr:** Professional Football Player, Carolina Panthers, 800 Mint St, Ericsson Stadium, Charlotte, NC 28202, (704)358-7000.

KING, STACEY (RONALD STACEY)
Professional basketball player. **Personal:** Born Jan 29, 1967, Lawton, OK. **Educ:** Univ of Oklahoma, Norman, OK, 1985-89. **Career:** Chicago Bulls, 1989-94; Minnesota Timberwolves, 1994-. **Honors/Awds:** NBA All-Rookie Second Team, 1990. **Business Addr:** Professional Basketball Player, Minnesota Timberwolves, 600 First Ave, N, Minneapolis, MN 55403.

KING, STANLEY OSCAR
Sports agent. **Personal:** Born Mar 21, 1958, Bronx, NY; son of Ellridge and Alberta King; divorced; children: Stanley O II, Stephanie N. **Educ:** Oglethorpe University, BA, 1981; Rutgers Univ School of Law, JD, 1994. **Career:** CIGNA Corporation, course designer, 1981-85; Xerox Corporation, major accounts sales manager, 1985-89; American Business Alternatives, president, 1989-92; First Round Sports Inc, exec vice president/COO, 1989-. **Orgs:** Negro Baseball League Celebrations, chairman, 1994; Philadelphia Youth Entrepreneurs Institute, youth mentor, 1994; Philadelphia Sports Congress, board member, 1994. **Honors/Awds:** Concerned Black Men, Sponsor's Award, 1994; National Black MBA Assn, Philadelphia Chapter, 1988. **Business Addr:** Exec VP, CEO, First Round Sports, 1000 White Horse Road, Ste 700, Glendale Executive Campus, Voorhees, NJ 08043, (609)782-1113.

KING, TALMADGE EVERETT, JR.
Physician, educator. **Personal:** Born Feb 24, 1948, Sumter, SC; married Mozelle Davis; children: Consuelo, Makaika M. **Educ:** Gustavus Adolphus Coll, BA 1970; Harvard Med School, MD 1974. **Career:** Emory University Affiliated Hospitals, residency, 1974-77; University of Colorado Health Sciences Center, pulmonary fellowship, 1977-79, professor of medicine, 1991-97, vice chairman for clinical affairs, 1993-97; National Jewish Medical and Research Center, senior faculty member, 1990-97, executive vice president for clinical affairs, 1992-96; San Francisco General Hospital, chief, medical services, currently; Dept of Medicine, Univ of CA San Francisco, professor and vice chair. **Orgs:** American Board of Internal Medicine, member, subspecialty board on pulmonary disease, 1995-; Gustavus Adolphus College, board of trustees, 1993-; American Lung Association of Colorado, board of directors, 1986-; American Thoracic Society, pres, 1997-98; American College of Chest Physicians; American College of Physicians; American Federation for Clinical Research; American Lung Association; ALA National Council, 1993-; Colorado Pulmonary Physicians; National Medical Assn; Natl Inst of Health, Lung Biology & Pathology Study Section, 1997; Pulmonary Fellowship, advisory bd, 1994-. **Honors/Awds:** Gustavus Adolphus College Alumni

Association , First Decade Award for Early Achievement, 1980; American College of Chest Physicians, Pulmonary Physicians of the Future, 1983, Fellow, 1984; American College of Physicians, Fellow, 1986; American Lung Association of Colorado, James J Waring Award for Outstanding Leadership in the Treatment of Lung Disease, 1992; Western Society for Clinical Investigation, Elected Mem, 1989; Western Assn of Physicians, Elected Mem, 1993; The Best Doctors in America, Woodward/White, Inc, Publications, 1992, 1994; The Best Medical Specialists in North Amer, Town & Country, 1995; The Best Doctors in America: Central Region, 1996-97, Woodward/White, Inc, Publications; The Best Doctors in America, American Health, 1996; The Fleischner Society, 1997; Constance B Wofsy Distinguished Professor, Univ of CA, San Francisco. **Special Achievements:** Co-editor of two medical textbooks; author of over 200 articles. **Business Addr:** Medical Services, San Francisco General Hospital, 1001 Potrero Ave, Rm 5H22, San Francisco, CA 94110, (415)206-8317.

KING, THOMAS LAWRENCE
Academic librarian. **Personal:** Born Feb 21, 1953, Medina, OH; son of Mozella King and Thomas King; married Toni King; children: Maria Louise King. **Educ:** University of Akron, Akron, OH, BA, geography, 1979; University of Colorado, Boulder, CO, MA, geography, 1983; University of Pittsburgh, Pittsburgh, PA, MLS, 1986; Doctoral candidate, LIS; Simmons College, Graduate School of Library & Information Science. **Career:** Library of Congress, Geography and Map Division, Washington, DC, reference librarian, 1987-88; State University of New York at Binghamton, Binghamton, NY, science reference/maps librarian, earth sciences bibliographer, 1989-96; Thomas L King, head librarian & assistant professor, currently. **Orgs:** Association of College and Research Libraries, Bibliographic Instruction Section, Black Caucus, American Library Association, 1997. **Honors/Awds:** Graduate Fellowship, National Science Foundation, 1979. **Home Addr:** 608 Boulder Dr, Delaware, OH 43015.

KING, W. JAMES
Company executive. **Personal:** Born Aug 26, 1945, Evergreen, AL; son of Vergie Smith and John D King; married Shirley (divorced 1984); children: Monica, Sean. **Educ:** University of Cincinnati, Cincinnati, OH, 1963-66. **Career:** Mutual of New York, Cincinnati, OH, sales representative, 1970-74; Jaytag Inc, Cincinnati, OH, vice president/operations, 1974-78; J King Contractors, Cincinnati, OH, owner/president, 1974-80; Avondale Redevelopment Corporation, Cincinnati, OH, executive director, 1980-. **Orgs:** Executive board, Historic Conservation Board, 1980-; executive baord, Boys & Girls Club of America, 1989-; chairperson, National Congress for Community Economic Development, 1983-; chairperson, Xavier Community Advisory Committee. **Honors/Awds:** Bi-Centennial Medal, 200 Greater Cincinnatians, 1990; Gonze L Twitty Award, National Congress for Community Econ Dev; Xavier University Presidential Citation, Xavier University; 100 Black Portraits of Excellence, Bicentennial Celebration. **Military Serv:** US Air Force, Staff Sergeant, 1970-74; Good Conduct Award. **Business Addr:** Executive Director, Avondale Redevelopment Corporation, 3460 Reading Road, Cincinnati, OH 45229.

KING, WARREN EARL
Management consultant. **Personal:** Born Jul 9, 1947, Durham, NC; son of Alice Mae Umstead King and Leroy Lesley King; married Hiawatha Mechall Jackson King, Apr 8, 1972; children: Justin Christopher. **Educ:** Purdue Univ, BSE 1976; Indiana Univ, MBA 1987. **Career:** US Postal Svcs, distrib clerk 1970-72; Delco Remy Div of GMC, Anderson, IN, engineering project manager, 1976-87; Hewlett Packard Co, Sunnyvale, CA, national accounts manager, 1987-88; Crown Consulting Group, Indianapolis, IN, president/owner, 1988-. **Orgs:** Life mem NAACP 1984; chmn rules & bylaws comm CASA/SME 1984, 1985; mem Natl Black MBA Assoc 1985; board of directors, Indianapolis Professional Assn, 1990-. **Honors/Awds:** Consortium Fellow Grad Study in Mgmt Indiana Univ 1985-87. **Military Serv:** USMC staff sgt 1966-70; Avionics Communications/Navigation Meritorious Commendations; Vietnam Combat Air Crewman. **Business Addr:** President, Crown Consulting Group, 7934 N Richardt St, Indianapolis, IN 46256.

KING, WESLEY A.
Surgeon. **Personal:** Born Sep 25, 1923, Napoleonville, LA; son of Dr & Mrs Wesley King Sr; married Barbara Johnson; children: Robin, Wesley, Jan, Erik. **Educ:** Dillard Univ, AB 1943; Howard Univ, MD 1951. **Career:** Meharry Med Coll Inst of Surgery, surgeon 1955-57; USC Med School, assoc prof clin surgery 1974; LA Cty USC Med Ctr, attending surgeon 1967-. **Orgs:** Mem LA County Med Assn, Amer Med Assn; mem bd mgrs Crenshaw YMCA 1972; past junior warden Christ the Good Shepherd Episcopal Church; founding bd mem The Good Shepherd Manor; mem Phi Beta Sigma; fellow Amer Coll Surgeons. **Honors/Awds:** Better Businessman's Awd 1962; Certified by Amer Bd of Surgery 1958. **Military Serv:** AUS sgt 1943-46.

KING, WILLIAM CARL
Dentist. **Personal:** Born Nov 29, 1930, Albany, GA; married Rosaria Thomas; children: Sarita, Sarmora. **Educ:** Paine Coll, BA; Meharry Med Coll, DT, DDS. **Career:** Val Comm Coll, adv dentl hyg 1977; Private Practice, dentist. **Orgs:** Mem Central Dist Dental Soc, ADA, NDA, FL Med Dental Phar Assoc, FL Dental Assoc; bd of trustees Valencia Comm Coll 1971-75; treas Goodwill Ind of FL; Handicap advis bd FL; pres Handicap Wrkshp; KC first clncl dentist in Health Dept 1966-67. **Honors/Awds:** Acad of Dentstry Aw Am Soc of children 1966; Excell Schlrshp Alpha Omega Frat 1966; Schlrshp Aw Chi Delta Mu Frat 1966; Certificate of Appreciation Awd FL Dept of Educ 1977. **Military Serv:** AUS capt 1960. **Business Addr:** 809 Goldwyn, Orlando, FL 32805.

KING, WILLIAM CHARLES
Attorney. **Personal:** Born Sep 4, 1952, Pensacola, FL; son of Mr & Mrs Howard O King, Sr; married Gayle Surles King, Jan 12, 1973; children: W Charles, Kristen Noel. **Educ:** Lincoln Univ, Pennsylvania, BS, 1973; N Virginia School of Law, JD, 1984; Antioch School of Law, attended. **Career:** District of Columbia Govt, retirement examiner, 1973-82, personnel management specialist, 1982-89, general counsel, 1989-91, assistant corp. counsel, 1991-95; US Department of Housing & Urban Development, assistant general counsel, 1995-. **Orgs:** Lincoln Univ, bd of trustees, chair, evaluations committee, 1994-; National Bar Association, 1984-; Washington Bar Association, 1984-; DC Bar Association, 1984-; American Bar Association, 1984-; Blacks In Government, 1995-; Shiloh Baptist Church, 1983-. **Honors/Awds:** District of Columbia Govt, Employee of the Year, 1985. **Home Addr:** 10012 Tenbrook Dr, Silver Spring, MD 20901-2151, (301)681-6807. **Business Addr:** Assistant General Counsel, US Department of Housing & Urban Development, 451 7th St SW, Ste 10170, Washington, DC 20410-3087, (202)708-3087.

KING, WILLIAM FRANK
Chemist, personnel administrator. **Personal:** Born Dec 13, 1938, Bluffton, GA; son of Eulalia Bankston King and Marcellus King; married S V Edwards Debourg (divorced 1971); children: William Jr, Kristina N; children: Julian, Isaac, Jason (stepson). **Educ:** Lincoln University, BA, chemistry, 1961; Fisk University, MA, organic chemistry, 1963; Utah State University, PhD, organic chemistry, 1972. **Career:** Atomic Energy Commission, Oak Ridge TN, New Brunswick NJ, tech intern, chemist, 1963-67; University of Utah, Salt Lake City, faculty, intern, post doctoral fellow, 1972-73; University of North Florida, Chemistry Dept, asst professor, 1973-75; Chevron Chemical Co, Richmond CA, sr research chemist, 1975-90; Chevron Resear ch & Technology Co, Richmond CA, human resources representative, 1990; Chevron Corp, San Francisco CA, human resources representative, 1990-92; Chevron Chemical Co, Oronite Technology Division, Additive Synthesis & Processing, sr research chemist, 1992-; College of Marin, chemistry instructor, currently. **Orgs:** Natl Organization for Professional Advancement of Black Chemists & Chemical Engineers; American Chemical Society; NAACP; AABE; American Assn of Blacks in Energy; ACLU, Marin County CA; Concerned Parents of Novato; Novato Community Hospital, bd of trustees, 1993-. **Honors/Awds:** Thirty US and foreign Patents, Chevron Corp, 1980-88; NIH Research Assistantships, Fisk University, 1962, University of Utah, 1968; NSF, Summer Post Doctoral Fellow, University of Utah, 1975; Martin Luther King Fellowship, Utah State University, 1972. **Home Addr:** 1205 Lynwood Dr, Novato, CA 94947. **Business Addr:** Sr Research Chemist, Chevron Chemical Co, Oronite Technology Div, 100 Chevron Way, Bldg 71, Rm 7540, Richmond, CA 94802-0627.

KING, WILLIAM J.
Clergyman, educator. **Personal:** Born Jul 21, 1921, Selma, AL; son of Lillian King and Joseph King; married Clarice Robinson King, Aug 15, 1952; children: Judy Thornton, Eric King, James King. **Educ:** Talladega Coll, AB 1943; Howard Univ School of Religion, MDiv 1946; Eden Theological Seminary, exchange student from Howard Univ 1946; Chapman College, Family Therapy Institute of Marin. **Career:** Shiloh Baptist Church, pastor; private practice, licensed counselor; Third Baptist Church, pastor 1946-51; Antioch Progressive Church, interim pastor; Trinity Missionary Baptist Church, interim pastor; Solano Community College, faculty, currently. **Orgs:** Progressive National Baptist Convention; Amer Assn of Marriage & Family Counselors; CA State Assn of Marriage Counselors; mem Natl Alliance for Family Life Inc; Alpha Phi Alpha Fraterity; NAACP. **Military Serv:** US Air Force, chaplain, Col, 1951-73.

KING, WILLIAM L.
Minister. **Personal:** Born Jun 15, 1933, Jacksonville, FL; son of Ellawese Jackson King and Theodore King, Jr; divorced; children: Kendall, Theodore, III, Kyleen. **Educ:** Rutgers Univ, New Brunswick NJ, AB, 1972; Lutheran Theological Seminary, Philadelphia PA, MA, 1984, MA Div, 1985; Lancaster Theological Seminary, Lancaster PA, DMin, 1989. **Career:** Mt Calvary Baptist Church, Camden NJ, asst minister, 1963-64; Shiloh Baptist Church, Bordentown NJ, minister, 1965-73; NJ Dept of Labor, Camden NJ, counselor, 1967-89; Calvary United Church of Christ, Philadelphia PA, minister, 1974-. **Orgs:** Pres, Young Peoples Dept, pres, parent body, New Light Missionary Baptist Union; pres Baptist Training Union, Bethany Baptist Assn; sec/treasurer, United B lack Christian United Church of Christ; pres, Camden County Branch NAACP; sec, NJ State Conference NAACP Branches; mem, bd of dir, Urban League of PA; mem, bd of dir, UNCF bd of dir; chairman, bd of dir, OIC, Southern NJ; secretary, board of directors, Big Brothers/Big Sisters of Camden CO, 1989-91; member, board of directors, United Way of Southern New Jersey, 1989-91; member, Howard W Brown Y's Men, Camden YMCA, 1988-91. **Honors/Awds:** US Wiggins Presidential Award, NAACP, 1984; Outstanding Membership Award, NAACP, 1988; Award of Appreciation, NAACP, 1989; Citation NJ State Senate, 1989; Citation NJ General Assembly, 1989; Distinguished Leadership Award, UNCF, 1989. **Military Serv:** US Army, PFC, 1953-56. **Home Addr:** 3041 Mickle Street, Camden, NJ 08105.

KING, WILLIAM MOSES
Physician. **Personal:** Born Jul 13, 1927, Philadelphia, PA; children: Renee Delores, William Michael, Eric William. **Educ:** Univ of MI, BS1952; PA Coll Osteopathic Med, DO 1962. **Career:** Gemedco Family Med Ctr, physician; Nat Heart, biochemist. **Orgs:** Mem AOA 1964-; mem PA Osteo Assn 1964-; mem Philadelphia Osteo Assn 1964-; mem NAACP; mem Alpha Phi Alpha. **Honors/Awds:** Army Commendation Ribbon AUS 1947-48; Honor Soc Phi Eta Sigma MI Univ 1949; Honor Soc Phi Kappa Phi MI Univ 1952; Honor Soc Phi Beta Kappa MI Univ 1952. **Military Serv:** AUS tech 4 3yrs. **Business Addr:** Gemedco Family Med Center, 5801 Chew Avenue, Philadelphia, PA 19138.

KING, WOODIE, JR.
Film/play producer, director. **Personal:** Born Jul 27, 1937, Alabama; son of Ruby and Woodie King; married Willie Mae, Nov 4, 1959; children: Michelle, Woodie Geoffrey, Michael. **Educ:** Will-O-Way Sch of Theater, grad. **Career:** Detroit Tribune, drama critic 1959-62; Concept E Theatre Detroit, founder, mgr, and director, 1960-63; Mobiliz for Youth, cultural arts dir 1965-70; Henry Street's New Federal Theatre of NY, founder/dir, 1970-; Woodie King Assn, pres; Natl Black Touring Circuit, founder and producer. **Orgs:** Natl Theatre Conf; Soc of Stage Dirs & Choreographers; Audelco; Theatre Communications Group; Assn for Study of Negro Life & History; Black Filmmakers Found; Directors Guild of America. **Honors/Awds:** John Hay Whitney Fellowship for directing 1965-66; Ford Found Grant for filmmaking; Theatre Award, NAACP; Audelco Award for best dir; dir of 35 plays; producer of more than 20 plays; dir & co-producer of film, The Long Night, 1976; author or co-author of 6 screenplays; author, Black Theatre: Present Condition, 1982; author of feature articles in magazines; editor of 5 books of plays, short stories & poems. **Home Addr:** 417 Convent Ave, New York, NY 10031.

KING, YOLANDA D.
Actress, producer, educator, lecturer. **Personal:** Born Nov 17, 1955, Montgomery, AL; daughter of Martin Luther King, Jr and Coretta Scott King. **Career:** Higher Ground Productions, pres, currently; Fordham Univ, Theatre Dept, visiting prof. **Orgs:** Lecturer on civil rights, politics, and the arts before various organizations. **Honors/Awds:** Numerous awards, honors, and citations from community organizations, educational, and religious institutions throughout the country. **Special Achievements:** Theatrical credits include: The Owl and the Pussycat, 1971; Funny House of a Negro, Five on the Black Hand Side, The Amen Corner, Willie & Esther, 1993, Trippin: A Journey Home, 1995; television credits include: King, 1978; America's Dream, 1995; Ghosts of Mississippi, 1996; creator of multimedia work Tracks: A Celebration of the Words and Spirit of Dr Martin Luther King, Jr, 1992; Achieving the Dream, 1996. **Business Addr:** PO Box 92446, Atlanta, GA 30314.

KINGDOM, ROGER
Athlete. **Personal:** Born Aug 26, 1962, Vienna, GA. **Educ:** University of Pittsburgh. **Career:** Track and field hurdler. **Orgs:** New Image Track Club. **Honors/Awds:** Olympic Games, gold medal, 110-meter hurdles, 1984, 1988. **Special Achievements:** Set Olympic records in 110-meter hurdles, 1984, 1988; set world record, 110-meter hurdles, 1989. **Business Addr:** Member, 1984, 1988 Teams, US Olympic Committee, 1 Olympic Plaza, Colorado Springs, CO 80909, (719)632-5551.

KING-HAMMOND, LESLIE
Educational administrator, art historian/critic. **Personal:** Born Aug 4, 1944, Bronx, NY; daughter of Evelyne King and Oliver King; divorced; children: Rassaan-Jamil. **Educ:** Queens College CUNY, BA 1969; Johns Hopkins Univ, MA 1973, PhD 1975. **Career:** Performing Arts Workshops of Queens, New York, NY, chair dept of art, 1969-71; HARYOU-ACT, Inc, Harlem, NY, program writer, 1971; MD Institute, College of Art, lecturer 1973-, dean of grad studies 1976-; Corcoran School of Art, lecturer 1977, visiting faculty 1982; Howard Univ, Dept of African Studies, doctoral supervisor, 1977-81; Civic Design Commission Baltimore City, commissioner 1983-87; Afro-Amer Historical & Cultural Museum, art consultant, 1990-96; Philip Morris Scholarships for Artists of Color, project director, 1985-. **Orgs:** Panelist, Natl Endowment for the Humanities 1978-80; panelist Natl Endowment for the Arts 1980-82; mem bd Baltimore School for the Arts 1984-; mem, Natl Conf of Artist; College Art Association; mem bd Community

Foundation of Greater Baltimore 1984-87; consult MD Arts Council 1985-; mem bd Art Commission, Baltimore City, Office of the Mayor, 1988; bd of drs, CAA, 1991-99, pres, 1996-98; bd, Alvin Ailey Dance Theatre Found of Maryland, 1990-93; bd of overseers, School for the Arts, Baltimore, 1996-99. **Honors/Awds:** Horizon Fellowship, 1969-73; Kress Fellowship, John Hopkins Univ, 1974-75; Guest curator, Montage of Dreams Deferred, Baltimore Museum of Art 1979; published Celebrations: Myth & Ritual in Afro-American Art, Studio Museum in Harlem, 1982; Mellon Grant for Faculty Research, MD Institute, College of Art, 1984; guest curator, The Intuitive Eye, MD Art Place 1985; Trustee Award for Excellence in Teaching 1986; co curator, Woman of the Year 1986, Women's Art Caucus, 1986; Mellon Grant for faculty research, 1987; curator, 18 Visions/Divisions, Eubie Blake Cultural Center and Museum, 1988; co curator, Art as a Verb: The Evolving Continuum, 1988; curator, Black Printmakers and the WPA, Lehman Gallery of Art, 1989; coordinated Hale Woodruff Biennial, Studio Museum in Harlem, 1989; Masters, Makers and Inventors, Artscape, 1992; MCAC, 1992; Tom Miller Retrospective, Baltimore Museum of Art & Maryland Art Place, 1995; Hale Woodruff Biennale, Studio Museum in Harlem, 1994; Co-curator, Three Generations of African-American Women Sculptors, African-American Historial and Cultural Museum, Philadelphia, Equitable Gallery, NY, The Smithsonian, 1996-98; Exhibiting Artist, Artist-Scholar: In Search of A Balance, Ctr for African American History & Culture; The Smithsonian, 1997. **Business Addr:** Dean of Graduate Studies, Maryland Inst Coll of Art, 1300 W Mt Royal Ave, Baltimore, MD 21217, (410)225-2306.

KINGI, HENRY MASAO
Stuntman, actor. **Personal:** Born Dec 2, 1943, Los Angeles, CA; son of Henriella Dunn Wilkins-Washington and Masao D Kingi; children: Henry Jr, Deanne, Dorian, Alex. **Career:** Stuntman, actor, model. **Orgs:** Mem bd dirs founder Black Fashion Mag "Elegant" 1963; mgr 1st major Black Pvt Key Club Maverick's Flat, CA; Organizer mem The Coalition of Black Stuntman's Assn Hollywood; sec mem Soc 10th Cavalry Buffalo Soldiers; NAACP chmn Labor & Industry Com co-chmn Motion Picture Com; PUSH; CORE Worked with Image. **Honors/Awds:** Awards to get Blacks in motion pictures; Image Award 10th Cavalry Cowboy Hall Fame; Image Award Black Stuntman's Assn; stunt award, Most Spectacular Sequence, "To Live and Die in LA," Stuntman Award Show, 1986. **Business Addr:** Stuntman, PO Box 8861, Universal City, CA 91618, (213)462-2301.

KINLOCH, JEROME
Community developer. **Personal:** Born Mar 28, 1943, Charleston, SC. **Educ:** College of Charleston, broadcasting school. **Career:** Community developer, currently. **Orgs:** Charleston Council, Shaws Boy Club; Grassroot Coalition; Natl Black Social Workers; Charleston Industrial Education Bd; Committee Against Racism & Political Repression; Charleston Lib Pty. **Honors/Awds:** Award for Political Action, Mu Alpha 1976; Outstanding Young Man, CIEC. **Business Addr:** Community Developer, 86 Drake St, Charleston, SC 29403.

KINNAIRD, MICHAEL LEON
Educational administrator. **Personal:** Born Jul 12, 1945, Indiana; son of Thelma Renfroe; children: Eric Michael. **Educ:** Scottsbluff Coll, AA 1967; Chadron State Coll, BS Educ 1969; No AZ U, MA 1973. **Career:** Opportunity Sch Clark Co Sch Dist, prin 1977-81; Jim Bridger Jr H Clark Co Sch Dist, asst prin 1973-78, admin asst 1972-73, dean 1971-72, tchr 1970-71; Clark County School Dist, Las Vegas, NV, Secondary Principal 1981-; Brinley MS, 1981-92; Area Technical Trade Center, 1993-94; Advanced Technologies Academy, 1994-. **Orgs:** Treas PDK Chap 1113 1979-80; pres Clark Co Assn of Sch Adminstrn 1977-78; treas Clark Co Secondary Prin Assn 1976-77; mem Phi Delta Kappa Chap 1113 1974; mem Nat Assn of Secondary Prin 1973. **Honors/Awds:** Appreciation for Continued Support Am Afro Unity Festival Las Vegas, NV 1978; Nevada Secondary Principal of the Year, 1996. **Business Addr:** Advanced Technologies Academy, 2501 Vegas Dr, Las Vegas, NV 89106.

KINNEBREW, LARRY D.
Professional football player. **Personal:** Born Jun 11, 1960, Rome, GA. **Educ:** Tennessee State Univ, attended. **Career:** Cincinnati Bengals, 1983-87; Buffalo Bills, fullback, 1989-. **Business Addr:** Professional Football Player, Buffalo Bills, One Bills Dr, Orchard Park, NY 14127-2296.

KINNIEBREW, ROBERT LEE
Real estate company executive. **Personal:** Born Feb 13, 1942, Manhattan, NY; son of Daisy Crawford Cobb and Covton Kinniebrew; married Raymona D Radford, Nov 30, 1963; children: Robertina, Rolanzo. **Educ:** Acad of Aeron NY; Commun School AUS; Non-Commiss Officers Acad Bad Toelz West Germany; Officers Candidate School Commiss Second Lt Artillery Ft Sill OK; Ins Underwriter's School PA; MW Funk Sales Inst Real Estate NJ; South Jersey Realty Abstract Sales School NJ; Grad Realtors Inst NJ; Natl Assoc of Independent Fee Appraisers NJ; Mgmt Devel Course Washington DC. **Career:** Veterans Admin, mgmt broker; Fed Housing Admin, mgmt broker; Vet Admin, appraiser; Mutural of NY Ins Co, dir sales underwriter; Protect A Life Burglar Alarm Co, dir sales; jewelry store chain, dir sales; Gen Sound in Philadelphia, customer relations mgr; Westinghouse, mgr lighting dept; Fort Dix NJ, post signal, oper & commanding officer; Fort Bliss TX & Viet-Nam, battalion commun officer; AUS West Germany, pole lineman, fixed station transmitter repairman 1963-65; Lockheed Aircraft Co Idlewild Airport, flight line mechanic; Century 21 Candid Realty Inc, pres 1972-. **Orgs:** Mem Edgewater Park Jaycees, Burlington Cty Draft Bd, Burlington Cty Chamber of Commerce, Masonic Lodge, Century 21 Brokers' Council of South Jersey, Beverly Rotary Club, Boy Scouts of Amer, Make Amer Better Comm, Natl Assn of Realtors; bd mem, chap chmn, exec comm, chmn, Burlington Cty Red Cross; rep Century 21 Natl Brokers' Commun Congress; pres, dir Burlington Cty Bd of Realtors; dir NJ State Bd of Realtors; legal action comm, Natl Assn of Realtors; nominating comm, equal opportunity comm, library comm, legal action comm, New Jersey Assn of Realtors. **Honors/Awds:** Community Serv Awd Burlington Cty Bd of Realtors 1983; Realtor of the Year Awd NJ State Assoc of Realtors 1983. **Military Serv:** Comm Chf 101st Airbn Div 327th Battle Grp; 10th Spec Forces Bad Toelz, Germ 1962; Comm 2nd Lt Battal Comm Ofcr 1st Battal 44th Artillery Ft Bliss. **Business Addr:** Pres, Century 21 Candid Realty Inc, Route 130, South Edgewater Park, PO Box 567, Beverly, NJ 08010.

KINSEY, BERNARD
Company executive. **Personal:** chilDren: Khalil. **Career:** Xerox Corporation, beginning 1971, regional general manager, Los Angeles, beginning 1983, vice president voice systems division, currently.

KINSEY, JIM
Professional sports official. **Career:** NBA, referee, currently. **Business Addr:** NBA Official, National Basketball Association, 645 5th Ave, 15th Fl, New York, NY 10022-5986.

KIRBY, JACQUELINE
Physician. **Personal:** Born Dec 17, 1946, Atlanta, GA; married Edward G Helm; children: Lisa. **Educ:** Spelman Coll, BA 1968; Meharry Med Coll, MD 1973. **Career:** Emory Univ Affiliated Hosps, fellow rheumatology 1977-, internal med 1974-76, med internship 1973-74; externship 1972; Harvard U, rsrch & fellow 1971; Crawford W Long Hosp, emergency room physician 1976-77. **Orgs:** Mem YWCA 1973; asso mem Am Coll of Physicians. **Honors/Awds:** Research Fellow Harvard Univ 1971; honor Dept of Pharmcacology 1971; fellow Emory Univ 1977.

KIRBY, MONEY ALIAN
Clergyman, author. **Personal:** Born Aug 8, 1914, Biscoe, AR; married Ann Ida Wall; children: Mattye Jo Willis, Ollie L, Scott. **Educ:** Philander Smith Coll, BA Mus 1950; So Univ Baton Rouge, La, Spec-Std-M Us 1953; UAPB Pine Bluff, AR Spec Std-Media 1968; SAU Magnolia AR 1965-84. **Career:** S AR-Conf CME Chch, exec-secty 1974-84; Foster High Schl Lewisville AR, bnd dir 1960-64; Walker High Schl Magnolia AR, bnd-soc stds 1965-84; author: "Seven Great Attributes of God", "Dr Jesus Christ and the Sick World", "Perspectives of an African-American Indian", "Arkansas At A Glance", "A 20th Century Book of Proverbs". **Orgs:** Pres Columbia-cty Techers Assoc 1966; dir Evangelism CME Church So-conf 1980-82; Special Edu Teachers AEA 1983-84; dir Socials-Concern-CME Ch-So-AR Conf 1983-85; pres Walker Schl Dist "AEA Techr" 1982-84; pres Philander Smith Coll "Magnolia Alumni" 1980-85; pres Columbia Cty NAACP 1985-. **Honors/Awds:** Special recog awd NEA-PAC Fundg 1981-82; outstndg cont ed, 1984; awd Peake High Schl Classes 1957-59; outstndg teach serv awd Walker Schl Brd and admin, 1984. **Military Serv:** USNA duty corp T-5 4-7 mo; Good-Conduct, Sharp Shooter, Service Strips 1941-45. **Home Addr:** 615 Gantt St, Magnolia, AR 71753. **Business Addr:** Social Services Consultant, Southern Conference CME Church, 615 Gantt St, Magnolia, AR 71753.

KIRBY, NANCY J.
Educational administrator. **Personal:** Born Apr 20, 1940, Haddonfield, NJ. **Educ:** Bennett Coll, BA Psych 1960; Bryn Mawr Coll, MSS 1965. **Career:** Temple Univ Med Ctr, chief social worker outpatient medicine 1966-69; Planned Parenthood of SE PA, dir of soc serv 1969-71; Beaver Coll, asst prof 1971-79; Bryn Mawr Coll, asst dean, dir of admissions 1979-. **Orgs:** Bd of dirs Planned Parenthood of SEPA 1974-78; bd of dirs Family Planning Council of SEPA 1979-85; bd of dirs Spectrum Health Serv 1978-; bd of dir Natl Assn of Social Workers (PA Chapt) 1986-91. **Business Addr:** Asst Dean, Director of Admission, Bryn Mawr College, Graduate School Of Social Work, & Social Research, Bryn Mawr, PA 19010.

KIRBY, TERRY GAYLE
Professional football player. **Personal:** Born Jan 20, 1970, Hampton, VA. **Educ:** University of Virginia, bachelor's degree in psychology. **Career:** Miami Dolphins, running back, 1993-95; San Francisco 49ers, 1996-. **Business Addr:** Professional Football Player, San Francisco 49ers, 4949 Centennial Blvd, Santa Clara, CA 95054, (415)562-4949.

KIRBY-DAVIS, MONTANGES (TAN)
President, human resources/strategic diversity consulting firm. **Personal:** Born Jan 6, 1953, Wadesboro, NC; daughter of Minnie Allen Kirby and Archie William Kirby (deceased). **Educ:** Winston-Salem State University, Winston-Salem, NC, BA, sociology, 1975. **Career:** Sara Lee, Winston-Salem, NC, personnel specialist, 1978-83, mgr, management employment, 1983-88; American Society for Personnel Administration, certified trainer, accredited personnel specialist in recruiting; Sara Lee Products, Winston-Salem, NC, mgr, training & development, 1988-91, dir of workforce diversity, 1991-97; The Kirby Resource Group, pres, 1997-. **Orgs:** Member, American Society for Training and Development; co-chair, First Piedmont Triad Professional Development Conference for Women, 1990-; chairman, United Way Training & Development Committee, 1990-91; pres, Forsyth County YWCA, 1982-83; board of directors, Winston-Salem Personnel Assn, 1980-85; board of directors, Battered Women's Shelter, 1980-85; board of directors, YWCA, 1980-85; NC Governor's Commission on Workforce Preparedness, 1994; Winston Salem State Univ, bd of trustees, 1994. **Honors/Awds:** Winston-Salem Leadership; featured, 1991, Women Who Make a Difference, published article, 1990, Minorities & Women Magazine; Outstanding Woman Achiever Award, Professional Business Women, 1982; Cooperative Ed Individual Leadership Award, Winston-Salem University, 1984; YWCA Volunteer Leadership Award, 1993; Leadership America, 1996. **Business Addr:** President, The Kirby Resource Group, 535 North Pleasantburg Dr, Ste 202, Greenville, SC 29607, (864)241-9900.

KIRCHHOFER, WILMA ARDINE LYGHTNER
Beverage company executive. **Personal:** Born Sep 30, 1940, Mason City, IA; daughter of Tressie Traylor Lyghtner and William Lyghtner; married Kirk Kirchhofer (divorced 1974); children: Gregory Luther, Douglas Bernard. **Educ:** Iowa State Univ, Ames, IA, BS, 1963; Emory Univ, Atlanta, GA, MPH, 1977; University Missouri, Columbia, MO, PhD, 1986. **Career:** Georgia State Univ, Atlanta, GA, assistant professor, 1977-81; Univ Missouri, Columbia, MO, assistant professor, 1984-86; Lincoln Univ, Jefferson City, MO, assistant professor, 1982-86; Ross Laboratories, Columbus, OH, associate director medical education, 1986-87; Coca-Cola Co, Atlanta, GA, manager, health promotion, 1987-. **Orgs:** Chair, Public Relation Atlanta Dietetic Association, 1989-91; editor, Newsletter Georgia Nutrition Council, 1989-91; member, board, Georgia Partners of Americas, 1988-91. **Honors/Awds:** Leadership Atlanta Class, 1991. **Business Addr:** Mgr, Health Promotion, Coca-Cola Company, PO Drawer 1734, Atlanta, GA 30301.

KIRK, LEROY W.
Real estate company executive. **Personal:** Born Apr 12, 1924, Tulsa, OK; son of Mary Payne and Leroy W Kirk Sr; married Annie M Brown; children: Leroy W III, Annette. **Educ:** Langston Univ, BS 1948; Univ IL, MS 1949. **Career:** Moton HS, principal 1949-50; Ponca City, math dept head 1950-53; Dunbar Jr HS, principal 1953-56; Tinker AFB, computer programmer/system analyst 1956-67, discrimination complaints officer 1967-82; State Bd Corrections, sec 1971-79, pres 1985-87, member 1971-91; Real Estate Rentals 1982-. **Orgs:** Oklahoma City Human Rights Commission, 1992-96; Pres OK City Urban League 1978-81; active Local Boy Scouts of Amer; deacon St John Baptist Church; life mem NAACP; life mem Langston Univ Alumni Assn, YMCA, Langston Univ Boosters Club. **Honors/Awds:** Outstanding Performance Awards 1967, 1976; Achievement Awards Kappa Alpha Psi Fraternity; chief EEO couns Dept Air Force 1979-82; OK Fed Employee of the Year 1982; Testimonial Dinner, 1991. **Military Serv:** USN 1943-46. **Home Addr:** 5717 N Everett Ave, Oklahoma City, OK 73111-6731.

KIRK, ORVILLE
Educator. **Personal:** Born Mar 5, 1936, St Louis, MO; married Joyce; children: Orville Jr, Gerald, Ronald. **Educ:** Wiley Coll, BA 1953-57; Harris Tchrs Coll, MO elem cert 1965; St Louis U, MO Spl Educ Cert 1967, MEd 1970, post masters work educ splst degree 1972, resident student 1973, supt cert 1973-. **Career:** MO Dept of Elementary & Secondary Educ, supvr Title I ESEA 1976-, speciall educ consult 1972-76; Univ of MO, rsch tech 1971-72; St Louis Baby Study Project CEMREL, resch tech 1968-71; St Louis Public School Sys, tchr 1961-72; Urban Behav Rsch Asso, consult 1973-77; Acad of Urban Serv, consultant 1973-77. **Orgs:** Pres Chap 103 Counc for Except Children 1975-76; mem Counc of Admnstr of Spl Edn; mem Counc of Children with Behav Disorders; mem Counc for Execpt Children; bd of dir The Annie Malone Children's Home; mem Counc of Mental Retardation CEC-MR. **Military Serv:** AUS spec 4 c 1959-61. **Business Addr:** PO Box 480, Jefferson City, MO.

KIRK, RON
City official. **Personal:** Born in Austin, TX; married Matrice Ellis Kirk; children: Elizabeth Alexandra, Catherine Victoria. **Educ:** Austin Coll, BA, political science/sociology, 1976; University of Texas School of Law, JD, 1979. **Career:** US Senator Lloyd Bentsen, legislative asst, 1981-93; City of Dallas, asst city attorney and chief lobbyist, 1983-89; Johnson & Gibbs PC, shareholder, 1989-94; State of Texas, 98th secretary of state,

1994-95; Gardere & Wynne, LLP, partner; City of Dallas, mayor, 1995-. **Orgs:** General Services Commission of Texas, 1992-94, chairman, 1993; Dallas Zoological Society, pres, 1992-94; Dallas Assembly, 1990-; Leadership Dallas Alumni Assn, 1986-; Austin Coll Bd of Trustees, 1991-; Museum of African American Life and Culture, 1991-; State Fair of Texas Bd, 1993-; Cotton Bowl Athletic Assn, 1991-; State Bar of Texas; American Bar Assn; Natl Bar Assn; J L Turner Legal Assn. **Honors/Awds:** J L Turner Legal Assn, C B Bunkley Community Service Award, 1994; Omega Psi Phi Fraternity, Citizen of the Year, 1994; Big Brothers/Big Sisters of Metropolitan Dallas, Volunteer of the Year Award, 1992; Austin Coll Alumni Assn, Distinguished Alumni Award, 1992. **Special Achievements:** First African American mayor of city of Dallas; first African American mayor of any big city in Texas. **Business Addr:** Mayor, City of Dallas, Mayor's Office, 1500 Marilla, Rm 5E North, Dallas, TX 75201, (214)670-4054.

KIRK, SARAH VIRGO
Educator, social worker. **Personal:** Born Oct 19, 1934, Kingston, Jamaica; daughter of Velmon Eaton Virgo and David Clarke Virgo; married Dr Wyatt Douglass Kirk. **Educ:** St Augustines Coll Raleigh NC, BA 1955; Atlanta Univ School of Social Work, MSW 1957; Univ of Pittsburgh School of Public Health, MPH, 1972; Univ of Pittsburgh School of Social Work, PhD Social Work 1975. **Career:** Meml Hospital Univ of North Carolina, med soc worker 1957-60; Johns Hopkins Hosp, med soc worker 1960-63; Public Health Grant, rsch team mem 1964-66; Dept of Public Welfare Work Training Ctr, soc work supv 1967, soc work supv public health adolescent program 1967, chief soc worker orthopedic prog 1968; Howard Univ School of Soc Work, asst prof 1969-71; School of Work Univ of Pennsylvania instr 1972-74; Three Rivers Youth, rsch asst 1975; School of Soc Work Virginia Commonwealth Univ, asst prof 1975-77; Western Michigan Univ School of Soc Work, asst prof 1977-78; North Carolina A&T State Univ, assoc prof, field coord 1978-79, prof social work, chairperson Dept of Sociology & Social Work 1982-. **Orgs:** Triad Assoc of Human Serv 1978-84; chairperson North Carolina Council on Social Work Education 1983-84; mem Womens Professional Forum 1986-; bd mem Family Life Council Greensboro North Carolina 1986-87; bd mem Commiss on the Status of Women; chair Guelford County DSS Bd; Women Improving Race Relations, founder, 1990-. **Honors/Awds:** Inducted into Departments Hall of Fame 1989. **Special Achievements:** Co-editor, "Student Athletes: Shattering The Myths and Sharing the Realities," with Dr. Wyatt Kirk,1993; co-author "Counseling, Black Family Involvement," Journal of Elementary School Guidance and Counseling, with Dr. Wyatt Kirk, 1981. **Business Addr:** Director Joint MSW, NC A&T State Univ, Dept of Sociology, Social Wrk, 1601 E Market St, Greensboro, NC 27401-3209.

KIRK-DUGGAN, CHERYL ANN
Cleric, musician, educator. **Personal:** Born Jul 24, 1951, Lake Charles, LA; daughter of Naomi Ruth Mosely Kirk (deceased) and Rudolph Valentino Kirk (deceased); married Michael Allan Kirk-Duggan, Jan 1, 1983. **Educ:** University of Southwestern Louisiana, BA 1973; University of Texas at Austin, MM 1977; Austin Presbyterian Theological Seminary, MDiv 1987; Baylor University, PhD, 1992. **Career:** Univ of Texas at Austin, music of Black Amers coach accomp 1974-77; Austin Community College, music of Black Amers 1976-77; Prairie View A&M Univ, teacher 1977-78; The Actor's Inst, teacher 1982-83; Williams Inst CME Church, organist, choir dir 1979-83; Self-employed, professional singer, voice teacher, vocal coach 1980-85; Christian Methodist Church, ordained minister, deacons orders 1984, elders orders 1986; Baylor University, Institute of Oral History, graduate asst, 1987-89, Dept of Religion, teaching asst, 1989-90; Meredith College, assistant professor, 1993-96; Center for Women & Religion, dir, Graduate Theological Union, asst prof, 1997-; Editorial Bd, Contagion: Journal of Violence, Mimesis & Culture, 1994-; Assn for Black Awareness, Meredith College, advisor, 1994-. **Orgs:** Pi Kappa Lambda, 1976-; Omicron Delta Kappa, 1977-; associate pastor, Trinity CME Church, 1985-86; president, Racial Ethnic Faith Comm, Austin Seminary, 1986-87; Golden Key Honor Society, 1990; Colloquim On Violence & Religion; Society of Biblical Literature; American Academy of Religion; Center for Black Music Research; Society of Chritian Ethics; American Society for Aesthetics; Sigma Alpha Iota. **Honors/Awds:** University of Southwestern Louisiana, Magna Cum Laude; University of Texas at Austin, University Fellowship, 1975-77; Fund for Theological Education, Fellowship for Doctoral Studies, 1987-88, 1988-89. **Special Achievements:** Carnegie Hall debut, 1981; featured: "Life, Black Tress, Das Goldene Blatte, Bunte," 1981, 1982; recording: "Third Duke Ellington Sacred Concert," Virgil Thompson's Four Saints in Three Acts, EMI Records, 1981-82; author: Lily Teaching Fellow, 1995, 1996; Collidge Scholar with Assoc for Religion & Intellectual Life, 1996; "African-American Spirituals: Exorcising Evil Through Song," A Troubling in My Soul: Womanist Perspectives on Evil and Suffering, Orbis Press, 1991; "Gender, Violence and Transformation," Curing Violence: The Thought of Rene Girard, Polebridge Press, 1991; African-American Special Days: 15 Complete Worship Services, Abingdon Press, 1996; It's In the Blood: A Trildgy of Poetry Harvested from a Family Tree, River Vision, 1996; Exorcizing Evil: A Womanist Perspective on the Spirituals, Orbis, 1997. **Business Addr:** Director, Center for Women, Religion, Graduate Theological Union, 2400 Ridge Rd, Berkeley, CA 94709-5298, (510)649-2490.

KIRKENDOLL, CHESTER ARTHUR, II
Cleric (retired). **Personal:** Born Jun 3, 1914, Searcy, AR; son of Mattie Wyatt Kirkendoll and Chester Arthur Kirkendoll; married Alice Elizabeth Singleton; children: Chester Arthur III, Loretta Jean, Leland Kapel. **Educ:** Lane Coll, BA 1938; Northwestern Univ Evanston IL, MA 1941; TX Coll Tyler, LittD 1957; St Andrews Seminary London England, DD 1962; MS Industrial Coll, DD 1971; Lane Coll Jackson, LHD 1972; Interdenominational Theol Ctr, DD 1982; Miles Coll, Hon Doctorate 1984. **Career:** Natl Youth Work CME Church, dir 1935-40; Natl Leadership Training School, dir, assoc ed church school publ 1940-50; Lane Coll, pres 1950-70; Christian Methodist Episcopal Church, bishop, 1970-86, sr bishop 1982-86 (retired). **Orgs:** Mem, bd of dir United Negro Coll Fund Inc 1950-70; mem TN Council of Human Relations 1961-70, Jackson Comm Relations Bd 1964-70, Natl Advisory Councilon Student Aid to the US Dept of Health Ed & Welfare 1966-70, TN Higher Ed Comm 1966-70; delegate World Methodist Conf 1966,71,76,81; chmn bd of trustees Miles Coll 1970-82; delegate 5th Assembly World Council of Churches 1975; recording sec Governing Bd Natl Council of Churches 1978-81; mem 33 Degree Masonic Order 1983; mem Christian Meth Episcopal Church, Natl Assoc for the Advancement for Colored People; bd of trustees Phillips School of Theol Interdenom Theol Ctr; Natl Advisory Council Amer Bible Soc, Natl Council Birm Area Boy Scout of Amer; recording sec Natl Council of Churches of Christ; mem Central Comm WorldCouncil of Churches; n v chmn Gen Bd of Evangelism CME Church; mem Governing Bd Natl Council of Churches of Christ in Amer; mem bd of dir Birm Big Brothers of Greater Birmg Inc,Travelers Aid Soc, Volunteer Bureau of Greater Birmingham Inc. **Honors/Awds:** Community Chest Campaign Awd 1951; Man of the Year Awd Omega Psi Phi Frat 1953; Citation by Amer LFW 1953; Award of Merit The Clara Maas Found 1962, Citation by West TN Teachers Conf 1964; Col-Aide-De Camp Governor's Staff TN 1967; author of, "The Obligation of the Church in the Field of Higher Ed During the Current Revolution" 1967; Citation by City of Jackson TN 1970; Citation by State of TN as Disting Citizen 1970; Disting Serv Awd Booker T Washington Business Coll 1971; Isaac Lane Awds Lane Coll Alumni Assoc 1971; Disting Serv Awd Boy Scouts of Amer 1975; B Julian Smith Awd for Disting Serv in Christian Ed 1976; Beaver Awd Boy Scouts of Amer 1980. **Home Addr:** 10 Hurtland, Jackson, TN 38305.

KIRKLAND, GWENDOLYN VICKYE
Financial industry executive. **Personal:** Born Apr 24, 1951, Chicago, IL; daughter of Warren & Gwendolyn Smith Kirkland. **Educ:** Bradley University, BS, 1972; DePaul University, MEd, 1976. **Career:** Chicago Public Schools, teacher-primary grades, 1972-80; AJ Nystron Inc, sales rep, 1980-82; Dean Witter Reynolds, assoc vice pres, investments, 1983-90; The Chapman Company, branch mgr, 1990-94; American Investment Services, Inc, CFP/investment broker & branch mgr, 1994-. **Orgs:** Delta Sigma Theta, 1971-; National Assoc of Security Professionals, past vice pres, 1985-; Village West Grauhomes Assn, pres, 1987-92; South Suburban Family Shelter, bd of dirs, 1989-91. **Special Achievements:** Black Enterprise Networking, Financial Forum Spokesperson, 1986; Dean Witter Reynolds, Natl Campaign Rep, 1986. **Business Addr:** Branch Manager, American Investment Services Inc, 600 Holiday Plaza Dr, Ste 236, Matteson, IL 60443, (708)481-8787.

KIRKLAND, JACK A.
Educator. **Personal:** Born Oct 28, 1931, Blythedale, PA; son of Anna Mae Kirkland and Aaron Kirkland; married Iris; children: Jack Jr, Adrianne, Kelly. **Educ:** Syracuse Univ, BA 1959; Syracuse Univ, MSS 1961. **Career:** Peace Corps, Training for Community Development, Honduras, dir, 1964-67; St Louis University, Social Group Work Program, chair, 1964-70; Washington University, assoc prof, social work, 1970-, dir, co-founder, African-American studies, 1974-76; State of Missouri, dir of transportation, 1976-78; Washington University, Economic Development Concentration, School of Social Work, founder, 1980-89. **Orgs:** Phi Delta Kappa End Honorary Soc. **Honors/Awds:** Educator of the Year, Omicron Eta Omega, Alpha Phi Alpha, 1992. **Special Achievements:** National consultant in Multicultural Education; National/International consultant in Economic Development. **Business Addr:** Assoc Prof of Social Work, Washington University, Campus Box 1196, St Louis, MO 63130.

KIRKLAND, KENNY DAVID (DOCTONE)
Musician. **Personal:** Born Sep 28, 1955, Brooklyn, NY; son of Arcadia Cannales Kirkland and Frank Kirkland. **Educ:** Manhattan School of Music, BA, 1976. **Career:** MCA Records, recording artist/studio musician; The Tonight Show, band mem, currently. **Business Addr:** Band Member, c/o NBC, The Tonight Show, 3000 W Alameda, #2104, Burbank, CA 91523, (818)840-2222.

KIRKLAND, LEVON
Professional football player. **Personal:** Born Feb 17, 1969, Lamar, SC. **Educ:** Clemson, attended. **Career:** Pittsburgh Steelers, linebacker, 1992-. **Honors/Awds:** Pro Bowl, 1996. **Business Addr:** Professional Football Player, Pittsburgh Steelers, Three Rivers Stadium, 300 Stadium Circle, Pittsburgh, PA 15212, (412)323-1200.

KIRKLAND, THEODORE
Educator. **Personal:** Born Jan 1, 1934, Camden, SC; married Winona; children: Sharon, Adrianne, Cynthia. **Educ:** State Univ of NY, BA 1976; State Univ of NY at Buffalo, MS 1984. **Career:** Buffalo Police Dept, police Ofcr 1962-78; WKBW-TV, Buffalo, TV host & producer of "Kirkland & Co" 1974-78; NY State Parole Brd, comm 1978-85; Hunter College & Cora P Maloney Coll Buffalo, prof, currently. **Orgs:** Senior Editor, Buffalo Black Newspaper (Challenger) 1985; bd mem Harlem Restoration Proj 1985; brd mem NY State Civil Liberties Union 1985; mem Natl Assn of Blacks in Criminal Justice 1985; pres & fndr Afro-Amer Police Assn of Buffalo 1969-71; chrtr mem Natl Black Police Assoc 1972; fellow Buffalo State Coll Comm 1984; Host, Radio Program Kirkland's Corner WUFO Radio. **Honors/Awds:** Testimonal dinner by Concern Citizens in 1973 & 1983; published article A Black Policemans Perspective on Law Enfrcmnt 1977; more than 30 Awards & Citations between 1970 & present; Presidential Citation for Exceptional Service 1972. **Military Serv:** USAF airman first class 1952-56; United Nations Service Medal, Natl Defense Medal, Good Conduct Medal, Korean Service Medal 1952-56. **Home Addr:** 352 Pratt St, Buffalo, NY 14204. **Business Addr:** Professor, Hunter College, 68th & Lexington, Rm 1111, West Bldg, New York, NY 10021, (212)772-5035.

KIRKLAND-BRISCOE, GAIL ALICIA
Orthodontist. **Personal:** Born Apr 12, 1960, Tuskegee, AL; daughter of Mrs Mary L Pratt Kirkland and Dr Levi S Kirkland Sr. **Educ:** Vanderbilt Univ, BS (Cum Laude) 1982; Howard Univ Coll of Dentistry, DDS (class rank #1) 1986, Certificate in Orthodontics 1986-88. **Career:** Orthodontist. **Orgs:** Mem Alpha Kappa Alpha Sor 1979-; mem Alumni Assn of Student Clinicians of Amer Dental Assn 1985; mem Omicron Kappa Upsilon 1986-, Natl Dental Assn 1986-; American Assn of Orthodontics 1986-. **Honors/Awds:** Deans Award Alpha Omega Natl Soc 1986; Scholarship Award for #1 Class Rank 1986; Intl Coll of Dentists Award 1986; Harold S Fleming Memorial Award for Dental Rsch 1986; Orthodontic Award for Superior Performance in Research, Howard Univ 1988; author of Forensic Dentistry: Solving the mysteries of identification, General Dentistry, 35:120, 1987; Changing Anatomical Developments in Permanent 1st Bicuspid Teeth, Journal of Dental Research, 65 (Abstracts):188, 1986; Featured on Working Woman Television Show. **Business Addr:** 3012 18th Street, NE, Washington, DC 20018, (202)526-4060.

KIRKLAND-HOLMES, GLORIA
Educator. **Personal:** Born Aug 29, 1952, Charleston, SC. **Educ:** Fisk U, BA 1974; IN State U, MS 1975, PhD 1978. **Career:** Univ of No IA, asst prof early childhood educ & dept of tching 1978-; Rose Southside Child Care Cntr, dir 1976-78; IN State U, adj asst prof 1976-78; IN State Lab Sch, nursery tchr 1978; Maehling Terrace Day Care Cntr, dir tchr 1976; Margaret Ave Child Care Center, asst dir parent coord 1975-76. **Orgs:** Mem Nat Assn for the Educ of Young Children 1975-; mem IA Assn ofr the Educ of Young Children 1975-; chairperson sec IA NE State Conf NAACP 1979-; chairperson program com Proj headstart 1979-; mem Black Child Devel Inst 1977; bd mem Logandale Urban Housing Corp 1979-; youth adv Black Hawk Co NAACP Youth Group 1979-. **Honors/Awds:** Achievement of Knowledge Afro-Am Cultural Cntr & Black Student Union IN State Univ 1977; 10 Top Min Women in IA appointed by Gov Ray 1980; Alpha Kappa Alpha Sor Pi Chap Fisk Univ 1971. **Business Addr:** Associate Professor, Price Lab School 102, University of Northern Iowa, 1222 W 27th St, Cedar Falls, IA 50614.

KIRKLIN, PERRY WILLIAM
Scientist. **Personal:** Born Feb 28, 1935, Ellwood City, PA; son of Martha Peek Kirklin and Perry Kirklin; married Betty Jean Lampkins; children: Cheryl Hawkins, Perry Kirklin III, Pamela June. **Educ:** Westminster Coll, New Wilmington, PA, BS, 1957; Univ of Minnesota, Minneapolis, MN, PhD, 1964. **Career:** Rohm & Haas Co, analyst group leader 1964-70; Mobil Research & Dev Corp, sr research chemist 1970-78, assoc chemist 1978-91; Aviation Fuels Research Leader, 1978-91; Bloomfield College, associate professor of chemistry, 1991-95; Cheyney Univ of Pennsylvania, adjunct prof, 1996-97. **Orgs:** Adjunct Prof Bucks County Comm Coll 1976-77; chmn Amer Soc for Testing and Materials Aviation Fuel Stability 1984-91; chmn Buckes County Health Planning 1968-72; bd of dir Ph Regional Comprehensive Health Planning 1968-74; mem PA State Health Planning Council 1970-74; vice pres Salem Fed Credit Union 1972-79; bd of dirs Bucks County Comm Center 1965-74; mem Salem Baptist Church Jenkintown PA 1968-; Natl Org Black Chemists & Chem Engineers, 1979-92; pres, Salem Federal Credit Union, 1986-. **Honors/Awds:** Numerous technical articles published; numerous technical journals 1964-; PA Regional Introduction of Minorities to Engineering Award, 1988; ASTM Award of Appreciation, American Society Testing & Mtls, 1990. **Home Addr:** 1860 Hillside Rd, Southampton, PA 18966.

KIRKSEY, M. JANETTE
Purchasing administrator. **Personal:** Born Apr 15, 1946, Brownsville, PA; daughter of Johnnie L Williamson (deceased) and George A Williamson; married Edward M Kirskey, Jun 8, 1966; children: Scott M (deceased), Daniele B. **Educ:** Franklin University, BA, 1981. **Career:** Ross Laboratories, associate buyer, buyer, senior buyer, contact manager, 1996-. **Orgs:** Delta Sigma Theta; Advent United Church of Christ, financial secretary; African-American Action Alliance, vice pres; Junior Achievement, project business volunteer counselor. **Business Addr:** Contact Manager, Ross Laboratories, 625 Cleveland Ave, Columbus, OH 43215, (614)624-6692.

KIRVEN, MYTHE YUVETTE
City government administrator. **Personal:** Born Jun 12, 1956, Dallas, TX. **Educ:** TX Tech Univ, BS 1977; Atlanta Univ, MPA 1980. **Career:** City of Dallas, admin asst. **Orgs:** Mem NAACP; recording sec Delta Sigma Theta Dallas Chap 1980-84; mem Conf of Minority Public Admin 1978-; vice pres South Dallas Club Natl Assn of Negro Bus & Professional Women's Clubs 1985-; mem Urban Mgmt Assistants of N TX 1983-; mem TX City Mgmt Assn 1983-; mem Intl City Mgmt Assn 1983-. **Business Addr:** Administrative Assistant, City of Dallas, 1500 Marilla St 2BS, Dallas, TX 75201.

KIRWAN, ROBERTA CLAIRE
Journalist. **Educ:** Manhattanville College, Purchase, NY, BA, Russian; Fordham Univ Graduate School of Business, New York, NY, MBA, marketing, 1978. **Career:** Doyle Dane Bernbach, New York, NY, personnel mgr, 1972-76, assistant account executive, 1978-80; freelance photographer and market research coordinator, 1980-82, 1984-88; Merrill Lynch, New York, NY, account executive, 1982-83; freelance market research coordinator, 1984-88; Time-Warner, Money Magazine, New York, NY, staff reporter, 1989-. **Orgs:** Member, National Assn of Black Journalists, 1990-; member/secretary, Black Alumnae of Manhattanville College, 1972-80. **Business Addr:** Staff Reporter, MONEY Magazine, 1271 6th Ave, 32nd Floor, New York, NY 10020.

KISNER, ROBERT GARLAND
Physician. **Personal:** Born Jun 15, 1940, Lexington, KY; married Gloria Hinmon; children: Robert, Angela. **Educ:** Morgan State Coll, BS 1964; Meharry Med Coll, MD 1969. **Career:** Univ of Pittsburgh, asst prof 1973-; Magee Womens Hosp, resd 1973-; Family Planning Cncl of Western PA, med dir 1973-77. **Orgs:** Mem Gateway Me Grp pres 1976-; mem Keystone Med Soc; Nat Med Assn; Allegheny Co Med Soc; AMA; fellow Am Coll of Ob Gyn Civic Ser mem NAACP. **Honors/Awds:** Recpt Cultural Critique Award World Comm of Islam in the W 1977; Upjohn Achvmt Award Meharry Med Coll 1969. **Military Serv:** AUSR capt 1970-76. **Business Addr:** 211 N Whitfield St, Pittsburgh, PA 15206.

KISPERT, DOROTHY LEE
Association executive (retired). **Personal:** Born Dec 10, 1928, Detroit, MI; daughter of Pearl Priestley and Leo Priestley; married Wilson G Kispert; children: Kimberly A, Cynthia L Kispert. **Educ:** Univ of MI, BA 1950; Wayne State Univ, MA 1971. **Career:** Merrill-Palmer Inst, faculty 1975-80; Parent Child Devel Center, dir 1975-80; Parent Child Center, dir 1980-81; Parents and Children Together, dir 1981-91; Detroit Family Project, direct services coordinator 1991-94. **Orgs:** Lay rep Children's Hospital of MI 1978-88; consultant Spelman College 1979; mem/tech review panel CDA Bank St Coll 1981; pres Metro Detroit Day Care Assn. **Honors/Awds:** Publications, "PACT, A Partnership with Parents," Contemporary Parenting 1983, co-author "Teaming Social Services with Education Cooperative," Journal of Cooperative Educ 1986; 4C Child/Family Advocate Award, 1989; Detroit Assn for Infant Mental Health, Esther Dean Collard Award, 1991; WSU School of Social Work Alumni Assn, Citizen of the Year Award, 1993. **Home Addr:** 19310 Woodingham, Detroit, MI 48221.

KITCHEN, WAYNE LEROY
Educational administrator. **Personal:** Born Sep 7, 1948, Sedalia, MO; son of Imogene Nurse Kitchen and Edgar Roy Kitchen. **Educ:** Lincoln Univ, BS, business educ 1970; Univ of MO, MEd, College administration 1977. **Career:** Admissions Dept, Cogswell Coll, asst dir 1978-80; Marketing Division, St Mary's Coll, program coord 1980-82; Marketing Div, Univ of San Francisco, assoc dir 1982-84; Bay Area Urban League Training Ctr, dir 1984-85; Peralta Comm Coll Dist, educ consultant; Mills Coll, upward bound asst dir 1986-90; Cal State-Hayward, director upward bound 1990-. **Orgs:** Phi Delta Kappa 1983-; bd of dirs, Lincoln Univ Natl Alumni Assn 1984-88; pres, Lincoln Univ of MO Alumni Assn 1984-88; vice pres, Phi Beta Sigma 1984-86; chmn, Comm to elect Lloyd Vann for School Bd 1985; bd of directors, Oakland Ensemble Theatre; UNCF Inter-Alumni Council; national vice pres, Lincoln University National Alumni Association. **Honors/Awds:** President's Serv Awd, Phi Beta Sigma Frat, Alpha Nu Sigma Chap 1984; Distinguished Lincoln Univ Alumni Awd 1987; Distinguished Alumni Award, Local Chapter, Lincoln Univ 1989. **Military Serv:** US Army, E-4, 1970-72; Good Conduct Medal, Natl Defense Serv Medal, M-16SS Medal 1972. **Home Addr:** 44 Oak Hill Circle, Oakland, CA 94605. **Business Addr:** Director, Upward Bound, Cal State Hayward, 25800 Carlos Bee Blvd, Rm LI2158, Hayward, CA 94542.

KITHCART, LARRY E.
Legislator. **Personal:** Born Jul 25, 1939, Glasco, NY; married Audrey; children: Larry, Jr. **Career:** Ulster Co, 1st Black legislator 1975; Co Legislator, elected 4th consecutive term. **Orgs:** Mem & pres Kingston City Recreation Com 1968-77; comnr recreation 1977; past pres Kingston Dem Men's Club, mem Sheriff's comm; pub health- Indus devel; taxbase & study; bridge & hwy; program for aged; conser Vation com Chmn Mayor's policy making bd Kingston Rondout Neighborhood Center; ward chmn; YMCA; United Way; Cancer com; Jaycees; NAACP; com pres Ulster Cnty Community Action Adv Bd; Finance Com Co Legis; Audit & Ins Com, Legis, Finance Com of Co Legis, Municipal Power Study Commn of Co Legis. **Military Serv:** USAF 4 yrs.

KITT, EARTHA MAE
Actress, singer. **Personal:** Born Jan 26, 1928, North, SC; divorced; children: 1 daughter. **Career:** Katherine Dunham Dance Group, soloist 1948; Night Clubs France, Turkey, Greece, Egypt, New York City, Hollywood, Las Vegas, London, Stockholm, singer 1949-; Stage play Dr Faust Paris 1951, New Faces of 1952, Mrs Patterson 1954, Shinbone Alley 1957, Timbuktu 1978, performer; Motion pictures New Faces 1953, Accused 1957, Anna Lucasta 1958, Mark of the Hawk, St Louis Blues, Synanon 1965, Up the Chastity Belt 1971; RCA, Victor, recording artist. **Honors/Awds:** Author "Thursday's Child" 1956, "A Tart Is Not A Sweet", "Alone With Me", Confessions of A Sex Kitten; Woman of the Year, Natl Assn of Negro Musicians, 1968; Several command performances before the Queen of England; 1 Grammy Award; 2 Tony Nominations. **Business Addr:** c/o Eartha Kitt Productions, 888 Seventh Ave, Fl 37, New York, NY 10106-3799.

KITTLES, KERRY
Professional basketball player. **Personal:** Born Jun 12, 1974, Dayton, OH. **Educ:** Villanova. **Career:** New Jersey Nets, guard, 1996-. **Special Achievements:** NBA Draft, First round pick, #8, 1996. **Business Addr:** Professional Basketball Player, New Jersey Nets, Brendan Byrne Arena, 405 Murray Hill Pkwy, East Rutherford, NJ 07073, (201)935-8888.

KLAUSNER, WILLETTE MURPHY
Theatrical/film producer. **Personal:** Born Jun 21, 1939, Omaha, NE; daughter of Gertrude Jones Murphy and William Murphy; married Manuel S, Feb 1, 1969. **Educ:** UCLA, BA economics 1957-61; Tobe-Coburn Sch for Fashion Careers NY, honors cert 1961-62. **Career:** Edgework Productions, producer, "Twist," Walnut St Theatre, 1992; "George Street Playhouse," 1996; "The Apprentice," The Richard Pryor Theatre, Hollywood, 1991, "Hurlyburly," Westwood Playhouse, 1988-89; Universal Studios Inc CA, vice pres marketing research and marketin g, 1974-81; Audience Studies Inc, research 1972-74, research unit dir, 1968-72, proj dir, 1966-88, research analyst, 1965-66; Carnation Co, research analyst, 1965. **Orgs:** Mem Gold Shield UCLA Alumni Assn, 1974-; mem The Trusteeship 1980-; founding mem Amer Inst of Wine & Food, 1982- ; mem bd dir Constitutional Rights Found, 1982; vice pres, bd of dir, Los Angeles County Music Center Operating Co, 1987; mem bd of dir, Audrey Skirball-Kenis Theatre Inc 1991-; mem bd of dir, Individual Rights Found 1994; mem bd of dir, American Cinema Found 1995. **Honors/Awds:** Mehitabel Award for outstanding Professional Achievement, Tobe-Coburn Sch for Fashion Careers 1978. **Business Addr:** President, Edgework Productions, 5538 Red Oak Drive, Los Angeles, CA 90068.

KLEVEN, THOMAS
Law professor. **Personal:** Born Aug 30, 1942, Cambridge, MA; married Ella Faye Marsh Kleven, Nov 24, 1972; children: Deborah, Aaron. **Educ:** Yale University, New Haven, CT, BA, 1964; Yale Law Sch, LLB, 1967. **Career:** Thurgood Marshall School of Law, Houston, TX, professor, 1974-. **Orgs:** Member, Conference of Critical Legal Studies, 1988-. **Home Addr:** 4914 N Braeswood, Houston, TX 77096. **Business Addr:** Professor, Thurgood Marshall School of Law, Texas Southern Univ, 3100 Cleburne, Houston, TX 77004.

KLINE, JOSEPH N.
County official. **Personal:** Born Oct 8, 1948, Dale, SC; son of Eddie & Frances Kline; married Audrey Annette Wheelwright, 1969; children: Marwin, Mikima, Miesha. **Educ:** Hartford Data Institution, computer oper & programming, 1967-68. **Career:** Senior analyst programmer, Savannah-Chatham County Public School, 1984-; Beaufort County, SC, councilman, 1979-. **Orgs:** Black Elected Officials of Beaufort County, bd mem, 1979-; Burton-Dale-Beaufort Branch of the NAACP, bd of dirs, 1979-; Mt Carmel Baptist Church, deacon, 1984-; Dale-Lobeco Community Org, bd of dirs, 1975-; Beaufort Marine Inst, bd of dirs, 1987-; Beaufort Jasper EOC, bd of dirs, 1984-; Low Country Council of Governments, board of directors, 1979-94; One of a Million Man Marcher; Beaufort County Local Organizing Committee, coordinator. **Honors/Awds:** Black Arise, Most Oputstanding Young Ma, 1973; Jaycees, New Brittai, CT, Jaycee of the Year, 1973; Beaufort County, Recreation Commission, Plaque of Appreciation, 1977; Beaufort Jasper ECON Oppor Comma, Certificate of Appreciation, 1991; Omega Psi Phi Frat, Citizen of the Year, 1992; Beaufort County Dr King Day Comm, Outstanding Contribution in Politics Award, 1993. **Home Addr:** 42 Kline Circle, Seabrook, SC 29940.

KLINE, WILLIAM M.
Educational administrator (retired). **Personal:** Born Feb 24, 1933, Paterson, NJ; married Lillian Thomas; children: Wayne, Michelle, William Jr, Wesley. **Educ:** William Paterson Coll, BS 1954, MS 1959. **Career:** Paterson Bd of Educ, teacher 1957-65, dir neighborhood youth corp 1965-68, vice prin sch #6 1968-71, prin Eastside hs 1971-79, dir curriculum & spl educ proj 1979, asst supt. **Orgs:** F & AM commr Bd of Recreation City of Paterson 1962-64; alderman City of Paterson 1965-67; NAACP; Omega Psi Phi; Phi Delta Kappa; IBPOE of W Integrity Lodge; 4th Ward County Committeeman; Paterson Rotary Club; municipal chairman, Democratic Party; mem, Bd of Education Paterson, NJ, 1996-97, chmn, 1997-98. **Honors/Awds:** Freedom Campaign Awd NAACP Paterson 1963; Cert of Merit Passaic Co Med Soc 1964; White House Conf Pres Lyndon Johnson 1965; Comm Serv Awd NAACP Paterson 1967; Educ Leadership Awd Lambda Kappa Mu Passaic Co 1971; DECA Serv Awd Distributive Educ Club Paterson 1973; Educ Awd New Polit Alliance Paterson 1976; Sci of Creative Intelligence Educ Awd NY 1976; Unity Serv Awd 1982; Hinton Comm Serv Awd 1983; Comm Bettermant Awd SECA Inc 1983; Morris Co Serv Awd NJ State Elks 1984; PH Grand Lodge Awd 1985; Amer Lodge Education Awd 1985; Passaic Cty Coll Awd 1985; NAACP Golden Heritage, 1989; Southern Poverty Law Center Award, 1992; American Indian Relief Council, Appreciation Award, 1992; Paterson Young Men's Assn, Education Award, 1993; Westend Warriors, Appreciation Award, 1994; Van Resalier Award for Education, 1997. **Military Serv:** US Army pfc 1955-57; Good Conduct Medal. **Home Addr:** 346 Ninth Avenue, Paterson, NJ 07514.

KLUGE, PAMELA HOLLIE
Economics and business journalism educator. **Personal:** Born Apr 17, 1948, Topeka, KS; daughter of Frances Hollie and Maurice Hollie; married P F Kluge, Feb 14, 1977. **Educ:** Washburn Univ, Topeka KS, BA English, 1970; Columbia Univ, New York NY, MS Journalism, 1971; Univ of Hawaii, Honolulu HA, Asain Studies, 1977; Columbia Univ, American Studies, 1987-. **Career:** Wall Street Journal, 1969-75; Honolulu Advertiser, Pacific correspondent, Saipan, 1975-76; Trust Territory of the Pacific Island, economics dept Micronesia, 1976; New York Times, natl correspondent in Los Angeles, foreign correspondent in Manilla, financial columnist in NY, 1977-87; NY Stock Exchange, New York NY, media consultant, 1987-, Knight Bagenot Fellowship in Economics & Business Journalism, Columbia Univ Graduate school of Journlism, dir, currently. **Orgs:** Dir, The Newspaper Foundation, 1973-75; contributor, Encyclopdeia Americana, 1985-; advisory board, The Kansas Center for the Book, 1988-; consultant, The Paragon Group, 1989-; visiting faculty, Poynter Institute, 1989-. **Honors/Awds:** Distinguished Service Award, Washburn Univ, 1981; Topeka High School Hall of Fame, 1988; Fulbright Fellow to Malaysia, 1988; Best in the Business, Washington Journalism Review, 1985; Editor, The Knight-Bagehot Guide to Business and Economics Journalism, Columbia Univ Press, 1990. **Business Addr:** Director, The Knight-Bagehot Fellowship in Economics and Bus, Columbia University, Graduate School of Journalism, 116th and Broadway, New York, NY 10027.

KNABLE, BOBBIE MARGARET BROWN
Educational administrator. **Personal:** Born May 20, 1936, Knoxville, TN; daughter of Jacqueline Jordan Brown (deceased) and Isaac Brown; married Norman Knable, Dec 21, 1963; children: Jacob. **Educ:** Oberlin Conservatory, Oberlin OH, BMus, 1958. **Career:** Tufts Univ, Medford MA, asst prof of English, 1970-76, dir of continuing educ, 1974-78, dean of freshmen, 1978-79, dean of students, 1979-. **Orgs:** Mem, New England Deans, 1978-; mem steering comm, New England Coll Alcohol Network, 1980-; trustee, Vermont Academy, 1983-85; mem 1986-, recording sec 1988-89, Massachusetts Assn of Women Deans, Administrators and Counselors; mem, Deans of the Round Table, 1988-; mem, Student Affairs Think Tank, 1988-; trustee, Pine Manor Coll, 1989-; commr, New England Assn of Schools and Colleges, 1989-95; governing board member, Massachusetts Institute of Psychoanalysis, 1990-96; trustee, Bennington College, 1997-. **Business Addr:** Dean of Students, Tufts Univ, Ballou Hall, Medford, MA 02155.

KNIGHT, ATHELIA WILHELMENIA
Reporter. **Personal:** Born Oct 15, 1950, Portsmouth, VA; daughter of Adell Virginia Savage Knight and Daniel Dennis Knight. **Educ:** Norfolk State University, Norfolk, VA, BA, 1973; Ohio State University, Columbus, OH, MA, 1974; Harvard University, Cambridge, MA, Nieman Fellow, 1985-86. **Career:** DC Cooperative Extension Service, Washington, DC, summer aide, 1969-72; Portsmouth Public Schools, Portsmouth, VA, substitute teacher, 1973; The Virginian-Pilot, Norfolk, VA, summer relief reporter, 1973; The Chicago Tribune, Chicago, IL, summer relief reporter, 1974; The Washington Post, Washington, DC, metropolitan desk reporter, 1975-81, investigative reporter, 1981-. **Orgs:** Member: Women in Communications; National Association of Black Journalists; Washington-Baltimore Newspaper Guild; Investigative Reporters and Editors. **Honors/Awds:** Mark Twain Award, Associated Press, 1982, 1987; National Award for Education, National Education Writers Association, 1987; Front Page Award, Washington/Baltimore Newspaper Guild, 1982; Nieman Fellowship for Journalists, Harvard University, 1985-86; Ohio State University

Fellow, Ohio State University, 1973-74; Maryland, Delaware District of Columbia Press Association, First Place, Public Service Award, 1990; Maryland/Delaware, District of Columbia Press Assn, First Place, Local Govt; Washington Chapter of the Society of Professional Journalists, Dateline Award for General News, 1993. **Business Addr:** The Washington Post, 1150 15th Street N.W., Washington, DC 20071.

KNIGHT, BREVIN
Professional basketball player. **Personal:** Born Nov 8, 1975; son of Melvin and Brenda. **Educ:** Stanford, BA in sociology, 1997. **Career:** Cleveland Cavaliers, guard, 1997-. **Honors/Awds:** Frances Pomeroy Naismith Award, 1997. **Business Addr:** Professional Basketball Player, Cleveland Cavaliers, One Center Ct, Cleveland, OH 44115-4001, (216)659-9100.

KNIGHT, BUBBA
Singer. **Career:** Singer with Gladys Knight and the Pips, 1952—; member of entertainment firm Shakeji, Inc. **Business Addr:** c/o MCA Record, 70 Universal City Plaza, Universal City, CA 91608.

KNIGHT, CAROLY ANN
Educator, minister. **Personal:** Born Aug 7, Denver, CO; daughter of Ed & Dorothy Knight. **Educ:** Bishop Coll, Dallas, TX, BA, 1977; Union Theological Seminary, New York City, MDiv, 1980; United Theoligical Seminary, Dayton, OH, DMin, 1995. **Career:** Canaan Bapt Ch, NYC, asst pastor, 1978-87; Philadelphia Bapt Ch, NYC, pastor, 1988-93; Union Theological Seminary, NYC, asst prof, 1989-93; ITC, Atlanta, asst prof, 1995-. **Orgs:** Delta Sigma Theta, golden life mem, 1982-; NAACP, 1980-. **Honors/Awds:** Ebony Magazine, 15 Greatest Black Women Preachers, 1997; Morehouse Coll, Coll of Preachers, 1996; United Negro Coll Fund, Alumni Award, 1993; Natl Coun of Negro Women, Bethune Award, 1991; Negro Professional Women Comm Svc, Laurelton Chap, 1987. **Special Achievements:** "If The Worst Should Come!," sermon, 1997; "When You Talk to Yourself!," sermon, 1997; "How To Deal With Failure," Sister to Sister, devotional, 1993. **Business Phone:** (404)527-7748.

KNIGHT, DEWEY W., JR.
Government official. **Personal:** Born Apr 7, 1930, Daytona Beach, FL; married Clara Brown; children: Dewey III, Patrick. **Educ:** Bethune Cookman Clg, BS 1947-51; Atlanta U, MSW 1955-57; MA Inst Tech, Urban Exec Pgm 1970. **Career:** Dade Cty Childrens Hm, dir prfsnl serv case spvr casewrkr 1960-64; Dade Cty Dept Pblc Welfare, dir 1967-70; Dade Cty Dept Housing & Urban Dev, dir 1970; Metropolitan Dade Cty, asst cty mgr & dir dept human resources 1970-75, interim cty mgr 1976-, deputy county mgr 1970-. **Orgs:** Natl Acad Pblc Admn; Acad Cert Soc Wrkrs; pres Am Soc Pblc Admn; mem C of C Advsry Bd Natl Assc Businessmen; bd dir James E Scott Comm Assc; bd dir Am Red Cross; bd dir United Way; bd dir Kappa Alpha Psi Frat; sire archon-pres Sigma Pi Phi Frat; prof advsry cmt Barry Clg Grad Sch Soc Work; chtr mem Miami Vrsty Clb; bd trustee FL Memrl Clg; bd trustee Stillman Clg; bd dir Chase Fed & Loan Assc; mem Natl Forum Black Admn. **Honors/Awds:** Natl pblc serv awrd; natl acad pblc admn & am soc pblc admn 1983; natl ldrshp awrd Natl Forum Blck Pblc Admn 1984; man of the yr Miami Chptr Rinky Dinks 1967; prod of a dream awrd Miami-Dade Chptr Bethune Cookman Alumni Assc 1975; comm serv awrd James E Scott Assc 1975; comm serv awrd Dade-Monroe Manpower Area Plng Cncl 1974; man of the yr Iota Phi Lambda 1976; distgshd serv awrd Miami-Dade C of C 1975; awrd serv rendered to frat Kappa Alpha Psi Frat; comm serv awrd Minrty Cntrctrs Assc 1972; otstndg comm serv awrd Frontier Intrl Miami Clb; dstgshd comm serv awrd Natl Conf of Christians & Jews 1977; man of the yr Zeta Phi Beta; dstgshd serv awrd Natl Assc of Soc Wrkrs 1977; kappa of the month natl; pblc admn of the yr Am Soc Pblc Admn S FL 1982; natl pblc servawrd Natl Acad Pblc Admn &PA 1983; natl forum Black Admn Ldrshp Awrd 1984. **Military Serv:** USAF stf sgt. **Business Addr:** Deputy County Manager, Metropolitan Dade Cty Govt, 111 NW 1st, Ste 2910, Miami, FL 33128.

KNIGHT, FRANKLIN W.
Educator. **Personal:** Born Jan 10, 1942; son of Irick M Sanderson Knight and Willis J Knight; married Ingeborg Bauer; children: Michael, Brian, Nadine. **Educ:** Univ Coll of WI London, BA (honors) 1964; Univ of WI Madison, MA 1965, PhD 1969. **Career:** SUNY at Stony Brook, asst/assoc prof 1968-73; Johns Hopkins Univ, assoc prof 1973-77, prof 1977-; Leonard & Helen R Stulman Prof of History, 1991-; Latin Amer Studies Program, dir, 1992-95. **Orgs:** Visit prof Univ of TX at Austin 1980; bd dirs Social Sci Rsch Council 1976-79; consultant NEH 1977-85; comm mem Inter-American Found 1984-86; rsch comm Amer Historical Assn 1984-86; chmn Intl Scholarly Relations Comm Conf of Latin Amer Historians 1983-86; exec comm Assn of Caribbean Hist 1982-85. **Honors/Awds:** Fellow Natl Endowment for Humanities 1976-77; Fellow Center for Adv Study in Behav Sciences 1977-78; author, "Slave Society in Cuba During 19th Century" 1970; "The Caribbean, Genesis of a Fragmented Nationalism" 1990; Fellow Natl Humanities Center 1986-87. **Home Addr:** 2902 W Strathmore Ave, Baltimore, MD 21209. **Business Addr:** Dept of History, Johns Hopkins Univ, 3400 N Charles St, Baltimore, MD 21218.

KNIGHT, GLADYS MARIA
Singer. **Personal:** Born May 28, 1944, Atlanta, GA; daughter of Elizabeth Woods Knight and Merald Knight Sr; married Barry Hankerson, Oct 1974 (divorced 1979); children: Kenya, Jimmy, Shanga-Ali; married Les Brown, Aug 29, 1995 (divorced 1997). **Career:** Morris Brown Choir, singer 1950-53; concert appearances in England 1967, 1972, 1973, 1976, Australia, Japan, Hong Kong, Manila 1976; Pipe Dreams (movie); Gladys Knight & The Pips, singer 1953-90, solo artist, 1990-; Charlie & Company; Kenya's Cakes To The Stars, co-own; Gladys and Ron's Chicken & Waffle Restaurant, co-own. **Honors/Awds:** Winner Grand Prize Ted Mack Amateur Hour 1952; 1 Gold Album; 1 Platinum Album; four Grammy Awards (two in 1972, one in 1989 for best group); Top Female Vocalist, Blues & Soul Mag 1972; Spec Awd for Inspiration to Youth WA City Council; Rolling Stone Awd; Ladies Home Jrnl Awd; author I Don't Want To Do Wrong, Do You Love Me Just a Little Honey, Daddy Could Swear I Declare, Me & My Family, Way Back Home; Winner 6 Gold Buddah Records; NAACP Image, Ebony Music, Cashbox, Billboard, Record World Awds 1975; American Music Awd (with Pips) 1984, 1988; produced and appeared in Sisters in the Name of Love (HBO) 1986; hits (with Pips) include Every Beat of My Heart, I Heard It Through the Grapevine, Midnight Train to Georgia; honorary doctor of humane letters, Morris Brown College, 1990; album: Just for You, MCA Records, 1995; Trumpet Awards, special honoree, 1997. **Special Achievements:** Star, Hollywood Walk of Fame, 1995; Author, Between Each Line of Pain and Glory, 1997. **Business Addr:** Singer, c/o Shakeji Inc, 2700 East Sunset Rd, Ste 31 D, Las Vegas, NV 89120-3506.

KNIGHT, JOHN F., JR.
Educational administrator. **Personal:** Born Jun 7, 1945, Montgomery, AL; son of Ruth Bateman Knight and Johnnie F Knight Sr; divorced; children: Tamara, Tehrik. **Educ:** AL State Univ, BS 1974. **Career:** AL State Univ, dir public relations 1976, dir of communications and public affairs, currently; AL PSC, exec asst to pres; postal serv, clerk 1969-74. **Orgs:** Pres adv council AL Dem Conf Young Dem 1973; Students Affairs Com 1973; pres AL State Univ Student Govt Assn 1972-73; mem St Dem Exec Com 1975; chmn, Montgomery County Democratic Conference, 1979-; commissioner, Montgomery County Commission, 1980-; bd mem, Montgomery Housing Authority Bd, 1975-. **Honors/Awds:** Highest ranking black in AL State Govt 1974; Presidential Citation, NAFEO, 1991; Man of the Year, Kappa Alpha Psi Fraternity, 1991. **Military Serv:** AUS 1967-69; Silver Star, 1964, Vietnam Service Medal, Natl Defense Medal, Vietnam Campaign Medal, Combat Infantryman Badge. **Home Addr:** PO Box 6148, Montgomery, AL 36106.

KNIGHT, LYNNON JACOB
Electronics engineer. **Personal:** Born Jan 13, 1920, Ernul, NC; married Louise Dixon. **Educ:** Lincoln U, BS 1941; Univ of PA, Postgrad 1942-44; Univ of AZ, 1959-61; Univ of CA at Los Angeles, 1968-72. **Career:** Radar/Electronics Defense Dept SE Asia, staff engr 1946-58; Army Dept Ft Huachuca, AZ, supv electronics engr 1958-62; Navy Dept Los Angeles, staff engr electronics 1962-65; Def Supply Agency Pasadena, tech mgr chief engr 1965-; Knight-dixon Co Los Angeles, pres 1971-. **Orgs:** Mem Power Source Com Army Dept 1961-62; AASS; IEEE; Armed Forces Communications & Elec Assn; mem Omega Psi Phi. **Business Addr:** 125 S Grand, Pasadena, CA 91105.

KNIGHT, MURIEL BERNICE
Educator, consultant. **Personal:** Born Apr 21, 1922, Hartford, CT; daughter of Rosena Burnett Williams and Oscar Milton Williams; widowed; children: Leo M Knight (deceased), Philip A Knight (deceased), Muriel Virginia, William Knight, Sheila Eileen Knight. **Educ:** AS Northeastern Univ, AS 1970; Northeastern Univ, BS 1972; Harvard Grad Schl of Ed, Ed M 1973; Suffolk Univ, certificate, consumer law, 1979; Northeastern Univ, Ed D, 1988. **Career:** Northeastern Alumni, mem 1973-; Harvard Grad Alumni, mem 1974-; Harvard Chap Phi Delta Kappa, histrn-elect 1985-86; New England Woman's Press Assoc, pres-elect 1985-86; Beaver Country Day School, instructor; Ward 5 Precinct 7 Warden, election department, 1980-88; Northeastern Univ, Graduate School of Education, teaching asst, 1977-78; Boston State College, lecturer, 1979-81; Massachusetts Bay Community College, lecturer, 1985. **Orgs:** Vice pres New England Woman's Press Assoc 1983-85; brd mem S End Neighborhood Action Prog 1985; brd mem Dimock St Health Cntr 1983-85; warden Election Dept City of Boston 1983-. **Honors/Awds:** Awarded Kennedy Fdn Schlrshp; Northeastern Univ Martin Luther King Schlrshp; Comm Serv Award; Citation for Civic Endeavors, Comm Work, Media Work, Comm Endeavors, Public Relations Work; Professional Award, Educator's Award, Negro Business and Professional Women, Boston Chapter; Merit Media Award, Lambda Kappa Mu Sorority; Selective Service Board Number 32, member. **Home Addr:** 31-C Village Court, P O 18366, Boston, MA 02118.

KNIGHT, NEGELE OSCAR
Professional basketball player. **Personal:** Born Mar 6, 1967, Detroit, MI. **Educ:** Dayton, 1990. **Career:** Phoenix Suns, guard, 1990-93; San Antonio Spurs, 1993-. **Business Addr:** Professional Basketball Player, San Antonio Spurs, 600 E Market St, Ste 102, San Antonio, TX 78205, (512)554-7787.

KNIGHT, RICHARD, JR.
Company executive. **Personal:** Born May 31, 1945, Fort Valley, GA; son of Freddie Knight and Richard Knight; married Mavis Best; children: Richard L, Marcus E, Nolan C. **Educ:** Fort Valley State Coll, BA 1968; Univ of NC, MPA 1976. **Career:** Carrboro NC, town mgr 1976-80; Gainesville FL, deputy city mgr 1980-82; City of Dallas, asst city mgr 1982-86, city manager, 1986-90; Caltex Petroleum Corp, dir, total qual & envir mgmt, 1990-. **Orgs:** Mem Rotary Intl; mem Free and Accepted Mason (3rd) Degree; past comm Cub Scout MAWAT Durham Dist Boy Scouts; mem Intl City Mgmt Assn; chmn Dallas Regional Minority Purchasing Council 1984-85; vice chair Dallas Alliance 1985; mem, Salesmanship Club of Dallas, 1989; bd of dirs, Comerica Bank, TX, 1990-; bd of dirs, Dallas Intl Sports Comm, 1990-; bd of dirs, Dallas Zoological Soc, 1990-. **Honors/Awds:** Perspectives of a Black City Mgr published in Popular Govt 1979; Observations from a Mgr in Local Govt published in Public Management 1982; vice pres Intl City Mgmt Assn 1982. **Military Serv:** AUS staff sgt 1969-71; Honors/Commendations. **Business Addr:** Director, Total Quality & Environmental Mgmt, Caltex Petroleum Corp, PO Box 619500, Dallas, TX 75261-9500.

KNIGHT, ROBERT S.
Dentist, educator. **Personal:** Born Aug 10, 1929, Montgomery, AL; married Patricia Tyler; children: Lynn, Robert, Joan, Stephen. **Educ:** Talladega Coll, BA 1949; Meharry Med Coll, DDS 1954. **Career:** Bridgeport, CT, private practice 1964; Howard Univ Coll of Dentistry, asst prof 1965-71, asso prof 1972-, asso dean for Student Affairs 1975-, professor 1978-. **Orgs:** Mem Amer Dental Assn; Natl Dental Assn; DC Dental Soc; Robert T Freeman Dental Assn; Amer Acad of Oral Pathology; Amer Assn of Dental Sch; Soc of Tchr of Oral Pathology; Capitol Order of Oral Pathologist; mem Natl Urban League; com chmn Explorer Scouts, BSA; Howard Univ Coll of Med Post; mem Sigma Xi 1971; mem Omicron Kappa Upsilon Honorary Dental Soc 1974. **Honors/Awds:** Recip Amer Cancer Soc Fellow in Oral Pathology New York Univ 1963; Fellow, Amer College of Dentist 1981. **Military Serv:** AUS dental corps 1954-61; USAR col. **Business Addr:** Professor, Howard University, College of Dentistry, Washington, DC 20059.

KNIGHT, SAMMY
Professional football player. **Personal:** Born Sep 10, 1975. **Educ:** USC, attended. **Career:** New Orleans Saints, defensive back, 1997-. **Business Addr:** Professional Football Player, New Orleans Saints, 5800 Airline Hwy, Metairie, LA 70003, (504)733-0255.

KNIGHT, THOMAS
Professional football player. **Personal:** Born Dec 29, 1974. **Educ:** Univ of Iowa, attended. **Career:** Arizona Cardinals, defensive back, 1997-. **Business Addr:** Professional Football Player, Arizona Cardinals, 8701 S Hardy, Tempe, AZ 85284, (602)379-0101.

KNIGHT, TOM
Professional football player. **Educ:** Iowa. **Career:** Arizona Cardinals, 1997-. **Special Achievements:** NFL Draft, First round pick, #9, 1997. **Business Addr:** Professional Football Player, Arizona Cardinals, P O Box 888, Phoenix, AZ 85001-0888, (602)379-0101.

KNIGHT, W. H., JR. (JOE)
Educator. **Personal:** Born Dec 5, Beckley, WV; son of Frances Knight and W H Knight; married Susan L Mask, Jun 6, 1981; children: Michael Joseph Mask Knight, Lauren Louise Mask Knight. **Educ:** Univ of NC at Chapel Hill, BA 1976; Columbia Univ Sch of Law, JD 1979. **Career:** Colonial Bancorp, assoc counsel and asst sec, 1979-83; Univ of IA Coll of Law, associate professor, 1983-88, professor, 1988-91; associate dean, 1991-93; Duke Univ Law School, Durham, NC, visiting professor, 1991; Wake Forest Univ Law School, Winston-Salem, NC, guest professor, 1989; Washington University, School of Law, St Louis, MO, visiting professor, 1992; vice Provost, Univ of Iowa, 1997-. **Orgs:** Bd adv mem CT Economic Development Authority 1982-83; consultant Knight Financial Enterprises 1982-; mem Lawyers Alliance for Nuclear Arms Control 1983-, Amer & Iowa Civil Liberties Union 1983-; pres Iowa City NAACP 1986-90; mem Natl Conference of Black Lawyers; IA Natl Bar Assoc; mem Society of American Law Teachers 1988-; member, National Bar Assn; member, American Bar Assn; Amer Law Instit, 1993-; board member, Willowwind School, 1992-; board member, Mid-Eastern Council on Chemical Abuse, 1992-; board member, State Farm Fire and Casualty Co, 1995-; board member, State Farm Mutual Automobile Co, 1996-. **Honors/Awds:** Woodrow Wilson Administrative Fellowship 1979; Univ of IA Old Gold Fellowship Grants 1984, 1985-87; Distinguished Teaching Award, Duke Law School, 1990-91; Co-author, "Weep Not Little Ones: An Essay for Our Children About Affirmative Action," African Americans and the Living Constitution, eds, JH Franlin, JR McNeil, Smithsonian Press, 1995; Co-Author, Commercial Transactions Under the Uniform Commercial Code, 5th edition, Matthew Bender, 1997; Author, Iowa Bar Review Materials on Contracts 1985-89; Author, book review "In Banks We Trust," P Lernoux Vol 10 IA Journal Corp Law 1095, 1985," International Debt and

the Act of State Doctrine: Judicial Abstention Reconsidered,'' 13 North Carolina Journal of International Law & Commercial Regulation 35-72 (1988), book brief, ''Black Robes, White Justice,'' Bruce Wright 10 UCLA National Black Law Journal 366-369 (1988), '' Loan Participation Agreements; Catching Up With Contract Law,'' 1987 Columbia Business Law Review 587-631, '' To Thine Own Self Be True,'' St. Louis Public Law Review, 1991. **Home Addr:** 10 Brickwood Knoll, Iowa City, IA 52240. **Business Addr:** Vice Provost, Univ. of IA, 111 Jessup Hall, Iowa City, IA 52242.

KNIGHT, WALTER R.
City official, association executive. **Personal:** Born Aug 16, 1933, Camden, AR; married Sadie M Brown; children: Harriet, Vicki, Sabrena, Michelle. **Educ:** Univ WI; Univ MN. **Career:** City Councilman; Un Steelworkers Am Local 1533, pres 1975-; USWA, vice pres 1969. **Orgs:** Bd dirs Gr Beloit Assn Commerce; mem City Ambassadors Club; exec com Black Res Personnel; Beloit Improv Coalition; bd dirs WI Equal Employ Oppor Assn 1967-; Rock Co Manpower Plng Council 1974. **Honors/Awds:** Serv award Salvation Army 1966; Soul Fest 1972; Beloit Coll Pres Counc. **Business Addr:** 614 Broad St, PO Box 1219, Beloit, WI 53511.

KNIGHT, WILLIAM ROGERS
City official (retired). **Personal:** Born Jan 8, 1945, Halifax Co, NC; married Nelma Kaye Johnson; children: Lisa, Kimberly, Ida Michelle, William II, Karen. **Educ:** Wilberforce U, BA 1968. **Career:** Raleigh City Dist C, councilman; St Augustines Coll, dir pub relat; Raleigh Comm Relat Com, asso dir 1969-73; Wake Co Oppor Inc, manpower coord 1968-69. **Orgs:** Mem Assn of Am Colls; Nat Assn of Fed Relat Ofcls; mem Shriners Masonic Lodges; NAACP; Un Ways of Wake Co; LQC Lamar Soc; Raleigh Cits Assn; Black Dem Caucus of Wake Co; Team for Progress; NC Comm Action Assn; Omega Psi Phi Frat; Nat Black Caucus of Local Elected Ofcls. **Honors/Awds:** Recip cert of merit US Jaycees; speak-up award Raleigh Jaycees; outst cit in field of pub relat 6th Dist Omega Psi Phi; outst cit award Jack & Jill Inc 1974; outst cir award Phi Beta Sigma.

KNIGHT-PULLIAM, KESHIA
Actress. **Personal:** Born Apr 9, 1979, Newark, NJ. **Career:** First show business job appeared in ad for baby care products (8 months old); appeared in several TV commercials; semi-regular on children's program Sesame St 1982; film, The Last Dragon; The Cosby Show, 1984-92. **Honors/Awds:** Emmy nomination for Outstanding Supporting Actress in a Comedy Series.

KNOTT, ALBERT PAUL, JR.
Manufacturing company executive. **Personal:** Born Mar 23, 1935, Pittsburgh, PA; son of Fannie Merideth Scott Knott and Albert Paul Knott; married Lynda Steenberg; children: Albert Paul Knott III, Olivia Merideth Knott. **Educ:** Yale Coll, AB 1956; NJ Coll of Medicine, MD 1960; DC Gen Hosp, Internship 1961; Michael Reese Hosp Chicago, Cardoiology Fellowship 1961-63; VA Hosp Hines IL, Med Res 1961-65. **Career:** Tabernacle Community Hospital, medical dir, 1972-77; Bethany/Garfield Park Hospital, medical dir, 1977-81; Statevl Cortl Inst, med dir 1981-83; Metpl Correctional Center, med dir 1984-85; Luxury Yachts Ltd, Miami, FL and Chicago, IL, president, 1984-; CHA Ltd. Chicago Illinois, president 1985-; Communication Equipment Consultants, president, 1987-; Marine Cellular Specialists Chicago and Fort Lauderdale, vice pres 1988-; Knott Lock Corporation, president 1988-. **Orgs:** Am Coll of Phys 1968-; dir Inner Cty Ind 1967-; dir Lux Yachts LTD 1980-; dir Reg Ind 1980-; dir St Johns Entp 1970-; dir Kings Bay LTD 1972-. **Military Serv:** US Navy, Lt Cmdr, 1965-67. **Business Addr:** c/o CHA LTD, Suite 1506, 53 West Jackson Blvd, Chicago, IL 60604.

KNOTT, MAY
Procurement officer. **Personal:** Born Feb 24, Montgomery, AL; daughter of Julia Kyle Alexander Mayberry and Joseph Paige (both deceased); married Gerald Jordan (divorced 1995); children: Deborah L Jordan, Gerald Jordan Jr. **Educ:** Sinclair College, Dayton, OH; University of Dayton, OH. **Career:** Wright Patterson Air Force Base, Dayton, OH, reports control clerk, 1953-55; Gentile Air Force Depot, Dayton, OH, executive secretary, 1959-72; Defense Electronic Supply Center, Dayton, OH, contract administrator/negotiator, 1972-74, Columbus, OH, procurement analyst, 1974-77; Digital Equipment Corp, Nashua, NH, buyer, 1977-80; Air Force Acquisition Center, Hanscom Air Force Base, Lexington, MA, small business specialist, 1982-91, Federal Women's Program, retired manager, 1989-93; Jazz Ensemble - May Knott, mgr. **Orgs:** Chairperson, YWCA Swim-In for Mentally Handicapped, 1980-82. **Honors/Awds:** Outstanding Performance, DLA, 1965, 1980; Letter of Commendation, DLA, 1974; Nominated for NAACP Roy Wilkins Award, 1989; Letter of Outstanding Federal Service, 37 years from AF.

KNOWLES, EDDIE (ADENOLA)
Educational administrator. **Personal:** Born May 3, 1946, New York, NY; son of Maggie Knowles and Ephraim Knowles; divorced; children: Alisa, Themba. **Educ:** Lincoln Univ PA, BA 1970; Columbia Univ Tchr Coll, MA 1973; SUNY, Rockefeller College, PhD candidate, currently. **Career:** Bronx Community College, assistant director of college discovery program, 1970-73, director of college discovery program, 1973-74; Hostos Community College, assistant professor, 1974-75; Rensselaer Poly Institute, assistant dean of students/foreign student advisor, 1977-79, dean of minority affairs, 1979-82, dean of students, 1982-. **Orgs:** Consult Exxon Ed Found 1984; consult NY Edtl Oppty Ctrs 1984; writer consult Blk Coll Mag 1980-; vice pres brd of dir Sponsors for Ed Opp 1970-. **Honors/Awds:** Martin Luther King awd Ren Poly Inst 1983; sevc awd Minty Stud Ldr RPI 1982; unity awd in media Lincoln Univ MO Ntl Media Comp 1981. **Home Addr:** 2115 Burdett Ave, Troy, NY 12180. **Business Addr:** Dean of Students, Rensselaer Polytechnic Inst, Troy Building RPI, Troy, NY 12180.

KNOWLES, EM CLAIRE
Educational administrator. **Personal:** Born Jun 6, 1952, Sacramento, CA; daughter of Almeana Early Knowles (deceased) and Sidney S Knowles. **Educ:** Univ of CA, Davis CA, BA, 1973, Univ of CA, Berkeley CA, MLS, 1974, Certificate/Mgt, 1975; CA State Univ, Sacramento CA, MPA, 1986; Simmons Coll, Boston MA, Doctor of Arts, 1988. **Career:** Univ of CA, Davis CA, reference librarian, 1975-82; soc science librarian, 1982-85; Wentworth Inst of Tech, Boston MA, archives librarian, 1982; Simmons Coll, Boston MA, circulation librarian, 1982; Univ of CA, Davis CA, coordinator of bib instr, 1985-88; Simmons Coll, Boston MA, asst dean, 1988-, freelance proofreader, reviewer, 1988-. **Orgs:** Life mem, Amer Library Assn, 1984-; councillor, 1978-90, mem, 1975-88, CA Library Assn; mem, MA Black Librarians Network, 1988-; chairman, Librarians' Assn of the Univ of CA, Davis CA, 1985-86; member NAWE, AAHE, 1990. **Honors/Awds:** Fellow, Wentworth Institute of Tech, 1982; Outstanding Black Staff, Sacramento Observer, 1981; Outstanding Service, Ethnic Minority Students, Delta Sigma Theta Sorority, Inc; Lambda Xi, 1980; mem, CA Governor's Conference on Library and Information Science, 1979; author of ''How to Attract Ethnic Minorities to the Information Profession,'' Special Libraries; ''Fulbright Scholars offered a Glimpse of American Academic Libraries,'' CA Clearinghouse of Library Instruction Newsletter, 7(2):1-2 May 1987; Dual Career Couple Relationships: An Annotated Bibliography. University of CA, Women's Resources and Research Center. Working paper series No 7, April 20, 1980; Black Women in Science and Medicine: A Bio- Bibliography, with Mattie T Evans, Affirmative Action Council, 1977. **Special Achievements:** Co-author: ''Recruiting the Underrepresented; Collaborative Efforts between Library Educators and Library Practitioners,'' Fall, 1991; ''Recruiting the Underrepresented to Academic Libraries,'' College & Research Libraries, 1990. **Business Addr:** Assistant Dean, Simmons College, Grad School of Library & Info Science, 300 The Fenway, Boston, MA 02115.

KNOX, DOROTHY DEAN
Law enforcement official. **Personal:** Born Mar 10, 1940, Jayess, MS; daughter of Robert Earl & Juanita Jones; married Stanley R., Oct 23, 1960. **Educ:** Wayne State University, BS, criminal justice, 1975. **Career:** Detroit Police Dept, policewoman, 1969-74, sergeant, 1974-77, lieutenant, 1977-80, inspector, 1980-86, commander, 1986-93, deputy chief, 1994; Wayne County Prosecutor, chief investigator, 1994-. **Orgs:** Children's Aid Society, board sec, 1985-; Old Newsboys Goodfellows of Detroit, board member, 1992-94; Child Care Coordinating Council, board member, 1986-92; Detroit Police Athletic League, board member, 1985-91; Black Family Dev, board member, 1984-91; Leadership Detroit, trustee, 1994-. **Honors/Awds:** Detroit City Council, Spirit of Detroit Award, 1994; Boys Town Of Italy, Inc, Woman of the Year, 1994; Women Police of Michigan, Detroit Honoree, 1993; Payne Pulliam School of Trade & Commerce, Honoree, 1993; Michigan Senate Resolution No 473, 1994; Detroit Police Dept, Chief's Citation No 498, 1994. **Special Achievements:** FBI Law Enforcement Bulletin, Apr 1980; A Procedural Model for Processing Citizen Complaints; International Society of Poetry, A Space Between & Best Poems of 1995.

KNOX, GEORGE F.
Attorney. **Personal:** Born Oct 17, 1943, Cleveland, TN; son of Iris Long Knox and George Knox; married Odette Curry Knox, Oct 12, 1985. **Educ:** MI State Univ, BS Zoology 1966; Univ of Miami School of Law, JD 1973. **Career:** Univ of Miami School of Business Admin, lecturer 1973-74; City of Miami, FL, asst city attorney 1974-75; Univ of AR Fayetteville, asst prof of law 1975-76; Univ of Miami School of Law, lecturer 1978-80; Nova Univ Center for the Study of Law, lecturer 1980-82; City of Miami, FL, city attorney and dir of law dept 1976-82; Paul, Landy Beiley & Harper PA, partner 1982-84; Long & Knox, partner 1984-; Kubicki Draper Gallagher, Miami, FL, attorney 1990-. **Orgs:** Mem FL, Natl, Amer, DC Bar Assns; mem, Natl Inst of Municipal Law Officers; mem Assn of Amer Law Schools, Black Lawyers Assn, FL League of Cities, Assn of Amer Trial Lawyers, Acad of FL Trial Lawyers; mem US Dist Court Southern Dist of FL, US Court of Appeals for Fifth Circuit, United States Supreme Court; mem NAACP; bd dirs Miami-Dade Community College Foundation Inc; mem Greater Miami Chamber of Commerce; mem FL Memorial College Ctr of Excellence; bd dirs YMCA of Greater Miami; Member Dade County Blue Ribbon Committee; member of board of trustees, Florida Memorial College; board of directors, United Way; member, The Miami Coalition for a Drug-Free Community. **Honors/Awds:** Jaycees Outstanding Young Men of Amer 1976; Miami-Dade Chamber of Commerce Awd of Outstanding Contribution to Social and Economic Development 1977; Black Lawyers' Assn Virgil Hawkins Achievement Award 1977; Alpha Phi Alpha Fraternity Achievement Award 1977; participant ''Law and Justice in Today's Society'' seminar sponsored by Natl Endowment for the Humanities Harvard Univ 1978; FL Jr Coll at Jacksonville Community Awareness Award; Beta Beta Lambda Chap Alpha Phi Alpha Fraternity Community Service Award 1981; NAACP Appreciation Award 1981; Northwest Council of Jacksonville Chamber of Commerce Jacksonville Achiever Award 1986; numerous publications. **Business Addr:** Head, Commercial Law Division, Kubicki, Draper, Gallagher & McGrane, 25 W Flagler St, Penthouse, Miami, FL 33130.

KNOX, GEORGE L., III
Corporate executive. **Personal:** Born Sep 6, 1943, Indianapolis, IN; son of Yvonne Nee Wright and George L Knox II; married B Gail Reed, Jan 1, 1979; children: Reed, Gillian. **Educ:** Tuskegee Univ, Tuskegee AL, BS, 1967; Harvard Business School, Boston MA, MBA, 1975; attended American Univ, Washington DC. **Career:** US Dept of State, Washington DC, Tokyo, foreign service officer, 1968-73; McKinsey & Co, New York NY, associate, 1975-77; Philip Morris, New York NY, mgr internal mgmt consultant, 1977-79, mgr financial relations, 1979-83, dir financial relations and administration, 1983-85, dir corp communications, 1985-87, vice pres, public affairs, 1987-95, vice pres corporate affairs strategy and communications, 1995-. **Orgs:** Studio Museum in Harlem, trustee; Franklin & Eleanor Roosevelt Inst, dir; Civilian Public Affairs Committee: US Military Academy; Southern Ctr for International Studies, dir; American Ballet Theatre, dir. **Military Serv:** US Air Force, 2nd Lt., 1967. **Business Addr:** Vice Pres, Corporate Affairs Strategy & Communications, Philip Morris Companies, Inc, 120 Park Ave, New York, NY 10017.

KNOX, STANLEY
Former police chief. **Personal:** Born 1939, Summerville, GA; son of Doris; married Dorothy Brent Knox, 1960. **Educ:** Wayne State University, Detroit, MI, BA, criminal justice, 1976. **Career:** Detroit Police Dept, Detroit, MI, police officer, 1966-, lieutenant, 1977, inspector, 1978, head of traffic section, 1980, commander, 1986, chief of police, 1991-93. **Orgs:** International Association Chief of Police; Michigan Association Chiefs of Police. **Military Serv:** US Army, sergeant, 3 years.

KNOX, WAYNE D. P.
Community developer. **Personal:** Born Jun 19, 1947, West Reading, PA; son of Mary V Peagram Knox and John W Knox; children: Latina Marie. **Educ:** Cheyney State Coll, BA 1970; Pennsylvania State Univ, M 1984. **Career:** City of Reading, dir of orientation & training USAC project 1974-75; Bureau of Planning City of Reading, urban planner 1973-78; Neighborhood Housing Serv of Reading, assoc dir 1978-80, exec dir 1980-82; Neighborhood Reinvestment Corp, field serv officer 1982-92. **Orgs:** Committee mem Reading Downtown Adv Comm 1980-; dir Old Bethel Cultural Serv Ctr 1985-91. **Honors/Awds:** Elected to Natl Coll Poetry Publications 1969,70; pres Youth Employment Serv 1970; Outstanding Serv Awd Cheyney State Coll 1970. **Military Serv:** US Army, E-5 2 yrs; Letter of Commendation, 1st Infantry Div 1971. **Business Addr:** Director of Planning and Comm Dev, PO Box 266, Dinwiddie, VA 23841.

KNOX, WAYNE HARRISON
Company executive. **Personal:** Born Apr 26, 1942, Atlanta, GA; son of Lessie Heard and Nazareth Knox Sr (deceased); married Isabel Houston, Jun 14, 1968; children: Michelle, Vanessa, Meredith. **Educ:** Clark-Atlanta University, BS, physics; Georgia Institute of Technology, MS, nuclear engineering, health physics. **Career:** Western Electric, electrical engineer, 1966-67; Clemson University, graduate teaching asst/student, 1971-72; Clark College, instructor, 1972-74; Westinghouse Hanford, operational health physics supervisor, 1974-77; Battelle Norhtwest, radiation safety auditor, research scientist, 1977-80; Institute of Nuclear Power Operations, project manager, 1980-81; Advanced Systems Technology Inc, president, chief executive officer, 1981-. **Orgs:** Health Physics Society. **Honors/Awds:** Atlanta Minority Business Development Center, Minority Service Firm of the Year, 1991; Inc Magazine, #195 of privately held corporations in US, 1991, #108 fastest growing privately held corporations in US, 1992; Atlanta Public School System, Entrepreneur of the Year, 1993. **Special Achievements:** First physics graduate at Clark-Atlanta University. **Military Serv:** US Air Force, captain; US Army Reserve, major. **Business Addr:** President, Advanced Systems Technology, Inc, 3490 Piedmont Rd NE, Ste 1410, Atlanta, GA 30305-4810, (404)240-2930.

KNOX, WILLIAM ROBERT
Business executive. **Personal:** Born Jun 19, 1951, Alba, AL; son of Johnnie Finch Knox and Henry Knox; divorced; children: Jerett, Rashard, Rachelle. **Educ:** Purdue Univ, BS 1974.

Career: Chicago Bears, defensive back, 1974-77; Correct Piping Co Inc, estimator 1978-83; W R Knox Corp, president, 1980-. **Orgs:** Pres, Purdue Club of Lake Co, 1983. **Honors/Awds:** Mem of East Chicago Sports Hall of Fame; Red Macky Award, Purdue Univ. **Business Addr:** President, W R Knox Corp, PO Box 6351, Gary, IN 46406.

KNOX-BENTON, SHIRLEY
Educational administrator. **Personal:** Born Aug 8, 1937, Carthage, TX; daughter of Rhoberdia Goodwin Byrdsong and Napoleon Byrdsong; married Sammy L Benton; children: Reginald Jerome Knox. **Educ:** Huston-Tillotson Coll, BA 1959; TX A&M Univ, summer study 1965; TX Women's Univ, Masters 1978; Harvard Univ, Ed Spec 1984. **Career:** Southwest High School, asst principal, counselor, music teacher. **Orgs:** Pres Neighborhood Club 1971-; delegate NEA, TSTA, FWCTA 1974-; consultant High School Workshops 1982-; vice pres, pres Ft Worth Counselors Assoc 1983-84, 1984-85; consultant B&B Assocs 1984-; consultant Links Sororities 1984-85; NAACP, Zeta Phi Beta; Texas Assn of Secondary School Principals, Ft Worth Admin Women, Phi Delta Kappa; Camp Fire Girls Board of Dir; member, FWASSP. **Honors/Awds:** Honorary Life Mbrshp PTA 1975; Outstanding Teacher Awd H Ross Perot 1975; Fellowship Harvard Univ 1984; Outstanding Counselor of Yr North Texas CounselingOrganization 1985; Television Talk Shows KTVT Ch 11 1985; appeared in Jet Magazine article on Outstanding Counselor 1985. **Home Addr:** 5901 Eisenhower Dr, Fort Worth, TX 76112.

KNUCKLES, KENNETH J.
City government official. **Career:** City of New York, Dept of General Services, commissioner, 1990-. **Honors/Awds:** First black commissioner of New York City's Dept of General Services. **Business Addr:** Commissioner, Dept of General Services, City of New York, Municipal Building, One Center St, 17th floor, S, New York, NY 10007.

KOGER, LINWOOD GRAVES, III
Physician. **Personal:** Born Feb 21, 1951, Baltimore, MD; son of Margaret Pigott Koger and Linwood G Koger Jr Esq; married Iantha Angela Hill Koger, Jul 4, 1987; children: Brian Anthony Koger, Kelsey Alexandria. **Educ:** Howard Univ, Coll of Liberal Arts BS 1974, Coll of Medicine MD 1978. **Career:** Howard Univ, Dept of General Surgery, resident 1983; private practice Baltimore, physician 1983-85; Meharry Medical Coll, asst prof of surgery 1985-89; Alvin C York VA Med Center, asst chief of surgery, 1985-; Morehouse Medical College, Atlanta, GA, professor of surgery, 1989-. **Orgs:** Fellow, American College of Surgeons 1988-; mem, Assn of Academic Surgeons 1988-; member, Society for Black Academic Surgeons, 1990-. **Honors/Awds:** Diplomate Amer Bd of Surgery 1984; Clinical Sciences Faculty Member of the Year Meharry Med Coll Pre-Alumni Council, 1985-86; Mesenteric Ischemia; The York VA Experience, presented at the NMA Convention, 1989; Outstanding Surgical Faculty Member, Morehouse Medical School, Class of 1994.

KOGER, MICHAEL PIGOTT, SR.
Physician. **Personal:** Born Jan 20, 1953, Baltimore, MD; son of Margaret Pigott Koger and Linwood Koger Jr; children: Michael Pigott, Jr. **Educ:** Fisk Univ; MIT; Meharry Medical Coll, MD 1979. **Career:** Franklin Square Hospital resident physician 1979-82; Provident Hospital, medical staff 1982-85; North Charles General Hospital, medical staff 1982-85; Jai Medical Center, internist 1982-84; Constant Care Medical Center, internist 1984; Basil Health Systems, internist 1985; St Joseph Hospital, physician 1985; Lutheran Hospital, house physician 1985; Hancock Memorial Hospital, internist 1985-86; Sparta Health Care Center, internist 1986; Veterans Administration Medical Center, internist 1986-88; Central State Hospital, medical staff, 1988-92; Northwest Georgia Regional Hospital, physician, 1992-96; South DeKalb Family Health Svcs, 1997; Complete Wellness Medical Ctr, 1997. **Orgs:** Certified in Basic Cardiac Life Support 1981, 1985, 1986, 1988-92; certified in Advanced Cardiac Life Support 1981, 1985; mem Baltimore City Medical Soc 1983-, Medical and Chirurgical Faculty of MD 1983-; chmn Hancock Co Bd of Health Sparta GA 1985-86; mem Medical Assn of GA 1985-86; chmn Dept of Utilization Hancock Memorial Hosp Review and Quality Assurance 1985-86; chmn physician's peer Utilization Review Comm Hancock Memorial Hospital 1985-86; vice pres of medical staff Hancock Memorial Hosp 1986; mem, Amer Society of Internal Medicine 1988-. **Honors/Awds:** Physician's Recognition Award Amer Medical Assn for Continuing Medical Educ 1985; publication ''Your Health,'' a weekly column in The Sparta Ishmaelite newspaper 1985-86; Physician's Recognition Award, Amer Medical Assn for Continuing Medical Educ 1988; Physician's Recognition Award, The American Medical Assn for Continuing Medical Education, 1991. **Home Addr:** PO Box 675832, Marietta, GA 30067, (404)215-0412.

KOKO. See TAYLOR, CORA.

KOMUNYAKAA, YUSEF
Educator. **Personal:** Born Apr 29, 1947, Bogalusa, LA; married Mandy Sayer, 1985; children: one. **Educ:** Univ of Colorado, BA, 1975; Colorado State Univ, MA, 1979; Univ of California, Irvine, MFA, creative writing, 1980. **Career:** Univ of New Orleans, English instructor; New Orleans public schools, poetry instructor; Indiana Univ, Bloomington, assoc prof of English, beginning 1985, full prof, currently. **Honors/Awds:** Claremont Grad School, Kingsley Tufts Poetry Award, 1994; Pulitzer Prize for Poetry, 1994; Kenyon Review Award for Literary Excellence, 1991; San Francisco Poetry Center Award; Natl Endowment for the Arts, two creative writing fellowships. **Special Achievements:** Poetry collections include: Dedications and Other Darkhorses, RMCAJ, 1977; Lost in the Bonewheel Factory, Lynx House, 1979; Copacetic, Wesleyan Univ Press, 1983; I Apologize for the Eyes in My Head, Wesleyan Univ Press, 1986; Dien Cai Dau, Wesleyan Univ Press, 1988; Neon Vernacular, Wesleyan Univ Press, 1993. **Military Serv:** US Army, beginning 1969; awarded Bronze Star; ''Southern Star,'' correspondent, editor. **Business Addr:** Professor of English, Department of English, Indiana University - Bloomington, Bloomington, IN 47405, (812)855-4848.

KONDWANI, KOFI ANUM
Consultant. **Personal:** Born Mar 11, 1955, Dayton, OH. **Educ:** Maharishi Intl Univ Fairfield IA, attended 1976-77; Canada Coll Redwood City CA, attended 1978-79; Univ of CA Dvais, attended 1979-80. **Career:** AUS, admin asst Korea 1972-75; Canada Coll Redwood City CA, recruitment consult 1976-78; TMC Inc San Francisco, transcendental meditation tchr 1977-; Univ of CA Davis, recruitment consult 1979-80; James E Tolleson, public relation rep for home study training course; Dayton & CA, syndicated columnist; Univ of CA, affirmative action officer. **Orgs:** Mem NAACP 1978-; vice pres Black Health Sci 1979-80. **Honors/Awds:** Awd of Gratitude Maharishi Intl Univ 1977; Eula Dyer Awd E Palo Alto CA 1979; Citizens Against Racism Scholarship Redwood City CA 1979. **Military Serv:** AUS E-4 1972-75. **Business Addr:** Affirmative Action Officer, Univ of CA, Davis, CA 95616.

KORAM, M. JAMAL
Educator. **Personal:** Born Nov 30, 1949, Valhalla, NY; son of Margaret Ellease Shephard Aponte-Codero and James Coram; married Binta Ida Denise; children: Anika-Kai, Nilaja, Khente, Omari. **Educ:** SUNY-New Platz, BA, 1975; SUNY-Albany, MS, 1978; Univ of Virginia, EdS, 1989. **Career:** Univ of Maryland, counselor/adviser, 1985-91; Catonsville Community College, counselor, 1985-90; Morgan State Univ, counselor/instructor, 1986-89; Insight and Attitudes, vice pres, educational programs, 1987-96; Sea Island Information Group, vice pres, product development, 1988-; African-American Storyteller's Retreat, prog dir, 1990-; African American Storytelling Arts Institute, director, 1992-; African-American Heritage Educ Drumming camps, dir, 1993-. **Orgs:** Natl Assn of Black Storytellers, president, 1992-94; Friends of Benjamin Banneker Historical Park, president, 1990-92; Griots Circle of Maryland, festival chairperson, 1990-. **Honors/Awds:** The African Liberators Award, Ancestors Roots, 1991; AESOP:Tales of Aethiop the African, Sea Island Information Group, 1990-91; When Lions Could Fly, Sea Island Information Group, 1989; Featured Teller, In the Tradition, Natl Black Storytelling Festival, 1989, 1991, Tribute to Unknown Ancestors, 1990; National Storytelling Festival, 1995; Frederick Douglass Award, Communication, 1997. **Home Addr:** 6120 Rich Avenue, Catonsville, MD 21228, (410)455-9119.

KORNEGAY, HOBERT
Dentist. **Personal:** Born Aug 28, 1923, Meridian, MS; married Ernestine Price; children: Carmon Kateena, X, Donna, James. **Educ:** Morehouse Coll, BS 1945; Meharry Med Coll, DDS 1948; Brooke Army Med Ctr, 1952; Walter Reed US Army Inst of Dental Res. **Career:** Dr of Dental Surgery, Dentist, pvt prac 1948-; Myricks Meridian Nursing Home, dental cons; Volt Tech Corp, dental surgeon 1970-72; Westinghouse Learning Corp, 1971-72; Riley's & St Joseph's Hosp, mem staff; MS Head Start Univ PR Dental Sch, consult preventive dentistry 1970-71; MS UI Prgm, cons. **Orgs:** Lauderdale County Board of Supervisors, bd pres; City of Meridian, city councilman Precinct IV, 1977-89; Meridian Area Dental Society, Mississippi Dental Assn; American and Natl Dental Assns, Academy of Dentistry; Red Cross Board; Salvation Army Board; Boy Scouts, Choctaw Area Council; 4-H Club, advisory council; Toastmasters, Intl Central Optimist Club; Masons; Shriners; Elks; Omega Psi Phi Fraternity; MCCSA; New Hope Baptist Church, trustee; Riley Hospital, staff; Selective Service System, local bd; District Appeal, Southern Judicial Dist, bd chairman; Mississippi Council on Aging, advisory bd; Natl League of Cities, Human and Community Development Steering Committee. **Honors/Awds:** Meharry Med Coll, Outstanding Alumnus, 1988; awards granted from various groups including: Mississippi Dental Assn, Headstart, Daughters of Isis, NAACP; Morehouse College, Candle In the Dark Bennie Achievement Award, 1996; and others. **Military Serv:** US Army, capt 1953-55. **Business Addr:** PO Box 1247, Meridian, MS 39301.

KORNEGAY, WADE M.
Chemical physicist. **Personal:** Born Jan 9, 1934, Mt Olive, NC; son of Estelle Williams Kornegay and Gilbert Kornegay; married Bettie Joyce Hunter; children: Melvin, Cynthia, Laura. **Educ:** NC Central Univ, BS (Summa Cum Laude) 1956; Bonn Univ Germany, 1957; Univ of CA Berkeley, PhD 1961; MIT Sloan School of Mgmt, 1979. **Career:** Univ of CA, postdoctoral fellow 1961-62, rsch assoc 1962; MIT, tech staff mem 1962-71; MIT Radar Signature Studies, tech group leader 1971-86; MIT, assoc div head 1986-93; MIT, Radar Measurements, div head, 1993-. **Orgs:** Mem Amer Physical Soc 1959-; Sigma Xi Sci Rsch Soc 1960-; vice president Humphrey's Task Force on Youth Motivation 1964-68; mem Exec Council of United Church of Christ 1971-77; mem bd dir Natl Consortium for Black Professional Devel 1976-80; Boston City Missionary Soc 1977-; mem YMCA MA & RI Camp Comm 1977-; YMCA Black Achievers Assn 1979; NYAS 1984-; American Institute of Aeronautics and Astronauts 1986-; Alpha Phi Alpha; chairman, board of directors, Two State YMCA 1990-94; mem US Army Science Board 1990-. **Honors/Awds:** Fulbright Fellowship US State Dept 1956-57; Grad Fellowship Danforth Found 1956-61; Natl Sci Found Postdoctoral Fellowship 1961-62; Hon ScD Lowell Univ 1969; Black Achiever Award, Boston YMCA 1979; ML King Jr Achievement Award, Mass Institute of Technology 1980; Scientist of the Year, National Society of Black Engineers 1990. **Business Addr:** Division Head, Massachusetts Inst of Tech, 244 Wood St, Lexington, MA 02173.

KORNEGAY, WILLIAM F.
Personnel director. **Personal:** Born Mar 9, 1933, Apalachicola, FL; married Dorothy L Little; children: Bill, Jr. **Educ:** Bethune-Cookman Coll, BS 1954; FL A&M U, MEd 1961; Univ of IL, PhD 1970. **Career:** General Motors Corp, Flint, MI, dir, personnel, 1985-; General Motors Corp, Detroit, MI, dir, org, res & devt, 1982-85; Fisher Body Div, dir Quality of Work Life 1979-82; Gen Motors Inst, dean of student affairs 1974-79; Bethune-Cookman Coll FL, acad dean of instr 1970-74; Univ of IL, coord of math tchrs 1967-70; Bethune-Cookman Coll FL, asst prof math 1966-67; Hampton Jr Coll, instr sci & math 1961-66; Rosenwald HS FL, head of sci dept 1957-58; Univ HS FL, head sci dept 1958-61. **Orgs:** Bd of trustees Jr Achvmt 1975-80; bd of trustees Flint Urban Leag 1977-79; bd of trustees United Way Chpn Allocations Com 1978-80; life mem Alpha Phi Alpha Frat. **Honors/Awds:** Ford Fellow 1967; Phi Delta Kappa Educ Frat 1965. **Military Serv:** AUS corpl 1954-56. **Home Addr:** 1486 Kennebec, Flint, MI 48507.

KOTTO, YAPHET
Actor, director, producer. **Personal:** Born Nov 15, 1944, New York, NY; son of Gladys Maria Kotto and Yaphet Manga Bell; married Antoinette Pettyjohn, Jan 29, 1975; children: Natasha, Fredrick, Robert, Sarada, Mirabai, Salina; married Tessie Sinahon, 1997. **Career:** Appeared in Off-Broadway and Broadway productions including Great White Hope, Blood Knot, Black Monday, In White America, A Good Place to Raise a Boy; films: Nothing But a Man 1964, Liberation of Lord Byron Jones 1968, The Thomas Crown Affair 1968, Man and Boy 1972, Live and Let Die 1973, Across 110th St 1973, Report to the Commissioner 1974, Sharks Treasure 1975, Monkey Hustle 1975, Drum 1976, Blue Collar 1978, Alien 1979, Brubaker 1980, Fighting Back 1981, Hey Good Looking 1982, Star Chamber 1983, Eye of the Tiger 1986, Prettykill 1987, Midnight Run, 1988; TV appearances: Losers Weepers 1967, The Big Valley 1967, High Chaparral 1968, Daniel Boone 1968, Hawaii Five-O 1969, Mannix 1969, The Name of the Game 1970, Gunsmoke 1970 Night Chase 1970, Doctors Hospital, 1975, Raid on Entebee 1977; Death in A Minor Key 1979, Women on San Quentin 1983, For Love and Honor 1983, Rage 1984, Harem 1986, In Self Defense 1987, Badge of the Assassin; TV credits include: Homicide, currently. **Business Addr:** Actor, Homicide, c/o NBC-TV, 30 Rockefeller Plaza, New York, NY 10012, (212)664-4444.

KOUNTZE, MABRAY (DOC)
Government employee (retired). **Personal:** Born Mar 22, 1910, Medford, MA. **Educ:** Univ Ext (Harvard) Night School Jour, Certificate 1930-40; Natl Tech School (Hts) Home Study Correspondence Course Elec; since 1970's FCC Comm Lic 2nd Class 1930-40; ICS 2nd other radio home studies (Inst Boys Radio Class Roxbury YMCA and West Medford Ctr). **Career:** Assoc Negro Press (ANP), sports gen news reporter 1929-50; Boston Chronicle, sports assoc editor newspaper 1930-40; Natl Negro Newspaper All Amer Assn, founder and dir sports editors 1930-40; Family Comm City Medford Historic Soc, hist 1930-; Boston Guardian, sports & assoc editor 1940-58; freelance writer 1929-. **Orgs:** Shiloh Bapt Church (West Medford) 1920; NAACP Natl, Local 1930; West Medford comm ctr mem since founding 1930; Carter Woodson Assn; Smithsonian Inst Assn; Boston Museum Afro-American History; Monroe Trotter Natl Equal Rights League; charter mem New England Sports Museum; Medford Historic Soc. **Honors/Awds:** Comm serv of journalism awd, West Medford Comm Ctr 1978; Dr Martin Luther King Jr Awd, Medford NAACP 1982; Greater Boston Black Historian Griot Award, Boston Coll 1984; life mem Natl Baseball Hall of Fame Museum 1984; Life Mem Award, Soc Radio Operators, New England, 1985; Negro Natl OMIK group of radio hams 1985 at OMIK convention; Honorary Member Tuskegee Airmen, East Coast Chapter, 1990; Negro Baseball Leagues Memorial Museum, 1990; Black American West Museum, 1983; Journalism & Historian Proclamation Certificate from Mayors of Cambridge & Medford, 1992. **Special Achievements:** Amateur radio operator, 1954-87; author: This is Your Heritage: 50 Sports Years along Memory Lane; special

papers in several colleges, including Harvard and Howard: ''History of Colored Press in Massachusetts,'' ''A Second Sketch of the Boston Guardian,'' ''Monroe Mason and Monroe Trotter''; history tapes on Tuskegee: Medford Public Library. **Home Addr:** 65 Arlington St, Medford, MA 02155.

KOUNTZE, VALLERY J.
Video company executive. **Personal:** Born in Cambridge, MA; daughter of Alberta M Yearwood Jackman and Wallace H Kountze. **Educ:** Chamberlain School of Retailing, Boston, MA, 1975; USC Graduate School of Business, Los Angeles, CA, CME, 1986. **Career:** Mainstreet Communications, Los Angeles, CA, vice pres, 1981-83; RCA/Columbia Pictures Home Video, Los Angeles, CA, vice pres, mktg, 1983-85, vice pres/gen mgr mm/div, 1985-86; Republic Pictures Home Video, Los Angeles, CA, vice pres, marketing, 1986-87, sr vice pres sales/mktg, 1987-89, president, 1989-91; Mainstreet Marketing, Los Angeles, CA, president, 1991-92; ITC Home Video, Los Angeles, CA, executive vice pres, general manager, 1992-. **Orgs:** Board of directors, AIDS Project Los Angeles, 1990-; president & steering committee, Video Industry AIDS Action Committee, 1989-; member, Video Software Dealers Association IAB, 1990-. **Honors/Awds:** Gold Merchandising Achievement Award, 1985, Bronze Merchandising Achievement Award, 1984, Point of Purchase Advertising Institute; National Superior Achiever Award, RKO General Broadcasting, 1977.

KRAFT, BENJAMIN F.
Educational administrator. **Personal:** Born Jan 15, 1948, Baton Rouge, LA; married Yanick Douyon; children: Benjamin Robeson, Phillip Fouchard, Guileine Frances. **Educ:** Rutgers Coll, AB 1970; Northeastern Univ, JD 1973; Amer Univ, MBA 1978. **Career:** Natl Labor Relations Bd, staff attorney 1973-77; Caribsun Export-Import Inc, pres 1977-79; Big Ben Hardware Haiti, owner/general mgr 1979-86; Florida Memorial College, assoc dir ctr for comm change 1986-87, chairperson, Division of Business Administration, 1988-89, 1990-91, associate dean of faculty, 1989-90; director, Government Relations & Sponsored Programs, 1992-. **Orgs:** Mem DC Bar Assoc 1974-; credit comm mem NLRB Fed Credit Union 1975-77, Haitian Foundation for Aid to Women 1985-86; bd mem treas Haitian Amer Chamber of Commerce 1984-86; bd mem Carib America Enterprises of Florida Inc 1986-; Alpha Phi Alpha Fraternity Inc, Beta Beta Lambda 1989-; NAACP; 100 Black Men of South Florida Inc, 1990-; board member, Center for Family and Child Enrichment, 1988-90. **Honors/Awds:** ACE Fellow, American Council on Education, 1991-92. **Military Serv:** USAF Reserves capt 4 yrs. **Business Addr:** Director, Government Relations & Sponsored Programs, Florida Memorial College, 15800 NW 42nd Ave, Miami, FL 33054.

KRAVITZ, LENNY
Vocalist. **Personal:** son Of Roxie Roker (deceased) and Sy Kravitz; divorced; children: Zoe. **Career:** Singer-musician, currently. **Special Achievements:** Albums include: Let Love Rule, 1989, Mama Said, 1991, Are You Gonna Go My Way, 1993, Circus, 1995; Songs include: ''Rock'n Roll Is Dead'', ''Don't Go and Put a Bullet in Your Head'', ''Thin Ice'', ''God Is Love'', ''Can't Get You Off My Mind''. **Business Addr:** Vocalist, ''Circus'', c/o Virgin Records America, 1790 Broadway, 20th Fl, New York, NY 10019-1412, (212)332-0400.

KRIGGER, MARILYN FRANCIS
Educator. **Personal:** Born Mar 27, 1940, St Thomas, Virgin Islands of the United States; daughter of Mary Augusta Skelton Francis and Charles Adolphus Francis; married Rudolph E Sr; children: Rudolph E Jr. **Educ:** Spelman Coll Atlanta GA, BA Social Sci 1959; Columbia Univ NY, NY, MA History 1960; Univ of DE, Newark, DE, PhD-History 1983. **Career:** Charlotte Amalie High Schl St Thomas, soc stud tchr 1960-66; University of the Virgin Islands St Thomas, history prof 1967-. **Orgs:** Mem Virgin Islds Histl Soc mem Assoc of Caribbean Histn; mem Phi Alpha Theat; consult Virgin Islds Dept of Ed; mem Virgin Islds, Hum Coun; mem VI State Rev Brd for hist; Pres Founder Virgin Island 2000; mem VI Brd of Ed 1974-76; co-chair, VI Status Commission, 1988-93. **Honors/Awds:** Grd flw John Hay Whitney Found Flwshp 1959-60; study-travel flw African Am Inst Ed-to-Africa Prog 1972; Natl Endowment for the Humanities, Summer Fellowships, 1976, 1988. **Home Addr:** Crown Mountain Rd, PO Box 4099, St Thomas, Virgin Islands of the United States 00803, (809)776-8342. **Business Addr:** Professor of History, University of the Virgin Islands, St Thomas, Virgin Islands of the United States 00802, (809)693-1273.

KROON, MARC JASON
Professional baseball player. **Personal:** Born Apr 2, 1973, Bronx, NY. **Career:** San Diego Padres, pitcher, 1995, 1997-. **Business Addr:** Professional Baseball Player, San Diego Padres, PO Box 2000, San Diego, CA 92120, (619)283-4494.

KUGBLENU, GEORGE OFOE
Educational administrator. **Educ:** Shaw Univ, BA 1973; NC State Univ, MPA 1975; Atlanta Univ, PhD 1983. **Career:** Shaw Univ, lecturer 1975-76; Atlanta Univ, asst prof 1979; Dept of Publ Admin Atlanta Univ, chairperson 1983-. **Orgs:** Co-chair/program com COMPA-Atlanta Chap 1982-84; vice pres arts & sci AU Natl Alumni Assoc Atlanta Chap 1984; asst vp, mem SID Atlanta Chap 1985; mem Amer Soc for Public Admin, Natl Forum for Black Publ Admin. **Honors/Awds:** Mem Alpha Chi Honor Soc 1973; Outstanding Facility Awd Dept of Publ Admin Atlanta Univ 1983; Outstanding Svd Awd Natl Forum for Black Publ Admin 1984.

KUMANYIKA, SHIRIKI K.
Dietician, educator. **Personal:** Born Mar 16, 1945, Baltimore, MD; daughter of Catherine Victoria Williams Adams and Maurice Laphonso Adams (deceased); married Christiaan Morssink, Jun 19, 1986; children: Chenjerai. **Educ:** Syracuse Univ Coll Arts & Scis, BA Psychology 1965; Columbia Univ, MS Social Work 1969; Cornell Univ, PhD Human Nutrition 1978; The Johns Hopkins Univ Sch of Hygiene & Publ Health, MPH Epidemiology 1984. **Career:** James Weldon Johnson Mental Health Clinic/Bird S Coler Hospital/Windham Child Serv, caseworker 1965-69; Natl Urban League, dir family planning proj 1969-70; Addiction Rsch and Treatment Corp Dept Educ & Prevention, community organizer 1970-71; Naomi Gray Assoc NY, proj dir 1971-72; Cornell Univ Ujamaa Residential Coll, resident dir 1973-74; Cornell Univ Div Nutritional Sciences, asst prof 1977-84; The Johns Hopkins Univ School of Hygiene & Public Health, asst prof 1984-89, assoc prof, 1989; The Pennsylvania State Univ, University Park, PA, associate professor, 1989-. **Orgs:** Assn of Black Cardiologists; Black Caucus of Health Workers; Soc for Nutrition Educ; Soc for Epidemiologic Rsch; Fellow, Amer Coll of Nutrition; Amer Public Health Assn, 1976-; Amer Dietetic Assn, 1979-; member, Amer Inst of Nutrition, 1990-; mem, Amer Soc for Clinical Nutrition, 1990-. **Honors/Awds:** Delta Omega Natl Public Health Honor Soc elected 1984; Natl Rsch Serv Award Cardiovascular Epidemiology Trainee Johns Hopkins Univ 1983-84; Quaker Oats Fellowship Cornell Univ Div of Nutritional Scis 1976-77; General Mills Fellowship Cornell Univ Div of Nutritional Scis 1974-76; publications & abstracts include: ''Towards a Lower Sodium Lifestyle in Black Communities,'' Journal of the Natl Medical Assn, 1985; ''Obesity in Black Women,'' Epidemiologic Reviews, 1987, ''Beliefs about High Blood Pressure Prevention in a Sample of Black and Hispanic Adults,'' AmerJournal of Preventive Medicine, ''Designing Sodium Reduction Strategies: Problems and Solutions,'' Clinical Nutrition 1989; ''Diet and Chronic Disease Issues for Minority Populations,'' Journal of Nutrition Educ, 1990; ''Association between Oity and Hypertension in Blacks,'' Clinical Cardiology, 1989; ''Theoretical and Baseline Considerations for Diet and Weight Control of Diabetes among Blacks,'' Diabetes Care, 1990. **Business Addr:** Associate Professor, Pennsylvania State University, Dept of Nutrition, South-126 Henderson Building, University Park, PA 16802-6597.

KUMBULA, TENDAYI SENGERWE
Educator. **Personal:** Born Nov 3, 1947, Epworth, Harare, Zimbabwe; son of Mandinema Edna Mungate Kumbula and Isaac Sengerwe Kumbula; married Barbara Ann Jackson Kumbula, May 8, 1971; children: Mandinema R, Runako T, Tendayi S Jr. **Educ:** San Diego State University, San Diego, CA, BA (w/honors) journalism, 1968; University of California, Los Angeles (UCLA), Los Angeles, CA, MA journalism, 1969, MA, poli science, 1970; Univ of South California, Los Angeles, CA, PhD, education, 1976. **Career:** Los Angeles Times, Los Angeles, CA, reporter, 1968-82; The Sunday Mail, Harare, Zimbabwe news editor, 1982-83; The Herald, Harare, Zimbabwe, assistant editor, 1984-86; California State Univ, Long Beach, CA, lecturer, 1987-89; Ball State Univ, Muncie, IN, journalism prof and news editorial sequence coordinator, 1989-. **Orgs:** Member, National Assn of Black Journalists, NABJ, 1990-; founder/faculty advisor, NABJ Student Chapter, Ball State Univ, 1990-; member, Society of Professional Journalists, 1989-; member, Association for Educators in Journalism and Mass Communication, 1990-; member, African Studies Association, 1991-; Motivate Our Minds, bd of trustees, 1992, board member, president, 1996-; Muncie Chapter of Indiana Black Expo; mem, International Platform Assn; overseas dir, M'pisaunga, Mutandiro and Assocs, Harare, Zimbabwe; chair, Ball State Journalism Dept, Multicultural Affairs Advisory Committee. **Honors/Awds:** DuMont Scholarship to attend UCLA graduate school of Journalism, 1968-69; Top Student Reporter, San Diego State University, 1968; Sigma Delta Chi Golden Press Card, 1968; Phi Delta Kappa, Education Honor Society, 1976. **Special Achievements:** Research in Southern Africa on the drought in summer 1993 and publish articles; adviser The Muncie Times, newspapers; co-writer, The Muncie Times; contributor LA/Accent Newspapers; North American contributor to the Southern African Political of Economic Monthly, Harare, Zimbabwe; Coauthor, The Process of Media Writing, 1997. **Business Addr:** Professor, Ball State University, Journalism Department, West Quad 306, Muncie, IN 47306.

KUNES, KEN R.
Insurance company executive. **Personal:** Born Feb 7, 1932, Maywood, IL; son of Emily M Kunes and Arthur F Kunes; divorced; children: Ken, Leigh Ann, Jeff. **Educ:** Univ of AZ, Undergrad 1949; NE Univ, BSBA 1955. **Career:** Maricopa Co, assessor 1968-81; Phoenix-Am Ins Agy, fdr 1965-85; Mid-City Glass & Mirror, owner 1986-; Security Reliable Ins, pres/CEO, currently. **Orgs:** Indep Ins Agents Assn; Phoenix Jaycees; vice pres, Kiwanis; state rep, International Assn of Assessing Officers; past pres, Arizona Assn of Assessing Officers; chairman, Maricopa Cty Sheriff's Religious Comm; licensed preacher, North Phoenix Baptist Church; Alpha Tau Omega Fraternity; Moon Valley Country Club; Phoenix Chamber of Commerce. **Honors/Awds:** Boss of yr Phoenix Midtowners Bus & Professional Women's Club 1975; rec Cert Appraisal Evaluator (CAE) professional desig for Intl Assn of Assessing Ofcrs. **Military Serv:** US Army, sgt. **Business Addr:** President & CEO, Security Reliable Insurance, 8686 North Central Ave, Phoenix, AZ 85020.

KUNJUFU, JAWANZA
Author, consultant. **Personal:** Born Jun 15, 1953, Chicago, IL; son of Mary Snyder Brown and Eddie Brown; married Rita Archer Kunjufu, Jun 1, 1985; children: Walker, Shik. **Educ:** Illinois State Univ, Normal, IL, BA, 1974; Union Graduate Institute, Cincinnati, OH, PhD, 1984. **Career:** African American Images, Chicago, IL, president, 1980-; Full feature film ''Up Against The Wall,'' executive producer. **Orgs:** Board of directors, Hales High School, 1990-; director, Church State Group, 1984-; board of advisors, Project Image, 1988-. **Honors/Awds:** Kool Achiever Award, R J Reynolds, 1989; Man of the Year, Omega Psi Phi, 1990; Communicator of the Year, Alpha Kappa Alpha, 1991; Educator of the Year, Phi Delta Kappa, 1991. **Special Achievements:** Author of 15 books. **Business Addr:** President, African American Images, 1909 West 95th St, Chicago, IL 60643, (312)445-0322.

KUYKENDALL, CRYSTAL ARLENE
Educator, attorney. **Personal:** Born Dec 11, 1949, Chicago, IL; daughter of Ellen Campbell Logan (deceased) and Cleophus Avant; married Roosevelt Kuykendall Jr, Apr 10, 1969 (deceased); children: Kahlil, Rasheki, Kashif. **Educ:** So IL Univ, BA 1970; Montclair State Univ, MA 1972; Atlanta Univ, EdD 1975; Georgetown Univ Law Ctr, JD 1982. **Career:** Seton Hall US Orange NJ, Montclair State Univ, instr 1971-73; DC Publ School, admin intern plnng rsch & eval 1974-75; Natl Comm for Citizens in Ed, dir 1975-77; Natl School Bds Assoc Wash DC, dir urban & minority rel dept 1978-79; PSI Assoc Inc Wash DC, dir ed devel 1979-80; Natl Alliance of Black School Ed, exec dir 1980-81; Roy Littlejohn Assoc Inc, sr assoc 1982-; KIRK Inc (Kreative and Innovative Resources for Kids), president and general counsel. **Orgs:** Chpsn Natl Adv Council Continuing Ed 1978-81; consult Natl Teachers Corp Proj 1978-79; cons, mem Natl Transition Team for the Office of Elem Secondary Ed 1980; mem Amer Assn of School Admin 1974-; mem ed task force Martin Luther King Jr Ctr for Soc Change 1977-; mem Black Amer Law Students Assn 1978-; mem, Amer Bar Assn, Natl Bar Assn, DC Bar Assn, 1988, assoc supvr and curriculum developer, 1992-. **Honors/Awds:** Awd for Outstanding Comm Serv to Women & Minorities, Natl Coalition of Esea Title I Parents 1979; ''50 Leaders of the Future'' Ebony Mag 1978; Hon Citizen New Orleans State of LA, Outstanding Serv Natl Caucus of Black School Bd Mems 1979; Presidential Appointment to The Natl Advisory Council on Continuing Educ, US Pres, Jimmy Carter 1978-81, chairperson 1979-81; Black Excellence Award, Black Alumni Association of Southern IL Univ 1981; Urban League of Greater Muskegon, Service Award; Natl Assn of Blacks in Criminal Justice, Service Award. **Special Achievements:** Author, ''Comm Serv & School Bd,'' Publ Cross Reference Journal of Multicultural Ed 1979; You/Yours: Making the Most of this School Year, motivational calender, 1987; booklet published: ''Improving Black Student Achievement Through Enhancing Self-Image,'' , Amer Univ Mid-Atlantic Equity Center, 1989; ''From Rage to Hope: Strategies for Reclaiming Black and Hispanic Students,'' National Education Service Inc, 1992. **Home Addr:** 8925 Harvest Square Ct, Potomac, MD 20854.

KWAKU-DONGO, FRANCOIS
Chef. **Career:** Spago Chicago, executive chef, currently. **Business Addr:** Executive Chef, Spago Chicago, 520 N Dearborn Pkwy, Chicago, IL 60610, (312)527-3700.

KYLE, GENGHIS
Organist, bandleader. **Personal:** Born Jun 7, 1923, Los Angeles, CA; married Dorothy F; children: Alfred C, Marie J. **Educ:** Los Angeles City Coll; USC Ext. **Career:** Vultee Aircraft Co, sub assembler 1942; City of Los Angeles CA Dept of Water & Power, storekeeper 1954-82 (retired); Genghis Kyle Enterprises, band leader, personal manager. **Orgs:** Mem Broadcast Music Inc; mem Local 47 Musicians Union; mem shop co-dirSignature Music Pub Co Imperial Youth Theater Work; mem Coaches & Mgr Assoc LA. **Honors/Awds:** Salute to Stars Award 1963; Recorded For Many Record Co 1963-73. **Military Serv:** AUS pfc 1943-46; AUS sgt ES 1950. **Business Addr:** Genghis Kyle Enterprises, 1544 W 93 St, Los Angeles, CA 90047.

KYLE, ODES J., JR.
Engineer. **Personal:** Born Jan 30, 1931, Toledo, OH; son of Etta Green Kyle and Odes James Kyle; married Bobbie McClelland; children: Odes, Lewis, Vickie, Lora, George. **Educ:** Mech Engr IN Inst of Tech, BS 1962. **Career:** Timken Co, ind eng 1962, mgmt trainee 1964, foreman 1965, gen foreman 1967, manager of admin 1982, supervisor of training & education &

safety-Canton dist 1986. **Orgs:** Past pres Canton Bd of Educ 1974; mem Recreation Bd; Draft & Bd #109; trustee St Paul AME Canton OH; grand orator of PH Grand Lodge of OH; past grand master Prince Hall Grand Lodge. **Honors/Awds:** Canton Man of Yr 1967; 33 Deg Mason 1975. **Military Serv:** USMC, CPL 1951-53; 3 battle stars. **Home Addr:** 1409 Lawrence Rd NE, Canton, OH 44705.

KYLES, DWAIN JOHANN
Lawyer. **Personal:** Born Aug 25, 1954, Chicago, IL; son of Gwendolyn Kyles Griffin and Rev Samuel Billy Kyles; married Theresa Cropper Kyles, Jun 19, 1988; children: Chad Joseph Kyles. **Educ:** Lake Forest Coll, BA Econ Urban Study 1976; Georgetown Univ Law Center, JD 1979. **Career:** Congressman Harold Ford 9th Dist TN, staff aide 1976-78; Office for Civil Rights Dept Health Educ & Welfare, law clerk 1978-79; Johnson Products Co, staff attny 1979-83; Office of Mayor Harold Washington, special counsel for minority bus devel 1983-84; McCormick Place Convention Center, house counsel, mgmt & intergovt liaison 1984-88; Dept of Economic Devel, special counsel to commissioner 1989-; Heroes A Sports Bar: Grill, Inc, owner, 1987-. **Orgs:** Mem Amer Bar Assoc 1979-, Natl Bar Assoc 1979-, Cook Cty Bar Assoc 1979-; bd mem Forum for Evolution of Progressive Arts 1983-; found & 1st pres mem New Chicago Comm; mem Operation PUSH, NAACP. **Honors/Awds:** Dean's List Jr & Sr Years; 1st recipient of Mentor of the Year Urban Focus 1984.

KYLES, JOSEPHINE H.
Educator. **Personal:** Born Sep 6, 1900, Lynchburg, VA; married Bishop Lynwood W Kyles (deceased); children: 2. **Educ:** Oberlin Coll, MA; Columbia Univ, MA; Union Theol Seminary, MRE; D Adult Educ. **Career:** Lynchburg VA, teacher; VA State Coll and Hampton Inst, instructor; Dept of Christian Educ for the Cncl of Churches of Greater Washington Area, dir; GradSch of Religion of Howard Univ, instructor; Metro Detroit MI Cncl of Churches, dir of christian educ, dir serv dept; Arthritis Foundation Project at Washington Hospital Ctr, social health educator. **Orgs:** Trainer/consultant Covenant for the Natl Ctr on Ministry with the Aging; mem Natl Adv Comm Interfaith Volunteer Caregivers Prog; vstg lecturer in Religious Educ Seminary for Black Ministries in Philadelphia PA; five certificates from the Psychiatric Inst on Stress, Crisis Prevention, Values and Ethics, Alcoholism; mem adv bd DC Village, adv bd Robert Wood Johnson Foundation; delegate Conf of the Soc for Intl Develop in Abijon West Africa; staff mem White House Conf on Aging. **Honors/Awds:** Sojourner Truth Awd.

KYLES, SHARRON FAYE
Police officer. **Personal:** Born Jan 3, 1950, Jackson, MS; daughter of Bennie Lee Lewis Catchings and Willie Lee Catchings; married James Tyrone Kyles, Aug 9, 1978 (divorced); children: Darrell Augustues Kyles, La Keista Renee Kyles. **Educ:** Jackson State Coll, Jackson MS, 1968-69; Jackson Police Training Academy, Jackson MS, 1975. **Career:** Jackson Police Department, patrol sergeant, 1975-. **Orgs:** Pres, Smith Chapel Freewill Baptist Church Choir, 1975-85; pres, Jackson Concerned Officers for Progress, 1980-88; Committee on Administration, YWCA, 1984-; mem, Natl Black Police Assn, 1986-; mem, New Mount Zion Inspirational Choir, mem, NAACP; mem, Mississippi Mass Choir. **Honors/Awds:** Outstanding Bravery, North Jackson Kiwanis Club, 1983; Lawman of the Year, LA/MS/West Tenn Dist of Kiwanis, 1983-84; Distinguished Service Award, Jackson Police Dept, 1984; Police Officer of the Month, Jackson Assn of Life Underwriters, 1984; J-Cop Silver Shield Community Service, Jackson Concerned Officers for Progress, 1985; Outstanding Heroic Performance Award, Lanier Class of 1965, 1985; The Mississippi Mass Choir Live Gospel Recording, 1988. **Business Addr:** Sergeant, Jackson Police Dept, City of Jackson, 327 East Pascagoula Street, Jackson, MS 39205.

L

LABAT, ERIC MARTIN
Oceanographer, scientist. **Personal:** Born May 8, 1962, Bay St Louis, MS; son of Geraldine T and Rudolph H Labat; married Katrina R Lane, Jun 5, 1993; children: Arielle. **Educ:** University of Southern Mississippi, BS, 1985; Naval Post Graduate School, 1987; University of New Orleans, attended. **Career:** Naval Oceanographic Office, physical science trainee, 1980-83, computer science trainee, 1983-85; mathematician, 1986-91, oceanographer, 1991-. **Orgs:** Alpha Phi Alpha Fraternity Inc, Zeta Mu Lambda, president, 1991-94; St Rose de Lima Catholic Church Pastoral Council, vp, 1991-93; Magic's AYSE Program, chairman, 1992-95; Naval Oceanographic Office EEOC, black employment program coordinator, 1990-; Marine Technology Society, 1992-; NAACP, 1990-; Blacks In Government (BIG) Stennis Chapter. **Honors/Awds:** Alpha Phi Alpha Fraternity Inc, Walter "Duke" Williams Alumni Brother of the Year, 1992; North Gulfport Civic Club, Community Service Award, 1991; Dollars and Sense Magazine, America's Best & Brightest Business and Professional Men, 1991; Doctor of Laws, Faith Grant Coll, Birmingham, AL, 1994; Honoris Causa. **Home Addr:** 7914 Lanai Court, Diamondhead, MS 39525, (228)255-7098. **Business Addr:** Oceanographer, Naval Oceanographic Office, 1002 Balch Blvd, Code N333, Stennis Space Center, MS 39529-5001, (228)688-4389.

LABAT, WENDY L.
Business owner. **Personal:** Born Jul 24, 1957, Chicago, IL; daughter of Ruby J. Martin White and Edward G. White Jr.; married Terry Abernathy (divorced 1983); children: Erika, Craig. **Educ:** Fisk University, Nashville, TN, 1974-76; San Diego State University, San Diego, CA, BS, 1978; National University, San Diego, CA, MBA, 1980; Amos Tuck at Dartmouth, Hanover, NH, MBEP, 1988. **Career:** Southern Belk Business Systems, president/CEO, 1984-91; Labat Enterprises, president, 1991-. **Orgs:** Vice-chairperson, Executive Committee, Georgia Minority Supplier Development Council, 1988-; Exec Committee, Coweta Communities in Schools Inc, vice chairperson. **Honors/Awds:** Supplier of the Year, National Minority Supplier Development Council, 1990; Woman on the Move, Austin Business Resource Center, 1990.

LABELLE, PATTI (PATRICIA LOUISE HOLTE)
Singer, actress. **Personal:** Born May 24, 1944, Philadelphia, PA; daughter of Henry Holte; married Armstead Edwards, 1969; children: Stanley, Dodd, Zuri. **Career:** Began career as lead singer of Patti LaBelle & the Bluebelles 1961-70; Sang with The Ordettes; Formed new group LaBelle, 1970-77; solo artist, 1977-; participant Live AID Benefit Rock Concert; TV specials: "Sisters in the Name of Love" 1986, "Motown Returns to the Apollo"; actress: Working (PBS production), 1981, Your Arms Too Short to Box with God (gospel musical), 1981-82, A Soldier's Story, (film), 1985, Unnatural Causes (TV film), 1986; Television: Out All Night, 1992-93. **Honors/Awds:** Eight Grammy nominations; three Emmy nominations; B'nai B'rith Creative Achievement Award; Image Award for Musical Excellence, NAACP; Congressional Black Caucus Medallion; Entertainer of the Year Award, NAACP, 1986; Special Citation from President Ronald Reagan, 1986; Platinum album, "Winner in You", 1986; Grammy Award for Best R & B Vocal performance, 1992; (Heritage) Soul Train, Career Achievement Award, 1996; Berklee College of Music, Honorary Doctor of Music Degree, 1996; Essence Award, 1998. **Special Achievements:** Collaborated with Fiori Roberts Cosmetics to create a new line of lip and nail color products. **Business Addr:** Vocalist, Gems, c/o MCA Records, 100 Universal City Plaza, Universal City, CA 91608.

LABRIE, HARRINGTON
Elected official. **Personal:** Born Oct 6, 1909, Lebeau, LA; married Ernestine (deceased); children: Dolores Fischer, Ann Marie McCune, Theron, Kenneth J, Willard, Doris Matthew, Janice Domechet. **Educ:** Immaculate Conception High School 1927. **Career:** St Landry Parish School Bd, school bus driver 1952-75; Cattle, Cotton, farmer 1932-; Williams Progressive Life Ins Co, insurance agent 1951-; St Landry Parish Ward 4, justice of peace 1972-; Labrie Realty, chmn of bd 1979-. **Orgs:** Grand knight Knights of Peter Claver 1932-; mem NAACP 1956-, LA Justice of Peace Assoc 1972-; advisory bd mem First Natl Bank 1978-. **Home Addr:** PO Box 395, Lebeau, LA 71345.

LACEY, BERNARDINE M.
Nursing education director. **Personal:** Born Jul 28, 1932, Vicksburg, MS; daughter of Katie & Leroy Jackson; married Dr Wilbert Lacey, Apr 27, 1970; children: Amando Gomez, Elthon, Jacinta. **Educ:** Gilfoy School of Nursing, Mississippi Bapt Hosp, Jackson MS, Nursing Diploma, 1962; Georgetown Univ, School of Nursing, BSN, 1968; Howard Univ, MA, sociology, 1985; Teachers Coll, Columbia Univ, New York, NY, EdD, 1991. **Career:** Howard Univ, Nursing Grad Prog, College of Nursing, asst prof, 1986-94; W K Kellogg-Howard Univ, Coll of Nursing, Homeless Project, proj dir, 1988-94; Univ of VA, clinical asst, 1991-95; Johns Hopkins School of Nursing, lecturer, 1991-93, adjunct asst prof, 1991-93; Howard Univ, Coll of Medicine, nurse dir, 1993-94; Western Mich Univ, dir, school of nursing, 1994-. **Orgs:** Fellow of Amer Academy of Nursing; Amer Nurses Assn; District of Columbia Nurses Assn; Natl Black Nurses Assn; Sigma Theta Tau Intl Nurses Honor Society; Natl League of Nursing; Society for Nursing History. **Honors/Awds:** New York Univ-Sch of Educ, Div of Nursing, Health Policy & Legislative Award, 1994; Amer Nurses Assn, Pearl McIver Public Health Nurse Award, 1994; AKA Sorority Inc, Iota Gamma Omega, Bowie State Univ, Bowie MD, Community Svc Award, 1994; Goergetown Univ, School of Nursing, Distinguished Alumna Award, 1993; James Madison Univ, Dept of Nursing, Distinguished Scholar Lecturer, 1992. **Special Achievements:** "Hands on Health Care: Taking the Classroom to the Street," The ABNF Journal, Spring 1993; Definition of Poverty, Needs Rethinking, Guest Editorial, Nursing & Health Care, Feb 1992; Caring for the Homeless, Arkansas League for Nursing, annual meeting, Little Rock, Arkansas, 1994; An Innovative Approach To Homelessness, Urban Initiatives Conference, Marquette Univ, 1994; Souls On Fire, Recognition Ceremony, Georgetown Univ School of Nursing, Washington DC, 1993. **Business Addr:** Director, School of Nursing, Western Michigan University, Kalamazoo, MI 49008, (616)387-2883.

LACEY, MARC STEVEN
Journalist. **Personal:** Born Nov 11, 1965, New York, NY; son of Jean Lilian Moran Lacey and Earle Milton Lacey. **Educ:** Cornell University, Ithaca, NY, BA, 1987. **Career:** The New York Times, New York, NY, stringer, 1986-87; The Washington Post, Washington, DC, intern, summer, 1987; The Buffalo News, Buffalo, NY, journalist, 1987-89; The Los Angeles Times, Los Angeles, CA, journalist, 1989-. **Orgs:** Member, Natl Assn of Black Journalists, 1988-; member, Cornell University Alumni Assn, 1989-. **Honors/Awds:** National Merit Achievement Scholarship, 1983-87; Quill & Dagger Senior Honor Society, Cornell University, 1987; Cornell Tradition Academic Scholarship Cornell, 1983-85; Summer Research Exchange Program, Univ of California-Berkeley Summer, 1985. **Business Addr:** Staff Writer, The Los Angeles Times, Washington Bureau, 1875 Eye Street, NW #1100, Washington, DC 20006.

LACEY, WILBERT, JR.
Psychiatrist. **Personal:** Born Dec 1, 1936, Washington, DC; married Bernardine Jackson; children: 4. **Educ:** Howard U, BS 1959; Howard Univ Coll of Med, MD 1968. **Career:** Howard Univ Coll of Med, clinical asst prof 1975-; Howard Univ Hlth Serv, Univ psychiatrist 1973-. **Orgs:** Mem DC Me Soc; Nat Med Assn; Am Inst of Hypnosis; Am Coll Hlth Assn; Metro WA Soc for Adolescent Psychiatry; Joint Cncl of WA Psyc Soc; life mem Kappa Alpha Psi Frat; mem Fox Ridge Civic Assn 1977. **Honors/Awds:** Cert Am Bd of Psychiatry & Neurology Inc 1977. **Military Serv:** AUS 1st lt 1960-62. **Business Addr:** Howard Univ, Washington, DC 20059.

LACHMAN, RALPH STEVEN
Physician, educator. **Personal:** Born May 12, 1935; married Rose Katz; children: Nicole, Monette. **Educ:** Temple Univ, BA 1957; Meharry Med Coll, MD 1961; Bronx-Lebanon Med Cntr NYC, rotating intern 1961-62; Mt Sinai Hosp NYC, ped resident 1962-64, radiology 1966-68; Children's Hosp Boston, ped radiology 1969-70. **Career:** US Army Hosp Bad Kremznach, Germany, Cpt USMC 1964-66; UCLA, asst prof radiology & ped 1970-73, assoc prof 1973-79, prof 1979-. **Orgs:** Chmn Equal Opp/Academic Affirm Action Comm UCLA 1981-83; mem Soc Pediatric Radiol; Am Coll Radiology; LA Pediatric Soc; AAAS; Western Soc for Pediatric Rsrch; Am Fedn Clinical Rsrch. **Honors/Awds:** Fellowship Am Coll of Radiology 1983; to date 165 scientific articles published, 3 books, 10 book chapters. **Military Serv:** AUS Capt Med Corps 1964-66. **Business Addr:** Prof Radiology & Pediatrics, UCLA, HGH/UCLA Med Center, Torrance, CA 90509.

LACKEY, EDGAR F.
Association officer. **Personal:** Born Mar 9, 1930, Ennis, TX; son of Thelma K Lackey and Sam Lackey; children: Anglyn, Anita, James, Mia, Ronald, Tammy. **Educ:** Texas Coll, BA 1963; Ball State Univ, MBA; Univ of Oklahoma, MLS. **Career:** Hamilton Pk High School, educator & coach; Dallas Industrial School, educator; USAF, criminal investigator; Lynn's Enterprises Private Investigators, owner; National Conference of Christians and Jews, executive officer, currently. **Orgs:** Asst dir OIC; dir Law Enforce Minority Manpower Proj; mem Fed Exec Assn; NAACP; Urban League; Negro C of C Dallas. **Military Serv:** USAF Special Investigator 1947-60. **Business Phone:** (214)374-8540.

LA COUR, LOUIS BERNARD
Attorney. **Personal:** Born Aug 12, 1926, Columbus, OH; son of Cleo Carter La Cour and Louis La Cour; married Jane McFarland; children: Lynne Denise, Avril R La Cour-Hartnagel, Cheryl Celeste La Cour-Belyn. **Educ:** OH State Univ, BA 1951; Franklin Univ Law School, LLB 1961; Capital Univ, JD 1967. **Career:** City of Columbus, OH, land acquisition ofcr 1959-62; Capital Univ Law Sch, adjunct prof 1975-80; Private Practice, attorney; US District Court, special master 1981-84; GreenBern Mgmt, Inc, president. **Orgs:** Past vp, devel code adv comm United Comm Council; Columbus Bar Assn, past pres Columbus Urban League; past sec Mid-OH Reg Planning Commission; past vice pres, Columbus Area Intl Prog; mem Columbus Leadership Conf, Selective Serv Appeals Bd, Fed Bar Exam Comm, So Dist, E Div; past vice chmn Columbus Civic Ctr Comm; steering comm Devel Com Greater Columbus; adv bd Bishop Hartley HS; adviser, Univ Area Civic Assn, Eastland Area Civic Assn, Kensington Park Area Civic Assn, Blendon Meadows Civic Assn, Model Cities Neighborhood Rev Bd, Bethany Homes Devel Corp, Bide-A-Wee Pk Civic Assn; spec master US Dist Ct 1975-80; fed bar examiner US Dist Ct 1980-84; spec counsel Columbus City Atty 1984-91; trustee Jazz Arts Group 1984-85; trustee, Greater Columbus ArtsCouncil; trustee, Ohio Citizens Comtee for the Arts; American Planning Assn Task Force; The Capitol Club; New Albany Country Club. **Honors/Awds:** Most Influential Men in Columbus 1972. **Military Serv:** US Air Corps 1944-45. **Home Addr:** 1809 N Cassady Ave, Columbus, OH 43219. **Business Addr:** Attorney, 400 E Town St, Suite B-30, Columbus, OH 43215-4700, (614)221-5373.

LACOUR, NATHANIEL HAWTHORNE
Educational administrator. **Personal:** Born Feb 11, 1938, New Orleans, LA; married Josie Brown; children: Carey Renee,

Carla Cenee, Charlette Jene. **Educ:** So Univ A&M Coll Baton Rouge, BS 1960; So Univ A&M Coll Baton Rouge, MSTB 1965. **Career:** United Teachres of New Orleans, pres 1970-; Carver Sr HS, biology teacher 1961-70. **Orgs:** Officer various tchr assns; chmn New Orleans Manpower Adv Planning Council; mem Am Inst of Biologists; mem exec bd Greater New Orleans AFL-CIO; mem YMCA; mem NAACP; exec bd New Orleans Urban League; bd of dirs New Orleans Pub Library. **Business Addr:** President, United Teachers of New Orleans, 4370 Louisa Dr, New Orleans, LA 70126.

LACOUR, VANUE B.
Attorney (retired). **Personal:** Born Sep 10, 1915, Natchez, LA; son of Ernestine Prudhomme and Ernest Lacour; married Arthemise Wilson; children: Vanue B Jr, Leonard J, Cynthia Marie, Bernard L, Elaine Theresa, Michael M, Anthony G. **Educ:** Xavier Univ New Orleans, AB 1938; Howard Univ, JD 1941. **Career:** Private Practice Kansas City, MO, attorney 1942-47; Southern Univ Law School Baton Rouge, LA, educator 1947-70, dean law school 1970-71; Lacour & Calloway, retired atty. **Orgs:** Past chmn LA Commn Govtl Ethics; advisory mem Istrouma Area Boy Scout Council; mem Alpha Phi Alpha; past mem LA Commission of Ethics for Public Employees. **Honors/Awds:** Alpha Eta Honor Soc; Silver Beaver Boy Scouts Amer; past vice pres Natl Bar Assn; past sec MO Conf of Branches-NAACP; Baton Rouge Legal Secretaries Assn, boss of the yr 1980-81; past bd mem Blundon Home-Family Counseling Serv; Branch Chapter American Red Cross.

LACY, EDWARD J.
Educator (retired). **Personal:** Born Sep 13, 1922, Dallas, TX; married Freddie J Slusher; children: Charles M. **Educ:** A&T Coll, BS 1947; Columbia Univ, MA 1952; Springfield Coll, further study 1953; Indiana Univ, further study 1954-55. **Career:** Voorhees Jr Coll Denmark, SC, teacher & coach 1947-50; Bladen Cnty Schools Elizabethtown, NC, teacher & coach 1950-56; St Paul's Coll Lawrenceville, VA, teacher & coach 1956-57; Booker T Washington HS Tulsa, OK, teacher & coach 1957-74; Tulsa Publ Schools, dir of athletics/phys ed, retired 1990. **Orgs:** Bd mgmt Hutcherson YMCA Tulsa 1960-; adv bd St John's Hospital Tulsa 1981-; mem Kappa Alpha Psi Frat 1946-; consult Am Football Coaches Assn 1971; OK Coaches Assn 1970; NE Dist HS Coaches Miami, OK 1972; mem Natl HS Coaches Assn; Am All Health Phys Educ & Rec; mem N Tulsa Optimist Club; Tulsa Pk & Rec Bd; St Monica Cath Par Counc. **Honors/Awds:** Physical Fitness Award Southeast Tulsa Jaycees 1968; Coach of the Year Dist 5 Natl HS School Coaches Assn 1972; Coach of the Year OK Coaches Assn 1968, 1971, 1973; OK Hall of Fame OK Coaches Assn 1979. **Military Serv:** AUS Sgt served 10 months. **Home Addr:** 21 E Woodrow Pl, Tulsa, OK 74106.

LACY, HUGH GALE
Attorney. **Personal:** Born Mar 23, 1948, Huntsville, AL; son of Mary Crean Berry Lacy and Leo Marshuetz Lacy; married Paulette Nettles, Feb 12, 1977; children: Kenitra Irma, Hugh Shomari. **Educ:** Alabama A&M University, BA, 1972, MEd, 1974; Miles Law School, JD, 1989. **Career:** Huntsville City Board of Education, teacher corps intern, 1972-74; US Army Ballistic Missle Defense Systems Command, supply management assistant, 1974-75; US Army Ordnance Missile & Munitions Center & School, education specialist, 1975-92; Hugh G Lacy, PC, attorney, 1990-; US Army Corps of Engineers, education specialist, 1992-. **Orgs:** St Bartley P B Church, building & education committees, 1986-; Alpha Phi Alpha Fraternity, Inc, area director, 1982-, associated editor to Sphinx, 1990-; Alabama Lawyers Association, 1989-; Alabama Trial Lawyers Association, 1990-; American Bar Association, 1990-; National Bar Association, 1990-; NAACP, 1972-; Special Education Action Committee, counselor, 1989-; Huntsville/Madison County Bar Association, legislative committee, 1990-. **Honors/Awds:** 4-H Club Leadership Award, 1974; US Army Ordnance Missile & Munition Center & School, Performance, 1985-92, Letters of Appreciation, 1982, 1988-91; US Army Missile Command, Equal Employment Opportunity Counselor Appreciation Certificate, 1992; Alpha Phi Alpha Fraternity, Inc, Brother of the Year, State of Alabama, 1990, Brother of the Year, Delta Theta Lambda, 1991. **Special Achievements:** Great American Family Award, 1990; Role Model of the Week, Speaking Out Newspaper, 1990. **Home Addr:** 146 Lauros Dr, Harvest, AL 35749-9468. **Business Addr:** Attorney, PO Box 18341, 300 E Clinton Ave, Ste 2, Huntsville, AL 35804, (205)536-1849.

LACY, VENUS
Professional basketball player. **Personal:** Born Feb 9, 1967. **Educ:** Louisiana Tech Univ. **Career:** Seattle Reign, center, 1997-98; Long Beach Stingrays, 1998-. **Honors/Awds:** US Basketball Writers, Player of the Year, 1990. **Business Addr:** Professional Basketball Player, Long Beach Stingrays, One World Trade Center, Ste 202, Long Beach, CA 90831-0202, (562)951-7297.

LACY, VERSIA LINDSAY
Educator. **Personal:** Born Mar 15, 1929, Houston, TX; married JW; children: Lindsay Keith, Elizabeth Juliene. **Educ:** Huston-Tillotson Coll, BS 1944-48; Atlanta Univ, MS 1948-50; Univ of TX, 1952,55-56; Univ of OR, 1958; TX Womans Univ, PhD 1966-73. **Career:** Paul Quinn Coll, instr, dean of women 1950-55; Tyler Jr Coll, asst prof 1956-66; TX Womans Univ, grad rsh asst 1966-69; Bishop Coll, assoc prof 1969-77; TX So Univ, guest prof 1971; Dallas ISD, sci/health coord 1977-82; Dallas ISD Sci/Engrg Magnet, prof 1977-. **Orgs:** Mem Radiation Rsch Soc, AAAS, AIBS, NIS, SW Photobiol Group, TARR, TAS, NTBS, BBB Biol Soc, BKX Sci Hon Soc, TWU Club of Sigma Xi Soc, Third Natl Anti-Basileus Zeta Phi Beta Sor Inc 1952-54; gov S Central Dist Natl Assoc of Negro Bus & Professional Womens Clubs Inc; 2nd natl vice pres NANB & PH Clubs Inc 1979-81; chpsn Amer Heart Assoc Spec Task Force; bd dir Amer Heart Assoc Dallas Chapt; bd dir YMCA Moorland Br; natl ed of Crown; mem SME Comm Mustang Dist, Circle 10 Counc, BSA, PTA, David W Carter & DA Huley Schools. **Honors/Awds:** Top Ladies of Distinction Inc; Woman of the Year Psi Chap Iota Phi Lambda Sor So Reg 1976; 1st Runner-up Natl Liola P Parker Awd; Woman of the Year United for Action Dallas Black C of C 1976; Outstanding Achievement Awd Zeta Phi Beta 1974; Outstanding Achievement Awd, Top Ladies of Distinction 1973; Sojourner Truth Natl Meritorious Awd 1982; Total Images Awd Mountain View C 1983. **Business Addr:** Professor, Dallas ISD, Science/Engineering Magnet, 3434 So RL Thornton Fwy, Dallas, TX 75224.

LACY, WALTER
International program management specialist. **Personal:** Born Nov 14, 1942, Huntsville, AL; son of Lelia Acklin Lacy (deceased) and Jessie Lacy Sr (deceased); married Julianne White, Sep 5, 1964; children: Lorraine Lacy Young, Walter Marcellus, Julian Crishon. **Educ:** Alabama A&M University, BS, 1966, MS, 1972. **Career:** US Army Msl & Mun Cen & School, electronics instructor, 1966-70; General Electric Co, equipment specialist, 1970-71; Safeguard Logistics Command, equipment specialist, 1971-73, equal opportunity specialist, 1973-74; US Army Missile Command, equipment specialist, 1974-85, logistics management specialist, 1985-92, intl prgm management specialist, 1992-. **Orgs:** Free and Accepted Masons, 1968-82; Seminole Service Center, tutor, board of directors, 1989-; Blacks in Government, parliamentarian, first vp, 1990-93; Alpha Phi Alpha Fraternity, various committees, 1991-; American Poetry Assn, 1989, 1990. **Honors/Awds:** American Poetry Society, Honorable Mention, poem, 1991; US Army Missile Command, Exceptional Performance Awards, 1990-97. **Special Achievements:** Poetry published: American Poetry Anthology, 1989. **Home Addr:** 1724 Millican Pl, Huntsville, AL 35816, (205)837-9034. **Business Phone:** (205)313-6889.

LACY-PENDLETON, STEVIE A.
Journalist. **Personal:** Born Apr 19, 1956, Oklahoma City, OK; daughter of Robert & Bette J. Lacy. **Educ:** Case Western Reserve University, BA, 1974. **Career:** Xenia Daily Gazette, reporter, 1975-79; Dayton Daily News, reporter, 1979-80; SI Advance, columnist, Sunday prespective editor, currently. **Orgs:** Society of Seamen's Children, board of directors; National Council of Negro Women, board of directors. **Honors/Awds:** Three Associated Press Awards (NY State); Numerous Community Service Awards in past 15 years; Deadline Club Award; Front Page Award. **Business Addr:** Editor/Columnist, Staten Island Advance, 950 Fingerboard Rd, Staten Island, NY 10305.

LADAY, KERNEY
Office equipment executive. **Personal:** Born Mar 14, 1942, Ville Platte, LA; son of Lillius Laday and Sampson; married Floradese Thomas; children: Marucs K, Kerney Jr, Anthony D. **Educ:** Southern Univ, BS 1965; Louisiana State Univ, MS 1970; Southern Methodist Univ, MBA 1982. **Career:** Southern Univ, asst placement dir 1968-71; Xerox Corp, vice pres 1971-, vice pres/region general mgr. **Orgs:** Bd of dir Eltrex Corp 1982-86, United Way of Dallas 1987-; bd of dir North TX Commn; trustee Shiloh Bapt Church Plano TX; assoc bd of dirs SMU; bd of dir African American Museum; mem Dallas Transportation "Thing Tank"; bd of dir Dallas Chamber of Commerce; bd of dir Dallas Citizens Council; bd of dir North Carolina Natl Bank of Texas. **Honors/Awds:** Renowned Graduate Southern Univ; Presidential Citation Natl Educ for Equal Opportunities. **Military Serv:** Signal Corp capt 1965-68. **Home Addr:** 6001 Jericho Court, Dallas, TX 75248. **Business Addr:** Vice Pres/Regional Genl Mgr, Xerox Corporation, 222 W Las Colinas Blvd, Irving, TX 75039.

LADD, FLORENCE CAWTHORNE
Association executive, educator, psychologist. **Personal:** Born Jun 16, 1932, Washington, DC; daughter of Eleanor Willis Cawthorne and William Cawthorne; married; children: Michael Cawthorne Ladd. **Educ:** Howard Univ, BS 1953; Univ of Rochester, PhD 1958. **Career:** Age Center of New England, rsch assoc 1958-60; Simmons Coll, asst prof 1960-61; Robert College (Istanbul), asst prof 1962-63; Harvard Graduate School of Educ, lecturer & rsch assoc 1965-70; Radcliffe Inst, fellow 1970-72; Harvard Graduate School of Design, assoc prof 1972-77; School of Architecture & Planning MIT, assoc dean 1977-79; Wellesley Coll, dean of students 1979-84; S African Educ Program, consultant 1984-85; WEB DuBois Inst, visiting scholar; Oxfam Amer, dir of educ & outreach 1985-87, assoc exec dir, beginning 1987; Mary Ingraham Bunting Institute of Radcliffe College, dir, 1989-. **Orgs:** Mem Black Women for Policy Action; mem TransAfrica; bd mem Overseas Development Network, United Natl Intl Rsch & Training Inst for the Advancement of Women; Natl Council of South African Programs; Association of Women in Development; Trustee, Bentley College; Institute of Contemporary Art (Boston), board member; Overseer, WGBH (Boston), board member; National Council for Research on Women, board member. **Honors/Awds:** Hon mem Amer Inst of Architects, Wellesley Alumnae Assn, Phi Beta Kappa, Sigma Xi. **Home Addr:** 82 Larch Rd, Cambridge, MA 02138. **Business Addr:** Director, Mary Ingraham Bunting Institute, Radcliffe College, 34 Concord Ave, Cambridge, MA 02138.

LADNER, JOYCE A.
Educational administrator. **Educ:** Tougaloo Coll, 1964; Washington Univ, master's degree and doctorate, sociology. **Career:** Howard Univ, Academic Affairs, vp, until 1994, university pres, 1994-. **Business Addr:** President, Howard University, 2400 6th St NW, Washington, DC 20059, (202)806-6100.

LADNER, TERRIA ROUSHUN
Advertising executive. **Personal:** Born Jun 7, 1962, Torrance, CA; daughter of Geraldine Ladner. **Educ:** Columbia College, BA, 1985; Northwestern University, MS, 1989. **Career:** Burrell Communications Group, assistant account executive, 1988-89, account executive, 1989-91; Lockhart and Pettus Advertising, account executive, 1992-. **Orgs:** Women's Advertising Club of Chicago, Education Committee, 1985-90.

LADSON, LOUIS FITZGERALD
Pharmacist. **Personal:** Born Jan 3, 1951, Georgetown, SC; son of Susan Smith Ladson and Henry Ladson; married Sharon Harris; children: Eric, Tisha. **Educ:** St Olaf Coll, BA History 1978; Creighton Univ, BS Pharmacy 1981; Central Michigan Univ, MA Business 1982. **Career:** James A Haley VA Hosp, resident pharmacist 1982-83; SuperX Univ Sq Mall, pharmacy mgr 1983-84; Lincourt Pharmacy, pharmacy mgr 1984-. **Orgs:** Mem Amer Soc of Hosp Pharm 1979-, Kappa Psi Frat 1980-, Natl Assoc of Retail Druggists 1982-, FL Pharmacy Assoc 1982-; pharmacy consultant Adult Care Living Facilities 1984-; mem Chamber of Commerce Clearwater 1985-, NAACP Clearwater Chap 1985-; mem, Alpha Phi Alpha Frat 1988-; member, Professional Compounders of America; cub master, Boy Scouts, Pack #52, 1991; advisory board member, care one, 1990; advisory board member, Mt Zion AME Church, 1990; advisory board, Pharmacy Mag, Drug Topics; CCH Homecare, advisory bd. **Honors/Awds:** Outstanding Leadership Certificate Creighton Univ 1981; Outstanding Serv Awd Creighton Univ Black Faculty 1982; Pharmacy Consultant Bd of Pharmacy 1982; Lincourt Pharmacy Newsletter 1984-. **Military Serv:** US Army, Major; Certificates of Appreciation 1977, 1980, Commission 1981. **Business Addr:** Dir of Pharmacy, Lincourt Pharmacy, 501 S Lincoln Ave, #20, Clearwater, FL 34616.

LAFAYETTE, BERNARD, JR.
Educational administrator. **Personal:** Born Jul 29, 1940, Tampa, FL; married Kate Bulls; children: 2. **Educ:** Amer Baptist Theological Seminary, BA 1961; Harvard U, EdM 1972, EdD 1974. **Career:** American Baptist Coll, pres, 1993-; Lindenwood Coll Four, dir; Exce Inst, adm chief prog ofc dep dir PUSH, 1979-80; Gustavus Adolphus Coll, dir prof 1974-76; SCLC, natl prog admin 1976; SNCC AL Voters Regist Project, dir, 1962-63. **Orgs:** Nat coor Poor People's Campaign 1968; founder chmn of exec bd Inst of Human Rights & Resp 1979-; natl chmn Founder Nat Black Christian Student Leadership Consult 1979-; chmn Consortium on Peace Research Educ & Devel 1975; bd mem Ministries to Blacks in Higher Educ 1977; treas & past pres Phi Delta Kappa. **Honors/Awds:** Hon Prof Frat Harvard Chpt; Underwood Fellowship Danforth Found; Full Fellowship Nat Council of Negro Women; Award for Settling Sch Strikes The Group ofConcerned Students St Louis; Fact-finding Visit to Panama with Congressman Andrew Young 1973. **Business Addr:** Chief, Academic Dean, American Baptist College, 1800 Whites Creek Park, Nashville, TN 37207.

LAFONTANT, JULIEN J.
Educator. **Personal:** Born in Port-au-Prince, Haiti; married Blandine. **Educ:** SUNY Binghamton, MA (distinction) 1974, PhD 1976. **Career:** Exec Mansion Morovia Liberia, translator 1961-63; Ivory Coast Embassy Monrovia Liberia, translator 1963-66; Cuttington Coll Suakoko Liberia, asst prof 1966-72; SUNY Binghamton, teaching asst 1972-76; Univ of NE Lincoln, asst prof 1976-77; Acting Chair Black Studies UNO, asst prof 1977-78; Univ of NE, assoc prof 1978-82, full prof French Chair Black Studies UNO 1983-85; full prof French and Black Studies 1986-. **Honors/Awds:** Great Teacher Awd Univ of NE Omaha 1982; book on Montesquieu; book entitled Understanding A Culture; several articles dealing with the Black exper in general and the French encounter with Blacks. **Home Addr:** 5301 Ida St, Omaha, NE 68152. **Business Addr:** Dept of Foreign Languages, Univ of Nebraska-Omaha, Omaha, NE 68182-0001.

LAGARDE, FREDERICK H.
Clergyman. **Personal:** Born Apr 10, 1928, Teaneck, NJ; son of Claudia LaGarde and Floville Albert LaGarde; married Frances Frye; children: Frederica, Francine, Francella, Frederick Jr.

Educ: Grand Music Acad, 1948; VA Union Univ & Sem, AB, MDiv 1953-59. **Career:** 1st Bapt Church, pastor 1956-58; Providence Bapt Church, pastor 1958-66; Community Bapt Church of Love, pastor 1966-; president & founder of comeunity & the annual greater Youth Crusade of Paterson vicinity 1980. **Orgs:** Founder United Neighborhood for Indust Training & Econ Devel 1967, Housing Oppty Provided for Everyone 1969, House of Action 1970, Paterson Community Schools 1983; mem NAACP, Reg Rep SCLC; mem ASCAP; mem Alpha Phi Alpha; active in civil rights movement; co-writer & producer of the Martin Luther King video/song 1986. **Honors/Awds:** Awd IBPO Elks of the World 1965; Black & Poor Citizens Awd 1966; Citizens of Paterson Awd 1967; NJ Council Churches Social Ed & Action Awd 1969; co-writer Official Song of Paterson 1983; Paterson pastors workshop award 1986. **Military Serv:** AUS 1950-52. **Business Addr:** Pastor, Comm Bapt Church of Love, 6 Auburn St, Paterson, NJ 07501.

LAGUERRE, MICHEL S.
Educator. **Personal:** Born Aug 18, 1943, Lascahobas, Haiti; son of Anilia Roseau and Magloire Laguerre. **Educ:** University of Quebec, Trois-Rivieres, BA, Philosophy, 1971; Roosevelt University, Chicago, MA, Sociology, 1973; University of Illinois, Champaign-Urbana, PhD, Anthropology 1976. **Career:** Fordham University, New York City, NY, assistant professor of anthropology, 1977-78; University of California, Berkeley, CA, associate professor of anthropology and Afro-American studies, 1978-82, professor, 1990-; Harvard University, visiting professor/scholar, 1991-92. **Honors/Awds:** Barbara Weinstock Lectureship, 1994. **Special Achievements:** Author, American Odyssey: Haitians in New York City, Cornell University Press, 1984; author, Urban Life in the Caribbean, Schenkman Publishing Co, 1982; author, Urban Poverty in the Caribbean, Macmillan (London), 1990; author, The Military and Society in Haiti, The University of Tennessee Press, 1993; author, The Informal City, Macmillan (London) 1994; Author, Minoritized Space: An Inquiry Into the Spatial Order of Things, Institute of Government Studies Press, 1997; author, Diasporic Citizenship; Haitian Americans in Transnational America, Macmillan (London), 1997. **Business Addr:** Professor, University of California at Berkeley, Afro-American Studies Department, Berkeley, CA 94720.

LAHR, CHARLES DWIGHT
Educator, mathematician. **Personal:** Born Feb 6, 1945, Philadelphia, PA; married Beatriz Pastor; children: Elena, Maria, Emilio, Sonia. **Educ:** Temple Univ, AB (Magna Cum Laude, Math) 1966; Syracuse Univ, MA 1968, PhD 1971. **Career:** Bell Labs, mathematician 1971-73; Savannah State Coll, visiting prof/math 1973-74; Amherst Coll, visiting prof/math 1974-75; Dartmouth Coll, asst prof/math 1975-79, assoc prof/math 1979-84, assoc dean sciences, dean of grad studies 1981-84, prof math & CS 1984-, dean of faculty 1984-89, prof of mathematics and computer science, currently. **Orgs:** Consultant Alfred P Sloan Fndtn 1982-; reviewer Mathematical Reviews; mem Amer Mathematical Soc; mem Mathematical Assoc of Amer; mem Amer Assoc for Advancement of Sci. **Business Addr:** Prof of Mathematics and Computer Science, Dartmouth Coll, 6188 Bradley Hall, Hanover, NH 03755.

LAINE, CLEO
Singer. **Personal:** Born Oct 28, 1927, Southall, Middlesex, England; daughter of Minnie Bullock Campbell and Alexander Campbell; married John Philip William Dankworth, 1958; children: Stuart, Alec, Jacqueline. **Career:** Singer, John Dankworth's Jazz Band, popularized Gimme a Pigfoot & It's a Pity to Say Goodnight, 1952; record albums: A Beautiful Theme, Pierrot Lunaire All About Me, Born on a Friday, Day by Day, That Old Feeling, Cleo Sings Sondheim, Woman to Woman, Feel the Warm, I'm a Song, Live at Melbourne, Best Friends, Sometimes When We Touch & many others; actress, Seven Deadly Sins, Showboat, The Roman Spring of Mrs Stone, 1961, Colette, 1980, A Time to Laugh, Hedda Gabler, The Women of Troy, The Mystery of Edwin Drood, 1986; guest singer, One Man's Music, Marvelous Party, Talk of the Town, Not So Much a Programme, The Sammy Davis Show, Merv Griffin Show 1974, Cotton Club 1975, and Dinah. **Honors/Awds:** Golden Feather Award, Los Angeles Times, 1973; Grammy Award for Best Female Jazz Vocalist, 1985; Singer of the Year, TV Times, 1978; Show Business Personality of the Year, Variety Club, 1977; honorary degrees: Open Univ, MA, 1975; Berkee Coll, MusD, 1982.

LAING, EDWARD A.
International judge, educator, ambassador, attorney. **Personal:** Born Feb 27, 1942; son of Marjorie Laing and Edward Laing; married Margery V Fairweather, Apr 5, 1969; children: Obi Uchenna, Nyasha Rufaro. **Educ:** Cambridge, BA 1964; Cambridge, LLB 1966; Columbia, LLM 1968; Barrister at Law 1966; Atty at Law IL 1969. **Career:** Belize, magistrate & crown counsel 1966-67; Baker & McKenzie, assoc 1968-69; Univ of West Indies, Barbados & Jamaica, sr lectr 1970-74; Notre Dame Law School, asst prof 1974-76; Univ of Maryland, associate law prof, 1976-81; Howard Univ School of Law, professor/director of graduate program, 1980-85; Embassy of Belize, ambassador, 1985-90; New York Law School, visiting professor, 1990-93. **Orgs:** Evaluated Jamaica Legal Servs Clinic for Inter-Am Found; arbitrator, American Arbitration Association; brd mem, Westchester NY, Community Opportunities Program; member, American Society of International Law; founder, Consortium for Belizean Development; Chamber for Fisheries Disputes, Intl Tribunal; ambassador/perm rep, Belize to UN, 1993-97; rep on exec bd, UN Development Prog, 1995-97; consultant, UNDP, 1997-. **Honors/Awds:** Publ Intro to Sources & Sys of the Common Law Caribbean 1974; numerous articles on international law, devel countries, trade law & electoral law. **Business Addr:** Judge, International Tribunal for the Law of the Sea, Wexstrasse 4, 20355 Hamburg, Germany, 49 40 35607110.

LAIRET, DOLORES PERSON
Educator. **Personal:** Born Dec 27, 1935, Cleveland; widowed; children: Christine, Evin. **Educ:** Wheaton Coll, AB 1957; Middlebury Coll, AM 1958; Univ of Paris; Case Western Reserve U, PhD 1972. **Career:** Cleveland State Univ, assoc prof 1972-77, instructor 1971-72, lecturer 1969-71; City of Cleveland, sr personnel asst 1969-71; Western Reserve Univ, teaching fellow lecturer 1965-67; John Marshall HS, French teacher 1963-65; Fox Lane Sch Bedford NY, educator 1960-62; Southern Univ Baton Rouge, instructor 1959. **Orgs:** Mem Am Assn of Tchrs of French 1971-; Am Assn of Univ Prof 1971; Am Council on Tching of Foreign Lang 1972-; NE Modern Lang Assn 1974-; African Lit Assn; Music Critics Assn; OH Mod Lang Tchrs Assn; past sec & pres Cleveland Chap Tots & Teens Inc 1963-73; mem of bd Glenville Health Assn 1974-; mem Champs Inc 1964-; Am Spec Lctr for US Dept of State in Niger Mali Upper Volta Senegal & Togo. **Honors/Awds:** Publ The Francophone African Novel Perspectives for Critical Eval Presence Africaine; Various Art on Jazz Cleveland Press Showtime; Recipient of various Fellowships. **Business Addr:** E 24 St & Euclid Ave, Cleveland, OH 44115.

LAISURE, SHARON EMILY GOODE
Deputy city manager. **Personal:** Born Sep 3, 1954, Wiesbaden; daughter of Mr & Mrs Robert A Goode; married W Floyd Laisure. **Educ:** Univ of NC Chapel Hill, BA 1976, MPA 1979. **Career:** City of Winston-Salem, admin asst to dep city mgr 1977-78, admin asst to asst city mgr 1978-79, personnel analyst 1979-80; City of Petersburg VA, personnel dir 1980-85; County of Durham, NC, personnel director, 1985-86; City of Richmond, VA, dir, human resources and employee relations, 1986-89, deputy city manager, 1990-. **Orgs:** Mem Amer Soc of Publ Admin 1979; mem bd of dir Southside Chap Amer Red Cross 1980, United Way of Southside VA 1982, 1983; pres elect Southern Reg IPMA, 1984; International City Management Assn; National Forum for Black Public Administrators. **Honors/Awds:** Natl Assoc of Schools of PA Fellowship UNC At Chapel Hill 1980; City Manager's Outstanding Achievement Award, 1987-. **Business Addr:** Deputy City Manager, City of Richmond, 900 E Broad St, Rm 201, Richmond, VA 23219.

LAKE, ALFREEDA ELIZABETH
Educator. **Personal:** Born Jan 7, 1923, Hickory Valley, TN; divorced; children: Neeley Jr. **Educ:** LeMoyne Coll, BA 1943; Univ of TN, MS 1967; Memphis State U; Grambling State U, Pre-serv Trng; Lane Coll. **Career:** Hardeman Co Schs, supr of instructor 1964-; Bolivar Indsl School, primary teacher 1950-64; Prospect School, elementary school prin 1945-50; Washington School, primary teacher 1943-45. **Orgs:** Mem St Paul Christian Meth Epis Ch; past pres Delta Sigma Theta Sor Inc; NAACP; Nat Counc of Negro Women; exec bd of dirs W TN Hlth Improve Assn; Bolivar Housing Auth Bd; contrib to the pub Toward the Prep of Elem Sch Tchrs 1969; consult lectr Num Colls Univ & Pub Sch Sys Civic & ReligiousGroups. **Honors/Awds:** Publ A Study of 15 Black Students Enrolled in Formerly All White Schs in Hardeman Co 1965-66; Author Handbook for Parents of Pre-Sch Children 1974. **Business Addr:** Courthouse 2nd Floor, Bolivar, TN 38008.

LAKE, CARNELL AUGUSTINO
Professional football player. **Personal:** Born Jul 15, 1967, Salt Lake City, UT; married Monica; children: Siena. **Educ:** UCLA, degree in political science, 1993. **Career:** Pittsburgh Steelers, safety, 1989-. **Honors/Awds:** Pro Bowl appearances, 1994-96. **Business Addr:** Professional Football Player, Pittsburgh Steelers, Three Rivers Stadium, 300 Stadium Circle, Pittsburgh, PA 15212, (412)323-1200.

LAMAR, CLEVELAND JAMES
Association executive. **Personal:** Born Apr 21, 1924, Atmore, AL; married Annie Ruth Wilkerson; children: Cleveland James, Mona Lisa, Torlorf Pinzo, Ave Maria, Arturo Laertes, Alvino Degoge, Caruso Noel. **Educ:** AL State U, BS 1949, MEduc 1954. **Career:** Eutaw, instr 1949-58; GW Carver Br YMCA Shreveport, sec boys work 1959; Samuel F Harris Br YMCA, %Exec dir 1962-63; YMCA Mobile Dearborn St, exec dir 1964; Mobile Area Com for Training & Devel, vice pres bd of dirs 1965-70. **Orgs:** Mem AL Tchrs Assn Bd of Dirs; NAACP; Manna House YMCA Blue Ridge Assembly; mem Phi Beta Sigma; Century Mobile Club. **Honors/Awds:** Recipient Cert of Achvmnt in Phys Educ SE Region YMCA 1960; Cert of AchvmnNat Bd YMCA 1965; YMCA Cert Springfield Coll 1965. **Military Serv:** AUS 1943-46. **Business Addr:** 309 Washington, Mobile, AL 36603.

LAMAR, JAKE
Author, educator. **Personal:** Born Mar 27, 1961, Bronx, NY; son of Jouce Marie Doucette Lamar and Jacob V Lamar Sr. **Educ:** Harvard University, BA, 1983. **Career:** Time Magazine, staff writer, associate editor, 1983-89; University of Michigan, adjunct lecturer, Communications Dept, 1993-. **Honors/Awds:** Lyndhurst Foundation, Lyndhurst Prize, 1992. **Special Achievements:** Bourgeois Blues, Summit Books, 1991.

LAMAR, WILLIAM, JR.
Company executive. **Personal:** Born Apr 25, 1952, Chicago, IL; son of Jeanette Jarrett Lamar and William Lamar Sr; married Kathy Amos Lamar, Aug 28, 1976; children: Brian William, Andrew Marcus. **Educ:** Univ of Illinois, Chicago IL, BS, 1973; Northwestern Univ, Kellogg School of Mgmt, Evanston IL, MBA, 1976. **Career:** Quaker Oats Co, Chicago IL, brand mgr, 1976-81; Burrell Advertising Co, Chicago IL, vice pres, account supvr, 1981-82; United Airlines, Elk Grove Village IL, market mgr, 1982-84; McDonald's Corp, Oakbrook IL, dir of mktg, Bloomfield NJ, dir of operations, vice pres, national mktg, 1984-. **Orgs:** Board Member, Oak Park Education Foundation; bd mem, New York Ronald McDonald House, 1986-88, Harlem Boys Choir, 1987-; trustee, bd mem, New Hope Baptist Church, 1988-. **Business Addr:** Vice Pres, National Mktg, McDonald's Corporation, One McDonald Plaza, Oak Brook, IL 60521.

LAMARR, CATHERINE ELIZABETH
Attorney. **Personal:** Born Jan 27, 1960, Chicago, IL; daughter of Sonya Frances Saxton LaMarr and Carl Leonard LaMarr. **Educ:** Cornell University, Ithaca, NY, BA, 1982; Howard University, School of Law, Washington, DC, JD, 1985. **Career:** US Dept of Justice/Antitrust Division, Philadelphia, PA, intern, 1984; Murtha, Cullina, Richter & Pinney, Hartford, CT, attorney, 1985-87; Tarlow, Levy & Droney PC, Farmington, CT, attorney, 1987-. **Orgs:** Current chair, Community Service Committee; member, Committee to Promote Minorities; Connecticut Bar Assn, 1985-; current treasurer, past president, past board member, George W Crawford Law Assn, 1985-; board of director, member, Legal Aid Society of Hartford, 1989-; advisory committee on small business, Connecticut Department of Economic Development, 1991; mentor, 2 Hartford High School students, 1987-; mentor, University of Connecticut Law student, 1989-. **Honors/Awds:** Frequent lecturer to small business people; frequent judge of moot court & speaking competitions. **Business Addr:** Attorney, Tarlow, Levy & Droney, PC, 74 Batterson Park Road, Farmington, CT 06032.

LAMAUTE, DENISE
Tax attorney. **Personal:** Born Mar 14, 1952, St Louis, MO; daughter of Josephine Carroll and Frederick Washington, Sr; married Daniel Lamaute, May 14, 1980. **Educ:** Brandeis Univ, Waltham, MA, BA, (Magna cum Laude) 1973; Washington Univ, St Louis, MO, JD, 1977, LL.M. (tax) 1980. **Career:** Teachers Insurance & Annuity Assn, sr tax attorney, 1978-82; Ernst & Whinney, New York, NY, supvr, 1982-85; Lamaute Tax & Financial Servs, New York, NY, owner, 1985-; Lamaute Capital, Inc, pres, currently. **Orgs:** Mem, US Tax Ct, 1981-; mem, Nzingha Soc, 1987-88; co-chmn, Natl Bar Assn, 1988-89; mem volunteer, Jr Achievement, 1989. **Honors/Awds:** Author "Tax Loopholes for Investors" to be published by Tab Books NY, 1989; natl speaker for "Black Enterprise" networking Forum; frequent speaker on tax & financial matters at confs around the country; frequent contributing writer to magazines, newspapers on financial issues.

LAMBERT, BENJAMIN FRANKLIN
Patent attorney. **Personal:** Born Mar 6, 1933, Lowell, MA. **Educ:** Boston Univ, BA 1955; Brandeis Univ, MA 1959; Seton Hall Univ Sch of Law, JD 1968. **Career:** Ciba Phar Co Inc, rsch chem 1957-66; Ciba Ltd, rsch asst 1962-63; Merck & Co Inc, atty 1966-70; Fitzpatrick, Cella, Harper & Scinto, atty 1970-72; Johnson & Johnson, patent atty 1973-. **Orgs:** Mem NJ Bar Assn; Reg US Patent Ofc 1968, NJ Bar, 1969; NY Bar 1972; US Ct of Customs & Patent Appeals 1977; US Dist Ct Dist of NJ 1969; Dist Ct So Dist NY 1972; Dist Ct Eastern Dist NY 1972; NJ Patent Law Assn; Amer Patent Law Assn; NAACP 1977. **Honors/Awds:** Delta Hon Soc; Scarlet Key Hon Soc; Student Fac Asmbl; Augustus Howe Buck Schlr; Tchng Fellow Brandeis Univ; num publ. **Military Serv:** US Army, Sgt, 1962. **Business Addr:** Patent Attorney, Johnson & Johnson, One Johnson & Johnson Plaza, New Brunswick, NJ 08933.

LAMBERT, BENJAMIN J., III
Optometrist. **Personal:** Born Jan 29, 1937, Richmond, VA; son of Mary Frances Warden Lambert and Benjamin T Lambert Jr; married Carolyn L Morris, May 14, 1966; children: Benjamin IV, David, Charles Justin, Ann Frances. **Educ:** Virginia Union Univ, BS 1959; MA College of Optometry, OD 1962. **Career:** Private Practice, optometrist 1963-; VA General Assembly, senator; Consolidated Bank & Trust Co, director, currently. **Orgs:** Mem general assembly House of Delegates 1977-85; sec bd of trustees VA Union Univ 1977-87; Corporate Bd of Virginia Power; Chairman of Senate Sub Committee on Higher Education. **Home Addr:** 3109 Noble Ave, Richmond, VA 23222. **Business Addr:** Senator, Virginia General Assembly, 904 N First St, Richmond, VA 23219.

LAMBERT, CHARLES H.
Educational administrator. **Personal:** Born May 14, 1948, Mobile, AL. **Educ:** Kentucky State Univ, BS 1970; Miss State Univ, Mgmt Training Cert 1971; Eastern Kentucky Univ, MPA 1972; Michigan State Univ, Natl Assn of Reg Utility Comm Cert 1979; Univ of Arizona, Cert in Reg Economics 1979. **Career:** KY Dept of Economic Security, technical service rep, 1970-72; Whitney M Young Jr Job Corps Center, asst dir of programs, 1972-74; KY Legislative Research Comm, legislative fiscal analyst, 1974-75; KY Dept of Finance/Policy & Budget, senior policy advisor, 1975; Kentucky Dept of Finance & Admin, executive assist 1975-76, deputy secretary 1976-79; Energy Regulatory Comm State of Kentucky, commissioner/vice chairman 1979-81; Kentucky State Univ, asst, 1981-82, Vice President for University Relations, 1982—. **Orgs:** member of board of directors, The Lincoln Foundation, 1982—; exec secretary, KSU Foundation, Inc, 1982—. **Business Addr:** Vice President Univ Relations, Kentucky State University, E Main St, Frankfort, KY 40601.

LAMBERT, JEANETTE H.
Librarian. **Personal:** Born Nov 29, 1949, Detroit, MI; daughter of Adeline Small Bell and Horace Bell; married Edward Lambert, Jun 30, 1973; children: Charisse. **Educ:** Wayne State University, Detroit, MI, BS, 1971; Atlanta University, Atlanta, GA, MSLS, 1972. **Career:** Richmond Public Library, Richmond, CA, librarian, 1975-79; United Airlines, McLean, VA, reservations, sales support, 1979-82; Oakland Public Library, Oakland, CA, librarian, 1982-83; Sequoia Union High School District, Redwood City, CA, librarian, 1983-86; Albuquerque Public Library, Albuquerque, NM, librarian, 1987-88; LaVega Independent School District, Waco, TX, librarian, 1988-92; Nashville Metro Schools, Nashville, librarian, 1992-. **Orgs:** Awards committee, American Library Assn, 1989-91; member, Society of School Librarians International, 1989-; member, Delta Sigma Theta, Inc, 1984-; member, Links, Inc, 1990-; secretary, treasurer, American Heart Assn/McLean Co (Texas) Division, 1989-. **Honors/Awds:** Summer Seminar for Secondary Teachers, National Endowment of Humanities, 1986; Educators' Institute, National History Day, 1990.

LAMBERT, JOSEPH C.
Business executive. **Personal:** Born Jul 4, 1936, Vaux Hall, NJ; married Joan E Cross; children: Kim, George, Joseph Jr. **Educ:** VA State Coll. **Career:** St Bank of Plainfield NJ, teller trainee 1961-64; Security Nat'l Bank Newark NJ, chief clerk 1964-66; Nat'l State Bank Linden NJ, adminstrv asst 1966-68; Nat'l State Bank Elizabeth NJ, asst br mgr 1968-70; Nat'l State Bank Plainfield NJ, asst chashier & br mgr 1970-72; East Orange Comm Bank, vice pres & treas 1972-; Deryfos Consumer Bank, sr vice pres & treas. **Orgs:** Mem Plainfield Area Urban Coalition; Plainfield Kiwanis; bd dir So Second St Youth Cntr YMCA; finance chmn Plainfield Bd of Edn. **Honors/Awds:** Apptd first Black Jury Commr Union Co 1974. **Military Serv:** AUS 1958-60; AUSR 1960-62; discharge 1966. **Business Addr:** Sr Vice President & Treasurer, Dreyfus Consumer Bank, 554 Central Ave, East Orange, NJ 07018.

LAMBERT, LECLAIR GRIER
State government public information administrator, writer, consultant. **Personal:** Born in Miami, FL; son of Maggie Grier Lambert (deceased) and George F Lambert (deceased). **Educ:** Hampton Univ, BA 1959; Harvard Univ, further study communications 1958-59; Univ Munich, Germany, art history 1966; Grantsmanship Cntr-Pgrm Planning & Mgmt, Cert 1981; coursework People Management of MN 1985. **Career:** Time-Life Books, writer, researcher, 1961-63; US Dependent Schools Overseas, teacher, 1964-65; Holt, Rinehart and Winston, biology editor 1966-68; Faraday Press, editor translator Russian and biology monographs 1971-72; Natl Foundation March of Dimes, public relations writer 1972; St Paul Urban League, asst to dir/comm officer 1972-80, 1985-86; African-American Museum of Art and Hist, dir 1980-85; Palestinian Legislative Coun/Birzeit Univ Palestine, consultant ARD/USAID, 1997; MN State House of Representatives, dir public information, 1996-; Minnesota House of Representatives, Educational Programs, coordinator/sergeant-at-arms, Officer of the House, 1987-96. **Orgs:** Co-founder Summit Univ Free Press St Paul MN 1974; board member HEART 1978-88; Dr Martin L King Jr Bust Comm Minn State Capitol 1983; consultant/writer/designer Black History Exhibits 1984-94; board member Twin Cities Cable Arts Consortium 1984-86; board member City of Golden Valley Human Rights Commission Black History Month Celebration 1984-87; National African-American Museums Association Exec Council and Midwest Regional Rep 1984-89; City of St Paul Roy Wilkins Aud Dedication Commission 1984; St Paul Urban League, board member, 1992-, Urban League Volunteers 1972-; St Paul Civic Center Authority, representative, City Public Arts, Operations and Personnel Committee, 1985-91; America's Smithsonian Exhibition, plan committee, 1996; vice chair, executive committee, bldg committee, 1991-97; board member, St Paul Convention Bureau, 1990-92; MN Museum of Amer Art, task force committees, 1990-91, pres, 1993-94, chairman, 1994-95; University of MN, Archie Givens Sr African-American Rare Books Collection, 1990-; Dr Martin Luther King Jr State Holiday Celebration, 1987-94; bd mem, Coll of Visual Arts, 1997; advisory bd mem, YMCA Youth in Government, 1997. **Honors/Awds:** St Paul Ministerial Alliance Awd 1974; Certificate of Appreciation Univ of MN Black Students 1981; Minneapolis St Acad Appreciation Awd 1983; Special Apprec Award Cultural Awareness Roosevelt HS Minneapolis 1985; Natl African Amer Museums Assoc Appreciation Awd 1985; 50th Anniversary Guest Speaker and Awardee Liberty Square Tenant's Assoc Miami FL 1986; author/editor Minnesota's Black Comm; editor Art in Development A Nigerian Perspective 1984; various articles/speeches Twin Cities Courier, Summit Univ Free Press, Miami Herald 1986; Volunteer Service Award, St Paul Urban League 1988; A Learning Journey Through Black History 1982. **Special Achievements:** Leclair Grier Lambert Day, proclaimed in city of St Paul, Sept 29, 1997. **Military Serv:** US Army, 1st lt, 1959-61. **Home Addr:** 590 Simpson, St Paul, MN 55104. **Business Addr:** Director, Public Information Office, Minnesota State House of Reps, 175 State Office Bldg, St Paul, MN 55155, (612)296-8905.

LAMBERT, LEONARD W.
Attorney. **Personal:** Born Oct 27, 1938, Henrico Co, VA; married Sylvia Jeter; children: Leonard Jr, Ralph, Linda, Brice, Mark. **Educ:** VA Union Univ, BA 1960; Howard Univ Sch of Law, JD 1963. **Career:** Private Practice, attorney. **Orgs:** Vice pres bd Metro YMCA; Jewish Comm Ctr; Children's Home Soc; Travelers Aid Soc; Richmond Chap Amer Red Cross; Neighborhood Legal Aid Soc; Old Dominion Bar Assn; VA Adv Council Com on Youthful Offenders; VA State, Richmond Criminal Bar Assns; VA Trial Lawyers Assn; Natl Assn of Defense Lawyers; Natl Bar Assn; Richmond Trial Lawyers Assn; Focus Club; Club 533; substitute Judge of Juvenile & Domestic Relations Ct of City of Richmond VA; mem Omega Psi Phi Frat; selective appeal bd Eastern Dist of VA; chmn trustee bd Westwood Baptist Church; Natl Bd YMCA; Natl Prog Chmn YMCA; vice pres VA Ctr for thePerforming Arts; vice pres Federated Arts Council. **Business Addr:** Attorney, 2025 E Main St, Richmond, VA 23223.

LAMBERT, ROLLINS EDWARD
Clergyman. **Personal:** Born Mar 3, 1922, Chicago. **Educ:** Univ of Chicago, AB 1942; St Mary of the Lake Sem, STL 1949. **Career:** US Catholic Conf, priest; Parish Ministry Chicago, 1949-61, 1968-70; Univ of Chicago, campus Ministry 1961-68, 1970-75. **Orgs:** Pres Comprehensive Health Planning Inc 1974-75. **Business Addr:** 1312 Massachusetts Ave NW, Washington, DC 20005.

LAMBERT, SAMUEL FREDRICK
Engineer. **Personal:** Born Jul 8, 1928, Monroville, AL; son of Nannie Howard Lambert and Frederick Lambert; married Florence Mickings; children: Carla, Pamela Roberts, Samuel II, Michele, Wanda. **Educ:** Armstrong School of Engrg, Marine Engrs License 1953; Pace Univ, Bachelor 1978. **Career:** 1st Army Headquarters AUS, SP 3/C 1954-56; Military Sea Transport Service, marine engr 1956-60; New York City Bd of Educ, custodian engr 1962-74, supervisor of custodian/engrs 1974-. **Orgs:** Engr-consultant WEBB & Brooker Inc; past natl pres Natl Assoc of Power Eng 1982; elected mem Comm School Bd 11 1980-. **Honors/Awds:** Trinity Baptist Church, Community Service Award; Outstanding Custodial Administrator, Morrisania Education Council; Certificate of Appreciation, Board of Education. **Military Serv:** AUS spec 2nd class 1954-56; USN Reserve Lt jg while serving as merchant marine engrg officer. **Home Addr:** 4071 Edson Ave, Bronx, NY 10466.

LAMONT, BARBARA
Company executive officer, journalist. **Personal:** Born Nov 9, 1939, Hamilton, Bermuda; daughter of Muriel Aird Alcantara and Theophilus Alcantara; married Ludwig Gelobter; children: Michel, David, Elisabeth. **Educ:** Sarah Lawrence Coll, BA 1960; Harvard Univ Sch of Business Admin, MPA 1985; Attended, Kennedy Sch of Govt, Harvard Business School. **Career:** WINS Radio NY, reporter 1970-73; WNEW TV NY, reporter/anchor 1973-76; CBS News NY, reporter/writer 1976-82; Columbia Sch of Journalism, assoc prof 1980-84; Nigerian TV Authority, sr producer 1982-83; ABC News, 1985-86; WCCL-TV New Orleans, 1987-; Crescent City Comms, pres; New Orleans Teleport, pres 1987-. **Orgs:** Dem dist leader Democratic Party 1970; bd mem NARAL 1975; bd mem Planned Parenthood 1975; editorial bd, Amsterdam News 1986-. **Honors/Awds:** Author "Journey to Nigeria" 1984; Associated Press Awd NY State 1974; Front Page Awd News Women's Guild 1975; Reporter of the Yr New York City Retired Detectives Assn 1976; book "City People" Macmillan 1975.

LAMOTHE, ISIDORE J., JR.
Physician. **Personal:** Born Feb 12, 1924, New Orleans; married Grace Cooper; children: Michelle Alicia, Isidore J. **Educ:** Xavier U, BS 1944; Howard U, MD 1947. **Career:** HG Phillips Hosp St Louis, internship 1947-48; VA Hosp Tuskegee, jr staff physician 1948-49; Marshall TX, gen practice med 1949-53, 1955-; Webb AFB,chief med serv 1953-55. **Orgs:** Hosp Med Staff Chief, General Practice Section; Natl Med Assn; past pres, East TX Med Dental & Pharm Assn; vice pres Lone Star State Med Assn; adv com TX Heart Assn; pres Harrison Ct Med Soc; TX Med Assn; Amer Heart Assn; St Joseph Parish Council; pres Parish Sch Bd; past pres St Joseph Home; past pres Sch Assn; bd dir NE TX Hlth Sys Agcy; mem at large Nat Coun Boy Scouts of Am; adv bd So Central Reg Boy Scouts of Am; consumer rep Food & Drug Admin; past pres Marshall Reg Fellow Club; past natl comptroller, Alpha Phi Alpha; Marshall Human Rels Comm; life mem Ch Educ Com Harrison Co Branch NAACP; Harrison Ct Progrssv Vot League; bd of trsts Wiley Coll; Ch Finance & Fiscal Affairs Com; dir Mrshl Allli for Justice; Boy Scouts of America, natl exec bd. **Military Serv:** AUS pfc 1944-46; USAF capt 1935-55. **Business Addr:** PO Box 1558, 1407 University, Marshall, TX 75670.

LAMOTTE, JEAN MOORE
Director. **Personal:** Born Sep 2, 1938, Shreveport, LA; divorced. **Educ:** CA State Univ Sacramento, attended; Amer River Clge Sacramento, attended; Central State Univ Wilberforce OH, attended. **Career:** KXTV-10 Corinthian Broadcasting, host moderator daily pub srv talk show 1973-; Human Rights Comm, proj dir/Affirmative action prog 1970-73; Affirm Act Prog for underutilizing employers, writer; Campbell Soup Co, voc spec 1966-70. **Honors/Awds:** Comm Serv Award Golden Empire Chap Amer Heart Assc 1977-80; Woman of Year Sacramento Observer Newspaper 1977; Sacramento's Most Influential Black Woman Sacramento Observer 1978; Outstanding Comm Serv Award Women's Civic Improvement Ctr 1980. **Business Addr:** KXTV 10, 400 Broadway, Sacramento, CA 95818.

LAMPKIN, CHERYL LYVETTE
City official. **Personal:** Born May 16, 1961, Brunswick, GA; daughter of Cynthia L Lampkin and William T Lampkin Sr. **Educ:** Attended Intl School of Kenya, 1976-78; Univ of Maryland, BA, 1983; Carnegie Mellon Univ School of Urban and Public Affairs, certificate of participation, summer, 1982; Harvard Univ School of Govt, certificate of participation, summer, 1983; State Univ of New York at Stony Brook, Harriman Coll, MPA, 1985. **Career:** Waxter Sr Center, Baltimore, MD, social work intern, summer, 1980; City of Brookhaven, Brookhaven, NY, consultant, 1984; City of New York Department of Correction, New York, NY, management intern, summer, 1984; City of Kansas City, Kansas City, MO, management intern, 1985-86; Montgomery County Govt, Rockville, MD, personnel specialist, 1986-88; City of Rockville, Rockville, MD, asst to city mgr, 1988—. **Orgs:** Mem 1985—, Natl Forum for Black Public Admin; mem 1988—, Natl Accoc of Female Exec; mem 1989—, Intl City Mgr Assoc. **Honors/Awds:** Scholastic achievement cash award, Links Inc, 1980; Outstanding Young Woman of America, 1983 and 1984.

LAMPKINS, LILLIAN ERNESTINE
Reading specialist, association administrator (retired). **Personal:** Born Jun 2, 1920, St Petersburg, FL; daughter of Sally Dawson Parker and Sebastian L Parker; married Samuel H Lampkins, Dec 18, 1943 (divorced); children: Linda Combs, Sandra Wynn. **Educ:** Florida Memorial College, BS, 1962; Barry University, MS, 1965; Miami University, 1979; University of District of Columbia, 1965-79. **Career:** US Federal Government, statistical clerk, 1943-58; Broward County Schools, teacher, 1962-64; Montgomery County Schools, teacher, 1964-66; District of Columbia, reading specialist, 1966-79. **Orgs:** NAACP, 1962-; Broward County Retired Teachers Association, secretary, 1981-85, president, 1986-88; AARP, 1989-90, state coordinator for Florida Retired Educators Association, 1990-; Girl Scouts of America, nominating committee and board of directors, 1985-88; Broward County Election, clerk, 1985-91; Broward County Schools Credit Union, nominating committee, 1988-. **Honors/Awds:** District of Columbia Public Schools, Achievement, 1964; Broward County Retired Educators Association, Recognition, 1982; Florida Retired Educators Association, Recognition, 1990; AARP, Recognition, 1992; Broward County Schools Credit Union, Recognition, 1992. **Special Achievements:** Original skit on America Health System, 1991-92; Keynote Speaker at Various Retirements aqeccles, 1990-; monthly contributions, Retired Educators Association of Florida, AARP, local chapters, 1990-93.

LAMPLEY, CALVIN D.
Educator. **Personal:** Born in Dunn, NC. **Educ:** NC A&T State U; Juilliard Sch of Music, Dip; Peabody Conservatory, MusM. **Career:** Morgan State Univ, prof of music; Columbia Records, producer; RCA Victor Records, producer; Warner Brothers, producer; Prestige Records, producer; WCBM-AM Baltimore, classical/Jazz disc jockey; Peabody Conservatory of Music, composition faculty; Concert Pianist. **Orgs:** Mem Am Soc of Univ Composers; Broadcast Mus Inc; Met Opera Guild; mus critic for Public Television.

LAMPLEY, EDWARD CHARLES
Physician. **Personal:** Born Jun 21, 1931, Hattiesburg, MS; son of Elma Wilson Lampley and Willie Lee Lampley Sr; married Dr Norma Jean Mosley, Sep 11, 1959; children: Edward, Marguerite, Karl. **Educ:** Alcorn Coll, 1953-54; Wayne Univ, AB 1956; Howard Univ, MD 1960. **Career:** Detroit Receiving Hosp, intern 1960-61; Provident Hosp Chicago, resident 1961-63; Harlem Hosp New York, resident 1963-66; Private Practice Oakland, CA, physician spec in obstetrics & gynecology 1966-; Memorial Hosp, sr md, chmn dept ob/gyn. **Orgs:** Mem staff Highland Hosp; mem Herrick Meml Hosp; mem Providence Hosp; mem Merrick Hosp; mem Meml Hosp; former clin med

dir E Oakland Planned Parenthood Clinic; diplomate Amer Bd Observ & Gyne; fellow Amer Coll Obst & Gynecol ACS; mem AMA; mem CA, Alameda Cnty & Natl Med Assns; Golden State Med Assn; Sinkler-Miller Med Soc; Alameda Cnty Gynecol Soc; Amer Fertility Soc; re-cert Amer Bd Obs-Gyn 1978; Am Assn Planned Parenthood Physicians; mem Alpha Psi; cofounder E Oakland Med Cntr Oakland, CA; chmn bd dir Comm Devel Inst E Palo Alto, CA 1984-85; chmn bd dir Community Devel Inst East Palo Alto CA 1984-86; mem Kappa Alpha Psi; chmn scholarship comm Downs Memorial Church; chmn Boy Scout Troup 33; councilman Alameda Contra Costa Med Soc,1985-; mem, House ofdelegates Calif Med Assn, 1985-. **Honors/Awds:** Man of the Year Awd Ravenswood School Dist; Soloist Downs Memorial Church Chapel Choir. **Military Serv:** USAF s/sgt 1949-52. **Business Addr:** 9925 International Blvd, Ste 1, Oakland, CA 94603-0097.

LAMPLEY, PAUL CLARENCE
Educator. **Personal:** Born Dec 12, 1945, Louisville, MS; married Fannie; children: Samantha. **Educ:** Tougaloo Coll, BS 1967; Atlanta U, MS 1971, NSF Grad Trainee; Howard Univ; Memphis St Univ; Univ of MS, PhD 1981. **Career:** Rust Coll, asst develop dir; Harris Jr Coll, instr; Rust Coll, div of social sciences chair, academic dean. **Orgs:** Mem NAACP; Yacona Area Council BSA; Omega Psi Phi; Nat Assn of Fed Rel Officers; Phi Delta Kappa; Sigma Pi Phi. **Honors/Awds:** Outstanding Young Man in Am 1972; UNCF distinguished professor 1985-86. **Business Addr:** Academic Dean, Rust College, Develop Office, Holly Springs, MS 38635.

LANCASTER, GARY LEE
Judge. **Personal:** Born Aug 14, 1949, Brownsville, PA; son of Ester Arabelle Lancaster and Paul L Lancaster. **Educ:** Slippery Rock University of Pennsylvania, 1971; University of Pittsburgh, School of Law, JD, 1974. **Career:** Pennsylvania Human Relations Commission, 1974-76; District Attorney of Allegheny Co Pennsylvania, 1976-78; private practice of law, 1978-87; US Magistrate Judge, 1987-93; US District Judge, 1993-. **Orgs:** Natl Bar Assn; American Inns of Court; Homer S Brown Association; Allegheny Co Bar Association. **Business Addr:** US District Judge, United States District Court, Western District of Pennsylvania, 911 US Post Office and Courthouse, Pittsburgh, PA 15201, (412)644-6489.

LANCASTER, HERMAN BURTRAM
Law consultant. **Personal:** Born Mar 6, 1942, Chicago, IL; son of Louise Lancaster and Eddie Lancaster; married Patricia L Malucci; children: Lauren E, Rachel J, Meredith E. **Educ:** Chicago State Univ, BS 1965; Rosary Coll, MA 1968; DePaul Univ, JD 1972. **Career:** Chicago Bd of Ed, teacher 1965-66; DePaul Univ Law School, asst dir law library 1966-70; Univ of Chicago, psychiatric dept dir of info 1970-72, legal counsel 1972-73; Glendale Univ Law School, prof, dir of research 1973-; The Legal Inst, law consultant, 1976-. **Orgs:** AAA, arbitrator, 1986-; The Subcontractors Inst, advisor, 1984-; Glendale Law Review 1976-; NAACP 1975-. **Honors/Awds:** Omega Psi Phi Scholarship 1963; Grad Fellowship 1966; DePaul Law School Scholarship 1968; DePaul Law Review Scholarship 1969-72; Blue Key Law Hon Soc 1968; Man of the Year Omega Psi Phi 1966; has published numerous articles.

LANCASTER, JOHN GRAHAM
County commissioner. **Personal:** Born Jan 31, 1918, Farmville, VA; son of Annie Moss Lancaster and John W Lancaster; married Albertine Thomas, Nov 21, 1971; children: John G Jr, Shirley Lancaster Gholston. **Educ:** Hampton Univ, BS 1940; George Washington Univ, MA 1964; Univ of MD, AGS 1974. **Career:** VA Coop Extension Svcs, extension agent 1940-55; NC Mutual Life Ins Co, salesman 1956-57; Univ of MD Coop Extension Serv, state 4H prog 1957-79; St Marys Co MD Govt, county commissioner 1986-. **Orgs:** Dir MD 4H Foundation 1981-86; mem Bd of Educ St Marys Co 1984-87; pres LOTT Enterprises Inc 1986-; dir So MD Business League of NBL 1986-; mem IBOEN, NAACP, Masons, Toastmasters; chmn St Marys Co Housing Authority. **Home Addr:** PO Box 26, California, MD 20619. **Business Addr:** County Commissioner, St Mary's County, PO Box 653, Leonardtown, MD 20650.

LAND, CHESTER LASALLE
Health services administrator. **Personal:** Born Apr 29, 1938, Jacksonville, TX; son of George Ann Price Land and Peary Land; married Shirley Walker; children: Celeste, Chrystal. **Educ:** CA State Univ LA, BS 1972; CA State Univ Northridge, MS 1980. **Career:** Olive View Med Center, supervisor recreational therapy 1964-81; Rancho Los Amigos Med Ctr, dir recreational therapy 1981-95; West Los Angeles Veterans Administration Health Ctr, chief of recreational therapy, 1995-. **Orgs:** Chair recreational commn Los Angeles City Council on the Disabled 1977-; dir CA Park & Recreation Soc 1979-81; vice chair Los Angeles City Council on the Disabled 1981; chair Certification Review Board Natl Council for Therapeutic Recreation 1987-89; President - National Therapeutic Recreation Society 1988-90. **Honors/Awds:** Citation Award CA Park & Recreation Society 1984; Employee of the Month Los Angeles County 1985; Employee of the Year Rancho Los Amigos Medical Center 1985; Outstanding Therapeutic Recreation CA Park & Recreation Society 1987; Distinguished Service Awd, National Therapeutic Recreation Society, 1991. **Home Addr:** 15210 Riviera Ln, La Mirada, CA 90638. **Business Addr:** Chief, Recreation Therapy, West Los Angeles, VA Medical Ctr, 11301 Wilshire Blvd, Los Angeles, CA 90073.

LAND, DANIEL
Professional football player. **Personal:** Born Jul 3, 1965, Donalsonville, GA; married; children: two. **Educ:** Albany State (Ga.). **Career:** Tampa Bay Buccaneers, defensive back, 1987; Oakland Raiders, 1989-. **Business Addr:** Professional Football Player, Oakland Raiders, 1220 Harbor Bay Pkwy, Alameda, CA 94502, (510)615-1875.

LANDER, C. VICTOR
Attorney, judge. **Personal:** Born Jun 29, 1954, Columbus, GA; son of Agnes Levy Lander and Fred L Lander III. **Educ:** Morehouse College, BA, with honors, 1975; University of Texas School of Law, JD, 1978. **Career:** Texas Attorney General's Office, legal intern, law clerk, 1976-78; Federal Communications Commission, attorney, 1978-86; Lander and Associates PC, attorney, managing partner, 1986-; City of Dallas Texas Municipal Court, associate judge, 1991-96, municipal judge, Court 7, 1996-; City of Balch Springs, Texas Municipal Court, municipal judge, 1993-96. **Orgs:** NAACP, legal redress committee chairman, nominations committee, election supervising committee, 1986-90, 1994-96; YMCA, board of directors, 1989-; National Bar Association, government lawyers division chairman, board of governors, 1977-89; Dallas Urban League, board of directors, 1996-. **Honors/Awds:** National Judicial College, Reno, NV, Certificate of Achievement, 1997. **Special Achievements:** Periodic writer, Dallas Weekly Newspaper, 1990-94; Frequent speaker on employment, legal, and judicial issues, 1986-; Participant and co-founder of CAW Clark Legal Clinic, 1989-; American Inns of Court; College of the State Bar of Texas. **Business Addr:** Managing Partner, Lander & Associates, PC, The Lander Bldg, 1447 Plowman Ave, Dallas, TX 75203, (214)942-1073.

LANDER, CRESSWORTH CALEB
City official (retired). **Personal:** Born May 15, 1925, Tucson, AZ; son of Julia Belle Watson Lander and James Franklin Lander; married Linda C Hill Lander, Mar 3, 1979; children: Melodie Lynette, Rochelle Elaine. **Educ:** Univ of Arizona Los Angeles State Coll, BS Business Admin 1958; MIT Sloan Business School, summer course 1975; Harvard Business School & Kennedy School of Govt, 1979. **Career:** City of Tucson's Dept Human & Comm Dev, dir 1974-78; Univ of AZ Urban Planning Dept, lectr 1976-78; Civil Aeronautics Bd, managing dir 1979-81; Comm Dev Training Inst, consultant 1983-; Dept Housing City of Tucson, dir, until 1992. **Orgs:** Dir City of Tucson's Dept Urban Resource Coord (Model Cities) 1969-74; dep dir Pima-Santa Cruz Co CEO 1968-69; real estate business 1959; dep assessor LA Co Assessor's Office Business Div 1958-59; bd trustees Public Housing Authority Directors Assn; bd mem Pima Council on Aging; bd mem Tucson Airport Authority; vice pres bd mem Tucson Urban League; Arizona Multibank Community Development Corp., board of directors, 1992-; Tucson Urban League, chairman of the board, 1992-; The Community Development Training Institute, president, 1992-. **Honors/Awds:** Comm Leadership Award Jack & Jill of Amer Tucson Chap 1985; Par Excellence Award AZ Black C of C 1984; US Govt Charter Sr Exec Serv 1979; Meritorious Serv Civil Aeronautics Bd 1981. **Military Serv:** USMC Gunnery Sgt served 3 yrs. **Home Addr:** 1424A 12th St N, Arlington, VA 22209-3664. **Business Addr:** Dir, Dept of Housing, City of Tucson, PO Box 27210, Tucson, AZ 85726.

LANDER, FRED LEONARD, III
Attorney, counselor. **Personal:** Born Apr 19, 1927, Charlotte, NC; son of Georgia Goldsberry Lander and Fred Leonard Lander Jr; married Bobbie Bolds Lander, Nov 14, 1964; children: Fred Leonard IV, Chauncey Victor. **Educ:** Howard University, College of Liberal Arts, BA, 1948, School of Law, JD, 1952. **Career:** US Government, IRS, revenue officer, computer analyst; US Government, NARS and FPC, management specialist; Office of Crime Analyst, assistant director; Pilot District Project, executive director; US Department of Justice, courts specialist; Dallas District Office, senoir trial attorney; Dallas Civil Service Bd, admini law judge, 1994; Landers & Associates, PC, senior partner, currently. **Orgs:** JL Turner Legal Association, former vice pres; National Bar Association, Government Section, former chairman; Omega Psi Phi Fraternity, former basilius; Dallas Urban League, former vice pres, board member; Regular Fellow Club of Dallas, Inc, former president; Dallas Kiwanis Club, former president; NAACP, former board member; Park South YMCA of Dallas, board member. **Honors/Awds:** Omega Psi Phi Fraternity, Omega Man of the Year, 1979; Committee of 100, Plaque for Outstanding Achievement in Law, 1977; J L Turner Legal Society, CB Burnkly Award in Law, 1989; Dallas Fort Worth Government, Hononary Accomplishment Award, 1986; Barrister Sources, Achievement Award for CW Clark Legal Clinic, 1991. **Special Achievements:** As We See it, Dallas Weekly; As I See It, Dallas Weekly. **Military Serv:** US Army, 1952-54. **Home Addr:** 712 Meadow Heath Ln, Dallas, TX 75232, (214)376-8956. **Business Addr:** Senior Partner, Lander & Associates, PC, The Lander Bldg, 1447 Plowman Ave, Dallas, TX 75203, (214)942-1073.

LANDERS, NAAMAN GARNETT
Project director. **Personal:** Born Oct 23, 1938, Anderson, IN; married Stephanie E Cox; children: Naaman III. **Educ:** Purdue Univ, BSCE 1966; Univ of Chicago, MBA 1969. **Career:** Amoco Oil Co, engr 1966-69; Esso Chem Co, trans analyst 1969-71; Amoco Oil Co, material mgr 1972-76; Standard Oil Co, coord inventory contr 1977-79; Amoco Technology Corp, proj dir. **Honors/Awds:** Presidential Citation Reconnaissance over Cuba. **Military Serv:** USN 1959-63. **Business Addr:** Project Dir, Amoco Technology Corp, 200 E Randolph Dr, Chicago, IL 60601.

LANDERS, RENEE M.
Educator. **Personal:** Born Jul 25, 1955, Springfield, IL; daughter of Marvel Neal Landers and Robert E Landers; married Thomas L Barrette Jr, Aug 2, 1980. **Educ:** Radcliffe Coll of Harvard Univ, AB, 1977; Boston Coll Law School, JD, 1985. **Career:** Massachusetts Secretary of State, Bookstore Div, program development specialist, 1978, admin asst to secretary of state, 1979-80, deputy secretary of state, 1980-82; Supreme Judicial Court of Massachusetts, law clerk, 1985-86; Ropes & Gray, associate, 1986-88; Boston Coll Law School, asst prof, 1988-93; Office of Policy Development, US Department of Justice, deputy assistant attorney general, 1993-96; US Department of Health & Human Services, deputy general counsel, 1996-. **Orgs:** Harvard Univ, bd of overseers, 1991-95, pres bd of overseers, 1996-97; Massachusetts Eye and Ear Infirmary, dir, 1993-96; Metropolitan District Commission, assoc commissioner, 1991-93; Big Sister Assoc of Greater Boston, vp and dir, 1988-93; Massachusetts Supreme Judicial Court, gender bias study committee, sub-committee chair, 1986-1989, racial and ethnic bias study, 1990-94; Boston Bar Assoc, council member, 1988-91, chair committee on gender and justice, 1989-93. **Honors/Awds:** Radcliffe College Alumnae Assn, Distinguished Service Award, 1992; Elected Honorary Mem, Iota of Massachusetts Chap, Phi Beta Kappa, Radcliffe College, 1995. **Business Addr:** Deputy General Counsel, US Department of Health & Human Services, 200 Independence Ave, SW, Washington, DC 20201, (202)690-6318.

LANDREAUX, KENNETH FRANCIS
Professional baseball player (retired). **Personal:** Born Dec 22, 1954, Los Angeles, CA; divorced; children: Kenneth Antoine, Todd Xavier. **Educ:** Arizona State Univ, Tempe, AZ, attended; Arizona School of Real Estate, 1992. **Career:** California Angels, outfielder, 1977-78; Minnesota Twins, outfielder, 1979-80; Los Angeles Dodgers, outfielder, 1981-87. **Orgs:** Comm Affairs, Los Angeles Dodgers. **Honors/Awds:** Led team in triples (5) 1984; tied for club in triples with Steve Sax (7), errorless streak snapped at 142 games 1982; longest hitting streak in majors in 1980 (31 games); 1980 tied mark for triples in a game (3); 1979 tied a mark with two doubles in same inning; American League All-Star Team, 1980.

LANDRUM, TITO LEE (TERRY)
Professional Baseball Player (retired). **Personal:** Born Oct 25, 1954, Joplin, MO; married Theresa; children: Melissa, Julie. **Educ:** Eastern Oklahoma State, Wilburton, OK, attended. **Career:** St Louis Cardinals, outfielder, 1980-83; Baltimore Orioles, outfielder, 1983; St Louis Cardinals, outfielder, 1984-87; Los Angeles Dodgers, outfielder, 1987; Baltimore Orioles, outfielder, 1988; Hydro-Tone Sports and Medical Equipment, director of research and development, 1992-94; Play It Again Ltd, team consultant, 1994-. **Honors/Awds:** Committed only 3 errors in 5 yr big league career; member of the Baltimore Orioles World Series Championship Team, 1983.

LANDRY, DOLORES BRANCHE
Business executive. **Personal:** Born Oct 9, 1928, Philadelphia, PA; daughter of Wilma Brown Branche (deceased) and Merwin Edward Branche (deceased); married Lawrence A Landry, Apr 16, 1966 (died 1997); children: Jennifer E, Michael H. **Educ:** Fisk Univ, BA 1950; Den Intl Hojskole Elsinore Denmark, diploma 1950-51; Univ of Chicago, MA 1960. **Career:** Sci Rsch Assocs, editor/guidance dir 1954-60, proj dir rsch & devel 1960-61; Chicago Commn on Youth Welfare, acting dir citywide youth serv 1961-63; Joint Youth Develop Comm, youth employment consul 1963-64; Horizons Employment Counselors Inc, founder/pres 1964-66; Chicago Commn on Urban Oppor, chief planner 1964-65; private consultant, 1965-71; Associate Consultants Inc, co-founder/vice pres 1971-. **Orgs:** Mem Chicago Guidance & Personnel Assn 1955-66; mem bd dirs Elliott Donnelly Youth Ctr 1961-63; mem Assn of Women Business Owners 1971-; chmn child guidance comm vice pres Murch Home & Sch Assn 1973-78; vice pres Howard Univ Faculty Wives Assn 1974-75; vice pres mem bd dirs DC assn for Children w/Learning Disabilities 1974-87; mem Alpha Kappa Alpha; board of directors, Glenbrook Foundation for Exceptional Children, Bethesda, MD, 1980-81; chair, budget/planning committee, DC Juvenile Justice Advisory Group, 1987-; National Foundation for Teaching Entrepreneurship, DC, advisory board, 1994-96; International Network of Women Business Owners, 1990-. **Honors/Awds:** Woman of the Year Award, Sigma Gamma Rho Sorority, Chicago, 1960; Outstanding Volunteer Award, DC Public Schools, Washington DC, 1979; Outstanding Commitment to Fisk Univ, NE Regional Alumni Award, 1990; author of over 200 articles & pamphlets

in field of vocational guidance for Sci Rsch Assocs Chicago; author/editor of Handbook of Job Facts. **Home Addr:** 2936 Davenport St NW, Washington, DC 20008.

LANDRY, L. BARTHOLOMEW
Sociologist, educator. **Personal:** Born Apr 28, 1936, Milton, LA; married. **Educ:** St Mary's, BA 1961; Xavier U, BA 1966; Columbia U, PhD 1971. **Career:** Purdue Univ, asst prof 1971-73; Univ of MD, asst prof 1973-. **Orgs:** Member, African Studies Assn; American Sociology Assn; Caucus of Black Sociologists; Law Sociology Assn; Population Assn of American Publs in field; Columbia Univ & Faculty Fellow, 1966-67. **Honors/Awds:** –IMH Flw 1967-69; NIH Dissertation Flw 1969-71; Rsrch Contract 20th Century Fund 1975-77. **Business Addr:** University of Maryland, Dept of Sociology, College Park, MD 20742.

LANDRY, LAWRENCE ALOYSIUS. See Obituaries section.

LANDSMARK, THEODORE CARLISLE
Association executive. **Personal:** Born May 17, 1946, Kansas City, MO; married Karen Rheinlander. **Educ:** St Paul's Sch Concord NH, 1964; Yale Coll, BA 1969; Yale Architecture Sch, 1973; Yale Law Sch, JD 1973. **Career:** Contractors' Assn Boston, exec dir; Hill & Barlow Law Firm Boston, asso; Yale Coll Polit Sci Dept New Haven CT, tchng asst; Quinnipiac Coll PolitSci Dept Hamden CT, instr; 540 Chester Park Limited, gen partner; Yale Law Sch New Haven CT, dir media wrkshp, film soc 1970-73; Hill Cinema Wrkshp,dir. **Orgs:** Mem New England Soc Assn Execs; mem Yale Alumni Bd; governing bd Episcopal Ch Yale; dir Yale Civil Rights Council. **Honors/Awds:** John Hay Whitney Opportunity Fellow; Nat Sci Found Res Fellow. **Business Addr:** 227 Roxbury St, Roxbury, MA 02119.

LANE, ALLAN C.
Urban planner. **Personal:** Born Dec 21, 1948, Akron, OH; son of Mable Farrior Lane (deceased) and Sanford Lane; married Nancy McClendon. **Educ:** Hiram Coll, BA 1971; Univ of Cincinnati, MCP 1973. **Career:** City of Cincinnati, city planner 1972-73; Cincinnati Comm Action Agency, asst project dir 1972; Model Cities Housing Corp, deputy planning dir 1973-75; City of Dayton, sr city planner 1975-89; City of Atlanta, urban planner 1989-92; GRASP Enterprises, director of community development, 1992-94; Atlanta Committee for the Olympic Games, project coord, 1994-96. **Orgs:** Founder/artistic advisor The Creekside Players 1978-89; bd mem Dayton Contemporary Dance Co 1984-86; bd mem OH Theatre Alliance 1984-87; presenting/touring panelist 1984-86, theatre panel 1989-91, OH Arts Council; Fulton County Arts Council, theatre panel, 1993-95; Ballethnic Dance Co., board member, 1991-; Project Interconnections, board member, 1996-. **Honors/Awds:** Employee of the Year Dayton Dept of Planning 1981; Outstanding Serv to Project Alpha, Alpha Phi Alpha Frat 1985-86; Service to Gifted Children Dayton Public Schools 1986. **Home Addr:** 3150 Key Dr SW, Atlanta, GA 30311.

LANE, CHARLES
Filmmaker. **Personal:** Born Dec 26, 1953, New York, NY; son of Albertha Nelson and Charles; married Laura Lesser, Jul 8, 1984; children: Nicole Alysia, Julien Michael. **Educ:** SUNY, Purchase, BFA, 1980. **Career:** Filmmaker since 1976; films include: A Place in Time, 1976, Sidewalk Stories, 1989, True Identity, 1991. **Orgs:** National Black Programming Consortium; Black Filmmakers Foundation; Academy of Motion Pictures Arts and Sciences; Independent Film Program, advisory board. **Honors/Awds:** Prix du Publique award, Cannes Film Festival, 1989; Best Director and Best Film awards, Upsalla Film Festival, Sweden, 1989; Grand Prix and 2nd Prize, Journalise Jury, Chamrousse, France, 1989; numerous other national and international awards. **Business Addr:** Filmmaker, 110 E 59th St, 6th Fl, New York, NY 10022.

LANE, DAVID PULASKI, SR.
Dentist. **Personal:** Born Nov 5, 1912, Raleigh, NC; married Vivian Tate; children: Deborah, David Jr, Victor. **Educ:** St Augustine's Coll, BS 1935; Howard Univ Dental School, DDS 1942. **Career:** Private practice, dentist 1946-. **Orgs:** Mem Chi Delta Mu Med Frat; Old N State Dental Soc; Natl Dental Soc; mem Raleigh Citizens Assn; NAACP; St Embrose Episcopal Church; St Augustine's Alumni Assn; adv comm, The Raleigh Downtown Mall; Howard Univ Alumni Assn; charter mem Meadowbrook Country Club. **Honors/Awds:** Distinguished Alumni Award, Natl Alumni Assn of St Augustine's College, 1975; Humanitarian Award, Gen Baptist State Convention, 1977. **Military Serv:** AUS capt 1942-45.

LANE, EDDIE BURGYONE
Educational administrator, clergyman. **Personal:** Born Aug 8, 1939, Providence, LA; son of Cleo Lane and John Lane; married Betty Jo Washington; children: Felicia, Carla, Eddie II. **Educ:** Barber Coll, M, 1960; So Bible Inst Dallas Theol Sem, ThM Bible Diploma 1974; Univ of TX at Dallas, BA 1980; Dallas Theological Seminary, ThM, 1980. **Career:** Bibleway Bible Ch, founder, pastor, 1969-; Dallas Theol Sem, administrative asst to pres, 1975-77, asst to pres 1977-80; Dallas Bible Coll, prof 1975-76; So Bible Inst, prof 1975-76; Dallas Seminary, asst dean of students, 1980-85, asst prof, pastoral ministry, 1980-90, assoc dean of students, american minorities, 1985-, assoc prof, pastoral ministry, 1990-. **Orgs:** Co-founder vice pres Black Evangelistic Enterprise Dallas 1974-; bd mem Dallas Nat Black Evangelical Assn 1974-; dir Black Chr Lit Am Tract Soc 1978-85; founder, pres, Institute of Black Family Renewal; pastor, Bibleway Bible Church. **Special Achievements:** Author: The African-American Christian Single, 1995; The African-American Christian Family, 1996; The African-American Christian Parent, 1997; The African-American Christian Man. **Business Addr:** Assoc Prof, Pastoral Ministry, Dallas Theological Seminary, 3909 Swiss Ave, Dallas, TX 75204.

LANE, ELEANOR TYSON
Educator. **Personal:** Born Feb 14, 1938, Hartford, CT; married James Perry Lane Jr; children: Randall P, Hollye Cherise. **Educ:** St Joseph Coll, BA 1960; Univ of Hartford, MEd 1975. **Career:** Hartford Bd of Educ, teacher 1960-72; Amistad House, acting dir 1973-75; Univ of CT, asst dir 1966-. **Orgs:** Mem New England Minority Women Administrators Annual Conf Wellesley Coll 1985; panelist Assoc of Social & Behavorial Scientists Inc 1985; participant Successful Enrollment Management Seminar sponsored by Consultants for Educational Resource & Rsch Inc 1986; mem New England Minority Women Administrators, Assocof Social and Behavorial Scientists, Urban League of Greater Hartford, Natl League of Business and Professional Women, Delta Sigma Theta Sor Inc, Univ of CT Professional Employees Assoc, CT Assoc of College Admissions Officers, Natl Assoc for Women Deans Administrators and Counselors, Natl Assoc for College Admissions Counselors, New England Assoc of Collegiate Registrars and Admissions Officers. **Home Addr:** 113 Vernwood Dr, Vernon, CT 06066. **Business Addr:** Asst Dir of Admissions, University of Connecticut, 28 North Eagleville Rd, Storrs, CT 06268.

LANE, GEORGE S., JR.
Dental surgeon. **Personal:** Born Dec 28, 1932, Norfolk, VA. **Educ:** BS Biology 1958; BS Chem 1959; MS Endocrinology 1960; DDS 1963; Cert in Oral Surgery 1969; post grad training in oral surgery, First Dist Dental Socof NYC; Albert Einstein Sch of Med; Northwestern U; Roosevelt Hosp of NYC; Walter Reed Army Hosp; Walter Reed Inst of Dental Research. **Career:** VA State Dental Health Prog, dental clinician. **Orgs:** Mem Am Dental Assn; Royal Soc of Health of London; Acad of Gen Dentistry; VA State Dental Soc; Virginia-Tidewater Dental Assn; bd mem YMCA; life mem NAACP; mem Alpha Phi Alpha; Shiloh Bapt Ch; Norfolk C of C; diplomate Nat Bd of Dental Examiners; elected for fellowship confirmation Acad of Gen Dentistry. **Military Serv:** USAF capt. **Business Addr:** 1419 E Brambleton Ave, Norfolk, VA 23504.

LANE, JANIS OLENE
Journalist. **Personal:** Born Jan 4, Kansas City, KS; daughter of Henrietta Perry Lane and Charles Thomas Lane. **Educ:** University of Missouri, Kansas City. **Career:** KCPT-TV, Kansas City, MO, reporter/assoc producer, 1978-83; KBMT-TV 12, Beaumont, TX, anchor/producer, 1984; KCMO 81 AM, Kansas City, MO, anchor/reporter, 1984-86; KCTV 5, Kansas City, MO, talk show host/reporter, 1985-88; Power 95 FM, Kansas City, MO, news director/anchor, 1986-88; WTOL-TV 11, Toledo, OH, weekend anchor/reporter, 1988-. **Orgs:** Member, National Assn of Broadcast Journalists, currently; member, Women Alive, currently, member, prayer intecessor, Toledo Covenant Church, currently. **Honors/Awds:** First Place, Assn of News Broadcasters of KS, 1987; Crystal Award, News Reporting, 1989.

LANE, JEROME
Professional basketball player. **Personal:** Born Dec 4, 1966, Akron, OH. **Educ:** Univ of Pittsburgh, Pittsburgh, PA, 1985-88. **Career:** Forward: Denver Nuggets, 1988-91, Indiana Pacers, 1992, Milwaukee Bucks, 1992, Cleveland Cavaliers, 1992-. **Honors/Awds:** Led NCAA Division I in rebounds per game (13.5), 1987. **Business Addr:** Professional Basketball Player, Cleveland Cavaliers, 1 Center Ct., Cleveland, OH 44115-4001.

LANE, JOHN HENRY
Clergyman. **Personal:** Born Apr 7, 1924, Brookfield, GA; son of Lou Ellen Lane; married Donneter Elizabeth Dean Lane; children: DeEtta Patricia, Gwendolyn Tempie. **Educ:** Albany State Coll, 1940-41; Univ of San Francisco, 1951-1954, BS, 1965; SF State Coll, 1963-65; Univ CA Ext, 1968; San Francisco Theological Seminary, MAV , 1990. **Career:** US Post Office, San Francisco, clerk; self-employed insurance broker, 1955-58; Golden State Life Insurance Co, life underwriter; State of California, toll-collector, 1959-61; Bayview Br Dept of Emp, asst mgr 1960-71; US Dept of Housing & Urban Devel, suprv spec 1971-; Grace Bapt Church, pastor 1973-; Hunters Point Ecumenical Ministries, pres 1976-; certified fraud examiner, 1990-. **Orgs:** Mem NAACP, Commonwealth Club of CA, APGA, Franklin Mint, Smithsonian Inst, Ecumenical Inst, Republican Residential Task Force; member, National Assn of Certified Fraud Examiners, 1990-; member, American Assn of Retired Persons, 1984-; member, Assn of Federal Investigators, 1976-; member, American Assn for Counseling & Development, 1966-. **Honors/Awds:** Roger Williams Fellowship Cert of Accomplishment "The Black Break", Black Urban Studies, Grad Theo Union; Cert of Apprec Amer Bapt Ch of W; Cert of Apprec Outstanding Citizenship City of LA CA, Cert of Apprec 5 Yrs Serv to the Nation Pres Nixon 1973; Certificate of Honor, Officers for Justice, 1985; Certificate of Honor, Board of Supervisors, San Francisco, CA, 1985, 1989; Honorary Doctor of Divinity, Technical Institute for Biblical Studies, 1990. **Military Serv:** US Navy, 1941-47. **Business Addr:** President, Hunters Point Ecumenical Min, 450 Golden Gate Ave, San Francisco, CA 94102.

LANE, JOHNNY LEE
Educator, percussionist. **Personal:** Born Dec 19, 1949, Vero Beach, FL; son of Anna Lee Lane and Alfred A Lane; married Claudia Hickerson Lane, Aug 11, 1973; children: Latoya T, Maxine A, Johnny A. **Educ:** Southern University, 1971; Southern Illinois University, MM, 1972; University of Illinois, advanced study; Bobby Christian School for Percussion, advanced study. **Career:** Johnny Lane Percussion Sextet Ensemble, conductor, 1971-72; Accent on Music, percussion instructor, 1971-72; Tennessee State University, University Percussion Ensembles, director, 1972-74, assistant director of bands, 1972-74; Johnny Lane Percussion Enterprises, president, 1980-83; MIDCO International, percussion consultant, 1983; University Baptist Church, director of music, 1978-; Eastern Illinois University, director of percussion studies, 1974-. **Orgs:** Percussive Arts Society, Illinois State Chapter, board of directors, 1979-1985, international board of directors, 1979-88, 1991-92, second vp, 1981-83, membership committee chairman, 1986-90; Percussive Notes Magazine of the Percussive Arts Society, editor, 1978-86; National Association of Rudimental Drummers; Kappa Kappa Psi, National Band Fraternity; Phi Mu Alpha, National Music Fraternity; Pi Kappa Lambda, National Music Honors Society; Sigma Alpha Iota, faculty advisor. **Honors/Awds:** Honorary Artist Diploma, Musikschule, Bad Nauheim, Germany, 1986; EIU Faculty Excellence Award, 1988-89, 1994, 1996; Friend of the Arts Award, Sigma Alpha Iota, 1992. **Special Achievements:** Co-author with Samuel A Floyd, Four-Mallet Independence for Marimba, forthcoming; author, Stick Control Exercises for Snare Drum; Rudiments in Slow Motion; My 30 Minute Workout; percussion workshops, Frankfurt, Germany, 1986; Music School, Detmold, Germany, percussion workshops and recital, 1986; Florida A & M University, percussion clinic, 1987; Southwestern Louisiana University, percussion clinic, 1987; Mississippi Valley State University, percussion clinic, 1987; Southern University, percussion clinic, 1987; North Carolina A & T University, percussion workshop, 1992, 1993; Delaware State College, percussion clinic, 1992; Founder and Host of the United States Percussion Camp; Percussion Clinic at Jackson State University, 1994, Elizabeth City State University, 1992, Northwestern State University of Louisiana, 1994, Morris Brown College, 1994, Tennessee State University, 1993. **Business Addr:** Professor, Department of Music, Eastern Illinois University, College of Fine Arts, Charleston, IL 61920, (217)581-3817.

LANE, JULIUS FORBES
Army officer (retired), fashion museum director. **Personal:** Born Sep 9, 1918, Portsmouth, VA; son of Lillian Forbes Lane and Julius F Lane; married Lois Kindle Alexander, Nov 17, 1971; children: Juliette Lane Hailey, Julius Lane Jr, Sylvia Adele, Lawrence Lane, Nichola Martin. **Educ:** Univ of Omaha, Omaha, NE, AB, l962; Temple Univ, Philadelphia, PA; Art Students League, New York, NY; New York University, New York, NY; Natl Academy School of Fine Arts, New York, NY. **Career:** US Army, Camp Craft, SC, enlisted army, l942-44; US Army, Ft Benning, officer-candidate l944; US Army, Ft Dix, NJ, retired lieutenant Colonel, l962; Bd of Educ of New York City, New York, NY, teacher; admin, Harlem Inst of Fashion, l970-; deputy dir, Black Fashion Museum, l979-. **Orgs:** Mem, Riverside Church NYC, 1980-; mem, 555 Parachute Infantry Assn, 1984-. **Honors/Awds:** "White Vase with Apples and Oranges" oil on canvas, l962; "Our Little Girl" oil on canvas, l988. **Military Serv:** US Army, Lieutenant Colonel, 1942-62; received master parachutist badge, l948.

LANE, NANCY L.
Vice Pres. **Personal:** Born Sep 3, 1938, Boston, MA; daughter of Gladys Pitkin Lane and Samuel M Lane. **Educ:** Boston Univ, BS Public Relations 1962; Univ of Pittsburgh Grad School of Public & Intl Affairs, Master of Public Admin 1967; Univ of Oslo, Norway, undergrad studies; Harvard Univ Grad School of Business Admin Prog for Mgmt Devel, certificate 1975. **Career:** Chase Manhattan Bank, second vice pres 1972-73; Off-Track Betting Corp, NYC, vice pres 1973-75; Johnson & Johnson Corp, corporate personnel staff 1975-76; Ortho Diagnostic Systems Inc Div of Johnson & Johnson, dir of personnel 1976-78, vice pres personnel & admin and mem bd of dirs 1978-89; Johnson & Johnson Worldwide Headquarters, vice pres, 1989-. **Orgs:** Black Exec Exchange PRog, advisory bd, prog founder, 1970; Benedict Coll, trustee, 1974-84; Harvard Bus School, Club of Greater NY, pres, 1990-92; Bennett Coll, chair of bd of trustees, 1989-90; Rutgers Univ, bd of governors, 1990-; Studio Museum in Harlem, bd of trustees, 1969-; NAACP, bod, 1996-; Women's Forum, bd mem; United Way of Tri State, bod; The Woodrow Wilson Natl Fellowship Foundation, bod, 1987-; Wilson Coll, trustee, 1975-78; Catalyst, bod, exec

comm, 1972-80; Harvard Bus School Alumni Assn, secy/trea, 1986-90; Ronald McDonald House of New York City, bod, 1995-; Natl Black MBA Assn, bod, 1972-75; Natl Comm on Working Women, 1980-84; A Better Chance, bod, vice chair, 1982-86. **Honors/Awds:** Living Legends in Black, JE Bailey III, 1976; Distinguished Awd, Harvard Bus School African-American, 1985; Distinguished Alumni Awd, Boston Univ School of Public Communications, 1987; Graduation Speaker, Univ Coll, Rutgers Univ, 1992; Chairman's Awd for Distinguished Service, Studio Museum in Harlem, 1996; Leadership Awd, New York City Support Group, 1996; YWCA Intl Twin Awd, 1978; Distinguished Alumni Award, Boston Univ, 1997; published numerous articles. **Business Addr:** Vice Pres, Johnson & Johnson Worldwide Headquarters, 1 Johnson & Johnson Plaza, New Brunswick, NJ 08933.

LANE, PINKIE GORDON
Educator (retired), poet. **Personal:** Born Jan 13, 1923, Philadelphia, PA; daughter of Inez Addie West Gordon (deceased) and William A Gordon (deceased); married Ulysses Simpson Lane, May 1948 (deceased); children: Gordon Edward. **Educ:** Spelman Coll, Atlanta GA, BA 1949; Atlanta Univ, Atlanta GA, MA 1956; Louisiana State Univ, Baton Rouge LA, PhD 1967. **Career:** Southern University, instructor, asst professor, associate professor, 1959-86, professor, 1967-86, chairperson dept of English 1974-86, professor emerita, 1986. **Orgs:** Poetry Society of Amer; Natl Council for Teachers of English; Modern Language Assn; Coll Language Assn; contributing & advisory editor, The Black Scholar; poetry editor, Black American Literature Forum; Delta Sigma Theta Sorority; Capita Area (Baton Rouge) Network of Executive and Professional Women; YWCA. **Honors/Awds:** Natl Award, Achievement in Arts & Humanities, Spelman Coll, Washington DC Alumnae Chapter 1983; among 57 LA Women included in the Women's Pavilion, World Exposition held in New Orleans LA 1984; Tribute to Black Women Writers at the Inaugural Celebration of Johnetta Cole, Spelman Coll, Atlanta GA 1988; Natl Award for Achievement in Poetry, Coll Language Assn 1988; Louisiana State Poet Laureate, State Governor Roemer 1989-92; numerous other honors and awards. **Special Achievements:** Poet, volumes of works include: Wind Thoughts, South & West Inc, 1972; The Mystic Female, South & West Inc, 1975; I Never Scream, Lotus Press Inc, 1978; Girl at the Window, Louisiana State University Press, 1991; works in numerous magazines, including: Callaloo; Black ALF, formerly Negro American Literature Forum; The Southern review; Nimrod; Obsidian; Ms; The Black Scholar; first African-American female to receive a PhD from Louisiana State University. **Home Addr:** 2738 77th Ave, Baton Rouge, LA 70807. **Business Phone:** (504)356-3450.

LANE, RICHARD (DICK NIGHT-TRAIN)
Director, athlete. **Personal:** Born Apr 16, 1928, Austin, TX; divorced; children: Richard Ladimir, Richard Walker. **Educ:** Southern U, 1972-73; Central State U. **Career:** Pol Athl Leag, exec dir 1975-; Det Lions, staff asst 1965-72, pro football player 1960-65; Chicago Cardinals, 1954-59; LA Rams, 1952-53; Southern U,coach 1972-73; Central U, 1973-74; Redd Foxx, consult 1974-75; Police Athletic League, exec dir. **Orgs:** Dir Mayor Daley's youth prgms 1954-57; dir Youth Opp Detroit 1963-65; Armed Forces Draft Bd; mem NFL Alumni Assn; past pres Detroit Varsity Club; fdr MI Yth Devel Found; mem Mason Cotillion Club; bd Boy's Club of Metro Detroit; Foursome Golf Club; Booker T Washington Bus Men's Assn; Detroit Optimist Club; Ring 32 Vet Boxing Assn. **Honors/Awds:** All-Time Player of the Century 1968; Football Hall of Fame 1974; Cert of Recognition West Lake JCC; Man of Yr Metro Boy's Clubs; Black Athl Hall of Fame 1977; One of the Best Ever Played in LA Colosseum voted by fans 1985. **Military Serv:** AUS corpl 1948-52. **Business Addr:** Executive Dir, Police Athletic League, PO Box 21013, Detroit, MI 48235.

LANE, VINCENT
Public housing administrator, real estate development. **Personal:** Born Mar 29, 1942, Mississippi; divorced; children: 3 sons. **Educ:** Roosevelt Univ, BS, 1966; Univ of Chicago, MBA, 1973. **Career:** Tuesday Publications, comptroller, 1970-72; The Woodlawn Comm Development Corp, sr vp, 1970-72; IL Dept of Public Aid, consultant, 1970-92; Urban Services & Development Inc, 1976-88; LSM Venture Assn, general partner, 1980-; Chicago Housing Authority, chairman, bd of commissioners, 1988-; Amer Comm Housing Assn, pres, 1991-. **Orgs:** Leadership Council for Metropolitan Open Communities, bd mem; Chicago Dwellings Assn, sec of the bd; United Charities, bd mem; Corp for Supportive Housing, bd of dirs; Council for Large Public Housing Authorities, steering comm; ETA Creative Arts Foundation, bd of dirs; Natl Trust for Historic Preservation, bd of trustees; Windows of Opportunity, Inc, chairman of the bd. **Honors/Awds:** US Dept of Housing & Urban Development, Regional Award Minority Developer of the Year; Anti-Defamation League, Distinguished Public Service Award; The Boys & Girls Clubs, Visionary Award; Governing Magazine, Public Official of the Year, 1994; The Jewish Natl Fund's Shalom Peace Award, 1992. **Special Achievements:** Appointed by the Bush Admin to serve on Natl Commission on Severely Distressed Public Housing, 1990; Appointed by Mayor Eugene Sawyer to serve on Mayor's Navy Pier Dev Corp; Appointed by mayor Harold Washington, Mayor's Advisory Council to CHA; Appointed, by Mayor Richard M Daley to Mixed Income New Communities Strategy, 1992; Appointed President's Commission on Model State Drug Laws, 1992.

LANEUVILLE, ERIC GERARD
Actor, director, producer. **Personal:** Born Jul 14, 1952, New Orleans, LA; son of Alexander and Mildred Laneuville; children: Sean. **Educ:** Santa Monica City College, 1971-73; UCLA Extension, 1974. **Career:** MTM Production, actor, director; PBS, producer; Lorimar Productions, director, producer; Universal City, director; 20 Century Fox, director; Citadel Productions, director. **Orgs:** Directors Guild of America; Screen Actors Guild; Academy of Television Arts and Sciences; Directors Guild Education and Benevalent Foundation; American Diabetes Association. **Honors/Awds:** Academy of Television Arts & Sciences, Emmy, 1992; Directors Guild of America, Outstanding Director, 1987, 1992; The Christophers, Christopher Award, 1987, 1996. **Special Achievements:** Nominated for Emmy for Drama and Comedy Series, dir, 1993; On Ballot for Emmy, acting, 1968; Three nominations for Emmy for directing, 1989, 1992, 1993. **Home Addr:** 5138 W Slauson Ave, Los Angeles, CA 90056-1641, (213)293-1277.

LANEY, ROBERT LOUIS, JR.
Educator. **Personal:** Born Sep 23, 1956, Conway, SC; son of Thillian Moore Laney and Robert L Laney Sr. **Educ:** SC State Coll, BA 1976; Atlanta Univ, MPA 1979; Clark-Atlanta Univ, Atlanta GA, EdD, 1990. **Career:** Morris Coll, dir career planning placement & coop educ & instructor 1982-84; GA Institute of Tech, Atlanta, GA, admissions officer, assist director, 1984-. **Orgs:** Mem Kappa Alpha Psi Frat 1976-; mem Amer Assoc of Coll Registrars & Admission Officers 1984-; mem Phi Delta Kappa Educ Frat 1986-.

LANG, ANDREW CHARLES
Professional basketball player. **Personal:** Born Jun 28, 1966, Pine Bluff, AR. **Educ:** Univ of Arkansas, Fayetteville, AR, 1984-88. **Career:** Phoenix Suns, center, 1988-92; Philadelphia 76ers, 1992-93; Atlanta Hawks, 1993-95; Minnesota Timberwolves, 1996; Milwaukee Bucks, 1996-. **Honors/Awds:** Athletes International Ministries, NBA Man of the Year, 1994. **Business Addr:** Professional Basketball Player, Milwaukee Bucks, 1001 N 4th St, Bradley Center, Milwaukee, WI 53203, (414)227-0500.

LANG, ANTONIO
Professional basketball player. **Personal:** Born May 15, 1972, Mobile, AL. **Educ:** Duke Univ. **Career:** Phoenix Suns, 1994-95; Cleveland Cavs, 1995-. **Business Addr:** Professional Basketball Player, Cleveland Cavaliers, 1 Center Ct., Cleveland, OH 44115-4001, (216)659-9100.

LANG, CHARLES J.
Educator. **Personal:** marrIed Agatha Daniel; children: Angele, Lori, Keith, Twyla. **Educ:** Tuskegee Inst, BA; Xavier U; Citrus Comm Coll; UCLA, MEd, EdD. **Career:** W Los Angeles Coll, dir educ prgm; Watts Skill Ctr, assoc dir; LA City Sch, tchr, prin; NASA Space Shuttle Prgm, recruiter, black astronauts & women. **Orgs:** Bd mem Our Authors Study Club; Mayor's African Sister City Com; vp, dir educ tutorial prgm Lang's Learning Lab; cert Scuba Diver & Underwater Photographer; consult Fgn Travel; adv French Lycee Sch of LA; hon mem PTA. **Honors/Awds:** Recip Audio Visual Grant; prod pioneer black sound filmstrip, Equal Oppor in Space Flight; rsrch gifted in Can, Mexicao, US; commd Motivating Black Yth to Achieve, LA City Council; Black Hist Week Award. **Military Serv:** AUS infantry offr 1948-51. **Business Addr:** Director, Dept of Education, West Los Angeles College, 4800 Freshman Dr, Culver City, CA 90230.

LANG, ISAAC, JR.
Manufacturing company executive. **Career:** Black River Manufacturing Co. Inc, CEO, currently. **Honors/Awds:** Co. is ranked 96th on Black Enterprise's Top 100 Industrial/Service Companies, 1992. **Business Addr:** Chief Executive Officer, Black River Mfg Co, Inc, 2625 20th St, Port Huron, MI 48060, (313)982-9812.

LANG, KENARD
Professional football player. **Personal:** Born Jan 31, 1975. **Educ:** Miami (Fla.), attended. **Career:** Washington Redskins, defensive end, 1997-. **Special Achievements:** NFL Draft, First round pick, #17, 1997. **Business Addr:** Professional Football Player, Washington Redskins, 13832 Redskin Dr, Herndon, VA 22071, (703)471-9100.

LANG, MARVEL
Educator. **Personal:** Born Apr 2, 1949, Bay Springs, MS; son of Rev & Mrs Otha Lang Sr; married Mozell Pentecost, Sep 15, 1973; children: Martin, Maya. **Educ:** Jackson State Univ, BA, 1970; Univ of Pittsburgh, MA, 1975; Michigan State Univ, PhD, 1979. **Career:** Lansing Community Coll, 1976-78; Jackson State Univ, assoc prof, 1978-84; US Census Bureau, research geographer, 1984-86; Michigan State Univ, Center for Urban Affairs, 1986-. **Orgs:** Steering comm mem, Southeastern Assoc of Amer Geographers, 1980-81; consultant, Mississippi Institute for Small Towns, 1980-84; bd mem, Catholic Social Services-St Vincent's Children's Home, 1986-89; Boys and Girls Clubs of Lansing, 1986-89; advisory bd mem, Michigan Legislative Black Caucus Found, 1987-90; Governing board member, Urban Affairs Association. **Honors/Awds:** Candidate, US Air Force Acad, 1966; Governor's Council on Selective Service (MS), mem, 1969-70; Natl Youth Advisory Council on Selective Ser, mem, 1969-70; Meritorious Serv Award, Michigan Legislative Black Caucus, 1988; Black Student Retention in Higher Educ (book) co-editor w/Clinita Ford, 1988; editor Contemporary Urban America, 1991; editorial board member, Journal of Urban Affairs, Urban Affairs Quarterly. **Business Addr:** Center for Urban Affairs, Michigan State University, W-31 Owen Hall, East Lansing, MI 48824.

LANG, WINSTON E.
City official. **Personal:** Born Dec 20, 1929, Detroit, MI; son of Althea Lang and Ernest Lang; married Annie Lois Lee; children: Mark, Andrea, Paul. **Educ:** Wayne State U, BA 1952, MSW 1968. **Career:** Neighborhood Serv Orgn, soc serv Admin 1967-70; City of Detroit, psychiatric soc worker 1962-67, human rights department director, currently. **Orgs:** Kappa Alpha Psi Social Fraternity; Wayne State University School of Social Work Alumni Assn; board of dirs, American Lung Assn; executive secretary, Detroit Central branch, NAACP; deputy dir, Detroit Urban League, 1970-79. **Honors/Awds:** Father of Yr Second Bapt Ch 1964; Outstanding Serv Award, Am Cancer Soc 1974; Man of Yr Second Bapt Ch 1975; Spirit of Det Award, Det City Council 1979; Equal Employment Opportunity Award, Greater Detroit Round Table, National Conference of Christians and Jews; A Phillip Randolph Community Services Award, Metropolitan Detroit Chatper. **Military Serv:** US Army, Cpl, 1952-54; Good Conduct Medal, 1954. **Business Addr:** Director, Human Rights Department, City of Detroit, 150 Michigan, 4th Flr, Detroit, MI 48226.

LANGE, LAJUNE THOMAS
Judge. **Personal:** Born Jan 29, 1946, Kansas City, MO; daughter of Thomas P Lange; married. **Educ:** Augsburg College, BA, psychology, 1975; University of Minnesota Law School, JD, 1978; Minnesota Institute of Criminal Justice, 1979; Harvard Law School, advanced training program for law school, trial advocacy instructors, 1984; Harvard Law School, employment discrimination, 1985, Judicial Scholar's Program, 1987; National Judicial College, advanced general jurisdiction, 1985, drugs and the courts, 1989. **Career:** Twin Cities Opportunities Industrialization Center, counselor, 1967; Minnesota Department of Civil Rights, field rep, 1968-70; Harry Davis Mayoral Campaign, media and public relations staff volunteer, 1971; Dorsey, Marquart, Windhorst, West & Halladay, legal assistant, 1971-73; self-employed, civil litigation matters, 1973-74; Oppenheimer, Wolff, Foster, Shepard & Donnelly, legal assistant in litigation, 1974-75; Hennepin County Public Defender's Office, law clerk, 1976-78, assistant public defender, 1978-85; Natl Institute of Trial Advocacy, faculty, 1980; William Mitchell College of Law, adjunct professor, civil rights clinic, 1984-, adjunct professor, trial advocacy, 1983-; Hennepin County Municipal Court, judge, 1985-86; Fourth Judicial District, judge, 1986-. **Orgs:** Minnesota Minority Lawyers Association, founding member, 1980-, vice pres, 1982; Minnesota Women Lawyers, board of directors, co-chair public relations committee, 1977-; Minnesota Civil Rights Commission, commissioner, 1979-84, chairperson, standards and procuedures committee hearing officer; Natl Bar Association, judicial council, intl law committee, criminal law & juvenile justice committee; Governor's Select Committee, impact of drugs on crime, education and social welfare; Natl Association of Women Judges, chairperson, minority affairs committee, nominating committee, liaison to National Bar Association judicial Council; Penumbra Theatre Company, board of directors; University of Minnesota, chancellor advisory council. **Business Addr:** Judge, Hennepin County Government Center, 300 S 6th St, Rm 951, Minneapolis, MN 55487, (612)348-5474.

LANGE, TED W., III
Actor, director. **Personal:** Born Jan 5, Oakland, CA; married Sherryl Thompson; children: Ted IV, Turner Wallace. **Educ:** Attended, San Francisco City College, Merritt Junior College. **Career:** Made Broadway debut in the hit musical ''Hair''; portrayed Isaac Washington on ABC-TV's ''The Love Boat''; film credits include ''Wattstax'', ''Trick Baby'', ''Blade'', ''Larry''; has written screenplays, plays and Love Boat segment ''Starmaker'' 1981; taught at San Francisco City College, Univ of CA, George Washington Univ; produced, directed, and starred in ''Othello''; play, ''Driving Miss Daisy''; made guest appearance on ''Family Matters''. **Orgs:** Mem Amer Film Institute. **Honors/Awds:** Donated an annual cash prize to each winning actor/actress in the adult division of the Ira Aldridge Acting Competitions; Bartender of the Year 1983; accepted at Royal Acad of Dramatic Art in London sponsored by Lynn Redgrave 1984; Certificate of Achievement, Black Filmmakers Hall of Fame, 1989.

LANGFORD, ANNA RIGGS
Attorney. **Personal:** Born Oct 27, Springfield, OH; divorced; children: Lawrence W Jr. **Educ:** Roosevelt U, attended 1946-48; John Marshall Law Sch, LlB, JD 1956. **Career:** Robinson

Farmer & Langford, attorney, 1959-69; attorney, private practice, currently. **Orgs:** Bd dir, Cook Co Bar Assn 1973-75; mem, Nat Bar Assn 1958-75; mem, NAACP; Chicago Urban League; Chicago Chap SCLC; founder, Pride Comm Cntr Inc; bd mem, Am Civil Liberties Union 1970-71; bd mem, Operation Breadbasket & PUSH; chmn, bd dir, IMPACT drug abuse prgm; one of first two women elected to Chicago City Council, 1971; delegate-at-large, Nat Dem Conv, 1972; mem, Sparling Commn; del, Pres Johnson's Conf "To Fulfill These Rights," 1968; mem, IL Gov Olgilvie's Com for Sr Citizens; del to Pres Nixon's Conf on Aging, 1971; del, World Congress of Peace Forces, Moscow, 1973; mem Commn of Inquiry into conditions in Chile, 1974; invitee to Intl Commn of Inquiry into Crimes of Military Junta in Chile, Helsinki, Finland, 1974. **Honors/Awds:** Written about in many articles; citation Cath Interracial Council; Interracial Justice & Brotherhood Award 1970; Civil Rights Award, Cook Co Bar Assn; Special Achievement Award, Cook Co Bar Assn 1971; Mahatma Ghandi Centennial of Greater Chicago Award 1969; IOTA Bus Week Award, Alpha Chpt, Iota Phi Lambda 1969; James B Anderson Award for Outstanding Achvmt in field of politics, Montford Point Marine Assn 1971; Achievement Award, 7th Ward Ind Polit Orgn 1971; Outstanding Serv in Govt for human outstanding & equal justice in performance as Alderman, SCLS's Operation Breadbasket 1971; Certificate Award Intl Travellers Assn 1971; Woman of Distiction, Etta Moten Civic & Educ Club 1970; Am Friendship Club Award of Distinction 1971; Afro-American Patrolmen'sAssn Testimonial Award 1971; WBEE Ro Comm Aard 1971; Operation Bootstrap Award 1971; hon mem Chicago Police Capt Assn 1974; & numerous others.

LANGFORD, ARTHUR, JR.
State senator. **Personal:** Born Oct 3, 1949, Atlanta, GA; married Susan Elaine Pease; children: Sarah Elizabeth. **Educ:** Morris Brown Coll, Political Sci 1971. **Career:** United Youth-Adult Conf, pres 1972; Atlanta City Council, councilman 2 - 4 yr terms; Rush Memorial Congr Church, pastor 1981; Georgia State Senate, state senator 1984-. **Orgs:** Lecturer; mem/pres United Youth-Adult Conf (UYAC) 1972-; mem NAACP; mem Southern Christian Leadership Conf (SCLC); mem Phi Beta Sigma Fraternity. **Honors/Awds:** Author of play "Life of a King" drama on the life of Martin Luther King 1969. **Business Addr:** State Senator, State of Georgia, 123-B State Capitol, Atlanta, GA 30334.

LANGFORD, CHARLES D.
Attorney. **Personal:** Born Dec 9, 1922, Montgomery, AL. **Educ:** TN State A&I Univ, BS; Cath Univ of Am, LLB 1952, JD 1967. **Career:** State of AL, legal advisor; Gray, Langford, Sapp, McGowan, Gray & Nathanson, partner/attorney. **Orgs:** Mem Senate State of AL; Elks; IBPOE of W; Alpha Phi Alpha Fraternity. **Honors/Awds:** Recipient Cert of Appreciation Ofc of Econ Opportunity Montgomery Comm Action Agency. **Business Addr:** Attorney, Gray, Langford, Sapp, McGowan, Gray & Nathanson, 352 Dexter Ave, Montgomery, AL 36104.

LANGFORD, DARIA
Record company executive. **Educ:** University of Illinois at Chicago. **Career:** Junior high school teacher; RCA, regional promotions mgr; Virgin Records, promotions and sales; Mercury Records, promotions and sales; LaFace Records, sr vice pres of promotions and marketing, currently. **Business Addr:** Senior VP, Promotions & Mktg, LaFace Records, 3350 Peachtree Rd NE, Ste 1500, Atlanta, GA 30326.

LANGFORD, DEBRA LYNN
Television programming executive. **Personal:** Born Mar 27, 1963, Los Angeles, CA; daughter of Barbara Jean Wilkins Langford and Roland Langford. **Educ:** University of Southern California, BS, business administration, 1984. **Career:** Golden Bird, director of marketing & advertising, 1984-86; Hanna-Barbera Productions, director of development, 1986-89; Warner Brothers Television, director of current programs, 1989-92, vice pres of current programming, 1992-93; Quincy Jones Entertainment, vp of television, 1993-. **Orgs:** NAACP, 1989-; African American Film & TV Assn, 1989-; Natl Assn of Female Executives, 1988-; Kwanza, 1989-; Black Entertainment Alliance, steering community, 1990-.

LANGFORD, JEVON
Professional football player. **Personal:** Born Feb 16, 1974, Washington, DC. **Educ:** Oklahoma State Univ, attended. **Career:** Cincinnati Bengals, defensive end, 1996-. **Business Addr:** Professional Football Player, Cincinnati Bengals, One Bengals Dr, Cincinnati, OH 45202, (513)621-3550.

LANGFORD, JOHN W.
Attorney. **Personal:** Born Mar 20, 1914, Montgomery, AL. **Educ:** Clark Coll Atlanta GA, AB 1936; NC Central Law School, LLB 1947. **Career:** Private practice, attny. **Orgs:** Mem, High Point Bar Assn, NC Assn of Black Lawyers, Amer Civil Liberties Union, So Poverty Law Ctr, St Marys United Methodist Church; NC State Bar Nat'l Assoc of Civilian Conservation Corps Alumni; Nat'l Assoc Against Discrimination in Housing; Africare; North Carolinians Against Racist and Religious Violence; mem, High Point N.C. City Council; mem, TransAfrica. **Military Serv:** USAAF s/sgt 1942-46. **Business Addr:** Attorney, 414 Cedar St, High Point, NC 27260.

LANGFORD, VICTOR C., III
Clergyman. **Personal:** Born Aug 6, 1939, Detroit, MI; son of Charlotte Langford and Victor Langford Jr; married Luana Calvert; children: Tanya, Natalie, Kineta, Victor IV. **Educ:** Seattle Pacific Coll, BA 1970; Concordia Sem, BD 1970, MDiv 1975. **Career:** Bethel Lutheran Church New Orleans, founder/pastor 1962-64; Holy Cross Lutheran Church Houston, pastor 1965-68; Good Shepherd Lutheran Church Seattle, pastor 1968-76; St Mark's Lutheran Church Seattle, minister 1976-; Nu-Life Enterprises, pres 1979-86. **Orgs:** Treas Black United Clergy for Action 1969-76; chmn exec com Emerg Feeding Prgm Seattle 1977-86; chmn Proj People of Seattle 1970-72; bd dir Seattle Opportunities Industrial Center 1969-86; mem NAACP 1969-; exec bd Assn for Black Lutherans 1983-87; instr Seattle Pacific Univ 1978; instr Seattle Univ 1978, 1980; exec comm bd dir Church Council of Greater Seattle 1983-86; organizer & chmn Filling the Gap Conf March 26 & 27, 1982; assoc ed Lutheran Partners Magazine 1985-; exec bd PNW Synod Lutheran Church in Amer 1986-87 Northwest Washington Synod Council 1988-89; founding bd chairman Emerald City Bank Seattle WA 1988; The African-American Luthern Association, president, 1991-93; president, Aid Assn for Lutherans, 1983-; editorial associate, Lutheran Partners Magazine, 1985-; dean, Cluster 8, Northwest Washington Synod, ELCA, 1994; president, Faith Ministries, 1996-. **Honors/Awds:** Juneteenth Fathers Day Awd Future Production of Seattle 1977. **Military Serv:** Washington Army NG COL, chaplain 1972-; STARC Chaplain. **Business Addr:** Minister, St Mark's Lutheran Church, 6020 Beacon Ave So, Seattle, WA 98108, (206)722-5165.

LANGFORD-MORRIS, DENISE
Judge. **Educ:** Wayne State Univ, guidance & counseling, cum laude, MA, 1978; Univ of Detroit, School of Law, JD. **Career:** Child welfare worker; Oakland County, trial attorney, asst prosecuting attorney, secretary of child abuse and neglect council; Sixth Judicial Circuit Court of Michigan, US Attorney's Office, asst US attorney, judge, 1992-. **Orgs:** Federal Bar Assn; Natl Bar Assn; Natl Assn of Women Judges; Amer Bar Assn, participant in commission on legal problems of the elderly; MI Judges Assn, bd of dirs; Black Judges Assn. **Honors/Awds:** Amer Bar Assn, Judicial Admini Division Certificate of Recognition; Southeastern MI Assn of Chiefs of Police, Certificate of Recognition; Women's Survival Center, Wonder Woman Award, 1993; Pontiac Urban League, Break the Glass Ceiling Award; NAACP, Judicial Award, 1994. **Special Achievements:** First African American judge to serve at Oakland County Circuit Court; First African American elected to a county position. **Business Addr:** Judge, 6th Judicial Circuit of MI, 1200 N Telegraph, Department 404, Pontiac, MI 48341, (313)858-0363.

LANGHAM, ANTONIO (COLLIE ANTONIO LANGHAM)
Professional football player. **Personal:** Born Jul 31, 1972, Town Creek, AL; son of Willie (deceased) and Deborah. **Educ:** Univ of Alabama, attended. **Career:** Cleveland Browns, defensive back, 1994-95; Baltimore Ravens, 1996-. **Honors/Awds:** Jim Thorpe Award, 1993; National Football League Players Assn Defensive Player of the Year, 1994; Football Digest, Defensive Player of the Year, 1994. **Business Addr:** Professional Football Player, Baltimore Ravens, 11001 Owings Mills Blvd, Owings Mills, MD 21117, (410)654-6200.

LANGHAM, JOHN M.
Business executive. **Personal:** marrIed Carvine; children: John Jr, Jimmy. **Educ:** Alabama State Coll, Alabama A&M, Univ of Southern Alabama, attended & received certificates; Univ of Southern Alabama, further studies in physical science. **Career:** Prichard Trading Post, self-employed, present. **Orgs:** Pres, PTA Mobile Co; pres, Toulminville Recreation Ctr; mem, 8 yrs, pres, 3 yrs, Prichard City Council; mem, Alabama & Amer Teachers Assns; bd dir Commonwealth Natl Bank; mem adv bd, Bishop State Jr Coll; pres, Prichard NAACP; mem, Supervisory Comm, Mobile Co Personnel Bd; mem, Mobile United, Natl League of Cities, Joint Ctr Political Action; mem, Southern Black Caucus of Elected Officials; mem, Natl Democratic Party. **Honors/Awds:** Prichard C of C Citizen of Week; Kappa Citizen of the Year; The John M Langham Auditorium, Prichard, AL; Prichard Senior Citizen Org; ACT Educ Prog. **Military Serv:** AUS. **Business Addr:** Prichard City Hall, PO Box 10427, Prichard, AL 36610.

LANGHART, JANET
Communications company executive. **Personal:** Born Dec 22, 1941, Indianapolis, IN; daughter of Louise Gillenwaters & Floyd Stamps; married William S Cohen, Feb 14, 1996. **Educ:** Attended, Butler University, Indiana University. **Career:** New England's Good Day, ABC Affiliate, talk show host, 1981-85; nationally syndicated You Asked for It, overseas correspondent, 1985-86; The Boston Herald, columnist, 1986-88; Home Show, ABC, guest host, 1990; Entertainment Tonight, correspondent, 1991; Nationally Syndicated America's Black Forum, co-host, 1991-96; Personal Diary with Janet Langhart, host, 1993-94; On Capitol Hill with Janet Langhart, host, 1995-96; MediaWise, gen partner, 1995-; Invest America, creator, developer, 1996-; Langhart Communications, pres, 1996-. **Orgs:** US News and World Report; Digital Equipment Corp., Avon Cosmetics, spokesperson; US Senate Spouses; New England White House Fellow, judge; Miss America Pageant, judge; United Negro College Fund, bd mem; US National Arboretum, bd mem. **Honors/Awds:** Boston's Junior Chamber of Commerce, Outstanding Young Leader Award; Israel Cultural Award; City of Indianapolis, The Casper Award; Glamour Magazine, One of Boston's Brights; Emmy Nomination for writing, producing and hosting "Janet's Special People.". **Special Achievements:** Featured in Francesco Scavullo's, Scavullo Women; Portrayed self in the movie adaptation of John Dean's "Blind Ambition," CBS-TV; acted in Haskell Wexler's movie, "Medium Cool.". **Business Addr:** President, Langhart Communications, 701 Pennsylvania Ave NW, Ste 1023, Washington, DC 20004, (202)393-5158.

LANG-JETER, LULA L.
Government administrator. **Personal:** Born May 19, Pickens Co, AL. **Educ:** Central State Univ, BS 1951; Wright State Univ Grad Sch, 1968-69; Central State Univ Grad Sch 1969-70. **Career:** Central State Univ, super of acctg 1968; Internal Revenue Svcs, auditor & super 1963-71, branch chief 1971-78, sr exec 1979-. **Orgs:** Co-chairperson N VA Minority Task Force for the Amer Cancer Soc; mem Amer Inst of Parliamentarians; participant Natl Urban League's Black Exec ExchangeProg; mem Soc of Women Accountants; local pres Alpha Kappa Alpha Sor Inc; mem League of Women Voters; life mem Natl Council of Negro Women; bd of dir YM-YWCA 1962-83; Natl Adv Bd Assn for Improvement of Minorities 1981-; natl treas Alpha Kappa Alpha Educ Advancement Found 1982-; natl treas Alpha Kappa Alpha Sor Inc 1982-; Natl Adv Bd Federally Employed Women 1983-; public relations Arlington Chap of Links Inc 1984-. **Honors/Awds:** Top Ten Women Dayton Daily newspaper 1969; Fed Employee of the Yr Fed Exec Bd Cincinnati 1971, Detroit 1974, Indianapolis 1982; Grad Leadership Awd Alpha Kappa Alpha 1981; IRS Comm EEO Awd IRS Washington 1982; Outstanding Black Women in State of IN. **Home Addr:** 1001 S Queen St, Arlington, VA 22204. **Business Addr:** Asst Director/Sr Exec, US Treasury-IRS, 1111 Constitution Ave NW, Washington, DC 20224.

LANGSTON, ANDREW A.
Salesman. **Personal:** Born May 12, 1929, Coleman, GA; married Gloria Muir; children: Andre M. **Educ:** Morris Brown Coll, attended 1947; Morehouse Coll, attended 1948; City Coll NY, BA 1949; NY Univ, MBA 1954. **Career:** CBS, continuity/copywriter 1950; Aglaw Corp, efficiency/comptroller 1953-56; Chase Manhattan Bank, mgmt trainee 1956-60; Prudential Ins Co, spl agent 1960-; Genesee Funeral Home Inc, owner/treas 1973-; Radio Station WDKX-FM, owner/gen mgr/sales mgr 1974-. **Orgs:** Trustee Rochester C of C; bd of dir Otetiana Council Boy Scouts of Amer; bd of dir William G Crimm Inst of Music; bd dir Eltrex Industries; bd dirDavid Hochstein Memorial Sch of Music; bd dir Natl Assn of Broadcasters Medium Markets; founder/past pres current chmn of bd Natl Assn Black Owned Broadcasters; pres Club Honor Guard. **Honors/Awds:** Comm Serv Awds, Pres Citations, Acad of Honor Prudential Ins Co of America; life & qualifying mem Million Dollar Round Table. **Business Addr:** General Manager/Sales Manager, WDKX-FM Radio, 160 Allen's Creek Rd, Ste 103, Rochester, NY 14618.

LANGSTON, ESTHER J.
Educator. **Personal:** Born Jun 20, 1939, Shreveport, LA; daughter of Daisy and Frank Jones. **Educ:** Wiley Coll, BA 1963; San Diego State Univ, MSW 1970; Univ of S CA, 3rd Yr Cert Social Work/Gerontology 1974; Univ of TX, PhD 1982. **Career:** Univ of Nevada Las Vegas, BSW, assoc prof, 1970-; Nevada State Welfare Dept, child specialist 1965-70. **Orgs:** Pres Undergrad Faculty, assoc mem bod, Cncl of Social Work Educ 1984-85; pres LV Chap Natl Assn of Black Social Workers 1983-84; pres, Nevada Chapter, NASW, 1996-98; mem Faculty Senate UNLV 1984-85; pres Les Femes Douze, 1990-94, 1996-; bd of dirs, BACC Program Directors, 1997-2000; Legal Defense Comm, NASW, 1997-2000; bd mem Oper Life Comm Develop Corp 1977-79; proj dir Minorities Public Policies & Laws & Their Effect on Serv Delivery 1977; vice pres, bd of directors, Aids for AIDS of Nevada 1988-90; vice chair, Governor's Commission on Mental Health M/R 1985-89. **Honors/Awds:** Co-recipient Univ Rsch Cncl Grant for Cross Cultural Comparison of Informal Support Systems for the Elderly, 1983; Fulbright Hays Scholar, USSR 1989; Social Worker of the Year, NABSW, 1982-, NASW, 1994. **Special Achievements:** Author: "The Family & Other Informal Supports," Campanile Press, 1983; "Care of the Terminally Ill, A Look at the Hospice Movement," Indian Journal of Social Services, 1986; "AIDS and the Black Church," 1990. **Home Addr:** 3618 Anthony, Las Vegas, NV 89121. **Business Addr:** Associate Professor, Univ of NV Las Vegas, 4505 Maryland Pkwy, Box 455032, School of Social Work, Las Vegas, NV 89154.

LANGSTON-JACKSON, WILMETTA ANN SMITH
Educator (retired). **Personal:** Born Sep 16, 1935, Burlington, IA; daughter of Inez Jane Wallace Smith and William Amos Smith, Sr (deceased); married Charles N Langston Jr (divorced 1966); children: Charles N III; married Robert Jackson; children: Robert Jackson Jr., (stepson). **Educ:** Fort Valley State College, Fort Valley, GA, BS, 1966; Atlanta University, Atlan-

ta, GA, MLS, 1976. **Career:** Fort Valley State College, Division of Vocational Home Economics, intermediate stenographer, 1960-64, Division of Education, secretary, 1965-67; Houston County Board of Education, Perry, GA, media specialist, teacher, librarian, 1967-88; Civil Service, Warner Robins, GA, computer programmer asst, 1988-94. **Orgs:** Pres, Pink Ladies, Peach County Hosp; leadership team member, Delta Sigma Theta Sorority, Inc, 1989-91; recording secretary, Georgia Council on Auxiliaries, 1989-91, central district dir, 1996-98 ; Middle Georgia Girl Scout, 1989-92, board of directors, 1993-97; Fort Valley State College National Alumni Association, board of directors, asst sec & sec, historian, 1990-93, 1994-98; Peach County Public Libraries, bd of trustees, 1992-98; board member, Peach County Unit, American Heart Association; Sunday school superintendent, youth director, Trinity Baptist Church, 1954-; Atlanta University National Alumni Association, Fort Valley Area Alumni Chapter, charter member, pres; life mem, NAACP; life mem, Georgia Retired Teachers Assn; life mem, GSUSA; life mem, Natl Educ Assn; life mem, GAE; Ft Valley Area Alumni Chapter, sec; sec, Peach County Health Education & Wellness Coalition, 1990-; charter mem, Women in Military Service for America. **Honors/Awds:** Four Year Honors Convocation Awardee, Fort Valley State College; One of 75 Delta Diamonds, Delta Sigma Theta Sorority, Inc, 1988; Certificate of Appreciation & Plaques, Middle Georgia Girl Scout Council, 1986, 1990; 30 Years of Service pin, US Girl Scouts of America, 1997; 4 Appreciation Plaques, Fort Valley State College National Alumni Association, 1982, 1990-92; Alpha Kappa Mu National Honor Society, 1955-. **Military Serv:** US Army, cpl, 1957-60; Proficiency P-1 Rating. **Home Addr:** PO Box 1413, Fort Valley, GA 31030-1413, (912)825-8675.

LANIER, ANTHONY WAYNE
Newspaper graphics editor. **Personal:** Born Aug 13, 1957, Louisville, KY; son of Ida Mae Smith Lanier and Austin Lanier; married Grace Foreman, Sep 13, 1997. **Educ:** Western Kentucky University, BFA, 1980; Univ of Louisville, 1982-84. **Career:** The Courier-Journal, Louisville, KY, news artist, 1984-90; The Patriot Ledger, Quincy, MA, graphics editor, 1990-. **Orgs:** The Club, mentor, 1990-93; Boston Assn of Black Journalists, treasurer/membership chair, 1990-95; New England Society of Newspaper Editors, 1990-; New England Press Assn, bd of dirs, 1993-96; Society of Newspaper Design, 1990-, board of directors, 1996-, Natl Assn of Black Journalists, Region One, treasurer, 1993-96; Natl Assn of Black Journalists, 1984-; Concord Baptist Church, middle adult ministry coordinator, 1994-95. **Honors/Awds:** The Club, Outstanding Service Award, Mentor, 1991, 1992, 1993; Chestnut Street Branch, YMCA, Black Achiever Volunteer Service Award, 1990, Black Achiever Award, 1987; Natl Assn of Black Journalists, Inst for Journalism Education Fellowship, 1992; American Press Inst, Newspaper Design Seminar Participant, 1985. **Special Achievements:** The JB Speed Museum, 10th Annual Black Artists Exhibition, 1990. **Home Addr:** 3 Douglass Park, #319, Boston, MA 02118-1076, (617)445-8681. **Business Addr:** Graphics Editor, The Patriot Ledger, Graphics Dept, 400 Crown Colony Dr, Quincy, MA 02169, (617)786-7284.

LANIER, DOROTHY COPELAND
Educator. **Personal:** Born Aug 19, 1922, Pine City, AR; married Marshall Alee; children: Frederick Delano, Adrien Copeland, Vanessa King. **Educ:** Henderson State Tchr Coll, BSE 1965; E TX State U, MS 1968, EdD 1974. **Career:** Jarvis Christian Coll, chmn div of humanities, prof of English 1977-; E AR Comm Coll, instr of English 1975-77; Jarvis Christian Coll, asst prof English, public relations assoc 1960-75; Sparkman Training School, elementary teacher 1957-60; Universal Life Insurance Co, sec-cashier 1952-54. **Orgs:** Mem Zeta Phi Beta Sor Inc 1941-; exec com mem Linguistic Assn of the SW 1974-77; talent file Nat Council of Tchr of Engl 1974-; mem AR Philol Assn 1976. **Honors/Awds:** Zeta of the Year, Zeta Phi Beta Sor Inc 1973; Outstanding Tchr, Jarvis Christian Coll 1974; publ "Selected Grammar Patterns in the Lang of Jarvis Students", Sociolinguistics in the SW 1974; Outstanding Professional Serv, Jarvis Christian Coll 1975; publ "Black Dialect grammar in fact & fiction", AR Philol Assn Publ 1976; Outstanding Contributor to Edn, Zeta Phi Beta Sor Inc 1977; publ "Textual Puzzle Technique", ERIC 1977. **Business Addr:** Jarvis Christian Collee, Hawkins, TX 75765.

LANIER, FRAN. See STRONG, HELEN FRANCINE.

LANIER, HORATIO AXEL
Education association executive. **Personal:** Born Feb 7, 1955, Augusta, GA. **Educ:** Univ of GA, AB Journalism 1977; Georgetown Univ Law Center, JD 1987. **Career:** Southern Bell Telephone Co, business office mgr 1977-79; Xerox Corp, marketing rep 1980-82; Sears Business Systems Ctgr, marketing rep 1982-84; US Justice Dept Office of Legal Counsel, legal editorial asst 1984-85; H Lanier Small Business Develop Consultant, pres 1985-86; Natl Black Alumni Assoc, natl president 1986-. **Orgs:** Pres Univ of GA Black Alumni Assoc 1980-82; mem Univ of GA Bicentennial Planning Comm 1984-85; exec producer UHURU Performing Arts Ensemble Georgetown Law Ctr 1985-87; vice chair Black Law Students Assoc Georgetown Law Ctr 1985-86; mem Amer Bar Assoc 1986-, Natl Bar Assoc 1987-. **Honors/Awds:** Disting Serv Awd Black Law Students Assoc 1985; WEB DuBois Awd Georgetown Law Ctr 1987.

LANIER, JESSE M., SR.
Food service company executive. **Personal:** Born May 2, 1941, Bath, NC; son of Beather O Lanier and Daniel Lanier Sr; married Barbara M Lanier, Nov 2, 1968; children: Audrey, Jesse Jr, Lucinda. **Educ:** North Carolina A&T State University, BS, business administration, 1968; University of New Haven, MBA program, 1971-73. **Career:** Lanier Trucking Co, partner, operator, 1959-69; C W Blakeslee & Sons Construction, accountant, 1968-70; Southern New England Telephone Co, staff accountant, administrative services staff assistant, community relations manager, purchasing manager, 1970-83; Springfield Food System, Inc, president, chief executive officer, 1983-. **Orgs:** Greater Springfield Chamber of Commerce, board of directors, 1988-92; Urban League of Springfield, MA, board of directors, 1987-, bd chairperson, 1997-; KFC Minority Franchisee Association, board member, 1989-; Association of Kentucky Fried Chicken Franchisee, Inc, 1985-; Junior Achievement of Western Massachusetts, Inc, board member, 1992-; North Carolina A&T Alumni Association, Connecticut Chapter, 1975-, past president; National Association of Purchasing manager, 1980-; NAACP, life mem 1972-. **Honors/Awds:** Greater New Haven Business & Professional Association, Business Man of the Year, 1992; Greater Springfield Business Association, Business Man of the Year, 1991; KFC, Promise Pride Operator, 1996-98; Million Dollar Store Operator, Top Sales Award, 1985-98; Connecticut Chapter of North Carolina A&T Alumni, Business Man of the Year, 1988. **Business Addr:** President, Chief Executive Officer, Springfield Food System, Inc, 644 State St, Springfield, MA 01109, (413)733-4300.

LANIER, MARSHALL L.
Educator (retired). **Personal:** Born Jan 12, 1920, Halifax Co, VA; son of Mary S Lanier and Parish L Lanier; married Dorothy Copeland; children: Frederick D, Adrien C, Vanessa C. **Educ:** Tuskegee Univ AL, BSA 1948, MSA 1950; TX A&M, PhD 1971. **Career:** Marvell Independent Sch Dist, instr of vets 1950-51; County Agr Agent, Texarkana, Ark, 1951-54; Sparkman Training Sch Sparkman AR, prin & teacher 1957-60; E AR Community Coll, dir spec serv 1976-77; Jarvis Christian Coll Hawkins, TX, dir student teaching 1977-85. **Orgs:** Mem Assn of Tchr Educators; mem TX State Tchrs Assn; mem Phi Delta Kappa; mem Assn for Supervision & Curriculum Devel; mem Kappa Delta Pi; mem Omega Psi Phi Frat. **Honors/Awds:** Recipient plaque for Outstanding Advisor, Jarvis Christian Coll 1975; Blue & Gold Plaque, Jarvis Christian Coll 1978. **Military Serv:** AUS sgt 1941-45. **Home Addr:** 18667 FM 2015, Tyler, TX 75706.

LANIER, SHELBY, JR.
Police officer (retired). **Personal:** Born Apr 20, 1936, Louisville, KY; son of Florine Bridgeman Lanier and Shelby Lanier; married; children: Michael, Ricardo, Stephanie, Rasheedah, Ciara. **Educ:** University of Louisville, Louisville, KY, BS, 1975; Central State University, Wilberforce, OH, 1955-56. **Career:** Louisville Division of Police, Louisville, KY, detective, 1961-92. **Orgs:** Chairman, National Black Police Association, 1990-92; president, Louisville Black Police Officers Org, 1990-92; president, Louisville Branch NAACP, 1988-92; Commissioner Metro Junior Football Leaue, 1980-89. **Honors/Awds:** Renault Robinson Award, National Black Police Assn, 1989; Community Service Award, Louisville Defender Newspaper, 1989; Outstanding Community Involvement, World Community of Islam, 1986; Citizen of the Year, Omega Psi Phi Fraternity, 1984; Equality Award, Louisville Urban League, 1972. **Military Serv:** US Air Force, Airman, 1956-60. **Business Addr:** Owner, Sarl Enterprises, 4906 Red Oak Ln, Louisville, KY 40218, (502)966-4211.

LANIER, WILLIE
Professional football player (retired). **Personal:** Born Aug 21, 1945, Clover, VA. **Educ:** Morgan State Univ, degree business administration. **Career:** Kansas City Chiefs, linebacker 1967-77; Wheat First Butcher and Singer, sr vice pres, currently. **Orgs:** Virginia State Univ, bd mem, bd of visitors; United Way of Greater Richmond; YMCA; The Garfield Child's Fund; WCVE Public TV, Central Virginia; Industrial Development Authority of Chesterfield Cty; Huddle House, Inc, bd of dirs. **Honors/Awds:** NFL Man of the Year, 1972; NFL Player's Assn, Linebacker of the Year, 1970-75; Chiefs' Super Bowl IV, Defensive Star; All AFL/AFC, seven times; played in two AFL All Star Games; six Pro Bowls; elected to Kansas City Chiefs, Hall of Fame, 1985; Pro Football Hall of Fame, 1986; Virginia Sports Hall of Fame, 1986; NFL 75th Anniversary Team, 1995; Virginian of the Year, 1986. **Business Addr:** Senior Vice President, Wheat First Butcher Singer, 901 E Byrd St, 5th Flr, Richmond, VA 23219, (804)649-2311.

LANKFORD, RAYMOND LEWIS
Professional baseball player. **Personal:** Born Jun 5, 1967, Modesto, CA. **Educ:** Modesto Junior College. **Career:** St Louis Cardinals, outfielder, 1990-. **Business Addr:** Professional Baseball Player, St Louis Cardinals, 250 Stadium Plaza, St Louis, MO 63102, (314)421-3060.

LANKSTER, BARROWN DOUGLAS
District attorney. **Personal:** Born Mar 14, 1950, Linden, AL; son of Velma Lankster Jones and Albert Lankster; married Marcia Swain; children: Kristina, Nakieta, Barrown Douglas II. **Educ:** Selma University, AA, 1970; Livingston University, BS, 1972; Howard University School of Law, JD, 1975. **Career:** City of Birmingham, assistant city attorney, 1977-80; Legal Aid Society of Birmingham, sr staff attorney, 1975-77; City of Uniontown, municipal judge, 1983-86; 4th Judicial Circuit of Alabama, assistant district attorney, 1983-92; Sumter County, county attorney, 1983-92; 17th Judicial Circuit, district attorney, 1992-. **Orgs:** Alabama State Bar Association; Alabama Lawyers Association; Seventeenth Judicial Circuit Bar; Alabama District Attorneys Association, associate mem. **Honors/Awds:** NAACP Legal Defense Fund, Herbert Lehman Scholar, 1972, Earl Warren Scholar, 1973; Howard University School of Law, American Jurisprudence Award for Excellence in the Study of Evidence, 1974. **Home Addr:** 801 Arcola Rd, Demopolis, AL 36732. **Business Phone:** (205)289-2244.

LANSEY, YVONNE F.
Bank executive. **Personal:** Born Sep 9, 1946, Baltimore, MD; daughter of Priscilla Phillips-Lansey and E Gaines Lansey, Sr. **Educ:** Morgan State Univ, Baltimore, MD, BS, 1969; Long Island Univ, Brooklyn, NY, MBA, 1974. **Career:** Fed Reserve Bank of NY, New York, NY, credit analyst, 1969-74; Xerox Corp, Rochestr, NY, financial analyst, 1974-76; Westinghouse Electric Rorp, Hunt Valley, MD, financial analyst, 1976-79, project dir, 1979-85; Ideal Fed Savings Bank Baltimore, MD, vice pres, 1985-88, pres, 1988-. **Orgs:** Trustee, Florence Crittenton Servs, 1986; trustee, Girl Scouts of Central MD, 1987; trustee, Combined Health Agencies, Inc. 1987; Governor's Task Force to Study & Revise the Inheritance & Estate Tax Law of the State of MD, 1987; financial sec, The Links, Inc,Harbor City Chapter, 1987-89; bd of dir & sec, Amer League of Financial Insts, Washington DC, 1988; trustee, Baltimore Museum of Art, 1989; Alpha Kappa Alpha Sorority. **Honors/Awds:** Women on the Move, Sigma Gamma Rho, 1986; Booker T Washington, Business League of Baltimore, 1989. **Home Addr:** 3303 Glen Ave, Baltimore, MD 21215.

LAPEYROLERIE, MYRA EVANS (MYRA LYNN EVANS)
Business executive, consultant. **Personal:** Born Jun 10, 1959, Cleveland, OH; daughter of Mary C Mahone Evans and John S Evans Sr; married Jeffrey C Lapeyrolerie, Sep 5, 1987; children: Sydney Adair. **Educ:** Yale Univ, BA Chem 1981. **Career:** Standard Oil of OH, asst chem engr 1977-79, asst chemist 1980; Columbia Presbyterian, biomedical rsch asst 1979; Goldman Sachs & Co, financial analyst 1981-83; Gelato Modo Inc, pres, 1983-86; Bankers Trust, assoc, 1986-88; Hibernia Natl Bank, 1989, trust investment officer; Wedgewood Capital Mgmt, exec vice pres, 1989-91, consultant, 1991-. **Orgs:** Financial Analyst Assn; Chem Engr Soc at Yale; mem Yale Club; mem Laurel Alumni Assn; mem/treas Black Church at Yale; mem, NASP, 1989-. **Honors/Awds:** Business Awd Natl Assn of Negro Bus & Prof Women; Youth Awd Avon Natl Black Leadership Round Table; Natl Achievement Semifinalist; Laurel School Disting Alumnae Awd Miller Brewing Calendar 1985; Entrepreneur of the Year, Links, 1985.

LARA, EDISON R., SR.
Beer company executive. **Personal:** marrIed Genevieve; children: Cecelia E, Valencia Ann, Edison Jr, Alysanne. **Career:** Country Club Malt Liquor, regional manager; Westside Distributors, chief executive, 1974-. **Orgs:** Black Business Association; YMCA; Cal State University Advisory Board; UNCF Leadership Council; Los Angeles Urban League; 100 Black Men; Tee Masters Golf Club; CBWWA; NBWA. **Honors/Awds:** United Negro College Fund, Mind Fires Award, 1981, Frederick D Patterson Award; Los Angeles Area Council Boy Scouts of America, Good Scout Award; 100 Black Men of America, Most Outstanding Black Businessman in the Nation, 1988. **Special Achievements:** Company ranked #26 on Black Enterprise's list of top 100 black businesses; company is among the top ten percent of Anheuser-Busch wholesalers in the nation. **Business Addr:** President/Owner, Westside Distributors, 2405 Southern Ave, South Gate, CA 90280, (213)758-3133.

LARGE, JERRY D.
Journalist. **Personal:** Born Jan 15, 1954, Clovis, NM; son of Viola Bailey; married Carey Gelernter, Jul 30, 1982. **Educ:** New Mexico State University, Las Cruces, NM, BA, 1976. **Career:** The Farmington Daily Times, Farmington, NM, reporter, 1976-77; The El Paso Times, El Paso, TX, reporter, 1977-80; The Oakland Tribune, Oakland, CA, copy editor, 1980-81; The Seattle Times, Seattle, WA, assistant city editor, 1981-. **Orgs:** Member, National Assn of Black Journalists, 1983-; treasurer, Black Journalists Assn of Seattle, 1989-90; member, Society of Professional Journalists, 1977-. **Business Addr:** Assistant City Editor, The Seattle Times, PO Box 70, Seattle, WA 98111.

LARK, RAYMOND
Artist, lecturer. **Personal:** Born Jun 16, 1939, Philadelphia, PA; son of Bertha Lark and Thomas Crawford. **Educ:** Philadelphia Museum School of Art, 1948-51; Los Angeles Trade Tech Coll, 1961-62; Temple Univ, BS 1961; University of Colorado, Boulder, LHD 1985. **Career:** Museum & Gallery exhibitions include: Library of Congress Washington, DC; Guggenheim Museum; Smithsonian Inst; Ava Dorog Galleries Los Angeles &

Munich; LaGalerie Mouffe Paris; Nader's Art Gallery Port-au-Prince, Haiti; Galleria d'Arte Caglairi Naples, Italy; Centre Intl D-Art Contemporain Paris France; Accademia Italia Parma, Italy; Honolulu Acad of Arts Hawaii; Museum of African & African-Amer Art & Antiquities Buffalo, NY; Portsmouth Museum VA; CA Museum of Sci & Industry Los Angeles; NJ State Museum Trenton; UCLA Ctr for Afro-Amer Studies LA; Stanford Univ Museum; Exec Mansion Vice Pres Nelson A Rockefeller NY; Santa Barbara Museum CA; Univ of Colorado Museum Boulder; Utah Museum of Fine Arts, Salt Lake City; Triton Museum of Fine Arts, CA, DickinsonUniv North Dakota; CA Museum of African Historical & Cultural Soc San Francisco; San Diego Museum CA; Museum of African Amer Art Santa Monica in conjunction with 1982 Natl Urban League Annual Conference; Gallery Vallombreuse Biarritz France; Smith-Mason Gallery of Art Washington, DC; Phillip E Freed Gallery of Art Chicago; Playboy Club Century City CA; Dalzell Harfield Galleries Ambassador Hotel Los Angeles; Diplomat Hotel Florida; Sheraton Park Hotel Washington, DC; Griffon's Light Gallery Denver, Co; Phoenix Art Gallery Atlanta, GA; Multi-Cultural Arts Inst San Diego, CA; Lyzon Galleries Nashville, TN; Ames Art Galleries & Auctioneers Beverly Hills; over 60 other exhibitions; lectured, various educational institutions throughout theUS; Art Commissions include work for "All in the Family"; "The Carol Burnett Show"; "Maude"; "Young and the Restless"; Univ City Studios Movie Land Wax Museum; Blue Cross Insurance Co; Museum exhibitions include Springfield Art Museum, Missouri, Washington County Museum of Fine Arts, Maryland; Peninsula Fine Arts Center, Virginia; Greenville Museum of Art, Inc, North Carolina. **Honors/Awds:** A succession of citations, honors, salutes, commissions, advertising endorsements, headlined billings, & Best-of-the-Show Cash Awds & Gold Medals; Citations from Pres Jimmy Carter, Gerald Ford, Richard Nixon, Gov Jerry Brown of CA, & mayor Tom Bradley of LA, NAACP, etc; over 50 "first" accomplishments; Grants, Natl Endowment for the Arts, ARCO, Coors Beer Co, Colorado Humanities Prog, the students at the Univ of Colorado, etc; author & contributor to over 50 scholarly treatises on art, education, historical development of black Amers, which are used as textbooks translated & subscribed to by institutions & individuals in nearly every country of the world;lectured & debated at many museums, colleges, & universities throughout the US. **Business Addr:** The Art of Raymond Lark, PO Box 76169, Los Angeles, CA 90076-0169.

LARKE, CHARLES
Educational administrator. **Career:** Richmond County Public Schools, interim superintendent, asst superintendent for vocational services, superintendent, currently. **Special Achievements:** First African American superintendent of the Richmond County Public Schools.

LARKIN, BARRY LOUIS
Professional baseball player. **Personal:** Born Apr 28, 1964, Cincinnati, OH. **Educ:** Univ of Michigan, attended. **Career:** Cincinnati Reds, infielder, 1986-. **Honors/Awds:** Tied for Ntl League lead, double plays (86) by shortstops, 1990; shortstop, Sporting News Natl League All-Star Team, 1988, 1990; shortstop, Sporting News Natl League Silver Slugger Team, 1988-90; member, 1984 US Olympic baseball team; named to Ntl League All-Star Team, 1988-91; member of World Series Championship Team, Cincinnati Reds, 1990. **Business Addr:** Professional Baseball Player, Cincinnati Reds, 100 Riverfront Stadium, Cincinnati, OH 45202, (513)421-4510.

LARKIN, BYRDIE A.
Political scientist, educator. **Personal:** Born in Tuskegee Inst, AL; daughter of Lula Berry Larkin and Rev Charles Haile Larkin; divorced; children: Seve, Mwangi Leonard. **Educ:** AL State Univ, BS, 1973; Atlanta Univ, MA, 1975, PhD, 1982. **Career:** Atlanta Jr Coll, part time instructor, 1975-77; Atlanta Public School System, assigned supply teacher, 1977; AL State Univ, Dept of Political Sci, assc professor, 1977-82, acting chairperson, 1982-85, assoc prof, currently. **Orgs:** Alpha Kappa Mu Natl Honor Soc; Alpha Kappa Alpha Sorority; charter mem Black Women Academicians; Phi Gamma Mu International Social Science Honorary Society; Consortium of Doctors, advisory cncl, appointee, 1995-96; Rodney Higgins Best Paper Award Comm, chairperson; Natl Conference of Black Political Scientists, 1994-96; council rep, Executive Comm of the Alabama Assn of Political Scientist, 1997; scy, Coll of Arts and Sciences, 1995, 1996. **Honors/Awds:** 4 year Valedictorian Scholarship AL State Univ; Grad Scholarships & Fellowships Atlanta Univ, Notre Dame & OH State Univs; Outstanding Grad Student Awd Atlanta Univ Dept of Political Sci, 1975; AL State Univ Study Grant, 1979; Dept of State Scholar, Diplomat Conf on Europe, 1981; Summer Inst on the Amer Judicial System, Amer Judicial Soc, 1984; Fulbright Scholar to Israel 1985; Leadership Montgomery Participant, 1986-87; Ford Found Fellowship for seminars on Southern studies at the Univ of Mississippi, 1989; AL State Univ, Clg of Arts & Sciences, Outstanding Faculty Award for Community Service, 1991; Alabama State Univ Student Government, Outstanding Faculty Award, 1993; Troy United Women's League, Outstanding Pike, countian, 1993. **Special Achievements:** Political commentator for local radio stations; participant: founding and structuring of the Consortium on National Voting Rights and Political Empowerment, 1991; attendance at July 5-7, 1996 Symposium of Minority Scholars and Voting Rights; represented AKA Inc's Supreme Basileus, Mary Shy Scott, National Coalition of Black College Students, Feb 10, 1991. **Home Addr:** 114 Mountain Laurel Rd, Prattville, AL 36066. **Business Addr:** Associate Professor of Political Science, Alabama State Univ, 915 S Jackson St, Montgomery, AL 36195.

LARKIN, MICHAEL TODD
Advertising agency director. **Personal:** Born Mar 7, 1963, Cincinnati, OH; son of Shirley J Larkin and Robert L Larkin; married Sharon Denise Dean, May 23, 1992. **Educ:** University of Notre Dame, BA, economics, 1985. **Career:** Hameroff, Milenthal Spence Inc, sports promotion director, currently. **Special Achievements:** Personal manager, Cincinnati Reds shortstop Barry Larkin. **Business Addr:** Director, Sports Promotion, Hameroff, Milenthal Spence Inc, 10 W Broad St, Columbus, OH 43215, (614)221-7667.

LARKINS, E. PAT
Mayor-commissioner. **Career:** Mayor-commissioner of Pompano Beach, FL. **Business Addr:** PO Drawer 1300, Pompano Beach, FL 33061.

LARKINS, JOHN RODMAN
Director. **Personal:** Born Dec 24, 1913, Wilmington, NC; married Marian; children: Sandra. **Educ:** Shaw U, AB; Atlanta Univ Sch of Soc Work, MSW; Sch of Serv Adminstrn Univ of Chgo, adv study. **Career:** Div of Youth Dev, dir 1973-; NC Probation Commn, asso dir 1968-73; Dept Soc Svc, coord of civil rights 1942-68. **Orgs:** Mem bd trustees Shaw U; NC Cntrl U; mem bd adv Raleigh Bus Coll; mem NC Adv Coun on Librs; mem NC Bd Juv Correc; adv bd, vice pres NC Coun on Human Rels; bd dirs So Regional Coun, Atlanta; aptd NC Recreation Commn, Adv Com of Thirty, Steering Com, Cit Com 1961; first vice pres Family Life Coun of NC Exec Com 1962; aptd Govs Com on Juv Delin & Youth Crime 1962; aptd Cit Adv Coun of Pres Com on Juv Delin & Youth Crime 1962; aptd NCGood Neighbor Council 1963; Gov Com on Demon Proj for Youth 1963; Family Svc, Travelers Aid Assn of Raleigh 1965-66; mem Nat Adv Coun of Upward BoundProj; Gov Law & Order Com 1973-; Juv Jus Adv Com of Gov & Order Com 1973-; Criminal Just Educ & Training Sys Coun 1973-. **Honors/Awds:** Recip Cert of Merit for pub svc, Bus & Professional Mens Club 1957; Man of Year, Negro Progess 1958; Cert for Merit Christ & Civic Serv to people of state, NC Fed of Negro Wom Club. **Business Addr:** Div of Youth Devel, 116 W Hargett St, Raleigh, NC 27602.

LAROCHE, GERARD A.
Educator. **Personal:** Born Oct 3, 1927, Cap Haitien, Haiti; married Carolyn Mae Seese; children: 2. **Educ:** SD State Coll, BS 1955; Bethel Sem, 1960; Roosevelt U, MA 1967; Univ of Strasbourg, Doc 1971; Tchr Coll, 1968; Univ of MN, 1961-63, 69, 72; Sioux FallsColl, 1950-53. **Career:** Bethel Coll & Seminary, prof 1969; SW HS, teacher 1968-69; Oaklawn HS, teacher 1967-68; Dusable Jr HS, teacher 1966-67; Zion Baptist Church, assoc minister 1961-64; Haiti, miss 1956-57; Shiloh Baptist Church, assoc minister 1973- 75; Amer Baptist Conv, ministry 1961; Family Tie Daily Dev Guide, 1974. **Orgs:** Chmn Minorities & Intl Com 1973-76; vice pres Spanish Evang Educ Crusade 1971-75; found Black French Club in St Paul 1973-74; mem Alln Francaise of TwinCities; Am Tchrs of French; rep MN Cncl of Chs 1963-64. **Business Addr:** 3900 Bethel Dr, Arden Hills, MN 55112.

LAROSILIERE, JEAN DARLY MARTIN (J. D)
Attorney. **Personal:** Born Feb 4, 1963, Port-au-Prince, Haiti; son of Lucitania S St Dic and Bernadotte Larosiliere; married Valerie Lynett Yearwood, Aug 20, 1988. **Educ:** Fairfield University, AB, 1985; Tulane University School of Law, JD, 1988; Georgetown University Law Center, LLM, 1990. **Career:** Georgetown University Law Center, graduate teaching fellow, 1988-90; Seton Hall University School of Law, adjunct professor of law, 1992-; US Department of Justice, assistant US attorney, 1990-. **Orgs:** US Department of Justice, hiring committee, 1992-; Garden State Bar Association, 1990-; American Bar Association, 1988-; Natl Bar Assn, 1985-. **Honors/Awds:** Tulane University, senior trial competition finalist, 1988; Black Law Students Association, Frederick Douglass Moot Court Champion, 1988. **Military Serv:** US Marine Corps, 1st lt, 1986-89. **Home Phone:** (201)584-1948.

LARRIE, REGINALD REESE. See Obituaries section.

LARRY, CHARLES EDWARD
Marketing executive. **Personal:** Born Dec 23, 1944, Dallas, TX; son of Ruby Myrtle Clausell-Hayes (deceased) and John Farrell Newton (deceased); married Elizabeth Wamboi Seaton (divorced 1984); children: Charles Kent, Cheryl Kristen, Felicia Wanjui. **Educ:** Tennessee State University, Nashville, TN, BS, civil engineering, 1969. **Career:** Genesco, Nashville, TN, production scheduler, 1965; IBM, Nashville, TN systems engineer, 1965-68; Exxon Company, USA, coordinator/consumer affairs, 1969-. **Orgs:** Senior fellow, American Leadersip Forum, 1988-; board member, past pres, Family Service Center of Houston, 1982-; board member, Boys & Girls Club of Houston, 1988-; national board member, Society of Consumer Affairs Professionals, 1989-; former board member, Houston Area Urban League, 1987-88.

LARRY, JERALD HENRY
State representative. **Personal:** Born Jul 29, 1944, Dallas, TX; son of Amy Beasley Larry and Jeff Larry; children: Jerald Andre, Jerrod Enrique. **Educ:** Attended, NTSU, Denton, TX, 1962-64, El Centro, Dallas, TX, 1969-71, Bishop Coll, Dallas, TX, 1972-77. **Career:** Regional Admin of Natl Bank Office of Comptroller of the Currency, US Treasury, asst natl bank exec, 1974-75; Interracial Council for Business, Dallas, loan serv officer, 1975-76; Jessie's Nursing Facility, business mgr, 1976; Larry's 4-J's/Professional Business, owner/mgr, 1977-83; Texas State Treasury, supvr, investigator, 1983-86; State of Texas, representative, currently. **Orgs:** Bd mem, Dallas Black Chamber of Commerce, 1976-; bd mem, VNA, 1979-83; chmn, budget & finance, Texas Coalition of Black Democrats, 1983-. **Home Addr:** 2430 Marfa Ave, Dallas, TX 75216. **Business Addr:** State Representative, Texas House of Representatives, PO Box 2910, Austin, TX 78769.

LARTIGUE, ROLAND E.
Company executive, engineer. **Personal:** Born Mar 3, 1951, Beaumont, TX; son of Emily and Homer Lartigue Sr; married Dell Malone, Jul 12, 1980; children: Jason. **Educ:** Michigan State University, BS, mechanical engineer, 1973; Xavier University, advanced business studies, 1979-84. **Career:** Eastman Kodak, research engineer; Rockwell International, research engineer, sales engineer, purchasing mgr and commodity mgr; Columbus Auto Parts, vice pres, materials; Stahl Manufacturing, executive vice pres, general mgr; United Technologies, vice pres, purchasing & legistics, currently. **Business Addr:** Vice Pres, Purchasing/Logistics, United Technologies Automotive Inc, 5200 Auto Club Dr, Dearborn, MI 48126, (313)593-9450.

LARVADAIN, EDWARD, JR.
Attorney. **Personal:** Born Aug 18, 1941, Belle Rose, LA; son of Maxine Larvadain and Edward Larvadain Sr; married Patricia Dorsett, 1965; children: Edward III, Malcolm X. **Educ:** Southern University, BA, 1963, Law School, JD, 1966. **Career:** Ernest Morial, attorney, 1966-67; self-employed, attorney, currently. **Orgs:** State, NAACP Education, chairman, 1985-; YMCA Black Achiever, committee member, 1989-; Alexandria Branch NAACP, 1968-; Louisiana State Bar Association, 1968-; Louisiana Trial Lawyers Association, 1970-. **Special Achievements:** Outstanding Contributions, Sickle Cell Anemia, 1984, 1992; Outstanding Contributions, Girl Scouts, 1992; Outstanding Service, Sickle Cell Anemia, 1990; Education, State NAACP, Service Award, 1984; Outstanding Service, 1988. **Business Addr:** Attorney, 626 Eighth St, Alexandria, LA 71301, (318)445-6717.

LASALLE, ERIQ
Actor. **Career:** Appeared in the films, Coming to America; Drop Squad; appears in the television series "ER". **Business Addr:** Actor, "ER", c/o NBC-TV, 3000 W Alameda Ave, Burbank, CA 91523.

LASANE, JOANNA EMMA
Theatrical director. **Personal:** Born Jul 24, 1935, Atlantic City, NJ; daughter of Viona Marie Foreman and John Westley Foreman; married Karlos Robert LaSane, Aug 29, 1955; children: Karlos Robert LaSane Jr. **Educ:** Katherine Dunham Schol of Dance NY, 1953-55; Martha Graham School of Modern Dance NY, 1953-55; Amer School of Ballet & Intl School of Dance, 1957; Montclair State Coll for Theatre Arts & Speech 1970; Negro Ensemble Co NY, 1971; New Lafayette Theatre NY, 1972-73. **Career:** Ebony Fashion Fair Johnson Publishing, Chicago, high fashion model 1965-66; Atlantic City Bd of Ed, comm agent 1972-75; Stockton Performing Arts Ctr, rep to the arts & lecture series 1983-85; Atlantic City Childrens Theatre, dir 1973-; Atlantic Human Resources, Atlantic City, NJ, drama consultant, 1973-; Atlantic City Board of Education, Atlantic City, NJ, drama consultant, 1983-; Center for Early Childhood Education, Atlantic City, NJ, drama consultant, 1983-. **Orgs:** Allied Arts; NAACP; Urban League; NJ Educ Assn; Natl Educ Assn; Stockton State Coll Friends Assn; advisory council Dr Martin Luther King Jr School Complex; NJ State Council on the Arts; NJ Speech and Theatre Assn; committee chairman Boy Scouts of America 1988-89; board of directors, Atlantic City Education Foundation, 1987-; commissioner, New Jersey-Atlantic City Coordinating Council, 1990-; Board of Dirs, Police Athletic League; Atlantic County Cultural and Heritage Advisory Board; Atlantic City Fine Arts Commission; South Jersey Stage Company, board of trustees; Childrens Cultural Arts Foundation. **Honors/Awds:** 1st Black model to do an intl ad for Pepsi Cola 1967; NJ Senate Citation for Excellence in the Cultural Arts 1981; Creating New Pathways for Youth Distinguished Award Gentlemen of Sports NJ 1981; Cultural Arts Award Atlantic City Magazine 1981; Leadership in the Arts 101 Women Plus NJ 1983 and 1994; Delta Sigma Theta Appreciation Awd for Serv at 37th Natl Convention Detroit MI 1983; Outstanding Citizen NAACP & Civic Betterment Assoc 1984; member of the NJ State Council on the Arts (1st Black woman);

Theta Kappa Omega Arts Award 1986; Alpha Kappa Alpha Comm Serv Award 1986; Omega Psi Phi Fraternity Upsilon Alpha Chapter Inspiration & Leadership Award 1986; apptd to serve as a commissioner of the Atlantic City US Constitution Bicentennial Commn 1987; role model award Sun Newspaper 1989; achievemenward National Conference of Christians and Jews 1988-89; people to watch award Atlantic City Magazine 1989; Mary Church Terrell Award, 1992; NJ State Legislature Superlative Accomplishment in the Arts Award, 1994; Atlantic County Women's Hall of Fame, 1996; The Omega Psi Phi Award for Arts Excellence, 1996; Educ Foundation Achievement Awd, 1997; Kiwanis Club Key Awd, Excellence in the Arts, 1997. **Business Addr:** Drama Consultant, Atlantic City Public Schools, Dr Martin Luther King Jr School Complex, Dr Martin Luther King Jr Blvd, Atlantic City, NJ 08401.

LASLEY, PHELBERT QUINCY, III (PHIL)

Musician, composer, arranger, teacher. **Personal:** Born Mar 27, 1940, Detroit, MI; son of Josephine Wooldridge Lasley and Phelbert Quincy Lasley; married Trudy Diana Norresi, Oct 15, 1973; children: Felicia, Nagira. **Educ:** Institute of Musical Arts, Detroit, MI, 1957-58. **Career:** Self employed, saxophonist, composer, 1958-. **Orgs:** Jazz Heritage Society, 1975-; Citizens Committee to Save Jazz, 1975-; Greenpeace, 1986; Detroit Jazz Orchestra, alto saxophonist, 1983-; Guerilla Jam Bank, alto saxophonist, 1987. **Honors/Awds:** Best Alto Sax, Honorable Mention, Metro Times, Detroit, 1989-90; Jazz Hall of Fame, Graystone Jazz Museum, 1990.

LASSITER, JAMES EDWARD, JR.

Dentist. **Personal:** Born Feb 12, 1934, Newport News, VA; children: Teri, Tina, James III, Judi. **Educ:** Howard Univ, B Music Ed 1957, DDS 1963. **Career:** Overlook Hosp Summit NJ, assoc attendant 1967-; Martland Hosp, assoc attendant 1972; Coll of Medicine & Dentistry, assoc prof 1972-73; Coll of Dentistry Fairleigh Dickenson, asst prof 1974-78; Coll of Medicine & Dentistry, asst prof 1982-84; Private Practice, dentist 1965-. **Orgs:** Numerous lectures; consul Union Co Vocational Sch 1975-; adv comm Coll of Medicine & Dentistry 1977-79; consul Piedmont Rsch Ctr 1979; consul Dept of Health Educ & Welfare 1979; adv comm Natl Health Professional Placement Network WK Kellogg Found 1979; adv comm to Review Coll of Med & Dentistry Dental Sch 1979; bd mem Group Health Ins of NY 1981-; mem Amer Dental Assn 1965-; mem Natl Dental Assn 1965-; mem NJ Dental Assn 1965-; mem Commonwealth Dental Soc 1965-; mem Amer Analgesia Soc 1976-; mem Acad of Medicine of NJ 1969-; mem NJ Dental Group PA 1970-; mem Morristown Dental Assocs 1973-78; mem Paterson Dental assocs 1974-; mem Acad of Genl Dentistry 1976-; mem Amer Soc of Dentistry for Children 1977-; Fellow Acad of Dentistry Intl 1977-; Fellow Amer Coll ofDentists 1978-; acting execr Natl Dental Assn 1981-; sr consul Natl Dental Assn 1981-; mem ADA's Special Comm of "The Future of Dentistry" 1982; chmn & pres Natl Dental Assn Found 1982-; life mem Golden Heritage mem NAACP; Kappa Alpha Psi Frat; Wallace AME Chapel. **Honors/Awds:** Citation Head Start Prog 1969; Citation Children's Dental Health Prog Summit NJ Bd of Heath 1972; Comm Serv Awd Greater Newark Urban Coalition 1975; Outstanding Serv Awd Natl Dental Assn 1976; President's Awd Natl Dental Assn 1977; Citation Giant of Excellence in the Health Care Arena 1979; Alumni Achievement Awd Howard Univ Coll of Dentistry 1981; Bergen/Passaic Howard Univ Alumni Awd 1981; President's Awd Natl Dental Assn 1982; Outstanding Achievement Awd Commonwealth Dental Soc of NJ 1983; Outstanding & Valuable Contrib to 70th Scientific Session Natl Dental Assn Baltimore MD 1983. **Business Addr:** President, James E Lassiter DDS PA, 475 Springfield Ave, Summit, NJ 07901.

LASSITER, JOHN

President. **Personal:** Born Apr 18, 1937, Chicago, IL; son of Ethel and John Sr; married Rosielyn Utley; children: John Randall, Eric Winston. **Educ:** Univ of IL, BS Econ 1959; Am Coll of Life Underwriters, CLU 1969. **Career:** Prudential Insurance Co, agent 1963-66, sales mgr 1966-69, district mgr 1969-81, div mgr 1981-84. **Orgs:** Pres Chicago Assn of Life Underwriters; bd mem Chicago General Agents & Mgrs Assn; bd mem Chicago Chap Amer Soc of CLU; bd mem, bd dirs South Chicago Comm Hosp; bd mem, bd dirs Operation PUSH. **Honors/Awds:** Pres's Citation Prudential Ins Co of Amer 1964-74; Pres' Trophy Prud Ins Co of Am 1968; Mid-Am Trophy Prudential Ins Co of Amer 1970; Nat Mgmt Awd General Agents & Mgrs Conf 1976-80. **Military Serv:** AUS 2nd lt 1960-65.

LASSITER, KWAMIE

Professional football player. **Personal:** Born Dec 3, 1969, Hampton, VA. **Educ:** Univ of Kansas, attended. **Career:** Arizona Cardinals, running back, 1995-. **Business Addr:** Professional Football Player, Arizona Cardinals, 8701 S Hardy, Tempe, AZ 85284, (602)379-0101.

LASSITER, WRIGHT LOWENSTEIN, JR.

College president. **Personal:** Born Mar 24, 1934, Vicksburg, MS; son of Ethel F Lassiter and Wright L Lassiter Sr; married Bessie Loretta Ryan; children: Michele Denise, Wright Lowenstein III. **Educ:** Alcorn State Univ, BS 1955; Tuskegee Inst, Certf Institutional Bus Mgmt 1956; IN Univ, MBA 1962; Auburn Univ, EdD 1975; CA Western Univ, PhD 1977. **Career:** Hampton Inst, investments accountant 1956; Tuskegee Inst, sr accountant 1958-61; Tuskegee Inst, dir aux Enterprises 1962-76; asst prof mgmt 1962; IN Univ Bloomington, research assoc 1961-62; Morgan State Univ, vice pres business & finance 1976-80; Schenectady County Community Coll, pres 1980-83; Bishop Coll, pres 1983-86; El Centro Coll, pres, currently. **Orgs:** Mem Counil Educ Facility Planner, Soc for Advancement Mgmt; board of directors, Dallas Urban League; board of directors, United Way of Metro Dallas; member, Dallas Black Chamber of Commerce; board of directors, Dallas Symphony Assn; member, Dallas County Youth Services Commission; member, Dallas AIDS Education Commission; board of directors, YMCA of Metropolitan Dallas; board of directors, Dallas Urban League; board of governors, Dallas Model United Nations; member, Downtown Dallas Rotary Club; board of directors/vice pres, Dallas Black Chamber of Commerce. **Honors/Awds:** Martin Luther King Disting Leadership Awd SUNY 1981; NAACP Leadership Awd 1982; Outstanding Conribs in Educ Awd Alpha Phi Alpha 1983; Disting Serv Awd Hamilton Hill Neighborhood Assoc 1983; Appreciation Awd State of NY 1983; Apprec Awd Alpha Phi Alpha 1984; Disting Achievement & Serv Awd 1984; Meritorious Serv Awd United Way of Metro Dallas 1984,85; Disting Serv Awd in Christian Educ TX Baptist Conv 1984; Disting Serv Awd InterFirst Bank 1984; Disting Serv Awd Interdenominational Ministerial Alliance 1984; Man of the Year Awd So Dallas Bus & Professional Women's Club Inc 1984; Brotherhood Awd New Jersulaem Bapt Church 1984; Cert of Appreciation Vet Admin Reg Med Ctr 1985; Cert of Special Congressional Recognition US Congressman James Armey 1985; Certof Appreciation Dallas Reg Office USpt of Ag 1985; Appreciation Awd in Educ Office of Civil Rights Dallas Reg 1985; Cert of Recognition Natl Republican Congressional Comm 1985; Black Portfolio Excellence Awd in Educ 1985; Disting Serv Awd New Birth Baptist Church 1985; Disting Serv Awd in Educ Arlington Assoc of Concerned Citizens 1985; Outstanding Serv Awd in Educ Most Worshipful St Joseph Grand Lodge 1985. **Military Serv:** US Army, Lt Col, 1956-62. **Business Addr:** President, El Centro College, Lamar & Main St, Dallas, TX 75202.

LATCHOLIA, KENNETH EDWARD

Administrator. **Personal:** Born Jun 17, 1922, Beaumont, TX; married Ruth Johannetta Weber; children: 2. **Educ:** Prarie View Univ Prairie View TX, Cert 1941-42; Univ of Wash, BA 1952-56. **Career:** Rural Development USDA, dep admin 1969; US Peace Corps Nigeria, dir 1967-69; Econ Devel Adminstrn Dept of Commerce & Seattle, project officer 1966-67; Jackson St Community Council Seattle, exec dir 1963-66; Wash State Bur of Rehab Seattle, asst supt 1960-63; King Co Juvenile Ct Seattle, asst supt 1954-60; EDA US Dept of Commerce Seattle, econ devel spec 1969-72; EDA US Dept of Comm, dep reg dir 1972-77; FMHA US Dept of Agr Wash DC, dep adminstr 1977. **Orgs:** Bd mem Seattle Urban League 1972-74; area council mem Greenbelt Cooperative Greenbelt MD 1978. **Honors/Awds:** Silver medal US Dept of Commerce 1973; cert fed employee of year Region 10 Seattle 1973; cert natl urban league Nat Mfg Atlanga GA 1975; commendation letter Pres Carter 1978. **Military Serv:** AUS PFC 1942-43. **Business Addr:** 14th at Independence SW, Washington, DC 20250.

LATEEF, YUSEF

Musician, composer, artist. **Personal:** Born Oct 9, 1920, Chattanooga, TN. **Educ:** Manhattan School of Music, BM & MM; Univ of Massachusetts, PhD 1975. **Career:** Borough of Manhattan Community Coll, assoc prof, 1971-76; musical compositions include Nocturne (Ballet), 1974, & Yusef's Mood; numerous TV & theater appearances; quartet leader, New York City, 1960; featured with Charles Mingus, 1960-61; Babatundi Olatunji, 1961-62; featured with Cannonball Adderley Combo on European tour, two yrs; combo leader; saxaphone teacher, Stan Kenton Summer Jazz Clinics, 1963; lecturer at various colleges; recordings on Impulse Prestige and other labels; Univ of Massachusetts, Amherst, MA, visiting prof; YAL Records, owner. **Orgs:** Local 802, NY; Local 5, MI. **Honors/Awds:** Author, Yusef Lateef's Flute Book of the Blues; Repository of Scales and Melodic Patterns. **Business Addr:** YAL Records, PO Box 799, Amherst, MA 01004.

LATHAM, CHRIS

Professional baseball player. **Personal:** Born May 26, 1973, Coeur D'Alene, MD. **Career:** Minnesota Twins, outfielder, 1997-. **Business Addr:** Professional Baseball Player, Minnesota Twins, 501 Chicago Ave S, Minneapolis, MN 55415, (612)375-1366.

LATHAM, WELDON HURD

Attorney. **Personal:** Born Jan 2, 1947, Brooklyn, NY; son of Avril Latham and Aubrey Latham; married Constantia Beecher; children: Nicole Marie, Brett Weldon. **Educ:** Howard Univ, BA business admin 1968; Georgetown Univ Law Ctr, JD 1971; George Washington Univ Natl Law Ctr, advanced legal courses 1975-76; Brookings Inst, exec educ prog 1981. **Career:** Checchi & Co, mgmt consultant 1968-71; Covington & Burling, atty 1971-73; Howard Univ Sch of Law, adj prof 1972-82; The White House Ofc of Mgmt & Budget, asst genl counsel 1974-76; Hogan & Hartson, atty 1976-79; Univ of VA Law Sch, guest prof 1976-91; US Dept of Housing & Urban Develop, genl deputy asst sec 1979-81; Sterling Systems Inc, vice pres genl cnsl 1981-83; Planning Research Corp, executive assistant, counsel to the chairman and CEO, 1983-86; Reed Smith Shaw & Mc Clay, managing partner, McLean VA office 1986-92; Minority Business Enterprise Magazine, columnist, 1991-; Civilian Aide to the Secretary of the Army, 1994-; Shaw, Pittman, Potts & Trowbridge, Natl Law Firm, senior partner, 1992-. **Orgs:** Bd dirs Washington Hosp Center Foundation, 1996; Capital Area Advisory Board of First Union National Bank, 1995-; Burger King Corp Diversity Action Council, 1996-; Small Business Administration National Advisory Council, 1994-; Maryland Economic Development Commission, 1996-; general counsel, National Coalition of Minority Businesses, 1993-; Decomcratic National Committee, 1996; Platform Drafting COmmittee, 1996; managing trustee, Democratic National COmmittee, 1995-; bd dirs District of Columbia Foundation, Inc, 1982-88; Bar Association membership, 1972-: American District of Columbia Natl Federal Virginia; Washington; Natl Contract Mgmt Assn 1982-; legal counsel MD Mondale/Ferraro Campaign Com 1984; apptee VA Gov's Business Adv Comm on Crime Prevention 1983-86; apptee VA Gov's Regulatory Adv Bd 1982-84; Washington steering comm NAACP Legal Defense & Educ Fund 1976-96; Professional Services Council, board of directors 1984-88; editorial advisory bd Washington Business Journal 1985-88; VA Commonwealth Univ, board of directors 1986-89; Democratic Natl Committee Business Council 1986-90, and vice chair, 1994-; Washington Urban League, board of directors 1986-90; numerous others. **Honors/Awds:** Advocate of the Year, Minority Enterprise Development Week, US Department of Commerce, 1996; Small Business Administration, Private Industry Advocate of the Year, 1992; Northern VA Min Business & Professioal Assn Award, 1990; National Association of Equal Opportunity in Higher Education Achievement Award, 1987; Outstanding Performance Award, US Department of HUD, Sr Exec Serv Washington DC, 1980. **Military Serv:** Cap/atty, Honors Prog Ofc of the Sec of the Air Force; Genl Counsel's Office 1973-74. **Business Addr:** Senior Partner, Shaw, Pittman, Potts & Trowbridge, 2300 N St NW, Washington, DC 20037.

LATHEN, DEBORAH ANN

Attorney. **Personal:** Born Mar 28, 1953, St Louis, MO; daughter of Olean Lathen and Levi Lathen. **Educ:** Cornell University, AB (magna cum laude), 1975; Harvard Law School, JD, 1978. **Career:** Foley and Lardner; Keck, Mahin and Cate, attorney, 1978-82; The Quaker Oats Co, litigation attorney, 1982-88; TRW Inc, sr counsel, 1988-91; Nissan Motor Corp USA, managing counsel, 1991-93, mgr consumer affairs, director consumer affairs, currently. **Orgs:** Nissan Foundation, board of directors; Leadership California, bd of dires; ABA; Black Women Lawyers Association; Los Angeles Black Women Lawyers, mem. **Honors/Awds:** The Quaker Oats Co, Chairman's Award, 1988, Volunteer Award, 1992; YWCA Women Leadership Award, 1987; Commendation from Mayor Thomas Bradley for Riot Relief Efforts, 1992; Selected for Americas Best & Brightest, 1993. **Special Achievements:** Admitted to Illinois Bar Association, Wisconsin Bar Association, California Bar Association; Selected by Dollars & Sense Magazine, Best and Brighest in America Issue, 1993. **Business Addr:** Director, Natl Consumer Affairs, Nissan Motor Corp in USA, 18501 S Figueroa, PO Box 191, GIG, Gardena, CA 90248-0191, (310)719-5675.

LATHON, LAMAR LAVANTHA

Professional football player. **Personal:** Born Dec 23, 1967, Wharton, TX; children: Octavia, Madison. **Educ:** Univ of Houston, education major, four years. **Career:** Houston Oilers, linebacker, 1990-94; Carolina Panthers, 1995-. **Honors/Awds:** Pre-season First Team All-Southwest Conference, senior year; Pro Bowl, 1996. **Business Addr:** Professional Football Player, Carolina Panthers, 800 Mint St, Ericsson Stadium, Charlotte, NC 28202, (704)358-7000.

LATIF, NAIMAH (DOREEN ALICIA CHARLES)

Newspaper publisher. **Personal:** Born Apr 15, 1960, Chicago, IL. **Educ:** Univ of NE-Lincoln, BA Journalism 1982. **Career:** Operation PUSH, youth comm 1982-84; Chicago Black United Comm, youth chmn 1982-84; Black United Front, sec 1982-83; Task Force for Black Political Empowerment, sec 1982-83; Intl Communications Corp, president, 1986-89; Latif Communications Group Inc, vp 1989-. **Orgs:** Mem PUSH Intl Trade Bureau 1984-, Intl Black Writers 1984-, NAACP 1985-, Urban League 1985-; delegate Natl Small Business Conference 1985-86. **Honors/Awds:** Outstanding Leadership Award, Afrikan People's Union, 1982; Certificate of Achievement, Operation PUSH Political Education, 1983; published book "Til Victory is Won," book of political poetry, 1984; wrote/acted in one-woman show, "Sojourner Truth," 1986; Co-author, Slavery: The African American Psychic Trauma, 1993. **Business Addr:** Vice Pres, Latif Communications Group Inc, 6 N Michigan Ave, Ste 909, Chicago, IL 60602.

LATIMER, ALLIE B.

Attorney. **Personal:** Born in Coraopolis, PA; daughter of Bennie Comer Latimer and L S Latimer. **Educ:** Hampton Inst Hampton VA, BS; Howard Univ Washington DC, JD; Cath Univ Washington DC, LLM; Am U, Study Towards Doctorate;

Howard University, MDiv, DMin. **Career:** Chief counsel atty 1960-71; General Services Administration, Washington, DC, assistant general counsel, 1971-76; Natl Aeronautics & Space Administration, asst general counsel, 1976-77, general counsel, 1977-87, special counsel, 1987-96. **Orgs:** Vol work Am Friends Serv Com in Europe; sec Nat Bar Assn 1966-76; co-chmn bd of dirs Presbyterian Economic Devel Corp 1974-80; pres Nat Bar Found 1974-75; pres DC Mental Health Assn 1977-79; mem Supreme Ct of US; US Ct of Appeals DC; NC St Ct of Appeals; mem Am Bar Assn; Fed Bar; Nat Bar, NC Bar, DC Bar, Washington Bar Asso; fndr 1st pres Federally Employed Women 1968-69; vice pres Links Inc 1976-80; mem bd of gov Nat Cncl of Ch USA 1978-84; mem NAACP & NAACP Legal Def Fund DC Steering Com. **Honors/Awds:** Pub Serv Award & GSA 1971; GSA Exceptional Serv Awards 1976-79; Humanitarian Award Sigma Delta Tau Legal Frat 1978; Outstanding Achievement Award; Kiwanis Club Award DC 1978; Presidential Rank Award, 1983, 1995; Distinguished Service Award, GSA, 1984.

LATIMER, CHRIS. **See LATIMER, DAVID CHRISTOPHER.**

LATIMER, DAVID CHRISTOPHER (CHRIS LATIMER)
Marketing company executive. **Personal:** Born Dec 25, 1968, White Plains, NY; son of Sudie Hardy & Benjamin Latimer. **Educ:** Howard Univ, 1987-90. **Career:** The Source Magazine, tour coord, 1990-91; Amer Coll Alliance Inc, promotions, 1990-91; DA Streetz, Inc, pres, currently. **Honors/Awds:** Thomas H Slater Inc, Mentor Award, 1997; The Source Magazine, Designer/Co-Owner, 1997; And 1, Recognition Award, 1995. **Business Addr:** President, DA Streetz Inc, 550 Broadway, Ste 406, New York, NY 10012.

LATIMER, FRANK EDWARD
Plastics company executive. **Personal:** Born Aug 28, 1947, Tulsa, OK; son of Wilda Dupree Latimer and Frank Edward Latimer Sr; married Connie Latimer-Smith (divorced 1989); children: Tomitra, Chelsea, Patrice, Tina, Ann. **Educ:** Univ of Maryland, College Park, BA, 1973; Harvard Univ, Cambridge, MA, MBA, 1976. **Career:** Brown And Williamson, Louisville, KY, product manager, 1976-77; International Paper, New York, NY, plant controller, 1977-80; Atlantic Richfield, Louisville, K, division controller, 1980-85; Regal Plastics, Roseville, MI, vice president & CFO, 1986-93, pres, 1993-. **Honors/Awds:** Certified Management Accountant, Natl Assn of Accountants, 1985; YMCA Black Achiever's Award, Louisville YMCA, 1983. **Business Addr:** President/CFO, Regal Plastics Co, 15700 Common Rd, Roseville, MI 48066.

LATIMER, INA PEARL
Educator. **Personal:** Born Oct 19, 1934, Okeechobee, FL; married Harold A Latimer; children: Cynthia L. **Educ:** Tuskegee Inst, BS Nursing 1956; N IL Univ, MS Education 1979. **Career:** Univ of IL, staff nurse charge 1958-60; St Mary of Nazareth Sch of Nursing, instruc medical-surgical nursing 1960-70; Triton Coll, instruc 1970-73, chairperson prac nursing prog 1973-. **Orgs:** Mem Homemaker-Home Health Aide Comm IL Council of Home Health Svcs; mem Natl League for Nursing; mem IL Voc Assn; mem Bd of Review Natl League for Nursing Council of Prac Nursing Progs 1979-84; eval Dept of Voc & Tech Educ 1981; accreditation site visitor Natl League for Nursing 1978-. **Honors/Awds:** Undergrad mem Delta Sigma Theta Sor; undergrad mem Alpha Kappa Mu Natl Honor Soc. **Business Addr:** Dept Chrprsn Practical Nrsg, Triton College, 2000 5th Ave, River Grove, IL 60171.

LATIMER, JENNIFER ANN
Educational administrator. **Personal:** Born Apr 29, 1953, Gastonia, NC; son of Susie M Kithcart Grier and Robert E Grier; married Steven Latimer Jr, Dec 1989; children: Faith G. **Educ:** Univ of Rhode Island, BA 1975; Rhode Island Coll, MA 1983; CAGS 1990. **Career:** Atlanta Bd of Educ, comm organizer 1977-78; Rhode Island Educ Oppt Center, follow-up counselor 1980; Comm Coll of Rhode Island, counselor access prog 1981-83; Rhode Island Coll, coord minority prog 1983-86, asst dir of student life/minority affairs 1986-, Cornerstone Counseling and Consulting Counselor 1989-. **Orgs:** Mem NAACP, CPARI; Providence Christian Outreach Ministries, 1988-; vice president, URI Minority Alumni Council, 1987-89; member, Minister's Wives & Widows of RI, 1989-. **Honors/Awds:** Wrote and directed gospel play, "Thy Will Be Done", 1985; co-wrote and directed gospel play, "Tis The Season", 1987. **Home Addr:** 160 Calla St, Providence, RI 02905. **Business Addr:** Asst Dir, Student Life for Minority Affairs, Rhode Island Coll, 600 Mount Pleasant Ave, Providence, RI 02908.

LATIMER, STEVE B.
Research director. **Personal:** Born Nov 4, 1927, Okla City; married Louise Cunningham; children: Steve, Jr, Ronald, Gail. **Educ:** Tuskegee Inst, BS Chem 1953; Tuskegee Inst, MS 1955; NC State U, PhD 1967; Fed Exec Inst, 1972. **Career:** Langston Univ 1966, chmn physical science dir div of arts & sciences, res & coord CSRS progs, USDA, marc visiting faculty, OK med res found; NC State Univ, chief control chem, res Asst 1962-66; Fries & Fries Chem Co, 1956; Shaw Univ, chmn chem 1955-62. **Orgs:** Fellow Am Inst Chem; Sigma Xi; Nat Inst of Sci; Am Chem Soc; OK Acad of Sci; Nat Geographic; Am Assn Advancement of Sci; Pre-med Adv 1968-72;prog dir MBS Lic Lay Reader; charter mem Langston Lions Club 1973; Guthrie Kiwanis Club 1975; Mason Shriner; Alpha Phi Alpha Frat. **Honors/Awds:** First black to receive Doctoral Degree from NC State Univ 1967; XXII Cert; 3 NSF Scholarships; PHS Trainee 1962; NIH Marc Faculty Fellowship 1975-77; Carver Found Fellow 1953; Alpha Phi Omega, Alpha Mu Gamma; Sigma Xi; Beta Kappa Chi.

LATNEY, HARVEY, JR.
Attorney. **Personal:** Born May 26, 1944, Caroline Co, VA. **Educ:** VA Union U, BA 1966; Howard Univ Sch Law, JD 1969. **Career:** US Dept Transp, legal intern June 1969-July 1969 & Aug 1971-Sept 1972; Richmond Comm Sr Cntr, dir Oct 1972-July 1973; Greene & Poindexter Inc, atty beginning 1973; Commonwealth Attorney, Carolina County, VA, 1978-. **Orgs:** Mem Nat Bar Assn; Am Bar Assn; VA Bar & Assn; VA Trial Lawyer's Assn; Old Dominion Bar Assn. **Military Serv:** AUS sgt 1969-71. **Business Addr:** 521-523 N Adams St, Richmond, VA 23220.

LATSON, DONALD
Computer company executive.

LATTIMER, AGNES DOLORES
Physician. **Personal:** Born May 13, 1928, Memphis, TN; daughter of Hoetense M Lewis Lattimer and Arthur O Lattimer; married Bernard Goss, Jan 10, 1952 (deceased); children: Bernard C Goss Jr. **Educ:** Fisk Univ, BS (Magna Cum Laude) 1949; Chicago Medical School, MD 1954. **Career:** Michael Reese Hosp, dir amb peds 1966-71; Cook County Hosp, dir amb peds 1971-84, dir Fantus Clinic 1984-85; Cook Co Hosp, med dir 1986-95; Dept of Pediatrics, Univ of Health Sci/Chicago Med School, professor. **Orgs:** Mem Ambulatory Ped Assoc 1974-; pres IL Chap Amer Acad of Pediatrics 1983-86; mem Physician's Task Force on Hunger 1984-86; mem Amer Assoc Public Health; fellow, American Academy of Pediatrics, 1960-; mem of bd of trustees Childserv; mem bd of trustees The Family Institute; mem Chicago Pediatric Society. **Honors/Awds:** Pediatrician of the Year Awd IL Chap AAP 1985; Tsang Award, Outstanding Teaching, 1966, Outstanding Alumnus, 1971, The Chicago Med School; Outstanding Alumnus, Fisk University, 1990; Archibald Hoyne Award, Outstanding Service to Children, Chicago Ped Society, 1990; Community Service Award, 1992; Women of Achievement Award, by the Consortium of Doctors, 1994; Distinguished Alumnus Award, Michael Reese Hosp, 1994. **Home Addr:** 1700 E 56th St, #3709, Chicago, IL 60637.

LATTIMER, ROBERT L.
Associate partner. **Personal:** Born Jul 16, 1945; son of James & Maryagnes Lattimer; married Sarah, Apr 5, 1997; children: Ebony, Isoador, Hope, John. **Educ:** Rutgers University, BA, Economics, 1973; Columbia University, Grad School of Business, Executive MBA Management Program, Arden House, 1978. **Career:** J Walter Thompson Co, vp, dir, 1976-81, Corporate Operating Comm, 1976-81; The Lattimer Group, CEO, sr consulting partner, 1981-90; Towers Perrin, global practice leader, 1990-96; Andersen Consulting, associate partner, 1996-. **Orgs:** Zoo Atlanta, vice chair, bd of dirs, 1993-; Atlanta Neighborhood Devel Partnership, exec comm, chmn of Strategic Planning and Human Resources Comm, 1993-; Congressional Black Caucus Foundation, advisory bd of dirs, 1996. **Honors/Awds:** American Society for Competitiveness, Global Strategy Formulation & Execution, 1997; US Jaycees, One of the Ten Outstanding Young Men of America, Honored with VP Albert Gore, Jr, 1987. **Special Achievements:** Quoted in significant management books, journals, newspapers, and magazines such as: Fortune Magazine, Atlanta Journal Constitution, Atlanta Tribune; completed book chapter, "Redefining Diversity," in book Beyond Affirmative Action, 1996. **Military Serv:** US Marine Corp, recog off, 1968-70; Bronze Star Medal with Combat V, 1969; Purple Heart, 1969. **Home Addr:** 210 East Court Dr, Atlanta, GA 30331, (404)696-0837.

LATTIMORE, CAROLINE LOUISE
Educational administrator. **Personal:** Born May 12, 1945, Winston-Salem, NC; daughter of Mary Rhodes Lattimore and Earl R Lattimore Sr. **Educ:** Hampton Inst, BS 1967, MA 1973; Duke Univ, PhD 1978. **Career:** Richmond Public School, Virginia, English teacher, 1967-74; State Univ, coord sr citizens program Winston-Salem, 1974; Duke Univ, psychological testing intern, 1974-75, educ consult & spec couns, 1978, dean of minority affairs/asst provost, 1978-83, academic dean, 1987-; NTS Research Corp, Washington, coord, 1978. **Orgs:** Mem, pres, Council on Black Affairs, 1984-; mem, Reggie B Howard Scholarship Selection Comm, 1985-; mem, NAACP, 1985-; mem, Natl Council of Negro Women, 1985-; WTVO-11 Television Committee Chairman, 1997; natl chair, AKA International Program, 1996-98; judge, JC Penny's Golden Rule Award, Durham, NC, 1990-91; talk show host, In Times Like These, Durham Cable 8, 1990-91; Duke ROTC Committee, 1997. **Honors/Awds:** Award of Merit for Outstanding Achievement Winston Salem Jr C of C 1963; Kappa Delta Pi Hon Soc Duke Univ 1975; Natl Fellow Ford Foundation, 1976-78; Regional Graduate Leadership Award AKA 1986; Concepts China Experience, 1996. **Business Addr:** Academic Dean, Duke University, 213 West Duke Bldg, Durham, NC 27708.

LATTIMORE, HENRY
Football coach. **Educ:** Jackson State University, graduated 1957. **Career:** North Carolina Central University, head coach; Virginia Union University, head coach, currently. **Special Achievements:** Coached teams that earned two Southern Division CIAA championships, one CIAA championship and an appearance in the NCAA Division II playoffs. **Business Phone:** (804)257-5600.

LAUDERBACK, BRENDA JOYCE
Retail wholesale company executive. **Personal:** Born Apr 25, 1950, Pittsburgh, PA; daughter of Dorothy Lauderback and Clayton Lauderback (deceased); married Boyd Wright, Jul 5, 1980; children: Phallon, Adam. **Educ:** Allegheny Community College, AS, marketing, 1970; Robert Morris College, BA, marketing, 1972; University of Pittsburgh, graduate studies, vocational education, 1972-73. **Career:** Gimbels, assistant buyer, buyer; Dayton's Department Store, assistant buyer, 1975-76, buyer, 1976-79, DMM, 1979-82; Dayton-Hudson Corp., vice pres, general merchandise manager, beginning 1982; 1993-95, US Shoe Footwear, Wholesale Group, president; Nine West Gp Inc., Wholesale/Retail Group, president, currently. **Orgs:** NAACP, 1975-; Urban League, 1989-; Committee of 200, 1989-; Links Inc; Jack & Jill of America; Executive Leadership CNL, 1993; bd mem: Arthur Ashe Institute of Urban Health, 1996-97; Irwin Financial, 1996; Consolidated Stores, 1997; Hord Foundation, 1997; For All Kids Foundation Advisory Comm, 1998. **Honors/Awds:** Ford Foundation, Scholarship, 1972; YWCA, Women's Leader, 1977-79; Minnesota Women's, Second Edition, 1984-85; Intimate Apparel Industry, Femme Award, 1987; Outstanding Retail Achievement Bragg Award, 1987; YWCA Career Woman of Achievement, 1995, Outstanding Young Women of America, 1995. **Business Addr:** President, Wholesale Group, Nine West Group, 58 Good Hill Road, Weston, CT 06883.

LAUDERDALE, PRIEST
Professional basketball player. **Personal:** Born Aug 31, 1973, Chicago, IL. **Educ:** Central State Univ (OH), 1994. **Career:** Peristeri Nikas (Greece), 1995-96; Atlanta Hawks, center, 1996-97; Denver Nuggets, 1997-. **Business Addr:** Professional Basketball Player, Denver Nuggets, 1635 Clay St, Denver, CO 80204-1743, (303)893-6700.

LAUTENBACH, TERRY
Computer company executive. **Personal:** Born Aug 10, 1938, Cincinnati, OH; son of Frances M. Herbert Lautenbach and Robert C. Lautenbach; married Carole Wuest; children: Jennifer, Susan, Julie, Martha, Mary, Anne. **Educ:** Xavier University, BS, physics, 1959. **Career:** IBM Corporation, Data Processing Division, White Plains, NY, president, 1976-78, World Trade Ams, Far East Corp, Mt Pleasant, NY, president, 1978-83, Marketing Division, Purchase, NY, vice president, 1984-85, Communications Products Division, White Plains, NY, president, 1985-86, group exec vp, Information Systems & Communications Group, 1986-88, IBM US, Armonk, NY, senior vice president, 1988-. **Orgs:** Member, board of directors, Arkwright Mutual Insurance Co, Xavier University; vp, Darien Library, CT. **Honors/Awds:** Honorary Doctor of Laws, Xavier University, 1977.

LAVAN, ALTON
Football coach. **Personal:** Born Sep 13, 1946, Pierce, FL; married Bessie Lavonia Jewell; children: Travis Alton, Douglas Milo, Maeleeke. **Educ:** CO State Univ Ft Collins, BS Sociology 1966-68; GA St U, 1971. **Career:** Philadelphia Eagles, def back 1968; Atlanta Falcons, def back 1969-70; CO State Univ, offensive rec coach 1972; Univ of LA, def backfield coach 1973; IA State Univ, offensive receivers coach 1974; Atlanta Falcons, def backfield coach 1975-76; GA Tech, offensive receiver coach 1977, offensive backfield coach 1978; Stanford Univ, offensive backfield coach 1979-80; Dallas Cowboys, offensive backfield coach 1980-. **Orgs:** Mem, Natl Football Coaches of America, 1971-. **Honors/Awds:** 1st Black Coach Dallas Cowboys & Atlanta Falcons. **Military Serv:** AUS sp 4 1969-71. **Business Addr:** Offensive Backfield Coach, Dallas Cowboys, 1 Cowboys Parkway, Irving, TX 75063.

LAVEIST, THOMAS ALEXIS
Educator. **Personal:** Born Feb 3, 1961, Brooklyn, NY; son of Eudora Ramos LaVeist and William Thomas LaVeist; married Bridgette LaVeist, May 25, 1996. **Educ:** University of Maryland Eastern Shore, Princess Anne, MD, BA, 1984; University of Michigan, Ann Arbor, MI, MA, 1985, PhD, 1988, PDF, 1990. **Career:** Johns Hopkins Univ, Baltimore, MD, assoc prof, 1990-. **Orgs:** Associate regional director, Phi Beta Sigma Fraternity, 1983-84; member, Maryland Commission on the Status of Black Males, Health Sub-committee, 1991-; member, Association of Black Sociologists, 1985-; member, American Public Health Association, 1988-; member, American Sociological Association, 1984-. **Honors/Awds:** Best Dissertation in Medi-

cal Sociology, American Sociological Association, 1989; Brookdale National Fellow, The Brookdale Foundation, 1991; Paul B Cornely Fellow, The Univ of Michigan, School of Public Health, 1988-90; Alain Locke Presidential Futures Award, Phi Beta Sigma Educational Foundation, 1984; National Deans List, 1984; Distinguished Alumni Award, Natl Assn for Equal Opportunity in Education, 1994; Outstanding Young Alumnus Award, Univ of Maryland Eastern Shore, 1994. **Business Addr:** Associate Professor, The Johns Hopkins University, School of Hygiene and Public Health, 624 N Broadway, Baltimore, MD 21205, (410)955-3774.

LAVELLE, AVIS
Public relations executive. **Personal:** Born Mar 5, 1954, Chicago, IL; daughter of Mai Evelyn Hicks & Adolph Eugene Sampson; divorced. **Educ:** University of Illinois, BS, 1975. **Career:** WLTH Radio, news director, 1978-79; WJJD/WJEZ, reporter, anchor, 1979-84; WGN-Radio/TV, chief political reporter, 1984-88; Richard M Daley for Mayor, campaign press secretary, 1988-89; Office of the Mayor, Chicago, mayoral press secretary, 1989-92; Clinton/Gore Campaign, national press secretary, 1992; Presidential Transition Team, special asst to chairman, 1992-93; US Dept of Health & Human Services, asst sec, public affairs, 1993-95; Waste Mgmt Inc, vice pres of communications and community relations, currently. **Orgs:** Project Image Inc, board member, 1988-89; Black Adoption Task Force of Ill, steering committee, 1987; Delta Sigma Theta Public Service, 1973; Human Resources Development Inst, board member, 1988. **Honors/Awds:** Dollars & Sense, African American Business/Professional Women, 1989; Associated Press, 1st Place Team Reporting Award, 1984; National Commission on Working Women, 1980. **Special Achievements:** "Should Children Be Tried as Adults?," Essence Magazine, September 1994; Jet, July 31, 1995. **Business Phone:** (773)242-4317.

LAVELLE, ROBERT R.
Banking executive. **Personal:** Born Oct 4, 1915, Cleveland, TN; son of Mary Anderson Lavelle and Franklin P Lavelle; married Adah Moore Lavelle, Jul 25, 1942; children: Robert Moore, John Franklin. **Educ:** Univ of Pittsburgh, Pittsburgh, PA, BS, 1951, Masters, 1954. **Career:** Pittsburgh Courier, Pittsburgh, PA, asst auditor, 1935-56; Lavelle Real Estate Inc, pres, 1951-; Dwelling House S&L Assn, exec vp, CEO, 1957-. **Orgs:** Elder, Grace Memorial Presbyterian Church, 1963-; life member, NAACP, 1957-; certified property mgr, Inst of RE Mgmt, 1972-. **Honors/Awds:** Honorary Doctor of Laws: Geneva Coll, PA, 1984, Gordon Coll, MA, 1989. **Military Serv:** US Army, 1st Lt, 1943-46. **Home Addr:** 4331 Andover Terr, Pittsburgh, PA 15213. **Business Addr:** Exec Vice Pres, Dwelling House S&L Assn, 501 Herron Ave, Pittsburgh, PA 15219.

LAVERGNE, LUKE ALDON
Judge, attorney. **Personal:** Born May 7, 1938, Lawtell, LA; son of Ida Nero LaVergne and Adam LaVergne Jr; married Catherine A Malveaux, Oct 15, 1960; children: Lance A, Cynthia A. **Educ:** University of Nebraska, BS, 1969; Southern Illinois University, MS, 1974; Louisiana State University, Law School, JD, 1982. **Career:** Louisiana State University, assistant professor, aerospace studies, 1975-79; assistant district attorney, 1982-84, assistant parish attorney, 1991-92; EBR Family Court, judge, currently. **Orgs:** Louis A. Martinet Legal Society, president, 1989-92; Baton Bar Association, board of directors, 1990-92; Louisiana State Bar Association, delegate, 1989-91; Lions Club, board of directors, 1989-96; Phi Beta Sigma Fraternity, state director, 1984-88, regional legal counsel, 1987-92; YMCA, board of directors, 1989-96; Boy Scouts of America, board of directors, 1990-96, scout show chairman, 1992-94; 100 Black Men of BR LTD. **Military Serv:** US Air Force, captain, 1956-79; Good Conduct, 1959; Presidential Unit Citation, 1960; Air Force Commendation, 1972, Meritorious Service Award, 1979. **Home Addr:** 5956 Valley Forge Ave, Baton Rouge, LA 70808, (504)924-0590. **Business Addr:** Judge, EBR Family Court, 222 St Louis St, Rm 948, Baton Rouge, LA 70801, (504)389-7657.

LAVERGNEAU, RENE L.
Administrator. **Personal:** Born Nov 4, 1933, New York, NY; son of Myrtle Lavergneau and Armando Lavergneau. **Educ:** CCNY, BA 1958, MS 1963, MA 1974. **Career:** WNYE-TV, NY Ed TV, TV instr 1965-67; Bureau of Audio-visual Instr NYC, writer & voice-over 1966-68; New York City Bd of Ed, bd of examiners 1968; Fairleigh Dickinson Univ in PR, grad instr 1969; Univ of PR, Bayamon, instr, 1974; Hackensack Public Schools, dir bureau of foreign languages, bilingual ed and English as a second language, 1986-. **Orgs:** Consult, Princeton Conf for Foreign Language Curriculum Devel 1967; chair NE Conf on the Teaching of Foreign Languages 1974; chair Statewide Committee on Bilingual & Teaching English as a Second Language Ed Cert NJ 1974; keynoter Amer Assoc of Teachers 1974; chair NJ Bilingual Minimum Standards 1978; com mem Bergen City Health & Welfare Council 1980; chmn bd of dirs Teatro Duo 1986-87; bd dir Hackensack Public School Historical Society, 1986-; mem selection committee, American Council on the Teaching of Foreign Languages/National Textbook Company Award for Building Community Interest in Foreign Language Education, 1987-. **Honors/Awds:** Careers Comm & Publ Awareness Awd NE Conf Rept Publ 1974; actor "The Wiz" 1977; Natl Awd for Bldg Comm Interest in Fgn Lang Ed Amer Council on Teaching of Fgn Langs & Natl Textbook Co 1983. **Business Addr:** Dir, Hackensack Public Schools, Bureau of Foreign Language & Bilingual Educ, 355 State St, Hackensack, NJ 07601.

LAVIZZO-MOUREY, RISA JUANITA
Physician, government official. **Personal:** Born Sep 25, 1954, Nashville, TN; daughter of Blanche Sellers Lavizzo and Philip V Lavizzo; married Robert J Mourey, Jun 21, 1975; children: Rel, Max. **Educ:** University of Washington, attended, 1972-73; SUNY at Stony Brook, attended, 1973-75; Harvard Medical School, MD, 1979; Wharton School, University of Pennsylvania, MBA, 1986. **Career:** Brigham and Women's Hospital, medical resident, 1979-82; Temple University Medical School, clinical instructor, 1982-84; University of Pennsylvania, associate professor, 1984-92; Agency for Health Policy and Research, deputy administrator, 1992-. **Orgs:** Association of Academic Minority Physicians, 1990-; National Medical Association. **Honors/Awds:** University of Pennsylvania, Class of 1970 Term Professor, 1992; American College of Physicians, fellow; American Geriatric Society, fellow. **Special Achievements:** Author: "Invasive Gynecologic Oncology," 1979; "Dehydration in the Elderly," 1987; "Amantadine-related adverse reactions among African-American elderly nursing home residents," 1991; numerous others. **Business Addr:** Deputy Administrator, Agency for Health Care Policy and Research, US Department of Health and Human Services, 2101 E Jefferson St, Ste 600, Rockville, MD 20852.

LAW, M. EPREVEL
Educator, company executive. **Personal:** Born Aug 19, 1943, Chicago, IL; married Marlene Ann; children: Martin Peter, Michelle Allison. **Educ:** NSF Fellow, BS; NSF Fellow Univ of MN, MS 1969; Univ of MN, PhD 1970. **Career:** Minneapolis Public Schools & Univ of MN, teacher & research 1966-88; Kenney Real, real est 1971-74; H & R Block, tax consultant 1970-71; Pact Real Inc, pres 1974-77; Law & Associates, inv analyst, tax consultant 1974-; Archer & Law Inc, pres 1976-77; Law & Associates, Southside Community Center Inc, co-owner; The Three "M" Realty Co, broker, mgr 1977-; Law & Associates Professional Financial and Tax Services, 1977-; Twin City Property Management Maintenance & Improvement Co, 1978-. **Orgs:** Kappa Alpha Psi Fraternity; Association of Afro-American Educators; National Association of Realtors; National Education Association; American Federation of Teachers; Citizens United for Responsible Education; bd mem Southside Comm Center; MN Assn for Retarded Children; MN Hist Soc; mayor's appointee City Wide City-wide Adv Com; co-chmn CW-CAC Phys Imp & Hous Asst Task Force; cap Long-range Imp Comm Hum Dev Task Force; proj acct St of MN Coun on Qual Educ; Cit Unit for Resp Educ Steer Comm; MN Urban Leag; Citizen League; NAACP; natl Women's Polit Caucus; MN DFL Feminist Causus; MI Environmental Educ Bd; So MN Comunity Fed Credit Union; chpsn 60th Sen Dist 1976; assoc chmn 60th Sen Dist 1974-76. **Business Addr:** 3722 W 50th St, Ste 375, Edina, MN 55410.

LAW, THOMAS MELVIN
Educator, educational administrator. **Personal:** Born Sep 23, 1925, Bristol, VA; son of Rebecca Law and Thomas K Law; married Katherine Tillar; children: Thomas Fenimore. **Educ:** St Pauls Coll, BS (summa cum laude) 1950; NY Univ, MA 1953; Cornell Univ, EdD 1962. **Career:** James Solomon Russell High School, instructor, 1950-54; Hampton Inst, dir div of business 1965-67; St Pauls Coll, dean of coll & prof of business 1967-69; WA Tech Inst, vice pres acad affairs 1969-71; Penn Valley Community Coll, pres 1971-76; VA State Univ, pres 1976-82; SUNY, dep to the chancellor for special progs 1982-86, deputy to chancellor for Community Colleges 1986-87, associate vice chancellor for contracts & purchasing 1987-89; St Paul's College, Lawrenceville, VA, pres, 1989-. **Orgs:** Cornell Univ Council, appointee; School of Human Ecology, Cornell Univ, board of directors; past member, Southside VA Commission on Business and Education, gubernatorial appointee; Council of Independent Colleges in Virginia, board of directors; American Council on Education, Commission on Leadership Development; Virginia Chamber of Commerce, Virginia Emissary appointee; Brunswick County, VA, Industrial Development Authority; advisory board, Essex Savings Bank, Emporia, VA; United Negro College Fund, government affairs committee, executive committee/member institutions; National Association for Equal Opportunity in Higher Education, board of director; licensed lay reader St. Paul's Memorial Chapel; Rotary Intl; American Voc Coop Education Assn, bd of trustees; VA Manufacturing Extention Partnership; NAACP, life member; National Association of Independent Colleges and Universities, Commission on Campus Concerns; Brunswick County (VA) Museum, board of directors; United Negro College Fund, past member, Natl Ctr for Higher Ed Mgmt Syst; VA State Fair; sire archon elect Beta Psi Boule Sigma Pi Phi 1985-; board dir Living Resources Corp, Albany NY; board dir Child's Nursing Home, Albany NY; past member, National Center for Higher Education Management, board of directors. **Honors/Awds:** Central Inter-Collegiate Athletic Assn Officials Hall Of Fame, appointee; Southeastern Universities Research Association, Board Resolution of Praise; Distinguished Alumni Award St Pauls Coll Natl Alumni Assn 1978; Martin Luther King Community Serv Awd Southern Christian Leadership Council 1980; St Pauls Coll, first grad from to receive highest academic honors (summa cum laude), first 4-yr degree grad to receive an earned doctorate degree, St Pauls College; Distinguished Trustee Awd; Alpha Phi Alpha Fellow; United Negro Coll Fund Grad Fellow; Alpha Kappa Mu, Phi Delta Kappa, Sigma Gamma Rho Community Serv Award; Distinguished Alumni Award St Pauls Coll 1974; St Pauls Coll, Hon Degree, 1982. **Military Serv:** US Army, ssgt, veteran; Civilian Distinguished Service Award, 1979. **Business Addr:** President's Residence, Saint Paul's College, Lawrenceville, VA 23868.

LAW, TY
Professional football player. **Personal:** Born Feb 10, 1974, Aliquippa, PA. **Educ:** Michigan. **Career:** New England Patriots, defensive back, 1995-. **Special Achievements:** 1st round/23rd overall NFL draft pick, 1995. **Business Addr:** Professional Football Player, New England Patriots, 60 Washington St, Foxboro Stadium, Foxboro, MA 02035, (508)543-7911.

LAW-DRIGGINS, ELLEN T.
Educator. **Personal:** Born Jul 10, 1918, Stephens, AR; married William Jefferson. **Educ:** Univ OR, BS 1941, MEd 1962, Secondary Admin Cert 1974. **Career:** Bennett Coll for Women, teacher 1941-42; Seattle Port-Embarkation, clerk 1942-43; Comm Center, Vanport City, dir 1943-44; Better Housing Assn, sec; Roch Branch NAACP, acting dir; Amer Natl Red Cross, 1944-46; Providence Hospital School of Nursing, registar instr 1950-54; George Elementary School, teacher 1954-56; Jefferson Ins in Phys Ed, 1956-61, counselor 1961-68, vice prin 1968-71; Thomas Jefferson HS, acting prin 1971-74; Franklin HS, vice prin. **Orgs:** Delta Sigma Theta, far west dir, 1959-64, Natl Finance Comm, 1967-69; NW Sec Am Bar Assn, vice pres, 1975-79; mem numerous offices, comm bds, professional religious and civic organizations. **Honors/Awds:** Woman of Yr Beta Psi 1968; 10 of achievement portland 1964.

LAWES, VERNA
Data company executive. **Personal:** Born in Philadelphia, PA; daughter of Jessie Lee Grier Jones and Thomas Jones; married Sylvester; children: Anthony, David. **Educ:** Temple Univ, BS. **Career:** US Treasury Dept, data coord; IBM, librarian; Sperry Univac Corp, rsch mgr; Certified Data Serv Inc, pres; Natl Political Congress of Black Women, exec secty; pres, Certified Data Services Inc, 1970-. **Orgs:** Member, Howard County Housing Alliance; member, Howard County Drug & Alcohol Advisory Board; Wilde Lake Village, bd mem. **Home Addr:** 6200-D Foreland Garth, Columbia, MD 21045.

LAWHORN, JOHN B.
Educator. **Personal:** Born Apr 2, 1925, Youngstown, OH; married Phyllis Jane; children: Michael John. **Educ:** Youngstown U, BS 1950; Columbia U, MA 1953. **Career:** Allen U, dept chmn band dir 1950-57; Albany State Coll, acting chmn, dept music, band dir 1957-62; Atlanta Pub Schs, band dir tchr 1961-66; GA StateDept Edn, consult 1966-73; Metro Cooperative Educ Serv Agy, music coodinator 1973-74; Newton Co Schs, 1974-75; Basic Instructional Concepts Inst Nat, concert pianist founder dir; The Child & Leisure Com White House Conf on Children, chmn 1970. **Orgs:** Mem Leadership Atlanta; Govs Adv Council for the Arts; Atlanta Symphonyd Bd; State Adv Commn on Correctional Recr%Eation Publs in Field. **Honors/Awds:** Mrs Fred W, petterson award. **Military Serv:** USN 1943-46. **Business Addr:** Newton County Bd Educ, 2109 Newton Dr, Covington, GA 30209.

LAWHORN, ROBERT MARTIN
Military officer. **Personal:** Born Jan 8, 1943, Camden, SC; married Jacqueline Carter; children: Bridgett Tiffany, Brandon Tilman. **Educ:** NC A&T State Univ, BS 1965; Natl Univ, M Bus Admin 1985. **Career:** Aviation Officer Candidate Sch, officer cand 1966; Basic Naval Aviation Trng, aviation trnee 1966; Advanced NFO Trng, student 1967; VF-101 NAS Oceana VA & Key West FL, student 1967; VF-41 Oceana VA, power plants div off & asst admin off 1967-70; Navy Recruiting Dist St Louis, exec officer minor recruitingofficer 1970-72; VF-124 Miramar CA, student 1972-73; VF1 NAS Miramar, nfo training officer administrative officer 1973-77; VF 124 Miramar, asst operations ofcr instr 1977-79; VF 1 NAS Miramar CA, maintenance ofcr safety ofcr 1980-81; USS Range CV 61 San Diego, weapons officer co-dept head 1981-83; Commander Naval Base San Diego, asst chief of staff for admin 1983-. **Orgs:** Mem Natl Naval Officers Assn 1972-. **Military Serv:** USN commander 18 yrs; Natl Def Medal; Navy Expiditionary Medal; Meritorious Unit Commen; Humanatrian Serv Medal; Sea Serv Ribbon; Armed Forces Exp Medal.

LAWING, RAYMOND QUINTON. **See Obituaries section.**

LAWLAH, GLORIA GARY
State official. **Personal:** Born Mar 12, 1939, Newberry, SC; married John Wesley Lawlah III; children: John Wesley IV, Gloria Gene, Gary McCarrell. **Educ:** Hampton Univ, BS 1960; Trinity Coll, MA 1970. **Career:** Washington DC Public

Schools, administrator; Maryland General Assembly, delegate, 26th dist, 1986-90, senator, 26th dist, 1991-. **Orgs:** Mem bd dirs Coalition of Black Affairs 1980-; life mem Natl Council of Negro Women; mem Oxon Hill Democrats; co-chair PG Govt Review Task Force Public Safety 1982; mem Democratic State Central Comm 1982-86; mem bd of dirs Hillcrest-Marlow Planning Bd 1982-; bd dirs Family Crisis Ctr 1982-84; mem Alpha Kappa Alpha Sor 1982-; delegate Democratic Natl Convention 1984; mem bd of dirs Natl Political Congress of Black Women 1984-; mem Black Democratic Cncl 1985-; mem John Hanson Women's Democratic Club 1985-; mem bd Ctr for the Aging Greater SE Comm Hosp 1985-; State of Maryland legislative committees: Economic and Environmental Affairs Committee, Senate-House Joint Committee on Investigation; The Child Care Administration Advisory Council; The Educational Block Grants Advisory Committee; The Transportation Planning Board ofWashington, advry board; Prince George's County Alliance of Black Elected Officials Inc. **Honors/Awds:** Prince George's County Women's Hall of Fame, inductee. **Home Addr:** 3801 24th Ave, Hillcrest Heights, MD 20748. **Business Addr:** State Senator, Maryland State House, Annapolis, MD 21401.

LAWRENCE, ANNIE L.
Nurse, educator. **Personal:** Born Feb 14, 1926, Virginia; widowed. **Educ:** Freedman's Hosp of Nursing; Loyola Univ, cert of pub hlth nursing; DePaul Univ, BSNE, MSNEd; Sarsota Univ, EDd; Illinois Stat Univ, EDd. **Career:** Division of Nursing and Health Sciences, chair; Gov's State Univ, prof nursing; nursing educ coord; St of IL Dept of Registration & Educ, asst nursing educ coord; Evangelical School of Nursing, asst dir; Mt Sinai Hospital School of Nursing, nursing educ; Provident Hospital School of Nursing, sup instr dir of nursing educ. **Orgs:** Treas Depaul Nursing Sch Alumni Assn; Northeastern League for Nursing; chmn Adv Student Sect Am Nurses Assn; Nat League ofr Nursing; parliamentarian N Assn of Lawyers Wives; aux vice pres immediate past pres N Assn of Lawyers Wives; N Ethical Guideline Com; United Ch of Christ; lay moderator, Park Manor Congregational UCC; pres Women's Fellowship Park Manor Congressional Ch; Am Inst of Parliamentarians; consult educ & civic coms; cororate mem bd of Homeland Ministries; past pres Sigma Gamma Rho Sor; bd dir Evangelical Hosp Assn Publ; Natl League of Nursing, NC, site visitor, panel reviewer; Bethany Hosp, Advocate Health Care, vice chair, governing council. **Honors/Awds:** Publ Adminstrn & Its Effectiveness; "Can an Evaluation Tool be Meaningful to Studies & Tchrs?"; "Professional Leadership"; The Scope of Nursing Prac, listed The Ebony Success Library; Successful Blacks.

LAWRENCE, ARCHIE
Attorney. **Personal:** Born Jun 21, 1947, East St Louis, IL; son of Addie Lawrence and Charlie Lawrence; married Ernestine King; children: Chiestine, Crystal, Candace. **Educ:** Southern Illinois University-Carbondale, BA, 1970; St Louis University School of Law, JD, 1975. **Career:** Legislative Reference Bureau, bill drafting agency, 1975-80; Internal Revenue Service, estate tax attorney, 1980-82; Illinois Department of Revenue, staff attorney, 1982-90; Illinois Attorney General's Office, assistant attorney general, 1990-. **Orgs:** NAACP, Springfield Branch, bd of dir, 1996-, first vice pres, 1990-92, board of directors, 1988-90, president, 1984-88. **Honors/Awds:** Sprinfield Illinois Urban League, Equal Opportunity Award, 1986; NAACP, Springfield Branch, President's Award, 1988, Political Action Award, 1989. **Special Achievements:** Elected representative, Sangamon County Board, 1986-92; named plantiff, voter's rights lawsuit against city of Springfield, Illinois, 1984-86. **Military Serv:** US Army, spc4, 1971-73; Meritorious Service Award, 1973. **Business Addr:** Assistant Attorney General, State of Illinois, 500 South Second St, Springfield, IL 62706, (217)782-9055.

LAWRENCE, AZAR MALCOLM
Jazz musician. **Personal:** Born Nov 3, 1952, Los Angeles; children: Daneka, Azar Malcolm III, Aisha. **Educ:** W LA Jr Coll; CA State U; USC. **Career:** Mccoy Tyner's Quintet, jazz musician. **Orgs:** Mem of various prominent quarters & bands; currently recording on Prestige Label Serv. **Honors/Awds:** Currently recording on Prestige Label Serv to Sickle Cedd Fdn; Urban League Guild; Black Awareness Programs; featured in Downbeat Mag 1973; Esq Mag 1975; Montreaux Jazz Festival 1973.

LAWRENCE, BRENDA
Educational administrator. **Career:** Southfield School Bd, bd member, currently. **Business Addr:** Bd Member, Southfield School Bd, 24661 Lasher, Southfield, MI 48034, (810)746-8500.

LAWRENCE, EDWARD
Association executive. **Personal:** Born Jan 8, 1935, Gasden, AL; married Marion Winn; children: Rita, Edward Jr, Jill, Lawrence. **Educ:** Empire State Coll, BA 1957; Studio Theatre Sch. **Career:** African-am Cultural Ctr, prof actor, exec dir 1968-. **Orgs:** Mem Actors Equity; Studio Arena Theatre 1966-68; Buffalo Urban League; Community Action Orgn; Buffalo & Build Orgn. **Honors/Awds:** Community serv award Black Harmony. **Business Addr:** 350 Masten Ave, Buffalo, NY 14209.

LAWRENCE, EILEEN B.
Librarian (retired). **Personal:** Born Apr 11, 1919, Centralia, IL; daughter of Essie Sherrod Barnett (deceased) and George Levi Barnett (deceased); widowed; children: Trumagne Fleming, Stephanie Pearson. **Educ:** Loyola U, PHB 1950; Wilson State Coll L & A Chicago T Chr Coll, attended 1964-65. **Career:** Fredrick A Douglass Br Library, br librarian 1964-75; Oakland Br Washington Park Sub-br, librarian; Dusable HS & Englewood HS, 1st asst; library asst ch pianist & choir & dir 1939-62; St Mark Amez Ch & Kelly Meth Ch; Chicago Public Library, South Shore Branch, librarian grade IV, until 1994. **Orgs:** Bd dir Lawndale Homemakers 1971-75; mem Model Cities Educ Task Force; mem Intl Platform Assn; mem Old Friends of Greater Chicago Recipient Mayoral Citation Model Cities Subcom; Chicago Commn on Human Relations 1971-74. **Honors/Awds:** Claude D Pepper Distinguished Service Award (for special accomplishment after age 55); DuSable High School Wall of Honor, 1989. **Business Addr:** Librarian Grade IV, Chicago Public Library, South Shore Public Library, 2505 E 73rd St, Chicago, IL 60649.

LAWRENCE, ELLIOTT
National sales manager. **Personal:** Born May 27, 1947, Mt Vernon, NY; son of Muriel and Milford Brown; divorced. **Educ:** Albany State University, BA, 1973. **Career:** Events Plus, vice pres of sales, 1989-91; Themes and Schemes, dir of sales and mktg, 1991-92; San Diego Convention and Visitors Bureau, national sales mgr, 1992-. **Orgs:** National Coalition of Black Meeting Planners; Religious Conference Management Association; Meeting Professionals Intl; Jackie Robinson YMCA, San Diego, bd mem; National Black MBA Association. **Honors/Awds:** National University, Multicultural Award, 1997. **Special Achievements:** CMP Designation, Centifies Meeting Planner, 1996; Former Broadway Singer/Dancer. **Military Serv:** Navy, 3rd class petty officer, 1964-68. **Business Addr:** National Sales Manager, San Diego Convention & Visitors Bureau, 401 B St, Ste 1400, San Diego, CA 92101, (619)557-2839.

LAWRENCE, ERMA JEAN
Business executive. **Personal:** Born Jul 12, 1926, Arkansas; married Joseph; children: Ronald, Gloristene, Imogene, Michelle, Valerie. **Educ:** Nat Inst of Prac Nurs, 1953; WA U, com dev training 1967-68; Urban Training Cent HDC, 2 yrs trng; WA U, cert in mngmt 1971; MO U, soc minority student; MO Univ WA U, org training sem; dev training sem econ 1970; MO U, econ dev sem 1970; GEO Grant CAP, 1970. **Career:** West Educ Cong, 3rd vp; Block Unit, chmn 10 yrs; Urban League, leadership trng; precinct capt 13 yrs; Main Post Office, mail clerk 1950-62; Firmin Des Lodge Hosp, prac nurse 1953-63; Coll of Rev, tax collector, auditor processor 1963-66; HDC, com dev 1966; West End Gateway Cent Sub Station, com dev 1966-; West End Dev Corp, dir 1972-79; Northside Preservation Commn Inc, exec dir 1979-. **Orgs:** Mem Urban League; Police Comm Rel Commn; YMCA; coorgan of Poor People Camp; coord Mat Blk Health Causus; Mental Health Task Force; bd mem ARCH; col People Guide; bd mem West End Dev Corp; Met Ten Orgn; West End Com Conf; Blk Women of Unity; Blk Women Com Dev Found; consult Youth Adv Coun; St Louis City Bd of Dn 1975; mem Baptist Ch of Good Shephard; org Blk People Coun; mem Kinder Cottage Women for City Living; pers comm Freedom of Resident; Mayors Coun on Aging; mem Educ Com to Study Dropouts; PTA; adv com Of Univ Year in Action Univ of Univ of MO; treas WA Univ Com Action Alumni; bd mem West End Comm Conf; past chmn West End Neighborhood Adv Comm; bd mem Dignity Reading Clinic; found pres Operation Challenge; mem appointed by Gov Teasdale The Neighborhood Commn; mem St Louis-Round TabHousing & Brain Thrust of St Louis Round Label St Louis Black Leadership; charter mem Scott Joplin Soc Constr Emp Prgm. **Honors/Awds:** Outstanding Supv; Aid of Delinq; Beautification Blocks Awd; Spec Awd Dinner West End Adv Comm; Spec Awd Bd of Educ Svc; Awd for Vol Serv on Coms Mayor James F Conway St Louis; Awd for Training 200 Youth & Adults in Work Experience Progs Operation Challenge Inc; Awd for Active Block Unit Chairmanship & Vol Serv St Louis League. **Business Addr:** Executive Dir, Northside Preservation Commiss, 5647 Delmar, St Louis, MO 63112.

LAWRENCE, GEORGE CALVIN
Physician. **Personal:** Born Apr 11, 1918, Greene County, GA; son of Lozie Ann Favors Lawrence and Noel Lawrence; married Pauline Blockshear (deceased); children: Brenda Jean Lawrence Harris, Montrois, George Calvin Jr. **Educ:** Meharry Med Coll, MD 1944; FACOG, 1972. **Career:** Private practice, obstetrics/gynecology. **Orgs:** Pres Atlanta Med Assn; sec GA State Med Assn; pres Atlanta Guardsmen; mem & 32nd degree Mason; Omega Psi Phi Frat; Ebenezer Baptist Church. **Honors/Awds:** Recpt recog awrd 25 yrs med serv Morehouse Coll & Meharry Med Coll; fellow, Amer Coll of Obstetrics-Gynecology. **Military Serv:** USNR MC comdr 1953-56. **Business Addr:** 550 Fairburn Rd SW, #A-5, Atlanta, GA 30331.

LAWRENCE, HENRY
Professional football player (retired), company executive. **Personal:** Born Sep 26, 1951, Danville, PA; son of Geneva Isom Thomas and Julius Lawrence; divorced; children: Dina Geneive, Starlin Le Ron, Juliet Elana, Itanzia Saras. **Educ:** Florida A&M Univ, BS, political science, 1974; Travelers Insurance, Tampa & Hartford, life, health & disability, 1975; Univ of Pennsylvania, Wharton School, real estate strategies, 1987. **Career:** Oakland Raiders (later, Los Angeles Raiders), 1974-86; Manatee Growers Packing Co Inc, pres and chairman of the board; Henry Lawrence Productions Inc, pres; L & S Farms, vice pres; Solid Rock Realty, vice pres; solo vocal entertainer and recording artist; Latco Technologies Inc, pres, office and computer supplies, currently. **Orgs:** Mem, Manatee County Sickle Cell, 1976-78; bd dir, Amer Cancer Soc, 1976-80; mem, NAACP; life mem, Alpha Phi Alpha Fraternity, 1973-; mem, Masonic Lodge Prentice Hall, 1971-; founder/producer, Miss Black Manatee County Scholarship Beauty Pageant Inc, 1978-; Henry Lawrence Youth Football Camps; fund raiser, United Negro Coll Fund; fund raiser, The Sonance Ear Institute; president, Henry Lawrence Youth Foundation. **Honors/Awds:** Comm Contrib Awd FL State Women's Assn 1978; Comm Image & Serv Awd NAACP 1979; played in three Super Bowls 1976, 1980, 1983; All American Teams 1973-74; played in Pro Bowl, 1983, 1984; NFL All Pro; nominated for Humanitarian Awd by The Southern California Alm Institute, 1987. **Home Addr:** 2110 Third Ave E, Palmetto, FL 34221-3320.

LAWRENCE, JACOB A.
Artist, educator. **Personal:** Born Sep 7, 1917, Atlantic City, NJ; married Gwendolyn Knight. **Educ:** Harlem Art Workshop NYC, attended 1934-48; Amer Artists Sch NYC, attended 1938-39. **Career:** Harlem YMCA, Columbia Univ, Baltimore Museum, work shown 1938-40; work Migration of the Negro reproduced 26 of the paintings in Fortune Magazine in 1941; started work on "Struggle, From the History of the American People" 1955; taught at Pratt Institute starting in 1955 for 15 years; 1967 Simon & Schuster published a children's book, Harriet and the Promised Land, and did a series of 17 paintings based on the life of Harriet Tubman; 1972 designed posters for Olympic Games in Munich; 1973 produced a series of paintings for the Washington State Capital Museum; commissioned by Limited Edition Books to illustrate a special edition of John Hersey's Hiroshima 1982; Univ of Washington, full prof 1970-. **Orgs:** Elected to Amer Acad of Arts & Letters 1984; mem Natl Inst Arts & Letters; Washington State Arts Commn; mem Natl Acad Design 1971. **Honors/Awds:** Rosenwald Fellowship 1940-42; Guggenheim Fellowship 1946; Spingarn Med 1970; exhibition sponsored by Ford Found 1960; retrospective exhibition Whitney Museumof Amer Art sponsored by IBM 1974; Washington State Governor's Awd of Special Commendation 1981; Washington State Governor's Arts Awd 1984; Citation by Washington State Senate 1985. **Special Achievements:** Author, Jacob Lawrence: The Migration Series, Rappahanock Press, 1994. **Military Serv:** USCG 1943-45. **Business Addr:** Professional Artist, Seattle Art Museum, Volunteer Park, Seattle, WA 98112.

LAWRENCE, JAMES FRANKLIN
Journalist. **Personal:** Born Aug 19, 1949, Orlando, FL; son of Ethel L Lawrence and James Lawrence; married Betty A Lawrence (divorced 1986); children: Terrance, Jamil, Ebony. **Educ:** Howard University, Washington, DC, BA, 1971. **Career:** Cleveland Coll & Post, Cleveland, OH, reporter, 1972-73; United Press International, Denver, CO, reporter/editor, 1973-85; Orlando Sentinel, Orlando, FL, editorial writer, 1985-87; Gannett Westchester Newspapers, White Plains, NY, associate editor, 1987-. **Orgs:** Treasurer, Alpha Phi Alpha (Eta Chi Lambda), 1989; member, National Association of Black Journalists. **Honors/Awds:** Beat Commentary, 2nd Place, The Orlando Sentinel, 1986; Mighty Pen, (4 firs t place, 2 second), Gannett Westchester Newspapers, 1987-91. **Business Addr:** Associate Editor, Gannett Westchester Newspapers, One Gannett Dr, White Plains, NY 10604.

LAWRENCE, JAMES T.
Business executive. **Personal:** Born Nov 20, 1921, Madison, GA; married Carrie B Dorsey; children: Sylvia L. **Educ:** Morris Brown Coll, attended; LUTC Grad. **Career:** Pilgrim Health & Life Ins Co, agent, mgr, state supr, state mgr, special claims controller, special ordinary supr, asst dean training school, asst vice pres chief acct 1947-. **Orgs:** Mem, Natl Accountants Assn, 1961-; SE Trainers Dir Assn, 1971-; mem, YMCA; NAACP; Urban League; bd dir, Pilgrim Employees Fed Credit Union; bd mem Amer Cancer Soc, 1973-. **Honors/Awds:** Cancer crusade chairman awards 1967; mgmt idea award 1969; 6 NIA certificates. **Military Serv:** AUS 1 lt 1942-45. **Business Addr:** Vice Pres, Chief Accountant, The Pilgrim Life & Health Insurance Co, 1143 Laney-Wolkey Blvd, Augusta, GA 30901.

LAWRENCE, JOHN E.
Educator. **Personal:** Born May 11, 1941, Durham, NC; married Virginia Landers; children: John II, Jason. **Educ:** NC Central Univ, BS; FL A&M Univ, M. **Career:** Lincoln HS, 1963-67; Godby HS, tchr 1967-69, asst prin 1969-73, prin 1973-78; FL Dept of Educ, bureau chief adult & comm educ 1979-. **Orgs:** Mem Comm Educators; Natl Comm Educ Assn NAPCAE; FAEA; Leon Dist Adv Com; mem Kappa Delta Pi; Phi Delta Kappa; Frontiers Intl; bd dir Capital City Tiger Bay Club; Tallahassee Urban League; mem NAACP. **Honors/Awds:** Frontiersman of the Yr Awd 1975. **Business Addr:** Bureau Chief Adult & Comm Educ, Florida Dept of Educ, Knott Bldg, Tallahassee, FL 32301.

LAWRENCE, LEONARD E.
Association executive. **Personal:** Born Jun 27, 1937, Indianapolis, IN; son of Elizabeth M Lawrence and Leonard A Lawrence; married Barbara Ann Price; children: Courtney, L Michael, David. **Educ:** IN Univ, BA 1959; IN Univ School of Med, MD 1962. **Career:** IN Univ School of Med, psych resident 1965-68, chief psych res 1967-68, child psych fellow 1967-69; Child Psych Serv Wilford Hall USAF Med Ctr, chief 1969-72; San Antonio Childrens Ctr, assoc med dir; Univ of TX Health Sci Ctr, prof of psych pediatrics & fam practice, assoc dean student affairs. **Orgs:** Cert Amer Bd Psych & Neurology 1970-71; TX Juvenile Corrections Master Plan Adv Council, mem 1974-75; Council on Children Adolesc & Their Families AmerPsych Assoc 1976, 1978-83; Natl Med Assoc; Amer Acad of Child Psych; Amer Ortho Psych Assoc; Amer Psych Assoc; Kappa Alpha Psi; ed bd Jrnl Amer Acad Child Psych; National Medical Assn, president-elect, 1992-93, president, 1993-94; Texas Youth Commission, 1992-97, chair 1995-. **Honors/Awds:** Co-author with J Spurlock ''The Black Child'' Basic Handbook of Child Psych vol 1 JB Noshpitz Ed-in-Chief Basic Books Inc NY 1979. **Military Serv:** Lt col 1963-72. **Business Addr:** Associate Dean Student Affairs, Univ of Texas, Health Science Center, 7703 Floyd Curl Dr, San Antonio, TX 78284.

LAWRENCE, LONNIE R.
Law enforcement director. **Personal:** Born Jun 11, 1946, Miami, FL; married Carol Walker Lawrence, Feb 14, 1987; children: Derek, Jonathan. **Educ:** Miami-Dade Comm Coll 1972; St Thomas Univ 1979; Barry University, Miami, FL, professional studies, 1989; Harvard University, JFK School of Government, sr executivec, 1990. **Career:** Metro-Dade Police Dept, patrolman 1968-80, sgt 1980, commander 1981-83, dist commander 1983-85, major 1985-87; Metro-Dade HUD, assistant director 1987-89; Metro-Dade Corrections, director 1989-. **Orgs:** Board of dirs, Leadership Miami Alumni Assn, Big Brothers/Big Sisters, Informed Families of Dade; bd of dir/treas, Miami-Dade Chamber of Commerce; Florida Criminal Justice Executive Institute, 1990-; chairman, Youth Activities Dade County Association of Chiefs of Police, 1984-; American Correctional Association, 1989-. **Honors/Awds:** Officer of the Year, Richmon-Porrine Jaycees, 1982; Public Serv US Dept of Justice, 1984; Officer of the Year, MIK Devel Corp, 1985; Outstanding Participation Award, Hialeah-Miami Springs Chamber of Commerce, 1991; Award of Honor, The Alternatives Programs Inc, 1990; Certificate of Commendation, Board of County Commissioners, 1991. **Military Serv:** US Marine Corps, corporal, 1965-68.

LAWRENCE, MARGARET MORGAN
Physician. **Personal:** Born Aug 19, 1914, New York, NY; daughter of Mary Elizabeth Smith Morgan (deceased) and Sandy Alonzo Morgan (deceased); married Charles R II (deceased); children: Charles R III, Sara Lightfoot, Paula Wehmiller. **Educ:** Cornell U, AB 1936; Coll of Physicians & Surgeons Columbis U, MD/MS pub health 1940-43, cert in psychoanalytic med 1951. **Career:** Harlem Hosp Center, supervising child psychiatrist & psychoanalyst 1963-84; Coll of P&S Columbia, assoc clinical prof of psychiatry 1963-84; Pomona NY, practicing child psychiatrist psychoanalyst 1951-; Child Devel Center, dir 1969-74; Sch Mental Health Unit, dir 1957-63; Children's Therapy Rockland Co Center for Mental Health, assoc dir 1954-57; Northside Child Devel Center City Coll Educ Clinic, psychiatrist 1951-57; Pediatrics Meharry Med Coll, asso prof 1943-47. **Orgs:** Life fellow Am Psychoanalytic Assn, life fellow Am Psychiatric Assn, Am Acad of Psychoanalysis, Am Orthopsychiatric Assn; life mem Nat Med Assn/Black Psychiatrists Of Am; life mem Med Soc Co of Rockland; Rosenwald Fellow 1942-43; Nta Research Council Fellow 1947-48; US Pub Health Serv Fellow 1948-50; Licentiate Am Bd of Pediatrics 1948; honorary member, Alpha Kappa Alpha Sorority, 1990. **Honors/Awds:** Publ ''Mental Health Team in the Schools'' Human Sci Press 1971; publ ''Young Inner City Families the development of ego strength under stress'' human Sci Press 1975; Joseph R Bernstein mental health award Rockland Co NY 1975; EY Williams MD Clinical Scholars of Distinction Awd 1984; Outstanding Women Practioners in Medicine Awd of the Susan Smith McKinney Steward Med Soc 1984; Honorary Doctor of Civil Law, University of the South, 1987; Honorary Doctor of Science, Connecticut College, 1989; Honorary Doctor of Divinity, General Theological Seminary, 1990; Honorary Doctor of Humane Letters, Marymount College, 1990; Honorary Doctor of Education, Wheelock College, 1991; Cornell Black Alumni Award, 1992. **Business Addr:** 34 Dogwood Lane, Pomona, NY 10970.

LAWRENCE, MARTIN
Actor, comedian. **Personal:** Born Apr 16, 1965, Frankfort, Germany; son of John Lawrence and Chlora Lawrence; married Patricia Southall, Jan 1995; children: one. **Career:** Actor, films include: Do the Right Thing, 1989; House Party, 1990; House Party II, 1991; Talkin' Dirty After Dark, 1991; Boomerang, 1992; You So Crazy!, 1994; Bad Boys, 1995; Thin Line Between Love and Hate, 1996; television shows include: What's Happening Now!; Russell Simmon's Def Comedy Jam, HBO, host; Martin, 1992-97. **Honors/Awds:** NAACP, Image Award, 1993, 1994.

LAWRENCE, MERLISA EVELYN
Sports writer. **Personal:** Born Oct 14, 1965, Winter Haven, FL; daughter of Esther Mae Martin Lawrence-Blue and Robinson Louis Lawrence. **Educ:** University of South Florida, Tampa, FL, BA, journalism, 1987. **Career:** Tampa Tribune, Tampa, FL, sports writer, 1987-88; Staten Island Advance, Staten Island, NY, sports writer, general assignments, 1988-90; Pittsburgh Press, Pittsburgh, PA, sports writer, 1990-92; Sports Illustrated, reporter, 1992-. **Orgs:** Member, National Association of Black Journalists, 1988-; member, Garden State Association of Black Journalists, 1992; editor, NABJ Sports Task Force Newsletter, 1990-. **Honors/Awds:** Outstanding Achievement on Brain Bowl Team, 1985; Public speaking to high school and college students, 1990-; Involved with local job fairs and workshops for minority high school and college students. **Business Addr:** Reporter, Sports Illustrated, Time & Life Bldg, Rockefeller Center, New York, NY 10020.

LAWRENCE, MONTAGUE SCHIELE
Surgeon (retired). **Personal:** Born Apr 22, 1923, Laurel, MS; married Melbahue Green; children: Michael, Julie. **Educ:** Alcorn A&M Coll, BS 1943; Meharry Med Coll, MD 1946; Homer Phillips Hosp, intern 1946-47, resd 1947-51. **Career:** Homer Phillips Hosp, supr sur 1953-54; Univ IA, chest surg resd instr assoc 1954-56, rsch asst prof 1956-57, asst prof 1957-59, assoc prof surgery 1959-65, prof surgery 1965-71; VA Hosp, vis surgeon 1962-71; Univ of IA, chmn div vascular surg 1970-71; private practice, surgeon, retired 1989. **Orgs:** Mem AMA; Natl Med Assn; fellow Amer Coll of Surgeons; Amer Coll of Chest Physicians; mem Amer Assn for Thoracic Surgery; Soc of Thoracic Surgeons; Western Surg Assn; Central Surg Assn; Amer Heart Assn; Amer Thoracic Socl; IA Thoracic Soc; IA Acad of Surgery; IA State Med Soc; Linn Co Med Soc; Alpha Omega Alpha; Kappa Pi Med Soc; Sigma Xi; diplomate Amer Bd of Surgery; Amer Bd of Thoracic Surgery; mem NINDB Prog Proj Comm; consult Thoracic & Cardiovascular Surgery; mem Joint Com for Stroke Facilities; gov Amer Coll of Chest Physicians; mem Central Adv Com Cncl on Cardiovascular Surgery; pres IA Acad of Surgery; IA Thoracic Soc; bd mem Human Experimentation & Rsch; mem House Staff Affairs Com; Med Sch Admission Comm. **Military Serv:** US Army, capt 1951-53. **Home Addr:** 4333 Fox Meadow Dr SE, Cedar Rapids, IA 52403.

LAWRENCE, OLLIE, JR.
Airline executive. **Personal:** Born Aug 3, 1951, Chicago, IL; son of Minnie Lawrence and Ollie Lawrence; married Robin Warr-Lawrence, Dec 30, 1989 (deceased); children: Nicole. **Educ:** University of Connecticut, BS, business administration, 1973; University of New Haven, 1976-78; George Washington University, 1979-90. **Career:** Pratt & Whitney Aircraft, compensation analyst, personnel counselor, 1973-78; USAir, Inc, Human Resources, vp. **Orgs:** Washington Personnel Association; American Compensation Association; Black Human Resource Network, bd mem; USAir Management Club; National Association of Securities Dealers, Inc, public arbitrator; American Stock Exchange, public arbitrator; Society for Human Resources Management, vp chapter; International Assn of Bus Communicators; Capital Press Club; VA Chamber of Commerce, bd mem; Arlington Chamber of Commerce; bd mem. **Honors/Awds:** Black Human Resources Network, Minority Human Resources Professional Award, 1992; USAir, USAir's Management Achievement Award, 1990. **Special Achievements:** Black Belt in Tae Kwon Do. **Business Addr:** VP, Human Resources, USAir, Inc, 2345 Crystal Dr, Crystal Park IV, Arlington, VA 22227, (703)418-7420.

LAWRENCE, PAUL FREDERIC
Consultant. **Personal:** Born Mar 20, Paterson, NJ; son of Louise Lawrence and Joshua Lawrence; married Vivian Ann Hall; children: Katherine Louise, Robin Ann. **Educ:** Newark State Tchrs Coll, BS Educ 1935; Stanford Univ, MA Educ 1946, EdD 1947. **Career:** Howard Univ, assoc dir counseling 1948-56; Willowbrook Sch Dist, supt of schs 1956-60; CA State Coll, assoc dean counseling 1960-63; CA State Dept of Educ, assoc state supt 1963-67; US Office of Educ, regional comm of ed 1967-73, dept asst comm regional off 1973-79, dir postsecondary liaison 1979-82; Consultants in Educational Policy and Admin, chief exec officer 85-; Self-Employed, private consultant; settlement team mem, federal court monitor in case of NAACP vs San Francisco School District & California State Department of Education. **Orgs:** Mem Phi Delta Kappa 1946-; bd mem Fair Play Council Palo Alto CA 1946-48; dir Southern Field Proj Natl Scholarship Serv Found 1949-54; bd mem Natl Conf Christians & Jews LA Region 1956-60; bd mem Scholastics Mag Adv Bd 1964-68; bd mem Coll Placement Bureau 1966-70; chmn pre-coll Council Natl Acad Sci Engrg Council 1975-80; bd mem Stanford Univ Alumni Assn 1984-; fed court monitor in case of NAACP vs SF Sch Dist & CA State Dept of Ed. **Honors/Awds:** Hon Doctorate Kean Univ NJ 1965; Keys to City Riverside CA 1966-70; Citations (3) CA State Legislator (Assembly & Senate) 1967-68; Serv Awd US office of Ed Washington 1970; Distinguished Educator Natl Alliance Black Sch Educators 1974; Publications, College Primer for Negro Youth 1946; co-author, Negro American Heritage (textbook) 1964; Primer for Compliance Monitoring 1989. **Military Serv:** US Army, USAF lt col 22 yrs; numerous medals. **Home Addr:** 4837 Crestwood Way, Sacramento, CA 95822.

LAWRENCE, PHILIP MARTIN
Company executive. **Personal:** Born Nov 12, 1950, Evansville, IN; son of Pilar Lawrence and William H Lawrence; married Cheryl Darlene Moore, Jun 6, 1971; children: DeVonna Marcel Lawrence, Philip M Lawrence II, Shane Kiwan Lawrence. **Educ:** ISUE, Evansville, IN. **Career:** People's Voice, Evansville, IN, editor, Black Newspaper, 1969-71; WJPS, Evansville, IN, radio announcer; City of Evansville, Evansville, IN, contract compliance officer (business devel supvr); Tomorrow's Treasures, CA, regional mgr; Heritage, New Jersey, regional/mgr; Community Action of Evansville, Evansville, IN, senior aide dir; ATSCO Inc, Evansville, IN, chief exec. **Orgs:** Bd mem, Council on Aging, 1984-87; Steering Comm Head, 1986-89, treasurer, 1987-89, Evansville Area Minority Supplies Devel Council; mem, State Chamber of Commerce, 1986-89; mem, Rotary Intl, 1987-89; mem, bd of dir, Private Industry Council, 1987-89; treasurer, NAACP, 1983-86; MIC chairman, IRMSDC, 1984-85; president, Grace Lutheran Church, 1990-. **Honors/Awds:** Played the beast in ''Beauty & the Beast'' on local TV station, 1982; Master of Ceremonies for Black History Talent, 1978-88; Freedom Award, NAACP, 1990; Evansville Chamber of Commerce & NAACP Minority Business Leadership Award, 1992; Black Enterprise Magazine, Certificate for Outstanding Business Achievement, 1990; Downtown Master Plan Steering Committee, Certificate of Appreciation, 1995. **Business Addr:** Pres, ATSCO, Inc, PO Box 3912, Evansville, IN 47737.

LAWRENCE, PRESTONIA D. (ANNU PRESTONIA)
Salon owner. **Personal:** Born Mar 26, 1957, Portsmouth, VA; daughter of Barbara Newsome and Preston Newsome; married Wayne Lawrence, Sep 13, 1985. **Career:** Khamit Kinks, president, 1977-. **Orgs:** International Braiders Network, curriculum committee mem. **Honors/Awds:** National Braiders Guild, Recognition Award, 1989; Uhuru Sasa, best conrows, 1979; Robert Fiance Beauty School, best creation, 1986; Bronner Brothers, trend setters, 1990-91. **Special Achievements:** Cover of Essence Magazine, Angela Bassett's hair, Dec 1992; Converse sneaker commercial, En Vogues hair, 1993; Clairol styling for their black market, 1992; Hype Hair, September cover, 1994. **Business Addr:** President, Khamit Kinks, 4 Leonard St, New York, NY 10013-2917.

LAWRENCE, RODELL
Business executive. **Personal:** Born Feb 19, 1946, Apopka, FL; son of Estella Richardson Lawrence and Adell Lawrence; married Cedar Lavern Evans; children: Christopher, Debora, Biram, Raegena. **Educ:** South Carolina State Coll, BSEE 1970. **Career:** North Amer Rockwell Missile System Div, mem tech staff 1970-73; Xerox Corp, test engr, sr engr field engr, regional product serv mgr midwest region headquarters, project mgr I II III, multinatl serv opers mgr, product support mgr, product serv mgr; Xerox Corp, Mgr, Multinational Configuration Mgmt, 1988-; Integrated Supply Chain, mgr, Office Document Systems Division, currently. **Orgs:** Bd of dirs CARI 1980-85; dean of educ Omega Psi Phi Frat 1984, 1985, 1987; athletic dir, Irondequoit Football League 1985-86; bd of dir Lewis St Settlement 1986-87; Bd of Visitor, Claflin Coll, 1988-; Advisory Council, SC State Coll, 1988-, chm, engineering, 1991-94; vice president, Rochester Chapter NAACP, 1991-92; vice pres, 2nd District Scholarship Foundation, Omega Psi Phi, 1990-91. **Honors/Awds:** Distinguished Corporate Alumni Citation NAFEO 1983; Houston Engrs Soc Awd SC State Coll 1986; 1989 Benjamin E Mays Most Distinguished Grauate Award, SC State Coll, 1989; Outstanding Performance Award, Xerox, 1989; Leadership through Quality Award, Xerox, 1989; honorary doctor of law degree, SC State University, 1992; President Award, Claflin College, 1992. **Military Serv:** AUS; staff sgt E-6 2 yrs; Bronze Star, Silver Star, Purple Heart, Army Accomodations.

LAWRENCE, SANDRA
Interior designer. **Personal:** Born Jan 28, 1938, New York, NY; daughter of Lossie Lawrence and George Lawrence; married Paul Evans Jr (divorced 1990). **Educ:** NY School of Interior Design, BFA; Parsons, attended 1983-84. **Career:** Batakari Ltd NY, pres int designer 1973-81; Sandra Lawrence Assocs Inc, pres/director. **Orgs:** Allied Board of Trade, 1980-. **Business Addr:** President, Sandra Lawrence Inc, 337 Convent Ave, New York, NY 10031.

LAWRENCE, THOMAS R., JR.
Personnel executive (retired). **Personal:** Born Sep 2, 1929, Waycross, GA; son of Thelma Sue Williams Lawrence and Thomas Reid Lawrence; married Caroline Barbosa, Nov 16, 1952; children: Lisa Frazier, Dwayne, Damon, Rene. **Educ:** Suffolk University, BA, 1960, MA, 1962; American University, graduate study, 1963-64. **Career:** Office of Economic Opportunity, educ specialist, 1963-65; Urban League of Springfield, exec dir, 1965-68; Information Systems, mgr of EEO, N Amer Operations, 1970-73; Honeywell Inc, Corporate Employee Relations, mgr of corporate EEO programs, 1973-75; Information Systems-Field Engineering Div, mgr of Distribution and Priority Control, 1975-77, mgr of natl accounts, 1977-79; Avionics Division-Product Support Logistics, mgr of systems and procedures, 1979-80; Controls Systems-Honeywell Plaza, staff asst, 1980-82; Honeywell Inc, Corporate Employee Relations, re-

tired mgr of univ relations and minority recruitment, 1983-92. **Orgs:** Mem, Minneapolis NAACP, 1972-; mem, Minneapolis Urban League, 1972-; bd mem, Industry Advisory Council NAACP ACT-SO, 1985-; bd mem, Natl Consortium for Minority Engineers, 1985-; bd mem, Natl Soc of Black Engineers, 1988-. **Honors/Awds:** Meritorious Service Award, Florida A & M Univ, 1988; Honeywell Focus Award, 1988; Black Engineer of the Year Award, Affirmative Action, 1989; National Black Heritage Observance Council Award, 1990; North Carolina A&T University, Distinguished Service Award, 1992; Awarded Honorary Doctrate of Laws, NC A&T Univ, 1993. **Military Serv:** U.S. Army, master sgt, 1948-52; received Bronze Star. **Business Addr:** Mgr, Univ Relations & Minority Recruitment, Honeywell, Inc, Honeywell Plaza, Minneapolis, MN 55408.

LAWRENCE, VIOLA POE
Librarian (retired). **Personal:** Born Aug 30, 1926, Burlington, NC; daughter of Hattie Hunter Poe and Burham Poe; married Aug 6, 1965 (divorced 1982). **Educ:** North Carolina Central University, Durham, NC, BA, 1948, BLS, 1950, MSLS, 1955. **Career:** West Badin High School, Badin, NC, librarian, 1950-52; Albany State College, Albany, GA, asst librarian, 1952-53; Stanford L Warren Public Library, 1953-62, 1962-65; Gentry Jr High School, Erwin, NC, media specialist, 1965-88; Merrick-Moore Elementary School, Durham, NC, media specialist, 1967-88. **Orgs:** Secretary, Durham City/County Retired School Personnel, 1990-; North Carolina Central University, School of Library and Information Science, president, 1978, visiting lecturer, currently; treasurer, Durham County Assn of Classroom Teachers, 1969; chairman, Piedmont District, North Carolina Assn of Educators, Library Division, 1954; president, Stanley County Assn of Classroom Teachers, 1964; chairman, nominating committee, North Carolina Assn of School Librarians, 1973; life member, North Carolina Assn of Educators and Retired School Personnel; Appalachian State University, visiting lecturer. **Honors/Awds:** Two NDEA Scholarships. **Home Addr:** 2215 Curtis St, Durham, NC 27707.

LAWRENCE, WILLIAM WESLEY
Educator. **Personal:** Born Jan 27, 1939, Whiteville, NC; son of Mary Lawrence and Horace Lawrence; married Queen E Wooten; children: William Wesley Jr, Lori Elecia. **Educ:** NC Coll, BS Chem 1962; St Josephs School of Med Tech Tacoma WA, Cert Med Tech 1967; NC Central Univ Durham, MA Counseling 1971; Univ of NC ChapelHill, PhD Counseling Psych 1974. **Career:** Liggett & Myers Inc, rsch chem 1969-71; Univ of NC Chapel Hill, counselor 1972-73; NC Central Univ Durham, assoc dir inst rsch & eval 1973-74; NC A&TState Univ Greensboro, chmn educ psych & guidance 1974-78; Natl Inst of Environ Health Sci, counseling psych/dir human resource devel; Fayetteville State Univ, prof of education 1978-87. **Orgs:** Med lab consult Hospitals & Scientific Labs 1967-72; consult Bus Educ Government 1975-85; public notary Durham Cty 198-85; real estate broker & instr Century21 NC Comm Coll 1982-85. **Honors/Awds:** Ray Thompson Humanitarian Awd NC Personnel & Guidance Assoc 1973; Ed Leadership Awd Afro-Amer Soc of Transit Employees NY 1978; Outstanding Work Performance Awd US Dept of Health & Human Serv 1983. **Military Serv:** AUS E-4 lab spec 2 yrs; Outstanding Recruit Awd, Platoon Leader 1963-65. **Home Addr:** 308 Wayne Circle, Durham, NC 27707.

LAWS, RUTH M.
Educator. **Personal:** Born Jul 25, 1912, Gatesville, NC; married William J Laws; children: Cherritta Matthews. **Educ:** Hampton Inst, BS 1933; Cornell Univ, MS 1943; NY Univ, EdD 1956. **Career:** Peabody Acad, teacher 1933-34; Rural Soc, caseworker 1934-36; Wilmington, adult educ supr 1936-37; Smyrna, teacher 1937-41; State Dept Pub Instr Home Econ, dir asst supr 1942-56, supr 1956-68; Adult & Continuing Educ, state dir 1968-71; DE Tech & Comm Coll, asst to pres 1971-77, vice pres 1977-78; L & M Educ Resources Ltd. **Orgs:** Mem numerous offices; consult numerous professional civic orgns; mem Natl Bd YMCA 1979-83. **Honors/Awds:** Merit Awd Natl Bd New Homemakers Amer 1954; Merit Awd DE Assn New Homemakers Amer 1961; Woman of Yr Dover Alumni Chap Delta Sigma Theta 1964; Commendation Cert Vet Admin Serv 1970; Outstanding Voc Educ Awd DE Dept Pub Instr 1972; recognition Adult Educ Assn USA 1974; Diamond State Awd Gov DE 1974; YMCA Citizen of the Yr 1980; Del Council of Women Hall of Fame 1981; Philadelphia Freedom Day Awd (Ed) 1981; Del Coll Personnel Assn Leadership in Educ Awd 1981; Brandywine Professional Assn Outstanding Achievers Awd (Educ) 1982; DE State Bar Assn Law Day Liberty Bell Awd 1983; Delaware Mother of the Year 1986; Delaware Ecumenical Awd 1986; Honorary Degree, Del Tech & Community College, 1994. **Business Addr:** L&M Educ Resources Ltd, 844 Forest St, Dover, DE 19904.

LAWSON, ANTHONY EUGENE, SR.
Engineering company executive. **Personal:** Born Nov 15, 1954, Martinez, CA; son of Inez Lawson and Ardell Lawson Sr; married Gazelle Williams Lawson, Apr 27, 1979; children: Tony, Danielle. **Educ:** University of Arizona, BS, pubic administration, 1977; University of LaVerne, MS, business & organizational management, 1985. **Career:** Rockwell International Space, supervisor, quality, reliable assurance, test quality engineer, 1980-85; Rockwell International NAAO, supervisor quality assurance, 1985; Northrop B-2 Division, beginning 1985, quality assurance manager, product inspector manager, major, final inspection operations manager, vice pres, production, vice president, site operations, currently. **Honors/Awds:** NCAA, All-American, indoor track, 1975. **Business Addr:** VP, Site Operations, Northrop Corp, 8900 E Washington Blvd, Dept 2000/MI, Pico Rivera, CA 90660, (805)272-8430.

LAWSON, BRUCE B.
Telephone company executive. **Personal:** Born Mar 30, 1948, New Orleans, LA; son of Josephine Hirsch Lawson and Henry Lawson; married Ruth Charles Lawson, Nov 15, 1969; children: Rachel, Roxanne. **Educ:** Southern University, Baton Rouge, LA, BSEE, 1969; University of Chicago, Chicago, IL, 1974-76. **Career:** AT&T, Morristown, NJ, international marketing director, 1969-. **Orgs:** Chairperson, Commission for Black Ministries, Diocese of Paterson, NJ, 1988-91. **Home Addr:** 2 Thompson Way, Morris Plains, NJ 07950.

LAWSON, CASSELL AVON
Educator. **Personal:** Born Mar 29, 1937, Little Rock, AR; married Amy Davison; children: Cassell, Cassandra, Roderick, Nikki, Joi. **Educ:** Langston U, BA 1959; IN U, MSED 1970; Univ of Notre Dame, PhD 1974; IN State U, postdoctoral 1975-76. **Career:** Erie Comm Coll, vice pres cty campus; Coppin State Coll, vice pres acad affairs; Coppin State Coll, former dean of educ; Morgan State Univ, asst to vice pres dir 1976-77; IN State Univ, rockefeller fellow 1975-76; Univ of MA, asst prof & dir 1974-75; Off Campus Student Activities & Min Student Affairs Univ of Notre Dame, dir 1973-74; S Bend Urban League, exec dir 1968-70; Grand Rapids Urban Leag, dir 1956-68. **Orgs:** Pres Toxbur Es Roxbury Comm Coll 1974; staff asso Inst for Urban Studies Univ of Notre Dame 1974; postdoctoral fellow Lab Comm Psychiatry Harvard Med Sch 1972-73; intern Univ of MA 1972-73; mem Kappa Alpha Psi Frat; Phi Delta Kappa; chpsn Black Student Afrs 1973-74; chpsn S Bend Black Caucus 1973-74; NatEduc Assn 1965; Am Personnel & Guid Assn 1974-75; Am Assn for Higher Educ 1975-76; chpsn IN Counc of Urban Leag Exec 1967-68; chpsn Midwestern RepUrban Leag Exec 1968-69; Jaycees 1966-67; Area Plan Commn 1968-69; Black Ldrshp Counc. **Honors/Awds:** Nat urban leag schlrshp 1968; rockefeller fellow IN State Univ 1975-76; comm serv award Suburban Club 1967; comm serv award Lamba Kappa Mu 1968; outst yng man of yr award 1968; publ Quality Educ a view from the top notre dame jour of educ 1971; instnl power a view from the top Contemp Educ Jour 1976. **Military Serv:** USAF a/1c 1959-63. **Business Addr:** VP City Campus, Erie Community College, 121 Ellicott St, Buffalo, NY 14203.

LAWSON, CHARLES H., III
Association executive. **Personal:** Born Nov 20, 1931; married Marie; children: Kim, Linda. **Educ:** Tuskegee Inst, BS 1954, advanced study in Industrial Educ 1955, secondary Tchr Certificate Holder in IL 1974. **Career:** Manual Arts & Indus Therapy at VA Hospital, Jefferson Barracks & John Cochran Div, St Louis MO, chief 1967-; E St Louis NAACP Br, pres 1969-; IL State NAACP Conf of Br, regional dir 1971-. **Orgs:** Mem Kappa Alpha Psi Frat; Elks; past canister chmn March of Dimes in E St Louis & St Clair Co; mem Greater New Hope Bapt Ch of E St Louis; mem Reserve Officers Assn of US; Am Federation of Govt Employees; life mem Nat NAACP Recipient of Awards for Comm Serv & Leadership from E St Louis Model Cities Agy, Sigma Gamma Rho Soroity, NAACP Nat Ofc St Luke AME Ch & others. **Military Serv:** USAFR lt col. **Business Addr:** PO Box 301, East St Louis, IL 62202.

LAWSON, CHARLES J.
Airline executive. **Personal:** Born Jul 13, 1948, Jackson, GA; son of James & Eliza Lawson; married Jackie. **Educ:** Savannah State College. **Career:** Delta Airlines, cargo service agent, Atlanta, 1971-73, passenger service agent, Philadelphia, 1973-77, zone manager, New York, 1977-81, sales manager, Cleveland, 1981-87, sales manager, Detroit, 1987-90, regional manager, Atlanta, 1990-93, director sales, Atlanta, 1994-95; Civic and Promotional Affairs, dir, 1996. **Orgs:** Atlanta Convention & Visitors Bureau, board member, 1994-; Atlanta Sports Council, board member, 1994-; French American Chamber, board member, 1994-; British American Chamber, board member, 1994-; Dekalb County Chamber, board member, 1995-; Cobb County Convention & Visitors Bureau, board member, 1996-; Atlanta Touchdown Club, board member, 1996-; Atlanta Tip-Off Club, board member, 1996-. **Honors/Awds:** American Cancer Society, Crusade Award, 1983; United Negro College Fund, Distinguished Leadership, 1983; UNCF Telethon, Appreciation Award, 1984; Corp Member of the Year, ACUB, 1997. **Military Serv:** US Army, sgt, 1968-71; Distinguished Service Award, Army Commmendation. **Business Addr:** Director of Civic & Promotional Affairs, Delta Air Lines, Inc, 1201 W Peachtree St, 49th Fl, Atlanta, GA 30309, (404)881-2541.

LAWSON, DEBRA ANN
Television broadcasting executive. **Personal:** Born Oct 25, 1953, Detroit, MI; daughter of Purvis & Lois Marie Patterson; divorced; children: Christina Marie. **Educ:** Wayne State University, BFA, 1975. **Career:** WJBK-TV, part-time switchboard operator, 1972-76, typist clerk, accounting, 1976-77; administrative secretary, accounting/personnel, 1977-78, secretary to news dir, 1978-81, community affairs coordinator, 1981-86, public affairs dir, 1987-92; assistant program dir, 1993-96, public relations director, 1996-. **Orgs:** American Heart Assn of MI, affilate bd of dir, 1991-94; Gleaners Comm Food Bank, bd of dir, 1991-92; Boys & Girls Clubs of Southeastern MI, corp leadership group, 1989-92; Detroit Chapter-NAACP, 1987-; Nat Academy of TV, Arts & Sciences- MI chapter, 1979-; Greater Det Chamber of Commerce, bus contributions comm, 1988-92; MADD, advisory bd, 1991-92; Substance Abuse Prevention Coalition for Southeast MI, community advisory bd, 1990-92. **Honors/Awds:** United Negro College Fund, Distinguished Service Award, 1987; American Women in Radio & TV, Detroit Chapter, Outstanding Woman in Televison, Middle Management, 1991. **Special Achievements:** Graduate, Leadership Detroit Program, Greater Detroit Chamber of Commerce, 1989.

LAWSON, ELIZABETH HARRIS
Educator. **Personal:** marrIed Harris Lawson; children: Dr Clyde H, Carol H Cuyjet, Dr Leonard J. **Educ:** IIT Chicago, BS; Chicago State Univ, MS 1961; Univ Chicago, post grad work, Hon PhD 1974. **Career:** City of Chicago, hs & univ counselor, teacher 20 yrs; Chicago State Univ, dir intensive educ prog 1968-72, asst dir admiss & foreign student adv 1974-. **Orgs:** Mem NAFSA, Natl Assn of Women Deans Couns & Admins; Natl Guidance & Personnel Assn; mem & sec Master Plan Com for Chicago State Univ; chmn CSU's 5th Div Univ Senator 1968-74; mem Amer Assn Sch Educators; IL Guidance & Personnel Assn; mem & rsch ch Delta Kappa Gamma Intl Soc; Alpha Kappa Alpha Sor; consult SC Desegregation Ctr 1968-69; served N Cntrl Bd for accreditation of HS's 1970-80; served as IL del & co-chair White House Conf on Lib & Inf Serv Washington DC 1979; bd gov's ICOLA 1983-84; vol coord for Natl Conf of Christians & Jews 1980-84. **Military Serv:** USAF; Citation 1965.

LAWSON, HERMAN A.
State official, consultant. **Personal:** Born Dec 25, 1920, Fowler, CA; son of Frances Lawson and Herman Lawson; married Pearl Lee Johnson; children: Betty, Patricia, Gloria, Yvonne, Thomas, Tracey. **Educ:** Fresno State Univ CA, attended; Univ of the Pacific; Sacramento State Univ; Chapman Coll. **Career:** State Employment Devel Dept, minority employment rep, manpower consultant 1963-; Sacramento, councilman 2nd dist 1973-75. **Orgs:** Mem, Del Paso Heights Library Comm; Coll Awareness Bd, Amer River Coll; mem, adv to the president on programs for the disadvantaged at Amer River Coll; City Amendments Study Comm; Sacramento Businessman's Adv Coun; 99th Fighter Squad Flight Leader Frt Pilot; bd dir, Tuskegee Airmen Inc 1974-75 & 1978-80; mem, NAACP; commodore Port of Sacramento. **Honors/Awds:** Awarded Distinguished Flying Cross Air Medal, Commendation Medal, Unit Cit Medal, Award of Valor; campaign medals. **Military Serv:** USAF major 1942-63. **Business Addr:** State Manpower Planning Ofc, 800 Capitol Mall, Sacramento, CA 95814.

LAWSON, JAMES M., JR.
Clergyman. **Personal:** Born Sep 22, 1928, Uniontown, PA; married Dorothy Wood; children: John, Morris, Seth. **Educ:** Baldwin-Wallace Coll, 1952; Boston Univ, STB 1960; Vanderbilt Univ Nashville, grad work 1960. **Career:** Centenary United Meth Ch Memphis, pastor 1962-74; Nonviolent Educ So Christian Leadership Conf, dir 1960-67; Student Nonviolent Coordinating Com, advisor 1960-64; Fellowship of Reconciliation So Region, field sec 1957-69; Hislop Coll Hagpur India, chmn dept of physical educ 1953-56. **Orgs:** Mem working com of ch and soc World Coun of Ch 1966-; mem Theological Comm of Nat Com of Black Churchmen 1969-; adv com aclu Amnesty Prof 1972-; chmn Black Meth for Ch Renewal 1968-71; bd mem SCLC 1973-; bd NAACP Memphis Br 1964-74; chmn educ com NAACP Memphis 1963-65 1974-; Nat Coun 1960-66; A Phil Randolph Inst bd 1971-; West TN ACLU bd 1969-74. **Honors/Awds:** Distinguished Alumnus Award Boston 1970; Russwurm Award 1969; Elk Award 1960; civic award Mallory Knights of Memphis 1974; Man of the Yr Cath Interracial Coun Memphis 1969; Cit of the Yr Prince Hall Lodge of TN 1969; NAACP award Memphis 1965 & 1974; Outstanding Witness to Christ award AME Nat Laymen's Assn 1971; Spec award AFSCME Intl 1968. **Business Addr:** 3320 W Adams Blvd, Los Angeles, CA 90018.

LAWSON, JASON
Professional basketball player. **Personal:** Born Sep 2, 1974. **Educ:** Villanova. **Career:** Orlando Magic, center, 1998-. **Business Addr:** Professional Basketball Player, Orlando Magic, 1 Magic Pl, Orlando, FL 32801, (407)649-3200.

LAWSON, JENNIFER KAREN
Television producer. **Personal:** Born 1946; daughter of Velma Lawson and William Lawson; children: two. **Educ:** Tuskegee Institute, pre-med studies, attended; Columbia University, undergraduate degree, masters degree, filmmaking. **Career:** Student Nonviolent Coordinating Committee, special education project dir, staff member, 1964-67; Natl Council of Negro Women, 1968-69; Quitman County, MS, adult education program, director; William Greaves Productions film company, ed-

itor; The Film Fund, executive director; Brooklyn College, film instructor; Corp. for Public Broadcasting, TV program fund director, 1980-89; Public Broadcasting Service, executive vice president for programming and promotional services, 1989-95. **Honors/Awds:** One of "101 Most Influential People in Entertainment Today," Entertainment Weekly Mag, Nov 2, 1990; Honorary Doctorate, Teikyo Post University.

LAWSON, JOHN C., II
Attorney. **Personal:** Born Jul 17, 1961, Nashville, TN; son of Dorothy & James Lawson Jr. **Educ:** Oberlin College, BS, 1983; Howard University School of Law, JD, 1986. **Career:** Los Angeles County Public Defenders Office, attorney, 1987-. **Orgs:** Los Angeles Black Public Defenders Assn; John M Langston Bar Assn; ABA. **Business Addr:** Attorney, Los Angeles County Public Defenders Office, 210 W Temple St, 19th Fl, Los Angeles, CA 90012.

LAWSON, LAWYER
City official. **Personal:** Born Aug 29, 1941, Cincinnati, OH; son of Fannie M Grant Lawson (deceased) and Lawyer Lawson; married Mary Bates Lawson, Jun 25, 1989; children: Mary Adale Hall, Kenneth L, George, Robert. **Educ:** Ohio Coll of Applied Sci, Associate; Pre-Med Xavier Univ; Univ of Cincinnati. **Career:** Village of Woodlawn, mayor. **Orgs:** Trustee Hamilton Co Development Co, 1985-87; mem OH Mayors Assn 1980-; mem Natl League of Cities 1980-; bd of dirs Natl Conf of Black Mayors 1984-; pres OH Chap of Black Mayors 1985; 2nd vice president of Natl Conf of Black Mayors 1990; President, Hamilton County Municipal League. **Business Addr:** Mayor, Village of Woodlawn, 10141 Woodlawn Blvd, Cincinnati, OH 45215.

LAWSON, MARJORIE MCKENZIE
Attorney. **Personal:** Born 1912, Pittsburgh, PA; daughter of Gertrude Stiver McKenzie and T Wallace McKenzie; married Belford V Jr; children: Belford, III. **Educ:** Univ of MI, BA; Univ of MI, cert in social work; Columbia Univ Sch of Law, JD. **Career:** Lawson & Lawson Law Firm Washington, atty; DC Juvenile Ct, asso judge 1962-65. **Orgs:** Mem Pres's Commn on Equal Employment Opport 1962; pres vP Com on Crime DC 1965; UN Commn for Social Devel 1965-69; Pres's Task Force on Urban Renewal 1969; Commn on Orgn of Govt of DC 1970; dir Nat Bk of Washington DC Tax Revision Com; Fed City Counc; Mayor's Com on Econ Devel Washington Urban Leag Housing Opport Counc of Met Washington; found trust Educ Found of Nat Council of Negro Women; founder Model Inner-City Comm Orgn.

LAWSON, QUENTIN ROOSEVELT
Government official, educator. **Personal:** Born Jan 7, 1933; married Helen Louis Betts; children: Rosilend, Quentin II. **Educ:** Wv State Coll, BA; Univ MD, MEd; Morgan State Coll, MSc; Inst, NSF; Morgan State, 1958; Vassar Coll, 1960; State Univ Coll, 1962. **Career:** City of Baltimore, human devel dir present; Baltimore, former mayor; Baltimore City Schs MD State Dept of Edn, tchr unit head, unit prin, dir, dropout prevention program 1958-71; Accountability in the Inner City, cons; am psychol assn conf 1971; OH, FL, AL, cons, dropout prevention programs; Public Tech Inc, exec vice pres. **Orgs:** Pres PTA; Phi Delta Kappa; Gov Task Force State Sch Constrn; Mental Health Support System; mayor's rep Nat League of Cities; Cen MD Health Systems Agy; retail study Soc Serv Commn; John F Kennedy Inst for Handicapped Children; Med Eye Bank; United Fund CICHA; Bay Coll of MD; Dept of HEW; steering comMet Communications System Study; YMCA; pres Comm Orgn Notable Ams 1976-77; developed dropout prevention proposal 1st 10 funded by US Office of Educ; Congressional Black Caucus Foundation, exec dir, 1992-. **Home Addr:** 7902 Audubon Ct, Baltimore, MD 21207.

LAWSON, ROBERT L.
Educational administrator. **Personal:** Born Feb 24, 1950, Gallipolis, OH; children: Robert L Jr. **Educ:** Rio Grande Coll, BS 1973; Marshall Univ, MA 1978; Nova Univ, DEd expected 1988. **Career:** Gallia Acad HS, teacher 1973-76; Marshall Univ, admin asst 1977-83, dir of continuing ed 1984-. **Orgs:** Consult Continuing Ed/SUCCESS 1978-; speaker SUCCESS 1980-; mem Com Coll Council 1982-, Com Serv Roundtable 1983-; mem bd of dir Opportunity Indust Ctr1983-; chmn Affirmative Action Advisory Com 1984-; co-authur of "The Black Pursuit Study Guide"; tape published "The Power of Creative Genius"; author of "The Cutting Edge, A Study Guide for Achievers". **Honors/Awds:** Trophy for Oral Interpretation of Poetry OH Univ 1969; Outstanding Coll Athletes of Amer Rio Grande Coll 1970; Affirmative Action Plaque President's Cabinet/Marshall Univ 1984. **Home Addr:** PO Box 5524, Huntington, WV 25703. **Business Addr:** Dir of Continuing Ed, Marshall University, Huntington, WV 25701.

LAWSON, WILLIAM DANIEL
Educator. **Personal:** Born Nov 5, 1948, Alpine, AL; married Nora Davenport; children: Sonya Danette, Nicole Danielle. **Educ:** Knoxville Coll, BA 1964-68; Atlanta Univ, MA 1968-70; IA State Univ, PhD 1975-78. **Career:** AL State Univ instructor of soc 1971-74; USAF, race relations spec 1974-75; NC A&T State Univ, asst prof rural sociology 1978-79; AL State Univ, assoc prof of sociology 1979-85, chmn dept of sociology. **Orgs:** Consultant AL Center for Higher Educ 1982-83; licensure monitor Amer Sociological Assoc 1984-; polemarch Montgomery Alumni Chap Kappa Alpha Psi 1984-; pres Tuskegee Area Knoxville Coll Alumni Assoc 1984-; bd of dirs Montgomery Area Council on Aging 1985. **Honors/Awds:** Amer Sociological Assn Fellow 1977-78; Kappa Man of the Year Kappa Alpha Psi Frat Inc 1985. **Home Addr:** 142 Elm Dr, Montgomery, AL 36117. **Business Addr:** Chmn Dept of Sociology, Alabama State University, 915 S Jackson St, Montgomery, AL 36195.

LAWSON, WILLIAM EMMETT
Optometrist. **Personal:** Born Nov 24, 1922, Detroit, MI; son of Florence A Lewis-Lawson and Dr William H Lawson (deceased); divorced; children: Diane C Lawson-Taylor, William W. **Educ:** IL College of Optometry, graduated 1943; Wayne State Univ, attended 1947. **Career:** Optometric Inst & Clinic of Detroit, co-fndr/bd mem/former pres 1965-; Ferris State Coll of Optometry, clinical assoc instr 1980; private practice, doctor of optometry, currently. **Orgs:** Life mem Amer Optometric Assoc, MI Optometric Assoc charter mem Contact Lens Section; mem Metro Detroit Optometric Soc; clinical assoc Optometric Extension Prog 1963 special section on children vision; mem White House Conference on children and youth 1970; charter mem 1979, honorary mem 1986 Lafayette Clinic Adv Council; mem Alpha Phi Alpha Frat, gen convention entertainment chair, 1953; Detroit Bd of Commerce and Sports Comm; co-founder, charter mem, chmn, Debutante Ball Committee Cotillion Club 1949-50. **Honors/Awds:** Detroit Public School Comm Serv & Human Relations Awd Region 8 1968; Comm Serv Awd Wayne Co Comm Coll 1979; Awd of Merit for Disting Serv Greater Christ Baptist Church 1981, 1984; Griffith Award, Optometric Institute and Clinic of Detroit 1988; Robert Shorr Award, 1991; Michigan Optometric Society, Key Person Award; Cert Theraputic Pharmacology & Management of Ocular diseases; Honorary Clan Chief, Kpella Tribe, West Africa 1974; Certificate, Diagnostic Pharmaceutical Aids 1984; Police/Community Service Award, 1993; Amer Optometric Assn Award for 50 years of Loyal & Faithful Service, 1993; World Contact Lens Conference, Tokyo. **Military Serv:** USAF. **Business Addr:** Optometrist, 1450 Broadway, Detroit, MI 48226.

LAWSON, WILLIAM R.
Architect. **Personal:** Born Mar 8, 1943, Washington, DC; son of Charlotte Hughes Lawson and LaMont Harris Lawson; married Carol Cloud Lawson, Aug 17, 1964; children: Derrick Mark, Leslye Michelle. **Educ:** Howard University, Washington, DC, BA, architecture, 1966. **Career:** General Services Administration, Region 3, Washington, DC, architect/project manager, 1966-70, assistant commissioner for design and construction, Headquarters, 1971-87; United States Postal Service, Washington Region, Washington, DC, chief, design section, 1970-71; HTB, Inc, Washington, DC, vice president; McDevitt Street Bovis, vice president, 1987-93, assistant commissioner for planning, PBS; ARA for PBS, NCR, GSA, 1993-. **Orgs:** Member, Committee on Public Architecture, American Institute of Architects, 1971-; member, American Institute of Architects, DC Chapter, 1987-; member, National Trust for Historic Preservation, 1987-; member, American Consulting Engineers Council, 1988-; member, Medals and Awards Committee, juror, Air Force Design Awards Program, Society of American Military Engineers, 1988-; past president, Society for Marketing Professional Services, DC Chapter, 1988-89; member, National Association of Industrial and Office Parks, 1988-; member, Urban Land Institute, 1988-; member, Consultative Council, National Institute of Building Sciences, 1990-; member, Greater Washington Board of Trade, 1988-; past member, Executive Committee, Leukemia Society of America,National Capitol Area Chapter, 1988. **Honors/Awds:** Award for Exemplary Leadership, 1982, Outstanding Performance Certificates, 1971-87, General Services Administration; Architect of the Year, DC Council of Engineers and Architects, 1972; Alpha R Chi Medal, 1966, Gold Medal for Design, 1966, Howard University. **Home Addr:** 11005 Saffold Way, Reston, VA 22090. **Business Addr:** Asst Regional Admin, PBS, GSA-NCR, 7th & D Svs SW, Washington, DC 20407.

LAWSON ROBY, KIMBERLA
Author. **Personal:** Born May 3, 1965, Rockford, IL; daughter of Willie & Arletha Stapleton; married Will M Roby, Jr, Sep 14, 1990. **Educ:** Rock Valley College, Business Associate, 1988; Cardinal Stritch Univ, BBA, 1993. **Career:** Sundstrand Corp, asst repair admin, 1985-89; State of IL, welfare caseworker, 1989-91; Greenlee Textron, human resources admin, 1991-93; First Financial Bank, customer svc rep for loans, 1993-94; City of Rockford, finance analyst for housing, 1994-96; author/novelist, 1996-. **Orgs:** Womanspace, advisory bd, 1997-. **Special Achievements:** Published 2 novels: "Behind Closed Doors," 1997; "Here and Now," 1998 expected. **Business Addr:** Author/Publisher, Lenox Press, PO Box 17016, Rockford, IL 61110-7016, (815)965-7461.

LAWSON-THOMAS, ALTHEA SHANNON
Educator. **Personal:** Born Jan 16, 1953, Ft Gaines, GA; married Eddie Walden Thomas; children: Shadrin, Jasil. **Educ:** Hampton Univ, BA 1973; Univ of TN, MS 1975; Attended, Troy State Univ 1983-84. **Career:** Wallace State Comm Coll, counselor/instructor 1975-82, instructor 1982-. **Orgs:** Mem AL Personnel & Guidance Assoc 1975-82; pres Young Women's Serv Club 1977-79; chair Henry Co Bd of Educ Bi-racial Comm 1978-80; mem Natl Council of Negro Women 1979-; Delta Sigma Theta Sor Inc, president, Dothan Alumnae Chapter, 1992-; sec Wallace Coll Educ Assoc 1986-88. **Business Addr:** Instructor, Wallace College, Rte 6, Box 62, Dothan, AL 36303.

LAWSTON, MARJORIE GRAY
Clergyman. **Personal:** Born Aug 26, 1928, Weakley Co Martin, TN; married Sylvester Ralph Gray; children: Michael. **Educ:** Univ of TN at Martin, BS 1975. **Career:** Burdette Chapel United Meth Ch Memphis, pastor 1980-; Andrews United Meth Ch Memphis, pastor 1978-79; Union City Sch TN, tchr 1978-79; Key's Chapel Circuit Lexington TN, pastor 1975-78; Beaver Elem Schl Lexington TN, tchr 1975-78. **Orgs:** Sem Schlrshp Bd of Global Ministries United Meth Ch New York City 1979-80. **Business Addr:** United Meth Church, 4953 Malone Rd, Memphis, TN 38118.

LAWTON, MATTHEW, III
Professional baseball player. **Personal:** Born Nov 3, 1971, Gulfport, MS. **Educ:** Gulf Coast Community College. **Career:** Minnesota Twins, outfielder, 1995-. **Business Addr:** Professional Baseball Player, Minnesota Twins, 501 Chicago Ave S, Minneapolis, MN 55415, (612)375-1366.

LAWYER, CYRUS J., III
Educator. **Personal:** Born Sep 21, 1943, Vicksburg, MS; married Vivian Moore; children: Lenaye Lynne, Sonya Denise. **Educ:** Tougaloo Clge, BS 1966; Bowling Green Univ, MS 1969; Univ Toledo, PhD 1974. **Career:** SBowling Green Univ, grad asst & tchr asst 1967-69; Univ Toledo, 1969-71; Univ Toledo, admin intern 1971-72, asst dean adj instr 1972-73, asst dean & housing dir 1973-75, sr prog assoc Inst for Srvs to Educ. **Orgs:** Mem Amer Chem Soc; Orgn Black Scientists; Amer Assc Univ Profs; Phi Delta Kappa; Assc Clge & Univ Housing Officers; mem Alpha Phi Alpha Frat; NAACP. **Honors/Awds:** Outstanding Young Men Amer 1975. **Business Addr:** 2001 S St NW, Washington, DC 20009.

LAWYER, VIVIAN
Educational coordinator. **Personal:** Born Jan 6, 1946, Cleveland; married Cyrus J Lawyer III; children: Lenaye Lynne, Sonya Alyse. **Educ:** Bowling Green State Univ, BS 1967; Green State Univ, MEd 1968. **Career:** Natl Council Teachres Eng, coord human resources 1967-68; OH Assn Women Deans & Counselors 1968-; Bowling Green Sate Univ, asst dean students 1968-72. **Orgs:** OH Affirmative Action Officers Assc 1973-; Natl Assc Womens Deans, Admin & Cnslrs 1972-; Natl Council Negro Women 1972-; Delta Sigma Theta Sor Toledo Alumnae 1973-; bd trustees Toledo YWCA 1974-77; Lucas Ct Health Srv Comm NW OH Health Planning Assc 1971-72. **Honors/Awds:** Dist Srv to Univ Award BGSU 1967; Delta Sigma Theta Midwest Region's Adv Award 1972. **Business Addr:** Bowling Green State Univ, 231 Administration Bldg, 901 Rye Beach Road, Huron, OH 44839.

LAY, CLORIUS L.
Attorney. **Personal:** Born Sep 1, 1940, Mound Bayou, MS; son of Laddel & Arzzie Lay; divorced; children: Rosmond M, Cloe R. **Educ:** Indiana Univ, BS, 1966; Univ of Chicago; Brunel Univ, England, 1973; Valparaiso Univ, JD, 1974; John M Marshall Graduate School of Law; Indiana Continuing Legal Education Forum's Program, 1995; Harvard Univ, John F Kennedy School of Government, 1996. **Career:** Inland Steel Co, corporate internal auditor and procedure designer; New Careers, project dir, 1968-69; East Chicago Hts Comm Ctr, exec dir, 1969; Black Ctr for Strategy, vp, 1969-71; Univ National Bank, vp, 1971-72; Northwest Sickle Cell Foundation, exec dir, 1972-75; Clorius L Lay, attorney/owner, 1975-. **Orgs:** National Alliance of Black School Educators; Valparaiso Univ School of Law, recruiter; Northwest Indiana Alliance of Black School Educators; Lake County Med Ctr, bd mem; Indiana School Bd Assn, liaison; Northwest Sickle Cell Foundation, honorary bd mem; Urban League of Northwest Indiana Inc, sustaining mem; NAACP, life mem; Indiana Univ Northwest Medical School Scholarship Committee; Gary City Council, councilman-at-large, 1996-. **Honors/Awds:** Woodrow Wilson Fellowship Foundation, National Fellow, 1972-74; Council for Legal Education Opportunity, Cleo Appointee, 1973; American Pool Checkers Assn, US Top Master; Northwest Indiana Sickle Cell Foundation Inc, Service Award; Kiwanis International, Certificate of Appreciation; Program of Senior Executives in State & Local Government, Cambridge MA. **Military Serv:** USAF, sgt, 1958-62. **Home Phone:** (219)882-5243. **Business Addr:** Attorney, Clorius L Lay, 1277 Broadway, PO Box M886, Gary, IN 46401, (219)883-8538.

LAYMON, HEATHER R.
Banker. **Personal:** Born Nov 10, 1948; daughter of Beryl O Harris Sealy and Ellis W Sealy; married John Laymon, Dec 22, 1973; children: Shawn M Laymon, Nasya H Laymon. **Educ:** Northeastern Univ, MA, BA, 1968-72; Natl School of Savings

Banking, CT, 1978-80; Cambridge Coll, MA, MED, 1981-83. **Career:** Suffolk Franklin Savings Bank, Boston, MA, mgr, 1972-80; Mutual Bank for Savings, Boston, MA, asst treasurer, 1980-82; Bank of Boston, Boston, MA, asst vice pres, 1982-87; Boston Bank of Commerce, Boston, MA, vice pres, 1987-. **Orgs:** Mem, Boston Bankers Urban Forum, 1980-; trustee, Cambridge YWCA, 1983-87; pres, Boston & Vicinity Club of the Natl Assn of Negro Business & Professional Women, 1986-89; mem, Plan Giving Comm, Andover Newton Theological Seminary, 1988-; mem 1988-, treasurer 1990-91, Roxbury Multi Serv Center; member, Massachusetts Mortgage Bankers Assn, 1990-; member, Massachusetts Young Mortage Bankers Assn, 1990-. **Honors/Awds:** Pres Award, Natl Assn of Negro Business & Professional Women, 1988; Prof Award, Women Serv Club of Boston, 1988, Black Achiever's Award, YMCA, 1981. **Business Addr:** Vice Pres, Dir of Business Devel, Boston Bank of Commerce, 133 Federal St, Boston, MA 02110.

LAYTON, BENJAMIN THOMAS
Army officer (retired). **Personal:** Born Dec 24, 1917, Hanover, VA; son of Mary Amanda Sully Layton and William Brown Layton; married Marguerite Charron, Nov 1, 1958; children: Isabelle Marie Solange, Catherine Marguerite. **Educ:** Virginia Union Univ, BSCh, 1939; Howard Univ, 1940-41; Univ of Chicago, 1941. **Career:** US Army, private to lt colonel, 1941-63; US Department of Agriculture, criminal investigator, 1966-85. **Orgs:** NAACP, Richmond Chapter; Boy Scouts of America; Amer Federation of Musicians; National Red Cross; Reserve Officers Assn, Richmond Chapter; Sons of King Solomon, Lodge 358; Omega Psi Phi Fraternity; Omega Psi Phi Fraternity, life mem; The Smithsonian Assoc, natl mem; Univ of Chicago Alumni Assn; Assn of Former Intelligence Officers, life mem; Reserve Officers Assn of the United States, life mem; Natl Council of Sr Citizens, Inc, life mem; Veterans of Foreign Wars, life mem; Natl Assn of Retired Federal Employees, life mem; Assn of the US Army, life mem; Freedomways, life mem; Capital District Kiwanis Foundation Inc, life mem; Natl Intelligence & Counterintelligence Assn, life mem; Natl Military Intelligence Assn, life mem; Natl Congress of Amer Indians, life mem; Natl Museum of Women in the Arts, charter mem; numerous others. **Military Serv:** US Army, lt col, 1941-63; Bronze Star. **Home Addr:** 10700 Brunswick Ave, Kensington, MD 20895, (301)933-5766.

LAYTON, WILLIAM W.
Lecturer. **Personal:** Born Jul 17, 1915, Hanover, VA; son of Mary Amanda Sully and William Brown Layton (both deceased); married Phoebe Anderson; children: Andree, Mary, Serena. **Educ:** Lincoln Univ, grad 1937; Fisk Univ, MI State Univ, post-grad study. **Career:** Columbus Urban League, indus relations dir 1943-51; Greater Muskegon Urban League, exec dir 1951-59; Lansing Fair Employment Practices Commn, reg dir 1959-64; MI OEO, assoc dir 1965; US Dept Agri, dir contract compliance 1965-71; EEO Bd Govs Fed Reserve System, dir 1971-78 (retired); Americana Originals, proprietor, lecturer, exhibitor, retail sales of framed original letters & documents. **Orgs:** Collector original abolitionist & civil war documents over 1500 items; collection on microfilm at Natl Archives; mem Muskegon Bd Social Welfare 1955-59; Mayor's Human Relations Comm 1962-64; founder 1st vice pres Greater Lansing Urban League 1964-65; pres Lansing Torch Club 1964; pres Muskegon Co Council Chs 1955; chap chmn Washington NAIRO 1969; mem Sigma Pi Phi; mem bd chmn Tri County VA 1984-86; mem bd Grafton School 1984-; bd mem, US Capitol Historical Society 1987-; bd mem, Shenandoah Arts Council 1987-. **Honors/Awds:** Comm Serv Citation Lansing 1965; lectr & exhibitor including TV presentations US Abolitionist Movement & Mil Serv of Blacks in the Civil War; Awd of Merit Natl Afro-Amer Museum & Cultural Center 1982; Poet-Author of A Paul Robeson Retrospective and My Bridge; Literature Award Shenandoah Arts Council, 1992; President's Community Svc Awd, Shenandoah University, 1994. **Special Achievements:** Author: Layton Looks at Life, Book of Essays on Living in America, 1996. **Business Addr:** Proprietor, American Originals, 1311 Delaware Ave SW, Washington, DC 20024.

LAZARD, BETTY
Banking executive. **Career:** WR Lazard, vice chairperson, currently. **Special Achievements:** Company ranked #3 on the Black Enterprise Investment Banking list, 1995. **Business Addr:** Vice Chairperson, WR Lazard, 14 Wall St, New York, NY 10005, (212)406-2700.

LEA, JEANNE EVANS
Educational administrator. **Personal:** Born Jul 2, 1931, Washington, DC; daughter of Edna Jenkins Evans and John Evans; divorced; children: Anne Richele Wharton, Jewa Maria. **Educ:** Miner Teachers College, BS 1953; Trinity College, MAT 1970; Virginia Tech, EdD 1975. **Career:** Federal City College, curriculum specialist 1969-71, associate prof 1971-76, acting dean, continuing ed 1976-78; University of DC, prof 1976-, vice pres student affairs 1984-88; Edward Waters College, Academic Affairs, dean 1989-. **Orgs:** President Adult Ed Assn Metropolitan Wash 1976-77; co-founder Wash Women's Forum 1977; member Network on Female Offenders, Women's Bureau 1979-; vice president, Region II Amer Assn for Adult/Cont Ed 1983-85; board member Met Wash Assn for Adult/Cont Ed 1983-85; bd mem/mem Wash Correctional Fdn; Potomac Chapter, LINKS, Inc 1984. **Honors/Awds:** Outstanding Young Educators DC Jaycees 1968; Outstanding Educator Black Men's Salute to Black Women 1977; Co-host, Knowledge Series NBC-TV "Man to Woman" 1977 5 28 min segments 1977; "Continuing Ed for Women" 1981. **Business Addr:** Edward Waters College, 1658 Kings Rd, Jacksonville, FL 32209.

LEACE, DONAL RICHARD
Educator. **Personal:** Born May 6, 1939, Huntington, WV; married Jakki Hazel Browner. **Educ:** Howard Univ, BFA 1966; George Washington Univ, MFA 1978; Georgetown Univ, MA, 1984. **Career:** The Howard Univ Players, pres 1965-66; Roanoke VA Total Action Against Poverty, dram/music consult 1966-67; Duke Ellington School of the Arts, Theatre Department, chair, 1979-86, teacher, Theatre Department, chair, 1990-; Georgetown Univ, adjunct faculty, 1992-. **Orgs:** Mem Amer Fed of Music 161-710 1960-; mem Amer Fed of TV & Radio Artists 1979-; bd dir Tokama Theatre WA DC 1983-85. **Honors/Awds:** Presidential Scholars Program Cert of Excellence, Presidential Scholars Prog Commission 1983; judge Helen Hayse Awds The Washington Theatre Awds Soc 1986-88; solo recording artists Atlantic Records Co, Gateway Records, Franc Records Co. **Special Achievements:** Conducted an Arts Assessment of the Federated Union of Black Arts Academy, Johannesburg, South Africa, 1991; proposed for a Fulbright Teacher Exchange, 1994-95; Recording, Leace on Life, JBL Records. **Business Addr:** Chair, Teacher, Duke Ellington School of Arts, Theatre Department, 3500 R St NW, Washington, DC 20007.

LEACOCK, FERDINAND S.
Physician. **Personal:** Born Aug 8, 1934, New York, NY; married; children: 4. **Educ:** Columbia Coll, BA 1956; Howard Medical Coll, MD 1960. **Career:** San Joaquin Hosp, rotating internship 1961; Ft Howard VA Hosp, residency 1961-65; Univ of MD Hosp, thoracic surgery residency 1967-69; UCLA Sch of Med, asst prof of surgery 1972-76; Martin Luther King Jr Gen Hosp, chief div thoracic & cardiovascular surgery 1973-74; Charles R Drew Postgrad Med Sch, asst prof of surgery 1972-76, v chmn dept of surgery 1974-75; CMA/CHA Educ Patient Care Audit Workshop Prog 1974-76; private practice, thoracic & cardiovascular surgery 1975-; Bon Secours Hosp, chief thoracic & cardiovascular surg 1987-; MD Gen Hosp, chief thoracic surg 1987-92. **Orgs:** Mem Univ of MD Surgical Soc, Baltimore City Medical Soc, Amer Coll of Surgeons, Amer Coll of Chest Physicians, The Soc of Thoracic surgeons, The Baltimore Acad of Surgery. **Honors/Awds:** 3 publications; 1 abstract. **Military Serv:** AUS 2 yrs. **Business Addr:** Chairman, Department of Surgery, Liberty Medical Center, 2600 Liberty Heights Ave, Baltimore, MD 21215.

LEACOCK, STEPHEN JEROME
Educator. **Personal:** Born Oct 28, 1943; married Phyllis Otway; children: Natasha, Talitha, Baron. **Educ:** CNAA, BA 1970; Garnett Coll, grad cert educ 1971; Council for Natl Acad Awds London, MA 1971; King's Coll, LLM 1971; Barrister Middle Temple 1972. **Career:** City Univ, visting lecturer 1971-72; SW London Coll, 1971-72; Hugh Wooding Law Sch, assoc tutor 1974; Coll of Law DePaul Univ prof law. **Orgs:** American Society of International Law. **Honors/Awds:** Publications include "Public Utility Regulation in a Developing Country"; "Lawyer of the Americas"; "Fundamental Breach of Contract & Exemption Clauses in the Commonwealth Caribbean"; Anglo-Amer Law Review; "Essentials of Investor Protection in Commonwealth Caribbean & US"; honorary member, British Inst of Securities Laws. **Business Addr:** Professor of Law, DePaul University Law School, 25 E Jackson Blvd, Chicago, IL 60604.

LEAGUE, CHERYL PERRY
Director of equal opportunity. **Personal:** Born Nov 29, 1945, New York, NY; daughter of Alberta Johnson and Robert Johnson; children: Anthony, Robeson, Assata. **Educ:** Merritt Coll, Oak, CA, AS, 1977; San Francisco State Univ, BA, 1979; Candidate for Masters at USF in Human Resources and Organization Development. **Career:** Legal Aid Soc, Alameda County, CA, contract compliance officer, beginning in 1975; US Dept of Commerce, Minority Business Development Agency, minority business program specialist, beginning in 1980; Management Professional Services, Oakland, CA, principle partner, beginning in 1982; Port of Oakland, CA, contract compliance officer, beginning in 1983, equal opportunity manager, beginning in 1986; dir of equal opportunity, 1991, founding mem of California Affirmative Action Council. **Orgs:** Natl Assn for the Advancement of Colored People; scy/treas natl bdm National Forum of Black Public Admin; California Assn of Affirmative Action Officers; pres, Bay Area Contract Compliance Officers Assn; bd mem, Bay Area Black United Fund; women's advisory comm mem, Oakland Police Dept; bd mem, Northern CA Minority Bus Opportunity Comm; steering comm mem, CA Bus Council Organization for Equal Opportunity. **Honors/Awds:** Minority Advocate of the Year Award, US Dept of Commerce, San Francisco, CA, 1988; Special Recognition Award for the Port of Oakland for outstanding contribution to the minority business community, Minority Business Devel Agency, San Francisco, CA, 1988; Outstanding Achievement Award on Behalf of Minority Entrepreneurs, Minority Enterprise Devel Week Committee, Oakland, CA, 1988; Community Service Award for outstanding service to the city of Oakland and for valuable service to the profession of public admin, Oakland/San Francisco Bay Area Chapter of the Natl Forum for Black Public Admin, 1989. **Business Addr:** Director of Equal Opportunity, Port of Oakland, 530 Water St, Oakland, CA 94604.

LEAK, LEE VIRN
Research scientist, educator. **Personal:** Born Jul 22, 1932, Chesterfield, SC; son of Lucille Elizabeth Moore Leak and Robert Lincoln Leak; married Eleanor C Merrick; children: Alice Elizabeth, Lee Virn Jr. **Educ:** SC State Coll, BS 1954; MI State U, MS 1959, PhD 1962. **Career:** MI State Univ, teaching asst cytology electron microscopist div biol sci, res assoc biol sci 1961, asst prof biol sci 1962; Brookhaven Natl Lab, rsch asst dept biol 1960, collabor biol 1968; Harvard Med School MA Gen Hosp, rsch fellow surgery 1962-64, asst surgery 1964, asst biol, surgery 1965, instr anatomy 1965-67; MA Gen Hosp, Shriners Burns Inst, dir lab biol structure 1967-70; Harvard Med School, asst prof anatomy 1968-70, prof, chmn anatomy, 1971-81; Howard University, dir, cellular & molecular biology, 1985-90, founder, dir, Ernest E Just Laboratory of Cellular Biology, 1972-, prof, Graduate School of Arts & Sciences, 1976-, res prof 1983-. **Orgs:** Sr investigator NIH 1982; vice pres Howard Univ Chap Sigma Xi 1974-75; exec comm Assn of Anatomy Chmn 1976-78; cancer biol & diagnosis bd sci couns Natl Cancer Inst NIH 1979-82; exec comm Amer Assn of Anatomists 1980-84; panel on basic biomed sci Natl Res Cncl Natl Acad of Sci 1980-85; adv bd lung diseases Natl Heart Lung & Blood Inst NIH 1982-86; AmerAssn of Anatomists, Amer Physiol Sci, Amer Soc for Cell Biol, Amer Soc of Zoologists, Intl Soc of Lymphology, Marine Biol Lab, NYAS, NY Soc for Electron Microscopy, Tissue Culture Assn, Microcirculatory Soc Inc; ed bd Jrnl of Microvascular Rsch 1975-, Jrnl of Microcirculation 1980-; exec com NA Soc Lymphology; member, research committee, American Heart Assn, Nation Capitol Affiliation, 1989-91. **Honors/Awds:** Cert, 1965, Medal, 1968, Scientific Exhibit 23rd Annual Meeting of the Electron Microscopy Soc of Am; Outstanding Fac Res Awd Howard Univ 1976; Outstanding Faculty Awd Grad School of Arts & Sci Howard Univ 1979-80; Outstanding Faculty Res Awd Howard Univ, 1981; res grant support, Lymphatic Capillaries During Early Inflammation NIAID 1966-74, Role of the Lymphatic System in Health & in Inflammation NIAID 1979-84, A Comparative Ultrastructural & Cytochem Study of Vertebrate Heart Tissue Amer Heart Assn 1967-70, Lymphatic Capillaries During Early Inflammation NIH Natl Heart Lung &Blood Inst 1970-75, Ontogeny, Ultrastructure & Function in the Lymphatic Syst Natl Heart Lung & Blood Inst NIH 1976-86; training grant support, Grad Training in the Anatomical Sci Natl Inst of Gen Med Sci Dept of Anatomy Coll of Med 1974-79, Multi-Disciplinary Biomed Rsch Training Natl Inst of Gen Med Sci Dept of Anatomy & Microbiology Coll of Med 1979-84; Adelle Melbourne Award, American Med Assn 1989; Research Grant, Control of Cell Mobility, National Science Foundation, 1990-93; Research Grant, Lymphatic Endothelium In Vitro, Natl Inst Gen Med Sci, NIH, 1994-98. **Special Achievements:** Wrote chapters: Handbuch der Allgemeine Pathologie, 1972; Inflammatory Process, 1974; Respiratory Defense Mechanisms, 1977; Blood Vessels and Lymphatics in Organ Systems, 1984; The Lungs, Scientific Foundations, 1st ed, 1991, 2nd ed, 1997. **Military Serv:** AUS 1st lt 1954-56. **Business Addr:** Research Professor, Howard University, College of Medicine, Anatomy Dept, 520 W St NW, Washington, DC 20059.

LEAKE, WILLIE MAE JAMES
Mortician. **Personal:** Born Mar 13, 1932, Philadelphia, PA; daughter of Eula Jones (deceased) and Joseph Jones (deceased); married Willie Ralph Leake. **Educ:** Ekels Coll of Mortuary Science; Univ of Pittsburgh. **Career:** City Treasurer, City of Chester 1982; City Council, City of Chester 1983; Mayor City of Chester 1986-91; W M James Leake Funeral Home, currently. **Orgs:** Nat'l Funeral Dir & Embalmers Assoc; member, NAACP. **Honors/Awds:** Delaware Cnty Womens Commission, Distinguished Leadership Awd 1986; Chester Scholarship Fund, Comm Service Awd 1983. **Home Addr:** 10th & Pusey St, Chester, PA 19013. **Business Addr:** W M James Leake Funeral Home, NE Corner of 10th & Pusey Sts, Chester, PA 19013.

LEAPHART, ELDRIDGE
Engineer. **Personal:** Born Sep 2, 1927, Sims, NC; married Audra Lane; children: Eldridge, Jr, Eldon Gerrald. **Educ:** Howard U, BS 1953; OH State U, 1964; UCLA, 1967; Air U, 1965, 1966, 1973. **Career:** TN Valley Authority, electrical engr 1953-55; Air Force Logistics Command 1955-58; Air Force Systems Command, electronics engr 1958-. **Orgs:** Mem Assn Old Crows 1962-; treas Kittyhawk Toastmasters Club 1108-40 1974-; cmn, supr com Bethel Bapt Fed Credit Union 1972-; supr Bethel Bapt Ch Sch 1969-70. **Honors/Awds:** Air Force Systems Command Certificate Merit Award 1974. **Military Serv:** USN 1945-47; USAR 2nd lt 1953-55. **Business Addr:** Air Force Avionics Lab, Wright Patterson AFB, Dayton, OH 45433.

LEATHERWOOD, LARRY LEE
State transportation official. **Personal:** Born Sep 7, 1939, Peoria, IL; son of Helen Moody Brown and Larry Leatherwood; married Martha; children: Jeffrey, Stacy. **Educ:** Kellogg Comm Coll, AA 1967; Western MI Univ, BS 1969, Masters of Publ Admin 1982; Harvard University, Boston, Senior Executive Fellow 1985. **Career:** Battle Creek Area Urban League, exec dir 1970-73; MI Dept of Commerce, spec asst 1973-77; MI State Minority Bus Office, dir 1977-83; MI Dept of Transportation, liaison officer 1983-85, asst deputy dir for admin 1985-92. **Orgs:** Vice chmn Lansing Urban League 1982-83; chmn Minority Tech Council of MI 1983-; vice chmn State Advisory Council for Voc Ed; mem Conf of Minority Trans Officials, Amer Public Works Assoc; President, Lansing YMCA 1991-92; President YMCA, 1992-93; Midwest Representative, Harvard Black Alumni Assoc 1989-; executive director, Citizens Council for Michigan Public University. **Honors/Awds:** Man of the Year Natl Assn of Black Women Entrepreneur 1980; Presidential Small Business Recognition 1980; MI Small Business Advocate 1985; Wall of Distinction Selected Western Michigan Univ and Alumni Assn 1986; Recognition by the MI Council of NAACP Branches for Contributions to Black Economic Development 1986. Public Servant of the Year, Capitol Chapter, ASPA 1990-; Partner In Community Service Award, Black Caucus Foundation of MI, Inc. **Military Serv:** USAF sgt 4 yrs. **Business Addr:** Asst Deputy Dir, Michigan Dept of Transport, PO Box 30050, 425 W Ottawa, Lansing, MI 48909.

LEATHERWOOD, ROBERT P.
Advertising executive. **Personal:** Born Jun 10, 1920, Forrest City, AR; married Pauline; children: 1 Stepdaughter. **Educ:** Fisk Univ Nashville, BA 1942; Wayne State Univ Detroit, marketing courses 1957-58. **Career:** MI Chronicl Pub Co Detroit, advertising exec 1945-59; Seymour Leatherwood Cleveland Detroit 1959-64; aide ot Congressman Diggs; Leatherwood Co, 1964-. **Orgs:** Founder Detroit Chapter Nat Asso Market Dev; consult Negro Manufacturers Dist Br Asso Detroit; consult MI State Senator Arthur Cartwight 1975. **Honors/Awds:** Pub numerous articles; NAMD honor 1974. **Business Addr:** PO Box 608, Detroit, MI 48206.

LEAVELL, ALLEN
Basketball player. **Personal:** Born May 27, 1957, Muncie, IN. **Educ:** Okla City Univ, 1975-79. **Career:** Houston Rockets, 1979-89; Tulsa Fast Breakers, 1989-. **Honors/Awds:** Chosen to 2nd All-Rookie team; 1st team by Bsktbl Digest.

LEAVELL, DOROTHY R.
Publisher, editor. **Personal:** Born Oct 23, 1944, Pine Bluff, AR; married Balm L Leavell Jr (died 1968); children: Antonio, Genice. **Educ:** Roosevelt Univ IL, 1962. **Career:** Crusader Newspaper, publisher, currently; Holy Name of Mary Sch Bd, pres. **Orgs:** Natl Newspaper Publishers Assn, head, 1995-97; Past bd dir, mem, Washington Park YMCA, 1974; past asst sec, Natl Newspaper Pub Assn, 1976; sec, PUSH; comm div bd mem, Directions Schlshp Found. **Honors/Awds:** YMCA Aw; PUSH Aw; Holy Name of Mary Awd. **Business Addr:** Editor/Publisher, Chicago Crusader, 6429 S King Dr, Chicago, IL 60637, (312)752-2500.

LEAVELL, WALTER F.
Educator. **Personal:** Born May 19, 1934; married Vivian; children: Pierce, Pierre. **Educ:** Univ of Cincinnati College of Pharmacy, BS 1957; Meharry Medical Coll, MD 1964; Univ of Cincinnati Coll of Law, Scholar-in-Residence 1981. **Career:** Cincinnati General Hosp, assoc chief of staff 1977-79, assoc administrator for professional affairs 1977-79; SUNY Upstate Medical Ctr Coll of Medicine, assoc dean 1971-75, vice dean and tenured assoc prof of medicine 1975-82; Meharry Medical Coll, dean school of medicine and dir medical affairs Hubbard Hosp 1982-. **Orgs:** Consultant AAMC on Minority Affairs 1972-; mem AAMC/GSA Steering Comm 1974-; natl chairperson AAMC/GSA Minority Affairs Section 1976-; consultant EDUCOM 1979-; mem Hubbard Hospital Attending Staff 1982-; mem Council of Deans 1982-; mem adv bd Natl Fund for Medical Educ 1983-; mem AAMC Ad Hoc MCAT Review Comm 1985-; mem AAMC Spring Meeting Program Comm 1985-; mem LCME Accreditation Review Team Council of Free Standing Medical Schools 1985-; mem Amer, Natl, Cincinnati Medical Assocs; mem Natl Assoc of Medical Minority Educators; mem Amer Assoc of Medical Colleges. **Honors/Awds:** AAMC Service Recognition Awd 1979; NAMME Presidential Citation 1985. **Military Serv:** USAF major. **Business Addr:** President, Charles R. Drew University, 1621 E 120th St, Los Angeles, CA 90059.

LEBER, MARIANN C.
Nursing administrator. **Personal:** Born Oct 1, 1921, Hamtramck, MI; divorced. **Educ:** Wayne State U, BS 1951; Harlem Sch of Nursing NYC, grad 1943. **Career:** Detroit Gen Hosp, gen staff nrse 1944; hd hosp nrse 1949; nrsng supr 1955; asst dir of nrses 1963; Detroit Gen Hosp, dir of nurses; Wayne St U Coll Nrsng, adj instr 1970. **Orgs:** Advsry Com Wayne Co Comm Coll Dept Nrsng; vol tutrng serv nrsng schl grads; Advis Com Highland Park Comm Coll Dept of Nurs. **Honors/Awds:** Elected to Hamtramck Hall of Hon 1977. **Business Addr:** Detroit Gen Hosp, 1326 St Antoine, Detroit, MI 48226.

LEBLANC, MICHAEL J.
Human resources manager. **Personal:** Born Feb 16, 1950, New Orleans, LA; son of Genevieve LeBlanc and Andrew LeBlanc; divorced; children: Andrew, Tashelle. **Educ:** Duke University, BA, 1971; University of Pittsburgh, MBA, 1972; Columbia University, 1987. **Career:** Polaroid Corp, financial analyst, sr int's finance mgr, national operations mgr of distribution, national operations mgr of customer service, national sales mgr; Entertainment Imaging, assistant to the president, corporate vice pres, currently. **Orgs:** Omega Psi Phi, 1989-; Polaroid Corp, chairman, education sub-committee, 1987-91; Board of Bar Overseers, 1992-; United Way Board Member, chair-public relations committee, 1992-; Inner City Board of Directors, 1990-; HR Roundtable, 1991-; B U Policy Inst, 1991; Roxbury Community College, board member, 1992-; Maynard School Mentor Program, 1991-; U-Mass Advisory Board, 1991-. **Honors/Awds:** National Achievement, Finalist, 1967; Duke University, Scholarship, 1967-71; University of Pittsburgh, Fellowship, 1972; YMCA, Black Achievers Award, 1985. **Business Addr:** Corporate Vice Pres, Human Resources, Polaroid Corp., 549 Technology Sq, 3, Cambridge, MA 02139, (617)577-2543.

LECESNE, TERREL M.
Educational administrator. **Personal:** Born Apr 13, 1939, New Orleans; married Gale H; children: Terrel, Jr, Haydel. **Educ:** Xavier U, BA 1961; Eastern MI U, MA 1967, EdS 1973; University of Michigan, PhD, 1979. **Career:** City of Inkster, MI, former mayor, counclmn; teacher, 1961-66; jr high school counselor, 1966-68; Willow Run/Romulas Schools, elem principal, 1968-79; Romulus Schools, assistant supt, 1979-95; Inkster Schools, supt, 1995-. **Orgs:** Pres Romulus Assn of Sch Bldg Adminstrs; past pres Inkster Jaycees; Dearborn-Inkster Human Relat Counc. **Honors/Awds:** Named outst yng man of yr Inkster Jaycees 1970. **Business Addr:** Supt, Inkster Public Schools, 3250 Middlebelt, Inkster, MI 48141.

LECHEBO, SEMIE
Educational administrator. **Personal:** Born Apr 5, 1935, Addis Ababa, Ethiopia; married Sandra Nettles-Lechebo; children: Monique Thomas, Shena Thomas, Meskeram. **Educ:** Univ of WI, BS 1964, MS 1967; SUNY at Albany, EdS 1975, EdD 1975; Harvard Univ, Higher Educ Mgmt diploma summer 1982. **Career:** Haile Selassie I Day School (Addis Ababa), School admin 1956-60; Ministry of Educ (Addis Ababa), dir 1964-66; Milwaukee Public School, teacher 1967-68; Jimma Teacher Training, dir 1968-69; College of Teacher Educ (Addis Ababa), vice principal 1969-71; Comm Agency in Albany, rsch fellowship 1975; NY State Educ Dept, rsch assoc 1976-77; SUNY at Albany, coord of tutorial prog 1976; SUNY Coll at Brockport, coord of academic affairs; Baden Street Settlement, Inc, dir of education development, currently. **Orgs:** Consultant NY Educ Dept 1975-76, Rochester City School Dist 1978-82; mentoring doctoral students SUNY Albany, Buffalo, Brockport 1976-86; mem Faculty Senate SUNY Brockport 1980-86; mem Coll Affirmative Action Bd SUNY Brockport 1982-83; chair Rochester Inst of Tech Adv Bd on Minority and Female Recruitment 1984-86; chair, Education Committee, County of Monroe Human Relations Commn 1985-; supervising interns SUNY Brockport 1986; chair mentoring programs Urban League of Rochester 1986; mem Coll Academic Council SUNY Brockport 1986-; member, Youth Service Quality Council, 1996-; member, Black Leadership Commission on AIDS of Rochester, 1996-. **Honors/Awds:** UNESCO Fellowship 1967-68; AFGRAD Fellowship 1971-75; Outstanding Award for Service 1984-85; Black Scholars Sponsor Award, Urban League of Rochester, 1985; Naturalized United States Citizen 1985; Outstanding Professional Service Award, SUNY Brockport, 1992; Cert of Appreciation for Service, Monroe County, Human Relations Commission, 1991-94, Song Writer, "Do More Than" & "Letting Go", Hilltop Records, 1997. **Home Addr:** 10-E Whitney Ridge Rd, Apt 8, Fairport, NY 14450-1617. **Business Addr:** Director, Education and Development, Baden Street Settlement, Inc, 152 Baden St, Rochester, NY 14605.

LECOMPTE, PEGGY LEWIS
Educational network executive, TV hostess. **Personal:** Born Oct 7, 1938, St Louis, MO; daughter of Winnie Penguite Lewis and Obadiah Lewis, Sr; married Larry Ferdinand LeCompte Sr, Nov 22, 1962; children: Larry F Jr. **Educ:** Lincoln Univ, BS 1960; Sangamon State, MS 1985; Natl Coll of Educ, Evanston IL, MS 1990. **Career:** E St Louis School Dist 189, educator 1962-; USAF, librarian 1968; E St Louis School Dist 1889, educator 1970-; Channel 13 E St Louis, TV host 1983-; Time Network; Impact Associates, president; E St Louis News Journal, Pure News, columnist. **Orgs:** Ed Adv Found 1982-86; Boys Club of Amer Planning Commission 1985-90; bd pres Boys Club of E St Louis 1978-86; pres, Area III dir, organizer, Top Ladies of Distinction, natl workshop chmn, natl parliamentarian, 1987-91; Language Arts Dept Head, District 189, 1988-; secretary, bd of dir Girl Scouts of Amer 1990-93; pres, Comp Mental Health Center; pres, St Clair County, YWCA; Natl YWCA Bd, Natl Policy Comm, Natl Constitution & Bylaws Comm; pres, board of directors, GEMM, 1990-; Racial Harmony, board of directors; AKA Sorority International mem chmn, past natl secretary; Alpha Kappa Alpha Sorority, central regional dir, 1997-98. **Honors/Awds:** Boys Club Medallion Boys Clubs of Amer 1984; Youth Awd YMCA 1984; Media Awd Shriners Aahmes Temple 112 1983; Leadership Alpha Kappa Alpha Sor 1983; Teacher of the Year Awd Zeta Phi Beta Sor 1977; Outstanding Serv Awd NAACP E St Louis 1978; Key to the City E St Louis 1978-79; Most Outstanding Jill Past Pres Awd Jack & Jill of Amer in E St Louis 1980; YMCA Communications Awd 1986; Boys Clubs of America Natl Serv Medallion; Metro St Louis Most Outstanding Speaker Toastmasters 1982; Top Lady of Distinction of Area III 1986; Master Teacher School District 189, 1988; Protocol: A Guide; YWCA Volunteer of the Year, 1990; Carol Kimmel Comm Service Leadership Award, 1991; Key to City, Waterloo, Iowa, 1992; Suburban Journal Woman of Achievement, 1995; AKA Women of Achievement in Leadership, 1997. **Home Addr:** 212 Bunker Hill Rd, Belleville, IL 62221.

LEDAY, JOHN AUSTIN
Janitorial company executive. **Personal:** Born Sep 11, 1931, Basile, LA; son of Edna Papillian LeDay and Alsay LeDay; married Christine Sandoval; children: Anna, Angela. **Career:** Southend Janitorial Supply Inc, owner/pres 1961-; People Chem Co, sales mgr 1954-61, warehouseman 1948-52. **Orgs:** Pres, Amer Enterprises Inc; pres, MTM Corp; mem, Natl Assn of Black Mfrs; Sanitary Supply Assn of Southern California; Los Angeles C of C; bd of dir Black Businessmen's Assn of Los Angeles; exec comm, Los Angeles Office Urban Devel; commissioned by Gov Brown Adv Council on Econ Business Devel State of California, 1978; dir, Equip Bank; bd dir, Pickett Enterprises; Natl Community Business Devel. **Honors/Awds:** Businessman of Year Award, BBA, 1977; Top 100 Black Businesses in US, Black Enterprise, 1974. **Military Serv:** AUS 1952-54. **Business Addr:** 11422 S Broadway, Los Angeles, CA 90061.

LEDBETTER, RUTH POPE
Health services consultant, nurse. **Personal:** Born in Indianapolis, IN; married Wilbur E Ledbetter (deceased); children: Mark F (deceased). **Educ:** Indiana Univ, Bloomington, pre-nursing, 1939-41; Amer Univ, Washington, BSNE, 1958; Marion County Gen Hospital, RN, 1958; Catholic Univ UDC, grad studies, 1974-80. **Career:** St Elizabeth Hospital, supvr training instructor, 1950-69; Area B Alcoholism Center, mental health nurse specialist, 1969-70; Congress Heights Health Center, community mental health specialist, 1970-73; Employee Counseling Serv, sr comm mental health specialist, 1973-76; Dept of Human Resources, trans analysis instr 1975-77; DHR Bureau of Alcohol RX, state prevention coord, 1976-80; Woodson Sr High, sex educ, alcohol, drug abuse, 1978-80; Trifax Corp, dir research & devel, exec vice pres, currently. **Orgs:** Speakers bureau Chi Eta Phi Sor Inc; 2nd vice pres, Amer Assn Black Women Entrepreneurs; certified sex educ; past pres, Hughes Mem Toastmistress Club. **Honors/Awds:** Incentive Serv Award, DHR, 1971; Mayors Serv Award, Dist of Columbia, 1980; Outstanding Achievement Award CIC Alcoholism Program, 1980; Dedicated Serv Award, Dist of Columbia Task Force on Alcoholism, 1981; Outstanding Comm Serv, Woodson Sr High, 1981; Cert of Recognition for Outstanding Serv to the Ward 7 Community from Councilmen HR Crawford, 1984; Spirit of Business Award Amer Assn of Black Women Entrepreneurs Inc, 1985; Partner Award, Marshal Heights Community Development Organization, 1996. **Home Addr:** 72-54th St SE, Washington, DC 20019. **Business Addr:** Executive Vice President, Trifax Corp, 4121 Minnesota Ave NE, Washington, DC 20019.

LEDE, NAOMI W.
Educational administrator. **Personal:** Born Mar 22, 1934, Huntsville, TX; married; children: Susan, Paul. **Educ:** Bradley U, BA, MA; Mary Allen Coll; TX So U; Univ TX, EdD 1979. **Career:** Lifson Wilson & Ferguson Houston; Survey Research Ctr Ann Arbor; Juvenile Delinquency Survey Univ Houston; Race Relations Inst Survey Fisk Univ Nashville; Reg Transportation Study Arlington TX; Consumer Opinion Inst NY; SRDS DATA Inc NY; Batten Barton Drustine & Orborne NY; Louis Harris & Asso; Inst for Social Research Univ SC; Natl Urban League St Louis; St Louis Urban League, dir research; St Louis Univ; lecturer; Washington Univ; Urban Intern Arlington TX; City of St Louis, program analyst & research cons; Bishop Coll Dallas TX, asst prof & dir research; Texas Southern Univ, prof of transportation and urban planning, dean and dir, Center for Urban Programs, vice pres for institutional advancement, 1990-. **Orgs:** Mem Amer Assn Univ Prof; Natl Council of Univ Research Administrators; Asso Study Negro Life & Hist; TX Assn Coll Tchrs; Nat Assn Social Science Tchrs; Am Sociological Soc; Research & Consult Dallas Urban League & Dallas Negro C of C; Soc Study Negro in Dentistry; Delta Sigma Theta Sor; Iota Phi Lambda Bus Sor; World Future Soc; Soc Research Administrators; Council of Univ Inst Urban Affairs; bd mem Urban Affairs Corp; Transportation Research Bd; Nat Acad Political & Social Sci; Smithsonian Inst; asso mem AIP; State Educ Comm AIP; mem Mayor's Manpower Adv Council. **Honors/Awds:** Received special recognition for participation in program Operation Champ from Vice Pres Hubert Humphrey; publ "Extensive Research in Trans Planning & Citizen Participation/Mental Hlth Services/Feasibility of Housing". **Business Addr:** Vice President, Institutional Advancement, Texas Southern Univerity, 3100 Cleburne Ave, Houston, TX 77004.

LEDEE, ROBERT
Consultant. **Personal:** Born Aug 20, 1927, Brooklyn, NY; son of Mary Godfrey Ledee and Reginald Ledee; married Victoria Marzan; children: Yvonne Alvarez, Robert Jr, Reginald, Anthony. **Educ:** John Jay Coll of Criminal Justice, AS 1971; BA 1973; MPA 1976; Fed Bur of Narcotics Training Sch, grad 1967; FBI Nat Acad 1968. **Career:** Sea Gate NY Harbor Police Dept, chief 1979-81; New York City Housing Police Dept, dep chief 1970-78; insp 1970; dep insp 1967-70; capt 1964-67; lt 1960-64; sgt 1958-60; apptd 1955;Fed Funded Comm Serv Ofcr Prgm, adminstr; Hispanic Law Enforcement Training Inst of Justice, cons; New York City Dept of Personnel, cons. **Orgs:** Guest lctr FBI Nat Acad; rep Housing Pol Dept; 1st Nat Symposium on Law Enforcement Tech 1967; 13th Annueal Inst on Polic & Comm MI Stae Univ 1967; Crive Prevention Sem 1968; Insterst Conf on Delinq Control 1965; adminstr Model Cities Comm Serv Ofcr Prgm. **Honors/Awds:** 1st black mem to hold rank of lt, capt, dep insp, dep chief New York City Housing Police Dept; 3 dept commendations for outst police work; awards from, Upper Pk Ave Bapt Ch 1963; Fedn of Negro Civil Serv Orgns 1964; Bronx Dective Unit 1965; Counc of Police Orgns 1966; Hispanic Soc 1966, 1970; Anti-Crime Com 1969; Grand Counc of Hispanic Soc 1971; Nat Police Ofcrs Assn 1972; Comm Relat Unit 1973; NY Club 1974; John Jay Coll Alumni Assn 1976; Nat Conf of Christians & Jews 1977; author article FBI Bull 1975; manual High Rise Policing Tech US Merchant Marine 1945-55. **Military Serv:** US Merchant Marine, AB, 1945-55; received Atlantic War Zone, Pacific War Zone Bars & Victory Medal. **Business Addr:** Consultant, PO Box 657, Jamaica, NY 11434.

LEDOUX, JEROME G.
Theologian. **Personal:** Born Feb 26, 1930, Lake Charles, LA. **Educ:** Divine Word Sem, Ordained 1957; Ponitifical Gregorian Univ Rome, Italy, MST 1961, Dr of Ch Law 1961. **Career:** Divine Word Theol Bay St Louis MS, prof of Moral Theol & Canon Law 1961-67; MS History Divine Word HS Sem, instr English civics 1967-69; Xavier UnivNew Orleans, 1st black chpln the only predominantly black Cath Univ in the US 1969-71; Xavier Univ, assoc prof of Theol 1971-80; pastor, St Augustine Church; Author, weekly synd colmn carried in 6 cath diocesan papers & 3 black weeklies; Author, montly clmn in natl cath paper. **Home Addr:** 1210 Governor Nicholls St, New Orleans, LA 70116.

LEDUFF, STEPHANIE CARMEL
Marketing director publishing company. **Personal:** Born Apr 30, 1953, Columbus, OH; daughter of Esther Winkfield and Dallas Winkfield; children: Eric Jason Wallace. **Educ:** Ohio State Univ, BS 1975; Attended, Harvard Univ 1981-82, MIT 1981-82. **Career:** Community Action Agency New Orleans, dir of program planning & develop; Real Estate Publication, managing editor 1984-86; News-Press Publishing Co, marketing dir. **Orgs:** Mem FL Public Relations Assoc 1986-87, Evaluation Rsch Soc 1986-87, Intl Newspaper Mktg Assoc 1986-87; bd mem Barbara Mann Performing Arts Ctr 1986-87, Abuse Counseling & Treatment Ctr 1987; bd of directors, Lee Mental Health.

LEE, AARON
Business executive. **Personal:** Born Aug 29, 1948, Hinds Co, MS; married Frances Jackson; children: Aaron Brennan. **Educ:** Utica Jr Coll, AA 1970; Jackson State Univ, BS 1975, MS 1976. **Career:** Major Associates Construction Co, estimator 1975-77; Natl Business League, construction mgr 1977-80; Town of Edwards, alderman 1977-, fed prog coord 1982-; Jackson State Univ, super building serv 1981-83; asst dir physical plant 1983-. **Orgs:** Mem Phi Beta Sigma Frat 1976-; mem bd of dirs NAACP Bolton-Edwards Branch 1981-; mem Amer Mgmt Assn 1984-. **Honors/Awds:** Outstanding Achievement in Public Serv MS Valley State Univ Social Sci Dept 1977; Outstanding Dedicated Serv Natl Business League 1980; Outstanding YoungMan of Amer-Outstanding Young Men of Amer 1984. **Military Serv:** AUS sgt 1st class 14 yrs; Meritorial Serv Awd USAR 1978. **Home Addr:** PO Box 88, Edwards, MS 39066.

LEE, ALLEN FRANCIS, JR.
Educator, scientist. **Personal:** Born Apr 12, 1943, Notasulga, AL; married Lula M Wheat; children: Allen F III, Aryanna F. **Educ:** Tuskegee Inst AL, DVM 1967; Univ of GA Athens, PhD 1978. **Career:** Univ of GA, post-doctoral rsch asst 1967-69, rsch assoc 1969-71; Emory Univ, NIH spl post-doctoral fellow 1971-72; Univ of GA, instr 1972-73; LA State Univ, assoc prof 1973-. **Orgs:** Mem Amer Vet Med Assn 1967-; mem Amer Soc of Vet Physiologists & Pharmacologists 1969-; mem AAAS; mem Kappa Alpha Psi Frat 1965-; mem Amer Radio Relay League 1977-; bd dir Campus Fed Credit Union 1978-; bd of dir Kenilworth Civic Assn 1980-. **Honors/Awds:** Schol in Vet Medicine Tuskegee Inst 1965; Outstanding Sr Vet Student Womens Aux AVMA 1967; NIH Post Doctoral Fellowship Emory Univ 1971; disertation "Evaluation of Ulnar Nerve Conductio Velocity in the Dog" Univ of GA 1978; researcher nerve/muscle physiology electromyography. **Business Addr:** Associate Professor, LA State Univ, School Vet Med, Dept Physiology Pharm & Tox, Baton Rouge, LA 70803.

LEE, AMP (ANTHONIA WAYNE)
Professional football player. **Personal:** Born Oct 1, 1971, Chipley, FL. **Educ:** Florida State. **Career:** San Francisco 49ers, running back, 1992-93; Minnesota Vikings, 1994-96; St Louis Rams, 1997-. **Business Addr:** Professional Football Player, St Louis Rams, One Rams Way, St Louis, MO 63045, (314)982-7267.

LEE, ANDRE L.
Educational administrator, healthcare administrator. **Personal:** Born Aug 14, 1943, Detroit, MI; son of Laura Lee and Clyde Lee; divorced; children: Andre, Bryan, Tracey, Robin. **Educ:** MI State Univ, BS 1966; Cornell Univ, MPA 1972; Nova Univ, DPA 1978. **Career:** Highland Park Gen Hosp MI, dir 1972-76; Sidney Sumby Hosp MI, dir 1976-78; St Joseph Hosp Ft Wayne IN, asst dir 1978-81; Hubbard Hosp TN, dir 1981-88; president Urban Health Associates Inc; Friendship Hospice of Nashville Inc, president, currently; United Community Hospital, pres/CEO, currently. **Orgs:** Pres Natl Assoc of Health Serv Exec 1985-87; state dir Amer Acad Med Admin IN & TN 1983-85; chmn Mgmt Housing Scholarship Comm; mem Alpha Phi Alpha, NAACP; tech Sinai Hosp Detroit 1966-67; propr Health Care Fin Sys; mem Amer Professional Mgmt Ltd, Amer Coll of Hosp Admin, Amer Publ Health Assoc, Amer Acad of Med Admin, MI Publ Health Assoc; bd mem Comprehensive Health Ctr, Model Neighborhood Health Ctr, Resd Manpower Ctr, MI C of C Ed Sub-Com, Reg Emergency Room Task Force, Cty Emergency Room Task Force. **Honors/Awds:** Publ over 60 articles; COGME Fellowship Awd 1970-72; Whitney Young Award, Boy Scouts of America, 1989; Silver Beaver Award, Boy Scouts of America, 1991. **Military Serv:** AUS capt 2 yrs active, 4 yrs reserve. **Business Addr:** President, Friendship Hospice of Nashville, Inc, 1326 8th Ave, Nashville, TN 37208.

LEE, ANDREA
Writer. **Personal:** Born 1953, Philadelphia, PA. **Educ:** Harvard University, MA. **Career:** Writer; staff writer for New Yorker magazine, New York NY. **Honors/Awds:** American Book Award nomination, 1981, for Russian Journal; Jean Stein Award, American Academy and Institute of Arts and Letters, 1984. **Business Addr:** New Yorker, 25 West 43rd St, New York, NY 10036.

LEE, ANTHONY OWEN
Airline industry executive. **Personal:** Born Jun 28, 1962, Seattle, WA; son of Owen G & Vivian O Lee. **Educ:** Brown University, ScB, 1984; Massachusetts Institute of Technology, ScM, 1987; PhD, 1990. **Career:** SABRE Decision Technologies, consultant, 1990-. **Orgs:** Informs, 1984-; AGIFORS, 1990-; Black Alumni of MIT, 1990-; Brown University Alumni, NASP, 1984-; Institute for International Public Policy, advisory bd, 1995-. **Honors/Awds:** Brown University, Rohn Truell Premium for Achievement, 1984; Dollars & Sense, America's Best & Brightest African-Americans, 1993; Ft Worth Business Press, Top 40 under 40 Business people, 1993. **Special Achievements:** Holiday & Special Event Forecasting, ORSA/TIMS, 1994; Reservations Forecasting for Yield Management, ORSA/TIMS, 1990; Airline Reservations Forecasting, AGIFORS Proceedings, 1987; Nested Decomposition Methods, ORSA/TIMS, 1987. **Home Addr:** 1022 San Jacinto Dr, #718, Irving, TX 75063. **Business Addr:** Senior Consultant, SABRE Decision Technologies, PO Box 619616, Dallas, TX 75261, (817)931-2170.

LEE, AUBREY WALTER, SR.
Banking executive. **Personal:** Born Oct 26, 1934, Huntington, WV; married Jeane F Lee, Apr 13, 1956; children: Aubrey Jr, David, Mark. **Educ:** Morehouse College, 1951-52; WV State Coll, BA, political science, economics, 1955; Marshall Univ, MA political science, economics, 1956; Univ of Wisconsin Graduate School of Banking, diploma, 1969. **Career:** NBD Bank teller, trainee, 1957-, asst mgr, branch mgr, asst vp, regional mgr, vp, head of minority & commercial lending, first vp, regional banking ctr dir, municipal banking group, sr vice pres, currently. **Orgs:** William Beaumont Hosp, bd of dirs, vice chmn, treas, chmn of finance comm; Walsh Coll, bd of trustees, chmn of organization & compensation comm; Bloomfield Hill Country Club; Troy Chamber of Commerce, former pres; Economic Club of Detroit; NAACP; Outer Dr Faith Lutheran Church, past pres. **Honors/Awds:** Pi Sigma Alpha Honor Fraternity, National Honor Society; YMCA Minority Achiever Award in Industry; City of Detroit, Medallion; Urban Bankers Forum, Distinguished Banker's Award; Marshall Univ, Distinguished Graduate Student Alumnus Award. **Military Serv:** US Army Reserves, captain, 1957-65. **Business Addr:** Senior VP, NBD Bank, 611 Woodward Ave, 3rd Fl South, Mail Ste 8078, Detroit, MI 48226.

LEE, AUBREY WALTER, JR.
Financial consultant. **Personal:** Born Oct 14, 1956, Ashland, KY; son of Aubrey W Lee Sr & Jeane F Lee; married Janice D Lee, Dec 2, 1989; children: Aubrey Bejamin, Lauren Nicole, Natalie Ann Booker, Nathan Alexander McGhee. **Educ:** University of Michigan Dearborn, 1974-76; University of Michigan Ann Arbor, 1976-78. **Career:** Booth American Co, radio announcer, 1978-81; Manufacturers National Bank of Detroit, branch assistant mgr, 1980-87; Inner City Broadcasting, radio announcer, 1981-83; Amaturo Group Inc, radio announcer, 1983-85; Booth American Co, radio announcer, 1987-90; Merrill Lynch, financial consultant/assistant vice pres, 1987-; Evergreen Media, radio announcer, 1990-; CBS Radio, WVMV-FM, radio announcer, 1997-. **Orgs:** National Association of Securities Professionals, Detroit Chap, vice pres, 1996; Men of Faith, Outer Dr Faith Lutheran Church, vice pres, 1996, assistant minister, 1996; Golightly Vocational School, internship committee, 1996-97; Promisekeepers, 1996; Michigan Minority Business Develop Council, Merrill Lynch, corporate liaison, 1996; Penn Center-Michigan Support Group, 1996. **Honors/Awds:** YMCA, Father & Son Footsteps Award, 1985. **Business Addr:** Assistant Vice Pres, Merrill Lynch, 290 Town Center Dr, Ste 1100, Dearborn, MI 48126.

LEE, BERTRAM M.
Entrepreneur. **Personal:** Born Jan 21, 1939, Lynchburg, VA; son of Helen Harris Lee and William T Lee Sr; married Laura Murphy; children: Paula, Elaine, Bertram M Jr. **Educ:** North Central Coll, BA 1961; Roosevelt Univ, graduate studies 1963-65. **Career:** Various city agencies in Chicago, dir 1961-67; OIC of Greater Boston, exec dir 1967-68; EG & G of Roxburgy, Inc, gen mgr & vice pres 1968-69; Dudley Station Corp, president 1969-81; BML Assoc, Inc, chairman, 1969-; New England TV Corp, president 1982-86; Albimar Mgmt Inc, chairman, 1983-; Mountaintop Ventures Inc, treas 1984-; Kellee Communications Group Inc, pres 1986-; Denver Nuggets Corporation, Denver, CO, chairman, 1989-92. **Orgs:** Exec committee, chairman, Boston Bank of Commerce; board of trustees, Martin Luther King, Jr Center for Non-Violent Social Change, Inc; dir, Jackie Robinson Foundation; dir, Natl Assn of Sickle Cell Inc, 1987-; board of directors, Congressional Black Caucus Foundation 1987-; board of directors, Joint Center for Political & Economic Studies, 1990-.; board of directors, Reebok International Ltd, 1990-; chairman, TransAfrica Forum, 1990-; Howard Univ, bd of trustees, 1993-. **Honors/Awds:** NAACP, Image Award 1982; American Heritage & Freedom Award 1983; New England Telephone/Minority Management Assoc, Recognition Award 1983; Recognition Award, Museum of Afro-American History; Recognition Award, Maryland/District of Columbia Minority Supplier Dev Council; CIAA Award, Friends from Norfolk. **Military Serv:** US Army, 1963-65. **Business Addr:** Chairman, BML Associates Inc, 4001 Nebraska Ave NW, Washington, DC 20016.

LEE, BILL. See LEE, WILLIAM JAMES EDWARDS, III.

LEE, CARL, III
Professional football player. **Personal:** Born Apr 6, 1961, South Charleston, WV. **Educ:** Marshall Univ, attended. **Career:** Minnesota Vikings, cornerback, 1983-. **Honors/Awds:** Sporting News NFL All-Star Team, 1988; post-season play: NFC Championship Game, 1987, Pro Bowl, 1988, 1989. **Business Addr:** Professional Football Player, Minnesota Vikings, 9520 Viking Dr, Eden Prairie, MN 55344-3825.

LEE, CHANDLER BANCROFT
Automobile dealer. **Career:** Chandler Lee Motors, Inc, Southern Pines, NC, chief executive officer, beginning 1986; Classic Pontiac-Buick-GMC Inc, pres, 1991-. **Special Achievements:** Company is ranked #100 on Black Enterprise magazine's 1997 list of Top 100 Black businesses. **Business Addr:** Owner, Classic Pontiac-Buick-GMC, 330 Old Country West Old Country Rd, Hicksville, NY 11801.

LEE, CHARLES GARY, SR.
General contractor. **Personal:** Born Sep 29, 1948, Jacksonville, FL; married Claudia Pittman; children: Charles, Marcus, Cedric. **Educ:** H Council Trenholm Jr Coll, A Masonry 1969; Westfield State Coll, Certificate Occ Ed 1974; Univ of MA, BA Occupational Educ 1984. **Career:** Springfield Sch System, adult educ instructor 1973-80; Lee-Hamilton Construction Co, pres/genl mgr 1974-78; Neighborhood Housing Svcs, asst dir 1978-80; Charles Gary Lee Inc, owner/president 1980-. **Orgs:** 3rd Degree Master Mason FAM of AL Prince Hall 1967-; dir Corporate Mem Springfield Girl's Club Family Ctr Inc 1979-; pres Big Will Express Athletic Club 1983-; certified mem Minority Business Enterprise 1983-; affiliate mem Western MA Contractor's Assoc 1985-; consultant shareholder Lee-Brantley Inc 1986-. **Honors/Awds:** Man of the Year Awd Big Will Express AA 1984; Outstanding Citizen Awd MA Black Caucus 1986; Letter of Recognition Mayor City of Boston 1986. **Home Addr:** 32 Briarwood Ave, Springfield, MA 01118. **Business Addr:** President, Charles Gary Lee Inc, PO Box 90953, Springfield, MA 01139.

LEE, CHARLIE
Professional sports administrator. **Career:** Denver Broncos, dir of player and community relations, currently. **Business Addr:** Director of Player and Community Relations, Denver Broncos, 13655 Broncos Pkwy, Englewood, CO 80112-1415.

LEE, CHARLOTTE O.
Educator. **Personal:** Born Jul 13, 1930, Boligee, AL; married Ralph Hewitt Lee; children: Krystal, Karla, Rachel, Rosalind. **Educ:** Knoxville College, BS 1953; Tuskegee Institute, MS 1955; The University of Kansas, PhD 1959. **Career:** Nassau Community College, asst prof chemistry 1970-71; St Louis Univ, rs assoc 1971-72; Southern IL Univ at Edwardsville, assoc prof 1972-78; Triton College, instructor 1979-. **Orgs:** Asst prof nutrition Univ of Kansas 1963; prof chemistry Alabama A&M Univ 1964-69; parks commissioner City of University City, MO 1976-78; community chest dir Oak Park River Forest Community Chest 1982. **Honors/Awds:** AAUW Research Fellowship Amer Assn of Univ Women 1958-59; American Men & Women of Science 1960; research grant Natl Institute of Health 1964-67; research grant NASA 1965-68; Women in Science Project NSF 1977-78; proposal review panelist Natl Science Foundation 1978, 1979. **Home Addr:** 333 N Cuyler, Oak Park, IL 60302.

LEE, CLARA MARSHALL
Educator. **Personal:** Born Feb 14, 1946, Mobile, AL; daughter of Clara Mae Marshall and Edward J Marshall Sr; married Marion Sidney Lee Jr, Jul 10, 1971; children: LaToia Ejuan Marius Sidward. **Educ:** Bishop State Jr Coll, 1963-65; AL State Univ, Montgomery Al, BS 1967; Natl Coll of Educ, Chicago IL, MA 1983. **Career:** Harvey Park Dist, commissioner 1981; Delta Sigma Theta Sor Inc Joliet Area Alumni Chapter, finance sec 1984; Harvey Publ Schools Dist 152, history teacher. **Orgs:** Bd mem People Organized to Secure Election Equalities 1982; mem IEA, NEA, NPRA, IPRA, The Natl Sor of Phi Delta Kappa Inc.

LEE, CLIFTON VALJEAN
Physician. **Personal:** Born Jan 21, 1929, New York, NY; married Irene Warner; children: Marquetta C, Michele C, Jeanine C. **Educ:** Howard Univ Washington DC, BS 1951; Howard U, MD 1955. **Career:** Univ of So CA Med Sch LA, physician/asst clinical prof ob-gyn 1968-; CA Coll of Med LA, clinical instr ob-gyn 1963-; Western Res Med Sch Cleveland OH, demonstrator ob-gyn 1962-63. **Orgs:** Mem numerous ob-gyn socs; consult Numerous Ob-gyn Dept Hosps; Nat Med Fellowship 1960-63; diplomate Am Bd of Ob-gyn. **Military Serv:** USAF capt 1956-58. **Business Addr:** 4361 Western Ave, Los Angeles, CA 90062.

LEE, CODY M.
Clergyman. **Personal:** Born Aug 3, 1910, Sparkman, AR; married Amanda; children: Cody, Maeola, Ada C. **Educ:** AR Bapt Coll, AA 1948; Rust Coll, AB 1957; AR Bapt Coll, DD 1958. **Career:** AR & TN, barber 1929-45; Pilgrim Rest Bapt Ch Memphis, minister 1948-. **Orgs:** Pres TN Bapt Sch of Religion Memphis, TN; mem bd dir Nat Bapt Conv USA Inc; state dir TN BM & E State Congress; co-chmn Shelby Rep Party Shelby Co TN 1965-66. **Honors/Awds:** Sermon writer; publisher of Poem Book for all occasions; publisher of Chair Handbook.

LEE, CONSELLA ALMETTER
Journalist. **Educ:** Wayne State University, Detroit, MI, journalism, 1989. **Career:** Michigan Chronicle, Detroit, MI, staff writer, 1990-. **Business Addr:** Staff Writer, Michigan Chronicle, 479 Ledyard, Detroit, MI 48201.

LEE, DANIEL
Physician. **Personal:** Born Apr 28, 1918, Pinehurst, GA; son of Leila Lee and Amos Lee Jr; married Thelma Ragin (deceased); children: Daniel Jr, Kenneth, Sharon. **Educ:** Lincoln University, BA 1940; Howard University, College of Med, MD 1945; Harlem Hospital, internship 1946. **Career:** Lincoln University College of Hygiene, school physician/asst professor 1946-48; Pine Forge Inst, school physician 1948-55; Coatesville Hospital, medical staff 1960-; Coatesville Area Schools, school physician 1968-; Coatesville Senior High, varsity football, 1968-; physician, private practice. **Orgs:** Grand asst medical director, IBPOE of W 1983-; coord council, Southeastern PA High Blood Pressure Control Program 1983-; charter member, US Defense Comm 1983-; president, Club XV 1972-; president, Western Chester County Chamber of Commerce; bd dir, W Chester Co Industrial Development Corp & Auth; Coatesville Red Cross; AMA; Fellowship Comm, Philadelphia, PA; commission on admissions & allocations United Way; bd dir, Chester Co OIC Inc; Mount Vernon Lodge #151; IBPOE of W; NMA; Boy Scout Council; NAACP, 1976-; Philadelphia Urban League; Coatesville Hall of Fame, selection committee; bd of dirs, United Cerebral Palsy Assn of Chester Co 1985-; Health & Welfare Council; dir, Health Dept, Improved Development ProtectiveOrder 1988; bd dir, Atkinson Memorial Community Center 1989-. **Honors/Awds:** Diplomate, Natl Board of Medical Examiners; honoree, Coatesville Hall of Fame 1976; fellow, American Academy of Family Physicians 1975; honoree, Man of Year Award, S Eastern Business & Professional Women of Chester Co, 1979; Kappa Alpha Psi, 1969-, 50 Year membership award, 1989; Paul Harris Fellow, Rotary Intl 1989; community service award, Veterans of Foreign Wars 1989; life member, American Academy of Family Practice 1989; honoree, Kappa Alpha Psi, Epsilon Chapter, 1991; Elks Diamond Ebony Award, Pennsylvania State Association, IBPOE of W, 1991. **Military Serv:** AUS Maj 1959. **Business Addr:** 723 Merchant St, Coatesville, PA 19320.

LEE, DEBRA LOUISE
Attorney. **Personal:** Born Aug 8, 1954, Columbia, SC; daughter of Delma L Lee and Richard M Lee; married Randall Spencer Coleman; children: Quinn Spencer Coleman Ava Coleman. **Educ:** Brown Univ, AB 1976; Harvard Law School, JD 1980; Harvard Kennedy School of Govt, MPP 1980. **Career:** US Dist Ct Judge Barrington Parker, law clerk 1980-81; Steptoe & Johnson, attorney 1981-86; Black Entertainment Television, vice pres/general counsel 1986-92, executive vice pres, general counsel and secretary 1992-96, pres and chief operating officer currently; Publisher, YSB Magazine, president. **Orgs:** Mem Minority Recruitment Comm Federal Comm Bar Assoc 1982-; mem Public Service Activities Comm DC Bar 1983-; bd of dirs Legal Aid Soc of DC 1986-. **Honors/Awds:** National Achievement Award, Washington DC Area Chapter of the National Alumnae Assn of Spel College, 1992; Eva A Mooar Awd Brown Univ 1976. **Business Addr:** President/COO, Black Entertainment TV, One BET Plz, 1900 W Place, NE, Washington, DC 20018-1211.

LEE, DERREK LEON
Professional baseball player. **Personal:** Born Sep 6, 1975, Chicago, IL. **Career:** San Diego Padres, infielder, 1997; Florida Marlins, 1998-. **Business Addr:** Professional Baseball Player, Florida Marlins, Pro Player Stadium, NW 199th St, Miami, FL 33169, (305)356-5848.

LEE, DETROIT
Business executive (retired). **Personal:** Born Aug 22, 1916, Daingerfield, TX; son of Lou Ella Rivers Lee (deceased) and Jessie lee (deceased); divorced; children: Detroit Jr, David M, Mary E Davis, Anthony T, Henry A. **Educ:** Tuskegee Inst Coll, 1936-42. **Career:** Civilian Conservation Corps, asst clerk & sr leader 1937-42; Tuskegee Army Air Field, clerk-typist II & III 1942-44; VA Hosp AL, clerk typist II & admin clerk 1944-65; Tuskegee Inst Comm Educ Program, admin asst & comm organizer 1965-67; Tuskegee Inst, res dir 1967-72; Pardon & Parole Bd, clerk typist III 1973; ABC Bd, store clerk & cashier 1974-78; AL Ind Relations, clerk typist III super 1980-81; Lee & Sons Enterprises Inc, pres, 1971-85. **Orgs:** Organizer & 1st pres Tuskegee Br NAACP 1944; vice-pres Tuskegee Civic Assn 1940's; organizer & promoter school desegregation 1956, 1963. **Honors/Awds:** Americanism Awd for Voter Registration Amer Vet Comm 1964; Serv to Fellow Alabamians AL Sec of State 1983; Awd for Outstanding Leadership Westminster Presbyterian Church 1983; author "Christianity Democracy or Communism" 1985, "Lee v Macon" Cty & State of AL 1985; won job discrimination suits: Lee v State of Alabama Personnel Dept, 1984, 1989; Lee v Robert White, 1985; Lee v ABC Board, 1987; Lee v Dept of Health and Human Services 1988; Lee v Darris, 1988; Lee v SCADC and City of Tuskegee, 1989. **Military Serv:** AUS pvt 1945. **Home Addr:** H-109 Sojourner Apts, Tuskegee, AL 36083.

LEE, DON L. See MADHUBUTI, HAKI R.

LEE, DOROTHEA
Association executive. **Personal:** Born Dec 13, 1930, Yonkers, NY. **Educ:** Seton Hall U, BS 1956; Seton Hall U, MA 1964. **Career:** Planned Prnthd Wrld Pop NY, dir fld dept 1972-; Nat Urban Lgue Inc NY, proj dir 1972; NJ St Hosp Marlboro, asst dir nrses 1969-70; NJ St Hosp Marlboro, proj spec 1964-69; NJ Rehab Comm, voc rehab cnslr 1964; St Barnabas Med Ctr, stf nrse 1962-64; Chaumont Air Frce Bse, nrse 1961-62; Newark Bd Ed, sch nrse 1960-61; NJ St Hosp Marlboro, instr 1957-60; Newark Cty Hosp, surg clin instr 1955-57; Newark Cty Hosp, asst supr nrses 1953-55; Newark Cty Hosp, stf nrse 1951-53. **Orgs:** Mem Am Persnnl & Guidnc Assn; Nat Rehab Assn; Newark Cty Hosp Sch of Nrsng alum Assn; Am Nrs Assn; Nat Lgue for Nrsng; Amer Pub Hlth Assn; Am Mngmt Assn; chmn NJ St Nrs Assn; pres Club Cicuso Inc 1965-67; fin secy Nat Assn Neg B & PW Club Inc 1970-74; mem NAACP; Nat Pol Caucus; Womns Po Caucus Essex Cnty NJ. **Honors/Awds:** NJ Med of Merit 1958; prof whmn of yr 1971; achvmnt Pubctn in Jrnl Psychtrc Nrsng & Mntl Hlth Serv 1968. **Military Serv:** USAF captn 1961-62; NJ Air Nat Gd 1957-68; USAFR mjr 1957-69. **Business Addr:** 810 7 Ave, New York, NY 10019.

LEE, DOROTHY A. H.
Educator. **Personal:** Born Jan 22, 1925, Columbia, MO; daughter of Helen Lee & Victor Hicks; married George E, Jun 18, 1950 (deceased); children: George V, Helen Elaine. **Educ:** Wayne State Univ, BA, 1945, MA, 1947; Radciiffe College, MA, 1948; Radcliffe College & Harvard Univ, PhD, 1955. **Career:** Wayne State Univ, asst professor, 1952-62; Henry Ford Comm College, instructor, 1963-72; Univ of MI-Dearborn, professor, 1972-93. **Honors/Awds:** Univ of MI-Dearborn, Susan B Anthony Award, 1985; Distinguished Teaching Award, 1985; MI Assn of Governing Boards of Colleges & Universities, Distinguished Facility Award, 1987; F Cousens Retired Person Award, U of M-Dearborn, 1993. **Special Achievements:** Essays published in Michigan Quarterly Review, Black Women Writers; Callaloo Black American Literary Forum; College Language Assn Journal; Journal of Spanish Studies-Twentieth Century; Critique; Modern Drama. **Home Addr:** 939 Green Hills Dr, Ann Arbor, MI 48105-2721, (313)213-6015. **Business Addr:** Professor Emeritus, The University of Michigan - Dearborn, 4901 Evergreen Rd, Dearborn, MI 48128.

LEE, EDWARD S.
Former city official. **Personal:** Born May 12, 1935, Phila; married Fay E Jones; children: Michael, Eric. **Educ:** Cheyney State Coll, BS 1968; Univ PA Fels Inst & State Govt 1969-70. **Career:** US PO; HELP Inc, exec dir 1967-69; Philadelphia Urban Coalition, exec staff mem task force coordinator & chmn 1969-71; City Phila, elected clerk quarter sessions 1971-; Nat Assn Postal & Fed Employees, former union rep; Regional & Community Treatment Centers Women, appointed attys 1967; elected ward leader 1970; Black Political Forum, exec dir 1968-70; Cheyney State Coll, adjunct prof 1974; appointed PA Gov's Justice Com. **Orgs:** Bd mem Nat Assn Court Adminstrs; Ile-Fe Black Humanitarian Center; Greater Germantown Youth Corps; mem bd trustees Canaan Bapt Ch; Ralph Bunche Club Phila; NAACP; Urban League Phila; elected delegate Dem Nat Mini Conv 1974; exec asst chmn Second World & Conf Arts & Culture; bd dir Police Athletic League; bd dir Community Services & Development Corp. **Honors/Awds:** Outstanding achievement award Inter Urban League PA; chmn bd trustees Cheyney State Coll 1974; light weight boxing champion 1956. **Military Serv:** USAF 1952-56. **Business Addr:** 673 City Hall, Philadelphia, PA 19107.

LEE, EDWIN ARCHIBALD
Physician. **Personal:** Born Jan 12, 1914, Indianola, MS; married Geraldine Elizabeth Dobisson; children: Edwin, Jr, Harold, Edith, Rhandie. **Educ:** Morehouse Coll Atlanta, GA, BA 1937; Meharry Med Coll Nashville, TN, MD 1941. **Career:** Pvt Practice St John's Hosp Springfield, IL, med staff; Meml Med Center, med staff; Comm Hosp, med staff 1949-; So IL Univ Med Sch, clinical asso1949-; St Mary's Infirmary, resident 1945-49; Homer Phillips Hosp St Louis, MO, intern 1941-42. **Orgs:** Pres Sangamon State Univ Found; mem NAACP; mem Alpha Omega Alpha Nat Med Hon Soc; bd of dir Peoples Nat Bank 1969-; pres St John's Hosp Staff 1969-; organizer/co-chmn Springfield Citizens for Effective Voter Participation & Communication 1978; mem Springfield Bd of Educ 1965-71; pres Springfield Bd ofEduc 1969-70; trustee chmn Zion Bapt Ch 1979-. **Honors/Awds:** Springfield merit award Springfield Bd of Educ 1969-70; hon life membership IL Congress of PTA's 1971; copley first citizens award Copley Press 1972; external serv award Frontiers of Am Intl 1976; hon cert Morehouse Coll 1977; man of the year Omega Nu Chap Omega Psi Phi Frat 1979. **Military Serv:** AUS maj 1941-45. **Business Addr:** 501 S 13th St, Springfield, IL 62703.

LEE, FELICIA R.
Journalist. **Personal:** Born Nov 11, 1956, Chicago, IL; daughter of Sarah Crawford Lee and Felix Lee. **Educ:** Northwestern University, Evanston, IL, BSJ, 1978. **Career:** Fort Worth Star-Telegram, Fort Worth, TX, reporter, 1978-79; Cincinnati Enquirer, reporter, 1979-82; USA Today, Washington, DC, reporter, 1982-85; Cincinnati Enquirer, Cincinnati, OH, assistant metro editor, 1985-86; Miami Herald, Miami, FL, reporter, 1986-88; New York Times, New York City, NY, reporter, 1988-. **Orgs:** National Association of Black Journalists, 1982-. **Honors/Awds:** Harvard University, Nieman fellowship, 1996. **Business Addr:** Journalist, Metro Desk, New York Times, 229 W 43rd St, 3rd Fl, New York, NY 10036.

LEE, FORREST A., SR.
Business executive. **Personal:** Born Nov 19, 1937, Boley, OK; son of Harriett Anderson Lee and Maurice W Lee Sr; married Joyce A Kirksey; children: Forrest, Carole, Catherine, Brian, Gregory, Michael, Rachael, Reginald, Crystal, Lee Otis. **Educ:** OK City Univ, BA 1961. **Career:** Liberty Tower Co OK City, draftsman 1959; Central State Hospital Norman, OK, psychiatric aide 1960-61; MW Lee Mfg Co, plant supvr 1961-68; Leefac Inc Boley, OK, pres 1963-70; Smokaroma Inc, vice pres 1974-; Farmers Home Adm Okemah, FHA loan committeeman 1970-73, chmn 1973; Smokaroma, Inc, vice president. **Orgs:** Exec com mem Central OK Criminal Comm 1970-73; public Chapter Boley Chamber of Commerce 1962-; councilman Town of Boley 1961-73; mem Natl Assn Black Mfgrs 1972-, bd of dir 1972-76; comm State of OK Human Rights Comm 1973-; bd trustees, treas Ward Chapel AME Church Boley; Wewoka Alumni Chapter Kappa Alpha Psi Fraternity; national assoc of food equipment mfgrs 1980-; national restaurant assoc 1977-. **Home Addr:** Drawer 7, Boley, OK 74829. **Business Addr:** Vice President, Smokaroma, Inc, Drawer 25, Boley, OK 74829.

LEE, FRED D., JR.
Automobile dealer. **Personal:** Born Apr 26, 1947, Tallahassee, FL; son of Maude Sneed Lee and Fred Douglas Mosley Lee Sr; married Patricia Mosley Lee, Aug 26, 1971; children: Ronald, Adrienne Dionne, Fred Douglas III. **Educ:** FL A&M Univ, Tallahassee, FL, BS Music, 1964-69, postgard studies, guidance counseling, 1970-71; Ford Motor Co, Detroit, MI, dealer training program, 1984-85. **Career:** Ford Motor Co, Jacksonville, FL, market analyst, 1971-74; Ford Motor Co, Memphis, TN, dist sales representative, 1974-78, business mgmt mgr, 1978-79, truck merchandising, 1979, fleet/leasing/rental mgr, 1979-82, vehicle dist mgr, 1982-84; Shoals Ford, Inc, Muscle Shoals, AL, pres/owner, 1986-. **Orgs:** Black Ford Lincoln Mercury Dealer Assn, 1986-; vice-chmn, Area New Car Dealers Association, 1988-89; bd of dir, Amer Heart Assn, 1988-; exec comm,

United Way of the Shoals, 1988-; Sheffield, Alabama, Rotary Club, 1988-; chairman, Alabama Commn on Higher Educ, 1988-: Sheffield Rotary Club; Alabama Commission on Higher Education, appointed by Gov Guy Hunt to nine-year term, vice chairman, 1992-. **Honors/Awds:** Distinguished Achievement Award for Quality, Ford Motor Co, 1988; Black Enterprise Magazine, Top 100 Auto Dealers in the Nation, 1988-; Chamber of Commerce of Shoals, Small Business Person of the Year Award, Retail Category, 1992. **Special Achievements:** Performed a musical variety show to benefit the Tennessee Valley Art Association, 1992; recorded an album during Operation Desert Shield for US Air Force. **Business Addr:** President, Shoals Ford, Inc, PO Box 820399, Dallas, TX 75382-0399.

LEE, GABRIEL S., JR.
Clergyman. **Personal:** Born Jul 6, 1922, Junction City, AR; son of Mollie Elder Lee (deceased) and Gabriel S Lee, Sr (deceased); married Leona Jean Williams. **Educ:** Bishop Coll Marshall TX, AB 1949; Howard Univ, MDiv 1954; St Andrews Univ St Andrews Scotland, special certificate 1970; McCormick Theological Seminary, DMin, 1987. **Career:** Fellowship New Land Baptist Churchs Lillie LA, pastor 1948-51; Westminster House Buffalo, dir boys' work 1954-55; Hollywood Heights Presbyterian Church Shreveport, stated supply minis 1955-60; Beacon Reformed Church Beacon NY, co-pastor 1960-61; pastor 1961-62; Erie Ct Dept Public Welfare Buffalo, caseworker 1963-65; Nazareth Baptist Church Washington PA, pastor 1965-71; Fellowship Baptist Church Christ Cleveland OH, pastor 1971-. **Orgs:** Treas UABA Con Christ Educ Pittsburgh 1969-71; vice moderator Allegheny Union Baptist Assn Pittsburgh 1969-71; instructor Penna Con Christ Educ 1968-71; pres Washington PA Council Churches 1970-71; pres Washington PA Ministerial Asso 1971; staff mem Natl SS & BT Univ Cong 1970-; instructor Cleveland Ext Unit Ameri-Baptist Theological Seminary Nashville; sec Greater Clevland Ministerial Assn Cleveland 1974-; mem Mayor's Comm Human Relations Washington PA 1966; advisory bd Washington Ct Dept Child Welfare; mem Washington Ct Mental Health Assn 1966-71; exec bd Bldg Com Washington YMCA 1970-71; life mem NAACP; exec com Clevleand Branch; Phi Beta Sigma Rat 1960-; Ions Intl Serv Org 1962-; mem, Executive Board Cleveland Baptist Assn, 1989-93;mem, Executive Board Greater Cleveland Interchurchuncil, 1989-93; pres, Cleveland Host Lions Intl, 1989-91. **Honors/Awds:** McKinley Theological Seminary, Doctor of Divinity, 1980. **Military Serv:** AUS staff sgt 1942-46.

LEE, GERALD E.
Educational administrator. **Personal:** Born Jan 11, 1958, Los Angeles, CA; son of Erma Willis Lee and Eugene Lee; married Tonya Marie Durley, Jul 22, 1978; children: Dawn Racquel, Gerald Eugene II, Darryl Eugene, Dennis Edward. **Educ:** Southwestern Christian Coll, AS 1978; Oklahoma Christian Coll, BS 1980; Amber University, Garland, TX, currently. **Career:** First & Euclid Church of Christ, minister 1976-78; Eastside Church of Christ, minister 1978-81; Florence St Church of Christ, minister 1981-84; Metropolitan Church of Christ, minister 1984-87. **Honors/Awds:** GP Bowser Bible Awd Southwestern Christian Coll 1978; Outstanding Young Men in Amer 1981,82,83. **Business Addr:** Dir of Admissions/Recruitment, Southwestern Christian College, 200 Bowser Circle, Terrell, TX 75160.

LEE, GLORIA A.
Entrepreneur. **Personal:** Born Mar 10, 1940, Cumberland, VA; daughter of Florence Allen Logan and Reginald Logan; divorced; children: Rhonda Michelle, Leroy E Jr. **Educ:** Univ of MD, BS 1978; Johns Hopkins Univ, MBA 1984. **Career:** Social Security Admin, supervisor 1976-80; Equal Employ Oppor Commn, eeo specialist 1980-86, investigator 1987-; Ward AME Church, admin/consultant 1986-87; Easy Transitions, pres 1986-87; Scarfs by Annlee, pres/owner, 1988-. **Orgs:** Presenter Black Family in Amer Conf 1985-89; mem Natl Black MBA Assoc 1985-89; non-affiliated pres Amer Assoc Black Women Entrepreneurs 1986-88; treasurer, Christian Elite Ensemble, 1988-.

LEE, GUY MILICON, JR.
Educator (retired). **Personal:** Born May 24, 1928, East Chicago, IN; married Trevor J Lee; children: Kim Valerie, Rodney, L Smith. **Educ:** Roosevelt Univ, BA, 1954; Inidana Univ, MS, 1959; Ball State Univ, EdD, 1969. **Career:** Gary Comm Schools IN, public school teacher 1956-64, administrator 1964-70; Saginaw Valley State Coll, dir of student teaching 1970-73, assoc dean sch of educ prof 1973-75, admin asst to the pres 1975-78, asst to the pres 1978-82, dean sch of educ 1982-86, prof of educ 1986-95, prof emeritus, 1995-. **Orgs:** Mem, Assn Supervison & Curriculum Devel; mem, Natl Org on Legal Problems in Educ; mem, Amer Assn of School Admin; rep, United Way of Saginaw Co; mem, Assn Teach Educ; mem, Amer Asoc Higher Educ; mem, Assn of Super and Curr Devel; bd of dir League of United Latin Amer Citizens, 1982-95. **Honors/Awds:** High Scholastic Achievement Award IN Univ Bloomington 1953; Doctoral Fellowship Ball State Univ Muncie IN 1968-69; Citizen of the Age of Enlightement Award for Educ Am Found for the Sci of Creative Intelligence 1976; Keyman Award for community Serv United Way of Saginaw Co MI 1979. **Military Serv:** AUS technician 1946-48.

LEE, HELEN ELAINE
Writer. **Personal:** Born Mar 13, 1959, Detroit, MI; daughter of Dorothy Ann Hicks Lee and George Ernest Lee. **Educ:** Harvard College, BA, 1981; Harvard Law School, JD, 1985. **Career:** Various law-related and attorney jobs, 1985-94; Univ of Michigan, Dearborn, adjunct lecturer, 1995; Massachusetts Institute of Technology, assistant professor in writing & humanistic studies, currently. **Honors/Awds:** American Library Assn, Black Caucus, First Novel Award, 1994, 1995; DC Commission on the Arts and Humanities, $5,000 Grant-in-Aid Award, 1991; Phi Beta Kappa. **Special Achievements:** Author, novel, The Serpent's Gift, Atheneum Publishers, 1994, London Headline Press, 1994; Marriage Bones, The African Diaspora in Short Fiction, ed; Charles Rowell Westview Press, 1995; Silences, The Best Short Stories by Black Writers vol II, ed, Gloria Naylor, Little, Brown and Co, 1995; novel Water Marked, Scirbner, forthcoming, 1998. **Business Addr:** Assistant Professor, Program in Writing and Humanistic Studies, MIT, Rm 14E-303, Cambridge, MA 02139-4307.

LEE, HELEN JACKSON. See Obituaries section.

LEE, HOWARD N.
City official. **Personal:** Born Jul 28, 1934, Lithonia, GA; married Lillian Wesley; children: Angela, Ricky, Karin Alexis Lou Tempie. **Educ:** Clark Coll, 1953-56; St Coll Ft Valley, BA 1959; Univ NC, MSW 1966; Acad of Cert Social Workers, ACSW 1968; Shaw U, LLD 1971. **Career:** Juvenile Comestic Rel Ct Savannah, prob off 1961-64; Yth Prog Duke U, dir 1966-68; NC Central U, vis asst prof 1967-68; Employee Rel Duke U, dir 1968-69; Lark Cinemas Inc, pres; Lee Dist & Mfg Co; Lark Entertainment Enter, pres chmn bd; Plastiwood Prod Inc, pres; Shaw Univ adj prof; office of human devel duke u, dir; chapel hill NC, mayor 1969-75. **Orgs:** Numerous professional mem. **Honors/Awds:** Recip GA St Tchrs Hon Student's Awd; honor student's awd St Coll; hunt fellow awd Ft Valley St Coll; achmnt awd Atlanta Br NAACP; achmnt awd Phi Beta Sigma Frat 1969; Nat Urban Leag Equal Oppor Day Awd 1970; publs in field. **Military Serv:** AUS 1959-61.

LEE, IVIN B.
Police chief. **Personal:** Born in Beard's Fork, WV; divorced. **Educ:** Bachelor's degree in criminal justice. **Career:** Charleston WV Police Dept, sergeant; Dunbar Police Dept, chief, currently. **Special Achievements:** First woman and the only African American to be appointed chief of the Dunbar Police Dept. **Business Addr:** Chief, Dunbar Police Department, 100th Block Myers Ave, City Bldg, Dunbar, WV 25064.

LEE, JAMES E.
Dentist. **Personal:** Born Mar 5, 1940, Conway, SC; son of Ophelia Buck Lee and Richard Allen Lee; married Patricia Ponds, Apr 21, 1973; children: James E Jr, Allen Earlington, Arrington Patrick. **Educ:** SC State College, 1963; Howard University, College of Dentistry, DDS, 1971. **Career:** Private practice, dentist, 1973-; Franklin C Fetter Comprehensive Health Care Clinic Charleston, staff dentist, 1971-73; Appalachian Reg Health Policy & Planning Council Anderson, SC, staff dentist, 1970-71; Dental Serv, Howard Univ Upward Bound Program, dir, summer 1971; private practice, dentist. **Orgs:** Chmn, Salvation Army Adv Bd, 1980; Palmetto Med Dental & Pharm Assn; Pee Dee Dist Dental Soc; SC Dental Soc; Am Dental Assn; Conway C of C; Nat Dental Assn; Conway Alumni Chap, Kappa Alpha Psi; chmn, Conway Housing Authority, 1980-81; Bethel AME Church Young Adult Choir; exec committee, Palmetto Med Dental & Pharm Assn; Grand Strand Dental Soc; pres, Pee Dee Medical Dental & Pharmaceutical Assn; Chmn, 1992-93, past pres, council pres, Palmetto Medical Dental & Pharmaceutical Assn, 1984-; health adv comm, Waccamaw Econ Oppty Council; Mental Health Assn of Horry County; Steward Board, Bethel AME Church; SC State Board of Dentistry, vice pres, pres, 1994; Intl College of Dentists, 1993. **Honors/Awds:** Howard Univ, Dental Award, 1958; Palmetto Medical Dental & Pharmaceutical Assn, Doctor of the Year, 1989. **Military Serv:** AUS, sp5, 1964-67. **Business Addr:** Dentist, 611 Highway 501, Conway, SC 29526.

LEE, JEFFERI K.
Business executive. **Career:** Black Entertainment Television, Network Operations, exec vp, currently. **Business Phone:** (202)608-2000.

LEE, JOHN C., III
Chief executive. **Career:** J C Lee Construction and Supply Co, Butler, PA, chief exec, 1977-. **Business Addr:** J C Lee Construction and Supply Co, Inc, RR 1, Box 216A, Petrolia, PA 16050-9312.

LEE, JOHN M.
Bank executive. **Career:** Standard Savings Bank, pres, currently. **Business Addr:** President, Standard Savings Bank, 888 North Hill St, Los Angeles, CA 90012, (213)617-8688.

LEE, JOHN ROBERT E.
Business executive. **Personal:** Born Jul 11, 1935, Tallahassee, FL; children: John Robert E Lee IV. **Educ:** FL A&M Univ, BA 1959; Boston Univ, MA 1961; Univ of KS, Doctorate 1973. **Career:** Communications Transportation & Real Estate Devel, pres, owner, entrepreneur; Silver Star Commun Corp, pres. **Orgs:** Dir of athletics TN State Univ 1985; mem Natl Assoc of Broadcasters 1985; pres Natl Assoc of Black Owned Broadcasters; chmn fund raising YMCA 1985; committee mem Boy Scouts of Amer 1985; mem Natl Coll Athletic Assoc 1985, ford Mercury Lincoln Minority Auto Assoc 1985. **Honors/Awds:** Outstanding Serv Awd Albany State 1970; Humanitarian of the Year NAACP 1977; Broadcaster of the Year HABOB 1983; Outstanding Comm Serv Hella Temple #105 1984. **Business Addr:** President, Silver Star Commun Corp, 1945 S Martin L King Dr, Tallahassee, FL 32301.

LEE, JOIE (JOY LEE)
Actress. **Personal:** daugHter of Jacquelyn Shelton Lee (deceased) and William James Edwards Lee III. **Educ:** Sarah Lawrence College. **Career:** Actress, films include: She's Gotta Have It, 1986; School Daze, 1988; Do the Right Thing, 1989; Mo' Better Blues, 1990; A Kiss Before Dying, 1990. **Business Addr:** Actress, c/o 40 Acres and a Mule Filmworks, 124 DeKalb Ave, #2, Brooklyn, NY 11217, (718)624-3703.

LEE, KERMIT J., JR.
Educator, architect. **Personal:** Born Mar 27, 1934, Springfield, MA; son of Lillian B Jackson Lee and Kermit James Lee Sr; married Lore Leipelt; children: Karin Justine, Jason Anthony. **Educ:** Syracuse Univ, BArch (Magna Cum Laude) 1952-57; Technische Hochschule Braunschweig Germany, Fulbright 1958, 1959. **Career:** Amer Inst of Arch, medary fellow 1959-60; Afex, Wiesbaden Germany, chief arch hq 7480th sup gp 1960-63; P Zoelly Arch Zurich Switzerland, assoc arch 1963-66; Syracuse Univ, prof of arch 1973-; SU Institute for Energy Research, faculty assoc 1978-; Syracuse Univ Pre-College Prog, appoint dir 1986-; Energenesis Development Corp, vice pres 1983-; Kermit J Lee Jr, AIA architect, principal 1989-. **Orgs:** Vice pres arch Skoler & Lee Arch 1969-; principal, CEO Chimaera Energy Tech Corp 1979-; mem NY Bd for Arch 1979-, Gov Cultural Adv Comm for Time Square, Natl Council Arch Regional Bd ARE 1985; mem NY Coalition of Black Arch 1977; adj assoc prof urban design Columbia Univ 1974; consultant Urban Designer Model Cities Springfield MA 1969-75; dir Campus Plan Group Syracuse Univ 1970; mem Amer Inst of Arch; mayors comm Revise City Charter 1972-74; bldg code bd of appeal 1970-; graphic exhibit Proj for Energy Syracuse Univ School of Arch 1979; technical consultant Onondaga County Citizens Energy Comm 1979-; Syracuse Univ, mem steering comm for accreditation 1987, Advisory Board for Human Development 1987; chmn, New York Board for Architecture, 1986-87; mem Citizen'sCultural Advisory Comm, Ti Square Development 1985-. **Honors/Awds:** Honor Diploma Swiss Natl Exposition 1964; Fulbright Fellowship US State Dept 1958; Medary Fellowship Amer Inst of Arch 1959; Rsch Grant Natl Endowment for the Arts 1980; Civ/Non-Appropriated Funds; School Medal AIA 1957; Luther Gifford Prize Design 1967; Class Marshal 1957; Phi Kappa Phi Hon 1957; Alpha Rho Chi Medal 1957; NY State Soc of Arch Medal 1957; Appt AIA Natl Comm on Design; Syracuse Black Leadership Council, Black Pioneer Award 1986; invitation to publish manuscript, International Forum for Design ULM, Germany 1989; Elected College of Fellows, American Institute of Architects, 1990. **Military Serv:** AF Exchange gs12 2 yrs. **Home Addr:** 301 Houston Ave, Syracuse, NY 13224-1755.

LEE, KEVIN BRIAN
Human resources executive. **Personal:** Born Aug 15, 1967, Philadelphia, PA; son of Grenthian Lee and William Keith. **Educ:** Pennsylvania State University, BS, 1990, MEd, 1995. **Career:** Pennsylvania State Univ, admissions assistant, 1990-91, human resources assistant, 1991-92, staff development and training coordinator, 1992-96; TRW Systems Integration Group, mgr human resources, 1997-. **Orgs:** American College Personnel Assn, 1994-; Pennsylvania College Personnel Assn, 1994-95; NAACP, Education Committee, 1988-90; Groove Phi Groove Social Fellowship, Inc, Penn State, president, 1990-91, advisor, 1991-92; Penn State Univ, Black Graduate Students Assn, 1994-96, University Libraries Diversity Council, exec asst, 1991-96, Graduate Students Assn, 1994-96. **Honors/Awds:** Penn State University, Black Caucus, Community Service Award, 1989, Homecoming King, 1989-90. **Business Addr:** Human Resources Manager, TRW Systems Integration Group, 1 Federal Systems Dr, Fairfax, VA 22033, (703)803-5759.

LEE, LARRY DWAYNE
Sports administrator. **Personal:** Born Sep 10, 1959, Dayton, OH; son of Charles V & Evolia Lee; married Daphne Y Lee, Jan 16, 1982; children: Dayna, Danielle. **Educ:** UCLA, BS, 1981. **Career:** Detroit Lions, player, 1981-85; Denver Broncos, player, 1987-89; Mel Farr Ford, used car manager, 1987-91; Miami Dolphins, player, 1991-93; While Allen Honda, general manager, 1991-93; Detroit Lions, vice pres of football administration, 1993-. **Orgs:** Kappa Alpha Psi; Dayton Pro Stars Football Camp, board member, 1981-. **Honors/Awds:** Kappa Alpha

Psi, Man of the Year, 1981; UCLA, Football All American, 1980. **Business Addr:** Vice Pres, Football Administration, Detroit Lions, Inc, 1200 Featherstone Rd, Pontiac, MI 48342, (810)335-4131.

LEE, LAVERNE C.
Educator. **Personal:** Born Dec 19, 1933, Bayonne, NJ; daughter of Violet M Grayson Churn and Charles H Churn; widowed; children: Juvia A. **Educ:** Morgan St Coll, BS 1955; Loyola Coll, MEd 1969; Johns Hopkins U, advanced study. **Career:** Baltimore Co Bd of Educ, instr reading spl; tchr of physically handicapped for 19 yrs; Battle Monumental School Eastwood Ctr, principal; Baltimore County Public Schools, coord of recruitment, currently. **Orgs:** Treas 1970-74, vice pres 1974-75 CEC; sec Teacher Assn Baltimore Co 1973-; pres Baltimore Co Chap Council for Excep Children 1974-76; del NEA Conv; del CEC Conv; mem Orton Soc; hon life mem PTA; exec bd TABCO; Phi Delta Kappa; Delta Kappa Gamma; member, Phi Delta Kappa, 1988-. **Honors/Awds:** Recip Tchr of the Year Awd. **Business Addr:** Coordinator of Recruitment, Personnel, Baltimore County Public Schools, 6901 N Charles Street, Towson, MD 21204.

LEE, LENA S. KING
Lawyer, educator, business executive (retired). **Personal:** Born Jul 14, Alabama; widowed. **Educ:** Morgan State Coll, BA 1939; NYU, MA, 1947; MD Univ of Law, LLB 1951, JD. **Career:** Citizens Commn on Recreation 1956; Urban Renewal and Housing Com 1955-61; Redevel Com 1955; Kennedy's Civil Rights Conf, pres 1961; Pres's Com on Govt Contractors & Conf 1958; Commn on Mfg Tax 1958; Justice of the Peace 1959-61. **Orgs:** House of Delegates, MD, 1982; Mem MD Gen Assembly House of Dels 1966-; mem Am Judicature Soc, Monumental, Baltimore Bar Assns, Center for Dispute Settlement, Nat Assn of Parliamentarians; coms Herbert M Frisby Hist Soc, Intl Platform Assn, Lambda Kappa, Sigma Gamma Rho, Bus & Professional Women's Club, Du Bois Circle, MD League of Women's Clubs, Cheyney Alumni Assn; alumni Univ MD Law School; univ club mem Univ of MD; gov comm on Criminal Justice 1968; gov comm on Juvenile Justice 1970; joint comm on Corrections 1973; comm Family Court & Domestic Relations 1973; comm on Chesapeake Bay Affairs 1980-83. **Honors/Awds:** Numerous awards and honors; inducted into Hall of Fame Women's Commission of Maryland, 1989; Charter member of Thurgood Marshall (Legal) Society, 1992; Honored as "Living Legend" by (Thelma Cox) Heritage Society, 1995, contributed article to MD Univ, Law School Journal. **Home Addr:** 1830 Madison Ave, Baltimore, MD 21217, (410)669-6446.

LEE, LERON
Company executive, former professional baseball player. **Personal:** Born Mar 4, 1948, Bakersfield, CA; son of Jewel Williams Lee and Leon Lee; married Vicquie Tanaka Lee, Oct 31, 1982; children: Juliet M, Vivian Y. **Career:** St Louis Cardinals, St Louis, MO, player, 1969-71; San Diego Padres, San Diego, CA, player, 1971-73; Cleveland Indians, Cleveland, OH, player, 1973-75; Los Angeles Dodgers, Los Angeles, CA, player, 1975-76; Lotte Orions Baseball Club, Tokoyo, Japan, player, 1977-88; Oakland Athletics, Oakland, CA, coach, 1989-90; Pro-Elite Sports Inc, pres; BoldTech Corp., owner, currently. **Honors/Awds:** Holds records for foreign players who played in Japan: Most Home Runs (283) RBI's (912) Hits (1579) Highest Lifetime Batting Average .320. **Business Addr:** President, Pro-Elite Sports,Inc, 1223 High Street, Auburn, CA 95603.

LEE, M. DAVID, JR.
Architect, educator. **Personal:** Born Aug 31, 1943, Chicago, IL; son of Mae Thomas Lee and M David Lee Sr; married Celeste E Reid, Apr 27, 1991; children: M David III, Aron Ford, Raquelle Yvette. **Educ:** University of Illinois, BA, 1967; Harvard University, MA, 1971. **Career:** Candeub, Flessig and Associates, planning draftsman, 1962-64; Roy D Murphy Architect, draftsman, 1965-67; David A Crane Architects, urban design draftsman, 1967-69; Stull Associates Inc, Architects, arch/urban designer, 1969-83; Stull and Lee Architects, partner, 1983-; Harvard University, adjunct professor, 1988-. **Orgs:** The Boston Society of Architects, president, 1992; The Institute for Urban Design, fellow; National Endowment for the Arts, Mayor's Institute Faculty; Boston Chamber of Commerce, board of directors, Boys and Girls Clubs (Boston), board of directors; Massachusetts Institute of Tech School of Arch, visiting committee; Berklee College of Music, trustee. **Honors/Awds:** The American Institute of Architects, fellow, 1992; National Endowment for the Arts, Presidential Design Award, 1988; John Hay Whitney Foundation, fellow, 1970; The Massachusetts Council for the Arts and Humanities, Regional and Statewide Governor's Design Award, 1986; The Boston Society of Architects, Von Moltke Urban Design Award, 1988; Boston Historic Neighborhoods Foundation Award for Excellence, 1990; American Institute of Architects, New England Council Design Award, 1991; American Planning Association, Social Advocacy Award, 1996. **Special Achievements:** Guest editorialist, Progressive Architecture Magazine, Oct, 1992. **Business Addr:** Partner, Stull and Lee, Architects, 38 Chauncy Street, Ste 1100, Boston, MA 02111, (617)426-0406.

LEE, MARGARET CAROL
Educator. **Personal:** Born Oct 3, 1955; daughter of Carol Rae Carruthers Lee and Charles Henry Lee Sr. **Educ:** Spelman College, Atlanta, GA, BA, 1976; University of Pittsburgh, Pittsburgh, PA, MPIA, 1981, PhD, 1985. **Career:** Lake Forest College, Lake Forest, IL, lecturer in politics, 1986; Tennessee Tech Univ, Cookeville, TN, associate professor of political science, 1986-; associate professor of political science, Spelman College, 1994-. **Orgs:** Member, African Studies Association, 1988-. **Honors/Awds:** SADCC, The Political Economy of Development in Southern Africa, Winston-Derek, 1989; Resource Guide to Information on Southern Africa, Winston-Derek, 1988; Black Faculty of the Year, Black Students Organization, Tennessee Tech, 1990.

LEE, MARGARET S.
Association executive. **Personal:** Born Mar 31, 1936, Ocean City, NJ; daughter of Mary Roberta Outen and Theodore Scott. **Educ:** Temple University, Philadelphia, PA, 1955-57; Taylor Business Institute, New York, NY, 1968-70. **Career:** City of Philadelphia, Philadelphia, PA, zoning clerk, 1954-60; Bankers Trust Company, New York, NY, credit clerk, 1964-68; Leitner & Goodman, Esqs, Brooklyn, NY, legal secretary, 1969-74; National Bowling Assn, New York, NY, executive secretary, 1974-. **Orgs:** Member, National Coalition Black Meeting Planners, 1989-; member, National Association for Female Executives, 1991; Trustee, National Bowling Hall of Fame & Museum, 1990-. **Honors/Awds:** Received the NBA Mary L Wilkes Award, Outstanding Service, 1974; received numerous local, regional and national NBA Awards and citations for outstanding service from 1974-; Inducted into Local Chapter Hall of Fame, 1990. **Business Addr:** Executive Secretary-Treasurer, National Bowling Association, Inc, 377 Park Ave S, 7th Fl, New York, NY 10016.

LEE, MARK ANTHONY
Professional football player. **Personal:** Born Mar 20, 1958, Hanford, CA. **Educ:** Univ of Washington, attended. **Career:** Green Bay Packers, cornerback, 1980-. **Honors/Awds:** Led or shared with Packer secondary in knocking down opponent passes; Packers leading punt returner during 1981 season. **Business Addr:** Green Bay Packers, 1265 Lombardi Ave, Green Bay, WI 54304-3997.

LEE, MICHAEL WARING. **See Obituaries section.**

LEE, MILDRED KIMBLE
Educator. **Personal:** Born Jan 2, 1919, New York, NY; daughter of Ernestine Mildred Scott Kimble (deceased) and Ural Kimble (deceased); married Granville Wheeler Sr, Nov 9, 1940; children: Granville Wheeler, Jr. **Educ:** Hunter Coll, New York, NY, AB cum laude, 1938; City College, (Baruch), New York, NY, MBA, 1943; further graduate study at Hunter Coll, 1943-60, City College of New York, 1960-64, State Univ Humanistic Educ Center, Albany, NY, 1971-72; Fordham Univ, New York, NY, EdD, 1977. **Career:** Morris High School Bd of Educ, New York, NY, teacher, guidance counselor, AP in guidance, 1949-66; District 8 Bd of Educ, New York, NY, supervisor of guidance, 1966-77; Fordham Univ, Lincoln Center Campus, New York, NY, asst and assoc prof, 1977-84; City Univ of New York Graduate Center, Center for Advanced Study Educ (CASE), New York, NY, project dir, 1984-; worked as adjunct prof, 1966-77, at Adelphi Univ Urban Center, City Coll of New York, and Teachers Coll at Columbia Univ; mem of Retired School Supervisors and Admin (RSSA), NYC Bd of Educ, 1977-; mem of Assoc of Black Women in Higher Educ (ABWHE), 1979-; partner of Lee & Lee Financial Mgmt, 1982-; evaluator for Fordham Univ, Day Care Council, 1984-95; consultant for Adult Basic Educ, NYC Bdof Educ, 1984-94. **Orgs:** Mem, Natl Urban Educ Assoc, 1981-85; mem, contributor, NAACP; mem, contributor, Natl Urban League; contributor, United Negro Coll Fund; membership chairperson, Wistarians of Hunter College, 1980-; member, Fordham University Alumni Association, 1977-. **Honors/Awds:** Sarah Ollesheimer Scholarship, Hunter Coll, 1939; plaque for "outstanding achievements in education," Natl Council Negro Women, 1978; plaque for "outstanding guidance supervisor," Morrisania Community Council, 1978; author of articles published in periodicals, including Forum, Educ Technology, Journal of Black Studies, and Educ Forum; Hunter College Hall of Fame, 1983; MENSA, 1985. **Home Addr:** 2 Fordham Hill Oval, #8EF, Bronx, NY 10468. **Business Addr:** Graduate School & University Center, City Univ of New York, Center for Advanced Study in Education, 25 West 43 St, Rm 620, New York, NY 10036.

LEE, NATHANIEL
Attorney. **Educ:** Florida College; Morehead State University, BA, 1977, MA, 1978; Univ of GA, JD, 1982. **Career:** Wilson, Coleman Roberts, 1981-83; Nathaniel Lee & Assocs, 1983-86; Watkins & Lee, partner, 1986-91; Lee & Clark, sr partner, 1991-. **Orgs:** Police Athletic League, bd mem, 1993-96; Ronald McDonald House, bd mem, 1985-; Marion Co Bar Assn, chairman of bd, 1988-91, officer, 1984-88; NAACP, Indianapolis Branch, vp, 1986-88; Indianapolis Urban League, golf chairman, 1992-94. **Honors/Awds:** Community Service Award, Marion County Bar Association, 1992; Special Contributor Award, Wheelers Boys Club; Captains Club; PAL Club. **Business Addr:** Senior Partner, Lee & Clark, 151 N Delaware, Ste 2025, Indianapolis, IN 46204, (317)631-5151.

LEE, OLIVER B.
Educator. **Personal:** Born Sep 27, 1926, Cleveland, OH; married Isis Edna; children: Brenda, Linda, Jacquelyn, John. **Educ:** Springfield Coll Springfield MA, BS 1953; Springfield Coll Springfield MA, MS 1957. **Career:** Cleveland YMCA, dir pe 1954-59; Cleveland, Vocational Rehab Cleveland, counselor supr 1959-64; OH Bur of Vocational Rehab Cleveland 1964-66; Rehab Serv Cleveland Soc for Blind Cleveland, dir 1966-67; Counseling & Placement Aim-Jobs Cleveland, dir 1967-69; Comm Extension Program Cleveland State U, dir 1969-73; Cleveland State U, asso dean 1973-; Youth Program Dir, Salvation Army, Superior Corps, Cleveland 1963-. **Honors/Awds:** United Area Citizens Agency Leadership Devel Award 1972; Kiwanis Club Serv to Youth Award 1973; Lincoln HS Football Hall of Fame Hinton WV 1972. **Military Serv:** USAF sgt 1946-48. **Business Addr:** Div of Continuing Ed, Cleveland State Univ, Cleveland, OH.

LEE, OTIS K.
Restaurateur. **Personal:** Born in Detroit, MI. **Career:** Mr FoFo's Deli and Restaurant, owner, president, 1973-. **Honors/Awds:** 14th/15th District Democratic Party Annual Fundraiser, honoree, 1993. **Special Achievements:** Commissioned by Kentucky Fried Chicken to create a sweet potato pie for mass marketing, 1993-; donates frozen turkeys each year for Thanksgiving. **Business Addr:** Owner, Mr FoFo's Deli, 8902 Second Ave, Detroit, MI 48202, (313)873-4450.

LEE, PAULINE W.
Library director. **Personal:** Born Nov 6, 1933, Simsboro, LA; daughter of Mionia Williams Willis and Clinton Willis; married Melvin Lee, Oct 3, 1963. **Educ:** Southern University, Baton Rouge, LA, BA, social studies/library science (cum Laude), 1955; University of Michigan, Ann Arbor, MI, MALS, 1961; California State College, Los Angeles, CA, 1966; Louisiana Tech University, Ruston, LA, 1971-72. **Career:** St Tammy High School, Louisiana, school librarian, 1955-58; GSU, Grambling, LA, circulation librarian, 1958-62, education librarian, 1962-76, coordinator of public services, 1975-77, acting dir, 1977-78, dir of the library, 1978-. **Orgs:** Member, Academic Library Administrators of Louisiana; member, American Library Assn; member, Library Development Committee of Louisiana; life member, Grambling State University Alumni Assn; member, Louisiana Library Assn; member, Trail Blazer Library System; member, Ruston-Grambling League of Women Voters; member, Black Caucus of the American Library Assn. **Honors/Awds:** Service Award, New Rocky Valley Baptist Church, 1981; Certificate of Merit, Gov Edwin Edwards, 1978; Awards of Recognition, Alpha Kappa Alpha Sorority, 1976; Certificate of Appreciation, Future Business Leaders of America, 1973; Certificate of Recognition, Lewis Temple CME Church, 1972; Task Force on Academic Libraries/Library Master Plan, 1980; author, Courage Through Love: A Story of a Family, Ruston Daily Leader, 1982. **Special Achievements:** Staff Development Workshop, SUSBO, consultant, 1980; Journal of Interlibrary Loan and Information Supply, consulting editor, 1989. **Home Addr:** PO Box 456, Grambling, LA 71245. **Business Addr:** Director, A C Lewis Memorial Library, Grambling State University, University Library, PO Box 3, Grambling, LA 71245.

LEE, RITTEN EDWARD
Business executive. **Personal:** Born Jun 25, 1925, Brighton, AL; son of Mattie Hogue Lee and Ritten Lee; married Betty Allen; children: Anthony Edward, Juliana Hogue. **Educ:** Earlham Coll, BA 1950; Univ of CT School of Soc Work, MA 1953. **Career:** Rutgers University, Newark, NJ, adjunct professor, 1965-81; Hudson Guild NYC, exec dir 1972-77; adj lecturer, Hunter Coll Sch of Social Work, 1977-78; United Neighborhood House NYC, dir manpower 1977-80; Natl Charities Info Bur NYC, asst dir 1980-81; Seneca Ctr, exec director, 1982-. **Orgs:** Publ BLACFAX Mag 1982-85; jazz disc jockey WCVI, WENY, WHRC 1981-84; consult New York City Dept of Law 1981-82; trustee Comm Church of NY 1973-77; bd mem RENA-COA Multi-Serv Ctr; trustee Earlham Coll 1970-79; publisher, BLACFAX Calendar 1989-. **Honors/Awds:** Sarah Addington Awd Earlham Coll 1950; Hon Mention Poetry Mag 1950-51; Poetry Publ Span, Botteghe Oscure Crisis, Flame, Crucible & others; Commiss NCNCR Appt Newark Comm for Neighborhood Conserv 1968; Cert of Apprec RENA-COA Multi Serv Ctr 1979. **Military Serv:** AAF sgt 2 yrs 4 mo; Good Conduct; Amer Theatre Victory 1943-46. **Home Addr:** 214 W 138th St, New York, NY 10030.

LEE, ROBERT EMILE
Oil company executive. **Personal:** Born Aug 19, 1948, New Orleans, LA; son of Mae Louise Lee and Robert Emile Lee Sr; married Glendarene Beck; children: Joseph. **Educ:** Tulane Univ, BS 1970; Univ of Chicago, MBA 1973. **Career:** Martin Marietta Aerospace, engineering admin specialist 1973-75; Tenneco Oil, planning analyst 1976-78, supply coord 1978-80, mgr product distribution 1980-84, mgr mktg & planning 1984-86; sr crude oil representative 1986-87. **Orgs:** Mem NBMBA

Assn Houston Chapter 1986-. **Home Addr:** 2318 Sugarline Dr, Sugar Land, TX 77479. **Business Addr:** Sr Crude Oil Rep, Tenneco Oil Co, PO Box 2511, Houston, TX 77001.

LEE, RONALD B.

Business executive. **Personal:** Born May 26, 1932, New York; son of Lillian B (Jackson) Lee and Kermit J Lee; married Nancy Jean (Knowalk), Oct 10, 1985; children: Dean E, Brett M. **Educ:** US Military Acad West Point, BS 1954; US Defense Language Inst, attended 1962; Indsl Coll Armed Forces, attended 1962; Syracuse Univ, MBA 1964; Syracuse Univ, Army Comptrollership School 1964; Western New England Coll, LLD (Hon) 1969; American Univ, PhD (ABD) 1971, MA 1977; Center for Urban Affairs, dir; Lawrence F O'Brien, asst provost. **Career:** White House Fellow, staff 1965-66; US Postal Serv, dir planning & syst analysis 1966-68; Michigan State Univ, prof 1968-69; US, asst postmaster gen 1969-72; Xerox Corp, dir mktg analysis 1972-73, region manager tech serv NE reg 1973-75, reg mgr branch operations 1975-78, mgr govt/educ & med mktg Rochester 1978-79, mgr bus & comm affairs Arlington VA 1979-82; Energy Intl Corp, pres; Marc London Ltd, chmn; Phoenix Group Intl Ltd, pres 1982-89; Development Management Group Inc, Chicago IL, exec vice pres 1989-. **Orgs:** Assn West Point Grads; Assn of Syracuse Army Comptrolles; Amer Soc Public Admin; Alpha Phi Alpha; White House Fellows Assn; life mem, NAACP; life mem, Natl Urban League; Amer Acad Pol & Soc Sci; bd trustees, Western New England Coll; bd trustees Natl Acad Public Admin; bd trustees Natl Inst Public Admin; bd advisors Natl Assn Sickle Cell Diseases; Natl Alliance of Business DC; Natl Inst of Public Affairs; Greater Washington Bd of Trade; DC Private Indus Counc; chmn bd of trustees, Capital Children's Mus; bd dir United Way Inc Rochester; bd dir Jr Achievement of Greater Washington; bd dir Natl Conf of Christians & Jews Washington; bd dir, Comm Found of Greater Washington DC; bd dir Metro Washington Min PurchasingCouncil; 1st pres Okinawa Coll Club 1958-59; 1st pres White House Fellows A 1966. **Honors/Awds:** Arthur S Fleming Awd 1 of 10 Most Outstanding Young Men in Govt 1968; Dept Army Outstanding Civilian Serv Med 1968; Miles Kimball Awd Contrib Bus Mailers 1971; numerous publications & speaking appearances; elected Beta Gamma Sigma (Bus Hon); pres Universal Postal Union Special Study Group Berne Switzerland; 20-25 publications & chapters of books. **Military Serv:** AUS 1954-67, Vietnam Veteran, major.

LEE, ROTAN

Physician (retired), hospital administrator. **Personal:** Born Nov 6, 1906, Bushkill, PA; married Bessie; children: Terry, Rotan. **Educ:** PA State U, BA 1928; Howard U, MD 1938; Columbia U, post grad 1932-33. **Career:** Med Audit Com, chmn; Utilization Rev Com, co-chmn; Ctr City Hosp, co-chmn 1976-; Diamond Family Med Ctr, dir 1974-75; Dist Health Ctr City of Phila, adminstr 1947-73; sch physician 1941-42; surg resd 1939-40; Mercy Hosp, med internship 1938-39; pvt med prac gen surgeon 1946-75; Center City Hosp, med staff 1960-77; Bushkill Water Co. **Orgs:** Mem HM Club of Am 1972-; Philadelphia Co Med Soc PA State Med Soc; AMA; Nat Med Assn; Chi Delta Mu; Omega Psi Phi. **Honors/Awds:** Articles on Twins & Twinning; Human Mastoid Process. **Military Serv:** AUS med corps capt 1942-46.

LEE, SHAWN SWABODA

Professional football player. **Personal:** Born Oct 24, 1966, Brooklyn, NY. **Educ:** North Alabama, communications major. **Career:** Tampa Bay Buccaneers, defensive tackle, 1988-89; Miami Dolphins, 1990-91; San Diego Chargers, 1992-. **Orgs:** Two Tons of Fun/San Diego Chargers Players Community Resource Center, co-founder. **Business Addr:** Professional Football Player, San Diego Chargers, Qualcomm Stadium, 9449 Friars Rd, San Diego, CA 92108, (619)280-2111.

LEE, SHEILA JACKSON

Congresswoman. **Personal:** Born Jan 12, 1950, Queens, NY; married Elwyn Cornelius Lee; children: Erica Shelwyn, Jason Cornelius Bennett. **Educ:** Yale University, BA (honors), political science, 1972; University of Virginia, School of Law, JD, 1975. **Career:** Mudge Rose Guthrie & Alexander, associate, summer 1974; Wld Harkrader & Ross, atty 1975-78; US House of Reps & Select Comm on Assasinations, staff counsel 1977-78; Fulbright & Jaworski, atty 1978-80; United Energy Resources, atty 1980-87; Brodsky & Ketchand, partner 1987-; City of Houston, associate judge 1987-90; private practice, attorney, 1988-; Houston City Council, Position Number Four, council member-at-large, 1990-94; US House of Representatives, congresswoman, 1994-. **Orgs:** Bd dirs John Courtney Murray Found Yale Univ New Haven 1972-73, John Courtney Murray Traveling & Rsch Fellowship, Houston Area Urban League 1979-, Episcopal Ctr for Children 1976-78, WA Council of Lawyers 1976-78; State Bar of TX, Bar Jour Com 1980; bd dir Amer Assn of Blacks in Energy 1980; chairperson Black Women Lawyers Assn 1980; pres Houston Lawyers Assoc 1983-84; dir TX Young Lawyers Assoc 1986; pres Houston Metro Ministries 1984-85; dir Children's Museum 1985-; dir Sam Houston Area Council Boy Scouts of Amer 1987-; Alpha Kappa Alpha Sorority Inc; Alpha Kappa Omega Chapter, Houston TX, mem 1988-. **Honors/Awds:** Outstanding Young Lawyer Pampered Lady Boutique Awards Luncheon NY 1977; Women's Day Speaker Award Linden Blvd Seventh-Day Adven Ch NY 1978; Rising Star of TX Awd TX Bus Mag 1983; Outstanding Young Houstonian Awd C of C 1984; Houston Lawyers Association Outstanding Serv Awd 1984; nominated Outstanding Young Lawyer of Houston 1985; Named one of Houston's 20 Most Influential Black Women 1984; Named Outstanding History Maker (Legal) Riverside General Hosp Awds Prog 1987; selected as fellow TX Bar Found for Outstanding Legal and Community Serv 1986. **Business Addr:** Congresswoman, US House of Representatives, 410 Cannon HOB, Washington, DC 20515.

LEE, SHIRLEY FREEMAN

Association executive (retired). **Personal:** Born May 6, 1928, Cleveland, OH; daughter of Marvin & Vivian Salvant Freeman; married Douglas F Lee (deceased); children: Vivian, Durriyya (deceased). **Educ:** Notre Dame Coll, BA, 1950; Boston Coll, School of Social Work, MSW, 1952; Case Western Reserve, 1980-; Baldwin-Wallace, 1986. **Career:** Com of Massachusetts Div of Child Guardianship, foster home, 1954-58; Head Start, supvr, 1965; Boston Redevel Authority, relocation spec, 1968-71; De Paul Infant Home, admin, 1981-83; Ohio Licensed Independent Social Worker, 1986; Catholic Soc Serv of Cuyahoga City, administrator day care ctr, counseling, outpatient mental health, until 1997. **Orgs:** Mem, Delta Sigma Theta; bd of dir, Long Beach & Van Nuys School of Business, 1977-89. **Home Addr:** 14221 Kingsford Ave, Cleveland, OH 44128.

LEE, SILAS, III

Educator. **Personal:** Born Jul 24, 1954, New Orleans, LA; son of Henrietta Johnson Lee and Silas Lee Jr; divorced. **Educ:** Loyola Univ, BA 1976; Univ of New Orleans, MS 1979, pursuing PhD, urban studies, currently; Local & National Media, public opinion pollster & analyst. **Career:** Silas Lee & Assoc, pres 1982-; Xavier University, New Orleans, LA, sociology instructor, 1988-; Public opinion pollster and analyst for local and national media. **Orgs:** Pres Silas Lee & Assoc first Black Opinion Pollster 1982-; consultant Ed Found 1984-; Published, The Econ Profile of Blacks & Whites in New Orleans; vice chairman Natl Black Tourism Assn 1989. **Honors/Awds:** Honorary Secretary of State for LA 1984; Court Certified Expert on the Social and Economic Status of Blacks and Public Opinion Research, Eastern District of Louisiana Court and Federal District Court. **Business Addr:** 400 Poydras St, Ste 2620, New Orleans, LA 70130.

LEE, SPIKE (SHELTON JACKSON LEE)

Film director. **Personal:** Born Mar 20, 1957, Atlanta, GA; son of Jacquelyn Shelton Lee (deceased) and William James Edwards Lee III; married Tonya Lewis, 1993; children: Satchel Lewis, Jackson. **Educ:** Morehouse College, BA, 1979; New York University, MA, filmmaking, 1983. **Career:** Film producer, writer, director, currently; Harvard University, instructor, 1991-. **Honors/Awds:** Writer/director of films: She's Gotta Have It, 1986; School Daze, 1988; Do the Right Thing, 1989; Mo' Better Blues, 1990; Jungle Fever, 1991; Malcolm X, 1992; Crooklyn, 1994; Clockers, 1995; Get on the Bus, 1996; 4 Little Girls, 1997; author: Spike Lee's Gotta Have It: Inside Guerilla Filmmaking, Simon & Schuster, 1987; Uplift the Race, Simon & Schuster, 1988; Best Seat in the House, 1997; Student Academy Award for Joe's Bed-Stuy Barber Shop: We Cut Heads, Academy of Motion Picture Arts aND Sciences, 1982; New Generation Award, LA Film Critics, for She's Gotta Have It; Prix de Jeunesse, Cannes Film Festival, for She's Gotta Have It, 1986; starred in commercials for Nike sport shoes; has directed music videos for Anita Baker, Miles Davis, and Branford Marsalis. **Business Addr:** President/CEO, Spike/DDB, New York, NY.

LEE, STRATTON CREIGHTON

Business executive. **Personal:** Born Apr 17, 1920, Tarrytown, NY; married Yvonne Holder; children: Stratton C Jr. **Educ:** Coll of the City of NY, BS 1942, MBA 1952. **Career:** Licensed real estate broker NY State 1955-; Adelphi Univ & Queens Coll, instr Afro-Am History 1967-70; Urban Home Ownership, vice pres 1970-71; Natl Corp for Housing Partnerships, dir of mgmt 1971-72; Natl Center for Housing Mgmt, exec assoc 1972; Inst of Real Estate Mgmt, prop mgr 1974-; Creighton Housing Mgmt, pres 1974-77; Pratt Inst vice pres campus mgmt 1977-82; Arco/Metro Prop Mgmt corp, pres 1982-; Freeport Housing Authority, chairman, 1990. **Orgs:** Mem Natl Assn of Housing & Redevel Ofcrs 1950-; mem Nassau Cnty Econ Opportunity Commn 1969-70; mem Assn of Phys Plant Adminstrs 1980; Ny State Legislative Aide 32nd AD Congr Dist 1974-76. **Honors/Awds:** CPM of the Year Inst of Real Estate Mgmt 1976; mem HUD-IREM natl Com Natl Assn of Realtors 1976-78. **Military Serv:** ROTC Sgt 1938-39. **Business Addr:** Real Estate Manager & Devel, 196 Delaware Ave, Freeport, NY 11520.

LEE, VAN SPENCER

Government official (retired). **Personal:** Born Mar 2, 1942, Morristown, TN; married Beulah Annette Arnett; children: Eric M, Melissa R, Steven M. **Educ:** Knoxville Coll Knoxville TN, 1961-63; TVA Pub Safety Serv Sch, cert 1971; Walters State Coll, AS (cum laude) 1972. **Career:** City of Morristown TN, vice mayor; TVA, pub safety officer 1971-77, equal employment investigator 1973-77, lt unit supv 1977-84, asst chief. **Orgs:** Mem TN Law Enforcement Officers Assn 1967; mem Fraternal Order of Police 1967; life mem Nat Rifle Assn 1970; mem, Bethel United Methodist Ch; mem Morristown Area C of C 1972; mem, past pres W Elem PTA 1973-74; mem, sec Morristown City Council PTA 1973-74; mem bd of dir Morristown-Hamblen Day Care Ctr 1972-76; mem adv com Morristown City Schs 1973-77; mem Lincoln Heights Middle Sch PTA 1977-; mem Morristown-Hamblen HS W Band Boosters 1977-; speaker Emeritus TVA Pub Safety Serv Sch 1971. **Honors/Awds:** 1st black patrolman Morristown Police Dept 1967-71; 1st black operator Am Enka 1965-67; 1st black commr Morristown Housing Authority 1975-77; 1st black councilmember Ward 1 City of Morristown 1977; 1st black commr Hamblen Co Work Release Program 1978-79; 1st black chmn Hamblen Co Am Cancer Soc 1980; 1st black mem Morristown Kiwanis Club 1976; 1st black mem bd of trustees Morristown-Hamblen Hosp 1977-; Outstanding Young Man of Am 1973; Charter Pres Award Lincoln Heights Middle Sch PTA Morristown 1974; Outstanding Defensive Course Instr Award TVA Nat Safety Council 1977; Meritorious Serv Award TVA Pub Safety Serv Knoxville TN 1978; Outstanding Comm Serv Award Morristown Coll 1978; award Morristown Honor Club 1980.

LEE, VIVIAN BOOKER

Federal health services administrator (retired). **Personal:** Born Jan 28, 1938, Spring, TX; daughter of Alvirita Wells Little; children: Anthony. **Educ:** Registered Nurse Cert, 1958; Public Health Cert, 1959; Univ of WA, BS, nursing, 1959, Master's Degree in Nursing Administration, 1961; School Nurse Cert, 1967; Univ of Puget Sound, M Pub Admin, 1980. **Career:** VA Hosp Seattle, psychiatric nurse 1959-60; Group Health Corp Puget Sound, outpatient clinic nurse 1961-66; Seattle Public Sch, sch nurse 1966-68; Renton Sch, supr group health hosp & title I health supr 1968-72; Health Care Consultant & Comm Volunteer, 1994-; Office of Women's Health, Office of Regional Health Admin, US Public Health Service, Region X, Seattle, founding dir, 1993-94, Regional Mgr of the Title X Family Planning Prog, 1980-; Title X Family Planning Prog in US PHS, Region X, Seattle, regional mgr, 1980-93, Regional Women's Health Corrd, 1984-93; Region X in Family Planning & Maternal & Child Health Programs, public health advisor, 1975-80, Region X Adolescent Health Coord, 1975-91, first PHS Region X Minority Health Corrd, 1987-92, PHS EEO investigator; US PHS, Region X, PHS EEo Officer, prog management officer, 1972-75; Emer Rm Nursing, Virginia Mason & Univ Hosp; Psychiatric Nursing at Veterans Administration Hospital; Public Health Nursing with Seattle/King Co DPH; School Nursing in Seattle & Renton School Districts; relief supervisor, Outpatient Clinical Services; Hosp Nursing Supervisor at Group Health Cooperative, Puget Sound; Nurse instructor, 50th Gen Hospital Army Reserve Corp, 1960-64. **Orgs:** Univ of WA Nurses Alumnae Assn; mem Found for Intl Understanding through Students; mem Delta Sigma Theta; mem Girls Club of Puget Sound; participant White House Conf on Civil Rights 1966; Food Nutrition Health & Children 1969-70; mem Natl Family Planning and Reproductive Health Assn, Washington State Family Planning Cncl; member, Washington Alliance Concerned With School Age Pregnancy; UW Minority Community Advisory Comm; United Methodist Church, UW Alumni Assn, exec committee bd, Diversity Committee chair; Multicultural Alumni partnership Club of the UWAA; Highline/West Seattle Mental Health Ctr bd mem; Mary Mahoney Professional Nurses Organization, Natl Family Planning & Reproductive Health Assn; Washington State Assn of Black Health Professionals; Alan Guttmacher Inst. **Honors/Awds:** Dept HEW Outstanding Performance Awd for Promoting Women's Equality 1975; DHHS Sustained Superior Performance Awds 1973-90; HRSA Awd for Excellence 1982; Washington Sch Nurse of Yr 1972; Outstanding Dedication Awd Washington State Cncl on Family Planning 1978; Annual Awd of Family Planning Advocates of Oregon State 1983, 1987, 1990; Region X Clinician Awd is named ''The Vivian O Lee Clinician of the Year Awd'' 1987; WACSAP Award, 1988; NFPRHA Award, 1991; Chief Nurse Officer's Award US Public Health Service, 1993; Cert of Recognition, Mary Mahoney Prof Nurses Organization, 1995; Featured in book ''The Path We Tread'' Mary Elizabeth Carnegie, Blacks in Nursing, 1986, 1995; Irving Kushner Award, Natl Family Planning & Reproductive Health Assn, 1995; Cert of Appreciation from US PHS, Region X, African-American Women's Health Care, 1994; Exemplary Service Award, Surgeon General of the US, Dr Joycelyn Elders, 24 yrs public service, 1994; Distinguished Service Award, US PHS Deputy Asst Secy, Population Affairs, Washington DC, 1994; Special Honors, nationwide group of RPC's for FPS; Deputy Asst Secy, Women's Health & the Dir of the PHS Office on Women's Health, US PHS, DHHS, 1994; PHS Region X Office Women's Health Annual Award, 1996; UWAA Volunteer of the Year, 1996. **Special Achievements:** Co-author of eight publications; Family Planning Services for Southeast Asians, Chlamydia, 1990 Health Objectives for the Nation, Title X Family Planning Prog, Pap Smear quality assurance. **Military Serv:** 50th Gen Hosp Reserve Corps 1959-63. **Home Addr:** 6323 Sand Point Way, NE, Seattle, WA 98115, (206)524-1312.

LEE, VIVIAN O.
Government official. **Career:** US Public Health Service, regional program mgr, currently. **Business Addr:** Regional Program Mgr., US Public Health Service, 2201 6th Ave., RX29, Seattle, WA 98121, (206)615-2469.

LEE, WILLIAM H.
Publisher. **Personal:** Born May 29, 1936, Austin, TX; son of Rev & Mrs Charles R Lee; married Kathryn Charles; children: Roderick Joseph, William Hanford, Jr, Lawrence Charles. **Educ:** Univ of CA, AB 1957; Sacramento State Coll, 1953-55. **Career:** Lee Sacramento Observer, pres, publisher; Lee Publishing Co, pres. **Orgs:** Pres, West Coast Black Publishers Assn, 1974-; sec, bd dir, Natl Newspaper Publishers Assn, 1970-73; mem, Delta Sigma Chi Journalism Frat; commr, Sacramento County Welfare Commn; founder, past pres, Men's Civil League of Sacramento; bd dir, Sacramento NAACP Credit Union; United Christian Center; dir, Sacramento Central YMCA; Sacramento Urban League; United Way; Sacramento County, Amer Cancer Soc; bd chmn, Sacramento Business Coordinating Council; co-founder, Sacramento Area Black Caucus; vice-chmn, Cancer Fund Drive; life mem, NAACP; mem, Sacramento Comm for Urban Renewal; Statewide Comm on Voter Registration. **Honors/Awds:** Sacramento's Outstanding Young Man of Year, 1965; received Sacramento C of C Distinguished Serv Award twice; Carl Murphy Plaque for community serv, 1974; John B Russwurm Trophy, 1973, 1975; Media Award, Western Regional Conf of Black Elected Officials, 1973; United Negro Coll Fund, 1975; Natl Media Appreciation Award; numerous natl & local newspaper awards; other civic leadership citations. **Military Serv:** USAFR 1959-65. **Business Addr:** PO Box 209, Sacramento, CA 95812.

LEE, WILLIAM JAMES EDWARDS, III (BILL LEE)
Musician, writer. **Personal:** Born Jul 23, 1928, Snow Hill, AL; son of Alberta Grace Edwards Lee and Arnold W Lee III; married Jacquelyn Shelton, Jun 7, 1954 (deceased); children: Shelton, Chris, David, Joie, Cinque; children: Arnold Tone Kaplan-Lee VI. **Educ:** Morehouse College, BA, 1951. **Career:** Self-employed jazz musician, 1950-; Folk Jazz Opera, Village Vanguard, 1968; Theatre in the Street, Youth In Action, Children's Folk Jazz Opera, Little Johnny, director/writer, 1971; Folk Jazz Opera, Alice Tully Hall, 1972; Folk Jazz Opera, Hampton University, 1973; Folk Jazz Opera, various college campuses, 1975; Essex County Community College, bass violin and Afro-American literature teacher, 1979-80; 9-B Folk Jazz Opera, 1981; College College Folk Jazz Opera, 1986; Westchester Community College, Lecture, Movie Music, 1992. **Orgs:** The New York Bass Violin Choir, founder, president, musical director, 1968-; The Brass Company, co-founder, co-musical director, 1970; The Desendents of Mike and Phoebe, founder, musical director, 1971-77; The Natural Spiritual Orchestra, founder, director, 1982-; Noah's Ark, co-founder, musical director, 1989-; Bill Lee and the Mo' Betta' Quartet, 1990; Jacobs Ladder, founder, children's chorus, 1991; His Wonders to Perform, musical director, umbrella group, 1991. **Honors/Awds:** The National Endowment of the Arts, Composing Grant, 1979, 1982; The LA Critics Awards, Best Movie Picture Score, Do the Right Thing, 1988; Columbia Records Citation, 300,000 record sales, Mo' Better Blues, 1990; Borough of Brooklyn, Howard Golden Citation for Service, 1991. **Home Addr:** 165 Washington Park, Brooklyn, NY 11205, (718)522-5802.

LEE, WILLIAM THOMAS
Labor official. **Personal:** Born Mar 27, 1942, Philadelphia, PA; son of Thelma Harper Lee and Walter Lee; married Celestine Tolbert Lee, Mar 25, 1978; children: Marie, Thomas, Melissa Cora. **Educ:** Temple University, Philadelphia, PA, BA, accounting, 1966. **Career:** Budd Company, Philadelphia, PA, cost accountant, 1966-67; Philadelphia Dress Joint Board Street, Philadelphia, PA, assistant manager, business agent, organizer, 1967-85; Local 132-98-102, ILGWU, New York, NY, manager/secretary, 1985-96; New York-New Jersey Regional Joint Board, manager, 1996-. **Orgs:** Board of directors, Empire Blue Cross/Blue Shield, 1988-; life member, NAACP, 1988-; member, Jewish Labor Committee, 1978-; member, Temple Varsity Club, 1966-; board member, A. Philip Randolph Institute, 1988-. **Honors/Awds:** Achievement Award, NAACP, 1988; Achievement Award, Philadelphia So. Jersey Dist. Council, 1985; Recipient of "Spirit of Life Award" from City of Hope Medical Ctr, 1991. **Business Addr:** Manager, Local 132-98-102, ILGWU, 275 7th Ave, 11th Floor, New York, NY 10001.

LEEK, EVERETT PAUL
Attorney. **Personal:** Born Jun 8, 1929, Canton, IL; son of Viola Petross Leek and James H. Leek; married Doreen A Dale; children: Everett Craig, Jennifer Ann, Paul Scott. **Educ:** MI State Univ, BS 1957, MS 1964; Univ of Detroit Law Sch, JD 1976. **Career:** US Treas Dept, agent 1957-60; Chevrolet Div Gen Motors, labor relations rep 1960-67; polygraph examiner/private consultant 1973-; Delta Coll, prof, 1967-92. **Orgs:** Mem NAACP, Alpha Phi Alpha, MI Assn of Polygraph Examiners; mem Amer, MI, Bar Assns; mem MI Trial Lawyers Assn. **Honors/Awds:** Professional Man of the Year, Negro Business & Professional Women's Assn 1970; Outstanding Educators of Amer 1972. **Military Serv:** USN 1949-53. **Business Addr:** Attorney, 330 S Washington, Saginaw, MI 48604.

LEEK, SANDRA D.
State official. **Personal:** Born Oct 8, 1954, Durham, NC; daughter of Inez Rempson Anderson and J Donald Leek. **Educ:** Tufts Univ, Medford, MA, BA Political Science, 1976; Indiana Univ, Bloomington, IN, JD, 1979. **Career:** Legal Services Org of Indiana, Inc, Indianapolis, IN, staff atty, 1979-81, managing atty, 1986-90; Indiana Legal Serv Support Center, dir, 1981-86; Indiana Dept of Employment & Training Services, chairperson review board member, unemployment insurance, 1990-92. **Orgs:** Mem, Delta Sigma Theta Sorority, Inc, 1979-; mem, Amer Bar Assn, 1979-; mem, Indiana State Bar Assn, 1979-; mem, Indianapolis Bar Assn, 1979-; Civil Cmt Representative, Natl Legal Aid & Defender Assn, 1981-89; mem, Natl Bar Assn, 1982-; chmn, Public Affairs/Indy YWCA, 1983-86; chmn, Political Action/Coalition of 100 Black Women, 1986-88; 2nd vice pres, bd of mgrs, Fall Creek YMCA, 1987-88; pres, Marion City Bar Assn, 1987-88; exec comm, NAACP, Indianapolis Branch, 1988-; mem, Links, Inc, 1988-; corp atty, Indiana Black Expo, Inc, 1988-. **Honors/Awds:** Exec editor, "You and the Law," 1983, 1985, 1992; moderator, Law for Laymen TV series, 1983, 1984, 1985; Woman of Achievement, Indy YWCA, 1985; Outstanding Contribution, Legal Services Org of Indiana, Inc, 1986, Outstanding Commununity Serv, Marion County Bar Assn, 1989. **Business Addr:** Director, Indiana Civil Rights Commission, 100 N Senate Ave, Room N 103, Indianapolis, IN 46260.

LEEKE, JOHN F.
Educator, organizational development. **Personal:** Born May 19, 1939, Indianapolis, IN; married Therese Gartin; children: Michael, Madelyn, Mark, Matthew. **Educ:** IN St U, BS 1961; Univ MI, MS 1966; Union Grad Sch, PhD 1977. **Career:** NEA, instrtn & prof devel spec 1968-85; Flint Comm Schools, teacher 1963-68; DC Public Schls, teacher 1962-63; IN State & Penal Frm, counselor 1962; Natl Training Lab of App Behavoral Science, consultant; Johnson & Johnson Pharmaceutical Core-States; US Dept Agriculture Grad School; Corning, Inc.; Kodak; Natl School Bds Assn; Natl Inst Drug Abuse; Consumer Product Safety Comm; Bell Labs; GSUSA; IN State Dept Instruction; numerous school systems; John F Leeke Associates, Inc, organizational development consultant, president, 1985-. **Orgs:** Mem St Joseph Ch Landover MD; Neighborhood Civic Orgnzn; Pi Lambda Phi. **Honors/Awds:** Achvmnt recgntn Pi Lambda Phi. **Business Addr:** President, John F. Leeke Associates, Inc, 11305 Indian Wells Lane, Mitchellville, MD 20721.

LEEKE, MADELYN CHERYL
Communications company executive. **Personal:** Born Dec 18, 1964, Flint, MI; daughter of John and Therese Leeke. **Educ:** Morgan State Univ, BA, 1986; Howard Univ School of Law, JD, 1989; Georgetown Univ Law Center, LLM, 1991. **Career:** Commodities Futures Trading Commission, legal advisor, 1989-90; John F Lecke Associates Inc, research policy analyst, 1990-93; Sunsum Communications, exec director, 1992-; DC Office of the Treasurer, debt manager, 1993-. **Business Phone:** (202)332-5767.

LEEPER, LUCIUS WALTER
Physician. **Personal:** Born Jan 9, 1922, Baltimore, MD; married Shirley Jenkins; children: Yvette, Fern, Frederick. **Educ:** Morgan State Univ, BS 1945; Howard Univ, MD 1948. **Career:** Resident Trng, 1948-52; Private Practice, physician 1954-66; MD State Helth Dept Div Voc Rehab, med adv comm 1960-66; State of MD Bd Mental Health, mental hygiene rev bd 1960-63; Occupational Medicine, 1977-79; Social Security Administration, dir employee health and occupational safety 1974-79. **Orgs:** Bd dir Amer Diabetes Assn 1974-; mem Cncl of Fed Med Dir 1969-; mem AEAONMS; tb & cancer bd Imp Cncl AEAONMS 1969-71; bd of dirs Lynn Cosmetics. **Honors/Awds:** First person operating iron lung via USAF plane 1953. **Military Serv:** AUS pvt 1943-46; USAF capt 1952-54.

LEEPER, RONALD JAMES
Government official. **Personal:** Born Dec 14, 1944, Charlotte, NC; married Phyllis Mack; children: Rhonda, Atiba. **Career:** LRT & Assoc Consultant Firm, pres; L&S Housing Corp, pres; Charlotte City Council, former council mem 10 yrs; RJL Reper Construction Co, president. **Orgs:** Chmn city council Community Devel Committee 1979-87; past pres NC Black Elected Municipal Official Assoc 1982-; former mem of bd of dir Urban League 1983-; chmn Charlotte-Meck Lenburg Black Elected Office 1984-85; organizer Westpark Youth Athletic Assoc; organizer Colony Acres Home Owners Assoc; former bd of dir Natl Conf Christians & Jews; bd mem Visitors of Boys Town NC; organizer of Vote Task Force; mem, past pres, St Mark's United Methodist Church; bd mem, Habitat for Humanities; past chmn, bd of dirs, C W Williams Health Ctr; former bd mem, Z Smith Reynolds; organizer, Save the Seed; former bd mem, Metropolitan YMCA. **Honors/Awds:** Certificate of Appreciation St Mark's United Methodist Church 1978, 1980; Sr Citizen United for Serv Christian Social Concern 1980; Certificate of Appreciation Black Political Awareness League Winston-Salem NC 1984; Meritorious Awd NAACP Outstanding Comm Serv 1984; Selected as one of ten Outstanding Men in America, 1979-81; Award of Appreciation for Services to Senior Citizens and the Handicapped, Senior Citizens United, 1981; Outstanding Community Service Award, Alpha Kappa Alpha Sorority, 1980; Recognized as Chart Pres, NC-BEMCO, 1982; YMCA Outstanding Service Award, Community Services Program, 1987; Honorary Neighbor of the Year Award, Charlotte Organizing Program, 1987; Award of Appreciation, Charlotte Civic League for Leadership, 1987; Award of Appreciation, Natl Assn of Negro Business and Professional Women's Club, 1987; Martin Luther King Gold Medallion, Charlotte-Mecklenburg Community Relations Committee, 1991; Community Pride Mazina, Citizen of the Year, 1994.

LEE SANG, SHARON NOLAN
Administrative law judge, lawyer. **Personal:** Born Mar 26, 1946, Kansas City, KS; daughter of Mary Louise Davis-Nolan & James Dewitt Nolan; divorced; children: David Lee Nolan. **Educ:** Metropolitan Jr College, AA, 1966; University of Missouri at Kansas City, BA, 1968; Howard University, School of Law, JD, 1972. **Career:** US Virgin Islands & United States, private law practice, 1973-89; New York City Board of Education, impartial hearing officer, 1987; Abyssinian Baptist Church, New York City, lawyer/council, 1987-89; New York State Department of Motor Vehicles, 1989-. **Orgs:** Association of Administrative Law Judges of NY State Department of Motor Vehicles, president, 1992-; NY State Public Employees Federation, AFL-CIO, council leader, 1996-; Brooklyn Bar Association, trustee, 1995-; Metropolitan Black Bar Association, board of directors, 1986-; National Bar Association, Region II, former secretary, associate director, 1984; Medical Malpractice Bd, panel mem, 1986-89; Metropolitan Black Bar Scholarship Fund, board member, 1986-; NY Civil Court Abritrator, 1986. **Special Achievements:** American Diabetes Assn, Harlem Coalition, lay mem, 1996-; Abyssinian Baptist Church, Chancel Choir, soloist; Carole King's background singer; Saundra Reeves's background singer, 1995-; gospel singer since age 5. **Business Addr:** Administrative Law Judge, New York State Department of Motor Vehicles, 2116 Adam Clayton Powell Jr Blvd, 2nd FL, New York, NY 10027.

LEE-SMITH, HUGHIE
Artist. **Personal:** Born Sep 20, 1915, Eustis, FL; son of Alice Williams and Luther Smith; married Patricia Ann Thomas. **Educ:** Cleveland Inst of Art, Cert of Grad 1938; Wayne State Univ, BS Art Edn. **Career:** Artist; Art Students League, instr of painting; Grosse Pointe War Memorial Assn, Grosse Pointe Farms, MI, instructor in painting, 1955-66; Howard Univ, Washington, DC, artist-in-residence, 1969-71; Trenton State College, Trenton, NJ, adjunct professor of history, 1972. **Orgs:** Council member, Natl Acad of Design, 1986-89; board mem, 1983-85, vice pres, 1985-88, Artists Fellowship Inc; pres, 1980-82, vice pres, 1984-85, Audubon Artists Inc; bd dir Artists Equity Assn 1982-84; Natl Adv Cncl Studio Museum Harlem, NYC; mem Grand Central Art Galleries 1967-80; Adv Commn High Sch of Art & Design New York City 1976-80; MI Assn of Pub Sch Adult Educators; MI Acad of Sci, Arts & Letters; The Century Assn NYC; The Lotos Club NYC; lectures & panel discussions: Princeton Univ, Univ of Chgo, Coll Art Assn Wash, DC, Montclair State Coll, NC Central Univ, Voorhees Coll, Morgan State Coll, The Walden Sch, Pub TV Channel 13 1979, Cleveland Inst of Art, Cleveland State Univ. **Honors/Awds:** Audubon Artists Inc The Ralph Fabri Award 1982, The Binny and Smith Award 1983, The Emily Lowe Award 1985; Bronze Plaque MD Commn on Afro-Amer Hist & Culture 1981; Art Achievement Award Wayne St Univ 1983; Key to the City of Hartford 1984; "Hughie Lee-Smith Day," Cleveland OH, Oct 19, 1984; numerous collections incl, Metropolitan Museum of Art/Det Institute of Arts/ Philadelphia Museum, The Natl Mus of Amer Art Wash, DC; Chase Manhattan Bank NYC; Univ of MI; Howard Univ; Barnet-Aden Coll Corcoran Gallery, Wash, DC; Alain Locke Soc Princeton Univ; US Post Office NYC; Schomburg Coll NYC; numerous one man shows incl, Snowden Gallery Chicago 1945; Janet Nessler Gallery New York City 1960, 1962, 1964; Western MI Univ Kalamazoo 1977; CRT's Craftery Gallery Hartford, CT 1984; Malcolm Brown Gallery Cleveland 1984-88; Century Assn of NY 1984;Butler Inst of Amer Art, 1989; VA Polytechnical Univ, 1989; publications incl, Crisis Mag 1970, 1983; Amer Artist Mag Oct 1978; Scholastic Mag HS Art Exhib Catalogue 1981; Represented in Cleveland Inst Art "The First Hundred Years" 1983; num other exhib; Len Everette Memorial Prize Audubon Artists Inc 1986; Honorary Doctorate, Maryland Institute, College of Art, 1995; Medal of Merit, Lotos Club, New York, NY, 1996; Benjamin West Clinedinst Medal, Artists Fellowship, Inc, New York, NY, 1996. **Military Serv:** USN Seaman 1st Class 1943-45; Cert of Commendation 1974. **Home Addr:** 3741 Altez, NE, Albuquerque, NM 87111.

LEEVY, CARROLL M.
Educator, physician, researcher. **Personal:** Born Oct 13, 1920, Columbia, SC; son of Mary Kirkland Leevy and Isaac S Leevy; married Ruth S Barboza; children: Carroll B, Maria S. **Educ:** Fisk Univ, AB 1941; Univ of MI, MD 1944; NJ Inst of Techn, ScD 1973; Univ of Nebraska, ScD, 1989. **Career:** Jersey City Med Cntr, dir clinical invest 1947-56; Harvard Med Sch, assoc in med 1959-60; NJ Med School, assoc prof/prof med 1960-; Veterans Medical Center, East Orange, NJ, chief of medicine, 1966-71; Sammy Davis Jr Natl Liver Inst, med dir & chm bd 1984-; NJ Med Sch, distinguished prof/chmn dept med 1975-91; University Hosp, Liver Transplant Prog, medical director, 1989-; NJ Med School Liver Ctr, dir, 1990-. **Orgs:** NASA, con-

sult, 1966-70; World Health Organization, 1978; Consult Food & Drug Admin 1970-; consult Natl Inst Health 1966-; consult VA 1966-; Consult Health Care, finance adm, 1991-; pres Am Assn for Study of Liver Disease; pres Intl Assn for Study of the Liver; Natl Commn on Digestive Disease 1977-79; NIH Alcohol & Addiction Found; chmn faculty Conf on Stand of Diagnostic Criteria & Methodol in Liver Disease; Soc for Experimental Biol; Amer Coll of Phys; chmn Faculty Orgn 1970-72; bd Concerned Citizens 1971-75; president, 1986-88, chairman board of trustees, 1988-, Assn for Academic Minority Physicians; chairman, Int Committee on Information in Liver Disease, 1992-; CapeTown Uni, fund, 1980-; UNOS, 1989-. **Honors/Awds:** Author and co-author of 6 books and over 500 scientific articles 1946-; 2 patents; mem Phi Beta Kappa; mem Alpha Omega Alpha; Modern Medicine Award, 1971; Achievement Award Natl Med Assn, 1989; master, Amer Coll of Physicians, 1991; Robert Williams Award, Assn of Professors of Medicine, 1991; Special Achievement Award, American Assn for Study of Liver Disease, 1991; NJ Med School, 40th Anniversary Honoree; editorial board, American Journal of Medicine; D Hon, Fisk University, 1981. **Military Serv:** US Navy, Cdr, 1954-60. **Home Addr:** 35 Robert Dr, Short Hills, NJ 07078.

LEFFALL, LASALLE DOHENY, JR.

Oncologist, educator. **Personal:** Born May 22, 1930, Tallahassee, FL; son of Martha Leffall and LaSalle D Leffall, Sr; married Ruth McWilliams; children: LaSalle III. **Educ:** FL A&M Univ, BS 1948; Howard Univ, MD 1952. **Career:** Howard Univ Coll Med, asst dean 1964-70, acting dean 1970, prof chmn dept surgery 1970-95, prof of surgery, 1995-. **Orgs:** Natl Med Assn 1962; SE Surg Congress 1970; Soc of Surg Chmn 1970; Alpha Omega Alpha 1972; Inst of Med Natl Acad of Sci 1973; Amer Surg Assn 1976; pres Amer Cancer Soc 1979; Natl Urban League; NAACP; YMCA; Alpha Phi Alpha; Sigma Pi Phi; Natl Cancer Adv Bd 1980; Amer Bd of Surgery 1981; Cosmos Club; Comm on CA; sec Amer Coll Surgeons 1983; president, Society of Surgical Oncology, 1978-79; president, Society of Surgical Chairmen, 1988-90; executive committee chairman, United Way of America, 1989-92; American Coll of Surgeons, pres, 1995-96. **Honors/Awds:** 1st prize Charles R Drew Fundamental Forum 1954; Outstanding Young Man of Yr 1965; Outstanding Educator in Am FL A&M 1971, 1974; William H Sinkler Meml Awd 1972; Star Surgeon Newsletter of NMA 1973; St George Medal & Citation Amer Cancer Soc 1977; had a street in Quincy, Florida, and a hospital surgical wing named in his honor, 1989; named Charles R Drew Professor of Surgery as first incumbent of this chair with Howard University College of Medicine. **Military Serv:** US Army, captain, 1960-61. **Business Addr:** Prof, Dept of Surgery, Howard Univ Hosp, 2041 Georgia Ave, NW, Washington, DC 20060.

LEFLORE, LARRY

Educator, counselor, federal and state official. **Personal:** Born Oct 1, 1949, Cuba, AL; married Amanda L Collins. **Educ:** William Carey College, BA 1971; Univ So MS, IMS 1974, MS 1980; FL State Univ, PhD 1984. **Career:** Columbia Training Sch, inst soc worker 1971-72; MS Dept Youth Serv Forrest Cty Youth Court, youth ct cnslr 1972-74, intake cnslr 1974-76, reg supr 1976-77; Univ of Southern Mississippi, instructor, 1977-, assistant professor, prof, 1994-; private practice, marriage & family therapist 1982-; Univ of Southern Mississippi, assistant professor 1982-; US Department of Health & Human Services, Center for Substance Abuse Prevention, grant reviewer, 1989-; US Department of Justice, Office of Juvenile Justice and Delinquency, grant reviewer, 1990-; Mississippi Children's Justice Act Program, administrator, 1991-; Forrest General Hospitals, Pine Grove Life Focus Center, marriage and family therapist, 1992-. **Orgs:** Mem Natl College Juvenile Ct Judges; commnr Gov's Commn For Standards & Goals in Crim Justice; bd dir Spl Serv Prog William Carey College; Opport House; consult Jackson County Dept of Public Welfare 1987-; curriculum comm mem MS Judicial College 1984-; adv comm Gov's MS Juvenile Justice 1984-; bd dir Hattiesburg MS Main St Project 1987-88; adv bd mem Grad School of Social Work Univ of So MS 1987-89. **Honors/Awds:** Faculty Excellence in Service Award, 1989; Harding Faculty Leadership Award, 1992; William Carey College, Heritage Award for Community Service, 1992, Outstanding Alumus Award, 1992. **Special Achievements:** First African-American elected President, University of Southern Mississippi Faculty Senate, 1990-91; First African American asst vp for acad affairs, Univ of Southern MS, 1994. **Business Addr:** Professor, University of Southern Mississippi, P O Box 9203 SS, Hattiesburg, MS 39406, (601)266-4509.

LEFLORE, LYAH

Television executive. **Personal:** Born 1970?. **Career:** Nickelodeon Network, assistant; Fox TV, ''New York Undercover,'' assoc producer, currently. **Business Addr:** Assoc Producer, ''New York Undercover'', c/o Fox-TV, 205 E 67th St, New York, NY 10021, (212)452-5555.

LEFLORE, WILLIAM B.

Educator, research scientist. **Personal:** Born Feb 22, 1930, Mobile, AL. **Educ:** St Augustine's Coll, BS 1950; Atlanta Univ, MS 1952; Univ of Southern California, MSc 1961, PhD 1965. **Career:** Bennett Coll, instructor in biology 1952-57; Spelman Coll, asst to prof biology 1964-; North Carolina A&T Univ, visiting prof of biology 1966; College of St Teresa, exchange prof of biology 1968-69; Spelman Coll, prof & chmn biology dept. **Orgs:** Consul Office of Educ USPHS 1968 1970-74; ad hoc consul MBS Prog USPHS 1975; consul Kellogg Found Univ of AR Pine Bluff 1981; consul Biol Dept Savannah State Coll 1984; mem Helminthological Soc of Washington, Amer Soc of Parasitologists, Amer Microscopical Soc, Amer Soc of Zoologists, Amer Physiological Soc. **Honors/Awds:** United Negro College Fund, Distinguished Scholar Award, 1982-83; Missouri Beale Scroll of Merit, Mobile Press Register, 1978; MARC Research Fellowship, Univ of Leeds, England, 1978; published over 30 scientific articles in Journal of Parasitol and other journals. **Military Serv:** AUS e-5 2 yrs. **Home Addr:** 864 Victoria Place, Atlanta, GA 30310. **Business Addr:** Prof & Chmn, Biology Dept, Spelman College, 350 Spelman Lane, SW, Atlanta, GA 30314.

LEFLORES, GEORGE O., JR.

Educational administrator. **Personal:** Born Jul 2, 1921, Mobile, AL; children: Victoria Gray, Willie J, George Jr, Claira. **Educ:** Vernon Sch of Real Estate, AA 1962. **Career:** Sacramento Black Alcohol Center, bd mem 1979-82; Project Area Comm, elected bd mem 1974-82; Delpaso Heights School Dist, elected bd mem 1981-; Faith Deliverance Center, bd mem 1972-; Delpaso Hts School Dist, clerk school bd. **Orgs:** Trustee bd mem Co-op Group 1977-81; trustee bd mem Elks Lodge #587 1948-85; bd mem Faith Deliverance Serv 1972-85. **Honors/Awds:** Recog & Outstanding Valuable Serv to the Young People Search for Solution Awd 1973; Comm Serv Awd Delpaso Heights Project Area Comm 1974; Outstanding Serv & Bd Mem Awd SCARE 1973; Comm Involvement Awd City of Sacramento Parks & Recreation Dept 1981. **Business Addr:** Clerk School Board, Del Paso Elem Sch Dist, 575 Kesner Ave, Sacramento, CA 95838.

LEFTWICH, NORMA BOGUES

Attorney. **Personal:** Born Aug 8, 1948, New York, NY; married Willie L Leftwich Jr; children: Curtis. **Educ:** Univ of Pittsburgh, BA 1969; Harvard-Kennedy Sch of Govt, Sr Govt Mgrs Prog 1982; Georgetown Univ, Law Ctr, JD, 1992. **Career:** Boone Young & Assoc, sr consultant 1977; Dept of Commerce, special asst 1978-79; Dept of Defense, dir; Howard Univ, gen counsel, 1995-. **Orgs:** Mem Delta Sigma Theta Sor 1968. **Honors/Awds:** Black Business Assn of LA, Outstanding Achievement, 1982, 1986; SBA Awd of Excellence 1984; Dept of Defense Special Achievement Awd 1985; The Roy Wilkins Meritorious Serv Awd NAACP 1985; Governor's Awd Commonwealth of Puerto Rico 1985. **Business Addr:** General Counsel, Howard University, 2400 6th St NW, Ste 321, Washington, DC 20059.

LEFTWICH, WILLIE L.

Attorney. **Personal:** Born Jun 28, 1937, Washington, DC; married Norma. **Educ:** Howard University, BSEE, 1960; George Washington Univ Sch of Law, JD, 1967, LLM, 1972. **Career:** Hudson Leftwich & Davenport, atty; George Washington Univ Sch of Law, prof; Tech Media Sys Inc, vp/gen counsel; Dept of Transportation FAA, patent atty; Naval Air Systems Command, advisor, research engineer; research electro-optical engineer; NASA, research aero instrumentation engineer; Leftwich Moore & Douglas, managing partner, currently; Potomac Surety Insurance Co. Inc, president, chief executive officer, currently. **Orgs:** Mem DC Bar Assn; dir PA Ave Devel Corp; DC Redevel Land Agy; mem Commerce Tech Adv Bd DC Judicial Nomination Commn; mem numerous political affiliations. **Military Serv:** 1st lt 1960-62. **Business Addr:** 1101 15 St NW, Washington, DC 20005.

LEGALL, TERRENCE GEORGE

Insurance financial consultant. **Personal:** Born Apr 26, 1954, Georgetown, Guyana; son of Waveney LeGall Williams and Benjamin Knobbs; married Portia Evans LeGall, Oct 27, 1984; children: Terrence George Michael, Tara Patrice. **Educ:** Indian Ed Trust College, Georgetown, South America, AA, economics, 1969; University of London, England, BA, history, 1972; Kean College, Union, NJ, political science, economics, finance, 1978-80. **Career:** United Insurance Co, Crawford, NJ, sales mgr, district mgr, 1980-90; LeGall & Evans Co, Linden, NJ, sales rep, president, 1985-; Family Seven Inc, Piscataway, NJ, vice president/president invest corp, 1985-. **Orgs:** Vice president, Morning Star Church, Linden, NJ, 1986-; trustee, Morning Star Church, Linden, NJ, 1984-86; vice chairman, Morning Star Day Care, Linden, NJ, 1980-. **Honors/Awds:** Sales mgr of Year, United Insurance Co, 1983; Black Enterprise Magazine, Earl Graves Publ, 1990.

LEGENDRE, HENRI A.

Business executive. **Personal:** Born Jul 11, 1924, New York, NY; married Ruth E Mills; children: Renee, Laurette, Jacques. **Educ:** Howard Univ, Civ Engrg ASTP 1943; CCNY, Liberal Arts 1949; Pratt Inst, Deploma Arch 1952. **Career:** Designs for Business, designer 1962; Ifill & Johnson Arch, partner 1963-67; Henri A LeGendre & Assoc; LeGendre Johnson McNeil Arch & Planners, private arch pract 1978. **Orgs:** Mem Amer Inst of Arch, NY State Assn of Arch, NY Soc of Arch, Natl Orgn of Minority Arch, Amer Arbitration Assn, US Gen Serv Admin Adv Panel onA/E Selections 1977, 100 Black men Inc, Bd of Educ Valhalla, Alpha Phi Alpha, 369th VA, US Powerboat Squadron, The Promeatheans Inc, Rotary Intl, St George Assn B&P Chap DAV, Order of St Vincent, Euclid Lodge 70 F&AM; reg Arch State of NY; mem NAACP, Westchester Coalition; 9th & 10th Cavalry Horse Association. **Honors/Awds:** Concrete Ind Awd of Merit Riverside Park Com & IS #95 1977; World Serv Awd YMCA Housing Devel 1979; Bldrs Inst Mr Vernon Nghbrhd Fac & Theatre Westchester/Putnam Co 1979; Honorable Mention Grant Park Housing Proj Mnpls Chap AIA; Certificate of Merit 139th St Playground NY Assn of Arch. **Military Serv:** AUS 9th Calvary WW II. **Business Addr:** Vice Pres, LeGendre, Purse Architects, PC, 7218 Bevington Woods Lane, Charlotte, NC 28277.

LEGETTE, TYRONE

Professional football player. **Personal:** Born Feb 15, 1970, Columbia, SC; married Reginene. **Educ:** Univ of Nebraska, attended. **Career:** New Orleans Saints, defensive back, 1992-95; Tampa Bay Buccaneers, 1996-. **Business Addr:** Professional Football Player, Tampa Bay Buccaneers, One Buccaneer Place, Tampa, FL 33607, (813)870-2700.

LEGGETT, RENEE

Communications marketing manager. **Personal:** Born Oct 7, 1949, Cleveland, OH. **Educ:** Fisk Univ, BA (Magna Cum Laude) 1972; Northwestern Univ, MA 1973; New York Univ, MBA 1980. **Career:** Cleveland State Univ, instructor (summer) 1973; Lincoln First Bank, mktg analyst 1973-76; Fortune Magazine, reporter 1976-79; Mobil Corp, mktg analyst 1979-81; The New York Times, mktg analyst 1981-82, planning mgr 1982-83, circulation marketing mgr 1983-86, advertising mktg & promo mgr. **Orgs:** Mem NY Univ Black Alumni Assoc, Natl Black MBA Assoc, Black Reps in Adv of NY; tutor First World Alliance Childrens Ctr; volunteer fund raiser Boy Choir of Harlem; speaker New Alliance of Public Schools; speaker Urban League's Black Exec Exchange Prog 1983. **Honors/Awds:** Wall St Journal Student Achievement Awd 1972; numerous articles published at Fortune Magazine 1976-79. **Business Addr:** Marketing Manager, The New York Times, 229 West 43rd St, New York, NY 10036.

LEGGETTE, VIOLET OLEVIA BROWN

Mayor, educator. **Personal:** Born in Tallula, MS; daughter of Theresa Gary Bowman Brown and Alfred Rufus Brown; married Clyde Lamar Leggette Sr, Jul 21, 1957 (divorced); children: Clyde, Melanye, Eric, Terrell. **Educ:** Natchez Jr College, AA 1955; Tougaloo College, BS elem educ 1957; University of IL, MLS 1974. **Career:** Bob Woods Elem Sch, teacher 1957-74; West Bolivar School District, Rosedale, MS, media specialist, 1957-78, 1989-; Bolivar Co Sit, elementary library supr 1974-78; Town of Gunnison, mayor, 1977-97; Delta Pace Preschool, dir 1978-79; Bolivar County Head Start, educ dir 1979-89; West Bolivar School District, curriculum/staff development coordinator, 1996-. **Orgs:** Vice chairperson MS Democratic Party; chairperson Bolivar Co Democratic Comm; pres Bolivar Co Sch Dist I Tch Assn 1977; vice pres MS Conf Black Mayors 1978-88; mem NAACP; chmn Legislative Com MCBM 1978-88; chairman MS Inst of Small Towns Board 1980-; mem MS Assn of Educators; mem NEA, Alpha Kappa Alpha Sor; mem Natl Council of Negro Women. **Honors/Awds:** Outstanding Achievement Award Alcorn Coll Chapter/Negro Business & Professional Women Club 1978; Community Service Awd MS Valley St Univ 1978; Leadership Awd Black Genesis Found 1979; Mother of the Year 1988, First Baptist Church.

LEGGON, HERMAN W.

Systems analyst, mathematician. **Personal:** Born Sep 20, 1930, Cleveland, OH; married Zara M. **Educ:** BS Chemistry 1953; MS Chemistry 1966. **Career:** Union Carbide Corp, systems analyst & mathematician; Dyke Coll, part-time instr, bus math, computer sci & applied quantitative techniques; Systems & Computer Techology Corp, supervisor of tech support for micro computers. **Orgs:** Life mem Alpha Phi Alpha Frat; mem Juvenile Delinquency of the ACLD; bd chmn Am Sickle Cell Anemia Assn; chmn ASTM Com E31-01; scoutmstr Troop 370; Ada; NAACP; Urban League; former serv dir, councilman, pres Council of Oakwood Village. **Home Addr:** 3470 Belvoir, Beachwood, OH 44122.

LEGRAND, BOB (SNAKE)

Educator. **Personal:** Born Aug 28, 1943, Nashville, TN; son of Sarah H Joyner; married Gloria Jean Young; children: Lisa, Robert III, Christopher, Brianna, Brian. **Educ:** St Mary's Univ TX, BA 1970; Southwest TX State Univ, MA 1973, Professional Certificate in Guidance & Counseling 1974. **Career:** Jefferson HS San Antonio, TX, head coach 1970-75; Univ of TX Arlington, asst coach 1975-76, head coach 1976-87, Irving High School, Irving TX 1988-; Sport 'n' Goods, owner-. **Orgs:** Chmn Dist 6 Editorial Comm Natl Assn of Basketball Coaches; chmn Dist 6 Membership Comm Natl Assn of Basketball Coaches; chmn United Way Campaign Univ TX Arlington 1980; mem bd dir Arlington Boys Club 1978-82; Arlington Noon Optimist Club; Texas Assn of Basketball Coaches. **Honors/Awds:** Man of the Year Omega Psi Phi 1980; Award for Outstanding Achievement Omega Psi Phi 1977; Coach of the Year Southland Conf 1981; News Maker of the Year Fort

Worth Press Club 1981; Honorary Commissioner Tarrant Cnty Commissioners 1980. **Military Serv:** USAF E-4 served 4 years. **Home Addr:** 3112 Westwood Dr, Arlington, TX 76012. **Business Addr:** Owner-Sport 'n' Goods 4 U, 3112 Westwood Dr, Arlington, TX 76012.

LEGRAND, ETIENNE RANDALL

Executive. **Personal:** Born Sep 1, 1956, Philadelphia, PA; children: Justin Alan. **Educ:** Boston Univ, BS 1978; Northeastern Univ, MBA 1981. **Career:** United Mine Workers of Amer, asst cash mgr 1981-82; Finalco Inc, cash mgr 1982-86; Children's Defense Fund, dir of finance 1986-87; Howard Univ Small Business Develop Ctr, deputy dir 1987-. **Orgs:** Pres, vice pres Delta Sigma Theta Inc 1976-; mem Big Sister Assoc 1978-80; prog co-chair NBMBAA Natl Conf 1985; fund develop chair Washington DC NBMBAA 1986; mem DC Coalition of Black Professional Org 1986-; sponsor Jr Achievement 1986-; pres Washington DC Natl Black MBA Assoc 1987; bd mem Owl School 1987-. **Honors/Awds:** Dr Martin Luther King Jr Fellowship Northeastern Univ 1979-81; Disting Serv Awd Natl Black MBA Assoc 1985-87.

LEGRAND, YVETTE MARIE

Management consultant. **Personal:** Born Nov 8, 1950, Chicago, IL. **Educ:** Loyola Univ Chicago, bA History 1971; Univ of Chicago, MBA 1975. **Career:** Intl Mgmt Asst United Way of Met Chicago, dir 1977-; First Natl Bank Chicago, loan ofc 1977; First Natl Bank, acct mgr 1975-77, first schlr mgmt trainee 1972-75. **Orgs:** Mem Natl Black MBA Assc Chicago Chap 1974-77; vice pres Chicago Jr Assc of Commerce & Industry Found 1979-80; first black pres Chicago Jaycees 1980-81 Vol; Lois R Lowe Women's Div United Negro Clge Fund 1972-79; vice pres pub rel Chicago Jaycees 1977-78; dir Chicago Jazz Gallery 1978-80. **Honors/Awds:** Pres Award of Honor Chicago Jaycees 1975-76; Outst Chap Ofc Chicago Jaycees 1978; Outst Young Woman of Amer 1979. **Business Addr:** 72 W Adams, Chicago, IL 60603.

LEHMAN, PAUL ROBERT

Educator. **Personal:** Born Apr 18, 1941, Mansura, LA; son of Frances Revare Lehman and Kermit Lehman; married Marion W White; children: Christopher Paul, Karlyn Elizabeth, Jeffrey Robert. **Educ:** LA City Coll, AA 1966; Central State Coll, BA 1969; Central State U, ME 1971; Lehigh U, PhD 1976. **Career:** Central State U, dean of grad coll 1985-88, prof dept of English 1984, 1988-, assoc prof dept of eng 1976-; NCACC, adjunct prof 1974-76; CSU, instr 1971-73;CSU, lecturer 1969-71; KWTV, newsman reporter writer editor photographer producer & weekend anchorman 1968-70; KOFM radio, music newsman 1968-69; Standard Oil of CA, credit dept 1966-67; Western Electric Co, tester insptct 1963-66; Northampton Co Area Community Coll, dev co-ordinated coll orientation wkshp for minority stud 1975; Blk Am Lit, vol lecturer coll pub private sch (Jr & Sr) churches on Radio/TV News 1974-75; member, Edmond Arts & Humanities, 1991-; board member, Oklahoma Arthritis Foundation, 1991-; board member, Oklahoma Alliance for Art Education, 1989-. **Orgs:** Natl Jay-Cees; NAACP; Urban League; Heart Assn Natl Assn of Press Photographers; stud exec officer LACC 1966; mem NEA, OEA, CSEA, NCTE; vice chmn, Oklahoma Foundation for the Humanities 1988-89; treasurer, Oklahoma Alliance for Arts Education 1988-; Oklahoma Folklife Council; Edmond Community Housing Resource Board; Afro-American Southern Assn; Edmond Arts & Humanities, 1991-; Oklahoma Arthritis Foundation, 1991-. **Honors/Awds:** Best actor in minor roll CSC 1968; dean's honor roll CSC 1968; 1st blk Am to rec PhD in Eng from Lehigh 1976; 1st blk Am to teach at CSU 1969; 1st blk in OK to anchor weekend TV news 1969; listed in Contemporary Authors for 1977-78; Lehigh Univ Fellowship 1973-76; 1st dissertation on John Oliver Killens 1976; 2nd place all-coll speech contest 1965; Awd for Serv to Urban League of Greater Okla City 1984; Awd for Serv to Boy Scouts of Amer 1985. **Military Serv:** USN 3rd cl petty off 1959-63. **Business Addr:** Dept of English, Central State University, 100 University Drive, Edmond, OK 73034.

LEIGH, FREDRIC H.

Association executive (retired). **Personal:** Born Mar 29, 1940, Columbus, OH; son of Cathrine A Lee Leigh and William F Leigh Sr; divorced; children: Tracey, William. **Educ:** Central State University, BA, history, 1963; Syracuse University, MS, journalism/public relations, 1972; US Army Command & Staff College, MMS, 1973; National War College, graduate, 1982; University of Chicago, Executive Development Program, certificate, 1986; Center for Creative Leadership, Eckerd College, FL, certificate, 1990; Harvard Univ, JFK School of Government Sr Exec in government program, Cert, 1993. **Career:** Office of the Secretary of the US Army, senior military assistant, 1982-83; Office of Chief of Staff, US Army, deputy director of the army staff, 1983-85; 19th Support Command, 8th US Army, Korea, chief of staff, 1985-87; 1st Brigade, 101st Airborne Division (Air Assault), Fort Campbell, KY, commander, 1987-89; Senior Leadership Research, Army War College, director, 1989-90; 7th Infantry Division (Light), Fort Ord, CA, assistant division commander (support), 1990-91; National Military Command Ctr, deputy director, 1991-93; Chief of Staff, Army Office, director of management, 1993; Joint Center for Political & Economic Studies, exec vp, currently. **Orgs:** pres, Rocks, Inc; The New Initiatives Committee for Historically Black College ROTC Assistance, chairman; Korean-American Friendship Association, board member, 1985-87; Big Brothers Inc, Clarksville, TN, 1977-78; Boy Scouts, Syracuse, NY, leader, 1971-72. **Honors/Awds:** Central State University, Hall of Achievement, 1991; Korean-American Friendship Society, Outstanding Friendship Award, 1987; Taegu Korea Labor Union, Labor Development Award, 1987; Command & Staff College, Commandant's List Graduate, 1973; Northern New York Public Relations Society of America, Outstanding Graduate in Public Relations 1972; Newhouse School of Communications, Syracuse University, Faculty Award to Most Outstanding Graduate Student, 1972. **Military Serv:** US Army, Major General, 1963-94; Army Distinguished Service medal, Defense Superior Service Medal; Legion of Merit (with 3 oak leaf clusters), Bronze Star Medal (with 4 oak leaf clusters), Bronze Star Medal with V Device, Meritorious Service Medal (with 2 oak leaf clusters), Army Commendation Medal (with oak leaf cluster); numerous others; Natl Military Command Ctr, deputy dir, 1991-93; Office Chief of Staff, dir of management, 1993. **Business Addr:** Executive Vice President, Joint Center for Political & Economic Studies, 1090 Vermont Ave NW, Ste 1100, Washington, DC 20005.

LEIGH, JAMES W., JR.

Educator. **Personal:** Born Jun 1, 1927, Detroit, MI; son of Pauline Leigh and James Leigh. **Educ:** Wayne State Univ, BA 1952; Wayne State Univ Sch of Social Work, MSW 1954; Smith Coll Sch for Social Work, third yr cert 1961. **Career:** Dept Pub Welfare Detroit, social worker 1952-54; Wayne Co Juvenile Court Detroit, probation officer 1954-60; Family Serv of the Cincinnati area, social worker 1960-67; Sch of Social Work Univ of WA, asst prof 1967-70, assoc prof 1970-. **Orgs:** Vice pres Natl Assn Black Soc Worker WA State Chap 1975-77; bd mem Smith Coll Sch for Social Work 1979-; mem NAACP; mem Urban League; mem Council on Social Work Educ. **Business Addr:** Associate Professor, Univ of Washington, School of Social Work, Seattle, WA 98105.

LEIGH, WILLIAM A.

Contractor, developer. **Personal:** Born Sep 12, 1929, Dayton, OH; children: William, Cornell, Bernard. **Educ:** Attended, Miami-Jacobs Business Coll, Sinclair Comm Coll. **Career:** Fleetline Cab Co, owner 1950-61; Main Auto Parts & Glass Co, sales rep 1960-68; Madden Inc, president, currently. **Orgs:** Bd mem Newfields Comm Authority; treasurer, bd mem, Amer Business Council; chmn Black Contractors & Business Assn; Dayton Housing Advisory Bd; bd mem Miami Valley Cncl of Boy Scouts; United Fund Agency; Miami Valley Child Devel; vice pres, Dayton Fund for Home Rehab; bd mem SCLC; president, Ohio Real Estate Investors Assn; board member, Montgomery County Child Development Corporation; board member, Unity State Bank; past president, Greater Dayton Real Estate Investor Assn; facilitator, Barbara Jordan Committee on Race Unity; mem Dayton City Schools Advisory Bd. **Honors/Awds:** Frontiersman of the Year, 1972; listed as 1 of top 100 Black Businesses, Black Enterprise Magazine; recognized by Professional Builders Magazine for Outstanding Land Use & Design, 1972; recognized by President Jimmy Carter as one of the nation's outstanding black businessmen, 1978; WS McIntosh Achievement Award, 1980. **Special Achievements:** Developed more than $195,000,000 in low & moderate income housing units; Redeveloped the Madden Hills Community, once referred to as the state's worst slum area. **Business Addr:** Chairman and President, Madden Investment Inc, 2305 Heartsoul Dr, Dayton, OH 45408.

LEIGHTON, GEORGE NEVES

Attorney, federal judge (retired). **Personal:** Born Oct 22, 1912, New Bedford, MA; son of Annay Sylvia Garcia Leitao and Antonio Leitao; married Virginia Berry Quivers, Jun 21, 1942; children: Virginia Anne, Barbara Elaine. **Educ:** Howard Univ, AB, 1940; Harvard Univ, LLB, 1946; Elmhurst Coll, LLD, 1964; John Marshall Law School, 1973; Southeastern Massachusetts Univ, 1975; New England Univ School of Law, 1978; Loyola Univ, LLD, 1989. **Career:** Moore, Ming & Leighton, Chicago, IL, partner, 1951-59; McCoy, Ming & Leighton, Chicago, IL, partner 1959-64; Circuit Court of Cook County, IL, judge, 1964-69, appellate court, 1st District, judge, 1969-76; US District Court, Northern Dist of Illinois, judge, district judge 1976-89, senior district judge, 1986-87; Earl L. Neal and Associates, of counsel, 1987-. **Orgs:** Member, Massachusetts Bar Association, 1946-; member, Illinois Bar Association, 1947; Chicago Bar Association; US Supreme Court Bar, 1958; member, various committees, American Bar Association; commr, 1955-63, chairman, 1959-63, Character and Fitness Committee, 1st Appellate Dist Supreme Court of Illinois; member, Joint Committee for Revision of Illinois Criminal Code, 1964; bd dirs United Ch Bd for Homeland Ministries, United Ch of Christ, Grant Hosp; member, American Bar Foundation; mem Howard Univ Chicago Alumni Club; chairman, Legal Redress Committee, NAACP, Chicago Chapter; council, Natl Harvard Law Sch Assn; Phi Beta Kappa;trustee, 1979-83, trustee emeritus, 1983-, Univ Notre Dame; bd overseers Harvard Coll 1983-. **Honors/Awds:** Recip Civil Liberties Award IL Div Am Civil Liberties Union 1961; named Chicagoan of Yr in Law & Judiciary Jr Assn Commerce & Industry 1964; author of numerous articles on the law. **Military Serv:** US Army, Capt, 1942-45; Bronze Star. **Business Addr:** US District Judge, Northern District of Illinois, Dirksen Federal Building, 219 South Dearborn St, Chicago, IL 60604.

LELAND, JOYCE F.

Deputy chief of police. **Personal:** Born Sep 8, 1941, Washington, DC; married John Watkins. **Educ:** Howard Univ, BA Sociology 1965. **Career:** Metropolitan Police Dept, lieutenant 1975-78, capt 1978-83, eeo inspector 1983-85, deputy chief 1985. **Orgs:** Bd dirs MPDC Boys and Girls Club, Police Mgmt Assoc; consultant Police Foundation, Ctr for Youth Svcs. **Honors/Awds:** Crime Reduction Awds; numerous awds from citizens, law enforcement agencies, churches, business establishments. **Business Addr:** Deputy Chief of Police, Metropolitan Police Department, 1324 Mississippi Ave, SE, Washington, DC 20032.

LEMEH, DOROTHA HILL

Dentist, educator. **Personal:** Born in Knoxville, TN; daughter of Mary Lucille Evans Hill and William Edward Hill; married Dr. Charles N. Lemeh, Jun 15, 1956 (deceased); children: Wayne, Dorotha, Eva, Carol. **Educ:** Fisk Univ, BA 1947; Morgan State Coll & Howard Univ, postgrad 1948-50; Howard Univ Coll of Dentistry, DDS 1954; Univ of Michigan School of Dentistry, MS Pediatric Dentistry 1958, MPH 1970. **Career:** Forsyth Dental Infantry for Child, intern 1954-55; Mott Found Dental Clinic, res 1957-58; Enugu Nigeria, minister of health dentistry div 1965-67; Meharry Med Coll School of Dental, assoc prof 1970-79, vice chmn 1971-76, act chmn dept of preventive dentistry & comm health 1976-79, prof 1979-, chmn dept of preventive dentistry & comm health 1979-. **Orgs:** Amer Acad Oral Med; Amer Assn of Dental Schools; Amer Assn of Public Health Dentists; TN Assn of Public Health Dentistry; Natl Dental Assn; Pan TN Dental Assn; Cap City Dental Soc; Delta Sigma Theta; rec sec Cap City Dental Soc; Intl Assn of Dental Rsch; Amer Assn of Dental Research. **Honors/Awds:** Louise C Ball Scholarship; CS Mott Found Scholarship; US Pub Health Serv Special Traineeship; author of numerous articles. **Business Addr:** Prof/Chairperson, Meharry Med Coll, School of Dentistry, 1005 D. B. Todd Blvd, Nashville, TN 37208.

LEMELLE, TILDEN J.

Educational administrator. **Personal:** Born Feb 6, 1929, New Iberia, LA; married Margaret Guillion; children: Joyce Marie, Stephanie Marie, Therese Marie. **Educ:** Xavier Univ New Orleans, AB 1953, MA 1957; Univ of Denver, PhD 1965. **Career:** Grambling Coll LA, asst prof 1957-63; Fordham Univ NY, assoc prof 1966-69; Ctr Intl Race Rel Univ Denver, prof, dir 1969-71; Hunter Clge NY, prof & acting dean 1971-, provost, vice pres, currently; Amer Com on Africa, treas 1973-; Univ of the District of Columbia, past pres. **Orgs:** Trustee Africa Today Assoc Inc 1967-; editor/publ Africa Today 1967-; bd office pres Amer Comm on Africa 1973-; trustee New Rochelle Bd of Educ 1976-;mem Cncl on Foreign Rel 1978-; trustee Social Sci Found 1979-; trustee Africa Fund 1979-; trustee Intl League for Human Rights 1980-; trustee Nurses Educ Fund 1984-; Council For International Exchange of Scholars, Fulbright, 1991-. **Honors/Awds:** John Hay Whitney Fellow NY 1963-65; The Black Coll Praeger NY 1969; Hon Consul-Senegal Denver CO 1969-71; Race Among Nations Heath-Lexington MA 1971. **Military Serv:** AUS sp4 1953-56; Special Agent Counterintelligence. **Business Addr:** President (former), Univ of District of Columbia, 4200 Connecticut Ave, NW, Washington, DC 20008.

LEMELLE, WILBERT JOHN

Educator. **Personal:** Born Nov 11, 1931, New Iberia, LA; son of Theresa Francis LeMelle and Eloi LeMelle; married Yvonne Tauriac; children: Patrice DiCioccio, Wilbert Jr, Gerald, Edward. **Educ:** Notre Dame Seminary, BA 1955, MA 1956; University of Denver Grad School of Intl Studies, PhD 1963. **Career:** Ford Foundation, held various positions 1965-77; US Dept of State, ambassador to Kenya and the Seychelles 1977-80; SUNY, system assoc vice chancellor 1981-85; Mercy Coll, president 1985-90; Phelps-Stokes Fund, president, 1990-. **Orgs:** Dir, Council of Amer Ambassadors 1983-; dir, PBS; dir, Chase Manhattan Regional Bd 1986-; trustee, Phelps-Stokes Fund 1986-; dir, Council on Foreign Relations; dir, Borden Inc, 1987-; trustee, Carnegie Endowment for Intl Peace, 1989-; trustee, Woodrow Wilson National Fellowship Foudation. **Honors/Awds:** Honorary Doctor of Laws (LLD) Cuttington Univ, Liberia 1978; Gold Medallion Awd, Black Catholic Ministries and Laymen's Council 1978; Honorary Doctor of Humane Letters (HDL), Mercy College, 1990; Honorary Doctor of Letters, California School of Professional Psychology, 1996. **Military Serv:** US Army, 1957-59. **Business Addr:** President, Phelps-Stokes Fund, 10 E 87th St, New York, NY 10128.

LEMMIE, VALERIE

City official. **Personal:** marrIed Olan Strozier. **Career:** Manager, City of Dayton (OH), 1996-. **Special Achievements:** First African American city manager in Dayton; First woman city manager in Dayton. **Business Addr:** Manager, City of Dayton, 101 West Third St., Dayton, OH 45402, (513)443-3600.

LEMMONS, HERBERT MICHAEL
Clergyman. **Personal:** Born Sep 25, 1952, Little Rock, AR; son of Deliah A Herron-Lemmons and Herbert G Lemmons; married Karenga Rashida Hill, Aug 31, 1974; children: H Michael II, Malcolm R. **Educ:** Univ of Detroit, Detroit, MI, BA, 1973; Interdenominational Theological Center, Atlanta, GA, Master of Divinity, 1976; Howard Univ School of Law, Washington, DC, Juris Doctor, 1979. **Career:** Seaton Memorial AME Church, Lanham, MD, pastor, 1977-84; US Small Business Admin, Washington, DC, attorney advisor, 1979-81; Univ of MD, College Park, MD, chaplain, 1982-84; Congress of Natl Black Churches, Washington, DC, deputy dir, 1984-85; Mount Moriah AME Church, Annapolis, MD, pastor, 1984-89; Congress of Natl Black Churches, Washington, DC, exec dir, 1989. **Orgs:** Mem, Human Relations Commn Annapolis, MD, 1986-88; mem, Mayor's Task Force on Substance Abuse, 1987-89; mem, Bd of Commrs, Annapolis Housing Authority, 1988-. **Honors/Awds:** Walder G Muelder Student Lectureship in Social Ethics, Interdenominational Theological Center, 1976; Clergy Award, Annual Kunte Kinte Celebration, 1990. **Business Addr:** Exec Dir, The Congress of Natl Black Churches, Inc, 1225 I St, NW, Suite 750, Washington, DC 20005.

LEMMONS, KASI
Director, writer, actress. **Personal:** Born 1961; married Vondie Curtis-Hall; children: Hunter. **Educ:** Attended New York Univ, UCLA, New School for Social Research. **Career:** Director, actress, writer, currently. Films (acting): School Daze, 1988; Vampire's Kiss, 1989; The Five Heartbeats, 1991; The Silence of the Lambs, 1991; Candyman, 1992; Fear of a Black Hat, 1993; Hard Target, 1993; Drop Squad, 1994; Gridlock'd, 1997; 'Til There Was You, 1997; Liars' Dice, 1998. TV (acting): 11th Victim, 1979; The Court-Martial of Jackie Robinson, 1990; The Big One: The Great Los Angeles Earthquake, 1990; Under Cover (TV series), 1991; Afterburn, 1992; Zooman, 1995. Wrote and directed film Eve's Bayou, 1997. **Honors/Awds:** National Board of Review, Best Debut Director Award (for Eve's Bayou), 1997; Independent Spirit Award, Best First Feature (for Eve's Bayou), 1998. **Business Addr:** Director, Trimark Pictures, 2644 30th St, Santa Monica, CA 90405, (310)314-2000.

LEMON, ANN
Financial executive. **Career:** PaineWebber Inc, vp of investments, currently. **Orgs:** National Black MBA Association; Financial Women's Association; Smith College Alumnae Association, treasurer; National Structured Settlement Trade Association. **Honors/Awds:** NBMBAA, Connecticut Westchester Chapter, Member of the Year, 1994. **Business Addr:** Vice President of Investments, PaineWebber Inc, 1251 Ave of the Americas, 2nd Fl, New York, NY 10020.

LEMON, CHESTER EARL
Professional baseball player (retired). **Personal:** Born Feb 12, 1955, Jackson, MS; married Valerie Jones; children: Geneva, Chester Jr, David. **Educ:** Pepperdine Univ, Malibu, CA, attended; Cerritos College, Norwalk, CA, attended. **Career:** Chicago White Sox, outfielder, 1975-81; Detroit Tigers, outfielder, 1982-90; Chet Lemo's Baseball Camp, founder. **Honors/Awds:** American League All-Star Team, 1978, 1979, 1984.

LEMON, MEADOWLARK
Professional athlete. **Personal:** Born Apr 25, 1932, Wilmington, NC; married Willie Maultsby (divorced); children: George, Beverly, Donna, Robin, Jonathan. **Career:** Harlem Globetrotters, 1954-78; The Bucketeers, basketball group 1978-; appeared in TV series Hello Larry 1979; films, The Fish That Saved Pittsburgh, Sweepstakes. **Military Serv:** AUS 1952-54.

LEMON, MICHAEL WAYNE, SR.
Police officer. **Personal:** Born Nov 2, 1953, Detroit, MI; son of Mary Strong Lemon and Primus Lemon; married Valerie Mennifee Lemon, Apr 2, 1978; children: Michael Wayne Lemon Jr, Ashlee Michelle Lemon. **Educ:** Wayne County Community Coll, associate, 1988; Wayne State Univ. **Career:** Detroit Police Dept, Narcotics Div, sergeant, currently; Michigan Bell Telephone, consultant, 1987-. **Orgs:** Bd mem, Community volunteer, 1986-; mem, Task Force on Drug Abuse, Detroit Strategic Plan, 1987-91. **Honors/Awds:** Appreciation Award, Michigan Bell Telephone, 1986; Community Serv Award, Detroit Chamber of Commerce, 1988; Man of the Year Award, Minority Women Network, 1988; Spirit of Detroit, Detroit Common Council, 1989, Heart of Gold Award, United Found, 1989. **Business Addr:** Police Officer, Detroit Police Dept, Narcotic Div, 1300 Beaubien, Detroit, MI 48226.

LEMUWA, IKE EMMANUEL
Investment executive. **Personal:** Born Oct 1, 1961, Mband, Nigeria; son of Ononiwu Lemuwa & Cyrina Adim Lemuwa; married Chioma N Lemuwa, Apr 7, 1997. **Educ:** The University of the District of Columbia, BA, Economics, 1993. **Career:** Dickinson & Co, stockbroker, 1995-96; RAF Financial Corp, investment exec, 1996-. **Orgs:** The Intl Assn of Friends of Africa Inc, IAFA, pres, founder.

LENARD, VOSHON KELAN
Professional basketball player. **Personal:** Born May 14, 1973, Detroit, MI. **Educ:** Minnesota. **Career:** Oklahoma City Calvalry (CBA), 1995; Miami Heat, guard, 1995-. **Business Addr:** Professional Basketball Player, Miami Heat, 721 NW 1st Ave, Miami Arena, Miami, FL 33136, (305)577-4328.

LENHARDT, ALFONSO EMANUEL
Military officer. **Personal:** Born Oct 29, 1943, New York, NY; son of Mary Mackey and Alfonso Emanuel Lenhardt; married Jacqueline Hill, Oct 2, 1965; children: Robin, Tracey, Kimberly. **Educ:** Univ of Nebraska, Omaha, NE, BS, 1972; Witchita State Univ, Witchita, KS, MS, 1976; Central Michigan Univ, Mt Pleasant, MI, MA, 1976. **Career:** US Army, various positions, 1966-, brigadier general, currently. **Military Serv:** US Army Military Police, 1966-; brigadier general, currently; Combat Infantry Badge; Defense Superior Service Medal; Legion of Merit; Bronze Star Medal; Meritorious Service Medal (3); Purple Heart; Air Medal; Joint Service Commendation Medal; Army Commendation Medal (3); Army Achievement Medal; Humanitarian Service Medal; Good Conduct Medal; Natl Defense Service Medal; Vietnamese Cross of Gallantry w/palm; Army Service Ribbon; Overseas Service Ribbon; Vietnamese Civil Action Medal; Vietnamese Campaign Medal; Vietnamese Service Medal; Parachustist Medal.

LENIX-HOOKER, CATHERINE JEANETTE
Business administrator. **Personal:** Born May 10, 1947, Camden, SC; daughter of Annie Lenix and Frank; divorced; children: Frank R Jr. **Educ:** Univ of MD, MLS 1970; Howard Univ, BA 1968. **Career:** Washington DC Public Library, chief, black studies div 1970-77; Anaheim CA Public Library, dir of public servs 1977-81; Schomburg Ctr for Research in Black Culture, asst chief, 1981-90; Krueger-Scott Mansion Cultural Center, executive director, currently. **Orgs:** Mem Harlem Tourism Assn; chairperson S CA Chap Howard Univ Alumni Scholarships 1980-81; mem Amer Library Assn 1970-; mem Black Caucus 1970-; chmn Harlem Hosp Ctr Comm Adv Bd 1981-90; Victorian Soc of Northern NJ. **Honors/Awds:** HEW Title II Fellowship Univ of MD 1969-70; Comm Serv Awd NY Chap of Negro Business and Prof Women's Club 1985; Community Service Award, Alpha Kappa Alpha Sorority, Beta Alpha Omega Chapter, 1992. **Business Addr:** Executive Director, Krueger-Scott Mansion Cultural Center, c/o City Hall, Room 204, 920 Broad Street, Newark, NJ 07102, (973)733-3748.

LENNON, PATRICK ORLANDO
Professional baseball player. **Personal:** Born Apr 27, 1968, Whiteville, NC. **Career:** Seattle Mariners, outfielder, 1991-92; Kansas City Royals, 1996; Oakland Athletics, 1997-. **Business Addr:** Professional Baseball Player, Oakland Athletics, 7677 Oakport St, 2nd Fl, Oakland Coliseum Complex, Oakland, CA 94621, (510)638-4900.

LENOIR, HENRY
Association executive. **Personal:** Born Sep 25, 1912, Philadelphia, TN; married Teri; children: Michael, Kip, Barry, Keith. **Educ:** Knoxville Coll, BA 1936; Univ WI, post grad work; Univ Cincinnati. **Career:** Ninth St YMCA, youth work dir 1945-51; exec dir 1951-57; Moreland YMCA, 1957-61; Page Park YMCA, 1961-68; St Louis YMCA, asst metro dir 1968-70; HarlemYMCA, exec dir 1970-75; YMCA of Greater NY, vice pres 1975-. **Orgs:** Mem Omega Psi Phi Frat; Dallas Comm Council; St Louis Council for Black People; NAACP; Ethical Practices Commn; Assn Professional Employees of YMCA; Banwys. **Honors/Awds:** Hon Citizen Dallas; Omega Man of Yr Dallas Chap 1961; Jack & Jill Award St Louis; Awards in Black Harlem. **Business Addr:** 422 9 Ave, New York, NY 10001.

LENOIR, KIP
Attorney. **Personal:** Born Apr 27, 1943, Knoxville, TN; son of Teri Adkins Lenoir and Henry Lenoir; married Richelle Guilmenot Lenoir, Jun 8, 1967. **Educ:** Howard University, Washington, DC, BS, 1966; Howard University, School of Law, Washington, DC, JD, 1969; New York University, Graduate School of Law, criminal justice. **Career:** Legal Aid Society Criminal, New York, NY, 1971-73; Supervising Attorney, Mayor's Office, New York, NY, 1973-75; New York State Attorney General's Office, New York, NY, assistant attorney general, 1975-77; Lenoir & Bogan, PC, New York, NY, partner, 1977-85; Malcolm/King College, law instructor, 1980; Bronx Community College, City University of New York, adjunct professor/criminal law, 1987-88; Kip Lenoir, Professional Corporation, New York, NY, president, 1985-. **Orgs:** Mayor's Graffiti committee, New York, 1974-75; former board member, Metropolitan Black Bar Association, 1987-88; Counsel to Harlem Interfaith Counseling Service Inc, 1980-; New York State Bar Association, 1975-; New York County Lawyers Association, 1975-. **Honors/Awds:** Outstanding Achievement, Harlem Interfaith Counseling Service Inc, 1984.

LENOIRE, ROSETTA
Business executive, performer. **Personal:** Born Aug 8, 1911, New York City, NY; widowed; children: William M. **Educ:** Attended, Hunter Coll Amer Theatre Wing. **Career:** ABC TV Ryan's Hope, role; John F Kennedy Ctr for Performing Arts & Brooklyn Acad of Mus, toured with "The Royal Family"; AMAS Repertory Theatre, artistic dir and co-founder, 1968-. **Orgs:** Mem Screen Actors Guild; Amer Fedn of TV & Radio Artists; Actor's Equity Assc; nom com SAG, AFTRA, AEA; chmn Welfare Dance Com Negro Actors' Guild; adv bd Off Off Broadway Alliance; vice chrmn Concerned Cit for the Arts; bd trustees The Actors Fund of Amer; bd dir The Cath Acts Guild of Amer; Natl Endowment For The Arts Policy & Small Grants Panel; life mem Cath Actors' Guild Com Woman NY State Re Party; Theatre Communications Group. **Honors/Awds:** Spl Citation, Tribute to Greatness Award Ceremony, 1975; Harold Jackman Award; appeared film version "The Sunshine Boys"; broadway credits, "God's Favorite"; "A Streetcar Named Desire"; "I Had A Ball" plus many more; TV appearances, The Nurses, The Doctors & the Nurses; Kraft Theatre; Studio One; Lamp Unto My Feet; Calucci Dept; Guess Who's Coming To Dinner; conceived "Bubbling Brown Sugar," first prod at AMAS Repertory Theatre, then on Broadway; "Thank You Ma'am" docum on Langston Hughes; founder of AMAS 1968; Bd of Directors Awd, Frank Silvera Writer's Workshop 1977; Tribute to Greatness Awd 1980; Hoey Awd, Catholic Interracial Cncl 1985; City Cncl Citation 1985; Richard Coe Awd, New Playwrights 1986; Cecilia Cabiness Saunders Awd YWCA, 1986;Woman of the Year, Caribbean Cultural Assn86; Mayor's Awd of Honor for Art and Culture 1986; Sojourner Truth Awd, Negro Professional Women 1986. **Business Addr:** Director, AMAS Repertory Theatre, Inc, 1 East 104th St, New York, NY 10029.

LEON, TANIA J.
Composer, conductor. **Personal:** Born May 14, 1943, La Habana, Cuba; daughter of Dora Ferran and Oscar Leon de Los Mederos; married Francisco Javier Perez (divorced 1985). **Educ:** National Conservatory, La Habana, CU, MA, music education, 1965; New York University, BS, music education, 1973; New York University, MA, composition, 1975. **Career:** Conductor/composer, numerous symphonies, operas, festivals, etc, 1969-; Brooklyn Coll, prof, 1993-; Harvard Uni, visiting lecturer, 1994; New York Philharmonic, revson composer, 1993-; Yale Univ, visiting prof, 1993. **Orgs:** ASCAP; American Music Center Inc; Composers Forum Inc, NY, Local 802, AFL-CIO; New York Foundation for the Arts, board member; American Composers Orchestra, board member; Meet the Composer, board member; Amer Academy of Poets, bd mem. **Honors/Awds:** American Academy and Institute of Arts and Letters, Academy-Institute Award in Music, 1991; Yaddo, John D and Catherine T MacArthur Foundation Annual Residency for Artists, 1991; New York State Council On The Arts, 1988; Manhattan Arts, 1985; Dean Dixon Achievement Award, 1985; ASCAP Composer's Awards, 1978-89; Meet the Composer, 1978-89; Queens Council on the Arts, 1983; Key to the City of Detroit, 1982; Byrd Hoffman Foundation, 1981; National Council of Women of the United States Achievement Award, 1980; CINTAS Award in Composition, 1976, 1979; National Endowment for the Arts Commission, 1975; New York Univ, Distinguished Alumni Award, 1994; BMW Music Theater Prize for best composition, Munich Biennale, 1994; Natl Endowment for the Arts Recording Award, 1993; Meet the Composer/Reader's Digest Commission Award, 1992. **Special Achievements:** Publications: "Ritual," for solo piano, Southern Music Publishing Co, 1991; "Parajota Delate," for mixed quintet, Southern Music Publishing Co, 1992; recordings: "De Orishas, The Western Wind," Newport Classic; Leonarda Records, Momentum, piano solo; Chamber works by Tania Leon, Composers Recordings Inc, Indigena; The Western Wind, Western Wind Records, Batey; Ana Maria Rosado, Albany Records, Paisanos Semos; Louisville Orchestra, First Edition Records, Bata, Carabali. **Business Addr:** Professor, Brooklyn College, Brooklyn, NY 11210.

LEON, WILMER J., JR.
Consultant. **Personal:** Born Mar 6, 1920, Louisiana; married Edwina T Devore; children: Valerie, Wilmer III. **Educ:** So Univ, BS 1949; Univ of CA Berkeley, MA 1954. **Career:** CA Adult Auth, admin officer; CA Dept of Educ, Bureau of Intergroup Relations, Sacramento, consultant; CA Dept of Corrections, parole agent; asst dist parole supr; State Dir of Corrections, consultant; CA State Univ Sacramento, lecturer in Criminal Justice. **Orgs:** Mem CA Probation & Parole Assn; Proj Safer CA Ofc of Criminal Justice Planning; Sacramento Reg Area Planning Comm CA Coun on Criminal Justice; mem Am Sociological Soc; bd dir Cath Welfare Bureau; exec bd CYO; Golden Gate Psychotherapy Soc; NAACP; Sacramento Com for Fair Housing; Sacramento Unified Sch Dist Adult Educ Group; educ coordinator Urban League Formation Com.

LEONARD, CAROLYN MARIE
Educational administrator. **Personal:** Born Nov 20, 1943, Portland, OR; daughter of Grace Ruth Searcie Probasco and Kelly Miller Probasco; divorced; children: Cherice M, Chandra M. **Educ:** Portland State Univ, BS 1976, MS Educ 1979. **Career:** Oregon Assembly for Black Affairs, vice pres 1979-86; Alpha Kappa Alpha, treasurer 1982-; Oregon Commn for Black Affairs, 1986-; Oregon Council for Excellence in Educ, sec 1987-; Portland Public Schools, Portland OR, evaluator 1979-85, coordinator of multicultural educ 1985-. **Orgs:** Mem Natl Alliance of Black School Educ; mem City Club of Portland 1984-; sec Black United Fund of Oregon 1987-; bd mem Oregon Commn

on Black Affairs 1984-, Natl Council of Black Studies 1986-, Metro Human Relations Commn 1987-, chair, 1990-91. **Honors/Awds:** President's Award, Oregon Assembly for Black Affairs 1984; Community Leadership Award, Skanner Newspaper 1987; Merit Award, Skanner Newspaper 1987; Cheik Anta Diop Award, Outstanding Scholarly Achievement in Multicultural Educ 1988; Education Award, Delta Sigma Theta Sorority 1988; editor African-Amer Baseline Essays 1987; editor, Hispanic-Amer Women 1988; chair Martin Luther King Jr Street Renaming Committee 1989. **Home Addr:** 2015 NE Ainsworth, Portland, OR 97211.

LEONARD, CATHERINE W.
Business executive. **Personal:** Born Aug 26, 1909, Greensburg, LA; married. **Educ:** Leland Coll, BA 1943; Tuskegee Inst, MEd 1958. **Career:** St Helena Parish Greensburg LA, tchr; Day Care Center Union Bethel AME Ch, dir; Elementary Principals Assn, pres 1952-54; Sixth Dist Educ Assn in St Helena Parish, two terms pres. **Orgs:** Mem Natl Educ Assn; mem Parish Educ Assn; mem JB Poew Crescent City Temple No 185 New Orleans LA GWM; Queen Elizabeth Grand No 11 OES; State of Louisiana F&AA York Masons; Natl Compact; Alpha Gamma Zeta Chap, Zeta Phi Beta Sorority Inc; Union Bethel AME Ch; asst SS Sunday Sch; tchr pres Missionary Soc; class leader, mem Steward Bd; chmn Natl Council of Negro Women Inc. **Honors/Awds:** Tchr of Yr 1969; Mayoralty of New Orleans Certif of Merit for Outstanding Comm Serv 1973; Moon Landrieu Mayor Outstanding Layman of AME Ch LA Conf; PTA Award Helena HS 1969; honor award Union Bethel AME Ch for Outstanding Chairmanship of Women's Div of United Effort 1973; trophy award for Speaker of Yr for Women's Day Program Bethel AME Ch 1973. **Business Addr:** 2310 Peniston St, New Orleans, LA 70115.

LEONARD, CURTIS ALLEN
Educational administrator. **Personal:** Born Aug 18, 1939, Philadelphia, PA; son of Henry and Rhebena Castteberry; married Jacqueline, Jun 20, 1964; children: Laurent C. **Educ:** Temple Univ, BSEd, 1961; University of Pennsylvania, MSW, 1963; Temple University, PhD, 1979. **Career:** VA Family Care Program, director, 1965-68; Temple Univ, professor, 1968-90, prof/dean, 1990-. **Orgs:** American Political Science Assn, 1979-; National Assn of Soc Work, 1965-; Council on Social Work Education, 1968-; National Assn Black Social Work, 1965-; National Assn of Deans/Directors, 1990-. **Honors/Awds:** NIMH, Fellowship, 1961-63. **Special Achievements:** Race, Class, Bureaucracy BLK Caucus J, 1978; The BLK Male in Amer J Soc Issue, 1977; Perspectives on African American Soc Work; Housing, Support, and Comm, Families in Soc, 1994; Admin Appointment at the Academy, chapter, 1995. **Business Addr:** Dean, School of Social Admin, Temple University, Ritter Annex, 5th Fl, 13th St. & Cecil B Moore Ave, Philadelphia, PA 19122.

LEONARD, GLORIA JEAN
Library administrator. **Personal:** Born Jan 12, 1947, Seattle, WA; daughter of Katie Mae Stratman Ashford and Charles Ratliff Jr; children (previous marriage): Melanie Renee Smith; children: James Oliver Leonard Jr. **Educ:** Fisk University, Nashville, TN, 1965-67; University of Washington, Seattle, WA, BA, 1969-71, MLS, 1973; City University, Seattle, WA, MBA, 1985. **Career:** University of Washington, Seattle, WA, reference/outreach librarian, 1973-79; Seattle Public Library, Seattle, WA, south region services development librarian, 1979, mobile services and bookmobile dept head, 1981, special assistant to the city librarian, 1989, south region manager, 1990, advocate & director, neighborhood library service, 1990-. **Orgs:** Member/past president, Seattle Chapter, Jack and Jill of America, Inc, 1981-; member, American Library Association, 1973-; executive board & member, Black Caucus of the American Library Association, 1975-; member, Washington Library Association, 1973; membership committee member, Public Library Association, 1990-. **Honors/Awds:** Reading Aloud: A Good Idea Getting Better by Tom Watson, Wilson Library Bulletin, volume 61, February, 1987, p 20-22; Articles: "Bias Busting: Valuing Diversity in the Work Place," Library Administration & Management, Vol 5, No 4, Fall 1991; "Learning to Get Along with Each Other," Library Personnel News, Vol 5, No 2, March-April, 1991. **Home Addr:** 5716 S Hawthorn Rd, Seattle, WA 98118. **Business Addr:** Advocate for Neighborhood Library Services, Seattle Public Library, 1000 4th Ave, Seattle, WA 98104.

LEONARD, JEFF
Professional baseball player (retired). **Personal:** Born Sep 22, 1955, Philadelphia, PA. **Career:** Los Angeles Dodgers, outfielder 1977; Houston Astros, outfielder 1978-81; San Francisco Giants, outfielder 1981-88; Milwaukee Brewers, outfielder, 1988; Seattle Mariners, outfielder, 1989-90. **Honors/Awds:** Tied career high with 21 homers; team leading 86 RBIs 1984; set record for Giants left fielders with 17 assists, 1983. **Business Addr:** Professional Baseball Player, Seattle Mariners, PO Box 4100, Seattle, WA 98104.

LEONARD, SUGAR RAY (RAY CHARLES)
Professional boxer (retired), business executive. **Personal:** Born 1957, Rocky Mount, NC; married Juanita Wilkinson (divorced 1990); children: Sugar Ray Jr, Jarrel. **Career:** Amateur Fights Olympics, team capt, boxer 1976; professional boxer, retired in 1988; Sugar Ray Leonard Inc, pres, currently; HBO, commentator, currently. **Honors/Awds:** Won Light Welterweight Gold Medal, Olympics, Montreal, 1976; regained WBC Welterweight Champion Title, 1980; defeated Marvin Hagler to win middleweight crown, 1987; record: 36 wins, two losses, one draw; DARE America, Future of America Award, 1997.

LEONARD, WALTER FENNER. See Obituaries section.

LEONARD, WALTER J.
Educator. **Personal:** Born Oct 3, 1929, Alma, GA; married Betty E Singleton; children: Anthony Carlton, Angela Michele. **Educ:** Savannah State Coll, 1947; Morehouse Coll Atlanta, 1959-60; Atlanta Univ Grad Schl of Business, 1961-62; Howard Univ Sch of Law, JD 1968; Harvard Univ Inst of Educ Mgmt, 1974; Harvard Univ, AMP 1977. **Career:** Ivan Allen Jr Atlanta, asst campaign mgr 1961; The Leonard Land Co Atlanta, owner/operator 1962-65; Sam Phillips McKenzie, campaign asst 1963; Dean Clarence Clyde Ferguson Jr Sch of Law Howard Univ, legal rsch asst 1966-67; Washington Tech Inst, admin asst to pres 1967-68; Howard Univ Sch of Law, asst dean & lectr 1968-69; Harvard Univ Law Sch, asst dean/asst dir admiss & finan aid 1969-; US Office of Econ Oppty, hearing examiner 1969-70; Univ of CA/ Univ of VA, visit prof summers 1969-72; Harvard Univ, asst to pres 1971-77; Fisk Univ, pres 1977-84; Howard Univ, disting sr fellow 1984-86; US Virgin Islands, executive assistant to governor, 1987-89; private consulting, 1989-90; Cities in Schools, Inc. (National/International), executive director, 1990-94. **Orgs:** Mem Assn of Amer Law Schs; Council on Legal Educ Oppty; Law Sch Admissions Council; Amer Assn of Univ Prof; Howard Univ Law Sch Alumni Assn; bd of visitors USN Acad; bd trustees Natl Urban League; bd trustees Natl Pub Radio; Intl Assn of Y's Men's Club Inc; NAACP; pres Natl Bar Assn; consult The Ford Found NY 1969-71; Committee on Policy for Racial Justice, Joint Center for Economic and Political Studies; Harvard Alumni; NAACP life member; Omega Psi Phi Fraternity; Sigma Pi Phi Fraternity; board of trustees, US Naval Academy Foundation; board of directors, Cities in Schools, Inc. **Honors/Awds:** Award for Disting Serv to Assn & Office of Pres 1972; Apprec Award Harvard Black Students' Assn 1971; Walter J Leonard Day and key to city of Savannah, GA 1969; 1st Annual Melnea A Cass Comm Award Boston YWCA 1977; New England Tribute Dinner to Walter J Leonard spons by Hon Thomas P O'Neill Jr, Hon Edw M Kennedy, Hon Edw W Brooke, Pres Derek Bok of Harvard Univ 1977; Paul Robeston Award Black Amer Law Students Assn 1977; Frederick Douglass Pub Serv Award Greater Boston YMCA 1977; Special Orator Celebration of 50th Birthday of Martin Luther King Jr Boston, MA 1979; Alumni Achievement Award Morehouse Alumni Club of New England 1977; Apprec Dinner and Award Urban League of Eastern MA 1977; Exemplary Achieve Award Faculty Resolution Grad Sch Educ Harvard Univ 1976;numerous published works l, "Our Struggle Continues-Our Cause is Just" The Crisis, May 1978; "Reflecting on Black Admissions in White Colleges" The Morning After A Retrospective View, 1974; articles in, The Boston Globe, USA Today, The Harvard Law School Bulletin; Service Award and Appreciation Citation, Governor of US Virgin Islands; Oxford Scholar, 1997; more than 250 other awards, citations, and 5 honorary degrees. **Special Achievements:** Two books and more than two dozen published articles. **Military Serv:** USCG 1945-46.

LEONEY, ANTOINETTE E. M.
Attorney. **Personal:** Born Jul 22, 1950, Boston, MA; daughter of Marie E Cardoza McLean and Calvin McLean; children: Dasan C. **Educ:** Lesley College, Cambridge, MA, BS, 1980; New England School of Law, Boston, MA, JD, 1984. **Career:** Commonwealth of Massachusetts, Dept of Social Services, Legal Counsel, Boston, MA, 1984-86; Dept of the Attorney General, Boston, Ma, assistant attorney general, 1986-87; Governor Michael S Dukakis, Boston, MA, deputy chief counsel, 1987-90; Brandeis University, Waltham, MA, director of the office of government regulation compliance, 1990-91; McKenzie & Edwards, PC, sr associate, 1991-. **Orgs:** Trustee, Lesley College, Cambridge, MA, 1989-; vice president, Massachusetts Black Women Attorneys, 1990-; executive board member, Massachusetts Black Lawyers Assn, 1990-; Massachusetts Bar Association, 1991-; Boston Bar Association, 1991-; director, Massachusetts Pension Reserve Investment Management, Board 1990-92; director, Massachusetts Crime & Justice Foundation, 1990-92. **Honors/Awds:** Young Alumni Award, Lesley College, 1990; New England School of Law, Women's Law Caucus, Outstanding Achievement Award. **Business Addr:** Attorney, McKenzie & Edwards PC, 1 Bulfinch Pl #501, Boston, MA 02114-2915.

LESLIE, LISA
Professional basketball player, model. **Personal:** Born Jul 7, 1972; daughter of Christine Leslie-Espinoza. **Educ:** USC, attended. **Career:** Atlanta Glory, center, 1996-97; Los Angeles Sparks, 1997-; Wilhelmina Models, model, 1996-. **Honors/Awds:** USA Basketball Player of the Year, 1993; National Player of the Year, 1994; US Women's Olympic Basketball Team, Gold Medal, 1996; All-WNBA First Team, 1997. **Special Achievements:** Guest appearances on the television shows "Hangtime," "Moesha," and "NBA Inside Stuff.".

LESLIE, MARSHA R.
Editor. **Personal:** Born Apr 16, 1948, Lexington, MS; children: Michaela Leslie-Rule. **Educ:** Univ of Missouri, BJ Journalism, 1970; Columbia Univ, MS in Journalism, 1974. **Career:** Journalist, 1970-; has worked at KMOX Radio; The Associated Press; The Houston Chronicle; The Seattle Times; KCTS-TV; The Rochester Democrat and Chronicle. **Special Achievements:** Editor, The Single Woman's Companion, Seal Press, 1994. **Business Addr:** Editor, The Single Mother's Companion, c/o Seal Press, 3131 Western Ave, Ste 410, Seattle, WA 98121, (206)283-7844.

LESTER, BETTY J.
Judge. **Personal:** Born Oct 14, 1945, Bristol, PA; daughter of Ollie Kimbrough Johnson and John Johnson; married Althear; children: Alyse Renee. **Educ:** Howard Univ, BBA 1968; Rutgers Univ, JD 1971; Marymount Manhattan, LLD (Honors) 1983. **Career:** Public Defenders Office, asst dep public def 1972-74; Public Advocates Office, asst dep public advocate 1974-76; Supermarkets Gen, staff attny 1976-77; Newark Municipal Court, judge 1977-80, presiding judge 1980-85; Superior Court of NJ, superior court judge 1985-96; Judge of Superior Court, presiding judge, criminal division, 1996-. **Orgs:** Mem EC Bar Assoc 1971-, Natl Bar Assoc 1971-; mem Natl Assoc of Negro Business & Professional Women's Club 1977; bd of dir The Joint Connection 1978; bd of dir, gov NJ State Bar Assoc 1978-80; mem, treas EC Mun Ct Judges Assoc 1982-; mem Natl Assoc of Women Judges 1982-, NJ Coalition of 100 Black Women 1983-. **Honors/Awds:** Outstanding Achievement Assoc of Black Women Lawyers 1980; mary Philbrook Awd Rutgers Law School 1986; Woman of the Year Zonta Club Intl 1986. **Business Addr:** Superior Court Judge, Superior Court of NJ, Essex County New Courts Bldg, Room 604, Newark, NJ 07102.

LESTER, DONALD
Educator. **Personal:** Born Sep 20, 1944, Detroit, MI; married; children: Tarik. **Educ:** Wayne State Univ, BS 1967; Western MI Univ, EdM 1972. **Career:** Detroit Public School System, teacher; Wayne County Community Coll, instructor; Univ of Detroit, instructor; Western MI Univ, instructor; Shaw Coll, assoc prof. **Orgs:** Natl dir Basic Trng, Black Christian Nationalist Church; vchmn Reg #1; bd ed Detroit Schools; southern reg bishop Shrines of the Black Madonna of the Pan-African Orthodox Christian Church; chmn Atlanta Housing Auth.

LESTER, ELTON J.
Attorney. **Personal:** Born Sep 28, 1944, Bronx, NY; married Sandra Hight; children: Eric, Shawne. **Educ:** Atlantic Union Coll, BA 1966; Howard Univ, JD 1969. **Career:** US Dept of Housing & Urban Devel, atty & adv; Ofc of Mgmt & Budget, examiner. **Orgs:** Mem Fed Bar Assn; DC Bar Assn; Nat Bar Assn; mem Omega Psi Phi; Urban League; Concerned Black Fathers. **Honors/Awds:** Recip Ford Foundation Scholarship 1966; guest speaker at annual conv for Urban Econ Devel.

LESTER, GEORGE LAWRENCE (LARRY)
Company Executive, author, historian, memorabilia collector. **Personal:** Born Dec 11, 1949, Charleston, AR; son of George Lester & Casteline Williams; married Valcinia Marie Boyd, Jul 3, 1976; children: Tiffany, Marisa, Erica Joi. **Educ:** Columbia College, BA, 1978. **Career:** Negro Leagues BB Museum, cofounder and research dir, 1990-95. **Orgs:** Negro Leagues BB Museum, treasurer, 1990-95; Midwest Afro American Genealogy Interest Coalition, vp, 1995; NAACP; Assn for the Study of Afro American Life & History; Society for American Baseball Research; American First Day Cover Society; American Topical Assn; Black American Philatelic Society. **Honors/Awds:** Black Collectors Hall of Fame, 1992. **Special Achievements:** The Negro Leagues Book, 1994; Silhouettes Newsletter, 1992-95; Discover Greatness Yearbook, 1993-95; Programmer & Creator of DataBall; Natl Baseball Hall of Fame, Blue Ribbon Committee. **Home Addr:** PO Box 37046, Kansas City, MO 64138, (816)358-0475. **Business Addr:** President, Noir Tech Research, Inc, 8212 Ash Ave, Raytown, MO 64138, (816)737-8806.

LESTER, JACQUELINE (JACCI)
Government official. **Personal:** Born Sep 27, 1949, St Louis, MO; daughter of Alma Constance Epps Allen and Ezell Allen; married Earle H Lester (divorced 1976); children: Sean Anthony, Marco Shay, Damon Lamarr. **Educ:** St Louis University, St Louis, MO, 1982-83. **Career:** Bi-State Transit Co, St Louis, MO, information specialist, 1974-81; State of Missouri, Jefferson City, MO, director, human relations, 1981-. **Orgs:** Chair, Northside Preservation Comission, 1986-90; regional director, American Contract Compliance Association, 1989-91; member, Leadership St Louis, 1987-88; vice chair, Structural Unemployment, Confluence St Louis, 1987-89; regional director, American Association for Affirmative Action, 1987-. **Honors/Awds:** Certified Compliance Administrator, American Contract Compliance Association, Boston University, 1989; Certificate of Achievement, Stockton, State College, NJ, 1990; 18 Hours of Continuing Ed, Compliance-EEOC & AA.

LESTER, JULIUS
Writer, educator. **Personal:** Born Jan 27, 1939, St Louis, MO; son of Julia B Smith Lester and Woodie Daniel Lester; children: Jody, Malcolm, Elena Grohmann, Lian Brennan (stepdaughters), David. **Educ:** Fisk Univ, Nashville, TN, BA, 1960. **Career:** Univ of Massachusetts, Amherst, MA, prof, 1971—. **Honors/Awds:** Newbery Honor Award, Amer Library Assn, 1969; Natl Book Award finalist, Amer Publishing Assn, 1972; author: Look Out, Whitey! Black Power's Gon' Get Your Mama, Dial Press, 1968, To Be A Slave, Dial Press, 1968, The Seventh Son: The Thought & Writings of W E B Dubois, 2 vols, Random House, 1971, All Is Well: An Autobiography, Morrow, 1976, Lovesong: Becoming A Jew, Holt, 1988; author of fiction, including Black Folktales, Baron, 1969, Long Journey Home: Stories from Black History, Dial Press, 1972, This Strange New Feeling, Dial Press, 1982, The Tales of Uncle Remus: The Adventures of Brer Rabbit, Dial Press, 1987, More Tales of Uncle Remus: The Further Adventures of Brer Rabbit, Dial Press, 1988, Do Lord Remember Me, Dial Press, 1984, How Many Spots Does a Leopard Have, Dial Press, 1989, Falling Pieces of the Broken Sky, Arcade Publications, 1990; author of poems, Who I Am, Dial Press, 1974; Massachusetts State Professor of the Year, 1986; National Jewish Book Award Finalist, 1988; Revolutionary Notes, 1969; Search for the New Land, 1969; Two Love Stories, 1972; The Knee High Man & Other Tales, 1972; The Last Tales of Uncle Remus, 1994; And All Our Wounds Forgiven, 1994; John Henry, 1994; The Man Who Knew Too Much, 1994; Boston Globe, Horn Book Award, 1995; Othello: A Novel!, 1995; Caldscott Honor Book, 1996; Sam & The Tigers, 1996. **Business Addr:** 306 Old Springfield Rd, Belchertown, MA 01007.

LESTER, NINA MACK
Journalist, consultant. **Personal:** Born Oct 16, Fort Davis, AL; married Eugene A; children: Rev Adlai, Valinda, Regina. **Career:** WGPR-TV, variety show hostess 1976; Consumer Guardian Newspaper, co-organizers 1972; Detroit Courier, adv & gen mgr; L & T Adv Specialties Gifts, founder. **Orgs:** Mem Consumer Educ Consultant; trustee bd mem RAYA; bd mem Estsd C of C 1963; Samaritan Hosp Divisional Bd Quality Assurance; mem Women Comm United Negro Coll Fund; League of Women Voters; Adv Comm Expl of Negro Hist & Educ; mem Deaconess Emeritus Plymouth United Church of Christ; natl & area publicist; past pres, Top Ladies of Distinction; past trustee Met Assn United Church of Christ; 2nd co-editor E Area News of the United Church of Christ; Booker T Washington Business Assoc, bdm; Specialty Advertising Assoc of Michigan; chp for benefit of school drop-outs; Urban League Guild; Chamber of Commerce; Eta Phi Beta, past prs; NAACP, life member; Million Dollar Club, 1991; co-chairperson, NAACP Freedom Fund Dinner, 1997; Women's Assn Detroit Symphony Orchestra. **Honors/Awds:** Hon Un Comm Svcs; Serv Awd March of Dimes 1966; Recog Cert Un Comm Negro Hist 1967; Town Crier Bell Awd & Citizen of Yr Awd Ford Motor Co; 1983 Honorary Doctorate Journ Humanities Shaw College; Woman of the Year 1971; Top Lady of the Year 1983; National Top Lady of the Year, 1991-93; Highland Park YMCA Outstanding Mother of the Year 1983; Detroit Urban League Guild Initiative awd 1985; Budweiser Community Award, 1993; Michigan Legis House Concurrent Resolution for distinguished contrib of service to community; Spirit of Detroit Award, 1992; Detroit City Council Testimonial Resolution 1985; United Negro College Fund, Inc, Meritorius Service Award, 1994; Eta Phi Beta, Past President Award, 1995; Edith Gamble Awd, Outstanding Community Svc; UNCF 1993-95, Volunteer Recognition Award.

LESTER, TIM LEE
Professional football player. **Personal:** Born Jun 15, 1968, Miami, FL; married Kendra; children: Brandi, Breanna. **Educ:** Eastern Kentucky. **Career:** Pittsburgh Steelers, running back, 1995-. **Business Addr:** Professional Football Player, Pittsburgh Steelers, Three Rivers Stadium, 300 Stadium Circle, Pittsburgh, PA 15212, (412)323-1200.

LESTER, WILLIAM ALEXANDER, JR.
Educator, chemist. **Personal:** Born Apr 24, 1937, Chicago, IL; son of Elizabeth Frances Clark Lester (deceased) and William Alexander Lester (deceased); married Rochelle Diane Reed; children: William Alexander III, Allison Kimberleigh. **Educ:** Univ of Chicago, BS 1958, MS 1959; Catholic Univ of Amer, PhD 1964. **Career:** Theoretical Chem Inst Univ WI, research assoc/asst dir 1964-68; Univ of WI Dept Chem, lecturer 1966-68; IBM San Jose Research Lab, research staff mem/mgr 1968-81; IBM TJ Watson Research Lab, techn planning staff 1975-76; Lawrence Berkeley Lab, assoc dir 1978-81; Natl Resource for Computation in Chem, dir 1978-81; Univ of CA Berkeley, prof chem, 1981, associate dean, College of Chemistry, 1991-95; Natl Sci Foundation, Human Resource Development, sr fellow for sci and engineering, asst to the dir, 1995-96. **Orgs:** Volunteer instr Project SEED (Spec Elem Educ for the Disadvantaged) 1970-72; chmn Black Liason Comm San Jose Unified Sch Dist 1971-72; mem Chem Eval Panel Air Force Off Sci Research 1974-78; chmn Div Phys Chem Amer Chemical Soc 1979; mem US Natl Comm of Internatl Union of Pure and Applied Chemistry, 1976-79; mem Natl Research Council Panel for Chemical Physics of Natl Bureau of Standards, 1980-83; mem Chem Adv Panel Natl Science Found 1980-83; mem Comm to Survey Chem Sciences Natl Acad Sciences 1982-84; bd mem Marcus Foster Educ Inst 1982-86; Comm on Recommendations for US Army Basic Research, 1984-87; Chmn Div of Chemical Physics, Amer Physical Society, 1986-87; committee on nominations, 1988-91; National Board, 1993-; American Assn for the Advancement of Science; advisory board, Science Y, World Book, Inc, 1989-; Federal Networking Council Advisory Committee, 1991-95; Army Research Laboratory Tech Assessment Bd, 1996-. **Honors/Awds:** Outstanding Contrib Award IBM Corp 1974; Chmn Gordon Conf on Atomic and Molecular Interactions 1978; Percy L Julian Awd Natl Organization of Black Chemists and Chemical Engineers 1979; Alumni Award in Sci Catholic Univ of Amer 1983; Elected Fellow Amer Phys Soc 1984; mem editorial brd, Journal of Physical Chemistry, 1979-81, Journal of Computational Chemistry 1980-87, International Journal of Quantum Chemistry 1979-87, Computer Physics Communications 1981-86; Outstanding Teacher Awd, Natl Organization of Black Chemists and Chemical Engineers 1986; Prof Achievement Award Northern CA Council of Black Prof Engineers 1989; Elected Fellow, American Assn for the Advancement of Science, 1991; California Academy of Sciences, Elected Fellow, 1994. **Business Addr:** Professor of Chemistry, Univ of California-Berkeley, Dept of Chemistry, Berkeley, CA 94720, (510)643-9590.

LETT, GERALD WILLIAM
Entrepreneur. **Personal:** Born Sep 28, 1926, Lansing, MI; married Ruby Truitt; children: William, Gerald, Debra. **Career:** Letts Fashions Inc, owner 1952-; Lansing C of C, bd dir. **Orgs:** Mem MI Retailers Assn Bd; dir YWCA; mem Lansing Econ Devel Corp; past pres Lansing Sexton HS PTA; mem NAACP; mem Urban League. **Honors/Awds:** Sales & Idea Book Citation Award Intl Newspaper Advertising Exec; Boss of Yr Professional Women's Club; Man of Yr Negro Professional & Bus Women's Club; 1st black retail owner to have story written on him Women's Wear Daily. **Business Addr:** 119 N Butler, Lansing, MI 48915.

LETT, LEON
Professional football player. **Personal:** Born Oct 12, 1968, Mobile, AL; children: Shanavia. **Educ:** Emporia State, attended. **Career:** Dallas Cowboys, defensive end, 1991-. **Honors/Awds:** Pro Bowl, 1994. **Business Addr:** Professional Football Player, Dallas Cowboys, One Cowboys Pkwy, Irving, TX 75063, (214)556-9900.

LEVELL, EDWARD, JR.
Airport commissioner. **Personal:** Born Apr 2, 1931, Jacksonville, AL; son of Gabrella Williams Levell (deceased) and Edward A Levell, Sr (deceased); married Rosa M Casellas, Aug 3, 1951; children: Edward A III (deceased), Ruben C, Kenneth W, Raymond C (deceased), Randy C ,Cheryl D Levell Rivera, Michael K. **Educ:** Tuskegee Inst, Tuskegee, AL, Bachelor of Science, 1953; US Air Force, Bryan AFB, TX, USAF Pilot Training, 1953-54; Univ of Northern CO, Greeley, CO, MA Urban Sociology, 1972; Industrial Coll of the Armed Forces, Washington, DC, MA Mgmt, 1973; Air War Coll, Maxwell AFB, AL, Leadership/Mgmt, 1973-74. **Career:** US Air Force, USAF Academy Commander, CO Springs Cadet Group 1, 1970-72, deputy commandant of Cadets, 1972-73; US Air Force, Hurlburt AFB, FL, commander 1st Special Operations WG Wing, 1976-77; US Air Force, Luke, AFB, AZ, commander 58th Tactical Training Wing, 1977-78; US Air Force, Langley AFB, VA, commander 20th Air Div, 1978-83; Chicago, IL, director of aviation, 1984-89; New Orleans Airport, dep dir of aviation, 1989-92, dir of aviation, 1992-. **Orgs:** Life mem, Kappa Alpha Psi Fraternity; life mem, The Retired Officers Assn (TROA); life mem, The Daedalian Found; life mem, The Tuskegee Airman, Inc (TAI). **Honors/Awds:** Winner of USAFE "Top Gun" Award, 1961; Tactical Air Command (TAC) "Top Gun" (F-100 Super Sabre) 1961, 1965, 1969; Distinguished Service Award, Jacksonville, AL, 1974; Air Force Assn Special Citation of Merit, State of FL, 1977; State of FL Commn of Human Relations Award for Special Recognition, 1977; over 5500 hours of flying time as a command pilot. **Military Serv:** US Air Force, Colonel, 1953-83; received Legion of Merit Award, 1983, Distinguished Flying Cross, 1969, Meritorious Serv Medal, 1970, Air Force Commendation Medal, 1966, Air Medal (eight awards) 1970, Vietnam Campaign Medals, 1965-69; Tuskegee University Hall of Fame, November 1991. **Business Addr:** Director of Aviation, New Orleans International Airport, PO Box 20007, New Orleans, LA 70141, (504)464-3536.

LEVENS, DORSEY
Professional football player. **Personal:** Born May 21, 1970, Syracuse, NY. **Educ:** Georgia Tech, attended. **Career:** Green Bay Packers, running back, 1994-. **Business Addr:** Professional Football Player, Green Bay Packers, 1265 Lombardi Ave, Green Bay, WI 54304, (414)494-2351.

LEVER, LAFAYETTE (FAT)
Professional basketball player. **Personal:** Born Aug 18, 1960, Pine Bluff, AR. **Educ:** Arizona State Univ, Tempe, AZ, 1978-82. **Career:** Portland Trail Blazers, 1982-84; Denver Nuggets, 1984-90; Dallas Mavericks, 1990-. **Orgs:** NBPA, vice pres, 1987-. **Honors/Awds:** All-NBA Second Team, 1987; NBA All-Defensive Second Team, 1988; All Star, 1988, 1990. **Business Addr:** Professional Basketball Player, Dallas Mavericks, Reunion Arena, 777 Sports St, Dallas, TX 75207-4499.

LEVERMORE, CLAUDETTE MADGE
Educational administrator. **Personal:** Born Feb 28, 1939, St Andrew, Jamaica; daughter of Herbert Willacy; married Oswald Burchell Levermore; children: Monique Althea, Jacqueline Maureen. **Educ:** McGill Univ, Certificate 1968; Univ of Miami, BBA 1978; Wharton Univ, Certificate 1981; Nova Univ, MBA 1984. **Career:** Government of Jamaica, civil servant 1958-64; Geigy Pharmaceuticals, admin asst 1964-68; McGill Univ, admin asst 1968-71; Univ of Miami, dir admin serv 1971-; Miami Dade South Campus, instructor, 1984-. **Orgs:** Natl Black MBA Assn; bd mem Black Cultural Art Ctr, Black South Florida Coalition for Economic Develop; Nursing School Business Officers Assn; mem Woodson Williams Marshall Assn 1978-; bd mem & treas United Nations Florida Chapter. **Honors/Awds:** Outstanding Achievement in Accounting Univ of Miami; Outstanding Achievement in Business Consulting Univ of Miami. **Home Addr:** 14865 SW 166th St., Miami, FL 33187. **Business Addr:** Dir Admin Serv, University of Miami, 1755 NW 12th Ave, Rm 412, Miami, FL 33101.

LEVERT, EDDIE
Singer. **Personal:** chilDren: Gerald, Sean. **Career:** The O'Jays, singer, currently.

LEVERT, FRANCIS E.
Engineer. **Personal:** Born Mar 28, 1940, Tusculoosa, AL; married Faye Burnett, 1965; children: Francis, Gerald, Lisa. **Educ:** Tuskegee Inst, BS, 1964; Univ of MI, MS, 1966; Pennsylvania State Univ, PhD, nuclear eng, 1971. **Career:** Tuskegee Inst, Schl of Engr, acting head mech engr, 1972-73; Commonwealth Edison Co, principal engr, 1973-74; Argonne Natl Lab, nuclear engr applied physics div, 1974-79; Tech Energy Corp, chief scientist, 1979-85; KEMP Corp, vice pres, 1985-. **Orgs:** American Nuclear Soc; Plant Maintenance Division, executive comm; American Soc Mech Engrs; Phi Kappa Phi; Pi Tau Sigma; Beta Kappa Chi; Amer Soc for Engr Educ; Ford Found Fellow; National Society of Professional Engineers. **Honors/Awds:** Inventor: 16 US Patents; author of two books & 63 technical journals, articles; Atomic Energy Commission; Univ of Michigan, fellow; DNEA, Fellow Pennsylvania State Univ; American Men & Women of Science, 1988.

LEVERT, GERALD
Vocalist, production company executive, composer. **Personal:** son Of Eddie Levert. **Career:** LeVert trio, lead singer, 1985-; albums include: Bloodline, 1986; The Big Throwdown, 1987; Just Coolin, 1988; Rope a Dope Style, 1990; singles include: Casanova; Just Coolin; solo albums; Private Line, 1991; Groove On, 1994; solo singles include: Baby Hold on to Me; Trevel Productions, owner; Club LeVert, owner, 1991-; album LSG with Keith Sweat and Johnny Gill, 1997. **Honors/Awds:** Private Line, gold and platinum album; group has three gold albums, seven top hits. **Special Achievements:** Writes and produces songs for Anita Baker, Stephanies Mills, James Ingram, Miki Howard; manages and produces five groups, including The Rude Boys, Men at Large. **Business Addr:** Singer, Groove On, c/o East West Records, 74 Rockefeller Plaza, New York, NY 10019, (212)484-6000.

LEVERT, SEAN
Vocalist. **Personal:** son Of Eddie Levert. **Career:** Singer, group Levert, solo; Songs include: Casanova, I'm Ready, Same One with Eddie and Gerald Levert; Album: The Other Side, 1995. **Business Phone:** (212)275-2000.

LEVINGSTON, CLIFFORD EUGENE
Professional basketball player. **Personal:** Born Jan 4, 1961, San Diego, CA. **Educ:** Wichita State Univ, Wichita, KS, 1979-82. **Career:** Forward: Detroit Pistons, 1982-84, Atlanta Hawks, 1984-90, Chicago Bulls, 1990-92, Paok, Greece, 1992-93; Denver Nuggets, 1994-. **Business Addr:** Professional Basketball Player, Denver Nuggets, Brendan Byrne Arena, East Rutherford, NJ 07073, (201)935-8888.

LEVISTER, ERNEST CLAYTON, JR.
Physician. **Personal:** Born Feb 4, 1936, New York, NY; son of Ruth Amos Levister and Ernest Clayton Levister Sr; married; children (previous marriage): E Clay, Michelle Nicole. **Educ:** Lincoln Univ, AB 1958; Lafayette Coll, BS Chem Eng 1958; Howard Univ Coll of Med, MD 1964. **Career:** Norfolk VA, internal medicine/cardiology private practice 1974-78; Embassy of USA Lagos Nigeria, medical attache 1978-79; Private Practice, internal/occupational med San Bernardino CA 1979-; Univ of California-Irvine, asst clinical prof of occupational and environmental medicine 1989-. **Orgs:** Asst prof Inst Sch of Engr Tuskegee Inst 1958-59; asst prof medicine George Washington Medical Sch 1973-74; asst prof medicine Eastern VA Medical Sch 1974-81; radio host Medical Talk Show Norfolk 1980-81; mem Los Angeles Council of Black Professional Engrs 1982-; columnist (medicine) Voice News Riverside CA 1986-; commissioner, Environmental Protection Commission, Riverside CA 1989-91. **Honors/Awds:** Fellow Amer Coll of Physicians 1977; Fellow, American College of Preventive Medicine, 1991. **Special Achievements:** Certified American Board of Internal Medicine. **Military Serv:** AUS Medical Corps major 1969-72; Vietnam, Unit Citation. **Business Addr:** 1738 N Waterman Ave, San Bernardino, CA 92404.

LEVISTER, WENDELL P.
Judge. **Personal:** Born May 14, 1928, Rocky Mount, NC; divorced; children: Degna P, Drew F. **Educ:** Hampton Inst, BS 1950; NY Univ, MBA 1951; NY Univ Law Sch, JD 1958; Stanford Univ, certificate Stanford Exec Prog 1973. **Career:** Greenup Golar & Levister Esqs, co-founder 1960-63; New York City Law Dept, asst corp counsel 1963-67; Borough of Brooklyn NYC, dir office of spec proj city planning comm 1970-74; Dept of Parks & Recreation, deputy commr revenue devel & park policy 1979-; Civil Court NYC, judge. **Orgs:** Chief Internal Review DAC HQ Ft Wadsworth USARADCOM SI NY; assoc Amer Inst of Planners 1973-; Bedford Stuyvesant Lawyers Assn 1960-; Brooklyn Bar Assn 1964-65; Omega Psi Phi 1949-; bd dir Stuyvesant Comm Ctr Brooklyn 1964-65; NAACP NY 1958-; exec bd United People's Com of Brooklyn UPC 1973-. **Honors/Awds:** Merrill Foundation Fellowship. **Military Serv:** USAF 1946-47. **Business Addr:** Judge, Bronx Criminal Court, 215 East 161st, Bronx, NY 10451.

LEVY, VALERIE LOWE
Government employee. **Personal:** Born in New York, NY; married Edward J Levy Jr; children: Vanessa Lynn, Edward Joseph III. **Educ:** NY Univ, BA; CCNY, grad studies; New Sch for Social Research, masters candidate. **Career:** New York City Dept for the Aging, dir Manhatten field office 1969-79, dir minority affairs 1979-. **Orgs:** Bd mem Natl Caucus and Center on the Black Aged Wash, DC 1974-; mem Gerontological Soc of Amer 1973-; mem Amer Pub Health Assn 1979-; Delta Sigma Theta Sor; one of orig organizers & coord of the Harlem Interagency Coun on Aging. **Honors/Awds:** Has written and pres many papers on aging and the elderly in the US; Is a recognized authority on the minority elderly. **Business Addr:** Dir of Minority Affairs, New York City Dept for the Aging, 2 Lafayette St, New York, NY 10007.

LEVY, VICTOR MILES, JR. (VIC MILES)
TV anchorman (retired). **Personal:** Born Nov 7, 1931, Philadelphia, PA; divorced; children: 3. **Career:** WCBS-TV rptr anchorman, retired 1995; KDKA-TV, corr; NBC monitor-Radio press internat, voice of am 1966-71; WHOA radio, prgm news dir. **Orgs:** Mem The Inner Circle. **Honors/Awds:** Comm Serv Award; Pittsburgh Guardian Soc 1970; Responsive Environ Found & Awd; ''Serv to Children'' 1970; Black Achiever Award; Harlem YMCA 1972; Ministerial Interfaith Assn Media Award 1977; 1st Black to Anchor Sched News Prgrm in Pittsburgh; WCBS-TV, 3 Emmy Awards, 1976, 1991, 1993; Several nominations; Deadline Feature Award, WY Society of Professional Journalists; Women in Communications, ''Clarion Award;'' AP & UPT Awards. **Military Serv:** USAF 1950-54.

LEWELLEN, MICHAEL ELLIOTT
Public relations/public affairs manager. **Personal:** Born Jan 16, 1960, Marianna, AR; son of Mildred King Lewellen and Herman L Lewellen; married Merle Williams, Aug 6, 1983; children: Elliott. **Educ:** Arkansas State University, Jonesboro, AR, BS, journalism, 1982. **Career:** Pine Bluff Commercial, Pine Bluff, AR, sports reporter, 1982-85; Bloom Tennis Center, Pine Bluff, AR, tennis pro, 1983-85; Southwestern Bell Telephone, St Louis, MO, public relations manager, 1985-91; Nike Inc, urban and minority affairs director, currently. **Orgs:** President, International Assn of Business Communicators, St Louis Chapter, 1990; treasurer, St Louis Assn of Black Journalists, 1987-88; board of directors, St Louis Journalism Foundation, 1990; board of directors and national advisory council, National Assn of Partners in Education, 1989-. **Honors/Awds:** Yes I Can (Role Model for Minority Youth), St Louis Metro Sentinel Newspaper, 1986; Accredited Business Communicator, International Association of Business Communicators, 1989; Corporate Volunteer Award, St Louis Affiliate National Black Child Development Institute, 1990; Certified Professional, US Professional Tennis Association, 1986-; Accredited Public Relations Professional, Public Relations Society of America, 1991. **Business Addr:** Director, Urban and Minority Affairs, Nike Inc, 1 Bowerman Dr, Beaverton, OR 97005-0979.

LEWIS, ALBERT RAY
Professional football player. **Personal:** Born Oct 6, 1960, Mansfield, LA. **Educ:** Grambling State Univ, attended. **Career:** Kansas City Chiefs, cornerback, 1983-93; Oakland Raiders, 1993-. **Honors/Awds:** Sporting News NFL All-Star Team, 1989; Pro Bowl, 1987, 1988, 1989, 1990. **Business Addr:** Professional Football Player, Oakland Raiders, 1220 Harbor Bay Pkwy, Alameda, CA 94502, (510)615-1875.

LEWIS, ALMERA P.
Educator. **Personal:** Born Oct 23, 1935, Chicago; married Thomas P Lewis; children: Tracy, Todd. **Educ:** Univ of WI, BS 1957; Loyola Univ, MSW 1959. **Career:** Day Care Cntrs & Sch, cons; Mental Hlth Cntr, psychiatric & sco worker 1959-65; Crittenton Comprehensive Care Cntr supr of professional staff 1966-68; Park Forest Sch Sys, social worker 1968-69; Chicago Circle-jane Adams Sch of Soc, work prest; Univ of IL, prof/ dean of students, social work. **Orgs:** Mem, natl bd od dir Nat Assn of Soc Workers; Il Assn of Sch Soc Workers; Academy of Certified Soc Workers; Am Assn of Univ Prof Bd; mem Women's Com of United Cerebral Palsy of Greater Chicago; Chicago Urban League PUSH; The Art Inst of Chicago.

LEWIS, ALONZO TODD
Health services administrator. **Personal:** Born Jun 29, 1969, Detroit, MI; son of Alonzo and Vera Lewis. **Educ:** Univ of Michigan, BA, sociology, 1991; Univ of Michigan School of Public Health, MHSA, 1993. **Career:** Mercy Health Services, management fellow, 1993-94; Mercy Hospital, director, senior services, 1994-. **Orgs:** American College of Healthcare Executives, assoc, 1991-; Alpha Phi Alpha, Fraternity Inc, 1989-; National Association of Health Services Executives, 1991-. **Business Addr:** Dir, Senior Services, Mercy Hospital, 5555 Connor Ave, Admin Servs Bldg, Detroit, MI 48213, (313)579-4228.

LEWIS, ALVIN
Church agency executive. **Personal:** Born Oct 1, 1935, Chicago, IL; married Dr Juanita L; children: Alvin, Lydia, Lystrelle. **Educ:** Northern Bapt Seminary, theological studies 1959-62; KS State Univ, MS 1970, PhD 1975; Garrett Evangelicol Theological Seminary, MDiv, 1993. **Career:** First Ch of God, pastor prof dir minorities resources ctr family consult 1966-74; KS State Univ, instr 1970-74, asst prof 1975; Minor Resources & Rsch Ctr, dir 1973-75; Bd Christian Educ Ch of God, assoc sec 1975-1989; National Association, Church of God, CEO, 1989-1992; Vernon Park Church of God, minister of administration and special programmer, 1992-. **Orgs:** Mem Natl Coun Family Rel; dir Natl Met Black Family Conf; Amer Assn Univ Profs; vice chmn & commr Family Life Nat Council of Ch; supervisor & clinical mem Natl Acad of Counselors & Family Therapists Inc; cert leader marriage enrichment Assn Couples for Marriage Enrichment; former pres Junction Manhattan NAACP 1967-71; vice chmn Madison Co Urban League 1985-86; mem Phi Alpha Theta 1969-71; served as ed consult in Africa Caribbean & Europe. **Honors/Awds:** Omicron Hon Soc 1968. **Business Addr:** Minister of Administration & Special Programs, Bd Christian Educ Ch of God, PO Box 2458, Anderson, IN 46011.

LEWIS, ANANDA
Television personality. **Educ:** Howard Univ, BA cum laude. **Career:** BET, host of TV show Teen Summit; MTV, video jockey, currently. **Honors/Awds:** NAACP Image Award for interview with Hillary Rodham Clinton. **Business Addr:** Video jockey, MTV, 1515 Broadway, New York, NY 10036, (212)258-8000.

LEWIS, ANDRE
Banking executive. **Personal:** Born May 4, 1960, Walterboro, SC; son of Clara Lee Martino Lewis and William Lewis; married Queen E Govan Lewis, Oct 15, 1983; children: Shana Nicole, William Andre. **Educ:** South Carolina State College, Orangeburg, SC, BS, accounting, 1982. **Career:** First Union National Bank, Columbia, SC, branch management, 1983-87; South Carolina National Bank, Columbia, SC, associate vice president of corporate banking, 1987-88; Victory Savings Bank, Columbia, SC, president, 1988-. **Orgs:** Board member, Committee of 100, 1990-; committee member, United Way of the Midlands, 1989-; board member, Greater Columbia Chamber of Commerce, 1989-90. **Honors/Awds:** Outstanding Business Achievement, Black Enterprise Magazine, 1990; Outstanding Alumnus, Upper Dorchester Alumni of South Carolina State College, 1989; Business Person of the Year, Phi Beta Lambda, 1988. **Home Addr:** 2212 W. Branch Rd., Columbia, SC 29223-6822.

LEWIS, ANNE A. See Obituaries section.

LEWIS, ANTHONY HAROLD, JR.
Computer company executive. **Personal:** Born Aug 31, 1953, Baton Rouge, LA; married Sonja Marie Newkirk; children: Kirsten Sonja, Kira Antoinette. **Educ:** Harvard Coll, AB (Cum Laude) 1975; Harvard Grad Sch of Business Admin, MBA 1977. **Career:** Touche Ross & Co, mgmt consultant 1977-79; Raychem Corp, business planner 1979-83; Headquarters Companies, mgr new business 1983-84; Bank of Amer, vice pres 1984-86; Tandem Computers, mgr corporate financial planning. **Orgs:** Treas trustee Katherine Delmar Burke Sch 1984-. **Business Addr:** Tandem Computers Inc, 5300 Stevens Creek Blvd, LOC 219-30, San Jose, CA 95129-1033.

LEWIS, ARTHUR A., JR.
Tax accountant, auditor. **Personal:** Born Nov 4, 1925, Los Angeles, CA; son of Verna Deckard Williams and Arthur A Lewis; married Elizabeth, Aug 1, 1970; children: Ivy, Derek, Cornell, Arthur III, Jeffrey, Jason. **Educ:** UCLA, BS 1947. **Career:** Dept of Energy, audit investigator (retired); Defense Contract Audit Agy; Vending Machine Bus Los Angeles, owns & operates, 1954-; Lewis Tax Serv, Los Angeles, owner; Golden State Mutual Life Ins Co 1947-52. **Orgs:** Board of directors, Southeast Symphony Assn; mem Fed Govt Accountants Assn; mem NAACP; Urban League; Alpha Phi Alpha Frat; Trustee for Lincoln Memorial Congregational Ch of Los Angeles. **Honors/Awds:** IRS Enrolled Agent; Certificate Certified Internal Auditor. **Military Serv:** AUS e-5 1952-54. **Business Addr:** Owner, Lewis Tax Service, 2415 W Martin Luther King Blvd, Los Angeles, CA 90008.

LEWIS, ARTHUR W.
Senior consultant. **Personal:** Born Jul 1, 1926, New York, NY; son of Marlon Lewis and Arthur Lewis. **Educ:** Dartmouth Coll, AB 1966, AM 1969; Foreign Serv Inst, Postgrad 1969-70. **Career:** USIA, fgn serv, US Embassy, cultural affairs officer Bucharest, 1970-72, counselor for pub affairs Lusaka, 1972-74, Addis Ababa, 1974-77, Lagos 1977-79, dir African Affairs 1979-; US ambassador, Republic of Sierre Leone, 1983-86; Edward R Murrow fellow, Fletcher School of Law & Diplomacy, 1986-87; Nord Resources Corp, sr consultant, currently. **Military Serv:** US Navy, 1943-45, 1950-.

LEWIS, AUBREY C.
Business executive. **Personal:** Born 1935, Montclair, NJ; son of Edna Lewis and Clem Lewis; married Ann; children: Lauren, Aubrey Jr, Lisa, John, Gary. **Educ:** Notre Dame Univ, BS; FBI Acad; Cornell Univ; New York Univ. **Career:** ACL Enterprises, Inc, Developers of Inner City Homes, chairman & CEO; Woolworth Corporation, vp, 1967-94; FBI, special agt; Chicago Bears, player and scout; New Jersey High School, football & track coach. **Orgs:** Board member, Independence Savings Bank; Midlantic Corporation, Midlantic Bank; board member, US Naval Academy Foundation; board member, University of Notre Dame; board member, YMCA of Greater New York; board member, 100 Black Men of New York; board member, Mentors International, Inc. **Honors/Awds:** Univ of Norte Dame, Man of the Year, 1994. **Military Serv:** US Army, ROTC cadet, 1955-58. **Business Addr:** 122 Brighton Avenue, East Orange, NJ 07017.

LEWIS, BILLIE JEAN
Librarian. **Personal:** Born Dec 6, 1947, Eden, NC; daughter of Darnella Blackstock Worthington and William Manns; married Jerome M Lewis Jr, Aug 6, 1966; children: Jerome V, Jill Renee. **Educ:** Corning Community College, AAS, 1983; Cornell University, Certificate, industrial relations and human services, 1984; Florida A&M University, BS (summa cum laude), 1988; University of Michigan, MS, 1989. **Career:** Corning Glass Works, quality, administrative aide, 1984-85; Florida State University, administrative aide, 1985-88; Michigan State University, GEAC operator, 1988; Wayne State University, research assistant, 1989; Detroit Public Library, children's librarian, 1989-92, asst manager, children's librarian, 1992-. **Orgs:** American Library Association, 1989-94; Association of African-American Librarians, 1992-; Detroit Public Library Children's Services: chairperson, African-American Children's Book Committee, chairperson, Fund-Raising Committee, Children's Book Committee, 1990-. **Business Addr:** Librarian, Detroit Public Library, Bowen Branch, 3648 W Vernor Hwy, Detroit, MI 48216-1441, (313)297-9381.

LEWIS, BYRON E.
Business executive. **Personal:** Born Dec 25, 1931, Newark, NJ; son of Myrtle Evelyn Allen and Thomas Eugene Lewis; divorced; children: Byron Eugene Lewis Jr. **Educ:** Long Island U, BA 1953; NY U, Grad Study; City Coll NY; King Meml Coll, hon DHL. **Career:** Uniworld Group Inc, chmn/ceo; Afro Mkt Co, pres, publ 1968-69; Tuesday Publs, vice pres 1964-68; Amalgamated Publs, asst ad mgr 1963-64; Urbanite Mag, co-fdr 1961-62. **Orgs:** Lectr Black Coll; Black Exec Exch Prgm Nat Urban League. **Honors/Awds:** Creator ''This Far by Faith'' 1977; exec Prodcr ''Sounds of the City'' 1974-75; Minority Bus Man of the Yr ICBO New York City 1980; exec producer, Americas Black Forum Television Show 1989. **Military Serv:** AUS pfc 1953-55.

LEWIS, CARL
Track and field athlete. **Personal:** Born Jul 1, 1961, Birmingham, AL. **Educ:** University of Houston, communications, 1979-. **Career:** Began running at age 8; Jesse Owens Youth Prog Meet, long jump winner, 1973; amateur athlete throughout high school and college career; US Olympic Team, track and field competitor, numerous Olympics; professional track and field athlete, currently. **Honors/Awds:** Top ranked HS track athlete in US; All Amer in 200 meters & long jump 1978; Natl HS long jump/100 yd record 1978; Ranks #1 in the world in the 100 meterrace & long jump, #2 in the world in 200 meters; Third fastest time ever in 100 meters; Long jump indoor world record; Duplicated Jesse Owens feat at 1936 Berlin Olympics; 1984 Olympics won 4 Gold medals, 100 meters, 200 meters, long jump, 4x400 meter relay; World Championship, 1st place long jump, 1st place 400m relay, 2nd place 100m, 1987; 1988 Olympics, 1st place, 100m & long jump, 2nd place 200m, 1988; World Champs, 1st place 100m World Record, 1st place 400 relay, 2nd place long jump, 1991; Olympics 1st place long jump, Gold Medal, 1st place 400m relay World Record, Gold Medal, 1992. **Business Addr:** c/o Tom Tellez, Unv of Houston/ Athletic Dept, 4800 Calhoun Blvd, Houston, TX 77004.

LEWIS, CARMEN CORTEZ
Educator. **Personal:** Born Jul 26, Detroit, MI; daughter of Maggie M Farris and John E Farris; married Thomas J Lewis, Jan 17, 1975. **Educ:** University of Detroit, BA, 1973; Wayne State University, MEd, 1987. **Career:** Detroit Board of Education, Ruddiman Middle School, teacher, 1974-. **Orgs:** Zeta Phi Beta, vice pres; State of Michigan treasurer; NAACP, Women's Committee, Detroit Branch; March of Dimes Organization, Re-

tirement Committee, Detroit Branch; Greater Ebenezer Baptist Church, Usher Board #2, president; The Ladies of Distinction, committee mem; The National Association of Business Women, committee mem; Greeters Ministry of Greater Ebenezer Church. **Home Addr:** 9190 Dale St, Redford, MI 48239, (313)532-1462.

LEWIS, CARY B., JR.
Educator, attorney. **Personal:** Born Sep 13, 1921, Chicago, IL; married Mary S; children: Cheryl, Cary B III. **Educ:** Univ of IL, AB 1942; Univ of Chicago, MBA 1947; Univ of IL, CPA 1950; DePaul Univ, JD 1966; Harvard Univ, AMP 1971; Teaching Certificates & Licenses, HS 1951, Jr Coll 1967, Coll 1958, Supervisory 1967. **Career:** KY State Univ, asst prof 1947-50; So Univ, assoc prof 1950-; CPA, 1950-75; MT Washington & Co CPA's Chicago, sr auditor 1951-53; Chicago Pub Sch, 1951-57; Collier-Lewis Realty Co, auditor 1953-71; Chicago Tchrs Coll, 1957-65; AA Rayner & Sons, auditor 1960-72; Budget Coord, 1966-67; Atty at Law, 1966-; Chicago State Univ, spec asst to vice pres 1967, prof law & acctg 1957-. **Orgs:** Budgetary consult office of econ oppor 1967-69; educ consult to dept hlth educ & welfare 1968-69; auditing consult to dept of labor 1967-69; mgmt consult to Black Econ Union 1969; chmn educ adv comm Chicago NAACP; mem Amer Bar Assn, IL Bar Assn; Chicago Bar Assn; Cook Co Bar Assn; Amer Judicare Soc; Amer Bus Law Assn; Amer Inst CPA's; IL Soc CPA's; Natl Soc CPA's; Amer Acct's Assn; Amer Assn of Univ Prof's; City Club of Chicago. **Honors/Awds:** Wisdon Hall of Fame, 1972; Worldwide Acad of Scholars 1975; Natl Hon Soc 1938; Sachem 1941; first black to practice as CPA LA 1951; first black atty & CPA State of IL 1966. **Military Serv:** USEAC bombardier & navigator 1942-45.

LEWIS, CHARLES GRANT
Designer. **Personal:** Born Mar 12, 1948, Los Angeles, CA. **Educ:** ELA Coll, AA 1973; Univ So CA, BS 1977. **Career:** Edward C Barker & Asso, proj designer 1977-; AIA, asst vice pres 1977-; Benito Sinclair PE, engr 1974-77; John D Williams, draftsman 1971-74; Charles Grant Orgn, prin 1974-77. **Orgs:** Alpha Phi Alpha Building Found 1972-74; assoc Urban Workshop 1967-77; Alpha Phi Alpha Frat 1971-73; stu rep Nat Orgn of Minority Architects 1974-77; comm Design Ctr Planning & Arch for Urban grps. **Honors/Awds:** Leadership Award Am Soc of Engrs & Arch 1973; outst serv to sch; comm Order of Omega Hon Frat; num articles publ by local & natl jours. **Business Addr:** 3123 W 8th St, Los Angeles, CA 90005.

LEWIS, CHARLES H.
Dentist. **Personal:** Born Dec 31, 1923, Vicksburg, MS; married Dorothy Foote; children: Stephen A, Brenda A, Phyllis G. **Educ:** Howard Univ Wash DC, BS Chem 1949; Meharry Med Coll Nashville, DDS 1955. **Career:** Alpha Phi Alpha Frat Inc, SW regional vp; Dentistry, priv pract 1955-70, 1973-; Morton-neighborhood Health & Ctr, dir 1970-73. **Orgs:** Mem Am Dental Assn 1955-; sec-tres Moton Meml Hosp 1958-; pres Oil Capital SW Reg Golf Assn 1958-; mem NAACP; YMCA 1958-; pres Greenwood C of C1977-79. **Honors/Awds:** Ribbon for campaigns ''Invasion of Borneo & China Coast'' 1944; Honorary Dental Soc; hon mem Omicron Kappa Upsilon Honor Dent Soc 1955-; twice rec ''Serviceto Humanity'' Award Langston Univ 1978-79; Tourn named ''Charles H Lewis Classic'' Oil Capital Golf Club 1979. **Military Serv:** USN signalman/2/c 1942-45. **Business Addr:** 5050 N Peoria, Tulsa, OK 74126.

LEWIS, CHARLES HENRY
Leisure consultant. **Personal:** Born Nov 22, 1930, Bessemer, AL; son of Charles M Lewis (deceased) & Erline Mills Carter; married Joyce Jean Hale Lewis, May 25, 1952; children: Joyce Rene Rich, Donna Kay (deceased), Charles Michael. **Educ:** Langston University, BS, 1953; Wayne State University, MA, 1967; Michigan State University, MBA, 1974. **Career:** City of Detroit Recreation Dept, rec instructor, center supvr, 1956-64; Detroit Public School, school-community agent, 1964-66; City of Detroit Commission on Children and Youth, project dir, 1966-69; City of Detroit Recreation Dept, recreation instructor, 1969-71; Blvd Gen Hospital, dir, personnel services, 1971-74; Wayne State Univ, assoc professor & chair, rec & parks serv, 1974-83; City of Detroit Recreation Dept, supt recreation div, 1983-93; Creative Holistic Leisure Services, leisure consultant/owner, currently. **Orgs:** Natl Rec & Park Ethnic Minority Soc, president, 1981-83, mem, 1974-; Natl Rec & Park Assn, 1974-; Mich Rec & Park Assn, 1974-; Amer Academy of Park & Rec Admin, fellow, 1991-; World Future Soc; Detroit Local 836 AFSCME, professional rec employees, president, treasurer; Alpha Phi Alpha Fraternity; Langston University Alumni Assn. **Honors/Awds:** Natl Rec & Park Ethnic Minority Soc, Ernest T Atwell Award, 1991, Citation Award, 1978, 1984; Michigan Rec & Park Assn, Fellowship Award, 1985; State of Michigan 84th Legislature, Special Tribute, 1988; Several awards from local community groups and organizations. **Special Achievements:** First African-American Chairman, Wayne State Univ Rec & Park Services Dept; First African-American Superintendant, Rec Div, Detroit Rec Dept; Established Leisure Resource Center & Charles H Lewis Collection, Detroit Gray Branch Library, 1992; MI Council for Humanities Grant, Urban Rec Conference with R B Fuller, 1975; Co-Chair, Community Analysis Committee UCS Report, ''Looking At Leisure: A Study of the Negative Aspects''; numerous articles, papers and proposals written. **Military Serv:** US Army, spec-5, 1953-56; graduate, Guided Missile School, All-Star Baseball. **Home Addr:** 3202 Waverly, Detroit, MI 48238, (313)868-1592.

LEWIS, CHARLES MCARTHUR
Information systems planner. **Personal:** Born May 29, 1949, Fitzgerald, GA; married Katrinda McQueen. **Educ:** Fort Valley State Coll, BS Math 1971; Univ of GA, MA Math 1973; GA State Univ, MBA 1984. **Career:** Southern Bell Telephone & Telegraph, engr 1973-78, management skills assessor 1978-80, staff engr 1980-86; Bell South Services Inc, information systems planner 1986-. **Orgs:** Mem Church Affiliated Orgs 1983-87; mem Natl Black MBA Assoc 1986-87. **Honors/Awds:** Alpha Kappa Mu Honor Soc Fort Valley State Coll 1970; Speakers Awd 1986. **Home Addr:** 3424 Boring Rd, Decatur, GA 30034. **Business Addr:** Staff Manager, BellSouth Services, 37F57 SBC, 675 W Peachtree St NE, Atlanta, GA 30375.

LEWIS, CHARLES MICHAEL
Corporate affairs manager. **Personal:** Born Jul 17, 1949, Columbus, OH; son of Irene V Lewis Fisher (deceased) and Charles W Lewis; married Anita Graham Lewis, Feb 25, 1978; children: Michael Jr, Christopher Morgan, Anicca. **Educ:** Central State Univ, Wilberforce, OH, BS, business, 1971. **Career:** Wilmington College, Wilmington, OH, admissions counselor, 1972-74; Bliss Business College, Columbus, OH, instructor, 1974-78; Huntington Bank, Columbus, OH, Branch Load Service, 1978-79; Anheuser Busch Cos, Columbus, OH, area mgr, 1979-82, district mgr, 1982-87, Anheuser Busch Cos, Houston, TX, regional manager of corp affairs, 1987-. **Orgs:** Board member, Houston Area Urban League, 1988-; board member, Houston Sun Literacy Academy, 1988-; member, Alpha Phi Alpha Fraternity Inc; member, NAACP, New Orleans, currently, member, Urban League, Oakland, CA, currently. **Honors/Awds:** Black Achievers in Business & Indsutry, Harlem Branch YMCA, 1983; 2nd Degree Black Belt Karate,1971-. **Business Addr:** Regional Manager, Corporate Affairs, Anheuser-Busch Co Inc, PO Box 130399, The Woodlands, TX 77393.

LEWIS, CLARENCE K.
Automobile dealer. **Career:** Pryor Ford Lincoln-Mercury Inc, owner, currently. **Special Achievements:** Co. is ranked #95 on Black Enterprise's list of Top 100 Auto Dealers, 1992. **Business Addr:** Owner, Pryor Ford Lincoln-Mercury Inc, PO Box 129, Pryor, OK 74362, (918)825-7373.

LEWIS, CLEVELAND ARTHUR
Senior industrial engineer. **Personal:** Born Apr 21, 1942, Selma, AL; son of Elsie Lewis and Levi Lewis; married Betty Faye Harris; children: Aisha, Jahmilla. **Educ:** Purdue Univ, AAS 1972, BS 1976; Indiana Wesleyan University, Marion, IN, MS, 1991. **Career:** Chrysler Corp, industrial engr 1972-76; Allison Transmission Div, senior product engineer, sr industrial engineer, currently. **Orgs:** Mem Inst of Industrial Eng 1970-; pres Clevetech Work Systems Inc 1975-; bd of regents Concordia College 1986-; board of directors, Purdue University Board of Alumni. **Honors/Awds:** Outstanding Achievement General Motors 1984; Distinguished Alumni Purdue Univ 1986. **Military Serv:** USAF airman 2nd class 4 yrs; Outstanding Performance Awd. **Home Addr:** 5085 Knollton Rd, Indianapolis, IN 46208. **Business Addr:** Sr Industrial Engineer, Allison Transmission, 4700 West 10th St, Indianapolis, IN 46206.

LEWIS, COLSTON A.
Lawyer, employment recruiter. **Personal:** Born Jan 23, 1914, Lynchburg, VA; married Glenyce Davis; children: Colston A, Jr. **Educ:** VA Union U, AB 1939; Howard Univ Law Sch, JD 1948. **Career:** Atty, gen pract 1949-70; Equal Employment Opport Commn, commr 1970-. **Orgs:** Mem VA St Bar Assn; Old Dominion Bar Assn; Nat Bar Assn; VA Trial Lawyers; World Asson of Lawyers of the World; Peace Through Law Center. **Honors/Awds:** Rep NAACP Urban League; bd dir United Way Washington DC Bicenntenial Commn for Black Am; Hon LlD 1973; Hon Colonel 1974; Cit of the Yr 1957; AchievAward Old Dominion Bar & Nat Bar Assns 1975. **Military Serv:** AUS 1942-46. **Business Addr:** 2401 E St NW, Washington, DC.

LEWIS, DANIEL
Justice. **Personal:** Born Apr 22, 1946, New York, NY; son of Anna Lewis Copeland and Matthew Gray; married Vernice Jackson-Lewis, Aug 15, 1982; children: Sharon Elaine. **Educ:** New Lincoln Sch, Acad Deg 1963; Brown Univ, BA 1967; PA Law Sch, JD 1970. **Career:** New York State Supreme Court, justice, 1996-; New York City Criminal Court, judge, 1992-95; New York State Supreme Court, principal law clerk to Justice Browne, 1977-91; New York State Div of Criminal Justice Services, civil rights comp officer, 1975-77; New York State Dept of Law, Harlem Office, assistant attorney-general-in-charge, 1975; Dist Atty Office, assistant district attorney 1970-75; Harlem Commonwealth Coun NYC, writer, 1969; Nat CORE, researcher 1968; Am Emb Rome, intern 1967; State Dept Bur of African Affairs, Wash DC, intern 1966. **Orgs:** Vol SCLC SCOPE Project AL, 1966; mem One Hundred Black Men; Am Civil Lib Union; former trustee Professional Children's Sch; president, Association of Law Secretaries, 1988-91; arbitrator, Small Claims Court, 1986-91; parliamentarian, Epsilon Sigma Chapter, Phi Beta Sigma, 1982-. **Honors/Awds:** Citation for Excellence, Mayor Wagner, 1960; Outstanding Young American Award, 1975; Certificate of Recognition, Small Claims Court, 1990; Brandies Assn Award, 1992; Assoc of Law Secretary's Award, 1992. **Business Addr:** Justice, New York State Supreme Court, 125-01 Queens Blvd, Rm 509, Kew Gardens, NY 11415.

LEWIS, DARREN JOEL
Professional baseball player. **Personal:** Born Aug 28, 1967, Berkeley, CA. **Educ:** Chabot College, CA; University of California. **Career:** Oakland A's, CA, 1990; San Francisco Giants, outfielder, 1990-. **Business Addr:** Professional Baseball Player, San Francisco Giants, Candlestick Park, San Francisco, CA 94124, (415)468-3700.

LEWIS, DARYLL LAMONT
Professional football player. **Personal:** Born Dec 16, 1968, West Covina, CA; married Stacey, Jun 13, 1992; children: Ari Elan. **Educ:** Univ of Arizona, BA in sociology. **Career:** Houston Oilers, defensive back, 1991-96; Tennessee Oilers, 1997-. **Honors/Awds:** Pro Bowl, 1995. **Business Addr:** Professional Football Player, Tennessee Oilers, c/o Baptist Sports Park, 7640 H 70-5, Nashville, TN 37221.

LEWIS, DAVID BAKER
Attorney. **Personal:** Born Jun 9, 1944, Detroit, MI; son of Dorothy Florence Baker Lewis and Walton Adams Lewis; married Kathleen Louise McCree; children: Aaron McCree, Sarah Susan. **Educ:** Oakland Univ, BA 1965; Univ of Chicago, MBA 1967; Univ of MI, JD 1970. **Career:** Northern Trust Co, administrative dept, 1966; Morgan Guaranty Trust Co, corporate research analyst, 1967; Lewis & Thompson Agency Inc, 1968; Miller Canfield Paddock & Stone, summer law clerk 1969; Univ of MI, lectr Afro-Am and African Studies Dept 1970; Hon Theodore Levin US Dist Ct, law clerk 1970-71; Patmon Young & Kirk, assoc atty 1971-72; Detroit College of Law, associate professor, 1972-78; David Baker Lewis Atty at Law, sole practitioner 1972; Lewis, White & Clay, president, 1972-82, chairman of the board, founding shareholder, director, 1972-. **Orgs:** Institute of American Business, executive committee, board of directors, 1985-; Lewis & Thompson Agency Inc, board of directors, 1967-; Consolidated Rail Corp., board of directors, 1989-, audit committee, 1989-, chairman, 1992-, ethics committee, 1992-95; Michigan Opera Theatre, board of trustees, 1982-; Center for Creative Studies, board of directors, 1983-96; Music Hall Center for the Performing Arts, board of directors, 1983-94; Detroit Symphony Orchestra Inc, board of directors, 1983-; Metropolitan Affairs Corp., board of directors, 1984-92; Booker T Business Association, board of directors, 1988-90; National Conference on Christians and Jews, board of directors, 1990-; SEMCOG-Regional Development Initiative Oversight Committee, 1990-92; Greater Detroit and Windsor Japan-American Society, board of directors, 1990-92; Arts Commission of the City of Detroit, board of directors, 1992-97; American Bar Association, 1970; American Bar Foundation, 1987-; State Bar of Michigan, 1970-; Client Security Fund, 1988-; Wolverine Bar Association, 1970-; Detroit Bar Association, 1970-; National Association of Securities Professionals, 1985-; Oakland University Foundation, board of trustees, 1985-; National Association of Bond Lawyers, 1979-; life member: Judicial Conference of the US Court of Appeals for the Sixth Circuit; University of Michigan Law School, Committee of Visitors; National Bar Association; NAACP. **Honors/Awds:** University of Detroit-Mercy, honorary LHD, 1991. **Business Addr:** Chairman, Lewis & Munday, PC, 1300 First National Bldg, Detroit, MI 48226, (313)961-2550.

LEWIS, DAVID LEVERING
Educational chairman. **Career:** Rutgers University, Martin Luther King Jr chair in history, currently. **Honors/Awds:** Pulitzer Prize for ''WEB DuBois: Biography Of a Race 1868-1919,'' 1994. **Business Addr:** Martin Luther King, Jr. Chair in History, Rutgers University, Department of History, New Brunswick, NJ 08903, (908)932-1766.

LEWIS, DAWNN
Musician, actress. **Personal:** Born Aug 13, Brooklyn, NY; daughter of Joyce Lewis and Carl Lewis. **Educ:** University of Miami, BA (magna cum laude), 1982. **Career:** Actress, currently; television appearances include: Stompin' at the Savoy TV movie, Kid-N-Play Cartoon, voice of Lela, A Different World, series regular, Hangin' with Mr Cooper; feature films include: I'm Gonna Git U Sucka; Your Love, co-writer; A Different World, theme song, singer; HBO's Dream On; composer of songs for artists such as Grover Washington, Jr and Nancy Wilson; The Cherokee Kid; Bad Day on the Block, 1997; How to Succeed in Business Without Really Trying; voices for several animated TV series: C Bear & Jamal, Mortal Kombat, Bruno the Kid, Wayne's Head, and Spider Man. **Orgs:** Campfire Boys & Girls, board of directors, spokesperson; Morning Jewel Inc, Production Co, president; National 4H Club, spokesperson; Planned Parenthood, spokesperson; UNICEF, spokesperson; Institute for Black Parenting, spokesperson; Arnold Schwarzenegger's Inner City Games, dir of the speakers bureau. **Honors/Awds:** University of Miami, Illustrious Alumni Award,

1991; American Lung Association, Outstanding Service, 1991; NAACP, Act-So Award; American Dental Association, Smile of the Year; UNCF, Outstanding Service Award, 1988, 1990, 1991; Howard University, Excellence in Achievement, 1992; ASCAP Award and four BMI Honors for Best Song; Grammy, Handel's Massiah: A Soulful Celebration; Gold Record, on the Take 6 Album, So Much To Say. **Special Achievements:** University of Miami, first graduate to receive musical theatre degree.

LEWIS, DELANO EUGENE
Broadcasting company executive. **Personal:** Born Nov 12, 1938, Arkansas City, KS; son of Enna W Lewis and Raymond E Lewis; married Gayle Jones; children: Delano Jr, Geoffrey, Brian, Phillip. **Educ:** Univ of KS, BA 1960; Washburn Sch of Law Topeka KS, JD 1963. **Career:** US Dept of Justice, genl atty 1963-65; US Equal Employment Oppor Commn, staff analysis & advice 1965-66; US Peace Corps Nigeria/Uganda, assoc dir/country dir 1966-69; Office of Sen Edward W Brooke, legislative asst 1969-71; Office of Rep Walter E Fauntroy, admin asst 1971-73; C & P Telephone Co, vice pres 1973-88; C & P Telephone of Washington DC, pres 1988-93, CEO, 1990-93; National Public Radio, president, 1993-. **Orgs:** Bd dirs Comm Found of Greater Washington 1978-; president The Greater Washington Bd of Trade 1987; Military Order of the Knights of Malta 1987-; board of directors, Hallburton Co.; Colgate-Palmolive Co, Guest Services, Apple Computer, BET. **Honors/Awds:** Washingtonian of the Yr Washington Mag 1978; comm Serv-Pres Medal Catholic Univ of Amer 1978; chmn Mayor's Transition Commn mayor Marion Barry Jr 1978-79; Distinguished Community service Award, Washburn Univ 1989; Honorary Degree, Marymount Univ 1988; Washburn University Distinguished Alumnae Award, 1990; Citizenship Award, National Council Christians & Jews, 1989; Cultural Alliance of Wash Community Service Award, 1991; Hon Degrees: Loyola Coll Baltimore, Barry Univ Miami. **Special Achievements:** First African-American president of National Public Radio, 1993. **Business Addr:** President, National Public Radio, 635 Massachusetts Ave, NW, Washington, DC 20001.

LEWIS, DIANE
Public administrator. **Personal:** Born in New York, NY; daughter of Alyce Morris Lewis and George A Lewis; divorced; children: 1 daughter. **Educ:** Beaver Coll, Glenside PA, BA, 1969; Columbia Univ, New York NY, MS, 1977; Hastings College of the Law, JD, 1995. **Career:** Natl Urban League, New York NY, project dir, 1970-73; Center for Urban Educ, New York NY, liaison, 1970-71; Trans Urban East, New York NY, consultant, 1972-73; Jamaica Urban Devel Corp, Kingston, Jamaica, West Indies, social planner, 1974-76; City of Oakland, Oakland CA, sr urban economic analyst, 1977-82, div mgr, 1982-92. **Orgs:** Consultant, Trans Urban East Org, 1972-73; vice pres, Progressive Black Business & Professional Women, 1983-86; assoc mem, Urban Land Inst, 1984-; chair, Economic Devel Comm, BAPAC, 1984-86; past vice pres & sec, chmn nominations comm, Citicentre Dance Theatre, 1985-89; mem, Niagara Movement Democratic Club, 1977-80, Natl Assn of Planners, 1978-, Black Women Organized for Political Action, 1983-84, Natl Forum for Black Public Admin, 1985-, Amer Soc of Public Admin, 1988-; membership chair, Assn of Black Families, 1989-92; loan committee member, Womens Initiative for Self Employment, 1990-93; Assn Symposium editor, West Northwest Environmental Law Journal; staff, Hastings Law News; Charles Houston Bar Assn; American Bar Assn; American Inns of Court; 2nd yr rep Hastings BLSA; Phi Alpha Delta. **Honors/Awds:** William F Kinne Fellowship, Columbia Univ, 1972, 1977; Intl Fellow, Columbia Univ, 1972-73; Intl Intern, Ford Found, 1973-74; speaker, Council of Minority Public Admin, 1988, Southeastern Conf of Public Admin, 1988, Amer Soc of Public Admin, 1989; Wiley F Manuel Law Foundation Scholarship, 1994. **Business Addr:** Hastings College of The Law, 200 Mt Allister St, San Francisco, CA 94102-4978.

LEWIS, DIANE CLAIRE
Government official. **Personal:** Born Jul 14, 1945, Bronx, NY; married Julius Wilson. **Educ:** Econ City Coll of NY, BA Econ 1968; Princeton U, MA 1971; Georgetown Univ Law Cntr, 1971-74. **Career:** Educ Office of the Mayor Wash DC, spl asst to the Mayor 1979-; Inter Govt Rel Bd of Educ DC, dir 1975-79; Bd of Educ DC, spl & asst to the pres 1974-75; Dept of Labor Ofc of Policy Eval & Resch,research analyst 1972-73; Ford Found Tanzania E Africa, cons-research 1970. **Orgs:** Fld supr grad work Incentives Exper Princeton 1968-69; Task Force chair DC Coalition for the Appointment of Women; chair-judiciary com DC Women's Polit Caucus.

LEWIS, EDWARD T.
Publisher. **Personal:** Born May 15, 1940, Bronx, NY. **Educ:** Univ NM, BA 1964, MA 1966; NY Univ, postgrad 1966-69; attended Harvard Business School. **Career:** Peace Corps Univ NM, lecturer 1963; City Mgr's Office Albuquerque, admin analyst 1964-65; First Natl City Bank NYC, fin analyst 1966-69; Essence Mag NYC, publisher 1969-. **Orgs:** Bd dir Vol Urban Consult Group, Black Counil on Africa, Fund for New Horizons for Retarded Inc, 21st Century Found, Rheeland Found, Negro Ensemble NYC, School Vol Prog; trustee Coty; mem 100 Black Men, Inc, Uptown C of C, New York City Commerce & Industry; Magazine Publishers of Amer, chmn, 1997-; TransAfrica Forum, chmn; Tuskegee Univ, Teachers Coll at Columbia Univ, trustee; NYC Partnership; Times Sq Business Improvement Dist; Lincoln Ctr for Performing Arts, bd; Jazz Comm; Intl Peace Comm; Greater Harlem Chamber of Commerce. **Honors/Awds:** Recipient Decision Maker Awd Natl Assn Media Women 1974; Natl IGBO Awd for Minority Businessman of the Year 1979; Named Businessman of the Year Blackafrica Promotions Inc 1974; Ellis Island Medal of Honor; Boy Scouts of Amer, Good Scout Awd; United Negro Coll Fund, Lifetime Achievement Awd; Dow Jones, Our World News Awd, Entrepreneurial Excellence; Democratic Womens' Political Caucus, Good Guy Awd; Amer Advertising Federation, Diversity Achievement Role Model Awd, 1997; NY's Assoc Black Charities, FL Yates Ruffin Ridley Awd; Black Women's Forum, The Men Who Dare Awd; Ernst & Young, Entrepreneur of the Year Awd, 1994; Natl Assn of Black Journalists Awd, 1995; AG Gaston Lifetime Achievement Awd, Black Enterprise Mag, 1997. **Special Achievements:** Featured with other prominent businessmen on the cover of Black Enterprise Magazine as one of the ''Marathon Men'' for 25 yrs of Entrepreneurial Excellence, June 1997; first African American to chair Magazine Publishers of America. **Business Addr:** Publisher and CEO, Essence Communications, 1500 Broadway, New York, NY 10036.

LEWIS, ELMA I.
Educator. **Personal:** Born Sep 15, 1921, Boston. **Educ:** Emerson Coll, BLI 1943; Boston U, MEd 1944. **Career:** Elma Lewis Sch Fine Arts, founder/dir 1950-; Robert Gould Shaw House Chorus, staged dir chorgrpd 21 Operas & Operettas; Harriet Tubman House, fine arts wrkr; MA Mental Health Habit Clinics Boston/Woodward Sch Quincy, teacher; Doris Jones Sch of Dance Boston, teacher; Roxbury Memorial HS for Girls, speech therapist; Natl Educ Assoc, consultant; Natl Endowment of the Arts, consultant; Natl Ctr Afro-Amer Artist, founder/dir 1968-. **Orgs:** Overseer Museum of Fine Arts; fellow Black Acad of Arts & Letters; trustee WGBH; mem Corp of Northeastern U; fellow Am Acad of Arts & Sci; Black Professional &Bus Women Arts Commn; bd mem Theater Commn Group; bd mem 2nd World Festival of Black Art in Nigeria; mem Meco Cultural Alliance; mem numerous offices,coms numerous civic orgns groups & councils; trustee MA College of Art, Boston Zoological Soc; mem Joslin Diabetes Foundation. **Honors/Awds:** Samuel Adams Bicentennial Comm Awd; NAACP Gold Cert Awd; Lambda Kappa Mu Cit; NE Theatre Conf Awd; Woman of Yr Awd; Zeta Phi Beta Sor 1969; Mayor'sCitation City Boston 1970; Omega Psi Phi Frat Awd; Negro Bus & Professional Women's Awd Boston & Vic; Black Womanhood Awd Black Big Bro Assn 1970; Hon degrees Boston Coll 1971, Anna Maria Coll 1974; Dr of Fine Arts Colby Coll 1972; many other hon degrees from various colls & univs; listed Contemporary Black Amers vol 1, Living Legends in Black; several other listings; MacArthur Prize Fellow Awd 1981; Presidential Citation and Medal President's Comm on the Arts & Humanities Washington DC 1983; Alumni Awd for Disting Public Serv to the Comm Boston Univ Alumni Assoc 1984; induction intoAcad of Disting Bostonians Greater Boston Chamber of Commer1985; author ''Let Minorities Interpret Their Own Culture'' Baystate Feb 1978; author ''Celebrating Little People'' Boston Review of the Arts 1972; various newspaper art written about her. **Business Addr:** Artistic Dir, Natl Ctr Afro-American Artists, 122 Elm Hill Ave, Boston, MA 02121.

LEWIS, EMMANUEL
Actor, singer, dancer. **Personal:** Born Mar 9, 1971, Brooklyn, NY; son of Margaret Lewis. **Career:** Theater appearance: A Midsummer Night's Dream, 1982; television appearances include: Webster, 1983-87; Lost in London, 1985; The Tonight Show; The Phil Donahue Show; The World's Funniest Commercial Goofs, host, 1983-85; Salute to Lady Liberty, 1984; Mr T and Emmanuel Lewis in a Christmas Dream, 1984; Secret World of the Very Young, 1984; Life's Most Embarassing Moments, 1986; Candid Camera: The First Forty Years, 1987; Emmanuel Lewis: My Own Show, 1987; numerous specials; Emmanuel Lewis Entertainment Enterprises Inc, owner; actor in over fifty tv commercials; singer and dancer. **Orgs:** American Federation of Television & Radio Artists; Screen Actors Guild; Actors Equity Assn. **Honors/Awds:** People Choice Awards, 1985, 1986. **Business Addr:** Actor, c/o Monica Stuart, Schuller Talent/New York Kids, 276 Fifth Ave, Rm 1001, New York, NY 10001.

LEWIS, EPHRON H.
Rice processing company executive. **Personal:** son Of Adline Mathis Lewis (deceased) and Jasper Lewis (deceased); married Doris; children: Ephron Lewis Jr. **Educ:** Arkansas AM&N Coll, Graduate. **Career:** Lewis and Son Rice Processing Co, owner. **Orgs:** Former mem Natl Rice Advisory Comm; pres, AR Land & Farm Devel Corp, 1980-92. **Honors/Awds:** Persistence of the Spirit, Univ of AR Pine Bluff, 1987; Distinguished Alumni of Year, Univ of Arkansas, Pine Bluff/National Assn Equal Opportunity for Higher Education, 1986; Minority Contractor of the Year, US Dept of Agriculture, ASCS, 1989. **Military Serv:** US Army, PFC, 1956-58.

LEWIS, ERMA
Association executive. **Personal:** Born Feb 7, 1926, Ft Worth, TX; married James Edward Jr. **Educ:** Dillard Univ TX. **Career:** Sojourner Truth Players Inc, exec prod 1972-75; HEW-ESAA, proj dir; HEW-ESAA, camp dir 1960-71; YWCA, dir num proj 1958-71; Highland Park YWCA, only prof staff 1971-72; Greater St James Bapt Ch, sec 1951-58. **Orgs:** NAACP Nom comm 1955; supv Youth Coun 1957-59; Voter Regis 1969; Life mem YWCA Assn 1959; Life mem Nat Coun of Negro Women 1976; mem numerous ofcs,coms, civic, poltl, rel orgns. **Honors/Awds:** Woman of Yr Awd F Brooks & Gray Literary Art Charity Club 1973; Gold Star Awd Better Infl Assn 1973; Image Awd Mayor's Coun on Youth Opport 1973; Outst Cit Awd Jack & Jill 1973; 15th Ann Celeb Plaque Jr Debutants 1973; plaque Nolan Robert Monseigneur HS Black Awareness Club 1973; Woman of Yr Mildred M Anderson 1974; nominee Sojourner Truth Awd 1974; Dist Serv Awd Com of 100 1974; Hidden Heroines Hall of Fame Girl Scouts 1975; Merit Comm Serv Am Revol Bicentennial Comm 1976; cert of Recogn Am Revol Bicentennial Comm 1976; Comm Awd Cert TX Ministers & Cit Leadership Coun 1976; Natl Cult Arts Fest Awd Sojourner Truth Players Inc 1976; chmn Ft Worth Black Cit for Fest 1976; Mary McLeod Bethune Bicent Achiev Awd Nat Counof Negro Women 1976. **Business Addr:** 1060 E Terrell Ave, Fort Worth, TX 76104.

LEWIS, FELTON EDWIN
Educational administrator. **Personal:** Born Oct 2, 1923, New Orleans, LA; son of Ethel Martin Lewis (deceased) and Felton B. Lewis (deceased); children: Ronald, Anthony, Felton III, Marita, Karen. **Educ:** Xavier Univ, BA (cum laude) 1955; Univ WI-Madison, MA 1956; Universite d'Aix-Marseille France, diplome 1956-58; Fordham Univ, professional diploma 1968-69; Universidad Interamericana Mexico, PhD 1970. **Career:** New York City Bd of Educ, teacher 1958-66; Foreign Language Dept JHS, acting chmn 1963-66; Jr High Spec Serv Sch, acting asst prin 1966-67; Title I New York City Bd of Educ, ESEA coord 1967-68; New York City Bd of Educ, student & intern of educ admin & super prin intern 1968-69, dep dist supt, District 12, 1969-71, acting comm supt District 12, 1971-72, comm supt dist 12 1972-78; comm supt dist 16 1978-82; New York State Dept of Education, Albany, NY, asst commissioner of education, 1985-86. **Orgs:** Member, Phi Delta Kappa, American Association of School Administrators, New York City Association of Superintendents, Doctoral Associaton of New York Educators, International Reading Association, Association for Supervision and Curriculum Development, NAACP, National Urban League, Bronx Boys Clubs. **Honors/Awds:** Alpha Epsilon Partial Grad Scholarship Middlebury Coll 1955; French Teaching Assistantship WI Univ 1955-56; Maison Francaise Scholarship WI 1956; Fulbright Scholar 1956-57; Fulbright Grant 1957-58; Ford Found Fellowship Fordham Univ 1968-69; numerous awds & testimonials S Bronx NAACP, WIN Adult Council, JFK Library for Minorities, Bronx NAACP, Fairmount Sch, Prin of Dist 12, CSA of Dist 12, Bronx Boys Club, Behaviorial Rsch Lab, Drug Abuse Prevention Project, Dr Martin Luther King Com, numerous certifications in teaching & admin. **Military Serv:** US Army, Sgt, 1942-45, Bronze Star.

LEWIS, FLOYD EDWARD
Corporate director. **Personal:** Born Nov 23, 1938; married Ruth M Lewis. **Educ:** S IL U, BS 1961; M Urban Affairs Bus St Univ 1972. **Career:** Anheuser-Busch Co Inc, dir equal oppor affairs 1975-; Monsanto Co, mgr equal oppor 1974-75; Urban League of St Louis, dir personnel 1972-74; United Way of St Louis, agency relations assn 1970-72. **Orgs:** Bd mem Carver House Assn 1977; bd mem Assn of Black Psychologist 1977; bd mem Annie Malone Children's Home 1978, St Louis Minority Council. **Business Addr:** Director, Corporate Affairs, Anheuser Busch Cos Inc, 1 Busch Plaza, St Louis, MO 63118.

LEWIS, FRANK ROSS
Librarian. **Personal:** Born Jul 13, 1931, Seale, AL; son of Bertha Simpson Lewis and Willie Lewis Sr; married Laura Scott, Aug 17, 1958; children: Jason. **Educ:** NC Central Univ, AB Pol Sci 1957; Atlanta Univ, MLS 1969. **Career:** LaGrange Sr HS, librarian 1969-73; LaGrange Coll, asst librarian 1973-74, library dir. **Orgs:** Treas GA Library Assn 1980; past dir bd of dirs Council on Aging 1978; mem adv bd West Central GA Regional Hosp Adv Council three year term ending in1990; past pres Alpha Phi Alpha Frat Theta Nu Lambda Chap 1979; 100 Black Men of West Georgia Inc, charter member. **Honors/Awds:** Mem Georgia Council for the Arts; reapptd to second term by Gov Joe Frank Harris for term ending in 1989, 3 yr appts. **Military Serv:** AUS pvt 1952-54. **Home Addr:** PO Box 667, La Grange, GA 30241.

LEWIS, FREDERICK CARLTON
Administrator. **Personal:** Born Jul 1, 1961, Birmingham, AL. **Educ:** Univ of Houston, 1979-82. **Career:** American Heart Assn, honorary chairman 1984-; Carl Lewis Foundation, chairman. **Orgs:** Peoples Workshop 1984-. **Business Addr:** c/o Tom Teller, Athletic Dept, Univ of Houston, 4800 Calhoun Ave, Houston, TX 77004.

LEWIS, GEORGE RALPH
Business executive. **Personal:** Born Mar 7, 1941, Burgess, VA; son of Edith Pauline Toulson Lewis and Spencer Harcum Lewis; married Lillian Glenn; children: Tonya, Tracey. **Educ:** Hampton Univ, BS 1963; Iona Coll, MBA 1968. **Career:** Gen Foods Corp, sales analyst 1963-64, profit planning analyst 1964-65, product analyst 1965-66; WR Grace Co, financial analyst 1966-67; Philip Morris Inc, corp analyst 1967-68, sr planning analyst 1968-70, mgr investor relations 1970-72, mgr financial serv 1972-73, asst treas 1973-74, vice pres financial & planning & treas 1975-82; Seven-Up Co, vice pres finance, 1982-84; Philip Morris Cos, Inc, vice pres, treas, 1984-97; Philips Morris Capital Corp, pres/CEO, currently. **Orgs:** Bd mem Central Fidelity Bank 1984, Natl Urban League 1986, Hampton Univ 1985, Kemper Natl Ins Co, 1993, Ceridian Corp, 1994; board of directors of The Professional Golfers' Assn of America in 1995. **Honors/Awds:** Arthur A Loftus Achievement Awd Iona Coll 1980; Outstanding Twenty Year Alumnus Awd Hampton Inst 1982. **Business Addr:** President/CEO, Philip Morris Capital Corporation, 200 First Stamford Place, Stamford, CT 06902.

LEWIS, GREEN PRYOR, JR.
Organized labor official. **Personal:** Born Apr 27, 1945, Columbus, GA; son of Minnie Jones Lewis and Green Pryor Lewis Sr; married Christine McGhee Lewis, Dec 22, 1967; children: Raquel, Green III, LeKeisha. **Educ:** Fort Valley State College, Fort Valley, GA, BS, 1967; American University of Fort Benning, 1968-69. **Career:** Buckner Contruction Company, Columbus, GA, bricklayer apprentice, student, 1963-64; American Toy Company, Columbus, GA, asst dept manager, 1965-67; Muscogee County School System, Columbus, GA, teacher/coach, 1967-69; American Federation of Labor and Congress of Industrial Organizations, asst dir, 1969-, dir, currently. **Orgs:** Keeper of records, Columbus Alumni Chapter, Kappa Alpha Psi, 1968-69; President, Proud Neighbors of South De Kalb, 1973-75; 1st vice president, Field Representative Federation AFL-CIO, 1979-84; vice-chair, 4th district, Democratic Party De Kalb County Georgia, 1982-84; executive committee, A Philip Randolph Institute, 1985-. **Honors/Awds:** High Achievement Award, Kappa Alpha Psi, 1963; High Achievement Award, Lewis Family Reunion, 1988; Distinguished Service, Houston Organizing Project, 1984; Distinguished Service, Field Representative Federation, 1985; A Philip Randolph Achievement Award, 1992; Histadrut Menorah Award, 1989; Labor Award Outstanding Service, Service Employees Local 579, 1987; Keeper of Flame Award NAACP, 1992. **Business Addr:** Director, Dept of Community Services, AFL-CIO, 815 16th St NW, Suite 509, Washington, DC 20006.

LEWIS, H. RALPH
Physicist. **Personal:** Born Jun 7, 1931, Chicago, IL; married Renate J. **Educ:** Univ of Chicago, AB 1951, SB 1953; Univ of IL, MS 1955, PhD 1958. **Career:** Univ of Heidelberg, rsch assoc 1958-60; Princeton Univ, instr 1960-63; Los Alamos Natl Lab, rsch physicist 1963-90, Laboratory Fellow 1983-; St John's College of Santa Fe, tutor, 1991; Dartmouth College, professor, 1991-. **Orgs:** Mem Amer Physical Soc; pres Student Concerts Inc 1973-75; mem Los Alamos Sinfonietta 1963-84. **Honors/Awds:** Univ Fellow Univ of IL 2 yrs during 1953-58; Fellow of American Physical Society. **Business Addr:** Professor, Department of Physics and Astronomy, Dartmouth College, Hanover, NH 03755.

LEWIS, HAROLD T.
Cleric, educator. **Personal:** Born Feb 21, 1947, Brooklyn, NY; son of Muriel Kathleen Worrell Lewis and Frank Walston Lewis (deceased); married Claudette Richards, Feb 7, 1970; children: Justin Craig. **Educ:** McGill Univ, BA, 1967; Yale Divinity School, M Div, 1971; Cambridge Univ, research fellow, 1972-73; University of Birmingham (Eng), PhD, 1994. **Career:** NYC Dept of Social Serv, social worker, 1967-68; Overseas Missionary, Honduras, 1971-72; St Monica's Church, rector, 1973-92; St Luke's Episcopal Church, assoc priest, 1983-; Mercer School of Theology, prof of homiletics, 1988-; Episcpal Church Cent, staff officer, 1983-94; NY Theological Seminary, prof of Homiletics, 1995-. **Orgs:** Sigma Pi Phi, sec, 1991-; Prophetic Justice Unit, Natl Council of Churches, exec committee, 1988-; Racial Justice Working Group, Natl Council of Churches, 1986-. **Honors/Awds:** Berkeley Divinity Schhol at Yale, Doctor of Divinity, 1991; Episcopal Church Foundation, Research Fellowship, 1978; Yale Univ, Research Fellowship, 1990; Operation Crossroads Office, Distinguished Alumnus Award, 1985. **Special Achievements:** Editor, Recruitment, Training & Devel of Black Clergy, 1980; Lift Every Voice and Sing II, 1993; Author, In Season, Out of Season, A Collection of Sermons, 1993. **Home Addr:** 138 Penham Ln, Pittsburgh, PA 15208-2637.

LEWIS, HELEN MIDDLETON
Clergyman. **Personal:** Born Apr 25, 1905, Crystal River, FL; daughter of Rosa Hunter Middleton and Luke Middleton; married Felix Early; children: 9. **Career:** The Church of the Living God the Pillar & Ground of the Truth Inc, chief overseer & pres 1968-; The Church of the Living God, West Palm Beach FL pastor & presiding bishop 1952-68, Nashville TN pastor 1940-50, sec/treas 1937, Sanford FL asst chief overseer 1937, KY IN dist bishop 1935, Sanford FL ordained to bishopric 1932, Daytona Beach FL pastor 1930. **Honors/Awds:** Outstanding leadership award The Ch of the Living God 1973; publications award "75th Anniversary Year Book" 1978. **Business Addr:** The Church of the Living God, Hydes Ferry Pike, Nashville, TN 37218.

LEWIS, HENRY, III
Educator, educational administrator. **Personal:** Born Jan 22, 1950, Tallahassee, FL; son of Evelyn P Lewis and Henry Lewis Sr; married Marisa Ann Smith, Dec 1990. **Educ:** Florida A&M University, BS, 1972; Mercer University, PharmD, 1978. **Career:** Florida A&M University, assistant dean, 1974-90; Texas Southern University, dean, professor, 1990-94; Florida A&M Univ, Coll of Pharmacy and Pharmaceutical Science, dean, professor, 1994-. **Orgs:** NIGMS, board of advisors, 1992-96; AMHPS, president, 1992-95; MHPF, president, 1994; AACP, 1974-; NPHA, president, 1988-90; APHA, 1980-; ASHP, 1978-; Rho Chi Honor Society, 1975-; Texas Pharm Association, 1990-; Board of County Commissioners, Leon County, 1986-90, Alpha Phi Alpha, 1985-. **Honors/Awds:** Texas Senate, Meritorius Service Award, 1994; Florida A&M University, Meritorious Achievement Award, 1992; HELP Inc, Outstanding Young Black Houstonian, 1990; Merck, Sharpe, Dohme, Leadership Achievement Award, 1990; National Pharmaceutical Association, Pharmacist of the Year, 1988. **Special Achievements:** Numerous publications. **Business Addr:** Dean, Coll of Pharmacy & Pharmaceutical Science, Florida A & M University, Dyson Pharmacy Bldg, Rm 201, Tallahassee, FL 32307, (904)599-3301.

LEWIS, HENRY S., JR.
Counselor, clergyman. **Personal:** Born Sep 26, 1935, Chester County, SC; son of Marie S Lewis (deceased) and Henry S Lewis Sr (deceased); married Savannah D Winstead; children: Robin Anita, Kenneth W, Jonathan H, Karen E. **Educ:** Winston-Salem State Univ, BS 1957; Andover Newton Theol School, MDiv 1961; Wake Forest Univ, further study; School of Pastoral Care Boston City Hosp, 1959; School of Pastoral Care North Carolina Baptist Hospital, 1977; Univ of Kentucky Coll of Med RBT Ctr, 1977. **Career:** Shiloh Bapt Church, student asst 1957-59; Wentz Memorial United Church of Christ, summer minister 1958-; Winston-Salem State University, university chaplain and James A Gray asst prof of religion and sociology, 1960-77; Mt Pleasant Bapt Church, pastor 1966-77; Winston-Salem Forsyth Cty Schools Urban Affairs Inst, human relations consultant 1967, 1969; Zion Bapt Church, 1959; Wake Forest Univ, part-time instr dept religion 1970-72; RJ Reynolds Tabacco Co, Winston-Salem NC, senior employee counselor 1977-; Wentz Memorial United Church of Christ, pastor, 1992-. **Orgs:** Clinical mem Amer Assn for Marriage & Family Therapy, Natl Inst of Business & Industrial Chaplains, North Carolina Chaplains Assn; mem Phi Beta Sigma, Winston- Salem Chap NAACP; North Carolina Licensed Marital & Family Therapist; bd of dir, Society for the Study of African-American History; mem, North Carolina Assn for Marital & Family Therapy; Employee Assistant Professional Association. **Business Addr:** Senior Employee Counselor, Department of Employee Counseling, RJ Reynolds Tobacco Company, Reynolds Bldg, 2nd Fl, Winston-Salem, NC 27102.

LEWIS, HENRY W.
Business administration. **Personal:** Born Nov 10, 1927, Meridian, MS; married Sarah N; children: Henry W Jr, Deborah, Barry, Deshawn. **Educ:** Jackson State Univ, 1949-52; Univ Ctr of Harrisburg, 1964. **Career:** Carpen's Fed Credit Union, vice pres 1973-85; NAACP Harrisburgh Cty Tri-Cty Affirm Action, pres, coord, currently. **Orgs:** Trustee St Paul Baptist Church 1961-75, Carpenter's Local Union #287 1968-, Delegate to Council 1968-; vice pres Dauphin Cty Dem Party 1977-83; mem Harrisburg School Adv Bd 1977-85, Harrisburg Incinerator Authority 1978-80; chmn Harrisburg Parking Auth 1980-82; mem P Hall Masonic Families 1977-83; mem Harrisburg Adv Bd, Harrisburg Downtown Devel Comm 1983-85; vice pres Himyar Temple Partrol #17 PHA 1983; affirm action officer Harrisburg School Dist 1984-; mem Harrisburg Comm Coll Bd 1984-85; trustee Carpenters Local Union #287; vice pres Harrisburg Br of NAACP 1987-88; pres Himyar Temple #17 Patrol Drill Team 1987. **Honors/Awds:** Man of the Year AASR of Free Masonry NJ USA Corp PHA 1983; Awd Himyar Temple 17 AEAONMS Patrol PHA 1984; Awd Life Mem NAACP, Golden Heritage 1984; Awd for 30 yrs Caprenters Local Union 30 Yr Pin 1985; received 33 Final Degree United Supreme Council Ancient and Accepted Scottish Rite of Free Masonry Prince Hall Affiliation 1987. **Military Serv:** Infantry pfc military policeman 1946-47; Awd for Outstanding Military Policeman 1947.

LEWIS, HOUSTON A.
Dentist. **Personal:** Born May 4, 1920, Bonham, TX; married Clara Houston; children: Ruth Ann Collins, Pamela Brinkley. **Educ:** Xavier Univ 1941-42; Fish Univ 1946-47; Meharry Med Coll Sch of Dentistry, DDS 1951. **Career:** Self employed gen dentistry present; Girl Scouts, dir 1958-67; Gtr Wheeling Cncl of Chs, dir 1955-64; Children & Fam Serv Assn, dir 1956-62 ; United Way, dir 1967-60. **Orgs:** Mem Nat Den Assn; Am Den Assn; pres WV Med Soc Inc 1977-78; mem Am Soc of Endodontics; Acad of Gen Den Mem Civitan Club of Wheeling 1963-; dir Moundsville Wheeling Chap Am Red Cross 1963-66; dir Urban Renewal Auth 1966-71; ran for WV House of Del 1968; dir wheeling Area Blue Cross-Blue Shield1969-. **Honors/Awds:** One of outst W Virginians 1965-66; %Mem Intl Plat form Assn. **Military Serv:** Mil Serv enlisted man 1942-45; commnd duty Den Corps 1951-53; 1951-53; col active res. **Business Addr:** Ste 402, Med Tower, Wheeling, WV 26003.

LEWIS, HYLAN GARNET
Sociologist, educator. **Personal:** Born Apr 4, 1911, Washington, DC; son of Ella Lanier Wells Lewis and Harry Wythe Lewis; children: Carole Ione Bovoso, Guy Edward. **Educ:** VA Union Univ, AB 1932; Univ of Chicago, AM 1936, PhD 1951. **Career:** Howard Univ Washington, instr sociology 1935-41; Talladega Coll, prof soc sci 1941-42; OWI, info spec 1942-45; Hampton Inst, assoc prof 1945-48; Inst for Rsch in Social Sci Univ of NC, research assoc 1947-48; Atlanta Univ, assoc prof sociology 1948-56, prof 1956-57; Unitarian Serv Com Inc, assoc dir comm serv 1957-59; Health & Welfare Council Washington, dir child rearing study 1959-64; Brooklyn Coll, prof sociology 1967-77; Met Applied Rsch Center, sr vice pres 1968-75; City Univ NYC, prof grad cntr 1967-; Brooklyn Coll, prof emeritus 1977-; CUNY Grad Center, prof; Queens College, CUNY, Flushing, NY, Michael Harrington prof, 1990-91. **Orgs:** Mem delinq grants review comm Natl Inst Mental Hlth 1963-67; mem Soc Problems Rsch Review Comm 1969-73; mem Dev Behavioral Sci Study Sect Natl Inst of Health 1974-76; sr consult Clark Phipps Clark & Harris Inc 1975-86, KBC & Assoc 1986-; consult Volta River Proj Prep Commn Gold Coast 1954; Ashmore Project Fund for Advance of Educ 1953; So Regional Cncl 1955-57; Commn on Race & Housing 1956-57; consult Disaster Study Comm NRC 1955; mem adv com grants prog US Children's Bur 1962; mem adv panel small grants prog US Dept Labor 1963-83; chief consult family panel White House Conf Civil Rights Planning 1965; mem review panel US Office Educ 1965-67; mem head start research adv com Office Econ Opport 1965-67; mem grants adv com natl Endowment for the Humanities Natl Found Arts & Humanities 1967; mem Amer Social Soc; mem, fellow AAAS; Sociological Research Assn; Alpha Phi Alpha. **Honors/Awds:** SSRC Grant, 1932-33; Rosenwald Fellow 1939-41; author Blackways of Kent 1955; Fund for Advancement of Educ Fellow 1956; DuBois-Johnson-Frazier Award 1976; Merit Award Eastern Sociological Soc 1979; visiting scholar Russell Sage Found 1974-75; Revson Fellow, City College, CUNY, 1988-89; Fellow, American Assn for Advancement of Science, 1967-; National Alliance of Black School Educators Silver Anniversary Award, 1995; Assn of Black Sociologists, 1997; Long Island Univ, Doctor of Humane Letters, 1997. **Home Addr:** 372 Central Park W, New York, NY 10025.

LEWIS, IDA ELIZABETH
Publisher, editor. **Personal:** Born Sep 22, 1935, Malverne, PA. **Educ:** Boston Univ School of Public Communications, BS, 1956. **Career:** Amsterdam News, financial and business writer, 1956-59; New York Age, financial editor, 1960-63; Life Magazine, writer, 1964-65; BBC, writer/broadcaster, 1967; Jeune Afrique Magazine, correspondent, 1968-71; Essence Magazine, editor-in-chief, 1970-71; Tanner Publishing Co, president, 1972-American and Worldwide News Magazine, publisher/editor, currently. **Orgs:** Trustee Tougaloo Coll; bd dir Am Com Africa; mem Commn Inquiry Into HS Journalism; mem Nat Council Negro Women; mem Alpha Kappa Alpha Soc; mem Amer Management Assn. **Honors/Awds:** Citizen of the Year, Omega Psi Phi, 1975; Intl Benih Award for Contribution to Black People throughout the world, 1975; Media Executive Award, National Youth Movement, 1975; Bicentennial Award, 1975; Journalism Award, Assn for the Study of Afro-American Life and History, 1974; Scarlet Key, Boston Univ, 1956. **Business Addr:** 515 Madison Ave, New York, NY 10022.

LEWIS, J. B., JR.
Funeral service business executive. **Personal:** Born Oct 22, 1929, Clifton Forge, VA; son of Mattie E Douglas Lewis (deceased) and J B Lewis Sr (deceased); married Mary Louise Colbert; children: Aaron. **Educ:** Eckels Coll of Mortuary Sci, grad 1957. **Career:** Insurance underwriter 1958-63; Greyhound Lines, optr 1964-65; Mt View Terr Apts, mgr/agent 1970-; JB Lewis Funeral Service, owner. **Orgs:** Adv bd Coreast Savings Bank 1972; VA Funeral Dir Assn 1976; Natl Funeral Dir Assn 1976; VA Mortic Assn 1959; councilman City of Lexington 1969; v mayor City of Lexington 1976; vice pres Rockbridge Area Housing Corp 1967-70; vice pres Human Relat Counc 1968; pres Lylburn Downing PTA 1962-63; treas sec Cub Scouts 1963; mem NAACP; American Legion Post 291. **Honors/Awds:** Eye Enucleat Cert 1976. **Military Serv:** AUS 1954-56. **Business Addr:** Owner, JB Lewis Funeral Service, 112 N Randolph St, Lexington, VA 24450.

LEWIS, JAMES, JR.
Educator, author. **Personal:** Born Mar 7, 1930, Newark; married Valdmir M; children: Michael, Patricia, Terrence. **Educ:** Hampton Inst, BS 1953; Columbia U, MS 1957; Harvard U, Alfred North Whitehead Flwshp for Adv Study in Educ 1970; Union Grad Sch, phD 1972. **Career:** Wyandanch School Dist, teacher act asst, HS prin 1957-66; Elem prin 1966-67; Dist prin

1967-72; Villanova Univ, assoc prof 1972-73; City Univ of NY, prof of educ, chmn of div of teacher educ 1972-74; Central Berkshire Regional School Dist, supt of schools 1974-; Educ Improvement Center NE, exec dir 1974-. **Orgs:** Mem Am Assn Univ Profs; Am Assn Sch Adminstrs; Nat Educ Assn; Nat Alli Black Sch Educators; Mass Assn Sch Supr; Assn for Suprvsn & CurriculumDevel; NJ Assn of Sch Adminstr; Am Soc of Training & Devel; Am Mgmt Assn; Nat Soc of Corp Plnrs. **Honors/Awds:** Outst ldrshp award Sch Dist 1968; author of 14 Professional Books. **Military Serv:** AUSR maj 1955-67. **Business Addr:** EIC/NE 2 Babcock Pl, West Orange, NJ 07052.

LEWIS, JAMES B.
Government official. **Personal:** Born Nov 30, 1947, Roswell, NM; son of Dorris Lewis and William Reagor; married Armandie Lillie Johnson; children: Teri Seaton, James Jr, Shedra, LaRon. **Educ:** Bishop College, BS, educ, 1970; Univ of NM, MPA, 1977; Natl College of Business, AS, business, 1980, BS (magna cum laude), business, 1981. **Career:** Univ of Albuquerque, Afro-studies adminis/instr, 1974-77; District Attorney's Office, investigator/purchasing dir, 1977-83; Bernalillo Co, treasurer, 1983-85; New Mexico State Govt, state treasurer, 1985-91; Chief of Staff to Governor Bruce King, 1991-94; NM State Land Office, director, Oil, Gas, Minerals Division, 1995-. **Orgs:** Past state housing chair, mem, NAACP, 1980-; bd mem, finance comm, Victims of Domestic Violence, 1983-; past treas, mem, Amer Soc for Public Admin, 1983-; mem, Natl State Treasurers, 1985-; mem bd, State Investment Council NM, 1985, Public Employee Retirement Bd, 1985, Educ Retirement Bd, 1985; mem, Amer Legion PO 99, 1985; mem, Kiwanis Club of Albuquerque, Masons, American GI Forum, Intl Alumni Assn Bishop College, Taylor Ranch Neighborhood Assn; life mem, Omega Psi Phi Frat; pres-elect, New Mexico Chapter, Amer Society for Public Admin, 1989; mem, New Mexico State Bd of Finance; mem, Educ Foundation Assistance Board; mem, Ad-Hoc Committee (Oil & Gas), State Investment Council, 1989. **Honors/Awds:** Outstanding Young Men in Amer, Natl Jaycees, 1980; Citizen of Year, Omega Psi Phi, 1983; Outstanding County Treasurer, Co Treasurer's Assn, 1984; hon mem, Beta Alpha Psi, CPA hon soc, 1989; commencement speaker, Zuni High School Zuni NM 1989; member, President Bill Clinton Transition Team, 1992-; commencement speaker, University of New Mexico, Department of Public Administration, 1992. **Military Serv:** AUS E-4 2 yrs. **Business Addr:** Director, Oil, Gas, Minerals Division, New Mexico State Land Office, PO Box 1148, Santa Fe, NM 87504-1148.

LEWIS, JAMES D.
Publisher. **Career:** Minority Business Journal, publisher, president, currently. **Business Addr:** President/Publisher, Minority Business Journal, PO Box 3543, Pittsburgh, PA 15230, (412)682-4386.

LEWIS, JAMES EARL
Engineer, physicist. **Personal:** Born Jun 2, 1931, Jackson, MS; son of Willie Mae Lewis (deceased) and Martin L Lewis Sr (deceased); married Annette Moody, Jun 20, 1959; children: Janice, Tamara, Jacquannette. **Educ:** Howard U, BSEE 1955; Physics Howard Univ, MS 1976. **Career:** Bendix Communication Div, sr staff engineer; "A" Westinghouse Elect Co, sr engineer 1969-75; Lockheed Electronics Co, sr elec engr 1966-69; US Naval Research Lab, elec scientist 1987-91; Raytheon Corp, principal engineer, currently. **Orgs:** Mem IEEE Co-founder Naylor-Dupont Community Assembly 1973; neighborhood commr Boy Scouts 1969-71; bd of dir Jr Citizen Corp, pres of DC Striders. **Honors/Awds:** US patent holder "Microwave Antenna Feed for Two Coordinate Radars" 1968; pub paper "Automatic Electronic Polarization Control for Satellites" Intl Conf on Communications 1972; invention award "Technique for Reduced Sidelobes on Radar Antennas" Westinghouse 1972.

LEWIS, JAMES EDWARD. See Obituaries section.

LEWIS, JAMES R.
Dentist. **Personal:** Born Aug 3, 1938, Asheboro, NC; married Barbara Walker; children: Krista, Erica. **Educ:** Chem NC Central University, BS 1963; Howard University, DDS 1968; McGill University, Montreal, Canada, rotating dental internship; VA Hosp, Albany 1968-69. **Career:** Lincoln Health Cent Durham NC, dental dir 1971-75; Univ NC Sch Dent, asst prof dep ecology 1969-71. **Orgs:** Mem Am Dent Assn; Acad Cent Dent; NC Dent Soc; Am Endodontic Soc; Chi Delta Mu Med & Dent Frat Bd Mem NC Health Plan Agcy; mem Highest Order Mystic Shrine 32nd deg Mason; health prof coun for Black Stud int in dent First black as mem Adm Comm for Sch of Dent UNC 1969-71. **Military Serv:** USN HM3 3rd class hospitalman 1956-59. **Business Addr:** P O Box 427, Lincoln Health Center, Durham, NC 27707.

LEWIS, JANNIE
Judge. **Career:** Legal Services Corp, attorney; attorney in private practice; Circuit Court, judge, currently. **Special Achievements:** First African American judge in two of the counties in the district.

LEWIS, JEFFREY MARK
Global management consultant. **Personal:** married; children: two. **Educ:** Rutgers University, BS, economics, BA, business administration, 1980; Northwestern University, JL Kellogg Graduate School of Mgt, masters of mgt, 1981. **Career:** Sands Hotel & Casino, acountant, 1980; Anheuser-Busch, Special Projects/Corp Investments, mgr, 1985; SmithKline Beckman, Financial Planning & Analysis, mgr, 1981-85; The Business Improvement Forum, executive director, 1986; Mars Inc, associate, 1986-91; Northwest Airlines, Inc, Intl Treasury, dir, 1991-93; Lewis & Co Inc, pres, 1993-. **Orgs:** Rotary International. **Honors/Awds:** Omicron Delta Epsion, Intl Economics Honor Society, 1981; Chase Manhattan Bank, Fellow, 1981. **Special Achievements:** Language Proficiency: Spanish, French, Japanese, Chinese; Professional Speaking Engagements: World Trade Institute Intl Finance Programs, chmn/lecturer, Arkansas State University, Intl Treasury Mgt Principles, US Department of Commerce, Intl Opportunities for Women & Minorities in Business; Professional Papers: Foreign Trade & Investment Review, Intl Trade Considerations in European Russia, 1995 Edition; Trade & Culture, South Africa: How to Use Investment & Trade Incentives; Treasury Mgt Assn, Derivatives Rick Mgt Compendium; numerous others. **Business Addr:** President, Lewis & Co, Inc, 1565 Cliff Rd, Ste 3268, St Paul, MN 55122, (612)707-8571.

LEWIS, JERMAINE EDWARD
Professional football player. **Personal:** Born Oct 16, 1974, Lanham, MD. **Educ:** Univ of Maryland, attended. **Career:** Baltimore Ravens, wide receiver, 1996-. **Business Addr:** Professional Football Player, Baltimore Ravens, 11001 Owings Mills Blvd, Owings Mills, MD 21117, (410)654-6200.

LEWIS, JESSE CORNELIUS
Educational administrator. **Personal:** Born Jun 26, 1929, Vaughan, MS; son of Mr & Mrs Jefferson Lewis; married Emma Goldman; children: Valerie. **Educ:** Tougaloo Coll, BS 1949; Univ of IL, MS 1955, MA 1959; Syracuse Univ, PhD 1966. **Career:** Southern Univ Baton Rouge, instructor math 1955-57; Prairie View Coll, 1957-58; Syracuse Univ, rsch asst computer center 1963-66; Jackson State Coll, prof math, dir computer center 1966-84; Norfolk State University, Norfolk, VA, vice pres, academic affairs, 1984-. **Orgs:** Consultant, lecturer, member, American Math Assn, 1971; proj dir, National Science Foundation Computing Network, 1973-, National Science Foundation Science Faculty Fellow, 1958, 1961; member, American Assn Computing Mach; member, Math Soc; chmn, Faculty Senate, Jackson State Coll, 1970-73; mem Alpha Phi Alpha. **Business Addr:** Vice Pres, Academic Affairs, Norfolk State Univ, 2401 Corprew Ave, Norfolk, VA 23504.

LEWIS, JESSE J.
Business executive. **Personal:** Born Jan 3, 1925, Tuscaloosa, AL; married Helen Merriweather; children: James, Jesse Jr. **Educ:** Miles Coll Birmingham AL, BA 1951-55; Troy State Univ Montgomery AL, MS 1976-77. **Career:** The Birmingham Times Newspaper, pres 1963-64; Office of Hwy Traffic Safety Montgomery, dir 1974-78; Lawson State Comm Coll, pres 1978-. **Orgs:** Mem Law Enforcement Plnng Agency, Birmingham Urban League; life mem Alpha Phi Alpha. **Honors/Awds:** Citation for Outstanding Serv Gov of AL 1975; Outstanding Acad Excellence Awd Miles Coll 1975, Ctr to Promote Safety in AL State of AL 1978. **Business Addr:** President, Lawson State Community Coll, 3060 Wilson Rd SW, Birmingham, AL 35221.

LEWIS, JOHN ROBERT
Government official. **Personal:** Born Feb 21, 1940, Troy, AL; son of Eddie Lewis; married Lillian Miles. **Educ:** Am Bapt Theol Sem, BA 1961; Fisk U, BA 1967. **Career:** Voter Educ Project Inc, exec dir 1970-; So Regional Council, comm orgn proj dir 1967-70; Field Found, assoc dir 1966-67; Nonviolent Coord Com Chmn, student 1963-66; Atlanta City Councilman-At-Large; Congressman, 1986—. **Orgs:** Amer Civil Liberties Union; Afro-Am Inst; Adv Com Biracial Com Atlanta Bd Edn; Adv Bd Black Enterprises; mem Martin Luther King Jr Ctr for Social Change; Life mem NAACP; SCLC; various others; mem Leadership Atlanta 1974-75; leading speaker organizer and worker in the Civil Rights Movement; apptd by Pres Johnson to White House Conference "To Fulfill These Rights" 1966; Speaker's Bureau during Sen Robert Kennedy's campaign. **Honors/Awds:** Named "One of Nation's Most Influential Black" Ebony Mag 1971-72; "One of America's 200 Rising Leaders" by Time Mag 1974. **Business Addr:** 501 Cannon House Office Bldg, Washington, DC 20515.

LEWIS, KENNETH DWIGHT
Engineer, clergyman. **Personal:** Born Aug 11, 1949, Newark, NJ; son of Carrie Attles & Joseph Lewis, Sr; married Pamela Josephine Masingale, May 27, 1978; children: Caleb, Sarah. **Educ:** Rutgers University, AB physics, 1971; Lehigh University, MS physics, 1972; Stanford University, MSE, Nuc E, 1974; University of Illinois at Urbana, AM (applied Math), 1979, PhD Nuc E, 1982; Trinity Theological Seminary, Newburgh IN, ThD, 1986; Moody Bible Institute of Chicago, Certificate, 1992. **Career:** Lockheed Martin Energy Systems, sr engineer, 1982-88, dev staff mem I, 1988-90, engineering specialist, 1990-95, sect manager, nuclear calculations sect, 1994-, sr staff engineer, 1995-, corporate nuclear criticality safety manager, 1995-. **Orgs:** Little Leaf Baptist Church, TN, associate pastor & youth director, 1993-; Second Baptist Church, Stockton CA, associate pastor, 1988-90; First Baptist Church, Chillicothe, OH, assistant pastor/trustee, 1983-87; Salem Baptist Church, Champaign IL, deacon, 1979-82. **Honors/Awds:** University of Illinois Black Alumni Association, Outstanding Achievement Awd, 1992; Lockheed Martin Cash Awds, Technical Achievement, 1992, 1994; Ohio House of Representatives, Certificate of Recognition for PE Licensure Exam, 1983; Graduate College Fellow, University of Illinois, 1977-78; Black Engineer of the Year President's Award, 1998. **Special Achievements:** Sigma Xi Honorary Society; Pi Mu Epsilon Mathematics Honor Society; Licensed Professional Engineer; Certificate of Merit, Ohio Society of Professional Engineer, highest grade on exam, 1983; Letter of Appreciation, President Clinton, participation in the Sapphire Project, 1995; Delegate to People's Republic of China Radiation Protection Conference, 1987; Session Chair, American Nuclear Society Annual Meeting, PA, 1995; Over 20 Technical Publications; Visiting Professor of Mathematics, University of the Pacific, 1989-90. **Business Addr:** Sr Staff Engineer & Section Manager, Lockheed Martin Energy Systems Inc, PO Box 2009, Bldg 9110, MS 8238, Oak Ridge, TN 37831.

LEWIS, LAURETTA FIELDS
Educator. **Personal:** Born in Chattanooga, TN; daughter of Lula Ballard Fields-Hogue and Mark Fields Sr; divorced; children: Jeffrey L, Mark F Lewis. **Educ:** Univ of TN Chattanooga BSW 1971; Univ of TN, MSSW 1974; Univ of MI Inst of Geron, Cert Aging 1982; North Carolina A&T State Univ, Summer Inst on Aging 1986. **Career:** Family Serv Agency, social worker aide 1966-68; Community Action Program TN, out reach soc worker 1968-70; Neighborhood Youth Corp, youth counselor 1972; Clover Bottom Dev Ctr Nashville TN, social worker 1973; Florence Crittenton Home TN, social worker aide 1973-74; East Carolina Univ, assoc prof of social work, instructor, Univ Geroutology Ctr, currently. **Orgs:** Consult Long Term Care 1976-; vice chmn, treas, 1980-82, chmn 1983 NC Council on Social Work Ed; past pres, exec bd Pitt Co Mental Health Assn 1983-92; chmn bd Pitt Cty Council on Aging 1983-85; mem exec comm & chap rep to state bd Pitt Co Mental Health Assn 1987; mem exec bd Creative Living Ctra Day Prog for Geriatric Patients; grants & research comittee member, Southern Gerontological Society, 1990-92; chair, personnel action, Pitt County Council on Aging, 1989-92; scholarship liaison, School of Social Work & Pitt Co Mental Health Assn, 1985-93; Greenville/Pitt County Habitat for Humanity, PORT Adolescent Substance Abuse Program, MH/Pitt County, bd member; Pitt County Coalition on Adolescent Pregnancy Prevention, Inc, committee member; East Carolina Organization of Black Faculty and Staff, program committee member; Hospice Volunteer with Home Health and Hospice Care, Inc; Certified Clinical Practitioner, recertified CCSW, 1994; Book Review Published in Intl Journal: Educational Gerontology: v 18 #5 Jul-Aug, 1992, Serving the Elderly: Skills for Practice, edited by Paul K H Kim, NY: Aldine de Gruyter, Inc, 1991; Chi Zeta - Phi Alpha - ECU - School of Social Work Chapter of Phi Alpha the National Social Work Honor Society, faculty adviser. **Honors/Awds:** Received Alumni Upper Classman Awd 1971; Danforth Assoc Danforth Found 1980; Awds of Appreciaiton NC Dept Human Serv MR 1981; Teacher of the Year Student Assoc Social Work Dept 1983; Outstanding Service Mental Health Assoc 1984-85; Appointee Reg Faculty Liaison Natl Assoc Soc Works; Minority Leadership Devel Fellowship Awd School of Public Health Univ of NC Chapel Hill 1985; Certificate of Appreciation from Undergrad Student Org 1987; Training Assistantship in Geriatric Educ & Leadership Dev from the Univ of NC at Chapel Hill Sch of Social Work & Geriatric Educ Ctr Summer Inst 1987; Merit Awd Mental Health Assoc Pitt Co 1987; inducted into "The Carolinas Associates" Excellence in Higher Educ as Charter Mem 1987; Reviewer for Educational Gerontology International Journal; Pitt County Chabitat for Humanity Family Selection Committee; Natl Assn of Social Workers, Faculty Liaison Service Award, 1995. **Home Addr:** PO Box 21061, Greenville, NC 27858.

LEWIS, LEO E., III
Professional football player (retired), sports administrator. **Personal:** Born Sep 17, 1956, Columbia, MO; son of Leo Lewis. **Educ:** Univ of Missouri, received education degree; Univ of Tennessee, received master's degree; received Doctorate in Kinesiology, Univ of Minnesota, 1997. **Career:** Minnesota Vikings, wide receiver, 1981-91; University of Minnesota Department of Kinesiology and Leisure Studies, instructor, 1986-94. **Orgs:** Board Member, Minneapolis Childrens Theatre. **Honors/Awds:** Played in NFC Championship Game, post-1987 season; University of Missouri All-Century Team, Hall of Fame. **Business Addr:** Player Relations Coord, Minnesota Vikings, 9520 Viking Dr, Eden Prairie, MN 55344-3825, (612)828-6500.

LEWIS, LEROY C.
Podiatrist (retired). **Personal:** Born Jun 23, 1917, Mason City, IA; married Elizabeth L Harris; children: Ronald. **Educ:** Buena Vista College; Illinois College of Podiatric Medicine 1946. **Career:** Podiatrist. **Orgs:** American Podiatry Assn; Missouri Podiatry Assn; Kansas City Podiatry Society; Martin Luther King

staff, bd dir, Urban League; YMCA; Midwesterners Inc; St Andrew Methodist Church; Sigma Ph Phi. **Honors/Awds:** Man of the Year; Distinguished Service Award. **Military Serv:** US Army, 1943-46.

LEWIS, LILLIAN J.
Social services. **Personal:** Born Apr 20, 1926, Chicago, IL; widowed; children: Robert, Gloria, Benjamin, Vivian. **Career:** US Naval Hosp, 1955-63; DeWitt Army Hosp, nurs div 1963-65; Group Health Assoc, clinical asst 1966-70; Manpower Admin, chief support serv 1971-. **Orgs:** Mem Natl Org for Women, Natl Polit Womens Caucus, MA State Dem Steering Comm 1976, NWPC Affirm Action Task Force; vice pres NAACP; mem Comm Rel Deseg Task Force; adv bd Model Cities Fellowship, League of Women Voters, Prince Georges Pol Womens Caucus & Affirm Action Coord, Prince George Cty Publ School ESAP 1971, Prince George Ment Health Assoc; comm to elect Marvin Mandel; chmn Comm Affairs 1970-72; bd of dir So Christian Leadership Conf MD Chapt, Prince Georges Cty MD Black Dem Council. **Honors/Awds:** Cert of Apprec for Meritiroius Asst US Dept of Commerce 1970; Cert of Merit NAACP 1973; deleg at large Dem Conv State of MD 1976.

LEWIS, LLOYD ALEXANDER, JR.
Clergyman, educator. **Personal:** Born Nov 12, 1947, Washington, DC; son of Alice Christine Bell and Lloyd Alexander Lewis. **Educ:** Trinity College, AB, 1969; Virginia Theological Seminary, MDiv, 1972; Yale University, MA, 1975, MPhil, 1981, PhD, 1985. **Career:** St George's Church, curate, 1972-74; General Theological Seminary, tutor, 1977, visiting professor, 1989; Virginia Theological Seminary, assistant professor of the New Testament, 1978-86, associate professor of New Testament, 1986-91; George Mercer School of Theology, dean, 1991-. **Orgs:** Society for the Study of Black Religion; Society of Biblical Literature; Programme for Theological Education, World Council of Churches, commissioner; Union of Black Episcopalians; Standing Liturgical Commission, The Episcopal Church, consultant. **Honors/Awds:** Virginia Theological Seminary, Honorary Doctorate in Divinity, 1992; Cathedral of the Incarnation, Canon Theologian, 1991; Rockefeller Doctoral Fellowship, Fellow, 1974-76. **Special Achievements:** Author, "An African-American Appraisal of the Philemon Paul Onesimus Triangle," Stony the Road We Trod, 1991; author, "The Law Courts at Corinth: An Experiment in the Power of Baptism," Christ and His Communities, 1990. **Home Addr:** 200-16 Hilton Ave, Hempstead, NY 11550, (516)565-3844. **Business Addr:** Dean, George Mercer School of Theology, 65 4th St, Garden City, NY 11530, (516)248-4800.

LEWIS, LLOYD E., JR.
Utility company executive. **Personal:** Born Nov 17, 1926, Xenia, OH; son of Ruth Hamilton Lewis and Lloyd Edward Lewis; married Edythe Mulzac; children: James D, Crystal M. **Educ:** Univ of Dayton, BS Business Admin 1948; Central MI Univ, MA Public Admin 1976. **Career:** Lloyd Lewis Sales & Serv Inc, vice pres 1950-66; SCOPE, program developer 1966; Rikes, general mgr 1966-75; City of Dayton, asst city mgr 1975-80; The Dayton Power & Light Co, asst vp. **Orgs:** Pres Dayton City Plan Bd 1967-75; dir Dayton Area Chamber of Comm 1978-84; treas Montgomery Cty Devel Corp 1980-85; trustee Miami Valley Auto Club 1980-; chmn St Elizabeth Med Ctr 1984-85; trustee, Franciscan Health System of Dayton 1987-; secretary, Citywide Development Corp 1985-; trustee, The Dayton Foundation, 1988-. **Honors/Awds:** Outstanding Civic Achievement Univ of Dayton Alumni Assn 1971; Outstanding Public Affairs Citizens Amer Soc of Public Admin 1973; Outstanding Achievement Awd OH Planning Conf 1978; Marketeer of the Year Amer Mktg Assn 1983; Citizens Legion of Honor, President's Club of Dayton 1988; Archon of the Year, Sigma Boul, Sigma Pi Phi Fraternity, 1988. **Military Serv:** US Army, capt, 2 yrs active, 14 yrs reserve. **Home Addr:** 800 Oak Leaf Dr, Dayton, OH 45408. **Business Addr:** Assistant Vice President, Dayton Power & Light Company, PO Box 8810, Dayton, OH 45401.

LEWIS, LOIDA NICOLAS
Food company executive. **Personal:** Born Dec 23, 1942, Sorsogon, Philippines; married Reginald F Lewis, 1969 (died 1993); children: Leslie, Christina. **Educ:** St Theresa's College, Manila; University of Philippines, law degree. **Career:** Attorney; TLC Beatrice International Holdings, Inc., chief executive officer, currently. **Business Addr:** CEO, TLC Beatrice Intl Holdings Inc., 9 W. 57th St., 48th Fl., New York, NY 10019, (212)756-8900.

LEWIS, LONZY JAMES
Scientist, educator. **Personal:** Born Aug 29, 1949, Sharon, GA; son of Joseph & Lillian (Seals) Lewis; married Cynthia Patterson Lewis, Jun 30, 1973; children: Lillianne Marie, Brianna Nicole, Adrianne Zanetta. **Educ:** Morehouse College, BS, 1971; Georgia Institute of Technology, MS physics, 1973; State University of New York at Albany, PhD, 1980. **Career:** Deutsches Elektronen-Synchrotron, (DESY), work study fellow, 1970; GA Inst of Tech, EPA trainee, Physics dept, ChE dept, 1972-73; Coll of State Rose, HCOP prog, math instr, 1979-80; State Univ of NY-Albany, research sci, atmos sci research ctr, 1974-80; GA Inst of Tech, Sch of Geophysi Sci, research sci II, 1980-83; State of MS, Dept of Environ, consultant, quality, pollut, control off, 1983-93; Jackson State Univ, Dept of Phy & Atmos Sci, assoc prof, 1983-93, chair, 1983-87; Clark Atlanta Univ, Dept of Physics, assoc prof & chair, 1993-. **Orgs:** Natl Soc of Black Phys, NSBP science ambassador, 1997-, treas, finance comm chair, 1990-95, conference chair, 1991-92, 1994-95, pres-elect, vice chair, 1995-96, pres, chair, 1996-98; Amer Meteorological Soc, mem bd of meteor & ocean ed in univ, 1983-87; Project Kalleidoscope, faculty assoc, 1994-; Ronald E McNair Foundation, curriculum supvsr, mentor, Sci Resource Agt, 1994-. **Honors/Awds:** Natl Soc of Black Phys, Charter Fellow, 1992; Sigma Pi Sigma, Fellow, 1993. **Special Achievements:** "Multiple Excitation of Neon by Photon and Electron Impact," Phys Ltrs, p 31A, 1970; Certificate of Proficiency in the German Language, Zeugnis, 1970; Certificate of Proficiency in Air Pollution Control Technology, 1973; "Terrestrial Solar Spectra Data Sets," Solar Energy, p 30, 1983; Proceedings of the XIX Day of Scientific Lectures and 15th Annual Meeting of NSBP, 1993; Proceedings of the XXII Day of Scientific Lectures and 18th Annual Meeting of NSBP, 1996. **Business Addr:** Associate Professor & Chairman, Department of Physics, Clark Atlanta University, 223 James P Brawley Dr, SW, Atlanta, GA 30314, (404)880-8798.

LEWIS, LYN ETTA
Educational administrator. **Personal:** Born Oct 1, 1947, Monroe, LA; daughter of Mr & Mrs Rufus & Onita Lewis. **Educ:** Grambling State Univ, BA, 1965-68; Univ of Tennessee, MA, 1968-70; Wayne State Univ, PhD, 1972-78. **Career:** Spelman Colorado, instructor of Sociology, 1969-72; Univ of Detroit, assoc prof, 1973-90; Univ of Detroit-Mercy, chair, assoc prof, 1990-. **Orgs:** Boysville of Michigan, pres Detroit advisory coun, 1993-. **Honors/Awds:** Wayne State Univ, Ctr for Black Studies, Distinguished Alumnae Award, 1981; Grambling State Univ, Distinguished Alumnae Award, 1990, Faculty Award for Excellence. **Special Achievements:** Published book review in publication of Michigan Psychological Association. **Home Addr:** 14368 Warwick, Detroit, MI 48223, (313)836-1877. **Business Addr:** Chair, Sociology Department, University of Detroit-Mercy, 4001 W McNichols, PO Box 19900, Briggs Bldg, Ste 315, Detroit, MI 48219-9000, (313)993-1094.

LEWIS, MARGARET W.
Administrator, educator. **Personal:** Born in Oviedo, FL; daughter of Margaret Ellis Williams and Morris T Williams; married Howard E Lewis, May 15, 1959. **Educ:** Florida A&M University, Tallahassee, FL, BSN, 1958; Ohio State University, Columbus, OH, MSN, 1968; Florida State University, Tallahassee, FL, PhD, 1977. **Career:** Florida A&M University Hospital, Tallahassee, FLl, staff nurse, 1958-59, Florida A&M University, Tallahassee, FL, instructor, 1959-61, asst professor, 1966-78, dean, school of nursing, 1982-; Centre County Hospital, Belafonte, PA, supervisor, 1961-66; Albany State College, Albany, GA, asoc professor, 1978-79; Winston-Salem State Univ, Winston-Salem, NC, director of div of nursing, 1979-82. **Orgs:** Board member, Florida League for Nursing, 1983-84, 1991; board member, Big Bend Deaf Center, 1989-; member, American Nurses Association, 1958-; member, National League for Nursing, 1975-; Florida League for Nursing, president, 1992-. **Honors/Awds:** Outstanding Alumnus Award in Administration, Florida A&M University School of Nursing Alumni Assoc, 1990; Outstanding Dean Award, Florida A&M University, 1988. **Military Serv:** US Army, cpl, 1951-54. **Home Addr:** 1805 Skyland Dr, Tallahassee, FL 32303. **Business Phone:** (904)599-3017.

LEWIS, MARTHA S.
Administrator. **Personal:** Born Feb 24, 1924, Kensett, AR; divorced. **Educ:** Univ of AR, BA 1944; Atlanta Univ Sch of Soc Work, MSW 1947. **Career:** Natl NY Dept of Soc Srv, dep commr 1976-; NYS Dept of Soc Srv, dep commr 1975-76; Dept of Soc & Comm Srv New York City Housing Auth, dir 1972-76, 1972-75; Maternity Ctr Assc, mgmt consult spl asst to dir 1971-72; Maurice W Perreault & Assc, consult 1971; Martha Lewis & Assc Mgmt Consult Firm, established 1970; Operation Better Block, dir 1968-71; Dept of Soc & Comm Srv New York City Housing Auth, dep dir 1964-68; New York City Housing Auth, chief tenant org tenant educ div 1961-64; New York City Youth Bd 1954-61; New York City Bd of Educ, soc wrkr 1951-54. **Orgs:** Soc Welfare Forum; Natl Assc of Soc Workers; Natl Assc of Housing & Redev Officials; mem Zonta Intl; Natl Urban League Guild; NAACP; mem Women Unitedfor NY Steering Comm; found mem exec bd Coalition of 100 Black Women; Black Women's Communications Hookup; mem Congr Black Caucus Dinner Plnng Comm 1976. **Honors/Awds:** Woman of Yr; Phi Beta Sigma Sor 1961; Founders Day speaker AM&N Clge 1962; nom Incentive Award New York City Housing Auth 1962; hnrd by Women's Advertising Counc of NY 1964; Regl Com of Pres Com on Consumer Afrs 1964; Comm Leaders of Amer Award 1972, publ in Comm Ldrs of Amer 1972; Night Owl Mayor City of NY 1974. **Business Addr:** 40 N Pearl St, Albany, NY 12243.

LEWIS, MARTIN
Professional basketball player. **Personal:** Born Apr 28, 1975, Liberal, KS. **Educ:** Butler County Comm College; Seward County Comm College. **Career:** Toronto Raptors, 1995-. **Business Addr:** Professional Basketball Player, Toronto Raptors, 150 York St, Ste 110, Toronto, ON, Canada M5H 3S5, (416)214-2255.

LEWIS, MATTHEW, JR.
Editor, photographer. **Personal:** Born Mar 8, 1930, McDonald, PA; son of Alzenia Heath and Matthew Lewis; married Jeannine Wells; children: Charlene, Matthew, Kevin. **Career:** The Washington Post, asst mgr, editor, photographer (retired); Morgan State Coll, inst 1957-65; photographer, currently. **Orgs:** White House New Photograph Assn; National Press Photograph Assn; National Assn of Black Journalists. **Honors/Awds:** Pulitzer Prize for Feature Photograph 1975; 1st prize Natl Newspaper Publs Assn 1964; White House News Photograph Assn 1968 & 71; Bill Pryor Award Washington-Baltimoer Newspaper Guild 1971-72; one of 12 African-Americans Pulitzer Prize Winners honored at NABJ's new "Hall of Fame" which inducted its first 7 members, 1990. **Military Serv:** USN 1949-52. **Home Addr:** 2 Clark St, Thomasville, NC 27360.

LEWIS, MAURICE
Journalist. **Personal:** Born Aug 23, 1943, Chicago, IL; children: Stephanie, Kevin. **Career:** WBZ-TV 4, news anchrmn rprtr 1976-; WHYY, guest journ 1976-77; WNAC-TV, coanchrmn 1975-76; WNAC-TV, anchrmn rprtr 1974-76; WBZ Radio News, rprtr 1969-74; CNL Radio, mgr 1965-67; AF Radio, rprtr commentator. **Orgs:** Chmn & co-fdr The Afro Am Media Assn 1975-; bd of dir Elma Lewis Sch of Fine Art 1977; bd of dir Family Serv Ctr 1976; bd dir Urban League 1976; bd trustees Graham Jr Coll 1977. **Honors/Awds:** Outst serv to comm award Jan Matzlinger 1974; news rprtr of yr MA Afro Am Patrolman's Assn 1977; Who's Who Boston's 100 Influential Black Citizens 1976-77; outst achvmt MA Sec of State Paul Guzzi 1976; outst citizen of yr MA State Senate 1976; outst citizen Congrsnsl Record 1976; outst contbns City of Bonston 1976; outst min broadcaster MA House of Rep 1976; black achvr in bus award Grtr Boston YMCA 1976; man of yr Nat Assn of Negro Bus & Professional Women's Club Inc; black achvr of yr Boston 200's Victorian Exhib & Gilette Co; outst commun serv award area of media Boston Chptr NAACP; 10 outst yg ldrs Boston Jaycees 1975. **Military Serv:** USNR seaman 1960-62, 65-67. **Business Addr:** 1170 Soldiers Field Rd, Boston, MA 02134.

LEWIS, MEHARRY HUBBARD
Educator. **Personal:** Born Aug 2, 1936, Nashville, TN; son of Helen M Lewis and Felix E Lewis; married Floretta I Williams; children: Karen Anita, Arlan David. **Educ:** TN State Univ, BA 1959; TN State Univ, MS 1961; IN Univ, PhD 1971. **Career:** IN Univ, NDEA fellow 1966-67; Student Activities Office IN Univ, frat affairs adv 1967-69, lecturer 1970, visiting asst prof 1970-72; Macon Cty Bd Ed, coord rsch & eval 1972-73; Natl Alliance of Black School Educators, dir rsch proj 1973-74; School of Educ, prof of educ, asst dean Tuskegee Inst, dir institutional rsch & planning 1974-84; MGMT Inc, pres, dir 1984-; Bullock County Bd of Education, counselor, currently. **Orgs:** Mem natl Alliance Black School Ed, Kappa Delta Pi, Phi Delta Kappa Intl, Alpha Kappa Mu Natl Honor Soc, Amer Personnel & Guid Assoc, ACES Div & Assoc for Non-White Concerns; general sec, trust Church of the Living God, Pillar & Ground of the Truth Inc; mem youth comm YMCA 1963-66; mem Beta Kappa Chi. **Honors/Awds:** Publisher of several poems & articles; Presidents Awd Natl Alliance of Black School Educators 1974. **Business Addr:** Counselor, Bullock County Board of Education, PO Box 5108, Union Springs, AL 36089.

LEWIS, MELANIE
News reporter. **Personal:** Born Dec 19, 1964, Wilmington, DE; daughter of F Pearle Lewis Saulsberry and Leurhman Saulsberry. **Educ:** University of Delaware, Newark, DE, BA, 1986. **Career:** Univ of Del, Newark, DE, resident assistant, 1983-84, hall director, 1984-86; WILM-AM, Wilmington, DE, public affairs reporter, 1984, 1985, traffic reporter, 1986; Des Moines Register, Des Moines, IA, staff writer, 1986-90; Dallas Morning News, Dallas, TX, staff writer, 1990-. **Orgs:** Natl Assn Black Journalists, 1990-; Delta Sigma Theta, 1990-; Dallas-Fort Worth Association of Black Communicators, 1990-. **Honors/Awds:** Member, Omicron Delta Kappa, 1985-; member, Mortar Board, 1985.

LEWIS, MO
Professional football player. **Personal:** Born Oct 21, 1969, Atlanta, GA; married Christy; children: Mo. **Educ:** Univ of Georgia. **Career:** New York Jets, linebacker, 1991-. **Honors/Awds:** Miller Lite Player of the Year, 1994. **Business Addr:** Professional Football Player, New York Jets, 1000 Fulton Ave, Hempstead, NY 11550, (516)560-8100.

LEWIS, ORA LEE
Business executive. **Personal:** Born Apr 27, 1930, Port Huron, MI; married Cornelius W; children: 5. **Educ:** Erie Comm Coll. **Career:** Langston Hughes Ctr for Visual & Performing Arts, exec dir 1971-; NY State Div for Yth, super couns 1975-; Westminster Comm House, admnstrv asst 1967-71; Comm Yths Boys Town, couns 1968-; YWCA, chaperone 1956-67; United

Mutual Life Ins Co, sec 1947-51; Mrs Sims, sec atty 1951-54; Frienship House, prgm asst 1947-49; Buffalo Criterion Press, rptr clmnst 1947-65; Ora-Lee's Sec Svc, owner 1955-. **Orgs:** Human Serv Assn 1974-; E Side Coalition 1975-; Review & Referral Bd 1972-74; Consortium of Human Serv 1975-77; Westminster Comm House 1972-74; Buffalo Sister City to Ghana 1974-77; rep City of Buffalo meet Ghanian Ambassdr 1975; vice pres Embassy Educ Culture Com Model Cities 1972-74. **Honors/Awds:** Cert of completion Erie Comm Coll 1976; outst achvmt in the Arts Comm Univ 1976; cert of award Victoria Sch of Sch Reporting 1976; comm serv award Westminster Comm House 1975; hon mem award vol serv Friendship House 1949; picture exhib Top Blacks in Buffalo for Comm Serv in Photography 1976; exhib Buffalo Savings Bank 1976; dev Langston Hughes Educ Coloring Book for Children 1975. **Business Addr:** 25 High St, Buffalo, NY 14203.

LEWIS, PEGGY
Government official. **Career:** The White House, special assistant to the president, media affairs, currently. **Business Addr:** Special Asst to the Pres, Media Affairs, 1600 Pennsylvania Ave, The White House, Office of Communications, Washington, DC 20500, (202)456-1414.

LEWIS, PERCY LEE
Clergyman, educator. **Personal:** Born May 11, 1937, Monterey, LA; son of Zula Lewis and Ather Lewis; married John Evelyn Hilleard; children: Twila. **Educ:** Bay Ridge Christian Coll, Ministry D 1966, BTh 1973. **Career:** Rockport Church of God, pastor, currently; Bay Ridge Christian Coll, exec vice pres 1975-80, dean of students 1971-80; Austin Pl Church of God, pastor 1969-70; Maple Grove Church of God, pastor 1965-68. **Orgs:** Chmn Southern Assn of Churches 1970-76; Head Coach Bay Ridge Christian Coll 1978-80; mem soc concerns Church of God Anderson, IN 1973-80; mem business comm Church of God Anderson, IN 1974-79; mem School Bd Kendleton ISD 1977-80; chairmaa, board of trustees, Bay Ridge Christian College; chairman, Arkansas County Minister's Alliance; vice chairman, South Texas District Church of God. **Honors/Awds:** Southwest Region Coach of the Year, Bay Ridge Coll Kendleton, TX 1978-79.

LEWIS, POLLY MERIWETHER
County official. **Personal:** Born Aug 16, 1949, Clarksville, TN; daughter of Viola Elliot Meriweather and Virgil Meriweather; married Joseph B Lewis; children: J Barry, Justin L. **Educ:** Austin Peay State Univ, 1967-69; GA State Univ, BS 1973; Georgia State University, MBA, 1991. **Career:** DeKalb Cty Comm Devel Dept, program monitor 1975-79; GA Dept of Comm Affairs, prog mgmt consult 1979-80; DeKalb Comm Relations Comm, exec dir 1981-. **Orgs:** Former chap basileus Alpha Kappa Alpha 1973-; chairperson, bd of dir DeKalb EOA Inc 1980-; mem Leadership Atlanta 1981-82; bd of dir YWCA of Greater Atlanta 1984-; Jr League of DeKalb County, Inc; steering committee chair, Leadership DeKalb, 1987-88; board of directors, Black Women's Coalition of Atlanta, 1986-; board of directors, Decatur/DeKalb Coalition of 100 Black Women, 1989-; board of directors, Citizens for South DeKalb, 1986-. **Honors/Awds:** Woman of the Week DeKalb News Sun 1984; Woman of Achievement, Atlanta Urban BPW; Women of the Year, DeKalb EOA; Outstanding Service Award, Toney Gardens Civic Assn, 1988; Volunteer Service Award, DeKalb Branch, YWCA of Greater Atlanta, Inc, 1989. **Business Addr:** Exec Dir, Community Relations Commission, DeKalb County Government, 1300 Commerce Dr, 6th Fl, Decatur, GA 30030.

LEWIS, PRINIC HERBERT, SR.
Clergyman. **Personal:** Born Mar 13, 1930, Camden, AL; married Alice Grady; children: Prinic H, Jr, Kenneth H. **Educ:** Daniel Payne Coll & Payne Theol Sem Birmingham AL, BA, BTh, DD 1957. **Career:** Bethel AME Ch, minister; Social Act Com Tuscaloosa, orgn 1962; Brown Chapel AME Ch, pastor 1963-70; Dallas Co & Voter Leag, vice pres 1963-70; March from Salem to Montgomery by Dr Martin L King, host. **Orgs:** Mem NAACP; Black Causeus; Master Mason; trust Daniel Payne Coll; mem Bd dir B&P Supermarket; pres AME Ministerial Alliance; candidate for Bishopric in Atlanta GA 1976; mem bd dir Good Samaritan Hosp 1968; mem bd dir Commonwealth Bank 1974.

LEWIS, RAMSEY EMANUEL, JR.
Musician. **Personal:** Born May 27, 1935, Chicago, IL; son of Pauline Richards Lewis and Ramsey Emanuel Lewis (deceased); married Janet Tamillow Lewis, Jun 1990; children: Vita Denise, Ramsey Emanuel III, Marcus Kevin, Dawn, Kendall, Frayne, Robert; married Geraldine Taylor (divorced 1989). **Educ:** Chicago Music Coll, student 1947-54; Univ of IL, 1953-54; DePaul Univ, 1954-55; priv music study. **Career:** Hudson-Ross Inc Chicago, mgr record dept 1954-56; Ramsey Lewis Trio, organizer/mem 1956-; 1st professional appearance 1957; Randalls' Island Jazz Fest New York City 1959; Saugatuck, MI Jazz Fest 1960; Newport Jazz Fest 1961 & 1963; jazz concerts at numerous univs; toured with Free Sounds of 1963; numerous TV appearances; rec artist Argo-Cadet records; CBS Records, 1971-90; Black Entertainment Television, BET on Jazz with Ramsey Lewis, host, 1990-; WNUA-FM Jazz, Ramsey, and Yvonne, co-host, 1990-97, Morning show, host, 1997-; lecturer on music at numerous universities, 1990-; Legends of Jazz with Ramsey Lewis, host, 1990-; Ravinia Festival ''Jazz at Ravinia'' series, Chicago, IL, artistic dir, 1992-. **Orgs:** Bd of dirs, Merit, 1986-; bd of dirs, CYCLE, 1987-; bd of dirs, Gateway Foundation, 1990-; bd of dirs, Ravinia Mentor Prog, 1995-; bd of dirs, Cares for Kids Foundation, 1997-. **Honors/Awds:** Albums include: Gentlemen of Swing, 1956; Gentlemen of Jazz, 1958; Down to Earth (Music From the Soil), 1959; An Hour With the Ramsey Lewis Trio, 1959; Stretching Out, 1960; More Music From the Soil, 1961; Sound of Christmas, 1961; Bossa Nova, 1962; The Sound of Spring, 1962; Pot Luck, 1963; Barefoot Sunday Blues, 1964; Bach to the Blues, 1964; More Sounds of Christmas, 1964; At the Bohemian Caverns, 1964; Country Meets the Blues, 1964; The In Crowd, 1965; Choice! The Best of Ramsey Lewis Trio, 1962-64; Hang On Ramsey, 1965; Wade in the Water, 1966; The Movie Album, 1966; The Groover, 1966; Goin' Latin, 1967; Dancing in the Street, 1967; Up Pops Ramsey Lewis, 1967; Maiden Voyage, 1968; Mother Nature's Son, 1968; Live in Toyko, 1968; Another Voyage, 1969; The Piano Player, 1969; Them Chas, 1970; Back to the Roots, 1971; Upendo Ni Pamoja, 1972; Funky Serenity, 1973; Solar Wind, 1974; Sun Goddess, 1974; Don't It Feel Good, 1975; Salongo, 1976; Love Notes, 1977; Tequila Mockingbird, 1977; Legacy, 1978; Ramsey, 1979; Routes, 1980; Blues for the Night Owl, 1981; Three Piece Suite, 1981; Live At the Savoy, 1982; Chance Encounter, 1982; Les Fleurs, 1983; Reunion, 1983; The Two of Us (with Nancy Wilson), 1984; Fantasy, 1985; Keys to the City, 1987; A Classic Encounter, 1988; Urban Renewal, 1989; We Meet Again, 1989; Grammy Award for The In Crowd, 1965, Hold It Right There, 1966, Hang On Sloopy, 1973; ACE Awds, nominated for Jazz Central, BET, 1991, 1992; numerous gold records. **Special Achievements:** ''Person of the Week'', ABC Nightly News, 1995; White House Performance, 1995; CBS Sunday Morning, Billy Taylor Jazz Segment, 1997. **Business Addr:** 180 N LaSalle St, #2200, Chicago, IL 60601-1538.

LEWIS, RAY ANTHONY
Professional football player. **Personal:** Born May 15, 1975, Lakeland, FL; children: Ray Anthony Jr. **Educ:** Univ of Miami FL. **Career:** Baltimore Ravens, linebacker, 1996-. **Honors/Awds:** The Sporting News, All-America second team, 1995; USA Today, All-Rookie Team, 1996. **Business Addr:** Professional Football Player, Baltimore Ravens, 11001 Owings Mills Blvd, Owings Mills, MD 21117, (410)654-6200.

LEWIS, RETA JO
Attorney. **Personal:** Born Sep 22, 1953, Statesboro, GA; daughter of Charlie & Aleathia Lewis; married Carlton, Sep 11, 1993. **Educ:** University of Georgia, BA, 1975; American University, MSAJ, 1978; Emory University, JD, 1989. **Career:** Democracy For South Africa, Nelson Mandela USA Tour, trip dir, 1991; Verner Liipfert Bernhard McPherson & Hand, attorney, 1989-91; DC Government, DC Department of Public Works, chief of staff, 1992-93; Executive Office of the President, The White House, special asst to the president, political affairs, 1996-97; Arter & Hadden, counsel, 1996-97; Greenberg Traurig, partner, 1997-. **Orgs:** Emory Law School Council, 1998; Delta Sigma Theta, 1997; A Broader Image, Inc, 1997; Women's Information Network, advisory council, 1997; NFTE/Adopt an Entrepreneur, 1997. **Business Addr:** Partner, Greenberg Traurig Hoffman Lipoff Rosen & Quentel, 1300 Connecticut Ave NW, Ste 1000, Washington, DC 20036, (202)331-3155.

LEWIS, RICHARD JOHN, SR.
Former government official and computer consultant (retired). **Personal:** Born Jun 7, 1936, Manheim, WV; son of Ida McLane Carroll and Thomas Ellington (deceased); children: Richard Jr, Thomas. **Educ:** Numerous Government, Commercial Institutes and Computer Manufacture Sponsored Training, 1965-83; Liberty University, Lynchburg, VA, 1989-91. **Career:** Dept of Health and Human Services, Washington, DC, from clerk/typist to computer programmer, 1964-70, senior computer systems programmer, 1970-80, chief, software management division, 1980-84; Advanced Management, Inc, McLean, VA, computer security consultant, 1984-91. **Orgs:** Past chairman, Audit Committee, Pittsburghers of Washington, DC, Inc, 1985-90; life member, American Legion, 1972-; Marine Corps Assoication, life mem. **Honors/Awds:** Lifesaving Bronze/Medal, Carnegie Hero Fund Commission, 1968; Secretary's Special Citation, Dept of Health and Human Services, 1968; many other awards for superior government service performance. **Military Serv:** US Marine Corps, sergeant (E5), 1953-63. **Home Addr:** 3214 SE Quay St, Port St Lucie, FL 34984.

LEWIS, RICHARD U.
Government official. **Personal:** Born Oct 3, 1926, W Field, AL; married Avial; children: 3. **Educ:** Morehouse Coll. **Career:** Brighton, AL, mayor 1972-; Brighton, cnclmn 1968-72. **Orgs:** Mem Dem Com Jefferson Co; mem Ust Bapt Ch. **Military Serv:** AUS WW II. **Business Addr:** 3700 Main St, Brighton, AL 35020.

LEWIS, ROBERT ALVIN, JR.
Aircraft company executive. **Personal:** Born Jul 10, 1945, Henderson, NC; son of Dorothy A Lewis and Robert A Lewis Sr; married Joanne Mangum, Sep 2, 1967; children: Derek Robert. **Educ:** North Carolina State University, BS, aero space engineering, 1966; University of Connecticut, MS, aerospace engineering, 1969, MBA, 1975. **Career:** Pratt & Whitney, director, sales & service, 1995-. **Orgs:** AIAA, 1966. **Honors/Awds:** UTC, Outstanding Contributor to Corporation, 1992. **Special Achievements:** ''Propfan Power,'' Association of Singapore Licensed Aircraft Engineers, 1988; ''Choosing Propulsion Technology,'' Alfred Wegener Institute, Germany 1988; ''Advances in Commercial Aviation,'' Indian Aeronautical Society, 1990; ''High Thrust Engines for Middle East,'' Abu Dhabi, 1994. **Home Addr:** 197 Fairview Dr, South Windsor, CT 06074, (203)644-8780.

LEWIS, ROBERT EDWARD
Educational administrator (retired). **Personal:** Born Apr 27, 1903, Sturgis, KY; son of Mary Ann Wynn Lewis and George Graham Lewis; married Virginia Frances Lewis, Nov 29, 1929. **Educ:** Fisk Univ, AB 1926; Chicago State Univ, Teaching Certificate 1927; Northwestern Univ, MA 1939; Harvard Univ, EdD 1960. **Career:** Chicago Public Elementary Schools, teacher 1927-35, high school teacher/counselor 1935-45, asst principal 1945-48, elementary school principal 1948-61, high school principal 1961-65, dist 13 supt 1965-68; General Learning Corp, Womens Job Corps Center, consultant, 1968-69; Encyclopaedia Britannica, associate, 1968-78. **Orgs:** First African-American male administrator in Chicago Public Schools 1948; educ consultant Job Corps Ctr Clinton IA; supervisor M degree candidates Harvard Univ; consultant for develop of Middle Schools Chicago Bd of Educ; principal of adult evening schools (Carver, Dunbar & Phillips HS Chicago); vice pres Property Owners Assoc Madison Park Chicago; mem Kappa Alpha Psi Frat, Sigma Pi Phi, Phi Delta Kappa; life mem Natl Educ Assoc; mem AASA, Chicago 40 Club, Druids, Nomads Golf Club, Good Shepherd Church, NAACP, Urban League, Fisk Club, Tee Birds, Scufflers; lecturer, DePaul Univ Grad School of Educ, 1969-72. **Honors/Awds:** Alumni Commencement Week Speaker Fisk Univ; Jubilee Day Speaker Fisk Univ; speaker Intl Reading Assoc Natl Conf on English Educ NDEA Inst of Western IL Univ and Tuskegee Inst. **Home Addr:** 4650 54th Ave South, #308 W, St Petersburg, FL 33711.

LEWIS, ROBERT LOUIS
Pastor, city official. **Personal:** Born Mar 10, 1936, Gilbert, LA; married Lendy Mae Neal; children: Gregory B, Keith A, Steven J, Christine M, Gerald W, Pamela V. **Educ:** SIU, BA 1980. **Career:** USAF tsgt E-6 1955-75; Sears, salesman 1978-83; Pulaski Cty Spec School Dist, sub teacher 1975-; Mt Pisgah Baptist Church, asst pastor 1980-; City of Jacksonville, alderman. **Orgs:** Scout master Boy Scouts of Amer 1956-60; short order cook Grand Forks AFB Exchange 1967-70; eoa rep USAF 1972-74; minister Base Chapel 1973-74; childrens church minister Mt Pisgah Baptist Church 1982-. **Military Serv:** USAF tsgt E-6 20 yrs; AFM 900-3; AF/SA W/4; AFM 900-3; AFGCM W/40LC 1973. **Home Addr:** PO Box 692, Jacksonville, AR 72076.

LEWIS, RODERICK ALBERT
Professional football player. **Personal:** Born Jun 9, 1971, Washington, DC; married Becky. **Educ:** Univ of Arizona, attended. **Career:** Houston Oilers, tight end, 1994-96; Tennessee Oilers, 1997-. **Business Addr:** Professional Football Player, Tennessee Oilers, c/o Baptist Sports Park, 7640 H 70-5, Nashville, TN 37221.

LEWIS, RONALD ALEXANDER
Professional football player. **Personal:** Born Mar 25, 1968, Jacksonville, FL. **Educ:** Florida State Univ, communications major, 1986-89. **Career:** San Francisco 49ers, wide receiver, 1990-92; Green Bay Packers, 1992-.

LEWIS, RONALD C.
City official (retired). **Personal:** Born Jun 15, 1934, Philadelphia, PA; married Leslie Annette Williams; children: Terri Anne, Anita Marie Lewis, Audrey Yvonne. **Career:** Philadelphia Fire Dept, fire fighter, fire lt, fire capt 1956-78, fire battalion chief 1974-78; Valiants Inc IABPFF Local, pres 1970-74; Intl Assoc of Black Prof Firefighters, reg vice pres 1974-77, affirm action officer 1978-82; City of Richmond, director Department of Fire and Emergency Services. **Orgs:** Bd of dir Offenders Aid & Restoration 1979-81, Muscular Dystrophy Assoc 1979-81, Alcohol & Drug Abuse Prevention & Treatment Serv 1984-90; life mem NAACP 1960-; mem IABPFF 1970-, Intl Assoc of Fire Chiefs 1978-, Bldg Officials & Code Admin 1979-; board of directors, Rich Chapter American Red Cross, 1989-. **Honors/Awds:** S Singleton Awd of Excellence Valiants IABPFF Philadelphia 1977; Outstanding Serv Awd NE Reg IABPFF 1978; Outstanding Achievement Awd NAACP Richmond Chap 1978; Outstanding Firefighter Phoenix Soc Hartford CT 1979; State of Virginia EEO Person of Year, 1991; Freedom Award, NAACP, 1994. **Business Addr:** Director, Department of Fire & Emergency Services, City of Richmond, 501 N 9th St, Room 131, Richmond, VA 23219.

LEWIS, RONALD STEPHEN
Substance abuse counselor, producer. **Personal:** Born Sep 3, 1950, Raleigh, NC; son of Beatrice H Lewis and Thomas J Lewis; married Veronica Nichols Lewis, Jul 29, 1978; children: N'Zinga Monique, Preston Stanford-Hashim. **Educ:** North Carolina Central University, BA, sociology, 1973. **Career:** Wake County Opportunities Inc, social services coordinator, 1973-78; Rhodes Furniture, collection officer, credit counselor, 1978-81; K-Mart, mgmt, 1981-82; Virginia CARES, pre/post release counselor, 1982-83; Small Business Broadcasting Service, studio supervisor, 1983-89; St Augustine's College, WAUG-TV, producer, host, 1990-; Drug Action Inc, Awareness Center, coordinator, substance abuse counselor, 1990-; Chapel Hill/ Carrboro School System, dir of fam resource ctr, 1994-; Shaw Univ (WSHA)/NC Central Univ (WNCU), radio programmer, 1990-. **Special Achievements:** Produced a four-part television series on substance abuse recovery, 1992; co-produced additional programming for local base origination such as: The Black Male, Are we an Endangered Species?. **Home Phone:** (919)571-8719.

LEWIS, SAMELLA
Art historian, artist, editor. **Personal:** Born Feb 27, 1924, New Orleans, LA; daughter of Rachel Taylor and Samuel Sanders; married Paul G Lewis, Dec 22, 1948; children: Alan, Claude. **Educ:** Hampton Inst, BS 1945; OH State Univ, MA 1948, PhD 1951; Postdoctoral studies, Tung Hai Univ, NYU, Univ of Southern CA. **Career:** Art Hist Scripps Coll, prof; LA Co Museum of Art; Coordinator of Educ, CA State Univ; Univ State of NY; FL A&M Univ; Morgan State Univ; Hampton Inst. **Orgs:** Mem, Expansion Arts Panel, NEA 1975-78; pres Contemp Crafts Inc; bd mem Museum African Amer Art; Art Educ Black Art Intl Quarterly Natl Conf of Artists; Coll Art Assn of Amer; Pres, Oxum Intl, 1988-; Dir/founder, Museum of African Amer Art, 1976-80. **Honors/Awds:** Published, Art African Amer, 1978; "Black Artist on Art," volumes I & II, 1969-71; Permanent collections, Baltimore Museum Art, VA museum fine arts, palm springs museum, high Mus Atlanta; Delta Sigma Theta Scholarship, Dillard Univ; Art Scholarship Hampton Inst; Amer Univ Fellowship OH State; Fulbright Fellowship Chinese Studies; NDEA Fellowship; NY Ford Found Grant; Honorary Doctorate, Chapman Coll, 1976; Fellowships, Fulbright Found, Ford Found; Published, "Art: African Amer", 1978. **Business Addr:** The Intl Review of African American Art, 3000 Biscayne Blvd, Suite 505, Miami, FL 33137.

LEWIS, SAMUEL, JR.
Mass transit administrator. **Personal:** Born Jul 19, 1953, Philadelphia, PA; son of Georgianna Johnson and Samuel Lewis Sr. **Educ:** Penn State Univ, BA 1976; Community Coll of Phila, AS Mgmt 1986; MS, Administration Info Resource Mgmt, 1998. **Career:** WPHL-TV Phila, broadcast dir 1976-77; Consolidated Rail Corp, operations mgr 1977-83; New Jersey Transit Rail Operations, revenue analyst 1983-85, sr operations planner 1985-. **Orgs:** Mem Conf of Minority Transportation Officials, Amer Public Transit Assn Minority Affairs Comm, Omega Psi Phi Frat, F&AM, The Brain Trust, Penn State Alumni Assn, Concerned Black Men of Philadelphia, Natl Assn of Watch and Clock Collectors, Black Music Assn; mem HBCU Transportation Consortium; transportation research bd Natl Acad of Sciences; mem Columbia Univ MBA Conf; Wharton School Black MBA Conf. **Honors/Awds:** Outstanding Young Men of Amer 1984, 1986, 1987; Honorary Doctorate of Humane Letters, Faith Grant College, 1995. **Home Addr:** 1643 Cobbs Creek Pkwy, Philadelphia, PA 19143. **Business Addr:** Sr Operations Planner, New Jersey Transit Rail Opers, 1 Penn Plz, E, Newark, NJ 07105.

LEWIS, SHERMAN
Professional football coach. **Personal:** Born Jun 29, 1942, Louisville, KY; married Toni; children: Kip, Eric. **Educ:** Michigan State Univ, M educ admin 1974. **Career:** MSU, assistant head coach/defensive coord 1969-82; San Francisco 49ers', running back coach, 1983-89; receiver coach, beginning 1989; Green Bay Packers, offensive coordinator, currently. **Honors/Awds:** Football News College Player of the Year 1963. **Business Addr:** Offensive Coordinator, Green Bay Packers, 1265 Lombardi Ave, Green Bay, WI 54304.

LEWIS, SHIRLEY A. R.
Educational administrator. **Personal:** Born in West Virginia; married Dr Ronald Lewis; children: Mendi. **Educ:** University of California at Berkeley, bachelor's degrees in Spanish and speech, master's degree in social work; Stanford University, doctorate, 1979; Ghana and Univ of London, certificate, African studies. **Career:** General Board of Higher Education and Ministry of the United Methodist Church, educational executive, 1986-; Paine College, president, 1994-. **Orgs:** Board of Directors: UNCF; Augusta United Way; GA Bank & Trust; National Association of Ind Colleges; Assoc of Governing Boards. **Special Achievements:** First woman president of Paine College. **Business Addr:** President, Paine College, 1235 15th St., Augusta, GA 30901, (706)821-8200.

LEWIS, STEPHEN CHRISTOPHER
Business executive. **Personal:** Born Aug 19, 1950, Chicago, IL; son of Elizabeth Stewart Lewis and Robert Lewis; married Stefanie Woolridge. **Educ:** Bradley Univ, BSIE 1972; Marquette Univ, MBA 1975. **Career:** Jos Schlitz Brewing Co, superintendent for production scheduling 1974-78; Ford Motor Co, Escort/Lynx plng analyst 1978-82, Taurus/Sable plng analyst 1982-83, small car import mgr 1983-86, Ford Motor Co, Dearborn, MI, advanced product mgr, 1988-91; Ford Motor Co. Associate Director New Market Development, currently; Success Guide, Cleveland, OH, regional dir, 1990-. **Orgs:** Omega Psi Phi, baselius 1971-72; NAACP, mem 1978-; Nat'l Technical Assoc, mem 1983-85; Nat'l Black MBA, detroit chapter pres 1984, nat'l scholarship chairperson 1984-, nat'l vice president 1985-; Assoc of MBA Executives; Detroit Economic Club, 1989-; Engineering Society of Detroit, 1989-. **Honors/Awds:** Omega Psi Phi, Omega Man of the Year 1971; YMCA of Greater New York, Black Achievers in Industry 1976; Natl Black MBA-Detroit Chapter, President's Award 1984; Natl Black MBA, Outstanding MBA of the Year, 1990.

LEWIS, STEVE EARL
Track and field athlete. **Personal:** Born May 16, 1969, Los Angeles, CA; son of Stella Lewis. **Educ:** UCLA, BA (with honors), history, 1992. **Career:** Track and field athlete, currently. **Orgs:** Santa Monica Track Club, 1987-93. **Honors/Awds:** Olympic Games, Gold Medal, 400m & 4x400m relay, 1988, Gold Medal, 4x400m relay, 1992, Silver Medal, 400m, 1992.

LEWIS, SYLVIA AUSTIN. See Obituaries section.

LEWIS, TERRY
Record producer, songwriter, record company executive. **Personal:** Born Nov 24, 1956, Omaha, NE; married Karyn White, Mar 31, 1991; children: Tremayne, Chloe, Ashley Nicole. **Career:** Producer, has produced hit songs for Cherelle, Alexander O'Neal, The SOS Band, The Time, Force MD's, Thelma Houston, Karyn White, Janet Jackson, Boyz II Men, numerous others; Flyte Tyme Productions, owner, 1982; Perspective Records, owner, 1991-. **Honors/Awds:** Grammy Award for Producer of the Year. **Business Addr:** Flyte Tyme Productions, Inc., 4100 W. 76th Street, Edina, MN 55435.

LEWIS, THEODORE RADFORD, JR.
Clergyman. **Personal:** Born Jul 23, 1946, Galveston, TX; son of Carrie Ann Eaton Lewis and Theodore Radford Lewis Sr; married Martha Fox, Nov 29, 1968; children: Geoffrey Bernard, Carrie Elizabeth. **Educ:** University of Houston, BA, 1970; Sam Houston State University Graduate School, 1971-74; University of Houston Continuing Education Center, certificate, 1977; Episcopal Theological Seminary of the Southwest, MDiv, 1982. **Career:** Federal Pre-Release Center, assistant counselor, 1970-71; Harris County Adult Probation Department, probation officer, 1971-75; US Probation & Parole Office, probation & parole officer, 1975-79; St James Episcopal Church, assistant rector, 1982-83; St Luke Episcopal Church, rector, 1983-91; Texas Southern University, Episcopal chaplain, 1983-91; Calvary Episcopal Church, rector, 1992-; Charleston Youth Leadership League, elder, 1997-. **Orgs:** NAACP, health committee, 1990-91; Union of Black Episcopalians, 1982; Mu Alpha Chapter, Omega Psi Phi Fraternity, chaplain, 1992; Nu Phi Chapter, Omega Psi Phi Fraternity, chaplain, dean of education, Keeper of Records and Seal, membership committee chair, 1987-91; Bd of Education Redirection, 1991-; Bd of Crisis Ministries, Inc, 1991-; Homeless Shelter of Crisis Ministries, chaplain, volunteer, 1997-; Charlestowne Academy, governing bd, 1997-. **Honors/Awds:** Trinity United Methodist Church, Minister of the Year, 1988; Nu Phi Chapter, Omega Psi Phi Fraternity, Omega Man of the Year, 1990; Mu Alpha Chapter, Omega Psi Phi Fraternity, Scroll of Honor, 1992; Assault on Illiteracy Program, Service Award, 1989. **Business Addr:** Rector, Calvary Episcopal Church, 106 Line St, Charleston, SC 29403-5305, (803)723-3878.

LEWIS, THERTHENIA WILLIAMS
Educator. **Personal:** Born Mar 1, 1947, Dayton, OH; daughter of Mattie Williams and Alexander Williams; married Dr Jerry J Lewis. **Educ:** Sinclair Comm Coll, A Liberal Arts, A Early Childhood Educ 1974; Univ of Dayton, BS 1975; Ohio State Univ, MS 1978; Atlanta Univ, MSW 1986; Univ of Pittsburgh, MPH, 1992. **Career:** Ohio State Univ, grad admin asst 1976-78; Wernle Residential Ctr, adolescent therapist 1978-81; Georgia State Univ, Coll of Arts & Sci, asst to the dir 1982-84; Bureau of Planning City of Atlanta, HUD fellow intern 1984-85; Univ of Pittsburgh, grad student asst 1986-87; Children's Hospital, Family Intervention Ctr, Pittsburgh, PA, 1988-92; Clark Atlanta Univ, School of Social Work, Kellogg Project, 1992-94, School of Social Work, asst prof, 1994-. **Orgs:** Adv comm mem Big Sisters/Big Brothers Adv Bd 1977-78; mem Amer Soc of Public Admin 1984-; mem Natl Assoc of Black Social Workers 1987, Amer Home Economics Assoc 1987, Black Child Develop Inst 1987; Council on Social Work Education, 1988; American Public Health Assn, 1988; American Assn of Univ Professors, 1994; American Assn of Mental Retardation, 1994. **Honors/Awds:** Outstanding Young Women of Amer 1978; HUD Fellowship Atlanta Univ 1984-86; Honor Soc Alpha Kappa Delta Intl Soc 1985; Maternal and Child Health Fellow, Grad School of Public Health, Univ of Pittsburgh, 1986-88; Child Abuse and Neglect Fellow, Univ of Pittsburgh Graduate School of Public Health, 1989; Council on Social Work Educa-tion Fellow, Univ of Pittsburgh, 1988-89. **Business Addr:** Asst Prof, Clark Atlanta Univ, School of Social Work, Dept of Health/Mental Health, JP Brawley St at Fair St, Atlanta, GA 30314.

LEWIS, THOMAS
Professional football player. **Personal:** Born Jan 10, 1972, Akron, OH. **Educ:** Indiana, attended. **Career:** New York Giants, wide receiver, 1994-. **Business Addr:** Professional Football Player, New York Giants, Giants Stadium, East Rutherford, NJ 07073, (201)935-8111.

LEWIS, THOMAS P.
Business executive, educator. **Personal:** Born Mar 17, 1936, Chicago, IL; married Almera P; children: Tracy, Todd. **Educ:** Kentucky State Coll, BS Business Admin 1959. **Career:** South Side Bank Chicago, pres & chief exec officer 1973-; Independence Bank of Chicago, sr vice pres 1972, vice pres 1970-72; Professional Opportunity Inc, pres 1969-70; Mgmt Opportunity Inc Northfield, pres 1968-69; Commonwealth Edison Co, market rsch & sales rep 1963-65; Chicago Housing Authority, 1961-63; Horner School Chicago, teacher 1959-61. **Orgs:** Chmn Commrcl Div Operation PUSH; mem Bd dir YMCA Hotel; Chicago Urban League; bSA; Chicago Forum; Chicago Assn of Commerce & industry. **Business Addr:** South Side Bank, 4659 S Cottage Grove Ave, Chicago, IL 60653.

LEWIS, TOM
Community service, executive director. **Personal:** Born Aug 7, 1939, Chadborn, NC; son of Martha & Gaston Lewis; married Lucille Lewis, Aug 22, 1970; children: Jason, Patrick, Tisha. **Educ:** American University, BS, 1975. **Career:** Metropolitan Police Dept, DC, police officer, 1965-86; Hope Village Comm Treatment Ctr, vocational counselor, 1986; Lutheran Social Svc, counselor, 1987-89; For Love of Children, coordinator, child & family svc, 1989-93; The Fishing School, founder, executive director, 1990-. **Orgs:** Leadership Washington, 1996-; Juvenile Justice Advisory Group, chair, 1988-97; Mid NE Collab, steering comm governance, 1996-97; Hands Across DC, 1996-; PTA, pres, chair safety comm, 1974-86; Fraternal Order of Police, chief steward, 1978-86; Lifers of Lorton, counselor, 1970. **Honors/Awds:** National Bapt Convention, Youth Sports Director Award, 1983; The Doll League Award, 1986; One and Only 9 Award, 1995; Institute for Public Service, Jefferson Award, 1995; Noble National Organization of Black Law Enf Executives, Public Service Award, 1997; Washingtonian, Washingtonian of the Year, 1997. **Special Achievements:** Wrote article in Channel 32 Magazine, 1994; Recorded 5 Gospel Albums, 1982; Philanthropic work has been highlighted on CBS This Morning, Hard Copy and several news channels. **Military Serv:** US Army, sp/4, 1963-65. **Home Addr:** 6110 7th Pl, NW, Washington, DC 20011, (202)723-1522.

LEWIS, VINCENT V.
Executive/consultant. **Personal:** Born Oct 1, 1938, Wilmington, DE; son of Matilda Janet Lewis and Vincent Lewis; married Babirette Babineaux (divorced 1974); children: Dawn C, Duane A. **Educ:** Upper Iowa University, Fayette, IA, BA, 1980, Loyola College, Baltimore, MD, MBA, 1983. **Career:** Wilmington Housing Authority, Wilmington, DE, vice president/ executive director, 1972-77; National Center for Community Dev, Washington, DC, 1978-79; HUD Headquarters, Washington, DC, housing management officer, 1979-85; Coopers & Lybrand, Washington, DC, manager, 1982-85; Vinelle Associates, Inc, Washington, DC, president, 1985-. **Orgs:** Member, American Society of Public Admin, member, American Management Association; member, Assn for MBA Executives, member, NAHRO. **Military Serv:** US Marine Corps, 1956-69. **Business Addr:** President, Vinelle Assocs Inc, 717 D St, NW, Suite 309, Washington, DC 20004.

LEWIS, VIOLA GAMBRILL
Educator. **Personal:** Born Feb 5, 1939, Baltimore, MD; divorced; children: Robin, Van Allen. **Educ:** Morgan State Coll, BS 1959; Loyola Coll, MA 1978. **Career:** Psychohormonal Unit Johns Hopkins School of Medicine, rsch asst 1960-62, asst med psychol 1962-74; instructor 1974-. **Business Addr:** Asst Prof Med Psych, Johns Hopkins Medical Inst, Baltimore, MD 21205.

LEWIS, VIRGINIA HILL
Process control specialist. **Personal:** Born Feb 13, 1948, Berria Co, GA; daughter of Mary Hill and H B Hill; married Robert Lewis; children: Michael, Roslyn. **Educ:** Albany State Coll GA, BS Chemistry 1970; UOP Stockton CA, MS 1972. **Career:** Grad Sch Univ of Pacific, lab asst 1972; Albany State Coll, advanced chemist; 3M Co, process control specialist, 1973-. **Orgs:** Summer training prog Argonne Natl Lab Argonne IL 1969; Sunday Sch Tchr Mt Olivet Bapt Ch St Paul MN 1973 & 1975-76; active in social affairs 3M & community; Step Program, 3M; Visiting Tech Women, 3M. **Honors/Awds:** Alpha Kappa Mu Honor Soc Albany State Coll GA 1967-70; Affiliate ACS 1968-70; "This Is Your Life" Awd & mem Delta Sigma Theta Sor 1969. **Business Addr:** Process Control Specialist, 3M Center, 236-GC, Industrial Chemical Products, St Paul, MN 55144.

LEWIS, VIVIAN M.
Physician. **Personal:** Born in Pensacola, FL; daughter of Dr Edward C Moon & Vivian L Crawley Moon (deceased); married Billie Lewis MD; children: Vivian V Sanford MD, William P, Beverly Gooden. **Educ:** Fisk Univ, BA 1952; Univ of OK Sch of Medicine, MD 1959; Hurley Hosp, rotating intern 1959-60, pediatric residency 1961-63. **Career:** Mott Childrens Health Ctr, pediatric staff 1963-69; Dept of Maternal & Infant Health Mott Childrens Health Ctr, chairperson 1967-69; Hurley Med Ctr & St Joseph Hosp, mem teaching staff; McLaren Hosp, courtesy staff; MI State Univ Dept of Human Medicine, asst prof clinical pediatrics; Univ of MI Medical Sch, preceptor for the interflex prog; Lewis Medical Svcs, pediatric practice 1970-. **Orgs:** Life mem Alpha Kappa Alpha Sor Inc; mem bd of dirs Girl Scouts of Amer; mem bd of dirs Flint Inst of Arts; mem Flint Women Business Owners' Council; mem MI State Med Soc; mem Amer Med Assn; mem Natl Med Assn; mem Amer Acad of Pediatrics; mem Genesee Valley March of Dimes Med Adv Comm; med advisor Flint Easter Seal Soc; bd mem Genesee Valley Chap Amer Lung Assn 1969-78; chairperson Genesee Co March of Dimes Campaign 1971; mem Flint Acad of Medicine; co-chair of the 1975 Flint United Negro College Fund Dr; adv comm Univ of MI-Flint; pres Flint Chap Links Inc 1983-; citizens adv comm Univ of MI-Flint; pres, Greater Flint Pediatric Assoc; pres, Prof Med Corp of Hurley Med Ctr; Genesee County Med Society, 1963-; Family Services Bd, 1990-; Whaley Children's Comm Bd, 1993-; Univ of MI Corp, advirosry bd, 1986-; MI Natl Bank, Flint, advisory bd, 1976-; bd treasurer, Hurley Foundation, 1993-; vp, Flint Inst of Arts Bd. **Honors/Awds:** Comm Serv Awd Flint Chap Negro Bus & Prof Women's Club 1973; Liberty Bell Awd Genesee Co Bar Assn 1975; Pan Hellenic Woman of the Yr 1978; Woman of the Yr Zeta Beta Omega Chap Alpha Kappa Alpha Sor Inc 1978; Nana Mills Award, YWCA, 1985; Outstanding Citizen Award, Gamma Delta Boule, Sigma Pi Phi Fraternity, 1985; Behold the Woman Award, Top Ladies of Distinction, 1987; Urban Coalition Service Award, 1989; Recognized as an Outstanding African American Woman Physician in pulication, Alpha Kappa Alpha Sorority, Heritage Series, 1993; Paul Harris Award, Rotary Club of Flint, 1994.

LEWIS, W. ARTHUR
Clergyman, housing administrator. **Personal:** Born Dec 13, 1930, Princeton, NJ; son of Blanche E Taylor Chase and George Peter Lewis Sr; married Rose Marie Dais, Jun 20, 1970; children: Adrienne Richardson, Andrea Lewis. **Educ:** Trenton Jr Coll, AA 1957; Rider Coll, BS 1959, MA 1977; Harvard Univ John F Kennedy School of Government, Cert 1982; Lutheran Theol Sem, MAR 1985; Luthern School of Theology, DMin, 1992. **Career:** United Progress Inc, personnel dir 1966-68; OIL Intl, prog advisor 1968-69; Economic & Manpower Corp, project mgr 1969-71; NJ Dept of Comm Affairs, div dir & asst commiss 1972-82; Philadelphia OIC, exec dir 1982-85; Lutheran Children & Family Svcs, clergy/administrator 1985-; Evangelical Lutheran Church in America 1988; NJ Dept of Comm Affairs, housing administrator, 1990-; Calvary Lutheran Church, Philadelphia, PA, pastor, 1990-. **Orgs:** Consult Natl Urban Coalition 1974; chmn Natl State Econ Oppty Office Dir Assn, 1976-77; bd of trustee Glassboro State Coll 1979-; vice pres NJ Chap of ASPA, 1980-82; bd mem Evesham Twp School Dist 1981-; mem Alpha Phi Alpha 1983-; consult NJ Synod Lutheran Church in Amer 1985; board of trustees, New Jersey Prison Complex, 1991-. **Honors/Awds:** Man of the Year Somerset Cty Comm Action 1976; Man of the Year Burlington Cty NAACP 1977; Philadelphia Liberty Bell City of Philadelphia 1984. **Military Serv:** USAF Airman 2nd class 1951-54; Natl Defense Medal, Good Conduct Medal, European Defense Medal. **Home Addr:** 41 Country Club Lane, Marlton, NJ 08053.

LEWIS, W. HOWARD
Automobile company executive. **Career:** Chrysler Corp, program mgr, viper coupe and prowler, currently.

LEWIS, WENDELL J.
Government administrator. **Personal:** Born Mar 22, 1949, Topeka, KS; son of Bonnie Lewis and Bryon Lewis. **Educ:** KS State Teachers Coll, BS Ed 1972, MS 1973. **Career:** Disability Determination Servcs, disability examiner I 1974-80, disability examiner II 1980-85, quality assurance speciality 1985-88; unit manager 1989-91, section administrator, 1991-. **Orgs:** Exec sec Great Plan Wheelchair Athletic Conf 1974-76; advisory bd Vocational Rehabilitation 1978-79, Shawnee County Affirmative Action Program 1979-80, KS Council on Devel Disabilities 1982-; chairperson, KS Council on Developmental Disabilities, 1991; chairman, Advisory Board, Accessible Transportaion, 1992; bd of dirs, NADDC, 1993-94, vp, 1994-. **Honors/Awds:** Inductee Natl Student Reg 1970-72; 2nd Place 100 yard dash Rocky Mountain Wheelchair Games 1975; 1st Place table tennis Rocky Mountain Wheelchair Games 1975; Delegate White House Conf Handicapped 1977; Leadership Award KS Advocacy & Protective Serv 1980; John Peter Loux Award, Cerebral Palsy Research Foundation, 1993; Muscular Dystrophy Assn, Personal Achievement Award, KS, 1994. **Home Addr:** 1619 SW 28th Terrace, Topeka, KS 66611. **Business Addr:** Section Administrator, Disability Determination Serv, D50B, 915 Harrision St, 10th Fl, Topeka, KS 66612.

LEWIS, WENDY
Human resources manager. **Career:** Chicago Cubs, director of human resources, 1989-95; Major League Baseball, executive director of human resources, 1995-.

LEWIS, WILLARD C. (CHUCK)
Banker. **Personal:** Born Apr 9, 1961, LaGrange, GA; son of Willard & Dora Lewis; married Patricia, Dec 31, 1986; children: Charles, Camille. **Educ:** Morehouse College, BA, banking & fin, 1983. **Career:** Citizens Trust Bank, controller, 1983-91; First Southern Bank, EVP & COO, 1991-. **Orgs:** YMCA, chairman of the bd, 1992-94; Kennesaw State College, advisory bd, 1993-; AUBA, 1995; Dekalb Medical Center Foundation Bd, 1997-; Lithonia Chamber of Commerce, economic development bd, 1996-. **Honors/Awds:** Georgia Trend Magazine, Top 40 Executives Under 40 in Georgia. **Business Addr:** Executive Vice Pres/COO, First Southern Bank, 2727 Panola Road, Lithonia, GA 30058, (404)593-6367.

LEWIS, WILLIAM A., JR.
Attorney. **Personal:** Born Aug 15, 1946, Philadelphia, PA; son of Constance Merritt Lewis and William A Lewis; married Deborah Cover; children: Ryan. **Educ:** Amer Univ, 1967-68; Susquehanna Univ, BA 1968; Boston Univ Law School, JD 1972. **Career:** City of Philadelphia PA, asst dist attorney 1972-75; US Civil Rights Commission, attorney 1975-80, dir cong lia div 1980-85, dir congressional & community relations div 1985-86, acting asst staff dir for congressional & public affairs 1987, counsel senate judiciary committee 1987-; Senate Judiciary Committee, Washington, DC, counsel, 1987-89; Equal Employment Opportunity Comm, Washington, DC, supervisory atty, 1989-92; Office of Admin and Mgt, US Dept of Energy, exec asst to dir, 1992-94; Office of Science Education Programs, director, currently. **Orgs:** Pres, Blacks in Govt US Civil Rights Comm 1977-80; exec comm Susquehanna Univ Alumni Assoc 1980-83, 2nd vice pres 1987; mem PA Bar Assoc 1972-, Eastern Dist Court PA 1974-; del Legal Rights & Justice Task Force White House Conf on Youth Estes Park Co 1970; pres Susquehanna Univ Alumni Assoc 1988-91; board of directors, Susquehanna Univ, 1988-. **Honors/Awds:** Legal Defense Fund Scholarship NAACP 1971-72; publ "Black Lawyer in Private Practice" Harvard Law School Bulletin 1971. **Military Serv:** AUSR sgt e-5 1968-75. **Business Addr:** Office of Science Education Programs (ET-30), US Dept of Energy, Washington, DC 20585.

LEWIS, WILLIAM M., JR.
Acquistions consultant. **Educ:** Harvard University, bachelor's degree (cum laude), economics, 1978; Harvard Business School, until 1982. **Career:** Morgan Stanley Group Inc, all positions in the Mergers and Acquisitions Dept, New York City, analyst, 1978, 1982-88, Midwest M&A Dept, Chicago, head, 1988, managing director, 1989-91, New York City, managing director, 1992-. **Orgs:** Morgan Stanley Group Inc, task force member, examining recruiting techniques for better retaining African American talent. **Business Addr:** Managing Director, Mergers & Acquisitions Dept, Morgan Stanley Group Inc, 1251 Avenue of the Americas, 29th Fl, New York, NY 10020, (212)703-4000.

LEWIS, WILLIAM SYLVESTER
Editor. **Personal:** Born Aug 31, 1952, Manhattan, NY. **Educ:** Columbia Univ Coll, BA Sociology 1974; Columbia Graduate School of Journalism, MS Journalism 1975-76. **Career:** Black Sports Magazine, contributing editor 1977-78; Encore Magazine, sports ed 1979-80; Good Living Magazine, sr editor 1979-80; Black Agenda Reports, producer, writer 1979-81; Touro Coll SGS, adjunct prof English. **Orgs:** Consulting Comm School Bd 9, 1978-; consulting coordinator, Bronx Area Policy Bd, 4 1982-87; sec, Legacy Intl Inc 1982-; chairperson Morrisania Ed Council Jrnl Comm 1978-; mem bd of dir, Columbia Coll Class of 1974, 1979-; founding mem, Columbia Univ Club of NY 1980-; mem Amer Athletic Union Distance Running Div 1978-; co-chairperson Morrisania Educ Council Journal Comm 1978-. **Honors/Awds:** Pulitzer Scholarship, Columbia Univ 1970; Bennett Certificate Award Writing Columbia Univ 1974; CBS Fellowship Columbia Univ Graduate School of Journalism 1976; Presidential Citation for Excellence Dist 9 Comm School Bd 1983, 1984; Loyal & Outstanding Serv Award Morrisania Educ Council, Bronx NY 1978. **Home Addr:** 348 West 123rd St, New York, NY 10027. **Business Addr:** Adjunct Professor of English, Touro College SGS, 1178 Washington Avenue, Bronx, NY 10456.

LEWIS, WOODROW
Government official. **Personal:** Born in Brooklyn, NY; married Ruth; children: 2 Sons. **Educ:** Brooklyn Coll, BA; Brooklyn Law Sch, LLD. **Career:** Bklyn, state assmblymn 1972-; City NY Dept Transp, admin atty; Pvt Prac. **Orgs:** Chmn Election Law Com; mem Brown Meml Bapt; Bedford Sty Lawyers Assn. **Business Addr:** 1293 Dean St, Brooklyn, NY 11216.

LEWIS-KEMP, JACQUELINE
Company executive. **Personal:** daugHter of James O. Lewis (deceased). **Career:** Lewis Metal Stamping & Manufacturing Co, prod control mgr, 1985-93, pres/CEO, 1993-. **Honors/Awds:** Enterprise magazine, Rising Star award, 1996. **Business Addr:** President, Lewis Metal Stamping & Manufacturing Co., 33 Midland Ave., Highland Park, MI 48203, (313)867-7350.

LEWIS-LANGSTON, DEBORAH
Judge. **Career:** 36th District Court, judge, currently. **Business Addr:** Judge, 36th District Court, 421 Madison Ave, Detroit, MI 48226.

LEWTER, ANDY C., SR.
Clergyman. **Personal:** Born Oct 6, 1929, Sebring, FL; son of Mary Lee Lewter and Rufus Cleveland Lewter Sr (deceased); married Ruth Fuller; children: Rita Olivia Davis, Cleo Yvette, Veda Ann Pennyman, Andy C Jr, Rosalyn Aaron, Tonya Marie. **Educ:** Morris Brown Coll, BA 1954; Atlanta U, Addl Stud; Biblical Seminary NY; James Teamer's School of Religion, BD 1964; NY Theol Seminary, MDiv 1985. **Career:** St John Bapt Ch Ft Myers, asst minister 1951-52; Morris Brown Coll, asst to coll pastor 1953-54; Zion Grove Baptist Church Atlanta, asst minister 1953-54; Stitt Jr HS, teacher 1954-60; First Bapt Ch Rockaway, asst minister 1954-59; AC Lewter Interdenom Sch of Religion, founder pres 1975; Pilgrim State Psychiatric Hosp, chaplain; Suffolk Co Office for the Aging, adv bd; Hollywood Bapt Church of Christ Amityville, pastor 1959-. **Orgs:** Mem past vice pres NAACP; past chmn mem Interfaith Hlth Assn; mem Bd Gov Interfaith Hosp of Queens; pres Interdenominational Ministerial Fellowship of Amityville; trustee of Long Island Health & Hosp Planning Council; vice pres Lewter-Scott Travel Assn; supr Ushers Nat Bapt Conv USA; adv bd Suffolk Co Office for the Aging; mem Amityville Taxpayers Assn; vice moderator, Eastern Baptist Assn, 1990-; pres, Noth Amityville Ministerial Alliance and Vicinity, 1989-. **Honors/Awds:** Hon DD Friendship Coll 1962; Hon LLD T School of Religion 1975. **Business Addr:** Pastor, Hollywood Baptist Church of Christ, 3504 Great Neck Road, Amityville, NY 11701.

LEWTER, ANDY C., JR.
Television station executive, cleric. **Personal:** Born May 11, 1954, Brooklyn, NY; son of Ruth Fuller Lewter and Andy C Lewter Sr; children: Stephine Diane, Andy C III. **Educ:** Oberlin College, BA, 1976; Harvard University, MDiv, 1979; Oxford University, certificate, 1980. **Career:** Union Church, drama director, 1976-78; Boston City Public Schools, teacher, 1977-78; Star of Bethlehem Baptist Church, pastor, 1978-85; New York Theological Seminary, prof, 1982-85; Mercy College, adjunct prof, 1983-85; Oakley Baptist Church, pastor, 1985-; WO8BV TV-8, chief executive officer, 1991-. **Orgs:** Central Ohio Operation PUSH, president, 1988-90; New Life Fellowship of Churches, executive director, 1990-; Oakley Christian Academy, principal, 1986-88; Westchester Council for Church & Social Action, executive director, 1983-85; Central Hudson Baptist Association, financial secretary, 1983-85; Empire Baptist State Convention, director of communications, 1982-85; Harambee, president, 1976-78; Abusua, president, 1974-76. **Honors/Awds:** Jaycees, Outstanding Young Men of America, 1978; Fund for Theological Education, Benjamin E Mays Award, 1977; Central Hudson, Award of Distinction, 1985. **Special Achievements:** Organizer, Westchester County Activist Group, 1983; founder, Christian Academy, 1986; organizer, major gospel concerts in Columbus, 1988; published only Black church newspaper, 1989; spearheaded the acquistion of first Black tv station in Ohio, 1991. **Business Phone:** (614)351-1636.

LIAUTAUD, JAMES
Computer company executive. **Career:** Capsonic Group Inc, chief executive officer, currently. **Special Achievements:** Company is ranked #31 on Black Enterprise's list of top 100 companies, 1994. **Business Addr:** CEO, Capsonic Group Inc., 460 S. Second St., Elgin, IL 60123, (708)888-7300.

LIDE, WILLIAM ERNEST
Educational administrator. **Personal:** Born Feb 14, 1950, Darlington, SC; married Cheryl Anita Leverett-Lide, Dec 22, 1980; children: Desiree Danielle, Amber Nicole, Lindsey Koren, Kristin Regina. **Educ:** Johnson C Smith Univ, Charlotte, NC, BS, 1973; The Univ of North Carolina, Charlotte, NC, MEd, 1976; The Ohio State University, Columbus, OH, PhD, 1980. **Career:** Johnson C Smith Univ, Charlotte, NC, physical education, 1975-78, 1980-84; Winston-Salem State Univ, Winston-Salem, NC, chair, physical education, 1984-87; Salisbury State Univ, Salisbury, Md, director of athletics/chair of physical education and recreation, 1987-. **Orgs:** National secretary, The Natl Roundtable for Parks, Conservation & Recreation, 1982-; member, board of dirs, NCAA Council, 1989-; chair, NCAA Council Postgraduate Scholarship Committee, NACDA Postgraduate Scholarship Committee, 1993-; Dist II, currently; president, Easterm State Athletic Concerence, 1989; The Roundtable Association, president elect, 1994; mem, Boule, 1989, Division III Steering Committee, NCAA, 1990. **Honors/Awds:** Award of Achievement, Amer Business Women's Assn, 1980; Awards of Tenure, Johnson C Smith Univ, 1977; Awards of Tenure, Salisbury State University, 1990; All Pro-Countdown Team, Calgary Stampeders (CFL), 1974. **Business Addr:** Director of Athletics, Physical Educ, Recreation & Athletics, Salisbury State University, 1101 Camden Ave, Salisbury, MD 21801.

LIGHTFOOT, JEAN DREW
Government official, association executive (retired). **Personal:** Born in Hartford, CT. **Educ:** Howard Univ, BA 1947; Univ of

MI, MPA 1950. **Career:** Coca Cola WA, publ relations 1954-55, asst dir 1959-61; Comm Rel Conf So CA LA, dir 1961-62; Dept of State, fgn serv reserve ofcr 1962-69; Consumer Protection & Environ Health Serv HEW, chief consumer spec sect 1969-70, asst dir publ affairs 1970-71; EPA intl affairs ofcr 1971, spec asst Training &Upward Mobility, dep dir eeo 1978-. **Orgs:** Women's aux bd Northwest Settlement House; former bd mem West Coast Reg Natl Negro Coll Fund, NAACP, Urban Laeague, Fred Douglass Mus African Art, Legal Def Fund, Intl Club Wash Inc; Indian Spring Country Club; Women's Intl Religious Fellowship, Univ of MI Club, Common Cause, Publ Citizen, Circle-Lets Inc, Neighbors Inc, Carroll Valley Cit Assoc, Crestwood Cit Assoc. **Honors/Awds:** NAACP Comm Serv Awd 1975; Natl Council Negro Women Mary McLeod Bethune Awd 1962; Comm Relations Conf So CA Comm Serv Awd 1962; Natl Assoc IntergroupRelations Fellowship 1958; Daughters of the Amer Revolution Good Citizenship Awd 1940; Hartford Publ HS Ideal Girl Awd 1940. **Home Addr:** 2000 Trumbull Terr NW, Washington, DC 20011.

LIGHTFOOT, JEAN HARVEY
Educator. **Personal:** Born Nov 29, 1935, Chicago, IL; divorced; children: Jaronda. **Educ:** Fisk Univ, BA 1957; Univ of Chgo, MA 1969; Northwestern Univ Evanston IL, PhD 1974. **Career:** Chicago Public Schools, English teacher 1957-69; Kennedy King Campus Chicago City Coll, prof English 1969-; Citizens Comm on Public Educ, exec dir 1975-76; Comm on Urban Affair Spec Projects AME Church, exec dir 1978-80; The Neighborhood Inst, educ coordinator 1979-. **Orgs:** Counselor Hillcrest Ctr for Children NY 1958-61; asst prof ed Northeastern Univ Chicago 1974-76; consult Prescription Learning Inc 1977-; featured soloist Park Manor Cong Church 1958-, John W Work Chorale 1959-; staff dir, convener The S Shore Schools Alliance 1979-80. **Honors/Awds:** Outstanding Young Women of Amer 1968; Ford Fellowship Univ of Chicago 1968-69; TTT Fellowship Northwestern Univ 1972-73. **Business Addr:** Education Coordinator, The Neighborhood Inst, 1950 E 71st St, Chicago, IL 60649.

LIGHTFOOT, SARA LAWRENCE
Educator. **Career:** Harvard Graduate School of Education, professor, currently. **Honors/Awds:** Author: I've Known Rivers: Lives of Loss and Liberation, 1994; Balm in Gilead: Journey of a Healer, 1988; The Good High School: Portraits of Character and Culture; ''Portraits of Exemplary Secondary Schools: Highland Park,'' Daedalus, Fall 1981, p. 59; ''Portraits of Exemplary Secondary Schools: George Washington Carver Comprehensive High School,'' Daedalus, Fall 1981, p. 17; ''Portraits of Exemplary Secondary Schools: St Paul's School,'' Daedalus, Fall 1981, p. 97. **Business Addr:** Professor, Harvard Graduate School of Education, Dept of Educational Administration, Harvard University, Cambridge, MA 02138.

LIGHTFOOT, WILLIAM P.
Physician. **Personal:** Born Sep 12, 1920, Pittsburgh, PA; married Edith Wingate; children: William, Philip. **Educ:** Lincoln Univ, AB 1943; Howard Univ Med Coll, MD 1946. **Career:** John F Kennedy Memorial Hospital, Philadelphia, attending surgeon; Temple Univ Hospital & Med School Faculty, prof of surgery. **Orgs:** Mem, Amer Coll of Surgeons, Philadelphia Acad of Surgery, Philadelphia Coll of Physicians; mem, AMA, Natl Med Assn, Philadelphia Co Med Soc; mem, Amer Soc of Abdominal Surgeons. **Honors/Awds:** Amer Bd of Surgey; Amer Bd of Utilization Review and Quality Assurance. **Military Serv:** AUS cpat 1953-55. **Business Addr:** Prof of Surgery, Temple Univ, 3401 N Broad St, Philadelphia, PA 19140.

LIGHTFOOTE, WILLIAM EDWARD, II
Physician, neurologist. **Personal:** Born Oct 6, 1942, Tuskegee, AL; son of Mary Johson Lightfoote and William Edward Lightfoote; married Marilyn Frances Madry; children: Lynne Jan-Maria. **Educ:** Grinnell Coll, AB 1963; Howard Univ, MD 1967. **Career:** Natl Inst of Health, rsch officer 1975-77; FDA Neurologist & Analgesic Drugs, group leader 1977-79; self-employed neurologist, 1979-. **Orgs:** Mem, Alpha Phi Alpha Frat 1965-, Medical Soc of District of Columbia 1969-, Amer Acad of Neurology 1972-, Assoc for Research in Nervous and Mental Diseases 1976-, Foundation for Advanced Educ in the Sciences 1977-; medical consultant to law firms in metro DC area 1979-; mem, Natl Medical Assoc 1980-, Medical-Chirurgical Soc of the District of Columbia 1980-, Amer Medical Assoc 1981-, Dist of Columbia Assoc for Retarded Citizens Inc 1981-, Amer Soc of Internal Medicine 1982-; assoc mem Eastern Assoc of Electroencephalographers Inc 1983-; mem Amer Soc of Law and Medicine 1983-, Southern medical Assoc 1983-, New York Acad of Sciences 1985-; mem bd of trustees of Office Serv corp 1985-. **Honors/Awds:** Mem, Alpha Omega Alpha Honor Medical Soc; publ 15 bibliographies, 14 abstracts/presentations; fellow, Amer Acad of Neurology, 1988-; American College of Physicians, fellow, 1991-. **Military Serv:** USAF major 2 yrs; USPHS, LCM, 2 yrs. **Home Addr:** 827 Swinks Mill Rd, Mc Lean, VA 22102. **Business Addr:** 1328 Southern Ave SE, Washington, DC 20032.

LIGHTNER, CLARENCE E.
Mortician. **Personal:** Born Aug 15, 1921, Raleigh, NC; married Marguerite Massey; children: Bruce, Lawrence, Debra, Claire. **Educ:** Echols Coll, Mortuary Sci; NC Central U, Grad 1975. **Career:** Lightner Funeral Home & Ins Agency, pres gen mgr; City of Raleigh, city council, 1967-75, mayor pro-tem, 1971-73, mayor, 1973-75. **Orgs:** Past pres Nat Funeral Dirs & Morticians Assn; past mem US Conf Mayors' Bicentennial Com; bd of dirs Nat League Cities; steering com Public SafetyNat League Cities; exec bd Occoneechee Council Boy Scouts Am; natl life mem NAACP; chmn NC Black Ldrsp Dem Caucus; mem N Raleigh Exchange Club; memOmega Psi Phi Frat; Shriners; Nat Business League; Masonic, Elk Lodges; board of trustees, NC State University Raleigh NC, 1984-, St. Agustine College Raleigh NC, 1974-; vice chairman NC Democratic Party, 1984-; Ruling Elder Davie St Presbyterian Church, 12 yrs service. **Honors/Awds:** Raleigh C of C Hon; man of yr award Mid-Atlantic Region Alpha Kappa Alpha Sor 1975; NC Central University, LLD, 1973; Shaw University, LLD, 1972. **Military Serv:** AUS, 1943-44. **Business Addr:** 312 Martin Luther King Blvd, Raleigh, NC 27601.

LIGON, CLAUDE M.
State commissioner. **Personal:** Born Jun 28, 1935, Baltimore, MD; married Doris Hillian; children: Claude M Jr, Carole Ann. **Educ:** Morgan State Univ, BS Math 1957; Univ of IL, BS Civil Engrg 1965; Univ of MD, MS Civil Engrg 1971, PhD Civil Engrg 1984. **Career:** US Army Corps of Engrs, Lt Col 1957-79; AMAF Industries Inc, mgr civil engrg and transp sys div 1979-85; MD Pub Serv Comm, commissioner 1985-. **Orgs:** Regist prof engr VA/MD/DC; fellow Inst of Transportation Engrs Washington, DC Sect (pres 1982); mem Amer Soc of Civil Engrs; indiv assoc Transportation Research Bd; mem NAACP, Baltimore Urban League, Kappa Alpha Psi Frat, Morgan State Univ Alumni Assn, Univ of IL Alumni Assn; Univ of MD Alumni Assoc; bd dir Howard Arts United; mem Howard Co Arts Grants Comm 1983-85; mem Columbia, MD Resident's Transportation Comm; mem Howard Co Public Transportation Bd 1976-79; mem Baltimore City Public Schools Industrial Arts Adv Comm 1983-85; co-founder (1980)/mem MD Museum of African Art; mem bd of dir Columbia Festival Inc. **Honors/Awds:** Chi Epsilon Natl Civil Engrg Hon Frat; Publications include, Arrow Panel Placement at Urban and Freeway Work Zones slide tape presentation Fed Highway Adm 1985; Development of the Highway Safety Improvement Decision Model doctoral dissertation 1984; Pedestrian Accommodation in Highway Work Zones report 1982; ''Pedestrian and Bicycle Issues and Answers'' FHWA 1981. **Military Serv:** RA Corps of Engineers Lt Col served 23 years. **Business Addr:** Commissioner, Maryland Public Serv Commission, 6 St Paul St, Baltimore, MD 21202.

LIGON, DORIS HILLIAN
Museum executive. **Personal:** Born Apr 28, 1936, Baltimore, MD; married Dr Claude M Ligon; children: Claude M Jr, Carole Ann. **Educ:** Morgan State Univ, BA Sociology (Summa Cum Laude) 1978, MA Art Hist/Museology 1979; Howard Univ, PhD courses African Hist. **Career:** Natl Museum of African Art Smithsonian Inst, docent (tour guide) 1976-88; Morgan State Univ, art gallery rsch asst 1978-79; Howard Cty MD School Syst, consultant African art & culture 1980-; MD Museum of African Art, founder/exec dir 1980-. **Orgs:** Mem Assn Black Women Historians, African-American Museums Assn; charter mem Eubie Blake Cultural Center 1984; charter mem Columbia (MD) Chap Pierians Inc 1983; mem Morgan State Univ Alumni; mem NAACP; mem Urban League; mem Arts Council of the African Studies Assn. **Honors/Awds:** Goldseeker Fellowship for Graduate Studies MSU 1978-79; Phi Alpha Theta (Natl History Hon Soc); Alpha Kappa Mu; Nirmaj K Sinha Award for highest honors in Sociology 1978. **Business Addr:** Director/Founder, African Art Museum of Maryland, 5430 Vantage Point Rd, Columbia, MD 21044, (301)596-0051.

LILLARD, KWAME LEO (LEO LILLARD, II)
Industrial engineer, social activist. **Personal:** Born Sep 16, 1939, Tampa, FL; son of Louise Taylor (deceased) and Leo Lillard, I (deceased); married Evelyn Downing Lillard, Mar 11, 1970; children: Leo III, Jessica, Joshua, Nyleve, Troy-Chiffonda. **Educ:** Tennessee State University, Nashville, TN, BS, Mechanical Engineering, 1961; City College, New York, NY, MS, Mechanical Engineering, 1965; Hunter College, New York, NY, MS, Urban Planning, 1971. **Career:** Malcolm X University, Greensboro, NC, engineering instructor, 1972; Weyerhaeuser, Plymouth, NC, industrial engineer, 1972-76; Nashville City Planning Dept, Nashville, TN, senior planner, 1976-80; Textron, Nashville, TN, industrial engineer, 1981-91; C21 Architects/Engineers, planning analyst TN Department Environment & Conservation, environmental specialist, currently. **Orgs:** President, African American Cultural Alliance, 1984-; co-founder, Men of Distinction Youth Development, 1989-; program coordinator, Nashville Peace Coalition, 1990-; executive board, Nashville NAACP Chapter, currently; executive board, Council of Community Service, currently. **Honors/Awds:** Martin Luther King Award, Nashville Martin Luther King Celebration, 1989; Black Expo Education Innovator, Black Expo Inc, 1980. **Home Addr:** 2814 Buena Vista, Nashville, TN 37218.

LILLARD, LEO, II. **See LILLARD, KWAME LEO.**

LILLIE, VERNELL A.
Educator. **Personal:** Born May 11, 1931, Hempstead, TX; married Richard L Lillie Jr (deceased); children: Charisse Lillie McGill, Hisani Lillie Blanton. **Educ:** Dillard Univ, BA (cum laude) 1952; Carnegie-Mellon Univ, MA 1970, DA 1972. **Career:** Julius C Hester House, group work spec 1952-56; Houston Indep School Dist Phillis Wheatley HS, chmn & teacher speech, drama & debate 1956-59; TX So Univ Project Upward Bound, English coord, dir drama workshop 1965-69; Carnegie-Mellon Univ Proj Upward Bound, dir student affairs 1969-71; Kuntu Repertory Theatre, founder/dir, 1974-; Univ of Pittsburgh, chair, dept of Africana Studies, 1997-, assoc prof Black studies, currently. **Orgs:** Mem Amer Soc Group Psychotherapy & Psychodrama, Natl & PA Counc Teachers of Engl, Speech Assoc of Amer, NADSA, ATHE, Afro-Amer Educators; bd dir Julius C Hester House Houston 1965-69, Earnest T Williams Meml Ctr, Pittsburgh Ctr Alterntive Ed 1972-78; Women in Urban Crisis 1973-80; coord curriculum & staff devel mem Hope Devel Houston; dir, founder The Hester House Exper Theatre, The Black Theatre, Scenario Theatre Concept, The Kuntu Repertory Theatre; Black Theatre Network. **Honors/Awds:** Awd for Outstanding Contrib to Arts Delta Sigma Theta 1969; Awd for Ed Achievements Carnegie-Mellon Univ Proj Upward Bound 1972; Pittsburgh Outstanding Ed Black Cath Ministeries 1973; Spec Achievements include curriculum & staff devel models for various schools & comms; Univ of Pittsburgh, Distinguish Teacher Awd 1986; Arts and Letter Awd, Alpha Kappa Alpha Sorority, 1987; Women of Color Caucus, 1985; Performances, Fringe Festival, Edinburgh Univ, Scotland, 1989, 1994; Dillard Vernell Andrew Watson Lillie Scholarship, Smith College. **Business Addr:** Associate Professor, Univ of Pittsburgh, Dept of Africana Studies, 230 S Bouquet St, Pittsburgh, PA 15260.

LIMA, GEORGE SILVA
Government official. **Personal:** Born Apr 4, 1919, Fall River, MA; married Selma Elizabeth Boone; children: Anna Maria Lima Bowling, George II, Robert. **Educ:** Brown Univ, AB 1948; Harvard Business Sch, Trade Union Labor Relations Mgmt 1958. **Career:** Amer Federation of State County & Municipal Employees New England, regional dir 1950-64; US Govt Action Dept of Vista, Older Amer Volunteer Progs, dir 1979-84; State of Rhode Island, state rep; 1986-87. **Orgs:** Vice chairman East Providence Comm Develop Corp 1978-82; natl bd mem Natl Blacks in Govt 1980-84; chmn Steering Comm New England Gerontology 1984-85;bd mem RI AFL-CIO; chmn East Providence Coalition for Human Rights; mem RI State Employees Retirement Commn; mem Amer Assoc of Retired Persons; mem Intl Sr Citizens Org; chmn of steering comm of SENE Gerontology Ctr at Brown Univ; mem RI Black Caucus of State Legislators; mem Comm to Study State of RI Affirmative Action; vchmn RI Commission of Needs of Cape Verdean Community; mem House Labor Comm; Ex Director, RI Black Caucus of State Legislators. **Honors/Awds:** NAACP Membership Enrollment Awd 1961; Delta Sigma Theta Comm Serv Awd 1978; Achievement Awd 274 Business Club 1986; Omega Man of the Year Sigma Nu Chap 1987; NAACP, Joseph Lecourt Medal, Distinguished Svc & Achievement, 1989; National Black Caucus of State Legislators, Nation Builder Award, 1991. **Military Serv:** AUS Air Corps 1st lt 4 1/2 yrs; Tuskegee Army Air Base 477th Bom B Gp.

LINCOLN, ABBEY. **See MOSEKA, AMINATA.**

LINCOLN, C. ERIC
Educator. **Personal:** Born Jun 23, 1924, Athens, AL; son of Mattie Lincoln and Less Lincoln; married Lucy Cook; children: Cecil, Joyce Godfrey, Hilary, Less II. **Educ:** LeMoyne Coll, AB 1947; Fisk Univ, AM 1954; Univ of Chicago, BD 1956; Boston U, MEd, PhD 1960; Carleton Coll, LLD 1968; St Michael's Coll, LHD 1970. **Career:** Duke Univ, prof of religion 1976-; Fisk Univ, prof & chmn 1973-76; Union Theol Sem, prof 1967-73; Portland State Univ, prof 1965-67; Clark Coll, prof 1954-65; Dartmouth Coll, lectr 1962-63; Vassar Coll, adj prof 1969-70; State Univ of NY, visiting prof 1970-72; Queens Coll, visiting prof 1972; Vanderbilt Univ, adj prof 1973-76; Change Magazine, consultant; Rev of Religious Research Soc, assoc editor for scientific study of religion. **Orgs:** Amer Sociol Assn; Authors League of Amer; founding pres, emeritus, Black Acad of Arts & Letters; NY Acad of Arts & Scis; Soc for Study of Black Religion; American Academy of Arts asnd Sciences; 32 Degree Mason; life member, NAACP; life member, Kappa Alpha Psi; Boule, Sigma Pi Phi; Fellowship of Southern Writers. **Honors/Awds:** Fellow Amer Acad of Arts & Sciences; Lilly Ednowment Grant; author of The Black Church Since Frazier 1974, The Black Experience in Religion 1974, A Profile of Martin Luther King Jr 1969, The Black Americans 1969, Is Anybody Listening? 1968, Sounds of the Struggle 1967, The Negro Pilgrimage in America 1967, My Face is Black 1964, The Black Muslims in America 1961; co-author of A Pictorial History of the Negro in America 1968; Lillian Smith Book Award, 1989, for first novel, The Avenue, Clayton City; author, This Road Since Freedom, poetry, 1989; author, The Black Church in the African American Experience, 1990-; William R Kenan, Jr Distinguished Professor, 1991; Teacher of the Year, Duke Univ; 11 hon degrees. **Special Achievements:** Co-author, The Black Church in the African-American Experience, 1991; author, Coming through the Fire: Surviving Race and Place in

America, 1996; Hymnodist; hymns appear in "United Methodist Hymanl," "Songs of Zion, (UMC)," "Lift Every Voice, (Episopalian)," etc. **Military Serv:** USN hosp corp 1944-45. **Business Addr:** William R Kenan Jr Prof, Duke University, Dept of Religion, Durham, NC 27706.

LINCOLN, JEREMY ARLO
Professional football player. **Personal:** Born Apr 7, 1969, Toledo, OH; married Lisa. **Educ:** Univ of Tennessee. **Career:** Chicago Bears, defensive back, 1993-95; St Louis Rams, 1996; Seattle Seahawks, 1997-. **Business Addr:** Professional Football Player, Seattle Seahawks, 11220 NE 53rd St, Kirkland, WA 98033, (206)827-9777.

LINDO, DELROY
Actor. **Career:** Appearances in television shows and films including: "First Time Felon," and "Ransom.". **Business Addr:** Actor, ICM (International Creative Management), 8942 Wilshire Blvd, Beverly Hills, CA 90211, (310)550-4000.

LINDO, J. TREVOR
Psychiatrist. **Personal:** Born Feb 12, 1925, Boston, MA; son of Ruby Ianty Peterson and Edwin Lindo; married Dr Thelma Thompson Lindo, Sep 23, 1962 (deceased). **Educ:** Boston Latin Sch; Boston Coll; NY Univ, AB 1946; Columbia Univ; Univ of Freibourg Switzerland, certificate 1953; Univ of Lausanne, MD 1957; attended Univ of Paris, State Univ of NY-Kings County Hosp Ctr 1957-61; Yale Univ, Neuropathology seminars. **Career:** St John's Episcopal Hosp, assoc attending psychiatrist; Columbia Univ NY, clinical instructor psychiatry; Brooklyn Bureau of Comm Svcs, psychiatric consultant; Ct Valley Hosp, supr psychiatrist 1961-64; Harlem Hosp, asst visiting psychiatrist 1964-66, senior psychiatrist, 1966-; Bedford Stuyvestant Comm Mental Health Ctr, psychiatrist 1976-; Columbia Univ, asst clinical prof of psychiatry 1981-,assoc clinical prof of psychiatry 1983-85; Marcus Garvey Manor, psychiatric consultant 1983; Bedford Stuyvestant Comm Mental Health Ctr, med dir 1986-. **Orgs:** Mem Natl Med Assn, Provident Clinical Soc; bd of dir Lyndon B Johnson Health Ctr; mem Amer Psychiatric Assn, World Federation for Mental Health; co-chmn Com for Dr Thomas Matthew Crown Heights Civic Assn; mem Black Psychiatrist of Amer, Caribbean Fed for Mental health; chmn NAACP Freedom Fund Dinner; mem Amer Assn of French Speaking Health Profls, Amer Assoc of Comm Mental Health Ctr Psychiatrists, Adv in Psychiatry Medical Soc County of Kings, Brooklyn Psychiatric Soc; mem educ comm NAACP; mem NY Acad of Sciences, Amer Assn for Advancement of Science. **Honors/Awds:** Fellow Amer College of Intl Physicians 1983; Distinguished Physician of America, 1990; life member, American Psychiatric Assn, 1991. **Military Serv:** US Merchant Marine 1948-51. **Home Addr:** 1265 President St, Brooklyn, NY 11213. **Business Addr:** Medical Director, Bedford-Sturyvestant Community Mental Health Ctr, 1406 Fulton St, Ste 201, Restoration Center Plaza, Brooklyn, NY 11216.

LINDSAY, BEVERLY
Educational administrator. **Personal:** Born Dec 21, 1948, San Antonio, TX; daughter of Ruth Roberts Lindsay. **Educ:** St Marys Univ, BA (magna cum laude) 1969; Univ of MA, MA 1971, EdD 1974; Amer Univ, PhD 1986. **Career:** PA State Univ, asst prof 1974-79; Natl Inst Ed Amer Council on Ed, fellow 1979-81, sr rsch & mgr 1981-83; US Info Agency, dir teacher text tech 1983-86; PA State Univ, spec asst vice pres 1983-86; Univ of Georgia, associate dean for academic affairs and professor beginning 1986; Hampton University, executive director, strategic planning, currently. **Orgs:** Business mgr, sec Compar Ed Soc 1976-79; faculty council, senate PA State Univ 1976-79; prog reviewer Amer Ed Rsch Assoc 1976-; bd mem Fairfax Comm Assoc 1982-84; treas Winston-Beers Comm School 1980-83; pres elect Comparative Ed Soc 1987-88; pres Compar Ed Soc 1988-89. **Honors/Awds:** Co-author, editor: "Comparative Perspectives of Third World Women"; "Migration & Natl Development in Africa"; Distinguished Doctoral Student Amer Univ 1984, 1985; published over 60 articles, chapters and reviews; Outstanding Educator Recognition, State Senate of Georgia, 1991. **Business Addr:** Executive Dir, Strategic Planning, Hampton University, Hampton, VA 23668.

LINDSAY, EDDIE H. S.
Business executive. **Personal:** Born Oct 23, 1931; married Joyce McCrae; children: Paul, Lisa. **Educ:** Attended, London Polytechnic Coll London, Queens Coll NY, Am Inst of Banking NY, Hofstra Univ. **Career:** Ins Salesman, 1968; Manufacturers Hanover Trust Co, credit officer; Broadway Bank & Trust Co, dir urban affairs, loan officer commercial minority economic devel, br mgr main ofc, asst vp. **Orgs:** Mem Nat Bankers Assn; New Jersey Bankers Urban Affairs Com; EDGES NY Professional Assn; dir Cath Diocese Com for Human Devel; dir Planned Parenthood of Passaic Co; finance chmn mem Boys Club of Paterson-Passaic; mem Legal Aid Soc; YMCA; United Way.

LINDSAY, GWENDOLYN ANN BURNS
Federal government official. **Personal:** Born Nov 13, 1947, Baltimore, MD; daughter of Lucinda Bowman Burns (deceased) and Robert Burns (deceased); divorced; children: Brock A. **Educ:** Coppin State College, BA, summa cum laude, 1975; University of Baltimore, MPA, 1977. **Career:** Bureau of Program Operation Prospective Reimbursement Branch, social science research analyst, 1975-77; Bureau of Program Operation Program Iniatives Branch, program analyst, 1977-79; Office of Executive Operation Program Liaison Branch, program liaison specialist, 1979-82; Department of Health & Human Services Health Care Financing Administration, Office of Regulations, health insurance specialist, 1993-97, Office of Communications and Operations Support, 1997-. **Orgs:** Baltimore Chapter of Continental Societies, Inc., corresponding secretary, 1994-; Delta Sigma Theta, Inc., regional journalist, 1997-; Baltimore Metropolitan Chapter of the Natl Black Women's Health Project, mem, workshop facilatator, 1993-; Delta Sigma Theta Sorority, Inc, president, 1991-93; Baltimore Alumnae Chapter, 1st vp, 2nd vp, 3rd vp, financial secretary, ebony, budget & finance, 1977-91; Maryland State Board of Dietetic Practices, board member, 1988-92; Towson Catholic Advisory Board, board member, 1989-94; YWCA of Greater Baltimore, board member & personnel committee, 1986-92; National Council of Negro Women, 1980-. **Honors/Awds:** Fullwood Foundation, Inc, "The Valued Hours Award," 1994; YWCA of Greater Baltimore, Helen Clapp Service Award, 1992; Mayor of Baltimore, Mayor's Citation, 1988, 1993, 1994; Governor of Maryland, Governor Citation, 1992, 1994; Associated Black Charities, Award for Volunteerism, 1988; Maryland Council of Deltas, Presidential Continued Service Award, 1986; Delta Sigma Theta, Outstanding Public Service Award, 1983. **Home Addr:** 12 Garobe Court, Baltimore, MD 21207.

LINDSAY, HORACE AUGUSTIN
Telecommunications company executive. **Personal:** Born Mar 1, 1938, New York, NY; son of Cecelia T Mitchell Lindsay and Horace A Lindsay Sr; married Donna McDade; children: Gloria, Horace. **Educ:** Prairie View A&M Univ, BS 1959; CA State Univ, MS 1969. **Career:** Boeing Co, rsch engr 1961-63; Martin Co, sr engr 1963-64; Bunker Ramo, prog mgr, 1964-68, mktg dir 1969-73, program dir 1973-77, mktg vice pres 1977-84; Eaton Corp, plans & bus devel vice pres, 1984-89; Contel Corp, vice pres & gen mgr, 1989-91; GTE Government Systems, IIPO, vice pres & gen mgr, 1991-93; GTE Airfone, president, 1993-96; GTE Corp, vice pres technology marketing, currently. **Orgs:** Mem, Armed Forces Communications & Electronics Assn. **Military Serv:** US Army 1st lt 1959-61. **Home Addr:** 6639 Hampton View Place, Mc Lean, VA 22101. **Business Addr:** Vice President, Technology Marketing, GTE Corp, 1001 N 19th St, Arlington, VA 22209, (703)247-9214.

LINDSAY, REGINALD C.
Attorney, government official. **Personal:** Born Mar 19, 1945, Birmingham, AL; son of Louise Lindsay and Richard Lindsay; married Cheryl Elizabeth Hartgrove. **Educ:** Univ of Valencia Spain, Certificate 1966; Morehouse Coll, BA (Hon) 1967; Harvard Law School, JD 1970. **Career:** Hill & Barlow, attorney, 1970-75; MA Department of Public Utilities, commissioner, 1975-77; Hill & Barlow, attorney, partner 1978-. **Orgs:** Board of directors, Morgan Memorial Goodwill Industries, Inc; board of directors, National Consumer Law Center; board of directors, 1867 Corp; board of directors, United Way of MA Bay, 1981-85; board of trustees, Thompson Island Education Center, 1975-86; MA Commission on Judicial Conduct, 1983-89; Commercial Arbitration Panel, American Arbitration Association; board of directors, Disability Law Center, 1989-90.

LINDSEY, JEROME W.
Educator. **Personal:** Born Apr 7, 1932, Phoenix City, AL; son of Willie Mae Harper Swinton and Jerome W Lindsey II. **Educ:** Howard U, BArch 1956; MIT, MArch 1960, MCity Planning 1961. **Career:** Howard Univ, dean, prof, 1971-, chmn 1969-70, assoc prof 1962-68; Harvard Univ, assoc dean, 1970-71; Yale Univ, visiting prof 1967-68; Washington DC, dir planning 1964-68; Providence Redevelopment Agency, sr planner 1961-62; Jose Luis Sert, planner 1959-61; Samuel Glaser, planner 1958-59; John Hans Graham, planner 1956-58; Harold M Lewis, planner 1955-56. **Orgs:** Reg architect MA/WASH DC/VA/MD/PA/MI; mem AIA; mem Bd of Edn; consult World Bank Urban Development Proj. **Honors/Awds:** NCARB Certificate. **Home Addr:** 501 Aspen St NW, Washington, DC 20012. **Business Addr:** 390 Cedar St NW, Washington, DC 20012.

LINDSEY, S. L.
City official, clergyman. **Personal:** Born Aug 23, 1909, Swiftwater, MS; widowed. **Educ:** MS Baptist Seminary Jackson MS, B Theol. **Career:** Ordained Minister 37 yrs; Town of Metcalfe, mayor. **Orgs:** Pres Metcalfe Devel Assoc 1975-; mem South Delta Planning 1977-; bd mem Washington Cty Oppty 1978-; mem Black Mayors Conf 1978-; pres Metcalfe Indust Dev Found 1981-; pastor at 4 churches. **Honors/Awds:** Outstanding Achievements Delta Council on Aging 60 1980. **Business Addr:** Mayor, Town of Metcalfe, PO Box 250, Metcalfe, MS 38760.

LINDSEY, TERRY LAMAR
Federal prosecutor. **Personal:** Born Jul 16, 1950, Gainesville, GA; children: Kevin. **Educ:** Clark Coll, BA 1972; So Univ Sch of Law, JD 1975. **Career:** Atty Gen State of LA, staff atty 1976-77, legal rsrch asst 1973-75; Gov Office of Consumer Protection, consumer protection mediator 1972-73; Shreveport LA, asst dist atty 1977-86; Miami FL, asst US atty 1986-. **Orgs:** Mem LA State Bar Assn 1976; Am Bar Assn; Nat Bar Assn; LA Dist Atty Assn; mem Fed Bar Assoc, So Dist of FL; member, The National Black Prosecutors Association, 1985-. **Honors/Awds:** Alpha Kappa Delta Hon Soc. **Business Addr:** Asst US Attorney, US Attorney So Dist of FL, 201 S Biscayne Ave, Miami, FL 33131.

LINER, LAMONT
Insurance broker. **Personal:** Born Nov 2, 1958, Chicago, IL; son of William & Willer Liner. **Educ:** University of Michigan; University of N AL. **Career:** Canaan Insurance Agency, owner, currently. **Orgs:** Phi Beta Sigma Frat, 1980; Mt Pleasant MB Church, minister, 1975. **Military Serv:** USAR, spec-4, 1989-97. **Home Addr:** 934 W College St, Florence, AL 35630. **Business Addr:** Sole Proprietor, Canaan Insurance Agency, 412 S Court St, Ste 412, Florence, AL 35630.

LINK, JOYCE BATTLE
Attorney. **Personal:** Born Dec 24, 1956, Columbus, OH; daughter of Dorothy L Battle and William R Battle; married Michael D Link, Mar 21, 1981. **Educ:** Washington University, BA, education, psychology, 1978; Ohio State University, College of Law, JD, 1983. **Career:** Assistant city prosecutor, 1983-85; asst attorney general, 1985-89; Bricker & Eckler, associate, 1989-. **Orgs:** Columbus Bar Association, ethic committee member, 1990-94, unauthorized practice of law committee; Action for Children, board member, 1990-, chairperson, insurance subcommittee; Westside/Eastside Child Care, associate board member, 1990-94; First Church of God, chairperson, Homeless Project Initiative. **Business Addr:** Attorney, Bricker & Eckler Law Firm, 100 S Third St, Columbus, OH 43215-4291, (614)227-2300.

LINSEY, NATHANIEL L.
Clergyman. **Personal:** Born Jul 24, Atlanta, GA; son of L E Forney Linsey (deceased) and Samuel Linsey Sr (deceased); married Mae C Mills; children: Nathaniel Jr, Ricarldo Mills, Julius Wayne, Angela Elise. **Educ:** Paine Coll, BS 1949; Howard Univ Sch of Religion, BD 1951; Scarritt Coll, Masters degree with distinction 1974; Texas Coll, honorary doctorate. **Career:** CME Church, natl youth dir 1951-52; Rock of Ages CME Church Walterboro, SC, natl youth dir 1952-53; Columbia Dist Columbia, SC, presiding elder 1953-55; Vanderhorst CMECh, pastor 1955-56; Mattie E Coleman CME, pastor 1956-62; Thirgood CME Church, pastor 1962-66; CME Ch, gen sec of evangelism 1966-74; CME Church, elected the 39th Bishop May 1978; Christian Meth Episcopal Ch, presiding bishop 9th district. **Orgs:** Pres K'ville branch NAACP 1957; chmn Bd of Lay Activities CME Ch 1974-82; pres Southern CA Ecumenical Council of Churches 1984; chmn Bd of Finance CME Church 1982-; chmn College of Bishops CME Ch 1984-; mem World Meth Council; board member, Miles College; chairman, Department of Evangelism, Missions and Human Concerns, CME Church. **Honors/Awds:** Presidential citation Natl Assoc for Equal Oppor in Higher Educ 1979; Alumni Achievement Awd Paine Coll Natl Alumni Assn 1983; Disting Serv Awd Govt of the District of Columbia 1984; Public Serv Awd TX Coll 1984; Honorary Doctorate, Miles College, 1975; Honorary Doctorate, Texas College, 1985; Honorary Doctor of Laws, Paine College, 1990; established telephone ministry in Atlanta and Washington DC. **Home Addr:** 2059 W Cedar Lane SW, Atlanta, GA 30311.

LINTON, GORDON J.
State representative. **Personal:** Born Feb 26, 1948, Philadelphia, PA; son of Alberta James Linton and James Linton; married Jacqueline Flynn; children: Sharifah, Sabriya. **Educ:** Peirce Junior College, AS, 1967; Lincoln University, PA, BA, 1970; Antioch Univ, MEd, 1973. **Career:** School Dist of Philadelphia, comm consult 1971-74; Baptist Children's House, educ dir 1974-78; Philadelphia Child Guidance Ctr, psych-ed spec 1978-80; Dept of Auditor General, reg dir 1980-82; Pennsylvania House of Representatives, state representative, currently. **Orgs:** Mem Natl Black Caucus State of Legislators 1982-, Minority Bus Enterprise Council 1982-; Trustee Lincoln Univ 1982-; mem Philadelphia Economic Roundtable 1983-; pres reg II Conf of Minority Transportation Officials 1984. **Honors/Awds:** Community Service Award, Hill Youth Assn, 1982; Community Service Award, Leeds Middle School, 1982; Community Service Award, Crisis Intervention Network, 1984; Appreciation Award, New Penn Del Minority Purchasing Cncl, 1985; Appreciation Award, Independent Minority Businessmen of Central Pennsylvania, 1985; Outstanding Civic Leadership Award, Entrepreneurial Club-Business and Technology Ctr, 1985; Dedicated Service to Higher Educ Lincoln Univ 1986; Pride of Peirce, Peirce Jr Coll, 1989; Adv of the Year Award, Natl Assn Women Business Owners, 1989. **Business Addr:** State Representative, District 200, Pennsylvania House of Representatives, 1521 E Wadsworth Ave, Philadelphia, PA 19150.

LINTON, SHEILA LORRAINE
Educator. **Personal:** Born Dec 19, 1950, Philadelphia, PA; daughter of Elvera Linton Boyd and Harold Louis Linton (deceased). **Educ:** Pennsylvania State Univ, BS 1972; Drexel

Univ, MS 1976. **Career:** School Dist of Philadelphia, teacher 1972-78; The Pew Charitable Trusts, program officer 1979-87; School District of Philadelphia, teacher 1988-. **Orgs:** Mem Alpha Kappa Alpha 1970-; natl sec Bullock Family Reunions 1978-85; adv comm Jack & Jill of Amer Found 1981-87; volunteer United Negro Coll Fund 1982-87; mem Women in Philanthropy 1983-87; bd of dir Assoc of Black Found Execs 1984-87; bd of dir Jack & Jill of Amer Foundation 1989-; board of directors, Friends of the Free Library of Philadelphia, 1989-96; board of directors, Kearsley Retirement Community 1992-; board of directors, Family Reunion Institute of Temple Univ, 1990; mem, Natl Coalition of 100 Black Women. **Honors/Awds:** Presidential Award for Distinguished Serv Jack & Jill of Amer Found 1984. **Home Addr:** 14 S Ruby St, Philadelphia, PA 19139.

LINTZ, FRANK D. E.
Landscaping contractor. **Personal:** Born Feb 5, 1951, Ottumwa, IA; son of Margaret E Lintz and Franklyn E Lintz; married Lisa M Campos, Jun 27, 1992. **Career:** Mid-Continent Meats, union leader, 1972-79; Circle C Beef Co, union leader, 1979-83; Swift & Co, lead butcher, 1983-86; Nebraska Turf Co, co-owner, currently. **Orgs:** Amalgamated Meat Cutters & Butcher Workmen, 1972-79, chief steward, 1979-83; United Food & Commercial Workers, 1983-86. **Special Achievements:** BET News Network, Drought in Midwest, television interview, 1989; Des Moines Register, farming article, 1968. **Military Serv:** US Army, spec-7, 1969-71; basic service awards, campaign medals. **Home Phone:** (402)571-3251. **Business Addr:** Co-Owner, Nebraska Turf Co, PO Box 24508, Omaha, NE 68114.

LINYARD, RICHARD
Banker. **Personal:** Born Nov 16, 1930, Maywood, IL; married Maggie; children: Linda, Lance, Timothy. **Educ:** Northwestern Univ, attnd; Amer Inst of Banking standard & advance cert; grad schl of banking univ of wI, diploma. **Career:** Seaway Natl Bank Chicago, exec vice pres bd dir cashier 1964-; Oak Park Trust & Savs Bank, janitor, elevator Oper, savs bookkeeper, teller, gen bookkeeper, savs dept, asst mgr, asst cashier; 1950-64. **Orgs:** Pres Chicago Chap Amer Inst of Banking. **Business Addr:** 645 E 87 St, Chicago, IL 60619.

LIPPETT, RONNIE LEON
Professional football player. **Personal:** Born Dec 10, 1960, Melbourne, FL. **Educ:** Univ of Miami (FL), attended. **Career:** New England Patriots, cornerback, 1983-. **Honors/Awds:** Post-season play, 1985: AFC Championship Game, NFL Championship Game. **Business Addr:** Professional Football Player, New England Patriots, Sullivan Stadium, Rt One, Foxboro, MA 02035.

LIPPMAN, LOIS H.
Government employee (retired). **Personal:** Born Jan 13, 1925, Boston, MA; daughter of Hilda Richards Higginbotham and George C. Higginbotham; married Romeyn V Lippman Jr; children: Marc R. **Educ:** Harvard Univ Extension School. **Career:** NY State Senate, asst to state senator, 1977; Gilbert A Robinson Inc Special Project, public relations consultant, 1979; Public Relations Bd Inc, vice pres; Intercontinental leisure Inc, vp; Alaska Airlines Inc, sales mgr; The White House, secretarial asst, sec; political consultant. **Orgs:** Active in political and civic activities; volunteer in arts and cultural affairs. **Special Achievements:** 1st African-American assigned to White House above level of messenger or domestic, served under Pres Dwight D Eisenhower 1953-59; one of the 1st women in a managerial position at a scheduled airline. **Home Addr:** 788 Columbus Ave, Apt 3E, New York, NY 10025.

LIPPS, LOUIS ADAM
Professional football player. **Personal:** Born Aug 9, 1962, New Orleans, LA. **Educ:** Univ of Southern Mississippi. **Career:** Wide receiver: Pittsburgh Steelers, 1984-92, New Orleans Saints, 1992-93. **Orgs:** Honorary chairman, Big Brothers & Sisters Bowl for Kids; chairman, MS Read-a-thon; chairman, Variety Club Golf Tournament, Ronald McDonald House; owner, Halls Mortuary, Hattiesburg, MS; drug and alcohol educ prog, Blue Cross of Western Pennsylvania, 1986-. **Honors/Awds:** NFL Rookie of the Year, 1984; first Steeler rookie since Franco Harris to be named to AFC Pro Bowl; Professional Athlete of the Year; MS Professional Athlete of the Year, 1984; Joe Greene Great Performance Award, 1984; Steeler MVP, 1985; Pittsburgh's Man of the Year in Sports; Louisiana Professional Athlete of the Year, Sugar Bowl's Sports Awards Committee, 1985; played in Pro Bowl, 1984, 1985. **Business Addr:** Former Professional Football Player, New Orleans Saints, 1500 Poydras St, New Orleans, LA 70112.

LIPSCOMB, CURTIS ALEXANDER
Publishing company executive. **Personal:** Born Mar 23, 1965, Detroit, MI; son of Mary Salley & Lester Lewis. **Educ:** Parsons School of Design, BFA, 1987. **Career:** Dagger Group, knitwear designer, 1987-89; Bonaventure, knitwear designer, 1989-90; Chelsea Young, knitwear designer, 1990; Ruff Hewn, knitwear designer, 1990-91; Banana Republic, knitwear designer, 1991-92; Kick Publishing Co, pres/CEO, currently. **Orgs:** Men of Color Motivational Group, Detroit, 1992-; editorial board, Between The Lines; editorial board, Michigan's Community News for Lesbians, Gays, Bisexuals, and Friends; co-chair, Michigan Clinton/Gore Lesbian Gay Leadership Council to re-elect President Clinton, 1996. **Honors/Awds:** Adolf Klein Scholarship Award, 1986; Roz & Sherm Fashion Award, 1983; SBC Magazine, Brother of the Year Award, Community Service, 1996. **Special Achievements:** Traveled to Europe/UK, 1990; Traveled to Far East, 1990; Publications: Kick! Magazine, The Motivator, Detroit Pride Guide, The Official Resouce Guide to Hotter Than July 1996 & 1997. **Business Addr:** President & CEO, Kick Publishing Company, PO Box 2222, Detroit, MI 48231.

LIPSCOMB, DARRYL L.
City official. **Personal:** Born Jan 18, 1953, Chicago, IL; son of Mary C Lipscomb; married Kathryn Gregor-Lipscomb. **Educ:** Univ of Wisconsin-LaCrosse, BS, journalism, 1977, MS, education, 1979. **Career:** Univ of Wisconsin, admissions counselor 1979-82; COE Coll, asst dir admissions 1982-83, assoc dean of admissions 1983-87; Cedar Ridge Publishing, dir of marketing 1986-89; City of Cedar Rapids, civil rights compliance officer 1989-; adjunct counselor, Student Development, Kirkwood Community College, 1994-; president, Lipscomb & Associates, 1995-; commissioner, Iowa Commission on the Status of African-American, 1996-. **Orgs:** Equal Opportunity Prog Personnel 1985-89; life mem Kappa Alpha Psi Frat; mem, IC/CR Alumni Chapter Kappa Alpha Psi; life member, NAACP; board member, Equal Employment Opportunity/Affirmative Action; advisory committee, Kirkwood Community College, 1991-; board of directors, Friends of Unity Inc, 1996-. **Honors/Awds:** Keeper of Records, Kappa Alpha Psi IC/CR Alumni Chapter 1988-94, Keeper of Exchecquer, 1996-. **Home Addr:** 2601 Meadowbrook Dr SE, Cedar Rapids, IA 52403, (319)363-9225. **Business Addr:** Civil Rights Commission, City of Cedar Rapids, City Hall, 2nd Fl, Cedar Rapids, IA 52401, (319)398-5036.

LIPSCOMB, WANDA DEAN
Administrator. **Personal:** Born Jan 29, 1953, Richmond, VA; married Keith N Lipscomb; children: Nicholas K, Victoria N. **Educ:** Lincoln Univ, BA 1974; Washington Univ, MA 1975; Michigan State Univ, PhD 1978. **Career:** MI State Univ Coll of Human Medicine, director of center of excellence, associate professor. **Orgs:** Mem bd dirs Assoc for Multiculture Counseling and Development 1980-88; mem bd dirs Amer Assoc for Counseling and Develop 1982-85; mem Assoc of Black Psychologists 1984-; mem bd dirs Natl Bd of Certified Counselors 1985-90; pres Lansing Alumnae Chap Delta Sigma Theta Sor Inc; mem Natl Program Planning Comm Delta Sigma Theta Sor Inc; mem bd dirs MSU Black Alumni Assoc. **Honors/Awds:** John L Lennon Awd for Disting Professional Service Assoc for Multicultural Counseling 1984; Sisterwood Awd Delta Sigma Theta 1985; Mich State Univ, Diversity Award, 1995; Professional Service Award, 1992; O'Hana Award for Multiculturalism, 1994. **Home Addr:** 3422 Penrose Dr, Lansing, MI 48911. **Business Addr:** Director, Center of Excellence, Michigan State University, College Of Human Medicine, A236 Life Science Bldg, East Lansing, MI 48824.

LIPSCOMB, WENDELL R.
Psychiatrist. **Personal:** Born Jun 9, 1920, Berkeley, CA; divorced. **Educ:** San Diego State Coll, AB 1947; Univ CA, MD 1951; Univ MI, MPH 1953. **Career:** Bur Chronic Diseases State CA Dept Pub Health, supr 1955-57; Div Alcoholic Rehab, sect chief 1957-59, asst chief 1959-61; Mendocino State Hosp, resident psychiat 1961-64; Cowell Mem Hosp, psychiat resident 1964-65; Mendocino State Hosp, chief research 1965-72; Gen Research Corp, prin cons/Study dir 1972-73; Westside Comm Mental Health Ctr, chief research 1972-74; Drug Abuse Prog Berkeley Health Dept, chief clin serv 1973-75; W Oakland Health Ctr, staff psychiat 1974-; E Oakland Mental Health Ctr, consult med clin dir 1975-; Source Inc Cons, exec dir, physician. **Orgs:** Mem N CA Psychiat Soc; Pacific Sociological Soc; Amer Assn for Advancement of Sci; Pan Amer Med Assn; Amer Acad Polit & Social Sci; Amer Med Soc on Alcoholism; Amer Therapeutic Soc; Amer Social Health Assc; Acad Psychosomatic Med; Biofeedback Research Soc; Intl Council on Alcohol & Addictions; Amer Soc Clin Pharmacology & Therapeutics; Black Psychiatrists of N CA; CA Soc for Treatment of Alcoholism & Other Dependencies. **Honors/Awds:** Prin investigator ''An Assessment of Alcoholism Serv Needs & Alcoholism Serv Utilization of CA Black Population''. **Military Serv:** USAF 1953-55. **Business Addr:** Psychiatrist, Source Inc, 1713 Martin Luther King Jr Way, Berkeley, CA 94709.

LIPSCOMBE, MARGARET ANN
Educator. **Personal:** Born Dec 12, 1939, Alabama. **Educ:** NY Univ, MA 1960; Univ MN, BS 1957; Columbia Univ 1968; CT Clge, 1967; Juilliard, 1970; New York City Studios 1975. **Career:** Instr of Dance W CT State Clge, professional dance wrkshps 1967-; City Clge of NY, instr 1964-67; Spelman Clge, instr 1959-64; Hunter Clge HS, instr 1959-60; Vassar NY, choreography performance under Mary Jean Corvele 1965-68; Dancers of Faith, performer 1971-72; Valmar Dance Co, performer 1958-59; Women's Dance Proj Henry St Playhouse NY, performer 1960. **Orgs:** Mem Assc for Mental Health; Amer Assc for Health Physical Educ & Recreation; Natl Tchrs Assc; Univ Professional Women; Music Fedn Inc.

LISTER, ALTON LAVELLE
Professional basketball player. **Personal:** Born Oct 1, 1958, Dallas, TX; married Elaine; children: J. Ross, Alton. **Educ:** AZ State Univ, 1978-81. **Career:** Milwaukee Bucks, center-forward, 1981-86, 1994-95; Seattle SuperSonics, 1987-89, Golden State Warriors, 1990-93; Boston Celtics, 1995-97; Portland Trailblazers, 1997-. **Orgs:** Named to 1980 Olympic team that played a series of games vs NBA All-Stars called the Gold Medal games. **Special Achievements:** NBA Draft, First round pick, #21, 1981. **Business Addr:** Professional Basketball Player, Portland Trailblazers, 1 Center Court, Ste 200, Portland, OR 97227, (503)234-9291.

LISTER, DAVID ALFRED
Educational administrator. **Personal:** Born Oct 19, 1939, Somerset; son of Etoile Johnson Lister and James Lister; married Anita Louise Browne, Dec 29, 1962; children: Mimi, Gigi. **Educ:** Central State Univ, BA 1962; Stetson Univ Coll of Law, JD 1977. **Career:** Johns Hopkins Medical Institutions, dir affirmative action 1978-79; Univ of MA Medical Center, assoc vice chancellor 1979-82; Inst of Intl Educ, dir of personnel 1982-86; Fairleigh Dickinson Univ, univ dir/human resources 1986-87, asst vice pres for admin 1987-88; Univ of Medicine and Dentistry of New Jersey, vice pres for human resources 1988-. **Orgs:** President's Advisory Comm Morgan State Univ 1978; NAACP; Society for Human Resources Administration; Coll & Univ Personnel Assn; Alpha Phi Alpha Fraternity Inc; bd mem, chmn Program Comm, mem Exec Comm, Comm of the Newark Private Industry Council; Amer Assn of Affirmative Action; Intl Personnel Mgmt Assn; Amer Mgmt Assn; Amer Hospital Assn; Amer Compensation Assn; Assn of Hospital Personnel Administrators; New Jersey Coll and Univ Personnel Assn; New Jersey Assn of Hospital Personnel Administrators; Greater Newark Chamber of Commerce; Urban League; Central State Univ Alumni Assn. **Business Addr:** Vice President for Human Resources, Univ of Medicine and Dentistry of New Jersey, 30 Bergen St, Newark, NJ 07107.

LISTER, VALERIE LYNN
Sports writer. **Personal:** Born Jun 21, 1961, Niagara Falls, NY; daughter of Espinetta Griffin Dorsey and Valentine Jonathan Dorsey. **Educ:** University of Texas at El Paso, El Paso, TX, BA, 1983. **Career:** Athens Daily News, Athens, GA, sports writer, 1984; Pensacola News Journal, Pensacola, FL, sports writer, 1984-88; USA Today, Arlington, VA, sports writer, 1988-. **Orgs:** Member, Natl Assn of Black Journalists, 1987-; steering committee, NABJ Sports Task Force, 1989-; regional director, Assn of Women in Sports Media, 1990-; member, Delta Sigma Theta Sorority Inc, 1982-. **Business Addr:** Sports Writer, USA Today, 1000 Wilson Blvd, Arlington, VA 22229.

LISTER, WILLA M.
Community services executive. **Personal:** Born Jan 16, 1940, Charleston, SC; daughter of Beatrice Coaxum and Willie Coaxum Sr (deceased); married L Venice. **Educ:** Dillard Univ, BA 1962; N TX State Univ, MEd 1978, Doctoral Candidate; East Texas State Univ Commerce TX, attended. **Career:** New Orleans Sch, phys educ tchr 1962-63; Ft Worth Sch, tchr 1964-73; Highland Park YWCA, ballet & modern dance instr 1964-71; Community Action Agency, activities dir 1967-70; Episcopal Found for Youth, dir Top Teens Tune In 1968-70; City of Fort Worth, personnel analyst training div HRD 1986-88, asst to city mgr, 1989-90, human services admin, 1990-91. **Orgs:** Mem Astro Rangers Riding Club 1980-; mem Ft Worth Comm Devel Fund 100 Com; pres Delta Sigma Theta Sor Ft Worth Chapter; secretary, Tarrant County Youth Collaboration, 1991-93; board member, American Heart Assn, 1991-94; National Forum for Black Public Admin, 1990-; US Conference of Human Services Officials, board member. **Honors/Awds:** Henry Armstrong Awd for Coll Sr Dillard Univ 1962. **Home Addr:** 4008 Freshfield Rd, Fort Worth, TX 76119. **Business Addr:** Supt, community services, City of Fort Worth, 4200 S Fwy, Fort Worth, TX 76115.

LITTLE, BENILDE ELEASE
Author. **Personal:** Born in Newark, NJ; daughter of Clara & Matthew Little; married Clifford Virgin III, Jun 13, 1992; children: Baldwin. **Educ:** Howard University, BA, undergrad, 1981; Northwestern University, Grad School, 1982. **Career:** The Star Ledger, reporter, 1982-85; People Magazine, reporter, 1985-89; Essence Magazine, sr editor, 1989-91; author, currently. **Honors/Awds:** Go On Girl Book Club, National, Best New Author, 1996; NAACP Image Award, Finalist, 1996. **Special Achievements:** Book Good Hair, National Bestseller, 75,000 copies; Los Angeles Times, One of 10 Best Books, Good Hair, 1996.

LITTLE, BRIAN KEITH
Workplace diversity coordinator, human resources. **Personal:** Born Apr 5, 1959, Peoria, IL; son of Georgia Gordon Little and James A Little; married Anise D Wiley Little, Jun 23, 1984. **Educ:** IL State Univ, BS 1981, MS 1983. **Career:** IL State Univ, teaching asst 1981-82; Eastern Broadcasting, adv consultant 1982-83; Public Serv Co of CO, specialist career planning/training. **Orgs:** Educ chmn PSC Black Employees Council 1986-; promotions chmn PSC Employee Volunteer Comm 1987-; safety chmn PSC Human Resource Div 1987-. **Honors/**

Awds: Outstanding Achievement in Pluralism (an effort by PSC to help people of different cultures & races understand each other).

LITTLE, CHESTER H.
Appraiser. **Personal:** Born Oct 12, 1907, Paducah, KY; married Leone Bryson; children: Michael Armistead. **Educ:** Wilberforce Univ, attnd 1927; IN Christian Univ, hon degrees 1971. **Career:** Eli Lilly Pharm Co, tech biols 1949-72; Malleable Foundry Indpls, 1926-45. **Orgs:** First vice pres Employees Credit Union Malleable Foundry; capt aux police Indpls; WWII chmn adv Com Marion Co Foster Grandparent Prog 1974-80; mem Central IN Council On Aging; chrmn Personnel Com/ Evaluation Com 1979-80; pres Marion Co Council on Aging 1980-81; first vice pres Fedn of Assc Clubs 1956-78; bd dir Indianapolis Urban League 1972-78; bd dir Operation Late Start 1975-. **Honors/Awds:** TSP Award Women in Communications; Best Regards Award Urban League; SRE PAC Com 1979. **Business Addr:** Indianapolis, IN.

LITTLE, GENERAL T.
Physician. **Personal:** Born Sep 10, 1946, Wadesboro, NC; married Barbara McConnell; children: Christopher, Adrienne, Kimberly. **Educ:** NC A&T State Univ, BS 1967; Meharry Med Clge, MD 1969-71; Walter Reed Gen Hosp, attnd 1975. **Career:** Cardio-Pulmonary Assc Charelston, md; Kimbrough AUS Hosp, chief internal medicine 1975-76; Am Bd of Internal Medicine, diplomate 1975. **Orgs:** Mem Natl Med Assc 1971-; consult internal med Sea Island Health Care Corp 1976-77; mem Amer Soc of Internal Medicine 1978-; bd trustees Charleston Co Hosp 1979-; bd trustees Charleston Area Mental Health Bd 1979-; mem Omega Psi Phi Frat Inc. **Military Serv:** USMC maj 1971-76. **Business Addr:** 696 Rutledge Ave, Charleston, SC 29403.

LITTLE, HELEN R.
Radio broadcasting co. executive. **Personal:** Born Feb 3, 1962, Salisbury, NC; daughter of Meriam S Little and Harlee H Little, Sr. **Educ:** The University of North Carolina at Chapel Hill, 1980-84. **Career:** WGIV, continuity director, 1984; WFXC, account executive, 1985; WRAL, account executive, 1985; WQOK, production director, 1986; WPEG, music director, 1987; WCKZ, news director, 1989; KJMZ, music director, 1992-. **Orgs:** Women on the Air, founder-co-chair, 1992. **Home Addr:** PO Box 141351, Irving, TX 75014. **Business Addr:** Music Director, KJMZ 100 3 Jamz, 545 E John Carpenter, 17th Fl, Irving, TX 75062, (214)556-8100.

LITTLE, HERMAN KERNEL
Educational administrator. **Personal:** Born Jan 25, 1951, Wadesboro, NC; son of Margie Little and Bryant Little; married H Patricia; children: Kentrell, Karlton. **Educ:** Anson Tech Coll, AAS Acctg 1980, AAS Retailing & Mktg 1980; Wingate Coll, BA Bus Admin Mgmt 1984. **Career:** Anson Tech Coll, asst proj dir 1977-83, proj dir 1983-, ed admin. **Orgs:** Bd of dir Morven Area Med Ctr 1978-, Anson Cty Red Cross 1978-; mem NC Comm Coll Adult Ed Assoc 1978-; bd of dir Anson Cty Bd of Adjustment 1980,Anson Cty Waste Mgmt Bd 1981-, Savannah AME Zion Church 1982-; mem Amer Soc for Personnel Admin 1982-; pres Political Action Comm for Concerned Citizens 1982-, Anson Cty Young Democratic Party 1982-83; mem Phi Beta Lambda Wingate Coll 1982-; Grace Sr Center Advisory Council 1983-; mem Anson Cty Personnel Assoc 1983-; bd of dir Anson Cty Art's Council 1984-, PDCOG Emergency Med Serv Advisory 1984-; elected first black Anson Cnty Commissioner 1986; Anson Cnty Health Bd 1987; board member, North Carolina United Way, 1991. **Honors/Awds:** Governor's Volunteer Awd State of NC 1983; Outstanding Service Award, 1991, President's Award, 1991, Anson County United Way. **Military Serv:** USAF E-4 1972-77; NDSM, AFOUA, AFLSA, AFGCM, AFM 900-3. **Home Addr:** Rte 1, Box 325, Wadesboro, NC 28170.

LITTLE, LARRY CHATMON
Head football coach. **Personal:** Born Nov 2, 1945, Groveland, GA; son of Ida Mae Little and George Little; married Rosa De Jesus, Apr 15, 1978; children: Damita, Learon. **Educ:** Bethune-Cookman College, BS, 1967. **Career:** San Diego Chargers, professional football player, offensive guard, 1967-69; Miami Dolphins, offensive guard, 1969-80; Miami Edison High School, athletic director, 1981-83; Bethune-Cookman College, head football coach, 1983-92; Ohio Glory, World Football League, head coach, 1992; North Carolina Central University, head football coach, 1992-. **Honors/Awds:** Natl Football League, All-Pro Football Team, 1971-76; NFL Players Assn, Offensive Lineman of the Year, 1971-73; Biscayne College, honorary doctorate, science and human relations, 1972; Florida Sports Writers, Florida Hall of Fame, 1978; Pro Football Hall of Fame, 1993. **Business Addr:** Head Coach, North Carolina Central University, PO Box 19705, Walker Complex, Durham, NC 27707, (919)560-5315.

LITTLE, LEONE BRYSON
Educator. **Personal:** Born Aug 4, 1924, Indianapolis, IN; married Chester H Bryson; children: Michael Armistead. **Educ:** Butler Univ Indpls, BS 1972, MA 1972; IN Univ Purdue Univ, grad work Social Studies 1972, 76, 77, 79; Notre Dame Univ, grad work admin 1977; Boston State, attnd 1980. **Career:** Thomas Carr Howe HS, chmn social studies dept 1979-; Forest Manor Schl Indpls, dept chmn soc studies 1976-79; Robert Browning Jr HS, tchr 1968-73;US Civil Srv Army Finance Ctr, examiner 1952-67. **Orgs:** Mem Natl Council for Soc Studies Com Sexism & Social Justice 1974-78; chmn IN Council for Soc Studies Jr High Comm 1975-78; pres IN Council for SocStudies 1979-80; pres Central IN Council for Soc Studies 1979-80; chmn League of Women Voters Gov Comm 1975-80; first vice pres Amer Assc Univ Women 1976-78; pres Indianapolis Br Amer Assc of Univ Women 1978-80; pres life mem Guild Natl Council Negro Women 1970-74; Outst Soc Studies Educ IN Council Soc Studies Supt of Pub Instr 1976; mem Indianapolis Pub Schs Black History Com 1977-79; mem Natl Sci Found Team of Soc Studies Educators who worked on proj at IN Univ 1978. **Business Addr:** Thomas Carr Howe HS, 4900 Julian Ave, Indianapolis, IN 46219.

LITTLE, MONROE HENRY
Educator. **Personal:** Born Jun 30, 1950, St Louis, MO; married Shelia Maria Josephine Parks; children: Alexander. **Educ:** Denison Univ, BA 1971 (magna cum laude); Princeton Univ, MA 1973, PhD 1977. **Career:** MIT, instructor 1976-77, asst prof 1977-80; Indiana Univ-Purdue Univ, Indianapolis, asst prof 1980-81, asst prof dir afro-amer studies 1981-. **Orgs:** Mem Amer Historical Assn; mem Organization of American Historians; mem Natl Urban League; mem Assoc for Study of Afro-Amer Life & History; consultant Educ Develop Ctr 1980; consultant CSR Inc US Dept of Labor 1981; consultant Black Women in the Mid-West Project Purdue Univ 1983. **Honors/ Awds:** Elected Omicron Delta Kappa Men's Leadership Honorary 1971; Fellowship Rockefeller Fellowship in Afro-Amer Studies 1972-75. **Business Addr:** Asst Prof History, Indiana University, Purdue University-Indianapolis, History Dept, Indianapolis, IN 46206.

LITTLE, REUBEN R.
Operations supervisor. **Personal:** Born Sep 1, 1933; married Margaret Jean Davis. **Educ:** Alabama A&M, BS 1957; Univ of Texas, grad study 1963; Kansas State Univ, 1964; Western Illinois Univ, 1965; Indiana Univ, MSS 1966. **Career:** DHHS/ SSA, Meridian MS, oper supvr, currently; DHEW/SSA, Tuscaloosa AL, mgmt trainee 1974-75; teacher admin at jr high school level; Neighborhood Youth Corp Prog, dir. **Orgs:** Mem Natl Bus League 1970; NAACP 1968; Natl Council for Geography Tchrs 1964; Natl Assc of New York City Dirs 1970; vol Youth Court Couns 1972; EEO Assc 1970; lay minister trustee chmn Bd of Elders Good Shepherd Luthern Ch Meridan MS; mem Kappa Alpha Psi 1954; Rescue Lodge 439 3rd Deg Mason 1958; IBPO Elk of W 1960; charter mem Cloverleaf Toastmaster Club 1967; past pres & area gov Toastmasters Intl 1973-74; Choctaw Area Council BSA 1965; div chmn Lauderdale Co March of Dimes 1968-70; Central Meridian Optimist Club, charter member, 1984, past president, 1990-91; board of directors, retired sr volunteer program, past president, 1990-; Meridian Area Toastmasters, president, 1989-93, Area VI Governor, 1985-86-; Recipient of the Able Toastmasters Award; Zoning Board, City of Meridian, 1978-92;past chairman, Lauderdale CounPlanning and Airport Zoning Commission, 1992-; life mem NAACP; president of the Sandwedge Golfers Association, Meridian, 1982-92-; finance committee Meridale Girl Scouts. **Honors/Awds:** Recipient Ldrshp Award Outst Achievement Toastmasters 1969; Hall of Fame Award 1973 Keyman 1974 Toastmasters; Able Toastmaster 1974; Recipient of the NAACP, Man of the Year Award, 1990; Distinguished Service Award, RSVP, 1989; Superior Performance Award, SSA, 1988-91; Outstanding Club Award as President, optimist, 1990. **Business Addr:** PO Box 5377, Meridian, MS 39301.

LITTLE, ROBERT BENJAMIN
Physician. **Personal:** Born Apr 25, 1955, Dublin, GA; son of Druzy Perry Little and William Albert Little. **Educ:** Morehouse Coll, BS (with departmental honors) 1977; Meharry Medical Coll, MD 1982. **Career:** Harlem Hospital, internship and 2 years residency, general surgery, 1983-85; US Navy, general medical officer, 1986-89; Morehouse Medical School, Atlanta, GA, family medicine intern, resident, 1989-92, chief resident, 1991-92; Family Medicine & Emergency Medicine, independent contractor, 1992-. **Orgs:** American Academy of Family Physicians; Amer Medical Assn; Amer Coll of Emergency Physicians; Assn of Emergency Physicians; AMSA; Atlanta Medical Assn; GA State Medical Assn; Amer Assn of Physician Specialists. **Honors/Awds:** Board Certification, Family Medicine, 1992. **Military Serv:** US Navy, lt cmdr, 1986-89; Sharp Shooters Medal 1988. **Business Addr:** Physician, 225 Canaan Glen Way SW, Atlanta, GA 30331.

LITTLE, RONALD EUGENE
Surgeon. **Personal:** Born Jun 29, 1937, Chicago, IL; married Jane Mclemore; children: Ronald Jr, Kevin, Bryan, Jennifer. **Educ:** Wayne State U, BS 1965; Howard Univ Coll Med, MD 1970. **Career:** Wayne State U, orthopedic Surgeon clinical instr 1975-. **Orgs:** Mem Am Acad of Orthopedic Surgeons 1977; AMA; Nat Med Assn; MI State Med Soc; Wayne Co Med Soc; Detroit Med Soc; diplomat Am Bd of Orthopedic Surgeon; Detroit Acad of Orthopedic Surgeons; mem Alpha Omega Alpha Hon Med Frat 1970. **Military Serv:** AUS spec 4 1955-58. **Business Addr:** 3750 Woodward, Detroit, MI 48201.

LITTLE, WILLIE HOWARD
Educator, coach. **Personal:** Born Aug 20, 1949, Greenwood, MS; married Janice Lynn Franklin. **Educ:** IA Wesleyan Coll, BA 1972. **Career:** Hugh Manley HS Chicago Bd of Educ, teacher, basketball coach 1975-; Calhoun N Elementary School Chicago, teacher 1972-75. **Orgs:** Mem Operation PUSH Chicago. **Honors/Awds:** Chicago City coach of the yr Chicago Pub League Coaches Assn 1977-78; coach of the yr Com on Urban Athletics & Educ 1978; IL State coach of the yr DistOne IL Basketball Coaches Assn 1978-79; basketball coach of the yr Chicago PUSH ofr Excellance 1979; IL State Basketball Champs IL State Basketball Class AA 1980.

LITTLEJOHN, BILL C.
Judge. **Personal:** Born Jan 25, 1944, Gaffney, SC; son of Elviry Geter; married Gail A Hodge; children: Erica A, Shai A, Eric. **Educ:** Central State University, BS, accounting, 1969; Ohio Northern Law University, JD, 1972. **Career:** Montgomery County Public Defender, criminal defense attorney, 1974-75; City of Dayton, prosecutor, 1975-76, traffic court referee, 1978-80, acting judge, 1978-91; Austin, Jones, Littlejohn & Owens, trial attorney, 1980-85; Littlejohn & Littlejohn, president, 1985-91; Dayton Municipal Court, judge, currently. **Orgs:** Natl Business League, board member, 1985-, regional vice pres, 1986, treasurer, 1990-93; Private Industry Council, board member, 1985; chairman of board, Central State University, Gleksto Inc, 1986; Neighborhoods USA, president, 1986; 32 Degree Prince Hall Mason; Optimist Intl, distinguished president; United Cerebral Palsy Foundation, board member. **Honors/Awds:** Wrote a column for media on entertainment law; Young Republican of the Year, State of Ohio, 1978; over 100 awards & certificates. **Military Serv:** US Army, 1st lt, 1966-75. **Business Addr:** Judge, Dayton-Montgomery County Court Bldg, 301 W Third St, Rm 313, Dayton, OH 45402.

LITTLEJOHN, EDWARD J.
Attorney, educator. **Personal:** Born May 5, 1935, Pittsburgh, PA; son of Crystal Hudson-Littlejohn and Chester W Littlejohn; divorced; children: Martin, Victor. **Educ:** Wayne State Univ, BA 1965; Detroit Coll of Law, JD (cum laude) 1970; Columbia Univ Law Sch, LLM 1974, JSD 1982. **Career:** City of Detroit, varied Gov serv 1959-70; Detroit Coll of Law, prof 1970-72; Wayne State Law Sch, assoc prof & assistant dean 1972-76, assoc dean & prof of law 1976-78, prof of law 1972-96, prof emeritus of law, 1996-; Univ of Utrecht Netherlands, visiting prof, 1974; Wayne State Center for Black Studies, faculty research assoc; The Damon J Keith Law Collection for History of African-American Lawyers and Judges of Wayne State University, founder/director. **Orgs:** Apptd to Bd Police Commrs Detroit 1974-78, chmn 1977-78; mem MI Bar Assn, NBA, ABA, Wolverine Bar Assn, Alpha Phi Alpha; ed bd The Urban Educator and the Coupleat Lawyer; hearing officer MI Dept of Civil Rights; consult Police Civil Liability and Citizen Complaints; reporter Amer Bar Assoc; task force on Minorities in the Legal Profession; chair, City of Detroit Board of Ethics, 1994-; trustee, Kurdish Museum and Library of NY, 1990-96; Michigan Correctional Officers, training council, 1990-93; Michigan Committee on Juvenile Justice, 1987-90. **Honors/ Awds:** Charles Evans Hughes Fellow Columbia Univ Law School 1973-74; WEB Dubois Scholarship Awd Phylon Soc Wayn State Univ 1986; Special Alumni Awd Wolverine Student Bar Assoc Detroit Coll of Law 1986; Trailblazer Award, Wolverine Bar Assn 1988;Black Educator of 1991 (MI & Ohio), Detroit Peace Corps; Alumni Faculty Service Award, Waynest Alumni Assn, 1991; DH Gordon Excellence in Teaching Award, Alumni and Friends of the Law School, 1994; Champion of Justice Award, State Bar of Michigan, 1995; publications in various legal journals. **Military Serv:** USA 1957-59. **Business Addr:** Professor Emeritus of Law, Wayne State Law Sch, 468 W Ferry Mall, Detroit, MI 48202-3620, (313)577-3957.

LITTLEJOHN, JOHN B., JR.
Government official. **Personal:** Born Mar 17, 1942, Chicoda, TX; son of Hattie Brown and J B Littlejohn; divorced; children: Cheryl Ann, David Alan ''J B'' III. **Educ:** Dodge City Coll, AA 1958; Kansas State Univ, BS 1961; Kansas Univ, MSW Cand. **Career:** Marin Tractor Co, dir public affairs, 1973-78; urban renewal negotiator 1972-74; Topeka Corrugated Container Corp, owner, vice pres, gen mgr 1970-73; Greater Topeka C of C, div mgr 1969-70; Juvenile Ct, chief couns 1964-69; Topeka Upward Bound, guidance dir 1968-69; State Banking Bd, dir 1976-81; Blue Cross/Blue Shield, adv bd; Mental Health Prog for Kansas, adv council; Topeka Club, dir; Greenbay Packers, player 1961; 52nd Dist, state rep 1976-81. **Orgs:** Chmn of bd Topeka Boy's Club 1976-; dir YMCA; co-fdr Big Bro/Big Sister; cofdr The Villages Inc; dir Topeka United Way. **Honors/Awds:** Football All-Am 1957-58; all big 8 hon mention 1959; outst young man of Am 1970-71. **Military Serv:** AUS sp 5 1961-64. **Home Addr:** 2014 Regency Parkway, Topeka, KS 66604. **Business Addr:** Regional Director of Sports & Culture, US Department of Housing & Urban Development, 400 State Ave, Gateway Tower II, Rm 400, Kansas City, KS 66101-2406.

LITTLEJOHN, JOSEPH PHILLIP
Educational administrator. **Personal:** Born Aug 31, 1937, Hackensack, NJ; divorced; children: Mavis, Marc. **Educ:** Rut-

gers Univ, BS Sociology 1960; NY Univ, MPA 1972. **Career:** Steward AFB NY, eeo officer & fed women's progs coord 1968-70; NAACP NY, asst dir housing prog 1970; Interreligious Found for Comm Organ Amilcar Cabral Inst, asst dir for admins 1972-73; Natl Council of Churches, coord 1973; New York City Human Resources Admin, prog mgr 1973-75; Jersey City State Coll, dir of affirmative action 1975-78; Fairleigh Dickinson Univ, dir of affirmative action 1978-. **Orgs:** US Army Signal Corps 1960-68; bd of dirs Orange Co United Fund 1968-71; EEO Officer Region II Genl Serv Admin 1970-71; bd of dirs Jersey City Branch NAACP 1977-83; bd of dirs Hudson Co Opportunities Ind Ctr 1978-82; 1st vice pres Amer Assoc for Affirmative Action 1984-. **Honors/Awds:** Student Council Rutgers Univ 1958-60; Martin Luther King Scholarship NY Univ 1969. **Military Serv:** AUS Signal Corps major 8 yrs. **Home Addr:** 66 Madison Ave, Jersey City, NJ 07304. **Business Addr:** Dir of Affirmative Action, Fairleigh Dickinson Univ, 1000 River Rd, Teaneck, NJ 07666.

LITTLEJOHN, SAMUEL GLEASON
Educational administrator (retired). **Personal:** Born Sep 4, 1921, Gaffney, SC; son of Mamie Gleason Littlejohn and Cleo Littlejohn; married Juanita Price, Aug 6, 1946; children: Samuel G Jr. **Educ:** A&T State Univ Greensboro, NC, BS MS 1942; Appalachian State Univ, Educ Specialist Degree 1974. **Career:** Richmond County School, retired school prin; city council 1972-77; pro-tem, mayor 1973-74. **Orgs:** Past master Masonic Order; NAACP; past dir NC Teachers Assn; NC Educ Assn; pres NC Principals Assn; dir Scotland Meml Hosp; dir Laurinburg-Maxton Airport; dir United Way; NEA; past chmn Scotland Co Br NAACP 1959-69; dist pres Dist 8 NC Educ Assn 1972-74; past pres Richmond County Teachers Assn 1959-65, 1967-69. **Home Addr:** 218 Center St, Laurinburg, NC 28352.

LITTLEJOHN, WALTER L.
Educator. **Personal:** Born Mar 5, 1932, Pine Bluff, AR; son of Beatrice Littlejohn and Ed Littlejohn; married Virginia Lowery. **Educ:** BS 1954; MEd 1957; EdD 1966. **Career:** Magnolia, AR, teacher 1954; Magnolia AR, principal 1965-58; Magnolia, AR, public school supt 1958-64; AM&N, prof 1966-74, dean of educ 1975-91, coordinator of graduate programs, 1991-. **Orgs:** Mem Phi Delta Kappa; Alpha Kappa Mu; life mem Omega Psi Phi Frat; Natl Educ Assn; past pres State Tchrn Assn. **Business Addr:** Coordiantor of Grad Programs, School of Education, Univ of AR at Pine Bluff, University Dr, Pine Bluff, AR 71601.

LITTLE RICHARD. See PENNIMAN, RICHARD WAYNE.

LITTLES, GENE
Coach. **Personal:** Born in Washington, DC; married Loredana; children: Darren, Travis, Gino. **Educ:** High Point Coll, 1965-69. **Career:** ABA, basketball player, six years; Appalachian State, asst, 1975-77; North Carolina A & T, head coach, 1977-79; Utah Jazz, asst coach, 1979-82; Cleveland Cavaliers, asst coach, 1982-86; Chicago Bulls, asst coach, 1986-87; Charlotte Hornets, various positions, beginning 1987; Denver Nuggets, asst head coach, currently. **Orgs:** High Point University, board of trustees. **Business Addr:** Asst Head Coach, Denver Nuggets, 1635 Clay Street, Denver, CO 80204, (303)893-6700.

LITTLES, JAMES FREDERICK, JR.
Physician. **Personal:** Born Nov 7, 1960, Florence, SC; son of James & Ella Littles; married Barbara Moultrie Littles, Jun 15, 1985; children: Jessica, Elena. **Educ:** South Carolina State University, BS, 1982; Howard University, MD, 1986. **Career:** Univ of MI Med School, clinical instructor, 1990-; Veterans Affairs Med Center, chief, radiation oncology service, 1991-. **Orgs:** One Hundred Black Men of Greater Detroit; Diplomate of the American Bd of Radiology; NAACP; South Carolina State Univ Alumni Assn; MI Society of Therapeutic Radiology; Straight Gate Church, deacon. **Special Achievements:** The First African-American Faculty Member, Dept of Radiation Oncology, Univ of MI Med School; The First African-American Clinical Service Chief, Veterans Affairs Med Center, Ann Arbor, MI. **Business Addr:** Chief, Radiation Oncology Service, Veterans Affairs Medical Center, 2215 Fuller, Ann Arbor, MI 48105, (313)769-7426.

LITTLETON, ARTHUR C.
Research psychologist. **Personal:** Born Sep 25, 1942, St Louis, MO; married Paula; children: Stephen, David, Jeffrey, Dennis. **Educ:** Univ of MO, BA 1962, MEd 1963; St Louis Univ, PhD 1969. **Career:** Univ of MO St Louis, instr 1968-69, asst prof of ed, research psych 1969-71; Urban Behavioral Rsch Assoc, pres. **Orgs:** Former cons, rschr, youth counselor, publ school teacher; lecturer, numerous natl conf of professional orgs. **Honors/Awds:** Co-author "Black Viewpoints"; contrib articles in various scholarly jrnl; chmn black caucus Amer Ed Rsch Assoc 1972; bd mem Bi State Transit Agency. **Business Addr:** President, Urban Behavioral Rsch Assoc, 1210 Washington Ste 100, St Louis, MO 63101.

LITTLETON, RALPH DOUGLASS. See Obituaries section.

LITTLETON, RUPERT, JR.
Auto dealer. **Personal:** Born Jul 26, 1950, Fort Gaines, GA; son of Trava L Reynolds and Rupert Littleton, Sr; married Carolyn Dixon, Aug 29, 1981; children: Shaeyna, Zogko, Maceo, Michael, Duane. **Career:** Sunbelt Ford-Mercury Inc, Quincy, FL, owner/gen mgr, currently. **Orgs:** Black Ford-Lincoln-Mercury Dealers Assn; Natl Auto Dealers Assn.

LIVELY, IRA J.
Realtor. **Personal:** Born Apr 18, 1926, Memphis, TN; children: Illona D Threadgill Jones. **Educ:** Monterey Peninsula Coll, AS 1970; Golden Gate Univ, Bachelor degree 1974, MA 1978. **Career:** Seaside Police Dept, juvenile officer 1956-82; MPC & Gavilan Coll, instructor 1972-; Bell's Real Estate, realtor assoc 1984-; Seaside City Council, seaside council mem; Monterey Peninsula USD, school bd mem; Seaside City Council, mayor pro-tem 1986-88; Monterey Peninsula USD, realtor assoc. **Orgs:** Pres MPUSD 1982-84; notary public Bell's Real Estate 1984-. **Honors/Awds:** Officer of the Year Seaside Amer Legion 1971. **Business Addr:** 440 Harcourt Ave, Seaside, CA 93955.

LIVERPOOL, CHARLES ERIC
Budget analyst. **Personal:** Born Mar 14, 1946, Ann's Grove Village, Guyana; son of Ivy Thomas Liverpool (deceased) and Eric C Liverpool (deceased); married Joan Ann Paddy; children: Charles Jr, Dionne, Euisi, Jamal. **Educ:** Bronx Comm Coll, AA 1978; Bernard M Baruch Coll, BBA 1982; Long Island Univ, 1986-88; Central MI Univ, MSA, master of general admin, 1995. **Career:** Navy Resale Serv Spt Office, acctg/liab ins asst 1974-83, program analyst 1980-86; HQ 77th US Army Reserve Cmd, budget analyst 1986-89; Fulton County Government, Atlanta, GA, financial budget evaluation specialist, 1990-. **Orgs:** Educ vp/secty Navresso Toastmasters #2285 1978-82; vice chmn supv comm 1980-85, mem bd of dirs 1985-89, CGA Federal Credit Union Brooklyn NY; literacy volunteer tutor Queens Boro Public Library 1984-89; mem New York Urban League 1985-89; mem Natl Black MBA Assoc 1986-; program committee member/tutor support coordinator, Literacy Vol Amer, 1990-; Amer Assoc St Budget & Program Analysts, (AABPA), mem, 1994-. **Honors/Awds:** Sigma Iota Epsilon (Scholastic MGT Society). **Special Achievements:** Author/Publisher: A Brother's Soul: Writings of a Country Boy-Poetry, 1992; Another Days Journey-Poetry, 1996. **Military Serv:** AUS Reserve master sgt 17 yrs; Army Achievement Medal, Army Reserve Comp Achm Medal 1979; Meritorious Service Medal, 1988, 1989. **Home Addr:** 424 Orchards Walk, Stone Mountain, GA 30087. **Business Addr:** Financial Budget Evaluation Specialist, Fulton County Government, 141 Pryor St, Suite 7027, Atlanta, GA 30303-3453, (404)730-7650.

LIVERPOOL, HERMAN OSWALD
Cleric (retired). **Personal:** Born Feb 12, 1925, Georgetown, Guyana; son of Hilda Beatrice Hinds Liverpool and Joseph Nathaniel Liverpool; married Lucille Joycelyn Cleaver, Jun 1, 1953; children: Lorraine Janet, James Nathaniel, Lynda Aleathea. **Educ:** University of London, Avery Hill College, teacher's certificate, education, 1971; University of the West Indies, BA, theology, 1977; International Seminary, ThM, 1985, DMin, 1990. **Career:** The Inner London Education Authority, teacher, 1971-73; The Bishop, Anglican Diocese of Guyana, clergyman, 1977-80; The Bishop, The Episcopal Diocese of Florida, vicar, 1983-; St Cyprian's/St Mary's Episcopal Church, vicar, beginning 1983-. **Orgs:** St Hilda's Anglican Church, Brockley Rise, England, vestry member, 1971; Community Relations Council, London, England, executive mem, 1971-73; Holy Redeemer Boy Scouts, Guyana, founder, 1977-80; East Coast Musical Church Festival, Diocese of Guyana, initiator, 1980; St Cyprian's Annual Church Festival, founder, 1984-; Friends of St Cyprian's, founder, 1984; St Augustine Ministerial Alliance, 1983, president, 1987-88; Vicar's Landing, Life Pastoral Care Services, board member, 1988-91. **Honors/Awds:** Awarded symbolic gavel by St Augustine Ministerial Alliance, 1986; plaque and letter of appreciation, Vicar's Landing, 1991. **Special Achievements:** A Brief History of the Anglican Church in Guyana, unpublished, 1826-70; Collection of Poems, unpublished. **Home Addr:** 8125 SW 24th St, Davie, FL 33324-5701, (904)797-5831.

LIVINGSTON, JOYCE
Librarian, educator. **Personal:** Born in Houston, TX; daughter of Jessie M McKelvey Wilson and C W Gunnells; married Ulysses Livingston (divorced); children: Deanne, Ronald, Kevin. **Educ:** Univ of Southern California, BA, 1974, MLS, 1975. **Career:** Los Angeles County Public Library, Los Angeles, CA, librarian-in-charge, 1980-81; Los Angeles Trade Technical Community College, Los Angeles, CA, reference librarian, 1980-91, department chairperson, library, 1991-. **Orgs:** Member, California Black Faculty and Staff Assn, 1981-; member, Black caucus, California Library Assn, 1985-; member, Black caucus, American Library Assn, 1989-90; member, American Library Assn, 1989-90; elected member of executive board, American Federation of Teachers for Los Angeles Community College District, 1988-. **Honors/Awds:** Ford Foundation Honoree, Los Angeles Community College District, Southwest College, 1972; Dean's List, Univ of Southern California, 1973-74; Phi Alpha Theta, 1973; cum laude, Univ of Southern California, 1974. **Business Addr:** Department Chairperson, Library Services, Los Angeles Trade-Technical College, 400 W Washington Blvd, Los Angeles, CA 90015.

LIVINGSTON, L. BENJAMIN
Psychologist. **Personal:** Born Jul 1, 1931, Eufaula, OK; married Margaret Juanita Johnson; children: David, Harvey, Lawrence. **Educ:** Univ of AZ, BA 1958; AZ State U, MA 1968; AZ State U, PhD 1971. **Career:** Univ of CA Riverside, psychologist; AZ State U, couns psychol 1969-71; Booker T Washington Sch, Instr 1967-69; Youth Oppor Ctr AZ State, supv couns; Employment Svc, 1965-66; St Mary's HS, dir music 1963-65; Maricopa Co Detention Home, home couns 1961-63; Whiteriver Pub Sch, supr 1959-61. **Orgs:** Couns to many schools private & govtl agencies; workshops & group facilitator; Mental Health Affirmative Action Com; consult Prof Sch of Psychology LA; adj faculty Univ of Redlands CA; dist rep Omega Psi Phi 1974-; western reg rep Assn of Black Psychologists 1973-; mem NAACP; MENC western reg bd dir Migrant Programs; Urban League; OIC; APGA; Omega Head Start; Phi Mu Alpha 1957; Phi Delta Kappa 1968. **Honors/Awds:** 12th dist Omega man of the year 1967; jaycee recognition & award 1968. **Military Serv:** US Army, e-3 1954-56. **Business Addr:** 3974 Jurupa Ave, Ste 305, Riverside, CA 92506.

LIVINGSTON, RANDY ANTHONY
Professional basketball player. **Personal:** Born Apr 2, 1975, New Orleans, LA. **Educ:** Louisiana State. **Career:** Houston Rockets, 1996-97; Atlanta Hawks, 1997-. **Business Addr:** Professional Basketball Player, Atlanta Hawks, One CNN Center, Ste 405, Atlanta, GA 30335, (404)827-3800.

LIVINGSTON-WHITE, DEBORAH J. H. (DEBI STARR-WHITE)
Consultant, educator, model. **Personal:** Born Nov 21, 1947, DuQuoin, IL; daughter of Tressie May Gaston-Livingston and Jetson Edgar Livingston; married Dr William Tyrone White. **Educ:** Southern IL Univ, BS Ed 1968, MS Ed 1971; Northern IL Univ, EdD Admin 1975; MI State Univ, Post-Doctoral Studies 1980-82; Univ of MI, Post-Doctoral Studies 1981-84. **Career:** Dansville Ag Schools, teacher/consultant, 1976-78; Management Recruiters, account executive, 1976-78; Michigan Dept of Education, special education consultant, 1978-; Michigan State Univ, asst professor, 1980-; Yale Univ, guest lecturer, 1984; Affiliated Models & Talent Agency, Full-Figure Model, 1987-; Talent Shop, Model, Actress, 1987-; Oak Park School Dist, Dir of Special Educ, 1987-96; East Detroit Public Schools, director of spec education, 1996-; Intl Consultants/The People's Network public relations, personal development & marketing consultant, motivational keynote speaker executive director, travel agent, currently. **Orgs:** Consultant, evaluator, US Dept of Educ 1979-; adv comm mem Black Notes MSU Media Prod 1980-83; pres, exec dir Intl Consultant 1981-; vocational chairperson Altrusa Intl 1982-83; reg coord Volunteers in Special Educ 1982-; trainer Project Outreach MDE 1984; Habitat for Humanity fund raising comm, Detroit; Public & Media Relations, chair for Archer, McNamara, 1995; Mental Health Educ Exhibit Treasurer; Alternative Living for Positive Handicapped Adults, pres, 1992-; The Tressie Found, founder & pres; Michigan Assn of Artists & Songwriters, 1989-; International Photographers Assn, 1990-; National Assn of Black Journalists, 1990-; Self-Esteem Institute, 1990-, Musicians', Entertainers', Composers' Creative Association, secretary, vice pres, 1992-. **Honors/Awds:** IL Congress of Parents & Teachers Scholarship 1968; Natl Ford Found Fellowship 1970-75; Phi Kappa Phi Honor Soc 1971; Self Magazine-Chrysler "Fresh Start Award" 1986; Publ "The Vicky Caruso Story, A Miracle in Process" 1979, "Use of the Optacon by Visually Impaired Persons in MI", 1980; Follow-up Study of Visually Impaired Students of the MI School for the Blind "Journal of Visual Impairment & Blindness" 1985; poem "Black Glass" in World's Most Cherished Poems 1985; poem "White Pearl Satin, Pink Orchid Lace" in World's Best Poets 1985; Intl Model & Talent Award, 1987; "Kids Are Special" PTA Service Award, 1991; author, Lyrics From Life by Livingston-White, The Early Years 1969-1989, 1991; author, Transition Life Planning: A Handbook, Oakland Schools, 1991; Transition Planning: A Manual for Students & Parents, 1995-96. **Home Phone:** 800-771-3330. **Business Addr:** Executive Director/President, International Consultants, 6261 St James Ct, West Bloomfield, MI 48322.

LIVINGSTON-WILSON, KAREN
Insurance company executive. **Personal:** marrIed Mark Wilson. **Educ:** Univ of Michigan, bachelor's degree in political science; Wayne State Univ, JD. **Career:** Citizens Insurance Company of America, vice pres, general counsel, secretary, currently. **Special Achievements:** First woman and first African American to hold the posts of vice president, general counsel and secretary of Citizens Insurance Company of America in Howell, MI. **Business Addr:** Vice President, General Counsel, Secretary, Citizens Insurance Company of America, 645 W Grand River, Howell, MI 48843.

L L COOL J (JAMES TODD SMITH)
Actor, Rap singer. **Personal:** Born 1969, Queens, NY. **Career:** Def Jam, music arranger, rap artist, 1985-; discography includes: Radio, 1985; Bigger and Deffer, 1987; Walking With A Panther, 1989; Mama Said Knock You Out, 1990; 14 Shots To The Dome, 1993; Phenomenon, 1997; Actor, Movies: Toys, Hard Way, Krush Groove, Out of Sync; Television: In the House (w/Debbie Allen), 1995-. **Honors/Awds:** Radio went

platinum and considered to be one of the pioneering albums to launch the rap era, 1985; Bigger and Deffer remained on Billboard's Top Ten list for two months, 1987; Received Grammy Award for Best Rap Solo performance for the single, Mama Said Knock You Out, 1992. **Special Achievements:** Cameo appearance in the movie Krush Groove. **Business Addr:** Rap Artist, c/o Def Jam Records, 652 Broadway, New York, NY 10012, (212)979-2610.

LLEWELLYN, JAMES BRUCE
Business executive. **Personal:** Born Jul 16, 1927, New York, NY; married Shahara; children: Kristen Lisa, Alexandra, JayLaan. **Educ:** CCNY, BS; Columbia Grad School of Business; NYU School of Public Admin; NY Law School, LLB, JD. **Career:** Coca Cola Bottler of Philadelphia, chmn, currently; Overseas Private Investment Corp, pres 1977-81; Fedco Food Stores NY, pres 1969-82; New York City Housing & Devel Admin, dep commr 1968-69; Small Business Devel Corp, exec dir 1967-68, dir mgmt training 1966-67, prog officer 1965-66; Small Business Admin, regional dir 1965; Upper Manhattan Office of Small Business Devel Corp, exec dir 1965; Housing Div Housing & Redevel Bd, asst dir 1964-65; Evans Berger & Llewellyn, atty 1962-65; NY Co Dist Atty Office, student asst 1958-60; Retail Liquor Store, proprietor, 1952-56; Queen City Broadcasting Inc, chief exec, currently. **Orgs:** Mem Harlem Lawyers Assn; NY State Food Merchants; pres 100 Black Men Inc; past pres bd of Riverpoint Towers Coop; chmn of bd Freedom Nat Bank; past co-chmn NY Interracial Council for Bus Opportunity; vice pres bd mem Bd of Fedn of Protestant Welfare Agencies; chmn Bd of NY Urban Coalition Venture Capital Corp; mem Bd of NY Urban Coalition; bd dir Flower 5th Ave Hosp; bd trustees City Coll; bd trustees Grad Center City Univ of NY; mem Bd of Nat Interracial Council for Bus Opportunity; dir Amer Can Co, Amer Capital Mgmt Rsch. **Honors/Awds:** Wagner Coll Staten Island Hon PhD; City Univ of NY Hon PhD; Atlanta Univ Hon PhD. **Military Serv:** US Corp of Engrs, 1st lt 1944-48.

LLEWELLYN-TRAVIS, CHANDRA
Organization executive. **Personal:** Born Jun 11, 1960, New York, NY; daughter of Jenny Cody Llewellyn & Gilbert Metcalfe Llewellyn, Sr; married Jack Travis, Sep 28, 1996. **Educ:** City University of New York-Lehman College, BA, 1986; Norwich University-Vermont College, MA, 1992; City University of New York-Graduate Ctr, PhD candidate, 1993-. **Career:** New York City Department of Health, health resource coord, 1984-86; Canaan Baptish Church, project director, living consortium, 1986-89; Colonial Park Community Svcs, family counselor, 1986-89; Malcolm King College, adjunct professor, 1989; New York Urban League, associate and director of education, 1989-91; The National Urban League, director of youth svcs, 1991-95; The Korea Society, director, intercultural outreach, 1995-97; College of New Rochelle, adjunct, 1997. **Orgs:** White Wave Rising, board member, 1995-; Intercultural Alliance, committee mem, 1995-; NY Board of Education-Multicultural Task Force, committee chair, 1989-91; Tri-State Parent Advisory Council, 1992-94; Educational Priorities Panel, 1989-91; NY State Board of Regents, downstate advisory mem, 1989-91; Memorial Baptist Church-AIDS Ministry, pr committee chair, 1996-; Walks of Life, professional volunteer, 1996-. **Honors/Awds:** Outstanding Young Women of America, Awardee, 1987; NY Board of Education, Partner in Education, 1990; Miss Black America, Judge, 1994; Countee Cullen School Parent Association, Community Svc Awd, 1988. **Special Achievements:** "The African-American Male: A Second Emancipation," co-editor, 1992; "African-American Male Immersion School: Segregation? Separation? or Innovation," proj director, 1992; "Rap: Good? Bad? or Both?," executive producer, 1994. **Business Phone:** (212)722-9070.

LLOYD, BARBARA ANN
Educator (retired). **Personal:** Born Sep 21, 1943, Fairfield, AL; daughter of Alberta Salley Lloyd (deceased) and Arthur Lee Lloyd (deceased). **Educ:** Tuskegee Institute (University), Tuskegee, AL, BSN, 1965; Univ of Alabama, Birmingham, Birmingham AL, MSN, 1975; Univ of Alabama, Tuscaloosa, AL, EdD, 1986. **Career:** Univ of Alabama Hospital, Birmingham, AL, staff nurse, 1965; Veterans Admin Hospital, Birmingham, AL, staff nurse, 1966-68; Tuskegee Institute, Tuskegee, AL, instructor, 1968-70; Jefferson St Jr College, Birmingham, AL, instructor, 1970-72, Lawson State Jr College, instructor, 1972-74; Univ of Alabama, Birmingham, AL, instructor/asst prof/assoc prof, 1975-95. **Orgs:** President, Tuskegee University National Nursing Alumni Assn, 1987-90; member, Kappa Delta Pi Honor Society in Education, 1982; member, Sigma Theta Tau International, Hon Society in Nursing, 1975; life member, Chi Eta Phi Sorority Inc, 1975; member, Order of Eastern Stars, 1983-; Board of Education, Fairfield City School System, AL, 1992-97. **Honors/Awds:** Author: Articles, Journal of Gerontological Nursing, 1979; The Glowing Lamp (journal), 1980, 1989; Association of Black Nursing Faculty Journal, 1994. **Home Addr:** 204 Westmoreland Circle, Fairfield, AL 35064.

LLOYD, GEORGE LUSSINGTON
Clergyman. **Personal:** Born Aug 9, 1931, Valley. **Educ:** Alma White Coll, BA 1959; Moravian Theological Seminary, MDiv 1962; Iona Coll, MSEd 1969; San Francisco Theological Seminary, DMin 1984. **Career:** Moravian Church, Guyana, S America, minister 1962-65; United Moravian Church, minister 1965-; pastoral counselor; licensed marriage counselor State of NJ, 1986. **Orgs:** Board president Harlem Interfaith Counseling Service 1966-70; fellow Amer Assn of Pastoral Counselors 1967-; president dept Pastoral Care Council of Churches City of NY 1983-; member board of directors Council of Churches City of NY 1983-; member Christian Assn for Psychological Studies 1984; vice pres, Eastern District Executive Board of the Moravian Church; The American Association of Christian Counselors. **Honors/Awds:** Special Contribution NYVA Med Center 23 St at 1st Ave 1983; Performance Award NYVA Med Center 23rd at 1st Ave NY 1984; Recognition Award NY Healing Community, NY 1984. **Military Serv:** AUS PFC 1953-55. **Business Addr:** Minister, United Moravian Church, 3357 Palmer Ave, Bronx, NY 10475-1510.

LLOYD, GREGORY LENARD
Professional football player. **Personal:** Born May 26, 1965, Miami, FL; married Rhonda; children: Gregory Lenard II, Tiana Cassandra, Jhames Isaac. **Educ:** Fort Valley State. **Career:** Pittsburgh Steelers, linebacker, 1988-. **Honors/Awds:** Pittsburgh Steelers, Ed Block Courage Award, 1988; Pittsburgh YMCA, Man of the Year Award, 1994; UPI, Defensive Player of the Year, 1994; Kansas City 101 Club, Defensive Player of the Year, 1994; Pro Bowl appearances, 1991-95. **Business Addr:** Professional Football Player, Pittsburgh Steelers, Three Rivers Stadium, 300 Stadium Circle, Pittsburgh, PA 15212, (412)323-1200.

LLOYD, JAMES
Business executive. **Personal:** Born Jul 13, 1932, Hensley, WV; son of Evangeline Lloyd and James Lloyd; divorced. **Educ:** WV State Coll Inst, attended 1950, graduate. **Career:** James Lloyd Ins Agency Inc, owner; CLM Development & Consturction Co, pres; CLM Trucking Inc, vice pres. **Orgs:** Bd dir Rochester-Genesee Reg Transportation Auth; mem NAACP; Urban League; chmn Adv Bd for PUSH Excel; bd mem Genesee Health Care Assn. **Honors/Awds:** Black Student's Awd St John Fisher Coll 1975; Outstanding Man in the Comm Rochester NY.

LLOYD, LEONA LORETTA
Judge. **Personal:** Born Aug 6, 1949, Detroit, MI; daughter of Naomi Chisolm Lloyd and Leon Thomas Lloyd. **Educ:** Wayne State Univ, BS 1971, JD 1979. **Career:** Lloyd & Lloyd Law Firm, senior law partner; 36th District Court, judge, 1994-. **Orgs:** Mem Amer Bar Assoc, Wolverine Bar Assoc, Mary McLeod Bethune Assoc of MI; past mem Natl Conf of Black Lawyers, Natl Assoc of Negro Business & Prof Women; Admitted to US District Court 1983, Michigan Supreme Court 1985, US Supreme Court 1988; National Assn of Recording Artists. **Honors/Awds:** Scholarship Bd of Governors Wayne State Univ, 1970,75; Fred Hampton Image Awd 1984; Black Women Hall of Fame Found 1985; Kizzy Image Awd 1985; Black Women in MI Exhibit 1985; Nat'l Coalition of 100 Black Women Achievement Awd 1986; comm serv awd presented by Wayne Cnty Exec 1986; Univ of Detroit Black Law Students Assn, cert of merit 1986; Wayne St Univ Assn of Black Business Students, minority business of the year awd 1986; 100 Top Black Lawyers in Detroit, Native Detroiter, 1990; Spirit of Detroit Award, 1991; Martin Luther King Award, 1995; State of MI Special Tribute, 1995; Resolution from Wayne County, 1995; City Clerks Certificate of Appreciation, 1995; Testimonial from the Det City Council, 1995. **Business Addr:** Judge, 36th District Court, 421 Madison Ave, Detroit, MI 48226.

LLOYD, LEONIA JANNETTA
Judge, performing artist manager, attorney. **Personal:** Born Aug 6, 1949, Detroit, MI; daughter of Naomi Lloyd and Leon Lloyd. **Educ:** Wayne State Univ, BS 1971, JD 1979. **Career:** Lloyd & Lloyd, sr law partner; Double L Management, partner; 36th District Court, judge, currently. **Orgs:** Past mem Natl Conference of Black Lawyers 1975-79; mem Friends of the Afro-American Museum 1983-; mem Amer Bar Assn; mem Wolverine Bar Assn; mem Mary McLeod Bethune Assn; past mem Natl Assn of Negro Business and Professional Women; mem, Assn of Black Judges of Michigan; mem, National Judicial Council. **Honors/Awds:** Scholarship Bd of Governors Scholarship/Wayne State Univ 1970, 1975; Certificate of Appreciation bestowed by Mayor Coleman Young 1977; Kizzy Image Award 1985; Fred Hampton Image Award 1984; IL Black Woman's Hall of Fame; Black Women in MI Exhibit 1985; Natl Coalition of 100 Black Women Award 1986; ABBS Minority Business of the Year 1986; Wayne County Exec Community Serv Award bestowed by William Lucas 1986; negotiated recording contracts for, Arista's recording artist, "KIARA" and MCA's recording artist, "Ready for the World" and RCA's recording artists, "David Ruffin" and "Eddie Kendricks"; Keep The Dream Alive Award, 1995; B'NAI B'RITH Award, 1993; Special Tribute, State of Michigan from Sen Michael J O'Brien, 1995. **Business Addr:** Judge, 36th District Court, 421 Madison Ave, Ste 3075, Detroit, MI 48226.

LLOYD, LEWIS KEVIN
Professional athlete. **Personal:** Born Feb 22, 1959, Philadelphia, PA. **Educ:** Drake Univ, 1979-81; New Mexico Military Jr Coll, 1977-79. **Career:** Golden State Warriors, guard, 1981-83; Houston Rockets, 1983-1989, 1990-; Cedar Rapids (CBA), 1988-89; Philadelphia 76ers, 1990;. **Business Addr:** Professional Basketball Player, Houston Rockets, PO Box 272349, Houston, TX 77277.

LLOYD, MARCEA BLAND
Attorney. **Personal:** Born Oct 12, 1948, Chicago, IL; daughter of Beatriz Bland and Ralph Bland; children: Randy Jr, Shomari, Malaika. **Educ:** Knox College, BS, BA, 1968; Northwestern University, JD, 1971. **Career:** Montgomery Wards Co, senior antitrust counsel, 1974-77; University of Minnesota, assistant attorney, 1977-78; Medtronic, Inc, international counsel, 1978-83, senior legal counsel, 1983-91, vp & assistant general counsel, 1991-. **Orgs:** Jack & Jill of America, Inc, currently; Links, Inc, currently; dir, Health Partners Health Maintenance Organization; Natl Bar Assn, 1971-; Turning Point Inc Foundation, president, currently; American Bar Association, currently; Minnesota Minority Lawyers Association, currently; Minnesota State Bar Association, currently; vp, MN Assn & Corporate Counsel; Trustee Episcopal Community Services. **Business Addr:** VP & Assistant General Counsel, Medtronic Inc, 7000 Central Ave NE, MS 300, Minneapolis, MN 55432, (612)514-3284.

LLOYD, PHIL ANDREW
Automobile dealer. **Personal:** Born Jun 24, 1952, Buffalo, NY; son of Mable Spivey Lloyd and Otis Lloyd; divorced; children: Phil A Lloyd, Jr. **Educ:** Erie Community, Buffalo, NY, AAS, 1972; Buffalo State, Buffalo, NY, BS, 1975. **Career:** Manufacture Trader Trusts, Buffalo, NY, collector, 1975; Wicks Lumber, Orchard Pk, NY, sales mgr, 1976-80; Ed Mullinax Ford, Amherst, OH, salesman, 1981-86; Western Ford-Mercury, Clyde, OH, pres, 1987-. **Orgs:** Mem, Phi Beta-Lamba, 1971-73; mem, Environmental Pollution Control, 1972-73; mem, Clyde Business Assn, 1987-; pres, Twin City Kiwanis, 1980-81; trustee, Clyde Kiwanis, 1988-89. **Honors/Awds:** Distinguished Service, Ford Motor, 1981-86; Salesman of the Year, Mullinas Ford, 1985; Sales Quality and Service, Lincoln-Mercury Div, 1988; Marketshare Pacesetter, Black Ford-Lincoln Mercury Assn, 1988; Quality Commitment, Black Ford-Lincoln Mercury Assn, 1988. **Business Addr:** President, Western Ford-Mercury Inc, 1036 W McPherson Hwy, Clyde, OH 43410.

LLOYD, RAYMOND ANTHONY
Physician, educator. **Personal:** Born Nov 25, 1941; married Eveline Moore; children: Raymond, Rhea, Ryan. **Educ:** Jamaica Coll, 1958; Howard Univ, BS 1962; Howard Univ Coll Med, MD 1966; Freedmen's Hosp, resident 1967-68; VA Hosp, Children's Hosp & NIH, fellow 1969-71. **Career:** Howard Univ Coll Med, asst prof of med 1971-; Comm Group Health Found, consultant 1971-76; Narcotics Treatment Admin, assoc admin treatment 1972-73; Div of Prevention, Natl Inst of Alcoholism & Alcohol Abuse, initial rev comm 1972. **Orgs:** Mem DC Med Soc; Caribbean Am Intercultural Orgn; Nat Assn of Intern & Residents; AMA; Nat Capital Med Found Inc; DC C of C; Am Heart Assn; AmFedn of Clinical Rsrch; Am Professional Practice Assn; flw Intl Coll of Angiology; mem WA Heart Assn; sub-com for CPR; Nat Capital Med Found; sub-com on Cardiovascular Diseases; pres L&L Hlth Care Assn; adv bd Hemisphere Nat Bank; mem Bata Kappa Chi 1962; Phi Beta Kappa 1962. **Honors/Awds:** Hon in chem 1962; hon pediatrics 1966; Daniel Hale & Williams Award; intern of yr 1967; BKX Award in Chem 1961. **Business Addr:** 1613a Rhode Island Ave NE, Washington, DC 20018.

LLOYD, WALTER P.
Government official. **Career:** State of South Carolina, state representative, currently. **Business Addr:** State Representative, State of South Carolina, Blatt Bldg, PO Box 11867, Columbia, SC 29211, (803)734-3028.

LLOYD, WANDA
Editor. **Personal:** Born Jul 12, 1949, Columbus, OH; married Willie Burk; children: Shelby Renee. **Educ:** Spelman Coll, BA 1971. **Career:** The Providence Evening Bulletin, copy editor 1971-73; Columbia Univ, instr 1972; The Miami Herald, copy editor 1973-74; The Atlanta Jrnl, copy editor 1974-75; The Washington Post, copy editor 1975-76; Univ of MD, instr 1978; Los Angeles Times-WA Post News Svc, dep editor; USA Today, senior editor, currently. **Orgs:** Mem WA Assoc of Black Journalists, Natl Assoc of Black Jrnlst, Amer Assoc of Sunday & Feature Editors; bd mem, consult Howard Univ Urban Jrnl Workshop; vice pres WA Spelman Alumnae Assoc 1984-86; mem Delta Sigma Theta; guest lecturer Univ of MD 1977, Booker T Washington Jr HS 1974; mem So Reg Press Inst. **Business Addr:** Senior Editor, USA Today, Gannett Co Inc, One Gannett Dr, White Plains, NY 10604-3498.

LOCHE, LEE EDWARD
Business executive. **Personal:** Born Feb 17, 1926, Collinston, LA; married Opeary Mae Hill; children: Veronica Tappin, Howard D, Edward C. **Educ:** Univ of Sipan, 1943-45; Atlanta Coll of Mortuary Science, 1949; Spaulding Business Coll, 1952. **Career:** Loche's Mortuary, Inc, mortician 1964; Purple Shielf Life Ins Co, manager 1966; Loche's Mortuary, Inc, presi-

dent, currently. **Orgs:** Treasurer S Louisiana Conf EME 1962-; pres Loche's Mortuary, Inc 1965-; mem Fidelity Lodge No 53 1966-; Police Jury mem 1972-, vice pres 1983-; vice pres Morehouse Police Jury 1983-; Police Jury, pres, 1994-98. **Honors/Awds:** Cert of Merit Natl Insurance Assn 1981. **Military Serv:** Transportation pfc 2 yrs. **Home Addr:** 412 Cyrstal St, Bastrop, LA 71220. **Business Addr:** President, Loche's Mortuary, Inc, 412 W Hickory, Bastrop, LA 71220.

LOCKARD, JON ONYE
Artist, educator, lecturer. **Personal:** Born Jan 25, 1932, Detroit, MI; divorced; children: John C, Carlton E. **Educ:** Wayne Univ, 1949-50; Fields' Sch of Art, Cert 1951-52; Meinzinger Art Sch, Cert 1951-52. **Career:** Natl Conf of Artists, exec bd 1972-83; Washtenaw Comm Coll, faculty 1979-; Acad of Creative Thought, dir; Natl Conf of Artists, pres; Univ of MI Center for Afro-American & African Studies, artist & asst prof art & Afro-Amer Hist. **Orgs:** Intl coord First World Cultural Feltival Bahia, Brazil 1980; exhibiting artist Suriname Festival of the Diaspora 1980-81; artist/curator Asubuhi Cultural Center Univ M 1984; numerous art exhibitions throughout country & abroad - Africa, Brazil, Suriname; sponsor Sandy Sanders Basketball League Ann Arbor 1983-85; consult "The State of Black America" channel 56 PBS Detroit 1983-84; consult "Suriname" a documentary channel 56 PBS Detroit 1984 (won 3 Emmys). **Honors/Awds:** NCA Disting Award of Honor Natl Conf of Artists Dakar, Seneyal 1985; Af Am mural "Continium" Wayne State Univ Detroit 1979; mural "Tallest Tree in the Forest" Central State Univ Wilberforce, OH 1981; City of Detroit Proclamation Detroit City Cncl 1980. **Home Addr:** 2649 Wayside Dr, Ann Arbor, MI 48103.

LOCKE, DON C.
Educator. **Personal:** Born Apr 30, 1943, Macon, MS; son of Carlene Locke and Willie Locke; children: Tonya E, Regina C. **Educ:** TN A&I State Univ, BS 1963, MEd 1964; Ball State Univ, EdD 1974. **Career:** South Side HS, social studies teacher 1964-70; Wayne HS, school counselor 1971-73; Ball State Univ European Program, asst prof 1974-75; NC State Univ, asst/assoc prof/prof 1975-89, dept head 1987-93; Director, NCSU Doctoral Program at the Asheville Graduate Center, 1993-. **Orgs:** Mem Alpha Phi Alpha Fraternity Inc; mem New Bern Ave Day Care Center Bd, 1978-86; pres NC Counseling Assoc 1979-80; chairperson S Region Branch ACA 1983-84; mem Carroll Comm Schools Advisory Council 1984-87, ex director, 1987-1991; chairperson NC Bd of Registered Practicing Counselors 1984-87; sec Assn for Counselor Educ & Supervision 1985-86; pres Southern Association for counselor Educ and Supervision 1988-89, member board dir, Asheville -Buncombe United Way, 1997-. **Honors/Awds:** Summer Fellow Center for Advanced Study in Behaviorial Sciences 1979, 1992; ACA Professional Development Award, 1996; co-author "Psychological Techniques for Teachers"; author Increasing Multicultural Understanding; author or co-author of more than 50 articles in professional journals. **Business Addr:** Director, Doctoral Program in ACCE, Asheville Graduate Center, 143 Karpen Hall, Asheville, NC 28804.

LOCKE, DONALD
Artist, educator. **Personal:** Born Sep 17, 1930, Stewartville, Demerara, Guyana; son of Ivy Mae Locke and Donald Locke; married Leila Locke Nee Chaplin (deceased); children: Hew, Jonathan, Corinne Rogers; married Brenda Stephenson, May 23, 1981. **Educ:** Bath Academy of Art, England, certificate in education, 1956, certificate in visual arts w/music and drama, 1957; Edinburgh University, Scotland, MA (with honors), fine art, 1964, ceramic research, 1969-70. **Career:** Aljira Arts, critic-in-residence, 1988; Arizona State University, artist-in-residence, 1979-80; University of California at Santa Cruz, assistant professor, fine art, 1987; Augusta College, assistant professor, fine art department, 1990-91; Georgia State University, fine art dept, interim assistant professor, 1991-92, assistant professor, 1992-. **Honors/Awds:** Mid-Atlantic Arts Foundation Fellowship, Aljira Arts Critic-in-Residence, 1988; Studio Museum of Harlem, Biennial Purchase Award, 1986; Guggenheim Foundation, Fellowship, 1979; British Council, Exhibition Grant, 1978, Travelling Grant to USA, 1977. **Special Achievements:** One of seven painters, official US representation, International Bienal, Equador, 1993; one-man show, Chastain Gallery, Cultural Affairs Bureau, 1994; Atlanta Biennial, Nexus Gallery, 1992; one-man exhibition, Spelman College, 1991; "Afro-Asian Art in Britian, since the War," Arts Council, Great Britian, Hayward Gallery, London, 1989. **Home Addr:** 97 Mobile Ave NE, Atlanta, GA 30305, (404)262-2249.

LOCKE, HENRY DANIEL, JR.
City official, journalist. **Personal:** Born Nov 16, 1936, Greenville, SC; son of Josephine Locke and Henry Locke Sr; married Audrey Marie Harris; children: Daniel Leroy, Tara Yvonne, Henry III. **Educ:** Univ of MD, attended 1955-58; Univ of Buffalo NY, attended 1958-61; American Press Inst Reston VA, completed editing sch 1979. **Career:** MI Ave YMCA Buffalo, weekend exec 1959-63; Buffalo Courier-Express, dist mgr 1960-72; Buffalo, youth counselor 1964-78; Black Enterprise Mag NYC, contrib (corr) 1979-; Buffalo Courier-Express, columnist/reporter 1972-82; The Natl Leader Phila, columnist/reporter 1982-83; Chicago Defender, natl reporter 1983-89, managing editor, 1988-92; Mayor's Office, City of Chicago, Dept of Human Svcs, director of public affairs, freedom of information officer, currently. **Orgs:** Mem Comm Assn of Black Journalists; bd dir MI Ave YMCA 1960-64; bd trustees Lloyd's Meml United Ch of Christ 1962-63; state pr dir NAACP Conf of Br 1976-77; mem Alpha Phi Alpha Frat, NAACP, Buffalo Urban League, Operation PUSH, Black Communications Assn, Black Social Workers/No Region Black Political Caucus; mem NY State Affirmative Action Com; mem BUILD; vice chmn Local 26 Amer Newspaper Guild 1975-; member, CABJ; Headlines Club; Marycrest Homeowners Assn. **Honors/Awds:** Nominee Pulitzer Prize 1977; 6 awds, page-one competition, newspaper articles; 1st place On the Spot Newspaper Reporting AP Wire Serv 1977; 38 Awds Outstanding Comm Serv various orgns; Pulitzer Prize nominee, 1978, 1986, 1987; Man of the Year Award, Chicago, IL, 1988. **Military Serv:** USAF A/1c 1954-58; Good Conduct Medal; Occupation of France; Germany Occupation; Natl Defense Medal. **Business Addr:** Freedom of Information Officer, Department of Human Services, 510 N Peshtigo Ct, Ste 801, Chicago, IL 60611-4309.

LOCKE, HUBERT G.
Educator, educational administrator. **Personal:** Born Apr 30, 1934, Detroit, MI; son of Willa Locke and Hubert H Locke; married; children: Gayle, Lauren. **Educ:** Wayne Univ, BA 1955; Univ of Chgo, BD 1959; Univ of MI, MA 1961; Payne Theological Sem, DDiv, 1968; Chicago Theol Sem, DDivChC, 1971; University of Nebraska, DLitt, 1992. **Career:** Wayne State Univ, asst prof, ed soc 1967-72; Univ of NE Omaha, dean public affairs 1972-76; Univ of WA, assoc dean arts & sci 1976-77, vice provost acad affairs, 1977-82, dean, prof public affairs, 1982-95. **Orgs:** Admin asst to commiss Detroit Police Dept 1966-67; exec dir Citizens Comm for Equal Oppty 1962-65; bd of dir Police Found 1970-71; dir Wm O Douglas Int 1972-; exec vice pres Inst for the Study of Contemp Soc Problems 1972-. **Honors/Awds:** Liberty Bell Awd MI Bar Assoc 1966; publ "The Detroit Riot of 1967" Wayne State Univ press 1969, "The Care & Feeding of White Liberals" Paulist Press 1970, "The Church Confronts the Nazis" 1984, "Exile in the Fatherland" 1986; The Black Antisemitism Controversy, 1994. **Business Addr:** Professor, Univ of Washington, Grad School of Public Affairs, Box 353055, Seattle, WA 98195.

LOCKE, MAMIE EVELYN
Educational administrator. **Personal:** Born Mar 19, 1954, Brandon, MS; daughter of Amanda McMahon Locke and Ennis Locke. **Educ:** Tougaloo College, Tougaloo, MS, BA, 1976; Atlanta University, Atlanta, GA, MA, 1978, PhD, 1984. **Career:** Dept of Archives & History, Jackson, MS, archivist, 1977-79; Atlanta Historical Society, Atlanta, GA, archivist, 1979-81; Hampton University, Hampton, VA, associate professor, 1981-, assistant dean, 1991-96, dean, 1996-. **Orgs:** National Conference of Black Political Scientists, 1976-, executive council, 1989-92, president elect, 1992-93, president, 1993-94; Alpha Kappa Alpha Sorority Inc; American Political Science Association, 1990-; Southeastern Women's Studies Association, 1987-; advisor, member, Alpha Kappa Mu National Honor Society, 1990-; editorial board, PS: Politics and Political Science, 1992-95; editorial board, National Political Science Review, 1994-; Hampton City Council; commissioner, Hampton Planning Commission; commissioner, Hampton Roads Planning District Commission; commissioner, Hampton Redevelopment & Housing Authority; VA Municipal League, Government Affairs Committee; National Black Caucus of Local Elected Officers; Women in Municipal Government, bd mem, 1998-99. **Honors/Awds:** Lindback Award for Distinguished Teaching, Hampton University, 1990; Rodney Higgins Award, National Conference Black Political Scientists, 1986; Fulbright-Hays Award, Department of Education, 1986; Ford Foundation Grant, College of William & Mary, 1988; Ford Foundation Grant, Duke University, 1987; NEH Fellowship, National Endowment for the Humanities, 1985. **Home Phone:** (804)722-5302. **Business Addr:** Dean, Hampton University, School of Liberal Arts & Education, 119 Armstrong Hall, Hampton, VA 23668, (804)727-5400.

LOCKE-MATTOX, BERNADETTE
Women's basketball coach. **Personal:** Born Dec 31, 1958, Rockwood, TN; daughter of Alfred M Locke. **Educ:** Roane State Community College, Harriman, TN, AS, 1977-79; University of Georgia, Athens, GA, BS, education, 1979-82. **Career:** Univ of Georgia, Athens, GA, academic advisor, 1982-83; Xerox Corp, Atlanta, GA, customer service rep, 1984-85; Univ of Georgia, Athens, GA, asst coach, 1985-90; Univ of Kentucky, Lexington, KY, asst coach, 1990-94, asst athletics dir, 1994-95, Head Women's Basketball Coach, 1995-. **Honors/Awds:** Academic Award, Univ of GA, 1980; Academic All-American, Univ of GA, 1981; National Honor Soc, Univ of GA, 1981. **Special Achievements:** First Black woman to head coach the woman's basketball team at Univ of KY. **Business Addr:** Head Coach, Women's Basketball, University of Kentucky, Lexington Ave Memorial Coliseum, Lexington, KY 40506-0019.

LOCKERMAN, GENEVA LORENE REUBEN
Educator. **Personal:** Born Nov 4, 1928, Silverstreet, SC; married Joseph H Lockerman; children: Joseph H Jr. **Educ:** Benedict Coll, BA 1949; Columbia Univ, MA 1950; NY Univ, Columbia Unvi, post-grad study. **Career:** FL A&M Univ, counselor freshmen women 1951-53; NY Telephone Co, serv rep 1954-55; Jersey City Bd of Educ, hist tchr 1959-64; Jersey City Comm & Neighborhood Devel Orgn, educ specialist 1965-68; Dartmouth Coll Educ Ctr, lectr in educ/adjunt 1971-74; Jersey City State Coll, counselor counseling & psychol svc. **Orgs:** Mem Alpha Kappa Mu Hon Soc; mem Phi Delta Kappa; mem Amer Personnel & Guid Assn; chairperson/hon soc mem Jersey City Educ Ctr; bd dir I Jersey City Bd of Personnel Practices; mem Natl Cncl of Negro Women; bd dir Sr Companion Prog Alpha Kappa Alpha Sor; past mem Jersey Cty Br NAACP; mem Bayview Ave Black Assn; mem Jersey City Planning Bd; mem NJ Assn for Affirmative Action; mem Assn for Non-White Concerns. **Honors/Awds:** Jersey Journal Woman of Achievement 1967; NJ Outstanding Citizen 1969; Sr Companion Awd Action Agy; Sojourner Truth Awd 1984 Action for Sickle Cell Anemia of Hudson Co Inc; Mary McLeod Bethune Awd for Black Women Achievers 1983 Com-Bi-Nations.

LOCKET, ARNOLD, JR.
Clergyman. **Personal:** Born Oct 6, 1929, Bethel, NC; married Jeffie Bernadine; children: Gwendolyn E. **Educ:** No AZ Univ Flagstaff, BA 1971f No AZ U, MA 1975. **Career:** Coconino Co & Flagstaff NAACP Br, reverend 1977-; Coconino Comm Guidance Cntr Inc, prog dir 1974-77; AZ State Dept of Econ Security, vocat rehab couns 1973-74; AZ State Dept of Econ Security, correctional rehab couns 1971-73. **Orgs:** Mem Nat Assn of Vocational Couns 1971-; adv counc mem AZ State Dept of Econ security 1977-; chmn plan devel com No AZ Health Systems Agency 1979;br pres Flagstaff NAACP Br 1976-; chmn of Mayor's Human Rel Com City of Flagstaff 1976-80. **Honors/Awds:** 1st Worshipful Master F&AM Prince Hall Lodge Killeen TX 1963; Ust Black Dept Head Coconion Co Flagstaff AZ 1977; recipient of Bronze Star & Army Commendation Medal AUS. **Military Serv:** AUS sfc-e7 1948-68. **Business Addr:** County Courthouse, San Francisco Birch, Flagstaff, AZ 86001.

LOCKETT, ALICE FAYE
Program analyst. **Personal:** Born Sep 6, 1944, Linden, TX; daughter of Bernice Fisher Lockett and Eddie Lockett. **Educ:** Prairie View A&M University, BS, 1968; University of Iowa, certificate, 1972; Colorado State University, MS, 1974; Montreal Diet Dispensary, certificate, 1975. **Career:** Denver Department of Health & Hospitals, public health nutritionist, 1969-73; L&L Health Care Associates, community nutritionist, 1974-76; Community College of Denver, nutrition instructor, 1973; Department of Human Services, public health nutritionist, 1976-81; DC General Hospital, Maternal and Child Nutrition, chief, beginning 1981-; USDA, Food and Consumer Svc, program analyst, currently. **Orgs:** American Dietetic Association, 1969-; DC Metropolitan Dietetic Association, 1974-; March of Dimes, Health Advisory Board, 1978-; Society Nutrition Education, 1990-. **Honors/Awds:** DC General Hospitals, Outstanding Performance Award, 1983-92, Outstanding Woman of Division, 1984, Employee of the Month, 1985, Outstanding Woman of Colorado, Nominee, 1972. **Special Achievements:** Presentation, "The Impact of Drug Abusers on Prenatal and the Unborn," 1991; author: Preliminary Results from a Study to Examine the Effects of Breastfeeding on Neonatal Intensive Care Cost, 1991; Prenatal Nutrition for Substance Abusing Women: Reaching the Unreachable, 1991; Perspectives on Breastfeeding for the High Risk Neonate, 1992; Nutrition Offset Drugs, 1993. **Home Addr:** 5300 Holmes Run Pkwy, #1007, Alexandria, VA 22304. **Business Phone:** (703)305-2730.

LOCKETT, BRADFORD R.
Designer, tailor. **Personal:** Born Sep 26, 1945, Norfolk, VA; married Brendale Joyce; children: Belinda Joyce. **Educ:** TX Southern Univ, BS 1968; Natl School of Dress Design, 1966. **Career:** JC Penney Co Tucson, AZ, head tailor 1970-71; Brotherhood Assn of Military Airmen Tucson, vice pres 1971-72; Tucson, master mason 1971-72; Research & AnalysisDMAFB Tucson, AZ, clothing counselor for USAF 1970-72; Joe Frank of Houston, Asst fashion designer 1973; Mr Creations Inc & Battlesteins, fashion designer & master tailor. **Orgs:** Mem Gulf Coast Fashion Assn; Small Bus Administrn; Basilus of Omega Psi Phi Frat 1966-67; master mason 11th Degree Pima Lodge #10 Tucson. **Honors/Awds:** Spl air force Documentary (AFN Series #38-ON Preparatory Mgmt) Film of the Fashion Entertainment of Brad Lockett 1972; man of yr award Ohega Psi Phi 1967; outstanding clothing design award The Yardley Co 1969; award to study fashion design under Italian Designer Emilio Pucci 1966; outstanding Military Achievements 1972. **Military Serv:** USAF e-5 staff sgt. **Business Addr:** Mr Creation Inc, Pima Co, Tucson, AZ.

LOCKETT, HAROLD JAMES
Physician, medical administrator. **Personal:** Born Jul 17, 1924, Wilmington, DE; son of Annie Colbert Lockett and Jesse Lockett; married Betty Griffin Lockett, Jun 11, 1950 (deceased); children: Cherie. **Educ:** IN Univ, AB 1948; Meharry Med Coll, MD 1952; LA County Gen Hosp, internship, 1952-53; Univ of MI Med Ctr, Psych 1956; Hawthorn Ctr, Child Psych 1958. **Career:** Hawthorn Center, Northville, MI, staff psychiatrist, 1958-71, asst dir, 1971-90, dir, 1990-; Univ of Michigan Medical

School, clinical asst professor. **Orgs:** Bd dir Spaulding for Children 1968-, mem Amer Psych Assn; fellow Amer Acad of Child & Adolescent Psych; fellow Amer Ortho Psych Assn; Black Psychiatric Assn; Natl Med Assn. **Honors/Awds:** Several articles in professional jrnls & books. **Military Serv:** Infantry s/sgt 1943-45; Med Corp 2nd lt 1950.

LOCKETT, JAMES D.

Educator. **Personal:** son Of Elvie Thomas Lockett and J D Lockett. **Educ:** Morehouse Coll, BA, pol sci; Atlanta Univ, MLS, DA, history, humanities; Case Western Reserve Univ, MA, political science. **Career:** Allen Univ, natl teaching fellow, 1966-67; TN State Univ, asst prof, political sci and history, 1967-69; Tuskegee Inst, asst prof, 1969-70; St Augustine Coll, acting chmn, Dept of history political sci, black studies, social scis, 1970-72; MS Valley State Univ, asst prof in the TCCP, 1972-74; Opportunities Industrialization Ctr, staff; Stillman Coll, assoc prof, history, pol sci & geography, 1977-91, prof, 1991-. **Orgs:** Pres, West AL Chap, Assn for the Study of Afro-Amer Life & History, 1983; apptd mem, Economic Adv Council, AL Conf of Black Mayors Inc, 1984; chmn of the bd, AL Afro-Amer/Black Hall of Fame, 1985; appointed mem, Economic Devt Comm, AL Conf of Black Mayors Inc 1985; appointed mem, advisory bd, AL Historical Commn, 1985; NEA; Amer Library Assn; Assn of Higher Educ; Amer Historical Assn; Southern Historical Assn; Org of Amer Historians; Assn for the Study of Afro-Amer Life and History; Birmingham Astronomical Soc; Advisory Bd, AL History Comm; associate commissioner, AL Election Comm; Executive Comm, W AL Oral History Assn; campus coordinator of Kettering Public Leadership; coordinator of SREB; editorial advisory bd, The Collegiate Press, 1993-94. **Honors/Awds:** Certificate of Appreciation, Atlanta-Fulton Co Dist Social Sci Fair, 1983; one of principal founders and first pres, West AL Chap, Assn for the Study of Afro-Amer Life and History; one of principal founders AL Afro-Amer/Black Hall of Fame; first chmn of bd of dirs, AL Afro-Amer Hall of Fame; articles published in US Black and the News, Negro History Bulletin, Presbyterian Survey, Aerospace Historian; compiled bibliography of all works by and about Dr Martin Luther King Jr and the Civil Rights Movement for Dr Martin Luther King Jr Ctr for Social Change, Atlanta, GA; nominated for NAFEO Achievement Awd; articles published in US Black and the News, Negro History Bulletin, Presbyterian Survey, Aerospace Historian; books James A Garfield and Chester A Arthur in vols 1 & 2 of a five volume work, ed by Frank N Magill, Great Lives from History, A Biographical Survey Pasadena CA, Salem Press Inc 1987; saluted as Great Black Alabamian by Govenor's AL Reunion; nominated for Stillman College Faculty Merit Incentive Award, 1988, 1989, 1990; fellow Royal Geographic Society, 1991. **Special Achievements:** The Negro and the Presbyterian Church of the South from the Antebellum Through the Postbellum Period, The Griot, 1992; Presented a paper on "Civil Rights, Law, Social Movements, and African-American," Univ of Alabama at Birmingham, 1994; "Lucius Davenport Amers on: the First Black Sheriff in the South since the Reconstruction Era," Alabama Sheriffs Star, v 17, n 1, pp. 143-47, April 1996; "Stillman College and Brewst er Hardy," The Christian Observer, v 174, n 16, pp. 24-25, August 16, 1996. **Business Addr:** Professor, Stillman College, PO Box 1430, Tuscaloosa, AL 35403.

LOCKETT, SANDRA BOKAMBA

Librarian. **Personal:** Born Nov 18, 1946, Hutchinson, KS; daughter of Dorothy Bernice Harrison Johnson and Herbert Wales Johnson; married James C Lockett, 1979 (divorced 1983); children: Eyenga M Bokamba, Madeline B Lockett; married Eyamba B. Bokamba, 1969 (divorced 1972). **Educ:** Hutchinson Community Jr College, Hutchinson, KS, associate of arts, 1966; University of Kansas, Lawrence, KS, BS, education, 1968; Indiana University, Bloomington, IN, MLS, 1973. **Career:** Gary Public Library, Gary, IN, Alcott Branch, librarian, 1973-76, asst dir for pr and programming, 1976-78, head of extension services, 1978-79; University of Iowa Law Library, Iowa City, IA, head gov docs dept, 1979-84; Milwaukee Public Library, Milwaukee, WI, branch mgr, 1984-88, extension services coordinator, 1988-91; assistant city librarian, 1991-. **Orgs:** Board of directors, Milwaukee Council on Adult Learning, 1990-; board of directors, Greater Milwaukee Literacy Coalition, 1986-; committee appointment, Public Library Association/American Library Association, 1988-; board of directors, Metropolitan Milwaukee Chapter, National Forum for Black Public Administrators, 1989-90; member, Alpha Kappa Alpha Sorority, 1967-. **Honors/Awds:** Librarian of the Year, Bookfellows, Milwaukee Public Library, 1987; Management Merit Award, Milwaukee Public Library, City of Milwaukee, 1988; delegate, Pre White House Conference on Libraries and Information Serv, 1991. **Special Achievements:** Author, "Adult Programming...," The Bottom Line, 1989. **Business Addr:** Assistant City Librarian, The Milwaukee Public Library, 814 W Wisconsin Ave, Milwaukee, WI 53233.

LOCKETTE, AGNES LOUISE

Educator. **Personal:** Born Apr 21, 1927, Albany, GA; daughter of Wessie McIntee Pollard (deceased) and Fred Pollard (deceased); married Emory W Sr; children: Sharon Anita, Emory W Jr. **Educ:** Albany State Coll, Albany, GA, BS, 1948; Univ of Nevada, Las Vegas, MEd, 1967; Univ of Arizona, Tucson, EdD, 1972. **Career:** Carver HS Dawson, GA, teacher, 1948-49; Clark County School Dist, Las Vegas, NV, teacher, 1952-70; Univ of Nevada, Las Vegas, prof of educ, 1972-84, prof, 1971-. **Orgs:** Kappa Delta Pi; Delta Kappa Gamma Soc; Natl Concil of Teachers of English; Amer Assn Univ Women; mem, Phi Kappa Phi; Assn of Childhood Educ Intl; Natl Soc of Profs; Natl Educ Assn; Grace Community Church, Boulder City, NV, church council, mem, financial section, 1989-; chairperson, Clark Co Air Pollution Hearing Bd, Las Vegas, NV. **Honors/Awds:** Honors Hazard Training School, Albany State Coll, GA; diploma, Albany State Coll HS Albany State Coll, GA; class valedictorian; first woman appointed to Clark County Air Pollution Hearing Bd, 1972-; Keynote speaker Annual Honor Convocation Univ of NV Las Vegas 1984; Disting Teaching Awd Coll of Educ Univ of NV Las Vegas 1984; Outstanding Service Award, Westside School Alumni Assn, 1988. **Business Addr:** Prof Emeritus of Education, University of Nevada, Las Vegas, 4505 Maryland Parkway, Las Vegas, NV 89154.

LOCKHART, BARBARA H.

Health services executive. **Personal:** Born Apr 1, 1948, Cleveland, OH; daughter of Estelle Lockhart and Willie Lockhart. **Educ:** Cleveland State University, BS, 1972; Central Michigan State University, MSA, 1987. **Career:** Aetna Casualty and Surety Insurance, senior underwriter, 1972-77; Blue Cross of Northeast Ohio, underwriting specialist, marketing research analyst, 1977-80; The Mead Corporation, HMO & cost control coordinator, 1980-83; Ohio Dept of Health, health care cost analyst, 1983-84; Physicians Health Plan of Ohio, vice pres, government programs, 1984-94; Medmetrix Group, Inc, senior consultant, currently. **Orgs:** Ohio HMO Association Human Services Committee, past chair, 1986-89, bd of trustees, 1991-; Ohio Medical Care Advisory Committee, 1990-; National Academy of State Health Policy, 1992-; American Managed Care Association's Medicaid Advisory Committe, 1992-; HCFA Medicaid Coordication Care Industry Group, 1992-; Association of Black Insurance Professionals, 1992-. **Honors/Awds:** Ohio House of Representatives, Community Service Proclamation, 1992. **Special Achievements:** Appointed, State Legislators Medicaid Oversight Committee, 1986; appointed, Governor's Commission on Ohio Health Care Costs, 1983. **Business Addr:** Senior Consultant, Medmetrix Group, Inc, 1001 Lakeside Ave, Cleveland, OH 44114, (216)523-1300.

LOCKHART, EUGENE, JR.

Professional football player, restaurateur. **Personal:** Born Mar 8, 1961, Crockett, TX; married Sharon; children: Bryan, Brandon, Eugene III. **Educ:** Univ of Houston, BA, marketing, 1983. **Career:** Dallas Cowboys, linebacker, 1984-91; New England Patriots, 1992-93; Lockhart One-Hour Photo, Dallas, TX, co-owner, currently; Cowboys Sports Cafe, Irving, TX, partner, currently; Lockhart Custom Pools. **Honors/Awds:** Sporting News NFL All-Star Team, 1989; active in a program that provides glasses to needy Dallas children; five-dollar donation to Natl Paralysis Foundation for every tackle made, 1990; Natl Cancer Society Golf Tournament. **Business Addr:** Lockhart 1 HR Photo, 515 W Campbell Rd, Richardson, TX 75080.

LOCKHART, JAMES B.

Attorney, insurance executive. **Personal:** Born May 27, 1936, New York, NY; son of Margaret Blakely and Edgar Lockhart; married Ruth Yvonne Douglas, Oct 30, 1976; children: Marc Blakeley, Diallo Henry. **Educ:** Palmer Meml Inst, 1954; Boston Univ Coll of Bus Adminstrn, BS 1957; Boston Univ Sch of Law, JD 1959. **Career:** Transamerica Corp, vice pres pub affairs, 1979-; Budget Rent A Car Corp, sr vice pres 1971-79; Rivers Lockhart Clayter & Lawrence Attys at Law Chicago, partner 1967-71; City of Chicago, asst corp counsel 1965-67; Office of Chief Counsel US Treas Dept, atty adv 1963-65. **Orgs:** Bd of dirs Pub Affairs Council; deputy CA Business Roundtable; mem Illinois & SC Bar Assns; mem Sigma Pi Phi Boule & Kappa Alpha Psi Frats; Episcopalian; former mem bd dir & v chmn of Legal Legislative Com Intl Franchise Assn; Car & Truck Rental & Leasing Assn; former mem bd trustees & exec com Episcopal Charities Diocese of Chicago; mem Standing Com Episcopal Diocese of Chicago; mem Com on Legislation of the Conv of the Episcopal Diocese of Chicago; vice pres & exec com Lawrence Hall Sch for Boys; pres, Downtown Assn of San Francisco; past chair, Bay Area Urban League; dir, vice chair, Public Broadcasting Service; dir, Oakland Private Industry Council; Bohemian Club; dir, past chair, City Club of San Francisco; president board of port commissioners, Port of Oakland, 1989-; trustee, emeritus, Fine Arts Museums of SF, 1986-95; board of governors, San Francisco Tennis Club, 1988-91. **Honors/Awds:** Outstanding contbns to the comm WBEE (Radio) Comm Serv Citation 1973; San Francisco Planning and Urban Research Associates Award for creative corporate community leadership, 1988. **Military Serv:** US Army, Capt, asst army staff judge advocate, 1960-63. **Business Addr:** Vice President-Public Affairs, Transamerica Corp, 600 Montgomery St, San Francisco, CA 94111.

LOCKHART, KEITH E.

Advertising agency executive. **Career:** Lockhart & Pettus, advertising executive, currently. **Special Achievements:** Ranked #60 on Black Enterprise's list of the top 100 industrial/service companies, 1993. **Business Phone:** (212)633-2800.

LOCKHART, ROBERT W.

Dental surgeon. **Personal:** Born Jul 19, 1941, Houston, TX; married Betty J Moore; children: Robert III, Chris, Lisa. **Educ:** Univ of TX, BA 1962, DDS 1966, MPH 1973. **Career:** Harris Co Hosp Sunnyside Clinic, dir dept serv 1973-74; CA George Dental Soc, vice pres 1974-76; Private practice, dentist 1968-. **Orgs:** Mem Amer & Natl Dental Assoc, Acad Gen Dentistry, Amer Assoc Publ Health Dentists, Alpha Phi Alpha, NAACP, Urban League. **Military Serv:** AUS Dental Corps capt 1966-68.

LOCKHART, VERDREE, SR.

Educator, counselor. **Personal:** Born Oct 21, 1924, Louisville, GA; son of Minnie B Roberson Lockhart and Fred D Lockhart; married Louise Howard, Aug 5, 1950; children: Verdree II, Vera Louise, Fernandez, Abigail. **Educ:** Tuskegee University, BS 1949; Atlanta Univ, MA 1957; George Peabody Coll, 1960; Atlanta Univ, PhD 1975. **Career:** Jefferson County HS, teacher 1949-58, counselor 1958-63; GA Dept of Edn, education consultant 1963-80; Atlanta Univ, vice pres 1981-82; Phillips College, dean of educ 1984-85; Regional Asbestos Inspector 1985-86; North Fulton High School, counselor 1986-92; West Fulton Middle School, counselor 1992-. **Orgs:** Alpha Phi Alpha Fraternity, 1949-; Former state pres, Assn of Counseling & Devel 1963-65; mem exec bd, Atlanta Area Cncl, Boy Scouts of Amer 1965-; treas, Atlanta Br NAACP 1972-90; trustee, Atlanta Univ 1975-81; mem, Tuskegee Univ Forest Resource Cncl 1978-88; vice pres, Tuskegee Univ Natl Alumni Assn 1980-84; Parlimentarian, Eta Lambda Chapter, Alpha Phi Alpha Fraternity, 1980-88; Amer Counseling Assn 1960-; Phi Delta Kappa 1981-; mem board of directors, Economic Opportunity of Atlanta Inc 1985-88; spec asst to Gen Pres of Alpha Phi Alpha Fraternity; Amer Vocational Assn; GA Adult Educ Assn; GA Educ Artic Com; GA Assn of Educators; National Education Association; former mem, Youth Employment & Planning Cncl, Atlanta CETA Office; mem, Mayor's Task Force on Public Education 1986-92; pres, Atlanta Univ Consortion Chapter, Phi Delta Kappa 1988-89; asst parlimentarian, Tuskegee University National Alumni Assn, 1990-92; board member, Atlanta Assn of Educators, 1990-95; Clark Atlanta Univ Natl Alumni Assn, executive bd; Amer School Counselor Assn; Fulton Atlanta Community Action Authority Inc, treas, exec bd mem, 1995-; pres, Tuskegee Univ, Coll of Agricultural, Environmental & Natl Sciences Assn, 1997-. **Honors/Awds:** Alumni Merit Award, Atlanta Univ Alumni Assn 1972; Silver Beaver Award, Atlanta Area Council, Boy Scouts Amer 1968; GA Governor's Medallions, Gov State of GA 1967-68; Alumni Brother of the Year, Alpha Phi Alpha Frat 1980; Presidential Award Atlanta Univ Consortium Chapter of Phi Delta Kappa 1989; George Washington Carver Outstanding Alumni Award, Tuskegee University Alumni Association; A Heritage of Leadership Plaque, Atlanta Area Council, Boy Scouts of America; Presidential Citation, National Association for Equal Opportunity in Higher Education. **Military Serv:** AUS retired M/Sgt 20 years; WW II Victory Medal; Good Conduct Medal 1943-45; Amer Serv Medal; Asiatic Pacific Service Medal w/2 Bronze Stars. **Home Addr:** 2964 Peek Rd NW, Atlanta, GA 30318.

LOCKHART-MOSS, EUNICE JEAN

Business executive. **Personal:** Born Nov 28, 1942, Mt Olive, MS; daughter of Eunice O Lockhart and Ernest L Lockhart; divorced; children: Tracy, Cory. **Educ:** Univ of WI Milwaukee, BS 1963; Univ of WI Milwaukee, Ms 1975. **Career:** E Inc Milwaukee, pres 1977-; CS Mott Found Flint, prog off 1976-77; The Johnson Found Racine, program assoc 1972-76; Dominican Coll Racine, instr 1971-72; Racine Eviron Com Educ Trust, admin 1969-71. **Orgs:** Bd of dirs Council on Founds 1974-80; pres, E Incorporated, 1977-; bd of dirs Found Cntr 1979-82; pension & annuity bd City of Milwaukee 1979-82; bd of dirs United Way of Greater Milwaukee 1978-82; personnel bd st of WI 1979-82; mem pres Commn on US Liberian Relations 1980; bd dir Maryville Coll TN 1984-; author In Seach of Partnerships; publisher, E Publications, 1988-; mem DC Commission on the Arts, 1988-; mem, Mayor's Advisory Board for the Howard Theater, 1989-. **Business Addr:** President, E Inc, 1201 Pennsylvania Ave NW, Ste 720, Washington, DC 20004.

LOCKLEY, CLYDE WILLIAM

Law enforcement. **Personal:** Born Jul 14, 1938, Jacksonville, FL; married Mary Frances Jordan; children: Rhonda M, Karen P, Larry K, Brian K, Darrell W, Rodney A. **Educ:** Liberal Arts LA SW Coll, AA 1971; CA State U, BA Pol Sci 1974; USC, Masters of Pub Adminstrn 1976; CA Highway Patrol Academy, Completion 1965; CA Specialized Inst, Completion Certificate 1976; Univ of VA, Cert of Completion Criminal Justice 1978; FBI Academy Quantico VA, Completion 1978. **Career:** CA Highway Patrol, lieutenant; Compton Comm Coll, part-time instr criminal justice. **Orgs:** V chmn Environmental Commn City of Cars on CA; mem FBI Nat Academy Asso; mem CA Assn of Hwy Patrolman LA Co Peace Officers Assn; life mem USC Alumni Assn; mem CA State Employees Assn. **Honors/Awds:** Outstanding Airman-Special Honor Guard VIP Guard March AFB CA 1959; %Certificates basic training, intermediate, advance, supervision, administrative CA State Commn of Peace Office Standards & Training; full-time Comm Coll Tching; credentials in Police Science, Political Science, Public Adminstr, Administrative-Supervision. **Military Serv:** USAF airman second 1956-60. **Business Addr:** California Highway Patrol, 4520 S Sepulveda Blvd, Culver City, CA 90230.

LOCKLIN, JAMES R.
Marketing executive. **Personal:** Born Jan 20, 1958, Monroe, GA; son of Geneva Malcolm Locklin and Orell Locklin; married Sherry Jackson-Locklin, Nov 23, 1981; children: Jacques, Kimberly. **Educ:** Clark Coll, BA 1980. **Career:** WCLK-FM, announcer/reporter/promo mgr 1978-80; WAOK-AM, admin asst 1979-80; WORL-AM, news, public affairs dir 1980; Clarke Cty GA, probation officer 1980-82, WXAG-AM, gen mgr 1982-83; First Class Mktg Ltd, pres 1984-; Leon Farmer & Co, vice pres marketing 1983-. **Orgs:** Athens Ad Club 1983-; bd mem Morton Theatre Corp 1984, Hope Haven School 1985, Athens Tutorial Prog 1985; exec comm Athens Area Human Rel Cnc; Zeta Beta Beta Chap of Omega Psi Phi Frat Inc; Athens Business Council; Huntington Park Homeowners Assn; Georgia Planning Assn; American Planning Assn; Greater Athens Jazz Assn; NAACP; Northeast Georgia Business League; Athens Area Chamber of Commerce; commission member, Athens Clarke County Planning Commission; commission member, Athens Clarke County Clean and Beautiful Commission. **Honors/Awds:** Leadership Athens Participant, 1985; Man of the Year, Omega Psi Phi Fraternity, 1989; Local Business Person of the Year, NAACP, 1990. **Home Addr:** 151 Chesterfield Rd, Bogart, GA 30622. **Business Addr:** Vice President, Marketing, Leon Farmer & Co, PO Box 249, Athens, GA 30603.

LOCKMAN, NORMAN ALTON
Journalist. **Personal:** Born Jul 11, 1938, Kennett Square, PA; son of Olive White Lockman and Norman James Lockman; married Virginia Trainer; children: Holly Beth, Carey Paige, Sarah Elizabeth. **Educ:** Kenneth Consolidated Sch, 1956; Penn State, 1957-58; Dept of Defense Sch of Journalism, 1963. **Career:** Edwards AFB, spts edtr/co-edtr 1962-64; WCOJ Coatesville, PA, announcer 1965-66; Kennett News, columnist 1965-68; DE Dept Mental Health, therapist/social worker 1967-69; Wilm News-Jour, reporter/WA Corresp 1969-75; WILM Wilmington, DE, talk show host 1972-73; The Boston Globe, state house bur chief 1975-84; The News-Journal Papers, managing editor, assoc editor, Editorial Pages, 1991-. **Orgs:** Bd mem UUA Mass Bay Dist 1979; trustee Unitarian- Univ Assn 1983-84; mem natl Press Club 1972-73; mem Capitol Press Club 1974; mem The Monday Club 1985; MA St House Press Assn; NAACP; National Assn of Black Journalists; National Conference of Editorial Writers; Associated Press Managing Editors Assn. **Honors/Awds:** MD/DE/DC Press Assn Awards for Loc Col 1968-69; Pulitzer Special Local Reporting The Boston Globe 1984; Black Achievers, Wilmington YMCA, 1990; Brandy wine Professional Assn Achievement Award, Industry, 1991. **Military Serv:** USAF 1961-65.

LOCKWOOD, JAMES CLINTON
Educator. **Personal:** Born May 22, 1946, Philadelphia, PA; son of Signora and William; married Carolyn Francina McGowan; children: Jason Perry, James Andrew. **Educ:** West Chester University, BS, 1968; Salisbury State University, attended 1972-76; University of Maryland College Park, MA in Sociology Expected Aug 1997. **Career:** Oxford Area School Dist PA, fifth grade teacher 1968-70; Lincoln Univ PA, asst in financial aid 1970-71; Salisbury State MD, dir of financial aid 1971-77; Coppin State Coll MD, dir of financial aid 1977-78; Univ of MD Eastern Shore, dir of financial aid 1979-89; Montgomery College MD dir of financial aid, 1989-97. Sociology University of MD Eastern Shore, instructor, 1983, 1985-89. **Orgs:** Mem Natl Appeals Panel US Dept of Educ 1981; MD chairperson 1985-86, pres 1982-84, vice pres 1982; chairperson Federation Relations Com, 1981-82; DE, DC, MD Association of Student Financial Aid Administration Inc; mem Middles States Sociology Univ of MD Eastern Shore 1983, 1985-89 (part time); mem Natl Regional Assembly, 1994-96; MD Trainer, college board, 1983-84; National Association of Student Financial Aid Administration & the US Department of Education, student financial aid Trainer, 1981, 1983, 1989, 1993; Eastern Association of Student Financial Aid Administration, trainer, executive cncl, 1996; Moton Consortium on Admissions & Financial Aid, instructor, 1986; US Chess Federation, life mem. **Home Addr:** 1404 Timberwolf Dr, Frederick, MD 21703, (301)696-1893.

LODGE, HERMAN
County official. **Personal:** Born Nov 8, 1928, Midville, GA; son of Bessie Lodge and John Lodge; married Anna Roberts; children: Terri Patrice. **Educ:** Ft Valley State Coll, BS 1951; Med Field Serv School, Cert 1952. **Career:** Corry HS, teacher, coach 1953-54; VA Hosp, corrective therapist 1953-84; Burke Cty Bd of Commissioners, currently. **Orgs:** Exec sec Burke Cty Improvement Assoc Inc 1961-; pres bd of dir Burke Cty Housing Improvement Inc 1979-; bd mem GA Housing Coaltion 1980-; pres of bd of dir GA Legal Serv 1981-85; past pres Burke Cty Black Coalition Inc 1982-83; steward, Mt Olive AME Church, Waynesboro, GA, 1972-; pres, Georgia Legal Services Program, 1981-85; chairman, Burke Co Economic and Industrial Committee, 1986-. **Honors/Awds:** Econ Devel Phi Beta Sigma 1982; Bill of Rights Awd Amer Civil Liberties Union of GA 1982; Outstanding Comm Service Mt Olive AME Church 1983; Pres Citation NAEOHE 1984; Alumni Hall of Fame (in politics), Fort Valley State College, 1987. **Military Serv:** AUS corpl 1951-53. **Home Addr:** 1139 Quaker Rd, Waynesboro, GA 30830.

LOEB, CHARLES P., JR.
Educator. **Personal:** Born Dec 6, 1927, Eunice, LA. **Educ:** Leland Coll, BA 1954; So U, MEd 1960; Univ TX, LSU; Univ SW LA, Further Study; Univ OK; Xavier U; Nicholls U. **Career:** St Landry Parish Sch Bd, supr 1954-67; Carter G Woodson HS prin 1966-68; st landry parish sch bd, supr 1966; asst supt; emergency sch Aid, dir. **Orgs:** Act chmn LA State Dept Educ Adult Educ Adv Council; chmn LA Educ Assn Adult Educ Sect; mem Adv Com Spl Serv LSU; bd dirs United Progressive Investment Corp; ARC; LA State Dept Edn; Am Legion Post #519; Satellite Civic & Social Club; Frontiers Intl Opelousas Club. **Honors/Awds:** Citizen of yr award 1965; frontiers Intl distinguish award 1973. **Military Serv:** AUS pfc 1946-47. **Business Addr:** PO Box 310, Opelousas, LA 70570.

LOFTON, ANDREW JAMES
City official. **Personal:** Born Oct 16, 1950, Longstreet, LA; son of Ethel M Peyton Lofton and Junius E Lofton; married Verda J Minnix, May 30, 1970; children: Junius, Lamar. **Educ:** Univ of Puget Sound, Tacoma, WA, BA, 1972; Univ of Washington, Seattle, WA, MUP, 1974. **Career:** City of Seattle, WA, Office of Policy Planning, human resource planner, 1974-76, capital improvement planner, 1976-78, Dept of Comm Devel, block grant advisor, 1978-80, deputy dir, 1980-87, Dept of Licenses & Consumer Affairs, dir, 1987-89, Office of Management & Budget, director, 1990-92, deputy chief of staff, mayor's office, 1992-94, deputy dir, Department of Comm Trade and Economic Development, 1994-95; deputy superientendent, Customer Services, Seattle City Light, 1995-. **Orgs:** Mem, Natl Forum for Black Public Admins, 1983-90; Region X Council mem, Blacks in Govt, 1983-87; pres, Seattle Chapter, Blacks in Govt, 1983-86; bd mem, Seattle Mgmt Assn, 1986-87, bd mem, Rainier High Boys & Girls Club, 1987-; Region IX Representative, Conf of Minority Public Administrators, 1989-. **Business Addr:** Deputy Superintendent, Customer Services, Seattle City Light, 700 5th Ave, Seattle, WA 98104.

LOFTON, DOROTHY W.
Educator. **Personal:** Born Jun 22, 1925, Marlin, TX; married Donald D; children: Ronald, Deanne Michelle. **Educ:** Baylor U, BA 1971. **Career:** Marlin Independent Sch Dist, tchr. **Orgs:** Mem TX Classroom Tchrs Assn; Falls County Tchrs Assn; TX State Tchrs Assn; pres City Fedn Women's Clubs; vice pres Strivette Club; sec Falconer- stamps Comm Center; sec-treas Marlin Parents Orgn; treas Carrie Adams Dist TX Women & Girls' Clubs. **Honors/Awds:** Adult leader certificate 4-H Council 1974.

LOFTON, ERNEST
Union official. **Personal:** Born Feb 25, 1932, Detroit, MI; children: Terry, Penny Holloway. **Career:** Dearborn Iron Foundry, water tester, 1950; Ford Motor Company, Specialty Foundry Unit, bargaining committeeman, president, 1967-76; UAW Local 600, second vice president, 1976-81, first vice president, 1981-82; UAW International Executive Board, Region 1A director, 1983-89, international vice president, 1989-; UAW Michigan Community Action Program Department, director, currently. **Orgs:** Blue Cross and Blue Shield of Michigan, board of directors; United Foundation, board of directors; New Detroit Inc, board member; Detroit Police Athletic League, board of directors; Transafrica, board member; Save Our Sons and Daughters, board member; Metropolitan Realty Corporation, board of directors; Detroit Economic Growth Corporation, board member; Detroit Repertory Theatre, advisory board; Economic Policy Council of the United Nations Association of the USA; Coalition of Black Trade Unionists, national secretary; NAACP, Detroit chapter, vice president. **Military Serv:** US Army, staff sergeant, 1950-52. **Business Addr:** Vice President, UAW National, Ford Department, 8000 East Jefferson, Detroit, MI 48214, (313)926-5391.

LOFTON, KENNETH
Professional baseball player. **Personal:** Born May 31, 1967, East Chicago, IN. **Educ:** Arizona. **Career:** Houston Astros, outfielder, 1991; Cleveland Indians, 1992-96, 1998-; Atlanta Braves, 1997. **Business Addr:** Professional Baseball Player, Cleveland Indians, 2401 Ontario, Cleveland, OH 44115, (216)420-4200.

LOFTON, MELLANESE S.
Attorney. **Personal:** Born Aug 24, 1941, Houston, TX; married Jimmy Dale; children: Frederick Douglas, Robin Mellanese. **Educ:** Univ of TX, BA 1962; Univ of CA Boalt Hall Sch of Law, JD 1974. **Career:** Lofton & Lofton, attorney, currently; Siemens Corp, 1989-92; Tel Plus Communications 1984-89; US Steel Corp, atty 1974-82; Jacobs Sills & Coblentz, law clerk 1973-74; Contra Costa Co, social worker 1969-73; Alameda & Co, social worker employ couns 1963-69; Univ Of TX, photographic tech 1961-62. **Orgs:** Mem PA Bar; CA State Bar; mem Alpha Kappa Alpha Sor; Publ Project Future. **Business Addr:** Attorney, Lofton & Lofton, 110 E D St, Ste A, Benicia, CA 94510.

LOFTON, MICHAEL
Public relations associate, athlete. **Personal:** Born Dec 10, 1963, Montgomery, AL; son of Inez Lofton. **Educ:** New York University, BA, 1988. **Career:** Shearson Lehman Hutton, broker, 1988-90; Ernest & Young, public relations associate 1990-. **Orgs:** Peter Westbrook Founadation, director of business affairs, 1990-. **Honors/Awds:** NYU Varsity Club, Sid Tanenbaum Award, 1989; NYU, Chancellors Award for Leadership, 1988, Chancellors Award for Volunteerism, 1987. **Special Achievements:** Olympian, 1984, 1988, 1992; Pan Am team member, 1987 (1 silver medal), 1991 (1 silver medal, 1 bronze medal); national sabre champ, 1991, 1992; NCAA sabre champ, 1984, 1985, 1986, 1987. **Business Addr:** Public Relations Associate, Ernst & Young, 787 Seventh Ave, 19th flr, Rm 1944, New York, NY 10019, (212)773-6467.

LOFTON, STEVEN LYNN
Professional football player. **Personal:** Born Nov 26, 1968, Jacksonville, TX. **Educ:** Texas A&M. **Career:** Phoenix Cardinals, defensive back, 1991-93; Carolina Panthers, 1995-96; New England Patriots, 1997-. **Business Addr:** Professional Football Player, New England Patriots, 60 Washington St, Foxboro Stadium, Foxboro, MA 02035, (508)543-7911.

LOGAN, ALPHONSO
Government official, educator (retired). **Personal:** Born Aug 15, 1908, Hot Springs, AR; son of Elaine Lee Logan and Abraham Logan; married Dorothy Lynne Lockhart Logan, Sep 23, 1942; children: Sybil Buford, Rachael Top, Mildred Summerville, Eloise Natl. **Educ:** Knoxville Coll, BS, 1933; Univ of Oklahoma, Counseling, 1966; Henderson State, Hrs on Masters, 1967. **Career:** Hot Springs School System, math teacher, coach, 1934-42; Employment Security Div, counselor, 1966-79; Justice of the Peace, Garland County. **Orgs:** Pres, NAACP, 1938; secretary, NAACP, 1942; secretary, Lamplighters Black Caucus, 1948, 1984; pres, Business & Professional Men's Club, 1980. **Honors/Awds:** Plaque Sangston Alumni Assn 1983; plaque Sharon Seventh Day Adventist Church 1984; Bankhead Award for Community Service, 1980. **Military Serv:** USAF Sgt 3; Good Conduct Amer Theatre 1942. **Business Addr:** Justice of the Peace, Garland Co Dist 3, Hot Springs, AR 71901.

LOGAN, BENJAMIN HENRY, II
Judge, attorney. **Personal:** Born Jun 25, 1943, Dayton, OH; son of Jeanne Ross Logan and Ben H Logan Sr; married Creola Logan (divorced 1983); children: Fonda, Benjamin M, Barry; children: Bradford, Benjamin W. **Educ:** Ohio Northern Univ, Ada, Ohio, BA, 1968; Ohio Northern Law School, Ada, Ohio, JD, 1972. **Career:** Ben's Enterprise, Dayton, Ohio, manager, 1960-68; Dayton Tire & Rubber, Dayton, Ohio, cost acct, 1968-69; Dayton Board of Education, Dayton, Ohio, sub teacher, 1969-70; G R Legal Aid, Grand Rapids, Michigan, staff attorney, 1972-74; Logan and Beason, Grand Rapids, Michigan, partner, 1974-88; 61st district judge, Grand Rapids, Michigan, 1988-94, chief judge pro tem, 1994-95. **Orgs:** American Bar Association, 1974-, judicial administration division, board member, 1992-, task force on opportunities for minorities, and ABA Standing Committee Judicial Selection, Tenure Compensation, 1995-96, and Commission on Minorities, 1997-; co-chair; National Bar Association, 1974-, board member, 1989-92, judicial council chair, 1994-95, board director, 1991-94; Grand Rapids Bar Association, 1973-, board member, 1991-94; Grand Rapids Urban League, 1973-; Press Club, 1975-; board of directors member, A Philip Randolph, 1978-; Grand Rapids Junior College President's Committee, 1984-; Michigan Supreme Court History Society, 1989-; founding member, executive board, vice chairman, Citizens for Representative Government, 1985-88; Boy Scouts of Western Shores, 1983-, vice pres, board member, 1986; Lions Club, 1986-, board member, 1991-94; Dispute Resolution, 1990-; Fair Housing Bd, 1992-; Leadership Grand Rapids, 1993-; Economic Club, 1990-; Arkon City Club, 1994-; US Supreme Court History Society, 1992-; Fellow State Bar of Michigan, 1995; YWCA Tribute Commission, 1993-; NAACP, Grand Rapids Chapter, board member, 1972, life mem, 1985; YMCA, general council, 1980-88, board of directors, 1993-; Sigma Pi Phi Fraternity, charter mem, 1982-, pres, 1986-87, 1993-95; Kappa Alpha Psi Foundation, national board member, general council 1996-; Pan Hellenic Council, national board member, 1996-; Kappa Alpha Psi, life mem. **Honors/Awds:** Role Model of the Year, NAACP, 1989; Distinguished Citizen, Muskegon, MI, 1989; Don Black Award, GRJC, 1989; Lawyer of the Year, Floyd Skinner Bar Assoc, 1987; Kappa Distinguished Member, Kappa Alpha Psi, 1990; Boys Scouts of America, Whitney Young Award, 1991; Ohio Northern Law, Honorary Doctorate Degree, 1992; Giant of Giants Award, 1996; UNCF, College Fund Distinguished Award, 1997; Grand Rapids Community College, Roastee Award, 1994; Judge Benjamin Logan Day, Grand Rapids, MI, 1994; Trailblazer Award, 1994; Renaissance Group Volunteer of the Year Award, 1995; NAACP, nominated for Spingarn Medal, 1995; NAACP, William Ming Award, 1997; Judge Benjamin Logan Day, Baltimore MD, 1995; Judge Benjamin Logan Day, Milwaukee, WI, 1995; awarded keys to following cities: Dayton, OH; Las Vegas, NV; Huntington, WV; Bay City, MI; Muskegon, MI; Muskegon Heights, MI; Baltimore, MD; Seattle, WA; Saginaw, MI; Dowagiac, MI; Cincinnati, OH; Kansas City, MO; Milwaukee, WI; inducted into Distinguished Hall of Fame, Alumni Chaminade High School, 1995. **Special Achievements:** Admitted to practice in Michigan, 1973-, Washington, DC, 1975-; member to US Supreme Court, 1976; panelist, Racism in the Courts, C-SPAN, 1996; Meet the Judge,

1996; State Bar Michigan panelist, 1995. **Home Addr:** 2243 Breton SE, Grand Rapids, MI 49506, (616)942-9519. **Business Addr:** Judge, 61st District Court, City of Grand Rapids, State of Michigan, Hall of Justice, 333 Monroe NW, Grand Rapids, MI 49506, (616)456-3802.

LOGAN, CAROLYN ALICE
Technical information specialist. **Personal:** Born Sep 14, 1949, Philadelphia, PA; daughter of Charlotte Mathews Logan and Roger William Logan; children: Ahmed, Ademola. **Educ:** Rutgers University, New Brunswick, NJ, BA, 1971; Rutgers Univ School of Information Science, New Brunswick, NJ, MLS, 1973. **Career:** Rutgers University, New Brunswick, NJ, Piscataway audio visual specialist, 1971-72, Piscataway assistant reference librarian, 1972-73; Newark Public Library, Newark, NJ, reference librarian tech info, 1973; AT&T, New Jersey, information, manager & librarian, 1976-85; Ogden Projects, Fairfield, NJ, librarian, 1988-89; Roy F Weston Inc, Edison, NJ, technical information specialist manager, 1989-. **Orgs:** Trustee, Plainfield Public Library, several offices, 1985-; coordinator, Langston Hughes Lecture Series, 1987-.

LOGAN, CAROLYN GREEN
State trooper. **Personal:** Born Jul 5, 1957, Asheville, NC; daughter of Mack & Gladys Green; married Karl Logan, Sep 20, 1987; children: Christopher Green, Morgan, Taelor. **Career:** Asheville Police Department, police officer II, 1977-84; NC Hwy Patrol, master trooper, 1984-. **Orgs:** Onyx Optimist Club, friendship chmn, 1995-96; First Mayfield Memorial Baptist Church, infant & toddler counselor, 1995-96. **Honors/Awds:** Central Asheville Optimist, Dedicated Svc, 1983; Asheville Police Dept, Dedicated Svc Awd, 1984; Hidden Valley Optimist, Law Enforcement Awd, 1985; Asheville Optimist Club, Dedicated Svc, 1985; Meck Co Rotary/Boy Scouts of Amer, HP Trooper of the Year, 1995; Northstate Law Enforcement, First Black Female Pioneer Trooper, 1996. **Special Achievements:** Advanced Law Enforcement, certificate, 1992; General Instructor, 1996; Radar-Vascar Instructor, first female NCSHP, 1997. **Business Addr:** Master Trooper, NC State Hwy Patrol, 8446 N Tryon St, Charlotte, NC 28262, (704)547-0042.

LOGAN, DAVID
Professional football player (retired). **Personal:** Born Oct 25, 1956, Pittsburgh, PA. **Educ:** Univ of Pittsburgh, BA/BS, urban and black studies, 1979. **Career:** Tampa Bay Buccaneers, nose tackle 1979-86. **Honors/Awds:** Named to The Sporting News NFL All-Star Team, 1984.

LOGAN, ERNEST EDWARD
Professional football player. **Personal:** Born May 18, 1968, Fort Bragg, NC; married Diana; children: Ernest III. **Educ:** East Carolina. **Career:** Atlanta Falcons, nose tackle, 1993; Jacksonville Jaguars, 1995-96; New York Jets, 1997-. **Business Addr:** Professional Football Player, New York Jets, 1000 Fulton Ave, Hempstead, NY 11550, (516)560-8100.

LOGAN, FRENISE A.
Educator (retired). **Personal:** Born Sep 30, 1920, Albany, GA; married Mary Esther Whitfield; children: Jewel, Frenise II. **Educ:** Fisk Univ, BA 1943; Case Western Reserve Univ, MA 1957, PhD 1953; Univ of Bombay India, Post-doctoral study 1954. **Career:** Univ of Zambia, visiting prof 1968-70; Amer Embassy Lusaka Zambia, 1st sec Cultural Affairs 1968-70; Bur of Educ & Cultural Affairs US Dept of State Wash DC, chief East Central & So Africa 1970-73; Amer Embassy Nairobi Kenya, 1st sec cultural affairs 1973-77; Museum of African Art WA DC, assoc dir 1977-78; Amer Consulate Kaduna Nigeria, 1st consultant & br public affairs officer 1978-80; NC A&T State Univ, prof of history 1980-91. **Orgs:** Mem Amer Hist Assoc, So Hist Assoc, Assoc for Study of Afro-Amer Life & Hist, Alpha Phi Alpha, East African Acad, Indian Hist Congress; mem Carolinas Symposium on British Studies. **Honors/Awds:** Author ''Negro in NC 1876-1894''; num articles in scholarly publs in US & India; num hons, awds, fellowships & grants including Commendation for Outstanding Achievements in Intl & Educ/Cultural Exchanges from the United States Dept of State, Bureau of Educ and Cultural Affairs 1977. **Military Serv:** USAAF 1943-45. **Home Addr:** 10069-6 Windstream Dr, Columbia, MD 21044.

LOGAN, GEORGE, III
Attorney. **Personal:** Born Dec 23, 1942, Elizabeth, NJ; married Sheila Jacqueline Miller; children: Natalie, Camille, George Spencer. **Educ:** Rutgers Coll, BA 1964; Rutgers Sch of Law, JD 1967. **Career:** Logan Marton Halladay & Hall, atty 1978-; atty self-emp 1976-78; Lindauer & Logan, 1975-76; Lindauer & Goldberg, asso atty 1975; Karl & N Stewart, 1973-74; Deprima Aranda & de Leon, 1972-73; USAF, asst staff judge advoc 1968-72; Ctr for Constl Rights, staff atty 1967-68. **Orgs:** Pres AZ Black Lawyers Assn; mem Phoenix Urban League; Nat Bat Assn; Am Civil Liberties Union; bd of dir Casa Linda Lodge; former pres Comm Legal Serv; City of Phoenix Com on Aging; Joint Legis Comm Conflict of Interest. **Military Serv:** USAF cpt 1968-72. **Business Addr:** Asst Dir, Management Review, AZ Dept of Econ Sec, 1140 E Washington, Phoenix, AZ 85034.

LOGAN, HAROLD JAMES
Publishing company executive. **Personal:** Born Feb 27, 1951, Washington, DC; son of Jean Rhodes Logan and Harold Green Logan; married Etienne Gabrielle Randall, Sep 10, 1988; children: Justin, Gabrielle Randall. **Educ:** Harvard Univ, Cambridge, MA, AB, 1973; Stanford Univ, Palo Alto, CA, MBA, 1980. **Career:** The Washington Post, Washington, DC, reporter, 1973-78, mgr, electronic publishing, 1980-84; Dow Jones & Co, Princeton, NJ, deputy dir, business dev, 1984-88; Pacific Bell Directory, San Francisco, CA, dir, business dev, 1988-. **Orgs:** Mem, minority caucus, New Oakland Comm, 1991-; mem, bd of dir, Crossroads Theatre, 1986-88; mem, bd of dir, Princeton Nursery School, 1986-88; mem, Natl Black MBA Assn, 1980-; founding mem, Black Harvard Alumni, Washington, DC, 1982-84.

LOGAN, JAMES
Professional football player. **Personal:** Born Dec 6, 1972, Opp, AL. **Educ:** Memphis. **Career:** Cincinnati Bengals, linebacker, 1995; Seattle Seahawks, 1995-. **Business Addr:** Professional Football Player, Seattle Seahawks, 11220 NE 53rd St, Kirkland, WA 98033, (206)827-9777.

LOGAN, JOSEPH LEROY
Physician. **Personal:** Born Feb 24, 1922, Mansfield, OH; children: Leanora, JoAnn. **Educ:** OH State Univ, BA 1947; Howard Univ Med Sch, 1951; special training Montefiore Hosp; post-grad Columbia Univ, Univ Chicago, OH State Univ, Harvard Univ; Civil Aero Med Inst. **Career:** Staff mem, Trumbull Memorial Hosp; St Joseph's Del Ohio State Medical Assn; Trumbull Co, dep coroner; Warren School Dist, athletic physician; Ohio State Univ, mem athletic medical team; Miami Dolphins, Cleveland Browns, asst med physician; private practice, physician 1952-. **Orgs:** Lifetime mem NAACP; mem Piltos Intl Assn; mem Air Force Assn; sponsor of Paul Warfield through high school, college, and professional career to Hall of Fame; physician in charge of Sickle Cell Testing in Warren OH 1973; appeared on the Dorothy Fuldheim TV show, Cleveland OH, to discuss venereal disease; sponsored a building & recreation prog for children in Warren OH; past interviewer for Northeastern Ohio Coll of Medicine & advisor for minority students; mem Med Intl Assistance; mem Med Staff, Ohio State Univ Athletics; mem Pilots Intl Assn; mem Air Force Assn; mem Buckeye Medical Assn; mem Amer Coll of Gen Practice; mem Science Group of Natl Inst of Health; mem Trumbull Co Metro Housing Authority; bd dir Planned Parenthood Assn; mem OSU Med Assn, NMA, AMA, Aerospace Med Assn,Civil Medsn, Amer Acad Gen Practice, NY Acad Sci; fellow Amer Geriatric Soc; mem Intl Coll Angiology, Flying Physicians Assn, British Med Assn; author ''Venereal Disease: Problems in Schools, Rural Areas & Among Juveniles,'' Archives of Environmental Health; American Society of Bariatric Physicians, special deputy sheriff, currently. **Honors/Awds:** Civic Award for Man of the Year, Urban League, 1973; Volunteer Serv Award, 1973; Outstanding American, 1976; United Negro College Fund Award, 1985; Award of Merit, Ohio Planning Comm; Trumbull Memorial Hospital delegete to the Amer Med Assn; elected to Amer Coll of Physicians. **Military Serv:** AUS s/sgt 1943-46; WW II Victory Ribbon; Good Conduct Medal; Amer Theater Ribbon; Three Bronze Stars. **Business Addr:** Special Deputy Sheriff, American Society of Bariatric Physicians, 1129 Youngstown Rd, Warren, OH 44484.

LOGAN, JUAN LEON
Artist. **Personal:** Born Aug 16, 1946, Nashville, TN; married Geraldine Johnson; children: Kim, Sidney, Jonathan. **Educ:** Howard Univ; Clark Coll. **Career:** Selected One-Man Exhibitions, Rowe Gallery Univ of NC at Charlotte 1983; Natl Museum of African Art Wash,DC 1980; Winston-Salem Univ Art Gallery 1979; SC State Coll 1976; Winthrop Gallery Winthrop Coll 1974; Davidson Coll Art Gallery 1973; Charlotte Arts and Cultural Soc 1970; Jefferson Gallery 1969; Selected Juried and Invit Exhibitions, Drawing Invitational Somerhill Gallery 1984; Six North Carolina Artists Pfeiffer Coll Gallery 1984; Afro-Amer Artists of NC Center/Gallery 1984; LA Watercolor Soc's 14th Annual Intl Exhibit 1984; 1984 Invitational/Black and White Spirit Square Arts Center 1984; St John's Museum of Art, 1994; Mint Museum of Art, 1994; Jerald Melberg Gallery, 1994; Wilmer Jennings Gallery at Kenkeleba, 1993; Isobel Neal Gallery, 1993; The McIntosh Gallery, 1993; Potsdam Coll of the State Univ of NY, 1993; The Tubman Museum, 1992; Lincoln Cultural Ctr, 1992; VA Polytechnic Inst & State Univ, 1991; NC State Univ, 1990; Marita Gilliam Gallery, 1990; Green Hill Ctr for NC Art, 1987; Afro-Amer Cultural Ctr, 1986; Gaston Cty Museum of Art & History, 1986; Deborah Peverall Gallery, 1985; Selected Group Exhibitions, Southeastern Ctr for Contemporary Art, 1995; Cleveland Ctr for Contemporary Art, 1995; Montgomery Museum of Art, 1994; Diggs Gallery Winston-Salem State Univ, 1994; Southeast Arkansas Arts & Sci Ctr, 1993; GA Southern Museum, 1993; Asheville Art Museum, 1993; Univ of IL at Chicago, 1992; Gainesville Coll, 1992; Greenville Museum of Art, 1991; Lawton Gallery Univ of Wisconsin Green Bay, 1990; Hodges Taylor Gallery, 1989; Johnson C Smith Univ, 1988; The Waterworks Visual Arts Ctr, 1988; NC Central Univ, 1987; Hickory Museum of Art, 1986; Museum of Science & Industry, 1986; Portsmouth Museum, 1986; Spirit Sq Ctr for Art & Education, 1985. **Honors/Awds:** NC Arts Council Artist Fellowship, 1991-92; 1st Place Award LA Watercolor Society's 14th Ann Intl Exhibit New Orleans; 1st Place Award LA Watercolor Society's 14 Ann Intl Exhibit New Orleans 1984; The Romare Bearden Award for Creativity/Innovation of Medium Carnegie Inst 1972; Honorable Mention-PIC Award/Nonprocess Educ Posters Assoc Printing Co Charlotte, NC 1974. **Military Serv:** USAF. **Home Addr:** 305 Henry's Chapel Rd, Belmont, NC 28012-9695.

LOGAN, LLOYD
Pharmacist (retired). **Personal:** Born Dec 27, 1932, Columbia, MO; married Lottie A Pecot; children: Terri, Connie, Gerald, Michael, Kevin. **Educ:** Purdue Univ 1951-52; Belleville Jr Coll 1953-54; St Louis Coll of Pharmacy, BS 1958. **Career:** Daughter of Charity National Health System, asst vp contracts, 1970-95; Rhodes Med Supply Inc, sec 1968-72; Mound City Pharmacy, owner; Dome Pharmacy, owner, dir pharmacy & purchasing 1966-69; chief pharmacist 1959-67; St Louis Univ Hosp, staff pharmacist 1958-59. **Orgs:** Mem Shared Servs Adv Panel Am Hosp Assn, 1971-73; pres People Inc 1967-68; sec 1967-69, pres 1973-74, Chi Delta Mu Med Frat; mem YMCA; adv com Help Inc; treas Page Comm Devel Corp 1971-77; trustee Lindell Hosp 1974-78; mem Am Pharmaceutical Assn; Nat Pharm Assn; pres Mound City Pharm Assn 1964; Nat Assn of Retail Druggists; Patentee; mem St Engelbert Sch Bd 1969-76; pres 1973-76; pres St Louis Archdiocesan Sch Bd 1977-79; mem bd St Louis Urban League 1980-. **Military Serv:** USAF 1952-56. **Home Addr:** 6055 Lindell, St Louis, MO 63112.

LOGAN, MARC ANTHONY
Professional football player. **Personal:** Born May 9, 1965, Lexington, KY; children: Marc Anthony II, Allegra. **Educ:** Univ of Kentucky, BS in political science, 1987. **Career:** Cincinnati Bengals, running back, 1987-88; Miami Dolphins, 1989-91; San Francisco 49ers, 1992-94; Washington Redskins, 1995-. **Business Addr:** Professional Football Player, Washington Redskins, 13832 Redskin Dr, Herndon, VA 22071, (703)471-9100.

LOGAN, THOMAS W. S., SR.
Episcopal minister. **Personal:** Born Mar 19, 1912, Philadelphia, PA; son of Mary Harbison Logan and John Richard Logan Sr; married Hermione Hill, Sep 3, 1938; children: Thomas Jr. **Educ:** Johnson C Smith Univ 1930-33; Lincoln U, AB 1935; Gen Theol Sem, cert 1935-38; Philadelphia Div Sch, STM 1941; Mansfield College, Oxford, England, cert, 1974; St Augustine's College, Raleigh, NC, LHD, 1984; Durham College, Durham, NC, DD, 1984; Lincoln Univ, LLD, 1985. **Career:** Calvary Epis Ch, Philadelphia PA, rector & canon 1945-84, rector, emeritus, 1984-; St Michaels, vicar 1940-45, rector, 1945; St Augustine, NY, vicar 1938-39; St Philips, New York NY, curate 1938-39; First Colonel Wesley Church, Philadelphia, PA, intern, 1984-86; Historic St Thomas Church, Philadelphia, PA, intern, 1990-92; Annunciation Church, Philadelphia, PA, intern, 1993-94. **Orgs:** Past pres Tribune Chrtrs 1945-69; past pres Nat Ch Wrkrs conf 1951-61; chpln Philadelphia police 1968-; trustee Haverford St Hosp 1970-84; fndr Parkside YMCA 1945; past pres Philadelphia YMCA 1946-47; life mem Central HS; life mem Lincoln U; life mem NAACP; bd mem Darby NAACP; past pres Hampton Min conf 1960-61; dean smr sch St Paul, Laurenceville, VA; pub dir Blk Cler Dir Epis Ch; past grnd mstr Prince Hall Masons 1968-69; life mem Alpha Phi Alpha; past grnd chpln 1973-74; past imp chpln Inperial Coun Shrinedon 1970-71, 1982-84, 1996-97; 1st asst grnd chpln IBPOEW 1968-; past grnd chpln Frontiers Int 1971; fndr/past & pres/chpln Philadelphia Chptr of Frontier 1945, 1965-67; 33rd degree Mason. **Honors/Awds:** Afro-Am aw 1944; Philadelphia Tribune Char aw 1968; Demolay consult aw 1966; hon mem Cornish Post 292 1944; bd Eme Philadelphia USO 1944; LHL, St Augustine's College, Raliegh, NC, 1982; LLD, Lincoln Univ, Chester Cty, PA, 1985, VA Seminary, 1989; LLD, Lynchburg, VA; author, chapter, Voices of Experiences, M L King Fellow Press, 1985; ThD, Episeopal Semenary, Cambridge, Mass, 1994-. **Home Addr:** 46 Lincoln Ave, Yeadon, PA 19050.

LOGAN, WILLIE FRANK, JR.
State representative. **Personal:** Born Feb 16, 1957, Miami, FL; son of Ruth Logan and Willie Logan; married Lyra Blizzard, Jan 23, 1993. **Educ:** Miami Dade Community College, AA, 1976; University of Miami, BBA, 1977. **Career:** Opa Locka Community Developement Corp., consultant; Florida House of Representatives, state representative, currently. **Orgs:** Democratic Party Executive Committeeman; National Association of Colored People; Urban League; National Conference of State Legislators. **Honors/Awds:** Opa locka Community Corp Award; Greater Miami Chamber Legislative Award; FEA/UTD Award; Metro-Dade Legislative Award; United Teachers of Dade TIGER Award. **Business Addr:** State Representative, House of Representatives, 490 Opa Locka Blvd, #21, Opa Locka, FL 33054, (305)681-0008.

LOGAN, WILLIS HUBERT
Executive director. **Personal:** Born Nov 23, 1943, Springfield, IL; married Joyce A Day; children: Gennea, Andre. **Educ:** Western IL Univ 1943; Sangamon State U, BA 1972. **Career:** Dept of Community Devel & Programs Springfield IL, exec dir present; Dept of Conservation, employ coord 1979; IL Nat Bank, bank teller 1967; Allis Chalmers, machine operator 1963;

Springfield Recreation Commn, youth supr 1962. **Orgs:** Mem Frontiers Intl 1976; v chmn Spfld Planning Commn 1979; chmn Spfld Sangamon Co Reg Planning Commn 1980; bd mem United Fund 1976; pres Springfield E Assn 1977; sec Alpha Phi Alpha Mu Delta Lambda 1980. **Honors/Awds:** Community serv award NAACP 1977; community serv award United Way 1978. **Military Serv:** AUS sgt e-4 1965-67. **Business Addr:** Dept of Community Devel Progs, 601 E Jefferson St second floo, Springfield, IL 62701.

LOGAN-TOOSON, LINDA ANN
Transportation executive. **Personal:** Born Aug 7, 1950, Cincinnati, OH; daughter of Amelia Logan and Harold Logan. **Educ:** Fisk Univ, BA 1972; Xavier Univ, MBA 1975. **Career:** Frigidaire/General Motors, mktg analyst 1972-75; IBM, mktg trainee 1975-76; Drackett Co/Bristol Myers, project dir 1977-82, mgr consumer rsch 1982-84, sr mgr consumer rsch 1984-92; West Shell Coldwell Banker, realtor, 1993-; Tucson Limousine Service Inc, vp, 1991. **Orgs:** Life mem Alpha Kappa Alpha Sorority, Inc, 1970-, chap vp, 1996-97, pres, 1998-00; vp, Greater Cincinnati Limousine Assn, 1994-96; visiting prof Natl Urban League Black Exec Exchange Program 1978-; mem Natl Assoc of Female Execs 1982-; youth prog chairperson YMCA Black Achievers Program 1983-84; bd mem Gross Branch YMCA 1984-85; vice pres membership bd of dirs Amer Mktg Assn 1985-86; exec adv bd Amer Mktg Assn 1986-89; mem Natl Black MBA Assn 1986-; account mgr United Way Campaign 1987, 1989, 1990; executive secretary/board of directors, 1986-88, president, 1990-91, Cincinnati Scholarship Foundation; Ohio Bd of Realtors, Natl Assn of Realtors, bd of realtors, 1993-. **Honors/Awds:** YMCA Black Achiever Award 1981; Outstanding Alumni Black Achiever YMCA 1982. **Home Addr:** 7624 Castleton Place, Cincinnati, OH 45237. **Business Addr:** VP, Tucson Limousine Service, Inc, 7624 Castleton Place, Cincinnati, OH 45237-2636, (513)821-4515.

LOGUE-KINDER, JOAN
Business executive. **Personal:** Born Oct 26, 1943, Richmond, VA; daughter of Helen Harvey Logue and John Thomas Logue; married Lowell A Henry Jr, 1963 (divorced 1983); children: Lowell A Henry III, Catherine Dionne Henry, Christopher Logue Henry; married Randolph S Kinder, Dec 1987. **Educ:** Wheaton Coll, attended 1959-62; Adelphi Univ, BA 1964; Mercy Coll, Certificate in Educ 1971; New York Univ. **Career:** TWA NYC, ticket agent 1964-65; US Census Bureau, admin asst to dist mgr 1970; Bd of Educ Yonkers, social studies tchr/admin 1971-75; Natl Black Network, dir public relations 1976-83; NBN Broadcasting Inc, vice pres 1983-90; The World Inst of Black Communication Inc, co-dir, co-founder, 1978-90; Mingo Group/Plus Inc, senior vp; Edelman Public Relations Worldwide, vice pres, currently. **Orgs:** Bd dirs Girl Scout Council of Greater NY 1985-; bd dirs Natl PUSH 1985; bd dirs NY Chap PUSH 1983; consultant KLM Royal Dutch Airlines 1976; consultant Kentucky Fried Chicken 1976; consultant ATESTA Spanish Natl Tourist Bd 1977; asst coord Howard Samuels for Gov NY 1974; advance pers Rep Morris Udall 1976; bd dirs Nigerian-Amer Friendship Soc; mem 100 Black Women; del White House Conf on Small Business; coord Natl Assn of Black Owned Broadcasters 1977-; counsultant, The Sony Corporation; sr black media advisor, Dukakis-Bentsen. **Honors/Awds:** Excellence in Media Award Inst of New Cinema Artists Inc 1984; co-pub "Communications Excellence to Black Audiences" CEBA Exhibit Awards Journ 1978-90; creator and developer The Action Woman Radio Prog 1979-. **Business Addr:** Vice President, Public Affairs Group, Edelman Public Relations Worldwide, 1500 Broadway, New York, NY 10036.

LOKEMAN, JOSEPH R.
Accountant. **Personal:** Born Jul 24, 1935, Baltimore, MD; son of Beulah V Lokeman and Joseph Miles Lokeman; married Shirley M Morse; children: Pamela, Kimberly, Sherre, Shereen. **Educ:** AS 1967; BS 1969. **Career:** Bureau Public Debt Treasury, auditor 1968-70; Bureau Accounts Treasury, staff accountant 1971-73; Bureau Govt Financial Operations Treasury, systems accountant 1973-, chief general ledger branch, treasury 1984-90; public accountant, enrolled agent, private practice 1967-. **Orgs:** Mem Fed Govt Accountants Assn; Nat Soc Public Accountants; Nat Soc Black Accountants; Nat Soc Enrolled Agts; MD Soc Accountants, Notary Public; Mem White Oak Civic Assn Silver Spring. **Honors/Awds:** Gallatin Award-Treasury, 1990. **Military Serv:** AUS 1957-59. **Business Addr:** Public Accountant, 4022 Edmondson Ave, Baltimore, MD 21229.

LOMAS, RONALD LEROY
Educator. **Personal:** Born May 21, 1942, Rock Island, IL. **Educ:** Western IL Univ, BA 1965, MA 1967; Bowling Green State Univ, PhD 1976. **Career:** Western IL Univ, grad asst dept of speech 1965-66; Bowling Green State Univ, grad asst dept of speech 1969-70; Lorain Cty Comm Coll instr speech & dir forensics, reg adv 1969; Bowling Green State Univ, instr speech & ethnic studies 1970-, asst to dir of ethnic studies 1970-75; Univ of Cincinnati Med School, coord of supportive serv 1975-76; TX So Univ Houston, assoc prof speech comm. **Orgs:** Chmn faculty eval comm Lorain Cty Comm Coll 1968-69; chmn Minority Affairs Comm 1968-69; adv Black Progressives 1968-69; consult & lectr Black Culture St Pauls Episcopal Church Maumee OH 1972-73; leadership consult B'nai B'rith Youth Org S Euclid OH 1972-73, Lorain Council 1970-71, MI Council 1973; communication consult Title I Grant Toledo Minority Businessmen 1974-75; mem Intl Commun Assoc, Speech Commun Assoc; producer Black Perspectives WBGU Channel 70 1971;producer, host & writer of prog WBGU Channel 57 1973. **Honors/Awds:** Foreign Serv Scholar 1964; Omicron Delta Kappa 1973; Disting Faculty Awd 1974; Outstanding Instr TSU 1980. **Business Addr:** Assoc Professor Speech Comm, Texas Southern Univ, 3201 Wheeler St, Houston, TX 77004.

LOMAX, DERVEY A.
Electronic specialist, mayor. **Personal:** married. **Career:** Naval Electronic Systems Command, electronic splst; City Council of Coll Park, elected 1957-65; City Council, re-elected 1967-73; Coll Park MD, elected mayor 1973. **Orgs:** Mem Mat Washington Council of Gov't Policy Com on Pub Safety; mem City Univ Liason Com; founder Lakeland Civic Assn; founder Lakeland Boy Scout Troop; former mem Am Legion; former mem bd dir Coll Park Boys Club; former vice pres Coll Park Boys Club; former mem Prince George's Boys Club; basketball coach for Boys Club of Coll Park 7 yrs; founded Local Civil Air Patrol Unit. **Business Addr:** Ofc of the Mayor, 4500 Knox Rd, College Park, MD 20740.

LOMAX, MICHAEL L.
Educational administrator. **Personal:** married Cheryl Ferguson Lomax; children: 3 daughters. **Educ:** Degrees from Columbia Univ, Morehouse College, Emory Univ. **Career:** Morehouse College, prof; Spelman College, prof; Dillard Univ, pres, currently. **Orgs:** The National Faculty, pres; Board of Commissioners of Fulton County, board chair, 1981-1993. **Business Addr:** President, Dillard University, 2601 Gentilly Blvd, New Orleans, LA 70122.

LOMAX, MICHAEL WILKINS
Business executive. **Personal:** Born in Philadelphia, PA; married Dr A Faye Rogers; children: Lauren. **Educ:** St Josephs Univ, BS Soc 1973; Ins Inst of Amer. **Career:** Allstate Insurance Co, dist claim mgr 1977, div claim mgr 1978-79, asst reg claim mgr 1979-83, reg claim mgr 1983-84. **Orgs:** Mem Insurance Ed Dir Soc 1982-; Black Exec Exchange Prog Urban League 1982; bd of dir Brockport Found 1983-84. **Business Addr:** Regional Claim Manger, Allstate Insurance Company, 1111 Old Eagle School Rd, Valley Forge, PA 19482.

LOMAX, WALTER P.
Physician. **Personal:** Born Jul 31, 1932, Philadelphia; married; children: 3 girls, boys. **Educ:** Lasalle Coll, AB 1953; Hahnemann Med Coll 1957. **Career:** Pvt practice 1958. **Orgs:** Mem Med Soc E PA; AMA; Philadelphia Co Med Soc. **Business Addr:** 1300 S 18 St, Philadelphia, PA 19146.

LOMAX-SMITH, JANET E.
Broadcast journalist. **Personal:** Born Jan 18, 1955, Louisville, KY; daughter of Sedalia M Lomax and James A Lomax; married Charles V Smith, Aug 31, 1986; children: Erica Claire Smith, Charles Lomax Smith. **Educ:** Murray State University, BS, 1976. **Career:** WAVE-TV, journalist, 1976-80; WHEC-TV, journalist, 1980-. **Orgs:** Natil Association of Black Journalists, 1978-; Rochester Association of Black Communicators, founding president, 1982; Delta Sigma Theta, 1975-; Community Heating Fund, board of directors. **Honors/Awds:** Rochester Advertising Association, Communicator of the Year, 1989; Delta Sigma Theta, Communications Award, 1987; numerous civic & community awards, Rochester, NY, 1980-; numerous awards, Louisville, KY, 1976-80. **Business Addr:** Co-Anchor, News 10, WHEC-TV, Viacom Broadcasting Inc, 191 East Ave, Rochester, NY 14604, (716)546-0794.

LONDON, CLEMENT B. G.
Educator. **Personal:** Born Sep 12, 1928; son of Henrietta Myrtle Simmons-London and John London; married Pearl Cynthia Knight; children: Al Mu' min, Chet, Sharon, Shawn, Tamika. **Educ:** City Clg City Univ of NY, BA 1967, MA 1969; Tchr Clg Columbia Univ NY, EdM 1972, EdD 1973. **Career:** Toco & Morvant EC Elem Schs Trinidad-Tobago Sch Systm Trinidad, W Indies, asst prncpl 1953-60; St Augustine Parochial Sch Brooklyn, NY, tchr 1960-61; Harlem Hosp Sch of Nrsng New York City, sec/registrar 1963-66; Development & Training Ctr Distrbtv Trades Inc NYC, instr math & engl 1967-70; Crossroads Alternative HS East 105th St NYC, assc prncl dean stdnt 1970-71; Tchr Clg Columbia Univ NYC, grad asst & instrctnl asst 1971-73; Intermediate Sch 136 Manhattan NYC, substitute tchr math 1974; Fordham Univ at Lincoln Center, Graduate School of Educ, asst prof of educ 1974-82, assoc prof of educ 1982-91, professor of education, currently. **Orgs:** Natl Alliance Black Sch Educators 1975; Editorial Bd College Student Journal, editor Curriculum for a Career Ed & Dev Demonstration Proj for Youth 1978; editorial consultant Natl Council Negro Women 1978; Assn Teacher Educators 1979; summer chmn Div Curriculum & Teaching 1979; bd elders Council of Mwamko Wa Siasa Educ Institute 1980; Natl Sch Bd Assn 1980-; Org Amer Historians 1980; Assn Caribbean Studies 1980-; Amer Assn for Advancement of Humanities 1980; American Academy Political & Social Sci 1980-; rprtr bd dir Kappa Alpha Psi 1980-; faculty secretary Sch of Educ Fordham Univ 1981; Journal of Curiculum Theorizing 1982-; dir Project Real, 1984; bd dir Solidaridad Humana 1984; faculty adv, exec comm memPhi Delta Kappa; Kappa Delta Pi; adv bd, curriculum consultant La Nueva Raza Half House program; bd mem African Heritage Studies Assn; Schomburg Corp., Center for Research in Black Culture, board member, 1992-. **Honors/Awds:** Project Real, Special Recognition, Award for Outstanding Quality, 1983; Toco Anglican Elementary School, Clement London Day, Celebrant, 1977; Salem Community Service Council of New York City, 1981. **Special Achievements:** Author, numerous research publications & professional activities including: On Wings of Changes, 1991; Through Caribbean Eyes, 1989; Test-taking Skills: Guidelines for Curricular & Instructional Practices, 1989; A Piagetian Constructivist Perspective on Curriculum, 1989; "Multicultural Curriculum Thought: A Perspective," 1992; "Multicultural Education and Curriculum Thought: One Perspective," 1992; "Curriculum as Transformation: A Case for the Inclusion of Multiculturality," 1992; "Afro-American Catholic School NYC", Black Educator in the Univ Role as Moral Authority Clg Stdnt Jrnl Monograph 18(1 Pt 2), Career Ed for Educational Ldrs, A Focus on Decision Making 1983, "Crucibles of Caribbean Conditions, Factors of Understanding for Teachg & Learng Caribbean Stdnts Am Ed Settings" Jrnl of Caribbean Studies, 2&3, p 182-188, Autumn/Winter 1982; "Career & Emplymnt, Critical Factors in Ed Plng," African-American Jrnl Res & Ed, 1981; "Black Women of Valor," African Heritage Studies Assn Nwsltr, p 9, 1976; "Conf Call, The Caribbean & Latin Am," WABC Radio, 3 hr brdcst, 1979-80; 2 video-taped TV appearances: Natl TV Trinidad, W Indies, featuring emotionally oriented issues, 1976-77; Parents and Schools: A sourcebook, Garland Publishings, Inc, 1993; A critical perspective of multiculturality as a philosophy for educational change, Education, 114(3), p 368-383, 1994; Three Turtle Stories, New Mind Productions, Inc, 1994; Linking cultures through literacy: A perspective for the future, In NJ Ellsworth, CN Hedley and AN Baratta (Eds), Literacy: A redefinition, Lawrence Erlbaum Associates, 1994; Queens Public Access Television, discussing Fordham University Graduate School of Education and its leadership role in Language, Literacy, and Learning, 1994. **Business Addr:** Professor of Education, Graduate School of Education, Fordham University, 113 W 60th St, New York, NY 10023-7471.

LONDON, DENISE
Marketing executive. **Educ:** Glassboro State College, bachelor's degree; Texas A&M Univ, graduate studies; Univ of Cambridge. **Career:** Patrol officer; Broadcast station account executive; Ford Motor Company, zone manager; Texas State Aquarium, director of marketing; Natl Aquarium in Baltimore, vp of marketing, currently. **Orgs:** Amer Mktg Assn; Amer Zoological Aquarium Assn; Amer Ass of Museums; Public Realtions Soc of Amer. **Honors/Awds:** Texas Public Relations Soc, Best of Texas and Silver Spur Award; YWCA of Amer, Honoree; Ford Motor Co, Gold Key Award; Mayor's of Baltimore Citation, Comm Service; 100 Black Women, Torchbearers Award. **Special Achievements:** First African American to be named senior director of marketing for The National Aquarium in Baltimore; first female patrol officer in Camden County New Jersey. **Business Addr:** Vice Pres of Mktg, National Aquarium in Baltimore, 111 Marketplace, Ste 800, Baltimore, MD 21202, (410)576-1438.

LONDON, EDDIE
Company executive. **Personal:** Born Nov 25, 1934, Morgan City, LA; children: Lori B. **Educ:** AA; BA; MBA. **Career:** London Enterprise Information Systems, president, 1990-; Pacific Missile Center Division Head, analyst, 1974-90; Navy, operations research analyst 1971-73; Navy, mgmt analyst 1970-71; design technician 1965-70, teacher, currently. **Orgs:** Pres Oxnard-Ventura NAACP; bd of Professional Employees; past chmn Grass Roots Poverty Program; pres, San Luis Obispo County NAACP, 1992-. **Honors/Awds:** Federation Executive Board Outstanding Management, 1983. **Military Serv:** US Army, Sgt, 1953-56. **Home Addr:** PO Box 1798, Atascadero, CA 93423.

LONDON, EDWARD CHARLES
Real estate executive. **Personal:** Born Aug 18, 1944, Memphis, TN; son of Juanita S London and James London Sr; married Nell R London; children: Edwin C, Torrick. **Educ:** LeMoyne-Owen Coll, BA 1967; Atlanta Univ, MBA 1972; John Marshall Law School, JD 1975. **Career:** Metropolitan Atlanta Rapid Transit Authority, federal grants/sr accountant 1973-75, sr contracts admin 1975-79, mgr of contracts 1979-81; Edward C London & Assocs Real Estate and Mgmt Consultants, pres 1981-; Real Estate Mgmt Brokers Inst/Natl Assoc of Real Estate Brokers, natl dir 1984-; Cornelius King & Son, Inc, Atlanta, GA, CEO, mng broker, 1988-94; Empire Real Estate Board, Inc, pres, CEO, 1989-90; Empire Real Estate Board, Inc, chairman, 1993-95. **Orgs:** Chmn bd of dirs Reach-Out Inc 1979-84; comm mem GA Real Estate Commn Educ Adv Comm 1983-87; coord Pastor's Higher Ground Task Force Antioch Baptist Church 1984-86; bd mem GA Chapter Natl Soc of Real Estate Appraisers 1986-87; mem Real Estate Educators Assoc 1987; mem bd of dirs 1st vice pres Empire Real Estate Bd Inc 1987;

mem Alpha Phi Alpha, NAACP, The Atlanta Business League, The Atlanta Exchange, The Progressive Alliance, The Minority Purchasing Council of the Atlanta Chamber of Commerce; sr mem & certified real estate appraiser Natl Assoc of Real Estate Appraisers 1987; certified senior mem, National Society of Real Estate Appraisers 1989-; mem, Board of Zoning Appeals, Fulton County GA 1987-; mem, bd of dirs, Community Housing Resources Board of Atlanta 1987-; chairman, board of trustees, Antioch Baptist Church North; US Dept of HUD, Regional Advisory Board, 1991-95; Georgia Real Estate Commission Task Force on Brokerage Industry; bd of dirs, Atlanta Urban Residential Finance Authority/Atlanta Development Authority, 1993-. **Honors/Awds:** Outstanding Leadership Awd Reach-Out Inc 1981; Assoc Partner Awd, Century Club Awd Butler St YMCA 1986; Outstanding & Dedicated Serv Awd Empire Real Estate Bd Inc 1986; publications Principles of Apartment Management, 1983, Basic Budgeting & Accounting for Property Management, 1986; Real Estate Broker of the Year, Empire Real Estate Board Inc 1988; Local Board President of the Year, National Assn of Real Estate Brokers, 1989; GA Real Estate Commission Task Force on Brokerage Industry; National Associate of Real Estate Brokers, Inc, Realtist of the Year, 1992; Realtist of the Year, Empire Real Estate Board, Inc, 1994; Outstanding Alumnus Award, United Negro College Fund (UNCF), 1995. (UNCF), 1995; Presidential Citation, National Association For Equal Opportunity in HIS HER Education, 1997. **Military Serv:** AUS E-5 2 yrs; Superior Cadet Awd, Expert Rifleman Badge, Bronze Star, USRVN Serv Medal, Good Conduct Medal 1968-70. **Business Addr:** CEO/Principal, EC London & Associates, PO Box 1885, Atlanta, GA 30301-1885, (404)688-6607.

LONDON, GLORIA D.
Savings and loan officer. **Personal:** Born Jul 24, 1949, Clinton, LA; daughter of Georgia Lee London-Hampton; children: Kenna Elizabeth. **Educ:** Southern University, A & M College, BS, business management, 1971. **Career:** Premier Bank NA, various positions, 1971-91; Life Savings Bank, chief operations officer, 1991-92, chief administrative officer, 1992-. **Orgs:** Alpha Kappa Alpha Sorority Inc, philacter; Pi Gamma Mu Honor Society; Phi Beta Lambda Honor Society. **Honors/Awds:** Alpha Kappa Alpha Sorority Inc, Outstanding Soror, 1985; YMCA, Black Achievers Award, 1992. **Business Addr:** Chief Administative Officer, Life Savings Bank, 7990 Scenic Hwy, Baton Rouge, LA 70807, (504)775-6133.

LONDON, ROBERTA LEVY
Construction company executive. **Personal:** Born in New York, NY; daughter of Carrie Belle Calier Levy and Henry Edward Levy; married Lester London Jr, Jul 30, 1955. **Educ:** Nassau Community Coll, Garden City, NY, AA, 1972; Hunter Coll, New York, NY, BA, 1977; Queens Coll, Flushing, NY, educl credits, 1978; Adelphi Univ, Garden City, NY, Graduate Certificate, 1988. **Career:** Presbyterian Church, New York NY, mgr Human Resources, Program Agency, 1981-89; Turner/Santa Fe Construction Co., Brooklyn NY, coordinator of Local Laws 49/50, 1989-. **Orgs:** Dist Clerk, Lakeview Public Library; mem, One Hundred Black Women of Long Island, 1979-83; Governor, Northeast Dist, Natl Assn of Negro Business and Professional Women's Clubs, Inc, 1987-91; mem, Delta Sigma Theta Sorority, Inc; mem, bd of trustees, Union Baptist Church, Hempstead, NY. **Honors/Awds:** Community Service Award, Long Island Black History Comm, 1981; Finalist, Long Island Woman of the Year, 1986; Sojourner Truth Award for Meritorious Serv, Brooklyn Club, Natl Assn of Negro Business and Professional Women's Clubs, Inc, 1989. **Home Addr:** 425 Columbia Ave, Rockville Centre, NY 11570.

LONEY, CAROLYN PATRICIA
Banking executive. **Personal:** Born Jun 16, 1944, New York, NY; daughter of Edna Loney and Daniel Loney. **Educ:** Morgan State Univ, BS 1969; Columbia Univ, MBA 1971. **Career:** Royal Globe Ins Co, rater 1962-65; NY NAACP, br mgr 1965; Human Resources Admin, field auditor 1967; NY State Senate, rsch worker 1967; Citibank, corp lending officer 1969-77; Federal Research Bank of NY, special asst; Citibank, vice pres. **Orgs:** Bd dir New Harlem YWCA 1975-76; mem 100 Black Women 1977-; adv bd Columbia Univ Alumni 1971-; mem Urban Bankers Coalition 1973-80; mem Natl Assn of Accountants 1973; mem Natl Credit & Financial Women's Org 1972-74; founder Carolyn P Lonely Schlrsp Awd Morgan State Univ; mem Amer Mgmt Assn 1977-; Uptown C of C 1977-. **Honors/Awds:** Outstanding Instr of Yr ICBO 1974; Black Achiever Awd Harlem YMCA 1973.

LONG, ANDU TRISA
Education Administrator. **Personal:** Born May 13, 1958, Akron, OH; daughter of Pauline Long and George W Long Jr. **Educ:** Univ of Akron, BS 1981, MS 1987. **Career:** Spelman College, associate vice pres for Institutional advancement, 1996-; Major Gifts, campaign dir, 1993-96; Univ of Akron, associate dir development & dir annual giving, beginning, 1988, assistant dir asst dir alumni relations 1983-85, associate dir 1985-88. **Orgs:** YWCA of Cobb County, bd of trustees; Antioch Baptist Church North, mem; Junior League of Atlanta, 1995; Delta Sigma Theta Sorority. **Honors/Awds:** Outstanding Employee, Univ of Akron Board of Trustees 1985; Woman of the Year, Akron Women's History Project 1988; Delta Sigma Theta Service Award, 1988; Delta Sigma Theta Sisterhood Award, 1990. **Business Addr:** Spelman College, 350 Spelman Lane, SW, PO Box 1303, Atlanta, GA 30314.

LONG, BARBARA COLLIER. **See COLLIER-BRIDGEFORTH, BARBARA.**

LONG, CHARLES H.
Educator (retired). **Personal:** Born Aug 23, 1926, Little Rock, AR; son of Geneva Diamond Thompson and Samuel Preston Long; married Alice M Freeman; children: John, Carolyn, Christopher, David. **Educ:** Dunbar Jr Coll, Diploma 1946; Univ of Chicago, BD 1953, PhD 1962; Dickinson Coll, LHD 1971. **Career:** Univ of Chicago, instr 1956-60, asst prof 1960-64, assoc prof 1964-70, prof 1970-74; Duke Univ, prof history of religion 1974-88; Univ of NC Chapel Hill, Wm Rand Keenan jr prof 1974-88; Jeanette K Watson prof, history of religions, Syracuse Univ. **Orgs:** Past pres Amer Acad of Religion; mem Soc for Religion in Higher Edn; Intl Assn of Historians of Religion; Soc for Study of Black Religion; American Society for Study of Religion. **Honors/Awds:** Guggenheim Fellowship 1971; mem bd of govs Univ of NC Press Natl Humanities Faclty; consult Encyclopaedia Brittanica; Alumni of Year, Divinty School University of Chicago, 1985; Distinguished Alumni Award, University of Chicago, 1991. **Military Serv:** USAAF Sgt 1944-46.

LONG, EARNESTEEN
Nurse, educator. **Personal:** Born Feb 13, 1939, Eutaw, AL; daughter of Cora Barnes Gordon and Johnnie Wright Gordon; married James Edgar Long, Jul 18, 1961; children: Eric Vincent, Amy Christine. **Educ:** Capital University, BSN, 1960; University of Cincinnati, MSN, adult psychiatric nursing, 1973; Miami University, PhD, higher education administration, 1985; University of Pennsylvania, Post-Doctorial Fellow, psychosocial oncology, 1989-92. **Career:** The Jewish Hospital School of Nursing, instructor, 1973-74; University of Cincinnati, College of Nursing & Health, instructor, 1974-78; Wright State University, assistant professor, 1978-80; University of Cincinnati Hospital, Psychiatric ER, clinician/therapist, 1981-84; Indiana University, BSN program, faculty coordinator, 1986-88; Auburn University, administrative coordinator, 1988-89; University of Illinois, clinical assistant professor, 1992-. **Orgs:** Association of Black Nursing Faculty in Higher Education, 1987-, journal editorial review board, 1989-, newsletter editor, 1991-; American Nurses Association, conference delegate, 1960-90; American Cancer Society, Philadelphia Division, Cancer & the Poor, advisory committee, 1990-92; Indiana University, College of Nursing, BSN program, steering committee, 1987. **Honors/Awds:** Sigma Theta Tau International, Honorary Member, 1985-; Phi Delta Kappa, Honorary Member, 1984-89; University of Pennsylvania, National Center for Nursing Research, National Institutes of Health Psychosocial Oncology, Post-Doctoral Fellowship, 1989-92; Association for Cancer Researchers International, Minority Travel Award, 1990; American Cancer Society, 2nd National Conference, Nursing Research Award, 1992; National Institute of Mental Health, Traineeship for Masters, 1971-73; National League for Nursing, Adult Psychiatric Nursing, Division of Accreditation, Administrative Internship. **Special Achievements:** Thesis: A Study of Black Students Who Entered One Baccalaureate Nursing Program, 1973; Dissertation Abstracts International: ''The Effects of Diagnosis Related Group Prospectives,'' 1986, ''Payment on Nursing Practice & Education,'' 1986; ''A Study of the Reponses of African-American Women to Breast Cancer,'' Ethnoscience 1991; ''Reponses of African-American Women to Breast Cancer Diagnosis,'' American Cancer Society 2nd National Nursing Research Conference, 1992; Breast Cancer in African-American Women: A Ten Year Review of Life Sciences Cancer Nursing, 1993. **Business Addr:** Clinical Assistant Professor, Psychiatric Nursing, University of Illinois at Chicago, College of Nursing, 845 S Damen Ave, 10th Flr, Chicago, IL 60612, (815)395-5625.

LONG, EDDIE
Cleric. **Personal:** marrled Vanessa; children: four. **Career:** New Birth Missionary Baptist Church, pastor, 1987-; Full Gospel Baptist Convention, bishop. **Special Achievements:** One of first among Baptist clergy appointed to office of Bishop in the newly formed Full Gospel Baptist Convention.

LONG, GERALD BERNARD
Accountant. **Personal:** Born Oct 19, 1956, Bessemer, AL; son of Ruby Stein Long and Edward Beckon Long Sr; married Darlene Gillon Long, Oct 20, 1980; children: Claudia Miranda. **Educ:** Bessemer Technical College, associate, 1978; University of Alabama-Birmingham, BS, 1983; Michigan State University Graduate School of Business Administration, attended, 1989. **Career:** Peat Marwick Main, assistant accountant, 1983-84, staff accountant, 1984-85, senior accountant, 1985-86, level 1 supervisor, 1986-87, level 2 supervisor, 1987-88; Booker T Washington Insurance Co, director of internal audit, 1988; State of Alabama Public Service Commission, advisory staff cpa, 1988-. **Orgs:** American Institute of CPA's, 1988-; Alabama Society of CPA's, 1985-. **Honors/Awds:** Goldstein Foundation, Goldstein Scholarship, 1982; Alabama State University, Scholastic Achievement Award, 1978. **Home Addr:** 216 Seaton Cir qqqqq, Montgomery, AL 36116, (205)288-4380. **Business Phone:** (205)242-5025.

LONG, GRANT ANDREW
Professional basketball player. **Personal:** Born Mar 12, 1966, Wayne, MI; married Nikki; children: Garvis, Gavar, Abagayl. **Educ:** Eastern Michigan Univ, Ypsilanti, MI, 1984-88. **Career:** Miami Heat, forward, 1988-94; Atlanta Hawks, 1994-96; Detroit Pistons, 1996-. **Business Addr:** Professional Basketball Player, Detroit Pistons, 2 Championship Dr, Auburn Hills, MI 48326, (248)377-0100.

LONG, IRENE
Physician. **Personal:** Born in Cleveland, OH. **Educ:** Northwestern Univ Evanston IL, attended; St Louis Univ School of Med, attended. **Career:** Cleveland Clinic, internship gen surgery; Mt Sinai Hosp, resd; Wright State Univ, Dayton OH, resd aerospace med; NASA, chief of med oper 1982-. **Honors/Awds:** 1st black woman chief of med at NASA. **Business Addr:** Chief of Medical Operations, NASA, Kennedy Space Center Office, MD-MED, Orlando, FL 32899.

LONG, JAMES, JR.
Company executive. **Personal:** Born Apr 26, 1931, St Francis County, AR; son of Almamie Gray Long and James Long, Sr; married Patricia Hardiman, Apr 18, 1954; children: Karen R Long, Kathryn C Long, Kaye Patrice H Long Allen, James, III. **Educ:** Lincoln Univ of MO, BS Educ/Commn ROTC Corp Engineers, 1954; attened MO at Kansas City, MO, 1965-66; Northeastern Univ, Boston, MA, Graduate School MBA, 1976. **Career:** US Govt Army, Ft Belvoir, officer/US Army, 1954-57, Ft Riley, KS, officer/US Army Corp Engineers, 1954-57; Lincoln Univ of Jefferson City, MO, asst instructor & dir student union, 1957-61; Lincoln Sr High School, Kansas City, MO, teacher/coach, 1961-64; Western Elec Co, Lee's Summit, MO, supv mfg & safety dir, 1964-69; Gen Electric Co, Lynn MA, mgr mfg manpower devel, mgr personnel practices, 1970-74, mgr employee relations LUO, 1974-81, mgr EO & compliance, 1982-. **Orgs:** Chmn, Lynn Corp Advisory Bd Salvation Army, 1982-86; dir, Private Industry Council, 1983-; dir, Private Industry Council, 1983-; dir, Action for Boston Community Devel, 1984-; dir, vice pres, Industrial Relations MA Pre-Engineering Program, 1985-; dir, Lynn, MA Historical Soc, 1986-. **Honors/Awds:** Developed a group of black square dancers for TV, 1957; No 1 Safety Program, Western Electric's Parent Body, 1964; Omega Man of the Year, Beta Omega Graduate Chapters, 1967; Past Basileus Award, Beta Omega Chapter Omega Psi Phi Fraternity, Inc, 1988; co-founder, The Henry Buckner School, St Paul AME Church Cambridge, MA, 1973; Hall of Fame ROTC, Lincoln Univ of MO, 1975; Others Award, Salvation Army, 1986; organized ''The Soulful Squares'' during black history month, 1988; Gen Electric Managerial Award, 1989; co-organized Minority Mentor's Program at Gen Electric, 1989. **Military Serv:** US Army Corp Engineers, 1st Lieutenant, 1954-57; No 1 Student, Ft Riley, KS, Fifty Army Physical Training Instructors Academy, 1955.

LONG, JAMES ALEXANDER
Communications executive. **Personal:** Born Dec 26, 1926, Jacksonville, FL; son of Ruby Hawkins Long and Willie James Long; married Ruth Beatrice Mitchell; children: John Alexander. **Educ:** North Carolina A&T State Univ, BS 1950; Univ of MI, MA 1962; Wayne State Univ, post grad study. **Career:** North Carolina A&T State Univ, instructor of English and journalism 1950-52; St Paul's College, instructor of English and journalism 1952-57; Foch Jr High School, teacher of English & social studies 1957-62, English dept head 1962-65; Cooley High School, guidance counselor 1965-67, asst principal 1967-70; Northwestern High School, principal 1970-72; Storer Broadcasting Co, general exec and coord of training programs 1972-74, mgr of personnel development 1974-80; Storer Communications Inc, corp vice pres of personnel development 1980-87; executive director, American Civil Liberties Union of Florida, 1987-88; American Civil Liberties Union of Florida, exec dir, 1987-88; Dade County Public Schools, educational specialist, 1988-. **Orgs:** Mem Amer Mgmt Assn 1973-; mem Amer Soc of Personnel Admin 1975-; mem Administrative Mgmt Soc, Phi Delta Kappa Educ Frat; mem Industry Labor Council Human Resources Ctr Albertson NY; mem Dade's Employ the Handicapped Comm Miami; exec bd Goodwill Industries Miami; mem Lafayette Park Kiwanis Club; mem Church of the Open Door United Church of Christ; mem Alpha Phi Alpha Frat Inc; mem Alpha Rho Boule Sigma Pi Phi Frat Inc; bd dirs Family Counseling Serv Miami; chairperson employment comm Private Industry Council Miami. **Honors/Awds:** North Carolina A&T State Univ Gate City Alumni Chap Awd; Achiever's Awd Family Christian Assoc of Amer Inc Miami 1986; Presidential Citation Natl Assn for Equal Opportunity in Higher Educ Washington DC 1986. **Military Serv:** US Army Air Force. **Home Addr:** 20 NW 89th St, Miami, FL 33150-2432. **Business Addr:** Educational Specialist, Dade County Public Schools, 1500 Biscayne Blvd, Ste 225, School Bd Admin Bldg, Annex 1, Miami, FL 33132.

LONG, JAMES L.
Judge. **Personal:** Born Dec 7, 1937, Wintergarden, FL; son of Susie L Long and James J Long. **Educ:** San Jose State Coll, BA, 1960; Howard Univ Law School, JD, 1967. **Career:** Legislative Counsel Bureau CA State Legislature, grad legal asst; Legal Aid Soc of Sacramento Co, grad legal asst; NAACP Western Region, special counsel; Private Practice, atty; Superior Court Bar Assn Liaison Comm, mem; Superior Court, judge; California State Univ, Sacremento, CA, asst prof, criminal justice. **Orgs:** Hon mem, Wiley W Manual Bar Assn, Sacramento, CA; mem, Appellate Dept Superior Court of Sacramento Co, 1987; mem, Sacramento City/County Commn of the Bicentennial of the US Constitution. **Honors/Awds:** The Law and Justice Award Sacramento Branch NAACP; Outstanding Contribution Award in the Field of Civil Rights Riverside Branch NAACP; sat as Pro Tem Justice of the Supreme Court Dec 9, 1985; assigned Justice Pro Tem to the Court of Appeal Third Appellate Dist 1987; co-author ''Amer Minorities, The Justice Issue,'' Prentice Hall Inc, 1975. **Military Serv:** AUS Reserve Corps 2nd lt. **Business Addr:** Judge, Sacramento County Superior Court, 720 9th St, Sacramento, CA 95814.

LONG, JERRY WAYNE
Computer company executive. **Personal:** Born Jun 6, 1951, Murfreesboro, TN; son of Delois Long and Ernest Long; married Marjorie E Russell, Aug 1, 1987; children: Julian, Jamaal, Khalilah. **Educ:** Middle Tennessee State University, BS, 1972; University of Tennessee, MBA, 1980. **Career:** General Electric, program mgr; CG/Aetna, project mgr; Hartford Insurance Group, mgr data architecture planning; P C Consultants, president, currently. **Orgs:** Black Data Processing Associates, Hd Membership Committee, 1988-. **Home Addr:** 6 Breezy Knoll Dr, Bloomfield, CT 06002, (203)242-1073. **Business Addr:** President, P C Consultants, 2 Barnard Lane, Ste 2B, Bloomfield, CT 06002, (203)242-3299.

LONG, JOHN
Professional basketball player. **Personal:** Born Aug 28, 1956. **Educ:** Detroit Mercy. **Career:** Toronto Raptors, currently. **Business Addr:** Professional Basketball Player, Toronto Raptors, 150 York St, Ste 110, Toronto, ON, Canada M5H 3S5, (416)214-2255.

LONG, JOHN BENNIE
Educator (retired). **Personal:** Born Apr 4, 1923, Landis, NC; daughter of Effie Mae Brewer Long and Allen Cephus Long; married Esther Clark; children: Sheila Long Kelly, Robert A, Glenn E. **Educ:** Livingstone Coll, BS (Honors) 1949; North Carolina A&T State Univ, MS 1957. **Career:** Army 93rd Infantry Div, 1942-46; North Warren High School, teacher coach & athletic dir 1946-50, 1954-66; Salisbury Rowan Comm Serv Council, ctr coord 1966-69; Kannapolis City Schools, classroom teacher 1969-82. **Orgs:** Post commander, 1970-79, veterans serv officer, 1984-87 Amer Legion Post 413, 1970-79; pres, Rowan Veterans Council, 1982; life mem, The Retired Officers Assn; life mem, Reserve Officers Assn of the US; comm chmn BSA Troop 373 Sandy Ridge AME Zion Church Landis NC; Kappa Alpha Psi Frat; supt Church school, Sandy Ridge AME Zion Church; pres, Charlotte Chapter, The Reserve Officers Assn of the US, 1985-; district commander, 19th district, The American Legion, Dept of North Carolina, 1989; district dir, Boy Scouts of America, Salisbury Dist Western NC Conference; AME Zion Church; Military Order of the World Wars, Commander Charlotte Chap, perpetual mem, 1993-94. **Honors/Awds:** Beta Kappa Chi Natl Hon Scientific Soc Inc; Dist Awd of Merit BSA Rowan Dist 1976; Veterans Serv Office of the Yr Rowan Veterans Council 1985; Silver Beaver Award, Central North Carolina Council, BSA, 1989. **Military Serv:** US Army, col 37 yrs Commissioned Serv, 1950-54, Reserves, 1954-83 (retired); Meritorious Serv Medal, Asiatic-Pacific Campaign Medal, Army Reserve Components Achievement Medal; Educ, Ord Co Officers Course, QM Co Officers Course, QM Adv Officers Course Command and Genl Staff Coll; Assoc Logistics Exec Develop Course, Industrial Coll of the Armed Forces. **Home Addr:** PO Box 785, Kannapolis, NC 28082.

LONG, JOHN EDWARD
Educator. **Personal:** Born Mar 16, 1941, Philadelphia, PA; married Carolyn Yvonne Wakefield. **Educ:** Temple U, BA 1963; Theol Sem of the Reformed Episcopal Ch, BD 1966; Westminister Theol Sem, Th M 1970; Brandeis U, MA PhD 1978. **Career:** Western KY Univ, assoc prof of religious studies present. **Orgs:** Mem Am Assn of Tchrs of Arabic 1979; mem Middle East & Studies Assn 1975; mem Middle East Inst 1975; Dissertation Research Fellowship Fulbright-Hays Research Fellow in Algeria 1974-75; Grad Study Fellowship Ford Found Advanced Study Fellowship for Black Am 1972-73; Fellowship to Study Arabic in Tunisia N African Cntr for Arabic Studies 1972. **Honors/Awds:** Dissertation Research Fellowship Fulbright-Hays Research Fellow in Algeria 1974-75; Grad Study Fellowship Ford Found Advanced Study Fellowship for Black Am 1972-73; Fellowship to Study Arabic in Tunisia N African Cntr for Arabic Studies 1972. **Business Addr:** Western KY Univ, Dept of Philosophy & Religion, Bowling Green, KY 42101.

LONG, JUANITA OUTLAW
Educator. **Personal:** Born in Philadelphia, PA; divorced; children: Thomas Marshall Jr. **Educ:** Boston City Hosp, Nursing Diploma, 1943; Washington Univ, BS, Nursing, 1956, MS, Nursing, 1958; Northeastern Univ, Cert of Advanced Grad Studies, 1974; Harvard Univ, Grad Study, 1975; Boston Univ, EdD, 1981. **Career:** Boston City Hosp, private duty 1943-44, head nurse 1944-46; Norfolk Comm Hosp, dir of nursing 1944-46; Homer G Phillips School of Nursing, instr 1958-59, clinical coord 1958-59, dir nurs ed 1961-65; Beth Israel Hosp School of Nurs, assoc dir 1965-67; Northeastern Univ, asst prof coord 1967-68; Coll of Nursing Northeastern Univ, acting dean 1968-69, dean & prof 1969-. **Orgs:** Bd of dirs MA Nurses Assoc 1975-77; corporator Lawrence Meml Hosp Medford 1976-78; bd of dirs Med Found Boston 1978-; chmn serv comm Zonta Intl Medford Club 1975-. **Honors/Awds:** Achievement Awd Dept of Health & Hosp Boston 1970; Black Achievers Awd YMCA 1977. **Military Serv:** ANC 1st lt 1948-52. **Business Addr:** Dean, Professor, Northeastern Univ, Coll of Nursing 102 RB, 360 Huntington Ave, Boston, MA 02115.

LONG, MONTI M.
Automobile dealer. **Personal:** Born Sep 24, 1957, Chicago, IL; son of Edna Phillips Long Carlson and Curtis Long; married Dana L Lucas Long, Nov 22, 1980; children: Tiffany Nicole, Tonya Renee. **Educ:** Glen Oaks Community College, attended, 1975-77; Ford Dealer Training, 1988; Chrysler Dealer Seminar, attended, 1989; Chrysler Financial Seminar, 1990. **Career:** Clark Equipment, quality control, 1979-82; Monti Long's Automobile Referral Service, president, owner, 1980-81; M & M Dodge-Honda Inc, salesman, 1982-85; Dick Loehr's Auto Mart, business manager, 1985-87; Brighton Ford-Mercury Inc, vice pres, general manager, 1988-90; Vicksburg Chrysler-Plymouth-Dodge Inc, president, general manager, 1989-. **Orgs:** Chrysler Minority Dealers Association, vice pres, Jeep Eagle Division; private capitol dealers chairman, 1982-; Chrysler Dealer Advisory Council, 1992-; Chamber of Commerce, 1988-; Better Business Bureau, 1988-; Chrysler Advertising Association, 1989-; Michigan Automobile Dealers Association, 1988-; National Association of Minority Auto Dealers, 1988-; Ford Black Dealers Association, 1988-. **Honors/Awds:** Chrysler, Pentastar Club, 1990, 1991, 1992, 1993 Just the Best Award, 1990, 1991, 1993, 1994, Sales Professionals, 1983, 1984; Marcellus High School, Hall of Fame Award, 1991. **Business Addr:** President/General Mgr, Vicksburg Car Sales, 13562 Portage Rd, PO Box 200, Vicksburg, MI 49097-0200, (616)649-2000.

LONG, NIA
Actress. **Personal:** Born in Brooklyn, NY. **Career:** Actress, films include: Boyz N The Hood, 1991; Made in America, 1993; Friday, 1995; Love Jones, 1997; Soul Food, 1997; TV: The Guiding Light; The BRAT Patrol; Fresh Prince of Bel-Air, role of Lisa, until 1996. **Honors/Awds:** Image Award Nomination, Guiding Light, 1993. **Business Addr:** Actress, c/o 20th Century Artists, 15315 Magnolia Blvd, Ste 429, Sherman Oaks, CA 91403-1174, (818)788-5516.

LONG, OPHELIA
Hospital administrator. **Personal:** Born Dec 5, 1940; married Henry Long; children: Donald, Celeste, Camille. **Educ:** Los Angeles City Coll, AA 1962; California State Univ, BS 1971; Univ of Southern California, MA in progress. **Career:** Kaiser Foundation Hospital, nursing care coord 1966, supervisor ICU 1966, asst dir of CCU 1972-81, dir of nursing 1981-84, Alameda County Med Center, hospital admin starting 1984; Meharry Med College, senior vp for admin. **Orgs:** Mem CA Nurses Assoc 1970-71; pres Council of Black Nurses Inc 1974-75; mem Black Congress on Health & Law 1979, Congressional Black Caucas Health Brain Trust 1979, Adv Com WLACC, CA State LA 1979-; bd of dir Natl Black Nurses Assoc 1982-83; pres Natl Black Nurses Assoc 1983-. **Honors/Awds:** Outstanding Awd Council of Black Nurses 1973; Merit Employees Assoc Kaiser Found Hosp 1974-75; Outstanding Nurse of the Year Awd Council of Black Nurses 1983; Outstanding Alumna Los Angeles City Coll 1984. **Business Addr:** Senior VP, Administration, Meharry Medical College, 1005 DB Todd Blvd, Nashville, TN 37208.

LONG, RICHARD A.
Educator. **Personal:** Born Feb 9, 1927, Philadelphia, PA; son of Leila Washington Long and Thaddeus Long. **Educ:** Temple Univ, AB 1947, MA 1948; Univ of PA, Grad Study 1948-49; Oxford, 1950; Paris, 1954; Univ of Paris, Fulbright Scholar 1957-58; Univ Poitiers, D 1965. **Career:** Morgan State Coll, instr, assoc prof 1951-66; Univ Poitiers, lectr 1964-65; Hampton Inst, prof, mus dir 1966-68; Atlanta Univ, prof, 1968-87; Harvard Univ, lectr 1969-71; Atticus Haygood Prof of Interdisciplinary Studies, Emory University, 1987-. **Orgs:** Conducted numerous symposiums, exhibitions, confs; past pres Coll Language Assoc, SE Conf Linguistics; ed bd Phylon. **Special Achievements:** Black Americana (cultural history) 1985; African American Writing (anthology) 1985; The Black Tradition in American Dance. **Business Addr:** Atticus Haygood Prof of Interdisciplinary Studies, ILA, Emory University, Atlanta, GA 30322.

LONG, STEFFAN
Business executive. **Personal:** Born Oct 6, 1929, Philadelphia, PA. **Educ:** Hward U; Univ of Mex; Univ of Bridgeport; Am Inst of Banking. **Career:** CT Nat Bank, vice pres & mgr present. **Orgs:** Past treas Family Serv of SE Fairfield Co; Gtr Bridgeport Heart Assn; bd mgrs YMCA; present exec bd mem Gtr Bridgeport-Stratford NAACP; treas Hall Neighborhood House; bd mem St Marks Day Care Cntr; mem UNA; Nat Negro Coll Fund; 2nd pres UNA of Fairfield Co; pres Japanese Schlrshp Com Univ of Bridgeport; treas Gr Bridgeport Opera Co; treas Gr Bridgeport Vis Nurses Assn; bd mem Italian Comm Cntr Guild. **Honors/Awds:** Barnum Festival Soc Award, 1968; Rotary Club of Newtown, 1952; Bureau of Naval Personnel Award, 1946; Spec Guest & Soloist Ch of England; formal invitation to White House; citations Mayor of Bridgeport NAACP & Natl Negro Business Women. **Business Addr:** Vice President, Connecticut Natl Bank, 777 Main St, Hartford, CT 06115.

LONG, WILLIAM H., JR.
Associate judge. **Personal:** Born Jun 7, 1947, Daytona Beach, FL; married Diann C; children: William III, Cherylen. **Educ:** Univ of Miami, BA 1968; Univ of Miami Law Sch, JD 1971. **Career:** Opa Locka Mun Ct, apptd assoc judge 1972; Long & Smith PA, partner; Counc on Legal Educ Oppor Univ of Miami Law Sch, instr 1970. **Orgs:** Founder United Black Students Univ of Miami 1968; pres Black American Law Students Assn 1971; chmn adv com Dade Co Comprehensive Offender Rehab Program Inc; Phi Alpha Delta. **Honors/Awds:** Recipient James E Scott Comm Serv Award 1973. **Business Addr:** 1 Biscayne Tower, Miami, FL 33131.

LOPES, DAVEY (DAVID EARL)
Professional baseball coach, professional baseball player (retired). **Personal:** Born May 3, 1945, East Providence, RI; married Linda Bandover. **Educ:** Washburn Univ, BS, education, 1969; Iowa Wesleyan College. **Career:** Los Angeles Dodgers, infielder/outfielder 1972-81; Oakland Athletics, infielder/outfielder/designated hitter 1982-84; Chicago Cubs, infielder/outfiel der 1984-86; Houston Astros, outfielder/infielder, 1986-87; Texas Rangers, coach; Baltimore Orioles, first base coach, 1992-. **Honors/Awds:** Top number of fan votes for the 1980 All-Star team; named to The Sporting News AP and UPI All-Star squads in 1979; Gold Glove winner; led the National League in stolen bases 63 for second consecutive year, 1976; stole 77 bases a career high in 1975; National League All-Star Team, 1978, 1979, 1980, 1981. **Business Addr:** First Base Coach, Baltimore Orioles, Oriole Park at Camden Yards, 333 W Camden St, Baltimore, MD 21201.

LOPEZ, MARY GARDNER
Director, educator. **Personal:** Born Apr 30, 1920, Nashville, TN; daughter of Jean Chandler and Kossie Gardner Sr; married George; children: Sharon, Adrienne. **Educ:** TN State Univ BS; Univ MI MBIA; Fisk Univ; Newark State Teachers Coll, MA; Columbia Univ; Yeshiva Univ. **Career:** Natl Bus Coll Meharry Med Coll, inst; New York City School System, inst 1962-64; NY State Consumer Protection Bd, dir consumer educ & rsch; Queens Div, NY State Div of Human Rights, dir 1964-84, reg mgr, currently. **Orgs:** Mem Natl Media Women; Alpha Kappa Alpha Sorority; NAACP; Negro Business & Professional Womens Clubs Inc; NAIRO; Notary Public; mem East Elmhurst Civic Assn; Ditmars Blvd Block Assn; Doll League Inc; Contempos. **Honors/Awds:** Special Cutty Sark Editorial Award; Good Neighbor Award; Journalism Award; radio sta WWRL award in Communications. **Business Addr:** Regional Manager, State Div Human Rights, 105-11 Ditmars Blvd, East Elmhurst, NY 11369.

LORD, CLYDE ORMOND
Physician. **Personal:** Born Aug 10, 1937, Brooklyn, NY; son of Mildred Agatha Lord and F Levi Lord; married Barbara; children: Sharon, Clyde Jr, David. **Educ:** Univ of VT, BA 1959; Meharry Med Coll, MD 1963. **Career:** Kings County Hospital, internship 1963-64; Columbia Presbyterian Med Mtr, resd 1964-66, fellow pharmacology 1966-67; AUS Hosp, chief of anesthesia 1967-69, asst prof dept of anesthesia 1969-70; SW Comm Hosp, staff physician 1970-; Westside Anesthesia Assoc, anesthesiologist. **Orgs:** Elder Westend Presbyterian Church 1973-; mem AMA, Natl Med Assoc, Amer Soc of Anesthesiologist; fellow pharmacology 1966-67; Alpha Omega Alpha Hon Med Soc; mem Amer Bd Anesthesiology; fellow Amer Coll of Anesthesiology; diplomate, American Academy of Pain Management. **Honors/Awds:** AUS maj 1967-69. **Business Addr:** Westside Anesthesia Assoc, 510 Fairburn Rd SW, Atlanta, GA 30331.

LORTHRIDGE, JAMES E.
Educational administrator. **Educ:** Prairie View A&M Univ, BS 1964; CA State Univ Long Beach, MA 1970; Claremont Grad School, PhD 1974; Rockefeller Found, Post Doctoral 1978. **Career:** Mt Pleasant School Dist, asst supt 1978, supt 1978-79; West Valley Comm Coll, dir, personnel 1979-83; Stockton Unified School Dist, supt 1983-86; Ithaca City School District, superintendent, currently. **Orgs:** Bd mem Mt Pleasant School Bd; mem CA Assn of Secondary School Admin, Amer Assn of Secondary School Admin, Assoc of CA School Admin, Phi Delta

Kappa, NAACP; hon life mem PTA. **Honors/Awds:** Hon Serv PTA; Panel Mem Amer Arbitration Assn. **Business Addr:** Superintendent, Ithaca City School District, PO Box 459, Ithaca, NY 14851.

LOTT, GAY LLOYD
Attorney. **Personal:** Born Mar 12, 1937, Chicago; children: Gay Lloyd, Jr. **Educ:** Univ IL; Roosevelt Univ 1962; John Marshall Law Sch 1964. **Career:** IRS, 1960-65; Peterson Johnson & Harris, 1965; Chicago, asst corp counsel 1965-67. **Orgs:** Pres chmn Civil Service Commn Met Sanitary Distr 1967; Weston Lott & William Ltd 1969-70; atty Lott, Powell & Williams Ltd 1970-78; Alpha Phi Alpha Inc; Phi Alpha Delta Law Frat; Am Bar Assn; regional dir Nat Bar Assn; mem bd of governors IL State Bar Assn; past pres Cook County Bar Assn; spkrs bureau Chicago Bar Assn; Defense Lawyers Assn; Trial Lawyers Assn. **Business Addr:** 33 N Dearborn St, Chicago, IL.

LOTT, RONNIE
Professional football player (retired). **Personal:** Born May 8, 1959, Albuquerque, NM. **Educ:** Univ of Southern CA, BA, public admin, 1981. **Career:** San Francisco 49ers, cornerback, 1981-84, free safety, 1985-90; Los Angeles Raiders, strong safety, 1991-93; New York Jets, beginning 1993; Kansas City Chiefs, until 1996. **Honors/Awds:** Named all-pro 1983; hnrd NFL Alumni Assn as Defensive Back of the Year 1983; estbl team record Most Career TDs on Interceptions; runner-up for NFL Rookie of the Year; 1981 made every all-star team from rookie to all-pro; All-Pac 10 performer; USC's 1980 MVP & Most Inspirational Player; mem NFL 1987 Pro Bowl team; All Pro, 1990; member of all four 49ers' Super Bowl Champ teams; 49ers' all-time leader in interceptions (51), interception yard returns (643), and interception touchdowns (five), 1991; voted to nine Pro Bowls. **Business Addr:** Professional Football Player, New York Jets, 1000 Fulton Ave, Hempstead, NY 11550.

LOUARD, AGNES A.
Educator (retired). **Personal:** Born Mar 10, 1922, Savannah, GA; daughter of Agnes Anthony and Joseph Anthony; married V Benjamin, Sep 2, 1950 (deceased); children: Rita, Diane, Kenneth. **Educ:** Univ of PA, BA 1944; Fisk Univ, MA 1945; Columbia Univ, MS 1948; NY Univ Add Studies. **Career:** The Manhattanville Neighborhood Ctr, suprv childrens div 1948-52; Union Settlement Assoc, dir rec & ed 1952-57; The E Harlem Proj, dir 1958-59; Speedwell Serv for Children NYC, sr caseworker 1959-61; Leake & Watts Children's Home, sr caseworker 1962-63; Patterson Home for Aged, suprv 1964-65; Columbia Univ, asst prof 1965-72, assoc prof 1972-. **Orgs:** Bd mem Harriet Tubman Comm Ctr 1965-; mem, vice pres Pleasant Ave Day Care Ctr 1971-; bd mem 1972-, pres 1985-88 Peninsula Counciling Ctr; consultant Spence Chapin Service for Families & Children 1974-; exec comm State Manpower Services Council 1977; mem NY State Employment & Training Council 1977-82; consultant Harlem Teams 1979-82; mem Alumni Assn Columbia Univ; adv bd JW Jr Comm Mental Health Bd 1982-84; panel chmn staff mediation comm Columbia Univ 1984-89; consultant Brooklyn Bureau of Community Services 1988-; bd mem Schomburg Corp 1988-; mem NY Coalition of 100 Black Women 1988-; mem ACLU, NAACP, Common Cause, Urban League, The Cottagers; trustee Union Chapel Marthas Vineyard; mem NASW. **Honors/Awds:** Award for dedicated service, Peninsula Counseling Center and Town of Hempstead, NY, 1988; Class of 1968 Columbia Univ School of Social Work, Outstanding Teacher Award, 1993. **Home Addr:** 560 Riverside Drive #6L, New York, NY 10027.

LOUCHIEY, COREY
Professional football player. **Personal:** Born Oct 10, 1971, Greenville, SC; married Nicole. **Educ:** South Carolina. **Career:** Buffalo Bills, tackle, 1994-. **Business Addr:** Professional Football Player, Buffalo Bills, One Bills Dr, Orchard Park, NY 14127, (716)648-1800.

LOUIS, JOSEPH
Chemical operator, manager. **Personal:** Born Apr 4, 1948, Vacherie, LA; son of Albertha Davis Louis and Marshal Louis; divorced; children: Crystal Michelle, Jeremy Allen. **Educ:** Southern Univ, 1966-70. **Career:** CJ's Ins Agency, mgr, owner 1985-. **Orgs:** Mem NAACP 1964-; mem Health & Phys Ed Club 1966-70; mem Southern Univ Alumni Federation 1970-; mem Hiram Lodge #12 of Free & Accepted Masons 1974-. **Military Serv:** ROTC E-5 1966-68.

LOUIS, SUCHET LESPERANCE
Educational administrator. **Personal:** Born Dec 23, 1935, Port-au-Prince, Haiti; son of Anaida Lesperance Louis and Joseph Louis; married Mathilde Clerge Louis, Aug 31, 1965. **Educ:** Faculty of Agronomy & Veterinary Medicine, Damien, Haiti, BS, 1963; Interamerican Institute of Agric w/Fural Sciences, Turrialba, Costa Rica, MS, 1967; University of California, Davis, CA, PhD, 1973; University of California, Berkeley, CA, Post Doctoral Studies, 1974-75. **Career:** University of California, Berkeley, CA, research associate, 1974-75; Tuskegee University, Tuskegee, AL, assistant professor and associate professor, 1975-83; Tufts University, North Grafton, MA, visiting associate professor, 1983-86; Tuskegee University, Tuskegee, AL, professor & associate director of international programs, 1986-89; associate provost & director of international programs, 1989-. **Orgs:** Member, American Association of Animal Science, 1970-; liaison officer, National Association for Equal Opportunity, 1986-; trustee, South East Consortium for International Development (SECID), 1989-; member, International Advisory Council/International, 1986-89; chairperson, Interdisciplinary Working Committee/International, 1989-. **Honors/Awds:** Best Student Agricultural Award, Faculty of Agronomy, 1962; Fellow, Organization of American States, 1965; Permanent Membership, Sigma Xi Scientific Assn, 1977; Outstanding Teacher Award, Tuskegee University, 1978; Outstanding Faculty Performance Award, Tuskegee University, 1988. **Business Addr:** Associate Provost & Director, Office of International Programs, Tuskegee University, Kresge Center #219, Tuskegee Institute, AL 36088.

LOUISTALL-MONROE, VICTORINE AUGUSTA
Educator (retired). **Personal:** Born Aug 19, 1912, Cumberland, MD; daughter of Malinda Waller Smith Louistall and Campbell McRae Louistall; married Ernest E Monroe, Oct 21, 1981. **Educ:** WV State Coll, BS 1936, MA 1945; West Virginia Univ, MALS 1963; Univ Pittsburgh, adv work. **Career:** Kelly Miller HS, teacher 1937-66; Roosevelt-Wilson HS, librarian 1956-66; WV Univ, asst prof 1966-74, assoc prof 1974-78, assoc prof emerita, Dept LibrarySciences, starting 1978 until retirement. **Orgs:** Consultant & instructor WV Univ 1964-66; consultant WV St Dept Libr Workshop at Morris Harvey Coll 1970; treas Harrison County Citizens Comm for Educ 1962-66; mem Pres Advisory Comm on Civil Rights 1960; vice pres WV Young Republicans 1953-55; bd dir Harrison County United Fund 1963-66; life mem NEA; mem Amer Library Assn; AAUW; NAACP; Alpha Kappa Alpha; WV Library Assn; treas Harrison County Citizens Comm 1960-64; Assn for Educ Communication & Technology; advisory comm; WV Library Commn 1971; chmn Certification Comm WV State Dept of Educ; mem Clarksburg-Harrison Public Library 1978-; bd mem Clarksburg Human Rights Commn 1978-; hon mem Delta Kappa Gamma Intl Soc 1980; appointed to WV Library Comm 1980; reappointed 1984; appointed to Pres Adv BdWV Univ 1982, reappointed 1986; mem Phi Beta Kappa WV Univ 1973-; Clarksburg-Harrison Public Library, re-appointed to Trustee Bd 1984, trustee emerita, 1985. **Honors/Awds:** 1st black woman to receive MA from WV Univ 1945; 1st black to receive acad appointment in Coll of Arts & Sci 1966; Citation Harrison County Bd of Educ 1960; Woman of the Year 1958; Achievement Award, Woman's Club 1981; Achievement Award, Library Skills Institute 1989; Certificate of Appreciation-Cause of Education, Literacy and Library Service, Woman's Club of Clarksburg, 1989; Inducted in Order of Vandalia, West Virginia University, 1992; Black Caucus, ALA Trustee Award, 1991. **Business Addr:** Associate Professor Emerita, West Virginia University, Main Library, Room 101, Morgantown, WV 26506.

LOURY, GLENN CARTMAN
Educator. **Personal:** Born Sep 3, 1948, Chicago, IL; married Linda Datcher; children: Lisa, Tamara, Glenn II, Nehemiah. **Educ:** Northwestern Univ, BA Mathematics 1972, Outstanding Graduate Dept of Mathematics 1972; MA Inst of Tech, PhD Economics 1976. **Career:** Northwestern Univ, asst prof dept of economics 1976-79; Univ of MI, assoc prof dept of economics 1980-82, prof 1980; Harvard Univ John F Kennedy Sch of Government, prof 1982. **Orgs:** Mem rsch adv bd Joint Center for Political Studies Washington; mem rsch adv bd Southern Center for Policy Studies Clark Coll; mem rsch adv bd DuBois Inst Harvard Univ; assoc editor Journal of Urban Economics; referee for various journals; Publication Comm, "The Public Interest". **Honors/Awds:** "One by One Forum, The Inside Out," 1995; Books and articles "From Children to Citizens" 1987; "The Family, The Nation and Senator Moynihan", commentary, 1986; "Who Speaks for American Blacks?", commentary 1987; "Why Should We Care About Group Inequality?" Social Philosophy and Policy, 1987; IntergenerationalTransfers and the Distriion of Earnings Econometrica 1981; Ford Found Doc Fellow 1972-76; Guggenheim Fellow 1985-86, Winner Leavy Awd for Excellence in Free Enterprise Education 1987; "Will Affirmation Action Eliminate Nigative Stereotypes," American Economic Review, 1993; American Book Award, 1996. **Business Addr:** Institute on Race & Social Divison, Boston University, 704 Comm Ave, Boston, MA 02215-1403.

LOVE, BARBARA
Educator. **Personal:** Born Apr 13, 1946, Dumas, AR. **Educ:** AR AM & N, BA 1965; Univ of AR, MA 1967; Univ of MA, PhD, EdD 1972. **Career:** Univ of MA Amherst Campus, assoc prof; Fellowship House, exec dir; Kansas City, teacher 1969-70; Center for Urban Educ, Univ of MA, grad asst 1970-71, instructor 1971-72, asso prof, chmn. **Orgs:** Mem Phi Delta Kappa 1974; Nat Alliance Black Sch Educators 1973; Am Educ Studies Assn 1974; Panel Am Women 1968-70; Urban Coalition Task Force on Educ 1968-70; comm rep Nat Tchrs Corps 1969-70; tast force Nat Alternative Schs Prgm 1971-73. **Honors/Awds:** Leadership Found Scholarship 1965-66; Jr League Award 1967. **Business Addr:** Professor, University of Massachusetts, Furcolo Hall, Amherst, MA 01002.

LOVE, BOB
Sports administrator. **Personal:** married Rachel Dixon. **Educ:** Southern University. **Career:** Chicago Bulls, dir of community relations, currently. **Business Addr:** Dir, Community Relation, Chicago Bulls, 1901 W Madison St, Chicago, IL 60612, (312)455-4000.

LOVE, CLARENCE C.
State representative (retired). **Personal:** Born Feb 24, 1922, Weir, KS; married Travestine Myers; children: Marva C Roberson, Cheryl C Thompson, Travestine Freeland, Terri Foreman, Clarence Jr. **Career:** State of Kansas 35th Dist, rep, 1966-88, (retired). **Orgs:** Mem, Allen Chapel AME Church, St James Masonic Lodge 59, Orient Consistory 19, 33 Degree Mason, 1971. **Military Serv:** AUS sgt 1944-45. **Business Addr:** State Representative, State of Kansas 35th Dist, State House, Topeka, KS 66612.

LOVE, DARLENE
Entertainer. **Personal:** Born Jul 26, 1941, Los Angeles, CA; daughter of Ellen Wright and Joseph Wright; married Alton A Allison, Jun 28, 1984; children: Marcus Peete, Chawn Peete, Jason Mitchell. **Career:** Singer, actress, currently. **Orgs:** Make a Wish. **Honors/Awds:** NAACP, Image Award, 1972; City of Atlanta, Key to the City-Honorary Citizen, 1985. **Special Achievements:** Darlene Love Day, Tocca, GA, Aug 3, 1991. **Home Addr:** PO Box 762, Nanuet, NY 10954, (212)242-9551.

LOVE, EDWARD A.
Visual artist, educator. **Personal:** Born Sep 21, 1936, Los Angeles, CA; son of Alyce and Edward Leon; married Monifa Atungaye; children: Edward Scott, Nia, Taifa Murry. **Educ:** Los Angeles City College, 1958-59; University of Southern California, 1960-61; California State University at Los Angeles, BFA, 1966, MFA, 1967; University of Uppsala, Sweden, 1967-68. **Career:** North American Aviation Corp., sr engineering draftsman, 1961-65; Howard University, professor of art, director of sculpture program, 1968-87; Interim Assistance Project Design of Parks/Outdoor Recreational Centers, architectural designer, 1969; Workshops for Careers in the Arts, artist-in-residence, 1973-74; Washington Project for the Arts, board of advisors, 1981-82; New World School of the Arts, Visual Arts Division, founding dean, 1987-90; National Foundation for the Advancement of the Arts, board of advisors, 1988-90; Florida State University, director of undergraduate studies, professor of art, 1990-. **Orgs:** Brotherhood of Pride, 1992-95; American Association of University Professors, 1985-; National Conference of Artists, 1980-89; The Box Project, 1988-; Habitat for Humanity, 1991-. **Honors/Awds:** The Florida State University Teaching Award, 1992; The California State University Distinguished Alumni Award, 1991; U.S. Department of Education, Certificate of Appreciation, 1991; The Pratt Institute, Art Educator Recognition Award, 1990; John Simon Guggenheim Memorial Foundation Fellowship, 1987-88; District of Columbia Awards in the Arts, 1987; District of Columbia Committee on the Arts Individual Fellowship, 1986-87. **Special Achievements:** Numerous exhibitions including: The Arkestra, 1991; Parallels, 1989; numerous speaking activities, lectures, catalogues, books, essays, and presentations. **Military Serv:** US Air Force, airman first class, 1954-58. **Business Addr:** Professor, School of Visual Art & Dance, Florida State University, Fine Arts Bldg, Tallahassee, FL 32306-2037, (904)644-6474.

LOVE, ELEANOR YOUNG
Educator (retired). **Personal:** Born Oct 10, Lincoln Ridge, KY; daughter of Laura R Young and Whitney M Young, Sr; children: Laura, David Whitney. **Educ:** KY State Univ AB 1944; Atlanta Univ, BLS 1946; Univ Louisville, med 1965; Univ IL, DED 1970. **Career:** FL A&M Univ, library 1946-51; Bergen Jr Coll, head librarian 1951-53; Lincoln Inst, librarian, prin, counselor 1953-66; Univ Coll Univ Louisville, asst dean, prof of educ psychology & counseling 1966-70, asst prof assoc prof 1970-78, full prof 1978-97. **Orgs:** Mem Presbyterian Ch; Urban League; YMCA; AKA; Moles Inc; Les Belles; consult Head Start & Sickle Cell Anemia; pres Adult Student Personnel Assn 1974-75; mem bd Vis Nurses; JADD; Health Licensure & Needs; Lincoln Found; Red Cross; Educ Commn of States; pres Lincoln Foundation 1987-; counselor Human Development EAP consultant 1987-; Human Relations Commissioner for Louisville and Jefferson County; chair, Louisville Public Library. **Honors/Awds:** Numerous scholarships, fellows. **Business Addr:** Professor Emeritus, University of Louisville, School of Education, Belknap Campus, Louisville, KY 40292.

LOVE, FAIZON
Actor. **Career:** Comedian, actor, currently. **Business Addr:** Comedian/Actor, The Artists Group, 10100 Santa Monica Blvd, Ste 2490, Los Angeles, CA 90067, (310)552-1100.

LOVE, GEORGE HAYWARD
Educator (retired), educational consultant. **Personal:** Born Oct 15, 1924, Philadelphia, PA; son of Daisy Gripper Love and Samuel H Love; married Hettie Simmons; children: George Hayward Jr, Karen Love Alford. **Educ:** Univ of Pennsylvania, BA 1948, MS Educ 1950, EdD 1973. **Career:** Philadelphia Sch Dist, teacher/admin 1952-71; Pennsylvania Dept of Educ, asst

commissioner 1971-75; Appalachia Educ Lab, assoc dir 1975-81; Harrisburg Sch Dist, biology teacher, 1981-84; dir of personnel 1984-88; dir, division of special projects, 1988-92; educational consultant, 1992-. **Orgs:** Consultant PA Dept of Educ 1981-; bd mem and chairman Camp Curtin YMCA 1981-; founder/past sire archon Beta Pi Boule, Sigma Pi Phi 1983; bd mem Children of Playroom, 1992; chmn Cities in Schools, 1992; chmn Dept of Christian Educ Diocese of PA 1984-; pres Greater Harrisburg Area Branch NAACP 1986-; president Harrisburg Bridge Club 1989; lay reader and vestryman, St Paul Episcopal Church. **Honors/Awds:** Service Awd Frontiers Intl 1973; Outstanding Citizenship Awd Omega Psi Phi Frat 1981; Judge Awd Pennsylvania Junior Acad of Science 1987; YMCA Award 1988. **Military Serv:** USAF pvt 1943-45. **Home Addr:** 3757 Chambers Hill Rd, Harrisburg, PA 17111.

LOVE, J. GREGORY
Fire chief. **Educ:** Wayne County Community College, AS; University of Detroit-Mercy, BA; Wayne State University, ME. **Career:** Jackson Fire Dept, fire chief, 1996-; Royal Oak Township Public Safety Dept, fire chief, 1995-96; Detroit Fire Dept, firefighter, captain-instructor, 1971-95. **Honors/Awds:** Numerous citations for bravery and rescue. **Special Achievements:** First African American fire chief in Jackson, MI. **Business Addr:** Fire Chief, Jackson Fire Department, 518 N Jackson St, Jackson, MI 49201, (517)788-4150.

LOVE, JAMES O., SR.
Law enforcement official. **Personal:** Born Jan 12, 1957, Chicago, IL; son of Henrietta Love and Jerry L Love; divorced; children: James O Jr, Jerry L II. **Career:** Chicago Police Department, police officer, 1985-. **Orgs:** Fraternal Order of Police; Carter Harrison/Lambert Tree Society; Illinois Police Association; IL Drug Enforcement Officers Assn. **Honors/Awds:** City of Chicago, Carter Harrison Award, 1991, Blue Star, 1991, Life Saver Award, 1991; Chicago Police Department, 53 Honorable Mentions, 1985-91, Department Commendation, 1987, 1995; Episode 401, Top Cops, CBS, Oct 15, 1993; Unit Meritorious Award, 1996; US Department of Justice, Certificate of Appreciation, 1997; US Attorney Letter of Recognition, 1997. **Special Achievements:** Author, Bleeding Blue, The James Love Story; profiled in "Sacred Bond," by Keith Brown, Little Brown & Co Publishing. **Business Addr:** Police Officer, Chicago Police Department, 1121 S State St, Chicago, IL 60609, (312)747-6216.

LOVE, JAMES RALPH
Business executive. **Personal:** Born Apr 2, 1937, Hahira, GA; married Bernice Grant; children: Rhita V, James R II, Gerald K, Reginald. **Educ:** KY State Coll, BS 1958; Tuskegee Inst, MS 1968. **Career:** Project MARK Jackson MS, job developer 1968; Natl Alliance of Bus Denver C of C, mgr 1968-71; Mt Bell, public relations 1971-74; Mutual Benefit Life, ths agt 1974-79; James R Love & Assocs Inc, pres 1980-86; Pyramid Financial & Insurance Services Inc, president, chief executive officer, 1986-. **Orgs:** Pres Delta Psi Lambda 1971-74; treas Denver Bd Mentally Retarded & Physically Handicapped 1972-78; vice pres Park Hill Br NAACP 1979-80; advisor to Gov Love Govt CO 1969-71; dir UNCF CO 1971-72; mem ethics comm Denver Area Life Underwriters 1978-79. **Honors/Awds:** Agent of the Yr Mutual Benefit 1974-75; Man of the Yr AA 1975-76; article pub "Prospecting Through My Board of Directors" Life Insurance Selling vol 52 1978. **Business Addr:** President, CEO, Pyramid Financial & Insurance Services Inc, 1901 Peoria St, Ste 200, Aurora, CO 80010.

LOVE, JON
Telecommunications company executive. **Personal:** married; children: two. **Career:** AT&T, sales specialist; Network Operations, engineer; Access Financial Management, engineer; AT&T, Federal Systems Division, manager, General Business Systems, manager, Federal Government Sales, branch manager; Lucent Technologies, Large Business Product Division, general manager of sales, 1996-. **Orgs:** Spearheaded Lucent's involvement in the United Negro College Fund, Lou Rawls Telethon, and Habitat for Humanity; Mayor's Scholarship Ball, steering committee mem. **Business Addr:** General Manager Large Business Product Division, Lucent Technologies, 24800 Denso Dr, Ste 250, Southfield, MI 48034, 800-356-0226.

LOVE, KAREN ALLYCE (KAREN A. WISE-LOVE)
Administrative assistant. **Personal:** Born May 22, 1946, River Rouge, MI; daughter of Ruth Lee McIlwain and Joseph William Wise; married John L Love, Nov 5, 1975; children: Schari Alana Dixon, Lloryn Ruth Love. **Educ:** Ferris State College, 1964-65; College of DuPage, 1973-75; Los Angeles City College, 1976-78; Wayne County Community College, 1990-91. **Career:** Commonwealth Edison Co, System Security Division, 1972-76; Los Angeles Times Co, account executive, 1976-78; Western States Association of Los Angeles, regional account executive, 1978-79; Chicago Tribune Co., account executive, 1979-86; Security Bank & Trust, accounting department, 1986; Associated Newspapers, retail manager, 1986-89; Michigan Chronicle Newspaper, executive administrative assistant, 1989-. **Orgs:** NAACP, lifetime member, publicity committee, 1990-; Urban League, publicity committee, 1992-; Order of the Eastern Star, grand officer, 1975-; Heroines of Jericho, officer, 1984-; Ladies of the Circle of Perfection, 1990-; Life Directions, publicity committee, 1992-. **Honors/Awds:** City of Chicago, Black Achievement Award, 1981; Benjamin Hooks, Outstanding Black Leader, 1991; National Political Congress of Black Women, Woman of the Year, 1992. **Business Addr:** Executive Administrative Assistant, Michigan Chronicle Newspaper, 479 Ledyard St, Detroit, MI 48201, (313)963-5522.

LOVE, LAMAR VINCENT
Sales and operations executive. **Personal:** Born Oct 20, 1964, Columbus, OH; son of Marie C Love and Lamar E Love. **Educ:** Ohio State University, BA, BS, 1989. **Career:** Banc Ohio, crt operator, 1981-83, group leader, 1983-86; Foster & Assoc, sales representative, 1988-90, sales and operations manager, 1991-92, vp, 1993-. **Orgs:** Ohio State Entrepreneur Network, vice pres, 1988-89. **Military Serv:** US Army Reserves, US Army National Guard, sgt, 1982-92; Army Achievement Medal, 1989. **Business Addr:** Vice President, Foster & Associates, Inc, 3761 April Ln, Columbus, OH 43227, (614)239-1064.

LOVE, LYNNETTE ALICIA
Coach, instructor. **Personal:** Born Sep 21, 1957, Chicago, IL; daughter of Dolores Merritt. **Educ:** Wayne State Univ, BFA, 1983. **Career:** Maryland Federal Savings, asst manager, 1986-89; City of Alexandria, recreation supervisor, 1993-94; Love's Taekwondo Academy, president, 1994-. **Orgs:** United States Taekwondo Union, vice chairperson, 1988-96; Women's Sports Foundation, 1988-. **Honors/Awds:** AAU, Sullivan Award for outstanding sports performance, nominated 1988; United States Taekwondo Union, Outstanding Female Player, 1984, 1988; Cass Technical High School, Alumni Award, 1988. **Special Achievements:** Female Coach, World Championships, 1993; Female Coach, PanAmerican Games, 1995; Ten-Time National Champion, 1979-87, 1990; Five-Time Pan American Champion, 1982, 1984, 1986, 1988, 1990; Two-Time Olympic Medalist, Gold, 1988, Bronze, 1992; Team Captain, 1989-92; Three-Time World Champion, 1985, 1987, 1991. **Business Addr:** President, Love's Taekwondo Acad Inc, 9018 A Clinton St, Clinton, MD 20735, (301)856-0224.

LOVE, MABEL R.
Educator. **Personal:** Born Jun 27, 1908, Hampton, VA; married Dr T A. **Educ:** Hampton Inst, BS 1929; Columbia U, MA 1933; Syracuse U, summer work; CT Coll for Women, summer work. **Career:** Fisk Univ, prof health physical educ; AL State Teachers Coll; Leynoyne Coll; Fisk Univ, dance prof; Dance Eductors of Amer, summer work for 15 yrs. **Orgs:** Bd mem Friends of Chamber Mus City of Nashville; sec TN Arts Commn 2 terms; mem AAUP; AAUW; TN St Dance Assn; life mem Am Tchr Assn; pres Delta Sigma Theta Sor three terms; golden life mem Girl Friends Inc. **Honors/Awds:** Spl awd Lieg for dedication in field of performing arts; orgn of "Orchesis" Coll Dance Group Fisk U.

LOVE, MILDRED L.
Administrator. **Personal:** Born Oct 25, 1941, Ringgold, LA. **Educ:** So U, BA 1963; Univ of Pittsburgh, MA 1969; Columbia U, MBA 24 credits 1979. **Career:** Nat Urban League Inc, dir career training & econ resources 1979-; Nat Urban League Inc, dir Eastern reg ofc 1976-79; Nat Urban League Inc, asst dir eastern reg ofc 1973-76; Harlem Teams for Self Help, instr & counselor 1965-72; New York City Dept of Social Svc, case worker 1964-65; Manhattan State Hosp, rehab counselor 1970; Cowles Publ Co, editorial consult 1971-72. **Orgs:** Volunteer ATC Domestic Peace Corps 1963-64; commr Nat Commn on Unemployment Compensation 1980-82. **Honors/Awds:** Ford Found Fellowship Award 1968-69. **Business Addr:** Vice Pres Programs & Field Service, Natl Urban League, Inc, 500 East 62nd St, New York, NY 10021.

LOVE, ROOSEVELT SAM
Business executive. **Personal:** Born Jun 11, 1933, Bulloch Co, GA; widowed; children: Katheleen, Patricia, Bonnie, Julia, Sandra. **Career:** Love's Fina Serv Sta, operator; JP Stevens, cement mixer; Gulf Inc, serv sta atdnt. **Orgs:** Mem Comm Rels Cncl 1975-77; DUSO Devel Uique Serv Ourselves; Comm Action Club; SCWC; mem Negotiations Com Textiles Wrkrs Unoin 1974; rep JP Stevens Empl Twisting Dept 1971; pres Bulloch Co Br NAACP 1973-; mem Bethel Primitive Bapt Ch. **Honors/Awds:** Outsndg serv awd NAACP 1977.

LOVE, RUTH BURNETT
Educational Administrator, newspaper publisher. **Personal:** Born Apr 22, 1939, Lawton, OK; daughter of Burnett C Love and Alvin E Love. **Educ:** San Jose State Univ, BA, 1958; San Francisco State Univ, MA, 1961; US International Univ, Cal Western, PhD, 1969. **Career:** Oakland Unified School District; CA State Dept of Education, bureau chief; Oakland Unified School District-Ford Foundation, consultant; US Office of Education, Washington, DC, national director, Right to Read; Oakland Unified School District, superintendent; Chicago Board of Education, general superintendent; Operation Crossroads Africa, Ghana, project director; Ruth Love Enterprises LTD, president, currently; California Voice, publisher, currently; Distintuished Professor SF State Univ; Ex-publisher of 9 weekly Black Newspapers. **Orgs:** American Assn of School Administrators, 1974-; Assn for Supervisors & Councilor Development, 1979-; Morehouse Medical School, bd of trustees, 1976-; Cities In Schools, board of directors, 1977-; Presidential Commission on HBUC, 1989-92; President's Mental Health Commission, vice chair, 1976-79; Natl Urban League, board of directors, 1977-82; Links Inc, chair, scholarship committee; National Newspaper Publishers Assn, board of directors, 1988-. **Honors/Awds:** Marquette Univ, Honorary Doctorate; Library named in honor; Dept of Health, Education and Welfare, Certificate of Recognition. **Special Achievements:** Author: Hello World, Field Publications, 1975; Strengthening Counseling Services for Disadvantaged Youth, 1966; Johnny Can Read, So Can Jane, Addison Wesley, 1982; The Paideia Proposal: An Educational Manifesto, w/Moeriwe Adler, MacMillan, 1982; The Paideia Proposal: Questions and Answers, MacMillan, 1983; numerous articles; traveled & lectured extensively around the world; Motivational Speaker. **Business Phone:** (510)635-2657.

LOVE, THOMAS CLIFFORD
Editorial director. **Personal:** Born Jul 23, 1947, New Rochelle, NY. **Educ:** Howard Univ, BA 1969. **Career:** WRC-TV AM-FM Washington, employment spec, publ serv dir 1969-71; WABC-AM Rdio New York City publ serv dir 1971-72, dir comm affairs 1972-73; WABC AM-Radio NY, ed, community affairs dir 1973-79; St Johns Univ, adj prof 1976-78; Montclair State Coll, vstg spec 1978-; WABC-TV, ed dir 1979-. **Orgs:** Mem Natl & Intl Radio & TV Soc, Natl Broadcast Ed Assoc, Alpha Phi Alpha. **Honors/Awds:** NY Emmy Awd 1980; Andy Awd of Merit Ad Club of NY 1978; NY State Broadcasters Awd 1979,84; UPI & AP Awd 1974; YMCA Black Achievers in Indust Awd 1974. **Business Addr:** Editorial Dir, WABC-TV, 7 Lincoln St, New York, NY 10023.

LOVELACE, DEAN ALAN
Government administrator. **Personal:** Born Jan 31, 1946, Kittaning, PA; married Phyllis Jean Rutland; children: Leslie Denise, Laeina Deandra, Dean Nyerere. **Educ:** Sinclair Comm Coll, AS, business, 1971; Univ of Dayton, BSBA, 1972; Wright State Univ, MS, Econ, 1981. **Career:** Univ of Dayton, dir of neighborhood dev; City of Dayton NW Office of Neighborhood Affairs, coordinator/dir 1979-80; City of Dayton NW Office of Neighborhood Affairs, comm serv adv 1977-79; City of Dayton Dept of Planning, neighborhood planner 1973-79; Nat Cash Register, lathe operator 1965-71. **Orgs:** Mem Citizens Avd Council Model Neighborhood Comm Center 1977-; mem Econ Resources Com Miami Valley Regional Planning Council 1977-; chmn Dayton OH Black Polit Assembly 1977-; trustee Housing Justice Fund Inc 1978-; pres Edgemont Neighborhood Coalition Inc 1980-; 1st vice pres Dayton Urban League 1982-; adv bdDayton Found Neighbor to Neighbor 1983-; council mem Montgomery County Human Serv Levy 1984-; chmnDayton-Montgomery County Rainbow Coaltion 1984-, Dayton Anti-Apartheid Comm 1985-. **Honors/Awds:** Comm Serv Awd Concerned Citizens of Dayton View 1977; Employee of the Year City of Dayton Div of Neighborhood Affairs 1978; Disting Serv Awd OH State Leg1979; Outstanding Young Man of Amer US Jaycees 1979; NAACP Freedom Fund Dinner Civil Rights Awd 1985. **Business Addr:** Dir of Neighborhood Dev, University of Dayton, 300 College Park Ave, Dayton, OH 45408.

LOVELACE, GLORIA ELAINE
Personnel executive. **Personal:** Born Jan 24, 1945, Danville, VA; daughter of Sara Thomas Lovelace and Theodore R Lovelace; children: Jabrie Daverand. **Educ:** VA State Univ, BS Health/Phys Ed/Biology 1968; Univ of IL, MS Kinesiotherapy 1971. **Career:** Scovill Mfg Co, employ asst 1974, asst to the dir of marketing 1974-75, coord of marketing systems 1975-76; Xerox Corp Info Systems Group, br internal control mgr 1976, Mid-Atlantic reg personnel admin 1976-77, affirm action/personnel relations 1977-78, personnel relations mgr 1978-79; Office Prod Div, midwest region personnel mgr 1979-81, mgr compensation affirm action safety/security & health serv 1981-83, mgr of human resources 1983; Old Stone Bank, sr vice pres Human resources 1983-85; owner and business counselor General Business Service 1985-88; National Captioning Institute, Falls Church VA, dir personnel 1988-89; US Sprint, Reston VA, dir human resources 1989-. **Orgs:** Bd of dirs Family Svcs, Urban League, Council for Aging, Visiting Nurses; personnel comm YWCA Rochester; mem Prof Women's Network; participant Chicago Forum 1980-81; mem Black Career Women Inc; corp advisor Bishop Coll; bd mem YMCA Providence 1984-; comm mem Providence Chamber of Commerce 1984-85; mem of, Natl Assn of Bank Women 1984-; Personnel Executives Club 1984-; Natl Assn of Urban Bankers 1984-85; Washington DC Chamber of Commerce, Nat'l Federation of Independent Businesses, Small Business Federation. **Honors/Awds:** Selected as one of the Outstanding Young Women of America; Guest Faculty Williams Coll Sch of Banking. **Home Addr:** 1531 Hemlock St NW, Washington, DC 20012.

LOVELACE, JOHN C.
Business executive. **Personal:** Born Mar 4, 1926, West Point, GA; married Mary Jean Roebuck; children: Juan Carlos, Carlita Joy. **Career:** Pittsburgh Plate Glass Industrial Inc, employee. **Orgs:** Mem Drug & Alcoholic Comm; numerous offices local NAACP; bd dirs Kiski Valley Med Facilities Inc 1974-75; plan-

ning comm Gilpin Township 1973-75; mem Youth Comm 1968; mgr Valley Choraliers Leechburg 1960-75. **Honors/Awds:** Thalheimer Award, NAACP, 1970; citation, Pennsylvania House of Rep, 1970; 1st place, Pennsylvania State Conf Brs 1974. **Military Serv:** USN 1944-46.

LOVELACE, ONZALO ROBERT
Business executive. **Personal:** Born Mar 20, 1940, Homestead, PA; son of Dorothy Louise Brown Lovelace and Onzalo Wilbert Lovelace; divorced; children: Caroline. **Educ:** Univ of Pittsburgh, BS Indus Engrg, 1964; New York Univ, MBA, 1972. **Career:** IBM, indus engr 1966-67; Trans World Airlines, mgr quality assurance 1967-72; Pan Am World Airways, dir corporate indus engrg 1972-77; Pan Am World Airways, dir corporate budgets 1977-78, system dir indus engrg 1978-82, division controller 1982-86, corporate budget dir 1986-87; First Nationwide Bank, vice pres/div controller 1987-89; vice pres/sr finance manager, 1991-. **Orgs:** Mem Amer Inst for Indus Engrs 1966-80; mem Assn for Systems Mgmt 1972-80; ''Mgmt System for Maintenance'' Plant Engrg Magazine 1975. **Military Serv:** AUS spec 5 1964-66. **Home Addr:** 451 Rich St, Oakland, CA 94609. **Business Addr:** Vice President/Senior Finance Manager, First Nationwide Bank, Loan Division, 355 Gellert Dr, Daly City, CA 94015.

LOVELACE, STACEY
Professional basketball player. **Personal:** Born Dec 5, 1974. **Educ:** Purdue Univ, bachelor's degree in organizational leadership and supervision. **Career:** Atlanta Glory, forward, 1996-. **Business Addr:** Professional Basketball Player, Atlanta Glory, 2100 Powers Ferry Rd, Ste 400, Atlanta, GA 30339, (770)541-9017.

LOVELESS, THERESA E.
Organization executive. **Career:** Girl Scout Council of Greater St Louis, executive dir, 1996-. **Orgs:** Missouri Botanical Garden Subs District Comm; Regional Hrts Commission. **Honors/Awds:** Woman of Achievement, 1992. **Special Achievements:** First African American to take helm of Girl Scout Council in St Louis. **Business Addr:** Executive Director, Girl Scout Council of Greater St. Louis, 2130 Kratky Rd, St Louis, MO 63114.

LOVETT, LEONARD
Clergyman. **Personal:** Born Dec 5, 1939, Pompano Beach, FL; son of Cassie Lovett and Charles Lovett; married Marie Bush; children: Laion, Lamont, Lamar, Mandon. **Educ:** Saints Jr Coll, AA 1959; Morehouse Coll, BA 1962; Crozer Theological Seminary, MDiv 1965; Emory Univ Candler's Grad Sch of Theology, PhD 1979. **Career:** Meml COGIC, pastor 1962-70; Health & Welfare Council Philadelphia New York City Proj, coord 1965-67; Stephen Smith Towers 202 Senior Citizens, proj mgr 1967-70; Ch Mason Theological Seminary, pioneer pres 1970-74; Fuller Theological Seminary, assoc dir Black Ministries 1977-81. **Orgs:** Pres Soc for Pentecostal Studies 1975; mem Soc for the Study of Black Religion 1972-; reactor Vatican-Pentecostal Dialogue W Germany 1974; visit prof Grad Theological Union Berkeley 1975; prof of Ethics & Theology Ecumenical Cntr for Black Church Studies 1978-; prof of Ethics & Theology Amer Bapt Seminary of the West 1984; visiting fellow Human Behavior Amer Inst of Family Relations 1982-85; bd mem, Watts Health Foundation, United Health Plan 1985-; columnist, Black Perspective, Ministries Today Magazine 1988-. **Honors/Awds:** Conditional Liberation Spirit Journal 1977; What Charismatics Can Learn from Black Pentecostals Logos Journal 1980; Tribute to Martin Luther King in Outstanding Black Sermons Vol 2 Judson Press 1982; contrib Aspects of the Spiritual Legacy of the Church of God in Christ in Mid-Stream An Ecumenical Journal Vol XXIV No 4 1985, Black Witness to the Apostolic Faith Eardmans 1988; Black Holiness-Pentecostalism, Black Theology, Positive Confession Theology, Dictionary of the Pentecostal Charismatic Movement, Zondervan 1988; Doctor of Laws, Saints Jr College, 1972.

LOVETT, MACK, JR.
Educator. **Personal:** Born Aug 31, 1931, Shreveport, LA; married Marlene; children: Alice, Pamela, Michelle, Albert. **Educ:** Oakland City Coll, AA 1959; CA State Univ, BA 1965, MPA 1970. **Career:** Municipal Court, court clerk 1956-65; Litton Indus, instr 1965-66, admin 1966-68; CA State Univ, asst to pres 1968-72, dir instruct serv 1972, asst vice pres 1978-. **Orgs:** Consult Hayward Uni Sch Dist 1966-73; consult Chabot Comm Coll 1969; consult CA Employ Serv 1968; dir & treas Ebony Constr Co 1972-73; dir Plnd & Appl Rescrs Inc 1967-68; Gr Hayward Kiwanis Serv Club; bd dir So Alameda Co Econ Oppor Orgn 1965-67; chmn Polit Actn Com NAACP So Alameda Co Chap 1958-64; pres NAACP 1964-68; bd dir New Lady mag 1965-70; Reg Adult Voca Educ Advis Com; bd mgrs YMCA Eden area. **Honors/Awds:** Publ ''How to File Your Income Tax'' Litton Indus Educ Sys Div. **Military Serv:** AUS 1954-56. **Business Addr:** Asst Vice President, CA State Univ, 25800 Carlos Bee Blvd, Hayward, CA 94542.

LOVICK, CALVIN L.
Magazine publisher. **Personal:** Born Aug 6, 1950, Belhaven, NC; son of Mr and Mrs Nathan Lovick; divorced; children: Scott, Christian, Jeannie. **Educ:** Kean College of NJ, BS, 1974. **Career:** CL Lovick and Associates, ceo/publisher, 1979-. **Military Serv:** US Airforce, sgt, 1968-71.

LOVILLE, DEREK KEVIN
Professional football player. **Personal:** Born Jul 4, 1968, San Francisco, CA; children: Derek II. **Educ:** Univ of Oregon. **Career:** Seattle Seahawks, running back, 1990-91; San Francisco 49ers, 1994-96; Denver Broncos, 1997-. **Business Addr:** Professional Football Player, Denver Broncos, 13655 Broncos Pkwy, Englewood, CO 80112, (303)649-9000.

LOVING, ALBERT A., JR.
Accountant. **Personal:** Born Mar 16, 1920, Chgo; divorced; children: Karyn L, Alan H. **Educ:** De-Paul U, BSC 1950; grad sch 1950-51, 1971. **Career:** US Atomic Energy Commn, accountant auditor asst br chief budget examiner 1957-66; Chicago Land Clearance Commn; asst comptroller 1951-57; Chicago Bd Edn, tchr 1950-51; Parkway Sec & Accounting Svc, proprietor 1948-51; G Stevens Marchman & Co, asst to pres 1947-48; Audit US Dept Labor, special asst to inspector genl-audit 1966-80; Executive Service Corps of Chicago, exec consultant 1980-. **Orgs:** Mem Army Finance Assn 1953-73; exec sec Jr Assn Commerce & Industry 1955-57; sec Jaycee Senate Toastmasters 1955-57; Fed Govt Accountants Assn 1959-;So Shore Commn 1961-71; Reserve Officers Assn US 1969-; Am Accounting Assn 1970-; Inst of Internal Auditors 1973-; Fed Exec League 1974-; bd trusteesJackson Towers Condo Assn 1974-78; bd of trustees Hyde Park Hosp 1983-. **Honors/Awds:** Certified Internal Auditor 1983-; Natl Assn of Minority CPA Firms Outstanding Serv Awd 1975; US Dept of Labor Office of the Reg Dir Commendable Serv Awd 1976; Chicago St Univ President's Awd 1979; Jones Commerical High Sch Afro American Hist Cert of Appreciation 1981. **Military Serv:** AUS lt col 1939-46; Reserve 1946-70.

LOVING, JAMES LESLIE, JR.
Business executive. **Personal:** Born Aug 14, 1944, Boston, MA; son of Wauneta Barbour Loving and James Leslie Loving; married Leebertha Beauford, Jul 1, 1967; children: Robyn Leslie. **Educ:** Boston Bus School, Diploma 1964; Harvard Univ, EdM 1974, CAS 1975; Univ of S CA, DPA. **Career:** City of Boston, spec asst to mayor 1972-77; US Dept of HHS, spec asst 1977-81; Student Natl Med Assoc, exec admin 1981-83; Data Processing Inst, vice pres 1983-86; The Career Business Academy, pres 1986-. **Orgs:** Natl coord Dr King 51st Celebration 1980; chmn Roxbury Cancer Crusade 1974; treas Boston Br NAACP 1972; dir Boston Legal Asst Proj 1972; hew fellowUS Dept of Health Ed & Welfare 1977; trustee Emmanuel Temple Church 1977. **Honors/Awds:** Finalist White House Fellows Prog 1977; Outstanding Leader JC's Boston Chap 1978; Outstanding Young Men of Amer 1976; 100 Black Influentials 1976; United Student Oakwood Coll Huntsville 1975. **Home Addr:** 8717 Baskerville Place, Upper Marlboro, MD 20772. **Business Addr:** President, The Career Business Academy, Inc, 1001 Connecticut Ave, NW, Suite 625, Washington, DC 20036.

LOVING, PAMELA YVONNE
Educational administrator, personnel administrator. **Personal:** Born Sep 28, 1943, Detroit, MI; married William Copeland; children: Gregory McKay, Michelle McKay. **Educ:** Mott Comm Coll, Associate Degree (honors) Registered Nurse 1967; Univ of Detroit, BA 1978; Univ of MI Flint, MBA prog. **Career:** GMI Eng & Mgmt Inst, coord health serv 1972-80, salaried personnel rep 1980-81, mgr personnel serv 1981-82, personnel admin 1982-. **Orgs:** Appointed Project Self-Reliance by Gov Blanchard 1984; mem Prison Ministry & Huron Valley Women's Facility Milan FCI 1982-; historian Hist Chap Top Ladiesof Distinct 1982-; consult Flint Bd of Educ Vocational Adv Comm 1982-; mem at large Flint Environ Action Team 1984-86; asst treas Flint Area Personnel Assn 1985-87. **Honors/Awds:** Author/editor GMI Employee Handbook 1st edition 1985; Except Volunteer Serv Award State Correct Facilities. **Business Addr:** Personnel Administrator, GMI Engineering & Mgmt Inst, 1700 W 3rd Ave, Flint, MI 48502.

LOW, PATRICIA ENID ROSE
Educator. **Personal:** Born Jun 4, 1932, Somerset, Bermuda; daughter of Nina Smith and Arnim Smith; divorced; children: Doris, Sharon, William, Jacquelyn. **Educ:** Morgan State Coll Baltimore, BS 1956; Bryn Mawr Coll, Bryn Mawr PA, MA 1958; Univ of MD School of Medicine, attended 1964-67. **Career:** Morgan State Univ, asst prof in physicial science 1968-, instructor in chemistry 1961-64; MD State Coll Div of Univ of MD, instructor in chemistry & math 1958-60. **Orgs:** Consulting Instructor for Serv to Educ Inc 1975; 1st presiding officer Faculty Advisory Com to State Bd for Higher Educ in MD 1977-80; bd of Trustees Graduate School of Innovative Studies 1979-; Spiritual Frontiers Fellowship Conf 1979; intuitive perceptor Integrated Awareness 1980; trained in NLP neurolinguistic programming Soc of NLP 1980, contextual therapy, spiritual therapy. **Honors/Awds:** NSF research fellow Princeton Univ 1960; research fellow in biochemistry Nat Inst of Mental Health 1964-67; coll research fellow NASA Goddard Space Flight Center 1970; a personalized system of instruction Workshop Published by Inst for Serv to Educ Inc 1975.

LOWE, AUBREY F.
Comptroller. **Personal:** Born Jul 7, 1940, Suffolk, VA; married Anne L Pulley; children: Gary, Brandon. **Educ:** NC Central U, BS Accounting 1960; NC Central U, SJD 1963. **Career:** Eli Lilly & Co, marketing financial analyst 1973-; Indianapolis Bus Investment Corpd pres 1971-73; Eli Lilly Co, financial analyst 1967-71; Fed Housing & Adminstrn, staff atty 1963-67; Citizens Health Corp, comptroller, 1994-. **Orgs:** Mem NAACP; Omega Psi Phi; St Paul's PE Church, Indianapolis Urban League. **Business Addr:** 1650 N College Ave, Indianapolis, IN 46202.

LOWE, EUGENE YERBY, JR.
Clergyman, educational administrator. **Personal:** Born Aug 18, 1949, Staten Island, NY; son of Miriam V Lowe and Eugene Y Lowe Sr; married Jane Pataky Henderson, Nov 4, 1989; children: Benjamin, Sarah. **Educ:** Princeton Univ, AB 1971; Union Theol Sem, MDiv 1978, PhD 1987. **Career:** Northwestern Univ, assoc provost for faculty affairs, sr lecturer in religion, currently; Princeton Univ, dean of students, 1983-93; Union Theol Sem, tutor 1979-82; Gen Theol Sem, tutor 1978-80; Parish of Calvary & St George's, asst minister 1978-82; Chase Manhattan Bank, 2nd vice pres 1973-76; St Agatha Home for Children, soc work asst 1971-73. **Orgs:** Dir Forum for Corp Responsibility 1976-80; mem Com on Soc Responsibility & Investments, Exec Council of the Episcopal Ch 1976-81; mem Council on Foreign Relations 1977-81; trustee Princeton Univ 1971-83; trustee Elizabeth Seton Coll 1972-83; trustee Berea College, 1995-; trustee Seabury-Western Seminary, 1996-. **Honors/Awds:** The Harold Willis Dodds Prize, Princeton Univ 1971; Phi Beta Kappa, Princeton Univ 1971; fellow, Fund for Theol Educ 1976-77; fellow, Episcopal Ch Found 1978-80. **Business Addr:** Assoc Provost for Faculty Affairs, Northwestern Univ, 633 Clark St, Rebecca Crown Ctr, 2-147, Evanston, IL 60208-1101, (847)491-5255.

LOWE, HAZEL MARIE
Federal official (retired). **Personal:** Born Aug 4, 1936, La Grange, NC; daughter of Musetter Gardner Rouse (deceased) and George Rouse (deceased); married Earl C Lowe; children: Katrina E Lombre, Cassandra Eileen. **Educ:** Barnes Business Coll, diploma 1955; Attended, US Agriculture Dept School of Business 1963-64, Univ of the District of Columbia 1982-83. **Career:** Interstate Commerce Commn, secty/stenographer 1977-78, secty/admin asst 1978-79, secty/admin officer 1982-84, confidential asst, ending 1995. **Orgs:** Mem Frink HS Alumna 1982-; member, Lake Arbor Civic Assn, 1989-. **Honors/Awds:** Outstanding Performance Awd Interstate Commerce Commn 1965, 1977, 1978, 1981, 1983-90. **Home Addr:** 10334 Sea Pines Dr, Mitchellville, MD 20721.

LOWE, JACK, JR.
Law enforcement official. **Career:** Etowah County Sheriff's Department, chief, currently. **Special Achievements:** First African American police chief in Etowah County; highest ranking African American official in Etowah County; First African American to run for sheriff in Etowah County. **Business Addr:** Chief, Etowah County Sheriff's Department, 3200 W Maighan Blvd, Gadsden, AL 35904, (205)549-5403.

LOWE, JACKIE
Actress. **Personal:** Born Dec 14, Bamberg, SC. **Educ:** Rider Coll, 1973. **Career:** Film, The Wiz; TV, The Guiding Light, Edge of Night, Ryan's Hope, The Merv Griffin Show, Easter Seals Telethon; Theatre, Daddy Daddy, The First, Ain't Misbehavin, Eubie, Best Little Whorehouse in TX, Storyville, Selma, West Side Story, Sweet Charity, Pippin, Daddy Daddy; J Walter Thompson Advertising, prod asst 1973-76; The Tap Dance Kid, actress. **Orgs:** Coord Mothers March March of Dimes 1972; mem AFTRA, SAG, AGVA, Equity Unions. **Honors/Awds:** Nominated Best Supporting Actress Santa Monica Theatre Guild 1977; 1st recipient of Capitol City Dance Awd in Recog for accomplishments in dance and/or fine arts Trenton NJ 1985. **Business Addr:** The Tap Dance Kid, 200 W 45th St, New York, NY 10036.

LOWE, JAMES EDWARD, JR.
Physician. **Personal:** Born Dec 5, 1950, Warsaw, NC; son of Alice Mae Gavins Lowe and James Edward Lowe; married Philamina Lucy Lozado Lowe, Oct 7, 1989; children: James Edward III. **Educ:** Harvard Univ, Health Careers Program 1970; Livingstone Coll, BS 1971; Univ of NC Chapel Hill, Health Careers Program 1971; Meharry Medical Coll, MD 1975. **Career:** Downstate Medical Ctr, resident in surgery 1975-78; Lutheran Medical Ctr, resident & chief resident 1978-81; Lutheran Medical Ctr, teaching fellow general surgery 1981-82; Maple Medical Ctr, co-director; Long Island College Hosp, asst attending plastic & reconstructive surgery; Lutheran Medical Ctr, asst attending plastic & reconstructive surgery; Cabrini Medical Ctr, asst attending plastic & reconstructive surgery; Lenox Hill Hospital, plastic surgery residency 1982-84, asst attending plastic and reconstructive surgery, 1985-. **Orgs:** Mem Phi Beta Sigma Frat 1968-, NAACP 1985-; CORE 1985-; New York County Medical Soc 1985-, Natl Medical Assoc 1986-; mem, Amer Society of Plastc and Reconstructive Surgeons, 1986-. **Honors/Awds:** Physician Recognition Awd AMA 1986; publications ''Adriamycin Extravasation Ulcers,'' Amer Soc of Plastic & Recons Surgery Meeting, 1983; ''Non-Caucasian Rhinoplasty,'' Plastic and ENT Surgical Group Lutheran Medical Ctr 1986; ''Common Pressure Ulcers and Treatment,'' Natl Medical Assoc Convention New Orleans, LA 1987; History of the Carter-Morestin Soc presented at Natl Medical Assoc Convention New Orleans LA 1987.

LOWE, SCOTT MILLER
Physician. **Personal:** Born Sep 2, 1942, Charlottesville, VA; married Sharon Brewer. **Educ:** VA Unoin U, BS 1964; Meharry Med Coll, MD 1970. **Career:** Ob-gyn chf resd physician 1974-75; Albany Med Ctr, ob-gyn sr resd 1973-74; ob-gyn jr resd 1971-73; Harlem Hosp Ctr, intern 1970-71; Richmond Dept of Hlth, insp 1964-66. **Orgs:** Bd dir Tidewater Area Bus & Contractors Assn 1975; attdb physician Norforlk Comm Hosp; Norfolk Gen Hosp; Bayside Hosp; Leigh Meml Hosp; mem Norfolk Med Soc; Norfolk Acad of Med; VA Ob-gyn Soc; jr fellow Am Coll of Ob-gyn; mem Med Soc of VA Omega Psi Phi; Zeta Chap Busileus 1963-64; Delta Chap Basileus 1969-70; VA Unoin Univ Alumni Assn 1970-; Meharry Med Coll Alumni Assn 19720. **Business Addr:** 555 Fenchurch St, Norfolk, VA 23510.

LOWE, SIDNEY ROCHELL
Professional basketball coach. **Personal:** Born Jan 21, 1960. **Educ:** North Carolina State University. **Career:** Indiana Pacers, professional basketball player, 1983-84; Detroit Pistons, Atlanta Hawks, professional basketball player, 1984-85; Charlotte Hornets, professional basketball player, 1988-89; Minnesota Timberwolves, professional basketball player, 1989-90, asst coach, 1990-93, interim/head coach, 1993-94; Cleveland Cavaliers, asst coach, 1994. **Special Achievements:** Natl Basketball Assn's youngest head coach, 1993. **Business Addr:** Asst Coach, Cleveland Cavaliers, 1 Center Ct., Cleveland, OH 44115-4001, (216)659-9100.

LOWE, SYLVIA ONEICE
Engineer. **Personal:** Born Nov 1, 1946, Detroit, MI. **Educ:** Wayne St U, BS 1972; Cent MI U, MA 1977; Dale Carnegie Human Rela & Efective Speaking Course, 1979; Dale Carnegie Sales Course, 1980. **Career:** General Motors Assmbly Div Central Office GM Corp, sr ins enr 1978; Ford Motor Co, product design engr 1977-78; Ford Motor Co, sys engr 1976-77; NI-GAS, dev engr 1976; NI-GAS, aquifer engr 1975; Catepillar Tractor Co, ind engr 1975; Ford Motor Co, auto body desgn 1968-74; Fruehauf Corp, sales engr 1967-68; USATACOM, draftsman 1966-67. **Orgs:** Sec Soc of Ind & Voc Educ Wayne St Univ 1971-72; SAE Jr Chptr Wayne St Univ 1964-68; Soc Mech Engr Wayne St Univ 1965; sec instr grp leader coord Gen Educ Wkshp 1968-77; sec Thompson Court Area Block Club 1964; Dale Carnegie Graduate Asst 1980; mem Engineering Soc of Detroit; mem Ind Ambassador Com 1978-80. **Business Addr:** GM Assem Div Cent Offc Gmc I, Dept 30009 Van Dyke, Warren, MI 48090.

LOWE, WALTER EDWARD, JR.
Company executive. **Personal:** Born Aug 20, 1951, Milford, VA; son of Fraulein C Lowe and Walter E Lowe Sr; married Sheryl Ferguson, Oct 28, 1978; children: Ashley Patrice, Walter Edward III. **Educ:** University of Virginia, BA, 1976. **Career:** Ford Motor Co, buyer, 1976-83; General Dynamics, buyer specialist, 1983, chief, procurement, 1983-85, manager, procurement, 1985-90, director, procurement, 1990-93, director, material acquisition, 1994-. **Orgs:** Institute of Certified Professinal Managers, certified manager, 1985-; United Way Allocation Panel, chairman, 1990-; Henry Ford Health System, board of trustees, 1992-; American Management Assoc, 1983-; NAACP 1988-; Electronic Industries Assn, material steering committee, 1995-. **Honors/Awds:** Dollars and Sense Magazine, America's Best and Brightest Young Business and Professional Man Award, 1988. **Special Achievements:** Feature article, ''Buying More Bank for the Buck,'' Electronics Purchasing Magazine, July 1992. **Military Serv:** US Army, spec 4, 1972-74. **Business Addr:** Director, Material Management, General Dynamics Land Systems Division, PO Box 2071, Warren, MI 48090, (313)825-4247.

LOWERY, BIRL
Educator. **Personal:** Born Dec 24, 1950, Starkville, MS; son of Katie Collins Lowery and Clem Lowery; married Ester Hamblin Lowery, Feb 24, 1973; children: Ramona C, Tyson B. **Educ:** Alcorn Univ, Lorman, MS, BS, 1973; Mississppi State Univ, Starkville, MS, MA, 1975; Oregon State Univ, Corvallis, OR, PhD, 1980. **Career:** Univ of WI, Madison, WI, asst prof, 1980-86, assoc prof, 1986-92; prof, 1992-. **Orgs:** Soil Science Society of America; International Soil Tillage Research Organization; Soil & Water Conservation Society. **Business Addr:** Department of Soil Science, University of Wisconsin-Madison, 1525 Observatory Dr, Madison, WI 53706-1299.

LOWERY, BOBBY G.
Cleaning service executive. **Personal:** Born Nov 26, 1932, Blacksburg, SC; son of Eliza Morgan Lowery and Garance Lee Lowery; married Betty Mason, Oct 16, 1955; children: Regina Jones, Reginald, Revonsia Dozier, Robert. **Educ:** Carver College, liberal arts, 1957. **Career:** US Post Office, letter carrier, 1957-70; Better Cleaning, president, 1970-. **Orgs:** Building Service Contractors Association International, director, 1985-88; Charlotte Business League, president, 1981-82; National Minority Supplier Development Council, Minority Input Committee, vice chairman, 1978-79; Charlotte Chamber of Commerce, executive committee, 1985-86; University of North Carolina at Charlotte, trustee, 1987-95; St Paul Baptist Church, chairman, board of deacons, 1982-. **Honors/Awds:** Sigma Gamma Rho Sorority, Outstanding Citizen Award, 1978; Charlotte Chamber of Commerce, Minority Business Enterpriser of the Year, 1985. **Military Serv:** US Army, cpl, 1951-54; US Army Occupation, Germany, 1952.

LOWERY, CAROLYN T.
Organization executive. **Personal:** Born Jul 7, 1940, New Iberia, LA; daughter of Genivie Thomas Davis and Eldridge Thomas; divorced; children: Donald Jr, Valencia, Michael, Peter, Donald Wayne. **Educ:** Maricopa Technical College, AA, 1978; Arizona State University, School of Social Work. **Career:** Palmade School, teacher's aide; Motorola Plant, assembly worker; Ebony House (rehabilitation program for men), 1977-81; Wesley United Methodist Church, black community developer, 1981-85; Arizona Black United Fund, Inc, executive director, 1985-; Kid's Place, founder and director 1989. **Orgs:** Co-chairwoman, Arizona New Alliance Party, 1985-; co-chairwoman, Westside Neighborhood Community Center, 1988-; board member, Arizona Future Forum Program, Phoenix, AZ; board member, Arizona Regional Public Transportation Authority; co-founder, Arizona Black Cultural Museum, 1981-; co-founder, Arizona Stop Police Brutality Organization, 1981-; AZ New Alliance Party, co-founder, 1986. **Honors/Awds:** Outstanding community service citations: City of Phoenix, 1984, Black Engineers and Scientists, 1986, Nation of Islam, 1983, Black Community, 1988, Masons, 1982; Leadership Award, 1995, Black Women Task Force; As They Grow Awards, Parents Magazine, Ceremony at the White House, May 22, 1997; Az National Assn of Blacks in Criminal Justice, Foot Soldier Award, 1997. **Business Addr:** Executive Director, Arizona Black United Fund, PO Box 24457, Phoenix, AZ 85074.

LOWERY, DONALD ELLIOTT
Investment banker. **Personal:** Born Jan 6, 1956, Chicago, IL; son of Annie Lowery and R D Lowery. **Educ:** Wesleyan University, Middletown, CT, BA, economics, 1977. **Career:** Landmark Newspapers, reporter, 1977-79; Arizona Republic, Phoenix, AZ, reporter, 1979-80; The Boston Globe, Boston, MA, reporter, 1980-82; WHDH-TV, Boston, MA, dir, public affairs & editorials, 1982-91; First Albany Corp, vp, currently. **Orgs:** Board of directors, Bay State Games, 1990-; past pres, National Broadcast Editorial Assn, 1982-; Natl Assn of Black Journalist, 1980-; Business Associates Club, 1984-. **Honors/Awds:** Emmy, National Academy of Television Arts & Sciences, 1985, 1986; UPS Tom Phillips Award, 1985; Lincoln University Unity Award, 1988, 1989, 1991. **Business Addr:** VP, First Albany Corp, 53 State St, 25th Fl, Boston, MA 02109.

LOWERY, JOSEPH E.
Association executive (retired). **Personal:** Born Oct 6, 1924, Huntsville, AL; married Evelyn Gibson; children: Yvonne, Karen, Cheryl. **Educ:** Clark Coll, AB, BD, DO, DD 1975; Chicago Ecumenical Inst, Garrett Theological Seminary, Payne Theological Seminary, Knoxville Coll, AL A&M, Payne Coll, Wayne Univ, attended; Morehouse Univ, DD; Atlanta Univ, LLD; Dillard Univ, LittD. **Career:** Warren St Church Birmingham AL, pastor 1952-61; Bishop Golden, admin asst 1961-64; St Paul Church, pastor 1964-68; Emory Univ Candler School of Theology & Nursery School, instructor 1970-71; Enterprises Now Inc, pres; Central United Methodist Church, minister 1968-86; Cascade United Methodist Church, minister 1986-92. **Orgs:** Founder, vice pres SCLC 1967; natl chmn, bd dir SCLC Mobile AL 1967-77; natl pres SCLC 1977-97; mem Comm on Race Relations of United Methodist Church 1968-76, United Methodist Comm on Relief of United Methodist; bd dir Global Ministry 1976; mem, bd dir MARTA 1975-78; past vice chmn Atlanta Comm Relations Comm; mem General Bd of Publ United Methodist Public Housing 1960-72; mem Mayors Comm on Human Relations; chmn Civil Rights Coord Comm; past pres Interdenominational Ministry All Nashville TN; pres OEO Comm Act Agency; del, general conf United Methodist Church World Methodist Council Birmingham AL; mem, bd dir United Way, Martin Luther King Jr Center for Social Change; mem bd dir Urban Act Inc; mem Natl Leadership Council on Civil Rights; mem bd trusteesPaine Coll; founder, pres Cascade Fst Comm Asson. **Honors/Awds:** Awards from Natl Conf Black Mayors, Ebony; Medal of Honor Moscow Theological Seminary 1971; twice named Citizen of the Year OEO Award Atlanta Urban League 1975; Outstanding Comm Serv Contr; Honoree 1985 Religion Award for accomplishments as pastor of Central United Methodist Church in Atlanta, and for leadership as Natl Pres of SCLC. **Business Addr:** President, Southern Christian Leadership Conference, 334 Auburn Avenue NE, Atlanta, GA 30303-2604.

LOWERY, MICHAEL
Professional football player. **Personal:** Born Feb 14, 1974. **Educ:** Univ of Mississippi, attended. **Career:** Chicago Bears, linebacker, 1996-. **Business Addr:** Professional Football Player, Chicago Bears, 1000 Football Dr, Halas Hall at Conway Park, Lake Forest, IL 60045-4829, (847)295-6600.

LOWERY, ROBERT O.
Fire commissioner (retired), educator. **Personal:** Born Apr 20, 1916, Buffalo, NY; widowed; children: Lesie Ann Strickland, Gertrude Erwin. **Educ:** Attended, Coll of City of NY, MI State Univ, Natl Inst on Police & Comm Relations. **Career:** New York City Fire Dept, fireman 1942, lt fire marshal, fire commr retired. **Orgs:** 1st black apptd adminstr of a fire dept in a major city; founder of progs to educate people about fires & encourage better relations between the dept & the pub; attempting to recruit more blacks into dept. **Honors/Awds:** Received numerous awds & citations from various civic orgns. **Business Addr:** Department of Minority Studies, Indiana University Northwest, 3400 Broadway, Gary, IN 46408.

LOWERY, TERRELL
Professional baseball player. **Personal:** Born Oct 25, 1970, Oakland, CA. **Educ:** Loyola Marymount. **Career:** Chicago Cubs, outfielder, 1997-. **Business Addr:** Professional Baseball Player, Chicago Cubs, Wrigley Field, 1060 W Addison St, Chicago, IL 60613, (312)404-2827.

LOWERY-JETER, RENECIA YVONNE
Organization executive. **Personal:** Born Jul 2, 1954, Detroit, MI; daughter of Harold & Sarah Lowery; married Darrell Jeter, Sep 3, 1993. **Educ:** Wayne State University, BA, 1976; Marygrove College, MA, 1992. **Career:** United Way Community Svcs, director of human resources, 1993-. **Orgs:** American Society for Training & Development, president, 1997-98; Junior Achievement, volunteer; Spaulding for Children, board member, 1993-96. **Home Phone:** (313)531-2509. **Business Addr:** Director, Human Resources, United Way Community Svcs, 1212 Griswold, Detroit, MI 48226, (313)226-9375.

LOWMAN, CARL D.
Airline executive. **Personal:** Born Dec 1, 1962, Philadelphia, PA; son of Carl N & Delores Guy-Lowman; divorced. **Educ:** University of Massachusetts at Amherst, BBA, 1984. **Career:** The Gillette Co., budget analyst assistant, 1984-85, administrative & controls analyst, 1985-86, budget analyst, 1986-87; Continental Airlines, Inc, financial analyst, 1987-89, sr financial analyst, 1989-91, manager of budgers & forecasting, 1991-95; Western Pacific Airlines, Inc, director of financial svcs, 1995-, treasurer, 1995-. **Honors/Awds:** Outstanding Young Men of America Awd, 1987; YMCA of the Pikes Peak Region, Multicultural Achievers in Business & Industry Awd, 1996. **Home Addr:** 4230-C Autumn Hts, Dr, Colorado Springs, CO 80906. **Business Addr:** Treasurer, Western Pacific Airlines, Inc, 2864 S Circle Dr, Ste 1100, Colorado Springs, CO 80906.

LOWMAN, ISOM
Physician. **Personal:** Born Jun 3, 1946, Hopkins, SC; married Irma Jean Smith; children: Joye Katrese, Isom Batrone, Robin Patrese. **Educ:** SC State Coll, BS Prof Chem 1968; Meharry Med Coll, MD 1972; Wm Beaumont Army Med Center, Bd Internship 1972-75, Bd Residency 1978-80. **Career:** Ft Benning, chief of medicine 1975-78; Wm Beaumont Army Med Center, nuclear fellowship 1978-80; Moncrief Army Hospital Ft Jackson SC, chief of nuclear med 1980-82, deputy commander, chief of nuclear med & med 1983-. **Orgs:** Mem Alpha Phi Alpha Fraternity 1965-, Palmetto Med Soc; pres Cong Med Soc; fellow Amer Coll of Physicians; mem Soc of Nuclear Med, Amer Med Assoc. **Honors/Awds:** Outstanding Alpha Alpha Phi Alpha Fraternity; Distinguished Grad Hopkins High School 1984. **Military Serv:** AUS col; military medal of merit award. **Home Addr:** 51 Running Fox Rd, Columbia, SC 29223.

LOWNES, MILLICENT GRAY
Educational administrator. **Personal:** Born Dec 24, 1951, Philadelphia, PA; daughter of James & Mildred Gray; married Dr Arthur Jackson, Sep 1995; children: Robert Jr, Monique. **Educ:** Fisk University, BA, 1972; Vanderbilt University, MBA, 1975, PhD, 1981. **Career:** Tennessee State University, professor, 1976-, assoc dean, 1995-. **Orgs:** Phi Kappa Phi Honor Society, 1995-; Beta Gamma Sigma Honorary Bus Fraternity, 1995-; Interdenominational Svcs, Organization of America, ISOA, founder, 1990-; Business Exchange for the Entrepreneurially Minded, BEEM, founder, 1995-; The Women's Institute for Success Entrep, WISE, founder, 1995-; 100 Black Women 1994-; Links, Inc, 1994-; Jack & Jill of America. **Honors/Awds:** JC Penney, Golden Rule Award, Community Service, 1993, Golden Rule Award for Educators, 1994; Nashville Jaycees, Distinguished Service Award, 1994; National Association of Negro, Distinguished Professionalism, 1994; Black Expo, Business Leader of Nashville Award, 1995. **Special Achievements:** Author of 13 entrepreneurial books; conducted over 200 workshops & seminars, entrepreneurial empowerment; impacted lives of over 3,000 youth and 1,000 women, through non-profit organization; established ISOA to economically & entrepreneurially empower youth and women, 1990. **Business Addr:** Associate Dean, College of Business, Tennessee State University, 330 10th & Charlotte, Nashville, TN 37203, (615)963-7127.

LOWRY, DONNA SHIRLYNN (REID)
Television news reporter. **Personal:** Born May 19, 1957, Pittsburgh, PA; daughter of Alma M Lowry and Walter J S Lowry; married Bennet W Reid Jr; children: Nicole Fuller, Lakisha Reid, Sparkle Reid. **Educ:** Chatham College, BA, 1979; Northwestern University, MSJ, 1981. **Career:** WEEK-TV, news anchor, reporter, 1981-83; WESH-TV, news anchor, reporter, 1983-86; WXIA-TV, news reporter, 1986-. **Orgs:** Save The

Children, advisory board, 1991-; West End Boys and Girls Clubs, board of directors, 1992-; Old National Christian Academy, bd of dirs, 1994-; South Fulton PTA, honorary chairperson, 1991; Atlanta Association of Black Journalists, 1987-; Alpha Kappa Alpha Sorority Inc; Links, Inc, Magnolia Chap, 1994-; Statewide Safety Belt Task Force, 1994-; Georgia Assn of Family Daycare, advisory bd, 1994; Georgia Assn of School-Age Care, bd of dirs, 1996-. **Honors/Awds:** Dollars and Sense Magazine, Outstanding Business and Professional Award, 1992; The Minority Recruiter Newspapers, Positive Image Award, 1993; Georgia Psychological Association, Media Award, 1992; various Child Care Media Awards, 1991; YWCA, Salute to Women of Achievement, 1987, 1990. **Business Addr:** News Reporter, WXIA-TV, 1611 W Peachtree St NE, Atlanta, GA 30309, (404)873-9190.

LOWRY, JAMES E.
Business executive. **Personal:** Born Jul 8, 1942, Wyoming, OH; son of Mamie Lowry and Henry Lowry. **Educ:** Xavier Univ Cincinnati, BS Bus Admin 1975. **Career:** General Electric Co, adminstr equal oppor minority relations 1970-71; Lincoln Heights OH, mayor 1972-74; General Elec Co, mgmt trainee 1975-78, buyer machined parts 1978-79, manager of specialty parts, 1979-84, materials administrator, 1984-89, manager sourcing advanced technology, 1989-93; Indirect Materials & Services, mgr, 1993-95; Business Practices, mgr, 1995-. **Orgs:** Bd dir Comm Action Commn Cincinnati 1972-74; bd dir Lincoln Heights Health Clinic 1972-74; consult Comm Chest Cincinnati 1972-74; bd dir People United to Save Humanity 1972-74; bd dir Freedom Farm Ruleville MS 1972-74; bd dir OH Black Polit Assembly 1972-74; board of directors, General Electric Credit Union, 1984; member, Union for Experimenting Colleges and Universities, 1986; member, City of Forest Park Civil Service Commission, 1989-94; chairman, Forest Park Civil Service Comm, 1994; AECU Credit Union, chairman, 1993. **Honors/Awds:** Key to City Cincinnati 1972; KY Col State of KY 1972; Awd of Appreciation City of Fayette MS 1973; Extra Step Awd Gen Elec Co 1980; Extra Step Award, General Electric Corporation, 1980; GE Purchasing Gold Cup Award, 1982; Outstanding Political Service to the Community, Ohio Black Political Assembly, 1973. **Business Addr:** Manager, Sourcing Advanced Technology, General Electric Co, Mail Drop H75, Evendale, OH 45215.

LOWRY, JAMES HAMILTON
Company executive. **Personal:** Born May 28, 1939, Chicago, IL; children: Aisha. **Educ:** Grinnell Coll, BA 1961; Univ of Pittsburgh, MPIA 1965; Harvard Univ, Prog for Mgmt Development (PMD) 1973. **Career:** Bedford-Stuyvesant Restoration Corp Brooklyn, spl asst to pres proj mgr 1967-68; Peace Corps Lima, Peru, assoc dir 1965-67; McKinsey & Co Chicago, sr assoc 1968-75; James H Lowry & Assoc, pres 1975-. **Orgs:** Inst of Mgmt Consult, 1980-85; Natl Black MBA Assn, 1981-85; prinicpal Chicago United, 1982-85; Harvard Alumni Assn, 1980-85; pres Chicago Publ Library Bd, 1981-85; bd of trustees, Northwestern Meml Hosp, 1980-85; bd of trustees, Grinnell Coll, 1971-85; bd dirs, Independence Bank/Chicago, 1983-85; bd of dirs, Johnson Product. **Honors/Awds:** John Hay-Whitney Fellow, Univ of Pittsburgh, 1963-65; pres of class, Harvard Business Sch, 1973; Travel Fellowship Grinnell Coll, 1961-62; Honor Scholarship Grinnell Coll, 1958-61. **Business Addr:** President, James H Lowry & Associates, 211 W Wacker Dr, Ste 950, Chicago, IL 60606.

LOWRY, WILLIAM E., JR.
Steel company executive (retired). **Personal:** Born Feb 16, 1935, Chicago, IL; son of Camille Lowry and William Lowry; married Teri; children: Kim Maria, William Andre. **Educ:** Kenyon Coll, AB 1956; Loyola Univ of Chgo, MSIR 1969. **Career:** Francis W Parker School, athletic dir, coach 1960-62; Inland Steel Co, suprv 1962-65; Inland Steel Container Co, personnel mgr 1965; Inland Steel Co, personnel mgr 1968-76; Opportunity Line WBBM TV, host TV series 1967-82; Objective Jobs WBBM TV, host TV series 1982-; Jos T Ryerson & Son Inc, mgr human resources 1976-86; Personnel Administration, dir 1986-88; Inland Steel Industries, dir, personnel and recruitment, 1988-93. **Orgs:** Human Resources Association Chicago 1965-; sec Midwest College Placement Association 1967-; Children's Home and Aid Society of Illinois, board of directors; vp, bd of dir Chicago Boys & Girls Clubs 1967-; mem bd of dir, trustees Lake Forest College 1984-88; bd of dir Donors Forum, 1996; bd of dir, Rehabilitation Institute of Chicago 1988-; bd of dir, United Way/Crusade of Mercy, 1996-; bd of dir, trustees Kenyon College; member, Chicago United, 1975-93; chairman, Chicago Private Industry Council, 1990-. **Honors/Awds:** George Foster Peabody Awd 1968; TV Emmy Natl Acad TV Arts & Sci 1968-69; Human Relations Mass Media Awd Amer Jewish Comm 1968; 10 Outstanding Men of Chicago 1969; Blackbook's Black Bus Man of the Year 1981; Distinguished Journalism Award, AICS 1984. **Military Serv:** USAF 1st lt 3 yrs. **Business Addr:** Vice President, Human Resources and Administration, 140 S Dearborn St, Chicago, IL 60603.

LOYD, WALTER, JR.
Utility company manager. **Personal:** Born Dec 23, 1951, Tampa, FL; married Lavader E Taylor; children: Stacey, Tracey, Symon, Samuel. **Educ:** Univ of AR-Pine Bluff, BS 1974. **Career:** Arkansas Power & Light, sales rep 1974-77, adm rate analyst 1977-78, procedures analyst 1974-78, contracts administrator 1979-84, mgr 1984-; Entergy Corp, mgr, 1991-. **Orgs:** Mem & treas Amer Assoc of Blacks in Energy; century club and leadership mem Quapaw Area Boy Scouts of Amer; mem ad hoc comm on Business Dev AR Develop Comm; bd of dirs Arkansas Regional Minority Supplier Development Council; chair Little Rock Bd of Housing & Appeals. **Honors/Awds:** US Dept of Commerce, Minority Business Advocate of the Year, Dallas Region, 1989; Small Business Administration, Minority Business Advocate of the Year, 1990; Publication: Minority Business Enterprise, Enlightened Interest, 1993. **Business Addr:** Director, Business Development, Entergy Corp, 425 West Capitol, PO Box 551, Little Rock, AR 72203-0551.

LUCAS, C. PAYNE
Association executive. **Personal:** Born Sep 14, 1933, Spring Hope, NC; son of Minnie Hendricks Lucas and James Russel Lucas; married Freddie Emily Myra Hill Lucas, Aug 29, 1964; children: Therese Raymonde, C Payne Jr, Hillary Hendricks. **Educ:** Maryland State College, Princess Anne, MD, 1951-53, BA, 1959; American University, Washington, DC, MA, 1961. **Career:** Peace Corps, Washington, DC, asst dir, Togo, 1964, dir Niger 1964-66, dir, Africa Region 1967-69, dir, off/returned volunteers, 1969-71; Africare, Washington, DC, exec dir, 1971-. **Orgs:** Mem Bd of dir Overseas Development Council, 1977-; mem bd of dirs Interaction; Educ Fund; Intl Develop Conf; board member, Environmental Energy Institute, 1986-; member, Council on Foreign Relations, 1983-; board member, Population Action International, 1990-. **Honors/Awds:** Disting Fed Serv Awd for Peace Corps 1967; Honorary Doctorate of Law Univ of MD 1975; Capitol Press Club's Humanitarian of the Yr 1980; Presidential Hunger Awd Outstanding Achievement 1984; Phelps-Stokes Fund Aggrey Medal, 1986; Officers of the Order of Distinguished Service Award, 1986; Recognition from the National Order of the Republics of Niger, Zambia, and Ivory Coast, 1988; Land Grant Colleges Distinguished Bicentennial Award, 1990; First Black Recipient of the American Political Science Association's Hubert H Humphrey Public Service Award; National Order of Merit Award from the Government of Senegal, 1990. **Military Serv:** US Air Force, airman first class, 1954-58. **Business Addr:** Executive Director, AFRICARE, 440 R St NW, Washington, DC 20001.

LUCAS, DAVID EUGENE
State representative. **Personal:** Born Apr 23, 1950, Byron, GA; son of Beatrice Lucas and David Lucas; married Elaine Huckabee; children: David Jr, Leonard, Aris. **Educ:** Tuskegee Inst, BS 1972; Atlanta Law School. **Career:** State of Georgia, state representatives, currently; owner, Lucas Supply Company, Macon, GA; Northeast High Sch, Macon GA, social studies teacher, coach, 1972-73; Bibb Tech High Sch, Macon GA, social studies teacher & varsity girls, basketball, 1973-74; Barney A Smith Motors, Macon GA, car salesman, 1974-75; independent insurance agent, 1980-86; Horace Mann Companies, insurance agent, 1986-88; TBL Inc, pres, 1988-. **Orgs:** Vice pres, Macon Chfs Amtr football team; mem Black Eagles Motorcycle Club; C of C Macon; Fellowship of Christian Athletes; GA Assn of Black Elected Officials; Natl Conf of Black State Elected Officials; bd mem, Boys Club of Macon; Coalition of Political Awareness; bd mem, Small & Minority Bus Council, City of Macon; bd of governors, appointed to Mercer Univ School of Medicine, 1994. **Honors/Awds:** Distinguished Service Award, Columbia Univ, 1979; Comm Service Award, Macon Courier Newspaper, 1986; Inducted into the 1993 Tuskegee Univ Athletic Hall of Fame;. **Special Achievements:** Youngest African-American to be elected to the GA General Assembly at age 24, 1974.

LUCAS, DOROTHY J.
Physician. **Personal:** Born Nov 27, 1949, Lambert, MS; daughter of Elizabeth Killebrew Lucas and Garvie Lucas Sr; divorced 1981. **Educ:** Kennedy-King Coll, AA (w/Honors) 1971; Roosevelt Univ, BS 1973; UHS/The Chicago Medical Sch, MD 1977; Univ of IL, Public Health, MPH, 1993. **Career:** Mercy Hosp Medical Ctr, asst atten 1986-87; Columbus Cuneo Cabrini, resident 1977-81, assoc attending 1981-; senior attending 1986-. **Orgs:** NAACP; Alpha Kappa Alpha 1986-; mem CMC, AMA, ISMA; diplomate Amer Bd Ob-Gyn; fellow Amer Coll of Ob-Gyn; instructor Roosevelt Univ; American Medical Assn. **Honors/Awds:** ACOG Amer Coll of Ob-Gyn 1985; AMA Physician recognition Amer Medical Assoc 1985; Chicago Jaycees Ten Outstanding Young Citizens 1987; Distinguished Alumni City Colleges Trustee Award 1987; Push-Andrew Thomas Health Award 1987. **Business Addr:** Sr Attending Physician, Columbus-Cabrini, 65 E 75th, Chicago, IL 60619, (773)874-1776.

LUCAS, EARL S.
City official. **Personal:** Born Jan 1, 1938, Renova, MS; married Marilee Lewis; children: Eric, Vicki, Carla, Tina, Mark, Kendric. **Educ:** Dillard Univ, BA 1957; further study DePauw Univ & Beloit Coll. **Career:** Bolivar County Sch System, teacher 1958-65; Star Inc, exec dir 1965-73; City of Mound Bayou, mayor 1969-. **Orgs:** Treas So Conf of Black Mayors; dir Mound Bayou Devel Corp; dir Fund for Educ & Comm Devel; mem Com Delta Ministry Natl Council Chs; dir Delta Found; mem Alpha Phi Alpha Frat; mem Conf Black Mayors. **Business Addr:** Mayor, City Mound Bayou, PO Drawer H, Mound Bayou, MS 38762.

LUCAS, GERALD ROBERT
Federal senior executive. **Personal:** Born Sep 18, 1942, Washington, DC; son of Sylvia Coats Lucas-Jiles and Mack Lucas; married Patricia Selena Jones, Jan 19, 1975; children: Gerald R Jr, Kenya, Kimberlee. **Educ:** Brandeis U, 1968-71; State Univ of NY Stoney Brook, MSW 1973; Univ of MN, PhD 1976. **Career:** US Dept of Commerce, special assistance to the asst sec for adminstrn 1978-; Univ of Cincinnati, assoc prof 1976-78; Minneapolis Urban League, proj dir 1974-76; US Dept HEW, personnel mgmt specialist 1969-71; Waszh Urban League, program Dir 1967-69; US Dept of Commerce, dir office of civil rights 1982-; US Department of Commerce, Eastern Administrative Support Ctr, director, 1994-. **Orgs:** Mem bd of dirs Minneapolis Zion Group Home 1975-76; mem Nat Assn of Black Social Workers Minneapolis Chap 1973-76; mem Am Soc for Pub Adminstrs Nat Capital Area Chap 1979-80; mem Cincinnati Title XX Adv Comm 1975-76; mem Barnaby Manor Civic Assn 1978-80; mem Conference of Minority in Pub Adminstrn 1979-80. **Honors/Awds:** DHEW secretary's special citation Dept of HEW 1969; urban coalitation fellowship Minneapolis Urban Coalition 1976; article pub 1977; commendation award AUS. **Military Serv:** AUS specialist 1964-66. **Home Addr:** 12006 Hazem Court, Fort Washington, MD 20744. **Business Phone:** (757)441-6865.

LUCAS, JAMES L.
Educator. **Personal:** Born Oct 20, 1923, Canton, OH; divorced; children: Carol Brynne. **Educ:** Boston Univ, AB 1947; Cornell Univ Law School, LLB 1950; Univ of Chgo, MA English 1965; Univ of Chicago Divinity School, MA 1970; No IL Univ, PhD 1980. **Career:** OH Indust Commiss, atty examiner 1953-57; Wittenberg Univ Springfield OH, instr english & humanites 1957-60; Harper Coll Palatine IL, instr english 1967-; TV Coll Chicago City Coll,TV instr 1970-74,84-; Chicago City Coll Wilbur Wright Coll, prof english 1965-. **Orgs:** Mem Bar of US Supreme Court 1955-, US Court of Military Appeals 1955-, Supreme Court of OH 1952-; lecturer fine arts, lit, humanites Chgo-Area Orgs 1965-; mem United Lutheran Church of Amer 1960, Sigma Tau Delta Natl English Honors Soc; Modern Lang Assoc 1975-, Natl Council of Teachers of English 1980-. **Honors/Awds:** Listed in Directory of Amer Scholars 1982; Martin Luther Fellow United Lutheran Church of Amer 1950; author 2 manuals in Amer Literature for televised college courses publ by Chicago Ed TV Assoc 1970-,71; author The Religious Dimension of Twentieth-Century & Amer Lit publ by Univ Press of Amer 1982-; listed in Men of Acheivement 1977; author Executive Seizure Power Constitutional Power of the President to Seize Private Industry publ JAG Bulletin USAF 1959. **Military Serv:** AUS sgt 1943-45; USAFR capt, judge advocate gen 1951-53. **Business Addr:** Professor, Wilbur Wright College, Chicago City Colleges, 3400 N Austin Ave, Chicago, IL 60634.

LUCAS, JOHN (COOL HAND LUKE)
Professional basketball coach, business executive. **Personal:** Born Oct 31, 1953, Durham, NC; married DeEdgra; children: Tarvia, John, Jai. **Educ:** Univ of MD, BBus 1976; Univ of San Francisco, M Second Educ. **Career:** Golden Gaters World Tennis Team, 1977, New Orleans Nets World Tennis Team, 1978; Houston Rockets, 1976-78, 1985-86, 1989-90; Golden State Warriors, 1978-81; Washington Bullets; 1981-83, San Antonio Spurs, 1983-84; Milwaukee Bucks, 1987-88, Seattle SuperSonics, 1989; John Lucas Enterprises, pres, currently; San Antonio Spurs, coach, 1993-94; Philadelphia 76er's, coach, general manager, 1994-. **Orgs:** Natl Council on Alcoholism and Drug Dependence, Inc, bd of dirs. **Honors/Awds:** NBA All Rookie Team 1977; All-Amer Tennis Player; won Atlantic Coastal Conf Singles Title Twice (Tennis). **Special Achievements:** Author: Winning A Day At A Time, Hazelden Publishing Group, 1994. **Home Addr:** Coach/GM/VP, Philadelphia 76er's, Philadelphia, PA 19147, (215)339-7600. **Business Phone:** (713)935-9294.

LUCAS, JOHN HARDING
Educator. **Personal:** Born Nov 7, 1920, Rocky Mount, NC; son of Rebecca Bowles Lucas and John William Lucas; married Blondola O Powell; children: Cheryl, John Harding, Jr. **Educ:** Shaw Univ NC, BS 1940; NC Central U, MA 1951; NYU, certificate of advanced study in education; NYU, Univ of NC, Duke U; Appalachian State University; Durham Technical Community College. **Career:** Adkin HS NC, sci tchr guidance dir coordinator of diversified occupations coack admin asst 1940-44, 1946-52; Orange St Elementary School Oxford NC, prin 1952-57; Mary Potter HS Oxford NC, prin 1957-62; Hillside Sr HS Durham NC, prin 1962-86; Shaw University, pres, 1986-87; Durham City Board of Education, 1987-; Durham Public Schools Board of Education, 1992-96. **Orgs:** Pres NC Assn of Educators 1974-75; pres Kinston Tchr Assn 1942-44, 1948-50; adv com Gov Commn on Study of Pub Sch in NC 1967-68; bd dir NC Assn of Educators 1970-72; dir for NC Nat Educ Assn 1961-72; Liaison Com NC Tchr Assn NC EdnAssn; US Delegate to World Assembly of World Confederation of Orgn of Tchr Profession in Africa, Asia British Columbia & Ire-

land 1965-73; consult Race Relations; contr Educational & Professional Journals; chmn NC Delegationsto Annual Conv NC Assn of Educators at Nat Educ Assn Nat Rep Assemblies; editor Beta Phi Chap Omega Psi Phi Frat Inc; deacon trustee White Rock Bapt Ch Durham NC; Task Force on NC Mental Health Cntr 1970; Nat Commn for TX Educ Assn Evaluation 1970; adv com White House Conf on Children & Youth 1970; chmn DurhamHuman Relations Commn 1973; bir Learning Inst of NC 1971-; bd dir Nat Found for Improvement of Educ 1970-; NC Cit Com on Sch; Durham Civic Conv Cntr Commn 1972-; honorary mem bd dir NEA 1973; Boy's Adv Council Salvat; chair, board of deacons, White Rock Baptist Church, 1990-; member, board of directors, NC Public School Forum; member, board of directors, Durham Public School Fund; board of trustees, Shaw University, 1978-; life member, NAACP; Governors Advisory Council on Aging. **Honors/Awds:** Man of the Year Award, Citizen's Welfare League NC 1951; Distinguished Service Award, NC Teachers Assn 1968; Meritorious Award, NC Resource Use Educ 1969; Honor Award, NC State Fair 1969; Distinguished Service Award, Durham City Assn of Educators 1971-72; Durham's Father of Year 1972; Honorary Citizen, Durham NC 1974; Hall of Distinction, Shaw University, 1990; Martin Luther King, Jr Meritorious Award, General Baptist Convention of North Carolina, 1987; Citizen of the Year, Omega Phi Psi Fraternity, 1988; Wachovia Principal of the Year, 1984; Above and Beyond Award, NCAE, 1986; NCAE Lobby named Lucas-Radar Lobby, NCAE Equity Award, 1995. **Military Serv:** WWII veteran 1944-46. **Business Addr:** Educator, Durham Public Schools Board of Education, PO Box 30002, Durham, NC 27702-0002.

LUCAS, LEO ALEXANDER
Business executive, certified public accountant. **Personal:** Born Sep 29, 1912, Woodbine, GA; son of Lydia Belle Lucas and Davis Lucas; married Alyce Downing; children: Lea Ann. **Educ:** FL A&M Univ, BS 1937; Miami Univ (Oxford, OH), MA 1951, LLD 1979. **Career:** Dayton, OH, teacher 1944-57; Dade Co FL Public Schools, tchr 1937-39; LA Lucas & Co, Inc, pres/chmn 1944-; Dayton Mesbic, Inc, pres, CEO 1973-81; Public School Governance, consultant 1973-; LA Lucas & Co Inc, sr accountant. **Orgs:** American Association of Mesbics Inc, past natl pres 1976-78; Natl Association of SBICS past mem/bd of dir 1976-78; Greater Dayton, OH Public Television Inc, secretary-treasurer 1980-88; Greater Dayton, OH Private Industry Council, vice pres 1981-; Accreditation Council of Accountancy 1974-; Natl Soc of Public Accountants Inc 1956- Natl Association of Black Accountants 1972; Ohio SOC of CPA's; OH Schl Bds Association, board of trustees 1972-88; co-chair Dayton Elected Officials, Inc 1973-; past pres Dayton Bd of Educ 1965-88; founder, past natl pres Natl Caucus of Black School Bd Members 1967-; American Assn of Mesibs Inc; NAACP Dayton 1989; Dayton Urban League 1989; treasurer, bd of trustees, Creekside Players Inc 1987-; Dayton Community Affairs Council, 1967-; Ohio Council for the Aging, 1985; Large City Commission of Ohio, 1972-, past chair; Alpha Phi Alpha, life member, 1934-. **Honors/Awds:** Sire archon Sigma Pi Phi 1980-; Man of the Year Frontiers International & Alpha Phi Alpha; Natl Award Outstanding Service in Education Governance NABSE 1974; 33 degree Prince Hall Mason/trustee-Bethel Baptist Church; Distinguished Daytonian Award, Miami Jacobs College 1989; Distinguished Elected Official, Dayton School Board for 23 years, 1988; "Dr Leo A Lucas Day," by the Ohio General Assembly and Mayor of Dayton Ohio. **Business Addr:** CPA, L A Lucas & Co, Inc, 736 Argonne Dr, Dayton, OH 45407-1238, (937)263-3219.

LUCAS, LINDA GAIL
Guidance counselor. **Personal:** Born Jul 18, 1947, Charleston, SC; married Henry Lucas Jr (deceased); children: Ayoka L. **Educ:** Herbert Lehman Coll, BA 1969; The Citadel, MEd 1984. **Career:** Rockland Children Psych Ctr, sr speech pathologist 1972-80; Dorchester Co Schools III, speech correctionist 1980; Chas Co Sch Dist, speech correctionist 1980-84; Hunley Park Elem, guidance counselor 1984-85; Buist Acad, guidance counselor 1985-. **Orgs:** Sec Tri-County Foster Parents Assoc 1982; adjunct staff mem Dorchester Mental Health Ctr 1984; guardian ad litem GAL Program 1985-; delegate Alice BirneySchool Bd 1986-87. **Honors/Awds:** News & courier article on single parent survival 1985; Licensed professional counselor State of SC 1986. **Business Addr:** Guidance Counselor, Buist Acad for Adv Studies, 103 Calhoun St, Charleston, SC 29403.

LUCAS, MAURICE
Professional basketball player. **Personal:** Born Feb 18, 1952, Pittsburgh, PA; married Rita Lyles; children: Maurice II, David. **Educ:** Marquette Univ, 1970-74. **Career:** Basketball player, Carolina-St Louis ABA 1974-75, Kentucky Colonels ABA 1975, Portland Trail Blazers, 1976-80, 1988, New Jersey Nets 1980-81, New York Knicks 1981-82, Phoenix Suns 1983-85, Los Angeles Lakers, 1986, Seattle SuperSonics, 1987. **Honors/Awds:** Portland's World Championship Team, 1977; NBA All-Star Performer all 3 years while a Portland Trail Blazer and was named to the NBA's All-Defensive Team, 1977-78, All-Defensive Second Team, 1978-79; Named to the All-NBA Second Team, 1978; Voted to starting position on West All-Star Team, 1983.

LUCAS, MAURICE F.
Government official. **Personal:** Born Oct 10, 1944, Mound Bayou, MS; son of Glady Collins Lucas and Julius Lucas; married Carolyn Cousin Lucas, Feb 3, 1968; children: Maurice F Lucas, Jr. **Educ:** Delta State Univ, Cleveland, MS, BBA, 1971. **Career:** Cleveland School Dist, sec & trustee, 1987-; Town of Renova, Renova, MS, mayor, 1978-. **Orgs:** Deputy grand master, PH Masons of MS, 1984-; dir, Industrial Devel Found, 1985-; dir, Chamber of Commerce, 1985-; dir, United Way, 1985-. **Special Achievements:** First Black President of Cleveland Chamber of Commerce. **Military Serv:** US Army, sergeant, 1962-65.

LUCAS, RENDELLA
Social worker. **Personal:** Born Oct 30, 1910, Cheriton, VA; widowed. **Educ:** VA Union Univ, BA, 1932; Hampton Inst, MA, 1943. **Career:** PA Dept of Public Welfare, retired caseworker supvr admin asst 1945-73; Fauquier HS, teacher 1932-36. **Orgs:** Youth ldr Salem Bapt Ch 1937-55; supr yth dept No Bapt Missionary Unoin 1940-55; vice pres Woman's Aux Easternbapt Keystone Assn 1945-48; vice pres Woman's Aux Sub Bapt Ch Assn 1951-53; pres Bapt Ministers' Wives Unoin 1943-45; corrs sec Nat Assn of Ministers Wives Inc 1943-55; pres Nat Assn of Ministers' Wives Inc 1957-70; fdr 1st edtr Newsette 1965; mem Philadelphia NAACP; exec sec Nat Assn of Ministers' Wives Inc 1970-74; mem Salem Bapt Ch; mem Ch Women United; life mem Nat Assn of Ministers' Wives Inc; mem exec bd No Bapt Missionary Unoin & Woman's Aux to Suburban Bapt Chs Assn; schlrshp sec No Bapt Missionary Unoin; recording sec Interdenom Ministers' Wives Flwshp of Philadelphia; vice pres PA Bapt Bus & Professional Women; vice pres Bapt &Women's Ctr of Philadelphia; comunist Minirs' Wives Herald; mem ML Chepard Chap VA Unoin Univ Alumni; mem Commn Disadvantaged Students Eastern Sem & Coll;vol Leukemia Soc of Am; mem adv counc Rose Butler Brown Fund RI Coll of Edn; coord Ministe. **Honors/Awds:** Testimonial & Distinguished Achvmt Award Philadelphia Ch Comm 1957; cert of merit VA Union Univ, 1958; Distinguished Service Award Philadelphia NAACP 1961; disting serv award Bapt Ministers' Wives of Philadelphia 1961; natl achvmnt award Salem Bapt Ch 1965; cert of achvmnt Bapt Ministers' Wives Unoin 1967; cert of award PA Batp Assn 1968; comm serv award Chapel of 4 Chaplains 1968; cert of hon life membership VA Assn of Ministers' Wives 1966; Elizabeth Coles Beueymeml ldrshp trophy Nat Assn of Ministers' Wives 1962; ousts natl chwmn plaque Bapt Ministers' Philadelphia Conf 1967; outst serv award plaques NY &Rose City Portland Ministers' Wives 1969; outstn serv cit PA Dept of Welfare 1973; Shrinre's Woman of the Yr Award 1970.

LUCAS, RUBYE
Broadcasting company executive. **Personal:** Born Sep 26, 1935, Fort Myers, FL; daughter of Viola Hendley & Booker T Mims; married William Lucas, Apr 27, 1958 (deceased); children: William Jr, Wonya, Andrea. **Educ:** Florida A&M University, social science degree; Atlanta Univ, MEd. **Career:** Florida Public School System, teacher; Atlanta Public School System, teacher; Turner Broadcasting System , Inc, hr admini/mgmt training, 1990-91, dir, The Atlanta Project, 1991-. **Orgs:** Atlanta Braves Natl Leagues Baseball Club, bd of dir; Bill Lucas Scholarship Foundation, bd of dirs; Bill Lucas Branch of the Butler Street YMCA, bd of dirs; Alliance Theatre, bd of dirs; Hank Aaron Rookie League, co-founder; GA World Congress Center Authority, sect; Fulton County Commission on Children & Youth; Turner Broadcasting System Inc, bd of dirs. **Honors/Awds:** AKA Sorority, Inc, Humanitarian Award, 1994; 20th Judicial Circuit, Florida, Outstanding Achievement Award, 1994; Butler Street YMCA, Youth Foundation Award, 1994, Service Award, 1994; The Atlanta Project, Award of Appreciation, 1994. **Special Achievements:** Fine & Performing Arts and Talent Center, 1993. **Business Addr:** Dir, The Atlanta Project, Turner Broadcasting System, Inc, 1 CNN Center, Box 105366, Atlanta, GA 30348-5366.

LUCAS, VICTORIA
Public relations executive. **Personal:** Born Feb 2, Chicago, IL. **Educ:** Malcolm-King Clg; Chicago, IL, Liberal Arts; Clg of the Univ NY, Bus Admn. **Career:** Amer Museum of Immigration, public relations asst 1955-57; Natl Council on Alcoholism, mgr publications dept 1957-63; Norman Craig & Kummel, copywriter/acct exec 1964-66; Cannon Advertising, public relations dir/copywrtr 1966-67; Victoria Lucas Assc, pres/owner. **Orgs:** Former mem bd of dir Publicity Clb NY; mem Pblc Rel Soc of Am; Natl Assc Media Women; conduct workshop Understanding The Basics of Public Relations,new school for Social Research, New York City 1977-. **Honors/Awds:** Natl assc of media women Media Woman of Yr awrd; among women honored achvmnt bus Intrl Womens Year Com Operation PUSH Chicago, IL 1975; D Parke Gibson Outstanding Mentor awd; NY chap Committee on Minorities; Public Relations Society of Amer 1985.

LUCAS, WILLIAM
Former judge. **Personal:** Born Jan 15, 1928, New York, NY; son of Charlette Hazel Lucas and George Lucas; married Evelyn Daniel Lucas. **Career:** Has worked as teacher, social worker, policeman, civil rights investigator, and FBI agent; lawyer; Wayne County Michigan, Detroit MI, county executive; US Govt, Washington DC, director of the office of liaison services, beginning 1989; Recorder's Court, judge, 1993-94. **Business Addr:** Former Judge, Recorder's Court, 1441 St Antoine, Detroit, MI 48226.

LUCAS, WILLIAM S.
Educator. **Personal:** Born Oct 31, 1917, Hampton, GA; married Doris Anderson; children: Yolande, Deborah, William. **Educ:** Morris Brown Coll, AB 1942; Univ Pittsburgh, MEd 1951. **Career:** Thomaston Training School, teacher 1946-47, prin 1947; A Leo Weil School, teacher 1949-50; So Fulton HS, teacher coach 1963-64; Fairburn HS, prin 1964-70; admin asst 1970-73; Fed Programs, Fulton County Schools, dir 1973. **Orgs:** Mem NEA; AFT; AASA; Natl Alliance Black Sch Educators; Phi Beta Sigma Frat; vice pres Morris Brown's Tay Club; recorder Knights of Columbus, pursuer; mem Summer Youth Employment Planning Comm; Title I Parents Adv Council; mem YWCA; Official Black Caucus of NEA. **Honors/Awds:** Tchr of Yr 1963; PTA Council Award 1963; Fulton County Tchrs Assn Pres's Award 1966-67. **Military Serv:** S/sgt 1942-46. **Business Addr:** 580 College St, Hapeville, GA 30354.

LUCAS, WILLIE LEE
Educational administrator, librarian. **Personal:** Born Dec 17, 1924, Jacksonville, FL; daughter of Maude Roberts Joyner and William Lavert Joyner; married Elcee R Lucas, Jul 23, 1948 (divorced 1980); children: Kim. **Educ:** Tennessee A&I University, BS, 1944; University of Michigan, AMLS, 1952; University of Florida, EdS, 1977, EdD, 1982. **Career:** Office of Price Adm, Washington, DC, stenographer, 1944-45; Afro-American Life Insurance Co, stenographer, 1945-46; McGill & McGill Law Firm, stenographer, 1946-47; Duval County Board of Public Instruction, teacher/librarian, 1947-74; Florida Community College, librarian/dept chair, 1974-. **Orgs:** Charter member, Jacksonville Alumnae Chapter, Delta Sigma Theta Sorority, 1947-; American Library Assn; Jacksonville Board of Realtors; advisory committee, Education and Research Foundation, Florida Real Estate Commission; Altar/Rosary Society, St Pius V Catholic Church. **Honors/Awds:** Outstanding Faculty Award, Florida Community College, 1990; Kappa Delta Pi, 1977; Alpha Kappa Mu. **Home Addr:** 1774 Shoreview Dr W, Jacksonville, FL 32218. **Business Addr:** Librarian, Learning Resources, Florida Community College, North Campus, 4501 Capper Rd, #D301, Jacksonville, FL 32218.

LUCAS, WILMER FRANCIS, JR.
Playwright, writer, journalist, producer-director, educator. **Personal:** Born Sep 1, 1927, Brooklyn, NY; son of Inez Williams and Wilmer Francis; married Cleo Melissa Martin, Feb 18, 1969 (deceased); children: Alain Francis. **Educ:** New York Univ, 1945-48. **Career:** Playwright, 1965-; writer, 1973-; New School for Social Research, New York City, lecturer in comparative Afro-American literature, 1962-68; University of Tennesse, Knoxville, instructor in humanities, 1971-; founder of Carpetbag Theater, Knoxville, 1971-, producer and director of "Carpetbag Theater Presents," 1972-. **Honors/Awds:** Natl Endowment for the Arts award and grant, 1973, for perpetuation of the Carpetbag Theater; author of Bottom Fishing: A Novella and Other Stories, Carpetbag Press, 1974, Patent Leather Sunday: And S'More One Act Plays, Carpetbag Press, 1975. **Home Addr:** 1936 Prospect Pl, Knoxville, TN 37915.

LUCK, CLYDE ALEXANDER, JR.
Surgeon. **Personal:** Born Mar 3, 1929, Danville, VA; son of Dr & Mrs Clyde Luck Sr; children: Kelli. **Educ:** Howard Univ, BS 1950; NY Univ, MA 1952; Howard Univ, MD 1959. **Career:** St Joseph Mercy Hospital & Detroit Receiving Hospital, resdent in general surgery 1960-64; Kaiser Found Hospital LA, 1 yr fellowship 1964-65; Crenshaw Hospital, chmn dept of surgery 1974-78. **Orgs:** Mem Omega Psi Phi, NAACP, Urban League, LA Cty Med Soc; fellow Amer Coll of Surgeons, Intl Coll of Surgeons. **Military Serv:** USAF 1st lt 1952-54. **Business Addr:** P O Box 34877, Los Angeles, CA 90034-0877.

LUCKEY, EVELYN F.
Educator, educational administrator. **Personal:** Born Apr 30, 1926, Bellefonte, PA; daughter of Agnes A Haywood Foreman and Arthur R Foreman; divorced; children: Jennifer, Carolyn. **Educ:** Central State Univ, 1945; OH State Univ, BA, BsEd, English, Psych 1947, MA English 1950, PhD Ed 1970. **Career:** Columbus Public Schools, teacher 1957-66, evaluation asst 1965-67; OH State Univ, asst prof 1971-72; Columbus Public Schools, exec dir 1972-77, asst supt 1977-90; Otterbein College, Westerville, OH, asst prof, 1990-. **Orgs:** Mem Amer Assoc of School Admin 1977-, Adv Bd of Urban Network of No Central Reg Ed Lab 1985-90, Assoc for Suprv & Curriculum Devel 1972-93, Natl Alliance of Black School Ed 1978-, Central OH Mktg Council 1984-89, Bd of Planned Parenthood of Central OH 1984-87; trustee, pres Bd of Public Libr of Columbus & Franklin Cty 1973-89; member, Links, Inc, 1988-; trustee, pres, board, Columbus Metropolitan Library, 1973-89; trustee, Central Ohio Marketing Council, 1984-89. **Honors/Awds:** Outstanding Educator Awd Alpha Kappa Alpha 1978; Woman on the Move Moles 1978; Woman of the Year Omega Psi Phi 1980; Distinguished Kappan Awd Phi Delta Kappa 1981; Disting Alumnae Awd OH State Univ 1982; Certificate

of Honor City of Columbus 1984; YWCA Woman of Achievement Award 1987, 1991; United Negro College Fund Eminent Scholar, 1990. **Home Addr:** 404 Brookside Drive, Columbus, OH 43209-7019. **Business Addr:** Assistant Professor, Education, Otterbein College, Department of Education, Westerville, OH 43081.

LUCKEY, IRENE

Educator. **Personal:** Born May 29, 1949, New York, NY. **Educ:** North Carolina Agric & Tech State Univ, BA 1971; Univ of Chicago,Schl of Soc Serv Administration MA 1973; City Univ of New York, The Graduate Schl, DSW 1982. **Career:** Metropolitan Hosp New York City, medical social worker 1973-76; NC Agric & Tech State Univ, asst prof social work 1976-78; Brookdale Ctr of Aging-Hunter Coll, dir of educ prgms 1979-81; LeMoyne Owen Coll, visiting prof 1981-82; Clark College, asst prof 1982-84; Univ of West Florida, asst prof of social work, assoc dir ctr on aging 1985-89; The University of Michigan, Ann Arbor, postdoctoral research fellow, 1987-89; State University of New York, Albany, asst professor, 1989-90; Rutgers, The State University of New Jersey, assistant professor, 1990-. **Orgs:** Consultant; Admin on Aging 1981; Atlanta Reg Comm on Aging 1984; Clark Coll Soc Work Prgrm 1985-86; Natl Assoc of Black Social Workers, Chair Educ Prgm 1985- ; Mental Health Assoc of Escambia Cnty, Advisory Member 1985-; State of Florida Long Term Care Council, Governor Appointed 1986-; Board of Directors, Northwest Florida Area Agency on Aging 1986; Geriatric Residential & Treatment of NW Florida 1986-; Phi ALpha, Kappa Alpha Kappa; Alpha Kappa Mu; Rutgers University, Undergraduate Social Work Program, advisory board; Geronotological Task Force, Gerontological Society Social Research, Planning and Practice; Task Force on Minority Issues, Subcommittee on Policy and Service/Practice; National Social Science Journal Gerontological Society, referee/reviewer. **Honors/Awds:** NIA Postdoctoral Research Fellow; Brookdale Center on Aging Fellow; GSA Postdoctoral Fellowship Program in Applied Gerontology; Appreciation Award, Association of Minority Affairs, School of Social Welfare, SUNY: Alpha Kappa Mu Honor Society; Kappa Alpha Psi Scholastic Achievement Award; Phi Alpha National Social Work Honor Society. **Special Achievements:** Author, with Johnson, H R, Gibson, R C, Health and Social Characteristics: Implications for Services, in Z Harel, E McKinney, & M Williams (eds), The Black Aged: Understanding Diversity and Service Needs, Calif, Sage Publications, Inc, 1969-81, 1990; with Taylor, R J, and Smith, J M, The Church's Ministry With Families: A Practical Guide, in D Garland and D Pancoft (ed), Churches and Families, Dallas, TX: Word Publishing, 194-209, 1990; Impact of Race on Student Evaluations of Faculty, article published 1986. **Home Addr:** 2 Redcliff Ave, Highland Park, NJ 08904. **Business Addr:** Assistant Professor, Rutgers Univ, School of Social Work, 536 George St, New Brunswick, NJ 08903.

LUCUS, EMMA TURNER

Educational administrator. **Personal:** Born Feb 5, 1949, Meridian, MS; children: Kamilah Aisha. **Educ:** Tougaloo Coll, BA 1970; Purdue Univ, MA 1972; Univ of Pgh, MSW 1978, PhD, 1986. **Career:** Planned Parenthood, counselor 1973-75; St Francis Hosp, rehab specialist 1975-76; Chatham Coll, dir of Black studies 1976-79, assoc vice pres for academic affairs 1979-. **Orgs:** Pennsylvania Blacks in Higher Education, 1987-; Pittsburgh Council on Public Education, board secretary; Girl Scouts of SW Pennsylvania, 1988-; Pres, Pittsburgh Chapter, Assn for the Study of Afro-Amer Life and History 1983; consultant, Presbyterian Home for Children 1982-; bd of dirs, YWCA Pittsburgh, 1982-86; bd of dirs, Training Wheels Childrens Ctr 1984-88. **Honors/Awds:** Pittsburgh Professional Award Talk Magazine, 1982; TV prod, Career Trends for the 80's, 1983; HJ Heinz Foundation Grant, 1983; Faculty Development Grant, Chatham Coll 1983-85; Girl Scouts 1992, Fulbright Hays Grants, 1987, 1989.

LUCY, WILLIAM

Engineer. **Personal:** Born Nov 26, 1933, Memphis, TN; son of Susie B Gibbs and Joseph Lucy; married Dorotheria; children: Benita Ann, Phyllis Kay. **Educ:** Univ of CA Berkeley; Contra Costa Jr Coll Richmond. **Career:** Am Fedn State Co Municipal Employees, intern sec treas; AFSCME AFL-CIO, exec asst to pres; Contra Costa Co CA, asst mat & research eng. **Orgs:** Bd of trustees African Am Inst; bd of trustees Transafrica; vice pres Indsl Union Dept AFL-CIO; vice pres Maritime Trades Dept AFL-CIO bd of dir Am for Dem Action; bd of dir Nat Laws of Black Aged; pres Coalition of Black Trade; mem Judicial Nomination Commn Wash DC; bd of trustee Martin Luther King Center for Social Change. **Honors/Awds:** Hon Doctorate of Humane Letters Bowie State Coll. **Business Addr:** American Federation of State County & Municipal Employees, AFL-CIO, 1625 L St NW, Washington, DC 20036.

LUDLEY, RICHARD

Educator. **Personal:** Born Oct 18, 1931, Grambling, LA; son of Marzella Younger Ludley and Arthur Ludley Sr; married Sadie Pearl Allen; children: Gregory, Karen, Valerie, Patrick. **Educ:** BS 1957; MS 1974. **Career:** Pinevew HS Lisbon, LA, public school teacher 1960-64; Hopewell HS Dubach, LA, 1964-68; Dubach HS, 1968-69; Ruston HS Ruston, LA, 1969-; Town of Grambling, alderman, mayor. **Orgs:** Mem LA Educ Assn, Nat Educ Assn, Grambling Voters League, Phi Delta Kappa, Optemist Intl, NAACP, Grambling State Univ Alumni Assoc, Prince Hall Mason 33degree, Lewis R Price Consistory No 173, Jomadi Temple No 171, bd of dir Grambling Federal Credit Union; mem Grambling Chamber of Commerce. **Honors/Awds:** Teacher of the Year Hopewell High School 1965; Thunderbird Dist Awd Boy Scouts of Amer 1984; Romeo of the Year Sigma Gamma Rho Sor Intl 1986; Top Scouter of the Year Boy Scouts of Amer 1986.

LUE-HING, CECIL

Civil & environmental engineer. **Personal:** Born Nov 3, 1930, Jamaica, West Indies; married 1952; children: Cecil Barrington, Robert James. **Educ:** Marquette University, BS, civil engineering, 1961; Case Western Reserve University, MS, sanitary engineering, 1963; Wash Univ, St Louis, doctorate, environmental & sanitary engineering, 1966. **Career:** Univ of Wisconsin, College of Med, chief technician, 1950-55; Mt Sinai Hosp, school medical tech, WI, instructor of histol & cytol chem & lab supervisor, 1955-61; Huron Rd Hosp, WI, res assoc clin biochem, 1961-63; Washington Univ, res assoc, environ eng, 1963-65, assistant prof, 1965-66; Ryckman, Edgerley, Tomlinson & Associates, 1966-68, senior assoc, 1968-77; Metrop Sanit Dist, Chicago, dir of research & devt, 1977-. **Orgs:** AAAS; ASCE; Natl Acad of Scis Task Force; Water Pollution Control Fedn; American Water Works Assn; American Public Works Assn; Sigma Si. **Honors/Awds:** Washington University, Fellowship; pub 30 tech articles; published chapters in 6 books. **Business Addr:** Director, Research & Development, Water Reclamation Dist, 100 E Erie St, Chicago, IL 60611.

LUIS, WILLIAM

Educator. **Personal:** Born Jul 12, 1948, New York, NY; married Linda Garceau; children: Gabriel, Diego, Tammie, Stephanie. **Educ:** SUNY at Binghamton, BA 1971; Univ of WI Madison, MA 1973; Cornell Univ, MA 1979, PhD 1980. **Career:** Bd of Educ NYC, tchr 1971-72, tchr 1973-74; Handbook of Latin Amer Studies, contrib editor 1981-, consul 1981-; Latin Amer Literary Review, mem editorial bd 1985-; Natl Endowment for the Humanities, reader 1985; Natl Research Cncl/Ford Fndtn Fellowship Panel, 1986; Dartmouth Coll, asst prof of latin amer & caribbean, assoc prof 1985-88; visiting assoc, Washington Univ, 1988; assoc prof, dir, Latin Amer and Caribbean Area Studies Prog, 1988-91; Vanderbilt Univ, assoc prof, 1991-96, prof, 1996-. **Orgs:** Mem Modern Lang Assn; Assn of Caribbean Studies; Amer Assn of Tchrs of Spanish & Portuguese; mem adv bd Comm on Spec Educ Projects; mem Ad Hoc Comm to Study Hispanic Admissions & Recruitment; mem Minority Educ Council; mem Black Caucus; mem African Afro-Amer Studies Steering Comm; mem Literary Criticism Seminar; mem Latin Amer Literary Seminar; co-dir Latin Amer Literary Seminar; faculty advisor Phi Sigma Psi; mem African & Afro-Amer Studies Seminar; mem exec comm Assn of Caribbean Studies; mem Screening Comm for the Dir & Adjunct Curator of Film DC; mem Native Amer Studies Steering Comm; mem exec comm of the Faculty of DC; mem Agenda Subcomm of the Exec Comm of the Faculty of DC; mem Library Search Comm for the Humanities Bibliographer. **Honors/Awds:** Deans List SUNY at Binghamton 1968-71; Vilas Fellowship UW 1972; Grad Sch Fellowship UW 1973; Grad Sch Fellowship CU 1974-76; Berkowitz Travel & Rsch Fellowship CU 1974-76; Sigma Delta Pi 1975; Latin Amer Studies Prog Travel Grant CU 1977; Edwin Gould Awd Aspira 1974-76-78; Tchng Asst CU 1976-78; Summer Rsch Fellowships CU 1975-79; Special Grad School Fellowships CU 1975-79; Amer Coun of Learned Society's, Fellowship, 1994; Directory of Amer Scholars 1982; ed Voices from Under, Black Narrative inLatin Amer & the Caribbean 1984; Literary Bondage and Slavery in Cuban Narratives, 1990; Modern Latin Amer Fiction Writers, Vols 1&2, 1992, 1994; Dance Between Two Cultures: Latino-Caribbean Literature Written in the US, 1997; and numerous lectures, publications, articles. **Business Addr:** Professor of Latin American Literature, Vanderbilt University, Nashville, TN 37235.

LUKE, SHERRILL DAVID

Judge. **Personal:** Born Sep 19, 1928, Los Angeles, CA; son of Venye Luke Corporal and Mordecai Luke; divorced; children: David, Melana. **Educ:** Univ of CA at Los Angeles, BA 1950; Univ of CA at Berkeley, MA 1954; Golden Gate Univ, JD 1960. **Career:** District of Columbia Govt, dir prog dev 1967-69; Aetna Life & Casualty, dir urban affairs 1969-71; ConnVal Dev Corp, pres/dir 1971-73, Pacht Ross of Counsel, 1973-76; Jacobs Kane Luke, partner 1976-78; Los Angeles County, chief deputy assessor 1978-81; Los Angeles Municipal Court, judge 1981-88; superior court judge 1989-. **Orgs:** Cabinet sec CA Governor's Office 1964-65; consultant Ford Foundation 1966-67; pres LA City Planning Commn 1975-76; bd of trustees UCLA Foundation 1976-; adjunct prof Loyola Law Sch 1979-81; pres (first black) UCLA Alumni Assoc 1988-90; regent Univ of CA 1988-90; board of visitors, UCLA, 1991-94. **Honors/Awds:** Outstanding Senior Award UCLA Alumni Assn 1950; Outstanding Achievement Awd Kappa Alpha Psi, 1963-; Justice Pro Tem CA Court of Appeal 1985-86, 1995. **Military Serv:** USAF 1st lt 1954-56. **Business Addr:** Judge, The Superior Court, 111 North Hill Street, Los Angeles, CA 90012.

LUMBLY, CARL

Actor. **Career:** Appearance in the film "Buffalo Soldiers.". **Business Addr:** Actor, 1033 Miller Ave, Berkeley, CA 94708.

LUMPKIN, ADRIENNE KELLY (ADRIENNE LORRAINE KELLY)

Consultant, business owner. **Personal:** Born Apr 12, 1957, Bronx, NY; daughter of James and Lorraine Kelly; married Kelly M. Lumpkin, Aug 9, 1986; children: Amelia Janine, Samantha Moriah. **Educ:** Wesleyan University, BA, 1979; Harvard University, MBA, 1983. **Career:** IBM, systems engineer, 1979-81; Hewlett-Packard, marketing manager, 1983-92; Alternate Access, president, 1993-. **Orgs:** National Black MBA Association, Raleigh/Durham Chapter, vp, 1994-96, board of directors, 1997-99; National Assoc of Women Business Owners, 1995-; Council for Entrepreneurial Development, 1993-. **Honors/Awds:** National Black MBA Association, Raleigh/Durham Chapter, MBA of the Year Award, 1993, Oustanding MBA Award, 1997; Greater Raleigh Chamber of Commerce, Future 30 Award, 1997; Entrepreneurial Education Foundation, Super Gazelle, southeast region, 1997. **Business Addr:** Owner, Alternate Access, Inc., 4205 City of Oaks Wynd, Ste 350, Raleigh, NC 27612-5314, (919)781-8371.

LUNDY, GERALD

Public relations executive. **Career:** University of Michigan, public relations staff; Chrysler Corporation, public relations staff; Frank Seymour Associates, public relations staff; Anthony M Franco Inc, senior vice president; Casey Communications Management Inc, senior vice president, currently. **Orgs:** United Way of Southeastern Michigan, Community Relations Committee, chairman, 1991; Public Relations Society of America: Detroit chapter, past president, national, task force on minorities, head, East Central District, regional secretary; Children's Aid Society; Your Heritage House; Detroit Strategic Plan, Image Task Force; Project Pride Inc, board of directors. **Honors/Awds:** Recipient of numerous honors and awards for public relations programming. **Business Phone:** (313)423-4600.

LUNDY, HAROLD W.

Educational administrator. **Career:** Grambling State University, vice pres for administration and strategic planning, until 1991, president, 1991-. **Business Addr:** President, Grambling State University, PO Drawer 607, Grambling, LA 71245, (318)274-3811.

LUNDY, LARRY

Food industry executive. **Personal:** Born in New Orleans, LA; married; children: three. **Educ:** Dillard Univ, bachelor's degree, accounting; Pepperdine Univ, master's degree, bus adm. **Career:** Peat, Marc & Mitchell; Alexander Grant & Co; Pizza Hut, controller, beginning 1983, vp/controller, vp of restaurant development, beginning 1988; Lundy Enterprises, pres/CEO, currently. **Honors/Awds:** Gambit Newspaper, New Orleanian of the Year, 1993. **Special Achievements:** Controller of the largest minority owned fast food franchise in America; company is ranked #69 on the Black Enterprise list of Top 100 businesses, 1994. **Business Addr:** CEO, Lundy Enterprises, 10555 Lakeforest, Ste 1J, New Orleans, LA 70127, (504)241-6658.

LUPER, CLARA M.

Educator. **Personal:** Born May 3, 1923, Okfuskee Co; married Charles P Wilson; children: Calvin, Marilyn Luper Hildreth, Chelle Marie. **Educ:** Langston Univ Langston, OK, BA 1944; OK Univ Norman, MA 1951. **Career:** Talent USA, pres dir 1974-80; consult various coll u 1959-80; OK City Bd of Edn, tchr history 1959-79; Choctaw Bd of Edn, tchr history 1961-78; Radio, commentator Clara Luper Radio Show 1960-93; Soul Bazaar, founder 1970-93; Miss Black Oklahoma, state promoter 1970-93; Amigos Club Grayhoff & Woods Neighborhood Club, co-founded 1949-. **Orgs:** Youth adv NAACP 1957-80; past basileus Zeta Phi Beta Sor Chi Zeta Chap 1962-; pres Freedom Center Inc 1968-93. **Honors/Awds:** Alumni Award Langston Univ 1969; Woman of Year Zeta Phi Beta Chi Zeta Chap 1970; nominee Nat Award Delta Sigma Sor 1975; Serv to Mankind Award Sigma Gamma Rho 1980; winner of 430 awards; author "Behold the Walls"; writer/director/producer "Brother President" a movie about Rev Martin Luther King Jr; Builder of Black History Wall, Black History Monument & Black History Garden.

LUSTER, JORY

Hair care products company executive. **Career:** Luster Products Co., president, currently. **Special Achievements:** Co. is ranked #20 on Black Enterprise magazine's list of top 100 industrial/service companies, 1992. **Business Addr:** President, Luster Products Co, 1631 S Michigan Ave, Chicago, IL 60616, (312)431-1150.

LUTCHER, NELLIE

Composer, arranger, recording artist. **Personal:** Born Oct 15, 1915, Lake Charles, LA; daughter of Susie Garrett and Isaac Lutcher; married Leonel Lewis, 1936 (divorced); children: Talmadge Lewis. **Career:** Composer, arranger, and recording artist; work includes He A Real Gone Guy, Hurry Down, and Fine

Browny Frame; appeared on the Ed Sullivan Show; Town Hall, Paramount Theater, Apollo Theater, Barney Josephson's Cafe Society. **Orgs:** Mem local 67 Musicians Union; ASCAP, AFTRA, AGAC; NAACP. **Honors/Awds:** Subject of This Is Your Life with Ralph Edwards, 1951; Honoree, Tiffany Guild of Los Angeles for work with handicapped children; Honoree, Los Angeles Bench and Bar Affiliates.

LUTEN, THOMAS DEE
HR/business consultant. **Personal:** Born Mar 12, 1950, Youngstown, OH; son of Christine Motley Luten and Ernest D Luten (deceased); married Nedra Farrar Luten, Jun 18, 1983; children: Thomas David, Christian Douglas. **Educ:** Kenyon College, Gambier, OH, 1968-69; Ohio State Univ, Columbus, OH, BS, MA, 1969-74; Michigan State Univ, East Lansing, MI, 1976-82; Univ of North Carolina, Chapel Hill, NC, 1983-84. **Career:** Michigan Dept of Commerce, admin analyst, 1977-78; Michigan Dept of Mental Health, personnel specialist, 1978-80; Univ of North Carolina, assoc dir, univ career planning and placement, 1980-83; GTE of the South, organizational effectiveness spec, 1984; North Carolina Central Univ, dir, career counseling, placement & cooperative educ, 1984-88; Michigan State Univ, dir, career devt & placement, 1988-1991; self-employed, education and human resource consultant, 1991-93, 1995-; Wayne County Community College, vp for student development, 1993-95. **Orgs:** Member, AACD, ACPA, 1972-81, 1984-92; member, SCPA, 1984-91; member, MCPA, 1988-91; member, ASCUS, 1985-86, 1988-91; member, IMPA, 1978-81, 1985-88; Natl Council of Student Dev, 1993-; Southeastern Assn of Student Personnel Admin, 1993-96. **Honors/Awds:** Presentations: Building a Global Workforce for a Competitive Edge, fall conference, Midwest College Placement Association, 1990; The Employment Outlook for Physical Science Professionals in the 1990's, American Institute of Physics, 1990; Making a College Relations Program Work, EDS Corporation, 1990; numerous others, articles published in Black Enterprise, 1985, 1991. **Home Addr:** 4328 Dutch Garden Ct, Raleigh, NC 27613, (919)782-7255.

LUTHER, LUCIUS CALVIN
Cleric. **Personal:** Born Feb 19, 1929, Mound Bayou, MS; divorced; children: Shirl Taylor, Elaine Taylor, Carol K, Lucius C Jr, Jacqueline F, Rev Byron E. **Educ:** Boliver County Training Sch, JL Campbell Sch of Religion, Religious Law; Brewster Sch of Theology, TN Reg Bapt Sch of Rel, B Theol, LLD, M Theol. **Career:** Brewster's School of Theol, teacher, assoc dean; Natl Bapt Convention USA Inc Dept of Christian Educ, instr of stewardship; EC Morris Inst of AR Bapt Coll, instr of christian educ; Thomas Chapel MB Church, pastor 1963-65; New Wrights Chapel MB Church, pastor 1963-65; Mt Zion MB Church, pastor 1965-68; Greater First Baptist MB Church, pastor 1967-68; First Baptist Church, pastor 1968-87; First Fellowship Baptist Church, pastor, currently. **Orgs:** V chmn Stewardship Bd 1976-, Natl Bapt Conv USA Inc; bd of dirs Chicago Baptist Inst; moderator New Fellowship Baptist Dist Assoc; mem of bd of evangelism Natl Bapt Convention USA Inc; vice pres United Baptist State Convention IL; vchmn of the bd EC Morris Inst at AR Baptist Coll Little Rock; chmn of loan dept, chmn of fed housing dept Natl Bapt Convention USA Inc; bd mem Natl Bapt Convention USA Inc. **Honors/Awds:** Mayor's Key to the City for Soul Saving Citywide Revival Tacoma WA; Mayor's Key to the City Gary IN, Baton Rouge LA; Hon Dist Atty of Baton Rouge LA; Hon Council Mem of Baton Rouge, Hon Mayor of Baton Rouge; Hon Degrees Brewster's School of Theology DD, JL Campbell School of Religion DD, TN Regular Baptist School of Religion DL. **Military Serv:** AUS 1954-56. **Home Addr:** 1819 Elizabeth Ave, North Chicago, IL 60064-2034. **Business Addr:** Pastor, First Fellowship Baptist Church, 2302 MLK Jr Dr, North Chicago, IL 60064.

LYDA, WESLEY JOHN
Educator. **Personal:** Born Apr 10, 1914, Terre Haute, IN; married Minnie V Davis; children: Meredith, Kimberly. **Educ:** Depauw Univ Greencastle, IN, AB 1935; INSTATE Univ Terre Haute, AM 1936; IN Univ Bloomington, PhD. **Career:** Center for Afro-Am Studies & IN State Univ, dir & prof of educ 1968-; Central State Univ OH, dean graduate studies acting pres 1966-68; Ft Valley State Coll GA, dean grad div prof of educ 1957-66; Atlanta Univ GA, dean grad sch dir summer school 1950-57; TX State Univ, dean coll of arts & sci, prof of educ & math 1948-50; Morgan State Coll MD, head dept of educ dir curriculum study 1945-48; Phelps Stokes Found NYC, natl consult on curriculum & evaluation 1952-57; Cleveland Job Corps Center for Women, educ dir 1966; EOA Bd of Dir, mayor's rep 1980-. **Orgs:** Mem Omega Psi Phi Social Frat; mem Kiwanis Club Terre Haute 1974-; pres Terre Haute Br of the NAACP 1979-. **Honors/Awds:** Recipient Outstanding Educator of Am Award 1972-73; recipient Distinguished Alumni Award Depauw Univ 1973; recip IN Black Expo Dist Serv Award & Plaque in Educ 1978; Scholastic Hon Societys Kappa Delta Pi Phi Delta Kappa Pi Mu Epsilon. **Business Addr:** Stalker Hall, Room 203, Terre Haute, IN 47809.

LYGHT, TODD WILLIAM
Professional football player. **Personal:** Born Feb 9, 1969. **Educ:** University of Notre Dame. **Career:** Los Angeles Rams, defensive back, 1991-94; St Louis Rams, 1995-. **Business Addr:** Professional Football Player, St Louis Rams, One Rams Way, St Louis, MO 63045, (314)982-7267.

LYLE, FREDDRENNA M.
Attorney. **Personal:** Born Jun 1, 1951, Chicago, IL; daughter of Delores Murphy Harris and Fred Lyle. **Educ:** Univ of Illinois-Chicago, BA, 1973; The John Marshall Law School, Chicago, IL, JD, 1980. **Career:** Cornelius E Toole & Assocs, Chicago, IL, associate, 1980-83; F Lyle & Assocs, Chicago, IL, partner, 1983-85; Smith & Lyle, Chicago, IL, partner, 1985-. **Orgs:** Pres, Cook County Bar Assn, 1980-; bd mem, Natl Bar Assn, 1981-; bd mem, Constitutional Rights Foundation, 1985-; mem, Natl Black Child Devt Inst, 1989-. **Honors/Awds:** William Ming Award, Cook County Bar Assn, 1987.

LYLE, KEITH ALLEN
Professional football player. **Personal:** Born Apr 17, 1972, Washington, DC. **Educ:** Univ of Virginia, attended. **Career:** St Louis Rams, defensive back, 1995-. **Business Addr:** Professional Football Player, St Louis Rams, One Rams Way, St Louis, MO 63045, (314)982-7267.

LYLE, PERCY H., JR.
Sales representative. **Personal:** Born Oct 15, 1947, Detroit; married Glenda Wilhelma (divorced); children: Kipp E, Jennifer B, Anthony S. **Educ:** Communications Univ Colo, BA 1970; Webster Univ, MA 1972; Univ of Denver, Phd, 1997. **Career:** Intl Business Machines, systems marketing rep; Community Coll of Aurora, instructor, dir for diversity, advisor to Black Student Allicance; Red Rocks Community Coll, instructor; Community Coll of Denver, instructor; Radio Talk Show Host. **Orgs:** Mem Park Hill Businessmens Assn; Optimist Club; Blessed Sacrament Ch; Com to Elect George Brown for Lt Gov; exec bd Malcolm X Mental Health Ctr; mem YMCA; Park Hill Improvement Assn. **Business Addr:** 2490 W 26 Ave, Denver, CO 80217.

LYLE, ROBERTA BRANCHE BLACKE
Educator (retired). **Personal:** Born Jul 20, 1929, Glasgow, VA; widowed; children: Valerie, Robert Jr, Carl. **Educ:** VA State Coll, BS 1966; Univ of VA, MEd 1972. **Career:** Town of Glasgow, councilperson 1972-75, 1972-; Rockbridge Cty School Bd, teacher. **Orgs:** Past mem, bd of dir Stonewall Jackson Hosp 1972-78; scholarship comm Burlington Indust Glasgow 1976-77; Grand Ass matron bd Grand Chap OES VA 1976; mem REA, VEA, NEA 1958, Order of Eastern Star 1952, secretary NAACP, PTA, Ann Ellen Early #209 OEA; usher bd, sr choir, past teacher Sunday School, Union Bapt Church; past sec Mt Olivet Cemetary Comm; secretary, Concerned Citizens Inc, Glasgow. **Honors/Awds:** Teacher of the Year Awd 1975.

LYLE, RON
Athlete. **Personal:** Born 1943, Denver, CO. **Career:** Boxer. **Orgs:** Mem US Boxing Team. **Honors/Awds:** 7 1/2 yrs CO prison & became outsdng athlete; Nat AAU Title; N Am Title Intl Boxing League. **Home Addr:** c/o Rev William H Lyle, 1590 Syracuse, Denver, CO 80220.

LYLES, DEWAYNE
Educational administration. **Personal:** Born Mar 8, 1947, Clanton, AL; married Michelle Billups; children: Raquel Lynn, Ryan Milton, Roderic. **Educ:** Miles Coll, Sociology & Ed 1969; Univ of AL Birmingham, Counseling & Guidance 1975; Marshall Univ, Mgmt 1981. **Career:** Miles Coll Special Prog, counselor 1971-75, instr 1975; Emergency School Aide Act Prog Miles Coll, asst dir 1975-76; Miles Coll, dir admissions 1976-77; Marshall Univ, dir minority student affairs. **Orgs:** Test suprv 1973-75, principal suprv 1975-76, Natl Assessment of Students; consult WV School of Osteopathic Med 1983; prog comm Fairfield West Comm Ctr Jobs 1983-84; mem Progressive Black Men's Assoc 1983-; treas Omega Psi Phi; vice pres Men's Assoc Church. **Honors/Awds:** Volunteer Serv Awd Joint Action in Community Serv 1973; Cert of Appreciation for Outstanding & Dedicated Serv Miles Coll Student Govt Assoc 1974-77; 1st Place Winner, 1st Awd Miles Coll Alumni Tennis Tournament 1977; Cert of Apprec OIC Help Our Youth Week Tri-State Oppty Indust Ctr 1979; Cert of Apprec for Outstanding Serv Student Activities; 1st Place Publ Spec Student Svcs. **Military Serv:** AUS E-4 1969-71; Commendation Medal w/2 OLC 1970-71. **Business Addr:** Asst Dean for Educ Services, Dentson University, Granville, OH 43023.

LYLES, LESTER EVERETT
Professional football player. **Personal:** Born Dec 27, 1962, Washington, DC. **Educ:** Univ of Virginia, attended. **Career:** New York Jets, 1985-87; Phoenix Cardinals, 1988; San Diego Chargers, safety, 1989-. **Business Addr:** Professional Football Player, San Diego Chargers, Jack Murphy Stadium, 9449 Friars Rd, San Diego, CA 92108.

LYLES, MADELINE LOLITA
Association executive. **Personal:** Born Sep 27, 1953, New York, NY; daughter of Mable Pendergrass Lyles and Gilbert H Lyles. **Educ:** Morris Brown College, BA 1971-75; Howard Univ, Master of Social Work 1979-81. **Career:** Kennedy Institute, program coordinator 1981-83; PSI Associates, program dir 1983; Roy Littlejohn Associates, consultant 1979-; Urban Shelters & Health Care Systems, Inc, dir of admin 1983-89, vice pres Residential Treatment Services, 1989-; president/ceo Health Resources Development Company, currently. **Orgs:** Consultant Roy Littlejohn Associates 1979-; member Natl Assoc of Black Socialworkers 1980-; member Group Health Assoc Advisory Council 1984-; volunteer Center for Youth Services; member NAACP; consultant, Multi-Therapeutic Services, 1987-; practicum instructor, Howard Univ School of Social Work, 1988-; bd sec, DC Institute of Mental Health, 1988-. **Honors/Awds:** Merit Scholar; Natl Dean's List 1971-81; Scholarship Award Howard University School of Social Work 1980; volunteer appreciation Center for Youth Services 1984.

LYLES, MARIE CLARK
Educator, city official. **Personal:** Born Oct 12, 1952, Sledge, MS; daughter of Mary McCoy Clark and Dave Clark; married Eugene D Lyles, Oct 1977; children: Jamaal Ventral Lyles, Justin Eugene Lyles, Jessica Marie Lyles. **Educ:** Coahoma Jr Coll, AA, 1972; MS Valley St Univ, BS, 1974. **Career:** Quitman Caenties School, Marks, MS, teacher, 1970-89; Town of Crenshaw, Crenshaw, MS, mayor 1987-. **Orgs:** Natl Teacher Org, 1970-89; Crenshaw Community Builders, treasurer, 1985; Troop Leader, Brownie Troop (Girl Scouts,) 1986; vice pres, Ebonette, 1988. **Honors/Awds:** Outstanding Religion Leader, Quitman County, 1978; Outstanding Young Women, 1988.

LYLES, WILLIAM K.
Psychologist, educational administrator. **Personal:** Born in Winston-Salem, NC; children: Don L. **Educ:** Univ of NC, BS 1939; New York Univ, MS 1947, PhD 1958. **Career:** Queens Coll, assoc dean of students 1972-73; West Harlem-Inwood Mental Health Ctr, exec dir 1973-74; Childrens Aid Soc, coord of mental health 1974-79; Bronx-Lebanon Hosp, assoc chief psychologist 1978-83; Harlem-Dowling Childrens Services, coord mental health servs 1984-. **Orgs:** Pres Richmond Co Psychological Assoc 1974; mem NY Urban League Adv Bd 1980-83; pres Natl Assoc of Black Psychol 1983; pres NY Assoc of Black Psychol 1983; mem Natl Black Leadership Round Table 1983; mem Natl Task Force on Black Race Homicide 1984. **Honors/Awds:** President's Awd Natl Assoc of Black Psychol 1984; President's Awd NY Assoc of Black Psychol 1984. **Business Addr:** Coordinator, Mental Health Services, PO Box 257, Staten Island, NY 10301.

LYMAN, WEBSTER S.
Attorney. **Personal:** Born Sep 24, 1922, Columbus, OH; son of Madie A Lyman and Webster S Lyman Sr; married Marion E Newman; children: Bonita L Logan, Alisa K. **Educ:** OH State Univ, BS 1944, LLB 1949, JD 1949. **Career:** OH Civil Rights Comm, hearing examiner 1970-78; Common Pleas Ct, chmn/med arbitration 1982-; private practice attorney 1950-. **Orgs:** Parliamentarian OH Assn of Black Attorneys 1975; pres Lawyers Christian Fellowship 1981; pres Robert B Elliott Law Club 1955-56; nominating comm Natl BarAssn 1977-78; commander Amer Legion 690 before 1956; legal advisor Franklin Lodge of Elks 203; legal advisor Past Exalted Rulers Council Elks 1978-; pres Inner City Lions Club 1984-85; treas Columbus Urban League before 1960; pres Isabelle Ridgway Home for Aged before 1970; vice pres Project Linden 1980; pres Mu Iota Chapter Omega Psi Phi Frat 1954-55; charter mem Good Shepherd Baptist Church 1976; vice pres Franklin County Forum 1985-87; past pres Buckeye Bridge Club 1982-84; past pres Second Community Bowling League 1981-82. **Honors/Awds:** 40 Year Pin Omega Psi Phi Frat Inc 1982; Family Award Second Baptist Ch before 1970; Charter Mem OH Assn of Black Attorneys 1975; Charter Mem Lawyers Christian Fellowship 1966; Humanitarian Award Gamma Phi Delta Sorority Inc 1984. **Military Serv:** AUS S/Sgt 1944-46. **Business Addr:** Attorney, 1313 E Broad St, Ste 17, 1313 E Broad St, Columbus, OH 43205-3510.

LYNCH, ERIC
Professional football player. **Personal:** Born May 16, 1970, Woodhaven, MI. **Educ:** Grand Valley State Univ. **Career:** Detroit Lions, 1992-. **Business Addr:** Professional Football Player, Detroit Lions, 1200 Featherstone Rd, Pontiac, MI 48342, (313)335-4131.

LYNCH, GEORGE DEWITT, III
Professional basketball player. **Personal:** Born Sep 3, 1970, Roanoke, VA. **Educ:** University of North Carolina. **Career:** Los Angeles Lakers, forward, 1993-96; Vancouver Grizzlies, 1996-. **Special Achievements:** NBA Draft, First round pick, #12, 1993. **Business Addr:** Professional Basketball Player, Vancouver Grizzlies, 788 Beatty St, Ste 311, Vancouver, BC, Canada V6B 2M1, (604)688-5867.

LYNCH, HOLLIS R.
Educator. **Personal:** Born Apr 21, 1935, Port-of-Spain, Trinidad and Tobago; divorced; children: Shola Ayn, Nnenna Jean, Ashale Herman, John Benjamin. **Educ:** British Columbia, BA 1960; Univ of London, PhD 1964. **Career:** Univ of IFE Nigeria, lecturer 1964-66; Roosevelt Univ Chicago, assoc prof 1966-68; State Univ of NY at Buffalo, assoc prof 1968-69; Columbia Univ, prof 1969-; Inst of African Studies Columbia Univ, dir 1971-74, 1985-90. **Orgs:** Fmem African Studies Assn; Assn for Study of Afro-Am Life & History; Am Historical Assn. **Hon-**

ors/Awds: Recipient Commonwealth Fellow London Univ 1961-64; Hoover Nat Fellow Stanford Univ 1973-74; fellow Woodrow Wilson Intl Ctr for Scholars 1976; ACLS (Am Council of Learned Soc) Fellowship 1978-79; author Edward Wilmot Blyden Pan Negro Patriot 1967 & The Black Urban Condition 1973; Black Africa 1973; ''Black Am Radicals & Liberaton of Africa'' 1978; ''Black Spokesman'' 1970; ''Selected Letters of Edward W Blyden'' (with a foreword by Pres Leopold Sedar Senghor) 1978. **Special Achievements:** Apartheid in Historical Prespective: A Case For Divestment, Columbia College Today, 1985; The Foundation of American-Nigerian Ties: Nigerian Students in the United States, 1939-48, Black Ivory, The Pan-African Magazine, 1989. **Business Addr:** Inst of African Studies, Columbia University, New York, NY 10027.

LYNCH, LEON
Union executive. **Personal:** Born Jun 4, 1935, Edwards, MS; children: Tina, Sheila, Tammy, Maxine. **Educ:** IN Univ, attended; Purdue Univ, attended; Roosevelt Univ Chgo, BS 1967. **Career:** Youngstown Sheet & Tube Co, loader 1956; United Steelworkers of Amer, staff rep, 1968; United Steelworkers of Amer, intl rep, 1973, intl vice pres human affairs 1976-. **Orgs:** Trustee Natl Comm for Coop Ed; chair, USWA Intl Civil Rights Comm; chair, USWA, Constitution Comm; USWA, Political Action Comm, chair; AFL-CIO Civil Rights, Public Employee, & Housing Coms; chmn, Natl A Philip Randolph Inst, Natl Steelworkers Oldtimers Found, pres, Workers Defense League; former, Natl Comm Against Discrimination in Housing; review comm City of Pgh's Job Training Partnership Act; Labor Partic Com of SW United Way; life mem NAACP 1981; Dem Natl Comm; Dem Party Commiss on Pres Nominations; mem natl exec comm Am for Dem Action, NBCSL Labor Roundtable; President's Adv Council on Unempl Comp. **Honors/Awds:** 1st A Philip Randolph Achievement Awd A Philip Randolph Inst 1977; A Philip Randolph Labor Awd Negro Trade Union Leadership Council 1977; Chicago Conf for Brotherhood Awd 1979; Apprec Awds APRI Chattanooga Chapt, NAACP Perth Amboy Br 1980; Declaration as Hon Mem in Good Standing of Local Union 5298 Dist 9; Local Union 1011 Awd of Gratitude & APRI Calumet Chap Grateful Recog Awd 1981; APRI Chicago Chap Henry Harrison Awd, Cert of Apprec from the VocationalRehab Ctr, NAACP IN State Awd for Outstanding Contribs to the Labor Movement 1982; ADA 35th Annual Roosevelt Day Dinner Awd & Dist 29 Cert of Apprec Awd for Outstanding & Dedicated Serv in Saving Jobs at McLouth Steel 1983; APRI Youngstown Chap Awd for Dedicated Serv to Mankind Careers Inc;Humanitarian Awd Local Union 1011 Awd in Recogr Outstanding Serv & Achievements in USWA. **Military Serv:** US Army, sgt, 1 yr. **Business Addr:** International Vice President, United Steelworkers of America, 5 Gateway Center, Pittsburgh, PA 15222.

LYNCH, LILLIE RIDDICK
Educator (retired). **Personal:** Born in Gatesville, NC; daughter of Rosa Riddick and Lee Riddick; divorced. **Educ:** Hampton Inst VA, BS 1941; Univ of MI Ann Arbor, MPH 1949; NY Univ, PhD 1971. **Career:** NC Public Schools, tchr of sci & social studies 1944-46; VA Public Schools, tchr of elem grades 1947, tchr biology & chem 1947-48; Portsmouth VA Public Schs, tchng high sch & elem sch levels 1951-57; New York City Public Schs, health educ & testing 1957-64 1964-67; Jersey City State Coll, asst prof of health educ 1964-69, assoc prof & coord of comm health educ 1969-76; Univ of MA, assoc prof of pub health 1972-73; Jersey City State Coll, prof health scis 1976-87; North Carolina Central University, adjunct prof, 1989-; consultant, health education and health program planning. **Orgs:** Fellow Amer Sch Health Assn; Amer Alliance for Health Physical Educ & Recreation; Royal Soc of Health London; Amer Fed of Tchrs AFL-CIO 1974-76; Amer Public Health Assn; Amer Assn of Univ Profs; Natl Soc of Public Health Educators; Tri State Soc of Public Health Educators; mem Constitution & Bylaws Comm Amer Sch Health Assn 1968-72; dept rep Amer Fed of Tchrs AFL-CIO 1974-78; mem SOPHE Ad Hoc Comm. **Honors/Awds:** Alpha Kappa Alpha; Kappa Delta Pi Beta Pi Chapt; Pi Lambda Theta Rho Chap; Alpha Kappa Delta Mu Chap NY Univ Founder's Day Awd 1972; Zonta Club; Intl Inst of Jersey City & Bayonne NJ; Natl Found for Infantile Paralysis for study in Health Educ at Univ of MI Fellowship 1948-49; Fellowship Found Field Study Public Health Educ in MI Kellogg Found; auth of many books & articles. **Home Addr:** 1725 Alfred St, Durham, NC 27713.

LYNCH, LORENZO
Professional football player. **Personal:** Born Apr 6, 1963, Oakland, CA. **Educ:** Sacramento State Univ. **Career:** Chicago Bears, defensive back, 1987-89; Arizona Cardinals, 1990-95; Oakland Raiders, 1996-. **Business Addr:** Professional Football Player, Oakland Raiders, 1220 Harbor Bay Pkwy, Alameda, CA 94502, (510)615-1875.

LYNCH, LORENZO A., SR.
Clergyman. **Personal:** Born in Oak City, NC; married Lorine Harris; children: Lorenzo A Jr, Loretta E, Leonzo D. **Educ:** Shaw University, BA 1955, Divinity School, BD, 1957; Boston U, grad student 1957-58, 1967-68; Univ NC Chapel Hill, 1957; Duke Univ Divinity School, 1962-65; Southeastern Theol Sem, 1958-59. **Career:** White Rock Bapt Church Durham, pastor, 1965-; Davis Chapel Washington; Endstreet Bapt Ch, Scotland Neck; Mt Zion, Arapahoe; St Delight, Nashville; Reid's Chapel, Fountain; Mt Olive, Ayden; Bazzel Creek, Fuquay Springs; Providence Bapt Ch, Greensboro, former pastor; Lynch Chapel, Oak City; Jones Chapel, Palmyra; Peoples Bapt Ch, Boston, past assistant pastor; Religious Educ Program, sponsored by Boston Council of Week-day Religous Edn, former tchr; Baptist Student Union, A&T College, former advisor; Palmer Meml Inst, Sedalia, preacher; former counselor. **Orgs:** President Durham Minister's Assn 1967-68; Durham's Clergy Hosp Chaplain's Assn; Greensboro Br NAACP; bd dir United So A&T College; bd dir Cumberland Ct Inc; bd dir Edgemont Comm Center 1968-71; adv bd Durham Co Mental Health Center 1968-74; bd dir Triangle Kidney Found 1975-; vis instr Duke Divinity Sch; Gen Bapt Conv of NC Inc; critic Interdenominational Minister's Alliance 1975; exec bd Durham NAACP; chmn Com on Econ Devel; Durham's Com on Affairs of Black People; unsuccessful candidate Durham's Mayor 1973. **Honors/Awds:** Shaw Divinity School, Honorary DD, 1982. **Business Addr:** Pastor, White Rock Baptist Church, 3400 Fayetteville St, Durham, NC 27707.

LYNCH, M. ELIZABETH
Equipment and machinery company executive. **Personal:** Born Jan 4, 1947, Dayton, OH; daughter of Elizabeth M Wood Lynch and Ulice C Lynch. **Educ:** Sinclair Community College, Dayton, OH, AS, 1977; University of Dayton, Dayton, OH, BS, 1979; Amos Tuck School of Business, Dartmouth College, Hanover, NH, MBA, 1982. **Career:** Delco Products Div, GMC, Dayton, OH, buyer, 1974-82; FMC Corp, Chicago, IL, senior business planner, 1982-83; FMC Corp, Minneapolis, MN, materials manager, 1983-85; Honeywell Inc, Minneapolis, MN, manager, strategic planning; 1985-87, program manager, 1987-88, manager, strategic planning, 1988-90; Hughes Aircraft Co, Tuscon, AZ, director business ops, 1990-92; Harnishfeger Corp, director of mining materials, 1992-. **Orgs:** Member, NAACP, 1990; president, Hughes Tucson-Black Professional Network, 1989-90; president, Arizona Women in Defense, 1989-90; board member, Harriet Tubman Battered Women's Shelter, 1988; board member, Tucson Community Food Bank, 1990-92; board member, Sahuaro Girl Scouts, 1990-92; YWCA, 1991-92; president/owner, JPT Associates (consulting firm), 1990-; United Way of Greater Tuscon, 1990-91. **Honors/Awds:** Salute to African-American Females, Dollars & Sense Magazine, 1989; Speaking of People, Ebony Magazine, 1990; 1991 Alumni of the Year, Black Board of Directors Project. **Business Addr:** Director, Mining Materials, Harnishfeger Corp, 4400 West National Ave, PO Box 310, Milwaukee, WI 53201.

LYNCH, ROBERT D.
Educator. **Personal:** Born Sep 4, 1933, Greensburg, PA; son of Martha Dickson Lynch and Robert E Lynch; married Dolores Cruse Lynch, Apr 16, 1960. **Educ:** Indiana Univ of Pennsylvania, BS, 1956, MEd, 1965; Duquesne Univ, MME, 1966; Pennsylvania State Univ, DEd candidate. **Career:** Hempfield Area Sch Sys, dept head 1958-65; Duquesne Sch of Music, instr 1965-66; PA State Univ, grad asst to dept chmn 1966-67; Fine Arts Component, asst proj dir coord; PA Reg J Title III, 1967-69; Upward Bound, proj dir; Lock Haven Univ, assoc prof 1969-71, dir supr coord 1971-, dir of development & special programs 1974-83, asst to vice pres for admin & development, affirmative action officer 1983-; Lock Haven University, Lock Haven, PA, asst to the pres for administration, 1989-. **Orgs:** Life mem, Music Educ Natl Conf; mem, PA Music Educ Assn; Natl Sch Orchestra Assn; PA Black Higher Educ Conf; Assn for Inst Rsch; Natl Council Univ Rsch Admin; Amer Assn Univ Admin; Amer Coll Pub Relations Assn; PA Assn Trio Program Admin; Phi Beta Mu; Phi Delta Kappa; Phi Mu Alpha; gov, Rotary Intl Dist 737, 1985-86; pres, PA Black Conf on Higher Educ, 1984-90; pres, Phi Beta Mu, 1980-82; pres, Phi Delta Kappa, 1973-81; conductor Lock Haven Univ Symphony Orchestra and Chorus, pres 1983-94, board of directors 1984-95, Tourist Promotion Agency. **Honors/Awds:** Lock Haven Citizen of the Year; TV Station WFBG ''People Are Great Awd'' Rotary Intl Paul Harris Fellow; Mary Davis Baltimore Awd by PA BCOHE for State & Community Svc; Hon Lt Colonel Aide-De-Camp to the Gov State of AL; Distinguished Educator, Phi Delta Kappa, Lock Haven, 1990; Frank D O'Reilly Jr, Memorial Award, Bcohe Student Leadership Dev Inst, (now The Robert Lunch SLDI). **Military Serv:** US Army, 1956-62. **Home Addr:** RR 4, Box 848, Cedar Heights, Mill Hall, PA 17751-9737, (717)726-6270. **Business Addr:** Asst to Pres for Admin/ Dir of Social Equity, Lock Haven University of Pennsylvania, N Fairview St, 301 Sullivan Hall, Lock Haven, PA 17745, (717)893-2455.

LYNCH, RUFUS SYLVESTER
Forensic social worker. **Personal:** Born Nov 30, 1946, Baltimore, MD; son of Rufus and Marie Lynch (biological parents) and Ned and Zelma Harvey (foster parents); married VeRita Amelia Barnette; children: Marie Rachel, Kirkland Alexander. **Educ:** Morgan State Univ, BA, sociology, 1968; Univ of Pittsburgh School of Social Work, MSW, 1970; Univ of PA School of Social Work, advanced certificate, social work administration, 1971, DSW, social work administration and policy, 1973; National Gerontological Society, research fellow, 1978; National Center for State Courts, Institute for Court Management, graduate fellow, 1990. **Career:** Westinghouse Defense & Space Ctr, urban soc scientist 1967-68; Catholic Diocese of Pittsburgh, prog dir & consult 1969; Ford Motor Co, staff coord 1969; Philadelphia Health Mgmt Corp, res dev & outreach specialist 1973-74; Comm Coll of Phila, dir serv for aging 1975-76; Office of Lt Gov of PA, sr human svcs policy adviser 1975-76; Office of Majority Leader PA H of R, ex asst chief of staff 1976-77; Office of Speaker of PA H of R, ex asst chief of staff 1977-78; MLB Inc, pres 1978-84; Temple Univ, sen exec mgmt cons, spec asst to exec vp for univ admin 1984-85; Admin Off of Supreme Court of PA, asst court admin 1986-87, director of court management, 1987-94; University of Pennsylvania School of Social Work, adjunct faculty; Cheyney Univ of Pennsylvania, asst prof, 1994-; Center for Studying Social Welfare & Community Development, Philadelphia Pennsylvania, pres, 1994-; Lincoln Univ Multidisciplinary Centr on Aging, assoc prof; Chestnut Hill Coll, adj criminal justice faculty; Ctr for Studying Social Welfare and Comm Devel, pres, 1994-. **Orgs:** Bd of dir, Blacks Educating Blacks about Sexual Health Issues, 1996-; bd of dir, West Philadelphia YMCA and Family Ctr, 1996-; pres, Fresh Start Comm Devel Corp, 1995-; project dir, Philadelphia Juvenile Ctr, Inc, 1995-; pres, PA Chap Natl Assn of Social Workers (NASW), 1994-98; mem, Adjudication Program Issues Advisory Grp, 1993-95; PA Rep Natl Delegate Assembly, 1992-95; mem, Continuing Ed Comm, PA Chap NASW, 1992-94; Natl Comm on Inquiry, NASW; 1991-94; Black Caucus/African-American Network, NASW, convenor, 1990; National Center for Social Policy and Practice, founding mem, 1986; Bicentennial Commission on the US Const 1985; congressional delegate, White House Conf on Aging, 1981; Center for Studying Social Welfare and Community Devel, founder, chairman of the board, 1979; The Justice System Journal, editorial bd; Natl Assn of Court Management; American Bar Assn, Judicial Administration Division; Association of Black Social Workers; Amer Bar Assn, Criminal Justice Div; Council on Social Work Educ, mem; Natl Ctr for State Courts, mem. **Honors/Awds:** Social Worker of the Year NASW PA 1978; Cert of Appreciation City of Philadelphia Personnel Dept 1980; Alumni of Year Awd Univ of Pittsburgh School of Soc Work 1981; PA Assn of Special Courts Special Award, 1988; President's Friendship Award, PA State Constable's Assn, 1988; Distinguished Service Award, Natl Constable's Assn, 1989; Distinguished Minority Scholars in Residents Prog, Pennsylvania State University, 1991; Pennsylvania State Constables Assn, Man of the Year Award, 1991; Natl Assn for Court Mgmt, President's Award, 1991. **Special Achievements:** 1st African American elected President of Pennsylvania Chapter of National Assoc of Social Workers, 1995; federal advisory appt as technical consultant for the Maternal and Child Health Bureau, US Office of Adolscent Health; author, numerous papers and presentations; serves as guest lecturer; ''Social Workers and the Judicial System: Looking for a Better Fit,'' with Edward Allan Brawley, DSW, Journal of Teaching in Social Work, Vol 10, No 1/2, 1994; ''Institutionalizing The Roles of Court Social Workers,'' with Jacquelyn Mitchell, Journal of Law & Social Work, Oct, 1992; ''An Analysis of the Reorganization & Automation of the Philadelphia Traffic Court by PA's AOPC,'' Institute for Court Management, Court Exec Development Prog, May 14, 1990 (unpublished). **Military Serv:** US Army. **Home Addr:** 1013 S St Bernard Pl, Philadelphia, PA 19143-3312.

LYNN, ANTHONY RAY
Professional football player. **Personal:** Born Dec 21, 1968, McKinney, TX; married Cynda; children: D'Anton, Danielle. **Educ:** Texas Tech. **Career:** Denver Broncos, running back, 1993, 1997-; San Francisco 49ers, 1995-96. **Business Addr:** Professional Football Player, Denver Broncos, 13655 Broncos Pkwy, Englewood, CO 80112, (303)649-9000.

LYNN, JAMES ELVIS
Government official. **Personal:** Born Feb 16, 1920, Highbank, TX; married Zona Mae Hunnicutt; children: Wanda E, James E. **Educ:** Paul Quinn Coll Waco, TX, BS 1950; Prairie View Coll Prairie View, TX, MS 1957. **Career:** Falls Co Marlin, TX, commr pct 2 1978-88; Hubbard Sch Hubbard, TX, counselor 1976-; Marlin Pub Sch Dist, principal 1955, tchr 1950. **Orgs:** Pres Marlin Falls Co Br NAACP 1974;scout master troop 320 Marlin, TX 1950-65; deacon & ss supt Zion Rock Bapt Ch 1960; mem Marlin C of C 1978; Sci Inst (2) Prairie View Coll 1958-59. **Honors/Awds:** Numerous honors and awards. **Military Serv:** AUS spc 5 1942-45. **Business Addr:** Falls County, Marlin, TX 76661.

LYNN, LOUIS B.
Research scientist. **Personal:** Born Mar 8, 1949, Bishopville, SC; son of Dorothy Evans Lynn and Lawton Lynn; married Audrey Johnson; children: Adrienne, Krystal, Bryan. **Educ:** Clemson Univ, BS Horticulture, (honors) 1970, MS Horticulture, 1971; Univ of Maryland, PhD Horticulture, 1974. **Career:** Elanco Product Co, field scientist 1976-80; Monsanto Agr Co, product mgr 1980-83, sr scientist 1983-88; Enviromental Affairs Mgr, 1988-90; Ebony Agricultural Associates, Inc, pres, 1985-90; ENVIRO AgScience, Inc, pres, 1990-. **Orgs:** Mem Clemson Univ Alumni Assoc, Weed Science Soc of Amer; pres, South Carolina Horticultural Society 1987-88; Amer Soc for Horticulture Sci; South Carolina Agricultural Study Committee; board of trustees, Clemson University. **Military Serv:**

AUS Capt 5 years. **Business Addr:** Field Rep, PO Box 23285, Columbia, SC 29224.

LYONS, A. BATES
State official. **Personal:** Born Nov 20, 1944, Philadelphia, PA; son of Irma Bates Lyons and Archie Lyons; divorced; children: Joanna, Daniel, Ashley. **Educ:** Central State Univ, Wilberforce, OH, BS, 1966; Columbia Univ, New York, NY, MBA, 1972. **Career:** US Army, captain, 1966-69; Atlantic Richfield, Philadelphia, PA, mgr, 1969-72; Philip Morris, New York, NY, mgr, 1972-79; Heublein, Farmington, CT, mgr, 1977-78; Office of Policy Mgmt, Hartford, CT, under sec, 1978-87; State Technical Colls, Hartford, CT, deputy exec dir, 1987-92; consultant, 1992-. **Orgs:** Pres, Fed of Black Democrats, 1982-84; polemarch, Kappa Alpha Psi Fraternity, 1982-84; State Retirement Commn, 1985-. **Military Serv:** US Army, captain, 1966-69. **Home Addr:** 212 Carriage Ln, Torrington, CT 06790.

LYONS, CHARLES H. S., JR.
Educator (retired). **Personal:** Born May 3, 1917, Athens, GA; son of Ophelia M Derricotte Lyons and Charles H S Lyons Sr; children: Lottie, Charles III, Charlotte, Collins, Beatrice, Faye. **Educ:** Savannah State Coll, BSE 1939; Attended, Univ of Hawaii 1944-45, Hampton Inst 1948, Univ of CA 1978-79. **Career:** Richmond County, math teacher, 1947-79. **Orgs:** Mem VFW 3910. **Honors/Awds:** Teacher of the Year Oglethorpe Co 1960. **Military Serv:** AUS corpl 3 1/2 yrs; Army Medal. **Home Addr:** 232 Rhodes Dr, Athens, GA 30606.

LYONS, DONALD WALLACE
Athletic director. **Personal:** Born Dec 11, 1945, Lexington, KY; married Myra Briggs. **Educ:** KY St U, AB 1968; Univ of KY, MSLS 1971. **Career:** KY State Univ, athletic director, currently, dir of library, asst librarian, teacher, supvr Adult Educ; Am Libr Assn, tchr; Amer Assn of Univ Prof; KY Library Assn. **Orgs:** NEA Alpha Phi Alpha frat. **Honors/Awds:** Publ "Afr & Afr Am Hsty & Cult a biblio"; "follow-up of on the job training plcmnts"; "blazer bugle". **Business Addr:** Athletic Director, Kentucky State University, Frankfort, KY 40601.

LYONS, HENRY J., SR.
Organization executive. **Personal:** Born 1942, Gainesville, FL; married Deborah; children: Derrick, Stephanie, Vonda. **Educ:** Morehouse College, bachelor's degree; Cincinnati Baptist College, DDiv; Hebrew Union Univ, PhD, 1972. **Career:** Abyssinia Baptist Church, pastor; Macedonia Baptist Church, pastor; Cincinnati Baptist College, academic dean; Bethel Metropolitan Baptist Church, pastor; Florida General Baptist Convention, pres, 1981-; National Baptist Convention USA, pres, 1994-.

LYONS, JAMES E., SR.
Educational administrator. **Career:** Bowie State Univ, pres; Jackson State University, president, currently. **Orgs:** American Association of Colleges for Teacher Education; American Association of State Colleges and Universities; American Council on Education; National Association for Equal Opportunity in Higher Education; 100 Black Men of Jackson Inc; Phi Delta Kappa; Phi Kappa Phi. **Honors/Awds:** Prince George's County Public Schools, Leadership in Public Education Award; American Council on Education Fellows Program, Service Award; Maryland Federation of Business and Professional Women, Employer of the Year; University of Connecticut, Distinguished Alumni Award; Maryland Legislative Black Caucus, Outstanding Leadership Award; Maryland Association of Community Action Agencies, Leadership Award; Puerto Rican Service Award; Jewish War Veterans' Brotherhood Award; Bowie State University National Alumni Association, Dedication and Service Award; numerous others. **Special Achievements:** Metropolitan Life Foundation Grant to study White students on African-American college campuses. **Business Addr:** President, Office of the President, Jackson State University, 1400 J R Lynch St, Jackson, MS 39217.

LYONS, LAMAR
Banker. **Career:** Rideau Lyons & Co Inc, CEO, currently. **Special Achievements:** Company is ranked #15 on the Black Enterprise list of top investment banks, 1994. **Business Addr:** CEO, Rideau Lyons & Co. Inc., 911 Wilshire, Ste. 2030, Los Angeles, CA 90017, (213)895-5900.

LYONS, LAURA BROWN
Motivational trainer. **Personal:** Born Jul 15, 1942, Birmingham, AL; daughter of Annie M Brown and Jesse Brown; married Edward Lyons, May 16, 1970; children: Kobie. **Educ:** Dillard University, New Orleans, LA, BA 1963; New York University, MSW. **Career:** Kaiser Corp, asst personnel manager, 1975-80; BVI Govt, Road Town, Tortola, BVI, asst community development officer, 1980-81; Career Dynamics International, Tortola, BVI, president, 1981-; WBNB-TV, CBS Affiliate, former TV talk show hostess. **Orgs:** Caribbean Executive Woman's Network, 1985-; American Society for Training and Development, 1985-; International Professional Practice Assn, 1989-. **Honors/Awds:** ASTD, Multi-Cultural Trainer of the Year Award, 1990; Virgin Islands Business Journal, Outstanding Business Person, 1988; CEWN, Outstanding Female Executive, 1990, 1997; US Virgin Islands Business Journal, Educator of the Year, 1988; American Express Recognition Award for Excellence in Motivational Training, 1989; British Virgin Islands Hotel and Commerce Association, Business Person of the Year, nominee, 1990; Black Career Women's Assn, "Legacy Messenger," Cincinnati, OH, 1997. **Special Achievements:** Author, Lyon's Guide to the Career Jungle, Odenwald Connection Publishing, 1989. **Business Addr:** President, Career Dynamics Intl, PO Box 3468, Charlotte Amalie, St Thomas, Virgin Islands of the United States 00803, (284)494-3185.

LYONS, LLOYD CARSON
Business executive. **Personal:** Born Aug 1, 1942, New Castle, PA; children: Lloyd Jr, Shannon, Christopher. **Educ:** IN U, AB 1966; IN Central U, MBA. **Career:** IN Nat Bank, sr vp, dir personnel 1966-; INB Financial Corp, senior vp, currently. **Orgs:** Mem Am Soc of Personnel Adminstrs; mem United Negro Coll Fund; bd mem Day Nursery Assn of Indpls; United Way Allocations & Admissions Com. **Business Addr:** Sr Vice President, INB Financial Corporation, One Indiana Square Suite 475, Indianapolis, IN 46266.

LYONS, ROBERT P.
Business executive (retired). **Personal:** Born Nov 18, 1912, Kansas City, MO; married Claudia Mae Hopkins. **Educ:** Attended, Univ of KS. **Career:** Universal Life Ins, dist mgr Kansas City 1949-55; Crusader Life Ins Co, agency dir 1957-69; American Woodmen's Life Insurance Co, past board chairman. **Orgs:** Past pres Millionaires Club Natl Ins Assn; Beta Lambda chap Alpha Phi Alpha; past chmn Agency Sect Natl Ins Assn; past chmn pro-tem, Bethel AME Trustee Bd; mem Bethel AME Ch; co-incorporator Bethel AME Ch Not-For-Profit Found; pres & founder Soft & Sweet Music Club; past dir Region 2 Natl Ins Assn; past mem Bd Mgmt Paseo-Linwood YMCA; past mem, KS City Area C of C; life mem Alpha Phi Alpha. **Honors/Awds:** Certificate of Achievement Millionaires Club Natl Ins Assn 1958-71; elected to Midwestern Hall of Fame; Alpha Phi Alpha Fraternity, Inc. **Special Achievements:** Author "The Life of a Black Salesman from Selling Newspapers to Serving as Chairman of a Board of Directors.". **Home Addr:** 600 E 8th St, Kansas City, MO 64106.

LYTE, M. C. (LANA MOORER)
Rap singer. **Personal:** Born 1971, Queens, NY. **Career:** Rap singer, currently. **Special Achievements:** Albums include: Lyte as a Rock, 1988; Eyes on This, 1989; Act Like You Know; 1991; Ain't No Other, 1993; Singles include: I Cram to Understand You, 1988; Cha Cha Cha, 1989; Ruffneck, 1993.

LYTHCOTT, JANICE LOGUE
Entertainment executive. **Personal:** Born Jun 19, 1950, St Albans, NY; daughter of Helen Harvey Logue and John Thomas Logue; married Michael Lythcott, Jun 1983; children: Omi, Shade. **Educ:** Simmons College, Boston, MA, 1968-69; Lehman College, Bronx, NY, 1969-71; Howard University, Washington, DC, BA, 1975. **Career:** WHUR, Washington, DC, special assistant to the general manager, 1976; Gil Scott Heron, New York, NY, manager, 1977-78; CBS Records, New York, NY, manager, adminstration, 1978-80; CBS Records, New York, NY, associate director programs and project development, 1980-88; Sony Music/CBS Records, New York, NY, director, project development, 1988-. **Orgs:** Committee chair, Jackie Robinson Foundation, 1982-89; board member, Alvin Ailey American Foundation, 1987-; board member, Jamison Project, 1988-89. **Honors/Awds:** Volunteer of the Year, Jackie Robinson Foundation, 1990; Award for Distrinction, CEBA Award, 1987; Award of Excellence, CEBA Award, 1984; Black Achiever, YMCA, 1983; Award for Excellence, American Women Radio & TV, 1975.

LYTLE, ALICE A.
Judge. **Personal:** Born in Jersey City, NJ. **Educ:** Hunter Coll, AB; Hastings Coll of Law, JD 1973. **Career:** Albert Einstein Coll of Medicine, medical rsch tech 1961-70; Univ of CA San Francisco Cardiovascular Rsch Inst; Gov Edmund G Brown Jr, dep legal affairs sec 1975-77; Dept Indus Relations Div Fair Employee Practices, chief 1977-79; State & Consumer Serv Agency (Cabinet Office in admin of Gov Brown), sec 1979-82; Sacramento Municipal Court, judge, currently. **Honors/Awds:** Hall of Fame Hunter Coll NYC. **Business Addr:** Judge Municipal Court, Sacramento Municipal Court, 720 9th St, Sacramento, CA 95814.

LYTLE, MARILYN MERCEDES
Organization executive. **Personal:** Born May 10, 1948, Mound Bayou, MS; daughter of Pauline J Thompson Holmes and C Preston Holmes; married Erskine Lytle III, Jun 26, 1971; children: Brandon Kyle, Kiera Danine. **Educ:** Fisk University, Nashville, TN, BS, 1969; Stanford University, Palo Alto, CA, MAT, 1970. **Career:** Washington High School, San Francisco, CA, music teacher, 1970-71; Jordan High School, Durham, NC, choral music teacher, 1972-78; INROADS Inc, Nashville, TN, coordinator, asst director, 1979-83, director, 1983-86, regional director, 1986-88, regional vice president, 1988-93, vice president, 1994-95, exec vp, 1995-. **Orgs:** Board member, United Way, 1987-94; head, allocations committee, United Way, 1984-86; board member, St Mary's Villa, 1984-87; member, selection committee, Bootstraps Scholarships, 1988; member, Leadership Nashville, 1986-; member, Alpha Kappa Alpha Sorority Inc; board member, executive committee mem, Nashville CARES, 1994-; exec committee mem, YWCA, 1995-. **Honors/Awds:** Selected to 100 Top African-American Business & Professional Women, Dollars and Sense Magazine, 1989; selected, Phelps Stokes West Africa Heritage Tour, Phelps Stokes Fund, 1978; St Peters AME Church, Community Role Model Award, 1994; Alpha Kappa Alpha Sorority, Alpha Delta Omega Chapter, Outstanding Community Leadership and Service Award; Project Cherish Honoree, Delta Sigma Theta Sorority Inc, 1995; President's Citation for Excellence, INROADS Inc, 1995; Executive in Residence, University of Tennessee at Knoxville, 1997. **Business Addr:** Exec VP, INROADS, Inc, 315 Deaderick, Box 97, Nashville, TN 37238, (615)255-7397.

M

MABEN, HAYWARD C., JR.
Physician. **Personal:** Born Jun 3, 1922, Augusta, GA; married Carrie M Harris; children: Hayward III, Burton, Michael. **Educ:** Wayne State Univ, BS 1942; Meharry Med Coll, MD 1945. **Career:** Wayne State Univ School of Med, clinical asst prof; private practice, cardiovascular & thoracic surgeon, currently. **Orgs:** Bd cert Amer Coll of Surgeons, Amer Bd of Surgery, Amer Bd of Thoracic Surgery; fellow Amer Coll of Chest Physicians; mem Soc of Thoracic Surgeons; life mem NAACP; mem Natl Med Assoc. **Honors/Awds:** 1st black thoracic surgeon in state of MI. **Military Serv:** AUS 1943-45. **Business Addr:** Cardiovascular & Thoracic Surgeon, 868 Fisher Bldg, Detroit, MI 48202.

MABIN, JOSEPH E.
Chief executive. **Career:** Mabin Construction Co, Inc, Kansas City, MO, chief exec, 1980-. **Business Addr:** Mabin Construction Co, Inc, 3101 E 85th St, Kansas City, MO 64132-2529.

MABREY, ERNEST L., JR.
Engineering company executive. **Personal:** Born Oct 1, 1937, Bristow, OK; son of Jemima House Mabrey and Ernest Mabrey; divorced; children: Ernest T Mabrey III. **Educ:** George Washington Univ, BS, mathematics, 1968, MS, engineering, 1978, Ap Sc degree, 1982. **Career:** US Dept of the Navy, mathematician, 1963-70; Natl Oceanic and Atmospheric Adm/Dept of Commerce, operations research analyst, 1970-77; Bureau of Census, supv math statistician, 1977-78; Dept of Energy, supv math statistician, 1978-82; Bowie State Univ, asst prof of math and computer science, 1982-87; LOGI-TECH Engineering Resources Inc, pres/CEO, currently. **Orgs:** Tower Club, bd of govs, 1992-95; Northern Virginia Minority Bus Assn, bd of dir, 1989-92; Math Assn of America, regional vice chair, 1980-82; Joe Gibbs Charities, 1991-; AFCEA, 1993-; IEEE, 1990; Northern Virginia Technology Counsel, 1992-. **Honors/Awds:** George Washington Univ, Pi Mu Epsilon, Natl Math Honors Society, 1968; Natl Aeronautics and Space Adm, Faculty Summer Internship, 1981; Dept of Energy, Research Grant, 1985; KPMG Peat Marwick, Entrepreneur of the Year Nominee, 1991, 1992. **Special Achievements:** "General Purpose Programs for CAL/COMP Platters," IR No 69-65, 1969; "Participation in Marine Recreational Fishing, SE US, Current Fishery Statistics," No 733, 1977; "Applied Analysis Model Summaries," TR DOE/EIA 018316, 1979; Copernicus Software/Final Report, SPAWAR Contract, 1991. **Military Serv:** US Army, SP4, 1959-62. **Business Addr:** Pres/CEO, LOGI-TECH Engineering Resources, Inc, 801 N Fairfax St, Ste 312, Alexandria, VA 22314, (703)684-3790.

MABREY, HAROLD LEON
Military official (retired), consulting company executive. **Personal:** Born May 24, 1933, Pittsburg, TX; son of Ethelyn E Brown and Horace L Mabrey; married Barbara J Johnson; children: Vicki Lynn, Lesley Harold, Kevin Frank. **Educ:** Lincoln Univ, BS Business Admin 1955; George Washington Univ, MBA 1971; Indus Coll of the Armed Forces, Grad 1978; Harvard Univ, diploma in national & international security affairs 1987. **Career:** US Army Avn Res & Dev Cmd, GM-15 suprv contract specialist/chief proc div 1977-83, GS-14 supv contr spec 1973-77, GS-13 supv contr spec 1969-73, GS-12 supv contr spec 1966-69, GS-11 supv contr spec 1964-66, aviation systems command, 1983-86, GM-15 supv cont sp; US Army, troop supp comd, senior exec service-04, SES-04, 1986-91, Avn Sys Cmd, GM-15, supr cont sp/div chief, 1983-86, director of proc and prod, 1985-91; Mabrey and Associates, Inc, currently. **Orgs:** NBMBAA; Natl Contract Mgmt Assn 1975-; mem Minority Bus Oppor Comm 1979-; vice chmn EEO Working Group AUS 1980; mem Omega Psi Phi Frat 1953-; mem Lincoln Univ Alumni Assn 1955-; Berea Presbyterian Church 1978-. **Honors/Awds:** Marksman, Good Conduct Medal US Army 1955-57; sustained superior performance award US Army Transp Cmd 1962; Meritorious Civilian Serv Award US Army 1970, 1976, 1977, 1980, 1991; outstanding performance award US Army 1971, 1977 & 1980; honor grad def adv proc mgmt US Army 1973; Cert of Achievement US Army 1977; Distinguished Alumni Award 1986; Secretary of Defense Supe-

rior Management Award 1989; Presidential Rank Meritorious Service Award, 1989; Exceptional Civilian Service Award, US Army, 1990. **Military Serv:** US Army corpl 1955-57. **Business Addr:** Mabrey & Associates, Inc, 4363 Keevenshore Dr, Florissant, MO 63034-3452.

MABREY, MARSHA EVE
Educator, orchestra conductor, administrator. **Personal:** Born Nov 7, 1949, Pittsburgh, PA; daughter of Ella Jones Mabrey and Theodore R Mabrey. **Educ:** Univ of MI School of Music, BM 1971, MM 1972; Univ of Cincinnati Coll Conservatory of Music. **Career:** Univ of Cincinnati Coll Conservatory of Music Orch, asst conductor 1973-76; Winona State Univ Symphony Orch, instr of music 1978-80; Grand Rapids Symphony Orch, asst conductor 1980-81; Grand Valley State Coll Symphony Orch, asst prof of music 1980-82; Interlochen All State Music Prog, conductor for All State Orchestra Concer Prog 1982; Eugene Chamber Orch, music dir, conductor comm orchestra 1984-91; Univ of OR Symphony Orch, asst prof of music 1982-89; Univ of Oregon School of Music, asst dean, 1989-91; Detroit Symphony Orchestra Hall, vice pres of educational affairs, 1991-. **Orgs:** Guest conducting MI Youth Symphony Orch 1977; coord, dir West Coast Women Conductor/Composer Symposium 1984-85; orchestra chmn OR Music Ed Assoc 1984-86; keynote speaker OR String Teacher Assoc 1984; guest conducting Music Ed Assoc All-Star Orchestras in Pennsylvania, Oregon, Arkansas and Utah; mem Natl School Band & Orchestra Assoc, Coll Music Soc; mem Amer Symphony Orchestra League, The Conductors Guild, MENC, OMEA; guest conductor, Utah All-State Orchestra, 1990; guest conductor, Oregon Symphony, 1988, Sinfonietta Frankfort, Germany, 1988; Savannah Symphony Orchestra, 1991; Allen Park Symphony, 1992. **Honors/Awds:** $10,000 Grant for West Coast Women Conductor/Composer Symposium Ctr for the Study of Women in Soc 1974; Grant for Amer Women Conductor/Composer Symposium Ctr the Study of Women in Soc. **Home Addr:** 1514 102nd Ave NE, Bellevue, WA 98004-3505. **Business Addr:** Vice President of Educational Affairs, Detroit Symphony Orchestra Hall, 400 Buhl Bldg, 535 Griswold St, Detroit, MI 48226.

MABRIE, HERMAN JAMES, III
Physician. **Personal:** Born Jul 10, 1948, Houston, TX; married Linda; children: David, Herman IV, Brent. **Educ:** Howard U, BS 1969; Meharry Med Coll, MD 1973. **Career:** Otorhinolaryngologist, pvt prac; Baylor Affiliated Hosp, otorhino resd 1975-78, gen surg resd 1973-75. **Orgs:** Mem Houston Med Forum; Alpha Phi Omega Serv Frat; The Deafness Rsrch Found; AMA; Nat Medc Assn; Harris Co Med Assn; TX Med Assn; Am Cncl Otolaryn; Houston Otolaryn Assn. **Honors/Awds:** 1st black otolaryn resd Baylor Affiliated Hosp 1975-78, Houston 1978; publ Archives of Otolaryn; 1 of 1st 10 Nat Achvmt Schlrsp 1965. **Business Addr:** 1412 Med Arts Professional Bldg, Houston, TX 77002.

MABRY, EDWARD L.
Educator. **Personal:** Born Nov 21, 1936, Brownsville, TN; son of Mary Palmer Mabry and Charlie Mabry. **Educ:** Millikin Univ, BA 1966; Princeton Theol Sem, MDiv 1969; Princeton Theol Sem, PhD 1982. **Career:** Millikin Univ, dir relgious activity 1969-70; Princeton Theol Sem, master in resd 1970-73; NJ State Home for Girls, chaplain 1971-72; Talladega Coll, dir of religious action & asst prof of religion 1973-75; OK School of Religion, dean; Millikin Univ, visiting professor, 1988; Richard Community College, instructor, evening coordinator, 1988-90; Augustana College, associate professor, 1990-, chairman, religion dept, 1995-. **Orgs:** Dir Christian Ed OK Bapt State Conv 1975-; mem AAUP 1973-; minister of ed Morning Star Bapt Church Tulsa 1975-; organist Morning Star Bapt Church 1975; lifetime member of NAACP; assoc minister, Second Baptist Church, Rock Island, IL. **Honors/Awds:** Student Senate Apprec Awd Talladega Coll 1974; Swank Prize in Homiletics, Princeton Theol Seminary, Rockerfeller Fellow 1967-69. **Military Serv:** AUS sp4 1960-63. **Business Addr:** Assoc Prof, Religion Dept, Augustana College, 639 38th St, Rock Island, IL 61201.

MABSON, GLENN T.
Production sound mixer. **Personal:** Born Feb 23, 1940, Tulsa, OK; son of Lowell and Ozella Mabson; married; children: Athena, Darvell, Kimberly, Daniel. **Educ:** Calif Inst of Technology, BEE, 1966; National Tech Schools, Mast Sci, 1968. **Career:** MGM/Sony Studios, prod sound mixer, 1968-75; Burbank Studios, prod sound mixer; 20th Cent Fox, West LA, prod sound mixer; Paramount Studios, prod sound mixer; NBC News, prod sound mixer; CBS News, prod sound mixer; ABC News, prod sound mixer; Universal Studios, prod sound mixer; Mabson Audio Engineering, prod sound mixer, currently. **Orgs:** Maui Epi-Leptic Assn, founder. **Honors/Awds:** Community Leader of Achievement of Volunteers. **Special Achievements:** First African-American to be in charge of production sound for a motion picture TV series; First African-American to be hired as a Audio-Engineer in the TV industry; First African-American to produce a perfect sound track for a TV series, Emmy Winner ''Reflections,'' 1981; First person to produce a perfect sound track for a motion picture ''Car Wash','' 1981; ''The Greatest, Muhammed Ali Story,'' 1982. **Business Phone:** (808)879-8999.

MAC, BERNIE
Comedian. **Personal:** Born in Chicago, IL; married; children: one. **Career:** Comedian; actor; Def Comedy Jam, host. **Special Achievements:** Movie appearances include: Above the Rim; Who's the Man; Mo Money; House Party 3; The Shaman; Friday; Moesha, recurring role, 1996-; HBO, Don King: Only In America, 1997. **Business Addr:** Host, Def Comedy Jam, c/o HBO, 1100 Avenue of the Americas, New York, NY 10036, (212)512-1000.

MACK, ALLY FAYE
Educational administrator. **Personal:** Born Apr 6, 1943, Marthaville, LA; married Dr Robert Mack; children: Robert III, Ryan, Renfred, Jessica. **Educ:** Grambling State Univ, BA 1963; Atlanta Univ, MA 1964; TX A&M Univ, further study 1971; Univ of So MS, PhD 1979. **Career:** Prairie View A&M Univ, asst prof 1968-69; TX A&M Univ, instr 1969-71; Langston Univ, asst prof 1971-74; Jackson State Univ, dept of political science, prof, acting chpsn beginning 1974, chair, currently. **Orgs:** Consult TN Valley Auth 1979-; trainer Natl Womens Ed Fund 1980-; mem Hinds Co Dem Exec Domm 1975-; distr chair Dem Women 1982-; mem MS Council on Human Rel 1976-, MS Health Systems Agency State Bd 1978-79, MS R&D Bd 1980-. **Honors/Awds:** Plaque NAACP Citizen Participation Awd 1977; Publ Serv Awd Fannie Lou Hamer Awd 1980. **Business Addr:** Professor, Chairperson, Jackson State Univ, Dept of Pol Sci, 1400 J R Lynch St, Jackson, MS 39217.

MACK, ASTRID KARONA
Educator. **Personal:** Born Aug 21, 1935, Daytona Beach, FL; son of Meta Marietta Mack; divorced; children: Astrid Kyle, Kristen Nichole. **Educ:** Bethune-Cookman Coll, BS (Magna Cum Laude) 1960; Univ of MN, MS (Zoology) 1965; MI State Univ, PhD (Human Genetics) 1974. **Career:** Dade Co FL Public Schls, tchr Biol & Chem 1960-66; Miami-Dade Comm Coll, instr asst prof 1966-73; Univ Miami Schl of Med, asst assoc prof 1973-; UMSM Associate Dean for Minority Affairs 1988-. **Orgs:** Mem Amer Soc of Human Genetics 1969-; mem Amer Assn for the Advancement of Sci 1974-; mem Amer Genetics Assn 1978-; exec dir Dade County Sickle Cell Fdn 1978-; 1st v dist rep Omega Psi Phi Frat Inc 1982-85; district rep Omega Psi Phi Frat Inc 1985-89. **Honors/Awds:** NSF Fellowship Earlham Coll 1962, Bowdin Coll 1964; acad yr fellowship Univ of MN (NSF) 1964-65; EO fellowship MI State Univ 1970-72; pres citation Natl Assn for Equal Opportunity in Higher Educ 1979; Pinnacle Award, Outstanding Achievement, Bethune-Cookman College, 1995. **Military Serv:** AUS sp5 1955-58. **Business Addr:** Research Associate Prof Med, Univ of Miami Sch of Med, 794 NW 18th St, Miami, FL 33136.

MACK, C.
Banking executive. **Personal:** Born Mar 8, 1959, Canton, OH; son of Henry Mack; married Tenetia, Sep 21, 1985; children: Lauren, Sean, Ryan. **Educ:** University of Cincinnati, BA, 1982; Indiana University, Bloomington, IN, MBA, 1984. **Career:** Procter & Gamble, brand mgr, 1984-91; Ryder System Inc, dir of consumer trade rental mktg, 1991-92, group dir of consumer truck mktg and mktg svcs, 1992-93, vp consumer track rental mktg, 1994, vp worldwide, 1994-96; Citibank Florida, FSB, sr vp of branch sales and operations, 1986-97; Citibank FSB, president & CEO, 1997-. **Orgs:** Chicago United, Economic Development Comm, principal/co-chair, 1997-; Chicago Urban League, business advisory coun, 1997-; The Lincoln Foundation for Business Excellence, bd of trustees, 1997-; Neighborhood Housing Svcs of Chicago, Leadership Comm, 1997-; Steppenwolf Theatre, bd mem, 1997-; DePaul University, College of Commerce, advisory coun, 1997-; Super Bowl Mktg Comm, co-chair, 1995; National Black MBA Association, bd of dirs, 1987-95. **Honors/Awds:** Indiana University, Kelley School of Business, Academy of Alumni Fellows, 1998; Black Enterprise Magazine, Keepers of the Flame, 1997; Consortium for Graduate Study in Management, Fellowship, 1983. **Special Achievements:** Speaks fluent German and Portuguese. **Business Addr:** President, CEO, Citibank FSB, 500 W Madison St, 5th Fl, Chicago, IL 60661-2591, (312)627-3535.

MACK, CHARLES RICHARD
Educator. **Personal:** Born Oct 2, 1942, Clarke Co, GA; married Joan Jacqueline Thomas. **Educ:** Univ GA, BS, MEd. **Career:** Clarke County School System, teacher, asst prin; Macedonia Baptist Church Athens, GA, Baptist minister; City of Athens, ward 1 alderman. **Orgs:** Vp Clarke Chap NAACP; mem CCAE; GEA; NEA; sec NE GA Bapt Ministerial Union; 2nd vice pres 8 Dist Gen Missionary Bapt Conv of GA Inc; sec 8th Dist Layman Group; pres-elect Clarke Co Assn of Educators; mem Phi Beta Kappa.

MACK, CLEVELAND J., SR.
Chief executive officer. **Personal:** Born Dec 5, 1912, Alabama; married Mary Holly; children: Cleveland Jr, Mary, Clarence. **Career:** Detroit, MI, contractor. **Orgs:** Mem Asso Gen Contractors of Am; mem Met Contract Assn; mem BTWBA; mem Urban League; mem Prince Hall Masons. **Honors/Awds:** Recip MCA Award for Contractor of Yr 1973; laid out & poured found The Renaissance Ctr (worlds larges hotel & related bldgs) 1974; businessman of yr BTWBA 1975; man of yr award State of MI Dept of Commerce 1976; listed Top 100 Businesses of Nation 1977. **Business Addr:** 14555 Wyoming, Detroit, MI 48238.

MACK, DANIEL J.
Chief executive. **Career:** Virginia Mutual Benefit Life Insurance Co, Inc, Richmond, VA, chief exec. **Business Addr:** Virginia Mutual Benefit Life Insurance Co, Inc, PO Box 201, Durham, NC 27701.

MACK, DEBORAH LYNN
Curator, consultant. **Educ:** Univ of Chicago, BA, geography, 1976; Northwestrn Univ, MA, anthropology, 1977, PhD, anthropology, 1986. **Career:** Sociology/Anthropology, Lake Forest College, asst prof, 1986-88; Northwestern Univ, visiting scholar, 1988-89; School of the Art Institute of Chicago, visiting asst prof, 1989-90; Field Museum of Natural History, proj dir, sr exhibit developer, 1990-95; The Field Museum, research assoc, dept of anthropology, until 1999; Northwestern Univ, research assoc/curator, 1996-; Museum/Academic Consultant, currently; numerous others. **Orgs:** African-American Museum Association; African Studies Assn; American Anthropological Assn; Assn of American Museums; US Committee, Intl Committee on Museums; The Museum Group. **Honors/Awds:** ILL State Scholarship, 1970-74; Univ of Chicago, Fellowship, 1970-74; United Nations Association, Ralph Bunche Fellow, 1974-75; Northwestern Univ, Fellowship, 1976-77; Fulbright-Hays, US Department of Education, Group Proj Abroad, 1988; National Endowment for the Humanities, Field Museum Africa Exhibit, 1992; numerous others. **Special Achievements:** Film Review of ''The South-East Nuba,'' American Anthropologist, 1986; ''The Beni Amer,'' Greenwood Press, 1984; numerous papers presented.

MACK, DONALD J.
Publisher. **Personal:** Born Jun 1, 1937, Port Arthor, TX; married Gussie L Vinson. **Educ:** BS 1963. **Career:** TX So U, tchr 1964-66; Galveston Co CAA, asst dir 1966-67; Nghbrhd Action Inc, dir 1967-72; Comm Action Agy, dir 1972-74; Ft Worth Ctr for Ex-offenders, dir; Ebony Mart, publshr. **Orgs:** Chmn Nghbrhd Action Apts 1973-; bd mem Conf of Christians & Jews 1974-; mem Ldrshp Ft Worth 1974-. **Honors/Awds:** Cert of merit from Comm Action Agy; cert of accmplshmt Criminal Justice Sys; cert of completion Ldrshp Inst for Comm Devel. **Military Serv:** USN.

MACK, FAITE
Military officer. **Personal:** Born Jan 8, 1919, Stratham, GA; married Katie; children: Faite, Jr, Phillip, Gregory. **Educ:** Wilson Jr Coll, 1951; Aircraft & Engine Mech Course, Grad 1942 & 48; Army Helicopter Mech Course, 1956; Multi-engine Single-rotor Helicopter Mech Course, 1966; Air Frame Repair Extension Course, 1962; Shop-Foreman Sch, 1971; Ldrshp & Pers Mgmt Extensions Course, 1971; UH1 Extension Course, 1971; Radiological Monitoring Course, 1971; Command & Gen Staff Coll, 1973; num other military courses. **Career:** AUS, master sgt 1942-; IL Army Nat Guard, 1947; Sr Aircraft Mech; Communications Chief; Sec Ldr; Platoon Sgt; Tech Inspector; Sr Flight Ops Chief; Battalion Sgt Major; Command Sgt Major, current assign Nov 1975; Gov Dan Walker, selected as aide promoted to Bird Col; Gov James R Thompson Gov IL Military Aide, personal staff 1977; Army Aviation Maintenance Shop, civilian aircraft maintenance supvry 25 yrs; IL & Army Aviation Support Facility; Midway Airport; IL Army Nat Guard, racial relat recruiting & retention splst. **Orgs:** Pres IL Nat Guard Non-Command Ofcr Assn; mem Bd Elimination of Racial Imbalance in IL Nat Guard. **Honors/Awds:** Recip Am Theatre Ribbon; European, African, Middle Eastern Theatre Ribbon with 4 Bronze Stars; Good Conduct Medal; Victory Medal WW II; Rome-Arno Campaign; N Appennines Campaign; PO Valley Campaign; State of IL Long & Hon Serv Medal; State Active Duty Ribbon 9th Award; Sr Air Crewman Badge.

MACK, FRED CLARENCE
Financial administrator. **Personal:** Born Sep 1, 1940, Elloree, SC; married Mildred Elaine Oliver; children: Lennie B, Keith O, Erika L, Fred S. **Educ:** South Carolina State College, BS 1973. **Career:** Utica Tool Co, leadman 1968-72; NC Mutual Insurance Co, debit manager 1970-73; Family Health Center, Inc, assoc dir 1973-85; Orangeburg County Council, vice-chairman 1976-. **Orgs:** Member Chamber of Commerce 1980; member OCAAB Community Service Agency 1983-85. **Honors/Awds:** Executive Board NAACP Bowman Branch 1960-85; Treasurer Antioch Baptist Church 1970-85; Political Action Concerned Citizen Dist #94 1972-85; Chairman/Deacon Antioch Baptist Church 1983-85; Advisor Board Orangeburg-Calhoun Tec College 1983-85. **Business Addr:** Vice Chairman, Orangeburg County Council, PO Box 1125, Orangeburg, SC 29115.

MACK, GLADYS WALKER
Government official. **Personal:** Born Feb 26, 1934, Rock Hill, SC; daughter of Henrietta Alexander Walker and Zenith Walker; married Julius Mack, Jan 25, 1958; children: Geofrey, Kenneth, Johnathan. **Educ:** Morgan State Univ, Baltimore MD, BS, 1955; graduate study at Catholic Univ of America, Washington DC, 1956-58. **Career:** Urban Renewal Admin Housing and Home Finance Agency, Washington DC, budget analyst, 1955-65; Office of Economic Opportunity, VISTA Program, Washington DC, budget analyst, 1965-67, program analysis officer, 1967-69; Exec Office of the Mayor, Washington DC, senior budget analyst, 1969-72; Washington Technical Inst, Washing-

ton DC, dir of budget and finance, 1972-75; Exec Office of the Mayor, Washington DC, deputy budget dir, 1975-78, acting dir, 1978-79, asst city admin, 1979-82, dir of Office of Policy and Program Evaluation, 1983-85, gen asst to the mayor, 1985-86; DC Board of Parole, Washington DC, chairperson, 1986-91. **Orgs:** Pres, Assn of Paroling Authorities International; mem, United Planning Org; mem, Amer Public Transportation Assn; mem, Amer Correctional Assn; mem, Middle Atlantic States Correctional Assn; mem, Delta Sigma Theta. **Business Addr:** Chairperson, D C Board of Parole, 717-14th St NW, Suite 200, Washington, DC 20005.

MACK, GORDON H.
Educator. **Personal:** Born Jul 1, 1927, Chicago, IL; son of W Howard Mack; married Kay Bell; children: Melissa, Michael, Margot, Matthew. **Educ:** Southern Univ, BA; New York Univ, MA. **Career:** YMCA of USA, dir cultural diversity 1990-; Bank St College Field Serv Div, chmn 1970-; Ldrshp Resour Inc, sr asso 1970-; Nat Bd of YMCA, dir 1967-69; Ctrl Atlantic Area Counc of YMCA, asst dir 1964-67. **Orgs:** YMCA Chicago Metro Assn 1953-63; Ctrl Atlantic Area Nat Counc; unit supr JOBS YMCA; yth dir Hyde Park; spec advs Tuckagee MIOTA Proj; inst & field supr George Williams Coll; Am Soc for Training & Dev; Am Counc on Educ 1970-; Assn of Prof YMCA & Whats New in Recrtng; bd of dirs Amer Montessori Society. **Honors/Awds:** Human relat award Nat Conf of Christians & Jews. **Military Serv:** US Army 1st lt 1952-54. **Business Addr:** Director, Cultural Diversity, YMCA of USA, 101 N Wacker Dr, Chicago, IL 60606.

MACK, JOAN
News media professional. **Personal:** Born Nov 23, 1943, Charleston, SC; daughter of Harriet Robinson Gladden (deceased) and Alonzo Gladden (deceased); married Charles Henry; children: Dandria, Charles, Kashauna. **Educ:** SC State Coll, BS Biology 1964; Ccity Coll of NY, Cert 1965. **Career:** Manpower Training & Devel Ctr, teacher 1970-72; WCSC TV-5 Charleston SC, public serv dir/TV hostess 1972-77; WCBD-TV Charleston SC, news reporter 1977-1985; College of Charleston, media resources coord adjunct prof. **Orgs:** Mem Amer Women in Radio & TV 1972-80; bd mem Mayor's Comm on the Handicapped 1976-80; bd mem March of Dimes 1976-80; bd mem Charles Webb Ctr for Crippled Children 1977-80; Gov Comm on Physical Fitness 1980; mem Natl Federation of Press Women 1983-85, ITVA 1986-87; bd mem Charleston County Heart Assn 1986-87; mem speakers bureau YWCA; bd mem, Charleston County Substance Abuse Commn, 1987-; public relations comm, YMCA Auxiliary, 1988-. **Honors/Awds:** Communications award Omega Psi Phi Frat 1974; vol serv award United Negro Coll Fund 1974; Sch Bell Awards for reporting SC Educ Assn 1975-76 & 79; Outstanding Young Woman of Amer 1977,1978; YWCA Tribute to Women in Industry Awd 1981; SC Commn on Women Broadcast Awd 1981; Natl Federation of Press Women Awd 1983; 2 Silver Reel Awds Intl TV Assoc 1986; Merit Award, Intl Television Assn, 1988; Communicators Award, Carolina Assn of Businesses, 1987. **Business Addr:** Media Resources Coordinator, College of Charleston, 25 St Philip St, Charleston, SC 29424.

MACK, JOHN L.
Educator. **Personal:** Born Jul 25, 1942, Philadelphia, PA; son of Catherine Mack and Norman Mack; married Bettie Taylor; children: Monica, Michael, Mark, Gwendolyn. **Educ:** MIT, BS 1973; Suffolk Univ, MBA 1978. **Career:** MIT, assoc dir admin 1975-78, personel staff rec 1974-75; Brown Univ Providence RI, assoc dir of admissions 1978-79; Univ of TX Austin TX, post-grad course in intl finance 1979-80; Sonicraft Chicago IL, dep program mgr for control 1980-82; US State Dept Wash DC, admin officer 1982-83; US Embassy Abidjan Invory Coast, admin officer 1983-85; US Embassy Paris France, mgmt officer 1985-87, US State Dept, Washington DC; coordinator Regional Administrative Management Centers 1987-. **Orgs:** Elec consult fdr Dearborn Proj; mem bd dir Cambridge Comm Ctr; pres bd dir Cambridge Comm Ctr; mem MIT Comm Serv Fund; chmn MIT Urban Act Comm; mem MIT Rech Training Adv Com; mem bd dir Hope for Housing; co-chmn MIT Blk Stud Un; mem MIT Task Force on Educ Oppor; real est broker; mem Intl Assoc of Financial Planners; Intl Association of Black Professionals in Foreign Affairs. **Honors/Awds:** Amer Spirit Medal of Hon; Marron W Fort fellowship MIT; MENSA; assoc dir admin MIT 1977; selected as Outstanding Young Amer Jaycees 1977; US Patent #4596041 electronic device. **Military Serv:** USN elec petty off 1961-66. **Business Addr:** U S State Dept, A/ISO Room 1916, Washington, DC 20520.

MACK, JOHN W.
Civil rights administrator. **Personal:** Born Jan 6, 1937, Kingstree, SC; married Harriett Johnson; children: Anthony, Deborah, Andria. **Educ:** Agr & Tech, Coll of NC, BS; Atlanta Univ, MSW. **Career:** Camarillo St Hosp, P SW 1960-64; UL of Flint, MI, exec dir 1964-69; Los Angeles Urban League, pres 1969-. **Orgs:** Ldr Atlanta Student Civil Rights Protest 1960; co-fndr/v chrm Comm on Appeal for Human Rights 1960; co-fndr & Cochrp LA Black Ldrshp Coalt on educ 1977; bd mem KCET-TV-CHANNEL 28 1975-; v pres United Way Corp Cncl of Exects 1984; brd mem LA Cty & Cnty Priv Ind Cncl 1983. **Honors/Awds:** Annual Roving Mbrshp Trophy Comm Rel Conf of S CA 1984; Mary McCleod Bethune Nat'l Cncl of Negro Women 1984; outstanding pub serv award Assn of Blk Law Enfrcmnt Exec 1984; civil rights LA Basin Equal Oppor Leag Ue 1984; commsnr LA Brd of Zoning Appls 1984; mem CA's Atty Gen John Van DeCamp's Racila, Ethnic, Rel, & Minority Violence Comm. **Business Addr:** President, Los Angeles Urban League, 3450 Mount Vernon Drive, Los Angeles, CA 90008.

MACK, JULIA COOPER
Judge. **Personal:** Born in Fayetteville, NC; widowed; children: Cheryl. **Educ:** Hampton Inst, BS 1940; Howard Univ, LLB 1951. **Career:** Dept of Justice, trial atty appellate sect criminal div 1954-58; EEO Comm, assoc gen cnsl 1968-73, dep gen cnsl 1973-75; DC Ct of Appeals, assoc judge. **Honors/Awds:** Nominee Fed Women's Awd 1969; EEOC Awd for Disting Serv 1971; Outstanding Fed Career Lawyer Justice Tom C Clark Awd 1974; Alumnus of Yr Howard Univ Law Alumni Assn 1975; Disting Alumnus Awd Hampton Inst 1976; Hon Mem AKA Sor; Natl Bar Assn Disting Jurist Awd 1980; Howard Univ Awd for Disting Postgraduate Achievement 1981. **Business Addr:** Associate Judge, DC Court of Appeals, 500 Indiana Ave NW, Washington, DC 20001.

MACK, KEVIN (JAMES KEVIN)
Professional football player. **Personal:** Born Aug 9, 1962, Kings Mountain, NC; son of Mary Francis and Calvin Mack; married Ava Bassett, May 31, 1986. **Educ:** Clemson, attended. **Career:** Los Angeles Express (USFL) running back, 1984; Cleveland Browns, running back, 1985-. **Honors/Awds:** Co-Most Valuable Player of Year by Akron Browns' Backers; honored by Hometown of Kings Mountain with "Kevin Mack Day"; named NFL Offensive Rookie of Year by Football Digest; named UPI AFC Rookie of Year; first team UPI NFL All-Rookie squad; first team Football Digest All-Star team; Most Valuable Player on offense by Cleveland TD Club; PFWA All Rookie team; AFC Offensive Player of the Week 10/6/85; broke Jim Brown's rookie rushing record; 1986 Pro Bowl team; 1988 Pro Bowl team.

MACK, LEVORN (VON)
City official. **Career:** McBee, SC, town councilman, mayor, currently. **Special Achievements:** First African American mayor in Chesterfield County, SC. **Business Addr:** Mayor, City of McBee, PO Box 248, McBee, SC 29101, (803)335-8474.

MACK, LURENE KIRKLAND
Educational administrator. **Personal:** Born May 20, 1948, Graceville, FL; married Robert Eastmon Mack; children: Uhura Jamal, Niesha Rochet. **Educ:** Miami Dade Com Coll, AA 1970; Barry Coll, BS 1982. **Career:** Dade Cty, 1st Black female consumer protection agent 1970-74; Dade Cty Schools, 1st Black female investigator 1974-79, 1st Black female area supervisor 1980-; Early Advantage Kindergarden Inc, Miami, FL, president 1980-. **Orgs:** 1st black female student at Miami Dade Com Coll to join a sorority Gamma Delta Sor 1966; mem NAACP 1979-, Black Public Admin Assoc 1983-, Youth Crime Watch Advisory Bd 1982-, Exec Bd YEW 1984-; vice pres NOBLE-FL Chap Sect 6 1984-. **Military Serv:** AUS sp4 4 years. **Home Addr:** 18635 NW 38th Ave, Opa Locka, FL 33055. **Business Addr:** Area Supervisor, Dade County School Board, 2210 SW 3rd St, Miami, FL 33135.

MACK, LUTHER W., JR.
Resturant franchise owner. **Personal:** Born May 7, 1939, Sun Flower, MS; son of Luther & Frances Mack; married Eugeni Mack, Aug 26, 1978; children: Janelle Mack. **Educ:** Univ of Nevada, Reno; LaSalle Univ. **Career:** State of NV, dept of employment security, 1968, job coord, 1969, dept of highways, equal opportunity coord, 1970; US Small Business Admin, deputy contract compliance officer, 1971; McDonald's, owner, operator of 8 franchises, 1974-. **Orgs:** NV Television Corp, president & CEO; Pioneer Citizens Bank of NV, bd of dirs; Harvey's Casino, bd of dirs; Airport Authority of Washoe County, bd of trustees, chairman of affirmative action comm, chairman of architectural review comm; NV State Athletic Comm, commissioner; Univ of NV, Reno, bd of dirs, budget comm, foundations comm. **Honors/Awds:** Raymond I Smith, Civic Leader of the Year, 1990; Reno Police Dept, Appreciation Award; San Francisco Region McDonald's, Ronald McDonald Awards; Natl Conference of Christians & Jews, Humanitarian Award, 1984; Univ of NV, Reno, Distinguished Nevadan Award. **Business Addr:** Mack Associates, 321 Broadway Blvd, Reno, NV 89502, (702)323-0704.

MACK, NATE
Association executive. **Personal:** Born Oct 15, 1956, Detroit, MI; son of Dorothy Mack and Uler Mack; married Jamie Baker Mack; children: Ramone. **Educ:** Wayne State Univ, Detroit, MI, BS, management. **Career:** Syntex Labs, Palo Alto, CA, sales rep, 1979-84; Glaxo Inc, Research Triangle Park, NC, sales, 1984-89; Coalesce, co-founder, currently. **Home Addr:** 337 Kimberly Ct, Atlanta, GA 30311.

MACK, PEARL WILLIE
Educator. **Personal:** Born Aug 16, 1941, Laurel, MS; daughter of Delia Ann Jones Moncrief and Sammie Gilmer; married Tommie Lee; children: Dwayne Mack. **Educ:** Illinois State Univ, BA 1962; Roosevelt Univ, Graduate Work; Governor's State Univ, MA 1975. **Career:** Harvey Educ Assn, teacher 1962-; treasurer 1971-75, chair grievance comm 1987-; Illinois Educ Assn, resolutions comm 1972-74; IEZ/NEA Women's Caucus, planning comm 1974-; Minority Caucus, chairperson 1974-75; Natl Educ Assn, exec comm 1987-87, chair elections comm 1987-89, chairperson special comm on black concerns. **Orgs:** Mem Political Action Comm Natl Educ Assn 1976-, Political Action Comm Illinois Educ Assn 1975-; bd mem Natl Educ Assn 1975-; Grievance Com Harvey Educ Assn 1977-; mem PUSH, NAACP, Governers State Univ Alumni Assn 1977; del rep NEA; bd dir World Confederation Org of Teaching Profession 1976,78,84,86; delegate to Democratic Natl Convention 1980; mem Coalition of Labor Union Women 1980-, Women in Arts 1984-, Citizens Utility Bd 1984-. **Honors/Awds:** 1 of 100 Outstanding Women in Educ NEA 1975; co-writer Mini-grant Proposal for Cultural Studies Program 1974-75; Intl Business and Professional Women, Dollars & Sense Magazine 1987.

MACK, PHYLLIS GREEN
Librarian. **Personal:** Born Jul 1, 1941, Charleston, WV; daughter of Gladys Webster Green (deceased) and Leroy Stanley Green (deceased); married Arnold Rudolph Mack (died 1989); children: Stephanie Michele Mack, Nicole Renee Mack. **Educ:** West Virginia State College Institute, WV, 1963; Pratt Institute, Brooklyn, NY, MLS, 1967; Columbia University, New York, NY, advanced certificate, 1985. **Career:** New York Public Library, New York, NY, clerk, 1963-64, librarian/librarian trainee, 1966-68, sr librarian, 1968-73, supervising librarian, 1973-84, reg librarian, 1984-; Hunter College Library, New York, NY, jr librarian asst, 1965. **Orgs:** Chairperson 1989-90, member 1987-90, Community Board 10 Manhattan; member, Black Caucus-American Library Association, 1980-; 1st vice pres, Delta Sigma Theta, Inc, North Manhattan Alumnae Chapter, 1989-93; member, Upper Manhattan Rotary Club International, 1988-; trustee, School Bd, District 5, NYC, 1997-. **Honors/Awds:** Doctoral Fellowship, Columbia University, 1983-84; Special Performance Award, New York Public Library, 1988; Citation for Community Service, NYC Council, 1990. **Home Addr:** 1901 Madison Ave, #521, New York, NY 10035-2710.

MACK, RODERICK O'NEAL
Managing owner. **Personal:** Born Jul 30, 1955, Birmingham, AL; son of Irene Mack and Edward Mack; married Votura E Hendeson; children: Amrette, Shanta, Roderick Jr, Tamarka. **Educ:** Miles Coll, Birmingham, AL, BS, accounting, 1977; Jefferson St Jr Coll, Birmingham, AL, AAS, finance, 1981; Samford Univ, Birmingham, AL, MBA, 1981. **Career:** Liberty Natl Life Insurance Co, accounting intern 1975-76; Emergency Sch Aid Act, tutor 1976-77; Amer Inst of Banking, instructor 1982-83; Amer South Bank NA Birmingham, corporate accounting officer 1977-85; Mack & Associates, managing owner 1982-; Southern Junior Coll of Business, instructor 1986; Miles Coll, Birmingham AL, instr, 1991. **Orgs:** Treas 1985-87 pres 1988-89 Natl Black MBA Assoc Birmingham Chap; treas Family & Child Services A United Way Agency 1985-87; pres Birmingham Minority Business Adv Comm 1986-88; assoc dir Natl Assoc of Accountants Birmingham Vulcan Chap; mem Inst of Mgmt Accountants, Birmingham Inter Professional Assoc; co-chair Youth Leadership Forum of Birmingham 1987; Natl Soc of Tax Professionals; Birmingham Assn of Urban Planners; Edward Lee Norton, Bd of Advisors for Management & Prof Education, Birmingham-Southern Coll, 1990-93; Birmingham Public Schools Bus Education, advisory comm, 1992-95. **Honors/Awds:** Outstanding Member Award, Natl Assn of Accountants, 1983, 1985; Member of the Year, NBMBAA Birmingham Chapter, 1987; Birmingham Assn of Urban Bankers, Presidents Award, 1993. **Home Addr:** 801 Graymont Avenue, W, Birmingham, AL 35204. **Business Addr:** Managing Owner, Mack & Associates, PO Box 11308, Birmingham, AL 35202.

MACK, RUDY EUGENE, SR.
Airline pilot. **Personal:** Born Feb 9, 1941, Miami, FL; son of Flossie M Mack; divorced; children: Rudy Jr, Derek, Maurice, Jason. **Educ:** TN A&I, BS 1967. **Career:** Northwest Airlines, capt, currently; Prudential, ins agt 1967-71; Burnside OTT, flight instr 1968-71. **Orgs:** Mem Airline Pilot Assn; Orgn Black Airline Pilot; co-chmn com Rel com The Airline Pilot Union; aeromed chmn OBAP. **Business Addr:** Captain, Northwest Airline, Minneapolis-St Paul Airport, Minneapolis, MN 55406.

MACK, SAM
Professional basketball player. **Personal:** Born May 26, 1970, Chicago, IL. **Educ:** Iowa State; Arizona State; Tyler Junior College; Houston. **Career:** San Antonio Spurs, guard/forward, 1992-93; Rapid City Thrillers (CBA), 1993-94; Yakima Sun Kings (CBA), 1993-94; Fort Wayne Fury (CBA), 1993-94; Oklahoma City Cavalry (CBA), 1994-95; Rockford Lightning (CBA), 1995-96; Houston Rockets, 1996-97; Vancouver Grizzlies, 1997-. **Special Achievements:** CBA, All-League second team, 1996. **Business Addr:** Professional Basketball Player, Vancouver Grizzlies, 788 Beatty St, Ste 311, Vancouver, BC, Canada V6B 2M1, (604)688-5867.

MACK, SHANE LEE
Professional baseball player. **Personal:** Born Dec 7, 1963, Los Angeles, CA. **Educ:** UCLA. **Career:** San Diego Padres, outfielder, 1987-89; Minnesota Twins, 1990-94; Yomiuri Giants, 1995-96; Boston Red Sox, 1997; Oakland Athletics, 1998-. **Business Addr:** Professional Baseball Player, Oakland Athletics, 7677 Oakport St, 2nd Fl, Oakland Coliseum Complex, Oakland, CA 94621, (510)638-4900.

MACK, SYLVIA JENKINS
Educational administrator. **Personal:** Born Dec 22, 1931, Deal Island, MD; daughter of Violet Armstrong Jenkins and William E Jenkins; widowed; children: Dr Alphonso L DDS, Lt Comm Michael L US Navy, Don Frederick, Thomas Everett, Anthony Charles. **Educ:** Newmaan Coll, BS Prof Ed; Certified Trade & Indus Inst DE State Board of Ed; DE State Board of Cosmetology, licensed cosmetologist, licensed cosmetology instructor; St Joseph Univ Philadelphia PA, Masters Prof Educ. **Career:** Del Castle Tech HS Wilmington, DE, instr cosmetology & science 24 yrs; Mas Aivlis Academy of Cosmetology and Barbering, owner, currently. **Orgs:** Mem Brandywine Professional Assoc; elected school bd member Brandywine Sch Dist DE 1981-84, re-elected to same position 1984-89; mem Natl Assoc of Black School Bd Mem; vice pres, Brandywine School District Board of Education; National Associate of University Women; life mem, NAACP; National Political Congress Black Women. **Home Addr:** 2121 Jessup St, Wilmington, DE 19802.

MACK, TREMAIN
Professional football player. **Personal:** Born Nov 21, 1974. **Educ:** Miami (Fla.), attended. **Career:** Cincinnati Bengals, defensive back, 1997-. **Business Addr:** Professional Football Player, Cincinnati Bengals, One Bengals Dr, Cincinnati, OH 45202, (513)621-3550.

MACK, WILBUR OLLIO
Educator (retired). **Personal:** Born Aug 11, 1919, Seward, OK; son of Addie Lowe Mack and Collister Mack; married Martha Griffin Mack, Aug 11, 1970; children: Ronald Wilbur, Waymond Ollio, Larry Wayne, Wilma Denise, Meltonia. **Educ:** Langston Univ, BS 1947; OK State Univ, MS 1954. **Career:** Prairie View Coll, assoc prof 1953-57; So Univ Baton Rouge, assoc prof 1957-62; FL A&M Univ Tallahassee, asst prof engrg 1962-89. **Orgs:** Registered professional engr TX LA; mem Amer Soc Engrs; mem Natl Safety Council; Kappa Alpha Psi; Mason 32 degree; mem Soil and Crop Society 1970-; ASAE, Agrieng, 1955-. **Military Serv:** AUS 1st lt 1941-45. **Home Addr:** 710 Stafford St, Tallahassee, FL 32310.

MACK, WILHELMENA
Hospital administrator. **Personal:** Born Oct 1, 1951, Kendall, FL; daughter of Gladys Terry Brown and Eugene Brown; divorced; children: Shannon Lynnette. **Educ:** University of Miami, BA, 1972, MEd, 1973; Florida Atlantic University, EdS, 1983, EdD, 1988. **Career:** Dade County, personnel officer, 1973-74; Jackson Memorial Hospital, personnel officer, 1974-75, education coordinator, 1975-78; Memorial Hospital, assistant director for management training, 1978-79, training & development director, 1979-. **Orgs:** American Assn of University Women, 1991-; American Society of Health Educators and Trainers, 1989-; Broward Economic Development Council; Exec committee 1993-; Education Committee, 1994-; Dania Chamber of Commerce; board of directors, 1988-91, exec comm, 1989-91; Greater Ft Lauderdale Chamber of Commerce; board of directors, 1994-, Exec Comm, 1995-97; Leadership Hollywood, 1994; Hollywood Chamber of Commerce, Phi Delta Kappa, 1991-; BAND (Business Against Narcotics and Drugs) board of directors, 1994-; Browards County School Boards Blu Ribbon Committee, Business Coalition for Education Excellence; World Class Schools. **Honors/Awds:** National Association of Negro Business & Professional Women, Ft Lauderdale chapter, Woman of the Year, 1986; National Junior Achievement, Bronze Leadership Award, 1987; Price Waterhouse, Up and Comers Award, 1989; Outstanding Service Award, 1990; Dania Chamber of Commerce, President's Award for Outstanding Service, 1990; Council for Black Economic Development, Appreciation Award, 1990; Dollars and Sense Magazine, America's Up and Coming Business and Professional Women Award, 1991; Greater Ft Lauderdale Chamber of Commerce, Abraham S Fischler Award (Education), 1992. **Special Achievements:** Appointed, Council for Black Economic Development. **Business Addr:** Director, Training and Development, Memorial Hospital, 3501 Johnson St, Hollywood, FL 33021, (305)987-2000.

MACKEL, AUDLEY MAURICE, III
Orthopaedic surgeon. **Personal:** Born Dec 3, 1955, Natchez, MS; son of Nannie Love Mackel-Blassingame and Audley Maurice Mackel Jr; married Sharon White, Aug 14, 1982; children: Ashley Monique, Audley Maurice. **Educ:** Morehouse Coll, BS 1977; Meharry Medical Coll, MD 1981. **Career:** Northwestern Univ Medical Center, intern 1981-82, orthopaedic resident 1982-86; Kerlan Jobe Orthopaedic Clinic, orthopaedic surgeon, arthritis/joint implant fellow 1986-87; Charles Drew Medical School, Los Angeles, CA orthopaedic surgeon 1987-88; Associates in Orthopaedics, Cleveland, OH, orthopaedic surgeon, 1988-. **Orgs:** Member, National Medical Association, 1982-; fellow, American Academy of Orthopaedic Surgeons, 1991-; drug crew chief, United States Olympic Committee, 1990-; member, Cleveland Orthopaedic Club, 1989-. **Honors/Awds:** The Natl Dean's List 1981; Alpha Omega Alpha Medical Honor Soc 1981; Outstanding Young Men of Amer 1983; Anatomy Awd Dept of Orthopaedic Surgery 1984; Physician Recognition Award, American Medical Association. **Home Addr:** 23200 Lyman Blvd, Shaker Heights, OH 44122. **Business Addr:** Orthopaedic Surgeon, Associates in Orthopaedics, Inc., 11201 Shaker Blvd, Cleveland, OH 44104, (216)795-2050.

MACKEY, JOHN
Professional football player (retired), community activist, business executive. **Personal:** Born 1941. **Educ:** Syracuse University. **Career:** Tight end/offensive end: Baltimore Colts, 1963-71, San Diego Chargers, 1972; Community for Education Foundation, chairman of the board, 1993-. **Honors/Awds:** Five-time Pro Bowl participant; Pro Football Hall of Fame, inductee, 1992; NAACP, Paul Robeson Award. **Business Phone:** (213)892-1402.

MACKEY, MALCOLM
Professional basketball player. **Personal:** Born Jul 11, 1970, Chattanooga, TN. **Educ:** Georgia Tech. **Career:** Phoenix Suns, 1993-. **Business Addr:** Professional Basketball Player, Phoenix Suns, 201 E Jefferson St, Phoenix, AZ 85004, (602)379-7900.

MACKLIN, ANDERSON D.
Educator. **Personal:** son Of Alice Macklin and H R Macklin; married JoAnn White. **Educ:** BS 1954; MS 1956; EdD 1969. **Career:** Dept Fine Arts, Jackson St Univ, prof/chair, 1988-; Dept Fine Arts VA State Coll, prof chmn 1962-86; MS Valley State Coll, 1960-62; Wiley Coll, 1958-60; Lincoln U, instr art 1954-58. **Orgs:** NASAD program evaluator, Mississippi Art Education Assn; VP VA Art Educ Assn; past polemarch Petersburg Alumni Chpt; Kappa Alpha Psi Frat Inc; Delta Phi Delta Art Frat; Phi Delta Kappa Educ Frat; Nat Conf of Artists; AAUP; NAACP; pres Men's Fellowship Gillfield Bapt Ch; chmn Spl Frat Com for AP Hill Comm Ctr. **Honors/Awds:** So Found Fellowship Recip 1967; Syracuse Fellowship for Faculty Devel 1969-70; num awards for paintings incl Atlanta Univ Annum. **Business Addr:** Professor/Chairman, Dept of Art, Jackson State Univesity, PO Box 17064, Jackson, MS 39217.

MACKLIN, JOHN W.
Educator. **Personal:** Born Dec 11, 1939, Fort Worth, TX; son of Vera L Macklin; children: Marcus E. **Educ:** Linfield Coll McMinnville, OR, BA 1962; Cornell Univ, PhD 1968. **Career:** Univ of WA, asst prof of chemistry 1968-87, assoc prof 1987-. **Orgs:** Mem Amer Chem Soc 1966-; mem AAAS 1978-; NOBCCHE 1986-; member, ISSOL, 1984-. **Business Addr:** Associate Professor, University of Washington, Dept of Chemistry, Box 351700, Seattle, WA 98195.

MACLACHLAN, JANET A.
Actress, acting coach; dialogue director, producer. **Personal:** Born Aug 27, New York, NY; daughter of Ruby Iris South MacLachlan (deceased) and Dr James M MacLachlan (deceased); children: Samantha. **Educ:** Hunter Coll, BA. **Career:** Theatre-The Blacks; Tiger, Tiger Burning Bright; Nevis Mountain Dew, Eyes of the American, Hamlet; films-Sounder, The Man, Uptight, Halls of Anger, Heart & Souls; television-I Spy, Cagney & Lacey, Amen, Gabriel's Fire, Love Thy Neighbor, Tuskegee Airmen, Murder One. **Orgs:** Mem bd dirs Screen Actors Guild 1976-81; Academy of TV Arts & Sciences, bd of governors 1986-88, chairman, membership, 1989-94; treasurer Media Forum, Inc 1984-88; sec bd directors MagaLink, Inc 1982-88; Academy of Motion Picture of Arts & Sciences, chairman Scholarships and grants comm, 1992-95, 1997. **Honors/Awds:** Emmy Awd for Best Performance Los Angeles area Academy of TV Arts & Sciences 1982; NAACP Theatre Award: Best Actress in "Eyes of The American," 1986-87. **Home Addr:** PO Box 27593, Los Angeles, CA 90027.

MACON, MARK L.
Professional basketball player. **Personal:** Born Apr 19, 1969, Saginaw, MI. **Educ:** Temple University. **Career:** Denver Nuggets, 1991-93; Detroit Pistons, 1993-. **Honors/Awds:** NBA All-Rookie second team, 1992. **Business Addr:** Professional Basketball Player, Detroit Pistons, 2 Championship Dr, Auburn Hills, MI 48326, (810)377-0100.

MADDOX, ELTON PRESTON, JR.
Dentist, educator. **Personal:** Born Nov 17, 1946, Kingston, MD; son of Virginia Maddox and Elton Maddox; married. **Educ:** Morgan State Coll, BS 1968; Univ of MD Dental Sch, DDS 1972. **Career:** Team Clinic, clinical dir, acting dir 1976-77; Univ of MD Dental Sch, asst prof 1975-77, instr 1973-75, clinical asst prof 1977-82; private practice 1977-. **Orgs:** Chmm Minority Recruitment Comm 1974-77; admissions comm Univ of MD Dental Sch 1974-77; clinical competency comm 1975-76; mem Alpha Phi Alpha Frat Inc.; Jr C of C; MD State Dental Assn, Eastern Shore Dental Assn; pres Community Awareness Committee. **Honors/Awds:** Publ "A Guide to Clinical Competency," Jour of Dental Educ 1976; "Why Not?" Univ MD 1976. **Business Addr:** 1229 Mt Hermon Rd, Salisbury, MD 21801.

MADDOX, GARRY LEE
Professional baseball player (retired). **Personal:** Born Sep 1, 1949, Cincinnati, OH; married Sondra; children: Garry, Derrick. **Educ:** Harbor College, Wilmington, CA, attended. **Career:** San Francisco Giants, outfielder 1972-75; Philadelphia Phillies, outfielder 1975-86. **Orgs:** Mem bd dirs Philadelphia Child Guidance Clinic. **Honors/Awds:** NL All-Star Fielding Team 1975-79; played in Championship Series 1976-78; Young Leaders of Philadelphia Awd, 1984; shares LCS record for most consecutive games with one or more RBI's total series w/4; led NL in sacrifice flys with 8 in 1981; 8 Gold Glove Awds. **Military Serv:** AUS 1968-70. **Business Addr:** Philadelphia Phillies, PO Box 7575, Philadelphia, PA 19101.

MADDOX, JACK H.
Real estate broker. **Personal:** Born Jul 17, 1927, Detroit, MI; son of Wylma Maddox and John Maddox (deceased); divorced; children: 1 daughter. **Educ:** Wayne State Univ, BS; Univ of MI, Cert; MI State Univ, Cert. **Career:** Real estate & rel subj teacher; Assoc Ins Agency, pres & gen agent; Past Brokers Invest Co, past vp; JH Maddox & Co, proprietor real estate, currently. **Orgs:** Past sec & dir Ebony Dist Cty; mem Real Estate Alumni MI; chmn fund raising comm for local state natl pol candidates; chaired comm Alpha Phi alpha; guardsman Jaycees; mem NAACP Freedom Fund Dinner Comm; past dir Detroit NAACP; chmn Housing Comm; mem Detroit Real Estate Brokers Assoc, Pol Action Comm; dir Housing Owners of US Exchange; mem natl life membership comm NAACP; original chmn 1300 Lafayette E Co-op Bd of Dir; mem, Detroit Bd of Realtors, chmn, Govt Affairs Comm 1988-95. **Honors/Awds:** Past chmn 1300 Lafayette E Co-op Bd of Dir, which negotiated purchase of 9 million dollar luxury apt overlooking Detroit River from HUD; contracted erection 1st black individually owned medical office bldg Detroit; co-chaired, 1970 NAACP Freedom Fund Dinner; Million Dollar Club, NAACP 1975-88. **Military Serv:** US Navy, SK3, 1946-48; Victory Medal. **Business Addr:** Real Estate Broker-Owner, J H Maddox & Co, 1300 Lafayette E, Suite 2603, Detroit, MI 48207.

MADDOX, JULIUS A.
Association executive. **Personal:** Born Oct 9, 1942, Philadelphia, PA; son of Fannie Maddox; children: Marcus, Christopher. **Educ:** Wayne State University, BS; Oakland University, MA; Wayne State University, Education Specialist. **Career:** Highland Park Schools, educator, 1974-76; Pontiac Schools, educator, 1976-91; Michigan Education Association, president, 1991-. **Orgs:** Professional Standards Commission for Teachers, former mem; Michigan Department of Education Periodic Review Council; NAACP, life mem; Delta Dental of Michigan, board of directors; Phi Delta Kappa. **Honors/Awds:** One of Detroit's Fifteen Top Educations, Success Guide; Jefferson County Kentucky Teachers Association, Apple Awd; MEA Eomen's Caucus, Man of the Year, 1980. **Military Serv:** US Army, spc 5, 1966-68; Usaryis Soldier of the Month, 1967. **Business Addr:** President, Michigan Education Association, 1216 Kendale Blvd, PO Box 2573, East Lansing, MI 48826-2573, (517)332-6551.

MADDOX, MARGARET JOHNNETTA SIMMS
Public relations counselor. **Personal:** Born Aug 31, 1952, Clio, SC; married Rev Odinga Lawrence Maddox. **Educ:** Livingstone Coll, BA 1973; The OH State Univ, MA 1975, PhD, 1991. **Career:** TRW Marlin-Rockwell Div, systems analyst 1977-78; FL A&M Univ, prof 1978-80; Senator Wm F Bowen OH, admin asst 1980-83; MJ Simms and Assocs Inc, ceo/pres 1983-; Wilverforce University, Wilberfore, OH, professor, political science, 1991-. **Orgs:** Columbus Area C of C 1983-; mem Amer Mktg Assoc Central OH 1984-; mem Public Relations Soc of Amer 1986-; Livingston College Alumni Association, vice pres local chapter, president. **Honors/Awds:** Outstanding Young Women of Amer 1983; Certificate of Commendation The Ohio Senate 1983. **Business Addr:** President and CEO, M J Simms and Associates Inc, 815 E Mound St 1st Floor, Redwood Bldg, Columbus, OH 43205.

MADDOX, MARK ANTHONY
Professional football player. **Personal:** Born Mar 23, 1968, Milwaukee, WI. **Educ:** Northern Michigan. **Career:** Buffalo Bills, linebacker, 1992-. **Business Addr:** Professional Football Player, Buffalo Bills, One Bills Dr, Orchard Park, NY 14127, (716)648-1800.

MADGETT, NAOMI LONG
Poet, professor, publisher, editor. **Personal:** Born Jul 5, 1923, Norfolk, VA; daughter of Maude Salena Hilton Long and Clarence Marcellus Long Sr; married Leonard P Andrews Sr, Mar 31, 1972 (died 1996); children: Jill Witherspoon Boyer. **Educ:** VA State Coll, BA 1945; Wayne State Univ, MEd 1955; Intl Inst for Advanced Studies (Greenwich Univ), PhD 1980. **Career:** Poet and author, 1941-; MI Chronicle, staff writer 1946-47; MI Bell Tel Co, serv rep 1948-54; Detroit Pub Sch, teacher 1955-65, 1966-68; public speaker, poetry readings only 1956-; Oakland Univ, res assoc 1965-66; East MI Univ, assoc prof English 1968-73; Univ of MI, lectr 1970; East MI Univ, prof 1973-84, prof Emeritus 1984-; Lotus Press, publ & editor 1974-; sr editor, Lotus Poetry Series, MI State Univ Press, 1993-. **Orgs:** Coll Language Assn; Alpha Kappa Alpha Sor; NAACP; Detroit

Women Writers; Southern Poverty Law Center; Langston Hughes Society; Zora Neale Hurston Society. **Honors/Awds:** Distinguished English Teacher of the Year, Met Detroit; 1st recipient Mott Fellowship in English 1965; Disting Soror Award, Alpha Rho Omega Chap, Alpha Kappa Alpha Sor, 1969; papers being collected in Special Collections Libr Fisk Univ; Resolutions from Detroit Cty Cncl 1982 and MI State Legisl 1982 & 1984; Key to the City of Detroit 1980; Recognition by Black Caucus of Natl Cncl of Teachers of English 1984; Natl Coalition of 100 Black Women 1984; Induction into Stylus Society Howard Univ 1984; Disting Artist Award, Wayne State Univ, 1985; Robert Hayden Runagate Awd, 1985; Creative Artist Award, MI Council for the arts, 1987; Creative Achievement Award, College Language Assn, 1988; "In Her Lifetime" Award, Afrikan Poets Theatre Inc, 1989; Literature Award, Arts Foundation of Michigan, 1990; Honorary Degree, Loyola University, Chicago, 1993; Recognition by Black Caucus of American Library Assn, 1992; honorary degree, MI State Univ, 1994; MI Artist Award, 1993; Amer Book Award, 1993. **Special Achievements:** Editor of two anthologies including: Adam of Ife: Black Women in Praise of Black Men, 1992; eight books published including: Remembrances of Spring: Collected Early Poems, 1993; Octavia and Other Poems, 1988; Star by Star; Pink Ladies in the Afternoon; Exits & Entrances; poems widely anthologized & translated. **Home Addr:** 18080 Santa Barbara, Detroit, MI 48221. **Business Phone:** (313)861-1280.

MADHUBUTI, HAKI R. (DON L. LEE)
Association executive, editor. **Personal:** Born Feb 23, 1942, Little Rock, AR; son of Maxine Graves Lee and Jimmy L Lee; married Johari Amini; children: 2. **Educ:** Attended Wilson Jr Coll, Roosevelt Univ, Univ of Illinois, Chicago Circle; Univ of Iowa, MFA, 1984. **Career:** DuSable Museum of African Amer History, Chicago IL, apprentice curator, 1963-67; Montgomery Ward, Chicago IL, stock dept clerk, 1963-64; US Post Office, Chicago IL, clerk, 1964-65; Spiegels, Chicago IL, jr exec, 1965-66; Cornell Univ, Ithaca NY, writer-in-residence, 1968-69; Northeastern Illinois State Coll, Chicago IL, poet-in-residence, 1969-70; Univ of Illinois, Chicago IL, lecturer, 1969-71; Howard Univ, Washington DC, writer-in-residence, 1970-78; Morgan State Coll, Baltimore MD, 1972-73; Chicago State Univ, Chicago IL, assoc prof of English, 1984-; Third World Press, Chicago IL, publisher and editor, 1967-; Inst of Positive Educ, Chicago IL, dir, 1969-. **Orgs:** Founding mem, Org of Black Amer Culture, Writers Workshop, 1967-75; past exec council, Congress of African People; vice-chmn, African Liberation Day Support Comm 1972-73; pres, African-American Publishers', Booksellers', and Writers' Assn, 1990-. **Honors/Awds:** Published works include Think Black, Broadside Press, 1967; Black Pride, Broadside Press, 1967; For Black People (and Negroes Too), Third World Press, 1968; Don't Cry, Scream, Broadside Press, 1969; We Walk the Way of the New World, Broadside Press, 1970; Dynamite Voices I: Black Poets of the 1960s, Broadside Press, 1971; Directionscore: Selected and New Poems, Broadside Press, 1971; From Plan to Planet—Life Studies: The Need for Afrikan Minds & Institutions, Broadside Press, 1973; Book of Life, Broadside Press, 1973; Earthquakes and Sunrise Missions: Poetry and Essays of Black Renewal, 1793-1983, Third World Press, 1984; Say That the River Turns: The Impact of Gwendolyn Brooks, Third World Press, 1987; Black Men: Obsolete, Single,Dangerous?; Claiming Earth: Race, Rage, Rape, Redempti Blacks Seeking A Culture of Enlightened Empowerment, 1994. **Business Addr:** Editor, Third World Press, 7524 S Cottage Grove, Chicago, IL 60619.

MADISON, EDDIE L., JR.
Writer, editor, public affairs coordinator. **Personal:** Born Sep 8, 1930, Tulsa, OK; son of Laverta Pyle Madison and Eddie L Madison Sr; married Davetta Jayn Cooksey, Nov 17, 1956; children: Eddie III, Karyn Devette, David. **Educ:** Lincoln Univ of MO Jefferson City, MO, BJ 1952; Univ of Tulsa, MA Mass Communications (1st Black) 1959. **Career:** The Chicago Tribune, sect editor (1st Black full-time editorial staff mem) 1963-65; Info Div US Dept of Commerce, info spec (1st Black profl) 1965; Office of Publ & Info for Domestic & Intl Bus, dept dir publ div 1965-69; Wash Star Station Group, mgr comm serv (1st Black mgr) 1969-77; Wash Star Comm Inc Broadcast Div, mgr admin serv 1977-78; US Indsl Outlook-1979, chief editor 1978-79; US Dept of Commerce Bus Amer Mag, asst editor 1979-81; Congressman Gus Savage of IL, chief press asst 1981-82; Three Elms & Assocs, founder/pres; US Dept of Health & Human Svcs, writer/editor/public affairs coord 1982-. **Orgs:** Public relations/management consultant; founding pres Natl Broadcast Assn for Community Affairs 1974-76; public relations dir, Alpha Phi Alpha Fraternity; Intl Bus Serv; US Dept of Commerce; Natl Assn of Educ Broadcasters 1978-79; dir Opportunities Industrialization Cntr 1971-78; mem Commn on Human Rights DC 1970-75; dir DC United Way 1970-78; bd trustees Children's Hosp Natl Med Center 1975-78; mem & officer numerous organizations & committees. **Honors/Awds:** Outstanding Young Men of Amer 1966; Citation of Merit for Outstanding Performance in Journalism Lincoln Univ of MO 1971; Spl Citation Presidential Classroom for Young Amer 1973; Plaque/Appreciation/Thanks Natl Broadcast Assn for Community Affairs Columbus, OH 1977. **Military Serv:** AUS 1952-54; UN Defense Medal, Good Conduct Medal. **Home Addr:** 1120 Netherlands Ct, Silver Spring, MD 20905.

MADISON, JACQUELINE EDWINA
Librarian, information manager, entrepreneur. **Personal:** Born Jul 16, 1951, Darlington, SC; daughter of Lula Mack McLeod and John Brown; married Calvin Lee Madison, Aug 18, 1975; children: Jaquenette, Calexandria. **Educ:** Fayetteville State Univ, Fayetteville, NC, BS, 1972; Baylor University, Waco, TX, certificate, 1974; Kansas State University, Kansas, KS, 1986; Emporia State Univ, Emporia, KS, MLS, 1991. **Career:** FDA, Orlando, FL, food & drug inspector, 1972-73; US Army, Nurnberg, Germany, sanitary eng, 1974-77, sup appt clerk, 1977-79; Central Texas College, Fort Lewis, WA, substitute teacher, 1980-82; Fort Riley Library, Fort Riley, KS, library tech, 1987-90; Youth Services, Fort Riley, KS, secretary/personal administrative assistant, 1990-; Jaqcal's Infophone, parent/teacher/student communication line. **Orgs:** Member, Kansas Library Assn, 1989-; member, Black Caucus ALA, 1989-; member, Delta Sigma Theta, 1971-; member, Parent Teacher Assn, 1988-; member, SLA, 1989-. **Honors/Awds:** Golden Poet Awards, World of Poetry, 1990-91; Science Awards, Phi Beta Kappa, 1971-72; Scholarship, ESU, 1989; Gold Poet Awards, World of Poetry, 1992, Phi Kapa Phi, 1991; Woman of the Year, Nominee & Finalist, 1996. **Military Serv:** US Army, cpl, 1974-77; National Defense Service Medal 1977, Army Commendation Medal, 1977, Good Conduct Medal, 1979; Certificates of Appreciation. **Business Addr:** Wyeth Ayerst Research, Drug Safety Info, Ctr, 641 Ridge Rd, Chazy, NY 12921, (518)846-6394.

MADISON, JOSEPH EDWARD
Broadcast journalist. **Personal:** Born Jun 16, 1949, Dayton, OH; son of Nancy Madison and Felix Madison; married Sharon Madison; children: Shawna, Jason, Monesha, Michelle. **Educ:** Washington University, BA, 1971. **Career:** General Motors Corp, public relations 1969-70; St Louis Cardinal Football, statistician 1970-71; Seymour & Lundy Assoc, urban affairs 1971-74; Detroit Branch NAACP, exec dir 1974-77; Natl Political Dir, NAACP; Political Dir of SEIU; Dir of COTE; WXYZ-TV, Detroit, MI, host of public affairs program, 1975-76; WXYT Radio, Detroit, MI, host, 1978-89; WRC Radio, WWDB-FM, 1989; Washington, DC, radio show host, 1990-94; Natl Press Building, personality & dir of syndication, currently. **Orgs:** Bd of dir Operation Big Vote, 1978-; bd of advisors, US Census Bureau, 1985; national board member, life member, NAACP; mem, Intl Platform Assoc, 1985; pres, Michigan Leadership Conference. **Honors/Awds:** Americans Noteworthy Community Leaders, Jaycees, 1976, 1977, 1978; Man of the Year, Black American Women's Hall of Fame, 1980; Men to Watch in the 1980's, Detroit Monthly Magazine; Nation's 50 Leaders of the Future, Ebony Magazine; Top Ten Newsmaker, Crain's Detroit Business; Achievement in Radio Award for Best Non Drive Time Radio Show; Best Spot News Bdcast, Finalist, Best New Talent Award; Honorary Kentucky Colonel.

MADISON, LEATRICE BRANCH
Educator. **Personal:** Born Sep 5, 1922, Washington, DC; daughter of Julia Bailey Branch and Hayes Louis Branch; married Robert P Madison; children: Jeanne M Anderson, Juliette M Little. **Educ:** Miner Teachers Coll, BA 1943; Univ of Chicago, MA 1947. **Career:** Syphax Elementary Sch, teacher 1943-48; Miles Standish Elem Sch, teacher 1949-51; George Washington Carver Sch, teacher 1954-57; Case Elem Sch, teacher 1957-60. **Orgs:** Board member Federation of Community Planning 1967-85; United Way Services 1970-76; Blue Cross of Northeast Ohio 1974-84; Greater Cleveland Girl Scouts; Shaker Lake Regional Nature Center; Cleveland Child Guidance Center; Western Reserve Historical Society; YWCA; Planned Parenthood; University of Chicago Alumni Board of Directors; Case Western Reserve University Board of Overseers and Visiting Committees 1973-86; Cleveland Symphony Orchestra Advisory Council; president/founding member Harambee: Services to Black Families 1979-85; chairman NAACP Freedom Fund Dinner; Juvenile Court, Youth Services Advisory Board; Cleveland Heights Advisory Commission for HUD Block Grants; mem Cleveland Symphony Orchestra Women's committee; Cleveland Heights-University library board. **Honors/Awds:** Distinguished Serv Awd Blue Cross 1984; Citation City of Cleveland 1984; Distinguished Serv Awd Harambee 1985; President's Awd Federation of Community Planning; Pi Lambda Theta Honorary Education Sorority; Citation, Cuyahoga County Commissioners, 1993-94; Citation, Ohio State House of Representatives, 1994; Univ of Chicago Public Service Citation, 1994. **Special Achievements:** First African-American President of Cleveland Heights, Univ Heights PTA Unit, 1971; First Black Woman to serve as vice pres, Federation of Community Planning, 1977; vice chair of United Way Svcs Capital Campaign, 1974; first black person to serve as chairman of Federation of Community Planning Annual Health and Human Svcs Institute, 1981. **Home Addr:** 2339 North Park Blvd, Cleveland Heights, OH 44106.

MADISON, RICHARD
Government official. **Personal:** Born Dec 6, 1932, Camden, AL; married Edith Sauhing Ho. **Educ:** Morehouse Coll, BA 1953; Univ of PA, MGA 1958; Univ of Pittsburgh, PhD. **Career:** Gov's Ofc of Adminstr PA, dir of personnel 1972-; Inst for Minority Bus Educ Howard U, exec dir 1970-71; Nat Urban League Entrepreneurial Devel, natl dir 1969-70; Nat Urban League Field Operations, asst dir 1968-69; CARE E Pakistan, dir 1968; CARE Malaysia, acting dir 1967; CARE Hong Kong, asst dir 1965-68; CARE Honduras, asst dir 1963-65; Peace Corps Colombia, asso dir 1962-63; CARE Turkey, field rep 1961-62; Gov's Ofc Harrisburg PA, adminstr asst to dir of personnel 1960-61; Budget Bur Gov's Ofc Harrisburg, bdgt analyst 1958-60. **Orgs:** Mem Am Soc for Pub Adminstr; Intl Personnel Mgmt Assn; mem NAACP; Frgn Policy Assn; Omega Psi Phi Frat; Black Polit Assmbly. **Military Serv:** AUS 1953-55. **Business Addr:** Gov's Ofc of Adminstrn, 517 Finance Bldg, Harrisburg, PA 17120.

MADISON, ROBERT P.
Architect. **Personal:** Born Jul 28, 1923, Cleveland, OH; son of Nettie Josephine Brown and Robert James Madison; married Leatrice Lucille Branch, Apr 16, 1949; children: Jeanne M Anderson, Juliette M Little. **Educ:** Western Reserve Univ, BA 1948; Harvard Univ, MA 1952; Ecole Des Beaux Arts Paris, 1953. **Career:** Robert A Little Architects, designer 1948-51; Howard Univ, asst prof 1952-54; Robert P Madison Intl, president, chairman, chief executive officer, 1954-. **Orgs:** Trustee Case Western Reserve Univ 1969-81; dir Industrial Bank of Washington 1975-81; trustee Cuyahoga Metropolitan General Hospital 1982-; mem Ohio Bd of Building Standards State of Ohio 1984-; chairman Jury of Fellows Natl AIA 1985; trustee Cleveland Chap Amer Red Cross 1986-; trustee Ohio Motorists Assn 1986-; mem Cleveland Downtown Plan Steering Comm 1986; mem City Planning Commn Cleveland Heights OH 1987-; mem Alpha Phi Alpha, Sigma Pi Phi; trustee, Cleveland Opera, 1990-; trustee, University Circle, Inc, 1974-; trustee, Midtown Corridor, Inc, 1982-. **Honors/Awds:** Architect US Embassy Dakar Senegal 1965-77; Architect's delegation Peoples Republic of China 1974; Fellow Amer Inst of Architects 1974; Disting Serv Award BEDO State of Ohio; President's Award Cleveland Chap AIA; Distinguished Firm Award, Howard Univ, 1989; Distinguished Serv Award, Case Western Reserve Univ, 1989; Honorary Doctor of Humanities, Howard University, 1987; AIA Ohio, Gold Medal Firm Award, 1994. **Military Serv:** US Army, 1st Lt, 1942-46; Purple Heart, 1944. **Home Addr:** 2339 N Park Blvd, Cleveland Heights, OH 44106.

MADISON, RONALD L.
Electrical engineer. **Personal:** Born Feb 3, 1942, Detroit, MI; married Mamie; children: Monica, Jeffrey. **Educ:** Univ of MI, BSEE 1964; Univ of MI Dearborn, MSEE 1972. **Career:** Ford Motor Co, sr design engr, body & elec prod engr 1976-, serv proj devel engr 1974, prod design engr 1973-74; Ford Motor Co Serv Rsrch Ctr, serv opr coord 1974-76; GM Tech Ctr, sr proj engr 1969-73; Delco Elec Div GM, proj engr 1966-69; GM Proving Ground, jr engr 1964-66. **Orgs:** Vp Alpha Phi Alpha Frat Univ of MI 1961-63; mem Univ of MI Dearborn Assn of Black Students 1972; Engineering Soc of Detroit 1972-74; NAACP 1974-75. **Honors/Awds:** Fellowship Chapel Lay Rdrs; Fellowship Chapel Men's Club; hon grad Cass Tech HS 1959; Grant-in-Aid Schlrshp Sr Yr Univ of MI 1964. **Business Addr:** Body & Elec Prod Engr Ford Mot, 21500 Oakwood Blvd, Dearborn, MI 48121.

MADISON, SAM
Professional football player. **Personal:** Born Apr 23, 1974. **Educ:** Louisville. **Career:** Miami Dolphins, defensive back, 1997-. **Business Addr:** Professional Football Player, Miami Dolphins, 2269 NW 199th St, Miami, FL 33056, (305)620-5000.

MADISON, SHANNON L.
Engineer. **Personal:** Born Jun 21, 1927, Texas; married Ruth Jean; children: Earl Wayne, Michael Denard, Stephanie Annett, Sharon, Maria. **Educ:** Howard U, BS. **Career:** York Div Borg Warner Corp, devel engr 1954-59; Emerson Radio & Phonograph Co, chief test engr 1959-61; Whirlpool Corp, sr mfg rsrch engr 1965-; Delco Appliance Div GM, sr proj engr 1961-65. **Orgs:** Human Resources Counc 1965-68; Tri-Co Comm Action Commn 1965-71; mem SME; NTA; ASHRAE; Sigma Xi; SPE; written many articles; subj of many articles; Relat Adv Bd; pres Homes Berrien Co Families Inc 1968-; mem State Adv Bd Gov MI 1972-; Comprehen State Hlth Plng Adv Counc 1971-74; Commnty Twin City Area Human Relat Counc; Twin Cities Comm Forum; Model Cities; mem NAACP; Self Devel Com Chmn. **Business Addr:** Sr Mfg Res Engr, Whirlpool Corp, Monte Rd, Rm 2050, Benton Harbor, MI 49022.

MADKINS, GERALD
Professional basketball player. **Personal:** Born Apr 18, 1969, Merced, CA. **Educ:** UCLA. **Career:** NBA Record: Cleveland Cavaliers, 1993-; CBA Record: Grand Rapids Hoops, 1992-93. **Business Addr:** Professional Basketball Player, Cleveland Cavaliers, Gund Arena, One Center Ct, Cleveland, OH 44115, (216)659-9100.

MADLOCK, BILL, JR.
Professional baseball player (retired). **Personal:** Born Jan 12, 1951, Memphis, TN; married Cynthia; children: Sarah, Stephen, William Douglas, Jeremy Joseph. **Educ:** Southwestern Community College, Keokuk, IA, attended. **Career:** Texas Rangers, infielder, 1973; Chicago Cubs, infielder, 1974-76; San Francisco Giants, infielder 1977-79; Pittsburgh Pirates, infield-

er 1979-85; Los Angeles Dodgers, infielder, 1985-87; Detroit Tigers, infielder, 1987. **Orgs:** Cystic Fibrosis ''65 Roses'' Campaign. **Honors/Awds:** 4 NL batting titles, becoming 11th player in Major League hist to win the crown 4 times 1983; helped lead the Pirates to the World Championship 1979; mem The Sporting News All-Star Team 1975; National League All-Star Team, 1975, 1981, 1983.

MADU, ANTHONY CHISARAOKWU
Educator, research scientist. **Personal:** Born Jun 10, 1956, Ulakwo, Nigeria; son of John & Pricilla Madu; married Mary Ellis, Jun 14, 1986; children: Geoffrey, Theandra. **Educ:** Benedict Coll, BS, 1979; Meharry Med Coll, PhD, 1985; Univ of MI, Postdoc, 1985-90. **Career:** Univ of MI, lecturer, 1989, Dept of Biology, research fellow, 1985-89, sr assoc, 1989-90; Emory Univ, Dept of Biology, sr assoc, 1990-91; VA Union Univ, Dept of Biology, assoc prof, 1991-; Med Coll of VA, Dept of Surgery, faculty assoc, 1992-; VA Union Univ, MARC, prog dir, 1992-;. **Orgs:** Council on Undergraduate Research, 1994-; Amer Society for Microbiology, 1983-; Amer Assn for the Advancement of Sci, 1985-; Alpha Kappa Mu Honor Society, Kappa Pi Chapter, 1988-. **Honors/Awds:** VA Union Univ, Teaching Excellence Award, 1992-93; American Society for Microbiology, Visiting Scientist; NIH, Minority Faculty Supplement Research Award, 1992-95; VUU, Beneficiary Mobil Foundation Institutional Award, 1991; NIH, Post-Doctoral Fellowship Research Award, 1987-89. **Special Achievements:** Numerous publications, 1981-91. **Business Addr:** Assoc Prof, Virginia Union University, 1500 N Lombardy St, Ellison Hall, Rm 220-A, Richmond, VA 23220, (804)257-5614.

MAGEE, ROBERT WALTER
Family practitioner. **Personal:** Born Apr 23, 1951, New Orleans, LA; married Deborah Ketcheus. **Educ:** Southern Univ, BS 1973; Meharry Medical Coll, MD 1977. **Career:** Plasma Alliance, staff physician 1979-82; Mathew Walker Health Ctr, staff physician 1980-82; Meharry FP Program, asst prof 1980-82; New Orleans Health Corp, medical dir 1982-85; HMO, staff physician. **Orgs:** Staff physician Health America 1985-.

MAGEE, SADIE E.
Educator, coach. **Personal:** Born Oct 27, 1932, Mt Olive, MS. **Educ:** Alcorn State Univ, BS 1954; Jackson State Univ, MS Ed 1975. **Career:** Lanier HS Jackson Publ School, teacher, coach 1954-69; Central HS Jackson Publ School, teacher 1969-75; City of Jackson Allied Svcs, counselor 1971-73; Jackson State Univ, instructor of physical educ, head basketball coach for women 1975-. **Orgs:** Mem NAACP 1950-, YWCA 1954-. **Honors/Awds:** Alumnus of the Month Natl Alumni Assoc 1978; Coach of the Year Natl Sports Found 1978-, Natl Assoc of Womens Sports 1978; Beverly Saulcy Awd Natl Sports Found 1978; Natl Alumni Awd in Sports JSU Natl Alumni Assoc 1978; Outstanding Achievement Awd Dept of HPER JSU 1978-79; Outstanding Coaching Awd NatlAssoc of Women Sports 1979; Leadership Awd Dept of Athletics JSU 1979; Achievements in Coaching & Serv Dept of HPER JSU 1980; Coach of the Year Natl Assoc of Womens Sports 1980; Coach of the Year Jackson Daily News 1980; Activist Awd Women for Progress 1981; Winning Coach Awd Jackson State 1981; Notable Achievements Awd Nine Iron Golf Club 1981; Outstanding Accomplishmnets in Coaching & Serv HPER Dept JSU 1981; Outstanding Achievements in the Field of Ed & Sports Mbel CarneyChap Students NJSU 1981; Resolution Miss Leg 1981; Nominated for the Jackie Robinson Awd in Sports 1981; Resolution State Bd of Ed Inst of Higher Learning State of MS 1981; Winning Coach Jackson State 1982; Coach of the Year SWAC 1982-83, Miller Brewer Co 1983; Outstanding & Meritorious Serv HPER Dept JSU 1983; Devotion & Dedicated Serv JSU HPER Majors Club 1983; Winning Coach Roundball Club 1984; Resolution MS Leg 1984; Spec in Ed JSU 1981. **Business Addr:** Instructor of PE, Head Coach, Jackson State Univ, 1325 Lynch St, Jackson, MS 39217.

MAGEE, WENDELL ERROL
Professional baseball player. **Personal:** Born Aug 3, 1972, Hattiesburg, MS; married Ramonica; children: Joshua. **Educ:** Samford. **Career:** Philadelphia Phillies, outfielder, 1996-. **Business Addr:** Professional Baseball Player, Philadelphia Phillies, PO Box 7575, Philadelphia, PA 19101, (215)463-6000.

MAHAN-POWELL, LENA
Mayor, teacher, business executive. **Personal:** Born Dec 3, 1951, Myrlewood, AL; daughter of Anna Givan Mahan and Buster Mahan; married Willie Powell, Nov 22, 1978; children: Donyale Jones, Ricky Leyvahn Powell. **Educ:** Univ of South Alabama, Mobile AL, attended, 1970-71; Alabama State Univ, Montgomery, AL, BS, 1974, MEd, 1977; Univ of Alabama Tuscaloosa, Tuscalossa AL, attended, 1978; Auburn Univ Montgomery, Montgomery AL, attended, 1984-86. **Career:** Wilcox County Bd of Educ, Camden AL, teacher, 1974-89; Talladega Deaf and Blind, Montgomery AL, teacher, 1984-86; Town of Yellow Bluff, AL, councilmember, 1984-88, mayor, 1988-; LMP Office & School Supply Co, founder/owner, currently. **Orgs:** Church sec, Arkadelphia Baptist Church, 1978-; pres, Universal Brotherhood, 1980-; mem, Lewis Delight #598 OES, 1982-; bd of dir, Wilcox Human Resources Dept, 1984-; mem, Prepared Cities Org, 1986-; bd of dir, Wilcox Educ Assn, 1987-89; mem, Alabama Conf of Black Mayors, 1988-, Natl Conf of Black Mayors, 1988-; by laws comm, Central High School PTO, 1988-; mem, Volunteer Fire Dept Assn, 1988-, vice pres, Wilcox Educ Assn, 1989-; member Wilcox Women Development, 1990-. **Honors/Awds:** Outstanding American Award. **Home Addr:** Rte 1, Box 198, Pine Hill, AL 36769.

MAHIN, GEORGE E.
Business executive. **Personal:** Born Oct 18, 1914, Franklin, KY; married Marjorie J Hines; children: George Frederick, Jerome, Daniel, Philip, David. **Educ:** Municipal Coll; Simmons Univ. **Career:** Mammoth Life & Accident Insurance Co, assoc agency dir, admin asst dir, agency sec, supt agencies, asst agency dir, mgr Gary & Cleveland Districts, home rep; Herald-Post, district mgr; Courier-Journal & Times, dist mgr. **Orgs:** Mem NAACP bd; served coms for YMCA; Boy Scouts; American Legion; commnity orgns; active chr groups; Ordained Elder AME Zion Ch. **Honors/Awds:** Recip numerous awards Mammoth & Nat Ins Assoc. **Military Serv:** AUS.

MAHONE, BARBARA J.
Automobile company executive. **Personal:** Born Apr 19, Notasulga, AL; daughter of Sarah L Simpson and Freddie Mahone Sr. **Educ:** Ohio State University, Columbus, OH, BS, 1968; University of Michigan, Ann Arbor, MI, MBA, 1972; Harvard Business School, Boston, MA, certificate, 1981. **Career:** General Motors Corporation Headquarters, Detroit, MI, various positions, 1968-79; General Motors Rochester Products, Rochester, NY, dir personnel administration, 1979-82; General Motors Packard Elec, Warren, OH, mgr labor rels & safety, 1982-83; Federal Government, Washington, DC, chairman, federal labor rels auth, 1983-84; General Motors C-P-C Group, Warren, MI, director, HRM, 1984-86; General Motors Corp., Warren, MI, general director, employee benefits, personnel, 1986-93; GM Truck Group, group dir of human resources, 1993-. **Orgs:** Advisory board member, Univ of Michigan Business School, 1986-; board of directors, Urban League of Detroit, 1990-; board of directors, Merrill-Palmer Institute, 1990-; advisory board member, National Black MBA Assn, 1985-; advisory board member, Congressional Assistance Program, 1989-. **Honors/Awds:** Mary McLeod Bethune Award, Natl Council of Negro Women, 1977; One of eleven Women ''Making It Happen in MI'', Redbook Magazine, 1978; Young Woman of the Year, Natl Assn of Negro Business and Prof Women, 1978; Distinguished Business Award, Univ of MI, BBSA, 1978; Outstanding Member of the Year, National Black MBA Assn, 1981; Salute to America's Top 100 Black Business and Professional Women, Dollars and Sense, 1988. **Business Addr:** Group Director, Human Resources, GM Truck Group, 1999 Centerpoint Pkwy, Pontiac, MI 48341-3150.

MAHONE, CHARLIE EDWARD, JR.
Educational administrator, educator. **Personal:** Born Aug 26, 1945, Washington, DC; married. **Educ:** Wayne State University, BBS, 1976; University of Michigan, MBA, 1978, PhD, 1981. **Career:** Florida A&M University, assoc prof of intl bus, 1985-89; Howard University, assoc prof of intl bus, 1989-, dept chmn, 1994-. **Orgs:** Academy of Intl Bus Studies; Book Reviewer for Southwestern Publishing Co; Competitiveness Review, editorial committee; Intl Academy of Bus Disciplines; Intl Journal of Commerce & Mgt, reviewer; National Economic Association; Society of Intl Bus Fellows; Japan-American Student Conference, board of directors, 1996; Washington DC Alumni Chap, Kappa Alpha Psi, Inc, pres, 1996-, board of directors, 1992-95, vice pres, 1994-95, chmn social action committee, 1990-94, assistant keeper of the records, 1991-92; Kappa Scholarship Endowment Fund, Inc, chmn of the bd, 1996-, board of directors, 1991-95, vice pres, 1991-95. **Honors/Awds:** Delta Sigma Pi Fraternity; Kappa Alpha Psi Fraternity, Outstanding Educator Award, Outstanding Service to the Fraternity; Melville Diamond Scholars Program, Outstanding Service & Dedicated Services; Small Bus Development Ctr, Certificate of Appreciation; Japan-America Student Conference, Certificate of Appreciation; Maryland Division of Corrections, Certification of Appreciation; University of Michigan, Black Bus Student's Association, Outstanding Alumnus of the Year; Exxon Corp Fellow (twice); Chrysler Corp Academic Scholarship (three). **Military Serv:** USAF, airman first class, 1964-68. **Business Addr:** Assoc Prof of Intl Business, Howard University, Dept of Finance, Intl Business Ins, 2600 6th St, NW, Washington, DC 20059-0001, (202)806-1568.

MAHONEY, KEITH WESTON
Drug abuse prevention specialist. **Personal:** Born Jan 12, 1939, Montego Bay, Jamaica. **Educ:** Brooklyn Coll, BA Sociology 1960-68, MA Political Sci 1972-75, MSc Ed 1979-82. **Career:** Dept of Welfare, caseworker 1968-72; Sch Dist 22 Drug Prevention Prog, specialist 1972-. **Orgs:** Comm org Vanderveer Park Actions Council 1973-79; bd of dirs Amersfort Flatlands Dev Corp 1980-; mediator Childrens Aid Soc 1982-; mediator Brooklyn Coll Dispute Resolution Centre 1982-; health coord Caribbean Action Lobby 1983-; comm org Amersfort Junction Anti Drug Task Force 1983-; comm bd mem Comm Bd 14 1985-; mem Natl Assn of Black Counselors 1985-; Natl Assn of Jamaican & Supportive Organizations, (NAJASO), E Region vp. **Honors/Awds:** Service to Comm Amersfort Flatlands Dev Corp 1980-83; Excellence & Serv to Comm Brooklyn Coll Grad Guidance & Counseling Student Orgs 1982-83; Prof Friend Brooklyn Coll Grad Guidance & Comm Serv Org 1982-84; Outstanding Effort to Prevent Drug Abuse Sch Dist 22 Drug Prev Prog 1972-. **Military Serv:** US Army Medical Corps, PFC, two years. **Business Addr:** Drug Abuse Prev/Interv Spec II, Sch Dist 22 Drug Program, 2525 Haring St, Brooklyn, NY 11235.

MAHORN, RICK (DERRICK ALLEN)
Professional basketball player. **Personal:** Born Sep 21, 1958, Hartford, CT; married Donyale. **Educ:** Hampton Inst, BS, business administration, 1980. **Career:** Washington Bullets, forward, 1980-85; Detroit Pistons, 1986-89; Philadelphia 76ers, 1989-91; Il Messaggero, 1991-92; Virtus Roma, 1992; New Jersey Nets, 1992-96; Detroit Pistons, 1996-. **Orgs:** Active in numerous charities; spent week at Special Olympics Intl Games 1983. **Honors/Awds:** Career-high rebounds, 19, against Sixers; set career playoff high with 15 rebounds against Celtics 1984; 3-time NAIA All-American at Hampton Inst; played in 4 post-season All-Star games, including the Aloha Classic; NBA Champion, Detroit Pistons, 1989; NBA All-Defensive Second Team, 1990. **Business Addr:** Professional Basketball Player, Detroit Pistons, 2 Championship Dr, Auburn Hills, MI 48326, (248)377-0100.

MAITH, SHEILA FRANCINE
Government attorney. **Personal:** Born Sep 9, 1961, Baltimore, MD; daughter of Georgia Vinau Haddon Maith and Warren Edward Maith; married David Lloyd Douglass, Aug 17, 1985. **Educ:** Duke University, Durham, NC, AB, 1983; Harvard Law School, Cambridge MA, JD, 1987; Kennedy School of Government, Cambridge, MA, MPP, 1987. **Career:** Hill & Barlow, Boston, MA, associate, 1987-89; Boston Redevelopment Authority, Boston, MA, special assistant, 1989-. **Orgs:** Board directors, Tent City, 1987-; director, United South End Settlements, 1987-; Boston Bar Association/Young Lawyers Division, 1987-89; alumni advisory admissions committee, Duke University, 1989-. **Business Addr:** Special Assistant, Boston Redevelopment Authority, 1 City Hall Square, Boston, MA 02201.

MAITLAND, CONRAD CUTHBERT
Physician. **Personal:** Born Jan 17, 1947, Belmont St Georges, Grenada, West Indies; son of Mavis Maitland and Denis Maitland; children: Nicholas. **Educ:** University of Detroit, BS, 1973; Wayne State University School of Medicine, MD, 1978. **Career:** Self-employed, medical doctor, private practice, 1984-. **Orgs:** American Medical Association; Michigan State Medical Society; Wayne County Medical Society Legislation/Comm Aff; Southeastern Medical Society; Wayne State University Medical Alumni; Wayne County Medical Society Project HOW Volunteer Physician; Black Medical Alumni Association. **Honors/Awds:** WCMS-Project HOW, Certificate of Appreciation, 1991; US mem of Congress, Certificate of Appreciation, 1991. **Business Phone:** (313)865-2110.

MAITLAND, TRACEY
Bonds trader. **Personal:** Born in New York, NY. **Educ:** Columbia University, BA, economics, 1982. **Career:** Merrill Lynch & Co Inc: corporate intern, New York, corporate finance, securities research, Washington, DC, equities sales, Detroit, vice president, sales, director, convertible bond sales, New York, currently. **Special Achievements:** Listed as one of 25 ''Hottest Blacks on Wall Street,'' Black Enterprise, 1992. **Business Addr:** Director, Convertible Securities and Trading, Merrill Lynch & Co, World Financial Center, North Tower, 5th Fl, New York, NY 10281, (212)449-4040.

MAJETE, CLAYTON AARON
Educator. **Personal:** Born Apr 19, 1941, Woodland, NC; son of Doreather Jefferson Majete (deceased) and Barnabas Majete (deceased); divorced; children: Lisa, Kim. **Educ:** Morgan State Univ, BA 1964; New York Univ, MA 1965, PhD 1984; University of Pennsylvania, The Warton School, accelerated business training program for PhD's in human relations 1970. **Career:** CUNY John Jay Coll, instructor 1970-72; CUNY Baruch Coll, instr 1972-75, lecturer 1975-84, asst prof 1984-; New York Times and WCBS-TV, consultant and researcher 1985; Governor of State of Maryland, consultant 1986; State Univ of NY, Stonybrook, summer program for medical careers, dir. **Orgs:** Amer Assn of Univ Profs 1975-, Soc for Field Experience Educ 1978-; chmn bd dirs Inst for Urban Affairs 1978-; mem Natl Assoc of Black Social Workers 1980-, Amer Sociological Assoc 1981-. **Honors/Awds:** Alpha Kappa Delta; Fellowship Johns Hopkins Sch of Medicine; published ''Black Voting Behavior: The Effect of Locus of Control and Socio-economic Status,'' The Western Journal of Black Studies Vol II, No 3, 1987. **Special Achievements:** Presentation of Annual Lecture Series, Interrace Magazine, ASA Annual Convention; ''Bias on the Study of Interracial Relationships,'' round table, 1996; Appeared on PBS, Tony Brown's Journal, in a discussion on racial categories. **Home Addr:** 35 Hampton Pl, Brooklyn, NY 11213-2612, (718)774-1000. **Business Addr:** Lecturer, Sociology, Baruch College, City University of New York, 17 Lexington Ave, New York, NY 10010.

MAJOR, BENJAMIN
Physician. **Personal:** Born Sep 28, 1924, Keyport, NJ; son of Eliza Radcliffe Major (deceased) and Frank Major (deceased); married Henriette Pickett Major, Mar 23, 1949; children: Misa, Cyd, Mark, Carol. **Educ:** Fisk University, Nashville, TN, 1941-43; Meharry Medical College, Nashville, TN, MD, 1943-46; University of California-Berkeley, Berkeley, CA, MPH, 1970. **Career:** Private medical practice, Berkeley/Oakland, CA, 1953-87; Self-employed private consultant, 1987-. **Orgs:** Fellow, American College of Obstetrics/Gynecology, 1990-; president, Sigma Pi Phi Fraternity, 1990-92; instructor/guest lecturer, University of California-Berkeley School of Public Health, 1987-. **Honors/Awds:** Mid-Career Fellowship, Ford Foundation, 1969-70; Black Alumnus of the Year, University of California-Berkeley, 1985; American Medical Womens Assn Award, 1994. **Military Serv:** US Air Force, Capt., 1951-53. **Home Addr:** Seven Highland Blvd, Kensington, CA 94707.

MAJOR, CLARENCE
Novelist, poet, educator. **Personal:** Born Dec 31, 1936, Atlanta, GA; son of Inez Huff Major and Clarence Major; married Pamela Jane Ritter, 1980. **Educ:** James Nelson Raymond Fellowship, Art Inst of Chicago, 1953; State Univ of New York at Albany, BS; Union Institute, PhD. **Career:** Writer; Sarah Lawrence College, Bronxville, NY, lecturer, 1972-75; Howard University, Washington, DC, lecturer, 1975-76; University of Washington, Seattle, WA, assistant professor, 1976-77; University of Colorado, Boulder, CO, associate professor, 1977-81, professor, 1981-89; University of California at Davis, professor, 1989-; has held numerous other positions as visiting professor, consultant, and lecturer. **Honors/Awds:** Nat'l Council on the Arts Award, Assn of Univ Presses, 1970; Pushcart prize for poem ''Funeral,'' 1976; Fulbright-Hays Inter-Univ Exchange Award, Franco-Amer Comm for Educational Exchange, 1981-83; Western State Book Award for Fiction (My Amputations), 1986. **Special Achievements:** All-Night Visitors (novel), 1969; Dictionary of Afro-American Slang, 1970; Swallow the Lake (poetry), 1970; Symptoms and Madness (poetry), 1971; Private Line (poetry), 1971; The Cotton Club: New Poems, 1972; No (novel), 1973; The Dark and Feeling: Black American Writers and Their Work (essays), 1974; The Syncopated Cakewalk (poetry), 1974; Reflex and Bone Structure (novel), 1979; Emergency Exit (novel), 1979; Inside Diameter: The France Poems, 1985; My Amputations: A Novel, 1986; Such Was the Season: A Novel, 1987; Surfaces and Masks (poetry), 1987; Some Observations of a Stranger at Zuni in the Latter Part of the Century (poetry), 1988; Painted Turtle: Woman with Guitar (novel), 1988; Juba to Jive: A Dictionary of African-American Slang, Penguin, 1994; Calling the Wind, Anthology, 1993; The Garden Thrives, Anthology, 1996; Dirty Bird Blues, Novel, 1996; New and Selected Poems: 1958-1998; author of numerous articles, reviews and anthologies; editor. **Military Serv:** US Air Force, Airman 1955-57. **Business Addr:** Professor, Department of English, University of California at Davis, Davis, CA 95616.

MAJOR, HENRYMAE M.
Guidance counselor. **Personal:** Born Mar 9, 1935, Earle, AR; daughter of Clara Sims McCoy and Andrew McCoy; married Isadore; children: Kelly Dianne. **Educ:** Lincoln U, BS 1956; Wayne State U, MA Guidance & Counseling 1963. **Career:** Central High School Detroit, guidance dept head 1970-, guidance counselor 1965-70, health, phys educ tchr, bd of & educ tchr, bd of educ 1958-65; State of Illinois, recreational therapist 1957. **Orgs:** Mem, Detroit Counselor's Assn; Guild Assn of Metro Detroit; Orgn of Sch Admin & Supvrs; Assn of Black Admin; Future Tchrs of Amer Sponsor; mem Lincoln Univ Alumni Assn; Delta Sigma Theta Alum Chap; Women of Wayne State Univ Alumni Chap; established Coord Health Clinic, Spain Middle School health counseling socio-econ areas; mem NAACP, Hartford Memorial Baptist Church; mem Amer Assn of Counseling Development 1980-; mem Michigan Assn of Counseling Development 1980-; mem Michigan Assn of College Admissions Counselors; mem Natl Board of Certified Counselors 1979-; member, Phi Delta Kappa, 1988-. **Honors/Awds:** Co-author, Role of the Counselor. **Home Addr:** 19410 Stratford Road, Detroit, MI 48221. **Business Addr:** Dept Head, Guidance & Counseling, Central High School, 2425 Tuxedo, Detroit, MI 48206.

MAJORS, ANTHONY Y.
Automobile dealership executive. **Career:** Varsity Ford Lincoln Mercury, Inc, owner, currently. **Special Achievements:** Co. is ranked #29 on Black Enterprise magazine's list of top 100 auto dealers, 1992. **Business Addr:** Owner, Varsity Ford Lincoln Mercury Inc, 1351 East BYP, College Station, TX 77845, (409)779-0664.

MAJORS, EDITH SARA
Association executive, statistician. **Personal:** Born Jun 8, 1920, Columbia, SC; widowed; children: Major Charles Wesley Simmons, Dr Reginald Leigh Simmons. **Educ:** Allen Univ, BS 1939-42; Howard Univ, 1943; Univ of MI, 1944; Amer Univ, 1954-56; USDA, 1964-65. **Career:** Carver Jr High School, math teacher 1942-45; Fed Government, stat clk 1953-59; stat super 1959-62; stat MED 1962-74. **Orgs:** Pres Justamere Club 1957; exec sec Lambda Kappa Mu 1981-85; sec Northwest Boundary Civic Assn 1983; organizer Neighborhood Block Club 1984; Basileus Theta Chap Laubda Kappa Mu Sor 1984-; ward coord Older Adult Learning Ctr DC Office on Aging. **Honors/Awds:** Sustained Superior Awd Dept of Army Office of Surgeon Gen; Comm Awd Fourth Dist of Wash DC 1984. **Home Addr:** 433 Ingraham St NW, Washington, DC 20011.

MAJORS, MATTIE CAROLYN
Public relations executive. **Personal:** Born Jan 16, 1945, Waynesboro, GA; daughter of Carrie L Skinner Majors and Willis Van Majors; children: Brandon Matthew Quentin Van. **Educ:** Central St Univ, BA, chemistry 1970. **Career:** CWRU Cleveland, rsch lab tech 1970-72; WABQ Radio Cleveland, news reporter 1970; WJMO Radio Cleveland, news reporter acting news dir 1970-72; WKBN Radio-TV Youngstown OH, minority affairs coord 1972-77; WJKW-TV, reporter 1977-82; WJBK-TV, news reporter, PM Magazine, 1982-88; Simons Michelson Zieve Advertising, Troy, MI, 1991-; Ambrose Associates Inc, director of public relations, currently. **Orgs:** Pres mem Youngstown Sickle Cell Anemia Found 1973-76; MENSA, Cleveland Press Club 1980; Negro Business & Professional Women's Club 1980; Young Black Businessmen 1979; Youngstown Fedn Women's Clubs; Freedom Inc; United Negro Improvement Assn; Omega Psi Phi Frat; hon co-chmn 1986, hon chair 1987 Black United Fund Campaign 1986; bd mem local AFTRA Chap. **Honors/Awds:** Outstanding Achievement in Broadcasting Youngstown Comm Action Council; Proclamation Mattie Majors' Day Youngstown City Council Mayor of Youngstown 1977; Best Spot News Story Cleveland Press Club 1980; nom as Outstanding Female on Air Talent 1984-85; Award, American Cancer Society, 1990; Volunteer Award, State of Michigan, 1987. **Business Addr:** Director of Public Relations, Ambrose Associates Inc, 429 Livernois, Ferndale, MI 48220.

MAJORS, RICHARD G., III
Educator, psychologist. **Personal:** Born in Ithaca, NY; son of Fannie Sue Majors and Richard Majors II. **Educ:** Auburn Community College, AA, humanities, 1974; Plattsburgh State College, BA, history, 1977; University of Illinois Urbana, PhD, educational psychology, 1987. **Career:** University of Kansas, postdoctoral fellowship, 1987-89; Harvard Medical School, postdoctoral fellowship and clinical fellow, 1989-90; University of Wisconsin, Eau Claire, assistant professor, 1990-93; The Urban Institute, Washington DC, sr research assoc, 1993-96; Michigan State Univ, David Walker Research Institute, visiting fellow/scholar, 1996-; Georgetown Univ, Social Policy Program, honorary visiting scholar, 1996-97. **Orgs:** National Council of African American Men, chairman, 1990-92, board of directors, co-founder, 1990-, pres, CEO, 1995-; American Psychological Association, 1987; Society for the Psychological Study of Ethnic Minority Issues, 1989; American Orthopsychiatric Association, 1990; American Men's Studies Association, 1992; Greenpeace, 1988; Journal of African American Men, founder, deputy editor; Whitehouse Initiative on African American Males, co-chair, 1996. **Honors/Awds:** International Publications, Outstanding College Poet Award, 1979; University of Illinois Student Government Association, chosen as delegate to US Student Lobbyist Association, 1981; American Psychological Association, Pre-Doctoral Minority Fellow, 1984, selected to be one of five presenters at conference, 1986; State of Kansas, Presidential Congressional District Delegate, 1988; Plattsburg State College, Distinguished EOP Alumni Award, 1992; Recipient, Arturo Schomburgh Distinguished Service Award & Fred Hampton Image Award, 1994; American Psychological Association, Minority Achievement Award for Research in Psychology, 1995. **Special Achievements:** Author, ''Nonverbal Behaviors and Communication Styles among Black Americans,'' Black Psychology, Cobb & Henry, 1991; Co-author, Cool Pose: The Dilemmas of Black Manhood in America, Lexington Books, 1992; co-editor, The American Black Male: His Present Status & Future, Nelson Hall, 1994; ''Black Men,'' Journal of Men's Studies, 1993, ''Cultural Value Differences: Implications for the Experiences of African-American Males,'' Journal of Men's Studies, 1993; founder, deputy editor, Journal of African-American Men, 1992; appointee of Rep Major Owens' (NY) to the executive committee of The National Citizens Commission on African-American Education, 1991; appearences on numerous TV and radio programs; citations in numerous newspapers.

MAKOKHA, JAMES A. N.
Educator, city official. **Personal:** Born Jun 20, 1951, Kakamega, Western, Kenya; son of Anjema Mitungu Makokha and Ali N. Makokha; married Patricia Brown Makokha, Dec 26, 1977; children: Audrey, Jarrett, Justin. **Educ:** Albany State College, Albany, GA, BBA, 1975-78; Auburn University, Auburn, AL, MSc, 1978-79; Century University, Los Angeles, CA, PhD, 1985-87. **Career:** Genesee County, Flint, MI, director of elections, 1979-83, deputy county clerk, 1984-87; State of Michigan, Lansing, MI, economist, 1987-88; City of Flint, Flint, MI, director of parks and recreation, 1988-90; Detroit College of Business, Flint, MI, executive director of community relations, 1990-91; City of Flint, MI, director of policy and intergovernmental relations, 1991-. **Home Addr:** 2607 Circle Dr, Flint, MI 48507.

MALBROUE, JOSEPH, JR.
Chemical company executive. **Personal:** Born Aug 24, 1949, Grand Coteau, LA; son of Earline Key Malbroue and Joseph Malbroue Sr; married Joretta Leauntine Tyson. **Educ:** Univ of Southwestern LA, BSChE 1966-70. **Career:** Union Carbide Corp, prod engr 1970-73, tech sales rep 1973-76, asst customer serv mgr 1976-78, dist planner 1978-84, LPG supply mgr 1984-97; SAP Project Implementation Team, 1997-. **Orgs:** Gas Processors Assn. **Honors/Awds:** Chairman's Award Union Carbide, 1993; Dir cncl Union Carbide Corp 1975; E I Dupont schlrshp Univ of SW LA 1968. **Military Serv:** USMCR sgt 1970-76. **Business Addr:** LPG Supply Manager, Union Carbide Corp, 820 Gessner, Ste 600, Houston, TX 77024.

MALCOM, SHIRLEY MAHALEY
Science association executive. **Personal:** Born Sep 6, 1946, Birmingham, AL; daughter of Lillie Mae Funderburg Mahaley and Ben Lee Mahaley; married Horace Malcom, May 31, 1975; children: Kelly Alicia, Lindsey Ellen. **Educ:** University of Washington, Seattle, WA, BS, (with distinction) 1967; UCLA, Los Angeles, CA, MA, 1968; The Pennsylvania State University, Univ Park, PA, PhD, 1974. **Career:** Univ of NC-Wilmington, Wilmington, NC, assistant professor, 1974-75; Amer Assn for Advancement of Science, Washington, DC, res assoc, staff assoc, proj director, 1975-77; National Science Foundation, Washington, DC, program officer, 1977-79; Amer Assn for Advancement of Science, Washington, DC, head, office of opportunities in science, 1979-89, head, directorate for educ & human resources prog, 1989-. **Orgs:** Board member, National Center on Education & the Economy; board member, Science Service; trustee, Carnegie Corp of New York; American Museum of Natural History; Natl Science Board, 1994-; President's Committee of Advisors on Science & Technology. **Honors/Awds:** Doctor of Humane Letters, Coll of St Catherine, 1990; Humanitarian of Year Award, National Coalition of Title I/Chapter I Parents, 1989; Scroll of Honor, National Medical Assn, 1989; Black Women Who Make It Happen, National Council of Negro Women, 1987; Doctor of Humane Letters, College of St Catherine, 1990; Doctor of Science, NJ Institute of Technology, 1991; Doctor of Humane Letters, St Joseph College, 1992, Knox Coll, 1993, Bennett Coll, 1993, Hood College, 1994. **Business Addr:** Head, Directorate for Education & Human Resources Programs, American Assn for the Advancement of Science, 1333 H St, NW, Washington, DC 20005.

MALDON, ALPHONSO
Government official. **Career:** The White House, deputy assistant to the president for legislative affairs, currently. **Business Addr:** Office of Legislative Affairs, Deputy Asst to the President for Legislative Affairs, The White House, 112 East Wing, 1600 Pennsylvania Ave, NW, Washington, DC 20500, (202)456-6620.

MALLEBAY-VACQUEUR DEM, JEAN PASCAL
Automotive company executive. **Personal:** Born Apr 3, 1953, Paris, France; son of Raymonde Mallebay-Vacqueur and Oumar Dem; married Mada Dao, Sep 7, 1982; children: Alain Moussa, Nelhai Adama, Sara Macora, Alexandre Sega Oumar. **Educ:** Ivory Coast University, Baccalaureate, 1969; ESME, School of Mechanical & Electronical Engineering, BSME/MSME, 1973-74; INSEAD, European School of Business Administration, MBA, 1978; Pantheon Sorbonne, Paris University, Post Graduate, 1978. **Career:** Mauretania School System, technical assistant, 1974-76; Regie Renault, manufacturing engineering, 1978, manufacturing plant mgr, 1981-84, engineering operations general mgr, 1985-87, international operations projects executive, 1988; RUSA, assistant to executive vice pres, 1979-80; Chrysler, special projects engineering general mgr, 1989-93, Environmental Testing Laboratories, exec eng, environmental and emissions testing, exec eng, currently. **Orgs:** Engineering Society of Detroit, 1990-; INSEAD Alumni, 1978-; Chrysler African American Network, 1995. **Military Serv:** Foreign Technical Assistance, VSNA, 1974-76. **Business Addr:** Environmental and Emissions Testing Executive Engineer, Chrysler Corp, 800 Chrysler Dr E, 483-05-02, Auburn Hills, MI 48326-2757, (810)576-2769.

MALLETT, CONRAD L., JR.
State Supreme Court justice. **Personal:** Born Oct 12, 1953, Detroit, MI; son of Conrad L Mallett Sr; married Barbara Straughn Mallett; children: three. **Educ:** UCLA, Los Angeles, CA, BA, 1975; USC, Los Angeles, CA, MPA, 1979, JD, 1979. **Career:** Governor, State of MI, Lansing, MI, legal adv, dir of legis affairs, 1982-84; Mayor, City of Detroit, Detroit, MI, political dir, exec asst, 1985-86; Jaffe, Raitt, Heuer & Weiss PC, Detroit, MI, attorney, 1986-90; Michigan Supreme Court, Detroit, MI, associate justice, 1990-. **Orgs:** Mem, American Bar Assn; mem, MI State Bar Assn; mem, Detroit Bar Assn; mem, Wolverine Bar Assn; mem, Genesee County Bar Assn. **Special Achievements:** The third African American jurist to sit on Michigan's Supreme Court; One of only five African American chief justices in the country. **Business Addr:** Chief Justice, Michigan Supreme Court, 500 Woodward, 20th Fl, Detroit, MI 48226-3435.

MALLETT, ROSA ELIZABETH
Educator. **Personal:** Born Oct 1, 1940, Montezuma, GA; daughter of Fannie Bell Terry Harp and Jesse Lee Harp; wid-

owed; children: Denise T Hunter, Lapha D Hunter, William Neil Hunter Jr, Steven P Hunter, Raven R Harris. **Educ:** Highland Park Community College, AS, 1975; Michigan State University, BA, 1976; Wayne State University, MEd, 1982, EdD, 1991. **Career:** Detroit Public Schools, teacher, 1976-82, teacher-in-charge, 1982-87, department head, 1987-91; Wayne County RESA, adult & community education consultant, 1991-. **Orgs:** Phi Delta Kappa, U of D Mercy Chapter, president, 1992-93; Michigan Association of Adult & Continuing Education, president, 1994-95, 1996-97; Michigan Association of Adult & Community Education, board member, 1992-97; Detroit Literacy Coalition, board member, 1991-; Professional Women's Network; American Association of Adult & Continuing Education; NAACP; National Community Education Association. **Honors/Awds:** Honorable John Conyers, US Congressional Proclamation, 1986; Detroit Public Schools, Outstanding Adult Basic Education Teacher, 1982; Phi Delta Kappa, Services in Education, 1988, Services to PDK, 1989; Detroit Public Schools, Sector 7, Unforgettable Award, 1991. **Special Achievements:** Adult Learning, 1992 and 1994. **Home Phone:** (313)342-9462. **Business Addr:** Adult & Community Education Consultant, Wayne County Regional Educational Service Agency, 33500 Van Born Rd, Rm 326, Wayne, MI 48184-2497, (734)334-1377.

MALLETTE, CAROL L.
Educator. **Personal:** Born Dec 24, Philadelphia, PA; daughter of Florence Evans Moore and Lewis Moore; married Kenneth (divorced); children: Tashia, Sydney. **Educ:** Morgan State University, Baltimore, MD, BS, 1963; Kean College of New Jersey, Union, NJ, MA, 1971. **Career:** Board of Education, Pleasantville, NJ, teacher, 1963-65; District of Columbia Public Schools, Washington, DC, teacher, 1966-70; Kean College of New Jersey, Union, NJ, coordinator of college projects, 1971-79; Harristown Development Corporation, Harrisburg, PA, coordinator of community events, 1981-85; Penn State University, Middletown, PA, assistant to the provost/dean, special events coordinator, 1985-. **Orgs:** Member, Jack & Jill Inc; member, Delta Sigma Theta Sorority; member, Pennsylvania Legislative Black Caucus Foundation. **Honors/Awds:** Numerous community service awards; Patriot newspaper recognition for carrier judging panel. **Business Addr:** Assistant to the Provost & Dean, Special Events Coordinator, Penn State University-Harrisburg, Rt 230, CRO Office, Middletown, PA 17057.

MALLISHAM, JOSEPH W.
Business executive. **Personal:** Born Jun 14, 1928, Tuscaloosa, AL; married Sadie B Townsend; children: Sheila, Ivy, Darlene. **Educ:** Tuscaloosa County Tech Trade Sch, 1954. **Career:** Gulf Serv Station, owner. **Orgs:** Pres Druid HS PTSA 1974; chmn bd dirs Tuscaloosa Opportunity Program 1968-71; 1st chmn Tuscaloosa Community Relations Adv Bd 1969; mem bd mgmt Benjamin Barnes Br YMCA 1969; mem Human Rights Com for Bryce Hosp 1972; NAACP; hon mem ODK; pres Tuscaloosa Citizens for Action. **Honors/Awds:** Citizen of Year, W Alabama Unit, Natl Assn (Soc Work); Man of Year, Tuscaloosa Community Alpha Phi Alpha Frat, 1974; hon staff, Atty Gen, State of Alabama, 1972. **Military Serv:** Corpl AUS 1950-51. **Business Addr:** 3135 20th St, Tuscaloosa, AL.

MALLORY, GEORGE L., JR.
Attorney. **Personal:** Born Apr 13, 1952, Washington, DC; son of Anna P Mallory and George L Mallory, MD. **Educ:** Occidental College, BA, political science, 1974; Western State University Law School, JD, 1977. **Career:** Los Angeles City Attorney, deputy city attorney, 1979-86; Mallory & Brown-Curtis, partner, 1986-. **Orgs:** John M Langston Bar Association, president, 1991; Langston Bar Association, board member, 1982-; NAACP Los Angeles Branch, first vice pres, 1988-90, board member, 1982-; Center for Early Education, board member, 1988-. **Honors/Awds:** United States Congressinal Records, Recognition of Service, 1991; California State Legislature, Recognition of Service, 1991; Los Angeles District Attorney, Recognition of Service, 1990-91; City of Inglewood, Recognition of Service, 1991. **Special Achievements:** General chairperson of the NAACP (Los Angeles Branch); Roy Wilkins Dinner; 1986, 1987, 1991. **Business Addr:** Partner, Mallory & Brown-Curtis, 1925 Century Park East, 10th Floor, Los Angeles, CA 90067, (310)788-5555.

MALLORY, JAMES A.
Journalist. **Personal:** Born Aug 1, 1955, Detroit, MI; son of Gertrude P Mallory; married Frances, Nov 5, 1977; children: Allison, Allen. **Educ:** Western MI Univ, BBA, 1977; MI State Univ, MA, 1982. **Career:** Lansing State Journal, reporter, 1981-83; Grand Rapids Press, reporter, 1983-84; Detroit News, reporter, 1984-86, asst bus editor, 1986-88; Atlanta Journal & Constitution, reporter, 1988-89, asst bus editor, 1989-93, news personnel mgr, 1993-96, asst managing editor/nights, 1996-. **Orgs:** National Assn of Black Journalists, 1993-; Atlanta Assn of Black Journalists, 1984-; National Assn of Minority Media Execs, 1993-; Bd of Visitors, School of Journalism, Mass Media & Graphic Arts, FL A&M Univ, 1994-; Western MI Univ Alumni Assn, 1994-. **Honors/Awds:** GA Associated Press, 1st Place Bus Reporting, 1992; National Assn of Black Journalists, 1st Place Business Reporting, 1992. **Business Addr:** Assistant Managing Editor/Nights, The Atlanta Journal & Constitution, 72 Marietta St, NW, Atlanta, GA 30303, (404)526-5325.

MALLORY, WILLIAM HENRY
Association executive. **Personal:** Born Mar 30, 1919, Monroe City, MO; son of Rosie Doolin Mallory and Frank Mallory; married Mary Taylor; children: Wanda Florence, Raymond. **Educ:** Gem City Bus Coll Quincy IL; MO U, Equip Tech & Oxygen Therapy. **Career:** Mallory Trucking Serv, self-employed for 20 yrs; St Mary's Hosp Quincy, IL, equip tech 1964-74; Levering Hosp Hannibal MO, central supply supr (retired). **Orgs:** Chmn NE & Comm Action Coalition; Personnel Com for 11 Co on Comm Aff; chmn Marion Co Advisory Bd; chmn MO Comm-coord Child Care; vice pres, pres 1975-, NAACP, Hannibal Chapter; vice pres St Con; elected auditor 1975, chmn Deacons & Laymen Union North MO Bapt Assn; aptd mem Affirm Action Com; pres, Missouri State Conf, NAACP, 1983-; pres, Pro Tem, Senate, 1990; Missouri Silver Hair Legislative, 1984-. **Honors/Awds:** Hannibal Sp Award for aid in Head-start Schls 1972; life membership award in St 4-C's of MO for outs accomp 1973; Martin Luther King Award, NAACP, Hannibal Branch, 1991. **Business Addr:** President, NAACP, Hannibal Branch, 2019 W Gordon St, Hannibal, MO 63401.

MALLORY, WILLIAM L.
State representative. **Personal:** married Fannie; children: 5. **Educ:** Central State Univ; Univ of Cincinnati, graduate studies. **Career:** Cinn Publ School, teacher; Univ of Cinn, assoc prof; State of OH, state representative, 1967-. **Orgs:** National Federation Settlement Housing. **Honors/Awds:** Pioneer Award Hamilton OH Comm on Aging; Outstanding Citizen Award City Cinn. **Business Addr:** State Representative, State of Ohio, State House, Columbus, OH 43215.

MALLOY, H. REMBERT
Physician, director. **Personal:** Born Jul 19, 1913, Hamlet, NC. **Educ:** Johnson C Smuth U, BS 1934; Univ Chicago, MS 1935; Spartanburg Methodist Coll; Howard U, MD 1939; Reynolds Meml Hosp, MD 19639; Freedmen's Hosp, Resd; NY, post-grad. **Career:** Mt Zion UM Ch, pastor 4 yrs; Yellow Freight System, truck driver; Howard U, instr; Winston-salem State U, dir student hlth svcs; Bowman Grey Sch ofMed, clinical instr; Med Park Hosp, attending surgeon; Forsyth Meml Hosp, attending surgeon; Jour of Nat Med Assn, edt staff; John Hale Surg Soc, former pres; Reynolds Hosp, chf 13; Area Civil Def Hosp, chf of surgery. **Orgs:** Bd of dir 1st Union Nat Bank 1974; Old N State Med Soc; Forsyth Co Med Soc; NC Med Assn; Nat Med Assn; chmn AMA Chmn Hlth & Safty Com; Boy Scouts 1948-58; Scout Master 1956-60; Com of Mgmt YMCA 1945-58; bd trste United Met Bapt Ch 1945-77; bd dir Am Cancer Soc; Outst Citizen of Yr Urban League 1950; Brotherhood Award Urban League 1975. **Honors/Awds:** Author, Co-author 13 Med Publs Am Jour 1942, 45, 49; Jour Of Nat Med Assn 1946, 47-51, 54; Jour of Old N State Med Soc 1957. **Business Addr:** 801 Camel Ave NE, Winston-Salem, NC 27101.

MALONE, AMANDA ELLA
City official. **Personal:** Born May 30, 1929, Lafayette County, MS; daughter of Leona Ingrom and Jerry Ingrom; married James Malone; children: Lawrence, Malcolm L, Kenneth Leon, Kelsey Lee, Sheila Elaine, Cheryl Leona, Travis, James Roland (deceased). **Educ:** Rust Coll Holly Springs MS, AS. **Career:** Elementary School, sub teacher; Head Start, teacher, parent involvement coord, soc serv dir; Marshall & Lafayette Cty Soc Serv Org, pres; Marshall County Bd of Ed, vice chmn, currently. **Orgs:** Mem NAACP; counselor, Sunrise Chap Order of Eastern Star, 1989-91; mem, Sunday school teacher New Hope MB Church; mem Marshall Cty Bd of Ed; member, Marshall Co Hospital Advisory Board; member, Holly Springs Baptist Assn Banking Committee. **Honors/Awds:** Effort and Proficiency as county bd mem MS Indust Coll 1979; Outstanding Community Serv Galena Elementary School 1980; Citation Inst of Community Serv Head Start Agency 1980; Cert of Recognition as Outstanding African-American Elected Official Chulahoma MB Church. **Business Addr:** Vice Chairman, Marshall County Board of Education, Route 5, Box 81-AB, Holly Springs, MS 38635.

MALONE, CHARLES A.
Attorney. **Personal:** chilDren: Tony, Charles, Vicki, Keith, Kevin, Julian. **Educ:** Detroit Coll, JD Law. **Career:** Sura & Malone, Inkster MI, atty at law; Mobil Oil, analytical chemist 1966-72. **Orgs:** Mem MI & Detroit Bar Assns; charter mem MI State Bar Crim Law Sect NAACP; chmn Inkster & Elected Officers Compensation Bd; co-chmn Westwood Comm SchDist Ad Hoc Com; Elks; Golden Gate Lodge; IBPOE of W; Lions.

MALONE, CLAUDINE BERKELEY
Business executive. **Personal:** Born May 9, Louisville, KY. **Educ:** Wellesley Coll, BA; Harvard Business School, MBA (High Distinction). **Career:** IBM Corp, systems engr 1963-65; Raleigh Stores, controller, mgr dp 1966-70; Crane Co, sr systems engr 1966; Harvard Bus School, assoc prof 1972-81; Fin & Mgmt Consulting Inc, pres 1982-. **Orgs:** Trustee Dana Hall School 1974-77; treas Wellesley Coll Alumni Assoc 1977-80; trustee Wellesley Coll 1982-; dir Scott Paper Co, Campbell Soup Co, MTV Networks, The Limited, Dart Drug, Supermarkets Gen Corp, Houghton Mifflin Corp, Penn Mutual Life, The Boston Co. **Honors/Awds:** Candace Awd Natl Coalition of Black Women 1982. **Business Addr:** President, Financial Mgmt Consulting Inc, 7570 Potomoc Fall Road, Mc Lean, VA 22102.

MALONE, CLEO
Health services administrator. **Personal:** Born Mar 2, 1934, Athens, AL; son of Estelle Hereford-Malone and Phillip Malone Sr; married Judy Sue Lower, Aug 31, 1974; children: Pamela McKinley, Daniel, Karen Wade, Donald, Kaya Malone. **Educ:** Cleveland College Case Western Res Univ, psychology/sociology 1963-66; Urban Training Inst Chgo, theological training 1967-68; Cleveland State Univ, Grp Dynamics 1970-71; Union Institute, Health Plng PhD, philosophy, 1981. **Career:** United Church of Christ/Community Organization, United Area Citizens Agncy, consultant & expeditor 1969-71; UCSD Muir Coll LaJolla, CA, assc dean of stdnts 1971-75; Univ Hosp, asst director, comm liaison officer, 1975-80; S San Diego Health Ed Cntr, exec dir 1980-84; The Palavra Tree, Inc, San Diego, exec dir 1984-. **Orgs:** Campus mnstr Case Western Res Univ 1969-71; mem CA Cncl on Alcohol Problems; mem San Diego Cnty Alcohol Adv Bd; sec San Diego Assoc of Black Health Ser Exec; orgnzr Protestant Ministry to Poverty 1961-64; assoc mnstr E Cleveland Cong Church 1961-64; v pres San Diego Interdnmntnl Minstrl Alliance 1985; mem, board of directors San Diego Urban League; board of directors California Council on Alcohol Policy 1984-; board of directors National Black Alcoholism Council 1988-. **Honors/Awds:** Publication "Minority Participation in Health Planning" 1981; Black Fellowship Award; UCSD Black Faculty & Staff; Outstanding Achievement Award 1985-88; Outstanding Drug Service Provider Award, San Diego County 1987-90; Association of Drug and Alcohol Administration of California, Outstanding Achievement Award, 1992; San Diego Police Department, Outstanding Community Service Award, 1992; County of San Diego, Citizen Recognition Award, 1992; Eureka Fellowship, 1995. **Home Addr:** 6659 Thornwood St, San Diego, CA 92111.

MALONE, EUGENE WILLIAM
Educator. **Personal:** Born Aug 8, 1930, Washington, PA; married Roberta Joanne Miller; children: Gina Dawn. **Educ:** Central State U, Sociology AB 1957, BS Educ 1958; Kent State U, MEd Guid & Counseling 1962; Nova U, EdD 1976. **Career:** Cuyahoga Comm Coll, dean student services 1975-; Cuyahoga Com Coll, dir counseling adm & records 1972-75; Cleveland State Univ, dir student devel program 1970-72; Cleveland State Univ, coord stud devel proj 1968-70; Central State U, dean of men 1967-68; Cleveland Pub Schs, guidance cnslr 1965-67; Com Action for Youth, guidance counselor 1964-65; Cleveland Pub Schs, tchr 1959-64; Canton Pub Schs, tchr 1958-59; Cleveland Pub Sch, group discussion leader 1966-67; Curber Assoc, consult 1968-71; Shaker Heights Pub Schs, consult 1969-70. **Orgs:** Mem Vocational Educ Adv Bd 1979; mem OH Assn Staff Program & Organizational Devel 1979; mem Nat & Assn Student Pers Adminstr; mem Am Pers & Guidance Assn; mem OH Pers & Guidance Assn. **Honors/Awds:** Good Conduct Medal. **Military Serv:** USAF airman 1949-53. **Business Addr:** Dean, Cuyahoga Community College, 25444 Harvard Rd, Cleveland, OH 44122.

MALONE, GLORIA S.
Educator (retired). **Personal:** Born May 12, 1928, Pittsburgh, PA; daughter of Doris Harris Snodgrass and John H Snodgrass; married Arthur A; children: Merrick, Deanna, Myrna. **Educ:** Central State Wilberforce OH, BS 1949; Kent State, ME 1956, MA 1969, PHD 1979. **Career:** Alliance OH Public Schools, elementary teacher, 1949-53, high school teacher, 1953-69; Mt Union Coll, prof of English 1969-90; Ohio Northern Univ, visiting professor, 1990-91; Stark County Head Start Program, education coordinator, 1991-93. **Orgs:** Member, NAACP; Second Baptist Church; Natl Educ Assn; Amer Assn of Univ Prof; Delta Kappa Gamma Soc; grand worthy matron, Amaranth Grand Chapter OES PHA 1972-74; bd of dir, Alliance United Way; bd of dir, Alliance Community Conc Assn; bd of dir, Alpha Kappa Alpha Sorority; table leader, ETS essay readings, consultant, evaluator, North Central Assn of Schools & Coll, 1987-91. **Honors/Awds:** State Scholarship Awards, Delta Kappa Gamma, 1967, 1974; Teacher of the Year, Alliance High School, 1969; Outstanding Member, Al Kaf Court Dts of Isis Akron, 1970; frequent speaker, Religious Civic Fraternity Groups; Citizen of the Year, 1986; Martin Luther King Award, 1996.

MALONE, HERMAN
Communications company executive. **Personal:** Born May 25, 1947, Camden, AR; son of Emma Hunter Malone and Roy Malone; married Pauline Strong Malone, Aug 4, 1990; children: Leon, Miles, Pamela. **Educ:** Jarvis College, BS, 1965; Community College of Denver, 1969. **Career:** Montgomery Wards, department manager; RMES Communications Inc, president, chief executive officer, currently. **Orgs:** Colorado Black Chamber of Commerce, chairman, 1990-; Mayors Business Advisory Council, 1992-; Mayors Black Advisory Council, 1992-; State of Colorado Space Advisory Council, 1990-; Greater Denver Local Development Corp., board member, 1990-; Colorado Association of Commerce and Industry, board member, 1990-; Colorado African Carribean Trade, former president, 1991-; Colorado Black Roundtable, 1990-; Colorado World Trade

Commission, board of directors, 1990-. **Honors/Awds:** Martin Luther King Jr Social Responsibility Award, 1989; AT&T, Sales Excellence Award, 1991-92; Minority Enterprise Inc, Supplier of the Year, 1991; The Denver Post, Minority Business of the Year, 1990-91; Juanita Ross Gray Community Service Award, 1991; Entrepreneur of the Year, 1989. **Military Serv:** US Air Force, sgt, 1965-68. **Home Phone:** (303)863-1056. **Business Addr:** President, Chief Executive Officer, RMES Communications, Inc, 4585 Ironton St, Denver, CO 80239, (303)371-5200.

MALONE, J. DEOTHA
Educational administrator. **Personal:** Born May 27, 1932, Sumner County, TN; daughter of Sadie Malone and Harvey Malone. **Educ:** Fisk Univ Nashville, BA/MA 1950 and 1955; TN State Univ, MA Adult Educ 1973; AL State Univ, Montgomery, AL, EdD 1974; Univ of AL Tuscaloosa, PhD 1981. **Career:** Sumner County School System, teacher/librarian 1950-70, instructor supervisor of secondary education, 1970-; City of Gallatin, TN, vice-mayor 1969-; State Comm Coll, instr 1976-80; TN State Univ, instr 1982-83; Sumner County Schools, English as a second language, supervisor of intl students 1986. **Orgs:** NAACP; Gallatin Voter's League; Beacon Civic Club; Econ Dev Program; vice pres, Democratic Women's Club Sumner Cnty; notary public; NEA; TN Educ Assn, adv bd; Middle TN Educ Assn; Sumner Cnty Educ Assn; TN Assn for Publ Sch Adult Edn; Austin Peay Area Supvrs Council, TN Assn of Adult Educators; Phi Delta Kappa; TN Assn for Supvrs and Admin; adv, Gallatin Day Care Center; Human Serv Career Educ Adv Comm for Volunteer State Comm Coll; adv bd, TN Assn of Licensed Practical Nurses; bd dir, TN Educ Assn; adv bd, First & Peoples Bank Gallatin; Governor's Mgmt Team, TN Master Teacher Program; First Baptist Church; Rotary Club, Community Drug Awareness Program, rotarian chairman; Dept of Electricity Power Advisory Bd, 1990-; Gallatin Planning Commission. **Honors/Awds:** Invited to serve on US Comm for Civil Rights; mem Kappa Delta Pi Natl Honor Soc; mem Phi Delta Kappa Honor Soc; selected by the US Office of Educ and TN State Dept of Educ to travel and study in 17 foreign countries; Honorary Citizen of Indianapolis Richard Lugar Mayor; selected by former Pres Jimmy Carter to serve as adv for Comm Dev 1978-79; Descriptive Study of Formal Training and Career Patterns of Secondary Principals in a Southeastern State in the US 1981. **Home Addr:** 1000 Woodmont Dr, Gallatin, TN 37066. **Business Addr:** Supvr Secondary Education, Summer County Board Education, PO Box 1199, Gallatin, TN 37066.

MALONE, JAMES HIRAM
Graphic artist, writer. **Personal:** Born Mar 24, 1930, Winterville, GA; son of Sarah Lena Echols Malone and Ralph Malone; married Mary Louise Liebaert (divorced 1982); children: Andrew Ralph, Matthew Martin. **Educ:** Morehouse College, Atlanta, GA, AA, 1950-51; Center for Creative Studies College of Art and Design, Detroit, MI, AA, 1959-62. **Career:** Federals Dept Stores, Detroit, MI, graphic artist designer, 1964-69; Northgate Art Agency, Detroit, MI, graphic artist designer, 1969-75; Montgomery Ward, Detroit, MI, graphic artist designer, 1975-80; K-Mart International Hdqrs, Troy, MI, graphic artist designer, 1980-83; The Atlanta Journal/Constitution Newspapers, Atlanta, GA, graphic artist designer, beginning 1983; graphic artist/writer, currently; Atlanta News Leader, columnist, Street Beat, 1991-. **Orgs:** Center for Creative Studies Coll Alumni Assoc, 1963-; publicity, Ad Hoc Comm of Atlanta Art Council, 1990-; writer/contrib, Assoc of Amer Cultures, 1980-; promotions/gallery assoc, The Visual Vanguard Art Group, 1988-; board member: Atlanta/Fulton County Neighborhood Planning Unit J, 1984-; Grasp: Bankhead Hwy Revitalization Project Atlanta, 1990-; First World Writers, Inc, 1985-; Atlanta Mayor Jackson's Arts Task Force Committee, consultant, 1990-; Publicity, Literary Inc, 1988-; Georgia's Artists Registry, Atlanta College of Art, consultant, 1989-; President Carter's Atlanta Cluster Project, publicity consultant, 1992-; Intl Black Writers Assn, Inc, vp, 1993, pres, 1997; Atlanta Olympic Comm, arts consultant, 1993; Atlanta Mayor's Bicycle Planning Comm, NPU-J area chairperson, 1995; Atlanta Project, Douglass Cluster, arts consultant, 1995; Atlanta Project, West Fulton Cluster, arts chairperson, 1995; Atlanta/Fulton County Neighborhood Planning Unit J, bd mem, 1984, public safety comm, 1996; Intl Black Writers Assn, Inc, vp, 1993, pres, 1996; Atlanta/Fulton County Action Authority, Inc, bd mem, 1996; Buttermilk Bottom Comm Assn, Inc, vp, 1996; Individual Visual Artists Coalition Assn, bd mem, 1996. **Honors/Awds:** Bronze Jubilee Award, Channel 30 TV, 1986; Group-7 Mural, Arts Festival of Atlanta, 1987; Atlanta Employer's Voluntary Employment Association, Task Force on Youth Motivation Award, 1987, 1988, 1989; Art with a Southern Drawl Art Award, Mobile College, 1993. **Special Achievements:** Works appeared at various juried, invitational, and commissioned exhibitions, including: Atlanta Black Artists Exhibition, 1992; Trinity Art Gallery Festival Show, 1992; Walker Art Gallery Exhibition, 1992; works included in such collections as Atlanta University Gallery; Carnegie Art Institute Gallery; Salon International de la Caricature, Montreal, 1980-88; creator of literary drawings entitled SAY (Simply Apply Yourself), 1986-; author, No-Job Dad, 1992; Giving Back to the Community Art Show, Alma Simmons Gallery, 1994; Encore Exhibition, Atlanta Project Office, 1994; Celebrating the Peanut Art Show, Albany Museum, 1994; Ahh-h, to be a Writer Art Show, Downtown Atlanta Main Library, 1995; Original art, papers, photographs in such collection as Auburn Ave Research Library of African-American Culture and History, Atlanta, 1995; Buttermilk Bottom Comm Historical Art Markers, Atlanta, 1995, 1996; Alma Simmons Gallery Collections Show, 1995, 1996; Auburn Ave Research Library Gallery Visual Arts Legacy Exhibition, 1996; City Hall East IVAC Members Show, 1996; First Place Centennial Olympic Park Art Contest, 1997; ''Voices of Renewal,'' Atlanta's Historical Markers at 420 Blvd, 1997; Atlanta's Metro Lions Club Award, 1997. **Military Serv:** US Army, sfc, 1951-59. **Home Addr:** 1796 North Ave NW, Atlanta, GA 30318-6441.

MALONE, JEFF NIGEL
Professional basketball player. **Personal:** Born Jun 28, 1961, Mobile, AL. **Educ:** MS State, Educ Major 1983. **Career:** Washington Bullets, 1983-90, Utah Jazz, 1990-93; Philadelphia 76ers, 1993-. **Honors/Awds:** 3rd leading rookie scorer; led Bullets in scoring 10 times; a first team All-Rookie selection; Coaches All-Southeastern Conf team; SEC Player of the Year; named a first team All-Am by The Sporting News; mem 36th NBA All Star Team. **Business Addr:** Professional Basketball Player, Philadelphia 76ers, PO Box 25040, Philadelphia, PA 19147.

MALONE, KARL
Professional basketball player. **Personal:** Born Jul 24, 1963, Summerfield, LA; son of Shirley Turner; married Kay; children: Kadee Lynn, Kaylee Ann, Karl Jr. **Educ:** Louisiana Tech Univ, Ruston, LA, 1982-85. **Career:** Utah Jazz, forward, 1985-. **Honors/Awds:** All-NBA First Team, 1989, 1990; All-NBA Second Team, 1988; NBA All-Defensive Second Team, 1988; NBA All-Rookie Team, 1986; NBA All Star Team, MVP, 1989, 1993; NBA, MVP, 1997; NBA All-Star, 1988-97; NBA All-Defensive First Team, 1997; Salt Lake Tribune, Utahn of the Year, 1997. **Special Achievements:** US Olympic Basketball Team, 1992, 1996; Selected as one of the 50 Greatest Players in NBA History, 1996; NBA All-Star Game, top vote getter in Western Conference, 1998. **Business Addr:** Professional Basketball Players, Utah Jazz, 301 W South Temple, Salt Lake City, UT 84101-1216, (801)575-7800.

MALONE, MICHAEL GREGORY
Administrator. **Personal:** Born Oct 27, 1942, Evansville, IN; children: Malik LeRoi, Stephanie Nicole. **Educ:** Butler Univ, 1960-61; IN State Univ Evansville, 1967-71; Univ of Evansville, BS Pol Sci 1971-74. **Career:** Iglehart Opers, quality control tech 1966-68; CAPE, dir youth prog 1968-71, dir commun serv 1971-72, exec dir 1972-; Malone Assoc Inc, pres, mgr. **Orgs:** Mem Natl Assoc of Social Workers 1971-; charter mem bd of dirs Natl Council for the Transportation Disadvantaged 1975-; bd mem Govs Council on Addictions 1976-; mem Downtown Civitans 1976-; mem Lakeview Optimist 1976-; exec bd mem Boy Scouts of Amer Buffalo Trace Council 1976-; mem Southern IN Soccer Officials Assoc 1977-. **Honors/Awds:** Community Serv Awd Gov of IN 1976; Outstanding Man Awd for Commun Affairs Evansville Black Expo 1978. **Business Addr:** President, Manager, Malone Associates Inc, 906 Main St, Evansville, IN 47708.

MALONE, MOSES EUGENE
Professional basketball player. **Personal:** Born Mar 23, 1955, Petersburg, VA; married Alfreda (divorced); children: Moses, Michael. **Career:** Utah Stars ABA, 1974-76, Buffalo Braves, St Louis Spirits; Houston Rockets, 1976-82, Philadelphia 76ers, 1982-86, Washington Bullets, 1987-88, Atlanta Hawks, 1989-91; Milwaukee Bucks, 1991-93; Philadelphia 76ers, 1993-94; San Antonio Spurs, 1994-. **Honors/Awds:** Mem NBA Championship team 1973; named to ABA All-Rookie Team 1975; led NBA in rebounding 1979, 1981, 1982, 1983, 1984, 1985; NBA Most Valuable Player 1979, 1982, 1983; All NBA First Team 1979, 1982, 1983, 1985; All NBA Second Team 1980,81, 1984; NBA All Defensive First Team 1983; NBA All Defensive Second Team 1979; NBA Playoff MVP 1983; mem 36th & 37th NBA All Star Teams. **Business Addr:** Professional Basketball Player, Atlanta Hawks, One CNN Center NW S Tower Suite 405, Atlanta, GA 30335-0001.

MALONE, ROSEMARY C.
Law enforcement official. **Personal:** Born Jun 23, 1954, Detroit, MI; daughter of Jesse James (deceased) & Rosetta M Cook; divorced; children: LaNetha P. **Educ:** Univ of Detroit, MA, 1990; Univ of Detroit-Mercy, doctoral candidate, clinical psychology, currently. **Career:** Detroit Police Dept, police officer, 1974-. **Orgs:** Adopt-A-Cop, co-director, 1992-; NAACP, lifetime mem; WPOM, lifetime mem. **Honors/Awds:** Detroit Police Dept, Officer of Year, 1993, Chief's Unit Award, 1989, 15 Citations, 1979-90, 20 Letters of Appreciation, 1979-90. **Home Addr:** 14811 Rosemary Avenue, Detroit, MI 48213, (313)372-5069. **Business Addr:** Police Officer, Detroit Police Dept, 7th Precinct, Special Operations Unit, 3300 Mack Avenue, Detroit, MI 48207, (313)596-5710.

MALONE, SANDRA DORSEY
Educator. **Personal:** Born Oct 5, Mexia, TX; married Joseph L. **Educ:** MEd 1972; BS. **Career:** Dallas Independent Sch Dist, asst dir 1974-75; Accountability, asst dir 1972-74; Guaranteed Performance Proj Dallas, educ analyst 1970-71; Team TeachingSch Chattanooga, team ldr 1961-65. **Orgs:** Mem Dallas Sch Adminstr & Assn; Am Asn of Sch Adminstrs; Am Educ Research Assn State; orgainzer Nat Council of Negro Women 1973-75; pres Dallas Alumnae Chap Delta Sigma Theta 1973-75; pres RL Thornton PTA 1973-74; vice pres Hulcy Middle Sch PTA 1975-76. **Honors/Awds:** Pres's award Pan Hellenic Council 1973; Comm Serv Award; United for Action Dallas Negro C of C 1975; serv award Delta Omega Chap Delta Sigma Theta 1975; pres's award RL Thornton PTA 1974. **Business Addr:** 3801 Herschell Ave, Dallas, TX.

MALONE, THOMAS ELLIS
Scientist (retired). **Personal:** Born Jun 3, 1926, Henderson, NC; married Dolores; children: Shana, Thomas Jr. **Educ:** North Carolina Central Univ, BS, 1948; Harvard Univ, PhD, 1952. **Career:** North Carolina Cent Univ, Durham, prof zoology, 1952-58; Argonne Nat Lab, resident res assoc, 1958-59; Loyola Univ, Chicago, fac mem, 1959-62; Nat Inst of Dental Research, NIH, asst chief res grants sec, 1963-64, dep chief extramural progs, 1964-66, chief periodont dis & soft tissue studies, 1966-67; Am Univ Beirut, Lebanon, Biol Dept, prof & chmn, 1967-69, assoc dir extramural progs, 1969-72, assoc dir extramural res & training, dep dir, NIH, actg dir, 1972-86; Univ Md, Baltimore, assoc vice chancellor res, 1986-88; Assn of American Med Colleges, vice pres biomed res, 1988-93. **Orgs:** Inst Med-Nat Acad Sci. **Honors/Awds:** Harvard Fellow, 1950-52; NAS-NRC Research Fellow, 1958-59; Department of Health, Educ, & Welfare, Super Service Award, 1971, Distinguished Service Award, 1974; Am Col Dentists, Cert Merit, 1975; Presidential Merit Award, Sr Exec Serv, 1980, Distinguished Exec Rank Award, 1983; DHHS, Secretary's Recognition Award, 1986. **Military Serv:** AUS 1945-46.

MALONE, VAN BUREN
Professional football player. **Personal:** Born Jul 1, 1970, Houston, TX; married Nedra, May 20, 1995. **Educ:** Texas, attended. **Career:** Detroit Lions, defensive back, 1994-. **Business Addr:** Professional Football Player, Detroit Lions, 1200 Featherstone Rd, Pontiac, MI 48342, (248)335-4131.

MALONEY, CHARLES CALVIN
Medical technologist. **Personal:** Born May 24, 1930, W Palm Beach, FL; married Ethel Pearl Covington; children: Charda Corrie, Charles Calvin, III. **Educ:** FL A&M U, BS 1951;Franklin Sch, Med Tec 1956. **Career:** N Dist Hosp Inc, chief med tech; Christian Hosp Miami, Chief Tech 1956-58; Provident Hospital, 1958-62; Broward Gen Med Cntr, 1962-75; Gen Diagnostics Sci Prod, clinical spec. **Orgs:** Mem Am Med Tech; Omega Psi Phi; Boys Club; Jacs Inc; vice pres & sec Broward Med Cntr Credit Univ 1971; mem Jack & Jill of Am Inc; sec Omega Psi Phi 1962-65; Connecting Link; All Am Tackle FL Agr & Mech Univ 1950-55; Basilus 1970-71. **Honors/Awds:** Man of Yr Omega Psi Phi 1960-61 & 1961-62. **Military Serv:** USAF sgt 1951-54.

MALRY, LENTON
Legislator, educator. **Personal:** Born Sep 30, 1931, Shreveport, LA; married Joy. **Educ:** Grambling Coll, BS 1952; TX Coll, MEd 1957; Univ of NM, PhD 1968. **Career:** NM Legislature, rep Bernalillo County; Albuquerque Pub Schs, equal opportunity ofcr 1975; Albuquerque, co-commisioner; Albuquerque Schl System, jr highschl tchr & principal; Albuquerque Publ Schl, dir Cltrl Awareness. **Honors/Awds:** Legislative Achievements include passage of a drug abuse bill & an anti-bias bill.

MALVEAUX, FLOYD
Immunologist. **Personal:** son Of Inez Lemelle Malveaux and Delton Malveaux; married Myrna Ruiz Malveaux, Dec 27, 1965; children: Suzette, Suzanne, Courtney, Gregory. **Educ:** Creighton University, Omaha, NE, BS, 1961; Loyola University, New Orleans, MS, 1964; Michigan State University, East Lansing, MI, PhD, 1968; Howard University College of Medicine, MD, 1974. **Career:** Johns Hopkins University, Baltimore, MD, associate professor of medicine, 1989-; Howard University, Washington, DC, professor of medicine/microbiology, 1989-; Howard University College of Medicine, Washington, DC, chairman of microbiology, 1989-, dean; vp for Health Affairs. **Honors/Awds:** Medical Service Award, National Medical Association, 1986. **Business Addr:** Professor and Chairman, Department of Medicine/Microbiology, Howard University College of Medicine, 520 W St, NW, Washington, DC 20059.

MANAGER, VADA O'HARA
Press secretary. **Personal:** Born Nov 26, 1961, East St Louis, IL; son of Ethel Manager. **Educ:** Arizona State University, BS, political science, 1983; London School of Economics, graduate work. **Career:** Arizona Department of Commerce, special assistant, 1984-86; Office of the Governor, special assistant, 1986-87, press secretary, special assistant, 1988-91; Babbit for President, political advisor, special assistant to president, 1987-88; Young Smith Research, vice pres public finance, 1988; Office of the Mayor, press secretary, 1991-. **Orgs:** Arizona Board of Regents, past member, 1982-83; NAACP; Commission on

Presidential Debates, press, 1992; American Council on Germany, 1990; The Council for United States and Italy, 1992. **Honors/Awds:** Arizona State University Alumni Association, Young Alumni Achievement, 1989. **Home Addr:** 1304 R St, NW, Washington, DC 20009, (202)387-6513. **Business Addr:** Press Secretary, Executive Office of the Mayor, 441 4th St, NW, 11th Fl, Washington, DC 20001, (202)727-5011.

MANCE, JOHN J.
Consultant, aerospace engineer (retired). **Personal:** Born Mar 18, 1926, Chicago, IL; son of Anna Mance and S J Mance; married Eleanore Edson, Oct 9, 1949; children: Richard, David. **Educ:** CAL-AERO Tech Inst, AeroE 1949; UCLA, Indl Rel 1969; Univ of So CA, Exec Progs, 1972. **Career:** Lockheed Aeronautical Systems Co, 1966-90; Aerospace Engineer, 1966-68; Employment Interviewer, 1969; Lockheed Watts-Willowbrook Plant, indl rel dept mgr, 1970-72, asst to indl rel dir, 1973-79, employee transp mgr, 1980-85, personnel rel rep, 1986-88, human rel consl, 1988-90; San Fernando Valley Lutheran Hosp Assn Credit Union, asst trea/mgr, 1963-66; Don Baxter Inc, engineering designer, 1959-63; Marquardt Aircraft Co, wind tunnel engineer, 1956-59; So CA Coop, Wind Tunnel Tech, 1952-56; Frank Mayer Engineering Co, tool designer, 1950-52. **Orgs:** NAACP Golden Heritage, natl bd of dirs, 1976-84, 1988-96, pres, 1966-67; Nevada Housing Devel Corp, pres, 1085-; Natl Mgmt Assn and Lockheed Mgmt Club, 1966-; CA Credit Union League, San Fernando Valley Chap, pres, 1968. **Honors/Awds:** Man of the Month Lockheed Mgmt Club, Nov 1970; Cert of Appreciation, Indsl Coll of Armed Forces 1972; Several citations from various hum rel & civil rights organizations since 1980, including: Distinguished Black American Civil Rights Award; CA State Univ, Dominguez Hills Black Alumni Assn, 1981; Outstanding Service Award, NAACP Natl Bd of Dirs, 1985; Roy Wilkins Award, 1985; General Conferene Chmn, 1990. **Military Serv:** USN aviation metalsmith 3rd class 1944-46. **Home Addr:** 16257 Marilyn Dr, Granada Hills, CA 91344.

MANGUM, CHARLES M. L.
Attorney. **Personal:** Born Nov 13, 1933, Salisbury, NC; married Lovella W Brown; children: Rhia, Mark, Travis. **Educ:** NC A&T State Univ, BS 1956; Howard Univ, JD 1966. **Career:** Peterson & Mangum Funeral Home, funeral dir 1956-62; Private Practice, attorney. **Orgs:** Mem VA, Old Dominion & Natl Bar Assns; adv bd Law Ctr Constl Rights 1968-76; co-operating atty, legal staff VA, Golden Heritage mem NAACP; co-operating atty Legal Defense Fund; VA Trial Lawyers Assn; chmn of bd Hunton YMCA; pres & life mem Gamma Nu Lambda Chap of Alpha Phi Alpha Frat; pres LynchburgChap NAACP; mem bd of dir Lynchburg Chap OIC; vice chmn bd dir VA Legal Aid Soc; pres Old Dominion Bar Assn; pres Lynchburg VA Chap NCA&T Aggie Club; bd dir Lynchburg Comm Action; mem Central VA Criminal Justice Adv Com; mem Masonic Lodge; mem Amer Civil Liberties Union; pres Virginia State Conf NAACP; mem bd of dirs Lynchburg Chap Natl Conf of Christians and Jews; publisher Lynchburg Area Journal Newspaper. **Honors/Awds:** Recipient of numerous state, local and natl awds and certificates. **Military Serv:** AUS 1957-58. **Business Addr:** Attorney, 915 Main St Ste 310, Lynchburg, VA 24504.

MANGUM, ERNESTINE BREWER
Educator, librarian (retired). **Personal:** Born Aug 7, 1936, Durham, NC; daughter of Patti Brewer (deceased) and Robert Brewer (deceased); married Billy L Mangum, Jul 25, 1969. **Educ:** NC Central Univ, BA Spanish, Library Sci 1957; Rutgers Univ, MLS 1965; Fairleigh Dickinson Univ, MA Human Devel 1982. **Career:** NJ Ed Assoc, mem 1957-; Natl Ed Assoc, mem 1957-; Civil Rights & Human Rights Comm, mem & officer 1963-; Elmwood Presbyterian Church, mem 1964-74; Mt Ararat Baptist Church, mem 1975-; school teacher/librarian; retired 1998. **Orgs:** Mem NJ Historical Soc 1960, NJ Media Assoc, NC Central Univ Alumni Assoc 1960-, Rutherford Educ Assoc 1962-; mem & officer Mt Ararat Women's Club 1974-; volunteer counselor in various self-help groups 1980; interviewed by three editors during Black History Month 1984. **Honors/Awds:** Published article in NJEA Review 1970, 1994; Governor's Teachers Recognition Program 1986; Student Aide & Counseling Committee of Rutherford & East Rutherford NJ, Lifetime Achievement Award, 1996. **Business Addr:** Rutherford Board of Education, 176 Park Avenue, Rutherford, NJ 07070.

MANGUM, ROBERT J.
Judge. **Personal:** Born Jun 15, 1921, Petersburgh, VA; married; children: one. **Educ:** City Coll of NY, BS 1942; Brooklyn Law, LLB 1949; Brooklyn Law Sch, JD 1967; NY U, MPA 1957; Adm Med Columbia, MS 1964; St John U, dr humane letters 1969; City Coll of NY, DL 1977. **Career:** Beth Israel Med Cntr, legal counc 1978-; Ct of Claims NY, st judge 1971-78; New York City Pol Dept 1942-54; 7th Dept Pol Commr, patrolman; Licensing Yth, deputy commr 1954-58; Dept of Hosp NYC, 1st deputy commr 1958-66; OEO, NE reg dir 1966-67; NY St Div of Human Rights, commr 1967-71. **Orgs:** Mem spl study group Dept of Correct 1956; parole commn pol commn rep New York City 1958; mem of com to revise Prin & Prac of NY St Parole Syst 1957; chmnof steering com Interdept Hlthl Coun New York City 1964; lctr in pub hlth Columbia U; bd of trust past NY U; chmn bd of trust Harlem Preparatory Sch; bd trust legal couns Beth Israel Med Cent; found Guardians Assn Police Dept NYC; 100 Blackmen NY City. **Honors/Awds:** Frederick Douglass awd NY Urban Leg cit masonic group; dept of corr; man of yr New York City bd of trade; cert of merit hosp admin assn dept of hosp NYC; charter mem Prof Assn of Publ Exec. **Military Serv:** AUS 1st lt 1946. **Business Addr:** Beth Israel Medical Center, First Avenue & 16th Sts, Attn: Annie Wilson, New York, NY 10003.

MANIGAULT, WALTER WILLIAM
Business executive, elected official. **Personal:** Born Sep 26, 1939, Georgetown, SC; married Earlyne Derious Rand; children: Terrence, Troy, Tiffany. **Educ:** Howard Univ, BS 1960; Atlanta Univ, MS 1968; Univ of OR Med School, Post-Grad Study 1969-71. **Career:** Manigault & Son Morticians, Inc, mortician 1961-85. **Orgs:** Mem Georgetown Cty Bd of Ed 1976-84, Natl Bd of Funeral Svc, SC Morticians Assoc, 6th Dist Progressive Morticians, Natl Funeral Dir & Morticians Assoc; past mem bd of dir Georgetown Cty Chamber of Comm; trustee Bethel AME Church; mem bd of dir Georgetown Breakfast Rotary Club, Baksersvill Housing Development Corp. **Honors/Awds:** Public Serv Awd 6th Dist Omega Psi Phi 1976; 8 Yrs Serv Awd Georgetown Cty Bd of Ed 1984. **Military Serv:** AUS capt 1961-63. **Home Addr:** Martin Luther King PO Box 822, Pawleys Island, SC 29585.

MANIGO, GEORGE F., JR.
Clergyman. **Personal:** Born Nov 10, 1934, Bamberg, SC; son of Ertha M Ramsey and George F Manigo Sr; married Rosa L Lewis; children: Marcia B, George F, III. **Educ:** Claflin Coll, BS 1959; Gammon Theol Sem, BD 1962. **Career:** Trinity United Methodist Church, pastor; St Mark & St Matthew Chs Taylors SC, minister 1970-; Wesley Church St James, 1965-70; Market St United Methodist Church, 1962-65; Hurst Memorial United Methodist Church, 1960-62; United Methodist Church, Walterboro District,district superintendant, 1986-. **Orgs:** Mem SC Conf Merger Com 1973-; chmn bd dirs Greenville CAP Agy; NAACP; sec Greenville Urban Ministry; Phi Beta Sigma; Trustee of Columbia Coll, Columbia SC, 1978-. **Military Serv:** AUS sp/3 1953-56. **Business Addr:** District Superintendent, Walterboro District United Methodist Church, PO Box 829, Walterboro, SC 29488.

MANLEY, ALBERT EDWARD. See Obituaries section.

MANLEY, AUDREY FORBES
Educational Administrator. **Personal:** Born Mar 25, 1934, Jackson, MS; daughter of Ora Buckhalter and Jesse Lee; married Albert E Manley, Apr 3, 1970. **Educ:** Spelman Coll, AB (cum laude) 1955; Meharry Med Coll, MD 1959; Cook County Hosp, resident 1960-63; Abraham Lincoln Sch Med, fellow 1965; Johns Hopkins Univ School of Hygiene and Public Health, MPH 1987. **Career:** Spelman Coll, med dir family plan program/chmn health careers adv com 1972-76, org/prog consult family plan program & inst 1972-76; Emory Univ Family Planning Program Grady Memorial Hospital, chief of med svcs 1972-76; USPHS, comm officer/med dir/chief family health & preventive serv 1976-78, comm officer/chief sickle cell diseases 1978-83; Howard Univ Dept Pediatrics, clinical asst prof 1981; Natl Naval Med Center, Dept Peds, Court Clinical attend, 1981; NIH Inter-Inst Genetics Clinic, guest attending 1981; USPHS, capt 06/med dir assoc admin for clinical affairs 1983-85; Natl Health Serv Corps, dir 1987-89; US Public Health Service, asst surgeon general, 1988-97; USPHS, Dept of HHS, Washington, DC, deputy asst secretary for health, 1989-93; Deputy Surgeon General & Acting Deputy Asst Ser for minority health, 1993-95; Acting Surgeon General, 1995-97; Spelman College, president, 1997-. **Orgs:** American Academy of Pediatrics; National Medical Association; American Public Health Association; American Association of University Women; Institute of Medicine/National Academy of Science; American Association for the Advancement of Science; Commissioned Officers Association; American Society of Human Genetics; National Society of Genetic Counselors; New York Academy of Science; National Council of Negro Women; Association of Military Surgeons of the United States; UNICEF/WHO, committee on health policy, 1990-92. **Honors/Awds:** Woman of the Year, Zeta Phi Beta Sorority, in recognition as first Black woman and youngest person to be appointed Chief Resident of Cook County's 500 bed Children's Hospital, 1962; NIH Fellowship, 1963-65; Mary McLeod Bethune Achievement in Govt Award, Natl Council of Negro Women, 1979; Meritorious Serv Medal, 1981, Commendation Medals, 1986, Unit Commendation Award, 1989, Distinguished Service Medal, 1992; all from PHS; invited for launch of Space Shuttle Challenger Mission #7, 1985; Community Health Awareness Award, Natl Med Assn, 1988; Outstanding Contribution Award, Minority Women in Science, 1989; Achievement Award, Coalition of 100 Black Women, 1989; elected Honorary Member, Delta Sigma Theta Sorority, 1989; DHL, Tougaloo College, 1990; Spelman College, Honorary Doctor of Laws, 1991; Honorary Doctor Humane Letters Meharry Medical College, 1991; First African-American woman to achieve rank of asst surgeon gen USPHS, 1988; First African-American woman asst surgeon gen USPHS. **Military Serv:** PHS, RAdm. **Business Addr:** President, Spelman College, 350 Spelman Ln, SW, Atlanta, GA 30314.

MANLEY, BILL
Banker. **Personal:** Born Jul 18, 1944, New Bern, NC; son of Bernice Manley and Robert Manley; married Gloria Myers, Apr 19, 1967; children: Christi, Stewart, Lorin, David. **Educ:** North Carolina A&T State University, BS, 1966; Vanderbilt Business School, MBA, 1972. **Career:** United States Armed Forces, captain, 1966-70; Vanderbilt Business School, director admissions, 1972-75; NationsBank, manager, Bank LPO, 1984-88, sr vice pres, 1988-. **Orgs:** YMCA, Matthews, NC, board member, 1992-; United Negro College Fund, corporate board member, 1992-. **Special Achievements:** Commencement speaker at Owen School, Vanderbilt's Business School, 1990. **Military Serv:** Army, captain, 1967-69. **Business Addr:** Senior VP, NationsBank Corp. Bank, NationsBank Corp. Center, 100 N Tryon St, 8th Fl, MC: NC1-007-08-04, Charlotte, NC 28255-0086.

MANLEY, DEXTER
Professional football player (retired). **Personal:** Born Feb 2, 1959, Houston, TX; married Glinda Joy; children: Dexter Keith II, Dalis Joy, Derrick Keith. **Educ:** Attended, Oklahoma State. **Career:** Defensive end: Washington Redskins, 1981-89, Phoenix Cardinals, 1990, Tampa Bay Buccaneers, 1991, Ottawa Rough Riders (CFL), beginning 1992. **Orgs:** Honorary member, Comptex Assoc; owner, Mr D Enterprises; filmed commercial for The Washington Post; contributed time/money Easter Seals, Epilepsy Foundation; owner, professional automobile detailing co: Auto-Brite. **Honors/Awds:** Defensive Player of the Game honors twice in 1984, five times in 1985; Pro Bowl team, 1987; NFC Championship game, post-1982, 1983, 1986, 1987 seasons; Super Bowl, post-1982, 1983, 1987 seasons.

MANLEY, JOHN RUFFIN
Clergyman. **Personal:** Born Oct 15, 1925, Murfreesboro, NC; married Gloria Roysler. **Educ:** Shaw U, AB BD 1949; Duke Univ Durham NC, ThM 1967; Shaw U, DA 1955. **Career:** First Bapt Ch Chapel Hill NC, pastor 27 yrs; Hickory Bapt Ch, 23 yrs; New Hope Assn, moderator. **Orgs:** Vp & chmn of Political Action Com Gen Bapt Conv of & NC Inc; mem Chapel Hill-caraboro Sch Bd; mem Chapel Hill Planning Bd; mem NAACP; 2nd Masonic Lodge; vice chmn Governor's Coun on Sickle Cell Syndrone; chmn Proj Area Com of Redevel Comm; mem Task Force for Community Devel Act for Chapel Hill. **Honors/Awds:** Man of Yr Shaws Theol Alumni; delegate to World Bapt Alliance. **Business Addr:** First Baptist Church, Chapel Hill, NC.

MANLOVE, BENSON
Utilities company executive. **Personal:** Born 1943; married. **Educ:** Wayne State Univ, BBA, 1969. **Career:** Wayne State Univ, asst to pres, 1968-70; Amtask Inc, dir mktg, 1970-71; L & M Office Products, co-owner, 1970-79; Michigan Consolidated Gas Co, exec asst to pres, 1979-81, exec dir, mtl support services, 1981-83, vice pres, administration, 1983-, codirector, currently; Detroit Economic Growth Corp, acting pres, 1995. **Orgs:** Chairperson, board of directors, Detroit Urban League, 1989-. **Business Addr:** Vice President, Administration, Michigan Consolidated Gas Co, 500 Griswold, Detroit, MI 48226.

MANN, CHARLES
Professional football player. **Personal:** Born Apr 12, 1961, Sacramento, CA. **Educ:** Univ of Nevada at Reno, attended. **Career:** Washington Redskins, defensive end, 1983-. **Honors/Awds:** Post-season play: NFC Championship Game, 1983, 1986, 1987, NFL Championship Game, 1983, 1987, Pro Bowl, 1987-1989.

MANN, GEORGE LEVIER
Educator, attorney (retired). **Personal:** Born Dec 18, 1901, Harriman, TN; son of Lucy Mann and Jacob Mann; married Susie Haire; children: Doris Elise, Lucia Carol. **Educ:** OH State Univ, AB 1930, AM 1931; IN Univ, EdD 1949; St Louis Univ, JD 1955. **Career:** W KY Coll, prof 1931-32; US Consvtn Corps, educ adv 1934-37; Dunbar High & Grade Schs Madison IL, prin 1937-40; St Louis Public Sch Sys, prin 1940-71; retired 1971. **Orgs:** Mem MO Bar Assn; Natl Bar Assn; Mound City Bar; mem Samaritan United Meth Ch; Omega Psi Phi Frat; bd mem N Side YMCA; Union Sarah Comm Corp; Anniversary Club; Creve Coeur Demo Coalition; life mem NAACP. **Honors/Awds:** Omega Man of Yr in St Louis 1952; Unique Grad St Louis Law Coll 1955; Certificate Sr Counsellor MO Bar 1976; Awd for Serv to St Louis pupils Omega Psi Phi Frat 1972; Awd for Serv to Boy Scouts; author poetry; Elijah P Lovejoy Award 1989; Natl Assn of Univ Award 1989.

MANN, MARCUS LASHAUN
Professional basketball player. **Personal:** Born Dec 19, 1973, Carthage, MS. **Educ:** East Central Comm College; Mississippi Valley State. **Career:** Golden State Warriors, forward, 1996-. **Business Addr:** Professional Basketball Player, Golden State Warriors, 1001 Broadway, Oakland, CA 94607, (510)986-2200.

MANN, MARION
Educator. **Personal:** Born Mar 29, 1920, Atlanta, GA; son of Cora Casey Mann and Levi J. Mann; married Ruth R, Jan 16, 1943; children: Marion Jr, Judith R. **Educ:** Tuskegee Inst, BS 1940; Howard Univ Coll of Med, MD 1954; Georgetown Univ Med Ctr, PhD 1961. **Career:** Howard Univ, coll of med dean 1970-79, asst through full prof dept of pathology; associate vice pres, research, 1988-91. **Orgs:** Natl Med Assn, Inst of Med, Natl Acad of Sciences. **Honors/Awds:** DSc Honoris Causa, Georgetown Univ 1979; DSc Honoris Causa, Univ of Massachusetts 1984. **Military Serv:** AUS 1942-50; USAR 1950-54 1958-80; USAR brigadier general 1975-80 retired 1980. **Home Addr:** 1453 Whittier Pl NW, Washington, DC 20012.

MANN, PHILIP MELVIN
Business executive, clergyman. **Personal:** Born May 31, 1940, Richmond, VA; married Hazel Smith. **Educ:** Lincoln Univ, BA 1960; Union Theol Sem, Pace Univ, Grad Studies. **Career:** The Kahali Modeling Prog, founder 1971; Blessed Trinity Bapt Church, pastor; The Helping Hand Comm Ctr, exec dir. **Orgs:** Bd mem Crispus Attucks Found, Urban Crisis Task Force, Ctr for Youth Devel, Mt Hope Bapt Church; expert org & civil rights activist; bd mem Ecclesiastical Soc, Harlem Planning Bd #10, Area Policy Bd #10. **Honors/Awds:** Man of the Year Awd NY Civic Assoc 1975. **Business Addr:** Executive Dir, Helping Hand Comm Ctr, 131 W 129th St, New York, NY 10030.

MANN, RICHARD
Professional football coach. **Personal:** Born in Aliquippa, PA; son of Broadies Hughes; married Karen; children: Deven, Richard, Mario, Brittany. **Educ:** Arizona State, BS Elem Educ. **Career:** Aliquippa High School, teacher/coach, 1970-73; Arizona State Univ, receiver coach, 1974-79; Univ of Louisville, receiver coach, 1980-81; Baltimore/Indianapolis Colts, receiver coach, 1982-84; Cleveland Browns, receiver coach, 1985-. **Honors/Awds:** Inducted Aliquippa Sports Hall of Fame, 1982; Black Image Achievement Award, 1989; Honorary Chmn, Charlotte Housing Authority Scholarship Fund, 1990.

MANN, THOMAS J., JR.
State senator, attorney. **Personal:** Born Dec 15, 1949, Brownsville, TN; son of Flossie Mann and Thomas Mann; married Leala Ann Salter Mann; children: Nari, Kari. **Educ:** Tennessee State Univ, BS, political science, 1971; Univ of Iowa Law School, JD 1974. **Career:** State of Iowa, asst attorney genl 1974-76; Iowa Civil Rights Commn, executive director 1976-79; State of Iowa, asst attorney genl 1980-82, state senator, 1983-91; Mann & Mann Law Office, partner, 1983-92; Texas Commission on Alcohol and Drug Abuse, general counsel, 1993-95; Mann Law Office, partner, 1995-. **Orgs:** Mem IA State Bar Assn, Polk Co Bar Assn; bd mem Des Moines Br NAACP; mem Omega Psi Phi; Texas Bar Assn. **Honors/Awds:** Comm Appreciation Awd Omega Psi Phi 1978; The Iowa Civil Liberties Union, Civil Libertarian of the Year Award, 1990. **Home Addr:** 12606 Deer Falls Dr, Austin, TX 78729-7228.

MANNEY, WILLIAM A.
Broadcast executive. **Personal:** Born Jul 12, 1931, Springfield, AR; married Alice. **Educ:** Philander Smith Coll, Little Rock, BA. **Career:** WENN Radio, gen mgr; WBEE Radio, Chicago, gen mgr 1970-, acct exec 1966-70. **Orgs:** Mem Nat Assn of Market Developers; black media rep, bd dir Cosmopolitan C of C Chicago; second vice pres Jane Dent Home for the Aged. **Business Addr:** General Manager, WAGG-AM, 424 16 St N, Birmingham, AL 35203.

MANNIE, WILLIAM EDWARD
Business owner. **Personal:** Born Jan 19, 1931, Helena, AR; son of Sylvia Manney and Tony Manney; married Jessie A; children: Regina D, Lynnette A, Gregory A, Reginald K. **Educ:** Wilson Jr Coll, AA 1951; Roosevelt Univ, BSC Acctg 1957; Kent Coll of Law, attended 1967-68. **Career:** US Treas Dept IRS Criminal Investigation Div, supervisory criminal investigator 30 yrs retired 1984; Manney Badge and Credential Cases, Ltd, currently. **Orgs:** Mem Fed Criminal Investigators Assn, IL Police Assn, Natl Assn of Treasury Agents; Association of Former Special Agents of the IRS; Federal Law Enforcement Officers Assn. **Honors/Awds:** Received following awds from US Treas Dept, Superior Perf Awd 1964, Finalist Fed Employee of the Yr 1967; Spl Achievement Awd 1974, 1975, High Quality Step Increase 1973, Meritorious Serv Awd Criminal Investigation Div 1983, Albert Gallatin Awd 1984. **Military Serv:** USAF 1952-56. **Business Addr:** Manney Badge & Credential Cases, Ltd, PO Box 208010, Chicago, IL 60620.

MANNING, BLANCHE MARIE
Judge, educator. **Personal:** Born Dec 12, 1934, Chicago, IL; daughter of Marguerite Anderson Porter (deceased) and Julius L Porter (deceased); married William Manning. **Educ:** Chicago Tchrs Coll, BE 1961; John Marshall Law Sch Chicago, JD 1967; Roosevelt Univ Chicago, MA 1972; Univ of VA, Charlottesville, VA, LLM, 1992. **Career:** Chicago Bd of Educ, teacher 1961-68; Cook Co State's Attys Office, asst states atty 1968-73; Equal Employment Oppor Commn, supervisory trial atty 1973-77; United Airlines, gen atty 1977-78; US Attys Office, asst US atty 1978-79; Circuit Ct of Cook Co, assoc judge; 1st Municipal Dist Circuit Ct of Cook Co, supervising judge 1979-86, supervising circuit judge 1986-87; Justice of the Illinois Appellate Court, 1st District 1987-; Harvard Law School, Univ of Chicago Law School, Trial Advocacy Workshops, teaching team member, 1991-; De Paul University College of Law, adjunct professor, 1992-; Dept of Justice, Atty Gen Adv Inst, adj, 1979-. **Orgs:** Mem Natl Assn of Women Judges; Cook County Bar Association; Il Judicial Council; lecturer IL Judicial Conf New Judges Seminar, Professional Devel Prog for New Assoc Judges, IL Judicial Conf Assoc Judges Sem 1982-86; New Judges Seminar, faculty; mem Chicago Bar Assn Symphony Orchestra. **Honors/Awds:** Edith Sampson Meml Awd 1985; Awd of Appreciation The Intl Assoc of Pupil Personnel Workers 1985; IL Judicial Council; Kenneth E Wilson Judge of the Year Awd Cook County Bar Assn; Disting Alumna Awd Chicago State Univ 1986; Awd of Excellence in Judicial Admin Women's Bar Assn 1986; Black Rose Award, League of Black Women 1987; Thurgood Marshall Award, IIT Kent Law School BALSA 1988; Professional Achievement Award, Roosevelt Univ 1988; We Care Role Model Award, Chicago Police Department 1987-94; Distinguished Service Award, John Marshall Law School, 1989; We Care Outstanding Role Model Award, Chicago Public Schools & Chicago Police Dept, 1992-94; National Black Prosecutors Association, Distinguished Service Award, 1991; The Guardians Police Organization, Citizen's Award, 1991. **Business Addr:** Judge, United States District Court, Ste 2156, 219 S Dearborn St, Chicago, IL 60604.

MANNING, BRIAN
Professional football player. **Personal:** Born Apr 22, 1975. **Educ:** Stanford, BS in sociology. **Career:** Miami Dolphins, wide receiver, 1997-. **Business Addr:** Professional Football Player, Miami Dolphins, 2269 NW 199th St, Miami, FL 33056, (305)620-5000.

MANNING, DANIEL RICARDO
Professional basketball player. **Personal:** Born May 17, 1966, Hattiesburg, MS; son of Edward Manning; married Julie; children: Elizabeth, Evan. **Educ:** Univ of Kansas, bachelor's degree in communications. **Career:** Los Angeles Clippers, forward-center, 1988-94; Atlanta Hawks, 1994; Phoenix Suns, 1994-. **Honors/Awds:** College Basketball Player of the Year, 1988; NBA All-Star, 1993, 1994. **Business Addr:** Professional Basketball Player, Phoenix Suns, PO Box 515, Phoenix, AZ 85001, (602)379-7867.

MANNING, EDDIE JAMES
Administrator. **Personal:** Born Mar 19, 1952, Philadelphia, PA; married Carolyn; children: Eddie Jr, C Jamal. **Educ:** Cheyney State Coll, BS 1974; Temple Univ, MEd 1976, DEd 1985. **Career:** Chester Upland School Dist, teacher/guidance counselor; Ashbourne School, teacher; Temple Univ Special Recruitment & Admissions Program, counselor/academic advisor 1977-79; Act 101 Program Temple Univ, coord 1979-80, dir 1980-. **Orgs:** Mem Amer Assoc of Counseling and Develop, PA Counseling Assoc, Amer Assoc of Multi-Cultural Counseling and Develop, PA Assoc of Multi-Cultural Counseling and Develop; treas PA Chap of the Amer Assoc for Non-White Concerns in Personnel and Guidance 1982-; chmn Act 101 Eastern Regional Exec Comm 1982-83; chmn State Chapts Div of Amer Assoc of Multi-Cultural Counseling and Develop 1983-85; mem Temple Univ Sub-Comm for Academic Excellence in Athletics 1985-; mem Temple Univ Residency Review Bd 1985-. **Home Addr:** 7834 Williams Ave, Philadelphia, PA 19150.

MANNING, EVELYN. See HALL, EVELYN ALICE.

MANNING, HOWARD NICK, JR.
Attorney. **Personal:** Born Jan 7, 1943, Montgomery, AL; married Lois. **Educ:** Univ of MO Sch of Mines & Metallurgy, BSCE, 1967; UCLA Sch of Law, JD, 1974 . **Career:** Manning Reynolds & Roberts LA, sr partner 1976-; Fed Trade Commn LA, staff atty 1974-75; Mobil Oil Corp LA, proj engr 1969-71; Army Corps of Engrs, commd ofcr; Army of Thaild, constrn advr 1968-69; Engrng Div Procter & Gamble Co, civil tech engr 1967. **Orgs:** Am Soc of Civil Engrs; Am Bar Assn; LA Co Bar Assn; CA State Bar Assn; Langston Bar Assn; Natl Bar Assn; Beverly Hills Bar Assn; lectr, CA Luth Coll Sem; bd of dirs, Beverly Hills Bar Assn Schlrshp Found, 1974; vice pres, bd of dirs Beverly Hills Bar Assn Schlrshp Found 1976; LA Br NAACP; Alpha Phi Alpha Frat. **Honors/Awds:** Midwestern Hall of Fame, Alpha Phi Alpha Frat, 1966; founder, Epsilon Psi Chap, Alpha Phi Alpha Frat, 1965; outst advocate mem sec bd of judges Moot Ct Honors Prgm UCLA Sch of Law, 1973; schlrshp recipient Beverly Hills Bar Assn Schlrshp Found.

MANNING, HUBERT VERNON
Clergyman, college president. **Personal:** Born Aug 2, 1918, Cheraw, SC; married Ethel Braynon; children: June, Michelle. **Educ:** Claflin Coll, AB 1940; Grammon Theol Sem, BD 1945; DD 1957; Boston U, MA 1947; Bethune-Cookman Coll, LLD 1971; Univ MI, Postgrad. **Career:** Pub Schs SC, tchr 1940-43; Meth Ch, ordained to ministry 1944; Home Mission Council N Am, minister to migrants 1945-47; Rural & Urban Chs, pastor 1947-48; Claflin Coll, prof hist chaplain 1948-51; pres 1956-; Wesley Meth Ch Charleston, pastor 1951-56; Missions Meth Bd Edn, dean sch 1948-49. **Orgs:** Chmn bd educ SC Conf 1947-57; del World MI Conf 1960; chmn comm ecumenical Qaffairs SC Ann Conf; mem bd higher educ & ministry United Meth Ch; mem exec com higher educ & ministry exec com ordained ministry rep Southeastern Jurisdiction; dir newspaper Palmetto Leader; bd dirs Orangeburg Co United Fund; mem adv counci SC Higher Edn; Facilities Commn; chmn bd dirs Triangle Assn Colls; mem Orangeburg C of C; Phi Beta Sigma; Alpha Kappa Mu. **Honors/Awds:** Contrib articles to professional jours; recipient Alumni Merit Award Boston Univ 1969. **Business Addr:** Claflin Coll, Orangeburg, SC 29115.

MANNING, JANE A.
Educational administration. **Personal:** Born Mar 22, 1947, Wichita Falls, TX. **Educ:** TX Southern Univ Houston, BA Journalism 1969; Columbia Univ NY, MA Journalism 1970. **Career:** Press Enterpise, city reporter 1971-74; TX Southern Univ, instr of journalism 1974-79; Riverside City Coll, dir info serv 1979-84; Media Methods, owner &gen mgr 1981-; Truckee Meadows Comm Coll, part-time journalism inst 1985-; Univ of NV Reno, dir office of public info 1984-. **Orgs:** Mem Assn of CA Coll Admin 1979-85, Natl Council for Community Relations 1980-84; dir Oppty Indust Ctr of Inland Counties 1980-82, Friends of Inland Counties Legal Serv 1981-83; bd mem Publ Relations Soc of Amer 1982-83; mem Soc of Prof Journalists Sigma Delta Chi, Council for the Advancement & Supportof Ed, Silver State Chap Intl Assoc of Business Comm; NV State Press Assoc; WIN; AAHE; bd mem and UNR Rep, AAUW; bd of dir Nevada Women's Fund; mem Nat'l Assoc for the Advancement of Colored People; mem Alliance of Racial Minorities; mem Reno/Sparks Negro Bus and Prof Women's Club; bd of dir American Red Cross. **Honors/Awds:** City Resolution for Outstanding Contrib to Centennial Celebration 1983; Valuable & Disting Serv Awd City of Riverside 1983; Inspirational Awd UNR Black Student Org 1985. **Home Addr:** PO Box 8478, University Station, Reno, NV 89507. **Business Addr:** Dir Office of Pub Informn, Univ Nevada at Reno, Jones Visitor Center, Reno, NV 89557.

MANNING, JEAN BELL
Educator. **Personal:** Born Aug 14, 1937, LaMarque, TX; married Dr Reuben D Manning. **Educ:** Bishop Coll, BA (hon student Valedictoria Scholarship) 1958; N TX State Univ, MEd 1964, EDd 1970. **Career:** Douglas HS Ardmore OK, instr 1958-60; Reading Lab Jarvis Coll Hawkins TX; instr & dir 1961-64; TX So Univ Houston, vis prof 1964-65; Douglas HS OK, instr 1964-65, 1965-67; Univ of Liberia, Liberia, W Africa, prof of English 1973-74; Paul Quinn Coll Waco TX, chmn dept educ 1970-73, 1974-78; Langston Univ OK, assoc prof/dir resources 1978-86, vice pres for academic affairs 1986-. **Orgs:** Educ for Leadership in Black Ch Lilly Found Sponsored Houston TX 1975-77; curriculum devel Wiley Coll Marshall TX 1978; competency based educ Dallas Independent S Dist 1979; mem Alpha Kappa Alpha Sor 1956-; mem Links Inc 1974-; mem Phi Delta Kappa Sor 1956-. **Honors/Awds:** Ford Found Doctoral Grant 1969; Outstanding Sor of SW Phi Delta Kappa Sor 1978. **Business Addr:** Assoc Professor Dir Resources, Langston University, PO Box 907, Langston, OK 73050.

MANNING, RANDOLPH H.
Educator, educational administrator. **Personal:** Born Dec 18, 1947, New York, NY; son of Gertrude Webber Manning and Ruthfoy Manning; married Monica S McEvilley; children: Randolph, Craig C, Corey A. **Educ:** Suffolk Co Comm Coll, AA 1969; SUNY at Stony Brook, BA 1971, MA 1975. **Career:** R H Manning Enterprises, owner/operator 1973-; Suffolk Co Comm Coll, counselor 1971-80, prof of psy & sociology 1980-85, dean of instruction 1985-. **Orgs:** Educational consultant BOCES 1980-; adv bd mem Re-Rout Dept of Labor BOCES, SOCC, SC Correction 1980-; bd dirs LI Sickle Cell Inc 1981-; bd of dir Gordon Heights Federal Credit Union; Past President New York State Special Programs Personnel Assn; Suffolk Cty Youth Bd; Brookhaven Social Svcs, advisory comm; Long Island Assn of Black Counselors; Long Island Minority Educators; East End Guidance Assn; NYS Special Programs Personnel Assn, pres emeritus, former chairman of the supervisory & publicity comm; Gordon Hgts Federal Credi Union; Long Island Sickle Cell Project, mem/treas; Council of Intl Programs, co-dir; Amer Sociological Assn; SUNY Two year Academic Deans Assn; Suffolk Cty Probation Dept, Day Reporting Ctr, steering comm; Comm Coll General Educ Assn, natl pres; NYS, Bd of Prof Med Conduct, bd mem. **Honors/Awds:** Outstanding Young Men of Amer 1981; SUNY Distinguished Alumni Chancellor Awd State Univ of NY 1983; Proclamation for Service County of Suffolk 1986; US Department of Commerce, Bureau of Census, Certificate of Appreciation, 1970; Special Program Personnel Assn, Certificate of Appreciation, 1980; Alpha Beta Gamma Natl Business Honor Society, Membership, 1986; Suffolk County, Proclamation; NAACP Award; Halpin County Executive, Recognition of Service Award, 1991; Outstanding Young Men of America Award, Prof & Comm Service, 1981; SUNY Distinguished Alumni Chancellors Award, 1983; Recognition of Service Award, "Sunrise Fires," County Executive Gaffney, 1995; Cert of Special Recognition, US House of Reps, Dedication to Educational & Comm Excellence, Congressman Michael P Forbes, 1997. **Special Achievements:** Author: "A World Apart," Viewpoints, Newsday series, 1990; Eastern Campus Research Project article for ERIC,

1992. **Business Addr:** Dean of Instruction, Suffolk Co Community College, Speonk-Riverhead Rd, Riverhead, NY 11901.

MANNING, REUBEN D.
Educator. **Personal:** Born Mar 18, 1931, Waco, TX; married Jean Bell. **Educ:** Paul Quinn Coll, BS; TX So U, MS; N TX State U, EdD; UCLA; Univ of TX; Univ of OK. **Career:** Paul Quinn Coll, pres; Univ of Liberia, vis lectr 1976, vis prof 1973-74; Paul Quinn Coll, dean of instr 1970-; N TX State U, grad asst 1967-68; Langston U, asso prof, chmn, research prof 1966-69; TX Coll, vis prof 1962; Wiley Coll, vis prof 1961; Jarvis Christian Coll, asst prof, chmn 1959-64; Bishop Coll, instr 1965-58. **Orgs:** Am Assn of Sci; Nat Assn of Sci Tchrs; Nat Inst of Sci; Am Counc of Edn; Nat Educ Assn; TX Educ Assn; Nat Asst of Coll Deans & Registrars; Edwards Chapel AME Ch; Alpha Phi Alpha Frat Inc; Phi Delta Kappa Frat, Beta Kappa Chi Sci Soc; Rotary Internat; BSA; YMCA; NAACP; bd dirs Heart O'TX Boy Scout Counc; chmn training div, bd dir ALIVE; bd dir, vice pres McLennan Co Heart Assn; co-chmn E Waco Heart Fund Campgn; bd dir Caritas; steering com Waco Environtl Task Force; bd dir Waco Manpower Plng Counc; bd dir Grtr Waco United Fund; bd dir Waco Urban League; bd dir Waco Econ Oppty Advncmt Coop; bd chmn Waco Min Afrs Clearing House; tast force Goals for Waco Edn; bd mem Waco Creative Art Ctr; consult E Waco Merchants Assn; Minority Forum; Ministry of Edn, Rep ofLiberia; Waco Classroom Tchrs A; E TX Sch Men Assn. **Honors/Awds:** Acad cit Jarvis Christian Coll 1960; NSF Acad Yr Flwshp, Univ of OK 1964; NSF Rsrch Grant, Univ of OK 1965; Outst Tchr Award, Langston Univ 1966; NSF SumFlwshp, Am Univ 1967; Title III Grant 1967; Ford Found Study Grant, N TX State Univ 1968; Tchng Asstshp, TX State Univ 1969; Rsrch Grant, Langston Univ 1969. **Military Serv:** AUS 1952. **Business Addr:** Research Professor, Langston University, PO Box 730, Langston, OK 73050.

MANNING, SHARON
Professional basketball player. **Personal:** Born Mar 20, 1969. **Educ:** North Carolina State, BA in sociology. **Career:** Charlotte Sting, center-forward, 1997-. **Business Addr:** Professional Basketball Player, Charlotte Sting, 2709 Water Ridge Pkwy, Ste 400, Charlotte, NC 28217, (704)424-9622.

MANSELL, BUFORD H. L.
Clergyman. **Personal:** Born Mar 10, 1938, Dacusville, SC; married Ruby Smith. **Educ:** SE Univ Greenville, SC, ThD; Emory Univ Atlanta, GA, Certificate of Attainment (Theology). **Career:** Chesnee Circuit Chrg, pastor 4 yrs; Duncan Landrum Chrg, 1 yr; Mt Zion UM Ch 6 yrs; Yellow Freight System, truck driver. **Orgs:** F&AAYM Mtn City Masonic Lodge; Blue Ridge Royal Arch Chptr; Voorhees Commandery Knights Templar; Islam Temple AAONMS; OES patron; heroine of Jericho; Crusader & Daughter of Isis. **Military Serv:** USAF A1c 1956-64; Good Conduct Medal, Marksmanship Ribbon, Longevity Serv Awd.

MANSFIELD, ANDREW K.
Government official. **Personal:** Born Feb 17, 1931, Morehouse Parish, LA; married Mae. **Educ:** Grambling State, BS; Atlanta U, MEd; So U. **Career:** Grambling, LA, mayor 1977-. **Orgs:** Mem Lincoln Parish Police Jury 1972-; mem Am Personnell & Guidance Assn; NEA; LEA. **Business Addr:** PO Box 183, Grambling, LA 71245-0183.

MANSFIELD, CARL MAJOR
Physician, educator. **Personal:** Born Dec 24, 1928, Philadelphia, PA; married Sarah Lynne; children: Joel, Kara. **Educ:** Lincoln Univ, AB 1951; Temple Univ, 1952; Howard Univ, MD 1956. **Career:** Episcopal Hospital, resident intern 1956-58; USAF, radiologist 1958-60; Epis Hosp, resident 1960; Jefferson Med Coll Hosp, assoc radiologist, chief div, Chernicoff Fellow, instr radiologist, NIH post doct fellow, resident 1960-67; Jefferson Med Coll, adv clinical fellowship 1965-68, asst prof 1967-69; Univ of PA Sch Med, lectr 1967-73; Thomas Jefferson Univ Hosp, assoc prof 1970-74; Hahnemann Med Coll Hosp, visiting prof 1971; Thomas Jefferson Univ Hosp, prof, chief div 1974-76; Univ of KS Med Center, prof chmn dept radiation 1976-83; Jeff Med Coll & Thomas Jefferson Univ Hosp, prof & chmn dept radiation thermo & nuclear med 1983-. **Orgs:** Mem Amer Bd of Radiology 1962; Amer Bd of Nuc Med 1972; Amer Coll of Nuc Med; Amer Coll of Radiology; AMA; Amer Soc of Therapeutic Radiologists; Assn Univ Radiologists; British Inst Radiology; Amer Coll Nuclear Physicians; Natl Med Assn; Radiol Soc N Amer; Royal Soc Med; Soc Nuc Med Gardens Bd Mt Carmel Bapt Ch 1965-73; adv bd BSA 1965-66; Hall-Mercer Comm Mental Hlth & Mental Retardation Ctr of PA Hosp 1973-74; mem PAC Philadelphia Redevel Authority 1973-75; bd tsts St Peter's Sch 1975-76; mem Pharmacy Com 1965-66; Admiss Com 1968-72; Student Affairs Com 1968-71; Alt Judiciary Com 1971-72; Student Promotion Com 1973-75; Pharmacy & Therapeutic Com 1974-76; Radiation Safety Com 1974-76; Computer Com 1974-76; natl bd of Amer Cancer Soc; pres, Amer Radium Society, 1988-89; pres, Philadelp-American Cancer Society, 1989-90. **Honors/Awds:** Over 150 publications, exhibits, presentations; Natl & Intl meetings; doctor of science, Lincoln Univ, 1991; fellow, Amer College of Radiology, 1976; fellow, Amer College of Nuclear Medicine, 1989; fellow, Philadelphia College of Physicians, 1984; Bronze Medal, American Cancer Society, 1990. **Military Serv:** USAF Capt 1958-60. **Business Addr:** Chmn Dept Radiation Therapy, Jefferson University Hospital, 111 S 11th St, Philadelphia, PA 19107.

MANSFIELD, W. ED
Administration consultant. **Personal:** Born May 7, 1937, Clifton Forge, VA; married Maxine L; children: Amy, Yolanda. **Educ:** Dept of Def Info School, 1964; Univ of Denver, 1969-70. **Career:** Equal Employment Opportunities Commn, St Louis Dist Office, dist dir; Minority Affairs Corp for Public Broadcasting, dir 1976; Alternative Mgmt, consultant 1975-76; Affirmative Action Programs Dept, leader 1972-75; Gen Mills Inc, consultant to chmn of bd & pres 1972; marketing & enrollment, dir 1971-72; Natl Urban Coalition, asst dir field operations 1971; Univ of Denver, asst to chancellor 1969-71; CO Assn of Industrial Colleges & Universities, exec dir 1969-71; Public Relations, dir 1967-68; Radio Station KTLN, moderator, commentator, newscaster 1966-67; Lincoln Natl Life Insurance Co, special agent 1966-69. **Orgs:** Consult EEO Laws Affirmative Action; Gn Mills Inc; Nat Assn of Cos; Nat Civil Serv League; Intl Personnel Mgmt Assn; MN League of Cities; ND League of Cities; Am Compliance Soc & Inc; Intl Assn of Official Human Rights Orgns; City & Co of Denver; fdr past chmn of bd MN Affirmative Action Assn; chmn Hennepin Co Bicentennial Planning Commn; Affirmative Action Adv Com; Intl Personnel Mgmt Assn; 1st v chmn Minneapolis Urban Coalition; mem MN State Bd of Nursing; Abbot-Northwestern Hosp Copr; Minneapolis Citizens Concered for Pub Edn; Am Soc of Personnel Adminstrn; Nat Orgn for Women; NAACP; Nat Urban League; Exchange of Minneapolis. **Military Serv:** USAF 1954-66. **Business Addr:** 1601 Olive St, St Louis, MO 63103.

MANUEL, EDWARD
Public relations executive. **Personal:** Born Aug 8, 1949, Raleigh, NC; son of Eloise Manuel and George Manuel; married Marilyn K. Moore (divorced 1988). **Educ:** University of Wisconsin at Platteville, BS, 1971; University of Wisconsin at Madison, MA, 1975, PhD, 1979. **Career:** Madison Metropolitan School District, Madison, WI, teacher, 1971-79, department chairman, 1975-79; Madison Gas and Electric Co, Madison, WI, community relations manager, 1979-90; Madison Area Technical College, Madison, WI, instructor; University of Wisconsin at Madison, manager of corporate relations, 1990-. **Orgs:** Executive vice president, Pride Classic Inc, 1990-; citizen member, Board of Nursing, State of Wisconsin, 1989-; board member, American Red Cross, Dane County Chapter, 1987-89; baord member, Madison Urban League, 1987; president, Black History Month, Inc, 1986. **Business Addr:** Manager of Corporate Relations, University of Wisconsin-Extension, 3319 W Beltline Hwy, Madison, WI 53713.

MANUEL, JERRY
Professional baseball manager. **Personal:** marrIed Renette Caldwell; children: four. **Career:** Florida Marlins, bench mgr; Chicago White Sox, manager, 1997-. **Special Achievements:** First permanent African American manager in Chicago White Sox history. **Business Addr:** Manager, Chicago White Sox, 333 W 35th St, Chicago, IL 60616, (312)924-1000.

MANUEL, LIONEL, JR.
Professional football player. **Personal:** Born Apr 13, 1962, Rancho Cucamonga, CA. **Educ:** Attended: Citrus College, Univ of the Pacific. **Career:** New York Giants, wide receiver, 1984-. **Honors/Awds:** Post-season play, 1986: NFC Championship Game, NFL Championship Game.

MANUEL, LOUIS CALVIN
Physician. **Personal:** Born Jun 13, 1937, Cleveland, OH; married Idabelle Todd; children: Donna L, April D, Erika L, Louis C. **Educ:** Bowling Green State U, BA 1960; Meharry Med Coll, MD 1965. **Career:** Louis C Manuel MD Eye Serv Inc, ophthalmologist 1971-. **Orgs:** Sec & mem Kansas City Med Soc 1971-; past pres & current sec MO Pan Med 1971-; mem House of Delegates; mem Nat Med Soc 1971-; mem AMA; MO StateMed; Jackson Co Med; SW Med Assn; APPA KC Oph & Otol; Roman Barnes Soc; Castroviejo Soc; Am Soc of Con Oph 1971-; life mem NAACP; consult ophthal Model Cities Health Orgn KC MO 1971-80; deacon Covenant Presbyterian Ch KC MO 1977-; youth council career devel United Presbyterian Ch; bd of dir Civic Plaza Nat Bk KC MO 1979-; mem Alpha Phi Alpha; YMCA; Univ of MO Asso; Midwesterners of Greater KC Med Svc. **Honors/Awds:** Combat Citation; commendation Medal; vietnamese serv ribbon AUS; Morgagmi Soc Meharry Med Pathology 1963f spl citation Med Consult City of St Louis Boxing Tourn 1969; Bowling Green State Rep St Louis Univ 200th Anniversary 1970; fellow Royal Soc of Medicine 1973. **Military Serv:** AUS capt 1966-68. **Business Addr:** Louis C Manuel MD Eye Services, 1734 E 63rd St Ste 601, Kansas City, MO 64110.

MAPLE, GOLDIE M.
Educational administrator. **Personal:** Born Nov 21, 1937, Neptune, NJ; married Jesse Maple; children: Yolanda, Desiree, Jomo. **Educ:** Brooklyn Coll, 1955-56; New York City Comm Coll, 1956-58. **Career:** New York City Board of Education, asst accountant 1968-78, educ admin 1978-83, principal admin assoc 1983-, mem bd of ed 1980-. **Orgs:** Life mem NAACP 1966-; sec Rockaway Day Care Coalition 1976-80; mem Comm School Bd 1980-; pres Rockaway Democratic Coalition 1982-; asst clerk Comm Church of God in Christ 1983-; mem bd of dir Far Rockaway Revitalization Corp 1984-. **Home Addr:** 3226 Mott Ave, Far Rockaway, NY 11691.

MAPP, CALVIN R.
Judge (retired). **Personal:** Born Sep 10, 1924, Miami, FL; son of Edna Mapp and Herschel Mapp; married Catherine Nelson Mapp; children: Calvin Jr, Corey Ramon. **Educ:** Morris Brown Coll, BA; Howard Law School, LLB; Attended, North Dade Jr Coll, Bethune Cookman Coll, Natl Judicial Coll, Univ of FL, Alcohol Abuse Seminar, Harvard Univ. **Career:** Teacher, Math, Chemistry, 1951-52; City of Miami, police officer, 1952-60; Community Relations Bd, 1963-66; All State Courts, State of FL, attorney, 1965; State Attorney's Office, 1966-68; Matthews Braynon & Mapp, attorney, 1968-73; County of Dade, county court judge. **Orgs:** Mem FL, Amer, Natl Bar Assns; admitted to bar State of FL, FL Supreme Ct, US Supreme Ct S Dist of FL 1965; life mem Kappa Alpha Psi Frat; mem Milton Littman Memorial Found. **Honors/Awds:** Morris Brown Coll Hon Dr Laws degree 1974; included in the Black Archives photo section of Dade Co 1976; Certificate of Appreciation Supreme Ct 1980; selected as a delegate by People to People Org, 1981; Judge of the Month Awd Spotlight Club 1983; City of Opa Locka Commendation 1983; Commendation City of Hialeah Gardens FL 1983; Gwen Cherry Political Award Sigma Gamma Rho Sor 1983-84; Outstanding Commitment to Mankind & Continuous Support of Shrine Progs Award, 1984; Certificate of Appreciation Black History Month Lillie C Evens Elem Sch 1984; Disting Leadership Awd Conf of the Co Court Judges of FL; Certificate for participation in 1981 FL Judicial Coll as Instructor FL Supreme Ct; inventor, holds patents on disposable syringe 1977, electra hoop 1978, sliding glass door dustpan; written books entitled, Traffic, A Compilation of Florida Case Law; mem, Rotary Intl. **Military Serv:** AUS s/sgt 1943-46.

MAPP, DAVID KENNETH, JR.
Law enforcement. **Personal:** Born Nov 15, 1951, Norfolk, VA; married Cynthia Gaines; children: Shomarr, Patrice. **Educ:** Norfolk State Univ, BA Sociology 1973. **Career:** Norfolk Sheriff's Dept, recreation dir 1973-75, clafficiation officer 1975-78, dir of classification & rehabilitative progs 1978-80, sheriff 1981-. **Orgs:** Officer Norfolk State Univ Alumni Assoc 1973-; officer Eureka Lodge 1973-; officer Norfolk Jaycees; mem Natl Sheriff's Assn 1981-; mem VA State Sheriff'sAssn 1981-; mem VA Assoc of Law Enforce Const Officers 1981-. **Honors/Awds:** Citizen of the Year Alpha Phi Omega Frat 1983; chmn Norfolk United Way campaign 1983; Cardiac Arrest Awd Norfolk Heart Assn 1983-84; mem JJDP State Advisory Council 1982-. **Business Addr:** Sheriff, Norfolk Sheriff's Dept, 811 East City Hall Ave, Norfolk, VA 23510.

MAPP, EDWARD C.
Educator, educational administrator, writer. **Personal:** Born Aug 17, 1929, New York, NY; son of Estelle Sampson Mapp and Edward Cameron Mapp; children: Andrew, Elmer, Everett. **Educ:** City Coll of NY, BA 1953; Columbia Univ, MS 1956; NY Univ, PhD 1970. **Career:** NY City Bd of Educ, tchr 1957-64; NY City Tech Coll, dir of Library Learning Resources Center 1964-77; Borough of Manhattan Community Coll, dean of faculty 1977-82; City Colleges of Chicago, vice chancellor 1982-83; Borough of Manhattan Community Coll, prof 1983-92, prof emeritus, 1994-. **Orgs:** Dir Natl Serv Corp 1984-87; bd of dir United Nations Assoc of NY 1975-78; bd of trustees NY Metro Ref & Rsch Agency 1980-81; feature columnist Movie/TV Mktg 1979-91; 100 Black Men Inc 1975-85; bd mem (Brooklyn Region) Natl Conf of Christians & Jews 1975-81; treas City Univ of NY Fac Senate 1972-77; Brooklyn Borough Pres Ed Adv Panel 1981; commissioner, New York City Human Rights Commission, 1988-94, vice chair, 1992-94. **Honors/Awds:** Founders Day Award for Outstanding Scholarship NY Univ 1970; Distinguished Serv Award Borough of Manhattan Community Coll The City Univ of NY 1982; elected to NY Acad of Pub Educ 1978; Black Collectors Hall of Fame, 1992. **Special Achievements:** Author: Blacks in American Films, 1972; Puerto Rican Perspectives, 1974; Blacks in Performing Arts, 1978, 2nd edition, 1990; co-author: A Separate Cinema, 1992; curator: Edward Mapp African-American Film Poster Collection, presented to Center for Motion Picture Study of the Academy of Motion Picture Arts and Sciences, 1996. **Business Addr:** Prof Emeritus, Speech & Communication, Manhattan Community College, City Univ of New York, 199 Chambers St, New York, NY 10007.

MAPP, FREDERICK EVERETT
Educator. **Personal:** Born Oct 12, 1910, Atlanta, GA; son of Willie Anne Johnson Mapp and Thaddeus H Mapp; married Betty Lewis, Mar 31, 1963; children: Wm M Boyd, Robert A Boyd. **Educ:** Morehouse Coll, BS 1932; Atlanta Univ, MS 1934; Harvard Univ, MA 1942; Univ of Chicago, PhD 1950; Gen Ed Brd Flwshp 1946-48. **Career:** BT Washington HS (At-

lanta), instr 1933-40; Knoxville Coll, prof of biology-chrmn 1944-46; TN State Univ, prof of biology-chrmn 1951-52; Morehouse Coll, prof of Biology, 1952-, chmn, 1952-97. **Honors/Awds:** Gen Educa Bd Flwshp 1946-48; the David Packard Prof of Biology 1973-82; Phi Beta Kappa Delta of Georgia, 1971-. **Home Addr:** 703 Waterford Rd NW, Atlanta, GA 30318. **Business Addr:** Professor of Biology, Morehouse Coll, Atlanta, GA 30314.

MAPP, JOHN ROBERT
Physician, neonatology. **Personal:** Born Jan 26, 1950, Springfield, MA; son of Edna Royster Mapp and Alexander B Mapp, Sr; married Maria Mejia, Nov 13, 1981; children: Alexandra, Lorean. **Educ:** Hillsdale Coll Hillsdale, MI, BA 1971; Meharry Med Coll Nashville TN, MD 1975; Med Coll of PA Philadelphia, Residence in Pediatrics 1975-77; California State Univ, San Diego, Master in Public Health 1986-87. **Career:** Univ Southern California, Los Angeles County Medical School, neonatal pathologist 1979-80; Univ Southern California Medical School, clinical instr in pediatrics 1977-79; Pediatrics Los Angeles, CA, symposuim re neonatology AA 1978; Hosp Italiano Rosario South Amer, guest lectr neonatologist, consultant in neonatology, 1979; Glendale Hospital, co-chief of neonatology department, 1979-. **Orgs:** Co-founder pres Blacks United at Hillsdale Coll 1969-71; mem Amer Assn of Pediatrics 1976-. **Honors/Awds:** Natl TV Program "Lifeline" segment filmed at USC newborn/neonatology unit of Med Center at Los Angeles 1978. **Special Achievements:** Organized unit of Buffalo Soldiers, circa 1866-1890, cav unit in LA Calif, which appeared in TV show, Geronimo, 1993 and an episode of Dr Quinn, Medicine Woman, 1993 and rode in 1995 Rose Bowl Parade. **Home Addr:** 135 Thompson St, Springfield, MA 01109.

MAPP, RHONDA
Professional basketball player. **Personal:** Born Oct 13, 1969. **Educ:** North Carolina State, attended. **Career:** Charlotte Sting, center-forward, 1997-. **Business Addr:** Professional Basketball Player, Charlotte Sting, 2709 Water Ridge Pkwy, Ste 400, Charlotte, NC 28217, (704)424-9622.

MAPP, ROBERT P.
Company executive. **Career:** RPM Supply Co Inc, ceo, currently. **Special Achievements:** Company is ranked number 91 on Black Enterprise's list of top companies, 1993. **Business Addr:** CEO, RPM Supply Co Inc, 621 N 2nd St, Philadelphia, PA 19123, (215)627-7106.

MAPP, YOLANDA I.
Physician. **Personal:** Born Jun 26, 1930, New York, NY; daughter of Viola Jefferson Jones and Edward Jones; divorced; children: Donald, David, Douglas, Daniel, Dorothy, Darryl. **Educ:** Monmouth Jr Coll, AA 1951; NJ Coll for Women Rutgers Univ, BS, 1953; Howard Univ Coll of Med, MD 1957; DC Genl Hosp, internship 1957-58; Freedman's Hosp Washington DC, residency 1958-60; DC Genl Hosp, residency 1960-61; Hahnemann Med Coll & Hosp, fellowship clinical pharmacology; Temple Univ Hosp, fellowship hematology-oncology 1964-66. **Career:** Hahnemann Med Coll & Hosp Philadelphia, instr of med & dir of alcoholic clinic 1961-64; Emory Univ Coll of Med Atlanta, assoc prof of med & internist 1969-70; Temple Univ Hosp, physician 1967-; Temple Univ Coll of Med, assoc prof; Temple Univ, acting dir univ health serv, 1984-93. **Orgs:** Med adv Leukemia Soc of Amer Greater Atlanta Chap 1970; vol physician Thaler Meml Hosp Bilwaskarma Nicaragua 1972; med adv Amer Cancer Soc Philadelphia 1976-; licensure MD 1959, PA 1961, GA 1969; bd of trustees, Rutgers Univ, 1979-91; mem, American College of Physicians, 1977. **Honors/Awds:** Howard Whitfield Found Med Scholarship 1952-57; Schering Pharm Corp Hon Awd 1957; speaker "Honors & Awds Day" Howard Univ Coll of Med 1965; Certificate Amer Bd of Internal Medicine 1969, Recertified, 1977, 1987; Amer Coll of Physicians 1970; Disting Achievement at Douglass Coll Douglass Soc Rutgers Univ New Brunswick NJ 1973; The Four Chaplains Legion of Hon Membership for Humanitarian Serv Chapel of Four Chaplains Philadelphia 1973; Awd for Free Flight Soaring Entry Nordic A-2 Glider Aero Crafts Exhibit Civic Ctr Philadelphia 1974; third degree black belt in Judo, 1989; Courage Award, American Cancer Society, 1988; Distinguished Alumnus Rutgers Univ, 1992; Fellow, 1997. **Business Addr:** Temple University, Philadelphia, PA 19122.

MARABLE, HERMAN, JR.
Attorney. **Personal:** Born Oct 4, 1962, Flint, MI; son of Iris Butler Marable and Herman Marable Sr. **Educ:** Michigan State Univ, James Madison College, BA, 1984; Ohio State Univ, College of Law, JD, 1987. **Career:** NAACP, Washington Bureau, intern, 1983; 68th District Judge Lee Vera Loyd, law clerk, 1983-84; UAW-GM Legal Services, law clerk, 1985; Garan, Lucow, Miller, Seward, Cooper & Becker, summer associate, 1986; Riegle for Senate Cmte, regional coordinator, 1987-88; Attorney Kathie Dones-Carson, director of research, 1988-91; County of Allegheny, assistant district attorney, 1991-93; County of Genesee, Asst prosecuting attorney, 1993-. **Orgs:** NAACP, Flint Branch, second vice pres, 1988-94; Michigan Democratic Party, state central cmte mbr, 1989-93, 1995-; 9th Congressional District Democratic Exec Comm, 1995-97; Genesee County Black Caucus, treasurer, 1989-91, exec bd mem, 1995-, vice chair 1997-; Urban Coalition of Greater Flint, secretary, nominating cmte chair, 1987-91; MSU James Madison Clg Alumni Assn, bd of dirs, 1987-89, 1990-94; United Way of Genesee & Lapeer Counties, advisory bd chair, 1988-91; Boy Scouts of America, Tall Pine Council, vice-chmn of administration, 1989-91; Homer S Brown Law Assn, 1990-93; Natl Bar Assn, 1985-; Pennsylvania Bas Assn; Pennsylvania District Attorney's Assn, 1991-93; Natl Black Prosecutor's Assn, 1993-, By-law Committee, vice chair, 1994-95; Prosecuting Attorney's Assn of Michigan, 1993-, Prosecution Diversity Comm, 1997-; Allegheny County Bar Assn, 1990-93; Mallory-Scott-Van Dyne Bar Assn, 1987-; Genesee County Bar Assn, 1993-; Michigan NAACP, Legal Redress, co-chairman, 1994-; Urban League of Flint, 1991-; Flint Neighborhood Coalition, bd of dirs 1997-; Genesee County Democratic Party, officer-at-large, 1988-91, 1994-; Central Flint Optimist Club, 1997-. **Honors/Awds:** Natl NAACP Radiothon, Outstanding Service Award, 1994; Flint NAACP Service Award, 1992; Urban League of Flint, Olive R Beasley Volunteer Award, 1989; MSU Housing Programs Office, Student Leadership Award, 1983; Kappa Alpha Psi, MSU, Outstanding Black Student Scholarship, 1983; State Senate of Tennessee, Honorary Page, 1980; Black Law Students Assn, Frederick Douglass-Midwest Regional Moot Court Competition, Best Petitioner's Brief Award, 1986, Competition Semi-finalist, 1986; Outstanding Young Men of America, 1986, 1988, 1989, 1996. **Business Addr:** Assistant Prosecuting Attorney, County of Genesee, 200 Genesee County Courthouse, Flint, MI 48502.

MARABLE, JUNE MOREHEAD
Educational administrator, cleric. **Personal:** Born Jun 8, 1924, Columbus, OH; daughter of Minnie Martin (deceased) and Rev J W Morehead (deceased); married; children: Dr James Marable Jr (deceased), Dr Manning Marable, Madonna Howard. **Educ:** Central State Univ Wilberforce, OH, BS Educ 1948; Univ of Dayton, MS Educ 1965; Miami Univ Oxford, OH, PhD Educ 1974; United Theological Seminary, Dayton, OH, MDiv, 1989. **Career:** Payne Seminary, Wilberforce, OH, executive director of Alternative Theological Education Program, 1989-; AME Church, elder, minister, 1989; Dayton,Ohio; Miami Univ Oxford, OH, visiting assoc prof 1978-80; Wright State Univ Dayton, asst prof 1972-77; Dayton Bd of Educ, teacher, reading consultant 1954-72; KS City Bd of Educ KS City, MO, teacher 1952-54; Wright Patterson AFB Dayton, cartographic draftsman & clerk-typist 1948-52. **Orgs:** Educ dir Marable Early Childhood Educ Center Dayton 1960-77; admin asst Black Research Asso Dayton 1979-85; mem OH State Right to Read Commn State Dept Educ for OH 1970-80; educ consult & lectr Pub Schools Universities Comm Civic Orgns Churches 1970-; coordinator, Reading Improvement Prog, Alpha Kappa Alpha Sor 1974-78; Sen Mer Rek Honor Soc Wilberforce Univ Wilberforce, OH 1948; Alpha Kappa Mu Wilberforce Univ Wilberforce, OH 1948; Delta Kappa Gamma Intl Sorority, Dayton chap, pres. **Honors/Awds:** Outstanding Citizen Award, Optimist Club, Dayton 1978; Alumni Hall of Fame, Central State University, 1988; Annie Webb Blanton Award.

MARBURY, DONALD LEE
Broadcaster. **Personal:** Born Nov 26, 1949, Pittsburgh, PA; son of Susie Burroughs Marbury and Sherrill Marbury; married Sheila JoAnn King, Mar 24, 1973; children: Cara Jean, Evan Lee. **Educ:** Univ of Pittsburgh, BA English 1971. **Career:** Pittsburgh Post Gazette, general assignment reporter 1969-71; WQED-TV, news anchorman, producer/host, executive producer/ dir local programming, special asst 1971-80; Chatham College, instructor communications 1977-80; Corp for Public Broadcasting, assoc dir cultural & general programs, childrens programs 1980-90; Television Program Fund, dir 1990-; Univ District of Columbia, instructor screen playwriting 1984-85; freelance writer non-fiction, publishes articles, Pittsburgh Magazine, current magazines, Public Broadcasting Review 1973-. **Orgs:** Bd dirs Intercultural House 1971-; mem bd dirs Pittsburgh Black Media Coalition 1971-74; bd dirs WYEP-FM 1974-75; mem Steering Comm of Producer's Council 1976-80; mem bd dirs Natl Black Program Consortium 1978-80; mem exec steering comm Producers Council Natl Assoc Education Broadcasters 1978-80; mem Task Force on Public Participation 1978; bd dirs Louise Child Care Center; poet, featured in nationally syndicated radio series, "The Poet and the Poem"; bd of dir, Children's Advocacy Newspaper, 1989. **Honors/Awds:** Golden Quill (2) Western PA Journalism Honorary 1973; Pittsburgh Goodwill Ambassador Pittsburgh Goodwill 1975; Black Achiever of the Year Talk Magazine 1975; Founders Award Natl Black Programming Consortium 1983; US delegate public broadcasting to the European Broadcasting Unions working party on programs for children & youth, 1984-86; featured poet in performance, WPFW-FM, 1985-88; Certificate of Appreciation, Natl Black Programming Consortium, 1988; English speaking moderator, Prix Jeunesse, Intl, Munich (Intl Children's Program Festival,) 1988; Leokoeberlein Distinguished Alumnus Award in Journalism, Univ of Pittsburgh, 1990. **Home Addr:** One Tupelo Court, Rockville, MD 20855. **Business Addr:** Director, The Program Fund, Corp for Public Broadcasting, 901 E Street NW, Washington, DC 20004-2006.

MARBURY, MARTHA G.
Administrative officer. **Personal:** Born Nov 22, 1946, Morgantown, WV; daughter of Georgia Johnson Dobbs (deceased) and John Dobbs Jr (deceased); children: Anthony Vaughn. **Educ:** University of Maryland, College Park, MD, BS, 1980. **Career:** US Dept of Agriculture Soil Conservation Ser, Morgantown, WV, clerk steno, 1967-73; US Dept of Agriculture Soil Conservation, Ser College Park, MD, personnel clerk, 1973-75, personnel assistant, 1975-76, personnel management specialist, 1976-78, personnel officer, 1978-83; US Dept of Agriculture Soil Conservation Ser, Washington, DC, classification specialist, 1983-85, chief, employment branch, 1985-88, chief, EEO branch, 1988-92; Human Resources Mgmt Service, assoc dir, 1992-94; Natural Resources Conservation Service, admin officer, SE Region, 1994-. **Orgs:** National Organization of Prof NRCS Employees; Intl Pers Mgmt Assoc. **Honors/Awds:** Several Outstanding Performance Awards, US Soil Conservation Service, 1975, 1978, 1980, 1983, 1985, 1986, 1989, 1990, 1994, 1997; Honorable Mention Blue Pencil Award Blue Pencil Assn, 1989. **Business Addr:** Administrative Officer, Southeast Region, US Dept of Agriculture, Natural Resources Conservation Svcs, 1720 Peachtree Rd, NW, Ste 446N, Atlanta, GA 30309.

MARBURY, STEPHON
Professional basketball player. **Personal:** Born Feb 20, 1977, Brooklyn, NY. **Educ:** Georgia Tech. **Career:** Minnesota Timberwolves, guard, 1996-. **Honors/Awds:** NBA, All Rookie team, 1997. **Special Achievements:** NBA Draft, First round pick, #4, 1996. **Business Addr:** Professional Basketball Player, Minnesota Timberwolves, 600 1st Ave N, Minneapolis, MN 55403, (612)337-3865.

MARCERE, NORMA SNIPES
Educator (retired), author, psychologist. **Personal:** Born Oct 21, 1908, Canton, OH; daughter of Ida Rosella Evans Snipes and Norman Sherwood Snipes; married Percy Alluren Marcere (deceased); children: Norma Jean, Alluren Leonard. **Educ:** Kent State Univ, MA 1957. **Career:** Stark Co Welfare Dept Canton, soc caseworker 1938-42; Stark Co TB & Health Assn Canton, health educator 1944-56; EA Jones Jr HS, tchr/ counselor 1957-56; Human Engrg Inst, voc counselor 1962-66; Garfield HS Akron, guidance counselor 1966-71; Kent OH City Sch, sch psychologist 1971-72; Stoydale-Brunnerdale Summer Projects, dir 1972-73; Hilltop House, psychologist 1972-74; Stark Technical College, founder/director 1974-84; Prog for Academic Excellence: A Saturday Sch, 1979-84; PAX Saturday School for Underachievers, founder 1979-; Stark Technical College, Canton OH consultant/minority affairs 1984-86; St Mary Peace Pax Saturday School, asst dir & psychologist, 1989-. **Orgs:** Mem OH Educ Assn; OH Sch Counselors Assn; OH Sch Psychologists; mem Natl Council Cath Women 1940-; mem Panel of Amer Women 1965-; mem Adv Bd Walsh Coll 1974-; mem Alpha Kappa Alpha Sor 1972-; mem Phi Delta Kappa Frat 1970-; life mem NAACP. **Honors/Awds:** "Bridging the Gap Between the Races" Urban League; Mayor of Canton; Oldtimers & others; rec'd at White House for positive contributions toward race relations, 40 Panel of Amer Women 1979; Ohio Women's Hall of Fame, State of Ohio, Governor Celeste, 1987; Honorary bd mem Walsh College 1989; Woman of Distinction, Soroptimist International, 1991; Honorary Doctorate, Walsh College, 1980. **Special Achievements:** Author: "Genteel Violence," Good Housekeeping, May 1970; Round the Dining Table, a childhood autobiography, Daring Press, 1984; The Fences Between, a young adult autobiography, 1989; How to Start a Saturday School for Academic Excellence, 1989; Subject of Play, Fence Between: Based on the Life of Dr Norma Marcere, by Lois De Glacomo, 1995.

MARCH, ANTHONY
Automobile dealer. **Personal:** Born Feb 25, 1951, Brooklyn, NY; married Gail, Dec 21, 1974; children: Crystal. **Educ:** Howard Univ, Washington DC, BS Electrical Engineering, 1973; General Motors Dealer Academy, Flint MI, graduate, 1985. **Career:** Fisher Body Div of General Motors, Warren MI, engineering group man 1971-84; Tony March Buick, Hartford CT, pres, 1985-89. **Orgs:** Mem, NAACP, 1985-; founder, dir, Sentinel Bank, 1986-; dir, Univ of Hartford Assn, 1987-, Greater Hartford Better Business Bureau, 1987-, Greater Hartford YMCA, 1988-, Mount Sinai Hospital, 1988-. **Honors/Awds:** America's Best & Brightest, Dollars & Sense Magazine, 1987; Meritorious Award, United Negro Coll Fund; Best-In-Class, Buick Motor Div, 1987, 1988; Business Man of the Year, Univ of Hartford, 1987; Business Man of the Year, Upper Albany Merchants, 1987.

MARCHAND, MELANIE ANNETTE
Chemical engineer. **Personal:** Born Mar 12, 1962, New Orleans, LA; daughter of Mrs Sandra Baker Marchand and Mr Edward Janvier Marchand. **Educ:** Tulane Univ, New Orleans, LA, Bachelor of Science in Chemical Engineering, 1980-84. **Career:** Union Carbide Corp, Taft, LA, production eng, 1984-86; Air Products and Chemicals, Inc, New Orleans, LA, process eng, 1986-87; Air Products and Chemicals, Inc, Allentown, PA, process eng, 1988-. **Orgs:** Mem, LA Engineering Soc, 1984-; mem, Soc of Women Engineers, 1988-90; mem, Assn for Integrated Mgmt, 1988-; mem, Minority Community Advisory Bd-Muhlenberg Coll, 1989. **Honors/Awds:** Appreciation Award for Leadership and Dedication to the UCC Aerobics Class, Union Carbide Corp Family Safety & Health Comm, 1985; Quality Recognition Variable Compensation Award, Air Products and Chemicals Inc, 1989. **Home Addr:** 7416 Scottsdale Dr, New Orleans, LA 70127.

MARDENBOROUGH, LESLIE A.
Human resources executive. **Personal:** Born Mar 25, 1948, Bronx, NY; daughter of Dorothy Richards Mardenborough and Victor E Mardenborough (deceased); children: Adina N, Keith A Clark, Kevin A Clark. **Educ:** Albright Coll, Reading, PA, AB, 1968; Simmons Coll Graduate School of Management, Program for Developing Executives, Boston, MA, 1989. **Career:** Brooklyn Coll, career counselor, 1969-73; Wildcat Serv Corp, vice pres, Operations, 1978, other positions 1973-78; New Life Group Inc, exec dir, Career Center, 1979-81; The New York Times Co, project mgr, Human Resources, 1981-84, dir, Employee Relations, 1984-86, dir, Personnel, 1986-87, dir, Corporate Personnel, 1987-90, vice pres, Human Resources, 1990-. **Orgs:** Board mem, 1991, mem, Human Resource Planners Assn, 1982-; bd mem, membership officer, New York Human Resource Planners, 1986-88; mem, NAA Employee Relations Comm, 1988-, Newspaper Personnel Relations Assn, 1988-, bd of dir, New York Bd of Trade, 1989-92; bd of dirs, Westchester Residential Opportunities, 1989-; bd of dirs, Westchester Housing Fund, 1991-94; bd of dirs, United Neighborhood Houses, 1991-. **Honors/Awds:** Black Achievers in Industry, Harlem YMCA, 1986; Honorary Doctorate, Albright College, 1990; 100 of the Best and Brightest Black Women in Corporate America, Ebony, 1990; Rappaport Alumni Achievement Award, Simmons College GSM, 1992. **Business Addr:** Vice President, Human Resources, The New York Times Company, 229 W 43rd St, New York, NY 10036.

MARIEL, SERAFIN
Bank executive. **Career:** New York Natl Bank, president, currently. **Business Addr:** President, New York National Bank, 960 Southern Blvd, Bronx, NY 10458, (212)589-5000.

MARINER, JONATHAN
Sports administrator. **Career:** Florida Marlins, vice pres of finance and administration, currently. **Business Addr:** Vice Pres of Finance & Administration, Florida Marlins, Pro Player Stadium, NW 199th St, Miami, FL 33169, (305)356-5848.

MARINO, EUGENE ANTONIO
Former archbishop. **Personal:** Born May 29, 1934, Biloxi, MS; son of Irnen Bradford Marino and Jesus Maria Marino. **Educ:** Epiphany Apostolic Coll, Sem Edn; St Joseph Sem; Fordham Univ, MA, 1967; Catholic Univ; Loyola Univ. **Career:** Ordained to priesthood 1962; St. Joseph's Sem, dir, 1963; Auxiliary bishop of Washington DC; Josephites, vicar general, 1971; Archbishop Baum, ordained to episcopate by 1974; St Gabriel's Parish, res; Walla Walla WA, titular Bishop; Archdiocese of Atlanta, archbishop, 1988-90. **Orgs:** Mem, Josephite Gen Counc; dir, Spiritual & Educ Form Josephites; Bishop's Comm on Per Diaconate; US Cath Conf; bd trustees, Cath Univ of Am; episcopal bd, Word of God Inst Rsrch Found at Chldrn's Hosp; chmn, Bishops' Comm for Liaison with Natl Office Black Catholics; trustee, Cath Univ Amer; mem, Devel Comm Natl Shrine of Immaculate Conception; mem, Natl Conf Catholic Bishops. **Honors/Awds:** Hon DD 1974; first black Catholic archbishop, 1988. **Business Addr:** Former Archbishop, Archdiocese of Atlanta, 680 West Peachtree St N W, Atlanta, GA 30308.

MARION, BROCK ELLIOT
Professional football player. **Personal:** Born Jun 11, 1970, Bakersfield, CA; son of Jerry Marion; married Keri; children: Brianna, Olivia, Brock Jr. **Educ:** Nevada-Reno, attended. **Career:** Dallas Cowboys, defensive back, 1993-97; Miami Dolphins, 1998-. **Business Addr:** Professional Football Player, Miami Dolphins, 2269 NW 199th St, Miami, FL 33056, (305)620-5000.

MARION, CLAUD COLLIER
Educator (retired). **Personal:** Born in Fort Pierce, FL; son of Hattie Marion and James Marion; married. **Educ:** FL A&M Univ, BS 1936; Univ of MN, MS 1941; Cornell Univ, PhD 1948. **Career:** TN A&I Univ, guest prof of educ 1951-52, 1956-70; Univ of MD Eastern Shore, asst dir and coordinator of 1890 extension programs 1972-77, prof agricultural educ and teacher training, beginning 1948, administrator of 1890 extension programs 1977-80. **Orgs:** Mem UMES Extension Comm, Administrative Conf Comm, Personnel Coord Comm, Publications Comm; mem Foreign Relations Comm Amer Vocational Assoc; commissioner of Higher Educ Peninsula Conf United Methodist Church Dover DE 1970-; advisor Alpha Tau Alpha; mem Masonic Lodge, Elks Lodge, Alpha Phi Alpha Frat. **Honors/Awds:** Certificate of Appreciation for Serv to the Office of Admin by Pres Harry S Truman 1946; Honorary American Farmer degree Natl Org of FFA 1975; Teacher of Teachers Gold Award Natl Vocational Agriculture Teachers Assoc Inc 1976; Certificate of Award for Outstanding Citizenship Princess Anne Chapter of Links Inc 1976; member of Maryland agri team to Soviet Union, 1990. **Home Addr:** PO Box 399, Princess Anne, MD 21853.

MARION, FRED D.
Professional football player. **Personal:** Born Jan 2, 1959, Gainesville, FL. **Educ:** Univ of Miami (FL), attended. **Career:** New England Patriots, safety, 1982-. **Honors/Awds:** Postseason play, 1985: AFC Championship Game, NFL Championship Game, Pro Bowl. **Business Addr:** Professional Football Player, New England Patriots, Sullivan Stadium, Rt 1, Foxboro, MA 02035.

MARION, PHILLIP JORDAN
Physician. **Personal:** Born May 14, 1958, Albany, NY; son of Marie Marion and G W Marion; married Tanya C Lumpkins, May 21, 1990. **Educ:** SUNY at Purchase, BA, 1981; New York University School of Medicine, MD, 1985; New York University, MS, 1989; George Washington University, MPH, 1993. **Career:** Rusk Institute of Rehabilitation Medicine, chief resident, 1989; Howard University School of Medicine, assistant professor, 1990-; National Rehabilitation Hospital, assistant medical director, 1990-, Ambulatory Services, medical director, 1990-; Health Policy Fellow, Office of Senator Orrin G Hatch; Health Policy Fellow, Senate Judiciary Committee. **Orgs:** American College of Physician Executives, diplomate, 1993; American Academy of Physical Medicine/Rehab, fellow, diplomate, 1990; Concerned Black Men, 1992-; National Mentorship Program, 1989-; American Medical Assn, 1985-; Association of Academic Physiatrists, 1993-. **Honors/Awds:** Robert Wood Johnson, Health Policy Fellow, 1994-95. **Home Addr:** 1316 Tuckerman St NW, Washington, DC 20011, (202)726-1873. **Business Addr:** Medical Director, Ambulatory Services, National Rehabilitation Hospital, 102 Irving St NW, Washington, DC 20010, (202)877-1652.

MARIUS, KENNETH ANTHONY
Physician. **Personal:** Born Feb 22, 1937, New York, NY; son of Aldith and Edwin; married Esther Bailey; children: Kenneth Jr, Robert. **Educ:** Howard Univ, BSEE 1960; New Jersey Inst of Technology, MS 1965; Howard Univ Coll of Med, MD, 1970. **Career:** Comm Coop Corp, pres 1972; Tricities Progress for Women, consult 1972; New Jersey Coll of Medicine & Dentistry, clinical prof 1976-. **Orgs:** mem Essex Co Med Soc; Consult City of Newark; Orange Board of Education, medical director, team physician Weeguanic HS; spkr Essex Co Heart Assn; mem Alpha Omega Alpha Med Hon Soc; Tau Beta Pi Eng Hon Soc; pres North Jersey Med Soc, NJ Med Soc 1984; Natl Med Assn delegate 1981-; Sickle Cell Found Advisory Bd 1983-;. **Honors/Awds:** Award CMDNJ, 1992; Bd of Concerned Citizens Awd 1986; Distinguished Serv Award, Tricities Chamber of Commerce 1985; Distinguished Serv Award, Sports Physician, Weequahic 1983-86. **Military Serv:** USAF 1952-56; USAR med ofcr 1984-86. **Business Addr:** 202 Medical Group, Inc., Newark, NJ 07108.

MARKETTE-MALONE, SHARON
Legislative liaison. **Personal:** Born Feb 5, 1956, Montgomery, AL; daughter of Mary Chilton Markette and Edward Markette; married Columbus Malone Jr, Feb 25, 1989; children: Sharon Monique. **Educ:** Chicago State Univ, BS Corrections 1978. **Career:** 28th Ward Young Democrats, sec 1981-83; 28th Ward Reg Democratic Org, precinct capt 1981-83; 28th Ward Women on the Move, recording sec 1982-83; IL General Assembly, state representative, 1983-85; IL Dept of Employment Sec, exec III, 1985-. **Orgs:** Choir dir Original Providence Young Adult Choir 1971-81; mem Young Democrats of Cook Cty 1980-83; state rep IL House of Rep 1983-85; mem Natl Black Caucus of State Leg 1983-; sec Ray Hudson Scholarship Club 1982-84; pres Women's Aux Original Prov Bapt Church 1984-86; advisory council State of IL 1985; mem 1989, recording sec 1991, Sigma Gamma Rho Sorority Inc; trustee, Original Providence Baptist Church, 1988. **Honors/Awds:** Plaque Concerned Black Exec 1984. **Business Addr:** Executive III, Illinois Dept of Employment Security, 401 S State St, Rm 623, Chicago, IL 60605.

MARKHAM, HOUSTON, JR.
Educator. **Personal:** Born Dec 20, 1942, Brookhaven, MS; son of Ethel Tanner Markham and Houston Markham Sr; married Annie Davis Markham, Jan 14, 1968; children: Yolanda, Houston III. **Educ:** Alcorn State Univ, Lorman, MS, BS, physical ed, 1965; TN State Univ, Nashville, TN, MS, 1971. **Career:** Vicksburg High School, Vicksburg, MS, head football coach, 1967-75; Jackson State Univ, Jackson, MS, asst football coach, 1975-87; AL State Univ, Montgomery, AL, head football coach, 1987-. **Honors/Awds:** SWAC Coach of the Year, Southwestern Athletic Coach, 1990-1991; Coach of the Year, Pigskin Club of America, 1990-91; Coach of the Year, 100% Wrong Club, 1990-91; Coach of the Year, Sheridan Poll, 1987. **Business Addr:** Head Football Coach, Athletics, Alabama State University, 915 S Jackson St, Montgomery, AL 36101.

MARKS, KENNETH HICKS, JR.
Attorney. **Personal:** Born Sep 15, 1951, Lawrenceville, VA; son of Nethel H Marks and Kenneth H Marks Sr; married Fe Morales Marks, Jan 13, 1979; children: Kenisha Maria Morales. **Educ:** Columbia Coll, BA, 1974; Columbia Univ School of Law, JD, 1977. **Career:** Shearman & Sterling, assoc, 1977-80; Webster & Sheffield, assoc, 1980-84; Wickwire, Gavin & Gibbs PC, partner, 1984-1989; Ginsburg, Feldman & Bress, partner, 1989-91; Alexander, Aponte & Marks, partner, 1991-97; Reid & Priest LLP, counsel, currently. **Orgs:** American Bar Assn; Public Finance Committee of the Section of Urban, State, and Local Govt Law, co-vice chair, 1993-96; American Bar Found, fellow, 1993-; Ayuda Inc, bd of dir, 1984-89; District of Columbia Bar Assn Elections Committee, 1988-91; Hispanic Bar Assn of the District of Columbia, bd of dir, 1984-85, chair public relations committee, 1983-85; Natl Bar Assn; Hispanic Natl Bar Assn; New York Bar Assn; Natl Assn of Bond Lawyers; Municipal Securities Rulemaking Bd, public arbitrator, 1986-89; Reston Community Assn, planning and zoning committee, 1986-91; Turnbridge Cluster Assn, bd of dir, 1987-90, pres, 1989-90; Japan Society. **Honors/Awds:** Earl Warren Scholarship Fund, Earl Warren Scholar, 1974; Columbia Univ School of Law, Charles Evans Hughes Scholar, 1975. **Business Addr:** Counsel, Reid & Priest LLP, 701 Pennsylvania Ave, NW, Washington, DC 20004, (202)508-4009.

MARKS, LEE OTIS
Educator. **Personal:** Born Nov 17, 1944, Carthage, AR; married Karen Vaughn; children: Cynthia Lynne, Valerie Jeanne, Allison Marie. **Educ:** Sioux Falls Coll, BA 1966; Univ of IL Champaign-Urbana, MS 1974. **Career:** Rockford Guilford HS, Physical Educ teacher, head track coach asst football coach, 1967-; Lincoln Park Elementary School, teacher, 1966-67; Madison Mustang, football player, 1966-67; Rockford Rams, football player, 1969-70. **Orgs:** SFC Letterman Club Sioux Falls Coll Alumni Assn 1966; mem Rockford Educ Assn; IL Educ Assn; mem Natl Educ Assn; IL Health Physical Educ & Recreation Assn; IL Coaches Assn; Rockford Coaches Assn; exec bd of dir Rockford Educ Assn 1971-73; Natl Educ Assn Black Caucus; IL Human Relations Commn 1971-73; Natl Letterman Assn; bd dir Rockford Black Educators Assn 1971-73; program dir BT Washington Comm Cent 1966-70; Allen Chapel AME Church; bd dir Central Terrace Co-op 1972. **Honors/Awds:** Teacher of year Guilford HS Student Body 1971; delegate to Natl Educ Assn Conv 1971; co-captain MVP football Sioux Falls Coll 1965. **Business Addr:** Guilford HS, 5620 Springcreek Rd, Rockford, IL 61114.

MARKS, ROSE M.
Library technician. **Personal:** Born Mar 17, 1938, Chicago; children: Deborah, Charles. **Educ:** Sacramento City Coll, 1958; Sacramento State U. **Career:** Oak Park Branch Library, branch supr; Sacramento City-Co Library, libr clk 1961-77. **Orgs:** Past bd dir KVIE Educ TV; past bd dir Sacramento Reg Arts Council; past sec Oak Park Comm Theatre; Sacramento Black Women's United Front; mgr of Band & co-mgr of singing group; past vice pres Sacramento City Employees Assn; past pres Sacramento City Library Assn. **Business Addr:** Oak Park Branch Library 3301 5, Sacramento, CA 95817.

MARQUEZ, CAMILO RAOUL
Physician. **Personal:** Born Feb 25, 1942, New York, NY; son of Gloria Marquez and Cecil Marquez. **Educ:** Colby College, AB, 1963; Howard University School of Medicine, MD, 1976. **Career:** St Vincent's Hosp, resident in psychiatry 1977-79, chief resident 1978-79; Manhattan Psychiatric Ctr, rsch psychiatrist 1979-80; Harlem Hosp, staff psychiatrist 1980-82; North General Hosp, dir in-patient psychiatry 1982-84; Health Sci Ctr of Brooklyn SUNY, asst instructor; Harlem Hospital, attending physician div of child and adolescent psychiatry 1988-92; Columbia University, College of Physicians & Surgeons asst clinical professor psychiatry 1988-92. **Orgs:** American Psychiatric Assn, 1978-; Black Psychiatrists of American, 1979-; bd of trustees Wooster Sch 1986-92; mem Amer Acad Child and Adolescent Psychiatry 1986-; co-chmn Black Health Professionals for School Based Health and Sex Educ Programs 1986-88. **Honors/Awds:** Falk Fellow Amer Psychiatric Assoc 1978-79; "Diagnosis of Manic Depressive Illness in Blacks", in Comprehensive Psychiatry, Vol 26, No 4 1985. **Military Serv:** Sp 4 1963-70. **Business Addr:** 275 Fair St, Kingston, NY 12401.

MARR, CARMEL CARRINGTON
Attorney, energy consultant, (retired). **Personal:** Born Jun 23, 1921, Brooklyn, NY; daughter of Gertrude C Lewis Carrington (deceased) and William P Carrington (deceased); married Warren Marr II; children: Charles, Warren III. **Educ:** Hunter Coll, BA (Cum Laude) 1945; Columbia Univ Law School, JD 1948. **Career:** Dyer & Stevens Esqs, law asst 1948-49; Private Practice, attorney at law 1949-53; US Mission to the United Nations, advisor on legal affrs 1953-67; United Nations Secretariat, sr legal officer 1967-68; New York State Human Rights Appeal Bd, mem 1968-71; New York State Public Serv Comm, commr 1971-86 (retired); Consultant, energy 1987-90. **Orgs:** Chairperson adv council Gas Rsch Inst 1979-86; chairperson US Dept of Trans Tech Pipeline Safety Standards Comm 1979-85; chairperson Natl Assoc of Regulatory Utility Commnrs, NARUC, Gas Comm, 1984-86; pres NARUC's Great Lakes Conf of Public Utility Commn; Amistad Rsch Center, Tulane Univ, 1970-, chmn & pres, 1982-94; bd mem Natl Arts Stabilization Fund, 1984-93; mem Natl Cncl of UN Assn of the USA, 1983-94; bd mem, exec comm, Brooklyn Soc for the Prevention of Cruelty to Children, 1972-; Natl Council to Hampshire Coll; mem bd Prospect Park Alliance, 1983-97; mem, President's Council, Tulane Univ, 1989-96; Alpha Kappa Alpha Sorority. **Honors/Awds:** Outstanding Community Serv Brooklyn Urban League; plaques and other citations from Friends of Amistad, Brooklyn Home for the Aged, Barbados Nurses Assoc, Amer Caribbean Scholarship Fund, Gas Rsch Inst, NYS Public Serv Commn, Amer Red Cross, Natl Council of Churches, Mademoiselle Magazine, The Links; Club Ta-Wa-Ses; mem Phi Beta Kappa, Alpha Chi Alpha Honorary Societies; elected to Hunter Coll Hall of Fame; Honorary Citizen, New Orleans; Jamaica Club National Business & Professional Women's Clubs, Sojourner Truth Award. **Home Addr:** 831 Sherry Dr, Valley Cottage, NY 10989.

MARR, WARREN, II
Editor. **Personal:** Born Jul 31, 1916, Pittsburgh, PA; son of Cecelia Antoinette McGee Marr and Warren Quincy Marr; married Carmel Carrington, Apr 11, 1948; children: Charles Carrington, Warren Quincy III. **Educ:** Wilberforce Univ, Journalism, Printing. **Career:** St Louis Argus, linotype oper 1938-39; The Plaindealer KC KS, linotype oper, shop foreman, asst ed 1939-42; Concert Mgmt, 1942-48; James Lassiter & Sons Madison NJ, drapery maker & asst to decorator 1948-52; House of Marr Inc, proprietor 1952-60; United Church Bd for Homeland Ministries NY Div of Higher Ed & Amer Missionary Assoc, AMA Coll Centennials, secy, 1961-68; Amistad Awds, founder & dir 1961-. **Orgs:** NAACP; ed ''The Crisis Mag'' 1968-80; founder & president, Amistad Affiliates, Inc, 1991; founder & exec dir Friends of Amistad; bd mem So NY Div UN Assn USA, Brooklyn Arts & Cultural Assn, Brooklyn Boys Club, Medgar Evers Coll Comm Council; past hon Natl Chmn Pan-African Found Art Shows, photography exhibits, private art collections; commiss Art Commis of NYC; chmn Comm Art Comm York Coll; co-founder with Clifton H Johnson, Amistad Research Center, New Orleans, 1966; member, New York City Community Board #9; trustee, Natl maritime Historical Society, 1992; Brooklyn Culture Assn, 1993. **Honors/Awds:** Awds, Amer Assn for United Nations Eleanor Roosevelt 1955, Testimonial Luncheon Waltann School for Creative Arts 1967, JFK Awd JFK Library for Minorities 1972; Intl Key Women of Amer 1974; Pan-African Found 1974; Frederick Douglass Awd Afro-Amer Hist Assn 1975; Third Army ROTC Reg 1974; Black Heritage Assn 1974; Achievement Awd Detroit Friends of Amistad 1976; co-editor w/Maybelle Ward ''Minorities & Amer Dream, A Bicentennial Perspective'' NY Arno Press 1977; co-editor w/Harry Ploski ''Negro Almanac'' 3rd ed NY Bellwether Publ Co 1977; National Maritime Society, American Ship Trust Award, 1995.

MARRETT, CORA B.
Educator. **Personal:** Born Jun 15, 1942, Richmond, VA; daughter of Clorann Boswell Bagley and Horace S Bagley; married Louis E. **Educ:** VA Union Univ, BA 1963; Univ of WI, MA 1965, PhD 1968. **Career:** Univ of NC-Chapel Hill, asst prof 1968-69; Western MI Univ, asst to assoc 1969-74; Univ of WI-Madison, assoc to full 1974-. **Orgs:** Bd of governors, Argonne Natl Lab 1982-89, 1996-; bd of trustees Cntr for Adv Study in the Behavioral Sciences 1983-89. **Honors/Awds:** Fellowship, Center for Advanced Study 1976-77, Natl Acad of Sci 1973-74; edtr Research in Race & Ethnic Relation (JAI Press) 1985; Distinguished Teaching Award, University of Wisconsin 1989; inductee, African American Portrait Gallery, Natl Academy of Science, 1996. **Business Addr:** Professor, Dept of Sociology, University of Wisconsin-Madison, Madison, WI 53706.

MARRIOTT, SALIMA SILER
Educator. **Personal:** Born Dec 5, 1940, Baltimore, MD; daughter of Cordie Ayers Siler and Jesse James Siler (deceased); divorced; children: Terrez Siler Marriott, Patrice Kenyatta Siler Marriott. **Educ:** Morgan State Univ, BS 1964; Univ of MD, MSW 1972; Howard Univ, DSW 1988. **Career:** Baltimore City Public Schools, teacher 1964-65; Dept of Social Services New York City, social worker 1965-68; Dept of Social Service, city of Baltimore, social worker 1968-72; Morgan State Univ, Baltimore, MD, instructor 1972-90, chairperson 1981-87, asst prof 1990-96; Maryland General Assembly, delegate, 1991-. **Orgs:** Park Heights Devt Corp, chair, 1988-92; founding mem/vice pres African-Amer Women Caucus 1982-85; Delta Sigma Theta Sor Inc 1989-; chair, 1993-95; vice chmn, Maryland Chapter Natl Rainbow Coalition 1988-89; sec, Natl Rainbow Coalition, 1994-95; chair, Natl Black Women's Health Project, 1993; NAACP; MD Legislative Black Caucus, vice chair, 1994-95; Women Legislators; Natl Black Caucus of State Legislators, regional chair, 1994-. **Honors/Awds:** Editor Behold the Woman Journal 1981, US Policy Toward Southern Africa 1984; Community Service Awd Morgan State Univ 1984,86; workshop convener United Nation's Decade for Women Conference 1985; Outstanding Teacher, Dept of Social Work & Mental Health Morgan State Univ 1988; Baltimore's Black Women of Courage Exhibit 1988; Jesse Jackson Delegate, Democratic Natl Convention, 1988; Maryland Democratic Central Committee; organizer National Conference Women of African Diaspora 1984; deputy state dir, Dukakis/Bentsen Campaign 1988; elected to Maryland General Assembly; African American Humanitarian Award, 1991; Senator Verda Welcome Political Award, 1992; Consortium of Doctors, 1992; Delegate of the Year, (Middle Atlantic Division of American Assn of Marriage and Family Therapist), 1993; Sarah's Circle Award, Coll of Notre Dame of MD, 1994; Delta Sigma Theta Sorority, Natl Legacy Award, 1994; Chair Intl Health Conference, Women of African Diaspora, 1995; Fleming Fellow, 1995. **Home Addr:** 4515 Homer Ave, Baltimore, MD 21215.

MARROW-MOORING, BARBARA A.
Government official. **Personal:** Born May 4, 1945, Trenton, NJ; married Kelly Daniel Mooring, Oct 29, 1988; children: Carla, Paula, Connie, Venessa Culbreth, Kelly D Mooring Jr., Anthony Mooring, Shawn Mooring. **Educ:** Mercer County Community Coll, AA (cum laude) Social Science & Humanities, 1973; Trenton State Coll, BS (magna cum laude) Elementary Educ, 1975. **Career:** Educational Testing Serv, Princeton NJ, division mgr, 1982-83, asst to vice pres, 1983-86, field serv representative, 1982-89; Trenton Bd of Educ, teacher, 1983-88; New Jersey General Assembly, Trenton NJ, clerk, 1986-87; New Jersey Lottery, Trenton NJ, exec dir, 1987-. **Orgs:** Pres, Natl Assn of Univ Women, 1977-79; vice pres, mem, Lawrence Township School Bd, 1978-87; founder, past pres, Coalition of 100 Black Republicans; treasurer, mem, Mercer County Improvement Authority, 1983-88; trustee, Rider Coll, 1987-; mem, Capital City Redevelopment Corp, 1987-, New Jersey Job Training Coordinating Council, 1987-89; trustee, Urban League of Metropolitan Trenton Inc, 1988-. **Honors/Awds:** Outstanding Achievement, NJ State Fedn of Colored Women's Clubs Inc, 1986; Community Service Award, BAC Publishing Co, 1988; Women of Achievement Award, NJ Fedn of Business & Professional Women Inc, 1989. **Business Addr:** Executive Director, New Jersey Lottery, CN 041, Trenton, NJ 08625.

MARRS, STELLA
Actress, vocalist, writer, painter, counselor, activist. **Personal:** Born Mar 22, 1932; daughter of Stella Marrs; divorced; children: Lynda, Joseph, Walter, Tita, Joseph III, Shawn, Cortez, Freddie. **Educ:** Attended, CCNY, RCC, Hunter Coll. **Career:** Lional Hampton Orchestra, vocalist 1969-70,72-73;TV special with Toots Thielmans 1977; recorded album Belgium Dicovers Stella Marrs 1977; toured US, Australia, Europe, jazz artist; Stella Marrs Cable TV Show, hosted; WRVR Radio, jazz DJ; WNJR, bright moments in jazz; Jazz Festivals Belgium, France, Amsterdam, Holland; Martin Luther King Multi-Purpose Center Inc, exec dir. **Orgs:** Intl Jazz Fed; contributing editor African-Amer Classical Music/Jazz Publication; mem Jazz at Home Club 1972, Westchester Jazz Soc 1975, Bi-Centennial Jazz Citation Manhattan Boro Pres 1976; mem Rockland County on Womens Issues 1986; mem adv comm Cooperative Extension 4H Club 1986; mem Crystal Run Environmental Center Adv Bd 1986; mem Spring Valley NAACP Educ Comm 1987; mem adv council Village of Spring Valley Comm Develop Advisory Council 1987; Rotary Intl, 1989; Ramapo Housing Authority, bd mem, 1988; member, Jazz Federation of America Coalition for Jazz Musicians Health and Welfare; member, Jazz Interactions Audience Development; treasurer, People to People. **Honors/Awds:** Woman of the Year Kennedy Center in Harlem 1976; Consortium of Jazz Artists Award of Excellence 1981; wrote, produced, dir, performed ''I A Black Woman'' New Heritage Repertory Theatre; researching Amer Indian, African Amer, Hispanic, Asian Cultures for publ called ''History Not To Be Denied''; Certificate of Excellence, A proud Heritage; St Paul Honorary Black Belt; Certificate of Appreciation, 1989; Certificate of Appreciation, Rockland County Dept of Social Services, 1989; Distinguished Service Award, County of Rockland; Certificate of Appreciation, Bethune-Cookman College; Distinguished Service Award, Senator Joseph R Holland; Certificate of Appreciation, People to People. **Business Addr:** Executive Dir, M L King Multi-Purpose Ctr Inc, 110 Bethune Blvd, Spring Valley, NY 10977.

MARSALIS, BRANFORD
Jazz musician. **Personal:** Born Aug 26, 1960, New Orleans, LA; son of Dolores Ferdinand Marsalis and Ellis Marsalis II; married Teresa Reese, May 31, 1985 (divorced 1994); children: Reese Ellis. **Educ:** Southern Univ, 1978-79; Berkeley Coll of Music, 1979-81. **Career:** Musician with Lionel Hampton Orchestra, 1980, Clark Terry Band, 1981, Art Blakey and the Jazz Messengers, 1981, Herbie Hancock Quartet, 1981, 1986, Wynton Marsalis Quintet, 1982-85, Sting, 1985-86, English Chamber Orchestra, 1986; Buckshot LeFonque, band, two albums, 1995-; The Tonight Show, music dir, 1992-95; recording artist, has appeared in motion pictures including ''Bring on the Night,'' 1985, ''School Daze,'' 1987, ''Throw Momma from the Train,'' 1987. **Honors/Awds:** Grammy Award nominations, 1987, ''Royal Garden Blues,'' 1988, for best jazz instrumental solo performance on Duke Ellington album ''Digital Duke,'' Grammy Award, ''I Heard You Twice the First Time,'' 1993. **Special Achievements:** Own recordings include: ''Royal Garden Blues,'' ''Scenes in the City,'' ''Renaissance,'' ''Frio Jeepy,'' ''Random Abstract,'' ''Crazy People Music,'' ''The Beautiful Ones Are Not Yet Born,'' ''I Heard You Twice the First Time''. **Business Addr:** Former Music Director, The Tonight Show, c/o Wilkins Management, 260 Brookline St, Cambridge, MA 02139.

MARSALIS, ELLIS
Pianist, composer. **Personal:** Born Nov 14, 1934, New Orleans, LA; married Dolores Ferdinand, 1958; children: Branford, Wynton, Ellis III, Delfeayo, Mboya, Jason. **Educ:** Dillard University, BA, 1955; Loyola University, MA, music education, 1986. **Career:** First played professionally as a tenor saxophonist in high school; joined the modernist American Jazz Quartet as a pianist, mid-1950s; played piano in band of Marine Corps television variety show, ''Dress Blues,'' 1956-58; returned to New Orleans and played in a quartet with tenor saxophonist Nat Perrilliat and drummer James Black; taught music in New Orleans high schools, beginning in the early 1960s; played with Al Hirt's band, 1967-70; joined the French brothers' Storyville Jazz Band, 1971; led the ELM Music Company, 1972-; head of New Orleans Center for the Creative Arts, 1974-86; head of jazz studies program, Virginia Commonwealth University, 1986-89, and University of New Orleans, mid-1990s. **Orgs:** National Endowment for the Arts; Southern Arts Federation, board member. **Honors/Awds:** ACE award for musical performance on cable television, 1984; honorary doctorate from Dillard University, 1989. **Special Achievements:** Albums: ''The Monkey Puzzle,'' 1963; ''Gumbo,'' 1976; ''Fathers and Sons,'' 1982; ''Syndrome,'' 1984; ''Homecoming,'' 1986; ''The New New Orleans Music: Vocal Jazz,'' 1989; ''The Vision's Tale,'' 1989; ''Piano in E,'' 1991; ''Ellis Marsalis Trio,'' 1991; ''The Classic,'' 1992; ''Heart of Gold,'' 1993; ''Whistle Stop,'' 1994. **Military Serv:** US Marine Corps, 1956-58. **Business Addr:** Pianist, Composer, c/o Columbia Records, 550 Madison Ave, New York, NY 10022-3211.

MARSALIS, WYNTON
Jazz musician. **Personal:** Born Oct 18, 1961; son of Dolores Marsalis and Ellis Marsalis; children: Jasper Armstrong Marsalis. **Educ:** Studied with John Longo; New Orleans Ctr for Performing Arts; Berkshire Music Ctr, Juilliard School of Music 1979-81. **Career:** Trumpet soloist with New Orleans Philharmonic Orch 1975; recitalist with New Orleans orchs; with Art Blakey's Jazz Messengers from 1980; Herbie Hancock's VSOP quartet; formed own group, 1981; albums include Father and Sons, 1982; Wynton Marsalis; Think of One, 1983; Trumpet Concertos, 1983; Hot House Flowers, 1984; Black Codes from the Underground, 1985; Joe Cool's Blues, 1994; CITI Movement; Blood on the Fields, jazz oratorio, 1997; Jazz at Lincoln Center, artistic director. **Honors/Awds:** Named Jazz Musician of the Year Downbeat readers' poll 1982, 1984, 1985; Wynton Marsalis album named best jazz recorded, Downbeat readers poll 1982; best trumpet player Downbeat critics' poll 1984; Acoustic Jazz Group of Year Award 1984; Grammy Awds for solo jazz instrumental 1984, 1986, classical soloist with orchestra 1984, best trumpet player 1985, Group Award 1986; Honorary Degrees: Manhattan College, Yale Univ, Princeton Univ, Hunter College; Pulitzer Prize, 1997; Young STAR Award, 1998. **Business Addr:** Trumpeter, Van Walsum Management Ltd., 26 Wadhan, London SW15 2LR, England.

MARSH, ALPHONSO HOWARD
Engineering manager. **Personal:** Born Sep 22, 1938, Mobile, AL; son of Augusta Barney Marsh and Alphonso Howard Marsh; married June E Peterson (deceased); children: Preston Howard, Alphonso Van. **Educ:** Howard Univ, BSEE 1961. **Career:** Radio Corp of Amer, electrical engineer 1961-63; General Dynamics, electrical engineer 1963-66; Rochester Inst Syst, electrical engineer 1966-67; Raytheon Co, sr engineer 1967-73; Digital Equipment Corp, project engineer 1973-77; LFE Corp, engineering mgr 1977-87; Honeywell-EOD, engr supvr 1987-90; EG&G, Rocky Flats Inc, development associate engr, 1990-. **Orgs:** Mem, Inst of Electrical & Electronic Engrs, 1960-; mem, Tau Beta Pi Honor Soc 1960-; elected Town of Medway Planning Bd 1979-90, chmn 1986-87; membership comm, Natl Soc of Professional Engrs, 1984-86; natl dir, Natl Soc of Professional Engrs, 1984-86; state pres MA Soc of Professional Engrs, 1983-84; st PEI chmn, MA Soc of Professional Engrs, 1984-86; chapter pres, MSPE Western Middlesex Chapter, 1978-79; elected Town of Medway School Comm, 1984-89, vice chair, 1987-88; chmn MA Engrs Week Comm Proclamation, 1984-90; mem, Constitution and Bylaws Comm Natl Soc of Professional Engrs, 1986-88; Minuteman Natl Soc of Professional Engrs, 1988-; mem, Professional Engrs of CO, 1990-. **Honors/Awds:** Reg Professional Engr State of MA 1972-; Pres Award MA Soc of Professional Engrs 1984; Serv Award MA Soc of Professional Engrs 1982, 1984; Design Awards Professional Journals, Raytheon Co 1969-; 12 articles published professional journals 1968-; Govt Citations Governor of MA & House of Representatives 1983; Town of Medway School Committee Service Award, 1989. **Home Addr:** 8020 Bottlebrush Dr, Austin, TX 78750.

MARSH, BEN FRANKLIN
Government official. **Personal:** Born Feb 17, 1940, Holly Springs, MS; son of Lizzie Dawkins Marsh and Willie Marsh (deceased); married Jessie Floyd Marsh, Sep 30, 1967 (divorced); children: Kimberly; married Gloria, Aug 4, 1993. **Educ:** OH State Univ, Columbus, OH, BS, 1963; Boston Univ, Heidelberg, Germany, Masters, 1980. **Career:** Clayton County Bd of Education; Third Army, Ft McPherson, GA, programs/plans officer; Parking Co of America, shift manager, 1995-. **Orgs:** Pres, Clayton County Branch NAACP, 1990-92; co-chair, Clayton United Negro Coll Fund, 1985-; div lieutenant governor, GA Toastmasters Intl; bd mem, Clayton County Water Authority; communications comm, Clayton United Way, 1991; advisory comm, Clayton County Rainbow House; Georgia Agricultural Exposition Authority, 1992. **Honors/Awds:** Distinguished Toastmaster, Toastmaster's Intl, 5 yrs; Certificate of Appreciation, United Negro Coll Fund, 5 yrs. **Military Serv:** Army, major, 1963-83, Meritorious Service Award (20 years), Army Commendation (10 years). **Home Addr:** 4773 White Oak Path, Stone Mountain, GA 30088.

MARSH, DONALD GENE
Medical administrator. **Personal:** Born Oct 12, 1936, Ft Madison, IA; married Rose E Guy; children: David, Dianne, Donna. **Educ:** Parsons Coll, BS 1958; Univ of MN, Radiology 1968; Univ of IA, MD 1962. **Career:** Univ of MN, asst prof radiology 1968-78; St Croix Vly Hosp, chief of Radiology 1978—; NW WI Med Imaging (Mobile Nuclear Medicine & Ultrasound), pres1980-. **Honors/Awds:** Publication Traumatic Rupture of the Aorta 1977. **Home Addr:** 6810 Kingston Cir, Golden Valley, MN 55427.

MARSH, DOUG
Professional football player (retired). **Personal:** Born Jun 18, 1958, Akron, OH. **Educ:** Univ of Michigan, attended. **Career:** St Louis Cardinals, tight end, 1980-86.

MARSH, HENRY L., III
Attorney, government official. **Personal:** Born Dec 10, 1933, Richmond, VA; married Diane Harris; children: Nadine, Sonya, Dwayne. **Educ:** VA Union Univ, BS 1956; Howard Univ, LD 1959; VA Union Univ, Hon LD. **Career:** City of Richmond, former mayor; City of Richmond VA, councilman present; Hill Tucker & Marsh, partner, atty. **Orgs:** Mem US Conf of Mayors Spec Com on Decennial Census; chmn subcom on urban hwy syst US Conf of Mayors; adv bd Natl League of Cities; past pres NatlBlack Caucus of Local Elected Officials; mem Youth Task Force Natl League of Cities; chmn Income Security Com Natl League of Cities; mem Human Resources Steering Policy Com US Conf of Mayors; chmn Effective Govt Policy Com VA Municipal League; mem Judicial Council of Natl Dem Party; mem adv com State Dem party; mem Judicial Selection Comm US Court of Appeals for 4th Circuit, Alpha Phi Alpha; bd dir Voter Ed Project, Lawyers Com for Civil Rights Under Law. **Honors/Awds:** Selected a Laureate of VA Laureate Ctr of VA 1979-80; del US Conf of Mayors to People's Repub of China 1979; hon mem US China Peoples Friendship Assoc; Outstanding Man of the Year Kappa Alpha Psi; Outstanding Mason of the Year VA; Man of the Year Alpha Phi Alpha; bldg addition named in hon of Mr Marsh GeorgeMason Elem School 1980. **Business Addr:** Attorney, Hill, Tucker & Marsh, PO Box 27363, Richmond, VA 23261.

MARSH, MCAFEE
Insurance broker. **Personal:** Born Aug 29, 1939, Meridian, MS; married Ruby Putmon; children: Marcellus G. **Educ:** Wilson Coll; Life Underwriters Training Course, Grad; LIAMA Mgrs Sch, Grad. **Career:** Chicago Metropolitan Mutual Assurance Co, 1960-72; Supreme Life Ins Co, assoc agency dir vice pres 1972-79; Cosmopolitan Chamber of Commerce School of Business Mgmt, instr; Al Johnson Cadillac, 1979-80; United Ins Co, 1980-82; McAfee Marsh Ins Agency, pres, owner (represents 18 of the largest insurance companies in US) 1982-. **Orgs:** Past sec Chicago Ins Assn 1975; pres grad class LUTC 1969; vice pres Natl Ins Assn; Operation PUSH; mem Christ Universal Temple; pres Men of C.U.C. of Christ Universal Temple, Chicago IL, 1987-89. **Honors/Awds:** Cert of Merit Chicago Assn of Commerce; The Excellence Award, Time Ins Co 1989; Pres Award & trip winner to Hawaii, Hong Kong & Tokyo 1987, Hawaii, 1990; Leader's Circle, Time Insurance Co, 1991. **Military Serv:** AUS 1962-64. **Business Addr:** President, McAfee Marsh Insurance Agency, 2952 Polly Lane, Flossmoor, IL 60422.

MARSH, MICHAEL LAWRENCE
Track & field athlete. **Personal:** Born Aug 4, 1967, Los Angeles, Canada;son of Jonnie Brown and Thamas Brown. **Educ:** University of California Los Angeles, history, business, 1991. **Career:** US Summer Olympic Team, track and field team, athlete, currently. **Special Achievements:** Olympic Games in Barcelona, Gold Medal, track & field, 1992. **Home Phone:** (713)835-9821.

MARSH, PEARL-ALICE
Political scientist. **Personal:** Born Sep 6, 1946, La Grande, OR; daughter of Mary Patterson Marsh and Amos Marsh Sr. **Educ:** Sacramento State College, Sacramento, CA, BA, 1968; University of Californiaat Berkeley, Berkeley, CA, MPH, 1970, PhD, 1984. **Career:** Neighborhood Health Center Seminar Program, Berkeley, CA, coordinator, 1970-73; Alameda County Mental Health Services, Oakland, CA, associate director-planning, 1973-76; Association of Bay Area Government, Oakland, CA, researcher, 1984-85; University of California at Berkeley, Berkeley, CA, associate director African studies, 1985-93; Joint Ctr for Political & Economic Studies, Washington, DC, sr research fellow, 1993-97, Africa Policy Information Ctr, acting executive director, 1997-. **Orgs:** Commissioner, Berkeley Rent Stabilization Program, 1989-92; elected officer, board member, Association of Concerned African Scholars, 1989-; member, African Studies Association, 1984-; member, Political Science Association, 1989-. **Business Addr:** Acting Executive Director, Joint Center for Political & Economic Studies, Africa Policy Information Center, 110 Maryland Ave NE, Ste 509, Washington, DC 20002.

MARSH, SANDRA M.
Law enforcement official. **Personal:** Born Jan 14, 1943, Charleston, SC; daughter of Ethel Baker and William Baker; divorced; children: David. **Educ:** Brooklyn College, CUNY, BA, 1977; New York University School of Law, JD, 1981; NYU Wagner Graduate School, MS, 1995. **Career:** Public Education Association, staff attorney, 1981-82; New York State Education Department, Office of Professional Discipline, prosecuting attorney, 1982-85; New York Police Department, assistant trial commissioner, 1985-88, deputy police commissioner, executive director, 1988-. **Orgs:** NYU Law School Alumni Association, board member, 1993-; Association of Black Women Attorneys, 1981-; National Organization of Black Law Enforcement Executives, 1986-; MLK Jr High School Mentor's Program, mentor, 1987; Black Law Students Association, mentor, 1981-; Girl Scouts of America, lecturer/instructor, 1993-. **Honors/Awds:** NY University Law School, Alumna Award for Excellence, 1996. **Special Achievements:** First African-American female to head NYPD Civilian Complaint Review Board, 1988; first African-American female appointed trial commissioner, NYPD, 1985; first African-American to head NYPD OEEO, 1993. **Business Addr:** Deputy Commissioner/OEEO, NYPD - 1 Police Plaze, Rm 1204, New York, NY 10038, (212)374-5330.

MARSH, TAMRA GWENDOLYN
Insurance sales/social work. **Personal:** Born Oct 8, 1946, Philadelphia, PA. **Educ:** Temple Univ, BA Sociology 1972, MSW Admin 1976; Charles Morris Price School, journalism & advertising 1980. **Career:** Dept Public Welfare, caseworker/applications interviewer 1969-74; Delaware Co, asst comm serv coord 1975-76; YWCA Southwest Belmont Branch, branch admin1976-79; Horizon House, mgr/training consultation coord 1979-82; Arbor Inc, job develop 1984-85; Natl Liberty Corp, ins sales licensed ins sales agent1984-. **Orgs:** Natl promotion dir Delaware Valley Defender Newspaper; mem Amer Women in Radio & TV; publ relations chair Philadelphia Club NANB-PINC Inc; finance sec Mid-Atlantic Dist Women's Clubs Inc; natl dir for youth Natl Assn of Negro Business & Professional Women 1983-85; Natl Assn of Female Executives 1985. **Honors/Awds:** Assistantship for Graduate Study-Administration 1974-76; Comm Serv Awd Tau Gamma Delta Sor Inc 1978; State-wide and City-wide Awd for Excellence in Mental Health & Mental Retardation Serv Delivery 1981; numerous awds for progs implementation and leadership in volunteer organizations 1979-. **Home Addr:** 1225 N 53rd St, Philadelphia, PA 19131. **Business Addr:** Insurance Sales/Social Work, Natl Liberty Corp, Valley Forge, PA 19493.

MARSH, WILLIAM A., JR.
Attorney. **Personal:** Born Jan 31, 1927, Durham, NC; married Bernice Sawyer; children: William A, Jewel Lynn. **Educ:** NC Central U, BS 1949; NC Central U, LLB 1953; NC Central U, JD 1970. **Career:** Self-employed, attorney; Mechanics & Farmers Bank, general counsel; Mutual Community Savings Bank, general counsel; UDI-CDC Garrett Sullivan Davenport Bowie & Grant CPA's, attorney. **Orgs:** UDI Comm Devel Corp; Found for Comm Devel; Durham Opportunities Found Inc; Legal Redress Com, chairman; ABA; NBA; Durham Com on Negro Affairs; Durham Chap NAACP; Beta Phi Chpt; Omega Psi Phi; Durham C of C; NC Central Alumni Assn; Masonic Lodge; Shriners; NC Assn of Black Lawyers, historian; NC State Bd of Elections, chairman; 33 degree Mason. **Military Serv:** WWII veteran. **Business Addr:** Partner, Marsh and Marsh, Attorneys, 120 E Parrish St, Ste 310, Durham, NC 27701.

MARSH, WILLIAM ANDREW, III (DREW)
Attorney. **Personal:** Born Mar 6, 1958, Durham, NC; son of Bernice S Marsh and William A Marsh Jr; married Sonja Denalli, Jul 20, 1991; children: William Andrew IV, Kylie Alexandra Marsh. **Educ:** Hampton Institute, Hampton University, BA, 1979; University of North Carolina at Chapel Hill, School of Law, JD, 1982. **Career:** Marsh & Banks, associate, 1982-83, 1985-86; Office of the Governor of North Carolina, asst legal counsel, 1983-85; State of District of Columbia, Office of the Corp. Counsel, Juvenile Division, prosecuting attorney, 1987-92; Marsh & Marsh, general partner, 1993-. **Orgs:** Kappa Alpha Psi Fraternity, 1978-; American Bar Assn, 1983-; District of Columbia Bar, 1983-; North Carolina State Bar, 1984-; North Carolina Assn of Black Lawyers, 1984-; Durham Co Bar Assn, pres-elect; 14th Judicial District Bar of NC, pres-elect. **Business Addr:** Attorney, Marsh & Marsh, Attorneys at Law, 120 E Parrish St, The Law Bldg, Ste 310, Durham, NC 27701, (919)688-2374.

MARSHALL, ALBERT PRINCE
Publisher, writer, speaker. **Personal:** Born Sep 5, 1914, Texarkana, TX; son of Mary Bland Marshall and Early Marshall (deceased); married Ruthe Helena Langley; children: Satia Yvette Marshall Orange. **Educ:** Lincoln Univ MO, AB 1938; Univ of IL, BSLS 1939, MA 1953. **Career:** Lincoln Univ (MO), asst Librarian 1939-41; Winston-Salem State Univ, librarian 1941-50; Lincoln Univ MO, univ librarian 1950-69; Eastern MI Univ, dir of libry 1969-72; Eastern MI Univ, acting dir of library 1979-80; Eastern MI Univ, dean of academic serv 1973-77; EMU, prof emeritus 1980-; Marlan Publishers, (specializing in black historical subjects), organizer and pres, currently; Ypsilanti Press, columnist, 1989-. **Orgs:** Pres Missouri State Conference of Branches, NAACP, 1953-55; Consultant Library Serv, US Off of Educ 1965-80; Consultant on Library Resources N Central Assoc 1973-80; Natl Endowment for Humanities, 1975-80; dist gov, Rotary Intl, 1977-78; pres Missouri Library Assn, 1959-60; vice pres Amer Library Assn, 1971-72; Speaker and consultant in Black History. **Honors/Awds:** Distinguished Alumnus, Lincoln Univ MO 1956; distinguished librarian Black Caucus, Amer Library Assn 1978, MO Library Assn 1970; Hon Griot Washtenaw Community Coll 1984; Martin Luther King Jr Award Ann Arbor Public Schools 1985; Distinguished Career Citation, Assn of College & Research Libraries 1989; Community Service Award, Washtenaw Community College, 1991. **Special Achievements:** Author: Soldiers Dream: Pictorial History of Lincoln University, Lincoln University of Jefferson City MO, 1966, Martin Luther King Jr: A Synopsis, and Molders of Black Thought, 1780-1980; The Real McCoy of Ypsilanti, Marlan Publishers, 1989. **Military Serv:** USCG seaman first class 1943-45; 5 Area Ribbons, 1 Battle Star.

MARSHALL, ANITA (ANITA DURANT)
Librarian. **Personal:** Born May 30, 1938, Newark, NJ; daughter of Estelle Mitchell Marshall and Noah Willis Marshall; children: Harry Vaughn Bims. **Educ:** Newark State College, Newark, NJ, BS, education, 1959; Chicago State University, Chicago, IL, MS, education, 1974; University of Chicago, Chicago, IL, 1978-86; Michigan State University, East Lansing, MI, 1985-89; Garrett Evangelical Theological Seminary, 1996-. **Career:** Newark Board of Education, Newark, NJ, teacher, 1959-62; Peace Corps, Philippine Islands, TESL, science teacher, 1962-63; Chicago Board of Education, Chicago, IL, media specialist, ESEA, coordinator, workshop facilitator, 1964-82; Chicago State University, Chicago, IL, lecturer, library science, HEW project director, 1976-77; Michigan State University, East Lansing, MI, head, gift unit, ethnic studies & sociology bibliographer, 1982-95; Chicago Board of Education, head librarian, currently. **Orgs:** President, Gamma Zeta Chapter, Alpha Kappa Alpha Sorority, 1957-59; secretary, Theta Omega, Delta Tau Omega, Alpha Kappa Alpha Sorority, 1969-88; member, Phi Delta Kappa, 1981-; member, American Library Assn, 1968-; member, chair of Tech Services Caucus, Michigan Library Assn, 1988-89; planning committee, Black Caucus of American Library Assn, First National Conference, 1990-92; Michigan State University, Black Faculty and Administrators Association, secretary, 2nd vice president, 1st vice president; MSU Museum Associates Bd, 1992-96, co-chair, 1995-96; Christian Education Department of AME Church, Writers Guild Coordinator; Women's Missionary Society, Chicago Conference; Kresge Art Museum Docent, Lansing Public Library Advisory Bd, 1995-96. **Honors/Awds:** State Academic Scholarship, New Jersey, 1955-59; White House Conference, State of Illinois, 1978; member, Women's Advisory Committee to Provost, Michigan State University, 1988-91; Planning Committee, International Conference for Women Writers in the African Diaspora, 1985; Proposal Reviewer, Capital Area United Way, 1989, 1990; member, Mission & Ethics Committee, St Lawrence Hospital Exec Board, 1991; organized three libraries, Chicago Public Schools, 1966, 1973, 1981. **Business Addr:** Head Librarian, Nancy Jefferson Alternative School, 1100 S Hamilton Avenue, Chicago, IL 60612.

MARSHALL, ANTHONY DEWAYNE
Professional football player. **Personal:** Born Sep 16, 1970, Mobile, AL. **Educ:** Louisiana State, attended. **Career:** Chicago Bears, defensive back, 1994-97; New York Jets, 1998-. **Business Addr:** Professional Football Player, New York Jets, 1000 Fulton Ave, Hempstead, NY 11550, (516)560-8100.

MARSHALL, BETTY J.
Purchasing executive. **Personal:** Born Oct 15, 1950, Youngstown, OH; daughter of L V Sharpe Mitchell and Grant Mitchell; married Richard H Young (divorced 1982); children: Melanie D. **Educ:** Youngstown State University, Youngstown, OH. **Career:** Arby's Inc, Columbus, OH, director of purchasing, 1975-89; Rax Restaurants Inc, director of purchasing and distribution, 1989-90; Shoney's Inc, Nashville, TN, director of purchasing, 1990, director of corporate and community affairs, 1990, vice president of corporate and community affairs, 1990-. **Orgs:** Treasurer & steering committee member, National Restaurant Association, 1987-; Hospitality Management Advisory Board member, Eastern Michigan University, 1990-; Tourism Task Force member, Nashville Area Chamber of Commerce, 1990-; vice chair, Health and Rehabilitative Services Community Initiatives Steering Committee, United Way, 1990-; board of directors, Tennessee Minority Purchasing Council, 1991. **Honors/Awds:** Selected as 1 of 15 women that make a difference, Minorities-Women in Business, Jan/Feb 1991. **Business Addr:** Vice President, Corporate and Community Affairs, Shoney's Inc, 1727 Elm Hill Pike, Nashville, TN 37210.

MARSHALL, CALVIN BROMLEY, III
Clergyman. **Personal:** Born Jun 13, 1932, Brooklyn, NY; son of Edith Best Marshall and Evans B Marshall; married Delma Mann; children: Sharon Wallinger, Monica, Edythe, Chad. **Educ:** Anderson Coll, Anderson, IN, BA 1955; Anderson Theological Sem, BD 1958; Teamer School of Religion, NC, DD 1972, LHD 1973; Grasslands Hospital, Valhalla, NY, CPC 1963-65. **Career:** Park St AME Zion Church, Peekskill, NY, pastor 1960-68; Cumberland Hospital, dir of Pastoral care 1972-83; Varick Mem AME Zion Church, pastor 1968-; Woodhull Medical & Mental Health Center, dir of Pastoral Care. **Orgs:** Chief of Protocol AME Zion Church; vice chair, National Action Network; American Association of Christian Counselors US Chaplains Association; American Association of Pastoral Counselors; Association for Clinical Pastoral Education. **Special Achievements:** Articles: ''Living on the Left Hand of God,'' Theology Today, 1968; ''The Black Church-Its Mission Is Liberation,'' Black Scholar, 1970. **Military Serv:** USAF 1st lt 1951-53. **Home Addr:** 125 Fairway, Hempstead, NY 11550. **Business Addr:** Pastor, Varick Memorial AME Zion Church, 806 Quincy St, Brooklyn, NY 11221.

MARSHALL, CARL LEROY
Educator. **Personal:** Born Aug 23, 1914, Dayton, OH; son of Lora Marshall and M C Marshall; married Mary Ellen Jenkins; children: Betty Lewis, Donna McIntosh, Carl L Jr, Lora Marshall. **Educ:** Wilberforce Univ, BS in Ed 1935; OH State Univ, MA (English) 1947, PhD (English) 1954. **Career:** AR AM&N Coll, asst prof & chmn English 1947-51, prof & chmn English 1954-55; Southern Univ, prof of Engl 1955-69, chmn dept 1962-69, OH State Univ, prof of English 1969-82, prof emeritus 1982-. **Orgs:** Life mem Modern Lang Assn; mem Coll Lang Assn; life mem Alpha Phi Alpha Frat; officer OH State Univ Retirees Assn 1983-86; mem, American Legion, 1978-. **Honors/Awds:** Author "American Critical Attitudes toward the Fiction of W D Howells," CLAJ 1955, "Eliot's 'Sweeney Erect,'" Southern Univ Bull 1956, "Two Protest Poems by Albery Whitman," CLAJ 1975; "Albery A Whitman, a Rebellious Romantic," included in the ERIC system of the Clearinghouse on Reading & Communication Skills 1975; "In Defense of Huck Finn," Sphinx, 1986. **Military Serv:** Army Infantry 1st lt 1941-46; Commendation 366th Inf Reg 1945. **Home Addr:** 3296 Colchester Rd, Columbus, OH 43221.

MARSHALL, CARTER LEE
Educator. **Personal:** Born Mar 31, 1936, New Haven, CT; married Carol Paul; children: Wendy, Holly, Com. **Educ:** Harvard, BA 1958; Yale, MD 1962; Yale, MPh 1964. **Career:** Coll Hospital, dir ambulatory care 1977-; NJ Medical School Coll of Medicine & Dentistry, dir ofc PRICARE prof of medicine & prev medicine 1977-; Dept Comm Med Morehouse Coll School of Medicine, prof chmn 1976-77; Mt Sinai School Medicine, prof comm med 1975-76; Mt Sinai, assoc dean 1973-76; City Univ of NY, dean for health affairs 1973-75; Mt Sinai School of Medicine, assoc prof 1969-75; Univ KS Medical School, asst prof 1967-69; New Haven Health Dept, fellow 1965; Yale Univ, 1964. **Orgs:** Mem Intl Med Care Com 1967-70; vis asst prof Univ Antioquia Sch Med 1968; consult Hlth Serv Adminstrn 1970-71; mem Com on Minorities in Sci 1971-72; Panel on Black Sci 1972-75; consult Children's TV Workshop 1973-75; chmn Com of Helth Educ of Pub Am Coll of Preventive Med 1974; mem Hlth Adv Com 1974-76; Editorial Bd Jour of Comm Hlth Assn of Tchrs of Preventive Med 1974; Task Force on Hlth Educ of the Pub Fogarty Intl Ctr 1974-75; TaskForce on Minority Student Opprt 1976-; Hlth Care Technology Study Sect Nat Ctr for Hlth Serv Rsrch 1975-; Minority Recruitment Team Nat Ctr Hlth Serv Rsrch 1975-; Nat Air Quality Criteria Adv Com 1975; Expert Panel Hlth Educ Fogarty Ctr 1975-76; bd dir Assn of Tchrs of Preventive Med 1976-; pres Hew Haven, CT Br NAACP 1964-65; NewHaven City Planning Commn64-65; New Haven Redevel Adv Com 1964-65; bd tsts Williston-Northampton Sch 1970-73; bd dir Am Cncl for Emigres in the Professions 1972-73. **Honors/Awds:** Publ "Dynamics of Hlth & Disease" 1972; "Toward An Educated Hlth Consumer" 1978; 43 sci publ; commendation medal AUS 1967; flw Am Coll of Prev Med 1973. **Military Serv:** AUS capt 1965-67. **Business Addr:** Coll Med & Dept of New Jersey, New Jersey Med Sch, Newark, NJ 07103.

MARSHALL, CHARLENE JENNINGS
State inspector. **Personal:** Born Sep 17, 1933; married Roger Leon; children: Gwendolyn, Roger Jr, Larry. **Career:** WV Dept of Labor, state insp 1978-; Rockwell Internat, stores attendant 1975-78; Rockwell Internat, machine operator 1963-75; United Steelworkers of Am Local 6214, recording sec 1976; Mon-Preston Labor & Council 1968-78. **Orgs:** Dir WV Women's Bowling Assn 1971-; chairperson Morgantown Human Rights Commn 1974-79; past vice pres NAACP Morgantown Br 1973-76. **Business Addr:** WV Dept of Labor, 1900 Washington St E, Charleston, WV 25305.

MARSHALL, CONSUELO B.
Judge. **Personal:** Born Sep 28, 1936, Knoxville, TN; married George E Marshall Jr; children: Michael, Laurie. **Educ:** Howard Univ, BA 1958, LLB 1961. **Career:** City of LA, dep city attny 1962-67; Cochran & Atkins, pvt practice 1968-70; City of LA, superior ct commiss 1972-76, municipal cout judge 1976-77, superior court judge 1977-80; US Dist Court Central Dist CA, judge 1980-. **Orgs:** Mem Black Women Laywers Assoc, CA Women Lawyers Assoc, CA Judges Assoc; mem State Bar CA, Los Angeles Cty Bar Assoc, NAACP, Urban League, Beta Phi Sigma, Ch Religious Sci, Los Angeles Women Lawyers' Assn, Assn of Black Lawyers, Natl Assn of Women Judges; bd mem Legal Aid Found, YMCA, Beverly Hills WestLinks Inc; mem, bd dir Antioch School of Law Wash DC; mem 9th Circuit Court of Appeals Educ Comm 1984-86; faculty mem Trial Advocacy Workshop Harvard Law Sch 1984-85; mem 9th Circuit Court of Appeals Library Comm 1985-86; lecturer Continuing Legal Educ of the Bar "Discovery in Federal Court" 1986. **Honors/Awds:** Honoree Black Women Laywers Assoc 1976; Woman of the Year Zeta Phi Beta 1977; Honoree Angeles Mesa YWCA 1977; Honoree Natl Bus & Professional Women's Club of Los Angeles 1978; Grad of the Year Howard Univ 1981; Woman of the Year for Contribs to the Improvement of Soc, The Los Angeles Sentinal 1983; Presidential Awd in Recognition for Serv and Contribs in Improving Quality of Life for Mankind, Alpha Phi Alpha 1984; Honoree, Black Amer Law Students Assn, UCLA 1985; Honoree Verbum Dei Catholic Boys High School Los Angeles 1986; Honoree Econ Equal Oppty Prog for Black History Month 1986; Ernestine Stahlhut Awd Women Lawyers Assoc of Los Angeles; Certificate Dept of Treasury Economic Equal Oppor Prog for Black History Month 1986. **Business Addr:** Judge, US Dist Court Central Dist, 312 N Spring St, 155 US Courthouse, Los Angeles, CA 90012.

MARSHALL, DON A., SR.
Physician (retired). **Personal:** Born Mar 4, 1929, Frankfort, KY; married Roumania Mason; children: Donna Marya (deceased), Don A Jr., C Angela. **Educ:** KY St U, BS 1951, MA 1954; Meharry Med Coll, MD 1967. **Career:** Delco Prods (GM), med dir 1974-; KY St U, phys ed instr 1961-63; USPHS (Narcotic Farm Lexton KY), physchtrc aide 1950-56. **Orgs:** Mem Alpha Kappa Mu KY St Univ 1948; mem Phi Delta Kappa Univ of KY 1955; pres Gem City Med Dntl & Phrmcy Soc 1976.

MARSHALL, DONALD JAMES
Performer. **Personal:** Born May 2, 1934, San Diego, CA; son of Ernest & Alma Marshall; divorced. **Educ:** San Diego City Coll, engineering, 1956-57; LA City Coll, theater arts, 1958-60. **Career:** DJM Productions Inc, past actor/prodr pres, 1970-73; Bob Gist Group, Frank Silvera Thtr of Being, Thtr E Workshop, Richard Boone Repertory Co, 1960-67; Land of the Giants ABC-TV, co-star 1967-71; performed in num TV shows, features, stage shows, motion pictures; JoCo Intl Enterprises, Inc, distributor, licensing agent, 1984. **Orgs:** Mem Equity, Am Fedn of TV & Radio Artists, Screen Actors Guild, Nat Acad of TV Arts & Sci; natl mem Am Film Inst; charter mem fdr Negro Actors for Action; vice pres natl mem NAACP; num cons. **Honors/Awds:** Actor's Achvmt Award African Meth Epis Ch 1970; ABC Movie of the Week Award The Egghead on Hill 656 Aaron Spelling Prodns 1971; Black Achiever in US CA Mus of Sci & Indus 1976; films: Uptown Saturday Night, The Interns; tv appearances: Cheers, General Hospital, Alfred Hitchcock; stage work: Of Mice and Men, A Cat Called Jesus; 1984 copyright, World Hunger Project; 1985 patent, vehicle protection system. **Military Serv:** AUS, PFC, 1954-56. **Business Addr:** c/o Abraham, Ruballff, Lawrence, 8075 W 3rd St, Suite 303, Los Angeles, CA 90048.

MARSHALL, DONNY
Professional basketball player. **Personal:** Born Jul 17, 1972. **Educ:** Connecticut. **Career:** Cleveland Cavaliers, currently. **Business Addr:** Professional Basketball Player, Cleveland Cavaliers, One Center Ct, Cleveland, OH 44115-4001, (216)659-9100.

MARSHALL, DONYELL LAMAR
Professional basketball player. **Personal:** Born May 18, 1973, Reading, PA. **Educ:** Connecticut. **Career:** Minnesota Timberwolves, forward, 1994-95; Golden State Warriors, 1995-. **Special Achievements:** Selected in the first round, fourth pick, in the NBA Draft, 1994. **Business Addr:** Professional Basketball Player, Golden State Warriors, 1001 Broadway, Oakland, CA 94607, (510)986-2200.

MARSHALL, EDWIN COCHRAN
Optometrist, educational administrator. **Personal:** Born Mar 31, 1946, Albany, GA; children: Erin C, Erika H. **Educ:** IN Univ, BA/BS 1968/1970, OD 1971, MS 1979; Univ of NC, MPH 1982. **Career:** Natl Optometric Assn, pres 1979-81; InterAmer Univ of Puerto Rico, consultant 1982; IU Sch of Optometry, assoc prof, 1977-92, professor, 1992-; Cebu Drs Coll of Optometry Philippines, consultant, 1980-87; Natl Optometric Assn, exec dir 1981-89, 1993-; Natl HBP Educ Prog, coordinating comm mem 1984-; IN Sch of Optometry, chmn dept of clinical sciences 1983-92, associate dean for academic affairs, 1992-; National University of Malaysia, consultant, 1992. **Orgs:** Life mem Kappa Alpha Psi Frat; public health exam comm Natl Bd of Examiners in Optometry 1983-94; coun of academic affairs Assn of Schools and Colls of Optometry 1983-84; sec Black Congress on Health Law & Economics 1985-87; mem, Natl Advisory Council on Health Professions Education 1987-91; chmn, Vision Care Section, American Public Health Assn 1988-90; vice chmn, Black Congress on Health, Law & Economics 1987-92; pres, Eye Ski Inc 1986-; chair, Diplomate Program, Public/Health/American Academy of Optometry, 1990-93; chair, Task Force on Health Policy, Assn of Schools & Colleges of Optometry, 1991-92. **Honors/Awds:** Optometrist of the Year Natl Optometric Assn 1976; Delta Omega Natl Public Health Honor Soc 1982; Diplomate in Public Health, American Academy of Optometry 1987; Founders Award, National Optometric Assn 1987; Co-Editor: Public Health and Community Optometry, Second Edition 1990. **Business Addr:** Associate Dean for Academic Affairs, School of Optometry, Indiana Univ, Bloomington, IN 47405.

MARSHALL, ETTA MARIE-IMES
Educator (retired), community activist. **Personal:** Born Jul 16, 1932, Goldsboro, NC; married Michael J Marshall; children: Cheryl S. **Educ:** Bowie State Coll, BS , 1954; Minor Fed City Coll; MD Univ, Amer Univ, George Washington Univ of DC, attended workshop seminars. **Career:** Resource tchr 1973-84; Lamond-Riggs Civic Assoc Block Two, lt 1964; PGC Tr Assn of MD, faculty rep 1968-84; Advisory Neighborhood Commission, recording sec 1981, vice chairperson 1984, commissioner, chr gov operations 1985; ANCSA treas 1986; Orientation of New Com Committee Member 1987 MC Terrell Elem Tr. **Orgs:** Mem PGC Ed Assn Inc 1954-84, NEA 1954-84, MSTA 1954-84, CEC 1964-84; Leader Girl Scout Brownie Troop 107 1967; faculty rep PGC of MD 1968-84; treas Longfields Elem School PTA 1974; Lt Lamond-Riggs Civic Assn Block Two 1981-85; treas 1983, pres 1984-85 DC Chap Bowie Alumni 1983; mem NEA-R 1984-96, CEC-R 1985-96, PGRTA, 1996, MSTA-R, 1996-97; DC Chptr Alumni membership chrmn 1986-87; Census Bureau Worker, LRCA membership chmn, 1995-97; St Anthony Parish, council, 1996-97; PGCRTA, 1984-97; NEA-R, 1997; MSTA-R, 1997; Tonies Sec, 1997. **Honors/Awds:** Plaque PGC Ed Assn Interpersonal Com Relations 1972-84; Letter PG Bd of Ed 1984; Plaques PG Bd of Ed 1984; Plaque Family-Kings of PA 1984; Gold Watch &Chain Longfields Elem School 1984; recd class cup letters from Mayor Barry 1986 election; congratulatory letters from city cncl members; MC Terrell School, Reelected ANC Commission, 1997. **Home Addr:** 1014 Galloway St NE, Washington, DC 20011. **Business Addr:** Commissioner 5A-01, Advisory Neighborhd Comm of 5A, Slowe School Demountable, 14th & Irving St NE, Washington, DC 20011.

MARSHALL, FRANK BRITT, III
Graphic designer, company executive. **Personal:** Born Jan 18, 1943, Bronx, NY; married Katie Wynn; children: Sean, Stacey, Travis. **Educ:** Newark Sch of Fine & Indsl Arts, 1962-65. **Career:** Park Advertising Agy, asst art dir 1969-70; Silver Burdett Textbook Pub, asso book designer 1965-69; Park Advrt Agy, asst art dir 1969-70; Chem Bank of NY,graphic designer 1970-73; GAF Corp, supr & sr graphic designer 1973-; Frank Marshall Graphic design, president. **Orgs:** Bd of trustees Black Art Dir Group of NY 1978-; mem Soc of Illustrators; mem Art Dir Club of NY. **Honors/Awds:** 5 creativity awards Art Direction Mag 1977-79; 7 awards for excellence in Design Graphic USA/NY "Desi" Awards 1978; gold medal & bronze medal excellence of design Art Dir Club of NJ 1979; 3 awards for excellence in Design Advertising Club of North Jersey 1979. **Military Serv:** AUS sp-5 1966-68. **Business Addr:** President, Frank Marshall Graphic Design, 270 Park Ave So, Ste 2D, New York, NY 10010.

MARSHALL, GLORIA A. See SUDARKASA, NIARA.

MARSHALL, H. JEAN
Manufacturing company executive. **Personal:** Born Jun 7, 1945, Lake Providence, LA; daughter of William L & Thelma Jones Harden; divorced; children: Lyndon E, Tangie F. **Educ:** Univ of Cincinnati, BS, 1972. **Career:** St Leo School, teacher, 1976-78; Cincinnati Pub Schools, work training coor, 1978-82; Ohio Lottery, regional mgr & field coor, 1983-87; British Amer Banknote, acct exec, 1987-89; Ohio Dept of Rehab, consultant, 1989-90; Ohio Lottery, deputy dir of sales, 1990-92; Interlott, vp, 1992-. **Orgs:** Arts Consortium of Cincinnati, vp-board of trustee, 1993-; Interlott Inc, vp-board of directors, 1993-; United Way, commun chest-field of service, 1993-; Minority Bus Dev Center, sec-bd of directors, 1994-; Harriett Beecher Stowe Historical Cultural Assn, 1981-. **Honors/Awds:** Ohio House of Representatives, Outstanding Leadership, 1993. **Special Achievements:** "Developing Postive Retail Relations," Public Gaming Ins, 1991; "Let's Talk Job Search," Series of Articles, Cinti Herald, 1989; Author/Poet, "Beautiful Words, Hearts of Love", Cinti Enquirer, Drama of the Year, 1994. **Home Phone:** (513)729-2935. **Business Addr:** VP, Marketing, Interlott Inc, 6665 Creek Rd, Cincinnati, OH 45242, (513)792-7000.

MARSHALL, HENRY H.
Professional football player (retired). **Personal:** Born Aug 9, 1954, Broxton, GA. **Educ:** Univ of Missouri, attended. **Career:** Kansas City Chiefs, wide receiver, 1976-87.

MARSHALL, HERBERT A.
Educator (retired). **Personal:** Born Feb 17, 1916, Cleveland; married Hattie N Harrison. **Educ:** VA Union U, AB 1938; Case-Western Reserve U, MA 1939; The VA Coll, DA; Carnegie-Mellon U; Univ Ghana; Univ of So CA. **Career:** Norfolk Unit VA U, acting dir 1940-42; Norfolk Polytechnic Coll, dept head 1945-45; Case-Western Reserve U, research assoc 1946-48; VA Union U, visiting prof 1940-45; Hampton Inst, tchr corps 1969; instruction, dir 1956-68; Norfolk State Coll, dir & prof, professor emeritus, currently. **Orgs:** Pres VA Tchrs Assn 1960-62; co-chmn VA United Negro Coll Fund 1964-65; consultant Black Studies; mem Adult Educ Assn US & VA; YMCA; NEA; VA StateCouncil Higher Edn; evaluator So Assn 1972-; Assn Higher Edn; mem Pub Library Bd; Mayor's Youth Commn; Nat Achievement Week Proj; OIC. **Honors/Awds:** Distinguished serv award VA Tchrs Assn 1966f outstanding educator award 1969; leadership Award Lambda Omega; serv youth Award UMCA 1970; Omega man yr 1972; meritorious serv Award; silver beaver Award BSA; cit Award NCIE 1973; hon Award Student Govt Assn 1975; certificate appreciation Award AUS 1975; host & coordinator TV proj PRIDE 1972-. **Business Addr:** 2401 Corprew Ave, Norfolk, VA 23504.

MARSHALL, JONNIE CLANTON
Social worker (retired). **Personal:** Born Jul 24, 1932, Memphis, TN; married Kenneth Evans Marshall (deceased); children: James Kwame, Evan Keith Marshall. **Educ:** Morgan State Coll, BA 1956; Columbia Univ Sch of Social Work, MSW 1963; Fashion Inst of Tech, attended 1974-86. **Career:** Retreat for Living Hartford, psych aide 1958-59; YWCA New York City, group leader 1959-61; Grant Houses Comm Ctr, supervisor & dir 1964-67; Designer of Fine Millinery, 1980-; Bd of Educ Comm on Special Educ New York City, school social worker 1967-91. **Orgs:** Mem Alpha Kappa Alpha Sor Inc Tau Omega Chap 1954-; bd Friend of Children's Art Carnival 1968-; bd of dirs Harlem Comm Council Inc 1971-, Commonwealth Holding Co Inc 1971-; vice pres Natl Assoc of Milliners Dressmakers 1983-; instructor Harlem Fashion Inst New York 1983-; mem fashion show coord, pres Cottagers of Martha's Vineyard MA 1985-86. **Honors/Awds:** Fashions have appeared in numerous fashion shows at the Black Fashion Museum, Howard Univ Alumni Fashion Show, Cottagers, Salem United Methodist Church Affairs. **Home Addr:** 470 Lenox Ave, #17P, New York, NY 10037.

MARSHALL, JOSEPH EARL, JR.
Organization executive. **Personal:** Born May 12, 1947, Saint Louis, MO; son of Odessa and Joseph E. Marshall, Sr.; married; children: Malcolm, Sydney, Cassie. **Educ:** Univ of San Francisco, BA, political science and sociology; San Francisco State Univ, MA, education; Wright Institute, PhD, psychology. **Career:** San Francisco Unified School District, teacher, administrator; Omega Boys Club, executive director and co-founder, 1987-; KMEL-FM, host of "Street Soldiers" radio show, currently. **Orgs:** Harvard Univ, Community Violence Prevention Program, advisory board. **Honors/Awds:** National Crime Prevention Council, Spotlight on Crime Award; California State Assembly, Certificate of Recognition; MacArthur Foundation, Fellowship, 1994; Children's Defense Fund, Leadership Award, 1994; Essence Magazine, Essence Award, 1994; National Education Assn, Martin Luther King Jr Memorial Award, 1996; Congressional Freedom Works Award, 1997; Morehouse College, Candle in Community Service Award, 1998. **Special Achievements:** Author of Street Soldier: One Man's Struggle to Save a Generation, One Life at a Time, 1996. **Business Addr:** Executive Director, Omega Boys Club, PO Box 884463, San Francisco, CA 94188-4463, (415)826-8664.

MARSHALL, JULYETTE MATTHEWS
Organization executive. **Personal:** Born Oct 26, 1942, Port Arthur, TX; daughter of Dr & Mrs J B Matthews (deceased); married Robert James Marshall, Aug 17, 1966 (divorced); children: Nicole Yvette. **Educ:** Fisk University, BA, 1964. **Career:** Mayor's Office, asst dir special events, 1970-73; Governor's EEO Office, compliance officer, 1973-75; Univ of Texas, personnel officer, 1975-77; Houston Community Coll, personnel officer, 1977-78; Career Planning Ctr, counselor, 1978-80; Concepts Unlimited, dir, founder, 1980-90; Zamaani, culltural decor designer, owner, dir, 1990-. **Orgs:** POS, Chap 8, actor writer, 1969-70; TX Harlem Ren Comm, 1973-74; TX African Art Gallery, 1990-; TX Writer's Guild, 1995-; Houston Black Doll Assn, 1995-; Houston Culinary History Assn, 1995-. **Honors/Awds:** NAACP, Excellence Comm Svc, 1989, Comm Involvement, 1983; Friends of the Phoenix, Contribution to the Arts, 1987; Arts Comm of Austin, Special Arts Award, 1985; TX Writers Assn, Special Series for TX Newspaper, 1980; Fisk Univ, Outstanding Alumni for 25 Years, 1989. **Special Achievements:** Created a series of "Black History in Port Arthur Texas," 1980; assisted in an 18 part TV series on "Black History in Pt Arthur, TX," 1980-81; created and produced "Tribute to Twenty-Eight Black Women in PA," 1981-82; created and produced "Tribute to Twenty-Eight Black Women in Austin," 1984; developed and produced seminars for disabled persons in state of Texas, 1985; developed and designed 25th class reunion, Fisk Univ, 1989. **Business Addr:** Cultural Designer/Owner/Director, Zamaani, 2111 Hollyhall St, No 3019, Houston, TX 77054, (713)790-0012.

MARSHALL, LEONARD
Professional football player. **Personal:** Born Oct 22, 1961, Franklin, LA; son of Mr & Mrs L Marshall Sr; married Annette DiNapoli. **Educ:** LA State Univ, Sociology, Business Commun w/emphasis on Finance; Fairleigh Dickerson Univ, Teaneck, NJ. **Career:** New York Giants, 1983-93; New York Jets. **Orgs:** Natl sports chmn The Leukemia Soc in Westchester & Putnam Valley NY; work with Gary Carter on NY City Bd; work with March of Dimes, NAACP & Cystic Fibrosis. **Honors/Awds:** Three years as a starter, an all-Amer from LSU; MVP at LSU 1983; first team All-NFL 1985, first team NFC 1985; first team All-NFC 1986; second team All-NFL 1986; NFC Defensive Lineman of the Year by NFLPA 1985; mem Pro Bowl teams 1986, 1987; finished tied for tackles each season w/55. 57/ 51 consecutively; voted as a leader among defensive lines; co-author, The End of the Line. **Business Addr:** Professional Football Player, New York Jets, 1000 Fulton Ave, Hempstead, NY 11550.

MARSHALL, MARVIN
Professional football player. **Personal:** Born Jun 21, 1972; married LaScotia. **Educ:** South Carolina State, attended. **Career:** Tampa Bay Buccaneers, wide receiver, 1996-. **Business Addr:** Professional Football Player, Tampa Bay Buccaneers, One Buccaneer Place, Tampa, FL 33607, (813)870-2700.

MARSHALL, PATRICIA PRESCOTT
Educator, educational administrator. **Personal:** Born Apr 4, 1933, Houston, TX; daughter of Willie Mae Prescott and St Elmo Leonidas Prescott; married Cornelius Marshall, Aug 26, 1969. **Educ:** California State University, BA, 1955, MA, 1960; University of Southern California, EdD, 1980. **Career:** Los Angeles Unified School District, teacher, 1955-60; Berkeley Unified School District, teacher, 1960-63; Los Angeles Unified School District, training teacher, 1963-63, assistant principal, principal, 1966-79; Mount St Mary's College, instruction, part-time, 1972-76; Los Angeles Unified School District, program director, administrative coordinator, 1979-86, KCLS, station manager, assistant superintendent, 1986-. **Orgs:** National Museum of Women in the Arts, board of directors; Education Advisory of Los Angeles County Museum of Art, board of directors; YWCA of Greater Los Angeles, board of directors; UNICEF, board of directors; Academy of Television Arts and Science; American Women in Radio and Television; Women on Target; Pubic Broadcasting Service Advisory Committee, Elementary & Secondary Education. **Honors/Awds:** NAACP Legal Defense Fund, Black Women of Achievement, 1992; Phi Delta Kapa, Model Excellence Award, 1991; Children's Television International, William E Fagan, 1989; Los Angeles Black Media Coalition, Ida B Wells Achievement for Female Executives, 1986; Academy of TV Arts & Science, Emmy, 1985, 1988. **Business Addr:** Assistant Superintendent, Los Angeles Unified School District, 1601 W Temple St, Los Angeles, CA 90012, (213)625-6130.

MARSHALL, PAUL M.
Clergyman. **Personal:** Born Aug 17, 1947, Cleveland, OH. **Educ:** Univ of Dayton, BA 1969; Univ of St Michael's Coll, Toronto, ON, Canada. **Career:** Soc of Mary, religious bro; Formation Prog, Cincinnati Province, Soc of Mary, regional coord, 1972-74; Dayton Urban Corps City of Dayton, dir, 1970-73; Natl Urban Corps Assn, regional coord, 1972-73. **Orgs:** Bd dir, Natl Urban Corps Assn, 1971-73; bd dir Pub Serv Internship Programs, 1972-73; dir, bd of youth, Screen Printing Co, 1972-73; Social Action Commn, Archdiocese of Cincinnati, mem 1971-73, vice chmn 1973; chmn, Dayton Black Catholic Caucus, 1971-73; vice chmn, Archdiocese of Cincinnati Black Catholic Caucus, 1972-73; Natl Black Catholic Clergy Caucus, mem 1970-75, bd dir 1972; Natl Comm on Urban Ministry, Notre Dame. **Business Addr:** 95 St Joseph St, Toronto, ON, Canada.

MARSHALL, PAULE BURKE
Author. **Personal:** Born Apr 9, 1929, Brooklyn, NY; daughter of Ada Clement Burke and Samuel Burke; divorced 1963; children (previous marriage): Evan. **Educ:** Brooklyn Coll (now of City Univ of New York), BA, 1953; Hunter Coll, 1955. **Career:** Our World magazine, staff writer, 1953-56; Yale Univ, lecturer in creative writing, beginning 1970; Virginia Commonwealth Univ, prof of English, currently. **Honors/Awds:** Guugenheim fellow, 1960; Rosen Award, Natl Inst Arts and Letters, 1962; Before Columbus Foundn Amer Book Award, 1984; author of Brown Girl,Brownstones, Random House, 1959, Soul Clap Hands and Sing, Atheneum, 1961, The Chosen Place, The Timeless People, Harcourt, 1969, Praisesong for the Widow, Putnam, 1983, Reena and Other STories, Feminist Press, 1983; author of teleplay based on Brown Girl, Brownstones, 1960.

MARSHALL, PLURIA W., SR.
Association executive, photographer. **Personal:** Born Oct 19, 1937, Houston, TX; married Corbin Carmen; children: Pluria Jr, Mishka, Jason, Natalie, Christopher. **Educ:** Texas Southern University. **Career:** Professional photographer; Operation Breadbasket of TX, exec dir 5 years; responsible for proj that produced nation's first Black franchise in Burger King Corp; Natl Black Media Coalition, natl organizer, treasurer, chairman 1975-. **Orgs:** TX State Adv Com, US Commn on Civil Rights; Natl Black Media Coalition. **Honors/Awds:** Outstanding Ex-student Award, TX So Univ, 1974; Community Service Award, Natl Assn of Mkt Developers, 1973; Marketeer of Yr Award, Houston Chap NAMD, 1974; Community Service Award, Omega Psi Phi, Houston Chap, 1973; others. **Military Serv:** USAF E-3 1956-60. **Business Addr:** KHRN-FM, 219 Main N. #600, Bryan, TX 77803.

MARSHALL, PLURIA WILLIAM, JR.
Broadcasting company executive. **Personal:** Born Jan 17, 1962. **Educ:** Clark Coll, Atlanta, GA, BS, l984. **Career:** KTRE-TV, Lufkin, TX, sales/marketing, l982, sales/accounting exec, l983; WTBS/Turner Broadcasting, Atlanta, GA, research, 1982-83; WLBT-TV, Jackson, MS, Mgmt devel/sales, 1983-84; WLBM-TV30, Meridan, MS, station mgr/sales mgr, l985-86, vice pres/ gen mgr, beginning 1986; KHRN-FM, general manager, currently. **Orgs:** Natl Black Media Coalition; Natl Assn of Broadcaster; Natl Assn of TV Programming Execs.

MARSHALL, REESE
Attorney. **Personal:** Born Sep 3, 1942, Fort Lauderdale, FL; married Leonora Griffin; children: Dara Isabelle, Kemba Lee, Reese Evans. **Educ:** Morgan State Coll, BA 1963; Howard Univ-Law, LLB 1966. **Career:** Jacksonville Urban League, chrmn; FL Comm on Human Relations, chrmn; FL Chapter NBA, pres; Regnl Brd of Dir-MBA, mem; Johnson & Marshall, prtnr 1971-79; Reese Marshall Law Office, attorney, 1979-. **Orgs:** Mem Kappa Alpha Psi Frat, Inc. **Home Addr:** 9100 Westlake Circle, Jacksonville, FL 32208. **Business Addr:** Attorney, 214 E Ashley St, Jacksonville, FL 32202, (904)354-8429.

MARSHALL, THURGOOD, JR.
Federal official. **Personal:** Born Aug 12, 1956, New York, NY; son of Cecilia S Marshall and Thurgood Marshall; married Colleen P Mahoney, Sep 24, 1983; children: Thurgood William III, Edward Patrick. **Educ:** Univ of Virginia, BA, 1978; Univ of Virginia School of Law, JD, 1981. **Career:** Judge Barrington D Parker, law clerk, 1981-83; Kaye Scholer Fierman Hays & Handler, attorney, 1983-85; Senator Albert Gore Jr, counsel & staff dir, 1985-87, deputy campaign mgr, 1987-88; Senate Judiciary Committee, Senator Edward M Kennedy, counsel, 1988-92; Clinton-Gore Campaign, Senator Al Gore Traveling Staff, senior policy advisor, 1992; Office of the vp, deputy counsel, director of legislative affairs, 1993-97; White House, asst to president Clinton, Cabinet secretary, 1997-. **Orgs:** Amer Bar Assn; District of Columbia Bar; Bars of the US District Court for the District of Columbia and the Second Circuit Court of Appeals; Commission for the Advancement of Policy Affecting the Disadvantaed, 1978-80; bd mem, Federal Bar Assn, DC Chapter, 1984-86; American Council of Young Political Leaders, board member; Supreme Court Historical Society, bd of trustees. **Honors/Awds:** University of Virginia Student Legal Forum, president, 1980-81; Lile Moot Court Competition, semifinalist, 1981. **Special Achievements:** Co-author: The Sony Betamax Case, Computers & The Law, 1984; contributing editor, The Nicaragua Elections: A Challenge of Democracy, 1989. **Business Addr:** Cabinet Secretary/Asst to the President, The White House, 1600 Pennsylvania Ave, Washington, DC 20510.

MARSHALL, TIMOTHY H.
Consultant, ethnomusicologist. **Personal:** Born Dec 8, 1949, Aiken Co, SC. **Educ:** Lone Mtn Coll San Francisco, BA 1974; Lone Mtn Coll San Francisco, Grad Studies. **Career:** Nat United Com to free Angela Davis & all Pol Prisoners Communications Fund raising, natl staff mem 1971-72; The Black Scholar Speakers Bureau, natl dir; Black World Foundation The Black Scholar, promotional dir 1973-74; Comm Lieson Cinema Lone Mountain Coll San Francisco, promotional coord 1974-. **Orgs:** Creator-director "In Concert for Angela" 1972; mem Black Expo Concert Prod Staff 1972; prof musician Episcopal Diocese Augusta, GA 1970-71; musical dir "Jr League Follies" Extravaganza 1970; mem Black World Foundation; Afro-Am Music Opportunites Assn; Nat Alliance Against Racist & Pol Repression; Inst BlackWorld; African-Am Historical & Cultural Soc; founder & pres Black Students Union Agusta Coll 1968-69; Nat Coordinator Elayne Jones Defense Com; founding mem pres & min affairs Progressive Black Organization 1967-70. **Honors/Awds:** Exclusive interview with James Baldwin France 1973; published The Blak Scholar Black History Issue 1974; Investigative Research Berlin 1973; silver ring presented by Loatian Delegation; fraternal pin deleg Guinea Bissau Africa 1973; outstanding service trophy Laney HS Agusta, GA 1968; Omega Psi Phi Scholarship 1967; Augusta Chronical Newspaper Gold Plaque 1966-67. **Business Addr:** Box 6285, C/o KEAL, San Francisco, CA 94101.

MARSHALL, TOM, SR.
Law enforcement official. **Personal:** Born Jan 5, 1927, Memphis, TN; son of Margaret Conley Marshall (deceased) and Robert Marshall (deceased); married Hazel James Marshall, Mar 29, 1974; children: Thomas Jr, Alan, Robert. **Career:** Memphis Police Dept, deputy chief, 1951-84; Shelby County Sheriff's Dept, deputy chief, 1986-. **Business Addr:** Deputy Chief, Shelby County Sheriff's Dept, 201 Poplar Ave, 9th Floor, Room 926, Memphis, TN 38103.

MARSHALL, WARREN
Association executive. **Personal:** Born Mar 7, 1922, Mobile City, AL; married Genevieve L Garner; children: Braden, Cynthia, Verda. **Educ:** Psychol Long Isl Univ Brooklyn, BS 1952; Columbia U, MA 1963; Columbia Univ Tchrs Coll, Attending. **Career:** City School Dist of NY; bd of edn; Bureau for child with retarded mental devel, supvr; USAF Rome & NY, civ 1943; US Maritime Serv, 1943-46; Natl Maritime Union CIO, 1942-65; US Post Office, 1948, 1959-62; Bd of Educ Newark, teacher 1956-58; Bd of Educ Englewood, NJ, teacher 1958-59; Bd of NY, teacher 1959-66; Methodist Church Manokin, MD, pastor 1956; E Shore Chs of Meth Ch, other. **Orgs:** Prof mem Assn for CRMD; Assn for Help of Retarded Child; United Fedn of Tchrs; NY United Tchrs; NEA; AFT; AFL-CIO 1947-57; educ consult pres Borough of Manhattan; St John #29 F & AM; pres Caribbean Voca Educ Fudn Inc; reg dir reg 2 Assn for Study of Afro-am Life & Hist; educ consult West Educ Sym Orch. **Honors/Awds:** Eli Tractenberg Award UFT 1964; Smal-

lheiser Award UFT 1966; spl hon Award NY Br Assn for Study of Afro-am Life & Hist; spl serv Award SW Harlem Addict Serv Agcy; sev Award Dist 20k1 Kings & Queens of Emp State Lions. **Military Serv:** AUS pfc psy tech 1946-47. **Business Addr:** 65 Court St, Brooklyn, NY.

MARSHALL, WILBER BUDDYHIA
Professional football player. **Personal:** Born Apr 18, 1962, Titusville, FL. **Educ:** Univ of Florida, attended. **Career:** Linebacker: Chicago Bears, 1984-87; Washington Redskins, 1988-. **Honors/Awds:** Lombardi Awd Finalist (only junior among 12 finalists); first team All-American, AP, UPI, NEA, Football Coaches, Walter Camp; selected 1st team All-Amer by Parade Mag & Natl HS Athletic Coaches; All-Southern Player-of-the-Year & Acad All-Amer as senior; played in Pro Bowl, 1986, 1987.

MARSHALL, WILFRED L.
Government official. **Personal:** Born Dec 11, 1935, Annemanie, AL; son of Pollye Ross Marshall and Felix Marshall; married Emma Jean Gregory Marshall, Mar 18, 1967; children: Michael Gregory. **Educ:** Tuskegee University, Tuskegee AL, BS, 1958; California State Univ, Los Angeles, CA, MS, 1969. **Career:** Veterans Administration, Los Angeles CA, assistant director, recreation therapy, 1961-69; NASA-WSO, Los Angeles, CA, public affairs officer presidential appointment, 1967-69; Economic Development, Admin Dept of Commerce, Los Angeles CA, program manager, 1969-81; City of Los Angeles, Mayors Office, Los Angeles, CA, special assistant to Mayor Tom Bradley, director business & ecomonic development, 1981-. **Orgs:** Member, Critical Urban Affairs Committee, 1967-69; vice president, California Therapeutic Recreation Society, 1964-66; member/board of directors, CALED, 1983-86, 1991-; mem board of directors, Through Children Eyes; mem board of directors, The Chapman Fund; mem, board of directors, Pan-African-American Organization. **Military Serv:** US Army, Sp-4, 1959-61.

MARSHALL, WILLIAM HORACE
Actor. **Personal:** Born Aug 1924, Gary, IN; son of Thelma Edwards Marshall and Vereen Marion Marshall; children: Claude, Malcolm, Gina, Tariq. **Educ:** Chicago Art Inst; Art Students League NY; Amer Theatre Wing NY; Observer Actors Studio NY; Master Class Lee Strasberg UCLA; studied mime with Etienne Descroux; studied voice with J Scott Kennedy, Abby Mitchell, Emma Otero, Gladys Lee & Alan Greene in NY, Jeanne Filon in Paris, & Robert Sellon in Los Angeles; studied French language & civilization at the Alliance Francaise in Paris; studied blues with Hazel Scott; Governors State Univ IL, BA 1978; Golden State Univ CA, PhD Theatre Arts 1983. **Career:** Busboy; steelworker; commercial artist; longshoreman; Harlem YMCA, prog dir; appeared in numerous stages plays including Carmen Jones, Lost in the Stars, Peter Pan, The Green Pastures, Oedipus Rex, Othello, Time To Go, Toys In the Attic, The Bear & the Marriage Proposal, When We Dead Awaken; numerous motion pictures including Lydia Bailey, Demetrius & the Gladiators, Shelia; TV guest star include Bonanza, Rawhide, Ben Casey, Star Trek, Tarzan; in London The Green Pastures (television), Interpol, the Magic Ring; directed 1st English language production of The Tragedy of King Christophe (of Haiti) 1970; CA State Northridge Smithsonian Inst, A Ballad for Americans as a tribute to Paul Robeson 1986; Enter Frederick Douglass, SmithsonianInst (one man 2 act play with spirituals); translated e Cesaires, The Tragedy of King Christophe (of Haiti); directed Oedipus Rex and In White America. **Honors/Awds:** Composer Gospel & Poetry; US Tour with Mahalia Jackson 1966; Poetry & Prose of Black Writers with UGMAA Watts Music Group at Univ CA LA 1968; Benjamin J Hooks Distinguished Achievement Award NAACP 1983; Roy Wilkins Award NAACP 1983; Hon Degree of Doctor of Human Serv Univ Without Walls 1984. **Business Addr:** Actor, Teacher, Lecturer, Devel of Black Heritage Drama, 11351 Dronfield Ave, Pacoima, CA 91331.

MARSHALL-WALKER, DENISE ELIZABETH
Teacher consultant. **Personal:** Born Oct 27, 1952, Detroit, MI; daughter of Alice Elizabeth Stevenson Middlebrooks and Donald Alexander Webb; married Donald Lawrence Marshall (divorced 1982); children: Dawn Elizabeth Marshall. **Educ:** Central State Univ, Wilberforce, OH, BA, 1974; Univ of Detroit, Detroit, MI, MA, 1976, 1978. **Career:** Detroit Public Schools, Detroit, MI, teacher, 1974-78, teacher consultant, 1978-. **Orgs:** Mem, Alpha Kappa Alpha Sorority, 1971-; chairperson of sr citizens program, Alpha Kappa Alpha Sorority, 1978-82; pres, Alpha Kappa Alpha Sorority, Beta Chapter, 1972-74; pres of Omega Wives, Omega Psi Phi Fraternity, Nu Omega Chapter, 1988-; pres of Detroit Chapter, Natl Coalition of 100 Black Women, 1989-; troop leader, Girl Scouts of Metro Detroit, 1988-. **Honors/Awds:** Outstanding Coalition Mem, Natl Coalition of 100 Black Women, Detroit, 1989; Outstanding Social Graces Instructor, Finishing Touches, Etc Charm School, 1988. **Home Addr:** 18905 Marlowe, Detroit, MI 48235.

MARSHBURN, EVERETT LEE
Television executive. **Personal:** Born Jan 4, 1948, Baltimore, MD; son of Theresa G. Marshburn and William A. Hall. **Educ:** Morgan State University, Baltimore, MD, BA, 1976. **Career:** Maryland Public TV, Owings Mills, MD, director regional productions begin 1993, vice pres broadcast productions, currently. **Orgs:** Member, Maryland Humanities Council, 1987-; member, Black Mental Health Alliance, 1990-; charter member, Beta Omega Epsilon Fraternity, Inc, 1965-; member, National Association of Black Journalists, 1985-. **Honors/Awds:** Alfred I. Dupont Award, Columbia School of Journalism, 1989; Frederick Douglass Award, National Association of Black Journalists, 1990; John R. Haney Award, SECA Award, 1990. **Business Addr:** Vice President, Broadcast Productions, Maryland Public TV, 11767 Owings Mills Blvd, Owings Mills, MD 21117.

MARTIN, ALBERT LEE
Professional baseball player. **Personal:** Born Nov 24, 1967, West Covina, CA. **Educ:** Southern California. **Career:** Pittsburgh Pirates, outfielder, 1992-. **Business Addr:** Professional Baseball Player, Pittsburgh Pirates, PO Box 7000, Pittsburgh, PA 15212, (412)323-5000.

MARTIN, AMON ACHILLES, JR.
Dentist. **Personal:** Born May 21, 1940, Anderson, SC; married Brenda Watts; children: Jocelyn, Amon III, Theodore. **Educ:** Fisk Univ, BA; Howard Univ, DDS. **Career:** Dentist, currently. **Orgs:** Amer Dental Assn, Natl Dental Assn, Palmetto Medical Dental & Pharmaceutical Assn, Omega Psi Phi Inc; past pres, Anderson Dental Soc; Seneca Advisory Board, Wachovia Bank; bd of visitors, Clemson Univ 1984-86; Sigma Pi Phi. **Honors/Awds:** International College of Dentists, Fellow. **Military Serv:** US Air Force, lt colonel, retired; Primary Duty LO of the Year, 1991. **Business Addr:** Dentist, 208 N Walnut, Seneca, SC 29678.

MARTIN, ANGELA M. COKER
Government professional. **Personal:** Born Jun 2, 1953, Baltimore, MD. **Educ:** Morgan State Univ, BS 1975; The OH State Univ, MS 1976; Univ of Dayton, MBA 1984. **Career:** Enoch Pratt Library, traveling info/retrieval agent 1977-78; Rehab Serv Commn, vocational rehab counselor 1979-80, personnel officer 1980-83, EEO Supvr, 1983-85; Mass Transit Admin, EEO officer 1986-. **Orgs:** Acting pres 1982-83, vice pres programs 1983-84 Amer Soc for Personnel Admin (Franklin Univ Chapt) 1980-86; mem Assoc of MBA Execs 1984-86; asst sec Conf of Minority Transportation Officials 1986-87; mem Natl Black MBA Assoc 1986-87, NAACP 1986-87. **Honors/Awds:** Departmental Honor Scholar Morgan State Univ 1974-75; Minority Master's Fellowship OH State Univ 1975-76.

MARTIN, ANNIE B.
Association executive. **Personal:** Born Dec 20, 1925, South Carolina. **Educ:** Allen Univ Columbia, SC, BA; NY U, MSW; Cornell Rutgers PA State U, Cert Labor Edn. **Career:** NY State Dept Labor, asst indsl commr 1972-; Cornell U, sr extension asso; Fordham U, asst adjunct prof; ER Squibb & Sons Brooklyn, chem. **Orgs:** Mem Intl Assn Personnel Employment Security; New York City Guidance Adv Coun; Am Assn Univ Women; chmn NY State Advisory Coun Voc Edn; Soroptimist; charter mem 1st vice pres Black Trade Unionists Ldrship Com New York City Cent Labor Coun AFL-CIO; bd dirs NY Lung Assn; exec bd New York City Cent Labor Council AFL-CIO; life mem Nat Coun Negro Women; NAACP; Bethel AME Ch. **Honors/Awds:** Comm serv award New York City Cent Labor Coun 1961; dist serv award 1971; woman of yr NY Brn NAACP 1976; award of merit Black Trade Unionists Ldrshp Com 1977; NY City Central Labor Cncl AFL-CIO; awards in Black 1973; woman of yr award Priv Voc Schs 1973. **Business Addr:** Rm 7384, 2 World Trade Cntr, New York, NY 10047.

MARTIN, ARNOLD LEE, JR.
Health services administrator. **Personal:** Born Jan 10, 1939, Hartford, CT; married Mary Remona Garner; children: Zena Monique, Arnold Lee III. **Educ:** Attended, FBI Natl Acad 1981; New Hampshire Coll, BS 1983. **Career:** Hartford Police Dept, chief's advisor 1962-83; WTIC 1080 Corp, chmn adv comm 1974-82; American Red Cross Hartford, bd of dirs 1975-84, exec dir 1986-. **Orgs:** Chmn Project 90 US Navy Recruiting Team 1974-75; bd dir NAACP 1975; 1st vice pres CT Assoc Police Comm Rel Off 1979-81; mem Hartford Hosp Public Relations Bd 1981-83; 1st vice pres West Hartford Lions Club 1982; mem Urban League 1982; rhetoricos Sigma Pi Phi Frat 1985-; pres Alpha Phi Alpha Frat 1986-. **Honors/Awds:** Hartford Man of the Month CT Mutual Life Ins Co 1974; Outstanding Serv Awd march of Dimes 1977; US Air Force Commendation Medal Westover AFB 1980; Lions Intl Dist Gov Serv Awd 1980; Director's Awd FBI Natl Academy 1981; Chairman's Awd Amer Red Cross 1984; Hartford Guardians Outstanding Community Serv Awd 1985. **Military Serv:** AUS Reserve sgt 1st class 3 yrs; Non-Commissioned Officers Achievement Ribbon 1987. **Home Addr:** 626 Park Rd, West Hartford, CT 06107.

MARTIN, BARBARA ANITA. **See BLACKMON, BARBARA ANITA.**

MARTIN, BARON H.
Judge, attorney. **Personal:** Born Sep 14, 1926, Boston; married. **Educ:** Suffolk U, AA BA JD; Univ of Chicago Exec Mgmt Training, 1972. **Career:** Wareham Dist Ct, judge; Comm of MA, former spl justice; Comm of MA, spl asst atty gen 1972; asst gen counsel 1973; sr atty; 1970; MA Bay Transp Authority, clerk 1951; MA Bay Transp Authority, atty 1958. **Orgs:** Mem MA Bar Assn; Am Bar Assn; MA Trial Lawyers; Am Judges Assn; Admitted to US Dist Ct 1959; US Supreme Ct 1966f Am Jud Soc; Intl Acad Law & Sci; mem Urban League; NAACP; chmn Dem Ward Com 1950-64; alternate delegate Dem Nat Conv 1968. **Honors/Awds:** Recip Alpha Phi Alpha Sigma Chtp Outstanding Achievement 1948. **Business Addr:** Wareham Dist Court, Wareham, MA 02571.

MARTIN, BASIL DOUGLAS
Oral surgeon. **Personal:** Born Oct 18, 1941, Roanoke, VA; son of Beulah Martin and Basil Martin; married Geneva Gail Allen; children: Basil D Jr, Shoan Beaufort Orell. **Educ:** Central State Univ, BS 1963; Meharry Medical Coll, DDS 1969; Baltimore City Hospitals, Johns Hopkins Univ, Univ of MD, Certificate Oral Surgery; New York Univ, Certificate Orthodontics. **Career:** Private practice, doctor of dental surgery, currently. **Orgs:** Worshipful master Mason 32nd F&AM of PA 1979-87; bd mem YMCA 1979-86; consistory 32nd Position Sublime Prince Pittsburgh St Cyprian #4 1982-87; shriner Pittsburgh Sahara #2 1982-87; mem Chamber of Commerce 1987; Omega Psi Phi Fraternity 1961. **Honors/Awds:** Publication "The Canadian Geese - Spirocete-Patuxent," Dept of Int 1963-65; clinical instructor, Pittsburgh Univ School of Dental Medicine 1974-75.

MARTIN, BERTHA M.
Dentist. **Personal:** Born Apr 5, 1926, Pulaski, TN; daughter of Fannie Martin Jones (deceased); divorced; children: Beryl (deceased). **Educ:** Howard Univ, BS 1947, DDS 1951; Holyoke Hosp, Internship 1951-52; Univ of MI, Cert, Pediatric Dentistry 1955-56. **Career:** Berkley, CA, private practice 1959-62; Los Angeles, CA, dental consultant 1963-66; Washington, DC, pediatric dentist 1966-97. **Orgs:** Amer Dental Assn; Amer Acad of Pediatric Dentistry; Alpha Kappa Alpha Sor; DC Dental Society; Robert T Freeman Dental Society; Amer Society of Dentistry for Children; St Mark's Church Vestry; bd of trustees, Dean Junior College, Franklin Massachusetts 1988-91; bd of advisors, Burgundy Farm Country Day School, Alexandria, Virginia, 1987-93. **Home Addr:** 3547 Texas Ave SE, Washington, DC 20020.

MARTIN, BLANCHE
Dentist. **Personal:** Born Jan 16, 1937, Millhaven, GA; divorced; children: Gary, Steven, Michael. **Educ:** MI St U, BS 1959; Univ of Detroit, DDS 1967. **Career:** Self Emp, dentist. **Orgs:** Mem MI St Univ bd of trsts 1969-76, 77-84; chmn bd 1975-76; mem Am Den Assn; MI Den Assn; Cen Dist Den Asso 1969-76 & 77-84; past mem River Rouge Youth Commn; mem bd of deacons Pentecostal Miss Baptist Ch; Omicron Kappa Upsilon Nat Den Hon 1967. **Honors/Awds:** Recpt award for excel in Gen Dent. **Business Addr:** 201 1/2 E Grand River, East Lansing, MI 48823.

MARTIN, CARL E.
Government official. **Personal:** Born Feb 14, 1931, Birmingham, AL; married Patricia; children: Ennis, Joel, Carla, Dana. **Educ:** Miles Coll, BA 1953; Pepperdine U, MPA 1973; LA Coll of Law, JD 1978. **Career:** LA Co Human Relat Commn, exec dir; CA Youth Auth, grp supr; CA Youth Auth, parole agt; LA Co Probation Dept, sr dep prof ofcr; LA Inglewood Culver City Duarte Sch Dist, cons; Univ of So CA UCLA CA State Univ Sys, cons. **Orgs:** Bd of dirs Econ & Youth Opptys Agy; pres Fedn of Black History & Arts Inc; bd of dir HELM Schlrshp Found; bd of dir RAKESTRAW Educ & Comm Ctr Wesley United Meth Ch; mem Employ Devel Com LA Urban League; bd of dir Westminster Neighborhood Assn. **Honors/Awds:** Num awards from orgns in Grtr LA areas. **Military Serv:** AUS sp-4 1953-55. **Business Addr:** 320 W Temple St, 1184 Hall of Records, Los Angeles, CA 90012.

MARTIN, CAROL (FRANCES MARTIN)
Reporter. **Personal:** Born Jul 15, 1948, Detroit, MI. **Educ:** Wayne State U, BA 1970. **Career:** WCBS-TV, NY, gen assignment news correspondent 1975-; WMAL-TV, Washington, DC, gen assignment reporter 1973-75; Detroit Free Press, ed features dept, feature writer 1971-73; WWJ-TV, Detroit, dept asst public affairs 1970-71. **Orgs:** Mem Amer Fed of TV & Radio Artists; US Sen & House of Representatives Radio/TV Gallery; mem adv bd Natl Child Day Care Assn 1974-75. **Honors/Awds:** Wayne State Univ Scholarship for Academic Achievement 1966-70. **Business Addr:** C/O WCBS-TV, 524 W 57th St, New York, NY 10019.

MARTIN, CAROLYN ANN
Educator. **Personal:** Born Aug 14, 1943, Versailles, MO. **Educ:** Lincoln Univ of MO, BS Phys Ed, Psych 1968; CA State Polytech Univ Pomona, MS 1974; Univ of CA Riverside, grad courses 1969-72; Pepperdine Univ, Los Angeles, CA, 1984-. **Career:** Lincoln Univ of MO Dept of Phys Ed, teaching asst 1964-68; Perris High School Dist, instructor phys ed 1968-78,

phys ed teacher, nursing women's athletic dir 1968-74; Perris Jr HS, chmn phys ed 1970-74; CA State Univ Summer Upward Bound, recreation coord 1976; San Bernardino HS head coach women's varsity softball 1981-84; CA State Univ Univ, associate prof phys ed, beginning 1974, prof of phys ed, currently. **Orgs:** Amer Alliance of Health; CA Teachers Assn; pres, CA Faculty Assn; Natl Bowling Council, Natl Assn for Sport & Phys Ed, Natl Assn of Girls & Womens Sports, CA Assn of Black Faculty & Staff; pres, CA Assn Health Phys Ed Recreation & Dance 1973-74, 1979-80; sec Delta Kappa Gamma; selected by State School Supt Wilson Riles to serve as mem of State Task Force on Athletic Injuries 1976-77; arbitrator BBB; pres 3 Sports Inc 1977-; proj ace coord, Amer Alliance for Health Phys Ed Rec & Dance 1979; Natl Girls & Womens Speedball Guide Comm 1980-82; chmn NatlGirls & Womens Sports Speedball Guide Comm 1982-84; bd mem San Bernardino Sexual Assault Serv Ctr 1983-84; mem Joint Comm of Amer Assoc of Leisure & Rec, Amer Alliance for Health Phys Ed Rec & Dance, Natl Assessment of Elem School Playgrounds85. **Honors/Awds:** Publ Workbook, Fundamentals of Basketball Officiating 1978, Games Contests & Relays 1981, Teaching Softball 1985; Softball Coach of the Year Perris HS 1970; Teacher of the Year 1973; Perris Jr HS Teacher of the Year 1973; Teacher's Advocate Awd San Bernardino Teachers Assoc 1974; Kiwanis Intl of San Bernardino Cert of Appreciation 1976; Mini Grant Awd CA State Univ Comm on Improvement of & Innovations in Ed 1978, 1980; San Bernardino Affirm Action Fac Devel Awd State Univ 1981; rsch "The Personality Characteristics of Black Female HS Athletes"; "Teaching Blind Students to Bow" 1981-83; editor Natl Girls & Womens Sports Speedball Rules Publ 1982-84; "Playing the Net Aggresively" 1979. **Business Addr:** Professor of Physical Ed, California State Univ, 5500 University Pkwy, San Bernardino, CA 92407.

MARTIN, CHARLES EDWARD, SR.
Association executive. **Personal:** Born Aug 3, 1943, Jackson, TN; son of Lavinia Martin and James Martin; married Paricia Ann Johnson; children: Charles Jr, Jenell, Rodrick. **Educ:** Ball State Univ Muncie, BS Social Science, 1967; Indiana Univ South Bend, 30 hrs towards MS. **Career:** YMCA Met S Bend, exec dir 1972-; YMCA Met S Bend, youth dir 1970-72; S Bend Com Sch Corp, teacher coach 1967-70. **Orgs:** Member, Kiwanis Club of South Bend; member, Indiana Black Expo Scholarship Committee; member, Parkview Juvenile Diversion Advisory Board; board of directors, Youth Facilities, Inc; founder/president, Black Community Scholarship Fund, Inc; admissions advisory council member, Ball State University; member, Kappa Alpha Psi National Fraternity; board of directors, South Bend School Boosters. **Honors/Awds:** Presented the Key to the City of South Bend, 1979, 1990; Sagamore of the Wabash Award, 1987, 1990; Outstanding Service to Youth Award, US Senator Richard Luger; Distinguished Alumni Award, Outstanding Black Alumnus Award, Ball State University; Outstanding Leadership Award, John Adams High School Cultural Awareness Society; Lewis Hine Award, National Child Labor Committee in New York; Community Service Award, Urban League of St Joseph County; Prince Hall Lodge Freedom Award; Martin Luther King Jr Community Service Award, LaSalle High School Black Culture Society; Exemplar Award, Community Education Roundtable of South Bend. **Business Addr:** Executive Dir, Urban Youth Services, YMCA of Michiana, South Bend, IN 46615.

MARTIN, CHARLES HOWARD
Attorney. **Personal:** Born Nov 13, 1952, Washington, DC; son of John & Hestlene. **Educ:** Harvard College, BA, 1974; University of California, Berkeley, JD, 1977. **Career:** State of Florida, assistant attorney general, 1982-84; Florida State University, assistant professor of law, 1984-85; Villanova University, assistant professor of law, 1985-87; Sallie Mae, assistant general counsel, 1987-. **Business Addr:** Assistant General Counsel, Student Loan Marketing Association, 1050 Thomas Jefferson St, NW, Washington, DC 20007, (202)298-3154.

MARTIN, CHARLES WESLEY
Insurance company executive. **Personal:** Born Apr 23, 1937, Middlesboro, KY; son of Allen & Cora Martin; married Ella K Martin, May 1, 1972; children: Tracy M Cargo, Charla M Sturdivant, Katheryn & Angela Martin. **Educ:** Kentucky State Univ, 1956-60. **Career:** Proctor & Gamble Co, sales rep, 1970-71; Eastern Life Zone, vp, 1981-82; Allstate Insurance Co, sales agent, 1971-72, sales management, 1972-80, reg vp, Denver, CO, 1982-86, reg vp Southern CA, 1986-94, vp, sales corp office, 1995-. **Orgs:** Zion Baptist, Denver, CO, bd of trustees, bd of deacons, 1984-86; Urban League, Orange County, CA, bd, 1991-94; Prison Fellowship Ministry, Inland Empire, Orange Cty, CA, 1992-94; CA Ins Commissioners, anti discrimination task force, 1993-94; Kappa Alpha Psi Fraternity; NAACP, 1st vp, Waukegan, IL chapter, 1967; Shaker Hts Comm Church Christ, Ohio, bd of trustees, 1980-81; Second Baptist Church, Santa Ana, CA, bd of trustees, 1988-91. **Honors/Awds:** Governor Commonwealth of Kentucky, Kentucky Colonel, 1979; YMCA of Metropolitan Chicago, Black Achievers of Industry, 1976. **Military Serv:** US Navy, E6, 1960-70; Navy Unit Commendation Award, Navy Achievement Award.

MARTIN, CHRISTOPHER (PLAY)
Actor, vocalist. **Career:** Kid n Play, group member, currently; actor, movies include: House Party, 1990; House Party 2, 1991; Class Act, 1992. **Business Addr:** Singer, Kid n Play, c/o Select Recording Co, 16 W 22nd St, New York, NY 10010, (212)691-1200.

MARTIN, CLARENCE L.
Attorney. **Personal:** Born Sep 5, Baxley, GA; married Annie D; children: Anthony L, Bernard E. **Educ:** Savannah St Coll, BS (cum laude) 1970; Emory U,; Notre Dame Law Sch, 1973. **Career:** City of Savannah, asst city atty, judge pro temporo recorders court; C & S Bank; SS Kresge Co; Hill, Jones & Farrington; Whitcomb & Keller Mortgage Co; Martin, Thomas & Bass PC, attorney. **Orgs:** Mem Savannah, Georgia & Amer Bar Assocs; mem NAACP; Operation Push. **Honors/Awds:** Martin Luther King Fellow Woodrow Wilson Fnd. **Military Serv:** USAF staff sgt 1962-67. **Business Addr:** Attorney, Martin, Thomas & Bass PC, 109 W Liberty St, Savannah, GA 31402.

MARTIN, CORNELIUS A.
Auto dealer. **Career:** Martin Olsmobile-Cadillac-Subaru-Isuzu, Bowling Green, KY, chief exec, 1985-91; Saturn Corp, auto dealer, 1991-. **Business Addr:** Auto Dealer, Saturn Automobile Dealership, 995 Miamisburg Centerville Rd, Dayton, OH 45459.

MARTIN, CORTEZ HEZEKIAH
Educator. **Personal:** Born Jul 25, Jacksonville, FL; daughter of Julius Neals Hezekiah (deceased) and Sam Hezekiah (deceased); married John Timothy Martin; children: Sonijia, Latacha. **Educ:** Tenn A&I Univ, BS 1955, MS 1957; Howard Univ, MSW 1980, Doctor of Social Work 1984. **Career:** 18th Ave Comm Center, program dir 1955-57; Tenn A&I State Univ, instructor, social work 1956-57; Edward Waters Coll, instructor, soc sci; Memphis City Schools, teacher, counselor, school social worker 1959-78; Comm Action Agency, eval coord, program dir 1967-70; US Dept of Agriculture, student intern, co-project mgr 1978-81; Howard Univ Sch of Soc Work, grad assist 1981-82; Congressman Harold E Ford, staff assist 1982-83; US Dept Health & Human Svcs, evaluator/reviewer 1984; Lemoyne-Owen Coll, assoc prof of rsch social sci dept, dir, social work program, 1989-. **Orgs:** Member Memphis Ed Assn 1960-78; member Natl Ed Assn 1960-78; member Tenn Ed Assn 1960-78; member Alpha Kappa Alpha Sorority 1972-; treasurer (Grad Chapter Tenn A&I Univ) 1972-74; Natl Assn of Social Workers 1978-; Natl Assn of Black Social Workers 1978-; Ford's Foundation Assn 1983-; bd of dirs, Porter Leath Children's Center, 1984-; res team, Free-the-Children; Alpha Kappa Alpha Soroity, historian, 1989-. **Honors/Awds:** Trustee Scholarship Award Howard Univ 1978-82; The Dean's List Honor Society Howard Univ 1978-82; Natl Institute of Mental Health Doctoral Training Grant 1981-82; Alumni Student Doctoral Rep Committee, Howard Univ 1981; Community Services Award, St Joseph's Hospital, 1988; editorial bd, Social Science Assn, 1988; author, "The Lack of Communication within the Office of Safety & Health, DA," 1980, "The Relationship Between the Level of Self Concept and Drinking Patterns of Black Youth" Dec 1984; co-author, "The Role of Top Management in the Implementation of the US Dept of Agriculture Employee Assistance Program," 1979; author, "Mary Had a Baby and Don't Know How She Got It," 1989; author, "Family Violence: Please Tell She Hit Me: Husband Abuse,"1989. **Business Addr:** Dir, Social Work Program, Lemoyne-Owen College, 807 Walker Ave, Memphis, TN 38126.

MARTIN, CURTIS
Professional football player. **Personal:** Born May 1, 1973, Pittsburgh, PA; children: Diamond. **Educ:** Univ of Pittsburgh, attended. **Career:** New England Patriots, running back, 1995-. **Honors/Awds:** Pro Bowl, 1995, 1996; Rookie of the Year, 1995. **Business Addr:** Professional Football Player, New England Patriots, 60 Washington St, Foxboro Stadium, Foxboro, MA 02035, (508)543-7911.

MARTIN, CURTIS JEROME
Educator. **Personal:** Born Nov 16, 1949, Kansas City, MO; married Valerie Joy Smith. **Educ:** USAF Acad, BS Humanities 1967-71; MI St U, MA Eng 1975-76. **Career:** USAF Acad Actvties Grp, chief congr liaison br 1980-; USAF Acad, asst prof of Eng 1976-80; Lowry Air Force Base Denver, dir drug/alcohol abuse prgm1972-75; USAF Acad CO, asst ftbll coach 1971-72. **Orgs:** Mem Nat Counc of Tchrs of Eng 1975-; course dir Blk Lit, Minority Lit, African Lit USAF Acad Eng Dept 1978-80; acad liaison ofcr mem USAF AcadWay of Life Com 1976-80; alcohol abuse rehab couns SW Denver Mntl Hlth Ctr 1973-74; parliamentarian Lowry AFB Chap Brthrhd Assn for Blk Svcmn & Svcwmn 1973-75; mem Aurora CO Drug Alcohol Abuse Counc 1973-75; Spkrs Bur Lowry AFB 1973-75; Spkrs Bur USAF Acad 1976-80. **Honors/Awds:** Outst yng man of Am US Jaycees 1977; dist grad Squadron Ofcr Sch Maxwell AFB 1978; jr ofcr of yr USAF Acad Faculty 1979; recip Clements award "MilEducator of Yr" USAF Acad 1980; recip of Cmmndtn Medal USAF 1975. **Military Serv:** USAF capt 1971-. **Business Addr:** HQ USAF/MPPA Pentagon, Washington, DC 20330.

MARTIN, DANIEL E.
Judge. **Personal:** Born Apr 14, 1932, Bluffton, SC; son of John Henry and Rena Johnson Martin; married Ruby Nesbitt, 1960; children: Daniel E Jr, Max Maurice. **Educ:** Allen Univ, BS Health & Phys Educ 1954; SC State Coll, JD 1966. **Career:** Wallace HS, phys educ dept 1959-62; Gresham Meggett HS, math tchr 1962-63; Neighborhood Legal Asst Prog, dir 1968-72; 9th Jud Circuit, asst solicitor First Black; SC House of Rep, vice chair judicial committee; Ninth Judicial Circuit of South Carolina, presiding judge, 1992-. **Orgs:** Mem ABA, SC Bar Assn, Charleston Co Bar Assn, Judges Selection Com for state of SC only Black lawyer; mem Gov Energy Commn; mem State Bd of Voc Rehab US Tax Ct; US Ct Customs & Patent Appeals; Fed Dist Ct Dist of SC; US Supreme Ct Trustee Emanuel AME Ch; mem turst bd Allen Univ; mem Neimiah Lodge #51 Free & Accepted Masons, past potentate Arabian Temple 139, Grand Inspector General; charter mem Choraliers Music Club; life mem, Alpha Phi Alpha; mem, Downtown Charleston Rotary International Club; mem, Charleston Business and Professional Association. **Honors/Awds:** Alpha Phi Alpha Frat Scroll of Honor Omega Psi Phi Frat 1969; Cert of Achieve Alpha Phi Alpha Frat 1970; Cert of Apprec Charleston Sym Assn 1970; Dist Serv Awd Alpha Phi Alpha Frat 1973; Apprec Awd Clara D Hill Mission Club 1974; Apprec Awd BSA 1974; Juris Prudence Achieve Awd Omega Psi Phi Frat 1974; Charleston Business and Professional Assn, Man of the Year, 1975; Phi Beta Sigma Fraternity, Recognition Award for Social Action, 1976; Selective Service System, Certificate of Appreciation, 1976; SC Vocational Rehabilitation Assn, Certificate from Gov James B Edwards, 1976; Alpha Phi Alpha Fraternity, Certificate of Achievement, 1979; Arabian Temple #139, Appreciation Award, 1979; Thelma F Murray Appreciation Award; Mary Ford School Award-Black History Contribution, 1987; AKA Debutante Award-Distinguished Service, 1988; Burke High School, American Education Award, 1988; Benedicat College, Resolution of Honor, 1989; University of Charleston, Honorary Doctor of Humane Letters, 1992. **Military Serv:** AUS corpl 1955-57. **Business Addr:** Attorney, 61 Morris St, Charleston, SC 29403.

MARTIN, DANIEL EZEKIEL, JR.
Attorney, former magistrate. **Personal:** Born Jan 21, 1963, Charleston, SC; son of Ruby N Martin and Daniel E Martin Jr; married Reba Hough-Martin, Apr 29, 1989. **Educ:** Howard University, Washington, DC, BA, 1985; Univ of South Carolina, Law, Columbia, SC, JD, 1988. **Career:** House of Representatives, Columbia, SC, law clerk, 1986-88; Martin, Gailliard & Martin, Charleston, SC, attorney/partner, 1988-; Charleston County, Charleston, SC, magistrate, 1989-93. **Orgs:** President, Network of Charleston, 1989-; treas, South Carolina Black Lawyer Assn, 1990-; exec bd, Charleston, NAACP, 1991-; corresponding scy, Beta Kappa Lambda Chapter, Alpha Phi Alpha, 1990-; bd of trustees, Emmanuel AME Church, 1990-; Cannon St YMCA, executive board member; Mayor's Committee of 12; Charleston Comm for Children; Masonic Lodge No 51; George Washington Carver Consistory No 162; Arabian Temple No 139; Owl's Whist Club; 100 Black Men of Charleston. **Honors/Awds:** Community Service, Charleston Chapter, 1990; Celebrity Reader, Charleston Co Library Assn, 1990. **Business Addr:** Attorney, Martin, Gailliard & Martin Law Offices, 61 Morris St, Charleston, SC 29403.

MARTIN, DARNELL
Filmmaker. **Personal:** Born in New York, NY; daughter of Marilyn; married Giuseppe Ducrot. **Educ:** Sarah Lawrence College; New York University. **Career:** Filmmaker, currently. **Special Achievements:** Film: "I Like It Like That". **Business Phone:** (310)280-8000.

MARTIN, DARRICK
Professional basketball player. **Personal:** Born Mar 6, 1971, Denver, CO. **Educ:** UCLA. **Career:** Played with Magic Johnson All-Stars, 1993-94; Sioux Falls Skyforce (CBA), guard, 1994-95; Minnesota Timberwolves, 1995-96; Los Angeles Clippers, 1996-. **Honors/Awds:** CBA, All-League second team, 1995. **Business Addr:** Professional Basketball Player, Los Angeles Clippers, 3939 S Figueroa St, Los Angeles Sports Arena, Los Angeles, CA 90037, (213)748-8000.

MARTIN, DOUG
Professional football player (retired). **Personal:** Born May 22, 1957, Fairfield, CA; married Audrey. **Educ:** Univ of Washington, attended. **Career:** Minnesota Vikings, defensive end, 1980-89.

MARTIN, D'URVILLE
Performer. **Personal:** Born Feb 11, 1939, New York, NY; married Lillian Ferguson; children: Jacques, Kala. **Career:** Producer dir actor over 36 Maj TV shows 16 Films; most recent The Omen, The System Shady Lady Disco 9000. **Orgs:** Mem Black Businessman's Assn of Atlanta; chmn Am Cancer Soc; bd of dir DiscO 9000. **Honors/Awds:** Hon citizen of Tusckeke. **Business Addr:** 1101 S Alfred St, Los Angeles, CA 90035.

MARTIN, EDWARD
Clergyman. **Personal:** Born Jun 30, 1936, Grove Hill, AL; divorced. **Educ:** AL State U, BS 1969; Carver Bible Inst, BTh; Interdenom Theological Cntr and Horehouse Sch of Rel Atlanta, mDiv (honor roll) 1973. **Career:** Bethel Bapt Ch Montgomery, AL, pastor 1967-; Union Acad Bapt Ch; Selma Univ Sch of Rel, instr. **Orgs:** Pres Montgomery-Antioch Dist SS and Bapt Training Union Congress 1970; mem Natl Bapt Conv USA Inc; Am Beatury Lodge 858; Charlie Garrett Chapter Royal Arch No 78a; United Supreme Council 32; Prince Hall Affil Grand Orient Wash, DC; NAACP 1958-; YMCA 1966-; Montgomery Improvement Assn Inc 1967-; Phi Beta Sigma 1969-. **Honors/Awds:** Nat Fndtn March of Dimes awd 1971.

MARTIN, EDWARD ANTHONY
Podiatrist. **Personal:** Born Dec 25, 1935, Mason City, IA; married Barbara C Payne; children: Gail Ingrid, Edward Brian, Stephen Vincent. **Educ:** Mason City Jr Coll, 1953054; IL Coll of Podiatric Medicine, DPM 1958. **Career:** Dr E A Martin , podiatrist 1958-. **Orgs:** First natl pres Acad of Ambulatory Foot Surgery 1973-74; diplomate Am Bd of Amubulatory Foot Surgery 1976; past pres Nat Podiatry Assn 1977-78; mem AmPodiatry Assn 1960-80; pvt pilot Single Engine-land 1974-; podiatry examiner IL Dept of Registration/Educ 1978. **Honors/Awds:** Henri L DuVries Award Proficiency in Clinical Surgery 1958; pectr foot surgery Nationally & Canada 1973-80; "Podiatry A Step Toward Healthy Happy Feet" EbonyArticl 1978; instr in surger-instructional movie on ambulatory surgery 1979. **Business Addr:** 2301 Lincoln Ave, San Jose, CA 95125.

MARTIN, EDWARD WILLIFORD
Administrator. **Personal:** Born Nov 29, 1929, Sumter, SC; son of Frances Martin and Eddie Martin; married Pearl Evelyn Sewell; children: Andrea Michelle, Debra Yvette, Christopher Edward. **Educ:** Fisk Univ, BA 1950; Univ of IN, MA 1952; Univ of IA, PhD 1962. **Career:** Prairie View A&M Univ, instr of biology 1952-56, asst prof of biology 1956-59, chmn div of natl sci/prof of biology 1968-81, dean college of arts & scis 1981-. **Orgs:** Mem Amer Soc of Zoologists, Soc of Sigma Xi, Amer Men of Science; adv bd Baylor Coll of Medicine; mem Omega Psi Phi Frat, Sigma Pi Phi Frat Nu Boule. **Honors/Awds:** Natl Sci Faculty Fellowship Natl Sci Found 1961-62; Beta Kappa Chi Distinguished Awd Beta Kappa Chi Sci Hon Soc 1965; Piper Prof for Teaching Excellence Minnie Stevens Piper Foundation 1979. **Business Addr:** Dean, Coll of Arts & Sciences, Prairie View A&M Univ, PO Box 878, Prairie View, TX 77446.

MARTIN, ELMER P.
Educator. **Personal:** Born Oct 31, 1946, Kansas City, MO; son of Harriet Cason Martin (deceased) and Elmer P Martin (deceased); married Joanne Mitchell Martin, Jul 29, 1972. **Educ:** Lincoln Univ, Jefferson City MO, BA Sociology, 1968; Atlanta Univ, Atlanta GA, MA Sociology, 1971; Case Western Reserve Univ, Cleveland OH, PhD Social Welfare, 1975. **Career:** St Louis Dept of Welfare, caseworker, 1968-69; Cleveland State Univ, asst prof, 1975-76; Morgan State Univ, Baltimore MD, professor, 1976-, chairperson Dept of Social Work and Mental Health, 1985-. **Orgs:** Mem, Natl Assn of Social Workers, 1980-; founder, "For Our People" Food Program, 1983-; mem, Natl Assn of Black Social Workers, 1984-; mem, Sandtown-Winchester Neighborhood Improvement Assn, 1984-85; bd pres, The Great Blacks in Wax Museum, 1988-. **Honors/Awds:** Co-author, The Black Extended Family, Univ of Chicago Press, 1978; co-author, Perspectives of the Black Family (in Family in Transition), Little Brown and Co, 1980; co-author, The Helping Tradition in the Black Family and Community, Nation Assn of Social Workers, 1985; Outstanding Achievement City of Baltimore, 1985; co-author, The Black Woman: Perspectives on Her Role in the Family in Ethnicity and Women, Univ of Wisconsin, 1986; Teacher of the Year, Morgan State Univ, 1986. **Special Achievements:** Co-author, "Social Work and the Black Experience," Natl Assn of Social Workers Press, 1996. **Business Addr:** Co-Founder, The Great Blacks in Wax Museum, Inc, 1601 East North Avenue, Baltimore, MD 21213.

MARTIN, EMANUEL
Professional football player. **Personal:** Born Jul 31, 1969. **Educ:** Alabama State. **Career:** Ottawa Rough Riders (CFL), 1994-95; Buffalo Bills, defensive back, 1996-. **Business Addr:** Professional Football Player, Buffalo Bills, One Bills Dr, Orchard Park, NY 14127, (716)648-1800.

MARTIN, ERNEST DOUGLASS
Physician, educator (retired). **Personal:** Born Oct 26, 1928, Petersburg, VA; married Aurelia Joyce Dent; children: Shellye, Erika, Tia. **Educ:** Lincoln Univ, PA, AB, 1951; Howard Univ Med School, Wash DC, MD. **Career:** VA Hospital, Washington DC, consultant, 1964-74; Dist of Columbia General Hospital, med officer; Howard Univ Medical School, asst prof, 1964-. **Orgs:** Bd of dir, Community Group Health Found, Wash DC, 1979-80; Omega Psi Phi, Frat Fellow; Amer Academy of Orthopedic Surgeons, 1973. **Military Serv:** US Navy, lt, 1957-59. **Home Addr:** 1807 Sudbury Ln NW, Washington, DC 20012.

MARTIN, EVELYN B.
Educator, educational administrator. **Personal:** Born Oct 12, 1908, Concord, NH; daughter of Alice A Bacon and James E Bacon; married Anatole Emile Martin Jr, Dec 31, 1935. **Educ:** Hampton Inst, BS; Columbia Univ, MA, EdD. **Career:** USOE Dept HEW, panelist 1974-77; Coll of Educ FL A&M Univ, acting dean 1978; FL A&M Univ, prof dept chmn 1947-, dir center for comm educ. **Orgs:** Gov bd Natl Assn Admin; AASA Adv Com on Higher Educ 1977-79; appointed by gov of FL Leon Co Sch Bd 1979; appointed by governor of FL Regional Adv Council Dept of Corrections; elected first vice pres Leon Co United Way 1980; mem Kappa Delta Pi; Delta Kappa Gamma; Phi Delta Kappa; Pi Gamma Mu. **Honors/Awds:** Distinguished Serv Award Amer Assoc of School Administrators 1983; Award for Women in Power Citation, National Assn of Jewish Women, 1985; Meritorious Achievement Award, Florida A&M Univ, 1986; Outstanding Community Women, AAUW, Tallahassee, FL, 1991. **Business Addr:** Dir, Center for Community Education, Florida A&M Univ, Box 153, Tallahassee, FL 32307.

MARTIN, FRANCES. See MARTIN, CAROL.

MARTIN, FRANK C., II
Curator, educator, administrator, choreographer. **Personal:** Born Aug 17, 1954, Sumter, SC; son of Leola Glisson Martin and Frank C Martin; married Shirley Fields, Jun 19, 1989. **Educ:** Yale University, BA, 1976; City University of New York, Hunter College, MA, 1990; New York University, Institute of Fine Arts, currently. **Career:** Metorpolitan Museum of Art, curatorial assistant, education associate, 1979-87, Office of Education Services, assistant manager, 1988-89, associate manager, 1989-91; IP Stanback Museum & Planetarium, South Carolina State University, exhibitions & collections curator, 1991-. **Orgs:** Artists of Color of South Carolina; The Renaissance Society of America, 1988-91; The College Art Association, 1988-91; Eboni Dance Theatre, executive board; Orangeburg Arts Council; Grants in Aid Panel, South Carolina Arts Commission, visual arts chairperson, 1992; Orangeburg Arts League. **Honors/Awds:** City University of New York, Hunter College, William Graf Grant for Travel and Study Abroad, 1986; Yale University, Yale National Scholar, 1976; Kiwanis of America, Key Club Scholarship Award, 1972; Educational Testing Service, National Achievement Commended Scholar, 1972; Scholastic Arts Awards Committee, Honorable Mention, 1970. **Special Achievements:** Author: "The Museum as an Artists' Resource," American Artist Magazine, 1991; "Cultural Pluralism: A Challange for the Arts in South Carolina," Triennial Exhibition Catalogue, 1992; "The Acacia Historical Collection," American Visions Magazine, 1992; "Art, Race, and Culture: Context and Interpretive Bias in Contemporary African-American Art in Transcendence and Conflict: African-American Art in South Carolina 1700-Present," 1992. **Business Addr:** Curator, Exhibitions and Collections, South Carolina State University, The I.P. Stanback Museum and Planetarium, 300 College St NE, Orangeburg, SC 29117, (803)536-7174.

MARTIN, FRANK T.
Transportation executive. **Personal:** Born Jul 24, 1950, Nashville, TN; son of Maureen Kimbrough Martin and William Henry Martin; married Pamela Johnson Martin, Nov 1, 1980; children: Jessica Maureen. **Educ:** Tennessee State University, BS, business administration, 1973; Fisk University, MURP, 1974. **Career:** North Central Florida Region Planning Council, local assistance and mass transit planner, 1974-77; Greater Richmond Transit Co., operation planning director, 1978-80; Birmingham Jefferson County Transit Authority, assistant general manager, 1980-81, general manager, 1981-84; ATE, Ryder Systems Inc, vice pres, gen mgr, New Orleans, Transit Management Southeast Louisiana, 1984-87; Metro-Dade County Transit Agency, deputy director, 1987-89, rail operations assistant director, 1989-. **Orgs:** Conference of Minority Transportation Officials, bd mem, 1992-; Tennessee State University, Alumni Association Miami Chapter, president, 1990-93, 1997-; American Public Transit Foundation, board member, 1991-97; New Miami Group, board member, 1991-97; National Forum for Black Public Administration, 1987-. **Honors/Awds:** American Society of Public Administration, Alabama Administrator of the Year, 1983; ATE, Ryder, President's Special Achievement Award, 1982. **Business Addr:** Assistant MDTA Director, Rail Operations, Metro-Dade Transit Agency, 6601 NW 72nd Ave, 2nd Fl, Miami, FL 33166, (305)884-7520.

MARTIN, FRANKLIN FARNARWANCE
Printing company executive. **Personal:** Born Jun 22, 1950, Cleveland, OH; son of Mozelle Marie Chatman Martin and General Ellis Martin; married Barbara Joyce Branic Martin, Jan 8, 1972 (divorced); children: Tiona Camille. **Educ:** Cuyahoga Comm Coll, AA 1968-69; Cleveland Plain Dealer Publ Co, journeyman printer degree 1968-75; Cleveland State Univ, attended 1969-70. **Career:** Parkview Fed S/L Assoc, printing systems dir 1976-85; Cleveland Plain Dealer Publ Co, asst composing room foreman 1968-85; Frandon Printing Inc, pres, CEO 1983-. **Orgs:** Vp Disabled Amer Vets 1974-, Urban League of Cleveland 1983-, Shaker Towne Ctr 1984-; bd mem Shaker Towne Ctr Adv Bd for the Mayor of Shaker Hts 1986-; bd mem Black Profls Assoc, 1986-; bd of directors Rotary Intl 1987-; bd mem Shaker Heights Youth Center 1987-; Human Relations Commission City of Shaker, 1989-. **Honors/Awds:** Bus Person of the Year C of C Eastern Suburbs 1988-89; one half page story in Cleveland Plain Dealer on Successful Entrepreneurship 1986; Making It Black Enterprise 1987; nominated Black Professional of the Year, Cleveland Growth Assn; Regional Minority Purchasing Council, 1989; Heights Chamber of Commerce Bus Person of the Year, 1989-90; Topic Bus Person to Succeed, Cleveland Magazine, 1990; Natl Assn of Black Journalists, Best Sports Story, 1991-92. **Military Serv:** USAF staff sgt 1969-72; Two Commendation Medals, Vietnam Vet Citation, Disabled Amer Vet.

MARTIN, GEORGE ALEXANDER, JR.
Administrator. **Personal:** Born May 4, 1943, New York, NY. **Educ:** Parsons Coll, BS 1966; City Univ of NY, MPA 1977. **Career:** Bedford-Stuyvesant Alcoholism Treatment Ctr, special asst to admin; Marlin Enterprises, pres 1973-; New York Univ Grad School of Public Admin, clinical asst prof of public admin 1972-73; Univ Year for ACTION Proj, New York City & Urban Corps, dir 1972-73; Herald-Bridge House, admin 1970-72. **Orgs:** Amer Soc for Public Admin; Amer Soc for Political Science; Conf of Minority Public Admin; dir, Public Mgmt Sys Inc; consultant, VISTA Region III, 1971; ATAC Inc 1972; Williamsbridge NAACP; Williamsburg Taxpayers Assn; Citizens Comm for Children; Brooklyn Comm on Alcholism; co-chmn, Achievement Week Comm, Omega Psi Phi Frat; adv bd, New York City Urban Corps/Acad Credit Internship Prog 1973; dir, Independent House Inc, Publ Professional Studies in Public Mgmt NYC/Compa Forum 1975. **Business Addr:** 1121 Bedford Ave, Brooklyn, NY 11216.

MARTIN, GEORGE DWIGHT
Professional football player (retired). **Personal:** Born Feb 16, 1953, Greenville, SC; married Diane; children: Teresa Michelle, George Dwight II, Benjmain Dean, Aaron. **Educ:** Univ of Oregon, attended. **Career:** New York Giants, defensive end, 1975-87. **Orgs:** Former rep United Way Pblc Serv TV Commercial. **Honors/Awds:** Five career touchdowns (most in club history by defensive lineman); five time winner, Byron "Whizzer" White Award; elected defensive captain, 1981.

MARTIN, GERTRUDE S.
Public relations executive. **Personal:** Born Apr 21, Savannah, GA; daughter of Laura McDowell Scott (deceased) and Walter S Scott (deceased); married Louis Emanuel Martin, 1937; children: Trudy Hatter, Anita Martin, Toni Martin, Linda Purkiss, Lisa Martin. **Educ:** OH State Univ, Columbus, OH, BA, (cum laude with honors in French), 1934, MA, 1936. **Career:** United Planning Organization, Washington, DC, education coordinator, 1963-66; Willmart Services, Washington, DC, coordinator, 1966-68; Univ of Chicago, Dept of Education, editor, 1970-74; Integrated Education Assoc, Evanston, IL, editor, 1974-78; Calmar Communicatons, Chicago, IL, vice pres, 1978-. **Orgs:** Bd mem, IL Child Care Society, 1955-58; bd of governors, American Red Cross, 1966-72; commitee, A Better Chance, Washington, 1983-85; life mem, Natl Council of Negro Women; Black Women's Agenda, Washington, DC, board member, 1989-92. **Honors/Awds:** Natl Council of Negro Women; New Horizons, George Washington Univ. **Business Addr:** Vice President, Calmar Communications, 850 N State St, 4F, Chicago, IL 60611.

MARTIN, GWENDOLYN ROSE
Union staff representative (retired). **Personal:** Born Dec 12, 1926, Cleveland, OH; daughter of Rosa M Johnson Fuller (deceased) and Monroe Fuller (deceased); married Aaron Martin; children: Jeffrey A. **Educ:** OH State Univ, 1946-48; Case Western Reserve Univ, real estate 1952; George Washington Univ, Ext Course 1976. **Career:** Commun Workers of Amer, CWA rep 1972, dir 1975, admin asst to vice pres 1976-87; State of Illinois, Department of Labor, dir 1987-91; Communications Workers, Itasca, IL, CWA rep 1991-92. **Orgs:** Delegate Dem Natl Conv 1976, 1978, l982, l984; vice pres Leadership Council Comm 1978-81; conf pres IL AFL-CIO 1978-87; chmn United Way New Appl 1980-81; mem Dem Natl Comm; vice chmn Dem Natl Comm Women's Caucus 1980-84; bd dir Amer Red Cross 1982-84; exec bd member Natl Assn Govt Labor Officials l988-91; exec bd mem Women Executives in State-Govt l987-88. **Honors/Awds:** Sojourner Truth Awd MI Women Trial Lawyers Assoc 1974; Harriet Tubman Awd Coalition of Black Trade Unionist 1975; Resolution #1161 IL House of Rep 1978; Florence Criley Awd Coalition of Labor Union Women 1980. **Home Addr:** 219 Hickory, Arlington Heights, IL 60004.

MARTIN, HAROLD B.
Dentist (retired). **Personal:** Born Oct 26, 1928, Petersburg, VA; married Dolores H; children: Harold, Lisa, Gregory. **Educ:** Lincoln U, AB 1950; Howard U, DDS 1957; John Hopkins U, MPH 1971. **Career:** Private practice, dentist, 1959-; Howard University College of Dentistry, Department of Comm Dentistry, professor, 1959-87, associate dean for advanced education and research, 1987-96; Dept of Corrections, DC, 1960-70. **Orgs:** Vp Nat Dental Assn; Century Ltd Inc; bd dir E of River Health Assn; mdm Am Dental Assn; Nat Dental Assn; DC Med Care Adv Com; Nat Review Com for Guidelines for the Expanded Function Training Prgm, HEW; mem Midway Civic Assn, US Youth Games Comm; NAACP; Urban League;

Omega Psi Phi; past pres Huntsmen Inc; bd dir Ionia Whipper Home for Unwed Mothers; bd dir Pigskin Club of WA; American Public Health Association; Sigma Xi, 1975; Howard University Chapter, president, 1984-85; Omicron Kappa Upsilon, 1976. **Honors/Awds:** American College of Dentists, Fellowship, 1978; International College of Dentists, Fellowship, 1985. **Military Serv:** AUS Med Corp, Dental Sec 1951-53.

MARTIN, HELEN DOROTHY
Actress. **Personal:** Born Jul 28, St Louis, MO; daughter of Amanda Frankie Fox Martin and William Martin. **Educ:** Fisk University; A&I State College. **Career:** Actress. **Orgs:** Actor's Equity Assn; Screen Actors Guild; American Federation of Television and Radio Artists; original member, American Negro Theatre, 1940-. **Honors/Awds:** Theatrical appearances include: Hits, Bits and Skits, 1940; Native Son, 1941; Mamba's Daughters, 1943; There's A Family, 1943; Chicken Every Sunday, 1944; Deep Are the Roots, 1945; On Strivers Row, 1946; The Little Foxes; The Petrified Forest, 1951; Take A Giant Step, 1953; Major Barbara, 1954; You Can't Take It With You, 1954-55; Juno and the Paycock, 1955; Anniversary Waltz, 1955; King of Hearts, 1956; A Land Beyond the River, 1957; Fever for Live, 1957; The Ballad of Jazz Street, 1959; The Long Dream, 1960; Period of Adjustment, 1960; The Blacks, 1961; Purlie Victorious, 1961; Critics Choice, 1962; My Mother, My Father and Me, 1963; The Amen Corner, 1964; The Cat and the Canary, 1970; Raisin, 1973; appeared in the films Phoenix City Story, 1955;A Matter of Conviction, 1960; Where's pa?, 1970; Cotton Comes to Harlem, 1970; The Anderson Tapes, 1971; Death Wish, 1974; Rose McClendon scholarship, 1959; numerous television and radio appearances, including Roots, tv, 1977; Black Filmmakers Hall of Fame, 1992.

MARTIN, HERMAN HENRY, JR.
Investment banker. **Personal:** Born Dec 29, 1961, Dayton, OH. **Educ:** Florida A&M Univ, BS 1984; The Wharton Sch Univ of PA, MBA 1986. **Career:** Hoffman LaRoche, pharmaceutical sales rep 1981-82; Cabot Corp, intl audit intern 1982; Chase Manhattan Bank, credit analyst intern 1983; Johnson & Johnson Products, mktg intern 1984-85; Salomon Bros Inc, fixed income rep. **Orgs:** Mem Kappa Alpha Psi Frat 1982-, Natl Black MBA Assoc 1986-, Natl Florida A&M Univ Alumni Assoc 1987-; mem The Wharton Business School Club of NY 1987-. **Honors/Awds:** Leadership Fellowship Johnson & Johnson 1985-86; Wharton Intl Exchange Student (Institut Superieur Des Affaires) Paris France 1985.

MARTIN, HOSEA L.
Marketing communications executive. **Personal:** Born Aug 10, 1937, Montezuma, GA; son of Marion Cannon and H L Martin. **Educ:** University of Chicago, BA, 1960; University of Chicago Graduate School of Business, 1965-66. **Career:** Prudential Insurance Co, advertising specialist, 1966-67; Coca-Cola Co, natl promotions mgr, 1967-75; Safeway Stores, Inc, marketing mgr, 1975-86; University of California, editorial specialist, 1986-89; United Way of San Francisco, vice pres, 1989-. **Orgs:** San Francisco Media Alliance, 1986-; National Association of Market Developers, 1967-75. **Honors/Awds:** American Advertising Federation, National 1st Place, Direct Mail Development, 1968. **Special Achievements:** Articles, Harper's, 1992; Essence, 1992; Wall Street Journal, 1991. **Military Serv:** US Army, Spec 4, 1960-63; Soldier of the Month, 1962. **Business Addr:** VP, Marketing & Communications, United Way of the San Francisco Bay Area, 50 California St, Ste 200, San Francisco, CA 94111, (415)772-4394.

MARTIN, HOYLE HENRY
Government official. **Personal:** Born Oct 21, 1921, Brooklyn, NY; son of Mattie Garrett Martin and Jesse T. Martin (deceased); married Mary Campbell Martin, Jun 28, 1951; children: Hoyle Jr, Michael C, David E, Cheryl L. **Educ:** Benedict College, Columbia, SC, BA, 1957; Syracuse University, Syracuse, NY, MA, 1961. **Career:** College educator, North Carolina and South Carolina, teaching, 1958-66; Charlotte Concentrated Employment Program, CEO, executive director, 1967-71; University of North Carolina-Charlotte, Charlotte, NC, associate director, Urban Institute, 1972-76; Charlotte Post, Charlotte, NC, chief editorial writer, 1974-89; City of Charlotte, Charlotte, NC, housing development administrator, 1977-88, city council member, 1989-95; Mecklenburg County Commissioner, currently. **Orgs:** Advisory board member, Habitat for Humanity, 1987-94; board member, Charlotte Civilian Club, 1989-98; board member, Reachline Inc, 1989-92; advisor, WBTV Black Advisory Committee, 1983-89; board member, West Charlotte Business Incubator, 1990-. **Honors/Awds:** Meritorious Service, National Alliance Businessmen, 1978; Dedicated Service Award, Southern Piedmont Health System Agency, 1977-78; Devoted Service Award, University of North Carolina-Charlotte College of Business, 1969-77; Meritorious Service Award, Charlotte Concentrated Employment Program, 1967-71; Volunteer Service Award, Joint Action in Community Service, 1970. **Military Serv:** US Army, Staff Sgt., 1950-51; U.S. Merchant Marines, 1945-49, 1952. **Home Phone:** (704)392-4623. **Business Addr:** County Commissioner, Mecklenburg County, 600 E 4th St, Charlotte, NC 28202, (704)336-2472.

MARTIN, I. MAXIMILLIAN
Chief executive. **Career:** Berean Savings Assn, Philadelphia, PA, chief exec. **Business Addr:** Berean Savings Assn, 5228 Chestnut St, Philadelphia, PA 19139.

MARTIN, IONIS BRACY
Artist, educator. **Personal:** Born Aug 27, 1936, Chicago, IL; daughter of Hattie O Robinson Bracy and Francis Wright Bracy; married Allyn A Martin; children: Allyn B, Martin. **Educ:** Fisk Univ, BA, 1957; Univ of Hartford, MEd, 1968; Pratt Inst, MFA, 1987. **Career:** YWCA Y-Teen Assoc, dir, 1957-59; Artist's Collective Inc, artist/educator, 1970-73; WFSB-TV/Wadsworth Atheneum, produced art segments for children's program, 1972-75; Northwestern CT Community Coll, lecturer 1985-90; The Hartford Courant, illustrator 1986-90; Hartford, Bloomfield Public Schools, art teacher 1961-; Central CT State Univ, lecturer, 1985-; Getty Center for Education in the Arts, Los Angeles, CA, consultant, 1990-93. **Orgs:** Co-trustee, Burr McManus Trust, chairman, 1990-; former commissioner, Hartford Fine Arts Comm; former dir, Greater Hartford Arts Council, Charter Oak Temple Cultural Center and Hartford Stage Co; co-founder, 2nd vice pres & dir, Artists Collective, 1970-; trustee, Wadsworth Atheneum 1977-85, 1986-96; mem adv comm CT Bd of Educ 1986-87; NAEA, CAEA, Delta Sigme Theta; pres Artworks Gallery 1986-87; Romare Bearden/Jackie McLean ''Sound Collages & Visual Improvizations'' 1986; curator/producer Cotra Gallery ''Five From CT'' exhibit 1987. **Honors/Awds:** CT State Comm on Arts Grant 1970; Outstanding Community Serv Award, University of Hartford, BPU, 1974; Honored by CT Historical Soc, 1984; 200 Years of Achievement Against the Odds Black Women of CT; JP Getty Trust Curriculum Devel Inst, 1988-; Skidmore Coll, Art Fellow, 1987; exhibitor, since 1968 solo and group shows; One Woman Show, Christ Church Cathedral, Hartford, 1990; One Woman Show, Wethersfield Historical Society, 1991; Best in Show, Pump House Gallery, 1990; One Woman Show, Lindgren Gallery, Manchester, 1990; One Woman Show Northampton Arts Center, Northampton MA, 1990; Jubilee, One Woman Show, Fisk University, 1992; Solo exhibit, Univ of Vermont, Burlington, VT, 1993; Group shows Artworks Gallery, The CRT Gallery and Pump House Galley, 1993-94; Consultant, Gale Research, 1992. **Special Achievements:** Secondary Art Educator of the Year, CT Art Ed Assn, 1993-94; Fellow, the WEB Dubois Institute, Harvard University, 1994. **Business Addr:** Artist, Teacher, Bloomfield High School, 7 Huckleberry Lane, Bloomfield, CT 06002.

MARTIN, JAMES LARENCE
Dentist. **Personal:** Born Sep 3, 1940, Dubuque, IA; son of Ada Martin and James Martin; married Willie Mae; children: Linda, James Larence III, John Lance. **Educ:** Loras Coll, BS 1959; TN State Univ, MS 1960; Meharry Med Coll Sch of Den, DDS 1966; Univ MI, MPH 1975; D. Litt., Loras Coll. 1982. **Career:** Meharry Med Coll, prof 1977-, assoc prof 1977-, coord 1975-, asst prof, dept pediatrics 1972-, asst prof, dept of operative 1974-75, dir 1973-75; Comprehensive Health Care Program for Children & Youth Promotion, proj dir 1972-73; Meharry Med Coll, assoc prof 1969-72, dental dir 1967-72, instr 1967-69,instr 1960-62. **Orgs:** Mem Amer Dental Assn; Natl Dental Assn; Amer Pub Hlth Assn; Intl Assn for Dental Rsrch, 1973; Amer Assn for Dental Rsrch; Amer Acad of Oral Med; Amer Acad of Gold Foil Operators; AAAS; Amer Assn of Dental Schs; Amer Assn of Med Schs; TN Pub Hlth Assn; Capitol City Dental Soc; Human Rights Commn; Alpha Phi Alpha; St Vincent DePaul Men's Club; Boy Scouts of Amer; Meharry Century Club; Nashville Area C of C; 50 Critics Orgn; Civitan Intl St Vincent DePaul Church Council. **Honors/Awds:** Numerous awards honors & recognitions; numerous manuscripts & publications. **Business Addr:** Professor, Meharry Medical Coll, 1005 18th Ave N, Nashville, TN 37208.

MARTIN, JAMES TYRONE
Physician, clergyman. **Personal:** Born Aug 17, 1942, Elkhorn, WV; son of Mr & Mrs Henry Martin. **Educ:** Bluefield St Coll Bluefield WV, BS 1960-66; Meharry Med Coll Nashville TN, MD 1969-73. **Career:** Tri-Dist Comm Hlth Serv; med dir; McDowell Co, teacher, 1966-69; US Army, 1980-88; med dir, Comm Health Serv, Raleigh County, Beckley, WV, 1988-95. **Orgs:** Mem Beta Kappa Chi Hon Sci Frat; mem IBPOOE of WV; F&AAY; Royal Arch Masons; asst pastor Emmanuel Tabernacle Bapt Ch, 1965-88, pastor, 1992-; mem Amer Acad of Family Physicians; WV Acad of Family Physicians. **Military Serv:** US Army, major, 1980-88; Army Serv Medal, 1980; Army Commendation Medal 1986; Army Achievement Medal, 1988. **Home Addr:** 108 Springwood Lane, Stanaford Acres, Beckley, WV 25801-9242. **Business Addr:** Community Health Serv, Raleigh County, 252 Rural Acre Dr, Beckley, WV 25801, (304)252-8555.

MARTIN, JAMES W.
Administrator. **Personal:** Born Nov 1, 1932, Cleveland, NC; married Marie Sanders; children: Dawn Martin. **Educ:** Claflin Coll, BS Biology 1954; SC State Coll Orangeburg, BS Ed 1960; Univ of SC Columbia, MS biology 1969; Univ of SC Columbia, PhD Biology 1971. **Career:** Emmett Scott HS Rock Hill SC, sci teacher, coach 1956-61; Voorhees Coll Denmark SC, acting pres, exec vice pres, dean of acad affairs 1961-76; Area Health Ed Center Med Univ of SC, dir of minority affairs state coor of minority affairs 1976-80; Affirmative Action & Minority Affairs Med Univ of SC, exec asst to pres 1980-. **Orgs:** Mem Mycological Soc, Mycrobiology Soc of Amer, Central Assoc of Sci & Math Teachers, So Assoc of Biologist, AAAS, Amer Assoc of Higher Ed, Amer Council on Higher Ed, Natl Assoc of Deans Registrars & Admiss Off, SC Ed Assoc, Alpha Kappa Mu Natl Hon Soc, Alpha Chi Natl Hon Soc, Sigma Xi Natl Rsch Hon Soc; off Univ Affirm Action 1978; elected chmn of bd Affirm Action 1978; elected chmn exec comm Affirm Action Bd 1978; bd mem Carolina Youth Devel 1982-; consult United Negro Coll fund 1979-; coord Morris Brown AME HS Tutorial Prog; consult United Negro Coll Fund ISATIM 1979-; dir Smal Bus Enterprise prog 1980-; consult Natl Sci Found Summer Inst; bd mem Equal Employment Oppty Commiss. **Honors/Awds:** Publ ''Devel Morphology of Apothecium of Trichophawa Abundans Karst An Epigean Operaculate Discomycete'' Mycrobiological Rschr Jour 1969; publ ''Structure &Function of Hardwood Litter & Soil Subsystems After Chronic Gamma Irradiation'' Third Nat Symposium on Radioecology 1970; Outstanding Educators 1971; Outstanding Alumni Awd Claflin Coll 1971; Achievement Awd Alpha Phi Alpha Frat 1971; Palmetto Awd State of SC 1985; Alpha Chi Natl Honor Soc, Sigma Xi Natl RschHonor Soc, Alpha Phi Alpha Frat Acheivement Awd. **Military Serv:** AUS Med Corp spec 4 1954-56. **Business Addr:** Exec Assistant to President, Medical Univ of So Carolina, 171 Ashley Ave, Charleston, SC 29425.

MARTIN, JANICE R.
Judge. **Educ:** University of Louisville, BS (with honors), political science; University of Louisville Law School, JD. **Career:** Instructor, Univ of Louisville; Private practice, attorney; Jefferson County Attorney's Office, Juvenile Division, head; Jefferson County District Court, district judge, 1992-. **Orgs:** Kentucky Task Force on Racial Bias; Women's Lawyers Assn; NAWJ. **Honors/Awds:** Distinguished Law School Alumni Award, 1992; Continuing Legal Educ Award, 1994, 1996; Kentucky Women's Leadership Class, 1994. **Special Achievements:** First African American female judge appointed and elected in the State of Kentucky. **Business Addr:** Judge, Jefferson County District Court, Hall of Justice, 600 W Jefferson Ave, Louisville, KY 40202, (502)595-4431.

MARTIN, JOANNE MITCHELL
Educator. **Personal:** Born Jun 12, 1947, Yulee, FL; daughter of Bessie Russell Mitchell and Jeremiah Mitchell; married Elmer P Martin, Jul 29, 1972. **Educ:** Florida A&M, Tallahassee FL, BA French, 1969; Atlanta Univ, Atlanta GA, MA French, 1971; Case Western Reserve Univ, Cleveland OH, MA Reading, 1976; Howard Univ, Washington DC, PhD Educational Psych, 1985. **Career:** Nassau County Bd of Educ, Fernandina Beach FL, teacher, 1969-70; Coppin State Coll, Baltimore MD, dir learning skills center, 1977-92. **Orgs:** Mem bd of dir, The Great Blacks in Wax Museum, 1985-; mem, African American Heritage Tour Assn, 1987-. **Honors/Awds:** Co-author, The Black Extended Family, Univ of Chicago Press, 1978, Perspectives of the Black Family (in Family in Transition), Little Brown and Co, 1980; Teacher of the Year, Coppin State Coll, 1984; Co-author, The Helping Tradition in the Black Family and Community, Natl Assn of Social Workers, 1985; Author, The Effects of a Cooperative, Competitive and Combination Goal Structure on the Math Performance of Black Children from Extended Families, 1985; Co-author, The Black Woman: Perspectives on Her Role in the Family in Ethnicity and Women, Univ of Wisconsin, 1986; Pace Setter Award, Balto City Urban Services, 1988. **Special Achievements:** Co-author, ''Social Work and the Black Experience,'' Natl Assoc of Social Workers Press, 1996. **Business Addr:** Executive Director, Co-Founder, The Great Blacks in Wax Museum, Inc, 1601 East North Avenue, Baltimore, MD 21213, (410)563-3404.

MARTIN, JOHN THOMAS
Military officer (retired). **Personal:** Born Apr 29, 1920, NYC, NY; son of Bertha Howard Martin and John Thomas Martin; married Hestlene Lee Brooks; children: Joan M Teaiwa, John Thomas, III (dec), Alan, Theresa M Roberson, Charles. **Educ:** Howard Univ, AB 1940; Sch Law, student 1940-41; Univ WI Sch Jour, student 1962. **Career:** Sec Defense Washington, exec to counselor's office 1952-53, 1956-62, 1965-66 ret 1968; AUS, commd 2nd lt 1940 advanced through grades to Col 1966-68; Selective Serv Washington, dir, 1966-79; Met Capital Corp, dir, currently; US Army, retired col. **Orgs:** Mem Retired Officers Assn, Assn US Army, Reserve Officers Assn, Capital Health & Welfare Council 1969; dir Capitol USO 1967-70; dir Natl Capitol Area Council BSA 1968-69; Met Capital Corp; Greater Southeast Comm Hosp Found; mem Kappa Alpha Psi; member of the board, National Historical Intelligence Museum, 1991-. **Military Serv:** AUS col retired; Legion of Merit; Bronze Star Medal w/one Oak Leaf Cluster; Combat Infantryman's Badge. **Home Addr:** 5026 10 St NE, Washington, DC 20017.

MARTIN, JOHN W.
Educator. **Personal:** Born Feb 15, 1924, Johnson City, TN; widowed. **Educ:** Knoxville Coll, BA 1948; Atlanta U, MA 1949; IN U, PhD 1959. **Career:** Univ of IL, asso prof emeritus of soc, 1992; IL Inst of Tech, Chicago, 1964-65; IL Wesleyan U, 1961-64; Dillard U, New Orleans, 1957-61; Miles Coll, 1949-57. **Orgs:** Mem IL Sociological Assn; Am Sociological Assn; Midwest Sociological Soc. **Military Serv:** USN 1944-46.

MARTIN, JOSHUA WESLEY, III
Judge. **Personal:** Born Sep 14, 1944, Columbia, SC; son of Bernice Baxter Martin and Joshua W Martin Jr; married Lloyd E Overton; children: Victoria, Alexis. **Educ:** Case Inst of Tech, BS 1966; Drexel Univ, 1971-73; Rutgers Schl of Law-Camden, JD 1974. **Career:** EI DuPont DeNemours & Co, sr physicist 1966-71; Hercules Inc, sr patent atty 1974-82; DE Pub Serv Comm, chmn 1978-82. **Orgs:** Mem DE Bar Assn 1975-; Natl Bar Assn 1975-; Philadelphia Patent Law Assn 1976-82; trustee Goldey Beacom Coll 1982-; Better Business Bureau of DE 1978-82; advisory comm Univ of DE Legal Asst Program 1982; trustee, Delaware Community Foundation 1988-. **Honors/Awds:** Alpha Man of Year Alphi Phi Alpha Frat Wilmington, DE 1978; Citizen of Year Omega Psi Phi Frat Wilmington, DE 1982; Outstanding Achievement Sigma Pi Phi Wilmington, DE 1983; Comm Serv Award Rutgers Univ-Camden BLSU Camden, NJ 1974; Adjunct Professor, Delaware Law School, 1988-89; Adjunct Professor, Wilmington Coll, 1984-89. **Business Addr:** Resident Associate Judge, Superior Court of Delaware, Public Building, Wilmington, DE 19801.

MARTIN, JULIA M.
Educator (retired). **Personal:** Born Nov 9, 1924, Snow Hill, MD. **Educ:** Tuskegee Inst, BS 1946, MS Chem 1948; PA State Univ, PhD Biochemistry 1963. **Career:** Tuskegee Inst, instr of chem 1948-49; FL A&M Univ, asst prof of chem 1949-59; Tuskegee Inst, assoc prof of chem 1963-66; So Univ, prof of chem 1966-, spec asst to the dean 1973-74, acting dean of grad sch 1974-76, dean coll of sci 1978-retirement. **Orgs:** Mem Amer Chem Soc; Amer Assn for Advancement of Science; Amer Inst of Chemists; LA Acad of Scis; NY Acad of Scis; Natl Assn of Coll Women; Amer Assn of Univ Women; Alpha Kappa Alpha; YWCA; NAACP; mem Alpha Kappa Mu, Beta Kappa Chi, Iota Sigma Pi, Sigma Delta Epsilon, Gamma Sigma Delta; lectr United Negro Coll Fund Disting Lecture Series in Chemistry 1976, 1984; cncl mem LA Univ Marine Consortium (LUMCON); mem LA Cncl of Deans of Arts Science & Humanities 1978-, mem exec comm 1979-85, chmn 1983-84; mem exec comm Cncl of Colls of Arts & Scis 1982-85; Marine Div NANGUSC. **Honors/Awds:** Citation Outstanding Educ of Amer 1974-75; Urban League Fellow Union Carbide 1968; Fellow Hoffmann-LaRoche 1969. **Business Addr:** PO Box 9608, Southern University, Baton Rouge, LA 70813.

MARTIN, KIMBERLY LYNETTE
Community service coordinator. **Personal:** Born Sep 5, 1963, Detroit, MI; daughter of Eldon & Linda Martin. **Educ:** Univ of MI, BA, marketing mgt, 1985; Atlanta Univ, MBA, marketing/information systems, 1988; Wayne State Univ, PhD candidate, higher education, 1993-. **Career:** Highland Park Board of Educ, adult educ instructor, 1990-; Wayne State Univ, community services dir, 1992-. **Orgs:** Univ of MI Alumni Assn, 1985-; Atlanta Univ Alumni Assn, 1988-; Amer Assn of University Professors, 1992-; Natl Black MBA Assn, 1986-; Alpha Kappa Alpha Sorority Inc, 1983, Graduate Advisor, 1982-84. **Honors/Awds:** Wayne State Univ, Outstanding Contributor Award, 1994; Alpha Kappa Alpha Sorority, Inc, Outstanding Graduate Advisor for Great Lakes Region, 1994; State of MI Governor's Office, Nominee, State Community Service Award, 1993. **Business Addr:** Community Service Dir, Wayne State Univ, Student Center Bldg, Rm 351, Detroit, MI 48202, (313)577-3444.

MARTIN, LAWRENCE RAYMOND
Clergyman. **Personal:** Born Sep 4, 1935, Archie, LA; married Barbara Thompson; children: Lawrence II, Perry, Chantel. **Educ:** Grambling State U, BS 1959; United Theo Seminary, BTh 1973; Interdenom Theo Cntr & Morehouse Sch of Religion, MDiv 1973. **Career:** Monroe City Edu Assn, pres 1971-; NAACP Monroe, LA, pres 1973-74; Tenth Dist Assn, Bible Instr 1970-; United Theo Sem Am Bapt Exten Classes, tchr. **Orgs:** Mem Monroe City Educ Assn; LA Educ Assn; Nat Educ Assn; LA Bapt Conv; Nat Bapt Conv USA Inc; mem LA Bicentennial Comm; mem bd on Drug Abuse & Alcoholism Co hon col on staff, Gov Edwin Edwards.

MARTIN, LEE
Educator. **Personal:** Born Aug 4, 1938, Birmingham, AL; married Nora White; children: Lee, Jr, Kristi, Dia. **Educ:** Eastern MI U, BS, MA; Univ of MI, PhD. **Career:** Romulus Sch, dir 1974-; Metro Learning & Mental Health Clinic, co-dir 1974-; Univ of Detroit, instr 1973-74. **Orgs:** Mem Task Force 1977; mem MI Dept of Mental Health 1976; mem Cncl for Exceptional Children 1975-; mem MI Soc of Mental Health 1976-; mgmt bd Western Wayne Cnty YMCA; trustee Peoples Comm 1975; bd of dir Northwest Guidance Clinic 1975-; trustee Inkster Sch Bd 1973-; pres Annapolis Park Homeowner's Asso 1965-67; aiding fellow-minorities MI Asso for Retarded Citizens. **Honors/Awds:** Achvmt Spec Educ. **Business Addr:** 36540 Grant Rd, Romulus, MI 48174.

MARTIN, LEROY
City law enforcement official. **Personal:** Born Jan 29, 1929, Chicago, IL; son of Lela Burts and Henry Lee Martin; married Constance Bertha Martin, Jun 20, 1954; children: Ronald, LeRoy, Dawn. **Educ:** Northwestern University, Chicago, IL, police supervision, 1965; University of Illinois, police supervision, 1968; Roosevelt University, Chicago, IL, BA, psychology, 1972, collective bargaining, personnel administration, 1975, MPA, 1976; Illinois State Police Academy, Dimensional Management II, 1986; numerous courses from the Chicago Police Department. **Career:** Chicago Police Department, Chicago, IL, patrolman, 1955-64, sergeant, vice control and gambling, 1965-67, sergeant, internal affairs, 1967-70, patrol sergeant, 1970-71, supervising sergeant, 1971-75, lieutenant, 1975, inspector, 1976-79, commander, 1979-81, captain, 1981, director of public and internal information, 1981-82, commander of detectives, 1982-83, deputy chief of patrol, 1983-87, superintendent of police, 1987-. **Orgs:** Member, National Organization of Black Law Enforcement Executives, 1987-; advisory board member, Illinois Criminal Justice Information Authority, 1988-; advisory board member, YMCA, 1989-; chairman of advisory board, Chicago City-Wide Colleges, 1990-; advisory board member, Boy Scouts of America, Chicago Chapter, 1989-; National Association of Juvenile Officers; Roosevelt University Alumni Association; United Negro College Fund; Illinois Police Association; International Association of Chiefs of Police; Northwestern Traffic Institute; Chicago Assocaition of Commerce and Industry; Major City Chiefs; National Executive Institute; Salvation Army. **Honors/Awds:** Distinguished Service Award, Chicago Assn of Commerce and Industry, 1990; Outstanding Contribution to the Law Enforcement; Recognition Award for Support and Assistance, Chicago Housing Authority, 1990; City of Chicago Recognition Award to Make Chicago's Communities Drug Free, Mayor Richard Daley, 1990; We Care Role Model, Chicago Board of Education, 1986, 1987, 1988, 1989, 1990; Law Enforcement Man of the Year, Chicago Area Council, Boy Scouts of America, 1988; author, "Chicago Drug Enforcement Administration Task Force," Intl Assn of Chiefs of Police Magazine, February, 1984; profile, "Interview with Chicago Police Superintendent LeRoy Martin," Law Enforcement News, April, 1990; profile, "Interview Chicago Police Superintendent LeRoy Martin,"N'digo Magazine, July, 1990. **Business Addr:** Superintendent of Chicago Police, Chicago Police Dept, 1121 S State St, Rm 500, Chicago, IL 60605.

MARTIN, MAXINE SMITH
Educational administrator. **Personal:** Born Aug 9, 1944, Charleston, SC; daughter of Emily Simmons Smith and Henry W Smith; married Montez C Jr, Mar 8, 1974; children: Emily Elise; Montez C III. **Educ:** Hampton Inst Hampton, VA, BS 1966; Atlanta U, MA 1973. **Career:** Coll of Charleston, student prog coord/advisor Center for Continuing Educ 1985-; Charleston County School Dist & Trident Tech Coll, English instr 1980-85; Coll of Charleston, dir of coll relations 1979-80, public inf specialist 1973-79; Morehouse Coll, fed relations coord 1972-73; Atlanta U, pub relations asst 1971-72; Supplementary Educ Cntr, publ specialist 1970-71; Charleston County School District, reading consultant II 1988-89. **Orgs:** Mem Charleston Chap Hampton Univ Alumni Assoc 1966-, Delta Sigma Theta 1969-, YWCA 1971-, Council for the Advancement & Support of Educ 1973-80, Coll News Assoc 1973-80; mem, comm chmn Charleston Chap of Links Inc 1974-; bd mem Charleston Area Mental Health Assoc 1976-80; mem Univ & Coll Designers1977-80; bd mem Charleston Civic Ballet 1983-85, Florence Crittenton Home 1983-85, SC Assoc of Higher Continuing Educ 1985-; bd of dirs, Young Charleston Theatre Company 1988-. **Honors/Awds:** Cert for Pub Relations Serv, Delta Sigma Theta 1975; Cert for Pub Relations Serv, YWCA 1975; Cert for Pub Relations Serv, Am Freedom Train Found 1977; YWCA Public Relations Awd 1984, YWCA Twin Women Awd 1985; WPAL Radio Community Serv Awd 1986. **Business Addr:** Student Prog Advisor/Coord, College of Charleston, 25 St Philip St, Charleston, SC 29424.

MARTIN, MCKINLEY C.
Educational administrator. **Personal:** Born Dec 2, 1936, Clarksdale, MS; married Willie Beatrice Burns; children: McKinley C II, Myron Craig, Marcia Corteze. **Educ:** Coahoma Jr Coll, AA (Magna Cum Laude); Jackson State Univ, BS (Cum Laude) 1961; Delta State Univ, ME 1967; FL State Univ, PhD (Summa Cum Laude) 1972. **Career:** Sandy Bayou Elementary School, principal 1962-65; Coahoma Jr Coll, registrar 1965-66; FL State Univ, instructor/admin asst 1970-72; Coahoma Jr Coll, dir continuing educ, 1973-80, pres 1980-92; LeMoyne-Owen College, Memphis TN, professor, Graduate Div, assistant to the president and dean, 1992-; Northside High School, counselor. **Orgs:** Exec bd mem Coahoma Cty Chamber of Commerce; planning com Governor's Office of Job Devel & Training; spec steering com US Dept of the Interior-Historically Black Coll & Univ; state chmn Child Devel Assoc, Delta Agency for Progress; mem Coahoma Cty Port Com, Hira #131 Shrine Temple, HW Nichols Lodge #556-Elk, Prince Hall Mason, Alpha Phi Alpha Fraternity; Mem, Planning Committee of the US Dept of Educ, Office of Student Financial Assistance; US Dept of the Interior's Natl Parks Services; Coahoma County Committee on the Lower Mississippi Delta Development Act; Leadership Clarksdale Bd of Dir; Mississippi Junior & Community coll Economic Council, Vice Pres of the Mississippi Assn of Community & Junior Colleges; vice chmn, Mississippi Assn of Community & JuniorColl Legislative Committee; M Univ of Mississippi Minority Advisory Bd; Black Business Association of Memphis; president, Mississippi Association of Community and Junior Colleges; pres, guidance division, TN Vocational Association. **Honors/Awds:** Citizen of the Year, Clarksdale Coahoma County, 1990. **Military Serv:** AUS 1955-58.

MARTIN, MONTEZ CORNELIUS, JR.
Construction engineer, county official. **Personal:** Born Jun 11, 1940, Columbia, SC; married E Maxine Smith; children: Tanya Elayne, Terrie Lanita, Emily Elise, Montez Cornelius III. **Educ:** Hampton Inst, BS 1963; Polytech Inst Brooklyn, grad studies 1967. **Career:** WSB-TV, acct exe, 1970; WSOK Radio, dir of operations 1973-74; Coll of Charleston, dir constrn 1974-80; Montez Real Estate, broker-in-charge 1976-92; Charleston County Housing and Redevelopment Authority, executive director, 1992-. **Orgs:** SC Chap Natl Assn Real Estate Brokers 1977-; Greater Charleston Bd of Realtors 1979-; Charleston Citywide Local Development Corp., president; Natl Assn of Community Clg Trustees; South Carolina Assn of Technical Clg Cmsners, president; Trident Technical Clg, Area Cmsn, chairman; South Carolina Cncl on Economic Ed, director; South Carolina Cmte for Excellence in Ed, business ed subcmte; City of Charleston Headquarters Cmte; Trident Urban League Formation Cmte; Leadership South Carolina Alumni Assn. **Honors/Awds:** Marketeer of the Yr Atlanta Chap Natl Assn Market Developers 1972; Certificate Am Freedom Train Found 1977; Cert of Achievement Beta Kappa Lambda Chap Alpha Phi Alpha Frat Inc 1978; Living the Legacy Awd Columbia Sect Natl Council of Negro Women, 1980; Leadership South Carolina, Class of 1982; Charleston Business & Professional Assn, Community Involvement Award, 1985. **Special Achievements:** Contributing editor, The Business Roundtable Participation Guide: A Primer for Business on Education, 1990; "Business Education Partnerships," South Carolina Business Journal, South Carolina Chamber of Commerce, 1989. **Military Serv:** US Army, maj, 1963-70; Presidental Unit Citation, 1967; Army Commendation w/Oak Leaf Cluster, 1967, 1969; Meritorious Service Medal, 1970. **Business Addr:** Executive Director, Charleston County Housing and Development Authority, 2106 Mt Pleasant St, Charleston, SC 29403, (803)722-1942.

MARTIN, PATRICIA ELIZABETH
Law enforcement official. **Personal:** Born May 29, 1951, Brooklyn, NY; daughter of Helen Elizabeth Smith Martin and Malverse Martin Sr; children: Linese Antoinette Martin. **Educ:** New York Community College, Brooklyn, NY, AAS, nursing, 1972; City College, New York, NY, BS, nursing, 1990; NY City Technical Coll, AAS hospitality, 1995. **Career:** St. Vincent's Hospital, New York, NY, registered nurse, 1973-81; New York City Police Department, New York, NY, sergeant, 1981-91; lieutenant, 1991-. **Orgs:** Member, Guardians Association, 1982-; member, National Org. Black Law Enforcement Executives, 1989-; member, Police Women Endowment, 1984-; member, NOBLWE, 1985-; member, International Association of Women Police, 1986-; St George Association, 1987; church usher, Bentel Tabernacle AME Church; Northeast Association of Women Police, 1988. **Home Addr:** 204-04 45th Rd, Bayside, NY 11361.

MARTIN, PAUL W.
Dentist. **Personal:** Born Dec 4, 1940, Columbus, OH; son of Pauline Locke Martin and Emmeal Martin; married Barbara Burts, Jun 30, 1973; children: Todd Christopher Emmeal. **Educ:** Indiana Univ Sch of Dentistry, BS, DDS 1958-62; IN State Teachers Coll, 1955-58; Harlem Hospital, oral surgery residency, 1969-72; NY Univ Coll of Dentistry, 1978. **Career:** Indiana Univ School of Dentistry, instructor, 1965-69; Prison Health Serv, dir 1973-75; Hostos Community College, asst professor, 1975-76; private practice, oral surgery 1976; North Gen Hospital, acting chief of oral surg 1985; Harlem Hospital Ctr, assoc attending surgery 1986-; Mt Sinai School of Medicine, clinical instructor, 1986-; Gov Hospital, staff oral surgeon; 223 W 80th St Corp, pres 1983-. **Orgs:** Mem Frontiers Intl 1963-; co-founder/mem exec comm Natl Dental Acupuncture Soc 1984-; member, American Dental Assn, 1962-; member, National Dental Assn, 1963-; member, National Society of Oral & Maxillofacial Surgeons, 1990-; member, American College of Oral & Maxillofacial Surgeons, 1989-; member, International Society of Plastic, Aesthetic & Reconstructive Surgery Inc, 1990-. **Honors/Awds:** Topical Antibiotic Maintenance of Oral Health 1968; Supraorbital Emphysema 1972; Phencyclidine (PCP) Abuse 1986; Crack Abuse 1987; Fellow, American College of Dentists, 1990; fellow, American College of Acupuncture, 1991; fellow, Royal Society of Health, 1962. **Military Serv:** USNR lt 1963-69. **Business Addr:** President, 223 W 80th St Corp, 2 W 86th St, New York, NY 10024.

MARTIN, RALPH C., II
County official, attorney. **Career:** Suffolk County District Attorney's Office, district attorney, 1992-. **Special Achievements:** First African American district attorney named to Suffolk County. **Business Addr:** District Attorney, Suffolk County, New Court House, Pemberton Square, Boston, MA 02108, (617)725-8600.

MARTIN, RAYFUS
Educator (retired). **Personal:** Born Jan 12, 1930, Franklinton, LA; married Elnora Lowe; children: Mechelle Denise. **Educ:** Leland College, BA 1956; Southern Univ, 1973; Southeastern LA Univ, MEd 1974. **Career:** St Tammary HS, teacher, English, 1957; Washington Parish HS, History teacher, 1962-90; Franklinton HS, English teacher 1969-90. **Orgs:** First African-American council member Town of Franklinton 1975-. **Hon-**

ors/Awds: Received a Plaque, Mayor of Franklinton for having served on the Council for 20 Years, 1996. **Special Achievements:** Poems: A Readers Creed, 1995; Twenty Frogs, 1995. **Military Serv:** US Army, corpl 1951-54. **Home Addr:** PO Box 93, Franklinton, LA 70438.

MARTIN, REDDRICK LINWOOD
Real estate agent. **Personal:** Born Jul 20, 1934, Anderson, SC; son of Mamie Lee Martin and Reddrick B Martin; married Ernestine Heath. **Educ:** Allen Univ, BS 1962. **Career:** Winnsboro SC Pub Schs, tchr 1962-63; Lancaster SC Public Schs, tchr 1963; Columbia Coca-Cola Bottling Co Columbia SC, sales & Mktg rep 1963-73; Miami Coca-Cola Bottling Co, regional market mgr 1973-76; Coca Cola USA, area mktg mgr 1976-82, market develop mgr 1982-83; Martin Real Estate Investment Co, pres, currently; real estate agent, 1989-. **Orgs:** Bd mem Palmetta Businessmen Assn 1970-73; bd mem OIC Columbia, SC 1972-73; adv bd mem Bus Dept Ft Valley State Coll 1980; mem Industry Cluster A&T State Univ 1980; mem NAACP; mem Urban League; bd mem Natl Assn of Market Developers 1983-. **Honors/Awds:** Outstanding Serv Award in Community Affairs, Save Our Community Club Columbia, SC 1970; Meritorious Serv Award in Pub Affairs, So Regional Press Inst Savannah State Coll 1980; Richmond Perrine Optimist Club, Community Service Award, 1974; MEAC Conference, Service Award, 1981; Ft Val State Coll, Business Department, Service Award, 1987. **Military Serv:** USAF airman 1st class 1954-57. **Business Addr:** President, Martin's Real Estate Inv Co, 1123 Braemar Ave SW, Atlanta, GA 30311.

MARTIN, RICHARD CORNISH
Cleric. **Personal:** Born Oct 15, 1936, Philadelphia, PA; son of Virginia Lorette Bullock Martin and Leon Freeman Martin. **Educ:** Pennsylvania State Univ, BA in Science 1958; Episcopal Theolgical Seminary in VA, Master of Divinity 1961; St Augustine's Coll, Canterbury; Howard Univ, Washington DC, DMin 1988. **Career:** PA State Univ, chaplain 1961-64; St Andrew's Church State Coll PA, assoc rector 1961-64; George Washington Univ, Washington DC, chaplain 1964-66; St Paul's Parish, Washington DC, assoc rector 1966-73, rector 1989-96; St George's Parish, Washington DC, rector 1973-89; The Church of the Advent, interim vicar, 1996-. **Orgs:** Superior Soc of Mary Amer Region 1966-; pres Prevention of Blindness Soc 1982-84; mem Studia Liturgica; dir Comm Outreach Ministry; mem Inter-Church Club; board, Hospice DC; chr, Americans Friends of Anglican Centre in Rome; Anglican International Liturgical Consultation; bd of trustees, Nachotah House Seminary. **Honors/Awds:** Editor Studies & Commentaries I & IV; editor The Dragon; composer Liturgical Music. **Home Addr:** 135 Mt Vernon St, Boston, MA 02108. **Business Phone:** (617)724-2174.

MARTIN, ROBERT E. (BOB)
Broadcast journalist, producer. **Personal:** Born Dec 17, 1948, Bronx, NY; son of Mary Martin and Robert Martin; divorced; children: LeRonne. **Educ:** RCA Inst, graduated 1973. **Career:** WABC-TV, assoc producer 1971-72; Capital Formation Inc, dir of comm 1972-75; WNEW-TV, producer 1976-83; WNBC-TV, producer 1983-88; Fox-TV, reporter/producer, ''A Current Affair,'' 1988-93, self-employed; MSNBC, currently; Unified Force Zujitsu-Ryu Martial Arts, chief instructor, currently. **Orgs:** Writers Guild of Amer East; former mem Council of Concerned Black Exec; YMCA; former dir Male Echoes 1st Union Bapt Ch; AFTRA; NYAJB; NABJ. **Honors/Awds:** Emmy Awd ''Like It Is'' spl on Attica NY 1972; Spl Awd for Promotion of Orgn NY Jaycees 1973; Serv Awd Salvation Army 1977; CEBA Award 1988. **Military Serv:** AUS, sgt-E5, 1969-71.

MARTIN, ROSETTA P.
Librarian. **Personal:** Born Jun 20, 1930, Charleston, SC; daughter of Della Scott Poaches and Phoenix Poaches, Sr; married George E Martin. **Educ:** Morgan State Coll, BA 1953; Boston U, adv grad work in Educ 1957; Simmon Coll, MS 1962. **Career:** Trident Technical College, Main Campus, Charleston, SC, librarian 1978-; Tufts U, ref Librarian 1970-78, supr curriculum lab 1965-, asst ref librarian 1963-70; Manning HS, tchr 1954-55; Boston Public Lib, children's librarian 1958-63. **Orgs:** Mem Am Library Assn; Special Library Assn; New England Library Assn; Am Assn of Univ Profs; Librarians in Educ & Research in The NE; mem NAACP; Civic Assn; Black Bibliographer; Assn for Study of Negro Life & Hist; member, South Carolina Library Assn; member, Charleston Library Consortium; member, Bibliographic Instruction Section. **Home Addr:** 2346 Brevard Rd, Charleston, SC 29414. **Business Addr:** Reference Librarian/Coordinator of Bibliographic Instruction, Trident Technical College, PO Box 10367, Main Campus LR-M, Charleston, SC 29411.

MARTIN, RUBY JULENE WHEELER
Administrator. **Personal:** Born Jan 24, 1931, Charleston, SC; daughter of Pearl Gladys Dunn Wheeler and Coleman James Wheeler; married Edward Alfred Martin, Sep 6, 1952 (divorced); children: Angela Zora, Edward Alfred Jr. **Educ:** Bennett College, BA 1952; SC State College, MS 1959; Syracuse University, EdD 1968. **Career:** Bonds Wilson High School, instructor of English & French 1953-55; SC State College, asst prof of English 1959-64, asst prof of reading 1964-68, professor of reading 1969-; Learning Resources Reading Center, TN State Univ, dir; TN State Univ, head dept Teaching and Learning 1986-, head dept Reading & Special Educ 1979-. **Orgs:** Consultant, Inst for Serv to Educ, Washington DC 1972-74; ed adv bd, Intl Reading Assn 1973-77; Natl Reading Conf Yearbook 1973-74; consultant, State of MS First Annual Reading Conf 1975; consultant, Dr Mary F Berry Asst Sec for Dept of HEW 1978; chmn, TSU, First & Second Natl Basic Skills Conf 1978-79; field reader, Tech Serv Dept of HEW Office of Educ 1980; consultant, Southern Assn of Coll & Schools Atlanta GA 1980-; public comm, Intl Reading Assn 1984-85; Girl Friends, Inc 1972-; president Nashville Chapter, Girls Friends, Inc 1989-91; Delta Sigma Theta; International Reading Association 1966-. **Honors/Awds:** Published ''Current Issues-The Public College'' Journal of Reading vol 16 #3 1972, ''Realities & Fallacies of Tea Rea to Black High School Students'' Journal of Reading vol 18 1975; reviewer of books for young people Journal of Reading 1977; listed in 2000 Women of Achievement Melrose Press, London and Dartmouth 1970-71. **Business Addr:** Head Teaching & Learning Department, Tennessee State University, PO Box 850, Nashville, TN 37203.

MARTIN, RUSSELL F.
Dental consultant, dentist. **Personal:** Born Aug 18, 1929, Hartford; married Jean E Procope. **Educ:** Howard U, BS 1950, DDS 1955; Yale U;; MPH 1970. **Career:** Pvt Practice Hartford, 1957-58; St Dept of Hlth, operated Mobile Dental Trailer Unit in Rural CT 1957-58; Hartford Dispensary;; staff dentist 1958-68; Univ of CT Hlth Cntr, staff dentist 1968-69; Univ of CT Hlth Cntr research assoc 1969-70; Hlth Action Survey proj dir 1969-70; Cit Hlth Action Coun HEW, proj dir 1971-72; Hlth Planning Coun Inc assoc dir 1972-74; Pvt Practice; Dept of Corrections, staff dentist; Aetna Ins Co, dental cons; Dept of Comm Dentistry Univ of CT, clinical assoc 1974-. **Orgs:** Mem Am Dental Assn; CT St Dental Assn; Hartford Dental Soc; Am Pub Hlth Assn; CT St Pub Hlth Assn; bd dir Comm Hlth Serv Inc Hartford, pres bd; mem pub hlth & welfare comm Urban League of Greater Hartford; Sickle Cell Anemia & Com Bloomfield CT; adv com on Occupational Therapy, Manchester Comm Coll; Ambulatory Hlth Care Coun Inc; chp NW Hartford Hlth Care Task Force ; bd dir Urban League of Greater Hartford; Minority Involvement in Higher Educ Com Hew Haven CT Co-author ''Health & Health Care in Hartfords N End'' 1974. **Military Serv:** AUS Dental Corps capt 1955-57. **Business Addr:** Aetna Life & Casualty Dntl Cla, 151 Farmington Ave, Hartford, CT 06105.

MARTIN, SAMUEL
Business executive. **Personal:** Born Sep 20, 1918, Newport, AR. **Educ:** Prairie View St Coll 1938-39; KCK Jr Coll. **Career:** Atlanta Life Ins Co KC KS, staff mgr; hd stockman & union ldr AFL-CIO; Nat Bellas Hess KC MO; rec dir KC Recreastion Dept; vice pres Atlanta Life Agency Group 1972-74; vP Greater & KC Underwriters 1971-72; pres Greater KC Underwriters 1973-74. **Orgs:** Introduced Boys Club of Am Prog KC KS 1972-74. **Honors/Awds:** Recpt Sales & Serv Awd Atlanta Life Ins Co 1972; Sales & Serv Awd Nat Ins Assn 1971-73; grad Agency Mgmt Assn 1973; Silver Tray Otstndng Sales 1973; Staff Mgr Cert 1974. **Military Serv:** AUS 1943-45. **Business Addr:** 4725 Paseo, Kansas City, MO.

MARTIN, SHEDRICK M., JR.
Government official. **Personal:** Born Jan 5, 1927, Savannah, GA; son of Hattie Mew Martin and Shedrick Martin; married Laura B Randolph, Jan 10, 1956; children: Beverly Anne, Brenda Annette. **Educ:** Savannah St Coll, BS biology, 1951; FBI Nat Acad 1970. **Career:** Special Deputy US Marshall, court security officer, 1994-; City of Savannah, Savannah, GA, dir of code enforcement, 1988-94; dept of pub serv adminstr 1972; Savannah, personnel asst training 1971-72; Savannah GA Police Dept, detective 1957-70; Chatham Co Bd of Educ Savannah, tchr 1952-57; US Postal Service, Atlanta, GA, railway postal clerk, 1951-52. **Orgs:** Mem Am Public Works Assn; Fraternal Order of Police; NAACP; Cath Holy Name Soc; Wolves Social Club; vice pres, Chatham South Lions Club, 1988-. **Military Serv:** AUS 1945-46. **Home Addr:** 17 Stillwood Circle E, Savannah, GA 31406. **Business Addr:** Dir of Code Enforcement, City of Savannah, PO Box 1027, Savannah, GA 31402.

MARTIN, SHERMAN THEODORE
Senior programmer/analyst. **Personal:** Born Mar 8, 1954, Detroit, MI; son of Floyd A and Inez C Martin; married Valencia Mic, Aug 22, 1981; children: DaNita Pattie, Raytheon Mahari, Nekia Danielle. **Educ:** Wayne State University, BA, 1977; Focus Hope Machinist Institute, certificate, 1991. **Career:** Merit Systems Inc, programmer, 1978-82; System Management Consultant, programmer analyst, team leader, 1982-83; Grand Trunk Western RR, data base analyst, 1984-89; Computer and Engineering Svcs, consultant, 1989-89; Focus: Hope, programmer, 1991-93; Eastern Michigan University, senior programmer analyst, 1993-. **Orgs:** IEE, Computer Society. **Business Addr:** Senior Programmer/Analyst, Eastern Michigan University, 127 Pray Harrold, Ypsilanti, MI 48197, (313)487-1288.

MARTIN, STEVEN ALBERT
Professional football player. **Personal:** Born May 31, 1974, St Paul, MN. **Educ:** University of Missouri. **Career:** Indianapolis Colts, defensive tackle, 1996-. **Business Addr:** Professional Football Player, Indianapolis Colts, PO Box 535000, Indianapolis, IN 46253, (317)297-2658.

MARTIN, SYLVIA COOKE
Government official, human resource manager. **Personal:** Born May 2, 1938, Baltimore, MD; daughter of Clara M Evans Cook and Emanuel Levi Cook; married Lawrence P Groce; children: Donald E K Martin, Marcia Lauren Martin. **Educ:** Univ of Maryland, College Park MD, BA, 1972, MPS, 1978; Univ of Virginia, Charlottesville VA, cert, 1975; Bowie State University, cert 1987. **Career:** Social Security Admin, Baltimore MD, file clerk, 1963-66, health insurance analyst, 1966, mgmt intern, 1968-70; Social Security Admin and Health Care Financing Admin, Baltimore MD, career devel specialist, 1970-78; Bowie State College, Bowie, MD, instructor, 1986-89; lecturer; Library of Congress, Washington DC, chief of staff training and devel, 1978-; self-employed mgmt consultant, 1979-. **Orgs:** National Pierians Inc, parlimentarian, 1985-89, recording secretary, 1989-91; historian, Natl Assn of Negro Business and Professional Women's Clubs, Inc, 1978-89; Daniel Murray African-American Culture Association, president, 1984-85, 1987-88; historian, 1984-85, parliamentarian, 1985-88, pres, 1988-90, African-American Historical and Genealogical Soc; Maryland Historical Soc, 1980-89; Oral History Assn, 1984-89; Natl Council of Negro Women; life mem, NAACP; Delta Sigma Theta, 1983-91; Maryland Genealogical Society, 1980-91; Harriet Tubman Genealogical Society. **Honors/Awds:** Commissioner's citation, Social Security Admin, 1972; Health Care Financing Administration, Director's Citation, 1978; distinguished achievement award, Conference of Minority Public Administrators, 1980; distinguished service award, 1983, Sojourner Truth Award, 1985, Natl Assoc of Negro Business and Professional Women's Clubs Inc; special achievement awards, Library of Congress, 1987, 1988; dedication and leadership award, Afro-American Historical and Genealogical Soc, 1989. **Special Achievements:** Author: Another Cook Book, A Family History, 1989; /editor, Just For You Cook Book, 1986; developer/designer, African-American history month exhibits. **Home Addr:** 6375 Shadowshape Place, Columbia, MD 21045. **Business Addr:** Chief, Staff Training and Development, Library of Congress, Washington, DC 20540.

MARTIN, TONY
Educator. **Personal:** Born Feb 21, 1942, Port-of-Spain, Trinidad and Tobago; son of Vida B Scope Martin and Claude G Martin. **Educ:** Hon Soc of Gray's Inn, Barrister-at-Law 1965; Univ of Hull England, BSc Economics (honors) 1968; MI State Univ, MA History 1970, PhD History 1973. **Career:** St Mary's Coll Trinidad, teacher 1962-63; Univ of MI Flint, asst prof 1971-73; Wellesley Coll, assoc prof 1973-79, full prof 1979-. **Orgs:** Mem Negro Historical Assn of Colorado Springs; vice pres Natl Council for Black Studies New England 1984-86; exec bd mem African Heritage Studies Assn 1982-88; exec bd Assn of Caribbean Historians; mem Assn for the Study of Afro-Amer Life History; Association for the Study of Classical African Civilizations. **Honors/Awds:** Numerous publications including ''Race First: The Ideological and Organizational Struggles of Marcus Garvey and the Universal Negro Improvement Assn'' 1976; Literary Garveyism: Garvey, Black Arts and the Harlem Renaissance, 1983; African Fundamentalism: A Literary & Cultural Anthology of Garvey's Harlem Renaissance, 1991. **Business Addr:** Professor, Dept of Africana Studies, Wellesley College, Wellesley, MA 02181, (781)283-2564.

MARTIN, TONY DERRICK
Professional football player. **Personal:** Born Sep 5, 1965, Miami, FL. **Educ:** Mesa College, business management major. **Career:** Miami Dolphins, wide receiver, 1990-93; San Diego Chargers, 1994-. **Business Addr:** Professional Football Player, San Diego Chargers, Qualcomm Stadium, 9449 Friars Rd, San Diego, CA 92108, (619)280-2111.

MARTIN, WALTER L.
Operations manager. **Personal:** Born Apr 15, 1951, New York, NY; son of Elizabeth Monterio Brito Martin and Robert Martin; married Regina Marvel Montgomery; children: Shalya Mekeela Kelly, Merissa Tarla Mekeshia. **Educ:** Northeastern Univ, BS 1975; Atlanta Univ, MBA 1977. **Career:** Pyramidwest Develop Corp, financial analyst/accountant 1979-82; Mobil Chem Co, financial analyst 1982-83; Federal Express Corp, sr financial analyst 1983-86, station oper mgt 1986-. **Orgs:** Dir Changes the Full Arts Production Co 1977-82; chairman allocation comm Youth Services United Way Atlanta 1985-; dir membership Natl Black MBA Assoc Atlanta 1985-86; dir student affairs Natl Black MBA Assoc Atlanta 1987; partner East Coast mgmt Group. **Business Addr:** Station Operations Mgr, Federal Express Corp, 2441 Cheshire Bridge Rd, Atlanta, GA 30324.

MARTIN, WAYNE
Automobile dealer. **Personal:** Born Dec 31, 1949, Boston, MA; son of Helen N Martin and Harry K Martin; married Millie Christmas Martin, Jun 7, 1969; children: Charmaine, Shondalyn, Michael. **Career:** Weisenberger Motor Co, sales manager,

1978-86; Bob Hoy's World Auto Market, general sales manager, 1986-89; Vision Ford Lincoln Mercury, Inc, president/owner, 1989-. **Orgs:** NAACP, Alamogordo Chapter; Children in Need of Services, board member; Alamogordo Chamber of Commerce; Adult Basic Education, board member; Ford, Lincoln Mercury Minority Dealer, Board of Directors (FLMMDA). **Honors/Awds:** City of Alamogordo, Business of the Year Award, 1996; New Mexico, Governor's VIVA Award 1995-. **Military Serv:** Army, e-4, 1970-71. **Business Addr:** President, Vision Ford Lincoln Mercury, Inc, 1500 White Sands Blvd, Alamogordo, NM 88310, 800-669-8474.

MARTIN, WAYNE (JERALD)
Professional football player. **Personal:** Born Oct 26, 1965, Forrest City, AR; married Gladys; children: Wayne Jr, Whitley. **Educ:** University of Arkansas, bachelor's degree in criminal justice, 1990. **Career:** New Orleans Saints, defensive tackle, 1989-. **Honors/Awds:** Ed Block Courage Award, 1991; Pro Bowl, 1994. **Business Addr:** Professional Football Player, New Orleans Saints, 5800 Airline Hwy, Metairie, LA 70003, (504)733-0255.

MARTIN, WILLIAM R.
Chemist. **Personal:** Born Dec 19, 1926, Washington, DC; married Mildred Dixon; children: William R, Jr, Janice Y. **Educ:** Morgan St Coll, BS 1951; PA Southeastern U, MBA 1976. **Career:** Food & Drug Adminstrn, chemist drug mfg controls 1963-; Howard U, reseasrch proj 1962-63; Nat Inst Mntl Hlth research neurochem 1960-62; Walter Reed Ins, reseasrch biochem 1955-60; NIH, biologist 1952-55. **Orgs:** Mem Am Soc Qual Control 1972-; Plymouth Cong United Ch Christ; past chmn Bowie St Coll Bd Of Visitors 1973-78; mem exec bd Prince George Co; NAACP 1979; Chillum-ray Citizens Assn; imed past pres Morgan St Univ Nat Alumni Assn; mem DC Metro Chptr NCCJ; Org Black Sci; mem Omega Psi Phi Frat; Dem. **Military Serv:** USN 1944-46. **Business Addr:** 5600 Fishers Ln, Rockville, MD 20852.

MARTIN CHASE, DEBRA
Entertainment company executive. **Educ:** Mount Holyoke Coll, AB, 1977; Harvard Law School, JD, 1981. **Career:** Butler & Binion, assoc, 1981-82; Mayor, Day & Caldwell, assoc, 1982-83; Tenneco Inc, atty, 1984-85; Columbia Pictures, motion picture dept, atty; Mundy Lane Entertainment, sr vice pres; BrownHouse Productions, exec vp, producing partner, currently. **Special Achievements:** Produced Devil In A Blue Dress; Courage Under Fire; "Hank Aaron: Chasing The Dream;" The Preacher's Wife; "Rodgers & Hammerstien's Cinderella," 1997. **Business Addr:** Executive Vice President, BrownHouse Productions, 8439 Sunset Blvd, Ste 106, West Hollywood, CA 90069, (213)650-2670.

MARTIN-CROSS, DENISE L.
Attorney, government official. **Personal:** Born May 16, 1953, Cincinnati, OH; daughter of Paul & Julia Martin; married Edward H Cross, IV, Apr 16; children: Vashon, Danielle, Hewitt. **Educ:** Wilberforce Univ, BA, 1975; Univ of Akron Law School, JD, 1978. **Career:** Erie County Pennsylvania, public defender, 1979-87; Montgomery Cty Prosecutors Office, asst cty prosecutor, 1988-90; Montgomery Cty Juvenile Ct, chief magistrate, legal director, 1990-. **Orgs:** Child Protection Task Force for Montgomery County; Delta Sigma Theta Sorority Inc; Thurgood Marshall Law Society; Ohio Bar Association; Ohio Association of Magistrates. **Business Addr:** Attorney, Legal Director, Montgomery County Juvenile Court, 303 W 2nd St, Ste 1125, Dayton, OH 45422, (937)225-4252.

MARTINEZ, RALPH
Chief executive. **Career:** Town and Country Chrysler-Plymouth Inc, Milwaukie, OR, chief exec. **Business Addr:** Town and Country Chrysler-Plymouth Inc, 16803 SE McLoughlin Blvd, Milwaukie, OR 97267.

MARTINEZ, RAMON JAIME
Professional baseball player. **Personal:** Born Mar 22, 1968, Santo Domingo, Dominican Republic. **Career:** Los Angeles Dodgers, pitcher, 1988-. **Honors/Awds:** Member of the Dominican Republic Olympic baseball team, 1984; National League All-Star Team, 1990. **Business Addr:** Professional Baseball Player, Los Angeles Dodgers, 1000 Elysian Park Avenue, Los Angeles, CA 90012-1199.

MARTIN-OGUNSOLA, DELLITA LILLIAN
Educator. **Personal:** Born Oct 27, 1946, New Orleans, LA; daughter of Wilma M Martin (deceased) and Ret Sgt Wellie Martin (deceased); married David Olajire Ogunsola, Aug 22, 1979; children: Oludare Ajayi-Martin Ogunsola, Oladimeji Ade-Olu Ogunsola. **Educ:** Louisiana State Univ, New Orleans, BA, 1968; Ohio State Univ, MA, 1971, PhD, 1975. **Career:** St Mathias High School, instructor of Spanish/French, 1975-76; Univ of Alabama-Birmingham, asst prof of Spanish, 1976-82, assoc prof of Spanish, 1982-, chair of dept of foreign langs, 1993-. **Orgs:** Afro-Hispanic Association, consulting and contributing editor, 1990-; Alabama Association of Teachers of Spanish, 1977-; Association of Caribbean Studies, liaison sec, 1979, 1982-84; College Language Association, 1977-; Hispanic Conf of Greater Birmingham, 1984-; Modern Language Association, 1976, sec 1977-78, chair Afro-Am ex com, 1979; South Atlantic Modern Lang Assn, 1979-; Alabama Humanities Foundation, sec exec sub-committee 1978-80, chair nominations sub-committee, 1979. **Honors/Awds:** Faculty Rep to the Bd of Trustees, Univ of Alabama System, 1994-95; Phi Beta Delta, Beta Nu Chapter, Charter Member Honor Soc for International Scholars, 1992; Alpha Lambda Delta, UAB Honorary Faculty Member, 1992; UAB-Univ College, Ingalls Finalist for Teaching Excellence, 1979-80, 1983, 1989; Sigma Delta Pi, Omicron Mu Chapter, UAB Faculty/Assoc Member, 1985; Dir of Amer Scholars Listings, 1978, 1982. **Special Achievements:** Selected Poems of Langston Hughes and Nicolas Guillen, Doctoral Dissertation, Ohio State Univ, 1975; "West African & Hispanic Elements in NG's La cancion del bongo," South Atlantic Bulletin, 45:1, p 47-63, 1980; "Langston Hughes & the Musico-Poetry of the African Diaspora," in Langston Hughes Review, 5:1, p 1-17, 1986; "Translation as a Poetic Experience/Experiment: Short Fiction of Quince Duncan," Afro-Hispanic Review, 10:3, p 42-50, 1991; Las mejores historias/The Best Short Stories of San Jose: Editorial, Quince Duncan, Costa Rica, 1995. **Business Addr:** Assoc Prof of Spanish/Chair of Dept of Foreign Langs & Lits, University of Alabama at Birmingham, 900 S 13th St, Arts & Humanities Bldg Rm 407-B, Birmingham, AL 35294-1260, (205)934-1834.

MARTS, LONNIE
Professional football player. **Personal:** Born Nov 10, 1968, New Orleans, LA; married Gionne; children: Gilone, Lonnie III. **Educ:** Tulane, BA in general studies. **Career:** Kansas City Chiefs, linebacker, 1991-93; Tampa Bay Buccaneers, 1994-96; Tennessee Oilers, 1997-. **Business Addr:** Professional Football Player, Tennessee Oilers, c/o Baptist Sports Park, 7640 H 70-5, Nashville, TN 37221.

MARVE, EUGENE RAYMOND
Professional football player (retired). **Personal:** Born Aug 14, 1960, Flint, MI. **Educ:** Saginaw Valley State College, attended. **Career:** Linebacker: Buffalo Bills, 1982-87; Tampa Bay Buccaneers, 1988-89. **Honors/Awds:** Named to Football Digest and Pro Football Weekly All-Rookie teams and was fourth in balloting for AP Defensive Rookie-of-the-Year; two-time NAIA All-Amer at Saginaw Valley State College; two-time MVP; three-time All-Great Lakes conf pick; named to the Amer Football Coaches Assn All-Amer Team, 1981; Bills' candidate for Lite/NFL Man of the Year 1984-85.

MARYLAND, MARY ANGELA
Nurse, educator. **Personal:** Born Sep 27, 1953, Cincinnati, OH; daughter of Christine Nero and James Pearl. **Educ:** Elmhurst College, Elmhurst, IL, BA, psychology, 1975; Malcolm X College, Chicago, IL, AAS, nursing, 1977; Chicago State University, Chicago, IL, BSN, 1980; Governors State University, University Park, IL, MSN, nursing admin, 1983. **Career:** Mount Sinai Hospital Medical Ctr, Chicago, IL, staff nurse II, 1977-83; Evangelical Health Systems, Oak Brook, IL, management engineer, 1983-85; City Colleges of Chicago, Chicago, IL, nursing faculty, 1985-87; University of Illinois at Chicago College of Nursing, Chicago, IL, coord, urban health program/recruiter, admissions counselor, 1987-90, research assistant, 1990-. **Orgs:** Member, Nominating Committee, Medical Surgical Nursing, American Nurses Assn, 1989-92; member, steering committee, Illinois Nurses Assn, 1989-91; member, Assn of Black Nursing Faculty, 1988-; member, American Assn of Critical Care Nurses, 1980-; member, People to People International, 1988-. **Honors/Awds:** Certified Medical Surgical Nurse, American Nurses Assn, 1981-; Outstanding and Dedicated Service Award, Chicago Public Schools, 1989; Service Award, Illinois Council for College Attendace, 1990; Co-Investigator, I'm Ready Minority Recruitment Program, Robert Wood Johnson Foundation, 1990; Principal Investigator, Health Behavior of African-American Eighth Graders, Sigma Theta Tau International, 1992. **Military Serv:** US Air Force Reserve, capt, 1986-. **Home Addr:** 420 Home Ave Apt 307-N, Oak Park, IL 60302-3716.

MARYLAND, RUSSELL
Professional football player. **Personal:** Born Mar 22, 1969, Chicago, IL; married. **Educ:** Miami (Fla.), bachelor's degree in psychology, 1990. **Career:** Dallas Cowboys, defensive tackle, 1991-95; Oakland Raiders, 1996-. **Business Addr:** Professional Football Player, Oakland Raiders, 1220 Harbor Bay Pkwy, Alameda, CA 94502, (510)615-1875.

MASHBURN, JAMAL
Professional basketball player. **Personal:** Born Nov 29, 1972, New York, NY. **Educ:** Kentucky. **Career:** Dallas Mavericks, forward, 1993-96; Miami Heat, 1996-. **Special Achievements:** NBA Draft, first round, fourth pick, 1993. Multimillion dollar endorsement contract, Fila, 1993. **Business Addr:** Professional Basketball Player, Miami Heat, 721 NW 1st Ave, Miami Arena, Miami, FL 33136, (305)577-4328.

MASK, SUSAN L.
Educational administrator, attorney. **Personal:** Born Oct 30, New York, NY; daughter of Joseph C & Eleanor G Mask; married W H Knight, Jun 6, 1981; children: Michael Joseph Mask Knight, Lauren Louise Mask Knight. **Educ:** City Univ of NY, BA, 1975; New York Univ, JD, 1978. **Career:** Univ of Iowa, asst to the pres/dir, Office of Affirmative Action, currently. **Business Addr:** Asst to the President, Dir, Office of Affirmative Action, Univ of Iowa, 202 Jessup Hall, Iowa City, IA 52242, (319)335-0705.

MASON, ANTHONY
Professional basketball player. **Personal:** Born Dec 14, 1966, Miami, FL. **Educ:** Tennessee State. **Career:** NBA career: New Jersey Nets, 1989-90; Denver Nuggets, 1990; New York Knicks, 1991-96; Charlotte Hornets, 1996-; CBA career: Tulsa Fast Breakers, 1990-91. **Business Addr:** Professional Basketball Player, Charlotte Hornets, One Hive Dr, Charlotte, NC 28217, (704)357-0252.

MASON, B. J.
Writer. **Personal:** Born Oct 31, 1945. **Educ:** Grambling St Univ, BS 1963; Colorado State Univ, MA 1965. **Career:** The Chicago Sun Times, features writer & novelist. **Orgs:** Writers Guild of Am W; Chicago Newspaper Guild. **Honors/Awds:** 1st place Unity Awd for Minority Journalism, Operation PUSH, 1975; Black Film Critics Awd 1973. **Business Addr:** c/o Ebony Magazine, 820 S Michigan Avenue, Chicago, IL 60605.

MASON, BILLY JOSEPHINE
Educator. **Personal:** Born Aug 2, 1918, Wheeling, WV; daughter of Hattie Harrison Anderson and William Anderson; married Louis Mason, Dec 15, 1965 (died 1973). **Educ:** West Virginia State College, Institute, WV, 1934, 1935, 1937; University of Dayton, Dayton, OH, BS, Education, 1965, master's, supervision education, 1973. **Career:** City of Dayton Public Schools, Dayton, OH, teacher/supervisor of elementary math department. **Orgs:** National president, National Sorority of Phi Delta Kappa, Inc, 1977-81, national secretary, 1971-77, regional director, 1967-71, member, 1935-. **Honors/Awds:** International Honorary Member, Gamma Phi Delta, 1968. **Home Addr:** 747 Mount Clair Ave, Dayton, OH 45408-1535.

MASON, BRENDA DIANE
Counselor. **Personal:** Born Nov 6, 1947, Paris, TX. **Educ:** Chapman Coll, (Honors Sem) 1969; Univ of NV, BA 1974, MS 1977; McGeorge Sch of Law Sacramento; Stdnt. **Career:** N V Indust Commin, indus rehab coun 1975-77; St of NV, Univ regent 1974-76; Tchrs Corp, coord 1971-75; GED Stlud, lab Instr 1971; Westinghouse Cred, cred clk; VISTA Vol Trustee Higher Educ Commin NV; Mntl Hlth Tech Children 1975; Child Dvlp Ctr, tchrs aide 1967-68; Friendly Ctr for Span Am, tutor 1966-67; Op Indep, tutor 1965-66. **Orgs:** Nat Hnr Soc 1960-66; NAACP 1962-66; Fr Soc 1963-64; Std of Serv Abrd 1968; Blk Voters Assn 1975-76; NLV Dem Club 1974-; trustee Act Refrl Serv 1975-77; Univ regent 1974-82; hghr Educ Com L1974-82; Ebony shwcse Lthtr for Actng 1965; Guy Ctr Actors Wrkshp 1971. **Honors/Awds:** Nat Mer Sch Fin 1965-66; schlrshp Chapman Coll & World Campus Afloat 1966-69; 6 Cert in Mus 1959-64.

MASON, CHERYL ANNETTE
Physician. **Personal:** Born Jul 2, 1954, McAlester, OK; daughter of Helen M Stuart and Lucious C Mason, III; married Mack Henderson, Feb 14, 1988; children: Alisha Dixon; Samuel Dixon. **Educ:** Univ of CA-San Diego, BA 1977; Howard Univ Coll Med, MD 1981. **Career:** San Pedro & Peninsula Hospital, family practice intern 1983; Georgetown Univ Hosp, resident Ob-Gyn 1983-87; The Memorial Hospital Danville VA Staff Physician 1987-89. **Orgs:** Mem Amer Business Women's Assn 1988-1990; mem Pittsylvania County Medical Society 1988-; bd mem American Cancer Society. **Business Addr:** Medical Doctor, The Memorial Hospital, 326 Taylor Drive, Danville, VA 24541.

MASON, CLIFFORD L.
Playwright. **Personal:** Born Mar 5, 1932, Brooklyn; married. **Educ:** BA 1958. **Career:** Freelance writer; playwright; Manhattanville Clge, tchr; Rutgers Univ NEH Grant Theatre Res 1978; Grant for Playwriting NEH Grant 1979. **Honors/Awds:** Pub article on Black Theatre NY Times Mag 1979; authored novel "When Love Was Not Enough" Playboy Press 1980. **Business Addr:** c/o Bertha Klausner, 71 Park Ave, New York, NY 10016.

MASON, DONNA S.
Educator. **Personal:** Born Jan 15, 1947, Mount Vernon, NY; daughter of Alexander & Olga Spence; married Charles L Mason Sr, Jun 30, 1973; children: Charles L Mason Jr. **Educ:** Howard Univ, BA, 1969, MEd, 1972; Univ of Maryland, College Park, AGS, 1975, PhD, 1987. **Career:** District of Columbia Public Schools, classroom teacher, building resource teacher, computer camp teacher, computer curriculum writer, computer teacher trainer, computer education instructor/lab coordinator, 1969-. **Orgs:** Maryland Instructional Computer Co-

ordinators Assn; Univ of Maryland Alumni Assn; International Society for Technology in Education; Special Interest Group for Computing Coordinators. **Honors/Awds:** Electronic Learning's, Educator of the Decade, 10 Who Made A Difference Award, 1991; Washington Post, Agnes Meyer Outstanding Teacher Award, 1991; Learning Magazine/Oldsmobile, Professional Best Teacher Excellence Award, 1991; Apple Computer, Thanks to Teachers Award, 1990; Business Week, Award for Innovative Teaching, 1990; University of MD Distinguished Alumni Award, 1995; Freedom Foundation at Valley Forge Award, 1995. **Special Achievements:** US Office of Education, Christa McAuliffe Fellowship, 1988, 1994; IBM/Classroom Computer Learning, Teacher of the Year for the District of Columbia, 1988; The Cafritz Foundation, Cafritz Foundation Teacher Fellowship, 1988; The Washington Post, The Washington Post Mini-Grant Award, 1986; ''A Teacher's Place To Work and Learn,'' Teaching & Computers 1986; ''Multimedia Applications in the Curriculum: Are Schools Preparing Students for the 21st Century?'' NASSP Curriculum Report, 1997; ''Display Word Processing Terms'' The Computing Teacher, 1986; ''Ten Computers-One Thousand Students'' Sigcc Bulletin for Computing Coordinators, 1987; ''Factors that Influence Computer Laboratory Use in Exemplary Junior High/Middle schools in the District of Columbia'' UMI's Dissertation Abstracts, 1988. **Business Addr:** Computer Ed Instructor/Lab Coordinator, Alice Deal Junior High School, Fort Drive & Nebraska Ave, NW, Room 201, Washington, DC 20016-1886, (202)282-0009.

MASON, EDWARD JAMES

Surgeon. **Personal:** Born Jul 31, 1923, Greenville, AL; married Rae; children: James, III. **Educ:** Youngstown Univ; Howard Univ, Clge of Med 1949. **Career:** DC General, surgeon self-emp, 1st black internship 1949-50; VA Hosp Tuskegee; Homer Phillips St Louis, residencies in gen surg; VA Hosp Pittsburg, 1st Black chief res 1959-60. **Orgs:** Diplomate Amer Bd of Gen & Abdominal Surgery; bd dir Forest Ave Hosp Dallas; BSA. **Honors/Awds:** Natl Hon Soc 1942; Undergrad Hon Soc 1944; AOA Kappa Pi Med Hon Soc 1949; Trailblazer Award 1974. **Business Addr:** 2516 Forest Ave, Dallas, TX 75221.

MASON, FELICIA LENDONIA

Journalist, writer. **Personal:** Born May 8, 1962, Pittsburgh, PA; daughter of Rev William L Sr and G Bernice Mason. **Educ:** Hampton Institute, BA, 1984; Thomas Nelson Community Coll, paralegal course work; Ohio State Univ, MA, 1986. **Career:** Pittsburgh Post Gazette, reporter, 1984-85; Hampton Univ, asst professor, 1986-90; Daily Press, copy editor, 1989-90, associate editor, 1990-92, asst metro editor, 1992-94, columnist, night metro editor, 1994-. **Orgs:** National Association of Black Journalists; Romance Writers of America; Chesapeake Romance Writers; Virginia Romance Writers; Voice of the Peninsula. **Honors/Awds:** Poynter Institute for Media Studies, Media Management Fellow, 1988; Hampton Univ, Print Alumni Award, 1991; WICI, Leadership Award, 1983; United Way, Loaned Executive, 1991; Romantic Times, Reviewer's Choice Award; Affaire de Coeur, Best Contemporary Ethnic Novel; Waldenbooks, Best-selling Multicultural Title. **Special Achievements:** For the Love of You, Pinnacle Books, 1994-95; Body and Soul, Pinnacle Books, 1995; Poetry and short romantic fiction published in refereed journal and national magazine; Seduction, Pinnacle Books; A Valentine Kiss, Pinnacle Books; Rhapsody, Pinnacle Books, 1997. **Home Addr:** P O Box 1438, Yorktown, VA 23692. **Business Addr:** Columnist, Daily Press Inc, 7505 Warwick Blvd, Newport News, VA 23607, (757)247-4776.

MASON, GILBERT RUTLEDGE

Physician. **Personal:** Born Oct 7, 1928, Jackson, MS; married Natalie Lorraine Hamlar. **Educ:** TN State Univ, BS 1947; Howard Univ, MD 1954. **Career:** Homer G Phillips Hosp St Louis, intern 1954-55; Biloxi, gen prac med 1955-; Harrison Co Head Start, med dir 1969. **Orgs:** Mem tissue & drug consult Howard Meml Hosp Biloxi 1967; chief family prac sect 1971; Fellow NY Research Found; diplomate Amer Bd Family Prac; fellow Amer Acad Family Phys; mem AMA; Natl Med Assc v chmn bd Greater Gulf Coast Sand Devel Corp 1970-; dir MS Indsl Spl Serv Inc; pres NAACP Biloxi 1960-; chmn USO 1959-60, 1970-; chmn Comm Action Prog 1966-69; mem city planning commn 1969-; mem state adv com Cabinet Com on Pub Educ 1970; mem state adv com Div Comprehensive Health Planning 1969-; v chrmn Harrison Co Regl Econ Commn 1973; Scoutmaster BSA 1959-72; pres Biloxi Civil League 1960-69; mem Harrison Co Dem Exec Com 1968-72; mem Alpha Phi Alpha; Elk Mason 32 Deg. **Honors/Awds:** Recip Sivler Beaver Award BSA 1963; outst Alumnus citation Semi-Centennial Celebration TN State Univ 1962; Citizen of Year 1959, 64; Outst Citizen 1970. **Business Addr:** 433 E Division St, Biloxi, MS 39530.

MASON, HERMAN, JR. (SKIP)

Archivist, historian. **Personal:** Born Jul 14, 1962, Atlanta, GA; son of Deloris Harris Hughes and Herman Mason Sr. **Educ:** Morris Brown College, Atlanta, GA, BA, mass communications, 1984; Jimmy Carter Presidential Library, Atlanta, GA, archival management, 1989; Atlanta University, Atlanta, GA, MS, library science, 1989. **Career:** The Herndon Home Museum, Atlanta, GA, historian, interpreter, 1983-86; The Martin Luther King National Historic Site, Atlanta, GA, historian, 1986; Atlanta-Fulton Public Library, Atlanta, GA, archivist, historian, 1988-. **Orgs:** President, African-American Family History Association, 1988-91; chairman, Southern Region Historical Commission, 1989-; historian, Eta Lambda Chapter of Alpha Phi Alpha Fraternity Inc, 1985-1990; board member, Georgia Association of Museums and Galleries, 1988-91; member, Outstanding Atlanta; founder, corr sec, African-American Male Study Group, 1990-; president, WestSide Community CME Church Senior Usher Board, 1988-. **Honors/Awds:** Curator/Author, Hidden Treasures: African-American Photographers in Atlanta, 1870-1970, an exhibition and publication; Author, Alpha In Atlanta: A Legacy Remembered, 1920-1987; National Alumni Brother of the Year, Alpha Phi Alpha Fraternity Inc, 1989; Volunteer Service Award, United Negro College Fund, 1988-91; Distinguished Alumni Citation, National Council of Negro Women, 1987-89; Distinguished Alumni Citation, NAEFEO, 1989. **Business Addr:** Archivist, Black Studies Collection, Atlanta-Fulton Public Library, 1 Margaret Mitchell Square, Atlanta, GA 30303.

MASON, HILDA HOWLAND M.

City official. **Personal:** Born Jun 14, Campbell County, VA. **Educ:** Miner Teachers College, graduate; District of Columbia Teachers Coll, MA; SUNY Plattsburgh, Catholic Univ, Graduate work. **Career:** District of Columbia Public Schools, teacher, counselor, supervising instructor and asst principal; District of Columbia City Council, member-at-large 1977-; DC Bd of Education, council to the district of columbia, 1977-. **Orgs:** Voting rep apptd by Council of the District of Columbia Washington Metro Area Transit Authority Bd of Dirs; present and past mem Amer Personnel & Guidance Assoc, District of Columbia Educ Assoc; Amer Federation of Teachers, DC CounselorsAssoc; DC Citizens for Better Public Educ; Washington Urban League; NAACP; Women Strike for Peace; The District of Columbia and Natl Women's Political Caucus; Nat Org for Women; Natl Cncl of Negro Women. **Honors/Awds:** Authored research and professional studies and served as an educ consultant and lecturer. **Home Addr:** 1459 Roxanna Rd NW, Washington, DC 20012.

MASON, HOWARD KEITH

Physician. **Personal:** Born Mar 19, 1949, Harrisburg, IL; married Adrienne Marie Murfree. **Educ:** Wayne State Univ, BS 1971; Univ of MI, MD 1974. **Career:** Pvt prac 1977-; USN Med Corps, gen med ofcr 1976-; USC Med Ctr, psychiat residency 1975-76; internship 1974-75. **Orgs:** Amer Psychiat Assc Conv 1975-77; Interstate Postgrad Med Assembly 1976 DC Med & Soc; Alliance for Psychiat Prog; Black Psychiat of CA. **Military Serv:** USN lt 1976-. **Business Addr:** 7711 Greenfield, Detroit, MI 48228.

MASON, JOHN

Radio personality. **Career:** WJLB-FM, morning disc jockey, currently. **Business Addr:** Air Personality, WJLB-FM, 645 Griswold, Ste 633, Detroit, MI 48226, (313)965-2000.

MASON, LUTHER ROSCOE

Elected official & business executive. **Personal:** Born Feb 21, 1927, Georgetown, KY; married Anne Nutter; children: Gregory K, Kurt D. **Educ:** Ed Davis High School, 1945. **Career:** Amer Red Cross, dir 1975-; KY School Bds, dir 1979-; Scott Bd of Educ, chmn 1983-84, mem 1976-. **Orgs:** Council mem Scott Cty Agr Extension Serv 1981-. **Honors/Awds:** Treas Scott Cty NAACP 1984-85. **Military Serv:** AUS corpl 1947-49. **Home Addr:** 1290 Delaplain Road, Georgetown, KY 40324.

MASON, MAJOR ALBERT, III

Research associate. **Personal:** Born Jul 15, 1940, McKeesport, PA; married Ann Mathilde Floberg; children: Major Albert IV, Arianna Melany. **Educ:** Univ of Pittsburgh, MEd 1976, PhD 1984. **Career:** Comm Clge of Allegheny Co, research assc 1974-; NOW Enterprises Inc, exec dir 1968-73; Comm Clge of Allegheny Co, reseach planning consult 1974-75. **Orgs:** Bd mem Allegheny OIC 1972-76; bd mem United Mental Health Inc 1973-75; radio show host WEDO Radio 1973-75; African-American Caucus, 1990-; Community College Convener, 1995-97; Program to Aid Citizen Enterprise (PACE), board member, secretary, 1990-96; InforMason Association, founder, 1995. **Honors/Awds:** Outst Young Men of Amer 1971. **Military Serv:** USN musician first class 1960-66. **Home Addr:** 1409 Bailey Ave, Mc Keesport, PA 15132.

MASON, RONALD EDWARD

Human resources executive. **Personal:** Born Aug 22, 1948, New York, NY; son of Eleanor Pierce Mason and Thurman Mason; married Louise Orazio Mason, Aug 10, 1980; children: Brian, Jonathan. **Educ:** Utica College of Syracuse University, Utica, NY, BA, 1974; Long Island Institute of Mental Health, New York, NY, certificate, 1976; City College of New York, New York, NY, MEd, 1978; Baruch College, New York, NY, certificate, 1979. **Career:** State University of New York, Brooklyn, placement director, 1974-76; Fordham University, New York, director of HEOP, 1976-79; State University of New York, Brooklyn, dean of students, 1979-80; SCM Corp, New York, asst manager, AA/EEO, 1980-81; NBC, New York, director, personnel, 1981-89; Reader's Digest, Pleasantville, human resources director, 1989-92; BBDO Worldwide, New York, human resources executive vice pres, board of directors, 1992-. **Orgs:** Board member, La Guardia Community College, 1978-; board member, New York, Metro Assn for Develop Education, 1989-; council member, Westchester Academy, 1990-; American Assn for Personnel Admin, 1979-; member, National Urban Af fairs Council, 1974-; NYC Technical College Foundation, bd mem, 1993-; NY Urban League, bd mem, 1993-; Edges Group, exec bd mem, 1993-; Amer Red Cross, Rockland Cty Chapter, bd mem, 1993-; Rockland Comm Coll Foundation, bd mem, 1995-; Amer Advertising Foundation, EEO/AA Committee, bd mem, 1994-. **Honors/Awds:** Black Achiever Award, Harlem YMCA, 1984; Presidential Award, NBC, 1988, 1989; Outstanding Young Men of America, National Jaycee, 1983; Outstanding Minority Human Resources Professional of the Year, Black Human Resources Network, 1994. **Business Addr:** Executive Vice Pres, Human Resources, BBDO Worldwide, New York, NY 10019.

MASON, TERRY

Physician, surgeon. **Personal:** Born Sep 13, 1951, Washington, DC; divorced; children: Terry Jr, Shaakira. **Educ:** Loyola Univ, BS, 1974; Univ of IL, MD, 1978, general surgery residency, 1978-80; Michael Rsses Med Ctr, urology residency, 1980-83. **Career:** Comprehensive Urology SC, pres, 1986-; Prairie Med Assoc, pres, 1994-; Mercy Hosp-Chicago, Dept of Urology, chairman, currently; Univ of IL School of Med, asst prof, currently. **Orgs:** Amer Coll of Surgeons, fellow; Amer Urological Assn; Chicago Urological Assn, exec comm mem; Chicago Med Society; Amer Med Assn; Natl Med Assn; R Frank Jones Urological Society of the Natl Med Assn; IL State Med Assn; North Central Section Amer Urological Assn; Cook County Physicians Assn; Impotence Inst of America, regional dir; NAACP, life mem. **Honors/Awds:** Human Resources Development Inst, On the Move In Med, 1988; Chicago Health & Med Careers Program, IL Inst of Technology Award, 1981; City of Chicago, Teen Opportunity Award; Dollars & Sense, Men In Med; Monarch Awards Foundation, Men in Med, 1988. **Special Achievements:** Surveillance Study of Diltiazem Use in Black & Non-Black Patients, Journal of Natl Med Assn, 1988; Making Love Again, Renewing Intimacy & Helping Your Man Overcome Impotence, Valarie Contemporary Books, 1988. **Business Addr:** President, Comprehensive Urology, SC, 8541 S State, Ste 9, Chicago, IL 60619, (312)846-7000.

MASON, WILLIAM E.

City official. **Personal:** Born Mar 12, 1934, Shuqualak, MS; married Catheryn; children: Terry, William, Jr. **Educ:** TN State U, BS 1952; So IL U, MS; Univ of St Louis, PhD 1975. **Career:** Institutional Research & Assoc, pres; Dist 189, tchr, prin, personnel dir, dist supt; E St Louis, IL, former mayor, former precinct committeeman; State of IL, human rights splst. **Orgs:** Mem E St Louis C of C; first pres, exec bd Comprehensive Educ Com; mem original Model Cities Planning Com; mem, bd dir Madison, St Clair Urban League; mem Phi Delta Kappa; Alpha Phi Alpha; Friendshp Bapt Ch. **Business Addr:** President, Institutional Research & Assoc, 1800 Tudor, East St Louis, IL 62207.

MASON, WILLIAM THOMAS, JR.

Attorney. **Personal:** Born Jul 27, 1926, Norfolk, VA; son of Vivian Carter Mason and William T Mason. **Educ:** Colby Coll, BA 1947; Howard Univ, LLB 1950. **Career:** William T Mason Jr Atty, private practice 1951-63; Dept of Justice ED of VA, asst US atty 1963-72; Mason & Robinson Attys, partner 1972-79; Robinson Eichler Zaleski & Mason, partner 1980-87; Robinson, Zaleski & Lindsey, counsel, 1987-92; Robinson, Madison, Fulton & Anderson, counsel, 1992-95; Robinson, Banks & Anderson, counsel 1995-97; Robinson, Shelton & Anderson, counsel, 1997. **Orgs:** Mem, vice chmn, chmn bd of dir Norfolk Comm Hospital 1975-; bd mem Planning Council 1976-; sec, vice pres & pres bd of dirs Norfolk State Univ Foundation 1980-; overseer Colby Coll 1982-94; mem & sec Bd of Visitors Norfolk State Univ 1969-73; sec, vice pres, pres, newsletter editor, Old Dominion Bar Assn, 1969-90. **Honors/Awds:** Award for Devoted Serv Old Dominion Bar Assn 1983. **Business Addr:** Counsel, Robinson, Shelton, & Anderson, 256 W Freemason St, Norfolk, VA 23510.

MASS, EDNA ELAINE

Company executive. **Personal:** Born Mar 17, 1954, Escatawpa, MS; children: Edward Juwan. **Educ:** Tougaloo Coll, BS 1976, Jackson State Univ, MEd 1978. **Career:** AT&T Network Systems, supervisor software tools develop. **Home Addr:** 1251 Folkstone Ct, Wheaton, IL 60187. **Business Addr:** Supervisor Software Tools Dev, AT&T Network Systems, 2600 Warrenville Rd, Lisle, IL 60532.

MASSAQUOI, HANS J.

Editor. **Personal:** Born Jan 19, 1926, Hamburg, Germany; divorced; children: Steve, Hans, Jr. **Educ:** Univ of IL, BS 1957; Northwestern Univ Medill Sch of Journalism, grad studies 1958. **Career:** Ebony Mag, mng ed 1967-, asst Mng ed 1964-67, assc ed 1959-64; Jet Mag, assc ed 1958-59; Natl Assc of

Educ Broadcasters, ed 1947; West Africa, travel 1948-50; Brit Occupation Forces in Germany, interpreter 1945-47. **Honors/Awds:** Receip Outst Immigrant Award Travellers Aid Soc & Immigrant Serv League 1970. **Military Serv:** AUS parachutist 1951-53. **Business Addr:** 820 S Michigan Ave, Chicago, IL 60605.

MASSE, DONALD D.
Physician. **Personal:** Born Dec 9, 1934, Lafayette, IN; son of Frances Maxine Johnson Masse and Otto Masse; married Mary Perkins; children: Stephanie, Mark. **Educ:** Purdue Univ, BS 1956; Marquette Med Schl, MD 1964; Wayne State Schl Med Post Grad Trng, Ob Gyn 1969. **Career:** Catholic Soc Serv Wayne Co, mem brd of dir 1970-84; Kirwood Hosp, chmn dept OB/GYN, 1974-77; St Joseph's Mercy Hosp, chmn dept OB/GYN 1978-80; SW Detroit Hosp, chmn dept OB/GYN 1977-80; Wayne State Univ School of Medicine Dept of Obstetrics & Gynecology, instructor. **Orgs:** Fincl sec Detroit Medical Soc 1973-75; instr Wayne State Univ Schl of Med dept OB/GYN; diplomat Amer Bd of Ob/Gynecology 1971; mem Wayne Co Med Soc, Detroit Med Soc, Wolverine State Med Soc, MI State Med Soc, Amer Fertility Soc, Amer Assn of Gynecologic Laparoscopists. **Military Serv:** AUS. **Business Addr:** Physician, Vincent, Combs, Masse, Shade Medical Group, 22255 Greenfield, Ste 411, Southfield, MI 48075.

MASSENBURG, TONY ARNEL
Professional basketball player. **Personal:** Born Jul 13, 1967, Sussex, VA; children: Tony James. **Educ:** Univ of Maryland, bachelor's degree in human ecology. **Career:** San Antonio Spurs, forward, 1990-91; played in Italy, 1991; Charlotte Hornets, 1991-92; Boston Celtics, 1992; Golden State Warriors, 1992; Unicaja-Mayoral (Spain), 1992-93; Barcelona (Spain), 1993-94; LA Clippers, 1994-95; Toronto Raptors, 1995-96; Philadelphia 76ers, 1996; New Jersey Nets, 1996-97; Vancouver Grizzlies, 1997-. **Business Addr:** Professional Basketball Player, Vancouver Grizzlies, 788 Beatty St, Ste 311, Vancouver, BC, Canada V6B 2M1, (604)688-5867.

MASSEY, ARDREY YVONNE
Association coordinator. **Personal:** Born Feb 18, 1951, Charlotte, NC; daughter of VeElla Massey and LeRoy Massey; divorced. **Educ:** National University, BBA, marketing, computers, and business, 1988. **Career:** Royal Globe Insurance Co., assistant underwriter, 1975-78; National University, academic advisor, 1984-86, assistant education coordinator, 1986-88, field coordinator, 1989-94; Roots and Wings, Unlimited, owner, 1994-; Charlotte Mecklenburg Urban League, placement specialist, special employment service, 1994-. **Orgs:** Sugar Creek Church of Christ; Rockwell AME Zion, Youth Development Program, chairperson, 1992-94; Carolinas Minority Supplier Development Councils Inc, field services committee, 1991-94, Business Opportunity Conference, education and registration committees, chairperson, 1991-94; Hemphill Heights Comm Organization, vp; Family Outreach and Counseling Center, vp; Boy Scouts of America Nominating Committee, 1996; Diversity Council of Carolinas, 1995-; One Accord of Charlotte Gospel Group, manager, 1995. **Honors/Awds:** Rockwell AME Zion Church, Fruit of the Spirit Award, 1990; Most Outstanding Woman of the Year Award, 1994. **Special Achievements:** Writer, "The Way Things are Now Won't Always Be," American Poetry Anthology, volume II, number 1-2, p 16, Spring/Summer 1983. **Business Addr:** Charlotte-Mecklenburg Urban League, 915 E 4th St, Charlotte, NC 28204, (704)376-9834.

MASSEY, CARRIE LEE
Business executive. **Personal:** Born Apr 23, 1922, Newberry, SC. **Educ:** Almanello Beauty Inst, grad diploma 1940; New York Univ 1941-43; Benedict Coll, 1943-44. **Career:** Massey's Beauty Shoppe, owner/oper 1950-; Tryon City Schools, currently. **Orgs:** Membership chairperson Polk Co NAACP 1960-; bd mem Roseland Comm Ctr 1961-; mem Tryon City Bd of Educ 1972-; bd mem Habitat for Humanity Inc 1982-; bd mem Polk Co Unit Amer Heart Assn 1978-; charter mem Polk Co Bus & Professional Women's Assn 1977; mem Polk Co Juvenile Task Force 1981-. **Honors/Awds:** All State Sch Bd NC Sch Bd Assoc, 1984; Hall of Fame, comm service award; recipient, "Friend of Education Award," 1989; special honors, Tryon High School, 1985. **Home Addr:** PO Box 693, Tryon, NC 28782.

MASSEY, HAMILTON W.
Chief executive. **Career:** Tropical Ford, Inc, Orlando, FL, chief exec. **Business Addr:** Tropical Ford Inc, 11105 S Orange Blossom Trail, Orlando, FL 32821.

MASSEY, JACQUELENE SHARP
Educational program director. **Personal:** Born Oct 8, 1947, Jackson, MS; married James Massey; children: Jermane Edward, Jamie Patrice. **Educ:** Knoxville Coll TN, BA Sociology 1979; DC Teacher Coll, Washington, Cert, 1970; College of Notre Dame of MD Baltimore, MS Gen Mgmt courses. **Career:** Univ of MD-Baltimore, assoc dir, special prog, 1978-; Baltimore City Public Sch; Baltimore; 1977-78; Fed Educ Prog/Direct Search for Talent MD, admin prog coord 1973-77; Delta Sigma Theta Inc/Public Serv Sorority, Mem office, 1970-71; DC Public School, teacher; US Dept Housing & Urban Devel Washinton, DC, summer coordinator, 1970; US Dept of Labor, Job Corps, vocational specialist, 1994-97; Office of Employment Development, School-To-Work Educational Alternative Learning program, manager, 1997-. **Orgs:** 2nd vice pres, Delta Sigma Theta Inc, Public Serv Sor, 1965-67; cons/decision making prog Coll Entrance Exam Bd, NY, 1976; vice pres, Girl Scouts of Central MD, 1977-; Speakers Bureau, United Fund of Central MD 1977-78; cons/cosmetic Business Fashion Two-Twenty Co 1978-; mem, chmn Hebbville Elementary School PTA, 1979-; Svc Academy Review Bd, 7th Congressional Dist, 1996; Echo House Multi-Svc Ctr, 1995-; Governor's Commission on Svc, 1996. **Honors/Awds:** Ldrshp Award White House Natl Youth Conf on Natural Beauty & Conservation 1965; Mayoral Award/ldrshp Mayor City Council Baltimore 1978; Thanks Badge Mgmt Ldrshp Award Girl Scouts of Central MD 1979. **Business Addr:** Mayor's Office of Employment Development, 101 W. 24th Street, Baltimore, MD 21218.

MASSEY, JAMES EARL
Cleric, educational administrator, educator. **Personal:** Born Jan 4, 1930, Ferndale, MI; married Gwendolyn Inez Kilpatrick. **Educ:** Detroit Bible Coll, BRE, BTh 1961; Oberlin Grad School of Theol, AM 1964; Asbury Theol Seminary, DD 1972; Pacific School of Religion, addit study 1972; Univ of MI; Boston Coll Grad School; Ashland Theological Seminary, DD, 1991; Huntington Coll, DD, 1994; Tuskegee Univ, Hum D, 1995; Warner Pacific College, DD, 1995; Anderson University, Litt D, 1995; Washington & Jefferson College, DD, 1997. **Career:** Church of God of Detroit, assoc minister 1949-51, 1953-54; Metro Church of God, sr pastor 1954-76; Anderson Coll, School of Theol, campus minister, prof of religious studies 1969-77; Christian Brotherhood, speaker 1977-82; Anderson University, School of Theol, prof of new testament 1981-84; Tuskegee Univ Chapel & Univ Prof of Religion, dean 1984-89; Anderson University, School of Theology, dean, professor of preaching and Biblical studies, 1990-95, dean emeritus & prof at large, currently. **Orgs:** Lecturer Gautschi Lectures Fuller Theol Sem 1975-1986; Freitas Lectures Asbury Theol Sem 1977, Rall Co-Lecturer Garrett-Evangelical Sem 1980, Mullins Lectures So Bapt Sem 1981, Swartley Lectures Eastern Baptist Sem 1982, Jameson Jones Lecturer Iliff School of Theol 1983, Rom Lectures Trinity Evangelical DivSchool 1984; northcutt lectures Southwestern Bapt Theol Sem 1986;l bd of dir Detroit Council of Churches; theol study commiss Detroit Council of Churches; corp mem Inter-Varsity Christian Fellowship; matl comm Black Churchmen; mem Wesleyan Theol Soc; ed bd Christian Scholars Review; bd of dir Warner Press Inc; vchmn Publ Bd of the Church of God; ed adv Tyndale House Publisher 1968-69; comm chmn Christian Unity; mem Natl Assoc of Coll & Univ Chaplains; bdof dir Natl Black Evangelical oc; life mem NAACP; Lausanne Continuation Comm 1974-; pres Anderson Civil Serv Merit Commiss 1975-81; ed bd Leadership Mag; bd of dir Natl Religious Broadcasteers; ed bd Preaching Mag 1987; Resource Scholar, Christianity Today Inst 1985; sr editor, Christianity Today, 1993-95. **Honors/Awds:** Danforth Foundation, Underwood Fellow, 1972-73; Staley Foundation, Staley Distinguished Christian Scholar, 1977; Wesleyan Theological Society, Lifetime Achievement Award, 1995. **Military Serv:** US Army, corpl, 1951-53. **Business Addr:** Dean Emeritus & Distinguished Prof-at-Large, School of Theology, Anderson University, Anderson, IN 46012-3462.

MASSEY, REGINALD HAROLD
Cleric. **Personal:** Born Jun 23, 1946, Rowan Co; married Arletta Bingham MD; children: Angela, Marc, Reginald, Jr. **Educ:** Livingstone Coll, BS Sociology; Hood Theological Sem Livingstone Coll, MDiv; Rowan Tech Coll, Cert Crisis Counseling; Baptist Hospital, Winston Salem, CPE certification. **Career:** Town of East Spencer Police Dept, police officer 1971-73; Town of East Spencer, mayor 1973-76, 1977-81; Salisbury Rowan Community Serv Council Inc, asst planner 1976-78, asst dir 1978; Herndon Chapel AME Zion Church, pastor 1979-81; Ezekiel AME Zion Church, 1979-83; VA Med Center Salisbury, chaplain 1984-; Center Grove AME Zion Church, 1983-89; Hood Memorial AME Zion Church, pastor, 1989-. **Orgs:** Mem E Spencer Planning Bd; Aux Police 1971-73; mem C of C; So Conf of Black Mayors; com chmn NC League of Municipalities Com; Boy Scout Troup 383; mem Am Legion Post 107; E Spencer Civic League; Salisbury-Rowan Civic League; Livingston Coll Alumni Assn; bd trustees So City AME Zion Ch; mem Nat League of Cities, Nat Conf Black Mayors; exec com Durham Coll; vice pres NC Conf of Black Mayors; intergovt relations comm NC League of Municipalities 1980; water quality policy adv comm Gov's Appointment 1st term 1980; mem Masonic Lodge Western Star #9. **Honors/Awds:** Martin Luther King Jr Humanitarian Award. **Military Serv:** AUS, sgt, 1966-69; Cert of Accomplishment at General Supply Ft Bragg. **Home Addr:** 3275 Jake Alexander Blvd, Salisbury, NC 28144.

MASSEY, ROBERT LEE
Professional football player. **Personal:** Born Feb 17, 1967, Rock Hill, SC; married Adrienne, Jun 1, 1996. **Educ:** North Carolina Central, BA in history, 1990. **Career:** New Orleans Saints, defensive back, 1989-90; Phoenix Cardinals, 1991-93; Detroit Lions, 1994-95; Jacksonville Jaguars, 1996; New York Giants, 1997-. **Honors/Awds:** Pro Bowl, 1992. **Business Addr:** Professional Football Player, New York Giants, Giants Stadium, East Rutherford, NJ 07073, (201)935-8111.

MASSEY, SELMA REDD
Association executive. **Personal:** Born Sep 8, 1953, Fort Campbell, KY; daughter of Gaynelle A Redd; divorced. **Educ:** Univ of Detroit, BA (summa cum laude), 1974, MA, education, 1975; Western Michigan Univ, EdD, organization and leadership, 1993. **Career:** Children's Aid Society, social worker, 1974-75; State of Michigan, social worker, 1975-79; Wayne County Community College, instructor, 1977-; Detroit's Most Wanted, producer/host, 1986, CEO/host, 1995; Project Start, CEO/executive director, 1981-. **Orgs:** American Correctional Association, 1983-; WDTR Educational Broadcasting, 1986-; Urban League, Detroit, 1994-; Michigan Assn Community Corrections Advancement, 1987-; Project BAIT (Black Awareness in Television), host, 1994-; For My People, host, 1994; University of Detroit Alumni Assn, 1974; Western Michigan University Alumni Assn, 1993. **Honors/Awds:** IBM Leadership Development, Leadership Commitment, 1992; Detroit Public Schools, Excellence Recognition, 1993, Certificate of Participation, 1994; Urban League, Teen Violence Accomplishment, 1994. **Special Achievements:** "Continue the Fight Against Crime," Michigan Chronicle, 1994; "We Cannot Afford Short-Sightedness," Michigan Chronicle, 1994; "A Study Needed to Understand Behavior," Michigan Chronicle, 1994; "I Don't Care," 1994; "Hurry Up! Bring it Back Home," 1995. **Home Addr:** 19250 Afton Rd, Detroit, MI 48203, (313)368-3023. **Business Addr:** CEO, Project Start Inc, 1035 St Antoine, Detroit, MI 48226, (313)965-3517.

MASSEY, WALTER EUGENE
Educational administrator. **Personal:** Born Apr 5, 1938, Hattiesburg, MS; son of Essie Nelson Massey and Almar Massey; married Shirley Anne Streeter, Oct 29, 1969; children: Keith, Eric. **Educ:** Morehouse Coll, BS 1958; Washington Univ, MS, PhD 1966. **Career:** Argonne Natl Lab, postdoctoral fellow, 1966-68, staff physicist, 1966-68, dir 1979-84; Univ of IL, assistant prof 1968-70; Brown Univ, associate prof 1970-75, prof, dean, 1971-79; Univ of Chicago, prof, 1979-93; vice pres for research, 1984-91; National Science Foundation, director, beginning 1991-93; Univ of California-Systemwide, provost and svp of academic affairs, 1993-95; Morehouse College, president, 1995-. **Orgs:** Review committee, Natl Science Foundation, 1971; review committee Natl Academy of Science 1973; American Association of Physics Teachers; Natl Science Bd 1978-84; fellow, bd of dir, 1981-85, pres elect, 1987, pres, 1988, American Association for the Advancement of Science; American Nuclear Society; American Physical Society; NY Academy of Sciences; IL Governor's Commission on Science and Technology; IL Governor's Science Advisory Committee; Sigma Xi; bd of dirs Amoco, Argonne-Chicago Development Corp, Motorola, Chicago Tribune Co, Continental Materials Corp, First Natl Bank of Chicago; Bank of Amer, Hewlett Foundation Commonwealth Fund; bd of fellows Brown Univ; bd of trustees, Rand Corp, Museum of Science & Industry, Chicago Orchestral Association; bd of governors, JF Symphony. **Honors/Awds:** Numerous science publications; NDEA fellowship, 1959-60; American Council on Education fellowship, 1974; Natl Science Foundation fellowship, 1961; Distinguished Service Citation, American Association of Physics Teachers, 1975; recipient of 21 honorary Doctor of Science degrees; New York Academy of Sciences, Archie Lacey Memorial Award, 1992; Morehouse College, Bennie Trailblazer Award, 1992; Morgan State University, Distinguished Achievement Award, 1992; Golden Plate Award, 1992. **Business Addr:** President, Morehouse College, 830 Westview Dr, Attn: President's Office, Atlanta, GA 30314-3773.

MASSIE, SAMUEL PROCTOR
Educator. **Personal:** Born Jul 3, 1919, N Little Rock, AR; married Gloria Thompkins, 1947; children: Herbert, James, Samuel III. **Educ:** Dunbar Jr Coll, AA, 1936; AM&N Coll, BS, 1938; Fisk University, MA, 1940; Iowa State University, PhD, 1946. **Career:** AM&N College, Arkansas, associate math professor, 1940-41; Iowa State Univ, research associate, chemistry, 1943-46; Fisk Univ, instructor, 1946-47; Langston Univ, department head & professor, 1947-53; Fisk Univ, assoc prog dir, 1953-60; Howard Univ, assoc prog dir, 1962-63; North Carolina Coll, Durham, pres, 1963-66, chmn dept, 1977-81; US Naval Academy, chemistry professor, 1966-. **Orgs:** Sigma Xi; Am Chem Soc; Swathmore College, board of trustee, 1957; Col of Wooster, board of trustees, 1966-68; Maryland State Bd Comm Col, chmn, 1968-69; Div Chem Ed, 1976; Gov Sci Adv Coun, MD, 1979-89; PFR Adv Bd, 1981-86; Dillard Univ, 1984-85; UMES, 1986-88; Smithsonian Exhibit Adv Comm, 1989-; IIT, 1991. **Honors/Awds:** MCA Award, Excellence in Teaching, 1961; Iowa State Alumni, Merit Award, 1964; Univ of Arkansa, Honorary LLD, 1970; NAACP, Freedom Fund Award, 1975; Virginia State Univ, Distinguished Visiting Professor, 1983-84; NOBCHCE, Outstanding Prof Award, 1985; Lehigh Univ, Honorary DSc, 1985; White House Initiative Lifetime Achievement Award, 1989; Natl Black Col Hall of Fame in Science, 1989; Bowie State Univ, MD, Honorary LHD, 1990; Chemical and Engineering News Magazine, One of 75 Outstanding Scientists in the Country, 1998. **Business Addr:** Professor, Chemistry, Department of Chemistry, US Naval Academy, Annapolis, MD 21402.

MATABANE, SEBILETSO MOKONE
Educational administrator. **Personal:** Born Oct 26, 1945, Johannesburg, Republic of South Africa; married William N Matabane. **Educ:** Syracuse Univ, BA 1969, MS 1970; Univ of TX Austin, PhD 1986. **Career:** Cook Productions, asst to pres 1974-75; Austin Comm Coll, media coord 1975-76; Austin Comm Coll, acting campus admin 1984-, dir learning resources 1976-. **Orgs:** Admin asst Chamba Prod 1970-71; instr TV Grahm Jr Coll 1971-72; oper asst United Nations Devel Prog 1974; bd mem Austin Comm TV 1977-80; adv bd mem KLRU-TV Comm Adv Bd 1980-; commr Cable Commn City of Austin 1984-; pres, Zakhele found; 1987-; bd mem, Texas Assn for Educ Technology, 1987-; chair, Assess Comm, Cable Commn, Austin TX, 1985-; mem, community advisory bd, KLRU-TV, 1984-. **Honors/Awds:** Outstanding Young Women of Amer 1979; pres Zakhele Foundation 1987-; bd mem Texas Association for Educational Technology 1987-; chair Access Committee Cable Commission Austin TX 1985-; mem Community Advisory bd KLRU-TV.

MATCHETT, JOHNSON, JR.
Telecommunications company executive. **Personal:** Born Oct 17, 1942, Mobile, AL; son of Johnson Matchett Sr. **Educ:** Alabama State Univ, BS 1963; Univ of Alabama, MA 1969; Univ of Southern MS, EdS 1975. **Career:** Anniston Public Schools, teacher 1963-64; Mobile Public Schools, teacher 1964-69; Miles Coll, dir of teacher educ 1969-73; Alabama State Univ, part-time instructor 1972-75; Univ of So Alabama, curriculum consultant 1974; BellSouth Services Inc, mgr/training 1974-. **Orgs:** Mem Amer Soc for Training and Develop 1975-, Phi Delta Kappa Hon Educ Frat 1975-, Natl Soc for Performance and Instruction 1982-, NAACP 1983-; mem exec bd AL State Univ General Alumni Assoc 1985-89; mem Natl Black MBA Assoc 1986-, AL Initiative for Black Coll Recruitment and Retention Birmingham Chapt, 1987-89, Holy Family HS Bd of Dirs 1987; Academic Affairs Committee, National Society for perf and instr, 1992-; President of the Birmingham Chapter of the National Black MBA Association, 1992-. **Home Addr:** PO Box 752, Birmingham, AL 35201.

MATEEN, MALIK ABDUL
Firefighter, association executive. **Personal:** Born Oct 19, 1949, Hialeah, FL; son of Zula M Jackson and Rubbie L Laughlin; married Fern Troupe Mateen, Sep 19, 1977; children: Africa, Clifford. **Career:** Life of Georgia Insurance Co, insurance agent, 1973-73; Dade County Solid Waste Department, truck driver, 1973-81; Metro Fire Rescue, firefighter, 1981-. **Orgs:** Progressive Firefighters Association, president, 1989. **Military Serv:** Army, sgt, 1969-72. **Business Addr:** President, Progressive Firefighters Association, 926 Rutland Britton St, Opa Locka, FL 33054.

MATH, JOHN
Professional sports administrator. **Personal:** Born in San Gabriel, CA; married Maxine; children: John Jr, Gayle, Wanda, Nancy, Cathy. **Educ:** Univ of California, 1950-54. **Career:** Los Angeles Rams, director of player personnel, currently.

MATHABANE, MARK JOHANNES
Author, lecturer. **Personal:** Born Oct 18, 1960, Alexandra Township, Republic of South Africa; son of Geli Mabaso Mathabane and Jackson Mathabane; married Gail Ernsberger, Aug 1, 1987; children: Bianca Ellen, Nathan Phillip, Stanley Arthur. **Educ:** Limestone College, 1978; St Louis University, 1979; Quincy College, 1981; Dowling College, BA, economics, 1983; Columbia University, 1984. **Career:** Author, lecturer, 1985-; works include: Kaffir Boy: The True Story of a Black Youth's Coming of Age in Apartheid South Africa, 1986; Kaffir Boy in America, 1989; Love in Black & White, co-author with Gail Ernsberger, 1992; African Women: Three Generations, 1994. **Orgs:** Authors Guild. **Honors/Awds:** Christopher Award, 1986; Robert Kennedy Memorial Award, finalist. **Home Addr:** 341 Barrington Park Ln, Kernersville, NC 27284, (336)996-1703.

MATHES, JAMES R.
Educator. **Personal:** Born Feb 7, Philadelphia; married Ann Higgs; children: Sjonia, Ngina. **Educ:** Shaw U, BA 1964; Rutgers U, completion credits for Masters Deg in Educ 1975; Tenton State Coll, grad work 1967-68. **Career:** Rutgers Univ Camden, dir proj talent search 1973-; Camden City, tchr 1964-69; Rutgers U, coor of curriculum urban uni prog 1969-70; Bur of Comm Serv, deputy dir 1970-73; Rutgers U, hd coach bsbl team 1970-. **Orgs:** Trea BPUM Devel Corp 1972-; vice pres Camden City Bd of Educ 1973-; Alpha Phi Alpha; Beta Rho Chap 1960; bd of dir BPUM Day Care; chmn Educ Com 1969-72; bd dir Centerville Liberty Park Fbl Assn 1970-; EOF Adv Bd Rutgers; v chmn EOF Adv Bd Camden Co Coll; adv bd Univ in Act Glassboro StateColl; Mayor's Open Space & Recrea Task Force; bd dir S Jersey Opport Indsl Ctr; Kappa Delta Phi Nat Hon Soc in Educ 1977; bd of dir Comm AdvocacyCoun of Camden Co. **Honors/Awds:** Concerned Citizen Award Club Athens 1969; for outstndg work dedic to BPUM Day Care 1970; candid for tchr of year award Camden Jaycees 1968; Outstndg Young Men of Am 1973. **Business Addr:** Bd of Education, Camden, NJ 08101.

MATHEWS, GEORGE
Business executive. **Career:** WGPR Inc, Detroit, MI, chief executive officer, currently. **Orgs:** International Free and Accepted Modern Masons Inc. **Honors/Awds:** Honorary LHD. **Business Addr:** CEO, WGPR TV-62 and Radio, 3140 E Jefferson, Detroit, MI 48207.

MATHEWS, KEITH E.
Judge. **Personal:** Born Mar 2, 1944, Steubenville, OH. **Educ:** Morgan State U, BS 1966; Univ of Baltimore, JD 1972. **Career:** US Dept of Justice Antitrust Div, atty 1974-75; Congressman Parren Mitchell, legislative asst 1973-74; Legal Aid Br of Baltimore, atty 1972-73; Foster Mathews & Hill, atty 1975-82; States Atty Office Baltimore, asst states atty 1978-83; District Court of MD, judge 1983-. **Orgs:** Bd of govs Univ of Baltimore Alumni Assn 1973; vchmn Consumer Affairs Adb Bd for Howard Co 1978; mem Monumental Bar Assoc, Natl Bar Assoc. **Honors/Awds:** Editorial Staff Law Review Univ of Baltimore 1972; Validictorian Police Acad Baltimore City 1968. **Business Addr:** Judge, District Court of Maryland, 5800 Wabash Ave, Baltimore, MD 21215.

MATHEWS, LAWRENCE TALBERT
Financial administrator. **Personal:** Born Oct 12, 1947, Michigan City, IN; married Beverly Ann Hoze; children: Gerald. **Educ:** Univ of MI Flint, AB 1969; Univ of Detroit, MBA 1975. **Career:** Arthur Young & Co, sr audtr 1972-75; Comm Credit/Mc Cullagn Lsng, cntrlr/treas 1975-78; MI Penisula Airwys, vice pres fin 1978-80; Clipper Intl Manuf, vice pres fin 1980-82; Comprehensive Hlth Serv of Detroit, dir of fin oper; Wellness Plan, vice pres, CFO, currently. **Orgs:** Pres, Natl Assn Blk Acctnts; MI Assn Health Maintence Org Finance Comm; asstexec dir Detroit Area Agncy on Aging 1984. **Honors/Awds:** Dstngshd Serv Natl Assn Blk Accts 1985; CPA State of MI 1975. **Military Serv:** AUS 1st lt 3 yrs; Disngshd Mltry Grad/Off Cand Sch 1973.

MATHIS, DAVID
Employment company executive. **Personal:** Born Sep 16, 1947, Riverhead, NY; son of Freddie Mae Thompson; married Dorothy; children: Darren, David, Denise, Doreen. **Educ:** Mohawk Valley Comm Coll, AAS 1970; Uitca Coll of Syracuse Univ, BS 1972. **Career:** Mohawk Valley Oppor Indus Ctr, dir of training 1972-73, exec dir 1973-74; Career Develop Ctr, dir of manpower serv 1974-79, dir of job develop 1979-80; Oneida Co Employment & Training, dep dir 1980-86, dir 1986-. **Orgs:** Bd of dirs Cosmopolitan Comm Ctr; bd of trustees Hope Chapel AME Zion Church; adv bd Oneida Co Youth Bureau; bd of trustees Mohawk Valley Comm Coll; mem; Assoc of Governing Bds of NY State Comm Colleges, board of directors; Utica Coll Ed Bass Black Students Scholarship Fund, chmn; bd of dirs Ferre Institute 1988; bd of dirs Neighborhood Center of Utica 1988; bd of trustees, Munson-Williams-Proctor Institute 1988; bd of dirs, Assn of Community College Trustees, 1990; bd of dirs, Utica Foundation, 1989; bd of dirs, Mohawk Valley Community College Alumni Assn, 1990; Commit, 1991; mem, Rotary Club of Utica, 1989; Utica Neighborhood Housing Services, board of directors; Utica Head Start, president, board of directors; American Red Cross, Northeast Regional Committee, mem, 1994; ARC of Oneida & Lewis Counties, board of directors, 1993; Fleet Bank of New York, CRA, advisory bd, mem, 1993; SUNY Alumni Confederation, board of directors, 1995; New York State Affirmative Action Officers, president, 1995. **Honors/Awds:** Outstanding Comm Serv Awd Mohawk Valley Frontiersman 1977; Man of the Yr Awd St Time 1978; 10th Yr Outstanding Grad Higher Educ Oppor Prog 1980; Outstanding Alumnus Mohawk Valley Comm Minority Union 1981; Citizen of the Yr Awd League of Women Voters Utica/Rome 1984; United Way of Greater Utica, Hero Awd; Utica Coll, Outstanding Alumnus; Len Wilbur Awd, Utica Kiwanis Club 1986; Outstanding Service Award Lambda Kappa MU 1987; Achievement Award, Oneida County NAACP 1987; Community Achievement Award, Aleppo #140 1988; Outstanding Community Service Award Utica Salvation Army 1987; Martin Luther King Jr Humanitarian Award, Mohawk Valley Psychiatric Center, 1990; Alumni of Merit, Mohawk Valley Community College, 1990; Utica-Rome Black Ministerial Alliance, Community Service Award, 1992; New York State Governor's Office, African-Americans of Distinction Award, 1994; America Red Cross, Presidents Fund Award for Cultural Diversity, 1996. **Home Phone:** (315)797-8069. **Business Addr:** Dir, Oneida Co Employment & Training, 800 Park Ave, Utica, NY 13501, (315)798-5543.

MATHIS, DEBORAH F.
Journalist. **Personal:** Born Aug 24, 1953, Little Rock, AR; daughter of Rachel A Myers and Lloyd H Myers; divorced; children: Meredith Mathis, Allison Mathis, Joseph Mathis. **Educ:** University of Arkansas at Little Rock, 1972. **Career:** KTHV-TV, general assignment reporter, 1973-74; WTTG-TV, weekend anchor, 1974-76; KARK-TV, assistant news director, 1976-82; KATV-TV, "Live at Five," anchor, 1983-88; Arkansas Gazette, associate editor, 1988-91; The Clarion-Ledger, columnist, 1992-93; Tribune Media Services, syndicated columnist, 1992-; Gannett News Service, White House correspondent, 1993-. **Business Addr:** White House Correspondent, Gannett News Service, 1000 Wilson Blvd, T1-10, Arlington, VA 22209, (703)276-5804.

MATHIS, DEDRIC
Professional football player. **Personal:** Born Sep 26, 1973, Cuero, TX. **Educ:** University of Houston. **Career:** Indianapolis Colts, defensive back, 1996-. **Business Addr:** Professional Football Player, Indianapolis Colts, PO Box 535000, Indianapolis, IN 46253, (317)297-2658.

MATHIS, FRANK
Church official. **Personal:** Born Aug 4, 1937, Fort Valley, GA; son of Laura B Lockhart Mathis-Gibson and Otis Mathis, Sr (deceased). **Educ:** Fort Valley State Coll, Fort Valley, GA, BS Zoology; Natl Exec Inst, Mendham, NS, professional scouter-BSA. **Career:** Boy Scouts of Am, dist scout exec 1954-72; Savannah Area Minority Contractors Assn Inc, dist dir 1972-; Catholic Diocese of Savannah, Savannah, GA, director office of black ministry, 1986-. **Orgs:** Mem Natl Assn Minority Contractors; charter mem Natl Greene Sertoma Club; Alpha Phi Omega Frat; Natl Council Christian & Jews; owner, Mathis & Assoc-Advertising/Business Consultant, 1980-; advisory board, Citizens Crime Commission, 1991-; member, Peace & Justice Commission, 1991-; consultant, National Plan & Strategy for Catholic Evangelization in the US, 1991. **Honors/Awds:** Boy of Yr Award 1955; Virgil Honor Order of the Arrow Natl Camping Soc 1967; Benedictine Medal 1971; St George Award Diocese of Savannah 1971; Leadership Award More Pure Heart of Mary's Parish 1972; Outstanding Citizen Award GA State Beauty Culture League 1974; DPC Service Award, Diocese of Savannah, 1981; Black Amer Hall of Fame, 1984; Masjid Jihad Award, 1985; Tought Love For Teenager, Salt Publication, 1985; Black Achievement Award, Urban Christian Academy, 1990. **Home Addr:** 911 W 37th St, Savannah, GA 31401. **Business Addr:** Director of Black Ministry, 601 E Liberty St, Diocese of Savannah, Savannah, GA 31401-5196.

MATHIS, GREGORY
Judge. **Personal:** Born Apr 5, 1960, Detroit, MI; married Linda Mathis, Jun 1, 1985; children: Camara, Gregory, Amir. **Educ:** Eastern Michigan University, BS, 1984; University of Detroit, JD, 1988. **Career:** Detroit City Council, admin asst to councilman Clyde Cleveland, 1984-88; Office of the Mayor, City of Detroit, mgr, neighborhood city hall, 1989-93, lawyer private practice, 1993-95; State of Michigan, 36th District Court, judge, 1995-. **Orgs:** Reclaim our Youth Crusade, chairman, 1993-; Young Adults Asserting Themselves, founder and chairman, 1986-; National Rainbow Coalition, special asst to Rev Jesse Jackson, 1994-. **Honors/Awds:** Southern Christian Leadership Conference, Man of the Year, 1995; Detroit City Council, Testimonial Resolution, 1995; Office of the Mayor, City of Detroit, Proclaimation from Mayor, 1995; Michigan Legislature, Special Tribute Proclaimation, 1995. **Special Achievements:** Co-author, "Inner City Miracle," 1995. **Business Addr:** Judge, 36th District Ct, 421 Madison, Ste 5075, Detroit, MI 48226.

MATHIS, JOHNNY (JOHN ROYCE MATHIS)
Singer. **Personal:** Born Sep 30, 1935, San Francisco, CA. **Educ:** San Francisco St Coll, attended. **Career:** San Francisco Night Clubs, singer informal jam sesions; numerous recordings, film, stage & TV appearances; singing tours Europe, Australia, South America, the Orient, Canada. **Honors/Awds:** Over 50 gold and platinum albums and singles. Hits include: Chances Are; It's Not for Me to Say; Twelfth of Never; Too Much, Too Little, Too Late; Small World; "In a Sentimental Mood: Tribute to Duke Ellington," 1990-; nominated for a Grammy, 1961, 1992. **Business Addr:** Singer, c/o Rojon Productions, 3500 W Olive Ave #750, Burbank, CA 91505.

MATHIS, KEVIN
Professional football player. **Personal:** Born Apr 9, 1974. **Educ:** East Texas State, attended. **Career:** Dallas Cowboys, defensive back, 1997-. **Business Addr:** Professional Football Player, Dallas Cowboys, One Cowboys Pkwy, Irving, TX 75063, (214)556-9900.

MATHIS, ROBERT LEE
Health services administrator (retired). **Personal:** Born Apr 21, 1934, Concord, NC; son of Minnie V Mathis; married Margaret Miller; children: Calven, Rodney, Jeffery, Kim West. **Educ:** US Navy, Cooks & Bakers School 1956; Central Piedmont Comm Coll, AS Political Science 1976; NC State Univ, Personnel Mgmt Diploma 1978; St Louis Univ, Food Serv Diploma 1978. **Career:** Cabarras Memorial Hospital, cook spec diets 1958, cook & baker supvr 1965, asst food serv dir, 1979-94; Concord, NC, mayor pro-team, 1995. **Orgs:** Dir Cabarrus Cty Boys Club 1979-; mem Mt Zion Lodge 26 Concord NC 1980-, NC Chapter of Amer Soc Hospital; Food Serv 1980; advisory bd Salvation Army 1981-; leader Boy Scouts 1983; dir Cab County United Way 1983; mem bd of visitor Barber-Scotia Coll Concord NC 1984; delegate for the city NC Centralina Council of Government; elder First Christian Church; bd of dir Life Center and Logan Day Care; Bd of Corrections, 1994; chmn, Cabarrus Cty, elected offical assoc, 1994. **Honors/Awds:** Represented the largest ward in NC 1980; first black elected Bd of Alderman Concord Bd of Alderman 1980-; Outstanding Citizen of the Year Kannpolis Daily Independence 1981; Co-Founder Fourth Word Devel Corp 1982; Citizen of the Year by Phi Chi 1985. **Military Serv:** USN third class commissaryman 5 1/2 yrs; Natl Defense, Korean Serv 1951-56.

MATHIS, SALLYE BROOKS
Councilwoman. **Personal:** Born in Jacksonville, FL; widowed. **Educ:** Benedict Coll; Bethune Cookman, AA; Tuskegee Inst, BS; FL A&M U, M. **Career:** Dist 11 Jacksonville City Coun, city counwm; Duval Cty Sch, tchr; Matthew Gilbert Sch, dean of girls. **Orgs:** Mem city coun bd dir Leag of Women Voters; bd of dir City Mission Ashley St; bd of dir Health Maintenance & Operation (HMO); pres Minority Women's Coalition; mem Bethel Bapt Ch; Llongest tenure of 19 mem on council (13 yrs) elected 4 times two without opposition; com Citizens for Better Edn; bd dir Oppty Indsltn Ctr; bd dir YWCA; Delta Sigma Theta Sor; Alcoholic Advis Com; Chan 7 TV trustee; FL State NAACP bd; Meth Hosp Fnd; Prbtnrs Res Bd. **Honors/Awds:** One of 1st 2 blk women elec cty coun; FL Publ Cmpy's Eve Aw 1973. **Business Addr:** 10th Fl City Hall, Jacksonville, FL 32202.

MATHIS, SHARON BELL
Educator (retired), author. **Personal:** Born Feb 26, 1937, Atlantic City, NJ; daughter of Alice Mary Frazier Bell and John Willie Bell; married Leroy Franklin Mathis, Jul 11, 1957 (divorced 1979); children: Sherie, Stacy, Stephanie. **Educ:** Morgan State Coll, BA, 1958; Catholic Univ of America, MLS, 1975. **Career:** Childrens Hosp of District of Columbia, Washington DC, interviewer 1958-59; Holy Redeemer Elem School, Washington DC, teacher 1959-65; Stuart Junior High School, Washington DC, special education teacher, 1974-75; Chas Hart Junior High School, 1966-74; DC Black Writers Workshop, founder/writer-in-charge of childrens lit div; Howard Univ, Washington DC, writer-in-residence, 1972-73; Benning Elem School, Washington DC, librarian 1975-76; Patricia Roberts Harris Educational Center, librarian 1976-95. **Orgs:** Mem bd advisors, lawyers comm of District of Columbia Commn on the Arts, 1972; mem, Black Women's Community Development Foundation, 1973; American Library Association, 1995-. **Honors/Awds:** Author: Brooklyn Story, 1969, Sidewalk Story, 1971, Teacup Full of Roses, 1972, Ray Charles, 1973, Listen for the Fig Tree, 1974, The Hundred Penny Box, 1975, Newbery Honor Book of the Amer Library Assn, 1976, Cartwheels, 1977, Red Dog/Blue Fly: Football Poems, 1991; Coretta Scott King Award, 1974; Arts and Humanities Award, Archdiocese of Washington, 1978; Running Girl (Harcourt Brace), 1997. **Home Addr:** PO Box 44714, Fort Washington, MD 20744.

MATHIS, TERANCE
Professional football player. **Personal:** Born Jun 7, 1967, Detroit, MI. **Educ:** New Mexico. **Career:** New York Jets, wide receiver, 1990-1993; Atlanta Falcons, 1994-. **Business Addr:** Professional Football Player, Atlanta Falcons, Two Falcon Place, Suwanee, GA 30174, (404)945-1111.

MATHIS, THADDEUS P.
Educator. **Personal:** Born Sep 8, 1942, Americus, GA; married Christine Harris; children: Latanya, Evan, Talani. **Educ:** Bluefield State Coll, BS (Cum Laude) Secondary Ed 1965; Bryn Mawr Coll, MS Social Work 1968; Temple Univ, PhD Political Sci 1985. **Career:** Dept of Public Welfare, group leader 1965-66; Child Study Center of Philadelphia Temple Univ Hospital, social work intern 1966-68; Dept of Public Welfare, social worker 1968; Philadelphia Model Cities Program, planning coordinator 1968-70; Temple Univ, prof of social admin 1970-. **Orgs:** Exec comm Philadelphia Congress of Racial Equality 1971-75; chairperson Philadelphia Black Political Convention 1971-80; presiding officer Natl Black Independent Political Party 1981-83; chairperson School of Soc Admin Grad Dept 1981-84; pres Philadelphia Alliance of Black Soc Workers; bd mem Housing Assoc of Deleware Valley; Philadelphia Alliance of Black Social Workers; board member Housing Association of Delaware Valley; chairperson Institute for African-American Development; director Institute for Afrocentric Social Work. **Honors/Awds:** Shapp Found Scholar Shapp Foundation Philadelphia 1961-65; PEP Fellow State of PA Office of Children & Youth 1966-68; Fellow Urban Affairs Inst Amer Univ 1971; Bernard C Watson Awd 1985. **Home Addr:** 163 W Wyneva St, Philadelphia, PA 19144. **Business Addr:** Professor, Social Administration, Temple Univ, RA 539 13th & Columbia Ave, Philadelphia, PA 19122.

MATHIS, WALTER LEE, SR.
County official. **Personal:** Born Feb 2, 1940, Columbus, MI; married Patricia E Grier; children: Walter, Tracy, Daryl, Melissa. **Educ:** Davenport Coll MI, ceret acctng. **Career:** Meijer Inc, shpng clerk mgr trainee; Mathis Tax Serv, owner; Party Store, owner; Co, comm. **Orgs:** Past mem Grand Rapids Hsng Bd of Appeals; past bd mem Freedom Homes Inc; mem NAACP; mem Kent-CAP Gob Bd. **Honors/Awds:** Named VIP of Grand Rapids Press 1972. **Military Serv:** AUS pfc 1959-62. **Business Addr:** 1014 Franklin SE, Grand Rapids, MI 49507.

MATHIS, WILLIAM LAWRENCE
Attorney. **Personal:** Born Feb 27, 1964, Albany, GA; son of Eliza Mathis Goree and William L Reynolds. **Educ:** Morehouse Coll, Atlanta GA, BA, 1985; Boston Coll Law School, Newton MA, JD, 1989. **Career:** US House of Representatives Select Comm on Narcotics Abuse & Control, Washington DC, staff asst, 1985-86; New York County District Attorney's Office, New York City NY, legal intern, 1987; Smith, Somerville & Case, Baltimore MD, summer assoc, 1988; The Honorable David Mitchell, Baltimore MD, judicial clerk, 1989-90; State's Attorney Office of Baltimore City, asst state's attorney, juvenile division, 1990-. **Orgs:** Mem, Morehouse Coll Alumni Assn, 1985-; natl chmn, Natl Black Law Students Assn, 1986-89; Northeast Regional dir, Natl Black Law Students Assn, 1987-88; bd mem, Natl Conference of Black Lawyers, 1988-, Natl Bar Assn, 1988-89; mem, consultant, Natl Assn of Public Interest Law, 1988-89; bd mem, Natl Alliance Against Racism and Political Repression, 1988-89; mem, Boston Coll Black Alumni Network, 1989-; member, Baltimore City Bar Assn, 1991-; member, Maryland State Bar Assn, 1991-; member, American Bar Assn, 1991-; mem, Monumental Bar Assn, 1991-. **Home Addr:** 719 Washington Place, 4th Floor, Baltimore, MD 21201.

MATHUR, KRISHAN
Educator. **Personal:** Born Apr 22, 1928, Hyderabad, India; son of Sarjo Rani and Shiv Dayal; married Erica Laufer (divorced 1965); children: Leila Rani, Roy. **Educ:** Osmania University, Hyderabad, India, BS, physics, chemistry, biology, MS, zoology; George Washington University, Washington, DC, MA, government, PhD, political science, 1958. **Career:** University of Maine at Presque Isle, ME, assistant professor, 1960-63; Library of Congress, Washington, DC, science division, beginning 1963; University of the District of Columbia, Washington, DC, professor, 1971-. **Orgs:** Department of Political Science at University of the District of Columbia, chairman, 1983-87; National Republican Indo-American Federation, founder and chairman, 1982-86. **Honors/Awds:** George Washington University, Pi Gamma Mu, 1957; Lions Club, Roaring Lion, 1973; Osmania University, Scholarship. **Home Addr:** 3442 Little Hunting Creek Dr, Alexandria, VA 22309.

MATLOCK, KENT
Advertising manager, consultant. **Personal:** Born in Chicago, IL. **Educ:** Morehouse Coll, BA 1982. **Career:** Anheuser-Busch Inc, public relations rep 1979-80; Visual Persuasion Inc, accts exec 1980-81; Garrett/Lewis/Johnson, accts exec 1981-83; Georgia Pacific Corp, mgr adv & sales promo. **Orgs:** Mem NAACP 1977-78; co-chair publicity United Negro College Fund Inc 1984-85; mem Atlanta Adv Club 1984-85. **Honors/Awds:** Lt Col Aide DeCamp Governors Staff 1982-85; Meritorious Serv Awd UNCF 1985. **Home Addr:** 1133 Scott Blvd, Decatur, GA 30030.

MATNEY, WILLIAM C., JR.
Federal official (retired), communications consultant. **Personal:** Born Sep 2, 1924, Bluefield, WV; son of Jane A Matney and William C Matney Sr; widowed; children: Alma, Angelique, William III. **Educ:** Wayne State Univ, 1940-42; Univ of Michigan, BA, 1946. **Career:** The Michigan Chronicle, reporter, sports editor, city editor, mng editor, 1946-61; Detroit News, reporter, writer, 1962-63; WMAQ-NBC, TV and radio reporter, 1963-65; NBC Network Television, correspondent, 1966-72; ABC Network News, correspondent, 1972-78; Who's Who Among Black Americans, founding editor 1974-88, consulting editor, 1988-93, advisory bd mem, 1993-; US Bureau of Census, deputy director of 1990 Census Promotion Office, 1989-90, sr public affairs specialist, 1979-93. **Orgs:** Mem, Big Ten Championship Track Team, 1943; pres, Cotillion Club, 1962-63; mem, NAACP, AFTRA; Alpha Phi Alpha; Natl Acad of Television Arts and Sciences. **Honors/Awds:** Natl Achievement Award, Lincoln Univ, 1966; Man of the Year, Intl Pioneers, 1966; Sigma Delta Chi Citation, 1967; Outstanding Achievement Citation (Emmy), Natl Acad of Television Arts and Sciences, 1967; Natl Award, Southern Press Inst, 1976; Hon Dr Jour, Benedict Coll, 1973; Outstanding TV Correspondent, Women in Media, 1977; Outstanding Natl Corres Serv Award, Michigan Minority Business Enterprise Assn, 1977; Natl Advisory Comm, Crisis Magazine, NAACP, 1981-91. **Special Achievements:** First Black exec sec, Michigan State Ath Assn, 1950-61; First Black reporter, Detroit News, 1960-63; First Black network news correspondent, NBC-News, 1965-70; First Black correspondent permanently assigned to the White House, Washington NBC News, 1970-72. **Military Serv:** USAAF, 1943-45.

MATORY, DEBORAH LOVE
Clinical psychologist. **Personal:** Born Apr 20, 1929, Norfolk, VA; daughter of Nannie Reid Love and David C Love; married William Earle Matory, Jul 26, 1949; children: William Earle Jr MD, Yvedt Love MD, James Lorand PhD. **Educ:** Howard Univ, BS 1950, MS 1955. **Career:** DC Public School, clinical psychologist 1959-66; WA Tech Inst, assoc prof psych 1969-71; NMAF, rsch assoc, clin psych; Mod Cit Health Outreach Health Welfare Council, dir 1971; DHR DC, planning dir 1973-75; private practice, cons, clinical psych; DC Public Schools Handicap Svcs, coord. **Orgs:** Consultant, Albert Deutsch Rehab Ctr, Shaw Comp Health Ctr, Stanford Univ, Univ of Pacific, School of Educ; prog dir Phizer Pharm Co; plnd progs & conf Lederle Pharm Co, Natl Med Assoc, DC Men Health Assoc; mem US Civil Rights Comm; bd dir SAC; mem Inst of Mental Hygiene, Soc Hygiene Soc, Mental Health Assn, Epilepsy Foundation, Howard Univ Alumni, Amer Assn of Univ Women, Womens Auxiliary to the Med Chirurgical Soc; founder, pres Ward Four Dem Inc; bd mgr PTA Cong; ed chprsn Women's Natl Med Assn 1964-66; pres, Civic League of North Portal Estates; pres, Women's Auxiliary to Medico-Chirurgical Society, Inc. **Honors/Awds:** Natl Hon Soc; Psi Chi Hon Soc; Fellowship to Grad School; Woman of the Year Awd Womens Aux to Med Chirurgical Soc 1967; Woman of the Year Afro-Amer Newspaper & Greyhound Bus Lines 1967; numerous citations, plaques for outstanding community involvement; NAACP Humanitarian Awd 1987.

MATORY, WILLIAM EARLE, JR.
Plastic surgeon. **Personal:** Born Nov 20, 1950, Richmond, VA; son of Deborah Matory and William E Matory; married Yvonne Marie Johnson, Aug 1, 1989. **Educ:** Yale, BS, 1972; Howard Univ, MD, 1976; Harvard Univ, Fellow, 1981. **Career:** Univ of Massachusetts Medical Center, Worcester MA, assoc prof, plastic surgery, anatomy, surgeon, 1984-. **Orgs:** Member, American Society of Plastic Reconstructive Surgeons, 1985-; member, American College of Surgeons, 1987-; American Assn of Plastic Surgeons; American Society of Aesthetic Plastic Surgeons. **Honors/Awds:** Fellow, Amer Soc Plastic Reconstruction Surgeons, 1985; author of Rhinoplasty in The African American, 1985; Fellow, Amer Coll of Surgeons, 1987; Cine Clinic Award, 1988; author of Aging in the African-American, 1989; Achievement Award, Upjohn, 1974; Excellence of Research, Student Amer Med Assn, 1975; NMA Surgical Section Award, 1991; Edward J Mason Award, 1994. **Business Addr:** Plastic Surgeon, Univ of Massachusetts Medical Ctr, 55 Lake Ave N, Worcester, MA 01655.

MATORY, YVEDT L.
Surgeon. **Personal:** Born Oct 31, 1956, Misawa, Japan; daughter of Deborah Matory and William Earle Matory; married Randall Kennedy, Jun 15, 1985. **Educ:** Yale University, BA, 1977, School of Medicine, MD, 1981. **Career:** Brigham & Women's Hospital, associate surgeon, 1992-; Dana Farber Cancer Institute, associate in surgery, 1992-; Veteran's Administration, associate in surgery, 1992-. **Honors/Awds:** Intl College of Surgeons Fellowship, 1993; Natl Medical Assn, Surgical Residents' Research Comp, first prize, 1983, second prize, 1986; American Cancer Society Fellowship, 1990; American College of Surgeons, diplomate, 1991. **Special Achievements:** American Cancer Society Fellowship, Immunology, Memorial Sloan-Kettering Cancer Center, 1990-92; Natl Institutes of Health, Medical Staff Fellowship, 1983-85; contributor in numerous professional journals in the field of medicine. **Business Addr:** Associate Surgeon, Brigham & Women's Hospital, 75 Francis, ASB II, 3rd Fl, Dept of Surgical Oncology, Boston, MA 02115, (617)732-6806.

MATSON, OLLIE GENOA
Professional football player (retired). **Personal:** Born May 1, 1930, Trinity, TX; married Mary Paige; children: Lesa, Lewis, Ollie III, Bruce, Barbara. **Educ:** San Francisco City Coll, 1948; Univ of San Francisco, BS, 1952. **Career:** Halfback: Chicago Cardinals, 1952-59; Los Angeles Rams, 1959-62; Detroit Loins, 1962-63; Philadelphia Eagles, 1964-66; professional scout, 1966-68; Swinger Golf Club, president. **Orgs:** Kappa Fraternity, Olympic Track Team, 2 medals, silver & bronze, 1952. **Honors/Awds:** Professional Football Hall of Fame, 1972; College Hall of Fame, 1976. **Military Serv:** US Army, Cpl, 1953-54. **Business Addr:** Los Angeles Sports Arena, 3911 Figueroa, Los Angeles, CA 90037.

MATTHEW, CLIFTON, JR.
Educator. **Personal:** Born Sep 25, 1943, Brooklyn, NY; married Claraleata Cutler; children: Darryl, Adrian. **Educ:** NC A&T State Univ, BS 1966; Rutgers Univ, MEd 1973. **Career:** Baltimore Orioles, professional baseball player 1966-71; Camden Sch Sys, tchr 1966-71; Trenton State Coll, head baseball coach 1974; Upward Bound, dir; Educ Oppty Fund Trenton St Coll, asst dir 1971-74; Camden City Bd of Edn, supr recreation 1974-79; Pleasantville Pub Sch, dir comm educ 1979-83; Lower Camden Cnty Bd of Ed, asst principal 1983-. **Orgs:** Mem Kappa Alpha Psi; mem Natl Assoc of Secondary Sch Principals, NJ Principals and Supervisors Assoc; Phi Delta Kappa Fraternity. **Business Addr:** Principal, Edgewood Junior High School, 200 Coopers Folly Rd, Atco, NJ 08004.

MATTHEWS, ALBERT D.
Retired judge. **Personal:** Born Feb 19, 1923, Oklahoma City, OK; son of Della Matthews and Samuel Matthews; married Mildred; children: Angela M. **Educ:** Howard Univ School of Law, LLB 1954; Howard Univ, 1941-43, 1950-51. **Career:** State of CA, superior court judge, 1973-89 (retired); municipal court judge, 1968-73; Pro Tempr, superior court commr, 1962-68; Dept Employment, state referee hearing officer, 1960-62; LA County, deputy district attorney, 1958-60; private practice, 1955-58. **Orgs:** Mem LA Bar Assn; Langston Law Club, Natl Conf Trial Court Judges; Amer Bar Assn; mem, bd of dir, Henderson Community Center, S LA; bd mgrs, Amer Baptist Pac SW; chmn, MATE; deacon, church school admin, 2nd Baptist Church, LA; exec bd, Amer Baptist Churches, USA Valley Forge, PA; Sunday School Teacher, past 48 years, christian educator. **Honors/Awds:** Graduated cum laude, Howard Univ, 1954. **Military Serv:** AUS sgt 1943-45.

MATTHEWS, AQUILLA E.
Business executive. **Personal:** Born in Danville, VA. **Educ:** Columbia U, BS; Northwestern U, MS. **Career:** Guest Houses, owner 1985; VA State Coll, prof music edn; So U, prof music edn;; USO Hattiesburg MS Witchita Falls TX, dir; Mobile Serv AZ CA NE, dir; Atlantic City Parking Authority, sec 1985; US Pres Bd of Edn, 1st black women 1985. **Honors/Awds:** Many Plaques & Awards For Disting Serv to Edn, Tchrs Assn, Youth Activites & Counseling; NAACP Citations.

MATTHEWS, BILLIE WATSON
Professional football coach. **Personal:** Born Mar 15, 1930, Houston, TX; son of Love Jones Matthews and Adolph Matthews; married Gene Woods Matthews, Mar 5, 1961; children: Jacquelyn McMillon, Kenneth Adams, Kennette Hatcher, Karen Kaufman. **Educ:** Southern Univ, Baton Rouge, LA, BS, 1952; Texas Southern Univ, attended. **Career:** UCLA, coach 1971-78; San Francisco 49'ers, running back coach 1979-82; Philadelphia Eagles, running back coach 1983-84; Indianapolis Colts, offensive coord, 1985-86; Kansas City Chiefs, coach, 1987-88; Detroit Lions, assistant coach, 1989-. **Honors/Awds:** Hall of Honor, Phillis Wheatley High School, 1989; Hall of Honor, Southern Univ, 1988. **Military Serv:** US Army, Pfc, 1954-56. **Business Addr:** Assistant Coach, Detroit Lions, 1200 Featherstone Rd, Pontiac, MI 48342.

MATTHEWS, CHRISTY
Foundation administrator. **Career:** Colonial Williamsburg Foundation, dir, Black History Dept, currently. **Business Addr:** Dir, Black History Dept, Colonial Williamsburg Foundation, 134 N Henry St, Williamsburg, VA 23187-1776, (757)220-7212.

MATTHEWS, CLAUDE LANKFORD, JR.
Television news producer. **Personal:** Born Jun 18, 1941, High Point, NC; son of Georgianna Matthews and Claude Matthews; married Cynthia C Clark; children: Georgeanne N. **Educ:** Howard Univ, BA 1963; Georgetown Univ Law Ctr, JD 1978. **Career:** WTOP-TV, reporter 1968-70, host of talk show ''Harambee'' 1970-74; NBC News, editor network radio 1976-77, editor network TV 1977-80, Washington producer weekend nightly news 1980-. **Orgs:** Mem Pennsylvania Bar Assn; mem American Bar Assn; mem District of Columbia Bar Association. **Honors/Awds:** Host of Emmy Awd winning talk show ''Harambee'' on WTOP-TV Washington DC 1970-74. **Home Addr:** 2805 31st Pl NE, Washington, DC 20018. **Business Addr:** Producer, NBC News, 4001 Nebraska Ave NW, Washington, DC 20016.

MATTHEWS, CYNTHIA CLARK
Attorney. **Personal:** Born Aug 27, 1941, Nashville, TN; married Claude Lankford. **Educ:** Wellesley Coll, attended 1959-61; Howard Univ, BA 1965; George Wash Univ Nat Law Center, JD 1973. **Career:** Housing Com Council of DC, exec asst to council mem & atty 1976-79; Onyx Corp, vice pres for marketing & contract mgr 1975-76; US Comm on Civil Rights, equal opportunity specialist 1973-75; United Planning Orgn, pub information ofcr 1970-72; Hon John Conyers US Congress, legislative & press asst 1965-69; US Equal Employment Opportunity Comm, atty advisor to dir, chair, management dir, 1980-92, dir, currently. **Orgs:** Mem DC Bar 1975; mem Supreme Court Bar 1980; mem US Dist Ct for DC Bar 1980; mem Nat Assn of Black Women Atty/Am Bar Assn/Anacostia Mus Bd of Dir. **Business Addr:** Equal Employment Opportunity C, 1801 L St NW, Washington, DC 20507.

MATTHEWS, DAVID
Clergyman. **Personal:** Born Jan 29, 1920, Indianola, MS; son of Bertha Henderson Matthews and Albert Matthews; married Lillian Pearl Banks; children: Denise D. **Educ:** Morehouse Coll, BA 1950; Attended: Atlanta Univ, Memphis Theological Seminary, Delta State Univ, Reformed Seminary. **Career:** Ordained Baptist minister, 1946-; Sunflower Cty & IN Public Schools, teacher 1950-83; Mt Heroden Baptist Church Vicksburg MS, pastor 1951-53; St Paul Baptist Church, pastor 1953-58; Bell Grove Baptist Church, pastor, currently; Strangers Home Baptist Church, pastor, currently. **Orgs:** Community Relations Committee of Indianola; Phi Delta Kappa; Mississippi St ate Dept of Education Task Force; Sunflower County Baptist Assn, moderator; Gene ral Missionary Baptist State Convention of Mississippi, pres, 1974-; National B aptist Convention USA Inc, vice-pres, 1971-94, oratorical contest supervisor. **Honors/Awds:** Honorary Doctor of Divinity, Natchez Junior College, 1973, Mississippi Industrial College, 1977, Morris Booker Memorial College, 1988. **Military Serv:** AUS pfc 1942-45; Good Conduct Medal, APTO Medal 1945. **Home Addr:** PO Box 627, Indianola, MS 38751.

MATTHEWS, DENISE. See VANITY.

MATTHEWS, DOLORES EVELYN
Educational administrator. **Personal:** Born Jul 23, 1938, DuBois, PA; daughter of Evelyn Goodrich Matthews and Daniel Matthews. **Educ:** New York City Comm Coll of AA&S, Associate 1961. **Career:** Columbia Univ Coll of Physicians & Surgeons Dept of Psychiatry, program coordinator, postgraduate education; officer, Columbia Univ Dept of Psychiatry, 1979-. **Orgs:** Mem, EDGES Group Inc; mem, national president, 1993-, Continental Societies Inc; mem Natl Assn of Negro Musicians; mem Guild, Aaron Davis Hall, City College of New York; NCNW, mem board of directors; Continental Societies, Inc; Natl Pres, 1993-; Natl Political Congress of Black Women, Inc, 1996-; Commission, Presidential Appointment of African-American Women, Second Clinton Administration. **Honors/Awds:** Grant recipient Natl Endowment of the Arts 1977; Merit Award, Presbyterian Hosp Comm Adv Council 1978; President's Award, Continental Societies Inc 1982, 1984; Distinguished Music Alumnus Award, DuBois Area High School Musical Department, 1985; Community Advisory Council Award, Columbia Presbyterian Medical Center, 1979; Psychiatric Residents' Award, Columbia University College of Physicians & Surgeons, 1988; DuBois Area High School Alumni Associate Guest Speaker, 1990; DuBois Area High School, Distinguished Music Alumnus Award, 1985; The Presbyterian Hospital's Community Advisory Council Award, 1979; Harlem Hospital Pastoral Care Service Award, 1986-93; Columbia Univ Coll of Physicians & Surgeons, Graduating Psychiatric Residents' Award, Class of 1988; EDGES Group, Inc, Consultant to NYC Mayoral Administration: Honorable Edward Koch and Honorable David Dinkins. **Home Addr:** 790 Riverside Drive, New York, NY 10032. **Business Addr:** Program Coordinator, Postgraduate Education, Department of Psychiatry, Columbia University, 722 W 168th St, New York, NY 10032.

MATTHEWS, DOROTHY
Advertising manager. **Personal:** Born Jan 21, 1962, St Louis, MO. **Educ:** Maryville Coll, BA 1983. **Career:** NY Ins, salesperson 1983; Channel 4 Newsroom, rsch person 1984; School Bd Dist 188, sec. **Orgs:** Mem Elks Purple Temple 126, Black Media Coalition St Louis, First Freewell Baptist Church, United Parcel Holiday Club. **Honors/Awds:** Citizenship Lovejoy School 1979; Best Essay First Freewill Bapt Church 1979; Valedictorian Lovejoy HS 1979. **Home Addr:** 412 Jefferson St, Lovejoy, IL 62059.

MATTHEWS, GREGORY J.
Business administrator. **Personal:** Born Oct 25, 1947, Baltimore, MD; married Paula Allen. **Educ:** Morgan State Univ, BA Sociology 1970; Coppin State Coll, MA Counseling 1973. **Career:** Adult Ed Economic Manpower Devl, instr 1970; Conciliation & Compliance-MD Comm on Human Rel, dir 1970-75; Intl Assn of Ofcl Human Rgts Agcies , EEO consultant 1975; Affirmative Action-Great Atlantic Pacific Tea Co, dir 1975-78; GJ Matthews & Assoc, mgng prtnr 1984-; Staffing and Equal Opp Prog, dir 1978-85; American Express Travel Related Servics, Co, Inc, dir employee relations 1985-. **Orgs:** Chrmn Natl Urban Affrs Cncl 1983-; chrmn Fed of Corporate Profsnls 1983-; brd mem Assoc Black Charities; life mem NAACP; bd mem Natl Assoc Market Dev; mem Edges Group. **Honors/Awds:** Key to the City Kansas City, MO 1984; Herbert H Weight Awd 1985; distinguished serv citation Natl Black MBA Assoc 1984. **Business Addr:** Dir Employee Relations, American Express Travel, World Financial Center, New York, NY 10285.

MATTHEWS, HARRY BRADSHAW
Educational administrator. **Personal:** Born Mar 1, 1952, Denmark, SC; son of Lucretia Killingsworth Parler Matthews and James Edgar Matthews; married Pamela Davis. **Educ:** SUNY Coll at Oneonta, BA 1974; Carnegie Mellon Univ, 1979; Northern MI Univ, MA 1981. **Career:** NYS Minority Ways & Means Rsch Div, trainee, intern 1973-74; SUNY Coll Oneonta, asst dean in rsch 1974-78; Northern MI Univ, dir black student serv 1978-81; Hobart & William Smith Coll, asst to deans 1981-85; Gettysburg Coll, dean of intercultural advancement 1985-. **Orgs:** Mem MI Gov & Bd Educ Task Force 1980-82, Human Rights Commission Geneva NY 1983-85; consultant The Matthews Plan 1984-; fellow Coll of Preceptors UK 1985-, Royal Commonwealth Soc UK 1985-; Pennsylvania Historical & Museum Commission's Black History Advisory Comm, l989; dir & founder, Minority Youth Educ Inst, l988-; co-chairman, Annual Conference, Afro-American Historical & Genealogical Society, 1991. **Honors/Awds:** Presidential Classroom for Young Amers 1970; Amer Legion Leadership Award SUNY Oneonta 1974; Distinguished Visitor US 8th Air Force 1979; WEB DuBois Dist Lecturer Hobart & William Smith Coll 1986; Certificate of Merit, AAHGS, l989; The Matthews Method in African Amer Genealogy, essay published by Univ of SC, l989; founder & dir, Intercultural Resource Center; essay, ''Intercultural Diversity and its Effects Upon the Education of African American Youths or The Island of Philae: A Contribution to the African American Identity,'' 1991; author, The Historical Portrait Collection, 1991. **Home Addr:** 140 W Broadway, Gettysburg, PA 17325. **Business Addr:** Dean of Intercultural Advance, Gettysburg College, Box 2248, Gettysburg, PA 17325.

MATTHEWS, HEWITT W.
Educator, educational administrator. **Personal:** Born Dec 1, 1944, Pensacola, FL; son of Jestine Matthews and Hewitt Matthews; married Marlene Mouzon; children: Derrick, David. **Educ:** Clark Atlanta Univ, BS 1966; Mercer Univ School of Pharmacy, BS Pharmacy 1968; Univ WI Madison, MS 1971, PhD 1973. **Career:** Center for Disease Control, research chemist 1976, visiting scientist, summer 1987, 1988; TX Southern Univ, visiting assoc prof 1979; Mercer Univ School of Pharmacy, asst dean 1980-83; Mercer Univ Atlanta, prof & asst provost; Mercer Univ School of Pharmacy, prof, assoc dean 1985-89; Mercer Univ Atlanta, School of Pharmacy, Hood-Meyer Alumni prof, dean 1990. **Orgs:** AACP, NPhA; ASHP; AphA; Rho Chi; Sigma Xi; Phi Kappa Phi; Georgia Pharmacy Association, bd of dirs; Commission on Pharmaceutical Care, chmn; Science & Technology Dev, governor's advisory coun; Natl Assn of Chain Drugstores, education comm; Natl Community Pharmacist Assn. **Honors/Awds:** Fellow, Amer Found for Pharmaceutical Educ, 1968; Natl Inst of Health, predoctoral fellow, 1970-76; Prof of the Year, Mercer Univ School of Pharm, 1980; Hood-Myers Alumni Chair, Mercer Univ School of Pharmacy, 1983-; Teacher of the Year, 1991; Outstanding Teacher Award, Southern School of Pharmacy; Rennebohm Teaching Assistant Award, Univ of Wisconsin. **Business Addr:** Professor & Dean, School of Pharmacy, Mercer Univ, 3001 Mercer University Dr, Atlanta, GA 30341.

MATTHEWS, IRVING J.
Company executive. **Career:** Prestige Ford Inc, CEO, currently. **Special Achievements:** Company is ranked number 61 on BE's list of Top 100 Auto Dealer's, 1994. **Business Addr:** CEO, Prestige Ford Inc, 351 Plaza Dr, Eustis, FL 32726, (904)357-5522.

MATTHEWS, JAMES VERNON, II
Roman Catholic priest. **Personal:** Born Oct 25, 1948, Berkeley, CA; son of Yvonne Feast Matthews and James Vernon Matthews. **Educ:** St Patrick's Coll, Mountain View, CA, BA Humanities, 1970; St Patrick's Seminary, Menlo Park CA, MDiv, 1973; Jesuit School of Theology, Berkeley CA, DMin (candidate), 1977-79. **Career:** St Louis Bertrand Church, Oakland CA, assoc pastor, 1974-78; All Saints Church, Hayward CA, admin, 1978-80; St Cyril Church, Oakland CA, admin, 1980-83; Diocese of Oakland, Oakland CA, vicar of Black Catholics, 1983-87; St Cornelius Church, Richmond CA, admin, 1987-89; St Benedict Church, Oakland CA, pastor, 1989-. **Orgs:** Knights of St Peter Claver Third and Fourth Degrees, 1971-; mem, past bd mem, Natl Black Catholic Clergy Caucus, 1973-; review bd, Alameda County Revenue Sharing, 1975-76; bd of dir, Campaign for Human Devel, 1979-84; commr, Oakland School District, Comm on Educ and Career Devel, 1982-83; Bay Area Black United Fund Religious Task Force, 1982-; bd of dir, Catholic Charities: Parish Outreach Program, 1983-87; advisory bd, Oakland Mayor's Task Force on Hunger, 1984-87, Oakland Mayor's Task Force on black/Jewish Relations, 1984-87; Diocesan coord, Natl Conference on Interracial Justice, 1984-; member, Oakland Mayor's Advisory Council, 1991-; member, Oakland Strategic Planning, 1991-; chaplain, African-American Catholic Pastoral Center, 1990-. **Honors/Awds:** Outstanding Black Sermons, Judson Press, Publishers, 1975; Rose Casanave Serv Award, Black Catholic Vicariate, Oakland CA, 1982; Martin Luther King Jr Award, United East Oakland Clergy, 1984; Marcus Foster Distinguished Alumni Award, Marcus Foster Educ Inst, 1984; Religion Award, Alameda/Contra Costa Chapter of Links Inc, 1985; Service Award, Xavier Univ Alumni Assn, 1985. **Home Addr:** 2245 82nd Ave, Oakland, CA 94605.

MATTHEWS, JESSIE L.
Librarian. **Personal:** Born Aug 18, 1935, Charleston, WV. **Educ:** Kutztown State Coll, BS 1958; Univ IL, MS 1959; State Coll, Reference Libr Cheyney 1959-60; Morristown Coll, Libr 1960-62; Rutgers Univ Law Sch Library 1962. **Career:** Mem Am Assn Law Libraries 1962-; chmn Directories Com 1972-74; editor co-author Indexer. **Business Addr:** 5 Penn Sts, Camden, NJ 08102.

MATTHEWS, LEONARD LOUIS
Educator/principal. **Personal:** Born Dec 4, 1930, New Orleans, LA; married Dolores; children: Mallory Louis. **Educ:** Southern Univ, BS/BA 1952-59; CA State Univ, Crdntl Psych 1964-65; Univ of CA Los Angeles, Crdntl Psych 1970-72, Pepperdine Univ Los Angeles, Crdntl Educ 1973-74; CA State Univ, MA Educ 1972-74. **Career:** St John School Dist, elem principal 1952-59; LA Unified School Dist, drama spec/master teacher 1959-70, counselor 1970-74; Inglewood Unified School Dist, secondary principal 1974-. **Orgs:** Organizer Citizens Against Prostitution 1982-84, Dr Martin L King Jr Memorial 1983-86, Citizens Against Crime & Drugs 1984-86; mem/officer Parents Teachers Assoc 1985-86, Young Men Christian Assoc 1985-86, Inglewood Mgmt Assoc 1986; mem CA Continuation Educ Assoc. **Honors/Awds:** Awd of Recognition Project Investment 1978; Proclamation City of Inglewood 1980,82; Service Awd Assoc of CA Administrators 1982; Commendation City of Inglewood 1985. **Military Serv:** AUS act/sgt 1976-78. **Home Addr:** 9626 5th Ave, Inglewood, CA 90305. **Business Addr:** Teacher, CCEO Youth Build-Americare, 17216 Figueroa, Gardena, CA 90248.

MATTHEWS, MARY JOAN
Educator. **Personal:** Born Dec 19, 1945, Boley, OK; married H Carl Matthews. **Educ:** Langston Univ, BS Elem Ed 1967; CA State Coll Dominguez Hills, MA Learning Disabilities 1976; Univ of OK, Cert Psychometry 1980. **Career:** Paramount Uni-

fied School Dist, teacher 1st grade 1968-70; Sapulpa City School, teacher 5th grade 1971-74; Boley Public Schools, teacher LD 1976-79; OK State Dept of Ed, psychometrist 1979-. **Orgs:** Sec Greater Boley Area NAACP Branch 1981; mem OK Council for Vocational Ed 1982-; sec Boley Chamber of Commerce 1983-, Bd of Dir CREOKS Mental Health 1983-; Grammateus, Epsilon Rho Omega Chapter of Alpha Kappa Alpha Sorority, 1989; treasurer, Self Culture Club of Okla Federated Colored Women's Club. **Home Addr:** PO Box 352, Boley, OK 74829.

MATTHEWS, MERRITT STEWART
Physician. **Personal:** Born Jul 8, 1939, Atlantic City, NJ; son of Bessie Stewart Matthews and George Matthews; married Patricia Anne Delgado; children: Shari, Luis, Merritt Jr, Michael, Marguerite. **Educ:** Howard Univ, BS Liberal Arts 1961, MD School of Medicine 1965. **Career:** St Joseph's Hospital, intern, 1965-66, resident, 1966-68, chief resident family practice, 1967-68; Otay Medical Clinic SD CA, 1971-74; USAF Medical Corps, 1968-70; San Diego Acad of Family Physicians, pres, 1984-85; Family Practice Comm Paradise Valley Hospital, chairperson, 1983-86, 1993-96; Skilled Nursing Facility of San Diego Physicians & Surgeons Hospital, med dir, 1983-87; private practice, physician. **Orgs:** Physician, San Diego County Jails, 1976-92; bd of dir, San Diego Acad of Family Physicians, 1982-, Jackie Robinson YMCA San Diego, bd of dirs, 1983-85; co-dir, Western Medical Group Lab, 1982-87; member, Task Force SD Police Dept, 1983; dir 1988-95, CA Acad of Family Physicians; alternate delegate, CA Medical Assn, 1987-93; Comm on Minority Health Affairs of AAFP, 1992-95, chair, 1995; board of directors, San Diego AIDS Foundation, 1992-94. **Honors/Awds:** Certified, Amer Bd of Family Physicians, 1970, recertified 1976, 1982, 1988, 1995; Delegate, CA Medical Assn, 1994-; fellow, Amer Acad of Family Physicians, 1974; published article "Cholelithiasis: A Differential Diagnosis in Abdominal Crisis of Sickle Cell Anemia," Journal of NMA, 1981; Special Achievement Award, Jackie Robinson YMCA, 1985; Competitive Award for Practicing Phys, Fam Practice, NMA, 1993, 1994. **Military Serv:** USAF capt 1968-70. **Business Addr:** 995 Gateway Center Way, #201, San Diego, CA 92102.

MATTHEWS, MIRIAM
Librarian, historian, consultant (retired). **Personal:** Born Aug 6, 1905, Pensacola, FL; daughter of Fannie Elijah Matthews and Reuben H Matthews. **Educ:** Univ of CA, AB 1926; Univ of CA, Cert of Librarianship 1927; Univ of Chicago, MA 1945. **Career:** South Central Region Los Angeles Pub Lib, reg librarian, 1949-60; NY Pub Lib, exchange Libr 1940; Lib, br 1929-49; Los Angeles Pub Lib, libr 1927-29; LA Pub Lib, radio book reviewer 1927-35. **Orgs:** Life mem Am Lib Assn, council 1947-51; Intellectual Freedom Com; CA Lib Assn; chmn Intellectual Freedom Com 1946-48; nominating com 1950; Youth Commn LA Co 1938-40; adv bd Nat Youth Adminstrn 1938-39; Mayor's Birthday Fiesta Com 1954-61; Mayor's Comm Adv Com 1961-65; pres vp Exposition Comm Coord Conc 1951-60; exec bd Nat Intercoll Christian Counc 1937-38; CA City Educ Adv Counc 1935-36; exec bd NAACP Legal Def Fund for So CA; lfe mem NAACP; bd of trustees, California Afro-Amer Museum Found, El Pueblo Park Assn, & Roy Wilkins Found; Los Angeles City Historical Soc. **Honors/Awds:** LA Fellshp League 1935; LA Urban League 1948; LA Co Bd of Supr 1960; LA Sentinel 1960; Nat Cong of Parents & Tchrs 1960; Expo Com Coord Counc 1965; Nat Assn of Media Women 1975; Fedn of Black Hist & Arts 1974; Award of Merit, California Historical Soc, 1982; Woman of the Year Award, Women on Target, 1985; Distinguished Service Award, Black Caucus of the Amer Library Assn & California Librarians Black Caucus, 1987; Miriam Matthews Award inaugurated at California State Univ at Dominguez Hills, 1988; Elected Fellow, Historical Soc of Southern California, 1988; contrib to professional journals. **Home Addr:** 4423 Victoria Park Dr, Los Angeles, CA 90019.

MATTHEWS, ROBERT L.
Educational administrator. **Personal:** Born Jun 2, 1930, Tonganoxie, KS; son of Suzie Jane Brown Matthews and Mark Hanna Matthews; married Ardelle Marie Dunlap, Aug 26, 1952; children: Mark Douglas, Brian Louis, Scott Wallace. **Educ:** KS State Teachers (Emporia, KS), BS 1952; Columbia Univ, MA 1955; US Internatl Univ, PhD 1971; UCLA, Stanford, San Diego State Univ, Advanced Studies. **Career:** San Diego City Schl, tchr 1955-64, princpl 1965-72, dir of elem ed 1972-83, princpl 1983-84; Educ Cultural Complex, pres 1984-86; Continuing Education Centers San Diego Comm Coll Dist; pres 1986-92; self-employed, educational consultant, currently. **Orgs:** Mem, Education Committee, San Diego Zoological Society 1973-; member and officer, San Diego Urban League, 1965-; NAACP; pres, Zeta Sigma Lambda Alpha Phi Alpha 1984-85; pres Elem Inst of Sci 1983-84; bd of dir Museum of Natl Hist 1984-. **Honors/Awds:** Humanities Fellowship, Natl Endowment for Humanities 1976; fellowship Rockefeller Foundation 1971-72; NDEA fellowship US Govt 1965. **Military Serv:** AUS cpl; Peace Medal, Marksmanship 1952-54. **Home Addr:** 4931 Dassco Court, San Diego, CA 92102-3717.

MATTHEWS, ROBERT L.
Law enforcement official. **Personal:** Born Oct 8, 1947, Wilmington, DE; married Elsie Nichols, Aug 26, 1972; children: Miel, Amne. **Educ:** Florida A&M University, BA (magna cum laude), sociology, 1972; Indiana State University, MS, criminology, 1973. **Career:** Bureau of Prisons, USP Leavenworth, associate warden, 1980, warden, 1981; Bureau of Prisons, FCI Ashland, warden, 1981; US Marshals Service, District of Columbia, US marshal, 1983; Bureau of Prisons, FCI Lexington, warden, 1985; Bureau of Prisons, USP Atlanta, warden 1990; Bureau of Prisons, regional director, 1991-94; Federal Bureau of Prisons, asst dir; Bureau of Prisons, Southeast Region, regional director, currently. **Orgs:** American Correctional Association, 1981-; Correctional Employees Committee for ACA, executive member, 1992; Federal Executive Board, San Francisco, 1991-; Federal Executive Board, Atlanta, 1990-91; National Association for Blacks in Criminal Justice, 1982-. **Honors/Awds:** Attorney General's Award, Distinguished Service, 1983; Bureau of Prisons Director's Award, Public Service, 1989; National Association of Blacks in Criminial Justice, Correctional Service Award, 1990; Department of Justice, Senior Executive Service Meritorious Service, 1990-92; American Federation of Government Employees, Labor Management Distinguished Service Award, 1991. **Special Achievements:** Appointment to Leavenworth Civil Service Commission, 1990; Department of Justice, Senior Executive Service Outstanding Performance Rating, 1990-92. **Military Serv:** US Air Force, sgt, 1965-69. **Business Addr:** Regional Director, Southeast Region, Bureau of Prisons, 523 McDonough Blvd, SE, Atlanta, GA 30315, (404)624-5201.

MATTHEWS, VINCENT
Athlete. **Personal:** Born Dec 16, 1947, Queens, NY. **Educ:** Johnson C Smith Coll. **Career:** Olympic Track Runner. **Orgs:** Mem Olympic Teams 1968, 1972; Ran 440 yd in 444. **Honors/Awds:** Won Silver Medal Pan-Am Games 1967; AAU 1968; ran on US 1600-m relay team which set world record; Founded Brooklyn Over the Hill Athletic Assn; won Gold Medal Munich Olympics 1972. **Business Addr:** c/o Essex County Comm College, 303 University Avenue, Newark, NJ 07102.

MATTHEWS, VIRGIL E.
Scientist, educator (retired). **Personal:** Born Oct 5, 1928, Lafayette, AL; son of Izetta Roberta Ware Matthews (deceased) and Virgil Edison Matthews (deceased); married Shirley McFatridge Matthews, Jan 23, 1960 (divorced); children: Brian Keith, Michael Andre, Deborah Michelle. **Educ:** Univ of IL, BS, chem, 1951; Univ of Chicago, SM, chem, 1952, PhD, chem, 1955. **Career:** Univ of Chicago, teaching asst 1951-52; WV State Coll, instr part time chem 1955-60, prof part-time chem 1960-70; Union Carbide Corp, rsch chemist 1954-67, proj scientist 1967-75, develop scientist chem & plastics div 1975-86; WV State College, Dept of Chemistry, prof and chmn 1986-94. **Orgs:** Councilman-at-Large Charleston 1967-83; mem Municipal Planning Commn Charleston 1971-83; chmn Planning Comm of City Council Charleston 1971-83; mem NAACP, vice pres Charleston Branch 1964-72; mem Charleston Bus & Professional Men's Club pres 1965-66; mem Amer Chem Soc; Fellow Amer Inst of Chemists; Fellow AAAS; mem Sigma Xi; Phi Lambda Upsilon; del Dem Natl Conv from WV 1968; Dem nominee for state senate 8th Dist of WV 1970; Amer Men of Sci; alternate delegate, Dem Natl Convention from West Virginia 1980; Democratic Nominee for City Treasurer of Charleston WV 1983; mem, Alpha Phi Alpha Frat, 1967-. **Home Addr:** 835 Carroll Rd, Charleston, WV 25314, (304)343-0724.

MATTHEWS, WESTINA LOMAX
Company executive. **Personal:** Born Nov 8, 1948, Chillicothe, OH; daughter of Ruth Matthews and Wesley Matthews. **Educ:** Univ of Dayton, BS 1970, MS 1974; Univ of Chicago, PhD 1980. **Career:** Mills Lawn Elem Sch, teacher 1970-76; The Chicago Comm Trust, sr staff assoc 1982-85; Merrill Lynch & Co Inc, first vice pres corporate responsibility, 1985-; Merrill Lynch & Co Foundation, Inc, secretary, 1985-. **Orgs:** Director, Coalition of 100 Black Women, New York City, 1992-95; director, Women's Forum, 1993-96; trustee, Wilberforce University, 1994-; director, Arthur Ashe Institute, 1994; trustee, New York Theological Seminary, 1995-; Board of Education, The City of New York, 1990-93. **Honors/Awds:** Postdoctoral Fellow Northwestern Univ 1980-81, Univ of WI-Madison 1981-82. **Business Addr:** First Vice Pres, Corporate Responsibility, Merrill Lynch & Co, Inc, World Financial Ctr, S Tower, New York, NY 10080-6106.

MATTHIS, JAMES L., III
Beer marketing executive. **Personal:** Born Mar 21, 1955, Chicago, IL; son of Doris Buckley Matthis and James L Matthis; married Michelle Englander Matthis; children: Jordan. **Educ:** Alabama A&M University, Huntsville, AL, BS, 1977. **Career:** Miller Brewing Co, Chicago, IL, merchandiser, 1977-78; Miller Brewing Co, Bloominton, IN, area sales manager, 1978-81; Miller Brewing Co, St Louis, MO, area sales manager, 1981-85; Miller Brewing Co, Milwaukee, WI, talent and video marketing manager, 1985-. **Orgs:** Member, American Marketing Assn, 1984-; member, NAACP, 1978-; member, World Tae Kwon Do Federation, 1980-. **Home Addr:** 9656 S Damen, Chicago, IL 60643. **Business Addr:** Talent & Video Marketing Manager, Event Marketing Dept, Miller Brewing Company, 3939 W Highland Blvd, Milwaukee, WI 53201.

MAULE, ALBERT R.
Business administrator (retired). **Personal:** Born Feb 18, Philadelphia, PA; son of Jessie R Maule and Albert D Maule; married Yvonne D; children: Albert C. **Educ:** Hillyer Jr Coll, AS Accounting 1944; Wharton School of Finance Univ of PA, BSE Accounting 1947, MBA Personnel & Indus Mgmt 1949; Command & General Staff Coll (US Army), Diploma 1969; Industrial Coll of Armed Forces, Diplma 1976. **Career:** Amer Garages, Inc Parking Mgmt, mgr 1953-62; Hartford Housing Authority, project mgr 1962-67; Vietnam Bonus Div Off of State Treasurer, deputy dir 1967-70; Univ of CT Law School, asst to dean for fiscal affairs 1970-84; State of CT, Banking Commr, exec asst 1984-89. **Orgs:** Exec bd Long Rivers Council Boy Scouts of Amer 1970-; pres Rocky Hill Civitan Club 1980-; club pres Res Officers Assoc Hfd Chapter 1967-1970; mem Res Officers Assn 1967-; mem Natl Guard Assn 1975-; dist pres Omega Psi Phi Fraternity Inc 1974-74; commr Human Relations Comm Rocky Hill 1976-80. **Honors/Awds:** Aide Camp Governor's Military Staff 1975-; Silver Beaver, Long Rivers Council, Boy Scouts of Amer 1987. **Military Serv:** US Army 1949-53, US Army Reserve 1953-75, Connecticut Army Natl Guard 1975-82, brigadier general. **Home Addr:** 7 Mark Lane, Rocky Hill, CT 06067.

MAULTSBY, DOROTHY M.
Community organization director. **Personal:** Born Feb 22, 1927, Wilmington, NC; divorced; children: James T Jr, Myra L, Wanda J (dec). **Educ:** Wilberforce Univ, BS 1947; Dist of Col Tech & Coll UDC, 1971; US Civil Serv Mgmt Serv Ctr DC, 1976; US Dept Ag Grad School, 1972; George Washington Univ Grad School, 1973; Antioch School of Law, 1988. **Career:** US Navy Dept, phys sci tchr 1951-61; Dist of Columbia Pub Schl, pub schl tchr 1961-66; Dist of Columbia Gov, coord of volunteers 1966-67; Natl Conf of Chrstns & Jews Natl Capital Area, assoc dir 1968-1969; Un Plng Comm, spcl asst oper 1969; United Plng Org, exec rep for admin 1969-71; Dept Health, Ed & Welfare (US Govt), admnstrv ofcr 1971-76, sr mgmnt analyst 1976-78; Dist of Columbia Gov, comm org consult 1980-82; District of Columbia Superior Court, legal intern 1987; African Methodist Epicsopal Zion Church, dir of lay activities, reg I. **Orgs:** Mem Alpha Kappa Alpha Sor Xi Omega Chaptr 4 1982-; former dir of lay activities Philadelphia & Balt Conf AME Zion Church 1981-84; co-govnr Fed EMA Women Dept of HEW 1972-74; tchr Sligo Jr HS Montgomery Co, MD 1984. **Honors/Awds:** Community Serv Ldrshp NAACP Dist of Columbia Chap 1971; Woman of the Year Grey Hound Bus Co & Afro Amer Newspaper 1976; ldrshp Lamond Riggs Citizens Assoc, Washington, DC 1976; Woman of the Year DC Women's Dem Club, Washington, DC 1976; Comm Serv Dist of Columbia Govt Washington DC 1982. **Home Addr:** 214 Oneida St NE, Washington, DC 20011.

MAULTSBY, PORTIA K.
Educator. **Personal:** Born Jun 11, 1947, Orlando, FL; daughter of Valdee C Campbell Williams and Maxie Clarence Maultsby, Sr. **Educ:** Mount St Scholastica Coll, Atchison, KS, BM, piano/theory composition, 1968; Univ of WI, Madison, WI, MM, musicology, 1969, PhD, ethnomusicology, 1974. **Career:** IN Univ, Bloomington, IN, prof, Afro-American Studies, 1971-. **Orgs:** Exec bd, Int Assn for the Study of Popular Music, 1987-95, editorial bd, 1989-; council mem, Society for ethnomusicology, 1973-76, 1977-80, 1988-91. **Honors/Awds:** Selected as one of 8 American performers/scholars to participate in workshop/conference on African American Sacred Music in Havana, Cuba, 1990; selected as one of 6 American ethnomusicologists to participate in an American-Soviet Research Conference in the Soviet Union, 1988; Awarded Honorary Doctor of Music Degree, Benedictine, KS, 1985; Portia K Maultsby Day proclaimed by the Mayor of Orlando, FL, 1975; Utrecht Univ, Netherlands, apptd prof to "Belle van Zuylen" Chair, Distinguished Visiting Professor, 1997-98. **Special Achievements:** Delivered keynote address for GATT Conference on the exchange of culture between America and Europe in Tilburg, The Netherlands, 1994. **Business Addr:** Prof, Dept of Afro-American Studies, Indiana Univ-Bloomington, Memorial Hall East, Bloomington, IN 47405, (812)855-2708.

MAULTSBY, SYLVESTER
Government officer. **Personal:** Born Oct 24, 1935, Whiteville, NC; son of Reather Maultsby; married Mildred Baldwin; children: Jerome, Hilda, Thimothy. **Educ:** Atlanta Coll, Mortuary Science, graduate, 1959; Penn Univ, 1973; Hampton Inst (CT Sch Rel), Cert 1978; Liberty Univ, attended 1985; Liberty Bible Coll, Lynchburg, VA Th G, 1989-; CT Institute of Christian Religion, School of Theology VA Union University, bd, 1981; Liberty University, Bible College, Th G, 1989-; Wheaton College, School of Evangelism, 1992; Shaw Divinity School, Doctor of Divinity Degree, 1990; Liberty Univ, PhD, 1995. **Career:** Edwards Co, expediter 1960-62; Norwalk Police Dept, patrolman 1962-68; Norwalk Area Ministry, youth dir 1968-70; New York Life Ins Co, underwriter 1970-75; General Motors Finance Div, 1973-75; CT State Police, chaplain 1985-; Prudential Life Ins Co of Amer, district agent 1975-; State of Connecticut, justice of the peace, 1993-. **Orgs:** Assoc minister Calvary Baptist Church, Norwalk, CT 1976-; vice president Greater Norwalk Black Democratic Club 1976-; city sheriff City of Norwalk 1977-80; councilman City of Norwalk 1981-; exec board NAACP; 32 degree Prince Hall Masonic Order; William

Moore Lodge #1533 (Elks) IBPOEW; past patron Eastern Star PHA; founding bd of dir PIVOT (alcoholic and drug rehab center); founder/dir Norwalk Interdenom Youth Movement; First Black Democrat for State Senator from Fairfield County, CT 1980; Natl Black Caucus of Local Elected Officials 1976; Hampton Univ Minister Conf 1976; CT Baptist Missionary Conv; chmn Political Affairs Conn Missionary Baptist Convention 1987-; mem The Baptist Ministers Conference of Greater New York and Vicinity 1986-; The American Association of Christian Counselors, 1992-; Intl Conference of Police Chaplains, 1993. **Honors/Awds:** Distinguished Achievement Greater Norwalk Black Dem Club; Outstanding Citizen Norwalk Area Improvement League; US Jaycees Spoke Award Junior Chamber of Commerce; Service Award United Way; Holy Order of Past High Priesthood Award 1974; The Norwalk Youth Comm Concert Choir Man of the Yr Award 1983; CT Gen Assembly Official Citation for Presidential Campaign of Jesse Jackson 1984; Realities of Empowerment Awd CT State Fed of Black Dems 1985. **Military Serv:** AUS paratrooper Cp Jumpmaster 1953-56; Sr Jumper; Good Conduct; Serv Medal; Leadership Medal Korean War. **Business Addr:** Insurance Broker, Prudential Ins Co of America, PO Box 601, Norwalk, CT 06856.

MAUNEY, DONALD WALLACE, JR.
Business executive (retired). **Personal:** Born Oct 16, 1942, New Castle, PA; divorced; children: Michael A, Dawnya M, Donovan T. **Career:** Diversified Payments & Loan Servicing Br, chief 1985; Tenant Ledger Br DC Dept of Housing & Comm, chief, 1988; Gen Accounting Br DC Land Agency, chief 1970-75; Robert Hall Store, asst mgr 1969-70; State Dept Fed Govt, budget analyst 1962-69; The DM Products Corp, CEO, 1994-. **Orgs:** Pres Tri-State Enterprises Inc 1974-; proprietor Tri-State Engraving Co 1969-70; state pres DC Jaycees 1975-76; 1st Blacknat; vp, US Jaycees 1976-77; 1st African-American mem US Jaycees Exec Com; 1st African-American USA Elected Jaycess Intl World Vice Pres Johannesburg S Africa 1977; chmn of bd DC Council on Clothing for Kids Inc; exec com DC Vol Clearing House; bd dir DC Jacyee Youth Devel Trust; trustee Plymouth Congregational United Ch of Christ; treas Commerce Dept Toastmasters 1976-77; Jaycee International Senate, Washington DC, pres, 1987-; Assoc for Renewal in Educ Inc, acting secretary; NE/SE Regional Bd of Dirs for Greater Washington Boys & Girls Clubs, bd of dirs, 1994-95. **Honors/Awds:** Spl DC City Council Comm Award Resolution 1976; Jaycee of Year 1973; Hon Citizen Baton Rouge LA. **Military Serv:** AUS 1965-67; AUS Reserves 1967-76; DC NG 1977-94. **Business Addr:** 2811-12th St, NE, Washington, DC 20017-2402.

MAUPIN, JOHN E., JR.
Dentist, educational administrator. **Personal:** Born Oct 28, 1946, Los Angeles, CA; married Eilene; children: Deanne, Henry, Virgil. **Educ:** San Jose State College, pre-dentistry/business administration, 1964-68; Meharry Medical College, DDS, 1972; Loyola College, MBA, 1979. **Career:** United States Army Dental Corps, captain, 1972-81; West Baltimore Community Health Care Corporation, dental director, 1976-81; Baltimore City Health Department, assist commissioner for health services, 1981-84, deputy commissioner for medical services, 1984-87; Southside Healthcare Inc, chief executive officer, 1987-89; Morehouse School of Medicine, executive vice president, 1989-94; Meharry Medical College, president & CEO, 1994-. **Orgs:** National Dental Assn; National Medical Assn; American Assn of Higher Education; Assn of American Medical Colleges; National Assn of Health Service Executives; National Assn of Community Health Centers; American Dental Assn; North Georgia Dental Assn. **Honors/Awds:** North Georgia Dental Society, Dentist of the Year; National Dental Assn, President's Award; City of Baltimore, Mayor's Citation; City Council of Baltimore, President's Citation; Honorary Doctor of Laws Degree, Virginia Union University; Honorary Doctor of Science Degree, Morehouse School of Medicine. **Military Serv:** Retired US Army Dental Corps Active Reserve, lt col; The Army Commendation Medal; The Army Achievement Medal; Meritorious Service Medal. **Business Addr:** President & CEO, Meharry Medical College, 1005 D B Todd Blvd, Learning Resources Center Building, 5th Floor, Nashville, TN 37208.

MAUSI, SHAHIDA ANDREA
Arts director. **Personal:** Born Dec 27, 1954, Detroit, MI; daughter of Joyce Finley Garrett and Nathan T Garrett; divorced; children: Dorian, Sulaiman, Rashid, Malik. **Educ:** Univ of Detroit, Detroit, MI, BA, 1976. **Career:** Arts in Public Places, coordinator/dir, Detroit, 1976-78; Detroit Public Library, program specialist, 1978-81; Detroit Council of Arts, Detroit, MI, exec dir, 1982-93; Greater Detroit YWCA, exec dir, 1993-. **Orgs:** Producer, Capricorn Enterprises, 1979-80; Michigan Democratic Party, 19 85-; board mem, Museum of African American History, 1984-; Detroit People Mover Art Commission, 1986-; New Detroit Art Committee, 1982-; panel mem, Natl Endowment for the Arts, 1985-; bd mem, Jamison Project/Repertory Dance America Foundation, 1989-. **Honors/Awds:** Produced: "Amen Corner," 1980, "Nina Simone in Concert," 1985, "Fela in Concert," 1986, Debut of Jamison Project, 1988. **Business Addr:** Executive Director, Greater Detroit YWCA, 607 Shelby, Suite 700, Detroit, MI 48226, (313)961-9221.

MAXEY, BRIGITTE LATRECIA
Journalist. **Personal:** Born Aug 8, 1967, Detroit, MI; daughter of Edith Virginia Holmes Maxey and Holbert Alonzo Maxey. **Educ:** Howard University, Washington, DC, BA, 1989. **Career:** The Journal of Commerce, New York, NY, reporter, 1990-. **Orgs:** Vice president, Mary Church Terrell Chapter, National Assoc of Colored Women's Clubs, 1987-88; member, YMCA Youth Program, 1987-89; member, National Association of Black Journalists, 1990. **Honors/Awds:** Youth of the Year, New Prospect Baptist Church, 1985; Recognition Service, Journalism Dept, Howard University, 1988.

MAXEY, CARL. See Obituaries section.

MAXEY, MARLON LEE
Professional basketball player. **Educ:** University of Minnesota; University of Texas-El Paso. **Career:** Forward: Minnesota Timberwolves, 1992-. **Business Addr:** Professional Basketball Player, Minnesota Timberwolves, 600 1st Ave N, Minneapolis, MN 55403, (612)337-3865.

MAXIE, PEGGY JOAN
Business executive. **Personal:** Born Aug 18, 1936, Amarillo, TX; daughter of Reba Harris M. Jackson and Cleveland Maxie. **Educ:** Seattle U, BA 1970; Univ of WA, MSW 1972. **Career:** Seattle Urban Le ague, housing counselor; State of Washington, state representative, 1971-82; House Higher Education Committe, chair, 1972-76; Joint Committee on Higher Education, officer, 1972-76; Central Area Council on Alcoholism, exec dir/consultant, beginning 1972; Peggy Maxie & Associates, pres, 1978-; Permanent Professional Staff Employment Committee and Session Staff Employment Committee, 1979-84. **Orgs:** League of Women Voters; Capitol Hill Business and Professional Women's Club; Munic League; Madrona Community Council; Seattle Chamber of Commerce; Seattle Executives Assn; Self-Insured Organization. **Honors/Awds:** Honorary LLD, St Martin's College, 1975.

MAXWELL
Vocalist. **Career:** The Coffee Shop, waiter; vocalist, currently. **Special Achievements:** Albums include: Maxwell's Urban Hang Suite; Maxwell Unplugged. **Business Addr:** Singer, c/o Columbia Records, 550 Madison Ave, New York, NY 10022-3211, (212)833-8000.

MAXWELL, ANITA
Professional basketball player. **Personal:** Born Apr 7, 1974. **Educ:** New Mexico State, BA in international business, 1996. **Career:** Cleveland Rockers, forward, 1997-. **Business Addr:** Professional Basketball Player, Cleveland Rockers, One Center Ct, Cleveland, OH 44115, (216)263-7625.

MAXWELL, BERTHA LYONS
Educator. **Personal:** Born in Seneca, SC. **Educ:** Johnson C Smith U, BA 1954; UNC Greensboro, MEd 1966; Union Grad Sch, PhD 1974; Cath U, Howard U, Univ of SC, further study. **Career:** Alexander St Sch, tchr 1954-60; corrective reading tchr 1960-67; Villa Heights Elem Sch, asst prin 1967; Morgan Elem Sch, prin 1967-68; Albemarle Rd Elem Sch, prin 1968-70; Univ of NC at Charlotte, asso prof edn, dir of black studies program 1970-. **Orgs:** Organized & coordinated Charlotte's first Volunteer Tchr Corps; provided first readiness program for 87 disadvantaged children at First Ward Sch 1964; consHead Start Winthrop Coll Rock Hill SC 1965; visiting com So Assn Accreditation of Gastonia City Sch System 1967; local consult ACE Workshop UNCC 1969; consult So Regional Educ Bd Regional Conf 1971; chmn, visiting com Harrisburg Sch; So Assn Accreditation of Cabarrus Co Sch 1972; chmn visiting com Greensboro City Sch 1973; mem NEA; Nat Assn of Elem Sch Prin; Afro-Am Study Assn; African Heritage Study Assn; mem Resolutions Com 1970; chmn Resolutions Com 1971; sec Charlotte-Mecklenburg Elem Pring Unit; mem Intl Reading Assn; mem bd dir 1969-72; Greater Charlotte Coun Intl Reading Assn; mem Intl PlatformAssn; mem League of Women Votes; mem, chmn Charlotte-Mecklenburg Human Resources Com League of Women Voters; bd dir Johnston Memorial YMCA; mem Jack & Jill Inc; past pres Merry Makers Inc. **Honors/Awds:** Outstanding Community Services Award Las Amagis Inc 1967; outstanding leadership Sigma Gamma Rho Sorority 1969; outstanding comm leader 1971; outstanding educator Las Amagis Inc 1973. **Business Addr:** National First Vice President, Delta Sigma Theta Sorority, Inc, Route 1, Box 305, Catawba, SC 29704.

MAXWELL, HAZEL B. (DELORIS)
Educator (retired). **Personal:** Born Oct 30, 1905, Chicago, IL; daughter of Katherine Bramlette and John Bramlette; widowed; children: Anna Diggs-Taylor, Lowell D Johnston. **Educ:** Howard Univ, BA, education, 1935. **Career:** Milwaukee School of Engineering, part-time sec 1978-86; DC Public Schools, jr high school teacher 1944-59. **Orgs:** Pres bd of trustees Milwaukee Pub Library 1965-79; pres bd dirs YWCA of Greater Milwaukee 1968-71; pres auxiliary Natl Med Assn 1974-75; Co-Founder, Milwaukee Chapter of Links, Inc. **Honors/Awds:** Headliner Award Milwaukee Press Club 1971; Pro Urbe Award Mt Mary Coll 1974; distinguished serv award Milwaukee Metro Civic Assn 1976; Hall of Fame YWCA of Greater Milwaukee 1979. **Home Addr:** 8620 N Port Washington Rd #311, Milwaukee, WI 53217-2205.

MAXWELL, MARCELLA J.
Educator & government official. **Personal:** Born Nov 6, 1927, Asbury Park, NJ; daughter of Ethel Click and William B Redwood; married Edward C Maxwell, Apr 10, 1968 (deceased); children: Deborah Young. **Educ:** Long Island Univ, Brooklyn NY, BS 1956, MS 1958; Fordham Univ, New York NY, EdD 1972. **Career:** New York City Comm on Status of Women, asst acad dean; Publ School Dist 20, elem sch teacher, teacher trainer 1958-63; Puerto Rico School Dist, exchange teacher 1963; Bank State Coll, curriculum coord; Medgar Evers Coll, City Univ, dean 1972-; NY City Commission on Human Rights, chairperson 1984-88; Board of Higher Education Medgar Evers College 1971-84. **Orgs:** Bd mem Women's Forum; vice pres Natl Council of Women 1989-; chairperson New York City Commn on the Status of Women 1978-84, 1988-. **Honors/Awds:** Natl Achievement Awd Natl Assn of Negro Bus & Professional Women's Club; Exxon Scholarship Harvard Bus School; Keynote Speaker Older Women's League; NCCJ Human Rel Awd; Doctor of Law Pratt Instutute Brooklyn NY 1985; Doctor of Humane Letters Marymount Manhattan College 1984. **Home Addr:** 35 Prospect Park W, Brooklyn, NY 11215.

MAXWELL, RAYMOND ANTHONY
Publisher. **Personal:** Born Sep 23, 1963, Washington, DC; son of Elaine L Cockrell and Walter Cockrell. **Educ:** American Business Institute, certificate, word processing. **Career:** Marriott Hotels, various duties, 1987-88; May Co, credit analyst, 1988; Telcom Group, phone operator, 1989; Trans American Entertainment Corp, secretary, 1989; Telcom Communications, phone opertor, 1990-; ANKH Enterprises, proprietor, currently. **Honors/Awds:** Upscale Magazine, 30 Under 30 Contest, honorable mention, 1992.

MAXWELL, ROGER ALLAN
Affirmative action officer, composer. **Personal:** Born Jul 31, 1932, Marshalltown, IA; married Arenda; children: Jennifer, Courtney, David, Matthew. **Educ:** Univ of N IA, BA 1954. **Career:** IA State Bd of Regents, affirmative action officer 1969-. **Orgs:** Nat pres Nat Assn of Affirmative Act Officers 1979-80. **Honors/Awds:** Composer "Twelve Weeks to a Better Jazz Ensemble" pub CL Barnhouse Co 1978; composer "Fourteen Weeks to a Better Band" Books I & Ii pub CL Barnhouse Co1973-74; composer "Mass in Honor of the Uganda Martyrs" 1964. **Military Serv:** AUS asst counductor AUS Band Pacific Honolulu HI 1956-58. **Business Addr:** Lucas State Office Building, Des Moines, IA 50319.

MAXWELL, STEPHEN LLOYD
Judge (retired). **Personal:** Born Jan 12, 1921, St Paul, MN; married Betty Rodney. **Educ:** Morehouse Coll, BA, BSL 1951; St Paul Coll of Law, JD 1953. **Career:** IRS, auditor 1945-48; St Paul Auditorium, accnt 1948-51; OPS, investigator 1951-53; Private practice, 1953-59; Ramsey Court, asst attny 1959-66; City of St Paul, corp counsel 1964-66; US Congressional Rep Candidate, 1966; Municipal Court, judge 1967-68; Dist Court State of MN, judge 1968-87. **Orgs:** Trustee,MN State Colleges and Universities. **Military Serv:** USCG WWII; USNR capt retired.

MAXWELL, VERNON
Professional basketball player. **Personal:** Born Sep 12, 1965, Gainesville, FL. **Educ:** Univ of Florida, Gainesville, FL, 1984-88. **Career:** San Antonio Spurs, 1988-89; Houston Rockets, 1989-95; Philadelphia 76ers, 1995-96; San Antonio Spurs, 1996-. **Business Addr:** Professional Basketball Player, San Antonio Spurs, 600 E Market St, Ste 102, San Antonio, TX 78205, (512)224-4611.

MAXWELL REID, DAPHNE ETTA
Business executive, actress. **Personal:** Born Jul 13, 1948, New York, NY; daughter of Rosalee Maxwell and Green Maxwell; married Timothy L Reid; children: Christopher Tubbs; Tim Jr, Tori. **Educ:** Northwestern Univ, BA 1970. **Career:** Screen Actors Guild, bd mem 1974-76; Screen Actors Guild, co-chmn, conservatory committee 1977; Daphne Maxwell, Inc, pres; Timalove Enterprises Inc, vice pres, currently; New Millennium Studios co-founder, currently. **Honors/Awds:** 1st Commercials 1967; Selected by Ladies Home Jrnl as 1 of 14 Most Beautiful Women 1970; Starred in Frank's Place, Snoops, The Tim & Daphne Show, Exposed; Fresh Prince of Bel Air; Home Sewing & Crafts Assn, Best New Product Award, 1993; Norfolk State University Honorary Degree, 1996. **Special Achievements:** Created and produced videotape package with the McCall Pattern Company, "Suddenly You're Sewing"; created pattern line at the McCall Pattern Company; "The Daphne Maxwell Reid Collection."; first African American homecoming queen at Northwestern Univ, 1967; first African American on the cover of Glamour Magazine, 1969. **Business Addr:** Vice President, Timalove Enterprises, Inc, 16030 Ventura Blvd, #380, Encino, CA 91436.

MAY, CHARLES W.
Songwriter, entertainer. **Personal:** Born Jun 13, 1940, Macon, MS. **Educ:** So IL U, BA 1962; So IL U, presently working on MA. **Career:** Ft Wayne IN, tchr pub sch; 1963; Los Angeles, tchr elementary sch including the mentally retarded 1966-70; club Harlem Atlanta City, performed 4 months 1970; Fairmont Hotel San Francisco, staed & vocally arranged Freda Payne's act 1970; Sands Hotel Las Vegas, played piano for Lola Falana's engaement 1 month; wrote title songs for movies, Wonder Women, Class of 74, Detroit 9000; numerous TV & radio appearances; produced wrote & sang several albums with Annette May Thomes & The 21st Century Ltd. **Orgs:** Formed group The 21st Centry Ltd; mem AFTRA. **Honors/Awds:** Winner Quarter Finals of the Annual Song Writer Festival "If I Thought He Didn't Care". **Business Addr:** PO Box 43402, Los Angeles, CA 90043.

MAY, DERRICK BRANT
Professional baseball player. **Personal:** Born Jul 14, 1968, Rochester, NY. **Career:** Chicago Cubs, outfielder, 1990-94; Milwaukee Brewers, 1995; Houston Astros, 1995-96; Philadelphia Phillies, 1997; Montreal Expos, 1998-. **Business Addr:** Professional Baseball Player, Montreal Expos, PO Box 500, Station M, Montreal, PQ, Canada H1V 3P2, (514)253-3434.

MAY, DICKEY R.
Corporate accounting administrator. **Personal:** Born Dec 14, 1950, Dublin, GA; son of Zelma Smith May and Clarence W May Sr; married L Yvonne Fambrough, Jul 3; children: Andrea Lynette May, Ronald Maurice May. **Educ:** Fort Valley State Coll, Fort Valley GA, BBA, 1972. **Career:** Church's Fried Chicken, Atlanta GA, exec mgr candidate, 1972-73, mgr to area mgr, 1973-75, San Antonio TX, auditor, 1975-80, regional liason, 1980-84; Ron's Krispy Fried Chicken, Houston TX, regional controller, corporate controller, 1984-86; Church's Fried Chicken Inc, San Antonio TX, dir Corporate Planning, 1986-89, dir Operatoinal Acct, 1989-. **Orgs:** Mem, Inst of Internal Auditors, 1975-, Long Range Planning Comm, Northminister Presbyterian Church, 1988-. **Business Addr:** Director of Operational Accounting, Church's Fried Chicken Inc, 355 Spencer Ln, San Antonio, TX 78250.

MAY, FLOYD O'LANDER
Government official. **Personal:** Born Dec 2, 1946, Kansas City, MO; married Connie S Brown; children: Cheriss Dachelle, Floyd O'Lander Jr. **Educ:** Kansas State College at Pittsburg, BS 1970, MS 1971. **Career:** Missouri Dept of Vocational Rehab, counselor 1971-75; US Dept of HUD, investigator 1975-77, mgmt liaison officer 1977-85, dept dir/dir of comp beginning 1985, regional director Office of Fair Housing and Equal Opportunity, Region VII, currently. **Orgs:** Mem City of Lee's Summit Chamber of Commerce, Urban League of KC; president Channel 19 Public TV Comm Adv Bd, Heart of America Pop Warner Football Assoc; Urban League; NAACP Board mem, Kansas City, MO, Chapter; KC Civil Rights Consortium. **Honors/Awds:** Outstanding Performance Awd US Dept of HUD 1977, 1985; Pride in Public Service Award, 1991; Distinguished Service Award, 1992; Outstanding Performance Award, 1991, 1992. **Military Serv:** AUS capt 7 yrs; Outstanding Military Graduate. **Home Addr:** 5223 SW Raintree Pkwy, Lees Summit, MO 64063.

MAY, JAMES F.
Educator, mayor. **Personal:** Born Feb 10, 1938, Millry, AL; married Bessie Hill; children: Keita, Katrice. **Educ:** Alabama A&M Univ, BS 1962; Tuskegee Inst, MEd 1968. **Career:** May's Plumbing & Elec Serv, owner; Uniontown AL, mayor pro tem; Perry County Bd of Educ, teacher; former city councilman. **Orgs:** Mem Uniontown Civic League; keeper of records Omega Chi Chap Omego Psi Phi; mem AVATA Perry Co Tchr Assn; AEA; NEA; Pride of AL Elks #1170. **Honors/Awds:** First Black Councilman Award 1972. **Military Serv:** AUS pfc 1956-58. **Business Addr:** P O Box 24, Uniontown, AL 36786.

MAY, JAMES SHELBY
Educator, judge, trial attorney. **Personal:** Born Jun 2, 1934, Louisville, KY; son of Arlee Taylor May and Shelby May; married Patricia Lynn Hunter; children: Angela Collen Weaver, James S May Jr, Sarita Maureen, Shara Lavorn Dickerson, Regina Grace. **Educ:** Cornell Univ, BA Amer Studies 1971; Yale Univ Law School, Juris Doctor 1977, (distinction in all subjects); Natl Judicial Coll, trial judge course 1980; Georgetown Univ Law School, enrolled Master in Law Program. **Career:** USMC, infantryman 1953-60, officers candidate school 1960, officers basic course 1960-61, financial admin 1961-64, logistics officer 1964-69; US Naval Academy, history instructor 1972-74; Navy Marine Corps Court of Military Review, appellate judge; Marine Corps Base Camp Pendleton, staff judge advocate. **Orgs:** Mem Amer Trial Lawyers Assn; mem CA, FL, DC Bar Assns; mem Alumni Exec Comm Yale Law Sch 1982-85; mem Assn of Afro-Amer Life & History 1980-; mem Marine Corps Historical Foundation 1983-; mem Secondary Sch Comm Cornell Club of Washington 1983-; chmn Military Judges Comm Judiciary Sect Fed Bar Assn 1984-. **Honors/Awds:** Woodrow Wilson Fellowship Finalist Cornell Univ 1971; White house Fellowship Finalist 1981; numerous published appellate court opinions in military law; first Black judge appointed to highest Navy Military Court (Ebony Jan 1983). **Military Serv:** USMC col 1953-; Navy Commendation Medal; Meritorious Unit Commendation; Vietnamese Cross. **Home Addr:** 3305 S Stafford St, Arlington, VA 22206. **Business Addr:** Administrator, Naval Council of Personnel Boards Petachment, Regional Physi, Naval Medical Center, Bldg 1, Tower 9, Bethesda, MD 20814.

MAY, LEE ANDREW
Professional baseball player (retired). **Personal:** Born Mar 23, 1943, Birmingham. **Educ:** Miles College, Birmingham, AL, attended. **Career:** Cincinnati Reds, infielder/outfielder 1965-71; Houston Astros, 1st baseman 1972-74; Baltimore Orioles, infielder, 1975-80, hitting coach, 1995-; Kansas City Royals, infielder, 1981-82; Kansas City Royals, first base and hitting coach, 1984-86, 1992-94; Cinti Reds, 1st base coach, 1988, 1989. **Honors/Awds:** Named Nat League Rookie Player of Yr 1967; 1st baseman Sporting News & Nat League All-Star Team 1971; leader Nat League 1st baseman double plays 1970; tied following major league records: most home runs in 3 consec games 1969; most total bases (8) one inning & most home runs in one inning 1974; hit 3 home runs in one game 1973; led NL first basemen total chances & double plays 1972; led AL first basemen total chances & double plays 1975; National League All-Star Team, 1969, 1971, 1972. **Business Addr:** Baltimore Orioles, Camden Yards Park, Baltimore, MD.

MAY, MARK
Professional football player. **Personal:** Born Nov 2, 1959, Oneonta, NY; married Kathy; children: Abra. **Educ:** Univ of Pittsburgh, four years. **Career:** Washington Redskins, guard, offensive tackle, beginning 1981; San Diego Chargers, 1991; Phoenix Cardinals, 1992-. **Honors/Awds:** Outland Trophy, 1980; offensive tackle, Sporting News College All-America Team, 1980; post-season play: NFC Championship Game, 1982, 1983, 1986, 1987, NFL Championship Game, 1982, 1983, 1987, Pro Bowl, 1988; offensive MVP, DC Touchdown Club, 1988; NFL's USO tours to South Korea (1985, 1988), Germany (1984); has worked closely with Children's Hospital; Honorary Chairperson, Americans Helping Americans program, Christian Relief Services, 1989; assisted in food distribution program, Appalachia, Thanksgiving 1989; has helped raise about $1,000,000 for Juvenile Diabetes Assn during career. **Business Phone:** (602)379-0101.

MAYBERRY, CLAUDE A., JR.
Publisher, entrepreneur. **Personal:** Born Feb 17, 1933, Detroit, MI; son of Anna Johnson Riley and Claude A. Mayberry Sr.; divorced; children: Lawrence, Karen, Cheryl, Claude III, Eric. **Educ:** Purdue University, West Lafayette, IN, BS, 1961-65, MS, 1967-68; Columbia University, Teachers College New York, NY, PhD, 1971-73. **Career:** University of Pennsylvania, Philadelphia, PA, dean of students, 1973-76; Colgate University, Hamilton, NY, provost, 1976-81; US Dept of Education, Washington, DC, special assistant to secretary for math and science, 1981-84; Science Weekly, Inc, Silver Spring, MD, president, 1984-. **Orgs:** National chairperson, National Conference on Educating the Black Child, 1990-92; member, National Alliance of Black School Educators, 1975-; chair, Minority Entrepreneurs Committee, 1987-; president, alumni advisory committee, Teachers College, Columbia University, 1990-93; member, alumni associations, Columbia University, 1973-; member, alumni associations, Purdue University, 1965-; chairman, Black Entrepreneurs Educational Publishers 1984-; Natl Citizens Commission on African American Education, president, 1994-. **Honors/Awds:** School of Science Distinguished Alumni Award, Purdue University, 1991; Marcus Foster Distinguished Black Educator Award, National Alliance of Black School Educators, 1988; African-American Businessman Award, Montgomery County, MD, 1990; Teacher of the Year Award, Indiana State Junior Chamber of Commerce, 1968; Hammond Achievement Award, 1992. **Military Serv:** US Air Force, Airman First, 1952-56. **Business Addr:** President, Science Weekly Inc, 2141 Industrial Parkway, Suite 202, Silver Spring, MD 20904, (301)680-8804.

MAYBERRY, JERMANE
Professional football player. **Personal:** Born Aug 29, 1973, Floresville, TX. **Educ:** Texas A & M-Kingsville. **Career:** Philadelphia Eagles, tackle, 1996-. **Honors/Awds:** National Football League, Extra Effort Award, 1996. **Special Achievements:** NFL Draft, First round pick, #25, 1996. **Business Addr:** Professional Football Player, Philadelphia Eagles, 3501 S Broad St, Philadelphia, PA 19148, (215)463-2500.

MAYBERRY, LEE (ORVA LEE JR.)
Professional basketball player. **Personal:** Born Jun 12, 1970, Tulsa, OK; married Marla; children: Taleya, Kaylan. **Career:** Milwaukee Bucks, guard, 1992-96; Vancouver Grizzlies, 1996-. **Special Achievements:** NBA Draft, First round pick, #23, 1992. **Business Addr:** Professional Basketball Player, Vancouver Grizzlies, 788 Beatty St, Ste 311, Vancouver, BC, Canada V6B 2M1, (604)688-5867.

MAYBERRY, PATRICIA MARIE
Attorney. **Personal:** Born Aug 25, 1951, St Louis, MO; daughter of Shirley Mayberry Hawkins and Samuel Mayberry; divorced. **Educ:** University of Missouri, BA, 1973; University of Houston, MSW, 1976; Thurgood Marshall School of Law, Texas Southern University, JD, 1979. **Career:** US Air Force, attorney/assistant staff judge advocate, 1980-84; Alvin Dillings, PC, attorney, 1984-87; private practice, attorney, 1987-89; Immigration & Naturalization Service, trial attorney, 1989-93; CA Unemployment Ins Appeals Bd, admin law judge, 1993-96; Dept of Air Force, labor law attorney, 1996-. **Orgs:** State Bar of Texas, 1979; Colorado Bar, 1985; Top Ladies of Distinction, 1990; Phi Alpha Delta, 1977; NAACP, executive board, 1990; AME Church, judicial council member, 1992; California Conference, trustee, 1991; Fellowship Manor, board of directors, 1992; Delta Sigma Theta Sorority, 1973-. **Honors/Awds:** American Jurisprudence, Contracts, 1977, Domestic Relations, 1977; Dollars and Sense, 100 Outstanding African-American Women, 1991. **Military Serv:** US Air Force, lt colonel (select), 1980-84, reserves, 1984-; Commendation Medal, 1981, 1984, 1996; Achievement Medal, 1984, 1990. **Business Addr:** Dept of Air Force, 5219 Arnold Ave, McClellan AFB, CA 95652-1082.

MAYBERRY-STEWART, MELODIE IRENE
Health services administrator. **Personal:** Born Sep 4, 1948, Cleveland, OH; divorced; children: George, Jay. **Educ:** Union College, BS, business administration and sociology; University of Nebraska, MA, sociological research and statistics; Pepperdine University, MBA; Claremont Graduate School, MA, executive management, PhD, philosophy. **Career:** IBM Corporation, various positions, ended career as western area telecommunications marketing manager; Saint Thomas Hospital, vice pres/chief information officer; Beth Israel Hospital, vice pres/chief information officer, currently. **Orgs:** Tennessee Sportsfest, board of directors/treasurer; Limited Way of Middle Tennessee, board mem; Nashville NAACP, executive committee mem; SunTrust Bank, board mem; Cumberland Valley Girl Scout Council, finance committee chairman; National Assn of Female Executives; National Black MBA Assn; National Council of Negro Women; Healthcare Information and Management Systems Society; American Hospital Assn; College of Healthcare Executives; National Assn of Healthcare Executives. **Honors/Awds:** Legal Defense Fund of the NAACP, Women of Achievement Award; Peter F Drucker Management Center, Alumni Award for Extraordinary Service. **Special Achievements:** Co-authored two publications on network management and network design; first African American vice president and chief information officer at Beth Israel Hospital; first African American vice president at St Thomas Hospital. **Business Addr:** Vice Pres/Chief Info Officer, Beth Israel Medical Center, 733 3rd Ave, 2nd Fl, New York, NY 10017, (212)692-5134.

MAYDEN, RUTH WYATT
Social work educator. **Personal:** Born Dec 20, 1946, Baltimore, MD; daughter of Wilhelmenia Outerbridge Mayden and John Clifton Mayden Jr. **Educ:** Morgan State Univ, Baltimore, MD, BA, 1968; Bryn Mawr Coll, Bryn Mawr, PA, MSS, 1970. **Career:** Day Care Assn of Montgomery County, Blue Bell, PA, social serv coordinator, 1970-72, exec dir, 1972-79; Bryn Mawr Coll Grad School of Social Work and Social Research, Bryn Mawr, PA, asst dean, 1979-81, associate dean, 1981-86, dean, 1987-. **Orgs:** Bd, exec comm, United Way of Southeastern PA, 1986-91; treas, PA Chapter, Natl Assn of Social Workers, 1989-91; chair, Child Welfare Advisory Bd, 1985-91; Natl Assn of Deans and Directors of Schools and Social Work, 1987-; American Assn of Black Women in Higher Education, 1989-91; bd mem, Natl Assn of Social Workers. **Honors/Awds:** Service Appreciation, PA Chapter, Natl Assn of Social Workers, 1986, 1987-89; Service Appreciation Award, Montgomery County Mental Health/Mental Retardation Bd, 1974-84; Service Appreciation Award, Community Services Planning Council, 1978-84. **Business Addr:** Dean, Graduate School of Social Work and Social Research, Bryn Mawr College, 300 Airdale Rd, Bryn Mawr, PA 19010, (610)527-8215.

MAYE, BEATRICE CARR JONES
Educator, librarian. **Personal:** Born Apr 23, Warren County, NC; daughter of Ellen Brown Jones and James S Jones; married John W Maye Sr, Jul 13, 1938 (deceased); children: John Walter Jr, Mamie Ellene Maye-Bryan. **Educ:** NC A&T State Univ, BS, English, French; NC Central Durham, BS, MS, library science; East Carolina Univ, post graduate study. **Career:** WH Robinson School, librarian, 1947-68; EB Aycock Jr High School, media specialist, 1968-81; Greenville City Bd of Sheppard Memorial Public Library, 1972-74, dept of library science, library science consultant, 1972-; selected member of Elections Study Comm by mayor, 1981; Pitt/Greenville Media Soc, former pres, 1981-82; The Carolinian, columnist; columnist, The "M" Voice; Pitt Community Coll, teacher, resource person on Black History Month. **Orgs:** American Assn of Retired Persons, 1981-; Delta Sigma Theta Aux, 1937-; North Carolina Association of Educators, 1981-. **Honors/Awds:** Southeastern Black Librarian 1976; 25 Most Influential Black Women in Greenville/Pitt City 1983; Volunteer-of-the Year by the Greenville Pre-Release 1983; Citizen of the Year Award for Community Serv 1984; author, Personalities in Progress, Biographies of Black North Carolinians, Treasure Bits, An Anthology of

Quotes 1984; editorials in We The People, The Daily Reflector, The News & Observer, The Wilson Library Bulletin, NC Libraries, Greenville Dispatch, The Carolinian & Bethel Herald; host, "Talk Show," WOOW Radio, Greenville Pre-Release & After-Care Center; Citizen of the Year, Mu Alpha Chapter, Omega Psi Phi Fraternity, 1984; Outstanding Senior Citizen, Greenville-Jaycees, 1988; Co-host, "M" Voices of Eastern North Carolina University WITN, Channel 7, TV Station. **Home Addr:** 1225 Davenport St, Greenville, NC 27834.

MAYE, RICHARD

Clergyman. **Personal:** Born Oct 26, 1933, Uniontown, AL; married Rose Owens; children: Darryl Kermit, Byron Keith. **Educ:** Sangamon State U, BA/MA 1972; Univ of IA, PhD pending. **Career:** Pleasant Grove Baptist Church Springfield, IL, pastor 1970-; IL State Univ Normal, lecturer political science 1973-77; IL Dept of Corrections Springfield, admin asst 1970-72; Chicago Baptist Inst IL, faculty 1968-70; City of Springfield, commr civil serv 1979-72. **Orgs:** Mem Mayor's Complete Count Com Springfield 1980; bd of dir Morgan-Wash Sch for Girls 1977; mem Sch Integration Commn Springfield 1977-79; bd of dirLincoln Lib; grad dean fellow So IL Univ Carbondl 1975-76. **Honors/Awds:** Citizen of the Year Award, NAACP Springfield 1976; Grad Fellow, Univ of IA 1977-80; Pub Serv Award, US Dist Ct Springfield, IL 1978. **Military Serv:** AUS spec/3 1954-56. **Business Addr:** 908 S 18th St, Springfield, IL 62707.

MAYES, CLINTON, JR.

Chief executive. **Career:** State Mutual Federal Savings and Loan Assoc, Jackson, MS, chief exec. **Business Addr:** First American Bank, PO Box 23518, Jackson, MS 39225-3518.

MAYES, DERRICK

Professional football player. **Personal:** Born Jan 28, 1974, Indianapolis, IN. **Educ:** Univ of Notre Dame, BA in communications. **Career:** Green Bay Packers, wide receiver, 1996-. **Business Addr:** Professional Football Player, Green Bay Packers, 1265 Lombardi Ave, Green Bay, WI 54304, (414)494-2351.

MAYES, DORIS MIRIAM

Concert artist, operatic performer, vocal technician. **Personal:** Born Dec 10, 1928, Philadelphia, PA; daughter of Evelyn Bulter Mayes and James Mayes; married Jurgen Ploog, Jun 21, 1960; children: Flavia Miriam. **Educ:** Philadelphia Conservatory of Music, Philadelphia PA, BM, teaching cert; attended Hochshule Fur Musik, Munich, Germany; attended Juilliard School of Music, New York NY. **Career:** Syracuse Univ, Syracuse NY, assoc prof, 1966-68; Oberlin College, Oberlin OH, asst prof, 1968-74; Western Reserve Univ, Hudson OH, voice technician, 1974-80; Univ of the Arts, Philadelphia, Pa, teacher in conservatory division, 1982-; Lincoln Univ, Lincoln PA, lecturer, voice technician, 1988-. **Orgs:** Scholarship chair, Pro Arts Soc, 1983-. **Honors/Awds:** Key to city of Philadelphia PA, 1961; Presidential Commendation, Lincoln Univ, 1989; citation, Philadelphia City Council, 1989; Congressional citation, 1989; Philadelphia Orchestra Award; Bell Isle Award, Detroit Symphony; John Hay Whitney award; Fulbright fellowships; winner of Munich Intl Competition and Geneva Intl Competition; winner of Grande Prix at Toulouse Internationa Competition; debut at Carnegie Hall, New York, NY; performances with Philadelphia and Cleveland orchestras and Detroit, Wiesbaden, Paris, Delaware, and Akron symphonies; opera performances in Europe and the United States. **Business Addr:** Department of Music, Lincoln University, Lincoln University, PA 19352-0999.

MAYES, HELEN M.

College official (retired). **Personal:** Born May 28, 1918, Waycross, GA; daughter of Mary Woodson Moody (deceased) and Oscar Moody (deceased); married Nathaniel H Mayes (deceased); children: Nathaniel H Mayes Jr. **Educ:** Savannah State Coll, BS 1938; New York Univ, MA 1961. **Career:** Albany State Coll, GA, emeritus dir of admissions & records, ret 1976. **Orgs:** Exec sec Natl Assn of Coll Deans Registrars & Admissions Officers 1963-; first black pres GA Assn of Collegiate Registrars & Admissions Officers 1971-72; mem GA Teachers & Educ Assn; Natl Educ Assn; mem Alpha Kappa Alpha; mem Amer Assoc of Collegiate Registrars and Admissions Officers; mem selection comm Natl Merit Achievement Scholarship Program; mem United Way of Dougherty County Bd; bd of dirs Albany Symphony Assoc; director finance Semper Fidelis Club 1980-; steward Bethel AME Church. **Honors/Awds:** Honorary membership GA Assn of Collegiate Registrars and Admissions Officers and Natl Assoc of Coll Deans, Registrars and Admission Officers; Top Leadership Awd Alpha Kappa Alpha Sor and Women of Distinction; Community Serv Awd Iota Phi Lambda Sor. **Business Addr:** 917 Dorsett Ave, Albany, GA 31701.

MAYES, MCKINLEY

Government official. **Personal:** Born Oct 7, 1930, Oxford, NC; son of Julia Mayes and Henry Mayes; married Mattie Louise Dupree, Aug 22, 1959; children: Byron Christopher Mayes. **Educ:** North Carolina A&T State Univ, BS, 1953, MS, 1956; Rutgers Univ, PhD, 1959. **Career:** Southern Univ, Baton Rouge LA, prof, 1959-76; US Dept of Agriculture, Cooperative State Research Service, Washington DC, 1976-. **Orgs:** Mem, Amer Soc of Agronomy, 1959-, Sigma Xi, 1959-; global ministries, VA Conference, United Methodist Church, 1986-; vice chair, admin bd, Roberts United Methodist Church, 1987-; mem, USDA/1890 Task Force, 1988-. **Honors/Awds:** American Society of Agronomy, fellow. **Military Serv:** AUS corporal, 1953-55. **Business Addr:** Director, US Dept of Agriculture-Coop State Research, Edu & Ext., Service (CSREES) South Bldg., Rm 3345, 14th & Independence Ave, Washington, DC 20250-2209.

MAYES, NATHANIEL H., JR.

Consultant, educator. **Personal:** Born Aug 22, 1941, Waycross, GA; married Constantina; children: Nathaniel III, Muriel, 009136. **Educ:** Howard U, MS 1966, BS 1962. **Career:** Multicultural Progs, Gr Boston Area Pub Schs, Inst for Learning & Tchg Univ MA, consult trainer 1971-; Soc Dynamics Inc Boston, prog mgr 1970-71; Organizational Dev Consltnt 1968-70; Clark Clg Atlanta, instr psychlgy 1966-68. **Orgs:** Co-founder mem Inter-Culture Inc Cambridge; mem SIETAR; Soc for Inter-Cultural Ed; Training & Rsrch. **Honors/Awds:** Co-author booklet on Multi-Cultural Tchr Training 1974; recip outst tchng cert Clark Clg 1965. **Business Addr:** Inst for Learn & Teach Univ MA, Boston Harbor Campus, Dorchester, MA.

MAYFIELD, CURTIS

Entertainer. **Personal:** Born Jun 3, 1942, Chicago, IL; children: Tracy, Curtis, Todd, Sharon, Tymphani, Kirk. **Career:** Curtom Record & Pub Co, Chgo, singer, composer, recording artist, owner 1970-; The Impressions, lead singer 1958-70; The Alphatones & gospel groups & choirs. **Honors/Awds:** Wrote & sang theme mus for 1972 film "Super Fly"; score for film "Sparkle" 1975; wrote score & appeared in "Short Eyes" 1977; compositions include "gypsy woman", "keep on pushing", "this is my country", "amen", "people get ready". **Business Addr:** Collectors Record Club, GHB Jazz Foundation Bldg, 1206 Decatur St, New Orleans, LA 70116.

MAYFIELD, JOANN H.O.

City official. **Personal:** Born Jul 1, 1932, Jackson Co; divorced; children: Joyce, Barbara, Theresa. **Educ:** Louise Beauty Clg, Grad. **Career:** Cosmetology, active in. **Orgs:** Cnclwoman Cty of Commerce GA; unit pres Am Legion Aux 1963-64, dist pres Am Legion Aux 1965-66; chmn Cit Training Dist A B C 1966-67; unit Pres Am Legion Aux 1967-68; usher bd sec Am Legion Aux 1972; chmn Ed & Schlrshp 9th Dists; mem Celebrity Clb 1970; dist pres Am Legion Aux 1963-64. **Business Addr:** 324 S Elm St, Commerce, GA 30529.

MAYFIELD, WILLIAM S.

Attorney, educator. **Personal:** Born Mar 2, 1919, Gary, IN; son of Elnora E Williams-Mayfield (deceased) and William H Mayfield Sr; married Octavia Smith (deceased); children: Pamela L, William E, Stephanie K. **Educ:** Detroit Inst of Technology, AB 1946; Detroit Coll of Law, JD 1949. **Career:** Lewis Rowlette Brown Wanzo & Bell Detroit, atty pvt law pract 1949-51; US Office of Price Stabilization, atty 1951-53; Friend of the Court Detroit, referee 1953-72; Southern Univ Sch of Law, prof of law; LA State Univ Law Ctr, Baton Rouge, LA, visiting prof, summer 1979. **Orgs:** Mem Natl Bar Assn; State Bar of MI; Amer Bar Assn; Wolverine Bar Assn; Louis A Martinet Legal Soc; World Assn of Law Prof of the World Peace through Law Ctr; Detroit Coll of Law Alumni Assn; The Retired Officers Assn; former vice pres Cotillion Club Detroit; mem Assn Henri Capitant; mem Delta Theta Phi Law Frat; past pres Krainz Woods Prop Owners Assn; former mem Regional Bd Boy Scouts of Amer; active in religious & civic affairs. **Honors/Awds:** Outstanding Professor Awd of the Delta Theta Phi Law Frat 1982-83; Hall of Fame, Natl Bar Assn, 1989; Hall of Fame, LA State Univ Law Ctr, 1988. **Military Serv:** US Army, lt col, ret. **Business Addr:** Professor of Law, Southern Univ Sch of Law, Southern Branch Post Office, Baton Rouge, LA 70813, (504)771-4900.

MAYNARD, EDWARD SAMUEL

Educator. **Personal:** Born Jul 16, 1930, Brooklyn, NY; son of Robertine Maynard and Samuel Maynard; married Ernestine Gaskin; children: Jeanne, Charles. **Educ:** Brooklyn Coll, BA (Cum Laude) 1958; Columbia Univ, MA 1967; New York Univ, PhD 1972; Graduate Center City Univ of NY, PhD 1984. **Career:** NY City Bd of Educ, teacher 1958-67; Brooklyn Coll, lecturer 1967-69; Medgar Evers Coll, dir of public relations 1970-71; Hostos Comm Coll, professor 1971-; Psychologist, private practice, 1980-. **Orgs:** lecturer various civic & professional organizations 1970-; mem NAACP 1980-, Amer Psychological Assoc 1984-; minister of counseling, Howells Congregational Church. **Honors/Awds:** Founders Day Award NY Univ 1972; mem NY Academy of Sciences 1983. **Military Serv:** USMC corpl 2 yrs; Natl Defense Serv Medal 1951-53. **Home Addr:** 52 Mine Rd, Monroe, NY 10950. **Business Addr:** Professor of Humanities, Hostos Community College, 500 Grand Concourse, Bronx, NY 10451-5307.

MAYNARD, VALERIE J.

Artist, educator, curator. **Personal:** Born Aug 22, 1937, New York, NY; daughter of Willie-Fred Pratt Maynard and William Austin Maynard Sr. **Educ:** Museum of Modern Art NY, Drawing & Painting 1954-55; Elaine Journet Art School New Rochelle NY, apprentice 1955-60; The New School NY, printmaking 1968-69; Goddard Coll Plainfield VT, MA 1977. **Career:** Studio Museum NY, instructor printmaking, artist-in-residence, 1969-74; Langston Hughes Library NY, instructor sculpture, 1971-72; Howard Univ Wash DC, instructor sculpture, 1974-76; Jersey City State Coll NJ, instructor sculpture, 1977-78; Baltimore School for the Arts, instructor sculpture, 1980-81; Coll of the Virgin Islands St Thomas, instructor sculpture, 1984-85; Northeastern Univ Boston MA, Goddard Coll Plainfield VT, Rutgers Univ NJ, Harlem State Office Bldg NY, St Thomas, Coll of the Virgin Islands St Thomas, lecturer, 1979-85; "Orie's Potpourri," St Thomas Cable TV, "Newscenter 10," WBNB-TV St Thomas, "AMVI," WBNB-TV St Thomas, "Sunday Morning," CBS-TV NY, films & videos 1985-86; University of the Virgin Islands, St Thomas, sculpture instructor, 1984-88; artist-in-residence: Women's Studio Workshop, 1986-87, Blue Mouin Center, 1987-91, McDowell Colony, 1991, Massachusetts Institute of Technology, 1992, Brandywine Workshop, 1992, Bob Blackburn Printing Workshop, 1992-93; University of Rochester, Susan B Anthony Center for Women's Studies, Rockefeller Humanities Fellow, currently. **Honors/Awds:** Travel Grant FESTAC Lagos Nigeria 1977; CEBA Design Award World Inst of Black Communication NY 1978; Citation of Merit Seward Park Alumni NY 1979; Living History Award NY Urban League Westchester 1980; Bedford-Stuyvesant Arts Award Brooklyn NY 1980; Finalist Natl Sculpture Competition Columbus OH 1980; Finalist Independence Monument Antigua West Indies 1981; Public School 181, Brooklyn, NY, commission; New England Foundation for the Arts, grant, 1992; Brandywine workshop, artist-in-residence grant, 1992; LifeAmerica, MacDowell Colony, fellowship, 1991; National Endowment for the Arts, grant, for a stage set for play, "Nzinga," 1992; Womens Studio Workshops, residency, 1989-; Sculpture Award, Atlanta Life Insurance Co., 1990. **Special Achievements:** One woman exhibitions: Reichhold Center for the Arts, St Thomas, US Virgin Islands, 1983; First PA Bank, St Thomas, US Virgin Islands, 1984; "No Apartheid Anywhere," Compton Gallery, MIT, 1992; two person exhibit, "Works in Progress," Valerie Maynard & Carol Byard Gallery 1199, 1978; travelling exhibits: "Impressions/ Expressions," Black American Graphics Studio Museum, NY, 1979-84; "Tradition & Conflict, Images of a Turbulent Decade 1963-73," Studio Museum, NY, 1985-87; Caribbean Center, NY, 1989; NY Community College, 1989; creator/designer: Communications Excellence to Black Audiences Award, statuette, 1978.

MAYNOR, KEVIN ELLIOTT

Opera singer. **Personal:** Born Jul 24, 1954, Mt Vernon, NY. **Educ:** Manhattan School of Music, Diploma 1972; Bradley Univ, BME 1976; Northwestern Univ, MM 1978; Moscow Conservatory, MMV 1980; IN Univ, DM 1987; Indiana University, doctoral candidate, currently. **Career:** Chicago Lyric Opera, soloist 1978; Sante Fe Opera, soloist 1979; Bolshoi Opera, soloist 1980; VA Opera, soloist 1984; New York City Opera, soloist 1986; Alice Tully Hall, soloist 1985; Avery Fischer Hall, soloist 1985; Carnegie Hall, 1986; Nashville Opera, soloist 1986; Long Beach Opera, soloist 1986; Mobile Opera, soloist 1986; Orlando Opera, soloist 1986; Metropolitan Opera-Netherlands Dance Theatre, soloist 1986-87; Triangle Music Theatre Assn/Durham NC, soloist 1987; Opera Company of Boston, soloist 1988; Alice Tully Hall, New York NY, soloist 1988; Valparaiso Univ, soloist/recitalist 1988; Fort Worth Symphony, soloist 1988; Knoxville Symphony, soloist 1988; Music Under The Stars Festival, soloist 1988; Opera Music Theatre International, soloist, 1989-90; Skylight Opera Theatre, 1990-91; Scottish Opera, 1991-92; Connecticut Opera, 1992-93; Cincinnati Opera, 1992-93; Chattanooga Symphony, 1993-94; Greensboro Opera, 1994-95. **Orgs:** NAACP, 1983-85; Edler G Hawkins Foundation Inc, board member, 1989. **Honors/Awds:** Fulbright Awd Fulbright-Hays Act of Constitution 1979; Sullivan Awd William M Sullivan Found 1983; Recitalist Awd Natl Endowment for the Arts 1984; Winner 1st Prize, Intl Singing Competition South Africa 1984; Natl Assn Teachers of Singing Award 1984; Richard Tucker Award 1985; George London Awd NIMT 1986; Tito Gobbi Awd 1986. **Special Achievements:** Soloist: Carnegie Hall 1983-84; Academy of Music, Philadelphia, 1984; Wolf Trap Festival, 1984; TX Chamber Symphony 1985; New Orleans Symphony, 1985; Long Island Philharmonic, 1985; Amer Symphony, 1985; Shreeveport Symphony, 1986; Artpark Festival, 1986; Buffalo Philharmonic, 1986; Baltimore Choral Arts, 1986; New Haven Symphony, 1987; Spoletto USA, 1987; Atlanta Symphony; appearances include: Morehouse College, Bennett College, Merkin Hall, Connecticut Opera, Cincinnati Opera, Opera Carolina, Greensboro Opera, New York's Little Orchestra Society, Scottish Opera, New Jersey State Opera, Opera Music Treasurer International of New Jersey; numerous others. **Home Addr:** 32 Howard Court, Newark, NJ 07103.

MAYNOR, VERNON PERRY

Entrepreneur, accountant. **Personal:** Born Feb 8, 1966, Mount Vernon, NJ; son of Josephine Maynor and Godfrey Maynor; married Shevella Brown Maynor, Dec 28, 1992. **Educ:** Hampton University, BS, finance, 1988. **Career:** Johnson & Johnson Consumer Products Inc, Cooperative Education Program, 1987-

88; Johnson & Johnson Corporate, accounting management trainee, 1988-90, financial accountant, 1990-, Me-2-You Inc, president, currently. **Orgs:** Omega Psi Phi Fraternity, editor; National Association of Black Accountants. **Special Achievements:** Urban Profile Magazine, 1992 Top 30 Under 30 Black Professionals, 1992. **Business Addr:** President, Me-2-You, Inc., PO Box 394, Dayton, NJ 08810, (908)940-3000.

MAYO, BARRY ALAN

Broadcasting company executive. **Personal:** Born Jun 30, 1952, Bronx, NY; son of Anne Lewis Mayo and Charles C Mayo; divorced 1992; children: Barry A II, Alana Aisha, Alexander. **Educ:** Howard University, radio, 1974-76. **Career:** WRAP, Norfolk, prog dir 1978; WMAK, Nashville, prog dir 1978; WGCI-FM, Chicago, prog dir 1978-81; WJLB-FM, Detroit, prog consultant 1981-84; WDMT-Cleveland, prog consultant 1984; WRKS-FM, New York, vice pres, gen mgr 1984-88; Broadcasting Partners Inc, president, 1988-; WVAZ-FM, president, gen mgr 1988-95. **Orgs:** Bd of dirs, sec NY Market Broadcasters; board member, Providence St Mel High School, 1990-; board of directors, Black United Fund. **Honors/Awds:** Black Achiever Awd NY Harlem YMCA 1983; Radio Awd Natl Black Media Coalition 1985. **Business Addr:** President, Broadcasting Partners Inc, 800 South Wells, Chicago, IL 60607.

MAYO, BLANCHE IRENE

Educational administrator. **Personal:** Born Jan 24, 1946, Woodstock, OH; daughter of Gertrude E Wilson (deceased) and William E Wilson; married Terry, Dec 30, 1965; children: Terry Jr. **Educ:** Central State Univ, BS, 1976, MBA, 1980, CMI diploma, 1989. **Career:** Central State University, fed credit union treasurer/manager, 1976-78, assistant to vice pres academic affairs, assistant Title III, 1978-85, assistant to vice pres academic affairs, Title III coordinator, 1980-85, executive assistant to president, Title III coordinator, 1985-87, vice pres administrative support services, currently. **Orgs:** Ohio Student Loan Commission, commissioner, 1987; Middle Run Baptist Church, chaplain, senior usher board, 1991-92; Executive Committee Central Association of College & University, business officer, 1991-93; CACUBO Management Institute, steering committee, 1990-93; North Central Association of Colleges and Schools, consultant, evaluator, 1992-93. **Honors/Awds:** National Association for Equal Opportunity, Distinguished Alumni of the Year, 1992; Award of Scholarship, Winning Team of CACUBO, 1987; YWCA Salute to Career Women, Special Recognition, 1980. **Business Addr:** VP, Administrative Support Services, Central State University, 1400 Brush Row Rd, Room 211, Wilberforce, OH 45384, (513)376-6334.

MAYO, HARRY D., III

Financial advisor. **Personal:** Born Aug 28, 1939, Brooklyn, NY; son of Lillie Mae CLark Mayo and Harry D Mayo Jr; married Joan Etta Bradley. **Educ:** Pace Univ, BBA Finance 1968, MBA Exec Mgmt 1978; Harvard Univ, Cert Exec Educ Prog Harvard Business School 1978; various other mgmt, computer and communications courses, certificates. **Career:** Sperry & Hutchinson Co Inc, standards admin, Sr Systms Analyst, sr programmer, oper 1958-68; Facts, Inc (JP Morgan & Co), mgr financial serv 1968-69, dir mktg 1969-70; Borden's Inc, proj mgr 1970-73; Arthur Young & Co, mgr 1973-76; Intl Paper Co, mgr sys devel 1976-80; Merrill Lynch & Co Inc, dir MIS 1980-82; Peters, Mayo & Co, pres & chief oper officer 1983-85; SRI Intl, mgr info serv & systems div NY 1985-86; HD Mayo & Assoc, chmn/founder 1982-. **Orgs:** Mem seminar chrmn guest spkr Amer Mgmt Assc; prin mem Amer Natl Standards Inst 1967-70; mem Assc for Systems Mgmt; guest spkr Data Process MgmtAssc IBM Process Indstry Users Grp NY Univ; mem MENSA; asst vice pres Eastern Rgn, Chap pres, Pledge Line pres Alpha Phi Alpha Frat NC 1963-66; sec & mem Plng Bd of Township North Bergen 1979-87, vice chmn 1988-; pres & dir Parker Imperial Assc Inc 1975-; chmn & guest spkr Natl Inst for Management Rsch 1986-87; chmn, Planned Giving Comm, St Luke's Episcopal Church, 1996-; director & mem, Development, Strategic Planning & Search Comms, Youth Consultation Services, 1995-; trustee and chmn, Investment Comm, St Lukes Foundation, 1994-. **Honors/Awds:** Designated info systems expert Amer Natl Standards Inst 1967, Amer Mgmt Assc 1967; pres 1st vice pres treas dir Pace Univ Alumni Assc 1977-80; mem pres adv comm Pace Univ 1981-; chmn Stonehenge Tenants Comm 1969-72. **Military Serv:** US Army Natl Guard pvt e2; Grad Trainee Ldrshp Schl 1962; Squad Ldr, Platoon Guide 1962. **Home Addr:** 7855 Boulevard East, North Bergen, NJ 07047. **Business Addr:** Chairman, HD Mayo & Associates, 7855 Blvd East, North Bergen, NJ 07047.

MAYO, JAMES WELLINGTON

Educator, director. **Personal:** Born Mar 2, 1930, Atlanta, GA; married Sandra Bratton; children: Joanna, Janell, Jamila. **Educ:** MIT, PhD 1964, MS 1961; Howard U, SM 1953; Morehouse, BS 1951. **Career:** Dept of Sci Ed Rsrch, Natl Sci Fnd, dep dir 1975-77; Natl Sci Foundation, sec hd 1973-75; NSF, pgm dir 1971-73; Morehouse Clg, prof chmn 1964-72; MA Inst of Tech, tutor 1961-63; MIT, rsch asst 1957-63; Howard U, instr 1955-57; Natl Bur of Stndrds, physicist 1952-53; Howard U, Rsrch asst 1951-52; DOE, Energy Storage Systems Division, division director, 1978-81; Consultant, 1981-82; AMAF, Research Group, marketing manager, 1982-83; Sonicraft, Washington Program, manager, 1983-88; Pailen-Johnson Associates, director, technical services, 1988-89; Computer Technology Group, vp, marketing, 1989-90; Catholic University of America, assistant academic vp for research, 1990-. **Orgs:** Mem Natl Rsrch Cncl CHR 1975-; mem Sloan Found 1975; Mem BEEP Natl Urban League 1972-; pres Brown Station Sch PTA 1971; mem Natl Sci Found AdComm 1969-71; mem Ctr for Rsrch 1969-71; consult Atlanta Sci Cong 1969-71; commr Commn on Clg Physics 1968-71; mem Beta Kappa Chi; Sigma Pi Sigma; Sigma XI; Phi Beta Kappa; mem Am Phy Soc; Am Assc of Physics Tchrs; mem Am Assc for the Advcmt of Sci; mem GA Admy of Sci; mem Natl Inst of Sci. **Honors/Awds:** DOE, Achievement Award; Department of Army, Outstanding Service Award.

MAYO, JULIA A. (JULIA MAYO JOHNSTON)

Sociologist. **Personal:** Born Aug 16, 1926, Philadelphia, PA; daughter of Mamie Clark and Henry Mayo; married William E Johnston, Dec 28, 1958 (deceased); children: Wilvena. **Educ:** Univ of PA, BA 1947; Bryn Mawr Clg, MS 1949; Univ of PA, PhD 1958. **Career:** St Vincents Hosp & Med Ctr NY, chief clncl stds & evaluation 1966-; NIMH St Elizabeth Hosp Wash DC, chief psychosocial stds 1960-66; Mental Hygiene Clinic VA Hosp Wilmington, DE, asst chief 1953-60; Psychotherapy, indiv/group part time pvt prac 1966-; DHew Ofc of Ed, consult 1975-; South Beach Psycho Ctr NY, consult rsrch 1978-; Medical College, New York, NY, assoc professor clinical psychiatry, 1989-91; New York Medical College and St Vincent's Hospital and Medical Ctr, clinical prof of psychiatry emeritus, 1991-. **Orgs:** Mem ASA; APPA; AAP; AAMFT; NASW; AGPA. **Honors/Awds:** Numerous scientific publ. **Business Addr:** St Vincent's Hosp & Med Center, 203 West 12th St, New York, NY 10011.

MAY-PITTMAN, INEVA

Educator. **Personal:** Born Jul 6, 1934, Jayess Lawrence Co, MS; married Joe; children: Albert Jefferson, Davion Jamaal. **Educ:** BS 1956; MS 1973; AA 1974. **Career:** Local NAACP; 1st vice pres 1965; Natl Council Negro Women, pres 1974; Bus & Professional Women's Club, 2nd vice pres; CSA, bd mem poverty program; Jackson School System, first grade teacher. **Orgs:** Pleasant Hill Missionary Bapt Ch; 1st vpres N Jackson Comm Boy's Club; chmn trst bd NCNW; bd mem Jackson Golden Heritage; NAACP; vol voter registrtn & edn; asst tchr Jackson Missionary Bapt Dist Assn; life mem JacksonState Univ Nat Alumni Assn; MS Tchrs Assn; Nat Counc Negro Women; Bus & Professional Women's Club; life mem Nat Educ Assn; chairperson, Thriftco of Mississippi, Inc. **Honors/Awds:** Tchr of yr 1959; pres of yr Jackson Dist missionary 1970; NAACP Fight for Freedom Cert of Merit 1973.

MAYS, ALFRED THOMAS

Health care research & development executive. **Personal:** Born Dec 29, 1947, East Meadow, NY; son of Marjorie (Stewart) Bamberg and Benjamin L Mays; married Deatrice Ward, Sep 7, 1969; children: Oneika, Ashley, Alexander. **Educ:** Hampton Univ, Hampton VA, BA Chemistry, 1970. **Career:** Chicopee, Dayton NJ, project dir, mgr scientific serv, dir new technology, dir absorbent technology, vice pres, dir, beginning 1970, vp, research and development, 1987-90, president, 1990-. **Orgs:** Mem, Amer Chemical Soc, 1973-89; advisor, bd of dir, Parents Anonymous, 1985-89; mem, Industrial Research Inst, 1987-89. **Honors/Awds:** Philip B Hoffman Award for Scientific Achievement, 1976; Johnson Medal, 1984; Black Achievers Award, 1985; Honorary Chairperson, Big Brothers/Big Sisters, Middlesex County, 1988. **Military Serv:** New Jersey Natl Guard, 1970-76. **Home Addr:** 33 Willis Dr, Ewing, NJ 08628.

MAYS, CARRIE J.

Funeral director. **Personal:** Born Aug 30, 1928, Lincoln Cnty, GA; widowed; children: Willie H III. **Career:** WH Mays Mortuary, self-employed funeral dir. **Orgs:** Mem Augusta Plng & Zoning Comm; mem Augusta Waterworks Com; mem Recorders Ct & Stockade Com; chmn Cemetery Parks Trees Com; mem Augusta Recreation Comm; rep Ofc of Equal Opp Bd 1971; co-chmn Paine Clg Build It Back Dr 1972; mem GA Alcoholism Adv Com; mem Expansion Com Augusta YM-YWCA's; votingdel Natl YWCA Conv 1967; chmn of bd Phyllis Wheatly Br YWCA; bd of dir Green St YWCA; mem Augusta Lib Bd; mem Dem Party; sec State Dem Party; natl voting electorate State of GA; mem exec bd State Dem Party; mem Augusta OIC; mem Sickle Cell Anemia Bd Med Clg of GA; city adv bd Med Clg ofGA; mem Augusta Black Caucus/ NAACP/SCLC/PAINE Clg Alumni Assc; Methodist Clb; Pinnacle Clb; GABEO. **Honors/Awds:** Woman of yr Lincoln League 1971; Topsy Eubanks 1973; Augusta OIC Awrd 1973; comm serv awrd 1973; citizen awrd 1973; citizen of yr Augusta News Review 1973; outst serv 1970-74; mortician of yr GA State 1977; mortician of yr Eight Dist GFSPA 1977; comm serv awrd Civic Women's Clb 1979; GA State Comm Serv Awrd. **Business Addr:** PO Box 754, Augusta, GA.

MAYS, DAVID

Dentist, professional football player (retired). **Personal:** Born Jun 20, 1949, Pine Bluff, AR. **Educ:** TX So U, BA 1971; Univ So CA, DDS 1976. **Career:** Los Angeles, dentist pvt prac 1978-; Comm Dentistry Dept & Pedodontic Dentistry Dept Univ of CA, clncl prof 1978-; Buffalo Bills, qtrbck/punter/place kicker 1978; Cleveland Browns, 1976-77; The Hawaiians, 1975; Houston Texans/Shreveport Streamer 1974. **Orgs:** Mem Western Dental Soc; Angel City Dental Soc; ADA; mem Alpha Phi Alpha Frat. **Honors/Awds:** Named All-Amer, TX So Univ (Football) 1971; All-conf (SWAC) 4 Yrs. **Business Addr:** 1414 Fairchild St, Baton Rouge, LA 70807.

MAYS, DEWEY ORDRIC, JR.

Physician. **Personal:** Born Dec 24, 1929, Wichita Falls, TX; married Ruby; children: Dewey, Archie, Ealy, Jones, Ruby, Quintence. **Educ:** Bishop Coll, BS 1949; Howard U, MD 1967. **Career:** Self-Employed, physician; tchr hs sci 1959-62; instr aircraft mech 1956-57; prin coach hs 1952-56; Smithville TX, tchr, coach, sci 1949-52. **Orgs:** Mem AMA; NMA. **Honors/Awds:** Good Samaritan Hospital, Certificate of Merit; Dayton Third District Ohio Boxing Association, Commemorative Plaque. **Business Addr:** 2114 Salem Ave, Dayton, OH 45406.

MAYS, JAMES A.

Physician, educator. **Personal:** Born May 1, 1939, Pine Bluff, AR; children: James Arthur Jr, James Anthony, James Ornett, James Eddie. **Educ:** Univ AR, BS, MD 1960; Univ CA Sch of Med, intern 1965; Wadsworth VA, Internal Medicine; UCLA Irvine, Cardiology. **Career:** Martin Luther King Hosp, cardiologist self chf comm ed; United High Blood Pressure Found, med dir 1974; LA & Chap Alumni Assc, pres 1972-73; AHA, gov cncl 1973; Merrill HS, stdnt cncl 1965; Stdnt Gov UAPB, vice pres 1960; owner of five medical clinics in Los Angeles County. **Orgs:** Mem State Cncl of Hypertension Cntrl CA 1975; publ edtrl LA Times 1974; chmn PUSH LA 1981; founder Adopt-a-Family; creator Black Super Heroes Radianand Radiance; chmn NY Public Serv Foundation; mem Philantropee Assoc; bd of dir Watt & Health Foundation; mem steering comm President Reagan's Comm onTax Reform. **Honors/Awds:** News Maker Natl Assc of Media 1975; ANA Awd 1975; Citation CA State Senate 1976; WA Human Rels Com 1977; songs Baby Coy 1977, Resing Wright 1977, Disco Bill Happy Birthday 1977; Senator Natl Holder 50 Awrd; George Washington Medal Freedom Foundation Valley Forge; appeared on Donahue, Today Show; publ "Methods to Make Ethnic Foods Safer" 1976, "Monogram on High Blood Pressure" 1976, "Chameleon Released" 1977, "Circle of Five", "Blink of an Eye", "Doctor Dan-Man of Steel"; write-ups in Washington Post, Jet, Ebony, LA Times, LA Harold, Life, Look, Newsweek, CBS News, CNW News, ABC News, USA Today, AMA News, Christian Serv Monitor; spoke before comm of US Senate and House of Reps. **Military Serv:** AUS capt 1966-68; Bronze Star, Combat Medic's Badge. **Business Addr:** 9214 So Broadway, Los Angeles, CA 90003.

MAYS, TRAVIS CORTEZ

Professional basketball player. **Personal:** Born Jun 19, 1968, Ocala, FL. **Educ:** Univ of Texas, Austin, TX, 1986-90. **Career:** Sacramento Kings, 1990-.

MAYS, VICKIE M.

Educator. **Personal:** Born Jan 30, 1952, Chicago, IL; daughter of Ruth Mays and Leonard Mays. **Educ:** Loyola Univ of Chicago, IL, BA, psychology and philosophy, 1973, MA, clinical psychology, 1979; University of Massachusetts, Amherst, MA, PhD, clinical psychology, 1979; RAND Corporation Health Policy Program/University of California at Los Angeles School of Public Health, health services research/epidemiology, 1987-89. **Career:** Loyola Univ Department of Psychology, Chicago, IL, research assistant, 1972; University of Massachusetts, Amherst, MA, teaching assistant, 1973-74, instructor/dorm counselor, 1974, lecturer, 1974, teaching assistant/clinical supervisor, 1976-77, acting intake coordinator/clincial supervisor, 1977, research assistant, 1978; George Washington University, Washington, DC, instructor, 1975-76; Univ of CA at Los Angeles, asst to professor of clinical psychology, 1979-; UCLA Academic Senate, vice chair, chair, 1997-99; consultant and advisor to government and educational institutions. **Orgs:** Member, American Psychological Assn, 1970-; member, Western Psychological Assn, 1981-; member, American Public Health Assn, 1986-, Black Caucus of Health Workers Program Committee, 1991-; American College of Epidemiology, 1996-. **Honors/Awds:** Author, "The Impact of Racial and Feminist Attitudes on the Educational Achievement and Occupational Aspirations of College Level Black Women," UCLA Center for Afro-American Studies Newsletter, May, 1980; author with L.J. Beckman, "Educating Community Gatekeepers About Alcohol Abuse in Women: Changing Attitudes, Knowledge and Referral Practices," Journal of Drug Education, 15 (4), 1985; author with T. Becker, W. Batchelor, J. Jones, "Introduction to the Special Issues: Psychology and AIDS," American Psychologist, 43 (11), 1988; author of numerousother research reports, review articles, abstracts, book chapters, and articles on psychology and AIDS; editorial board member of Clinical Psychology of Women, AIDS Education and Prevention, and Journal of Homosexuality; Journal of Cultural Diversity & Mental Health, Outstanding Woman of the Year, Board of Outstanding Young Women, 1984, 1986; Women and Psychotherapy Research Award, Div of the Psychology of Women, American Psychological Assn, 1985, American Psychological Assn, Master Lecture, 1997. **Business Addr:** Professor, UniversidadV of California at Los Angeles, 1285 Franz Hall, PO Box 951563, 405 Hilgard Ave, Los Angeles, CA 90024, (213)206-5159.

MAYS, W. ROY, III
Attorney. **Personal:** Born Jul 19, 1946, Atlanta, GA. **Educ:** Fort Valley State Coll, BS 1967; Atlanta Univ, MA 1968; Temple Univ School of Law, JD 1972. **Career:** Commonwealth of Pennsylvania, deputy atty general 1972-75; City of Atlanta, assistant city attorney, 1976-83, deputy city attorney, 1983-88; Mays & Slayton PA, attorney, currently. **Orgs:** Member Kappa Alpha Psi, Inc 1964-; board of trustees Shiloh Missionary Baptist Church 1975-; president Gate City Bar Assn 1983; board member Natl Bar Assn 1984; parliamentarian Natl Bar Assn 1984-85. **Honors/Awds:** Presidential Scholarship Atlanta Univ 1968; Distinguished Serv Award Fort Valley State College 1981. **Military Serv:** AUS 2nd Lt served 2 years.

MAYS, WILLIAM, JR.
Executive director. **Personal:** Born Oct 12, 1929, Detroit, MI; married Marilouise; children: Elisabeth, Adrienne. **Educ:** Eastern MI Univ, BA 1954; Univ of MI, MA 1958. **Career:** Ann Arbor Pub Schs, speech therapist 1958-66, elem prin 1966-72, asst supt 1972-74, dir elem educ 1974-75; MI Elem & Middle Sch Prin Assn, exec dir 1975-. **Orgs:** Bd trustees Washtenaw Comm Coll 1974; mem E MI Univ Alumni Assn; pres E MI Univ Track Alumni. **Honors/Awds:** Churchmanship Awd 1st United Meth Ch 1969; article pub MI Assn of Sch Bds Journ 1976. **Business Addr:** Executive Dir, MI Elem & Middle Sch Prin Assn, Rm 210 Manly Miles Bldg, 1405 S Harrison, East Lansing, MI 48823.

MAYS, WILLIAM G.
Company executive. **Career:** Mays Chemical Co Inc, CEO, currently. **Special Achievements:** Company ranked number 20 on BE's list of Top 100 Company's, 1994. **Business Addr:** CEO, Mays Chemical Co Inc, 5611 E 71st St, Indianapolis, IN 46222, (317)842-8722.

MAYS, WILLIAM O.
Physician, business executive. **Personal:** Born Dec 21, 1934, Little Rock, AR; married Deborah Easter; children: William III, Ryan Easter, Eric Easter. **Educ:** Howard U, BS 1956; Univ of AR, MD 1960. **Career:** Wayne Co Gen Hosp, internshp 1960, residency 1965; Southwest Medical Plaza, physician, currently. **Orgs:** Pres & chmn of bd MI Hlth Maint Org Plans Inc; pres chmn of bd Detroit Medical Found; vice pres Harris Mays & Assc PC; mem NMA; AMA; Detroit Med Soc; Wayne Co Med Soc; MI State Med Soc; Wolverine Med Soc; mem bd dir & exec com & tres CHPC, SEM; mem bd dir Blue Shield of MI; pres Detroit Med Soc 1972-74; American Coll of Physician Executives. **Military Serv:** AUS Med Corps 1962-63. **Business Addr:** Physician, Southwest Medical Plaza, 2401 20th St, Detroit, MI 48216.

MAYS, WILLIE HOWARD, JR.
Professional baseball player. **Personal:** Born May 6, 1931, Westfield, AL; married Mae Louise Allen; children: Michael. **Career:** Birmingham Black Barons Baseball Team, mem 1948-50; NY now San Francisco Giants System, mem 1950; Trenton Team, mem 1950-51; Minneapolis Millers, mem 1951; Giants, mem capt 1951-72; NY Mets, mem 1972-73 retired from maj league baseball 1973; Bally Park Place Atlantic City, asst to pres; Ogden Corp & Gruntal & Co, public relations; SF Giants, asst to the pres; Say Hey Foundation, president, currently. **Honors/Awds:** Voted Black Hall of Fame 1974; elected Baseball's Hall of Fame 1979; San Francisco Bay Area Hall of Fame 1980; George Mosone Meml Awd Big Bros 1980; A Phillip Randolph Awd 1980; played in 24 All Star Games; Rookie of Yr 1951; League's Stolen Bases Champion 1956-59; led Natl League in homeruns 1955, 1962, 1964-65; named Natl League's MVP 1954, 1965; named Player of Yr Sporting News 1954; Baseball Player of Decade 1970; named Male Athlete of Yr AD 1954; Hickock Belt 1954; 1st Commr's Awd 1970; author "Willie Mays, My Life In and Out of Baseball" 1966. **Military Serv:** AUS 1952-54. **Business Addr:** President, Say Hey Inc, 51 Mount Vernon Lane, Menlo Park, CA 94027.

MAZIQUE, FRANCES MARGURITE
Educator. **Personal:** Born Oct 12, Washington, DC; married Dr Edward C; children: Adrienne Biesemeier, Shari Harper. **Educ:** Hampton Inst; NY U; BS, MA, PhD. **Career:** US Dept HEW, dir, acad prgms; psychologist; Early Childhood Educ Spec, TV-Radio personality; HEW Fellows Prgm, dir; DC Commn on & Aging, chprsn; Child Devel Marriage & Family Life, cons; Child Serv Delta Sigma Theta, staff, currently. **Orgs:** Bd mem DC Med Soc; Aux Nat Med Assn; Proidence Hosp Womens Bd; Hosp for Sick Children; DC Arthritis Found; Doll League Inc; NAACP; Urban League; Am Civil Liberties; Afro Arts; Performing Creative Arts Assn Internatl. **Honors/Awds:** Womens year award 1976; Univ Women; Woman of Year; Commr DC. **Business Addr:** 330 Independence Ave SW, Washington, DC 20201.

MAZON, LARRI WAYNE
Educator. **Personal:** Born Dec 6, 1945, Roanoke, AL; son of Fannie Wilson and Dewey Wilson; married Dorothy Antrum Mazon, May 21, 1982; children: Jeffrey (stepson), Nikki. **Educ:** University of New Haven, West Haven, CT, BS, 1976; State University of New York-Stony Brook, LI, MSW, 1983; Nova University, doctoral candidate, currently. **Career:** Fairfield Hills Hospital, Newtown, CT, rehabilitation counselor, 1968-72; Regional Network of Programs, Bridgeport, CT, director, rehabilition services, 1972-78; Conntac-Wesleyan, Middletown, CT, counselor/coordinator, 1978-84; Fairfield University, Fairfield, CT, dir minority relations, 1984-, director, multicultural relations and student academic support services, currently. **Orgs:** Chairman, Association of Jesuit Colleges and Universities, Conference on Minority Affairs, 1990-91; chairman, Minority Advisory Council, Hamden Board of Education and Superintendent of Schools, 1989-90, 1990-91; steering committee member, African-American in Higher Eduction in Connecticut, 1988-90; member, Institute for Afro-American Scholarship, 1984-91. **Home Addr:** 15 Jayne Lane, Hamden, CT 06514. **Business Addr:** Director, Multicultural Relations and Student Academic Support Service, Fairfield University, North Benson Road, Fairfield, CT 06430.

MCADAMS, DAVID
United Nations official. **Personal:** Born Dec 6, 1931, Clermont, NC; son of Valerie Adams McAdams and John McAdams; married Dominique Ait-Ouyahia, Jun 19, 1990; children: Elsa Cecile, Alexandre Daniel. **Educ:** Adelphi University, Garden City, NY, BA, 1955; New School Social Research, New York, NY, MA, 1960. **Career:** United Nations Development Programme, resident representative, Lesotho, 1977-80, resident representative, Gabon, 1980-83, resident representative, Senegal, 1983-85, chief division southern Africa, New York, 1985-89, resident representative, Namibia, 1989-. **Orgs:** Member, Council on Foreign Relations, 1987-; member, board of trustees, Ralph Bunche Institute City University of New York, 1986-. **Military Serv:** US Army, Spec 5th Class, 1956-58. **Business Addr:** Resident Representative, Regional Bureau for Africa, United Nations Development Programme, Namibia, Grand Central Station, PO Box 1608, New York, NY 10163-1608.

MCADOO, BOB
Professional basketball player (retired), assistant coach. **Personal:** Born Sep 25, 1951, Greensboro, NC; married Charlina; children: Rita, Robert III, Ross. **Educ:** NC Univ, 1972. **Career:** Buffalo Braves, 1972-76, NY Knicks, 1976-79, Boston Celtics, 1979, Detroit Pistons, 1980, New Jersey Nets, 1980, Los Angeles Lakers, 1981-84, Philadelphia 76ers, 1985-86; Forli, Italy, 1992-; Miami Heat, asst coach, 1996-. **Honors/Awds:** Rookie of the Year 1973; All Star Team 1974-77; leading scorer in the NBA (130); ranks 20th on NBA's all-time scoring list with 17,803 career points; led NBA in scoring for 3 consecutive years 1973-76 averaging more than 30 points per game each season; All-Rookie Team 1973; MVP & 2nd team All-League Honors 1974-75. **Business Addr:** Assistant Coach, Miami Heat, 721 NW 1st Ave, Miami Arena, Miami, FL 33136, (305)577-4328.

MCADOO, HARRIETTE P.
Educational administrator. **Personal:** Born Mar 15, 1940, Fort Valley, GA; daughter of Ann Pipes and William Pipes; married John McAdoo PhD; children: Michael, John, Julia, David. **Educ:** MI State Univ, BA 1961, MA 1963; Univ of MI, PhD 1970; Harvard Univ, Post-doctoral 1974; Univ of MI, Post-doctoral 1982. **Career:** Milan/Ypsilanti HS, teacher 1964-67; Columbia Rsch System, rsch assoc 1976-77; visiting prof summer, Smith College, Washington Univ, Michigan State Univ, University of Minnesota; School of Social Work Howard Univ, prof/assoc 1970-, acting dean 1984-85. **Orgs:** Bd of dirs Natl Coun on Family Relations 1979-82; publications com Soc for Res in Child Develop 1979-85; gov council Soc for Res in Child Develop 1979-85; bd of dirs Groves Conf on Mar & Fam 1983-88; dir of conf VIII, XI, XII Empirical Conf on Black Psych 1985, 1987, 1988; prog vice pres Natl Council on Family Rel 1985; mem at large AERA Spec Interest Group in Early Educ & Child Devel 1985-87. **Honors/Awds:** Natl Adv Comm White House Conf on Families 1979-81; Outstanding Com Awd Howard Co Foundation for Black Educ 1980; Outstanding Soror Alpha Kappa Alpha Iota Lambda Omega Chap 1981; Marie Peters Awd Natl Coun on Family Relations 1984; Natl Acad of Science Comm on Status of Black Amers Demography & Health Panel; Researcher of the Year, 1982, 1987. **Home Addr:** 3034 Chestnut St NW, Washington, DC 20015. **Business Addr:** Professor, Howard University, School of Soc Work, 6th & Howard Place N W, Washington, DC 20059.

MCADOO, HENRY ALLEN
County official. **Personal:** Born Feb 9, 1951, Murfreesboro, TN; son of Doris Ann Wade McAdoo and John Allen McAdoo; married Gayle Elizabeth Howse McAdoo, Dec 3; children: Carol, Allen Jr, Lauren. **Educ:** Middle Tennessee State Univ, Murfreesboro TN, BS 1975; UTSI Tullahoma TN, graduate studies 1977; MTSU Murfreesboro TN, graduate studies 1979. **Career:** Sedrulp Technologies, application programmer 1972-82; NISSAN, sr analyst 1982-1986 sr systems analyst 1986-; Rutherford Co Comm, commissioner 18th Dist 1978-; Scales & Son Funeral Home, Inc. **Orgs:** Chmn Law Enforcement Rutherford Co 1978-79; chmn Economic Committee Rutherford Co 1983-84; Mason Murfreesboro Lodge #12; Elks EA Davis Lodge #1138; Kappa Alpha Psi Fraternity, Murfreesboro Alumni Chapter. **Honors/Awds:** Nominated & appointed Rutherford Co Bd of Governors Mid-Cumberland 1978-79, Bd of Zoning Appeals 1979-. **Home Addr:** PO Box 3132, Murfreesboro, TN 37133-3132.

MCAFEE, CARRIE R.
Educator. **Personal:** Born Dec 20, 1931, Galveston, TX; married Joshua McAfee. **Educ:** Lincoln Univ, BA 1951; Columbia Univ, MA 1963; Univ of CA Berkeley, TSU. **Career:** NYC, tchr 1955-64, coun 1965-68, asst prin 1968-73, coun & coord 1969, 1972; Houston Ind Sch Dist, exec dir, 1974-. **Orgs:** Mem TASSP, NASSP, ASCD, TSCD, HSCD; Natl Assn Women Exec; Natl Assn Sex Educ & Coun; TS&A Hon Prin Assn Bd Dirs; Amer Bridge Assn; mem YWCA; mem MacGregor Orioles Little League; state bd dirs American Lung Assn; bd dirs San Jacinto Lung Assn; Natl Coalition of 100 Black Women; chairman of bd, American Lung Assn of Texas; Greater Houston Foundation, Houston Federation of Professional Women; Zeta Phi Beta; VIL State Executive Committee; President, Texas Democratic Women of Harris County. **Honors/Awds:** Lady of Yr 1951; Outstanding Master Bridge Player 1969; ABA Lady 1974; Outstanding Journ Tchr 1962; Achieve in Educ TSU 1974; Professional Awd Natl Assn of Bus & Professional Women 1975; Outstanding Women YWCA 1977; Newspaper Fund Fellow 1964; Big E Award, Boy Scouts of America l989; Outstanding Women, Houston Woman Newspaper l989; Carrie Rochon McAfee Library, 1995; Sojourner Truth Awd, 1996. **Business Addr:** Executive Director, Houston Ind Sch Dist, 13719 Whiteheather, Houston, TX 77045.

MCAFEE, CHARLES FRANCIS
Architect. **Personal:** Born Dec 25, 1932, Los Angeles, CA; son of Willie Anna McAfee and Arthur James McAfee Sr; married Gloria Myrth Winston; children: Cheryl Lynn, Pamela Anita, Charyl Frena McAfee-Duncan. **Educ:** Univ of Nebraska, BArch, 1958. **Career:** Self-employed, architect, currently. **Orgs:** American Inst of Architects, fellow, 1963; National Business League, senior vice pres; Wichita Urban League; Wichita Chamber of Commerce; Phyllis Wheatley Children's Home; Excelsior Club; Kappa Alpha Psi Fraternity; Sigma Pi Phi Fraternity; National Assn of Minority Architects, founder, past president. **Honors/Awds:** American Institute of Architects, numerous Design Awards, 1964-96; National Organization of Minority Architects, Design Awards, 1983; Federal Housing Administration, Design Awards, 1964; University of Nebraska, Alumni Achievement Award, College of Architecture, Distinguished Alumni Award. **Special Achievements:** Joint Venture selected for program, construction and design management, Olympic Games facilities, Atlanta, 1996; developer, architect: Richmond Health Dept; McAfee Manufacturing Modular Housing Systems, pres. **Military Serv:** US Army, cpl, 1953-55. **Business Addr:** President, Charles F McAfee FAIA NOMA PA, Architects Planners, 2600 N Grove, Wichita, KS 67219, (316)686-2138.

MCAFEE, FLO
Government official. **Career:** The White House, Office of Public Liaison, special assistant to the president, currently. **Business Phone:** (202)456-2930.

MCAFEE, FRED LEE
Professional football player. **Personal:** Born Jun 20, 1968, Philadelphia, MS. **Educ:** Mississippi College, degree in mass communications. **Career:** New Orleans Saints, running back, 1991-93; Arizona Cardinals, 1994; Pittsburgh Steelers, 1995-. **Business Addr:** Professional Football Player, Pittsburgh Steelers, Three Rivers Stadium, 300 Stadium Circle, Pittsburgh, PA 15212, (412)323-1200.

MCAFEE, LEO C., JR.
Educator. **Personal:** Born Dec 15, 1945, Marshall, TX; married Sandra Wray; children: Leo III, La Ruth. **Educ:** Prairie View A&M U, BS 1966; Univ of MI, MSE 1967; Univ of MI, PhD 1970. **Career:** Univ of MI, asso prof of elect & computer engr; Semiconductor Group Electronics Dept Gen Motors Research Labs MI, asso sr research engr 1973-74; Univ ofMI IBM Thomas J Watson Research Labs NY, summer & faculty 1971-78. **Orgs:** Mem tech staff summer Bell Telephone Labs NJ 1968; mem Inst of Elect & Electronics Engr Inc; mem Eta Kappa Nu; Tau Beta Pi; Sigma Xi; Phi Kappa Phi; Alpha Kappa Mu. **Honors/Awds:** Outstanding engr student at Prairie View A&M Univ 1956-66; Nat Sci Found Trainee Univ of MI 1966-68; Univ MI Predoctoral Fellowship 1969-70. **Business Addr:** Elec Comp Engr, Dept Univ of MI, Ann Arbor, MI 48109.

MCALLISTER, LEROY TIMOTHY, SR.
Government official. **Personal:** Born Sep 1, 1918, Hamlet, NC; married Elizabeth Gwathmey; children: Leroy Jr, Ernest. **Educ:** VA State Univ, BS 1947. **Career:** VA Hosp, supv corrective therapy 1948-75; King Williams Cty, chmn bd of supv. **Orgs:** Treasurer & bd mem Eastern VA Health Sys Agency 1976-; chmn NN-MP Agency on Aging 1976-84; bd of dir VA State-

wide Health Coord Council 1976-; bd mem VA State Emerg Med Advisory Council 1980-; treas & bd dir VA Assoc of Counties 1981-; bd of dir Natl Assoc of Counties 1982-. **Honors/Awds:** Omega Man of the Year Phi Phi Chap Omega Psi Phi Frat 1971; Serv Awd Paralized Vets of Amer 1975; Comm Serv Awd VA State Univ Alumni Assoc 1983; Serv Awd & Founder NNMP Area Agency on Aging 1984; Serv Awd Third Union Baptist Church 1984. **Military Serv:** AUS sgt 3 1/2 yrs; Amer Defense & Good Conduct 1944.

MCALLISTER, SINGLETON BERYL

Attorney. **Personal:** Born Mar 25, 1952, Baltimore, MD; daughter of Ann Hughes McAllister and James Winfred McAllister. **Educ:** University of Maryland, BA, 1975; Howard University, School of Law, JD, 1984. **Career:** Parren J Mitchell, legislative assist, 1975-78; TransAfrica, Inc, assistant director, 1978-79; Congressman William H Gray, III, legislative director, 1979-81; Congressman Mickey Leland, special assistant, 1981-83; US Federal District Court, law clerk, 1984-85; US House of Representatives, budget committee counsel, 1986-88; Reed, Smith, Shaw & McClay, partner, 1988-92; Shaw, Pittman, Potts & Trowbridge, counsel, 1992-96; Agency for Intl Development, gen counsel, 1996-. **Orgs:** Women in Government Relations Inc, pres, 1994; Democratic Natl Committee Women Leadership Forum, 1994; Health Policy Advisory Committee, Joint Ctr for Political Studies, 1994; Federal Affairs Committee, Greater Washington Bd of Trade, 1994; Northern Virginia Minority Business and Professional Association, general counsel, 1992; Congressional Black Caucus Foundation, advisory board member, 1991; Virginia Small Business Financing Authority, board member, 1990; Women in Government Relations Inc, general counsel/board member, 1991; Virginia Local Anti-Trust Fund Drug Authority, board member, 1990; Capitol Ballet Guild, Inc, board member, 1988; African Development Foundation, board member of advisory board, 1987. **Honors/Awds:** American Federation of Government Employees Award from Local 1733, 1978; Amer Lung Assn of the District of Columbia, Recognition Award, 1992; Minority Bus Award. **Special Achievements:** Washington Technology, Commentary, 1992; National Medical Association News, Articles, 1991; Association of Black Cardiologist News, Articles, 1992. **Business Addr:** General Counsel, USAID, 6895 New State Bldg, Washington, DC 20523.

MCALPINE, ROBERT

Association executive. **Personal:** Born Jul 13, 1937, New Haven, CT; son of Mrs. Rachel Thomas Simpson; married Carole J Robinson; children: Monique, Angie. **Educ:** Southern CT State Coll, BS 1960, MS 1969; Yale Univ, Cert Urban Studies 1969; Occidental Coll, MA 1970. **Career:** Guilford Publ Schls, tchr 1960-67; New Haven Publ Schls, admin 1967-69; US Conf of Mayors, prog analyst 1970-74; Natl Urban League Inc, congressional liaison 1974-1989, director of policy and government relations 1989-. **Orgs:** NAACP; Washington Urban League. **Honors/Awds:** Natl Urban Fellows 1969-70; New Haven Jaycees Key Man of the Year 1969-. **Home Addr:** 11700 Old Columbia Pike, Silver Spring, MD 20904. **Business Addr:** Natl Urban League, Inc, 1111 14th Street, NW, Suite 600, Washington, DC 20005.

MCANDREW, ANNE E. BATTLE

Educator. **Personal:** Born May 28, 1951, Philadelphia, PA; daughter of Marian Louise Chester Battle and Turner Charles Battle III; married John McAndrew, Dec 3, 1983; children: Allison, Christina. **Educ:** Moore Coll of Art & Design, Philadelphia, PA, BFA, BS, 1972; Visual Studies Workshop, Rochester, NY, photography, 1972-74; Rochester Institute of Technology, Rochester, NY, MFA, 1983. **Career:** Panther Publishing House, New York, NY, researcher, 1971; Univ of Rochester, Rochester, NY, museum video asst, 1974-75; Rochester Institute of Technology, Rochester, NY, graduate asst, 1982-83; Wedge Newspaper, Rochester, NY, managing editor, 1985-86; Rochester City School District, Rochester, NY, art teacher, 1974-, lead teacher, 1988-. **Orgs:** Curriculum comm dir, Professional Practice Schools Design Team, American Federation of Teachers, 1990-; mem, School Based Planning Team, 1990-; designer, Professional Teaching Portfolio Format, Rochester City School District, 1989-. **Honors/Awds:** Fannie Knapp Allen Memorial Graduate Graphic Design Scholarship, Rochester Institute of Technology, 1982-83; Sara B Peters Art Education European Fellowship, 1971. **Business Addr:** Lead Teacher in Art, Rochester City School District, 131 W South Broad Street, Rochester, NY 14614.

MCARTHUR, BARBARA JEAN

Educator (retired), epidemiologist, writer. **Personal:** Born Jul 7, Dubuque, IA; daughter of Ada Boone Martin and James Laurence Martin; divorced; children: Michele Jean, William Michael. **Educ:** Provident Hospital & Training School, diploma in nursing; DePaul Univ, BSN, MS; Univ of Washington, MS, PhD 1976. **Career:** Knoxville Coll, nurse & asst prof Biology & Science Educ; Wayne State Univ, assoc prof, 1976-78, graduate program in institutional epidemiology, 1976-84, as soc dept Immunology & Microbiology Med School, 1976-, adj prof biology & liberal arts, 1980-88, prof of nursing, 1978-96. **Orgs:** Principal investigator Wayne State Univ Medical School, 1976-83; consultant Plymouth Center for Human Devel 1978; WSU Phylon Soc, bd mem, 1979-, co-chair 1980-82, 1990-92; bd mem United Condo Owners of MI 1979-81; bd mem Planned Parenthood League Inc 1982-88; bd mem WSU Minority Biomedical Support Program 1979-81; consultant CURN Proj Self Catheterization in Rehabilitation Care 1979; dir MI Soc for Infection Control 1979-81; bd mem editorial advisory bd Infection Control 1979-87; Oral Assessment Bd for Higher Educ; consultant MI Civil Serv Comm 1980; bd mem Total Health Care Inc 1981-84;Task Force Natl Council on Alcoholism & Chem Dependence, 1983-84; New Detroit Inc Health Comm, 1984-90; Founder's Soc Detroit Inst of Arts, 1984-86; Womens' Economic Club, 1984-85; chair Public Relations Committee, Southfield Alumnae Chapter Delta Sigma Theta Inc, 1984-86; keynote speaker Southwest Hospital Nurses Day, 1985; WSU Graduate Council, 1985-93; expert witness malpractice suites, 1984-; first assembly sec, governor, bd of regents, general comm, The Nightingale Soc, 1988-91; Coalition for Health Care, 1988-89; Friends of Southwest Hospital, 1988-91; board mem, Community Health Awareness Group, 1992-93; director, Consortium of Doctors, Ltd, 1993-94. **Honors/Awds:** A Wilberforce Williams Award Provident Hospital; Student Rsch Grant Sigma Theta Tau 1974; Nurse Traineeships from DePaul Univ & Univ of Washington 7 yrs; fellow Amer Acad of Nursing 1978; Sigma Theta Tau Nursing Honor Soc 1980; fellow NY Acad of Science 1980; numerous publications, chapters in books, journal articles, abstracts; biography in Dr Elizabeth Carnegie's History of Black Nursing 1986; AIDS presentation at second intl conf and exhibition on infection control, England, 1988; first African Amer faculty mem to win lawsuit against a predominantly white univ, 1987; First Editorial Review Board, The ABNF Journal, 1990-95; presenter, First Research Workshop, Michigan Nurses of VA, 1989; Key Note Address, Health Care Crisis in Black Community, U of Wis, 1990; Professor of-Week, WSU South E p 4, June 12, 1990; key note address, seventeenth annual state mtg, Alabama Dental Society, 1990; honoree, Consortium of Doctors, Ltd, 1993. **Home Addr:** 26500 Summerdale Dr, Southfield, MI 48034, (313)357-1161.

MCBEE, VINCENT CLERMONT

Criminalist. **Personal:** Born Nov 4, 1946, Greenville, SC; son of Scotia Marion Henderson McBee and Bozie C McBee; married Virginia Daniels (divorced); children: Vanessa Latasha, Victoria Simone. **Educ:** Johnson C Smith Univ, BS 1971; Florida Intl Univ, 1971; Univ of Miami, 1976. **Career:** Natl Brewing Co Southern Div, quality control chem dir 1971-75; Southland Corp Velda Farms, quality control supvr 1975-76; Metro-Dade Police Dept, criminalist 1976-. **Orgs:** Mem Southern Assn of Forensic Sci, Prince Hall Masons, Omega Psi Phi Frat Inc, Ordained Elder New Covenant Presbyterian Church. **Home Addr:** 3500 NW 171 St, Miami, FL 33056, (305)623-8237.

MCBETH, VERONICA SIMMONS

Judge. **Personal:** Born Feb 23, 1947, San Diego, CA; daughter of Judith LaBrie Jackson and Lemuel Jackson; divorced; children: Ashley, Alison. **Educ:** CA State Univ, BS 1972; Univ of CA, JD 1975. **Career:** Office of the Los Angeles City Attorney, trial deputy 1975-76, coordinator-domestic violence program 1976-78, special counsel to the city attorney 1978-79, supervising attorney 1979-81; Los Angeles Municipal Court, assistant presiding judge, currently. **Orgs:** Pres Black Women Lawyers Assn of CA 1979-80; mem Natl Bar Assn 1975-; bd mem LA-NAACP 1979-80; mem Natl Assn of Women Judges 1981-; dir UCLA Law Sch Exec Comm 1981-; exec comm LA Muni Court 1982-, chair pers comm 1985, 1987; sec Judicial Division CA Assn of Black Lawyers 1984-85, vice pres 1986-; dir Harriet Buhai Center for Family Law; bd of dir judicial cncl Natl Bar Assn 1985-; bd of dir Coalition of 100 Black Women 1985-; lecturer Natl Judges Coll, PA Trial Judges Conf, ABA Appelate Judges Seminar; pres judicial division CABL 1988-89; President Municipal Court Judges Association, 1988-89; chair elect 1989-90, chair 1990-91, judicial council National Bar Assn; board of directors Jack and Jill of America 1987-91. **Honors/Awds:** UCLA Law Review 1973-74; Editor in Chief Black Law Journal 1974-75; Bernard Jefferson Jurist of the Year Award, John Langston Bar Assn 1991; Raymond Pace Alexander Award, Judicial Council, National Bar Assn 1989; Presidential Award, National Bar Assn 1987; NAACP Thomas Griffith Award, 1991; Cal Association of Black Lawyers, Judge of the Year, 1991; Cal State Bar Public Law Section, Public Law Award, 1992; National Ctr for State Courts, Distinguished Svc Awd, 1996; Century City Bar Association, Municipal Court Judge of the Year, 1996. **Business Addr:** Assistant Presiding Judge, Los Angeles Municipal Court, 110 N Grand Ave, Los Angeles, CA 90012.

MCBETH-REYNOLDS, SANDRA KAY

Real estate/mortgage banker. **Personal:** Born May 7, 1950, Loma Linda, CA; daughter of Velma A Woods and Timothy L Woods; married James L Reynolds; children: Brandon Lincoln. **Educ:** Indiana University, Bloomington, IN, BA, psychology, 1970; Pepperdine University, Malibu, CA, MA, urban planning & development, 1972, MA, science, public administration, 1973; University of West Los Angeles, School of Law, JD, 1981. **Career:** Loyola Marymount University, Westchester, CA, dean student service, 1976-79; United International Mortgage & Investment, pres, 1980. **Orgs:** Coalition of 100 Black Women, 1988-; Jack & Jill of America, 1986-; Alpha Kappa Alpha Sorority, 1969-; National Association of Female Executives, 1987-. **Honors/Awds:** Black Women of Achievement, Legal Defense Fund, 1988; Top 100 Black & Prof Women, Dollars & Sense Mag, 1989; Top 50 Business Executives, LA Chamber of Commerce, 1985. **Business Addr:** President, United Intl Mortgage & Investment, 973 N LaBrea Ave, Inglewood, CA 90302.

MCBRIDE, BRYANT

Professional sports executive. **Personal:** Born in Chicago, IL. **Career:** National Hockey League, New Business Development, Diversity Task Force, dir, currently. **Business Addr:** Director of New Business Development, National Hockey League, 1251 Avenue of the Americas, New York, NY 10020, (212)789-2165.

MCBRIDE, FRANCES E.

Educator (retired). **Personal:** Born Nov 4, Athens, GA; married Willie; children: Reginald. **Educ:** Savannah St Coll, BS 1945; Atlanta U, MA 1953; Univ of GA, postgrad. **Career:** Alps Rd Elem Sch Clarke Co, tchr, 1954-83; Polk Co, 1949-53; Lagrange GA, 1946-47; Jones Co, 1945-46; Savannah St Coll Alumni Assn, 1976-77; Atlanta U Alumni Assn, 1976-77; Clarke Co Assn of Educs; GA Assn of Edn; Nat Assn of Educs. **Orgs:** Mem Resolution Comm NEA, 1973-74; Ebenezer Bapt Ch; Am Assn Univ Women Athens Br; NAACP; Delta Sigma Theta Sor; mem Eval Team for So Assn of Schs Habersham Co Sch, 1977; past pres Silhouette Club of Athens; chmn Kappa Alpha Psi Frat Clarke Co; state president, Georgia Retired Teachers Association, 1988-89. **Honors/Awds:** Tchr of Yr, 1970; regnl Tchr of Yr GA St C of C 1970; st Tchr of Yr 1970; st Tchr of Yr Assn of Classroom Tchrs 1975-76; runner up Tchr Hall of Fame 1975-76; editor, publr 1st ch newpaper, The Messenger 1976; elected to GA Assn of Educs Exec Com 1977; cert Ebenezer Bapt 1977; century asso cert Savannah St & Coll 1972-73; apprec cert GAE 1976-77; 1st black female pres of local Clarke Co Assn of Educ 1971; 1st black female pres of GA Assn of Classroom Tchrs 1972-73; 1st black female dir 10th dist GAE 1974-78. **Home Addr:** 284 Plaza St, Athens, GA 30606.

MCBRIDE, SHELIA ANN

Registered nurse. **Personal:** Born Aug 27, 1947, Albany, GA; married Mathis; children: William Alexander Corbett, Erica Monique Corbett. **Educ:** Albany State Coll, BS 1971. **Career:** ICU, Coatesville Vet Adminstrn Hosp, staff nurse 1976-77; ICU, Pheobe Putney Meml Hosp, charge nurse 1975-76; Albany Urban League Fam Planning Prgm, proj dir, nurse 1974-75; Orthopedics & Newborn Nursery, Pheobe Putney Meml Hosp, 1971-74.

MCBRIDE, ULLYSSES

Educator. **Personal:** Born Nov 27, 1938, Atmore, AL; son of Mamie McBride and George McBride; married Mabel Copridge; children: Valeri. **Educ:** Knoxville Coll, AB 1959; IN Univ, Masters Degree; Auburn Univ, Doctoral Degree 1974; Univ of NY Stony Brook, Coe Fellow; Troy State Univ, Post-Doctoral Studies; Alabama State Univ, Montgomery, AL, Doctoral Degree in Law, 1990. **Career:** Escambia Cty Training School Atmore AL, teacher, coach; No Norman HS Brewton AL, dir; James H Faulkner Coll, prof, secondary social sci, dean 1988. **Orgs:** Past pres Escambia Cty Teachers Assoc; pres Faulkner State Coll Ed Assoc; dist dir AL Council for Soc Studies; mem Polemarch So Province KAY, Kappa Delta Pi, Phi Delta Kappa, Alpha Kappa Mu; dir United Fund; bd mem AL Library; mem grand bd of dir Kappa Alpha Psi; mem pensions & security bd Escambia Cty; chmn bd of dir AL Dem Conf; reader Fed Grants Washington DC; dir self study Southern Assoc Coll & Schools Faulkner State Coll. **Honors/Awds:** Achievement Awds; Teacher of the Year Faulkner State Coll 1974, 1975; 100 Most Influential Black Americans, Johnson Publishers 1989; International President, Kappa Alpha Psi Fraternity 1989. **Home Addr:** 173 Dr Martin Luther King Jr Ave, Atmore, AL 36502.

MCBRIER, VIVIAN FLAGG

Music educator (retired). **Personal:** Born Apr 12, Lynchburg, VA; married Clyatt (deceased). **Educ:** VA State Coll, BS Music, BS El Educ 1937; Columbia U, MA Music 1941; Cath Univ of Am, PhD Musicology 1967. **Career:** DC Tchr Coll, prof, mnr Tchr 1944-72; Hampton Inst, tchr 1945-46; Pub Sch Lynchburg, VA, 1937-44; Cath Univ, lecturer 1971-72; Sch of Religion Howard U, lectr 1973-76. **Orgs:** Dir Coll Choir & num ch choirs in DC; lecturer Niagara Falls NY & Canada. **Honors/Awds:** Publ ''Finger Fun for Piano'' 1949; Meyer Fellowship for Superior Serv in DC Sch 1963; book, ''R Nathaniel Dett His Life & Works'' 1974; num articles; Alpha Kappa Alpha Achvmnt Award.

MCBROOM, F. PEARL

Physician. **Personal:** Born in Louisville, MS; daughter of Augusta Dooley and Thomas Riley; divorced; children: Lorelei, Durga Pamela. **Educ:** Univ of Chicago, BA 1946; Columbia Clge Physicians & Surgeons, BS 1949, MD 1953. **Career:** Bellevue Med Ctr NY, internship 1953-54; Columbia Univ Wing Goldwater Hosp NY, residency 1954-55; UCLA Los Angeles CA, residency 1955-57; USC Los Angeles CA, flwshp

Cardiology 1957-58; NIH Grants, resrch fellow 1958-62; F Pearl McBroom MD Inc, Marina Del Rey, spec intl med cardiology 1958-, director, 1980-; Cardiovascular & Preventive Med, indpendent rsrch 1962-87; West Los Angeles Medical Clinic, director, CA, 1970-80; Marina Del Rey, CA, medical clinic director, 1980-93; F Pearl McBroom, MD, Inc, physician, currently; SPA Revitalization Site, Nevis West Indies, Fiji Isle of Vulani, Cancun, Mexico, Malibu CA, Sandiego CA, Everglades, FL, med consultant, 1993-98. **Orgs:** Bd mem Frederick Douglas Child Dev Ctr 1958-62, EST Fnd 1972-82, Siddha Yoga Fnd 1974-80; Lotus Springs Enterprises, dir, 1985-98; mem Assoc AUM Soc Univ So CA 1986-87; medical consultant, Spa Revitalization Site, Nevis, West Indies, Fiji Ilse of Vulani, Cancun, Malibu, San Diego, Everglades, 1993-95. **Honors/Awds:** Fellow Assoc Clinical Investigators 1987; Medical Consultant for numerous Exec Spas, 1998; George Carver Award, Trailblazer Award, 1001 Women of Achievement. **Business Addr:** Physician, F Pearl McBroom MD Inc, 1515 Palisades Dr, Ste P, Pacific Palisades, CA 90272, (310)454-7227.

MCBURROWS, GERALD
Professional football player. **Personal:** Born Oct 7, 1973, Detroit, MI. **Educ:** University of Kansas, attended. **Career:** St Louis Rams, defensive back, 1995-. **Business Addr:** Professional Football Player, St Louis Rams, One Rams Way, St Louis, MO 63045, (314)982-7267.

MCCAA, JOHN K.
Broadcast journalist. **Personal:** Born Feb 24, 1954, Rantoul, IL; son of Margaret Britt McCaa and Johnnie McCaa; married Michele Moore McCaa, Oct 30, 1982; children: Collin. **Educ:** Creighton University, Omaha, NE, BA, Journalism, 1972-76. **Career:** WOWT-TV, Omaha, NE, reporter/anchor, 1976-84; WFAA-TV, Dallas, TX, reporter, anchor, manager, 1984-. **Orgs:** President, Dallas-Fort Worth Association of Black Communicators, 1984-; member, National Association of Black Journalists, 1987-. **Business Addr:** News Manager, WFAA-TV, 606 Young St, Dallas, TX 75202.

MCCABE, EUGENE LOUIS
Hospital president and administrator. **Personal:** Born May 18, 1937, New Haven, CT; son of Edna Dawson McCabe and Eugene Louis McCabe Sr; divorced; children: Kevin Louis. **Educ:** Southern Connecticut State Univ, New Haven CT, BA, 1965. **Career:** Booz, Allen & Hamilton, New York NY, 1972-75; Governor's Commission for New York Fiscal Crisis, New York NY, 1976; Deleuw/Cathers & Assoc, New York NY and Washington DC, 1976-81; North General Hospital, New York NY, 1981-. **Orgs:** Vice chair, Manhattan Empowerment Zone; vice chair, Apollo Theatre Foundation; vice chair and chief exec officer, North Geberak Service Corp; trustee, Natl Executive Service Corps (NESC). **Honors/Awds:** Honorary Doctorate, St Joseph's Coll, 1989; Frederick Douglass Award, NY Urban League, 1994; President's Medal, Hunter Coll, NY, 1996; Community Service Award, Citizens Housing and Planning Council, NY, 1996. **Military Serv:** US Marine Corps, corporal, 1954-58. **Home Addr:** 490 West End Ave, New York, NY 10024.

MCCABE, JEWELL JACKSON
Association executive. **Personal:** Born Aug 2, 1945, Washington, DC; daughter of Hal Jackson; married Eugene L McCabe Jr. **Educ:** Bard Coll, liberal arts 1963-66. **Career:** NY Urban Coalition, dir of pub affairs 1970-73; Special Serv for Children NYC, pub rel officer 1973-75; Women's Div Office of the Gov, NY State, assoc dir, pub info 1975-77; WNET-TV/Thirteen, dir gov comm affairs 1977-82; Natl Coalition of 100 Black Women, chair 1978-. **Orgs:** Bd dir Bus Mktg Corp, NY Urban League, New York City Planned Parenthood, Lenox Hill Hosp, Settlement Housing Fund Inc; mem Community Plng Bd 4; exec comm Assoc for a Better NY; bd dir Women's Forum; co-chair Women United for NY, Planned Parenthood of New York City Public Issues & Answers; mem Edges; bd dir Harlem Interfaith Counciling Svc, Comm Council of Gr NY; mem Policy Plng Comm NY Partnership David Rockefeller Chmn; mem Adv New York City Comm on Status of Women. **Honors/Awds:** Publs "Women New York" 1975-77, "Give A Damn" 1970-73; E Region Urban League Guild Awd 1979; Seagrams Civic Awd 1980; Links Civic Awd 1980; Dep Grand Marshal The Annual Martin Luther King Jr Parade New York City 1980; Outstanding Comm Leadership Awd Malcolm/King Coll 1980.

MCCAIN, ELLA BYRD
Librarian, media specialist (retired). **Personal:** Born Mar 8, 1925, Dothan, AL; daughter of Olivia Claudia Woods Byrd and Erskine Byrd; married John McCain, Jun 17, 1947. **Educ:** Alabama A&M Univ, Normal, AL, BS (magna cum laude), 1945; Univ of Michigan, Ann Arbor, MI, MLS. **Career:** East Street High School, Opelika, AL, teacher, 1945-47; Wenonah High School, teacher, 1947-52, librarian, 1952-72; Atlanta Univ School of Library and Sciences, Atlanta, GA, asst professor, 1956-82 (summmers); Rogers Area Vocational Center, librarian, 1972-87. **Orgs:** 2nd vice president, Birmingham Urban League Guild, 1989-; volunteer, American Red Cross, 1986-; parliamentarian, Alabama Instructional Media Assn, 1989; vice president, Progressive Action Club of Birmingham, AL, beginning 1986, pres, 1992-; board of directors, Birmingham International Educational Film Festival, 1985-; member, Alabama State Dept of Education Accreditation Committee, 1954-67; president, Alabama Assn of School Librarians, 1956-58; Jefferson County Retired Teachers Assn; Alabama Retired Teachers Assn; pres, Alabama Instructional Media Assn; American Assn of Retired Persons; American Vocational Assn; American Assn of School Librarians; Assn for Educational Communication & Technology; Phi Delta Kappa Fraternity; Friends of Alabama Libraries; Univ of Michigan Alumni Assn; Alabama A&M Univ Alumni Assn; Seasoned Performers. **Honors/Awds:** Leadership Award, Phi Delta Kappa Chapter, Univ of Michigan; Alabama Instructional Media Assn Award; Library Service Plaque, Atlanta Univ; Mental Health Assn Service Pin; Rogers Area Vocational Center Service Plaque; Alumni Plaque of the Year, Alabama A&M Univ; American Red Cross Volunteer of Year Award; Red Cross Service Medal. **Home Addr:** 1 Green Springs Ave, SW, Birmingham, AL 35211.

MCCALL, BARBARA COLLINS
Educator. **Personal:** Born Nov 17, 1942, Norfolk, VA; daughter of Gladys George Collins and Joseph Collins, Sr; children: Monsita McCall Allen, Monique Lavitia, Clifton III. **Educ:** Norfolk State Univ, BS 1965, MA 1982. **Career:** Norfolk State Univ, confidential sec/pres 1966-75, instructor evening coll 1970, asst dir couns upward bound 1975-76, dir asst instr irc 1976-81, instructor English/language skills ctr 1981-91, assistant director of writing center/English instructor, 1991-. **Orgs:** Secty/treas Natl Sorority of Phi Delta Kappa Alpha Lambda Chap 1985-87; mem The Natl Council of Negro Women, The Natl Assoc of Negro Business & Professional Women's Club Norfolk; charter mem Metropolitan Club; mem Sigma Tau Delta Natl English Honor Society 1987-; member, Delta Sigma Theta Sorority, Chesapeake-Virginia Beach Alumnae Chapter, 1990-; Citizens Drug Advisory Commission, appointed by Chesepeake, VA mayor Dr William Ward, 1991-. **Home Addr:** 3032 Sunrise Ave, Chesapeake, VA 23324. **Business Addr:** English Instructor, Norfolk State University, 2401 Corprew Ave, Norfolk, VA 23504.

MCCALL, EMMANUEL LEMUEL, SR.
Clergyman. **Personal:** Born Feb 4, 1936, Sharon, PA; son of Myra Mae Preston McCall and George McCall; married Emma Marie Johnson; children: Emmanuel Jr, Evalya Lynette. **Educ:** Univ of Louisville, BA 1958; So Bapt Theol Sem, BD 1962, MRE 1963, MDiv 1967; Emory Univ, DMinistry 1975. **Career:** Simmons Bible Coll Louisville, prof 1958-68; 28th St Bapt Church Louisville, pastor 1960-68; Cooperative Ministries w/Natl Bapt So Bapt Conv, assoc dir, 1968-74; So Bapt Theol Sem Louisville, adj prof 1970-96; So Baptist Convention, dir dept of black church relations home missions bd 1974-88; Black Church Extension Division, Home Mission Board, SBC, director 1989-91; Christian Fellowship Baptist Church, College Park, GA, pastor, 1991-; Mercer Univ School of Theology, adjunct prof, 1996-. **Orgs:** Bd of dir Morehouse Sch of Religion 1972-85; mem Amer Soc of Missiology 1975-80; bd of trustees Interdenominational Theol Ctr 1978-; president elect, National Alumni Assn SBTS 1990-91, president 1991-92; co-chairman, Interdenomenational Theological Center, 1990-93, chair, 1993-96; Atlanta University Center, trustee, 1993-96; Truett McConnell College, trustee, 1994-. **Honors/Awds:** Hon DD Simmons Bible Coll 1965; Ambassador of Goodwill City of Louisville 1967; Hon DD United Theol Sem 1977; Victor T Glass Awd Home Mission Bd So Bapt Conv 1979; E Y Mullins Denominational Service Award, Southern Bapt Theological Seminary, 1990, E Y Mullins Humanitarian Award; American Baptist College, 1990. **Business Addr:** 1500 Norman Dr, College Park, GA 30349, (770)997-4087.

MCCALL, H. CARL
Comptroller. **Personal:** married Joyce Brown; children: Marci. **Educ:** Dartmouth Coll, Grad; Univ of Edinburgh, attended; Andover-Newton Theol Sem, MDiv. **Career:** UN under Pres Jimmy Carter, ambassador spec political affair; WNET-TV, sr vice pres 1981; New York State, candidate for lt gov 1982-; State of NY, senator 1974-79; Brooklyn Board of Education, president; State of New York, comptroller, 1993-. **Orgs:** Founder, past pres Inner City Broadcasting Corp; past chmn, ed bd NY Amsterdam news; dep admin NY City Human Resources Admin; chmn NY City Council Against Poverty 1966-69; ordained minister United Church of Christ; preaching minister Met Comm Methodist Church in Harlem; trustee NY Med Coll; vchmn, bd Ctr for NY Affairs of the New School; dir Blue Hill Protestant Ctr 1961-63; dir church comm serv New York City Missionary SOC 1964-; proj dir Taconic Found Inc, 1964-66; mem Gamma Delta Chi; Alpha Phi Alpha. **Honors/Awds:** Hon Canon of Cathedral of St John the Divine. **Business Addr:** Comptroller, State of New York, Alfred E Smith Office Bldg, 6th Fl, Swan St, Albany, NY 12236, (518)474-4040.

MCCALL, LOUIS. See Obituaries section.

MCCALL, MARION G., JR.
Physician. **Personal:** Born 1930, Birmingham. **Educ:** Fisk U, BA; Univ of MI, MS, MD; Providence Hosp Detroit, intern, res int med; Kresge Eye Inst, Wayne Univ Detroit, ophthal. **Career:** Pvt prac Detroit 1964-; MD MI & CA; cert Am Bd Ophthal 1968. **Orgs:** Mem NMA; AMA; Det, Wayne Co & MI Med Socs; Am Acad Ophthal; Gr Det Area Hosp Council; bd dirs Blue Cross Blue Shield, MI; adv com DeptSoc Serv Medicaid; chmn Com Socioeconomics, Wayne Co Med Soc.

MCCALL, NATHAN
Journalist. **Personal:** divoRced; children: Monroe, Ian, Maya. **Educ:** Norfolk State Univ, BA. **Career:** Virginia Pilot/Ledger Star, reporter; Atlanta Constitution, rep, until 1989; Washington Post, rep, 1989-; writer. **Special Achievements:** Has written autobiography Makes Me Wanna Holler: A Young Black Man in America, 1994; What's Going On, 1997; numerous articles and essays.

MCCALL, PATRICIA
Civil rights compliance coordinator. **Personal:** Born Jul 29, 1948, Columbus, OH; daughter of Mildred L Hollingsworth (deceased) and Theodore Hollingsworth Sr (deceased); married Jun 1, 1970 (divorced); children: Stacie R. **Educ:** Franklin University, 1979-81. **Career:** State of Ohio Civil Rights Commission, secretary, typist, 1973-74, administrative assistant, clerk staff supervisor, 1974-80, civil rights compliance coordinator, compliance officer, 1980-; Mary Kay Cosmetics, beauty consultant, 1996-. **Orgs:** National Association for Human Rights Workers, 1989-; Christ the King Catholic Church, special communion minister, 1986-, women's club, 1980-; Eastgate Elementary School, tutor/math, reading, 1991-; OCSEA-AFSCME Chapter 2540, steward secretary/treasurer, 1986-; Christ The King Catholic School Board, secretary, 1983-86; Bishop Hartley Athletic Board, secretary, 1986-89; National Nominating Committee, Outstanding Young Americans, 1996-. **Honors/Awds:** D&W Alinatha Estello Modeling Agency, Model of the Year, 1977; San Kuy Ninjabudo Martial Arts, 3rd Degree Brown Belt, 1972; Outstanding Young Woman of America, 1984. **Home Addr:** 3469 Liv-Moor Dr, Columbus, OH 43227, (614)235-0099. **Business Addr:** Civil Rights Compliance Coordinator, State of Ohio Civil Rights Commission, 1111 E. Broad Street Ste 301, Compliance Department, Columbus, OH 43215, (614)466-7384.

MCCALLA, ERWIN STANLEY
Business executive (retired). **Personal:** Born Dec 10, 1928, New York, NY; son of Isma I Levy; married Ruth Elizabeth Thomas, Apr 1, 1956; children: Kim, Ruth, Christopher, Richard. **Educ:** Elec Tech Acad of Aerontcs NY, AAS 1958; Engr Sci CW Post Coll Brookville NY, BS 1971. **Career:** Grumman Aerospace Corp, Bethpage, NY, vice pres facilities mgmt, 1986-90, retired, dir, engr test oprtns 1976-85, mgr affirm act progs 1976, grp head 1972, lab mgr 1970, proj test engr 1966, test engr 1958. **Orgs:** Mem, 1975, assoc fellow, 1985-, AIAA 1975; mem Toastmasters Intl 1975; mem ITEA 1980; mem NY Pioneer Track Club 1947; mem 5th AF/FEC Champ Track Team 1950; mem Urban League of LI 1973; chairman, Long Island Section of AIAA, 1983-85. **Honors/Awds:** Honoree Black Achievers in Ind YMCA of NY 1979; Occuptn Medal, 5 Bronze Stars AUS 1948-52; Basil Staros Memorial Award, AIAA-LI Section, 1985-86. **Military Serv:** AUS e6 1948-52. **Home Addr:** 100 Columbus Ave, Central Islip, NY 11722.

MCCALLUM, LEO. See SALAAM, ABDUL.

MCCALLUM, WALTER EDWARD
Dentist. **Personal:** Born Mar 13, 1936, Hendersonville, NC; son of Lucy Lillian McCallum-Dausuel; married Dolores Johnson; children: Robin, Todd Jason. **Educ:** Univ of Pittsburgh, BS 1959; Univ of Pittsburgh Sch of Dentistry, DDS 1962. **Career:** Lake Cty Comm Action Proj, treas of bd dir 1966-71; Lake Cty Jr College Med Dental Adv Comm, mem charter comm 1973-; Lake County Urban League, pres bd dir 1971-73; VTU Dental 1314 Navy Reserves, commanding officer 1979-81; private practice; Naval Reserve Dental Unit 113, commanding officer 1986-88. **Orgs:** Mem adv comm Partnership for Health Clinic 1973-75; chapter mem Natl Naval Officers Assn 1971-; mem Amer Dental Assn 1962-, Lake Cty Health Dept Dental Adv Comm 1982-84, Senator's Adlai Stevenson & Alan Dixon's Acad Selection Bds 1978-, North Suburban Branch of Chicago Dental Soc 1969-; Senator's Adlai Stevenson & Alan Dixon's Academy Selection Bds 1978-88. **Honors/Awds:** Plaque VTV Dental 1314 presented by Adm C Schreier for serv as Commanding Officer Navy 1981-83; citation presentd by Capt R D Porter of US Naval Acad for serv to Acad 1976; plaque Dental Adv Comm of Lake County Health Dept, Senators A Stevenson & A Dixon 1982-84; letter of appreciation for serv on Military Acad Selection Bd 1975-85; Plaque for Outstanding Naval Reserve Dental Unit in Redcom 13 1987. **Military Serv:** USNR Capt. retired 1988 after 30 years service, 27 years reserve and 3 years active duty. **Home Addr:** 594 Audubon Pl, Highland Park, IL 60035. **Business Addr:** Private Practice, 1800 Grand Ave, Waukegan, IL 60085.

MCCAMPBELL, RAY IRVIN
Singer/songwriter. **Personal:** Born Jun 22, 1959, Flint, MI; son of Victoria McCampbell and Ellsworth McCampbell. **Educ:** Olivet Coll, Olivet MI, Music, 1979; Texas Southern Univ, Houston TX, Bachelor of Communications, 1982. **Career:** Self Employed, saxophonist, 1975-77, singer, 1977-82, singer/songwriter 1983-87; MCA Records, Los Angeles CA, singer/

songwriter, 1987-; Lorimar Productions, Los Angeles CA, actor, 1988. **Orgs:** Mem, Kappa Alpha Psi Fraternity, 1980-; mem, Oak Cliff Bible Fellowship, 1983-. **Honors/Awds:** Symphonic Award, Flint Northwestern High School, 1977; NBA Pre-Game Song, Dallas Mavericks, 1988; Appearance, Lorimar Productions, 1988; NBA Legend's Allstar Pre-Game Song, NBA, 1989; Soul Train Performance, 1988; McDonald's Commercial, 1989; Dallas City Proclamation, 1989; Houston City Proclamation, 1989; Arsenio Hall Show Performance, 1989; member of The MAC Band; debut album The MAC Band Featuring The McCampbell Brothers.

MCCANE, CHARLOTTE ANTOINETTE
Educator (retired). **Personal:** Born in Washington, DC; daughter of Margaret Perea McCane (deceased) and Charles A McCane (deceased). **Educ:** Albright Coll, BA Hist; Univ of Mysore India, Fullbright Grant 1964; Northwestern Univ, NDEA Grant 1968; Fairleigh-Dickinson Univ, MA Hist. **Career:** New London CT Bd of Ed, educator 1957; Red Bank NJ Bd of Ed, educator 1957-69; Ridgewood NJ Bd of Ed, educator 1969-94. **Orgs:** Group leader World Youth Forum Tour of Europe 1965, Oper Crossroads Africa Liberia 1966; mem eval comm Middle State Assn for Secondary School, Yorkers & Hempstead School; mem NASDTEC Eval Comm, Princeton Univ, Glassboro State; assoc inst, adv comm Racism & Social Justice Natl Council for Social Studies; sec, treas Multicultural Ed SIG; mem Life Assoc for Study of Afro-Amer Life & History; mem Amer Assoc of Univ Women, NAACP; life mem Natl Council of Negro Women; Falmouth Woman's Club, AARP; Falmouth Senior Center; Anti-Racism Task Force. **Honors/Awds:** Article "Social Ed" Book Review Natl Council for Soc Studies 1980; publ article "Definition of Democracy" NY Herald Tribune 1964; extensive travel thru Africa, Asia, Europe, Latin Amer Central America, 1966-92. **Special Achievements:** Volunteer: Falmouth Public Library; East Falmouth Elementary School; Falmouth Historical Society. **Home Addr:** 493 Old Meeting House Road, East Falmouth, MA 02536.

MCCANNON, DINDGA FATIMA
Artiste, author, educator. **Personal:** Born 1947, Harlem, NY; daughter of Lottie Porter and Ralph Miller; married Percival E McCannon, 1967; children: Afrodesia, Harmarkhis. **Educ:** Bob Blackburn Workshop, Nyumba Ya Sanaa Galleries, attended; studied under: Charles Aston, Richard Mayhew, Al Hollingsworth, Abdullah Aziz. **Career:** Artist, author/illustrator, fashion designer, quiltmaker, teacher, currently. **Orgs:** Where We At, Black Women Artists. **Home Addr:** 800 Riverside Dr, New York, NY 10032. **Business Addr:** 800 Riverside Dr, New York, NY 10032.

MCCANTS, COOLIDGE N.
Attorney. **Personal:** Born Nov 17, 1925, Mobile, AL; married Elaine J; children: Kevin, Gary, Lisa. **Educ:** NY U, BS; Brklyn Law Sch, LLB. **Career:** Wshington Pvt Pract, atty 1960-; Legal Aid, Sup Ct Br, atty. **Orgs:** Mem Nat Am Washington & DC Bar Assns; Alpha Phi Alpha; Neighbors Inc. **Military Serv:** USAF. **Business Addr:** 7826 Eastern Ave, NW, Washington, DC 20012.

MCCANTS, JESSE LEE, SR.
Business executive. **Personal:** Born Feb 13, 1936, Fairfax, AL; son of Rosie McCants and Gabe McCants; married Hettie Jane Lindsay; children: Sheree Yvonne, Jesse Jr, Jacinta Lariece, Jerel Lindsay, Janella Larose. **Educ:** TN St U, M Deg Admin 1966; AL St U, BS 1958; Columbia Pacific University, San Rafael, CA, PhD 1990. **Career:** Allstate Loan & Inv Co, pres, fdr 1985; Peoples Bk of Chattanooga, chmn, organizer 1972-76; City Govt, admin 1969-72; Security Fed Svngs & Loan Assn, bd chmn, pres, fdr 1971-74; City of Chattanooga, tchr 1961-68. **Orgs:** Bd dir Chatta Chap of Nat Bus Leag; Am Diabetes Assn; Chatta Area Vo Tech Sch; Chatta E 5th St Day Care Ctr; bd chmn, dir Allstate Loan & Inv Co Inc; chmn, bd dir McCants Dev Co Inc; mem Kappa Alpha Psi Frat; active Corps of Execs; mem NAACP; mem Big Bros Assn; mem Better Bus Bur of Chatta. **Honors/Awds:** Black Businessman of Yr Award 1975; Disting Serv Award Jaycees 1972; Commd by Gov Winfield Dunn of TN rank of Col 1972. **Military Serv:** US Army sp4 1959-61. **Business Addr:** President, Allstate Investment Co, PO Box 16214, Chattanooga, TN 37416.

MCCANTS, KEITH
Professional football player. **Personal:** Born Nov 19, 1968, Mobile, AL. **Educ:** Alabama, majored in general studies. **Career:** Tampa Bay Buccaneers, linebacker, 1990-. **Honors/Awds:** CBS-TV Defensive Player of the Year, 1989; first-team choice on all three All-SEC Teams by AP, UPI, football coaches, 1989; All-America selection by AP, UPI, football coaches, 1989; Sports Illustrated Defensive Player of the Week.

MCCANTS, ODELL
Medical doctor. **Personal:** Born Sep 5, 1942, Winnsboro, SC; married Laura; children: Odell, Jr. **Educ:** Howard Univ, BS 1965, MD 1970. **Career:** Howard Univ Hosp, resident 1975; Automobiles Intl, ceo 1984-; Greater SE Comm Hosp Washington, president/designate 1985-; Automobiles Intl, broker and founder 1984-; Odell McCants MD, PC, president 1975-. **Orgs:** Fellow Amer Coll of Obstetricians and Gynecologists 1977-, Intl Coll of Surgeons 1977-; mayor's task force Adolescent Health City of Alexandria VA 1986-; instructor Howard Univ Coll of Medicine; house specialist Alexandria Hosp, and Dept of Health Commonwealth of VA 1982-; former dir United Black Fund of WA; bd of dir Northern VA 1978-79; mem & bd of dir American Cancer Soc 1983-. **Honors/Awds:** Daniel Hale Williams Awd Assoc of former Residents & Interns Freedmen's Hosp. **Business Addr:** 1600-K Crystal Sq Arcad, Arlington, VA 22202.

MCCARRELL, CLARK GABRIEL, JR.
Mechanical engineer. **Personal:** Born Apr 13, 1958, Chicago, IL; son of Mrs Melva Lee Washington McCarrell and Mr Clark G McCarrell Sr. **Educ:** Wright Coll, Chicago IL, AA Engineering, graduated with honors, 1984; Washington Coll, Chicago IL, dipl Computer Science, 1986; Univ of Nevada, Las Vegas NV, BS Mechanical Engineering, 1991; MS Engineering Management Candidate. **Career:** Donohue & Assocs, Milwaukee, WI, engineering aide, 1978-80; Consulting Consortium, Chicago, IL, engineering apprentice, 1980-82; Dunham & Assocs, Las Vegas, NV, mechanical designer, 1986-87; Science Application Inter Corp, Santa Barbara, CA, CAE designer, 1987-88; Clark County School District, Las Vegasm, NV, CAD designer, 1989-90; Southwest Gas Corp, Las Vegas, NV, 1990-. **Orgs:** Amer Soc of Mechanical Engineering, 1977-, National Soc of Black Engineers, 1979-; asst to program coord, Ray Coll of Design, 1983-86; Diaconate Bd, The Congressional Church of Park Manor United Church of Christ, 1984-86, Natl Fire Protection Assn; procurement consultant, Nevada Economic Devel Co, 1986; Amer Nuclear Soc, 1987-88, Amer Soc of Plumbing Engineering, 1987, National Soc of Professional Engineering; pres, (UNLV Chapter) Amer Soc of Heating, Ventilation & Air Conditioning Engineers, 1989; Student Advisory Committee UNLV, 1990; Mountain Top Faith Ministries, pres; Operations & Maintanance Aux, Toastmasters International, pres, 1993; Gas House Gang. **Honors/Awds:** Phi Theta Kappa Award, Phi Theta Kappa Honor Frat, 1984; ASHRAE Scholarship, Amer Soc of HVAC, 1988; Registered Engineer-In-Training (EIT), State of Nevada, 1994, (ET-2633); Spirit of Southwest Award, Outstanding Design & Comm Service, Southwest Gas Corp, 1993; Southern Nevada Chapter of ASHRAE, Citizen of the Year, 1992; Young Engineer of the Year, Nominee, 1994; Nevada Society of Prof Engineer, Most Promising Engineer Nominee-Black Engineer of the Year, 1993-94; Outstanding Alumni Award, Halls Franciscan High School, Chicago IL, 1994; Southwesterner of the Month, Southwest Gas, 1995; Prof Engineer (PE) Candidate, State of Nevada, 1995; Outstanding Young Men of America, 1986, 1987. **Business Addr:** Southwest Gas Corp, 4300 W Tropicana, Las Vegas, NV 89193.

MCCARTHY, GREGORY O'NEIL
Professional baseball player. **Personal:** Born Oct 30, 1968, Norwalk, CT. **Career:** Seattle Mariners, pitcher, 1996-. **Business Addr:** Professional Baseball Player, Seattle Mariners, 83 King St, 3rd Fl, PO Box 4100, Seattle, WA 98104, (206)628-3555.

MCCARTY, WALTER LEE
Professional basketball player. **Personal:** Born Feb 1, 1974, Evansville, IN. **Educ:** Kentucky. **Career:** New York Knicks, 1996-97; Boston Celtics, 1997-. **Special Achievements:** NCAA-Division I, Championship, 1996; NBA Draft, First round pick, #19, 1996. **Business Addr:** Professional Basketball Player, Boston Celtics, 151 Merrimac St, Boston, MA 02114, (617)523-3030.

MCCASKEY, DAPHNE THEOPHILIA (DAPHNE MCCASKEY ROBINSON)
Physician. **Personal:** Born Sep 26, 1912; married Dr Algernon Robinson; children: George A. **Educ:** Washington Sq Coll NYU, AB 1936; Howard Med Sch HU, MD 1941; Am Acad of Family Practice, FAAFP 1976. **Career:** Pvt Practice, md 1985. **Orgs:** Mem Med Soc of Co of NY; mem AAFP; mem NMA. **Honors/Awds:** Sojourner Truth Award, Nat Negro B & P Women's Clubs 1968.

MCCAULLEY, JAMES ALAN, III
Health services administrator. **Personal:** Born May 22, 1948, Huntsville, AL; son of Geraldine McCaulley and Alan McCaulley; married Mary L Cassels; children: Chenessa Vay, James Alan IV. **Educ:** Gen Motors Inst, Flint MI, BIE 1971; Michigan State Univ Lansing, MBA 1971; California Western Univ Santa Ana, PhD 1976. **Career:** Chenita Nursing Homes & Twin Oaks Living & Learning Ctr, adminstr 1985; Buick Motor Div Flint, personnel dir salaried employees 1971; Ashland Coll, prof 1985; McCaulley Dairy Inc, pres, owner; McCaulley Care Center, pres, owner; owner 4 other nursing homes. **Orgs:** Vice pres Ped Ctr 1985; qualified mental retardation professional OH Dept of Mental Health & Retardation 1985; bd mdm North Central Tech Coll 1985; bd mem Richland Ind 1985; mem Beta Gamma Sigma Man Hon Soc 1985; mem Tau Beta Pi Engr Hon Soc 1985; Licensed Social Worker. **Business Addr:** President, Owner, McCaulley Care Center, 1670 Crider Rd, Mansfield, OH 44903.

MCCLAIN, ANDREW BRADLEY
Educational administrator, attorney. **Personal:** Born Nov 12, 1948, Akron, OH; son of Margaret L Greene McClain and Andrew H McClain; children: Andrew, Peter. **Educ:** Univ of Akron, Akron, OH JD 1984-88; Kent State Univ Kent, OH, M Ed 1976-78; Univ of Akron Akron, OH, BA 1966-70. **Career:** Akron Bd of Educ, English teacher 1970-73; Western Reserve Acad, dir upward bound 1973-87; The Univ of Akron, dir upward bound 1987; Western Reserve Academy, Hudson, OH, dir Upward Bound 1973-87; Univ of Akron, dir pre college programs, 1988, dir of Academic Achievement Programs, currently; private practice, atty. **Orgs:** Consultant A Better Chance 1975-86; dir School Scholarship Serv 1979-84; consultant Mid-South Assoc of Independent Schools 1981-83, Marquette Univ 1984; mem former dir and pres state chap MAEOPP; mem NAACP; consultant, Natl Council of Educational Opportunity Assn, (NCEOA); parlamentarian, NCEOA, 1993-94; treasurer, Education Foundation Mid American Assn, Educ Opportunity Probram Personnel (MAEOPP), 1992-95; mem, African Amer Male Commission, 1989-. **Honors/Awds:** Fellowship Natl Assoc of Independent Schools 1982; Fellowship Inst for Educational Leadership 1982-; Ohio Assn of Educational Opportunity Program Personnel OAEOPP, James Rankin Award, 1990. **Business Addr:** Director, Academic Achievement Program, Gallucci Hall 112, The University of Akron, Akron, OH 44325-7908.

MCCLAIN, DOROTHY MAE
Government official (retired). **Personal:** Born Jun 17, 1931, Hartsville, SC; daughter of Eloise Eltridge Hunter and Chester Hunter; married Thurman McClain, Mar 31, 1950 (died 1987); children: Thurman Jr, Roxcella McClain Brown, Vaness McClain Smith. **Educ:** Washington Tech Inst, Certificate 1972; Howard Univ, Univ Without Walls 1980; Morgan State Univ. **Career:** DC Govt, clerk-typist 1962-79; DC Govt Newspaper Recycling, program coord 1979-81; DC Govt Environmental Serv, office supvr 1975-79; DC Govt Dept Public Works Mayor's Beautification Comm, exec dir 1984-89; McClain & Associates, president, currently. **Orgs:** Dir Ander-Mac Video Production 1983-84; bd dir Combine Communities in Action 1975-; councilwoman Town of Cheverly MD 1974-86; bd dir MD Municpal League 1977-78; pres Iota Phi Lambda Sor Epsilon Delta Chapter 1979-81; Prince George's County Public Schools, Group Activity Leader for Gladys Noon Spellman Elementary School (Before and After School Program), 1991-; Prince George's County Housing Development Corporation, board member; Prince George's County Voluntary Action Center, South County Representative, 1989-91. **Honors/Awds:** Certificate of Appreciation Dept Environmental Serv Women's Prog 1984, Adams-Morgan Comm; Outstanding Job Performance Dept Environmental Serv 1974, 1975, 1979, 1980; plaque 25th Legislative Distinguished Alliance Club 1976, Sorority of Year Iota Phi Lambda Sorority 1984, Outstanding Community Serv Los Amigos Serv Club 1976.

MCCLAIN, EARSALEAN J.
Educator (retired). **Personal:** Born Jul 28, 1910, Lexington, MS; daughter of Paralee Huckleby McClain and Sam McClain; married; children: 3. **Educ:** Jackson State Univ, BS; Eastern Michigan Univ, Graduate Work. **Career:** Holmes Co Tchng Unit, IPS tchr 1985; Holmes Co, IPS tchr 1975-; MAM Heroines of Jericho Local 7th Dist, jr atty; Holmes Co, notary pub 1975-; FDD Lexington MS, soc wkr. **Orgs:** Holmes Lexington Br NAACP; mem St Sci & Math Club; Lebanon MB Ch Chorus; pres Lebanon Pastors Aide Club; pres Women Fed Club; Lebanon MB Ch Grp; grp capt, tchr Sun Sch; usher supervisor, Lebanon MB Church; pros, Lexington Branch, NAACP, 1982-. **Honors/Awds:** Recip 30 yr Tchrs Award; life mem certificate, NAACP in 1985.

MCCLAIN, JAMES W.
Educator, administrator. **Personal:** Born May 14, 1939, Southern Pines, NC; son of Mary McClain and Wilton McClain; married Mary E Rafferty; children: James W Jr, Ellen M, Elizabeth A, Kimberly A, Kara J, Matthew A. **Educ:** Providence College, BA 1962. **Career:** McClain, McDaniel, Sullivan & Fowler Inc, pres 1968-77; Ford Motor Co, dealer develop 1977-80; Arthur D Little Co, sr consultant 1980-81; Boston Univ, dir of equal oppor 1982-. **Orgs:** Faculty mem Wheeler College Boston 1968-72, Newton College; mem Cardinal's Commn on Peace and Justice; chmn bd dirs Community Ctr School Newton MA 1985-86; bd mem Community Change Inc Boston 1985-86; regional dir Amer Assoc for Affirmative Action 1986-; bd mem Massachusetts chapter of Amer Society for Training and Development. **Honors/Awds:** Stoughton, Massachusetts, Jaycee Man of the Year, 1972. **Home Addr:** 32 Massapoag Ave, North Easton, MA 02356. **Business Addr:** Dir of Equal Opportunity, Boston University, 25 Buick St, Boston, MA 02215.

MCCLAIN, JEROME GERALD
Banking executive. **Personal:** Born Jun 2, 1939, Cleveland, OH; son of Lavonne S McClain and Johnny McClain; children: Jenee, Jennifer. **Educ:** Central State Univ, BS, education, 1963; American Institute of Banking, certificate, 1969. **Career:** Society Natl Bk, mgmt trainee 1965, asst br mgr 1967, br mgr 1969, asst vp, br mgr 1972, manager, 1974-79, vice pres community relations 1979, manager, 1979-86, vice pres corporate commu-

nity relations 1986-90, senior vice president, 1990-. **Orgs:** Alpha Phi Alpha Frat Inc; Phi Alpha Theta Hon Hist Frat; Blacks in Management, 1990-91; trustee, Cleveland Chapter, American Red Cross, 1990-91; treasurer, Historic Warehouse District Development Corp, 1990-91; Diversity Task Force, United Way Services, board member. **Honors/Awds:** Martin Luther King, Jr Community Service Award, African American Archives Auxiliary, 1991; Distinguished Leadership Award, United Negro College Fund, 1983; Humanitarian Award, Mt Pleasant Community Council, 1980. **Military Serv:** US Army, 1st Lt, 1963-65. **Business Addr:** Senior VP, Corporate Community Development, Society National Bank, 127 Public Square, 7th fl, Cleveland, OH 44114-1306.

MCCLAIN, KATRINA
Professional basketball player. **Personal:** Born Sep 19, 1965. **Educ:** Univ of Georgia, attended. **Career:** Atlanta Glory, forward, 1997-. **Honors/Awds:** National Player of the Year, 1987; US Olympic Basketball Team, Gold Medal, 1988, Bronze Medal, 1992; ABL All-Star, 1998. **Business Addr:** Professional Basketball Player, Atlanta Glory, 2100 Powers Ferry Rd, Ste 400, Atlanta, GA 30339, (770)541-9017.

MCCLAIN, PAULA DENICE
Educator. **Personal:** Born Jan 3, 1950, Louisville, KY; daughter of Mabel T Molock McClain (deceased) and Robert Landis McClain, Annette Williams Mcclain (stepmother); married Paul Crane Jacobson, Jan 30, 1988; children: Kristina L McClain-Jacobson, Jessica A McClain-Jacobson. **Educ:** Howard University, Washington, DC, BA, 1972, MA, 1974, PhD, 1977. **Career:** Univ of Wisconsin-Milwaukee, Milwaukee, WI, asst prof, 1977-82; Arizona State University, Tempe, AZ, assoc prof, professor, 1982-91; University of Virginia, professor, 1991-, department chair, 1994-97. **Orgs:** President, National Conference of Black Political Scientists, 1989-90; executive council, American Political Science Association, 1985-87, vice pres, 1993-94; executive council, Western Political Science Association, 1989-92; executive council, Southern Political Science Association, 1992-95. **Honors/Awds:** Graduate School of Arts & Sciences, Howard, Univ, Distinguished PhD Alumni Award, 1993; Policy Studies Organization, Miriam Mills Award, 1994. **Business Addr:** Professor, Woodrow Wilson Department of Government and Foreign Affairs, University of Virginia, 232 Cabell Hall, Charlottesville, VA 22901, (804)924-3614.

MCCLAIN, SHIRLA R.
Educator. **Personal:** Born Feb 4, 1935, Akron, OH; daughter of Marcella Macbeth Robinson and Dumas Robinson; married Henry McClain, Apr 6, 1957; children: Kelli Shimabukuro, Scott McClain. **Educ:** Univ of Akron, Akron OH, BS, 1956, MS, 1970, PhD, 1975. **Career:** Akron Public School, Akron OH, teacher and supervisor, 1956-76; Kent State University, Kent OH, prof of education, 1976-87; Walsh University, North Canton OH, prof of education, 1987-; asst director of teacher preparation, 1990-. **Orgs:** Mem, Assn of Teacher Educators, 1984-87, 1989-; mem, Univ of Akron Black Cultural Center advisory board, 1987. **Honors/Awds:** Author of numerous monographs, book chapters, and reviews; achievement award, Akron Urban League, 1975; distinguished black alumna award, Black Alumna Assoc of Univ of Akron, 1986; lifetime achievement award, Black United Students, Walsh College, 1988; distinguished educator award, Multicultural Education Special Interest Group of the Assn of Teacher Educators, 1989; Akron Grassroots Activist Award, University of Akron's Afro-American Studies, 1991; Alumni Honor Award for Excellence in Professional Achievement, Univ of Akron, 1994; Inducted into the Consortium of Doctors, Savannah GA, 1994. **Home Addr:** 865 Packard Drive, Akron, OH 44320.

MCCLAIN, WILLIAM ANDREW
Attorney. **Personal:** Born Jan 11, 1913, Sandford, NC; son of Blanche Leslie McClain (deceased) and Frank McClain; married Roberta White. **Educ:** Wittenburg Univ, AB 1934, Univ of Michigan, JD 1937. **Career:** City of Cincinnati, asst city solicitor 1942-57; Berry & McClain, mem 1938-58; City of Cincinnati, deputy city solicitor 1957-63, city solicitor 1963-72, acting city mgr 1968, 1972; Keating, Muething & Klekamp, mem 1972-73; Cincinnati Branch Small Business Admin, general counsel 1973-75; Hamilton County Common Pleas Court, judge 1975-77; Hamilton County Municipal Court, judge 1977-1980; Manley, Burke, Fischer, Lipton & Cook, mem 1980-. **Orgs:** Mem bd of dir Cincinnati Chapter Red Cross 1975-; Natl Conf Christians & Jews Cincinnati 1975-; Cincinnati Bar Assn, Amer Bar Assn & Natl Bar Assn; Amer Judicature Soc; Amer Bar Fnd; Cincinnati Bar Fnd; Fed Bar Assn; Prince Hall Mason 33 Degree; Alpha Phi Alpha. **Honors/Awds:** Wilberforce Univ, LLD 1963; Univ of Cincinnati, LLD 1971; Wittenberg Univ, LHD 1972. **Military Serv:** Judge Advocate General USA 1st lt 1943-46; Army Commendation Award 1945. **Home Addr:** 2101 Grandin Rd, Apt 904, Cincinnati, OH 45208.

MCCLAIN, WILLIAM L.
Automobile dealer. **Personal:** Born Apr 25, 1958, Bronx, NY; son of Jacqueline Francis Jackson Winters and Willie Lee McClain; married Pamela Kay Johnson, May 18, 1985. **Educ:** Oregon State Univ, Corvallis OR, BS Business Admin, 1981. **Career:** Zale Corp, Salem OR, mgr; Westside Timber Inc, vice pres, 1985-; Stayton Motors Inc, dealer, owner, 1985-; Jackies Ribs Inc, vice pres, 1985-; Reedsport Motors Inc, dealer, owner, 1988-.

MCCLAMMY, THAD C.
College president. **Personal:** Born Oct 22, 1942, Evergreen, AL; son of Ukla Maye McClammy and T C McClammy; married Patricia Larkins McClammy, Jun 5, 1966; children: Christopher, Patrice. **Educ:** Alabama State Univ, Montgomery AL, BA, 1966; Auburn Univ, Montgomery AL, MS, 1977. **Career:** City of Montgomery, Montgomery AL, real estate officer/broker, 1967-68, developer, 1968-72; Lomax-Hannon Jr Coll, Greenville AL, devel officer, 1974; Trenholm State Technical Coll, Montgomery AL, instructor, 1974-77, coord Community Serv, 1977-81, pres, 1981-. **Orgs:** Mem, Omega Psi Phi Frat, 1963-, Phi Delta Kappa Professional Council; mem, President's Club, Natl Democratic Party, 1976-80; mem, bd of dir, Montgomery Area United Way, 1982; mem, Lion's Club, 1987-. **Honors/Awds:** Honorary LLD, Selma University, 1984. **Business Addr:** President, Trenholm State Technical College, PO Box 9000, Montgomery, AL 36108.

MCCLANE, KENNETH ANDERSON, JR.
Educator. **Personal:** Born Feb 19, 1951, New York, NY; son of Genevieve Dora Greene McClane and Kenneth A McClane; married Dr Rochelle Evette Woods. **Educ:** Cornell Univ, AB (with distinction) 1973, MA 1975, MFA 1976. **Career:** Colby College, instructor of English 1974-75; City Univ of New York, asst dir of SEEK 1977-78; Williams College, Luce visiting prof of English 1983-84; Cornell Univ, asst prof of English 1976-83, assoc prof of English 1983-89, prof of English, beginning 1989, WEB DuBois professor of English, currently. **Orgs:** Dir, Creative Writing Program, Cornell Univ 1983-86; editor, Epoch Magazine, 1984-86; script consultant, ''The Bluest Eye,'' 1984; college scholar adv bd, Cornell Univ, 1984-; bd of dir, Human Affairs Training Program, 1986-; delegate, Modern Language Assn, 1989-. **Honors/Awds:** Clark Distinguished Teaching Award, 1983; books of poetry include A Tree Beyond Telling, Poems, Selected and New, published 1983, and Take Five: Poems 1971-1986, published 1988; essays include ''A Death in the Family'' 1985 Antioch Review, ''The School'' 1985 Northwest Review, ''Walls, A Journey to Auburn'' 1987 Community Review; essay ''Walls'' selected for inclusion in Best American Essays of 1988, ed by Robert Atwan and Annie Dillard, Ticknor and Fields, 1989; author Walls: Essays 1985-90, Wayne State Univ Press, 1991. **Home Addr:** 114 Glenside Rd, Ithaca, NY 14850. **Business Addr:** Professor, Cornell University, Dept of English, Ithaca, NY 14853.

MCCLASKEY, WILLIAM H.
Attorney. **Personal:** Born Jun 24, 1912, Louisville, KY; married Belma D Pleasant; children: William H. **Educ:** Univ of Louisville (LMC), AB 1936; IN U, Bus Admin 1936-37; John Marshall Law Sch Chicago IL, JD 1950. **Career:** Priv Prac, atty 1985; Comm Serv Admin Chicago Reg Ofc, chief operatns div 1975-78; OEO/CSA Legal Serv Prog Chicago Reg, reg dir 1967-75; Ofc of Chief Cnsl IRS Philadelphia Reg Ofc, staff atty 1964-66; Purdue Univ Calumet Dev Found, atty 1960-62; Moore Ming & Leighton Chicago, atty 1950-59; Gary IN City Ct, spl judge 1963-64. **Orgs:** Dir Louiseville Urban Leag 1979-; life mem NAACP 1976; trustee Good Shepherd Cong Ch Chicago 1960-70; mem Kappa Alpha Psi Frat Louisville Alumni Chap 1978; %Dir Louisville Area Primary Care Consortium 1980-; KY Bar Assn Frankfort KY 1978; Louisville Bar Assn Louisville KY 1978; Plymouth Cong Ch Louisville KY 1980. **Honors/Awds:** Recip Am & Victory Awards USN 1946; Order of John Marshall Hon, John Marshall Law Sch Chicago 1950. **Military Serv:** USN av storekep 2c, 2 1/2 srvd.

MCCLEAN, VERNON E.
Educator. **Personal:** Born Sep 17, 1941, St Thomas, Virgin Islands of the United States; married Freda McClean; children: Malaika, Maliki, Macheo. **Educ:** St Augustine's Coll, BA 1965; Atlanta U, MA 1967; Columbia U, EdD 1975; Johns Hopkins U, Further Study; Yale U; University of Michigan. **Career:** Paine Coll, tchr 1966-67; William Paterson Coll NJ, professor, 1969-. **Orgs:** Life mem S Hist Assn; mem Assn for the Study of Negro Life & Hist; Assn Soc & Behavioral Scintsts; former natl pres Sigma Rho Sigma Hon Soc; found BASE; NOMAS, National Organization for Men Against Sexism. **Honors/Awds:** Pub UJAMAA, WPC Journal of Black Studies; estblshmnt of Vernon E McClean Award 1972; fellows Danforth Found 1971-72; inst in S & Black Hist 1967-69. **Special Achievements:** Author, Solutions to Problems of Race, Class, and Gender (with Lois Lyles), Kendall/Hunt Publishing Company, Dubuque, Iowa, 1993; editor, Brother: The Newsjournal of the National Organization for Men Against Sexism; Published articles in The New York Times, The City Sun, Brooklyn NY, The GlenRidge paper, GlenRidge, NJ, The Nutley Journal, Nutley, NJ, The Irvington Herald, Irvington, NJ, Dawn Magazine, Washington, DC. **Business Addr:** Educator, African-American & Caribbean Studies, William Paterson Univ, 300 Pompton Rd, Wayne, NJ 07470.

MCCLEARN, BILLIE
Community service activist. **Personal:** Born Aug 6, 1937, Cushing, TX; daughter of Ida G Smith and Charlie Smith; married Sylvester McClearn, Nov 30, 1957; children: Richard Kyle, Michael Anthony, Sylvester Darnell, Billy Cathel, Alex Bernard. **Career:** Black Community Development, Inc, executive director, 1979-. **Honors/Awds:** Newburgh Free Academy, Humanitarian Award, 1987; Newburgh City School District, Sojourner Truth Youth Community Service Award, 1987; NAACP, Distinguished Service Award, 1989; Black Ministerial Association, Distinguished Service Award, 1989; Coalition for People's Rights, Recognition Award, 1991. **Business Addr:** Executive Director, Black Community Development, Inc, Liberty St, #245, Newburgh, NY 12550, (914)561-2107.

MCCLEAVE, MANSEL PHILIP
Minister, educator. **Personal:** Born Aug 7, 1926, Rock Hill, SC. **Educ:** NC Agr & Tech Coll, BS 1950, MS 1959; NY School of Floral Design, Graduate 1953; NC St U; Univ of NC; Friendshp Coll Rock Hill SC, DD 1970. **Career:** First Bapt Ch Siler City NC, pastor 1957-70; Edwards Grove Church Liberty NC, pastor 1958-81. **Orgs:** Pres Deep River Bapt Training Union 1943-66; instr of horticulture NC Agr & Tech St Univ 1953-; pastor Edwards Grove Missionary Bapt Ch, Liberty NC 1958-; moderator Deep River Missionary Bapt Assn 1959-; mem Am Assn Univ Prof; mem gen bd Gen Bapt St Conv of NC; mem adv bd Hm Hlth Srvs, RandolphCo Hlth Dept; Intrntl Black Writers Conf, Greensboro Pulpit Forum; Liberty Ministerial Assn; Greensboro Ministers Flwshp; Am Horticultural Soc; org, found Liberty Imprvmnt Assn; committeeman BS of Am; mem Phi Beta Sigma Frat; Hayes-Taylor YMCA; Hampton Inst Alumni Assn. **Honors/Awds:** Honorary DD Frndshp Coll Rock Hill SC; Gamma Sigma Delta Hon Soc of Agriculture; author of publs, Murmurs of the Heart A Collection of Poems Vantage Press 1976, The Story of the Deep River Missionary Assn of NC & Its Auxiliaries, Deep River Missionary Baptist Assoc Ushers' History & Resource Manual. **Military Serv:** WW II staff sgt.

MCCLEAVE, MILDRED ATWOOD POSTON
Educator (retired). **Personal:** Born Dec 19, 1919, Memphis, TN; daughter of Ellen Winston Poston (deceased) and Carl Rivers Poston (deceased); married Ben F McCleaye Jr; children: Benjamin F III, Robert A, William S, Bruce P. **Educ:** LeMoyne Coll, BA 1941; Univ of Denver, MA 1971; postgraduate, Univ of Northern Colorado; postgraduate, Colorado University; Adams State. **Career:** Memphis Publ Schl, tchr 1941-52; Denver Publ Schl, tchr cnslr 1958-85; Hill Middle Schl, cnslr, retired. **Orgs:** Natl Educ Assn; CO Educ Assn; Denver Classroom Tchrs Assn; CO School Counselrs Assn; Amer Personnel & Guidance Assn; pres & charter mem Denver Chap Jack & Jill of Amer Inc 1954-; dist capt Denver Rep Party 1962-; alt delegate Natl Rep Conv 1972; secr CO Black Rep 1970-1980; Alpha Kappa Alpha Sor 1941-; appeared in nationwide NBC-TV movie The Case of the Long Lost Love, 1987, and The Case of the Murdered Madame. **Honors/Awds:** Distinguished Tchr Award Denver CO 1983; CO Tchr of the Year Special Recognition State of CO 1984; CO Educ Assn Human Rel Award State of CO 1984; Outstanding Serv in fld of Educ Epsilon Sigma Alpha Sor 1984; Award of Excellence Denver Chapter; by executive order of Richard D Lamm, Governor of Colorado, May 21, 1985 proclaimed Mildred McCleave Day. **Home Addr:** 1606 Jamison Pl, Longmont, CO 80501.

MCCLELLAN, EDWARD J.
Transportation company executive. **Personal:** Born Dec 12, 1921, Chicago, IL; son of Clara Moses McClellan and Jay McClellan; married Emma G Johnson McClellan, Apr 28, 1943; children: Kenneth Wesley McClellan. **Educ:** Governors State University, University City IL, BA, 1983. **Career:** City of Chicago Police Dept, patrolman, 1949-66; NAACP, Chicago IL, urban program dir, 1966-70; State of IL, Notary Public, 1970-; US Postal Service, Chicago IL, br mgr security, 1970-76, br mgr EEO, 1976-84; Willett Corporation, Chicago IL, pres Spears School Bus Div, 1984-86; EJ McClellan & Associates, pres, 1985-; Multi-Pure Corp, distributor, 1988-. **Orgs:** Mem, Salem Lutheran Church, 1953-; NAACP, Southside Chicago Branch, 1964-; mem, Museum of Science & Industry, 1983-; mem, Art Institute of Chicago, 1985-. **Honors/Awds:** Service Award, Chicago Boys Club, 1969; Leadership Award, NAACP, 1970; Service Award, Illinios Law Enforcement Comm, 1971; Employee of the Year (nominee), US Postal Service, 1974; Distinguished Service Award, Willett Corp, 1987. **Military Serv:** US Army, 1st Lt, 1942-48; received 4 campaign ribbons, combat infantryman badge. **Home Addr:** 5555 S Everett Ave, Chicago, IL 60637.

MCCLELLAN, FRANK MADISON
Attorney, educator. **Personal:** Born Feb 5, 1945, Marion, SC; married Linda J Hughey; children: Malik, Toussaint. **Educ:** Rutgers U, AB 1967; Duquesne U, JD 1970; Yale U, LLM 1974. **Career:** Duquesne U, prof of law 1985, asso prof of law 1974-76, asst prof of law 1972-74; Wilmer Cutler & Pickering, asso atty 1971-72; Chief Judge William H Hastie, US Ct of Appeals, law clerk. **Orgs:** Mem PA Bar Assn; mem DC Bar Assn; bd dir House of the Crossroads; law rev ed United Way Rev Com. **Honors/Awds:** Merit Award; Felix S Cohen Prize; publ Law Review Articles. **Business Addr:** 600 Forbes Ave, Pittsburgh, PA 15219.

MCCLELLAND, MARGUERITE MARIE
Educator (retired). **Personal:** Born Dec 6, 1919, St Louis, MO; daughter of Minnie Mae Marshall Hubbard and Brooks Manuel Hubbard Sr; married John Clyde McClelland, Sep 2, 1972. **Educ:** School of the Art Inst of Chicago, Chicago IL, BA, 1943; Wayne State Univ, Detroit MI, MA, 1949; postgraduate study at Temple Univ, Philadelphia PA, 1963, Univ of Michigan, Ann Arbor MI, 1975, and Wayne State Univ. **Career:** Chicago Public Schools, Chicago IL, art teacher, 1943-47; Detroit Public Schools, Detroit MI, student teacher and supervisor of Wayne State Univ teachers of art education, 1948-78, guidance counselor, 1963-78, guidance dept head, 1978-83. **Orgs:** Supreme basileus, Natl Sorority of Phi Delta Kappa, 1989-; mem, American Guidance Assn; mem, Natl Council of Negro Women; mem, Natl Assault on Literacy; life mem, NAACP; mem, Natl Assn of Univ Women; mem, Organization of School Administrators; mem, Michigan Personnel and Guidance Assn; mem, Michigan Assn for Career Education; mem, Detroit School Women's Assn; mem, United Methodist Women; mem, Top Ladies of Distinction; member, Alpha Kappa Alpha Sorority Inc, 1949-. **Honors/Awds:** Teachers Medal, Valley Forge Freedom Foundation; Teacher of the Year Award, Detroit Education Assn; Industrial Arts Award, Ford Motor Co; State of Mich, City of Detroit, and Detroit Board of Education resolutions; co-author of Art Education Guide, Grades 7-8-9 for Detroit Public Schools; author of The Language of Child Art; author of Education in Spain: A Comparative Report; author of A Handbook for Art Education Student Teachers; Assault on Illiteracy Service Award; Alpha Rho Chap ter Service Award; State of Tennessee, Outstanding Service Award, Aide De Camp Award, Certificate of Appreciation; Spirit of Detroit Award; Dorcas Society of Detroit, Exceptional Achievement, Outstanding Leadership; National Theological Seminary of the Commonwealth University, Honorary Doctorate of Humane Letters. **Home Addr:** 19211 Pennington Dr, Detroit, MI 48221.

MCCLENDON, CAROL A.
Public official. **Personal:** Born Aug 21, 1942, Cleveland; married William C; children: William Jr, Kelley. **Educ:** So U. **Career:** Cuyahoga Co Auditors Ofc, dep admnstr; NE OH Area Wide Asso Agy, prgm mgr/compliance ofcr; City of Cleveland, councilman. **Orgs:** Exec com Cuyahoga Co Dem Party 1972; apptd to state com 1972; first black elected Dem Nat Committeewoman in history of state of OH; elected v-chmn Cuyahoga Dem Party 1975.

MCCLENDON, KELLEN
Lawyer, educator. **Personal:** Born May 7, 1944, New Castle, PA; son of Sylest Butler McClendon and LeRoy McClendon; married Michele McClendon. **Educ:** Westminster Coll, BA 1966; Duquesne Univ School of Law, 1974. **Career:** PA Dept of Justice, asst attny gen 1974-79; Private practice, attny 1979-; City of Pittsburgh, asst city solicitor 1982-89; Robert Morris Coll Legal Asst Prog, instructor 1985-89; Duquesne Univ School of Law, adjunct prof 1987-89, visiting prof 1989-90, assistant professor, 1990-. **Orgs:** Mem Allegheny Cty Bar Assoc 1974-; minority bus enterprise review comm City of Pittsburgh 1982-; board of directors, Housing Authority of City of Pittsburgh, 1990-. **Military Serv:** USAF capt 1967-71; Bronze Star; Vietnam Serv Medal. **Business Addr:** Asst Prof, Duquesne University, School of Law, 900 Locust St, Pittsburgh, PA 15282.

MCCLENDON, LLOYD GLENN
Professional baseball player. **Personal:** Born Jan 11, 1959, Gary, IN; son of Hattie McClendon and Grant McClendon; married Ingrid Scott, Feb 14, 1981; children: Schenell, Beaudillio. **Educ:** Valparaiso University. **Career:** Cincinnati Reds, 1987-88; Chicago Cubs, 1989-90; Pittsburgh Pirates, 1990-. **Orgs:** Kappa Alpha Psi Fraternity. **Honors/Awds:** Valparaigo Univ, Alumni Achievement Award, 1993. **Special Achievements:** Batted 1000, all homeruns, for first all Black Team in Little League World Series, 1971; Little League Hall of Fame; All State in baseball in high school; Tied National League record for consecutive hits, 5, in National League Championship Series; played in four straight National League Championship Series; founded McClendon's Atheletes Against Crime, MAAC; Set Natl League record at 8 consecutive hits. **Business Addr:** Professional Baseball Player, Pittsburgh Pirates, c/o Sports Development Ltd, 8401-A Mayland Dr, Richmond, VA 23294.

MCCLENDON, MOSES C.
Materials engineer (retired). **Personal:** Born Dec 11, 1934, Graceville, FL; son of Virginia McClendon and Harry McClendon; married Grace Jones McClendon, Jun 24, 1962; children: Chantelle M, Michelle R, Moses C II. **Educ:** Edward Waters Coll, Jacksonville FL, AA, 1954; Morris Brown Coll, Atlanta GA, BA, 1957; North Carolina A&T State Univ, Greensboro NC, MS, 1967. **Career:** Washington Bd of Educ, Chipley FL, asst principal, math/science teacher, 1960-66; Bell Telephone Labs, Winston-Salem NC, assoc mem of tech staff, 1967-70; Western Electric, Greensboro NC, materials engineer, 1971-80; AT&T Technologies, Richmond VA, dept chief, Materials Engineering, 1980-88; AT&T Microelectronics, Richmond VA, sr materials engineer, beginning 1988. **Orgs:** Mem, The Soc of Plastic Engineers, 1975-87, The Amer Chemical Soc, 1980-86; instructor, Richmond Area Program for Minorities in Engineering, 1984-86; mem, YMCA, 1985-87, Amer Mgmt Assn, 1987-88, NAACP, 1987-, Black Exec Exchange Program, 1988. **Honors/Awds:** Beta Kappa Chi, Natl Science Soc, 1956; Reaction of Selected Hydrazino Phosphonate, Phrosphorium Bromides and Phosphorane, 1967; Evaluation of One Component Silicone Encapsulant, 1967; Cost Reduction of Power Transformers by Plastics Encapsulants, 1968; Differential Scanning Calorimetric Evaluation of B-Staged Epoxy Resin, 1972; Sigma Man of the Year, Phi Beta Sigma Frat Inc, 1980; Morris Brown Coll Athletic Hall of Fame, Morris Brown Coll, 1988. **Military Serv:** AUS, E4, 1957-60.

MCCLENDON, RAYMOND
Investment banker. **Educ:** Morehouse College, BA; Georgia State University, MBA. **Career:** Federal National Mortgage Association, Mutli-Family Activities, vice president; RL McClendon Capital Corp, founder; Pryor, McClendon, Counts & Co, vice chairman, CEO, currently. **Special Achievements:** Ranked second among African-American owned investment banks, Black Enterprise, 1992. **Business Phone:** (404)875-1545.

MCCLENIC, DAVID A.
Attorney, business executive. **Personal:** Born Mar 6, 1926, Akron, OH; married Zenobia; children: Lisa, Brian. **Educ:** Akron U, BS 1951; Akron Law Sch, JD 1956; Life Underwrtrs Training Cncl; CLU. **Career:** Det Bank & Trust Co, asst vp, trust dept 1971-, Asst trust ofcr 1968-71, trust adminstr 1967-68, trust consult 1965-67; Metropolitan & Life Ins Co, ins consult 1961-65; Richard H Austin & Co, acct 1958; W Howard Fost Law Off, legal clk 1957-58; Peavy Rlty Co, salesman, gen mgr 1953-58; Goodyear aircraft Corp, assemblyman 1952-57; Notary Pub, 1985. **Orgs:** Mem MI & Detroit Bar Assns; Am Arbitration Assn; Wolverine Bar Assn; CLU. **Military Serv:** AUS 1944-46.

MCCLENIC, PATRICIA DICKSON
Executive administrator. **Personal:** Born Nov 13, 1947, Akron, OH; children: Richard L Jr; Dennis K, Nicole M. **Educ:** Akron Univ, BA 1971-78. **Career:** WSLR Radio, dir of public affairs 1970-75; United Way of Summit Cty, dir of comm 1975-79; United Way of South Hampton, dir of comm 1979-83; Amer Cancer Society, state public information dir 1983-84; United Way of Amer, assoc dir 1984-. **Orgs:** Mem Public Relations Soc of America 1979-; mem Intl Assn of Bus Comm 1978-; mem Natl Press Club 1985. **Home Addr:** 6050 Haverhill Ct, Springfield, VA 22152. **Business Addr:** Associate Dir, United Way of America, 701 North Fairfax, Alexandria, VA 22314.

MCCLENNEY, EARL HAMPTON
Educational administrator. **Personal:** Born Mar 4, 1907, Marion, AL; married Fannie M; children: Earl Jr, Clifton, Gail, Neil, Henry Clay IV. **Educ:** A&T St U, BS 1930; Cornell U, MS 1938; PA St U, DD 1942; VA Theol Sem, LLD; St Paul's Coll, LLD. **Career:** Educ Admin, consult 1985; St Augustine's Coll, tchr 1938-47. **Orgs:** Pres Assn of Episc Coll 1970-83; coll pres Voorhees Coll St Paul's Coll 1947-49; mem St Bd Comm Coll VA 1985; mem VA Minority Commn 1985; chmn of bd Southside Sr Citizens Ctr Inc; vice pres PD XIII VA 1985; treas Univ of Black Episcopalian Inc.

MCCLEON, DEXTER
Professional football player. **Personal:** Born Oct 9, 1973. **Educ:** Clemson, bachelor's degree in management, 1996. **Career:** St Louis Rams, defensive back, 1997-. **Business Addr:** Professional Football Player, St Louis Rams, One Rams Way, St Louis, MO 63045, (314)982-7267.

MCCLESKEY, J.J.
Professional football player. **Personal:** Born Apr 10, 1970, Nashville, TN; married Susan. **Educ:** Tennessee, bachelor's degree in political science. **Career:** New Orleans Saints, defensive back, 1994-96; Arizona Cardinals, 1996-. **Business Addr:** Professional Football Player, Arizona Cardinals, 8701 S Hardy, Tempe, AZ 85284, (602)379-0101.

MCCLINTON, CURTIS R., JR.
Investment banker. **Personal:** Born in Muskogee, OK; married Devonne French MD; children: Tobi, Margot. **Educ:** Cntrl MI U, MPA; Univ of KS, BS; Univ of NE, Sch of bkng; Univ of MO, Real Est Law; Am Inst of Bkng; Weaver Sch of Real Est Pract Franklin Fin Serv Inst; Real Est Bd Inst; Wharton Sch, Univ of PA. **Career:** Black Ec Union of Gr KC, pres, fdr, xec dir 1985; Midwest Prog Svc, lectr 1974-; Franklin Fin Svcs, reg securities broker, dealer 1974-; Tech Fab Inc, gen mgr, pres 1972-; Swope Pky Nat Bk, fdr, exec vice pres 1969; Douglass St Bk, comm loan ofcr, asst cashier 1965-67; KPRS, tv, radio brdcstr 1965-66; Interstate Securities, loan ofcr, collector 1964-65; Franklin Life Ins Co, ins salesman 1963-; Professional Ftbl Club 1962-70; Professional Concert Singer;U of KS, asst ftbl coach, recruiter 1962-63. **Orgs:** Mem Am Mgmt Assn; Black Ec Union of Gr KC; C of C fo Gr KC; Nat Assn of Mkt Devs; Nat Bkrs Assn; Nat Security Dealers Assn; past pres Comm Ec Dev Congress; Cnsl on Urban Ec Dev; Mid-Am Reg Cncl; Planned Ind Expansion Com of City of KC; Univ of MO Ext Prog Adv Cncl Flwshp of Christian Athlts; Kappa Alpha Psi Frat; NAACP; Urban Leag; YMCA; mem, bd of dir Who's Who of Outstndng Young Men of Am; St Mary's Hosp; United Negro Coll Fund; Selec Cnsl Sch of Med Univ of MO at KC. **Honors/Awds:** All-Pro Fullback, KC Chiefs, World Champs 1970; All Am, Univ of KS; All Big 8 High Hurdle Champ 1960-61; recip C of C Ldr of Mon 1970; runner-up to MrKS Cit Annual C of C Hon 1970; Outst Cit Award, Presby Interracial Cncl; Outst Young Am 1971; Boss of Yr, KC Jr C of C 1975. **Military Serv:** AUS. **Business Addr:** 2502 Prospect, Kansas City, MO 64127.

MCCLINTON, SUZANNE Y.
Business owner. **Personal:** Born Sep 5, 1955, Chicago, IL; daughter of Essie McDonald and Willie B. McDonald; divorced; children: Jamila Makini. **Educ:** University of Illinois, BA, 1976; University of Chicago, MBA, 1978. **Career:** First National Bank of Chicago, portfolio manager, 1977, security analyst, 1978-79; CEDCO Commercial Credit, co-manager, 1979-81, manager, 1981-82; McClinton Management Services Inc, president, 1981-. **Orgs:** Probe Inc, 1982; Chicago Regional Purchasing Council, 1984-86; YWCA, director, 1987; Cosmopolitan Chamber of Commerce, treasurer, 1984-89. **Honors/Awds:** Black Women's Hall of Fame, Kizzy Award for Professional Achievement, 1985; Dollar & Sense, Chicago's Up and Coming Black Business and Professional Women, 1985; CCUP, Outstanding Professional Award, 1986; National Association of Negro Business and Professional Women's Club Inc, 1986; League of Black Women, Black Rose Award, 1988. **Special Achievements:** Author, "How to Finance Your Salon," 1984; co-author, "Family Networking Makes Good Business Sense," 1990; interviewed, "Are You Living Beyond Your Means?" 1991. **Business Addr:** President, McClinton Management Services Inc, 330 South Wells St, Ste 922, Chicago, IL 60606, (312)922-3194.

MCCLOMB, GEORGE E.
Educator. **Personal:** Born Apr 24, 1940, Long Island, NY; married Audrey Hamilton; children: George Jr. **Educ:** Colgate U, BA 1962; Univ of Pittsburgh, MSW 1964, MA Polit Sci 1974, PhD Polit Sci 1984. **Career:** Univ of Pittsburgh, assoc prof 1973-, guest lectr 1970, adj asst prof 1969; hlth care consult 1971-72; Hlth Sys, asst dir 1971-73; Homewood Brushton Hlth Ctr, proj dir 1968-71, asst proj dir 1967-68. **Orgs:** Pres, bd dir Lemington Hm for Aged 1971-83; bd dir W PA Comprehensive Hlth Plng Agy; W PA Reg Med Prog; Visiting Nrs Assn; Pittsburgh Model Cities Hlth Task Force; Urban Leag Hlth Com; Comprehensive Care Task Force, Sickle Cell Anemia; commr Pub Pkng Auth City of Pittsburgh; commr Prog to Aid Citizen Enterprise; delegate White House Conf on Aging 1981; del Penna State Conf on Aging 1984. **Honors/Awds:** Outstndng Vol Award, Allegheny Co United Way; Allegheny Co Med Soc Outstanding Citizens Awd 1981; Pittsburgh Fed Exec Bd 2nd Annual Black History Awd for Community Serv 1983. **Military Serv:** USAF 1st lt 1964-67. **Business Addr:** Assoc Prof, Chmn Admin, Univ of Pittsburgh, 2201 Cathedral of Learning, School of Social Work, Pittsburgh, PA 15260.

MCCLOUD, AARON C.
Educator. **Personal:** Born Oct 28, 1933, Saginaw, MI; married Doris Jean Godbee; children: Sylvia Lynn, Monica Delis. **Educ:** AA 1954; BA Pub Admin 1957; MA Guid & Cncl 1966-67; EdD Ldrshp in Curr 1973. **Career:** Eng & soc studies tchr 1960-68; cnslr 1968; evening adult ed 1967-69. **Orgs:** Pres MI Assn of Supv for Curr Dev 1969; mem Phi Delta Kappa 1972; pres, exec bd Hampton PTA 1971-72; exec bd Winterhalter PTA 1966-67; mem Concerned Cit for Action 1966-70; mem Messiah Bapt Ch; pres Mumford Constel Cit Grp 1968-71. **Honors/Awds:** Recip Whitney Young, Outstndng Contri Black Culture 1971; WJR Radio, Outstndng Comm Contrib 1970. **Military Serv:** US military 1958-59. **Business Addr:** 2470 Collingwood, Detroit, MI 48206.

MCCLOUD, ANECE FAISON
Educational administrator. **Personal:** Born May 29, 1937, Dudley, NC; daughter of Nancy Simmons Cole; married Verable L; children: Vernece Lynn, Carla D. **Educ:** Bennett Coll, BS 1959; Univ of NE at Omaha, MA 1989. **Career:** Lincoln Jr High School, teacher 1959-60; Univ of NE Med Ctr, asst registrar 1972-76, dir of minority affairs 1976-85, asst instructor med jurisprudence & humanities 1980-85; Washington and Lee Univ, assoc dean of students 1985-. **Orgs:** Peer reviewer health career oppor prog grant 1982-84; Div of Disadvantaged Assist Bureau of Health Prof HHS; consultant Life and Career Planning Workshop Urban League of NE 1985; mem bd dirs Rockbridge Comm Unit Amer Cancer Soc Virginia Div 1986; mem Natl Assn for Women Deans Admins & Counselors, Amer Assn for Counseling and Develop, Assn for Multicultural Counseling and Develop, Natl Assn for Foreign Student Advisors, The Assn of Amer Medical Colls. **Honors/Awds:** Certificate Black History Month Program Speaker Veterans Admin Medical Ctr Omaha 1984; Certificate Acknowledgement of Contribution to Educ Omaha Public Schools 1984; Plaque in Appreciation Minority Health Career Oppor 1984; Plaque in Appreciation Student Natl Medical Assoc UNMC Chap 1985. **Business Addr:** Assoc Dean of Students, Washington & Lee University, Payne Hall 3, Lexington, VA 24450.

MCCLOUD, GEORGE AARON
Professional basketball player. **Personal:** Born May 27, 1967, Daytona Beach, FL; son of George McCloud (deceased). **Educ:** Florida State Univ, Tallahassee, FL, 1985-89. **Career:** Indiana Pacers, forward, 1989-93; Scavolini Pesaro (Italy), 1993-94; Rapid City Thrillers (CBA), 1994-95; Dallas Mavericks, 1995-96; Los Angeles Lakers, 1996-97; Phoenix Suns, 1997-. **Special Achievements:** NBA Draft, First round pick, #7, 1989. **Business Addr:** Professional Basketball Player, Phoenix Suns, PO Box 515, Phoenix, AZ 85001, (602)379-7867.

MCCLOUD, J. OSCAR
Clergyman. **Personal:** Born Apr 10, 1936, Waynesboro, GA; married Robbie J Foster; children: Ann Michelle, Cassandra Anita, Tony Delancy. **Educ:** Warren Wilson Coll Swannanoa NC, AA 1956; Berea Coll Berea KY, BA 1958; Union Theol Sem NY, MDiv 1961. **Career:** Davis St Untd Pres Ch, Raleigh NC, pastor 1961-64; Untd Pres Ch, Atlanta GA, fld rep, bd christian ed 1964-67; Div of Ch & Race Bd Nat Missns, asso 1968-69; Untd Pres Ch NY, Div of Ch & Race Bd of Nat Missns, asso chrmn for opertns 1969-71; Gen Sec Comm on Ecumcl Missn & Rel, asso general sec, 1971-72; The Program Agency United Presbyterian Church NY, gen dir 1972-86; The Fund for Theol Educ New York, exec dir, 1986-95; Fifth Ave Presbyterian Church, currently. **Orgs:** Bd dir Sthrn Chrstn Ldrshp Conf; GA Cncl of Chs; Blk Pres Untd, Nat Conf of Blk; vchrprsn Div Overseas Ministries, Nat Cncl of Chs; mem Commn on World Mission & Evangelism, World Council of Churches, GZ Cncl on Hum Rel; mem NE Comnty OrgC Teaneck; Proj Eqlty Inc Nat; proj coord Am Forum for Intnl Stdy Tour to W Africa 1971; mem exec comm, central comm World Council of Churches; mem exec comm, governing bd Natl Council of Churches in the USA; Chair, Advisory Bd on Commun Relations, Teaneck, NJ. **Honors/Awds:** Hon Deg DD, Mary Holmes Coll, W Point MS 1974; Hon DHL, Whitworth Coll, Spokane WA; Black Congressional Caucus Comm Serv Awd 1978; 1st alumnus to receive Berea Coll Comm Serv Awd 1981; Berea College, board of trustees, 1990-; board of directors, Independent Sector, Washington District of Columbia. **Business Addr:** 7 West 55th, New York, NY 10019.

MCCLOUD, THOMAS HENRY
Association executive. **Personal:** Born Jul 29, 1948, Jersey City, NJ; son of Pearline McCloud and Robert McCloud Sr; married Georgia. **Educ:** Rutgers Univ, BA 1974, MPA 1977; Georgetown Univ Law Ctr, JD, 1989. **Career:** Rutgers Univ, counselor, special programs 1974-76; City of Newark, deputy dir PSE 1977, acting dir 1977-78; Natl League of Cities Wash DC, dir, employment & training proj 1978-81, dir, Urban Noise Programs 1981-82; Wash Convention Ctr, dir, human resources & bus services 1982-86, asst general manager 1986-87; Natl League of Cities, dir membership service 1987-91, dir, public affairs, 1991-; Network Fighting Back Partnership, executive director, 1993-96; 18th Congressional District, chief of staff, 1996; Public Technology Inc, vp, 1996-. **Orgs:** Chrmn EOF Comm Advisory Bd 1972; treas Rutgers Univ Alumni Assoc, NCAS 1976; pres MPA Alumni Assoc 1976-77; trustee Leaguers Inc 1977-78; mem Amer Society for Pub Admin 1978-; member, National Bar Assn; board member, National Forum for Black Public Administrators. **Honors/Awds:** Strauss Human Relations Schlrp 1972, Robert A Wynn Mem Awd 1974 Rutgers U; Pub Service Educ Fellow Dept of HEW Wash DC 1974; Manager of the Yr Wash Convention Ctr 1984. **Military Serv:** USMC, Sergeant, 1966-70. **Home Addr:** 1310 Merganser Ct, Upper Marlboro, MD 20774. **Business Addr:** Dir Public Affairs, Natl League of Cities, 1301 Pennsylvania Ave NW, Suite 600, Washington, DC 20004, (202)626-2413.

MCCLOUD, TYRUS KAMALL
Professional football player. **Personal:** Born Nov 23, 1974; son of Armie. **Educ:** Louisville, attended. **Career:** Baltimore Ravens, linebacker, 1996-. **Business Addr:** Professional Football Player, Baltimore Ravens, 11001 Owings Mills Blvd, Owings Mills, MD 21117, (410)654-6200.

MCCLUNG, WILLIE DAVID
Clergyman. **Personal:** Born Apr 3, 1939, Aliceville, AL; married Mary Jean Shamery; children: David, Rosemary, Bonita LaDawn, Rashawn. **Educ:** Wayne Co Comm Coll, AA 1970; Wayne St U, BS 1971; Univ Detroit, MA 1972; Wayne St U, PhD 1975. **Career:** Detroit Council Bapt Pastors, sec 1966-67; Comm Human Rel Highland Park, 1969-73; New Grace & Univ Detroit, minister. **Business Addr:** 25 Ford, Highland Park, MI 48203.

MCCLURE, BRYTON ERIC (BRYTON ERIC JAMES)
Actor. **Personal:** Born Aug 17, 1986, Fullerton, CA; son of Bette McClure and Eric McClure. **Educ:** Studies dance with instructor, choreographer, Michael Chambers, currently. **Career:** Lorimar TV/Warner Brothers, actor, currently; Television appearances: Family Matters, actor, Thirty Something, actor; Film appearances: See-Say; Commercials: Hershey, Mattel Toys, See-N-Say, LA Gear. **Orgs:** Screen Actors Guild of America; AFTRA Union. **Honors/Awds:** Youth in Films Award, 1992. **Special Achievements:** Has appeared in several national television commercials & print advertisements; by request, presented

Michael Jackson the NAACP Image Award's 25th Anniversary Lifetime Achievement Award on natl television, 1993. **Business Addr:** Actor, c/o Barbara Cameron and Associates, 8369 Squsalito Ave, Ste A, West Hills, CA 91304.

MCCLURE, DONALD LEON, SR.
Educational administrator. **Personal:** Born Nov 10, 1952, San Antonio, TX; son of Vera James McClure and Edmond McClure. **Educ:** Prairie View A&M University, Prairie View, TX, BS, education, 1974, MS, counseling, 1975; Our Lady of the Lake University, San Antonio, TX, MS, administration, 1982; Texas A&M University, College Station, TX, principalship institute, 1983-85. **Career:** San Antonio Independent School District, San Antonio, TX, J T Brackenridge Elementary, teacher, 1975-79, Tafolla Middle School, counselor, 1979-82, Douglass Elementary, principal, 1982-86, S H Gates Elementary, principal, 1986-90, M L King Middle School, principal, 1990-. **Orgs:** Texas Elementary Principals and Supervisor Association, 1983-; trustee, Alamo Community College District Board of Education, 1989-; trustee, I Have A Dream Scholarship Foundation, 1988-; founder, People Against Corruption, Anti-Drug/Crime Community Coalition, 1988-; founder, SAISD Black History Month Fine Arts Festival Scholarship Fund, 1983-; board chairman, Alamo Community College Dist; appointed, by Governor to the State Principals Incentive Board, 1996-97. **Honors/Awds:** TEPSAN of the Year-Region 20, 1989, 1990; Omega Psi Phi Fraternity Inc, Citizen of the Year Award, 1990-91, 1994-95; Texas Governor's Community Service Award - Sen Frank Tejeda, 1990; Texas PTA Community Life Membership Award, 1989; Luby Prize for Educational Leadership San Antonio, 1988; San Antonio Mind Science Award. **Special Achievements:** First African-American Chairman of the Alamo Community College Dist, trustee board, 1994, re-elected, 1996. **Business Addr:** Principal, Rodriguez Elem School, San Antonio Independent School Dist, 3626 W Durango, San Antonio, TX 78207.

MCCLURE, EARIE
Educator. **Personal:** Born in Atlanta. **Educ:** Clark Coll, AB, Atlanta U, MA; Wayne State U; Lund U, Lund Sweden; Univ London, London England; Union of Soviet Socialist Republics Educ Seminar, post grad. **Career:** Atlanta Pub Schs & Special Edn, educator; Clark Coll Alumni Assn Atlanta Chpt, vp; Atlanta Pub Schs Silverbow & Clark Coll Alumni Atlanta, resource specialist for exceptional children; First Southern Bank, Lithonia, GA, organizer, 1988, advisory bd, second branch, Decatur GA, 1993; Amer Communications Network, Southfield, MI, independent rep, 1995; grant facilitator. **Orgs:** Life mem NAACP; Nat Educ Assn; mem GA Assn of Retarded Children; Assn of Educators; chmn Pub Rel Assn of Classroom Tchrs; exec sec Nat Black Women's Polit Leadership Caucus Atlanta Chpt; chmn Program Com Atlanta Assn of Educators; comm organizer Citizens Rights; membership recruiter YWCA; precinct chmn Fulton Co Dem Party; mem GA Dem Party & Nat Dem Party; founder & assoc mem Museum of Confederacy; Am Forestry Assn; Museum of Nat Hist NY; public relations chairman, Annual Operatic Gala of the Cultural Educ Tour Inst; elected chairman, Fulton County Elderly Authority Committee; president, Metropolitan Atlanta National Community Economic Development Coalition Inc; co-chair, library-media center, Library Power AmeriCorp Project First. **Honors/Awds:** Plaque for outstanding serv in special educ parents; various awards from Clark Coll Alumni; Black Women saluted by Univ System of GA, Consortium of Doctors, Atlanta GA, 1992; Elected Bronze Woman of the Year, Community Service, Iota Phi Lambda Sorority Inc, Delta Chapter, Atlanta GA, 1994. **Business Addr:** PO Box 92336, Atlanta, GA 30314-0336.

MCCLURE, EXAL, JR.
Printing company executive. **Personal:** Born Mar 24, 1941, Proctor, AR; son of Dorothy McClure and Exal McClure St; married Bertha McClure, 1962; children: Marlon, Marilyn, Cheryl. **Career:** Custom Printing Company, pressman/owner, 1972-. **Business Addr:** Owner, Action Printing Co, 7232 W Florissant, St Louis, MO 63136, (314)381-2433.

MCCLURE, FREDERICK DONALD
Investment banker. **Personal:** Born Feb 2, 1954, Fort Worth, TX; son of Mayme Barnett McClure and Foster McClure; married Harriet Jackson McClure, Dec 17, 1977; children: Lauren Elizabeth, Frederick Donald Jr. **Educ:** Texas A&M University, College Station, TX, BS, 1976; Baylor University, Waco, TX, JD, 1981. **Career:** Reynolds, Allen & Cook, Houston, TX, trial attorney, 1981-83; Senator John Tower, Washington, DC, legislative director/legal counsel, 1983-84; Department of Justice, Washington, DC, associate deputy attorney general, 1984-85; The White House, Washington, DC, special assistant to the president for legislative affairs, 1985-86; Texas Air Corporation, Washington, DC, staff vice president, 1986-89; The White House, Washington, DC, assistant to the president for legislative affairs, 1989-92; First Southwest Company, Dallas TX, managing director, 1992. **Orgs:** President, National Capital A&M Club, Texas A&M University Association of Former Students, 1990-92; board of directors, Texas Lyceum, 1986-; board of directors, National Fraternity of Alpha Zeta, 1985-; international vice president, Texas A&M University Association of Former Students, 1984-88; 1993-; board of directors, Childrens

Medical Center of Dallas, 1992-; board of directors, United States Naval Academy, 1992-; member, American Council on Germany, 1988-. **Honors/Awds:** National FFA Hall of Achievers, National FFA Organization, 1990; Distinguished Alumnus, Texas A&M University, 1991; Outstanding Young Alumnus, Baylor University, 1991; Jon Ben Sheppard Outstanding Texas Leader, 1992. **Business Addr:** Managing Director, First Southwest Company, 1700 Pacific Avenue, Ste 500, Dallas, TX 75201.

MCCLURE, FREDRICK H. L.
Attorney. **Personal:** Born Oct 21, 1962, Chattanooga, TN; son of Carrie M Green and Howard McClure Jr. **Educ:** Earlham College, BA, 1984; University of Cincinnati College of Law, JD, 1987. **Career:** University of Cincinnati, instructor, 1986-87; Grant, Konvalinka & Grubbs, PC, attorney, 1987-. **Orgs:** Chattanooga Bar Association, Young Lawyers Division, president, 1987-; Tennessee Bar Association, Young Lawyers Division, board of directors, 1987-; American Bar Association, career issues committee, minorities in the profession committee, national confernece team, 1991-; Alpha Phi Alpha, 1988-; Phi Alpha Delta Legal Fraternity, 1984-, vice justice, 1985, justice, 1986. **Honors/Awds:** Alpha Phi Alpha, Man of the Year, 1990; Tennessee Young Lawyers Conference, Service Award, 1989; Ebony Magazine, Young Leader of the Future, 1991. **Business Addr:** Attorney, Grant, Konvalinka & Grubbs, PC, 633 Chestnut Street, 9th Floor, Republic Centre, Chattanooga, TN 37450, (615)756-8400.

MCCLURE, WESLEY CORNELIOUS
Educational administrator. **Career:** Virginia State University, Petersburg, VA, president; Lane College, pres 1992-. **Business Addr:** President, Lane College, 545 Lane Avenue, Jackson, TN 38301-4598, (901)426-7500.

MCCLURKIN, JOHNSON THOMAS
Business executive (retired). **Personal:** Born Sep 25, 1929, Chester, SC; married Evelyn Rudd; children: Gary. **Educ:** Morgan State U, BS 1958. **Career:** Nat Assn of Real Estate Brokers Inc, exec dir; Nat Corp for Housing, asst dir; Washington, DC, partner 1972-73; The Rouse Co, asst to dir of property mgmt 1970-72. **Orgs:** Bd dir Nat Assn Real Estate Brokers Inc; life mem NAACP; mem Ldrsp Conf on Civil Rights; Nat Bus League; mem St John Bapt Ch Columbia Interfaith Ctr; Columbia Assn; Am Soc of Assn of Execs. **Honors/Awds:** Pres's Award 1974, 1977; Lang & Speech Merit Award Morgan State Coll. **Military Serv:** AUS 1951-53.

MCCLUSKEY, JOHN A., JR.
Educator. **Personal:** Born Oct 25, 1944, Middletown, OH; son of Helen Harris McCluskey and John A McCluskey; married Audrey T. **Educ:** Harvard Univ, BA 1966; Stanford Univ, MA 1972. **Career:** Miles Coll Birmingham AL, English teacher; Valparaiso Univ IN, humanities teacher; Case Western Reserve Univ, assoc prof Afro-Amer Studies 1969-77; IN Univ, assoc prof Afro-Amer Studies 1977-83; adjunct prof English 1982-; prof and chair Afro-Amer Studies 1983-; assoc dean Graduate School 1984-88; dir CIC Minorities Fellowships Program 1983-88. **Orgs:** American Studies Association; Modern Language Association; Association of African-American Life & History. **Honors/Awds:** Author "Look What They Done to My Song" 1974, "Mr America's Last Season Blues" 1983, "Blacks in History Nine Stories", 1975 "City of Refuge, Collected Stories of Rudolph Fisher" 1987; Best Amer Short Stories 1976; Yaddo Fellowship Yaddo Corporation 1984, 1986; Blacks in Ohio History, 1976; co-editor with Charles Johnson, "Black Men Speaking", 1997. **Business Addr:** Professor & Chair, Indiana University, Dept of Afro-American Studies, Memorial Hall East M37, Bloomington, IN 47405.

MCCOLLUM, ALICE ODESSA
Judge. **Personal:** Born Feb 15, 1947, Oklahoma City, OK; daughter of Maryland Gear McCollum and Irving A McCollum. **Educ:** Univ of NC Greensboro, BA 1969; Univ of Cincinnati School of Law, JD 1972. **Career:** Reginald Heber Smith Community Lawyer Fellow, 1972-74; Legal Aid Society of Dayton, co-dir 1974-75; Wilberforce Univ, dir pre-law 1975-76; Univ of Dayton School of Law, asst prof, asst dir clinical legal 1976-79; Dayton Municipal Court, judge 1979-. **Orgs:** Bd member, United Theological Seminary, 1980-95, United Way, 1980-84, Dayton Contemporary Dance Co 1980-84; member, OH Municipal Judges Assn, Amer Judges Assn, Natl Bar Assn, OH State Bar Assn, Amer Bar Assn, Dayton Bar Assn, Thurgood Marshall Law Soc; member, ethics comm, Dayton Bar Assoc 1978-; Central State University, board of trustees, 1992-95; Ohio Criminal Sentencing Commission; Victoria Theatre, board of trustees, 1987-93; Children's Med Ctr, bd of trustees, 1993-. **Honors/Awds:** Outstanding Black Woman of 1979 Sinclair Community Coll Student Govt; Woman of the Year Iota Beta Lambda Sorority 1980; YWCA Salute to Career Women Special Achievement Award 1983; Woman of the Year, Unique Study Club 1985. **Business Addr:** Judge, Dayton Municipal Court, 301 W Third St, Dayton, OH 45402.

MCCOLLUM, ANITA LAVERNE
Business executive. **Personal:** Born Aug 20, 1960, Cleveland, OH. **Educ:** Kentucky State University, BS 1983; Atlanta University, MBA 1985. **Career:** IBM, admin asst 1981; NASA Lewis Rsch Ctr, procurement coordin Summers 1981,82,83; IBM, sales asst 1984; Atlanta Exchange, asst to the exec vice pres 1984-;AT&T Communications, spvsr in Residence Marketing. **Orgs:** Undergraduate member of Natl Bd of Directors Alpha Kappa Alpha 1982-84; member Toastmaster's Intl 1983-85; student member Natl Black MBA Assn 1985; memberNAACP. **Honors/Awds:** Soror of the Year Alpha Kappa Alpha 1982; Natl Dean's List KY State Univ 1981-83; Executive Management Scholarship AUGSBA 1983. **Home Addr:** 16512 Invermere Ave, Cleveland, OH 44128.

MCCOMBS, TONY
Professional football player. **Personal:** Born Aug 24, 1974. **Educ:** Eastern Kentucky, attended. **Career:** Arizona Cardinals, linebacker, 1997-. **Business Addr:** Professional Football Player, Arizona Cardinals, 8701 S Hardy, Tempe, AZ 85284, (602)379-0101.

MCCONNELL, CATHERINE ALLEN
Educator (retired). **Personal:** Born Aug 31, 1929, Asheville, NC; daughter of Felicia Allen & John Benjamin Taylor Jr; married Roland C McConnell, Jul 1983; children: Catherine Marie Howard, Charles Preston Howard III. **Educ:** Howard University, AB (cum laude), 1946-50; American University, Grad Stud, 1950-53. **Career:** Morgan State University, Cooperative Education Center, coordinator, 1975-77; Morgan State, instructor, Dept of Education, 1977; Baltimore City School System, secondary school librarian, 1963-71, media dept head, 1971-80, secondary unit principal, 1980-83. **Orgs:** Delta Sigma Theta Soority; Jack & Jill of America, Inc, Baltimore City Chapter, president, 1971-73; United Fund of Central Maryland, bd of directors, Womens Council; Boy Scouts of America, Troop 496, secretary; Continental Society, Baltimore Chapter, recording sec, 1968-70; NAACP, life mem; The Links Inc, Baltimore County Maryland Chapter, exec bd member at large, 1996-97; Howard University Alumni Assn, Baltimore Chapter, secretary, 1983-85; Afro-American Historical & Genealogical Society, national vice pres, 1988-90. **Honors/Awds:** Baltimore City Schools, Service Award, 1983; Jack & Jill of America, Baltimore Chapter, Outstanding Service and Leadership Award, 1982; United Way Community Service Award, 1981; Middle States Evaluation Team for High Schools, 1978. **Special Achievements:** Afro-American History Month Bibliography, yearly, 1971-80; Media Communications Dept Handbook, 1971; Media Curriculum for High Schools, Baltimore City Public Schools, 1971; Genealogy articles in The Journal of the Afro-American Historical & Genealogical Society, Andrew Dibble, Bonds Conway, Kershaw County, Vol 4, no 2, South Carolina, summer 1983; Naudin Dibble Family Directory, 1983; Afro-American Historical and Genealogical Society Annual Conferences; co-chair, 1988, 1990. **Home Addr:** 2406 College Avenue, Baltimore, MD 21214.

MCCONNELL, CONRAD (PETER)
Editor. **Personal:** Born Sep 2, 1952, Denver, CO; son of Geraldine Blanche Christian and Conrad N McConnell. **Educ:** University of Oregon, Eugene, OR, BS, journalism 1970-74. **Career:** The Oregon Journal, Portland, OR, reporter, 1975-82; The Portland Oregonian, Portland, OR, reporter, 1982-83; Seattle Post-Intelligencer, Seattle, WA, editor/reporter, 1983-. **Orgs:** Member, National Association of Black Journalists, 1983-; member, Seattle Youth-at-Risk, 1989-; member, Amnesty International, 1989-; member, Seattle Association of Black Journalists, 1983-. **Honors/Awds:** Fair Housing Award, Seattle Board of Realtist, 1987; St Matthew Award, The Northwest Harvest, 1986; Challenge of Excellence, Washington Press Assn, 1987; Pacific Northwest Excellence in Journalism, Society of Professional Journalists, 1986; C B Blethen Memorial Award, Blethen, 1985. **Business Addr:** Night Assistant City Editor, Seattle Post-Intelligencer, 101 Elliott Ave W, Seattle, WA 98119.

MCCONNELL, DOROTHY HUGHES
Educator (retired), consultant. **Personal:** Born Apr 19, Cleveland, OH; daughter of Genevieve Harris Hughes (deceased) and Harry Hughes (deceased); children: Jan Yvette Evans. **Educ:** Ohio State Univ, BS 1946; Western Reserve Univ, MA 1956; Loyola Univ, Admin Credential 1975. **Career:** Los Angeles Unified School Dist, training teacher 1960-79, school improvement coord 1979-80, integration coord 1980-81, lang arts spec 1982-90 (retired); Black Studies, specialist and consultant, 1990-. **Orgs:** State Comm of Credential State of CA Sacramento CA 1978-83; wrkshp org & ldr Parent Educ Workshops 1982-; Los Angeles Alumnae, life mem Delta Sigma Theta Sor; life mem NAACP, LA Branch 1995; pres Natl Assoc Univ Women, LA Branch, 1996-98; mem Angelus Mesa; adm bd YWCA. **Honors/Awds:** Recg spec cert Outstanding Tchr of the Year, Human Rel City of Los Angeles Human Rel Comm 1979; selected by USC & Dept Educ Wash DC as Research Participant in Egypt 1980; elected by LAUSD Tchrs as Mentor Tchr Evaluator in Mentor Tchrs Prog 1984-; National Assn of University Women, LA Branch, Woman of the Year, 1995, honoree, 1997. **Home Addr:** 5547 Secrest Dr, Los Angeles, CA 90043.

MCCONNELL, ROLAND C.
Educator (retired). **Personal:** Born Mar 27, 1910, Nova Scotia;son of Helen Viola Halfkenny McConnell and Rev Thomas Benjamin McConnell; married Catherine Allen Taylor (deceased). **Educ:** Howard Univ, AB 1931, MA 1933; NY Univ, PhD 1945. **Career:** Elizabeth City State Teachers College, Elizabeth City NC, hist dept instructor 1938-42; Natl Archives, Washington DC, archivist 1943-47; Morgan State Univ, prof 1948-78, hist dept chmn 1967-75, prof emeritus in history 1981-; editorial bd, African-American Historical and Genealogy Society, guest editor, AAHGS Journal, 1991; executive board, Morgan Christian Center, Morgan State University. **Orgs:** Chmn, Maryland Commn Afro-Amer History & Culture 1974-84; mem, Maryland Commn Afro-Amer History & Culture; Pub Comm Maryland Historical Soc 1981-; consultant, Maryland Branch Natl Hist Pub; Exec Council, Association for Study of Afro-Amer Life & Hist 1960-; Opera; Symphony; elder, Trinity Presbyterian Church. **Honors/Awds:** Outstanding Serv Plaque, Phi Beta Sigma Frat, 1978; Maryland Commn Afro-Amer Hist & Culture, Plaque 1984, 1991; Certificate for Patriotic Civilian Serv Dept of US Army, Morgan State Univ, 1972; Meritorious Plaque, State of Maryland & Morgan State Univ, 1972; Morgan State Univ, Morgan Heritage Award for Dedicated & Distinguised Service, 1993. **Special Achievements:** Author, Negro Troops of Antebellum Louisiana, The History of the Battalion of Free Men of Color, Louisiana State Univ Press, xii, 145, 1968; Louisiana Black Military History, 1729-1865, Louisiana Black Heritage, eds, Macdonald, Kemp & Haas; Louisiana State Museum New Orleans, chapter xxi, 1979; The Black Experience in Maryland, 1634-1900; The Old Line State A History of Maryland, ed by Morris L Radoff, Hall of Records Commission, State of MD, Annapolis, 1971; A History of Trinity; Presbyterian Church, Wells Printer, Baltimore, MD viii, 55, 1959-89; Audio visual, Frederick Douglass' Leadership & Legacy, Symposium for Black History Month, 1995; Maryland Commission on Afro American History, Annapolis, Dept of Housing & Community Development, Crownsville, MD. **Military Serv:** US Army, second lt, ROTC, 1931-37; WWII, pvt. **Home Addr:** 2406 College Ave, Baltimore, MD 21214.

MCCOO, MARILYN
Singer, actress. **Personal:** Born in Jersey City, NJ; daughter of Mary Ellen Holloway McCoo and Wayman Glenn McCoo; married Billy Davis Jr. **Educ:** Univ of CA, BS, business administration. **Career:** The Hi-Fi's, singer; The Fifth Dimension formerly the Versatiles, orgl mem 1965-75; Art Linkletters Talent Scouts, singer; formed duo with husband Billy Davis, Jr; Solid Gold, host. **Orgs:** Los Angeles Music Ctr, bd of governors. **Honors/Awds:** Grammy Awd with Billy Davis Jr for "You Don't Have to be a Star" 1977; 4 Grammy Awds for Up, Up & Away; 2 Grammy Awds for Aquarius w/The 5th Dimensions; Awarded the Prestigious Grand Prize at Tokyo Music Fest; 14 Gold Records and Albums with the 5th Dimension; 2 Gold Records and Albums with husband Billy Davis, Jr; Honorary Doctorate, Talladega College, AL; Harvard Foundation Award, Harvard University. **Business Addr:** Singer, Actress, 1900 Avenue of the Stars, Ste 1640, Los Angeles, CA 90067.

MCCORMACK, EDWARD G.
Educator, librarian. **Personal:** Born Apr 1, 1948; married. **Educ:** Ohio University, Athens, OH, MA, 1977; Indiana University, Bloomington, IN, MLS, 1981. **Career:** Ohio University, Athens, OH, teaching asst, 1977-80; Indiana University, Bloomington, IN, asst librarian, 1980-81; Newark Public Library, Newark, NJ, reference librarian, 1981-85; College of New Rochelle, New Rochelle, NY, prof/coordinator of campus library services, 1985-. **Orgs:** American Library Assn, 1980-; Black Caucus Assn, American Library Assn, 1980-. **Business Addr:** Professor/Coordinator of Campus Library Services, College of New Rochelle, New Rochelle, NJ 10805.

MCCORMACK, HURVIN
Professional football player. **Personal:** Born Apr 6, 1972, Brooklyn, NY. **Educ:** Indiana, attended. **Career:** Dallas Cowboys, defensive tackle, 1994-. **Business Addr:** Professional Football Player, Dallas Cowboys, One Cowboys Pkwy, Irving, TX 75063, (214)556-9900.

MCCORMICK, LARRY WILLIAM
Journalist. **Personal:** Born Feb 3, 1933, Kansas City, MO; married Anita Daniels; children: Alvin Bowens, Mitchell, Kitrina. **Educ:** Lincoln Jr Coll Kansas City, MO, AA 1951; Univ of Kansas City UMKC; CA State Los Angeles, BA & MA (in progress). **Career:** KGFJ Radio Los Angeles, music prog host 1958-63; KFWB Radio Los Angeles, music prog host-columnist 1964-67; KGFJ Radio Los Angeles, music prog host, prog dir 1967-71; KABC Channel 7 Los Angeles, weathercaster 1971; KTLA Channel 5 Los Angeles,TV newscaster 1971-. **Orgs:** Mem Los Angeles NAACP 1960-; vp, bd of dirs Los Angeles Urban League; bd of dir Ebony Showcase Theatre 1978-; bd of dirs Challengers Boys Club; 100 Black Men of Los Angeles; Cal-State LA Support Group; Black Journalists Assoc of So CA; USC Ebonics Long-Range Dev Comm. **Honors/Awds:** Outstanding Comm Serv Citation LA City LA Co Mayor Tom Bradley CA Senate CA Assembly 1976; Communicator of the Year Awd Nat Assn of Market Developers 1976; Nat Communication Award Nat Assn of Media Women 1977; LA Unified Sch Dist; So Christian Leadership Conf West; Women at Work; Los Angeles Lullaby Guild; Sons of Watts; Black Probation Officer's Assoc; Alpha Phi Alpha Frat; So CA Podiatry Assoc. **Business Addr:** KTLA Channel 5, 5800 Sunset Blvd, Los Angeles, CA 90028.

MCCORVEY, KEZ
Professional football player. **Personal:** Born Jan 23, 1972, Gautier, MS; married Loris; children: Imoni. **Educ:** Florida State, bachelor's degree in sociology. **Career:** Detroit Lions, wide receiver, 1995-. **Business Addr:** Professional Football Player, Detroit Lions, 1200 Featherstone Rd, Pontiac, MI 48342, (248)335-4131.

MCCOVEY, WILLIE LEE
Professional baseball player (retired), sports administrator. **Personal:** Born Jan 10, 1938, Mobile, AL. **Career:** San Francisco Giants, 1959-73; San Diego Padres, 1974-76; Oakland Athletics, 1976, San Francisco Giants, 1977-80, general manager, special assistant to president, currently; IBM, public relations, presents "Tale of the Tape" trophies, currently. **Orgs:** Chmn, Willie McCovey March of Dimes Annual Charity Golf Tournament. **Honors/Awds:** Natl League Rookie of the Yr 1959; led NL in home runs (36) & RBI 105 1968; NL in HR (45) & RBI (126) 1969; NL All Star Game 1963, 1966, 1968-71; leading left-handed home run hitter ever in NL; ranks 9th on baseball's all-time list of HR & 1st among active players; 18 grand slams 1st in NL & 2nd in history of major leagues; only player in baseball hist to hit 2 HR in same inning twice in career; NL Comeback Player of the Yr; Sporting News/UPI; NL MVP 1969; Hutch Award 1977; Willie McCovey Day Candlestick Park 1977; inducted into Natl Baseball Hall of Fame 1986. **Business Addr:** General Manager, Special Assistant to President, San Francisco Giants, Candlestick Park, San Francisco, CA 94124.

MCCOY, ANTHONY BERNARD
Professional football player. **Personal:** Born Jun 10, 1969, Orlando, FL; married Jodie; children: Anthony Bernard Jr. **Educ:** University of Florida. **Career:** Indianapolis Colts, defensive tackle, 1992-. **Honors/Awds:** Noble Max Award, 1994; Ed Block Courage Award, 1994. **Business Addr:** Professional Football Player, Indianapolis Colts, PO Box 535000, Indianapolis, IN 46253, (317)297-2658.

MCCOY, FRANK MILTON
Concert pianist, educator, lecturer. **Personal:** Born Sep 17, El Centro, CA; son of Henderson & Annie Lee McCoy. **Educ:** Mus & higher edn, BA, MA; Walden Univ, PhD, higher ed, 1980; Universidad de Valencia, Spain, 1958. **Career:** LA City Schs, edctr, lectr, Eurpoe, Mexico, CAN 67 other countries (First Am to Present Concert on French/Protectorate Islands of St Pierre et Miquelon Ofcly Received by Gov Gen Clarence Campbell of Jamaica), concert piano tours; Los Angeles Sentinel, music critic, 1988-; Job Corps, advisor. **Orgs:** Music drama critic El Centro CA, 5 Yrs; Intrnl Platform Assn; CA Music Tchrs Assn; Music Critics Association; M-2 Prison Reform Program; Southeast Symphony Association, bd of dirs Los Angeles; Social Public Art Resource Ctr, bd of dirs; Los Angeles Press Club; Natl Public Speakers Assn. **Honors/Awds:** Author "Black Tomorrow - A Portrait of Afro-Am Culture," "We Too, Are Americans," contributor of articles for professional journals; recip Leona M Hickman Awrd, Univ of WA; Rotary Clb Schlrshp, San Fran State U; featured in Ebony Mag 1960; featured in Sepia Mag 1960 & 1965; 1st African-American adjudicator Nat Piano Playing Auditions sponsored by Nat Guild of Piano Teachers San Jose Co & San Bernadino California; appeared on Canadian Broadcasting; TV debut from Halifax Nova Scotia; recip awrd Natl Negro Clg Women; recip & awrd Our Author's Study Clb LA; founder administrator of awrd honoring his mother: Annie Lee McCoy Chopin Piano Meml; pub articles "A Corner of France at Your Doorstep," Travel & Arts Mag 1980; Mayor Bradley, official commendation for work in and contributions to music in Los Angeles; only African-American selected for Early Music Fellowship, San Antonio, TX, 1991-92; "A Corner of France At Your Doorstep," Commendation from Mayor Tom Bradley. **Special Achievements:** First American to present piano concerts on the French Protectorate Islands of St Pierre et Miquelon; officially received by Gov Gen Clarence Campbell of Jamaica; concert piano tours presented in Europe, Mexico, Canada and 67 other countries on 5 continents; selected to attend San Juan Heineken Jazz Festival, 1994; selected as journalism intern for Kalamazoo Intl Piano Competition, 1994; selected to observe Musical Life of Philadelphia, 1994; toured Brazil, Costa Rica, Australia, New Zealand, 1993; participant in Dorothy Taubman Institute of Piano, 1995.

MCCOY, GEORGE H.
Administrator. **Personal:** Born Dec 10, 1930, Philadelphia, PA; son of Clara J Palmer McCoy and James Ross McCoy; married Louise (deceased); children: Eva, Hassan. **Educ:** City Coll of NY, BA Biology 1970; Bernard Baruch NY, MBA Bus Health 1973. **Career:** Albert Einstein Hosp Bronx NY, asst admin 1973-75, sr asst admin 1975-77; Kings County Hosp Brooklyn NY, deputy dir 1977-78; West Co Med Ctr Valhalla NY, first deputy comm 1978-86; Erie County Medical Ctr Buffalo NY, chief exec officer 1986-; Gov Juan Luis Hospital, St Croix, VI,

CEO, 1993-. **Orgs:** Mem Amer Coll Hosp Admin 1972-; Amer Hosp Assn 1970-; adj Prof Marymount Coll Terrytown 1979-86; mem bd dir West-Putnam March of Dimes 1984-86; chmn bd dir Congregations Concerned with City Mt Vernon 1983-86; Greater Buffalo Chamber of Commerce, Buffalo Urban League; Executive Bd, United Way; Autistic Bd of Buffalo; bd of dirs, Buffalo Eye Bank; executive comm, Natl Assn of Public Hospitals; National Association of Public Hospitals, president, 1993; Hospital Association of New York State; National Public Health and Hospitals Institute, treasurer. **Honors/Awds:** Comm srv Key Women of Amer Upper Westchester 1984; Professional of the Year, Buffalo Club, Natl Assn of Negro Business & Professional Women, 1988; SCLC Honoree 1989; Black Achievers Award, 1990. **Military Serv:** AUS capt 1951-59. **Business Addr:** Chief Executive Officer, Gov Juan Luis Hospital, 4007 Estate Diamond Ruby, C'std, St Croix, Virgin Islands of the United States 00820.

MCCOY, GLADYS

Government official. **Personal:** Born Feb 28, 1928, Atlanta, GA; daughter of Tillman Simms and Lucille Simms; married William McCoy; children: Krista, William, Paul, Mary, Cecilia, Peter, Martha. **Educ:** Talladega Coll, BA Sociology, 1949; Portland State Univ School of Social Work, MSW 1965-67; School of Work, Field Supvr, 1969-70. **Career:** Project Head Start Vancouver WA, dir of social serv 1967-70; Clark Coll, Pacific Univ, Portland Comm Coll, Intl Coll of Cayman Isle British WI, prof sociology & social work 1970-74; State of OR, ombudsman 1975-78; Multnomah County OR, commissioner 1979-84, chair/exec 1987-. **Orgs:** Planning/coordination specialist NW Regional Educ Lab 1978-79; bd mem Providence Medical Center Comm Bd Multnomah Co Ext Serv, KPBS Public Broadcasting, Sentinel Editorial Bd; trustee Amer Mothers Inc, Endowment Fund, mem, American Diabetes Assn, Oregon Affiliate; mem, American Institute of Parliamentarians; mem, Natl Assn of Counties; mem, Natl Assn of Social Workers; mem, Natl Organization of Black County Officials; member, Leaders Roundtable Executive Committee; mem, president's advisory council, Portland State Univ; mem, Natl Org of Black County Officials. **Honors/Awds:** Woman of Achievement Portland 1974; OR Mother of the Year 1980; Woman of Today Albina Womens League 1982, Abigail Scott Duniway Award, Women in Commun, 1984; OR Assembly of Black Affairs Political Devel Award, 1987; Community Serv Award, Natl Assn of Blacks in Criminal Justice Serv 1987. **Business Addr:** Chair/Executive, Multnomah County, 11205 W Fifth Ave, #1410, Portland, OR 97204.

MCCOY, JAMES F.

Librarian (retired). **Personal:** Born Aug 1, 1925, Clarkton, NC; son of Gertrude Smith McCoy and Frank McCoy. **Educ:** Lincoln Univ, AB 1952; Rutgers Univ, MLS 1956; Univ of Denver, advanced cert 1973; Appalachian State Univ HEW Inst, attended. **Career:** NJ St Library, ref librarian 1956; Elizabeth Public Library, ref librarian 1956; Mercer Co Comm Coll, chmn library dept 1956-74; Hudson Valley Comm Coll, dir learn resources 1974-84 (retired). **Orgs:** Nom com ALA-ACRL 1971-72; Ad Hoc Comm on Interns 1972-77; AV Com 1975; edtrl bd CHOICE 1974; chmn schlrshp com 1966-67, vice pres 1969-70, pres coll & univ sect 1964-65; pres AAUP Mercer Co Coll; NJLA Exec Bd 1968-70; sec NJ Exec Bd 1970-72; AAUP, pres Alumni Assn GSLS Rutgers 1958, 1975; sec, NJ Jr Coll Assn 1960, 1965; adv comm Grad Sch Library Serv Rutgers 1958-59, 1975-76; Mayor's Adv Comm Trenton Model Cities 1968-73; adv comm Trenton Urban Renewal 1966-68; pres Trenton Nghbrhd Hlth Ctr 1971-72; Trenton Historical Soc 1965-74; chmn Adv Assoc GLIS Rutgers Univ 1979; pres Alumni Assn SLIM Univ Denver 1979; chmn Intellectual Freedom & Due Process NYLA 1979; sec Council of Head Librarians SUNY 1977; contrib Biblio of Negro in NJ 1967; Basic Books for Jr CollLibraries 1963; Kappa Alphsi Frat; ALA; NJLA; NYLA; AAUP; NAACP; chair SUNY Cncl Head Librarians 1984; chair membership comm Amer Library Assn 1985; chair Comm & Jr Coll Lib Sect 1986; trustee, elder pres scholarship comm, Berean Presbyterian Church. **Honors/Awds:** Disting Serv NJLA Coll & Univ Sect Awd; Disting Alumni Awd Lincoln Univ; Cert of Achievement Trenton Model Cities; Founders Awd Black & Hispanic Faculty and Admins Assn 1984; Sire Archon Beta Psi Boule Sigma Pi Phi Frat 1984; 50th Anniversary Awd of Appreciation 1985; Appreciation Awd Beta Psi Boule, Sigma Beta Psi Fraternity 1986; Outstanding Contribution, Comm Org 1986. **Military Serv:** US Army Sgt 4th grade; 1944-46. **Home Addr:** 317 N Broad St, Apt 718, Philadelphia, PA 19107.

MCCOY, JAMES NELSON

Controller. **Personal:** Born Sep 18, 1955, Tallahassee, FL; son of Delores Tookes McCoy and Elihu McCoy; married Shari Myree McCoy, Jun 12, 1982. **Educ:** Florida A&M University, Tallahassee, FL, BS, 1976. **Career:** Central Foundry, Div of General Motors, Saginaw, MI, senior accountant, 1976-81; Michael Alan Lewis Company, Union, IL, accounting manager, 1981-83; Hometown Distributing Company, Chicago, IL, assistant controller, 1983-86; Adolph Coors Company, Golden, CO, distributor development controller, 1986-88; River North Distributing, Chicago, IL, controller, 1988-. **Orgs:** Member, Kappa Alpha Psi Fraternity, 1974-. **Honors/Awds:** America's Best & Brightest Young Business & Professional Men, Natl Publications Sales Agency Inc, 1989. **Business Addr:** Controller, Administration, River North Distributing, 1300 N North Branch St, Chicago, IL 60622-2412.

MCCOY, JESSIE HAYNES

Educational administrator. **Personal:** Born Nov 17, 1955, Mound Bayou, MS; divorced; children: Raven, Tameka. **Educ:** Coahoma Jr Coll, AA English 1975; Univ of S MS, BA Journalism 1976; MS State Univ, further study 1984; Bloomsburg Univ, further study 1985. **Career:** Hattiesburg Amer Newspaper, part-time reporter 1976; Delta Democrat-Times Newspaper, news reporter 1976-79; MS Valley State Univ, dir univ relations 1979-84; freelancer various print media; Bloomsburg Univ, univ relations dir 1984-86; J & R Enterprises, co-owner 1987-; Bloomsburg Univ, asst to city mgr, public info officer 1986-. **Orgs:** PTA pres Fulwiler & LS Roger Elem Schs 1978-1982; dist chairwoman MS Press Women 1981-83; pres College Public Relations Assn of MS 1982-83; public relations officer Amer Assn of Univ Women 1983; mem mgmt intern comm Bloomsburg Univ 1984-85; mem Columbia-Montour Tourist Promotion Agency 1984-85, Black Council on Higher Educ 1984-85; telecommun council, pres council Bloomsburg Univ; mayors task force War on Drugs; mayors bicentennial of the constitution comm, Jubilee Comm, C of C PR Comm, city hall grand opening comm, road bond referendum comm, mayors youth day comm; curricullum adv bd comm Tidewater Comm Coll; mem NAACP Chesapeake VA, Natl Forum for Black Public Admin, Intl City Mgrs Assoc, Public Relations Soc of Amer, Amer soc of Publ Admin, Amer MktgAssoc, VA Municipal League, Conf oinority Public Admin, PTA. **Honors/Awds:** Journalism Scholarship Univ of S MS 1976; Ford Fellow in Journalism Ford Found Washington 1979; CASE Fellow Council for Advancement & Support of Educ 1981;Exec Council MS Valley State Univ 1982-84; Outstanding Young Woman of America 1983; only Black non-academic mgr Bloomsburg Univ 1984-86; Regional Finalist President's Commission on White House Fellows.

MCCOY, WALTER D.

Public administrator. **Personal:** Born Mar 17, 1930, Damascus, GA; married Toni Moynihan (divorced); children: Jonathan D, Wanda D Noble. **Educ:** FL A&M Univ, BS 1951; Univ of TX El Paso, MS 1971; NM State Univ, ABD 1974; Univ of TX Arlington, PhD Admin 1980. **Career:** AUS, col 1950-70; Univ of TX El Paso, vice pres student affairs 1970-74; Univ of TX Arlington, dir of student serv 1974-76; Corpus Christi State Univ, assoc prof of mgmt 1975-85, dir public admin; School of Business, dean, asst provost. **Orgs:** Mem Acad of Mgmt 1981-; chmn allocation comm United Way of Corpus Christi 181-83; pres bd Women's Shelter of Corpus Christi 1984-; mem Federal Mediator and Mediation Services 1989-. **Honors/Awds:** Leadership Award United Way Coastal Bend 1970-80; Hon Soc Phi Kappa Phi 1974; Hon Soc Order of Omega 1974. **Military Serv:** AUS col 20 1/2 yrs; Meritorious Serv Medal, Bronze Star w/Devices, Commendation Medal w/4 OLC; Pres Unit Citation, Republic of Korea. **Business Addr:** Provost Office, Michigan Tech Univ, 1400 Townsend Dr, Houghton, MI 49931-1200.

MCCOY, WAYNE ANTHONY

Attorney. **Personal:** Born Nov 5, 1941, Louisville, KY; son of Martha Nuckolls McCoy and Herbert B McCoy; married Sharron Lynne Gulliford, Jul 18, 1964; children: Jay Brandon Todd, Kamilah Nneka. **Educ:** Univ of MI Law Schl, JD 1972; IN Univ, BS Bus Admin 1965. **Career:** General Dynamics Corp, graphic reprod 1962-63; RCA, distr & traffic 1963-65; Dow Chem Co, mrkt & sales mgr 1965-69; Schiff Hardin & Waite, 1972-, partner 1977-. **Orgs:** Dir Evanston Northwestern Healthcare (formerly Evanston Hosp Corp), 1980-; Dir, Evanston Business Investment Corporation, 1988-; mem Evanston IL Econ Dev Comm 1985-92; general cnsl Jesse Owens Fnd 1983-95; trustee, Chicago Historical Society, 1994-; director, First Evanston Bancorp, 1995-; director, First Bank & Trust of Evanston, 1995-; director, Michael Jordan Foundation, 1994-96; comm Evanston Human Rel Comm 1978-80; mem Evanston Comm on Schl Finance 1977-78; dir, American Judicature Society, 1989-92; trustees' associate, Northwestern University, 1988-; director, Research Park Inc, 1988-; vistors comm, University of Michigan Law School, 1977-; visiting committee, University of Miami School of Law, 1997-; visitors comm, Northwestern University School of Law, 1988-91; Evanston City Council Task Force on Police Serv 1973-1976; consult atty Evanston Fair Housing Review Bd 1972-73; trustee Evanston Environmental Assc 1977-79; mem Amer, Natl, IL, Cook Cty Chicago Lawyers Bar Assn; life mem Kappa Alpha Psi 1960-; Oper PUSH; NAACP; Natl Assc Sec Prof; member, National Assn of Bond Lawyers. **Honors/Awds:** Co-author "Advising Publicly-Held Corporation" Cont Legal Ed 1973, 1979; co-editor, IL State Bar Assc Newsletter on Corp & Sec Law 1973, 1974. **Business Addr:** Partner, Schiff Hardin & Waite, 7200 Sears Tower, Chicago, IL 60606, (312)876-1000.

MCCOY, WILLIAM

State senator. **Personal:** marrIed Gladys; children: Krista, William, Paul, Mary, Cecila, Peter, Martha. **Educ:** Univ Portland, BA, bus admin & political sci; Univ of OR, grad studies in public admin; Univ of So CA, grad studies in gerontology. **Career:** State of Oregon, state representative, 1972-74, state senator, 1975-. **Orgs:** Director Foster Grandparent Program. **Honors/Awds:** Honorary LLD, University of Portland. **Military Serv:** US Navy, 1942-46. **Business Addr:** State Senator, State of Oregon, S-219 State Capitol Bldg, Salem, OR 97310.

MCCRACKEN, FRANK D.

Clergyman, city offical. **Personal:** Born Jul 1, 1949, Reading, PA; son of Ada R Baxter McCracken and James McCracken; married Charlene Flowers; children: Alicia, Frank, Stephanie. **Educ:** PA State, 1967; Albright Coll, 1968; Kutztown State Univ, BA 1980; Lutheran Theological, attending. **Career:** Assoc Financial Svcs, mgr 1972-74; Police Athletic League, exec dir 1977-92; maternal Health Svcs, past pres, bd 1979-; NAACP Reading Branch, exec mem 1982-84; Berks County Resource Consortium, pres; St James Chapel COGIC, pastor; City of Reading, PA, city councilman, director of public safety, currently. **Orgs:** Past mem Berks Cty Children & Youth Serv 1981-82; mem bd Prokids, Reading Ministerium; pres Berks Cty Training Inst, Berks Cty Resource Inc; mem, adv bd PA State Berks Campus; chmn, bd of trustee Kutztown Univ; bd, Nation Family Planning Assn; bd treas, One Church One Child of PA; chairman Council of Trustees Kutztown University; executive director Police Athletic League 1977-92; international chairman Southern Agricultural Industrial Development Corp. of West Africa; board member Concern Inc child care and Adoption Services Program; president, Million Man March, of Reading; founder, St. James Christian Academy; treasurer, Victor Lodge #73, F.A.M. Prince Hall; executive vp Reading Broadcasting TV 51. **Honors/Awds:** Achievement IBPOEW Eastern Distr 1983; Honorary Doctorate, Christ Bible Coll, Madras, India, 1987. **Military Serv:** AUS Intelligence E-5 3 yrs; Army Commendation w/OLC 1969; Presidential Unit Citation. **Home Addr:** 1716 N Third St, Reading, PA 19601.

MCCRACKEN, QUINTON ANTOINE

Professional baseball player. **Personal:** Born Mar 16, 1970, Wilmington, NC. **Educ:** Duke. **Career:** Colorado Rockies, outfielder, 1995-97; Tampa Bay Devil Rays, 1998-. **Business Addr:** Professional Baseball Player, Tampa Bay Devil Rays, One Tropicana Dr, St Petersburg, FL 33705.

MCCRACKIN, OLYMPIA F.

Librarian. **Personal:** Born Jun 8, 1950, Tuscaloosa, AL; daughter of Susie Seltz Hines and Oliver G Hines Sr; married Mack A McCrackin, Jun 1, 1989. **Educ:** Stillman College, Tuscaloosa, AL, BA, 1972; University of Alabama, Tuscaloosa, AL, MLS, 1990. **Career:** Social Security Administration, Tuscaloosa, AL, claims representative, 1973-85; FBI, Birmingham, AL, rotor clerk, 1985-88; Tuscaloosa Public Library, Tuscaloosa, AL, librarian, 1988-90; Bryce Hospital, Tuscaloosa, AL, librarian, 1991-. **Orgs:** Board of directors, Hospice of West Alabama, 1985-87; member, anti basileus, Eta Xi Omega Chapter, Alpha Kappa Alpha Sorority, Inc, 1989-90; member, American Library Assn, 1989-; member, Alabama Public Library Assn, 1989-; member, Mental Health Assn of Tuscaloosa County, 1988-; deputy registrar, Tuscaloosa County Board of Registrars, 1987-; secretary, Eta Xi Omega Chapter, Alpha Kappa Alpha Sorority, 1986-88; co-moderator, Presbyterian Women, Brown Memorial Presbyterian Church, 1990-91, moderator, Presbyterian Women, 1991-95; Bosileus, Eta Xi Omega Chapter, Alpha Kappa Alpha Sorority, Inc, 1993-94. **Honors/Awds:** Alabama Public Library Assn Scholarship, Alabama Public Library Assn, Montgomery, AL, 1989; Louise Giles Minority Scholarship, American Library Assn, Chicago, IL, 1989; Elder, Brown Memorial Presbyterian Church, 1987-; Beta Phi Mu International Library Science Honor Society, 1991-; board mem, Alabama Advisory Council on Libraries; board mem, Library School Association, University of ALA. **Home Addr:** 1926 40th Ave, Tuscaloosa, AL 35401.

MCCRARY, FRED DEMETRIUS

Professional football player. **Personal:** Born Sep 19, 1972, Naples, FL. **Educ:** Mississippi State, attended. **Career:** Philadelphia Eagles, running back, 1995; New Orleans Saints, 1997-. **Business Addr:** Professional Football Player, New Orleans Saints, 5800 Airline Hwy, Metairie, LA 70003, (504)733-0255.

MCCRARY-SIMMONS, SHIRLEY DENISE

Attorney. **Personal:** Born Nov 7, 1956, Boston, MA; daughter of Eupha McCrary and Earlie McCrary; married Nathaniel O Simmons; children: Charity Denise Simmons. **Educ:** Brown Univ, AB 1978; Boston Univ School of Law, JD 1982. **Career:** Georgia Legal Servs, law intern 1982; Internal Revenue Servs, tax rep/revenue officer 1983-84, attorney, estate tax, 1984-90; attorney, 1990-93; Arrington and Hollowell, PC, attorney, 1993-. **Orgs:** Pres Black Amer Law Student Assn 1980-81; mem JD Curriculum Comm 1981-82; mem Natl Bar Assn 1983; deputy registrar Fulton Co GA 1983; mem State Bar of GA 1983-; mem Gate City Bar Assn 1985, 1987; union steward Natl Treasury Employees Union 1985-88; legal advisor Africare Atlanta Inc 1985-89; Georgia Association of Black Women Attorneys; Metropolitan Atlanta Chapter of 100 Black Woman; board of directors Joseph E Mertz Memorial Educational Foundation, Antioch Urban Ministries, Inc, Walton Management, Inc. **Honors/Awds:** First African-American female to be hired as an estate tax attorney in the Atlanta Dist; Superior Performance Award, IRS 1988, 1989. **Business Addr:** Attorney At Law, 191 Peachtree St NW, Ste 3350, Atlanta, GA 30303.

MCCRAVEN, CARL CLARKE
Business executive. **Personal:** Born May 27, 1926, Des Moines, IA; son of Buena Vista Rollins Alexander (deceased) and Marcus H McCraven (deceased); married Eva Louise Stewart; children: Carl Bruce, David, Larry, Maria. **Educ:** Howard Univ, BS Elec Engr 1950; CA State Univ Northridge, MS Health Svr Admin 1976. **Career:** Natl Bureau of Standards Wash DC, radiation physicist 1950-55; Lockheed CA Co Burbank, CA, sr research engr 1955-63; Space Elec Power Engr Dept TRW Systems Inc, mem tech staff 1963-72; CA State Univ Northridge, asst prof 1974-76; Pacoima Mem Hosp Inc Lake Vw Terr CA, assc admin vice pres 1972-73; Hillview Mental Health Ctr Lake View Terr CA, founder, president 1973-; Hillview Village Housing, general manager, 1992-. **Orgs:** Fellow Assc Mntl Hlth Admin 1984-90; mem Amer Publ Hlth Assc 1976-90; Am Mgmt Assc 1978-85; Natl Assc Hlth Serv Exec 1976-85; pres NAACP Southern Area CA Conf 1967-71; natl bd dir NAACP 1970-76; regent Casa Loma Clge Bd Dir 1970-85; bd dir San Fernando Valley Girl Scout Council 1980-82; past pres mem North San Fernando Valley Rotary 1981-85; mem Sigma Phi Xi Boule 1984-; pres, Los Angeles County Association of Community Mental Health Agencies, 1996-. **Honors/Awds:** Recipient Citation CA Senate 1971, CA Assembly 1971, City of Los Angeles 1971, 1978; Cert of Appreciation Councilman Bob Ronka 1st Dist 1979; Certificate of Appreciation, Los Angeles County Board of Supervisors. **Special Achievements:** Hillview Village Housing Project, developer, manager. **Military Serv:** AUS 1945-46. **Home Addr:** 17109 Nanette St, Granada Hills, CA 91344. **Business Addr:** President/CEO, Hillview Mental Health Ctr Inc, 11500 Eldridge Ave, Lake View Terrace, CA 91342.

MCCRAVEN, MARCUS R.
Business executive (retired). **Personal:** Born Dec 27, 1923, Des Moines, IA; son of Buena Rollins McCraven and Marcus H McCraven; married Marguerite Mills; children: Carol J, Stephen A, Paul A. **Educ:** Howard Univ, BSEE; Univ of MD; Univ of CA. **Career:** Naval Research Lab, engr; Lawrence Radiation Lab, engr group leader nuclear test; Phelps Dodge Commun Co, chief engr; Bridgeport Elec Co, vice pres; United Illuminating Co, vice pres. **Orgs:** Dir First Constitution Financial Corp; pres Middletown Ave Assn Real Est; dir Metrodata Inc Okla City; bd trustees CT State Colleges; chrmn bd So Central CT Amer Red Cross; Sigma Pi Phi Fraternity; exec comm EPA Science Adv Bd; bd of trustees, Quinnipiac Coll, The Graduates Club, Jr Achievement; chmn bd So Central Ct Health Planning; president, Yale Univ Peabody Museum Assoc; Quinnipiack Club; Golden Heritage Life Member NAACP; State of Connecticut Statewide Grievance Committee; associate fellow, Yale University. **Honors/Awds:** City Commissioner Menlo Park CA; Most Notable Citizen Award Hamden CT; pres North Haven CT Rotary; IRA Hiscock Award; mem Quinnipiack Club; New Haven Chamber of Commerce Award; Urban League; United Way; Junior Achievement, Free Enterprise & Spirit of Achievement Hall of Fame. **Military Serv:** US Army.

MCCRAW, TOM
Professional baseball coach. **Personal:** Born Nov 21, 1940, Malvern, AR; children: Bryan, Marla. **Career:** White Sox, first baseman 1963-70; Washington, 1971; Cleveland, 1972; CA, 1973; Cleveland Indians, infielder, 1974-75, coach 1975, minor league hitting instr, 1976-79, first-base coach 1980-82; San Francisco Giants, hitting instr 1983; New York Mets, hitting, first-base coach, currently. **Honors/Awds:** Am Assn, batting title, 326 mark; named circuits All-Star Team, 1962. **Military Serv:** USNG. **Business Addr:** Hitting/First-Base Coach, New York Mets, Shea Stadium, Flushing, NY 11368.

MCCRAY, ALMATOR FELECIA (ALMA)
Galley director. **Personal:** Born Sep 16, 1956, Charlotte, NC; daughter of Alma O McCray and Robert Lee McCray; children: Ryan Lamar. **Educ:** Queens College, BA, history, 1992. **Career:** Belk Stores Services, corporate buyer, 1975-88; Ubiquitous Art Space, president, 1988-. **Orgs:** National Association of Negro Business and Prof Women's Association; NC Museums of Art, African-American Advisory Board; UNCC, Art Advisory Board National Black Child Dev Institute; Natl Assn of Female Executives. **Honors/Awds:** Focus on Leadership, Arts Award, 1992; Optimist Club, Speaker's Award, 1991; Arts and Science Council Emerging Artist Grant. **Business Phone:** (704)376-6944.

MCCRAY, BILLY QUINCY
County government official. **Personal:** Born Oct 29, 1927, Geary, OK; son of Ivory B. McCray and John J. McCray; married Wyvette M Williams, Oct 12, 1952 (deceased); children: Frankeleen Conley, Anthony, Melodie Miller, Kent. **Educ:** Langston Univ Langston OK, 1945-47; CO Univ Boulder, 1949-50. **Career:** Boeing Co, Wichita, KS, industrial photographer, 1952-77; Govt of KS, Topeka, KS, state representative, 1967-72, state senator, 1973-84; KS Dept of Economic Development, Topeka, KS, dir, 1984-86; Sedgwick County Commissioner, 1987-93; McCray & Associates, consultant. **Orgs:** Pres, Wichita Ach Club, 1953-55; me, Wichita Human Relations Committee, 1963-66; KS Drug Abuse Council, 1972-74; dir, Wichita A Phillip Randolph Inst, 1976-78; US Small Business Advisors Council, 1977-80. **Honors/Awds:** Published Song of Autumn, 1948, and A Tree by the Highway, 1956; Outstanding Legislator, KS Association of Public Employees, 1977; plaque Outstanding Award, KS Credit Union League, 1975; Outstanding State Senator, KS Assc of Public Employees, 1983; Pres Award, Langston Univ Regl Alumni, 1982; Outstanding Service, Natl Advisory Council on Small Business, Pres Jimmy Carter. **Military Serv:** USAF s/sgt 1947-51. **Home Addr:** 2801 N Rock Rd, #901, Wichita, KS 67226.

MCCRAY, CHRISTOPHER COLUMBUS
Government official (retired). **Personal:** Born Sep 16, 1925, Waycross, GA; son of Pompey McCray (deceased) and Rosa Lee McCray (deceased); married Jewel Hollis; children: Cynthia, Linda Bacon, Christi. **Career:** CSX Railroad Co, equip operator, 1943-92; Waycross/Ware Co, co-chmn bi-racial comm 1966-71; Waycross GA, sch bd mem 1967-71; City of Waycross, mayor pro-tem. **Orgs:** Waycross Community Concert Association; John Sutton American Legion Post No 517; Keystone Voters League; NAACP, Waycross Chapter; Future Business Leaders of America; Supreme Grand Lodge Ancient and Accepted Scottish Rites Free Masons. **Honors/Awds:** Kiwanis Club Miller Medal Award, 1976; Gaines Chapel Merit Award of Civics; Waycross City School Board, Silver Bowl Award; Waycross College Appreciation Award; Keystone Voters and Civic League, Certificate of Appreciation; National Law Enforcement Community, Certificate of Appreciation; Jacksonville FL Urban League, Certificate of Appreciation; CSX Transportation, Certificate of Appreciation; Greater Mt Zion AME Church, Merit Award of Civics; Phi Delta Kappa Sorority, Delta Zeta Chapter Public School Award; Groveland Park Community Club, Public Service Award of Achievement in Community Service; Mt Zion AME Church, Sunday School Award for Civic and Christian Leadership; Morris Jacobson Award for Outstanding Achievement in Brotherhood and Community Relations; Southeast Georgia Area Planning and Development Commission, Certificate of Merit for Outstanding Service; NAACP, E E Moore Membership Award for Outstanding Solicitation of Members; National Guard of Georgia, Distinguished Service Award for Service Rendered; Future Business Leaders of America, Honorary Life Member; Northside Community Club, Award for Outstanding Service to the Community; Martin Luther King Jr Commission Award, 1994; Woodmen of the World, Waycross Chapter, Citizen of the Year, 1994. **Special Achievements:** First African American mayor of the city of Waycross. **Military Serv:** USN petty officer 2/c 1943-46.

MCCRAY, DARRYL K.
Fashion designer. **Personal:** Born Oct 3, 1963, Bronx, NY; children: Akira, D'Andra, Darryl II. **Career:** IBEW LU #3, purchasing agent, 1985-90; Midtown Electric Supply, purchasing agent, 1987-90; House of Nubian Inc, CEO, 1989-. **Special Achievements:** Started a retail business with $138.00 and grossed over a million dollars per year after seven years. **Military Serv:** USMC, cpl, 1981-85. **Business Addr:** CEO, House of Nubian Inc, 35 W 8th St, New York, NY 10011, (212)475-7553.

MCCRAY, JOE RICHARD
Business executive. **Personal:** Born Nov 12, 1928, Bucksport, SC; son of Vetus C McCray Sr; married Gertrude E Bellamy (deceased); children: Sidney, Richard, Rhonda. **Educ:** Univ MD, 1974. **Career:** Joe R McCray Enterprises Inc, pres. **Orgs:** Mem Washington Bd of Realtors DC; Prince George's Bd of Realtors MD; Kiwanis Club; E Branch, DC Life Fellow, Kiwanis Intl. **Honors/Awds:** Past pres awrd Disting Clb Kiwanis Intrnl 1973-74. **Military Serv:** AUS lt col 1946-72.

MCCRAY, MELVIN
Maintenance director. **Personal:** Born Aug 9, 1946, Ft Benning, GA; married Rosie M Thompson; children: Kimya Nicole, Keisha Michelle, Cora Danielle, Diedra Marie. **Educ:** GA State Univ, BS 1972. **Career:** Atlanta City Aviation, admin asst II 1975-76, admin asst III 1976-77, project coord 1977-80, dir of maintenance 1980-. **Orgs:** Fin field City of Atlanta City Hall 1972-; collector dep marshal 1975; mem Amer Assoc of Airport Exec, Southeastern Airport Mgrs Assoc, Conference of Minority Public Admin, Natl Forum for Black Public Admin; mem bd of dir City of Atlanta Credit Union. **Honors/Awds:** Cert of Appreciation ASPA 1982; Cert of Recognition GA Engrg Found 1982; Pres City of Atlanta Employees Club 1982; Cert of Merit City of Atlanta/Andrew Young 1983; Cert of Appreciation COMPA 1983 Christmas Fundraiser 1983. **Business Addr:** Dir of Maintenance, Hartsfield Atl Int'l Airport, Commissioners Office, Atlanta, GA 30320.

MCCRAY, NIKKI
Professional basketball player. **Personal:** Born Dec 17, 1972. **Educ:** Tennessee, attended. **Career:** American Basketball League, Columbus Quest, 1996-97; Washington Mystics, guard, 1998-. **Honors/Awds:** Univ of TN, Best Defensive Player, 1992; Southeastern Conf, College Player of the Year, Women's Basketball, 1994, 1995; US Olympic Basketball Team, Gold Medal, 1996; American Basketball League, Most Valuable Player, 1997. **Business Addr:** Professional Basketball Player, Washington Mystics, MCI Center, 601 F St NW, Washington, DC 20071, (301)622-3865.

MCCRAY, ROY HOWARD
Dentist. **Personal:** Born Mar 14, 1946, Birmingham, AL; son of Annie Cleggett and Maceo Cleggett; children: Kenja, Kendyl, Kennethia. **Educ:** AL A&M Univ, BS 1972; Meharry Medical Coll, DDS 1978. **Career:** Meharry Medical Coll, instructor operative dentistry 1978-81; AL Dental Soc, parliamentarian 1985-86; Private Practice, dentist. **Orgs:** Mem Huntsville Madison Co Dental Soc 1980-86; vice pres No AL Medical Assoc 1985-; mem NAFEO 1985. **Honors/Awds:** CV Mosby III Awd Meharry Dental Sch 1977; Dr Martin Luther King Awd Meharry Dental Sch 1977; The Intl Coll of Dentists 1978; Amer Assoc of Endodontists and Orthodontists 1978. **Military Serv:** AUS e-4/sp4 infantry 1967-69; Vietnam Overseas, Combat Infantryman, Unit Citation 1968. **Business Addr:** President, McCray DDS PC, 2510 Pulaski Pk NW, Huntsville, AL 35810.

MCCRAY, THOMAS L.
Cleric. **Personal:** Born Jan 1, 1928, Valdosta, GA; married Elizabeth Wafier; children: Lois, Teresa, Thomas. **Educ:** Wilberforce U, BA; Payne Theol Sem Wilberforce U, BD Candidate; Bucknell U, Extended Study; Cleveland State U, Western Reserve. **Career:** St Mathews AME Ch, pastor; Bethel AME Ch 1950-52; Milton PA, Circt pstr 1952-58; St James AME Ch Cleveland, assc pstr & dir chrstn ed 1958-67; MtMoriah AME Ch Maple Hghts, OH, pstr 1965-66; Avery AME Ch Clveland 1967-73; St James AME Ch Erie 1973; OH Civil Rights Commn, field Investigtr; Grtr Cleveland Interchr Cncl, dir. **Orgs:** Past pres Cncl of Chs of Christ Grtr Clvlnd; past pres Grtr Clvlnd Mnstrl Assc; past pres Clvlnd Cncl of Chs Chld Dev Pgm; mem Div Chrstn EdnDept of Yth Mnstry; exec com Natl Cncl of Chs of Chrst; mem Div of Ch & Witness & of Prog & Plng Comm oH pstrs assc; OH Cncl of Chs; alt del Grtr Clvlnd Intrch Cncl; vice pres Clvlnd Advsry Bd; OH Ldrshp Conf; mem Gov Com; Migrant Affrs; Clvlnd Brnch; NAACP; E Urbn Bd; YMCA; bd of trust Forest City Hosp; mem Cnsmrs Lgue of OH; past vice pres Untd Area Ctzns Agcy; mem Training Com. **Honors/Awds:** UACA Hon Degree DD Monrovia Clg Monrovia, W Africa 1972.

MCCREARY, BILL
Reporter, co-anchorman. **Personal:** Born Aug 18, 1933, Manhattan NYC, NY; married O'Kellon. **Educ:** Cty Clg NYC; NY Univ Schl of Commnctns. **Career:** Radio Sta WWRL Woodside Queens, stf ancr eng 1960, co-prodcr 1961; Night Pgm, mgr 1962; Radio Sta WLIB, nwscstr 1963; News Dir 1965; Metro Media Brdcstg Inc,TV nwscstr 1967; WNEW & TV'S 10 O'Clock News, co-anchorman; 1 Hour TV Newscast, anchorman; Black News, anchorman 1970, mng edtr & exec dir 1971; Gen Assgnmt Rptr; Fox Broadcasting Co, exec producer "McCreary Report", vice pres 1987-. **Orgs:** Mem Cambria Hghts Civ Assc Queens; vice pres Royal Crusdrs Bowling Clb; board member NY Urban League Lifetime Member-NAACP. **Honors/Awds:** Emmy Awd NY Chap Natl Acad TV Arts & Sci 1969-70; Citation of Merit 1971-72; Achievement Awd Bkly Chap Natl Assoc Negro Bus & Prof Wmns Clb Inc;Cambria Heights Serv Awrd 1975; Achievement Awd NAACP LI Chap 1975; Emmy Awd for co-anchoring 10 o'clock news 1980-81; Public Serv Awd FDA; Special Citation from the Commissioner; voted Most Watched and Belived Black Correspondent in Metro Area. **Military Serv:** AUS corpl 1953-55. **Business Addr:** Fox Broadcasting, 205 E 67th St, New York, NY 10021.

MCCREE, EDWARD L.
Clergyman. **Personal:** Born Feb 24, 1942, Quitman, MS; married Mae Lois Heath; children: Anita, Edward, Michele. **Educ:** Univ of Detroit, 1963; Detroit Bible Clg, 1961-62; Am Bapt Theo Sem, BA 1972. **Career:** Creeball Ice Cream Co, fndr 1961-62; Shell Oil Sta, Co-owner 1962; Cedar Grove Miss Bapt Ch Mt Juliet, TN, pastor 1968; Macedonia Bapt & Ch Pontiac, MI, pastor. **Orgs:** Mem Hoi Adelpos Frat; Ministerial Fellow; Gen Mtr Truck & Coach; Chapel Pontiac Gen Hosp; adv bd United Brotherhood; bd dirs Christians for Tomorrow;pres Boy of Hope Clb; Lecturer, cncl, advsr. **Honors/Awds:** Recip Most Progressive Young Business Man of Royal Oak Twnshp 1962; most oust young man of Ferndale 1963; big brother awrd Royal Oak Twnshp 1963; activities awrd 1964. **Business Addr:** 512 Pearsall Blvd, Pontiac, MI 48341.

MCCREE, SAMUEL W.
Clergyman, educator. **Educ:** Talladega College, Talladega, AL, BA, English, 1969; Colgate-Rochester Divinity School, Rochester, NY, MA, religious studies, 1971; SUC Brockport; Columbia University; University of Rochester. **Career:** Talladega College, instructor, upward bound program, dir, student activities, upward bound program, 1968-69; Colgate Rochester Divinity School, asst to the dean of black studies, 1969-71; Rochester City Schools, elementary teacher, 1971-75, media resource teacher, 1974-75; Division for Youth, rehab coord, 1978; Rochester City Schools, project supervisor, community schools council, 1975-78, helping teacher, cluster coord, 1979-80, magnet schools planning specialist, 1980-81, dir, community & parent involvement, 1981-; Zion Hill Baptist Church, Rochester, NY, pastor, currently; Colgate Rochester Divinity School Black Church Studies, instructor; Chamberlain & Assoc, Washington, DC, consultant. **Orgs:** Member, Baptist Ministries Alliance; member, Southwest Ministerial Assn; organizer, Bullshead Ministry to the Night People; chairman,

Black Leadership Forum; co-chair, Anti-Drug Task Force, Southwest Minister's Alliance; dir, Project Spirit/Southwest; founder, Minority Educator Assn of Rochester, forerunner to Black Educators Assn of Rochester, 1975; chair, Afro-American Sickle Cell Assn. **Honors/Awds:** Cited for meritorious achievement in community involvement, Community Schools Council, 1978; Urban League's Community Service Award, 1983; Man of the Year Award, National Assn of Negro Business and Professional Women's Club, 1986; author, Parents as Partners, Rochester City School District, 1983. **Business Addr:** Pastor, Zion Hill Baptist Church, 250 Bronson Ave, Rochester, NY 14611.

MCCRIMMON, NICKY
Professional basketball player. **Personal:** Born Mar 22, 1974. **Educ:** Univ of Southern California. **Career:** Seattle Reign, guard, 1997-. **Business Addr:** Professional Basketball Player, Seattle Reign, 400 Mercer St, Ste 408, Seattle, WA 98109, (206)285-5225.

MCCRIMON, AUDREY L.
Government official. **Personal:** Born Oct 21, 1954, Covington, KY; daughter of Letha Lewis Patrick and Arthur McCrimon. **Educ:** Northern Illinois University, DeKalb, IL, BS, educ, 1974, MS, educ, 1975. **Career:** Jewish Vocational Service, Chicago, IL, counselor, 1975-77; City Colleges of Chicago, Chicago, IL, coordinator, 1977-84; City of Chicago, Chicago, IL, deputy commissioner, 1984-90; Dept of Rehabilitation Serv, Chicago, IL, associate director, 1990-91; director, Department of Rehab Service, 1991-. **Orgs:** Member, Renaissance Women, 1990-; member, Illinois Association of the Deaf, 1978-; member, Coalition of Citizens with Disabilities, 1985. **Honors/Awds:** August Christmann, City of Chicago-Advocacy, 1990. **Business Addr:** Director, Department of Rehabilitation Services, 100 W Randolph, Suite 8-100, Chicago, IL 60601.

MCCROOM, EDDIE WINTHER
Attorney. **Personal:** Born Sep 11, 1932, Memphis, TN; married Shirley Kathryn Lewis; children: Darren Winther, Audrey Jay, Sandra Marguerite. **Educ:** University of Arkansas, BS 1955; Case Western Reserve Univ, LLB 1961. **Career:** OH Civil Rights Comm, fld rep 1961-63; US Dept of Justice, asst US atty 1964-69; State of OH Dept Adm Srv, state EEO coord 1972-74; E Winther McCroom & Associates, priv law prac 1976-. **Orgs:** Exec vice pres Industrial Fed S & L Assc 1969-70; lecturer bus law Univ Cincinnati 1971-72; legal cnsl Jaycee 1970-; Ohio Legal Advisor; NAACP 1970-; IBPOE of W Elks 1980-. **Military Serv:** USN seaman II 1955-57. **Business Addr:** Attorney, E. Winther McCroom & Associates, 402 Legal Arts Centre, Youngstown, OH 44503, (330)747-1163.

MCCROREY, H. LAWRENCE
Educator. **Personal:** Born Mar 13, 1927, Philadelphia, PA; son of Marian Dawley McCrorey and Henry Lawrence McCrorey Jr; married Constance Gilliam; children: Desiree, Lauren, Leslie, Larry. **Educ:** Univ MI, BS 1949, MS 1950; Univ IL, MS 1958, PhD 1963. **Career:** Univ VT, dept of physiology & biophysics, asst, assoc, full prof 1966-, School of Alied Health Sciences, dean, 1981-; Acad Affairs Univ VT, assoc vice pres 1973-77; Physiology Univ IL, asst prof 1963-66; Sharp & Dohme Phila, rsrch assoc 1951-55; Howard Univ, vis prof; Tuskegee Inst; Goddard Clg; Univ CA; Charles Drew Med Sch; Coll of VI FL A&M; Dillard Univ; Statistics Walter Reed Army Inst of Rsrch, vis prof 1967-70; University of Colorado Medical College, visiting prof 1978-79. **Orgs:** Mem Gen Rsrch Support Pgm Adv Com NIH 1973-78 & 1980-84; bd trustee VT-NY Proj 1968-70; bd dir Am Civil Liberties Union 1971-75; Surgeon Gen's Ad Hoc Com on Health of Americans 1968-69; corporator Burlington Savings Bk 1976-; bd dir Burlington YMCA 1976-. **Honors/Awds:** List of sci publ in Phsyiology; outst tchg awrds Coll of Nursing 1960,& 1964; Coll of Pharmacy 1965; Coll of Medicine, 1970, 1971, 1984; Univ of Vermont 1988. **Military Serv:** AUS nco 1944-46. **Business Addr:** Professor of Physiology & Biophysics and, Dean, School of Allied Health, Univ of Vermont, 301 Rowell Bldg, Burlington, VT 05405.

MCCUISTON, FREDERICK DOUGLASS, JR.
Automobile company executive. **Personal:** Born Nov 27, 1940, Wynne, AR; son of Erma McCuiston and Frederick McCuiston Sr; married Norma P; children: Frederick III, Marcus, Maia. **Educ:** TN State Univ, BS 1961; Univ of Cincinnati, MS 1970, PhD 1976. **Career:** General Motors, asst staff engr, currently. **Orgs:** Mem Amer Soc of Mechanical Engrs 1962-, Society of Automotive Engrs 1968-; mem NBCDI 1981-; pres Ann Arbor NAACP Branch 1982-92. **Honors/Awds:** Omega Psi Phi Comm Serv Awd 1984; Alpha Phi Alpha Man of the Year 1985; Region III (Midwest) NAACP Leadership Award, 1986, 1990. **Military Serv:** USAF capt 5 yrs. **Home Addr:** 1398 Wolverhampton Ln, Ann Arbor, MI 48105.

MCCUISTON, STONEWALL, JR.
Physician. **Personal:** Born Feb 23, 1959, Chicago, IL; son of Annie M McCuiston and Stonewall McCuiston. **Educ:** Grinnell Coll, BA 1981; Meharry Medical Coll, MD 1985. **Career:** Cook County Hospital, resident physician; private medical practice, internal medicine and pediatrics, currently. **Orgs:** President, Cook County Hospital House Staff Assn, 1988-; president, Cook County Hospital Black Physicians Assn, 1987-88; member, Cook County Hospital Union Coalition, 1988-; member, Cook County Hospital Executive Medical Staff, 1988-; member, American Medical Assn; member, Chicago Medical Society; member, Illinois State Medical Society. **Honors/Awds:** Research grant March of Dimes 1982-83; First place Research Day Medical Div Meharry Medical Coll 1983. **Home Addr:** 7810 South Ridgeland, Chicago, IL 60649. **Business Addr:** Physician, Med-Peds Associates, 401 N Wall St, Kankakee, IL 60901.

MCCULLERS, EUGENE
Beverage company executive. **Personal:** Born Jan 30, 1941, Garner, NC. **Educ:** Shaw U, BA 1962; Univ of Wisconsin and Univ of Puerto Rico, additional study. **Career:** US Peace Corps, volunteer, 1963-65; Capitol Coca-Cola Bottling Co, Raleigh, NC, special markets represetaive, 1965-67; Coca-Cola Bottling Co, Thomas, TN, acount executive, 1968-76; Coca-Cola USA, Atlanta, GA, marketing manager, 1976-81, manager of community affairs, 1981-. **Orgs:** Board of directors, trustee, Shaw University; board of directors, Grambling State University Athletic Foundation; board of directors, The National Black College Hall of Fame Foundation; board of directors, The Jacquelyn McClure Lupus Center; board of directors, National Association of Market Developers; life member, NAACP; member, Elks; member, Kappa Alpha Psi. **Honors/Awds:** Distinguished Alumni Award, Shaw University; Marketer of the Year Award, National Association of Market Developers; Inductee, Hall of Fame, Grambling University, 1986; inductee, Hall of Fame, Central Intercollegiate Athletic Association, 1987; Honorary Doctor of Humane Letters, Shaw University, 1992.

MCCULLOUGH, FRANCES LOUISE
Personnel adminstrator. **Personal:** Born Apr 5, 1941, Dermott, AR; married Leo McCullough; children: Nancy L. **Educ:** Contra Costa Jr Coll, AA 1962; San Francisco State Univ, BA 1975, MA 1977. **Career:** Comm Vol, 1972-80; Employment Specialist, 1980-. **Orgs:** Chmn Comm Housing Resources Bd of Pacifica 1979-80; commr/pres San Mateo Co Human Relations Commn 1977-80; bd mem N San Mateo Co League of Women Voters 1974; chmn League of Women Voters Pacifica CA 1973; educ consult CA Educ Compliance Com 1977; desegregation consult Fellow-Coro Pub Affairs Found 1978; adv Skyline Comm Coll; mem African Hist Soc San Francisco 1976-80; prog dir Friends of Pacifica's Library 1979; mem Fair Hearing Com Pacifica's Childcare; Conferee Pacifica Rep Regional Bar Assn Conf 1975. **Honors/Awds:** Fellowship Coro Pub Affairs Found San Francisco 1978; Manpower Fellowship San Francisco State Univ; producer/fndr First Black History Prog & Black Club inPacifica. **Business Addr:** Employment Specialist, 444 El Camino, San Mateo, CA 94401.

MCCUMMINGS, LEVERNE
Educational administrator. **Personal:** Born Oct 28, 1932, Marion, SC; son of Mamie McCummings and Henry McCummings; married Dr Betty L Hall; children: Gregory, Gary, Ahada. **Educ:** St Augustine's, BA 1960; Univ of PA, MSW 1966; Ohio State Univ, PhD 1975. **Career:** Competency Certification Bd, Bd of Health & Human Svcs, Futures Think Tank, chmn 1981-82; Natl Conf of Grad Deans/Dirs & Off Soc Work Progs, pres 1982-85; Cheyney Univ of PA, pres, currently. **Honors/Awds:** Outstanding Educators Awd Univ of KY 1971; Recognition Awd NASW Sixth Biennial Prof Symposium 1980; Distinguished Alumni Awd Univ of PA 1980; Recognition Awd Council of Intl Prog 1981; Institute for Educational Management, Harvard University, l989. **Military Serv:** AUS 1955-57. **Business Addr:** President, Cheyney Univ of Pennsylvania, Cheyney, PA 19319.

MCCURDY, BRENDA WRIGHT
Microbiologist. **Personal:** Born Jun 29, 1946, Richmond, VA; daughter of Alcie Taylor Wright and Rogers C Wright; married Howard Douglas McCurdy. **Educ:** Virginia Union Univ, BS (Magna Cum Laude) 1968; Virginia Commonwealth Univ School of Medicine, MS 1970; Wayne State Univ School of Medicine, PhD 1980. **Career:** Henry Ford Hospital Detroit, microbiologist III 1970-72; Wayne State Univ, rsch asst 1972-75; Wayne State Univ, adj asst prof of immunology & microbiology 1980-; Veterans Admin Med Ctr, section chief of microbiology 1979-. **Orgs:** Mem Amer Soc for Microbiology 1970-; mem South Central Assoc for Clinical Microbiology 1978-; chairperson Medical Ctr Adv Comm for Equal Employment Oppor 1983-; pres Windsor Black Coalition (Canada) 1983-85; mem Delta Sigma Theta. **Honors/Awds:** Graduate Professional Scholarship Wayne State Univ 1976-77; Natl Fellowship Awd 1977-78; Augusta T Calloway Fellowship Awd 1979.

MCCUTCHEON, LAWRENCE (CLUTCH)
Professional scout. **Personal:** Born Jun 2, 1950, Plainview, TX; son of Leanna Bell McCutcheon and Roland McCutcheon; married Myra Emerson, Dec 9, 1983; children: Adrian Campbell, Marcus McCutcheon. **Educ:** Colorado State University, Fort Collins, CO, 1968-72. **Career:** LA Rams, running back 1972-80, scout, currently; Denver Broncos, running back 1980-; Buffalo Bills 1981. **Orgs:** Only Six Times In Ram Hist has a Ram Ball Carrier Gained More Than 1,000 Yds in a Season; McCutchoen has Done it the Top Three of Those Only Needs 1,132 to Catch Ram Record of 5,417. **Honors/Awds:** NEA'S Third Down Awrd; 2nd Team ALL-NFC; UPI; Pro Bowl for 4th Staight Time; outst Ofnsv Back 1974; Daniel F Reeves Meml Awrd; MVP; All-Rookie Team UPI; All-Western Athletic Conf; CO State U; NFC All Star Team Sporting News 1974. **Business Addr:** Professional Scout, Los Angeles Rams, 505 N Tustin Ave, Ste 243, Santa Ana, CA 92705-3735.

MCDADE, JOE BILLY
Judge. **Personal:** marrled Mary Evelyn. **Educ:** Bradley University; University of Michigan, JD. **Career:** State of Illinois, Peoria, associate circuit judge, 1982-88, circuit judge, 1988-91; US District Court, Central District of Illinois, judge, currently. **Orgs:** Illinois Judges Association, bod; American Red Cross Central Illinois Chap, bod, 1991-94; Illinois Central Health Systems Agency, bod, 1975-82, prs, 1978-80; Peoria Chamber of Commerce Leadership School, guest lecturer, 1977; Court Counselors Prog, Inc, bod, 1968-75, 2nd term, 1983-86; Heart of IL United Fund, panel mem, 1974-77; Peoria YMCA, bod, 1975-77, 2nd term 1985-92, prog comm, 1989-92; Boy Scouts of America, WD Boyce, executive bd, 1984-86; Comprehensive Work & Training Prog, adv bd, 1975-83; Tri-County Peoria Urban League, bod, 1970-72; Peoria Chap NAACP, chrmn, legal action comm, 1966-67; Greater Peoria Sports Hall of Fame Inc, bod, 1980-82; St Peter's Catholic Church, trustee, 1980-85, chrmn, House of Prayer Comm, 1987-89; Creve Coeur Club, 1978-82, house comm, 1980-81; Central IL Bradley Alumni Club, bod, 1982-83; IL Eagle Scouts, Citizenship Prom Comm, 1988-94; Amateur Musical Club of Peoria, bod, 1988-92; Peoria Tri-Centennial, bod, 1990-92; SHARE Foods Inc, bod, 1987-92; Upgrade, a Non-Profit Housing Corp, bod, 1983-89. **Honors/Awds:** Bradley University AWDS, NIT Championship Team (Also All-NIT Team), 1957, 1959, Shriner's East/West All-Star Basketball Team, 1959, Outstanding Academic Athlete, 1959, Watonga Awd, Highest Student Awd Given by University, 1959, Hall of Fame, 1961, Honorary Coach Awd, 1980, Distinguished Alumnus Awd, 1990, University Centurion, 1990; First Presbyterian Church Youth Retreat, Leadership Awd, 1966; National Legal Aid & Defender Assn, Outstanding Svc Awd, 1971; City of Peoria Svc Commendation, Library Awd, 1977, Civic Ctr, 1982; Court Counselor Prog Inc, Founder's Awd, 1979; Boys Club of America Man of the Yr - Caho Club, 1982; UPGRADE Non-Profit Housing Corp, Svc Awd, 1982; Award of Merit, United Usher Bd, 1982; Awd of Merit, Peoria Citizens Comm for Economic Opportunity, 1982; Citizen of the Yr Awd, Omega Psi Phi Fraternity, 1983; Greater Peoria Sports Hall of Fame, 1984; Citation of Recognition, American Legion Dept of IL, 1987; Thank Youd Awd, Chamber of Commerce of Morton IL, 1988; Civic & Community Svc Awd, 1988; IL/WI States Assn, IBPO Elms of the World Achievement Awd, Bethel United Meth Men's Club, 1989; Recognition Awd, African-American Hall of Fame Museum, 1991; Cert of Appreciation, IL Dept of Children & Family Svcs, 1991; Cert of Recognition, Peoria Chirstian Leadership Council, 1992; Awd of Appreciation, Share Food Prog of Central IL, 1992; Awd of Recognition, Houston Area Urban League, 1994. **Business Addr:** US District Judge, US District Court, Rm 122, Federal Bldg, 100 NE Monroe, Peoria, IL 61602, (309)671-7821.

MCDANIEL, ADAM THEODORE
Dentist. **Personal:** Born Jun 8, 1925, Rock Hill, SC; married Lois Butler; children: Jenita, Frederic. **Educ:** NC Central Univ, BS 1946; Howard Univ, DDS 1947-51; Jersey City Med Ctr, Internship 1951-52; Friendship Jr Clge. **Career:** Dentist; Rahway Geriatric Cntr, dental consultant, currently. **Orgs:** Rahway Rtry Club; pres Rahway Mun Council Caucus of Elected Black Officials 1960-72; Union Co & NJ Dental Soc; 100 Black Men of NJ; Omega Psi Phi Frat; NJ Chap Natl Guardsmen Inc; state rep Rahway Housing Auth 1959-70; Correctional Hlth Serv Invest Comm of NJ State Prisons; Lay Comm Publ Schl Systems; Urban League. **Honors/Awds:** Beta Kappa Chi Hnr SJI Soc Honoree; Testimonial Dinner 1961, 1973. **Military Serv:** US Air Force, capt, 1953-54. **Home Addr:** 97 E Milton Ave, Rahway, NJ 07065.

MCDANIEL, BILLY RAY
Environmental coordinator, safety supervisor. **Personal:** Born Sep 13, 1943, Hearne, TX; son of Zelma McDaniel and James Lee McDaniel; married Marilyn Davis; children: Pamela, Billy Ray Jr, Franchesca. **Educ:** San Antonio Jr College, San Antonio, TX, Graduate, San Antonio Incarnate Word College; Prairie View College; University of Texas at San Antonio, San Antonio, TX. **Career:** GATX, Hearne, TX, supervisor, 1977-; City of Hearne, Hearne TX, Mayor, currently. **Military Serv:** US Air Force, 8 years, discharged 1969. **Home Addr:** 1108 W 9th St, Hearne, TX 77859. **Business Addr:** Mayor, City of Hearne, 210 Cedar St, Hearne, TX 77859.

MCDANIEL, CHARLES WILLIAM
Government administrator. **Personal:** Born Mar 17, 1927, Fairfield, AL; son of Willie V Seldon McDaniel and Charles Andrew McDaniel; married Rose L Bowen; children: Deborah Roberts, Charles F, Reginael. **Educ:** Miles Coll, attended 1946;

Civil Serv Comm, attended 1978; Coast Guard Acad, attended 1982; GA State Univ, attended 1981; US Army Logistics Mgmt Center, 1970-81; Exec Seminar Center, Kings Point NY, attended 1982; Exec Seminar, Denver CO, attended 1987. **Career:** US Army, Warren MI, system analyst 1967-70, budget analyst 1970-76; US Army, Washington DC, budget analyst 1976-80; US Army HQ FORSCOM, suprv budget analyst 1980-89; deputy dir Log Mgmt Div 1989, chief Mgmt Branch; Indiana Ave Baptist Church, administrative assistant to pastor, 1990-. **Orgs:** Pres Amer FED of Musicians #286 1965-73; church organist IN Baptist Church 1966-76; band leader Detroit MI 1968-76; mem NAACP 1970; bd mem Amer FED of Musician #15/286 1973-75; mem Amer Soc of Military Comptrollers 1981-; church organist Shiloh Baptist Church 1982-, treasurer 1987-; staff union negotiator US Army HQ FORSCOM Ft McPherson 1983; Mayor's Committee for Substance Abuse, 1990; New Hope Baptist Church, organist, 1990. **Honors/Awds:** Outstanding Award US Army 1973-75; Special Act US Army 1975; Letter from Pres Ford Cost Reduction US Army 1976; Outstanding Award US Army Pentagon 1980; Outstanding Award US Army Ft McPherson 1980; Outstanding Achievement US Army Ft McPherson 1983; Exceptional Performance, HQ FORSCOM, Ft McPherson GA 1986; Outstanding Chief Award Program & Budget Branch, HQ FORSCOM 1987; Department of Army, Commander's Award for Civilian Service. **Military Serv:** USN stewards mate III 2 yrs. **Home Addr:** 2412 Valley Brook Rd, Toledo, OH 43615-2956. **Business Addr:** Indiana Ave Baptist Church, 640 Indiana Ave, Toledo, OH 43602.

MCDANIEL, EDWARD
Professional football player. **Personal:** Born Feb 23, 1969, Batesburg, SC. **Educ:** Clemson, attended. **Career:** Minnesota Vikings, defensive back, 1992-. **Business Addr:** Professional Football Player, Minnesota Vikings, 9520 Viking Dr, Eden Prairie, MN 55344, (612)828-6500.

MCDANIEL, ELIZABETH
Health service/educational administrator. **Personal:** Born May 3, 1952, St Louis, MO; children: Paul. **Educ:** Forest Park CC, BA Arts 1981. **Career:** Forest Park Admin Bldg, work study 1978; Forest Park Comm Coll, work study 1981, student asst 1982; Coalition for School Desegration, sec 1982; St Louis Comp N Health Center, secty/clerk 1982; Visiting Nurse Assn, billing clerk 1984; Wellston School Bd, vice pres; St Louis Univ Hosp, lead clerk 1986; St Louis Regional Physician's Billing, 1987. **Home Addr:** 6562 Jesse Jackson Ave, St Louis, MO 63121.

MCDANIEL, EMMANUEL
Professional football player. **Personal:** Born Jul 27, 1972, Griffin, GA. **Educ:** East Carolina. **Career:** Carolina Panthers, defensive back, 1996; Indianapolis Colts, 1997-. **Business Addr:** Professional Football Player, Indianapolis Colts, PO Box 535000, Indianapolis, IN 46253, (317)297-2658.

MCDANIEL, JAMES BERKLEY, JR.
Physician. **Personal:** Born Aug 8, 1925, Pittsburgh, PA; son of Mr & Mrs James McDaniel Sr; widowed; children: James B III, Nancy Alben Lloyd. **Educ:** Howard Univ Wash DC, BS 1950; Howard U, MD 1957. **Career:** Physician OB GYN, prv practice 1962; State Univ of NY, asst clinical prof at Buffalo 1974; Geneva B Scruggs Community Health Care Center Inc, head, OB/GYN dept. **Honors/Awds:** First ach award Student Nat Med Assn & Buffalo 1972; ach award Buffalo Youth Bd; Chief Executive Officer's Lifetime Achievement Award, Geneva B Scruggs Center, 1989. **Military Serv:** USN musician 3/c 1944-46. **Home Addr:** 180 N Pearl St, Buffalo, NY 14202. **Business Addr:** Chief, OB/GYN, Geneva B Scruggs Community Health Care Center Inc, 543 Kensington Ave, Buffalo, NY 14215.

MCDANIEL, KAREN COTTON
University administrator, library director. **Personal:** Born Nov 16, 1950, Newark, NJ; daughter of Maude Smoot Cotton Bledsoe, Alphonso C Cotton Jr; married Rodney McDaniel, Sr, Aug 25, 1971; children: Rodney Jr, Kimberly Renee, Jason Bradley. **Educ:** Berea College, BS, 1973; University of Kentucky, MSLS, 1975. **Career:** KY State University, asst librarian, 1975-83; KY Department Public Advocacy, law librarian, 1983-85; KY Department for Libraries & Archives, prog coord, 1985-89; KY State University, director of libraries, 1989-. **Orgs:** KY Council on Archives, 1987-; Women's History Coalition of KY, chair, 1997-98, mem, 1993-; Amer Library Assn, 1989-; Assn Coll & Research Libraries, 1989-; KY Library Assn, section scy, 1990-91, mem, 1975-; SOLINET, bd of dirs, treas, 1995-96, scy, 1996-97, mem, 1994-97; 1890 Land Grant Lib Director's Assn, chair, 1994-98, vice chair, 1992-94, mem, 1989-; State Assisted Academic Library Council of KY, chair, 1992-93, scy, 1991-92, mem, 1989-; Black Caucus of the Amer Library Assn, 1991-; Assn of Agricultural Admin, chair, 1996-98, mem, 1989-. **Honors/Awds:** US Off of Education, fellow for studies in Librarianship, 1974-75; Outstanding Young Women in America, 1979-81; Alpha Delta Kappa, Intl Honorary Sorority for Women Educators, 1991-; Delta Sigma Theta Sorority, 1976-. **Special Achievements:** Author of numerous essays published in encyclopedias. **Business Addr:** Director, Libraries/Professor, Kentucky State University, 400 E Main St, Paul G Blazer Library, Frankfort, KY 40601, (502)227-6852.

MCDANIEL, MYRA ATWELL
Attorney. **Personal:** Born Dec 13, 1932, Philadelphia, PA; daughter of Eva Yores Atwell and Toronto C Atwell, Jr; married Dr Reuben McDaniel Jr, Feb 2, 1955; children: Diane, Reuben III. **Educ:** Univ of PA, English 1954; Univ of TX Law School, JD 1975. **Career:** Aviation Supply Office Philadelphia, mgmt analyst; Baldwin-Wallace Coll Berea OH, IN Univ Bloomington, admin asst jobs; Railrod Commiss of TX, asst spec counsel, asst atty gen in charge of taxation div; Gov Mark White, gen counsel; State of TX, sec of state 1984-87; Bickerstaff Heath & Smiley, partner 1987-. **Orgs:** Mem TX Bar Assoc, Amer Bar Assoc, Travis County Bar Assoc, Austin Black Laweyrs' Assoc, Travis County Women Lawyers' Assoc, Fellows of the TX Bar Found, Fellows of the Amer Bar Found; admitted to practice, State of TX, US Supreme Court, US Fifth Circuit Court of Appeals, US Dist Courts for the Eastern Western Southern & Northern Dist of TX; chmn atty sect Natl Assoc of Tax Admins 1980-81; mem Professional Efficiency & Econ Rsch 1978-84, Asset Mgmt Adv Comm State Treas 1984-86, Hobby-Lewis Joint Select Comm on Fiscal Policy 1984-86, Criminal Justice Policy Council State of TX 1984-86, Natl Assoc of Secretaries of State 1984-86; mem bd of dir Austin Consulting Group Inc 1983-86; mem bd trustees St Edward's Univ Austin 1986-, TX Bar Found 1986-89,Episcopal Found of Houston TX 1986-90; bd of trustees, Episcopal Seminary of the Southwest, 1989-; bd of dirs, Assn of Govering Bd of Colleges & Universities, 1992-; Lay Eucharistic Minister, St James Episcopal Church, 1993-, newsletter editor, 1991-, vestry bd, 1988-91, sr warden, 1990-91; Univ of TX, Law Alumni Assn, dir, 1992-94; Black Alumni Advisory Comm, Univ of TX, Ex-students Assn, mem, 1989-; Advisory Bd, Longhorn Assoc, Excellence in Women's Athletics, 1988-91; TX Ex-students Athletics Comm, co-chair, 1988-89. **Honors/Awds:** Woman of the Year, TX Natl Organization of Women, 1993; Hendrick Arnold Lifetime Achievement Award, TX African-American Heritage Organization, 1993; Honorary Doctorate Degree, Jarvis Christian Coll, Hawkins, 1986; Citizen of the Year, Mega Psi Phi Fraternity, Epsilon Iona Chapter, Austin, 1985; Woman of the Year, International Training in Communication, Austin Chaper, 1985; Woman of the Year, Longview Metro Chamber of Commerce, Longview, 1985.

MCDANIEL, PAUL ANDERSON
Clergyman. **Personal:** Born Jul 5, 1930, Rock Hill, SC; married Edna Carolyn Phillips; children: Paul Jr, Pamela Anita, Patricia Ann, Peter Adam. **Educ:** Morehouse Coll Atlanta, BA Hist Polit Sci 1951; Colgate Rochester Div Sch, MDiv 1955; Univ of Rochester, MA 1959. **Career:** Second Baptist Church Mumford, pastor 1952-56; Second Baptist Ch Rahway NJ, pastor 1956-66; Second Missionary Bapt Ch Chattanooga, pastor 1966-. **Orgs:** Former pres Clergy Assn of Greater Chattanooga; past pres TN Leadership Educ Congress; instr Natl Bapt Congress of Christian Educ; del TN Constitutional Conv 29th Dist Nashville 1977; chmn GA-TN Regional Health Commn 1978-80; chmn & past vice chmn Hamilton Co Commn Chattanooga 1979-. **Honors/Awds:** DD Friendship Jr Coll Rock Hill SC 1975; various serv awds comm orgs. **Business Addr:** Pastor, Second Missionary Baptist Ch, 2305 E Third St, Chattanooga, TN 37404.

MCDANIEL, RANDALL CORNELL
Professional football player. **Personal:** Born Dec 19, 1964, Phoenix, AZ; married Marianne. **Educ:** Arizona State, bachelor's degree in physical education. **Career:** Minnesota Vikings, guard, 1988-. **Honors/Awds:** Pro Bowl, 1989-96; Midwest Sports Channel, Most Inspirational Man of the Year, 1996. **Business Addr:** Professional Football Player, Minnesota Vikings, 9520 Viking Dr, Eden Prairie, MN 55344, (612)828-6500.

MCDANIEL, REUBEN R.
Educator. **Personal:** Born Jan 6, 1936, Petersburg, VA; son of Nannie Finney McDaniel and Reuben R McDaniel; married Myra Yores Atwell; children: Diane, Reuben R III. **Educ:** Drexel Univ, BMechEng 1964; Univ of Akron, MS Guidance Cnslng 1968; IN Univ, EdD Higher Educ 1971. **Career:** Baldwin-Wallace Clge, asst dean, asst prof educ, & dir div educ srv 1965-69; Indiana Univ, assoc instructor 1969-71; Florida State Univ, asst prof 1971-72; Univ of Texas at Austin, Jesse H Jones prof 1983-89, Tom E. Nelson, Jr. regents professor, 1989-91; Charles and Elizabeth Prothro Regents Chair in Heath Care Management, professor of management, 1991-. **Orgs:** Acting deputy commnr Texas Dept of Human Resources 1979; consultant Seton Medical Center Austin 1980-; bd of trustees Seton Medical Ctr Austin 1985-91; Priority Schools Comm, Austin Ind School District 1989-91; Advisory Comm, Banaker Honors Coll, Prairie View A&M Univ 1987-91. **Honors/Awds:** J D Beasley Grad Teaching Awd UT Austin 1982; Univ TX at Austin 1983-89; chmn Faculty Senate Univ of Texas at Austin 1985-87; Key D Award, Outstanding Alumni, Drexel University, 1988. **Home Addr:** 3910 Knollwood Dr, Austin, TX 78731, (512)345-0006. **Business Addr:** Professor of Management, Univ of TX at Austin, Dept of Management CBA 4246, Austin, TX 78712, (512)471-9451.

MCDANIEL, ROBERT ANTHONY (PETE)
Writer. **Personal:** Born Aug 2, 1952, Arden, NC; son of Mary Alice Spain McDaniel and Theodore Roosevelt McDaniel; divorced; children: Demayne Z Ginyard, Marc A McDaniel, Tristan S McDaniel. **Educ:** University of North Carolina, Asheville, NC, BA, English, 1974. **Career:** Asheville Citizen-Times, Asheville, NC, sports writer, 1974-75; Life of Georgia Ins Co, Asheville, NC, insurance agent, 1975-78; Piedmont Airlines, Asheville, NC, ticket agent trainee 1978-79; Times-News, Hendersonville, NC, sports writer, 1979-82, sports editor, 1982-93; Golf World Magazine, Trumbull, CT, sr writer, 1993-97; Golf Digest, 1997-. **Orgs:** Member, National Association of Black Journalists, 1989-; member, Associated Press Sports Editors, 1982-93; member, Golf Writers of America Assn, 1993-. **Honors/Awds:** Spot Sports News, 3rd Pl, NC Press Assn, 1981; Sports Feature, 2nd Pl, NC Press Assn, 1984; Sports Feature, 2nd Pl, NC Press Assn, 1985; 1st Place, Sports Reporting, NC Press Association, 1992; Black Achiever in Bus/Industry Award, 1997. **Special Achievements:** Co-Author of best-selling book "Training A Tiger.". **Business Addr:** Golf Digest, 5520 Park Ave, Trumbull, CT 06611.

MCDANIEL, SHARON A.
Arts administrator, music critic. **Personal:** Born Jan 3, 1950, Hampton, VA; daughter of Mae Hallie Payne McDaniel and James Cornelius McDaniel. **Educ:** Paris American Academy of Music, Paris, France, certificates in piano & French, 1967; College-Conservatory of Music, Cincinnati, OH, BA in music theory, 1971; Eastman School of Music, Rochester, NY, 1972-74, 1986-88. **Career:** General Telephone & Electronics, Los Angeles, CA, regional sales manager, 1974-78; Oakland Symphony Orchestra, Oakland, CA, orchestra manager, 1978-79; Dayton Contemporary Dance Company, Dayton, OH, general manager, 1982-84; Springfield Symphony, Springfield, OH, general manager, 1984-86; Hochstein Music School, Rochester, NY, director of communications, 1988-; about time Magazine, Rochester, NY, editorial assistant, 1991-. **Orgs:** Classical music announcer/host WRUR-FM, Rochester, NY, 1986-; singer, Rochester Bach Festival Choir, Rochester, NY, 1972-74 & 1987-; member, Rochester Association of Black Communicators, Rochester, NY, 1987-; board of directors, member, publicity, Madrigalia Ltd, Rochester, NY, 1987-; member fund raising committees, IBM-PC Club of Rochester, NY, 1988; member, Music Critics Assn, 1984, 1991. **Honors/Awds:** National Merit Scholar, 1967; Outstanding Junior Woman; Daisy Chain-University of Cincinnati, 1970; Educational Institute Fellow, Music Critics Association, 1991. **Business Addr:** Director of Communications, Hochstein Music School, 50 N Plymouth Ave, Rochester, NY 14614.

MCDANIEL, TERRENCE LEE
Professional football player. **Personal:** Born Feb 8, 1965, Mansfield, OH; married. **Educ:** Univ of Tennessee, attended. **Career:** Oakland Raiders, cornerback, 1988-. **Business Addr:** Professional Football Player, Oakland Raiders, 1220 Harbor Bay Pkwy, Alameda, CA 94502, (510)615-1875.

MCDANIEL, WILLIAM T., JR.
Educator. **Personal:** Born Sep 24, 1945, Memphis, TN; married Bernice Dowdy; children: William Theodore III. **Educ:** Morehouse Coll, BA 1967; Univ IA, MA 1968, PhD 1974. **Career:** School of Music, OH State U, prof; NC A&T State U, prof, chmn dept of music; Morehouse Coll, dir of bands 1968-72, chmn dept of Music, dir of bands 1974-77; Univ IA, instr blk music 1973-74. **Orgs:** Mem Mus Edtrs Nat Conf; Am Musclgcl Soc; Coll Mus Soc; Coll Band Dir Nat Assn; Nat Assn Coll Wind & Percsn Instrs; Nat Band Assn; mem Alpha Phi Alpha. **Honors/Awds:** Advncd Study Felwshp for Black Ams, Ford Found 1972-73; IBM Fclty Flwshp, Untd Negro Coll Fund 1972-73; grant, Nat Endowmt for Arts 1972; Nat Flwshp, Ford Found 1973-74. **Business Addr:** Professor, School of Music, Ohio State University, Room 313A, 1899 College Road, Columbus, OH 43210.

MCDANIEL, XAVIER MAURICE
Professional basketball player. **Personal:** Born Jun 4, 1963, Columbia, SC. **Educ:** Wichita State Univ, Wichita, KS, 1981-85. **Career:** Forward: Seattle SuperSonics, 1985-91; Phoenix Suns, 1991; New York Knicks, 1991-92; Boston Celtics, 1992-96; New Jersey Nets, 1996-. **Honors/Awds:** NBA All-Rookie Team, 1986. **Business Addr:** Professional Basketball Player, New Jersey Nets, Brendan Byrne Arena, East Rutherford, NJ 07073, (201)935-8888.

MCDANIELS, ALFRED F.
Track and field coach, educator. **Personal:** Born Sep 21, 1940, Muskogee, OK; son of Alvin McDaniels; married Cheryl McDaniels Kieser, Jun 11, 1971; children: Alfred Jr, Debbie. **Educ:** Bakersfield Jr Coll, AA 1961; Univ of NV, Reno, BS, 1965; Univ of NV, Las Vegas MED, 1971; Univ of NV, BS 1965, MEduc, 1972. **Career:** PE Health Educ, tchr 1965-70; Varsity Football, asst varsity head jr varsity asst track coach, 1965-67; Merced HS, head track coach 1968-80; Univ of NV, asst football coach 1970-72, asst track coach 1971-74, asst prof phys educ head track coach, 1975-92, teacher, Dept of Kinesiology, currently. **Orgs:** Mem NEA, NSEA, NAHPER, AAHPER; United Tching Profsn; US Track & Field Coaches Assn;

Women's Track & Field Coaches Assn; organized developed summer track & field prog for youths & adults 1971-75 (has more than 600 participants each summer); designed and developed the USA Youth Track & Field program in Nevada, 1980-93; trained and organized the Southern Nevada Track & Field Officials Assn, 1975-92. **Honors/Awds:** Most Outstanding Sr Athlete Univ of NV Reno 1965; Most Outstanding in Track 1963; Most Outstanding in Football 1964; 1984 Women's PCAA Team Champion Track & Field; 1984-86, 1989 Women's PCAA Coach of the Yr Track & Field, 1984-86, 1989; big west coach of year, PCAA 1989; Outstanding Athlete, Bakersfield H.S., 1960, Bakersfield Coll, 1959, Univ of NV, 1965; publication in athletic journals, speaker at numerous clinics; Las Vegas Black Sports Hall of Fame, 1991; Bakersfield College Track and Field Hall of Fame, 1993; USA Track and Field President's Award, 1993; NCAA District Eight Coach of the Year, 1989, 1991; Big West Coach of the Year, 1984-86, 1989. **Special Achievements:** Wrote a chapter on track and field in "Sports and Recreational Activities for Men and Women," January 1994. **Business Addr:** Dept of Physical Education, Univ of Nevada - Las Vegas, 4505 S Maryland Pkwy, Las Vegas, NV 89154-9900.

MCDANIELS, JEANEEN J.
Attorney. **Personal:** Born Mar 29, 1960, Canton, OH; daughter of Nadine Williams McIlwain and Albert H. McIlwain (deceased). **Educ:** Central State University, Wilberforce, OH, 1981; University of Akron, Akron, OH, JD, 1984. **Career:** County Prosecutor's Office, Canton, OH, assistant prosecuting attorney, 1985-86; City Prosecutor's Office, Canton, OH, assistant prosecuting attorney, 1986-90; The Timken Company, Canton, OH, senior personnel and logistics analyst, 1990-91, industrial relations representative, 1992-; Timken Co Gam Roller Plant, mgr of hr, 1992-; We'll Do It For You, Inc, owner. **Orgs:** Vice president, 1988-90, president, 1990-92, Stark County Delta Sigma Theta Inc; president, 1988-90, treasurer, 1990-92, The Mahogany Association; secretary, Canton City School Foundation, 1990-92; secretary, Canton Urban League, 1990-92; legal advisor, Indian River School, 1987-92. **Home Phone:** (330)588-8304. **Business Phone:** (330)471-4131.

MCDANIELS, JOHN EDWARD, SR. See Obituaries section.

MCDANIELS, PELLOM, III
Professional football player. **Personal:** Born Feb 21, 1968, San Jose, CA; married Nawab. **Educ:** Oregon State. **Career:** Birmingham Fire (WFL), 1991-92; Kansas City Chiefs, linebacker, 1993-; Pic N Cottin Inc, owner. **Special Achievements:** Established the Arts for Smarts Foundation, a program that acquaints disadvantaged children with theater and dance. **Business Addr:** Professional Football Player, Kansas City Chiefs, One Arrowhead Dr, Kansas City, MO 64129, (816)924-9300.

MCDANIELS, WARREN E.
Fire chief. **Educ:** Harvard Univ, John F Kennedy School of Government, fellow. **Career:** New Orleans Fire Dept, asst superintendent, 10 years, superintendent, currently. **Special Achievements:** First African-American Fire Chief in New Orleans. **Business Addr:** Superintendent, New Orleans Fire Department, 317 Decatur, New Orleans, LA 70130, (504)565-7800.

MCDEMMOND, MARIE V.
Educational admnistrator. **Career:** Florida Atlantic Univ, vp for finance/COO; Norfolk State Univ, pres-elect, currently. **Orgs:** Southern Association of College and University Business Officers (SACUBO), pres. **Special Achievements:** First African-American woman president of SACUBO.

MCDONALD, ALDEN J., JR.
Banking executive. **Career:** Liberty Bank and Trust Company, New Orleans, LA, president, 1972-.

MCDONALD, ANITA DUNLOP
Social worker (retired). **Personal:** Born May 11, 1929, Morgantown, WV; daughter of LaFronia Chloe Dunlop (deceased) and William J Dunlop (deceased); married James J McDonald, Dec 27, 1950; children: Janice-Marie McDonald. **Educ:** WV State Coll, BA 1951; WV Univ, MSW 1953. **Career:** Syracuse Memorial Hosp, med soc worker 1954-56; Family Serv of Jamestown, social worker 1975-79; Chautauqua Co Mental Health-Jamestown, psychiatric social worker 1980-94. **Orgs:** Mem AAUW Jamestown Branch 1968-; sec bd of trustees Jamestown Comm Coll 1969-78; pres Bd of Dirs of YWCA 1973-75; chmn public affairs bd of dirs YWCA 1984-85; financial sec & chairman trustee bd Emmanuel Bapt Church; president, Chaut Co American Baptist Women, 1990-; member, School Community Relations Council, 1989-91; Ebony Task Force, 1986-; adult leader, Emmanuel Baptist Church Youth Group, 1990-; nominating committee, Girl Scouts, Jamestown, 1991-94, mem, 1994-; Jamestown Chapter, Links, Inc, 1993-, vp; Amer Baptist New York State, bd of managers, 1994-; pres, Ebony Task Force, 1995. **Honors/Awds:** Lifetime Achievement Award, Western Division New York State Chapter NASW, 1994; 3rd VP, Girl Scouts, Jamestown, 1996. **Home Addr:** 40 W 22nd St, Jamestown, NY 14701.

MCDONALD, AUDRA ANN
Actress. **Personal:** Born Jul 3, 1970, Berlin, Germany; daughter of Anna & Stanley McDonald Jr. **Educ:** Juilliard School, BM, 1993. **Career:** Lincoln Center Theater, actress in Carousel, 1994; ATP/Dodger, The Secret Garden, actress; Great Performances, PBS, singer-Hammerstein Tribute, 1995; Whitehead Productions, master class, currently. **Honors/Awds:** American Theater Wing, Tony Antoinette Perry, Best Featured Actress, 1994; Outer Critics Circle, Outer Critics Circle Award, Best Actress, 1994; Drama Desk, Best Supporting Actress, 1994; Theater World, Outstanding New Talent in a Musical; Tony Award for Best Supporting Actress in a Play, 1996; LA Ovation Award, 1996.

MCDONALD, CHARLES J.
Physician, educator. **Personal:** Born Dec 6, 1931, Tampa, FL; married Maureen McDonald; children: Marc, Norman, Eric. **Educ:** NC A&T Univ, BS (distinction) 1951; Univ of MI, MS 1952; Howard Univ, MD (highest distinction) 1960. **Career:** Hosp of St Raphael New Haven, intern 1960-61, asst resident in med 1961-63; Yale Univ School of Med, asst resident 1963-65; US Public Health Serv, Special Rsch Fellow, Yale Univ School of Med, fellow & chief resident 1965-66; Yale Univ School of Med, Yale-New Haven Med Ctr, instr, assoc physician 1966-67, asst prof, asst attending physician 1967-68; Brown Univ Providence RI, asst prof 1968-69, assoc prof 1969-74; Rhode Island Gen Hosp head dermatology, assoc chief of med 1968; Brown Univ, dermatology prog dir 1970, prof of med sci, head subsect dermatology 1974-96, chair, dept of dermatology, 1996-. **Orgs:** Mem Amer Dermatology Assn, New England Dermatology Soc, Soc for Investigative Dermatology, Amer Fed for Clinical Rsch, Amer Acad of Dermatology, Natl Med Assn; chmn Sect of Dermatology 1973-75, AAAS, RI Dermatology Soc, Noah Worcester Dermatology Soc, Amer Soc for Clinical Oncology, Dermatology Found; mem Dermatology Coun, Assoc of Profs of Dermatology; consult Natl Inst of Arthritis Metabolism & Digestive Diseases; consult RI State Dept of Health; consult Providence Health Ctrs Inc; former chmn Health Task Force, RI Urban Coalition; former mem comm Governors Conf on Health Care Cost; mem bd dir, vice pres, pres RI Div Amer Cancer Soc, 1969-; board of directors, Natl American Cancer Society, 1983-Vice President and President elect National ACS 1997-; mem bd of trustees Citizens Bank Providence RI; mem, Alpha Omega Alpha, Med Society; vp and pres New England Dermatology Soc 83-85; mem bd dirs Amer Acad Dermatology 1986-90; Natl Inst General Med Sciences, Pharmaeological Sciences Review Ctr, 1978-82; FDA Damatology Advisory Ctr, 1970-75; Natl Inst of Arthrites, Musculoskeletal & Skin Diseases; mem, Natl Advisory Bd, 1992-95; residency review comm for dermatology, ACGME, 1991-97, vice chair, 1995-97; Assn Prof of Dermatology, bd of dirs, 1991-95; Noah Worcester Dermatological Society, bd of dirs, 1983-86; Howard Univ, bd of trustees, 1993-; chair, Medical Affairs, 1994-; Providence Public Library, bd of dirs, 1987-, secretary, 1990-96, chair nominating comm, 1990-96; Rhode Island Commodores, 1990-. **Honors/Awds:** Highest Academic Achievement Awd Coll of Medicine, Howard; 1st Annual Distinguished Serv Award Hosp Assoc of RI; Distinguished Alumni Award Coll of Medicine Howard Univ 1983; author, co-author of approx 150 sci articles; Honorary MS, Brown Univ, 1970; Certified Amer bd of Dermatology, 1966; Amer Cancer Society Natl Division Award, St George Medal, 1992; The Best Doctors in Amer, 1992, 1994, 1997; Eric Zwerling Memorial Lecturer & Outstanding Dermatology Professor, Natl Medical Assn, 1987; Firs Annual Distinguished Service Award, Hospital Assn Rhode Island, 1971. **Military Serv:** USAF mjr 4 yrs. **Business Addr:** Prof of Med Science, Rhode Island Hospital, Brown University, Dept of Dermatology, 593 Eddy St, Providence, RI 02903.

MCDONALD, CURTIS W.
Educator. **Personal:** Born Jan 29, 1934, Cedar Creek, TX; son of Virgie McDonald and Oscar McDonald; married. **Educ:** Huston Tillotson Coll Austin, BS 1955; TX Srthrn Univ, MS 1957; Univ TX, PhD 1962. **Career:** Alcorn A&M Coll Lorman MS, tchr 1961-63; AL State Univ Montgomery, 1963-68; Southern Univ Baton Rouge, 1968-73; TX Southern Univ Houston 1973-. **Orgs:** Mem Amer Chem Soc; Natl Inst Sci; Soc Applied Spectscpy; Soc Sigma Xi; TX Acad of Sci; Amer Inst Chemists. **Honors/Awds:** Publications in Anal Chem 1964, 1967, 1969, 1973, 1974; Mikrochim 1970, 1972, 1974; 40 publications from 1964-90. **Business Addr:** Professor, Texas Southern Univ, Dept of Chemistry, Houston, TX 77004.

MCDONALD, EDMUND MORRIS
Dentist (retired). **Personal:** Born Sep 30, 1917, Sumter, SC; son of Adelaide Palmer McDonald and Samuel J McDonald Sr; married Anna Louise Birnie; children: Edmund, Jr. **Educ:** Benedict Coll, BS 1938; Colum Univ, MA 1941; Meharry Med Coll, DDS 1948. **Career:** Howard HS, teacher & coach 1938-39; Booker Washington HS, teacher & asst coach 1941-44; McDonald and McDonald, dentist 1984-, dental private practice, 1948-88. **Orgs:** Mem Pee Dee Dental Soc; mem SC Dent Assn; relief comm SC Dental Assn; mem Amer Dental Assn; Congaree Denta; Soc; Palmetto Med Dent & Pharmac Assn; pres Palmetto Med Dental & Pharmacy Assn 1971; mem Natl Dental Assn; House of Delegates Natl Dental Assn 1970-; mem Omega Psi Phi Frat; chmn life mem Comm NAACP; mem adv bd Pee Dee Boy Scouts; steward trustee Emmanuel United Methodist Church; captain Benedict Coll Football Team 1937. **Honors/Awds:** 1st Benedict Coll football player to make Little All-Amer 1st team 1937; Dental Faculty Honor Med Meharry Med Coll 1948; mem Omicron Kappa Upsilon Hon Fraternity; mem Kappa Sigma Pi Hon Fraternity; elected to Benedict Coll Athletic Hall of Fame 1982; elected to Sumter SC Athletic Hall of Fame 1984.

MCDONALD, ELLA SEABROOK
Child welfare administrator. **Personal:** Born in Adel, GA. **Career:** Richard Allen Center on Life, exec dir, currently; registered nurse; health and human services specialist, currently. **Orgs:** Black Agency Executives; National Association of University Women; The Schomung Corp.; Black Administrators inChild Welfare. **Honors/Awds:** Black Health Research Foundation, Woman of the Year, 1992; International Black Woman Congress, Oni Award, 1991. **Home Addr:** 138 Manhattan Ave, New York, NY 10025. **Business Addr:** Executive Director, Richard Allen Center on Life, 1854 Amsterdam Ave, New York, NY 10031, (212)862-3799.

MCDONALD, G. MICHAEL
Automobile dealership executive. **Career:** Courtesy Ford Lincoln-Mercury Inc, chief executive officer, currently. **Special Achievements:** Company ranked #79 on BE's Top 100 Auto Dealers, 1990, #78, 1992. **Business Addr:** Chief Executive Officer, Courtesy Ford Lincoln-Mercury Inc, 231 W Main St, Danville, IL 61832, (217)442-1840.

MCDONALD, GABRIELLE KIRK
Judge. **Personal:** Born Apr 12, 1942, St Paul, MN; married Mark T McDonald; children: Michael, Stacy. **Educ:** Howard Univ, LLB 1966. **Career:** Legal Def Fund NYC, staff attny 1966-69; McDonald & McDonald Houston, partner 1969-79; TX So Univ Houston, asst prof 1970, adj prof 1975-77; Univ of TX Houston, lectr 1977-78; US Dist Court Houston, judge, beginning 1979; Mathews Branscomb, attorney; UN General Assembly, International War Crimes, Trial Chamber II, presiding judge, currently. **Orgs:** Bd dir Commun Serv Option Prog, Alley Theatre Houston, Natl Coalition of 100 Black Women, ARC; trustee Howard Univ 1983-; bd visitors Thurgood Marshall School of Law Houston; mem ABA, Natl Bar Assoc, Houston Bar Assoc, Houston Lawyers Assoc, Black Women Lawyers Assoc. **Business Addr:** Presiding Judge, Trial Chamber II, Intl War Crimes Tribunal, Aegon Bldg, 052-053 Churchill Plein I, 2517G The Hague, Netherlands.

MCDONALD, HERBERT G.
Architect. **Personal:** Born Feb 11, 1929, Jamaica, NY; son of Priscilla A Young McDonald and Herbert C McDonald; married Debra H; children: Gail Louise, Cathy Allison. **Educ:** Howard Univ, BArch 1953. **Career:** Gitlin & Cantor Architects, Wash DC, assoc 1959-60; Edwin Weihe, architect 1960-62; Herbert G McDonald & Assoc, architect 1962-65; McDonald & Williams AIA, architect, partner 1965-90; McDonald, Williams, Banks, 1990-. **Orgs:** Dir, Lawrence Johnson Assoc, Wash DC; vice pres, dir, Barkingside Devel Inc, Bahamas; dir, sec, Davis Const Co; adv, Independence Federal Savings & Loan, Wash DC; mem, Amer Inst of Archit; mem, DC Council of Black Archit; mem, Aircraft Owners & Pilots Assn; mem, Omega Psi Phi Archit Clifton Terrace Apts, 1969; DC Correctional Detention Facility, 1974; archit NECIP 1977, Lincoln Westmoreland Apts 1972; mem, DC Legislative Comm on Housing; dir, Natl Housing Rehab Assoc; vice pres, dir, CEO, H Bear Enterprises Inc. **Military Serv:** Corps of Engrs 1st lt 1954-56. **Business Addr:** Architect, McDonald, Williams, Banks, 7705 Georgia Ave, NW, Washington, DC 20012.

MCDONALD, JASON ADAM
Professional baseball player. **Personal:** Born Mar 20, 1972, Modesto, CA. **Educ:** Houston. **Career:** Oakland Athletics, outfielder, 1997-. **Business Addr:** Professional Baseball Player, Oakland Athletics, 7677 Oakport St, 2nd Fl, Oakland Coliseum Complex, Oakland, CA 94621, (510)638-4900.

MCDONALD, JEFFREY BERNARD
Company executive. **Personal:** Born Oct 12, 1952, Benham, KY; son of Nathan & Orya McDonald Jr; children: R Malik. **Educ:** Kentucky State Univ, BSBA, 1976; Boston Univ, MBA, 1978. **Career:** Monsanto, supervisor, internal audit, 1977-87; Ralston Purina, director, financial services, 1987-. **Orgs:** Natl Assn of Black Accountants; MBA Assn; Internal Audit Assn; Cash Management. **Special Achievements:** Fluent in Spanish. **Military Serv:** US Marine Corps, sergeant, 1970-72. **Business Addr:** Director, Financial Services, Protein Tech Intl Ralston Purina Co, Checkerboard Square, Tower Bldg 13, St Louis, MO 63164, (314)982-3845.

MCDONALD, JON FRANKLIN
Educator. **Personal:** Born Jun 28, 1946, Jackson, MS; son of Ruby Tripplet McDonald and Charles McDonald; married Mary Ann Davies, Jan 18, 1972; children: Gabriel Charles, Beau Richards. **Educ:** Kendall School of Design, Certificate 1969; San Francisco Art Inst, M Fine Arts 1972. **Career:**

Spungbuggy Works, asst animator 1974-75; Everywomans Village, teacher 1977-79; Kendall Coll of Art & Design, Grand Rapids, MI, prof, 1980-. **Orgs:** Visual arts advisor Frauenthal Center of Performing Arts/Muskegon MI 1986-89; comm mem Mayor's Advisory Comm on Art/Grand Rapids 1989-90; artist-in-residence Grand Haven Public Schools 1989-90. **Honors/Awds:** Ellen Hart Bransten Scholarship San Francisco Art Inst 1970-72; Moscow/Manhattan Connection, 48 paintings travelled in USSR & USA 1989-91. **Business Addr:** Assoc Prof Visual Communication, Kendall School of Design, 111 Division Ave N, Grand Rapids, MI 49503.

MCDONALD, LARRY MARVIN
Human resources executive. **Personal:** Born Mar 12, 1952, Louisville, KY; son of Angie V McDonald and Charles S McDonald; married Denise Harker McDonald (divorced 1989); children: Angie M, Ebeni M, Denisha I. **Educ:** University of Kentucky, Lexington, KY, BBA, 1974; University of Louisville, Louisville, KY, MBA, 1992. **Career:** Humana Inc, Louisville, KY, equipment specifier/buyer, 1982-85, mgmt development intern, 1985-87, personnel manager, 1987-89, director of EEO, affirmative action, 1989-. **Orgs:** Business consultant, Project Business, Junior Achievement, 1986-88; pres, steering committee, Project BUILD, 1985-; vice chairman, trustee board, First Congregational Methodist Church, 1981-; board member, Louisville Urban League, 1990-; board member, BETA Advisory Board, Univ of Louisville Speed Scientific School, 1986-; steering committee, Black Achievers Organization, 1983-89, 1992-; board member, Louisville Orchestra, 1992-; board member, Classical Roots, 1990. **Honors/Awds:** Honored Volunteer Spirit of Louisville Foundation Inc, 1989; Citizen of the Month, Louisville Jaycees, 1989; Outstanding Volunteer of the Year, YMCA of Greater Louisville, 1986; Black Achiever, Chestnut St YMCA, 1983; Leadership Louisville, honoree, 1987. **Business Addr:** Director of Equal Employment Opportunity, Affirmative Action, Humana Inc, 500 W Main St, Louisville, KY 40202.

MCDONALD, MARK T.
Attorney. **Personal:** Born Jun 20, 1935, Henderson, TX; married Babrielle Kirk; children: Mark T, Jr, Micheal K, Stacy Frances. **Educ:** Prairie View A&M Coll, BA hon 1956; TX So U, LlB 1962. **Career:** McDonald & McDonald Atty at Law, atty 1962; Legal Serv Div OEO, consult 1965; TX So U, asst prof law 1964-70; Prarie View A&M Coll, asso prof Polit sci 1963-64. **Orgs:** Mem State Bar of TX; Am Bar Assn; Assn of Trial Lawyers of Am; NatL Bar Assn; Am Judicature Soc; Natl Assn of Criminal Def Attys; TX Trial Lawyers Assn; Houston Bar Assn; Houston Trial Lawyers Assn; NAACP; Houston Bus & Professional Men's Club; ACLU of Houston; YMCA Century Club. **Business Addr:** 1834 Southmore Blvd, Houston, TX 77004.

MCDONALD, MIKE
Professional football player. **Personal:** Born Jun 22, 1958, North Hollywood, CA. **Educ:** Univ of Southern California, attended. **Career:** Univ of Southern California, grad asst coach, 1980, 1981; Burroughs (CA) High School, asst coach, 1982, 1983, 1985; Los Angeles Rams, linebacker, 1984, 1986-. **Honors/Awds:** NFC Championship Game, post-1989 season.

MCDONALD, R. TIMOTHY
Educational administrator. **Personal:** Born Sep 29, 1940, Pittsburgh, PA; married Beverly Clark; children: Lawana, Monica, Lanita, Patrick. **Educ:** Oakwood Coll, BS 1963; Atlanta Univ, MS 1968; Univ of Miami, EdD 1972. **Career:** AL A&M Univ, prof of educ 1972-78; Oakwood Coll, vice pres for develop 1975-78; Barber Scotia Coll, vice pres for academic affairs 1978-79; OH State Univ, develop officer 1979-83; Seventh-day Adventist Church, dir of educ 1983-. **Orgs:** Bd mem Columbus Mental Health Assn 1980-83; consultant Higher Educ Assns 1975-; proposal writer-reader Fed Govt 1975-; bdmem Columbia Union Coll 1983-. **Honors/Awds:** Higher Educ Fellowship Fed Govt 1969-72; Title III Grant Fed Govt 1972-78; Spec Serv Awd OH State Univ 1981. **Home Addr:** 10516 E Wind Way, Columbia, MD 21044. **Business Addr:** Dir of Education, Mid-Atlantic Region SDA Church, 5427 Twin Knolls Rd, Columbia, MD 21045.

MCDONALD, RICARDO MILTON
Professional football player. **Personal:** Born Nov 8, 1969, Kingston, Jamaica. **Educ:** Univ of Pittsburgh, attended. **Career:** Cincinnati Bengals, linebacker, 1992-. **Business Addr:** Professional Football Player, Cincinnati Bengals, One Bengals Dr, Cincinnati, OH 45202, (513)621-3550.

MCDONALD, TIMOTHY
Professional football player. **Personal:** Born Jan 26, 1965, Fresno, CA; married Alycia; children: Timothy Jr, Tevin, Taryn. **Educ:** USC, attended. **Career:** St Louis Cardinals, defensive back, 1987; Phoenix Cardinals, 1988-92; San Francisco 49ers, 1993-. **Honors/Awds:** Pro Bowl appearance, 1991, 1992, 1993, 1994, 1995. **Business Addr:** Professional Football Player, San Francisco 49ers, 4949 Centennial Blvd, Santa Clara, CA 95054, (415)562-4949.

MCDONALD, WILLIAM EMORY
Engineer. **Personal:** Born Mar 9, 1924, Detroit, MI; son of Willie Mae Burrill McDonald and Emory S McDonald; widowed; children: Varnell, William, Jeannette. **Educ:** Univ of Michigan, BS 1950. **Career:** Public Lighting Comm, jr engineer 1950-54; Detroit Arsenal, electronic scientist 1954-57; Farrara Inc, chief project engineer 1957-58; Chrysler Missile, design engineer 1958-59; Rockwell Intl, sr project engineer 1959-72; North Carolina Central Univ, physical plant dir 1972-. **Orgs:** Pres bd Urban Ministries 1970-71; Alpha Phi Alpha Fraternity; sec, treasurer, 1st black officer Southeastern Reg Assoc of Physical Plant Admin; treasurer Assn of Physical Admin (APPA) 1989-91; secretary/treasurer, South Eastern Reg APPA 1980-89; mem bd of Adjustment, City of Durham, NC 1981-91; mem NC Synod Council, Evangelical Lutheran Church in Amer 1988-;. **Honors/Awds:** Meritorious Serv Award SE Reg Assn of Physical Plant Admin 1987. **Military Serv:** USAF 1944-46. **Business Addr:** Physical Plant Dir, North Carolina Central Univ, Box 19735, Durham, NC 27707.

MCDONALD, WILLIE RUTH DAVIS
Educator. **Personal:** Born Nov 4, 1931, San Antonio, TX; married Freeman; children: Ava Yvonne, Arva Yvotte. **Educ:** Wiley Coll, BS 1952; TS U, MEd 1964. **Career:** Bonham Schl, elemen tchr 1954-77. **Orgs:** Dir SW Houston Tchrs Assn 1977-78; leg comm mem HTA; bd mem House of Bees Halfway House; vP Nat Council of Negro Women; mem Nat Conf of Christians & Jews; com mem Special Events for Senatorial Dist 7; asst coord Precinct Club 240; adv cncl bd mem Eliza D Johnson Home for the Aged; com mem Conf on Minority Concerns; com mem Human Relation for HISD; nom com Moderate Dem Orgn; group com Transportation for the Mayor of Housing & Citizens of Dist 19 1972-77; exec bd mem HTA 1976-78; polt educ comm Dist 4 TSTA 1976-78; Fac Rep HTA 1972-77. **Business Addr:** 4815 Ligonberry, Houston, TX 77033.

MCDOWELL, BENJAMIN A.
Dentist. **Personal:** Born Apr 12, 1939, Laurens, SC; son of Annie B McDowell and Jesse McDowell; married Bobbie Green; children: Robyn, Joy, Mark. **Educ:** Morehouse Coll, BS 1960; Howard U, DDS 1965. **Career:** VA Hosp Tuskeegee, intern 1965-66; Pvt Practice, dentist; Jefferson County AL, Dept of Health, currently. **Orgs:** Mem Nat Dental Assn; AL Dental Soc; Jefferson Co Dental Study Club; mem NAACP; Bessemer Cit Com; Assn Wmn's & Clubs Adv Bd; bd mem AG Gaston Boys Club of Am 1975-76; Boy Scouts of America. **Honors/Awds:** Dentist of the Year, Alabama Dental Society, 1990. **Business Addr:** Jefferson County Dept. of Health, 2201 Arlington Ave, Bessemer, AL 35020.

MCDOWELL, CLEVE. See Obituaries section.

MCDOWELL, HARRIETTE FOWLKES
Ontologist. **Personal:** Born Sep 21, 1938, New Rochelle, NY; daughter of Mary Alice Fowlkes and William Harry Fowlkes; divorced; children: Michelle Renee Coston, Tracey Anne, Curtis Alden Jr. **Educ:** Syracuse University, 1970-72; SUNY College of Environmental Science & Forestry, 1975-77; Landmark Education, Toronto, Canada, certified, 1992. **Career:** Onondaga County, employment & training program coordinator, 1977-80; McDowell & Company, principal, 1980; McDowell Group Corporation, principal, 1980-. **Orgs:** Landmark Education, transformation leader, 1989-; Onondaga County Industrial Development Agency, vice chair, 1984-; Regional Development Planning Board, 1992-; Partners of Americas, president, 1992-. **Honors/Awds:** Post-Standard-Newhouse Communications, Businesswomen of the Year, 1986; Greater Syracuse Chamber & General Motors, Athena, 1986. **Home Phone:** (315)469-4972. **Business Phone:** (315)476-2223.

MCDOWELL-HEAD, LELIA M.
Journalist. **Personal:** Born Jun 7, 1953, San Francisco, CA; daughter of Elenita McDowell and Steven Helmut Heims; married Anthony Head, Dec 30, 1980; children: Layla. **Educ:** New York Univ, New York NY, BFA, 1975. **Career:** Fenton Communications, Washington DC, senior account exec; WPIX TV, New York NY, reporter; WBLS-WLIB Radio, New York NY, reporter anchor; WHTM TV, Harrisburg PA, reporter; Natl Alliance of Third World Journalists, Washington DC, natl co-coordinator, 1989.

MCDUFFIE, DEBORAH
Music producer, composer. **Personal:** Born Aug 8, 1950, New York, NY; daughter of Nan Wood McDuffie and Thomas McDuffie; children: Kijana Saunders, Kemal Gasper. **Educ:** Western Coll for Women, Oxford, OH, BA, music, 1971. **Career:** McCann-Erickson Advertising, New York, NY, music producer, composer, 1971-81; The Mingo Group, New York, NY, music dir, 1981-90; Middleman Liaison Extraordinaire, New York, NY, exec vp, creative dir, 1990-; Jana Productions, Inc, New York, NY, pres, CEO, 1981-. **Orgs:** Bd of dir, NY Urban League, 1990-; mem, ASCAP, 1980; mem, American Federation Musicians, 1978; mem, Screen Actors Guild, 1982; mem, Amer Federation Television-Radio Artists, 1977-. **Honors/Awds:** Clio Award (Advertising), 1981; Ceba Awards (Advertising Black Consumer Market), 1982-90 (excluding 1984); Telly Awards (Advertising), 1986.

MCDUFFIE, DWAYNE GLENN
Illustrator, editor. **Personal:** Born Feb 20, 1962, Detroit, MI; son of Edna Earle Hawkins Gardner and Leroy McDuffie; married Patricia Younger McDuffie, Dec 23, 1990; children: Angel, Avshalom. **Educ:** New York University, 1984-85; University of Michigan, Ann Arbor, MI, 1980-83. **Career:** NYU, resident advisor, 1985-86; Investment Dealers Digest, copy editor, 1987; Marvel Comics, special projects editor, 1987-90; Harvey Comics, consultant, 1990-; Milestone Media Inc, editor-in-chief, currently. **Honors/Awds:** Creator of Damage Control, Marvel Comics, 1987-; Writer Captain Marvel 1st Black Female Character with Own Title, Marvel, 1988; Writer, Deathlok, Only Black Character with Continuing Series, 1989-; Editor, A Clockwork Orange Adaptation of Anthony Burgess Novel, Harvey Comics, Writer of Various Titles, Double Dragon, Road to Hell, Back to the Future, MC Hammer, Hellraiser.

MCDUFFIE, HINFRED
Educational administrator. **Personal:** Born Aug 8, 1949, Montgomery, AL; children: Paula, Barry, Toka. **Educ:** Tuskegee Inst, BS 1971; Alabama State Univ, MS 1982, MS 1986. **Career:** Tuskegee Inst, assoc dir 1971-72, dir 1972-77; Alabama State Univ, dir of planning 1977-83, dir title III & planning 1983-. **Orgs:** Bd of dirs Montgomery Co Comm Action Agency; mem Election Law Commr State of Alabama, Kappa Alpha Psi Fraternity, Kappa Delta Phi Honor Soc in Educ, Soc for Coll & Univ Planning. **Business Addr:** Dir, Alabama State University, 915 S Jackson St, Montgomery, AL 36195.

MCDUFFIE, JOSEPH DELEON, JR.
Certified public accountant. **Personal:** Born Nov 9, 1950, St George, SC; son of Ernestine Brownlee McDuffie and Joseph DeLeon McDuffie Sr. **Educ:** SC State Coll, BSBA 1972; Columbia Univ, MBA 1974. **Career:** Touche Ross & Co, CPA 1974-77; CBS Inc, financial exec mergers & acquisitions 1977-79; SC State Coll, asst prof 1979-81; J deLeon McDuffie & Co, CPA 1979-; McDuffie Bros Inc, Registered Investment Advisors, CEO, 1989-. **Orgs:** Bd mem Eushua Arts Found 1983-; life mem Kappa Alpha Psi 1971-; mem Amer Inst of CPA's 1975-; sec asst, exec sec 1st Natl City Bank 1969; exec sec mgmt trne Amer Bank & Trust Co 1970-72; consulting Financial Pkg Corp 1973; IBM opr Ebasco Nuclear Engrg 1973; student advisor, consulting Lt Gov SC; mem SC State Student Leg; mayors comm Human Devel; bd dir SC State Coll Devel Fund; bd trustee SC State Coll; mem Kappa Alpha Psi; mem SC State Coll Alumni Assoc, SC State Coll Founders Club, SC State Coll Career Consultant, Columbia Univ Alumni Assoc of Business School, Columbia Univ Alumni Career Consult Assoc; vol Big Bros of NY Inc, Canaan Baptist Church; mem Amer Inst CPA, Natl Assoc Black Acct, Natl Soc Public Acct, NY State Soc CPA's; council Concerned Black Exec; 100 Black Men of NYC. **Honors/Awds:** 100 Black Men of NY City IN; Provincial Achievement Awd Kappa Alpha Psi 1972.

MCDUFFIE, OTIS JAMES
Professional football player. **Personal:** Born Dec 2, 1969, Marion, OH. **Educ:** Penn State, BA in labor and industrial relations. **Career:** Miami Dolphins, wide receiver, 1993-. **Business Addr:** Professional Football Player, Miami Dolphins, 2269 NW 199th St, Miami, FL 33056, (305)620-5000.

MCDYESS, ANTONIO KEITHFLEN
Professional basketball player. **Personal:** Born Sep 7, 1974, Quitman, MS. **Educ:** Alabama. **Career:** Denver Nuggets, forward-center, 1995-97; Phoenix Suns, 1997-. **Honors/Awds:** NBA All-Rookie First Team, 1996. **Special Achievements:** NBA, First Round Draft Pick, #2 Pick, 1995. **Business Addr:** Professional Basketball Player, Phoenix Suns, PO Box 515, Phoenix, AZ 85001, (602)379-7867.

MCEACHERN, D. HECTOR
Banking executive. **Personal:** Born in Fayetteville, NC; married Brenda Britt; children: Todd, Natashia, Dorian, Brandon. **Educ:** Fayetteville State University, BA, English, 1969; North Carolina State University, graduate study in psychology, 1971; management study, supervisory management, American Management Association, 1977; Management Seminar, The Art of Motivation, 1976; Clemson University, Employment Seminar, How to Remain Non-Union, 1978; Management Seminar, Every Employee A Manager, 1978; Interaction Management Instructor Certification; Duke University, Manager Development. **Career:** The Fayetteville Observer Newspaper, news reporter, 1968-70; Cumberland County Mental Health Center, social worker, 1970-72; Mount Vernon Psychiatric Clinic, psychiatric social worker, 1972-74; Texfi Industries, Inc, plant personnel manager, 1974-78, group personnel director, 1978-90; Wachovia Bank & Trust Co, senior vp/mgr personnel services, 1980-87; Wachovia Bank of North Carolina, director of personnel/senior vp/group executive, 1987-. **Orgs:** United Way of North Carolina, board member, 1992; Work/Family Resource Center, board member, 1992; Leadership Winston-Salem, board member; Bank Administration Institute, Human Resources Commission, former chairman; Fayetteville State University, board of trustees; Winston-Salem Urban League, board of directors; Leadership Winston-Salem, Bi-Racial Committee; Fayetteville State University Alumni Association, foundation board member; Childrens Home Society. **Home Phone:**

(910)676-1466. **Business Addr:** Senior VP, Group Executive Director, Wachovia Bank of North Carolina, PO Box 3099, Winston-Salem, NC 27102.

MCEACHERN-ULMER, SYLVIA L.
City official (retired). **Personal:** Born Mar 24, 1934, New York, NY; married Joseph Ulmer; children: Patricia McEachern, Brian McEachern. **Educ:** Rutgers Extension School, certified as Registered Municipal Clerk, 1973-77. **Career:** Bd of Educ Passaic Co Voc & Tech Schl, commissioner, pres 1986-87; City of Paterson, city clerk, 1971-89. **Orgs:** Pres, Passaic Co Municipal Clerk's Assn, 1984; mem, New Jersey State Municipal Clerk's Assn, 1972-; member, International Municipal Clerk's Assn, 1980-; Natl Black Caucus Schl Bd, 1980-; vice pres, 1984-86, pres, 1986-87, NJ Cty Voc Schl Bd. **Honors/Awds:** Honored Mother Women Active in Comm Affairs 1983; Salute to Blk Men & Women spec award Comm for Black History Month 1984; Christian Srv Award Calvary Baptist Church 1983, Canaan Baptist Church 1983; plaques from various comm grps; Testimonial Dinner 1975. **Special Achievements:** First African American Municipal Clerk in the State of New Jersey.

MCEACHIN, JAMES
Actor. **Personal:** Born May 20, 1930, Rennert, NC; married Lois Davis; children: Alainia, Lyle. **Career:** Films include: Uptight; If He Hollers, Let Him Go, 1968; True Grit, 1969; Hello Dolly, 1969; The Undefeated, 1969; Play Misty for Me, 1971; Buck and the Preacher, 1972; The Groundstar Conspiracy, 1972; Short Walk to Daylight, 1972; Fuzz, 1972; appeared in numerous TV productions including: The FBI; Mannix; Hawaii Five-O; Marcus Welby MD; That Certain Summer; actor in numerous other television movies and films. **Orgs:** Screen Actors Guild; American Federation of Television and Radio Artists. **Military Serv:** US Army, 1947-53; Purple Heart. **Business Addr:** PO Box 5166, Sherman Oaks, CA 91403.

MCELRATH, WANDA FAITH
Musician, artist, educator, security officer. **Personal:** Born Jan 11, 1959, Sylacauga, AL; daughter of Josephine L McElrath and Danfort McElrath. **Educ:** Troy State University, BME, 1983. **Career:** Avondale Mills, winder operator, 1977-82; Troy State University, student secretarial assistant to dean of fine arts/arts & sciences, 1977-82; self-employed, private trumpet instructor/performer, 1983-, karate instructor, certified, 1988-, airbrusher, 1988-; security officer, 1994-. **Orgs:** Principal's Advisory Committee, 1971-72; Anchor Club, senior director, 1976; Women Band Director's National Association, 1979; Tau Beta Sigma National Honorary Band Sorority, elected regional secretary, 1981-83; Alpha Phi Omega National Service Fraternity, pledge class president, 1981, social chairman, 1981; Senior Scholastic Society, 1976, 1977; US Yoshukai Karate Association, 1976; Tau Beta Sigma and Alpha Phi Omega, life memberships, 1983-; Music Educators National Conference, president, 1980-81; The Troy State Karate Club-Dojo, founding president/instructor, 1978-82; Troy State University Band, elected lieutenant, 1980, elected band captain, 1981; NAACP, secretary, 1991-. **Honors/Awds:** All American Music Hall of Fame, 1976; Troy State University, Band Scholarship, 1977. **Special Achievements:** Feature article written and published on Dr Paul Yoder, 1979; feature soloist with Troy State's Concert, Marching, Jazz Bands, 1979; Anchor Club, first African-American voted in, 1976; Miss Sylacauga Pageant, first black to enroll, 1976; first African-American president-elect of the Troy State Alumni Band Assn, 1991, president, 1993-95. **Home Addr:** PO Box 462, Sylacauga, AL 35150, (205)249-0508. **Business Phone:** (205)249-6403.

MCELROY, CHARLES DWAYNE
Professional baseball player. **Personal:** Born Oct 1, 1967, Port Arthur, TX; son of Elizabeth Simmons Mayfield and Herman C McElroy; married Shari Lannette Cooper McElroy, Jan 19, 1991. **Career:** Philadelphia Phillies, pitcher, 1989-90; Chicago Cubs, 1991-93; Cincinnati Reds, 1994-96; Anaheim Angels, 1996-97; Chicago White Sox, 1997; Colorado Rockies, 1997-. **Orgs:** Professional Baseball Players Assn, 1986-. **Business Addr:** Professional Baseball Player, Colorado Rockies, 1700 Broadway, Ste 2100, Denver, CO 80290.

MCELROY, COLLEEN J.
Educator, writer. **Personal:** Born Oct 30, 1935, St Louis, MO; daughter of Ruth C Long Johnson and Jesse D Johnson; divorced; children: Kevin D, Vanessa C. **Educ:** Kansas State Univ, Manhattan KS, BS, 1958, MS, 1963; Univ of Washington, Seattle WA, PhD, 1973. **Career:** Rehabilitation Inst, Kansas City MO, chief, Speech & Hearing Serv, 1963-66; Western Washington Univ, Bellingham WA, asst prof, Speech, 1966-74; Univ of Washington, Seattle WA, supvr, EOP Composition, 1972-83, dir, Creative Writing, 1984-87, prof of English, 1983-. **Orgs:** Mem, Writers Guild of Amer East, 1978-, Dramatists Guild, 1986-, PEN Writers, 1989-; member, Author's Guild, 1989-; member, Writer's Union, 1989-. **Honors/Awds:** NEA Creative Writing Fellowship for Poetry, 1978; Fiction 1st place, Callalvo Magazine, 1981; Poetry 1st place, Cincinnati Poetry R, 1983; Creative Writing Residency, MacDowell Colony, New Hampshire, 1984, 1986; Before Columbus Amer Book Award, 1985; Women of Achievement, Theta Sigma Phi, 1985; Creative Writing Residency Yugoslavia, Fulbright Fellowship, 1988; Washington State Governor's Award for Fiction and Poetry, 1988; NEA Creative Writing Fellowship for Fiction, 1991; Rockefeller Fellowship to Bellagio Institute, Lake Como, Italy, 1991; DuPont Distinguished Scholar in Residence, Hollins College, Virginia, 1992; Fulbright Research Fellowship, Madagascar, 1993; Arts America, Jordan & Morocco, 1996. **Special Achievements:** The Wild Gardens of the Loup Garou, 1983; Queen of the Ebony Isles, 1984; Jesus and Fat Tuesday, 1987; Follow the Drinking Gourd, 1987; Driving Under the Cardboard Pines, 1990; What Madness Brought Me Here, 1990; A Long Way from St Louie, 1996. **Business Addr:** Professor of English, University of Washington, Dept of English GN-30, Padelford Hall, Seattle, WA 98109.

MCELROY, GEORGE A.
Journalist. **Personal:** Born May 25, 1922, Houston, TX; son of Philomena Woodley McElroy and Hugh G McElroy; married Lucinda Martin McElroy, Nov 27, 1951; children: Madeline Johnson, Toni, Linda, Kathleen, Sherri. **Educ:** TX Southern Univ, BA 1956; USAF Systems Command, Honorary Doctorate 1966; Univ of MO-Columbia, MA 1970. **Career:** Houston Independent Sch Dist, journalism teacher 1957-69; Univ of Houston, asst prof of communications 1970-76; Houston Post, columnist 1971-78; TX Southern Univ, assoc prof of Journalism 1976-; Houston Informer, publisher/editor. **Orgs:** Chapter adviser Soc of Professional Journalists 1979-; publicist 9th and 10th Cavalry Assn; lay adviser TSU Catholic Newman Center; publicity chair United Negro College Fund/Houston; National Assn of Black Journalists; National Newspaper Publishers Assn; Texas Press Assn; Omega Psi Phi; Press Club Houston; pres, Houston Breakfast Club, 1990-. **Honors/Awds:** Amigo de Guatemala Award govt of Guatemala 1977; Lynn C Eusan Serv Award Prof Amateur Boxing Assn 1979; Certificate of Recognition TSU Ex-Students Assn 1985; TSU Relays Service Award TX Southern Univ 1985. **Military Serv:** USN steward 1st class 1940-46; USAF Information Specialist 1950-52. **Home Addr:** 3307 Wentworth St, Houston, TX 77004. **Business Addr:** Publisher/Editor, Houston Informer, PO Box 3086, Houston, TX 77253-3086.

MCELROY, LEE A., JR.
Sports executive, educator. **Personal:** Born Mar 19, 1948; son of Ada Mae Ford and Lee A McElroy, Sr. **Educ:** Univ of California, Los Angeles, BA, 1970; Univ of Southern California, MS, 1974; Univ of Houston, TX, PhD, 1984. **Career:** Santa Monica Schools, Santa Monica, CA, coach, teacher, 1971-76; South Parks High School, Beaumont, TX, vice principal, 1976-81; Univ of Houston, TX, assoc ath director, 1981-88; Univ of the District of Columbia, athletic director, vice pres, student affairs, 1988-89; California State Univ, Sacramento, director of inter athletics, 1989-; Sacramento Sports Medicine, board of directors, 1989-; Comstock Magazine, board of directors, 1990-. **Orgs:** Public relations, Rotary, 1989-; board of directors, Doug Williams Found, 1988-; president, Natl Assn of Academic Advisors, 1986; consultant, Amer Institute of Research, 1987. **Honors/Awds:** An Analysis of the Relationships among Control Variables, Organizational Climate, Job Satisfaction and Turnover/Absenteeism in the Public Schools, Univ of Houston, 1984. **Home Addr:** 4410 Massachusetts Ave NW #396, Washington, DC 20016-5572.

MCELROY, LEELAND
Professional football player. **Personal:** Born Jun 25, 1974, Beaumont, TX; married Vinita. **Educ:** Texas A&M, attended. **Career:** Arizona Cardinals, running back, 1996-. **Business Addr:** Professional Football Player, Arizona Cardinals, 8701 S Hardy, Tempe, AZ 85284, (602)379-0101.

MCELROY, NJOKI
Educator, storyteller, writer, company executive. **Personal:** Born in Sherman, TX; daughter of Marion Hampton and J D Hampton; married Clenan C McElroy, Mar 1946 (deceased); children: Ronald, Phillip, David, Marian. Harry, Larry. **Educ:** Xavier Univ, BS, 1945; Northwestern Univ, MA, 1969, PhD, 1973. **Career:** Northwestern Univ, adjunct professor, 1970-; Black Fox Enterprises Ltd, president, 1972-; storyteller, performer, 1980-; Southern Methodist Univ, adjunct professor, 1987-. **Honors/Awds:** City of Dallas Cultural Affairs 1992, 1993; Ford Foundation, Travel Grant, 1972. **Special Achievements:** Author, works include: "Black Journey," play on African-American history, 1975; "The Gods Were Watching Them," play, Northwestern Univ, 1991; "La Bakaire," play, Northwestern Univ, 1992; stories published in: Common Bond, 1991; Spiritual Walks, 1993. **Business Addr:** President, Black Fox Enterprises, Ltd, 1700 20th St, North Chicago, IL 60064, (708)689-4437.

MCELROY, RAYMOND EDWARD
Professional football player. **Personal:** Born Jul 31, 1972, Bellwood, IL; married Michelle. **Educ:** Eastern Illinois. **Career:** Indianapolis Colts, defensive back, 1995-. **Business Addr:** Professional Football Player, Indianapolis Colts, PO Box 535000, Indianapolis, IN 46253, (317)297-2658.

MCELVANE, PAMELA ANNE
Insurance company executive. **Personal:** Born Sep 4, 1958, Stockton, CA; daughter of Charlene Penny. **Educ:** Univ CA Berkeley, BA 1981, MBA 1983. **Career:** US Dept of Labor, contract mgr 1980-82; Gelco-Cti Leasing Co, lease admin/sys supv 1982-84; Allstate Ins Co, market mgr 1984-88; Chubb Group of Ins Cos, dept manager/officer, 1988-92; Hanover Ins Co, dir of personal lines, 1992-. **Orgs:** Newsletter editor 1984-86, exec bd mem 1984-87, co-chair std affrs 1987, mgr editor 1987 SFMBA; coord Bay Blk Profls 1984-; bd mem, newsletter editor, vice pres UCB Alumni Assoc 1985-; recruiter Big Bros 1985-86; organizer March of Dimes 1986; pres, UCB Alumni Assn, 1988-89; Cinti MBA, 1989-90; chapter communications director, Mentor, 1989-91; member, Ins Professionals 1990-95; MBA, Boston Chapter, vp operations, 1995; NBMBAA, conference public relations dir, 1995. **Honors/Awds:** Coach of the Year Madeliene Sch 1984-86; Merit Awd Big Brothers 1984; Rosalie Stern Outstanding Comm Achiev UC Berkeley 1986; Community Serv Awd March of Dimes 1986; Mentor Award, Cincinnati Public Schools, 1989-90; Outstanding MBA, Unti Chapter, 1992. **Home Addr:** 1416 N Cleveland Ave, #2, Chicago, IL 60610.

MCEWEN, MARK
Broadcasting administrator. **Personal:** Born Sep 16, 1954, San Antonio, TX; son of Dolores McEwen and Alfred McEwen; married Judith Lonsdale. **Educ:** University of Maryland, College Park, 1972-76. **Career:** WWWW-FM Radio, Detroit, MI, music director, disc jockey, 1978-80; WLUP-FM Radio, Chicago, IL, research director, disc jockey, 1980-82; WAPP-FM Radio, New York, NY, disc jockey, 1982; WNEW-FM Radio, New York, NY, disc jockey, 1982-86; CBS, The Morning Program, weatherman, 1987, CBS This Morning, weatherman, music editor, 1987-92, enterainment editor, 1992-96, anchor, 1996-. **Orgs:** Natl Assoc of Black Journalists. **Honors/Awds:** Listed as one of the 10 Most Trusted Newspeople in TV Guide, Feb 1995. **Business Addr:** Anchor, "CBS This Morning", CBS Inc, 524 W 57th St, New York, NY 10019.

MCEWING, MITCHELL DALTON
Educational administration. **Personal:** Born May 16, 1935, Jacksonville, TX; married Verta Lee Ellis; children: Andre R, Veronica Lee. **Educ:** Wiley Coll Marshall TX, BS 1958; TX Southern Univ, degree credits summers 1964; North TX State Univ, MEd 1973, degree credits 1974-75; TX State Bd of Examiners of Prof Counselors, Licensure Prof Counselor 1982. **Career:** Bethlehem United Com Ctr, athletic dir 1958-63; IM Terrell Jr-Sr HS, teacher/asst coach 1963-67, teacher/head coach 1968-69; Tarrant Cty Jr Coll, counselor/instructor 1971-75, dean of students devel svcs. **Orgs:** Soc worker Bethlehem United Com Ctr 1971; vice pres United Com Ctrs of Ft Worth 1971-73; bd mem Advisory Council in Counseling Student No TX State Univ 1981-82; mem Phi Delta Kappa; mem The Council of Black Amer Affairs; sec/treas E St Paul Bapt Church. **Honors/Awds:** Dedicated Svs The Dukes 1975-76; Coach of the Year IM Terrell HS 1959-69; Serv Awd Phi Theta Kappa 1984. **Military Serv:** AUS Spec 4 3 years; Berlin Serv Awd, Second Team Army Quarterback 1959; Hon discharge from the Army 1960. **Home Addr:** 3445 Denbury Dr, Fort Worth, TX 76133. **Business Addr:** Dean, Student Devel Services, Tarrant County Junior College, South Campus, 5301 Campus Dr, Fort Worth, TX 76119.

MCFADDEN, ARTHUR B.
Cleric. **Personal:** Born Jan 5, 1940, Jacksonville, FL; married Marjesta Sanders; children: Anntoinette, Renee. **Educ:** Stillman Coll, BA 1962; Johnson C Smith U, BD 1965; Eden Theological Seminary, STM; D Min 1970, 1973; St Louis Univ, 1970-71; Southern IL Univ, 1984. **Career:** Calvary Presbyterian Church/Detroit, MI, asst minister 1965-66; Butler Memorial Church/Youngstown, OH, minister 1966-68; Third United Presbyterian Church/St Louis MO, minister 1968-. **Orgs:** Alumni bd dir, Stillman Coll 1973-79; adjunct prof, St Louis Univ 1974-82; bd const for blk clergy Eden Theological Seminary 1976-80; Omega Psi Phi Frat; bd dir King Fanow Mental Health Center 1985-; clergy support comm St Louis OIC; mem Men Organized Against Juvenile Crime. **Honors/Awds:** Community Serv, St Louis Univ; 25th Anniversary of Ordination to the Christian Ministry, 1990. **Special Achievements:** Co-author: "Together.. A Biblically based Evangelism Resource with Particular Focus on African-American Youth in the Presbyterian Church and Community," 1993; Moderator of Presbytery of Giddings-LoveJoy, 1995; Distinguished Alumnus of Johnson C Smith Theological Seminary, 1996. **Home Addr:** 7112 Forest Hill Dr, St Louis, MO 63121. **Business Addr:** Minister, 3rd United Presbyterian Church, 2426 Union Blvd, St Louis, MO 63113.

MCFADDEN, CORA C.
Government administration. **Personal:** Born Oct 3, 1945, Durham, NC; divorced; children: Lori Yvette, Larry Everette. **Educ:** North Carolina Central U, BA, MA; NC Chapel Hill U, post grad. **Career:** Durham County Dept of Social Services, social worker 1969-76, foster care supervisor 1976-78; City of Durham, community services supervisor 1978-81, affirmative action dir 1981-. **Orgs:** One of the founders NC Association of Black Social Workers 1972; board member Volunteer Services

Bureau 1980-83; board member YWCA 1983-84; state coordinator American Assn for Affirmative Action 1985; member Durham County Council for Women 1985; president Ebonettes Service Club, Inc 1985. **Honors/Awds:** Founders Award North Carolina Association of Black Social Workers 1984. **Business Addr:** Affirmative Action Dir, City of Durham, 101 City Hall Plz, Durham, NC 27701.

MCFADDEN, GREGORY L.
Physician. **Personal:** Born Jun 18, 1958, Tallahassee, FL; son of Alma L Johnson McFadden and Robert L McFadden; married Cynthia Williams, Dec 12, 1987; children: Desiree. **Educ:** Florida A&M Univ, BS 1980; Howard Univ Coll of Medicine, MD 1984. **Career:** Orlando Regional Medical Center, resident physician 1984-87; Cigna Health Plan, staff physician, 1988-. **Orgs:** Mem Amer Coll of Physicians, Amer Medical Assoc, Alpha Phi Alpha Fraternity Inc; diplomate Natl Bd of Medical Examiners. **Honors/Awds:** Natl Dean's List 1980; Physicians Recognition Award, Amer Medical Assn, 1987. **Home Addr:** 4308 Ellenville Pl, Valrico, FL 33594.

MCFADDEN, JAMES L.
Educator. **Personal:** Born Nov 9, 1929, Darlington, SC; married Gertha Moore; children: Dionne Jametta. **Educ:** Claflin Coll, AB 1954; NY U, MA; NY U, Further Study. **Career:** Morris Coll, Art instr 1954-56; Orangeburg City Sch Sharperson Jr HS, art tchr 1954-70; SC State Coll Orangeburg SC, prof of art 1970-; SC TextbookAdoption Com, selected to serve; Art & Music Texts, selected to serve 1969; Scholastic art awards in SC, regional adv comm 1969. **Orgs:** Treas SC Art Educ Assn 1971-Jan 1975; mem SC Educ Assn; Nat Educ Assn; Nat Art Educ Assn; mem Clafin & New York Univ Alumni Assn; Am Legion Post #210 1954; Edisto Masonic Lodge #39 AF&M 1966; Shriner Jeddah Temple No 160 1966; O-Burg IBOE of W Lodge #1627 Elks 1972; Orbg Alumni Chapter KAY; adv Alpha Lambda Chapter of KAY; Attend William Chapel AME Ch; mem NAACP; Honorable Mention & 3rd Place Sculpture Negro Nat Art Exhibition Atlanta 1950; grad Cum Laude Claflin Coll 1954; staff artist & asst mgr Post Theatre No 1 Ft & Benjamin Harrison IN 1951-53. **Honors/Awds:** Southeastern Province Achievement Award Kappa Alpha Psi Frat 1950; Outst Ldrshp & Dedication Award Alpha Lambda Chap of Kappa Alpha Psi Frat 1976; 25 yr award SE Province of Kappa Alpha Psi Frat; Honored as Chartered Mem & Speaker 25th Anniv of Gamma Nu Chapter Kappa Alpha Psi Frat 1974. **Military Serv:** AUS 1951-55. **Business Addr:** PO Box 1962, SC State College, Orangeburg, SC 29115.

MCFADDEN, NATHANIEL JAMES
Educational administrator, government official. **Personal:** Born Aug 3, 1946, Philadelphia, PA; married Rachel Tift; children: Nathaniel Jr, Byron, Devon Dodson. **Educ:** Morgan State Coll, AB 1968; Morgan State Univ, MS 1972. **Career:** Off-St Parking Commn Baltimore, 1983-; Jail Industries Adv Bd Baltimore City Jail, 1984-; Natl Youth Sports Prog Johns Hopkins Univ, adv comm 1984-; Sojourner-Douglass Coll, coord of comm affairs 1985-; Urban Serv Agency Baltimore, chmn 1985-; Morgan State Univ Dept of Educ, adv comm 1985-; City Council of Baltimore, councilmember; Baltimore City Public Schools, Baltimore, MD, facilitator, educ opportunity program, dept head, teacher, 1968-; State of Maryland, senator, currently. **Orgs:** Mem Assoc for the Study of Negro Life and History Baltimore City Chap 1980-82; mem Eastern Dist Police Community Relations Council Baltimore 1982-; mem adv bd Johns Hopkins Medical Plan 1985-; mem Optimist Club of East Baltimore 1985-; asst recordkeeper, Baltimore Alumni Chapter, Kappa Alpha Psi Fraternity, 1989-; board member, Eastside Democratic Organization, 1975-; member, Urban League; member, NAACP; member, Alpha Kappa Mu, 1968-; member, Kappa Delta Pi, 1968-; member, Phi Alpha Theta, 1967-; member, Gamma Theta Upsilon, 1963-; Alpha Phi Omega, Natl Service Fraternity, Baltimore Area Alumni; RAIDE-EOP Inc. bd of dirs; 100 Black Men of Maryland, Inc. **Home Addr:** 1033 N Central Ave, Baltimore, MD 21202. **Business Addr:** Facilitator, Community Outreach Activities, Baltimore City Public Schools #40, 2801 St Lo Dr, Baltimore, MD 21213.

MCFADDEN, SAMUEL WILTON
Physician. **Personal:** Born Jun 17, 1935, Newark, NJ; married Nancy A Peters; children: Jonathan, Jesse. **Educ:** NY University Coll, BA 1956; Univ Basel Switzerland, MD 1964. **Career:** BU Sch Med, pediatric radiologist/asst prof 1971-77; Child Abuse & Neglect Unit, chief 1973-75; Roxbury Comprehensive Comm Hlth Ctr, pediatrician 1973-77, chief radiology 1974-77; Eunice Kennedy Shriver Med Ctr, chief radiology 1974-83; Tobry Hosp, radiologist 1977-80, chief of radiology 1980-; Wareham Radiology Assoc, pres. **Orgs:** Pres New England Med Soc 1975-77; mem Bay State Peer Standards Rev Orgn 1976; treas New England Med Soc 1977-78; mem Am Coll of Radiology, Nat Med Assn; bd dir MA Radiol Soc; school comm ORR Regional HS 1981-; pres M & L Staff Toby General Hosp 1981-83; medical advisor Registry of Motor Vehicles 1983-; natl sec System Radiology Natl Medical Assoc 1987; medical advisor Marion UNA. **Business Addr:** President, Wareham Radiology Assoc, 295 Delano Rd, Marion, MA 02738.

MCFADDIN, THERESA GARRISON
Teacher, counselor. **Personal:** Born Jul 23, 1943, Philadelphia, PA; daughter of Barbara Campbell Prunty and Alvin Prunty; widowed; children: Roslyn Ballard, Theresa McFaddin. **Career:** Motown Records, Los Angeles CA, writer, producer; Christian Broadcasting Network, Virginia Beach VA, writer, producer; Terri McFaddin & Friends, Pasadena CA, teacher, counselor. **Honors/Awds:** Grammy Award, 1986; Citizen of the Year, Zeta Phi Beta Sorority, 1989.

MCFALL, MARY
Educational administrator. **Personal:** Born Aug 30, 1938, San Angelo, TX; children: Jeanette, Owen III. **Educ:** San Angelo Jr Coll, Honor Grad 1953-55; Univ of TX, BA Honor Grad 1957; Univ of TX, JD 1979; Cand. **Career:** Intercultural Devel So Meth U, dir 1971-; Tarrant Co YWCA, br exec 1969-71; Comm Action Agy, asst nghbrhd servs dir 1967-69; Soc Security Adm, serv rep 1965-66; Soc of Ethnic & Spec Studies, sec 1975-; TX Assn of Black Personnel in Higher Edn, co-founder 1st vice pres conf coord 1973-79; TX Assn ofBlack Personnel in Higher Edn, pres 1979. **Orgs:** Bd of dirs Family Guidance Assn 1979-; Coalition for Educ of Black Children; TX Assn of Coll; Univ Stu Personnel Adm Goals for Black Dallas Com 1976-77;vp Minority Cultural Arts Assn 1970-71; mem chmn Am Civil Liberties Union Ft Worth Chap 1968-70; mem Citizen's Plng Com Ft Worth 1971; co-fdr Students for Direct Action Univ of TX; del Nat Students Assn 1961; Alpha Kappa Alpha Sor. **Honors/Awds:** First Black Student Admitted to San Angelo Coll; 1st Black Student to Receive BA from Univ of TX Austin; Listed Golden Profiles of Dallas Ft Worth 1980. **Business Addr:** Box 355, SMU, Dallas, TX 75225.

MCFARLAND, ARTHUR C.
Attorney. **Personal:** Born Feb 5, 1947, Charleston, SC; married E Elise Davis; children: Kira Jihan, William Joseph. **Educ:** Univ Notre Dame, BA Govt 1970; Univ VA, JD 1973. **Career:** Private Practice, attorney 1974-; City of Charleston SC, municipal judge 1976-78, chief municipal judge 1978-. **Orgs:** Mem Natl, Amer Bar Assns 1974-; mem Natl Conf of Black Lawyers 1974-; mem Amer Judges Assn, NBA Jud Council 1976-; bd dir Trident United Way 1977-; pres Robert Gould Shaw Boys Club 1978-; mem Chas SC NAACP Exec Com 1978-; pres Charleston Bus & Professional Assn 1983-85; mem Charleston Neighborhood Legal Assistance Prog Bd of Dir 1984-86; mem Charleston Waterfront Park Comm 1983-; national advocate, Knights of Peter Claver, 1994-. **Honors/Awds:** Earl Warren Fellow NAACP Legal Defense Fund 1973-74; Earl Warren Fellowship NAACP Legal Defense & Educ Fund 1973-77. **Business Addr:** Chief Municipal Judge, City of Charleston, 1847 Ashely River Rd, Ste 200, Charleston, SC 29407.

MCFARLAND, CLAUDETTE
Lawyer, arbitrator, business executive. **Personal:** Born Dec 8, 1935, St Louis, MO; married Vernon Winstead; children: Vernon Jr, Claudette II. **Educ:** Roosevelt Univ, BA 1958; Univ NC, LLB; John Marshall Law School, LLM, JD; Univ of IL, MSW 1971, AM 1973, PhD. **Career:** Chicago Dwellings of Chicago Housing Auth, attny 1972; VAW Indust, corp lawyer, bus exec, exec vice pres 1975-; McFarland Enterprises, pres 1975-. **Orgs:** Member: Chicago Assn Commerce & Indust, Chamber of Commerce, Natl Assn Univ Women, PUSH, Chicago Urban Leaue, Wives Aux of Alpha Phi Alpha, YWCA, Chicago Community Devel Block Rep Comm, Alpha Kappa Alpha (treas, co-chair of Natl Grantsmanship Committee); life member: NAACP, Natl Council of Negro Women; life board member: Alpha Kappa Alpha, Amer Bar Assn, Natl Council of Jewish Women, Tau Gamma Delta; board member: Provident Hosp Womens Aux, Natl Bar Assn, Jack & Jill, Girl Scouts of Amer, Chicago Links, Chicago Beautiful Comm, Amer Assn of Univ Women, League of Women Voters, South Shore Committee;president: Chicago & Greater Chicago Sections of Natl Council of Negro Women, Chicago Chapter of Natl Council of Negro Women, SE Area Kiwanis; pres emeritus: Dr Claudette McFarland Ed Civic & tural Club of CNDA, Northern Dist Assn of Women & Girls Clubs of Amer, South Shore Natl Bank Bd; vice pres: Natl Assn of Women in Ministry, Chicago Econ Devel Comm; White House consultant, Women & Minority Affairs & Status of ERA, 1979; consultant & participant, White House Conf on Minority Human Experimentation, 1975; ordained as interdenominational minister, Universal Life Church, 1977; publisher/editor, Chicago South Shore Scene Newspaper. **Honors/Awds:** Outstanding Achievement Awd, Natl Council Negro Women, 1972, 73, 75; Public Serv Awd, WAIT Radio, Natl Council Jewish Women; Nationally Outstanding Woman Awd, Tau Gamma Delta, 1975; Outstanding Comm Serv Awd, Afro-Amer Patrolmen's League, 1975; Outstanding Prof & Civic Awd, Gamma Phi Delta, 1975; Outstanding Woman of the Year, Girl Scouts of Chicago, 1975; Guest at White House of Pres Ford, 1975; Outstanding Humanitarian & Comm Serv Awd, Intl Travelers Awd, 1979. **Business Addr:** President, McFarland Enterprises, 407 S Dearborn, Ste 950, Chicago, IL 60610.

MCFARLAND, OLLIE FRANKLIN
Educator. **Personal:** Born Oct 25, 1918, Jacksonville, FL; married William A McFarland (deceased); children: William Michael. **Educ:** Spelman Coll, BA 1940; Wayne State Univ, MM 1952; Columbia Univ, John Hay Fellow 1965-66. **Career:** Detroit Public Schools, music tchr Central High 1958-67, supvr music educ 1967-79, asst dir music educ 1979-81, dir music educ 1981-. **Orgs:** Life mem NAACP 1979-; singer Celeste Cole Opera Theatre; narrator Detroit Symphony Det Pub Schools Educ Concerts; concert/opera singer on radio/TV -St Joseph's Church; bd mem Detroit Comm Music Sch; bd mem Rackham Symphony Choir; mem Alpha Kappa Alpha Sor; mem Delta Kappa Gamma. **Honors/Awds:** Honoree Natl Assn of Negro Musicians 1985; Educator's Achievement Award Booker T Washington Business Assn 1983; Achievement Award Omega Psi Phi Frat 1977;author music textbook, "Afro-America Sings" Det Pub Schools 1973, revised 1981. **Business Addr:** Dir of Music Education, Detroit Public Schools, 5057 Woodward Ave, Room 850, Detroit, MI 48202.

MCFARLIN, EMMA DANIELS
Government official. **Personal:** Born Nov 14, 1921, Camden, AR. **Educ:** Philander-Smith Coll Little Rock, BA 1950; Univ of WI Madison, MS 1961; US Intl Univ San Diego, PhD 1975. **Career:** US Dept HUD, regional admisntr 1977-; Univ of CA LA, asso prof 1975-77; Ofc of the Mayor LA, spl asst 1974-75; Menlo Parl CA, asst city mgr 1973-74; US Dept HEW, regional rep 1970-73; US Dept HUD, spl rep 1965-70; San Francisco Unified Sch Dist, tchr 1964-65; Low Rent Housing Proj Little RockRedevel & Housing Authority, mgr 1952-64. **Orgs:** Mem Omicron Nu Nat Honor Soc 1961; mem Nat Assn of Media Woman 1975; chmn Pub Utilities & Tran Commn LA 1976. **Honors/Awds:** Cum laude Philander-Smith Coll 1949; recipient Emma McFarlin Day Award City of Menlo Park CAL 1974; newsmaker award Nat Assn of Media Women 1975; outstanding serv & achievement City Council LA 1975. **Business Addr:** US Dept HUD, 450 Golden Gate Ave, San Francisco, CA 94102.

MCFARLIN, KERNAA D'OFFERT, JR.
Long range planner. **Personal:** Born Oct 7, 1946, Jacksonville, FL; married Sandra Annette Williams; children: Kernaa D III, Brian Christopher, Patrick Allen. **Educ:** Hampton Univ, BS 1968. **Career:** MA Mutual Life Ins Co, systems analyst 1969-71; IBM Corp, marketing rep 1971-77; Hartford Insurance Group, systems specialist 1978-79; Travelers Insurance Co, manager telecommunications 1979-. **Orgs:** Pres bd of dirs W W Johnson Life Ctr 1979-; vice pres Springfield Symphony Orchestra Assoc Marketing Comm 1983-; pres bd of dirs Longmeadow A Better Chance Inc 1985-. **Home Addr:** 124 Green Meadow Dr, Longmeadow, MA 01106. **Business Addr:** Manager Telecommunications Div, Travelers Insurance Co, One Tower Square, Hartford, CT.

MCFERRIN, BOBBY
Singer, songwriter, musician. **Personal:** Born Mar 11, 1950, New York, NY; son of Sara McFerrin and Robert McFerrin; married Debbie Lynn Green, 1975; children: Taylor John, Jevon Chase. **Educ:** Sacramento State University; Cerritos College. **Career:** Singer, 1977-. **Honors/Awds:** Albums include: Bobby McFerrin, 1982; The Voice, 1984; Spontaneous Inventions, 1986; Simple Pleasures, 1988; sings theme song for the Cosby Show; appears regularly on Sesame Street; two Grammy Awards: best male jazz vocalist, best arranger, for Another Night in Tunisia, 1986; Grammy Award, best jazz vocalist, for 'Round Midnight (title song to the movie of the same name), 1987; four Grammy Awards: best male pop vocalist; best song; best male jazz vocalist, for Brothers; record of the year, Don't Worry, Be Happy, 1989. Total Grammy Awards received: nine. Best known for being able to use his voice as a musical instrument. **Business Addr:** Singer, c/o EMI-Manhatten, CEMA, 1750 N Vine St, Hollywood, CA 90028.

MCFERRIN, ROBERT
Educator. **Personal:** Born Mar 19, 1921, Marianna, AR; son of Mary and Melvin; divorced. **Educ:** Chicago Musical Coll, BA. **Career:** Roosevelt Univ, visiting professor of voice 1976-77. **Honors/Awds:** First black to perform regularly with Metro Opera; performed in Canada, Latin Amer, Germany, Belgium, England, Italy, Greece, recorded album "Porgy & Bess Sound Track." 1987 Honorary Doctorates; Stowe Teacher's College, St Louis, MO, 1987; University of Missouri, 1989.

MCFERRIN, SARA ELIZABETH COPPER
Educational administrator (retired). **Personal:** Born Sep 10, 1924, Washington, DC; daughter of Elizabeth and Charles; divorced; children: Robert, Brenda. **Educ:** Howard Univ, attended 1942; Attended, Univ So CA LA; Attended, UCLA; Attended, California State University, Los Angeles. **Career:** CBS-TV, Christmas specials; solo recitalist & oratorio soloist throughout USA; symphony soloist; appeared in films Porgy & Bess, Elmer Gantry; appeared in Broadway prod "Lost in the Stars," "Troubled Island"; NY City Ctr Opera Chorus, soloist; Hollywood Greek Theatre Opera Chorus, soloist; CA State Univ, Long Beach/Nelson Sch of Fine Arts Canada, Pasadena City Coll, Cerritos Coll, tchr; Fullerton Coll Music Dept, chmn voice dept 1973-90; University of Oklahoma, Norman, OK, visiting professor in voice 1986; Fullerton Coll Music Dept, chmn, 1990-93. **Orgs:** Mem, Natl Assn of Tchrs of Singing (NATS); Adjudicator Met Opera Western Region Auditions in CA, AZ, NV 30 yrs; mem Adjudicating Panels Vocal comp in So CA,

San Francisco Opera, South California Opera Guild; Los Angeles Master Chorale Assoc, bd of associates; Opera Pacific, Costa Mesa, CA, bd of dirs; Pacific Chorale, Costa Mesa Co, bd of dirs. **Honors/Awds:** Fullerton Coll, Staff of Distinction Award, 1993, Professor Emeritus Award, 1993. **Home Addr:** The Water Gardens, 2925 E Barrington Ct, Fullerton, CA 92631.

MCGATHON, CARRIE M.
Nurse. **Personal:** Born Feb 3, 1936, Mendenhall, MS; daughter of Lena Hays Smith (deceased) and James Smith Sr; married John A McGathon, 1954; children: Berlinda, Brenda, John Reginald. **Educ:** Dillard Univ, BSN 1964; College of Holy Names, PHN 1970; Jackson State Univ, MEd 1978. **Career:** Naval Regional Medical Ctr Oakland CA, clinical supervisor Ob/Gyn 1975-80; Health Care Services Inc, director/administrator; Alameda Community Hospital, Alameda, CA, RN, labor & delivery, 1980-; COGIOC, license, evangelist, 1980-; Healthforce, case mgr, nursing dept; Corp of Registered Nurses, staff ltd. **Orgs:** Mem Dillard Alumnus 1964-, NAACOG 1970-, Biblesway CIGOGC 1975-; member, California Nurses Assn, 1964-; member, Black Nurses Assn of Greater East Bay; member, Council of Black Women Female Executives; Order of Eastern Star #49A; Heroines of Jericho. **Honors/Awds:** Commendation, Juris Doctoral Bishop EE, Cleveland, COGIOC; JD Bishop Larry J McEathon, Woman of Boldness Award. **Special Achievements:** Certified herbalist, nutritional consultant, iridologist, 1994. **Military Serv:** US Navy, nurse representaive, 1967-80; Merit Award, 1975. **Business Addr:** Ob-Gyn Nurse, Alameda Community Hospital, 5801 Christie Street, Ste 309, Alameda, CA 94501.

MCGAUGHY, WILL
City official. **Personal:** Born Feb 23, 1933, Plantervills, MS; divorced; children: Felix Xavier. **Educ:** Mildred Louis Bus Coll, 1954. **Career:** Citizen Participation, dir 1969-72, 1973-75; Will McGaughy Health Ctr, dir 1972-73; Health Educ & Welfare, dir 1975-78; E St Louis Twp Citizen Prog, 1978-81; East St Louis Township, asst to town super 1981-89, supervisor, 1989-. **Orgs:** Adv to NAACP Youth Council 1966; pres Metro East Health Serv 1970-72; dir of Project Life 1970-73; precinct committeeman 1971-86; dir Dawson Manor Housing 1954-; chmn E St Louis Transit Bd 1975-; vice pres City Central Democrate 1978-; cty bd mem Spec Asst to the Mayor of E St Louis 1978-; pres Southend Neighborhood Improvement Assn 1982-; mem Amer Red Cross; taxation committee chairman, St Clair County Board, 1991. **Honors/Awds:** Outstanding Leadership Awd E St Louis 1975; Politician of the Year 1976; Citizen Participation Workshop 1977; Resolution of Commendation from mayor of E St Louis 1980; Arson Awareness 1981; Project Hope 1982; Man of the Year E St Louis Monitor Newspaper 1982; Dr Martin Luther King Jr Drum Major Award, GEMM Center, 1991. **Military Serv:** AUS corpl 3 yrs. **Home Addr:** 1402 So H, East St Louis, IL 62207.

MCGEE, ADOLPHUS STEWART
School administrator. **Personal:** Born Jan 29, 1941, Dos Palos, CA. **Educ:** Coalinga Coll, AA 1960; CA State U, BA 1963; CA State U, MA 1970; CA State U, MA Educ Adminstrn 1972. **Career:** Union High School Dist Sacramento, teacher math, head track coach football coach 1963-66; Luther Burbank High School Sacramento, teacher math science, track & football coach 1966-68; Sacramento City Unified School Dist, asst to supt 1968-70; inter-group relations adv 1969-70; Sacramento Sr High School, prin 1970-. **Orgs:** Mem Jount Legislative Com on Educ Goals & Evaluations Joint Task Force Goals & Evaluation For State of CA 1972-; pres Sacramento Sr High Sch Meml Scholarship Fund 1970-; Assn CA Sch Adminstrs; chmn Minority News Media Joint Task Force Urban Coalition 1969-71; mem YMCA; NAACP; Blue Key; Phi Delta Kappa; Omega Chi Delta. **Business Addr:** 2315 34 St, Sacramento, CA 95817.

MCGEE, ARTHUR LEE
Fashion designer. **Personal:** Born Mar 25, 1933, Detroit, MI. **Educ:** Wayne U, attended; Fashion Inst of Tech & Design, attended; Cybick Sch of Tailoring, attended. **Career:** Arthur McGee Designs, president, 1958-; Ulla, design dir 1971-72; Sir For Her, head designer 1969-71; Coll Town of Boston, head designer 1965-69. **Honors/Awds:** 1 of 2 Am Designers to Show in Intl Men's Show Europe 1965; contrib extrordinarie Oplehia Devore 1979; 1st Black Designer to work for a giant 7th Ave firm.

MCGEE, BENJAMIN LELON
Company executive. **Personal:** Born Feb 18, 1943, Booneville, MS; married Rose M Jackson; children: Ivy, Ben II, Brian, Holly. **Educ:** AR AM&N Coll Pine Bluff AR, Agronomy Sci 1967; Memphis State U, 20 hrs 1975. **Career:** Liquor Center, owner 1977-; GMAC, credit rep 1976-77; Dept of Agr ASCS, compliance supr 1967-75. **Orgs:** Bd mem Marion Sch Dist 1975-; vice chmn bd of trustees AR State Univ 1977-; state committeeman Dem Party 1979-; bd trustees AR State Univ Jonesboro 1980; bd of trustees AME Ch. **Business Addr:** The Liquor Center, 3109 E Broadway W, West Memphis, AR 72301.

MCGEE, BUFORD LAMAR
Professional football player. **Personal:** Born Aug 16, 1960, Durant, MS. **Educ:** Univ of Mississippi, BS, business, 1984. **Career:** San Diego Chargers, 1984-86; Los Angeles Rams, running back, 1987-92; Green Bay Packers, fullback, 1992. **Honors/Awds:** Played in NFC Championship Game, post-1989 season.

MCGEE, EVA M.
Educator. **Personal:** Born Jun 13, 1942, Nashvl, AR. **Educ:** AM & N Coll, BS 1963; Univ AR Fayetteville, MEd 1971. **Career:** AM & N Coll Pine Bluff, AR, educ sec 1963-69; Univ AR, instr, dir of institutional advancement 1969-86; Broadcast Media, director, 1986-. **Orgs:** Pres AR Bus Ed Assn 1973-74, sec 1972-73; mem AR Coll Tchrs of Ec & Bus; Sthrn Bus Educ Assn; pres Nat Bus Educ Assn 1972-74, treas 1970-72, st coordntr 1974-; Pine Bluff Alum Chap Delta Sigma Theta; mem, bd dir Pine Bluff OIC 1973-74; Nat Cncl Negro Wmn; Jeff Cnty Advsry Com, Blk Adptn 1973-74. **Honors/Awds:** Lstd Ldrs of Blk Amer 1973/74; named Outstndg Edtr of Amer 1974/75; Ldrshp Award, Pine Bluff Alum Chap Delta Sigma Theta 1973; Delta of the Yr 1974. **Business Addr:** Director, Broadcast Media, 1200 University Dr, Box 4145, Pine Bluff, AR 71601.

MCGEE, GLORIA KESSELLE
Nurse, psychotherapist. **Personal:** Born Jul 12, 1954, Monrovia, Liberia; daughter of Izola Lewis and Andrew Belton; married Waddell McGee, Feb 16, 1992. **Educ:** Wayne State University, BS, 1977; University of Michigan, MS, 1981. **Career:** Lafayette Clinic, clinical nurse specialist, 1981-87; VA Medical Center, Oklahoma City, OK, head nurse, 1987-90; VA Medical Center, Lincoln, NE, associate chief nurse, 1990-; Inner Visions Counseling Center Inc, chairman of the board, president, 1990-. **Orgs:** University of Michigan Alumni Association, 1981-; Lincoln Human Rights Commission, commissioner, 1991-; America Red Cross, board of directors, 1991-; Sigma Theta Tau International, 1980-; Altrusa International, 1992-; NAACP, board of directors, 1980-; American Nurses Association, 1980-. **Honors/Awds:** VA Medical Center, Special Advancement for Achievement, 1988, Special Advancement for Performance, 1991; Inner Visions Counseling Center Inc, Woman of the Year, 1991. **Special Achievements:** "Reducing and Controling Absenteeism in Nursing," 1991. **Business Addr:** Associate Chief Nurse, Veterans Affairs Medical Center, 600 S 70th, Mail Symbol #118, Lincoln, NE 68506, (402)489-3802.

MCGEE, HANSEL LESLIE
Attorney, judge. **Personal:** Born Jun 13, 1926, Miami, FL; son of Flossie McGee and Hansel L McGee; married Mildred E Wareham; children: Elizabeth Florence, Leland Scott. **Educ:** George Washington Law Sch, JD 1966; City Coll NY, BS 1952; Polytechnic Inst, MS 1960. **Career:** IBM, sr patent atty 1974-; IBM, pat atty 1966-74; Bronx Legal Svcs, chief atty proj dir 1972-74; IBM Rsrch, rstch staff mem 1960-63; NY Supreme Court, justice, currently. **Orgs:** Pres bd dir SE Bronx Neighborhood Ctr; v chmn bd dir Bronx Legal Svcs; mem Morris Educ Council; chmn Bronxwide Com for Voter registration; mem 100 Black Men; consult Women of Am; mem Bronx NAACP; mem Harlem Lawyers Assn; mem Bronx OIC; chmn African-American Legal Defense and Educational Fund; chmn Morrisania Revitalization Corp; chmn Southeast Neighborhood Centers. **Honors/Awds:** US Patents 3214460, 3342051, 3129104, 3214282; sev outst serv awards. **Military Serv:** USN 1943-45. **Business Addr:** Supreme Court Justice, New York Supreme Court, 851 Grand Concourse, Bronx, NY 10466.

MCGEE, HENRY W., JR.
Educator. **Personal:** Born Dec 31, 1932, Chicago, IL; son of Attye Belle Truesdale and Henry W McGee; married Alice; children: Henry III, Kevin, Byron, Gregory, Erik. **Educ:** NW Univ, BS 1954; DePaul Univ, JD 1957; Columbia Univ, LLM 1970. **Career:** Cook Co, asst state's atty 1958-61; Great Lakes Region USOEO, regional legal servs dir 1966-67; Univ of Chicago Ctr for Studies in Crim Justice Juv Delinq Rsch Proj, legal dir 1967-68; Wolfson Coll Oxford Univ England, visiting fellow 1973; Visiting Prof, Univ of Florence Italy Inst of Comparative Law 1976, Univ of Puerto Rico 1979, Univ of Madrid (complutense) 1982; Fed Univ Rio de Janeiro Brazil, grad planning prog 1987; National Autonomous University of Mexico, 1988; UCLA, prof of law, currently. **Orgs:** Mem Natl Bar Assn; mem Natl Conf of Black Lawyers; draftsman Natl Conf of Bar Examiners 1974-; consult City Poverty Com London England 1973; consult & lectr Urban Plng USIS Italy 1976; past editor in chief DePaul Law Review. **Honors/Awds:** Blue Key Natl Honor Frat 1957; num publ. **Business Addr:** Professor of Law, Seattle University School of Law, 950 Broadway Plaza, Seattle, WA 98122.

MCGEE, HENRY WADSWORTH, III
Television executive. **Personal:** Born Jan 22, 1953, Chicago, IL; married Celia; children: 1 daughter. **Educ:** Harvard University, Cambridge, MA, BA (magna cum laude), 1974; Harvard Business School, Cambridge, MA, MBA, 1979. **Career:** Newsweek Magazine, New York, NY and Washington, DC, reporter, 1974-77; HBO, New York, NY, manager of film acquisition, 1979-80, director of program acquisitions, Time-Life Television, 1980-81, director of budgeting and planning for Cinemax, 1981-82, manager, HBO family programming department, 1982-83, director, HBO Enterprises, 1983-85, vice president of Home Video, 1985-88, senior vice president, programming, 1988-95; HBO Home Video, pres, 1995-. **Orgs:** Board of directors, The New 42nd Street Inc, 1990-; treasurer, Film Society of Lincoln Center, currently; director, The Black Filmmaker Foundation, currently; Alvin Ailey Dance Theater Foundation, president, currently. **Business Addr:** President, HBO Home Video, 1100 Avenue of the Americas, New York, NY 10036.

MCGEE, JAMES H.
Attorney. **Personal:** Born Nov 8, 1918, Berryburg, WV; married Elizabeth McCracken, 1948; children: Annette, Frances. **Educ:** Wilberforce Univ, BS, 1941; Ohio State Univ Law School, LLB, 1948. **Career:** Self-employed attorney, 1949-; City of Dayton, city commissioner 1967-70, mayor 1970-82. **Orgs:** Mem bd dirs Town Affiliation Assn; Dayton Art Inst; mem OH Bar Assn; mem bd of dir Sister Cities Intl; mem adv bd, Natl League of Cities; mem Supvr Counc on Crime & Deliquency; mem bd Melissa Bess Day Care Center mem Dayton Natl Amer Bar Assn; Juvenile Ct Adv Council; member, NAACP. **Honors/Awds:** Honorary LLD Degree: Wilberforce University; Central State University; Dayton University; Friend of the Boy Award, Dayton Westmont Optimist Intl. **Military Serv:** US Army, 1942-45; Five Battle Stars.

MCGEE, JAMES MADISON
Association executive. **Personal:** Born Dec 22, 1940, Nashville, TN; married Mary Francis Wilkins; children: Andrea, LaSandra, James Jr. **Educ:** Fisk U, attended 1959-60; Mid-S Sch of Electronics Nashville, diploma 1968-70. **Career:** District Four, National Alliance of Postal & Federal Employees, vice pres, 1976-89, pres, 1989-; US Postal Service, LSM instr trainer 1973-76; US Postal Service, LSM operator 1967; US Postal Service, clerk 1965. **Orgs:** Treasurer NAPFE Nashville Local #410 1968-72; pres NAPFE Nashville Local #410 1972-78; mem TN Voters Counc 1967-80; mem NAACP 1968-80; mem Benevolent Protective Order of Elks TN 1970-80. **Honors/Awds:** Mem HJ Johnson Honor Soc 1955-59; all conf basketball team High Sch 1959; all freshman basketball team Fisk Univ 1959-60. **Military Serv:** USMC PFC 1961-65; Good Conduct Medal, 1961-62, All Marine Basketball Team, 1963-64. **Business Addr:** President, National Alliance of Postal and Federal Employees, 1628 11th St NW, Washington, DC 20001.

MCGEE, JOANN
Counselor. **Personal:** Born in Buffalo, NY; daughter of Verlene McGee Freeman and Rev Cephus McGee Jr. **Educ:** Elmira College, NY, BA, MEd, MEd, reading education, 1992; Univ of Scranton, MS, counseling, 1987; Columbia University Teachers College, MA, EdD, adult & continuing education, 1987-92; Bank Street College of Education, MEd, special education, 1992. **Career:** SUNY at Binghamton, NY, instr 1980-81; Arnot Art Museum, traveling artist, instructor, 1982-85; Southern Tier Office of Social Ministry, community residence counselor, 1985-86; Elmira Correctional Facility, supervisor of volunteer tutors, 1984-94; Elmira City School District and Corning City School District, home teacher, 1994-. **Orgs:** Chemung Area Reading Cncl 1984-; Assn for the Care of Children's Health, 1990-. **Honors/Awds:** Grad asstshp SUNY at Binghamton NY 1975-77. **Business Addr:** Child Life Consultant, 402 W Church St, PO Box 500, Elmira, NY 14901, (607)737-6777.

MCGEE, PAMELA
Professional basketball player. **Personal:** Born Dec 1, 1962; children: Javale, Imani. **Educ:** USC, bachelor's degree in economics and communications. **Career:** Sacramento Monarchs, center, 1997-98; Los Angeles Sparks, 1998-. **Honors/Awds:** US Olympic Basketball Team, Gold Medal, 1984. **Business Addr:** Professional Basketball Player, Los Angeles Sparks, 3900 W Manchester Blvd, Inglewood, CA 90306, 800-978-9622.

MCGEE, ROSE N.
Association coordinator. **Personal:** Born Jan 23, 1921, Steubenville, OH; widowed; children: Robert, John, Thaddeus, Patricia Williams. **Educ:** Steubenville Bus Coll, attended 1947; Univ of Steubenville, attended 1 yr. **Career:** OH Commn on Aging, area coordinator 1974-80; SSI OH Commn on Aging, dir 1970-74; Office City of Steubenville, clk treas 1968-70. **Orgs:** Area ldr Cancer Soc; area ldr ARC; area ldr Comm Chest Rec; steward Phillips Chapel CME; past pres life mem exec bd NAACP; vice pres League of Women Voters. **Honors/Awds:** Recipient Awd of Commendation & Recognition, WSTV-TV Inc 1962; Outstanding Serv Awd OH Conf of NAACP 1968; Cert of Commendation, Nat Council of Negro Women Inc 1975; Cert of Appreciation for Falued Contribution, Bus & Professional Women, 1976; Comm Awd, City of Steubenville, 1976. **Business Addr:** Area Coordinator, OH Dept of Aging, 50 W Broad St, 9th Floor, Columbus, OH 43266.

MCGEE, SHERRY
Business owner, educator. **Personal:** Born Nov 16, 1957, Honolulu, HI; daughter of Winnie R Johnson; children: Michael L. **Educ:** Wayne State Univ, BS, 1987, MBA, 1991. **Career:**

CDI Corp, division sales mgr, 1978-89; McGee & Co, sales training consultant, 1990-92; Bartech, Inc, dir of mktg, 1992-97; Apple Book Ctr, founder/president, 1996-. **Orgs:** Junior Achievement, volunteer. **Business Addr:** Founder/President, Apple Book Center, 7900 W Outer Dr, Detroit, MI 48235.

MCGEE, SYLVIA WILLIAMS
Educational administrator. **Personal:** Born Aug 5, 1952, Macon, GA; daughter of John Paul & Nora Cunningham Williams; married Terry D McGee, Sr, Mar 19, 1977; children: Terese Lynette, T Dwight Jr. **Educ:** Tift College, BA, 1974; University of Georgia, MSW, 1976. **Career:** Mercer University, Project Upward Bound, counselor, 1976-77; Bibb Cty Public Schools, School Social Svcs, dir, 1977-. **Orgs:** Jack & Jill of America, Inc, regional dir, 1991-93, natl vp, 1996-98; United Way of Central Georgia, chmn evaluation comm, 1997-; Jr League of Macon, corr sec, 1996; Family Counseling Ctr, bd of dirs, 1998-; Youth Leadership Bibb Cty, chmn of programs, 1996-97; Georgia Industrial Home for Children, exec comm, 1994-97; Macon 2000, comm chmn of resource svcs. **Honors/Awds:** Leadership Macon, Hatcher Leadership Awd, 1997; Jack & Jill of America, Macon Chap, Distinguished Mother, 1997; School Social Workers Assn of Georgia, Leadership Georgia, Social Worker of the Year, 1998. **Business Addr:** Director, School Social Svcs, Bibb County Public Schools, 484 Mulberry St, Ste 390, Macon, GA 31204.

MCGEE, TIMOTHY DWAYNE
Professional football player. **Personal:** Born Aug 7, 1964, Cleveland, OH. **Educ:** Univ of Tennessee, attended. **Career:** Cincinnati Bengals, wide receiver, 1986-93; Washington Redskins, 1993-. **Honors/Awds:** Post-season play, 1988: AFC Championship Game, NFL Championship Game.

MCGEE, TONY
Professional football player. **Personal:** Born Apr 21, 1971, Terre Haute, IN. **Educ:** Univ of Michigan, bachelor's degree in communications. **Career:** Cincinnati Bengals, tight end, 1993-. **Business Addr:** Professional Football Player, Cincinnati Bengals, One Bengals Dr, Cincinnati, OH 45202, (513)621-3550.

MCGEE, VONETTA (LAWRENCE VONETTA JR)
Actress. **Personal:** Born Jan 14, San Francisco, CA; daughter of Alma Irene Scott McGee and Lawrence McGee; married Carl Lumbly, May 29; children: Brandon Lumbly. **Career:** Film actress, currently.

MCGEE, WADDELL
Environmental consultant/engineer. **Personal:** Born Dec 13, 1946, Hattisburg, MS; son of Corine McGee and Ovell McGee Sr; married Gloria Kesselle, Feb 16, 1990. **Educ:** Alcorn State University, BS, 1968; Southern University, LLB, 1976; American University, School for Environmental Studies, MS, 1980, PhD, 1985. **Career:** US Army, nuclear and environmental engineer, 1968-73; Oil Field Environmental Safety, consultant, director of operations, 1977-86; administrative assistant to the mayor, law administrator, 1986-87; California Environmental Waste Management, consultant, vice pres, company executive operations, 1987-88; Mid-America Environmental Consultants/Engineers, chief executive officer, 1988-. **Orgs:** Society of American Military Engineers; American Bar Association, 1975-; Nebraska Environmental Commission, 1992-; Nebraska Energy Commission, chairman, 1991-; American Red Cross, board of directors, 1992-; Goodwill Industries, board of directors, co-chair, 1991-; NAACP, president, 1992-; International Society of Environmental Professionals, US president, 1991-; Clean in America Inc, chairman, 1989-. **Honors/Awds:** Clean in America Inc, Man of the Year, 1990; International Society of Environmental Professionals, Professional Award, 1991; Senatorial Citation, 1989. **Special Achievements:** Author, Blacks and the Environment, 1992. **Military Serv:** US Army, sgt, 1969-73. **Business Addr:** CEO, Mid-America Environmental Consultants/Engineers, Inc, 6100 Vine St, Ste Z-205, Lincoln, NE 68505, (402)465-4755.

MCGEE, WILLIAM TORRE
Journalist. **Personal:** Born Sep 3, 1966, Miami, FL; son of Betty Jean McGee and William McGee (deceased). **Educ:** Northwestern University, BS, journalism, 1988. **Career:** The Miami Times, copy editor, reporter, 1988-90; The Miami Herald, copy editor, living, 1990-92, reporter, action line, 1992-94, reporter, 1994-. **Orgs:** South Florida, Black Journalists Association, 1988-; NAACP. **Home Addr:** 2423 NW 179th St, Miami, FL 33056-3623, (305)626-8837. **Business Phone:** (954)985-4521.

MCGEE, WILLIE DEAN
Professional baseball player. **Personal:** Born Nov 2, 1958, San Francisco, CA. **Educ:** Diablo Valley Junior College, attended. **Career:** St Louis Cardinals, outfielder 1982-90; Oakland Athletics, outfielder, 1990; San Francisco Giants, outfielder, 1991-94; Boston Red Sox, outfielder, 1995; St Louis Cardinals, outfielder, 1996-. **Honors/Awds:** 17 consecutive steals; tied World Series record for outfielders with 24 putouts in the Series; set record for highest fielding average in 7 game series with most chances accepted; named to Howe News Bureau post-season All Star team 1981; Topps Chewing Gum All-Rookie team 1982; St Louis BBWAA Rookie of the Year; 3 Gold Glove Awds; Natl League MVP 1985; named to The Sporting News and UPI NL All Star teams 1985; Sporting News NL Player of the Year 1985; winner of BBWAA Natl League MVP 1985; voted to first Silver Slugger Team 1985; Sports Illustrated and Natl League's Player of the Week June 3-9 1985; NL Player of the Month August 1985; mem All Star Teams 1983 and 1985. **Business Addr:** Professional Baseball Player, St Louis Cardinals, 250 Stadium Plaza, Busch Memorial Stadium, St Louis, MO 63102.

MCGEHEE, MAURICE EDWARD
Educational administrator (retired). **Personal:** Born Aug 17, 1914, Chicago, IL; son of Dorcas Lucille Appleby McGehee and George E McGehee. **Educ:** Chicago Teacher Coll, BA, 1941; DePaul Univ, MA, 1953; Univ of Southern CA, postgraduate, 1954-55; Los Angeles State Teachers Coll, 1954-63; Juilliard School of Music, 1943; City Univ, EdD, 1981. **Career:** Wendell Phillips Evening High School, Chicago, asst principal counselor, 1950-54; Keith Elementary School, Chicago, asst principal, 1950-54; 96th St Sch Los Angeles, substitute vice principal, 1957-58, 1961-62; head thcr summer sessions 1961-62; Fremont Adult Sch Los Angeles, specialist 1966-67; Dorsey Adult School, head counselor 1957-67; Los Angeles Adult Sch, vice-principal, 1967-68; Watts Skill Center Los Angeles, manpower devel training acting principal, 1968-71; Principal, Manual Arts Community Adult School, 1972-74; Principal, Crenshaw-Dorsey Community Adult School, 1974-82 (retired). **Orgs:** Principal consultant curriculum div Career & Continuing Educ, Los Angeles Unified Sch District, 1972-73; mem, Commn on Evaluation of Language Arts Textbooks, Los Angeles 1957-; Adult Educ Guidance Counseling Commn, Los Angeles, 1964-; So Central Welfare Planning Comm, 1968-; mem Adult Educ Assn; Early Childhood Assn; Natl Assn Public School Adult Educ; NEA; Assn Classroom Teachers; CA Council Adult Educ Admin; CA Teachers Assn; CA Council Adult Educ; mem, Mayor's Comm Adv Com 1965-; Crenshaw Coordinating Council Los Angeles 1957-; 96th St PTA 1954-; exec dir Watts Summer Festival 1971; pres Negro History Assn 1961-; Nat CA Urban League; NAACP; Manpower Devel Assn Los Angeles Co Mus Assn; DePaul Univ Alumni Assn; Alpha Phi Alpha. **Honors/Awds:** Named outstanding community citizen, Los Angeles City Council 1971; Community Man of the Year, Westminister Presbyterian Church, 1971; State of California Certificate of Commendation for Outstanding Service, 1971; Mayor's Certificate of Appreciation, 1976; Award for Community Service, Los Angeles Police Dept, 1978; Recipient of the Congressman's Medal of Merit, presented by Augustus F. Hawkins, 1974. **Business Addr:** 430 N Grand Ave, Los Angeles, CA 90012.

MCGEHEE, NAN E.
Educational administrator, psychologist. **Personal:** Born Mar 9, 1928, Chicago, IL; daughter of Ethel Davis McGehee and Winston T McGehee. **Educ:** Univ of Chicago, BA 1947; Northwestern Univ, BSE 1958, MS 1959, PhD 1962; Harvard Univ, IEM Cert 1972. **Career:** Northwestern Univ Eve Div, instr 1960-61; Univ of IL Chicago Circle, instr 1961-62, asst prof 1962-66, assoc prof 1966-, dir univ honors progs 1967-70, dean of faculties 1970-72, assoc chancellor 1972-79 retired. **Orgs:** Sec, treas IL Psychol Assn 1968-70; consult US Civil Serv Comm, EEOC, FWP Reg & Training 1970-72; bd mem IL Reg Libr Council 1973; policy bd mem Natl Ctr for Study of Ed Policy Alternatives 1972; mem Sigma Xi, Alpha Kappa Alpha, Amer Psychol Assn, IL Psychol Assn, Midwest Psychol Assn, Amer Assn of Univ Profs, Alpha Lambda Delta, Phi Eta Sigma. **Honors/Awds:** NIMH Fellow 1959; Univ of IL Rsch Fellow 1962; co-author several articles. **Home Addr:** 14214 Glen Acres Rd SW, Vashon, WA 98070.

MCGHEE, GEORGIA MAE
Associate executive. **Personal:** Born Dec 9, 1934, Joiner, AR; daughter of Marge Young and Webb Young; divorced; children: Curits L, Steven Alan, Garry Lynn, Cheryl Densie Johnson, Rita Lorain, Kenneth G. **Educ:** Davenport Business Coll, 1958-59; Jr Coll, Data Processing, English 1973. **Career:** AFSCME AFL-CIO, vice pres council 07 1972-76, council vice pres 1977-79; pres local 261 1973-77, Coalition of Labor Union Women, convenor 1974, chap pres 1975; Coalition of Labor Union Women Natl Officers Council, 2nd vice pres 1977-80 & 1980-86; AFSCME AFL-CIO, intl vice pres 1977-80 & 1980-84 AFSCME Int vice pres two terms; MI Women's Commiss, commiss 1977-80 & 1980-84. **Orgs:** Pres Block Club 1969-70; intl vice pres AFSCME AFL-CIO 1977-80 & 1980-84; vice pres Coalition of Labor Union Women Natl Officers Council 1977-80; coalition of Labor Union Women term from 1984-86; was re-elected (3rd term); MI Women's Commiss 1977; AFL-CIO Comm Serv Committee 1978-86; audit & review comm Kent Cty United Way Committee 1978-81; pres AFSCME AFL-CIO local 261; exec bd mem United Way Kent Co 1978-82. **Honors/Awds:** Rosalyn Carter's Comm Plan Cert 1979; Kenneth W Robinson Comm Serv Kent Cty United Way 1982; Mary McLeod Bethune Awd Natl Council of Negro Women 1984; MI Women's Comm Disting Serv Awd MI Women's Commiss 1984; Martha Reynolds Labor Awd GR Giants Awd 1984; Coalition of Black Trade Unionist Trail Blazer Award, 1990. **Home Addr:** 612 Worden SE, Grand Rapids, MI 49507.

MCGHEE, JAMES LEON
Business executive. **Personal:** Born Mar 3, 1948, Wayne, IN. **Educ:** Univ of Puget Sound, BA 1974. **Career:** City Planning Commiss Tacoma WA, asst planner 1972-73; US Treasury Dept, asst bank examiner 1973-76; Housing & Devel Seattle, DC, dir 1977-78; Northwest Tech Inc, pres, chmn 1983-; Medsco Inc Med Supply Corp, pres, chmn 1983-. **Orgs:** Fin treas NW Black Elected Official Assoc 1973-85; founder United Trade Worker Assoc 1975; pres, chmn of bd WA State Bus League 1980-85; bd of dir NW Tech Inc 1981-85; plnng commiss City of Seattle 1981-85; asst reg vice pres Natl Bus League 1983-85; bd of dir Medsco Inc 1983-85; bd of dir UnitedNegro Coll Fund 1985. **Honors/Awds:** Pres Alpha Phi Alpha/Sphinx OH State 1968; co-founder Seattle Central Comm Coll Found 1978; Honors for Serv EFP Rhomania 1979; Community Black Leader of 1980 NW Conf of Black Public Official 1980. **Military Serv:** AUS sgt E-5 3 yrs; Hon Discharge; Viet Nam Medal; Serv Citation 1971. **Business Addr:** President, Medsco Inc, 22030 W Valley Hwy, Kent, WA 98032.

MCGHEE, NANCY BULLOCK
Educator (retired). **Personal:** Born Mar 19, 1908, High Point, NC; daughter of Mehala Bullock and Dr Oscar S Bullock; married Samuel. **Educ:** Shaw Univ, BA; Columbia Univ, MA; Univ of Chicago, PhD 1942; Univ of London; Cambridge Univ; Shaw Univ, HHD 1973. **Career:** Hampton Inst, dir, instructor in humanities 1964-69, chmn English dept 1967; Univ of Louisville, instructor; visiting prof of literature, Coll of William & Mary 1979; Hampton Inst, prof emeritus of English, commissioned by trustees to write history of Hampton Inst. **Orgs:** Exec comm member, Assn of Dept of English, 1972-75; sec bd dir, VA Found for Humanities & Public Policy, 1973-; pres, VA Humanities Conf, 1973-74; Grand Basileus Zeta Phi Beta Sorority Inc, 1948-54; bd chmn, Amer Council of Human Rights; vice pres, Natl Council of Negro Women 1954-56; comm member, Amer Assn of Univ Women, 1973-75. **Honors/Awds:** Gen Educ Bd Scholarship Rockefeller Found; Julius Rosenwald Fund Scholarship; Distinguished Alumni Award Shaw Univ 1965; Avalon Found Chair in Humanities (first endowed chair at Hampton Inst). **Business Addr:** Professor Emeritus, Hampton Univ, PO Box 6567, Hampton, VA 23668.

MCGHEE, REGINALD D.
Business executive. **Personal:** Born Jan 20, 1927, Detroit, MI; married Christine; children: Reginald, Kathleen. **Educ:** Detriot Inst of Technology, 1960. **Career:** Blue Cross-Blue Shield, spl rep 1964-. **Orgs:** V chmn first Dem Cong Dist Organization 1966-70; Precinct Delegate 1966-68; mem dist exec bd 1966-70; candidate Wayne Co Bd of Commissions 1968, lostby 7 votes; elected precinct delegate 1974; aptd to Zoning Bd of Appeals City of Detroit 1975; former pres Concerned Citizens for Action Inc; former pres Barton-MacFarlane Comm Coun; former speaker for New Detroit Inc; mem TV Study Com; mem UAW-CIO Local #1781, 1st vice pres; ruling elder Calvary Presbyterian Ch; former clerk of session Calvary Presbyterian Ch; former mem bd dir Metropolitan Detroit Coun of Ch; former chmn Pub Educ Com; chmn Com on Urban Crisis 1968. **Honors/Awds:** First black hired as a spl rep for Blue Cross-Blue Shield; certificat of recognition City of Detroit 1974.

MCGHEE, SAMUEL T.
Educator, government official. **Personal:** Born May 29, 1940, Jersey City, NJ; son of Lucile Bitten McGhee and Samuel T McGhee; children: Darren, Elissa, Samuel III, Jeffrey. **Educ:** Jersey City State Coll, BA 1962; Seton Hall Univ, MA 1965, postgrad study. **Career:** Jersey City State Coll, asst dir admissions 1971-72, assoc dir admissions 1972-76, dir of admissions 1976-; Hillside, NJ Finance Commissioner 1987; Hillside Township, Hillside NJ, mayor 1988; Hillside Township, Hillside NJ, police commissioner 1989-90, 1993-94, mayor, begin 1991, public works commissioner 1992, 1996, fire commissioner, 1995-96, mayor, 1997-. **Orgs:** Mem Omega Psi Phi Fraternity 1988-; mem Natl Conference of Black Mayors 1988-. **Honors/Awds:** Black Merit Acad E St Louis 1973; Jersey City State Coll, Distinguished Alumni Award 1981; Phi Delta Kappa, 1990; Omega Psi Phi Superior Service Award, 1991. **Business Addr:** Dir of Admissions, Jersey City State College, 2039 Kennedy Blvd, Jersey City, NJ 07305.

MCGHEE, WALTER BROWNIE
Musician, singer. **Personal:** Born Nov 30, 1915, Knoxville, TN; son of Zella Henley McGhee and George McGhee; married Ruth Dantzler McGhee (deceased); children: Vediazella E, Vilhelmina, George, Valerie, Colin Che'. **Career:** BMI, songwriter, publisher, 1950; Cat On A Hot Tin Roof, actor 1955; Face In The Crowd, musician & actor 1955; Simply Heavenly, actor, musician, singer 1958; Buck & The Preacher, music; films: The Jerk, musician, 1977; Angel Heart, actor, 1986; television appearances: Family Ties, actor, 1987; Matlock, musician, 1989. **Orgs:** Member, Local 802 Musician Union, 1944; member, AFTRA, Screen Actors Guild; patron & life mem, Melbourne Blues Appreciation Society, 1991. **Honors/Awds:** Inducted, Blues Hall of Fame, Bay Area Blues Society, 1989; Certificate of Appreciation, California Highway Patrol, 1989; song book, Oak Publishing Co; Lifetime Achievement Award from Bay Area Music Award, 1991. **Home Addr:** 688 43rd St, Oakland, CA 94609.

MCGILL, LENNY
Professional football player. **Personal:** Born May 31, 1971, Long Beach, CA. **Educ:** Arizona State, BA in criminal justice. **Career:** Green Bay Packers, defensive back, 1994-95; Atlanta Falcons, 1996-. **Business Addr:** Professional Football Player, Atlanta Falcons, Two Falcon Place, Suwanee, GA 30174, (404)945-1111.

MCGILL, MICHELE NICOLE JOHNSON
Newspaper columnist. **Personal:** Born Jul 14, 1966, San Diego, CA; daughter of Dianne Campbell Johnson and Leonard Johnson. **Educ:** University of Florida, Gainesville, FL, BS, Journalism, 1988; University of North Florida, Jacksonville, FL, currently. **Career:** Independent Florida Alligator, Gainesville, FL, layout editor, 1987-88; The Florida Times-Union, Jacksonville, FL, copy editor, 1988-90, columnist, 1990-. **Orgs:** President, Jacksonville Assn of Black Communicators, 1991-93; president, Soul Autonomy, Inc, 1991-; newsletter dir, Jacksonville Urban League Auxiliary, 1991-92; member, National Assn of Black Journalists, 1987-90; past president, University of Florida Assn of Black Communicators, 1987-88; First Baptist Church of Mandarin Youth Group. **Business Addr:** Call Box Writer, Editorial, Florida Times-Union, One Riverside Ave, PO Box 1949, Jacksonville, FL 32231.

MCGILL, THOMAS L., JR.
Attorney. **Personal:** Born Aug 13, 1946, Martinsburg, WV; son of Dorthy Kathryn Baylor McGill and Thomas L McGill, Sr; married Charisse R Lillie, Dec 4, 1982; children: Leslie Janelle, Thomas L III, Alison Charisse. **Educ:** Lincoln Univ, BA 1968; Occidental Coll, MA 1972; Notre Dame Law School, JD 1975. **Career:** Olney HS, teacher 1968-71; Hon Kenneth Gibson Mayor, mayor's aide 1971-72; Hon Paul Dandridge Judge, law clerk 1975-82; PA Human Relations Commn, commissioner 1981-90, chairperson 1986-90; McGill & Seay, attorney 1975-90; Clark, McGill, Newkirk & Seary, 1990-. **Orgs:** Mem Philadelphia Bar Assn 1975-, Amer Bar Assn 1975-; mem Natl Bar Assn 1977-; Recording Sec Barristers Assn 1977-78; pres Barristers Assn 1980-81; mem of bd Veritas Inc 1980-83, Germantown Boys Club 1982-84; bd of dirs West Mount Airy Neighbors 1986-87; bd of dirs, Friends Neighborhood Guild, 1995. **Honors/Awds:** All Conf Baseball Team Lincoln Univ 1967; Sr Class Awd for Creative Writing Lincoln Univ 1968; Natl Urban Fellow, Natl Conf of Mayors Yale Univ 1971-72. **Home Addr:** 7000 Emlen St, Philadelphia, PA 19119-2556, (215)842-9961. **Business Addr:** Attorney at Law, Fidelity Bldg, Ste 2542, 123 South Broad St, Philadelphia, PA 19109-1025, (215)735-5300.

MCGINEST, WILLIE
Professional football player. **Personal:** Born Dec 11, 1971, Long Beach, CA. **Educ:** USC, attended. **Career:** New England Patriots, defensive end, 1994-. **Honors/Awds:** 1776 Quarterback Club of New England, Rookie of the Year, 1994; Pro Bowl, 1996. **Business Addr:** Professional Football Player, New England Patriots, 60 Washington St, Foxboro Stadium, Foxboro, MA 02035, (508)543-7911.

MCGINNIS, JAMES W.
Educator, attorney. **Personal:** Born Jul 8, 1940, Fairfield, AL; son of Reatha Saunders Felton and James McGinnis; married Debra Hughes, Mar 16, 1988; children: Ayana Marie. **Educ:** Wayne State Univ, BS 1963; San Francisco State Univ, MA 1965; Yeshiva Univ, PhD 1976; Wayne State Univ Law School, JD 1977. **Career:** Coll Entrance Examination Bd, asst dir 1967-69; Univ of California Berkeley, instructor, 1970-72; Far West Lab for Educ Research, research assoc 1972-73; Oakland Univ, asst prof 1976-81; Private Practice, lawyer. **Orgs:** Pres Kappa Alpha Psi Frat Wayne State Univ 1961-62; mem Assn of Black Psychologist 1963-73; researcher Black Studies Inst Wayne State Univ 1975-76; office counsel Hall & Andary Law Firm 1982-84; chmn PAC 1982-85, mem 1982-, Natl Conf of Black Lawyers. National Bar Association 1989-. **Honors/Awds:** Fellowship Project Beacon, Yeshiva Univ 1965-66; Ford Found Fellowship Language Soc of Child, Univ of CA 1968.

MCGINTY, DORIS EVANS
Educator, musician, author. **Personal:** Born Aug 2, 1925, Washington, DC; daughter of Vallean Richardson Evans and Charlie Evans; married Milton Oliver McGinty, Sep 6, 1956; children: Derek Gordon, Dana Winston, Lisa Megan. **Educ:** Howard Univ, BMus Educ 1945, BA 1946; Radcliffe Coll, MA 1947; Oxford Univ (LMH), DPhil 1954. **Career:** DC Public Library, music librarian 1943-45; Howard Univ, instructor, prof 1947-; TX Southern Univ, assoc prof musicology summer 1956; Howard Univ, chmn dept of music 1977-85, prof of music. **Orgs:** Contributing editor, The Black Perspective in Music, 1975-; Educ & Community Outreach Comm, Natl Symphony Orchestra 1978-81; bd trustees exec comm, WETA radio & TV 1979-85; bd trustees, Cathedral Choral Soc 1983-86; bd trustees & chair, Comm on Status of Minorities, Coll Music Soc 1982-85; consul, Afro-Amer Arts 1983-84; consul, L Bolliger Assoc Filming 1984-. **Honors/Awds:** Gen Educ Bd Fellowship 1951-52; Fulbright Fellowship 1950-51, 1951-52; Caribbean-Amer Scholars Exchange Phelps-Stokes Fund 1974; Outstanding Teacher Awards 1973, 1976; Faculty Research Awards Howard Univ 1968-69, 1975-76; research grant Natl Endowment for the Humanities 1984, 1987. **Business Addr:** Prof Dept of Music, Howard Univ, Washington, DC 20059.

MCGLOCKTON, CHESTER
Professional football player. **Personal:** Born Sep 16, 1969, Whiteville, NC; married. **Educ:** Clemson. **Career:** Oakland Raiders, defensive tackle, 1992-. **Business Addr:** Professional Football Player, Oakland Raiders, 1220 Harbor Bay Pkwy, Alameda, CA 94502, (510)615-1875.

MCGLOTHAN, ERNEST
Business executive. **Personal:** Born Oct 25, 1937, Tuscaloosa, AL; married Willa Rean May; children: Wilma, Kecia, Corey. **Educ:** Tuskegee Inst Sch of Arch, 1971; Tuskegee Inst Sch of Arch, BS 1971. **Career:** Mac-Pon Co Gen Contractors, pres owner; Gaillard Constrn Co Birmingham; A H Smith Constrn Co Birmingham. **Orgs:** Mem Alpha Phi Alpha Frat; Mayor's Adv Com; Nat Assn of Minority Contractors; Birmingham Zoining Bd of Adjustments; Omicron Lambda; bd dir BSA; chmn Cooper Green Golf Course Com. **Honors/Awds:** Oustsnd bus men of yr Omega Psi Phi 1973; bus of the yr awd Dr Herman H Long 1977; licensed Minority Gen Contr AL. **Military Serv:** AUS 1971-73.

MCGLOTHEN, GOREE
City government official, electrician. **Personal:** Born Aug 17, 1915, Huntsville, TX; married Allie Mae Hightower; children: Goree, Jr, Mattie Grant. **Educ:** Indsl Educ Tuskegee Inst, BS 1937. **Career:** United Gas Corp, mstr gas meter repair 1941-45; State of TX, mstr electrical 1942-77, mstr plumber 1944-55; McGlothen Elect Co, owner; City of Huntsville, city councilman 1975-. **Orgs:** Sec Walker Co Negro C of C 1941-44; pres Coodgellows Club 1942-43; mem adult educ bd Huntsville HS 1975-76; chmn Janes Found 1976-77; deacon ss tchr fncl sec First Mission Bapt Ch; pres Cent Mission Bapt Assn of TX Brthd; mem NAACP Internt Bus Fellowship. **Honors/Awds:** Golden Eagle Awd BSA 1967; 1st black to defeat a white polit opponent since Reconstruct Days Huntsville TX 1975; Ldr Celeb Bicent Year 1976; Plaque Trinity River Authority 1978; Black History Awd from Pres Jimmy Carter 1979; Hon Fine Lighter of the Year 1980; Outstanding Male Alpha Phi Alpha 1984; Plaque Huntsville Housing Authority 1985; Outstanding Achievement Awd Natl Council of Org 1986; vice pres Grand Persons Bd 1987.

MCGLOVER, STEPHEN LEDELL
Business executive. **Personal:** Born Nov 8, 1950, Los Angeles, CA; son of Octavia Bell and Theodore McGlover; married. **Educ:** Woodbury College, intl business management, BS, 1978; University of Maryland, 1979; Intl Business Machines, 1980; Black Businessmen Assn, BS, business, 1981; Ohio State University, NOPA Cealer Management Institute, 1984; Natl Office Products Assn, IBM sales course, 1984; Southern Methodist University, Edwin Cox School of Business, 1984; Minister Training Institute, CCC, 1992-95; Golden Gate Baptist Sem, 1996; Amos Tuck Executive, Met Course, 1996. **Career:** Occidental Insurance, salesman, 1974-76; Inventory Data Supplies, shipping mgr, 1975, director/collections, 1976, general mgr, 1977-78; McGlover Incorporated, salesman, 1977-79; Oasis Office Supplies, president/partner, 1979-83; Oasis Office Products, Inc, president/ceo, 1983-. **Orgs:** Black Business Association, 1980-; Mayor's Small Business Adv Board, 1988-; National Office Products Association. **Honors/Awds:** Black Business Association, BBA Member of the Year Award, 1987; Mid-City Chamber of Commerce, Man of the Year, 1987; Small Business of the Year Award, 1996. **Military Serv:** US Air Force. **Business Addr:** President, Oasis Office Products, Inc, 4600 W Washington Blvd, Los Angeles, CA 90016, (213)938-6211.

MCGOODWIN, ROLAND C.
Dentist. **Personal:** Born Jul 15, 1933, Evansville, IN; married Lillian Pollard; children: Nina Marie, Roland Jr. **Educ:** Cntrl State Clge, BS 1955; Meharry Med Clge Sch Dentistry, DDS 1963; Hubbard Hosp, intern 1964; Albert Einstein Med Ctr, Resident 1965. **Career:** Cincinnati OH, pvt prac; Lincoln Hghts Health Ctr, staff; Bethesda Hospital. **Orgs:** Dentist crippled children; bd educ Amer Dental Assc; Natl Dental Assc; OH State Dental Assc; OH Valley Dental Soc; Cincinnati Dental Soc; Acad GenDentists Bd Mt Auburn Health Ctr; Walnut Hill Area Counc Adv; Health Manpower Linkage Sys; OH Dept Health. **Military Serv:** AUS 1st lt 1956-59; LTC KC USAR 1978-. **Business Addr:** 645 E Mc Millan St, Cincinnati, OH 45206.

MCGOWAN, ELSIE HENDERSON
Educator. **Personal:** Born Jul 3, 1947, Pell City, AL; daughter of Rannie Collins Henderson and Franklin Henderson; married James Oliver McGowan, Jan 3, 1970; children: Kenneth Eugene, LaCindra DeNae. **Educ:** Knoxville College, Knoxville, TN, BS, 1969; University of Alabama, Birmingham, AL, MA, 1982, EdS, 1989. **Career:** St Clair County Board of Education, Ashville, AL, business education teacher, 1969-83, assistant principal (elem), 1983-94, director of migrant education program, 1986-94; Headstart Prog, exec dir, currently. **Orgs:** President, St Clair County Education Association, 1979; coordinator, Substitute Teachers' Workshop, 1987. **Honors/Awds:** Member, Kappa Delta Pi Honor Society, University of Alabama, Birmingham, AL, 1980; Outstanding Woman of the Year, 1979; member, National, State, Local Education Associations in Alabama, 1969-; National Alumni Society, University of Alabama, 1981; Delta Sigma Theta Sorority, Anniston Alumnae Chapter. **Home Addr:** PO Box 268, Pell City, AL 35125.

MCGOWAN, THOMAS RANDOLPH
Director of religious ecumenism. **Personal:** Born Apr 19, 1926, Baltimore, MD; son of Mary McGowan and Robert McGowan; married Roedean Olivia Oden; children: James, Karen White, Terry V Stevens, Kevin, Kurt. **Educ:** Oakland City Coll, AA 1964; Attended, San Francisco State Coll 1964-66, Univ of CA at Berkeley 1966-67; Univ of MD, BS 1978. **Career:** San Francisco Procurement Agency, contract specialist 1963-68; US Army Harry Diamond Labs, branch chief 1972-79; US Army Yuma Proving Ground, dir proc directorate 1979-81; Roman Catholic Diocese of Oakland, dir for ecumenism 1983-. **Orgs:** Chmn of bd Columbia Found 1978-79; dir Youth for Serv 1985-. **Military Serv:** AUS pfc 1944-46. **Home Addr:** 139 Pinto Dr, Vallejo, CA 94591. **Business Addr:** Dir, Roman Catholic Diocese, 3014 Lake Shore Ave, Office of Ecumenical Affairs, Oakland, CA 94610.

MCGRADY, EDDIE JAMES
Supervisor (retired). **Personal:** Born Mar 6, 1928, Americus, GA; son of Ola Scott McGrady and Will McGrady; married Alice, Dec 26, 1952 (deceased); children: Broderick, Rodney, Valery McGrady Trice. **Educ:** US Army Admin School Germany, Admin 1951; US Const NCO Acad, Sr NCO 1951. **Career:** US Army 555th Parachute Infantry, sgt 1946-66; Americus & Police Dept, one of first black patrolmen 1966-71; Only Black Star Security Patrol, owner, mgr 1971; Campus Safety, lt, 1st black shift suprv 1973-, captain campus safety and asst dir, 1st black 1985-90. **Orgs:** Bd mem Americus City School Bd 1967-80, Natl Amer Council Amer Legion; chmn Seventh Dist Title 20 Council 1967-80; post commander CB Dowdell Amer Legion Post 558 1971-76; jr commander 3rd Dist Amer Legion Dept of GA 1976-80; adv Boy Scouts of Amer 1977; v chmn 3rd Dist of GA Assn of Black Elected Officials 1978; com mem GA Sch Bd Assn 1979; bd mem W Central GA Comm Act Councl 1979; commander The Amer Legion Third Dist Dept of GA 1979-80; Natl Membership Comm Amer Legion 1983; appt Patriotic Observance of Flag Etiquette Amer Legion State of GA 1984; chmn bd of directors of West Central GA Community Action Council, 1985-94; served on Americus-Sumter County Bi-Centennial Commission, 1987-88; chairman, board of trustees Flint Services, Inc 1988. **Honors/Awds:** Outstanding Dist Commander Natl Commander of Amer Legion for State of GA for Membership 1979-80; Mr legionnaire of the Year CB Dowdell Amer Legion 558 1976; Barnum Dosey-Comm Serv Awd Elks & Lodge 691 & BSAT 226 1977; Cert Black Youth in Action 1979; Awd Support of Delta Sigma Theta GA SW Coll 1980, Support of Kappa Alpha Kappa 1980, Assn of Women Students 1980, Support of SABU 1980, 3rd Dit of Amer Legion Aux 1980, CB Dowdell Amer Legion Post 558 1980, CB Dowdell Amer Legion Ladies Aux 558 1980; Proclamation from Gov George Busbee State of GA 1981; Resolution from GA House of Reps 1981; Outstanding Dist Commander Natl Commander of Amer Legion for State of GA for Membership 1979-80; Lt Col Aide De Campfrom gov JoeFrank Harris State of GA 1984; Comm SV and Region VI of Noble 1987; Outsting Leadership Award, West Central Georgia Community Action Council 1987; Community Service Award, United Holiness Church 1987; Life Achievement Award, Boy Scout Troup 226, 1988; Distinguished Service Award, Georgia Southwestern College, Campus Safety Dept 1973-90; Certificate of Appreciation, Fraternal Order of Police Lodge #72 1990; Certificate of Achievement, Alpha Kappa Alpha Sorority, Inc 1991; West Central GA CAC Inc, Appreciation for Devoted Leadership, 1996. **Military Serv:** AUS 1st sgt E-8 20 yrs active 24 retired reserve; Sr Parachutist Army Commendation Ribbon 1946; Commendation Ribbon with Metal Pendant; 3 Awds by Sec of the Army 1957-66. **Home Addr:** 112 Ashby St, PO Box 1305, Americus, GA 31709.

MCGRADY, TRACY
Professional basketball player. **Personal:** Born May 24, 1979. **Educ:** Mount Zion Christian Academy. **Career:** Toronto Raptors, forward-guard, 1997-. **Honors/Awds:** USA Today, Player of the Year; The Associated Press, North Carolina State Player of the Year. **Business Addr:** Professional Basketball Player, Toronto Raptors, 150 York St, Ste 110, Toronto, ON, Canada M5H 3S5, (416)214-2255.

MCGRATH, CLARICE HOBGOOD
Automobile dealer. **Personal:** Born Oct 30, 1951, Galveston, TX; daughter of Ruby Lee Ashford Hobgood and James R Hobgood; children: Clarice Nakia Mitchell, Byron Bernard Mitchell. **Educ:** Univ of Plano, Plano, TX, BS, 1974. **Career:** Higgins Lincoln-Mercury, Texas City, TX, sales; Westwood Ford, Lincoln-Mercury, pres, currently. **Business Addr:** President, Westwood Ford-Lincoln-Mercury, Inc., 11 N 25th St, Fort Dodge, IA 50501.

MCGREGOR, EDNA M.
Educational Administrator (retired). **Personal:** Born Jan 10, Ontario;daughter of Charlotte Maud Jackson McGruder and Walter Jay McGruder; married Albert (deceased). **Educ:** Howard Univ, BS 1945; Univ of Michigan, MA 1950; Michigan

State Univ; Univ of Detroit. **Career:** Detroit Schools, health & physical educ teacher 1945-52, science teacher 1952-66; Butzel Jr High School, guidance counselor 1966-68; Northeastern High School, guidance counselor, 1968-82; Osborn High School, guidance counselor 1982-85; Ivery's Professional Travel Agency, travel agent, 1985-. **Orgs:** Exec comm counselors Detroit Fed of Teachers 1970-; mem House of Delegates, Detroit Assn of Black Organizations; delegate to the Michigan Senate 1980; mem Metro Detroit Guidance Assn; Amer Assn of Univ Women; bd dir Detroit Assn of Univ of Michigan Women Alumnae; life mem NAACP; pres Detroit Urban League Guild; Alpha Kappa Alpha; Alpha Rho Omega; bd of mgmt YWCA; Howard Univ Alumni Club; exec comm Natl Howard Univ Alumni Council; Women's Day chairperson Second Baptist Church 1984; project coordinator Health-O-Rama 1984; volunteer Southwest Detroit Hospital 1984; registration staff Metro Detroit Convention & Visitors Bureau 1985; Women's Comm NAACP 1985; pres Howard Univ Alumni Club of Detroit 1986-88; prog chmnDetroit Assn Univ of Michigan Alumnae; board of directors, Univ of Michigan, 1989-; Museum African-American History, million dollar club member, 1988; Operation Big Vote, vice chair; Alpha Kappa Alpha Sorority, Alpha Rho Omega Chapter, Health Care Committee, chairperson. **Honors/Awds:** Human Relations Award, Detroit Roundtable of Protestants, Catholics & Jews, 1955; Detroit Urban League, Guilder of the Year, 1972; Alumni Meritorious Award, Detroit Howard Univ Alumni, 1975; Top Ladies of Distinction, 1984; Five-Year Pin for Volunteerism, Southwest Detroit Hospital, 1983. **Special Achievements:** NAACP, Fight for Freedom Dinner, Million Dollar Club Member, 1990, 1991, 1992; held a children's health fair at elementary schools, 265 were screened by professionals, follow-up in dental and nutritional areas. **Home Addr:** 17333 Muirland, Detroit, MI 48221.

MCGREGOR, ORAN B.
Business executive (retired). **Personal:** Born Oct 29, 1925, Marshall, TX; married Eulalia; children: Dietra Wade, Michelle. **Educ:** Bishop Clge, BS 1949; TSU, addtl study 1950-51; Prairie View Clge 1951; LUTC Ins Course, grad; LIAMA Sch in Agency Mgmt, grad. **Career:** FW Urban League, bd dir 1958-61; Ft Worth Tarrant Co United Way, bd dir 1971-73; YMCA, bd dir 1962-72; Atlanta Life Ins Co Ofc 2, retired mgr 1972-82; First Fed Equities Mortgage Corp, vice pres 1967-68; Ft Worth Public School, substitute educ spec 1982-. **Orgs:** Trustee Mt Gilead Glen Garden Apts 1967-70; appointee/Elect Dallas-Ft Worth Airport Bd 1980-; mem Omega Phi Psi Frat 1951-; mem YMCA 1952; bd dir FW Chap NAACP 1960. **Honors/Awds:** Good Cit Award KNOK Radio 1967; mem Atlanta Life Ins Co Exclusive Pres Club 1953, 1957, 1959, 1961, 1963, 1965, 1969, 1970, 1976, 1977. **Military Serv:** AUS 1944-46.

MCGRIER, JERRY, SR.
District attorney. **Personal:** Born Apr 4, 1955, Dallas, TX; son of Irve Leen Bass Looney and Joseph McGrier; married Diane Jones, Aug 21, 1982; children: Jerry McGrier Jr. **Educ:** The Coll of Wooster, Wooster OH, BA Political Science, 1977; SUNY, Buffalo NY, JD, 1980. **Career:** Neighborhood Legal Serv, Buffalo NY, staff attorney, 1980-82; Erie County District Attorney, Buffalo NY, asst dist attorney, 1982-. **Orgs:** Mem, Erie County Bar Assn, 1980-, Natl Dist Attorney's Assn, 1982-, Natl Bar Assn, 1984-, New York State Bar Assn, 1984-; chmn, Minority Bar Assn of Western New York, 1986-88; bd of dir, Grace Manor Nursing Home, 1987-. **Honors/Awds:** Special Faculty Award, SUNY Buffalo Law School, 1989; Lawyer's Serv Award, Minority Bar Assn of Western New York, 1988. **Business Addr:** Assistant District Attorney, Erie County District Attorney's Office, 25 Delaware Ave, Buffalo, NY 14204.

MCGRIFF, DEBORAH M.
Educational administrator. **Personal:** Born Jun 6, 1949, Portsmouth, VA; daughter of Everlena Madkins and Ernest Boyd Madkins; married Howard Fuller, Nov 16, 1995; children: Jacqueline Denise. **Educ:** Norfolk State Coll, Norfolk, VA, BS, 1970; Queens Coll, Flushing, NY, MS, 1975; Fordham Univ, New York, NY, PhD, 1985. **Career:** NY Public Schools, Brooklyn, NY, exec asst superintendent, 1983-85; Ctr for Educ Leadership, New York, NY, project mgr, 1985-86; Cambridge Public Schools, Cambridge, MA, asst supt, 1986-88; Milwaukee Public Schools, Milwaukee, WI, exec asst supt, 1988-89, deputy supt, 1989-91; Detroit Public Schools, Detroit, MI, general supt, 1991-93; The Edison Project, 1993-. **Orgs:** Advisory Panel of the Harvard Urban Superintendent's Program; the National Urban Alliance; the Educational Testing Services Board of Trustees; Children's Defense Fund Educ Task Force; , United American Healthcare Foundation, bd of trustees. **Honors/Awds:** Excellence in Education, Career Youth Devt, 1989, 1990; Woman of the Year, Pulaski High School, 1991; Crains Detroit Business, Newsmaker of the Year, 1992.

MCGRIFF, FREDERICK STANLEY
Professional baseball player. **Personal:** Born Oct 31, 1963, Tampa, FL. **Career:** Toronto Blue Jays, infielder, 1986-90; San Diego Padres, 1991-93; Atlanta Braves, 1993-97; Tampa Bay Devil Rays, 1998-. **Business Addr:** Professional Baseball Player, Tampa Bay Devil Rays, One Tropicana Dr, St Petersburg, FL 33705.

MCGRIGGS-JAMISON, IMOGENE
Attorney. **Educ:** Alcorn State Univ, bachelor's degree (summa cum laude), 1986; Bowling Green State Univ, master's degree in American literature, 1987; Univ of Mississippi College of Law, JD, 1991. **Career:** US Army Judge Advocate General's Corps, prosecutor, defense attorney, currently. **Orgs:** Delta Sigma Theta Sorority, Inc. **Honors/Awds:** American Bar Assn Outstanding Young Military Service Lawyer Award, nominee, 1996. **Business Addr:** Trial Defense Attorney, US Army, Trial Defense Service, Pike Hall, 3rd Ave, Fort Knox, KY 40121-5000.

MCGRUDER, CHARLES E.
Physician, educator. **Personal:** Born Jul 25, 1925, Alabama; married Curlie Haslip; children: Charles II, Jeffery. **Educ:** AL A&M Clge; Xavier Univ; Meharry Med Clge, MD 1952. **Career:** Meharry Med Clge, assc prof; Flw Amer Clge Ob/Gyn, physician 1956-; Amer Bd Ob/Gyn, diplomate. **Orgs:** Asst Scoutmaster Troop 77; mem exec com Middle TN Cncl BSA. **Honors/Awds:** Recpt Woodbadge Beads in Scouting; Long Rifle; Silver Beaver. **Business Addr:** 1005 18th Ave N, Nashville, TN 37208.

MCGRUDER, ROBERT G.
Managing editor. **Personal:** Born Mar 31, 1942, Louisville, KY; son of Nancy Tanner; married Annette Cottingham McGruder; children: Tanya Cottingham. **Educ:** Kent State Univ, BA, 1963. **Career:** Dayton Journal Herald, reporter, 1963; Cleveland Plain Dealer, reporter, 1963, military editor, managing editor, 1966-86; Detroit Free Press, dep managing editor, 1986-87, managing editor/news, 1987-93, managing editor, 1993-. **Orgs:** APME, pres. **Honors/Awds:** Kent State, Distinguished Alumni Award, 1984; Robert F. Kennedy Award, 1973. **Special Achievements:** First African American president of the Associated Press Managing Editors. **Military Serv:** US Army, public info specialist, 1964-66. **Business Addr:** Managing Editor, Detroit Free Press Inc, 321 W Lafayette, Detroit, MI 48226, (313)222-6400.

MCGUFFIN, DOROTHY BROWN
Counselor/educator. **Personal:** Born Jul 27, 1944, Metropolis, IL; daughter of Mary Brown and Lester Brown; married Robert McGuffin; children: Denise, Toni Greathouse. **Educ:** Southern Illinois Univ, Carbondale IL, BS 1965, MS 1968; Drake Univ, MS 1985. **Career:** Lawrence Adult Ctr, adult educator 1977-81; Des Moines Area Community College, adult educator 1981-84; Young Women's Resource Ctr, community outreach counselor 1984-86; St Louis Community College at Forest Park, assessment specialist 1986-87; St Louis Comm Coll Florissant Valley, counseling, assoc prof, 1991-. **Orgs:** Prog chair/sec/treas, Black Women's Coalition 1976-80; bd mem, Continuing Educ Comm, St Louis Assn for Counseling & Devel; licensed teacher and counselor in 4 states; Amer Counseling Association; troop leader/consultant/bd rep, Girl Scouts Council; St Louis Counseling Association, past president; Missouri Multicultural Counseling Association, past president. **Honors/Awds:** Workshop presenter, Drake Univ Career Develop; Conference presenter, English as a Second Language, Kansas City MO; Distinguished Service Award, Missouri Vocational Special Needs Assn, 1990; INROADS/St Louis Inc, Parent of the Year, 1992, 1996; Bd mem for Licensing Professor Counselors in Missouri. **Business Addr:** Asst Prof, St Louis Community College, Florissant Valley, 3400 Pershall Dr, St Louis, MO 63135, (314)595-4269.

MCGUIRE, CHESTER C., JR.
Educator. **Personal:** Born Oct 29, 1936, Gary, IN; married Julieivory; children: Michael, Angela, Gail. **Educ:** Dartmouth Coll, AB 1958; Univ of Chgo, MBA 1964; Univ Qof Chicago Grad Sch of Bus, PhD 1974. **Career:** Inland Steel Co, financial analyst 1962-64; Real Estate Res Corp, economist 1965-68; Wington A Burnett Const Co, vice pres, gen mgr 1968-70; Dept of Cty & Regional Planning Univ of CA Berkeley, faculty mem 1970-. **Orgs:** Mem Am Inst of Planner; Am Econ Assn Mem Bd Dirs Acameda-contra Costa Co Transit Dist; vice chrprsn Berkely Master Plan Revision Com. **Military Serv:** USN lt 1959-62. **Business Addr:** Dept City & Regional Planning, U of CA, Berkeley, CA 94720.

MCGUIRE, CYRIL A.
Labor leader. **Personal:** Born Apr 9, 1926, Lansing, MI; married Mary Jane Haithco; children: Cyril, Terence, Pamela. **Educ:** Lansing Bus Univ, 1954-56; MI State Univ, 1957. **Career:** UAW Intl Union, educ rep; Gen Motors, employee 1947-. **Orgs:** Pres UAW Local 652; 1972-77, vice pres 1969-72, chmn shop com 1965-69, shop & committeeman 1959-69, dist committeeman 1956-59; dE UAW Intl Convs 1966, 68, 70, 72, 74, 77; com sec Intl Credentials 1974, com Chmn 1977; instr Labor Rel Studies Lansing Comm Clge 1976-77; vice pres Lansing Labor News Bd 1971-75, pres 1975-77; rec sec Capitol Area Comm Action Progs; mem Genesee Co Comm Action Progs Council; pres vice pres treas sec PTA; bd mem Gtr Lansing Urban League; Gtr Lansing Council Against Alcoholism; treas Dem Bus & Professional Org; Salvation Army; Boy Scouts of Amer; Big Bros Inc; Vol Action Ctr; Health Cntrl; Gtr Lansing Safety Council; Model Cities & Woldumar Nature Ctr; treas Dem 6th Cong Dist; precinct del Ingham Co Dem Exec Com; NAACP; Dem Party; UrbanLeague; MI Labor History ; Labor Adv Com Lansing Comm Clge MI State Univ; liaison consult Region 1-C Big Bros of Lansing; state pres, Michigan Chapter A Philip Randolph Institute; Michigan Democrate State Central Committee, 8th District. **Honors/Awds:** Outst Serv award Lansing Model Cities; Man of Year Natl Assc of Negro Bus & Professional Women 1976-77; Distinguished Service Award, Flint Chapter, A Philip Randolph Inst, 1990; Distinguished Service Award, Natl Office, APRI, 1991; Distinguished Service Award, Ingham County; Edward Taylor Memorial Lifetime Achievement Award, 1991; State of Michigan, Special Tribute, 1991; US House of Representatives Congressional Record, 1991. **Military Serv:** AUS m sgt 1950-52. **Business Addr:** 1940 W Atherton Rd, Flint, MI 48507.

MCGUIRE, JEAN MITCHELL
Organization executive. **Personal:** Born Apr 11, 1931, Canton, MA; married Clinton McGuire; children: Johanna, David, Clinton Jr. **Educ:** Howard Univ, 1951; Boston State Coll, BS 1961; Tufts Univ, MEd 1963. **Career:** Boston Public Schools, pupil adjust counselor 1963-73; Simmons Coll, instr 1971-74; Boston School Comm, mem 1982-; Metro Council for Educ Opportunity, exec dir 1973-. **Orgs:** Mem, Boston Teachers Union 1962, Black Educ Alliance of MA, Negro Airmans Intl, Natl All Black School Educ; adv bd MA Womens Political Caucus; corporator Homes Savings Bank; mem bd MA Conf United Church of Christ; trustee Boston Children Museum; mem Negro Airmen's Intl New England Chpt; mem Delta Sigma Theta Sorority, Boston Alumnae Chapter; mem MA Black Political Task Force; life mem NAACP. **Honors/Awds:** Alice K Pollitzer Awd, The Encampment for Citizenship 1978; Zeta Phi Beta Sor Awd 1980; Black Achievers Awd Boston 1982; Fred Douglass Public Serv YMCA 1982; Doctor of Humane Letters Salem State Coll 1983; WGBH Community Achvmnt Award; Bristol Co Juvenile Court Award; Big Brothers Assn Award; Founders Award Omega Psi Phi Fraternity Inc, Eta Phi Chapter; MA Teachers Assn Award; Pride Citation Simmons Coll. **Business Addr:** Executive Dir, METCO, Inc, 40 Dimock St, Roxbury, MA 02119.

MCGUIRE, PAUL M., JR.
Business executive, clergyman. **Personal:** Born Jul 15, 1935, Chicago, IL; son of Callie McGuire and Paul McGuire; married Dorothy; children: Paul III, Andre, Tajuana, Gregory, Monee, Derrick. **Educ:** BS phy educ 1957; US Army Guided Mis Sch, 1958; Univ Chicago, 1972; Shaw Univ Seminary W/O Walls; New Brunswick Theological Seminary, 1989-90. **Career:** Sea-Land Serv Inc, corp director equal oppor affairs; Second Bapt Ch Freehold, NJ, pastor; Manpower Plan, mgr; Johnson & Johnson, employ; Minority Affairs, mgr 1969; spec proj mgr 1969; prod supvr 1968; RCA, prod supvr 1965-68; Fields Entpr, area mgr 1964-65; IL Nat Guard, fire con supr 1960-63. **Orgs:** Mem Chicago Assn of Commerce & Industry; mem Nat Assn of Market Dev; mem Chicago Urban Affairs Coun; Chicago Urban League; mem Alpha Phi Alpha Frat Inc; oper PUSH; Chicago bd edn; deacon trustee Mt Calvary Bapt Ch; North Carolina A&T Alumni; board of directors, Central New Jersey, Freehold YMCA. **Honors/Awds:** Inductee, NC A&T State Univ Hall of Fame; recip WGRT Great Guy Award 1973; WBEE Cit of Week Award May 1974. **Military Serv:** AUS capt 1957-60. **Business Addr:** PO Box 900, Edison, NJ 08818.

MCGUIRE, RAYMOND J.
Financial/banking services director. **Educ:** The Hotchkiss School, Harvard College, AB, 1979; Harvard Business School, MBA, 1984; Harvard Law School, JD, 1984; University of Nice, France. **Career:** First Boston Corp, associate, 1984-88; Wasserstein Perella & Co, managing director, 1988-94; Merrill Lynch, Mergers & Acquistions, managing director, 1994-. **Honors/Awds:** Rotary Fellowship recipient; Black Enterprise, one of the 25 Hottest Blacks on Wall Street, 1992-1997. **Special Achievements:** First African-American managing director at Wasserstein Perella; specialist in mergers and acquisitions. **Business Addr:** Managing Dir, Merrill Lynch, 250 Vesey St, World Finance Center, North Tower, 30th Fl, New York, NY 10281, (212)449-9334.

MCGUIRE, ROSALIE J.
Educator. **Personal:** Born Jan 27, Baltimore; married John McGuire; children: Elwyn Rawlings, Marsden Rawlings. **Educ:** Coppin Tchrs Clge, grad; Morgan State Clge, BS; NY Univ, MA; Columbia Univ, post grad studies; Johns Hopkins Univ, post grad studies; Cath Univ, post grad studies. **Career:** Elementary classroom teacher, demonstration teacher, supvr teacher; prin; asst prin; elementary school prin. **Orgs:** Natl pres Natl Assc of Negro Bus & Professional Women's Clubs Inc 1971-75; 1st vice pres NANB&PW 1967-71; 1st vice pres MD League of Women's Clubs; Basileus Natl Sor of Phi Delta Kappa Gamma Chpt; pres Baltimore Club NANB&PW; sec bd trustees Provident Hosp; asst sec United Fund of Cntrl MD; mem at-large Natl Council of Women of US; historian For-Win-Ash-Garden Club; mem Steering Comm Pres Comm on Employment of Handicapped; mem bd dir Comm Cntr Union Bapt Ch, Adv Comm for Day Care Ctr, Sr Choir; Woman Power Negro Clge Women Cits Planning & Hsng Assc MD Council on Educ; NAACP; NEA; Elem Schl Prins Assc; Eastern Star; Queen of Sheba Chpt; Natl Council of Negro Women.

Honors/Awds: Recip Sojourner Truth Award Baltimore Club NANBPW; Professional Award Philadelphia Club NANBPW; Century Club Award YMCA; GSA Award; Appreciation Award Westchester ClubNANBPW; Comm Serv Award B&P League Ldrshp Westbury Club NANBPW; Extension Award Natl Assc of Negro Bus & Professional Women's Clubs Inc.

MCGUIRT, MILFORD W.
Certified public accountant. **Personal:** Born Aug 15, 1956, Niles, MI; son of Vhuaness McGuirt and Milton McGuirt; married Carolyn J Sconiers; children: Shavonne, Andrea, Brittany. **Educ:** Western MI Univ, BBA (cum laude) 1978. **Career:** Coopers & Lybrand, audit mgr 1978-85; Peat Marwick Mitchell & Co, sr audit mgr 1985-90; KPMG Peat Marwick, partner, 1990-. **Orgs:** Bd mem South Bend IN Chapter of Urban League 1981-82; mem Amer Inst of CPA's 1980; MI Assoc of CPA's 1980; GA Soc of CPA's 1986; Natl Assoc of Black Accountants 1986; Financial Mgr's Soc 1986; Atlanta Chamber of Commerce President's Comm 1986; bd mem Atlanta West End Rotary Club 1986; bd mem UNICEF Atlanta, 1997; bd mem West End Boys & Girls Club, 1995. **Honors/Awds:** Beta Alpha Psi, Western Michigan Univ, Outstanding Alumni Award, 1995; KPMG Peat Marwick, Best Mentor, 1997. **Business Addr:** Audit Partner, KPMG Peat Marwick, 303 Peachtree St NE, Ste 2000, Atlanta, GA 30303.

MCHENRY, DONALD F.
Consulting company executive, former ambassador, educator. **Personal:** Born Oct 13, 1936, St Louis, MO; divorced; children: Michael Stephen, Christina Ann, Elizabeth Ann. **Educ:** IL State Univ, BS 1957; So IL Univ, MS 1959; Georgetown U, post grad studies 1962. **Career:** Howard Univ Washington, instructor, 1959-62; US State Dept, various positions, 1963-73; Brookings Inst, guest scholar 1971-73; Council on Foreign Relations, intl affairs fellow 1971-73; School of Foreign Serv Georgetown Univ, lecturer 1971-72; Carnegie Endowment for International Peace, humanitarin policy studies, project director, beginning 1973; American Univ Washington, lecturer 1975; US State Dept, Pres Jimmy Carter's transition staff, 1976; UN Security Council, appointed US deputy representative, 1977-79; United Nations, US permanent representative, 1979-81; Georgetown Univ, Distinguished Prof of Diplomacy & Int Affairs 1981-; IRC Group, president, currently. **Orgs:** UN Western Five Contact Group; dir: Intl Paper Co, Coca-Cola Co, SmithKline Beecham Corp, AT&T, First Natl Boston Corp; Amer Stock Exchange, former gov; Cncl Foreign Relations, director; Foreign Policy Magazine, editorial board member; American Academy of Diplomacy. **Honors/Awds:** Superior Honor Award, Dept of State 1966; Family of Man Awd NY Council Churches 1980; American Academy of Arts and Sciences, fellow. **Special Achievements:** US negotiator on question of Namibia; author, Micronesia: Trust Betrayed, 1975. **Business Addr:** Professor, Georgetown University, School of Foreign Service, ICC 301, Washington, DC 20057.

MCHENRY, DOUGLAS
Film producer, director. **Educ:** Harvard Business School, graduate; Harvard Law School, graduate. **Career:** BET, "New Attitude," producer, production asst; Columbia Pictures; motion picture credits include: Krush Groove, co-producer, 1985; House Party, co-producer, co-director, 1991; New Jack City, co-producer, co-director, 1991; Jason's Lyric; Jackson/McHenry Entertainment, co-founder, currently; The Walking Dead. **Honors/Awds:** World Institute of Black Communications Inc, CEBA Award, Pioneers of Excellence, 1991. **Special Achievements:** Landmark three-year production deal with Savoy Pictures. **Business Addr:** Co-Founder, Jackson/McHenry Entertainment, 4000 Warner Blvd., Producers Bldg 2, Ste 1106, Burbank, CA 91522, (818)954-3221.

MCHENRY, EMMIT J.
Systems integration company executive. **Career:** Network Solutions Inc, CEO, currently. **Special Achievements:** Co. is ranked #17 on Black Enterprise magazine's list of top 100 industrial/service companies, 1992. **Business Addr:** Chief Executive Officer, Network Solutions Inc, 505 Huntmar Park Dr, Herndon, VA 22070, (703)742-0400.

MCHENRY, JAMES O'NEAL
Administrator. **Personal:** Born Nov 11, 1940, Sterlington, LA; son of Rebecca McHenry and S O McHenry; married Esther C Johnson; children: Stephanie Diane, Ali Kenyatta. **Educ:** Grambling State Univ, BS 1963; Wayne State Univ, MEd 1970, DEd 1979. **Career:** Monroe LA Bd of Educ, music tchr, 1962-63; US Army Educ Center Europe, GED tchr, 1965; MI Bd Educ, res tchr, 1966-67; Wayne Cty Recdrs Ct, prob officer, 1967-73; Recorders Ct Probation Dept, asst supervisor, 1973-78; MI Dept Licensing & Reg, certified marriage counselor, 1975-80; Recorders Ct Drug Prog, director, 1978-80; Recorders Ct Pretrial Serv, director, 1980-82; Oakland Univ, lecturer, 1984-; US Pretrial Service Agency, Detroit, MI, chief officer, currently. **Orgs:** Mem Omega Psi Phi Frat 1960-. **Honors/Awds:** Special Award, NARCO 1983; Leadership Award, Recorders Ct Prob Dept 1983; President's Award, Grambling State Univ 1983. **Military Serv:** US Army, E-4. **Home Addr:** 17191 Pennington Dr, Detroit, MI 48221. **Business Addr:** Chief Officer, US Pretrial Serv Agency, US Courthouse, 231 W Lafayette St, Detroit, MI 48226.

MCHENRY, MARY WILLIAMSON
Educator. **Personal:** Born Jan 23, 1933, Washington, DC; children: Michael S, Christina A, Elizabeth A. **Educ:** Mt Holyoke Coll, AB 1950-54; Columbia Univ, MA 1955-60; George Washington Univ, 1962-65. **Career:** Howard Univ, instr in english 1960-62; George Washington Univ, asst prof of english 1964-69; DC Teachers Coll, guest lecturer in english 1967-68; Fed City Coll, asst prof of english 1969-74; Mt Holyoke Coll, assoc prof of english, assoc dean of studies 1974-. **Orgs:** Instr amer studies Peace Corps Training Prog 1962-63; adv bd Radcliffe Seminars Forum for Continuing Ed 1980; consult editor Univ MA Press 1978-79; mem Phi Beta Kappa MHC Chap 1954. **Honors/Awds:** Fellowship John Jay Whitney Oppty 1954-55,57-58; Fellowship Danforth Found 1961-62; Natl Endowment for the Humanities 1972-73. **Business Addr:** Associate Professor, Dept of English, Mt Holyoke College, South Hadley, MA 01075.

MCILWAIN, NADINE WILLIAMS
Educational administrator. **Personal:** Born Jul 29, 1943, Canton, OH; daughter of Mabel W Williams and Willie J Williams; married Albert H McIlwain (deceased); children: Jeaneen, Floyd. **Educ:** Malone Coll, BA 1970; Univ of Akron, MA 1978; Ashland University, MA 1990. **Career:** Canton City Health Dept, lab asst 1962-65; OH Bell Telephone Co, opr & consult 1967-70; Canton City Schools, teacher 1970-; Nefertiti Nuptials, owner/operator 1984-; Canton City Council, ward councilperson 1984-86; Canton City Schools, curriculum specialist; Alliance City Schools, principal; Allen Elementary School, principal, currently. **Orgs:** Pres Frontiers Intl Aux 1971; dir hs migrant program Canton City Schools 1975-82; pres Leila Green Educators Council 1978; sec Amer Business Womens Assoc 1980; state parliamentarian Natl Black Womens Leadership Caucus 1983-84; ward councilwoman Canton City Council 1984-; owner/operator Nadine's Nuptials 1984-. **Honors/Awds:** Theses, Social & Structural Determinants of Methodone Clinic Attendance 1978; Woman of the Year Canton Negro Oldtimers Athletic Assoc 1979; Political Awd Black Women's Leadership Caucus 1981; Woman of the Year Greater Canton Amer Bus Women's Assoc 1982; Milken Family Foundation, Natl Educ Award; Ohio Humanitarian Award for Education, Martin L King Jr Holiday Commission, State of Ohio. **Home Addr:** 1731 Newton Ave, Dayton, OH 45406.

MCINTOSH, ALICE T.
Management consultant. **Personal:** Born Jan 10, 1933, Miami, FL; daughter of Thelma M Jones and James S Jones; married William R McIntosh, Sep 22, 1979; children: Otis Edwards, Yvonne Edwards, Jaynie Edwards, Zigmond Robinson. **Educ:** Attended Savannah State College, Savannah GA, 1951; attended Indiana Business College, Muncie IN, 1953-56; attended Ball State Univ, Munice IN, 1980-81. **Career:** Action Inc, Muncie IN, manpower coordinator, 1968-70, executive dir, 1971-74, consultant, 1974-76; MSS Inc, Muncie IN, owner, consultant, 1976-83; Human Rights Comm, Muncie IN, executive dir, 1978-80; Muncie City Council, councilwoman, 1984-88; INC Inc, Muncie IN, Neighborhood Coordinator, 1986-. **Orgs:** Advisor, Black Achievers Inc, 1986-; mem, JTPA screening committee, 1987-. **Honors/Awds:** Author of govt proposals and projects. **Military Serv:** Women's Army Corps, private, 1951-52. **Home Addr:** 1412 East 8th St, Muncie, IN 47302. **Business Addr:** 1121 East 7th St, Muncie, IN 47302.

MCINTOSH, FRANKIE L.
Educator, educational administrator. **Personal:** Born Dec 15, 1949, Quitman, GA; daughter of Ida Hardy McIntosh (deceased) and Frank McIntosh (deceased). **Educ:** North Carolina Central Univ, Durham, NC, BA, 1968-72; Atlanta Univ, Atlanta, GA, 1972-73; Univ of Georgia, Athens, GA, MPA, 1981; Georgia State Univ, Atlanta, GA, ABD, 1993. **Career:** Social Security Administration, Atlanta, GA, claims representative, 1974-78, supervisor, 1978-80, manager, 1980-86; DeKalb College, Clarkston, GA, assoc professor, 1986-. **Orgs:** Southern Political Science Association, 1989-; Georgia Association of Women Deans, Administrators, and Counselors, 1988-91; National Education Assn/DCFA, 1987-; Georgia Political Science Assn, 1986-; National Conference of Black Political Scientists, 1986-; American Business Women's Assn, 1980-86; SSA Southern Regional Management Assn, 1980-87; NCCU Alumni Assn, Atlanta Chapter, 1972-; Alpha Kappa Alpha Sorority, 1970-. **Honors/Awds:** Selected as Instructor for Special Summer Seminar Program, Agnes Scott College, 1989-90; Selected as a Community College Leader, National Institute of Leadership Development, Phoenix, AZ, 1988; Inducted, Thousandaire Club, Alpha Kappa Alpha Sorority, 1988-; Nominated for Outstanding Teacher of the Year, Phi Theta Kappa Honor Society, DeKalb College, Central Campus, 1987; Outstanding Public Service Award, Social Security Administration, 1986-; Woman of the Year American Business Women's Association, Mableton Chapter, 1983; Superior Performance Award, Social Security Administration, 1976, 1980; Dekalb Coll, Teaching Excellence Award, 1995, Outstanding Faculty Award, 1996, NISOD Teaching Excellence Award, 1996. **Business Addr:** Associate Professor, Political Science, DeKalb College, 555 N Indian Creek Dr, Clarkston, GA 30021.

MCINTOSH, JAMES E.
Dentist. **Personal:** Born Jul 15, 1942, St Louis, MO. **Educ:** Univ MO, BA 1965; Meharry Coll, DDS 1969; Sydenham Hosp, rotating internship 1970, periodentics residency 1971; Columbia U, MPH 1975. **Career:** Sydenham Hosp, dir 1975-; Tri-State Eval of Accident Ins, consult 1974-; Assn of NY Nghbrhd & Hlth Ctrs, consult 1974-; Columbia U, asst prof 1974-; Pvt Practice, 1971-; Dental Clinic Sydenham Hosp, adminstr 1971-; dental Hlth educ 1970; Cloverbottom Ment Hlth Inst, 1969; Nashville Hlth Dept, rsrch 1968-69; Univ MO, fellow 1963-65; Fed Food & Drug Div, insp 1965. **Orgs:** Pres of Medical bd & execl com mem Sydenham Hosp med bd 1976-; Sydenham Hosp med bd exec com 1976-; MO Dental Soc 1972-; 1st Dist Dental Soc 1970-; NY State Dental So 1970-; Am Pub Hlth Assn 1974-; Nat Dental Assn 1969-; Nat Student Dental Assn 1956-69; NAACP 1965-; Black Am Med & Dent Assn of Students 1969-; Ewell Neal Dental Soc 1965-69; Rose Hill Bapt Ch 1958-; rep Nat Conclave of Kappa Alpha Psi 1964; diplomate Nat Dental Bds 1969-; bd Eligible Am Acad of Pub Hlth & Preventive Dentistry 1974-. **Honors/Awds:** Nat Hlth Professions Scholarship 1965-69; Omicron Sigma Nat Hon Ldrshp Frat 1976-; award for Table Clinic Presentation 1969; del Proctor & Gamble RsrchSymposium 1968; pres Student Faculty Rels Com Meharry Med Coll 1968-69; class pres Dental Sch 1967-69. **Business Addr:** Dir of Dentistry, Harlem Hospital, City of NY Health & Hosp Corp, 506 Lenox Ave, New York, NY 10037.

MCINTOSH, MARC
Financial services company executive. **Personal:** Born in Chicago, IL. **Educ:** De Paul University, graduate; Harvard Business School, graduate. **Career:** Goldman, Sachs & Co, corporate finance, vice pres, until 1989; PaineWebber Group Inc, managing director, Telecommunications Group, head, 1989-, Latin American group, head, 1991-. **Orgs:** Greater New York Council of Boy Scouts of America, board of directors, currently. **Honors/Awds:** Black Enterprise, one of the 25 Hottest Blacks on Wall Street, 1992. **Business Phone:** (212)713-2847.

MCINTOSH, RHODINA COVINGTON
Attorney. **Personal:** Born May 26, 1947, Chicago Heights, IL; daughter of Cora Jean Cain Covington and William George Covington; married Gerald Alfred McIntosh, Dec 14, 1970; children: Gary Allen, Garvey Anthony, Ayana Kai. **Educ:** MI State Univ, BA (Cum Laude) 1969; Univ Detroit, JD 1978. **Career:** MI State Univ Office of Equal Oppor, asst to dir 1969-70; Bell & Hudson PC Detroit, law clerk 1977-79; Covington McIntosh & Assocs Intl, pres Detroit MI, Washington DC, and Mbabane Swaziland 1980-83; Univ Swaziland and Botswana Kwaluseni Swaziland, lecturer 1981-83; US AID Office of Private and Voluntary Coop, chief information & tech assistance 1983-87, chief information & prog support 1987-88; Automation Research Systems, Limited, corporate counsel 1988-93; pres, Konsider It Done Mgmt Corp, 1993-. **Orgs:** Founding bd mem Women's Justice Ctr Detroit 1975-77; coord Women's Leadership Conf Wayne State Univ Detroit 1979; bd mem/counselor Awareness Inc Detroit 1979-80; consultant Polit Educ Workshops Detroit, Flint, Lansing, Saginaw, Grand Rapids MI 1979-80; speaker Ohio Republican Co Leadership Conf 1980; founding bd mem Wayne Co Chap MI Republican Women's Task Force Detroit 1980; speaker Detroit Urban League 1980; main rapporteur 1st All Africa Law Conf Univ Swaziland and Botswana Kwaluseni Swaziland 1981; bd mem Detroit Urban League 1981; chairperson foreign relations subcom Natl Black Women's Polit Caucus Washington 1984; bd mem Amer Oppor Foundation Washington 1984-; charter mem Natl Assn of Female Executives 1983-; mem GOP Women's Network 1986-87; Phi Alpha Delta Law Fraternity, 1977-; ent Teacher Association of Springbrook High School, 1986-90; Naval Academy Athletic Assn, 1987-90; Michigan State University Alumni Assn 1985-; St Teresa of Avila Roman Catholic Church, 1987-89; National Bar Association, 1989-; American Bar Association 1989-; Univ of California, Berkeley Booster Club Track 1990-93; vice chair Small Business Comm, ABA 1991-92; bd mem Suburban Recovery Center, Inc, 1996-; chair of bd, Christian Vision Center Homeless Shelter, 1995. **Honors/Awds:** Scholar Martin Luther King Jr Ctr for Social Change Atlanta 1976; Awd Detroit Women's Justice Ctr 1978; Awd Goodwill Charity Club Chicago Heights IL 1978; Awd Outstanding Volunteer Service Reagan/Bush Campaign 1980; Awd Detroit Edison 1980; Awd Wayne County Chap Republican Women's Task Force 1980; New Republicans MI 1981; mem Delta Sigma Theta Goodwill Charity Club; Publications The AID/PVO Partnership: Sharing Goals and Resources in the Work of Development l984, l987; Voluntary Foreign Aid Programs: Report on U.S. Private Voluntary Organizations Engaged in Relief and Development Registed by USAID l983-86; The Individual Under African Law 1984; Small Businesses 1988; Effective Management 1988; Managers and the Law 1989; Success and Your Business 1990; National Achievement Scholar Finalist National Merit 1965. **Business Addr:** 1020 Chicago Rd, No 10, Chicago Heights, IL 60411, (708)755-3900.

MCINTOSH, WALTER CORDELL
Educational administrator. **Personal:** Born Jul 26, 1927, Lake Forest, IL; married Bernice Clay; children: Ann Elizabeth, David, Jeffrey. **Educ:** Macalester Coll St Paul MN, BA Econ;

Natl Coll of Ed Evanston IL, MA Ed; Columbia Univ NY, EdD. **Career:** Cuyahoga Welfare Dept, caseworker; Chicago Dept of Welfare, vocational counselor; LA Unified School Dist, teacher 1958-68; W Los Angeles Coll, instr english, spec reading 1972-73, coord basic skills 1973-76, dean evening div 1976-77; LA SW Coll, pres 1977-. **Orgs:** Mem Kappa Alpha Psi, Kappa Delta Pi, Phi Delta Kappa, NAACP, LA Urban League; bd of dir S Central LA Reg Ctr, LA Police Commiss Adv Comm. **Honors/Awds:** Lifetime Awd Membership 10th Dist PTA LA 1968; Martin Luther King Fellow Columbia Univ NY 1968-71; Woodrow Wilson Fellow Columbia Univ NY; Social Sci Found Fellow Columbia Univ NY; Outstanding Teacher W LA Coll 1974. **Military Serv:** AUS corpl 1946-48; Good Conduct Medal. **Business Addr:** President, Los Angeles SW College, 1600 W Imperial Highway, Los Angeles, CA 90047.

MCINTOSH, WILLIAM E., JR.
Business executive. **Personal:** Born Jun 13, 1945, Minneapolis, MN; son of Thelma Mae Burrell McIntosh and William E McIntosh Sr; married Helen B; children: Brian Justin, Blair Jason, Blake Jamone. **Educ:** Metropolitan State Coll, AA 1970; MacAlester Coll, BA 1972; Univ of MN, 1973. **Career:** Chrysler Corp, staff exec to USAS vice pres 1982-83, USAS div 9 positions 1974-, mgr retail dealer devel prog 1983-; North Seattle Chrysler-Plymouth Inc, owner, currently. **Orgs:** Mem Urban League 1972-, Coll Alumni Bd 1972-, NAACP 1976-, Operation PUSH 1977-, Disabled Vets 1980-, Amer Prod & Inventory Control 1983-, Conf of Mayor's Auto Task Force 1985-; instructor Dale Carnegie Course 1983-84; pres Chrysler's Minority Dealer Assn 1986-; co-chairman Martin Luther King Memorial Comm 1987-; pes Natl Assn of Ministry Dealers 1988-. **Honors/Awds:** Dist Mgr of the Year Chrysler Corp 1976, 1977; Comm Excellence Awd Operation PUSH 1979; Black Achiever in Industry YMCA 1980; Chrysler Award for Excellence Chrysler Corp 1986, 1987; Be List of 100 Earl Graves Ltd 1986-89; Chrysler's Pacesetter Award Chrysler Corp, 1986-89. **Military Serv:** USMC sgt E-5 1962-67; Good Conduct Medal, Expeditionary Medals, Cuba & Vietnam 1966.

MCINTYRE, DIANNE RUTH
Choreographer. **Personal:** Born Jul 18, 1946, Cleveland, OH; daughter of Dorothy Layne McIntyre and Francis Benjamin McIntyre. **Educ:** Ohio State Univ, Columbus, OH, BFA, dance. **Career:** Choreographer, 1972-; Sounds in Motion, New York, NY, choreographer, 1972-88; Work with Sounds in Motion includes Memories; Deep South Suite; Life's Force; Eye of the Crocodile; Mississippi Talks, Ohio Walks; Gratitude; Take-Off From a Forced Landing; Their Eyes Were Watching God; How Long Brethren, 1991; theatre choreography work includes: King, The Musical; Miss Evers' Boys; In Dahomey; God's Trombones; Paul Robeson; 80 Days; Shout Up a Morning; Spell #7; The Great MacDaddy; Boogie Woogie Landscapes, Black Girl; Adam; The Last Minstrel Show; BeBop; Mule Bone; In Living Color; has collaborated with the Alvin Ailey American Dance Theatre, Cecil Taylor and Max Roach; choreographed the television programs Langston Hughes: The Dreamkeeper; For Colored Girls . . .;and Women of the Regent Hote. **Orgs:** Society of Stage Directors and Choreographers; American Federation of Television and Radio Artists. **Honors/Awds:** AUDELCO (Black Theatre Awards), United Black Artists of Cornell Univ, choreography, 1979; Bessie Award (New York Dance and Performance Award), 1989; Choreographer's Fellowship, National Endowment for the Arts, 1990-93. **Home Addr:** 580 St. Nicholas Ave, New York, NY 10030.

MCINTYRE, MILDRED J.
Clinical neuro-psychologist. **Personal:** Born in Boston, MA. **Educ:** Swarthmore Coll, BA 1965; Clark Univ, MA 1972, PhD 1975. **Career:** McLean Hosp, rsch asst 1966-68; Clark Univ, rschr 1968-72; Univ of MA, asst prof 1975-80, consulting psychologist 1977-. **Orgs:** American Psychological Association; International Neuropsych Society. **Honors/Awds:** Ford Foundation Fellow 1972-73; Natl Fellowships Fund Awd 1973-74. **Business Addr:** Neuro-Psychologist, PO Box 990124, Boston, MA 02199-0124.

MCIVER, EVERETT
Professional football player. **Personal:** Born Aug 5, 1970, Fayetteville, NC. **Educ:** Elizabeth City State. **Career:** New York Jets, guard, 1994-95; Miami Dolphins, 1996-. **Business Addr:** Professional Football Player, Miami Dolphins, 2269 NW 199th St, Miami, FL 33056, (305)620-5000.

MCIVER, JOHN DOUGLAS
Mayor, paper maker. **Personal:** Born Nov 7, 1941, Savannah, GA; son of Hagar Norman McIver and James McIver; married Gloria Grant, Mar 26, 1966; children: Andrea, Timothy, Anthony, Pamelia, Cassandra. **Career:** City of Riceboro, mayor, currently; Interstate Paper Corp Riceboro, GA, papermaker 1st asst 1968. **Orgs:** Mem Liberty Co Industrial Auth 1980; vice chmn Riceboro Comm Foundation 1982; chmn New Zion Baptist Church 1977-; pres Georgia Conference of Black Mayors 1989; board member, Coastal Georgia Community Action Agency, 1988-91; vice pres, GCBM, 1991-92; vice-chairman, New Zion Baptist Church, 1989. **Honors/Awds:** First Black Dorchester Credit Union 1978; comm leader Riceboro Comm Found 1983; Outstanding Achievement Award, Omega Psi Phi Fraternity Inc, 1992. **Military Serv:** US Army, spec-4. **Business Addr:** Mayor, City of Riceboro, PO Box 269, Riceboro, GA 31323.

MCIVER, MARGARET HILL
Educator. **Personal:** Born Jun 3, 1925, High Point, NC; married Conerlious W; children: Conerlious W, Jr, Deborah Ann. **Educ:** Bennett Coll Greensboro, NC, BA 1944; Atlanta Univ Sch of Social Work, MSW 1946; Harvard U, EdM 1967. **Career:** Douglass Middle Sch, guidance counselor 1969-; Douglass High Sch GA, tchr guidance counselor 1953-69; Morris Brown Coll, dean of women 1951-53; FL A&M U, counselor for women 1949-51; Clark Coll Atlanta, tchr counselor 1946-49; Proj Upward Bound Norman Park Coll GA, counselor 1968-70; GA Governor's Honors Program for Gifted Wesleyan Coll Macon, GA, guidance counselor 1972-74, 79. **Orgs:** Pres GA br Am Personnel & Guidance Assn 1968; pres GA Sch Counselors Assn 1973-74; dir district 2 GA Assn of Educators 1974-77. **Honors/Awds:** Alpha Kapa Mu Honor Soc Bennett Coll Greensboro, NC 1943; Tchr of the Yr Thomasville, GA Tchrs Assn 1962; Counselor of the Yr District 2 GA Sch Counselors Assn 1972; Women of the Yr Thomasville, GA C of C 1975. **Business Addr:** Douglass Middle School, Forrest St, Thomasville, GA 31792.

MCKANDERS, JULIUS A., II
Attorney, clergyman. **Personal:** Born Jun 21, 1941, Jackson, MS; married Yvonne Mclittle. **Educ:** Wayne St U, JD 1971; Henry Ford Comm Coll, 1962; Detroit Inst Tech, 1962; Eastern MI O, BS 1964; Univ MI Med Sch, 1966; Morehouse Scho of Religion, ITC 1976. **Career:** Metro Atlanta Rapid Transit & Auth, dir contracts & procur 1972-; Ebenezer Bapt Ch, asso minister; Council on Leg Ed Opp, deputy dir oper 1971-72; Detroit Bd Ed, mgr 1970-71; Price Waterhouse, sr mgmt 1969-70; IRS Detroit, sys analyst 1967-69; City of Detroit, sys analyst-programmer 1966-67; Univ MI Med Sch, research asst 1964-66; MI Bar, admitted 1972; GA Bar, 1974. **Orgs:** Mem Am Bar Assn; Detroit Bar Assn; Atlanta Bar Assn; Phi Alpha Delta; Purch Mgmt Assn #Of GA; Atlanta Jr C of C; bd dirs Martin L King Jr ChildDevelop Center; bd dirs NAACP Atlanta Br Program Comm Am Pub Transit Assn; adv council Martin L King, Jr Handicapped Child Project; bd mem Ebenezer Bapt Ch Charitable Found & life mem NAACP; ordained Bapt min. **Business Addr:** 101 Professional Bldg, 2192 Campbellton Rd SW, Atlanta, GA 30311.

MCKANDERS, KENNETH ANDRE
Attorney. **Personal:** Born Nov 18, 1950, Inkster, MI; son of Addye N. Norwood Smith and Julius Aaron McKanders; married Carolyn M. Welch McKanders, Aug 4, 1973; children: Kimberly, Karla, Kristal, Kenneth. **Educ:** Michigan State University, East Lansing, MI, JD, 1972; Wayne State University, Detroit, MI, BA, 1977. **Career:** Recorder's Court, Detroit, MI, probation officer, 1973-78; Wayne State University, Detroit, MI, assistant general counsel, 1978-86; Wayne County Community College, Detroit, MI, general counsel, 1986-87; Eastern Michigan University, Ypsilanti, MI, general counsel, 1987-. **Orgs:** Member, Michigan State Bar Association, 1978-; member, American Bar Association, 1980-; board member/past president, Renaissance Optimist Club, 1986-; board member/past president, Wayne State University Campus Ministry, 1984-; board member/past vice chair, Hartford Agape, Inc, 1984-90. **Business Addr:** General Counsel, Legal Affairs, Eastern Michigan University, 11 Welch Hall, Ypsilanti, MI 48197, (313)487-1055.

MCKANDES, DARNELL DAMON
Sports educator. **Personal:** Born Aug 26, 1966, Honolulu, HI; son of Dorothy Clark McKandes and Robert Henry McKandes Sr. **Educ:** South Carolina State College, 1984-88. **Career:** General Motors Corporation, Saginaw Division, security officer, 1986; Maple Hill Golf Club, assistant pro, 1991; Jackson State University, golf coach, girls golf team, 1992; golf professional, PGA, currently. **Orgs:** Kappa Youth Leadership League, sponsored by the Saginaw Alumnae Chapter of Kappa Alpha Psi Fraternity, Inc, 1983-84; Bethel AME Church, volunteer, Frontiers Annual Christmas Shopping Spree for Underpriviledged Children, 1982-84. **Honors/Awds:** Frontiers International, Community Leadership & Service Youth Award, 1983; South Carolina State College, Golf Scholarship, 1984; Alpha Phi Alpha Fraternity, Inc, Iota Chi Lambda Chapter Annual Golf Tournament, 1st place, 1989, 1990; Saginaw District Invitational Golf Tournament, medalist honors, 1989; Tri-City Chapter, The Links Inc, Scholarship Recipient, 1984; Black Honors Convocation, 1980-82; A Anton Pieritz Scholarship, nominee, 1984; Saginaw Valley League's All Conference Golf Team, runner-up, 1983; Hawaii Golf Tournament Players Assn, Hawaii Prince Course, First Place, 1994. **Special Achievements:** Lee Elder Golf Invitational, golf participant, Myrtle Beach, 1988; First Annual Natl Coll Minority Golf Championship Tournament, First Place, 1987; Second Annual South Carolina State Golf Team, First Place, 1988; Saginaw Valley All League Golf Honors. **Home Addr:** 1550 Seminole, Saginaw, MI 48603, (517)799-0796.

MCKANDES, DOROTHY DELL
Educator. **Personal:** Born Jul 5, 1937, Saginaw, MI; daughter of Katherine Halliday Clark and William Henry Clark; married Robert Henry McKandes, Jan 16, 1961; children: Robert Henry Jr, Darnell Damon. **Educ:** Leeward Community Coll, Pearl City, Hawaii, AA, 1974; Central MI Univ, Mt Pleasant, MI, BA, 1975, MA, 1977; Delta Coll, Certificate, Adult Literacy, 1986. **Career:** Leeward Community Coll, Pearl City, Hawaii, asst instructor, 1975; Public Schools of Saginaw, Saginaw, MI, elementary teacher, 1977-84; Student Task Force Program, job shadow coordinator, 1982; MI Child Care Ctr, asst dir, 1986-89; Kiddie Kingdom Pre-School Ctr, Saginaw, MI, dir, 1990-. **Orgs:** Co-founder, Tri-City Chap, Links, Inc, 1980-; bd mem, Bethel African Methodist Episcopal Church; mem, United Way of Saginaw County; fund distribution comm, Literary Task Force, 1991; life mem, Central MI Univ; bd mem, Saginaw County Foster Care, 1988-89; former co-owner, Cosmopolitan Roller Arena, 1978-83; bd of dirs, READ Assn, 1997; bd of dirs, Mitten Bay Girl Scout Council, 1997-98. **Honors/Awds:** Dedicated Service & Distinguished Service Awards, Tri-City Links, Inc, 1990; State Scholarship Recipient Hawaii Federation of Business & Professional Women's Club, 1977; Nominee, 1990 Kool Achiever Awards, Brown & Williamson Tobacco Corp, Kentucky, Certificate in Recognition; Nestle USA, Inc, Community Service Award, 1992; Certificate of Appreciation, Internal Revenue Service, 1992; J. C. Penney Golden Rule Nominee, 1995; Woman of Distinction, Mitten Bay Girl Scout Council, 1997. **Home Addr:** 1550 Seminole Ln, Saginaw, MI 48603.

MCKAY, PATTI JO
Judge. **Educ:** Univ of California-Irvine; Hastings Coll of Law. **Career:** City of Los Angeles, deputy city attorney, deputy public defender; Office of CA Governor Edmund ''Jerry'' Brown, deputy legal affairs secretary; Los Angeles Municipal Court, judge, 1980-. **Business Addr:** Judge, Los Angeles Municipal Court, Criminal Courts Bldg - Div 47, 210 W Temple St, Los Angeles, CA 90012, (213)974-6047.

MCKAYLE, DONALD COHEN
Choreographer, director, writer, educator. **Personal:** Born Jul 6, 1930, New York, NY; son of Eva Wilhelmina Cohen McKayle and Philip Augustus McKayle; married Lea Vivante, 1965; children: Gabrielle, Liane, Guy. **Educ:** Coll of the City of NY, 1947-49. **Career:** Dance instructor, Juilliard School of Music, Sarah Lawrence College, Bennington College, Neighborhood Playhouse, New Dance Group, Martha Graham School; advisor, Cultural Program of Tunisia, 1964; choreographer, 1950-, with Donald McKayle Dance Company, Alvin Ailey American Dance Theater, Batsheva Dance Company, Israel; Repertory Dance Theater; Dayton Contemporary Dance Co; Cleo Parker Robinson Dance Ensemble; Los Angeles Contemporary Dance Theatre, among others; choreographer of films including: The Jazz Singer, 1980; The Minstrel Man, 1975-76; Bedknobs & Broomsticks, 1970; choreographer of Broadway plays, including: Sophisticated Ladies, 1981; Dr Jazz, 1975; Golden Boy, 1964; The Last Minstrel Show, 1974, director/choreographer, Raisin, 1974; director/choreographer of TV shows including: The Annual Emmy Awds, 1979; Free to Be You and Me, 1974; The Hollywood Palace (with Diana Ross), 1969; The 49th Annul Academy Awards, 1977; Good Times, 1974; Komedy Tonite, 1977; The Richard Pryor Special, 1977; The 43rd Annual Academy Awards, 1973; choreographer/creator of numerous other TV shows, concerts, and ballets; Regional Theatre, Denver Center Theatre Company, Mark Taper Forum, director/choreographer; California Institute for the Arts, School of Dance, dean; Univ of California at Irvine, professor, fine arts, dance, artistic dir; UCI Dance, currently; Faculty: Inner City Cultural Center; University of WA; Portland State University; FL State University; Alvin Ailey Dance Center. **Orgs:** Bd dirs, Amer Dance Festival Durham NC, New Dance Group NYC; Clarke Cntr for Perform Arts NYC; Soc of Stage Dir & Choreog NYC; Modern Dance Found; The Dance Circle Boston, MA; Natl Cntr for Afro-Amer Artists Roxbury, MA; Irvine Barclay Theatre, St Joseph Ballet; National Endowment for the Arts Dance Panel; Natl Foundation for Advancement in the Arts, bd of trustees; mem Soc of Stage Dir & Choreog; Assn of Amer Dance Companies; ASCAP; AEA; AGMA; AFTRA; AGVA; fellow Black Acad of Arts and Letters; fellow Dir Guild of Amer. **Honors/Awds:** Natl Black Arts Festival, Living Legend Award, 1994; American Dance Guild Award, 1994; Samuel H Scripps/American Dance Festival Award, 1992; NAACP Image Award Writer/Concept & Best Stage Play for Sophisticated Ladies, 1981; Outer Circle Critics Award Choreography, Sophisticated Ladies, 1981; Drama League Critics Award Choreography, Evolution of the Blues, 1978; Capezio Award 1963; Emmy Nomination Choreography, The Minstrel Man, 1977; Tony Award nominations: director/choreography, Raisin, 1974; choreography, Golden Boy, 1964; Dr Jazz, 1975; Sophisticated Ladies, 1981; UCI Distinguished Faculty Lecturship Award for Research; Balasaraswati/Joy Ann Dewey Beineck Chair for Distinguished Teaching; numerous articles and publications including The Dance Has Many Faces, Columbia Univ Press, Modern Dance: Seven Points of View, Wesleyan Univ Press. **Business Addr:** Professor, Advanced Modern Technique, University of California, Irvine, MAB 300, Irvine, CA 92697, (949)824-7284.

MCKEE, ADAM E., JR.
Veterinarian. **Personal:** Born Apr 12, 1932, Fairfield, AL; married Barbara Nance; children: Adam III, Eric, Brett. **Educ:** Dillar Univ New Orleans, AB 1954; Tuskegee Inst, DVM 1958; Vet Path Armed Forces Inst Pathology, res 1963-66. **Career:** Naval Med Research Inst Nat Naval Med Cntr Bethesda, MD,

chmn Qqqexptl path dept 1969-; Biol & Med Scis Div Naval Radiological Defense Lab San Francisco, chief vet & path 1967-69; Lackland AFB, TX, chief altitude chamber unit aerospace path 1966-67, sentry dog clinician 1960-63; Istanbul, Turkey, vet 1958-60. **Orgs:** Mem Am Vet Med Assn; Intl Acad Pathology; Washington So Scanning Electron Microscopy; Am Soc Microbiology; mem Post Doctoral Res Asso Prog Com; chmn Naval Med Res Inst Policy Adv Council scientific & managerial bd 1975-76; Am Assn Lab Animal Scis; Omega Psi Phi mem pres Tuskegee Vet Med Alumni Assn 1975-; mem USAF Distinguished Unit 1960-64. **Honors/Awds:** Commendation medal USAF 1963; Special Merit Award Naval Med Research Inst 1976; keynote speaker 6th Annual Intl Scanning Electron Microscopy Symposium Chicago 1973; chrm Scanning Electron Cicroscopy Application in Med Microbiology 10th Annual Interna Scanning Electron Microsocpy Symposium Chicago 1977. **Military Serv:** USAF 1975. **Business Addr:** Naval Med Research Inst, Nat Naval Med Cntr, Bethesda, MD 20814.

MCKEE, CLARENCE VANZANT, JR.
Business executive, attorney. **Personal:** Born Nov 16, 1942, Buffalo, NY. **Educ:** Hobart College, BA 1965; Howard University School of Law, JD 1972. **Career:** Dept HEW, civil rights compliance officer 1966-67; Senator Jacob Javits, legal asst 1969-71; Senator Charles MacMathias, legal asst 1971-72; Office of Congressional Relations US Civil & Aeronautics Bd, acting dir 1972; Industry EEO Unit Office of General Council FCC, dep chief 1973-76; Federal Communications Commission, legal asst; Commissioner Ben Hooks FCC, legal asst 1976-77; Law, Murphy & McKee, attorney, 1978-79; Pepper and Corazzini, counsel, 1977-87; National Union for Total Independence of Angola, counsel, 1985-87; WTVT, Channel 13, co-owner, CEO, chairman, president, 1987-92; McKee Communications, McKee Holdings, McKee Acquistion Corp, chairman, CEO, president, 1992-. **Orgs:** Bd mem, DC United Way; American Bar Assn; Natl Conference of Black Lawyers; Federal Bar Assn; Unified Bar of DC; NY, PA, DC Bars; Washington commentator, FOX Broadcasting Co; board of directors: Florida Progress Corp; Florida Power Corp; American Heritage Life Insurance Co; Checkers Drive In Restaurants, Inc; Barnett Banks Inc; Florida Association of Broadcasters. **Honors/Awds:** Outstanding Alumni Public Service Award, Hobart College; Howard Univ School of Law, John Mercer Langston Award, Outstanding Achievement in Law and Public Service; Tampa Bay Business, Hall of Fame, Inductee, 1998. **Business Addr:** President/CEO, McKee Communications, 2701 N Rocky Point Dr, Ste 630, Tampa, FL 33607.

MCKEE, LONETTE
Actress, singer, writer, producer, director. **Personal:** Born 1959, Detroit, MI. **Career:** Theater appearances include: Lady Day at Emerson's Bar & Grill, 1986; Show Boat, 1983; film appearances include: Sparkle, 1976; Which Way Is Up?, 1977; Cuba, 1979; The Cotton Club, 1984; Brewster's Millions, 1985; 'Round Midnight, 1986; Gardens of Stone, 1987; The Women of Brewster Place; Jungle Fever, 1990; Malcolm X, 1992; tv shows: Miami Vice; Blind Faith, Showtime, 1998; record albums: Words & Music, Natural Love, Warner Brothers, Forty Acres and a Mule Music. **Orgs:** Actors' Equity Assn; American Federation of Television and Radio Artists. **Honors/Awds:** Tony nomination, Julie, pre-Broadway revival of Showboat, 1983. **Special Achievements:** First and only African Amercian female to star in the role of Julie on Broadway, Show Boat. **Business Addr:** Actress, Singer, Gersh Agency, 130 W. 42nd St., 24th Fl., New York, NY 10036.

MCKEE, THEODORE A.
Judge. **Personal:** Born in Rochester, NY; married Dr Ana Pujols. **Educ:** State Univ of NY, BA 1965; Syracuse Univ Coll of Law, JD (magna cum laude) 1975. **Career:** Wolf Block Schorr & Solis-Cohen, assoc 1975-77; Eastern Dist of PA, asst US atty 1977-80; Law Dept City of Phila, deputy city solicitor 1980-83; Court of Common Pleas Commonwealth of PA, judge; US Court of Appeals, circuit judge, 1994-. **Orgs:** Bd of dirs Crises Intervention Network. **Business Addr:** Circuit Judge, US Court of Appeals, 20614 US Courthouse, Philadelphia, PA 19106.

MCKELLAR, STEPHEN ALEXANDER
City official. **Personal:** Born Apr 26, 1956, Chester, PA; married Beverly Rice; children: Tamika, Jonee. **Educ:** VA State Univ, 1974-76; St Joseph's Univ, BS 1980. **Career:** Dept of Sts & Public Improvements, 1st exec asst 1978-81; Co of Delaware, mun energy coord 1981-83; City of Chester, dir of parks pub prop & rec, councilman, currently. **Orgs:** Mem St Michael Roman Catholic Church; mem NAACP; mem Franklin Lodge #58; F&AM chmn YMCA Bd of Mgrs; mem Republican Party of Chester PA 1974-; mem Del Co Republican Council 1984-; mem Alpha Phi Alpha; mem, Minaret Temple #174, AEAONMS 1987; mem, Charles E Gordon Consistory #65 Scottish Rite Freemasonry 1986. **Honors/Awds:** Outstanding Comm Contribution Awd YIA 1974; Comm Involvement Awd Club Amoebia 1982; Humanitarian Awd Chester Black Expo 1984; Outstanding Young Men of Amer Awd 1984.

MCKELLER, THOMAS LEE
Educator, cleric, law enforcement officer. **Personal:** Born Dec 31, 1940, Middletown, OH; children: Yolanda M, Monica L, Julia L. **Educ:** Monmouth Coll, AA, Business Law 1962-64; Univ of Toledo, BA, Business & Educ, 1969-73; MI State Correctional Special School, Certificate, 1977; MI Constr Training Council, Certificate, 1979. **Career:** Berrien City State Correction Center Counselor, 1978-81; Benton Harbor Elementary School Advisory Comm, chmn, 1982-83; The Church of Our Lord & Savior, minister, 1982-; Benton Harbor Area Schools Bd of Educ, trustee, 1983-84; Educ instructor; Benton Harbor Schools, security 1984-. **Orgs:** Sgt major, OH Explorer Scouts Drill Council, 1964-65; coordinator, OH Model Cities Signing Comm 1965-67; corner back Cincinatti Bengals Professional Football Team 1966-67; pres Silver Tax & Bookkeeping Serv 1978-80; finance chmn supt Educ Task Force 1983; dir Brotherhood of Christian Ministers 1983; assoc dir BH Marriage Counselors Assn 1984; bd of dir Full Gospel Businessmans Assn 1984; Local Selective Service Board #11, president appointee, 1992; AF&AM 32nd Degree Scottish Rite Masons; Mensa Intl, 1973-. **Honors/Awds:** Published "I Am Gods Child" Oh Methodist Youth Dept 1960, "Black Is" US Black Legion of Scholars 1967; chmn OH Hi-Y Council 1971; Pres Chosen Few Literary Soc 1974. **Military Serv:** USAF tech sgt 6 yrs; Pres Citation, Special Merit Award, Special Serv Medal, 1960-66; USMC 2 yrs sgt Pres Citation 1958. **Business Addr:** Public Service, Benton Harbor Area Schools, 870 Colfax, Benton Harbor, MI 49022.

MCKELPIN, JOSEPH P.
Educator. **Personal:** Born May 6, 1914, Leflore Co, MS; married Peggy A Jones; children: Joseph P Jr, Emmett O. **Educ:** SU, AB 1943; Univ WI, MS 1948, PhD 1952. **Career:** Fed City Coll, prof ed 1974-; Morris Brown Coll, dean 1973-74; S Assn Colls & Schs, dir resrch & eval 1967-73; SU, prof ed 1952-62. **Orgs:** Mem Phi Delta Kappa; Kappa Delta Pi; Kappa Phi Kappa; Omega Psi Phi. **Military Serv:** AUS 2nd lt 1943-46. **Business Addr:** 724 9 St NW, Washington, DC 20001.

MCKENNA, GEORGE J., III
Educational administrator. **Personal:** Born Sep 6, 1940, New Orleans, LA; son of Leah McKenna and George McKenna Jr. **Educ:** Xavier University, New Orleans, LA, BS, 1961; Loyola University, Chicago, IL, MA, 1962; Xavier University, New Orleans, LA, EdD. **Career:** Los Angeles Unified School Dist, Los Angeles, CA, teacher, 1962-70, principal, admin, 1970-88; Inglewood Unified School District, Inglewood, CA, superintendent, beginning 1988; Compton Unified School District, deputy superintendent, currently. **Orgs:** Former president, Los Angeles Unified Schools, Council of Black Administrators, 1981-82, 1986-87; board member, Los Angeles Southern Christian Leadership Conference, 1978-; commission member, National Drug Free Schools Commission, 1989-90. **Honors/Awds:** Congressional Black Caucus Chairman's Award, 1989; UNCF Achievement Award, 1988. **Special Achievements:** Subject of CBS television movie, "The George McKenna Story," starring Denzel Washington; Great Black Educators Calendar, 1988. **Business Addr:** Deputy Superintendent, Compton Unified School District, 604 S Tamarind Ave, Compton, CA 90220.

MCKENZIE, EDNA B.
Historian. **Personal:** Born Dec 29, 1923, Grindstone, PA; married Edmond (died 1986); children: Clyde Marc, Edmond Robert. **Educ:** Univ of Pittsburgh, BSEd 1968, MA History 1970, PhD History 1973. **Career:** Community Coll of Allegheny County, assoc prof of History 1973-, chairperson black minority & ethnic studies 1973-; Seton Hill Coll Greensburg PA, assoc prof History 1970-72; Pittsburgh Bd of Educ Sec Schools, teacher 1968-70; The Pittsburgh Courier Hm Off, staff writer 1942-50. **Orgs:** Mem exec council Assn for the Study of Afro-Amer Life & History 1978-; bd of dirs PA Higher Educ Assistance Agency 1985; advisory council PA Historical & Mus Commn 1985; trustee Univ of Pittsburgh 1987-90; exec comm mem Pennsylvania Higher Educ Assistance Agency 1988-. **Honors/Awds:** Outstanding Achievement Award, African Methodist Episcopal Church; Found Day Award Ministerial Alliance Pittsburgh 1975; pub "Freedom in the Midst of a Slave Soc" Univ Press Washington DC 1980. **Business Addr:** Dept of History & Govt, Allegheny County Community Coll, 808 Ridge Ave, Pittsburgh, PA 15212-6003.

MCKENZIE, ELI, JR.
Company executive. **Personal:** Born Dec 28, 1947, Byromville, GA; married Vera Lee Thomas; children: Jatun Kreatson, Eli III, Jennifer Ashley. **Educ:** Ft Valley State Coll, BS 1969; Univ of IL, MS 1971, PhD 1975. **Career:** Univ of IL, rsch asst 1969-74; Ft Valley State Coll, rsch sci 1975; Prairie View A&M Univ, dept head soil sci 1976-78; M&M products Co, dir of R&D 1978-83; EAR Enterprise, pres/CEO, currently. **Orgs:** Mem Soc of Cosmetic Chemist 1978, Amer Soc for Quality Control 1979. **Honors/Awds:** Rsch Grant Univ of IL 1969; "Effect of Pretreatment of Loss of Nitrogen" Soil Sci Soc Amer Proc 1976; "15-Labelled Fertilizer N from Waterlogged Soil During Incubation", "Phosphorus Fertility of Some Tropical Soils in Sierra Leone" Soil Sci Soc Amer Proc 1977. **Business Addr:** Pres/CEO, EAR Enterprises, 2528 Lantrac Ct, Decatur, GA 30035, (404)808-4499.

MCKENZIE, FLORETTA D.
Educational administrator, consultant. **Personal:** Born Aug 19, 1935, Lakeland, FL; daughter of Ruth J Dukes and Martin W Dukes Sr (deceased); children: Dona R, Kevin. **Educ:** DC Teachers Coll, BS History 1956, Postgrad 1967-69; Howard Univ, MA 1957; George Washington Univ, Amer Univ, Catholic Univ of Amer, Union Grad School Baltimore, Postgrad; George Washington Univ, EdD 1984. **Career:** Balt & WA Schools, teacher 1957-67; DC Public Schools, asst supt charge secondary schools to dep supt educ prog & servs; 1969-74; Montgomery Cty Public Schools, area asst supt 1974-77, dep supt schools 1978-79; State of MD, asst dep supt schools 1977-78; US Dept of Educ, 1979-81; Office School Improvement, dep asst sec 1980-81; Ford Found, educ consult 1981; WA Office Coll Entrance Exam Bd, adv com 1970-; Educ Products Info Exchange, trustee 1970; DC Public Schools, supt 1981-89; The McKenzie Group, pres, 1988-; Harvard Univ, Kennedy School of Education, visiting scholar, 1989-91; The American Univ Graduate School of Education, professor, 1991-. **Orgs:** Amer Assn of School Admin, Urban League, Gamma Theta Upsilon, Phi Alpha Theta, Phi Delta Kappa; hon life mem MD PTA; bd of trustees George Washington Univ; bd of dirs Natl Geographic Soc, Potomac Electric Power Co, World Book, Acacia Life Insurance; Delta Sigma Theta Inc; board of directors, Riggs Natl Bank; Marriott Hotels, board member. **Honors/Awds:** Honorary doctorates: Georgetown Univ, 1986, Catholic Univ, 1985, Columbia Univ Teacher's College, 1987. **Special Achievements:** First African American and female elected to the Marriott Hotels board, 1992. **Business Addr:** President, The McKenzie Group, 555 13th St NW, Suite 700, East Tower, Washington, DC 20001.

MCKENZIE, KEITH
Professional football player. **Personal:** Born Oct 17, 1973, Detroit, MI. **Educ:** Ball State, BS in history. **Career:** Green Bay Packers, defensive end, 1996-. **Business Addr:** Professional Football Player, Green Bay Packers, 1265 Lombardi Ave, Green Bay, WI 54304, (414)494-2351.

MCKENZIE, MIRANDA MACK
Brewing company executive. **Personal:** Born Jun 21, 1955, Atlanta, GA; daughter of Jewel Hillman Mack and Dennis Mack; married Therman McKenzie, Feb 15, 1992. **Educ:** Morris Brown Coll, BA 1977. **Career:** WAOK Radio, copy writer, 1977-79, account executive, 1979-80; City Beverage Co, director of market development, 1980-84; Coors Brewing Co, asst mgr, special mkts, 1984-85, field mgr, 1985-86, comm realtions regional mgr 1986-93; Atlanta Committee, Olympic Games, dir of communications, 1993-98; Anheuser-Busch Co, dir of local affairs, 1994-. **Orgs:** Natl pres, Natl Assn of Market Developers 1991-92; bd mem NAACP 1983-; bd mem, Atlanta Urban League, secretary, board member, 1987-95; bd mem, Atlanta Business League 1989-91; bd mem, Georgia Assn of Minority Entrepreneurs 1988-; Atlanta NAACP, board member, 1977-95; Coalition of 100 Black Women, founding board member, 1988; Friends of Morehouse College, steering committee, 1989-; Morris Brown Coll Athletic Foundation, 1989-95. **Honors/Awds:** Named 1 of 10 Outstanding Atlantans Outstanding Young People of Atlanta 1986; Media Woman of the Year Natl Assn of Media Women 1986; NAMD, Marketer of the Year, 1987; Leadership Awd Council of Natl Alumni 1986; Leadership America, 1989, 1992; Leadership Atlanta, 1986; 100 of the Best and Brightest Black Women in Corporate America, Ebony Magazine, 1990; Top African American Business and Professional Women, Dollars & Sense Magazine, 1987, 1992; Iota Phi Lambda, Bronze Woman of the Year, 1989; Morris Brown College, Athletic Hall of Fame, 1987; NAACP, C L Harper Award, 1986; Leadership Georgia, 1992. **Business Addr:** Director, Local Affairs, Anheuser-Busch Companies, 3400 Peachtree Rd, Ste 1025, Atlanta, GA 30326, (404)848-9236.

MCKENZIE, RALEIGH
Professional football player. **Personal:** Born Feb 8, 1963, Knoxville, TN; married Martha; children: Rachel, Raleigh Jr, Malcolm. **Educ:** Univ of Tennessee, bachelor's degree in marketing. **Career:** Washington Redskins, center, 1985-94; Philadelphia Eagles, 1995-96; San Diego Chargers, 1997-. **Business Addr:** Professional Football Player, San Diego Chargers, Qualcomm Stadium, 9449 Friars Rd, San Diego, CA 92108, (619)280-2111.

MCKENZIE, REGINALD
Professional sports executive. **Personal:** Born Jul 27, 1950, Detroit, MI; son of Hazel Mckenzie and Henry Mckenzie; married Ethellean Hicks (divorced). **Educ:** Univ of Michigan, BS, 1972. **Career:** Buffalo Bills, offensive guard, 11 yrs; Seattle Seahawks, offensive guard, 1983-84, dir of marketing and sales for Seattle Kingdome exec suites, offensive line coach; spokesman for United Way. **Orgs:** Comm Projects, Special Olympics, United Way, Boys Clubs of America; exec dir Reggie McKenzie Found Inc of Detroit; bd of dirs Central Area Youth Assoc Seattle; bd of dirs King County Boys and Girls Club. **Honors/Awds:** Unsung Hero Awd Detroit Sports Media 1986; Sportsman of the Year Detroit March of Dimes 1986; Outstanding Young Citizen Washington State Jaycees 1989; Brotherhood Awd BTWBA 1988. **Business Addr:** Seattle Seahawks, 1120 NE 53rd St, Kirkland, WA 98033.

MCKENZIE, THERMAN, SR.
Business executive. **Personal:** Born Jun 2, 1949, Byromville, GA; son of Sallie McKenzie and Eli McKenzie Sr; married Miranda Mack; children: Therman Jr, Carmisha Deniece, Christopher Bernard. **Educ:** Ft Valley State Coll, BS 1970; Mercer Univ, RPh 1973. **Career:** Reeds Drug Chain, pharmacist 1971; Grady Mem Hosp, pharmacist 1971-73; Revco Drug Chain, pharmacist 1973-74; M&M Prod Co, exec vice-pres 1973-, chmn chief opers officer, currently; McKenzie Masonry, Inc, pres, currently. **Orgs:** Mem Atlanta Bus League 1973-; mem, bd of dirs Amer Health & Beauty Aids Inst 1982-; vice-pres Intl Bus Fellows 1983-; trustee Mercer Univ 1983-; bdchmn Collections of Life & Heritage 1983-; treas Chamber of Commerce Atlanta 1984-; bd of trustees Leadership Atlanta 1984-; chmn CW Pettigrew Mem Endow Campaign; corp treas EAR Enterprises; apptd US Small Business Adv Comm, Morris Brown Coll Free Enterprise Inst; bd of dirs Citizen Trust Bank; mem natl bd Jr Entrepreneurial Traders Assoc; bd of dirs Citizen Banchares Corp; apptd to State Bd of Compensation and Postsecondary Vocational Educ Bd by Gov Joe Frank Harris; apptd to State Productivity Bd; bd of trustees Fort Valley State Coll; mem Natl Assoc for Equal Oppor in Higher Educ, Cncl of Natl Alumni Assocs; 100 Black Men of Atlanta. **Honors/Awds:** Entrepreneur of the Year Stanford Univ Grad Sch of Bus 1980; People to Watch-Fortune Magazine 1984; Hon Doctorate of Laws Morris Brown Coll 1984; 100 Top Atlantans Under 40-Atlanta Magazine 1984; Honorary Counsel General for the Republic of Sierra Leone West Africa, 1989-.

MCKENZIE, VASHTI
Cleric. **Career:** Payne Memorial AME Church, pastor, currently. **Special Achievements:** One of the first women to be ordained as pastor in the Afrcan Methodist Episcopal Church. **Business Addr:** Pastor, Payne Memorial AME Church, 1714 W Madison Ave, Baltimore, MD 21217, (410)669-8739.

MCKENZIE, WILFORD CLIFTON
Business executive. **Personal:** Born Apr 1, 1913; married Mercia; children: Wilfred, Rona. **Educ:** City Coll of NY, BA; Fisk U. **Career:** NY City Dept of Income Maint, admin mgr; HRA, emp 1985; Jamaica, civil srvnt 1933-45. **Orgs:** Mem 100 Black Men 1975; Managerial Empl Assn. **Business Addr:** 250 Church St, New York, NY 10013.

MCKERSON, EFFIE M.
Educator. **Personal:** Born Mar 16, 1924, Henderson, TX; married Hayward Cornelious; children: Hayward Alton. **Educ:** TX Coll, BA 1948; Univ WI, MS 1957; Boston U, Post Grad Study 1949; Sonoma St Coll, 1965; US Intrntl U, 1971-72; LaVern Coll Ctr, 1972; IGSE, 1973; Univ MN, 1973; Univ VA, 1974. **Career:** Longview TX, tchr 1948-59; Gary IN, 1959-68; Manilla Phillippine, 1968; Minn MN, 1968-69; Edina Pub Sch, 1969-. **Orgs:** Mem, pres Nat Adv Vo Rehab; Nat Cncl Soc Studies; Nat Ed Assn; Am Acad Pol & Soc Sci; Intl Assn Childhd Ed; Edina Historical Soc; rep Nat Cncl Soc Studies 1967, 1970, 1973-74; mem Nat Cncl Negro Women; vice chrwmn MN Rep; Minneapolis Girls Club Aux; past pres St Stephen Luth Ch Women. **Honors/Awds:** Attend 1974 Presdntl Clsrm Wrkshp; cert Apprec from SecCasper Weinberger; del to US Dept St Foreign Policy Conf for Ed. **Business Addr:** Creek Valley Sch, 6401 Gleason R, Edina, MN 55435.

MCKERSON, MAZOLA
Manager. **Personal:** Born Jan 10, 1921, Bluff, OK; married Alfred; children: 4. **Educ:** Grad HS; Many seminars 7 workshops related to restaurant bus. **Career:** Gourmet Rstrnt, mgr, owner 1962-. **Orgs:** Chrprsn Gov Commn St of Women; mem municipal bd St of OK; apptd commn on ed St of OK; chair Ardmore's 100th Birthday Centennial 1887-1987; adv bd Higher Educ Center. **Honors/Awds:** 1st Lady Mayor Ardmore OK 1979-80; 1st Black Elected to City Commn Ardmore 1977-83; Lady of Yr Zeta Phi Beta Sor 1976-77; Hon for Srvng as Chrprsn C of C Bicentennial Com 1976; Woman of the Yr YMCA 1980; hon mem Sigma Gamma Rho 1986. **Business Addr:** Manager, Owner, Gourmet Restaurant, 1606 McLish SW, Ardmore, OK 73401.

MCKEY, DERRICK WAYNE
Professional basketball player. **Personal:** Born Oct 10, 1966, Meridian, MS. **Educ:** Univ of Alabama, University, AL, 1984-87. **Career:** Seattle Supersonics, forward, 1987-93; Indiana Pacers, 1993-. **Honors/Awds:** NBA All-Rookie Team, 1988. **Business Addr:** Professional Basketball Player, Indiana Pacers, 300 E Market St, Indianapolis, IN 46204, (317)263-2100.

MCKIE, AARON FITZGERALD
Professional basketball player. **Personal:** Born Oct 2, 1972, Philadelphia, PA. **Educ:** Temple University. **Career:** Portland TrailBlazers, guard, 1994-96; Detroit Pistons, 1996-97; Philadelphia 76ers, 1997-. **Special Achievements:** NBA Draft, First round pick, #17, 1994. **Business Addr:** Professional Basketball Player, Philadelphia 76ers, One Corestates Complex, Philadelphia, PA 19148, (215)339-7676.

MCKINNEY, ALMA SWILLEY
Educator. **Personal:** Born Mar 4, 1930, Lamont, FL; children: Matthew M. **Educ:** FL A&M Univ Tallahassee, BA 1951; FL State Univ, MS 1966; Univ of MN, attended. **Career:** Madison Cty School Bd Madison FL, teacher 1951-60; Greenville Training School Greenville FL, math instr 1960-63; Suwannee River Jr Coll Madison FL; head mathdept 1963-67; N FL Jr Coll, assoc prof of math 1967-73; Univ of MN, teaching asst 1973-76; N FL Jr Coll, coord learning lab 1976-80; State Dept of Ed Tallahassee, ons. **Orgs:** Chmn math dept N FL Jr Coll 1981-; chmn reg adv council Dept of Corrections 1977-79; corp dir ACTT Inc of Madison 1978-80; bd of dir Madison Cty Meml Hosp 198-84; pol action comm NAACP; mem Zeta Phi Beta Sor; mem voters League, RECS Serv Club, Recreation Assoc Senatorial Scholarship FL State Senate 1948-51. **Honors/Awds:** Teacher of the Year Suwannee River Jr Coll 1964; Natl Sci Fellow NSF 1975-76; Citizen of the Year Iota Alpha Zeta Chap Zeta Phi Beta 1979. **Business Addr:** Consultant, State Dept of Educ, 530 Carlton Bldg, Tallahassee, FL 32301.

MCKINNEY, BILLY
Sports administrator. **Career:** Chicago Bulls, Denver Nuggets, Kansas City Kings, former professional basketball player; Billy McKinney Enterprises Inc, president; Minnesota Timberwolves, director of player personnel, until 1990; Detroit Pistons, vp of basketball operations, until 1995. **Orgs:** Detroit Urban League, bd mem; Harlem Globetrotters, advisory bd. **Business Addr:** Former VP of Basketball Operations, Detroit Pistons, The Palace, 2 Championship Dr, Auburn Hills, MI 48326, (810)377-0100.

MCKINNEY, CYNTHIA ANN
Congresswoman. **Personal:** Born Mar 17, 1955, Atlanta, GA; daughter of Leola and Billy McKinney; divorced; children: Coy Grandison Jr. **Educ:** University of Southern California, BA, 1978; Tufts University, Fletcher School of Law and Diplomacy, MA, PhD, candidate, 1993. **Career:** Spelman College, diplomatic fellow, 1984; Clark Atlanta University, instructor, political science; Agnes State College, educator; State of Georgia, House of Representatives, representative, 1988-92; US House of Representatives, congresswoman, 1992-. **Orgs:** Metro Atlanta, HIV Health Services Planning Council, past board member; Natl Council of Negro Women; NAACP; Sierra Club; Agriculture Committee; Congressional Black Caucus; Women's Caucus; Progressive Caucus; 103rd Congress Freshman Class, secretary. **Special Achievements:** First African-American woman elected to Congress from Georgia, 1992; only father-daughter team ever to serve in country, Georgia State House, 1988-92. **Business Addr:** Congresswoman, US House of Representatives, 124 Cannon House Office Bldg, Washington, DC 20515, (202)225-1605.

MCKINNEY, ERNEST LEE, SR.
Educator (retired). **Personal:** Born Nov 26, 1923, Chesnee, SC; son of Corrie C Dodd McKinney and Jaffer N McKinney; married Marion L Birdwell; children: Ernest Jr, Kevin. **Educ:** Tennessee State Univ, BS 1947; E Tennessee State Univ, MA 1964; Swift Mem Jr College, Cert, 1945. **Career:** Swift Jr Coll, teacher 1947-49; Rogersville AL, teacher 1949-53; Booker T Washington, principal 1953-56; Langston HS, teacher 1956-65; Science Hill HS, teacher 1965-70; So Jr HS, guid 1970-76; Science Hill HS, asst principal 1976-85 (retired); Washington County Bd of Educ, elected, 1988, re-elected, 1992-96; Washington County Bd of Education, elected 1988, 1992, 1996; Headstart Policy Council, 1991-94. **Orgs:** Alderman Town of Jonesborough 1968-73, 1976-84; mem/pres Jonesborough Kiwanis Club 1980; mem Omega Psi Phi Frat; mem First Tennessee Development Dist; secretary, Pro-To Club, 1986-; treasurer, Bethel Christian Church, 1965-95; chairman, Black Voters Alliance, 1990-; Iota Alpha Chap, 1968, other chapts, 1973, 1974, 1977, 1978, 1983; 5th Dist 1989; All TN School Bd, 1996. **Honors/Awds:** Omega Man of the Year, Iota Alpha Chap, 1968, 1973, 1974, 1977, 1978, 1983; 50 years Omega pen, Grand Conclave, Los Angeles, 1996. **Home Addr:** 119 N Lincoln Ave, Jonesborough, TN 37659.

MCKINNEY, GENE C.
Military officer. **Personal:** marrIed Wilhemina Hall; children: Zuberi. **Educ:** El Paso Community College, associate science degree in general management; Park College, BS, management/human resources. **Career:** US Army Europe, command sergeant major; US Army, sergeant major, currently. **Honors/Awds:** Bronze Star, Meritorious Service Medal. **Special Achievements:** First African American sergeant major.

MCKINNEY, GEORGE DALLAS, JR.
Clergyman. **Personal:** Born Aug 9, 1932, Jonesboro, AR; married Jean Brown; children: George, Grant, Gregory, Gordon, Glenn. **Educ:** AR State AM& N Coll Pine Bluff, BA (magna cum laude) 1954; AR State Univ Oberlin Coll, MA 1956; Univ of MI, Grad Studies 1957-58; CA Grad Sch of Theol, PhD 1974. **Career:** St Stephen's Ch of God in Christ, pastor 1962-; Private Practice, marriage family & child counselor 1971-; Comm Welfare Council, consult 1968-71; Econ Opportunity Com, asst dir 1965-71; San Diego Co Probation Dept, sr probation officer 1959-65; Family Ct Toledo, couns 1957-59; Toledo State Mental Hosp, prot chaplain 1956-57; Chargin Falls Park Comm Center, dir 1955-56. **Orgs:** Mem CA Probation Parole & Correctional Assn; founder & chmn of bd of dirs St Stephen's Group Home; mem Sandiego Co Council of Chs; bd of trustees Interdenominational Theol Center Atlanta; bd of dirs C H Mason Theol Sem Atlanta; bd of dirs Bob Harrison Ministries; bd of elders Morris Cerillo World Evangelism; mem Sigma Rho Sigma Social Sci Frat; mem San Diego Rotary Club (1st black); mem Alpha Kappa Mu Nat Hon Society; mem Operation Push; vol chaplain at summer camp BSA; mem San Diego Mental Health Assn; mem NAACP; mem YMCA; mem San Diego Urban League; bd of advs Black Communication Center San-Diego State U; mem CA Mental Health Assn. **Honors/Awds:** Recipient JF Kennedy Award for servs to youth; outstanding pastor award San Diego State Univ Black Students; award for servs to youth Black Bus & Professional Women of San Diego; listed in Contemporary Authors; social worker of the yr award San Diego Co 1963; one of the ten outstanding men in San Diego Jr C of C 1966; outstanding man ot the yr award Intenat Assn of Aerospace Workers Dist 50 1969; outstanding contributions to the San Diego Comm in Field of Religious Activities NAACP 1975; achievement award for Religion Educ & Dedicated Serv to Youth So CA Ch of God in Christ; pub "The Theol of the Jehovah's Witnesses" "I Will Build My Ch"; several other pubs; hon at Testimonial Dinner San Diego State Univ by the NewFriends of the Black Communications Center 1977; listed "Today" 1 of 20 hors Making Significant Contribution to Evangelical Christian Lit. **Business Addr:** Bishop, St Stephen's Church, 5825 Imperial Ave, San Diego, CA 92114.

MCKINNEY, JACOB K.
Publicist. **Personal:** Born Jun 10, 1920, Columbus, OH; married Marjorie Weiss; children: Jacquelyn Kyle. **Educ:** OH St U, 1 yr; LA City Coll, 1954-55. **Career:** Kyle Ldr mus variety act, 1940-50; UAW-CIO Local #927, pub dir 1950-53; LA Sentinel, adv mgr 1953-56; Bronze Am Mag, ed pub 1957-65; Columbia-Screen Gems, asst dir pub 1968-71; Am Intnl Pictures Inc, pub-comm rel dir 1972-80; Knott's Berry Farm, asst mgr pub rel; McKinney & Asso PR, pres. **Orgs:** Mem Nat Safety Coun 1950-52; mem bd dir Pub Guild Local 818; Elder Presb Ch 1963; bd dir Watts Comm Ctr 1969-70. **Honors/Awds:** 1st black pub Nat TV network 1965-68; cited by LA Bd Ed for Summer Seminar UCLA 1973; Campaign Mgr for Pat Paulsen's pseudo Pres Campaign 1968. **Military Serv:** USAAF pvt 1943-44. **Business Addr:** Mc Kinney & Asso PR, 6515 Susnet Blvd, Los Angeles, CA.

MCKINNEY, JAMES RAY
Vocational counselor. **Personal:** Born Apr 17, 1942, Arlington, KY; married Shirley J Bennett; children: James B, Zandra. **Educ:** Lane Coll, AB 1967; MI St U, MA 1971; MSU, Ed Spec 1979. **Career:** Ins salesperson; newspaper editor; Boy's Dorm Lane Coll, undertaker dir; TN Valley Auth, checker, pymstr; Comm Sch, dir Civic Rec Dept, playground supr; Dept of Interior Rocky Mt Nat Pk CO, ranger; Calhoun Area Vocational Center, Battle Creek Public Schools, special needs counselor 1985-. **Orgs:** Mem Battle Creek Ed Assn 1970-72; st rep Nat Ed Assn 1971; bd dir Family & Children Srv 1973-80; chmn Pub Rel Com 1975; mem Urban League 1965-72; NAACP 1965-72; tchr Black History 1972; co-pres Ann J Kellog Elem PTA 1971-79; mem Alpha Phi Alpha 1961-64, vice pres 1963, dean of pledges 1962, hstrn 1964; founder of Battle Creek Track Club 1979. **Honors/Awds:** Pres, Pre Alumni Club 1963-64; Hon Guard, Reclamation Tour UT. **Business Addr:** Special Needs Counselor, Battle Creek Publ School, 475 E Roosevelt Ave, Battle Creek, MI 49017.

MCKINNEY, JESSE DOYLE
Clergyman. **Personal:** Born Oct 9, 1934, Jonesboro, AR; son of osie L McKinney (deceased) and George D McKinney, Sr (deceased); married Mary Francis Keys, Aug 5, 1978; children: Antoinette, Patrick, Bruce, Gloria, Carla. **Educ:** Univ of AR, BA 1957; San Diego State Univ, MSW 1972. **Career:** San Diego State Univ/Grossmont Comm Coll, teacher/lecturer 1972-74; Southeast Counseling and Consultant Svcs, counselor/director 1974-76; San Bernardino Co Mental Health Dept, mental health clinician II 1977-79; Pleasant Place Group Home, dir 1979-82; licensed clinical social worker; St Stephen's Church of God In Christ, pastor/social service dir. **Orgs:** Bd mem Home of Neighborly Serv 1985-; mem Natl Assoc of Social Workers; founder/pastor St Stephen's Church Samaritan Shelter; psychiatric social worker Dept of Mental Health San Bernardino Cty; mem San Diego County Health Adv Bd, CA Personnel and Guidance Assoc, Assoc of Black Social Workers; bd of dirs San Diego Operation PUSH; mem, advisory board, Graduate School of Social Work, 1989-. **Honors/Awds:** Fellowship Grant Natl Inst of Mental Health. **Home Addr:** 1883 Myrtlewood St, Colton, CA 92324.

MCKINNEY, NORMA J.
Banking executive. **Personal:** Born Dec 30, 1941, Banks, AR; daughter of Lorene Fry Bizzell and Jesse Marks; married Herman McKinney, Aug 16, 1959; children: Kristal, Kevin, Kent. **Educ:** Northwest Intermediate Banking School, 1986; Babson Coll Human Resource School, 1989; Univ of WA School of Business Admin Mgmt School, graduate, 1990. **Career:** Security Pacific Bank, Seattle, WA, various poositions, 1968-78, vice pres & human resource specialist, 1978-89, vice pres & human

resource mgr, 1987-89, first vice pres & human resource mgr, 1989-. **Orgs:** Bd of dir, United Negro Coll Fund; bd of dir, First AME Headstart Program; mem, Natl Urban Bankers Associates; mem, First AME Church; facilitator, Diversity Training, Security Pacific Bank; comm, Seattle Human Rights Commission, 1990. **Honors/Awds:** National Urban Bank Award, 1988.

MCKINNEY, OLIVIA DAVENE ROSS

Educator (retired). **Personal:** Born May 14, 1931, Detroit, MI; daughter of Mary Olivia Brookins Ross and Solomon David Ross; married Robert Vassar McKinney Jr, Jun 14, 1953; children: David Ross, Mark Dennard. **Educ:** Eastern Michigan University, BS, 1952-53; Wayne State University, MEd, 1968, Education Specialist Certificate, 1973. **Career:** Inkster Board of Education, music teacher, 1953-54, teacher, 1955-70; Shiloh Baptist Church, organist, pianist, choir director, 1968-72, African-American workshop consultant, 1988-; Detroit Board of Education, teacher, 1970-86, black studies consultant, 1980-81. **Orgs:** Shiloh Baptist Church, organist, choir director, 1947, 1950, 1968-72, historian, 1988-; Young People's Department of the National Baptist Convention USA Inc, pianist, 1948-50; Fred Hart Williams Genealogical Association, board of directors, 1985-89; Michigan Council for the Social Studies, board of directors, 1984-88; Delta Sigma Theta, Inkster Chapter, president, 1972-74; Chairperson for Haitian International Project 1987-88, 1992-; Woman's Auxulary to the National Baptist Convention, chairperson of audio/visual, 1962-. **Honors/Awds:** Certificate of Honor for Directing a Tutorial Reading Program for the Greater Shiloh Baptist Church in Detroit, MI. **Special Achievements:** Co-author, Teaching Manuels for Inkster Public Schools, "Black Contributions in the World", "Black Contributions in the US," 1969; Correlated notes and statements to publish From Crumbs to Gravy, The Autobiography of Mary Olivia Brookins Ross, 1982-; Workshop Consultant of Black Studies, 1989-; Author, The Slide Picture of the American Revolution, 1968. **Home Addr:** 24505 Green Valley, Southfield, MI 48034, (810)352-8397.

MCKINNEY, RICHARD ISHMAEL

Educator (retired). **Personal:** Born Aug 20, 1906, Live Oak, FL; son of Sally R Ellis and George P McKinney; married Lena R Martin; children: George K, Phyllis McKinney Bynum. **Educ:** Morehouse Coll, AB 1931; Andover Newton Theological Sch, BD 1934, STM 1937; Yale Univ, PhD 1942; Post-Doctoral Study, The Sorbonne, Univ of Chicago, Columbia Univ. **Career:** Virginia Union Univ, Richmond, VA, professor, 1935-44; Storer College, Harpers Ferry, WV, president, 1944-50; Morgan State Univ, Baltimore, MD, chairman of philosophy dept, 1951-76; Medical College of Georgia, visiting professor, 1972; Univ of Pennsylvania, visiting professor, 1973; Univ of Ife, Nigeria, visiting professor, 1974; Morgan State Univ, acting dean Coll of Arts & Scis 1977-78; Virginia Union Univ, acting vice pres for academic affairs 1978-79; Morgan Christian Ctr interim dir 1980-81; Bethune Cookman College, visiting prof, 1981-82; Coppin State Coll, distinguished professor, 1983-95. **Orgs:** Mem Soc for Values in Higher Educ 1938-; mem Amer Philosophical Assoc 1951-; mem Soc for Phenomenology and Existential Philosophy 1951-; life mem Natl Educ Assoc, NAACP. **Honors/Awds:** Kent Fellow Soc for Values in Higher Educ 1938; Alpha Kappa Mu Honor Soc Pi Lambda Psi Chap 1955; DD St Paul's Coll 1978; Phi Beta Kappa Delta of GA 1981; 14 publications including "History of Black Baptists of Florida," Miami FL Memorial Coll Press 1987.

MCKINNEY, RUFUS WILLIAM

Business executive (retired). **Personal:** Born Aug 6, 1930, Jonesboro, AR; son of Rev & Mrs G D McKinney Sr (deceased); married Glendonia Smith; children: Rufus Jr, Frederick Warren, Ann Marie, Paula Elaine. **Educ:** U Univ AR, BS 1953; IN Univ School of Law, JD 1956. **Career:** US Dept Lbr, attorney 1956-69; Pacific Lighting Corp, atty 1969-71, sr atty 1971-72; Southern CA Gas Co, asst vice pres 1972-75, vice pres for natl public affairs 1975-. **Orgs:** Vice pres, Southern CA Gas Co 1975-92; vice pres, WA Chapter NAACP 1963-69; Natl Urban League; pres, Gas Men's Roundtable 1975; chmn, Amer Assn of Blacks in Energy 1980-81; CA and IN Bar Assns; Kappa Alpha Psi; Sigma Pi Phi Frat. **Home Addr:** 5832 Tanglewood Dr, Bethesda, MD 20817.

MCKINNEY, SAMUEL BERRY

Cleric. **Personal:** Born Dec 28, 1926, Flint, MI; son of Ruth Berry McKinney and Wade Hampton McKinney; married Louise Jones; children: Lora Ellen, Rhoda Eileen. **Educ:** Morehouse Coll, BA 1949; Colgate-Rochester Div Sch, MDiv 1952; Colgate-Rochester Div Sch, D of Ministry 1975. **Career:** Mt Zion Bapt Ch, pastor 1958-; Olney St Bapt Ch, pastor 1954-58; Antioch Bapt Ch, asst to pastor 1952-54; Aenon Bapt Ch, student asst 1950-52. **Orgs:** Life mem NAACP; mem Alpha Phi Alpha; Sigma Pi Phi Alpha Omicron Boule; Princehall Mason 33rd degree; mem Wash State Voc Educ Commn; past pres N Pacific Bapt State Conv; past pres Black Am Bapts; past pres Seattle Council of Chs; past bd exec com mem Am Bapt Bd of Natl Ministries; past bd exec com mem Amer Bapt Gen Bd ; fdr Seattle OIC; 2nd natl vice pres OIC of Amer; fdr past bd mem Liberty Bank of Seattle; mem bd trustee Wash Mutual Savings Bank;co-author Black Adminstrn in Black Perspective. **Business Addr:** Mount Zion Baptist Church, 1634 19th Ave & E Madison Street, Seattle, WA 98122.

MCKINNEY, VENORA WARE

Library administrator. **Personal:** Born Jun 16, 1937, Meridian, OK; daughter of Hazel Parrish Ware and Odess Ware; married Lafayette; children: Carole Louise, James Christopher. **Educ:** Langston University, Langston, OK, BS, 1959; University of Il, Urbana, IL, library science, 1965; University of Wisconsin-Milwaukee, Milwaukee, WI, 1974; Marquette University, Milwaukee, WI, 1980, 1982. **Career:** Milwaukee Public Library, Milwaukee, WI, librarian, 1963-69; Peoria Public Schools, Peoria, IL, librarian, 1970-71; Milwaukee Public Schools, Milwaukee, WI, librarian, 1972-79, branch mgr, 1979-83, deputy city librarian, 1983-. **Orgs:** Delta Sigma Theta Sorority; United Negro College Fund; Links Inc, Milwaukee Chapter; National Forum for Black Public Administrators; NAACP; Milwaukee Repertory Theater Board, 1990-; American Library Assn; Wisconsin Library Assn. **Honors/Awds:** Milwaukee Public Library, Librarian of the Year, 1990.

MCKINNEY, WADE H., III

Business administrator (retired). **Personal:** Born Sep 6, 1925, Flint, MI; married Sylvia Lawrence (died 1993); children: Wade Hampton IV. **Educ:** Western Reserve U, BA 1948. **Career:** Cleveland Press, copy editor/reporter 1949-53; Urban League, Fort Wayne, indus relations sec 1953-56; Denver, indus relations sec 1956-59; Milwaukee, indus relations dir 1959-61; Chicago, youth guidance project dir 1961-63, employment & guidance dir 1963-68, prog dir 1968-71; Natl Urban League Skills Bank, midwest rep 1963-66; Econ Devel Corp, vice pres 1965-68; Northwestern Univ Business School, Mgmt Assistance Class, dir, 1971-72; US Postal Serv Hdq, Washington, DC, 1972-92. **Military Serv:** USAAF 1943-46; USAFR, captain, 1946-67.

MCKINNEY-JOHNSON, ELOISE

Freelance Writer, lecturer. **Personal:** Born Dec 7, 1926, Greensboro, NC; divorced; children: Myron Herman Johnson Jr. **Educ:** Spelman Coll, AB 1947; Boston Univ, Coll of Lib Arts, AM 1948; Johnson C Smith Univ, 1950; Univ of WI 1950-51; Univ of CO 1953; Univ of CA 1966,67,70; Univ of Pacific 1970; San Fran City Coll 1971; San Fran State Univ 1976; Stanford Univ, cert publishing course 1986. **Career:** Winston Salem St Coll, instr 1948-52; Carver Mun Jr Coll, instr 1951; Morehouse Coll, instr, asst prof 1953-61; NC Agr Tech St Univ, assoc prof 1961-65; SF Un School Dist, ed 1965, eng reader 1965-67; John Adams Adult School, eng lecturer 1966; San Fran Comm Coll, teacher 1966-71; Peralta Coll, instr, chrpsn 1971-73; No Peralta Comm Coll, instr engl 1973-75; Laney Coll, instr of engl; freelance writer and lecturer, currently. **Orgs:** San Francisco Chapter, United Nations Association, executive board; San Francisco Academy of World Studies, board of directors; San Francisco Chapter of the English-Speaking Union, essay contest judge; Association for the Study of Afro-American Life and History; College Language Association; American Association of University Women; Friends of Johnson C Smith University; NAACP; Spelman College National Alumnae Association; Sanderson Trustee Board of the San Francisco African-American Historical and Cultural Society, Sanderson board; Black Women Stirring the Waters; San Francisco Bay Area Chapter, Association for the Study of Classical African Civilizations; Langston Hughes society; SF CAAAS; Charlotte Hawkins Brown Memorial State Historic Site; Alpha Kappa Alpha Sorority; Junos and Junos West. **Honors/Awds:** Junos "West"; Mothers Day Speaker Morehouse Coll 1959; Merrill Fac Fellowship Morehouse Coll 1959; NCTE Study Abroad Cert 1959; Hist PTA, Geo Washington Sr HS 1969-70; articles publ in JET Mag, Atlanta Daily World, Berkeley Post, San Francisco Sun Reporter, San Francisco Courier, CLA Jrnl, Black Art, IntlQuarterly, NAACP Crisis, Good News (Laney Coll Mag), other school pubs; African Heritage Course Univ of IFE 1970; Lge Fellowship Peralta Coll Dist 1972;Laney Coll Fac Sen Grants for studies in Greece, Crete, Egypt & Turkey, Laney Coll 1976; publ "The Jrnl of Negro History", "The Langston Hughes Review", "Black Women in Antiquity" Jrnl African Civilizations; "Unsung Hero" of SF Public Library, 1993. **Special Achievements:** Has written articles that have appeared in Black Art: An International Quarterly; Langston Hughes Review; Journal of Negro History; CIA Journal; Black Women in Antiquity; created a special collection of books, journals, articles, programs, and monographs at the African American Historical Society.

MCKINNON, DARLENE LORRAINE

Government official. **Personal:** Born Jul 28, 1943, Baltimore, MD; daughter of Ruth Estelle Thurston McClaine and Percy Otto McClaine Jr; divorced. **Educ:** University of Redlands, BA (summa cum laude), business management, 1984. **Career:** The Rouse Company, new projects, special assistant to director, 1973-75; Baltimore Council for Equal Business Opportunity, Procurement Services, director, 1975-79; US Small Business Administration, director, SCORE Program, women's representative, 1983-92, deputy district director, 1992-. **Orgs:** YWCA, board member, 1990; Scripps Hospital Women's Health Source, board member, 1990-; San Diego Community College District, advisory board, 1992-; San Diego Housing Commission, advisory board, 1992-. **Honors/Awds:** San Diego Business Journal, One of The San Diego 100 Business and Community Leaders, 1992; Soroptomist International, Woman of Distinction, 1992; Small Business Administration, Regional & District Employee of the Year, 1991, 1986, Women's Business Representative of the Year, 1988; Women's Times, Wonder Woman in Business, 1990. **Special Achievements:** Founding member, National Association of Women Business Owners, San Diego, 1990. **Business Addr:** Deputy District Director, US Small Business Administration, 455 Market St 6th Fl, San Francisco, CA 94105-2420, (415)744-8475.

MCKINNON, ISAIAH

Chief of police. **Personal:** Born Jun 21, 1943, Mongomery, AL; son of Cota & Lula McKinnon; married Patrice, Oct 18, 1975; children: Jeffrey, Jason. **Educ:** Mercy College of Detroit, BA, history/law enforcement, 1976; Univ of Detroit, MA, criminal justice, 1978; Michigan State Univ, PhD, administration/higher ed, 1981; FBI Academy, police mgmt & procedures, 1987. **Career:** Detroit Police Dept, inspector, 1965-84; Univ of Det, dir, public safety, 1984-89; Renaissance Center, dir of security, 1989-93; Det Police Dept, chief of police, 1994-. **Orgs:** Leadership, Management Advisory Bd; FBI National Academy Grads Org; International Assn of Chiefs of Police; American Society for Industrial Security; Citizens Crime Watch, pres; Detroit Police Officers Assn; Lieutenants & Sergeants Assn. **Special Achievements:** Michigan Trial Lawyers Assn, faculty member; Alabama State Univ, domestic violence; Natl Organization of Black Law Enforcement Officers, dom violence; Michigan Assn of Chiefs of Police, lectured on personal safety. **Military Serv:** US Air Force, sgt, 1961-65. **Business Addr:** Chief of Police, Detroit Police Department, 1300 Beaubien, Room 303, Detroit, MI 48226, (313)596-1800.

MCKINNON, PATRICE

County executive. **Personal:** marrIed Isaiah McKinnon; children: Jeffrey, Jason. **Career:** Wayne County, budget dir, currently. **Business Addr:** Budget Director, Wayne County, 304 Wayne Co Bldg, 600 Randolph, Detroit, MI 48226, (313)224-5061.

MCKINZIE, BARBARA A.

CFO, certified public accountant. **Personal:** Born Jan 2, 1954, Ada, OK; daughter of Johnnie M Moses Watson and Leonard T McKinzie. **Educ:** East Central OK Univ, BS (Cum Laude) 1976; Northwestern University, MM, 1997. **Career:** Touche Ross & Co, supervisor & health care coord 1976-83; DeLoitte Haskins and Sells, mgr 1983-85; Alpha Kappa Alpha Sor Inc, exec dir 1985-87; Coopers & Lybrand, mgr 1987-94; Whitman Corp, Internal Audit, dir, 1994-96; Illinois Toll Authority, chief of internal audit, 1996-. **Orgs:** Mem Amer Inst of Certified Public Accountants 1978; bd mem Natl Assoc of Black Accountants 1980; minority recruitment subcomm IL Soc of CPA's 1983; mem Amer Women's Soc of CPA's 1986. **Honors/Awds:** Outstanding Alumnae of East Central OK Univ 1976; Valuable Contribution Awd Oklahoma City 1983; Outstanding Young Woman of Amer 1980, 1985. **Home Addr:** 1635 East Hyde Park Blvd, Chicago, IL 60615. **Business Addr:** Illinois Toll Authority, 1 Authority Dr, Downers Grove, IL 60515.

MCKISSACK, FREDRICK LEM, SR.

Writer, researcher. **Personal:** Born Aug 12, 1939, Nashville, TN; son of Lewis Winter & Bessye Fiser McKissack; married Patricia C McKissack, Dec 12, 1964; children: Fredrick L II, Robert Lewis, John Patrick. **Educ:** TN State Univ, Nashville, BS, engineering, 1964. **Career:** Nimrod Corp, owner, 1972-80; All-Writing Servs, co-owner, currently. **Honors/Awds:** Univ of Missouri, honorary doctorate; C S Lewis Silver Medals (2), 1985; A Long Hard Journey—The Story of Pullman Porter won the Coretta Scott King Award for Text and the Jane Addams Peace Award; Ain't I a Woman won the Coretta Scott King Honor book, an ALA Notable title, a NCSS Notable title, and winner of the Boston Globe-Horn Book Awrd for Nonfiction; NAACP, Image Award, for work in children's literature, 1994. **Special Achievements:** Books include: Rookie Readers, Messy Bessey, Who is Coming?, Who is Who?, Bugs, and Constance, Stumbles, Its the Truth, Christopher and Abram, Abram, Where are We Going?; Flossie and the Fox; A Long Hard Journey—The Story of the Pullman Porter; Ain't I a Woman; numerous others. **Military Serv:** US Marine Corps, sgt, 1957-59. **Business Phone:** (314)725-6218.

MCKISSACK, LEATRICE BUCHANAN

Company executive. **Personal:** Born Jul 27, 1930, Keytesville, MO; daughter of Catherine Brummell Buchanan and Archie Buchanan; married William DeBerry McKissack, Oct 31, 1949 (deceased); children: Andrea McKissack Krupski, Cheryl, Deryl. **Educ:** Fisk University, BS, mathematics, 1951; Tennessee State University, MS, psychology, 1957. **Career:** Metropolitan Board of Education, teacher, 1952-69; McKissack and McKissack, chief executive officer, 1983-. **Orgs:** Federal Reserve Bank Board, advisory board member, 1990-95; State of Tennessee Employment Security, advisory board member, 1991-; Commissioner-Metro Planning Commission, board member, 1989-95; Nashville Chamber of Commerce, 1983-; United Way, board member, 1983-; National Conference of Christians and Jews, 1995-; Cheekwood Fine Arts Center, board member, 1991-; Nashville Symphony Guild, life member, 1975; Nashville Symphony Bd, 1997-; Tenn Bd of Economic Growth, governor's appointee, 1995-; Fisk Univ, bd of trustees, 1995-; Chamber of Commerce, bd of governors, 1995-;

YMCA advisory bd, 1994-. **Honors/Awds:** Department of Commerce, President Bush, National Female Entrepreneur, 1990; Howard University, Business Award, 1993; NAFEO, Distinguished Alumni Award, 1991; State of Tennessee, Business Woman of the Year, 1990, Women Owned Business of the Year, 1990. **Home Addr:** 6666 Brookmont Terrace, Nashville, TN 37205, (615)352-8546. **Business Addr:** Chief Executive Officer, McKissack & McKissack, 2014 Broadway, Ste 260, Nashville, TN 37203, (615)327-0455.

MCKISSACK, PATRICIA CARWELL
Writer. **Personal:** Born Aug 9, 1944, Smyrna, TN; daughter of Robert & Erma Carwell; married Fredrick L McKissack Sr, Dec 12, 1964; children: Fredrick L II, Robert, John. **Educ:** TN State Univ, BS, English, 1964; Webster Univ, MA, early childhood lit and media programming, 1975. **Career:** Concordia Publishing Co, editor, 1975-81; Nipher Jr High School, teacher, 1969-75; Forest Park Coll, instructor, 1977-84; Univ of Missouri, instructor, English, 1979-84; Lindenwood Coll, instructor, English, 1977-. **Honors/Awds:** Univ of Missouri, honorary doctorate; C S Lewis Silver Medals (2), 1985; A Long Hard Journey—The Story of Pullman Porter won the Coretta Scott King Award for text and the Jane Addams Peace Award; Ain't I A Woman won the Coretta Scott King Honor book, an ALA Notable title, a NCSS Notable title, and winner of the Boston Globe—Horn Book Award for Nonfiction; NAACP, Image Award, for work in children's literature, 1994; numerous others. **Special Achievements:** Books include: Rookie Readers, messy Bessey, Who is Coming?, Who is Who?, Bugs, and Constance Stumbles, Its the Truth, Christopher and abram, Abram, Where are We Going?, Flossie and the fox, A Long Hard Journey — The Story of the Pullman Proter; Ain't I a Woman; numerous others. **Business Phone:** (314)725-6218.

MCKISSACK, PERRI (PEBBLES)
Vocalist. **Personal:** Born 1965; married Antonio Reid, 1989; children: Ashley, Aaron. **Career:** Vocalist; recordings include: "Pebbles," "Always"; Savvy Records, pres, 1993-. **Special Achievements:** Two platinum albums: Always, Pebbles.

MCKISSACK, WILLIAM DEBERRY. See Obituaries section.

MCKISSICK, EVELYN WILLIAMS
Commissioner. **Personal:** Born Aug 19, 1923, Asheville, NC; married Floyd Bixler; children: Joycelyn, Andree, Floyd Jr. **Career:** Soul City Sanitary Dist, comsnr chmn; Educ Enrichment Prog, dir 1970-72; Pre Sch Educ & Rec Bd , dir. **Orgs:** Mem Soul City Cultural Arts & Hist Soc 1975-; bd mem Soul City Pks & Rec Assn 1976-; bd mem Interfaith Comm of Soul City 1975-; mem Durham Comm on Negro Affairs; mem CORE; mem Durham Rec Dept; Union Bapt Ch Youth Prog; NAACP; vice chrm Warren Cnty Rep Party; mem Black Elected Officials. **Business Addr:** PO Box 128, Soul City, NC 27553.

MCKISSICK, FLOYD B., JR.
Attorney. **Personal:** Born Nov 21, 1952, Durham, NC; son of Floyd B Sr and Evelyn Williams McKissick; married Cynthia Heath McKissick, Jun 29, 1990; children: Alicia Michelle, Floyd B III, and Graison Heath. **Educ:** Clark Univ, AB, 1974; Univ of NC at Chapel Hill, School of City and Regional Planning, MRP, 1975; Harvard Univ, Kennedy School of Government, MPA, 1979; Duke Univ School of Law, JD, 1983. **Career:** Floyd B McKissick Enterprises, asst planner, 1972-74; Soul City Com, director of planning, 1974-79; Peat, Marwick, & Mitchell, management consultant, 1980-81; Dickstein, Shapiro & Morin, attorney, 1984-87; Faison and Brown, attorney, 1987-88; Spaulding & Williams, attorney, 1988-89; McKissick & McKissick, attorney, 1989-. **Orgs:** Durham City Council, 1994-; NC Center for the Study of Black History, president; Land Loss Prevention Project, past chairman, board member; Durham City-Council Planning Commission; St Joseph's Historical Society, board member; Museum of Life and Science, board member; Durham City of Adjustments; Rural Advancement Foundation International, board member. **Special Achievements:** Co-author of Guidebook on Attracting Foreign Investment to the US, 1981; Author of When an Owner can Terminate a Contract Due to Delay, 1984; Author of Mighty Warrior, Floyd B McKissick, Sr, 1995. **Business Phone:** (919)490-5373.

MCKISSICK, MABEL F. RICE
Librarian, media specialist. **Personal:** Born Jun 12, 1921, Union, SC; daughter of Charity M Rice and Phillip H Rice; married Wallace T McKissick; children: Wallace T Jr. **Educ:** Knoxville Coll, AB 1943; SC State Coll, summer courses library science 1949-50; Tchrs Coll Columbia Univ, MA 1954; Sch of Library Serv Columbia Univ, MSLS 1966. **Career:** Sims HS, tchr/librarian 1943-48, librarian 1948-68; New London Jr HS, librarian/media specialist 1968-79; New London HS, librarian/media specialist 1979-90. **Orgs:** Nom comm Natl Cncl of Negro Women 1979-, Amer Assn of Univ Women 1978-; 2nd vice pres 1969-, pres 1988-90, Delta Kappa Gamma, Eta Chap 1969-; Delta Sigma Theta Sor 1943-; Educ Assns NEA, CEA, NLEA; Library Assns ALA, AASL,CEMA, NEEMA; founding mem CEMA 1976-; adv comm NLEA 1985-; mem CEA County Council Comm 1985-; mem New England Assn of Schools & Coll Evaluation Com 1986-. **Honors/Awds:** First black pres, Connecticut Sch Library Assn, 1973-74; "Black Women of CT, Achievements Against the Odds" Exhibit Hartford CT Historical Soc 1984; Outstanding Woman of the Yr Awd CT Div Amer Assoc of Univ Women 1982; Rheta A Clark Awd CT Educ Media Assoc 1980; Outstanding Library Media Svcs; Coretta Scott King Awd ALA/SRRT Comm 1974; Dr Martin Luther King Jr Community Serv Awd 1981; New Haven Alumnae Chap Delta Sigma Theta Educ Devel Awd 1985; Citation Office of the Mayor City of New London for Outstanding Educ Achievements in Educ 1985; State of CT General Assembly Official Citation in Educ Achievements 1985; Community Serv Awd as an Educator Miracle Temple Church 1985; Cert of Apprec NEASC Commiss on Public Schools as a Vstg Comm Mem 1986; CEMA Service Award,Connecticut Educationaldia Assn, 1988.

MCKITT, WILLIE, JR.
Law enforcement official (retired). **Educ:** Troy State University, criminal justice, psych, sociology. **Career:** Montgomery County Sheriff's Dept, jailer, 1968-70, Civil Division, 1970-77, asst jail administrator, 1977-81; Montgomery County Detention Facility, administrator, 1981-92. **Orgs:** FOP. **Special Achievements:** First African-American to be employed by the Montgomery County Sheriff's Department, 1968. **Military Serv:** US Air Force, twenty years. **Business Phone:** (205)832-4985.

MCKNIGHT, ALBERT J.
Financier, clergyman. **Personal:** Born Aug 8, Brooklyn, NY. **Educ:** St Mary's Sem, BA, BT; rcvd sem training under Holy Ghost Fathers in PA & CT. **Career:** So Cooperative Devel Fund Lafayette, LA, pres 1970-84; Southern Development Foundation 1972-. **Orgs:** Served on numerous LA econ devel task forces, So Consumers' Coop, Goals for LA Task Force, US Ofc of Econ Opty Task Force, People's Enterprise Inc 1970-; diocesan dir Credit Unions 1963; former assoc with Our Lady of Lourdes, Immaculate Heart of Mary & St Martin de Porres Chs in LA; helped organize over 10 credit unions in LA; bd mem of the Natl Consumer Coop Bank 1978-; chairperson of Consumer Coop Dev Corp; pastor of Holy Ghost Catholic Ch Opelousas, LA. **Business Addr:** President, So Development Foundation, PO Box 3005, Lafayette, LA 70501.

MCKNIGHT, BRIAN
Vocalist. **Personal:** marrIed; children: two. **Career:** Singer, currently. **Special Achievements:** Albums: Brian Mcknight, I Remember You; Anytime; Songs include: "One Last Cry", "On the Down Low", "Crazy Love", "Still in Love", "Love Is" (duet with Vanessa Williams), "You Will Know" (Black Men United), "I'll Take Her" with Ill Al Skratch. **Business Addr:** Vocalist, I Remember You, c/o Mercury Records, 17066 Oak View Dr, Encino, CA 91436, (818)752-6055.

MCKNIGHT, JAMES
Professional football player. **Personal:** Born Jun 17, 1972, Orlando, FL; children: David. **Educ:** Liberty Univ, criminal justice major. **Career:** Seattle Seahawks, wide receiver, 1994-. **Business Addr:** Professional Football Player, Seattle Seahawks, 11220 NE 53rd St, Kirkland, WA 98033, (206)827-9777.

MCKNIGHT, REGINALD
Author, educator. **Personal:** Born Feb 26, 1956, Furstenfeldbruck; son of Pearl M Anderson McKnight and Frank McKnight; married Michele Davis McKnight, Aug 25, 1985; children: 2. **Educ:** Pikes Peak Comm Coll, Colorado Springs, CO, AA, general studies, 1978; CO Coll, Colorado Springs, CO, BA, African Lit, 1981; Univ of Denver, Denver, CO, MA, English, 1984. **Career:** Univ of Pittsburgh, Pittsburgh, PA, asst prof of English, 1988-91; Carnegie Mellon Univ, Pittsburgh, PA, assoc prof of English, 1991-. **Orgs:** PEN American, 1989-; African Lit Assn, 1989-. **Honors/Awds:** O Henry Prize, 1990; Dr of Humane Letters, CO Coll, 1990; Kenyon Review Award for Literary Excellence, 1989; Special Citation: Pen Hemingway Foundation, 1989; Drue Heinz Prize for Literature, Univ of Pittsburgh, 1988; Bernice M Slate Award for Fiction, Univ of Nebraska, 1985; Thomas J Watson Fnd Fellow, 1981; Member, Phi Beta Kappa, 1981. **Military Serv:** USMC, corporal E-4, 1973-76. **Business Addr:** Professor, Dept of English, Carnegie-Mellon University, Baker Hall, Pittsburgh, PA 15213.

MCKOY, CLEMENCIO AGUSTINO
Editor. **Personal:** Born Sep 9, 1928, Oriente, Cuba; married Jean Delores Lewis; children: Andre, Clemencio II, Gregorio. **Educ:** Univ of London, BSc; London, FCI. **Career:** Minority News Digest Inc, editor-in-chief; PR Communications, pres 1975; Black Sports Inc, advertising dir 1972; Culinary Revs Inc, mgng editor 1968; Nat Publ House, exec vice pres dir 1961. **Orgs:** Mem Pub Relat Soc of Am; v chmn Black Athletes Hall of Fame 1975f dir Black Audio Network Inc; orgnzr coord Intl Inductions to Black Athletes Hall of Fame 1975; co-fdr 1st W Indian Standing Com African Afrs. **Honors/Awds:** Co-publr The Jamaican Housewife, The Jamaican Builder, The Jamaican Nat Trade Rev; author This Man Smith.

MCKYER, TIMOTHY BERNARD
Professional football player. **Personal:** Born Sep 5, 1963, Orlando, FL. **Educ:** Texas-Arlington. **Career:** San Francisco 49ers, defensive back, 1986-89; Miami Dolphins, 1990; Atlanta Falcons, 1991-92, 1996; Detroit Lions, 1993; Pittsburgh Steelers, 1994; Carolina Panthers, 1995; Denver Broncos, 1997-. **Business Addr:** Professional Football Player, Denver Broncos, 13655 Broncos Pkwy, Englewood, CO 80112, (303)649-9000.

MCLAREN, DOUGLAS EARL
Management consultant, attorney. **Personal:** Born Nov 3, 1948, Wilmington, NC; son of Huldah E McLaren and Austen E McLaren; married Rosemarie P Pagon; children: Damion Earl, Kaili Elizabeth. **Educ:** Univ of the West Indies, BSc Eng 1970; McGill Univ, MBA 1974; Harvard Law School, JD 1984. **Career:** Hue Lyew Chin, engr 1970-72; Peat Marwick Mitchell, management consultant 1974-76; Jamaica Natl Investment Co, project officer 1976-78; Exxon Intl Co, planning analyst 1979-84; ICF Kaiser Engineers, project manager, 1984-. **Orgs:** Admitted to NY and DC Bars 1985; mem Amer Bar Assoc 1985; mem Panel of Commercial Arbitrators of the Amer Arbitration Assn. **Home Addr:** 1825 Tulip Street, NW, Washington, DC 20012, (202)291-5383.

MCLAUGHLIN, ANDREE NICOLA
Educator, poet. **Personal:** Born Feb 12, 1948, White Plains, NY; daughter of Willie Mae Newman McLaughlin and Joseph Lee McLaughlin. **Educ:** Cornell Univ, BS 1970; Univ of MA-Amherst, MEd 1971, EdD 1974. **Career:** Medgar Evers College/CUNY, asst prof/project dir 1974-77, chairperson 1977-79, dean of administration and assoc prof, 1979-82, planning coord of Women's Studies Rsch & Develop 1984-89, professor of Humanities, 1986-; University of London Institute of Education, distinguished visiting scholar, 1986; Hamilton Coll, Jane Watson Irwin Visiting Prof of Women's Studies, 1989-91; Medgar Evers College/CUNY, prof of literature & language/ prof of interdisciplinary studies, 1992-, Office of International Women's Affairs, director, 1996-. **Orgs:** Bd mem, Where We At, Black Women Artists, 1979-87; mem Natl Women's Studies Assoc 1980-84, Amer Assoc of Univ Profs 1982-; founding intl coord, Intl Resource Network of Women of African Descent, 1982-85, founding mem Sisterhood in Support of Sisters in South Africa 1984-; adv bd mem Sisterhood of Black Single Mothers 1984-86; founding intl coordinator, Cross-Cultural Black Women's Studies Inst, 1987-; chair, Editorial Bd, Network: A Pan African Women's Forum (journal), 1987-91; mem, Policy & Publication Comm, The Feminist Press, CUNY, 1988-. **Honors/Awds:** Natl Endowment for the Humanities Fellow, 1976, 1979, 1984, 1989, 1993; 25 articles published; Amer Council on Educ, Fellow in Acad Admin, 1980-81; Andrew W Mellon Fellow, CUNY Graduate School & Univ Center, 1987; Co-editor, Wild Women in the Whirlwind: Afra-American Culture & the Contemporary Literary Renaissance, Rutgers Univ Press, 1990. Author, Double Dutch, poetry, 1989; author, "Black Women's Studies in America," 1989; author, "Urban Politics in the Higher Education of Black Women," 1988; author, "The International Nature of the Southern African Women's Struggles," 1988; author, "Unfinished Business of the Sixties: Black Women on the Front Line," 1990; author, "Black Women, Identity and the Quest for Humanhood and Wholeness," 1990; author, Through the Barrel of Her Consciousness: Contemporary Black Women's Literature and Activism in Cross Cultural Perspective, 1994. Susan Koppelman Book Award for Best Edited Feminist work in Popular/ American Culture Studies, 1990; author The Impact of the Black Consciousness and Women's Movements on Black Women's Identity: Intercontinental Empowerment, 1995. **Business Addr:** Professor, Medgar Evers College, City University of New York, 1650 Bedford Ave, Brooklyn, NY 11225.

MCLAUGHLIN, BENJAMIN WAYNE
Corporate manager. **Personal:** Born Feb 24, 1947, Danville, VA; son of Lucy S McLaughlin and Daniel S McLaughlin; married Gwen Stafford; children: LaShandra, Sonya. **Educ:** Johnson C Smith Univ, Charlotte NC, graduated 1969. **Career:** Lockheed Martin, buyer 1969-70, maintenance engineering tech asst 1970-76, ORGDP affirmative action coord 1975-79, wage and salary associate 1979, ORGDP employment dept supervisor 1979-81, barrier mfg div supt 1981-82, maintenance engrg dept supt 1982-83, ORGDP wage and salary dept head 1983-84, energy systems dir of minority prog devel 1984-86, personnel mgr Portsmouth OH gaseous diffusion plant 1986-95; admistrative support manager, 1995-. **Orgs:** President, Ross County (Ohio) Gideons; Commissioner, Chillicothe, Ohio, Civil Service Commission; mem, Omega Psi Phi; Ionic Lodge #6, F & AM. **Honors/Awds:** Distinguished Serv Award, State of Tennessee, 1980; Martin Marietta Energy Systems Community Serv Award, 1985; Omega Man of the Year Award, Zeta Gamma Gamma Chap of the Omega Psi Phi Frat, 1985; Light From the Hill Award, Knoxville College, 1985; Jefferson Award for Community Service, 1986. **Home Addr:** 1055 Edgewood Dr, Chillicothe, OH 45601.

MCLAUGHLIN, DAVID
Protozoologist, educator. **Personal:** Born Nov 1, 1934, Sumter, SC; son of Iris Ladson McLaughlin and Arthur S McLaughlin; divorced. **Educ:** Clark Coll, BS 1956; Howard Univ, MS 1962,

PhD 1965. **Career:** Howard Univ, research asst USPHS grantee; NSF, teaching & rsch supr; summer research participant for HS students 1957-58, 1958-64; USPHS grantee, research assoc 1962-65; supr summer undergrad rsch participation 1965-66; IN Research Lab, prof zoology 1965-; NASA Wallops Sta Bio-Space Tech, post-doctoral studies 1965. **Orgs:** Gemini Summary Conf NASA Manned Space Craft Ctr Houston; participant 3rd Intl Congress on Protozoology Leningrad, USSR 1969; mem Soc Protozoologist; NY Acad Sci; Amer Inst Biol Sci; AAAS; Amer Micros Soc; Amer Soc Zoologists; mem NAACP. **Honors/Awds:** Sigma Xi; Beta Chi Kappa; Omega Psi Phi; contrib articles to prof journals. **Business Addr:** Prof of Zoology, Howard Univ, E E Just, G-37A, 415 College St, Washington, DC 20059.

MCLAUGHLIN, DOLPHY T.
Attorney. **Personal:** Born Jul 10, 1922; married Nora Belle Facey; children: Norman Anthony. **Educ:** Northwestern Univ, 1949-52; Loyola Univ Sch of Law, LLB 1955. **Career:** Brown, Brown, Greene & McLaughlin, attorney 1956-73; Victory Mutual Life Ins Co, asst gen counsel & mem bd dir 1962-67; Met San Dist of Greater Chicago, mem civil serv bd 1966-67, prin asst atty 1967-73; Govt of Jamaica, consul of Jamaica 1969-; Met San Dist of Greater Chicago, head asst attorney 1973-. **Orgs:** Pres Amer West Indian Assn 1962-67; mem Cook Co Bar Assn 1956-; mem Natl Bar Assn 1973-; mem Amer Bar Assn; Phi Alpha Delta Legal Frat 1956-. **Honors/Awds:** Cert of Recognition Superior Pub Serv Award natl Civil Serv League 1971; Man of the Year Jamaican-Amer Caribbean Quarterly Mag 1982; Order of Distinction Govt of Jamaica 1983.

MCLAUGHLIN, EURPHAN
Government official. **Personal:** Born Jun 2, 1936, Charlotte, NC. **Educ:** Univ of MD Baltimore Coll of Commerce, 1958; Univ of Baltimore, AA 1963; Univ of Baltimore, LLB 1969; Univ of Baltimore, JD 1969; Univ of Baltimore, BS 1972; Univ of Baltimore, MBA (23 credits completed). **Career:** State of MD Dept of Personnel, asst sec for employee serv 1979-; MD Commn on Human Realtions, dep dir 1976-79; State of MD Dept of Health & Mental Hygiene, EEO supr 1975-76; MD Commn on Human Relations, intergroup relations rep 1973-75; Baltimore City Police Dept, intelligence div officer 1959-73. **Orgs:** Real estate asso & bd mem Century 21/Otis Warren & Co 1971-; mem NAACP; Nat Assn of Human Rights Workers; MD Assn of Equal Opportunity Personnel; Nat& MD Assn of Realestate Brokers; Baltimore Bd of Realtors. **Honors/Awds:** Nine accommendations commendations City Police Dept 1959-73; award of merit MD Commn on Human Relations 1978; award of merit Staff of MD Commn on Human Relations 1978. **Military Serv:** USAF a/2c 39 years. **Business Addr:** MD Dept of Personnel, 301 W Preston St, Baltimore, MD 21201.

MCLAUGHLIN, GEORGE W.
Educator. **Personal:** Born Feb 14, 1932, Petersburg, VA; married Sadie Thurston; children: Wesley, George Jr, Avis. **Educ:** St Paul's Coll, BS Educ 1957; VA State Coll, 1958; Univ of VA, MEd, EdD 1970; Bank St Coll Univ of PA; Amer Bible Inst, DD 1974. **Career:** DE State Coll, dir of student teaching 1966-72, chmn educ 1972-75; St Paul's Coll, chmn educ & psych. **Orgs:** Assoc Blvd Cab Co 1962-; pastor Wayland Baptist Church 1974-; pres L&M Const Co 1976-; v chmn Alberta Child-Care Ctr 1978-; mem LA Cty Law Enforcement Comm 1980; vice pres Lawrenceville Optimist Intl 1982-84; pres Epsilon Omicron Lambda, Alpha Phi Alpha 1980-85. **Honors/Awds:** Outstanding Citizen Awd LA Emancipation Org 1979; Faculty of the Year St Paul's Coll 1979; Alpha Man of the Year Alpha Phi Alpha Frat 1982; Disting Serv Awd Optimist Intl 1983. **Military Serv:** AUS maj 1952-72. **Home Addr:** Rt 3 Box 1635, Trevilians, VA 23170. **Business Addr:** Coordinator of Gifted Education, Mecklenburg County Public Schools, PO Box 190, Boydton, VA 23917.

MCLAUGHLIN, JACQUELYN SNOW
Educational administrator. **Personal:** Born Aug 12, 1943, Camden, NJ; daughter of Mr & Mrs Arlington Reynolds Sr; married Herman McLaughlin; children: Jevon, Jacques. **Educ:** Shaw Univ Raleigh NC, AB Sociology 1965; Univ of Bridgeport CT, couns cert 1965; Glassboro St Coll New Jersey, MA Couns 1972; Rutgers Univ New Jersey, DEd 1976. **Career:** Camden Co Coll, dean student affairs, 1975-, dir EOF program 1971-75, counselor 1970-71; Washington Elementary School, teacher 1966-70; Div New Jersey Employment Serv, counselor 1965-66. **Orgs:** Team mem Middle St Accrdtn Assn 1980-; pres NJ St Deans of Stud 1980-; Nat Assn for Foreign Students; Assn of Coll Admnstrs; Alpha Kappa Alpha Sor; Juvenil e Resource Center 1986-89; ad hoc comm mem, Affirmative Action 1989; board of directors, YWCA, 1990-93; board of directors, National Council on Black American Affairs Assn of College Admin, 1990-93; New England Accreditation Association, 1992. **Honors/Awds:** Plaque of Outstanding Serv to Educ Oppor Fund Program, Camden Co Coll 1976; Certif Cited in Bicentennial Vol, Comm Leaders & Noteworthy Amer, 1976; chosen Outstndng Woman in Amer 1977; mem Delta Kappa Pi Honor Soc; Exec Leadership Inst, League for Innovations in the Community Coll; Leaders for the 80s Inst for Leadership Devel; Honorary Mem of Phi Theta Kappa Honor Fraternity; Outstanding Educator of the Year, Camden Church Organization, 1978. **Business Addr:** Dean of Student Affairs, Camden County College, PO Box 200 Wilson Hall East 105, Blackwood, NJ 08012.

MCLAUGHLIN, JOHN BELTON
Physician (retired). **Personal:** Born Jul 3, 1903, Birmingham, AL; son of Hattie B McLaughlin and Amasa A McLaughlin; married Mildred Woods; children: John Jr, William A, Harriet Stafford. **Educ:** Talladega Coll, AB 1928; Fisk U, Advanced Study 1929; Meharry Med Coll, MD 1933. **Career:** Self-employed, retired physician; WW I promoting sale of US War Bonds, 4 minute speaker 1917-18; dr's aide influenza epidemic 1918; L Richard Meml Hosp, 2 yr intership 1933-35; med & surgery prac 1935; L Richard Meml Hosp, sec of med staff 1952-54; L Richardson Hosp Staff, pres 1962-63. **Orgs:** Mem Greensboro C of C 1965; Greensboro Men's Club 1942; sec pres 1950's; Hayes-Taylor YMCA 1948; Omega Psi Phi Frat 1926; mem Old N State Med Soc 1935-77; Natl Med Soc 1940-77; mem St James United Presbyterian Church of Greensboro; regular mem NAACP 1942-. **Honors/Awds:** Cert of award & honor for 40 yrs devotion & serv to Omega Frat 1965; cert of award Free Med Care given to poor & indigent patients Natl Med Assn 1963; received the Meharry Medical Coll President's Awd for 50 years of Serv to Mankind 1933-83; Greensboro Men's Club and Citizens of Greensboro, North Carolina, Certificate of Appreciation, 1988. **Business Addr:** Physician, 1709 S Benbow Rd, Greensboro, NC 27406.

MCLAUGHLIN, KATYE H.
Automobile dealer. **Personal:** Born Jan 31, 1943, Richland Parish, LA; daughter of Etta Stephens Harris and Johnnie Harris Sr; married Joseph C McLaughlin, Aug 27, 1955 (died 1984); children: Brian David, Bridget Diane. **Educ:** Kensington University, Glendale, CA, PhD, 1983; Antioch Grad School of Education, Washington, DC, MA, 1975; District of Columbia Teachers Coll, Washington, DC, BS, 1963. **Career:** District of Columbia Board of Education, Washington, DC, teacher, 1963-84; McLaughlin Olds Inc, Capitol Hgts, MD, pres/CEO, 1984-; Penguin Unity Enterprises, Inc, Washington, DC, pres/CEO, 1996-. **Orgs:** Member, Phi Delta Kappa Sorority, 1980-; board of directors, Langston University, 1992; member, International Club, 1991; National Political Congress of Black Women, 1992. **Honors/Awds:** Prince Georges Ed Support Advisory Council Inc, Outstanding Service bd of directors, 1989; Outstanding Black Business Leader in MD, The Baltimore Sun Newspaper, 1987-89; Business Woman of the Year, Prince Georges Minority Development Off, 1986; Ertha M M White, Women's Achievement Award, Natl Bus League, 1985; Chairperson United Negro College Fund Telethon, Washington Metro Area, 1985, 1986; Greeting Card Association, 1997. **Business Addr:** Pres/CEO, Penguin Unity Enterprises, Inc, PO Box 42642, Washington, DC 20015, (202)363-3884.

MCLAUGHLIN, LAVERNE LANEY
Educator, librarian. **Personal:** Born Jul 29, 1952, Ft Valley, GA; daughter of Gladys Slappy Laney and John Laney; married Frederick; children: Frederick Laney. **Educ:** Spelman Coll, BA (cum laude) 1974; Altanta U, MSLS (with honors) 1975. **Career:** Byron Elem Schl Bryon GA, tchr 1975-76; GA SW State Univ, Americus GA, assoc prof/librarian l976-. **Orgs:** Organist Allen Chapel AME Church 1977-81; pianist St John Baptist Church 1968-; bd of dir, Amer Cancer Soc; American Library Assn; Georgia Library Assn; Southeastern Library Assn; mem Sumter Co Chamber of Commerce/Education Committee 1989; organist, Bethesda Baptist Church, 1992-; Martin Luther King Jr State Holiday Commission of Georgia, 1991-; GA Public Television Advisory Board, 1980-85; Data Base Qualtiy Control Committee Southeastern Library Network, 1981-87. **Honors/Awds:** Andrew Mellon Fellow Atlanta Univ 1974-75; cum laude Spelman Coll 1974; Beta Phi Mu Atlanta Univ 1975; Outstanding Young Women of Amer l983. **Home Addr:** 536 E Jefferson St, Americus, GA 31709. **Business Addr:** Associate Professor, GA Southwestern Coll, James Earl Carter Lib, Americus, GA 31709.

MCLAUGHLIN, MEGAN E.
Social services agency director. **Personal:** chilDren: Afiya McLaughlin-White. **Educ:** Howard Univ, BA 1966, MSW 1968; The Graduate Ctr CUNY, Doctoral work in Cultural Anthropology 1970-72; Columbia Univ Sch of Social Work, Certificate in Advanced Social Welfare 1976, DSW 1981. **Career:** Columbia Univ Sch of Social Work, lecturer 1975-78; The New York Community Trust, prog officer 1978-83, sr program officer 1983-86; Federation of Protestant Welfare Agencies Inc, exec director/CEO, 1986-. **Orgs:** Adv council Columbia Univ Sch of Social Work; mem Caribbean Women's Health Assn; Dept of Social Serv Adv Comm, Health System Agency; Neighborhood Family Serv Continuing Crisis Implementation, Task Force on Human Svcs; Agenda for Children Tomorrow; member, Black Leadership Commission on AIDS; member, Interagency Task Force on Food & Hunger Policy; chair, New York State Assembly Braintrust on Children & Families; advisory committee, Human Resources Administration; advisory committee, New York Department on Aging; member, New York City Partnership; co-chair, Human Services Council. **Honors/Awds:** 8 publications including ''West Indian Immigrants, Their Social Network and Ethnic Identification'' Distribution Columbia Univ 1981. **Home Addr:** 404 W 149th St, New York, NY 10031. **Business Addr:** Executive Director/CEO, Fed of Protestant Welfare Agen, 281 Park Ave South, New York, NY 10010.

MCLAURIN, BENJAMIN PHILIP
Educational administrator. **Personal:** Born Apr 24, 1947, New York, NY. **Educ:** Morehouse College, BA 1969; Rutgers State University, 1970. **Career:** Morehouse College, Career Counseling & Placement, director, currently. **Orgs:** Bd mem, Southern College Placement Assn 1977-78; Georgia College Placement Assn, vice pres 1978, bd mem 1984-85. **Business Addr:** Director, Career Counseling & Placement, Morehouse College, PO Box 5, Atlanta, GA 30314.

MCLAURIN, DANIEL WASHINGTON
Business executive. **Personal:** Born Nov 24, 1940, Philadelphia, PA; son of Dorothy E Foster McLaurin and Abraham McLaurin; married Delores E White, Sep 9, 1961; children: Craig Blair, Brian Keith. **Educ:** LaSalle Coll, BS Marketing 1981. **Career:** Gulf Oil Corp, retail mktr 1970-73, EEO coord 1973-76, dir admin serv 1976-83; Chevron Gulf Oil Corp, dir security & safety 1983-85, supv bldgs mgmt 1985-; Chevron Real Estate Management Co, representative, building projects, 1994-. **Orgs:** Amer Soc for Industrial Security; Society Real Prop Admin; Building Owners & Mgrs Inst International. **Honors/Awds:** Chpl of Four Chplns 1973; Black Amer in Industry 1974. **Home Addr:** 1301 McKinney, Houston, TX 77010.

MCLAURIN, FREDDIE LEWIS, JR.
Educator, mathematician. **Personal:** Born Dec 6, 1943, Jackson, MS; son of Nora L Robinson McLaurin (deceased) and Fred L McLaurin; married Dorothy Loretta Turner, Jul 10, 1965; children: Freddie Lewis III, Tanya Lynn. **Educ:** CA State Univ, BA 1972, STC 1973; Webster Univ, MPA 1977; Univ of CO, MS 1978; Air Univ Air Command & Staff Coll Course, cert 1984-85; University of San Francisco, CA, EdD 1991. **Career:** USAF, electron syst spec 1964-73, auto flt cont syst tech 1973-74, electron syst ofcr 1974-75, logistics ofcr 1975-78; USAF Acad, asst prof dept math sci 1978-82; CA State Univ Fresno Dept Aerospace Studies, asst prof 1982-85; 2049 Comm Group, chf of operations 1985-88; Amer River College, mathematics instructor; Amer River College, math instructor, 1989-91, dean, math, engineering, drafting, 1992; Consumers River Coll, math instructor. **Orgs:** Commandant of Cadets Det 35 AF ROTC 1983-85; pres Black Faculty & Staff Assn 1983-84; The Mathematical Assn of America, 1992-, US Chess Federation, 1993-. **Honors/Awds:** Distinguished Grad Sch Mil Sci 1974; Educ Achievement Award Tactical Air Command USAF 1976. **Military Serv:** USAF Major 1964-88; USAF Meritorious Serv Medal 1982-85; 1st Oakleaf Cluster USAF Commendation Medal 1st Oak Leaf Cluster 1978-82; USAF Commend Medal 1975-77.

MCLAURIN, JASPER ETIENNE
Physician. **Personal:** Born Dec 12, 1927, Braxton, MS; son of Magdeline Hicks McLaurin Jenkins and Jasper McLaurin; married Doris Williams McLaurin, Nov 24, 1956; children: Karen, Pamela, Toni. **Educ:** Wayne State U, BA 1954; Meharry Med Coll, MD 1958; Harvard Med School, basic sci, neurology 1959-62; Univ MI, MS 1964; Mt Carmel Mercy Hosp, intern 1958-59; VA Hosp, resident 1959-62. **Career:** McLaurin Neurodiagnostic PC, ceo, 1993-; Family Rehabilition Clinic, neuologist, 1992-93; New Center Hospital, director of neurological service, 1990-92; private medical practice, 1964-90; Univ MI Med Center, assoc neurologist 1962-65; Univ MI Med Sch, instructor; chf neurology 1963-64; VA Hosp, asst chief neurology 1962; Wayne State Univ, asst prof present; Mt Carmel Mercy Hosp, staff mem; Grace NW; Hutzel; Harper; MI Children's; Receiving Hospital of Detroit, Samaritan Med Center. **Orgs:** Mem Wayne Co Med Soc; MI State Med Soc; AMA; Detroit Med Soc; Nat Med Assn; MI Neurological Assn; Am Acad of Neurology; Amer Neurology Assn; flw Am Coll of Angiology Amer Geriatrics Soc; Am Heart Assn; bd dir Epileptic Ctr MI; World Med Relief 1970, 1972; consult MI State Dept Edn; Detroit Bd Educ; MI Cripple Children's Soc; MI Neuromuscular Inst; Soc Security Admin; mem, Pres Adv Com on Strokes & Heart Disease; Life mem NAACP; Urban League; Omega Psi Phi Frat; mem Nat Yacht Racing Union; bd dir Huron River Heights Property Owners Assn; member, Knights of Columbus. **Military Serv:** USN lt commander, 1946-50. **Home Addr:** 2693 Laurentide, Ann Arbor, MI 48103.

MCLAWHORN, JAMES THOMAS, JR.
Association executive. **Personal:** Born Apr 27, 1947, Greenville, NC; son of Mr & Mrs James T McLawhorn, Sr; married Barbara Campbell; children: Karla, James III, Mark. **Educ:** North Carolina A&T State University, BS, political sci, 1969; Univ of NC Chapel Hill, MA, city & regional planning, 1971; Univ of Miami, MBA, 1977. **Career:** Model Cities, program planning coord 1971-74; City of Charlotte, program mgmt coord 1974-76; First Union Bank, loan devel analyst 1977-78; Democratic Natl Comm of Congressional Black Caucus, admin asst 1978-79; Columbia Urban League Inc, pres, CEO 1979-. **Orgs:** City of Columbia Comm on Minority & Small Bus, Seven Thirty Breakfast Club, Governor's Volunteer Awds Selection Committee, Crime Stoppers, Indian Waters Boy Scouts

of Amer Exec Council; chmn Governor's Primary Health Care Task Force for Richland County; National Black Family Summit, founder; Minority Professional Development Program, founder; Black Male Workshop, Midland, South Carolina, cofounder; Sanders Middle School Improvement Council; Columbia College, board of visitors; Richland County Private Industry Council; CHOICE, study committee; The Alliance for Carolina's Children; South Carolina Educational Policy Council. **Honors/Awds:** Ten for the Future Columbia Record; one of 60 civilian leaders in the nation invited to participate in the Joint Civilian Orientation Conf Sec of Defense 1985; presenter, The South Carolina Great American Family Tour, Aspen Institute, 1988; Governor of South Carolina, Order of The Palmetto 1992; Mayor of Columbia, JT McLawhorn Day Honoree, Nov 28, 1989. **Special Achievements:** Assisted in bringing national attention to the plight of the rural poor and small farmers who were devastated by Hurrican Hugo, 1989; publication: The State of Black South Carolina: An Agenda for the Future, founder. **Business Addr:** President & CEO, Columbia Urban League, Inc, 1400 Barnwell St, Drawer J, Columbia, SC 29250.

MCLEAN, DENNIS RAY
Manufacturing company executive. **Personal:** Born Dec 8, 1951, Fuquay, NC; son of Minnie Mae McLean and Mathew McLean Jr; married Hye Suk McLean Ohm, Jun 24, 1985; children: Louis, Enoch, Tiffany. **Educ:** Midlands Technical College, AA, 1978; Benedict College, BS, 1980. **Career:** US Air Force, air traffic controller, 1970-75; South Carolina Youth Services, family counselor, 1975-82; SKM3/Transax Inc, founder and president/CEO, 1982-. **Orgs:** Greater Columbia Tennis Association, co-founder/public relations officer, 1983-86; Greater Columbia Chamber, 1982-. **Honors/Awds:** Professional Black Women Association, Dr King Living the Dream, 1986; General Dynamics, Administrative Small Business Man of the Year, 1989. **Special Achievements:** Midlands Aviation, Private Pilot Certificate, 1984; Midlands Technical College, CAD Design, 1992; General Dynamics, Top Supplier of the Year, 1992. **Military Serv:** US Air Force, sgt, 1970-75. **Home Addr:** 1800 Broadview Ct, Columbia, SC 29212.

MCLEAN, HELEN VIRGINIA
Educational administrator (retired). **Personal:** Born Jul 23, 1933, Southern Pines, NC; daughter of Nora McLean Jackson and Mitchell McLean. **Educ:** NC Central U, BA 1954; Univ of PA, MA 1956; Univ of FL, EdD 1974. **Career:** St Petersburgh Junior Coll, dir div of communications beginning 1975-; St Petersburg Junior Coll, chairperson directed studies dept 1964-75; Gibbs Junior Coll, chairperson communications dept 1958-64; Wilberforce U, assoc prof languages 1956-58. **Orgs:** Am Assn of Univ Women; Modern Language Assn; Coll English Assn; FL English Assn; Council on Black Am Affairs So Region; various others YWCA; sec exec com Pinellas County Dist Mental Health Bd; mem NAACP; bd United Negro Coll Fund St Petersburg FL; mem The Greater St Petersburg Council on Human Rel; various others. **Honors/Awds:** Tangley Oaks Educ fellowship 1972-73; EDDA-E grad fellowships Univ of FL 1972-74; "Reading-A Total Faculty Commitment," "Career Educ and Gen Edn," "Every Tchr a Reading Tchr," "Teaching Strategies for a Developmental Studies Curriculum"; various other publs. **Home Phone:** (813)736-5143.

MCLEAN, JACQUELINE FOUNTAIN
City official. **Personal:** Born Mar 2, 1944; daughter of Marie Fountain and George Fountain; married James H McLean, 1968; children: Michelle D. **Educ:** American Institute of Banking, 1962-65; Institute of Computer Management, BS, 1968; LaSalle University, 1991-. **Career:** Four Winds & Seven Seas Travel Management, executive vice pres, 1975-1991; City Council, mem 2nd District, City of Baltimore, vice pres, 1987-93; City of Baltimore, city comptroller, 1991-. **Orgs:** Loyola College, trustee, 1985-92; March of Dimes, board mem, 1984-; Baltimore International Visitors Bureau, board mem, 1990-; Friends of Enoch Pratt Libr, board mem, 1982-85; NAACP, life mem, 1977-79; Kidney Foundation, board mem, 1981-83; Baltimore Neighborhoods, Inc, board mem, 1983-91; Girl Scouts of America, board member, 1977-79. **Honors/Awds:** Second Episcopal District, African Methodist Episcopal Church, Public Service Award, 1992; Beta Phi Beta Sorority, Alpha Zeta Chap, Woman of the Year in Government, 1992; Dollars & Sense Magazine, Salute to African-American Business & Prof Women, 1989; Greater Balitmore Board of Realtors, Legislative Achievement Award, 1991; United States Small Business Administration, Minority Business Advocate of the Year, 1990. **Business Phone:** (410)396-4755.

MCLEAN, JOHN ALFRED, JR.
Scientist, educator, educational administrator (retired). **Personal:** Born Nov 8, 1926, Chapel Hill, TN; son of Anna Belle Sheffield McLean and John Alfred McLean; married Esther Ann Bush; children: Jeffery, David, Linda. **Educ:** TN A&I State Univ, BS 1948; Univ of IL, MS 1956, PhD 1959. **Career:** State Bd for Pub Community & Jr Coll, chmn 1965-81; Univ of Detroit Mercy, prof of chem, chmn dept chem & chem engineering 1959-94. **Orgs:** Bd of directors, American Heart Association 1988-. **Honors/Awds:** Comm Service Awd Wayne County Comm Coll 1977; Amer Chemical Soc Certificate for Outstanding Leadership of Detroit Sect of ACS 1982; Annual Disting Serv Awd Detroit Sect of the ACS 1985; Univ of Detroit President's Awd for Excellence in Teaching and Research 1986; mem Phi Delta Kappa, Phi Lambda Upsilon, Sigma Xi. **Military Serv:** US Army, sgt, 1953-55.

MCLEAN, JOHN LENWOOD (JACKIE MCLEAN)
Musician, composer, educator, historian. **Personal:** Born May 17, 1931, New York, NY; married Clarice Simmons; children: Rene, Vernon, Melonae. **Educ:** Attended, A&T Coll. **Career:** The Living Theatre, actor musician 1959-63; played w/ Thelonious Monk, Miles Davis, Bud Powell, Charlie Mingus and others; travelled extensively in Europe & Japan playing concerts & teaching; Univ of Buffalo, teacher w/Archie Shepp; NY State Correctional Dept, bandmaster; recorded on Prestige, Blue Note, United Artists, Steeplechase, RCA & Columbia labels; Joseph Papp's prod "Unfinished Women", composer 1977; Univ of Hartford Hartt Coll of Music, prof 1978; RCA Victor, recording contract 1979; Artists Collective Hartford, creative consultant; Hartt Coll Univ of Hartford, fndr & chmn African-American music dept, professor, currently. **Orgs:** Honorary mem Omega Phi Epsilon Frat; panelist two Natl Endowment for the Arts Progs (expansion arts & jazz prog). **Honors/Awds:** Mobilization for Youth New York City Outstanding Band Leader 1966-67; Downbeat TDWR Awd 1964; Humanities Awd Omega Phi Epsilon Delta Chap 1972; NAACP Awd for Artists Collective; State of CT Arts Awd 1983; Afro-American Museum Philadelphia PA; Jazz Master Awd 1983; BMI Jazz Pioneer Awd 1984; New York Chap of Natl Black MBA Assn Inc Gold Note Jazz Awd 1985; Upper Albany Ave Hartford CT Merchants Assn Special Awd for Dedication to and Preservation of African-American Culture & Service to the Comm; Univ of CA Berkeley Roots Awd 1986; performed in Paris on the commemoration of the bicentennial of the French Revolution, under the patronage of Daniele Mitterand, wife of the President of France, 1989; received a medal as Officier de L'Ordre des Arts Lettres from the Minister of Culture, Jack Lang; honored by New York City's Lincoln Center's clical jazz series. **Special Achievements:** Recordings on Triloka Label, "Dynasty" and "Rites of Passage"; recordings on Polygram, Antilles Label, "Rhythm of the Earth"; noted educator, community activist, celebrated musician and composer. **Business Addr:** Professor, Hartt Coll Univ of Hartford, 200 Bloomfield Ave, West Hartford, CT 06117.

MCLEAN, MABLE PARKER
Educator. **Personal:** Born Mar 19, Cameron, NC; widowed; children: Randall P. **Educ:** Barber Scotia Coll; Johnson C Smith U; Howard U; NW U; Cath Univ of Am; Inst for Educ Mgmt Harvard Univ 1972; Johnson C Smith U, LHD 1976; Rust Coll, LHS 1976; Coll of Granada, LlD; Barber-Scotia, Pedu. **Career:** Barber-Scotia Coll, prof of educ and psychology, coordinator of student teaching 1969-71, chairman dept of elementary educ 1970-71, dean of college 1971-74, apptd interim president 1974, apptd acting president of college 1974, apptd president of the college 1974-. **Orgs:** Mem Assn for Childhood Edn; Assn for Student Teaching; Nat & St NC Assn for Supr & Curriculum Devel; St Coun on Early Childhood Edn; Delta Kappa Gamma Soc of Women Edn; NC Adminstrv Women in Edn; Am Assn of Univ Adminstr; Nat Coun of Adminstrv Women in Edn; mem exec com Metrolina Lung Assn; Dem Women's Org of Cabarrus Co; Alpha Kappa Alpha Sorority Inc; elder John Hall Presb Ch; elected bd of dir Children's Home Soc of NC; past pres United Presb Women's Org of John Hall United Presb Ch; pres Presidents Roundtable of UPC USA; bd dir NAFEO; mem United Bd for Coll Develop; mem United Way of Cabarrus Co; mem exec com NC Assn of Independent Colleges & U; mem exec com NC Assn of Colleges & U. **Honors/Awds:** 7 Honorary Degrees; numerous awds and citations among which are Johnson C Smith Alumni Outstanding Achievement Awd 1977; Disting Alumna Awd 1977; Alumna of the Year Johnson C Smith Univ 1980; Dedicated Service Citation-Consortium on Rsch Training 1982; Disting Service Awd Grambling State Univ 1984; Presidential Scroll for devotion to higher educ by promoting achievement of excellence 1986. **Business Addr:** Interim President, Barber Scotia College, Concord, NC 28025.

MCLEAN, MARQUITA SHEILA MCLARTY
Consultant, management, personnel, environment. **Personal:** Born Aug 5, 1933, Richmond, VA; daughter of Daisey B McLarty and William C McLarty; married Cecil P. **Educ:** VA State Univ, BA 1953; OH State Univ, MA 1956; Univ of Cincinnati, postgrad 1957-69. **Career:** Delaware OH, teacher 1954-57; Robert A Taft HS Cincinnati, teacher 1957-62; Sawyer Jr HS Cincinnati, counselor 1962-65; Withrow HS Cincinnati, counselor 1965-67; Cincinnati Public Sch, assoc guidance serv div 1968-73; Ofc Univ Commitment to Human Resources Univ of Cincinnati, dir 1973-77; Univ Personnel Serv Univ of Cincinnati, assoc sr vice pres 1978-83; OH Environmental Protection Agency, deputy admin 1983-85; McLean Olohan & Associates, principal-in-charge. **Orgs:** Mem Alumni Advisory Council OH State Univ 1971-; past trustee Cincinnati Tech Coll; mem OH Educ Assn; mem Cincinnati Personnel & Guidance Assn; mem Amer School Counselor Assn; mem OH Sch Counselor Assn; mem Nat Assn of Sch Counselors; mem Delta Sigma Theta; mem OH State Alumni Club; mem and vice chairperson Ohio Water Advisory Council, Governor appointee 1985-89; mem Leadership Steering Comm Cincinnati 1986-87; mem Natl & Cincinnati Women Political Caucus; mem Citizens Scholarship Foundation of Amer Inc, Natl Bd of Governors; public manager, State and Local Govt Council 1988-92; mem, Cincinnati Environmental Advisory Council 1988-; charter member, Withrow Dollars for Scholars 1988. **Business Addr:** Principal, McLean Olohan & Associates, 5324 Kenwood Road, Cincinnati, OH 45227.

MCLEAN, MARY CANNON
Special education adminstrator (retired). **Personal:** Born Sep 25, 1912, Cranford, NJ; daughter of Gertrude Moody Cannon (deceased) and Rev Dr David W Cannon Sr (deceased); married Dr Eldon George McLean, Sep 3, 1942; children: Eldon James McLean. **Educ:** Jersey City State Coll, Jersey City NJ, BS, 1935; Columbia Univ Teachers Coll, New York NY, MA, 1947, Professional Diploma, Supervisor of Work with the Mentally Retarded, 1948, Supervisor of Elementary Schools, 1949, PhD, Education, 1950. **Career:** Social Centers for Migratory Workers in Delaware and Maryland, Home Mission Council of Amer, New York City, organizer and director; Egg Harbor Township, Pleasantville NJ, primary grades teacher 1936-38; Springfield Public Schools, Springfield MA, teacher 1939, supervisor of special educ 1967-68, director of special educ 1968-79; Amer Intl Coll, Boston Coll, New York Univ, Queens Coll, Flushing LI, visiting professor and lecturer; Holyoke Public Schools, consultant 1980-85. **Orgs:** Bd dir: Massachusetts Blue Cross, Assn of Teachers of Children With Special Needs (Western Massachusetts), Massachusetts Special Class Teachers Assn, Springfield Day Nursery, Hampden County Assn for Retarded Children, Visiting Nurses Assn, Springfield Hearing League Highland Branch YMCA; adv bd, United Cerebral Palsy of Western Massachusetts; bd of managers, Massachusetts Congress of Parents and Teachers; commr, Educational Development, Commonwealth of Massachusetts; chmn, Lyceum Comm, St John's Congregational Church UCC, 3 years; exec comm, Educ Comm, Citizen Action Commn, Springfield MA; exec comm; Springfield Branch NAACP; exec comm, New England Regional Conf, NAACP; steering comm, Region II, NAACP. **Honors/Awds:** Distinguished Alumna, Jersey City State Coll, NJ, 1978; Hon Doctor of Humane Letters Degree, Westfield State Coll, Westfield MA, 1980; Hon Doctor of Laws Degree, Western New England Coll, 1981; Human and Civil Rights Award, Massachusetts Teachers Assn, Sturbridge MA, 1987; awarded commendations from the House of Rep, State Senate, Sec of State, Commonwealth Museum for contributions to the 350 years of African experience in Massachusetts, 1989; author of The History of St John's Congregational Church 1844-1962; author of "A Study of Occupational Opportunities for the Mentally Retarded in the City of Springfield, MA," School Dept, Springfield MA; contrib to Curriculum Guide for Auxiliary Classes in the Elementary Schools, Sprinfield Public Schools; author, "Easing the Load of the Limite Amer Journal of Mental Deficiency". **Home Addr:** 909 Roosevelt Ave, Springfield, MA 01109.

MCLEAN, RENE
Educator, composer, musician. **Personal:** Born Dec 16, 1946, New York, NY; son of Dollie McLean and Jackie McLean; married Thandine January; children: Rene Jr, Sharif, Thandine-Naima, Nozipho-Jamila. **Educ:** New York College of Music; University of Massachusetts. **Career:** Educator, band leader, 1965-; New York State Narcotic Control Comm, Melrose Center, band master, 1970-73; University of Hartford, Department of Afro-American Music, artist in residence, 1984-85; MMABANA Cultural Center, South Africa, music department head, 1986-90; Triloka Records, recording artist, producer, 1988-; The New School, visiting lecturer, jazz program, 1989-; Broadcast Music Inc, writer, publisher; Harry Fox Agency, publisher; Nordisk Copyright, publisher; self-employed, multi-reed instrumentalist, composer, currently. **Orgs:** AFM 802. **Honors/Awds:** Creative Artist Fellowship Award for Japan, Japan-US Friendship Comm/National Endowment for the Arts, 1986-87; Cultural Medallion, presented by Mayor of Karlstad, Sweden, 1977; Survival Black Artist Award, Howard University Fine Arts Festival, 1983; scholarship, Outward Bound Mountaineering School, 1963. **Special Achievements:** Recordings: In African Eyes, Triloka Records, CD, 1992; with Jackie McLean, Dynasty, CD, 1988; with Jackie McLean, Rights of Passage, Triloka Records, 1990; Watch Out, Steeple Chase, 1975; has performed with Lionel Hampton, Horace Silver, Dizzy Gillespie, Woody Shaw, and various others.

MCLEAN, ZARAH GEAN
Physician. **Personal:** Born Aug 28, 1942, Tallulah, LA; married Russell McLean; children: Paul, Crystal, Grant. **Educ:** Fisk Univ, BA 1964; Howard Univ Coll of Medicine, MD 1968. **Career:** Medical Coll of WI, assoc prof of pediatrics 1972-86. **Orgs:** Bd dirs Emma Murry Child Care Ctr 1982-86. **Honors/Awds:** Outstanding Community Service, St Mary's College Women of Color Alliance, 1990; Physician of Year, Cream City Medical Society, 1989. **Business Addr:** Physician, 2040 W Wisconsin Ave #580, Milwaukee, WI 53233.

MCLEMORE, ANDREW G.
Construction company executive. **Personal:** Born Dec 13, 1931, Memphis, TN; son of Belle McLemore and Benjamine McLemore; married Dorothy Ellison, 1954; children: Andrew

Jr, Raymond S. **Educ:** West Virginia State College, BS, 1953. **Career:** A-MAC Sales & Builders Co, president, currently. **Orgs:** Association of Black General Contractors. **Military Serv:** US Army, 1st lt, 1953-56. **Business Addr:** President, A-MAC Sales & Builders Co, 15780 Schaefer, Detroit, MI 48227, (313)837-4690.

MCLEMORE, LESLIE BURL

Educator. **Personal:** Born Aug 17, 1940, Walls, MS; son of Christine Williams McLemore and Burl McLemore; divorced; children: Leslie Burl McLemore II. **Educ:** Rust College, BA (summa cum laude), 1964; Atlanta University, MA, 1965; University of MA Amherst, PhD, 1970. **Career:** Atlanta Univ, research assistant, 1960-65; Southern University, instructor, 1965-66; Univ MA Amherst, teaching assistant, 1966-69; Mississippi State University, Department of Political Science, visiting professor, 1979-80; Harvard University, WEB DuBois Institute of Afro-American Research, research associate, 1982-83; Johns Hopkins University, post-doctoral fellow 1970-; Jackson State Univ, professor of political science, 1976-, founding chairman, 1976-84, dean of grad school, dir of research administration, 1984-90, acting director, 1990-. **Orgs:** President, Rust Coll Natl Alumni Association; past vice pres, So Political Science Association; former president, Natl Conference of Black Political Scientist; Jackson League Task Force on Local Government; executive committee, Black Mississippians Council on Higher Education; chair, liaison committee NCEA; chair, Task Force on Minorities in Graduate Education; 100 Black Men of Jackson, 1991-; Institute for Southern Studies, board of directors, 1991; American Association for Higher Education, 1992-. **Honors/Awds:** Hon Woodrow Wilson Fellow Rust Coll; Pi Sigma Alpha Polit Sci; Chancellor's Medal Univ of MA at Amherst 1986; appointed to the Comm on the Status of Black Americans, Natl Acad of Sci 1985-87; Rockefeller Foundation Research Fellowship 1982-83; Spotlight on Scholars Awd Jackson State Univ 1980-81; Mississippi Center for Technology Transfer, Certificate of Appreciation, 1992; Science and Engineering Alliance, Coordinator Award of Appreciation, first, 1992; US Secretary of Energy, Certificate of Commendation for Outstanding Service, 1990. **Home Addr:** 746 Windward Rd, Jackson, MS 39206. **Business Addr:** Professor of Political Science, Jackson State University, PO Box 18420, Jackson, MS 39217.

MCLEMORE, MARK TREMELL

Professional baseball player. **Personal:** Born Oct 4, 1964, San Diego, CA. **Career:** California Angels, infielder, 1986-90; Cleveland Indians, 1990; Houston Astros, 1991; Baltimore Orioles, 1992-94; Texas Rangers, 1995-. **Business Addr:** Professional Baseball Player, Texas Rangers, 1000 Ballpark Way, Arlington, TX 76011, (817)273-5222.

MCLEMORE, NELSON, JR.

City official (retired). **Personal:** Born Jan 29, 1934, Chicago, IL; married Ollie Stokes; children: Nelson III. **Educ:** TN A&I State U, BS 1955; Governors State Univ Park Forest S IL, MA 1978; Chicago Tchrs Coll & John Marshall Law Sch, addl study. **Career:** Kennedy King Coll, Chicago, IL, coordinator, transfer ctr, 1990-; Dept of Public Works, dir of programming 1985-90; Human Svcs, dep commr 1980, chief-of-staff; Human Svcs, dir of personnel & training 1979-80; Planning-Human Svcs, asst dir 1978-79; Chicago Dept of Human Resources, asst to Commr; coord of Comm Serv 1972-74; comm unit dir 1969-72; Chicago Commn on Youth Welfare, comm unit dir 1965-69; Chicago Pub Elem & Secondary Sch, tchr 1955-65. **Orgs:** Mem Nat Assn for Comm Develop; past pres & mem 2nd ard Reg Dem Organization Boosters Club; Kappa Alpha Psi; certified social worker. **Military Serv:** AUS pfc 1956-58.

MCLEMORE, THOMAS

Professional football player. **Personal:** Born Mar 14, 1970. **Educ:** Southern University. **Career:** Detroit Lions, tight end, 1992-. **Business Addr:** Professional Football Player, Detroit Lions, 1200 Featherstone Rd, Pontiac, MI 48342, (313)335-4131.

MCLENDON, JOHN B., JR.

Athletic adviser, educator. **Personal:** Born Apr 5, 1915, Hiawatha, KS; son of Effie and John McLendon Sr; married Joanna L Owens; children: Querida Banks, John III, Herbert Bryant, Nannette Adams. **Educ:** Univ of Kansas, BS, educ, 1936; Univ of Iowa, MA, 1937. **Career:** Cleveland State University, athletic consultant, 1991-; Converse Rubber Co, natl & promotional rep, 1975-91; Denver Rockets Am Basketball Assn, basketball coach 1969-70; Cleveland State Univ, 1966-69; KY State Coll, 1963-66; Cleveland Pipers, 1961-62; Cleveland Pipers Nat Indsl Bsktbl League, 1959-61; Tennessee A&I State University, 1954-59; Hampton Inst, 1952-54; NC Coll, 1937-52; Lawrence Memorial HS, 1935-36; Health & Phys Educ, North Carolina College, athletic dir, 1942-52; Athletics Hlth PE & Recreation Tennessee State A&I University, coordinator, 1962-63; Carolina Times, sports columnist, 1950-52. **Orgs:** US Olympic Bsktball Com 1965-72; chmn Martin Luther King Chicago Boys Club; bd dir 1974-77, World BB Rules Com 1972-76; chmn Nat AAU Basketball 1967-68; bd of trustees Naismith Memorial Basketball Hall of Fame, currently. **Honors/Awds:** Coaching Award of Merit, NABC, 1970; 25-yr coaching award, Natl Assn Basketball Coaches of US, 1970; top-four coach in 50 years, 1937-87, Natl Assn of Intercollegiate Athletics; Natl BB Championship, 1957-59; TN A&I State Univ; 1st team to win 3 Natl Championships consecutively; Natl AAU BB Championship, 1st Black Coach; Eastern ABA Championship, 1st black, 1962; Helms Athletic Hall of Fame, 1962; published, Fast Break Basketball, 1965; The Fast Break Game, 1974; Honorary DHL, North Carolina Central Univ, 1979, Jarvis Christian Coll, 1981; Alumni Award, Kansas Univ, highest honor given by University, 1979; life member, Central Intercollegiate Athletic Association; founder, Central Intercollegiate AA Basketball Tournament; author: with Milton Katz, Breaking Through: The Intergration of College Basketball in Postrld War II, 1987; The First Central Intercollegiate Championship Basketball Tournament, 1987; McBasket—Three on Three, 1988; writer, technical director of five sports films on basketball fundamentals, for Athletic Institute, first by a black basketball coach, 1982; Chicago Public League Sports Hall of Fame, 1990; number one contributor/coach in 100 years of basketball, Virginia State University HBCU Classic, 1992; TV Sports Analyst Billy Packer Named McLendon Top Ten Coach of the Century, 1992; NC Central University renamed gymnasium McLendon McDougald Gymnasium, 1992; Naismith Award by Atlanta Tip-Off Club Contributions to Basketball, 1992; Tennessee State University, Gentry Complex Arena Floor named McLendon Court, 1992; inductee, Tennessee Sports Hall of Fame, 1993; Sportsview Magazine, Coach of the Century, 1993. **Home Addr:** 3683 Runnymede Blvd, Cleveland Heights, OH 44121.

MCLEOD, GEORGIANNA R.

Social worker, health services administrator (retired). **Personal:** Born Oct 6, 1937, New York, NY; daughter of Annie Coles McLeod and George McLeod. **Educ:** NY Univ, BS 1959. **Career:** Morningside Comm Ctr Camp #41, group work/recreation 1952-; Rusk Inst, recreation therapist 1957-58; Neighborhood House, 1959; New York City Dept Soc Serv Emer Asst Unit/Bronx, director/social wkr, 1984-89; Willow Star II, Womens Shelter for Substance Abusers, director, social service; Social Services 68 Lex Womens Shelter, dir, retired 1996. **Orgs:** APWA; NCSW; NABSW; Am Chama Soc; SSEU; Amer Soc of Professional Exec Women; trustee, Eureka Grand Chapter, Ph-OES; past matron, Alpha Chap No 1 PH-OES; past pres, exec bd mem, New York City DSS NAACP 1960-; master activist, secretary, deacon, mem, Church of the Master 1947-; vp, National Black Presbyterian Caucus, New York City; founder/dir, NYS-NAACP Project THRESH, 1967-; chp, Consumer Education/Economic Development, NYS-NAACP, 1966-; under Gov Rockefeller served on Migrant Workers Comm; dir, Westchester County voter rep dir, St Compt Carl McCall; vice pres, Black Dems of Westchester, 1968-. **Honors/Awds:** Woman of the Yr Interboro Civic 5 1980; Comm Serv Awd DSS Branch NAACP 1983; Outstanding Serv Church of the Master 1983; Willow Star II, Employee of the Year, 1993; PhD in Humanities from Institute of Applied Research in London, England; Certificate of Appreciation, NYC-DHS and National Park Trust. **Home Addr:** 28 University Ave, Yonkers, NY 10704.

MCLEOD, JAMES S.

Mortician. **Personal:** Born Oct 14, 1939, Bennettsville, SC; married Shirley J Jeffries; children: Tracey, Maymia, Erica. **Educ:** A&T State U, attended 1 yr; NC Central Univ Durham NC, 2 yrs Eckels Coll Mortuary Science Philadelphia, grad. **Career:** Morris Funeral Home Bennettsville SC, mgr 1964-72, owner since 1972. **Orgs:** Mem 6 Dist Morticians Assn; SC State & Nat Morticians Assn; mem exec bd Pee Dee Regional Planning & Devel Coun Marlboro Co Betterment League; 6th Dist VEP bd dir Carolina Messenger Inc Mem Shiloh Bapt Ch trustee; Landmark Masonic Lodge #16; F&AM; CC Johnson Consistory #13-Cairo Temple #125 Shriners; Am Legion Post 213; Theta Phi Lambda Chap; dean of pledges Alpha Phi Alpha; NAACP. **Honors/Awds:** Recipient certificate of merit United Supreme Coun 1970; distinguished serv award Alpha Phi Alpha 1971; certificate of achievement Omega Psi Phi Frat 1971; certificate of pub serv Mayor of Bennettsville SC; dean's award Eckels Coll of Mortuary Science; first black since Reconstruction to be appointed to a Boardin Marlboro Co Social Services 1968 & to be elected to Bennettsville City Coun 1971 presently serving 2 terms. **Military Serv:** AUS signal corp 1962-64. **Business Addr:** PO Box 551, Bennettsville, SC.

MCLEOD, MICHAEL PRESTON

Dentist. **Personal:** Born Aug 16, 1954, Tulsa, OK; son of Jeanne McLeod and Wallace B McLeod, Jr; married Corlis Clay; children: Lauren Micah, Kathleen Blake. **Educ:** Howard Univ, BS (Cum Laude) 1976; Univ of OK, DDS 1980; Martin Luther King Genl Hosp, GPR 1981. **Career:** Private practice, dentist; Univ of OK College of Denistry, Oklahoma City OK, part-time faculty 1984-. **Orgs:** Mem Kappa Alpha Psi 1975-; mem Oklahoma City Med Dental-Phar 1982-; mem Citizen's Advisory Comm, Capital-Medical Center Improvement and Zoning Commn, 1984-. **Honors/Awds:** Amer Acad of Periodontology Awd 1980; Amer Soc of Dentistry for Children Awd 1980; Div of Comm Dentistry Awd 1980; Univ of OK Assoc of Black Personnel Awd 1980. **Business Addr:** Owner/Proprietor, Michael P McLeod Family Dentistry, 2216 N Martin Luther King Blvd, Oklahoma City, OK 73111, (405)427-0237.

MCLEON, NATHANIEL W.

Attorney. **Personal:** Born Jul 13, 1944, Jersey City, NJ; son of Mary McLeon; married Lee; children: Jennifer. **Educ:** Howard Univ, BA 1966; Howard Univ School of Law, 1970; NY Univ School of Law, LLM Taxation 1981. **Career:** Drew Hall Howard Univ Residence Hall Prog, grad asst 1967-70; Neighborhood Legal Serv, law intern 1969-70; Ernst & Ernst, staff atty 1970-71; Bank of Tokyo Trust Co NY, vice pres & dir of taxes 1979-84; Squibb Corp New York, tax atty; self-employed tax practitioner, 1984-. **Orgs:** Mem Natl Bar Assn; mem Omega Psi Phi Frat; Concerned Black Citizens Alliance; bd mem Jersey City Chap Operation PUSH. **Honors/Awds:** Outstanding Intern Award, Ctr for Clinical Legal Studies, Howard Univ School of Law, 1969-70; Harlem YMCA Black Achiever, 1973; 100 Outstanding Young Men in Amer, 1973. **Home Addr:** 1512 Palisade Ave, Palisade, NJ 07024.

MCLIN, LENA JOHNSON

Educator, composer. **Personal:** Born Sep 5, 1928, Atlanta, GA; married Nathaniel Mclin; children: Nathaniel G, Beverly. **Educ:** Spelman Coll, AB 1951; Conservatory, MA 1954; Roosevelt Univ Chicago State Coll. **Career:** Singer; composer of numerous works; clinician; Kenwood High Sch, Chicago, teacher, dir, head of music department; small opera co ''Mclin Ensemble'', founder, dir. **Orgs:** Mem Chicago Bd of Edn; TCI Educ Film Co Mem MENC; Nat Assn of Negro Musicians; NJE; Institute of Black Am Music. **Honors/Awds:** Outstanding composer VA Union Univ Award 1973; Tribune Newspaper article 1973; Best tchr of yr 1972-73; Critics Assn Outstanding Composer 1971; NANM Named Leading Black Choral Composer Sidney Alsop Critic 1970; outstanding musician NAACP; Gary Mayor Hatcher; hon degree HHD VA Union Univ 1975. **Business Addr:** Music Dept, Kenwood Academy, 515 S Blackstone, Chicago, IL 60615.

MCLINN, HARRY MARVIN

Dental specialist. **Personal:** Born in Huntsville, AL; married Angela; children: Teloca, Marvin, Jenol. **Educ:** Columbia Univ, Cert of Proficiency; Amer Bd of Orthodontics, diplomate; Howard Univ, DDS 1947. **Career:** Private Practice, dentist 1947-51; Howard Dental Sch, chmn dept orthodontics & dental anatomy 1948-50; New York City Dept of Hlth, panel 1950-60; NYC, orthodontics 1951-71; NJ City Med Dental Coll, assoc prof of orthodontics 1975-. **Orgs:** Mem ADA, NDA, NHDA, Columbia Univ Dental Alumni; NESO Amer Assn of Orthodontists; FICA Intl Coll of Dentists; mem Bd of Health; dir Englewood NJ Dental Prog for Sch Children; mem Longrange Hlth & Planning Com 1976-77; fellow Intl Coll of Dentists 1976; diplomate Amer Bd of Orthodontics 1958; mem Long Range Planning Comm of Englewood NJ Hosp serving 27 comms 1980; member IRB (Human Use) Committee 1988-. **Honors/Awds:** 1st Louise Ball Teaching Fellow Howard Univ, Columbia Univ 1948; 1st Howard Univ Diplomate of Amer Bd of Orthodontics; Fellow Intl Dental Coll; 2nd Black Diplomate, American Board of Orthodontics 1958. **Military Serv:** AUS Dental Corp WW II capt.

MCMICHAEL, EARLENE CLARISSE

Journalist. **Personal:** Born Sep 29, 1963, New York, NY; daughter of Norma Krieger and Earl McMichael. **Educ:** Cornell University, Ithaca, NY, bachelor's degree, 1984; Columbia University Graduate School of Journalism, New York, NY, master's degree, 1987. **Career:** The Oakland Press, Pontiac, MI, reporter, 1987; Kansas City Times, Kansas City, MO, reporter, 1987; Shoreline Newspapers, Guilford, CT, reporter, 1988; The Jersey Journal, Jersey City, NJ, reporter, 1988-. **Orgs:** Vice president, Brooklyn chapter, Zeta Phi Beta Sorority, 1986-87; secretary, New Jersey chapter, National Association of Black Journalists, 1988-90. **Honors/Awds:** WNBC-TV Minority Fellow Scholarship, 1986-87; participant in the Capital Cities/ABC Inc Minority Training Program, 1987-88. **Home Addr:** 163 Eastern Pkwy, #D4, Brooklyn, NY 11238.

MCMICKENS, JACQUELINE MONTGOMERY

Government official. **Personal:** Born Dec 10, 1935, Birmingham, AL; daughter of Flora B Walton Montgomery and Zollie Coffer Montgomery; married William McMickens; children: Lenell Myricks, Charles Maurice, Barry. **Educ:** John Jay Coll of Criminal Justice, BA Criminal Justice 1972, MPA 1976; Brooklyn Law School, attending. **Career:** Kings Cty Hospital, CEO; Adolescent Ctr on Rikers Island, dep warden for security, dir training acad; New York City Dept of Corrections, commissioner; NY Housing Authority, vice chairwoman. **Honors/Awds:** 1st woman to run security in a men's ward; 1st woman to head the dept acad; 1st woman to be named chief of King's Cty Hosp Prison Ward; 1st woman to be chief of oper; Hon DL St Joseph's Coll NY, Miles Coll Birmingham.

MCMILLAN, DOUGLAS JAMES

Clergyman, educator. **Personal:** Born Feb 8, 1947, New York, NY; son of Irene Wilson McMillan (deceased) and James McMillan (deceased). **Educ:** Community Coll Allegeny Co, AA (Eng) 1975; Univ Pittsburgh, BA (Lang Comm) 1977; Xavier Univ of Louisiana, New Orleans, LA, ThM, 1990. **Career:** Canevin High School, Pittsburgh, Pennsylvania, teacher, 1973-80; Assum Acad NY, tchr 1980-81; Bishop Grimes HS, NY, tchr 1981-89, 1997-; asst principal, 1989-90; Diocese of Syracuse, Syracuse, NY, dir, office of Black Catholic Ministry, 1990-. **Orgs:** Natl Black Catholic Clergy Caucus 1984-; bd mem, Office of Black Catholic Ministry for the Diocese of Syracuse; National Assn of Black Catholic Administrators, 1990-. **Honors/Awds:** Order Friars Minor Conventuals, member, 1968-. **Military Serv:** US Army, spec-5, 1966-68. **Home Addr:** 812 N Salina, Syracuse, NY 13208. **Business Addr:** 240 E Onandaga St, PO Box 511, Syracuse, NY 13201-0511.

MCMILLAN, ELRIDGE W.
Association executive. **Personal:** Born Aug 11, Barnesville, GA; son of Agnes Boatwright McMillan and Marion R McMillian Sr; divorced. **Educ:** Clark Coll, AB, English, 1954; Columbia University, MA, 1959, post graduate work, 1960-61. **Career:** Atlanta Public Schools, teacher, administrator, 1954-64; US Office of Economic Opportunity, program operations supervisor, 1965-67; US Office for Civil Rights, D/HEW, region IV, education branch chief, 1967-68; Southern Education Foundation Inc, assoc dir, 1968-78, pres, 1978-. **Orgs:** University System of Georgia Board of Regents, chairperson, 1986-87; Clark Atlanta University trustee; Southeastern Council of Foundations, board of directors; Alonzo F & Norris B Herndon Foundation, board of trustees; Tulane University, president's council; Omega Psi Phi; Free & Accepted Masonic Order of Prince Hall; 100 Black Men of Atlanta Inc; Atlanta Action Forum; Assn of Black Foundation Execs, mem; The Atlanta Committee for Public Educ, dir; Panel on Educ Opportunity & Post-Secondary Desegregation, co-chair. **Honors/Awds:** Claflin College, Doctor of Humanities, 1992; Clark College, Doctor of Humanities, 1980, Distinguished Alumni Achievement Award, 1988; Atlanta Black Male Achiever, Southern Bell's 1991-92 Calendar of Atlanta Black History, 1991; Atlanta Urban League, Distinguished Community Service Award, 1988; State Committee on Life and History of Black Georgians, Black Georgian of the Year Award, 1978; NAACP, Atlanta branch, WEB DuBois Award, 1982, 1987, 1992; Association of Social & Behavior Scientists, WEB DuBois Award, 1992; Outstanding Educator, Clark Atlanta Univ, School of Educ, 1994; Tuskegee Univ, Doctor of Laws Degree, 1994; Distinguished Service in Educ Award, GA Assn of Black Colls, 1995; Fifth James A Joseph Lecture Honoree, Assn of Black Foundation Execs, 1995. **Business Addr:** President, Southern Education Foundation Inc, 135 Auburn Ave NE, 2nd Fl, Atlanta, GA 30303, (404)523-0001.

MCMILLAN, ENOLIA PETTIGEN
Educator (retired). **Personal:** Born Oct 20, 1904, Willow Grove, PA; daughter of Elizabeth Fortune Pettigen and John Pettigen; married Betha D McMillan, Dec 26, 1935 (deceased); children: Betha D Jr. **Educ:** Howard Univ Washington, DC, AB 1926; Columbia Univ New York, MA 1933. **Career:** Denton & Pomonkey MD, high school teacher 1926-28; Pomonkey High Schl, princ 1928-35; Jr High School Baltimore, teacher 1935-56; Clifton Pk JHS & Cherry Hill JHS, v princ 1956-63; Dunbar Sr High Schl Baltimore, vice principal 1963-69; Baltimore City School System, apptd lifelong principal 1985-. **Orgs:** Secy MD Fed Clrd PTA's; pres D St Conf NAACP Brnchs 1938; reg vice pres Reg v Amer Teachers Assn 1939; pres Baltimore Brnch NAACP Trust Pub School Teachers' Assn 1948; bd mem & sec Bltmr Urban League; advisory com Dept of Juvnl Ser of MD; gov comm Strctr & Govrnce of Educ in MD; trust Calvary Baptist Church. **Honors/Awds:** NAACP Merit Medal 1938; mem Afro Roll of Honor 1941; Cert of Merit Kappa Chap Iota Phi Lambda 1957; Merit Ser Award Nat Assn Negro Bus & Prof Wmn Clubs 1970; Fndrs' Day Award Tau Gamma Delta 1970; Dist Ctzn Award Dem Ladies Gld 1971; Douglass HS Hall of Fame 1972; Hon DHumane Letters Sojourner-Douglass Coll 1984; 1986 Brotherhood Citation of Natl Conf of Christians & Jews MD Region; one of Top 100 Black Business & Professional Women of 1986.

MCMILLAN, HORACE JAMES
Physician (retired), health services administrator. **Personal:** Born Oct 30, 1919, Mineola, TX; son of Lemon Columbus (deceased) and Joann Aletha Zollars (deceased); married Jessie, Oct 21, 1942; children: Yvonne Camille, Michelle Louise. **Educ:** Prairie View A&M Coll, BS 1942; St Louis Univ, Graduate Work 1945-46; Meharry Med Coll, MD 1950; UCLA, Certificate in Health Maintenance Org, 1975. **Career:** Family Medical Ctr, Santa Barbara, CA, vice pres 1952-88, pres, 1988-92; private practice, physician 1952-88. **Orgs:** Founder/bd of dir, Goleta Valley Comm Hosp 1967-77; 1st chmn, Mayor's Adv Comm on Human Relations 1968; forerunner of Comm Relations Commn recommended the CRC; pres of the board, Comm Hlth Task Force 1973-81; pres, bd dir, Comm Nghbrhd Ctr; staff mem St Francis Hosp, Santa Barbara Cottage Hosp, Goleta Valley Comm Hosp; mem, Santa Barbara Acad of Family Practice, Natl Academy of Family Practice; life mem, NAACP; Amer Assn for Clinical Immunology and Allergy, 1982-88. **Honors/Awds:** Recognition Awd City of Santa Barbara as innovator of Franklin Neighborhood Serv Ctr on 10th Anniversary 1985; Recognition Awd Afro-Amer Comm Serv for the Martin Luther King Awd 1986; Resolution for Community Service, California Legislative Assembly, 1988; Resolution for Community Service, Board of Supervisors, Santa Barbara County, CA, 1988; 10th Anniversary Award of Appreciation, Franklin Neighborhood Center, 1988; 35 Years of Outstanding Community Service, NAACP; 25 Years Service to Mankind, Meharry Medical College, 1975; numerous other awards for community service and health care. **Special Achievements:** Personal papers received into the ethnic and multicultural archives at University of California at Santa Barbara, 1994. **Military Serv:** USCG chief pharmacist mate 1942-46; first African-American pharmacist mate in history of USCG. **Home Addr:** 3340 McCaw Ave #103, Santa Barbara, CA 93105.

MCMILLAN, JACQUELINE MARIE
Educator, business consultant. **Personal:** Born Dec 15, 1966, Jamaica, NY; daughter of Drs Margaret & Vincent Savage; divorced; children: De Morris Jourdan Baity. **Educ:** College of the Holy Cross, BA, 1989; Kent State University, MPA, 1993, PhD, 1997. **Career:** College of the Holy Cross, resident asst, 1987-89; Student Programs for Urban Development, co-director, 1986-89; New York City Child Welfare Admin, case mgr, 1990-92; Kent State University, academic advisor, 1992-95, research asst, 1995-. **Orgs:** Phi Delta Kappa, bd mem, 1995-; Children's Services Bd, mentor, 1994-; Women's Network, 1993-; World Bible Way Fellowship, 1995; National Forum for Public Administrators, 1992-; Black Graduate Student Assn, program advisor, 1994-; American Assn for Higher Education, 1994-95; Delta Kappa Pi, 1996-; Natl Assn of Women in Education, 1996-. **Honors/Awds:** College of Education, Service Award, 1995; Future Business Leaders of America Inc, Leadership Award, 1994; Phi Delta Kappa Dissertation Award, 1996. **Special Achievements:** "Financial Analysis of the City of Kent, Ohio," 1993; "Dealing with Fiscal Stress in the Twentieth Century," 1993; "Health Care Administration and the Budget Crunch," 1994; "A Review of the Prospective Health Care Plans," 1995; "Total Quality Management in Ohio Institutions," 1997. **Business Addr:** Program Coordinator, Kent State University, Office of Campus Life, 262 KSC, Kent, OH 44242, (216)672-2480.

MCMILLAN, JAMES BATES
Dentist. **Personal:** Born Jan 18, 1918, Aberdeen, MS; son of Rosalie Gay (deceased) and James Milton McMillan (deceased); married Marie Elizabeth Stever-Daly, Jun 20, 1964; children: Jarmilla, James Bates III, Michelle Caliendo (deceased), Jacqueline (deceased), John and Jeffrey. **Educ:** Univ of Detroit 1937-39; Meharry Med Coll, DDS 1944; Hospital L'Arriboissiere, Paris, France, 1966; Univ of Southern California, 1984; Univ of California at Los Angeles, 1986. **Career:** Detroit, pvt practice dentistry 1946-55; Las Vegas, NV, pvt practice 1956-. **Orgs:** Candidate US Senate 1964; mem Acad Gen Practice; Acad Implant Dentures natl & am dental assn; mem las vegas golf bd 1965-; clark co NV central Dem Com 1960-; NV State Dom Com 1960; pres NAACP 1956-60; mem Intl Golf Assn; Alpha Phi Alpha; Roman Cath; member, State Board of Dental Examiners, 1972-80; member, City of Las Vegas Block Grant Redevelopment, 1984-; Governor's Legislative Committee, 1990-; Clark County School Board, trustee 1994-; past president of the Black Chamber of Commerce Award for Vision and Direction. **Honors/Awds:** Meritorious Service, Nevada Association of School Boards; Elementary school named "Dr James B. McMillan". **Military Serv:** US Army, maj dental corps 1955-57. **Business Addr:** President, James B McMillan DDS, LTD, 2300 Rancho Rd, Ste 218, Las Vegas, NV 89102.

MCMILLAN, JAMES C.
Educator. **Personal:** Born Dec 23, 1925, Sanford, NC; son of Rev & Mrs J E McMillan; divorced; children: Eric Wesley, Frances Lynne. **Educ:** Howard Univ, BA Art 1947; Skowhegan School Art ME, Fellowship 1947; Acad Julian (Paris France), Certificate 1951; Catholic Univ Amer, MFA 1952; Syracuse Univ NY, Fellowship (adv study) 1960-61. **Career:** US Naval Air Station, art instructor, illustrator 1945-46; Bennett Coll Greensboro NC, chmn art dept 1947-50, 1952-53, 1956-59; Guilford Coll (Summers), dir London/European arts seminar, 1968-72; Guilford Coll, prof of art, painter, sculptor, professor of art emeritus, 1988-; Virginia State Univ, Petersburg, VA, eminent scholar in fine arts, 1990. **Orgs:** Dir cultural enrichment, EPDA Bennett Coll (summers) 1969-70; dir NY Art Sem Guilford Coll 1971-75; mem Coll Art Assn, 1984-85; mem DC Art Assn, 1985; mem Natl Conf Artists 1984-85; president, Afro-American Atelier Inc Gallery, Greensboro, NC, 1990-91. **Honors/Awds:** Skowhegan art fellowship Howard Univ Washington, DC 1947; Danforth teacher fellowship (Bennett Coll) Syracuse Univ NY 1960-61; Fresco Mural Skowhegan School of Art ME 1947; MFA and sculptor comm Catholic Univ (to LA Catholic Church) 1952; mural Providence Baptist Church Greensboro NC 1977. **Military Serv:** USN aviation mach mate 2nd class 1944-46; Pacific Theatre of Oiper, WWII, 1946. **Business Addr:** Professor of Art Emeritus, Guilford Coll, 5800 W Friendly Ave, Greensboro, NC 27410.

MCMILLAN, JOSEPH H.
Association executive, university administrator. **Personal:** Born Nov 17, 1929, Louisville, KY; married; children: Charles, Diane, Michael, Dwight, Joseph Jr. **Educ:** Univ of Louisville, AB 1950; Univ of MI, MA 1959; MI State U, EdD 1967. **Career:** Dir Dept of Human Relations for Academic Affairs Univ of Louisville, asst vice pres 1977-; MI State U, 1972-77; State U, 1972-; Dir Equal Opp Progs MI StateU, 1969-72; Wstrn MI U, part-time instr fall 1969; Inner-City Schs Dir of Human Relations Dir Grand Rapids Head Start Prog Grand Rapis Bd of Edn, supr 1966-69; MI State U, extension lectr 1965-; Sheldon Elem Sch Grand Rapids, prin 1960-66; Elem Educ MI State U, asst instr 1963-64; Sheldon Elem Sch, tchr 1956-60; Webber Sch Baldwin, MI, tchr prin 1954-56; Idlewild, MI, tchr 1950-54. **Orgs:** Consult Project Follow Through in NY, Harlem, Louisville, E St Louis Pub Schs; consult Parent Child Cntr Louisville 1974-; instr Pepperdine Univ 1974-77; consRoosevelt Comm Sch 1976-77; mem Adv Cncl to Bur of Pub Hlth 1977; instr Univ of No CO 1974; mem Conflict Mgmnt Workshops; Curriculum Workshops; consult SRA; Addison-Wesley Co; consult Behavioral Res Labs Proj Read; participated in deseg study Clairton PA 1968 Asso Educ Consult Inc; participated in SchoolReorgn Study Pontiac, MI 1969-70; participated in Elem Sch Decentralization Study at Detroit 1970-71 Title I Adv Bd Proposal 1970, 72, 73; testified as witness in Geo & Carolyn Higgins v Bd of Educ of City of Grand Rapids 1973; court appointed expert in Benton Harbor Schools Deseg Case 1978-;resourse personat Affirmative Action Worop Urban Research Corp 1972; pres Louisville Urban League; co-chrmn Community Consortium on Black survival in Louisville; bd mem N St Baptist Ch; mem Louisville NAACP; mem Gr Lansing NAACP. **Honors/Awds:** Recip Omicron Delta Kappa Award Univ of Louisville 1950; outstanding man of Yr Grand Rapids Elks Club 1963. **Business Addr:** 202 Adminstrn Bldg, Univ of Louisville, Louisville, KY 40292.

MCMILLAN, JOSEPH TURNER, JR.
Educational administrator. **Personal:** Born Jul 19, 1944, Valdosta, GA; son of Rev J T McMillan (deceased) and Olivia Cooper McMillan (deceased). **Educ:** Howard University, BS in psychology, 1965, MA in student personnel administration, 1970; Teachers College, Columbia University, doctorate in higher education administration, 1986; Harvard University, certificate in educational management, 1990. **Career:** United Church Board for Homeland Ministries, secretary for higher education relationships, executive secretary of the council for higher education, 1970-88; Huston-Tillotson College, Austin, TX, president, 1988-. **Orgs:** Texas Association of Developing Colleges, chairman, board of trustees, 1993-97; Pension Boards of the United Church of Christ, board of trustees; Amistad Research Center, board of directors; United Negro College Fund, board of directors; Congregational Church of Austin; Council of Higher Educ of United Church of Christ, chair; Big State Conf, Natl Assn of Intercolliegiate Athletics (NAIA), pres; Austin Regional Advisory Bd of Texas Commerce Bank; Alpha Phi Alpha Fraternity. **Honors/Awds:** Honorary degrees: Yankton College, 1978, Huston-Tillotson College, 1984; Austin Area Affiliates of the National Alliance of Black School Educators, Educator of the Year Award, 1990; Texas Legislative Black Caucus, Outstanding Texan Award in Education, 1993; Austin Area Urban League, Whitney M Young Jr Award, 1995. **Business Addr:** President, Huston-Tillotson College, 900 Chicon St, Austin, TX 78702, (512)505-3001.

MCMILLAN, LEMMON COLUMBUS, II
Corporation executive (retired). **Personal:** Born Apr 17, 1917, Mineola, TX; son of Joanna A Zollar McMillan (deceased) and Lemmon C McMillan Sr (deceased); married Vivian L Boyd, Sep 5, 1942; children: Lemmon III, Robert, Samuel. **Educ:** Prairie View A&M Univ, BA 1939, MA 1951; Univ of TX, Doctoral Study 1952-54; Univ of VA, special prog 1963. **Career:** Dallas Public Branch Library, branch librarian 1939-42; Prairie View A&M Univ, asst registrar 1946-54, registrar 1954-63; executive director, Association of Huntsville (AL) Area Companies, 1963-71; National Merit Scholarship Corp, Evanston, IL, vice pres, 1971-87. **Orgs:** Life mem/supporter of NAACP, NAACP Legal Defense Fund, Urban League, Southern Poverty Law Center; SCLC, UNCF, Alpha Phi Alpha Frat; member, Sigma Pi Phi Fraternity, 1990-; emeritus member, National Assn of Collegiate Deans, Registrars and Admissions Officers; life mem, Natl Prairie View Univ Alumni Assn; Trustee, Hobart Taylor, Jr. Fellowship Program, 1997-. **Honors/Awds:** Plans for Progress Awd Natl Assn of Market Developers 1965; Outstanding Alumnus Awd Prairie View A&M Univ 1965, 1988; Outstanding Comm Serv Awd JF Drake State Tech Sch 1966; Disting Serv Awd Jaycees Huntsville AL, 1971; Resolution of Commendation AL Legislature 1971; Distinguished Alumnus Citation, National Assn for Equal Opportunity in Higher Education, 1989; National Citation for Services to Youth, Delta Sigma Theta Sorority, 1985; Henry M Minton Fellow, Sigma Pi Phi Fraternity, 1994. **Military Serv:** AUS 1st Lt, field artillery, 1942-46; Asiatic-Pacific Campaign Medal with Bronze Star, 1946; American Theater Campaign Medal, 1946; Victory Medal, 1946. **Home Addr:** 2001 Sherman Ave, Apt 101, Evanston, IL 60201.

MCMILLAN, MAE F.
Physician, educator, psychiatrist. **Personal:** Born May 12, 1936, Austin, TX; daughter of Annie M Walker-McMillan and Ben S McMillan Sr. **Educ:** Wiley Coll Marshall TX, BS BA (summa cum laude) 1955; Meharry Med Coll, MD (honors) 1959; Wayne Co Genl Hosp MI, internship 1960; Baylor Univ Coll of Med Houston, affiliated hosp residency 1960-63 1963-65; Hampstead Child Therapy Course & Clinic London, postdoctoral Fellowship 1965-67. **Career:** Baylor Coll of Med Depts Psych & Child Psych, asst prof 1966; private practice, part time child psychiatry specialty pre-schoolers 1966-; TX

Rsch Inst of Mental Sci, asst dir div of child psych 1968-72, dir div of child psych 1972-74, dir early childhood therapy course & clinic 1974-; Univ of TX Med Sch at Houston, clinical assoc prof 1974-; Faculty for Advanced Studies Univ TX Sch of Biomedical Science, asst prof 1975; Univ of TX Health Sci Ctr at Houston, clinical assoc prof 1976; TX Woman's Univ Child Devel & Family Living, adjunct prof 1977-; Baylor Coll of Med Depts Psychiat & Child Psych, clinical assoc prof 1982-. **Orgs:** Bd mem CAN-DO-IT 1973-80; bd dirs Girls Clubs of Houston Sect 1983-; mem Natl Council of Negro Women, Delta Sigma Theta, Mental Health Assn; coord Child Care Cncl of Houston-Harris Co; United Methodist Women; treasurer, Texas Community Corporation, 1986-; chair, Child Advocacy Committee, Houston Psychiatric Society, 1992; American Psychiatric Association; Texas Society of Psych Physicians. **Honors/Awds:** Criminal Justice Award, Delta Sigma Theta; One Amer Proj, 1973; Distinction of Merit; Natl Council of Negro Women, 1977; Woman of Distinction Award, YWCA Houston Sect, 1980; Amer Psychiatric Assn, Fellow, 1982, life fellow, 1998; Notable Women of TX Award, Gov's Comm 1983. **Special Achievements:** Certified Lay Speaker, United Methodist Church, 1992; consultant, Depelchin Children's Services, Florence Crittenton Services. **Business Addr:** Child Psychiatrist, 503 1/2 N Loop West, Houston, TX 77018.

MCMILLAN, NAOMI. See GRIMES, NIKKI.

MCMILLAN, NATE (NATHANIEL)
Professional basketball player. **Personal:** Born Aug 3, 1964, Raleigh, NC; married; children: Jamelle, Brittany. **Educ:** Chowan College, Murfreesboro, NC, 1982-84; North Carolina State Univ, Raleigh, NC, 1984-86. **Career:** Seattle Supersonics, guard-forward, 1986-. **Business Addr:** Professional Basketball Player, Seattle SuperSonics, PO Box 900911, Seattle, WA 98109, (206)281-5850.

MCMILLAN, REGINA ELLIS
Attorney. **Personal:** Born Mar 27, 1964, Louisville, KY; daughter of Mary A Ellis and Geoffrey S Ellis; married Antonio B McMillan, 1993. **Educ:** University of Louisville, Summer 1981; Fisk University, BA, 1985; London School of Economics, England, Summer 1985; Georgetown University Law Center, JD, 1988. **Career:** Brown-Forman Distillers Corp, summer intern, 1984-1985; Georgetown University Law Center, research asst, 1987; Perpetual Savings Bank, law clerk, 1987; Wyatt, Tarrant & Combs, associate attorney, 1988-89; Thomas, Kennedy, Sampson & Patterson, associate attorney, 1989-95; Danley & Assocs, associate attorney, 1995-. **Orgs:** State Bar of Georgia, 1992-; Atlanta Bar Association, 1992-; National Bar Association, 1987; Georgia Association of Black Women Attorneys, 1990-; Gate City Bar Association, 1992-; NAACP; Natl Assn of Female Executives, 1993-; Atlanta Volunteer Lawyers Foundation, truancy project, 1993-. **Honors/Awds:** YMCA, Youth Achiever of the Year, 1981; Fisk University, National Dean's List, 1982-85, Rhodes Scholar State Finalist, 1984-85, Mortar Board, President, 1984-85; Phi Beta Kappa, 1985; YMCA, Adult Black Achievers Awards, 1989; National Council Education Opportunity Associations, TRIO Achiever Award, 1991. **Business Addr:** Danley & Associates, 6519 Spring Street, Atlanta, Douglasville, GA 30134, (404)942-2053.

MCMILLAN, ROBERT FRANK, JR.
Development officer. **Personal:** Born Jul 8, 1946, Glassboro, NJ; son of Kurt Yvonne McMillan (deceased) and Robert F McMillan, Sr; divorced; children: Ayisha Nell, Marcia Akillah. **Educ:** Temple Univ, BS Civil Engrg 1972; Northwestern Univ, MBA Prog; State of IL, Real Estate Broker License 1985. **Career:** Turner Construction, field engr, supt 1972-76; Hudson Corp, proj mgr 1976-80; Urban Investment & Devel Co, devel mgr 1980-85; Joseph J Freed & Assoc Inc, dir of development 1985-87; Wil-Freds Developments Inc, development officer, 1988-; McMillan Garbe Structures, Inc, owner/president, currently. **Orgs:** Charter mem Rotary Intl 1984-; board member, Greater Aurora Chamber of Commerce; bd mem, Aurora Crime Stoppers; bd mem, Merchants Bank. **Honors/Awds:** State of Wisconsin, real estate broker license, 1989-; candidate for commercial certified investment member desigination. **Military Serv:** AUS 1st lt 3 yrs; Bronze Star; Meritorious Achievement Vietnam 1969. **Business Addr:** Development Officer, Wil-Freds Developments Inc, 274 E Indian Trail Rd, Aurora, IL 60506.

MCMILLAN, TERRY L.
Novelist, educator. **Personal:** Born Oct 18, 1951, Port Huron, MI; daughter of Madeline Washington Tillman and Edward McMillan (deceased); children: Solomon Welch. **Educ:** Univ of California, Berkeley, BA 1979; Columbia Univ, MFA, 1979. **Career:** New York Times HERS column, guest columnist; book reviewer, New York Times Book Review, Atlanta Constitution, Philadelphia Inquirer; University of Wyoming, Laramie, WY, visiting prof, 1987-88; University of Arizona, Tucson, AZ, associate professor, 1988-; Stanford Univ, visiting prof. **Orgs:** PEN; Author's League; Harlem Writer's Guild. **Honors/Awds:** Natl Endowment for the Arts Fellowship, 1988; New York Foundation for the Arts Fellowship, 1986; Doubleday/Columbia Univ Literary Fellowship. **Special Achievements:** Author: Breaking Ice, Viking Penguin, 1990; Disappearing Acts, Viking Penguin, 1989; Mama, Houghton Mifflin, 1987; Waiting to Exhale, Viking Penguin, 1992; A Day Late and a Dollar Short, 1995; How Stella Got Her Groove Back, 1996. **Business Addr:** Author, c/o Molly Priest Literary Agency, 122 E 42nd St, Ste 3902, New York, NY 10168.

MCMILLAN, WILLIAM ASBURY, SR.
Educational administrator, educator (retired). **Personal:** Born Feb 29, 1920, Winnabow, NC; son of Lydia McMillan and James McMillan; married Mildred Geraldine Newlin; children: Pamela Jackson, Paula Jones, William Jr. **Educ:** Johnson C Smith Univ, BA 1942; University of Michigan, MA 1945, PhD 1954. **Career:** Gatesville NC, tchr 1942-44, 1946-47; Johnson C Smith Univ, asst dean of instr 1947-48; Pomeroy PA, counselor 1948-49; Wiley Coll, dir 1949-58; Bethune-Cookman Coll, acad dean 1958-64, 1966-67; Rust Coll, pres 1967-93, pres emeritus, 1993-. **Orgs:** Life mem NEA; ATA; Mid-S Med Assn; pres MS Assn of Pvt Coll 1977-78; Alpha Phi Omega; NAACP; Boy Scout Leader; chmn bd of educ N MS; Conf of United Meth Ch; Omega Psi Phi; UNCF chairman, membership & visitation committee, board of directors, vice chair of the members; board of directors Mississippi Methodist Hospital & Rehabilitation Center; Phi Delta Kappa. **Honors/Awds:** Hon LLD: Cornell Coll, Johnson C Smith Univ, Bethune-Cookman Coll; Pres of Yr, MS Tchrs Assn 1973-74. **Military Serv:** US Air Force, 1945. **Home Addr:** 672 Woodward Ave, Holly Springs, MS 38635.

MCMILLAN, WILTON VERNON
Educator. **Personal:** Born Jun 5, 1943, Hope Mills, NC; son of Eunice E McMillian; married Lenora W McMillian, Apr 13, 1974; children: Valerie Kay. **Educ:** St Paul's College, BS, 1973; George Mason University, MEd, 1979. **Career:** Fairfax County Public Schools, teacher, 1972-. **Orgs:** Phi Delta Kappa, foundation/chair, 1995-; Omega Psi Phi Fraternity, past Baseluis, 1995-; Prince Hall Mason, past Master, 1980-; FEA, VEA, NEA. **Honors/Awds:** Omega Man of the Year, 1989; Eastern NC Theological Institution, Doctor of Humanities, 1995. **Military Serv:** US Army, Sp 4, 1966-69. **Home Addr:** 3208 Norwich Terrace, Alexandria, VA 22309. **Business Phone:** (703)780-5310.

MCMILLIAN, FRANK L.
Chemist, educator. **Personal:** Born Jun 9, 1934, Mobile, AL; son of Walter J and Roberta E McMillian; married Ruby A Curry; children: Franetta L, Kecia L. **Educ:** Dillard Univ, BA 1954; Tuskegee Univ, MS 1956; Univ of KS, PhD 1965. **Career:** Ft Valley State Coll, instructor, 1956-58; NC Central Univ, instr chemistry 1959-60; Norfolk State Coll, asst prof of chemistry 1960-62; Dillard Univ, visiting assoc prof of chemistry, 1968-69; E I du Pont de Nemours & Co, rsch chemist/sr technical specialist 1965-. **Orgs:** Mem Sigma Xi 1967-; mem Phi Lambda Upsilon Chem Soc 1964-; mem Omega Psi Phi Frat 1954-. **Honors/Awds:** Natl Science Found Fellow 1963. **Home Addr:** 3117 Albemarle Rd, Wilmington, DE 19808.

MCMILLIAN, JOSIE
Labor union executive. **Personal:** Born Oct 21, 1940, Childersberg, AL; divorced; children: 1 son, 2 daughters. **Educ:** Cornell Univ, Trade Union Study/George Meany Labor & Women Studies 1977. **Career:** NY Metro Area Postal Union, sector aide, chief steward, shop steward 1969, ex dir of clerk 1975, org'l vice pres 1976, exec vice pres 1979, pres. **Orgs:** Labor adv council NY Natl Urban League; mem Coalition of Labor Union Women; mem Natl Org of Women; mem New York City Black Trade Leadership Comm; adv bd mem Cornells Sch of Indus & Labor Relations; mem bd of dirs United Way of New York City; bd mem New York City & NJ combined Federal Campaign; life mem NAACP; clerk craft rep NYS Amer Postal Workers Union; adv mem New York City Central Labor Council; mem bd of dirs NYC Arthritis Foundation. **Honors/Awds:** Hispanic Labor Comm Awd New York City Central Labor Council 1978; Outstanding Achievement Awd New York City Chap Coalition of Labor Union Women 1981; Mary McLeod Bethune Awd Natl Council of Negro Women 1981; Achievement Awd New York City Branch NAACP 1981; Distinguished Serv Awd New York City Central Labor Council 1981; Sojourner Truth Loyalty Awd NY Chap Blk Trade Unionist 1982; Hoey Ecumenical Awd NY Catholic Interracial Council 1982; Appted Admiral in the Great Navy of NE 1982; Awd of Appreciation NY Chap Arthritis Found 1983; Pacific Group Home Awd Little Flower Children's Serv 1983; Outstanding Labor Leader Awd Natl Assn of Negro Business & Prof Women's Clubs 1984; Citation of Appreciation Amer Legion Dan Tallon Post 678; Appreciation Awd Women for Racial & Econ Equality 1985; Citan of Appreciation Brooklyn Borough Pres H Golden 1984; Labor Leaders' Award New York City Arthritis Foundation, 1988; Women's Achievement Award, YWCA 1985; Leadership Award Borough of Manhattan Community College 1989. **Business Addr:** President, NY Metro Area Postal Union, 460 W 34th St, New York, NY 10001.

MCMILLIAN, MARK
Professional football player. **Personal:** Born Apr 29, 1970, Los Angeles, CA. **Educ:** Alabama. **Career:** Philadelphia Eagles, defensive back, 1992-95; New Orleans Saints, 1996; Kansas City Chiefs, 1997-. **Business Addr:** Professional Football Player, Kansas City Chiefs, One Arrowhead Dr, Kansas City, MO 64129, (816)924-9300.

MCMILLIAN, THEODORE
Judge. **Personal:** Born Jan 28, 1919, St Louis, MO; married Minnie E Foster. **Educ:** Lincoln Univ, BS 1941; St Louis Univ Law School, LLB 1949. **Career:** St Louis Univ Law School, lecturer; Webster Coll, faculty mem; State of MO, circuit judge; City of St Louis, asst circuit attny 1953-56; MO Ct of Appeals, judge 1972-78; US Circuit Court of Appeals for 8th Cir, circuit judge 1978-. **Orgs:** Former mem bd of trustees Blue Cross 1974; former mem Danforth Found Adv Council 1975; mem Pres Council of St Louis Univ; former bd chmn Human Devel Corp 1964-77; former mem Natl Legal Aid Adv Bd; mem Alpha Sigma Nu, Phi Beta Kappa. **Honors/Awds:** Alumni Merit Awd St Louis Univ; Awd of Honor Lawyers Assoc 1970; Man of the Year Awd 1970; Doctor of Humanities, University of Missouri-St Louis; Doctor of Laws, St Louis University; inducted to the National Bar Association Hall of Fame; Founders Award, Bar Assn of St. Louis, 1992; Distinguished Lawyer Award, Bar Assn of St. Louis, 1996; Honorary Dimplomate, American Board of Trial Advocates, 1996. **Military Serv:** Signal Corps lt 1942-46. **Business Addr:** Circuit Judge, US Circuit Court of Appeals for 8th Circuit, US Court & Customs Bldg, St Louis, MO 63101.

MCMILLON, BILLY (WILLIAM E)
Professional baseball player. **Personal:** Born Nov 17, 1971, Otero, NM. **Educ:** Clemson. **Career:** Florida Marlins, outfielder, 1996-97; Philadelphia Phillies, 1997-. **Business Addr:** Professional Baseball Player, Philadelphia Phillies, PO Box 7575, Philadelphia, PA 19101, (215)463-6000.

MCMORRIS, JACQUELINE WILLIAMS
Government official. **Personal:** Born Mar 18, 1936, Washington, DC; daughter of Mr and Mrs John D Williams; married James Oliver McMorris; children: Jameille Olivia, James Oliver Jr. **Educ:** Temple Univ, AB, 1958; Howard Univ Coll of Medicine, MD, 1962. **Career:** Office of Economic Opportunities, medical consultant, 1965; DC Public Health Department, medical officer for child health and school health services, 1965-69; Health Services for Children with Special Needs, clinic director, 1969-95, acting chief medical officer, health services for children with special needs, 1989-. **Orgs:** Church choir dir 1962-82; mem Howard Univ Med Alumni 1962-87; bd of dirs DC Special Olympics 1978-79; chairperson Mamie D Lee Neighborhood School Cncl 1982-86; Mayor's Devel Disabilities Council 1984-87, sec St Anthony's Grade Sch PTA 1984-86; Mayor's Developmental Disabilities and Planning Council, 1980-; Medical Adv Rehab Serv 1985-87, Mayor's Comm on Handicapped 1985-87, Amer Medical Women's Assoc 1985-86; Howard Univ Transgenerational Project for Children with Learning Disabilities 1986-87; Mayor's Committee on Early Child Development, 1990-; DC Early Intervention Consortium of Providers, 1990-. **Honors/Awds:** Institute for the Integration of Handicapped Children into Early Education Programs, Appreciation Award, 1974; DC Special Olympics, Award for Outstanding Service to Mentally Retarded Citizens, 1978; Easter Seals Society, Silver Lily Membership Club Award, 1986; Information, Protection and Advocacy Center for Handicapped Individuals, The Second Roland J Queene Sr Memorial Award, 1987;. **Home Addr:** 4304 10th St NE, Washington, DC 20017. **Business Addr:** Acting Chief Medical Officer, Health Services for Children with Special Needs, 1900 Massachusetts Ave, SE, Washington, DC 20003.

MCMULLINS, TOMMY
Business executive. **Personal:** Born Sep 15, 1942, Macon, GA; son of Mr & Mrs Alummer McMullins; married Gwendolyn Williams; children: Tommy, Tyrone, Timothy. **Educ:** Ft Vly State Coll, BS Social Sci 1964; Amer Inst Banking, Var Bank Courses 1969-75; Pepperdine Univ, 1972; Pacif Cst Banking School, Grad Cert 1980. **Career:** Ylwstn Natl Pk, seasonal pk rgr 1963-64; First Intst Bank, manager reg sales manager vice pres 1965-82; Crocker Natl Bank, vice pres 1982-85; Wells Fargo Bank 1985-94; Citibank, vp, 1994-. **Orgs:** Co-chrpsn Emerg Hispanic Mjty 1978-80; bd mem Pasadena NAACP 1979-82; bd mem Comm Bell Gdns Rotary 1981-85; bd mem Monrovia Kiwanis 1969-73; pres Pasadena Chptr Alpha Phi Alpha 1975; chmn, International Visitors Council of Los Angeles. **Honors/Awds:** Crusdr awd Am Cncr svcs 1973-74. **Military Serv:** USM corpl 2 yrs; Expert Riflmn 1967. **Home Addr:** 1245 Rubio Vista Rd, Altadena, CA 91001. **Business Addr:** Vice President, Citibank, 5077 Lankershim Blvd, North Hollywood, CA 91601.

MCMURRY, KERMIT ROOSEVELT, JR.
Educational administrator. **Personal:** Born Jul 31, 1945, Kansas City, KS; married Valerie M; children: James Patrick, Chris, Nikii, Kermetria, Justin. **Educ:** Univ CO, BS 1968, MS 1970; Univ NE, PhD 1975; Harvard U, Post-Dctrl Study 1979. **Career:** Dept Admin Serv Exec Brnh State Govt State of NE, asst to dir 1974-75; NE Coord Comm for Post Scndry Educ, exec dir 1975-77; Grambling State U, exec vice pres, beginning 1977; Nebraska Dept of Social Services, dir, 1986-90; Oklahoma State Regents for Higher Education, assoc vice chancellor,

academic affairs, 1990-. **Orgs:** Asst dir Leisure Serv Univ of NE 1970-74; vice chmn United Campus Mnstrs; mem Lincoln Total Com Action Prog. **Honors/Awds:** Outstanding Young Man NE Jaycees 1971; Pioneering Coord Awrd NE Coord Commsn for Post Scndry Educ 1977. **Business Addr:** Associate Vice Chancellor for Academic Affairs, Oklahoma State Regents for Higher Education, 500 Education Building, State Capitol Complex, Oklahoma City, OK 73105.

MCMURRY, MERLEY LEE
City official. **Personal:** Born Aug 20, 1949, Kansas City, MO; daughter of Andrew Jackson Owens III; married Murvell McMurry, Jul 1, 1989; children: Steven Andrew, Courtney Michelle. **Educ:** University of Missouri, Columbia, MO, BA, 1971; Central Michigan University, Mt Pleasant, MI, MA, 1974. **Career:** Missouri Employment Security, Kansas City, MO, employment counselor, 1972-74; Metro Community Colleges, Kansas City, MO, counselor, 1974-78, project coordinator, 1978-83, tutorial coordinator, 1983-85; American Nurses' Association, Kansas City, MO, education consultant, 1985-86; Greater Kansas City Chamber of Commerce, Kansas City, MO, vice president, 1986-. **Orgs:** Member, President's Advisory University of Missouri Extension Board, 1989-; member, University of Missouri Small Business Develop Advisory Board, 1990-; member, University of Missouri Jackson County Extension Board, 1988-; vice chair, Small/Minority Business Networking Committee, 1986-; secretary, Teenage Parent Center Advisory Board, 1989-. **Honors/Awds:** US Small Business Admin, Minority Business Advocate, District, State, Region, 1991; Minorities and Women's Magazine, Women Who Make A Difference Award, 1990.

MCMURRY, WALTER M., JR.
Business executive. **Personal:** Born Mar 21, 1934, Canton, MS; married Reesa Anita Motley; children: Walter S, Stacie, James Randolph. **Educ:** Univ of MI, BBA 1963. **Career:** Bank of the Commonwealth, loan officer 1965-68; Inner-City Bus Improvement Forum, exec dir 1967-71; COMAC Caribbean/West Indies, resident mgr 1969-70; Independence Capital Formation, pres 1973-; Inner City Bus Improvement Forum, pres 1971-. **Orgs:** Bd of gov Natl Assn of Small Bus Invest Co; chmn OMBE Reg 5 Adv Counc; chmn MI Dist 203 Adv Counc; mem bd dir MI Minority Tech Council; dir Detroit Housing Finance Corp; dir at large BSA Detroit Area Councl; founder Black United Fund. **Honors/Awds:** Black Journal's 100 Most Influential Friends; guest lecturer Univ of MI. **Business Addr:** President, Inner-City Bus & Improv Foru, 1505 Woodward Ave St #700, Detroit, MI 48226.

MCNAIR, BARBARA J.
Singer, actress. **Personal:** Born Mar 4, 1939, Racine, WI; widowed. **Educ:** Univ of Southern California. **Career:** Night club singer; theatrical appearances include the Body Beautiful, 1958; The Merry World of Nat King Cole, 1961; No Strings, 1962; films include Spencer's Mountain, 1962; Stiletto, 1969; Change of Habit, 1969; Venus in Furs, 1970; They Call Me Mister Tibbs, 1970; The Organization, 1971; star of TV show, The Barbara McNair Show. **Orgs:** American Guild of Variety Artists; Screen Actors Guild; Actor's Equity; American Federation of Television and Radio Artists. **Business Addr:** c/o Moss Agency Ltd, 113 N San Vicente Blvd, Beverly Hills, CA 90211.

MCNAIR, CHRIS
County official, judge. **Career:** Jefferson County Courthouse, county commissioner, judge, currently. **Business Addr:** County Commissioner, Jefferson County, District 2, Courthouse, 716 21st Street, Birmingham, AL 35263, (205)325-5555.

MCNAIR, STEVE
Professional football player. **Personal:** Born Feb 14, 1973, Mount Olive, MS. **Educ:** Alcorn State University. **Career:** Tennessee Oilers, 1995-. **Special Achievements:** Selected in the 1st round/3rd overall pick in the 1995 NFL Draft; one of nine African-American quarterbacks, largest number in NFL history, 1997. **Business Addr:** Professional Football Player, Tennessee Oilers, c/o Baptist Sports Park, 7640 H 70-5, Nashville, TN 37221.

MCNAIRY, FRANCINE G.
Educational administrator. **Personal:** Born Nov 13, 1946, Pittsburgh, PA; daughter of Gladys McNairy and F E McNairy. **Educ:** Univ of Pittsburgh, BA, Sociology, 1968, MSW, 1970, PhD, Comm, 1978. **Career:** Allegheny Co Child Welfare Servs supvr & soc worker, 1970-72; Comm Action Regional training, tech asst specialist, 1972; Clarion Univ of PA, assoc prof/counselor 1973-82, coord of academic devel & retention 1983, dean of acad support serv & asst to the acad vice pres, 1983-88; West Chester Univ, Assoc Provost, 1988-. **Orgs:** Presenter Natl Conf on the Freshmen Yr Experience Univ of SC 1982-86; advisor Clarion Univ Black Student Union 1973-; vice chair Clarion Co Human Resources Develop Comm 1983-86; presenter, Intl Conf on the First Year Experience England, 1986, Creative Mgmt in Higher Educ, Boston 1986; consultant, Univ of NE, Briar Cliff Coll, Marshall Univ 1986; St Lawrence Coll 1984, Wesleyan Coll 1983; mem, PA Advisory Bd to ACT; member, AAHE; member, National Assn of Black Women in Higher Education. **Honors/Awds:** Publications ''Clarion Univ Increases Black Student Retention''; co-authored ''Taking the Library to Freshman Students via Freshman Seminar Concept'' 1986, ''The Minority Student on Campus'' 1985. **Business Addr:** Assoc Provost, West Chester Univ, 151 E O Bull Center, West Chester, PA 19383.

MCNARY, OSCAR LEE
Artist. **Personal:** Born Mar 23, 1944, San Antonio, TX; married Maudene J; children: Omar. **Educ:** Attended San Antonio Jr Coll 1964-65; attended TX So Univ 1967-68; attended So Meth Univ; attended Hunters Sch of Art 1973-74. **Career:** Visual artist. **Orgs:** Mem Dallas Mus of Fine Arts 1974-81; mem Natl Conf of Artists 1975-81; bd of adv/mem Phoenix Cultural Arts Cntr 1975-81; mem TX Arts Alliance; state & local mem TX Fine Arts Assn 1975-81; assoc mem Amer Watercolor Soc 1976-81; natl mem Artists Equity Assn 1977-81; elect mem the Intl Platform Assn 1978-81; 1st Black vice pres & 1st Black bd mem Artists Coalition of TX 1979; bd of trustees & 1st Black pres Richardson Civic Art Soc 1979-81; committeeman Cub Scouts of Amer Pack 584 1979-81; mem PTA Heights Elem Sch 1979-81. **Honors/Awds:** Numerous Group exhibitions 1965-80; 1 Man Exhibit Promenade Natl Bank 1976; Man Exhibit Phoenix Cultural Arts Cntr 1979; 1 Man Exhibit Arthello's Gallery 1980. **Business Addr:** 1308 Timberlake Circle, Richardson, TX 75080.

MCNEAL, DON
Professional football player (retired). **Personal:** Born May 6, 1958, Atmore, AL; married Rhonda. **Educ:** Univ of Alabama, BS, social welfare. **Career:** Miami Dolphins, cornerback, 1980-89. **Honors/Awds:** NFL all rookie, Tommy Fitzgerald mem awrd outstanding rookie, 1980.

MCNEAL, JOHN ALEX, JR.
Educational administrator. **Personal:** Born Jun 18, 1932, Metter, GA; married Earlene Hazel; children: Lydia Tryphenia, Kezia Ruth. **Educ:** Fort Valley State Coll, BS 1961; Grace Theol Sem, BRE 1964; GA State Univ, MEd 1975; Carver Bible Coll, doctor of divinity 1986. **Career:** Fundamentalist Baptist Assn, publicity chmn 1964, pres 1975-77, vice pres 1977-80; Atlanta Bible Baptist Church, pastor/founder; Carver Bible Inst & Coll, rev & dean of students 1964-; Baptist Mission of North America, ethnic rep 1985. **Orgs:** Mem Fellowship of Baptist for Home Missions. **Honors/Awds:** Outstanding Educators of Amer 1972; Awd for Dedicated Serv Carver Alumni Assn 1972. **Military Serv:** USAF airman 1st class 1952-56; Good Conduct Medal; Service Awd. **Business Addr:** Rev & Dean of Students, Carver Bible Inst & Coll, 437 Nelson St SW, Atlanta, GA 30313.

MCNEAL, TIMOTHY KYLE
Television executive. **Personal:** Born Jun 27, 1960, Sacramento, CA; son of Homer and Carol McNeal. **Educ:** UCLA, BA, political science. **Career:** The WB Network, vice pres of drama development, currently. **Business Addr:** Vice Pres, Drama Development, The WB Network, 4000 Warner Blvd, Bldg 34R, Burbank, CA 91522.

MCNEELY, CAROL J.
Dentist, consultant. **Personal:** Born Jul 17, 1954, Chicago, IL; daughter of Jessie O Woodfin McNeely and Lewis W McNeely; divorced; children: Matthew Allan Ivy. **Educ:** Univ of IL College of Dentistry, DDS 1979; Kellogg School of Management Northwestern Univ, MM, 1995. **Career:** Tyrone Holiday DDS, assoc dentist 1979-80; Provident Dental Assocs, owner 1984-; Dr Carol McNeely & Associates, owner 1979-; Soulful Expressions (A Practice Promotion Co), owner, 1987; Dental Network of America, Consultant, 1988-. **Orgs:** Speaker Amer Assoc of Women Dentists 1982; treas Lincoln Dental Soc Natl Dental Soc 1982-83; assoc bd mem Chicago Child Care Soc 1982-85, American Academy of Cosmetic Dentistry 1988; American Dental Association; National Dental Association; co-chairperson, Chicago Urban League Sholarship Committee, 1989; member Taskforce on Women and Minorities, American Dental Association, 1992; president Chicago Metro Association of Black Women Dentists, 1992; American Assn of Dental Consultants; American Assn of Healthcare Executives. **Honors/Awds:** Partners in the Comm Natl Bar Assoc Chicago Chap 1985. **Business Addr:** Dentist, Dr Carol McNeely & Assocs, 7933 South King Dr, Chicago, IL 60619.

MCNEELY, CHARLES E.
Government official. **Personal:** Born Jun 24, 1951; son of Louise Johnson McNeely and Aubrey McNeely; married Rosalind Gulley McNeely, May 21, 1974; children: Leslie, Brian, Brandon. **Educ:** University of Kansas, Lawrence, KS, BA, political science, 1973, MBA, 1975. **Career:** City of San Diego, San Diego, CA, international relations intern, 1971; City of Palo Alto, Palo Alto, CA, adm. analyst, budget & staff services, 1974-75, personnel administrator, 1975-76, management assistant, 1976-78, assistant city manager, 1978-83; City of Seaside, Seaside, CA, city manager, 1983-. **Orgs:** Committee member, League of California Cities Housing & Community & Economic Development, 1991; board member, CRA, 1990; chairperson, Coalition of African American Men, 1990-91; committee member, League of California Cities Advancement of Minorities & Women, 1990-91; instructor, Golden Gate University, 1991. **Business Addr:** City Manager, City of Seaside, 440 Harcourt, Seaside, CA 93955.

MCNEELY, MATTHEW
State representative. **Personal:** Born May 11, 1920, Millen, GA; son of Nina Norton McNelly and Whaley McNeely; married Beatrice; children: Chris, Roy, Cloteele, Camille, Cynthia. **Educ:** Lansing Community College, AA. **Career:** Local 306 Dist, educ dir; 18 & 20 Wards, pres; Michigan State Board of Escheats, cons; Houston House of Representatives, member, 1964-80; State of Michigan House of Representatives, member, 1985-. **Orgs:** Mem, board of directors, Michigan Partners of the Americas; mem, Executive Committee, Natl Legislative Black Clearing House; adv bd Carmel Hall; Pine Grove Bapt Ch; first past pres & fndr NCBSL; del Educ Comm of the States Advanced Leadership Prog. **Honors/Awds:** Michigan International Certificate of Leadership Award, Natl Conf of State, 1978; delegate to African-Amer Insts 9th Conf Khartoum Sudan. **Business Addr:** State Representative 3rd Dist, MI House of Representatives, PO Box 30014, Lansing, MI 48909.

MCNEIL, ALVIN J.
Educator. **Personal:** Born Apr 12, 1920, Hinds Co, MS; son of Pamelia McGee McNeil and Charlie McNeil; married Ella Edith Holmes, Mar 18, 1951; children: Charles, Needha, Adrian. **Educ:** TN A&I State Coll, BA; Boston Univ, MA 1951; Univ Denver, EdD 1960; Univ of MO, post doctoral study. **Career:** Wynne, AR, asst prin/counselor 1947-49; MS Voc Coll, registrar/dean/dept head 1951-58; Grambling State Coll, prof/dept head 1958-68; Prairie View A&M, dean 1968-71; TX So Univ, prof/assoc dean/head dept of administration & higher educ. **Orgs:** City councilman Grambling 1965-68; past natl pres Phi Beta Sigma 1965-69; mem Lions Club; Prince Hall Masons; Shriner; Amer Legion; Kappa Delta Pi; Phi Delta Kappa; Alpha Kappa Delta; Sigma Delta Pi. **Honors/Awds:** Crusade fellowship grant 1957-58; Citation for Meritorious Serv Town of Grambling; Distinguished Serv Chap Phi Beta Sigma; Distinguished Educator Award, MS; Christian Serv Award Wheeler Ave Baptist Ch; Appreciation Award Sch of Educ TX So Univ; Amer Assn for Higher Educ Black Caucus; Pioneering Efforts in Higher Educ Doctoral Students Appreciation Awd. **Military Serv:** Military Serv WO-1 1942-45. **Home Addr:** 6008 Del Rio, Houston, TX 77021.

MCNEIL, DEEDEE
Songwriter, singer, poet, freelance journalist. **Personal:** Born Sep 7, Detroit, MI; daughter of Mary Virginia Elkins and Frank Lawton Elkins; divorced; children: Maricea Lynn McNeil, Harry Lawrence McNeil III, William A Chappell, Jr. **Educ:** Attended, Pasadena City Coll, Music, Journalism, one year. **Career:** Jobete Publishing Co, Motown Record Co, Detroit, contract songwriter 1968-71; Ala Record Co, Los Angeles, recording artist, 1971; The Watts Prophets, coll campus lecturer & traveling poet, 1971-77; A&M Record Co, Hollywood, first black publicist, 1972-73; United Artist Records, Hollywood, Natl Press & Media Coord, 1973-74; contributing writer, Soul & Jazz Records Magazine, various newspapers & magazines in US & Canada, 1974-75; The Soul & Jazz Record Magazine, assoc editor, co-publisher, 1975-77; songwriter, singer, freelance journalist, publisher 1971-. **Orgs:** Asst, David Gest & Assoc PR Firm, Hollywood; coll speaker, seminars for promotional publications & publicity; co-establisher, Al-Bait Haram Publishing Co, CA, 1971; co-publisher, operator, House of Haram Publishing Found; co-producer, Ar-Tee/Double Dee Production Co; consultant & public relations specialist, KWANZA Org; established Eddie Beal Scholarship Fund for Creative Youth; bd of dir and lifetime member, The Jazz Heritage Found; program coord, free program for children, ''Jazz & You'' sponsored by Jazz Heritage Found. **Honors/Awds:** The Outreach Award, Pasadena, 1976; Shreveport Reg Bicentennial Comm Award, KWANZA Org, 1976; named Dir of Publicity, NATRA, 1976-77; founder, fellow, Fellowship of Intl Poets Assn, London; dean's honor list, Pasadena City Coll Music Dept; Certificate of Merit, Amer Song Festival, 1977; nominee, Best Spoken Word Image Award, NAACP, 1972; published numerous articles, Black Stars Magazine, Essence, Soul & Jazz Record Mag; published numerous poems; wrote numerous songs, Kiki Dee, Gladys Knight, Diana Ross, Nancy Wilson; performed various coll concerts with Watts Prophets; various TV appearances; featured vocalist, recordings & concerts; listed as west coast rap originator in ''The Black Music History of Los Angeles, It's Roots,'' 1992.

MCNEIL, ERNEST DUKE
Attorney. **Personal:** Born Oct 9, 1936, Memphis, TN; married Sandra; children: 2. **Educ:** TN State Univ BS; Fisk U, BA 1957; Depaul U, JD 1965. **Career:** Mcneil Cheeks & Assoc, presently an atty. **Orgs:** Pres The woodlawn Organization; pres TWO Enterprises; pres woodlawn Redevel Assn; vice pres Cook County Bar Assn; Health Commr Cook Co Governing Comm; weekly columnist Chicago Defender Cook Co Dept of Pub Aid; interviewer & pub relations officer IL State Employment Serv; private investigator claimsadjuster Safeway Insurance Co; law clerk & defense atty Leo Gilfoy Attorneys; chmn Speaker Bureau Am Negro Emancipation Centennial Authority; adv youth

div Chicago Urban League; co-founder & treas Organization of Black Am Culture; co-founder & treas Legal Found; mem Phi Alpha Delta; Kappa Alpha Psi; bd dirMandel Legal Aid Clinic; bd dir Mid S Health Planning Coun; bd dir Gateway House IL Drug Abuse Prog; mem Jackson Park-Woodlawn Businessmen's Assn; ch-chmnCivil Rights Com; chmn Woodlawn Comm.

MCNEIL, FRANK
City treasurer. **Personal:** Born Jan 6, 1937, St Louis; married Annetta Cropp; children: Frank, Anita Louise, Patricia Ann, Betty Marie, Scott Kevin. **Career:** Wellston MO (1st Black Elected in MO), city treas; Block Mothers, dir 1973-. **Orgs:** Treas Wellston Youth League for Boys; FEPC Lincoln Eng Co Fair Employment Practices Com. **Honors/Awds:** Recipient plaque Wellston Block Mothers 1973-74; mem Natl Roster of Black Elected Officials 1974. **Military Serv:** AUS sp/4 hon discharge 1963. **Business Addr:** 1804 Keinlin, St Louis, MO.

MCNEIL, FRANK WILLIAM
Lobbyist. **Personal:** Born Dec 12, 1948, High Point, NC; son of Madge Holmes McNeil and Walter H McNeil; married Barbara Jean Curtain McNeil, Mar 17, 1977; children: Kwahme, Kofi. **Educ:** NC Central Univ, Durham NC, BA, 1971; JD, 1974. **Career:** IL Law Enforcement Committee, Springfield Il, legislative spec, 1974-76; State Board of Ethics, Springfield Il, admin asst, 1976-77; Secretary of State Corp Div, Springfield Il, corp spec, 1978-79, admin asst, 1979-81; Senate Democratic Staff Parleamentarian, Springfield IL, 1981-86; Chicago Urban League, govt rel coordinator, 1986-87; consultant/lobbyist, Springfield Il, 1987-. **Orgs:** Springfield Urban League Guild; Springfield Branch NAACP; Family Service Center Sangamon County Board of Directors; Boy's Club Board of Directors. **Honors/Awds:** Political Action Award, NAACP, 1986; Omega Psi Phi Man of the Year, 1986, 87; Webster Plaque, NAACP, 1987; Plaintiff in successful voting rights suit, McNeil vs City of Springfield; Elected Alderman Ward 2 City of Springfield, 1987. **Home Addr:** 2010 Brown Street, Springfield, IL 62703. **Business Addr:** Consultant/Lobbyist, Frank W McNeil & Associates, Inc, 1 West Old Capitol Plaza, Suite 501, Springfield, IL 62703.

MCNEIL, FREEMAN
Professional football player (retired). **Personal:** Born Apr 22, 1959, Jackson, MS. **Educ:** UCLA. **Career:** New York Jets, running back, 1981-93. **Honors/Awds:** Voted Most Valuable Player, New York Jets, 1981-84; holds New York Jets' rushing record, running back, 1984; Mackiey Award, 1981; named AFC Offensive Player of the Month, Sept 1986; All-NFL by AP, NEA, Football Digest; All-AFC by UPI; Pro Bowl, 1983, 1986. **Business Addr:** Former Professional Football Player, New York Jets, 1000 Fulton Ave, Hempstead, NY 11550.

MCNEIL, LORI MICHELLE
Professional tennis player. **Personal:** Born Dec 18, 1963, San Diego, CA; daughter of Doris McNeil and Charlie McNeil. **Educ:** Oklahoma State University, 1981-83. **Career:** Professional tennis player, 1983-. **Orgs:** Women Tennis Assn, 1983-; Wightman Cup Team, 1989. **Honors/Awds:** Singles Champion Suntory Open, Tokyo, Japan, 1991; Singles Champion Colorado Tennis Classic, Denver, CO, 1991; French Open Mixed Doubles Champion, Paris, France, 1988; Singles Champion Virginia Slims of Oklahoma, 1988; Big Eight No 1 Singles Champion, 1983; US Open Semifinalist, defeated Chris Evert, 1987; quarter finalist, Wimbledon, 1986; quarter finalist, Australian, 1987; Winner: singles, Albuquerque, 1989, doubles, Oklahoma (with Nagelson), Newport (with G Fernandez), Indianapolis (with K Adams), Brighton (with K Adams), European Open (with K Adams), 1989; United States Federation Cup Team, 1988-89; ranked as high as 9, 1988; Pilkington Glass Trophy, 1992. **Business Addr:** Professional Tennis Player, Tennis Div, International Management Group, One Erieview Plaza, Ste 1300, Cleveland, OH 44114.

MCNEIL, OGRETTA V.
Educator. **Personal:** Born Sep 2, 1932, Savannah, GA; married Kingsley R; children: John, Robert Vaughn. **Educ:** Howard Univ, BS magna cum Laude 1954; Clark Univ, MA 1959; PhD (Danforth fellowship) 1967. **Career:** Worcester Youth Guidance Cntr, psychologist 1967-68; Worcester Pub Schs, clin psychologist 1968-70; Assumption Coll, asst prof 1968-71; Clark Univ, visit lectr 1972; Anna Maria Coll, consult clin psychologist 1968-78; Holy Cross Coll, assoc prof psychology 1971-. **Orgs:** Mem Amer Psychol Assn; New England Psychol Assn; steering com 1980-89; exec com Assn Soc & Behav Scis 1978-; AAUW corp laison; bd of trustees Univ of MA 1976-81, 1992-97; bd of trustees LeMoyne Coll 1977-82; AAUP Phi Beta Kappa. **Honors/Awds:** Sigma Xi; USPHS fellow 1956-58; VA Clin intern 1958-60; Danforth assoc 1971-77; NSF 1971. **Business Addr:** Professor, Holy Cross Coll, College St, Worcester, MA 01610.

MCNEIL, ROBERT LAWRENCE, JR. (BOB)
Business Owner. **Personal:** Born Oct 3, 1969, Chicago, IL; son of Robert L & Yvonne McNeil, Sr.; married Stacey R. **Career:** Images USA, president. **Orgs:** American Marketing Association; Atlanta Ad Club; Georgia Minority Supplier Development Council.

MCNEIL, RYAN DARRELL
Professional football player. **Personal:** Born Oct 4, 1970, Fort Pierce, FL. **Educ:** Miami (Fla.). **Career:** Detroit Lions, defensive back, 1993-96; St Louis Rams, 1997-. **Business Addr:** Professional Football Player, St Louis Rams, One Rams Way, St Louis, MO 63045, (314)982-7267.

MCNEILL, CERVES TODD
Advertising executive. **Personal:** Born Jun 20, 1950, Jamaica, NY; son of Todd Cerves & Ella Mae McNeill; married Elizabeth Straka McNeill, Aug 15, 1972; children: Nigel Isaiah. **Educ:** NY University, Undergraduate Institute of Film & TV, 1968-71; University of California, Los Angeles, screenwriting, 1980-81, film production, 1985; private study with Bess Bonnier, Jazz Piano Improvisation, 1988-90; Continental Cable Public Access, production certification, 1993. **Career:** Self-employed, freelance bassist, guitarist, vocalist, composer, actor, 1965-; Young & Rubicam Inc, NY copywriter, 1976-79; Benton & Bowles Inc, NY sr copywriter, 1980; SSC&B Inc, Los Angeles, sr copywriter, 1980-81; Dancer Fitzgerald Sample Inc, Torrence CA, sr copywriter, 1982-84; Self-employed, freelance copywriter/screenwriter, 1984-; Campbell-Ewald Advertising, sr vice pres associate creative director, 1986-. **Orgs:** American Federation of Musicians, 1965-93; Christians In Advertising, board member, 1985-86; Raulerson Evangelistic Association, evangelist, board member, 1987-90; Broadcast Music Inc, writer, publisher affiliate, 1972-; Blacks in Advertising, radio & TV, 1997-. **Honors/Awds:** The World Institute of Black Communications, Inc, CEBA AWD, United Negro College Fund, Print Campaign, 1979, CEBA Awd, UNCF/Poster, 1980; Interagency Council on Child Abuse and Neglect, ANDY Merit Award, 1983; Art Directors Club of NY, Merit Awd, Chevrolet, 1987; International Film & TV Festival, NY Festival Bronze Detroit News/TV, 1990; Detroit Creative Directors Council, Caddy Awd of Merit, GMAC Financing/TV, United Way/TV, 1990; Delta Faucet/TV, Caddy Silver Award, 1991, ADDY Award, 1992; Continental Cable Access Award, Best Produced Show, 1993. **Special Achievements:** Bass player on movie soundtrack "Chaffed Elbows," 1965; Actor in motion picture "Putney Swope," 1969; Bassist on movie soundtrack, "The White Whore and the 2 Bit Player," 1970; Co-writer/bassist on 45 record "My Heart And I Don't Believe," (BMI), 1972; Model in Urban League Football Poster, "Make It to the Game That Will Knock You Off Your Feet," 1976; Writer, co-producer, actor in UNCF TV ad "Plantation," 1979; Co-writer, producer, director on Boy Scout Video, "The Great Steal," 1991; initiated Chevrolet's first and continuing Kwanzaa and Black History Month ad campaigns as creative director, writer, and co-producer, 1994-; writer and co-producer on Chevy Blazer radio campaign featuring comedian George Wallace, "Auntie," "Close Encounter," "No Preferences," "Stress," 1997. **Business Addr:** Senior VP, Associate Creative Director for Chevrolet Diversity Advertising, Campbell-Ewald Advertising, 30400 Van Dyke Ave, Warren, MI 48093-2316, (810)558-6318.

MCNEILL, SUSAN PATRICIA
Military officer (retired), attorney. **Personal:** Born Oct 3, 1947, Washington, DC; daughter of Lula M McNeill and Robert H McNeill. **Educ:** Wilson College, BA, 1969; Creighton University, JD, 1978; Pepperdine University, MBA, 1980. **Career:** US Air Force: Edwards AFB, Assistant Staff Judge Advocate, contract attorney, 1978-81; Norton AFB, Ballistic Missile Office, Asst Staff Judge Advocate, staff attorney, 1981-84; Lindsey Air Station, Germany, Staff Judge Advocate, chief legal officer, 1984-87; Dept of Justice, Defense Procurement Fraud Unit, trial attorney, 1987-89; Pentagon, Air Force Contract Law Division, trial attorney, 1989-91, Air Force General Counsel's Office, staff attorney, 1991-92; Defense Systems Management College, Acquisition Law Task Force, associate director, senior attorney, 1992-93; AF General Counsels Office, civilian staff attorney, 1993-95; Sawyer Myersburg, of counsel, currently. **Orgs:** Nebraska Bar Assn, 1978-; Big Sisters of Omaha, 1977-78; National Contract Management Assn, Wiesbaden, Germany, chapter president, 1985-87; Air Force Cadet Officer Mentor Program, executive board, 1991-; American Bar Assn, Government Contracts Section, 1991-. **Honors/Awds:** Judge Advocate, Big Sisters of Omaha, Big Sister of the Year, 1978; Natl Coalition 100 Black Women, VA Commonwealth Chapter, Serwa Award, 1993. **Special Achievements:** Highest ranking African-American female Judge Advocate in all branches of the Armed Forces, 1993. **Military Serv:** US Air Force, Col, 1970-93; Legion of Merit, 1993, Defense Meritorious Service Medal, 1993, Air Force Meritorious Service Medal, 1981, 1984, 1987, Air Force Commendation Medal, 1982.

MCNEILL-HUNTLEY, ESTHER MAE
Elected official, educator (retired). **Personal:** Born May 7, 1921, Fayetteville, NC; daughter of Margaret McNeill; widowed; children: Micheline E, Karen D, Frances M. **Educ:** NC A&T State Univ, BS Home Economics 1944; Bank St Coll NYC, teachers cert; NY Univ, Administration 1953; Fayetteville State Univ, Small Business Mgmt 1977. **Career:** NYC, postal clerk; day care teacher; Headstart teacher; Washington Ave Day Care Ctr, first dir; Rainbow Nursery Sch, proprietor/dir, currently. **Orgs:** Former mem Girl Scout Leader NYC 1970-72; 3rd Dist Chairwoman Women in Municipal Govt 1982-85; found bd Bladen Tech Coll; mem NC Black Leadership Caucus; mem Natl Black Caucus of Local Elected Officials; vice pres NC Minority Public Officials; former mem Bladen Co Improvement Assn; charter & former mem Bladen Co Arts Council; mem Mt Zion AME Zion Church. **Honors/Awds:** County Chmn LINC Children's 100 1974; 1st Black elected to Elizabethtown's City Council 1979; represented City of Elizabethtown in the Natl League of Cities; First woman to be elected to City Council; Lobbyist in Washington DC for Newtown Comm Block Grant awarded 1983; Outstanding Community Serv Zeta Phi Beta 1983; Cert of Appreciation Holshouser Jr; appointed by Gov James G Martin to serve on the Local Govt Advocacy Council 1985 (2 yr term); State of NC Human Relations Commission, Gov Jim B Hunt, Certificate of Appreciation, 1994; Rainbow Nursery School, Outstanding Service to Family & Community, 1994; NAACP, West Bladen Branch, 50 Years Service to Children, 1945-95, Humanitarian Awd, 1996. **Home Addr:** PO Box 1346, Elizabethtown, NC 28337.

MCNELTY, HARRY
Clergyman. **Personal:** Born Jan 5, E, TX; married Edna Crossley; children: Michael. **Educ:** Chicago Bapt Theo Sem; Chicago Baptist Institute, graduate; McKinley Theological Seminary, bachelor of thelogy. **Career:** First Bapt Church, Melrose Park, IL assoc minister, 1958-59, pastor, 1959-. **Orgs:** Pres Comm Orgn for Maywood; vice pres E Proviso Ministers Alliance; mem Black Men Moving Div SCLC Operation Breadbasket; tchr Ch Adminstrn Bapt Ministers' Conf of Chicago & vicinity; mem Adv Bd IL Citizens Conservation for Life Com Cook County Chpt; Am Soc Distinguished Citizens; pres, Proviso Ministers Alliance; vp, Maywood Branch, NAACP; Operation PUSH/Rainbow Coalition; Salem District Assn, Natl Baptist Convention USA, Inc; advisory bd mem, Cook County Chap, Citizens Conservation for Life. **Honors/Awds:** Honors SCLC Black Men Moving Div 1971; Foreign Mission Bd 1974; Certificate of Appreciation, Chaplain Svc, Westlake Comm; Outstanding Church of the Year Awd, 1977; Midwest Baptist Laymen Fellowship, Natl Baptist Convention USA, Inc, 1978; Certificate of Honor, Baptist Ministers Conference of Chicago and Vicinity; Certificate of Awd, Chicago Alumni Assn; Outstanding Leadership Awd, Fred Hampton Scholarship Fund; George E Stone Humanitarian Awd, Operation Uplift, 1992; Honorary Doctorate of Divinity, McKinley Theological Seminary; Honorary Doctorate of Divinity, Hamilton State Univ; MA Talley Awd, Sunday School Publishing Board of the Natl Baptist Convention USA, Inc, 1992. **Special Achievements:** Organized the H McNelty School of the First Baptist Church, 1981; Builder of the H McNelty School of the First Baptist Church, Completion and Dedication, 1991. **Business Addr:** Pastor, First Bapt Church, 2114 Main St, Melrose Park, IL 60160.

MCNORRIELL, MOZELL M.
Labor union executive. **Personal:** Born Oct 20, 1922, Marshall, TX; divorced; children: Robert, Jr. **Educ:** Wayne State Univ Labor Sch 1971. **Career:** Am Fed State Co & Municipal Employees AFL-CIO, intl vice pres 1975-; Wayne Co Local 409 AFSCME AFL-CIO, pres 1967-; Metro Cist Council 23, sec 1969-. **Orgs:** Life mem NAACP; mem Elliottorian Bus Women's Club 1952-; Plymouth United Ch Christ; natl coordinating com mem Coalition of Labor Union Women; dir CivilRights Trade Union Leadership Council; mem Coalition Blak Trade Unionists; First Black woman MI Intl vice pres major union AFSCME AFL-CIO. **Business Addr:** 24611 Greenfield, Southfield, MI.

MCNORTON, BRUCE EDWARD
Professional football player. **Personal:** Born Feb 28, 1959, Daytona Beach, FL. **Educ:** Georgetown (KY) College, BA, social work, 1982. **Career:** Detroit Lions, cornerback, 1982-.

MCPHAIL, IRVING P.
Educational administrator. **Personal:** Born Mar 27, 1949, New York City, NY; married Carolyn Jean Carver; children: Kamilah Carole. **Educ:** Cornell Univ, BS 1970; Harvard Univ, MAT 1971; Univ of PA, EdD 1976. **Career:** Morgan State Univ Baltimore, coord freshman reading prog 1971-73, assoc prof ed, chmn dept curr & instr 1977-80; The Johns Hopkins Univ Baltimroe, spec asst to pres & provost 1978-79; Univ of MD Coll Park, asst provost div of human & comm resrcs, assoc prof curriculum & instr; Baltimore City Public School, coo 1984-85; Kamilah Educ Enterprises Inc, pres, principal cons; DE State Coll, vp, dean of acad affairs, prof of educ 1985-. **Orgs:** Antioch Univ 1975-76,82-; co-found & pres Natl Assoc of Black Reading & Lang Ed; mem Natl Alliance of Black School Educators, Intl Reading Assoc, Amer Assoc for Higher Ed, Natl Council of Teachers of English, Phi Delta Kappa, Coll Reading Assoc; consult AID Prog Staff Devel School Dist of Philadelphia 1976; consult to off Right to Read Baltimore City Publ School 1977;author of over 25 articles chapters & menographs in professional lit; mem Alpha Phi Alpha, ZetaRho Lambda; vchmn DE Coalition for Literacy. **Honors/Awds:** Amer Counc on Ed Fellow in Acad Admin 1978-79; Natl Fellowships Fund Doctoral Fellow Phi Delta Kappa Univ of PA; Certs for Outstanding Contribs & Svcs, Morgan State Univ 1973, MD Reading Inst 1977,81,85, Baltimore City Public Schools 1977,85, IRA 1978,81,82,85, Teacher Corps 1979, DC Public Schools 1983, Copping State Coll 1984, MD State Dept

of Educ 1985, Concord Black Parents of Hartford Cty 1986; listed in Men of Achievement 1977; selected as Eminent Scholar Norfolk State Univ 1981, One of Amers Ten Outstanding Youn Men US Jaycees 1982. **Business Addr:** VP, Dean Academic Affairs, Delaware State College, Grossely Hall, Dover, DE 19901.

MCPHAIL, JERRIS
Professional football player. **Personal:** Born Jun 26, 1972, Clinton, NC. **Educ:** East Carolina. **Career:** Miami Dolphins, running back, 1996-. **Business Addr:** Professional Football Player, Miami Dolphins, 2269 NW 199th St, Miami, FL 33056, (305)620-5000.

MCPHAIL, SHARON M.
Attorney. **Personal:** Born Nov 6, 1948, Cambridge, MA; daughter of Natalie Fowler McPhail and Robson Bacchus McPhail; married David Snead, May 27, 1995; children: Angela, Erika. **Educ:** Coe College, Cedar Rapids, IA, 1966-68; Northeastern University, Boston, MA, BA, 1972; University of Michigan Law School, 1975-76; Northeastern University Law School, JD, 1976. **Career:** Ford Motor Company, staff attorney, 1976-80; assistant United States attorney, 1980-82; special assistant United States attorney, 1982-83; Dickinson, Wright, Moon, Van Dusen & Freeman, associate, 1982-84; Bushnell, Gage, Doctoroff & Reizen, associate, 1984-86; Wayne County Corporation Counsel, principal attorney, 1986-87; Wayne County Prosecutor's Office, chief of screening and district courts, 1987-94; Feikens, Vander Male, Stevens, Bellamy, and Gilchrist, partner, 1995-. **Orgs:** President, 1992, vice president, 1986-89, member, National Bar Assn; director, Natl Council of Northeastern University, 1988-; chairperson, member, Detroit Board of Police Commissioners, 1985-90; vice chair, State Officers Compensation Commission, 1988-; vice chair, member, Wayne County Neighborhood Legal Services, 1987-; director, Kirwood Mental Health Center, 1990; life member, Sixth Circuit Judicial Conference, US Court of Appeals; member, board of directors, Federal Bar Assn, 1988; member, board of directors, Music Hall Center for the Performing Arts, 1988-; member, board of directors, Detroit Branch, NAACP; president, Wolverine Bar Assn, 1985-86; member, Women Lawyers Assn of Michigan; member, Assn of Defense Trial Counsel; fellow, Michigan State Bar Foundation, 1988-; March of Dimes: Humanitarian of the Year, 1994. **Honors/Awds:** Cora T. Walker Award, National Bar Association, 1988; Academy of Honors, Northeastern University, 1972; Phi Kappa Phi, Northeastern University, 1972; National Poetry, Press for Poetry, 1968; Ladies Literary, Society for Poetry, 1968; faculty member of the Federal Bar Association, National Bar Association, Wolverine Bar Association, University of Michigan; First Woman in History to Win Primary for Mayor of Detroit, 1993. **Business Addr:** Partner, Feikens, Vander Male, Stevens, Bellamy & Gilchrist, 500 Woodward Ave, Ste 3400, Detroit, MI 48226, (313)962-5909.

MCPHATTER, THOMAS H.
Association executive. **Personal:** Born Oct 8, 1923, Lumberton, NC; married Genevieve R Bryant; children: Thomas, Doretha, Mary Elizabeth, Joseph, Neil. **Educ:** Johnson C Smith Univ Charlotte, NC, BA 1948; Johnson C Smith Univ Charlotte, NC, MDiv 1951; Program in Human Behavior Urban Devel PhD. **Career:** Newport News Shipyard, ship rigger 1941-43; Clothing Store, clk & mgr 1946-51; St Paul Presb Ch KC, MO, pastor 1951-58; navy chaplain 1958-69; LCDR Consult Religions & Race No CA 1969-70; Golden Hill Presb Ch, asso pastor, hon ret Presbyterian Mini, 1970-71. **Orgs:** Pres Omega Housing & Devel Co; project dir MDTA; Dept Labor; deputyequal Employment Opportunity Officer Dept of Def 1974-75; commr United Presb Ch Gen Assembly 1968; comm Synod of MO 1953 & 1955; Moderator Presbytery of KC 1957-58; vice pres Council of Ch of Greater KC 1956-57; mem MO Synod Council 12th Dist ; rep Omega Psi Phi Frat; vice pres MO State Conf NAACP 1969-70; bd mem YMCA 1954-55; pres Eisenhowers Minority Adv Com 1954-58; Urban League Bd 1957-58; pres Any Boy Can 1968-69; SD Dist Chaplain & Post Chaplain Am Legion KC, MO 1955-58; Life mem Urban League Omega Psi Phi. **Honors/Awds:** Key to City of San Diego 1963; listed in Who's What & Why in MO 1967-68; 12th Dist citizen of yr Omega Psi Phi Frat; honorary Life mem Council of CA PTA; Honorary Thomas H McPhatter (DD), Doctor of Divinity, Interdenomination Theological Ctr. **Special Achievements:** Author: "Caught in the Middle, A Dychotomy of An African-American Man" and "They Called Him Troublemaker". **Military Serv:** USMC sgt 1943-46; USN chaplain Capt 1958-83, Iwo Jima, Japan. **Business Addr:** 4297 Pacific Hwy, PO Box 80337, San Diego, CA 92138.

MCPHEETERS, ANNIE LOU
Librarian (retired). **Personal:** Born Feb 22, 1908, Rome, GA; daughter of Josiephine Dozier Watters (deceased) and William A Watters (deceased); married Alphonso Alonza McPheeters, Aug 26, 1940 (deceased). **Educ:** Clark Univ, Clark Atlanta Univ, Atlanta, GA, AB, 1929; Hampton Institute, Hmpton Univ, Hampton, VA, BSLS, 1933; Columbia Univ School of Library Science, New York, NY, MSLS, 1957; Georgia State Univ, Atlanta, GA, school journalism, 1974. **Career:** Clark Univ, Atlant, GA, acting librarian, 1930-31; Simpsonville High School, Simpsonville, SC, teacher, librarian, 1931-32; Phillis Wheatley Branch, Greensville, SC, librarian, 1933-34; Carnegie Library, Auburn Branch, Atlanta, GA, assistant librarian , 1934-40, librarian, 1940-49; Atlanta Public Library, West Hunter Branch, librarian/head of dept, 1949-66; Georgia State Univ, Atlanta, GA, reference librarian, 1966-75. **Orgs:** Member, Georgia Library Association; member, Retired Teacher Assn of Georgia; member, Warren M E Church, member, Utopian Literary Club, 1940-. **Honors/Awds:** Negro Progress in Atlanta, Georgia 1950-61; vol. 2, 1962-72; Library Service in Black and White, Scarecrow Press 1988; Ford Foundation Study Grant, (Adult Education), summer 1954; Bronze Woman of the Year & Woman of the Year in Education Phi Lambda Sorority, 1953; Woman of Excellence for Pioneering in Education, Alpha Kappa Sorority, 1983; Outstanding Woman Award, NAACP, 1981; honored by Atlanta Fulton Public Library Board of Trustees, 1991-92; Atlanta Tribune Newspaper, 1992. **Home Addr:** 1365 Mozley Pl, SW, Atlanta, GA 30314.

MCPHERSON, JAMES ALAN
Educator, writer. **Personal:** Born Sep 16, 1943, Savannah, GA; son of Mable Smalls McPherson and James Allen McPherson; divorced; children: Rachel Alice McPherson. **Educ:** Morris Brown Coll, BA English/History 1965; Morgan State Coll, 1963-64; Harvard Law Sch, LLB 1968; Univ IA, MFA 1971. **Career:** Atlantic Monthly, contrib ed 1968-; Univ of CA, tchr 1970-72; Morgan State University, Baltimore, MD, asst prof 1975-76; University of Virginia, Charlottesville, VA, assoc prof 1976-81; University of Iowa, Iowa City, IA, prof 1981-. **Orgs:** Judge lit panel Nat'l Endow for Arts 1977-79; judge Loft McKnight awd Mnpls 1981-82; judge CCLM General Elec Writing Aawds 1983-84; ACLU; NAACP; PEN; Authors Guild. **Honors/Awds:** Guggenheim Fellowship 1972-73; Pulitzer Prize 1978; MacArthur Prize Fellowship 1981; LLB Honorary, Morris Brown College 1979; The University of Iowa, Award for Excellence in Teaching, 1991. **Business Addr:** Professor of English, Univ of Iowa, 430 English Philosophy Bldg, Iowa City, IA 52240.

MCPHERSON, JAMES R.
Attorney, utilities co. manager. **Personal:** Born Mar 26, 1953, Fayetteville, NC; son of Annie R McPherson Wright and Willie D Wright; married Michelle Bagley McPherson, Jul 3, 1982. **Educ:** Fayetteville State University, BS (with honors), business administration, 1975; University of Wisconsin, Madison, MBA, 1980; Georgetown University Law Center, JD, 1985. **Career:** Scott Paper Co., personnel assistant, 1981-82; U.S. Department of Labor, program analyst, 1983-84; US Claims Court, legal intern, 1983-84; International Brotherhood of Teamsters, law clerk, 1984-85; Clark, Klein & Beaumont, associate, 1985-88; Carolina Power & Light Co., associate general counsel, 1988-92; human resource projects manager, assistant to vice president, employee relations department, area employee services manager, 1992-94; Area Human Resources, mgr, until 1994, ast to Northern Region vice pres, 1994-95; Sanford, district mgr, 1995-96; Sanford/Southern Pines, district mgr, 1996-. **Orgs:** Society for Human Resource Management, 1992-95; American Association of Blacks in Energy, 1989-; American Corporate Counsel Association, 1989-92; Wake County Bar Association, 1989-92; North Carolina Bar Association, Labor & Employment Section, council, 1989-91, Bar Exam Stipend Subcommittee, Minorities in the Profession Committee, chair, 1989-92; National Bar Association, 1989-92; North Carolina Association of Black Lawyers, 1989-92. **Honors/Awds:** Earl Warren Legal Scholarship, 1982; University of Wisconsin, Advanced Opportunity Fellowship, fellow, 1980; Consortium for Graduate Study in Management, fellow, 1979-80; Fayetteville State University, Delta Mu Delta National Honor Society in Business Administration, charter member, 1976. **Military Serv:** US Air Force Reserves, captain/1st lt, 1979-90; US Air Force, 1st Lt, 1975-79; Air Force Commendation Medal; Air Force ROTC Most Outstanding Cadet, Mid-Atlantic Region; Exceptional Performance Citation, North Carolina Air Force Association; Commander, Detachment 607th Air Force Reserve Officer Training Corp. **Business Addr:** Manager/District Manager, Carolina Power & Light Co, Southern Region Department, 1000 Carthage St, Sanford, NC 27330, (919)774-2600.

MCPHERSON, ROOSEVELT
Educator, editor, publisher. **Personal:** Born Nov 27, 1948, Fayetteville, NC; son of Clara Mae Hill McPherson and Arthur McPherson; married Carrie Lee Ratliff McPherson, Mar 5, 1977; children: Phillip Ratliff, Kenyatta Troy, Tameka McGilvary. **Educ:** Fayetteville State University, Fayetteville, NC, BA, 1967-69, 1972-74; Lafayette College, Fayetteville, NC, 1977; Fayetteville Technical Institute, Fayetteville, NC, 1978-80; Appalachian State University, Boone, NC, 1990; Fayetteville State Univ, Fayetteville NC, Educational Leadership Program, 1994. **Career:** Burlington Industries, Raeford, NC, production supervisor, 1974-76; Kane-Miller, Fayetteville, NC, administrative assistant, 1976-78; Sears Roebuck, Fayetteville, NC, credit correspondent, 1978-81; General Productions, Inc, Raeford, NC, publisher/editor, 1981-; Sandhills Community College, Raeford, NC, instructor, 1984-92, ERA Fowler Realtors, Fayetteville, NC, realtor, 1987-88; Fayetteville Technical Community College, Fayetteville, NC, instructor, 1988-90; West Hoke Middle School, Raeford NC, teacher, 1992-, associate principal, currently. **Orgs:** Board of directors, Sanctuary Deliverance Churches, Inc, 1986-89; associate minister, Mt Sinai Sanctuary Deliverance Church, 1985-88; minister/deacon, Mt Carmel Holy Church of God, 1978-83; member, Hoke County Black Caucus, 1985; member, Hoke County Branch, NAACP, 1981; member, Hoke County Civic League, 1981; member, National Newspaper Publishers Assn, 1985-; member, North Carolina Black Publishers, 1985-. **Honors/Awds:** Sunday School Superintendent of the Year, Holy Church of God, Inc, 1978-79; Top Salesman/lister, ERA Realtor, 1988; Special Awards of Recognition, Miss Black Teenage Pageants, 1982-85. **Military Serv:** US Army, E-5, 1969-71; North Carolina Army National Guard, 1985-; received Academic Achievement Award, 1990. **Home Addr:** 190 Major Evans Rd, Raeford, NC 28376. **Business Addr:** Associate Principal, West Hoke Middle School, Raeford, NC 28376.

MCPHERSON, VANZETTA PENN
Judge. **Personal:** Born May 26, 1947, Montgomery, AL; daughter of Sadie G Penn and Luther L Penn; married Thomas McPherson Jr, Nov 16, 1985; children: Reagan Winston Durant. **Educ:** Howard University, BA, 1969; Columbia University, MA, 1971; Columbia Law School, JD, 1974. **Career:** Legal Services for Elderly Poor, summer associate, 1972; Thatcher, Proffit & Wood, summer associate, 1973; Hughes, Hubbard, Reed, associate, 1974-75; State of Alabama, asst attorney general, 1975-78; self-employed, private practive, 1978-92; US Government, US Magistrate Judge, 1992-. **Orgs:** Alabama Lawyers Association, 1976-, president, 1980-81; Natl Bar Assn, 1981-; American Bar Association, 1981-; Montgomery County Inn of Court, Master Bencher, 1990-; National Council of Negro Women, 1989-; Alabama Shakespeare Festival, board member, 1987-; Leadership Montgomery, 1984-, chairman, 1985; American Association of University Women, 1975-85, fellow, 1974; Federal Bar Association, 1995-, pres, 1997-. **Honors/Awds:** NMSC, National Achievement Scholar, 1965-69; American Association of University Women, Fellow in Law, 1973-74; American Bar Association, Law Oficce Design Award, 1985; Montgomery Advertiser, Women of Achievement, 1989; SCLC, Legacy of the Dreamer Award, 1981. **Special Achievements:** "Introduction of Blood Tests in Paternity Litigation," ABA, 1986. **Business Addr:** Judge, United States District Court, PO Box 1629, Montgomery, AL 36102, (334)223-7061.

MCPHERSON, WILLIAM H.
Technical editor (retired). **Personal:** Born May 18, 1927, Ft Worth; married Olivia T Denmon; children: Valencia D, Olivette R. **Educ:** Morehouse Coll, BS 1948. **Career:** The Aerospace Corp El Segundo, CA, publications editor, supervisor; N Am Rockwell Corp Autonetics Div, tech writer 1967-68; N Am Aviation Space & Info Systems Div,tech writer 1963-67. **Business Addr:** 2350 E El Sequndo Blvd, El Segundo, CA 90245.

MCQUATER, PATRICIA A.
Attorney. **Personal:** Born Sep 25, 1951, Washington, DC; daughter of Margaret Jackson McQuater and Matthew McQuater. **Educ:** Boston Univ Coll of Busn Admin, BS 1973; Univ of San Diego Schl of Law, JD 1978. **Career:** San Diego City Cnsl, admin intern 1976-78; Cnty of San Diego, admin anlst 1979-82; Foodmkr Inc, corp cncl 1982-84; Solar Turbines Inc, sr attorney, 1984-. **Orgs:** Bd govs Earl B Gellium Bar Assn 1982-; mem Am Bar Assn, Natl Bar Assn, 1981-; CA Assn Blk Lawyers; San Diego Cnty Bar Assn; Am Arbtrtn Assn; sec, San Diego Urban League Bd Dir 1982-; EO-Chr Cnty San Diego Affirm Action Comm, 1983-; chairperson, San Diego Urban League Bd of Dir, 1988-89; vice pres, San Diego Convention Ctr Corp Bd of Dir, 1990-; mem, Univ of San Diego School Law Admin Bd of Dir, 1990-. **Honors/Awds:** Law Merit awd USD 1978. **Business Addr:** Senior Attorney, Solar Turbines, Inc, 2200 Pacific Highway, San Diego, CA 92138-5376.

MCQUAY, JAMES PHILLIP
Business executive. **Personal:** Born Nov 15, 1924, Baltimore, MD; married Doris; children: James Jr, Kevin, Jamal. **Educ:** NY Fashion Sch Design. **Career:** Retail & Wholesale, fur mfr; 12th Mt Vernon 100 Black Men Inc Conc Fur Flair, dist leader; Fur Wear Mt Vernon, businessmen. **Honors/Awds:** Fur Design Award 1972, 75, 76; spl fur showing for congressional black caucus Wash 1977; 1st place award for design Century Fur Trade Show 1980. **Military Serv:** AUS tech sgt. **Business Addr:** President, James McQuay Furs, Inc, 130 West 30th St, New York, NY 10001.

MCQUEEN, ANJETTA
Copy editor. **Personal:** Born Sep 12, 1966, Brooklyn, NY. **Educ:** University of North Carolina, Chapel Hill, NC, BA, journalism, political science, 1988. **Career:** News and Observer, Raleigh, NC, part-time copy editor, 1986-88; Philadelphia Inquirer, Philadelphia, PA, copy editor, 1988-. **Orgs:** Member, Natl Assn of Black Journalists, 1989-; member, Urban League, 1990-; member, Fleisher Art Memorial, 1988-; member, Carolina Alumni Assn, currently; member, Intl Society for General Semantics, 1989-. **Business Addr:** Copy Editor, Metro Desk, Philadelphia Inquirer, 400 N Broad St, Philadelphia, PA 19101.

MCQUEEN, KEVIN PAIGE
Banker. **Personal:** Born Jul 8, 1958, Brooklyn, NY; son of Constance Marie Jackson McQueen and Robert Paige McQueen. **Educ:** Brown University, Providence, RI, AB, 1976-80. **Career:** National Westminster Bank, USA, New York, NY, banking officer, 1980-82; Citibank, NA, New York, NY, relationship manager, 1982-85; National Congress for Community Economic Development, Washington, DC, program director, 1985-88; NCB Development Corp, Washington, DC, vice president, 1988-. **Orgs:** Board member, National Neighborhood Coalition, 1987-88; president, Brown University Club of Washington, DC, 1988-90; steering committee coordinator, Third World Alumni Network of Brown University, 1990-. **Business Addr:** Vice President, NCB Development Corp, 1401 I St NW, Washington, DC 20005.

MCQUEEN, MICHAEL ANTHONY
Journalist. **Personal:** Born Nov 3, 1956, Jacksonville, FL; son of Carolyn Eubanks McQueen and Otto McQueen; married Glenda Wright McQueen, May 31, 1981; children: Michael II, Otto III. **Educ:** Mercer University, Macon, GA, 1974-75; Florida State University, Tallahassee, FL, BA, 1976-78. **Career:** Tallahassee Democrat, Tallahassee, FL, reporter, 1978-79; Florida Times Union, Jacksonville, FL, reporter, 1979-80; Associated Press, Miami, FL, bureau chief, 1980-85; USA Today, Arlington, VA, national correspondent, 1987-90; Miami Herald, Miami, FL, assistant city editor, 1985-87, editor, 1990-. **Orgs:** Member, Kappa Alpha Psi Fraternity, 1975-; national board member, National Association of Black Journalists, 1981-87. **Business Addr:** Day City Editor, Miami Herald, One Herald Plaza, Miami, FL 33131.

MCRAE, BRIAN WESLEY
Professional baseball player. **Personal:** Born Aug 27, 1967, Bradenton, FL. **Career:** Kansas City Royals, outfielder, 1990-94; Chicago Cubs, 1995-97; New York Mets, 1997-. **Business Addr:** Professional Baseball Player, New York Mets, 126th St and Roosevelt Ave, Shea Stadium, Flushing, NY 11368, (718)507-6307.

MCRAE, CARMEN
Jazz singer. **Personal:** Born Apr 8, 1922, Brooklyn, NY; married Teddy Wilson (divorced). **Educ:** Private student in piano. **Career:** Benny Carter, pianist 1944; Count Basie, pianist 1944; Mercer Ellington Band, record debut 1946-47; made 1st records as solo singer during 1950's; appearances at, Ronnie Scott's in London, Lincoln Center, Carnegie Hall, Playboy Clubs, MGM Grand Las Vegas; jazz singer, currently. **Honors/Awds:** Albums include: As Time Goes By; I Am Music; Just A Little Lovin'; Of Carmen; For Once in My Life; Great American Songbook; It Takes A Whole Lot of Human Feelings; Ms Jazz; Carmen MaRae; Carmen's Gold; Live and Doin' In; Alive!; In Person; I Want You; You Can't Hide Love; Two for the Road; You're Looking At Me; Velvet Soul; Any Old Time; Ms Magic. **Business Addr:** Jazz Singer, c/o Abby Hoffer Enterprises, 223 1/2 E 48th St, New York, NY 10017.

MCRAE, EMMETT N.
Retaurant owner, city official. **Personal:** Born Feb 12, 1943, Rennert, NC; son of Katie Smith McRae and Donnie McRae; married Helen McLean McRae, Aug 5, 1962; children: David, Linda F, Lori A McRae Strickland. **Career:** CS&X Transportation Railroad, Florence, SC, cook, 1968-90; E & H BBQ Hut, Rennert, NC, owner & operator, 1984-; City of Rennert, NC, mayor, currently. **Orgs:** Deacon, 2nd St Matthew Baptist Church, 1970-; past master, St Pauls Masonic Lodge #354, 1987-; worship master, St Pauls Masonic Lodge, #354, 1979-87; member, Carpenters Consistory #164, 1975-; board member, Lumber River Council of Government, currently; president, Sunday School Convention, 1986-. **Honors/Awds:** Jefferson Award, Jefferson Broadcasting Co Channel 11 Durham, NC, 1986; Honorary Attorney General, Rufus L Edmisten Attorney General of NC, 1984; Certificate of Appreciation as a Special Volunteer, James B Hunt Governor of N C, 1984; Man of the Year, Carpenters Consistory #164, 1986; Service Award, St Matthew Baptist Church, 1985; Service Award, Rennert Volunteer Fire Department, 1990. **Home Addr:** Rt 1 Box 42, Shannon, NC 28386.

MCRAE, HAL (HAROLD ABRAHAM)
Former professional baseball manager. **Personal:** Born Jul 10, 1945, Avon Park, FL; son of Virginia Foster McRae and Willie James McRae; married Johncyna Williams; children: Brian, Cullen, Leah. **Educ:** Florida A&M University, Tallahassee, FL, 1963-66. **Career:** Minor Leagues, baseball player 1965-68; Cincinnati Reds, baseball player 1968-72; Kansas City Royals, baseball player 1973-87, hitting instructor 1987; Pittsburgh Pirates, Pittsburgh, PA, minor league hitting instructor, 1987-89; Montreal Expos, Montreal, Canada, hitting instructor, 1990-91; Kansas City Royals, manager, 1991-94; Cincinnati Reds, hitting instructor, 1995-96; Philadelphia Phillies, hitting instructor, 1997. **Honors/Awds:** Played in World Series 1970, 1972, 1985; played in League Championship Series 1970, 1972, 1976, 1977, 1978, 1985; Royals Player of the Yr 1974; Highest batting avg of DH in Amer League; Played All-Star Games 1975-76; Tied major league record most long hits in a doubleheader (5 doubles & 1 home run) 1974; Designated Hitter ''Sporting News'' All Star Team 1976-77; Led AL designated hitters in doubles (41), 1977; Led in doubles (39), 1978; Led AL designated hitters in runs (88) 1978.

MCRAE, HELENE WILLIAMS
Educator. **Personal:** Born in New York, NY; married Lemuel C. **Educ:** Trenton State Coll, BS 1945; Columbia Univ, MA 1948, Prof Diploma 1965; Lehigh Univ, EdD 1974. **Career:** Bates HS Annapolis, chmn math dept 1945-52; Teacher/reading coord/learning disability consult 1952-68; Trenton State Coll, prof/chairperson/grad supervisor dept of spl edn. **Orgs:** Past pres Trenton State Coll Chap of Amer Assn Univ Prof; past pres Lawrence Twp Educ Assn; mem Delta Kappa Gamma Intl Hon Soc; Kappa Delta Pi Hon Soc; Council for Except Children; Intl Reading Assn; mem Alpha Kappa Alpha Sor; Girlfriends Inc; Links Inc; field reader US Dept Educ, OSER. **Honors/Awds:** Recip Comm Serv Award Trenton State Coll 1971; Recip Faculty Teaching Awd, Mary McLeod Bethune Plaque Trenton State Coll 1987; Recip Merit Awds TrentonState Coll 1980,85,86. **Business Addr:** Prof/Grad Supervisor, Trenton State Coll, Dept of Special Education, Trenton, NJ 08625.

MCRAE, RONALD EDWARD
Salesman. **Personal:** Born Feb 7, 1955, Dillon, SC; son of Betty McRae Dudley. **Educ:** Macalester Coll, BA 1976; Northwestern Univ School of Management, MBA 1978; DePaul Univ School of Law, JD 1986. **Career:** The Toro Co, marketing intern 1976; Federal Savings & Loan Ins Corp, rsch asst 1977; Searle Pharmaceuticals Inc, asst product manager 1978-79, product manager 1979-84, key account hospital consultant 1984-88; Westwood Pharmaceuticals Inc, manager, new bus devel 1988-. **Orgs:** Mem Amer Management Assoc, Amer Bar Assn, Natl Black MBA Assoc, Midwest Pharmaceutical Advertising Club, Association of MBA Executives, Chicago Volunteer Legal Servs, Chicago Heart Assoc Church Based Hypertension Program; Licensing Exec Society. **Business Addr:** Mgr, New Business Devt, Westwood Pharmaceuticals Inc, 100 Forest Avenue, Buffalo, NY 14213.

MCRAE, THOMAS W.
Educator (retired), certified public accountant. **Personal:** Born Mar 7, 1924, Philadelphus, NC; son of Anna Line Buie McRae and James T McRae; married Dorothy Hilliard McRae, Apr 11, 1954; children: Ellen Coretta, Paul Hilliard, Lawrence David. **Educ:** Univ of Chicago, Chicago, IL, BA, 1952; Univ of Southern California, Los Angeles, CA, MBA, 1955. **Career:** Amer Inst of CPA, New York, NY, vice president, 1967-89; New York Univ, New York, NY, clinical professor, 1989-94. **Orgs:** Board of trustees, Home Corp, 1988-90; board of directors, National Assn of Black Accountants, 1972-80; bd of dirs, United Methodist Homes, 1993-. **Honors/Awds:** Beta Gamma Sigma, Univ of Southern California, 1955; Outstanding Member, National Association of Black Accountants, 1976; Journal of Accountancy, Annual Literary Award; American Institute of CPAs, 1982, Outstanding Achievement in Education, National Assn of Black Accountants, 1986; Outstanding Alumnus, Univ of Southern California, 1989. **Military Serv:** US Army, S Sgt, 1943-47. **Home Addr:** 124 Christopher St, Montclair, NJ 07042.

MCREYNOLDS, ELAINE A.
Federal official. **Personal:** Born Feb 5, 1948, Louisville, KY; married George R McReynolds; children: Jennifer, Jason, Julie. **Educ:** Attended Univ of Montpellier France 1965; attended Centre Coll of KY 1966-68; Univ of TN, BS 1975. **Career:** Natl Life and Accident Ins Co (became Amer General Life and Accident Insurance Co in 1983), computer programmer 1970-73, programmer analyst 1974-75, expense mgmt analyst 1975-76, adminstrv asst 1976-78, asst sec & mgr 1978-83, asst vice pres 1983-85; real estate 1985-87; commr Tennessee Dept Commerce & Insurance 1987-94; Federal Insurance Admini, 1994-96; AM Gen Life & Accid Ins Co, sr vice pres, 1996-. **Orgs:** Dir Crisis Intervention, Bd of Dirs 1977-78; trustee Univ of TN Bd of Trustees 1975-84; dir Cumberland Mus Bd of Dirs 1978-81; bd of dir Citizens Bank; bd of dir St Bernard Academy; bd of dir Harpeth Hall Middle School; LINKS. **Honors/Awds:** Presidential appointee, 1994; Top Ten Outstanding Grads Nashville Mag 1976; mem of 1st class Leadership Nashville 1976-; commencement speaker Univ of TN at Knoxville 1979; commencement speaker Univ of TN at Nashville 1979; reduced day care insurance rates in state; Woman of Achievement Award, 1993; March of Dimes, Person of the Year, 1994; Maryland Association, Independent Insurors, Insurance Person of the Year, 1996. **Business Addr:** Sr Vice Pres, AM Gen Life & Accid Ins Co., AM Gen Ctr, Nashville, TN 37250.

MCRIPLEY, G. WHITNEY
Government official. **Personal:** Born Nov 29, 1957, Detroit, MI; married Sandie Cameron; children: Marlena L; Gil Whitney McRipley Jr. **Educ:** Univ of Detroit, BA 1979; Univ of MI, MA 1983; Thomas M Cooley Law School, JD 1984. **Career:** Detroit Public Schools, teacher 1980-81; Waverly Public School, teacher 1981-83; City of Lansing, dir of div dept 1983-84; Charter Twp of Royal Oak, supervisor 1984-. **Orgs:** Mem Pi Sigma Alpha; Dem Party; pres Royal Oak Twp Bus Assoc, Royal Oak Twp Mainstream; sec MI Conf of Black Mayors. **Business Addr:** Supervisor, Charter Twp of Royal Oak, 21075 Wyoming St, Ferndale, MI 48220.

MCROY, RUTH GAIL
Educator. **Personal:** Born Oct 6, 1947, Vicksburg, MS; daughter of Lucille A McKinney Murdock (deceased) and Horace David Murdock (deceased); married Dwight D Brooks, Jul 16, 1988; children: Myra Louise, Melissa Lynn. **Educ:** Univ of Kansas, BA w/honors 1968, MSW 1970; Univ of Texas, PhD 1981. **Career:** Family Consultation Serv, social worker 1970-71; KS Children's Serv League, adoption worker 1971-73; Univ of Kansas, asst prof 1973-77; Prairie View A&M Univ, asst prof 1977-78; Univ of Texas, asst prof 1981-86, assoc prof 1986-90, Ruby Lee Piester Centennial Professor, services to children and families 1990-; Center for Social Work Research, dir, 1994-. **Orgs:** Bd pres Black Adoption Program & Services 1975-77; Council on Social Work Educ 1977-; Natl Assoc of Social Workers 1977-; bd pres Carver Museum 1983-86; Natl Assoc of Social Workers Steering Comm Austin 1986-90; bd mem Carver Museum 1987-90; Casey Family Advisory Comm 1989-; Adoptive Families of America Advisory Comm 1989-92; Marywood Board of Directors, 1991-94. **Honors/Awds:** Danforth Fellow 1978; Black Analysis Fellow 1978; Phi Kappa Phi 1979; Outstanding Dissertation Award Univ of Texas 1981; Lora Lee Pederson Teaching Excellence Award 1984; Ruby Lee Piester Fellow in Serv to Children and Families 1985; Phi Kappa Phi Scholar Awd 1985; Rishon Lodge Wilhemina Delco Award for Excellence in Educ 1987; Texas Excellence Teaching Award 1990, Leadership Texas, 1995. **Special Achievements:** Author: Transracial and Inracial Adoptees: The Adolescent Years, 1983; Emotional Disturbance in Adopted Adolescents, 1988; Openness in Adoption, 1988; Social Practice with Black Families, 1990. **Business Addr:** Professor, The Univ of Texas at Austin, 1925 San Jacinto Blvd, Austin, TX 78712.

MCSMITH, BLANCHE PRESTON
Researcher/writer. **Personal:** Born May 5, 1920, Marshall, TX; divorced; children: Kymberly Blanche Walton. **Educ:** Butler Jr Coll Tyler TX; Cert; Wiley Coll TX, BA Socio & Language; Univ of So CA, MSW; Wiley Coll, Hon Degree DL 1960. **Career:** Amer Red Cross, home serv consult 1944-49; AK, state legislator (first black) 1959-61; Mcsmith Enterprises TV Sales & Svcs, co-owner 1950-69; Anchorage Sch Dist, dir social serv Headstart prog 1968-70; Office of the Gov, state dir pub employ prog 1972-75; Self-Employed, rscher/writer. **Orgs:** Conducted weekly TV Show The NAACP Speaks; pres & organized Afro-Amer Hist Soc Inc 1975-; assoc ed Alaska Spotlight Newspaper. **Honors/Awds:** Amer Cancer Soc Awd 1956; Human Rela Awd NAACP 1956; MCA-USO Leadership Awd 1959; Daus of Elks Achievement Awd Chicago 1960; Hall of Fame Anchorage Daily News 1962; Sojourner Truth Club Awd LA 1965; Woman of the Yr No Lights Civic Club 1966; Comm Serv Awd NAACP 1966 & 1974; Older Persons Action Grp Awd 1973; ''Blanche McSmith Libr'' renamed City Libr City of Whittier 1973; AK Black Caucus Awd 1978; Juneau Chamber of Commerce Awd 1978-83, each yr; Visitor Prog Volunteer; Honored by Taku Toastmasters Club 1984. **Business Addr:** Researcher/Writer, 3456 Meander Way, Juneau, AK 99801-9607.

MCSTALLWORTH, PAUL
Educator (retired). **Personal:** Born Mar 4, 1910, Flatwoods, AL; married Charlotte Young; children: Ann M Wheeler, Carol M Higginbotham. **Educ:** Geneva Coll Beaver Falls, BA 1936; Howard Univ, MA 1940; OH State Univ, PhD 1954. **Career:** St Augustine Coll Raleigh, instr 1940-43; Central State Univ Willerforce, asst prof 1947-50, assoc prof, 1954-58, prof & dean of students, 1954-58, chair, History Dept & dean, 1960-69; Wright State Univ Dayton, prof & asst to pres 1969-76; Central State Univ, interim vice pres 1976-77; Wright State Univ, prof history, 1970-76, prof emeritus; Xenia Township, trustee 1980-88. **Orgs:** Consult North Central Accred Assoc 1972-73; prog chmn, life mem Optimist Intl Wilberforce Xenia 1973; bd mem Greene Cty Health, Mental Guidance, Afro-Amer Museum Task Force 1978-, Dayton-Tri Cty Red Cross 1981-; mem Sigma Pi Phi Frat, life mem Alpha Phi Alpha. **Honors/Awds:** Minority Outstanding Awd OSU Grad School 1978; Man of the Year Xenia-Greene Cty Sertoma Club 1982. **Military Serv:** AUS Infantry 1st lt, 1943-47. **Home Addr:** PO Box 235, Wilberforce, OH 45384-0235.

MCSWAIN, BERAH D.
Executive. **Personal:** Born Feb 6, 1935, Albany, NY; son of Willie McSwain and Berah McSwain; married Diane Bradd, Dec 25, 1966; children: Berah N McSwain. **Educ:** Univ of Rochester, BS, 1956, MS, 1962; Univ of California, Berkeley, PhD, 1968. **Career:** Northrop Aircraft Inc, Anaheim CA, lab manager, 1956-58; US Naval Ordnance Laboratory, Corona CA, researcher and designer, 1958-61; Univ of Rochester, Rochester NY, researcher, 1961-62; Univ of California, Berkeley, Berkeley CA, researcher, 1962-76, dir of professional devel program, 1976-79; Dow Associates, vice pres and chief scientist, 1979-81; Lawrence Berkeley Laboratory, visiting research scientist, 1979-81; TEM Associates Inc, president, 1981-; consultant to govt and private organizations. **Orgs:** Mem, Amer Chemical Soc; mem, Optical Soc of Amer; mem, Amer Soc of Plant Physiologists; mem, Soc of Photographic Scientists and Engineers; lecturer, Amer Inst of Biological Sciences. **Honors/Awds:** Author of book chapters, conference proceedings, and articles. **Home Addr:** 5333 Greenwich Ct, Newark, CA 94560-1936.

MCSWAIN, RODNEY
Professional football player. **Personal:** Born Jan 28, 1962, Caroleen, NC. **Educ:** Clemson Univ, attended. **Career:** New England Patriots, cornerback, 1984-. **Honors/Awds:** Post-season play, 1985: AFC Championship Game, NFL Championship Game. **Business Addr:** Professional Football Player, New England Patriots, Sullivan Stadium, Rt 1, Foxboro, MA 02035.

MCSWEEN, CIRILO A.
Business executive. **Personal:** Born Jul 8, 1929, Panama City, Panama; married Gwendolyn Amacker; children: Esperanza, Veronica, Cirilo Jr. **Educ:** Univ of IL, BA 1954, MA. **Career:** McSween Ins Counselors & Brokers, 1957-; McDonalds, bus exec. **Orgs:** Mem, vchmn Independence Bank of Chgo; owner, oper Cirilo's Inc McDonald Franchise; vp, natl treas So Christian Leadership Conf; mem IL Adv Bd tothe Dept of Ins; mem IL State Prop Ins Study Comm; natl treas, bd mem PUSH; vice pres Chicago Econ Devel Corp; bd King Ctr for Nonviolent Soc Change in Atlanta; mem Univ of IL Athletic Bd; rep Panama in Olympic Games in Track & Field. **Honors/Awds:** McDonalds Golden Arch Awd 1984; 1st Black Elected to State St Council 1984; 1st black in history to sell over $1,000,000 of life ins in 1 month; Life &Qualifying mem Million Dollar Round Table 1958-. **Business Addr:** McDonalds, 230 S State St, Chicago, IL 60604.

MCTEER, GEORGE CALVIN
Dentist. **Personal:** Born Mar 9, 1938, Barnwell, SC; son of Janie Elizabeth Williams McTeer (deceased) and Henry A McTeer (deceased); married Norma Jean Eaddy McTeer, Aug 17, 1963; children: Sonja Nichelle, Arlene Veronica, George Calvin Jr. **Educ:** South Carolina State Univ, BS 1960, MEd 1968; Medical Univ of SC Coll of Dental Medicine, DMD 1974. **Career:** Fairfield Co Schools, math & science teacher 1960-63; Charleston Co Schools, math teacher and adult school teacher 1963-69; Franklin C Fetter Family Health Ctr Inc, chief of dental serv 1974-76; George C McTeer DMD, private practice 1976-; Sea Island Health Care Inc Nursing Home, dental consultant, currently. **Orgs:** Mem Alpha Phi Alpha Frat 1958-, Psi Omega Dental frat 1974-; former chmn ad hoc comm on health Charleston Business and Professional Assoc 1981-; former pres Charleston County Medical Assoc 1982-86; former mem bd of dirs Sea Island Health Care Corp 1984-90; former mem of bd chmn Personnel Comm Cannon St YMCA 1986-87; state pres Palmetto Medical Dental & Pharmaceutical Assoc; SC Dental Assoc; Coastal Dist Dental Soc, Amer Dental Assoc; board of deacons Central Baptist Church; Charleston Dental Soc; The Acad of General Dentistry; The Charleston Mules; NAACP; Jack and Jill of Amer Inc; Owl's Whist Club; former secretary and pres, CBC Men's Club 1991-. **Honors/Awds:** First black graduate Coll of Dental Medicine Medical Univ of SC 1974; Management Devel Award Franklin C Fetter Family Health Center 1976; Certificate of Achievement Alpha Phi Alpha Frat 1982; Appreciation for Outstanding Leadership Charleston County Med Assoc 1984; Volunteer Award Coming St YWCA 1985; Volunteer Award Stono Park Elementary School PTA 1986; Merit Award for Outstanding Support of the Student Natl Dental Assn 1987; Recognition of Service in Dentistry, Sigma Gamma Rho Sorority, 1987; Distinguished and Exemplary Service, Delta Sigma Theta Sorority, 1988. **Home Addr:** 2942 Ashley River Rd, Charleston, SC 29414. **Business Addr:** PO Box 20940, Charleston, SC 29413-0940.

MCTIER, ROSELYN JONES
Educator, librarian (retired). **Personal:** Born Oct 4, 1916, Eufaula, AL; daughter of Cassie Brown Hughes (deceased) and Rueben Jones (deceased); married Eddie McTier II, Aug 30, 1959. **Educ:** Miles College, Birmingham, AL, AB, 1938; Alabama State College, Montgomery AL, MA, 1955; Atlanta University School of Library Science, Atlanta, GA, summers, 1965, 1966. **Career:** Russell County, Wenda AL, teacher, 1938-41; Russell County, Hurtsboro, AL, teacher, 1941-44; Jefferson County, Birmingham, AL, teacher/librarian, 1944-70, librarian, 1970-78 (retired); Ervin High School, asst librarian. **Orgs:** Member, Sixth Ave Baptist Church, 1927-, secretary, Mission #7, 1974-, member, usher board jr; president, 1947-52, teacher, 1966-86, treasurer, Jefferson Co PTA, 1950-65; president, Progressive 13 Social Saving Club, 1950-55, treasurer, 1956-64. **Honors/Awds:** Advisor to the Senior Classes for 22 years; Citizens Bank of Leeds, AL, 1970. **Home Addr:** 1604 1st St S, Birmingham, AL 35205.

MCTYRE, ROBERT EARL, SR.
Journalist. **Personal:** Born Aug 2, 1955, Detroit, MI; son of Barbara Shorter McTyre and Earl McTyre; married Carmela McTyre, Sep 22, 1990; children: Tamika Baldwin, DuJuan Robinson, Cornelius Fortune, Rob Jr. **Educ:** Wayne County Community, certificate, training emergency medical tech, 1976; Highland Park Community, liberal arts; Wayne State University, journalism scholarship, 1989. **Career:** Ambro Ambulance, Detroit, MI, attendant/driver, 1973-75; Detroit General Hospital, Detroit, MI, emergency room attendant, 1975-77; Detroit Fire, EMS, Detroit, MI, EMT, 1977-85; Metro Times, Detroit, MI, classified salesman, freelance writer, 1984-86; Citizen News, Detroit, MI, managing editor, general manager, 1985-87; Michigan Chronicle, Detroit, MI, reporter, associate executive editor, 1987-93, exec editor, 1993-. **Orgs:** Detroit Chapter, National Association of Black Journalists, 1985; Investigative Reporters and Editors Inc, 1990; Society of Environmental Journalist, 1991. **Honors/Awds:** Licensed Baptist Minister, New Resurrection MB Church.

MCWHORTER, GRACE AGEE
Agricultural scientist. **Personal:** Born Jan 15, 1948, Mobile, AL; married George R McWhorter MD; children: Kenya, Lia. **Educ:** Tuskegee Institute, BS (Honors) 1970, MS 1972; Univ of FL, PhD 1978. **Career:** Univ of FL, rsch assoc 1973-75; Univ of MO, vstg prof of biology 1976-77; Talladega Coll, asst prof of biology 1980; Jacksonville State Univ, asst prof of biology 1980-81; Univ of TX at San Antonio, lecturer-biology 1981-82; FL A&M Univ, assoc prof agriculture 1982-86; State Univ System of FL Bd of Regents, program review assoc 1986-. **Orgs:** Owner LaFontain Floral Design 1984-; vstg prof Farmers Home Admin USOA 1984-85; mem Delta Sigma Theta Sor, Jack & Jill Inc, Amer Assoc Higher Educ Black Caucus, United Faculty of FL Political Action Chmn; bd of volunteers Tallahassee Memorial Hospital; mem Toastmasters Intl, Tuskegee Alumni Club, Amer Assoc of Univ Women. **Honors/Awds:** BOR Rsch Fellow 1977; several publications on small farm issues and concerns 1977. **Home Addr:** 2421 Tempest Dr, Birmingham, AL 35211. **Business Addr:** Program Review Assoc, State Univ System of FL, FL Board of Regents, 117 W Gaines St, Tallahassee, FL 32308.

MCWHORTER, MILLARD HENRY, III
Physician. **Personal:** Born Nov 27, 1954, Hamilton, GA; son of Geneva C McWhorter and Millard H McWhorter Jr (deceased). **Educ:** Morehouse Coll, BS 1976; Meharry Medical Coll, MD 1981. **Career:** Morehouse Family Practice Prog, residency training 1981-84; Natl Health Serv Corp, staff physician 1986-; Red Level Medical Clinic, medical director; First Step Alcohol & Drug Treatment Center, consultant, 1986-. **Orgs:** Amer Acad of Family Physicians 1975-; NAACP 1984-; Amer Medical Assn 1986-, Covington Cty Medical Assn 1986-; Alabama Medical Assn 1986-; Alpha Phi Alpha. **Honors/Awds:** Beta Kappa Chi Natl Scientific Honor Soc 1975-.

MCWHORTER, ROSALYND D.
Account supervisor. **Personal:** Born Dec 19, 1960, Chicago, IL; daughter of Earnestine Pollard Triplett and Edward H Triplett; married Anthony Michael McWhorter, May 28, 1988. **Educ:** Univ of Illinois-Urbana, Urbana, IL, BA, English, 1982. **Career:** R J Dale Advertising, Chicago, IL, acct executive, 1984-88; Burrell Public Relations, Chicago, IL, acct group supervisor, 1988-. **Orgs:** Member, Natl Coalition of 100 Black Women, Chicago Chapter, 1991; member, Publicity Club of Chicago, 1990-; member, Black Public Relations Society, 1988. **Honors/Awds:** Certifications: McDonald's Corporation Media Relations Training Program; Publicity Club of Chicago. **Business Addr:** Account Group Supervisor, Burrell Public Relations, 20 N Michigan Ave, 2nd Floor, Chicago, IL 60602.

MCWILLIAMS, ALFRED E., JR.
Educator. **Personal:** Born Feb 3, 1938, Wewoka, OK; son of Elvira M Bowles McWilliams and Alfred E McWilliams Sr; married Wilmer Jean Bible; children: Kimberly Beatrice, Esther Gabriel Moten, Cassandra Gabriel, Kenneth Gabriel, Fredericka Gabriel Rice, Keith Gabriel. **Educ:** CO State Coll, BA 1959, MA 1960; Univ No CO, PhD 1970. **Career:** Denver Public School CO, teacher, counselor & admin asst 1960-68; Proj Upward Bound Univ No CO, dir 1968-70; Univ No CO, asst dean-special educ & rehabilitation 1970-72; Fed of Rocky Mt States Inc, consultant & career educ content coord 1972-76; Univ No CO, dir personnel AA/EEO 1976-79, asst vice pres admin serv personnel 1979-82; Univ of CO, asst to vice pres for admin 1982-84; Atlanta Univ, vice pres for admin 1984-85; Atlanta Univ, dean, School of Educ, 1985-87; GA State Univ, professor, educational policy studies, 1987-, coordinator, educational leadership program, 1995-. **Orgs:** Chmn/co-founder Black Educators United 1967-68; asst prof 1970-72, assoc prof educ 1976-82 Univ of No CO; bd mem CO Christian Home Denver 1977-; sec 1977-, chmn 1980-84 Aurora CO Career Serv Comm; bd mem Natl Brotherhood of Skiers 1978-79; mem 1978-, bd mem 1980-85 Amer Assn of Univ Admin; mem 1978-, Gov Lamm appointed chmn 1980-84 CO Merit System Council; council mem 1978-, chmn elect 1981-82 (EEO) Coll & Univ Personnel Assn; mem Am Soc for Personnel Admin 1979-; cons, trainer Natl Center for Leadership Development Atlanta Univ 1979-80; cons, trainer Leadership Develop Training Prog Howard Univ 1981-82; mem, Rotary Club of West End Atlanta, 1984-87, 1989-; mem & army committeeman, Greater Atlanta Chapter reserve Officers Assn of US, 1985-; mem & chairman ofbd of dir, APPLE Corps, 1986; mem, Professional Journal Committee, Assn of Teacher Educators, 1987-; member, Amer Assn for Higher Education, 1989-; member, Assn for Supervision and Curriculum Development, 1989-; Amer Assn of Univ Professors, 1995-. **Honors/Awds:** Appreciation Award Natl Brotherhood of Skiers 1979; Leadership Styles & Management Strategies, Management Education, series at Atlanta Univ, 1986; Review of KA Heller, et al Placing Children in Special Education: A Strategy for Equity, Natl Academy Press, 1987. **Military Serv:** AUSR, Col, 1961-68, 1977-93; Army Reserve Component Medal, Army Achievement Medal, Army Commendation Medal, with Oak Leaf Clusters, Meritorious Serv Medal, with Oak Leaf Clusters. **Home Addr:** 1221 Ashley Lake Dr, Marietta, GA 30062. **Business Addr:** Professor of Educational Policy Studies, Georgia State University, University Plaza, Atlanta, GA 30303.

MCWILLIAMS, ALFRED EDEARD
Educator clergyman. **Personal:** Born May 7, 1911, Guthrie, OK; married Elvira Minerva Bowles; children: Alfred E, Jr, Stanley Wilmax, Patricia Elaine Hunter. **Educ:** Lane Coll Jackson TN, AB 1933; Yale Divinity Schl New Haven CT, BD 1936; Lane Coll Jackson TN, DD 1958; Univ of MS Oxford, MS, MEd 1967. **Career:** Christian Meth Epscpl Ch KS OK, pstr 1936-40; TX Coll Tyler TX, prof 1940-43; AUS, chpln 1943-46; USAF, lt col 1946-64; Anderson Chpl CME Chrh,pastor 1964-67; MS Indust Coll, coll dean 1967-70; Head Start Prog, dir 1967-79; MS Indstrl Coll, prof 1970-80; Evnglsm 4th Epis Dist CME Chrh, sec 1966-67; Acad Policy Comm (MI Coll), chmn fclty forum mem. **Orgs:** Sec Grtr Memphis Christian Meth Episcopal Chrh Memphis TN 1982-; pstr Armstead/ St Paul CME Chrhs 1979- Oxford MS; mem Alpha Phi Alpha Frat; Thirty Second Degree Mason. **Honors/Awds:** 50th yr cert grad Lane Coll Jackson TN 1983; Memshp-at-large Gen Brd Christian Meth Episcopal Chrh 1982; delegate Gen Conf CME Chrh1952, 1978, 1982; ldr of E MS Delg 1982, Gen Conf. **Military Serv:** USAF lt col; Bronze Star 1952; Meritorious Serv 1964; Retired 1964. **Home Addr:** 181 Golf Club Cir, Memphis, TN 38109.

MCWILLIAMS, JAMES D.
Attorney. **Personal:** Born Dec 25, 1932, Fairfield, AL; son of Minnie McWilliams and James McWilliams; married Anne; children: Laura, Susan, Diana. **Educ:** Talladega Coll, Talladega, AL, BA, 1954; Univ of WI Law School, Madison, WI, JD, 1962. **Career:** Private practice, DC Govt Dept of Transp, asst dir 1979-91; Atty, pvt prac 1977-79; Opp Funding Corp, gen coun sec 1973-77; Coop Assistance Fund, asst sec; US Virgin Islands, asst att gen 1967-72; US Virgin Islands Port Authority, gen coun 1969-72; United Plng Organ, Wash DC CAP, asst gen coun 1966-67; US Dept of Interior, att adv 1962-66. **Orgs:** Mem Nat Bar Assn; Am Bar Assn; State Bar of WI 1962-; DC Bar Assn 1972. **Honors/Awds:** Drafted legislation which establshed US Virgin Islands Port Authority. **Military Serv:** AUS 1955-58. **Business Addr:** 5604 MacArthur Blvd NW, Washington, DC 20016.

MCWILLIAMS, TAJ
Professional basketball player. **Personal:** Born Oct 20, 1970, Austin, TX; daughter of Stephanie Wiggins; children: Michelle. **Educ:** St Edwards. **Career:** Philadelphia Rage, center, 1996-. **Business Addr:** Professional Basketball Player, Philadelphia Rage, 123 Chestnut St, First Flr, Philadelphia, PA 19106, (215)629-1976.

MCWORTER, GERALD A.
Educator. **Personal:** Born Nov 21, 1942, Chicago, IL; divorced; children: One. **Educ:** Ottawa Univ, BA Soc & Philosophy, 1963; Univ of Chicago, MA, 1966, PhD, 1974. **Career:** Ottawa Univ Dept of Philosophy, teaching asst, 1962-63; Univ of Chicago Natl Opinion Research Center, research asst, asst study dir, 1963-67; Fisk Univ Center for Afro-Amer Studies, asst prof of sociology, 1967-68; Inst of the Black World, asst prof of sociology, 1967-68; Fisk Univ, asst prof, assoc prof of sociology & Afro-Amer studies, 1969-75, dir, Afro-Amer Studies Program, 1969-75; Univ of Illinois at Chicago, assoc prof of Black studies, 1975-79; Univ of Illinois at Urbana-Champaign, assoc prof of sociology & Afro-Amer studies, 1979-87, dir Afro-Am Studies & Research Program, 1979-84; Twenty-First Century Books & Publications, sr editor, currently; State Univ of New York at Stony Brook, assoc prof of Africana studies, currently. **Orgs:** Founder & dir, Cooperative Research Network in Black Studies, 1984-; ed bd, Malcolm X Studies Newsletter, 1987-, Afro Scholar Newsletter, 1983-, Western Journal of Black Studies, 1983-, Black Scholar, 1969-; founder, chair, Org of Black Amer Culture, 1965-67. **Business Addr:** Assoc Prof, Africana Studies Program, State Univ of New York at Stony Brook, Social & Behavioral Sciences Bldg, Stony Brook, NY 11794.

MCWRIGHT, CARTER C.
Business executive. **Personal:** Born Feb 7, 1950; children: Carter, II. **Educ:** Southern Univ, BA 1972. **Career:** Saginaw Black Business Assn, vice pres, 1982-84; Saginaw East Side Lions Club, vice pres, 1983-84; Music Planet, owner. **Orgs:** Bd member, East Central Michigan Planners, 1984-87; member, NAACP, Joy Baptist Church. **Honors/Awds:** Businessman of the year, Saginaw Frontiers Club, 1983, Saginaw Black Business Assn, 1984; Lion of the year, Saginaw Eastside Lions, 1983. **Business Addr:** Music Planet, 517 W Carpenter Rd, Saginaw, MI 48601.

MCZEAL, ALFRED, SR.
Business executive. **Personal:** Born Mar 6, 1931, Ridge, LA; son of Olivia and Alzfall McZeal; married Virgis Mary Sampay, Jan 5, 1952; children: Olivia Figaro-McZeal, Myra Holmes, Alfred Jr, Janet Lynn. **Career:** Morgan & Lindsey, janitor, 1948-64; Southern Consumers, volunteer, 1962-64,

general mgr/CEO, 1964-. **Orgs:** Southern Consumers, 1962; St Paul's Credit Union, supervisor, 1961; NAACP, 1955; MLK Holiday Committee, 1991; Better Business Bureau, 1986; Institute of Karamic Guidance, Holy Family African Tour, 1992; Black Alliance for Progress, secretary; Louisiana Black Assembly; National Black Assembly. **Honors/Awds:** Southern Consumers Education Foundation, Lifetime Achievement, 1991; Acadiana Kiwanis, Outstanding Citizen Award, 1990; Federation of Southern Cooperatives, Dedicated Service Award, 1987; LA Beautician Association, Achieving Civic & Religious Improvement, 1985; Southern Consumers Education Foundation, Black Citizen Award, 1975; KJCB Radio Station, Service Award, 1990; Immaculate Heart of Mary, Support, 1988. **Special Achievements:** Traveled to Geneva Switzerland to speak on Human Development to the third world countries, 1975. **Business Addr:** Chief Executive Officer, Southern Consumers Cooperative, 1006 Surrey St, Lafayette, LA 70501, (318)232-1126.

MCZIER, ARTHUR
Management consultant. **Personal:** Born May 4, 1935, Atlanta; married Ruby Burrows; children: Sandra, Jennifer Rose. **Educ:** Loyola U, BS 1959, study towards M 1960-61. **Career:** Resources Inc, mgmt consult 1974-; Gen Bahamian Co, bus exec 1973-74; US Small Bus Admin, asst adminstr for minority enterprise 1969-73; US Dept of Commerce Office of Foreign Direct Investmts, 1968; Ford Motor Co, mktng analyst 1966-67; Seeburg Corp, intl sales & mktng rep 1962-66. **Orgs:** Adv Bd of Inst of Minority Bus Educ Howard U; Wash Bd of Couns Fed City Coll. **Honors/Awds:** Who's Who in Am Adv Bd; Robert Russo Moton Ldrshp Award, Natl Bus League 1971; hon dr laws degree Daniel Payne Coll 1971; gold medal disngshed serv USSmall Bus Admin 1969; award of merit Natl Econ Devel Admin 1971; spl achvmt award US Small Bus Admin 1969; recog award for outst contrib to minority econ dev Black Businessmen's Professional Assn 1971; recog award for outst serv to minority bus in TX & USA Pylon Salesmanshp Club 1971; hall of fame Loyola Univ 1972; cert outst perform Small Bus Adm 1972; city econ devel ctr award Miami 1972; pub serv award Houston Citizens C of C 1973; Arthur S Fleming award nominee Small Bus Adm 1972; key award Natl Assn Black Manufacturer's 1974. **Business Addr:** President, Natl Business Services, 1420 N St NW, Washington, DC 20005.

MEACHAM, HENRY W.
Physician. **Personal:** Born Apr 20, 1924, Jackson, TN; married Jean; children: Paul, Henry, Brian. **Educ:** Lane Coll, BS 1941; NYU, MS 1947; Howard Univ Med Sch, MD 1952. **Career:** Kings Co Hosp, hematology fellow 1955-56; Mt Sinai Hosp, attending physician internal med & hematology serv unit 1965-78; Carter Hlth Ctr, internist-hematologist 1968-80; Physician, prvt pract 1978-. **Orgs:** Mem NY Blood Soc 1970-80; bd mem Queens Urban League 1978-80; pres Empire State Med Assn NM Assn 1978-80; bd mem Am Cancer Soc Harlem Div 1980; pres Queens Clinical Soc Inc; chmn of the board Queens Alliance, IPA; mem board of directors, ACS, New York City Div. **Honors/Awds:** Past pres award Queens Clinical Soc Inc 1979. **Military Serv:** USN pharmacist mate 2/c 1944-46. **Business Addr:** 119-15 Sutphin Blvd, Jamaica, NY 11436.

MEACHAM, ROBERT B.
Educator, administration. **Personal:** Born Mar 21, 1933, Tuscaloosa, AL; son of Manarah Meacham and Armond Meacham; married Grace A; children: Anthony, Alexander. **Educ:** AB, EdM 1973; doctoral cand 1975. **Career:** Lecturer on Psychology; Univ of Cincinnati, counselor 1970-73; Univ of Cincinnati Coll of Applied Sci, asst dir 1973-74, dir student life & counseling 1974-, assoc vice provost minority programs & serv & intl serv, associate vice provost student services 1978-89, associate athletic dir 1989-. **Orgs:** Mem Amer Personnel & Guidance Assn; mem Assn for Non-White concerns; mem Assn for Counselor Educ & Supervision United Black Faculty Assn, treas 1973; mem Paddock Hills Assembly Inc 1970-; mem Comm Devel Adv Cncl City of Cincinnati. **Honors/Awds:** Affirmative action plan prepared for OH Coll of Applied Sci 1973; aided 200 Black students from 1971-80 in receiving industrial grant-in-aid scholarships. **Military Serv:** USAF A/1C 1952-56. **Home Addr:** 1228 Westminster Dr, Cincinnati, OH 45229. **Business Addr:** Associate Athletic Director, Univ of Cincinnati, 200 Armory Field House, Cincinnati, OH 45221.

MEADE, ALSTON B.
Research associate (retired). **Personal:** Born Jun 28, 1930; son of Hepsy Condell Meade and Frank I R Meade; divorced; children: Alston B Jr, Allison D, Jule Anne, Brandon D, Fred A. **Educ:** Fisk Univ, BA 1956; Univ MN, MS 1959, PhD 1962. **Career:** EI du Pont de Nemours Co, rsrch biolgst 1964, sr rsrch biolgst 1971, research associate, until 1992. **Orgs:** Mem Brd Ed W Chester Area Schl Dist 1970-80; v pres Brd Ed W Chester Area Schl Dist 1975-77; chrmn Joint Comm Spl Ed Chester Cnty PA 1974-80; mem Inter Unit Chester County PA 1974-80; pres, Intl Society of African Scientists, 1988-90; pres, Natl Assn of Jamaican & Supporting Organizations, 1993-; pres, NAACP-Southern Chester County Branch, 1965-75. **Home Addr:** 2014 Valley Dr, West Chester, PA 19382.

MEADE, MELVIN C.
Counselor. **Personal:** Born Jan 16, 1929, Aliquippa, PA; married Beverly Ann Carter; children: Carroll Ann, Melvin Carter, Yolanda Alike, Natalie Marie. **Educ:** W VA St Coll, BS 1953; Westminster Coll, MEd 1965; W MI U, 1967; Carlow Coll NSF, 1968-70; Boston Univ Pittsburgh Theol Sem, 1978, 1971. **Career:** Aliquippa Sch Dist, guidance couns; Aliquippa Sch Middle Sch, tchr 23 yrs. **Orgs:** Waterfront dir YMCA; dir Nghbrhd Yth Corp; dir Ch Bsktbll; dir YMCA Day Camp; mem Phi Delta Kappa; NEA; PA Educ Assn; Aliquippa Educ Assn; PA Sch Couns Assn; Midwstrn Couns Assn; Am Pers & Guid Assn; Assn for Non-White Concern; mem bd Christ United Beaver Co; Beaver Vly YMCA; Beaver Co Yth Serv Inc; Beaver Co Mental Hlth Red Cr; Alpha Phi Alpha; Phi Delta Kappa 1972; pastor Holy Institutional Bapt Ch; prgm coord Middle Sch 1974. **Honors/Awds:** Man of yr Aliquippa Club 1971; Eagle Scout 1947. **Military Serv:** AUS Corps eng PFC 1953-55. **Business Addr:** Aliquippa Middle Sch, Aliquippa, PA 15001.

MEADE, WILLIAM F.
Educator. **Personal:** Born Jan 4, 1925, Brooklyn, NY. **Educ:** Brooklyn Coll, BA 1954, MA 1956; Teachers Coll, Columbia Univ, Diploma Special Educ 1960; Certified NLP practitioner level 1986, trainer 1987. **Career:** Dept of Physical Med & Rehabilitation Kingsbrook Jewish Med Center, chief speech therapist 1954-65; Long Island Univ Speech & Hearing Clinic, dir; Brooklyn Center, Long Island Univ, Assoc prof speech pathology & audiology. **Orgs:** Nursing home consultant speech problems of neurologically impaired adults geriatrics 1971-74; assoc mem Bedford Stuyvesant Jaycees 1974-75; treas of dirs Hosp Programs in Speech Pathology Audiology 1975-76; pres 1975-76; mem Am Speech & Hearing Assn; mem NY State Speech & Hearing Assn. **Honors/Awds:** Recip Certificate of Appreciation for Civic Service Bedford Stuyvesant Jaycees 1975, Greenpark Care Center 1984. **Military Serv:** USMC 1943-46. **Business Addr:** Associate Professor, Long Island University, University Plaza, Brooklyn, NY 11201.

MEADE-TOLLIN, LINDA C.
Biochemist, educator. **Personal:** Born Aug 16, London, WV; daughter of Virginia Meade and Robert A Meade; married Gordon Tollin; children: Amina Rebecca. **Educ:** WV State Coll, BS cum laude 1964; Hunter Coll, MA 1969; City Univ of New York, PhD 1972. **Career:** Coll of Old Westbury, asst prof 1972-75; Rockefeller Univ, visiting asst prof, 1973-74; Univ of AZ, NIH postdoctoral fellow 1975-77, rsch assoc 1978-80; Coord Women in Science & Engrg Office 1980-82, visiting asst prof 1982-85; Morehouse Schl of Medicine, Faculty Development Fellow, 1985-86; Univ of AZ, Sr Lecturer/Asst Research Scientist, 1987-91, NIH Minority Special Investigator, 1987-89, 1990-93, research asst prof 1987-. **Orgs:** Natl Organization for the Professional Advancement of Black Chemists and Chemical Engineers, 1973-85, 1987-, chair exec bd 1981; consultant Amer Med Women's Assn 1977-85; bd of dir Ododo Theatre Foundation 1977-85; Alpha Kappa Alpha Sorority 1962-; Jack and Jill Inc, 1987-89. **Honors/Awds:** Finalist Natl Merit Scholarship Corp 1960; contributor What People Eat Harvard Univ Press 1974; NIH Rsch Fellow at Univ of AZ College of Medicine 1975-77; indv preceptorship Amer Medical Women's Assoc 1979; Awd for Excellence in Medicine Scimitar Temple 108 1981; Scientist of the Year AZ Council of Black Engrs & Scientists 1983; NIH-N HLBI Minority Faculty Career Development Award, 1996-2001. **Business Addr:** Research Assistant Professor, University of Arizona, College of Medicine, Surgery/Section of Surgical Research, PO Box 245084, Tucson, AZ 85724, (520)626-7019.

MEADOWS, CHERYL R.
City administrator. **Personal:** Born Sep 7, 1948, Cincinnati, OH; daughter of Ruth Pulliam and Jack Pulliam; children: Jerry C Wilkerson Jr. **Educ:** Tennessee State Univ, BA, 1970; Univ of Cincinnati, MS, 1975. **Career:** City of Cincinnati, planner, 1971-76, program mgr, 1976-82, asst to the city mgr, director, department of neighborhood svcs, currently. **Orgs:** Mem, AS Conference of Mayor/City Human Serv, 1976-; Natl Forum for Black Public Admin, 1986-; Amer Soc of Public Admin, 1989. **Honors/Awds:** Aspo Ford Found Fellowship, 1975; Univ Scholarship, 1975; Outstanding Young Women of Amer, 1982; Community Chest's President Award, 1983; Community Action Comm Award, 1986; Community Serv Award, 1987; Career Women of Achievement, 1992; City of Cincinnati Manager, Outstanding Manager Award, 1992.

MEADOWS, FERGUSON BOOKER, JR.
Educator. **Personal:** Born Jan 23, 1942, Charleston, WV; son of Mary and Ferguson; married Hildred Jean Hutcherson; children: Leslie Michelle, Stephanie Dawn, Kimberlie Elizabeth. **Educ:** West Virginia State College, BA Sociology 1962-67; West Virginia Univ, MA Counseling 1968-71; Virginia Polytechnic Institute & State Univ, EdD 1975. **Career:** West Virginia State College, dir of counseling 1968-71, dir guidance & placement 1971-72; Kanawha Co Bd of Education, dir project CARE 1972-73; VPI & State Univ, adjunct professor Summer 1975; Kent State Univ, assistant professor 1975-; Kent State Univ, Kent, OH asst dean Coll of Educ & Graduate School of Educ. **Orgs:** Bd of dir pres Portage County Housing Advocates 1981-82; member Amer Assn for Counseling & Devel 1971-; member Amer School Counselors Assn 1971-; member Assn for Non-White Concerns 1973-; member Assn of Counselor Educ & Supervision 1975-; bd of dir Portage County NAACP 1982-; bd of dir Portage County Headstart 1984-; bd of dir Portage County Comm Action Council 1984-; mem Amer Assn for Multicultural Counseling & Devel; pres Ohio Assn for Multicultural Counseling & Devel, 1988-89; Treasurer Ohio Assn for Counseling & Devel, 1988-90. **Honors/Awds:** Kent State University Distinguished Advisor Award 1981; published book, Using Guidance Skills in the Classroom Eds Charles Thomas 1982; 15 articles and book chapters. **Military Serv:** US Army Matl Guard, lieutenant colonel, 1960; Army Commendation Medal; Armed Forces Res Medal; Natl Defense Serv Medal; XO WV Military Acad; Army Achievement Medal. **Home Addr:** 1048 DeLeone Drive, Kent, OH 44240. **Business Addr:** Dept of Couns, Kent State Univ Main Campus, PO Box 5190, Kent, OH 44242-0001.

MEADOWS, LUCILE SMALLWOOD
Educator (retired). **Personal:** Born May 23, 1918, Glen Ferris, WV; daughter of Luvennia Galloway Smallwood and Solomon Smallwood; married Reginald Clinton (deceased); children: Benita Luanne. **Educ:** WV State Coll, graduated 1939. **Career:** Harlem Hgts Elem, princ 1957-67, teacher 1939-83, retired. **Orgs:** Mem WVEA Blk Caucus Strng Comm 1973-78; mem WVEA Polit Action Comm 1976-; chmn Fayette Co Blk Caucus 1974-95; chrpsn Tri Area Park Com; chrpsn Fayetteville Prop Owners Assn; spl adv com WV Tchrs Retirement Bd apptd by Gov Rockefeller; adv cncl WV Women's Commn; pub relat dir and vp Upper Fayette Co Chap NAACP; past sec Fayette Co Chap WV State Alum Assn; delegate Dem Midterm Natl Convention 1978; delegate Dem Natl Conv; apptd to Gov Judiciary Adv Comm 1983 by Gov Rockefeller IV;WV Dem Exec Comm; secretary Fayette Co Dem Women's Club; past mem Fayette Co Volunteer Steering Comm; district director, West Virginia Federation of Democrat Women, Inc, 1990-. **Honors/Awds:** Apptd WV for charter com 1976; Ten Persons of the Yr Fayette Co 1976; alt del 1976 Dem Conv; apptd Fayette Co Bicent Com 1976; Washington Carver Award, WV Dept of Culture, 1985; Mary L Williams Award, WV Educ Assn, 1982; appointed to WV Legislature, Governor Gaston Caperton, 1990; Mary Hatwood Futrell Award, Natl Educ Assn, 1991; Distinguished West Virginian by Governor Gaston Carperton, 1992; Outstanding Citizen Award by Mountain Bar Association, 1992; Tribute by Congressman Nick Joe Rahall II appearing in Congressional Record, 1992; West Virginia Ethics Commission, 1992; 1 of 356 Women included in Pressing Onward: The Women's Historical Biography of the National Education Association, 1996; Mary L Williams Award, West Virginia Education Association, 1996. **Home Addr:** 2205 Oakmont Court, Greensboro, NC 27407.

MEADOWS, RICHARD H.
Dentist. **Personal:** Born Dec 7, 1928, Roanoke, VA; married Dorothy M Magee; children: William C. **Educ:** VA Union U, BS 1951; Howard Univ Sch of Dentistry, DDS 1955; Freedman' Hospital, intern 1956. **Career:** Dentist, pvt prac. **Orgs:** Pres PBR Dent Soc 1961-68; pres Old Dominion Dent Soc 1968-71; mem Nat Dent Soc; mem Intl Endodontic Soc; mem Aircraft Owners & Pilots Assn; mem Omega Psi Frat; NAACP. **Honors/Awds:** Recip award in oral surg Beta Kappa Chi Nat Sci Soc Howard Univ 1955. **Business Addr:** 215 W Clay St, Richmond, VA 23220.

MEANS, BERTHA E.
Educator. **Personal:** Born May 1, 1920, Valley Mills, TX; married James H Means; children: Joan, Janet, James Jr, Patricia, Ronald. **Educ:** Huston-Tillotson Coll, AB 1945; Univ of TX, MEd 1955; Univ of TX Austin, attended. **Career:** Prairie View A&M Univ, vstg instr 1959-68; Austin Independent School Dist Austin TX, dir head start 1969-70; Univ TX Austin, instr 1971-72; Austin Independent School Dist, instr coord secondary reading, currently. **Orgs:** Mem Intl Reading Assoc; past pres Capitol Area Council; mem TX State Teachers Assoc; charter mem Ad Hoc Com for Enactment Human Relations Comm City of Austin; bd mem YWCA; mem Epsilon Kappa Chap Delta Kappa Gamma Soc for Women Ed Area Ch, United Fund, Austin & Travis Cts 1965-67; 1st vice pres Austin NAACP 1970-74; chmn voter Reg & Ed, City Council appointee to Parks & Rec Adv Bd 1967-74; citizens comm for A More Beautiful Town Lake 1972-75; mem Local Citizens Adv Comm TX Constitutional Adv Comm 1973; past pres, org Austin Chap Jack & Jill of Amer Inc 1956-58; mem Alpha Kappa Alpha Sor, St James Episcopal Ch; pres Episcopal Women St James 1966-67. **Honors/Awds:** Woman of the Year Awd Zeta Phi Beta Sor 1965; DeWitty Civil Rights Awd Austin Br NAACP 1966; selected 1 of Austins Outstanding Women of 1975; Austin Amer Statesman; NAACP Spec Awd for Serv to Parks & Rec Dept 1975; Comm Serv Awd Zeta Phi Beta 1976; Comm Leadership Cert Apprec Capital City Lions & Optimist Clubs 1972. **Business Addr:** Instructional Coordinator, Austin Independent School Dist, 6100 N Guadalupe, Austin, TX 78752.

MEANS, CRAIG R.
Educator, dentist (retired). **Personal:** Born Aug 16, 1922, Shreveport, LA; children: Stephanie. **Educ:** Southern U, BS 1950; Howard U, DDS 1954; OH State U, MSc 1963; Memorial

Hosp Cancer, Certif 1964. **Career:** Coll of Dentistry Howard U, asst prof 1961-66, assoc prof 1966-70; Dept Rmvbl Prost, chmn 1968-70, prof 1970-; Coll of Dentistry Howard U, assoc dean 1970-81; Continuing Dental Ed, dir 1982-85, retired, professor. **Orgs:** Consult ADA Comm Dental Accreditation 1982-85; mem Amer Dental Assn; mem Natl Dental Assn; mem Amer Assn of Dental Schools. **Honors/Awds:** Fellow Louise C Ball Fellowship Fund 1962-64; mem Omicron Kappa Upsilon Dental Honor Soc; fellow Amer Coll of Dentists 1971; alumni awd Howard Univ of Coll Dentistry 1984. **Military Serv:** AUS 1st lt 1941-46. **Home Addr:** 9823 Hedin Dr, Silver Spring, MD 20903.

MEANS, DONALD FITZGERALD
Government official. **Personal:** Born Dec 29, 1966, Tuscaloosa, AL; son of Mary Turner Means and Harry L Means. **Educ:** University of Alabama, Tuscaloosa, AL, marketing management, 1989. **Career:** Greene County Racing Commission, Eutaw, AL, chairman of commission, 1989-, financial management analyst, 1989-90. **Orgs:** Chairman, Greene County Water Authorty, 1990-; chairman, Agriculture Advisory Board, 1991-; president, Community Fire Department, 1990; member, Extension Service Advisory Board, 1990-. **Business Addr:** Chairman of Commission, Greene County Racing Commission, PO Box 542, Eutaw, AL 35462.

MEANS, ELBERT LEE
Elected official. **Personal:** Born Feb 3, 1945, Sandy Ridge, AL; married Harriet Ivory; children: Madelene, Jennifer, Kristen. **Educ:** Selma Univ, 1964; AL State Univ 1964-66 & 1968-69. **Career:** Station Help Inc, supervisor 1969-73; General Motors, shipping clerk 1973-75; Brockway Glass, laborer 1975-79; Lowndes County, lst Black tax assessor 1979-. **Orgs:** State exec member Alabama Democratic Conf; county coordinator Lowndes Cty Democratic Party; member advisory board Lowndes Cty Community Org; vice-pres Selma Univ Alumni-Chapter; honorary lieutenant colonel aide-de-camp in the Alabama State Militia. **Military Serv:** AUS E-5 sergant 1966-68; Bronze Star Vietnam Veteran. **Home Addr:** PO Box 69, Fort Deposit, AL 36032. **Business Addr:** Tax Assessor, Lowndes Co, PO Box 186, Hayneville, AL 36040.

MEANS, FRED E.
Educational administrator (retired). **Personal:** Born in Pacolet, SC; son of Lemor Tucker and Fred Means Sr; married Helen Pryor; children: Chad, Marc, Vincent. **Educ:** NY Univ, BS 1959; Trenton State Coll, MA 1963; Rutgers Univ, EdM 1973, EdD 1975. **Career:** NY City Schools, tchr 1959-60; Newark School System, tchr, administrator 1960-70; Rutgers Univ, lecturer & dir 1970-75; Jersey City State Coll, dir 1975-78, asst dean 1978-85, dean 1985-94, adjunct prof, 1995-. **Orgs:** Mem Newark Bd of Educ 1973-76; trustee Action for Sickle Cell Anemia of Hudson City 1982-88; mem bd dirs Research for Better Schools 1983-94; pres Org Newark Educators Newark 1967-70; trustee UCC Newark Anti Poverty Agency 1965-66; mem AACTE; mem AERA; mem ATE. **Honors/Awds:** Project PRIME (Program to Recruit Interested Minorities Educators), paper presented at Norfolk State Univ 1988; "The Process and Product of Restructuring an Urban Teacher Education Program," paper presented at Assn of Teacher Educators Conference, New Orleans, 1991. **Military Serv:** AUS Spec 3 1953-56.

MEANS, KEVIN MICHAEL
Physician. **Personal:** Born Jun 14, 1955, Brooklyn, NY; son of Muriel C and Phillip A Means Jr. **Educ:** State Univ of NY at Binghamton, BS Biology 1978; Howard Univ Coll of Medicine, MD 1978-82; Rehabilitation Inst of Chicago of Northwestern Univ, physical medicine and rehabilitation residency, 1982-85. **Career:** Veterans Admin Medical Center, staff physician 1985-88; University of AR for Med Science Dept of Physical Medicine and Rehab, asst prof, 1988-91, assoc prof, 1991-, interim chairman, 1997-; Univ Hospital of Arkansas, Staff physician, 1985-; Veterans Admin Medical Center, Little Rock, AR, asst chief; Rehab Medical Serv, 1988-96, chief, 1996-; medical director, Falls and Mobility Program, 1988-, staff physician, Rehab Medical Serv 1985-88. **Orgs:** Fellow, Amer Acad of Physical Medicine & Rehab 1986-; Assoc of Academic Physiatrists 1986-; Amer Geriatric Soc; Gerontol Society of America, 1987-; Geriatric Rehab, special interest group, chairman VA physiatrists subcommittee; Amer Acad of PM&R 1986-. **Business Addr:** Physical Medicine & Rehabilitation Service, Falls & Mobility Disorders Program (117), Veterans Administrations Medical Center, 2200 Fort Roots Dr, North Little Rock, AR 72114, (501)688-1619.

MEANS, NATRONE JERMAINE
Professional football player. **Personal:** Born Apr 26, 1972, Harrisburg, NC. **Educ:** Univ of North Carolina. **Career:** San Diego Chargers, running back, 1993-95; Jacksonville Jaguars, 1996-. **Business Addr:** Professional Football Player, Jacksonville Jaguars, One Stadium Place, Jacksonville, FL 32202, (904)633-6000.

MEARES, PAULA G. ALLEN
Educator, educational administrator. **Personal:** Born in Buffalo, NY; daughter of Mary T. Hienz and Joseph N. Allen; married Henry O. Meares, Jun 8, 1974; children: Tracey, Nichole, Shannon. **Educ:** State University of New York at Buffalo, Buffalo, NY, BS, 1970; University of Illinois at Urbana-Champaign, Jane Addams School of Social Work, MSW, 1971, PhD, 1975; Harvard University, Management Institute, Boston, MA, certificate, 1990; University of Michigan, management certificate, 1993-94. **Career:** Facilty University of Illinois School of Social Work, Urbana-Champaign, IL, 1978-84, associate professor, 1983-89, director of doctoral program, 1985-89; University of Michigan, dean, 1993-. **Orgs:** Editor in chief, Journal Social Work Education (CSWE), National Association of Social Workers, 1989-93; board of directors, Council on Social Work Education, 1989-91; communications board member, National Association of Social Workers, 1990-; elected member, steering committee, Group for the Advancement of Doctoral Education, 1987-88; chair, commission on education, National Association of Social Workers, 1982-88. **Honors/Awds:** Medallion of Honors, University of Illinois at Urbana-Champaign, 1990, Participant in the Committee on Institutional Cooperation Development Seminar, 1989-90; Delta Mu National Social Work Honor Society; Delta Kappa Gamma International Honor Society of Women Educators. **Business Addr:** Dean, Professor, School of Social Work, University of Michigan, 1065 Frieze Bldg, Ann Arbor, MI 48109.

MEASE, QUENTIN R.
Association executive. **Personal:** Born Oct 25, 1917, Buxton, IA; son of Cornelia Frances Mease and Charles Henry Mease; married Jewell Mary Chenault Mease, Sep 25, 1950; children: Barbara Ann Ransom. **Educ:** Des Moines U, BS 1939; George Williams Coll, MS 1948. **Career:** Crocker Br YMCA, exec dir 1939-42; Metro YMCA Chgo, asst prgm sec 1946-49; Bagby Br YMCA Houston, exec dir 1950-55; So Central YMCA, exc dir 1955-75; Human Enrichment of Life Programs, Inc, president, 1975-. **Orgs:** Chmn bd mgrs Harris Cnty Hosp Dist 1970-75; mem Rotary Club of Houston; bd mem TX Med Ctr; fdr pres Houston Area Urban League 1967-69; bd mem Alley Theater; Star of Hope Mission; exec sec Houston Bus & Professional Men's Club 1950-75; board member, Baylor College of Medicine, 1971-; board member, Sheltering Arms, 1987-89; board member, Lockwood National Bank, 1984-; bd mem, Institute of International Education, 1988-; life bd mem, South Central YMCA; bd mem, Rotary Club of Houston, 1987-89; chairman of the board, Hospital District Foundation, 1993-. **Honors/Awds:** Distinguished Service Award, Texas Peace Officers Assn, 1983; Distinguished Service Award, Baylor College of Medicine, 1985; First Annual Sheriff Johnny Klevenhagen Award, 1986; Community Service Award, Houston Area Urban League, 1989; Distinguished Service Award, 152nd Anniversary, City of Houston, 1989; Distinguished Service Award, Black United Fund, 1989; Distinguished Citizens Award, Metropolitan Transit Authority, 1991; Life Trustee Award, Texas Medical Center, 1991. **Military Serv:** USAF capt 1942-46. **Business Addr:** President, Human Enrichment of Life Programs, Inc, 2646 South Loop West, Suite 320, Houston, TX 77054.

MEAUX, RONALD
Artist, educator. **Personal:** Born Feb 15, 1942, Louisville. **Educ:** Univ of KY, BA Art 1965. **Career:** Cleveland Public Schools, art instructor; Artist. **Orgs:** Mem Nat Conf of Artists; mem NAACP; mem Metro Opera Guild. **Honors/Awds:** One man art show Karamu 1974; exhib work Clevelande Akron; recip Scholarshps Alpha Phi Alpha 1 yr; Mary E Johnston Art Sch 3 yrs. **Business Addr:** Art Instructor, East Technical High School, 2439 E 55th St, Cleveland, OH 44105.

MEDEARIS, VICTOR L.
Clergyman. **Personal:** Born Apr 3, 1921, Austin, TX; son of Pearl B Edgar Medearis and James Ever Medearis; married Gladys Lonell Alexander Medearis, Apr 3, 1943; children: Victor L, Pamela Faye, Charlotte Briana. **Educ:** City Coll of San Fran, AA 1958; San Fran Bapt Bible Coll, Std Theol 1948-53; San Fran U, Std Soc Sci 1959-61. **Career:** Federal Employment, mechanic hlpr, warehse foreman, heavy duty drvr trainer, drvr examnr, mech inspec, equal employmt spec 1949-; Double Rock Bapt Ch San Fran, pastor, 1948-. **Orgs:** Chmn San Fran Humn Rights Comm 1971-; sec bd instr Fellowshp Bible Inst; chmn Civic Com Bayview Bapt Min Fellowshp; past mod Bay Area Dist Assn; bd mem San Fran Chptr NAACP; bd mem Sickle Cell Anemia; West Bay Clergy Rep Northern CA Adv Bd of United Negro Coll Fund Bay Area Inter Alumni Com; ofcl Organist CA State Bapt Conven. **Honors/Awds:** Recip highest award of merit City San Fran 1971; hon award Pelton Jr HS 1973; hon award Quartett Singers Assn of Am 1972; Outstanding Community Achievement Award, San Francisco Bayview Hunters Point Multi-purpose Senior Services, 1989; 40th Pastoral Anniversary Commemoration, Senator Quentin Kopp, 1989. **Business Addr:** Pastor, Double Rock Baptist Church, 1595 Shafter Ave, San Francisco, CA 94124.

MEDFORD, ISABEL
Attorney. **Personal:** Born Mar 15, Louisiana; children: Richard Kevin. **Educ:** Univ of CA Berkley, BA Psych & Polit Sci 1972; Univ of CA Boalt Hall Sch of Law, JD 1975; Univ of CA, M Crim 1976. **Career:** Isabel Medford Law Firm, atty 1978-; Robert T Cresswell Inc, atty 1974-78; NAACP Legal Def Fund, law clerk 1974-75. **Orgs:** Bd dir A Safe Place 1979-; vice pres UC Black Alumni Assn 1979-; legal adv Oakland E Bay Chap Delta Sigma Theta 1979-; mem past chmn Memshp Com Niagra Movement Dem Club 1974-.

MEDINA, BENNY
Recording company executive, television producer. **Career:** Warner Brothers Records, artists and repertoire, vice pres, currently; "Fresh Prince of Bel-Air," co-producer, currently. **Business Phone:** (818)953-3277.

MEE, LAFARRELL DARNELL
Professional basketball player. **Personal:** Born Feb 11, 1971, Cleveland, TN. **Educ:** Western Kentucky. **Career:** Denver Nuggets, 1993-. **Business Phone:** (303)893-6700.

MEEK, CARRIE P.
Congresswoman. **Personal:** Born in Tallahassee, FL; divorced; children: Lucia Raiford, Sheila Davis Kinui, Kendrick Meek. **Educ:** Florida A&M University, BS, (honors), 1946; University of Michigan, MS, public health, physical education, 1948; Florida Atlantic University, doctorate courses. **Career:** Bethune Cookman College, physical educ, health instructor; Miami-Dade Community College, professor, 1961; Florida A&M Univ, asst prof, health-physical educ; Florida Legislature, seat, 1979; Florida State Senate, senator, 1982; US House of Representatives, congresswoman, currently. **Special Achievements:** First African-American elected to the US Congress from Florida this century, 1992. **Business Addr:** Congresswoman, US House of Representatives, New Jersey & Independence SE, Washington, DC 20515, (202)225-4506.

MEEK, KENDRICK
State representative. **Career:** Wackenhut Corp, development representative, currently; Florida House of Representatives, state representative, currently. **Orgs:** Greater Miami Service Corps Board; Focus Advisory Board.

MEEK, RUSSELL CHARLES
Educator, lecturer, consultant, director/producer. **Personal:** Born Sep 9, 1937, Springfield, IL; son of Josephine Snowden Meek and Albert Jackson Meek; divorced; children: 4. **Educ:** Milliken Univ Natl Coll LaSalle U, student 1960; Hwa Rang Do Martial Arts Acad, 1970, Universal Life Ch, DD 1975; Natl Coll of Chiropractic Med, Doct Religious Humanities; Temple Univ; CLC, computer programming, 1991; Chicago Access Corp, TV producer. **Career:** Univ of IL, instr radio TV prod Psycholinguistics & Philology; CETA V "Devel Educ & Employ Prog," proj dir; Malcolm X Coll, instr 1970-72; Northeastern ILU, rehab educ specialist 1974-75; Natl Black Writer's Workshop, lecturer 1973-75; Study Commn for Residential Schs IL, hearing coord 1974; Investigative Jour & Historical Rsch, writer; Malcolm X Coll bd dir, Parents Without Partners, comm adv commn; Cook Co Dept of Corrections, 1966-; Search for Truth Inc, pres, 1966-; Westside Art & Karate Center Inc, dir, 1968-; Radio Sta WVON, prod host, 1970-. **Orgs:** Instr Martial Arts; pres Black Karate Fed; mem Black United Front, Black Enpowerment Comm; pres Search for Truth Inc; radio commentator, talk show host WBEE Radio; leader, Dr Russ Meek's Jazz AllSTARS; bd of dir African American Clergy for Action 1988-. **Honors/Awds:** Songs "My Love," "You," and "Shadows of the Night," 1969; Blue Ribbon Panel Citizens for Police Reform, 1973-75; received 10 humanitarian, community, integrity, merit & special awards, 1972-75; Westside Citizen of the Year, 1972-76; starred in 2 documentary films, "Crisis in the Cities" (Emmy Award winner) and "A Letter to Martin"; produced and directed TV and radio shows since 1966, first black to do so in country; editor, Search for Truth News; Comm Integrity Award, 1973; doctoral candidate, Univ of the Pacific; publicist, co-sponsor, African-Amer Culture Center Imo State; The Can Do It Awd, 1973; Champion of Imprisoned Award, 1974; The Get It Done Award, 1973; Special Commendation Award for Community Interest and Support, El Centro de La Causa 1975; Natl Community Leaders; Gentlemen Distinction; Master of the Martial Arts; Outstanding Serv to the Martial Arts and Community; playwright, "The Message," 1976; co-author "Our Songs"; Image Makers Award, 1977; co-producer, actor, The Sinister Reign, Anna Lucasta, and Blues for Mr Charlie; author, Poems for Peace, Justice and Freedom, 1966; co-director "Mfundishi," Pan African Martial Ars Federation Inc. **Home Phone:** (312)995-8679. **Business Addr:** Search for Truth, Inc, 10937 S Lowe Ave, Chicago, IL 60628.

MEEKS, CORDELL DAVID, JR.
Judge. **Personal:** Born Dec 17, 1942, Kansas City, KS; son of Cellastine D Brown Meeks and Cordell D Meeks, Sr (deceased); married Mary Ann Sutherland, Jul 15, 1967; children: Cordell, III. **Educ:** Univ KS, BA Pol Sci 1964; Univ KS Law Schl, JD Law 1967; Univ PA Law Schl, Smith Fellowship 1968; Harvard Law Schl, Practicalities of Judging 1978; Natl Judicial Coll, Grad Gen Jrs 1981. **Career:** Wyandotte Cty Legal Aid Socty, staff counsel 1968-70; Meeks Sutherland McIntosh Law Firm, sr partner 1968-81; State of KS, special asst atty gen 1975; Kansas City KS, municipal judge 1976-81; 29th Judicial Dist of Kansas, dist court judge 1981-; National Institute for Trial Advocacy, faculty, 1986-. **Orgs:** Kansas Municipal Judges Assn, pres 1980-81; Univ of Kansas Alumni

Assn, chmn, 1997-; Gov Comm on Crime Prev 1982-91; Comm Ethics and Prof Resp, Natl Assoc of State Trial Judges 1984-; Bd Govr KS Univ Law Schl, pres 1984-85; Natl Conf of Christians & Jews (Greater Kansas City region), co-chair 1993-97, natl bd of trustees, 1990-94; natl bd, Amer Lung Assn, 1997-; Amer Lung Assn of Kansas, pres, 1988-89; El Centro, Inc, chmn, 1996-97; Kansas Bar Journal of Kansas Bar Assn, bd of editors 1989-97; United Way of Wyandotte County, chmn, 1991-92; Visiting Nurses Assn of Greater Kansas City, pres 1989-91; Midwest Bioethics Ctr, chmn, 1995-97; Substance Abuse Ctr of Eastern KS, pres 1985-87; KS Commission on Bicentennial of US Constitution, mem 1987-91; Kaw District, Heart of America Boy Scouts of America, chmn, 1994-95, vp of operations, 1996-. **Honors/Awds:** Omicron Delta Kappa 1964; Fellow Regn Heber Smith Comm Lawyer 1968; Mo-Kan Chapter of National Association of Social Workers, Kansas Citizen of the Year, 1994;United Way, outstanding services awd 1979; Yates Branch, Men of Distinction Awd 1982; 100 Most Influential Black Men, Greater Kansas City, The KC GLOBE 1992-; Kansas City Spirit Award, 1994; Distinguished Service Awd, Park Coll, 1995; Distinguished Service Award, Blacks in Government of Greater Kansas City, 1989; President's Award, Southern Christian Leadership Conference, 1990; Distinguished Service, Kansas City Assn for Mental Health, 1990; Sire Archon Pres, Theta Boule Chapter, Sigma Pi Phi Frat, 1995-97; Distinguished Service, Kansas City Chapter, NAACP, 1986; University of Kansas, Distinguished Service Citation, 1995; Silver Beaver Awd, Boy Scouts of America, 1996. **Military Serv:** US Army, NG col 30 years; US Army, active duty 1968-70; Army Commendation Medal 1969; Meritorious Service Medal, 1995; US Army Command & General Staff Coll, graduate 1980;US Army War Coll, gradcuate, 1997; 35th Infantry Div KS Natl Guard, staff judge advocate 1983-89, state judge advocate general, 1989-90, senior military judge, 1991-. **Home Addr:** 7915 Walker, Kansas City, KS 66112, (913)334-1879. **Business Addr:** District Court Judge, 29th Judicial Dist of KS, 710 N 7th St, Wyandotte County Courthouse, Kansas City, KS 66101, (913)573-2926.

MEEKS, LARRY GILLETTE
Syndicated columnist. **Personal:** Born Apr 11, 1944, Bakersfield, CA; son of Henrietta Meeks and Reuben Meeks; married Dinnie Jean Williams; children: Kimerley, Corey. **Educ:** Bakersfield Jr Coll, AA 1963; Univ CA Davis, BS 1970; Golden Gate U, MPA 1973; National University, MA, 1995. **Career:** State of California Office of Health Planning and Dev, director, 1983-92; Syndicated Columnist ''Ethnically Speaking'', 1991-; Radio, talk show host, 1991-; Los Rios Comm College, college professor, 1995-. **Orgs:** Prof Golden Gate U; mem Am Hlth Plnrs; chm trts Williams Meml Chrh God In Christ; life mem Natl Urban Leag; mem NAACP; pres, Natomes School Board, 1985-; bd mem, Univ of Southern California 1983-; bd mem, Golden Gate Univ 1989-; board mem, Mercy Hospital Board; Women Escaping a Violent Environment; Japanese American Civil Liberties; League of Women Voters. **Honors/Awds:** Honorary Doctorate of Humanity, Angeles Univ, Philippines, 1989; Certificate of Appreciation, Los Angeles County, 1990-. **Military Serv:** AUS 1st lt 1966-69; Army Cmndtn, Combat Infrymn, Vietnam Serv Medals.

MEEKS, PERKER L., JR.
Judge. **Personal:** Born Aug 6, 1943, Tallahassee, FL; married Patricia E Evans MD; children: Perker III, Alicia Nicole. **Educ:** FL A&M Univ, BS 1965, JD 1968. **Career:** Gov State of FL, administrative aide 1968-69; San Francisco Sch Dist, teacher 1970-72; San Francisco Pub Defender's Office, trial lawyer 1972-80; San Francisco Municipal Ct, judge. **Orgs:** Sec/bd mem Charles Houston Bar Assn 1977-80; pres/bd mem OMI Com Assn 1970-80; bd mem San Francisco Chap NAACP 1978-79. **Business Addr:** Judge, San Francisco Municipal Court, City Hall, San Francisco, CA 94102.

MEEKS, REGINALD KLINE
Elected official. **Personal:** Born Mar 21, 1954, Louisville, KY; son of Eloise Meeks and Florian Meeks; children: Nilaja Nurajehan. **Educ:** Wabash College, BA History (minor Third World studies) 1976; Univ of Iowa Coll of Law, JD 1979; Univ of Louisville, PhD candidate. **Career:** Legal Aid Society, community development unit 1981-82; Christian & Bynum Attorneys, law clerk 1982-83; Bleidt, Barnett & Shanks Attorneys, law clerk 1983-88; City of Louisville, 11th ward alderman 1982-; Jefferson County Public Schools, Louisville KY, career developer 1988-91; Univ of Louisville, assoc dir of admissions, 1991-. **Orgs:** Sec, board of directors Seven Counties Services 1983-88; board of directors Stage One - The Louisville Children's Theater 1983-87; Shawnee District chmn Old KY Home Council Boy Scouts 1984-87; NAACP; Natl League of Cities; KY Municipal League; mem Natl Bar Assn; Natl Black Caucus of Local Elected Officials 1982-; Chairman Museum Development Committee KY African American Museum 1987-; board of directors Farm & Wilderness Camps Plymouth VT 1987-90; advisory council Salvation Army Boy's & Girl's Clubs 1987-; Neighborhood Housing Services, bd of dirs, 1991-. **Honors/Awds:** Dean's List Wabash College; Black Achievers Award - YMCA 1983; One of Fifty Young Future Leaders - Ebony Magazine Sept 1983; Numerous local awards. **Home Addr:** 2301 Osage Ave, Louisville, KY 40210. **Business Addr:** Alderman Ward 11, City of Louisville, 601 W Jefferson, Louisville, KY 40202, (502)574-3919.

MEEKS, STEPHEN ABAYOMI (OBADELE)
Acupuncturist, educator, institution builder. **Personal:** Born Aug 31, 1958, Philadelphia, PA; son of Pearl A Moore & Clyde R Meeks; divorced; children: Oji K, Kumasi D O, Adeyemi O. **Educ:** Howard Univ, pre-med, BS, 1982; Institute of TCM of NYC, diploma of Acupuncture, 1986; Institute International D'Acupuncture et Medecine Chirois, Doctor of Acupuncture, 1988. **Career:** Professor Martial Arts, instructor, 1976-; Family Planning Council, health educator, 1983-84; MIC-FPP, Inc, Health Education, asst dir, 1984-89; professional musician, percussionist, vocalist, 1983-; professional speaker, health/cultural conferences, 1984-; Moyo Nguvu CAC, Inc, founder, director, 1990-97; Moyo Health Association Inc, pres, doctor of Asian medicine, 1988-. **Orgs:** Acupuncture Association of Colorado, 1990-; National Black Child Dev, 1994-97; Denver Black United Fund, charter mem, 1994-96; Qamada International Martial Arts Association, charter mem, 1989-; National Commission for the Certification of Acupuncturist. **Honors/Awds:** NYC, Outstanding Young Man of the Year, 1987. **Special Achievements:** Ikhalipha-ship, Black Belt 5th Degree, 1993; principal research/co-author, Amer Public Health Assn, published ''The Role & Needs of the Male Partner in Reproductive Health Care: A Survey of Low Income, Inner City Males,'' 1985; Music Director, ''Moyo Arts Ensemble,'' 1990-97; Recorded ''Afrikans in Amerika,'' as producer, writer, performer, 1996.

MEEKS, WILLIS GENE
Aerospace executive. **Personal:** Born Jan 19, 1938, Harlan, KY; son of Thelma Meeks and Maceo Meeks; married Magalene Powell, Aug 3, 1991; children: Larry, Pamela Moore, Eric, Shauna. **Educ:** Hancock College, AA, 1964; California State University, BS, 1975, MBA, 1977. **Career:** Jet Propulsion Laboratory, Helios Project engineer, 1972-75, seasat chief, mission operations, 1975-78, mission operations mgr, 1978-83, Ulysess Project mgr, beginning 1983; OAO Corporation, Corp Strategic Planning, sr vp, currently. **Orgs:** American Geophysical Union, 1990-; Urban League; LA Sickle Cell Foundation; NAACP; LA Council of Black Professional Engineers; CalTech Management Association. **Honors/Awds:** NASA, EEO Medal, 1984, Outstanding Leadership Medal, 1992; European Space Agency, Director/General's Certificate, 1990; City of Pasadena, Professional Award/Human Relations, 1991; County of Los Angeles, Commendation, 1991. **Military Serv:** US Air Force, ssgt, 1956-64. **Business Addr:** Senior VP, Corporate Strategic Planning, OAO Corp., 300 N Lake Ave, Ste 1105, Pasadena, CA 91101, (626)792-8836.

MEGGETT, DAVID LEE
Professional football player. **Personal:** Born Apr 30, 1966, Charleston, SC; children: Davin. **Educ:** Morgan State (then Towson State). **Career:** New York Giants, running back, 1989-94; New England Patriots, 1995-. **Honors/Awds:** Walter Payton Award, 1988; Pro Bowl, 1989, 1996. **Business Addr:** Professional Football Player, New England Patriots, 60 Washington St, Foxboro Stadium, Foxboro, MA 02035, (508)543-7911.

MEHLINGER, KERMIT THORPE
Psychiatrist. **Personal:** Born Jun 17, 1918, Washington, DC; married Lillian L Pettiford; children: Dianne, Bonnie, Renee, Jill. **Educ:** Oberlin Coll OH, AB 1939; Howard Univ Med Sch, MD 1950; Yale U, Past Grad Training 195153; Cook Co Grad Sch Clinical Neurology, 1959. **Career:** Mental Hlth Ctr Chgo, sr psychiatrist 1954-59; Circuit Ct Chgo, sr pshychtrst 1960-69; Martin King Nghbrhd Hlth Ctr Chgo, proj dir 1969-71; Div of Pshyctry Cook Co Hosp, dir 1972-73; Rush Med Coll, prof 1976; Pvt Prac; Div of Behavior Sci & Psycholdynamic Med Jackson Park Hosp & Med Ctr Chgo, dir 1978-; Chicago Med Sch, asso prof clinical pshych 1969-; Columbia Coll, prof communication 1973-; Div Vocatnl Rehab, psych consult 1967-; West Side Orgn, psych consult 1973-; Friendship Med Clinic, psych consult 1974-. **Orgs:** Fdr chmn Image & Indentifctn 1961-; pres Coal Black Enterprise Inc 1971-; mem IL Dangerous Drug Adv Coun 1966-73; mem Am Med Assn Com on Alcoholism 1975-; mem Chicago Found for Med Care 1974-; mem IL State Med Soc Com on Drugs & Hazrds Substance 1973-; bd dir Gateway Houses Inc 1971-; past pres Cook Co Physician Assn 1968-69; pres S Side Br Chicago Med Soc 1970-; med adv com IL Criminologcl Soc; IL Psych Assn; Nat Rehab Assn; mem Am Veteran's Com; Kappa Alpha Psi. **Honors/Awds:** Recip Fellow Inst of Med Chicago 1970; fellow Am Psych Assn 1973; distinctive award AMA 1969; diplomate Am Psych Assn 1961; author book ''Coal Black &The Seven Dudes''. **Military Serv:** AUS capt med reserve ret 1941-46. **Business Addr:** 7531 S Stoney Island Ave, Chicago, IL 60649.

MEHRETEAB, GHEBRE-SELASSIE
Corporate executive. **Personal:** Born Jun 29, 1949, Asmara, Eritrea; married Sarah Brill Jones. **Educ:** Haverford Coll, BA 1972. **Career:** Health & Welfare Council, staff assoc 1972-73; East Mt Airy Neighbors, dir 1974-76; YMCA of Germantown, assoc dir 1976-78; New World Foundation, assoc dir 1978-81; The Ford Foundation, program officer 1981-87; National Corp for Housing Partnerships, vice pres, president, CEO, currently. **Orgs:** Dir Assoc of Black Foundation Execs Inc 1980-86, NY Regional Assn of Grantmakers 1980-86; mem Columbia Univ Seminar on Philanthropy 1985-. **Honors/Awds:** Citation Senate of Pennsylvania 1979; Key to the City Savannah GA 1987. **Business Addr:** President/CEO, NHP Foundation, 1090 Vermont Avenue, NW, Suite #400, Washington, DC 20005.

MELANCON, DONALD
Educator. **Personal:** Born Nov 12, 1939, Franklin, LA; married Hortense Ferguson; children: Douglas Louis, Girard James. **Educ:** Southern Univ, BS, 1963; Univ of IL, MEd 1971, PhD 1976. **Career:** Kankakee Sch Dist, cent off adminstr 1971-72, sch psychol couns 1970; St Anne HS, tchr 1964-70; MO, tchr 1963; Nympum Mini-bike Prgm YMCA, consult 1972; Pembroke Consol Sch Dist, 1972; Opport Ind Ctr, 1972; Kankakee Boys Camp, 1972; UofIL, lab trainer 1972; Ofc of Edn,1979; Union Grad Sch, 1979; St Ann Sch Bd of Educ 1976; Kankakee Sch Dist, elem sch prin; Lemoyne-Owen College, professor, 1994-. **Orgs:** Bd of dir Kankakee Drug Abuse; Old Fair Pk Day Care; Kankakee Cult Prgm; YMCA Exten Dept; Cub Sct Mstr; Appt by Gov of IL Reg Manpwr Comm for CETA; mem NEA; IL Educ Assn; Humanist Assn; Sch Bd Assn of IL; Kankakee Co Adminstr Assn. **Honors/Awds:** Sel Phi Delta Kappa-Hon Soc in Edn; Bicent Declar for Serv to Cub Sct 1976; Ebony Esteem Aw 1976; Men of prgss Outst Educator Award 1978; publ articles ''As Stud See Things'' IL Educ Assn Jour 1969; ''Staff Dev on a Shoestring'' IL Princ Journl 1973; ''A System Apprch to Tension Monit & Tension Reduct in an Educ Setting'' Journl of Rsrch in Educ 1973; ''Model for Sch Commun Relat'' Phi Delta Kappan 1974. **Business Addr:** Lemoyne-Owen College, Memphis, TN 38126.

MELANCON, NORMAN
Educator. **Personal:** Born Nov 6, 1939, Paincourtville, LA; son of Mr & Mrs Alfred Melancon Sr; married Joyce Carr; children: Norman Jr, Latisha, Marlon. **Educ:** Dillard Univ, BA 1962; Nicholls State, MEd 1969; Loyola Univ, MSc 1972. **Career:** Assumption Parish, asst principal 1964-85; Ward 6, police juror 1976-85; Belle Rose Middle School, asst principal, currently. **Orgs:** 4-H Club sponsor; Boy Scout coordinator. **Business Addr:** Assistant Principal, Belle Rose Middle School, PO Box 518, Belle Rose, LA 70341.

MELLETTE, DAVID C.
Business executive. **Personal:** Born Dec 8, 1909, Sumter, SC; married Mary Way; children: Willie Wright, Gertrude M Ledbetter. **Career:** Comm Funeral Home, pres/owner 1950-. **Orgs:** Mem SC Mortician Assn; mem Dist 2 SC Mortician Assn; mem Natl Funeral Dir & Mortician Assn; masonic Corinthians Lodge #200; shriner YMCA of Sumter; mem Joint Stock of SC; mem Odd Fellows; chmn deacon bd Mt Zion Baptist Church; bd mem Sumter Sch Dist #17 1971-83. **Honors/Awds:** Awd for Outstanding Service to Sumter Co Career Ctr; Awd for Dedicated Serv to Sumter Sch Dist #17. **Home Addr:** 9 West Williams St, Sumter, SC 29150. **Business Addr:** Funeral Dir, Community Funeral Home, 353 Manning Ave, Sumter, SC 29150.

MELROSE, THOMAS S.
Electrical engineer, educator (retired). **Personal:** Born Nov 23, 1922, Charleston, SC; son of Lucy B Melrose and Samuel Melrose; married Shirley Chambers; children: Cassaundra T, Zhukov R, Thomas K. **Educ:** Howard Univ School of Engineering, BSEE 1952. **Career:** Tennessee Valley Auth, elec design engr 1952-56; USAF Aeronautical Sys Div, sr proj engr instrument & visual flight simulators 1956-79; Sinclair Comm Coll, instructor engrg techn 1981-85. **Orgs:** Assoc mem Inst of Elec & Electron Engrs; mem Tau Beta Pi Engrg Hon Soc; chairman, Publicity Committee NAACP; bd mem & 1976 Layman of the Yr Dayton Fifth St YMCA; chmn Kettering Bd of Com Relations; past club pres & 1970 Copenhagen delegate Intl Assn of Y's Men; founder & past pres Carillon Civic Cncl; Scholarship Com chmn & chap ed Omega Psi Phi Frat; treas Sr Choir Bethel Baptist Ch; vice pres Howard Univ Alumni Club of Greater Dayton; treasurer, mgr, Bethel Baptist Federal Credit Union; Chappie James/National Aviation Hall of Fame Committee chairman; National Technical Assn. **Honors/Awds:** Math Tutor with Distinguished Serv Award Dayton Public Schools VIPS Program 1980-84; Howard University Alumni Club; Kettering board of com rel awards; Cited for Outstanding Performances with Simulators; Volunteer of the Year Award, Miami Valley Chapter of Credit Unions, 1994. **Military Serv:** AUS WWII. **Home Addr:** 808 Cushing Ave, Dayton, OH 45429.

MELTON, BRYANT
State representative. **Personal:** Born May 9, 1940, Marion, AL; son of Bertha Bobyne Melton and Bryant Melton, Sr; married Emma Jean Holmes, 1962; children: Tony, Delisa, Emily. **Educ:** Alabama A&M University, 1958-60; Stillman College, Tuscaloosa, AL, BS, 1965; University of Alabama, 1968-70. **Career:** US Post Office, Tuscaloosa, AL, postman, 1965-69; Hale County Board of Education, Greensboro, AL, teacher, 1969-72; Protective Insurance Company, Tuscaloosa, AL, manager, 1972-75; BF Goodrich, quality control manager, 1976-; Alabama State House of Representatives, state representative, currently. **Orgs:** NAACP, Tuscaloosa County Chapter; Boy Scouts; Stillman College Alumni Assn; Alpha Phi Alpha; Masons. **Honors/Awds:** May of the Year, Charlie Green Award, Alpha Phi Alpha, 1977; Man of the Year, NAACP, 1978. **Military Serv:** US Army, SSgt, 1960-63; Army Reserve. **Business Addr:** State Representative, District 61, 5003 4th Ave, Tuscaloosa, AL 35405.

MELTON, FRANK E.
President/general manager. **Educ:** Stephen F Austin State Univ TX, BS Educ. **Career:** TX Dept of Mental Health & Mental Retardation, 1969-74; Angelina Coll Lufkin TX, part-time teacher 1974-85; KTRE-TV Lufkin, weekend news anchor 1974; KLTV-TVTyler TX, exec vice pres and general mgr 1976-81; WLBT-TV Jackson MS, president/general manager 1984-. **Orgs:** Former pres broadcast div Buford TV Inc Tyler; apptd by Gov Mark White to TX Bd of Mental Health & Mental Retardation 1985.

MELTON, FRANK LEROY (GLOBE)
Clergyman, international representative. **Personal:** Born May 26, 1921, Sumter, SC; married Gertrude Eleanor Van Dunk; children: Lawana Francine Mc Gee. **Educ:** Rutgers; New York City Coll; PA State; 1950-70. **Career:** Interchem Corp Inmont Corp, union local reg sec 1956-73; New AME Zion & Wm Chapel AME Zion Ch, pastor's asst 1955-58; Mt Olive AME Zion Ch, pastor 1958-62; St Mark AME Zion Church, rev 1962-; Oil Chem & Atomic Workers Intl Union, intl rep 1973-80; Williams Chapel AME Zion Ch Passaic NJ, pastor 1980-. **Orgs:** Mem NAACP Paterson Br 1950-80; bd mem Paterson CETA & Paterson P/C 1979; mem Inter-faith Westwood NJ 1979; coord of Safety Paterson Rotary; mem Passaic& Vicinity Minster Fellowship; pres North Jersey Ministerial Alliance. **Honors/Awds:** Plaque Labor Studies Seminar 1972; plaque 17 yrs of serv St Mark AME Zion Ch 1978; plaque OCAWIU Local 8-417. **Military Serv:** USAF pfc 1945-47. **Business Addr:** International Representative, Oil Chemical & Atomic Workers, 1155 W Chestnut St, Ste 1-A, Union, NJ 07083.

MELTON, HARRY S.
Judge. **Personal:** Born Apr 18, 1915, Philadelphia, PA; married Dorothy; children: 2. **Educ:** Pioneer Bus Inst, 1950; Temple U, 1969. **Career:** Ins Broker, 10 Yrs; Commwlth PA, reg dir liquor audits 8 yr; Mun Ct Commwlth PA, ret judge. **Orgs:** Fin sec Ch of Redeemer 3 yrs; treas Ch of Redeemer 3 yrs; chmn bd trustees Ch of Redeemer. **Military Serv:** Staff sgt 1943-45.

MENCER, ERNEST JAMES
Surgeon. **Personal:** Born Apr 24, 1945, Baton Rouge, LA; son of Maudra E Mencer and George E Mencer, Jr; married Thomasine Haskins; children: Melanie Lynn, Marcus Kinnard. **Educ:** Morehouse Coll, BS 1967; Meharry Medical Coll, MD 1972. **Career:** Our Lady of the Lake Regional Medical Ctr, chief of surgery 1983; Earl K Long Hosp LSU Medical Sch, asst prof of surgery 1984-; Baton Rouge General Medical Ctr, vice chief of surgery 1985-; Private Practice, general surgeon. **Orgs:** Diplomate Amer Bd of Surgery 1983; bd of dirs Baton Rouge Genl Medical Ctr 1984-; fellow Amer Coll of Surgeons 1985; bd of dirs East Baton Rouge Parish Amer Cancer Soc 1985-. **Business Addr:** Physician, 7777 Hennessy Blvd, Ste 306, Baton Rouge, LA 70808.

MENDENHALL, JOHN RUFUS
Professional football player. **Personal:** Born Dec 3, 1948, Cullen, LA. **Educ:** Grambling Coll. **Career:** Green Bay Packers, professional football player 1980-; NY Giants, ftbll plyr 1972-80.

MENDES, DONNA M.
Surgeon. **Personal:** Born Oct 25, 1951, Oceanside, NY; daughter of Bernice Smith Mendes and Benjamin Mendes; married Ronald E LaMotte, May 4, 1986. **Educ:** Hofstra Univ, Hempstead, NY, BA, 1973; Columbia Univ, Coll of Physicians & Surgeons, New York, NY, MD, 1977. **Career:** Self-employed surgeon, 1984-. **Orgs:** International Society of Cardiovascular Surgeons, 1992-; Advisory bd mem, Urban League, 1988-91; mem, Susan Smith McKinney, 1989-; mem, Manhattan Chapter NMA, 1986-; mem, American Medical Women's Assn, 1988-; mem, NY Cardiovascular Society, 1989-; mem, Society of Clinical Vascular Surgeons, 1990-; mem, Peripheral Surgical Society, 1986-. **Honors/Awds:** Fellow of Amer Coll of Surgeons, American Bd of Surgery, 1988; College of Surgeons, Of Surgery; Chief, Div of Vascular Surgery, St Lukes Hospital, 1990-. **Home Addr:** 311 Speer Ave, Englewood, NJ 07631. **Business Phone:** (212)636-4990.

MENDES, HELEN ALTHIA
Counselor, consultant. **Personal:** Born May 20, 1935, New York City, NY; daughter of Louise Davenport and Arthur Davenport; married Gregory R Love; children: Sheila, Leon. **Educ:** Queens Coll, BA 1957; Columbia Univ, MSW 1964; UCLA, DSW 1975; Fuller Theological Seminary 1987-. **Career:** Big Brothers Res Treatment Center, acting dir 1967-69; Albert Einstein Coll Med, mental health consultant 1969; Hunter Coll School Soc Work, lecture 1970-72 ; UCLA, assoc 1972-75; Univ of Southern California, assoc prof 1975-86; Mendes Consultation Serv, founder, pres, 1976-. **Orgs:** Distrib Success Motivation Inst 1985-89; bd dir Jenesse Center Inc 1985-86; alternate Private Indus Cncl LA 1984-86; chairperson Pastor Parish Rels Comm Wilshire Hm Church 1981-87; mem Natl Asso Black Soc Workrers; mem Black Womens Network; mem bd of dir House of Ruth 1985-89; vice pres Professional Dev NASW CA 1986-88; 1st vice pres NASW, California 1988-90; bd of dirs, SISCA; bd of dirs, West Angeles Church of God in Christ; bd of dirs, Hollygrove Children's Home. **Honors/Awds:** Outstanding Educ Zeta Phi Beta Sor Altadena Pasadena Chap 1985; published book, The Africian Heritage Cookbook MacMillan Publishers Professional Journals 1971; publ articles on Single Parent Families, Religion/Therapy, Black Families 1976-; Outstanding Serv Award LA Comm Coll 1974; mem Acad Certified Soc Workers Natl Assn of Soc Workers; licensed clinical social worker, California; Bd Certified Diplomate; Diplomate in Clinical Social Work; Award of Merit for Outstanding Service to USC School of Social Work, 1986; Women of Religious Achievement Award, 1995. **Home Addr:** 1543 S Stanley Ave, Los Angeles, CA 90019-3849. **Business Addr:** President, Mendes Consultation Services, 3660 Wilshire Blvd, Penthouse I, Los Angeles, CA 90010, (213)388-6668.

MENDEZ, HUGH B.
Educator, coach. **Personal:** Born Dec 16, 1933, E Orange, NJ; married Dorothy L; children: Robert Hugh. **Educ:** Springfield Coll, BS 1958; Whittier Coll, MEd 1975; Newark State Coll, Postgrad; Montclair State Coll; CA State Coll; UCLA. **Career:** Whittier Coll CA, instr afro-Am history & varsity bsbll coach; Long Beach, tchr bsbll coach 1968-70; Long Branch NJ, supvr elem phys educ 1960-66; Milwaukee Braves Bsbll Assn 1958-60. **Orgs:** Capt Springfield Coll Bsbll Team 1958. **Honors/Awds:** Led NCAA in stolen bases; signed bonus contract with Milwaukee Braves 1958; 1st black coach maj sport Whittier Coll. **Military Serv:** USN. **Business Addr:** Whittier Coll, Whittier, CA 90608.

MENEFEE, JUAN F.
Consultant. **Personal:** Born Jan 24, 1961, Chillicothe, OH. **Educ:** University of Cincinnati, BBA, 1984. **Career:** Procter & Gamble, sales management; Johnson & Johnson, mgr; Frito Lay, regional sales mgr; Juan Menefee & Associates, president, 1988-. **Orgs:** Omega Psi Phi Fraternity; National Black MBA Association; National Association of Black Sales Professionals, president. **Business Phone:** (708)848-7722.

MENEWEATHER, EARL W.
Educator. **Personal:** Born Sep 12, 1917, Marshall, TX; married Sarah E Thomas; children: Patricia, Earl, II, Leslie. **Educ:** San Fran St, Adminstrv Degree 1967, MA 1965; Humboldt St U, BA 1941. **Career:** Univ Ombudsman Humboldt St U, spl asst to pres 1971-; Ravenswood HS E Palo Alto, prin 1968-71; Peralta Jr Coll Dist, asst dean of stdnt prsnl serv 1968; Madison Jr HS, prin 1967-68; Lowell Jr HS, dept chmn tchr 1955-57; McClymonds HS Oakland, tchr head coach 1957-66; Kaiser Shipyard, foreman 1944. **Orgs:** Dir & coord VIP's Oakland Raider Professional Ftbll Club 1960-; pofl ftbll plyr Oakland Giants & San Fran Bay Packers 1943-44; past mem Urban Rehab Proj Oakland CA; bd mem YMCA; Scattered Housing Com Oakland; City Info Counc for E Palo Alto; El Cerrito Rec Commn; St Dept of Educ Commn; CA Tchr Assn Plng Commn for Currclm Svc; mem Alpha Phi Alpha; CA Coll & Univ Prof Assn; CA Scndry Adminstrn Assn; United Prof Assn; Ombudsman Caucus of CA; Coll & Univ Prsnl Assn; mem Actin Com Humboldt St U; consult Minority Afrs Com Humboldt; chmn Afrmtv Action Com; Univ Prof Assn; consult Minority Recruit & Hiring Atomic Enrgy Comm Livermore & Berkeley 1967; chmn Mnrty Outrch Prgm; mgr dir Boys Clubs of Am Oakland 1945-55; del Luth Chs of Am 1967; dir Adminstrn SeirraBckpck Prgm Luth Ch 1971; dir SummWrkshp Sequoia Union Sch Dist 1970; orgntr consult adv Blk Educ Corp Stanford 1970; mem Humboldt Co Hum Right Comm 1971; Ethinic Task Force Consult CA St Univ Humboldt. **Honors/Awds:** 1st blk dept chmn phys educ No CA HS 1963; 1st Blk HS Prin Sequoia Union HS Dist 1968; 1st blk Adminstr CA St Univ 1971; 1st Athl Hall of Fame mem Humboldt St Univ 1955; author num publs on minority & educ subjects. **Military Serv:** AUS 1st sgt 1942-45; Reserve 1945-50; Korean War 1950-51.

MENSAH, E. KWAKU
Accountant. **Personal:** Born Nov 1, 1945, Accra, Ghana; son of Bertha Mensah-Amuzu and Mensah Amuzu; married Linda May Mensah, Jul 27, 1974; children: Tonyo, Asanvi, Delali. **Educ:** St. Joseph's University, Philadelphia, PA, BS, 1974. **Career:** Hilton Hotels Corporation, comptroller, dir of finance, 1979-. **Business Addr:** Director of Finance, The Washington Hilton, 1919 Connecticut Ave, NW, Washington, DC 20009.

MENZIES, BARBARA A.
Physician. **Personal:** Born Oct 24, 1950, Memphis, TN; daughter of Mr & Mrs Simon Ledbetter; divorced; children: Simone Benai Williams. **Educ:** Michigan State University, BS, 1972; Wayne State University, MS, 1974, Medical School, MD, 1978; University of Wisconsin-Madison, MS, 1996. **Career:** Self-employed, physician, currently; Harper Hospital, chief of internatl medicine, currently.

MERCADO-VALDES, FRANK MARCELINO
Communications company executive. **Personal:** Born May 18, 1962, New York, NY; son of Lidia Valdes and Frank Mercado. **Educ:** Miami-Dade College, AA, 1983; University of Miami, BA, 1985. **Career:** Bush/Quayle, media asst, 1988; Alto-Marc Communications, African Heritage Movie Network, president, 1985-. **Orgs:** Kappa Alpha Psi Fraternity, 1983-; Golden Gloves of Florida Benefit Committee, 1987; Kappa Alpha Psi Scholarship Foundation, 1989-92; Dancer's Alliance; African-American Anti-Defamation Association, 1991-; African-American Film and Television Association; National Association of Television Program Executives. **Honors/Awds:** Golden Gloves Lightweight Champion of Florida, 1979; Junior Olympic Boxing Champion of Florida, 1978. **Special Achievements:** Quarter finalist 1980 Olympic trials, lightweight; Urban Profile "Under Thirty Entrepreneur of Excellence Award"; creator of Miss Collegiate African-American Pageant/Creator of "Stomp" television special; youngest black executive producer in television history. **Military Serv:** US Marine Corps, corporal, 1980-82. **Home Phone:** (212)281-1141. **Business Addr:** President, African Heritage Movie Network/Alto-Marc Communications, 721 5th Ave, #63C, New York, NY 10019.

MERCER, ARTHUR, SR.
Insurance salesman (retired). **Personal:** Born Mar 31, 1921, Pachuta, MS; married Mildred Pugh; children: Arthur II, Lillian A, Lori A. **Educ:** Attended, Laramie County Community Coll 2 yrs. **Career:** WY Private Industry Council, mem 1984-1989; US Army, 1942-47; USAF, 1947-74; Life/Hosp/Investment Ins, retired salesman 1974-85. **Orgs:** Pres Exchange Club of Cheyenne 1976-77; mem bd of dir Laramie County United Way 1976-82; commander Amer Legion Carter Brown Post #83 1976, 1977; life mem NCOA 1977; life member Air Force Assocation 1978; life member Retired Enlisted Association 1987; life member Air Force Sergeant Association 1985; member Cheyenne Rotary Club 1987; clerk Laramie County Sch Dist #1 Bd of Trustees 1978-85; re-elected to Laramie County School Dist #1 board of trustees for 4 yr term 1988- treasurer Laramie County School Dist #1 1988-, re-elected to Laramie County School Dist #1, board of trustees for 4 year term, 1992-, treasurer, 1992; Amer Legion Post #6 1992; bd of dir, mem WY School Bd Assoc 1980-82, re-elected Board of Directors, WY School Board Association, 1992-96; pres Rocky Mountain Dist Exchange Clubs 1981-82; 2nd vice pres School Bd Assoc 1983; 1st vice pres WY School Bd Assoc 1984; gov apptd mem WY Community Coll Commn 1984-89; WY School Bd Assoc 1985-87; mem Natl School Bds Assoc Resolutions & Policy Comm 1985; mem NSBA Delegate Assembly 1985, 1986; Multicultural Commission ELCA Rocky Mountain Synod 1988-. **Military Serv:** USAF chief master sgt 31 yrs; UN Serv Medal; Korean Serv Medal w/1 Bronze Star; AFGCM w/2 OLC; AFGCM w/1 Bronze OLC; AFGCM w/1 Silver Cluster; AF Commendation Medal; AF Missileman Badge; APTO Medal; Army Good Conduct Medal; World War II Victory Medal; New Guinea Campaign Medal. **Home Addr:** 5131 Syracuse Rd, Cheyenne, WY 82009-4749.

MERCER, RONALD
Professional basketball player. **Personal:** Born May 18, 1976. **Educ:** University of Kentucky. **Career:** Boston Celtics, 1997-. **Business Addr:** Professional Basketball Player, Boston Celtics, 151 Merrimac St, Boston, MA 02114, (617)523-3030.

MERCER, VALERIE JUNE
Journalist. **Personal:** Born Jun 5, 1947, Philadelphia, PA; daughter of Helen Kono Mercer and William Mercer. **Educ:** School of Visual Arts, New York, NY, 1971-74; New York University, New York, NY, BA, art history, 1979; Harvard University, Cambridge, MA, art history, 1982. **Career:** The New York Times, New York, NY, freelance art writer, 1988-91; The Brooklyn Paper, Brooklyn, NY, freelance art writer, 1990-91; American Visions, New York, NY, Washington, DC, 1991. **Orgs:** Member, National Association of Black Journalists, 1989-; member, College Art Association, 1985-. **Honors/Awds:** Teaching fellowship, Harvard University, 1982-86. **Home Addr:** 74 Rutland Rd, Brooklyn, NY 11225.

MERCER-PRYOR, DIANA
General purchasing agent. **Personal:** Born Dec 4, 1950, Detroit, MI; daughter of Dessie Hogan Walton and Elisha Walton; married Donald Pryor; children: Eleasha De Ann Mercer, Jason Thomas Mercer. **Educ:** Univ of Michigan, Ann Arbor, MI, BBA, 1972; Univ of Detroit, Detroit, MI, MBA, finance, 1975. **Career:** Chrysler Corp, Highland Park, MI, general purchasing agent, 1972-. **Orgs:** Board member, Univ of Detroit Alumni Board, 1989-; board of trustees, member, Franklin Wright Settlement, 1989-. **Honors/Awds:** High Profile Style, Essence Magazine, March 1991; 100 Most Promising Black Women in America, Ebony Magazine, Jan 1990, Jan 1991; YMCA Achievement Award, YMCA, 1988; Americas Top Black Business and Professional Women, Dollars & Sense Magazine, May 1988.

MERCHANT, JAMES S., JR.
Restaurant executive. **Personal:** Born Apr 28, 1954, Clarksburg, WV; son of Millie A Merchant and James S Merchant; married Joyce A Walton, Sep 27, 1975; children: Linel, Shelita, Ebony. **Educ:** West Virginia University, BS, business administration, 1976. **Career:** Bob Evans Farms Inc, manager trainee, 1977-78, 2nd assistant manager, 1978, 1st assistant manager, 1978-79, general manager, 1979-1983, area director, 1983-94, vp and regional director, 1994-. **Orgs:** Touchston Cafe, advisory board, 1988-; Omega Psi Phi, 1974-. **Honors/Awds:** Bob Evans Farms Inc, Central Zone Manager of the Year, 1982.

Special Achievements: Blue Chip Award, nominated, 1991. **Business Addr:** Vice President/Regional Director, Bob Evans Farms Inc, 3776 S High St, Columbus, OH 43207, (614)491-2225.

MERCHANT, JOHN CRUSE
Attorney. **Personal:** Born Apr 1, 1957, Lexington, KY; son of John and Thelma Merchant; married Debra Spotts Merchant, Aug 15, 1981; children: Leah Cruse. **Educ:** Morehead State Univ, BA, 1979; Univ of Kentucky, JD, 1982. **Career:** Shirley A Cunningham, law associate, 1982-83; Office of Lt Gov, admin asst, 1983-87; Wilkinson for Governor Campaign, staff worker, 1987; Office of Legal Services, finance cabinet, staff atty, 1988-91; Peck, Shaffer, and Williams, associate, OH, 1991-94, partner, 1994-. **Orgs:** National Assn of Securities Professionals, 1991-; Cincinnati Bar Assn, 1991-; National Forum for Black Public Administrators, 1985-; Black Male Coalition, 1992-; Junior Achievement of Cincinnati, exec board, head of state planning, 1992-; Cincinnati Youth Collaborative, mentor, 1992-; KY Bar Assn, 1982-; OH Bar Assn, 1992-; National Bar Assn, 1985-. **Honors/Awds:** Morehead State Univ, Alumni Award, 1989; Quinn Chapel AME Church, Black Business Award, 1995. **Home Addr:** 4156 Allenhurst Close, Cincinnati, OH 45241, (513)769-5088. **Business Addr:** Partner, Peck, Shaffer & Williams, 201 East Fifth Street, Ste 900, Cincinnati, OH 45202, (513)621-3394.

MERCHANT, JOHN F.
Attorney. **Personal:** Born Feb 2, 1933, Greenwich, CT; son of Essie L Nowlin Merchant and Garrett M Merchant; divorced; children: Susan Beth. **Educ:** VA Union U, BA 1955; Univ of VA, LLB 1958. **Career:** CT, atty 1962-; ABCD Inc, dep dir 1965-67; State Dept Community Affairs, dep commr 1967-71; legislative lobbyist; Fairfield U, visiting lecturer 1970-75; Gen Elec Corp & Candeub Fleissig Assoc, consultant; Peoples Bank, dir, mem loan & Trust Committees 1969-; Consumer Counsel, State of Connecticut, 1991-96; National Minority Golf Foundation Inc, president/ceo, currently. **Orgs:** Trustee, Univ of Bridgeport; partner Merchant & Rosenblum Attorneys At Law; mem Doric Lodge #4 F&AM; NAACP & other civic activities; pres Child Guidance Clinic; dir Regional Plan Assoc; pres Hartcom Inc; chmn Conn Council on Human Rights 1964-65; pres Brideport Area Mental Health Assn 1968; dir Bridgeport Hosp 1968-79; dir, Child Welfare League of America, chmn, Public Policy committee, 1986-92, president, 1993-; trustee St Vincent's College of Nursing; trustee, Fairfield University. **Honors/Awds:** 1st black grad, Univ VA law sch; Citizen of the Year, Omega Psi Phi 1983; Community Service Award, Sacred Heart Univ 1982; 1st black mem of United States Golf Association Executive Committee; Tree of Life Award from Jewish National Fund; First Black Pres, Child Welfare League of America, Inc. **Military Serv:** USN lt comdr 1958-61. **Home Addr:** 290 Alma Dr, Fairfield, CT 06430. **Business Addr:** President/CEO, National Minority Golf Foundation, Inc, 1140 E Washington St, Phoenix, AZ 85032.

MERCY, LELAND, JR.
Educator. **Personal:** Born Nov 1, 1942, Jacksonville, FL; married Holly Hamilton; children: Michael, Leanne, Ryan. **Educ:** Univ of MD, 1964-65; Boise St U, BBA 1971. **Career:** Boise State U, dir of affirmative action/Exec asst to pres 1981; USAF, staff sgt 1961-69; Salt & Pepper Enterprises Inc, pres, currently. **Orgs:** Pres ID Assn for Collegioat & Registars & Admissions Ofcrs; dir C of C of Boise; mem cmn Sped Student Srevs Com 1973-74; cmn Boise St Univ Affirmative Action Com 1974-75; cmn Boise St Univ Registration Task Force; mem Pacific Assn of Collegiate Registars & Admissions Ofcrs; v cmn Ada Cnty Planning Commn; Am Assn of Collegiate Registars & Admissions Ofcrs; v chmn & charter mem bd of dir Opptys Indsln Ctrs of Am of ID Fdr Salt & Pepper Soul radio prog KBBK; Webelo ldr BSA Boise; guest lectr Boise St U; guest spkr at num civic orgns. **Honors/Awds:** Outst Mktng Student Sales & Mktng Exec 1971; Speaking of People Ebony Mag 1974. **Military Serv:** USAF staff sgt 1961-69. **Business Addr:** President, Salt & Pepper Enterprises Inc, PO Box 9431, Boise, ID 83707.

MEREDAY, RICHARD F.
Government employee. **Personal:** Born Dec 18, 1929, Hempstead, NY; married Emma (divorced); children: Philip, Richard, Meta. **Educ:** Hofstra U, BA 1951; licensed NY Ins Broker 1961; Brooklyn Law Sch, LLB 1958. **Career:** Ofc of Manpower Programs, coordinator of educ serv nassau co govt 1975-; Nassau Co Bur of Career Planning & Devel Dep of Gen Svcs, former dir 1971-75; Town of Hempstead Dept of Pub Works, adminstr 1965-70; probation officer supr 1964-65; Charles Meredary Trucking Corp, vp; Tri-County Trucker Owners Assn, sec-scribe 1956-63; Nassau Co Met Regiona Council TV classes, speaker; Nassau Co, Office of Aff Action, executive director. **Orgs:** Rep exec Town Leader; former vp, Uptopia Comm Covoc Assn; past chmn Roosevelt United Fund; former institutional rep Nat Boy Scouts Counsils; past pres Lions Club; adv bd Salvation Army. **Honors/Awds:** Recip good neighbor award Nassau Co Press Assn 1973; active participant Rep Leadership Conf 1975; plaque Unselfish Serv to Comm of Roosevelt 1969; recognition certificate Dist 20 K-2 Lions Intl 1973. **Military Serv:** USN med corps 1951-53. **Business Addr:** 488 Hempstead Trnpke, Elmont, NY 11003.

MEREDITH, JAMES HOWARD
Business executive, lecturer. **Personal:** Born Jun 25, 1933, Kosciusko, MS; son of Roxie Meredith and Cap Meredith; married Judy Alsobrooks; children: John Howard, Joseph Howard, James Henry, Kip Naylor, Jessica Howard. **Educ:** Jackson State Univ, B 1962; Univ of MS, BA 1963; Ibadan Univ Nigeria, Certificate 1965; Columbia Univ Law Sch, JD 1968. **Career:** Meredith Enterprises, pres 1968-. **Military Serv:** USAF s/sgt 1951-60.

MERENIVITCH, JARROW
Human resources company executive. **Personal:** Born Jun 1, 1942, Alexandria, LA; son of Georgia N Merenivitch (deceased) and Audrey Merenivitch Sr (deceased); married Hazel R Wilmer; children: Jarrow Jr, Marion, Jonathan. **Educ:** Grambling State Univ, BA, political science, 1964; Inst for Applied Mgmt & Law, Certificate 1985. **Career:** Procter & Gamble Co, Green Bay, WI, team mgr 1969-72, Albany GA plant personnel relations mgr 1972-75, Cincinnati corporate personnel develop consultant 1975-78, employee/employer relations mgr 1978-80, personnel mgr, Macon, GA Plant, 1980-83, mgr industrial relations 1983-85, food mfg div human resources mgr 1985-90, associate director, food and beverage personnel sector, 1990-93; associate director, Human Resources Customer Service, Global, 1993-. **Orgs:** Vice pres Grambling Univ Alumni 1990; mem Omega Psi Phi Frat; mem NAACP; Grambling State University, student government president, 1963, 1964. **Honors/Awds:** Outstanding Serv to Eta Omicron Chap Psi Phi Omega 1975; publication "Toward a Multicultural Organization," 1979; Citation Outstanding Contribution to Procter & Gamble Beverage Div 1984; John Feldmann Diversity Leadership Award, 1988; Outstanding Contribution to Food PSS in the Diversity Area, 1989; Rosa Parks Award, Leadership in Diversity and Multiculturalism; Diversity Planning Initiative Award, 1996; Diversity Globe Award, 1996. **Military Serv:** USAF staff sgt 1964-68. **Home Addr:** 1817 Forester Dr, Cincinnati, OH 45240. **Business Addr:** Associate Director, Procter & Gamble, Human Resources, Customer Services, Global, 2 Procter & Gamble Plaza, Cincinnati, OH 45202-3315.

MERIDETH, CHARLES WAYMOND
Educator. **Personal:** Born Nov 2, 1940, Atlanta, GA; son of Ruth Wilson Merideth and Charlie Merideth; married Rebecca Little; children: Kelli, Cheryl. **Educ:** Univ CA Berkeley, PhD 1965; Morehouse Coll, BS 1961; Univ IL, post doctoral 1956-66. **Career:** Atlanta Univ Cen, provost 1976-; Atlanta Univ Cen, dir of engineering 1969; Morehouse Coll, prof 1965; Harvard Univ Institute for Educ Management. **Orgs:** Mem Phi Beta Kappa; Soc of the Sigma Xi; Beta Kappa Chi Sci Soc; Am Chem Soc; Am Physical Soc; Am Assn for the Advancement of Sci; NY Acad of Sci; bd of dir Blayton Bus Coll 1971; Chancellor Atlanta Univ Center Inc. 1978-90; vice pres 100 Black Men of Atlanta Inc. 1988-90. **Honors/Awds:** Woodrow Wilson Nat Fello 1961; Charles E Merrill Early Admission Schlrshp Magna Cum Laude 1961; appointment Danforth Faculty Asso 167; Fresman Achievement Award in Chem 1957; one of 10 outstanding young people of atlanta TOYPA 1956. **Business Addr:** President, New York City Technical College, 300 Jay St, Brooklyn, NY 11201.

MERIDITH, DENISE P.
Government official. **Personal:** Born Apr 14, 1952, Brooklyn, NY; daughter of Dorothy Sawyer Meridith and Glenarva Meridith. **Educ:** Cornell University, Ithaca, NY, BS, 1973; USC, Sacramento, CA, MPA, 1993. **Career:** Bureau of Land Management, Las Vegas, NV, wildlife bio/env spec, 1973-77, Silver Spring, MD, environmental spec, 1977-79, Washington, DC, wildlife biologist, 1979-80, Alexandria, VA, deputy state director, 1980-86, Santa Fe, NM, deputy state director, 1986-89, Sacramento, CA, associate state director, 1989-91, Alexandria, VA, state director, 1991-. **Orgs:** Board of directors, AZ Cactus-Pine Council Girl Scouts, 1996-; AZ Black board of directors, 1996-; Phoenix Federal Executive Association, pres, 1996; City of Phoeni Judicial Selection Advisory Board, 1997-; Cornell University, alumni state dir/area captain, 1986-95, council mem, 1989-; Society of Air Foresters, Forest Sciences & Technology Board, 1998-. **Honors/Awds:** Meritorious Award, Dept of Interior, 1987, Senior Executive Service Certificate, 1990. **Business Addr:** State Director, Bureau of Land Management, 222 N Central Ave, Phoenix, AZ 85004, (602)417-9500.

MERIWEATHER, MELVIN, JR.
Elected official. **Personal:** Born Oct 22, 1937, Hernando, MS; son of Virgie Meriweather and Melvin Meriweather; married Juliet Ilene Thomas; children: Kristel, Douglas, Dana. **Educ:** Isaac E Elston, grad 12th 1957. **Career:** Eastport Improvement Assn, pres 1971-73; Michigan City PTA Council, pres 1974-75; Riley School PTA, pres 1968-79; N Central Comm Action Aency, pres 1979-84; Michigan City School Bd, pres; Michigan City Area School, bd pres 1987-88; sec 1988-89; Midwest Steel, Portage IN, crew coordinator 1989. **Orgs:** Treas and deacon New Hope Baptist Church 1963-85; parents adv bd Rogers HS 1978-79; hlth & safety chmn 1980-82, 2nd vice pres 1982-84 IN Congress of Parents & Teachers; mem Daniel C Slocum Mem Found 1982-85; vol fireman Fire Brigade Midwest Steel 1970-85; IN Dept of Education "Parent/Community Involvement" task force. **Honors/Awds:** Mr Indiana IN AAU Amateur Bodybuilding 1966; Mr Most Muscular AAU Mid States Competition 1966; state life member IN Congress of PTA 1974; vice pres MI City Area School Bd 1982-86; School Board Pres 1986-87; IN Dept of Education certificate of merit. **Home Addr:** 616 Monroe St, Michigan City, IN 46360.

MERIWETHER, LOUISE
Author. **Personal:** Born May 8, 1923, Haverstraw, NY; daughter of Julia Golphin Jenkins and Lloyd Jenkins; married Angelo Meriwether (divorced). **Educ:** New York Univ, BA English; Univ of California at Los Angeles, MS, journalism, 1965. **Career:** Los Angeles Sentinel, Los Angeles, CA, newspaperwoman 1961-64; Universal Studios, N Hollywood, CA, story analyst, 1965-67; City College, New York, NY, Black studies teacher, spring 1979; Sarah Lawrence College, Bronxville, NY, creative writing teacher, undergraduate & graduate, 1979-88; University of Houston, Houston, TX (on leave from Sarah Lawrence), creative writing teacher, undergrads & grads, fall 1985; freelance writer, currently. **Orgs:** PEN. **Honors/Awds:** Fiction Grant, Rabinowitz Foundation, New York City, NY 1968; Fiction Grant, New York State Foundation of the Arts, 1973; Fiction Grant, National Endowment of the Arts, 1973; Fiction Grant, New York State Foundation of the Arts, 1977; Mellon Research Grant, via Sarah Lawrence College, 1983; Fiction Grant, New York State Foundation of the Arts, 1992, 1996. **Special Achievements:** Author, Daddy Was A Number Runner, 1970; The Freedom Ship of Robert Small, 1971; The Heart Man: The Story of Daniel Hale Williams, 1972; Don't Ride the Bus on Monday: The Rosa Parks Story, 1973; Fragments of the ARK, 1994; contributing editor of Black Review No 2, Morrow, 1972, Black-Eyed Susans, Anchor Press, 1975, confirmation: An Anthology of African-American Women, Morrow, 1983; Daughters of Africa, Pantheon, 1992; numerous other publications. **Business Addr:** Author, c/o Ellen Levine Literary Agency, 15 E 26th St, Suite 1801, New York, NY 10010.

MERIWETHER, ROY DENNIS
Pianist, producer, arranger. **Personal:** Born Feb 24, 1943, Dayton, OH; children: Tammi, Cyd. **Career:** Howard Roberts Chorale & Dayton Contempory Dance Co w/the Roy Meriwether Trio, composer arranger Black Snow 1976; Dayton Philharmonic Orchestra, guest artist 1980; Thomas A Edison State Coll, composer lyricist for college alma mater 1984; Gemini Records, producer arranger composer & recording artist 1985; Columbia-Capitol-Gambit-Stinger Recording Companies, pianist composer & recording artist 1960-. **Orgs:** Benefit performance of Black Snow for Wilburforce Univ & Central State Univ 1976; mem Amer Federation of Musicians Local 802 1960-; mem ASCAP 1960-. **Honors/Awds:** Grant recipient Natl Endowment for the Arts 1974; proclamation to honor Black Snow Mayor City of Dayton OH 1976; Significant Achievement Awd Black Snow Powell & Assocs 1976; Outstanding Jazz Instrumentalist Manhattan Association of Cabarets 1987. **Home Addr:** 7 W 87th St, #4D, New York, NY 10024.

MERKERSON, S. EPATHA
Actress. **Career:** Cast member of the television show "Law and Order," currently. Performed in the Broadway plays The Piano Lesson, I'm Not Stupid, and Three Ways Home; films: Terminator 2, Navy Seals; TV movies: Breaking Through, A Place for Annie, A Mother's Prayer; TV series: Here and Now, Mann and Machine. **Honors/Awds:** Obie Award, 1991; Tony Award Nomination. **Business Addr:** Actress, Law & Order, c/o NBC-TV, 30 Rockefeller, New York, NY 10112.

MERRICK-FAIRWEATHER, NORMA. **See SKLAREK, NORMA MERRICK.**

MERRITT, ANTHONY LEWIS
Automotive company executive. **Personal:** Born Sep 15, 1940, New Haven, CT; son of Bernadine Merritt; married Ann Sarver; children: Eric, Heather. **Educ:** Dodge City Jr Coll, AA 1958; Westminister Coll, BS 1964; Univ of UT, MBA 1966; Univ of Detroit, Post MBA 1968-70. **Career:** Pomona Unified School Dist, biology & business teacher 1966-67; Ford Motor Co, numerous mgmt assignments 1968-77, reg sales plnng & distribution 1977-78, gen field mgr 1978-81; Toyota Motor Sales USA, natl merchandising mgr 1981-; San Francisco Region Toyota Motor Distributors, gen mgr, currently. **Orgs:** Westminster College Alumnus & board member. **Honors/Awds:** Special recognition for group for exceeding assigned task United Way Coordinator Ford Motor Co 1972-73. **Military Serv:** AUS pfc 1961-63. **Home Addr:** 415 Shirlee Dr, Danville, CA 94526. **Business Addr:** General Manager, Toyota Motor Distributors Inc, 2451 Bishop Drive, San Ramon, CA 94583.

MERRITT, BISHETTA DIONNE
Educator. **Personal:** Born Dec 15, 1947, Greensboro, NC; married Owen Lee. **Educ:** Fisk Univ, Nashville TN, BA 1970; Ohio State Univ Columbus, MA 1972; Ohio State Univ, Columbus OH, PhD 1974. **Career:** Shaw Univ, assoc prof 1980-; Univ of North Carolina, asst prof 1974-80; Ohio State Univ, grad assoc 1972-73. **Orgs:** Adv bd, WTVD-TV Channel 11, 1976; mem, Congressional Black Caucus Brain Trust on Communications,

1977; mem, Southern Coalition for Responsive Media 1978; mem, NAEB, 1980; mem, Delta Sigma Theta Sorority Inc, 1967; mem, The Links Inc, 1975; pres, Danville VA Chap, The Links Inc, 1977-79; mem, Southeastern Black Press Inst, 1978; mem, North Carolina Central Univ Mus Bd, 1979. **Honors/Awds:** Graduate School Leadership Award, 1974; Motor Bd Honor Soc, 1975; published booklet, Stony the Way We Trod, 1976; received research grants from the Univ of North Carolina, 1976. **Business Addr:** Shaw Univ, 118 E South St, Raleigh, NC 27602.

MERRITT, JOSEPH, JR.
Business executive. **Personal:** Born May 24, 1934, Tunica, MS; divorced; children: Joseph, III. **Career:** Fillmore Taxi Svc, proprietor pres 1968-. **Orgs:** Black Men's Devel Found 1963; Buffalo Metro Bus Assn 1974; Buffalo C of C 1973; Better Bus Bur 1974; YMCA 1950; St John Bapt Ch 1961; NAACP 1963; Jefferson-Fillmore Revital Assn 1975; vice pres Dem Party 1976; apptd Civil Serv Commr Buffalo 1977; mem Local Devel Corp. **Honors/Awds:** Black Achvmt Awd 1976. **Business Addr:** Fillmore Taxi Service, 1000 E Ferry St, Buffalo, NY 14211.

MERRITT, THOMAS MACK
Insurance company executive. **Personal:** Born Jun 16, 1949, Homer, LA; son of Janelle Thomas Youngblood Merritt and Cordelus Merritt; married Rosa M White; children: Kimberly R. **Educ:** Grambling State Univ, BA 1971. **Career:** Liberty Mutual Ins, underwriter 1971-76, supervising underwriter 1976-78, asst mgr 1978-84, mgr large risks 1984-87, mgr reg risks 1987-88; dist underwriting mgr l988-92; Division Technical Director, 1992-. **Orgs:** Founder 1st pres, Grambling State Univ Alumni Assoc of Metro Atlanta; mem Phi Beta Sigma; member, Grambling State University Alumni Asosciation, Dallas Chapter; Society of CPCU. **Honors/Awds:** Honoree Presidential Citation Natl Assoc for Equal Opportunity in Higher Ed 1983; Chartered Property and Casualty Underwriter Designation, society of CPCU Malvern, PA; Associate in Risk Management designation, Insurance Institute Malvern, PA; qualified through 1993 in the Continuing Professional Development Program of the Society of CPCU and American Institute. **Business Addr:** Division Technical Director, Liberty Mutual Insurance Co, Business Accounts Underwriting, 2100 Walnut Hill Lane, Irving, TX 75038.

MERRITT, WENDY
Interior design coordinator. **Personal:** Born Mar 4, 1953, Shelby, NC; daughter of Nevada Merritt & Lucy Merritt-Buggs. **Educ:** North Carolina Central University, BS, 1974. **Career:** Montaldo's and Night Gallery, buyer, manager couture retail, 1974-80; Games Production, Inc, D.C. instant lottery sales executive, 1980-84; Condominium Rentals, Ltd, buyer/int design/ sales, 1984-87; TBS Inc Turner Properties, interior service coordinator, 1990-; Speakers Forum & Lotus, PSS, chief executive officer, speakers bureau & int design, 1980-. **Orgs:** S Phi S, Inc; Sisters with Interest Never Gone, proj manager; Atlanta Grad Chapter; United Negro College Fund, special events fundraiser, 1992-; Apex Museum, spec events coordinator, 1995; Black Adults of Action Section National Council of Negro Women, prog chair, 1985-88. **Honors/Awds:** UNCF Star Volunteer Award Atlanta Chapter, 1992, 1993. **Home Addr:** 704 Carriage Place Ct, Decatur, GA 30033, (404)294-9302.

MERRITT, WILLETTE T.
Association executive. **Personal:** Born in Reidsville, NC; married Dr Bishop (deceased); children: Dr Bishetta D. **Educ:** VA State Coll, BS 1935; Univ of NC, atnd; A&T State U; Univ of VA. **Career:** VA Polytechinic Inst & State U, extension agent home economist; Pittslvania Co VA VPI & SU Extension Div Blacksburg, extension agent; A&T State U, distsupvr 5 yrs; A&T U, subj matter specialist 2 yrs; Rockingham Co NC, extension agent 3 yrs; Reidsville NC, tchr pub sch 1935-37. **Orgs:** Mem Epsilon Sigma Phi Extension hon frat; Am Assn Univ Women; Am Home Economics Assn; pres Danville Chap Delta Sigma Theta Sor; organized Jack & Jill Inc; Danville Chap Links Inc; mem exec bd Mental Health Assn 1974-75; past mem exec bd Heart Assn 1973-74; past mem exec bd Cancer Assn 1973-74; past pres Wstrn Dist Home Economics Assn 1969; pres VA Home Economics Assn first black 1975; first vice pres Nat Assn of Extension 1974-75; deacon Holbrook St Presb Ch. **Honors/Awds:** Recip Distin Serv Award 1968; Danville Woman of the Day 1975; first black Virginian elected 1974-75 Nat ofcr of Nt Assn extension Home Economist. **Business Addr:** PO Box 398, Chatham, VA 24531.

MERRITT, WILLIAM T.
Association executive. **Career:** National Black United Fund Inc, Newark, NJ, president, CEO, currently. **Business Addr:** President, CEO, National Black United Fund Inc, 50 Park Pl, Ste 1538, Newark, NJ 07102, (201)643-5122.

MERRITT-CUMMINGS, ANNETTE (ANNETTE MERRITT JONES)
Marketing, advertising, public relations executive. **Personal:** Born May 14, 1946, Grady, AL; daughter of Virgie Mathews Dowdell and Henry W Merritt; married Iran Cummings, Aug 31, 1985; children: Michael O Jones, Angela J Jones. **Educ:** Cuyahoga Community College, AA, 1975; Cleveland State Univ, BA (magna cum laude), 1977; University of Detroit, MBA, 1993. **Career:** EI DuPont de Numours, Wilmington DE; Occidental Petroleum, Madison Hts MI, sr sales rep, 1979-81; Publisher's Rep, Detroit MI, independent contractor, 1981-82; NW Ayer Inc, Detroit MI, sr acct exec, 1982-88; Natl Board for Prof Teaching, Detroit MI, dir of devel & marketing, 1988-; National Board for Professor Teaching, 1988-92; Campbell & Co, vp, 1992-94; The Courier-Journal Newspaper, marketing communications mgr; Paul Werth Associates, vice pres, 1996-. **Orgs:** Adcraft Club of Detroit, 1985-; Literacy Volunteers of America, 1986-; Women's Economic Club of Detroit, 1987-; Natl Society of Fund-Raising Executives, 1988-; Detroit Rotary Club Intl, 1989-; National Black MBA Association, 1992; Public Relations Society of America; Strategies Against Violence Everywhere, board member. **Honors/Awds:** PRSA, Bronze Anvil, 1992. **Business Addr:** Vice Pres, Paul Werth Associates, 88 E Broad St, Columbus, OH 43215.

MERRIWEATHER, BARBARA CHRISTINE
Organization executive. **Personal:** Born May 11, 1948, Philadelphia, PA; daughter of Elizabeth Livingston Merriweather and Robert C Merriweather; married Frank Washington. **Educ:** Cheyney State Univ, BS Ed 1969; Beaver Coll, MA, Humanities, 1989. **Career:** Black Women's Ed Alliance, mem chair 1981-83, vice pres 1983, pres 1983-87; Philadelphia Fed of Black Bus & Professional Organizations, pres 1987-90; Frank Washington Scholarship Fund, executive director, 1990-. **Orgs:** Bd dir Minority Assoc for Student Support 1981-; co-chair public rel Salem Baptist Church 100 Anniversary 1983-84; chair public rel Philadelphia Fed of Black Bus & Prof Org 1984-87; recruiter Amer Fed Teachers 1985; task force mem Youth Serv Coord Commiss 1986-; mem planning comm AFNA Educ & Rsch Fund 1987; pres Philadelphia Fed of Black Businesses & Prof Org. **Honors/Awds:** Chapel of Four Chaplins 1970; Achievement Awd BWEA 1984, Women in Ed 1985; City Council Citation City of Philadelphia 1985; Outstanding Achievement BWEA 1986; House of Rep PA Citation for Outstanding Service 1987; Outstanding Serv Citation Commonwealth of PA House of Representatives 1987; PATHS Fellowship for Indep Study, Council for Basic Educ 1988; Teacher of the Year Award, Rose Lindenbaum Committee, 1990. **Home Addr:** 114 Benjamin Ct, Philadelphia, PA 19114.

MERRIWEATHER, MICHAEL LAMAR
Professional football player. **Personal:** Born Nov 26, 1960, Albans, NY; married Djuna Mitchell. **Educ:** Univ of the Pacific, BA, history, 1982. **Career:** Linebacker: Pittsburgh Steelers, 1982-87; Minnesota Vikings, 1989-. **Orgs:** Mem, Alpha Phi Alpha 1980-; Big Brothers Bowling for Kids, 1986-87. **Honors/Awds:** Twice named to All Pacific Coast team; NEA All-Amer team; played in East-West game; Olympia Gold Bowl; broke all-time Steeler sack record with 15 QB sacks ranking third in AFC and fifth in NFL 1983. **Business Addr:** Professional Football Player, Minnesota Vikings, 9520 Viking Dr, Eden Prairie, MN 55344-3825.

MERRIWEATHER, ROBERT EUGENE
Business consultant. **Personal:** Born Sep 1, 1948, Cincinnati, OH; son of Ruth Hawkins Merriweather and Andrew J Merriweather; married Augustine Pryor, Sep 19, 1970; children: Tinia, Andre, Tarani. **Educ:** Univ of Cincinnati, BA, mathematics, 1970. **Career:** Procter & Gamble Co, math consultant 1970-78, statistical analyst 1978-81, affirmative action mgr 1981-83, sr systems analyst 1983-89, personnel services mgr 1989-. **Orgs:** Bd mem Mt Zion Federal Credit Union 1980-88; trustee Mt Zion Baptist Church 1986-; Community Advisory Bd, University of Cincinnati 1988-; Project Alpha, chairperson Alpha Phi Alpha Fraternity 1989-91; member NAACP, Cincinnati Branch. **Honors/Awds:** Black Achiever YMCA 1983; Black Networking Award, Procter & Gamble 1986; Diversity Award, Procter & Gamble 1988; Unsung Hero Award, Procter & Gamble 1990. **Home Addr:** 9580 Heather Ct, Cincinnati, OH 45242.

MERRIWEATHER, THOMAS L.
Business executive. **Personal:** Born Nov 15, 1932, Chicago, IL; son of Mary Louise Merriweather and Thomas L Merriweather; widowed; children: Anita Lynn Williams. **Educ:** Chicago City Coll Am Cons, Music 1954; Roosevelt Univ/Loyola Univ, 1959-62; Chicago Conser Coll, BME, 1960; Columbia School of Broadcasting, 1971-72; United Inst Grad Coll of Performing Arts, DMA 1978. **Career:** Chicago Bd Educ, teacher, 1960-66; IL Dept of Labor, employment/training specialist, 1967-74; Chicago Urban League, trainee adv, counselor, 1974-76; The woodlawn Organ, vocational counselor, placement counselor/ supvr, 1976-80; Creative Career Assn, exec dir, 1979-80; United Christian Fellowship, lay minister, entertainer, writer; State of Illinois, Chicago, IL, income maintenance spec, 1981-86, 1987-; Merriweather Enterprises, Chicago, IL, pres, resident artist, author, 1988-. **Orgs:** Dir/res artist Indigo Prod Merriweather Ent, 1956-; Chicago Fed of Musicians, 1966-; asst mgr, recruitng/govt program, Natl Alliance Business, 1968-71; chmn admin bd, St James United Methodist Church, 1968-72; mem, Am Guild Musical Artists, 1970-; res artist Lyric Opera Chicago, 1970, 1972-73, 1977, 1985; dir music, 1975-81; lcnd lay speaker 1975-86; church lay ldr, St James United Meth Church, 1979-86; pres/exec dir, Creative Music Studies Inc 1979-; professional rep, Local 2000, American Fed of State, County & Municipal Employees, 1989-. **Honors/Awds:** Commendation for Dedicated Serv, Natl Alliance Business, 1971-72; Certificate of Recognition, Natl Alliance Business, 1971; Serv Award, Musical Direction, St James United Methodist Church, 1981. **Military Serv:** AUS pfc (e-3) 2; Natl Defense Serv Medal 1954-56. **Business Addr:** Regional Vice President, American Guild of Variety Artists, 184 5th Ave, New York, NY 10010.

MERTON, JOSEPH LEE
Association executive (retired). **Personal:** Born Oct 23, 1923, Chicago, IL; son of Harriet Brown Merton and Joseph Merton; married Valenia Olson; children: Joseph K, Geoffrey, David. **Educ:** Chicago City College, associates degree, 1941-43, 1946-47, 1961; Chicago School of Photography, graduate, 1948; Air Force University Ext, 1955-58; Southern Methodist University, 1986. **Career:** Univ of Chicago Rsch Inst, chief photographer 1948-58; Chicago Area Council BSA, dir urban rels & field dir dist exec field scout exec 1958-68; Boy Scouts of Amer, faculty natl exec inst 1968-70, regional deputy reg 2 1970-71, scout exec Newark 1971-74, admin asst to chief scout exec 1974-77, natl dir boy scout div 1977-85, natl dir rsch & eval 1985-90. **Orgs:** Club pres & lt gov IL Eastern Iowa Dist Kiwanis Intl 1962-68; adv Sigma Sigma Chap Alpha Phi Omega 1965-68; adv bd IL Youth Comm 1966-68; pres elect Chester Rotary Club NJ 1979; Commander, Texas Dept, Past Commander, Dallas Chapter; Military Order of the World Wars, Tuskegee Airman. **Honors/Awds:** Faculty Prof Training Africa Region Accra Ghana World Scout Organ 1969; Disting Serv Awd Order of the Arrow BSA 1983; Named Distinguished American Citizen by American Citizenship Center, 1992. **Military Serv:** US Army, Aircorps fighter pilot 1st lt 1943-45; Disting Unit Citation; Air Medal w/Clusters; Seven Campaigns. **Home Addr:** 3701 Ashbury Lane, Bedford, TX 76021.

MESA, MAYRA L.
Dentist, educator. **Personal:** Born Jul 20, 1949, Cuba. **Educ:** Univ of Puerto Rico, BS 1968; Univ of Puerto Rico Dental Sch, DMD 1972; Boston Univ Sch of Grad Dentistry, MSc 1974. **Career:** CMDNJ NJ Dental Sch, assoc prof ora pathology 1977-, asst prof oral pathology 1974-77; Commonwealth Dental Soc, sec 1977-79. **Orgs:** Mem Commonwealth Dental Soc NDA 1975-; mem Am Bd of Oral Pathology 1978-; mem bd dirs Act for Boston Comm Devel 1973; supv Black Coalition Hlth Law Fair 1977-79; Table Clinics Nat Dental Assn 1977-79. **Honors/Awds:** Hon mention Outstdg Young Women of Am 1978; various publ. **Business Addr:** Assoc Prof of Oral Pathology, Univ of Medicine & Dentistry, Dental Schl C-854, 100 Bergen St, Newark, NJ 07103.

MESHACK, LULA M.
Vocational counselor (retired). **Personal:** Born in Dallas. **Educ:** Univ of TX Ext Div, grad 1942; LA SW Coll Pasadena City Coll & UCAL Ext, certificate. **Career:** Fed Civil Serv Navy Dept Washington DC, 1945; employed LA County Assessor, 1948; Prog Spec Neighborhood Adult Part Proj, 1964-. **Orgs:** Charter mem, State Attorney General Advisory Bd; charter mem Dist Att Adv Bd; mem SC Vol Act Com; mem S Ctrl Reg Coun of Lung Assn; mem Martin Luther King Guild; coord 25 Candy Stripers; mem Vol Act Com Natl Baptist Convention Women's Aux; past pres Russel Elementary Sch PTA 1955-56, 1956-57; past pres Fremont Coun PTA 1959-61; past bd mem LA 10th District PTA 1961-65; past pres Interdenominational Ministers' Wives of LA 1966-68; past pres Florence-Firestone Coord Coun 1971-74; mem, pres, Bapt Ministers' Wives; mem bd dirs LA Chptr & S Cntrl Dist Barc; comm, LA County Children's Services Comm; Church Women United, LA Unit; LA County Regional Library Council of the A C Bilbrew Library; pastor, worthy matron, Order of Eastern Star; past high preceptress, New Beulah Tab #2 of Tabor. **Honors/Awds:** Recipient several Commendations from Co & city of LA for comm serv; vol serv award LA City Schools; Certificate of Merit, Baptist Ministers' Wives Union; LA Brotherhood Crusade; commr General Revenue Sharing LA Co; Business & Professional Club Sojourner Truth Award; Lifetime CA Adult Sch Couns Cred; American Lung Assn Merit Award; LA City Human Relations Comm Salute to Women of LA; LA County's Material Resources Award; Community Worker of the Year; Honorary Doctorate Degree, Pentecostal Bible Coll. **Home Addr:** 8214 1/2 Hooper Ave, Los Angeles, CA 90001.

MESHACK, SHERYL HODGES
Attorney. **Personal:** Born Feb 25, 1944, Boston; daughter of Florence Norma Clifton and Clyde H Hodges; married John L Meshack; children: Norman, LaJohn, Derrick, Myles. **Educ:** Howard Univ, BA 1965; USC Law School, JD 1972. **Career:** City of Los Angeles, CA, Dept of Airports asst city atty, currently. **Orgs:** CA State Bar; John M Langston Bar Assn; CA Women Lawyers Assn; Black Women Lawyers of So CA; bd of gov CA Assn of Black Lawyers 1979-81; CA Attorneys for Criminal Justice, 1972-76; Delta Sigma Theta Sorority; pres, Assn of Black LA City Attorneys, 1988-89. **Business Addr:** Assistant City Attorney, Dept of Airports, Los Angeles City Attorney's Office, 1 World Way, Los Angeles, CA 90045.

MESIAH, RAYMOND N.
Technical manager (retired), consultant. **Personal:** Born Sep 1, 1932, Buffalo; son of Marie Mesiah and Nicklos Mesiah; married; children: 2. **Educ:** Canisius Coll, BS 1954; MS 1960. **Career:** FMC Corp, Philadelphia, PA, sr environmental engr, 1977-90, eastern region environmental mgr, 1991-93, environmental mgr, 1993-95; private environmental consultant, 1995-. **Orgs:** Amer Chem Soc; bd educ Franklentown 1969-75; press 1972-73; treas Frederick Douglass Liberation Library 1969-70; Franklin Twp Jaycees 1963-68; pres 1965; chmn Franklin Twp Civil Rights Commn 1967-68; treas Franklin Twp Pub Library 1967-69; Alpha Phi Alpha; Presenting team Worldwide Marriage Encounter, 1977-, coordinator, Camden, NJ, 1985-87, coordinator, section #3, 1992-95. **Honors/Awds:** 1 of 5 outstanding mem of yr NJ Jaycees 1967. **Military Serv:** Corpl 1954-56f.

METCALF, ANDREW LEE, JR.
Government official. **Personal:** Born Feb 21, 1944, Muskegon, MI; married Elizabeth Jane Lamb; children: Andrea, Andrew III. **Educ:** Muskegon Comm Coll, AA, police sci tech, 1971; Grand Valley State University, BS, public service, 1972; Thomas M Cooley Law School, JD, 1987. **Career:** Muskegon Heights Police Dept, patrolman, juvenile officer, 1967-71; McCroskey, Libner, Van Leuven, Cochcrane, Kortering and Brock Law Firm legal investigator, 1971-78; US Dept of Justice, US marshal, 1978-81; Michigan Dept of Commerce, Liquor Control Commission, hearings commissioner, 1982-83, Finance Section, director of internal audit, 1983-84; Michigan Dept of Licensing and Regulation, Bureau of Commercial Services, division director of enforcement, 1987-89, Bureau of Occupational Professional Regulation, Office of Commercial Services, director, 1989-. **Orgs:** Nat Assn of Legal Investigators, asst regional director, 1973-78, 1976; mem W MI Law Enforcement Officer Assn 1978; charter mem Muskegon Hgts Lions Club 1975; treas Iota Phi Lambda Chap of Alpha Phi Alpha Fraternity, 1973-; NAACP Grand Rapids MI Chap, executive board member, 1980, Freedom Fund Chair, 1987; Grand Rapids Gentry Club, president, 1987-88; Citizens for Responsible Government, 1986. **Honors/Awds:** Academic scholarship (3.75 gpa) Ford Found NY 1971. **Military Serv:** USAF sgt 1962-66. **Business Addr:** Dir of Office of Commercial Services, State of MI Dept of Commerce, 611 N Ottawa, Lansing, MI 48909.

METCALF, DAVINCI CARVER (VINCE)
Librarian. **Personal:** Born Jul 1, 1955, Dayton, OH; son of Maggie Lee Blake Metcalf and Zubie West Metcalf Jr. **Educ:** Auburn University, Auburn, AL, BA, political science, 1977; East Carolina University, Greenville, NC, MA, community health, 1982; University of North Carolina, Greensboro, Greensboro, NC; MLS, 1985; Florida State University, Tallahassee, FL, MLS, 1988. **Career:** Library of Congress, Washington, DC, intern, 1984; West Virginia University,Main Library, Morgantown, WV, general reference librarian/college instructor, 1985-86; Jacksonville Public Library, Jacksonville, FL, business, science, documents reference librarian, 1989-. **Orgs:** Member, American Library Assn, 1985-; member, Florida Library Assn, 1985-; member, NAACP, 1988-; member, Black Caucus, Jacksonville Jaycees, 1992-94; American Library Assn; Jacksonville Jaguars Booster Club News, reporter 1995-. **Honors/Awds:** McKnight Fellowship Scholar, McKnight Foundation, 1987-88; Internship, Library of Congress, Library of Congress, 1984; Member, Pi Sigma Alpha Political Science Honor Society, Pi Sigma Alpha Society, 1981-83; National Catholic Scholarship for Negroes, National Catholic Scholarship Foundation, 1973-82; Vocational Rehabilitation Scholarship for Indiana, Indiana Vocational Rehab Dept, 1973; Vocational Rehabilitation Scholarship Alabama, Alabama Vocational Rehab Dept, 1974-77; Volunteer Service Award, Tuskegee Veteran's Administration Hospital, 1975-76; Member, Judge, Auburn University Debate Team, 1974-77; Certificate of Recognition, Outstanding Community Services, Delta Sigma Theta, Greenville, NC, 1987. **Home Addr:** 6090 Terry Rd, Randall Court Apts, #203, Jacksonville, FL 32216. **Business Addr:** Reference Librarian, Business, Science Documents Department, Jacksonville Main Public Library, 122 Ocean St, Jacksonville, FL 32202.

METCALF, ERIC QUINN
Professional football player. **Personal:** Born Jan 23, 1968, Seattle, WA; son of Terry Metcalf; married Lori. **Educ:** Univ of Texas, received liberal arts degree, 1990. **Career:** Cleveland Browns, wide receiver, 1989-94; Atlanta Falcons, 1995-96; San Diego Chargers, wide receiver, 1997-. **Honors/Awds:** Played in AFC Championship Game, post-1989 season; Pro Bowl appearances, 1993, 1994. **Business Addr:** Professional Football Player, San Diego Chargers, 9449 Friars Rd, Qualcomm Stadium, San Diego, CA 92108.

METCALF, MICHAEL RICHARD
Physician. **Personal:** Born Jan 4, 1956, Detroit, MI; son of Adele C Metcalf; married Ruth Chantell Holloman; children: Michael Jr, Leah, Jonathan, Christina. **Educ:** Dartmouth Coll, BA 1978; Howard Univ Coll of Medicine, MD 1982. **Career:** DC General Hospital, internship 1982-83, resident 1983-85, chief resident 1984; CW Williams Health Center, internist 1985-94, health services dir, 1991-94; Carolina Health Care Group, chief of internal medicine, 1996-; Carolinas Medical Center, assoc div, active staff, dept of internal med 1987-. **Orgs:** Mem Charlotte Medical Soc 1986-; mem, Mecklenburg Medical Society, 1991; Executive Committee, Department of Internal Medicine, Carolinas Medical Center, 1991-. **Honors/Awds:** Diplomate Amer Bd of Internal Medicine 1985. **Business Addr:** Carolina Health Care Group, 8420 University Executive Park, Ste 850, Charlotte, NC 28262, (704)547-0410.

METCALF, ZUBIE WEST, JR.
Educational administrator (retired). **Personal:** Born Jul 4, 1930, Ft Deposit, AL; son of Ella Louise Reasor Metcalf and Zubie West Metcalf Sr; married Maggie L Blake; children: DaVinci C, Caroletta A. **Educ:** Univ of Dayton, BS 1957; Miami Univ, MAT 1961; State Univ of NY Buffalo, EdD 1972. **Career:** Ball State Univ, dir acad oppty prog 1971-73; Tuskegee Inst, asst vice pres for academic affairs/dean of grad prog 1973-76; East Carolina Univ Sch of Med, assistant vice chancellor, assoc dean, dir med center student oppty and minority affairs 1976-92. **Orgs:** Dir Natl Sci Found Summer Inst FL A&M Univ 1966-69; coord Tchr Educ Prog State Univ of NY Buffalo 1969-70; consult US Dept of Health & Human Serv Div of Disadvantaged Asst 1983-84; bd mem Pitt-Greenville C of C 1983-87; chairperson Southern Region Minority Affairs Sect of Assn of Amer Med 1984-86; bd Centura Natl Bank 1986-92; vice president, Natl Assn of Medical Minority Educators 1987-89. **Honors/Awds:** Hon Soc in Ed Univ of Dayton OH 1957; Fellowship Natl Sci Found Washington DC 1960-61; Fellowship Ford Found NY 1970-71; Distinguished Service Award, Natl Assn of Med Minority Educators, 1992; Merit Award, 16 Institutions Health Sciences Consortium, 1993; Outstanding Leadership Award, 1992. **Home Addr:** 3518 Colonnade Dr, Tallahassee, FL 32308.

METHOD MAN
Rapper. **Career:** Rapper, currently. **Honors/Awds:** Award for "All I Need," with Mary J. Blige. **Special Achievements:** Part of rap group, Wu-Tang Clan; albums include: Enter the Wu; Wu-Tang Forever, 1997; solo albums include: Tical, 1995; rapped on "Ill Na Na," with Foxy Brown; appeared in "Next Lifetime" video, with Erykah Badu, Pete Rock; appeared in Copland, 1997. **Business Addr:** Rapper, c/o Def Jam Recordings Group Inc., 160 Varick St., New York, NY 10013, (212)229-5200.

METIVIER, MARION. **See TIMM, MARION ELEANOR.**

METOYER, CARL B.
Attorney. **Personal:** Born Aug 8, 1925, Oakland; married Coline Apperson; children: Carl, Ronald, Monique. **Educ:** Univ of CA, 3 yrs undergrad work econ; Hastings Coll, 1952. **Career:** Priv Prac Sole Practitioner, att 1968-; firm Metoyer & Sweeney, sen part 1959-68; Priv Prac Law Sole Practitioner, 1955-59; firm Fracois & Metoyer, partner 1953-55. **Orgs:** Vice-chmn exec com CA State Bar Conf of Del; mem State Bar of CA; mem Alameda Co Bar Assn; Lawyers Club of Alameda Co; Chalres Houston Law Club; mem Alameda Co Sup Cts Arbitration Panel; vice pres mem bd dirs CA Lawyers Serv; past vice pres Hastings Coll of Law Alumni Assn; past judge pro tem Oakland Mun Ct; past mem bd govs Alameda Co Comm Found; mem CA State Univ Hayward Adv Bd; vice pres mem bd dirs Family Serv Bur Alameda Co; mem NAACP; mem Urban-League; mem Sigma Pi Phi Frat; past chmn Manpower Comm City of Oakland; Past mem Oakland Eco Dev Coun; past mem bd dirs Children's Home Soc of CA; past pres Sen Div Hayward Little League; past mem exec bd San Fran Coun Boy Scts Am. **Honors/Awds:** Recip order of the coif Hastings Coll of Law 1952; mem thurston soc Hastings Coll of Law Hon Soc 1950-52; mem tower & flame Univ CA Berkeley Campus 1947-49. **Military Serv:** USNR 1943-46. **Business Addr:** 6014 Market St, Oakland, CA 94608.

METOYER, ROSIA G.
Librarian. **Personal:** Born Mar 2, 1930, Boyce, LA; daughter of Eloise Pannell Washingston and Horace Gilbert; married Granvel G; children: Renwick, Keith, Karlette, Toni Rosette. **Educ:** Grambling Coll, BS Edu 1951; Webster Coll, MA; Nrthwstrn State U, stdy 1964; Sthrn Univ Baton Rouge, stdy; TX Sthrn U; Nrthwstrn State U. **Career:** Acadian Elem Sch, libr; Lincoln Rd Elem Sch Rapides Parish Sch Bd, former school librarian; Rapides Parish Library, selections librarian. **Orgs:** Pres LA Classroom Teacher Assn LEA 1977-78; mem Exec Council of LA Assn of Educators 1978-80; mem United Teaching Professional LA Libr Assn, SW Libr Assn, Alexandria Zoning Bd of Adjustment & Appeals, Assn of Classroom Teachers, LA Libr Assn, YWCA, NAACP; negotiated the dedication of the Martin Luther King Jr Center; established the Black Awareness Resource Prog at Martin Luther King Jr Center; acquired $1200 from Jack & Jill Found to purchase resources for Center; secretary, Rapides Parish Democratic Executive Committee, 1988-92; 2nd vice-president, Louisiana Federation of Democratic Women, 1991-93; chairperson, National Political Congress of Black Women, Alexandria Chapter, 1990-92; Alapha Kappa Alpha Sorority, Zeta Lambda Omega Chapter, Basileus; member, Alexandria Chapter of Jack &l of America Inc, 1990-92; district coordinator, Louisiana Federation of Democratic Women, 1990-91; secretary, Louisiana Association for Sickle Cell Disease, 1986-; Huey P Long Medical Center Governoring Board; Louisiana Developmental Disabilities Council. **Honors/Awds:** Recipient 1st James R Hovall Award; LA Assn of Librarians Serv Awd; LA Beauticians Serv Awd; LA Assoc of Educators Outstanding Serv to Teachers Awd Zeta Lambda Omega; Alpha Kappa Alpha Sor Community Serv Awd; SE Kiwanis Community Serv Awd. **Home Addr:** 910 Papin St, Alexandria, LA 71301. **Business Addr:** Librarian, PO Box 206, Alexandria, LA 71309.

METTERS, SAMUEL
Telecommunications company executive. **Educ:** PhD. **Career:** Metters Industries Inc, chairman, chief executive officer, 1981-. **Special Achievements:** Company ranked #43 on BE's Top 100 Industrial/Service Companies, 1992. **Business Addr:** CEO, Metters Industries Inc, 8200 Greensboro Dr, Ste 500, Mc Lean, VA 22102, (703)821-3300.

MEYER, ALTON J.
Automobile dealership executive. **Career:** Al Meyer Ford Inc, president, currently. **Special Achievements:** Company ranked #76 on BE's list of Top 100 Auto Dealers, 1992. **Business Addr:** President, Al Meyer Ford Inc, 800 N Medford Dr, Lufkin, TX 75901-5222, (409)632-6611.

MEYERS, ISHMAEL ALEXANDER
Judge. **Personal:** Born Feb 3, 1939, St Thomas, Virgin Islands of the United States; son of Elvera L Meyers (deceased) and H Alexander Meyers (deceased); married Gwendolyn Lorraine Pate; children: Ishmael Jr, Micheline, Michael. **Educ:** Morgan State Univ, BS with high honors 1962; Amer Univ, MBA 1964; George Washington Univ, JD with honors 1972. **Career:** Interstate Commerce Commn, acct/auditor 1963-64; VI Dept of Housing & Comm Renewal 1964-69; VI Dept of Law, asst atty gen 1973; US Dept of Justice, asst US atty 1973-78, US atty 1978-82; Territorial Court of the VI, assoc judge 1982-. **Orgs:** Mem Bar of the Supreme Court of the US 1980-; mem DC Bar Assn 1973-; mem VI Bar Assn 1973-; mem Amer Bar Assn 1973-; charter mem St Thomas Lions Club 1968-; vice pres, historian, Theta Epsilon Lambda Chap, Alpha Phi Alpha Frat, Inc. **Honors/Awds:** Alpha Kappa Mu Natl Honor Soc Morgan State Univ 1960-62; John Hay Whitney Found Fellow 1962-64; US Atty Gen Special Achievement Award US Dept of Justice 1976; The Natl Alumni Assn of Morgan State Univ Special Achievement Award 1984. **Business Addr:** Associate Judge, Territorial Court of the Virgin Islands, PO Box 70, St Thomas, Virgin Islands of the United States 00804.

MEYERS, ROSE M.
Research scientist. **Personal:** Born Aug 18, 1945, Mt Pleasant, SC. **Educ:** Bennett Coll Greensboro, BS Chem 1966; NY U, MS Biochem 1972, PhD Biochem 1976. **Career:** Philip Morris Rsrch Ctr, rsrch sci 1978-; Univ of Louisville Med Sch, postdoctoral fllwshp & rsrch tchng 1976-78; NY Univ Med Sch, rsrch tech II cancer rsrch 1972-76, rsrch tech I cancer rsrch 1968-72; Yeshiva Univ NY, rsrch tech chem 1967-68; Howard HS Georgetown SC, math tchr 1966-67. **Orgs:** Mem Sister Cities Intl 1978-; mem Nat Assn Blk Chem 1978-; pres Bennett Coll Alumnae of Richmond 1980-82; mem Bus & Professional Wmn's Club Mus of African Art. **Honors/Awds:** Publ article "Studies on Nucleoside Deaminase" Jrnl Biol Chem 2485090 1973; publ "sialyltransferase in lympocytes" fdrtn prcdngs 351441 1976; Louisvillecitz awd Mayor Harvey Sloane Louisville 1976-77; publ "Immunosupprsn & Tobacco Smoke" Fdrtn Prcdngs 361230 1977.

MFUME, KWEISI
Association executive, former congressman. **Educ:** Morgan State Univ, (magna cum laude), 1976; Johns Hopkins Univ, masters degree, 1984. **Career:** Talk show host; radio station prog dir; Baltimore City Council member; US House of Representatives, congressman State of MD, until 1996; NAACP, president and CEO, 1996-. **Orgs:** Chairman, Congressional Black Caucus; member, Caucus for Women's Issues; member, Congressional Arts Caucus; member, Federal Government Service Task Force; board of trustees, Baltimore Museum of Art; member, Morgan State University Board of Regents. **Business Addr:** President, NAACP, 4805 Mt Hope Dr, Baltimore, MD 21215.

MICHAEL, CHARLENE BELTON
Associate director. **Personal:** Born in Heath Springs, SC; daughter of Cherryane Powe Belton and Charles Belton; married Joseph Michael Sr, Jul 29, 1941; children: Joseph M Jr, Charles B. **Educ:** Knoxville Coll, BA 1939; Teachers Coll, Columbia Univ, MaA 1955; Univ of TN, MS 1958; Univ of TN, PhD 1976. **Career:** Knoxville Cty Schls, tchr 1950-75; Knoxville Cty Schl & Univ TN, speech pathologist 1958-75; Knoxville/Knox Co Project Headstart, dpty dir 1965-66; Knoxville Coll-Upward Bound, assoc dir 1968-69 (summers); Educ & Training Adaption Serv Inc, ed dir 1971-75; MAARDAC/UNIV of TN, assoc dir 1974-; Univ Assoc, Johns Hopkins U, consultant 1979, 82-83; Mid Atlantic/Appalachian Race Desegregation Assistance Ctr, acting dir 1987. **Orgs:** Pres Phi Delta Kappa Univ of TN 1979-80; mem bd of trustees Knoxville Coll

1984; pres Knoxville Coll Natl Alumni Assoc Inc, pres Knoxville Educ Assoc, Delta Sigma Theta Sor Alumnae Chapt; bd of dirs Knoxville Women's Ctr, Matrix, Children's Ctr; mem Metropolitan Planning Commn. **Honors/Awds:** Publications, "Why I Teach", "The Effect of Parental Invlmnt on the Lrng Process", "Advantages of Lang-Experience Approach in the Teaching of Reading" "Coping with Stresses in the Classroom", "Student Team Learning, An Educational Equity Tool", "Workshop Participants' Perception Rankings of Second Gen Schl Desegregation Issues"; Cert of Recgntn Knoxville Coll SE Regnl & Natl Alumni Assoc 1977; lic speech pathologist State of TN; Citizen of the Year Award/For Serv & Contrib to Humanity 1984; Selwyn Awd Knoxville Women's Ctr 1985; YWCA Awd Tribute to Outstanding Women 1986. **Business Addr:** Acting Dir, Mid-Atlantic/Appalachian Race, 238 Claxton Addition, Knoxville, MS 37996.

MICHAEL, DALE R.
Attorney. **Personal:** Born Oct 1, 1942, St Thomas, Virgin Islands of the United States; son of Elizabeth Michael and Cyril Michael; married Emilie Kheil. **Educ:** Manhattan Coll, BChE 1962; Columbia Univ, MSChE 1967, LLB 1967, MBA 1968. **Career:** Robert S First, aup 1968-69; Coalition Venture Corp, exec dir 1969-72; NY Financial Serv, partner 1972-74; DPS Protective Systems, 1974-85; JD Asset Protection Group, owner 1985-89; Frydenhoj Estates Corp, 1987-. **Orgs:** Mem NY Bar; mem California Bar; patron Metropolitan Opera 1982-.

MICHAUX, ERIC COATES
Attorney. **Personal:** Born Sep 23, 1941, Durham, NC; married Della Dafford. **Educ:** Univ of NC, attended 1959; NC Central Univ Sch of Law, attended 1963-65; Boston U, BS Bus Adminstrn 1963; Duke Univ Sch of Law, B of Law 1966; Univ of Denver, attended 1968. **Career:** Eric C Michauz Law Firm, pres; 14th Solicitoral Dist, asst dist attorney 1973-75; Perason Malone Johnson & DeJormon, atty 1971-73; W G Pearson, atty 1967; Durham Coll Durham NC, tchr bus law 1965. **Orgs:** Vis prof N CA Central Univ 1971-73; adj asst prof Dept of Health Educ Univ of NC Chapel Hill 1972-73; %Congressional aide Congressman Nick Galifianakis 1971-72; pres Unoin Ins & Reality Co; vice pres Glenview Mem Park Washington Terr Apts Inc; bd of dir Harrison Constrn Realty Co; vchmn/bd of dir Cardinal Savs & Loan; mem Am Bar Assn; NAACP; So Christian Leadership Conf; mem Omega Psi Phi Frat; Phi Alpha Delta Legal Frat; Nat Soc of Perishing Rifles;Durham Com on the Affairs of Black People; mem United Citizens Against Drug Abusr; steward trustee treas St Joseph's African Meth Episcopal Ch; mem NC Bar Assn; bd of dirs Durham Chap of the Am Nat Red Cross. **Honors/Awds:** Recipient of Nat Defencs Serv Medal; Vietnam Serv Medal; Vietnam Campaign Medal; Bronze Star USAF 1967-69. **Military Serv:** USAF 1967-69. **Business Addr:** PO Box 1152, Durham, NC 27702.

MICHAUX, HENRY G.
Educator, sculptor. **Personal:** Born Jan 19, 1934, Morganton, NC; son of Mary Annie Phillips Michaux and Fred D Michaux Sr. **Educ:** TX So Univ, BFA (magna cum laude) 1959; PA State Univ, MEd 1960, DEd 1971, grad grant-in-aid 1959-60, grad asst 1966-67. **Career:** VA State Univ, tchr fine arts & art educ 1960-62; So Univ in New Orleans, 1962-67; Cntrl State Univ, 1967-68; TX So Univ, 1968-70; Coll of the VI, 1970; Appalachian State Univ, assoc prof art educ 1972-76; NC Central Univ, assoc prof art educ 1977-78; SC State University, associate prof art educ 1978-. **Orgs:** National Association of Schools of Art and Design; National Sculpture Center; NC Coalition of Arts; mem Amer Craftsmen Council 1964-; National Council on Education for the Ceramic Arts; Seminar for Research in Art Education; Amer Assn of Univ Profs 1962-71; natl Art Educ Assn 1974-87; Black Art Festivals; first pres Caldwell Arts Council Lenoir, NC 1976; designed and coord first indoor/outdoor regional (NC, GA, SC, TN, VA) Sculptors Competition Lenoir NC 1986 through Lenoir Parks & Recreational Dept & the Caldwell Arts Cncl; developed Black Studies (African-Amer Studies for Caldwell Comm Coll Lenoir NC) Project proposal; ETV (WXEX-TV) participant VA State Coll. **Honors/Awds:** Honorary mem Alpha Kappa Mu 1956-59; Jesse Jones Fine Arts Scholarship TX So Univ 1956-59; Selected Participant Japanese Seminar on Preserv of Cultural Continuity by SC Consortium for Intl Studies 1980; numerous exhibits; natl winner of competition for one-man shows; Madison Galleries, NY; work in Look Magazine; drawings owned by NC Arts Museum; "African American Artists, NC USA" NC Museum of Art 1980; interview and feature on "Carolina Camera" WBTV Charlotte 1981; apptd SC Acquisitions Comm a part of the SC Museum Commn 1982-84; NC Artist International, Hickory Museum of Art, 1987; Natl Invitationals "Dimensions and Directions, Black Artists of the South" Jackson MS 1983; "Changing Images,": Hickory Museum of Art, 1993 . **Business Addr:** Professor, South Carolina State College, 300 College St, NE, Orangeburg, SC 29117-0001.

MICHAUX, HENRY M., JR.
State official. **Personal:** Born Sep 4, 1930, Durham, NC; son of Isadore C Michaux and Henry M Michaux; children: Jocelyn. **Educ:** NC Central Univ, BS 1952; Rutgers Univ, 1954-55; NC Central Univ, JD 1952, 1964. **Career:** Michaux & Michaux, sr partner; real estate broker 20 years; Durham Cnty, chf asst dist atty 1962-72; NC Gen Assembly & House Rep 1972-76; Middle Judicial Dist NC, US atty 1977-81; NC Gen Assembly 1985-. **Orgs:** Trustee NC Central Univ; mem exec com 14th Judicial Dist Bar; N State Bar; NC Bar Assn; George H White Bar Assn; Black Lawyers NC; Amer Bar Assn; Judicature Soc; Criminal Code Commn State NC 1973-77; Steering Com Caucus Black Dem; NC Commn Human Skills & Resources; NC Com Law Focused Edn; NC Central Alumni Assn; bd dir NC Central Univ Found Inc; Durham Bus & Professional Chain; Durham C of C; Durham Merchants Assn; NAACP. **Honors/Awds:** Hon Dr Degree Durham Coll & NC Central Univ; Realist of Yr; Pub Affairs & Polit Achievement Award 1973-74 & 1976; Annual Award for Triad Sickle Cell Anemia Found 1973; Citiz Com Sickle Cell Syndrome Award 1976; Polit Achvmt Award NAACP 1975; Serv Award Phi Alpha Delta Law Frat; Achvmnt Award CA Real Estate Brokers 1974; Service Award 14th Judicial Dist Bar 1972; Triangle "J" Cncl Govt 1973; NC Bar Assn 1975; Pub Serv Award NC Chiropractic Assn 1977; NC Black Dem Leadership Caucus 1977. **Military Serv:** AUS MC 1952-54.

MICHEL, HARRIET RICHARDSON
Business organization executive. **Personal:** Born Jul 5, 1942, Pittsburgh, PA; daughter of Vida Richardson and John Richardson; married Yves Michel; children: Christoper, Gregory. **Educ:** Juniata College, Huntingdon, PA, BA. **Career:** Natl Scholarship Serv & Fund for Negro Students, director of special projects, 1965-70; Office of the Mayor of New York, assistant, 1971-72; New York Foundation, executive director, 1972-77; US Department of Labor, Washington, DC, director of youth employment, 1977-79; John Jay College, New York, NY, 1981; US Department of Housing and Urban Development, Washington, DC, consultant, 1982-83; New York Urban League, New York, NY, president, 1983-88; National Minority Supplier Development Council, New York, NY, president, 1988-. **Orgs:** Board member, African American Institute; board member, Citizens Committee of New York; board member, Juniata College; board member, New York City Partnership; board member, TransAfrica Forum. **Honors/Awds:** DHL, Baruch College, 1990; The First Nonprofit Leadership Award, New School, 1988; First Women on the Move Award, B'Nai B'rith, 1990; Ethnic New Yorker Award, 1985; Resident Fellow, Harvard University, 1988; Wall Street Journal Black Entrepenurial Award, 1994. **Business Addr:** President, National Minority Supplier Development Council, Inc, 15 W 39th St, 9th Fl, New York, NY 10018, (212)944-2430.

MICKELL, DARREN
Professional football player. **Personal:** Born Aug 3, 1970, Miami, FL. **Educ:** University of Florida, attended. **Career:** Kansas City Chiefs, defensive end, 1992-95; New Orleans Saints, 1996-. **Business Addr:** Professional Football Player, New Orleans Saints, 5800 Airline Hwy, Metairie, LA 70003, (504)733-0255.

MICKENS, MAXINE
Business executive. **Personal:** Born Dec 3, 1948, Clarksdale, MS; married Caesar Jr; children: Leonora. **Educ:** Univ of MI, AB 1974; Comm Film Workshop of Chicago, cert 1976; ICBIF Sma Business mgmt Detroit, cert 1978. **Career:** Max Belle & Asso, vice pres 1977-; Simpson's Wholesale Detroit, adv mgr 1977; WJLB Radio Detroit, merchandising & promotion dir 1976-77; Detroit Bd of Edn, vocational & adult educ tchr 1974-80. **Orgs:** Mem WXYZ-TC Women's Adv Com Detroit MI 1974-76; mem Black Communicators Assn Detroit 1979-; mem Nat Assn of Media Women Detroit; communications chairperson Triedstone Bapt Church 1972-73; communications chairpersons Jeffersn Chalmers Com Assn 1974-75. **Business Addr:** Max Belle & Associates, 1308 Broadway Ste 206, Detroit, MI 48226.

MICKENS, RAY
Professional football player. **Personal:** Born Jan 4, 1973, Frankfurt, Germany; children: Kamray. **Educ:** Texas A&M. **Career:** New York Jets, defensive back, 1996-. **Business Addr:** Professional Football Player, New York Jets, 1000 Fulton Ave, Hempstead, NY 11550, (516)560-8100.

MICKENS, RONALD ELBERT
Educator, researcher. **Personal:** Born Feb 7, 1943, Petersburg, VA; son of Daisy Mickens and Joseph P Mickens; married Maria Kelker; children: Leah, James. **Educ:** Fisk Univ, BA 1964; Vanderbilt Univ, PhD 1968. **Career:** MIT Center for Theoretical Physics, post doctoral researcher 1968-70; Fisk Univ Dept Physics, asst to prof 1970-81; MIT Dept Physics, visiting prof of physics 1973-74; Morehouse Coll/Atlanta Univ, visiting prof of physics 1979-80; Vanderbilt Univ Dept Physics, visiting scholar 1980-81; Joint Inst for Lab Astrophysics Boulder, CO, research fellow 1981-82; Atlanta Univ, chairperson 1984-86, Distinguished Callaway prof 1985-. **Orgs:** Consult work for, Natl Acad of Sciences, Los Alamos Sci Lab, Coll of Old Westburg; National Science Found, Dept of Energy, National Institutes of Health; mem Amer Assn of Physics Tchrs, European Phys Soc, Amer Phys Soc, Amer Assn for Advancement of Sci, Sigma Xi, Beta Kappa Chi, Soc of Black Physicists, Amer Math Assn; mem London Mathematical Soc, Soc of Mathematical Biologists, Soc for Industrial and Applied Mathematics; American Mathematical Society. **Honors/Awds:** Phi Beta Kappa, Fisk Univ Chap elect 1964; Woodrow Wilson Fellowship 1964-65; Danforth Fellowship 1965-68; Natl Sci Foundation Postdoctoral Fellowship 1968-70; Ford Foundation Postdoctoral Fellowship 1980-81; Joint Inst for Lab Astrophysics Fellowship 1981-82; research grants from Dept Energy, NASA, Natl Sci Found, GTE Found, Army Research Office; UNCF Distinguished Faculty Fellowship 1984-85; Callaway Professor 1985-; over 160 published papers, five books. **Business Addr:** Callaway Professor, Clark Atlanta University, Box 172, 223 James P Brawley Dr SW, Atlanta, GA 30314, (404)880-6923.

MICKENS, TERRY KAJUAN
Professional football player. **Personal:** Born Feb 21, 1971, Tallahassee, FL; children: Tyler Jarrod. **Educ:** Florida A&M. **Career:** Green Bay Packers, wide receiver, 1994-. **Business Addr:** Professional Football Player, Green Bay Packers, 1265 Lombardi Ave, Green Bay, WI 54304, (414)494-2351.

MICKEY, GORDON EUGENE
Educational administrator. **Personal:** Born in Chillicothe, OH; married Dr Rosie Cheatham; children: Miguel Eugene,Madganna Mae. **Educ:** Indiana Univ-Bloomington, BS 1962, MS 1966, EdD 1971; Cleveland State Univ, post doctoral work; The University of Akron, psychology school courses. **Career:** Indianapolis Public Schools, teacher/coach 1962-65; IN Univ Div of Univ Schools, instructor/coach 1966-69; New Castle Gunning Bedford Sch Dist, principal 1971-73; St Dept of Public Instruction (DE), state sup 1973-76; Mental Retardation Program-Lorain County OH, adm, consult 1976-77; Akron Public Schools-Akron OH, unit principal 1977-80; Stow City Schools-Stow OH, central office special educ supervisor 1981-89, consultant and special education instructor, 1990-. **Orgs:** Former vice chmn church trustee bd, church usher; Methodist Men's Organization, 1980-91; Second Baptist Church 1980-82; scholarship comm Beautillion Militaire 1980, 1981, 1983, 1985; founder/coord Minority Youth Recognition Programs 1982-84; vice pres Akron Frontiers Club 1982-84; chap consultant Jack and Jill of Amer Inc 1986; exec bd Neal-Marshall Alumni Club 1986; mem ASCD, NABSE, Phi Delta Kappa, Alpha Phi Alpha, Council for Exceptional Children. **Honors/Awds:** Masters Fellowship Indiana Univ 1965-66, Doctoral Fellowship 1969-71; Presidential Natl Awd Frontiers Intl 1981; Certificate of Commendation Stow City Schools 1985; President's Awd Akron Frontiers Club 1986; Kentucky Colonel Award for IU Neal Marshall Alumni Club, 1987; Chillicothe High School Hall of Fame Inductee, 1993. **Home Addr:** PO Box 33592, Indianapolis, IN 46203-0592.

MICKEY, ROSIE CHEATHAM
Educational administrator (retired). **Personal:** Born Jun 13, Indianapolis, IN; married Dr Gordon Mickey; children: Miguel Eugene, Madganna Mae. **Educ:** Indiana Univ Bloomington, BS 1970; The Univ of Akron, MS 1979, EdD 1983. **Career:** New Castle and Newark Sch Dists Delaware, business teacher 1971-76; Lorain City Schools OH, voc business teacher 1976-78; The Univ of Akron, grad asst 1978-80; Manfield City Schools OH, asst high school principal 1980-83; The Univ of Akron, asst dir fin aids 1984, asst dean & asst prof 1984-88; Indianapolis Public Schools, Indianapolis Indiana, consultant/admin, 1988-91. **Orgs:** Vice pres Akron Yokettes Club Aux of Frontiers 1983-84; mem exec bd Ecumenical Campus Ministry 1984-88; general chairperson Beautillion Militaire J & J 1985; coord Individualized Study Program C&T 1985-88; vice pres Pi Lambda Theta educ hon 1986-87; pres Jack and Jill of Amer Inc Akron Chap 1986-88; mem Phi Delta Kappa, NABSE, Natl Assoc Women Deans, Couns Admin, 1986-88; charter mem Neal-Marshall Alumni Club of Indiana Univ; mem Amer Assoc of Univ Women, United Way Allocations Panel Bd; urban consultation comm, steering comm United Methodist Churches; Indianapolis Black Expo Scholarship Committee; founder Anna H & Smith H Cheatham Book Scholarship Fund, 1990-91. **Honors/Awds:** Service Awd Vitiligo Symposiums Akron Frontiers Club 1983; Awd of Commendation House of Representatives of OH 1984; publication(s) from dissertation study 1983; papers presented Indianapolis, Atlanta, Chicago 1983, 1985, 1986; Community Service Award, Frontiers International Service Organization Sixth District; awards, Jack and Jill of America Inc; University of Akron, Board of Trustees, President, Outstanding Administrator recognition 1987; YWCA, Women's History Week Awards, 1987, 1988.

MICKINS, ANDEL W.
Educator. **Personal:** Born Oct 28, 1924, Central, SC; daughter of Estelle Jamison Watkins and Ernest Watkins; married Rev Isaac C Mickins, Jul 11, 1952; children: Isaac Clarence, II. **Educ:** Tuskegee Inst, BS; Columbia Univ, MA; Iowa State Coll, std; Univ of Miami. **Career:** Sr HS, head home econ dept 1946-52; Holmes Elem School, teacher 1953-62; Curr Liberty City Elementary, asst principal 1962-67; Univ of Miami, summer supr tchr 1965;RR Moton Elem, principal 1967-72; Rainbow Park Elementary, principal 1972-81 (retired); Memorial Temple Baptist Church, dir early childhood educ center 1983-. **Orgs:** Pres Friendship Garden Club; vice pres Baptist Women's Coun; former supt Sunday School; mem Temple Baptist Church; adv Bus & profes Women's Club; pres Ministers

Wivers Council of Greater Miami; spon Y-Teen; Comm Chr Boy Sct Troop 290; mem Alpha Kappa Alpha Sor; mem Phi Lambda Thet Honor Soc; mem Kappa Delta Pi Honor Soc; mem Amer Assoc of Univ Women; bd of dir Black Archives Foundation of Rsch of South FL; chmn exec bd Womens Aux Gen Baptist State Convention of FL; pres FL State Assoc of Ministers Wives. **Honors/Awds:** Recip Sarah Blocker award FL Mem Col; plaque Rainbow Park Elementary School & Friendship Garden & Civic Club; plaque Alpha Kappa Alpha Sorority; Citation City of Miami; Natl Conf of Christians & Jews. **Business Addr:** 15355 NW 19 Ave, Miami, FL 33054.

MICKLE, ANDREA DENISE
Educational administrator. **Personal:** Born Jul 26, 1952, Kershaw, SC; daughter of Mable Harris Mickle and John T Mickle. **Educ:** Hampton Univ, BA (Honor Graduate) 1974; Adelphi Univ, Certificate 1974; Howard Univ, MPA 1985. **Career:** Howard Univ, financial aid officer. **Orgs:** Conf participant, resource person Natl Assoc for Equal Oppor in Higher Educ 1975-; mem Amer Paralegal Assoc 1975-77; charter mem Lawyer's Assistants Inc 1975; pres Howard Univ Pi Alpha Alpha Honor Soc 1984-85; mem DE-DC-MD Assoc of Student Financial Aid Administrators; mem Amer Soc for Personnel Admin, Amer Soc for Public Admin, NAACP; speaker, coord of workshops for coll bound students sponsored by local organizations. **Honors/Awds:** Outstanding Serv Awd Howard Univ Liberal Arts Student Council 1979, Howard Univ Upward Bound 1986; Certificate of Service Howard Univ Chap of ASPA 1982; Certificate of Appreciation Howard Univ Financial Aid Crisis Comm 1989; editorial reviewer for Black Excellence magazine 1989. **Home Addr:** 7543 Newberry Lane, Lanham, MD 20706. **Business Addr:** Financial Aid Officer, Howard University, 2400-6th St NW, Washington, DC 20059.

MICKLE, ELVA L.
Business executive. **Personal:** Born May 18, 1949, Oakland, CA; daughter of Sadie Blanche Thomas Mickle and John C Mickle. **Educ:** Fisk Univ, BA (magna cum laude) graduated first in class 1971; Harvard Univ, Grad School of Business, MBA 1974. **Career:** Ford Div, Ford Motor Co, statistician-mgmt trainee 1971-72, financial analyst 1974-75; Michigan-Wisc Pipe Line Co, corp planning specialist/spvsr, financial modeling 1976-79; Michigan Bell Telephone Co, staff mngr Federal Issues & Analysis and Rates Proposals; University of TN at Chatanooga, instructor in Business Policy/Strategic Management and Planning 1988-89; LeMoyne-Owen College, Memphis, TN, assistant professor, division of business and management, 1989-91; U.S. Environmental Protection Agency (EPA), Region 10, Seattle, WA, personnel specialist, faculty fellows program 1991-. **Orgs:** Women's Economic Club, Detroit 1980-86; 2nd vice pres, Natl Black MBA Assn, Detroit chapter 1982, 1983, secretary 1982-84; Entrepreneur Conference Planning Comm 1983-85; Harvard Business Sch Alumni Assn of Detroit; moderator & speaker, Strategies Annual Women's Career Conference 1983, 1984; Engineering Soc of Detroit 1983-85. **Honors/Awds:** Outstanding Serv Award for leadership work on annual Banquet Committee, Detroit chapter, Natl Black MBA Assn 1981.

MICKS, DEITRA R. H.
Attorney, city councilwoman (retired). **Personal:** Born May 26, 1945, Bronx, NY; daughter of Mabel Handy and John Handy; divorced. **Educ:** Howard U, BA 1967; Howard U, JD 1971. **Career:** Jacksonville, legal aid 1971-73; Pvt Prac, atty; Jackson & Micks; Univ N FL, tchr; Duval Co, FL, city councilwoman. **Orgs:** Bd dir Legal Aid 1974-; life mem NAACP Jacksonville chpt; student articles Ed Howard Law Journal 1970-71.

MIDDLEBROOKS, FELICIA
Broadcast journalist. **Personal:** Born May 29, 1957, Gary, IN; daughter of Geraldine Rembert Middlebrooks and Raymond Middlebrooks Jr. **Educ:** Purdue Univ, Hammond IN, BA Mass Communications, 1982. **Career:** WBAA, anchor, 1976-77; WGVE Radio for Handicapped, anchor, 1978-81; Jones & Laughlin Steel, laborer, 1978-82; WJOB Radio, reporter, anchor, 1979-82; WLTH Radio, reporter, anchor, 1982-84; WBBM Radio, morning drive anchor, reporter, 1984-; Saltshake Productions, owner. **Orgs:** Honorary chairperson, March of Dimes WalkAmerica, 1985-88; mem, Chicago Assn of Black Journalists, 1987-; bd mem, Cris Radio (Chicagoland Reading Information Serv for the Handicapped), 1987-; mem, Sigma Delta Chi/Professional Journalists, 1987-; mem, Women in Communications Inc, 1989; bd of dirs, Chicagoland Radio Information Services of the Blind; Illinois News Broadcasters Assn; New Regal Theater Foundation, bd of dirs; Women in Film. **Honors/Awds:** Benjamin Hooks Distinguished Achievement Recognition, NAACP, 1987; featured in Washington Journalism Review, 1987; Salute to Chicago's Up & Coming Black Business & Professional Women, Dollars & Sense Magazine, 1988; Tribute to Chicago Women, Midwest Women's Center, 1988; Skyaward of Merit, Women in Communications, 1989; Outstanding Excellence Award, Women in Communications, 1989; Outstanding Communicator, Women in Communications, 1989; Best Reporter Award, Illinois Associated Press, 1989; Midwest Radio and Music Assn, Salute to Women in the Industry, 1992; Assn of Black Journalists, Best Radio Reporter, 1987; Chicago Jaycees, Outstanding Young Citizens Award, 1991; Natl Assn of Univ Women, Distinctive Imprint Award, 1993. **Business Addr:** Morning Drive Anchor, WBBM Newsradio 78, 630 N McClurg Ct, Chicago, IL 60611.

MIDDLETON, BERNICE BRYANT
Librarian, educator (retired). **Personal:** Born Nov 11, 1922, Orangeburg, SC; daughter of Gertrude Dangerfield Bryant and Alonzo Webster Bryant; married Earl Matthew Middleton, Feb 10, 1946; children: Anita Middleton Pearson, Kenneth Earl, Karen Denise. **Educ:** Claflin College, Orangeburg, SC, AB (summa cum laude), 1942; Atlanta University, Atlanta, GA, BSLS, 1944, MSLS, 1957; University of Pittsburgh, Pittsburgh, PA, advanced certificate in library and information sciences, 1968. **Career:** Granard High School, Gaffney, SC, teacher/librarian, 1942-43; Atlanta University, Atlanta, GA, assistant cataloger, 1944-46; South Carolina, State College, Orangesburg, SC, circulation librarian, 1946-52, assistant professor, Dept of Library Sciences, 1952-57, professor and chairman, Dept of Library/Media Services, 1957-84. **Orgs:** Former pres, South Carolina State College Chapter, AAUP; corporate representative, AAUW, 1983-84; member, Visiting Committees, Southern Assn of Colleges and Schools 1958-84; former member, ALA, Southeastern and the South Carolina Library Assn; member, Orangeburg Branch, member, AAUW, member, Delta Sigma Theta Sorority, member, The United Methodist Women. **Honors/Awds:** Summa Cum Laude, Claflin College, 1942; Fellowship, General Education Board, 1943-44; Beta Phi Mu National Honorary Fraternity, 1968. **Business Addr:** South Carolina State University, Box 7368, Orangeburg, SC 29117.

MIDDLETON, ERNEST J.
Educator. **Personal:** Born Dec 25, 1937, Franklin, LA; married Rosa Metz; children: Lance, Owen. **Educ:** Southern U, BA 1962; Univ of CO, EdS 1973; Univ of CO, EdD 1974. **Career:** Univ of KY, asso prof; Race & Sex Desegration Training Inst, dir 1974-; St Mary Par Publ Sch, prof 1962-63, 1965-70f St Mary Human Rel Cncl, vice pres 1966. **Orgs:** Pres St Mary Educ Assn 1967-70; chrm St Mary Comm Action Agency 1969; mem LA Educ Assn; Southern Univ Mrch Band 1958-62; Kappa Alpha Psi Frat; NAACP; Phi Delta Kappa Frat; Nat Alliance of Black Sch Educ. **Honors/Awds:** ASCD award Bowling Green Univ 1968; EPDA fellowship Souther Univ 1971; EPDA flwshp Univ of CO 1972; TDIS 1970-71; outstanding serv St Mary Par 1970-71; outstanding achvmnt LA Eudc Assn 1974. **Military Serv:** AUS 1963-65.

MIDDLETON, JOHN ALLEN
Educator. **Personal:** Born Nov 19, 1945, Hawthorne, FL; son of Marguerite Ivey Middleton and Theodore Agustus Middleton; children: Alicia, John II, LaTonya. **Educ:** Florida A&M University, BS, 1970; University of Florida, MEd, 1974, EdD, 1984. **Career:** PCR Inc, chemist, 1970-72; Alachua County School Board, teacher, 1972-78; University of Florida, director, 1978-79; Alachua County School Board, principal, 1979-85; Volusia County School Board, assistant superintendent, 1985-90; Columbus City Schools, superintendent, 1990-92; Ohio State University, associate professor, director of School Relations, 1992-. **Orgs:** United Way of Franklin County, board member, 1992-; YMCA of Columbus, Ohio, board member, 1990-; In-Roads Inc of Columbus, Ohio, board member. 1992-; Boy Scouts Central Ohio Council, board member, 1991-; American Association of School Administrators; Buckeye Association School Administrators; Sigma Pi Phi Fraternity; Alpha Phi Alpha Fraternity, life member. **Honors/Awds:** Florida A&M University, Science Hall of Distinction, 1988. **Special Achievements:** A model preparation program for first year substitute teachers without a bachlors degree, 1984; first African-American superintendent in Columbus, OH. **Military Serv:** US Air Force, e-4, 1963-67. **Business Addr:** Assoc Dean, College of Education, University of Central Florida, Orlando, FL 32816.

MIDDLETON, RICHARD TEMPLE, III
Educator. **Personal:** Born Jan 17, 1942, Jackson, MS; son of Johnnie Beadle Middleton and Richard T Middleton II; married Brenda Marie Wolfe; children: Jeanna E, Richard T IV. **Educ:** Lincoln Univ of MO, BS 1963, MEd 1965; Univ of Southern MO, EdD 1972. **Career:** Tougaloo Coll, instructor of educ 1967-70; Jackson State Univ, asst & assoc prof 1970-76, dir student teaching 1976-97; Episcopal priest, 1995-. **Orgs:** Bd mem Ballet Mississippi 1983-85, Security Life Ins Co 1985; pres Beta Gamma Boule Sigma Pi Phi Frat 1985-87; bd mem Opera/South Co 1986-90, Catholic Charities 1986-90; vice pres Mississippi Religious Leadership Conference 1988-89; mem Natl Executive Council The Episcopal Church 1987-88; vice chairman, Jackson, MS Planning Board, 1990-94; NCATE Board of Examiners. **Honors/Awds:** Woodrow-Wilson King Fellowship Doctoral Study 1969; selected as mem of leadership, Jackson MS Chamber of Commerce 1987-88. **Military Serv:** AUS 1st lt 2 yrs. **Home Addr:** 944 Royal Oak Dr, Jackson, MS 39209. **Business Phone:** (601)968-2355.

MIDDLETON, ROSE NIXON
Educational administrator, consultant. **Personal:** Born Jun 3, 1932, Gum Tree, PA; daughter of Margaret Black Nixon and Havard Downing Nixon; married C. T. Middleton, Mar 12, 1951; children: Karen Ann Nixon Middleton, Tanya Hope Nixon Middleton. **Educ:** University of Pennsylvania, Philadelphia, PA, AB, 1954; Bryn Mawr College, Bryn Mawr, PA, MSS, 1958. **Career:** Child Care Service of Chester County, West Chester, PA, child welfare worker, 1960-62; Child Study Center of Philadelphia, Philadelphia, PA, psychiatric social worker, 1962-66; Mental Health Center, West Chester, PA, senior psychiatric social worker, 1966-68; Chester County Intermediate Unit, Coatesville, PA, administrative assistant to the director of special education for preschool programs, 1968-89; Expertise and Assistance, Coatesville, PA, president, 1990-. **Orgs:** Communications Task Force member, Downingtown Area School District, 1991-; treasurer/board of directors, United Cerebral Palsy Assn, 1989-; president/board of directors, 1985-86, member, 1980-86, Chester County Head Start, Inc; board of directors/president, Handi-Crafters, Inc, 1971-73; secretary/board of directors, Brandywine Red Cross, 1983-84; founder, Chester County Local Children's Team, 1979; handicapped services committee chairperson, Rotary International, 1988-. **Honors/Awds:** Scholarship, Senate of Pennsylvania, 1950-54; Scholarship, National Institute of Mental Health, 1956-58. **Business Addr:** President, Expertise and Assistance, 1263 Lone Eagle Rd, Coatesville, PA 19320.

MIDDLETON, VERTELLE D.
Educational administrator. **Personal:** Born Aug 10, 1942, Charleston, SC; daughter of Nazarene Baldwin Graham and Michael Graham; married James Middleton Jr, Dec 21, 1963; children: Jamela V, Gloria Holmes, Tylon Taylor Middleton. **Educ:** Johnson C Smith Univ, BS Psych/Soc 1964; NYU, Adult Educ Certificate 1975; Bank Coll, Adult Educ Certificate 1975; Temple Univ, Admin Training Certificate 1981; Webster Univ, Charleston SC, MA 1989. **Career:** Immacuate Conception High School, teacher 1964-67; Charleston County OIC Inc, exec dir 1968-82; Trident Technical, Coll Fair Break Center, center dir 1982-84; Trident Tech Coll Manpower Skill Center, dir; Beaufort Technical Coll, Walterboro SC, dir Career Success, 1987; Trident Technical College, Berkeley Campus, Moncks Corner SC, JTPA director, 1987-90, minority affairs director, 1991-. **Orgs:** President, SCPAAE; mem SC Chapter of SETA 1984-; mem SC Tech Educ Assn 1984-; Natl membership comm So Atlantic region; Alpha Kappa Alpha Sorority 1982-86; sec Greater Bd Chapel AME Church 1980-90; sec Burke High School Advisory Bd 1983-; vice chmn Steward Bd Greater Bd Chapel 1980-90; South Atlantic Region-Cluster Coordinator 1988-90; chmn Burke High School Improvement Council 1988-90; Trident Technical Coll Employee Assistance Program Advisory Council 1989; South Atlantic regional director, Alpha Kappa Alpha Sorority Inc, 1990-94; member, American Jr College Women Assn, 1990-; president, South Carolina Professor Association of Access & Equity; president, Charleston Intercollegiate Consortium; mem, Charleston Speech & Hearing Advisory Bd, 1993. **Honors/Awds:** Outstanding Community Serv, WPAL Radio Station 1984; Tribute to Women YWCA 1980; Alpha Kappa Alpha Sorority Outstanding Award S Atlantic Region 1986; Tribute to TWIN Woman-YWCA, Trident Technical Coll 1989; Scholar-Key Leadership Award, Alpha Kappa Alpha, 1991; Frederica Wilson Sisterly Relations Award, Alpha Kappa Alpha, 1991; Women in SC Making a Difference, Alliance of Achievement Commendation Award; St Luke AME Church, Black History Recognition Award. **Home Addr:** 1861 Taborwood Cir, Charleston, SC 29407. **Business Addr:** Minority Affairs Director, Trident Technical College, PO Box 482, Moncks Corner, SC 29461.

MIKELL, CHARLES DONALD
Health administrator. **Personal:** Born Jan 12, 1934, McKeesport, PA; son of Sadie Bell Qualls and Eugene Mikell; married Jacqueline Henry, Oct 20, 1961; children: Michelene Wofford, Charles D II. **Educ:** Lincoln Univ, AB, 1960; Univ of Pittsburgh, Pittsburgh, PA, MPA, 1968, MPH, 1972. **Career:** Family Health Council Inc, project coordinator, 1989-; McKeesport Area Health System, asst administrator, 1978-89; Alcoholic Counseling & Recovery Prog CAP Inc, dir 1970-; Univ Pittsburgh, field supr grad students 1971-; Hill Rehab Center, dir 1968-70; Hill Rehab Center, asst dir 1967-68; Hill Emergency Lift Prog, supr 1966-67; Hill Dist Comm Action Program, asst coord 1965-66; neighborhood devel worker 1964-65; Allegheny Co Health Dept, pub health san 1960-64; academic & prof consult 1968-69. **Orgs:** Alcoholism Com United Mental Health Svc; former pres McKeesport Br NAACP 1964-74; Am Pub Health Assn; Am Legion Post 666; Booker T Wash Lodge 218 IBPOE of W; chairman, McKeesport Redevelopment Authority, 1984-; chairman, McKeesport Housing Authority, 1989-. **Honors/Awds:** Bronze Key Award, National Council on Alcoholism Inc, 1975. **Military Serv:** USNR 1950-52; USMC, Cpl, 1952-55; US Presidential Unit Citation. **Home Addr:** 1726 Eagle Ridge Dr., Monroeville, PA 15146-1769.

MILBOURNE, LARRY WILLIAM
Professional baseball player (retired). **Personal:** Born Feb 14, 1951, Port Norris, NJ. **Educ:** Cumberland County Junior College, attended; Glassboro State College, attended. **Career:** Houston Astros, infielder 1974-76; Seattle Mariners, infielder 1977-80; New York Yankees, infielder, 1981-82; Minnesota Twins, infielder, 1982; Cleveland Indians, infielder, 1982; Philadelphia Phillies, infielder, 1983; New York Yankees, infielder, 1983; Seattle Mariners, infielder, 1984-85.

MILBURN, CORINNE M.
Educator (retired). **Personal:** Born Sep 20, 1930, Alexandria, LA; daughter of Corinne Neal Martin Brown and Ramsey Martin (deceased); married Dr Sidney E, Jun 14, 1952 (deceased); children: Sidney E II, Deborah Anne. **Educ:** Marian Coll Indpls, BS 1950; Univ of SD, MA 1970, EdD 1976. **Career:** IN Univ Med Ctr, lab tech (clin biochem) 1950-53; Carver Found-Tuskegee Inst, tissue culture tech 1954-57; Elk Point Pub Sch, high school teacher 1969-73, teacher corps team leader 1973-75; grad intern sci consult AEA 12-Sioux City 1975-76; proj writer-HEW grant Univ of SD 1976-77; Univ of SD, asst prof/dir of outreach beginning 1977; assoc prof, C/I, beginning 1988, assoc –dean, school of education, 1990. **Orgs:** State pres Epsilon Sigma Alpha Int 1977-78; chap pres Phi Delta Kappa (USD chpt) 1979-80; state pres Assn of Tchr Educators 1979-80; exec director, South Dakota Assoc of Middle Level Education; international pres, Epsilon Sigma Alpha Int, 1986-87. **Honors/Awds:** Pub in ''Leaders of Amer Sec Educators'' 1972; voc educ ''A Challenging Alternative for the Gifted/Talented Student'' 1976; voc educ ''A New Dimension for the Gifted/Talented Student'' 1976; ''Education-A Lifelong Process'' ESA Jour 1980; Helping to make the transition from high school to College, 1988; The Effect of Assertive Discipline & Training, Reducing Anxiety and Stress in the Student Teaching Setting, The Teacher Educ Autumn, 1993; Implementing Middle School Concepts in Rural Areas, Problems & Solutions, Middle School Journal, Sept, 1994.

MILBURN, GLYN CURT
Professional football player. **Personal:** Born Feb 19, 1971, Santa Monica, CA. **Educ:** Stanford, bachelor's degree in public policy. **Career:** Denver Broncos, wide receiver, 1993-95; Detroit Lions, 1996-. **Honors/Awds:** Pro Bowl, 1995. **Business Addr:** Professional Football Player, Detroit Lions, 1200 Featherstone Rd, Pontiac, MI 48342, (248)335-4131.

MILBURN, RODNEY. See Obituaries section.

MILES, ALBERT BENJAMIN, JR.
Communications company executive. **Personal:** Born Jan 7, 1956, Brooklyn, NY; son of Marguerite & Albert Miles, Sr; married Susan J Burns Miles, Aug 23, 1981; children: A Benjamin III, Claire. **Educ:** Wesleyan University, BA, 1978, MLS, 1990; Northwestern University, Kellogg Executive Program, Certificate, 1987; RPI, MBA, 1992. **Career:** SNET, manager, corporate data ctr, 1988-94, director, corporate data network, 1994-95; Citizens Utilities, director, pinnacle project, 1995-96, director, corporate strategic architecture, 1997-. **Orgs:** Dixwell Community Ctr, board of directors, 1988-93; Guide, 1988-90; Share, 1988-90; New Haven Boys Club, board of directors, 1989-90; Meriden CT/SNET Business Partnership, founding mem, 1990-93; Community Health Ctr, board of directors, 1990-95; Lenua S Williams, MD, board of directors, 1991-; Special Olympics World Games, communications director, 1995. **Honors/Awds:** Dixwell Community Ctr, Service Awd, 1993. **Business Addr:** Director, Citizens Utilities, High Ridge Office Pk, Stamford, CT 06905, (203)595-6657.

MILES, CARLOTTA G.
Physician. **Personal:** Born Sep 19, 1937, St Augustine, FL; married Theodore A; children: Wendell Gordon, Cecily Allison, Lydia Carlotta. **Educ:** Wheaton Coll, AB 1959; Howard Univ Med Sch, MD 1964. **Career:** Pvt Practice, physician 1968-; Area B Children's Program, co-dir 1969-71. **Orgs:** Mem APA; Am Academy of Child Psychiatry; affiliate mem Am Psychoanalytic Inst; tching & supervising analyst Children's Hosp; asst prof psychiatry Howard Univ Coll of Med; faculty Washington Sch of Psychiatry; trustee Wheaton Coll; Black Student Fund of Washington The Potomac Sch; Woodley House. **Honors/Awds:** Clerkship Prize for excellence in psychiatry Howard Univ Med Sch 1964. **Business Addr:** 3000 Conn Ave NW, Washington, DC 20008.

MILES, E. W.
Educator. **Personal:** Born May 4, 1934, Hearne, TX; married Frances Winfield; children: Tony W, Christopher W. **Educ:** Prairie View Univ, BA 1955; IN Univ, AM 1960, PhD 1962. **Career:** Prairie View Univ, assoc prof 1962-65; Univ of NC, visiting faculty scholar 1965-66; IN Univ, visiting summer prof 1966; So Univ, 1967; Univ of TX, 1971; San Diego State Univ, prof polit sci 1966-. **Orgs:** Trustee, Center for Research and Development in Law Related Education, 1991-; president, San Diego & Imperial Counties, 1990-, delgate-at-large, Natl Bd, 1989-, American Civil Liberties Union; chmn of bd San Diego Urban League 1983-; bd of dirs Law in Amer Soc Found; chmn Com on Status of Blacks of the Amer Polit Sci Assn; past mem exec council Western Polit Sci Assn; adv panel CA Bd of Educ 1969-70; San Diego Blue Ribbon Com for Charter Review 1968; assoc edit West Pol Sci Quarterly; exec com CA State Assembly Fellowship Prog; State-Wide Anti-Discrim Com; Unit Prof of CA. **Honors/Awds:** San Diego State Univ, Distinguished Teaching Award, 1968. **Special Achievements:** Co-author: Vital Issues of the Constitution, 1975; author of various scholarly articles. **Military Serv:** US Army, 1st lt, 1955-57. **Business Addr:** Professor, San Diego State Univ, Dept of Polit Science, San Diego, CA 92182.

MILES, EDWARD LANCELOT
Educator. **Personal:** Born Dec 21, 1939; son of Louise Dufont Miles and Cecil B Miles; married Wanda Elaine Merrick (divorced); children: Anthony Roger, Leila Yvonne. **Educ:** Howard Univ, BA, w/honors, 1962; Univ of Denver Graduate School of Intl Studies, PhD, 1965. **Career:** Univ of Denver, instr 1965-66, asst prof, 1966-70; Univ of Denver Graduate School of Intl Studies, assoc prof 1970-74; Univ of WA, prof, Marine Studies & Public Affairs 1974-; dir, School of Marine Affairs, 1982-93; Virginia & Prentice Bloedel Professor of Marine Students & Public Affairs, 1994-99. **Orgs:** mem, Ocean Policy Comm, Natl Rsch Council, 1970-74, chmn 1974-79; mem, bd of editors intl org, 1969-77; exec bd, Univ of Hawaii-Law of the Sea Inst, 1971-; assoc ed, ''Ocean Devel & Intl Law Journal'' 1973-; joint appointee Micronesian Maritime Auth Fed States Micr, 1977-83; chief negotiator, Micronesian Maritime Authority, 1983-92; chmn, advisory comm on intl programs, Natl Science Foundation, 1990-93. **Honors/Awds:** Honors in history Phi Beta Kappa 1962; Intl Affairs Fellow Cncl on Foreign Relations Inc 1972-73; James P Warburg Fellow Harvard Univ 1973-74; Council on Foreign Relations, 1990. **Business Addr:** School of Marine Affairs, University of Washington, HF-05 3707 Brooklyn NE, Seattle, WA 98195.

MILES, FRANK J. W.
Business executive. **Personal:** Born Dec 18, 1944, Orange, NJ; married Brenda. **Educ:** Columbia U, MBA; Hampton U, BA. **Career:** State of NJ, major account relationships; Citibank NA Nat Black MBA Assn, vp; Urban Bankers Assn; NJ Real Estate Assn. **Orgs:** Vol Urban Consult Minority Bus; former Mayor's Appointee Exxex Co Econ Devel Corp Omego Psi Phi Frat. **Military Serv:** AUS capt. **Business Addr:** 100 Wood Ave, Iselin, NJ 08830.

MILES, FREDERICK AUGUSTUS
Psychiatrist. **Personal:** Born May 25, 1928, Boston, MA; married Cora Edythe; children: Frederick, Felix, Andre. **Educ:** VA St Coll, BS 1949; Columbia U, 1951; Army Lang Sch, 1952; Hunter Coll, 1955; Univ Basel Switzerland, 1958; Univ Freiburg, W Germany, MD 1964. **Career:** Brooklyn-Cumberland Med Cntr, internship & res pathology 1966-68; Brooklyn State Hosp, residency psychiatry 1969-72; Pvt Prac, psychiatrist; Brooklyn State Hosp, staff psychiatrist; Willia Hardgrow Mental Health Clinic, consult psychiatrist. **Orgs:** Mem AMA; APA; NY & Kings Co Med Soc; AAGP; ACEP; ACP; Provident Med Soc of Brooklyn; mem United Demo Club; Kappa Alpha Psi; bd trustees Redeemer Bapt Ch; AFAM. **Military Serv:** AUS German interrogator 1952-55. **Business Addr:** 808 New York Ave, Brooklyn, NY 11203.

MILES, JACOB
Toy executive. **Personal:** marrled Rosalind Bell. **Career:** General Electric; General Mills-Kenner Products, mgr of engineering, 1975-1985; Tonka Corp, sr dir of operations, 1985-91; Cultural Exchange Entertainment Corp./Cultural toys, pres/CEO, 1993-. **Honors/Awds:** Black Enterprise mag, Emerging Company of the Year, 1997. **Special Achievements:** First African American owned full-line toy company in the U.S.

MILES, JUNE C.
Judge. **Personal:** Born Jun 24, 1939, Boston, MA; daughter of Gladyce Satterwhite Miles and William D Miles; married Manuel (divorced); children: Monique Soares, Manuel. **Educ:** Northeastern Univ (cum laude), BA 1962; Northeastern Univ School of Law, JD 1973. **Career:** Boston Juvenile Court, associate justice, 1990-; Gonsalves, attorney, pvt prac 1979-90; Univ Lowell, assoc prof dept of criminal justice 1979-90; affirmative action offcr 1973-78. **Orgs:** Distngshd mem Affirmative Action Offcrs in MA Pub & Pvt Edn; mem Lowell Bar Assn/MA Bar Assn; mem MA Black Lawyers Assn; mem Black Genesis Found 1974-; bd of dirs Urban League of Eastern MA 1978-82; pres Greater Lowell YWCA 1980; pres Merrimack Valley NAACP 1985-90; mem Mass Black Women Attorneys; mem Mass Women Lawyers; bd of trustees, MA School of Law at Andover 1988-90; bd dirs, First Foundation 1986-90; chairperson, Lowell Human Rights Planning Committee 1987-90; mem, Mass Judges Conference; Mass Black Judge's Conference, pres, 1996-. **Honors/Awds:** Woman of the Yr Northeastern Univ 1962; Black Achievers Boston YMCA 1978; outstndg serv AAOMPHE 1979; Beulah Pierce Mem Award Greater Lowell Black Heritage Com 1980; Community Serv Awd YMCA 1985; Martin Luther King Jr Awd Univ of Lowell 1985; Certificate of Achievement, Tribute to Women in Industry, Lawrence YWCA 1988; Street Lawyers, Certificate of Appreciation; Mass Black Lawyer's Assn Achievement Award. **Business Addr:** Associate Justice, Boston Juvenile Court, Pemberton Square, Boston, MA 02108, (617)725-8570.

MILES, MARY P.
State government official. **Personal:** Born May 5, 1948, St Matthews, SC; children: Donald, Thaddeus, Handy Jr. **Educ:** Orangeburg Technical College, AA 1968; South Carolina State College, BS 1980; University of South Carolina, MEd. **Career:** South Carolina State Legislator, representative, District 93, currently. **Orgs:** Vice pres, Calhoun NAACP; advisor, Youth Council NAACP; bd mem, Citizens Against Sexual Assault; Zeta Phi Beta; South Carolina Personnel & Guidance Assn; School Guidance Committee; Assn for Counselor Education; South Carolina Mental Health Assn; Fed of Eastern Stars; pres, Citizens in Action. **Honors/Awds:** Concerned Citizen Award, Zeta Phi Beta 1982; Presidential Scholar, South Carolina State College; Key South Carolina Legislator, Ebony Magazine 1984; Woman of the Year, Alpha Kappa Mu 1984. **Business Addr:** Representative Dist 93, House of Representatives, 5000 Thurmond Mall, Ste 114, Columbia, SC 29201.

MILES, NORMAN KENNETH
Clergyman, educator. **Personal:** Born Dec 5, 1946, Toledo, OH; son of Sadie Miles and Mervin Miles; married Doris Calandra Goree; children: Erica Lynette, Norman Jr, Candace Renee, Kira Danette, Neal Mervyn. **Educ:** Oakwood Coll, BA Theology 1964-68; Andrews Univ Seventh Day Adventist Theological Seminary, MDiv 1972-73; Univ of Michigan, MA 1974, PhD 1978. **Career:** Economic Opportunity Planning Assoc, work counselor 1968-69; South Central Conf & 7th Day Adventists, pastor 1969-72; Lake Regional Conf 7th Day Adventists, pastor 1974-77; 7th Day Adventists, prof 1977-; Andrews Univ, prof Urban Ministry; Univ of Michigan, Ann Arbor MI, adjunct prof of religion 1977-; Hyde Park Seventh-Day Adventist Church, Chicago IL, pastor 1989-; Andrews Univ, Berrien Springs, MI, Chmn of Christian Ministry Dept, 1988-. **Orgs:** Mp Ministerial Alliance, Hattiesburg MS, 1969-72; bd of dir Southern Mississippi Chapter Amer Red Cross; mem Natl Black Pastors Conf 1980-; dir Inst of Human Relations 7th Day Adventist Church 1983. **Honors/Awds:** John Pierce Award, Historical Scholarship Univ of Michigan 1975. **Business Addr:** Professor of Urban Ministry, Chairman, Dept of Christian Ministry, Andrews University, Berrien Springs, MI 49104.

MILES, RACHEL JEAN
Educator. **Personal:** Born Sep 3, 1945, Memphis, TN; married Willie T; children: Lisa, Jason. **Educ:** Lemoyne-Owen Coll, BS 1967; Memphis State U, EdM guidance & counseling 1970; Memphis State Univ , post graduate 1971. **Career:** Shelby State Comm Coll, coor of counseling adv 1975-, prof coun 1972-75; Fairview Jr High Sch, coun engl tch 1971-72; Moorestown Township Coll Prep, guidance counselor 1971; Memphis State U, couns 1969-70; Memphis City Sch Sys, elem tchr 1967-68. **Orgs:** Pres bd of dirs Human Employment Resources Inc 1979-80; workshop presenter Am Personnel & Guidance Assn 1980; mem JUGS Charitable Orgn 1967-; mem Cherokee Com Civic Club 1969-; secr Westlawn-Galveston Block Club 1972-; bd of dirs Miss Black Memphis Pageant 1979-80. **Honors/Awds:** Deans List Lemoyne-owen Coll 1967; Kappa Delta Pi H Onor Soc Memphis State Univ 1970; Phi Delta Kappa Memphis State Univ 1971; Colonel Aide De Camp Gov Ray Blanton 1977-78; appointed Limited Constitutional Convention of the State of TN Pres JD Lee & Delegates Micheal Hooks & Roscoe Dixon 1977-78; Honorary Staff Mem TN House of Repr 1977-78. **Business Addr:** Shelby State Comm Coll, 737 Union Ave, Memphis, TN 38104.

MILES, RUBY A. BRANCH
Librarian. **Personal:** Born Sep 6, 1941, Houston, TX; daughter of Ernestine Phelps Branch and Richard Andrew Branch; widowed. **Educ:** Prairie View A&M University, BS, education, 1963; Atlanta University, MLS, 1969. **Career:** Atlanta Fulton Public Library, child/young adult librarian, 1969-71, Branch Head, 1971-77; Houston Independent School District, Houston Technical Institute, librarian, 1977-79, Gregory-Lincoln Education Center, librarian, 1979-85, Bellaire High School, librarian, 1986-90, DeBakey High School for Health Professions, librarian, 1990-; Houston Community College System, part-time campus librarian, 1985-92; Houston Academy of Medicine, Texas Medical Ctr Library, part-time librarian, 1997-. **Orgs:** American Library Association, 1984-, Young Adult Service Association Committee, 1984-88, 1992-96; American Association of University Women, 1971-; Texas Library Association, 1991-92. **Honors/Awds:** First Runner Up ''Librarian of the Year,'' 1993-94, Houston Ind School District. **Home Addr:** 4514 Connies Ct Ln, Missouri City, TX 77459. **Business Addr:** Librarian, Michael E DeBakey High School for Health Professions, Houston Independent School District, 3100 Shenandoah, Houston, TX 77021-1097, (713)746-5215.

MILES, STEEN
Broadcast journalist. **Personal:** Born Aug 20, 1946, South Bend, IN; daughter of Rose E Wheeler Davis (deceased) and Rev Austin A Davis (deceased); divorced; children: Kellie J King Middleton, Heather Lynne King. **Educ:** Ball St University, business education, English; Indiana University, communications; Daniel School of Management. **Career:** WNDU-TV, reporter/anchor/talk show hostess, 1969-73; WMAQ, NBC Radio, reporter/anchor, 1973-78; WGCI, news director, 1978-80; United Press International, broadcast editor, 1981-84; WXIA-TV, assignment editor, 1984-86, managing editor, 1986-89, reporter/anchor, 1989-. **Orgs:** SCLC, mentor, 1995-; Jack and Jill of America Stone Mountain, president, 1988-92; Dekalb County Chamber of Commerce, board member, 1988-91; Natl Academy of Television Arts and Sciences, board member, 1988-91; Victims Witness Assistance Advisory Board, board member, 1992-; Salvation Army Advisory Board, board member, 1988-92; Atlanta Assn of Black Journalists, 1989-;

Natl Association of Media Women, 1989-; Georgia Association of Broadcasters, 1982-84; Decatur-Dekalb Coalition of 100 Black Women, charter mem; Dekalb Academy of Leaders; Project Impact, board member, 1994-. **Honors/Awds:** National Association of Media Women, Pioneer Award, 1976; One Emmy; Three Emmy Nominations, Two Best Newscast, Best Feature, 1989-91; National Association of Black Journalists Award, Four Best TV Feature, 1989, 1992; United Press International, Best Spot News, 1976; Georgia Associated Press, Best Feature, 1991. **Special Achievements:** YWCA, 11 alive, Woman of Achievement, 1988; Dollars and Sense Magazine, 100 Best and Brightest Women, 1989; Toney Gardens Civic Association, Community Service Award, 1992; Bush Administration White House Luncheon, 1989; Carter Administration White House Briefing, 1979; AABJ, Pioneer Journalist of the Year, 1996. **Business Addr:** Reporter/Anchor, WXIA-TV, 1611 W Peachtree St, Atlanta, GA 30309, (770)873-9104.

MILES, VERA M.
Government official. **Personal:** Born Jan 3, 1932, Fostoria, OH; daughter of Luella Talmadge Jackson and Joseph Alexander Jackson; married Paul E Miles, Oct 20, 1951 (died 1989); children: Paul J, Ronald C, Linda A, Leah Miles-King, Lisa Miles Brady. **Educ:** Music Conservatory, Toledo; North West Tech, Archbold, photojournalism. **Career:** Paulding Village, Paulding, OH, council person; Paulding Village, Paulding, OH, mayor, 1988-. **Orgs:** Tri-County Mental Health, 1977-89; 5 County Alcohol & Drug Programs, 1984-89; board member, PIC JTPA Programs, 1984-88; council person, Village Council Member, 1984-87; CIC, president, 1992; Paulding County Governor's Safety Committee Network, chairperson; Paulding County Emergency (Disaster) Management Programs; Melrose United Methodist Church, teacher, song leader; County Mayors Association, president; AARP; Defiance District Officer, United Methodist Women as Christian Social Involvement, coordinator. **Honors/Awds:** Governor's Award for Excellence in Education Concerning Safety, nominated by Lt David D Myers, OSP Post #81, Van Wert, 1992. **Special Achievements:** Certified Lay Speaker. **Business Addr:** Mayor, Paulding Village, 116 S Main, Paulding, OH 45879.

MILES, VIC. See LEVY, VICTOR MILES, JR.

MILES, WILLIE LEANNA
Association executive. **Personal:** Born in Vienna, GA; daughter of Leanna Wood Miles and John Miles. **Educ:** Florida A&M Univ Tallahassee; Univ of District of Columbia, Washington, DC, BS, 1982. **Career:** Assn for Prog & Dev of Assn for Study of Afro-Am Life & Hist, 1943; Fed Gov Washington, DC, suprvr supply req officer 1942-57; ASALH Inc, admin asst 1957-72; Assn for the Study of Afro-American Life & History, associate for program & development, ASALH, 1973-81; Associated Publishers, managing director, 1981-. **Orgs:** Visited most major cities in US promoting work of Assn for the study of Afro-Amer Life & Hist. **Honors/Awds:** Recep num awds for educ achievement; Achieve Award Educ Assn 1968; Serv Award Assn for Study of Afro-Am Life & Hist 1971; Founder's Day Speaker Philadelphia Branch & Steadfast Devotion & outstanding service award Assn for the Study Of Afro-Am Life & History Inc May 17, 1975; Outstanding Service Honored at 75th ASALH Meeting, Chicago branch, 1990.

MILES-LAGRANGE, VICKI
Judge. **Educ:** Vassar Coll; Howard Univ, School of Law; Univ of Ghana. **Career:** TV news reporter; Speaker of the US House of Representatives, Carl Albert, congressional aide; Federal Court, District Judge Woodrow Seals, SD Tex, law clerk; Oklahoma County, asst dist attorney; Oklahoma Senate, state senator; US Attorney, Oklahama; US District Federal Judge, currently. **Orgs:** Kirkpatrick Museum & Planetarium, board of directors; Oklahoma Children's Museum; Alpha Kappa Alpha Sorority; Links Inc; Jack & Jill of America; Urban League, life mem; NAACP; Oklahoma Heritage Association; America Bar Association; Oklahoma Bar Association; Oklahoma Black Lawyers Association. **Honors/Awds:** Honorary Doctor of Laws, Oklahoma City University. **Business Addr:** US District Judge, 200 NW 4th St, Rm 5011, Oklahoma City, OK 73102, (405)231-4518.

MILEY, DEBRA CHARLET
Sales executive. **Personal:** Born Dec 8, 1963, Atlanta, GA; daughter of Leila Mae Williams Miley and Charles Miley Sr; children: Brandy. **Educ:** Georgia State Univ, Atlanta GA, BS Public & Urban Affairs, 1988. **Career:** Courtyard by Marriott, Atlanta GA, front desk supvr, 1986-89, sales coord, 1989-90; JW Marriott Hotel at Lenox, Atlanta, GA, sales assistant, 1990-. **Orgs:** Mem, Natl Coalition of Black Meeting Planners, 1987-. **Home Addr:** 1937 Smokey Rd, La Grange, GA 30240.

MILLARD, THOMAS LEWIS
Educator. **Personal:** Born Mar 8, 1927, Newark, NJ; son of Elizabeth Millard and James Millard; married P Anne Kelsic; children: Elizabeth Millard Reaves, Thomas Lewis Jr, James Edward. **Educ:** Rutgers Univ, AB 1952; Columbia Univ, MS 1956; New York Univ, MA 1960; Columbia Univ, 3rd Year Certificate 1969; The Drug Dependence Institute, Yale University School of Medicine 1971; Fairleigh Dickerson Univ, EdD 1976. **Career:** New York Youth Serv Bureau, youth parole officer 1956-59; United Parent Assoc, New York City Bd of Educ, consultant in comm school rel 1959-60; Irvington House, social worker 1960-61; Public Schools, school soc worker Newark Brd of Ed 1961-65; Montclair State Univ, prof of educ, social work and coord of school social work. **Orgs:** Bd of dirs Mental Health Assoc of Morris Cnty 1983-, The Mental Health Assoc in New Jersey; vice chmn bd of trustees New Jersey Neuro Psychiatric Inst 1977-79; bd of dir ALFRE Inc (Alcoholic Trmnt Fac) 1981-84; bd of dir New Jersey State Prison Complex 1979-81; fellow Amer Orthopsychiatric Assn 1982; pres, bd of educ Orange NJ 1968-71; delegate White House Conf on Children 1970; consulting editor The Clearing House Journal 1981-; consulting editor Int Journal of Adolesence and Youth 1990-; consulting editor Journal of Educators and Scholars 1985-. **Honors/Awds:** Diplomate in Prfsnl Psychotherapy Int, Academy of Behavioral Medicine and Professional Counseling, 1983; licensed Marital and Family Therapist, NJ 1983; Honored by NJ State Assembly in Resolution Citing Outstanding Teaching; appointed mem by Governor to New Jersey State Bd of Marriage Counselor Examiners; author of professional journal articles and chapters in textbooks; presented scholarly papers at conferences in US, Canada, Puerto Rico, Africa, Europe, Australia, Japan and Mexico. **Military Serv:** AUS lt col USAR-RET ACTIVE & reserve; WW II Ribbon, Occupation Ribbon (Japan), Victory Medal 1946. **Home Addr:** 5 Overlook Ave, Randolph, NJ 07869. **Business Addr:** Prof Educ & Soc Work, Montclair State Univ, Upper Montclair, NJ 07043.

MILLEDGE, LUETTA UPSHUR
Educational administrator. **Personal:** Born in Savannah, GA; children: Dr Marshall L Upshur. **Educ:** Ft Valley State Coll, BA English 1948; Atlanta Univ, MA English 1949; Univ Georgia, PhD English 1971. **Career:** Savannah State Coll, asst instructor 1949-, assoc prof, prof, chr div humn 1973-80, hd dept English 1972-80, hd dept humnl/fine arts 1980-84, head department of humanities 1984-91, professor emerita 1991-. **Orgs:** Brd mem GA Endowment for Humanities 1980-83; Elder Butler Presbytery Churh; mem Presid Comm Futr Savannah State Coll. **Honors/Awds:** Regent's Scholarship 1944-48; Ford Found Fellowship 1969-71; George Washington Honor Medal; Freedoms Found Valley Forge Speech Vital Spchs 1973; Phi Kappa Phi, Phi Beta Kappa, Univ of GA; Co-Teacher of the Year School of Humanities 1989. **Home Addr:** 918 Carver St, Savannah, GA 31401.

MILLENDER, DHARATHULA H.
Educational administrator (retired). **Personal:** Born Feb 4, 1920, Terre Haute; daughter of Daisy Ernestine Eslick Hood and Orestes Hood; married Justyn L Millender, 1944 (deceased); children: Naomi Estelle, Justine Faye, Preston (Isaac). **Educ:** Indiana State Univ, BS, 1941; Purdue Univ, MS, 1967; additional work several Universitys. **Career:** Dunbar-Pulaski School Gary, librn media specialist 1960-78; Houston Jr High School Baltimore, librn 1953-60; Lincoln Jr High Montgomery Co, teacher 1952-53; Serv Club#2 Indianatown & Gap Mil Reser, army librn 1944; Netherlands Stds Unit Libr of Congress, ref asst 1943-44; Pmoney HS, librn teacher 1942-43; Bettis Jr Coll, librn 1941-42; Black Exper Film News Mag, ed 1973-82; Gary School System, librarian/media specialist 1960-78, school radio station, 1978-83, reading lab coord 1979-82. **Orgs:** Chairperson, founder, Gary Hist & Cultural Soc 1977; Gary Precinct Committeewoman 1972-80; former organist St Philip Luth Church; pres NIMM Educ Media Serv Inc; Louis Armstrong - Rev Simon & Schuster, 1997; author 4 Books & num articles in journ & educ mags; libr Multi-Media Counsul Model Cities Dayton 1969-70; devel libr from storeroom using para-profes tchr help; libr Media Consul Model Cities Gary dev media cntr at Comm Research Cntr Gary; prog oord Cable TV Gary channel 3a 1973-; radio program Lift Every Voice & Sing sta WWCA, mat from Black Exper State dir Assn for Study of Afro-Am Life & Hist 1973; State Hist IN Black Pol Caucus 1973; hist Gary Chptr IN State Black Caucus 1973; former state chrmn Hist & Cul 1966-72; chrmn Gary NAACP Black Hist Com 1962-72; libr trustee Gary Pub Libr 1971-75, 1982-86; founder & CEO, Gary Historical & Cultural Society Inc, 1971-; historian, Natl Black Caucus - Natl League of Cities, 1984-92; consultant, Follow Through Cultural Linguistic Approach 1989-; mem, Gary City Council, 1980-92; historian, City of Gary; vp, Gary School Bd of Trustees, 1992-; organizer & secretary, Peace Lutheran Church of Gary, 1989-. **Honors/Awds:** Recip Commendable Book by an Indiana author Crispus Attucks Indiana Writers Conf 1966; outstanding serv Rendered to Comm Award Gary NAACP 1966; Media Women's Award, Natl Assn of Media Women 1974; Outstanding Women of Lake County, Indiana 1984; Brief Note on the Early Development of Lake County & Gary, Indiana, published by Gary Historical & Cultural Society, Inc 1988; History of Gary City Council, 1992; Revised, 1995. **Home Addr:** 2409 W 5 Ave, Gary, IN 46404.

MILLENDER, MALLORY KIMERLING
Editor, publisher & educator. **Personal:** Born Jul 11, 1942, Birmingham, AL; married Jacqueline Stripling; children: Mallory Jr, Marlon. **Educ:** Paine Coll, BA (cum laude) English Lit, 1964; Univ Toulouse (French), 1966; KS State Teachers Coll, MS Foreign Lang, 1969; Columbia Univ, MS Journalism, 1977. **Career:** Paine Coll, asst prof 1967-; Augusta News Review, editor & publisher 1974-; Paine Coll, coord foreign lang 1977-, dean admissions 1971-. **Orgs:** Tchr TW Josey High Schl 1964-67; mem Brd Trts of Paine Coll 1980-82; vice pres Brd Trts of Antioch Bpt Chrh 1971-; pres New Grow Inc 1971-. **Honors/Awds:** Best column Natl Nwspr Publs Assoc Merit Awd 1983; flw Time Inc 1977; fclty flw United Negro Coll Fnd 1976-77; french govt tchg asst, Fulbright US and French Govt 1968-69. **Business Addr:** Editor & Publisher, Paine Coll, 1235 15th St, Augusta, GA 30910.

MILLENDER-MCDONALD, JUANITA M.
Congresswoman. **Personal:** Born Sep 7, 1938. **Educ:** Univ of Redlands, BS, 1981; California State Univ, MEd. **Career:** Teacher; Carson City Council, 1990-92; California State Assembly, 1993-96; US House of Representatives, congresswoman, 1996-. **Business Addr:** Congresswoman, US House of Representatives, 419 Cannon House Office Bldg, Washington, DC 20515-0537.

MILLER, ANDREA LEWIS
Educator. **Personal:** Born Sep 10, 1954, Memphis, TN; married Robert A Miller; children: Meredith Mechelle. **Educ:** LeMoyne Owen Coll, BS 1976; Atlanta Univ, MS 1978, PhD 1980. **Career:** Univ of Cincinnati Coll of Med, postdoctoral fellow 1980-82; LeMoyne Owen Coll, prof of biol, assoc investigator 1982-83, pof biol, principal invest 1983-. **Orgs:** Mem Memphis Volunteer Placement Prog 1973, Alpha Kappa 1973, Amer Soc of Cell Biologist 1981; pres LeMoyne Owen Coll Faculty Org 1984-86; mem SoutheastElectron Microscopy Soc 1985, Electron Microscopy Soc of Amer 1985. **Honors/Awds:** Predcotoral Fellowship Natl Inst of Health 1977-80; Rsch Awd Lederle Labs 1980; Rsch Grant Natl Inst of Health 1983-86; Premed Ed Grant United Negro Coll Fund 1984-; Doe Research Grant. **Business Addr:** Assoc Professor of Biology, LeMoyne Owen College, 807 Walker Ave, Memphis, TN 38126.

MILLER, ANNA M.
Association executive. **Personal:** Born May 15, 1923, New Orleans; married Martin W; children: Walter P, Loretta E, Fatima M. **Educ:** Xavier Univ New Orleans, BS (cum laude) 1943; Cath Sch Soc Serv Wash, DC, 1944; Howard U, 1945. **Career:** Chester Cit Info Cntr, chmn steering com 1969-; NAACP, chmn voter reg 1963-; League Women Voters, chmn 1964-70; Centennial Com IHMC, co-chairperson 1971-74; Human Concerns Com YWCA, chmn 1971-. **Orgs:** Mem Chester Rep Theatre 1969. **Honors/Awds:** Comm Serv award 5th United Presb Ch 1967; Hum Serv award Chester Br NAACP 1973.

MILLER, ANTHONY (LAWRENCE ANTHONY)
Professional football player. **Personal:** Born Apr 15, 1965, Los Angeles, CA. **Educ:** Attended: San Diego State Univ, Pasadena City College, Univ of Tennessee. **Career:** San Diego Chargers, wide receiver, 1988-93; Denver Broncos, 1994-96; Dallas Cowboys, 1997-. **Honors/Awds:** Pro Bowl, 1989, 1990, 1992, 1993, 1995. **Business Addr:** Professional Football Player, Dallas Cowboys, One Cowboys Pkwy, Irving, TX 75063, (214)556-9900.

MILLER, ANTHONY
Professional basketball player. **Personal:** Born Oct 22, 1971, Benton Harbor, MI. **Educ:** Michigan State University, bachelor's degree in criminal justice. **Career:** Los Angeles Lakers, forward, 1994-97; Atlanta Hawks, 1997-. **Business Addr:** Professional Basketball Player, Atlanta Hawks, One CNN Center, Ste 405, Atlanta, GA 30335, (404)827-3800.

MILLER, ANTHONY GLENN
Cleric. **Personal:** Born Sep 24, 1959, Los Angeles, CA; son of Lillian Lois Gray-Miller and Isaac Nimrod Miller. **Educ:** Univ of Southern California, BA, 1984; General Theological Seminary, MDiv, 1988; Graduate Institute of Religion & Health, certified pastoral counselor, 1993; Yale Univ, STM, 1994. **Career:** Parish of Trinity Church, seminarian, 1985-86; St Philip's Episcopal Church, seminarian intern, 1986-87; Church of the Heavenly Rest, seminarian, 1987; Church of the Transfiguration, associate rector, 1989-91; Diocese of Long Island, executive officer to the bishop, 1988-92; St Andrew's Episcopal Church, vicar, 1993-. **Orgs:** Diocese of Long Island Commission on Ministry, 1993, Diocesan Epsicopal AIDS Committee, 1993; General Board of Examining Chaplains, GOE reader, 1993; Presiding Bishop's Fund for World Relief, Long Island representative Guatemala program, 1992; General Theological Seminary, dean's search committee, 1992, junior tutorial program, tutor, 1991. **Honors/Awds:** I Am Somebody, essay contest, 1973. **Business Addr:** President, The MillMoore Productions, 2350 S Merrick Ave, Merrick, NY 11566.

MILLER, ARTHUR J.
Management consultant. **Personal:** Born Oct 7, 1934, New York, NY; son of Rosalie White Miller and Theodore Roosevelt Miller; married Mary Lee, Feb 19, 1966 (deceased). **Career:** Chase Manhattan Bank, dividend clerk 1952, supvr 1961, sys planning ofcr 1968, 2nd vice pres 1970, vice pres banking 1974-87; AJM Assoc, Inc, pres l988; Business Systems Mgmt, Inc, principal, 1989, president, 1992-. **Orgs:** Chairman of the board

of directors, Reality House Inc. **Honors/Awds:** Angel Guardian Family Service, Man of the Year, 1997. **Military Serv:** AUS Corpl 1955-58. **Business Addr:** President, Business Systems Mgmt, Inc, 150 Broadway, Suite 812, New York, NY 10038.

MILLER, BERNICE JOHNSON
Educational administrator. **Personal:** Born in Chicago, IL; married George Benjamin Miller; children: Benita, Michael. **Educ:** Roosevelt Univ Chicago IL, BA; Chicago Teachers Coll, MA 1965; CAS Harvard Univ Grad School of Ed, 1968-69, EdD 1972; Harvard Univ Grad School of Ed, 1972. **Career:** Chicago Bd of Ed, teacher elem & hs 1950-66; The New School for Children Inc, headmistress 1966-68; Jackson Coll, assoc dean 1968-70; Radcliffe, instr1970-73; Harvard Grad School of Ed, assoc dir 1971-75; Boston Public Schools Lucy Stone School, principal 1977-78; Boston Public Schools, sr officer 1978-84; Harvard Grad School, dir high tech rsch proj 1983-84; City Coll of Chgo, pres, currently. **Orgs:** Bd mem, Children's World Day Care Ctr Boston 1972-84, Blue Cross/Blue Shield Boston, United Way; trustee, Brigham's & Women's Hosp Med Found; mem 1968-84, pres, United Commun Plng Corp 1983-85; bd mem, Chicago Metro History Fair Bd; mem, Mayor's Commiss on Women. **Honors/Awds:** Educator's Award Boston 350th Anniv of Boston MA 1980; Educator of the Year Urban Bankers Ed Awd Boston 1982; Woman of the Year Awd Assoc of Mannequins 1984; Woman in Ed Business & Professional Women Boston & Vicinity 1984; Freedom Awd Roosevelt Univ 1985; Disting Alumni of Chicago State Univ NABSE 1985; Outstanding Achievement Awd in Educ YWCA 1986; Minority Networking Org of Focus & Seana Mag Serv Awd 1986. **Business Addr:** President, Harold Washington College, 30 E Lake St, Chicago, IL 60601.

MILLER, BUBBA
Professional football player. **Personal:** Born Aug 29, 1973, Floresville, TX. **Educ:** Tennessee, attended. **Career:** Philadelphia Eagles, center, 1996-. **Business Addr:** Professional Football Player, Philadelphia Eagles, 3501 S Broad St, Philadelphia, PA 19148, (215)463-2500.

MILLER, C. CONRAD, JR. (CLARENCE)
Advertising executive. **Personal:** Born Jul 16, 1950, Little Rock, AR; son of Bernice Beatrice Jaudon Miller and Clarence Conrad Miller Sr; married Sherrin Ellen Johnson, May 24, 1980; children: Andrew, Lauren. **Educ:** Fort Hays Kansas State University, BS, 1973; University of Michigan, MM, 1974, doctoral studies, 1975-76. **Career:** Ortho Pharmaceutical Corp, sales representative, 1977-78, sales training manager, 1979-81, district sales manager, 1981-83, product manager, 1983-86, product director, 1986-88, sr product director, 1988-90; Dudnyk Co, account group director, 1990-91; vp, 1992-. **Orgs:** Healthcare Marketing and Communications Council, 1991-; Branchburg (NJ) Environmental Commission, 1985-86; Business Council for the Arts, volunteer, 1983-84. **Honors/Awds:** University of Michigan, Horace H Rackham Doctoral Fellow, 1973-76. **Business Addr:** VP, Planning/Business Development, Dudnyk Healthcare Communications, 100 Tournament Dr, Ste 100, Horsham, PA 19044, (215)443-9406.

MILLER, CARROLL LEE
Educational administrator. **Personal:** Born Aug 20, 1909, Washington. **Educ:** Howard U, BA (magna cum laude) 1929, MA 1930; Columbia Tchrs Coll, EdD 1952. **Career:** Miles Coll, instr 1930-31; Howard U, mem faculty 1931-, prof educ 1957-, chmn dept 1961-68; Coll Liberal Arts, asso dean 1961-64; Grad Sch, dean 1966-74, prof higher educ 1974-, dir summer session 1964-70; DC Pub Schs Winings, instr social studies 1933-40; Commonwealth, VA, research asst 1938-39; Nat Conf Problems Rural Youth OK, mem adv com 1963; Commn Civil Rights, part conf 1962. **Orgs:** Mem exec council Episcopal Diocese WA 1964-68; mem Dept Coll Work 1957-67; mem standing com 1967-68; chmn Interracial Task Force 1969-70; mem Comm on Ministry 1970-72; rev bd 1973-74; Episcopal Council Overseas Students & Visitors 1960-63; mem Grad Record Exams bd 1965-70; exec com Council Grad Sch US 1968-71; exec com Grad Deans African-Am Inst; bd dirs DC TB & Assn 1953-59, 65; DC Epis Cntr for Children 1964-70; trustee Absolom Jones Theol Inst; mem Am Personnel & Guid Assn, del assembly 1963-65, 68-69; Nat Assn Student Personnel Adminstr Nat Assn Univ Research Adminstrs; Am Assn Coll Tchr Educ liaison rep DC 1963-65; Am Coll Personnel Assn; Nat Vocational Guid Assn; Student Personnel Personnel Assn Tchr Educ pres 1971-72; Nat Soc Study Edn; Assn Higher Edn; SocAdvancement Edn; Adultuc Assn; AAAS; Assn for Gen & Liberal Edn; Nat Soc Coll Tchrs of Edn; Am Acad Polit & Social Scis; Phi Delta Kappa; Kappa Delta Pi Contrib ednl.

MILLER, CHARLES D., JR.
Company executive. **Personal:** Born Apr 13, 1952, Lexington, NC; son of Charles D Miller, Sr; married Loretta W, Mar 30; children: Charles D III, Kellen A. **Educ:** General Electric Corp, EDC/BMC; North Carolina A&T State Univ, BSME, 1974; Univ of Illinois, MBA, 1984. **Career:** John Deere, engineer, 1974-77; Ford, sr engineer, 1977; GE, dir of engineering, 1984-86, vp, marketing, 1986-91; Whirlpool Corp, vp, marketing, Kitchenaid, 1991-92, president, Kitchenaid, 1992-93, vp, marketing, 1993-. **Orgs:** Whirlpool Foundation, director, 1992-; Marketing Science Institute, trustee, 1994-; American Management Assn, 1992-. **Honors/Awds:** National YMCA, Achievers, 1993; American Marketing Assn, Organization of the Year, 1993; Baldridge, Gold Award, 1994. **Business Addr:** Vice President, Marketing-North America, Whirlpool Corp, 2000 M-63 North, Benton Harbor, MI 49022.

MILLER, CHERYL DE ANN
Coach. **Personal:** Born Jan 3, 1964, Riverside, CA. **Educ:** University of Southern California, BA, broadcast journalism. **Career:** Outstanding college and amateur basketball player; teams include: Junior National Team, 1981; US National Team, 1982; JC Penney All-American Five Team; World Championship Team, 1983; University of Southern California, Women's Basketball Team, player; US Olympics, Women's Basketball Team, player, 1984; ABC Sports, commentator; Univ of Southern California, head coach, women's basketball, 1993-95; Phoenix Mercury, head coach, 1997-; Turner Sports, TNT, TBS, NBA analyst, currently. **Honors/Awds:** Sports Illustrated Player of the Week, 1983; member of US Olympic Gold Medal Basketball Team, 1984; ABA/USA Female Athlete of the Year, 1986; Naismith Player of the Year, three consecutive years; Kodak All-American, four consecutive years. **Special Achievements:** Recipient of more than 1,140 trophies and 125 plaques; offered 250 scholarships to various college and university teams; participant in championship games including: CIF state championship, National Sports Festival, 1981, Pan Am Games, 1983; FIBA World Championships, Goodwill Games; player for US Olympic team winning first Gold Medal for women's basketball, 1984; first female analyst to call a nationally televised NBA game. **Business Addr:** Head Coach, General Manager, Phoenix Mercury, America West Arena, 201 E Jefferson St, Phoenix, AZ 85004, (602)252-9622.

MILLER, CONSTANCE JOAN (MILLER-ENGELSBERG)
Managing director. **Personal:** Born Sep 8, 1945, Frederick, OK; daughter of Esther Bell Herd Miller and Arthur Lee Miller; married Norman Engelsberg (divorced 1982); children: Braswell, Michelle. **Educ:** Community College of Philadelphia, 1966-70; Temple University, 1971; University of Washington, 1971-74; Goddard-Cambridge Graduate School, MA, 1974-76. **Career:** City of Seattle, administrator, 1979-81; The Phoenix Project, founder, 1982, managing director, 1982-89; Medical Legal Consultants of Washington, legal assistant, Dalkon Shield project manager, 1988-91; IUD Claim Information Service, ICIS, founder, 1989, managing director, 1991-. **Orgs:** International Dalkon Shield Victims Education Association, founding board member, 1986-. **Honors/Awds:** Co-author, From The Ashes, A Head Injury Self-Advocate Guide, The Phoenix Project Books, 1987-; author, Dalkon Shield Claims Information Guide, ICIS Books, 1989-; Dalkon Shield Claims Legal Guide, ICIS Books, 1990-; author, Dalkon Shield Claims Up-Date Service, ICIS Books; "Clap Your Hands . . .," Essence, May 1990, p 112; "Day of Reckoning," Ms. Magazine, June 1989, p 50; "Are You a Victim of this Nasty-Looking Thing?" Woman's World Magazine, April 25, 1989, p 6. **Business Addr:** Managing Director, IUD Claims Information Service, 600 1st Ave, 225 Pioneer Bldg, Seattle, WA 98104.

MILLER, COREY
Professional football player. **Personal:** Born Oct 25, 1968, Pageland, SC; married Lisa; children: Corey Jr, Christian. **Educ:** South Carolina, attended. **Career:** New York Giants, linebacker, 1991-. **Business Addr:** Professional Football Player, New York Giants, Giants Stadium, East Rutherford, NJ 07073, (201)935-8111.

MILLER, CYLENTHIA LATOYE
Attorney. **Personal:** Born Dec 13, 1962, Pine Bluff, AR; daughter of George Boyer Miller Jr & Sharon Elaine Bernard. **Educ:** Wayne State University, BA, 1988; Detroit College of Law at Michigan State University, JD Cum Laude, 1996. **Career:** Wayne County Neighborhood Legal Svcs, mediator, 1988-89; Michigan Credit Union League, regulatory specialist, 1989-93; Neighborhood Svcs Organization, emergency phone counselor, 1993-96; Gosset PLLC, associate, 1996-. **Orgs:** NAACP; Alpha Kappa Alpha Sorority Inc, 1984-; American Bar Association, 1993-; National Bar Association, 1996-; State Bar of Michigan, 1996-; Wolverine Bar Association, 1996-; Women Lawyers Association of Michigan, 1996-; Arkansas Bar Assn, 1997-; National Association of Female Executives, 1993-. **Honors/Awds:** Detroit College of Law, Book Awd - Probate Procedure, 1996, Book Awd RWA II, 1993, Honors - RWA I & II, 1992-93; Wolverine Bar Association, Scholarship, 1994; Wolverine Student Bar Association, Scholarship, 1993-94. **Special Achievements:** First African American female president of a graduating class, Detroit College of Law at Michigan State University, 1996. **Home Addr:** 620 Chrysler Dr, Apt 202, Detroit, MI 48207-3054. **Business Phone:** (313)568-6591.

MILLER, DENNIS WELDON
Physician. **Personal:** Born Mar 12, 1949, Roanoke, VA; son of Rosa Miller and Henry Miller; married Carol Miller; children: Damon, Jared. **Educ:** Fisk Univ, 1971; Meharry Med Coll, 1975; KC General Hosp & Medical Cntr, residency in Ob/Gyn 1975-76; Truman Medical Center 1976-79. **Career:** Private practice, physician; University of Kansas Medical Center Family Practice Dept, clinical professor, 1983-. **Orgs:** Mem Gynecological Soc, Southwest Clinical Soc, Natl Med Assn 1971-77; mem AMA 1971-77; mem NAACP; mem, sec/treasurer Kan Valley Med Soc, 1988-90; Amer Assn of Gynecological Laparoscopists, Wyandotte Co Medical Soc, KS Medical Soc, KS Foundation for Medical Care; Gyn Laser Soc; chairman, Dept OBG Providence; chairman St Margarets Health Center, 1987-89. **Business Addr:** MD, PA, 600 Nebraska, Ste 102, Kansas City, KS 66101.

MILLER, DEXTER J., JR.
Business executive (retired). **Personal:** Born Dec 10, 1934, Kansas City, MO; married Martha L; children: Maelyn, Sherri, Candace, Dexter, Marcus. **Educ:** Kansas City Univ, 1959-61; Rockhurst Coll, 1968-70; Natl Coll of Bus, BS Bus Admin 1975-76; completed both parts of LUTC Professional Sales Training Course 1959-61; completed 6 parts of CLU Prol Theoretical Ins Course 1969-72. **Career:** Atlanta Life Ins Co, life underwriter 1957-66, staff mgr, asst dist mgr 1966-68, dist mgr. **Orgs:** Mem MO Underwriters Assoc; mem exec com Underwriters Assoc of Gr KC; life mem NAACP; mem trustee bd Bethel AME Church; mem Laymans Org of AME Church, Millionaires Club, Natl Ins Assoc 1977-80; pres Ivanhoe Social Club 1978; pres Life Underwriters Hon Soc 1978; chmn bd of dir Blue Hills Comm Fed Credit Union 1978; mem Presidents Club Atlanta Life Ins 1978-80; appt chmn ins comm trustee bd Bethel AME Church 1980; mem exec comm Ivanhoe Soc 1980; elected fin sec Ivanhoe Club 1984; pres, Nonprofit Foundation, Bethel AME Church, 1984-. **Honors/Awds:** Salesman of the Year 1958,59; Awd for Outstanding Sales Achievement Natl Negro Ins Week 1958-66; Outstanding Asst Mgr in Sales Natl Negro Ins Week 1967;Outstanding Mgrs Perf Natl Negro Ins Week 1968-74; Exceptional Performance & Leading all Others in the Field of Life Insurance-Sales & Serv for Mgrs Hornsby Trophy Natl Ins Assoc 1980,81,82. **Business Addr:** District Manager, Atlanta Life Insurance Co, 4725 Paseo Blvd, Kansas City, MO 64110.

MILLER, DONALD LESESSNE
Company executive (retired). **Personal:** Born Jan 10, 1932, New York, NY; son of Mamie Johnson and John H Miller; married Gail Aileen Wallace, Jun 27, 1981; children: Lynn Ann, Mark L. **Educ:** University of Maryland, BA, 1967; Harvard Business School, 1969. **Career:** Inmont Corporation, New York, NY, assistant to the president, 1968-70; Seatrain Shipbuilding, New York, NY, vice president of industrial relations, 1970-71; US Dept of Defense, Washington, DC, assistant secretary of defense, 1971-73; Columbia University, New York, NY, vice president of personnel, 1973-78; International Paper, New York, NY, director of personnel, 1978-79; Con Edison, New York, NY, vice president of employee relations, 1979-86; Dow Jones & Company, New York, NY, vice president, employee relations, 1986-95. **Orgs:** Chairman of the board, Associated Black Charities, 1982-; director, United Way, Tri State, 1981-; director, Jackie Robinson Foundation, 1981-; trustee, Pace University, 1979-. **Honors/Awds:** Distinguished Civilian Medal, US Defense Department, 1973; Distinguished Alumnus Award, University of Maryland, 1977. **Military Serv:** US Army, Major, 1948-68; Legion of Merit, 1968, Commendation Medal, 1961. **Business Addr:** Former VP, Employee Relations, Dow Jones & Co Inc, 200 Liberty St, New York, NY 10281.

MILLER, DORIS JEAN
Educational administrator. **Personal:** Born Oct 13, 1933, River Rouge, MI; married Olie Miller; children: Carla A, Darryl S, Felicia C. **Educ:** Wayne State Univ, BA 1957; MI State Univ, Cert 1963; Wayne State Univ, MA 1968. **Career:** River Rouge Public Schools, teacher 1959-73, principal 1973-74, teacher 1974-79; MI Fed of Teachers and School Related Personnel, field rep 1979-96, assistant, 1996-; Wayne County Community Coll, trustee, 1978-88. **Orgs:** Mem Alpha Kappa Alpha Sor 1952-; mem bd of dir Downriver Guidance Clinic 1970-88; chmn Black Women's Task Force 1982-85; mem Greater Metro Det Guidance Assoc 1982-88; mem Women's Conf of Concerns 1982-89; mem bd of dir Wayne County Private Indus Council 1983-89; pres 1982-84, treas 1985 Wayne County Community Coll Found. **Honors/Awds:** Scholarship Ford Motor Co Fund 1951-55; Community Activist/Educ NAACP 1973. **Business Addr:** 2661 E Jefferson, Detroit, MI 48207.

MILLER, DORSEY COLUMBUS, JR.
Educator. **Personal:** Born Jan 7, 1943, Ocala, FL; son of Eudora J Miller and Dorsey C Miller Sr; married Betty J Samuel, Dec 16, 1967; children: Kim Y, Eric T, Dorsey C III. **Educ:** Morehoues College, BA, 1965; University of Florida, Masters, 1971; Florida Atlantic University, EdD, 1980. **Career:** The School Bd of Marion County, teacher, guidance counselor, 1965-68; The School Bd of Broward County, guidance counselor, 1972-73; Florida Department of Education, counsultant, 1973-75, regional coordinator, 1975-79; Southern Bell Telephone Co, manager, 1979-80; The School Bd of Broward County, migrant education coordinator, 1980-91, special programs director, 1991-. **Orgs:** Omega Psi Phi Fraternity Inc, grand basileus; Broward Community College, board of trustees chairman; Mt Olive Baptist Church, board of trustees; Greater Fort Lauderdale Chamber of Commerce, board of governors; National Conference of Chris-

tians and Jews, board of directors. **Honors/Awds:** US Jaycees, Outstanding Young Man of America, 1977; Omega Psi Phi Fraternity 7th District, Citizen of the Year, 1983; Presidential appointee, US Motor Carrier Ratemaking Study Committee, 1983; City of Lauderdale, Community Service Award, 1984; NAACP, Act-So Award, 1991. **Special Achievements:** Dissertation: The Impact of Race on a Desegregated School District as Perceived by Selected School Administrators, 1980; author, ''Migrant Student Record Transfer System,'' 1974. **Military Serv:** US Army, spec-4, 1968-70; Good Conduct Medal, 1969. **Home Addr:** 4765 NW 6th Place, Coconut Creek, FL 33063. **Business Addr:** President, DC Miller & Associates, Inc, 3701 NW 16th Street, Lauderhill, FL 33313.

MILLER, E. ETHELBERT
Author, educational administrator. **Personal:** Born Nov 20, 1950, New York, NY; son of Enid Marshall Miller and Egberto Miller; married Denise King, Sep 25, 1982; children: Jasmine Simone, Nyere-Gibran. **Educ:** Howard Univ, BA Afro-Amer Studies 1972. **Career:** African-American Resource Ctr Howard Univ, dir 1974-; University of Nevada, visiting professor, 1993; African American Review, poetry editor, currently. **Orgs:** Former bd mem PEN American Center; adv bd The Washington School 1984-; council member DC Comm Humanities Council 1984-; be mem Pen/Faulkner Found; board member Associated Writing Programs; bd mem The Inst for Policy Studies (IPS); bd mem NECA (Network of Educators on the Americas). **Honors/Awds:** Tony Taylor Award Cultural Alliance of Washington DC 1986; Mayor's Art Award for Literature 1982; Honorary Doctorate of Literature, Emory and Henry College, 1996. **Special Achievements:** New publication: In Search of Color Everywhere, Stewart Tabori & Chang, 1994; First Light, New and Selected Poems, Black Classic Press, 1994. **Business Addr:** Dir, African-American Resource Center, Howard Univ, PO Box 746, Washington, DC 20059, (202)806-7242.

MILLER, EARL VONNIDORE
Physician. **Personal:** Born May 9, 1923, Natchez, MS; married Rosalie; children: Miriam, Earl, Beryl, Kyle, Michael. **Educ:** Dillard U, BA 1943; Atlanta U, post-grad 1944; Medharry Coll, MD 1947. **Career:** Pvt Prac, physician urology 1959-; VA, chf resd urology 1958-59; Univ of IA Hosp, 1st urology resd 1957-58; Hubbard Hosp, 2nd yr surg resd 1956-57; VA Hosp, 1st yr surg resd 1955-57; Columbus, GA, gen prac 1948-55; St Agnes Hosp, intern 1947-48; Univ WA, asso clinical prof urology 1972-; Harvorbiew Med Ctr, urologist-in-chief 1968-70; The Dr's Hosp, chf urology 1967-71, med staff 1974-75. **Orgs:** Natl Medical Assn; Kings County Medical Society; AMA; NW Urological Society; American Urological Association, Western Section; American Urological Association. **Special Achievements:** Author, International College of Surgeons publications: ''Use of Intestines in Urology Surgery,'' 1959; ''Bladder Pouch for Tubeless Cystomstomy,'' Jour of Urology, 1960; ''Symtomatic Blindly Ending Bifid Ureter,'' Journal of Urology, 1964; ''Use of DMSO in Peyronie's Disease,'' 1967; ''Pseudocysts & of the Pancreas Presenting as Renal Mass Lsions,'' British Journal, 1971; ''Benign Testis Tumor,'' ''Epidermoid Testicular Cyst,'' Nat Med Assn; ''Epidermoid Cyst benign testicular tumor,'' intl sur; ''Simultaneous adrenal & multiple bilateral Renal Cysts,'' Journal of Urology. **Business Addr:** Urologist, 503 Medical Dental Bldg, Seattle, WA 98101.

MILLER, EDITH
Judge. **Personal:** Born in New York, NY; daughter of Florence Meyer and Earl Meyer; children: Janice, Brian. **Educ:** Hunter Coll, BA; St John's Univ Sch of Law, JD, Hon LLD. **Career:** New York Univ Sch of Law, adj assoc prof; Fordham Univ Grad Sch of Soc Svc, adj prof; New York City Family Court, admin judge; New York State Supreme Ct, associate supreme court justice. **Orgs:** New York State Association of Women Judges, vice pres; Practising Law Institute, board of trustees; New York Coalition of 100 Black Women, board of directors; Women's City Club of New York, representative; League of Women Voters; National Bar Association, life member; Hunter Coll Alumni Assn, bd mem; NAACP, life mem. **Honors/Awds:** Mem Hall of Fame Hunter Coll; Hon DL degree St John's Univ; executive mem Assoc of the Bar of the City of New York; Hon LLD, Long Island Univ; National Bar Assn, Hall of Fame, 1995. **Business Addr:** Associate Supreme Court Justice, NY State Supreme Court, 60 Centre St, New York, NY 10007.

MILLER, ERENEST EUGENE
Educator. **Personal:** Born Jun 13, 1948, Farmville, VA; son of Maria G. Miller and William C. Miller; married Alice Robinson, Jun 8, 1985. **Educ:** VA State Univ, BA 1970, EdM, 1978. **Career:** Gold Hill Elementary School, teacher 1970-71; Cumberland Co Schools, adult educ teacher 1973-; Longwood Coll Summer Inst for Talented & Gifted Students, facilitator 1979; Cumberland HS, educator 1971-92; Prince Edward Co Middle School, teacher, 1992-, assistant principal, 1993-. **Orgs:** Scout master Robert E Lee Scout Troop 6280 1971-74; dir proj VA Found for the Humanities & Public Policy 1979; pres Cumberland Co Branch NAACP 1976-80; bd mem VA State Conf NAACP 1978-; Sponsor SCA Cumberland HS; Dir, Summer Youth Employment and Training Program; Coach, Battle of the Brains, 1988; Coach, Social Studies AC Team, 1988; Vice pres, Virginia State NAACP, 1988; Vice Pres, Iota Tau Lambda Chapter, Alpha Phi Alpha, 1988; mem, Tearwallet and Sharon Baptist Church, Vice Pres, Inspirational Choir, Dir, Vocational Bible School; prs Virginia State Conference NAACP, 1992-; pres Iota Tau Lambda, 1991; board of directors, Southside YMCA. **Honors/Awds:** Trophy & Plaque Luther P Jackson Faculty 1966; Engraved Plaque Robt E Lee Scout Troop 6280 1974; Certificate, VA State Conf, NAACP 1976; Plaque, Cumberland High School, 1987; Plaque, Central Piedmont Action Council, 1989; Alpha Phi Alpha, Man of the Year, 1991; Southside and Central Chapters of Alpha Phi Alpha, Leon Monton Leadership Award, 1995. **Home Addr:** 1135 Plank Road, Farmville, VA 23901, (804)392-9929. **Business Addr:** Assistant Principal, Prince Edward Middle School, Route 5, Farmville, VA 23901.

MILLER, ETHEL JACKSON
Librarian (retired). **Personal:** Born Jul 20, 1916, Savannah, GA; daughter of Mr and Mrs Isaac M Jackson; divorced; children: Leroy Hebert, Jr. **Educ:** A&T State Univ Greensboro, NC, BS 1936; Hampton Inst Library Sch VA, BS in LS 1937; Columbia Univ Sch of Edn, 1951. **Career:** A&T State Univ Greensboro NC, asst librarian 1937-41; USMC Camp Lejeune NC, camp librarian 1942-45; VA Hosp Roanoke VA, hosp librarian 1945-50; Moultrie GA Publ School, hs librarian 1950-52; Tremont Branch NY Public Library, first asst 1953-70; Lane Library Armstrong State Coll, coord of reader serv 1971-78, acting dir 1978-79, retired coord of reader serv 1979-81. **Orgs:** Bd of dir Greenbriar Children's Center 1975-; mem Alpha Kappa Alpha Sorority; mem Am Library Assn; mem GA Library Assn.

MILLER, EVELYN B.
Association executive, author. **Personal:** Born in Atlanta, GA; daughter of Willie Groves Bailey (deceased) and Thomas F Bailey (deceased); married Charles R Miller, Aug 28, 1955 (deceased). **Educ:** Southeastern U, BA; Spelman Coll, Hunter Coll, Columbia Univ, studies; New Sch for Social Research. **Career:** YMCA of Gr NY Harlem Br, senior dir of membership, adult prog and pub relations, retired. **Orgs:** Mem Assn Black Social Workers; life member NAACP; Metro Comm of 100 Inc; Assn Professional Dirs; 5th pres Knickerbocker Intl Business & Professional Women Inc; past mem Commn on Personnel & Security Matters YMCA; past reg co-commr on white racism YMCA; past chair Communications Cabinet YMCA Gtr NY; mem League of Women Voters; deacon 2nd Presb Ch; charter mem, Childsville Inc; trustee, Alexander Robertson Elem School, New York City. **Honors/Awds:** Cert YMCA Sr Dir; 2nd place Woman of Yr Greyhound Bus Co 1967; Loyalty & Devotion Award Metro Comm of 100 Inc 1972; winner 3rd place poll taken by NY Daily Challenge newspaper ''Ten Leading Harlemites'' 1977; author ''Footsteps on the Stair'' under pen name ''Leslie Groves'' 1977; Youth Serv Award, Harlem Branch YMCA, 1984. **Home Addr:** 129 Parsons Place, SW, Atlanta, GA 30314.

MILLER, FRANK LEE, JR.
Military officer. **Personal:** Born Jan 27, 1944, Atchinson, KS; son of Evelyn A Wilson Miller and Frank L Miller; married Paulette Duncan Miller, Sep 28, 1968; children: Frank L III, Michael W, Toni K. **Educ:** Univ of WA, Seattle, WA, BA, 1973; US Army Command & General Staff Coll, Ft Leavenworth, KS, Distinguished Graduate, 1977; Troy State Univ, England, Masters, 1979; Naval War Coll, Newport, RI, Distinguished Graduate, 1984. **Career:** US Army, from private to major general, 1965-. **Orgs:** Mem, Assn of the US Army, 1966-; mem, Field Artillery Assn, 1988-. **Military Serv:** Received: Legion of Merit with 3 OLC; The Distinguished Flying Cross; The Bronze Star Medal with ''V'' and 2 Oak Leaf Clusters; Meritorious Service Medal; Air Medal with ''V'' and 19 Oak Leaf Clusters; Joint Service Commendation Medal; Vietnamese Cross of Gallantry with Silver Star; First black chief of staff of the free world's ctr for fire support at Fort Sill, OK; First black commanding general of the Army's largest and most diverse Corps Artillery. **Home Addr:** 7 Scenic Ter, Round Rock, TX 78664-9635.

MILLER, FRED
Professional football player. **Personal:** Born Feb 6, 1973, Aldine, TX; married Kim. **Educ:** Baylor, attended. **Career:** St Louis Rams, tackle, 1996-. **Business Addr:** Professional Football Player, St Louis Rams, One Rams Way, St Louis, MO 63045, (314)982-7267.

MILLER, FREDERICK A.
Management consultant. **Personal:** Born Nov 2, 1946, Philadelphia, PA; son of Clarice Gaines Miller and Frederick Miller; married Pauline Kamen Miller; children: Kamen Kaleel, Shay Clarice. **Educ:** Lincoln Univ PA, BA 1968. **Career:** CT Genl Life Ins Co, admin 1968-72, human devel consult 1972-76, asst dir training 1976-79; Kaleel Jamison Mgmt Consult Group, partner vice pres, 1979-85, pres 1985-. **Orgs:** Mem Kappa Alpha Psi Fraternity Inc, 1965-; bd of dir The Living Sch 1973-; mem Orgn Devel Network 1974-; mem Am Soc for Training & Devel 1974-; mem NTL Inst 1976-; bd of dir NTL Inst 1980-85; bd of dirs Orgn Devel Network 1986-94; board of directors, Ben & Jerry's Homemade. **Military Serv:** AUS sgt 1968-70. **Business Addr:** President & CEO, The Kaleel Jamison Consulting Group, Inc, 279 River St, Ste 401, Troy, NY 12180-3270.

MILLER, GEORGE CARROLL, JR.
Management consultant. **Personal:** Born Mar 3, 1949, Atlanta, GA; son of Beatrice Miller and George Miller; married Nawanna Lewis; children: George III, John Elliott, Mikah Alexis, Victoria Melissa. **Educ:** Amer Inst of Banking, 1971, 1975; GA State Univ, BBA 1971, MBA 1974; Univ of OK, 1975. **Career:** Trust Co of GA, commercial officer 1971-76; US Treasury Dept, exec asst 1977-79; Cooper & Lybrand, dir state & local govt practice, 1980-89; Spectrum Consulting, president, currently. **Orgs:** Fundraiser YMCA 1972-74, United Negro Coll Fund 1973-74, United Way 1973-74; v chmn, treas Atlanta Bus League 1974-75; bd dir Joint Action in Commun Serv 1982-; pres GA State Univ Natl Capital Alumni Club 1985-; bd dir DC Lung Assoc 1986-; Natl Asbestos Council; board of directors, Metropolitan Towers Inc; board of trustees, Metropolitan Baptist Church; bd of dirs, Jobs For Homeless People; bd of dirs, Capitol City Bank & Trust Co; chmn, The Messiah's Temple Ch. **Honors/Awds:** WSB Beaver Awd 1968; Herbert Leman Educ Grant 1968-71; GA State Univ Alumni Appreciation Awd 1976. **Military Serv:** USA ROTC 2 yrs. **Business Addr:** President, Spectrum Consulting Associates Inc, 1155 Connecticut Ave NW, Suite 521, Washington, DC 20036.

MILLER, GEORGE N., JR.
Business executive. **Personal:** Born Sep 12, 1951, Neptune, NJ. **Educ:** Bowling Green State Univ, BS 1973; Miami Jacobs Bus Sch, attended 1974; Norfolk State Univ, grad study. **Career:** Gem City Savings & Loan, mgr trainee 1973-74; Comm Svgs & Loan, mgr trainee 1974-75, asst mgr 1975-76, exec vice pres 1976-77, pres 1977-83; First Development Enterprises Inc, pres ceo 1983-. **Orgs:** Bd dirs/sec Whittaker Meml Hosp 1978-80; bd of dir/sec Amer Svgs & Loan League 1979-80; adv com Fed Home Loan Mortgage Corp; FHLBB 1980; bd of dir Amer Cancer Soc 1977-; vice chmn Peninsula Area Adv Council to HSA 1979-; bd dirs Comm Fed Svgs & Loan Assn 1977-83; chmn NAACP 1977-; participant US Conference for Business Leaders of Foreign Affairs; life mem Omega Psi Phi Frat. **Honors/Awds:** Alumni of the Yr Bowling Green State Univ 1982; Outstanding Contributions to the Comm & Business Alpha Phi Alpha Frat 1980; Scroll of Honor Omega Psi Phi Frat 1980; Outstanding Young Men in the Financial World in Amer American Svgs & Loan League 1978; Outstanding Citizen of the Yr Awd Zambda Lambda AOA Frat Inc 1977; Achievement Awd in Bus Office of Human Affairs 1978; Achievement Awd Under 30 Category Black Enterprise Mag NY 1980; Outstanding Achievement Bus & Commerce Heaven on Earth Restaurant Hampton VA 1980; Most Outstanding Man of the Yr Athenan Corp 1980. **Business Addr:** President, First Develop Enterprises Inc, 1512 27th St, Newport News, VA 23607.

MILLER, HELEN S.
Nurse, educator (retired). **Personal:** Born Mar 29, 1917, Atlanta, GA; daughter of Ola Sullivan and Floyd Sullivan; widowed; children: Ronald. **Educ:** Univ Hosp Augusta, GA; Med Coll of VA, RN; Tuskegee Inst Sch of Midwifery, BSNEd; Yale Univ Sch Nursing CNM, MSN; Sr Nurse Ofcr Resrv Corps Pub Health, MSN. **Career:** GA Dept Pub Health, staff nurse 1947-49; US Pub Health Serv, area suprv 1949-51; Army Nurse Corps, admin nurse 1951-53; City Philadelphia Dept Health, dist suprv 1953-54; FL A&M Univ, pub health coord sch of nursing 1954-56; NC Cntrl Univ, chmn dept nursing 1956-77, assoc prof nursing research 1977-82. **Orgs:** Sec Undergrad Cncl NC Cntrl Univ; mem Fac Exec Com NC Cntrl Univ; mem Long Range Planning Com NC Cntrl Univ; mem NC State Nurses Assn; mem Amer Nurses Assn; mem Com to Write Hist of Nursing in NC; NC State Nurses Assn; mem bd dir NC League for Nursing; mem Yale Univ Alumnae Assn; mem Amer Assn of Univ Women; mem Adv Com on Cont Educ Sch of Nursing Univ of NC at Chapel Hill; mem YWCA; former bd mem Local Chptr ARC; mem Exec Com NC Lung & Resp Assn; mem Health Careers Com NC Cntrs Univ Gubernatorial appt to NC Bd of Nursing 1966-70; natl pres Chi Eta Phi Sor Inc 1969-73. **Honors/Awds:** Mary Mahoney Award Amer Nurses Assn 1968; bd mem 1st vice pres Natl League for Nursing 1971-75; Disting Alumni Award Yale Univ 1978; life mem Natl Councl Negro Women; life mem Chi Eta Phi Sor Inc; listed in Minority Groups in Nrsg, Amer Nurses' Assn 1976, Historical Preservations of Amer 1975-76; author, two abstracts in Abstracts of Nursing Research in the South, Vol 1, 1979; author, The History of Chi Eta Phi Sorority Inc, Assn for the Study of Afro-American Life & History, 1968; co-author, Contemporary Minority Leaders in Nursing, American Nurses Association, 1983. **Military Serv:** AUS Nurse Corps 1st Lt 1951-53. **Home Addr:** PO Box 810, Durham, NC 27702-0810.

MILLER, HENRY B., JR.
Clinic director. **Personal:** Born Jun 3, 1940, San Diego; divorced; children: Holly, Amber. **Educ:** Antioch Coll, MA Prgm. **Career:** YMCA Drug Proj, group facilitator 1969; Drug & Narcotic Educ Hlth Serv Div San Diego City Schs, speaker 1969-70; IL Drug Abuse Prgm, comm serv aide, trainee 1970; San Diego Narcotic Treatment Prgm Dept Psychiat Univ CA, clinic head 1970-72; Harbison Out-Patient Full-Serv Clinic, clinic dir 1972-. **Orgs:** Mem Nat Assn Concerned Drug Abuse Workers; CA Conf Methadone Prgms. **Honors/Awds:** Poems publs Arx Mag; selected poems ''New Voices In Am Poetry'' 1977. **Business Addr:** Harbison Clinic, 5402 Division St, San Diego, CA 92114.

MILLER, HERBERT J.
Computer services executive. **Personal:** Born in Camden, SC. **Educ:** Clark College, mathematics; Howard University, MS, mathematics. **Career:** Lambda Corp, programmer, 1963-69; Hendrickson Co, 1969-78; Social & Scientific Systems Inc, chair, 1978-. **Special Achievements:** Company is ranked #81 on Black Enterprise magazine's 1997 list of Top 100 Black businesses. **Business Addr:** Chairman, Social & Scientific Systems Inc, 7101 Wisconsin, Bethesda, MD 20814, (301)986-4870.

MILLER, HORATIO C.
Pianist, music educator. **Personal:** Born Jan 8, 1949, Birmingham, AL; married Judith Willoughby; children: Allison. **Educ:** Univ of PA, BA 1970; Temple U, MusM 1973. **Career:** Cheyney State Coll, instr 1973-74; Community Coll of Philadelphia, asst prof 1974-. **Orgs:** Foundation for the Study of Cycles, mem. **Honors/Awds:** Concert pianist gave performances throughout US, JFK Center for Performing Arts, Lincoln Center Library Auditorium New York City, Acad of Music Philadelphia, Inaugural Concert President Carter Washington, DC 1976; rated in the top 10 market timers in the gold market for 1988 by Timer Digest, a natl ratings publication; Article, Eliott Wave and Gold, Stocks and Commodities Magazine, 1991; Rated number 3 gold market timer, 1990, Timer Digest. **Business Addr:** Assistant Professor, Music Department, Community College of Philadelphia, 1700 Spring Garden St, Philadelphia, PA 19130, (215)751-8295.

MILLER, INGRID FRAN WATSON
Educator. **Personal:** Born Jul 4, 1949, Washington, DC; daughter of Dempsey & Matilda Watson; married George E Miller, III PhD, May 3, 1980; children: Sean Gregory, Simon Geoffry. **Educ:** North Carolina Central Univ, BA, 1971; Howard Univ, MEd, 1983; Catholic Univ of America, MA, 1993; Univ of Maryland, College Park, 1994-96. **Career:** T Roosevelt SHS, Washingon, DC, Spanish teacher, 1973-88; Jackson State Univ, lecturer, 1983-85; Hampton Univ, asst prof of Spanish, 1988-96; Norfolk State Univ, asst pro of Spanish, 1996-. **Orgs:** Alpha Kappa Alpha Sorority, Inc, pres, vp, parl, reporter, 1968-; Jack & Jill of America Inc, rec sec, pres, regional dir, natl editor, 1985-; Coll Language Assn, 1985-, constitution comm, 1994-95; American Assn of Teachers of Span & Port, 1980-, workshop chair, 1991; American Council of Teachers of FL, 1975-; Phi Delta Kappa Educ Frat, 1987-; Natl Council of Negro Women. **Honors/Awds:** Greater DC Area Teachers of FL, Distinguished FL Educator of the Year, 1987; Jack & Jill of America, Chesapeake, Distinguished Mother of the Year, 1991; Howard Univ, Leadership in Afro-Hispanic Studies Award, 1998. **Special Achievements:** Publication, ''Afro-Hispanic Literature: An anthology of Hispanic Writers of African Ancestry,'' 1989; language proficiency, Spanish. **Home Addr:** 1101 Worthington Ct, Virginia Beach, VA 23464, (757)467-0474.

MILLER, ISAAC H., JR.
Administrator. **Personal:** Born Sep 26, 1920, Jacksonville, FL; married Effie; children: Isaac, III, Kevin, Eric, Keith, Kay. **Educ:** Livingston Coll, BS 1938; Univ of WI, MS, PhD 1948 1951. **Career:** Meharry Med Coll Nashville, former prof biochemistry; Bennett Coll Greensboro NC, past pres (retired 1987). **Orgs:** Mem Am Chem Soc; Botanical Soc of Am; Am Assn for Advncmt of Sci; Assn of Southeastern Biologists; former vis sci Oak Ridge Inst of Nuclear Studies; panelist Nat Sci Found Prgm on Rsrch Participation for HS Tchr. **Honors/Awds:** Recip Lederle Med Faculty Award Meharry Coll 3 Consecutive Yrs. **Business Addr:** Past President, Bennett Coll, 900 E Washington, Greensboro, NC 27401.

MILLER, JACQUELINE ELIZABETH
Library administrator, educator. **Personal:** Born Apr 15, 1935, New York, NY; daughter of Sarah Ellen Grevious Winslow (deceased) and Lynward Winslow; children: Percy Scott. **Educ:** Morgan State Coll, BA 1957; Pratt Inst, MLS 1960. **Career:** Brooklyn Public Library, 1957-68; New Rochelle Public Library, head extension serv 1969-70; Yonkers Public Library, branch admin 1970-75, dir 1975-; Queens College of the City of New York, adjunct prof, 1989-90. **Orgs:** Commr Commn on State-wide Library Devel 1980; NYS Government's Commission on Libraries, 1990-91; numerous other natl, state, county professional library org; Rotary of Yonkers; Chamber of Commerce. **Honors/Awds:** Honored Citizen of Yonkers, Church of Our Saviour 1980; Annual Award West County Club Natl Assn Negro Business & Professional Women's Clubs 1981; Mae Morgan Robinson Award, 1992; Women's Equality Day Award, 1992. **Business Addr:** Dir, Yonkers Public Library, Seven Main St, Yonkers, NY 10701.

MILLER, JAKE C.
Educator (retired). **Personal:** Born Dec 28, 1929, Hobe Sound, FL; son of Augustine White Miller-Paige and Jake Miller; married Nellie Carrol; children: Charles, Wayne, Warren. **Educ:** Bethune-Cookman Coll, BS 1951; Univ of IL, MA 1957; Univ of NC at Chapel Hill, PhD 1967. **Career:** Martin Co Sch Sys FL, instructor 1954-59; Bethune-Cookman Coll, asst prof 1959-64; Fisk U, assoc prof 1967-76; Bethune-Cookman Coll, prof 1976-96. **Orgs:** Amer Political Sci Assn; Intl Studies Assn; Caribbean Studies Assn; TransAfrica. Natl Conference of Black Political Scientists; Alpha Phi Alpha Fraternity. **Honors/Awds:** Fellowship Natl Endowment for the Humanities 1981-82; Prof of the Yr Finalist Cncl for Adv & Support of Educ 1984; book publ, Black Presence in Amer Foreign Affairs, Univ Press of Amer 1978; book publ, Plight of Haitian Refugees, Praeger 1984; Fellowship United Negro Coll Fund Distinguished Scholar 1986-87; Excellence in Research Award Bethune-Cookman College 1979, 1985, 1989; Ja Flo Davis Faculty member of the Year Bethune-Cookman College 1980, 1985, 1988; Distinguished Alumni Citation Natl Assn for Equal Opportunity in Higher Educ 1988; US Institute of Peace Fellowship 1989-90. **Military Serv:** USMC Cpl. **Home Addr:** 1103 Lakewood Park Dr, Daytona Beach, FL 32117. **Business Addr:** Professor of Political Science, Bethune-Cookman Coll, Daytona Beach, FL 32115.

MILLER, JAMES
Banker. **Career:** First Tennessee Bank, vp of commercial banking, currently. **Orgs:** 100 Black Men of Chattanooga, president. **Business Addr:** VP, Commercial Banking, First Tennessee Bank, 701 Market St, Chattanooga, TN 37402, (423)757-4495.

MILLER, JAMES ARTHUR
Educator. **Personal:** Born Aug 27, 1944, Providence, RI; son of Elease Miller and John Miller; married Edjohnetta Fowler; children: Ayisha, John. **Educ:** Brown Univ Providence, RI, AB 1966; State Univ of NY Buffalo, PhD 1976. **Career:** Trinity Coll Hartford, CT, prof English & Amer studies, 1990-, assoc prof English 1979-90, asst prof 1972-78; City Univ of NY Medgar Evers Coll, asst prof humanities 1971-72; State Univ of NY, dir black studies 1969-71; CT Pub Radio, humanities consult 1979-80; WGBH Radio Found Boston, consult 1978-80; Lafayette Coll Easton PA, distinguished visiting prof 1982-83; Wesleyan Univ Middletown CT, visting assoc prof Afro-Amer studies 1985-86; Wesleyan Univ Middletown CT, visiting assoc prof English & Afro-Amer studies 1988-89. **Orgs:** Pres Blue Hills Civic Assoc Hartford 1976-78; bd of dir Big Bro of Greater Hartford 1978-80; pres, bd dir Artists Collective Inc Hartford 1984-86; Connecticut Humanities Council 1985-91; trustee, Mark Twain Memorial, Hartford 1987-94. **Honors/Awds:** Outstanding Young Man of Am 1978; Fellowship, African Humanities Inst, Natl Endowment for the Humanities 1979; Fellow, WEB DuBois Inst, Harvard Univ, 1993; Scholar In Residence, Schomburg Ctr, 1994. **Business Addr:** Professor, Trinity College, English Department, Hartford, CT 06106.

MILLER, JAMES S.
Educator (retired). **Personal:** Born Feb 20, 1923, Gastonia, NC; married Anne E Grier. **Educ:** Howard U, BS 1949; A&T State U, MS 1956; NC Cntrl; Appalachian State U; UNC Extension Prog. **Career:** Arlington Elem Sch, principal 1970-88; CF Gingles Elem Sch, prin 1952-70. **Orgs:** Mem Nat Educ Assn; NC Assn of Educators; Gaston Co Educ Assn Elder Loves Chapel Press Ch; mem Omega Psi Phi Frat; ofcr Local Chap treas past 19 yrs; treas Gaston Co Prin Assn; past mem bd dirs Excelsior Credit Union; Gastopn Boys Club; Gaston Co Red Cross; mem Gaston Co Bicentennial; bd of dirs, Catherine's House; Community Share Food Program, sponsor; Mayors Task Force Against Crime; Presbytery Western NC Committee on Ministry; Commissioner to Gen Assembly in Witicka Kansas, 1994. **Honors/Awds:** Recip Omega Man of Yr 1965-93; cert of Appreciation outstndg serv as prin cited Best Prin Schs PTA 1974; plaque serv rendered as pres of Gaston Co Tchrs Assn; Alliance For Children, Caring Hands for Children & Youth Award, 1992; Guston County, NAACP, Community Service Award, 1992; Guston County, Community Service Award, 1994. **Military Serv:** USMC 1st sgt 1943-46.

MILLER, JAMES S.
Library director. **Personal:** Born Dec 23, 1924, Atlanta; married Nellie Jeter; children: Marilynn Maxine, James S. **Educ:** Morehouse Coll Atlanta, AB 1950; Atlanta U, MS in LS 1951. **Career:** FL Mem Coll, head librn 1951-56; FL A&M U, asst prof libr sci 1956-60; AL A&M Coll, head librn 1960-62; Norfolk State Coll, libr dir 1962-; Univ of Chgo, libr workshops 1957, 58. **Orgs:** Mem Libr Adv Com State Coun Higher Educ VA; mem Act Com VA Libr Assn 1973; mem ALA; SELA; VA LA; vice pres FL State LA 1954-57. **Military Serv:** USMC sgt. **Business Addr:** Norfolk State Coll, 2401 Corprew Ave, Norfolk, VA 23504.

MILLER, JAMIR MALIK
Professional football player. **Personal:** Born Nov 19, 1973, Philadelphia, PA; married Racquel; children: Ashlynn. **Educ:** UCLA, attended. **Career:** Arizona Cardinals, linebacker, 1994-. **Business Addr:** Professional Football Player, Arizona Cardinals, 8701 S Hardy, Tempe, AZ 85284, (602)379-0101.

MILLER, JEANNE-MARIE A.
Educator, author. **Personal:** Born Feb 18, 1937, Washington, DC; daughter of Agnes C Johns Anderson (deceased) and William Anderson (deceased); married Dr Nathan J Miller. **Educ:** Howard Univ, BA 1959, MA 1963, PhD 1976. **Career:** Howard Univ, instr English 1963-76, grad asst prof English 1977-79; Inst for the Arts & the Humanities Howard Univ, asst dir 1973-75, grad assoc prof of English 1979-92; asst for academic planning office of the vice pres for academic affairs 1976-90, grad professor of English, 1992-. **Orgs:** Ed Black Theatre Bulletin Amer Theatre Assoc 1977-86; mem exec council Black Theatre Prog Amer Theatre Assoc 1977-86; proposal reviewer Natl Endowment for the Humanities 1979-; adv bd WETA-TV Ed prog on Black Folklore 1976-77; mem Friends of JF Kennedy Ctr for Performing Arts, Amer Assoc of Univ Women, Amer Civil Liberites Union, Amer Film Inst; assoc mem Arena Stage, Washington Performing Arts Soc, Eugene O'Neill Memorial Theatre Ctr, Amer Soc of Business and Exec Women; assoc Art Inst of Chicago, Boston Museum of Fine Arts, Metropolitan Museum of Art, Corcoran Gallery of Art, Smithsonian Inst, Washington Performings Arts Soc, The Washington Opera Guild, World Affairs Council of Washington DC, Drama League of New York, Modern Language Assoc, Amer Studies Assoc, Coll Lang Assoc, Natl Council of Teachers of Engli Amer Assoc for Higher Educ, Natl Assoc for Women Deans Administrators and Counselors, Natl Women's Studies Assoc. **Honors/Awds:** Advanced Study Fellowship Ford Found 1970-72; Fellow So Fellowship Fund 1972-74; Grantee Amer Council of Learned Societies; 1978-79; Grantee Natl Endowment for the Humanities 1981-84; Grantee, Howard University Faculty Research Fund, 1994-95, 1996-97; edited book From Realism to Ritual: Form & Style in Black Theatre 1983; publ over 60 articles in various jrnls & mags; Pi Lambda Theta Natl Honor and Professional Assn in Education 1987. **Business Addr:** Prof, Dept of English, Howard University, 2400 6th St NW, Washington, DC 20059.

MILLER, JOHN H.
Clergyman. **Personal:** Born Dec 3, 1917, Ridgeway, SC; married; children: George F, John H Jr. **Educ:** AB, BD 1941-45; Hartford Sem Found Religious Ed, further study 1954. **Career:** African Methodist Epis Zion Church, AME Zion Church, bishop, currently. **Orgs:** Mem Alpha Phi Alpha 1941; past vice pres CT Council of Churchs 1955-60; mem Mayors Goodwill Comm Housing Comm Waterbury CT 1956; mem Winston-Salem NC Goodwill Comm deseg all publ facilities 1963; mem Natl Council of Churchs 1966; charter mem Louisville Jeff Cty Crime Comm 1967-71; past pres Louisville Area Council of Churchs 1969-71; sec treas Waterbury Ministers Assoc; mem exec bd NAACP, Urban League; dir Fed Fund for City of Winston-Salem; mem World Meth Council of Churchs; trustee Livingstone Coll Lomax-Hannon Coll. **Honors/Awds:** KY Col Civic Title Outstanding Citizen of Commonwealth of KY 1966; Livingstone Coll Alumni Merit Serv Awd 1971; AR Traveller Civic Title given by Gov of AR 1972; Greatest Hon Election to Episcopacy Mobile AL 1972; Citation City of Winston-Salem Outstanding Civic Contrib; Outstanding Contrib to Coll DD Livingstone Coll. **Business Addr:** Bishop, AME Zion Church, 8605 Caswell Ct, Raleigh, NC 27612.

MILLER, JOSEPH HERMAN
Insurance company executive. **Personal:** Born Mar 5, 1930, Port Gibson, MS; married Cleo L Baines; children: Darryl, Stephen, Carrington, Vicki, Scott. **Educ:** Talladega Coll, AB 1950; Howard Univ, JD 1957. **Career:** Miller Funeral Homes Inc, pres 1972-; Freedom Natl Ins Co, pres 1976-; Natl Ins Assoc, pres 1976-; Reliable Life Ins Co, pres. **Orgs:** Bd dir Monroe LA C of C 1976. **Military Serv:** USA corpl 1951-53. **Business Addr:** President, Reliable Life Insurance Co, PO Box 1157, Monroe, LA 71211.

MILLER, KEVIN D.
Access manager. **Personal:** Born Apr 9, 1966, New York, NY; son of Viera McAfee Miller and Lawrence Miller. **Educ:** Syracuse University, Syracuse, NY, communications, 1984-88; Fordham University, Graduate School of Arts and Science, MA, Liberal Studies, 1994. **Career:** Washington Arms, Syracuse, NY, work study, 1984-87; Roberto Clemente Park, Bronx, NY, filter room, summer, 1987; Campus Convenience, Syracuse, NY, work study, 1987-88; Salt City Productions, Syracuse, NY, producer, 985-89; Expressive People Prod, New York, NY, producer, 1988-; Paragon Cable Manhattan, New York, NY, assoc producer/producer, 1988-89, access manager, 1989-92, commercial use manager, 1992-93; ABC Sports, associate, 1994-. **Orgs:** Board member, American Cancer Society, NYC, 1991-; committee chairperson, Phi Beta Sigma Fraternity Inc, 1985-; liason, member, Harlem Week Inc, Uptown Chamber of Commerce, 1990-; member, National Academy Cable Programming, 1990-; member, Black Filmmakers Foundation, 1989-; Prince Hall FM & AM, 1990-. **Honors/Awds:** Service Award, Beta Psi Sigma Chapter, 1989; Brotherhood Award, Theta Xi Chapter, 1988; President's Award, National Pan-Hellenic Council, 1988; Sigma Man of the Year, Phi Beta Sigma-Theta Xi, 1985. **Business Addr:** President, Expressive People Productions, Inc, 240 Nagle Ave, #7B, New York, NY 10034.

MILLER, LAMAR PERRY
Educator. **Personal:** Born Sep 1, 1925, Ypsilanti, MI; married Deborah F Fox; children: LaMar Jr, Arianne E. **Educ:** Univ MI, PhD 1968; Univ MI, EdS 1965; Univ MI, MA 1958; Eastern MI U, BA 1954. **Career:** NY U, sec ed & prof of metro studies present; Inst of Afro-Am Affairs, educ rsrch dir; Inst for Tchrs of Disad Youth, dir; Educ Ypsilani MI, asso prof; English Dept Willow Run, chmn; dir forensic activ. **Orgs:** Chief consult Nat Inst of Educ Dept of HEW; dir Tchrs Corps; ons Union Carbide

Corp; NY Urban League; asso edit Am Educ Rsrch Jour AERA 1975-78; mem publ com Assn for Super & Curric Devel 1975-77; Nat Alliance of Black Sch Educ 1975-; edit bd NY Univ Quarterly 1972-75 ; sec Div G Am Educ Rsrch Assn 1972-74. **Honors/Awds:** Publs "equality of educ opport a handbook for rsrch" 1974; "the testing of black students a symposium" 1974; "edn for an open soc" 1974. **Military Serv:** AUS 1944-46. **Business Addr:** New York University, Press Building, Room 72, 32 Washington Place, New York, NY 10003.

MILLER, LAUREL MILTON
Deputy chief of police (retired). **Personal:** Born Apr 29, 1935, Richmond, VA; son of Dahlia and Alma Miller; married Betty Loggins; children: Yasmin, Nicole. **Educ:** VA Union Univ, BS 1972; NWU, attended 1974; Univ of Louisville, grad study 1975; Nova Univ, MS 1980. **Career:** Richmond Bureau of Police, patrolman 1961-68, detective 1968-69, sgt 1969-73, lt personnel officer 1973-76, capt 1976-77, major 1978, deputy chief of police. **Orgs:** Mem Police Benevolence Assn; bd mem Natl Organ of Black Law Enforcement Execs; alumni So Police Inst. **Honors/Awds:** First Black Traffic Sgt Richmond; First Black to Head Div in Bur of Police; First Black Capt of Bureau; First Black Major and Deputy Chief of Police; 36 Public Serv Commendations; Police Cit Certl 1963; Police Medal 1972; Merit Police Duty 1975. **Military Serv:** USAF a/1c 1953-57. **Business Addr:** Deputy Chief of Police, Richmond Bureau of Police, 501 N 9th St, Richmond, VA 23219.

MILLER, LAWRENCE A., JR.
Special projects coordinator, government official. **Personal:** Born Aug 17, 1951, Bronx, NY; son of Adella B Williams King and Lawrence A Miller; married Shirley; children: Keisha Yvette, Dahra Ayanna. **Educ:** York Coll, BA Publ Admin 1974; Brooklyn Coll, MPA 1989. **Career:** Dept of Juvenile Justice, juvenile counselor 1973-76; NY City Youth Bd, evaluation consult 1976-79; NYS Div for Youth, program mgmt spec, special projects coord 1980-89; NYC Health Hospitals Corp, director of EEO/affirmative action, 1989-94; Suffolk County Human Rights Commission, exec dir, 1994-. **Orgs:** Mem NAACP; bd mem Comm School Bd #28 1983-86, Comm Planning Bd #12 1983-, Rochdale Village Inc 1985-; vice pres Fred Wilson Regular Democratic Club 1987; chmn of the bd Youth Advocates through Educ & Sports 1987; producer and host of radio program WNYE Comm Trustees Report for the Borough of Manhattan; exec dir, Community Advocates for a Better Living Environment 1989. **Honors/Awds:** Cert of Apprec NY City Office of Serv Coord 1975; Outstanding Young Men of Amer US Jaycees 1980; Outstanding Serv Awd NYS Div for Youth 1981; Comm Serv Awd Elmcor Youth & Adult Activites 1984; Certificate of Appreciation Bd of Educ New York City 1986; Chancellor's Awd for Outstanding Alumni 1986; Natl Assn of Negro Business and Professional Women's Club Comm Serv Awd 1987; Honor Service Award, Assn of Black Educators of NY 1988; Oustanding Community Service, York College 1986; Columnist, New York Voice Newspaper 1988; Producer/Host, Comm Affairs Talk Show, Radio 91.5 FM & Cable TV 1986, 1989; NAACP, Central Islip Branch, Community Service Award, 1997. **Business Addr:** Executive Director, Suffolk County Human Rights Commission, 158 N County Complex, Hauppauge, NY 11788.

MILLER, LAWRENCE EDWARD
County official, association administrator. **Personal:** Born Aug 13, 1950, Columbia, SC; son of Mary E Miller and Ralph Carter. **Educ:** Hard Barger Jr Coll, Raleigh NC, AAS, 1969; A&T State Univ, Greensboro NC, BA, 1974; Natl Theological Seminary, MA, PhD, 1983. **Career:** Wake-Raleigh Headstart, Raleigh NC, teacher, 1975-79, asst execeptional children coordinator, 1979, transportation coordinator, 1980; Housing Opportunity Unlimited, Laurel MD, dir of social services, 1980-83; PG County Housing, Landover MD, rental specialist, 1983; Arlington County Housing, Arlington VA, housing asst, 1983-. **Orgs:** Mem, NC State Elks Assn, 1972-; bd mem, PG County Headstart Policy Council, 1981-83; Eastern Region secretary, Phi Beta Sigma Frat, 1987-91; Executive Council, United Church of Christ, 1987-90; Trustee, Alpha Sigma Chapter, Phi Beta Sigma Frat, 1988-90; mem, Columbia Elks Lodge; mem, Alpha Sigma Frat, Phi Beta Sigma Frat; mem, Peoples Congregational UCC. **Honors/Awds:** Brother Elk of the Year, Mississippi State Elks Assn, 1974; Director of the Year, Elks IBPOE of W, 1978; NC Longleaf, NC Governor, 1978; Doctor of Humane Letter, Natl Theological Seminary, 1982; Colonel Robert L Pollard Award, Alpha Sigma Chapter, 1989. **Home Addr:** 1631 New Jersey Ave NW, Washington, DC 20001-2407.

MILLER, LESLEY JAMES, JR.
State representative. **Personal:** Born Apr 21, 1951, Tampa, FL; son of Shaddie Alice Robinson Miller and Lesley James Miller Sr; married Gwendolyn O Martin Miller, Nov 27, 1982; children: Le'Jean Michelle, Lesley James III. **Educ:** Bethune-Cookman College, Daytona Beach, FL, 1969-70; University of South Florida, Tampa, FL, BA, political science, 1978, MPA, 1979. **Career:** Tampa Electric Co, Tampa, Fl, personnel service spec & customer relations rep, 1978-87; Lesley Miller Consultants, Tampa, FL, consultant, 1988-; Greater Tampa Urban League, Tampa, FL, vice president for programs/external affairs, 1989-90; Time Customer Service Inc, Tampa, Fl, recruiter, 1990-91; Florida House of Representatives, state rep, 1992-; Tampa General Healthcare, Tampa, FL Coordinator of Minority Business Enterprise, 1996-. **Orgs:** Member, Kappa Alpha Psi Fraternity Inc, 1975-; member, Hillsborough County City-County Planning Commission, 1978-91; member, City of Tampa Convention Facilities Board, 1987-91; member, Tampa-Hillsborough Cable TV Advisory Committee, 1983-91; member, Greater Tampa Urban League, 1977-. **Honors/Awds:** University of South Florida Distinguished Alumnus Award, 1983; Tampa Bay Area;s Most Influential Black, Black News, 1983; Outstanding Young Man in America, US Jaycees, 1978; George Edgecomb Memorial Award, Greater Tampa Urban League, 1977. **Military Serv:** Air Force, sgt, 1971-74. **Home Addr:** 2505 38th Ave, Tampa, FL 33610.

MILLER, LOREN, JR.
Judge. **Personal:** Born Mar 7, 1937, Los Angeles, CA; married Gwen Allain; children: Pamela Allain, Michael, Stephanie Allain, Robin, Nina, Gregory Allain. **Educ:** Univ of OR, BS 1960; Loyola Law School Los Angeles, JD 1962. **Career:** State of CA Dept of Justice, dep atty gen 1962-69; Western Ctr on Law & Poverty, dir of litigation 1969-70; Model Neighbor Legal Prog, dir 1972-73; Pacific Lighting Corp, asst gen counsel 1973-75; Los Angeles Municipal Court, judge 1975-77; Superior Court LA County, superior court judge. **Business Addr:** Judge Superior Court, Superior Court LA County, 400 Civic Center Plz, Pomona, CA 91766.

MILLER, LORI E.
Publicity executive, author. **Personal:** Born Mar 2, 1959, Detroit, MI; daughter of Mary Miller and Percy Miller. **Educ:** Univ of MI, BA 1981. **Career:** Carl Byoir & Assoc Public Relations, staff writer 1981-82; Metro Detroit Convention Bureau, communications asst 1982-83; Greater LA Visitors & Convention Bureau, public relations mgr; Ketchum/Bohle Public Relations, account exec 1985-86; Porter/Novelli, senior account exec 1986-90; Universal Studios Hollywood, mgr, publicity, 1992-. **Orgs:** Public Relations Soc of Amer 1985; Amer Women in Radio and TV, Amer Film Inst, Public Relations Soc of Amer, Publicity Club of Los Angeles, Black Journalist Assoc Los Angeles Chapter; Academy of Television Arts and Sciences; Travel Association of America, public relations committee; Society of American Travel Writers. **Honors/Awds:** LA Advertising Women's "Lulu Awards/Honorable Mention" for public relations. **Business Addr:** Manager of Publicity, Universal Studios, 100 Universal City Plz, Universal City, CA 91608.

MILLER, LORRAINE
Government official. **Career:** The White House, deputy assistant to the president for legislative affairs, currently. **Business Phone:** (202)456-1414.

MILLER, LOUISE T.
Educator. **Personal:** Born Mar 2, 1919. **Educ:** Univ MI, BS 1949; Syracuse U, MS 1951; Yale U, MPH 1961; Univ RI, PhD 1970. **Career:** Spelman Coll, asso prof Biology 1973-; Univ RI, res asso in Animal Path 1963-72, res asst 1962-63; Syracuse U, tchng res asst 1951-60. **Orgs:** Mem Ad Hoc Com for Disad Students 1968-69; coun Special Prgm for Talent Dev 1970; instr Ed 900 Bio Workshop for Elem Sch Tchrs 1965-66, 68, 72; coll French Textbook by Jean S Hyland PhD. **Honors/Awds:** Recip USPHS Trainee Grant Yale U, 1960-61. **Business Addr:** 350 Spelman La SW, Atlanta, GA 30314.

MILLER, LUVENIA C. See Obituaries section.

MILLER, M. SAMMYE
Administrator. **Personal:** Born Feb 23, 1947, Philadelphia, PA; son of Sammye Elizabeth Adams-Miller and Herman S Miller; married Gloria J Miller. **Educ:** Delaware State University, BA 1968; Trinity Coll Washington, MAT 1970; The Catholic Univ of Amer, PhD 1977; Stanford Univ, Post Doc Fellow 1983. **Career:** Natl Endowment for the Humanities, humanist admin & policy analyst 1978-80; Assn for the Study of Afro-Amer Life & History Inc, exec dir 1983-84; Bowie State Univ, dept chmn/prof of hist, currently. **Orgs:** Southern History Assn; Org of Amer Historian; The Amer Historical Assn; life mem Kappa Alpha Psi Fraternity Phi Alpha Theta Intl; Hon Soc in History; ASALH; Knights of Columbus. **Honors/Awds:** NAFEO Research Achievemnt Award Natl Assn for Equal Opportunity in Higher Educ 1984; fellowships Knights of Columbus 1970; Penfield Fellow; Bd Trustees Scholar, Catholic Univ. **Home Addr:** 7709 Wingate Dr, Glenn Dale, MD 20769.

MILLER, MAPOSURE T.
Dentist. **Personal:** Born Jul 17, 1934, Wadesboro, NC; son of Mary R Miller and Wade H Miller; married Bobbie J Grubbs; children: Teresa, Vickie, Gail. **Educ:** Bluefield State Coll, BS 1956; WV Univ Sch Dent, DDS 1965. **Career:** Dr MT Miller Inc, pres. **Orgs:** Mem Natl Dent Assn; Amer Dent Assn; Buckeye State Dent Assn; OH State Dent Assn; Cleveland Dent Soc; Forest City Dent Study Club (pres-elect 1975-76); sec-treas Lee road Dent Cntrs Inc; bd tr Olivet Institutional Bapt Ch; chmn health & welfare E Cleveland Bus Men Assn; Urban League; NAACP. **Honors/Awds:** Provincial Man of the Year Kappa Alpha Psi 1956; Beta Kappa Chi hon soc 1955-56. **Military Serv:** AUS Sp4 1957-59; USN Lt 1965-68. **Business Addr:** 13944 Euclid Ave, Cleveland, OH 44112.

MILLER, MARCIA M. See TRENT, MARCIA M.

MILLER, MARGARET ELIZABETH BATTLE
Business executive. **Personal:** Born Nov 19, 1934, Chapel Hill, NC; daughter of Johnnie M Battle and Ivy Battle; divorced; children: Lisa, Monica, William II. **Educ:** NC Central U, AB 1955; Univ of NC, MSLS 1961; NC Central U, JD 1982. **Career:** Highland Jr & Sr HS, librarian 1955-59; Swannee River Jr Coll, librarian 1959-66; Borgess Med Ctr, librarian 1968-79; Whitaker Sch, DHR administrator II 1981-90; MLM Svcs, pres 1986-89; Miller's ARTrium, owner, 1989-. **Orgs:** Asst editor Commnty Courier Newspaper 1971-73; columnist Kalamazoo Gazette Newspaper 1973-75; commr Kalamazoo Co Bd of Commns 1975-78; chmn Orange Co Rainbow Coalition Educ Comm 1984-85; mem NAACP; mem Am Re-Educ Assn. **Honors/Awds:** Fellow Newspaper Fund Fellowship 1965; fellow US HEW Fellowship 1967; recep of Mary M Bethune Award, Delta Sigma Theta Sor 1978; Liberty Bell Award, 1978. **Business Addr:** Owner, Miller's ARTrium, PO Box 413, Chapel Hill, NC 27514.

MILLER, MARGARET GREER
Educational Administrator. **Personal:** Born Jan 25, 1934, Indianapolis, IN; married Charles E; children: Gregory Charles, Jennifer Charmaine. **Educ:** Indiana State Univ, BS 1955; Indiana State Univ, MS 1965; Univ of Florida, Doctorate of Educ 1978. **Career:** Orange County Public Schools, speech clinician 1957-70; Univ of Central Florida, asst prof 1971-81; Orange County Public Schools, asst to supt for planning, research & testing 1981-83; Univ of Central Florida, assoc prof exceptional educ 1987-; Orange County Public Schools, assoc supt for personnel & office serv 1983-; Univ of Central Florida, dir of teacher educ center and extended studies 1989-91, dir office of multicultural issues, 1991-93, asst dean undergraduate programs and clinical experiences, 1993-. **Orgs:** Mem Alpha Kappa Alpha Sorority, Amer Speech & Hearing Assn, Amer Soc for Training & Devel, Florida Assn for School Admin, Council of Exceptional Children, Natl Sorority of Phi Delta Kappa; mem ACLD-Assn for Children with Learing Disabilities, Mental Health Assn, ASCD Assn for Supervised Curriculum & Devel, Phi Delta Kappa, Inc, AERA Amer Educ Research Assn, AASPA Amer Assn of School Personnel Admin (Nom Comm), FASPA Florida Assn of School Personnel Admin (Comm Mem, Merit Pay, Records); comm sec Orange County Advisory Comm to Bd of Educuation; committee member, Walt Disney Community Awards, 1990; Howard Phillips Fund Evaluation Committee, 1986-90, board member, 1991-; president, FASD, Florida Association for Staff Dev, 1994-95. **Honors/Awds:** Dr Emory O Jackson Memorial Journalism Award South Atlantic Regional Conf of Alpha Kappa Alpha Sorority 1983; Pioneer Award Black Student Union Org at Univ of Central Florida First Minority Full Time Instructor UCF, and Outstanding Leadership 1985; State Health, Rehabilitation Serv Award for Outstanding Work in Child Abuse 1987; Certificate of Appreciation for Outstanding Work and Contributions to the Comm and State from Gov Robert Graham 1987; Distinguished Black Educator, UCF, 1991-94; Summit Award, Pioneering Work in Community Svcs & Volunteerism, Women's Resource Ctr, 1991; I Dream a World Community Award, Outstanding Pioneer in Education & the Arts, County Commission & Orlando Historical Society, 1992; Outstanding Black Achiever, 1996. **Business Addr:** Asst Dean, Undergraduate Programs and Clinical Experiences, College of Education, University of Central Florida, Orlando, FL 32816.

MILLER, MARQUIS DAVID
Educational administrator. **Personal:** Born Jan 22, 1959, Charleston, WV; son of Fredericka Inez Sherrill Miller and Manuel Thurston Miller; married Jennifer Jean Kee Miller, Jul 10, 1982; children: Janae Latise. **Educ:** Ohio State University, BA, social behavioral sciences, 1981. **Career:** Buckeye Federal Savings & Loan, project specialist, 1981-83; Continental Office, account executive, 1983-90; Karlsberger Companies, business development representative, 1990-91; Ohio State University, associate director, Corp Foundaton, 1991-95; UNCF, natl dir of corp gifts, 1995-. **Orgs:** Ohio State University Alumni Association, 1981-; Ohio State University Black Alumni Society, 1987-; Varsity "O", 1981-; Omega Psi Phi Fraternity, 1990-; Columbus Focus Committee, founding member, 1990-. **Honors/Awds:** Columbus Jaycees, 10 Outstanding Young Citizens Award, 1987. **Business Addr:** Natl Director, Corp Gifts, United Negro College Fund, 8260 Willow Oaks Corp Dr, PO Box 10444, Fairfax, VA 22031-4511, (703)205-3466.

MILLER, MATTIE SHERRYL
Educational administrator. **Personal:** Born Jun 19, 1933, Adams, TN; daughter of Luetta Carney Washington and George Washington; married William Edward Miller, Sep 19, 1953; children: Kori Edwin. **Educ:** Tuskegee Inst AL, BS 1955; IN U, MS 1965, reading splst 1970; Univ of Evansville, adminstrn suprvsn 1975. **Career:** Evansville-Vanderburgh Sch Corp, Harper Sch principal, 1985-, guidance couns 1975-85, proj dir right to read 1972-75, reading clinician 1971-72, tchr 1959-71; Univ of Evansville, adjunct instr 1967-; IN Univ, practicum supv 1970-73; Vincennes U, field couns-upward bound 1975-77; Ball State Univ Muncie IN, part-time instr. **Orgs:** Bd of dirs Channel 9 WNIN 1975-; sec bd of dirs Ldrshp Evansville 1976-; bd of dir IN State Tchrs Assn & Evansville Tchrs Assn;

member, Rotary Club of America, 1988. **Honors/Awds:** Woman of yr in educ Evansville YWCA Ldrshp Award 1975; staff repr 8th dist Congressional Apptmnt 1975-78; black woman of yr in educ Evansville Comm Action Award 1978; Representative to France Sec Ed Schools, 1985, Representative to West African Countries, 1984, NEA. **Home Addr:** 517 S Boeke Rd, Evansville, IN 47714.

MILLER, MELVIN ALLEN
Public relations manager. **Personal:** Born Nov 24, 1950, Hattiesburg, MS; married Alfredia Dampier. **Educ:** U Univ of So Mississippi, BS 1972; Jackson State Univ, MS 1978. **Career:** Jackson Plant DeSoto Inc, communications asst 1975-76; Jackson State Univ, staff writer 1976-77, asst to dir of pub info 1977, acting dir of pub info 1977-78, dir of pub info 1978-86, dir of development 1987-. **Orgs:** Trustee, New Hope Baptist Church, Jackson, 1978-; 1st vice pres, Cystic Fibrosis Found, Mississippi Chap, 1980; unit commr, Boy Scouts of Amer, 1980; dean's list scholar, Univ of So Mississippi, 1970-72; Delta Omicron Hon Soc, Univ of So Mississippi, 1972; Phi Kappa Phi Natl Hon Soc, Jackson State Univ, 1978; pres, Coll Pub Relations Assn of Mississippi, 1979-80; bd mem, Jackson Chap of March of Dimes. **Military Serv:** AUS 1st lt 1972-75. **Business Addr:** Dir of Development, Jackson State University, 1400 Lynch St, Jackson, MS 39217.

MILLER, MELVIN B.
Publisher. **Personal:** Born Jul 22, 1934, Boston, MA; divorced. **Educ:** Harvard Coll, AB 1956; Columbia Law Sch, JD 1964. **Career:** US Justice Dept, asst US atty 1965-66; Unity Bank & Trust Co, conservator 1973-77; Bay State Banner, publ & editor 1965-; WNEV-TV, Inc, vice pres & genl counsel 1982-; Fitch Miller & Tourse, partner 1981-. **Orgs:** Trustee Boston Univ, Milton Academy, The Wang Center past trustee; New Eng Conserv of Music; James Jackson Putnam Children's Ctr, Family Serv Assn of Greater Boston, Family Couns & Guid Ctrs Inc; past dir Grtr Boston C of C; past dir MA Counc on Crime & Correc; past chmn Boston Comm Media Com; pastmem Visiting Comm; mem Overseers of Harvard Univ, MA Small Bus Adv Counc; NE Reg Area One Exec Com BSA; exec bd Minor Bus Oppor Com. **Honors/Awds:** Boston Ten Outstanding Young Men Boston Jr C of C 1967; Annual Achiev Awd NAACP 1971; Awd of Excell Art Dir Club of Boston 1970; 1st prize Gen ExcellNew Eng Press Assn 1970; 2nd prize Make-up and Typography New Eng Press Assn 1970; 2nd prize Spec Sect Awd New Eng Press Assn 1971; hon ment Gen Excell New England Press Assn 1975; Honorary Doctor of Humane Letters Suffolk Univ 1984. **Business Addr:** Publisher, Fitch Miller & Tourse, 189 State St, Boston, MA 02109.

MILLER, NATE
Professional football player. **Personal:** Born Oct 8, 1971. **Educ:** Louisiana State, attended. **Career:** Atlanta Falcons, tackle, 1997-. **Business Addr:** Professional Football Player, Atlanta Falcons, Two Falcon Place, Suwanee, GA 30174, (404)945-1111.

MILLER, NORMA ADELE
Dancer, author. **Personal:** Born Dec 2, 1919, New York, NY; daughter of Alma and Norman. **Career:** Dancer, writer, currently. **Orgs:** Society of Singers. **Honors/Awds:** Stompin at the Savoy, nomination for choregraphy. **Special Achievements:** Redd Foxx Encylopedia of Black Humor, 1977; Savoy Home of Happy Feet, Temple University, 1996. **Home Addr:** 4325 Bruce, Las Vegas, NV 89119.

MILLER, NORMAN L.
Postal executive. **Personal:** Born Apr 7, 1928, Cincinnati, OH; son of Edna O Finklea Mitchell and William A Miller; married Martha Marie Simmons Miller, Dec 29, 1951; children: Gregory E, Anthony J. **Educ:** Xavier University, Cincinnati, OH, BS, 1962; University of California, Los Angeles, CA, advanced management, 1972; Command & Gen Staff College, Fort Leavenworth, KS, MMS&T, 1975. **Career:** US Postal Service, Chicago, IL, manager opn req, 1975-80; US Postal Service, Milwaukee, WI, district manager, 1980-86; US Postal Service, St Paul, MN, postmaster/general manager, 1986-87; US Postal Service, Milwaukee, WI, postmaster/general manager, 1987-89; US Postal Service, Cincinnati, OH, postmaster/general manager, 1989-91; US Postal Service, Chicago, IL, postmaster/general manager, 1991-. **Honors/Awds:** Regional Postmaster General Special Achievement, 1986-89. **Military Serv:** Army, Colonel, 1952-77.

MILLER, OLIVER J.
Professional basketball player. **Personal:** Born Apr 6, 1970, Fort Worth, TX. **Career:** Phoenix Suns, 1992-94; Detroit Pistons, 1994-95; Toronto Raptors, 1995-. **Business Addr:** Professional Basketball Player, Toronto Raptors, 20 Bay St., Ste. 1702, Toronto, ON, Canada M5J 2N8, (416)214-2255.

MILLER, OLIVER O.
Business executive. **Personal:** Born Jul 23, 1944, Battle Creek, MI; son of Edith and Oliver; married Jeannette Claire Walker. **Educ:** Dartmouth Coll, BA 1966; Stanford Univ, MBA 1968. **Career:** Business Week, Advertising Sales 1984-; McGraw-Hill Broadcasting Co, vice pres plng 1974-84, dir of acquisitions 1977-79; MECCO, vice pres 1975-77; Mc-kinsey & Co, mgmt consult 1973-75. **Business Addr:** Business Week, 1221 Avenue of the Americas, New York, NY 10020.

MILLER, ORLANDO SALMON
Professional baseball player. **Personal:** Born Jan 13, 1969, Changuinola, Panama. **Career:** Kansas City Royals, shortstop, currently. **Business Addr:** Professional Baseball Player, Kansas City Royals, PO Box 419969, Kansas City, MO 64141-6969, (816)921-2200.

MILLER, RAY, JR.
Business chief executive. **Personal:** Born Apr 6, 1949, Hampton, VA; son of Inez Smith Miller and Inus Ray Miller; married Marlene Rose Phillips; children: Inus Ray III. **Educ:** Ohio State University, BA in political science, 1972, MA in public administration, 1974. **Career:** OH Legislative Serv Comm, research associate; former State Rep Richard F Celeste, legislative asst; Rep C.J. McLin Jr, admin asst; Correctional Inst Inspect Comm, exec dir; American Federation of State, County, and Municipal Employees, lobbyist; White House Staff of Pres Jimmy Carter, deputy spec asst; Columbus State Community College, vice president of minority affairs; Columbus Area Chamber of Commerce, vice president of community development; Ohio House of Representatives, state representative, 29th district, 1981-93; National Urban Policy Institute, president, 1993-. **Orgs:** Second Baptist Church; NAACP, life member; Alpha Phi Alpha Fraternity; AfriCare, Columbus Chapter, president; King Cultural Arts Complex, board of directors; Health Coalition of Central Ohio, board of directors; International Health Commission of the African, African-American Summit, board of directors. **Honors/Awds:** World Congress on the Family, International Pathfinder Award; Columbus Education Association, Dr Martin Luther King Jr Humanitarian Award; Ohio Commission on Minority Health, Chairman's Award; Akron Summit Community Action Association, Hubert H Humphrey Humanitarian Award; Alpha Phi Alpha Fraternity, President's Award; Columbus Urban League, Award of Excellence; Black Elected Democrats of Ohio, Distinguished Service Award. **Special Achievements:** Chief sponsor of legislation which established first time state funding for the Head Start program in Ohio; chief sponsor of some of the most significant health care legislation ever enacted in the state of Ohio, including the Indigent Health Care Act, Health Data Act, and the Mental Health Act of 1988. **Business Addr:** President, National Urban Policy Institute, 17 S High St, Ste 1015, The Huntington Bank Bldg, Columbus, OH 43215, (614)228-2220.

MILLER, REGINALD WAYNE
Professional basketball player. **Personal:** Born Aug 24, 1965, Riverside, CA; married Marita Stavrou. **Educ:** Univ of California at Los Angeles, Los Angeles, CA, 1983-87. **Career:** Indiana Pacers, guard, 1987-. **Honors/Awds:** NBA All-Star, 1990, 1995, 1996, 1998; All-NBA Third Team, 1995, 1996; won a gold medal with the US Olympic Basketball Team, 1996. **Special Achievements:** Became the first Pacer ever to start in an NBA All-Star Game, 1995; the first player in NBA history to hit 100 three-pointers in eight consecutive seasons, 1989-97; first player in Pacers' franchise history to top 15,000 career points. **Business Addr:** Professional Basketball Player, Indiana Pacers, 300 E Market St, Indianapolis, IN 46204, (317)263-2100.

MILLER, RICHARD CHARLES
Educational administrator. **Personal:** Born Jul 26, 1947, Ithaca, NY; son of Marjory Miller and Richard Miller (deceased); married Doris Jean Boyd, Jul 14, 1973; children: Carin Lea, Courtney Alison. **Educ:** Ithaca Coll, BS 1969, MS 1971; Springfield Coll, DPE 1976. **Career:** Tompkins Co Trust Co, bank teller 1965-70; San Francisco Giants Baseball Club, professional baseball player 1969-70; Springfield College, instructor, 1975-77; Bowie State University, assistant professor, 1975-77, director of physical education, 1976-90, associate professor, 1977-84, professor, 1984-90; Ithaca College, Ithaca, NY, School of Health Sciences and Human Performance, dean, 1990-. **Orgs:** American Alliance for Health, Physical Education, Recreation and Dance; National Association for Sport and Physical Education; Association for Research, Administration, Professional Councils and Societies; Association of Schools of Allied Health Professions; bd of dirs, Special Children's Ctr; bd of dirs, Ithaca YMCA; bd of dirs, Ithacare Sr Ctr; bd of dirs, Tompkins County Public Library; bd of dirs, Cayuga Medical Ctr. **Honors/Awds:** All Amer Baseball Team Ithaca Coll 1969; Sports Hall of Fame Ithaca Coll 1979. **Home Addr:** 142 Lexington Dr, Ithaca, NY 14850-1749. **Business Addr:** Dean, School of Health Sciences and Human Performance, Ithaca College, 320 Smiddy Hall, Ithaca, NY 14850.

MILLER, ROBERT, JR.
Librarian. **Personal:** Born Feb 27, 1947, New York, NY; son of Robert and Edythe Kitchens Miller; divorced; children: Nova Jean, Jennifer Ann, Robynn Marie. **Educ:** Wagner College, BA, 1972; Columbia University, MSLS, 1974. **Career:** New York Public Library, community liaison asst, 1972-74, librarian I, 1974-75; National College of Education, reference librarian, 1975-79; Memphis and Shelby County Public Library and Information Center, first asst, 1979-81; Atlanta-Fulton Public Library, communications officer, 1981-86; Chicago Public Library, curator, 1986-. **Orgs:** American Library Assn, 1972; Black Caucus of ALA, board member, 1987-91. **Honors/Awds:** Stephen A Douglas Association, Stephen A Douglas Award, 1992. **Special Achievements:** Memphis the old and new, Tennessee librarian, 1980; Genealogy Sources in the Vivian G Harsh Collection, Illinois libraries, 1989; Ben Burns and Horace Cayton Papers, Illinois libraries, 1988; Harold Washington, 1922-87, A Select Bibliography, 1987. **Business Addr:** Curator, Vivian G Harsh Res Collection of Afro-Amer Hist & Lit, Carter Godwin Woodson Regional Library, 9525 South Halsted street, Chicago, IL 60628, (312)747-6910.

MILLER, ROBERT LAVERNE
Professional athlete. **Personal:** Born Jan 9, 1953, Houston, TX; married Lennie; children: Robert II, Samuel, Tiffanie. **Educ:** Univ of KS Lawrence, B Bus Admin 1978. **Career:** James D Ryan Jr High, 1967; Jack Yates Sr High, 1968-70; MN Vikings, professional athlete 1975-80; CDC, admin 1981-. **Orgs:** Mem 9th St Missionary Baptist Church; deacon Church Org; asst tchr Sunday Sch; Campus Crusade for Christ; Fellowship of Christian Athletes; bd of reference Hospitality House. **Honors/Awds:** MVP 1969-70; most determined and inspirational player 1973; Jayhawk 1974; has missed only one game in five years. **Home Addr:** RR 3, 285 Holyoake, Box 200A, Northfield, MN 55057.

MILLER, RONALD BAXTER
Educator. **Personal:** Born Oct 11, 1948, Rocky Mount, NC; son of Elsie Bryant Miller and Marcellus C Miller; married Jessica Garris; children: Akin Dasan. **Educ:** NC Central Univ, BA (Magna Cum Laude) 1970; Brown Univ, AM 1972, PhD 1974. **Career:** Haverford Coll, asst prof English 1974-76; State Univ Coll of NY, lecturer 1974; Univ of TN, assoc prof, 1977-81, prof of English, 1982-92, dir of Black Literature Program, prof; Univ of GA, prof of English & African American studies, 1992-, dir of Institute for African American Studies, currently. **Orgs:** Consultant, NEH sponsor, TV Series "The South" 1977-78; advisor and contributing editor "WATU: A Cornell Journ of Black Writing" 1978-79, "Obsidian: Black Literature in Review" 1979-, "Callaloo" 1981-, "Black American Literature Forum," African American Review, 1982-, "Middle Atlantic Writers Assn Review" 1982-,"Langston Hughes Review" 1982-; evaluator Div of Publ Programs Harlem Exec Comm Afro-Am Lit Discuss Group MLA 1980-83; chr/founder/1st chr Div on Black Amer Lit and Culture 1982-84; mem MLA delegate Assembly 1984-86, 1997-99; participant/consultant Black Writers South (GA Cncl for the Arts and Humanities) 1980-; vice pres Black History Month Lecture Series 1980; reader Univ of TN Press 1980-; chr Black Studies CLA 1982-; pres The Langston Hughes Soc 1984-88; Zora Neale Hurston Review 1986-; Committee on Languages and Literatures of America, 1994-97. **Honors/Awds:** Black Scholar Lectures Le Moyne Coll 1985, Univ of UT 1985; ACLS Conf Grant Black Amer Literature and Humanism Research 1978; NEH Summer Research 1975; Haverford Coll Rsch 1975; Natl Fellowships Fund Dissertation Grant 1973-74; Univ of TN Committee Awards for Excellence in Teaching of English 1978-79; United Negro Coll Fund, Distinguished Scholar, Xavier Univ, 1988; Honored teacher, Alpha Delta Pi, 1988; Natl Rsch Council, Ford Found, Sr Fellowship, 1986-87; Irvine Foundation Visiting Scholar, University of San Francisco, 1991; author: Reference Guide to Langston Hughes and Gwendolyn Brooks, 1978; Ed & Contra Black American Literature and Humanism, 1981; Black American Poets Between Worlds, 1986; Author, Art and Imagination of Langston Hughes, 1989; Southern Trace of Black Critical Theory, 1991; co-author: Call and Response: Riverside Anthology in African American Literary Tradition, 1997; University of Tennessee, Golden Key Award for Excellence, 1990; American Book Award, 1991; ACOG Cultural Olympiad, 1994; University of Georgia, Golden Key Award for Excellence, 1995; Sr Lilly Teaching Fellowship, 1995-96. **Business Addr:** Professor of English & African American Studies, University of Georgia, Institute for African American Studies, Athens, GA 30602-3012.

MILLER, RUSSELL L., JR.
Educator, physician, administrator. **Personal:** Born Jun 30, 1939, Harvey, WV; son of Corinne Miller and Russel Miller; married Daryl Lawson; children: Steven, Laura. **Educ:** Howard Univ Coll of Liberal Arts, BS 1961; Howard Univ Coll of Med, MD 1965. **Career:** Howard Univ, dean of coll of med 1979-88, vice pres for Health Affairs 1988-90, senior vice president and vice president for health affairs, 1990-93; prof of internal med & pharm, 1979-93; Howard Univ Coll of Med, Assoc Prof, Internal Med & Pharm, dir, section of clinical pharm, 1974-79; visiting scientist, Natl Inst of Health, 1984-; Cardiovascular Rsch Inst, Univ of CA, Dept of Intl Med San Francisco Div of Clinical Pharm, rsch fellow, 1968-69, 1971-73; Univ of MI Med Center, Ann Arbor MI, summer fellowships intern/Internal Med Rsch, 1965-68; Natl Inst of Health Bethesda MD, summer fellowships, 1961-63; Dept of Cellular Biology Div of Pharm & Immunopharmacology Roche Inst of Molecular Biology Nutley NJ, visiting scientist, 1973-74; Howard Univ, assoc prof, 1974-79, College of Medicine, dean, 1979-88; vp for Health Affairs, 1988-93, senior vp, 1991-93; SUNY HSCB, Brooklyn,

NY, president, 1994-97; consultant, 1997-. **Orgs:** AAAS; Am Fed for Clinical Rsch; Am Soc of Internal Med; Am Soc for Clinical Pharm & Therapeutics; Reticuloendotheolial Soc; DC Med Soc; DC Natl Med Assn; Med Chirurgical Soc; Mem, DC General Hospital Commn 1984-88, Mayor's Advisory Commn on Post-Secondary Education 1987-, Natl Advisory Council on Aging 1988-; bd of dir, Natl Resident Matching Program 1988; chmn, Council of Southern Deans, 1987-88; member-at-large, National Board of Medical Examiners, 1988-91, executive board member, 1991-; member, Board of Trustees of the Educational Commission for Foreign Medical Graduates, 1991-; board of directors, Sight Savers International, 1989-. **Honors/Awds:** Fellow, Am Coll of Physicians & Coll of Clinical Pharm; elected to Phi Beta Kappa, Howard Univ Chapter, 1961; elected to Alpha Omega Alpha Hon Med Soc, Howard Univ Chapter, 1964; Diplomate, Natl Bd of Med Examiners, 1966; certified, Am Bd of Internal Med, 1971; scholar in Clinical Pharm Burroughs Wellcome Fund, 1977-82; awarded grants, Dept of Health Educ & Welfare Rsch Grant 1977-80; Burroughs Wellcome Found, 1977-82; certificate of honor, Natl Medical Fellowships, 1988. **Military Serv:** USAR, Major, 1969-71; received Bronze Star. **Business Addr:** 130 Jefferson Street NW, Washington, DC 20011.

MILLER, SAMUEL O.
Educator. **Personal:** Born Jun 8, 1931, La Boca, Panama; son of Germaine Harvey Miller and Hubert Miller; divorced; children: Larisa, Mark. **Educ:** Dakota Wesleyan Univ, BS (cum laude) 1957; Boston Univ School of Social Work, MSW (honors) 1961; Univ of Chicago Social Serv Admin, PhD 1970. **Career:** Family Serv Bureau Chicago, IL, social work 1959-62; Univ of Chicago Dept of Psy, instructor 1962-64; San Mateo County Mental Health Dept, sr social wkr 1964-67; Western MI Univ School of Soc Work, assoc prof 1970-73; Columbia Univ, prof of social work, currently. **Orgs:** Consult Mental Health Organization Council on Soc Work Educ Sch; bd mem Manhattan Country School; NAACP; Natl Assn of Social Workers. **Honors/Awds:** Natl Research Service Award, Natl Inst of Mental Health 1979; Fellowship Award, Whitney Young Found 1980; Career Tchr Natl Inst of Mental Health 1968-70; published various papers & chapters in social work books. **Business Addr:** Professor of Social Work, Columbia Univ, 622 W 113th St, New York, NY 10025.

MILLER, SAUNDRA CELIA
Counselor. **Personal:** Born Jul 4, 1943, New York, NY; daughter of Vivian Hedgepeth; widowed; children: Rodney, Anthony, Yvette. **Educ:** John Jay College Criminal Justice, Social Sciences, Criminal Law Cert; College of New Rochelle, Liberal Arts, 1982. **Career:** NYPD, invest counselor, 1973-76. **Orgs:** National Organization of Black Law Enforcement Executive, delegate, 1988-; National Black Police Association, trustee, 1989-; 100 Black Women, 1992-; Community Board #14 Queens Cty, 1979-; A Better Chance, NY-NJ Chap, 1980-. **Home Addr:** 353 Beach 57th St, #5A, Arverne, NY 11692.

MILLER, SHERRE. **See BISHOP, SHERRE WHITNEY.**

MILLER, SYLVIA ALBERTA GREGORY
Educator, librarian (retired). **Personal:** Born Dec 11, 1919, Snow Hill, NC; daughter of Rachel E Suggs Gregory and Albert Gregory; married Matthew Miller, Aug 20 (deceased); children: Muriel Kay, Sylvia Gay. **Educ:** Shaw University, Raleigh, NC, BS, 1949; North Carolina Central Univ, Durham, MS, 1959; Graduate Secondary Teacher's, certificate Class A, 1958. **Career:** Retired school personnel, secretarial service; Shaw Alumni Chapter, financial service; Grove Park Christian Church, financial service, librarian; Savanah H & M, Griffin, NC, clasroom instructor & counselor, librarian, 1953-83, (retired). **Orgs:** Member, ALA American Library, 1953-91; program committee, American Business Women, 1990-92; financial treasurer, Shaw Univ, Kinston Chapter, 1991-92; financial pledge treasurer, Grove Park Church, 1980-92. **Honors/Awds:** NCAE for Interest & Participation, 1983; Special Volunteer Certificate of Appreciation, 1984; Greatest Number of Years at School, Savannah School Faculty, 1981; Executive board, NCCU, Sister Alumni Assn Service, 1985; Alumni Assn, NCCU, Slis Award, 1985. **Home Addr:** 603 Beech Ave, Kinston, NC 28501.

MILLER, TEDD
Educator. **Personal:** Born Jan 4, 1946, Washington, DC; son of Ruby and Theodore; married Gail D Johnson-Miller, Feb 1, 1976; children: Tony, Tammy, Tyesha, Atiba. **Educ:** Bethune Cookman College, BA, 1968; Rutgers School of Law, JD, 1972. **Career:** Rutgers Univ, adjunct faculty, 1972-75; Essex County Legal Services, staff attorney, 1972-75; Council on Legal Education Opportunity, asst director, 1975-80; Georgetown Univ Law Center, director of admissions, 1980-92; Howard Univ School of Law, asst dean of director of admissions, currently. **Orgs:** Law School Admissions Council, board of trustees, 1994-97; Assn of American Law Schools, chair section on pre legal education and admission to law school, 1994-96. **Business Addr:** Assistant Dean & Director of Admissions, Howard University School of Law, 2900 Van Ness St NW, Ste 200, Holy Cross Mall, Washington, DC 20010.

MILLER, TELLY HUGH
Educator, clergyman. **Personal:** Born Jun 18, 1939, Henderson, TX; married Glory D Bennett; children: Alanna Camille. **Educ:** Wiley Coll, BA 1962; Interdenom Theol Cntr, MDiv 1965; Vanderbilt U, DMin 1973; Prairie View A&M Univ, EdM 1980. **Career:** St Paul Baptist Church St Albans WV, pastor 1965; WV State Coll, religious counselor 1967; Wiley Coll Marshall TX, coll minister 1968, financial aid dir 1970, assoc prof/chmn dept of religion 1973, vice pres for student affairs 1974, prof and chmn dept of religion and philosophy 1976-. **Orgs:** Relig consult Bapt WV St Coll Inst 1967; mem Am Assn Univ Profs; chmn Christmas Baskets for Needy St Albans 1967; bd dirs YMCA St Albans 1966-67; chmn mem drive NAACP 1967; mem exec com Kanawha Co chap 1967; v moder Mt Olivet Assn 1966-67; pres George Washington Carver Elem Sch PTA 1977; pres Gamma Upsilon Lambda Chap Alpha Phi Alpha Frat Inc 1977; mem Alpha Phi Alpha Frat Inc, Alpha Phi Omega Natl Serv Frat Kappa Pi Chapt, AAUP, Morgan Lodge No 10 St Albans WV, NAACP; fellowship of Christian Athletes; bd of dirs Harrison County United Way Fund Dr 1983, bd of dirs Harrison County Red Cross. **Honors/Awds:** East TX Educ Oppors Ctr Awd 1980; Kappa Alpha Psi Achievement Awd 1980; Omega Psi Phi Man of the Year Awd 1983; elected first Black Commissioner for Harrison County 1983; apptd by Gov of TX to East TX Regional Review Comm for the State's Comm Develop Block Grant Prog. **Business Addr:** Chmn, Dept of Religion/Philosophy, Wiley College, 711 Rosborough Springs Rd, Marshall, TX 75670.

MILLER, THEODORE H.
Engineer. **Personal:** Born Jan 27, 1905, Kansas City, KS; son of Otie B Miller and Harry W Miller; married Grace Eubank; children: Stanley E, Harry F. **Educ:** Univ of NV, BS Elec Engrg 1930; Attended, KS State Coll. **Career:** Westinghouse Elec Co, comml refrig sales div 1935-42; USN Mare Island Naval Shipyard, supvr elec design 1941-46; VA Engrg Div, asst head 1946-51; US Govt GSA 9th Region, chief elec engr 1951-72; Self-Employed, consulting engr, currently. **Orgs:** Licensed Professional Engr Elec State of CA; sr mem Inst of Elec & Electronic Engrs; instr part-time Radiological Defense Stanford Univ; pres Employees Assn 9th Region GSA 1962-66; Western Regional Dir Phi Beta Sigma Frat 1954-56; pres bd dirs Booker T Washington Comm Ctr San Francisco 1956-59; mem bd examiners US Civil Serv Commn 1949-52; Mason; Shriner. **Honors/Awds:** Merit Serv Awd GSA 1964; High Quality Perf Awd GSA 1963; Commendable Serv Awd GSA 1964; Sustained Superior Perf Awd GSA 1968; Man of Month Awd GSA 1972. **Home Addr:** 9403 Braewick Dr, Houston, TX 77096.

MILLER, THOMAS PATTON (TOM)
Artist. **Personal:** Born Oct 13, 1945, Baltimore, MD; son of Clarence Miller & Frances Miller. **Educ:** Maryland Institute, College of Art, BFA, 1963-67, MFA, 1985-87. **Career:** Artist, art educator. **Orgs:** Maryland State Arts Council, 1990. **Honors/Awds:** Baltimore Public schools, Merit Work Scholarship, 1963; Maryland State Arts Council, Ford Foundation Grant, 1986; Gov Wm Donald Schaefer, MD, Artistic Excellence Citation, 1990; Louisville Visual Arts Assn, Kentucky, Purchase Award, 1991. **Special Achievements:** Next Generation Exhibit, Winston Salem, NC, 1990; Retrospective Exhibit, Baltimore Museum of Art, 1995; Seeing Jazz Exhibit, Smithsonian Institute, Washington DC, 1997. **Business Addr:** Artist, 2010 McCulloh St, Baltimore, MD 21217.

MILLER, THOMASENE
Administrator. **Personal:** Born Dec 6, 1942, Newcastle, PA; married David Lamar; children: David. **Educ:** DePaul U. **Career:** City of Chicago, comm adminstr; Model Cities, asst comm adminstr 1970-76; Chicago Com on Urban Oppty, asst chief clk 1968-70, sec 1965-68. **Orgs:** Rua Consult Firm 1976-; Metro Home Hlth Adv Com 1976-; bd of mgrs Chicago Boys Club Martin Luther King Unit 1977; mem NAACP; mem Nat Assn for Comm Devel; mem Am Soc for Pub Adminstrn. **Honors/Awds:** Recog of merit Chicago Com on Urban Oppty; Englewood Childrens Club Award 1970; recog of merit Chicago State Univ 1970; recog of achvmt Model Cities/CCUO 1975. **Business Addr:** 10 S Kedzie, Chicago, IL 60612.

MILLER, WARD BEECHER
Banking executive. **Personal:** Born Jun 22, 1954, Kingstree, SC; son of Bertha McCray Miller and Clifton Miller; married Vicki Smith. **Educ:** College of Charleston, BA 1976. **Career:** Wachovia Bank, personal banker 1977-79, branch mgr 1979-81, field analyst 1981-83, branch mgr 1983-85, exec banker 1985-88, Main Office Branch Mgr, 1988-92, East and South Office Manager, 1992-. **Orgs:** Steward St James AME Church 1979-; bd mem Big Brothers/Big Sisters 1982-, March of Dimes 1983-, Lift Inc 1986-; financial partner Forsyth Investment Partners 1985-; at large mem Juvenile Justice Council 1986-; Inner City Council, Boy Scouts of America; member, Forsyth County Zoning Board. **Honors/Awds:** Campaign Award for Fund Raising March of Dimes 1984-86; YMCA Century Club Award, Big Brothers/Big Sisters Appreciation Award; Forsyth Investment Partners Appreciation Award; Oustanding Lay Leader Award. **Home Addr:** 2520 Treetop Ln, Winston-Salem, NC 27101. **Business Addr:** VP, Wachovia Bank & Trust Co NA, 701 Martin Luther King Jr Dr, Winston-Salem, NC 27101.

MILLER, WARREN F., JR. (PETE)
Educator. **Personal:** Born Mar 17, 1943, Chicago, IL; son of Helen R. Miller and Warren F. Miller; married Judith Hunter Miller, Feb 21, 1969; children: David, Jonathan. **Educ:** US Military Academy, West Point, NY, BS, 1964; Northwestern University, Evanston, IL, MS, 1970, PhD, 1972. **Career:** Northwestern University, Evanston, IL, assistant professor, 1972-74; Los Alamos National Laboratory, Los Alamos, NM, staff member, 1974-76, group leader, 1976-79, associate director, 1979-86, deputy director, 1986-90; University of California-Berkeley, Berkeley, CA, Pardee professor, 1990-92; Science & Technology Base Programs, Los Alama Natl Lab, dir, 1992-. **Honors/Awds:** New Mexico Eminent Scholar, 1988-; Martin Luther King Fellow, Woodrow Wilson Foundation, 1969-72; Merit Award, Northwestern Univ, 1993. **Military Serv:** US Army, Capt., 1964-69; received Bronze Star, 1968; Army Commendation Medal, 1969. **Business Addr:** Professor of Nuclear Engineering, University of California-Berkeley, 4161 Etcheverry Hall, Berkeley, CA 94720.

MILLER, WILBUR J.
Benefit authorizer, councilman. **Personal:** Born Feb 16, 1928, Wilkes-barre, PA; married Gertha Wallace; children: Wilbur J. **Educ:** BS 1975. **Career:** Roosevelt City, AL, city councilman; Soc Sec Admin SE Prgm Ctr Birmingham, benefit authorizer; AUS Ptr Pyramid Sporting Goods Co Inc Roosevelt City,1973-. **Orgs:** Pres Roosevelt Invest Corp; pres Citizens Econ & Ed Devel Corp; pres McDonald Chapel Sp Sch PTA; mem Civic League; Birmingham Grid Forecstrs. **Honors/Awds:** Purple Heart; Bronze Star; Army Commendation; Outst Councilmn of Yr 1971. **Military Serv:** AUS sgt 1945-66. **Business Addr:** 301 Brighton Ave, Bessemer, AL 35020.

MILLER, WILLIAM NATHANIEL
Association executive. **Personal:** Born Mar 15, 1947, Perry, GA; married Shirley Jones; children: Corbett Burgess, William Franklin. **Educ:** Ft Valley State College, BA Economics 1969; American Inst of Banking, Advanced 1971. **Career:** Natl Bank of Georgia, banking officer 1972-77; US Small Business Admin, disaster loan specialist 1977-78; Atlanta Regional Minority Purchasing Council, executive dir 1978-. **Orgs:** Member Phi Beta Sigma Fraternity 1966-; life member Atlanta Chamber of Commerce 1976-; chairman of board John Harland Boys Club 1976; member Ft Valley State Coll Alumni Assn 1978-; member Atlanta & Natl Business League 1979-; member NAACP 1980-; chairman business com United Negro College Fund 1982; member Natl Assn of Exhibition Mgrs 1985; graduate Leadership Atlanta 1985. **Honors/Awds:** Natl Top Achiever Atlanta Chamber of Commerce 1976; Business Dev Honors Collections of Life & Heritage 1984; Council of the Year Natl Minority Supplier DevCouncil 1984. **Business Addr:** Executive Dir, Atlanta Reg Minority Purch Co, 235 International Blvd, Atlanta, GA 30303.

MILLER, WILLIAM O.
Association executive. **Personal:** Born Apr 14, 1934, Philadelphia, PA; son of Ethel Reed Miller and Joseph M Miller (deceased); divorced; children: William C. **Educ:** Temple Univ, BS 1957; Antioch Univ, ME 1974. **Career:** Opportunity Indus Centrs Inc, instructor, 1965-73; Philadelphia Urban Coalition, instructor 1968-80; Fitzsimons Jr HS, dir publicity, 1968-70; Fellowship Commn Philadelphia, PA, dir educ, 1975-76; OIC/A Philadelphia, PA, asst dir funds devel, 1976-83, dir natl organization & special events, 1983-; Lincoln/Eagleville Program, l980-8l. **Orgs:** Mem bd dir Philadelphia Miniv; Temple Univ Downtown Club; Graduate Council of Antioch Univ; Philadelphia Tribune Charities; Voters Crusade; Delaware Valley Chapter of the Natl Soc of Fund Raisers; bd dir Philadelphia Civic Ballet; Serv Acad Select Bd-Congr Gray; Prince Hall Masons King David #52 F and A of Penna PHA; Alpha Phi Alpha Fraternity; Deacon Board Zion Baptist Church; Comm Leaderships Seminar; mem Amer League of Lobbyist, Archival Comm OIC/Temple Univ. **Honors/Awds:** Legion of Honor Award Chapel of Four Chaplins, 1967-75; Second Mile Award Prince Hall Masons PA, 1972; Distinguished Serv Award Philadelphia Chapter NAACP, 1965; published "Why Bus?" Urban Coalition Publication.

MILLER, YVONNE BOND
Educator, state government official. **Personal:** Born Jul 4, 1934, Edenton, NC; daughter of Pency Cola Bond and John Thomas Bond Sr; married Wilbert Roy Miller Jr (divorced). **Educ:** VA St Coll, BS 1956; Columbia Univ Tchrs Coll, MA 1962; Univ of Pittsburgh, PhD 1973. **Career:** Virginia Senate, senator 5th senatorial district, 1988-; VA House of Delegates, delegate 89th dist, 1984-88; Norfolk State Univ, prof of educ, 1976-, head, Dept of Early Childhood/Elementary Educ, 1980-87, assoc prof, 1973-76, asst prof, 1968-72; Mid-S Tchr Corps Network, dir exec com 1976; Tchr Corps Corpsmen Train Inst, fac mem 1976; Old Dominion U, adj asso prof 1975-76; Mid-Atlantic Tchr Corps Network Bd of Dir, sec 1974-75, dir 1974-76; Norfolk Tchr Corps Proj, dir 1975; Norfolk/Chesapeake Tchr Corps Proj, dir 1974-75, asso dir 1973; Headstart, educ dir 1969; Norfolk City Sch, tchr asst 1966-68; Young Park Sch, headstrt tchr 1965-66, tchr 1956-66. **Orgs:** Life mem NEA; Am Assn of Elem Kinder Nurs Edn; Assn for Supv & Curr Devel; Nat Assn for Educ of Yng Child; Assn for Child Educ Internat;

VA Assn of Early Child Edn; Tidewater Pre-Sch Assn; So Assn for Child Under 6; life mem Nat Alliance of Black Sch Edn; Am Assn of Univ Prof; VA Educ Assn; CH Mason Meml Ch of God in Christ; editor Viewpoint Newsletter of VAECE 1979-80; Am Assn of Univ Women; Chrysler Mus at Norfolk; VA Mus; Beta Theta Zeta Chap Zeta Phi Beta; life mem Zeta Phi Beta Kappa Delta Phi 1962. **Honors/Awds:** Academic Excellence Award, Zeta Phi Beta, 1974; Hall of Fame Induction, Virginia Commission of Women, 1991; SERWA Award, Virginia Commonwealth Chapter, National Coalition of 100 Black Women, 1989. **Business Addr:** The Honorable Yvonne B. Miller, General Assembly Bldg, Richmond, VA 23219.

MILLER-HOLMES, CHERYL
Library director. **Personal:** Born Sep 15, 1958, Detroit, MI; daughter of Elzenia Miller and Hubert Miller. **Educ:** Specs Howard School of Broadcast Arts, Southfield, MI; Oakland Community College, Farmington Hill, MI, AA; Spring Arbor College, Spring Arbor, MI, BA, 1988; Wayne State University, Detroit, MI, MLS, 1990. **Career:** Wayne County Department of Social Services, caseworker, beginning 1981; Michigan Department of Corrections, library director, until 1993; Wayne County Community College, library director, 1993-. **Orgs:** Board of directors, African American Reparations Committee, member, Wayne County Department of Social Service, Affirmative Action Advisory Committee. **Honors/Awds:** Paul Laurence Dunbar Award, Detroit Black Writers Guild, First Prize, Poetry Contest. **Home Addr:** P O Box 48127, Oak Park, MI 48237-5827.

MILLER-JONES, DALTON
Educational administrator, psychologist. **Personal:** Born Jul 6, 1940, St Louis, MO; married Cynthia L Miller; children: Dalton A Jones, Julie K Jones, M Luke Jones, Marcus N. **Educ:** Rutgers Univ, BA & BS 1962; Tufts Univ, MS Experimental Psy 1965; Cornell Univ, PhD Psychology 1973. **Career:** Cornell Univ Africana Studies, lecturer & rsch assoc 1969-73; Univ of Mass/Amherst, asst prof 1973-82; Williams Coll, Henry Luce assoc prof 1982-84; City Univ of New York Grad School, assoc prof 1984-. **Orgs:** Adjunct prof & fellow Inst Comparative Human Cognition Rockefeller Univ, NY 1974-76; member Soc for Rsch in Child Dev 1978-; empirical rsch consultant in Black psychology for New York Board of Ed, Am Can Co & Black community organizations 1980; Jean Piaget Society 1981-; Amer Psych Assn 1982-; Amer Ed Rsch Assn 1981-. **Honors/Awds:** NSF & Office Education Fellowships 1966-69; NSF 1972; Carnegie Corp New York Grant 1972-73; articles and book chapters on Black children's language & thought in J of Black Studies and Academic Press 1979-84. **Business Addr:** Associate Professor Psychology, Developmental Psychology Prog, GSUC/CUNY, 33 W 42nd St, New York, NY 10036.

MILLER-LEWIS, S. JILL
Art gallery owner. **Personal:** Born in Detroit, MI; daughter of Margie K Miller and Ruben H Miller; married James A Lewis, Dec 29, 1984; children: Alake-Asabi, Bakari Ogbonna Jahi, Makeda-Menen. **Educ:** Tuskegee Institute; Howard University, BS; Michigan State University, post-graduate studies; Wayne State University. **Career:** National Day Care Association, Washington, DC, educational consultant, 1978-80; Detroit Board of Education, Detroit, MI, teacher, 1980-82; Rosa Parks Center/Museum, Detroit, MI, program director/designer, 1983-84; Charming Shoppes Inc; Fashion Bug, Royal Oak, MI, assistant manager, 1985-86; Detroit Board of Education, Detroit, MI, teacher, 1986-; Jill Perette Gallery, Detroit, MI, owner, 1988-; Aida-Akante Designs and Manufacturing, owner, 1993-. **Orgs:** Network director, National Association of Female Executives, 1992; program director, Rosa Parks Center/Museum, 1983-84; chairperson, Walk-a-thon 84, 1984; fashion designer, Celebrity Fashion Extravaganza, Rosa Parks Center, 1983; member, Convention Bureau of Detroit, 1990-91; Michigan Retailers Association, 1992. **Honors/Awds:** Spirit of Detroit, City Council of Detroit, 1988; Certificate of Appreciation, Childrens Center of Wayne County, 1982-83. **Special Achievements:** Author, Dressing Successfully, 1984-85; African Pattern Design, 1993.

MILLER-POPE, CONSUELO ROBERTA
Association executive. **Personal:** Born in Ayer, MA; daughter of Harold G & Consuelo D Miller; divorced; children: Alexis Michelle-Dale Williams. **Educ:** Pennsylvania State University, BA, 1965; University of Chicago, MA, 1969; Chicago-Kent College of Law, currently. **Career:** Chicago Economic Development Corp, vice pres, 1969-81; Cosmopolitan Chamber of Commerce, president, 1982-. **Orgs:** Institute for Urban Economic Dev, vice pres; University of Illinois Ctr for Urban Business, board member; NAACP. **Honors/Awds:** Chicago Economic Dev Council, Svc Awd, 1987; League of Black Women, Econ Dev, Svc Awd, 1988; So Austin-Madison Dev Corp, Bridge-Builder Awd, 1988; National Sales Network, Appreciation Cert, 1995. **Special Achievements:** Published in Crain's Chicago Business; Dollars & Sense Magazine; Talking to the Boss Newspaper; Organizer for minority business participation in White House Conf on Small Business, 1995. **Business Addr:** President/CEO, Cosmopolitan Chamber of Commerce, 1326 S Michigan, Ste 100, Chicago, IL 60605, (312)786-0212.

MILLER-REID, DORA ALMA
Educator (retired). **Personal:** Born Mar 24, Montgomery, AL; daughter of Mary-Frances Ingersoll Miller (deceased) and George Miller (deceased); married Willie J Reid, Sep 28, 1949. **Educ:** Florida A&M Univ, Tallahassee FL, BS, 1954; Wayne State Univ, Detroit MI, EdM, 1959. **Career:** Escambia County Bd of Public Instruction, Pensacola FL, teacher, 1955-71; Detroit Bd of Educ, Detroit MI, teacher, 1971-81. **Orgs:** The Detroit Fedn of Teachers, AFL-CIO, 1971-; Amer Fedn of Teachers, 1971-; bd of dir, mem, Co-Ette Club Inc, Detroit Chapter, 1971-; Wayne State Univ Alumni Assn, 1975-; Natl Retired Teachers Assn, 1981-; Retirement Coordinating Council, 1981-; mem, United Foundation's Heart of Gold Awards Council, 1982-, Metro Detroit Teen Conf Coalition, 1983-; Women's Comm, NAACP, 1983-. **Honors/Awds:** Certificate of Merit, Detroit Bd of Educ, 1981; John F Kennedy Memorial Award, Co-Ette Club Inc, Detroit Chapter, 1987; Certificate of Appreciation, Detroit Bd of Educ, 1988; Governor's Volunteer Honor Roll, State of Michigan, Special Tribute, 1989; Certificate of Appreciation, Ronald McDonald House, 1989; Outstanding Service to Community and State Award, Editorial Board of Amer Biographical Institute, 1976-77; United Way, Heart of Gold Award, 1991. **Home Addr:** 9000 E Jefferson, Apt 11-8, Detroit, MI 48214.

MILLETT, KNOLLY E.
Physician. **Personal:** Born Aug 15, 1922; married Mavis DeBurg; children: Eileen, Mercedes, Denise, Maria, Jacques. **Educ:** Long Island Univ Brklyn, BS 1947; Univ of Paris Faculty of Med, MD 1959. **Career:** Brklyn Physicians, pvt prac. **Orgs:** Mem Nat Med Assn; AMA; Kings Col Med Soc; Provident Clinic Soc of Bklyn; Phi Beta Sigma; Gamma Rho Sigma; affil Brklyn-Cumberland Med Ctr Jewish Hosp of Bklyn; mem Urban League; NY Civil Liberties Union; Manhasset C of C; diplomate Am Bd of Family Practice. **Business Addr:** 453 Franklin Ave, Brooklyn, NY 11238.

MILLETT, RICARDO A.
Association executive. **Personal:** Born May 10, 1945, Panama City, Panama; son of Ometa Towers Millett and William G Millett; married Jan Stepto; children: Sundiata Madoda, Miguel Stepto, Maya Alegre. **Educ:** Brandeis Univ, BS Econ 1968; Florence Heller School Brandeis Univ, MA 1971, PhD 1973. **Career:** Atlanta Univ, assoc prof 1973-77; ABT Assoc, sr analyst, proj mgr 1977-80; Dept of Social Svc, dep asst comm mgr 1980-81; Boston Univ, dir, adj prof 1981-83; Roxbury Milti-Serv Ctr, exec dir 1983-85; Neighborhood Housing Development, asst dir 1985-. **Orgs:** Asst dir Boston Redevel Auth 1985-; bd mem, chmn Hillside Pre-Release Prog; mem, pres Black Political Task Force; mem Museum of Afro-Amer History African Meeting House Comm 1987; bd of overseers Florence Heller School, Brandeis Univ; bd of dirs Thomas Jefferson Forum; bd of dirs Social Policy Research Group. **Honors/Awds:** "St Corner Alcoholics" Alton Childs Publ 1976; "Widespread Citizen Participation in Model Cities and the Demands of Ethnic Minorities for a Greater Decision Making Role in Amer Cities" 1977; "Simmering on the Calm Presence and Profound Wisdom of Howard Thurman," 1981-82; "Racism and Racial Relations in Boston" 1982-83; Faces to Watch in 1986 Boston Mag 1986; "Urban Renewal and Residential Displacement in the South End" Boston Univ Afro-Amer Studies Dept 1987; "Enterprise Zones and Parcel to Parcel Linkage, The Boston Case" Univ of MA School of Public & Community Serv 1987; "New Players in Urban Development" Boston Redevelopment Authority 1989; "Monuments for Social Justice: A Commentary from the Black Perspective," in Toward Social & Economic Justice, edited by David & Eva Gil, 1985; "elopment & Displacement in the Black Community," in Journal of Health & Social Policy, Vol I, No 4, 1990. **Business Addr:** Sr Vice Pres for Planning & Resource Mgmt, United Way of Mass Bay, 245 Summer St, Ste 1401, Boston, MA 02210-1121.

MILLIARD, RALPH GREGORY
Professional baseball player. **Personal:** Born Dec 30, 1973, Sacramento, CA. **Career:** Florida Marlins, infielder, 1996-. **Business Addr:** Professional Baseball Player, Florida Marlins, Pro Player Stadium, NW 199th St, Miami, FL 33169, (305)356-5848.

MILLICAN, ARTHENIA J. BATES
Educator (retired), writer. **Personal:** Born Jun 1, 1920, Sumter, SC; daughter of Susan Emma David Jackson and Calvin Shepherd Jackson; married Noah Bates (deceased); children: Willie Louis Lee. **Educ:** Morris Coll Sumter, SC, BA (Magna Cum Laude) 1941; Atlanta Univ, MA 1948; LA State Univ Baton Rouge, PhD 1972. **Career:** Westside HS Kershaw, SC, English teacher 1942-45; Butler HS Hartsville, SC, civics/English teacher 1945-46; Morris Coll, head English dept 1947-49; Mary Bethune HS Halifax, VA, English teacher 1949-55; MS Valley State Univ, English instructor 1955-56; Southern Univ, English instructor 1956-59, asst prof 1959-63, assoc prof 1963-72, prof English 1972-74; Norfolk State Univ, prof English 1974-77; Southern Univ Baton Rouge, LA, prof English & creative writing 1977-80; researcher, writer, freelancer. **Orgs:** Mem Baton Rouge Alumnae Chap of Delta Sigma Theta; mem comm Arts and Letters Baton Rouge Sigma Alumnae Chapt; serve as poet prose reader and exhibitor of creative works for programs; mem Les Gayettes Civic and Social Club; executive committee member, Societas Docta, Inc, 1988-90; life member, College Language Assn, 1948-; member, Society for the Study of Southern Literature, 1986-; committee member, Louisiana Folklore Society, 1973-; Modern Language Assn of America; Natl Council of Teachers of English; Assn for the Study of Afro-American Life & History; Phillis Wheatley Club. **Honors/Awds:** National Endowment for the Arts Award, 1 out of 165 in the nation, 1976; Delta Sigma Theta Sorority Inc, Silver Anniversary Award, 1991, Baton Rouge Sigma Alumnae Chapter, first, Delta Pearl Award in Literature, 1989. **Special Achievements:** Author, works include: prize short story "Where You Belong" publ in "Such Things From the Valley" 1977; cover story Black World July 1971; cover picture and interview "Nuance" with Adimu Owusu March 1982; contributing author, James Baldwin, A Critical Evaluation; Sturdy Black Bridges, Visions of Black Women in Literature; author, The Deity Nodded 1973, Seeds Beneath the Snow, Vignettes of the South 1975, Journey to Somewhere 1986, Trek to Polaris 1989; contributing ed, Heath Anthology of American Literature; Prepared Black Culture Registry, Louisiana, a first, 1985; author, Hand on the Throttle, 1993; works have been included in several anthologies. **Home Addr:** PO Box 723, Sumter, SC 29151-0723.

MILLIGAN, RANDALL ANDRE (RANDY)
Professional baseball player. **Personal:** Born Nov 27, 1961, San Diego, CA. **Educ:** San Diego Mesa College. **Career:** New York Mets, 1987, Pittsburgh Pirates, 1988, Baltimore Orioles, 1989-93; Cincinnati Reds, 1993-94; Montreal Expos, 1994-. **Business Phone:** (514)253-3434.

MILLIGAN, UNAV OPAL WADE
Secretary. **Personal:** married Larry; children: Guren, Gary, Aaron, Mike, Gregory, Margarena, Ann. **Educ:** Jr Coll & Bus Mgmt, 2 yrs. **Career:** First Integrated Beauty Salon Jasper TX, owner oper 1977-; Charmetts Beauty Salon, owner 1962-74; Gen & Masonry Contractors, sec. **Orgs:** Pres NAACP Alameda 1973-75. **Honors/Awds:** Achvmt award fund raising NAACP 1973; recog award Alameda Unified Sch Dist 1976; apprectn award Alameda Br NAACP 1976; apprectn award Oakland Br NAACP1976; outst award Alameda Naval Airstation CA 1976. **Business Addr:** Unav's Beauty Salon, R #2 Box 280, Jasper, TX 75951.

MILLIN, HENRY ALLAN
Elected government official. **Personal:** Born Mar 17, St Thomas, VI; married Graciela Guzman; children: Leslie, Inez, Henry, Janet, Juliette. **Educ:** Inter-Am U; OH State U. **Career:** Govt of the Vi, lt gov 1978-; 1st PA Bank of N Am, vp; VI Housing Authority, exec dir; Tax Assessor's Office, chief clk; Police & Prison Dept, chief clk. **Orgs:** Commr Pub Serv Commn; mem Rotary Club; sr warden All Saints Ch. **Business Addr:** Govt of the VI, Box 450, St Thomas, Virgin Islands of the United States 00801.

MILLIS, DAVID HOWARD
Physician. **Personal:** Born Jun 26, 1958, Brooklyn, NY; son of Ena G Whitaker Millis and Clovis B Millis. **Educ:** Yale Univ, BS Psychobiology 1979; Howard Univ, MD 1983; New School for Social Research, Certificate Microcomputer Systems 1986. **Career:** Univ of IL Chicago, resident general surgery 1983-84; SUNY Downstate Medical Center New York, resident psychiatry 1984-88; Stanford Univ Medical Center, postdoctoral fellow, currently. **Orgs:** Mem AMA, ACM, AAAI.

MILLNER, DIANNE MAXINE
Attorney. **Personal:** Born Mar 21, 1949, Columbus, OH; daughter of Barbara Johnson Millner and Charles Millner; married Herb Anderson, Aug 15, 1986; children: Ashley Anderson, Tori Anderson. **Educ:** Pasadena City Coll, AA 1969; Univ of CA at Berkeley, AB 1972; Stanford U, JD 1975. **Career:** Hastings Coll of The Law, instructor 1977-78; Pillsbury Madison & Sutro Law Firm, attorney 1975-80; Alexander, Millner & McGee, atty, 1980-91; Steefel, Levitt & Weiss, attorney, 1991-94; CA Continuing Education of the Bar, atty, currently. **Orgs:** Dir Youth for Serv 1978-80; mem Commnty Redevel Agencys Assn 1983-94; Nat Bar Assn; Black Woman Lawyers Assn; Charles Houston Bar Assn; mem, American Assn of Univ Women, 1990-92; comm chair, Parents Division of the Natl Federation of the Blind, 1988-; mem, American Bar Assn; mem, CA State Bar. **Honors/Awds:** Pres Award Womens Div Nat Bar Assn 1980; Phi Beta Kappa UC Berkeley 1975. **Business Addr:** Attorney, California Continuing Education of the Bar, 2300 Shattuck Avenue, Berkeley, CA 94704.

MILLOY, LAWYER
Professional football player. **Personal:** Born Nov 14, 1973, St Louis, MO; son of Janice and Gary. **Educ:** Univ of Washington, attended. **Career:** New England Patriots, defensive back, 1996-. **Business Addr:** Professional Football Player, New England Patriots, 60 Washington St, Foxboro Stadium, Foxboro, MA 02035, (508)543-7911.

MILLS, ALAN BERNARD
Professional baseball player. **Personal:** Born Oct 18, 1966, Lakeland, FL. **Educ:** Polk Community College. **Career:** New York Yankees, pitcher, 1990-91, Baltimore Orioles, 1992-. **Business Addr:** Professional Baseball Player, Baltimore Orioles, Oriole Park at Camden Yards, 333 W Camden St, Baltimore, MD 21201, (410)685-9800.

MILLS, BILLY G.
Judge. **Personal:** Born Nov 19, 1929, Waco, TX; married Rubye; children: Karol, Karen, William Karl, John, James. **Educ:** Compton Coll, AA High Hon 1949; UCLA, BA 1951; UCLA Law Sch, LLB 1954; UCLA, JD 1958. **Career:** LA Sup Ct, Fam Law Dept, suprvsg judge 1979-, judge Superior Court; Sup Ct, State of CA, judge 1974; LA City Counc, city councmn 1963-74; Atty, pvt prac 1957-74; LA Co, dep probation ofcr 1957-60. **Orgs:** Chmn LA Co Dem Cntrl Com; mem Dept of Justice Adv Com; exec bd LA Co Bar Assn; mem CA State Bar Assn; com on cts & the comm Am Bar Assn; mem Am Judicature Soc; mem num other legal & law enforcement orgn mem Trinity Bapt Ch; bd of trustees United Ch of Rel Sci; mem S Cntrl LA & Watts C of C; consult USC Sch of Pub Adminstrn; mem League of CA Cities; United Negro Coll Fund; Sickle Cell Found; CA Black Corr Coalition; CA Fedof Black Ldrshp; Crippled Child Soc; Kiwanis Club; mem num other orgns. **Honors/Awds:** Outst grad Compton Comm Coll; outst achvmt S Cntrl Area Plng Counc United Way; IES Lamplighters Cert The Rdwy Ltg Forum; 2nd anniv comm serv award Met Gazette; cert of merit Un Supreme Counc Prince Hall Affil; outst cit of yr Jefferson Adult Sch; Hon D Humane Letters Un Ch of Rel Sci Schof Ministry; boss of yr Civic Ctr Women's Counc; num other certs plaques & awards. **Military Serv:** AUS 1955-57. **Business Addr:** Judge Superior Court, Los Angeles Superior Court, Family Law Dept, Los Angeles, CA 90012.

MILLS, CASSANDRA E.
Record company executive. **Personal:** Born Oct 21, 1959, Lonoke, AR; daughter of Charlene Allen and Rufus McCoy. **Educ:** San Jose State University, San Jose, CA, 1975-79. **Career:** Creative Star Management, Encino, CA, president, 1981-90; Giant Records, Beverly Hills, CA, head of black music, 1990-. **Business Addr:** President of Black Music, Giant Records, 8900 Wilshire Blvd #200, Beverly Hills, CA 90211.

MILLS, CHERYL
Government official. **Career:** The White House, associate counsel to the president, currently. **Business Addr:** General Counsel, Associate Counsel to the President, The White House, 1600 Pennsylvania Ave, NW, Washington, DC 20500, (202)456-1414.

MILLS, CHRISTOPHER LEMONTE
Professional basketball player. **Personal:** Born Jan 25, 1970, Los Angeles, CA. **Educ:** Kentucky; Arizona, bachelor's degree in communications/sociology. **Career:** Cleveland Cavaliers, forward, 1993-97; New York Knicks, 1997-. **Business Addr:** Professional Basketball Player, New York Knicks, 2 Pennsylvania Plaza, New York, NY 10121, (212)465-5867.

MILLS, DONALD
Entertainer. **Personal:** Born 1915, Piqua, OH; children: John. **Career:** Sang during intermissions with Harold Greenamier's Band in Piqua, OH in 1923; Worked as "Four Boys and a Guitar" for WLW radio in Cincinnati in 1928; Performances on CBS radion in NY; US and European tours include Copenhagens Tivoli Gardens and New York's Rainbow Grill; presently touring as "John and Donald Mills of the Mills Brothers". **Honors/Awds:** Between 1941 & 1946 recorded "Paper Doll" (more than 6 million copies sold), "I'll Be Around", "Till Then", "You Always Hurt the One You Love", "I'm Afraid to Love You", "Across the Alley from the Alamo"; to date The Mills Brothers have recorded over 1,264 songs. **Business Addr:** c/o General Artists Corp, PO Box 260185, Encino, CA 91426.

MILLS, DOREEN C.
Sales and marketing executive. **Personal:** Born Jan 5, 1959, New Haven, CT; daughter of Dolores Tyson & Marcus Mills. **Educ:** Hampton University, BS, Psychology. **Career:** Ramada Renaissance Hotel, sales mgr, 1985-88; Philadelphia Convention & Visitors Bureau, convention sales mgr, 1988-90; Los Angeles Convention & Visitors Bureau, dir, convention sales, 1990-97; Continental Plaza Hotel, dir of sales/mktg, 1997-. **Orgs:** Delta Sigma Theta, 1982-; American Society of Association Executives, 1996-; Meeting Professionals International, 1997-; Religion Conference Management Association, 1998-; Southern CA Society of Association Executives, chair; National Association of Black Hospitality Professionals, pres, 1995-; LA Chap Urban League, 1990-. **Business Addr:** Director, Sales/Mktg, Continental Plaza Hotel, 9750 Airport Blvd, Los Angeles, CA 90071.

MILLS, ERNEST LEE, III
Professional football player. **Personal:** Born Oct 28, 1968, Dunnellon, FL. **Educ:** Univ of Florida. **Career:** Pittsburgh Steelers, wide receiver, 1991-96; Carolina Panthers, 1997-. **Business Addr:** Professional Football Player, Carolina Panthers, 800 Mint St, Ericsson Stadium, Charlotte, NC 28202, (704)358-7000.

MILLS, GLENN B., JR.
Auditor. **Personal:** Born Jul 5, 1948, Oakland, CA; married Ernestine Pratt; children: Tasha, Glenn III, Lennard. **Educ:** Prairie View A&M Univ, Pol Sci 1969. **Career:** Transamerica Fin Corp, mgr, 1970-75; State of Texas Comptroller Office, senior auditor, 1974-. **Orgs:** Pres (state & natl), 1976-82, bd of dirs (local, regional, state & natl), Headstart; bd of trustees, Wilmer-Hutchins School District, 1980-; mem, NAACP; mem, Dallas Area Black Elected Officials; mem, Texas Black Employee Organization; master mason, Masonic Order, 1977-; deacon, Concord Missionary Baptist Church, 1976-. **Business Addr:** Senior Auditor, Comptroller's Office, State of Texas, 1331 E Highway 80, Suite 2, Mesquite, TX 75150.

MILLS, JOEY RICHARD
Make-up artist. **Personal:** Born Apr 2, 1950, Philadelphia, PA. **Educ:** Temple U, BA 1970. **Career:** Vogue, make-up artist; Harper's Bazaar; Glamour; Red Book; Mccalls; Ladies Home Journal; Family Circle; Essence; Town & Country; The Next Man, created make-up for Cornelia Sharpe & Sean Connery; "Eyes of Laura Mars", appeared in role of make-up artist; has appeared on countlesTV and radio programs; Nancy Wilson & Melba Moore, num others, record album covers; Valerie Harper, regular Clients; Raquel Welch; Diana Ross; Naomi Sims; Beverly Johnson; Cissy Houston; MelbaMoore; Nancy Wilson; Jodie Foster; Jill Clayburgh; Brooke Shields; Twyla Thorpe; Margot Kidder; Mariel Hemingway; Olivia Newton-John; Lauren Hutton. **Honors/Awds:** Guest appear WNBC Not For Women Only; For You Black Woman; appeared "Kenneth" Beauty Talk Show; appeared "AM New York"; appeared "PM New York"; appeared "The Morning Show" w/Regis Philbin; appeared "Today in New York"; appeared "The Barbara Walters Special" with Brooke Shields; 3 beauty books; cosmetic line 1978; designed make-up for Twyla Thorpe's first season on Broadway 1980; author of best seller, "New Classic Beauty"; introduced & created, The Joey Mills Makeup System, beauty compacts and sets in skin palettes of Ivory, Suntan, Bronze & Mahogany, 1994; Appearances on BET. **Home Addr:** One Lincoln Plaza, Apt 37M, New York, NY 10023.

MILLS, JOHN
Entertainer. **Personal:** Born 1956. **Career:** Performances as "John and Donald Mills of the Mills Brothers" at Copa Room of the Sands Hotel in Las Vegas, Fiesta Dinner Theater in San Diego, Carleton in Minneapolis; European tour including performance in Copenhagen, West Germany, Sweden, England. **Business Addr:** c/o General Artists Corp, PO Box 260185, Encino, CA 91426.

MILLS, JOHN HENRY
Professional football player. **Personal:** Born Oct 31, 1969, Jacksonville, FL. **Educ:** Wake Forest Univ. **Career:** Houston Oilers, 1993-96; Oakland Raiders, 1997-. **Business Addr:** Professional Football Player, Oakland Raiders, 1220 Harbor Bay Pkwy, Alameda, CA 94502, (510)615-1875.

MILLS, JOHN L.
Business executive. **Career:** DL&J Services, Chambersburg, PA, chief exec, currently.

MILLS, LARRY GLENN
Human resource vice pres, cleric. **Personal:** Born Oct 6, 1951, Monroe, LA; son of Catherine; married Bernice Perry, Sep 17, 1982; children: Erma, Larry, Larita, Larnell, Yolando, Larone, Lantz, Tracie, Milania. **Educ:** Wayne State University, 1974; Bethany College, BRE, 1990; Bethany Theological Seminary, MA, 1992; Bethany D MN, 1994. **Career:** OXY Metal Ind, mgr, pc, 1971-77; Portec Rail Car, supervisor, pc, 1977-82; General Dynamics, mgr, pc, 1982-84; Lockheed Martin, mgr, human resources, 1984-; Mt Sinai Baptist Church, pastor, 1988-. **Orgs:** SCLC, vp, currently; Private Industry Council, chairman, currently; TASTD; West Coast Baptist Association, past president; YMCA Black Achievers, currently; Citizen's Review Board, currently; APICS, 1973-90; Phi Beta Sigma Fraternity, 1974-. **Honors/Awds:** State of Florida, Attorney General, Crime Prevention Award, 1992; YMCA, Black Achievers Award, 1991; Martin Marietta, "Top 100" Meritorious Achievement Award, 1988; Masonic, Meritorious Youth Community Work, 1989; American Production & Inventory Society, Certified Practicioner, 1980; Urban League of Orlando, Community Support Award, 1992; Management Excellence Award, 1995. **Special Achievements:** Published chapter in book: Human Factors in Advanced Manufacturing, 1992; "Training Needs in CIM," Society of Manufacturing Engineers, 1989; Annual Conference Presenter, Society of Manufacturing Engineers, 1988. **Home Addr:** 6632 Crenshaw Dr, Orlando, FL 32835. **Business Addr:** Vice Pres, Human Resource, Lockheed Martin Corp, Info Systems, 12506 Lake Underhill, MP 610, Orlando, FL 32859-0385.

MILLS, LOIS TERRELL
Industrial engineer. **Personal:** Born Sep 24, 1958, San Francisco, CA; daughter of Lois M Terrell Clark and Warren C Terrell; married Roderick L Mills, Jul 21, 1990. **Educ:** University of Valencia, Valencia, Spain, 1978; Stanford University, Stanford, CA, BS indusrial engineering, 1980. **Career:** Procter & Gamble, Albany, GA, line & staff management, 1980-82, industrial engineer department manager, 1983-85; Procter & Gamble, Cincinnati, OH, corporate planning manager, 1985-88, corporate distribution planning manager, 1989-90; Ethicon Inc, division of Johnson & Johnson, Albuquerque, NM, industrial engineer, 1991-92; Total Associate Involvement, coordinator, 1992-. **Orgs:** National president, American Business Women's Association, 1990-91; member, Albuquerque Chamber of Commerce Board of Directors, 1991-92; member, Stanford University Black Alumni, 1982-; member, Toastmasters International, 1987-90; member, New Mexico Network for Women in Science and Engineering, 1991-. **Honors/Awds:** Top Ten Business Woman, Amer Bus Women's Assn, 1985; YMCA Black Achiever, YMCA, 1987; Highest Fund Raiser, Boys Club of Amer, Albany, GA, 1985. **Business Addr:** Industrial Engineer, ETO Starts, Ethicon, Inc, PO Box 26202, Albuquerque, NM 87125.

MILLS, MARY ELIZABETH
Educator. **Personal:** Born Jul 4, 1926, Franklin, TN; daughter of Daisy Johnson Knowles; married Latham L Mills, May 31, 1951; children: Latham L Mills, Joycelin M Blackman. **Educ:** Tennessee State Univ, Nashville TN, BS, 1946, MS, 1965, certificate in admin and supervision; attended George Peabody College for Teachers at Vanderbuilt Univ. **Career:** Williamson County School System, Franklin TN, teacher, 1953-55; Franklin Special School District, Franklin TN, teacher, 1955-77, asst principal, 1977-80, principal, 1980-. **Orgs:** Pres, Franklin City Teachers Assn, 1977; board of trustees, William Medical Center, 1983-; chair, Community Child Care Center, 1983-; sec, Williamson County Tourism, 1983-; Natl Education Assn; Tennessee Education Assn; Assn of Elementary School Principals; Assn of Principals and Supervisors; Franklin Special School District Education Assn; Phi Delta Kappa; regional director, National Sorority of Phi Delta Kappa Inc. **Honors/Awds:** Henry L. Hardison Humanitarian Award, Franklin Special School District Education Assn; Whitney M Young Jr Award, Boy Scouts of Amer; Helping Hand Award, Williamson County Chamber of Commerce; Black History Month Achievement Award; Outstanding Achievement in the Field of Education, Black Perspective Newspaper; Outstanding Chamber of Commerce Member of the Year; Soror of the Year, National Sorority of Phi Delta Kappa Inc; Educator of the Year. **Home Addr:** 1776 West Main St, P O Box 486, Franklin, TN 37065.

MILLS, MARY LEE
Nurse (retired), consultant. **Personal:** Born Aug 23, 1912, Wallace, NC; children: Lt Cmdr Robert S, David G. **Educ:** Lincoln Sch of Nursing, dipl 1934; Med Coll of VA, cert in pub hlth nursing 1937; Lobenstine Sch of Midwifery, cert midwifery 1941; NYU, BS, MA 1946; George Washington Univ, cert 1973. **Career:** US Public Health Service, Office of International Health, Agency for International Development, nurse, 1946-76. **Orgs:** Comm volunteer with Program on Aging in Pender Cnty; mem reg Adv Comm on Aging; chmn of fund raising Shiloh Columbia Volunteer Fire Dept; chmn Black History Cnty Comm; spec assignment on Natl Acad of Sci for Study of America's Role in Health and Sanitation in foreign aid; numerous speaking invitations toprofessional and comm groups; life membership, American College of Nurse Midwives; life member, National Organization of Public Health Nursing; life member, National College of Midwives; life member, Assn for the Study of Afro American Life and History; life member, National Assn for Uniformed Services; life member, NAACP. **Honors/Awds:** NC State Volunteer Award James Rufus Herring Award; Lakes Chapel Bapt Ch Award; Shiloh Columbia Volunteer Fire Dept Disting Serv Award; Pleasant Hill BaptChurch Centennial Award; Included in, "Contemporary Minority Leaders in Nursing, Afro-Americans, Hispanics, Native Americans Perspectives" 1983; "Hope and Dignity - Older Black Women in the South" 1983; Seton Hall University, Honorary Doctor of Laws; Tuskegee Institute, Honorary Doctor of Science; United States Public Health Service, Distinguished Service Award; Woodrow Wilson School of Public and International Affairs, Rockefeller Public Service Award; New York University Citation, 1996. **Special Achievements:** First woman to receive the Rockefeller Award.

MILLS, SAMUEL DAVIS, JR.
Professional football player. **Personal:** Born Jun 3, 1959, Neptune, NJ; married Melanie; children: Sam II, Larissa, Marcus. **Educ:** Montclair State, bachelor's degree in industrial technology. **Career:** New Orleans Saints, linebacker, 1986-94; Carolina Panthers, 1995-. **Honors/Awds:** Pro Bowl, 1987, 1988, 1991, 1992, 1996. **Business Addr:** Professional Football Player, Carolina Panthers, 800 Mint St, Ericsson Stadium, Charlotte, NC 28202, (704)358-7000.

MILLS, STEPHANIE
Singer, actress. **Personal:** Born Mar 22, 1959, New York, NY; married Jeffrey Daniels (divorced); married Michael Saunders,

1993. **Educ:** Juilliard School Music. **Career:** Singer/actress. The Wiz, 1975, 1984; Maggie Flynn; To Sir With Love; singles include "Never Knew Love Like This Before," "Whatcha Gonna Do With My Lovin'"; albums include: The Power of Love, Something Real. **Honors/Awds:** 2 Gold Albums; Grammy Award for Best Female R&B Vocal, 1980; American Music Award for Best Female R&B Vocal, 1981. **Business Addr:** Singer, c/o Casablanca Records, 810 7th Ave, New York, NY 10019.

MILLS, TERRY RICHARD
Professional basketball player. **Personal:** Born Dec 21, 1967, Romulus, MI; son of Emma Mills. **Educ:** Univ of Michigan, Ann Arbor, MI, 1986-90. **Career:** Denver Nuggets, forward, 1990-91, New Jersey Nets, 1991-92, Detroit Pistons, 1992-97; Miami Heat, 1997-. **Business Addr:** Professional Basketball Player, Miami Heat, 721 NW 1st Ave, Miami Heat, Miami, FL 33136, (305)577-4328.

MILNER, BILLY
Professional football player. **Educ:** Houston. **Career:** Miami Dolphins, 1995-. **Special Achievements:** 1st round/25th overall NFL draft pick, 1995. **Business Addr:** Professional Football Player, Miami Dolphins, 2269 NW 199th St, Miami, FL 33056, (305)620-5000.

MILNER, EDDIE JAMES, JR.
Professional baseball player (retired). **Personal:** Born May 21, 1955, Columbus, OH; married Retha Sims. **Educ:** Central State Univ, BS, business, 1978; Muskingum College, New Concord, OH, attended. **Career:** Cincinnati Reds, outfielder, 1980-86; San Francisco Giants, outfielder, 1987; Cincinnati Reds, outfielder, 1988.

MILNER, MICHAEL EDWIN
Banking executive. **Personal:** Born Mar 16, 1952, Atlanta, GA; son of Ethel M Minor Milner and Edwin R Milner; married Ocie Stiggers Milner; children: Kimberly, Michaelyn, Therron, Tasha. **Educ:** Morehouse Coll, BA 1974. **Career:** General Finance Corp, mgr 1974-78; Federal Reserve Bank of Atlanta, federal bank examiner 1978-90; SouthTrust Corporation, corp vice president, dir, community reinvestment, currently. **Orgs:** Bd of dirs, SouthTrust Reinvestment Corp; chairman, Alabama Bankers Assn Compliance Comm; member, The Brotherhood of St Andrews; mem, The Birmingham Assn of Urban Bankers; advisory board, Alabama Minority Supplier Development Council; board of directors, Birmingham Habitat for Humanity. **Honors/Awds:** Competent Toastmaster Toastmaster Intl 1985. **Home Addr:** PO Box 370172, Birmingham, AL 35237-0172.

MILNER, THIRMAN L.
Business executive. **Personal:** Born Oct 29, 1933, Hartford, CT; son of Grace Milner Allen and Henry Marshall Milner; divorced; children: Theresa, Gary, Thirman Jr. **Career:** All State Ins Co, acct rep; Gen Electric Bus Div, acct rep; New York City Council Against Poverty CAA, exec asst; Comm Devel NYC, dep asst admin; Comm Renewal Team Community Action Agency, pub relations dir; State of CT, rep; House of Reps, asst maj leader 1978-81; City of Hartford, mayor 1981-87; First Natl Supermarkets, Inc, dir, govt affairs, beginning 1987; Food Marketing Inst, chmn of govt rel, currently. **Orgs:** Sub-comm chmn, Finance Revenue and Bonding legislative Comm, 1979-80; sub-comm chmn, Planning and Devel legislative Comm 1979-80; northeast region liaison, Minority Energy Technical Assistance Prog, 1979-81; bd dir, Hartford Branch NAACP, 1979-81; regional coordinator, Natl Caucus of Black State Legislators, 1979-81; Natl Conf of Black Mayors, first vice pres 1985-86, assoc mem 1987-; bd dir, Massachusetts Food Assoc, 1989-; bd mem Connecticut Food Assoc, 1989-; life mem, NAACP; board of directors, New York State Food Merchants Assn. **Honors/Awds:** Comm Serv Awd Omega Phi Epsilon Frat 1980; Comm Serv Awd Guardians Afro-Amer Police 1980; Comm Serv Awd NAACP 1980; Comm Serv Awd Gr Hartford Black Soc Workers 1980; Jewish Tree of Life Award 1986; Univ of Hartford Chair-Establishing Thirman L Milner Scholar, 1987; dedication of Thirman L Milner Public Elementary School 1989; first African Amer mayor in New England popularly elected, 1981. **Home Addr:** 19 Colebrook St, Hartford, CT 06112.

MILSTEAD, RODERICK LEON, JR.
Professional football player. **Personal:** Born Nov 10, 1969, Washington, DC; son of Veronica E Milstead and Roderick L Milstead Sr. **Educ:** Delaware State College, BA, sociolgy, criminal justice, 1992. **Career:** Cleveland Browns, guard, 1993-94; San Francisco 49ers, 1994-. **Honors/Awds:** Member of San Francisco's Super Bowl championship team, 1994. **Business Phone:** (415)562-4949.

MILTON, DELISHA
Professional basketball player. **Personal:** Born Sep 11, 1974. **Educ:** Univ of Florida. **Career:** Portland Power, forward, 1997-. **Honors/Awds:** Wade Trophy, 1997. **Business Addr:** Professional Basketball Player, Portland Power, 439 N Broadway, Portland, OR 97227, (503)249-1130.

MILTON, ISRAEL HENRY
Government official. **Personal:** Born Aug 30, 1929, Marianna, FL; son of Lucille Barkley McRae and Rogene Milton; married Regina Wooden Milton, Apr 24, 1969; children: Addie, Otha, Charles, Israel I. **Educ:** Bethune-Cookman College, Daytona Beach, FL, BS, 1951; Atlanta University, Atlanta, GA, MSW, 1958. **Career:** Dade Co Model City Prog, Miami, FL, director, 1974-77; Dade Co Neighborhood Service Center Division, Miami, FL, director, 1977-80; Dade Co Dept of Human Resources, Miami, FL, deputy dir, 1980-82; Dade Co Dept of Human Resouces, Miami, FL, 1982-. **Orgs:** Member, & board nominee, National Forum for Black Public Administrators, 1982-; policy board member, Florida Assn of Social Serv Executives, 1982-; past chairman & member, YMCA/Family Christian Assn of America, 1974-; member, Bethune-Cookman College Alumni Assn, 1951-; member, Alcohol, Drug Abuse & Mental Health Council, 1987-90. **Honors/Awds:** JFK School of Government Program for Senior Executives, Harvard University, 1989; Volunteer of the Decade, YMCA, 1984; Citizen of the Year, Miami Chamber of Commerce, 1978. **Military Serv:** US Air Force, Airman 1st Class, 1951-55. **Business Addr:** Director, Dade County Dept of Human Resources, Metro-Dade Government, 111 NW First St, Suite 2210, Miami, FL 33128-1985.

MILTON, LEROY
Research analyst. **Personal:** Born Apr 7, 1924, Los Angeles, CA; married Alma M Melonson; children: James E, Angela H. **Educ:** Pepperdine U, BS 1949. **Career:** Avacaclo Grower, 1985-; Mental Health Dept, LA County, chief of admin serv, 1976-96; Potomac View Prop, fincl consultant, currently; LA Co, admin deputy coroner 1969-70; exec asst bldg serv 1968-69; LA Co, head coll invest 1963-68; Secured Div LA Co, chief 1961-63; real estate investor, 1950-96. **Orgs:** Pres Milton Enterprise 1960-; pres & dir Pub Ser Credit Union 1960-73; dir Eye Dog Found 1966-73; dir Beverly Hills Hollywood NAACP 1969-77; pres & mem Cosmos Club 1946-; Alpha Phi Alpha. **Military Serv:** USN 1942-46. **Business Addr:** Financial Consultant, Potomac View Properties, 17437 Tarzana St, Encino, CA 91316-3824.

MILTON, OCTAVIA WASHINGTON
Educational administrator (retired). **Personal:** Born Apr 30, 1933, Greensboro, NC; married Tilman C Cothran; children: James Jr, Lynne Michelle. **Educ:** Hampton Inst, BS 1954; Atlanta U, MA 1968, EdS 1971, Edd 1986. **Career:** Greensboro NC City Schools, speech therapist 1954-62; Atlanta Public Schools, speech therapist 1962-73, coordinator speech/hearing impaired 1973-83, dir/program for exceptional children 1983-. **Orgs:** Outstanding Elementary Teachers of Amer 1973; mem Amer Speech-Language Hearing Assn; mem Council for Exceptional Children; mem Delta Sigma Theta Sorority. **Honors/Awds:** Assist I & II Communication Skill Builders 1977, assist III 1981, assist combined 1983; grammarifics Imperial Intl Learning Corp 1980.

MIMMS, MAXINE BUIE
Educational administrator. **Personal:** Born Mar 4, 1929, Newport News, VA; married Jacques; children: Theodore, Tonie, Kenneth. **Educ:** VA Union U, BA 1950; Union Graduate Sch, PhD 1977. **Career:** Evergreen State Coll, prof 1972-; Women's Bureau Dept of Labor 1969-72; Seattle Pub Schs administrator 1964-69; Kirkland Public Schs tchr 1961-64; Seattle Public Schs, tchr 1953-61. **Orgs:** Mem Nat Consultances in Edn; mem New Approaches to Higher Edn; mem NAACP; mem Urban League; mem NEA (WEA). **Honors/Awds:** Women of the yr awards at several levels Seattle St Louis Tacoma. **Business Addr:** Evergreen State Coll, Tacoma Campus, 1202 South K St, PO Box 5678, Tacoma, WA 98405-0678.

MIMS, BEVERLY CAROL
Educator. **Personal:** Born Jan 29, 1955, Washington, DC; daughter of Barbara Crockett Mims and Oscar L Mims Sr; divorced; children: Michael Armwood-Phillips Jackson. **Educ:** Howard University, BS, pharmacy, 1977, doctorate, pharmacy, 1987. **Career:** Professional Pharmacy, pharmacist, manager, 1978-80; DC General Hospital, staff pharmacist, pharmacist-in-charge, 1980-85; Howard University, assistant professor of pharmacy practice, 1987-. **Orgs:** American Society of Hospital Pharmacists, 1980-; Washington Metropolitan Society of Hospital Pharmacists, 1980-; Rho Chi Society National Pharmacy Honor Society, 1986-; National Pharmaceutical Association, 1990-. **Special Achievements:** Quality Assessment and Improvement: Clinical Impact on Distribution . . ., 1992; Medicating the Elderly in Minority Aging, 1990. **Business Addr:** Assistant Professor of Pharmacy Practice, Howard Univ Coll of Pharmacy and Pharmacal Sciences, 2300 Fourth St NW, Washington, DC 20059, (202)806-7960.

MIMS, CHRISTOPHER EDDIE
Professional football player. **Personal:** Born Sep 29, 1970, Los Angeles, CA; married Dina. **Educ:** Tennessee, attended. **Career:** San Diego Chargers, defensive tackle, 1992-96; Washington Redskins, 1997-. **Business Addr:** Professional Football Player, Washington Redskins, 13832 Redskin Dr, Herndon, VA 22071, (703)471-9100.

MIMS, GEORGE E.
Social service director. **Personal:** Born May 14, 1932, Columbia, SC. **Educ:** Howard Univ Washington DC, BA (Magna Cum Laude, Dist Military Grad) 1959; Amer Univ DC, MA 1960; Miami Univ OH, attended 1963-65; Univ of HI, attended 1965-68; Neotarian Coll of Philosophy, DD 1980. **Career:** USAF Race Relations Ed/Equal Opport, Drug/Alcohol Abuse, major 1951-55, 1959-76; Royal Thai Air Force Base Thailand, chief social actions 1973; USAF School of Social Actions San Antonio TX, chief of training 1973-76; Community Action Agency Ft Worth TX, exec dir 1976-78; Community Ed Extension Headstart, chief exec office 1979-81; Youngstown Area Urban League, pres and CEO. **Orgs:** Vp NAACP Honolulu HI 1965-68; instr Creighton Univ Omaha NE 1969-71, Eastern Washington State Coll Spokane WA 1971-72, Los Angeles City Coll Extension Thailand 1973; exec founder dir Black Unity Coord Council 1974-76; instr San Antonio Coll San Antonio TX 1976; pres Oper PUSH Columbia SC 1981; exec dir Black Leadership Summit Council 1982-85. **Honors/Awds:** Disting Grad Squadron Officer School AL 1963; Military Man of the Year Owlers Mens Club Omaha NE 1969; Outstanding Achievement NAACP Honolulu HI 1968; Appreciation Awd Black Unity Coord Council San Antonio TX 1976; Youngstown/Warren Realtors Assoc, distinguished community serv awd 1986. **Military Serv:** USAF maj 1951-55, 1959-76; Bronze Star, Commendation 1972-73.

MIMS, GEORGE L.
Educational administrator. **Personal:** Born Feb 27, 1934, Batesburg, SC; son of Mary Aletha Corley and George W Mims; married Clara Ann Twigg; children: Cheryl Ann, Carla Aletha. **Educ:** FL A&M U, BS 1955; TC Columbia U, MA 1957, Prof Dip 1967; Rutgers U, EdD 1976. **Career:** Fisk U, head res counselor 1959-61; Volusia Co Comm Coll FL, dean of students 1961-63; Hunter Coll NY, asst placement dir 1963-67; Pace Univ NY, dir of special programs 1968-. **Orgs:** Mem editorial bd Journal, Educ & Psych Research 1983-86; mem adv comm Merck Sharp & Dohme 1983-; proposal reader US Ofc of Educ NY 1974-; pres AERA, Spec Int Group Black Educ 1982-86; chmn/designate AERA, Comm on Spec Int Groups 1984-87; res NY State Div of AACD 1982-83; pres Eta Theta Lambda Chap Alpha Phi Alpha 1980-87. **Honors/Awds:** Minority Alumni Award Pace Univ NY, NY 1983; HEOP Award 1980; Leadership Award HEOP 1975; Cert of Merit Big Bro of NY 1969; Brothers Award, Eta Theta Lambda Chap 1987; Community Service Award Central Nassau Club 1989; Humanitarian Award Howard University LI Alumni 1990; Youth Community Education Award Ministerial Alliance of N Amityville and Vicinity (LI) 1991; Mt Pleasant Bapt Church, The African-American Hall of Fame; Distinguished Comm Service Award, Natl Hampton Unin Alumni Assn, 1993; Special Interest Group: Amer Educ Research Assn, 1994; Outstanding Service Award, Dedication to Higher Educ; African Amer Youth Award, African Amer Heritage Assn of Long Island, 1993; Distinguished Service Award, Lakeview Branch, NAACP, 1994; Comm Service Award, Eta Theta lanbda Chapter, Alpha Phi Alpha Fraternity, Inc, 1995; Humanitarian Awd, Lakeside Family & Children's Services, Spring Valley NY, 1996; Gentleman of Distictnion Award, Holy Trinity Baptist Church, Amityville NY, 1996; Appreciation Awd, Hempstead School District, Hempstead NY, 1996. **Military Serv:** US Army sgt E5; Good Conduct 1957-59. **Home Addr:** 885 Seneca Rd, West Hempstead, NY 11552.

MIMS, MARJORIE JOYCE
Association executive. **Personal:** Born Sep 14, 1926, Chicago, IL; married Thomas S Mims; children: John, Raleigh. **Educ:** Univ of IL, BS in LAS 1949, MS Admin 1974; Univ of Chicago, advanced study 1974-76; DePaul Univ, advanced study 1978-81. **Career:** Jack & Jill of Amer Chicago Chapt, pres 1974-78; The Moles, natl vice pres 1978-82; The Links Inc, central area dir 1983-. **Orgs:** Mem Amer & Guidance Assn, 1970-; bd mem Ada S McKinley Assn, 1972-82, Assn for Family Living 1973-81; chmn Natl Nominating Comm of Jack & Jill of Amer 1978. **Honors/Awds:** Woman of the Year Radio Station WAIT 1974; Anti-Basielus Theta Omega Chap Alpha Kappa Alpha Sor. **Home Addr:** 7016 S Constance Ave, Chicago, IL 60649.

MIMS, OSCAR LUGRIE
Public administrator. **Personal:** Born Jun 7, 1934, Washington, DC; married Barbara C Crockett; children: Donna, Beverly Jackson, Oscar L Jr. **Educ:** Univ of DC, BS 1959; Bank St Coll of Edn, Cert 1963; Howard U, MA 1964; Univ of MA, EdD 1971; Fed Exec Inst, Cert Pub Admin 1974. **Career:** DC Pub Sch, educator 1959-68; DC Tchrs Coll, asst acad dean 1967-68; US Dept of HUD, pub admin 1968-, dir affirmative action. **Orgs:** Life mem NEA 1959-; mem Am Soc of Pub Admin 1968-; bd of dir DC Branch NAACP 1972-76; bd of dir Wash Urban League 1972-76; natl dir C Rodger Wilson Leadershp Conf 1982-; Kappa Alpha Psi Frat. **Honors/Awds:** Leadership Award Wash Urban League DC 1976; Nat Educ Fellow Bank St Coll of Educ 1963. **Business Addr:** Director, Affirmative Action, US Dept of HUD, 451 7th St SW, Washington, DC 20410.

MIMS, RAYMOND EVERETT, SR.
Container company supervisor, cleric. **Personal:** Born Apr 10, 1938, Bogalusa, LA; son of Hattie L Mims and Edward A Mims; married Shirley Humbles, Jun 26, 1971; children: Raymond E Jr. **Educ:** Southern University, BS, 1961; United Theological Seminary, BTh, 1984, MTheol, 1987. **Career:** Crown Zellerbach Corp, assistant safety & pers supervisor, 1969-74, schedule coordinator, production, 1974, logging foreman, 1974-79, supervisor, employee relations, 1979-82, employee relations manager, 1982-86; Gaylord Container Corp, personnel supervisor, 1986-; Greater Ebenezer Baptist Church, pastor, currently. **Orgs:** Good Samaritans Nursing Home, church affiliated, board chairman, 1987-92; Zellco Federal Credit Union, board member, 1980-91; Habitat for Humanity, board member, 1986-; American Pu lpwood Association, 1974-86; American Paper Institute, 1986-; Bogalusa City School board, 1992-; chairman of finance committee & transportation committee. **Honors/Awds:** American Pulpwood Association, HH Jefferson Mem Safety Award, 1981. **Military Serv:** US Army, sgt, 1962-64; Soldier of the Month. **Home Addr:** 1714 St Louis St, Bogalusa, LA 70427, (504)732-8407. **Business Addr:** Personnel Supervisor, Gaylord Container Corp, PO Box 1060, Bogalusa, LA 70429-1060, (504)732-8407.

MIMS, ROBERT BRADFORD
Physician, educator, scientist. **Personal:** Born Mar 24, 1934, Durant, MS; son of Laura Mims and Dawson Mims; married Eleanor Veronica Meeseburgh; children: Sharon Beverly, Valerie Tracy, Robin Eleanor, Bari Allen. **Educ:** Shorter College, 1952-54; Philander Smith Coll, BS 1956; Univ AR School Med, MD 1960; USC School Med, Res 1961-64, Fellow 1964-66. **Career:** USC School of Medicine, acad prof 1964-77; USN, LCDR 1966-68; John Wesley County Hospital, assoc med dir 1970-74; USC/LAC Med Center Home Health Servcs, dir 1974-78; Fndtn Med Center, pres/bd of dir 1978-82; USC School of Med, Associate Clinical Prof, 1978-86; Endocrine Metabolic Clinic of Santa Rosa, dir 1984-; CEO, Mims Enterprise Diversified; co-founder ACE-2000; independent senior exec, The Peoples Network. **Orgs:** Mem Pasadena Unified School Dist; CA Med Assn; Endocrinology Soc; AAAS; Amer Federation Clinical Research; Amer Coll Phys; Amer Geriatric Assn; founder, president Endocrine Society of the Redwoods 1987-; Natl Assn Home Health; vice pres bd dir Health Plan of Redwoods 1978-80; bd dir Sonora Co Diabetic Assn 1978-88; bd dir Tri-Co Found for Med Care; dir Dept of Internal Med for Family Practice Sonoma County Community Hospital 1984-86; director Department of Internal Medicine Santa Rosa Memorial Hospital 1984-86; bd dir VNA Sonoma Co; CA Assn for Health Care at Home; Amer Diabetes Assn; CA Political Action Assn 1984; dir BSA 1979-81; bd of dir Visiting Nurses Assn 1978-83; pres N CA Amer Diabetic Assn 1985-86; Altadena Family Serv; Altadena Neighbors; Pasadena Integration Plan; med admin advisor Southwest LA Comity Med Corp; med lecturer at various public educ meeting 1977-; served on numerous community and hospital committees; bd of dir, executive committee, CA Affiliate Amer Diabetes Assn, 1986-89; vice pres, bd of directors, Laura & Dawson Mims Educ Foundation & The Mims Research Institute, 1985-. **Honors/Awds:** Natl Honor Soc Philander Smith Coll 1952-56, Summa Cum Laude 1956; Honorary Life Membership CA & Natl Congress of PTA 1973; Natl Scientific Soc; numerous Collegiate Awards & Honors; Award & Scholarship Pasadena Unified School Dist by CA Congress of Parents & Teachers Inc 1971; Award for dedicated serv to Med-Cor Affairs at USC School of Med 1972-74; numerous scientific presentations & publications, 1964-. **Military Serv:** USN lt commander 1966-68. **Business Addr:** Director, Endocrine Metabolic Clinic, 4704 Hoen Ave, Santa Rosa, CA 95405.

MINCEY, W. JAMES
Association executive. **Personal:** Born Feb 27, 1947, Statesboro, GA. **Career:** NC Mut Life Ins, empl. **Orgs:** Pres Bulloch Co Chapt; SCLC 1970-; co-chmn Mcgovern campaign Bulloch Co 1972-72; pub dir NAACP 1969-70; youth coun pres NAACP 1967-68; memJ Wesley Lodge #161; Mason; Ins Underwriters Assn Thomas Grove Bapt Ch. **Honors/Awds:** Semifinalist Ford Found Ldrshp Dev Prog.

MINCY, CHARLES ANTHONY
Professional football player. **Personal:** Born Dec 16, 1969, Los Angeles, CA. **Educ:** Univ of Washington, attended. **Career:** Kansas City Chiefs, defensive back, 1992-94; Minnesota Vikings, 1995; Tampa Bay Buccaneers, 1996-. **Business Addr:** Professional Football Player, Tampa Bay Buccaneers, One Buccaneer Place, Tampa, FL 33607, (813)870-2700.

MINDOLOVICH, MONICA HARRIS
Book editor. **Personal:** Born Aug 2, 1968, Washington, DC; daughter of Benjamin L & Blanche R Harris; married Paul D Mindolovich, Oct 5, 1996. **Educ:** Carnegie-Mellon University, Literary & Cultural Studies, 1990, Professional Writing, 1990. **Career:** Dell Publishing, editorial asst, 1990-93; Kensington Publishing, asst editor, editor, sr editor, 1993-96; Carol Publishing Group, sr editor, 1996-. **Orgs:** Black Women In Publishing, 1990-93. **Honors/Awds:** NY Chap NAACP, Lifetime Achievement Award, 1996; Waldenbooks, Inc, Special Achievement Award, 1995. **Special Achievements:** Established ''Arabesque,'' the first African-American Romance line from a major publisher, 1994. **Business Addr:** Sr Editor, Carol Publishing Group, 120 Enterprise Ave, Secaucus, NJ 07094, (201)583-6551.

MINER, HAROLD
Professional basketball player. **Educ:** University of Southern California. **Career:** Miami Heat, guard, 1992-. **Business Phone:** (305)577-4328.

MINER, WILLIAM GERARD
Architect. **Personal:** Born May 12, 1950, Washington, DC; son of Charlotte Miner and George Miner. **Educ:** Princeton U, AB 1972; MA Inst Tech, March 1974. **Career:** US Dept of State, Foreign Bldgs Operations, chief, engineering support branch, 1990-, program mgr, 1985-90; CRS Sirrine Intl Group, training & res coord, 1983-85; Amer Inst of Architects, dir of practice pubs, 1978-83; Univ of MD School of Architecture, asst prof of architecture, 1977-81; Keyes Lethbridge & Condon, proj architect, 1974-77; MIT Sch Archt & Urban Planning, tchr asst 1973-74; Keyes Lethbridge & Condon, intern archt 1973; MIT Sch Archt, rehab consult 1973; Keene Interior & Systems, designer draftsman 1972; Peoples' Workshop, co-fndr, designer 1972-72; Irving Wasserman Gulf Reston Inc, asst head planner 1971; Princeton Univ Sch Arch & Planning, rsrch asst 1970-71; Princeton Alumni Cncl, trvlg rsrch 1970; Joseph Minor Nat Capital Housing Authority, asst sr archt, 1970. **Orgs:** Mem Student Planning Team Metro Dist Commn 1972; instr Trenton Design Ctr 1970-71; stud rep bd dir AIA 1972. **Honors/Awds:** Design competition finalist Nat Granite Quarry Assn 1974. **Business Addr:** Chief, BDE/ESB, US Dept of State, Foreign Buildings Operations, SA-6, Rm 335, Washington, DC 20520.

MINES, RAYMOND C., JR.
Company executive. **Personal:** Born Dec 18, Somerville, NJ; son of Helen M Miller & Raymond C Mines, Sr; married Joyce; children: Sean M, Kimara L. **Educ:** Academy of Advanced Traffic & Transportation, traffic transportation management. **Career:** McDonald's Corp, director of operations & training, 1982-84, regional manager, 1984-85, sr regional manager, 1985-86, regional vice pres, 1986-91, zone vice pres, 1991-93, senior vp/zone manager, 1993-. **Orgs:** Children's Memorial Hospital, board of directors; Links Unlimited, sponsor; DMSF, board of directors. **Business Addr:** Senior VP/Zone Manager, McDonald's Corp, Jorie Blvd, Oak Brook, IL 60521, (630)623-6230.

MING, DONALD GEORGE K.
Bishop. **Career:** African Methodist Episcopal Church, president of council of bishops, presiding bishop of 8th Episopal district. **Business Addr:** 28 Walmer Rd, Woodstock, Capetown 8001, Republic of South Africa.

MINGO, PAULINE HYLTON
Travel agent, real estate agent. **Personal:** Born Aug 8, 1945; daughter of Martha Correoso Hylton and Cecil Hylton; divorced; children: Martha Senetta, Elizabeth Joy, Nelson III. **Educ:** Univ of Hartford, 1964-67; nursing school, currently. **Career:** State of CT, social worker 1964-67, private sec to chancellor of higher ed 1969-71; real estate agent, 1970-; Natl Black Business & Professional Womens Org, chaplain 1971-74; Pan Am World Airways Eleuthera Bahamas, asst to base oper mgr 1972-74; Mingos World Travel Serv Hartford, owner, mgr 1974-; Brass Key Bar-B-Que/Soul Food Restaurant, owner. **Orgs:** Treas NW Family Day Care Ctr Hartford 1972-; vice pres Greater Hartford Bus Devel Corp Hartford 1975-78; member, Union Baptist Church, Hartford Conneticut; member, Elks. **Honors/Awds:** Published pictoral article ''The Watchman'' Philadelphia Spring 1977; A Woman Worth Knowing Awd Ujima Inc 1978; appointed mem Gov's Vacation Council 1978-80; publ ''Making It'' Black Enterprise Mag 1980; featured CT Bus Times 1980; writer Bi-Weekly Travel Article No Agents Newspaper 1980. **Business Addr:** Owner/Manager, Brass Key Restaurant, 829 Main St, Manchester, CT 06040.

MINION, MIA
Computer specialist. **Personal:** Born Nov 5, 1960, Washington, DC; daughter of Katherine Jackson Mills; children: Daryn. **Educ:** Coppin State Coll, BS 1985. **Career:** Coppin State Coll, clerk-typist 1981-85; Social Security Admin, computer systems analyst 1985-. **Orgs:** Vice pres Zeta Phi Beta Sor Inc 1984-85. **Honors/Awds:** Mem Alpha Kappa Mu Natl Honor Soc 1983; Natl Deans List 1983,84,85; Outstanding Young Women of Amer 1983,84,85; John S Sheppard Scholarship Baltimore Mktg Assoc 1983. **Home Addr:** 5801 Bland Ave, Baltimore, MD 21215. **Business Addr:** Computer Systems Analyst, Social Security Administration, 6401 Security Blvd, Baltimore, MD 21235.

MINOR, BILLY JOE
Educator. **Personal:** Born Nov 10, 1938, Pine Bluff, AR; married Mary McMillian; children: Billy, Devron, Darius. **Educ:** CA State Coll at Hayward, BA 1968; CA State Coll at Hayward, MS 1969; IN U, PhD 1974. **Career:** Oakland U, asso prof 1974; HRD department, chair; San Francisco Sch, sch psychologist 1969-71. **Business Addr:** Oakland Univ, Rochester, MI 48309.

MINOR, EMMA LUCILLE
Educator. **Personal:** Born Mar 16, 1925, Pollard, AL; daughter of Estella Dowell Walton and Berry Walton; married James H Minor, May 24, 1946; children: Dale Michael Minor, Gail Minor Christopher, Valerie E Minor Alloy. **Educ:** Kent State Univ, Kent OH, BS, 1971; Cleveland State Univ, Cleveland OH, MA Educ Admin, 1974; Bowling Green State Univ, Bowling Green OH, post graduate studies; John Carroll Univ, Univ Heights OH, post graduate studies. **Career:** Cleveland Public Schools, Cleveland OH, cadet teacher, 1968-72, consultant teacher, admin intern, asst principal, 1972-75, principal, 1975-85. **Orgs:** Natl Assn of Reading and Language Educ, 1975-85; mem, Phi Delta Kappa Educ Frat, 1976-89, Natl Alliance of Black School Educ, 1977-89; supreme basileus, natl officer, Natl Sorority of Phi Delta Kappa Inc, 1977-89; life mem, NAACP, 1977-89; local officer, Ohio Assn of School Admin, 1980-85; mem, Delta Sigma Theta Sorority, 1982-89; affiliate representative, Natl Urban League, 1985-89, Legal Council on Civil Rights, 1986-89, United Negro Coll Fund, 1986-89; affiliate pres, Natl Council of Negro Women, 1986-89; co-chairperson, Assault on Illiteracy, Professional Educ Comm, 1986-89; pres, Natl Sorority Phi Delta Kappa Perpetual Scholarship Foundation, Inc, 1997-2001. **Honors/Awds:** Distinguished Serv Award, City of Cleveland, 1982; Teaching Reading for Competency, 1984; Distinguished Serv, Cleveland Public Schools, 1985; Organizational Growth and Change, 1986; Mission to Make a Difference, 1987; Distinguished Serv, Natl Sorority of Phi Delta Kappa Inc, 1987; 100 Most Influential Black Amer, Ebony Magazine, 1987, 1988, 1989. **Home Addr:** 98 Gleneagles Drive, Fayetteville, GA 30214.

MINOR, GREG MAGADO
Professional basketball player. **Personal:** Born Sep 8, 1971, Sandersville, GA; children: Kira, Greg Jr. **Educ:** University of Louisville. **Career:** Boston Celtics, 1994-. **Special Achievements:** NBA Draft, First round pick, #25, 1994. **Business Addr:** Professional Basketball Player, Boston Celtics, 151 Merrimac St, 5th Fl, Boston, MA 02114, (617)523-6050.

MINOR, JESSICA
Psychotherapist, consultant. **Personal:** Born in Chicago, IL. **Educ:** Wittenberg Univ, BA, 1962; Univ of Chicago, MA, 1964; Univ of California, JD, 1988. **Career:** Mgmt consultant, corporate exec, & psychotherapist, 1970-; Minor & Co, pres, currently. **Orgs:** Mem, Phi Alpha Delta Law Fraternity, United Nations Assn, Commonwealth Club of California, Amer Women for Intl Understanding, The Planning Forum, Intl Visitors Center; San Francisco Opera Guild; Founders Comm, United Nations World Centre in San Francisco; charter mem, San Francisco Symphony League. **Honors/Awds:** Semifinalist, White House Fellows Program, 1973-74; Outstanding Professional in Human Services, 1974; Honorary Consul, Republic of Liberia, 1979-84. **Business Addr:** President, Minor & Co, PO Box 15505, San Francisco, CA 94115.

MINOR, JOHN S.
Construction executive. **Personal:** Born Apr 2, 1948, Morristown, NJ; son of Helen Nelson Minor (deceased) and George Minor (deceased); married Catherleen Webber, Jul 8, 1967; children: Jonn C, Keir S, Levar T, Maissha L. **Educ:** New Jersey Inst of Technology, BSET 1981. **Career:** ET Killam Assoc, construction manager 1971-80; McKee Assoc, project manager 1980-81; JS Minor Corp, pres, CEO 1981-; Jacmin Inc, chmn of the bd 1982-89; MV Construction Co, St Croix, Virgin Islands, vice pres, 1990-. **Orgs:** Esquire IBPOE-PON #93 1982-84; dir FSP Jaycees 1983,85; pres Sugar Bear Prod 1985-89; coach YMCA Youth Basketball 1986-87.

MINOR, TRACEY L.
Publisher. **Personal:** Born Nov 9, 1963, Philadelphia, PA; daughter of Evie R Minor and C Wes Minor. **Educ:** Temple University, BA, communications, 1988. **Career:** Expression Modeling Agency, model, 1982-87; Center for Social Policy, newsletter editor, intern, 1985-86; Click Modeling Agency, model, 1985-87; Horizon House, newsletter editor, intern, 1986-87; Atlantic Tech, newspaper associate editor, 1987-88; Saint Benedict's Day Care Center, assistant director, 1988-89; EMSCO Scientific Enterprises, sales representative, 1989-91; Delaware Valley Network, publisher, currently. **Orgs:** National Association of Black MBA's, 1992-; Poor Richard Club, 1992-; New Penn Del Minority Business Council, 1992-; Women in Communications, 1992-; Public Relations Society of America, 1987-89; Screen Actor's Guild, 1983-87; Harriet Tubman Historical Preservation Society, 1980-81. **Honors/Awds:** National Black MBA Association, Entrepreneur of the Year, 1992; Urban Profiles Magazine, Honored in 30 Under 30, Thirty Top Business Owners, 1992; Zeta Phi Beta, Woman of the Year Nominee, 1992. **Business Phone:** (215)849-5207.

MINOR, WILLIE
Educational administrator. **Personal:** Born Jan 31, 1951, Navasota, TX; son of Marjorie Williams and Carl Minor Jr. **Educ:** Prairie View A&M Univ, BS (magna cum laude), 1973, MS 1974; Univ of Phoenix, MA 1980; AZ State Univ, EdD 1976. **Career:** Faculty Assn, sec 1984-85; Admin Mgmt Soc, pres 1984-85; Phoenix Coll, prof of business; Phoenix Coll, admin intern 1989-, associate dean of instruction, currently. **Orgs:**

Mem & sec Delta Mu Delta 1972; grad co-op NASA Space Ctr 1974; sponsor Afro Amer Club 1977; mem & sponsor Phi Beta Lambda 1972-; mem Business Comm Assn 1976-85; mem & officer Delta Pi Epsilon 1976-; pres Admin Mgmt Soc 1977-; mem Phi Delta Kappa 1980-; arbitrator Better Business Bureau 1984-. **Honors/Awds:** Academic Recognition, Prairie View Faculty 1976. **Home Addr:** 6442 W Fremont Rd, Laveen, AZ 85339. **Business Addr:** Faculty Chair of Business and Applied Programs, Rio Salado College, 2323 West 14th Street, Tempe, AZ 85281-8519.

MINTER, BARRY ANTOINE
Professional football player. **Personal:** Born Jan 28, 1970, Mt. Pleasant, TX; married Shawyna; children: Gia, Bari. **Educ:** Tulsa, attended. **Career:** Chicago Bears, linebacker, 1993-. **Business Addr:** Professional Football Player, Chicago Bears, 1000 Football Dr, Halas Hall at Conway Park, Lake Forest, IL 60045-4829, (847)295-6600.

MINTER, ELOISE DEVADA
Educational administrator. **Personal:** Born Oct 24, 1928, Monroe Co, AL; children: Clifford B, Brenda Y. **Educ:** Tuskegee Inst AL, BS 1949; Tuskegee Inst AL, MA 1961; Wayne State & Merril Palmer Inst Detroit, attended 1970 & 1974. **Career:** Pershing High Sch Detroit, asst prin 1979-; City of Detroit, real estate salesman & appraiser 1975-80; Telegram Newspaper, writer 1970-80; Longfellow MiddleSch Detroit, unit head 1978-79; Jefferson Middle Sch, dept head 1968-78; Southside Jr High Sch Mobile, asst prin 1965-68. **Orgs:** Pub speaker religious occasions civic groups & youth progs 1960-80; dir Bd of Christian Educ Dexter Ave Bapt Ch 1968-80; mem Nat Orgn of Sch Adminstrs Suprs 1968-80;; mem Sunday Sch & BTU Congress 1970-80; mem Alpha Kappa Alpha 1949; Mem NAACP 1965-80; mem PUSH 1965-80; Marie Clair Block Club 1970-80. **Honors/Awds:** Pub audio presentation of Israel ''In the footsteps of Jesus''; pub ''A Drama for Your Ch'' 1980. **Business Addr:** Pershing High Sch, Detroit Bd of Educ, Detroit, MI 48202.

MINTER, KENDALL ARTHUR
Attorney. **Personal:** Born May 24, 1952, New York, NY; son of Jerolyn Minter and William Minter; married Revola. **Educ:** Cornell Univ, BA 1974, JD 1976. **Career:** Black Affairs Dept WVBR-FM, announcer, chmn 1970-71; WTKO, announcer, music dir, acct exec 1972-76; Cornell Univ, legal asst to vp, campus affairs 1975-76; Farichild Industries Inc, corp rep for broadcasting 1976-78; Burns Jackson Miller Summit & Jacoby NY, attny 1978-80; Private practice, attny; Minter & Gay, New York, NY, partner, 1988-. **Orgs:** Pres, chmn of bd Full Circle Enterprises Inc 1973-77; bd dir 100 Black Men Inc; bd of dir Amer Youth Hostels Inc; dir HS Talent Search Intl Inc 1977-; media cons, lawyer, entertainment lawyer, adv counc Amer Youth Hostels Metro NY Council 1976-; fdg com Cornell Black Alumni Assn 1977; mem Amer Bar Assn, NY St Bar Assn, Fed Comm Bar Assn, Comm Task Force Natl Conf of Black Lawyers, Natl Black Media Coalition; cofounder, exec dir, 1979-, Black Entertainment & Sports Lawyers Assn.

MINTER, STEVEN ALAN
Foundation executive. **Personal:** Born Oct 23, 1938, Akron, OH; son of Dorothy K Knox and Lawrence L Minter; married Dolores K; children: Michele, Caroline, Robyn. **Educ:** Baldwin-Wallace Coll, BE 1960; Case Western Reserve Univ School of Applied Soc Servs, M Soc Adm 1963. **Career:** Cuyahoga Co Welfare Dept, dir 1969-70; Commonwealth of MA, commr of public welfare 1970-75; US Dept of Educ Washington DC, under sec 1980-81; The Cleveland Found, assoc dir & program officer 1975-80, 1981-83, dir, beginning 1984, executive director, currently. **Orgs:** Director, Goodyear Tire and Rubber Co., 1985-; trustee Coll of Wooster 1978-; dir Key Corp 1987-; life mem NAACP; dir Society Corp 1987-; dir Consolidated Natural Gas 1989-; director, Rubbermaid, Inc, 1990-; board of overseers, Florence Heller Graduate School for Advanced Studies in Social Welfare, Brandeis University, 1990-; board of trustees, Foundation Center; board of trustees, Leadership Cleveland; North Coast Harbor Inc, board of directors; Cleveland Iniative on Education, board of directors. **Honors/Awds:** Hon PhD Humane Letters Baldwin-Wallace Coll 1974; Distinguished Serv Awd The Sch of Applied Social Sci Case Western Reserve Univ 1979; Hon PhD Humane Letters Findlay Coll 1984; Social Worker of Yr OH Chap of Natl Assoc of Soc Workers 1984; Black Professional of Yr Black Professional Assoc Cleveland 1985; Hon PhD Humane Letters Oberlin Coll 1988; Hon PhD Humane Letters Kent State Univ 1988; Hon PhD Humane Letters Case Western Reserve Univ 1989; Ohio Governor's Award for Education, 1991. **Business Addr:** Executive Director & President, The Cleveland Foundation, 1422 Euclid Ave, Suite 1400, Cleveland, OH 44115.

MINTER, THOMAS KENDALL
Educational administrator. **Personal:** Born Jun 28, 1924, Bronx, NY; married Rae Alexander; children: Thomas K Jr. **Educ:** NY U, MA 1950; Union Theol Sem NY, SMM 1950; Harvard U, EdD 1971. **Career:** Lehman Coll, City Univ of NY, dean of professional studies, currently; USOE, dep commr elem & secon edn; Wilmington Public Schs, supt 1975-77; Dist 7 Sch Dist of Phila, supt 1972-75; PA Advancement Sch, dir 1970-72;PA, adminstrv asst to supt 1968-70; Boston, adminstrv asst to dir of field serv 1967-68; Human Resources Adminstrn NY, consult 1967; Medford MA, arsrch asst 1967; Music Dept Benjamin Franklin HS, tchr acting chmn 1959-66; James Otis Jr HS, tchr 1955-59; MD State Tchrs Coll, inst 1949-53. **Orgs:** Coord Philadelphia Cluster Nat Ed D Prgm for Educ Leaders NOVA Univ 1973-76; coord Philadelphia Cluster Nat Ed D Prgm for Educ Leaders NOVA Univ 1973-76; consult Nat Alliance of Black Sch Educators; consult Nat EdD Prgm for Educ Leaders NOVA U; consult Rsrch for Better Schs PA; consult Supt of Schs Portland Learing Rsrch & Devel Ctr Rider Coll; Carter Mondale Transition Planning Group 1976; mem Assn for study of Afro-Am Life & History; memNAACP Fellow John HaySummer Inst in Humanities Williams Coll 1965; Phi Delta Kapp Hon Educ Frat 1966; Phi Mu Alpha Hon Music Educ 1949. **Honors/Awds:** Publs Intermediate Sch 201 Manhattan ctr of controversy 1967; a study of NY city bd of ed demonstration projs IS 201 2 bridges ocean hill Brownsville 1967; The Role of Conflict in Devel Operation of 2 New York City Decentralized Sch Projs 1968; Covering the Desegreation Story current Experiences & Issues 1976; Sch Desegregation Making It Work. **Business Addr:** Dean, Prof Studies, Lehman College/ City Univ of NY, Bedford Pk Blvd West, Bronx, NY 10468.

MINTER, WILBERT DOUGLAS, SR.
Administrator. **Personal:** Born Nov 17, 1946, Knoxville, TN; children: Wilbert Douglas, Jr. **Educ:** Knoxville College, 1965-67; Univ of Tenn, 1970-. **Career:** Association of Records Managers & Administrators, pres (local chapter) 1974-; Administrative Management Society, pres (local chapter) 1982; Martin Marietta Corporation, suprv of engineering records. **Orgs:** Pres Oak Ridge Comm Relations Council 1972-73, Atomic City Sportsmen Club of Oak Ridge 1975; mem Human Resources Bd of Oak Ridge 1980-82, Oak Ridge School Bd 1983-, State Adv Comm US Civil Rights Cimmiss 1983-85, Dept of Energy Contractors & Micrographics Assoc 1985; natl conf speaker Assoc of Records Mgrss & Admin. **Honors/Awds:** Distinguished service award Shriners of Knoxville 1973; outstanding chapter member Records Managers & Administrators 1975; outstanding certified records manager 1982. **Business Addr:** Suprv of Engineering Records, Martin Marietta Corporation, P O Box Y, Oak Ridge, TN 37830.

MINTZ, REGINOLD LEE
Real estate company executive. **Personal:** Born Sep 27, Alexander, VA; son of Dorothy Mintz and John H Mintz; children: Reginold Lee Lewis. **Educ:** Virginia State Univ, BS, 1983; IBM Programmers School, Dallas, TX, 1984; Century 21 Real Estate Mgmt Inst, 1988. **Career:** Natl Student Bus League, immed past natl pres 1981-83; MSP Landscaping Inc, vice pres 1983; IBM, program analy 1983-88; Investment Real Estate Annuity Corp, pres, 1988-; Century 21 Prestige Realty, realtor-assoc, currently. **Orgs:** Mem Natl Student Bus League Bus Advisory Comm; pres Minority Bus Assoc of VA 1984-85; mem Alpha Phi Omega Inc 1981-; bd mem, 1981-87, mem, currently, Natl Bus League; mem, Natl Assn of Real Estate Brokers, 1989-; mem, Natl Student Business League, 1981-; mem, Natl Assn of Realtors, currently. **Honors/Awds:** Leadership Award, Natl Business League, 1982; Community Service Award, IBM; Outstanding Service Award, Minority Business Assn, 1987; author, ''Buyer Beware,'' Real Estate Today, 1989.

MINUS, HOMER WELLINGTON
Dentist, cleric. **Personal:** Born Mar 21, 1931, Wyoming, DE; son of Luvenia Roberts Minus and George Greenfield Minus; married Barbara; children: Carla Michele Minus Lewis, Felicia Yvette Minus Lewis. **Educ:** Univ of Delaware, BS 1953; Temple Univ School of Dentistry, DDS 1959; Howard Univ School of Div, MDiv 1987. **Career:** Dentist; United Methodist Church, clergyman, currently. **Orgs:** Vestryman Dioc Counc Conv DE Prot Episcopal Church; school bd mem Dover DE 1967-70; life mem NAACP; life mem Alpha Phi Alpha Fraternity Inc. **Military Serv:** US Army, s/sgt, 1953-55; US Army Reserve Dental Corp, capt, 1959-66.

MINYARD, HANDSEL B.
Business executive. **Personal:** Born Mar 11, 1943, Phoenix, AZ; son of Vivian Minyard and Richard Minyard (deceased); married Karen Flavell; children: Stacey B, H Blair. **Educ:** Stanford U, AB 1964; Yale Law Sch, LlB 1967. **Career:** NLRB San Francisco, law clerk 1967-68; Fordham Univ NY, asst to exec 1968-69; Sullivan & Cromwell NY, assoc counsel 1969-72; Temple Univ School of Law Philadelphia, prof of law 1972-89; City of Philadelphia, city solicitor, 1986-88; Graimark Realty Advisors Inc, Philadelphia, PA, 1989-. **Orgs:** Mem CA Bar Assn 1968; mem NY Bar Assn 1970; mem Philadelphia Bar Assn 1979; bd mem N PA Sch Dist Authority 1975-79; dir N PA Chap ARC 1975-79; bd mem Friends Hospital 1981-; bd of overseers Widener Law School 1986-93; bd mem Franklin Institute 1988-; dir, Penns Landing Corp, 1989-92; board, Pennsylvania Intergovernmental Cooperation Authority, 1992-94; bd, Crime Prevention Assn, 1993-; trustee, Philadelphia College of Textiles & Science, 1996-. **Business Addr:** Executive Vice President, Graimark Realty Advisors Inc, 230 S Broad St, 10th Fl, Philadelphia, PA 19102.

MISSHORE, JOSEPH O., JR.
Insurance executive. **Career:** Gertrude Geddes-Willis Life Insurance Co, New Orleans, LA, chief executive. **Business Addr:** Gertrude Geddes-Willis Life Insurance Co, 2120 Jackson Ave, New Orleans, LA 70113.

MISTER, MELVIN ANTHONY
Business executive. **Personal:** Born Jun 18, 1938, Memphis, TN; son of Mattie A Cunningham Mister and Mack A Mister, Sr.; married Joan Devereux; children: 4. **Educ:** Carnegie Inst of Tech, BS 1958; Princeton Univ, MPA 1964. **Career:** US Conf of Mayors, assoc dir comm rel serv 1964-66; NW #1 Urban Renewal Area DC, proj dir 1966-68; Ford Found NY, prgm ofcr 1968-69; DC Redevelop Land Agency, exec dir 1969-75; US Conf of Mayors, dir office of prog develop 1975-80, dep exec dir 1980-82; Citibank NA, vice pres 1982-84; Security Pacific Bank NA, vice pres 1984-86; Chase Municipal Securities, vice pres 1986-91; Clayton Brown & Associates, vice pres, 1991-94; WR Laidlawy and Mead, senior vp, 1994-95; Twentieth Century Fund, fellow, 1991-; Melvin A Mister & Associates, consultant, president, currently. **Orgs:** Asst exec dir US Conf of Mayors 1977-; dir Urban Econ Policy League of Cities Conf of Mayors 1975-77; act dep dir DC Dept of Housing & Comm Dev 1974-75; exec dir DC Redevelop Land Agency 1969-74; Natl Assn of Housing & Redevelop Officials; Natl Urban Coalition Housing; BSA; bd Potomac Inst; bd Interfaith Medical Ctr, Urban Land Inst; bd Hispanic Devel Proj; bd Seedco; Mortgage Bankers Assn; bd, Taconic Foundation; bd, Institute for Public Administration. **Military Serv:** AUS corp of engrs 1st lt 1958-62. **Business Addr:** President, Melvin A Mister & Associates, 146 Maple St, Brooklyn, NY 11225.

MITCHAL, SAUNDRA MARIE
Marketing executive. **Personal:** Born Jun 3, 1949, Massillon, OH; daughter of Betty Jones Brown and Clyde Mitchal; married John Higginbotham (divorced 1988). **Educ:** Kent State University, Kent, OH, BBA, 1967-71; Indiana University, Bloomington, IN, MBA, 1971-73. **Career:** Bristol Myers Co., New York, NY, product manager, 1973-81; Hunt Wesson Foods, Fullerton, CA, marketing manager, 1981-84; Neutrogena Corporation, Los Angeles, CA, vice president of marketing, 1984-. **Orgs:** Member, Corporate Women's Network, currently; member, Delta Sigma Theta Sorority, 1968-. **Honors/Awds:** Women of Achievement, Essence Magazine, 1990; Motor Board Honor Society, Kent State University, 1971; Consortium for Graduate Studies Fellowship, Indiana University. **Business Addr:** Vice President of Marketing, Neutrogena Corporation, 5760 W 96th St, Los Angeles, CA 90045.

MITCHELL, ARTHUR
Artistic director. **Personal:** Born Mar 27, 1934, New York, NY. **Career:** Premier Danseur New York City Ballet, prin 1955-72; Dance Theatre of Harlem Everett Center for the Performing Arts, exec dir/choreographer/founder, currently. **Orgs:** Natl Conf on Soc Welfare 1973; US Dept of State Dance Adv Panel 1973; Natl Soc of Literature & The Arts 1975. **Honors/Awds:** First black dancer to become a principal artist in the New York City Ballet; first male recip Dance Award HS of Performing Arts 1951; Cert of Recog The Harold Jackman Memorial Com 1969; spl tribute Arthur Mitchell & Dance Theatre of Harlem Northside Cntr for Child Develop Inc 1969; The Changers Award Mademoiselle Mag 1970; North Shore Comm Arts Cntr Award 1971; 20th annual Capezio Dance Award 1971; numerous other awards & tributes to Arthur Mitchell & The Dance Theatre of Harlem; National Endowment for the Arts, ambassador at large, 1994; MacArthur Fellowship, 1994; School of American Ballet, Lifetime Achievement Award, 1995. **Business Addr:** Artistic Director, Founder, Dance Theatre of Harlem Everett Ctr for the Performing Arts, 466 W 152nd St, New York, NY 10031.

MITCHELL, AUGUSTUS WILLIAM
Physician. **Personal:** Born Apr 26, 1913, McKeesport, PA; married Dollie; children: Terrence, Wendell, A W Jr, Gail Jackson. **Educ:** Lincoln U; Howard U, BS 1946; Homer G Phillips Hosp, Rotating Internship 1946-47; Univ MI, Post Grad Studies 1949. **Career:** Physician, self-employed; Fed Govt, mail clerk 1937-39; City of Ecorse, hlth offcr; City of River Beuge, hlth offcr 1960; Sumby Hosp, chief of staff; Outer Hosp, chief of staff. **Orgs:** Mem AMA; MI State SOE; Detroit Med Soc; Wayne Co Med Soc; Nat Med Soc; com chmn Accreditation of Hosp by Joint Com; nominating com, bd dir Wayne Co Gen Pract; bd dir Council of Med Staff Of Gen Prac; charter fellow Acad of Family Physicians; MI Assn of the Profession; Nat Med Vets Soc; mem bd dir Down River Guidance Clinic 1955; Omega Psi Phi Frat; Chi Delta Mu. **Honors/Awds:** Recpt Award in Boxing Tennis; mem exec com Outer Hosp 1958; award in Med Nursing Com 1962. **Military Serv:** USN lt commdr. **Business Addr:** 12000 Visger, Detroit, MI 48217.

MITCHELL, B. DOYLE, JR.
Banking executive. **Career:** Industrial Bank, President/CEO. **Business Addr:** President, Industrial Bank, NA, 1900 John Hanson Ln, Oxon Hill, MD 20745-3111, (301)839-4600.

MITCHELL, BENNIE ROBERT, JR.
Clergyman. **Personal:** Born Apr 24, 1948, Edgefield, SC; son of Mr. and Mrs. Bernie R. Mitchell; married Betty Tompkins, 1974; children: Benita Roshaunda, Bendette Renee, Bennie III. **Educ:** Benedict Coll, BA 1970; Morehouse Sch of Religion, M of Div 1974. **Career:** Connors Temple Baptist Church, minister 1974-; Rock Hill Baptist Church, minister 1971-73; South Side Elementary, teacher 1970-71; NY City & Housing Authority, housing Officer, 1969; Mims Elementary, teacher 1969-70. **Orgs:** Mem, Exec Bd of General Missionary Baptist Convention of GA; Natl Baptist Convention; Natl Sunday School & Baptist Training Union; Savannah Baptist Ministerial Union; Political action Chmn of Interdenominatinal Ministerial Alliance; Spokesman of IMA Pilgrim Assn; Savannah Landmark Rehabilitation Project Inc; Savannah Emanicipation Assn; Chmn, MKL Jr Observance; bd mem, Savannah Chapter of PUSH; Life Mem, Omega Psi Phi Frat; Prince Hall Masonic Lodge; Volunteer Chaplain of Savannah Police Dept; bd of dirs, Natl Baptist Convention; bd of trustees, Morehouse school of religion; bd of trustees, Savannah Vocational & Technical School; Appointed to the MLK Jr State Holiday Commn. **Honors/Awds:** Man of the Year, Savannah Tribune Newspaper; Ivan Allen Humantarian Award, Natl Chapter, Morris Brown Coll Alumni; May 2nd, Bernie R. Mitchell Jr, Day, Chatham County; Chaplain of the Day, Georgia State Senate; Preacher of the Year, Gospel Music Workshop of Savannah; Citizen of the Year, Omega Psi Phi Fraternity; Chaired the Jesse Jackson Campaign for Savannah, 1988; Person of the Week, WJCL-TV; guest Evangelist for the FL Baptist Convention & Outstanding Communty Service Award, Gamma Sigma Omega Chapter, AKA Sorority; Community Service Award, West Broad SDA Church. **Business Addr:** Connors Temple Baptist Church, 509 W Gwinnette St, Savannah, GA 31401.

MITCHELL, BERT NORMAN
Business administrator. **Personal:** Born Apr 12, 1938; son of Edith and Joseph; married Carole Harleston; children: Tracey, Robbin, Ronald. **Educ:** City Coll of NY, BBA 1963, MBA 1968; Harvard Grad Sch of Bus, 1985. **Career:** JK Lasser & Co CPA'S, sr auditor 1963-66; Interam Ins Co, controller 1966-67; Ford Found, asst controller 1967-69; Lucas Tucker & Co CPA'S, partner 1969-73; Mitchell/Titus & Co, CEO 1973-; Ariel Mutual Funds Chicago, chm of bd. **Orgs:** Dir Greater NY Fund 1981-; treas 100 Black Men Inc 1976-90; trustee Baruch Coll Fund 1969-; Assn for a Better NY 1980-; pres elect NY State Soc of CPA'S 1986-; pres NY State Soc of CPA's 1987-88, dir/chmn 1970-; State bd of pub acctncy, dir/chmn 1974-; AICPA, dir 1977-80; NYSSCPA, dir 1977-80, 1982-83; Pres, Accountants Club of America 1991-; Harvard Business School, visiting committee; University of Southern California, School of Accountancy, board of advisors; The Consolidated Corporate Fund for Lincoln Center, committee member; Association of Black CPA Firms. **Honors/Awds:** Outstand Achievement Award Nat Assn of Black Accntnts 1977; Outstand Alumnus Award City Coll of NY 1982; CPA NY, NJ & DC; published over 50 articles in professional jour; Townsand Harris Medal, City College, NY 1991, Hon Doctor of Laws, Baruch College 1988; Hon Doctor of Letters Degree, Western New England College 1991; Human Relations Award, The Anti-Defamation League of B'Nai B'Rith 1991; Alumni Achievement Award, Harvard Univ Bus Sch 1995. **Business Addr:** Managing Partner, Mitchell/Titus & Co, 1 Battery Park Plaza, New York, NY 10004.

MITCHELL, BILLY M.
Saxophonist. **Personal:** Born Mar 11, 1926, Kansas City, MO. **Career:** Billy Mitchell Inc; worked with Lucky Thompson, Sonny Stitt, Julius Watkins, Mil Jackson, Nat Towles Orch Detroit, 1948, Jimmie Lunceford, Milt Buckner, Gil Fuller, Woody Herman 1949, Dizzy Gillespie 1956-57, Count Basie 1957; Nasau County in School Jazz Ensemble, composer, arranger, tchr, dir; Major Univ, tchr, lctr. **Honors/Awds:** Played a major role in devel of Detroit Jazz Wave; toured Middle East for State Dept 1956; Renowned as modern tenor saxophonist; downbeat's New Star Awd for small combo 1962; recorded with Clarke-Boland Orch in Europe on Atlantic Label; own LP's are on Smash Label; mus dir for Dizzy Gillespie, Della Reese, Sarah Vaughn, Stevie Wonder & Motown Recording Corp. **Business Addr:** 407 Yale Ave, Rockville Centre, NY 11570.

MITCHELL, BRENDA K.
Government official. **Personal:** Born Jan 9, 1943, New York, NY; daughter of Ola Mae King and William Franklin King; married William Nelson Mitchell (divorced 1974); children: Corrie Nelson Mitchell. **Educ:** Fordham University, New York, NY, BA, liberal arts, 1975; Hunter College, New York, NY, master's, urban affairs, 1976; Nova University, Fort Lauderdale, FL, doctorate, public administration, 1981. **Career:** Control Data Corp, Minneapolis, MN, director of control data business & technology center, 1983-87; Commonwealth of Pennsylvania, Dept of Commerce, Harrisburg, PA, deputy secretary of commerce, Governor's Office, special assistant, 1990-91; Department of State, secretary of the commonwealth, currently. **Orgs:** Vice president, Philadelphia Regional Port Authority; co-founder, former vice pres, Capitol Chapter, National Forum for Black Public Administrators; board of trustees, United Way of Southeastern Pennsylvania; board of directors, West Philadelphia Chamber of Commerce; vice president, West Parkside Philadelphia Business Assn; board of directors, Ben Franklin Partnership Advanced Technology Center for Southeastern Pennsylvania; member, Greater Philadelphia First Neighborhood Economic Development Task Force; board of directors, Philadelphia Fund for Community Development; board of trustees, Lincoln University; board of finance and revenue, PA Municipal Retirement System; PSU Economic Development Council; PA Economic Education Council. **Business Addr:** Secretary of the Commonwealth, Department of State, 302 N Office Bldg, Harrisburg, PA 17120.

MITCHELL, BRIAN KEITH
Professional football player. **Personal:** Born Aug 18, 1968, Fort Polk, LA; married Monica; children: Bria. **Educ:** Southwestern Louisiana, attended. **Career:** Washington Redskins, running back, 1990-. **Honors/Awds:** Pro Bowl, 1996; NFL Alumni, Special Teams Player of the Year, 1996. **Business Addr:** Professional Football Player, Washington Redskins, 13832 Redskin Dr, Herndon, VA 22071, (703)471-9100.

MITCHELL, BYRON LYNWOOD
Orthodontist. **Personal:** Born Mar 2, 1936, Miami, FL; divorced; children: Vanessa, Lynita, Patricia, Michael. **Educ:** Savannah State Coll, BS 1959; Howard Univ, DDS 1966; Howard Univ, Orthod degree 1969. **Career:** General dentistry, private prac 1966-69; Family Health Ctr, chf family dentist 1969-70, dental dir 1971-72; private practice, orthodontist 1970-. **Orgs:** Mem Alpha Phi Alpha Frat, Kiwanis Club, Elks, Dade Co Dent Soc, Dade Co Acad of Med, Grtr Miami Acad of Orthodon; mem Miami, E Coast, FL Dent Socs; mem So Soc of Orthodon; mem Amer Assn of Orthodon. **Honors/Awds:** First black specialist in dentistry to practice in state of FL; first black orthodontist to practice in FL; 2nd black orthodontist to practice in entire South. **Military Serv:** AUS 1959-61. **Business Addr:** Orthodontist, 4885 NW 7th Avenue, Miami, FL 33127.

MITCHELL, CARLTON S.
Banker. **Personal:** Born Sep 7, 1950, New York, NY. **Educ:** Howard University, BA 1972; Columbia University, MS 1984. **Career:** Marine Midland Bank, vice president, currently. **Orgs:** Natl Assn of Urban Bankers; Natl Bankers Assn; Long Island Assn. **Business Addr:** Vice President, Marine Midland Bank, One Old Country Rd, Carle Place, NY 11514.

MITCHELL, CAROL GREENE
Marketing research manager. **Personal:** Born Jul 22, 1960, Baltimore, MD; daughter of Thelma Stewart Greene Clardy; married A Stanley Mitchell, Sep 5, 1987. **Educ:** Fisk University, Nashville, TN, BA, Economics/Management, 1982; University of Wisconsin, Madison, WI, MBA, Marketing, 1983. **Career:** General Mills, Minneapolis, MN, marketing research assistant, 1983; RJ Reynolds Tobacco Co., Winston-Salem, NC, marketing research analyst, 1984-86, senior marketing research analyst, 1986-87, assistant marketing research manager, 1987-88, marketing research manager, 1988-91, sr marketing research manager, 1991-. **Orgs:** Financial secretary, Alpha Kappa Alpha Sorority-Phi Omega Chapter, 1988-90; member, NAACP, 1984-; member, Alpha Kappa Alpha Sorority, 1979-; member, Barrister's Wives, 1987-. **Honors/Awds:** Who's Who in the Beverage and Tobacco Industries, Dollars and Sense Magazine, 1990-92; Outstanding Business and Professional Award, Dollars and Sense Magazine, 1992. **Business Addr:** Sr Marketing Research Manager, RJ Reynolds Tobacco Co, PO Box 2959, Winston-Salem, NC 27102.

MITCHELL, CHARLES, JR.
Educational administrator. **Personal:** Born Apr 21, 1938, Detroit. **Educ:** Western MI U, BS 1959; Wayne State U, MEd 1965, EdS 1968; MA Inst Tech, MS 1970; Wayne State U, EdD 1972. **Career:** Fed & State Prog, div dir 1976-; Physical Edn, consult 1959-60; Detroit, tchr 1960-65; Highland Pk, coordinator 1965-67; Highland Pk, dir spl Proj 1967-69, asst supr personnel 1970-72; supt sch 1972-. **Orgs:** Mem Assn Sch Coll Univ Staffing; Am Assn Sch Adminstrs; Am Assn Sch Personnel Adminstrs; Assn Supervision Curriculum Devel; Acad Mgmt; Booker T Wash Bus Assn; MI Assn Sch Adminstrs; MI Assn Sch Bds; MI Assn Supervision Curriculum Devel; Nat Community Sch Educ Assn; Nat Alliance Black School Adminstrs; Black Causes Assn Inc; NAACP; YMCA; Rotary Internat; Civic League; Human Relations Com; Civic & Industrial Com; Jaycees; mem Caucus Club; Alumni Assn; MI Inst Tech Western MI Univ Wayne State; Varsity Club Inc; adv Mothers Club. **Honors/Awds:** Outstanding young man & yr 1968; sloan fellow MI Inst Tech 1969-70; Danforth NAES fellow 1975; Ford Found fellow 1973. **Home Addr:** 1130 3rd Ave, Apt 1703, Oakland, CA 94606. **Business Addr:** Oakland Unified School Distric, 1025 2nd Ave, Oakland, CA 94606.

MITCHELL, CHARLES E.
Attorney. **Personal:** Born Jul 7, 1925, Seymour, IN; married Julia Sarjeant; children: Charles L, Albert B. **Educ:** Temple Univ Sch of Law, JD 1954; Brooklyn Law Sch; NY U, BA 1949; Morehouse Coll. **Career:** Philadelphia Schl Dist, tchr 1954-55; Fin Dept Phila, mgmt trainee 1955-56; Att Phila, legal asst 1956-60; Ofc of Dist Att Phila, legal asst 1956-60; NY US Soc Sec Admin, claim rep 1960-64; Labor Mgmt Rel Exam Nat Labor Rel Bd Phila, E I DuPont DeNemours & Co Inc, att labor mgmt. **Orgs:** Mem Am Bar Assn; mem Com on Prac & Proc under the Nat Labor Rel Act; Corp Banking & Bus Law; Legal Educ & Adm to Bar; Philadelphia & PA Bar Assn; pres Fed Bar Assn, DE Chptr; Am Jud Soc; Barristers Club of Phila; Lawyers Club of Phila; DE St Bar Assn; mem Com to Promote Equal Opp for Entry Legal Profes in DE; mem Philadelphia Interalumni Coun; United Negro Coll Fund; Indsl Rel Res Assn; Philadelphia Chptr; West MT Airy Neighbors Assn; subchrmn Zoning; Morehouse Coll Club of Phila; YMCA fund raiser; United Way of DE solicitor; mem Interested Negroes Inc; NAACP; Rotary Club of Wilmington. **Military Serv:** USN 1944-46. **Business Addr:** Management Labor Counsel, E I DuPont DeNemours Co, Legal Department, 1007 Market St, Wilmington, DE 19898.

MITCHELL, CRANSTON J.
State corrections official. **Personal:** Born Aug 25, 1946, St Louis, MO; son of Elizabeth Mitchell and Monroe M Mitchell; married Aleta Grimes Mitchell, Jul 8, 1983; children: Leslie Barnes, Catherine J, Christie J. **Educ:** University of Missouri, St. Louis, MO, BS, political science, 1973; Harvard University, Boston, MA, program for senior executives in state and local government, 1988. **Career:** City of St. Louis, St. Louis, MO, police officer, 1967-74; Mitchum-Thayer Inc, St. Louis, MO, marketing representative, 1974-75; State of Missouri, St. Louis/Kansas City, MO, vocational rehabilitation counselor & supervisor, 1975-83; Jobs for Missouri Graduates, St. Louis, MO, regional supervisor, 1983-84; State of Missouri, Missouri Board of Probation and Parole, Jefferson City, MO, board member/chairman, 1984-. **Orgs:** Regional vice president, Association of Paroling Authorities International, 1988-90; member, American Probation and Parole Association, 1984-; member, American Corrections Association, 1984-; charter vice president, National Association of Blacks in Criminal Justice, 1984-; commissioner, Jefferson City Housing Authority, 1990-. **Business Addr:** Chairman, Board of Probation and Parole, State of Missouri Department of Corrections, 117 Commerce, Jefferson City, MO 65101.

MITCHELL, DANIEL B.
Executive director. **Personal:** Born Mar 19, 1941, Walterboro, SC; divorced; children: Jamal. **Educ:** Clark Coll, BA 1962; Syracuse Univ Maxwell Sch, MA 1965; Course Wrk of PhD Completed. **Career:** Black Econ Resrch Ctr, exec dir 1977; City of Mound Bayou, conslt 1969; Nat Bus Planning Team Black Eco Union, chrm 1969; Tufts Delta Hlth Ctr, dir1967-69; Tufts Med Sch, instr; Emergy Land Fund, vice pres dir; pres Minority Constrn Supply Co Inc; Drune Communications Inc WENZ AM Richmand VA, chmn; Unified Limousine Service Inc NYC, chmn & pres; Twenty First Cent Fndt, sec dir; Delta Enterprises Inc, dir; Delta Fndt, dir; Delta Ministry, dir. **Honors/Awds:** Fellow John Hay Whitney 1963; fellow Mellon 1969.

MITCHELL, DEAN LAMONT
Artist. **Personal:** Born Jan 20, 1957, Pittsburgh, PA; son of Hazel Mitchell. **Educ:** Columbus Coll of Art's Design, BFA, 1980. **Career:** Hallmark Cards, illustrator, 1980-83; artist, currently. **Orgs:** Amer Watercolor Society; Natl Watercolor Society; Allied Artist of America; Natl Society of Painters in Casein, Acrylic, mem; Knickerbocker Artist. **Honors/Awds:** TH Saunders International Artist in Watercolor, London, Top Prize, 1980; Allied Artist of America, Gold Medal, Oil, 1992, Gold Medal, Watercolor, 1990; American Artist Professional League, Newington Award for Best Painting; American Watercolor Society, Hardie Gramatky Award, 1990. **Special Achievements:** Columbus Coll of Art Design, Honorary Master's Degree, 1994; PBS Special, Living Canvas; PBS Special, Legacy of Achievement. **Business Addr:** PO Box 27085, Shawnee Mission, KS 66225-7085.

MITCHELL, DENNIS A.
Company executive, olympic athlete. **Personal:** Born Feb 20, 1966, North Carolina; son of Lenora Mitchell and Edward Mitchell; married Kristin Mitchell, Nov 14, 1992. **Educ:** University of Florida. **Career:** Mind, Body & Soul Inc, pres, currently; US Olympic Team, track and field, 1992. **Honors/Awds:** Olympic Games, Gold Medalist, 4 x 100 relay, 1992; Bronze Medalist, 100 meters, 1992; American Champion, 100M, 1992; Second in the World, 100M, 1992. **Business Addr:** Gold Medalist, 1992 Games, c/o US Olympic Training Center, 1 Olympic Plaza, Colorado Springs, CO 80909, (719)578-4500.

MITCHELL, DOLPHUS BURL
Optometrist. **Personal:** Born Sep 9, 1922, Birmingham, AL; son of Gertrude Mitchell; children: Dawn, Donald, Dori. **Educ:** Alcorn A&M Coll, 1943; Northern IL Coll of Optometry, OD 1949; Union Bapt Sem Inc, Hon LLD 1952; Optometry Ext Pgm; Workshop So Coll of Optometry, 1973; Sch of Nut Sci, Diploma 1980; Chicago Med Coll Calcutta, India, MD Homeopathy 1981, PhD Homeopathy 1986. **Career:** Birmingham, AL, private prac optometry 1949-73; Horner Rausch Optical of Huntsville, optomotrist 1986; Huntsville, AL, private prac optometry 1973-; Royal Optical Madison Square Mall 1988; self employed, money broker, currently. **Orgs:** Better Vision Inst;

Mason 1948; Shriners 1952; Boy Scout Comm 1952; part time asst prof opt Univ of AL Birmingham 1969-70; deacon, Sixth Ave Missionary Bapt Ch 1973-; NAACP; hon deputy sheriff Madison Co 1973; Amer Judicature Soc 1973-; assoc mem FOP Huntsville 1974; fellow Amer Biog Inst 1978; AL Assn of Optometry 1980-; Natl Optometric Assn 1980-; consult Amer Nutrition 1981; Chamber of Commerce Huntsville/Madison Ct 1984; life mem Natl Rifle Assn; mem Redstone Military Officer Club, 1990. **Honors/Awds:** Cert of Merit Dic of Int Biog; Cert of Award BT Wash Bus Coll 1971; recip Wisdom Award of Hon 1973; listed Lib of Human Resources 1973; hon lt col AL State Militia 1977; Appreciation Award USN Recruiting Command Huntsville, AL 1981; Certificate of Merit Pearle Vision Center 1985; mem Board Certified Diplomate in Nutrition 1991. **Military Serv:** AUS Inf pvt 1943-46; Good Conduct Medal, American Camp; USAF Civil Air Patrol, captain. **Home Addr:** 4013 Apollo Dr SW, Huntsville, AL 35805.

MITCHELL, DONALD
Actor. **Personal:** Born Mar 17, 1943, Houston, TX; married Judy Pace; children: Dawn Marie, Shawn Michelle, Julia Anette. **Educ:** Los Angeles City Coll, drama directing; Lee Strasberg Actors Studio; Los Angeles Reportory Co, Theatrical Mgmt; Beverly Hills Directors Lab, Directing; UCLAExt, Sculpture Ceramics; Tony Hill Ceramics, Ceramics Sculpture. **Career:** Don Mitchell Prodn, actor commr of Presidential Scholars; "Treemonisha" Los Angeles Opera Co, prod 1979; TV Series "Chips", actor 1979; "Police Story", actor 1978; "Perfume",co-dir movie 1977; Spl Proj for Theater, dir 1976; "Richard Pryor Live in Concert", pckgd movie 1976; "Medical Story", actor 1975; "The Blacks", prod & co-dir 1972; Mafundi Inst, tchr Acting 1971-72; The Watts Training Cntr, cofndr 1967; "Ironside", actor 1966-75; Los Angeles, actor; New York, actor 1963-65. **Orgs:** Mc spl prog & or guest spkr, The US Jaycees; Nat Assn of Negro Bus & Professional Women; Boy Scouts; Am Cancer Soc; New Sch of Soc Res; Mot Pic Assn; Media Women; CA Spl Olympics; Charles Drew Med Soc; Am Black Vet Adminstrn; Am Polit Sci Assn; Handicapped Assn; Boys Club; UCLA Dept of Theater Arts; Black Filmmakers Hall of Fame; Nat Park Serv US Dept of Int; Nat Counc of Negro Women; Involvement for Young Achievers Inc; LAPD Drug Abuse Prog; Los Angeles Urgan League; Intl Year of the Child; Screen Actors Guild; El Monte City Counc; Ward Meth Episcopal Ch; L A Thespians; Inner City Cult Ctr; CA State Los Angeles; FL A&M U; Grambling U; Univ of Houston; Alcorn U; Howard U; New Fed Theater; Negro Ensemble Co; Mouehouse; Rockefeler Found; United Negro Coll Fund; Los Angeles Unified Sch Dist; NAA AFTRA; Actors Equity Assn; numerous others; campaigned Los Angeles Mayor, Tom Bradley; campaigned TX Congresswoman Barbara Jordan; campaigned State Sen Nate & Holden; campaigned Pres Jimmy Carter; campaigned for numerous others. **Business Addr:** 939 S Serrano Ave, Apt 800, Los Angeles, CA 90006-1146.

MITCHELL, DOUGLAS
City official, electrical technician. **Personal:** Born Apr 10, 1948, Leslie, GA; son of Lula Mae Jenkins Winbush and Albert Joe Mitchell; married Velma Jean Floyd Mitchell, Jun 27, 1971; children: Rodney Purcell Mitchell. **Career:** Procter and Gamble, Albany GA, line technician, 1975-82, team leader, 1982-84, electrical technician, 1984-; City of Smithville, Smithville GA, mayor, currently. **Orgs:** Past mem, Albany Area Primary Health Bd of Dir, 1985-86; mem, Lee County Chamber of Commerce Task Force, 1989, Highway 19 Improvement Task Force, 1989. **Military Serv:** AUS, E-4, 1968-70. **Business Addr:** Mayor, City of Smithville, PO Box 180 Main St, Smithville, GA 31787.

MITCHELL, DWAYNE OSCAR
Health services administrator. **Personal:** Born Jul 13, 1959, Chicago, IL; son of Sylvia Norwood Mitchell and Willie James Mitchell; married Debra Clifton, Aug 2, 1986; children: Daninelle Ashley Mitchell. **Educ:** IL State Univ, BS 1982; Governor State Univ, MHA 1984. **Career:** Amer Cancer Society, asst youth coordinator 1982; Comm Mental Health, research assoc 1982-83; Cook County Hospital, lab admin 1984-85, Ob/Gyn admin 1985-. **Orgs:** Mem, Natl Assoc Health Care, 1982, treasurer, l988; Alpha Phi Alpha Inc, 1985, Natl Black MBA Assoc, 1986; adjunct clinical prof, Governon State Univ, 1987; mem, Amer Public Health Assn, l986; member, American College Health Care Executives, 1986; assoc bd member, Illinois University, 1989. **Honors/Awds:** Appreciation Award, Amer Cancer Society, Chicago, 1982; Certification, Community Mental Health Assn, 1989.

MITCHELL, EARL DOUGLASS, JR.
Educator. **Personal:** Born May 16, 1938, New Orleans, LA; married Bernice Compton; children: Karen, Doug, Mike. **Educ:** Xavier Univ of LA, BS 1960; MI State Univ, MS 1963, PhD 1966. **Career:** MI State Univ, research assoc 1966; OK State Univ, research assoc 1967-69, asst & assoc prof 1969-78, prof & asst dean 1978-82; NHLI of NIH, research chem 1978-79; OK State Univ, prof of biochemistry 1978-. **Orgs:** Mem Oklahoma State Advisory Committee to US Commn on Civil Rights 1969-; chrmn SAC of OK 1980-86; chmn OK State Personnel Bd 1980-82; chmn OK Ethics & Merit Comm 1982-84; mem consult Biochem Study Sect Natl Inst of Health 1984-87; chmn Merit Protection Commn 1986-88; mem bd of trustees OK High School of Sciences & Math 1986-; chair, Oklahoma Merit Protection Commission, 1985-91; chair, Oklahoma State Advisory Committee, US Commission on Civil Rights, 1989-; mem Minority Biomedical Research Support Program of National Institute of Health, 1988-92, chair committee, 1991-92. **Honors/Awds:** NIH & NSF Research Grants 1969-75; 40 research journal publications & 41 research abstracts 1969-92; project dir, Oklahoma Alliance for Minority Participation in Mathematics, Science, Engineering, and Technology. **Business Addr:** Assoc VP, Multicultural Affairs, Professor of Biochemistry & Molecular Bio, Oklahoma State Univ, 408 Whitehurst, Stillwater, OK 74078-0117.

MITCHELL, EDWIN H., SR.
Educator. **Personal:** Born Dec 21, 1921, Norfolk, VA; married Noella Pajaud; children: Tresa (Saxton), Kathryn, Cheryl (newsom), Edwin H. **Educ:** Meharry Med Coll, MD 1948; certification in radiology & nuclear med 1960. **Career:** Harlem Hosp, internship 1948-49; Sydenham Hosp NY, admitting physician 1949; Sydenham Hosp, dir of clinics 1950-51; Camden SC, pvt practice 1952-56; Nat Cancer Inst Meharry Med Coll, trainee 1956-59; Columbia Presb Med Center, fellow 1959-60; Meharry Med Coll, asst prof 1960-62; Meharry Med Coll, asso prof 1962-72; Meharry Med Coll, prof of Radiology 1972-. **Orgs:** Mem Alpha Omega Alpha Honor Med Soc; Nashville Academy of Med; R F Boyd Med Soc; TN Med Assn; volunteer Med Assn; TN Radiol Soc; Nat Med Assn; Middle TN Radiol Soc; Am Coll of Radiology; pres of staff Meharry Med Coll 1974-75; chief dept radiology/Activing Chief Nuclear Medicine VA Hosp Murfreesboro TN; original bd mem & pres Davidson Co Ind Polit Council 1962-72; mem TN Voters Council 1962-; treas 1974; chmn Met Human Relations Commn 1967-70; chmn coordinating com Model Cities 1969-72; bd mem NAACP Nashville Br 1966-73; bd mem Easter Seals Soc; bd mem Urban Projects Inc 1968-72; mem Davidson Co Ind Polit Council; TN Voters Council; bd mem treas Voters Educ Project; mem Phi Beta Sigma Fraternity; Sigma Pi Phi Fraternity;Alpha Omega Alpha Med HonorFraternity; Nat Assn of Human Rights Wors; Davidson Co Assn for Retarded Children. **Honors/Awds:** Cit of yr Frontiersman 1967; Nat Assn of Intergroup Relations Officials 1968; Middle TN Council of BSA 1968; Nat Assn of Negro & Professional Women's ClubsNashville Br 1968; Dept of History & Polit Sci TN & State Univ 1968; Agora Assembly 1969; Meharry Med Coll 1970; Met Human Relations Commn 1970; WelfareRights Orgn 1970; churchman of yr Religious Nashville Opportunities Industrialization Center 1970; citation Awards, POETS 1970; NAACP Youth Council1970; Model Cities Coordinating Com 1970; Phi Beta Sigma 1971; alumnus of yr Meharry Alumni 1971; pres award 25 yrs serv Meharry Med Coll 1973. **Military Serv:** Sgt 1942-43; 1st Lt 1951-52. **Business Addr:** Chief Radiology/Nuclear Med, A C York VAMC, Lebanon Road, Nashville, TN 37208.

MITCHELL, ELLA PEARSON
Theological educator, cleric. **Personal:** Born Oct 18, 1917, Charleston, SC; daughter of Jessie Wright Pearson (deceased) and Rev Dr Joseph R Pearson (deceased); married Dr Henry H Mitchell; children: Muriel, Elizabeth M Clement, Kenneth. **Educ:** Talladega Coll AL, BA 1939; Union Theological Seminary & Columbia Univ, MA 1943; The School of Theology at Claremont, DMin 1974. **Career:** Berkeley Baptist Div School, instructor Christian educ 1951-59; Sunset Unified School Dist CA, kindergarten instructor 1961-66; Compton Coll CA, instr early child educ 1967-69; Amer Baptist Seminary of West & LaVernue Univ, adjunct prof 1974-82; Claremont Unified School Dist CA, kindergarten teacher 1973-80; Second Baptist Church Los Angeles, CA, minister of church educ 1980-82; School of Theology VA Union Univ, assoc prof Christian educ/dir Continuing Educ 1982-86; Spelman Coll, Atlanta, dean of sisters chapel 1986-88; Interdenominational Theological Center, Atlanta, visiting professor of homiletics, 1988-95; visiting professor of Homiletics, United Theological Seminary, 1990-. **Orgs:** Mem Claremont City Human Resources Comm 1975-79; mem Gov Bd Natl Council of Churches 1971-75; mem (pres 1969-73) Bd of Educ Ministries Amer Baptist Churches 1959-73; mem General Bd of Amer Baptist Churches 1984-87; regional chaplain, Delta Sigma Theta Sorority, 1993-. **Honors/Awds:** Author/Editor Those Preachin' Women, Vols 1 1985 & 2 1988; Women: To Preach Or Not To Preach, 1991; Deputy Dir Martin Luther King Fellows Program 1972-75; Chaplain (life mem) Natl Delta Sigma Theta Sorority 1979; First Woman Dean of the Chapel, Sisters Chapel, Spelman Coll, Atlanta; Talladega College, LHD, Granted 1989. **Home Addr:** 411 Angier Court, Atlanta, GA 30312.

MITCHELL, EMMITT W.
Chief executive. **Career:** Mitchell Lincoln Mercury, Kansas City, MO, chief executive, 1982-. **Business Addr:** Mitchell Lincoln Mercury, PO Box 26084, Shawnee Mission, KS 66225.

MITCHELL, GEORGE L.
Chief executive. **Career:** Dyersburg Ford, Inc, Dyersburg, TN, chief exec, 1985-. **Business Addr:** Dyersburg Ford-Lincoln-Mercury, 920 Highway 51 By-Pass W, Dyersburg, TN 38024.

MITCHELL, HENRY B.
Clergyman. **Personal:** Born Nov 12, 1918, Ahoskie, NC; married Gertrude Phillips; children: Carolyn, H. **Educ:** Hampton Inst, BS; Protestant Episcopal Theol Sem, 1957; Yale Univ Schl Alcohol Studies, 1960. **Career:** Danville Cure, priest 1957-58; Trinity Episcopal Ch, vicar 1958; VTS Alexandria VA, adj prof; Diocese of MI, asst to bishop 1977; Seabury Press & Bd 1978. **Orgs:** Bd of Bishop Whipple Schs 1979; bd trustees VA Theol Sem 1973; chmn Charlottesvl City Sch Bd 1972; mem Omega Psi Phi; exec bd NAACP 1970; bd sec Anglican Council No Am & Caribbean 1974. **Honors/Awds:** Humanitarian award Secret 7 Soc, Univ of VA 1969; scroll honor VA State Assn Elks 1974.

MITCHELL, HENRY HEYWOOD
Theological educator, cleric. **Personal:** Born Sep 10, 1919, Columbus, OH; son of Bertha Estis Mitchell (deceased) and Orlando W Mitchell (deceased); married Ella Muriel Pearson; children: Muriel, Elizabeth M Clement, Kenneth. **Educ:** Lincoln Univ, AB (Cum Laude) 1941; Union Theol Sem NYC, MDiv 1944; CA State Univ, MA 1966; The School of Theol at Claremont, ThD 1973. **Career:** NC Central Univ, dean chapel instr 1944-45; Amer Bapt of Northern California, area staffer & editor 1945-59; Second Bapt Church Fresno, pastor 1959-66; Calvary Bapt Church Santa Monica, pastor 1966-69; Colgate Rochester/Bexley Hall/Crozer, black church studies 1969-74; Fuller Theol Sem Pasadena & Amer Bapt Sem of W Berkeley & LaVerne Coll, adj prof school of theology, Ecumenical Ctr for Black Church Studies of LA, prog dir 1974-82; CA State Univ Northridge, prof rel & pan-African studies 1981-82; VA Union Univ, dean school of theol 1982-86, prof history & homiletics 1986-87; visiting prof of homiletics, Interdenominational Theological Center, Atlanta, 1988-95; visiting prof of homiletics, United Theological Seminary, Dayton OH, 1989-. **Orgs:** Dir ML King Prog in Black Church Studies 1972-75; mem Soc for Study of Black Religion 1972-; pres North California Bapt Conv 1963; chmn bd 1964-65, pres Fresno Co Econ Oppor Commn 1966; mem Natl Comm of Black Churchmen 1968-75; chmn bd North California Bapt Conv 1964; pastor Calvary Bapt Church Santa Monica CA 1966-69, Second Baptist Church Fresno CA 1959-66; lit ed Martin Luther King Fellows Press 1975-; Lyman Beecher lecturer Divinity School of Yale Univ 1974. **Honors/Awds:** Author: Black Preaching 1970, Black Belief 1975, The Recovery of Preaching 1977, Soul Theology with Nicholas Cooper Lewter, 1986, Celebration and Experience in Preaching, Abingdon Press, 1990, Black Preaching: The Recovery of a Powerful Art, Abingdon Press, 1990; Preaching for Black Self-Esteem, with Emil M Thomas, 1994; numerous articles in books magazines & journals; Fellow Phelps-Stokes Fund E Africa 1973, 1974; Lyman Beecher Lecturer on Preaching Yale Divinity School 1974; Phi Kappa Epsilon Lincoln Univ Chap 1941; Phi Kappa Phi CA State Univ Fresno Chap 1966. **Home Addr:** 411 Angier Court, NE, Atlanta, GA 30312.

MITCHELL, HORACE
Educator. **Personal:** Born Oct 4, 1944, Lambert, MS; married Barbara J; children: Angela, Kimberly. **Educ:** Wash U, AB 1968; Wash U, MEd 1969; Wash U, PhD 1974. **Career:** Wash U, asst dean 1968-73; Educ Black Studies Wash U, asst prof 1973-76; Wash U, dir black studies 1976-. **Orgs:** Publ many art couns psycol; consult Midwest Cntr Equal Educ Opport 1974; mem APGA Com Standardized Testing Poten Disad; consult many sch dist; mem Kappa Delta Ph; Phi Delta Kappa; Phi Beta Sigma; Am Person & Guid Assn; Assn Black Psychol Assn; Non-White Concerns Person & Guid. **Business Addr:** Univ of California - Irvine, 260 Administration Building, Irvine, CA 92717.

MITCHELL, HUEY P.
Attorney. **Personal:** Born Dec 10, 1935, Bivins, TX; married Nelvia G; children: Huey, Jr, Janet H. **Educ:** TX So Univ Schl of Law, LLB 1960. **Career:** Law Firm of Mitchell & Bonner, atty; Reg Counsel US Dept HUD, asst 1967-73; City of Houston, asst city atty 1964-67; Office of Judge Advocate Gen; AUS FtHood, 1960-62; Pvt Prac Houston, 1962-64; Municipal Ct Ft Worth, sub judge 1973; TX Christian U, tchr Bus Law 1968-73. **Orgs:** Mem chmn of bd Tarrant Co Legal Aid Found 1972; mem & vice pres Ft Worth Chap Fed Bar Assn; mem Nat Bar Assn; Ft Worth Tarrant Co Sr Bar Assn; Hex Learning Cntr, prtnr; HPM Mgmt Devel & Co, owner & org; mem Nat Bd Dir Planned Parenthood Fedn of Am; Tarrant Co Hlth Plnng Cncl; orgnzng Com of Ft Worth Tarrant Comm Devel Fund. **Honors/Awds:** First black asst city atty in history of Houston Apptd 1964; first black Municipal Judge in Ft Worth apptd 1973. **Military Serv:** AUS splst e-5 62. **Business Addr:** 700 Baker Bldg, Fort Worth, TX 76102.

MITCHELL, IVERSON O., III
Attorney. **Personal:** Born Dec 20, 1943, Washington, DC. **Educ:** Georgetown U, BSFS 1965; Wash Coll Law Am U, JD 1968. **Career:** DC Corp Counsel, assistant, 1971-76; Wilkes & Artis, attorney, 1976-85; private practice, attorney, 1985; Speights & Mitchell, partner, 1986-. **Orgs:** DC Bar; Wash Bar Assn, president, 1982-84; Natl Bar Assn; DC Bd of Labor Relations, 1977-79, chairman, 1978-79; DC Bd of Equalization and Review, 1987-93, chairman, 1991-93. **Honors/Awds:** Cert apprctn YMCA 1973. **Military Serv:** US Army capt 1969-70.

Biographies

MITCHELL

MITCHELL, JACOB BILL
Business executive. **Personal:** Born Jun 19, 1932, Boswell, OK; married Erma Jean Davis; children: Waymon, Victor, Erik, Mark, Kayla. **Educ:** Armed Forces Inst, AE, 1953; UCLA, BSEE, 1958, MSEE 1963; City Univ of Los Angeles, Wichita State, PhD program, 1979. **Career:** Librascope Inc, sr engr analyst, 1956-60; North Am Aviation, sys design engr, 1960-62; Hughes Aircraft Co, sr electronic engr, 1962-64; NASA, sr research engr, 1964-68; Beech Aircraft, design engr, 1968-73; Cessna Aircraft, design engr, 1973-75; Jacob B Mitchell Assoc, engring consult, 1975-79; NCR, sys engr, 1979-81; Telemetry Sys Inc, pres. **Orgs:** IEEE, 1963-. **Military Serv:** AUS, communications chief, 1951-54; European Occupation Medal, Good Conduct Medal. **Home Addr:** 2210 E 13th St, Wichita, KS 67214. **Business Addr:** President, Telemetry Systems, Inc, 1601 E Harry, Wichita, KS 67211.

MITCHELL, JAMES H.
Automobile dealership executive. **Personal:** Born Sep 15, 1948, Danville, VA; married Linda T. **Educ:** VA State Univ, BS 1972. **Career:** Mel Farr Ford, used car mgr; Park Motor Sales, asst used car mgr; Crest Lincoln-Mercury, asst used car mgr; Ford Motor Dealer Training Prog; Detroit Lions Inc, pro football 1970-78; Lynchburg Ford Inc, chief executive, currently. **Orgs:** Children's Miracle Network. **Business Addr:** President, Lynchburg Ford, Inc, PO Box 11828, Lynchburg, VA 24506.

MITCHELL, JAMES WINFIELD
Scientist. **Personal:** Born Nov 16, 1943, Durham, NC; son of Eunice Hester Mitchell and Willie Mitchell; married Alice J Kea; children: Veronica, Duane, Tonya. **Educ:** Agr & Tech State Univ of NC, BS, 1965; IA State Univ Ames, PhD Analytical Chem 1970. **Career:** Bell Laboratories, mem technical staff 1970-72, supvr 1972-75, head analyst chem research dept 1975-85, AT&T Fellow 1985-. **Orgs:** Adv bd Analytical Chem 1977-80; adv bd Mikro Chim Acta 1978-82; mem NRC board, Chem Sci & Math, 1992-95; mem Omega Psi Phi Frat 1963-; bd of dir Essex County Community Coll NJ 1972-74; bd dir Plainfield Science Center NJ 1972-. **Honors/Awds:** Book, ''Contamination Control in Trace Element Analysis'' Wiley-Intersci Published 1975; Pharmacia Award in Analytical Chem; Editorial Bd Talanta 1978; 56 journal articles; 3 patents; Percey Julian Industrial Research Award 1980; IR100 Award 1982; Bell Labs Fellow 1985; Natl Academy of Engineering, 1989; Industrial Research Award, 1989. **Business Addr:** Head, Analytical Chem Research Dept, Bell Laboratories, MH 1D239, Murray Hill, NJ 07974.

MITCHELL, JOANN
University administrator. **Personal:** Born Sep 2, 1956, Augusta, GA; daughter of Alice King Mitchell and Earl Mitchell. **Educ:** Davidson Coll NC, AB 1978; Vanderbilt Univ Sch of Law, JD 1981. **Career:** Manson Jackson & Assocs, attorney/assoc 1981-86; TN Human Rights Comm, law clerk 1983-84; Vanderbilt Univ Opp Dev Ctr, asst dir 1983-86; Univ of PA, dir affirmative action 1986-. **Orgs:** Mem Amer Bar Assoc 1981-; treas bd of dirs Napier-Lobby Bar Assoc 1985, 1986; adv bd mem Vanderbilt Women's Ctr 1985, 1986; bd of dirs Assoc of Vanderbilt Black Alumni 1985, 1986; financial sec usher bd Mt. Oliver Miss Bapt Church 1985, 1986; deacon Mt Oliver Miss Baptist Church 1986-. **Honors/Awds:** Outstanding Young Women of Amer 1983-; Affirmative Action Awd Vanderbilt Univ 1986. **Business Addr:** Director, Affirmative Action, University of Pennsylvania, 1133 Blockley Hall, 418 Service Dr, Philadelphia, PA 19104-6021.

MITCHELL, JOANNE
Social worker. **Personal:** Born May 30, 1938, Evansville, IN; married Robert Bright; children: Howard Polk, Karen Polk. **Educ:** Roosevelt Univ Chicago, Sociology 1971; Univ of Chicago School of Social Serv Admin, AM SSA 1973. **Career:** IL Commn on Deliquency Prevention, exec dir; IL Law Enforcement Commn, assoc dir 1973-78; IL Dept of Corrections, community worker 1969-73; Brunswick Chicago Job Corps Center, admin asst 1966-69; IL Dept of Educ & Registration, social worker 1973; IL Dept of Financial Inst, asst director. **Orgs:** Acad of Certificate Social Workers; Natl Assn of Social Workers 1973; panelist Assembly of Behavioral & Social Science Natl Acad of Science 1979; mem League of Black Women 1976; mem NAACP; mem Natl Urban League. **Honors/Awds:** Appointment Gov Advisory Council on Criminal Justice Legislation 1978; Outstanding Leadership & Dedicated Serv IL Health & Human Serv Assn 1978. **Business Addr:** Assistant Dir, IL Dept of Financial Inst, 100 W Randolph, Ste 15-700, Chicago, IL 60601.

MITCHELL, JOSEPH CHRISTOPHER
Educational administrator. **Personal:** Born Oct 8, 1922, Albany, GA; son of Hattie Bell Mitchell (deceased) and Rischard Monroe Mitchell (deceased); married Julia Louise Craig; children: Joseph Clovis, Haazim Jawaad Abdullah, Michael Charles. **Educ:** Fort Valley State Coll, BS Natl Sci-Math, 1939-43; Atlanta Coll of Mortuary Science Inc, diploma (summa cum laude), 1945-46; Atlanta Univ, MS (cum laude), 1947-48; Univ of Michigan, certificates, 1955-60; Princeton Univ, Chemistry certificate, 1959; Duke Univ, Marine Biology certificate, 1961; Cornell Univ, PhD candidate medical entomology-parasitology, London School of Applied Rsch, ScD, 1972. **Career:** Albany & Mobile High School, head of science dept, head coach, 1943, 1946, 1948; Atlanta Coll of Mortuary Science, dir of labs, 1945-46; Fort Valley State Coll, asst prof of science, asst coach, 1949-52; Alabama State Coll Branch, asst prof of science, head of science dept, 1952-54; Albany State Coll, asst prof of biology, asst coach, 1954-63; Alabama State Univ, assoc prof of sci, head of science dept, 1963-65; Bishop State Community Coll, interim pres, 1981, chmn of div of science & math, dir of mortuary science, 1965-. **Orgs:** Science consultant, Phelps Stokes Found, 1954-57; science consultant, Region 9, Georgia Teachers Assn, 1954-63; ESEA Title III proj consultant, US Office of Health, Educ & Welfare, 1964-67; dir, Natl Science Found, Minority Inst Science Improvement Prog, Bishop State, 1975-78; evaluator, Natl Science Teachers Assn, 1978; science consultant, visiting comm for Southern Assn of Schools, 1980, 1982, 1983; chmn of selection comm, Assoc Degree Nursing Prog, 1982-; rsch assoc, Dept of Medical Entomology Parasitology, Cornell Univ; bd mem, United Cerebral Palsy Mobile Inc; bd mem, Alabama Interdenominational Seminary Assoc; mem, NEA, AEA, AAAS, AAJC, NAACP, NABT; bd mem, Amer Cancer Soc. **Honors/Awds:** Fellowships, Natl Science Found, Washington DC, summer 1959, summer 1961, 1961-62; acad fellowship, Ford Found, New York, 1969-70; plaque Outstanding Interim Pres, Faculty & Students of Bishop State, 1981; published, ''The Influence of Inhibitors on the Cytochrome System of Heterakis Gallinae,'' Transactions of Natl Inst of Science, Vol 45 No 1, 1952, ''A Study of Endoparasites & Ectoparasites of the Cotton Rat, Sigmodon Hispidus,'' 1964-66, ''A Cytogenetic Study of the Simuliidae of Tompkins County NY,'' 1969-71; founder, mortuary science program/funeral service education, Bishop State CommunityCollege, 1972; founder, associate degree nursing program, Bishop State Community College, 1970; Organized Ad Hoc Committee that changed the name of Mobile State to Bishop State. **Military Serv:** ERC of US Army, private, 1942-43. **Home Addr:** 712 Bishop St, Mobile, AL 36617. **Business Addr:** Chairman, Div of Science & Mathematics, Bishop State Community College, 351 N Broad St, Rm 102, Mobile, AL 36690.

MITCHELL, JOSEPH RUDOLPH
Physician. **Personal:** Born Aug 9, 1938, Chicago, IL; son of Vivian James Mitchell and Joseph R Mitchell; married Emi Yamashiro. **Educ:** Morehouse Coll, BS 1959; Meharry Medical Coll, MD 1964; Tulane Univ, MHA, 1992. **Career:** Santa Clara Valley Medical Ctr, internship 1964-65; Kapiolani Hospital, residency 1968-71; Mama Yemo Hospital Zaire Kinshasa, chief of gyn pav 1972-74; Deltal Health Ctr Mound Bayou MS, med dir 1974-75; Gulfport MS, private practice 1975-93; Cost Care Inc, Atlanta GA, 1993-. **Orgs:** Mem & vice chmn Mississippi Bd of Health 1980-86; bd of dirs Gulfport Area Chamber of Commerce 1984-86; mem Governor's Infant Mortality Task Force 1985-; mem Amer Coll of Obstetricians & Gynecologists, Natl and Amer Medical Assns, Coast Counties Medical Assn, Natl Perinatal Assn, MS Perinatal Assn, Southern Perinatal Assn, MS Medical & Surgical Assn, MS State Medical Assn; Mississippi State Board of Medical Licensure, 1990-93. **Honors/Awds:** Mem Alpha Omega Alpha Honor Medical Soc. **Military Serv:** AUS Capt 1965-67. **Business Addr:** Associate Medical Dir, Cost Care Inc, PO Box 724567, Atlanta, GA 31139-1567.

MITCHELL, JUDSON, JR.
Internal auditor. **Personal:** Born Oct 26, 1941, Jersey City, NJ; son of Lucy Barnes Mitchell and Judson Mitchell (deceased); married Patricia Roberts (deceased); children: Mark A, Judson (deceased), Steven C, Guy (deceased). **Educ:** Rutgers Univ Coll, BS, Accounting, 1975; Rutgers GSBA, MBA 1979. **Career:** Public Service Electric & Gas Co, sr plant analyst 1980-81, assoc accountant 1981-82, internal auditor 1982-, senior staff auditor, 1994. **Orgs:** Mem, Natl Black MBA Assn; Amer Inst of CPA's, NJ Soc of CPA's; Inst of Internal Auditors, Minority Interchange; Natl Assn of Certified Fraud Examiners; National Association of Black Accountants; past pres, Northern NJ Chapter of National Association of Black Accountants, 1987-881; Outstanding Member of the Year, 1992. **Honors/Awds:** Certified Public Accountant NJ 1982; Certified Internal Auditor Inst of Internal Auditors 1986; Certified Fraud Examiner, National Assn of Certified Fraud Examiners, 1989; Black Achiever of Business and Education, YMWCA of Newark and Vicinity, 1988. **Military Serv:** USMC lance corpl 4 yrs. **Home Addr:** 15 Holly Street, Jersey City, NJ 07305.

MITCHELL, JUDYLYNN
Educational administrator. **Personal:** Born Aug 19, 1951, Salisbury, MD; married Fred; children: Cortni Lee-Lynn. **Educ:** Bowie State Coll, BS 1969-72; Bowling Green State U, MEd 1973-74; Nova U, EdD (Expected) 1985. **Career:** Salisbury State Coll, academic cnslr 1974-79, project dir 1980-82, pgm splst 1982-83; Center for Human Svcs, educ spclst 1983-84, residential admin. **Orgs:** Mem Assn for the Study of Afro Life & Hist; bd of trustees Wicomico Co Lib; bd of dir Eastern Seals Soc; mem Wicomico Co Historical Soc. **Honors/Awds:** Black Heritage Articles, ''Salisbury Sunday & Daily Times'' Salisbury, MD 1979; religious black hist play, ''Yester-Days Women, Gone But Not Forgotten'' 1983; Outstand Young Women of The Yr 1982-83. **Home Addr:** Rt 5 106 Southbury St, Salisbury, MD 21801. **Business Addr:** Residential Administrator, Center for Human Serv, Univ of MD Eastern Shore, PO Box 1021, Princess Anne, MD 21853.

MITCHELL, JULIUS P.
Educational administrator. **Personal:** Born Nov 5, 1941, Rome, GA; son of Carrie Mitchell and Pryor Mitchell; married Gwendolyn McLeod; children: Toni L, Shaune. **Educ:** Clarkson Univ, Potsdam NY, Bachelor 1984; St Lawrence Univ, Canton NY, MED 1987. **Career:** US Army, special forces 1959-81; St Lawrence Univ, dir of HEOP/pres HEOP-PO; Clarkston Univ, Potsdam NY, dir of minority affairs, 1988-. **Orgs:** Pres Higher Educ Oppor Prog Prof Organ of NY State 1984. **Military Serv:** AUS 1st sgt 22 yrs; Bronze Star; Meritorious Serv Awd. **Home Addr:** PO Box 146, Potsdam, NY 13676. **Business Addr:** Dir of Minority Student Development, Clarkston Univ, Potsdam, NY 13676.

MITCHELL, KATHERINE PHILLIPS
Educator. **Personal:** Born Apr 16, 1943, Hope, AR; daughter of Parthenia Phillips and Clem Phillips; divorced; children: Jeffrey Allen. **Educ:** Philander Smith College, BA, English education; University of Wisconsin, 1965-66; Cleveland St ate University, MEd, reading education; University of Arkansas, EdD, higher education. **Career:** Cleveland Public Schools, teacher, 1967-73; University of Central Arkansas, assistant professor, 1977-78; City of Little Rock, grant manager, 1978-79, project director, 1979-81; Storer Cable, coordinator of Channel 14, 1981-89; Philander Smith College, division chair, education, 1986-89; Shorter College, president, 1989-. **Orgs:** Little Rock School Board, 1988-, immediate past president; Professional Counseling Associates, 1986-, past secretary; Central Arkansas Library System, 1988-; Delta Sigma Theta, 1962-, past chapter president; Independent Community Consultants, 1982-; Ouachita Council Girl Scouts, 1987-; Minority AIDS Task Force, 1987-; AAUW. **Honors/Awds:** Philander Smith College Alumni Association, Outstanding Contribution to Higher Education; Delta Sigma Theta, Delta of the Year; Mt Pleasant Baptist Church, Black Achiever's Award; Ward Chapel AME Church, Woman of the Year. **Home Addr:** 1605 Welch, Little Rock, AR 72202. **Business Phone:** (501)374-6305.

MITCHELL, KEITH
Professional football player. **Personal:** Born Jul 24, 1974. **Educ:** Texas A&M, attended. **Career:** New Orleans Saints, linebacker, 1997-. **Business Addr:** Professional Football Player, New Orleans Saints, 5800 Airline Hwy, Metairie, LA 70003, (504)733-0255.

MITCHELL, KELLY KARNALE
Clergyman. **Personal:** Born May 18, 1928, Newnan, GA; married Audrea Marie Martin; children: Kelyne Audrienne, Kelly Karnale Jr. **Educ:** Nashville Christian Inst, 1948; Fisk U, BA 1952; AL Christian Coll, ThB 1968; Missionary of the New Truth Schl, DD 1971; AL Christian Sch of Religion, MRE 1978. **Career:** Southside Ch of Christ Montgomery AL, minister 1972; WRMA Radio Sta Montgomery, religious Supr 1963-67; Christian Echo LA, staff writer 1958-65; Holt St Ch of Christ Montgomery, minister 1955-72; Green St Ch of Christ Nashville, minsiter 1951-55; Greenlea Weekly Paper Nashville, editor 1951-55; Lawrenceburg Ch of Christ TN, minister 1946-51; Phi Beta Sigma Frat Inc, chaplain. **Orgs:** Pres Nat Christian Inst Alumni Assn; pres Fisk Univ Debating Soc; pres Ecumenica Assn; chmn Car Pool Transp Montgomery Bus Boycott; chmn Montgomery Comm Action Bd. **Honors/Awds:** Leadership award Danforth Found 1948; cert of Appreciation Montgomery Community Action Agency 1970; outstanding Ministry Plaque S Berkeley CA Ch of Christ 1970; cert of merit Montgomery Heritage Movement 1975; Nat Summer Youth Sports Prog Award AL State Univ 1975; fndrs plaque AL Statewide Lectureship 1975; publ various religious books; spkr coll campuses, civic groups, frats. **Business Addr:** 4214 Cleveland Ave, Montgomery, AL 36105.

MITCHELL, KEVIN DANYELLE
Professional football player. **Personal:** Born Jan 1, 1971, Harrisburg, PA. **Educ:** Syracuse, bachelor's degree in sociology. **Career:** San Francisco 49ers, linebacker, 1994-. **Business Addr:** Professional Football Player, San Francisco 49ers, 4949 Centennial Blvd, Santa Clara, CA 95054, (415)562-4949.

MITCHELL, LEMONTE FELTON
Personnel director. **Personal:** Born Feb 19, 1939, Wake Forest, NC; married Emma Jean Hartsfield; children: LaMarsha, Muriel, Andrea. **Educ:** Johnson C Smith Univ, BA 1960; Loyola Univ in Chicago, graduate study, 1964; Government Executive Inst, Univ of NC, School of Business Administration, 1979. **Career:** Classification Specialist for the NC Dept of Human Resources And NC Dept of Transportation, 1980-92; NC Dept of Correction, personnel dir 1977; NC Dept of Admin, personnel analyst 1969-77; jr & sr high school teacher 1960-69. **Orgs:** Mem NC Chap IPMA; pres Wayne & Co Teachers Assn; Omega Psi Phi Frat; minister of music, Davie Street Presbyterian Church, The Committee on Ministries for The New Hope Presbytery. **Honors/Awds:** Outstanding Young Man of Amer 1971-72.

MITCHELL, LEONA
Soprano. **Personal:** Born Oct 13, 1949, Enid, OK. **Educ:** OK City Univ, MBA 1971, DMus (Hon) 1979. **Career:** San Francisco Opera, soprano 1973,74,77; Edinburgh Scotland Festival 1977, Sacria Umbria Festival, Australia 1978, various maj symphonies in US, European debut, Barcelona Spain 1974, Met Opera 1974, soprano; appeared in films &TV shows. **Orgs:** Mem Amer Guild Musicians Assoc, Sigma Alpha Iota, Alpha Kappa Alpha, Church of God in Christ. **Honors/Awds:** Named Ambassadress of Enid 1978; OK Hall of Fame 1983; performed for Pres Ford 1976, pres Carter 1978,79. **Business Addr:** Columbia Artists, 165 W 57th St, New York, NY 10019.

MITCHELL, LILYANN JACKSON
Public relations, promotion specialist. **Personal:** Born Jun 29, 1933, Greenville, MS; divorced; children: Craig, Claudia, Debra, Claude. **Educ:** Stowe Jr Coll, AA 1950; MO U, 1951; MO U; Wash U; Dhaw Coll Detroit; Marygrove Coll Detroit. **Career:** Shaw Coll of Detroit, dir spec projects & promotion; Intl UAW Rep 1973-74; WTVS TV Detroit, dir pub rel 1972-73; Highland Pk, MI, deputy to the Mayor; Dir Pub Ser Careers 1971; UPI Internat, staff writers 1970-71; Intl Brotherhood of Teamsters, asst dir of pub rel; MO Joint Council of Teamsters Newspapers St Louis IBT 1965-70; Anheuser-beusch Inc St Louis, exec sec 1961-65; St Louis Job Corp Ctr for Women, instr; St Louis Argus Newspaper, bus& clerical subjects & Pub Rel staff Writer 1966-70; St Louis Am Newspaper 1968-70. **Orgs:** Mem Am Women in Radio TV; Pub Rel Soc of Am; Media Women Inc; Women in Comm; NAACP; SCLC; Urban League; Womens Conf of Concerns; Black in Comm; Black-Comm Assn. **Honors/Awds:** Outstanding Journalism & Unique Writing Style, Newspaper Pub Assn 1967; award of Black Entrepreneurs 1970; Dis Comm Serv Award 1969; award for Outstanding Serv to Youth St Louis City; award for Promoter of Muhammad Ali Shaw Coll benefit matches Olympia Stadium June 1975, Detroit; various other awards for comm serv. **Business Addr:** 7351 Woodward Ave, Detroit, MI 48202.

MITCHELL, LOFTEN
Writer. **Personal:** Born Apr 15, 1919, Columbus, NC; married Helen March, 1948. **Educ:** City College, New York, NY, 1937-38; Talladega College, BA, 1943; Columbia University, MA, 1951; Union Theological Seminary; General Theological Seminary. **Career:** Worked as an actor in New York, NY; WNYC-Radio, New York, NY, writer of weekly program The Later Years, 1950-62; WWRL-Radio, New York, NY, writer of daily program Friendly Advisor, 1954; State University of New York, Binghamton, NY, department of theater and department of African-American studies, professor, 1971-85, professor emeritus, 1985—. **Honors/Awds:** Black Drama: The Story of the American Negro in the Theatre, 1967; playwriting award, Research Foundation, State University of New York, 1974; Voices of the Black Theatre, 1975; Outstanding Theatrical Pioneer Award, Audience Development Committee, 1979; Bubbling Brown Sugar, 1984; Guggenheim Award, 1958-59; 1977 Best Musical Award for Bubbling Brown Sugar, Musical of the Year; Bubbling Brown Sugar, nomiated for a Tony Award, 1976. **Special Achievements:** The Stubborn Old Lady Who Resisted Change and The Complete Works of Loften Mitchell, 1993. **Military Serv:** US Navy, served during WW II. **Home Addr:** 88-45 163rd St, Jamaica, NY 11432.

MITCHELL, MARIAN BARTLETT
Administrator. **Personal:** Born Oct 27, 1940, Elizabeth City, NC; daughter of Mrs Sarah Bartlett and Mr Paxton Bartlett (deceased); children: Lonzo Antonio Bartlett. **Educ:** Elizabeth City State Univ, BS 1970; Norfolk State Univ, further study toward MA-Communications. **Career:** Elizabeth City State Univ, dir alumni relations. **Orgs:** Ex-officio mem bd of dirs General Alumni Assoc 1976-; former sec Council of Natl Alumni Assocs; mem CASE; mem Professional Business Women, Natl Assoc of Univ Women, General Alumni Assn; Delta Sigma Theta Sorority, North Carolina Alumni Dir. **Honors/Awds:** Merit Awds from Tri-State Alumni Chapter 1986, Atlanta Alumni Chapter Alumni and Friends Coalition 1980, Class of 1946 1980; Woman of the Year Awd Natl Assoc of Univ Women 1981; Outstanding Service Awd General Alumni Assn 1971; Outstanding Service E A Johnson 1980; General Alumni Assn, Service Awards, 1994. **Business Addr:** Director-Alumni Relations, Elizabeth City State Univ, Weeksville Road, Box 977, Elizabeth City, NC 27909.

MITCHELL, MARTHA MALLARD
International communications company executive. **Personal:** Born Jun 11, Gary, IN; daughter of Elizabeth Allen Mallard and Louis B Mallard; divorced. **Educ:** Michigan State Univ, East Lansing MI, BA, 1963, MA, 1968. **Career:** Univ of District of Columbia, Washington DC, dir continuing educ for women, 1970-74; Drug Abuse Council, dir info services, 1974-77; US Government Exec Office of Pres, special asst to pres, 1977-79, Dept of Commerce, assoc dir, 1979-81; self-employed business consultant, 1981-84; Fleishman-Hillard Inc, St Louis MO, vice pres, 1985-87, sr vice pres, 1987-93, partner, 1993-. **Orgs:** Bd of trustees, Natl Urban League; Missouri Women's Forum; bd of dirs, VP Fair Foundaton; bd of dirs, Eugene Field House & Toy Museum; exec comm, St Louis Branch, NAACP; Links, Inc. **Honors/Awds:** Public Service Award, Capital Press Club, 1978; Distinguished Achievement Award, NAACP, Gary IN Branch, 1985; 100 Top Black Business & Professional Women, Dollar & Sense Magazine, 1988. **Business Addr:** Partner, Fleishman-Hillard Inc, 200 N Broadway, Suite 1800, St Louis, MO 63102.

MITCHELL, MELVIN J.
Clergyman (retired). **Personal:** Born Feb 29, 1904, Girdon, AR; married Katherin Lambert; children: Melvin Thomas, Beverly Ann, William James, Mary Jane, Nathaniel. **Educ:** Baltimore Coll of Bible, 1974. **Career:** Pilgrim Bapt Ch Columbus OH, pastor-emeritus. **Orgs:** Founder Columbus Area Devel Action Training Sch 1967; fndr Boy's Own Youth Shelter Inc 1969; pres Model Neighborhd Assy; mem Mayor's Adv Bd; mem Columbus Bapt Ministerial Alliance; mem OH Minister's Conf; pres OH Bapt State Conv; pres Mt Calvary Bapt Assn; worshipful grand master St John's Masonic Lodge; bd mem Cath Social Svc; bd mem Neighborhood Comm Ctr; mem other civic orgns. **Honors/Awds:** Recip Religious Achievement Award Gay St Bapt Ch 1972; Ather of the Week & One of Most Influential Black Men of Columbus WCOL 1973; One of Then Top Men of 1971 Citizen's Journal.

MITCHELL, MELVIN LESTER
Architect, educator. **Personal:** Born Aug 11, 1939, New Orleans, LA; married Geraldine Vaughan; children: Marcus Quintana, Michelle Violet. **Educ:** Howard U, B Arch 1967; Harvard Grad Sch of Design, M Arch 1970. **Career:** Howard Univ, asst prof of arch 1970-75; Univ of District of Columbia, associate prof of arch 1986-93; Melvin Mitchell Architects Washington DC, principal/sole owner 1979-. **Orgs:** Mem Am Inst of Architects; mem Nat Orgn of Minority Architects. **Honors/Awds:** Awarded total expenses stipend to Harvard Grad School of Design 1968-70; author "The Case for Environmental Studies at Black U" AIP Journal 1968; author "Urban Homesteading" Washington Post 1974. **Military Serv:** AUS spec 4 cl construction 1960-62, Thule Greenland & Fort Belvoir VA. **Business Addr:** Owner, Melvin Mitchell Architects, 413 Van Buren St NW, Washington, DC 20012.

MITCHELL, MICHELLE BURTON
Law enforcement official. **Personal:** Born Jun 30, 1963, Richmond, VA; daughter of Claudette Moore, Arthur Burton; married William Thomas Mitchell, Jun 30, 1984; children: Michael. **Educ:** Virginia Commonwealth Univ, BS, (w/honors), 1984. **Career:** Virginia Dept of Corrections, 1983-86; Richmond City Sheriff's Office, various positions, 1986-, sheriff, currently. **Orgs:** Virginia Sheriff's Assn; Willing Workers Ministry; Board of Corrections Liaison Comm; National Sheriff's Assn; NOBLE. **Honors/Awds:** Urban League Guild of Greater Richmond, Charlotte J Harris Washington Service Award, 1994; Natl Epicureans, National Service Award, 1994; VCU Psychology Dept, Outstanding Alumni Award, 1994; VCU Humanities & Sciences, Alumni Star for 1994. **Special Achievements:** Virginia's first female sheriff; Only one of fourteen female Sheriffs out of 3,095 in the United States. **Business Addr:** Sherriff, Richmond City Sheriff's Office, 1701 Fairfield Way, Richmond, VA 23223, (804)780-8035.

MITCHELL, MIKE ANTHONY
Professional basketball player. **Personal:** Born Jan 1, 1956, Atlanta, GA; married Diane; children: Kiah; Michael Jr. **Educ:** Auburn, studed Dstrbtv Educ 1978. **Career:** Cleveland Cavaliers, 1979-82, San Antonio Spurs, 1982-88. **Honors/Awds:** Had double pts in 74 of 79 games; had dougle pts-rebounds 16 times; career 47 pts 1984; twice was All-SEC selection.

MITCHELL, NELLI L.
Psychiatrist. **Personal:** Born in Jersey City, NJ; daughter of Eloise Casey Mitchell and Cullie Mitchell; children: Edward H Chappelle Jr. **Educ:** NYU, BA 1945; Columbia Univ, MA 1949; Howard Univ, MD 1950. **Career:** St Elizabeth's Hosp, staff psychiat 1956-57; Mental Hlth Cntr, med dir youth consultation serv 1963-65; Co of Monroe, 1966-; Hillside Children's Cntr, psychiat consult 1970-; Rochester Mental Hlth Cntr, training dir/child psychiat 1965-89, supervising psychiatrist, 1983-89; private practice, Rochester, NY, psiychiatrist, 1989-; Anthony Health Ctr, Rochester, NY, consultant, 1989-90. **Orgs:** Fellow Amer Psychiatric Assn 1956; mem Natl Med Assn 1956; Amer Orthopsychiatric Assn 1960; Hudson City Med Assn 1960; Amer Acad of Child Psychiatry 1970; asst prof psychiat Rochester Sch of Med; bd mem Camp Fire Girls Inc 1967-73; YWCA 1974-75; Monroe Co Bd of Mental Hlth 1976-80; mem NY State Bd Visitors Monroe Devel Ctr 1977-; Synod of the NE; UPC of the US 1975-79; Diplomate Amer Bd of Psychiatry & Neurology, Psychiatry 1961; Amer Bd of Psychiatry & Neurology, Child Psychiatry. **Honors/Awds:** Psi Chi Honor Society Psychology. **Business Addr:** Psychiatrist, 345 Highland Ave, Rochester, NY 14620-3027.

MITCHELL, ORRIN DWIGHT
Orthodontist. **Personal:** Born Oct 1, 1946, Jacksonville, FL; son of Ella Mae Mitchell and Arthur O Mitchell (deceased); married Patricia Hill; children: Derrick, Kia. **Educ:** Howard Univ, BS 1969, DDS 1973, Certificate of Orthodontics 1975. **Career:** Orrin D Mitchell DDS PA, orthodontist 1975-. **Orgs:** Mem, Amer Assn of Orthodontists, Amer Dental Assn, Natl Dental Assn, Acad of General Dentistry, Continental Orthodontic Study Club; Jacksonville Dental Soc, Northeast Dist Dental Assn, FL Medical, Dental & Pharmaceutical Assn, Southern Soc of Orthodontists, Jacksonville Medical Dental & Pharmaceutical Assn, Jacksonville Urban League; life mem Alpha Phi Alpha Frat; mem Chi Delta Mu Frat, Howard Univ Alumni Assoc, Sigma Pi Phi Frat; life mem NAACP; adv bd of dirs First Union Natl Bank of FL; mem FL Assoc of Orthodontists; trustee bd New Bethel AME Church; Fl Bd of Dentistry; Jacksonville Chamber of Commerce Bd of Governors, 1989; Stewart Bd of New Bethel AME Church; Secretary, Howard Univ Orthodontic Alumni Assn; Private Indus Council of Jacksonville; Pres, NorthwestCouncil, Jacksonvilleamber of Commerce; Bd of Dir, Jacksonville Urban League, 1988-90; Bd of Dir, Midas Touch Day Care Center; Pres, Continental Orthodontic Study Club. **Honors/Awds:** Diplomate Amer Bd of Orthodontics 1986; Alumni Achievement Awd Howard Univ Col of Dent 1986; Small Business Leader Jacksonville Chamber of Commerce Northwest Cncl 1986; Alpha Phi Alpha Frat Alumni Brother of the Year for the State of FL 1986, 1988; Achiever's Award, Northwest Council Chamber of Commerce, 1992. **Business Addr:** 1190 W Edgewood Ave, Suite A, Jacksonville, FL 32208.

MITCHELL, OSSIE WARE
Educational administrator. **Personal:** Born Oct 12, 1919, Uniontown, AL; widowed. **Educ:** Tuskegee Inst AL, BS 1939; Daniel Payne Coll Birmingham AL, D of Humane Letters 1972; AL State Univ Montgomery, MEd 1974. **Career:** Elberton Co Sch System, elem sch principal 1943; Palmer Meml Inst, instr 1945; Booker T Washington Bus Coll, asst dir, beginning 1947. **Orgs:** Mem Steering Com Urban Sch Bd 1979-82; dir AL Sch Bds Assn 1980-82; mem exec bd Comm Affairs Comm Operation New Birmingham 1982-, Women's Network 1982-. **Honors/Awds:** Life Membership Plaque NAACP 1981; Outstanding Serv Awd United Negro Coll Fund 1981; Black Heritage Awd 1983; Meritorious Serv Awd UNCF 1985; Certificate of Recog Metro Business and Professional Women's Club of Birmingham1985; Friend of Educ Awd 1985; Laymof Yr Awd 1984,85; Outstanding Contrib to Educ Birmingham Alumnae Chap Delta Sigma Theta Sor Inc 1986; Salute Silver Anniversary Celebration Alphi Xi Chap Gamma Phi Delta Sor Inc; Citizen of the Week, Anheuser-Busch/WAGE/WENN Radio, 1988; Aprreciation Award, Vocational Ed Birmingham School System, 1989; Soror of the Year, Alpha Eta Chapter Iota Phi Lambda Sorority, Inc, 1990; Outstanding Service Award, Imperial Club Ind, 1990; Award Meritorious Service to City of Birmingham, 1992; 50 years Service Award, UNCF, 1994; Service Award on 90th Anniversary of YWCA, 1994; Gallery of Neighborhood Leaders & Achievement, 1994; 20 years Service Recognition, Brown Springs Neighborhood, 1994; numerous others. **Business Addr:** Asst Dir, Booker T Washington Bus Coll, 1527 5th Ave North, Birmingham, AL 35203.

MITCHELL, PARREN JAMES
Company executive. **Personal:** Born Apr 29, 1922, Baltimore, MD; son of Elsie J Mitchell and Clarence Mitchell, Sr. **Educ:** Morgan State Univ, Baltimore MD, BA, 1950; Univ of MD, College Park MD, MA, 1952; additional studies, Univ of Connecticut. **Career:** MD Commission of Human Relations, dir, 1961-65; Baltimore Anti Poverty Agency, dir, 1965-68; US House of Representatives, 1971-87; Minority Business Enterprise, chair of bd, 1980-. **Honors/Awds:** Honorary Degrees: Lincoln Univ, Bowie State Coll, Univ of MD, Howard Univ, Coppin State, Morehouse Univ, VA Union Seminary, St Mary's Coll, Morgan State Univ; Natl and local consumer groups, civil rights groups, business and economic groups, fraternities, sororities, religious groups, and educational organizations have presented more than 1200 awards to Mr Mitchell; He has recieved awards from such diverse groups as: The Natl Alliance of Black Educators, The Southern Christian Leadership Conference, the Greater New Haven Business and Professsional Assn, The Minority Contractors, The Alaska Black Caucus. **Military Serv:** US Army, Infantry, Lieutenant, 1942-45; received Purple Heart.

MITCHELL, QUITMAN J.
Mayor. **Career:** City of Bessemer, AL, mayor, currently. **Honors/Awds:** First Black mayor of Bessemer. **Business Addr:** Mayor, City of Bessemer, 1800 3rd Ave, Bessemer, AL 35020-4999.

MITCHELL, ROBERT C.
Professional football executive. **Personal:** Born Jun 6, 1935, Hot Springs, AR; son of Avis Mitchell and Albert James Mitchell, Jr; married Gwendolyn E Morrow; children: Terri Sue, Robert Jr. **Educ:** Univ IL, BS 1958. **Career:** Pepsi Cola, marketing rep 1963-69; Bobby Mitchell Ins Agy, owner 1967-72; pro football scout 1969-72; Wash Redskins, dir of pro scouting 1972-78, exec asst to pres 1978-, asst gen mgr 1981-. **Orgs:** Member, University of Illinois Presidents Council; board of directors, University of Illinois Foundation; chairman, Metropolitan Washington DC Area Leadership Council; board member, American Lung Assn; member, Martin Luther King Federal Holiday Commission; member, NFL Alumni Executive Committee; member, Boys Club of Washington; board member,

Bike Foundation; advisory council, Variety Club of Greater Washington DC, Inc; advisory board, UNCF; advisory bd, Univ of IL Library; advisory bd, Horizon Bank of VA. **Honors/Awds:** 1st Black to play for WA Redskins 1962; All Big-Ten 1955-57; hon mention All-Amer 1955-57; mem Big-Ten Track Championship 1958; 5 times All-Pro NFL; Most Valuable Player All-Star Coll Game 1958; Rookie of the Year 1958; AR Hall of Fame 1977; Inducted in NFL Pro Football Hall of Fame 1983; DC Stars Hall of Fame 1979; Washington Touchdown Hall of Fame 1983; Hot Springs School District Hall of Fame, 1989; Univ of IL Foundation, National Network, Outstanding Leadership Award; Hot Springs, AR, Walk of Fame, 1997; IL Varsity, Illini of the Year, 1995. **Military Serv:** AUS 1958-59, 1961-62. **Business Addr:** Assistant General Manager, Washington Redskins, PO Box 17247, Dulles International Airport, Washington, DC 20041.

MITCHELL, ROBERT L.
Educational administrator. **Career:** Edward Waters College, Jacksonville, FL, president. **Business Addr:** President, Edward Waters College, 1658 Kings Road, Jacksonville, FL 32209.

MITCHELL, ROBERT LEE, SR.
Aircraft company employee. **Personal:** Born Nov 18, 1932, West Palm Beach, FL; son of Grace Mitchell and Hezekiah Mitchell; divorced; children: Verdette L, Marc A, Robert Jr. **Career:** Pratt & Whitney Aircraft, utility, currently. **Orgs:** Founder Afro-Amer Civ Action Unit Inc 1960-69; mem bd of dir Palm Beach Co Comm Mental Health Center 1979-81; state chmn FL Minority Conf of Repub Clubs 1980-82; pres Frederick Douglass Repub Club 1979-81; mem Black Citizen's Coalition PB Co 1979-84; NAACP; past gen bd mem Urban League; Black Professional Caucus; bd mem Concerned Alliance Progressive Action Inc (CAPA); mem Palm Beach co Repub Exec Comm 1970-80; mem Policy Comm/Platform Com Rep Party of FL 1975-77; organz/chmn FL black Repub Councl 1975; del GOP Conv 1976; bd mem Tri-Cnty Chapter Natl Business League 1984-; Palm Beach Cnty Reagan-Bush Campaign - co-chmn Blacks for Reagan 1984. **Honors/Awds:** Community Serv Award Tri-Cnty Natl Business League 1984; Accomp Pres Ford on historic riverboat trip down the MS river 1975; Man of the Year Professional Men's Bus League 1966; Official Particip FL Human Rel Conf 1977; Player KC Monarchs Baseball Team 1954-57; Man of the Year Omega Si Phi 1967; dep reg reg over 1000 persons.

MITCHELL, ROBERT P.
Public relations executive. **Personal:** Born Feb 28, 1951, Glenridge, NJ; son of Johanna Eason Mitchell and Robert Pleasant Mitchell. **Educ:** Quinnipiac College, Hamden, CT, BA, 1973; Syracuse University, Syracuse, NY, MA, 1975. **Career:** Univ of Pennsylvania, Philadelphia, PA, news officer, 1978-80; Office of the Mayor, Philadelphia, PA, press secretary, 1980-83; Hahnemann Univ, Philadelphia, PA, director, public affairs, 1984-86; Stevens Inst of Technology, Hoboken, NJ, dir public relations, 1986-87; Brandeis University, Waltham MA, director, news & media relations, 1987-. **Orgs:** Co-chairman, FYI-Consortium of Boston PR Directors, 1988-; member, National Assn of Black Journalists, 1987-; member, Boston Assn of Black Journalists, 1987-; chairman, Summit of African American Male Conference, 1991; chairman, Boston Ballet Fund Raising Committee, 1990.

MITCHELL, RODERICK BERNARD
Community development corporation executive. **Personal:** Born Aug 14, 1955, Reidsville, NC; son of Christine Odessa Dixon Mitchell and Hunter Lee Mitchell; married Monica Boswell, Aug 12, 1979; children: Marcus Galen Mitchell, Akia Lee Mitchell. **Educ:** UCLA, Los Angeles, CA, BA Economics, 1977; Columbia Univ, New York, NY, MBA, 1980. **Career:** Collins & Aikman Corp, Charlotte, NC, industrial eng, 1977-79; Celanese Corp, New York, NY, sr financial analyst, 1981-83; Bedford Stuyvesant Restoratoin, Brooklyn, NY, 1984-85, dir of operations, 1985-86, vice pres physical devel, 1987-88, pres, 1988-. **Orgs:** Treasurer, Men 'N' Ministries, 1986-; bd of dir, Brooklyn Academy of Cultural Affairs, 1988-; bd of dir, Brooklyn Chamber of Commerce, 1988-; bd of dir, Brooklyn Bureau of Community Serv, 1989; mem, 100 Black Men on Manhattan, 1989; Adult Sunday School Teacher, Bethel Gospel Assembly, 1989. **Honors/Awds:** NOMMO Outstanding Graduate, UCLA, 1983; Outstandig Businessman Award, Central Baptist Church; 1988 Achievement Award, Brooklyn Urban League, 1988; RF Kennedy Minority Business Award; Brooklyn Chamber of Commerce, 1988; Merit Award, Natl Assn of Negro Business & Professional Women's Club, Inc, 1989. **Business Addr:** Pres, Bedford Stuyvesant Restoration Corp, 1368 Fulton St, Brooklyn, NY 11216.

MITCHELL, ROSCOE E.
City official. **Personal:** Born Aug 27, 1934, Chicago, IL; son of Mary G Taylor Mitchell and Roscoe E Mitchell; married Jacqueline L Abrams; children: Karen, Roslyn, Valerie, Robert. **Educ:** Univ of IL Urbana, BS 1956; Univ of Chicago, MBA 1976. **Career:** Prudential Insurance Co of Amer, reg appraiser 1964-70; Talent Asst Program Business Consultants, exec dir 1970-73; Zenith Elec Corp, dir equal opportunity & admin serv 1973-87; Highland Community Bank, vice president, 1989; Chicago Transit Authority, Chicago, IL, general manager, 1990-. **Orgs:** Dir Chicago Community Ventures 1972-87; dir Chicago Regional Purchasing Council 1974-87; dir Cosmopolitan Chamber of Commerce 1976-90; exec comm Chicago Council Boy Scouts of Amer 1977-, council commr 1983-85; bd of dir Chicago Alumni Kappa Alpha Psi 1983-; vice pres Chicago Council Boy Scouts of Amer 1986-; Dads Association, University of Illinois, vice president. **Honors/Awds:** Silver Beaver Boy Scouts of Amer 1985; Beautiful People Chicago Urban League 1981; Black Book Business Black Book Magazine 1980. **Military Serv:** US Army, captain 1956-66. **Home Addr:** 8620 S Dante, Chicago, IL 60619. **Business Addr:** General Manager, Property and Admin Services, Chicago Transit Authority, PO Box 3555, Merchandise Mart Plaza, Chicago, IL 60654, (312)664-7200.

MITCHELL, SADIE STRIDIRON
Cleric. **Personal:** Born Jan 4, 1922, Philadelphia, PA; daughter of Lucinda Clifton and Joseph Alfonso Stridiron; married Charles Mitchell Jr, Aug 19, 1946 (deceased); children: Sadye Mitchell Lawson, Chas T III, Charlene Mitchell Wiltshire. **Educ:** Temple University, BS, education, 1942; University of Pennsylvania, MS, ed adm, 1968; Nova University, EdD, 1978; Lutheran Theological Seminary, MDiv, 1990. **Career:** Philadelphia Board of Education, teacher, 1945-68, principal, 1968-81; seminary, 1981-83; St Luke's, deacon & deacon in training, 1983-89; Christ Church, priest in charge, 1989-90; St Luke's, assistant rector, 1984-91; African Episcopal Church of St Thomas, assistant rector, 1991-. **Orgs:** NAACP, 1944-; Philadelphia Association of School Administrators, secretary, 1968-81; Black Women's Ed Alliance, founder, vp, 1975-; Diocesan Christian Ed Committee, 1981-92; Diocesan Phia Theol Institute; Episcopal Comm Services, board of council, 1990-; Union of Black Episcopalians, 1961-. **Honors/Awds:** Chapel of Four Chaplains, community leader, 1971, educational leader, 1973, community leader, 1978; PASA, Highest Achievement, Administrative, 1981; Mill Creek Comm Center, Community Service, 1978; Achievement Award to Women Clergy, 1994. **Business Addr:** Associate Rector, African Episcopal Church of St Thomas, 6361 Lancaster Ave, Philadelphia, PA 19151.

MITCHELL, SAMUEL E., JR.
Professional basketball player. **Personal:** Born Sep 2, 1963, Columbus, GA; married Anita; children: Morganne, Maya. **Educ:** Mercer Univ, Macon, GA, 1981-85. **Career:** Wisconsin Flyers (CBA), forward, 1985-86; Rapid City Thrillers, (CBA), 1986-87; played in France, 1987-89; Minnesota Timberwolves, 1989-92, 1995-, Indiana Pacers, 1992-95. **Business Addr:** Professional Basketball Player, Minnesota Timberwolves, 600 1st Ave N, Minneapolis, MN 55403, (612)337-3865.

MITCHELL, SHANNON LAMONT
Professional football player. **Personal:** Born Mar 28, 1972, Alcoa, TN. **Educ:** Georgia. **Career:** San Diego Chargers, tight end, 1994-. **Business Addr:** Professional Football Player, San Diego Chargers, 9449 Friars Rd, Qualcomm Stadium, San Diego, CA 92108, (619)280-2111.

MITCHELL, STANLEY HENRYK
Attorney. **Personal:** Born Sep 28, 1949, St Louis, MO; children: Stanley J P. **Educ:** Univ of MO St Louis, BS Spec Ed 1974; Washington Univ, MSW 1976; Temple Univ School of Law, JD 1979. **Career:** Solo Practicioner, attny 1980-; PA House of Reps, exec dir 1981-83; Elizabethtown Coll Soc Welfare, adj prof 1982-84; City of Harrisburg, solicitor 1984-; PA House of Reps, chief counsel; Shippensburg Univ, Adjunct Prof, criminal law, 1991-96. **Orgs:** Chmn Pro Bono Legal Redress City of Hbg NAACP 1981-; brother Omega Psi Phi Frat 1984-; committeeman 11th Ward City of Harrisburg. **Honors/Awds:** Recipient Amer Jurisprudence Awd Conract Remedies 1976-77; Democratic Nominee City of Harrisburg City Council 1985. **Business Addr:** Chief Counsel, PA House of Representatives, 34 E W, Main Capitol Bldg, Harrisburg, PA 17120.

MITCHELL, TEX DWAYNE
Supervisor. **Personal:** Born Nov 19, 1949, Houston, TX; married Deborah Ann Earvin; children: Tonya DiBonne, Tess Dionne. **Educ:** Lee Jr Coll, attended 1970; TX Southern Univ, BA 1977. **Career:** Courtesy Ford, parts delivery 1968-69; Petro-Tex Chem Corp, plant oper 1969; TX Petrochem, pumping suprv; Crosby ISD Trustee Bd, vp. **Orgs:** Pres Barrett-Crosby Civic League 1976-; mem Tenneco volunteers 1979-83. **Home Addr:** 407 Red Oak, Crosby, TX 77532. **Business Addr:** Vice President, Crosby ISD Trustee Bd, 8600 Park Place Blvd, Houston, TX 77017.

MITCHELL, THEO W.
State senator, attorney. **Personal:** Born Jul 2, 1938, Greenville, SC; son of Dothenia E Lomax Mitchell and Clyde D Mitchell; married Greta JoAnne Knight; children: Emily Kaye, Tamara JoAnne, Megan Dawn. **Educ:** Fisk Univ, AB 1960; Howard Univ Law Sch, JD 1969. **Career:** South Carolina General Assembly, state senator; attorney. **Orgs:** Pres Greenville Urban League Inc 1971-73. **Honors/Awds:** Senator of the Year, South Carolina Probation Parole & Pardon Service, 1989; Senator of the Year, South Carolina Education Assn, 1989; General Assembly Member of the Year, Transportation Assn of South Carolina, 1988. **Home Addr:** 522 Woodland Way, Greenville, SC 29607. **Business Addr:** State Senator, South Carolina Genl Assembly, Nine Bradshaw St, Greenville, SC 29601.

MITCHELL, WILLIAM GRAYSON
Editor. **Personal:** Born Mar 8, 1950, Mobile, AL; married Renee Grant. **Educ:** Univ of IL, BS 1970. **Career:** Johnson Pub Co, assoc editor Ebony-jet magazines 1973; Washington Post, gen assignment reporter 1972-73; Chicago Sun-times, 1970-72. **Orgs:** Nat Endowment for the Humanities Journalism Fellowship 1975-76. **Business Addr:** 1750 Pennsylvania Ave NW, Washington, DC.

MITCHELL, WINDELL T.
County official. **Personal:** Born Feb 28, 1941; son of Eveline V. Mitchell and Thomas T. Mitchell; married Myrtle J. Mitchell, Nov 22, 1964; children: Jonathan, Audrey. **Educ:** University of Washington, bachelor's degree, architecture and urban planning, 1971, MBA, 1973. **Career:** King County, Seattle, WA, special assistant to public works director, fleet manager, 1980-. **Orgs:** National membership chair, 1990-, chapter chair, 1988-89, National Association of Fleet Administrators; chapter chair, American Public Works Association for Equipment Services; member, Forum for Black Public Administrators, 1984-. **Business Addr:** Fleet Manager, King County Public Works, 400 Fourth Ave, 900 King County Administration Building, Seattle, WA 98104.

MITCHELL, ZINORA M.
Judge. **Personal:** Born 1956; married Michael L. Rankin; children: Lee, John Michael, Everett, Michael Joseph. **Educ:** Spelman College; George Washington University Law School, JD. **Career:** Civil Division, Commercial Litigation Branch, US Department of Justice, trial attorney; US Attorney's Office, Washington, DC, assistant US attorney; District of Columbia Superior Court, Washington, DC, judge, 1991-. **Orgs:** National Association Women Judges; Natl Bar Assn; Amer Bar Assn. **Business Addr:** Judge, Superior Court of Washington, DC, 500 Indiana Ave, NW, Chamber 2420, Washington, DC 20001.

MITCHELL-BATEMAN, MILDRED
Psychiatrist. **Personal:** Born 1922, Cordele, GA; married. **Educ:** Johnson C Smith U, BS 1941; Women's Med Coll of PA, MD 1946; NYC, intern; Menning Sch of Psychiatry, psychiatric residency cert 1957. **Career:** WV Dept of Mental Health, dir 1962; Philadelphia, pvt practice; Lakin State Hosp WV, phy Clinical dir & supt. **Honors/Awds:** First woman to head such a dept in the US; The first black in WV history to direct an exec dept. **Business Addr:** WV Dept of Mental Health, Charleston, WV 25305.

MITCHELL-KERNAN, CLAUDIA IRENE
Educational administrator. **Personal:** Born Aug 29, 1941, Gary, IN; married Keith Kernan; children: Claudia L, Ryan J. **Educ:** Indiana Univ, BA Anthropology 1963, MA Anthropology 1964; Univ of California Berkeley, PhD Anthropology 1969. **Career:** Harvard Univ, asst prof of anthropology 1969-73; UCLA, asst prof of anthropology 1973-77, assoc prof of anthropology 1977-83, prof of anthropology 1983-89, dir Center for Afro-American Studies, beginning 1977, vp, chancellor of grad programs, dean, grad div, 1994-. **Orgs:** Researcher Natl Inst of Mental Health 1971-75; consultant Natl Urban League 1973; fellowship review comm Natl Sci Foundation 1974; bd of trustees Ctr for Applied Linguistics Washington DC 1979-81; bd mem Crystal Stairs Inc 1980-; vice chancellor, Academic Affairs & Dean Grad Divison, UCLA, 1994-; National Science Board, (presidential appointment), 1994. **Honors/Awds:** Fellow Natl Inst of Mental Health 1965-66; fellow Social Science Rsch Council 1966-68; fellow Ford Found 1968-69. **Business Addr:** Vice Chancellor, Graduate Division, UCLA, 405 Hilgard Ave, #1237 Murphy Hall, Los Angeles, CA 90024.

MITCHEM, ARNOLD LEVY
Education council executive. **Personal:** Born Sep 17, 1938, Chicago, IL; son of DeV Levy Mitchem and Archie Mitchem; married Freda Kellams Mitchem, Apr 1, 1969; children: Nichelle, Adrienne, Michael, Thea. **Educ:** Pueblo Junior Coll, AA, 1959; Univ of Southern Colorado, BA, 1965; Haverford Coll, post bac study 1966; Univ of WI, grad Study 1968; Marquette Univ, PhD, 1981. **Career:** Marquette Univ, history dept instr, 1968-69, director, educ opportunity prog, 1969-86; Natl Council of Educational Opportunity Assns, Washington, DC, president, 1986-. **Orgs:** Pres, Mid-Amer Assn of Educational Opportunity Program Personnel, 1974-76; Inroads Natl Board, 1975-77; chair, Natl Coordinating Council of Educational Opportunity Assns, 1977-81; board of directors, trustee, College Board, currently. **Honors/Awds:** Citation for outstanding serv to higher educ Region V Ofc of Educ 1974; spl Woodrow Wilson fellowship 1967-68, 1966-67; honorary Woodrow Wilson fellowship 1965-66; Doctor of Humane Letters, Marycrest Coll, 1990; Doctor of Laws, Universty of Massachusetts, 1990. **Business Addr:** Executive Director, National Council of Educational Opportunity Associations, 1025 Vermont Ave, NW, Suite 310, Washington, DC 20005.

MITCHEM, JOHN CLIFFORD
Educational administrator. **Personal:** Born in Terre Haute, IN; son of Clara Mitchem and Clifford Mitchem; married Anna Maria; children: Terence, Melanie. **Educ:** Ball State Teachers Coll, Chem, Biol, BS Ed; State Univ of IA Iowa City, MA Phys Ed, PhD Phys Ed. **Career:** Northern IL Univ, spec asst to pres 1969-72; Baruch Coll, asst dean of faculty 1972-73, asst dean of acad affairs 1972-77; Bronx Comm Coll, prof, dean 1977-81; Univ of WI LaCrosse Coll of Health, PE & Rec, dean 1981-88. **Orgs:** Life mem Amer Alliance for Health, PE & Rec 1966-; ed Rsch Quarterly 1969-74; policy adv bd City Univ of NY Freshman Skills Assessment Prof 1977-; personnel & budget comm Dept of Compensatory Prog, Coll of Liberal Arts & Sci; univ council on instr, open admiss coord CUNY; middle state eval accred team; north central assoc accred team; southern dist accred team; life mem Phi Epsilon Kappa; mem Phi Delta Kappa, Amer Assoc of Univ Profs. **Honors/Awds:** Numerous publ incl ''Athletics:The Lab Setting for Character'' 1967; ''The Child that Bears Resentment'' 1968; ''Resolved that the Amer Acad of PE Support the Position that the Requirement of PE in Coll & Univ Should be Abolished'' 1974; IL Assoc for Health, PE & Rec Quarter Century Club Awd 1972; Fellow Amer Acad of PE 1973. **Business Addr:** Dean, Retired, Univ of Wisconsin-La Crosse, College of Health, Physical Educ,and Recreation, 1725 State, La Crosse, WI 54601.

MITCHEM-DAVIS, ANNE
Educator, educational administrator (retired). **Personal:** Born Dec 17, Boston, MA; daughter of Marian Franklin Mitchem and Robert T Mitchem; widowed; children: Leah Anne Davis-Hemphill. **Educ:** Lincoln Univ, BS 1950; IN Univ School of Nursing, Diploma 1950-53; Simmons Coll, MS 1960; Boston Univ, CAGS 1966. **Career:** Visiting Nurse Assn of Boston, staff nurse 1954-59, asst supvr 1960-62; Hampton Inst, asst prof 1962-65; Boston Univ, asst prof 1966-70; Mental Health/Retardation Center, public health nurse consultant 1970-71; Boston City Hospital, nursing dir out patient dept 1971-73; Howard Univ, asst dean Coll of Nursing 1973-75, chairlady, senior studies, currently; College of Nursing Chicago State Univ, acting dean 1982-83, chairperson 1983-84, assoc prof 1980-89. **Orgs:** Exec dir Alpha Kappa Alpha Sorority 1975-80; mem Amer Nurses Assn, Natl League for Nursing, Amer Public Health Assn, Alpha Kappa Alpha Sorority; North Atlantic Regional dir, 1970-74; Beta Kappa Chi; Sigma Theta Tau. **Honors/Awds:** Special Serv Award, Alumni Assoc of IN Univ School of Nursing 1979; Advisor of the Year, 1983; Outstanding Faculty of the Year, Chicago State Univ, 1984, 1985.

MITCHUM, DOROTHY M.
Radio station executive. **Personal:** Born Oct 7, 1951, Moncks Corner, SC; daughter of Frank & Laura Simmons; married Ronnie, Oct 21, 1973; children: Ronnie L, Melody. **Educ:** Denmark Technical College, Associate, 1969; Charleston Southern Univ, BS, 1990; Univ of SC, MA, 1995. **Career:** Dotty Sims Graphic Designs, owner, currently; WMCJ Radio, vp, gen mgr, currently. **Orgs:** Kids Who Care; Berkeley Chamber of Commerce. **Home Addr:** PO Box 1483, Moncks Corner, SC 29461, (803)899-7094. **Business Addr:** Vice Pres/General Manager, WMCJ Radio, 314 Rembert Dennis Blvd, Moncks Corner, SC 29461, (803)761-9625.

MIX, BRYANT LEE
Professional football player. **Personal:** Born Jul 28, 1972, Water Valley, MS; married Tonette, Feb 8, 1997. **Educ:** Alcorn State, attended. **Career:** Houston Oilers, defensive end, 1996; Tennessee Oilers, 1997-. **Business Addr:** Professional Football Player, Tennessee Oilers, c/o Baptist Sports Park, 7640 H 70-5, Nashville, TN 37221.

MIXON, CLARENCE W.
Executive director. **Personal:** Born Mar 7, 1934, Cleveland, OH; married Gayle; children: Rhonda Pheonix, Piper Gibson, William Gibson, Shelley Gibson, Donald, Heather, Lindsey. **Educ:** Kent State U, BS 1961; Base Western Reserve U, MS 1968; MI State U, PhD 1974. **Career:** Cleveland Scholarship Programs Inc, exec dir; Mixon's Barber Shop, barber 1950-; Cuyahoga Comm Coll, dir comm serv 1968-69; Vista US, dir 1968; Cleveland Pub Sch, asst prin counselor tchr 1961-68; Singer Sewing Machine Co, salesman 1953-54; Roy & Eva Markus Found, educ consult 1969-80; Nat Episcopal Ch NYC, chmn black desk 1976-80; Garden Valley Neighborhood House Cleveland, bd pres 1977-78; OH Instructional Grants Program, adv bd 1978-80. **Honors/Awds:** Kellogg fellow MI State Univ 1970-71; educator of year Alpha Phi Alpha Frat 1975; elected dep Nat Conv Episcopal Ch 1976 & 1979; ''Positive Cleveland'' Emerson Press 1977. **Military Serv:** AUS specialist 3rd 1954-56. **Business Addr:** Cleveland Scholarship Programs, 1380 E & Sixth St, Cleveland, OH 44114.

MIXON, VERONICA
Editor, writer. **Personal:** Born Jul 11, 1948, Philadelphia, PA; daughter of Bertha Goodwine Mixon and William Mixon. **Educ:** Long Island Univ, BA 1974. **Career:** Food Fair, bookkeeper 1966-68; Social Sec Admin, admin asst 1968-70; Doubleday & Co Inc, Starlight romance editor 1974-88. **Orgs:** Writer, VM Media Service 1985-; film reviewer Carib News 1983-. **Honors/Awds:** Co-editor, Freshstones, Women's Anthology 1979; Author,'' The World of Octavia Butler,'' Essence Mag 1979;'' Black Agents,'' Emerge Mag, 1993; ''Nick Gomez,'' The Independent Film & Video Mag, 1995. **Home Addr:** PO Box 694, Grand Central Station, New York, NY 10163-0694.

MIZZELL, WILLIAM CLARENCE
Data processing professional/mgr. **Personal:** Born May 29, 1949, Ahoskie, NC; son of Myrtle Burke Mizzell and Eddie Lewis Mizzell, Sr; married Jomare Bowers, Dec 30, 1981; children: Jomare Elizabeth Bowers Mizzell. **Educ:** Elizabeth City State Univ, Elizabeth City, NC, BS Mathematics, 1971. **Career:** Western Electric Co, Greensboro NC, spare parts analyst, 1971-73; Western Electric Co, Cincinnati OH, staff associate, 1973-74; Proctor & Gamble Co, Cincinnati OH, analyst/system analyst, 1974-77; Licoln National Corp, Fort Wayne IN, senior development analyst, 1977-80, senior programmer/analyst, 1980-82, project manager, 1982-83, senior project manager, 1983-87, lead project leader, 1987-. **Orgs:** Bd mem, Fort Wayne Branch, NAACP, 1980-; pres/host/founder, Minority Spectrum, Inc, 1982-; bd mem, WBNI Radio Community Advisory Bd, 1985-; mem, Fort Wayne Chapter Jack & Jill, Inc. 1985-; consultant, Business Assisted Summer Employment Program, 1986-; dir/bd mem, Al Stiles Talent Factory, 1987-; pres/found, Black Data Processing Assoc, Fort Wayne Chapter, 1987-. **Honors/Awds:** Million Dollar Club, NAACP Natl Office, 1981-84; President's Award, NAACP, Fort Wayne Branch, 1981; Marjorie D Wickliffe, NAACP, Fort Wayne Branch, 1983; Community Serv, NAACP, Fort Wayne Branch, 1984; Minority in Media, Indiana/Purdue Fort Wayne Univ, 1989. **Home Addr:** 1509 Channel Ct, Fort Wayne, IN 46825-5934.

MOANEY, ERIC R.
Educator. **Personal:** Born May 16, 1934, Easton, MD; children: Sara Elizabeth, Lucinda Jennifer. **Educ:** RI Sch of Design, BFA 1956; Syracuse U, MFA 1965; San Diego State U, MS. **Career:** Dept of Art CA State Univ San Diego, asst prof 1968-; Benton & Bowles Advertising Agy, asst art dir 1965-66; Syracuse & U, designer asst to dir of graphic arts 1963-65; freelance artist 1962-63; Darrel Prutzman Assoc,asst art dir 1957-62; Rustcraft Greeting Cards, designer 1956-57; Motown Record Corp, design consult 1968; NJ area library, 1966-70; Terry Phillips Enterprises, 1968-69; New Frontiers Corp, 1965; Four Guys Stores, 1969; Thomas Corp, 1970; Core Faculty ca Sch of Prof Psychology, series coordinator for the humanities 1973-76; San Diego Co Collegiate Council All Media. **Orgs:** Art Show 1975. **Honors/Awds:** Recip certificate of merit, CA Governor's com 1971; commn sculpture bust of Beethoven to be completed for Beethoven Bi-centennial NJ 1970. **Business Addr:** San Diego State Univ, San Diego, CA 92115.

MOBLEY, CHARLES LAMAR
Educator (retired), consultant. **Personal:** Born Oct 9, 1932, Winter Garden, FL; son of Mary Jayne Davis Mobley and Benjamin James Mobley. **Educ:** Morehouse Coll, 1953-55; Univ of Miami, BMus 1964, MMus 1971; FL Intl U, 1981-83; Barry U, 1984. **Career:** Mt Zion Baptist Church, organist/choir dir 1948-60; Beulah Baptist Church, organist/choir dir 1953-55; Fine Arts Conservatory, teacher 1963-64; Miami-Dade Community Coll, teacher 1971-79, dir choir 1971-80; Dade County Public Schools, teacher, consultant, 1994-. **Orgs:** Mem MENC, FMEA, DMEA, UTD, FEA, AFT 1964-; pub rel chmn Dade Co Music Educ Assn 1974-75; treas DMEA 1983-; founder & dir Liberty City Elem String Ensemble 1976-; chmn Tract II Model City Prog 1974-75; bd of dir Greater Miami Youth Symphony 1982-; vice president, Oakland Park Homeowners Assn, 1989-. **Honors/Awds:** Teacher of the Year, North Central Area, Dade Co FL 1977; recorded the liberty City Elementary String ensemble for the Dade County Florida Superintendent's Honors Music Festival 1983; Community Serv Award, Natl Assn of Negro Business and Professional Women's Clubs Inc, Miami Club 1985; Achievement Awd in Music Educ, Natl Sor of Phi Delta Kappa Inc, Gamma Omicron Chap 1987; Achievement Award Miami Alumni Chapter, Kappa Alpha Psi Fraternity 1989; Top Teens Award, Top Ladies of Distinction, 1990; Martin Luther King's Vision Award, Bayside Market Place, 1991; Teacher of the Year, Liberty City Elementary School, Dade County, FL, 1991; Outstanding Community Leader in Education, Zeta Phi Beta Sorority, Inc, 1991; Black Music Festival Vanguard Award, African Heritage Cultural Arts Center, Dade Cty, FL, 1992; Guest Conductor, Dade County, Florida Public Schools Superintendent's Honors Music Festival, Elem Orchestra, 1993; Unsung Hero Award, The Links Inc, 1993; Conductor, Liberty City Tri-String Ensemble, 1994. **Business Addr:** Teacher, Dade County Public Schools, 1855 NW 71st St, Miami, FL 33147.

MOBLEY, EMILY RUTH
Librarian. **Personal:** Born Oct 1, 1942, Valdosta, GA; daughter of Ruth Johnson Mobley and Emmett Mobley. **Educ:** Univ of MI, AB Ed 1964; Univ of MI, AM Library Sci 1967, additional coursework. **Career:** Chrysler Corp, engrg librarian 1965-69; Wayne State Univ, librarian 1969-75; Gen Motors Rsch Labs 1976-81; Univ of MI, adj lecturer 1974-75, 1983-85; GMI Engrg & Mgmt Inst, library dir 1982-86; Purdue University, assoc dir of lib 1986-89, dean of libraries, 1989-. **Orgs:** Resolutions committee 1969-71; rsch comm 1977-80; comm on positive action 1972-74; Mi Chap Bulletin ed 1972-73, ed comm 1974-76, prog comm 1976-80; pres elect 1979-80, pres 1980-81, career advisor 1980-83, program comm 1981-82, long range plnng comm chmn 1981-82; nominating comm chmn 1982-83; library mgmt div sec 1983-85; chap cabinet chmn elect 1984-85, chapter cabinet chairman 1985-86, president-elect 1986-87, pres 1987-88, past pres 1988-89, chmn, awards comm 1989-90, IFLA Rep, 1989-93; all with Spec Libraries Assn; bd of trustees Library of MI 1983-86; mem Alpha Kappa Alpha Sorority; bd of dir, Assn of Research Libraries, 1990-93; ACRL professional education comm, American Library Assn, 1990-92. **Honors/Awds:** CIC Doctoral Fellow in Library Sci Committee on Inst Cooperation 1973-76; Various publ including ''Special Libraries at Work'' Shoe String Press 1984, ''Library Operations within a Decentralized Corporate Organization'' Issues & Involvement 1983; Distinguished Alumnus, Univ of Michigan School of Information and Library Studies, 1989; Fellow, Special Libraries Assn, 1991. **Home Addr:** 1115 Trace Eleven, West Lafayette, IN 47906. **Business Addr:** Dean of Libraries, Purdue University, Libraries, Stewart Center, West Lafayette, IN 47907.

MOBLEY, ERIC
Professional basketball player. **Personal:** Born Feb 1, 1970, Bronx, NY. **Educ:** Allegany Community Coll; Pittsburgh. **Career:** Milwaukee Bucks, 1994-95; Vancouver Grizzlies, 1995-. **Special Achievements:** NBA Draft, First round pick, #18, 1994. **Business Addr:** Professional Basketball Player, Vancouver Grizzlies, 788 Beatty St, Ste 311, Vancouver, BC, Canada V6B 2M1, (604)688-5867.

MOBLEY, EUGENIA L.
Educator, dentist. **Personal:** Born Dec 21, 1921, Birmingham, AL; married Charles W Mcginnis. **Educ:** TN State U, BS 1943; Meharry Med Coll, DDS 1946; Univ Of MI, MPH 1948. **Career:** Sch of Dentistry Meharry Med Coll, interim dean 1976-; Dept of Prev Dent & Comm Health & Comm Health Sch of Dentistry Meharry Med Coll, assoc dean prof & chmn 1974-76; Div of Den Hygiene Meharry Med Coll, dir 1952-56; Meharry, pvt practice & part-time instr 1950-57; Jefferson Co Bd Health, staffdentist 1946-479. **Orgs:** Dental Health Res & Educ Adv Com; Nat Inst of Health PHS; mem TN State Dental Assn; Capital City Dental Soc,; Pan-TN State Dental Assn; Nat Dent TalAssn; Nashville Dental Soc; Council of Comm Agencies; Federation Intl Dentaire, mem various other prof orgns; mem Delta Sigma Theta; NAACP; Urban League; sec WA Bass Jr High PTA; St Vincent's Depaul Alter Soc & Ardent Gardners. **Honors/Awds:** Recipient of several research grants Omicron Kappa, Upsilon Hon Dental Soc 1952; Kappa Sigma Pi Hon Dental Soc 1954; outstanding educ Of Am 1972. **Business Addr:** 1005 18 Ave N, Nashville, TN 37208.

MOBLEY, JOAN THOMPSON
Physician. **Personal:** Born Jun 2, 1944, New York, NY; daughter of Gertrude Porcher Thompson and Alfonso Thompson; married Stacey J; children: Michele T. **Educ:** Fisk Univ, BA 1966; Howard Univ Coll of Med, MD 1970. **Career:** Thomas Jefferson Univ Hosp, resident 1971-75, staff pathologist 1975-77; Howard Univ Hosp, asst prof 1977-79; HHS Indian Health Svcs, dir of labs 1979-83; St Francis Hosp, dir of labs 1983-. **Orgs:** Coll of Amer Pathologists; dir Girls Clubs of DE; director, Blood Bank of Delaware, 1991; member, State Arts Council, 1989-; director, Neumann College, 1991. **Honors/Awds:** Fellow Coll of Amer Pathologists, Amer Soc of Clinical Pathologists. **Business Addr:** Dir, Dept of Pathology, St Francis Hospital, 7th & Clayton Sts, Wilmington, DE 19805.

MOBLEY, JOHN ULYSSES
Professional football player. **Personal:** Born Oct 10, 1973, Chester, PA. **Educ:** Kutztown State (PA). **Career:** Denver Broncos, 1996-. **Special Achievements:** NFL Draft, First round pick, #15, 1996. **Business Addr:** Professional Football Player, Denver Broncos, 13655 Broncos Pkwy, Englewood, CO 80112, (303)649-9000.

MOBLEY, SINGOR
Professional football player. **Personal:** Born Oct 12, 1972. **Educ:** Washington State, attended. **Career:** Dallas Cowboys, defensive back, 1997-. **Business Addr:** Professional Football Player, Dallas Cowboys, One Cowboys Pkwy, Irving, TX 75063, (214)556-9900.

MOBLEY, STACEY J.
Attorney. **Personal:** Born Nov 19, 1945, Chester, PA; married Dr Joan C Thompson; children: Michele. **Educ:** Howard Univ Coll of Pharm, BPharm 1968; Howard Univ Sch of Law, JD 1971. **Career:** Del Co Legal Asst Assn, atty 1971-72; EI DuPont DeNemours & Co, attorney 1972-76, Washington cnsl 1977-82, dir fed affairs 1983-86, vice pres of federal affairs 1986-92, vice pres of communications, 1992-. **Orgs:** DC Bar 1977; bd of dirs, DuPont Canada, Wilmington Trust Co; Wilmington Club. **Honors/Awds:** National Assn for Equal Opportunity in Higher Education, Distinguished Alumni Award, 1987. **Business Addr:** Senior VP, External Affairs, E I Du Pont de Nemours & Co, 1007 Market St, Wilmington, DE 19898-0001.

MOBLEY, SYBIL C.
Educational administrator. **Personal:** Born Oct 14, 1925, Shreveport, LA; daughter of Cora Collins and Melvin Collins; married James Otis (deceased); children: James Jr, Janet Yolanda Sermon, Melvin. **Educ:** Bishop College, BA, 1945; Wharton Sch Univ PA, MBA 1961; Univ IL, PhD 1964; State Of FL, CPA. **Career:** FL A&M Univ Sch of Business, prof 1963-, department head, 1971-74, dean, 1974-. **Orgs:** Mem Alpha Kappa Alpha; Intl Assoc of Black Bus Educators; mem bd dir Anheuser-Busch Co Inc, Champion Intl Corp, Hershey Foods Corp, Sears Roebuck & Co, Southwestern Bell Corporation; Dean Witter; Discover, Inc. **Honors/Awds:** Received hon doctorate degrees from Wharton School of Univ of PA, Babson Coll, Bishop Coll, Hamilton College, Washington Univ, Princeton Univ, University of Illinois. **Business Addr:** Dean, School of Business & Industry, Florida A&M University, 1 SBI Plaza, Rm 105, Tallahassee, FL 32307, (904)599-3565.

MOCK, JAMES E.
Educator. **Personal:** Born Oct 26, 1940, Tuscaloosa, AL; son of Elizabeth Jemison Jackson and Christopher Mock; married Lorna Thorpe, Dec 1980; children: Che, Tekalie. **Educ:** Marquette Univ, Milwaukee, WI, civil engineer, 1958-60; Memphis State Univ, Memphis, TN, BBA, economics, 1972; Joint Center, Nashville, TN, MPA, 1977; Univ of Tennessee, Knoxville, TN, PhD, 1981. **Career:** Austin Peay State Univ, Clarksville, TN, professor/former chairperson, currently . **Orgs:** Former chairperson, Department of Public Management, 1994-97; director, Public Management Programs, 1981-91; chair, Political Science, 1991-94. **Honors/Awds:** Direct study abroad in Africa. **Business Addr:** Chair, Public Management, Austin Peay State University, 138 Queens Ct, Clarksville, TN 37044.

MODESTE, LEON EDGAR
Association executive. **Personal:** Born Aug 19, 1926, Brooklyn, NY; son of Hattie Modeste and Leon Modeste; married Nettie C; children: Wendi, Leon III, Keith, Kharon, Joseph, Rhea. **Educ:** LI Univ, BA 1950; Columbia Univ Sch of Soc Work, MSW 1953; Columbia Univ, attended Grad Sch of Business. **Career:** NY Univ, assoc prof; Univ So MS & Univ KY, guest lectr; State Univ of NY, assoc prof; Medgar Evers Coll, prof; Youth Consultation Serv Assoc, asst dir; Gen Conv Special Prog, dir; Manhood Found, exec dir; Brooklyn Br NY Urban League; dir; Syracuse Univ, adjunct prof; Urban League Onondaga Co Inc, president. **Orgs:** Board Member Unity Mutual Life Ins Co 1982; mem Syracuse Black Leadership Congress 1982; Certified Social Worker NY State; Phi Beta Sigma Frat; Martin Luther King Commission; NY State JTPA Council; Onondaga County: Economic Development Task Force, Criminal Justice Task Force; Syracuse School District Strategic Planning Task Force. **Honors/Awds:** Humanities Awd St Augustine Coll; Citizens Awd Farragut Houses; Exceptional Serv Manhood Found; Educ Awd Phi Beta Sigma Frat; NAACP Award; Rev Lawrence Briggs Memorial Drum Major Award. **Military Serv:** USN 1945-46.

MOHAMED, GERALD R., JR.
Accountant. **Personal:** Born Oct 3, 1948, New York, NY; son of Helen Brown Mohamed and Gerald R Mohamed; children: Gerald R III. **Educ:** Duquesne Univ, BS 1970; Univ of Pittsburgh, MBA 1979. **Career:** Westinghouse Credit Corp, commercial receivable accountant 1971-72, internal audit 1972-75, supervisor genl ledger/accts payable 1975-77, mgr consumer receivables 1977-79, financial analyst/financial planning 1979-82, mgr general accounting 1982-84; Westinghouse Electric Corp, staff asst corp financial planning & procedures 1984-88, Westinghouse Broadcasting, mgr financial planning 1989-92; Westinghouse Broadcasting/Ad Value Network, controller, 1992-; UAAI, staff accountant, 1996-. **Orgs:** Mem Black MBA Assoc 1983-86; mem Omega Psi Phi Frat 1968-, basilius 1969-70, treas 1985-87; mem Free Masonry PHA 1985 Masonry PHA 1985-. **Honors/Awds:** Omega, Man of the Year, 1987. **Home Addr:** 4 Suttie Ave, Piscataway, NJ 08854. **Business Addr:** UAAI, 511 South Ave, Cranford, NJ 07016.

MOHR, DIANE LOUISE
Library administrator. **Personal:** Born Nov 24, 1951, Fairbanks, AK; daughter of Dean Burgette Mohr (deceased) and Mary Louise Leonard Mohr. **Educ:** Alliance Francais Brussels Belgium, Deuxieme degree 1971; CA State Univ Long Beach, BA Black Studies 1977; Univ of So Ca Los Angeles, M Science in Library Sci 1978. **Career:** Getty Oil Co, indexer-reviewer 1978-79; Woodcrest Public Library, librarian in charge 1979-82; View Park Public Library, librarian in charge 1982-83; Compton Public Library, sr librarian in charge 1983-87; District of Columbia Public Library, Martin Luther King Jr Branch, sociology librarian 1987-89, West End Branch, branch librarian 1990, assistant coordinator of adult services 1991-. **Orgs:** Life mem Univ of So CA Alumni Assoc 1978-; American Library Association 1980-; California Library Association, 1980-87; Vesta Bruner Scholarship Bd 1980-83; California Black Librarians Caucus 1981-87; Alpha Kappa Alpha Sor Inc 1981-; SEIU Local 660 1979-83; The Links Inc 1985-87; District of Columbia Library Association 1989-; Washington DC Film Society 1990-. **Honors/Awds:** President's Honor List Cal State Univ Long Beach CA 1975-77; mem Phi Kappa Phi Honor Soc CA State Univ Long Beach 1977-. **Business Addr:** Assistant Coordinator, Adult Services, District of Columbia Public Library, 901 G St NW, Rm 417, Washington, DC 20001, (202)727-1117.

MOHR, PAUL B.
Educator. **Personal:** Born Aug 19, 1931, Waco, TX; married Rebecca Dixon; children: Paul, Michelle. **Educ:** FL A&M Univ, BS 1954; Univ NM, MS 1969; OK State Univ, EdD 1969. **Career:** St St Petersburg Jr Coll FL, instr 1954-55; FL A&M Univ Tallahassee, acad dean 1969; Norfolk State Univ VA, acad vp; Talladega Coll AL, pres 1984-. **Orgs:** Consult So Assn of Colls & Schools 1971-; evaluator of proposals Natl Inst Educ & Dept HEW 1975-; mem So Regional Educ Bd 1975-, FL Council on TeacherEduc 1976-. **Honors/Awds:** Phi Delta Kappa Awd 1974; Recipient Liberty Bell Awd FL A&M Univ Natl Alumni Assn 1976. **Military Serv:** AUS 1955-57. **Business Addr:** President, Talladega College, 627 West Battle St, Talladega, AL 35160.

MOLAND, WILLIE C.
Educational administrator. **Personal:** Born Jan 19, 1931, Shamrock, OK; married Marianne; children: Charlotte, Debbie, Gary, Brent, Bryan. **Educ:** Denver Art Acad Denver CO, certificate 1958. **Career:** Metropolitan State Coll, affirmative action staff officer 1971-; Denver Commn on Comm relations, consult 1970; Metropolitan State Coll, coordinator of resources & Support 1968-69; Martin Luther King Young Adults Center, dir 1955-68; Air Force Accounting & Financecenter, data devel technician. **Orgs:** Chrpsn Black Faculty Staff Caucus Metro State Coll; state dir of youth Prince Hall Grand Lodge CO; copres Phillips Elem PTSA; sec Syrian Temple #49 Chanters Group; pres Syrian Temple #49 Arabic Patrol; exec bd mem Greater Park Hill Community Inc; dir of youth programs Greater Park Hill Community Inc. **Honors/Awds:** Citizens soldier of year 1959; man of year GPHC Tutorial Program 197 2; superior perf award USAF 1965; Golden Rule Award accounting & finance center. **Military Serv:** USAF AUS 1951-54. **Business Addr:** Metropolitan State Coll, 250 W 14 Ave Rm 208, Denver, CO 80204.

MOLDEN, ALEX
Professional football player. **Personal:** Born Aug 4, 1973, Detroit, MI. **Educ:** Univ of Oregon. **Career:** New Orleans Saints, cornerback, 1996-. **Business Addr:** Professional Football Player, New Orleans Saints, 5800 Airline Hwy, Metairie, LA 70003, (504)733-0255.

MOLETTE, BARBARA J.
Educator. **Personal:** Born Jan 31, 1940, Los Angeles, CA; daughter of Nora L Johnson Roseburr and Baxter R Roseburr; married Carlton W Molette, Jun 15, 1960; children: Carla E Molette, Andrea R Molette. **Educ:** Florida A&M, Tallahasse FL, BA, 1966; Florida State Univ, Tallahassee FL, MFA, 1969; Univ of Missouri, Columbia MO, PhD 1989-. **Career:** Spelman Coll, Atlanta GA, instructor, 1969-75; Texas Southern Univ, Houston TX, asst professor, 1975-85; Mayor's Advisory Committee on Arts & Culture, Baltimore MD, dir arts in educ programs, 1988-90; Baltimore City Community College, professor, 1990-93; Eastern Connecticut State Univ, 1993-. **Orgs:** Mem, Dramatist Guild of Amer, 1971-; president, Natl Assn For African-American Theatre, 1989-91; consultant for workshops in theatre and mass communications. **Honors/Awds:** Graduated with Highest Honors from Florida A&M, 1966; Graduate Fellowship, Florida State Univ, 1967-69; Graduate Fellowship, Univ of Missouri, 1986-87; author of Black Theatre, Wyndham Hall Publishers, 1986; Noahs Ark, published in Center Stage, 1981; Upstage/Downstage, column in Houston Informer, 1977-78; Rosalee Pritchett, performed at Negro Ensemble Company, 1971, published in Black Writers of America. **Home Addr:** 51C Eastbrook Heights Road, Mansfield, CT 06250. **Business Addr:** English Dept, Eastern Connecticut State Univ, Willimantic, CT 06226, (203)465-4583.

MOLETTE, CARLTON WOODARD, II
Educator, playwright, author. **Personal:** Born Aug 23, 1939, Pine Bluff, AR; son of Evelyn Richardson Molette and Carlton William Molette Sr; married Barbara Roseburr, Jun 15, 1960; children: Carla, Andrea. **Educ:** Morehouse Coll, BA 1959; Univ of KC, graduate study 1959-60; Univ of IA, MA 1962; FL State Univ, PhD 1968. **Career:** Little Theatre Div of Humanities Tuskegee Inst, asst dir 1960-61; Des Moines Comm Playhouse, designer tech dir 1962-63; Howard Univ Dept of Drama, asst prof of tech production & design 1963-64; FL A&M Univ, asst prof & tech dir 1964-67, assoc prof 1967-69; Spelman Coll, assoc prof of drama, 1969-75; Div of Fine Arts, chmn 1974-75; School of Communications TX So Univ, dean 1975-84; Lincoln Univ, dean College of Arts & Sciences, 1985-87; Coppin State College, vice pres Academic Affairs, 1987-91; University of CT, Department of Dramatic Arts, prof, Institute for African-American Studies, senior fellow, 1992-; guest dir Univ of MI Feb-Mar 1974. **Orgs:** Mem The Dramatists Guild; National Conference on African American Theatre, past president; Natl Assn of Dramatic & Speech Arts; past editor of ''Encore''; mem bd dir Atlanta Arts Festival; vice pres Greater Atlanta Arts Council; chmn bd trustees Neighborhood Arts Center, Miller Theatre Advisory Council; mem, bd dir, Young Audiences of Maryland, 1990-93. **Honors/Awds:** Graduate fellowship in theatre Univ of KC; Atlanta Univ Center Faculty Rsch Grant 1970-71; co-author with Barbara Molette, Black Theatre, Premise & Presentation Wyndham Hall Press, 2nd ed, 1986; Rosalee Pritchett (play) produced by Negro Ensemble Company, 1970; other plays: Dr B S Black (musical), Booji, Noah's Ark; Fortunes of the Moor produced by The Frank Silvera Writers' Workshop, 1995. **Military Serv:** AUS sp 5 1963. **Business Addr:** Department of Dramatic Arts, The University of Connecticut, 802 Bolton Rd, Storrs, CT 06268, (860)486-1634.

MOLETTE, WILLIE L.
Dentist. **Personal:** Born Feb 15, 1919, Camden, AR; married Hattie J Center; children: Dr. **Educ:** A M & N Coll, BS; Meharry Med Coll, DDS; Nat Dental & Chicago Dental Soc Mtgs, continuing educ dentistry. **Career:** Pine Bluff AR, dentist pvt prac 1947-; Univ of AR at Pine Bluff coll dentist, 1950-; hygiene a m & n coll, instr 1947-50. **Orgs:** Mem Nat Dental Assn 1949-; bd mem 1967-77; treas past pres AR Med Dental & Pharmaceutical Assn; mem SW Medical Dental & Pharmaceutical Assn; Am Dental Assn; Chicago Dental Soc; sec treas Delta Developers Inc; bd mem Union Enterprises Inc; bd mem Impex Corp; v chmn of bd Diversified Unlimited Corp; mem Educ Com Pine Bluff Hsng Authority 1968-; one of first four black men C of C; mem Pine Bluff Sch Bd 1968-69; first Black Mem; pres Nat Alumni Assn Univ Of AR at Pine Bluff 1970-74; treas of bd St John Apts; bd mem Cits Boys Club; past chmn Pine Bluff Boy Scout Div; mem Tau Phi Chap Omega Psi Phi Frat Inc; v chmn bd Pine Bluff & Opps Industrialization Cntr; mem trustee St John AME Ch; life mem NAACP; mem Adv Com City of Pine Bluff; commnr Pine Bluff Conv Ctr. **Military Serv:** AUS capt. **Business Addr:** 817 Cherry St, Pine Bluff, AR 71601.

MONAGAN, ALFRIETA PARKS
Educator. **Personal:** Born Nov 27, 1945, Washington, DC; daughter of Frances Gordon Parks-Reid; children: Venice Frances, Agra Charlotte. **Educ:** George Washington Univ, AB 1969; Princeton, MA 1971, PhD 1981. **Career:** Hamilton Coll, visiting asst prof 1974-75; Univ Erlangen-Nuremberg, Fulbright Jr lecturer Amer Studies 1975-76; Univ of IA, asst prof Afro-Amer studies & anthropology 1976-86, adjunct assoc prof anthropology 1986-; Cornell Coll, visiting asst prof, 1990-. **Orgs:** Mem NAACP, Amer Anthropology Assn, Assn of Black Anthropologists, Caribbean Studies Assn; Districtwide Parents Organization; Friends of International Students. **Honors/Awds:** Fulbright Alumni Assn Gillen Scholarship 1968; Univ Fellowship Princeton 1969-70, 1973-74; Research Grant Princeton 1970; NSF Transportation 1972-73; Research Grant NSF 1972-73; Fellowship Soc Women Geographers; Research Grant Latin Amer Studies Princeton 1974; Lectrsp Fulbright-Hays Program 1975-76; Award from Natl Assoc for Foreign Student Affairs 1982, 1987; Old Gold Summer Faculty Research Fellowship 1985. **Business Addr:** Adjunct Associate Professor, University of Iowa, Dept of Anthropology, Iowa City, IA 52242.

MONCRIEF, SIDNEY A.
Business executive. **Personal:** Born Sep 21, 1957, Little Rock, AR; married Debra; children: Jon, Jeffrey. **Educ:** Univ of Arkansas, BS, phys education. **Career:** Welch One on One Competition, spokesman; Milwaukee Bucks, 1980-89; Atlanta Hwaks, 1990-91; Sidney Moncrief Pontiac-Buick-GMC Truck Inc, president, currently; Glendale Mitsubishi, president, currently. **Orgs:** Partner with Arkansas basketball coach Eddie Sutton to conduct clinics for the Special Olympics; board of directors, Arkla Corp. **Honors/Awds:** SW Conference Player of the Year; broke the record of 504 FTM by Kareem Abdul-Jabbar in 1971-72 season; Sporting News All-American Second Team, 1979; All-American & SW Conference Player of the Year during senior season, Univ of Arkansas; NBA Defensive Player of the Year 1983, 1984; NBA All-Defensive First Team 1983, 1984, 1985, 1986; 36th NBA All-Star Team. **Business Addr:** President, Sidney Moncrief Pontiac-Buick-GMC Truck, Inc, 5700 Landers Rd, Sherwood, AR 72117.

MONCRIEFF, PETER
Broadcast company executive. **Career:** KQLX-FM, president, currently. **Business Addr:** President, KQLX-FM, Citywide Broadcasting Corp, 7707 Waco St, Baton Rouge, LA 70806, (504)926-1106.

MONCURE, ALBERT F.
Business executive. **Personal:** Born Apr 19, 1924, Lancaster, PA; married Dr Bennie Sue Morrison; children: Sheila Ann Belfon, Albert F Jr, Alexandria Marie. **Educ:** Long Island Univ, BS Acctng 1950; NY Univ Grad Sch Business Adm, MBA 1956. **Career:** The Port of NY Authority, various positions through asst mgr operations 1951-67; New York City Dept Soc Svcs, dep comm 1967-70; The Port Authority of NYand NJ, asst personnel dir 1970, dep dir of gen serv 1970-71, dir gen serv 1971-84; Arlington Cnty VA Dept Human Services, admin serv div chief 1984-. **Orgs:** Chmn Child Health Assurance Prgm Subcomm for Citizen's Comm for Children 1973-80; conf chmn Inflation and Impact on Soc Serv at Ford Found 1974; vice pres Community Council of greater NY 1974-82; pres Purchasing Mgmt Assn of NY 1979-80; chmn Ethics Bd the Port Authority of NY and NJ 1980-83; chr Logistics Comm for the 1983 Conf of the Amer Soc for Publ Admin 1983; mem

adv bd Sch of Busniess & Publ Admin Long Is Univ 1983; bd mem United Way of Tri-State. **Honors/Awds:** Natl Urban League Black Exec Exch Prog Award 1979; One of 3 Disting Publ Leaders honored by People's Alliance 1983; Harlem YMCA Black Achievers Award 1973. **Military Serv:** AUS Master Sgt 1943-46 and 1950. **Business Addr:** Admin Serv Div Chief, Arlington County, Dept of Human Services, 1800 N Edison St, Arlington, VA 22207.

MONK, ART
Professional football player(retired). **Personal:** Born Dec 5, 1957, White Plains, NY; married Desiree; children: James Arthur Jr, Danielle. **Educ:** Syracuse Univ, attended. **Career:** Washington Redskins, wide receiver 1980-94; New York Jets, 1994; Philadelphia Eagles, 1995; Record Den Inc, director of outside sales; Rich Walker's Scoreboard Restaurant, Herndon, VA, part owner; WRC-TV, broadcast; Cactus Advertising Associates, principal owner, currently. **Orgs:** Dir of Outside Sales for Record Den Inc; part owner Rick Walker's Scoreboard Restaurant Herndon VA; Good Samaritan Foundation, founder. **Honors/Awds:** Led Redskins in receptions, 1980, 1982, 1984, 1985, and in yards 1980, 1981, 1984, 1985; all-Pro selections by AP, UPI, Pro Football Weekly, Pro Football Writers Assoc and The Sporting News; Player of the Year, Washington Touchdown Club and Quarterback Club; named Offensive Player of the Game twice; voted Redskins MVP, 1984; played in Pro Bowl, 1984-86 seasons. **Business Addr:** Founder/Principal Owner, Good Samaritans Foundation, c/o Cactus Advertising Associates, 13930 Willard Rd, Chantilly, VA 20151-2953.

MONK, EDD DUDLEY
Business executive. **Personal:** Born Apr 25, Magnolia, NC; married Marie Allen. **Career:** Edd D Monk Farms, farmer; funeral dir, 1982, Rose Hill Funeral Home Rose Hill, NC, pres 1948-. **Orgs:** Life chmn trust bd Missionary Bapt Training Inst 1973-80; pres /organizer Duplin Co Coastal Growers Coop 1968-78; pres/organizer Stanford Burial Soc Magnolia, NC 1932-64; bd dir FHA Kenansville 6 terms; bd dir Neuse River Cncl of Govt 1968-79; bd trustees James Sprunt Tech Coll Kenansville 1971-80; v chmn Good Neighbor Cncl 5 yrs; bd of dir Duplin Co Farm Bur 10 yrs; chmn deacon bd Kenansville Bapt Ch 1953-76; pres Duplin Co PTA & EE Smith High PTA 1962-69; bd dir Duplin Co Planning Bd 1975-79; worshipful master Beulah Lodge #110 10 yrs. **Honors/Awds:** Leadership Award Stanford Burial Soc 1962; Citizen of the Yr Duplin Co Adv Bd Ext 1966; Disting Serv Award E E Smith HS 1967; Disting Serv Award Kenansville Bapt Ch 1974; Disting Serv Cup Duplin Co Good Neighbor Cncl 1976; Citizen of the Year Duplin Co 4-H Club 1978; Disting Serv Award FHA 1978; Disting Serv Award Newuse Cncl of Govt 1979. **Business Addr:** President, Rose Hill Funeral Home, PO Box 338, 302 W Church, Rose Hill, NC 28458.

MONROE, ANNIE LUCKY
Educator. **Personal:** Born Dec 6, 1933, Milledgeville, GA; married Semon V Monroe; children: Angela V, Michael V. **Educ:** Paine Coll, BA 1953; GA Coll, MEd 1977. **Career:** Boddie HS, tchr 1953-68; Baldwin HS, tchr 1968-76, asst prin 1976-77; GA Coll, instr of English 1977-80. **Orgs:** Mem GA Libr Assn 1976-80; mem GA Coll Alumni Assn 1977-80; mem GA Coll Women's Club 1978-79; trustee Mary Vinson Libr 1976-80; mem Trinity CME Ch; asst pianist Trinity CME Ch. **Honors/Awds:** Teacher of the Year Boddie HS 1967; First Black Instr of English Baldwin HS 1968; First Black Woman chosen Bd of Trustees Mary Vinson Libr 1976; First Black Instr of English GA Coll 1977; Most Effective Teacher in Classroom Students of Baldwin HS 1977; First Black Woman Asst Principal Baldwin HS 1976-77. **Business Addr:** Georgia College, Milledgeville, GA 31061.

MONROE, BRYAN K.
Newspaper company designer. **Personal:** Born Aug 22, 1965, Munich, Germany; son of Charlyne W Monroe and James W Monroe. **Educ:** University of Washington, BA, communications, 1987. **Career:** The Seattle Times; The Roanoke Times & World News; United Press International; University of Washington Daily, editor; The Poynter Institute for Media Studies, visiting lecturer; The Sun News, graphics editor, director of photography, 1988; Knight-Ridder Inc's 25/43 Project, assistant project director; San Jose Mecury News, design director, currently. **Honors/Awds:** Numerous journalism awards: The Society of Newspaper Design; National Press Photographers Association; The South Carolina Press Association; The Florida Press Association; The Washington Press Association. **Special Achievements:** Guest speaker on topics including newspaper design, graphics, photjournalism, technology, innovation and the future of American newspapers. **Business Addr:** Director of Design & Graphics, San Jose Mercury News, 750 Ridder Park Dr, San Jose, CA 95190, (408)920-5031.

MONROE, CHARLES EDWARD
Educational administrator. **Personal:** Born Dec 9, 1950, Laurel Hill, NC; married Edwina Williams; children: Jarrod, Keisha, Charles, Jr. **Educ:** Johnson C Smith Univ, BA (Summa Cum Laude) 1978; Univ of NC, MEd 1980; Univ of NC Greensboro, EdS 1989. **Career:** Greensboro City Schools, teacher 1980-84, asst principal 1984-86, principal 1986-. **Orgs:** Mem NC Assn of Educators 1981-, Natl Assn of Elementary School Principals 1986-, NC Assn of Administrators 1986-; teacher Cedar Grove Baptist Church 1985-; pres Alpha Kappa Mu Natl Honor Soc; vice pres Alpha Chi Natl Honor Soc; mem Pi Delta Tau Educ Honor Soc, Honors Program. **Honors/Awds:** James B Duke Academic Scholarship; Babcock Academic Scholarship; George W Gore Grad Scholarship; Teacher of the Year Reidsville City Schools; Outstanding Young Educator in Reidsville City Schools Reidsville Jaycees. **Military Serv:** AUS E-4 2 yrs; Purple Heart, Air Commendation Medal, Bronze Star, Soldier of the Month, Distinguished Graduate in Ranger School in Vietnam 1970-71. **Home Addr:** 2204 Cheltenham Blvd, Greensboro, NC 27407.

MONROE, EARL
Professional basketball player (retired), business executive. **Personal:** Born Nov 21, 1944, Philadelphia, PA. **Educ:** Winston Salem State, 1967. **Career:** Baltimore Bullets, 1968-72, New York Knicks, 1972-80; Pretty Pearl Entertainment Co, pres. **Orgs:** Mem Groove Phi Groove Frat. **Honors/Awds:** All star team 1969, 71, 75, 77; rookie of the year 1967-68. **Business Addr:** NY Knicks, Madison Square Garden, 4 Pennsylvania Ave, New York, NY 10001.

MONROE, JAMES H.
Newspaper publisher. **Personal:** Born Feb 23, 1946, Hartford, CT; son of Rosalee Brown Monroe and James H Monroe; married Sarah Jones Scott, Sep 30, 1979; children: Judy. **Educ:** Parsons Coll, 1964-66; Central CT State Univ 1968-73. **Career:** Travelers Ins Co, acct 1968-69; enterpreneur 1969-; Conn Minority News, publisher; New England Minority News, Hartford, CT, 1969-. **Orgs:** Mem NAACP, 1970-, pres CT Business League, 1970-85; past pres, dir Greater Hartford Business Devel Center, 1973-; dir Hartford Econ Devel Comm, 1979-; mem SBA Task Force on Energy New England, 1979-81; dir CT Petroleum Council, 1981-; pres Greater Hartford Black Democratic Club, 1984-; dir Hartford Capital Corp. **Military Serv:** AUS sgt E-5 2 yrs.

MONROE, JAMES W.
Military officer. **Personal:** Born Mar 12, 1942, Laurinburg, NC; son of Bessie Monroe (deceased) and Ed Monroe (deceased); married Charlyne Williams, Aug 31, 1963; children: Donya, Bryan. **Educ:** West Virginia State College, BS, 1963; University of Cincinnati, MA, 1973. **Career:** US Army, various positions, 1963-, major general, currently. **Military Serv:** US Army, major general, 1963-; Legion of Merit, with 2 Oak Leaf Clusters, Defense Meritorious Service Medal, Army Meritorious Service Medal (with three Oak Leaf clusters), Army Commendation Medal, National Defense Service Medal, Southwest Asia Service Medal, Army Service Ribbon, Overseas Service Ribbon. **Business Addr:** Major General, Commanding General, US Army Ordinance Ctrs, Schools & Chief of Ordiance, Aberdeen Proving Ground, MD 21005, (410)272-0377.

MONROE, LILLIE MAE
Educational administrator. **Personal:** Born Feb 15, 1948, Louisiana; married Egbert Thaddeus Lord; children: Alan Christopher Lord. **Educ:** SU Baton Rouge LA, BS 1969; Freedmen's Hosp Washington DC, RD 1970; Howard Univ Washington DC, PhD, MS 1978, 1971. **Career:** CHANGE Inc, dir of nutrition prog 1970-72; Admin on Aging Dept Hlth Educ & Welfare, aging prog spec 1972-73; Med Assoc of NE Washington, private pract 1972-77; Comm Grp Health Found Inc, dir nutrition serv 1973-77; Univ of MD Eastern Shore, chmn, asst prof 1977-. **Orgs:** Mem Omicron Nu 1970; mem Soc Sigma Xi 1971; vol proj FIND 1971; judge/nutrition prog Phyllis Wheatley YMCA 1971; hmn diet therapy comm DC Dietetic Assoc 1973; mem Comm Nutrition Com DC Dietetic Assn 1971; mem Beta Kappa Chi 1972; mem pub rels com DC Dietetic Assn 1975; ed potomac post mag DC Dietitic Assn 1977. **Honors/Awds:** Outstanding Young Dietitian of the Year 1973.

MONROE, ROBERT ALEX
Business executive. **Personal:** Born in Somerville, NJ. **Educ:** Attended, Westchester Comm Coll, Hofstra Univ 1964. **Career:** Calvert Distillers, asst eastern div sales mgr, eastern div mgr; General Wine, mgr western upstate NY, NY mgr, natl brand mgr; asst metro NY sales mgr, eastern div sales rep; Calvert Distillers Co, vice pres/dir marketing; Summit Sales Co/Perennial Sales Co, pres. **Orgs:** Bd of dir, Joseph E Seagram & Sons Inc. **Honors/Awds:** Outstanding Business & Professional Award, Blackbook Magazine, 1983; Man of the Year Award, Anti-Defamation League, 1985; first black to lead a major firm in the liquor industry; George M Estabrook Award, Hofstra Univ Alumni Assn, 1987. **Military Serv:** USMC, cpl, 1954-57.

MONTAGUE, CHRISTINA P.
County commissioner, educator. **Personal:** Born Dec 25, 1952, Inkster, MI; daughter of Mattie Lee Watson and Romo Watson; married Larry Montague, Jun 1976 (divorced); children: Teesha Fanessa. **Educ:** Washtenaw Community College, criminal justice, 1974; Eastern Michigan University, BSW, 1984; University of Michigan, MSW, 1988. **Career:** Joint Center for Political & Econ Studies, executive director for Michigan, 1984-85; Ann Arbor Public School, community agent, 1974-87, research assistant, 1987-88; Franklin Wright Settlement, case manager, 1989-90; Ann Arbor Public Schools, social worker, 1988-90, child and family therapist, 1990-91, family service specialist, 1991-. **Orgs:** Ann Arbor NAACP, 1st vice pres, 1987-89; Michigan Branches of NAACP, voter education chairperson, 1984-86; National Political Congress of Black Women, founding president, Washtenaw County chapter, 1989; The National Taxation and Finance Steering Committee for County officials; The Terry Scholarship Foundation, national president; Ann Arbor Democratic Party, 1st black to chair, 1988-90; State of Michigan Licensed Professional and Amateur Boxing, judge, 1984-88; Michigan Democratic Party, central committee, 1988-. **Honors/Awds:** National NAACP, Political/Education Award, 1985; National Political Congress of Black Women, Outstanding Achievement, 1989; Washtenaw County Democratic Party, Service to Washtenaw County; Saturday Academy for African American Youth, Certificate of Appreciation, 1991. **Special Achievements:** First African American woman ever elected Washtenaw County Commissioner, 1990; asked to submit speech, "Dare to Run Dare to Win," Journal of Exceptional African American Speeches, 1991; appointed, National Steering Committee, Taxation and Finance, National President of County Officials, 1991-. **Home Addr:** 1430 Broadway, Ann Arbor, MI 48105, (313)662-9908.

MONTAGUE, LEE
Educational administrator, clergyman. **Personal:** Born Apr 15, 1930, Philadelphia, PA; married Shirley Mae Demmons; children: Ricardo V, La Donna M, Michael A, Saunders L, Shirley M, Christina L, Deborah L, Denise A. **Educ:** Coll of Marin, CA, 1965; Glendale Comm Coll, 1966-67; AZ Bible Coll, BA 1967-71. **Career:** USAF, sergeant 1947-67; Maricopa Med Ctr, med asst 1967-71; New Chance Inner City Ministries, dir 1972-84; Canaan Bible Inst, pres/dean 1983-; Solid Rock Missionary Baptist Church, pastor, currently. **Orgs:** Scoutmaster Boy Scouts of Amer 1966-69; chaplain Disabled Amer Vets 1971-74; brigade chmn Christian Serv Brigade 1973-75; pastor Luke AFB Gospel Chapel 1973-; administrator/director Inner City Children's Camps 1974-. **Honors/Awds:** Recognition Black Chamber of Commerce; Meritorious Serv USAF 1966. **Military Serv:** USAR t/sgt 20 years; AFOUA, AFGCM, GCM/5bl, NDSM/1bss, KSM, UNSM, AFLSA/4bolc 1947-67. **Home Addr:** 4935 West Berkely, Phoenix, AZ 85035. **Business Addr:** President, Canaan Bible Institute, PO Box 1244, Phoenix, AZ 85001.

MONTAGUE, NELSON C.
Scientist, ministry administrator. **Personal:** Born Jul 12, 1929, Washington, DC; son of Rosmond P Montague and Nelson R Montague; married Nancy L; children: Lennis Lee. **Educ:** BS Elec Engr 1952. **Career:** Def Documentation Cntr, Def Logistics Agy, physical scientist, elec engr 1984 retired; Nat Bur of Standards, elec engr 1951-68; Virginia, marriage celebrant, currently. **Orgs:** Mem Inst of Elec & Electronics Engrs Inc 1950's; Fairfax NAACP; treas N VA Bapt Assn 1968-; mem exec bd NVB Assn; vice pres Commn on Hum Rights & Comm Rels, Vienna VA; Mayor's Adv Com 1966-70; coach Little Leag VA 1972-73; fin sec Northern VA Baptist Ministers & Laymen's Union 1985-94; life mem, NAACP, 1994. **Honors/Awds:** Recip Grp Award Nat Bur of Standards 1964; Outstndng Perf Rating QSI Def Documentation Ctr 1974; finished 4 in 7 man race for 3 seats on Vienna Town Cncl 1968; Achievement Awd Arlington Branch NAACP 1986; Faithful Service Award Fairfax NAACP Branch, 1988. **Military Serv:** AUS pfc 1952-54.

MONTAIGNE, ORTIZ. See WALTON, ORTIZ MONTAIGNE.

MONTEIRO, MARILYN D.S.
University administrator. **Personal:** Born Feb 22, 1941, Washington, DC; divorced; children: Chinyelu. **Educ:** Univ of MA-Boston, BA 1970; Harvard Univ, EdM 1973, EdD 1982. **Career:** Delta Oppors Corp, teacher/teacher trainer 1970-71; YWCA Roxbury Branch, prog dir 1973-74; MA College of Art, dir affirmative action 1980-83; Univ of Northern IA, dir affirmative action progs 1983-. **Orgs:** Chair Cedar Falls Human Rights Commn; regional dir Amer Assoc for Affirmative Action; consultant Waterloo Dept of Correctional Svcs, Waterloo Civil SvcsCommn, Wendy's Restaurant Cedar Falls; bd mem YWCA Waterloo IA; mem NAACP, Phi Delta Kappa of Harvard and Univ of Northern IA, Amer Assoc on Higher Educ; mem Inter-Institutional Equal Employment Oppors Comm. **Honors/Awds:** 2 publications; 8 articles published. **Business Addr:** Affirmative Action Dir, University of Northern Iowa, 126 Gilcrist Hall, Cedar Falls, IA 50613.

MONTEIRO, THOMAS
College professor. **Personal:** Born Oct 6, 1939, New York, NY; son of Lovely Peters and John Monteiro; married Joy Williams (divorced 1980); children: Thomas, Tod. **Educ:** Winston-Salem State University, Winston-Salem, NC, BS, 1961; Queens College of the City University of New York, New York NY, MA, 1966; Fordham University, New York, NY, professional diploma, 1968-69, PhD, 1971-74. **Career:** Board of Education, New York, NY, teacher, 1961-68, district curriculum director, 1969-70; Brooklyn College of the City University of New York, New

York, NY, professor, 1970-85, chairperson, dept of education administration and supervision, director, the principal's center at Brooklyn College, 1985-. **Orgs:** President, New York Jamaica Branch, NAACP, 1977, 1978; education co-chairperson, New York State, NAACP, 1976-1980. **Honors/Awds:** Congressional Achievement Award, Congressman Floyd Flake, 1990; Outstanding Educator Award, Success Guide George Fraser, Editor, 1991; Educator of the Year Award, New York Association of Black Educators, 1988; Educational Leadership Award, Council of Supervisors and Administrators of New York, 1991; Award of Excellence, New York, Alliance of Black School Educators, 1988. **Business Addr:** Chairperson, School of Education, Brooklyn College, Ave H & Bedford Ave, Brooklyn, NY 11210.

MONTEITH, HENRY C.
Nuclear engineer. **Personal:** Born May 10, 1937, Columbia, SC; son of Susie Elizabeth Monteith and Frank Hull Monteith; divorced. **Educ:** Milwaukee Sch of Engrg, BS 1965; Univ of NM, MS 1970, PhD 1975. **Career:** RCA Indianapolis, elec engr 1965-67; Sandia Labs Albuquerque, math computer programmer, elec engr, tech staff mem 1967-80; Sandia Labs Albuquerque, nuclear engr 1976-88; ITT Technical Institute, instructor, 1990-92; Albuquerque Academy, mathematics instructor, 1992-. **Orgs:** Writer & lecturer on scientific/philosophical subjects; priv res Parapsychology; mem Amer Assn for Advancement of Sci, Soc of Physics Students, Intl Assoc of Math Physicists. **Honors/Awds:** Sigma Pi Sigma Physics Honor Soc. **Military Serv:** USN Electron Tech 2nd Class 1958-62. **Business Addr:** Math Instructor, Albuquerque Academy, 6400 Wyoming Blvd NE, Albuquerque, NM 87109.

MONTEVERDI, MARK VICTOR
Public affairs executive. **Personal:** Born Jun 19, 1963, New York, NY; son of Marcella F Monteverdi-Monahan. **Educ:** Hiram Coll, Hiram OH, BA, 1985. **Career:** Small Business Admin, New York NY, public affairs specialist, 1985-87; Black Enterprise Magazine/Earl G Graves, Ltd, New York NY, natl networking forum coordinator, 1987-88; Mayor's Office, New York, NY, mgr of public communications & outreach, 1988-89; Westchester Minority Commerce Assn, exec dir, 1989-90; Philip Morris Companies Inc, public affairs coordinator, 1990-91, public programs specialist, 1991-. **Orgs:** Alpha Lamda Delta, 1981-; Omicron Delta Kappa, 1983-; Assn of Minority Enterprises of NY, 1985-; Caribbean-Amer Chamber of Commerce, 1985-; Natl Minority Business Council, 1985-; Self-Help Group, advisory board member, 1988-; Business Policy Review Council, membership & program development vice pres; Latin American Management Association, corporate advisory board secretary; Manhattanville College Entrepreneurial Council, board of directors; National Urban League's Black Executive Exchange Program, visiting professor; National Association of Market Developers; Queensborough Community College, project prize mentor; National Coalition of Black Meeting Planners. **Honors/Awds:** James A Garfield Memorial Award, Hiram Coll, 1981; Outstanding Political Science Major, Hiram Coll, 1985; Martin Luther King Jr Scholarship, Hiram Coll, 1985; received White House recognition for role as downstate coordinator for the 1985 White House Conference on Small Business, 1986; Award of Distinction, Communications Excellence to Black Audiences, 1992; President's Award, Association of Minority Enterprises of New York, 1991; Junior Fellow, US Small Business Administration, 1981-85. **Home Addr:** 23 S Elliot Pl, Brooklyn, NY 11217.

MONTGOMERY, ALPHA LEVON, SR.
Judge. **Personal:** Born Feb 1, 1919, Oklahoma; son of Melissa Montgomery and Emmett Montgomery; married Ann E; children: Alpha L Jr, Levonne, Adrien, Alain. **Educ:** Fisk Univ, BA 1941; Howard Univ, JD 1947. **Career:** Economist for fed govt, Washington, DC, 1945-47; Bussey, Montgomery & Smith 1948-49; Montgomery & Smith 1949-54; Montgomery & Rithcey San Diego, att 1964-79; Superior Court of San Diego, judge. **Orgs:** Mem Am Bar Assn; San Diego County Bar Assn; Am Arbitration Assn; bd architectural rev San Diego 1955-61; Legal Aid Soc 1958-59; psychology commn 1961-62; founder, San Diego Urban League; NAACP; Forum Am Freedoms 1961-; CA Adv Com US Commn Civil Rights 1962-66; vp Citizens Interracial Com San Diego 1963-64; interview bd San Diego Civil Serv Commn 1963; Gov's Commn Rumford Act 1966; state bd educ Moral Guidelines Com 1970-72. **Honors/Awds:** Fed ct serv certificate, San Diego Bar Assn 1959; certificate of appreciation San Diego 1963; superior accomplishment award, Federal Government, for work as an economist; participant in President Eisenhower's Conference for President's Commission on Equal Employment Opportunity, President Kennedy's Regional Conference of Community Leaders on Equal Employment Opportunity, and President Johnson's White Conference on Civil Rights; pub papers & booklets on economics and politics.

MONTGOMERY, CATHERINE LEWIS
Business executive. **Personal:** Born in Washington, DC; daughter of Catherine Branch Lewis Laster (deceased) and Lloyd Lewis (deceased); married Alpha LeVon Montgomery Sr (divorced); children: Alpha LeVon Jr. **Educ:** Howard Univ, attended 1944-46; Univ CA ext 1948-49; Natl Inst Pub Affairs 1968. **Career:** USN elect Lab San Diego, admin asst to tech dir 1950-62; Republican State Central Comm, admin asst to field dir Jan 1966-June 1966; Economic Oppor Comm San Diego Cnty, pers dir admin serv 1966-69; State of CA Fair Empl Practice Commn, commissioner 1969-75; USN Dept, mgmt cons/equal opportunity spec 1978-90, consult Urban Arrairs, 1972-. **Orgs:** San Diego Plang Commr 1966-73; Mental Hlth Serv Adv Bd 1968-72; President's Adv Cncl on Minority Bus Enterprise 1972-75; mem Western Gov Rsch Assn; Natl Assn of Planners; Amer Soc of Planning Officials; Commonwealth Club of CA; served on bds of Soroptimist Intl San Diego; pres Soroptimist Intl San Diego 1979-80; Natl Girls Clubs of Amer Inc; Urban League of San Diego Inc; Univ Hosp Adv Bd; mem NAACP; life mem Natl Cncl of Negro Women; League of Women Voters; San Diego Girls Club Inc; The Links, Inc; bd mem, SE Economic Devt Corp, 1987-94; life mem, Friends of VP Public Library, 1990; founder, bd mem, Women's Bank, 1974-78; gCvt/community relations comm, San Diego Convention/Tourist Bureau, 1989-90. **Honors/Awds:** Citizen of the Year Awd Omega Psi Phi 1977; Recognition Awd San Diego Br NAACP 1977; Cert of Apprec San Diego City Schools 1978; Natl Recognition Awd Lambda Kappa Mu 1978; Natl Trends & Serv Honoree The Links Inc 1978; Action Enterprises Devel Community Serv Awd 1979; Valuable Serv Awd Natl Fed Bus & Professional Women's Clubs 1980; Woman of Accomplishment Central City Assn & Soroptimist Intl of San Diego 1981; Woman of the Year, San Diego, Girls Clubs of Amer Inc, 1988; Woman of Achievement, Chamber of Commerce & Council of Women's Clubs, 1974; Profiles in Black, Congress of Racial Equality, 1976; Award of Merit, San Diego Sec, Amer Inst of Planners, 1973; Distinguished Community Service Award, Girls Clubs of America, 1972; Natl Sojourner Truth Meritorious Serve Award, Negro Bus & Profl Womens Assn, 1967; Woman of Valour, Temple Beth Israel Sisterhood, 1967; Celebrate Literacy Award, Valencia Park (Malcolm X), Library, Greater SD Reading Assn, 1992; Woman of Dedication, Salvation Army Door of Hope, 1944; Unsung Hero Award, SD NAACP, 1994; San Diegan of the Year, San Diego Home-Garden Magazine, 1994. **Business Addr:** Urban Consultant, Montgomery's Consulting Service, PO Box 740041, San Diego, CA 92174.

MONTGOMERY, DELMONICO
Professional football player. **Personal:** Born Dec 8, 1973, Dallas, TX. **Educ:** Indianapolis Colts, defensive back, 1997-. **Business Addr:** Professional Football Player, Indianapolis Colts, PO Box 535000, Indianapolis, IN 46253, (317)297-2658.

MONTGOMERY, DWIGHT RAY
Clergyman. **Personal:** Born Apr 8, 1950, Memphis, TN. **Educ:** Lane Coll, BA 1968-72. **Career:** New Zion Bapt Ch, minister 1985; Goodwill Ind, cnslr 1977; Memphis Reg Sickle Cell Cncl, dep dir 1973-76. **Orgs:** Kappa Alpha Psi Alumni Chap 1969; Masonic Lodge; 32 deg Scotish Rite; Elks; Shriners 1969-71; found, dir Coalition of Benevolent Yth 1974. **Honors/Awds:** Memphis Hall of Fame, Alpha Kappa Alpha Sor 1973-75; outstndng Young Men of Am 1975; Outstndng Citizen of Memphis, Tri-St Def Nwspr 1976; 50 Future Black Ldrs, Ebony Mag Chicago 1978. **Business Addr:** 1210 College St, Memphis, TN 38114.

MONTGOMERY, EARLINE ROBERTSON
Corporate executive. **Personal:** Born Aug 18, 1944, New Orleans, LA; daughter of Ella Jones Robertson and Harold C Robertson; married Murray Montgomery Jr, Jun 3, 1983. **Educ:** TX Southern Univ, Houston, TX, BS, 1977; Univ of Houston, Houston, TX, post graduate work, 1978. **Career:** City of Houston, Houston, TX, personnel mgr, 1974-88; Robertson & Assoc Inc, Houston, TX, owner & pres, 1988-; FamCorp USA Mktg, Houston, TX, vice pres, Human Resources, 1989. **Orgs:** Mem, Alpha Kappa Alpha Sorority, Inc, 1964-; mem, Amer Compensation Assn, 1978-; mem, Natl Forum for Black Public Admin, 1986-; commr, Mayor's Affirmative Action Advisory Commn, 1987-88; co-chmn of fund raising comm, Natl Urban League, 1988; chmn of membership comm, NFBPA, Houston Chapter, 1988; consultant, The Hackney Co, 1988; mem, Natl Urban League, 1988-; consultant, The Winning Edge, 1989; chmn of By-Laws Comm, NFBPA Houston Chapter, 1989; parlimentarian, NFBPA, Houston chapter, 1989. **Honors/Awds:** Outstanding Young Woman of Amer Award, 1978; author, "Clerical Training Manual, 1980"; author "Job Performance Appraisal Manual," 1981; 1st Women of Achievement Award, 100 Top Women of Achievement, 1989.

MONTGOMERY, EDWARD B.
Economist. **Educ:** Penn State Univ, grad; Harvard Univ, PhD, economics. **Career:** Univ of MD, tenured prof, currently; US Dept of Labor, chief economist, currently. **Special Achievements:** First African American chief economist at the US Dept of Labor. **Business Addr:** Chief Economist, US Dept of Labor, 200 Constitution Ave, Rm South 218, Washington, DC 20210, (202)219-5108.

MONTGOMERY, ETHEL CONSTANCE (CONNIE)
Telecommunications company executive (retired). **Personal:** Born Jul 10, 1931, Morristown, NJ; daughter of Aletha Mounter and Arnold Mounter; widowed; children: Byron, Lisa. **Educ:** Fairleigh Dickinson Univ. **Career:** AT&T Bell Labs, employment rep, 1987-90 (retired); supv 1985-87, grp supr 1978, prsnl rep, affirm act coord 1975; Wstrn Elec Co, salaried prsnl rels, prsnl results invtgtr, tech clk, sec, steno sec 1968-75; Bell Tel Co, typist 1968; Silver Burdette, Morristown Ship, 1967; Warner Lambert Inc, coder 1965; Morristown Neighborhood House, prog dir, coord, vol, grp worker, sec 1951-64. **Orgs:** Ldr Girl Scout 1952; pres PTA 1957; Carettes Inc 1959; sec, treas, vp, corrs sec Carettes Inc 1959-76; mem, vp, pres Morristown Bd Ed 1966-70; corrs sec Morris Co Sch Bd Assn 1969; mem Morristown Civil Rights Commn 1969; Morristown Comm Act Com 1969; Urban Leag & Family Srv 1970; Yth Empl Srv 1970; United Fund Adv Bd 1970; vice pres Morris Sch Dist Bd Ed 1972-74; mem St Bd Ed 1975; Juv Conf 1977; adv com Meml Hosp 1977; mem Gov Byrn's Govt Cost & Tax Policy Com 1977; mem 1982-, pres 1984, 1986, 1987 Morristown Council; newsletter chairperson, Concerned Citizens of the 2nd Ward, 1989-90; mem, Morris Count Democratic Comm , 1986-90; bd mem, Morristown Neighborhood Watch, 1987-90. **Honors/Awds:** Morris Co Urban League Award 1953, 1963; Outstndng Women of NJ, Fairleigh Dickinson Univ 1964; Morris Co NAACP Award 1970; Lambda Kappa Mu Sor Award 1970; Transcendental Meditation Award 1977; Nat Black Achiever 1979. **Home Addr:** 17 Liberty St, Morristown, NJ 07960.

MONTGOMERY, EVANGELINE JULIET
Business executive, artist. **Personal:** Born May 2, 1933, New York, NY. **Educ:** Los Angeles City College, AA 1958; CA State University, Los Angeles, attended 1958-62; University of CA Berkeley, attended 1968-70; CA College of Arts & Crafts, BFA 1969; museum studies and workshops, 1970-83. **Career:** Freelance artist 1960-62; EJ Associates, art consultant to museums, comm organizations and colleges 1967-; Montgomery & Co, exhibits specialist, freelance art consultant 1969-73; ARK Urban Systems Inc, vice pres/director 1973-78; American Assn for State and Local History, workshop coordinator 1979; WHMM TV Washington DC Community Affairs, dir, 1980; African American Museums Assn, Exhibit Workshops coordinator, 1982; Art Consultants and Gallery, Freelance artist represented by SAMJAL, Los Angeles, CA; Michigan Chapter NCA Gallery, Detroit; Parish Gallery, Washington DC; Arts America, program officer 1983-. **Orgs:** Art commissioner, San Francisco Art Commission 1976-79; natl coordinator of regions, Natl Conference of Artists 1973-81; natl fine arts & culture director, Natl Assn of Negro Business & Professional Women Clubs Inc 1976-78; president, Metal Arts Guild 1972-74; president, Art West Assn North Inc 1967-78; advisory bd, Parting Ways Ethnohistory Museum 1977-85; board member, Museum Natl Center Afro-American Artists 1974-85; American Museums Assn 1970-; DC chap co-chair, Fine Arts and Culture Comm; Coalition of 100 Black Women 1984-91; board of directors, DC Arts Center, 1989-; Michigan Chapter Natl Conference of Artists, 1990-; College Art Assn, 1983-; Womens Art Caucus, 1988-; mem, Brandywine Workshop, 1990-; bd mem, Natl, 1993, Year of the Craft Celebration, American Craft Council, 1989-94. **Honors/Awds:** Natl Program Award, NANB & P W Clubs Inc 1977; Service Awards, Natl Conference of Artists 1970, 1974, 1976; Museum Grant, Natl Endowment for the Arts, Smithsonian Prof Fellowship 1973; Grant, Third World Fund 1974; Special Achievement Award, Arts America, 1989. **Business Addr:** Artist, c/o Norman Parish Gallery, 1054 31st St, NW, Washington, DC 20007.

MONTGOMERY, FRED O.
Banking administrator. **Personal:** Born Jan 23, 1922, Oak Ridge, LA; married Hazel White; children: Daryl Young, Cynthia. **Educ:** Atlanta Coll, Mortuary Sci 1942. **Career:** Morehouse Funeral Home, mortician 1943-76; D&M Casket Co, owner, mgr 1959; Apex Vending Co, owner 1960-76; Ins Co, pres; Montgomery Funeral Home, owner; Security Natl Bank, dir. **Orgs:** Police juror Parish Governing Body 1974; pres Insurance Co 1976; dir Security Natl Bank 1985; treas, interim bd chmn 1987 Morehouse Concern Citizens Civil Club. **Military Serv:** AUS 1st sgt 3 years; Battle Star & Good Conduct Medal 1940.

MONTGOMERY, GEORGE LOUIS, JR.
Realtor, banker. **Personal:** Born Jul 13, 1934, St Louis, MO; children: Gay, Kelly. **Educ:** St Louis U, BS 1956; Wash U, AD 1968. **Career:** St Louis Redevelopment Authority, real estate spec 1974; Kraft Foods Inc, salesman 1963-68; Conrad Liquor, salesman 1962-63; Universal Life Ins Co, salesman 1961-62; Montgomery Real Estate, broker, 1968-. **Orgs:** Indpd Fee Appraisers Assn 1974-; Realtist Assn of St Louis 1974-; vice-chmn Gateway Nat Bank of St Louis 1977; Wayman Temple AME Ch; Frontiers Intl Inc, 1970-, president, 1980-84, board member Annie Malone Children's Home 1976-; Pres Council of St Louis Univ 1973-; St Louis Jr C of C 1961-63; Nat Assn of Mrkt Dev 1961-63; past chmn Sel Ser Bd 1974. **Honors/Awds:** Citizen of the Wk KATZ Radio 1961; Ebony Magz Most Eligible Bachelor 1964; Man of the Yr Frontiers Intl 1964; St Louis University, Alumni Merit Award, 1980; Top Ladies of Distinction, Distinguished Service Award, 1981. **Military Serv:** USNR seaman 1956-58. **Business Addr:** Broker, Montgomery Real Estate, 3412 N Union, St Louis, MO 63115.

MONTGOMERY, GREGORY B.
Attorney. **Personal:** Born Mar 23, 1946, McKeesport, PA; married Patricia A Felton. **Educ:** Rutgers Coll, AB 1968; Rutgers Law Sch Newark NJ, JD 1975. **Career:** Gregory B Montgomery PA, atty 1985; Forrestal Village Inc, corp sec 1978-79; S & E Const Corp, corp sec 1977-79; Fidelity First Corp, vice pres 1975-79. **Orgs:** Mem lwyr refferral & inform panel Nat Bar Assn; mem Am Bar Assn; mem Commercial Law Leag of Am; mem BA Law List; medm NJ Garden St & Camden Co Bar Assns; mem Nat Urban Leag. **Honors/Awds:** USAF Commendtion Medal 1972. **Military Serv:** USAF capt 1968-72. **Business Addr:** 108 North Seventh St, Camden, NJ 08102.

MONTGOMERY, JAMES C.
Clergyman. **Personal:** Born Feb 8, 1918, Lake, MS; married Mary I Roberts. **Educ:** Rust Coll Holly Spg MS, 1952. **Career:** Mt Sinai Missionary Bapt Ch, pastor; Radio Shop, owner. **Orgs:** Mem NAACP. **Honors/Awds:** Recip Award Comm Sch Improvement Prog 1961; Award of Apprec Metro Bapt Ch 1954; Award Dept of Christine Ed Nat Cncl Chs; Hon St of MI 68 Dist Ct Flint. **Military Serv:** AUS pfc 1940. **Business Addr:** Sinai Missionary Baptist Ch, 1215 Downey Avenue, Flint, MI 48505.

MONTGOMERY, JOE ELLIOTT
City official. **Personal:** Born Jul 10, 1942, Hemingway, SC; son of Emma Jane Montgomery and Elliott Montgomery; married Phyoncia Montgomery, Apr 30, 1969; children: Charles Montgomery. **Educ:** Allen Univ, Columbia, SC, BA, 1965, Univ of SC, graduate work. **Career:** City of New York, NY, counselor, 1965-66; Horry County Dept of Educ, teacher, 1966; Town of Atlantic Beach, Atlantic Beach, SC, mayor. **Orgs:** SC Educ Assn, Natl Educ Assn; Horry County Educ Assn; National Conference of Black Mayors, board of directors; South Carolina Conference of Black Mayors, president, 1988-90. **Honors/Awds:** Costa Carolina Coll, Certificate, 1979; Joint Center for Political Action, Certificate, 1979; Kappa Alpha Psi Fraternity, Certificate, 1982; Horry County Culture Assn, 1982; Natl Conf of Black, Certificate, 1984. **Home Addr:** PO Box 1374, North Myrtle Beach, SC 29582.

MONTGOMERY, KEESLER H.
Magistrate. **Personal:** Born Oct 15, 1917, Carrollton, MS; son of Jennie Goodwin Montgomery and Charlie Montgomery; married Josephine Chamberlain. **Educ:** Prairie View State Univ, AB 1941; Suffolk Univ Law School, JD 1950; Boston Univ, MA 1960; Suffolk Univ, LLM 1961. **Career:** State of MA, asst atty gen 1953-60; US Circuit Ct of Appeals 1954; US Supreme Ct 1957; Roxbury Municipal Ct Comm of MA, magistrate. **Orgs:** Life mem & past Grand Exalted Ruler IBPOE; past Master JJ Smith Lodge of Prince Hall Masons 33rd degree; trustee Ebenezer Bapt Ch; trustee Andover Newton Theol Sch; life mem NAACP; bd mem Roxbury YMCA; Resthaven Nurs Home; United So End Settlements, Greater Boston Fam Serv Assn; Visiting Nurses Assn. **Honors/Awds:** Elks Alumni Award 1954 & 1957; Alumni Award Prairie View State Univ 1954; Disting Legal Serv Boston Policemen's Assn 1972; Paul Revere Bowl Past Masters Club, Prince Hall Masons. **Military Serv:** USN Petty Officer 1943-45. **Business Addr:** Magistrate, Roxbury Municipal Court, 101 Tremont St, Boston, MA 02108.

MONTGOMERY, OLIVER R.
Research assistant. **Personal:** Born May 31, 1929, Youngstown, OH; married Thelma Howard; children: Darlene, Howard, Brenda, Oliver, Jr, Edwin. **Educ:** BS 1956. **Career:** Untd Steelworkers of Am AFL-CIO, assoc res asst present. **Orgs:** Nat bd mem Sec Nat Afro-Am Labor Counc 1970-75; vice pres Untd Steelworkers Local 3657; natl bd & exec counc mem Coalition of Black Trade Unionists; bdmem Gr Pittsburgh ACLU 1972-75; chmn labor & ind com NAACP 1960-63; mem Kappa Alpha Phi Frat. **Honors/Awds:** Recip A Philip Randolph Awd; awd cert of merit NAACP Urban League; Testimonial Dinner 1970; awds from Mayor, City Counc CAP ofcrs, OEO Progs. **Military Serv:** AUS military sci instr. **Business Addr:** Research Dept United Steelwork, Pittsburgh, PA 15222.

MONTGOMERY, OSCAR LEE
Educator. **Personal:** Born Jul 19, 1949, Chapman, AL; married Alfredia Marshall; children: Paula Onese, Renita Falana, Christa Ivana, Oscar Lee Jr. **Educ:** Alabama A&M Univ, BS 1972; Purdue Univ, MS 1974, PhD 1976; Trinity Theological Seminary, D Min, 1997. **Career:** Union Hill PB Church, pastor 1977-; Alabama A&M Univ, asst prof 1976-81, assoc prof 1981, vice president, professor. **Orgs:** Dir Alabama Ctr for Applications of Remote Sensing 1980-; pres GHIMF-Ministerial Fellowship 1980-; pres NAACP local chap 1982-84. **Home Addr:** 3800 Milbrae Dr, Huntsville, AL 35810.

MONTGOMERY, PAYNE
Educator, city official. **Personal:** Born Nov 24, 1933, Bernice, LA; married Rosemary Prescott; children: Janice, Eric, Joyce. **Educ:** Grambling Coll, BS 1956; Tuskegee Inst, MS 1969; NE LA U, 1969. **Career:** Morehouse Par Sch Bd, hum rel cnsl; City of Bastrop, city cnclmn; Morehouse HS, bsktbl coach 1959-69; Delta HS, soc stud tchr 1969-72. **Orgs:** Elec to City Cncl 1973; mem LA Ed Assn; Nat Ed Assn; Parish Rec Bd; C of C; Am Leg; bd dir Headstart; first pres Morehouse Comm Org; workedto increase black voter regist; evaluator Title VII Progs 1973-74. **Honors/Awds:** Spl recog Coaching Record; Coach of Yr 1961. **Military Serv:** AUS 1956-58. **Business Addr:** Human Relations Office, Bastrop HS, Bastrop, LA.

MONTGOMERY, ROBERT E.
Automobile dealer. **Personal:** Born Feb 1, 1948, Lake Wales, FL; son of Annie L Gadson; married Valorie A; children: Ryan, Raven. **Educ:** John B Stetson University, BBA, 1970; Columbia University, Graduate School of Business, MBA, 1972. **Career:** Ford Motor Co, analyst, 1972-73; Chevrolet Motor Co, analyst/supervisor, 1973-80; Gulf & Western, director, business planning, 1980-85; GM Dealer School, trainee, 1985-86; Self-Employed, consultant, 1986-88; Mountain Home Ford, president, 1988-. **Orgs:** Alpha Phi Alpha; Ford-Lincoln Mercury Minority Dealers Association, board of directors. **Military Serv:** US Army, 1st lt, 1970-74. **Business Addr:** President, Mountain Home Ford/Lincoln-Mercury Inc, 400 W 6th St S, PO Box 520, Mountain Home, ID 83647, (208)587-3326.

MONTGOMERY, TONI-MARIE
Educator, educational administrator. **Personal:** Born Jun 25, 1956, Philadelphia, PA; daughter of Mattie Drayton and Milton Montgomery. **Educ:** Philadelphia College of Performing Arts, Philadelphia, PA, BM, 1980; University of Michigan, Ann Arbor, MI, MM, 1981, DMA, 1984. **Career:** Western Michigan University, Kalamazoo, MI, asst director school of music, 1985-87; University of Connecticut, Storrs, CT, asst dean, 1987-89; Arizona State University, Tempe, AZ, assoc dean/asst professor, 1990-96; Arizona State Univ, School of Music, dir, 1996-. **Orgs:** Member, Tempe Arts Commission, 1991-93; president, Sister Friends: African-American Women, 1990-; member, board of directors, Faculty Women's Association, 1990-. **Honors/Awds:** Outstanding Keyboard Performer, American Keyboard Artists, 1988. **Business Addr:** Assoc Dean/Prof, Coll of Fine Arts, Arizona State University, Dixie Gammage Building, Tempe, AZ 85287-2102.

MONTGOMERY, TRENT
Educational administrator. **Career:** Southern University, School of Engineering, dean, currently. **Orgs:** IEEE; Eta Kappa Nu; ASEE. **Business Addr:** Dean, Southern University, School of Engineering, PO Box 9969, Baton Rouge, LA 70813.

MONTGOMERY, VELMANETTE
State senator. **Personal:** married William Walker; children: William Montgomery. **Educ:** New York University, MEd; University of Ghana. **Career:** New York City District 13 School Board, member, 1977-80, president, 1977-84; Child Care Inc, Advocacy Group, former co-director; New York Senate, 18th Senatorial dist, senator, 1984-. **Orgs:** Serves on many senatorial committees, including: Finance; Consumer Protection; Housing and Community Development; Comm on Children and Families, chief democrat; Democratic Task Force on Primary Health Care, chair; Robert Wood Johnson Foundation, Natl Advisory Comm. **Honors/Awds:** Institute of Educational Leadership, fellow, 1981; Revson Foundation, 1984; St. Joseph's College, hon doctor of law degree, 1991; Advocates for Youth, National Teen Leadership Award, 1994; The Visiting Nurse Assn of Brooklyn, Legislative Leadership Award; New York Therapeutic Communities, Inc, Legislative Leadership Award; named one of "America's Top 100 Black Business and Professional Women"; Parade Magazine, feature article, 1992. **Business Addr:** State Senator, State of New York, Legislative Office Bldg, Rm 306, Albany, NY 12247, (518)455-2800.

MONTGOMERY, WILLIAM R.
Consultant, educator. **Personal:** Born Dec 18, 1924, Uniontown; son of Emmie Jackson Montgomery and Lee Montomery; married Sara Nelliene Prioleau, Dec 18, 1984; children: Sharon, Myra, John, Kara, William. **Educ:** Wilberforce Univ, BA, 1950; Univ of Pittsburgh, MSW, 1955, PhD, 1973; Duquesne Univ, School of Business, certificate, management, 1964. **Career:** Duquesne Univ School of Business, Continuing Education, associate, 1964-66; PEP of HEA, planned parent consultant, 1966-68; Neighborhood Centers, associate executive director, 1968-70; Univ of Pittsburgh, asst to vice chancelor, assistant professor, 1970-75; PA Dept of Health, Public Health Program, deputy secretary, 1975-78; self-employed consultant, 1979-83; WRMCO, president, 1983-. **Orgs:** Allegheny County Port Authority, vice chairman, 1972-84; American Public Transportation Association, vice pres, 1982-84; American Public Health Association, 1964-; National Assn of Social Workers, 1955-; H/B Neighborhood HEA Center, chairman, 1974-75; Black Caucus of HEA Workers, national program chairman, 1970-78; National Association of Black Social Workers, 1969-78; Academy of Certified Social Workers, 1962-. **Honors/Awds:** BCHE of APHA, Hildrus A Poindexter Award, 1978; COM of PA, Governors Transportation Award, 1977; Univ of Pittsburgh, SNMA Award, 1975; Allegheny County, Service Merit Award, 1984; APTA, Service Award, 1984. **Special Achievements:** Author: Board Members Responsibilities and Legal Liabilities, 1979; Politics: The Magic Ointment of Health, 1974; Emotional Aspects of Sickle Cell Anemia, 1973; Conceptual Eclectism: A Black Prospective on Health, 1973; Social Work, The Black Community and Family Planning, 1971. **Military Serv:** US Navy, cm 2nd class, 1942-45. **Home Addr:** 1094 Cardinal Dr, Harrisburg, PA 17111. **Business Addr:** President, WRMCO, 2451 North 3rd St, PO Box 4335, Harrisburg, PA 17111, (717)238-8711.

MONTGOMERY, WILLIE HENRY
Association executive. **Personal:** Born Feb 20, 1939, Woodville, MS; married Thelma Johnson; children: Delores, Willie Jr, Monique. **Educ:** YMCA Sch of Commerce, 1964; Loyola U, 1965; Nat AFL-CIO Hdqrtrs, internship 1973. **Career:** AFL-CIO, field rep 1985. **Orgs:** Past mem sec Young Dems of New Orleans; past chmn Labor Adv Com United Way of Gtr New Orleans; past exec bd mem LA Assn of Mntl Hlth; org LA APhilip Randolph Inst 1973; NAACP; Urban Leag of Gtr New Orleans; Met Area Com; LA Adv Cncl on Voc Tech Ed; LA Coop Org Com AFL-CIO. **Honors/Awds:** Spl Serv Award Amalgamated Transit Union ALF-CIO; Testemonial Award LA A Philip Randolph Ins; Ldrshp Contrib Award New Orleans Chap A Philip Randolph Inst; Award United Way of Gtr New Orleans. **Business Addr:** 1016 Carondelet Bldg, New Orleans, LA 70130.

MOODIE, DAHLIA MARIA
Cable television communications executive. **Personal:** Born Dec 19, 1959, San Francisco, CA; daughter of Nancy L Myers-Moodie and Alfred G Moodie. **Educ:** Coll of the Holy Names, BA Organizational Soc, Bus & Indust, Indust Rec 1981; UC Berkeley, 1982-84, MSW 1984. **Career:** Inner City Youth Program, prog dir 1978-81; St Mary's Elderly Housing, retirement training asst 1980; Youth Employment Agency, work experience counselor, trainer 1980-83; Fairmont Hosp Psychiatric Day Treatment, treatment coord 1982-84; Holy Names High School, bus dept chair, school counselor 1984-85; City of Oakland, employee asst prog; Port of Oakland, employment resources devel coord 1985-. **Orgs:** Assoc mem Assn of Labor Mgmt Admin & Consult on Alcoholism 1985-; comm mem Women and Family Issues in the Work Place ALMACA 1985-; mem bd of advisors Turning Point Career Ctr 1986-; assoc mem Amer Soc for Training & Devel 1986-; employer adv bd mem Adelante/Asians for Job Oppty 1986-; classroom consultant Jr Achievement Project Business 1986; employer adv bd mem Local Employment Devel Dept 1987-; mem bd dir Youth Employment Corp 1987-; consultant, chair Job Preparation Sem. **Honors/Awds:** Intl Dean's List 1980; Annual Scholarship Chi Kappa Rho 1980; Plaque Intl Youth in Achievement 1980; life mem Soc Sci Hon Soc Pi Gamma Mu 1981-; Scholarship CA Recreation Soc 1981; UC Berk Minority Fellowship Prog Grant 1982-84; Image Builder Awd Coll Bounders Comm 1986; publ Employment Resources Devel Prog Quarterly Newsletter for Port of Oakland tenants; media co-host Educ Highlights; Fellowship in Cable Television, Walter Kaitz Foundation 1989.

MOODY, ANNE
Writer. **Personal:** Born Sep 15, 1940, Wilkerson County, MS; daughter of Elmire Williams and Fred; married Austin Straus, Mar 9, 1967 (divorced); children: Sascha. **Educ:** Natchez Junior College; Tougaloo College, BS, 1964. **Career:** Congress of Racial Equality, Washington, DC, organizer, 1961-63, fundaraiser, 1964; Cornell University, Ithaca, NY, civil rights project coordinator, 1964-65; writer. **Orgs:** International PEN. **Honors/Awds:** Brotherhood Award, National Council of Christians and Jews, 1969; Best Book of the Year Award, National Library Association, 1969; Coming of Age in Mississippi, 1969; Silver Medal, Mademoiselle, 1970; Mr Death: Four Stories, 1975. **Business Addr:** c/o Harper & Row, 10 East 53rd St, New York, NY 10022.

MOODY, CAMERON DENNIS
Engineer. **Personal:** Born Jun 17, 1962, Chicago, IL; son of Charles and Christella Moody. **Educ:** BS, Industrial Engineering. **Career:** Ford Motor Co, engineer, 1986-93; CD Moody Construction, engineer, 1991-92; Atlanta Olympic Committee, regional logistics mgr, 1994-96; Democratic Natl Convention, dep dir of trans, 1996; Presidential Inaugural, dep dir of trans, 1996-; Denver Summit of the Eight, dir of transportation, 1997; Sinbad Soul Music Festival, Aruba, transportation coordinator, 1997; DJ Miller & Associates, chief info officer, 1997-. **Orgs:** Omega Psi Phi; NABSE. **Home Addr:** 3521 Windemere Dr, Ann Arbor, MI 48105.

MOODY, CHARLES DAVID, SR.
Educator, university administrator. **Personal:** Born Aug 30, 1932, Baton Rouge, LA; son of Rosetta Ella Hall Moody and James Nathaniel Moody; married Christella Delois Parks; children: Charles David Jr, Corey Derrick, Cameron Dennis. **Educ:** Central State Univ, BS Biology 1954; Chicago Tchrs Coll, MA Sci Ed 1961; Univ of Chicago, Cert Adv Study 1969; Northwestern Univ, PhD Ed Admin1971. **Career:** Mentally Handicapped Chicago Schs, tchr of educable 1959-62; Dist #143 1/2 Posen-Robbins IL, tchr of sci & soc studies 1962-64; Sch Dist #65 Evanston, asst principal 1964-68; Sch Dist #147, supt 1968-70; Urban Fellows TTT Prog North WU, instr 1979-70; Div of Educ Specialist Univ MI, chmn 1973-77; Proj for Fair Admn Student Disc Univ MI, dir 1975-80; Univ MI, prof educ SOE 1970-, dir prog for educ oppor 1970-87, dir ctr for sex equity in schs 1981-87, vice provost for minority affairs 1987-. **Orgs:** Fndr/ex bd NABSE 1970-; pres/fndr CD Moody & As-

socs Inc 1981-; bd dirs Ann Arbor NAACP 1983-85; bd dirs NITV. **Honors/Awds:** Awd of Respect Washtenaw Comm Coll Ann Arbor MI 1984; Dr of Laws Degree Central State Univ 1981; Comm Leader Awd Ann Arbor Veterans Admn Med Ctr 1980; Professional of the Yr Awd Ann Arbor Chap of Natl Assn of Negro Businesses & Professional Women Inc 1979; Charter Inductee, Central State Univ, Wilberforce OH 1989. **Military Serv:** AUS capt 1954-56. **Business Addr:** Vice Provost for Minority Affairs, Office of Academic Affairs, The University of Michigan, 503 Thompson St, 3052 Fleming Admin Building, Ann Arbor, MI 48109-1340.

MOODY, ERIC ORLANDO
Attorney. **Personal:** Born Jul 16, 1951, Petersburg, VA; married Sherrie Y Brown. **Educ:** Lafayette Coll, AB Philosophy 1973; Univ of VA School of Law, JD 1976. **Career:** VA Beach Police Dept, uniformed police officer 1974; WINA/WOMC Radio, reporter & announcer 1974-75; Neighborhood Youth Corps, client counselor 1975-76; Norfolk State Coll, instr 1977-78;; Eric O Moody & Assoc PC, sr partner 1976-. **Orgs:** Mem Coll Bd of Trustees; mem VA State Bar, Portsmouth Bar Assoc, Old Dominion Bar Assoc, Amer Bar Assoc, Chesapeake Bar Assoc, Twin City Bar Assoc; bd of dir Chesapeake YMCA, NAACP, Chesapeake Men for Progress, Chesapeake Forward, Boy Souts of Amer; mem Fellowship United Church of Christ. **Honors/Awds:** Dean's List; George F Baker Scholar; Debate Team; Substitute Judge City of Chesapeke; Indust Devel Authority. **Business Addr:** Senior Partner, Eric O Moody & Assoc PC, PO Box 97, Portsmouth, VA 23705.

MOODY, FREDREATHA E.
Business executive. **Personal:** Born Dec 4, 1941, Washington, DC; daughter of Susie Baker Knight and Fred Arrington; divorced; children: Bruce L, Frieda D, Suzan C, Ron K. **Educ:** Howard Univ, attended 1960-61; Montgomery Coll, attended 1971-72; Amer Univ, attended 1972-73. **Career:** Georgetown Univ, supr keypunch div 1964-70; Vitro Labs, data proc coord 1970-78; Tab Products, mkt & sales spec 1973-79; Market Concepts Inc, vice president 1980-83; Affairs by Freddi, president; Seagull Publishing & Rsch Co Inc, pres 1984; Emphasis Magazine, editor 1982-; Entrepreneuring Women Magazine, publisher & editor 1982-; District of Columbia Govt Minority Business Opportunity Comm, Washington, DC, press sec, 1984-87; Litter & Solid Waste Comm, Washington, DC, exec dir, 1987-88. **Orgs:** Chap sec Washington DC Chap Natl Assn of Market Developers Inc 1978-80; natl bd mem Natl Assn of Market Developers Inc 1980-; com mem Mayor's Complete Count Com Wash DC 1979-; chairperson-pub relations Natl Council of Negro Women DC Chap 1980-; pres Forum for Women Bus Owners 1982-83; chair Task Force for Black Women Business Owners 1983; natl sec Natl Assn of Market Developers 1982-; pres Natl Assn of Market Developers DC 1984; in-house consul to dir of develop Congressional Black Caucus Found; cofounder, bd mem, American Assn Black Women Entrepreneurs, 1983-87; mem, Natl Coalition of Black Meeting Planners, 1988-91. **Honors/Awds:** Data Entry Rookie of the Yr TAB Prods Rockville MD 1974; Outstanding Sales Performance TAB Prods Rockville MD 1975-77; 80/20 Club (top sales) TAB Prods Rockville MD 1978; Cert of Appreciation Census Adv Com Office of the Mayor Washington DC 1980. **Home Addr:** 146 Majestic Cir, Virginia Beach, VA 23452-1700.

MOODY, HAROLD L.
Educator (retired). **Personal:** Born Sep 6, 1932, Chicago, IL; married Shirley Mc Donald; children: Michele Marcia. **Educ:** Chicago Teacher, BE 1954, ME 1961. **Career:** Williams Elem School, teacher 8 yrs; Ray Elem School, teacher 8 yrs; S Shore HS, audio visual con 1 yr; Deneen Elem School, principal 1970-90. **Orgs:** Bd of dir Elementary Press Assoc, Phi Delta Kappa, Chicago Principal Assoc, Chicago Area Reading Assoc, Intl Reading Assoc, Block Club, Steering Comm Police Comm Workshops 3rd dist; mem bd of dir Salem House Luth Soc Serv Agency; mem First Unitarian Church. **Honors/Awds:** Best Teacher Awd Chicago Bd of Ed; Scholarship Harvard Univ 1963; Serv Awd Park Manor Neighbors Comm Org 1979. **Military Serv:** USNG 2 yrs.

MOODY, WILLIAM DENNIS
Dentist. **Personal:** Born Jun 6, 1948, White Plains, NY; son of Ellen Rebecca Moody and William Moody Jr. **Educ:** North Central Coll, BA 1970; SUNY Buffalo, DDS 1974. **Career:** Private practice, dentist. **Orgs:** Program chmn Greater Metropolitan Dental Soc 1977-78; bd of dirs Greenburgh Neighborhood Health Center 1979-81, Greenburgh Comm Center 1982-83, Thomas H Slater Center 1984-91; mem White Plains Dental Forum, Scarsdale Dental Soc; bd of dir Union Child Day Care Center; mem Amer Dental Assn, Alpha Omega Frat, Natl Dental Assn, Greater Metro New York Dental Soc; pres, Greater Metropolitan Dental Society, 1987-89; corresponding secretary Greater Metropolitan New York Dental Society 1990-91. **Business Addr:** 48 Mamaroneck Ave, White Plains, NY 10601.

MOON, WALTER D.
Government official. **Personal:** Born Aug 10, 1940, Marietta, GA; married Winford G Strong; children: Sonja, Sonita. **Educ:** Kennesaw Jr Coll; Savannah State Coll; Inst Computer Tech 1967. **Career:** Mails US Postal Serv Marietta GA, foreman; part-time bldg contractor. **Orgs:** Treas Future Devel Assn Inc Pres Concerned Citizens of Marietta; mem NAACP; Mem Marietta Cobb Bridges Prog; v-chmn Marietta Bd Edn; only Black elected Marietta Civil Serv Commn; mem USN Manpower Speakers Team Freshman Scholastic Savannah State Coll USN 1960-64. **Military Serv:** USNR chief petty ofcr 1966-. **Business Addr:** 257 Lawrence St NE, Marietta, GA 30060.

MOON, WARREN
Professional football player. **Personal:** Born Nov 18, 1956, Los Angeles, CA; married Felicia Hendricks Moon; children: Joshua, Chelsea, Blair, Jeffrey. **Educ:** Univ of Washington. **Career:** Quarterback: Edmonton Eskimos (CFL), 1978-84; Houston Oilers, 1984-94; Minnesota Vikings, 1994-96; Seattle Seahawks, 1997-; Began Warren Moon's Chocolate Chippery while in Edmonton; has since sold stores and formed new corporation in Houston. **Orgs:** The Crescent Moon Foundation, founder. **Honors/Awds:** MVP in Rose Bowl victory over Michigan; career marks at WA, 142 of 496 for 3,277 yds passing and 19 TDs with career long of 78 yards in 1975; profl, holds two Oilers' passing records after one season - most yards gained passing 3,338, breaking old mark set by George Blanda and sharing with Blanda record for most 300 plus yard games passing in a season; pass attempts and completions are third best in Oilers history; named All NFL Rookie Team by Pro Football Writers, UPI, and Pro Football Weekly; Football Digest's Rookie All-Star Team; NFL Man of the Year, 1989; named to Pro Bowl, 1988-92; AFC Passing Leader, 1992; holds NFL single-season records for most passes attempted-665, 1991; holds record for most passes completed-404; one of nine African-American quarterbacks, largest number in NFL history, 1997. **Business Addr:** Professional Football Player, Seattle Seahawks, 11220 NE 53rd St, Kirkland, WA 98033, (206)827-9777.

MOONE, JAMES CLARK
Educator, project director. **Personal:** Born Aug 11, 1938, Fountain Inn, SC; son of Lillie Moone and Jimmie Lee Moone; married Rev Ruby Reese, Nov 20, 1960; children: Malaika (Ruby), Afua (Jamesa). **Educ:** SC State Univ, BS 1958; Morgan State Univ, MS 1967; Howard Univ, PhD 1976. **Career:** Pilgrim H&L Ins Co, asst mgr 1959-69; Washington DC Public Schools, principal 1965-72; Georgetown Univ, prof 1978-82, founding dir African Studies 1982-84. **Orgs:** Life mem, Montgomery County MD & Exec bd NAACP 1963-87; mem-at-large PUSH 1969-87; mem Rockville, MD, Pythagoras Lodge #74 33 degree PHA 1969-; bd dir SCLC Montgomery Co MD, chapter, 1980-; bd of appeals City of Rockville MD 1987-; dir communications & life mem, Alpha Phi Alpha 1976-; pred & vp, exec dir Intl United Black Fund Inc. **Honors/Awds:** 150 Awards, NSF Grants, Univ of Akron 1965-70; Human Rights Awd, City of Rockville 1979; Amer Leadership Awd, City of Denver 1987. **Special Achievements:** Author: The Physical Qualities of Life in Sub-Sahara Africa, Brunswick Publishing Co, 1985; 200 newspaper & journal articles. **Home Addr:** 1204 Potomac Valley Rd, Rockville, MD 20850, (301)762-1822.

MOONE, WANDA RENEE
Consultant. **Personal:** Born Oct 12, 1956, Greensboro, NC; daughter of Beulah Moone and Connell Moone; divorced; children: Dedrick L. **Educ:** NC A&T State Univ, BS (cum laude) 1982; Univ NC Chapel Hill, MSW 1983. **Career:** Bowman Group Sch of Medicine Amos Cotlage Rehab Hosp, social worker I 1983-85; St James Nursing Ctr Inc, dir social serv 1985-87; Rockingham Council on Aging, case manager 1987-89; Piedmont Triad Council of Governments, regional long term care ombudsman 1989-90; Youth Focus Psychiatric Hospital, director of social work, 1990-94; Guilford County Department of Social Services, child protection services supervisor, currently. **Orgs:** NASW 1982-; Alpha Delta Mu 1982-; field instructor Bennett Coll 1985-86, NC A&T State Univ & UNC Greensboro 1986-; NC Assn of Black Social Workers 1987-90; NAACP 1987-; NC Assn of Health Care Facilities 1987-88; Academy of Certified Social Workers, 1988; Alzheimer's Assn, 1989; advisory committee member United Services for Older Adults 1989-90. **Honors/Awds:** NC Dean's List 1979-80; Certificate Alpha Delta Mu Natl Social Work Hon Soc Rho Chap 1982-. **Business Addr:** Guilford County DSS, PO Box 2288, Greensboro, NC 27402.

MOORE, ACEL
Editorial board member. **Personal:** Born Oct 5, 1940, Philadelphia, PA; divorced; children: Acel Jr. **Educ:** Settlement Music Sch 1954-58; Charles Morris Price Sch 1966-64. **Career:** Philadelphia Inquirer, assoc editor 1981-, staff writer 1968-81, editorial clerk 1964; copy boy 1965. **Orgs:** Pres Philadelphia Assn of Black Journalists; founding mem Nat Assn of Black Journalists Sigma Delta Chi; mem Amer Soc of Newspaper Editors, Pulitzer Prize Juror. **Honors/Awds:** Mng editors award PA Assn of Press 1975-76; PA Prison Soc award; humanitarian award House of Umoja; comm serv award Youth Devel Ctr; journalism award Philadelphia Party 1976; Philadelphia Bar Assn award; paul robeson award Afro-Am History Mus 1976; Nat Headliners award; natl clarion award Women in Communication; Nat Bus League of Philadelphia award; N Philadelphia Mothers Concern award; achievement award White Rock Bapt Ch; yvonne motley mccabe award Swarthmore Coll Annual UpwardBound 1977; nieman flwshp Harvard Univ 1979-80; scales of justice award Philadelphia Bar Assn 1970; Pulitzer Prize 1976; Robert F Kennedy Jour Awd 1976; Heywood Broun Awd 1976. **Military Serv:** AUS 1959-62. **Business Addr:** Associate Editor, Philadelphia Inquirer, 400 N Broad St, Philadelphia, PA 19101.

MOORE, ALBERT
Public relations consultant, educational administrator. **Personal:** Born Feb 17, 1952, Johnsonville, SC; married Marie Durant; children: Porchia Atiya, Chelsey Maria. **Educ:** Friendship Jr Coll, 1970-71; Benedict Coll, BA Pol Sci 1974; Univ of SC, Publ Admin 1979-80; SC Criminal Justice Acad, Cert Correction Officer 1981-. **Career:** Crayton Middle School, sub techer 1974-75; Square D Co, prod coord 1975-76; US Auto Assoc, vice pres mktg & publ relations 1976-77; Al's Drive In Restaurant, owner 1976-77; Benedict Coll, equip mgr 1977-79, tech asst, dean of acad affairs 1979-82; Natl Conf of Black Mayors Prog, asst dir 1979-82; Central Correctional Inst, correction officer II 1981-83; Benedict Coll, coord of spec svcs, publ relations 1982-84; St Augustines Coll, dir public relations1984-. **Orgs:** Attend confs & workshops in vairous cities Natl Conf of Black Mayors 1979,80,81,82; seminar Robert R Morton Mem Inst 1980; panalist Amer Census Bureau Workshop 1980; participant Assoc of Records Mgrs 1981; mem Benedict Coll Jr Alumni Club, Drexel Lake Residents Civic Org, NAACP, SCARMA, SC Correction Officers Assoc; charter mem Benedict Coll Tiger Club. **Honors/Awds:** Alternate delegate Richland Cty Dem Convention 1984. **Home Addr:** 2020 Drexel Lake Dr, Columbia, SC 29223. **Business Addr:** Dir of Publicity & Pub Rel, St Augustines College, 1315 Oakwood Ave, Raleigh, NC 27611.

MOORE, ALFRED
Chief executive officer. **Personal:** Born Feb 24, 1956, Detroit, MI; divorced. **Educ:** Adrian College, Adrian, MI, BA, accounting, 1978; State of Michigan, certified public accountant; numerous seminars. **Career:** New Center Hospital, Detroit, MI, administrator, 1986-90; Central City Health Services, Inc, Detroit, MI, exec dir, 1984-; New Center Clinic-East, Detroit, MI, exec dir, 1986-; New Center Hospital, Detroit, MI, chief executive officer, 1990-. **Orgs:** Life time member, NAACP; president, Block Club. **Business Addr:** Chief Executive Officer, New Center Hospital, 801 Virginia Park, Detroit, MI 48202.

MOORE, ALICE EVELYN
Educator. **Personal:** Born Feb 16, 1933, Washington, NC. **Educ:** Tuskegee Inst, Social Studies 1950-55; NM Highlands Univ, History/Ed 1961-62; Johns Hopkins Univ, Certificate Negro & Sou Hist 1969-70; North TX State Univ, Certificate Aging Specialist 1979,82. **Career:** Young Women's Christian Assoc, teen-age dir 1955-56; Emerson Settlement House, group work 1957-58; Friendship Jr Coll, instr social sci 1962-71; Elizabeth City State Univ, instr social sci 1971-73; Claflin Coll, asst prof social sci 1974-80; Allen Univ, assoc prof social sci 1981-, interim dir academic affairs 1985-86, coord gerontology prog 1981-. **Orgs:** Counselor Epworth Children's Home 1981; mem/secty Resource Mobilization Adv Council Dept Social Serv of Richland Co 1981-84; founder/secty/treas Orangeburg Branch Assoc for Study of Life & History. **Honors/Awds:** Volunteer of the Year Epworth Children's Home 1986. **Business Addr:** Coord Gerontology Prog/Soc Sci, c/o Allen University, 1530 Harden St, Columbia, SC 29204.

MOORE, ALLYN D.
Automobile dealer. **Personal:** Born Aug 9, 1960, Chicago, IL; son of Buck & Elizabeth Moore; married Cheryl Moore, Oct 17, 1992; children: Cydney, Zackery. **Educ:** Bradley University, Peoria, Illinois, graduated. **Career:** Ford Motor Credit, Chicago/St Louis; Quality Ford-Mercury, owner, currently. **Orgs:** Southside Bapt Ch, business comm, long range planning comm; FLMMDA; NADA; Princeton Chamber of Commerce, bd mem; Optimist Club; United Way, past bd mem. **Honors/Awds:** KY-TN Lease, Contest Dealer of the Year, 1993; Paducah, KY, Minority Business Association, Minority Businessman of the Year, 1997; Dealer Development, Alumni Award. **Business Addr:** Owner, Quality Ford-Mercury Inc, 311 Hwy 62 W, Princeton, KY 42445, (502)365-3673.

MOORE, ALSTORK EDWARD
Airline executive. **Personal:** Born May 12, 1940, Washington, DC; son of Charles E Moore; married Geraldine L Hagens; children: Anthony, Robert, Shannon, Samuel. **Educ:** Montgomery Coll, Washington, DC, AA, 1967-71; Amer Univ, Washinton, DC, BS, 1971-73. **Career:** United Airlines, Philadelphia, PA, supvr passenger serv, 1977-78; New York, NY, operation mgr cargo, 1978-81, New York, NY, staff representative personnel, 1981-82, Lincoln, NE, mgr of station operations, 1982-85, Washington, DC, mgr cust serv, 1985-86, gen mgr, customer serv, 1986-. **Orgs:** Mem, United Methodist Men, 1982-. **Honors/Awds:** Award of Merit, United Airlines, 1977, 1980. **Military Serv:** US Air Force, sergeant, 1958-65; received Good Conduct, 1961, 1964, Outstanding Unit, 1964, Longevity, 1965.

MOORE, ANNIE JEWELL
Couturiere/fashion designer. **Personal:** Born Sep 20, 1919, Daytona Beach, FL; daughter of Ora Lee Moore Hall (deceased) and James Moore (deceased). **Educ:** Spelman Coll, AB 1943; Fashion Academy, Golden Pen Certificate 1951-52; Ecole Guerre-Lavigne, Paris France, Certificate 1954; Marygrove Coll, Certificate 1976. **Career:** Ann Moore Couturiere Inc, fashion designer, pres 1952-70; Detroit Public Sch System, teacher 1972-82; Atlanta Public Sch System, teacher 1985-86; Rich's Academy, couturiere teacher, 1986-91; Military Justice Clinic Inc, receptionist, 1991. **Orgs:** Past pres, Michigan Women's Civic Council; vice pres Detroit Chap of The NAASC 1980-82; chairperson of awds comm of the Atlanta Chap of NAASC 1986-87; mem, Ad Hoc Committee for Clothing and Textile, appointed 1965. **Honors/Awds:** Produced Cent Fash Focus Spelman's 100th Anniversary 1981; Michigan Women Civic Council Awd 1982; Certificates of Recognition, Detroit Chapter of the Natl Alumnae Assn of Spelman College. **Special Achievements:** Benefactors of Education, founders, 1990; Donated fashion designs created over a 40 year period; donated fashion designs to the Atlanta Historical Society; taught a practicum on costume design, Drama Department of Spelman College, 1983-84. **Home Addr:** 988 Palmetto Ave SW, Atlanta, GA 30314-3128.

MOORE, ANTHONY LOUIS
Business executive. **Personal:** Born Jan 10, 1946, Chicago, IL; married Joyce M Watson; children: Jason A. **Educ:** Southern Illinois Univ, BS 1971; DePaul Univ, Grad Study 1976; Univ of Illinois Chicago, Grad Study 1978. **Career:** Vince Cullers Advertising, media buyer 1971-73, media planner 1973-74; Proctor & Gardner Advertising, assoc media dir 1974-76, media dir 1976-78, vice pres advertising serv, sr vice pres advertising serv, 1990. **Orgs:** Bd mem Faulkner School 1984-; mem Amer Advertising Fed 1971-; mem Amer Mgmt Assn 1976-; mem Natl Assn Market Devel 1975-; advisory bd Chicago YMCA 1976-; Alpha Delta Sigma 1970-; mem Stepp School; mem Chicago Media Director's Council 1986; Target Adv Pros. **Honors/Awds:** Creative Advertising Certificate, Assn of Natl Advertisers; Black Media Merit, Black Media Inc; Employee of the Year, Proctor & Gardner; Achievement Award, YMCA. **Military Serv:** USMC E-4 1967-69; USMC Combat Corres Assn 1968-. **Business Addr:** Sr Vice Pres, Advertising Svcs, Proctor Communications Network, 980 N Michigan Ave, Chicago, IL 60611.

MOORE, ARCHIBALD LEE WRIGHT
Former light-heavyweight champion. **Personal:** Born Dec 13, 1916, Benoit, MS; married Joan; children: Anthony, D'Angelo, Hardy, Joanie, Rena, Billy. **Career:** Former Light-heavyweight boxing champion for ten yrs; dr training Any Boy Can Clubs; Dept of Housing and Urban Development, special assistant to Samuel Pierce, LA, 1980-89; trainer/advisor to George Foreman; boxing instructor, currently. **Orgs:** Mem NAACP; Urban League; Optimists Club; founder, dir ABC (Any Boy Can) Club 1965-. **Honors/Awds:** Winner of 194 out of 229 professional bouts; 2nd Greatest Light Heavyweight Champion Ring Mag; Light Heavyweight Champion 1952. **Business Addr:** Boxing Instructor, 3517 E St, San Diego, CA 92102.

MOORE, ARCHIE BRADFORD, JR.
Educator (retired). **Personal:** Born Jan 8, 1933, Montgomery, AL; son of Annie Ruth Jeter and Archie B Moore Sr; married Dorothy Ann Flowers; children: Angelo Juan, Kimberly D'Anna. **Educ:** AL State univ, BS 1959, MEd 1961; KS State Univ, PhD 1974. **Career:** Russell Co Public School System, teacher 1959-61; Montgomery Co Public School Sys, teacher 1961-69; Clarke Coll, asst prof of soc sci 1970-75; AL State Univ, dir of TCCP 1975-77; AL State Univ, coord of continuing educ 1977-78, dean of evening & weekend coll & public serv 1978-83, prof of educ & spec asst to dean of grad studies & cont educ 1983-91. **Orgs:** Mem Natl Educ Assn; mem AL Assn of Social Science & History Teachers; mem Amer Fed of Musicians Affiliated with AFL-CIO; mem Phi Beta Sigma Frat; mem Phi Delta Kappa Prof Educ Frat; mem Assn for Continuing Higher Educ; mem Natl Comm Educ Assn; chmn Catholic Charity Drive; mem Holy Name Soc; mem AL Center for Higher Educ Comm Serv Comm; mem College of Educ Curriculum Comm AL State Univ; mem AL State Univ Council of Academic Deans; chmn Resurrection Catholic School System Bd of Educ. **Honors/Awds:** Grant Natl Science Found 1965; Fellowship Natl Defense Educ Act 1967, 1968, 1969; Fellowship Educ Prof Develop Act 1972-74; State Awd AL Social Studies Fair Teacher Recognition 1968. **Military Serv:** USN petty officer 3rd class 1952-56. **Home Addr:** 2966 Vandy Dr, Montgomery, AL 36110.

MOORE, ARNOLD D.
Hearings officer secretary of state. **Personal:** Born Mar 31, 1916, Selmer, TN; married Emma; children: Joyce Parson, Barbara Rochelle. **Educ:** Springfield Jr Coll. **Career:** St Paul AME Ch Springfield, asst pastor; Allen Chapel AME Ch Taylorville, IL, pastor; State Office, claims examiner 1947-49; Dept Pub Welfare, pubrel 1949-59; juv prob officer 1959; Sec of State Titles & Regist Vehicle Sect, adminstr/hearings officer. **Orgs:** Mem bd Salvation Arym; Comm Action; Mental Health; USO; ARC; Ministrial Alliance; AME Coalition; 1st pres local chap NAACP. **Honors/Awds:** Outstanding Layman's Award 1965; Scouters Key. **Military Serv:** AUS Capt; Commendation Medal. **Business Addr:** Hearings Officer, Secretary of State, Centennial Bldg, Springfield, IL 62722.

MOORE, BEVERLY
Mayor, educational administrator. **Career:** City of Kalamazoo, mayor, currently; Western Michigan University, School of Social Work, director of admissions, currently. **Special Achievements:** First African-American female mayor of Kalamazoo. **Business Addr:** Mayor, City of Kalamazoo, 241 W South St, Kalamazoo, MI 49007, (616)337-8047.

MOORE, BOBBY. See RASHAD, AHMAD.

MOORE, BRENDA CAROL
Mortgage banker. **Personal:** Born Sep 6, 1945, Buffalo, NY; daughter of Anna York and James Evans; married Stanley Moore, Aug 17, 1974; children: Toi C Rice, Shana K Moore. **Educ:** State Univ of New York at Buffalo, Buffalo, NY, 1971-74. **Career:** Marine Midland Bank, Buffalo, NY, assistant vice president. **Orgs:** American Bankers; New York State Collectors Assn; Erie County Assessors Assn. **Honors/Awds:** Award of Excellence, Empire of America, 1986.

MOORE, CARMAN LEROY
Composer, music critic, educator. **Personal:** Born Oct 8, 1936, Lorain, OH; divorced; children: Martin, Justin. **Educ:** OH State U, BMus 1958; Juilliard Sch of Music, MS 1966. **Career:** Manhattanville Coll, asst prof of music/composer; New School for Social Research, Queens Coll, NY; Univ Yale Graduate School of Music; The Village Voice, music critic 1965-, NY Times; contributed since 1969; The Saturday Review; Master Composer-The American Dance Festival, rock lyricist; The Skymusic Ensemble, founder and conductor. **Orgs:** ASCAP. **Honors/Awds:** Compositions include "Mass for the 21st Century," commissioned by Lincoln Ctr for the Performing Arts; "African Tears"; "Drum Major"; "Wildfires & Field Songs" (commissioned by NY Philharmonic Orch); "Gospel Fuse" (commissioned by San Francisco Symphony Orch); Hit, A Concerto for Percussion and Orchestra "Wild Gardens of the Loup Garou" music theatre work "Paradise-Lost The Musical" and "Journey to Benares"; Opera, "The Last Chance Planet" and "Gethsemane Park" (libretto by Ishmael Reed). **Home Addr:** 152 Columbus Ave, New York, NY 10023.

MOORE, CHANTE
Vocalist. **Personal:** Born in San Francisco, CA. **Career:** MCA Records, vocalist, currently. **Special Achievements:** Albums include: "Precious," "A Love Supreme.". **Business Phone:** (615)244-8944.

MOORE, CHARLES W.
Educational administrator, business executive. **Personal:** Born Nov 2, 1923, Macon, GA; son of Rose Bud Cornelius Moore and Henry Moore; married Mary Agnes DuBose; children: Tallulah Ragsdale. **Educ:** Morris Brown Coll, AB 1950; NY U, MBA 1952; Univ of UT, MS 1975; Daniel Payne Coll, Dr of Humane Letters 1971; Morris Brown Coll, LLD 1980. **Career:** Morris Brown Coll, bus mgr 1951-66; US Dept of HEW, educ prog officer 1966-78; US Dept of HHS, financial mgr 1978-85; Morris Brown Coll, vice pres finance 1985-91; BMA Financial Services, vice pres, currently. **Orgs:** Treas Am Assn of Coll & Univ Bus Off 1960-66; mem Assn of Govt Accountants 1983-; treas Atlanta Investment Assoc Inc 1956-; chmn bd of dir Butler St YMCA 1979-81; natl treas Phi Beta Sigma Frat Inc 1970-93; pres Natl Alumni Assn Morris Brown Coll 1984-85; mem bd of stewards Big Bethel AME Ch 1955. **Honors/Awds:** Alumnus of the Yr Morris Brown Coll Natl Alumni Assn 1968 & 1975; Distinguished Serv Award Phi Beta Sigma Frat Inc 1978; Distinguished Serv Award Rust Coll 1971; Distinguished Leadership Award United Negro Coll Fund 1985; Special Achievement Award US Dept of Health & Human Serv 1984. **Military Serv:** AUS staff sgt; Good Conduct Medal. **Home Addr:** 734 Flamingo Dr SW, Atlanta, GA 30311.

MOORE, CHARLIE W.
Consulting engineer. **Personal:** Born Feb 16, 1926, Chattanooga, TN; son of Vallie Turner Moore and Simon Moore; married Elva M Stanley; children: Charlie W Jr, Kelli Noelle. **Educ:** Hampton Inst, BS 1950; Univ of AL, 1951; Villanova Univ, 1967-68; USAF Civil Engineering Officer, diploma, 1957. **Career:** USA Corps of Engr Anchorage AL Dist, struc engr 1951-52; AUS Corps of Engrs N Atlantic Div, constr mgmt engr 1952-55; USAF New Castle Co Airport, constr mgmt engr 1955-57; USAF Fifth AF Ashiya & Tokyo, Japan, gen engr 1957-58; Ankara Turkey USAFE HQ USLOG, maintenance engr 1958-61; AUS Corps of Engrs, civil engr 1962, Civil Defense Support Br, civil engr 1962-65, chief resident engr, support group 1975-79; Engrg Support Serv Corp, pres, 1981-; FEMA NY, suprv civil engr; Fed Civil Serv Reg II, retired. **Orgs:** Mem Amer Soc of Civil Engrs, Soc of Amer Military Engrs, PA Soc of Professional Engrs, Camphor United Meth Church; mem Natl Defense Exec Reserve, Frontiers Intl. **Honors/Awds:** Letter of Appreciation, Yahata Labor Mmgt Office 1st US civilian to receive a letter of apprec, Mssrs Schechet Kasparian Falcey support provided in connection with Mercer Cty Survey Briefing 1974, Mercer Cty CD Coord 1974; Outstanding Performance New England Div USC of E 1976; Outstanding Commendation DefenseCivil Preparation Agency 1978; Mr Lynch Comm Shelter Prog Jerry Vallery GSA Philadelphia Philadelphia Urban Coalition School Prog for Minority Contractors; Mr Duscha Qualified Instrs Briefing Conf New York City 1969. **Military Serv:** US Navy, MM3C, 1944-46. **Business Addr:** President, Engineering Support Serv Corp, 526 Main St, Darby, PA 19023-2514.

MOORE, CHRISTINE JAMES
Educational administrator (retired). **Personal:** Born Sep 9, 1930, Windsor, NC; daughter of Maude Boxley James and Henry James; married Marcellus; children: Lisa M Barkley. **Educ:** Morgan State Coll Baltimore, BA 1952; Columbia Univ New York, MA 1962; Johns Hopkins Univ Syracuse Univ. **Career:** Booker T Washington Jr HS, tchr 1952-59; counselor 1959-64; Balt Secondary Schs, specialist guidance 1965-69; Workshop Employment Opportunities for Disadvantaged Youth Johns Hopkins U, asst dir 1966; instr 1969-70; Dev Studies Community Coll Balt, dir 1969-74; Comm Coll Balt Harbor Campus, dean student services 1974-79; Comm Coll Balt, dean staff devel present; Comm Coll of Baltimore, retired exec asst to the pres 1979-83; House of Delegates of the MD Gen Assembly, reader; freelance actress. **Orgs:** Commn Higher Educ Middle States Assn Coll & Secondary Schs 1977-83; mem Am Personnel & Guidance Assn; Am Coll Personnel Assn; bd dir Mun Employees Credit Union of Baltimore 1975-83; bd dir Arena Players Comm Theater; bd of dir 4th Dist Dem Orgn 1980-82; Mayor's Steering Com Balt Best Promotional Camp 1976-87; NAACP; Nat Council Negro Women; Urban League Consult counseling & human relations; pub speaker; publs in periodicals; bd dir Baltimore MD Metro YWCA 1983-86; bd of examiners Speech Pathology 1983-85; commissioner Commission on Med Discipline for MD 1984-88; bd of trust City Temple of Balto Baptist Church 1986-87; mem Maryland State Bd of Physicians Quality Assurance 1988-94; mem Am Fed of Television and Radio Artists 1983-; regional dir Delta Sigma Theta 1968-70; Screen Actors Gui 1991-. **Honors/Awds:** Outstanding Educators of Am 1973; Outstanding Delta of Yr 1974; Arean Players Artistic Awd Community Theater Group 1979; 100 Outstanding Women in Baltimore Delta Sigma Theta Sor 1975; One Hundred Outstanding Black Women of Baltimore Emmanuel Christian Community Church 1988. **Home Addr:** 3501 Hilton Rd, Baltimore, MD 21215.

MOORE, CLEOTHA FRANKLIN
Association executive. **Personal:** Born Sep 16, 1942, Canton, MS; son of Luevenia Lee McGee Moore and Sam A Moore; married Normajo Ramsey Moore, Jun 26, 1965; children: Faith Veleen, Sterling Kent. **Educ:** IN Central Univ, BS 1960-64; Ball State Univ, Ed 1965-; IN Univ Purdue Univ Indpls, Bus Studies 1975-. **Career:** Wood HS Indianapolis Publ School Syst, teacher, coach 1964-69; IN Natl Bank, personnel admin 1969-74; RCA/Consumer Electronics, employee relations mgr 1974-90; United Way of Central Indiana, director of human resources, 1990-. **Orgs:** 1st vp, newsletter ed IN State Missionary Bapt Convention 1968-79; mem NAACP 1969-; trustee, asst treas S Calvary Bapt Church 1977-; pres Audubon Terr Neighborhood Assoc 1978-85; mem Mayor's Ridesharing Work Rescheduling Task Force 1979; bd mem Metro School Dist of Warren Twp (1st black to be elected to this post); bd of directors, Near East Side Multi Service Center, 1983-89; bd of directors, Indianapolis Day Nursery Assn, 1988-90; mentor, Business Encouraging Success for Tomorrow, 1990-; mentor, Indianapolis Public School System, 1990-. **Honors/Awds:** Work study Grant IN Central Coll 1960-64; IN State HS Wrestling Champion IN HS Athletic Assoc 1960; Coll Wrestling Championship Awds IN Little State Coll Conf 1962, 1964; Spoke Aws Indianapolis Jaycees 1971; Spark Awd Indianapolis Jaycees 1972; Serv Awd Indianapolis Headstart Prog 1974. **Business Addr:** Director of Human Resources, United Way of Central Indiana, 1828 N Meridian St, Indianapolis, IN 46202.

MOORE, COLIN A.
Attorney. **Personal:** Born Apr 24, 1944, Manchester Village, Berbice, Guyana; son of Olive Muriel Moore and Victor Emmanuel Moore; married Ela Babb, May 18, 1985; children: Simone Moore. **Educ:** Univ of the West Indies, Kingston Jamaica, BSc, 1963; Univ of London, London England, MA, 1968; doctoral study at Princeton Univ, Princeton NJ; Brooklyn Law School, Brooklyn NY, 1978. **Career:** Douglas College, Rutgers Univ, New Brunswick NJ, lecturer, 1971-75; Wachtell Lipton Rosen Katz, New York NY, paralegal, 1975-76; Attorney General, State of New York, New York NY, law clerk, 1976-78; Bronx County NY, New York NY, asst district attorney, 1978-79; self-employed attorney, Brooklyn NY, 1979-. **Orgs:** Legal Redress Committee, NAACP, Jamaica Chapter, chmn 1978-81, board mem 1979-82; St Albans Local Devel Corp, Queens NY, 1979-82; pres, Macon B Allen Bar Assn, 1980-83; pres, Carribean Action Lobby, 1981-82; board mem, Natl Bar Assn, 1981-83; mem, Natl Conference of Black Lawyers, 1982-84; board mem, Medgar Evers Center for Law & Social Justice, 1986-. **Honors/Awds:** Amer Jurisprudence Award, Lawyers Coop Publishing House, 1976; Leadership Award, Sesame Flyers Intl, 1987; Achievement and Community Service Award, Med-

gar Evers College, 1987; Distinguished Service Award, Jamaica Natl Movement, 1988; Humanitarian Award, Vidcap Inc, 1989; author of The Simpson-Mazzoli Bill: Two Steps Forward, One Step Backward, 1984; author of The History of African Liberation Movements from Os Palmares to Montgomery, 1989; author of collection of articles, 1989. **Business Addr:** Attorney-At-Law, 16 Court St, Ste 1212, Brooklyn, NY 11241.

MOORE, CORNELL LEVERETTE
Attorney. **Personal:** Born Sep 18, 1939, Tignall, GA; son of Luetta T Moore and Jesse L Moore; married Wenda Weekes; children: Lynne M, Jonathon C, Meredith L. **Educ:** VA Union Univ, AB 1961; Howard Univ Law School, JD, 1964. **Career:** US Treasury, staff attorney, 1962-64; Crocker Bank, trust admin, 1964-66; Comptroller of Currency, US Treasury, Regional counsel, 1966-68; NW Natl Bank of Minneapolis, asst vice pres & legal officer, 1968-70; Shelter Mortgage Co Inc, exec vice pres & dir 1970-73; Shelard Natl Bank, dir 1973-78; Hennepin Co Bar Found, pres 1975-78; Golden Valley Bank, dir 1978-; Lease More Equipment Inc, pres & CEO, 1977-86; Miller & Schroeder Financial Inc, sr vice pres & general counsel, 1987-95; Dorsey and Whitney, partner, 1995-. **Orgs:** Trustee, Dunwoody Inst; dir Greater Minneapolis Housing Corp; trustee VA Union Univ; trustee, Howard University; chairman, Greater Minneapolis Visitors & Convention Assoc; William Mitchell College of Law, trustee; Johnson C Smith Univ, trustee; Minnesota Better Bus Bureau, dir; Minneapolis Public Housing Authority, commissioner. **Business Addr:** Partner, Dorsey and Whitney, LLP, 220 S 6th St, #1900, Minneapolis, MN 55402, (612)340-6331.

MOORE, CYNTHIA M.
Journalist. **Personal:** Born Nov 11, 1963, Columbus, OH; daughter of Barbara Price Hughes and Jackie Moore. **Educ:** Ohio State University, Columbus, OH, BA, 1990. **Career:** WSYX, TV 6, ABC, Good Morning Columbus, producer, currently. **Orgs:** Member, National Association of Black Journalists. **Honors/Awds:** American Heart Association Media Award, 1992. **Home Addr:** 3751 Rosewell Dr, Columbus, OH 43227. **Business Addr:** Producer, Good Morning Columbus, WSYX-TV 6, ABC, 1261 Dublin Rd, Columbus, OH 43215.

MOORE, DAVID BERNARD, II
Educator (retired). **Personal:** Born Jul 13, 1940, Uniontown, AL. **Educ:** AL State Univ, BS 1960; Fordham Univ, Special 1962; Univ of AL, MA 1972. **Career:** Superior Graphics, dir 1973-79; RC Hatch HS, teacher 1981-90. **Orgs:** Pres Uniontown Civic League 1970-; city councilman 1972-. **Honors/Awds:** Versality Award, 1975. **Home Addr:** PO Box 635, Uniontown, AL 36786.

MOORE, DAVID M.
Food company executive. **Personal:** Born May 2, 1955, Chattanooga, TN; son of Clara S Moore and David Moore. **Educ:** Univ of Wisconsin, Eau Claire, WI, BA, business admin, 1986. **Career:** Miller Brewing Co, Milwaukee, WI, group manager, 1977-82; Miller Brewing Co, San Francisco, CA, area manager, 1982-85; Miller Brewing Co, Los Angeles, CA, marketing development mgr, 1986; Quality Croutons Inc, Chicago, IL, vice president, 1986-. **Business Addr:** Vice President, Quality Croutons Inc, 825-29 W 37th Place, Chicago, IL 60609.

MOORE, DERRICK
Professional football player. **Personal:** Born Oct 13, 1967, Albany, GA. **Educ:** Albany Junior College; Troy State; Northeastern Oklahoma State. **Career:** Detroit Lions, running back, 1993-94; Carolina Panthers, 1995; Arizona Cardinals, 1996-. **Business Addr:** Professional Football Player, Arizona Cardinals, 8701 S Hardy, Tempe, AZ 85284, (602)379-0101.

MOORE, DWAYNE HARRISON
Public housing. **Personal:** Born Oct 27, 1958, Joliet, IL; son of Patricia Moore and William Moore; children: Latasha Ann Davis, Bryan Dwayne. **Educ:** Joliet Jr Coll, AAS 1980; Northeastern Illinois Univ, BA (w/Honors) 1983; Univ of Chicago, Graduate Study 1984-85; Sangamon State Univ, MPA 1987. **Career:** Springfield Housing Authority, operations rsch & analysis. **Orgs:** Mem Amer Soc for Public Admin 1984-, Alpha Phi Alpha Frat Inc 1986-, Springfield Jaycees 1986-, Natl Black MBA Assoc 1987; Big Brothers KIDS & PALS Program 1988-89. **Honors/Awds:** HUD Local Govt Internship Prog Scholarship 1984-86; Outstanding Achievement in Comm & Public Serv Minority Svcs/Black Student Caucus Sangamon State Univ 1985-86; interviewed on public service cable TV on subject of black history 1987; United States Achievement Academy Collegiate Academic All-Amer 1987; US Achievement Academy Natl Collegiate Student Govt Awd Winner 1987; Outstanding Young Men of Amer 1988.

MOORE, EARL B.
Clergyman. **Personal:** Born Feb 2, 1930, Tulsa; married Cora Thornton; children: Julin, Jeanelle. **Educ:** MDiv 1956; MST 1969; DMin 1976. **Career:** NY State Dept Correctional Svc, dir of ministerial serv 1973-; St Paul Bapt Ch, minister 1965-; New York City Dept of Corr, chpln 1963; Shilo Bapt Ch, pastor 1960-63; New York City Mission Soc, chaplain 1956-60. **Orgs:** Mem NY State Crime Control Com; State Select Com on Institutions; Attica Observance; founder Central Harlem Assn of Neighborhood Chs; adjunct prof Union Theol Sem Feild Services Program; mem NAACP, SCLC; Ford Fellowship; SCLC Ministerial Training Prog; Am Bapt Black Churchmen; pres Bapt Ministers Conf ofGreater NY & Vicinity. **Honors/Awds:** History Makers Award; Ministerial Ser Award; Harlem Churchmen Award. **Business Addr:** Dept of Correctional Serv, State Campus, Albany, NY 12226.

MOORE, EDDIE N., JR.
Educational administrator. **Career:** State of Virginia, Department of the Treasury, state treasurer; Virginia State Univ, president, 1993-. **Orgs:** Omega Psi Phi Fraternity Inc; The Forum Club; The Virginia Heroes Inc. **Honors/Awds:** Dr Martin Luther King Jr Legacy Award, 1995. **Business Addr:** President, Virginia State Univ, PO Box 9001, Petersburg, VA 23806.

MOORE, ELIZABETH D.
Attorney. **Personal:** Born Jul 29, 1954, Queens, NY; daughter of M Doreen and William A; married Jimmy L Miller, Dec 21, 1984. **Educ:** New York State School of Industrial & Labor Relations at Cornell University, BS, 1975; St John's University School of Law, JD, 1978. **Career:** Consolidated Edison Company of New York, attorney, 1978-79; American Express Co, attorney, 1979-80; Equitable Life Assurance Society, mgr, equal opportunity, 1981; Office of Counsel to the Governor, assistant counsel, 1981-83, first assistant counsel, 1983-87; Governor's Office of Employee Relations, director, 1987-90; New York State Ethics Commission, chairperson, 1988-90; Office of Counsel to the Governor, counsel to the governor, 1991-. **Orgs:** Board of directors of the Center for Women in Government, vice chair; Task Force on the NYS Public Workforce in the 21st Century, co-chair; NYS/CSEA Committee on the Work Environment and Productivity, ch-chair; Board of Trustees of the Catholic Interracial Council; Governor's Executive Committee for Affirmative Action; International Personnel Management Association; National Association of State Directors of Employee Relations; National Forum for Black Pubic Administrators; National Public Employer Labor Relations Association; NYS Joint Labor/Management Committees; State Academy for Public Administration; Women Executives in State Government; Governor's Task Force on Work and Family; Governor's Special Prosecutor Screening Committee; Governor's Task Force on Bias-Related Violence. **Honors/Awds:** St John's University, Doctor of Civil Law (Honorary), 1989; National Council on State Governments, Toll Fellow, 1987; State University of New York, John E Burton Award, 1990; Westchester County Black Women's Political Caucus Leadership Award, 1989; NAACP/BYS, NAACP Legislative Mobilization Appreciation Award, 1986; Governor Mario M Cuomo, nominated for the 9th Annual Salute to Young Women Achievers Award, 1985. **Business Phone:** (518)474-8343.

MOORE, EMANUEL A.
Attorney. **Personal:** Born Nov 22, 1941, Brooklyn, NY; son of Hilda Waterman Moore and Hubert Moore; married Maria DoNascimento Moore, Aug 4, 1990. **Educ:** New York Univ, BS Willard J Martin Schlr, James Talcott Schlr 1963; NY Law Sch, JD Thurgood Marshall Schlr 1966. **Career:** Justice Dept Washington, atty civil rights div 1966-68; Queens Co NY, asst dist atty 1968; Ofc Gen Counsel AID Wash, legal adviser 1968-70; Eastern Dist NY, US atty 1970-72; US Atty Ofc Estrn Dist NY, chief consumer protect sec 1972-74; US Fed Energy Admin, dir compliance & enforcement 1974-77; private practice, attorney 1977-. **Orgs:** Mem NY Law Sch Alumni Assn; dir Natl Macon B Allen Black Bar Assn; Ed NY Law Forum 1965-66; Chinese American Lions Club, NY, Knighted Order of St George and Constantine 1986; pres, Atlantic Palace Condo Assn, 1989-; appointed to United States Magistrates Selection Committee, Eastern Distict, NY, 1992-. **Honors/Awds:** Amer Jurisprudence Awd Academic Excellence in Law of Evidence 1965; Amer Jurisprudence Awd Academic Excellence in Law of NY Prac 1965; Vice Pres Awd Academic Excellence 1966; mem dir NY Law Sch Alumni Assn. **Business Addr:** Attorney At Law, Emanuel A Moore & Associates, 89-17 190th St, Jamaica, NY 11423.

MOORE, EMERSON J.
Clergyman. **Personal:** Born May 16, 1938, New York City, NY. **Educ:** Cathedral Coll NYC, attended; St Joseph's Sem NY, attended; NY Univ, Columbia Univ School of Social Work, attended. **Career:** Curubi, aux bishop; Diocese of NY, aux bishop 1982-. **Honors/Awds:** Ordained priest Roman Catholic Church 1964.

MOORE, EVAN GREGORY
Psychiatrist. **Personal:** Born Sep 5, 1923, Lima, OK; son of Millicent Earl Taylor and Eugene Ralph; married June Elizabeth Gibbs; children: Colleen Moore Jones, Evan Jr. **Educ:** Meharry Medical Coll, MD 1948. **Career:** Harlem Hospital NY, intern 1948-49; Univ of IL, clinical asst prof psychiatry, 1958-70; Child Therapy Program, Inst Psychoanalysis Chicago, faculty 1968-85, faculty teacher training program, 1968-85; Erikson Inst Chicago, lecturer 1969-85; Cumberland Hall Nashville, attending staff 1985-88; Hubbard Hosp Nashville, attending staff 1986-88; Meharry Medical Coll, assoc prof, dept psychiatry and pediatrics 1985-88; clinical director, Children's Unit, HCA Montevista Hospital, 1989-90; Charter Hospital of Corona, Children's Unit, clinical director, 1990-92; Del Amo Hosp, clinical dir, 1993-, chief of med staff, 1995-96; Kedren Comm Mental Health Ctr, psychiatrist, 1995-96; Health Care Agency, 1997-. **Orgs:** Life Fellow, Amer Acad of Child Psychiatry; Life Fellow, Amer Psychiatric Assn; Life Fellow Amer Orthopsychiatric Assn; mem IL Council Child Psychiatry; Chicago Psychoanalytic Soc; Amer Medical Assn; Natl Medical Assn; IL State Psychiatric Soc; IL State Medical Soc; TN Psychiatric Assn; CA State Med Assn; assoc examiner Amer Bd of Psychiatry and Neurology 1978-; impartial medical testimony panel IL Medical Soc/IL Bar Assn Chicago 1980-86; consultant Provident Hospital Chicago 1985; mem Academic Affairs Council; honoray degree Comm Meharry Medical Coll 1986-88. **Honors/Awds:** Research, Longitudinal Study of Object Relations, Maternal Substance Abuse, Assault on Infant Morbidity and Mortality, Prenatal Head Start; numerous and varied informal presentations to staff students and public in a wide range of settings including radio and tv; Certified Amer Bd of Psychiatry and Neurology, General Psychiatry; Amer Bd of Psychiatry and Neurology, Child Psychiatry. **Military Serv:** AUS Medical Corps capt 2 yrs. **Home Addr:** PO Box 7046, Orange, CA 92613-7046.

MOORE, EVELYN K.
Agency executive. **Personal:** Born Jul 29, 1937, Detroit, MI. **Educ:** Eastern MI Univ, BS 1960; Univ of MI, MA 1960. **Career:** Natl Black Child Devel Inst Washington, DC, dir 1973-. **Orgs:** Mem bd dir Children's Lobby; mem N Amer Adoption Bd; adv com DC Citizens for Pub Edn; consult US Offc of Edn; mem Natl Assn for Educ of Young Children. **Honors/Awds:** Chosen Outstanding Young Woman of State of MI 1970. **Business Addr:** Executive Director, Natl Black Child Devt Inst, 1023 15th St, NW, Washington, DC 20005.

MOORE, FLOREESE NAOMI
Educator, educational administrator. **Personal:** Born Mar 15, 1940, Wilson, NC; daughter of Naomi Jones Lucas and Wiley Floyd Lucas; divorced; children: Lemuel Wiley, Lyndon Benjamin. **Educ:** West Chester State University, BS, 1974; University of Delaware, MI, 1979; Nova University, EdD, 1984; The Ohio State University, currently. **Career:** Red Cross, Japan, general office worker, 1961-63; Vita Foods Inc, bookkeeper, 1963-64; Chesapeake Potomac Telephone Co, operator, 1964-66; Doctors Bookkeeping, secretary, 1966-68; New Castle Co Delaware Public Schools, human relations sp, teacher, 1968-79; School Board of Alachua, FL, teacher, administrator, principal, assistant superintendent, 1979-90; Columbus Public Schools, assistant superintendent, 1990-. **Orgs:** Links Inc, arts committee, teens committee, 1985-; Phi Delta Kappa, secretary, 1983; Council for Exceptional Cnildren, executive board, 1980-84; Delta Sigma Theta Sorority; The Altrussa Club of Gainesville, international committee, 1982; Florida Organization of Instructional Leaders, 1984-90; Buckeye Association of School Administrators, 1990-; American Association of School Administrators, 1985-; Delta Sigma Theta. **Honors/Awds:** School Board of Alachua, School Board Merit Award, 1981; Florida Association of Exceptional School Administrators, Founder's Award, 1986; City of Gainesville, FL, The Ebony Appreciation Award, 1988; Mayor's Proclamation Award, 1988. **Special Achievements:** Founder, Florida Association of Exceptional School Administrators, 1984; author, ''Operant Treatment of Asthmatic Responding with the Parent as Therapist,'' Behavior Journal, 1973; ''Implementation of Residential School Age Children into the Public Schools,'' presented at the International Conference for the Council for Exceptional Children; ''Applying Business Management and Organizational Development Practices to a Public School Organization,'' presented at the Fourteenth Annual Conference of the National Council of States on Inservice Education, 1989; Peer Assistance and Review: Helping Entry Year & Veteran Teachers, Third Annual Natl Evaluation Inst, 1994; Is Your Organization Ready, Fifth Annual Nal Conference of the Natl Assn for Multicultural Educ. **Business Addr:** Assistant Superintendent, Columbus Public Schools, 270 E State Street, Columbus, OH 43215, (614)365-5715.

MOORE, FRED HENDERSON (DANNY)
Attorney. **Personal:** Born Jul 25, 1934, Charleston County, SC; married Louise Smalls; children: Fredena, Melissa, Fred, Louis, Rembert. **Educ:** SC State Coll 1952-56; Roosevelt Univ Chicago 1956; Allen U, BS 1956-57; Howard Episcopal, JD 1957-60; Teamers Sch of Religion, DD 1976; Stephens Christian Inst 1976; Reform Episcapal Seminary. **Career:** Atty self-employed 1977. **Orgs:** Corp cncl NAACP 1960; mem Black Rep Party; mem Silver Elephant Club; 1st Dist Coun SC Conf of NAACP; co-author ''Angry Black South'' 1960; asso pstr Payne RMUE Ch; asso cncl NC Mutual Ins Co; Mem Omega Psi Phy Frat. **Honors/Awds:** Youth award NAACP 1957; memorial award Charles Drew 1957; Youth March for Integrated Schs 1958; stud body pres SC State Coll. **Business Addr:** 39 Spring St, Charleston, SC 29403.

MOORE, GARY E.
Media specialist, educational administrator. **Personal:** Born Dec 8, 1962, Rochester, NY; son of Christine Enge Moore and Frank Lewis Moore; married Marva Elaine Nabors-Moore, Jul 1, 1989. **Educ:** Clarion Univ of PA, BS Accounting 1985, MS Communications 1988. **Career:** USAR, second lt, platoon leader, training & evaluation, equipment accountability 1984-; Clarion Univ, graduate asst; 1985-, admissions recruiter 1987-, project dir; Univ of PA, asst dir of admissiona; 332nd Eng Co (DT), Kittanning PA, company commander; GEM Presentation Graphics, pres/owner, presently/. **Orgs:** Graduate advisor Black Student Union 1985-87; chair, editor Amer Mktg Assn Newsletter 1986-87; chmn, editor Black Student Union Newsletter 1987; human relations subcomm Clarion Univ; mem Accounting Club, Amer Mktg Assn; Soc of Military Engineers 1987; Reserve Officers Assn 1989. **Honors/Awds:** Black Student Union Acad Achievement Award; Graduate Assistantship Clarion Univ of PA 1985-87. **Military Serv:** USA 2nd lt 4 yrs; Merit of Achievement 1986.

MOORE, GEORGE ANTHONY
Television producer. **Personal:** Born Feb 8, 1914, Cleveland, OH. **Educ:** Ohio State Univ, BA; Univ of Iowa, MA. **Career:** Gama Assn Inc, owner; US TV Station WEWS, first black prod & dir; Scripps-Howard Cleveland Press & Scripps-Howard's TV station, news dir to current position; actor in over a dozen live stage & prod. **Orgs:** Mem Nat Acad of TV Arts & Sci; found dir Cath Theater of Cleveland OH St Univ Playmakers; mem Karamu House; Proj Equal; found pres Proj Peace Cath Commn on Comm Action. **Honors/Awds:** The Dorothy Fuldheim prog which is his chief respons; Highlights of the News have been chosen as the outstndg Cleveland TV news show by many newspaper surv.

MOORE, GEORGE THOMAS
Scientist. **Personal:** Born Jun 2, 1945, Owensboro, KY; married Peggy Frances Jouett. **Educ:** KY State U, BS chemistry/math 1967; Univ of Dayton, MS inorganic chem 1971; Env Health Univ of Cincinnati Med Center, PhD 1978. **Career:** US DOE Pittsburgh Energy Tech Ctr, chief occupational health br 1979-; US DOE Pittsburgh Energy Tech Ctr, research indsl hygienist 1978-79; MonsantoResearch Corp Mound Lab, research chemist 1967-72. **Orgs:** Mem Am Chem Soc 1975-; mem Air Pollution Control Assn 1977-; mem Am Insl Hygiene Assn 1978-; Mem Unity Lodge #115 Price Hall Affiliation 1963-; memOmega Psi Phi Frat 1964-; supt Ebenezer Bapt Ch Sunday Sch 1980-. **Honors/Awds:** Hon French award Alpha Mu Gamma French Soc. **Business Addr:** PO Box 10940, Pittsburgh, PA 15236.

MOORE, GREGORY B.
Telecommunicator, dispatcher. **Personal:** Born Mar 27, 1962, New York, NY; son of Vera R Moore. **Educ:** Norfolk State Univ, BS, industrial ed, 1987. **Career:** Norfolk State Univ, head resident asst, 1982-86, electrical lab asst, 1986-87; Cox Cable Hampton Roads, repair dispatch operator, 1987-88, radio dispatcher,1988-89; signal leakage auditor, 1989-91; telecommunicator I, 1992-. **Orgs:** Natl Technical Assn, board of dirs, 1984-85, student director, 1984-85, 1987-89; Student Natl Assn, pres, 1984-85, 1987-89, student advisor, 1985-86; Norfolk State Univ, SNTA; Student Assn of Norfolk State Univ, co-founder, 1982-86. **Honors/Awds:** Black Engineer of the Year Award, nominee, 1989; Outstanding Young Men of American, 1989. **Business Addr:** Telecommunicator 1, Dispather, Cox Cable Hampton Roads, 5200 Cleveland St, Virginia Beach, VA 23462-0547.

MOORE, GWEN
Assemblywoman (retired), communications company executive. **Personal:** Born Oct 28, Michigan; married Ronald Dobson; children: Ronald Dobson II. **Educ:** CA State Univ LA, BA Tchng 1963; Univ S CA, MPA candidate. **Career:** LA County, deputy probation officer, 1963-69; Gr LA Comm Action Agency, dir, public affairs/dir of personnel, 1969-76; Social Action Rsch Ctr, LA, consultant, 1970-72; LA Comm Coll, bd of trustees, 1975; Compton Comm Coll, instr, 1975; Inner City Information System LA, consultant, 1976-77; CA State Assembly, 1978-94, chair, assembly subcomm on cable TV 1982, chair assembly utilities & commerce comm 1983-94; G & M Communications, president, currently. **Orgs:** Western regional chair Natl Black Caucus of State Legislators; reg v chair Natl Conf of Legislatures; mem CA Public Broadcasting Task Force; mem Commnon State Govt Orgn & Economy; platform comm of Dem Natl Comm; mem CA Elected Women's Assn for Educ & Rsch; mem Dem Women's Forum; mem LA Coalition of 100 Black Women; mem Natl Women's Political Caucus; mem YWCA, United Negro Coll Fund, CA Legislative Black Caucus; reg dir Women's Network of Natl Caucus o State Legislatures; sec Natl Org of Black Elected Legislative Women (Nobel/Women). **Honors/Awds:** Natl Alliance of Supermarket Shoppers Golden Shopping Cart Awd for Legislator of the Yr 1983; Natl Caucus of Black State Legislators Awd 1984; CA State Package Store & Tavern Owner's Assn Awd 1984; Meritorious Awd for Outstanding Serv Women for Good Govt; Newsmaker of the Yr Awd Natl Assn of Media Women 1983; Natl Assnn of Minorities in Cable's. **Business Addr:** President, G & M Communications Group, 4201 Wilshire Blvd, Ste 301, Los Angeles, CA 90010.

MOORE, HAROLD EARL, JR.
Physician. **Personal:** Born Sep 5, 1954, San Antonio, TX; son of Barbara Stewart Moore and Harold Earl Moore Sr. **Educ:** Florida A&M University, 1972-76; Morehouse College, BS, 1978; Morehouse School of Medicine, 1981-83; Howard University College of Medicine, MD, 1985. **Career:** FSU Department of Psychology & Neuro-Histology, lab technician, research, Dr Karen Berkley, 1974-75; Cornell University College of Pharmacology, lab technician, 1979-80; Georgia Regional Hospital at Atlanta, ER physician, 1988-89; Fulton County Teen Clinics, physician, 1988-89; Sterling Group, ER physician, 1989-95; Stewart-Webster Rural Health, Inc, physician, 1989-91; Southeastern Health Services, Inc, physician, beginning 1991; Emory Clinic Inc, physician, 1993-. **Orgs:** American Academy of Family Physicians, 1987-; GA State Medical Association, 1988-; American Medical Association, 1989-; Georgia Academy of Family Physicians, 1983-; Natl Medical Assn, 1987-; Morehouse School of Medicine National Alumni Association, 1983, president, 1993; Howard University College of Medicine Alumni Association, 1985-; Kappa Alpha Psi Fraternity, Inc, 1989-. **Honors/Awds:** Morehouse School of Medicine, Dean's Leadership Award, 1982; Fellow of American Academy of Family Physicians, 1994; Outstanding Young Doctor Award, Dollar & Sense Magazine, 1991. **Home Addr:** 3873 Brookwater Point, Decatur, GA 30034, (770)593-8759. **Business Addr:** Physician, Emory Clinic Inc, 2764 Candler Rd, Decatur, GA 30034, (404)778-8600.

MOORE, HAZEL STAMPS
School librarian (retired). **Personal:** Born Jan 10, 1924, Learned, MS; daughter of Seretha Hicks Stamps and Andrew Stamps; married Wilbur D Moore, May 30, 1948 (died 1984); children: Wibur Dexter, Debra M Carter, MD. **Educ:** Southern Christian Institute Junior College, certificate, 1945; Tougaloo College, BA (cum laude), 1947; Atlanta University, MS, library science, 1955; Washington University, St. Louis, MO; Xavier University; Louisiana State University; University of New Orleans; Tulane University. **Career:** Tougaloo College, librarian, 1947; Oakley Training School, teacher, librarian, 1947-49; Tougaloo College, Preparatory School, teacher, librarian, 1949-51, asst librarian, 1951-57; Booker T Washington High School, head librarian, 1957-61; St Louis Public Library, sr reference librarian, 1961-62; Booker T Washington High School, head librarian, 1962-66, 1967-72; New Orleans Public Schools, Projects 1089-B, 1095-A & 1200-G, asst supervisor, 1966-67; Marion Abramson High School, head librarian, 1972-91, New Orleans Public Schools, Adult Education Center, instructor, currently; One Church One School, Central Congregational United Church of Christ, director, 1990-93. **Orgs:** American Library Assn; American Assn of School Librarians; Louisiana Library Assn; Louisiana Assn of School Librarians; Catholic Library Assn, Greater New Orleans Unit 1958-91; Louisiana Assn for Educational Communications and Technology; Louisiana Assn Computer Users for Educators; United Teachers of New Orleans Retired Chapter; Southern Assn of Colleges and Schools Teams; National Council of Negro Women; Tougaloo Alumnae Club; Snacirema Club; numerous others. **Honors/Awds:** PTA Outstanding Service Award, Abramson; Guidance Department Award, Landry; author, How to Conduct a Dial-an-Author Program, LLA Bulletin, 1989; LA Library Association, Modisette Award; US Dept of Education, Special Citation. **Home Addr:** 5931 Congress Dr, New Orleans, LA 70126. **Business Addr:** Instructor/New Orleans Center for Adult Education, Library Science University, University of New Orleans, 5931 Congress Dr, New Orleans, LA 70126.

MOORE, HELEN D. S.
Educator (retired). **Personal:** Born Jan 21, 1932, Baldwyn, MS; married Elijah Moore; children: Michelle, Pamela, Elijah. **Educ:** MS Industrial Coll, BA 1951; TN State Univ, MS 1957; Delta State Univ, educational specialist, 1977. **Career:** Jr, Sr, HS, teacher 4 yrs; Primary Grades, teacher 1953-75; Greenville Municipal School District, elem principal 1975-90; AME Church, ordained minister, 1994. **Orgs:** Mem Voter Reg; Political Camp; Ad Hoc Comm; lectr Wash County Political Action Comm; past pres YWCA 1950-51; past pres Greenville Teacher Assn; pres MS Assn of Educ 1978-79; youth advisor St Matthew AME Church 1977; advisor Teenette Art & Civic Club; mem Modern Art & Civic Club, NAACP, Natl Fed Colored Women's Club; NEA, bd of dirs, 1984-88. **Honors/Awds:** NSF Grant, Eastern MI Univ, 1963; Citizen Award, NAACP, 1975; Citizenship Award, WB Derrick Masonic Lodge, 1976; Educ Award Civil Liberties Elks 1976; Comm Seventh Day Adventist Church Award.

MOORE, HENRY J.
Appointed government official. **Personal:** Born Jan 26, 1949, Philadelphia, PA; married Donna Morgan; children: Caprice. **Educ:** NC A&T State Univ, BS English 1971; Univ of MD, MA Urban Mgmt 1976. **Career:** Bur of Govt Rsch/ Univ of MD, public mgmt assoc 1974-76; Univ of MD, dir of student employment 1976-77; Seat Pleasant MD, city mgr 1977-79; Joint Ctr for Political Studies, dir of comm & eco dev 1979-81; City of Savannah, asst city mgr/public develop. **Orgs:** Mem Clean Comm Adv Council 1981-85; bd of dirs Neighborhood Housing Ser 1981-85; mem Amer Soc for Public Admin 1981-85; mem Leadership Savannah 1984-85; bd of dirs United Way 1984-85; mem Forum for Black Public Admin 1984-85. **Honors/Awds:** Man of the Year Alpha Phi Alpha Beta Phi Lambda Chap 1983-84. **Home Addr:** 518 E Maupas Ave, Savannah, GA 31401.

MOORE, HERMAN JOSEPH
Professional football player. **Personal:** Born Oct 20, 1969, Danville, VA; married Angela; children: Aaron, Ashton. **Educ:** University of Virginia, degree in rhetoric and communications studies, 1991. **Career:** Detroit Lions, wide receiver, 1991-. **Orgs:** Catch 84 Foundation, founder. **Honors/Awds:** Pro Bowl, 1994, 1995, 1996, 1997; Detroit Lions, Offensive Most Valuable Player, 1995; Detroit Lions, True Value/NFL Man of the Year, 1995, 1996. **Business Addr:** Professional Football Player, Detroit Lions, 1200 Featherstone Rd., Pontiac, MI 48342, (248)335-4131.

MOORE, HIRAM BEENE
Physician. **Personal:** Born Jan 1, 1914, South Pittsburg, TN; son of Clara Beene Moore and Levi Moore; married Stella M Epps, Dec 31, 1944; children: Clara Lynn Moore. **Educ:** TN State U, BS 1938; Meharry Med Coll, MD 1944. **Career:** Physician, self-employed. **Orgs:** Med advsr Marion County Draft Bd 1952-; mem Marion County Bd of Health; chmn City Beer Commn; mem City Planning Commn 1956-66; commr Local Housing Authority 1956-66; mem Natl Med Assn; Amer Med Assn; mem Chattanooga Hamilton County Med Soc; life mem Omega Psi Phi Frat; trustee Lay Leader Randolph Univ Meth Ch; mem 32nd degree Mason; life mem NAACP; mem Shriner. **Honors/Awds:** Family Doctor of the Year, Natl Med Assn 1964; Distinguished Alumni Natl Assn for Equal Opportunity in Higher Education 1989. **Military Serv:** ASTP 2nd Lieutant 1943-1944. **Business Addr:** 206 Elm Ave S, South Pittsburg, TN 37380.

MOORE, HOWARD, JR.
Attorney. **Personal:** Born Feb 28, 1932, Atlanta, GA; married Jane Bond; children: Grace, Constance, Kojo. **Educ:** Morehouse Coll, AB 1954; Boston Univ, LLB 1960. **Career:** Moore & Lawrence, attorney. **Orgs:** Admitted to practice MA 1961, GA 1962, CA 1973; admitted to practice before Supreme Ct of US all lower Fed Cts & US Tax Ct; mem Natl Conf of Black Lawyers; Charles Houston Law Club; Natl Lawyers Guild; Natl Emergency Civil Liberties Com; Amer Civil Liberties Union; Fedn of So Coop; former genl counsel Student Nonviolent Coord Comm. **Honors/Awds:** Martin Luther King Jr Awd Howard Univ 1972; Disting Son of Morehouse Coll 1973; Centennial Awd Boston Univ 1973; Disting Serv Natl Coll of Advocacy Assn of Amer Trial Lawyers 1975. **Military Serv:** AUS pfc 1954-56. **Business Addr:** Attorney, Moore & Lawrence, 445 Bellevue Ave 3rd Fl, Oakland, CA 94610.

MOORE, JAMES FREDRICK
Company executive. **Personal:** Born Nov 23, 1958, North Carolina; son of Jean Moore Williams and James Harold (deceased); married Jacqueline Howard Moore, May 29, 1983; children: Cameron James, Brady Sinclair. **Educ:** University of North Carolina at Chapel Hill, BS, 1981; University of Wisconsin, minority business program, 1992. **Career:** Policy Management Systems, analyst, 1981-83; United Carolina Bank, lending officer/branch manager, 1983-87; I Supply, vice pres, 1987-94; VIS Technologies, LLC, CEO, currently. **Orgs:** National Minority Suppliers Development Council Inc, Minority Business Southeast US, chairman, 1992-; Carolinas MSDC, minority business chairman, 1991-; Johnson C Smith University, corporate business advisory board chairman, 1989-; Charlotte Oratorio Singers, board of directors, 1992-; New St John Baptist Church, trustee board chairman, 1992-, usher, choir member, 1989-. **Honors/Awds:** Carolinas Minority Suppliers Development Council, Metrolina Chapter, Minority Business Person of the Year, 1992; Jaycees of America, Man of the Year, 1986; Boys Clubs of America, Volunteer of the Year, 1984; Bankers Educational Society Inc, Man of the Year, 1987; Alpha Phi Alpha Fraternity Inc, Man of the Year, 1982. **Business Addr:** CEO, VIS Technologies, LLC, 1300 Baxter St, Ste 428, Charlotte, NC 28204.

MOORE, JANE BOND
Attorney. **Personal:** Born Sep 1, 1938, Nashville, TN; daughter of Julia Washington Bond and Horace Mann Bond; married Howard Moore; children: Grace, Constance, Kojo. **Educ:** Spelman Coll Atlanta, AB 1959; Boalt Hall Univ of CA, JS 1975. **Career:** So Regional Council, research asst 1961-63; So Christian Leadership Conf, research asst 1963-64; Moore & Bell, assoc atty 1975-76; Open Road (a youth proj), admin 1976-77; Bank of CA, asst counsel 1977-80; Federal Trade Commission, San Francisco, CA, attorney 1980-83; Moore & Moore Attorneys at Law, Oakland, CA, partner 1983-90; Oakland Unified School District, Oakland, CA, assoc counsel 1990-, deputy general counsel, 1995-. **Orgs:** Mem, Charles Houston Bar Association. **Business Addr:** Deputy General Counsel, Legal Office, Oakland Unified School District, 1025 2nd Ave, Rm 406, Oakland, CA 94606, (510)879-8535.

MOORE, JEAN E.
Educational administrator. **Personal:** Born in New York, NY; daughter of Theodora Campbell and Hugh Campbell; married

Robert M Moore Jr; children: Robert III, Doreen Moore-Closson. **Educ:** Hunter Coll, BA; Bryn Mawr Coll, MSS; Temple Univ, EdD 1978. **Career:** Vet Admin PA, asst chief clinical social work service; Redevel Auth City of PA, social work spec; Model Cities US Dept Housing & Urban Devel, human services adv; Temple Univ, School of Soc Admin, assoc prof 1969-89, associate prof emerita; Cheyney Univ of Pennsylvania, Cheyney, PA, exec asst to pres, 1985-91; Univ of Maryland Eastern Shore, Princess Anne, MD, vice pres for institutional advancement, 1991-; Radio Program Host, WESM-FM. **Orgs:** Mem Natl Assoc Social Workers, Acad Cert Soc Workers, Council Soc Work Ed, PA Black Conf Higher Ed; team chairperson/team member, Commission on Higher Educ, Middle States Assoc of Coll & Schools; act 101 reviewer & eval Commonwealth of PA; past pres Spectrum Health Svcs; past bd dirs Comm Y Eastern DE Cty; mem Fair Housing Council DE Valley; elder Lansdowne Presbyterian Church; Delta Sigma Theta Sorority; Phi Delta Kappa; Phi Beta Kappa; former board of trustees, Community College of Phila, and Lackawanna Junior College; consultant. **Honors/Awds:** Bronze/Silver Medals for Writings; Outstanding Educator 1977; Educator Achievement Award 1979; Coll of Ed Alumni Award 1978; Award of Chapel of the Four Chaplains; Community Service Award, Cheyney Univ, 1990; Dedication Award, Cheyney Univ, 1991; Licensed Social Worker, Commonwealth of Pennsylvania; Appreciation Award from Spectrum Health Services, 1992. **Business Addr:** Vice President, Institutional Advancement, University of Maryland Eastern Shore, J T Williams Administration Bldg, Princess Anne, MD 21853, (410)651-6665.

MOORE, JELLETHER MARIE

Computer systems manager. **Personal:** Born Sep 4, 1949, Sacramento, CA; daughter of Artaive Daniels Moore and Oserine Moore; children: Cornealis N, Halima JJ. **Educ:** Wagsburn Univ Topeka KS, BA 1973; Attended, California State Univ, Sacramento City Coll, Cosumnes River Coll, Univ of California at Davis. **Career:** State of California, computer software applications programmer/analyst 1976-84; Crystal Lightworks, owner 1986-; State of California, Dept of Conservation, Farmland Mapping and Monitoring Program, land & water use analyst/computer systems manager 1984-. **Orgs:** Mem California Assn of Professional Scientists 1984-, California Geographers Soc 1985-, Southwestern Anthropological Soc 1985-, Assn of Women Entrepreneurs, Chamber of Commerce of Sacramento CA, Better Business Bureau of Sacremento CA; reviewer Digital Cartographic Standards 1985-86;mem Multi-cultural Comm SUSD 1986-87; partner in Mooncraft/Minds Eye Images. **Honors/Awds:** Superior Accomplishment Award for Excellence in Information Mgmt, State of California, Office of Information Technology 1988; Sustained Superior Accomplishment, State of California, Dept of Conservation 1988. **Business Addr:** Computer Systems Manager, State of California, Farmland Mapping & Monitoring, 1516 9th St, Room 400, Sacramento, CA 95814.

MOORE, JERALD

Professional football player. **Personal:** Born Nov 20, 1974, Houston, TX. **Educ:** Oklahoma, attended. **Career:** St Louis Rams, running back, 1996-. **Business Addr:** Professional Football Player, St Louis Rams, One Rams Way, St Louis, MO 63045, (314)982-7267.

MOORE, JERRY A., JR.

Clergyman. **Personal:** Born Jun 12, 1918, Minden, LA; son of Mal Dee Moore and Jerry A. Moore; married Ettyce Hill, Jan 14, 1946; children: Jerry III, Juran D. **Educ:** Morehouse Coll, BA, 1940; Howard U, BD, 1943, MA, 1957. **Career:** USO, New Orleans, asst dir, beginning 1943; YMCA, boys work sec 1944; 19th St Bapt Ch, pastor, 1946-. **Orgs:** Mem-at-large, DC City Council, 1970-84; past pres Bapt Conv Wash DC & Vincinity; past pres Intl Soc Christian Endwavor; past pres Wash Metro Area Council Govts; past chair public works Com DC Council; Rock Creek East Civic Assn; NAACP; Pigskin Club; Urban League; Capitol City Rep Club; past executive secretary, Home Mission Board, NBC, 1985-. **Honors/Awds:** Washington Area Contractors Award 1971; NAACP Serv Award 1972; Capitol City Rep Club Lincoln Award 1974; Minority Transportation Officials Award, 1986. **Home Addr:** 1612 Buchanan St NW, Washington, DC 20011.

MOORE, JESSE

Auto dealer. **Career:** Warner Robins Olds-Cadillac-Pontiac-GMC, owner, currently; full service auto body shops, owner. **Orgs:** Metropolitan Business League; General Motors Minority Dealer Development program. **Business Addr:** Owner, Warner Robins Olds-Cadillac-Pontiac-GMC, 741 Russell Pkwy, Warner Robins, GA 31088, (912)929-0222.

MOORE, JOHN WESLEY, JR.

Business executive. **Personal:** Born Mar 10, 1948, Martins Ferry, OH; married Brenda Scott; children: Kelly Shannon, Ryan Wesley, Johnathan Morgan, Nicholas Patrick. **Educ:** W Liberty State Coll, BA 1970; WV Univ Morgantown, MA 1972. **Career:** Bridgeport HS, tchr 1970-71; W Liberty State Coll, dir counseling ctr & asst dir financial aids 1971-76; WesBanco, Inc, vice pres personnel-human resources, supervisor, currently. **Orgs:** Mem bd trustees OH Valley Medical Ctr 1979; consult Ctr for Creative Comm 1974-75; consult No Panhandle Mental Health Ctr Wheeling 1977-79; bd of dir Big Bros/Big Sisters of Wheeling 1976-77; adv bd OH Co Bd of Vocational Educ 1977-; bd of dir Amer Inst of Banking Wheeling Chap 1979-; Ambassadors Club Wheeling Area C of C 1979-; adv com Upper OH Valley Employer Wheeling 1979-80; Salvation Army, president and board member, 1980; Ohio Valley Business Industrial Commission, board member. **Business Addr:** Sr Vice Pres Personnel-Human Resources, WesBanco Inc, Bank Plaza, Wheeling, WV 26003.

MOORE, JOHNNIE ADOLPH

Federal official (retired), public relations consultant. **Personal:** Born Sep 28, 1929, Cuero, TX; son of Eva Jones Moore and Nelson Moore; married Tommye Dalphine Jordan; children: Carmalie Budgewater. **Educ:** Tuskegee Inst AL, BS 1950; George Williams Coll, Grad Study. **Career:** Intl Personnel Mgt Assn Chgo, IL, editor 1963-66; US Dept of Labor Chgo, IL, pub aff ofcr 1966-67; US Civil Serv Commn Wash, DC, pub aff ofcr 1967-79; Bowie State Coll Bowie, MD, asst to pres 1980-82; US Office of Personnel Mgt Wash, DC, pub aff ofcr 1979-83; Am Nurses Assn, dir mrktng & pub aff div 1984-85; US Nuclear Regulatory Commission, public affairs officer 1985-90; US Dept of the Treasury, Bureau of Engraving and Printing, Washington, DC, public affairs manager, 1990-93, public relations consultant, currently. **Orgs:** Exec dir Nat Ins Assn 1961-62; info spclst Pres Comm on Gov't Contracts 1960-61; night editor Chicago Daily Defender 1959-61; bureau editor Norfolk Journal & Guide 1958-59; pres Capital Press Club Wash, DC 1972-74; visiting prof NUL Black Exec Exchange Pgm 1978-; mem Pub Rel Soc of Am 1977-; mem Kappa Alpha Psi Frat; AARP, mem, state legislative committee. **Honors/Awds:** Spcl Citation US Civil Serv Commn 1978; Pearlie Cox Harrison Award Capital Press Club 1974; Image Maker Award Nat Assn of Media Women 1976; Citation Bowie State Coll 1982; citation US Nuclear Regulatory Commission 1986-90; Treasury Department, Albert Gallatin Awd, 1993. **Military Serv:** USAF 1st Lt 1953-55. **Home Addr:** 2212 Westview Ct, Silver Spring, MD 20910. **Business Addr:** 2212 Westview Ct, Silver Spring, MD 20910.

MOORE, JOHNNY BRIAN

Basketball player. **Personal:** Born Mar 3, 1958, Altoona, PA; married Natalie. **Educ:** Texas, studied Phys Ed 1979. **Career:** San Antonio Spurs, 1980-88, New Jersey Nets, 1988, San Antonio Spurs, 1990; Tulsa Fast Breakers (CBA), 1990-. **Orgs:** Conducts youth camps. **Honors/Awds:** 14th with a 396 rating in Shick Pivotal Player contest; led NBA with 96 assists in 1981-82; his career 29 pts were 2/25/83 vs Kansas City; twice was All-Southwest Conf at TX; as jr led team to NIT title & was teams MVP.

MOORE, JOSEPH L.

Health services administrator. **Personal:** Born Nov 22, 1935, Ripley, TN; son of Alice Irons Moore and William Moore. **Educ:** St Louis Univ, BA 1959. **Career:** VA Med Ctr Lebanon PA, asst dir 1974-75; VA Med Ctr Louisville, asst dir 1975-76; VA Med Ctr Fresno, acting dir 1976; VA Med Ctr Cincinnati, asst dir 1976-79; VA Lakeside Med Ctr, dir 1979-. **Orgs:** Exec comm Chicago Fed Exec Bd 1979; bd of dir Mcgaw Med Center 1979; council of teaching hosp rep Assn of Am Med Coll 1979; comm Chicago Health Systems Agency 1979; chmn appropriateness rev com Chicago Health Systems Agency 1980. **Honors/Awds:** Prestigious Presidential "Distinguished Executive" Rank Awd presented in a White House ceremony Dec 8, 1986; Federal Executive of the Year, FEI Alumni Assn, 1990; Meritorious Service Award, Department of Veterans Affairs, 1990; Presidential Meritorious Executive Award, 1990. **Business Addr:** Director, 333 E Huron St, Chicago, IL 60611.

MOORE, JOSSIE A.

Educator. **Personal:** Born Aug 20, 1947, Jackson, TN; married Jimmy L Moore; children: Juan, Jerry. **Educ:** Lane College, BA 1971; Memphis State Univ, MEd 1975, EdD 1986. **Career:** Lane College, dir of audio visual 1970-74; Memphis State Univ/Memphis City Schools, teacher corps intern 1974-75; Lauderdale County Schools, resource teacher1975-76; Covington City Schools, spec ed teacher 1976-77; State Technical Institution, assoc prof reading, currently. **Orgs:** Secretary PTA Lincoln School 1973-74; Sigma Gamma Rho; AUA; TEA, SCETC; NEA, 1977-83; secretary/adm vice pres Stimulus Toastmasters 1978-84; consultant Fed Corrections Inst 1978-79; representative Parent Advisory Comm 1979-82; consultant Expert Secretarial Serv 1981-84. **Honors/Awds:** Honorable Mention Third World Writer's Contest 1979; Best Regional Bulletin Toastmasters Regional 1981-82; member Phi Delta Kappa 1982; publication co-author "Instructor Magazine" Feb 1984 issue. **Business Addr:** Assoc Professor of Reading, State Technical Inst at Memphis, 5983 Macon Cove, Memphis, TN 38134.

MOORE, JUANITA

Actress. **Personal:** Born 1922, Los Angeles, CA; married Charles Burris. **Educ:** Los Angeles City College, drama, grad. **Career:** Dancer, singer, night clubs, New York City, London, England (Palladium), Paris, France (Moulin Rouge); actress, stage credits include No Exit (Ebony Showcase production), Raisin in the Sun (London company); films: Lydia Bailey (1952), Witness to Murder (1954), Ransom (1955), The Girl Can't Help It (1957), Imitation of Life (1959), Walk on the Wild Side (1962), The Singing Nun (1966), Rosie (1968); television appearances: Wagon Train, Breaking Point, Going My Way. **Honors/Awds:** Oscar nomination, best supporting actress, Imitation of Life.

MOORE, JULIETTE R.

Educational Administrator. **Personal:** Born Sep 30, 1953, New Orleans, LA; daughter of Mr & Mrs Frank Moore. **Educ:** Xavier University in New Orleans, BS, 1975; University of West Florida, MS, 1977. **Career:** University of West Florida, graduate teaching assistant, 1975-76, sports club coord, 1975-76, assistant director of recreation & sports, 1976-84; Arizona State University, assistant director of recreation, intramurl sports & sports clubs, 1985-89; James Madison University, associate director of student activities for programming & recreation, 1989-91; Northern IL University, director of campus recreation, currently. **Orgs:** Zeta Phi Beta Sorority Inc, faculty advisor, 1991-; National Association of Campus Activities, 1989-91; Arizona College Personnel Association, 1988-89; National Association of Student Personnel Administrators, 1989; and numerous others. **Honors/Awds:** NIRSA, Outstanding Leadership & Svc Awd, 1996; Ruth Haddock Awd, Northern Illinois University, 1996; University of West Florida, Outstanding Alumni Awd, 1995; Northern Illinois University, Stacy Dolby Awd for Diversity, 1994; James Madison University, Women of Color of the Year, 1991; NIRSA, Outstanding Leadership & Svc Awd, 1989. **Special Achievements:** Diversity: Be a Part of the Solution, NIRSA Journal's, 1991; Melonball, NIRSA Journal, Fall 1985. **Business Addr:** Director, Campus Recreation, Northern Illinois University, Student Recreation Ctr, De Kalb, IL 60115, (815)753-9416.

MOORE, KATHERINE BELL

Trucking company executive, city government official. **Personal:** Born Nov 30, 1941, Norfolk, VA; daughter of Katherine Scott Bell-Webber and William Grant Bell; divorced; children: Ira Braswell IV, Katherine Larilee. **Educ:** University of North Carolina-Wilmington, BA, 1972. **Career:** Mechlesburg County Schools, teacher, 1972-73; Cape Fear Community College, teacher, 1973-74; Fairfax County Schools, teacher, 1974-77; Eastern Delivery Service Inc, president, 1977-; City of Wilmington, mayor pro-tem, 1992-. **Orgs:** New Hanover County Human Relations Committee, chairman, 1980-83; New Hanover Department of Social Services, vice chairman, 1980-82; Duke University LEAD Program, advisory board, 1980-82; Governor's Commission on Economic Development, board member, 1982-84; Lt Governor's Commission on Jobs, board member, 1984-86; UNC Center for Public Television, trustee, 1990-; Carolina Savings Bank, board of directors, 1986-. **Honors/Awds:** Links, Achievement Award, 1985; YWCA, Women of Achievement in Business Award, 1985; SBA, Minority Business, 2nd runner-up, 1986; Avon, Women of Enterprise, 1990; Connecticut Mutual, Blue Chip Award, 1991. **Home Addr:** 4311 Appleton Way, Wilmington, NC 28412, (919)395-1510. **Business Addr:** President, Eastern Delivery Service, Inc, 1704 Castle Hayne Rd, PO Box 1643, Wilmington, NC 28402, (919)763-1043.

MOORE, KENYA

Miss USA, model. **Personal:** Born in Detroit, MI. **Educ:** Wayne State University, Detroit, MI, child psychology, currently. **Career:** Miss USA, 1993. **Special Achievements:** Second African-American to gain both Miss Michigan and Miss USA titles, 1993. **Business Phone:** (213)965-0800.

MOORE, KERMIT

Cellist, conductor, composer, educator. **Personal:** Born Mar 11, 1929, Akron, OH; married Dorothy Rudd. **Educ:** Cleveland Inst Music 1951; NY Univ MA; Paris Conservatory 1956; Juilliard Sch Music. **Career:** Univ Hartford, formerly prof; numerous concerts throughout US, Europe, Africa & Far East; toured NY Philharmonic to Argentina & Dominican Repub 1978; Nat Opera Ebony, gst conductor; commd to compose several works "Viola Sonata"; classical Radio WQXR, premiered 1979; Brooklyn Philharmonic at Lincoln Center NY, conductor 1984-87, 1992; Detroit Symphony, guest conductor 1985, 1992; Berkeley CA Symphony, guest conductor 1986-88, 1990, 1992; commissioned by St Louis Arts Festival to compose work tor cello and piano, premiered work in Sheldon Hall 1986; Rud/Mor Publ Co, pres; Classical Heritage Ensemble, founder, conductor; Summer Chamber Music Conference at Bennington Coll, mem of faculty, 1988-; composed film score with Gordon Parks about Ida B Wells on American Experience Series, 1989. **Orgs:** Founder proj dir Symphony of the New World 1964-; founder Soc Black Composers 1968. **Honors/Awds:** Edgar Stillman Kelly Award State of Ohio; grant Knight Publs 1954; Lili Boulanger Award Paris 1953; found Riverside Symphony 1975; conducted concert UN Gen Assembly Hall 1976; composed "Many Thousand Gone"; special medal Queen Elizabeth of Belgium 1958. **Special Achievements:** Recital at Kennedy Center, 1992; played Washington Premiere of his composition, "Music for Cello and Piano"; lecturer for NY Philharmonic, 1992-93. **Business Addr:** President, Rud/Mor Publishing Co, 33 Riverside Drive, New York, NY 10023.

MOORE, KERWIN LAMAR
Professional baseball player. **Personal:** Born Oct 29, 1970, Detroit, MI. **Career:** Kansas City Royals, MO, outfielder, 1988-92; Florida Marlins, 1993-. **Business Phone:** (305)356-5848.

MOORE, LARRY LOUIS
Educator. **Personal:** Born Jul 21, 1954, Kings Mountain, NC. **Educ:** Western Carolina Univ, BA 1978; Univ of NC-Charlotte, Graduate School 1980-. **Career:** Cleveland Tech Coll, instructor in black history and world civilization 1979-81; Southwest Junior High School, teacher chmn/foreign language dept. **Orgs:** Mem NEA/NCEA 1982-84; mem NC Teachers of Math 1983-84; chmn Student Activities Comm 1984-85; sec Parents and Teachers Org 1985-87; mem NAACP 1987. **Honors/Awds:** Published articles on black topics in various newspapers. **Business Addr:** Teacher/Chmn Foreign Lang Dept, Southwest Junior High School, #1 Roadrunner Dr, Gastonia, NC 28052.

MOORE, LENARD DUANE
Literary consultant. **Personal:** Born Feb 13, 1958, Jacksonville, NC; son of Mary Louise Pearson Moore and Rogers Edward Moore; married Marcille Lynn, Oct 15, 1985; children: Maisha. **Educ:** Attended, Coastal Carolina Comm Coll 1976-78, Univ of MD 1980-81, NC State Univ 1985; Shaw Univ, BA (magna cum laude), 1995; NC A & T State Univ, MA, 1997. **Career:** Freelance Lecturer/Workshop Conductor, 1981-; The Black Writer Chicago, magazine consultant 1982-83; Pacific Quarterly Moana Hamilton New Zealand, acting advisor 1982-83; Intl Black Writers Conf Inc Chicago, regional dir 1982-83; Mira Mesa Branch Library San Diego CA, poet-in-residence 1983; NC Dept of Public Instruction, educational media technician, 1984-95; United Arts Council, Raleigh, NC, writer-in-residence, 1987-93; Enloe High School, Raleigh, NC, English teacher, 1995-96; NC State Univ, English dept, visiting lecturer, 1997-. **Orgs:** Mem Kuumba Festival Comm NAACP Onslow Co Branch 1982; bd of dirs Intl Black Writers Conf Inc 1982; mem Toastmasters Intl 1982-84; exec comm NC Haiku Soc 1983-; usher bd Marshall Chapel Missionary Bapt Church 1984-85; mem Poetry Soc of Amer, The Acad of Amer Poets, World Poetry Soc, NC Poetry Soc, Poets Study Club of Terra Haute, NC Writers Network, Intl Platform Assoc, The Poetry Council of NC Inc; The Haiku Soc of Amer; mem WV Poetry Soc; mem The Raleigh Writing Alliance; member, North Carolina Writers Conference, 1989-; member, Natl Book Critics Circle, 1989-; founder, executive director, Carolina African-American Writers Collective; chairman, The North Carolina Haiku Society, 1995-96; bd of dirs, La Jan Productions, 1995-. **Honors/Awds:** 1996 Indies Award; Haiku Museum of Tokyo Awd Haiku Soc of Amer 1983, 1994; CTM Awd Toastmasters Intl 1983; Dr Antonio J Waring Jr Memorial Prize The Poetry Soc of GA 1984; publishing grant NC Haiku Soc 1985; listed in Poets & Writers Inc; Alpha Chi Natl Coll Honor Scholarship Society, 1995; Gold Medal for Creative Writing Contest in West Germany; The Sallie Paschall Awd; Published in I Hear A Symphony: African Americans Celebrate Love, Anchor Books, 1994; In Search of Color Everywhere, Stewart, Tabori & Chang Inc, 1994; The Garden Thrives; Twentieth-Century African-American Poetry (Harper Collins), 1996; numerous works published including "The Open Eye," NC Haiku Soc Press 1985; "North Carolina's 400 Years, Signs Along the Way," The Acorn Press; "The Haiku Anthology," Simon & Schuster; Emerging Artist Grant, City of Raleigh Arts Commission, 1989; Role Model Experiences Award, St. Louis Public Schools, 1996-97; Margaret Alexander Creative Writing Award, College Lang Assn, 1997. **Special Achievements:** Author, Forever Home, 1992; Desert Storm: A Brief History, 1993; The Open Eye, 1985. **Military Serv:** AUS splst 4/E-4 3 yrs; Honorable Discharge, Good Conduct Medal. **Business Addr:** Division of Media & Technology, North Carolina Education Bldg, Raleigh, NC 27601-2825.

MOORE, LENNY EDWARD
State official. **Personal:** Born Nov 25, 1933, Reading, PA; son of Virginia and George; married Edith Randolph; children: Lenny, Leslie, Carol, Toni, Terri. **Educ:** PA St Univ 1956; LA. **Career:** Juvenile Serv Admin State of MD, prevention specialist, 1984-, program specialist, 1989-, crisis intervention counselor, 1991-; Baltimore Colts Ftbl Inc, promotions dir present; NW Ayer & Sons, field rep 1970-74; Baltimore Colts, professional ftbl 1956-67; WWIN Radio, sports dir 1962-64; pub relat for natl brewery 1958-63; WSID-RADIO, disc jockey sports dir 1956-58; resource consultant, 1984-. **Orgs:** Chmn Heart Assn; helped start "Camp Concern" following 1968 riots upon death of Martin Luther King; CBS Pro-Football analyst 1968; associate Leukemia, Kidney Found, Multiple Sclerosis, Muscular Dystrophy, Spec Olympics 1975-; adv council Juvenile Justice 1985-; board of directors, The Door, 1991; Governor's Advisory Committee on "Violence in Schools," 1994. **Honors/Awds:** Prof Ftbl Hall of Fame 1975; Pennsylvania Hall of Fame 1976. **Home Addr:** 8815 Stonehaven Rd, Randallstown, MD 21133. **Business Addr:** Ad of Special Projects, Maryland Dept of Juvenile Justice, 2323 Eastern Blvd, Baltimore, MD 21220.

MOORE, LEWIS CALVIN
Union official. **Personal:** Born Jun 22, 1935, Canton, MS; son of Louvenia McGee Moore and Sam A Moore; married Delores Thurman, Sep 29, 1956; children: Kelly, Thurman, Anderson. **Educ:** Manual HS Indianapolis IN, 1954. **Career:** OCAW Local 7-706, pres 1970-75; OCAW Dist Council 7, pres 1970-75; OCAW Dist 4 Houston, intl rep 1975-77; OCAW Washington Office, citizenship-legislative dir 1977-79; Oil Chem & Atomic Workers Intl Union, vp. **Orgs:** Labor instr Univ of IN; charter mem, natl bd mem A Philip Randolph Inst; mem NAACP; mem of bd Big Brothers of Amer; leader Boy Scouts of Amer; mem TX Black Alcoholism Council; instr Health & Safety Seminars in Kenya 1984, 1988. **Honors/Awds:** Recognition for serv in field of alcoholism & drug abuse. **Business Addr:** Vice President, OCAW Intl Union, PO Box 2812, Denver, CO 80201.

MOORE, LOIS JEAN
Health care executive. **Personal:** Born Oct 12, 1935, Bastrop, TX; daughter of Cecelia Wilson and Coronza Wilson; married Harold Moore, Nov 13, 1958; children: Yolanda E. **Educ:** Prairie View A&M University, Prairie View, TX, nursing diploma, 1957; Texas Woman's University, Houston, TX, BA, science nursing, 1970; Texas Southern University, Houston, TX, MA, education, 1974. **Career:** Harris County Hospital District-Ben Taub General Hospital, Houston, TX, shift supervisor, 1962-68, assistant director nursing services, 1968-69, director of nursing services, 1969-77; Harris County Hospital District-Jefferson Davis Hospital, Houston, TX, administrator, 1977-87; Harris County Hospital District, Houston, TX, executive vice president & CEO, 1987-89, president & CEO, 1989-. **Orgs:** Advanced fellow, American College of Healthcare Executives, 1987-; board member, National Association of Public and Non Profit Hospitals; board member, Texas Association of Public Hospitals, board member, March of Dimes Gulf Coast, chairperson, Houston Crackdown Treatment and Research Committee. **Honors/Awds:** Women on the Move, Medicine, The Houston Post, 1989; Outstanding Women of the Year, YWCA, 1989; Houston Women Leaders, Economic Summit, 1990; Distinguished Professional Woman's Award, Univ of Texas Health Science Center, 1990; Houston Nurse of the Year, Eta Delta Chapter, Sigma Theta Fraternity International, 1990. **Business Addr:** President, Chief Executive Officer, Harris County Hospital District, 726 Gillette 122, PO Box 66769, Houston, TX 77266-6769.

MOORE, M. ELIZABETH GIBBS
Librarian, library consultant (retired). **Personal:** Born in Boston, MA; daughter of Marece A Jones Gibbs (deceased) and Warmoth T Gibbs; divorced. **Educ:** NC A&T State Univ, 1940; Univ of Chgo, BLS 1945; Univ of Chgo, Grad Study 1948-49. **Career:** NC A&T State Univ, instr 1940-43; NC A&T State Univ, asst librarian 1943-44; Fisk Univ, cataloger 1945-48, Library Sci, instr 1945-46; Detroit Publ Library, cataloger 1945-53; Detroit Publ Library, ref librarian 1953-54; cataloging supervisor 1955-67; Burroughs Corp, Detroit area librarian 1967-71; Corp Library Burroughs Corp, 1971-79; Library MI Bell, human resources supervisor 1979-82, library consultant 1982-85 (retired). **Orgs:** Women's Econ Club, Special Libraries Assn; life mem Amer Library Assn, YWCA, Womens Natl Book Assn; bd dir Delta Home for Girls 1974-76; Friends of Detroit Publ Library 1970-76, 1980-82, Your Heritage House 1969-; bd dir Special libraries Assn 1981-84; mem Ctrl Adv Comm on Re-Accreditation of Wayne State Univ div of Libr Sci 1975-76; Adv Group for Selection of Head of Sci Libr Wayne State Univ 1976-77; life mem Delta Sigma Theta, NAACP; Guilford Cty Bd of Soc Serv 1984-87, 1988-90; bd dir Charlotte Hawkins Brown Historical Foundation 1985-; Women's Econ Club of Detroit 1967-82; bd dir Guilford Women's Network 1989-90; Library Serv & Construction Act Advisory Council to North Carolina State Library 1988-89; advisory council, North Carolina Central University, School of Library & Informan Service, 1981-88, member 1988-, recording secretary 1990-, Friends of the School of Education, North Carolina A&T State University. **Honors/Awds:** Saslow Medal for Scholarship in Soc Sci; Award for Meritorious Serv on Coll Newspaper; Alumni Award for Outstanding Serv 1969; Outstanding Grad in Field of Soc Sci Alumni Award 1973; Hall of Fame, Special Libraries Assn, 1986; Senior Citizen, Greensboro, NC, 1990. **Home Addr:** 1000 Ross Ave, Greensboro, NC 27406.

MOORE, MARCELLUS HARRISON
Physician. **Personal:** Born Apr 28, 1939, Griffin, GA; children: Marc, Michelle, Chris. **Educ:** Morehouse College, BS 1959; Meharry Medical College, MD 1966. **Career:** Mercy Hospital, attending physician 1975-; Michael Reese Hospital, attending physician 1975-. **Orgs:** American Medical Assn; Natl Medical Assn 1966-; American Academy Ophthalmology 1975-. **Honors/Awds:** Fellow, American Academy of Ophthalmology, 1979. **Military Serv:** US Air Force, capt, 1964-67.

MOORE, MARIAN J.
Former museum director, historian. **Personal:** Born in Saginaw, MI; daughter of Ann Moore and Eugene Moore. **Career:** National Afro-American Museum and Cultural Center, former director; Museum of African American History, Detroit, MI, director, 1988-93.

MOORE, MELANIE ANNE
Singer. **Personal:** Born Feb 7, 1950, Dayton, OH. **Educ:** Central State Univ Wilberforce OH, BS 1972. **Career:** Atlantic Records, singer; "The All Night Strut Boston Reperatory Theater," actress singer 1979; "The Autobiography of Lorraine Hansbery" Britanica Films Inc, actress 1976; Tymes RCA Records, singer 1975-78; Prudential Lines Inc, mgmt trainee 1976-77; JC Penney Co NY, asst buyer trainee 1972. **Orgs:** Mem AFTRA 1977; mem AGVA 1979; counselor adminstrv asst Veritas Therapeutic Drug Center 1976. **Honors/Awds:** Miss homecoming Central State Univ 1972; biography Black Stars Mag Tymes 1977; biography Kleeer Black Stars Mag 1980; "Black Tress" Magazine 1980.

MOORE, MELBA (BEATRICE HILL)
Actress, singer. **Personal:** Born Oct 29, 1945, New York, NY; daughter of Melba Smith Hill and Teddy Hill; married George Brewingston. **Educ:** Montclair State Teachers College, BA. **Career:** Acting experience includes: Cotton Comes to Harlem, 1970; Hair, 1979; Inacent Black, 1981; television appearances include: Comedy is King; Ed Sullivan Show; Johnny Carson Show; Melba, 1986; Ellis Island, 1984; Melba Moore-Clifton Davis Show, 1972; Hotel; The American Woman: Portraits of Courage; theater appearances include: Purlie, 1970; film appearances include: Lost in the Stars, 1974; albums include: Melba Moore; Peach Melba; This Is It; A Portrait of Melba; The Other Side of the Rainbow; Never Say Never; Read My Lips; A Lot of Love. **Honors/Awds:** First black to perform solo, Metro Opera House, 1977; Tony Award, Best Supporting Actress, Purlie, 1970; Drama Desk Award, Purlie, 1970; Antoinette Perry Award, Purlie, 1970; New York Drama Critics Award, Purlie, 1970; Grammy Award, nomination, Read My Lips, 1985; Grammy Award, nomination, This Is It. **Business Addr:** c/o Capitol Records, 1750 N Vine St, Hollywood, CA 90028.

MOORE, MILTON DONALD, JR.
Dermatologist. **Personal:** Born Aug 16, 1953, Aberdeen, MD; son of Dora Lee Moore; divorced; children: Rahmon, Justin. **Educ:** Xavier Coll of Pharmacy, RPh 1976; Meharry Medical Coll, MD 1980. **Career:** Hubbard Hospital, pharmacist 1976-80; Baylor Coll of Medicine, derm dept asst prof 1985-; private practice, physician 1985. **Orgs:** Bd mem Ensemble Theatre 1986. **Honors/Awds:** Outstanding Young Men of Amer; American Academy of Dermatology. **Business Addr:** Physician, 7553 South Freeway, Houston, TX 77021.

MOORE, MINYON
Organization executive. **Career:** Democratic National Committee, political director; White House, deputy asst to the president, deputy dir of political affairs, currently. **Special Achievements:** First African American political director of the Democratic National Committee.

MOORE, N. WEBSTER
Educator (retired). **Personal:** Born Mar 5, 1913, Claremore, OK; married Fordine Stone. **Educ:** KS State Coll of Pittsburgh, attended; Univ of KS, AB 1937, MA 1939; St Louis Univ, Washington Univ, Stowe Teachers, Harris Teachers Coll, Langston, attended. **Career:** Bristow OK Public Schools, teacher 1939-48; AR State AMN Coll, teacher 1947; Hadley Tech High School, teacher 1956-63; Vashon High School St Louis, teacher 1948-56, 1963-78. **Orgs:** Pres Missouri Council for Social Studies, 1975-76; acting pres, St Louis Public Library, 1979-80; vice pres bd of dir, Arts & Educ Council, 1978-80; chmn bd, Page Park YMCA, 1972-74; bd of mgr, YMCA of Greater St Louis, 31 years; bd of dir, St Louis Prog Teachers Credit Union, Jr Kindergarten 1978-, KS Univ 1978-, Wells-Goodfellow 1978-79, Carver House, AARP, NRTA, Retired Teacher Assn of MO 1980, Retired St Louis School Employees Assn, Boy Scouts; dir, St Louis Public Library, 1972; committeeman, NAACP; grand historian, Kappa Alpha Psi, 1944-47; sr member, Monsanto YMCA; member, Natl Council for Social Studies, Greater St Louis Council for Social Studies, MO Council for Social Studies, St Louis White House Conf on Educ, Historical Assn of Greater StLouis, MO Historical Soc, State Histcal Soc of MO, St Louis Teachers Assn, St Louis Teachers Union, United Churchmen, Metro Bd of YMCA, Urban League, Arts & Educ Council, US China Peoples Friendship Assn, Metro Dist & Branch YMCA Intl Program Comm, St Louis Westerners; former member, Natl Council of YMCA of the US; attended the World Council of YMCA in 1981. **Honors/Awds:** Kappa Alpha Psi, Outstanding Service Award, 1966, N Webster Moore Humanitarian Award, first, 1971, Mid-Western Province, Achievement Award, 1974, Lifetime Achievement Award, 1992; Young Men's Christian Association, St Louis Chapter, Award for 17 Years Service to Youth, 1965, J Clinton Hawkins Award for Volunteering, 36 Years of Service, 1992; Mayor's Proclamation, 50 Years of Community and Youth Services, 1991. **Special Achievements:** Author, several articles, Missouri Historical Society Bulletin.

MOORE, NAT
Professional football player (retired), business executive. **Personal:** Born Sep 19, 1951, Tallahassee, FL; son of Julia Mae Gilliam; married Patricia; children: Trellanee, Natalie, Melanie. **Educ:** Attended, Univ of FL. **Career:** Superstar Rollertheque,

owned; Inferno Lounge, owned; L&S Builders, past partner; Miami Dolphins, wide receiver, 1974-86; Nat Moore & Associates Inc, president, currently. **Orgs:** Bd mem Dade County United Way; bd mem Jackson Mem Children's Hosp; Boy Scouts of America; member, Orange Bowl Committee; board of governors, Doral Ryder Open; trustee, Greater Miami Chamber of Commerce; board member, University of Florida Foundation. **Honors/Awds:** All NFL Honors AP Pro-Football Writers 1977; All AFC Recognition; Tommy Fitzgerald Awd Outstanding Rookie in Training Camp 1974; Byron ''Whizzer'' White Humanitarian Awd NFL Players Assn 1986; inducted: Sports Hall of Champions, Florida Hall of Fame.

MOORE, NATHAN
Educator. **Personal:** Born Jun 26, 1931, Mayaro, Trinidad and Tobago; son of Eugenie Samuel Moore and William B Moore; married Mary Lisbeth Simmons, Jul 3, 1967; children: Christine, Serena. **Educ:** Caribbean Union Coll Trinidad, A 1958; Rockford Coll IL, BA 1963; Carleton Univ Ottawa, MA 1965; Univ of British Columbia, PhD 1972. **Career:** Barbados Secondary Sch, hs tchr 1958-61; Carleton U, sessional lecturer 1964-65, teaching fellow 1963-65; Barrier Sch Dist British Col, hs tchr, 1966-67; Walla Walla Coll WA, coll tchr 1967-79; AL State U, professor of English, 1979-, chmn dept of Engl 1980-. **Orgs:** Mem Modern Lang Assn 1965-; mem Am Soc for 18th Century Studies 1971-; mem South Atlantic MLA 1980-. **Honors/Awds:** Schlrshp Rockford Coll 1961; schlrshp Readers Digest 1962; Carleton Fellow Carleton Univ 1963-65. **Business Addr:** Chairman, Department of Languages and Literatures, Alabama State University, S Jackson St, Montgomery, AL 36101.

MOORE, NOAH WATSON, JR.
Bishop (retired). **Personal:** Born Mar 28, 1902, Newark, NJ; son of Eliza A Boyce Moore and Noah W Moore, Sr; married Carolyn W Lee Moore (deceased); children: Carolyn Moore Weddington. **Educ:** Morgan State Coll, AB 1926; LLD 1961; Drew Univ, BD 1931; Crozier Theol Sem, postgrad 1945-46; Grammon Theol Sch, DD 1951; So Meth Univ, 1968; NE, Wesleyan Univ, STD 1969. **Career:** Meth Ch ordained to ministry 1932; consecrated bishop 1960; NY State MD PA, pastor 1930-47; Eastern Dist MD, supt 1947-49; Tindley Temple Meth Ch Philadelphia, pastor 1949-60; New Orleans area, resident bishop 1960-64; SW area, bishop 1964-68; NE area, 1968-72. **Orgs:** Mem Meth Gen Overseas Relief 1952-60; del Gen Conf Meth Ch 1952, 56, 60; sec treas dir Philadelphia Housing Auth 1954-60; Gammon Theol Sem Houston-Tillotsen Coll Morriston Coll 1956-60; Hlth & Welfare Agency So Area Meth Ch Philadelphia 1957-59; pres Coll of Bishop Cntrl Juris 1956; mem Preaching Mission to AK 1956; study tour W Germany Berlin 1959; trustee Dillard Univ 1960-68; pres bd trustees Philander Smith Coll 1964-68; pres trustees Wiley Coll 1964-68; mem Gen Bd Educ pres United Meth Gen Bd Evangelism 1968-72; mem exec com World Meth Council; United Fund Philadelphia & vincinity; Bryan Meml Hosp; St Paul Sch Theol; Meth Kansas City MO; bd govs trustee NE Wesleyan Univ; bd dirs Urban League Philadelphia; NAACP; bd mgrs Christian St YMCAPhiladelphia; mem Frontiers of Am; Natl Co ul Chs; Omega Psi Phi; Mason; trustee Atlanta Comm Coll. **Honors/Awds:** Honorary LLD, Morgan State Coll, 1961.

MOORE, OSCAR JAMES, JR.
Physician, educator. **Personal:** Born in Griffin, GA; son of Minnie B Moore and Oscar Moore Sr; children: Frederick, Elna. **Educ:** Morehouse Coll, BS, 1955; Atlanta Univ, 1955-56; Howard Univ, MD, 1962, intern, 1963; Harvard Univ, Thorndike Memorial Lab, Boston City Hospital, resident, 1963-66. **Career:** US Navy Submarine Base Hospital, director of Medicine, 1966-68; St Francis Hospital, Hartford, CT, physician, 1968-69; Mt Sinai Hospital, physician, 1968-69; Mile Square Center, Chicago, IL physician, 1969-72; Michael Reese Hospital, Chicago, IL, physician, 1969-80; Presbyterian St Lukes Hospital, Chicago, IL, physician, 1969-80; Rush Medical College, assistant professor, 1969-79; Cedar Sinai Hospital, Los Angeles, CA, physician, 1970-91; University of California at Los Angeles School of Medicine, assistant clinical professor, beginning 1970, clinical professor, currently; KoMed Center, medical director, 1972-80; University of Chicago Pritzker School of Medicine, associate professor; California Hospital, Los Angeles, CA, physician, 1990-. **Orgs:** Board of directors, Chicago Urban League; board of directors, Olive Harvey College, Chicago Junior College Board; board of directors, Mid South Health Planning Organization; consultant to HEW Regional Planning; board of directors, Abraham Lincoln Center, Chicago, IL; board of directors, Hoover Institute, Stanford University, 1990-; Omega Psi Phi; Beta Kappa Chi. **Honors/Awds:** Citizen of the Year Award, Olive Harvey College, Junior College Board, 1976. **Military Serv:** US Navy, Lt Cmdr, 1966-70; Distinguished Service Award. **Business Addr:** Clinical Professor, UCLA Medical School, 1414 S Grand Ave #380, Los Angeles, CA 90015-1970.

MOORE, OSCAR WILLIAM, JR.
Clergyman, educator. **Personal:** Born Mar 31, 1938, White Plains, NY; son of Helen Moore and Oscar Moore Sr; married Vicki Renee Bransford, Feb 14, 1990; children: Derrick, John, Sean, Mahla, William. **Educ:** Southern IL Univ, BS 1969, MS 1970; graduate of Philadelphia Coll of The Bible; attending Trinity Coll of The Bible, Trinity Theological Seminary. **Career:** Southern Illinois Univ, asst dir 1969-71; Glassboro State Coll, asst prof, head track & field coach, currently; Mt Olive Baptist Church, Glassboro, NJ, assoc minister, currently. **Orgs:** Sec/treas New Jersey Track Coaches Assoc 1975-; faculty sponsor Alpha Phi Alpha, Sigma Sor; dir Glassboro Summer Martin Luther King; dir Manna Bible Institute, Glassboro campus. **Honors/Awds:** Teams have consistently placed in the top natl ranking including NCAA Div III Championships in 1980, 1981; recognized as one of the countries finest masters competitors; numerous speaking engagements in high schools; assists with Red Cross, Cancer Soc, YMCA fund raising campaigns; Track a Field Team, Five Time Natl Champions. **Special Achievements:** Olympian, track and field, 1964. **Military Serv:** USMC sgt 1956-60; Good Conduct Award 1957. **Home Addr:** 6 Harrell Ave, Williamstown, NJ 08094. **Business Addr:** Assistant Professor, Rowan College of New Jersey, Health & Physical Ed Dept, Glassboro, NJ 08028.

MOORE, PARLETT LONGWORTH
Educational administrator. **Personal:** Born Sep 17, 1907, Wetipquin, MD; married Thelma Crawford; children: Thelma Moore Smith, Parlett L Moore Jr, Daniel C Moore. **Educ:** Howard Univ, AB 1930; Teachers Coll Columbia Univ, MA 1935; Univ of Chicago, 1946; Temple Univ, EdD 1952; Stanford Univ, 1955. **Career:** St Clair HS, principal 1930-38; Lincoln HS Rockville, MD, principal 1938-50; Morgan State Coll-Summer School, instr 1938-43; Carver HS Rockville, MD, principal 1950-56; Coppin State Coll Baltimore, MD, pres 1956-70; Middle States Acrdtg Assoc, evaluation comm 1950-70; MD Assoc for Higher Educ, pres 1968; Coppin State Coll, pres emeritus 1970-. **Orgs:** Bd of dir MD Region Natl Conf Christians & Jews 1956-63; bd of dir MD Assoc of mental health (15 yrs); bd of dir Baltimore Metro YMCA (8 yrs); prlmntrn Frontiers Internatl Baltimore Club 1957-85. **Honors/Awds:** The Gnrl Alumni of Howard Univ Metitorious Award for Consipcuous Serv in the Field of Educ 1963.

MOORE, PENNY
Professional basketball player. **Personal:** Born Jan 25, 1969. **Educ:** Long Beach State, attended. **Career:** Charlotte Sting, forward, 1997; Washington Mystics, 1998-. **Business Addr:** Professional Basketball Player, Washington Mystics, MCI Center, 601 F St NW, Washington, DC 20071.

MOORE, QUEEN MOTHER. **See Obituaries section.**

MOORE, QUINCY L.
Educational administrator. **Personal:** Born Dec 31, 1949, Chicago, IL; son of Hannah Moore and N L Moore; widowed. **Educ:** Culver-Stockton College, BA, 1972; University of Nevada, Las Vegas, MS, 1975; University of Iowa, PhD, 1983; Harvard Graduate School of Education, MDP diploma, 1992. **Career:** University of Nevada, Upward Bound Program, director, 1973-76; Clark County Community College, CETA consultant, 1976-77; University of Nevada, Special Services Program, director, 1977-78; Virginia Commonwealth University, Educational Support Program, director, 1985-89, president's office administrative assistant, 1991, Office of Academic Support, director, 1989-. **Orgs:** Association for Multicultural Counseling & Development, president, 1992-93; Coalition for Access, Affordability & Diversity in Higher Education, vice chairman, 1992-93; Concerned Black Men of Richmond, 1990-94; American Counseling Association, Task Force on Black Males, chairman, 1991-92; Leadership Metro of Richmond, 1991-92; Richmond Jazz Society, advisory board member, 1989-94; Richmond Community High School, advisory board member, 1991-94; Richmond Javeline & Domestic Courts, advisory board, 1993-. **Honors/Awds:** United Negro College Fund, Distinguished Leadership Awards, 1985-88; American Counseling Association, ACA Legislative Award, 1992; Association for Multicultural Counseling & Development, John L Lennon Professional Success Award, 1992; Delta Sigma Theta, Virginia Commonwealth University, Faculty of the Year Award, 1992. **Special Achievements:** Co-author, Transcultural Counseling from an African-American Perspective, 1993. **Business Addr:** Assistant Professor, Director, Office of Academic Support, Virginia Commmonwealth University, 109 N Harrison St, PO Box 842500, Richmond, VA 23284-2500, (804)828-1650.

MOORE, RICHARD
Cleric, educator. **Personal:** Born Oct 19, 1956, Chicago, IL. **Educ:** Union Theological Seminary, MDiv. **Career:** Holy Unity Day Care, director; Holy Unity Baptist Church, pastor, currently. **Orgs:** NAACP; Youth Unlimited Inc, pres. **Business Addr:** President, Holy Unity, 167-10 137th Ave, Jamaica, NY 11434, (718)723-7353.

MOORE, RICHARD BAXTER
Attorney. **Personal:** Born May 26, 1943, Erie, PA; son of Jean Baxter Moore and Lewis Tanner Moore; divorced; children: Leonard, Richard Jr, Tiffiny. **Educ:** Central State Coll, BS 1965; Howard Univ School of Law, JD 1969. **Career:** City of Phila, asst jury commissioner, 1979-91; Private Practice, attorney; Philadelphia, PA asst district atty 1971-77. **Orgs:** IBPOEW; Mem Elks Chris J Perry Lodge 965, Phi Alpha Delta Law Frat, Omega Psi Phi Frat; NAACP; chmn Veterans Comm; vice chmn United Negro Coll Fund, City of Philadelphia; Juvenile Serv Sub Comm on Public Serv, vice chmn 1973-74; Compensation for Victims of Crimes Comm, sec 1974-75; Natl Bar Found, vice pres bd of dirs 1975-78; Philadelphia Bar Assn; Sigma Pi Phi Fraternity. **Honors/Awds:** Service Awd Chapel of Four Chaplains; Citation United Negro Coll Fund; Service Award, Boys & Girls Clubs of America. **Military Serv:** AUS capt 1969-71. **Business Addr:** Attorney at Law, 406 South 16th St, Philadelphia, PA 19146.

MOORE, RICHARD EARLE
Educational administrator. **Personal:** Born Apr 3, 1916, Marion, AL; married Rose Marie Greene; children: Richard E, Harriette M, Gwendelyn Tutt, Reginald E. **Educ:** Talladega Coll, AB cum laude 1939; Atlanta U, MS/MA 1961; Auburn Univ, EdS/EdD 1979. **Career:** Clayton Jr Coll, asst dean 1973-; JF Drake High Sch, high school prin 1949-71; Coffee Co Training School, high school prin 1945-49; Escombia Co Training School, high school science math teacher 1940-45. **Orgs:** Mem NAACP; Alpha Phi Alpha; NASSP; Phi Delta Kappa; Council on Black Am Affairs Commr; Fulton Co Voter Registration Bd 1977; 100 Black Men of Atlanta. **Honors/Awds:** NDEA fellow Amherst Coll 1965; NDEA fellow Davidsons Coll 1966; CPSDI fellow Auburn Univ 1971-73; blacks in white coll Council on Black Amer Affairs 1976. **Home Addr:** 4270 Sloop Way, College Park, GA 30349.

MOORE, RICHARD V.
Educator. **Personal:** Born Nov 20, 1906, Quincy, FL; married B J Jones. **Educ:** Knoxville Coll, AB; Atlanta Univ, MA; NY Univ, post grad work. **Career:** Pinellas HS, instr coach 1932-34; Unoin Acad, prin 1934-37; Rosenwald HS, prin 1937-44; Booker T Washington HS, 1944-45; Negro Secondary Schools, state supr 1945-47; Bethune-cookman Coll, pres 1947-. **Orgs:** Mem Rotary Club Dayton Beach; conf lay leader FL Conf; mem Halifax Bd Commnrs; bd dirs Whinn-dixie Stores Inc; vice chmn FL Fed Savs & Loan Assn; mem Civic League; Daytona Beach Chamber of Commerce; NAACP; dir Central FL United Negro Coll Fund Inc; sec Independent Colleges & Univ of FL; Afro-Am Life Ins Co; Halifax Area Citizen's Scholarships Found; trustee So Coll & Gammon Theol Sem. **Honors/Awds:** Lovejoy Award; St George Award; outstanding citizen of yr Daytona Beach; numerous hon degs honors. **Business Addr:** 640 2 Ave, Bethune Cookman Coll, Daytona Beach, FL 32115.

MOORE, ROB
Professional football player. **Personal:** Born Sep 27, 1968, New York, NY; married Drucilla; children: Dakota, Savoy. **Educ:** Syracuse University, degree in psychology, 1990. **Career:** New York Jets, wide receiver, 1990-94; Arizona Cardinals, 1995-. **Honors/Awds:** New York City Council, Role Model of the Year, 1991; Marty Lyons Award, 1992; Edge Man of the Year, 1992; Pro Bowl, 1994. **Business Addr:** Professional Football Player, Arizona Cardinals, 8701 S Hardy, Tempe, AZ 85284, (602)379-0101.

MOORE, ROBERT ANDREW
Broadcaster. **Personal:** Born Mar 12, 1953, Harrisburg, PA; son of Occie Belle Anthony Moore and Johnson Parker Moore. **Educ:** Northwestern University, Evanston, IL, BS, 1988; Medill School of Journalism, Evanston, IL, MSJ, 1989. **Career:** Centel, Des Plaines, IL, recruiter, 1976; Honeywell Inc, Schiller Park, IL, employment manager, 1977-79; Chicago Urban League, Chicago, IL, program manager, 1979-81; General Electric Company, Oak Brook, IL, employee relations specialist, 1981-83; US Dept of Defense, North Chicago, IL, management analyst, 1984-87; Hill & Knowlton, Chicago, IL, editorial assistant, 1988; Capital Cities/ABC Inc, Philadelphia, PA, producer, 1989-. **Orgs:** Member, Philadelphia Assn of Black Journalists, 1989-; member, Chicago Assn of Black Journalists, 1986-88; member, Natl Assn of Black Journalists, 1986-; member, Natl Academy of Television Arts and Sciences, 1991; founding pres, Northwestern Black Alumni Assn, 1986-88. **Honors/Awds:** Gannett Journalism Fellow, Gannett Educational Foundation, 1988-89. **Business Addr:** Producer, News, Capital Cities/ABC Inc, 4100 City Ave, Philadelphia, PA 19131-1610.

MOORE, ROBERT F.
Educator. **Personal:** Born Jan 30, 1944, Tuskegee Inst, AL. **Educ:** Fisk Univ, BS 1965; IN Univ, MS 1966; IN Univ, EdD 1969. **Career:** Fisk Univ Nashville; assoc prof educ 1971-; Coppin State Coll, asst Prof 1968-70. **Orgs:** Mem bd dirs TN Assn Retarded Citizens; Davidson Co Assn Retarded Citizens; TN Foster Grandparents Assn; Grace Eaton Day Home; Phi Delta Kappa 1966. **Business Addr:** Box 11, Dept Educ Fisk University, Nashville, TN 37203.

MOORE, RODNEY GREGORY
Attorney. **Personal:** Born Sep 1, 1960, Birmingham, AL; son of Jethroe Moore (deceased) & Tommie Moore; married Yaslyn Moore, Nov 20, 1994; children: Nyosha, Rodney G II, Imani. **Educ:** University of Washington, BA, 1982; University of Santa Clara School of Law, JD, 1985. **Career:** Washington

State Attorney General's Office, consumer protection claims rep, 1980-82; Bancroft Whitney Legal Pulications, associate editor, 1984-85; Law Offices of Williams, Robinson and Moore, partner/attorney, 1987-89; Lincoln Law School, professor, 1991-93; East Side Union High School District, school board member, 1994-97; Moore Law Firm, president/CEO, 1989-97; General Counsel, Eastside Union High District, 1997-. **Orgs:** California Association of Black Lawyers, president, 1993-94; National Bar Association, director region IX, 1993-94, general counsel, 1997-98; Santa Clara County Black Lawyers Association, president, 1989-91; Santa Clara County Bar Association, bd of trustees, 1989-91; Board of Visitors, Univ of Santa Clara Law School, 1993-; Chief Counsel, Santa Clara County Black Chamber of Commerce, 1991-97; California State Bar, 1987-; Santa Clara Computer & High Technology Law Journal, associate editor, 1984-85; National Black Law Students Association, western regional director, 1984-85; University of Washington, Black Student Union, president, 1980-82. **Honors/Awds:** California Legislature, Resolution, 1994; US House of Reps, Resolution, 1994; City of San Jose, Proclamation, 1994; California Legislature, Certificate of Recognition, Entreprenurial Spirit, 1994; Santa Clara County Black Chamber of Commerce, Order of the Golden Hand, 1991; CA Assn of Black Lawyers, "Loren Miller Award-Attorney of the Year", 1997. **Special Achievements:** International Monitor, Independent Elections Commission, Republic of South Africa, 1994. **Business Addr:** President, Moore Law Firm, APC, 1611 The Alameda, San Jose, CA 95126, (408)286-6431.

MOORE, RONALD
Professional football player. **Personal:** Born Jan 26, 1970, Spencer, OK; married Tammy; children: Ashlynn, Allison. **Educ:** Pittsburg State, attended. **Career:** Arizona Cardinals, running back, 1994, 1997-; New York Jets, 1995-96; St Louis Rams, 1997. **Business Addr:** Professional Football Player, Arizona Cardinals, 8701 S Hardy, Tempe, AZ 85284, (602)379-0101.

MOORE, ROSCOE MICHAEL, JR.
US health services veterinarian. **Personal:** Born Dec 2, 1944, Richmond, VA; son of Robnette Johnson Moore and Roscoe Michael Moore Sr; married Patricia Ann Haywood, Aug 2, 1969; children: Roscoe III, John H. **Educ:** Tuskegee Univ, BS 1968, DVM 1969; Univ of Michigan, MPH 1970; Johns Hopkins Univ, MHS 1982, PhD 1985. **Career:** Natl Insts of Health, veterinarian 1970-71; Centers for Disease Control, epidemic intelligence serv officer 1971-73; Ctr for Veterinary Medicine, sr veterinarian 1973-74; Natl Inst Occup Safety & Health, sr epidemiologist 1974-81; Center for Devices and Rad Health, sr epidemiologist 1981-92; Univ of Washington, Seattle, assoc prof, 1989-; Public Health Serv, chief veterinary medical officer, 1989-93; assoc dir, Office of International and Refugee Health, US Public Health Service, 1992-. **Orgs:** Mem Amer Veterinary Medical Assoc 1969-; mem bd of dirs FONZ 1979-; pres bd of dirs Friends of the Natl Zoo 1984-87; fellow Amer Coll of Epidemiology 1984-; adv comm Howard Univ Coll of Medicine 1985-; consultant, School of Veterinary Medicine, Tuskegee Univ 1988-; mem bd of governors, Univ of Michigan Public Health Alumni 1987-93; Omega Psi Phi Fraternity, 1995-; bd of dirs Montgomery General Hospital, 1992-. **Honors/Awds:** Commendation Medal US Public Health Serv 1976,83; USPHS Career Develop Awd to attend Johns Hopkins Univ 1977-79; Delta Omega Natl Honorary Public Health Society 1985; Honorary Doctor of Science, Tuskegee University, 1990; Surgeon General's Exemplary Service Medal, 1990. **Home Addr:** 14315 Arctic Ave, Rockville, MD 20853. **Business Phone:** (301)443-1774.

MOORE, SAM
Singer, entertainer, performer. **Personal:** Born Oct 12, 1935, Miami, FL; son of Louise White and John Richard Hicks; married Joyce McRae, Mar 26, 1982; children: Debra, Steven, Tangela, Lawanda Denise, Michelle Gayle, Vicky, JoAnn. **Career:** Singer, entertainer, performer, singles (with Dave Prater) include: "You Don't Know Like I Know," 1966; "Hold On, I'm Comin," 1966; "Soul Man," 1967; "I Thank You," 1968; albums (with Dave Prater) include: Sam and Dave, 1966; Best of Sam and Dave, 1969; Soul Men, 1992. **Orgs:** NARAS, currently; Society of Singers, currently; Rhythm & Blues Foundation, Artist Advisory Board, currently. **Honors/Awds:** NARAS, Grammy, 1967; Rhythm & Blues Foundation, Pioneer, 1991; Rock & Roll Hall of Fame, inductee, 1992. **Special Achievements:** Command performance for Queen of England, 1967; command performance for Jimmy Carter, White House, 1975; Presidential Inauguration of George Bush, 1989. **Business Addr:** Entertainer, c/o Joyce McRae, The Bubba Inc, 7119 E Shea Blvd, Ste 106, Scottsdale, AZ 85254, (602)996-0548.

MOORE, SHELLEY LORRAINE
Writer, corporate communications consultant. **Personal:** Born Mar 19, 1950, New York, NY; daughter of Sheppie Moore and Dr Marcus W Moore. **Educ:** Syracuse Univ, BA 1971; Columbia Univ, MA, EdM 1973. **Career:** Natl Urban League, asst dir 1976-80; Natl Urban League, program coordinator 1980-83; Burson-Marsteller, Inc, acct exec 1983-85; Shelley Moore Communications, principal, 1985-; Mobil Corporation, staff assoc, 1988-. **Orgs:** Chairperson comm on minorities Public Relations Soc of Amer NY Chapter 1979-80 dir public relations Council of Concerned Black Exec 1981-82; mem NY Assn of Black Journalists; mem, Brooklyn Communications Arts Professionals. **Honors/Awds:** Articles & photographs published in natl publications.

MOORE, SHEMAR
Actor, model. **Educ:** Santa Clara Univ. **Career:** Actor; TV appearances: The Young and the Restless, 1994-; Living Single; The Jamie Foxx Show; The Nanny. **Honors/Awds:** Emmy Award nomination, 1997; NAACP,Image Award, nominated, 1996, Daytime Drama Actor, 1998. **Business Addr:** Actor, Craig Agency, 8485-E Melrose Pl, Los Angeles, CA 90069, (213)655-0236.

MOORE, SUSIE M.
Government association executive. **Personal:** Born Sep 3, 1918, Washington, DC. **Educ:** Miners Tchr's Coll. **Career:** HEW Bur Comm Health Servs, training grant splst family planning; Fed Govt, employee 34 yrs; Vocational Rehab Serv, grants mgmt splst & adminstrv asst 22 yrs. **Orgs:** Mem dist pres Woman's Home For Miss Soc; AME Zion Ch 1961-; rec sec Nat Coun Negro Women 1971-73. **Honors/Awds:** Superior serv award Vocational Rehab Ofc 1957. **Business Addr:** 5600 Fishers Ln, Rockville, MD 20852.

MOORE, THELMA W. C.
Judge. **Career:** Superior Court, Fulton County, GA, judge, currently. **Orgs:** Natl Ctr for State Courts, bd of dirs, currently. **Business Addr:** Judge, Superior Court, 136 Pryor St. SW, Rm 108, Atlanta, GA 30303, (404)730-5300.

MOORE, THOMAS L.
Business executive. **Personal:** Born Jun 26, 1926, Burke Co, GA; married Alma Brown; children: Tommy, Yvonne, Dionne, Michael. **Educ:** Swift Meml Coll; Knoxville Coll. **Career:** TAM Inc Constrn Co, pres; Tommy Moore Enter; Moore's Package Store. **Orgs:** Bd dir City & Co Bank of Knox Co; chtr commn Knox Co Bd of Commr; pres Knoxville Nat Bus League; Bus Devel Ctr C of C; bd dir Jr Achmvt; bd dir BSA; pres Cncl on Yth Oppt YMCA. **Honors/Awds:** YMCA cert award Commonwealth of KY; KY Col Nat Soc of Vol of Am; TN Rep Capitol Club. **Business Addr:** 1312 Mc Calla Ave, Knoxville, TN 37915.

MOORE, TRUDY S.
Journalist. **Personal:** Born Jan 6, 1957, Paterson, NJ; daughter of Queen E Moore; children: Taylor S Moore. **Educ:** Howard Univ, Washington, DC, BS, 1979; Northwestern Univ, Evanston, IL, MS, 1980. **Career:** Chicago Sun-Times, Chicago, IL, gen assignment reporter, 1980; Jet Magazine, Chicago, IL, asst editor, 1980-83, assoc editor, 1983-89, feature editor 1989; Ebony Man, Chicago, IL, contributing editor, 1988-90. **Orgs:** Volunteer, Big Brothers/Big Sisters, Chicago, IL, 1982-85; mem, Chicago Urban League, 1986-; mem, NAACP, Women's Auxiliary, 1989; mem, bd of dir, NAACP, Chicago, South Side Branch, 1989, mem, Chicago Assn of Black Journalists. **Business Addr:** Feature Editor, Jet Magazine/Johnson Publishing Co, 820 S Michigan Ave, Chicago, IL 60605.

MOORE, UNDINE SMITH. See Obituaries section.

MOORE, WALTER LOUIS
Government official. **Personal:** Born Mar 14, 1946, Pontiac, MI; married Daisy Barber. **Educ:** Attended Ferris State Coll 1966-68, Oakland Univ. **Career:** City of Pontiac MI, firefighter; County of Oakland MI, commissioner 1978; City of Pontiac MI, mayor. **Orgs:** Campaign mgr, Coalition for a Modern Charter, City of Pontiac; organized I-75 Mayor's Conference; mem, US Conference of Mayors; mem, Natl Conference of Black Mayors; dir, Pontiac Youth Assistance; charter mem, Pontiac Optimist Club; mason, Gibraltor Lodge #19 Prince Hall; bd mem, Offender Aid and Restoration. **Honors/Awds:** America's Outstanding Young Men, Jaycees of Amer, 1984; Man and Boy Award, Boys and Girls Club of Pontiac, 1986; Community Serv Award, Oakland County NAACP; Community Serv Award, Natl Org of Negro Business and Professional Women's Clubs. **Home Addr:** 37 Ottawa Dr, Pontiac, MI 48341.

MOORE, WARFIELD, JR.
Judge. **Personal:** Born Mar 5, 1934, Chicago, IL; son of Sally Curry Moore and Warfield Moore, Sr; married Jeane Virginia; children: Warfield III, Sharon, Sally Anne, Janet. **Educ:** Univ of MI, AB 1957; Wayne State Univ, LLB 1960. **Career:** Private Practice, attorney 1961-78; Recorders Court, judge 1978-. **Orgs:** Michigan Bar Assn; Wolverine Bar Assn; Black Judge's Assn. **Honors/Awds:** Law Review, Wayne State Univ; editor 1958-60. **Business Addr:** Judge, Recorders Court, 1441 St Antoine #404, Detroit, MI 48226, (313)224-2430.

MOORE, WENDA WEEKES
Researcher. **Personal:** Born Dec 24, 1941, Boston, MA; daughter of Dr and Mrs Leroy R Weekes; married Cornell L Moore; children: Lynne, Jonathon, Meredith. **Educ:** Howard Univ, BA 1963; USC, grad work 2 years. **Career:** Gov Wendell R Anderson, staff asst; Wash, DC Library, researcher; Westminster Town Hall Forum, director, currently. **Orgs:** Mem League of Women Voters 1964, 1974; appointed by Gov Anderson to bd of regents Univ of MN 1973; elected by MN Legislature to bd of regents 1975; elected v chairperson bd of regents 1975; chmn bd of regents 1977-83; mem Univ of MN Found; bd mem MN bd of Continuing Leg Edn; elected dir Gamble-Skogm Inc 1978-82; leader First Educ Exchange Delegation Univ of MN to People's Republic of China 1979; Presidental appointee to Bd of Adv US Dept of Educ 1980; Adv Coun 1980-83; Natl Commn on Foreign Lang 1980; mem Alpha Kappa Alpha; mem, pres 1987-, Minneapolis/St Paul Chap of Links; Jacks and Jill; pres of the board of directors, Chart/Wedco 1989-90; trustee, Kellog Foundation, 1988-; bd mem, Amer Judicature Society, 1990. **Honors/Awds:** Torch & Shield Award 1982; Outstanding Woman in Education YWCA 1983; Outstanding Alumni Achievement Howard Univ 1989; Esther Crosby Contribution to Community, Greater Minneapolis Girl Scout Council, 1990. **Home Addr:** 2727 Dean Parkway, Minneapolis, MN 55416.

MOORE, WILL H.
Professional football player. **Personal:** Born Feb 21, 1970, Dallas, TX; married Phyllis. **Educ:** Texas Southern, bachelor's degree in business, 1992. **Career:** New England Patriots, wide receiver, 1995-96; Jacksonville Jaguars, 1997-. **Business Addr:** Professional Football Player, Jacksonville Jaguars, One Stadium Place, Jacksonville, FL 32202, (904)633-6000.

MOORE, WINSTON E.
Association executive. **Personal:** Born in New Orleans; married Mabel Lee Woods. **Educ:** WV State Coll, MA 1952; Univ LA, BA 1954. **Career:** Clinic IL Youth Commn Joliet, dir 1961-66; IL State Employment Serv Chicago, staff psychologist 1966-68; Cook Co Jail, supt cook 1968-70; Cook Co Dept-Corrections, exec dir 1970-. **Orgs:** Mem Am Correctional Assn; Cook Co Criminal Justice Commn; IL Dept Corrections Adult Adv; bd mem Rotary 1. **Military Serv:** AUS s/sgt 1945-49. **Business Addr:** 2600 S California, Chicago, IL 60608.

MOORE, YOLANDA
Professional basketball player. **Personal:** Born Jul 1, 1974; children: Courtney, Ashley. **Educ:** Mississippi, attended. **Career:** Houston Comets, forward, 1997-. **Honors/Awds:** Associated Press, Honorable Mention All-America, 1996. **Business Addr:** Professional Basketball Player, Houston Comets, Two Greenway Plaza, Ste 400, Houston, TX 77046, (713)627-9622.

MOOREHEAD, BOBBIE WOOTEN
Educator. **Personal:** Born May 26, 1937, Kelly, LA; daughter of Ora Lee Edwards Jones and Verdie C Wooten; married Erskine L Moorehead; children: Eric Lyn, Jennifer Lynne. **Educ:** Atlanta Univ, attended 1958-59; TX Southern Univ, BS 1958, MEd 1977; Certification, Administration Supervision, 1977. **Career:** Goose Creek Consolidated School Dist, teacher 1959-62; Houston Independent School Dist, teacher 1963-. **Orgs:** Comm on administration YWCA 1977-84; regional dir Zeta Phi Beta Sorority 1978-80; Natl Convention Chmn Zeta Phi Beta Sorority, 1978; mem Commn on Accreditation for the Schools of TX 1978-83; natl first vice pres Zeta Phi Beta Sorority 1980-84; natl pres Top Ladies of Distinction Inc 1983-87; natl bd convention chmn Natl Council of Negro Women 1985, 1987, 1989; mem Speakers Bureau, Houston Planned Parenthood Federation, Houston Urban League Guild; Natl Executive Bd, Natl Council of Negro Women, Natl Chrmn Social and Legislative Action for Top Ladies of Distinction, Inc; Natl Council of Negro Women, Inc, natl vice pres, 1991-95. **Honors/Awds:** Service to the State Award Gov Dolph E Briscoe 1977; Hon Bd Mem TSU Maroon and Grey Ex-Students Assn 1983, 1984; Woman of Achievement in Leadership Sigma Gamma Rho Sor 1986; Leadership Award Zeta Phi Beta Sorority 1986; Jack Yates High School Hall of Fame 1986; Distinguished Woman Award South Central Dist Women of Achievement Inc 1986; 1987 History Makers Award Educ Riverside Hospital; Gem, Blue Triangle Branch, YMCA, 1990; Natl Women of Achievement, Inc, Natl Achiever's Award, 1993; Kappa Alpha Psi, Community Leadership Award-Education, 1994; South Central Branch, YMCA, Community Leadership Award, 1993. **Business Addr:** Meeting Planner/Consultant, PO Box 131894, Houston, TX 77219, (713)748-3119.

MOOREHEAD, ERIC K.
Journalist. **Personal:** Born Jun 21, 1958, Baltimore, MD; son of Rose Marie Lewis Moorehead and Archie Clarence Moorehead; married Gemma Arlene Arrieta Moorehead, Dec 21, 1986; children: Eric Bradford Arrieta Moorehead. **Educ:** University of Central Arkansas, BA, 1980; University of Southern California, Graduate School, journalism, 1982-84. **Career:** Western Electric, New York, NY, intern public relations, 1980-80; City of Los Angeles, Los Angeles, CA, intern, press office of Mayor Tom Bradley, 1982-82; Los Angeles Business Journal, Los Angeles, CA, editorial intern, 1984-84; Arkansas Democrat, Little Rock, AR, copy editor/reporter, 1986-90; Arkansas State Press, Little Rock, AR, reporter, 1990-91; Little Rock In View Magazine, Little Rock, AR, editor, 1991. **Orgs:** Member,

National Association of Black Journalists, 1990-; member, Univ of Central Arkansas Alumni Association, 1985-. **Honors/Awds:** AEJ/NYU Summer Internship, Association of Education in Journalism, New York University, 1980; Dean's List, Univ of Central Arkansas, 1979. **Home Addr:** 3512 Wynne St, Little Rock, AR 72204.

MOOREHEAD, JUSTIN LESLIE

Banker. **Personal:** Born Oct 31, 1947, St Thomas, VI; married. **Educ:** Occidental Coll Los Angeles CA, BA History 1969; Woodrow Wilson School Princeton Univ, MPA Concentration, Econ Devel 1971; NY Univ Grad School of Bus Admin, Transp Econ 1974; Univ of MI Exec Acad, 1977; Bank of Amer, Municipal Credit & Money Mkt Instr 1978. **Career:** Government of Kenya, rural devel planner 1970; Government of the US Virgin Islands, economist office of the budget dir 1971-72; Virgin Island Dept of PublicWorks, admin 1972-73; Amerada Hess Corp, 1973-75; Virgin Island Office of the budget Dir, budget dir 1975-79; Lehman Brothers Kuhn Loeb Inc vice pres publ fin 1979-83; Dean Witter Reynolds Inc, managing dir public finance. **Business Addr:** Managing Dir, Dean Witter Reynolds Inc, 2 World Trade Center, New York, NY 10048.

MOOREHEAD, THOMAS

Automobile dealer. **Personal:** Born Apr 21, 1944, Monroe, LA; son of Minnie M Moorehead and Thomas E Moorehead; married Deborah J, Oct 3, 1972; children: Lawrence A. **Educ:** Grambling State University, BS, business administration, economics, 1966; University of Michigan, School of Social Work, MSW, 1971; University of Michigan, PhD, urban and regional planning, 1993. **Career:** Moble Oil Corporation, marketing analyst, 1966-67; Chrysler Corporation, Parts Division, systems analyst, 1969-70; University of Michigan, director, project community, 1971-72, School of Social Work, field instructor, 1971-83, director, community services, 1972-83; Jim Bradley Pontiac, Cadillac, GMC Inc, sales consultant, 1984-85, Cadillac sales mgr, 1985-88; Thomas A Moorehead Buick Inc, Sentry Buick-Isuzu, president/owner, 1988-. **Orgs:** Omaha Chamber of Commerce, board member; Norwest Bank Omaha, board member; Omaha Boy Scouts of America, board member; YMCA of Omaha, board member; Methodist Hospital, board of trustees; RH Davis Scholarship Fund, board member; The Salvation Army, Omaha, board member; Federal Reserve Bank of Kansas City's Tenth District, advisory council; City of Omaha Private Industry Council, board member; Rotary Club International, Omaha; Kappa Alpha Psi Fraternity, life member; Urban League of Nebraska, life member; University of Nebraska, Omaha, chancellor's advisory council. **Honors/Awds:** Pontiac Motors, Master Sales Guild, 1984-86; Cadillac Motors, Crest Club, 1986; Black Entreprise Top 100 Minority Business, 1988-91; Omaha Chamber of Commerce Business of the Year, 1989. **Military Serv:** US Army, sp4, 1967. **Home Addr:** 882 Jasons Way, Forsyth, IL 62535-9647. **Business Addr:** President, CEO, Moorehead Buick GMC, PO Box 2168, Forsyth, IL 62535.

MOORER, MICHAEL

Professional boxer. **Career:** Professional boxer, currently. **Honors/Awds:** World Heavyweight Boxing Champion, defeated Evander Holyfield, 1994. **Business Phone:** (708)897-4765.

MOORE-STOVALL, JOYCE

Physician. **Personal:** Born Nov 5, 1948, Washington, DC; daughter of Ida Barnes Moore and Joseph Samuel Moore; married Arthur J Stovall; children: Artis Jomar, Aaron Joseph, Arthur Jr, Kelly Ann. **Educ:** Fisk Univ, BA 1970; Meharry Medical Coll, MD 1974. **Career:** Veteran's Administration, diagnostic radiologist; Mallinckrodt Institute of Radiology, St Louis, MO, visiting fellowship, 1983; VA Medical Center, Kansas City, MO, visiting fellowship, 1984; Washington School of Medicine, Mallinckrodt Institute of Radiology, St Louis, MO, visiting fellowship, 1987; Wisconsin School of Medicine, Milwaukee, WI, visiting fellowship, 1990; Eisenhower Veteran's Affair Medical Center, diagnostic radiologist, currently. **Orgs:** Natl Medical Assn; Greater Kansas City Radiological Society. **Honors/Awds:** Board Certified Radiology, 1989; A Consortium of Doctors Honoree, 1993. **Special Achievements:** Author: "Parosteal Osteosarcoma," 1982; "Anorectal Abscesses," 1983, Journal of the Kansas Medical Soc; "Pneumatosis Coli," Journal of the Natl Medical Assn, 1983; "CT, Detecting Intraabdominal Abscesses," Journal of the Natl Medical Assn, 1985; "AIDS: The Role of Imaging Modalities and Infection Control Policies," Journal of the Natl Medical Assn, 1988; "Magnetic Resonance Imaging of an Adult with Dundy Walker Syndrome," Journal of the Natl Medical Assn, 1988; "Serial Nonenhancing Magnetic Resonance Imaging Scans of High Grade Glioblastoma Multiforme," Journal of the Natl Medical Assn, 1993; "Ruptured Pancreaticodyodenal Arterial Aneurysms: Diagnosis and Treatment by Angiographic Interventional," Journal of Natl Medical Assn, 1995. **Home Addr:** 1617 Ridge Rd, Leavenworth, KS 66048-6504. **Business Addr:** Diagnostic Radiologist, Eisenhower Veteran's Affair Medical Center, 1401 S 4th Trafficway, Leavenworth, KS 66048.

MOORHEAD, JOHN LESLIE

Food and beverage company executive. **Personal:** Born Oct 6, 1942, St Thomas, Virgin Islands of the United States; son of Valerie Leslie Moorhead and Dr John S Moorhead; married Ingela Carlestrom-Moorhead; children: Charles, Robynn. **Educ:** Otterbein College, Westerville, OH, BA, 1963; New York University, New York, NY, ABD, 1966; Harvard Business School, Boston, MA, MBA, 1973. **Career:** General Mills, Minneapolis, MN, assistant product manager, 1973-76, product manager, 1976-79; Frito Lay, Dallas, TX, director of marketing, 1979-81; Taco Bell, Irvine, CA, vice president marketing, 1981-85; Pepsi-Cola, Somers, NY, vice president, marketing services/public affairs, 1985-91; CPC International, vice pres, business management mktg services, 1992-. **Orgs:** Board member, Dance Theatre of Harlem, 1986-91; board member, National Consortium for Educational Access, 1988-92; board member, Association of National Advertisers, 1990-94; board member, Council of Better Business Bureaus, 1990-93; board member, Citizens Scholarship Foundation of America, 1985-92. **Military Serv:** US Air Force, Captain, 1967-71. **Business Addr:** Vice Pres, Best Foods, CPC International, 700 Sylvan Ave, Englewood Cliffs, NJ 07632.

MOORHEAD, JOSEPH H.

Physician. **Personal:** Born Mar 15, 1921, Frederiksted, St Croix, Virgin Islands of the United States; married Juanita; children: Joel, Karen, Frankie, James, Justina, Joseph, John. **Educ:** Fisk U; Meharry Med Coll; Homer G Phillips Hosp; Hubbard Hosp; Pittsfield Gen; W MA. **Career:** Pvt Prac, gynecologist; Am Bd Ob-Gyn, diplomate. **Orgs:** Mem Atlanta Ob-Gyn Soc; Nat Med Assn; mem Kappa Alpha Psi Frat; FL Cattleman Ass; diplomate Nat Bd of Med Examrs; flw Am Coll Surgeons; Am Coll Ob-Gyn. **Military Serv:** AUS capt 1952-55. **Business Addr:** 75 Piedmont Ave NE, Atlanta, GA 30303.

MOORING, KITTYE D.

Educator. **Personal:** Born Mar 18, 1932, San Antonio; married Leon. **Educ:** Prairie View A&M Univ, BA 1953, MS 1960; Univ Houston, EdD 1969. **Career:** Carver HS, dept head 1953-62; Prairie View A&M Univ, assoc prof 1962-68; Bus Educ & Off Administration TX Southern Univ, dept head 1970-; School of Business, assoc dean, 1990-93. **Orgs:** Nat & TX Bus Assn; chmn TX Bus Tchr Educ Council 1973-75; TX Assn Coll Tchrs; Amer Assn Univ Prof; YWCA; Chadwick Manor Civic Club; Commission on Standards, 1989-92; Univ Curriculum Comm, chairman, 1980-; Faculty Awards & Recognition Committee, chairman, 1985-. **Honors/Awds:** Many hon soc; State Service Youth Awd; Leaders Black Amer 1974; TBEA Collegiate Business, Teacher of the Year, 1983; McCleary, Teacher of the Year, 1993. **Business Addr:** Professor & Dept Head, School of Business, Texas Southern University, 30100 Cleburne, Houston, TX 77004.

MOORMAN, CLINTON R. (BOB)

Football scout. **Personal:** Born Mar 10, 1924, Cincinnati; son of Clinton and Thelma; married Tamiko Sanbe; children: Bobby, Kathy. **Educ:** Univ of Maryland, BS 1965. **Career:** National Football League, Officials' Scouting Program, scout, 1989-; Old Dominion Univ, special asst to the athletic director, 1989-91; Central Intercollegiate Athletic Assn, commissioner, 1976-89; San Diego Chargers, talent scout 1969-75; worked for the Packers, Cardinals, Browns, Falcons, Redskins, Giants, Patriots, working for CEPO area scouts, 1975-76; Wiley Coll, head football coach 1966-68. **Orgs:** Mem Alpha Phi Alpha Res Officers Assn; Fellowship Christian Ath 1969; Peninsula Sports Club 1973; Big Bros Inc 1973. **Military Serv:** US Army, Corporal 1943-46, Major 1949-66; Bronze Star, Purple Heart, US Army Commendation Medals.

MOORMAN, HOLSEY ALEXANDER

Military officer. **Personal:** Born May 18, 1938, Roanoke, VA; son of Grace O Walker Moorman (deceased) and Holsey James Moorman (deceased); married Carrie Boyd, Aug 3, 1963; children: Gary Wayne. **Educ:** Hampton Univ, 1956-58; Park Coll, BS, business administration, 1986; Command & General Staff Coll; US Army War Coll, senior reserve component officer course. **Career:** US Civil Service, training officer 1965-68, admin officer 1968-80, EEO officer 1980-86; Office of Dept Chief of Staff Personnel for the US Army, personnel policy integrator; Asst Sec of the Army, military asst, 1987-90; Asst Sec of the Army, Washington, DC, asst deputy, 1990-92; Army Reserve Forces Policy Committee, military executive, 1992-94; deputy adjunct general, 1994-. **Orgs:** Life mem, Natl Guard Assn of NJ 1964-, life mem, Natl Guard Assn of the US 1964-; mem, PHA, F&AM 1978-; EEO investigator Natl Guard Bureau 1982-86. **Honors/Awds:** NAACP, Roy Wilkens Renown Service Service Award, 1993. **Military Serv:** US Army col 1961-; Meritorious Serv Medal, Army Commendation Medal, Army Serv Ribbon, Armed Forces Reserve Achievement Medal, Armed Forces Reserve Medal, NJ Medal of Honor; Legion of Merit; (IOLC) National Defense Service Medal; Army Superior Unit Award; NJ Good Conduct Award; Desert Storm Ribbon; New Mexico Medal of Merit; Governor's Unit Award; Unit Strength Award; National Guard Bureau Eagle Award, 1994. **Home Addr:** 60 Drewes Ct, Lawrenceville, NJ 08648.

MOOSE, GEORGE E.

Foreign service officer. **Personal:** Born Jun 23, 1944, New York, NY; son of Ellen Amanda Lane Jones Moose and Robert Moose; married Judith Roberta Kaufmann. **Educ:** Grinnell Coll, BA 1966-; Syracuse Univ, postgraduate 1966-67. **Career:** Dept of State Washington DC, special asst to under sec for political affairs 1977-78, dep dir for Southern Africa 1978-79; Council For Relations NY, foreign affairs fellow 1979-80; US Mission to the UN NYC, dep political counselor 1980-83; Dept of State Washington DC, US ambassador to Benin 1983-86; deputy dir office of mgmt operations 1986-87, dir office of mgmt operations 1987-88; US ambassador to Senegal, 1988-91; US Alternate Representative in the UN Security Council, 1991-92; Assistant Secretary of State for African Affairs, 1993-. **Orgs:** Mem Amer Foreign Serv Assn 1967-; foreign affairs fellow Council on Foreign Relations NY 1979-80; mem Assoc of Black American Ambassadors 1985-, Policy Council Una Chapman Cox Foundation 1986-89; member, Council on Foreign Relations, 1991-; mem, board of directors, African Development Foundation, 1993-. **Honors/Awds:** Superior Honor Award Dept of State 1974; Meritorious Honor Award Dept of State 1975; Superior Honor Award Dept of State 1979; Senior Performance Pay 1985; Presidential Meritorious Serv Award, 1989, 1994; Doctor of Letters Honoris Causis, Grinnell College, 1990. **Business Addr:** Assistant Secretary of State for African Affairs, US Department of State, Rm 6234A, Washington, DC 20520.

MOO-YOUNG, LOUISE L.

Educator. **Personal:** Born Dec 29, 1942, Lexington, MS; married Ervin; children: Troy, Tiffany, Tricia. **Educ:** Nursing St Mary of Nazareth 1963; Roosevelt Univ, B Gen Studies 1974; Governors Univ BA; Roosevelt Univ, MPA 1975. **Career:** State Univ Instructor, Marion Adult Educ Center, com prof gov. **Orgs:** Pres Faulkner Sch Assn 1977-78; mem Bd Trustees Faulkner Sch 1977-78; beat rep 21st Dist Police; mem Gov Adv Cnc of Developmental Disabilites 1976-77; mem Comprehensive Sickle Cell Anemia Community Adv Cnc Univ of Chicago Neighborhood Health Cntr Adminstr Chicago Bd of Health Claude WB Holman Neighborhood Helath Cntr 1972-; pub health nurse supvr Chicago Bd of Health 1970-72; pub health field nurse Chicago Bd of Health 1964-70; staff nurse head nurse MI Ave Hosp Chicago 1963-64; part-time indu nurse Ryerson Stell; staff nurse Woodlawn Hosp; Past mem Am Nurses Assn; Economic & Gen Welfare Com; IL Nurses Assn; Pub Health Section IL Nurses Assn Sec 1975; ARC Nurse Active in Ch & Comm Affairs; chmn Health Task Force Chicago Urban League 1973-74; peer group educ com Loop JrColl; ex-oficio tdvisory Bd of Claude WB Holman Neighborhood Health Center; St Margaret Epis Church Vestery 1976-77; office mgr for Chicago Campaign Office 1975; mem Amer Soc of Pub Adminstrs; St Mary's Alumni; Roosevelt Univ Alumni. **Honors/Awds:** Awarded by Jr Assn of Commerce Indus one of Chicago's Ten Outstanding Young Cits 1973-74; outstanding achvmt aw 4th Ward Dom Orgnz; recip cert The Emerging Women in Mgmt Workshop.

MORAGNE, LENORA

Publisher, editor. **Personal:** Born in Evanston, IL; daughter of Linnie Lee Moragne (deceased) and Joseph Moragne Sr (deceased). **Educ:** IA State Univ, BS; Cornell Univ, MS, PhD 1969. **Career:** Comm Hosp Evanston IL, chief dietitian 1955-57; Cornell Univ, asst prof 1961-63; NC Coll, asst prof, 1965-67; Gen Foods Corp, publicist 1968-71; Columbia Univ, lecturer, 1971-72; Hunter Coll, prof, 1971-72; Food & Nutrition Serv USDA, head nutrition, ed & training 1972-77; Agr Nutrition & Forestry Comm US Senate, professional staff mem, first female, 1977-79; DHHS nutrition policy coord 1979-84; Nutrition Legislation Svcs, founder, pres, 1985-; founding editor, publisher, Nutrition Legislation News, The Nutritior Funding Report, 1986-; founding editor, publisher, Black Congressional Monitor, 1987-; National Academy of Sciences, senior project officer, Institute of Medicine, 1988-89; National Rainbow Coalition, consultant, 1990; Environmental Protection Agency, environmental officer, 1994-. **Orgs:** Mem, Amer Dietetic Assn, Soc Nutrition Ed, Amer Publ Health Assn, Cornell Club DC, Natl Council Women; mem Adv Council Major Univ, Cornell IA State, Univ of DE, Univ of MD; mem bd of dir Amer Dietetic Assoc 1981-84; mem APHA Prog Devel Bd 1984-87; nominee bd of trustees Cornell Univ 1984; pres Soc for Nutrition Educ 1987-88; mem adv council Meharry Med Coll Nutrition Center, 1986-; Chairman, Cornell University Federal Government Relations Committee, 1985-88. **Honors/Awds:** Co-author Jr HS nutrition text "Focus on Food"; co-authored baby record book for new parents "Our Baby's Early Years"; author num food-nutrition related articles in professional publication; Elected to Cornell Univ Council, 1981; Distinguished Alumni Award, IA State, 1983; Certificate of Appreciation, USDA, 1973; Special Appreciation Award, Natl Assoc of Business & Professional Women, 1971; traveled W Africa, Central Amer, Europe; Nominee, Cornell Univ, Bd of Trustees, 1984; Inducted into Gamma Sigma Delta Honorary Agriculture Soc, 1987; president, Society for Nutrition Education, 1987-88; founding mem, Joseph & Linnie Lee Monagne Memorial Scholarship Fund, 1992-. **Business Addr:** Founding Editor/Publisher, Black Congressional Monitor, PO Box 75035, Washington, DC 20013, (202)488-8879.

MORAGNE, MAURICE S.
Tobacco company executive. **Personal:** Born Jan 22, 1964, Washington, DC; son of Jacquelyn D Moragne; married Dana M Moragne, Mar 24, 1989; children: Mitchell M, Jordan A. **Educ:** Edinboro University of Pennsylvania, BA, 1986. **Career:** Brown & Williamson, sales rep, Orlando FL, 1987-89, div manager, Orlando FL, 1989-91, brand mktg associate, Louisville KY, 1991-94, district sales manager, Champaign IL, 1994, district sales manager, Milwaukee WI, 1994-95, section sales manager, Baltimore, 1995-96, director of human resources, 1996-. **Honors/Awds:** Black Achievers Award, Louisville, 1993. **Special Achievements:** Fluent in Spanish, 1977-80. **Business Addr:** Director, Human Resources, Brown & Williamson Tobacco Corp., 1500 Brown Williamson Tower, Louisville, KY 40202, (502)568-8270.

MORAGNE, RUDOLPH
Physican. **Personal:** Born Feb 5, 1933, Evanston, IL; married Kathlyn Elaine; children: Donna, Diana, Lisa. **Educ:** Univ IL, BS 1955; Meharry Med Coll, MD 1959; Cook Co Hosp, intern & resident 1961-65. **Career:** R Moragne, MD SC, physician. **Orgs:** Amer Coll Ob-gyn Surgeons; AMA; Nat'l Med Assn; IL & Chicago Med Soc; Cook Co Physicians Assn Univ Chicago Lying In Hosp staff; dir S Side Bank; memUrban League; Operation PUSH. **Honors/Awds:** Beautiful people awd Chicago Urban League 1973; co-author Our Baby's Early Years 1974. **Military Serv:** USAF capt 1961-63. **Business Addr:** 8044 S Cottage Grove, Chicago, IL 60619.

MORAN, GEORGE H.
Employment analyst. **Personal:** Born Jun 30, 1941, Chicago, IL; son of George H Moran & Wedell Johnson; divorced. **Educ:** IUPUI; Baker College, AAS; Detroit College, BA. **Career:** Instructor, data processing; Instructor, computer programming; Employment Svc (DVOW), Durable Veteran Outreach; Michigan Employment Security Commission, employment analyst, currently. **Orgs:** Vietnam Veterans Management Commission, chairman; VFW 3791; Southern Cross 39, free mason; International Association of State Employment; Black Association of State Employers; Black Data Processing Association, VVA, Vietnam, Vietnam Veterans of America. **Honors/Awds:** Henry; The Department of Michigan VFW Henry Wolfe Awd, 1994; Veterans VVA, VVA Retraining Awd, 1993; African-American Veterans Banquet, State of MI, 1994. **Military Serv:** US Army, ssgt, 1960-70. **Home Addr:** G-1055 W Harvard Ave, Flint, MI 48505. **Business Addr:** Employment Analyst, Michigan Employment Security Commission, 7310 Woodward, Detroit, MI 48202.

MORAN, JOYCE E.
Attorney. **Personal:** Born May 21, 1948, Chicago, IL; daughter of Irma Rhyne Moran and Theodore E Moran. **Educ:** Smith Coll Northampton MA, AB 1969; Yale Law School New Haven, JD 1972; Univ of Chgo, MBA 1981. **Career:** Sidley & Austin, associate attorney, 1972-78; Sears Roebuck & Co, vice pres, law, deputy general counsel, 1978-. **Orgs:** Bd of dirs, vice pres, president Legal Asst Found of Chicago 1974-88; chmn Lawyers Com Chicago Urban League 1980-82; vice pres Chicago League of Smith Coll Clubs 1972-; ed review team leader Mayor Washington Transition Comm Chicago 1983; Jr Governing Bd of Chicago Symphony Orchestra 1973-85; Chicago Symphony Chorus & Chorale Omega 1974-78; bd of dirs Alumnae Assn of Smith Coll 1984-87; vice pres Smith Coll Class of 1969, 1974-79; vp, treas Yale Law School Assoc of IL 1975-78; coordinator Coppin AME Church Enrichment Prog 1981-84, chair for public forums, 1992-93; bd of dir Chicago Area Foundation for Legal Serv 1982-95; bd of dir, vice pres ACLU of IL 1983-92; bd of dir, v chair Chicago Found for Women 1985-88, advisory council, 1989-92; bd of dir, vp, treas Chicago School Fin Auth 1985-93; Kennedy-King Community Chorus 1986-94; Illinois Judicial Inquiry Bd 1987-91; bd of trustees, vice chair, chair of pres search comm, chair of AD Hoc chaper, com, Smith Coll 1988-98; dir, ACLU 1987-89; bd of dir, sec Women's Association of the Chicago Symphony Orchestra 1991-97, exec leadership counsel, 1997. **Honors/Awds:** Distinguished Serv Awd Coppin AME Church Chicago 1972; Player of the Year Jr Master, Amer Bridge Assn 1977; Beautiful People Awd Chicago Urban League 1979; YMCA of Metro Chicago Black & Hispanic Achievers of Indust Recog Awd 1981; Ten Outstanding Young Citizen Awd Chicago Jr Assn of Commerce & Industry 1985. **Business Addr:** Vice President, Law and Deputy General Counsel, Sears Roebuck & Co, B6 222A, 3333 Beverly Rd, Hoffman Estates, IL 60179.

MORAN, ROBERT E., SR.
Clergyman, educational administrator (retired). **Personal:** Born Jul 24, 1921, Columbus, OH; son of Edna Carr and Herbert Williams; married Esther Quarles; children: Robert E Moran Jr. **Educ:** Ohio State Univ, BS 1944; Ohio State Univ, MA 1947; Ohio State Univ, PhD 1968; Harvard Summer School, Certificate 1971. **Career:** Palmer Memrl Inst, teacher 1944-46; Xenia E High, teacher 1947; Allen Univ, teacher dir student teaching 1948-59; Southern Univ, prof dean 1959-87; Southern Univ, dean coll of arts & humanities, retired; Bethel AME Church, asst pastor, 1989-. **Orgs:** Historian Assn of Soc & Behavrl Science 1981; edtr br jrnl of Negro history Assn for the Study of Negro Life & History 1982-; Omega Psi Phi Frat. **Honors/Awds:** One Hundred Yrs of Child Welfare in LA 1980.

MORANCIE, HORACE L.
Appointed official, management consultant. **Personal:** Born in San Fernando, Trinidad and Tobago. **Educ:** Polytech Inst of Brooklyn BSc Civil Engrg 1958; Cornell Univ, MSc Civil Engrg 1960; Brooklyn Law School, Harvard Univ, John F Kennedy School of Govt, Cert 1982. **Career:** Office of the Mayor City of NY, asst admin 1968-74; Rockland Comm Action Council Inc, mgmt consult 1974-80, exec dir 1976-80; State of NY Div of Econ Opport, dir 1980-82; City of Harrisburg Dept of Community & Econ Devel, dir; Horace L Morancie & Assocs, devel housing & mgmt consultant. **Orgs:** Teaching fellow Cornell Univ 1958-60; rsch & civil engr Port Authority of NY & NJ 1960-68; bd chmn Urban Resources Inst, Addiction Rsch & Treatment Corp; v chmn Harrisburg Redevel Auth; bd mem Natl Comm Devel Assoc; chmn Harrisburg Property Reinvestment Bd. **Honors/Awds:** HUD Scholarship John F Kennedy School of Govt 1982. **Business Addr:** Consultant, Horace L Morancie & Assocs, 469 Rockaway Parkway, Brooklyn, NY 11212.

MORANT, MACK BERNARD
Educator, publisher. **Personal:** Born Oct 15, 1946, Holly Hill, SC; son of Jannie Gilmore Morant and Mack Morant. **Educ:** Voorhees College, Denmark, SC, BS, business administration, 1968; University of Massachusetts, Amherst, MA, MEd Urban Education, 1972, CAGS, education administration, 1973, EdD, 1976. **Career:** Belcher Town State School, mental health assistant I, 1974-76; University Masachusetts, graduate student, research assistant, 1971-74; South Carolina Public School System, history, English, business teacher, 1968-71; Dillion-Marion Human Resources Comm, deputy director, 1977-81; South Carolina State College, Orangeburg, SC, director small business development ct, 1982-85; Virginia State University, Petersburg, VA, placement director, 1985-92; Augusta College, assistant professor, teacher, Georgia, 1992-96; Voorhees College, student support services program, dir, 1997-. **Orgs:** Vice-chairman, Virginia State University Assessment Committee, 1986-87; member, Prince Hall Mason, 1986-; member, American Philatelic Society, 1988-; member, Alpha Kappa Psi Fraternity, 1985-. **Honors/Awds:** SPA Articles Include: ''Identifying and Evaluation of Black History in Textbooks,'' The Journal of Secondary School Principals News; ''The Gigantic Asylumn,'' The Carolina Messenger, 1977; ''Blues, Jazz, and American Blacks,'' The Chronicle of Higher Education, 1978; The Insane Nigger, R&M Publishing Co, 1979; Publications include ''Demystification of Blackness,'' Exploration in Education, South Carolina State College, 1983; ''Bookselling: Direct Mail Marketing,'' Interlit, Dec, 1991. **Business Addr:** Publisher, R&M Publishing Co, PO Box 1276, Holly Hill, SC 29059.

MORCOM, CLAUDIA HOUSE
Judge. **Personal:** Born Jun 7, Detroit, MI; daughter of Glady Stuart and Walter House. **Educ:** Wayne State Univ, BA 1953; Wayne State Univ Law School, LLB-JD 1956. **Career:** City of Detroit Housing Commission, pub housing aid 1956-60; Law Firm of Goodman Crockett et al, atty/assoc mem 1960-66; Natl Lawyers Guild So Legal Com, so regional dir 1964-65; City of Detroit, dir neighborhood legal serv 1966-68; State of MI Dept of Labor, admin law judge 1972-83; Wayne County Circuit Court, judge 1983-. **Orgs:** Instr Afro-Amer Studies Univ of MI 1971-73; instr Inst of Labor Industrial Relations 1972-73; bd of mgmt YMCA & YWCA 1971-; adv Wayne State Univ Council on World Affairs - Cntr for Peace & Conflict Studies 1974-; exec bd natl Alliance Against Racist & Polit Repression 1974-; mem State Bar of MI; mem and delegate to conf in Nicaragua 1981, Granada 1983, Argentina 1985 Assoc of Amer Jurists; participant Human Rights Workshop Natl Conf on the Nicaragua Constitution held in NY 1986; bd mem Merrill Palmer Inst; chmn adv bd Renaissance Dist Boy Scouts of Amer; mem Detroit Police Dept, Jr Cadet Adv Comm, Detroit Strategic Plan Comm; bd of dir Renaissance Club, Harmony Park Playhouse; vice pres Millender Fund; Wilmington 10 Defense Committee; Alternatives for Girls; KIND; Michigan Democratic Black Caucus; life mem NAACP; Plymouth United Church of Christ; Michigan Black Judges Assn; National Bar Assn. **Honors/Awds:** Natl Shrine Scholarship Award Denver, CO 1953; Civil Rights Award Natl Negro Women 1965; Civil Rights Award Cook Cnty Bar Assn 1966; Human Rights Award Detroit Chap Amer Civil Liberties 1967; Human Rights Award Detroit Com on Human Rights 1969; MI State Legislative Cert of Merit 1977; Spirit of Detroit Award 1977; Cert of Recognition YWCA Met Detroit 1979; Damon J Keith Civic and Humanitarian Award 1984; Comm Leadership Awd Coalition of 100 Black Women; Women of Wayne Headliner Awd; Boy Scouts Appreciation Awd; John F Kennedy Awd of Co-Ettes Club; Heart of Gold Awd Boy Scouts of Amer; Natl Honor Soc Awd Cass Tech HS; Shaw College, Honorary Doctor of Humane Letters; Wayne County Neighborhood Legal Services, Liberty Bell Award; Cass Technical High School, National Honor Society Award; Wayne State University, The Woman of Wayne Award, Dauris Jackson Award, Outstanding Alumni Award; Eastern Market Business Assn, Service to the Handicapped Award; The Center for Constitutional Rights Award, 1990; Boy Scouts of America, Silver Beaver Award, 1994; Certificate of Special Congressional Recognition, 1996; Evergreen Children Services, Service Award, 1996; State Bar Of Michigan, Champion of Justice, 1996; Michigan Women's Hall of Fame, Life Achievement Award, 1996. **Business Addr:** Circuit Court Judge, Wayne County, 1607 City County Bldg, Detroit, MI 48226.

MORELAND, LOIS BALDWIN
Educator, educational administrator. **Personal:** Born in Washington, DC; daughter of Fannie Baldwin and Genis G Baldwin; married Charlie J Moreland; children: Lisa Carol Moreland Overton. **Educ:** Sarah Lawrence Coll, BA; Howard Univ, MA; Amer Univ Washington, PhD. **Career:** Howard Univ, asst & instr soc sci 1956-57; NAACP, SE reg youth field sec 1957-58; US Senator R Vance Hartke, legis asst 1958-59; Spelman Coll, instructor 1959-65, asst prof, chairman, pol sci dept, 1965-70, prof & chmn political science dept 1970-90, 1991-92, acting dean of instruction 1970-72, chmn soc sci div 1980-90, prof polit sci, dir of international affairs center, 1989-. **Orgs:** Charter mem & first treas Natl Conf Black Polit Sci; former mem Amer Assn Univ Women, NAACP, League Women Voters; former mem Fulton Co Bd Elections; Fulton Co Jury Commn; Gov's Council Human Rel; mem American Southern & GA Political Science Assoc, Assoc of Politics & the Life Sciences; Alpha Kappa Alpha; former mem advisory council, Natl Inst of Neurological, Communicable Disease and Stroke; former member advisory council on Deafness and other Communication Disorders; Natl Institutes of Health. **Honors/Awds:** Author, White Racism and the Law 1970; Amer Legion Award; Ford Foundation Fellow; The American Univ Govt Intern Fellow; Merit Achiev Amer Men of Sci; Outstanding Educator 1973; Amer Polit Sci So Conf Award; United Negro Coll Fund Fellow; Sarah Lawrence College Scholarship; honorary life mem, Natl Assoc of Business Women; Presidential Award for Excellence in Teaching, Spelman College, 1988-89; Nu Fambda Omega Chapter, Alpha Kappa Alpha Sorority, Professional Excellence Award, 1993; Editorial Bd, The Natl Political Science Review, 1993-. **Business Addr:** Dir, Intl Affairs Center, Spelman College, PO Box 359, Atlanta, GA 30314.

MORELAND, SALLIE V.
College president. **Career:** Clinton Junior College, Rock Hill SC, president, currently. **Business Addr:** President, Clinton Junior College, PO Box 968, Rock Hill, SC 29731.

MORELAND-YOUNG, CURTINA
Educator. **Personal:** Born Mar 5, 1949, Columbia, SC; daughter of Gladys Evelyn Glover Moreland and Curtis Weldon Moreland; married James Young, Jun 20, 1978 (divorced 1983); children: Curtis Jamel Turner Moreland-Young. **Educ:** Fisk University, Nashville, TN, BA, 1969; University of Illinois, Urbana, Il, MA, 1975, PhD, 1976; Harvard University, Cambridge, MA, post-doctoral, 1982. **Career:** Ohio State University, Dept of Black Studies, Columbus, OH, instructor asst prof, 1971-78; Jackson State University, Mississippi College & University Consortium for International Study, Dept of Political Science, coord for MA program, assoc prof, 1978-84, chair, public policy & administration dept, 1984-. **Orgs:** Chair, pres, The Conference of Minority Public Administrators, 1989-90; member, exec board, National Conference of Black Political Scientist, 1989; member, National Council of American Society for Public Administrators, 1989-90; chair, The Committee on Organization Review & Evaluation, ASPA, 1990-91; member, exec board, Jackson International Visitors Center. **Honors/Awds:** Kellogg National Fellow, Kellogg Foundation, 1989-92; Rockefeller Foundation Feller, Rockefeller Foundation, 1983; DuBois Scholar, DuBois Institute, Harvard University, 1983; John Oliver Killen Writing Award, Fisk University, 1969; Lilly Fellow, Lilly Foundation, 1979-80. **Business Addr:** Chair, Jackson State University, Public Policy & Administration Dept, 3825 Ridgewood Rd, Box 18, Jackson, MS 39211.

MORGAN, ALICE JOHNSON PARHAM
Mental health administrator. **Personal:** Born Jul 17, 1943, Richmond, VA; daughter of Fannye Mae Quarles Johnson and Elmore W Johnson Jr; married Wilson M; children: Weldon Leo, Arvette Patrice. **Educ:** VA Union Univ, BA 1965; VA Commonwealth Univ, MSW 1967; Univ of Southern CA (WA Public Affrs Cntr), MPA 1982. **Career:** Area D CMHC, supvr, soc worker 1981; St Elizabeth's Hosp, soc work prog 1981-82; Area D CMHC, soc worker 1982-83, dir special apt program, 1983-88, dir, Region IV Psychosocial Day Prog, 1988-91, Region 4 Housing, resource specialist, 1991-. **Orgs:** Program analyst, Public Health Serv, 1980-81; dir, comm placement office, Area D, CMHC 1980; ed & standards specialist, St Elizabeth's Hosp, 1979-80; dir, comm placement office, Area D, CMHC, 1972-79; chairperson (city of Alex, VA) Martin Luther King Planning Comm, 1973-; First Black Female City Council Candidate, Alex, VA, 1979; mem, First Black/First Female Planning Comm, 1971-79; bd of dir, Natl Conf of Christians and Jews, Alexandria Mental Health Assn. **Honors/Awds:** Dorothea Lynde Dix Award, St Elizabeth's Hosp, 1984; Human Rights Award, Alex Comm on Status of Women, 1984; Intergovtl Mgmt Appointee, Dept of Health & Human Serv 1980-81; Outstanding Comm Serv Award Alex Dept Pro Club, 1979; NAACP Community Serv Award, 1988; Community Serv Award, Alex Commn on Status of Women, 1986; Lorraine B. Funn Atkins Community Service Award, 1996. **Home Addr:** 1513 Dogwood Dr, Alexandria, VA 22302. **Business Addr:** Housing Resource Specialist, CMHC Allison Bldg, Region IV, 2700 M L King Ave, SE, Washington, DC 20032, (202)373-7082.

MORGAN, BOOKER T.
Educator. **Personal:** Born Sep 29, 1926, Boley, OK; married Ella L Parker; children: Travis W, Delois Jean. **Educ:** Langston U, BS cum laude 1954; OK State Ud addl study 1964. **Career:** Langston Univ, dir graphic arts center 1970-; Langston Univ, asst dean mem 1961-70; Local 1140 Omaha, labor steward 1958-60; State Training School Boys Boley OK, farmsupt 1955-57. **Orgs:** Mem OK Educ Assn 1961-74; Langston Univ Alumni Assn; deacon Mt Bethel Bapt Ch Rising Star Lodge #22; Jaycees; Langston Lions Club; polemarch Langston Alumni Chap of Kappa Alpha Psi. **Honors/Awds:** Undergrad adv Alpha Pi Chap Kappa Alpha Psi 1961-; Kappa adv of Yr awd 1969; estab Booker T Morgan Achiev Awad most outstanding grad sr Alpha Pi Chap 1969. **Military Serv:** AUS sgt 1949-52. **Business Addr:** Development & Public Relations, Langston University, Langston, OK 73050.

MORGAN, CLYDE ALAFIJU
Educator. **Personal:** Born Jan 30, 1940, Cincinnati, OH; son of Harriette Young and Lee Morgan; married Marie Lais Goes Morgan; children: Clyde G, Dyuna G, Lee Young G. **Educ:** Bennington College, Bennington, VT, professional certificate 1963-65; Cleveland State Univ, Cleveland, OH, BA, 1963. **Career:** Federal Univ of Bahia, Salvador Bahia Brazil, choreographer & artistic dir of the Contemp Dance Co UF BA; Univ of Wisconsin, Madison, WI, visiting artist, 1979-80; Univ of Wisconsin, Milwaukee, WI, assistant prof, 1980-85; Federal Univ of Bahia, Salvador, Brazil, Fulbright prof, 1985-86; Univ of Wisconsin, Milwaukee, assistant prof, 1987; State Univ of New York, Brockport, NY, associate profe ssor, 1987-. **Orgs:** Member, CORD (Congress on Research in Dance), 1985-; Dance History Scholars, 1991-; United University Professions, 1987-. **Honors/Awds:** Academic Scholarship, The Cleveland Foundation, 1961-62; Dance Fellowship, Bennington College VT, 1963-64; Leaders & Specialist Grant US IS, 1985; Fulbright Professorship, Brazil, 1986-87. **Business Addr:** Associate Professor of Dance, State University of New York, Dance Dept Hartwell Hall, College at Brockport, Brockport, NY 14420.

MORGAN, DEBBI
Actress. **Personal:** marrIed Donn Thompson. **Career:** Actress; starred in TV movie Roots; soap operas: All My Children, Generations, Loving, Port Charles; film: Eve's Bayou, 1997. **Honors/Awds:** Emmy Award for Best Supporting Actress, All My Children (first black actress to win the award).

MORGAN, DOLORES PARKER
Performer. **Personal:** Born in New Orleans, LA; daughter of Mabel Moton Parker and Joseph Parker; married E Gates Morgan MD; children: Melodie Morgan-Minott MD. **Educ:** Attended Chicago Musical Coll 1941; attended Wilson Coll. **Career:** Earl "Fatha" Hines, singer 1945-47; Duke Ellington, singer 1947-49; Solo Performer, singer 1949-56; Local Charity Events, singer 1960-; bd of dir Kent State Foundation 1987-. **Orgs:** Bd mem, corres secy OH Ballet 1983-87; exec bd of trust Vstg Nurses Serv 1984-; devel council Akron Art Museum 1984-; exec bd Boy Scouts of Amer 1986-; bd mem Akron Symphony 1986-. **Honors/Awds:** Hall of Fame Best Dressed Akron Beacon Jrnl 1971; Ebony Best Dressed List Ebony Mag 1972; Dolores Parker Morgan Endowed Scholarship in Music Kent State Univ1986; EL Novotny Award Kent State School of Art 1989; Internatioanl Honorary Member, Alpha Kappa Alpha Sorority, 1990; Dolores Parker Morgan Day, City of Akron, OH, 1990. **Home Addr:** 3461 S Smith Road, Akron, OH 44333.

MORGAN, ELDRIDGE GATES
Corporate medical director (retired). **Personal:** Born Jan 9, 1925, Petersburg, VA; son of Emma Gates Morgan and Waverly J Morgan; married Dolores, Aug 30, 1956; children: Melodie Morgan-Minott. **Educ:** VA State Coll, BS 1944; Meharry Medcl Coll, MD 1950; NY Univ Post Grad Surgery 1954; Harlem Hosp, NY City Res Surgery 1950-56. **Career:** St Thomas Hosp-Akron, staff surgeon 1956-78; Firestone Tire & Rubber Co, asst med dir 1978-82; Firestone Tire & Rubber Co, corp med dir 1982-90. **Orgs:** Pres, Summitt County Med Soc 1970-72; treasurer, Summit County Med Soc 1968-84; lay advisory bd Akron Univ 1970-85; bd mem Independent Med Plan 1983-85; mem AMA, OSMA, NMA, Alpha Phi Alpha, ACOEM, 1978-; mem Wesley Temple AME Church 1956-; vice pres, Med Serv Bureau 1986-; treasurer, Independent Med Plan, 1986-92; occupational medical consultant, currently. **Honors/Awds:** Fellow, Amer Coll of Surgery, Amer Coll of Med Hypnosis, 1958-; bd certified Hypnosis Analysis, Hypno Therapy 1968-; 14 articles published, 1952-74; Fellow, Amer Coll of Occupational Med, 1984-. **Military Serv:** Med Admin Corp, 2nd lt, 1944-46. **Home Addr:** 3461 S Smith Rd, Akron, OH 44313. **Business Addr:** Occupational Medical Consultant, 3461 S Smith Rd, Akron, OH 44333.

MORGAN, FLETCHER, JR.
Government administrator (retired). **Personal:** Born Oct 6, 1920, Bay City, TX; son of Ella Morgan and Fletcher Morgan; married Alice Mae Riggins; children: Nadine, Rita, Dennis L. **Educ:** Prairie View A&M U, BS 1943, MS 1947; Lasalle Inst & Wharton Co Jr Coll, addl study. **Career:** USDA Farmers Home Adm Bay City, TX, retired co supr 1970-86, asst co supr 1965-70; USDA FMHA Richmond TX Co, supr 1949-51; Vets in Agri, instr & supr 1946-49. **Orgs:** Mem bd dir Ft Bend Co Taxpayers Assn; Centennial Council Prairie View A&M Univ 1968-70; Nu Phi; Omega Psi Phi; TX Soc Farm & Ranch Mgrs & Appraisers; NAACP; AME Ch; 32 deg Mason; Shriner; Prairie View A&M Univ alumni assn; bd of dir Coastal Plain; Plains Soil & Water Conservation District; bd dirs #1772 AARP; bd dirs & sec treas, Sam Houston Conservation District; bd of dirs, Fort Bend Cty FSA Committee Minority Advisor; volunteer, Brazos Bend State Park; pres, Gulf Coast Assn of Soil & Water Conservation Dist; advis comm, Cty Agricultural Extension Prog. **Honors/Awds:** Alumni citation PV A&M 1969; dist Omega Man of Yr 1969; Omega Man of Yr Nu Phi Chap Houston 1973. **Military Serv:** MIL serv 1943-45. **Home Addr:** PO Drawer 9, Thompsons, TX 77481-0009.

MORGAN, GORDON D.
Educator. **Personal:** Born Oct 31, 1931, Mayflower, AR; son of Georgianna Madlock Morgan and Roosevelt Morgan; married Izola Preston Morgan, Jun 15, 1957; children: Marsha, Brian, Marian, Bryce (deceased). **Educ:** Arkansas AM & N College, BA (cum laude), soc, 1953; University of Arkansas, MA, soc, 1956; Washington State University, PhD, soc, 1963. **Career:** Pine St School, teacher 1956-59; AR AM & N College, instructor 1969-60; Washington State University, TA/RA, 1960-63; Teachers for East Africa Project, research asst 1963-65; Lincoln University, asst prof of soc 1965-69; University of Arkansas, assoc prof/prof 1973-91; Washington State Univ, visiting professor of sociology, 1991-. **Orgs:** Consultant to numerous education institutions including: S Regional Education Board, SW Minnesota State College, Philander Smith College, Arkansas Program on Basic Adult Education, Arkansas Tech Assistance Program, Quachita Baptist College, Natl Inst of Mental Health; fly-in prof, St Ambrose College, 1973, expert witness before Rockefeller Comm on Population & Future, 1971; expert witness on fed judge panel on at-large voting in AR, 1973; Washington Co Grand Jury, 1974; Rotary/Downtown, AR, 1980-. **Honors/Awds:** Guest on several programs dealing with topics as crime, human relations, and foreign language study; lecturer at numerous colleges and churches; author, "A Short Social History of the E Fayetteville Community," with Izola Preston Morgan, 1978, "The Training of Black Sociologists," Tolbert H Kennedy and Washington State University, Teaching Sociology, 1980, "African Vignettes, Notes of an American Negro Family in E Africa," New Scholars Press, 1967, America Without Ethnicity, Kennikat, 1981, "The Little Book of Humanistic Poems," 1981; Law Enforcement Asst Admin Award, SUNY, 1975; Ford Foundation Postdoc, Lincoln Univ, 1969; Am College Testing Postdoc, Lincoln Univ, 1969;Russell Sage Postdoc, Univ of AR, 1972; NEH, Univ of WI, 1980; NEH, Queens College SUNY, 1983; The Ghetto College Stut, ACT, 1970; Lawrence A Davis, AR Educator, Assoc Faculty Press, 1985; Fellowship in Southern Studio Mississippi, 1987-88; co-author, The Edge of Campus, A Journal of the Black Experience at the University of Arkansas, 1990; co-author, The History of the Southeast Fayetteville Community Action Committee, The Fayetteville Action Group, 1990; Ida Rowland Bellegorde: Master Teacher, Scholar, McGraw-Hill, 1992; Toward an American Sociology; Questioning the European Construct, Westport, CT, Greenwood, 1997. **Military Serv:** US Army, 1953; US Army Reserves, commission, 1959. **Business Addr:** Professor, Univ of Arkansas, Fayetteville, AR 72701.

MORGAN, HARRY
Educator. **Personal:** Born Jun 6, 1926, Charlottesville, VA; son of Cheyney Lewis and John Morgan; children: Parris, Lawrence. **Educ:** NY Univ, BS 1949; Univ of WI, MSW 1965; Univ of MA, Ed D 1970. **Career:** Bank St Coll, program coordinator 1966-69; Univ of NH, prof 1969-70; OH Univ, prof 1970-72; Syracuse Univ, prof 1972-84; State University of West Georgia, prof 1984-, chmn early childhood educ. **Orgs:** Astr fdn Pre-Teen Research Project 1960-64; US Govt dir Project Head Start North East Region 1964-66; mem AERA 1975-, NAEYC 1972-, AAUP 1980-; AACTE 1984; Phi Delta Kappa 1985. **Honors/Awds:** Fellowship Ford Foundation 1967-69; consultant US Govt "Black Aged" 1970-74; book, The Learning Comm pub Charles Merrill, OH 1972; numerous articles for learned journals. **Special Achievements:** Historical Prspectives on the Education of Black Children, Praeger, 1995; Cognitive Styles & Classroom Learning, Greenwood Publishing Group, 1997. **Home Addr:** 2284 Lakeview Parkway, Villa Rica, GA 30180. **Business Addr:** Chairman, Early Childhood Education, West Georgia College, Maple St, Carrollton, GA 30118, (770)836-4423.

MORGAN, HAYWOOD, SR.
Chemical company executive. **Personal:** Born Feb 6, 1936, Lakeland, LA; son of Eloise Weber Morgan and George Morgan Sr; married Brenda Hughes Morgan; children: Althea, Haywood Jr, April. **Educ:** Southern Univ, BS Educ 1968. **Career:** CIBA Geigy Corp, tech 1969-; West Baton Rouge Sch Bd, personnel & finance comm, trans & vocational skills comm, building equipt & maint comm 1972-84. **Orgs:** Mem Sunrise Baptist Church. **Honors/Awds:** First Black elected official in West Baton Rouge Parish 1971; Comm Serv Scotts United M Church 1978. **Home Addr:** 1117 Maryland Avenue, Port Allen, LA 70767.

MORGAN, HAZEL C. BROWN
Educator (retired). **Personal:** Born Oct 25, 1930, Rocky Mount, NC; daughter of Beulah McGee Brown (deceased) and Rollon Brown (deceased); married Charlie Morgan; children: Savoynne Fields. **Educ:** A&T State Univ, BS Nursing 1960; East Carolina Univ, MS Rehab Counseling 1977, MS Nursing 1980. **Career:** Wilson Mem Hosp, charge nurse 1964-66; Northern Nash High School, health occupations teacher 1966-73; Nash General Hosp, team leader pt care 1971-; East Carolina Univ School of Nursing, asst prof of nursing 1973-93; Veteran's Admin Hospital Richmond VA & E Orange NJ, staff nurse 1960-62; Landis State Hospital Philadelphia PA, asst head nurse & instructor 1963. **Orgs:** Mem Amer Nurses Assoc, NC Assoc of Black Educators, NC Nurse's Assoc Dist 20; ECU Org of Black Faculty & Staff; mem, Sigma Theta Tau 1988-; mem, The Assn of Black Nursing Faculty 1987-; health consultant, Wright Geriatric Day Care Center 1988-; supervisor & instructor, United Friendship Church Nurses Organization 1988-; Carrie Broadfoot Memorial Club, president; Carrie E Broadfoot Nurses Club, pres; Seasons Plus, Srs Organization, scy, 1995, pres; Leisurettes Club, prof regires, treas, 1997; East Carolina Retired Faculty Assn, mem; East Carolina Univ, School of Nursing Emeriti, comm/mem. **Honors/Awds:** 10 yr Serv Awd East Carolina Univ School of Nursing 1983; Serv Awd for Achievement, Black Fac Mem with Greatest Numbers of Yrs Serv Omega Psi Phi Frat 1984; Soc & Civic Awd Chat-a-While Civic Orgn LA State Univ Eunice 1984; Devel Slide-Tape Program, Creativity in Documenting Nursing Interventions 1989. **Home Addr:** 913 Beal St, Rocky Mount, NC 27801.

MORGAN, JANE HALE
Librarian, educator (retired). **Personal:** Born May 11, 1925, Dines, WY; daughter of Billie Wood and Arthur Hale; married Joseph C Morgan; children: Joseph Hale, Jane Frances, Ann Michele. **Educ:** Howard Univ, BA 1947; Univ of Denver, MA 1954. **Career:** Detroit Pub Library, staff, beginning 1954, exec asst dir 1973-75, dep dir 1975-78, dir 1978-87; Wayne State Univ, visiting prof 1989-91. **Orgs:** Amer Libr Assn; MI Library Assn; exec bd Southeastern MI Reg Film Libr; LSCA adv council Lib of MI; Women's Natl Book Assn bd of trustees; New Detroit Inc; bd dir Rehab Inst; United Way for Southeastern Michigan, vice pres; bd of dir YWCA; Assn of Municipal & Professional Women; Alpha Kappa Alpha; bd dir Univ Cultural Cntr Assn; Urban League; NAACP; bd of dir Women's Economic Club; bd dir United Community Svcs; brd dirs, Delta Dental Plan of MI; brd dirs, Metropolitan Affairs Corp; board of directors, New Detroit, Inc; Michigan Council for the Humanities; Michigan Women's Commission; Detroit Women's Committee. **Honors/Awds:** Recipient, "The Anthony Wayne Awd", Wayne St Univ, Coll of Ed 1981; Detroit "Howardite of the Year", 1983; Summit Award, Greater Detroit Chamber of Commerce 1989.

MORGAN, JOE (JOSEPH LEONARD)
Sports broadcaster, professional baseball player (retired). **Personal:** Born Sep 19, 1943, Bonham, TX; married Gloria Stewart Morgan; children: Lisa, Angela. **Educ:** Oakland City College; California State Univ, Hayward. **Career:** Houston Colt .45's (later Houston Astros), 1963-71; Cincinnati Reds, 1972-79; Houston Astros, 1980; San Francisco Giants, 1981-82; Philadelphia Phillies, 1983; Oakland A's, 1984; KTVU, broadcaster; ESPN, color analyst, currently; Joe Morgan Beverage Co, CEO, currently. **Honors/Awds:** National League Rookie of the Year, 1965; Most Valuable Player, All-Star Game, 1972; Gold Glove, 1973, 1974, 1975, 1976; National League Most Valuable Player, Baseball Writers' Association of America, 1975, 1976; Most Valuable Player, San Francisco Giants, 1982; Comeback Player of the Year, Sporting News, 1982; Hall of Fame, 1990. **Business Addr:** Color Analyst, ESPN, 935 Middle St, ESPN Plaza, Bristol, CT 06010, (203)585-2000.

MORGAN, JOHN PAUL
Dentist. **Personal:** Born Oct 23, 1929, Kokomo, IN; married Pauline Marie Jones; children: Angela Marie. **Educ:** IN Univ, pre-dental studies; Meharry Medical Coll, DDS 1960. **Career:** 6510 USAF Hospital Edwards AFB CA, officer-in-charge hospital dental 1960-64; 439th USAF Hospital Misawa AB Japan, oic security serv dental asst base dental surgery 1964-67; Lockbourne AFB OH, chief of prosthodontics 1967-71; 377th USAF Disp Tan Son Nhut AB Vietnam, chief of oral surgery 1971-72; USAF Hospital Kirtland AFB NM, asst base dental surgeon 1972-78; USAF Hospital Hahn AB Germany, base dental surgeon 1978-81; USAF Medical Center SGD Scott AFB IL, deputy dir of dental serv 1981-, independent contractor, currently. **Orgs:** Mem Natl Dental Assoc, Acad of General Dentistry, Assoc of Military Surgeons, Prince Hall Lodge; life mem NAACP, Alpha Phi Alpha. **Military Serv:** US Air Force, col, 28 yrs; Meritorious Serv Medal w/One Oak Leaf Cluster, Air Force Commendation Medal, Presidential Unit Citation AF Outstanding Unit Awd; Republic of Vietnam Gallantry Cross w/Palm; Republic of Vietnam Campaign Medal 1960-; The Legion of Merit, 1988. **Home Addr:** 4 Deer Run, O Fallon, IL 62269-1209. **Business Addr:** Independent Contractor, Dental Serv, USAF Medical Ctr/SGD, Scott Air Force Base, IL 62225.

MORGAN, JOSEPH C.
Deputy director. **Personal:** Born Jan 10, 1921, Douglas, GA; married Jane Hale; children: Joseph, Jane, Michele. **Career:** Detroit Zool Park, dep dir 1974-; Pub Serv Employment Detroit, dir 1974. **Orgs:** Pres Frame Div of UAW 1955-67; appointed Intl Rep as Recruiter Couns 1967-74; pres Detroit Chap Nat Negro Labor Council 1957-59. **Honors/Awds:** Recip of award for meritorious serv in field of soc econ leadership by UAW Assn 1974. **Military Serv:** AUS corp of eng 1946. **Business Addr:** 8450 W Ten Mile Rd, Royal Oak, MI 48068.

MORGAN, JOSEPH L.
Clergyman. **Personal:** Born Aug 9, 1936, Pittsboro, NC; son of Susie Morgan Bynum; married Caroldine Leake; children: Sharon, Susan. **Educ:** Johnson C Smith Univ Charlotte, NC, AB 1958; Shaw Univ Raleigh, NC, MDiv 1961. **Career:** First Calvary Bapt Ch, pastor; associate dean, Evening Programs, Central Carolina Community College, Sanford, NC, dir; Cntrl Hs, tchr English, 1968-74; First Bapt Dallas, NC Pleasant Grove Wendell, NC, New Light Hallsboro, NC, pastor. **Orgs:** Dir Gaston Boy's Club 1961-63; mem Sanford Redevel Comm 1968-; mem Lee Co Minister's Fellow 1964-74; mem ACT, NEA, NCEA; Gen Bapt State Conv; Lott Carey Foreign Miss Conv; Nat Bapt Conv USA mem NAACP, SCLC; inst rep BSA; mem Sanford Human Relations Coun & Coun on Aging. **Honors/Awds:** Doctor of Divinity, Shaw University, 1981; Citizen of the Year, City of Sanford, 1986. **Business Addr:** Associate Dean, Central Carolina Tech Inst, 1105 Kelly Dr, Sanford, NC 27330.

MORGAN, JUANITA KENNEDY
Teacher. **Personal:** Born Dec 16, 1911, Birmingham, AL; daughter of Viola Skipper Kennedy and William Kennedy; married William Morgan. **Educ:** Attended Alabama State Teachers' College, Montgomery AL, 1930-35; Terrell Law School, Washington DC, LLB, 1949; DC Teachers' College, Washington DC, BS, 1962; attended Howard Univ, Washington DC; attended George Washington Univ, Washington DC. **Career:** Tennessee Coal & Iron Co, Birmingham AL, teacher, 1935-41; Dept of Treasury, Washington DC, examiner, 1941-60; DC Public School System, Washington DC, teacher, 1961-83; Ultra Realty Service, Washington DC, real estate broker, 1952-89. **Orgs:** Parlimentarian, Business and Professional Women's Club, 1965-70; mem, Common Cause, 1970-80; exec sec and dir, National Black Women's Political Leadership Caucus, 1981-89; mem board of dir, Kiwanianne Club, 1985-87; mem, Kiwanis Club, 1987-89; mem, NAACP; mem, Urban League. **Honors/Awds:** Community Award, Urban League, 1965; Outstanding Grass Roots Community Leader Award, DC Civic Assn, 1968; Community Service Award, Southern Beauty Congress, 1977; Community Award, DC Citizens' Forum, 1983-87; Resolution, DC City Council, 1988; directly responsible for integrating cafeterias and restroom facilities in federal govt buildings during Roosevelt and Truman admins; author of A New Kind of Handbook in Retrospect: Informatives & Directives, Woodridge Civic Assn, 1967-68; lobbied for funding, conceived idea, and planned organizational structure of Federal City College (now Univ of the District of Columbia), 1966-68; delegate to numerous Methodist conferences. **Home Addr:** 630 11th Ct West, Birmingham, AL 35204.

MORGAN, MARY H. ETHEL
Educator (retired). **Personal:** Born Mar 11, 1912, Summerton, SC; married Dr C M; children: Carolyn Marie Brown-Geli Revelle. **Educ:** SC State Coll, BA 1951; Ball State Univ IN, MA Ed 1975; Anderson Coll Theological Sem, MA Religion 1979. **Career:** Brd of Ed, tchr SC 1935-40; Nursery Schl, tchr FL 1941-44; IN Church Schl, tchr 1960-70; Comm Schls, tchr Anderson, IN 1970-82; Retired Tchr Minister; Substitute Tchr Anderson Community School; Minister Sherman St Church. **Orgs:** Mbrshp NAACP Local & Natl 1985; Ladies Republican Club Local & Natl 1985; State Tchrs Retirmnt Club IN 1985; Madison Cnty retired Teachers organization; Women United; board of directors CCCV; board of directors, YWCA, 1987-; assoc minister, Church of God, 1990-; ordained Christian ministry, Indiana Ministry Assembly, 1984. **Honors/Awds:** Outstanding Tchr (Elem) of Amer 1974; "Love Award" 1987; Women Ministers Organization Award for faithful service; Outstanding Alumnus Award, Ball State University, 1989; Distinguished Alumnus Award, Anderson University Seminary, 1990. **Business Addr:** PO Box 2041, Anderson, IN 46018.

MORGAN, MELI'SA (JOYCE)
Singer, songwriter, record producer. **Personal:** Born 1964; married Shelly Garrett, Aug 28, 1993. **Educ:** Attended Juilliard School, New York NY. **Career:** Former backup singer for Chaka Khan, Kahsif, Whitney Houston, and Melba Moore; singer, songwriter, and record producer. **Honors/Awds:** Singer on two record albums, Do Me Baby, 1985, Good Love, 1987; three top five hit singles. **Business Addr:** c/o Capitol Records, 1750 Vine St, Hollywood, CA 90028.

MORGAN, MICHAEL
Conductor. **Personal:** Born 1957, Washington, DC. **Educ:** Oberlin College Conservatory of Music; master classes of Witold Rowicki, Vienna, Austria; Berkshire Music Center, Tanglewood, CA. **Career:** Buffalo Philharmonic, apprentice conductor; Chicago Symphony Orchestra, Exxon/Arts Endowment assistant conductor, 1980-87, affiliate artist conductor, beginning 1987. **Honors/Awds:** Has guest conducted numerous major orchestras; appeared with New York Philharmonic, 1986; Leonard Berstein Young American Conductors Concerts; New York City Opera, conducting La Traviata in New York, Wolftrap, Taiwan; has appeared with the Vienna State Opera, Deutsche Staatsoper, Vienna Symphony Orchestra, Warsaw Philharmonic Orchestra, Danish Radio Orchestra; First Prize, Hans Swarowsky International Conductors Comeptition, Vienna, Austria, 1980; First Prize, Gino Marrinuzzi International Conductors Competition, San Remo, Italy; First Prize, Baltimore Symphony Young Conductors Competition.

MORGAN, MONICA ALISE
Public relations specialist, journalist. **Personal:** Born May 27, 1963, Detroit, MI; daughter of Barbara Jean Pace. **Educ:** Wayne State Univ, Detroit MI, BS, 1985. **Career:** Domino's Pizza, Ann Arbor MI, promotional coordinator; Detroit Public Schools, Detroit MI, public relations coordinator; WDIV-TV, Detroit MI, production assistant; Palmer Street Productions, Detroit MI, host and public relations dir; WQBH-radio, talk show host; Michigan Chronicle, Detroit MI, columnist and photojournalist, 1987-; US Dept of Census, Detroit MI, Community Awareness Specialist, 1988-; photography studio, owner, photographer, currently. **Orgs:** Sec, Natl Assn of Black Journalists, 1981-; mem, Optimist Club, 1987-; board member, Manhood Inc, 1988-; mem, Elliottorian Business Women Inc, 1988-; Natl Assn of Black Journalists; National Association of Female Executives; National Press Photographers; Kindred Souls. **Honors/Awds:** Outstanding Young Woman of Amer, 1986, 1987; Civic and Community Award, Wall Street Inc, 1989; author of articles published in periodicals; Rosa and Raymond Parks Institute for Self Development, Certificate of Appreciation. **Business Addr:** Columnist/Photojournalist, Michigan Chronicle, 479 Ledyard, Detroit, MI 48201.

MORGAN, RALEIGH, JR.
Educator. **Personal:** Born Nov 12, 1916, Nashville, TN; son of Adrien Beasley Morgan and Raleigh Morgan Sr; married Virginia Moss Morgan, Dec 25, 1941 (deceased); children: Phyllis Adrian (deceased), Carol Morgan Russell, Jill Morgan Burrows. **Educ:** Fisk Univ, AB 1938; Univ of MI, AM 1939; Univ of MI, PhD 1952. **Career:** Sumner High School, St Louis, MO, teacher of French 1940-42; North Carolina College, Durham, NC, head, dept of French 1946-49; Amerika Haus, Cologne, dir 1956-57; US Embassy, Bonn, dep chief, cultural opns 1957-59; Center for Applied Ling, assoc dir 1959-61; Howard U, chair, prof of Romance languages 1960-65; Univ of MI, prof of Romance linguistics 1965-87, prof emeritus of Romance linguistics, 1987-. **Orgs:** Lecturer linguistics, Nicaragua, Haiti 1956, 8 countries of French speaking Africa 1964, US State Dept; conslting linguist MLA Materials Devel 1962; dir summer lang institute Howard Univ 1962, 1963, 1965; ins mem USIA Eng Teaching Advisory Panel 1964-67; visiting prof lingustics Cornell Univ 1973; mem visiting Comm Germanic Harvard Overseers 1972-80; consultant Proj on French as a World Language 1978-80; chair Michigan Council for the Humanities 1974-77; Assembly of Behavioral & Soc Sci of Natl Rsch Council 1973-. **Honors/Awds:** Regional French Of Cnty Beauce, Quebec (Mouton) 1975; alumnus mem Phi Beta Kappa Fisk Univ 1974-; Fulbright Sr Rsch Scholar France 1974; author of Old French Jogleor and Kindred Terms 1954. **Military Serv:** AUS 2nd lt 1942-46. **Home Addr:** 3157 Bluett Dr, Ann Arbor, MI 48105.

MORGAN, RANDALL COLLINS, SR.
Business executive. **Personal:** Born Aug 31, 1917, Natchez, MS; married Joyce Tatum; children: Randall C Jr MD. **Educ:** Rust Coll, AB 1938; Northwestern Univ, BS 1939; Northwestern Univ & IN Univ, grad studies;Loyola Univ; Grinnell Coll; Industrial Coll of the Armed Forces 1962-63. **Career:** Columbia & Gary, tchr; Vet Admin, voc counselor & supr 1946-51; Ironwood Drugs Inc, founder/pres 1950; Assoc Med Ctr, cofounder 1966; Eastside Med Ctr, pres/founder 1969-. **Orgs:** Alpha Phi Alpha 1947; Int'l Frontiers Serv Clb 1962-64 Pres; Nat'l Hlth Srvcs Exec 1972-76; Med Grp Mgmt Assn; Lay Leader Calumet dist United Meth Chrch 1976-82; Co-Chrmn NAACP, Life Membshp Comm; Spec Contrib Fund Brd Dir NAACP; Chtr Pres Gary East Chicago Serv Club; mem Ad Brd Bank of TN, adv comm In Univ; Brd DirMethodist Hosp; Brd of Trustees, Rust Coll, Grinnel Coll; Multi-racial Soc Comm trustee; Gary Chamber of Comm Trustee; NW Ctr for Med Educn;mem & chrmn Lake CO Med Ctr Deve Agncy; Med Grp Mgmt Assn; Nat'l Assoc Hlth Srvcs; past mem & pres & 1st Black Gary Police Civil Serv Comm; past co-chrmn Negro Coll Fund; vice chrmn United Fund Grtr Gary Campaign; brd dir Gary Joint Hosp Fund; co fndr & busns mgr Assocs Med Ctr; Lake Cnty Comm DevComm; Lake Area United Way Camp vice ChrmNW Ind Compr Hlth Plng Cncl; Gary Cancer Crusade; Mayors Adv Comm; Better Buss Breau Nw Ind; Bank One Advis Brd. **Honors/Awds:** Gary Est Chg Frontiers CLb Awd 1955; Chmb of Comm Certif of Apprectn 1961; Rust Coll Outstndg COntrib Awd 1966; NAACP Citation of Merit; Delaney United Meth Chrch Disting Serv 1967-68;Citizen Awd Chmb of Comm;1968;IU Gents Outstndg Citizen Awd 1967; United Fund Awd of Apprectn; 1968; Grinnell Coll Dr of Humane Ltrs 1971; NAACP Dist Ldrsp & Srvc Awd 1973; Greater Gary Arts Cncl Awd 1974; Gary Jaycees Outstndg Comm Awd 1976; Notable Americans 1st Ed 1976-77; Govrnrs Vol Actn Prgm Commendation 1977; Grinnell Coll Pres CLb 1978; Dist Ldrshp Awd NAACP 1983; Phi Beta Sigma Dist Citizen Awd 1984; The Cadre Awd of Recog 1984; Roy Wilkins Awd NAACP 1985; NAACP Nat'l Frdm Awd 1985; Rust Coll Trustee Emeritus Awd 1986; Great Garyite 4th Annual Awd 1986. **Military Serv:** AUS maj93rd Infantry Div 1942-46. **Business Addr:** Administrator, The Gary Professional Center, 3229 Broadway, Gary, IN 46409.

MORGAN, RICHARD H., JR.
Attorney. **Personal:** Born Feb 12, 1944, Memphis; married Olga Jackson; children: Darrin Allan, Heather Nicole, Nia Abena, Amish Adzua. **Educ:** Western MI U, BA, MA; Univ of Detroit Law Sch, 1973. **Career:** Western MI U, counselor; Oakland Univ Project Pontiac, dir; Student Center, asst dir, asso dir; Dean of Students, asst; Comm Serv Program Urban Affairs Center, dir 6 yrs; Hatchett Mitchell Morgan & Hall, atty; Morgan & Hall, sr partner. **Orgs:** Pmem APGA & MPGA; MI State Bar; Oakland Co Bar; Wolverine Bar; Am Bar & Wayne Co Bar Kappa Alpha Psi Frat; Big Bro of Kalamazoo; Pontiac Area Urban Force on hs dropouts; treas vice pres Black Law Student Alliance Univ of Detroit Law Sch; bd mem Heritage Cultural Ctr; Akan Priest. **Business Addr:** Attorney at Law, Morgan & Hall, 47 North Saginaw, Pontiac, MI 48342.

MORGAN, ROBERT, JR.
Transportation engineer, military officer (retired), trade development mgr. **Personal:** Born May 17, 1954, Donaldsonville, LA; son of Ruby Fields Morgan and Robert Morgan Sr; married Rowena Guanlao Morgan; children: Robyn Talana Morgan, Ryan Guanlao Morgan, Rubi Guanlas Morgan. **Educ:** Southern Univ, BS 1972; Old Dominion Univ, grad work 1976; Natl Univ, MBA 1982; Armed Forces Staff Coll, Certificate 1986; Fort Gordon Signal School, Augusta GA Certificate 1987; Univ of Maryland, Foreign Language Studies, 1989; Panama Canal College, AS, computer science, 1993; Texas Southern University, MS, Transportation technology, 1995. **Career:** USS America CV 66, Norfolk VA, deck/ASW officer, 1977-79; USS Cleveland LPD 7, San Diego CA, navigator/weapons officer, 1979-80; Surface Warfare Officer School, Coronado CA, instructor, 1981-83; USNS Ponchatoula FAO 108, Philippines Island, officer in charge, 1983-84; Naval Station Guam, Guam MI, operations officer, 1984-85; Central Texas College, Guam MI, instructor, 1984-85; HQ Central Command, Macdill AFB FL, comms staff officer, 1986-88; MSCO Korea, Pusan Korea, commanding officer, 1988-90; HQ US Southern Command, Quarry Heights, Panama, logistics staff officer, 1990-92; MSCO Panama, commanding officer, 1992-94. Port of Houston Authority, Operations Manager, 1994-. **Orgs:** Life mem Alpha Phi Omega Frat 1973-; life mem Omega Psi Phi Frat 1980-; mem Assoc of MBA Execs 1981, Accounting Soc 1982; St Joseph Masonic Lodge 1982; human resource mgmt instructor US Navy 1983; mgmt professor Central TX Coll 1985; master scuba diver Micronesian Diver Assoc 1985; Certified PADL and NAUL diver; mem Natl Naval Officers Assoc; mem NAACP; Armed Forces Communications and Electronics Association 1988-; American Chamber of Commerce in Korea 1988-; mem, Natl Defense Transportation Assn, 1987. **Honors/Awds:** Outstanding Black American Awd, Comnav Marianas 1985; Outstanding Citizens of the Year, 1992, Omega Man of the Year, 1993. **Military Serv:** US Navy, lt cmdr, 1976-; Surface Warfare Officer, Humanitarian Service Medal, Navy Achievement Awd; Expert Rifle and Pistol Marksmanship 1976-; Joint Service Commendation Medal 1988; Commanding Officer 1988-89; Defense Meritorious Service Medal, 1988; Navy Commendation Medal, 1990; Natl Defense Medal, 1991; Joint Specialty Officer, 1989; Joint Meritorious Unit Award, 1991; Meritorious Unit Commendation, 1988; Defense Meritorious Service Medal, 1992, Meritorious Service Medal, 1994. **Home Addr:** PO Box 890263, Houston, TX 77289-0263.

MORGAN, ROBERT LEE
Architect, business executive. **Personal:** Born Mar 6, 1934, Yazoo City, MS; married Janet Rogers; children: Allyson, Whitney, Peter. **Educ:** Lincoln Univ Jefferson City, MO; KS State U, BArch 1964. **Career:** Opus Architects & Engineers, 1984-; Adkins-Jackels Association Architects, executive vice pres partner, stockholder, architect, 1968-84; Hammel, Green & Abrahamson, architect, 1966-68; Cavin & Page Architects, architect, 1964-66. **Orgs:** Mem Comm on Architecture for Arts & Recreation, American Institute of Architects, 1974-77; MN Soc of Architects AIA; National Organization of Minority Architects; board of directors, National Council of Architectural Registration Bds, 1991-95; secretary, NCARB, 1993-95; MN Comm on Urban Envir, 1968-76; MN Schools Long-Range Facilities Planning Comm; president, MN CDC, 1971; MN Board of Architecture, Engineerings, Land Surveying & Landscape Architecture, 1983-91. **Honors/Awds:** Invested, College of Fellows, American Institute of Architects, 1995. **Business Addr:** 9900 Bren Rd E, Ste 700, Minnetonka, MN 55343.

MORGAN, ROBERT W., II
Educator. **Personal:** Born Sep 1, 1932, Poughkeepsie, NY; married Harriott V Lomax. **Educ:** Durham, JD 1961. **Career:** Ability Devel Dept Kutztown State Coll, dir 1977; Prentice

Hall, legal editor 1961-63; Flood & Purvin, defense counselor 1963-69; Univ Tech Corp, adminstr 1969-71; Morgan Assn & Urban Design Inc, adminstr 1970-74; Somerset Cnty Coll, adminstr 1970-72. **Orgs:** Mem Hlth Sys Coun 1977; mem State Coordin Coun on Health of PA 1977; mem State Allotment Com on Health of PA 1977; mem Black Conf on Higher Educ 1977; mem Nat Educ Assn 1977; mem Am Personal & Guidance Assn 1977; mem Natl Assn of Devel Studies 1977; chrprsn Ability Devel Dept at KSC 1977. **Military Serv:** AUS pvt 1953-55. **Business Addr:** Dept of Devel Studies Chair, Kutztown University, RM 152 Bukey Bldg, Kutztown, PA 19530.

MORGAN, ROSE
Business executive (retired). **Personal:** Born in Shelby, MS; daughter of Winnie Morgan and Chappel Morgan; divorced. **Educ:** Morris Beauty Academy of Chicago, attended. **Career:** Trim-Away Figure Contouring Ltd, franchiser; mail order bus natl & intl; Rose Morgan Enterprise, founder, pres. **Orgs:** Charter mem, Cosmetic Career Women; NY State Beauty Culturists Assn; Natl Assn of Negro & Professional Women; Natl Assn of Bank Women Inc; incorporator, Bethune Fed & Savings Loan Bank; dir, Freedom Natl Bank of NY; dir, Interracial Council for Bus Oppty; vice pres, Natl Council of Negro Women; Assn to Asst Negro Bus; life mem NAACP; Task Force Econ Adv Comm to Mayor of NYC; dir, Uptown Chamber of Commerce NYC, Mt Morris Park Hosp; pres, Continental Soc of NY; bd of dir, Kilamanjaro African Coffee; bd trustee, Arthur C Logan Meml Hosp; bd of trustee, Shaw Univ in Raleigh NC; Convent Ave Bapt Church; bd mem, Assn Black Charities; treas, Natl Coalition of 100 Black Women; New York City Partnership Inc. **Honors/Awds:** Outstanding Achievement Awd, NY State Beauty Culturists Assn.

MORGAN, RUDOLPH COURTNEY
Health service administrator. **Personal:** Born May 29, 1950, Buffalo, NY; son of Lillian Blue Donald and Rudolph Morgan; married Gwendolyn Young, Aug 12, 1973; children: Dawn J, Rudolph C Jr. **Educ:** Tuskegee Inst, Tuskegee, AL, BS Biology, 1973. **Career:** Univ Hosp, Cleveland, OH, dialysis technician, 1973-80; Organ Recovery Inc, Cleveland, OH, transplant coord, 1980-82, sr transplant coord, 1982-84; SC OPA, Charleston, SC, dir of procurement, 1984-85; Upstate New York Transplant Services Inc, exec dir, 1985-; Buffalo, Eye Bank, Buffalo, NY, exec dir, 1987-. **Orgs:** Chmn mem, N Amer Transplant Coor Org, 1982-89; bd of dir (sec,) Assn of Independent Organ Procurement Agencies, 1986-87; bd of dir (treasurer) N Amer Transplant Coordinator Org, 1987-89; bd of dir, United Network for Organ Sharing (UMOS) 1987-89; mem comm, Professional Standard United Network for Organ Sharing Comm, 1987-90.

MORGAN, STANLEY DOUGLAS
Professional football player. **Personal:** Born Feb 17, 1955, Easley, SC; married Rholedia; children: Sanitra Nikole, Monique. **Educ:** Univ of Tennessee, BS, education, 1979. **Career:** Industrial Natl Bank; wide receiver: New England Patriots, 1977-89, Indianapolis Colts, beginning 1990, Denver Broncos, until 1992. **Honors/Awds:** PFW All Rookie Team; Rookie of the Year, Patroits' 1776 Fan Club; Patriots' all-time leading reception yardage leader (1029 yards), 1981; played in Pro Bowl, 1979, 1980, 1986, 1987.

MORGAN-CATO, CHARLOTTE THERESA
Educator. **Personal:** Born Jun 28, 1938, Chicago, IL; daughter of Helen Juanita Brewer Morgan and Eleazar Jack Morgan; married John David Cato; children: One. **Educ:** Univ of Chicago, BA 1960; Haile Selassie I Univ Addis Ababa, Certificate of Attendance 1965; Columbia Univ, Sch of Intl Affairs M Intl Affairs 1967, Teachers Coll MEd 1976, EdD 1979. **Career:** Chicago Bd of Educ, high school Social Studies teacher 1961-65; African-Amer Inst, teacher at Kurasini School 1967-70; Phelps-Stokes Fund, asst for African programs 1970-71; Lehman Coll CUNY, associate prof 1972-, acting dir, Women's Studies Program, 1996-. **Orgs:** Mem adv comm adult learning Follett Publishing Co 1982-83; natl treasurer African Heritage Studies Assoc 1984-88; alternate rep United Nations NGO Alpha Kappa Alpha Sor Inc 1985-86; mem Amer Assoc Adult/Cont Educ, Assoc Study of African-Amer Life and History, Natl Council for Black Studies, Alpha Kappa Alpha Sor. **Honors/Awds:** Fulbright Award 1965; CUNY Faculty Fellowship Award 1978-79; Award Natl Fellowships Fund Emory Univ 1978-79; mem Kappa Delta Pi Honor Soc 1979; Research Grant Women's Research & Devel Fund CUNY 1986-87; published articles in Afro-Americans in NY Life and History, Grad Studies Journal (Univ DC); Historical Foundations of Adult Education. **Business Addr:** Associate Prof of Black Studies, Lehman Coll of CUNY, 250 Bedford Park Blvd West, Bronx, NY 10468, (718)960-7722.

MORGAN-PRICE, VERONICA ELIZABETH
Judge. **Personal:** Born Nov 30, 1945, Chas, SC; daughter of Mary Cross Morgan and Robert Morgan; married Jerome Henry Price; children: Jerome Marcus. **Educ:** TN State Univ, BS Eng 1966-69; Univ of Cincinnati Summer Law Scholarship, cert; TX So Univ, JD 1972; Univ of NV Natl Coll of Juvenile Judges, cert 1980. **Career:** Wade Rasmus & Washington, law clk & atty 1970-72; Baylor Coll of Med Alcoholism Prog, chief counselor coord 1972-75; Houston Comm Coll, law prof 1972-78; Harris Co Dist Atty Offices, asst dist atty 1975-80; TX Paralegal Sch, prof of law 1978-; Harris Co Juvenile Ct, associate judge, currently. **Orgs:** Mem Houston Lawyers Assn 1973-; mem Natl Bar Assn 1975-; mem adv bd Safety Council of Gr Houston 1979-; former chairperson Med Legal Child Advocacy Comm 1980; mem adv bd Criminal & Juvenile Justice Educ Prog 1980; Ford Found Council on Legal Educ; bd of dir Assoc for Community TV Channel 8; mem Natl Council of Juvenile & Family Court Judges; mem Metro Court Judges; committee member, Learning Disabilities and Juvenile Delinquincy, National Council of Juvenile & Family Court Judges; Judicial Leadership council, chair, Children's Defense Fund/Black Community Crusade for Children, 1997. **Honors/Awds:** Law school Scholarship 1969-72; first black woman prosecutor TX Harris Co Dist Atty 1975-80; Serv Distinction Plaques Phi Alpha Delta/Thurgood Marshall Sch of Law/Houston Lawyers Assn/Natl Council of Negro Women/Harris Co Dist Atty; Black Women Lawyers Assn; Thurgood Marshall School of Law Alumni Assn; speaker, Hooding Ceremony, Thurgood Marshall School of Law 1984; speaker, Commencement Exercise, Tennessee State Univ 1985; Hidden Heroine Award, Girls Scouts of the U.S.A., 1996. **Business Addr:** Judge, Harris Co Juvenile Court, Office of Referee, 3540 W Dallas, Houston, TX 77019, (713)512-4091.

MORGAN-SMITH, SYLVIA
Community relations manager. **Personal:** Born Dec 19, Alabama; married William Smith II; children: Shiva, Andre, Melody, Ramon Morgan. **Educ:** Tchnl Comm Coll, Nursing 1956; Univ of CO-Denver, Jrnlsm Major 1970; Signal Broadcasting, diploma, 1971; Real Estate College, diploma, 1976. **Career:** KBPI-FM Radio, radio producer & announcer 1970-72; KWGN-TV 2, anchorwomen, 1972-77; Champion Realty, realtor, 1975-; Rockwell Intl Rocky Flats, mgr pub afrs, 1977-80; Natl Solar Energy Resch Inst, mgr comm relations 1980-; KOA-TV, annoucner, 1981-. **Orgs:** Dir, First Interstate Bank of Golden 1979-; dir Childrens Hosp 1981-; commissioner, Denver Commission on Community Relations, 1973-; exec comm Jefferson Cnty Priv Indstry Cncl 1980-; pres, Citizens Appreciate Police 1981-; Natl Small Business Administration Advisory Council, vice chairperson. **Business Addr:** Manager of Community Relations, National Solar Research Laboratory, 1617 Cole Blvd 17/3, Golden, CO 80401.

MORGAN-WASHINGTON, BARBARA
Dentist. **Personal:** Born Nov 9, 1953, Richmond, VA; daughter of Florence Brown Morgan and Calvin T Morgan Sr (deceased); married Fred S Washington Jr; children: Bria Renee, Fredrica Samone. **Educ:** Virginia State Univ, BS 1976; Medical Coll of Virginia School of Dentistry, DDS 1980. **Career:** US Public Health Svcs, sr asst dental surgeon 1980-82; Private Practice, associate 1983-86; Beaufort/Jasper Comp Health Services, staff dentist 1982-. **Orgs:** Acad of General Dentistry 1980-; Tabernacle Baptist Church 1981-; Amer Dental Assn, 1982-, SC Dental Assoc 1982-; NAACP, 1986-. **Home Addr:** PO Box 325, Beaufort, SC 29901. **Business Addr:** Dentist, 1320 S Ribaut Rd, Port Royal, SC 29935, (803)986-0157.

MORGAN-WELCH, BEVERLY ANN
Arts executive. **Personal:** Born Sep 15, 1952, Norwich, CT; married Rev Mark RP Welch Jr; children: Michael, Dominique, Alexandra. **Educ:** Smith Coll, BA 1970-74. **Career:** Creative Arts Com, admin asst 1975-76; Amherst Coll asst to the dean 1976-77; Amherst Coll, asst dean of admission 1977-78; CT Mutual Life, consult corp responsibility 1979-83; Avery Theater, gen mgr; Wadsworth Atheneum, corp & museum serv officer 1983-86; Wads Worth Atheneum, development officer, 1986-87; Greater Hartford Arts Council, executive director, 1987-. **Orgs:** Chrpsn Urban Affairs Council 1981-82; sec CT Mutual Life Found 1981-83; charter bd mem CT Coalition of 100 Black Women 1982-85; mem United Way Allocations Com Capitol Area 1982-86; bd of dir Newington Children's Hospital 1983-86; bd dir, sec Jazz Inc 1983-86; bus assoc Gr Hartford C of C 1983-86; bd dir Amer Red Cross Gr Hartford Chap 1985-86; pres Goodwin Track Conservancy 1986-88; vice pres Horace Bushnell Management Resources, Inc 1985; executive committee, Hartford Downtown Council, 1988-; vice pres, Amistad Foundation, 1987-; corporator and director, Institute of Living, 1988-; Diaconate, First Church of Christ, Hartford, 1989-; regional advisory council, Capitol Community Technical College Foundation, 1991-; corporator, Hartford Seminary, 1991-. **Honors/Awds:** Recipient Gerald Penny Mem Awd 1979; producer co-founder PUSH Performing Ensemble 1980-82; recipient Big Brothers/Big Sisters Awd 1982; participant Leadership Greater Hartford Chair Poverty Task Force 1984; coord producer CPTV Video Ducumentary Paint by Mr Amos Ferguson 1985; Recipient, Greater Hartford Community College Recognition Award, 1990. **Business Addr:** Greater Hartford Arts Council, PO Box 231436, Hartford, CT 06123-1436.

MORIAL, MARC
Mayor. **Personal:** Born Jan 3, 1958, New Orleans, LA; son of Ernest "Dutch" (deceased) and Sybil Haydel. **Educ:** Univ of Pennylvania, BA, economics, 1980; Georgetown Univ, JD, 1983. **Career:** Barham & Churchill Law Firm, associate, 1983-85; Marc H Morial Professional Law Corp, managing partner, 1985-; Off of Civil Sheriff, Orleans Parish, LA, legal counsel auctioneer; Xavier Univ, adjunct prof, political science, 1988; State of LA, senator; City of New Orleans, mayor, 1994-. **Orgs:** Harare Inc, chmn, 1983-86; LA Assn of Minority and Women Owned Bus Inc, gen counsel; New Orleans Assn of Independent Cab Drivers Inc; Morial for Mayor of New Orleans, democratic campaign coord, 1977; Jesse Jackson for Pres, 1984; Russell Long for Senator, dep campaign mgr, 1980; Dem Natl Conv, delegate, 1988; LA Voter Registration Education Crusade Inc, 1986-; LA Special Olympics, bd of dirs, 1991-; Milne Boys Home, 1991-; American Bar Assn; Natl Bar Assn; LA Trial Lawyers Assn; Natl Conf of Black Lawyers; LA State Bar Assn. **Honors/Awds:** Pro Bono Award, 1988. **Business Addr:** Mayor, City of New Orleans, City Hall, Rm 2E10, 1300 Perdido St, New Orleans, LA 70112, (504)565-6400.

MORIAL, SYBIL HAYDEL
Educational administrator. **Personal:** Born Nov 26, 1932, New Orleans, LA; daughter of Eudora Arnaud Haydel and Clarence C Haydel; married Ernest Nathan Morial, Feb 17, 1955 (deceased); children: Julie, Marc, Jacques, Cheri, Monique. **Educ:** Boston Univ, BS Ed 1952, MEd 1955. **Career:** Newton Public Schools, teacher 1952-55; Baltimore Public Schools, teacher 1955-56; New Orleans Public Schools, teacher 1959-71; Xavier Univ, dir spec serv 1977-85, assoc dean Drexel Center for Extended Learning 1985-93; Xavier Univ, assoc vp, public and communications affairs, 1993-. **Orgs:** Founder, pres, pres emeritus LA League of Good Govt 1963-; mem 1967-, pres 1976-78 New Orleans Chap of Links Inc; bd of dir WLAE-TV Adv Bd 1979-81, 1984-; Natl Conf on Children Having Children, Black Women Respond 1983; co-chair 1983 Year of the Healthy Birth; founder, pres, chmn I've Known Rivers Afro-Amer Pavilion LA World Exposition 1982-85; dir Liberty Bank & Trust Co 1979-; bd of trustees Amistad Rsch Ctr 1980-; trustee Natl Jewish Hosp Natl Asthma Ctr 1983-; vice pres, International Women's Forum 1987-; president, Women's Forum of Louisiana, 1985-; bd of dirs, Greater New Orleans Foundation, 1993-; chair, Ernest N Morial Asthma & Respiratory Disease Ctr, LSU Med Ctr, 1994; Tulane University President's Fund, 1988-; member, Advisory Board, Tulane Medical Center, 1990-; bd of dirs, Leadership Foundation, 1993. **Honors/Awds:** Natl Hon Soc in Ed Pi Lambda Theta; Torch of Liberty Awd Anti-Defamation League of B'nai B'rith 1978; Whitney M Young Brotherhood Awd Urban League of Greater New Orleans 1978; Zeta Phi Beta Finer Womenhood Awd 1978; Arts Council Medal LA Council for Music & the Performing Arts Co 1979; Weiss Awd Natl Conf of Christians & Jews 1979; Woman of the Year Links Inc 1981; Citizen of the Year Spectator News Jrnl 1984; Martin Luther King Jr, Lifetime Achievement Award, 1995. **Business Addr:** Assoc VP, Public and Communications Affairs, Xavier University, 7325 Palmetto St, New Orleans, LA 70125.

MORISEY, PATRICIA GARLAND
Educational administrator. **Personal:** Born Aug 1, 1921, New York, NY; daughter of Dagmar Cheatum and Arthur L Williams (deceased); widowed; children: Paul Garland, Jean, Alex, Muriel Spence, Caranny Morisey. **Educ:** Hunter Coll, BA 1941; Columbia Univ School of Social Work, MSS 1947, DSW 1970. **Career:** Comm Serv Soc & NYANA, caseworker 1944-51; Louise Wise Adoption Servs, caseworker consultant 1951-59; Bureau of Child Welfare NY Dept Social Servs, proj dir, dir of training 1959-63; Youth & Corrections Comm Serv Soc, staff consultant 1963-64; Family & Child Welfare Fed of Protestant Welfare Agency, director, division on family & child welfare, 1966-68; Catholic Univ of Amer Washington DC, assoc prof 1968-69; Lincoln Center Fordham Univ Grad School of Social Science, asst dean, 1975-86, prof emeritus, 1970-91. **Orgs:** Mayor's Task Force on Child Abuse & Mayor's Task Force on Foster Care, 1980; New York City Department of Mental & Retardation-Task Force Youth & The Law, Council on Social Work Educ, Natl Assoc of Social Workers; vice pres Leake & Watts Childrens Svc; mem bd Citizens Comm for Children; bd of dir Fed of Protestant Welfare Agencies; mem Subpanel on Spec Populations; pres Comm on Mental Health 1977-78; Greater NY Committee Natl Council of Negro Women, 1984-; vice president, Leake & Wahs Children's Service, 1985-91; secretary, Fed of Protestant Welfare Agencies, 1988-91. **Honors/Awds:** Hall of Fame Hunter Coll 1975; Honoree Natl Assoc of Women's Business & Professional Club 1975; Bene Merente, Fordham University, 1989. **Home Addr:** 10 W 135th St, Apt 16F, New York, NY 10037.

MORMAN, ALVIN
Professional baseball player. **Personal:** Born Jan 6, 1969, Rockingham, NC; son of Hettie F Morman; married Pamela; children: Latydra Janae. **Educ:** Wingate Coll, BS, business adm, 1991. **Career:** Houston Astros, pitcher, 1996-97; Cleveland Indians, 1997-.

MORNING, JOHN
Graphic designer. **Personal:** Born Jan 8, 1932, Cleveland, OH; son of Juanita Kathryn Brannan Morning and John Frew Morning, Sr; divorced; children: Ann Juanita, John Floyd. **Educ:** Wayne State Univ, 1950-51; Pratt Inst, BFA 1955. **Career:** McCann Erickson, Inc, art dir 1958-60; John Morning Design, Inc, owner 1960-. **Orgs:** Director, Dime Savings Bank of NY, FSB 1979-; dir Henry St Stlmnt 1973-, chmn 1979-86; trustee The

City University of New York, 1997-; director, Charles E Culpeper Foundation, 1991-; chairman, Pratt Institute Board of Trustees, 1989-92; trustee, Wilberforce University, 1987-; vice chair, New York City Cultural Affairs Advisory Commission, 1994-; vice chair, Assn of Governing Boards of Universities and Colleges, 1996-; trustee, Brooklyn Academy of Music, 1993-; dir, Lincoln Center Theater, 1995-; trustee, The Museum for African Art, 1990-; dir, New York Landmarks Conservancy, 1985-. **Honors/Awds:** Alumni medal Pratt Inst 1972; Pres Recognition Award/White House 1984. **Military Serv:** AUS sp/3c 1956-58. **Business Addr:** President, John Morning Design Inc, 333 E 45th Street, New York, NY 10017-3417.

MORRIS, ARCHIE, III
Educator, manager. **Personal:** Born Mar 24, 1938, Washington, DC; married Irene Beatrice Poindexter; children: Giovanni, Ottiviani. **Educ:** Howard Univ, BA 1968, MUS 1973; Nova Univ, DPA 1976. **Career:** US Dept of Commerce, dep asst dir admin 1972-73; US Dept of Commerce OMBE, R& D spec 1973-74; DC Govt, rent admin 1974-76; The MATCH Inst, proj dir, cons 1976-79; US Dept of Agr, chief facilities mgmt 1979-82; US Dept of Agri, chief mail & reproduction mgmt 1982-. **Orgs:** Mem bd of dirs HUD Fed Credit Union 1971-76; instr Washington Ctr for Learning Alternatives 1976; instr Howard Univ Dept of Publ Admin 1976-77; pres Natl Capital Area Chap Nova Univ Alumni 1980-81; mem Amer Soc for Publ Admin; mem Natl Urban League. **Honors/Awds:** Honors & Plaque HUD Task Force Against Racism Washington 1972; Spec Achievement Awd OMBE Dept of Commerce Washington 1973; Outstanding Serv Awd HUD Fed Credit Union Washington 1976; Cert of Apprec Mayor Washington 1976. **Military Serv:** USAF a/1c 1955-59. **Business Addr:** US Dept of Agriculture, 12th & Independence Ave SW, Washington, DC 20250.

MORRIS, BERNARD ALEXANDER
Consultant, company executive, university teacher. **Personal:** Born Jun 25, 1937, New York, NY; son of Beryl Bernice Berry Morris and Herbert Anthony Morris; married Margaret Mary Taylor Morris, Jul 16, 1988; children: Myron, Michael, Loree V Smith, Quincy. **Educ:** Boston State Coll, BS 1975; Harvard Univ, EdM 1978. **Career:** MIT, academic admin 1971-77; New York City Bd of Educ, sr policy analyst 1979-80; Nolan Norton and Co, MIS consultant 1980-85; Morris Associates, president/consultant 1985-. **Orgs:** Mem Transafrica, Pi Sigma Alpha, Phi Delta Kappa. **Military Serv:** USAF electronics/radar 4 yrs. **Home Addr:** PO Box 358, Littleton, CO 80160-0358.

MORRIS, BYRON "BAM"
Professional football player. **Personal:** Born Jan 13, 1972, Cooper, TX. **Educ:** Texas Tech. **Career:** Pittsburgh Steelers, running back, 1994-95; Baltimore Ravens, 1996-. **Business Addr:** Professional Football Player, Baltimore Ravens, 11001 Owings Mills Blvd, Owings Mills, MD 21117, (410)654-6200.

MORRIS, CALVIN S.
Educator, minister. **Personal:** Born Mar 16, 1941, Philadelphia, PA; son of Dorothy Morris and Abner Williams; children: Dorothy Rebecca, Rachel Elaine. **Educ:** Friends Select Schl, Philadelphia, PA, Diploma 1959; Lincoln Univ, AB, Amer Hist 1963; Boston Univ, AM, Amer Hist 1964; Boston Univ Schl of Theology, STB 1967; Boston Univ, PhD, Amer Hist 1982. **Career:** SCLC Operation Breadbasket, assoc dir 1967-71; Simmons Coll, dir Afro-Amer Studies/Simmons Coll 1971-73; Urban Devel, Michigan State Univ, visitng lecturer 1973-76; Martin Luther King, Jr Ctr for Social Change, exec dir 1973-76; Howard Univ Divinity Schl, asst prof practical theology & dir min in church & soc 1976-82; Howard Univ Divinity Schl, assoc prof pastoral theology & dir Urban Ministries 1982-. **Orgs:** Mem Amer Historical Assn, Amer Soc of Church History, Assn for the Study of Negro Life & History, Assn for Theological Field Educ, Soc for the Study of Black Religion, Amer Civil Lib Union, Amer Friends Serv Comm Amnesty Intl, NAACP-Life Mem, Natl Urban League; mem Omega Psi Phi; Intl Peace Research Assn 1987-; bd mem, Arts in Action, 1988; bd mem, The Churches Conference on Shelter and Housing 1988. **Honors/Awds:** Distinguished Alumni Award, Friends Select HS 1974; Jr Chamber of Comm Award One of Chicago's Ten Outstanding Young Men 1970; Crusade Schlr United Methodist Church 1963-66; Rockefeller Protestant Fellow 1964-65; Whitney Young Fellow 1971-72; Grad Fellowship for Black Amer, The Natl Fellowship Fund 1979-80; Black Doctoral Dis The Fund for Theological Ed 1979-80; Distinguished Alumni Award, Lincoln Univ, Pennsylvania, 1988; Published Reverdy C. Ransom: Black Advocate of the Social Gospel Univ Press of America, 1990. **Home Addr:** 917 Hamlin St NE, Washington, DC 20017. **Business Addr:** Director of Urban Ministries, Howard University School of Divinity, 1400 Shepherd Street NE, Washington, DC 20017.

MORRIS, CAROLYN G.
Law enforcement executive. **Educ:** North Carolina Central Univ, bachelor's degree in mathematics; Harvard Univ, master's degree in mathematics. **Career:** FBI, asst director for information resources, currently. **Special Achievements:** Highest ranking African American female in FBI history.

MORRIS, CELESTE
Publisher. **Personal:** Born Oct 7, 1949, Brooklyn, NY; daughter of Edith Harding and Cuthbert Allsop; divorced; children: Oji, Kimya. **Educ:** Howard University, 1967-68; Brooklyn College, BS, 1980. **Career:** BHRAGS Home Care Programs, program director, 1980-85; New York City Transit Authority, government relations specialist, 1986-87; Congressman Major Owens, community specialist, 1987; Unlimited Creative Enterprises, president, 1987-. **Orgs:** National Minority Business Council; Caribbean American Chamber of Commerce; National Association of Market Developers, board of directors; Black Pages Publishers Assn, president; Workshop in Business Opportunities, instructor. **Honors/Awds:** Commendation, New York City, Controller, 1996; National Association of Market Developers, NAMDer Award, 1992; National Minority Business Council, Outstanding Minority Business, 1992; Medgar Evers College, Women of Color Entrepreneurs Award, 1991; Mosaic Council, Committee Service Award, 1990; Councilwoman Annette Robinson, Communicators Award, 1992; Revson Fellowship-Columbia University, 1993-94. **Special Achievements:** The Big Black Book, 1987-95. **Business Addr:** President/Publisher, Unlimited Creative Enterprises, PO Box 400476, Brooklyn, NY 11240, (718)638-9675.

MORRIS, CHARLES EDWARD, JR.
Educational administrator. **Personal:** Born Sep 30, 1931, Big Stone Gap, VA; son of Verta Edith Warner Morris and Charles E Morris; married Jeanne A Brown; children: David Charles, Lyn Elizabeth. **Educ:** Johnson C Smith Univ, BS 1952; Univ of IL, MS 1959, PhD 1966. **Career:** William Penn High School, teacher 1954-58; Univ of IL-Urbana, teaching/rsch assoc 1959-66; IL State Univ, assoc prof math 1966-, sec of the univ 1973-80, vice pres for admin 1980-90; Illinois Board of Regents, Springfield, IL, interim vice chancellor for academic affairs, 1990-91, vice chancellor, 1991-; CEM Associates, Inc, pres, currently. **Orgs:** Bd dirs Presbyterian Foundation 1974-83, Presbyterian Economic Develop Corp 1975-85, Western Ave Comm Ctr 1978-86; chairperson IL Comm on Black Concerns in Higher Educ 1982-88, chmn emeritus 1988-; adv bd College Potential Program Council for the Advancement of Experiential Learning 1984-; chairperson IL Consortium for Educ Oppor Bd 1986-. **Honors/Awds:** Distinguished Alumnus Johnson C Smith Univ 1976; Citizen's Awd for Human Rel Town of Normal 1979; Distinguished Alum of the Year Citation Natl Assn for Equal Oppor in Higher Educ 1979; numerous speeches and articles on topics including mathematics educ, univ governance, blacks in higher educ; Doctor of Humane Letters, Monmouth College, 1991. **Home Addr:** 1023 Barton Dr, Normal, IL 61761.

MORRIS, CHRISTOPHER VERNARD
Professional basketball player. **Personal:** Born Jan 20, 1966, Dawson, GA; son of Patricia Ann Pittman Walton and John Morris; married Felicia Michelle Hammonds Morris, May 10, 1986; children: Micheal Christopher, Brenden Re'Sean, William Patrick. **Educ:** Auburn University, Auburn, AL, 1984-88. **Career:** New Jersey Nets, forward, 1988-95; Utah Jazz, 1995-. **Honors/Awds:** NBA, All Rookie Second Team, 1989. **Special Achievements:** NBA Draft, First round pick, #4, 1988. **Business Addr:** Professional Basketball Player, Utah Jazz, 301 W South Temple, Salt Lake City, UT 84101-1216, (801)575-7800.

MORRIS, CLIFTON
Educator. **Personal:** Born Jun 21, 1937, Fredericktown, PA. **Educ:** Waynesburg Coll, BS (summa cum laude) 1959; WV Univ, MS 1961; OH State Univ, PhD 1968. **Career:** Whittier Coll, chmn biology dept 1979-; City of Hope Med Tech Training Program, lectr 1978; Whittier Coll, asso prof biology 1972; OH State Univ Lima, asst prof biology 1969; OH State Univ Columbus, teaching assn 1965-68; WV Univ, research fellow 1959-61; Natl Dental Aptitude Test Rev Course, consult & instr 1977-; Natl Med Coll Aptitude Test Rev Course, consult instr 1977-; Educ Testing Serv Advanced Placement, consult 1978. **Orgs:** Mem Xi Psi Epsilon Hon Scholastic Soc Waynesburg, PA 1959; treas Gamma Alpha Grad Sci Frat Columbus, OH 1963-65; appointed James Irvine Chair in Biological Sci Whittier Coll 1980. **Honors/Awds:** Rockefeller Found Grant WV Univ Physiology of Fung I 1959-61; NSF Cooperative Grad Fellowship OH State Univ 1961; NSF summer fellowships OH State Univ 1962-64; Muellhaupt Found fellowship OH State Univ 1964; Distinguished Tchr Award OH State ULima 1971; Distinguished Tchr Award Whittier Coll 1977-78; joint authorship "Hormone-like substances which increase carotenogenesis in plus & minus sexes of Choanephora cucurbitarum" Mycologia 1967;highest honors WV U; highest honors OH State U. **Business Addr:** 13406 Philadelphia St, Whittier, CA 90608.

MORRIS, DOLORES N.
Broadcasting company executive. **Personal:** Born Sep 11, 1948, Staten Island, NY; daughter of Norcie Allen Morris and William A Morris, Jr. **Educ:** Hunter Coll, BA Physical Anthology 1970. **Career:** Port Richmond HS, teacher/advisor curriculum develop 1971-73, dir of curriculum develop; Presidio Hill School, teacher 1973-78; Children's TV Workshop, coord 1979-80; ABC Television, dir children's programs, 1980-87; vice pres Magical World of Disney. **Orgs:** Mem Women in Film NY, Hunter Coll Alumni Assoc, Amer Film Inst; comm organizer VISTA Clovis NM 1970-71. **Honors/Awds:** Black Achievement Award Harlem YWCA 1985. **Business Addr:** Vice President, Creative Development/Television Animation, Walt Disney Television, 5200 Lankershim Blvd, Ste 600, North Hollywood, CA 91601.

MORRIS, DOLORES ORINSKIA
Clinical psychologist. **Personal:** Born in New York, NY; daughter of Gertude Elliott and Joseph Morris; divorced. **Educ:** CUNY, MS 1960; Yeshiva University, PhD 1974; New York University, certificate psychoanalysis, psychotherapy post doctoral program. **Career:** Children's Center, Dept Child Welfare, psychologist 1959-62; Urban League of Greater NY, staff psychologist 1962-65; Bureau of Child Guidance NYC, school psychologist 1965-74, supvr of school psychologists 1974-78; Urban Research Planning Conf Center, tech asst 1976; Bedford Stuyvesant St Acad, consultant 1977; Fordham Univ, asst prof 1978-87; New York City Public Schools Div of Special Educ, Clinical Professional Devel, educ admin 1987-92, supervisor of school psychologists, clinical administrator, 1992-95; NYU Postdoctoral Program, supervisor, psychoanalysis, psychotherapy, 1993-. **Orgs:** Amer Psychology Assn & E Psychology Assn; treasurer, NY Assn Black Psychologist 1967-75; co-chair, professional devel NY Assn Black Psychologists 1975-77; chair Schools & Mental Health Amer Orthopsychology Assn 1978-81, 1986-87; Natl Association School Psychology; NY State Psychology Association pres Div of School Psychology 1985-86; member Board of Psychology NYS Education Department, vice chairperson, 1988-; Diplomate in Psychoanalysis Psychology, 1996-. **Honors/Awds:** Yeshiva Fellowship, NIMH 1970-72; fellowship, Black Analysis Inc 1972-74. **Business Addr:** 290 Riverside Dr, Apt 11B, New York, NY 10025.

MORRIS, EARL SCOTT
Footwear/industrial designer. **Personal:** Born May 24, 1966, Waukegan, IL; son of Velma D Morris and Earle Morris. **Educ:** Michigan State University, BA, industrial design, 1989. **Career:** Hasbro Inc, toy designer, 1990; Reebok International, footwear designer, 1990-. **Orgs:** WIMA, Cultural Diversity Group for Reebok International, 1992; Association of Black Sporting Goods Professionals, 1992; Michigan State Alumni Group, 1990. **Honors/Awds:** Hasbro Inc, GI Joe action figure, codenamed Bulletproof, named after self, 1992. **Special Achievements:** Spoke as rep for Reebok at Association of Black Sporting Goods Professional's Career Awareness Program, 1992. **Military Serv:** US Marine Corps Reserves, sgt, 1985-93; Desert Storm veteran, Southwest Asia Campaign Medal, National Defense Medal, Naval Achievement Medal. **Business Addr:** Footwear Designer, Reebok International Limited, 100 Technology Center Dr, Annex 1 Bldg, Research Design and Development, Stoughton, MA 02072, (617)341-5000.

MORRIS, EFFIE LEE
Librarian, lecturer, consultant. **Personal:** Born Apr 20, Richmond, VA; daughter of Erma Lee Caskia Morris (deceased) and William Hamilton Morris (deceased); married Leonard V Jones, Aug 25, 1971 (deceased). **Educ:** Univ of Chicago 1938-41; Case Western Res Univ, BA 1945, BLS 1946, MLS, 1956. **Career:** Cleveland Publ Library, br children's librn 1946-55; Atlanta Univ, instructor, 1954; NY Public Library, br children's librn, 1955-58; Library of the Blind, children's spec 1958-63; Univ of San Francisco, lecturer 1974-76; San Francisco Publ Library, coord children's serv 1963-78; editor, Harcourt Brace Jovanovich, 1978-79; Mills College, lecturer 1979-89. **Orgs:** Consult reading proj San Francisco Chap Natl Council Chris & Jews 1967-70; OH, NY & CA Library Assns; American Library Assn; Newbery-Caldecott Award Comm 1950-56, 1966-67, 1967-71, 1975-79, 1984-85; Laura Ingalls Wilder Award Comm 1953-54, 1958-60; bd dir Natl Aid to Visually Handicapped; library adv bd New Book Knowledge 1966; con children's serv Chicago Public Library Study 1968-69, Oakland Public Library Study 1974; adv comm Title II ESEA State of CA 1965-75; del White House Conf on Children 1970; bd dirs YWCA San Francisco 1968-73; dir children's serv div 1963-66, council 1967-71, 1975-79, 1984-88 ALA; pres, Public Library Assn 1971-72; League Women Voters, 1958-; chap pres 1968-70, Women's Natl Book Assn; Natl Council Teachers English; pres Natl Braille Club 1961-63; CAbrary Serv Bd 1982-94, vice pres 1984-86; mem adv bd Center for the Book Library of Congress 1978-86; chair, Coretta Scott King Book Award, 1984-88; chair, mem, Art Force, 1984-; Commonwealth Club of CA 1972-; American Assn of University Women 1964-; Mayor's Advisory Council on Child Care, 1978-96; Chair High School Essay contest & board member, English-Speaking Union, 1985-89; board, Phoebe Hearst Nursery School, 1992-; Golden Soror, 1996, Alpha Kappa Alpha Sorority; life mem NAACP; Univ of CA at Berkeley Chancellor's, incentive award selection committee, 1993-. **Honors/Awds:** Lola M Parker Award, Iota Phi Lambda Sor 1978; Apprec Award, Jewish Bur of Ed, San Francisco 1978; Distinguished Serv to Librarianship, Black Caucus of AL 1978; Distinguished Serv Award, CA Librarians Black Caucus 1978, 1997; Distinguished Alumni Award, School of Libr Serv, Case Western Reserve Univ 1979; Outstanding Negro Woman, Iota Phi Lambda Sor 1964; EP Dutton-John Macrae Award, Advancement of Library Serv to Children & Young People 1958; Women's Natl Book Assn Award 1984; San Francisco Public Library, Effie Lee Morris Historical & Research Collection of Children's Literature 1982; June 12, 1984,

named Effie Lee Morris Day by Mayor Diane Feinstein; keynote addresses and workshops, Assn of Intl Schools in Africa, 1988; Grolier Foundation Award of ALA, 1992; Professional Award for Continuing Service and leadership in the Professional Black Caucus of ALA, 1992; San Francisco Chapter Links, Inc, Comm Service Award, 1994; Effie Lee Morris Annual Lecture Children's Literature to San Fran Public Library funded by Women's Natl Book Assn, 1996. **Home Addr:** 66 Cleary Ct, #1009, San Francisco, CA 94109, (415)931-2733.

MORRIS, ELISE L.

Educator. **Personal:** Born Oct 25, 1916, Deridder, LA; married John E; children: Monica Delphin, John T. **Educ:** Xavier Univ, BA 1937; Prairie View A&M Univ, MEd 1965; TX So Univ, Univ of Houston, Southwestern Univ, post grad study; Univ of St Thomas, religious educ. **Career:** Archditoches Parish Training School, teacher 1973; Our Mother of Mercy School, 1942; Our Lady Star of the Sea Day School, dir 1956; Galena Park Ind School Dist, teacher 1962-. **Orgs:** Life mem Natl Educ Assn; honorary life mem, Natl PTA & TX PTA; golden life mem Delta Sigma Theta Sorority; life mem TX State Teacher Assn; mem Natl Assn of Univ Women; chmn founder Natl Assn of Univ Women Houston 1965; Harris Co Grand Jury Adv Com 1974-75; supreme lady Knights of Peter Claver 1970-75; steering com on black participation 41st Intl Eucharistic Congress 1975. **Honors/Awds:** TSU listed Black Leader of Houston 1970, KOCH & TSU Newman; Dict of Intl Biog 1975; Silver Medal Award outstanding serv Knights of PC; outstanding citizenship & serv commendation Mayor of Houston; Woman Breaking New Ground Delta Sigma Theta 1974; outstanding Xavier Alumnae of Houston.

MORRIS, ELIZABETH LOUISE

Nurse (retired). **Personal:** Born Dec 3, 1924, Cincinnati, OH; daughter of Malcolm & Ethel Ruth Brown; married Laurence Morris, Sep 28, 1962 (deceased); children: Donna Louise Higgins. **Educ:** Practical School of Nursing, licensed practical nurse, 1954; pharmacology course completed, 1968. **Career:** Jewish Hosp of Cincinnati, staff development, 1978-89. **Orgs:** American Bridge Association; Gaines United Methodist church. **Home Addr:** 3469 Ruther Ave, Cincinnati, OH 45220-1809.

MORRIS, ELLA LUCILLE

Librarian. **Personal:** Born Mar 13, 1923, Beachton, GA; daughter of Maggie Thomas Glenn and Daniel Glenn Jr; married William Alexander (deceased); children: Daniel G. **Educ:** Ft Valley State Coll, BS 1944; Atlanta Univ Sch of Libr Sci, BS LS 1949; FL A&M U, MEd 1959; FL State Univ Sch of LS, MSLS 1970. **Career:** Thomasville HS GA, head librarian 1969-; AL State Coll, acquisitions 1952; Douglass HS Thomasville, GA, librarian 1946-69; Boston HS Boston, GA, English instr 1944-45; Glenn-Mor Home Inc, sec 1970-; Southwestern State Hospital Thomasvill GA Library Consultant 1985-; Glenn-Mor Home Inc, pres 1986-; Southwestern State Hospital Thomasville GA, library consultant 1986-. **Orgs:** Mem NAACP; Hostess TV show "Input" WCTV 1974-80; mem, Alpha Kappa Alpha; Thomas Coll, trustee 1984-; WAM Assoc Inc, bd of dir 1985-; pres Glenn-Mor Horne Inc 1986-; Historical Preservation Commission 1987-; mem Thomasville City Bd of Education 1987-; pres Natl Council Negro Women Thomasville Section 1987-; bd of dirs, Thomasville Cultural Ctr, Inc, 1989-; bd of dirs, Thomasville Landmarks, Inc, 1989-. **Honors/Awds:** Achievement Award in Communications, Ft Valley Atlanta Alumni Assn 1976; Beta Phi Mu Intl Hon Soc in LS FL State Univ 1970. **Business Addr:** President, Glenn-Mor Home, Inc, 308 W Calhoun, Thomasville, GA 31792.

MORRIS, ERNEST ROLAND

Educational administrator. **Personal:** Born Dec 15, 1942, Memphis, TN; son of Ernestine Edwards Morris and Benjamin C Morris; married Freddie Linda Wilson; children: Ernest Jr, Daniel. **Educ:** Rocky Mountain Coll, BS (cum laude) 1967; Eastern IL Univ, MS Educ (w/distinction) 1968; Univ of IL Urbana Champaign, PhD 1976. **Career:** Minneapolis Pub Sch, history tchr 1968-69; Eastern IL Univ, admissions officer 1969-71; Univ of IL at Urbana-Champaign, asst dean, assoc dean 1971-78, exec asst to the chancellor 1978-80; Univ of WA Seattle, spec asst pres 1980-82, vice pres for student affairs 1982-. **Orgs:** Chmn educ div 1983, 1984, mem admissions and review comm 1984-85, vice chmn bd of dirs 1985-88, first vice chair 1989, chairman elect, 1990, chairman 1991, Residential Care and Family Services Conference Panel, 1984-85; vice chmn planning and distribution comm 1986, chmn planning and distribution comm 1987-89, mem finance comm, 1993-; United Way Seattle/King Co; mem class of 1983-84, bd of dirs 1985-, exec comm 1986-, chmn selection comm 1987, vp, 1992, pres, 1993, exec comm, 1992-94, chair bd of dirs, 1994-95; United Way/Chamber of Commerce Leadership Tomorrow Prog; chmn Federal Emergency Mgmt Agency Local Bd Seattle/King Co 1984-86; founding trustee Seattle/King Co Emergency Shelter Foundation 1984-86; member, board of trustees, First Funds of America, 1990-93; mem bd of dirs, Central Puget Sound Council of Campfire, various bd committees, 1993-; YWCA Isabel Colman Pierce Award Committee, 1992-97; King County Redistricting Committee, Chair (nonpartisan) 1996. **Honors/Awds:** Clark Meml Scholar 1966; Outstanding History Student Awd 1966; Alumni Distinguished Achievement Awd Rocky MT Coll 1982; mem Natl Assoc of Student Personnel Administrators, Natl Assoc of State Univ and Land Grant Colls; Outstanding Alumnus Award Leadership Tomorrow 1988. **Business Addr:** Vice Pres for Student Affairs, University of Washington, Box 355831, Seattle, WA 98195-5831.

MORRIS, EUGENE

Advertising executive. **Personal:** Born Jul 25, 1939, Chicago, IL; son of Willie Mae Mitchell Morris and Eugene Morris, Sr; married Beverly Coley-Morris, Sep 3, 1988. **Educ:** Roosevelt Univ, Chicago Il, BSBA, 1969, MBA, 1971. **Career:** Foote, Cone & Belding, Chicago, IL, account exec, 1968-74; Burrell Advertising, Chicago, IL, sr vice pres, 1974-86; Morris & Co, Chicago, IL, pres, 1986-87; Morris/Randall Advertising, Chicago, IL, pres, 1987-88; E Morris, Ltd, Chicago , IL, pres, 1988-. **Orgs:** Bd chmn, Chicago Urban League Public Relations Advisory Bd, 1986-; vice chairman, Sickle Cell Disease Association of Illinois; director, Cosmopolitan Chamber of Commerce; board of directors, Junior Achievement, Chicago; bd mem, Bethune Museum, 1989-; board of directors, Traffic Audit Bureau. **Honors/Awds:** Blackbook Business & Professional Award, Natl Publications, 1984; Citizen Professional Award, Citizen Newspapers, 1985. **Military Serv:** US Army, E4, 1962-65. **Business Addr:** President, E Morris, Ltd, Communications, Inc, 820 N Orleans St, Ste 402, Chicago, IL 60610, (312)943-2900.

MORRIS, FRANK LORENZO, SR.

Educational administrator. **Personal:** Born Jul 21, 1939, Cairo, IL; son of Frankie Mae Taylor (Honesty) and Lorenzo Richard Morris, Jr; married M Winston Baker, Jan 2, 59 ; children: Frank Jr, Scott, Rebecca, Kristina. **Educ:** Colgate Univ, BA 1961; Syracuse Univ, MPA 1962; MIT, PhD, MS 1976. **Career:** US Dept Housing & Urban Devel, Seattle WA, urban renewal rep, 1962-66; US Agency for Intl Develop, reg coord 1966-72; Northwestern Univ, assoc prof 1972-77; US Community Serv Admin, chief of planning & policy 1978; USAID, deputy dir chief of operations 1979-83; Congressional Black Caucus Found, exec dir 1983-85; Colgate Univ, O'Connor prof 1986; Univ of MD School of Public Affairs, assoc dean 1986-88; Morgan State Univ, Baltimore MD, dean of graduate studies and research, 1988-. **Orgs:** Pres NAACP Tacoma 1963-66; vice pres NAACP Montgomery Cty 1977-79; trustee Lincoln Temple UCC 1984; moderator Potomac Assn, United Church of Christ 1987-; treas, bd of dir Global Tomorrow Coalition 1987-; mem Alpha Phi Alpha; bd of dir Center Immigration Studies, 1988-; bd of homeland ministries, United Church of Christ, 1988-; Council of Historically Black Graduate Schools, president, 1992-94; Graduate Record Examination, minority advisory committee, 1992-94. **Honors/Awds:** NDEA Fellow MIT 1971; Dissertation Fellow Russel Sage Found 1972; selected as Father of the Year Chicago Defender 1975; Educ Policy Fellow Inst for Educ Leadership 1977; three awards NAACP Evanston IN, Mont Cty MD; Superior Honor Awd Dept of State 1982. **Military Serv:** US AID sr foreign service officer 18 yrs. **Home Addr:** 1212 Hidden Rdg Apt 1048, Irving, TX 75038-3758. **Business Addr:** Dean of Graduate Studies & Research, Morgan State University, Baltimore, MD 21239.

MORRIS, FRED H., JR.

Company executive. **Personal:** Born Oct 15, 1925, Bristol, VA; son of Fred H Sr (deceased) & Estella Ruth Charles Morris; married Wilma J Booker Morris, Feb 4, 1957; children: Marvin L, Fred III, Karen, Kevin, Deborah. **Educ:** Univ of State of NY, accounting, 1952; Blackstone School of Law, LLB, 1969. **Career:** Univ of State of NY, Educ Dept, public accounting and taxation, 1960; Town of Babylon, comptroller, 1962; Suffolk County, commissioner, Human Rights Advisory Bd, 1985-; Morris Mgmt Consulting Co, chmn, CEO, currently. **Orgs:** Masonic Lodge, King of Tyre Affiliation, A F & AM; State of New York, Northern Hemisphere; Federation of Masons of the World, grandmaster, 1960-80; American Legion Post 1218; Cpl Anthony Casamento Memorial Post #46; Italian American War Veterans; Vet Mem Park, founder; Suffolk County Black History Assn Inc Museum, founder; St Andrew General Masonic Congress, founder, chmn. **Honors/Awds:** Newsday Editorial Award, 1979; 33 Degree Mason, honorary degrees (2). **Military Serv:** US Army, two years.

MORRIS, GARRETT

Actor, comedian, musician. **Personal:** Born Feb 1, 1937, New Orleans, LA; married Freda. **Educ:** Dillard University, BA; Juilliard School of Music; Manhattan School of Music. **Career:** Theater appearances include: The Bible Salesman, 1960; Porgy and Bess, 1964; I'm Solomon, 1968; Show Boat, 1966; Hallelujah, Baby!, 1967; Slave Ship, 1969-70; Transfers, 1970; Operation Sidewinder, 1970; In New England Winter, 1971; The Basic Training of Pavlo Hummel, 1971; What the Wine-Sellers Buy, 1974; Don't Bother Me, I Can't Cope, 1974; Sweet Talk, 1974; The World of Ben Caldwell, 1982; The Unvarnished Truth, 1985; film appearances include: Where's Poppa (also known as Going Ape), 1970; The Anderson Tapes, 1971; Cooley High, 1975; Car Wash, 1976; How to Beat the High Cost of Living, 1980; The Census Taker, 1984; The Stuff, 1985; Critical Condition, 1987; The Underachievers, 1988; Dance to Win, 1989; Husbands, Wives, Money, and Murder, 1989; television appearances include: Saturdaight Live, regular, 1975-80; It's Your Move, 1984-85; Hunter, 1986-; Married With Children, 1987, 1989; Who's the Boss?, 1988; Murder, She Wrote, 1985; singer and musical arranger, Harry Belafonte Folk Singers; writer, The Secret Place, 1972; Daddy Picou and Marie LeVeau, 1981. **Orgs:** ASCAP, 1963-; American Federation of Television & Radio Artists. **Honors/Awds:** Tanglewood Conductors Award 1956; Omega Psi Phi Nat Singing Contest Winner.

MORRIS, GERTRUDE ELAINE

Clergy administrator. **Personal:** Born Dec 20, 1924, Brooklyn, NY; daughter of Estelle Justina Taylor Morris (deceased) and Clifford Alphonso Morris (deceased). **Educ:** Grailville Community Coll, Loveland, OH, 1957-61; DeSales School of Theology, Washington, DC, Certificate in Pastoral Leadership, 1991. **Career:** Mobilization for Youth, New York, NY, office mgr, 1963-67; Human Resources Admmn, New York, NY, dir of clerical training, 1967-73; Natl Office for Black Catholics, Washington, DC, dir of culture & worship, 1973-78, dir of evangelization, 1980-85; Catholic Archdiocese of San Francisco, San Francisco, CA, dir of African Amer Cath affairs, 1986-. **Orgs:** Professed mem, The Grail, 1957-; comm mem, Campaign for Human Dev-San Jose, 1988-90, San Francisco, 1990-; mem, Natl Conf of Catholic Bishops Comunication Comm, 1980-84; bd of dir, Natl Council for Catholic Evangelization, 1981-85; allocations panel, United Way Natl Capitol Area, 1981-85. **Honors/Awds:** Named one of "People To Watch in the 90's," San Francisco Chronicle, 1990; Evangelist of the Year Award, Paulist Fathers, 1986; Imani Distinguished Service Award, Natl Office for Black Catholics, 1985; Outstanding Community Service, Pres of Brooklyn, City of NY, 1984; The Fr Norman Dukette Award for Natl Evangelization Efforts, Office of Black Ministry, Brooklyn, NY, 1984. **Home Addr:** The Grail, PO Box 3045, San Jose, CA 95156. **Business Addr:** Director, Office of African American Ministry, Archdiocese of San Francisco, 445 Church St, San Francisco, CA 94114.

MORRIS, HERMAN, JR.

Attorney. **Personal:** Born Jan 16, 1951, Memphis, TN; son of Reba Garrett Morris and Herman Morris; married Brenda Partee Morris, Oct 4, 1980; children: Amanda Elizabeth, Patrick Herman, Geoffrey Alexander. **Educ:** Rhodes College, Memphis, TN, BA, 1973; Vanderbilt University School of Law, Nashville, TN, JD, 1977. **Career:** Dixie Homes Boys Club, Inc, Memphis, TN, counselor, 1969; Porter Leath Children Center, Memphis, TN, counselor, 1970-73; RLS Assoc, , Charleston, SC, director of minority recruiting, 1973-74; Sears, Nashville, TN, retail salesman, 1975; Tennessee Commission on Human Development, Nashville, TN, law clerk, 1976; Ratner, Sugarmon and Lucas, Memphis, TN, law clerk, 1976; Ratner and Sugarmon, Memphis, TN, associate attorney, 1977-82, partner, 1982; Sugarmon, Salky and Morris, Memphis, TN, managing partner, 1982-86; Herman Morris and Associates, Memphis, TN, 1986-88; Morris and Noel, Attorneys at Law, Memphis, TN, partner, 1988-89; Memphis Light, Gas and Water Division, Memphis, TN, General Counsel, 1989-96, pres/CEO, 1997-. **Orgs:** Chairman, Shelby County Homerule Charter Commission; chairman of the board, Memphis Health Center, Inc; chairman of the board, Dixie Home Boys Club; exec bd, Southwestern at Memphis Alumni Assn: Primary Health Care Advisory Bd; pres, Ben Jones Chapter, Natl Bar Assn; bd of dirs, Memphis Public Educ Fund; bd of dirs, Natl Conference of Christians and Jews; president, Memphis Branch, NAACP; member, American Bar Assn; mem, Tennessee Bar Assn; bd mem, Memphis Bar Assn; member, American Trial Lawyers' Assn; bd of dirs, TN Trial Lawyer's Assn; bd of dirs, Judicial Criminal Justice Center Advisory Comm; vice chairman, TN Bd of Professional Responsibility. **Honors/Awds:** Best Lawyer in America 1994-96; PSI Inc, Executive of the Year, 1996; Legal Secretarys Association, Boss of the Year, 1992-93. **Special Achievements:** First African American president/CEO at Memphis Light, Gas and Water Division; first African American to lead the nation's largest three-service municipally owned utility company. **Business Addr:** President/CEO, Memphis Light, Gas and Water Division, 220 S Main St, Memphis, TN 38103.

MORRIS, HORACE W.

Association executive. **Personal:** Born May 29, 1928, Elizabeth, NJ; son of Evelyn Turner and Pringle Morris; divorced; children: Bradley, JoAnne, Horace, Jr, Bryan. **Educ:** Syracuse Univ Sch of Edn, BA 1949; Rutgers The St Univ Grad Sch of Edn, MEduc 1962. **Career:** Burlington Public Schools, teacher, admin 1956-64; NY Urban League, exec dir 1974-83; Intl Center of the Meridan Found, lecture on "Civil Liberties & Race Relations in Amer" 1966-69; Dade County Community Relations Bd, dep dir 1970; Dade County Model Cities Prog, dir 1971; Garmco Inc, pres/CEO 1968-70; Greater NY Fund/United Way, exec dir 1983-88; executive vice president, United Way of New York City, 1988-91. **Orgs:** Nat Conf of Soc Welf; NAACP; Alumni Assn Syracuse U; Alpha Phi Alpha Frat; Frontiers Internatl; Chrtr mem Civitan Internatl Springfield OH Chpt; AME Zion Ch; mem, bd dir New York City Partnership. **Honors/Awds:** Recip Pop Warner Serv to Youth Awd S Jersey area 1962; Outstanding Young Man of Yr Gr Burlington Area Jr C of C 1962; Father of Yr Burlington Jr HS PTA 1960; Four Yr Scholar Syracuse Univ 1945-49; Letterman of Distinction, Syracuse University, 1985; Frederick Douglass Awardee, New

York Urban League, 1992. **Home Addr:** 15 Ridgeview Pl, Willingboro, NJ 08046. **Business Addr:** HWM Associates, 15 Ridgeview Pl, Willingboro, NJ 08046.

MORRIS, JAMIE WALTER (JAMES)
Professional football player. **Personal:** Born Jun 6, 1965, Southern Pines, NC. **Educ:** Univ of Michigan, attended. **Career:** Washington Redskins, 1988-90; New England Patriots, running back, 1990-. **Business Addr:** Professional Football Player, New England Patriots, Sullivan Stadium, Rt 1, Foxboro, MA 02035.

MORRIS, JOE
Professional football player (retired). **Personal:** Born Sep 15, 1960, Fort Bragg, NC; married Linda; children: Samantha Ashley. **Educ:** Syracuse Univ, BS, 1982. **Career:** New York Giants, running back, 1982-90. **Honors/Awds:** Played in Senior Bowl, East-West Shrine and Blue-Gray games; set all of the all-time rushing records at Syracuse; set 5 all-time Giant records: 1,336 yards rushing, 21 rushing touchdowns, seven 100 yard plus games, three touchdowns in a game four times, back-to-back 1,000 yard seasons, 1985, 1986; played in Pro Bowl, 1985, 1986.

MORRIS, JOHN P., III
Shipping executive. **Personal:** son Of John P Morris Sr (deceased). **Career:** Red River Shipping, beginning 1988, owner, 1993-. **Special Achievements:** Red River Shipping is the first African-American controlled company to own and operate an oceangoing motor vessel under the US flag. **Business Addr:** Owner, Red River Shipping, 6110 Executive Blvd, Ste 620, Rockville, MD 20852, (301)230-0854.

MORRIS, KELSO B.
Educator. **Personal:** Born in Beaumont, TX; married Marlene Isabella; children: Kenneth Bruce, Gregory Alfred, Karen Denise, Lisa Frances. **Educ:** Wiley Coll, BS 1930; Cornell Univ, MS 1937, PhD 1940. **Career:** Wiley Coll, prof 1940-46; Howard Univ, prof 1946-77, dept head 1965-69; Atlanta Univ, visiting lecturer 1946, 1949, & 1951; NC Coll, 1957-59; Air Force Inst of TechWright Patterson AFB, prof sect head 1959-61; Amer Inst Chemists, fellow; TX Acad Sci; Washington Acad Sci; Amer Assn for Advancement of Sci; Wash Acad of Sci, sec 1977-78; Sci Achievement Awards Prgram Wash Acad of Sci, gen chmn 1974-78. **Orgs:** Mem Am Chem Soc; Nat Assn for Research in Sci Teaching; DC Inst Chemists pres 1974-75 Unitarian; mem Alpha Phi Alpha Frat; monographs in field; Sigma Xi. **Honors/Awds:** Distinguished Teaching Award Washington Acad Scis 1968; Gen Educ Bd Fellow 1936-37; Cosmos Club of Washington 1969-; United Negro Coll Fund Dreyfus Found 1974-80.

MORRIS, LATICIA
Professional basketball player. **Personal:** Born May 26, 1974. **Educ:** Auburn Univ. **Career:** Portland Power, forward, 1997-. **Business Addr:** Professional Basketball Player, Portland Power, 439 N Broadway, Portland, OR 97227, (503)249-1130.

MORRIS, LEIBERT WAYNE
Educational administrator. **Personal:** Born Nov 20, 1950, Cleveland, OH; married Cathy L. **Educ:** OH Univ, BGS 1973, MEd 1980. **Career:** OH State Univ Office of Minority Affairs, coord of recruitment 1974-75; Oberlin Coll, asst dir admissions 1975-77; Coll of Osteopathic Med OH Univ, assoc dir admissions 1977-79, asst to regional dean 1979-85; OH State Univ Coll Med, associate to the dean 1985-90, director of admissions, 1990-96; Columbus State Community College, director of admissions, 1996-, coord admin for enrollment svcs, 1998-. **Orgs:** Adv bd staff Builders Home Health Care Agency 1983-85; bd trustees Triedstone Missionary Baptist Church 1985-88; keeper of records & seal Omega Psi Phi Frat Inc 1984-85; natl nominations chair, Natl Assn of Medical Minority Educators, 1989-91; Ohio Commission of Minority Health 1989-92; member, New Salem Missionary Baptist Church. **Business Addr:** Coordinator-Administrator for Enrollment Svcs, Columbus State Community College, 550 E Spring St, Columbus, OH 43215.

MORRIS, LEWIS R.
Educator. **Personal:** Born Feb 17, 1926, Windsor, NC; son of Brulena Morris and Richard Morris; married Selena R Clark; children: Brenda J, Constance L, Lolita R, Richard J. **Educ:** NC A&T Univ, BS 1947; Univ MI, MA 1950; Howard Univ, PhD 1970; Mount Hope Bible Coll, ThD 1978; Detroit Urban Bible College, DD. **Career:** Morris Coll Sumter SC, dean dept chmn; TX Southern Univ, prof English chmn, currently. **Orgs:** Mem CLA; CCCC; MLA; NCTE; YMCA; Magnolia Lodge #3; Douglass Burrell Consistory (32); Doric Temple; Alpha Kappa Mu; Lambda Iota Tau; chaplain Nu Phi, Omega Psi Phi; United Supreme Council 33 degree PHA. **Military Serv:** Lt, WWII. **Business Addr:** Professor, Texas Southern University, 3300 Cleburne, Houston, TX 77004.

MORRIS, MAJOR
Educator (retired). **Personal:** Born May 12, 1921, Cincinnati, OH; son of Ellen Morris; married Anne-Grethe Jakobsen; children: Lia Jacqueline. **Educ:** Boston Univ, attended 1949-51; Harvard Univ Graduate School of Educ, EdM 1976. **Career:** MIT, rsch technician 1953-66; Tufts Univ, program dir officer 1969-76; Southeastern MA Univ, affirmative action officer 1977-79; Portland State Univ, dir equity programs 1979-87. **Orgs:** Photographer/administrator Education Develop Ctr 1966-68; dir Deseg Training Inst Univ of Delaware 1976-77; state coord MA Region I AAAA 1977-79; vice chair Tri-County AA Assoc Portland 1981-83; state coord Oregon Region X AAAA 1983-; Willamette Valley Racial Minority Consortium (WVRMC); dir/photographer Foto MaJac 1987-; bd mem Beaverton OR Arts Commission 1989-91. **Honors/Awds:** Monographs EEO/AA In Postsecondary Institutions, Concepts in Multicultural and Intergroup Relations Ed, Click and Tell, Our Street; contributor Intergroup Relations Curriculum. **Military Serv:** AUS staff sgt 1942-46; European Theatre; Po Valley; No Appenines; Good Conduct Medal; Victory Medal.

MORRIS, MARGARET LINDSAY
Educator. **Personal:** Born Dec 23, 1950, Princess Anne Co, VA; daughter of Lillie Mae Phelps Lindsay and George Alfred Lindsay; married Richard Donald Morris, Aug 24, 1984; children: Kristin Richelle, Tyler Donald. **Educ:** Norfolk State U, BA 1973; Iberian Am Univ Mexico City, 1975; Univ of IL Urbana-Champaign, MA 1974, PhD 1979; Univ of Madrid, summer 1982; Michigan State Univ, summer, 1991. **Career:** Lincoln U, asst prof of Spanish 1980-; Central State Univ Wilberforce OH, language lab dir 1980; Livingstone Coll Salisbury NC, asst prof 1981-85; Portsmouth City Schools, teacher 1986-; Hampton University, asst prof of Spanish. **Orgs:** Mem Am Assn of Tchr of Spanish & Portuguese 1976-80; mem Am Assn of Univ Prof 1976-80; mem Coll Language Assn 1980; life mem Alpha Kappa Mu Honor Soc 1972-; life mem Sigma Delta Pi Spanish Hon Soc 1974-; life mem Alpha Gamma Mu Spanish Hon Soc 1972-; mem Alpha Kappa Alpha Sor 1983-. **Honors/Awds:** Fellowship Univ of IL 1973-74; Fellowship Grad Coll Univ of IL 1975; 1st Black to Receive PhD in Spanish Univ of IL 1979; wrote proposal entitled "Personalizing Instruction in Modern Foreign Langugages" 1982-84; Ford Foundation Fellowship, 1992. **Business Addr:** Assistant Professor of Spanish, Hampton University, Hampton, VA 23668.

MORRIS, MARLENE C.
Staff chemist (retired). **Personal:** Born Dec 20, 1933, Washington, DC; daughter of Ruby Cook and Richard Cook; married Kelso B; children: Gregory A, Karen D, Lisa F. **Educ:** Howard Univ, BS 1955; Polytechnic Ins of NY, postgraduate. **Career:** AUS, research assoc High Temp Research Project 1953-55; NBS JCPDS Associateship, research assoc 1955-, dir & research assoc 1975-; Intl Centre for Diffraction Data, research chemist 1986-90. **Orgs:** Mem Amer Chemist Soc; Amer Crystallographic Soc; Amer Assn for Adv of Sci; Joint Comm on Powder Diff Stand; Intl Union of Crystallography; mem NBSSr Lunch Club; mem & fellow, Washington Acad of Sci Sigma Xi; Beta Kappa Chi Hon Sci Soc; mem Unitarian Church; mem, JCPDS-ICCD. **Special Achievements:** Published 69 articles in professional periodicals; author of 4 books.

MORRIS, MELVIN
Attorney. **Personal:** Born May 7, 1937, Chicago, IL. **Educ:** Univ WI, BS 1959; John Marshall Law Sch, JD 1965. **Career:** Prv Prac, atty; Gary, IN, city atty. **Business Addr:** 2216 Broadway St E, East Chicago, IN 46312.

MORRIS, ROBERT V., SR.
Communications company executive. **Personal:** Born May 13, 1958, Des Moines, IA; son of Arlene J Morris and James B Morris Jr; married Vivian E Morris, Jun 3, 1989; children: Jessica, Robert Jr. **Educ:** University of Iowa, 1981. **Career:** Iowa Bystander, editor/writer, 1968-83; Des Moines Register, editorialist, 1990-; Morris Communications International, Inc, CEO/president, 1983-. **Orgs:** Kappa Alpha Psi Fraternity, life membr, 1984; NAACP: Iowa/Nebraska State Conference, president, 1982; NAACP: Iowa City Chapter, president, 1979-81. **Honors/Awds:** State of Iowa, TSB Entrepreneur of the Year, 1989; NAACP Iowa/Nebraska Conference, Meritorious Service, 1990; NAACP Iowa City Chapter, President Emeritus, 1981, Chair's Award, 1980; University of Iowa, Black Hall of Fame, 1980. **Special Achievements:** Black Enterprise Magazine, Making It, 1990; Des Moines Register, Business Up and Comer, 1990. **Business Addr:** Chief Executive Officer and President, Morris Communications International, Inc, 1600 Hickman Rd, Des Moines, IA 50314-1543.

MORRIS, STANLEY E., JR.
Educational administrator. **Personal:** Born Nov 15, 1944, Brooklyn, NY; son of Bernice Lambert Morris and E Morris; married Sandra Brito; children: Brooke Brito. **Educ:** Howard Univ, BA 1968; Cornell Univ, public relations board, certification, natural training, 1990. **Career:** State Univ of NY, asso dean 1970-96, asst dir 1969-70; NY City Bd of Educ, teacher 1968-69. **Orgs:** Pres/chmn of bd, Elephant Ent Ltd 1975-; pres, SE Morris Mgmt Assn 1976-; mem, NY State Personnel & Guidance Assn; mem, Afro Am Tchr Assn; rep, Univ Negro Coll Fund 1970; rep, ASG; mem, Dist of Columbia Sociological Soc; member, National Association of Student Personnel Administrators, 1990-91; member, American Association for Higher Education, 1991; trainer, National Coalition Building Institute for Prejudice Reduction, 1990-91. **Honors/Awds:** Claude Mckay Award 1960; publ "Beyond the Blue" 1961; University Faculty Senate Award for Excellence in Affirmative Action/Equal Opportunity, SUNY Faculty Senate, 1991; Chancellor's Service Award for 20 years, SUNY, 1990; Distinguished Service Award, President's Committee on Minority and Traditionally Underrepresented Students, SUNY Oneonta, 1990. **Home Addr:** Upper West St, Oneonta, NY 13820.

MORRIS, WAYNE LEE
Contractor, horse ranch owner, professional football player (retired). **Personal:** Born May 3, 1954, Dallas, TX. **Educ:** Southern Methodist Univ, BA, 1976. **Career:** Running back: St Louis Cardinals, 1976-83; San Diego Chargers, 1984; Wayne Morris Enterprises Inc, chairman of the board; Landmark Northwest Plaza Bank, loan officer, 1978; Wayne Morris Quarter Horse Ranch, owner, 1979-. **Orgs:** Co-chmn YMCA. **Honors/Awds:** Player of Year, Golden Knights, 1975-76; Most Valuable Player, Shriners Children's Hospital, 1976; Most Improved Player, St Louis Quarterback Club, 1977. **Business Addr:** Wayne Morris Enterprises Inc, 5715 Old Ox Rd, Dallas, TX 75241.

MORRIS, WILLIAM H.
Financial co. executive, educator. **Personal:** Born Sep 7, 1960, Detroit, MI. **Educ:** Northwood Institute, BBA, 1982; The Wharton School of the University of Pennsylvania, MBA, 1988. **Career:** Peat Marwick, supervisor, 1982-86; Chrysler Corp, senior treasury analyst, 1988-90; Hillsdale College, professor of finance/accounting, 1991-; WILMOCO Capital Management, president/chief investment officer, 1990-. **Orgs:** State of Michigan Accountancy Board, secretary/treasurer, 1991-; American Institute of Certified Public Accountants, investment committee, 1992-93; National Association of State Board Accountants, finance/administration committee, 1992-93; Michigan Association of Certified Public Accountants, 1988; National Black MBA Association, 1987-; Financial Analysts Society of Detroit, Accounting Committee, 1989-. **Honors/Awds:** Northwood Institute, Outstanding Alumni Award, 1992; Crain's Detroit Business, Top 40 Business People Under 40 Years of Age, 1991. **Business Addr:** President/Chief Investment Officer, WILMOCO Capital Management, 300 River Place, Ste 5350, Detroit, MI 48207.

MORRISEY, JIMMY
Association executive. **Personal:** Born Mar 31, 1922, Raeford Hoke Co, NC; son of Besty Morrisey and Ceaser Morrisey; married Nina; children: Jo Belinda Morrisey, McPhatter Ben, John, Barbara. **Educ:** New York City Trade Sch, cert mens tailoring 1951; Cardinal Health Agy, cert 1979. **Career:** Scurlock Comm Orgn Inc, pres 1972-; Hoke Co Voter Registration Edn, dir 1968-70. **Orgs:** Bd mem Cardinal Health Agency Inc 1975-; pres Hoke Co Branch NAACP 1968-; pres Scurlock Community Orgn Inc 1972-; v-chmn Hillcrest-Scurlock Water System Inc 1972-. **Honors/Awds:** Achievement Award Hoke Co Branch NAACP 1975; cert for Volunteer Serv State of NC 1976. **Military Serv:** AUS sgt 5 yrs served, recipient 3 European Battle Stars. **Business Addr:** PO Box 501, Raeford, NC 28376.

MORRIS-HALE, WALTER
Educator. **Personal:** Born Jan 30, 1933, Chicago, IL. **Educ:** Univ of CA Berkeley, 1957; Univ of Stockholm Sweden, MA 1962; Univ of Geneva Switzerland, PhD 1969. **Career:** Smith Coll, asst prof 1969-75, assoc prof, full prof, currently. **Honors/Awds:** Publs "British Admin in Tanganyika from 1920-45, with Spec Reference to the Preparation of Africans for Admin Positions" 1969, "From Empire to Nation, the African Experience" in Aftermath of Empire Smith Coll Studies in History XIVII 1973; Conflict & Harmony in Multi-Ethnic Societies: An International Perspective, 1996. **Business Addr:** Full Professor, Smith College, Northampton, MA 01063.

MORRISON, CHARLES EDWARD
Beverage company executive. **Personal:** Born Jul 18, 1943, Longview, TX; married Geri Brooks; children: Constance, Rani, Kristi, Jennifer. **Educ:** Bishop College, BS 1964; Wichita State Univ, Grad work. **Career:** General Motors, accountant 1965-70; Procter & Gamble, sales/mktg 1970-72; Schlitz Brewing Co, sales/mktg 1972-77, 1979-81; Burrell Advertising, advertising acct sup 1977-79; Coca-Cola USA, dir black consumer marketing 1981-. **Orgs:** Consultant WCLK Adv Bd 1985-86; consultant Southern Arts Federation 1985; trustee Bishop Coll 1985-86; bd mem South DeKalb YMCA 1986; life mem NAACP, Urban League; bd mem Atlanta Boys Club; mem Grambling State Univ Industry Cluster; chairman, National Assn of Marketing Developers, 1991-92; trustee, Rust College; board member, Jackie Robinson Foundation. **Honors/Awds:** Top 10 Black Businessperson Dollar & Sense Magazine 1985; Beverage Exec of Year Cal-PAC Org 1986; several ad awards; CEBA's, CLIO's, Addy's; Honorary Doctorate, Rust College, 1988; Honorary Doctorate, Grambling State University, 1989. **Business Addr:** Vice Pres Black/Hispanic Mktg, Coca-Cola USA, One Coca Cola Plaza, Atlanta, GA 30313-1734.

MORRISON, CLARENCE CHRISTOPHER
Judge. **Personal:** Born Feb 17, 1930, Charleston, SC; son of Ida Morrison and Clarence Morrison; married Grace Fulton; children: Derricott M, Mark E. **Educ:** Howard Univ Coll of Liberal Arts, BS Psych 1954; Howard Univ School of Law, LLB 1959. **Career:** Judge Carl B Shelly, law clerk 1960-61; State of PA Auditor Gen, legal asst 1961-62; Commonwealth of PA Dept of Revenue, asst attny gen 1962-65; Dauphin Cty Prosecutor's Office, asst dist attny 1965-69; PA State Ed Assoc, staff counsel 1969-76; Marrison & Atkins, law partner 1972-80; Court of Common Pleas, Dauphin Cty Court House, judge 1980-. **Orgs:** Bd of dir, pres Harrisburg Housing Authority; mem Mayor's Comm on Human Relations; vice pres Yoke Crest Inc; mem, vice chmn of bd of trustees, legal advisor, Sunday school teacher Tabernacle Baptist Church of Harrisburg PA; co-chmn South Central PA Chap of Heart Fund; legal advisor, chmn of bd of dir Opport Indust Ctrs Inc; pres Harrisburg Club of Frontiers Intl; mem bd of dir Dauphin Cty NAACP; charter mem Optimist Club of Harrisburg; mem Omega Psi Phi Frat. **Honors/Awds:** Morrison Towers home for the elderly named after Clarence Morrison. **Military Serv:** AUS commiss officer 1964-56. **Business Addr:** Judge, Court of Common Pleas, Dauphin County Court House, Harrisburg, PA 17108.

MORRISON, CURTIS ANGUS
Attorney. **Personal:** Born Jun 4, 1945, Pinehurst, NC; married Christine. **Educ:** Rutgers U, BA deans list 1971; Rutgers Univ Sch of Law, JD 1974. **Career:** Prudential Ins Co of Am, asst genl counsel; St of NJ, deputy atty gen 1974-76. **Orgs:** Am Bar Assn; NJ Bar Assn; Garden St Bar Assn. **Military Serv:** AUS sgt 1967-70. **Business Addr:** 1111 Durham Ave, South Plainfield, NJ 07080.

MORRISON, GARFIELD E., JR.
Law enforcement officer. **Personal:** Born Apr 13, 1939, Boston, MA; son of Iona Blackman Morrison and Garfield E Morrison Sr; married Pearl P Johnson Morrison, Jul 27, 1963; children: Garfield E Morrison III, Melissa E Morrison. **Educ:** MA Bay Community Coll, Wellesley, MA, AS, 1978; Boston State Coll, Boston, MA, BS, 1981; Anna Maria Coll, Paxton, MA, 1982. **Career:** US Post Office, Boston, MA, letter carrier, 1966-74; Cambridge Police, Cambridge, MA, police officer, 1974-84, sergeant, 1984-. **Orgs:** Chmn, usher bd, Mass Ave Baptist Church, 1966-70; sec, Men's Club, Mass Ave Baptist Church, 1965-68; trustee, Mass Ave Baptist Church, 1968-72; treas, Cambridge Afro-American Police Assn, 1977-86, pres, 1990, 1992. **Honors/Awds:** WEB DuBois Academy Award, Recognition of Service, 1992; Boston Police Dept, Recognition of Outstanding Contribution in Aiding Police Service to the Citizens of Boston, 1992. **Military Serv:** US Air Force, A/3C, 1957-59; Unit Citation, 485th Communication Squadron. **Home Addr:** 50 Dorothy Rd, Arlington, MA 02174.

MORRISON, GWENDOLYN CHRISTINE CALDWELL
Educator. **Personal:** Born Dec 11, 1949, Cuney, TX; daughter of Josephine Pierce Caldwell Ellis and John Caldwell (deceased); married Ben Arnold Morrison, 1973; children: Paul, Brandon, Jonathan, Betsey. **Educ:** Stephen F Austin State Univ Nacogdoches TX, BS home econ 1970; Stephen F Austin State Univ, MEd 1971; Univ of North Texas, Denton, TX, Educational Leadership Post doctoral studies 1986-88; Texas Woman's Univ, Denton, TX, EdD Adult Educ 1986-88; Texas Womans Univ, Denton, TX, Doctor of Philosophy, 1981. **Career:** Radio Shack, employee relations counselor 1977-81; Property Management Co, admin asst 1973-77; Palestine ISD TX, homemaking teacher 1971-73; Fort Worth ISD Fort Worth, TX, classroom teacher, 1986-87, dir of Employee Staffing, 1988-90, dir of alternative certification, 1990-; E-Systems, Inc, Garland, TX, EEO specialist, 1987-88; dir of Personnel, City of Grand Prairie, TX 1982-84. **Orgs:** Trustee elected countywide Trrant Co Jr Coll Dist 1976-; mem appointed by gov Coordinating Bd TX Coll Univ System 1979-83; bd of dirs St Citizens Center Inc 1976-82; v gov S Central Dist Nat Assn Negro Bus Prof Women 1978-83; bd of dirs Ft Worth Girls Club 1979-82; President, Texas Alliance of Black School Educators; chair, NABSE Council of Affiliate Presidents, mem, bd of dirs. **Honors/Awds:** Trailblazer of the Yr Award Ft Worth NB & PW Club 1976; "Characteristics of Black Executive Females" 1981. **Home Phone:** (817)429-2726.

MORRISON, HARRY L.
Educator. **Personal:** Born Oct 7, 1932, Arlington, VA; married Harriett L; children: Vanessa L. **Educ:** Catholic Univ of Amer, AB, 1955, PhD 1960. **Career:** Natl Inst of Health, rsch chemist 1955-56; Natl Bureau of Standards, post doctoral fellow 1960-61; Lawrence Radiation Lab, rsch physicist 1964-72; Univ of CA Lawrence Hall of Sci, assoc dir 1970-75; Coll of Letters & Sci Univ of CA, asst dean 1985-; Univ of CA Berkeley, prof of physics 1972-. **Orgs:** Governing council APS 1971-75; visiting prof Univ of CO 1972-73, Howard Univ 1973, MIT 1975-76; mem Amer Math Soc, Intl Assn Math Physics; fellow Amer Physical Soc 1971; co-founder MESA Out-Reach Prog 1970-. **Honors/Awds:** Science Honor Soc Sigma Xi; edited book "Quantum Theory of Many Particle Systems". **Military Serv:** USAF 1st lt 3 yrs; Commendation Medal 1963. **Business Addr:** Professor, Physics, University of California, Department of Physics, Berkeley, CA 94720.

MORRISON, JACQUELINE
Association service administrator. **Personal:** Born Aug 9, 1951, Plainfield, NJ; daughter of Wisteria Ingram McKnight (deceased) and Caldwell McKnight (deceased); married Curtis Morrison Sr, Jul 1971 (divorced 1988); children: Curtis Morrison Jr (deceased). **Educ:** San Diego State University, BA, 1978; University of Michigan School of Public Health, MPH, 1983. **Career:** National Council on Alcoholism, public health consultant, 1984-86; Wayne State University, public health consultant, 1986-88; Detroit Urban League, vp, programs, 1988-. **Orgs:** Literacy Volunteers of America, advisory board member, 1992-96; Life Directions, board member, 1990-91; New Detroit, Inc, committee member; Sickle Cell Disease Association, board member; Brush park Dev Corp.; Workforce Dev Board. **Honors/Awds:** City of Detroit, Detroit City Council Youth Commission, 1987-89; Natl Council Negro Women, Community Service Award, 1994. **Home Addr:** 16152 Chapel, Detroit, MI 48219. **Business Addr:** Senior VP, Detroit Urban League, 208 Mack Ave, Detroit, MI 48201, (313)832-4600.

MORRISON, JAMES W., JR.
Consultant, lobbyist. **Personal:** Born Jan 14, 1936, Bluefield, WV; son of Winnie E Hendricks Morrison and James W Morrison Sr; married Marva Tillman Morrison, Aug 8, 1957 (divorced); children: Traquita Renee Morrison Arrington, James W. III. **Educ:** WV State Coll, BA 1957; Univ of Dayton, MPA 1970. **Career:** Dayton AF Depot Def Electronics Supply Ctr OH, inventory mgr 1959-63; AF Logistics Command Dayton OH, mgmt spec 1963-72; NASA Wash Dc, ex asst to dir mgmt sys 1972-74; Ex Ofc of Pres OMB Wash DC, sr mgmt assoc 1974-79; US Office of Personnel Mgmt Wash DC, asst dir econ and govt 1979, dir congressional rel 1979-81, assoc dir for compensation 1981-87; CNA Ins Co Rockville MD, sr mgr for prog support 1987-88; president, Morrison Associates, Washington, DC 1988-. **Orgs:** Visiting lecturer Publ Exec Proj State Univ NY Albany 1974-76; mem adv comm Dayton Bd of Educ 1971; mem Alpha Phi Alpha, Pi Delta Phi, Pi Alpha Alpha; member American League of Lobbyists, 1988-. **Honors/Awds:** Except Serv Award Exec Office of Pres OMB Wash DC 1977; Pres Cert Pres USA Wash DC 1979; Meritorious Serv Award US Office of Personnel Mgmt Washington, DC 1980; Pres Meritorious Exec Pres USA Wash DC 1983; Pres Distinguished Exec Pres USA Washington, DC 1985. **Military Serv:** US Army, 1st lt 1957-59. **Home Addr:** 11311 Morning Gate Dr, North Bethesda, MD 20852-3126. **Business Addr:** President, Morrison Associates, 1000 Potomac St NW, Ste 401, Washington, DC 20007.

MORRISON, JOHNNY EDWARD
Attorney, judge. **Personal:** Born Jun 24, 1952, Portsmouth, VA; son of Mary Bernard Morrison; married Cynthia L Payton, Aug 21, 1976; children: Melanie Yvette, Camille Yvonne. **Educ:** Washington and Lee Univ, Grad 1974; Washington and Lee Univ School of Law, Grad 1977. **Career:** Legal Aid Soc Roanoke Valley, staff atty 1977-78; Norfolk Commonwealth's Atty's Office, prosecutor 1978-79; Portsmouth Commonwealth's Atty's Ofc, prosecutor1979-82; Overton, Sallee and Morrison, partner 1982; Portsmouth Commonwealth's Atty's Ofc, atty 1982-91; Portsmouth Circuit Court, chief judge, 1993-94, judge, 1994-. **Orgs:** Mem VA State Bar Assc, VA Assc of Commonwealth's Atty's, Kiwanis Intl; bd mem Tidewater Legal Aid Soc, United Way, Effingham St Branch YMCA; pres Tidewater Legal Aid Society; mem Tidewater Alumni bd of dirs for Washington & Lee; mem Virginia Black Caucus; mem Central Civic Forum; Old Dominion Bar Assn; Twin City Bar Assn; Natl Criminal Justice Assn; Natl Black Prosecutors Assn. **Honors/Awds:** Young Man of the Year Eureka Club 1982; Reginald Heber Smith Flwshp Washington and Lee Schl of Law 1977; Man of the Year Disabled Amer Vets Portsmouth 1982; Outstanding Young Men of Amer Publ 1983; Man of Year, Eureka Club 1988; Martin Luther King, Jr Leadership Award, Old Dominion Univ, 1987. **Business Addr:** Chief Judge, Circuit Court, 601 Crawford St, Portsmouth, VA 23704.

MORRISON, JUAN LARUE, SR.
Educator. **Personal:** Born Mar 22, 1943, Springfield, IL; son of Margaret Morrison and Farries Morrison Sr; married Clementine Lorraine; children: Juan L Jr, Daryl G, Cheryl L. **Educ:** IL State Univ, BS Education 1969, PhD Higher Educ Admin 1980; IL State Univ, MA Ed Admin 1972; Sangamon State Univ, MA Human Dev/Counseling 1975. **Career:** Springfield School Dist #186, elemen teacher 1969-70, secondary teacher 1970-72; Prayer Wheel Church of God in Christ, co-pastor 1980-84; Emmanuel Temple Church of God in Christ, pastor 1984-; Lincoln Land Comm Coll, counselor and coordinator 1972-. **Orgs:** Test admin Amer College Test 1979-; test admin Amer Registry of Radiologic Technologists 1982-; test admin Natl Bd for Respiratory Care Mgmt Services Inc 1982-; publicity chmn Springfield Ministerial Alliance 1983-; test admin Educational Testing Serv 1984-; pres of music Dept for Central IL Jurisdiction of the Church of God in Christ 1984-. **Honors/Awds:** Published article A Look at Community College Testing Programs; IL Guidance and Personnel Assn 1982. **Home Addr:** 260 Maple Grove, Springfield, IL 62707. **Business Addr:** Counselor, Lincoln Land Comm College, Shepherd Rd, Springfield, IL 62708.

MORRISON, K. C. (MINION KENNETH CHAUNCEY)
Educator. **Personal:** Born Sep 24, 1946, Edwards, MS; son of Elvestra Jackson Morrison and Minion Morrison; married Johnetta Bernadette Wade; children: Iyabo Abena. **Educ:** Tougaloo Coll, BA 1968; Univ of WI Madison, MA 1969, cert in African Studies 1974, PhD 1977; Univ of Ghana, cert in African Studies 1972. **Career:** Tougaloo Coll, inst/asst prof 1969-71 1975-77; Hobart Coll, asst prof/coord 1977-78; Syracuse Univ, assoc prof 1978, chair afro-amer studies 1982-89; University of Missouri, Columbia, MO, vice provost, prof of political science 1989-97. **Orgs:** African Studies Assn; Natl Conf Black Political Scientists; Amer Pol Sci Assn; consultant/fellow Ford Foundation, Danforth Frost & Sullivan Huber Foundation 1968-84; NAACP; bd of dirs United Way. **Honors/Awds:** The Ford, NSF, NEH, and Huber Foundations, Fellowships & Grants, 1969-82. **Special Achievements:** Author: Housing Urban Poor in Africa, 1982; Ethnicity and Political Integration, 1982; Black Political Mobilization, 1987. **Business Addr:** Professor of Political Science, University of Missouri, Professional Building, Columbia, MO 65211.

MORRISON, KEITH ANTHONY
Educator, artist, educational administrator. **Personal:** Born May 20, 1942, Linstead, Jamaica; son of Beatrice McPherson Morrison and Noel Morrison; married Alexandra, Apr 12, 1989. **Educ:** School of Art Institute of Chicago, BFA 1963, MFA 1965. **Career:** Fisk Univ, asst prof of art 1967-68; DePaul Univ, chmn dept art 1969-71; Univ IL Chicago, assoc prof art 1971-79, assoc dean Coll of Art 1974-78; Univ of MD, chmn dept of art beginning 1987, prof of art 1979-93; San Francisco Art Institute, dean, 1992-94; San Francisco State University, College of Creative Arts, dean, 1994-. **Orgs:** Chmn of bd Washington Proj for the Arts 1984-85; adv bd New Art Examiner 1983-. **Honors/Awds:** Award for Painting Natl Assn for Equal Oppty in Educ 1984; Bicentennial Award for Painting City of Chicago 1976; Intl Award for Painting OAU Monrovia, Liberia 1978; Danforth Foundation Teaching Assoc 1970-71. **Business Addr:** Dean, San Francisco Art Institute, 800 Chestnut St, San Francisco, CA 94133-2299.

MORRISON, PAUL-DAVID
Office products company executive. **Personal:** Born Apr 28, 1965, Boston, MA; son of Paul E Morrison & Carole Vitale-Chase; married Nancy Morrison, May 28, 1994. **Career:** Digital Equipment Corp, mechanical engineering technology, 1983-88; Raytheon, supervisor, 1988-91; Motorola, sr packaging engineering technology, 1991-94; Hurricane Office Supply, president, 1995-. **Honors/Awds:** United States Patent Office, Patent # 5,381,039, 1994. **Business Addr:** Owner, Hurricane Office Supply, 600 S Bell Blvd, Ste 9, Cedar Park, TX 78613, (512)335-7173.

MORRISON, RICHARD DAVID
Educator. **Personal:** Born Jan 18, 1910, Utica, MS; married Ethel. **Educ:** Tuskegee Inst, BS 1931; Cornell U, MS 1941; State U, phD 1954. **Career:** AL A&M Univ in Normal, pres 1962-. **Orgs:** Former chmn Div of Agriculture; mem Joint Council on Food & Agr Sci; mem adv com of Marshall Space Flight Center AL A&M Univ 1937-62; affiliated withnumerous professional & civic groups. **Business Addr:** AL A&M Univ, Normal, AL 35762.

MORRISON, ROBERT B., JR.
Appointed government official. **Personal:** Born Jul 9, 1954, Orlando, FL. **Educ:** Loyola Univ, BA Pol Sci, Bus Admin 1975; Univ of FL, JD 1978. **Career:** Law Office of Warren H Dawson, attny 1978-79; Morrison Gilmore & Clark PA, partner 1986-; City of Tampa, exec asst to mayor. **Orgs:** Mem Amer Bar Assn, Natl Bar Assoc, FL Bar Assoc, FL Chap Natl Bar Assn 1979-; chmn Bi-Racial Adv Comm Hillsborough Cty School Bd 1978-81; chmn Mayor's Cable TV Advisory Comm 1979-83; pres St Peter Claver Parish Council 1979-83; mem Franklin St Mall Adv Comm 1979-, Tampa Org of Black Affairs 1979-; mediator Citizen Dispute Settlement Prog 1979-80; bd of dir Tampa Urban League 1980-, WEDU TV 1980-, March of Dimes of Hillsborough Cty 1980-; mem NAACP 1981; bd of dir Boy Scouts of Amer 1982-; mem State Job Training Coord Council 1983-, Rotary Club of Tampa 1983-; pres FL Chap Natl Bar Assoc 1986,87; mem Bi-Racial Commn 1987. **Honors/Awds:** Council of Ten Outstanding Law Student Group in Country 1976; Citizen of the Year Omega Psi Phi 1980; George Edgecomb Mem Awd for Outstanding Comm Serv at an Early Age Urban League 1981. **Business Addr:** Executive Asst To Mayor, City of Tampa, 306 E Jackson St, Tampa, FL 33602.

MORRISON, RONALD E.
Television producer/writer. **Personal:** Born Jun 26, 1949, Portland, OR. **Educ:** Portland State U; Portland Comm Coll. **Career:** TV Prod, indpt 1973-; KCET-TV Hollywood, assoc prod 1973; KCET-TV "Doin It At The Storefront," prodn asst, reporter 1972-73; Watts Writers Workshop LA, prod asst/video & instr 1972; KOAP-TV Portland OR "Feedback", floor dir, studio camerman 1971-72; KATU-TV "Third World", asst to producer 1971-72; Portland State Univ TV Programming, producer, dir writer, production asst 1971-72; KION-TV, news

film processor, news film careraman 1968-69. **Honors/Awds:** Recipient Cert of Appreciation City of LA 1973. **Business Addr:** Television Producer, 4067 Hardwick St, #268, Lakewood, CA 90712.

MORRISON, SAMUEL F.
Library director. **Personal:** Born Dec 19, 1936, Flagstaff, AZ; son of Ruth Morrison Genes and Travis B Morrison; divorced. **Educ:** Compton Junior College, AA, 1956; California State University at Los Angeles, BA, English, 1971; University of Illinois, Champaign, IL, MSLS, 1972. **Career:** Frostproof Living Learning Library, Frostproof, FL, director, 1972-74; Broward County Library, Ft Lauderdale, FL, administrative assistant, 1974-76, deputy director, 1976-87; Chicago Public Library, Chicago, IL, deputy commissioner and chief librarian, 1987-90; Broward County Libraries, library dir, 1990-. **Orgs:** National Urban League, 1972-; NAACP, 1972-; board member, Broward County Library Foundation, 1990; board member, Urban League of Broward County; board member, NFBPA, South Florida Chapter, 1990; American Library Association, 1971-; steering committee, Center for the Book, currently; Fontaneda Society, Fort Lauderdale, FL, currently; bd mem, United Way, 1995-97; bd mem, The National Conference; bd mem, Gold Coast Jazz Society; bd mem, FL Humanities Council. **Honors/Awds:** Dean's List CA State Univ 1971; English Honors Program CA State Univ 1971; Faculty Award Univ of IL Library School 1972; Employee of the Year Broward Co Library Advisory Bd 1977-78; NAACP Freeman Bradley Award, 1993; Urban League of Broward Service Award, 1993; The National Conference Silver Medallion Brotherhood Award, 1995; Leadership Broward Foundation Leader of the Year Award, 1996. **Military Serv:** US Air Force, Airman 1st Class, 1955-59; Good Conduct Medal, 1958; Air Force Longevity Award, 1959. **Business Addr:** Director, Broward County Libraries Division, Broward County Library, 100 S Andrews Ave, 8th Fl, Fort Lauderdale, FL 33301.

MORRISON, TONI (CHLOE ANTHONY WOFFORD)
Author, educator, editor. **Personal:** Born Feb 18, 1931, Lorain, OH; daughter of Ramah Willis Wofford and George Wofford; married Harold Morrison, 1958 (divorced 1964); children: Harold Ford, Slade Kevin. **Educ:** Howard University, BA, 1953; Cornell University, MA, 1955. **Career:** Texas Southern University, instructor, 1955-57; Howard University, instructor, 1957-64; Random House Publishing Co, senior editor, 1965-; author, 1969-; SUNY at Purchase, associate professor, 1971-72; Yale University, visiting professor, 1976-77; SUNY at Albany, Schweitzer Professor of the Humanities, 1984-89; Bard College, visiting professor, 1986-88; Princeton University, Robert F Goheen Professor of the Humanities, 1989-. **Orgs:** American Academy & Institute of Arts & Letters; Natl Council on the Arts; Authors Guild; Authors League of America. **Honors/Awds:** Nobel Prize, literature, 1993; writings include: The Bluest Eye, 1970; Sula, 1974; Song of Solomon, 1977; Tar Baby, 1981; Beloved, 1987; Jazz, 1992; Paradise, 1998; playwright: Dreaming Emmett, 1986; editor: Th Black book, 1974; contributor of essays and reviews to numerous periodicals; awards include: Natl Book Award nomination and Ohoana Book Award for Sula, 1975; Natl Book Critics Circle Award and American Academy & Institute of Arts & Letters Award for Song of Solomon, 1977; cover of Newsweek Mag, 1981; New York State Governor's Art Award, 1986; Natl Book Award nomination, 1987, Natl Book Critics Circle Award nomination, 1987, Pulitzer Prize for Fiction, 1988, Robert F Kennedy Award, 1988, all for Beloved; Elizabeth Cady Stanton Award, Natl Organization of Women; 1996 National Book Foundation Medal. **Special Achievements:** First African-American to win a Nobel Prize in literature, 1993. **Business Addr:** Robert F Goheen Professor of the Humanities, Dept of Creative Writing, Princeton University, Princeton, NJ 08544-1099.

MORRISON, TRUDI MICHELLE
Attorney, presidential aide. **Personal:** Born Jul 25, 1950, Denver, CO; daughter of Marjorie Morrison and George Morrison; married Dale Saunders, 1981. **Educ:** CO State Univ, BS 1971; The Natl Law Ctr, George Washington Univ, Georgetown Law Ctr, JD 1972-75; Univ of CO Denver, Doctorate of Publ Admin Candidate 1986. **Career:** States Atty Office Rockville MD, asst states atty 1975-76; Gorsuch Kirgis Campbell Walker & Grover, atty 1977; Denver Dist Attny Office, atty 1977-78; CO Div of Criminal Justice, criminal justice admin 1978-81; US Dept HUD, acting dep asst sec for policy & budget 1981-82; US Dept Health & Human Svcs, reg dep dir 1982-83; The White House, assoc dir office of publ liaison; US Senate, dep sgt at arms. **Orgs:** Exec sec of the student body CO State Univ 1969-71; bd of dir Natl Stroke Assoc 1983-87; mem Natl Council of Negro Women; founder CO Black Republican Council; mem Natl Urban League, NAACP. **Honors/Awds:** 1st Black Homecoming Queen CO State Univ 1970-71; Outstanding Young Women of Amer 1978,79,82; Young Careerist for the Natl Org of Bus & Professional Women 1978;Highest Ranking Black Woman in the White House 1983-; 1984 Black Republican of the Year 1984; William E Morgan CSU Alumni Achievement Awd 1984; 1st woman & 1st Black dep sgt at arms for US Senate. **Business Addr:** Deputy Sergeant at Arms, The Capitol of the US, United States Senate, United States Capitol, Washington, DC 20510.

MORRISON, YVONNE FLORANT
Computer company executive. **Personal:** Born Feb 9, 1929, New York, NY; daughter of Lorraine Heath and Charles Florant; married John A Morrison, Mar 21, 1947 (deceased); children: Bryan S, Eric M, Marilyn Morrison Tatum. **Educ:** Hunter College of City Univ of New York, BS, 1960; New York Univ, Graduate School of Bus, MBA, 1984. **Career:** Patterson Moos Research Labs, physicist; Intl Business Machines, systems analyst; American Express Co, senior EDP auditor,; Stanley Computer Systems Inc, founder, pres/CEO, currently. **Orgs:** Natl Minority Business Council, 1994; NYU Black Alumni Assn, 1994; Natl Assn of Counties, charter member, 1994; Small Business Mentor, 1993; Silver Birch Village Condo, bd member, 1993; Gateway Plaza Tenant Assn Bd, vp, 1992; Big Brother/Big Sister Assn, 1992. **Honors/Awds:** Small Business Adm, Reg II, New York District, Minority Business Person of the Year, 1990; Small Business Adm, Regional Minority Small Business Person of the Year, 1990, National Award, 1990. **Special Achievements:** KISS/FM Community Affairs Prog, speaker, 1984. **Business Addr:** Pres/CEO, Stanley Computer Systems, Inc, 395-19K South End Ave, Ste 19K, New York, NY 10280-1051, (212)321-2087.

MORROW, CHARLES G., III
Utility company representative. **Personal:** Born Jul 21, 1956, Chicago, IL; son of Lillian Morrow. **Educ:** Chicago Inst of Tech. **Career:** School Dist, driver's ed instructor 1971-74; Metro Sanitary Dist, bookkeeper 1975-76; Peoples Gas, customer serv rep 1977-. **Orgs:** Mem Boy Scouts of Amer, NAACP, Urban League.

MORROW, DION GRIFFITH
Judge. **Personal:** Born Jul 9, 1932, Los Angeles, CA; son of Anna Griffith Morrow and Virgil Morrow; married Glynis Ann Dejan; children: Jan Bell, Kim Wade, Cydney, Carla Cavalier, Melvin Cavalier, Dion Jr. **Educ:** Loyola Univ Law School, LLB 1957; Pepperdine Coll. **Career:** Los Angeles City Atty, asst city atty 1973-75; Los Angeles, atty at law 1957-73; Municipal Ct Compton CA, judge 1975-78; Superior Ct, judge, 1978-95, probate judge, currently. **Orgs:** Vice pres Gen Counsel dir Enterprise Savings and Loan 1962-72; pres John M Langston Bar Assc 1969-71; life mem NAACP; mem Natl Bar Assc 1969-. **Honors/Awds:** Langston Bar Association, Judge of the Year, 1992. **Business Addr:** Judge, Superior Court, Retired, 5101 Bedford Ave, Los Angeles, CA 90056.

MORROW, JESSE
Business executive. **Career:** Leader Lincoln-Mercury-Merkur, Inc, St Louis, MO, chief executive, 1983-. **Business Addr:** Leader Lincoln-Mercury-Merkur, Inc, 6160 S Lindbergh Blvd, St Louis, MO 63123.

MORROW, JOHN HOWARD, JR.
Educator. **Personal:** Born May 27, 1944, Trenton, NJ; son of Rowena Davis Morrow and Dr John H Morrow Sr; married Diane Batts; children: Kieran, Evan. **Educ:** Swarthmore Coll, BA, (with honors), 1966; Univ of PA Philadelphia, PhD history 1971. **Career:** Univ of TN Knoxville, asst prof to full prof & dept head 1971-; Natl Aerospace Museum Washington DC, Lindbergh prof of history 1989-90; University of Georgia Athens, GA Franklin prof of history 1989-, department chr, 1991-93, assoc dean of arts & science's, 1993-95. **Orgs:** Mem Amer Historical Assn 1971-; consult Coll Bd & Ed Testing Serv 1980-84, 1990-; chr, Coll Board Natl Academic ASN, 1993-95, mem Coll Board, bod of trustees, 1993-; mem AHA Comm on Committees 1982-85, AHA Prog Comm for 1984 Meeting 1983-84; mem edit adv bds Aerospace Historian 1984-87; and Military Affairs 1987-90; Smithsonian Inst Pr, 1987-93; chairman History Advisory Committee to the Secretary of the Air Force 1988-92. **Honors/Awds:** Author: Building German Airpower 1909-1914, 1976, German Airpower in World War I, 1982; The Great War in the Air, 1993; A Yankee Ace in the RAF, co-ed, 1996; Hon Soc Phi Kappa Phi 1980; Lindsay Young Professorship 1982-83; Outstanding Teacher UT Natl Alumni Assn 1983; UT Macebearer 1983-84; Univ Distinguished Serv Professorship 1985-88. **Home Addr:** 130 Pine Tops Dr, Athens, GA 30606. **Business Addr:** Franklin Professor of History, Univ of Georgia, Department of History, Athens, GA 30602, (706)542-2536.

MORROW, LAVERNE
Business owner. **Personal:** Born Mar 2, 1954, Kankakee, IL; daughter of Shirley Jackson Watson and George Morrow. **Educ:** Illinois State Univ, Normal, IL, BS, 1976; Washington Univ, St Louis, MA Ed, 1978. **Career:** Urban League, St Louis, MO, specialist, 1978-79; Midtown Pre-Apprenticeship Center, St Louis, MO, dir, 1979-82; Coro Found, St Louis, MO, trainer, 1983-85; Emprise Designs Inc, St Louis, MO, pres, 1985-, founder. **Orgs:** First vice pres, Coalition of 100 Black Women Program, St Louis, MO, 1981-84; White House Conf on Small Business Minority Caucus, national chairperson, 1986, 1995, rules committee, 1995; comm chmn, Jr League of St Louis, 1986. **Honors/Awds:** Appointed to the US Senate, Small Business Natl Advisory Council; featured and profiled as an Outstanding Business Woman in the September 1988 St Louis Business Journal. **Business Addr:** President, Emprise Designs Inc, 5353 Union Blvd, St Louis, MO 63115.

MORROW, PHILLIP HENRY
Development administrator. **Personal:** Born Sep 30, 1943, New Haven, CT; son of Viola English Morrow and Benjamin Morrow; married Ann Jordan Morrow, Feb 6, 1985; children: Nicole, Haleema, Germaine. **Educ:** University of Connecticut, Storrs, BA, 1965, MA, 1967; MIT, min developers program, 1992. **Career:** The Poor Peoples Federation, Hartford, CT, exec dir, 1968-71; The Greater Hartford Process, dir of social dev, 1971-75; The Upper Albany Com Org, Hartford, CT, exec dir, 1975-79; The US Dept of Housing & Urban Dev, Washington, DC, dir office pub pri, 1979-81; The Harlem Urban Dev Corp, New York, NY, dir of dev, 1982-. **Orgs:** Bd mem, The Intl Downtown Assn, 1987-94; bd mem, The North General Attendant Project, 1986-; vice chair, The 125st LDC, 1986-; pres, The 260-262 Corp, 1985-; treas, PACC Housing Assn, 1988-; Pratt Area Community Council, vice chair. **Honors/Awds:** All American City Juror, 1990. **Business Addr:** Director of Development, Harlem Urban Development Corp, 163 W 125th St, New York, NY 10027.

MORROW, SAMUEL P., JR.
Attorney (retired). **Personal:** Born Jan 29, 1928, Jackson, TN; son of Mrs Samuel P Morrow and Rev Samuel P Morrow; married Elizabeth B. **Educ:** Lane Coll, BS 1948; Boston Univ, LLB 1955. **Career:** Carrier Corp, sr attorney, currently. **Orgs:** Tennessee Bar Assns. **Military Serv:** USAF major 5 yrs. **Home Addr:** 2264 Connell Terr, Baldwinsville, NY 13027.

MORROW, W. DERRICK
Sales executive. **Personal:** Born May 26, 1964, Philadelphia, PA; son of Tammy Morrow & Ward Morrow. **Educ:** Howard University, 1983-87. **Career:** Washington Hilton & Towers, sales manager, 1987-92; Hyatt Regency Atlanta, associate director of sales, 1992-94; Hyatt Regency Bethesda, director of sales, 1994-95; Hyatt Regency Baltimore, director of sales & mktg, 1995-. **Orgs:** Black Professional Men Inc; Professional Convention Managers Association. **Honors/Awds:** Hyatt Hotels, Nominee for Director of Sales of the Year, 1994, 1995.

MORSE, ANNIE RUTH W.
Educator (retired), historical researcher. **Personal:** Born Mar 4, Pendleton, SC; daughter of Hester Lee Webb and Walter Webb; married Wilford Morse, Dec 27, 1947 (deceased); children: Harry B, Rejetta Ruth. **Educ:** SC State A&M College, Orangeburg, SC, BS Ed, 1937; Columbia University Teachers College, MA, 1958; Clemson Univ Graduate Prog, Dept of Ed, 1973-74. **Career:** Easley Elementary, Easley, SC, teacher, 1937-40; Whitmore High School, Conway, SC, teacher, 1940-42; East End Elementary, Seneca, SC, teacher, 1942-43; Lancaster Tr. School, Lancaster, SC, teacher, 1943-44; Pickens County, Jeanes Sup-Elem. Sup, 1945, supervisor, reading and special service, 1974. **Orgs:** Education Association, County, National, State, 1990; SC and National ASCD; SC State Adoption Textbooks; SC and NEA Retired Education Association; AACP, Anderson chapter; founder/member, Anderson chapter, Delta Sorority; advisory board member, SC Blacks and Native Americans, 1977; president/director, Pendleton Foundation for Black History and Culture, 1976-91; Historical Foundation, Humanities Council for the State of South Carolina, researcher involved in the production of an exhibit of the Jane E Hunter Club; South Carolina Department of Archives and History, 1992; Curriculum Council, District 4, 1992; South Carolina African American Heritage Council, Public Relations Committee, 1992-95; County comm Advisory Bd, Anderson County Museum, 1997. **Special Achievements:** With the Foundation, South Carolina Dept of Parks, Tours and Recreation Commission, involved in the production of brochures on Africa and the Afro American Arts and Crafts Festival, and a legacy of Pendleton, SC. **Home Addr:** PO Box 305 Morse, Pendleton, SC 29670.

MORSE, JOHN E., JR.
Judge. **Career:** Chatham County State Court, appointed judge, 1992-, Elected, 1994, appointe d superior court, 1995, elected, 1996. **Business Addr:** Judge, Chatham County Court, 133 Montgomery St, Rm 213, Savannah, GA 31401, (912)652-7236.

MORSE, JOSEPH ERVIN
Business executive. **Personal:** Born Jul 31, 1940, Tuskegee, AL; married S Edwina; children: Ronald Elliot, Richard Eric. **Educ:** Howard Univ DC, BArch 1964; Howard Univ, JD 1968; Howard Univ, MArch 1969. **Career:** JEMAR Assos, pres 1978-; So Consumers Conf, pres 1978-; Community Nutrition Inst, regl 1978-79; AL State & Community Serv Adminstrn, planning dir 1977-78; The Tuskegee Times & The Montgomery Times Wklys, founder & editor 1972-78; The Ford Found & PEDCO, consult 1972-76; Fedn of So Coops, consult 1976-; Nat Assn of Minority Consult & Urbanologists, dir & vP 1977. **Orgs:** Mem Shriners; 33 Masons; Wings USAF 1962-66; 1st Black Regional Comdr Arnold Air Soc. **Honors/Awds:** Outstanding Pub Serv Award AL Press Assn 1974; pub 5 natl newsletters JEMAR Publs 1980. **Military Serv:** USAF 2nd lt 1962-66.

MORSE, MILDRED S.
Communications company executive. **Personal:** Born Oct 20, 1942, Dermott, AR; daughter of Helen Wilson Sharpe and John Sharpe; married Oliver ''Reds'' Morse; children: Stacey, Kasey. **Educ:** Howard University, JD 1968; University of AR, BA 1964; Bowling Green State University, 1960-62. **Career:** Morse Enterprises Inc, Silver Spring, MD, pres, 1989-; Corporation for Public Broadcasting, Washington, DC, asst to the pres, 1980-89; Phase II White House Task Force on Civil Rights Presidents Reorganization Proj, deputy dir 1977-79; HUD, dir 1973-77 & 1979-80; HEW, staff asst to dir 1971-73; Civil Rights, spec 1968-71. **Orgs:** Natl Bar Assn; Nat Civil Rights Assn; steering com Dept of Justice Title VI Proj; member, Blacks in Public Radio, 1980-90; member, American Women in Radio & TV, 1980-90; member, National Black Media Coalition, 1982-; member, Americans for Indian Opportunity, 1989-91; board of directors, American Indians in Media Assn, 1982-91; Capital City Links Inc, 1981-; member, Delta Sigma Theta Sorority, 1983-; member, Arcousa of Sigma Phi Pi Fraternity, 1980-; Adv Comm on Minority Student Educ, Montg County School Bd, 1990-92, vice chair, 1991-92; Channel 32, advisory board, 1990-95; life mem, NAACP. **Honors/Awds:** Spec Achievement Award HUD 1980; Certificate of Service Award Fed Serv 1980; Presidential Award, Maryland Branch, NAACP, 1987; Extraordinary Record of Success, National Black Media Coalition, 1985; Award of Appreciation, Native American Public Broadcasting Consortium, 1984; National Black Programming Consortium, 1984; Certificates of Merit, Inside Public Relations, 1992, 1993; Proclamation City of New Orleans, Certificate of Recognition City of New Orleans, 1996; Proclamation City of Detroit, 1997. **Home Addr:** 98 Delford Ave, Silver Spring, MD 20904. **Business Addr:** President, Morse Enterprises Inc, 11120 New Hampshire Ave, Ste 204, Silver Spring, MD 20904, (301)593-4991.

MORSE, OLIVER (RED)
Educator (retired), business executive. **Personal:** Born May 17, 1922, New York, NY; son of Ethel Leftage Morse-Jackson and Hugh Morse; married Mildred; children: Stacey, Kasey. **Educ:** St Augustine's Coll, BS 1947; Brooklyn Law Sch, LLB 1950; NY U, LLM 1951; Brooklyn Law Sch, JSD 1952. **Career:** Howard Univ School of Law, acting dean, 1986, asso dean, prof (retired); Hunter Coll, instr 1959; So Univ School of Law, prof 1956-59; Brooklyn Law School, prof 1968-69; Morse Enterprises Inc, chairman, board of directors, 1989-97. **Orgs:** Vice-chmn HEW Reviewing Authority; Beta Lamba Sigma; Phi Alpha Delta; Omega Psi Phi; Am Assn of Law Schs; mem Nat Bar Assn; mem NY Bar Assn; 1st chmn of section on legal Educ of NBA 1971-72; sire archon, 1986-87, member, Sigma Pi Phi Fraternity, Maryland Boule, 1981-; board of trustees, St Augustine's College, 1991-. **Honors/Awds:** Most Outstdng Law Prof Howard Law Sch 1967, 70-72; written serveral publs including over 40 legal decisions of cases heard on appeal to HEW Reviewing Authority. **Military Serv:** AUS sgt 1943-46. **Home Addr:** 98 Delford Ave, Silver Spring, MD 20904. **Business Addr:** Morse Enterprises, Inc., 11120 New Hampshire Ave, Ste. 204, Silver Spring, MD 20904-3448.

MORSE, WARREN W.
Association executive. **Personal:** Born Jul 25, 1912, Newport News, VA; married Maizelle; children: Madeline, Valerie, Warren Jr. **Educ:** Wilberforce U, BS 1936. **Career:** Occupational Safety & Health Div W Conf of Teamsters, coord; Alameda Co, soc worker; Regnl Brewery, sales rep. **Orgs:** Mem Omega Psi Phi; bd dir Bay Area Urban League; bd dir Nat Housing Conf; Nat Adv Com on Agr Dept of Labor; No CA Med Pharm & Denatl Assn. **Honors/Awds:** Recipient Cert of Apprec Kiwanis Club. **Military Serv:** AUS lt col 1940-70. **Business Addr:** 1870 Ogden Dr, Burlingame, CA 94010.

MORSELL, FREDERICK ALBERT
Performer. **Personal:** Born Aug 3, 1940, New York, NY; son of Marjorie Ellen Poole Morsell and John Albert Morsell. **Educ:** Dickinson College, BA, 1962; Wayne State University, MA, 1974. **Career:** Fremarjo Enterprises Inc, president, currently. **Orgs:** Actor's Equity Association; Screen Actor's Guild; AFTRA; Dramatists Guild; ASCAP. **Special Achievements:** Performing nationally in a one-man show: ''Presenting Mr Frederick Douglass''. **Military Serv:** US Army, 1st lt, 1962-65. **Business Addr:** President, Fremarjo Enterprises, Inc, PO Box 382, Emigrant, MT 59027.

MORSE RILEY, BARBARA LYN
Broadcast journalist. **Personal:** Born Nov 15, 1958, Zanesville, OH; daughter of Sylvia Barbara Yancich Morse and Stanley LaVern Morse; married David N Riley, Jan 2, 1988; children: Maryssa Ann, David Marko, Sydney Elaine. **Educ:** Indiana University at Indianapolis, Indianapolis, IN, BA, 1983. **Career:** Indy Today Newspaper, Indianapolis, IN, columnist, 1984-86; Visions Magazine, Indianapolis, IN, staff writer, 1985-86; WNDE-AM, Indianapolis, IN, news anchor, reporter, 1986; WAND-TV, Decatur, IL, news reporter, 1987-88; WLNE-TV 6, Providence, RI, news reporter, 1988-89; WLVI-TV 56, Boston, MA, news reporter, 1989-94; WISH TV 8, Indianapolis IN, reporter, 1994-95; WJAR TV 10, Providence RI, 1995-. **Orgs:** National Association of Black Journalists, 1987-. **Honors/Awds:** Emmy Nomination, 1993. **Business Addr:** News Reporter, WJAR-TV, 23 Kenney Dr, Cranston, RI 02920.

MORSTON, GARY SCOTT
Educator. **Personal:** Born Oct 20, 1960, Queens, NY; son of Thelima Morston; children: two sons. **Educ:** City University of New York, AAS, child care, 1983, BS, education, 1985, MS, education, 1990; Bank Street College, educational leadership, 1992-. **Career:** United Cerebral Palsy, health aide, 1983-91; New York Board of Education, Central Park East II, kindergarten teacher, 1985-. **Orgs:** The City University Track Team; Mustang Track Club; New York City Technical College Theatre Works Performing Arts Group; Scholastic Inc, educational advisor, 1992-. **Honors/Awds:** City University of New York, Minnie Tibland Award, 1985; New York Technical College, Child Care Service Award, Theatre Works Skilled Craft Award, NYCTC Track and Field Team Award. **Special Achievements:** Colaborator: ''Recruiting New Teachers,'' national advertising campaign television commercial, 1991-. **Home Addr:** 468 W 141st St, New York, NY 10031, (212)281-7815.

MORTEL, RODRIGUE
Physician, educator. **Personal:** Born Dec 3, 1933, St Marc, Haiti; married Cecilia; children: Ronald, Michelle, Denise, Renee. **Educ:** Lycee Stenio Vincent, BS 1954; Med Sch Port Au Prince Haiti, MD 1960. **Career:** General Practice, physician; PA State Univ, consultant; Lancaster General Hosp, prof; Penn State Univ, chmn, dept of Ob-gyn; Penn State University Cancer Ctr, associate dean/director, 1995-. **Orgs:** Mem AMA; PA Med Soc; James Ewing Soc; Soc of Synecologic & Oncologist; Amer Coll Ob-Gyn; Amer Coll Surgeons; Amer Radium Soc; NY Acad of Sci OB Soc of Phila. **Honors/Awds:** USPHS Award 1968; Horatio Alger Awd 1985; Pennsylvania State Univ Faculty Scholar Awd for Outstanding Achievement in the Area of Life and Health Sciences 1986; Health Policy Fellow, Robert Wood Johnson Foundation 1988. **Home Addr:** PO Box 532, Hershey, PA 17033.

MORTIMER, DELORES M.
Financial aid officer. **Educ:** Howard University, Macalester College, BA 1971; Cornell University, masters, professional studies, 1973; Univ of MI, Intl Educ, doctoral studies, 1993-94. **Career:** Cornell Univ, grad asst 1971-72; African Bibliog Ctr, rsch coord-proj supr 1972-75, tech resource person/broadcaster 1973-76; Free-lance Consultant, 1973-89; Phelps-Stokes Fund Washington, adminis 1974-75; Smithsonian Inst, Rsch Inst on Immigration & Ethnic Studies, social sci analyst 1975-79; US Commn Civil Rights, social sci analyst 1979-81; US Information Agency, sr intl academic exchange specialist 1981-89; University of Michigan Center for Afro-American & African Studies, assistant director 1988-90; University of Michigan Rackham School of Gradute Studies, sr financial aid officer 1990-94; US Dept of State, Am Embassy Pretoria, foreign service officer, currently. **Orgs:** Natl Association of Female Execs 1981-; vice pres, Thursday Luncheon Group 1985-89; Intl Studies Association 1987; Black Professionals in International Affairs 1988-. **Honors/Awds:** Recipient Grant, Howard Univ, Sponsors for Educ Opportunity Scholarship 1967; Scholarship Award, Lambda Kappa Mu, Black Professional Womens Sorority 1969; Scholarship Award, Macalester Coll 1969; Scholarship Award, Sponsors for Educ Opportunity 1970; Fellowship Award Cornell Univ 1971; Elected Mem, Cornell Univ Senate 1971, 1972; Travel-study Grant Cornell Univ 1972; Elected Mem, Smithsonian Inst Womens Council 1976-79; pub various essays & book reviews in ''A Current Bibliography on African Affairs,'' 1970-74; pub ''Income & Employment Generation''. **Business Addr:** Foreign Service Officer, Am Embassy Pretoria (USIS), US Department of State, Washington, DC 20521-9300.

MORTON, CHARLES E.
Clergyman, educator. **Personal:** Born Jan 31, 1926, Bessemer, AL; married Jean Morton; children: Joan, Carla. **Educ:** Morehouse College, Atlanta, GA, BA, 1946; Union Theological Seminary, New York, NY, 1949; Heidelberg University, Heidelberg, Germany, 1955; Garrett Biblical Institute, Northwestern University, 1956; Columbia University, New York, NY, PhD, 1958; Shaw College, Detroit, MI, LHD, 1970. **Career:** Michigan Bd Edn, mem 1946-54; Div of Humanities & Philosophy Dillard Univ, former chmn; Albion Coll, assoc prof of philosophy; Ebeneze Baptist Ch Poughkeepsie, NY, minister; Metropolitan Baptist Church, Detroit, MI, pastor, 1963-; Oakland University, Rochester, MI, professor of philosophy, 1972-. **Orgs:** President, board of directors, Metropolitan Baptist Church Non-Profit Housing Corporation, 1969-; member, board of directors, First Independence National Bank, Detroit, MI, 1970-; chairperson emeritus, Inner-City Business Improvement Forum of Detroit, 1972-; member, board of directors, Brazeal Dennard Chorale, 1988-; president, Michigan Progressive Baptist State Convention, 1990-92; board member, Gleaners Community Food Bank, 1990-; pres, Michigan Progressive Baptist Convention, Inc; chairperson, board of trustees, Wayne County Community College, 1990-93. **Business Addr:** Pastor, Metropolitan Baptist Church, 13110 14th St, Detroit, MI 48238.

MORTON, CYNTHIA NEVERDON
Educator. **Personal:** Born Jan 23, 1944, Baltimore, MD; daughter of Hattie Neverdon and James Neverdon; married Lonnie George. **Educ:** Morgan State Univ, BA 1965, MS 1967; Howard Univ, PhD 1974. **Career:** Baltimore Public School Syst, tchr of history 1965-68; Peale Museum, rschr/jr archivist 1965; Inst of Afro-Amer Studies, instructor curr develop 1968; MN Lutheran Synod Priority Prog, consultant 1969; Univ of MN, admissions assoc 1968-69, coordinator special programs 1969-71; Coppin State Coll, asst dean of students prof of hist 1971-72, assoc prof of history 1972-81, chairperson dept of history, geography, international studies 1978-81; prof of history, 1981-; Historically Black Colleges and Universities (HBCU) Fellow, EEO/Special Emphasis Programs, summer 1989-93, Dept of Defense, 50th Anniversary of WWII Commemoration Comm, 1993-95; MI State Univ, Research for CD-ROM on Immigration and Migration in US 1900-1920, consultant, 1996. **Orgs:** Study grant to selected W African Nations 1974; participant Caribbean-Amer Scholars Exchange Program 1974; mem adv bd MD Commn of Afro-Amer Life 1977-; mem Assn of Black Female Historians 1979-; mem adv bd Multicultural Educ Coalition Com 1980-; mem Assn for the Study of Afro-Amer Life & History; reader & panelist Natl Endowment for the Humanities Smithsonian Inst Fellow 1986; Natl Forum for History Standards, 1992-94; reviewer, history dept, Howard Univ, 1995; mem MD State Dept of Educ Task Force on the Teacher of Social Studies, 1991, mem Accreditation Team; Nonstandard English and the School Environment Task Force, Baltimore County Public Schools, 1990; bd of editors Twentieth Century Black American Officials and Leaders; Great Blacks In Wax, bd mem. **Honors/Awds:** Publ ''The Impact of Christianity Upon Traditional Family Values'' 1978; ''The Black Woman's Struggle for Equality in the South'' 1978; NEH Fellowship for College Teachers 1981-82; publ ''Self-Help Programs as Educative Activities of Black Women in the South 1895-1925, Focus on Four Key Areas'' 1982; ''Blacks in Baltimore 1950-1980, An Overview'' with Bettye Gardner 1982; ''Black Housing Patterns in Baltimore 1895-1925'' publ MD Historian 1985; Annual Historical Review 1982-83, 1983-84; Ordnance Center & School Aberdeen Proving Ground 1986; mem consult ed bd Twentieth Century Black Amer Officials & Leaders publ Greenwood Press; recent publications book, ''Afro-American Women of the South and the Advancement of the Race 1895-1925'' Univ of TN Press 1989; essay,''Through the Looking Glass: Reviewing Bo about the African American Female Experience'' in Feminist Studies 1988; wrote eight chapters, African American History in the Press, 1851-1899, Gale Press, 1996; ''Securing the Double V: African-American and Japanese-american Women in the Military During World War II'' in A Woman's War Too: US Women in the Military in World War II, 1996; ''In Search of Equality: Maryland and the Civil Rights Movement, 1940-1970,'' Black Classic Press, 1997; guest editor, Negro History Bulletin, 1995-98; ''Interracial Cooperation Movement,'' The Readers Companion to US Women's History, Houghton Mifflin, 1998. **Business Addr:** Professor, Coppin State Coll, 2500 W North Ave, Baltimore, MD 21216.

MORTON, JAMES A.
Business executive. **Personal:** Born Dec 20, 1929, Ontario, VA; married Juanita; children: James A, David L. **Educ:** Am Acad of Mortuary Sci, 1950; Lincoln U, Howard U. **Career:** Morton & Dyett Funeral Homes Inc, first black owned funeral home in Baltimore, pres. **Orgs:** Past pres Funeral Dir & Morticians Assn of MD; past pres Opportunities Industrial Center; bd mem Nat Funeral Dir Mforticians Assn; chmn Tri-state Conv Comm; mem Adv com of Bus bd; bd mem Am Red Cross; committee man BSA; chmn House of Hope Financial Com; trustee Wayland Bapt Ch; adv bd Advance Fed Sav; bd mem YMCA; 3 times life mem NAACP; mem A Phillip Randolph Prince Hall Masons. **Business Addr:** 1701 Laurens St, Baltimore, MD 21217.

MORTON, JOE
Actor. **Personal:** Born Oct 18, 1947, New York, NY. **Educ:** Hofstra University, drama. **Career:** Accomplished actor appearing in A Month of Sundays, off broadway, 1968; Hai r, broadway; Stage: Salvation, 1969, Prettybelle, 1971, Charlie Was Here and Now He's Gone, 1971, Two if By Sea, 1972, numerous others; Film: And Justice for All, 1970, The Brother From Another Planet, 1984, Crossroads, 1985, Zelly and Me, 1988, There's City of Hope, 1991, Terminator 2, 1992; numerous others; Television: Another World, MASH, 1976, Equal Justice, A Different World, Miss Evers Boys, others. **Honors/Awds:** Theatre World Award, Best Actor in Musical, Raisin, 1974; nomination, Antoinette Perry Award, Best Actor in Musical, Raisin, 1974. **Business Addr:** Actor, c/o Judy Schoen & Associates, 606 N Larchmont, Ste 309, Los Angeles, CA 90004, (213)962-1950.

MORTON, JOHN, JR.
Professional basketball player. **Personal:** Born May 18, 1967, Bronx, NY; son of Anne Helen Jones Morton and John Lee Morton. **Educ:** Seton Hall University, BA, 1990. **Career:** Guard: Cleveland Cavaliers, 1989-91, Miami Heat, 1991-92.

MORTON, JOHNNIE JAMES
Professional football player. **Personal:** Born Oct 7, 1971, Inglewood, CA. **Educ:** Univ of Southern California. **Career:** Detroit Lions, wide receiver, 1994-. **Orgs:** Screen Actors Guild, membership; American Federation of Radio and Television Assn, membership; active in DARE, Athletes and Entertainers for Kids, and Big Brothers of America. **Special Achievements:**

Appeared in the film "Jerry Maguire," 1996; appeared in several episodes of "The Young and the Restless," 1996. **Business Addr:** Professional Football Player, Detroit Lions, 1200 Featherstone Rd, Pontiac, MI 48342, (248)335-4131.

MORTON, LORRAINE H.
City official. **Personal:** married James T Morton (died 1974); children: Elizabeth Morton Brown. **Educ:** Winston-Salem State Univ, BSEd; Northwestern University, MSEd. **Career:** Foster School, various other schools, teacher, 1953-77; Haven Middle School, principal, 1977-89; 5th Ward, alderman, until 1991; City of Evanston, mayor, 1992-. **Orgs:** Second Baptist Church, deacon. **Business Addr:** Mayor, City of Evanston, 2100 Ridge Ave, Evanston, IL 60201, (708)328-2100.

MORTON, MARGARET E.
State senator (retired), funeral director. **Personal:** Born Jun 23, 1924, Pocahontas, VA; married James F Morton; children: James III, Robert Louis, Gerald Woods, Dawn Margaret. **Career:** Funeral dir; Connecticut Gen Assembly, 1972-79; Connecticut State Senate, senator, 1980-92, asst majority leader, senate co-chmn Exec & Legislative Nominations Comm, deputy president pro tempore 1990-92. **Orgs:** Mem, vice pres 1970, exec bd 1971-76 NAACP; bd dir Gr Bridgeport YWCA 1970-72; mem Gr Bridgeport C of C 1973-79; bd dirs Hall Neighborhood 1973-76, St Marks Day Care Ctr 1974-76; mem United Dem Club Bridgeport, State Fed Black Dem Clubs, Fed Dem Women, Org Women Legislators; Greater Bridgeport Chap Coalition of 100 Black Women, Fairfield Co CHUMS. **Honors/Awds:** Sojourner Truth Awd Natl Council Negro Women 1973; Achievement Awd Barnum Festival 1973; Achievement Awd Bridgeport Chap Bus & Professional Women 1973; AMORE Ch Achievement Awd 1972.

MORTON, MARILYN M.
Company executive. **Personal:** Born Jan 20, 1946, New York, NY; daughter of Wilma Hayes Pegg and William Gaitha Pegg (deceased); married Louis H Morton, Jun 28, 1969; children: Louis-Hale, Khaim, Micah. **Educ:** Howard Univ, Washington, DC, BA, 1967; UCLA Extension, Los Angeles, CA, 1974-77. **Career:** Los Angeles 200 Bicentennial Committee, Los Angeles, CA, dir, public rels, 1979-81; Mixner, Scott & Assocs, Los Angeles, CA, associate, public affairs, 1981-83; Times-Mirror Cable TV, Irvine, CA, manager public affairs, 1983-84; Parsons Corp, Los Angeles, CA, manager community affairs, 1984-96, reg manager, gov't rels, 1987-96; Metro Transportation Authority, manager of external relations, currently. **Orgs:** Co-founder, Women of Color Inc, 1985-; president, Environmental Affairs Commission, appointed by Mayor Tom Bradley, 1987-93; The Ethnic Coalition, board of directors, co-chair, 1989-; So CA Economic Partnership, bd of dirs, 1994-. **Honors/Awds:** Environmental Affairs Commission, Appointed by Mayor Bradley, 1987; NAACP, Black Women of Achievement Award, 1992. **Business Addr:** Manager, External Relations, Los Angeles Cty, Metro Transportation Authority, 1 Gateway Plaza, Los Angeles, CA 90012, (213)922-2218.

MORTON, NORMAN
Computer systems analyst. **Personal:** Born Jul 27, 1938, Washington, DC; son of Bertha Morton (deceased) and Matthew Morton (deceased); married Robbie Clark Morton, May 26, 1967; children: Norman Jr, Mark. **Educ:** Grantham College of Engineering, ASET, 1989; University of Maryland, BS, mathematics, MA, mathematics. **Career:** Self-employed, professional tutor, 1965-; US Army, Finance & Accounting Office, computer programmer, 1966-68; Small Business Administration, computer programmer, 1968-74; Minority Business Development Administration, computer systems analyst, 1974-75; Economic Development Administration, computer systems analyst, 1975-88; Dept of Commerce, Census Bureau, computer programmer, systems analyst, 1988-. **Orgs:** MENSA, 98th percentile mbr, IQ, 1992-; INTERTEL, 99th percentile mbr, IQ, 1993; Boy Scouts of America, den leader, 1977-81, 1984-88; Good Shepherd Church, homeless shelter volunteer helper, 1986-87; Intl Soc of Philosophical Enquiry, 99.9th percentile IQ, mbr, 1994-; Prometheus Soc, 99.9th percentile IQ, mbr, 1994-. **Honors/Awds:** DC Teachers College, BKX Science Honor Fraternity, 1963, President of the Math Club, 1963; Small Business Administration, President of the SBA Statistical Club, 1972. **Special Achievements:** Volunteer tutor: Census Bureau, 1992-93; Crossland High School, 1991; instructor: COBOL programming class, SBA, 1973; copywrights: "CLOAK," cryptographic software, #TX 1675827, 1985; "Large Scale Number Manipulations on the PC," #TX 1705169, 1985; "Hide It/Find It," #TX 4-332-687; author: "Why Does Light Disappear in a Closed Room after the Switch is Turned Off?", Capital M, MENSA Publishing, 1993; scored at 99th percentile, IQ test, INTERTEL, 1993; scored at 98th percentile, IQ test, MENSA, 1993; IQ percentile of 99.997 ranks at 1 in 33,000 of the general population. **Home Addr:** 1600 S Eads St, #302, Arlington, VA 22202, (703)920-2678.

MORTON, PATSY JENNINGS
Advertising executive. **Personal:** Born Oct 2, 1951, Fauquier County, VA; daughter of Louise Dickson Jennings and Thomas Scott Jennings; married Allen James Morton Jr, May 28, 1978; children: Valerie, Allen Christopher, Douglas. **Educ:** Jersey Academy, Jersey City, NJ 1965-69; Oberlin Coll, Oberlin, OH, BA, 1969-73; Columbia Univ, New York, NY, 1973-75. **Career:** Earl G Graves Publishing, New York, NY, mktg mgr, 1973-75; The New York Times Co, New York, NY, sales representative, 1975-81, assoc group mgr, 1981-83; group mgr, 1983-87, advertising mgr, 1987-, classified advertising director, 1989-92; advertising managing director 1992-96; Education Allicances, dir, 1997-. **Orgs:** Mem, Business Comm, Admissions Comm, Oberlin Coll, 1986; mem, task force, Five Star Newspaper Network, 1988; bd dir, New York State Food Merchants, 1989; member, Association of Newspaper Classified Advtg Managers; exec council, NYU Metro Center, 1993-. **Honors/Awds:** Rookie of the Year, Jersey Academy, 1965; Dean's List, Oberlin Coll, 1970-73; Black Achievers Award, YMCA, 1989; Publisher's Award, 1994. **Business Addr:** Education Programs, The New York Times, 229 W 43rd St, New York, NY 10036, (212)556-8843.

MORTON, WILLIAM STANLEY
Attorney. **Personal:** Born Jul 18, 1947, White Plains, NY; son of Clara Worthy Morton and William Morton; married Mary; children: William Stanley Jr, Sydney Elaine. **Educ:** Coll of Arts & Sci, BS 1969; Coll of Law OH State U, JD cum laude 1974. **Career:** Procter & Gamble Co, sr counsel 1974-88, division counsel, 1988-, assoc general counsel, currently. **Orgs:** Cincinnati Bar Association, American Bar Association; bd of dir Am Civil Liberties Union Central OH 1973; mem OH Bar 1974-; mem Omega Psi Phi Frat; mem & bd of dir ProKids 1985-87; board member, Housing Opportunities Made Equal, 1990-; vice pres and board mem, Cincinnati Opera. **Military Serv:** AUS sp4 1970-72. **Business Addr:** Associate General Counsel, The Procter & Gamble Co, One Procter & Gamble Plaza, Cincinnati, OH 45202.

MOSBY, CAROLYN ELIZABETH
Community affairs manager. **Personal:** Born Nov 27, 1967, Gary, IN; daughter of John O & Senator Carolyn Mosby. **Educ:** Indiana State University, BS, Radio/TV/Film, 1990. **Career:** State of Indiana-Minority Business Development, administrative coordinator, 1990-94, Department of Administrative Communications, mgr, 1994-95; Indiana Black Expo, public relations mgr, 1995-96; Ameritech, market relations mgr, 1996-97; USX Corp, community affairs mgr, 1997-. **Orgs:** Indiana Black Expo, public relations committee, 1995-; Circle City Classic, executive committee, 1995-96, parade committee, 1996-; 1997 NCAA Final Four, public relations committee, 1996-; Mozel Sanders Thanksgiving Dinner Committee, 1995-96; National Association of Female Executives, 1994; Society of Government Meeting Planners, pres, 1994; Salvation Army, bd, 1997-; Hoosier Boystown, bd, 1997-; Gary Police Foundation, vp, 1997-. **Business Addr:** Community Affairs Manager, USX Corp, 1 North Broadway, Gary, IN 46402, (219)888-5677.

MOSBY, CAROLYN LEWIS
Educator. **Personal:** Born Mar 6, 1937, Lynchburg, VA; daughter of Nannie Jackson Lewis and William Lewis; married Alexander Mosby, Aug 17, 1963. **Educ:** The College of William & Mary, Williamsburg, VA, EdD, higher education, 1983; Morgan State University, Baltimore, MD, MA, math, 1970; Virginia Union University, Richmond, VA, BS, math, 1958. **Career:** East High School, Buffalo, NY, teacher, math, 1959-61; Blackwell Jr High School, Richmond, VA, teacher, math, 1961-65; John Marshall High School, Richmond, VA, teacher/assistant principal, 1965-74; Virginia Union University, Richmond, VA, director learning skills/genl education, 1974-76; John Tyler Community College, Chester, VA, division chair for mathematics, natural sciences allied health, 1978-91; Richmond Public Schools, staff dev & officer, part-time currently. **Orgs:** Charter member, James River Chapter, The Links Inc, 1983-; member, The Girl Friends Inc, Richmond, VA, 1983-; member, Delta Sigma Theta Sorority, 1955-; national pres, National Epicureans Inc, Richmond, VA, 1984-86; charter member, Coalition 100 Black Women, Richmond, VA, 1984-; chair, commission, pupil reassignment, Richmond Public Schools, 1985; board member, State Health Regulatory board, Commonwealth of VA, 1978-82; board member, United Giver's Fund, 1970. **Honors/Awds:** Outstanding Teacher of the Year, Richmond Jaycees, 1971. **Home Addr:** 3524 Bathgate Rd, Richmond, VA 23234, (804)271-0565. **Business Phone:** (804)780-7872.

MOSBY, NATHANIEL
County official (retired). **Personal:** Born Mar 24, 1929, Middletown, OH; son of Elsie Jackson Moore (deceased) and John Mosby (deceased); married Gwendolyn Mizell, Apr 15, 1953; children: Natalyn Mosby Archibong, David Nathaniel, Warren Frederick, Howard Alan, Phillip Anthony. **Educ:** Morehouse Coll, AB 1951; Atlanta Univ, MBA grad School of Bus Admin 1961. **Career:** Lockheed Aircraft Corp Marietta GA, 1955-58; SE Fidelity Fire Ins Co Atlanta, 1961-62; GSA, bldg mgmt prog (1 of 1st blacks hired) 1963, mgr fed ofc bldg 1964, area intergroup spec 1967, reg intergroup spec 1968-72; Fed Aviation Admin, personnel staffing spec 1972-77, serv difficulty specialist, 1977-88; DeKalb County, GA, commissioner, 1988-91. **Orgs:** Mem FL Coll Placement Assoc, So Coll Placement Assoc; charter mem Soc for Advancement of Mgmt Atlanta Univ Chapt; fed personnel council commiss Atlanta Reg Commn; commiss DeKalb Cty Comm Relations Commn; commiss, vchmn Commn, DeKalb Cty Comm Rel Commn; bd dirs Grady Homes Boys Club; bd mgrs, past pres of bd SE Br YMCA; Alpha Phi Alpha; Mason; elder Oakhurst Presbyterian Church, Inst Rep of BSA; past chmn Atlanta Council for Publ Ed. **Honors/Awds:** Outstanding Layman of the Year Atlanta YMCA 1973; Superior Achievement Awd for exemplary serv to FAA EEO 1983; Outstanding Fed Employee of the Year EEO 1984. **Military Serv:** AUS ofcr 1951-53; Korean Conflict. **Home Addr:** 618 Blake Ave SE, Atlanta, GA 30316. **Business Addr:** DeKalb County Commissioner, DeKalb County Govt, 434 Flat Shoals Ave SE, Atlanta, GA 30316.

MOSEBY, LLOYD ANTHONY
Professional baseball player. **Personal:** Born Nov 5, 1959, Portland, AR; son of Birdo Moseby and Terry Moseby; married Adrienne Brown Moseby, Sep 14, 1981; children: Alicia Antoinette, Lloyd II, Lydell Emanuel. **Career:** Toronto Blue Jays, outfielder, 1978-89, Pioneer League, 1978, Florida State League, 1979, Intl League, 1980; Detroit Tigers, outfielder, 1989-91; Tokyo Giants, outfielder, currently. **Honors/Awds:** Pioneer League All-Star, 1978; Florida State League All-Star Team, 1979; Topps Class A All-Star Team, 1979; co-winner, Labatt's Blue MVP, 1983; American Leauge All-Star Team, The Sporting News & UPI, 1983; Silver Slugging Team, 1983; American League, Player of the Week, 1983; Labatt's Blue Player of Month, July 1983, August 1986; American League Player of Month, August 1983; American League All-Star Team, 1986. **Business Addr:** Professional Baseball Player, Tokyo Giants, Tokyo, Japan.

MOSEE, JEAN C.
Physician, educator, administrator. **Personal:** Born Jun 6, 1927, Dallas, TX; married Dr Charles; children: Sheila Joan, Wren Camille, Meharry Med. **Educ:** Hoawrd U, BS 1947; Middlebury Coll, MA 1951; Meharry Med Coll, MD (highest honors) 1960. **Career:** Dept of Human Resources, chief of clinic 1963-; DC General Hospital, pediatric resident 1961-63, intern 1960-61; Fisk University, instructor, 1954-56; SC State College, asst prof of German 1951-54; VA Union University, instr of German 1948-51. **Orgs:** Bd of dirs DC Mental Hlth Assn; mem Med-Chi Society Soc DC Wash Chap of Acad of Pediatrics; particip Career Confs at Pub & Parochial Sch; lectrChild Abuse; bd of tsts Nat Children's Intl Summer Villages; bd of mgrs Nat Meharry Alumni Assn; bd of tsts Friendship Settlemnt House. **Honors/Awds:** Recip josiah macy rsrch flwshp Meharry Med Coll Pharm Dept; designated most outstndng stud in German Sch 1951; particip rsrch proj on Hypertension in Black Children; plaque fro otstndng alumna Meharry Med Coll. **Business Addr:** Dept of Human Resources, Benning Rd & 46th St SE, Washington, DC 20019.

MOSEKA, AMINATA (ABBEY LINCOLN)
Actress, director. **Personal:** Born in Chicago, IL. **Career:** The Girl Can't Help It, actress 1956; Nothing But a Man, lead role 1965; For Love of Ivy, title role 1968; A Pig in a Poke Prod Co, author, dir; African Amer Theatre CA State Univ, teacher. **Orgs:** Chairwoman, producers com Tribute to the Black Woman 1977. **Honors/Awds:** Best Actess Nothing But a Man 1st World Fest of negro Arts 1966; Best Actess Nothing But a Man Fed of of Italian Film Makers 1964; Most Prom Screen Person For the Love of Ivy All Amer Press Assoc 1969; Black Filmmakers Hall of Fame 1975; worked with Coleman Hawkins, Sonny Rollins, Thelonious Monk, John Coltrane. **Business Addr:** Teacher, California State Univ, African Amer Theatre, Northridge, CA 91324.

MOSELEY, CALVIN EDWIN, JR.
Educator, clergyman (retired). **Personal:** Born Jan 7, 1906, Demopolis, AL; married Harriet F Slater; children: Harriet Ann, Barbara Jean. **Educ:** Andrews Univ, BA, MA; Chicago Univ, Attended; Northwestern Univ, attended; Daniel Payne Coll, LLD. **Career:** Evanston & Springfield IL, pastoral minister 1929-31; St Louis KC, MO, pastor 1931-34; 7th Day Adventists Church Washington DC, gen field sec; ministerial workshops & field schools of evangelism 1951-71; Oakwood Coll, prof of religion 1934-51, chmn dept of religion 1943-51, teacher ministerial trainees 1934-51, 1972-74, part time teacher ministerial trainees 1974-90. **Orgs:** Columnist ed consult Message Mag. **Honors/Awds:** Author "The Lords Day" 1949; "Information Please" 1973. **Business Addr:** Oakwood Coll, PO Box 187, Huntsville, AL 35896.

MOSELEY, FRANCES KENNEY
Association executive. **Personal:** Born Mar 20, 1949, Cleveland, OH; married Monroe Avant Moseley; children: Gavin. **Educ:** Univ of Denver, BA Psych 1971. **Career:** State St Bank & Trust, security analyst 1974-77; Bank of Boston, trust officer 1977-79; WGBH-TV, dir of promo 1979-80; Boston Edison Co, sr publ info rep; John Hancock Financial Services Inc, sr manager of retail marketing and consumer affairs, until 1993; Boys & Girls Clubs of Boston, pres/CEO, 1992-. **Orgs:** Mem & former officer Boston Branch NAACP 1976; mem Amer Assoc of Blacks in Energy 1980-88; chmn of the bd Big Sister Assoc of Greater Boston 1984; pres of bd of Big Sisters Assn of Greater Boston 1982, bd mem since 1979; trustee, The Huntington Theatre; New England Aquarium; director PNC Bank, New England, 1996; director, Tufts Associateed Health Plans

Inc, 1996; Beth Israel Deaconess Medical Ctr; Wang Ctr for the Performing Arts; The Children's Hospital Board of Overseers; founding member, Boston Chapter of the Coalition of 100 Black Women; chair Bell Atlanta Consumer Advisory Panel; bd mem, Massachusetts Sports Partnership. **Honors/Awds:** The Urban League, 75th Anniversary President's Award; The College Club 1993 Career Award for Social Service; Honorary Doctorate of Public Service, Bridgewater State Coll, 1998; Named 1 of Boston's Most Powerful 100 People by Boston Magazine in 1997. **Business Addr:** President/CEO, Boys and Girls Clubs of Boston, 50 Congress St, Ste 730, Boston, MA 02109-4002.

MOSELEY BRAUN, CAROL ELIZABETH
Senator. **Personal:** Born Aug 16, 1947, Chicago, IL; daughter of Edna and Joseph Moseley; divorced; children: Matthew Braun. **Educ:** Univ of IL Chicago, Chicago, IL, BA 1969; Univ of Chicago, Chicago, IL, JD 1972. **Career:** Mayer Brown & Platt, law clerk 1970; Rose Hardies O'Keefe Babcock & Parsons, law clerk, 1971; Davis Miner & Barnhill, assoc 1972; US Dept of Justice, asst attorney 1973-77; Jones, Ware & Grenard, of counsel; 26th Legislative District, Chicago, state rep, beginning 1977; Cook County, recorder of deeds/registrar of titles; US Senate, senator, State of Illinois, 1992-. **Orgs:** Bar of the US Court of Appeals 7th Circuit, Bar of the US Dist Court Northern Dist of IL, Bar of the State of IL, IL State Bar Assn, Natl Order of Women Legislators, Dem Policy Commiss of the Dem Natl Conv, Cook County Bar Assn, Chicago Council of Lawyers, Amer Judicature Soc, Natl Conf of State Leg; comm on Courts & Justice; del Dem Natl Conv 1984; League of Black Women, Jane Addams Ctr for Social Policy & Rsch, Alpha Gamma Phi, Chicago Forum, DuSable Museum, Chicago Public Schools Alumni Assn, IL women's Political Caucus, Coaltion to Save South Shore Country Club Park, Urban League, NAACP, South Shore Commn. **Honors/Awds:** Awardee Attny Gen's Commendation; Woman of the Year Awd Lu Palmer Found 1980; Best Legislator Awd Independent Voters of IL 1980; Recog & Appreciation Cert IL Sheriffs Assoc 1981; Award of Distinction Networking Together 1981; Outstanding Woman of Struggle Awd Chicago Alliance Against Racist & Political Repression 1981; Dist Serv Awd Concerned Black Execs of Social Serv Org 1983; Outstanding Legislator Awd IL Public Action Council 1983; Leadership Awd Assn of Human Serv Providers 1984; Legislative Leadership Awd Chicago Public Schools & Coaltion to Save Our Schools 1985; Beautiful People Awd Urban League 1985; Legislator of the Year Awd IL Nurses Assn 1986; Cert of Appreciation Chicago Bar Assn 1986; Serv Awd IL Pro-Choice Alliance 1986; Best Legislator Awd, Independent Voters of IL Indepent Precinct Org 1986; Friends of Educ Award, IL State Bd of Educ 1988; "Day Breaker" Award, Mayor Harold Washington 1988; Chicago Black United Communities "Secrets" Award, St Mark's United Methodist Ch, 1989; Karunya Educational Award for Legislative Excellence; Certificate of Appreciation, PTA; Minority Economic Resources Corp, Woman of the Year, 1997; Interdenominational Ministerial Alliance of Chicago, Martin Luther King Jr Excellence Award, 1997; Bus & Professional Women, Magnificant 7 Award, 1996; and numerous honorary degrees and other awards. **Special Achievements:** First female African American US senator, 1992. **Business Addr:** US Senator, United States Senate, Capitol Building, Washington, DC 20510-0001.

MOSELEY-DAVIS, BARBARA M.
Computer specialist. **Personal:** Born Feb 12, 1938, NYC; married Alphonso Davis. **Educ:** BS Mathematics 1960. **Career:** M-Cubed Information System, Inc., sr project mgr; Computer Science, progmng with simulation team for commun network models. **Orgs:** Mem ACM; sec IBM Share Inc Graphics Group; mem Urban League; NCNW; Delta Sigma Theta Inc. **Business Addr:** 3206 Tower Oaks Blvd, Ste 200, Rockville, MD 20852.

MOSELY, KENNETH
Educator. **Career:** South Carolina State College, Health & Physical Education Department, professor, currently. **Business Addr:** Educator, Health & Physical Education Department, South Carolina State College, 300 College Ave, Orangeburg, SC 29117-0002, (803)536-7000.

MOSES, CHARLES T.
Government official. **Personal:** Born Oct 2, 1952, New York, NY; son of Grace Moses and Charles T Moses; divorced. **Educ:** Howard University, BS, 1975; Baruch College, MBA, 1985. **Career:** Newsday, reporter, asst business editor, strategic planning director, 1978-88; Bristol Myers-Squibb, communications executive, 1988-89; City of New York, Comptroller's Office, deputy press secretary, 1991; State of New York, Governor's Office, executive director, 1991-95. **Orgs:** National Association of Black Journalists, 1976-88; Leadership New York, fellow, 1991. **Honors/Awds:** Gannett Co, Frank Tripp Award, 1978; National Association of Black Journalists, Outstanding News Feature Award; Odyssey Institute, Media Award, 1980, 1988. **Special Achievements:** Fellowship in strategic planning from the American Newspaper Publishers Association, 1987.

MOSES, EDWIN
Olympic hurdler. **Personal:** Born Aug 31, 1955, Dayton, OH; son of Irving S. and Gladys H.; children: Edwin Julian. **Educ:** Morehouse College, BS, physics, 1978; Pepperdine University, MBA, 1994. **Career:** Olympic hurdler; The Platinum Group, partner; Robinson-Humphrey Company, Salomon Smith Barney, financial consultant, currently. **Orgs:** USOC, Substance Abuse Committee, chairman, exec comm, 1994-96, board of directors 1986-96; International Olympic Committee, Athletes Commission, 1982-96, Medical Commission, 1994-96; Intl Amateur Athletic Assn, pres, 1982-; Commission on White Fellowships, 1992-; US Olympic Foundation, vice chair, 1996-; 100 Black Men of Atlanta, 1997-. **Honors/Awds:** Worlds Top Ranked Intermediate Hurdler begin 1976-; holds world record 400 meter hurdle (47.02); 2 times Olympic Gold Medalist 1976, 1984, Bronze Medalist 1988; Sportsman of the Year US Olympic Comm; Sports Illustrated, Athlete of the Year, 1984; Sullivan Award, 1983; Track & Field, Hall of Fame, 1994. **Special Achievements:** First US athlete to be voted as delegate to Intl Amateur Athletic Federation; 122 consecutive victories in 400 hurdles, 1977-87; speaks fluent German & French. **Business Addr:** Financial Consultant, The Robinson-Humphrey Company/Salomon Smith Barney, 3333 Peachtree Rd NE, Ste 800, Atlanta, GA 30319, (404)266-6555.

MOSES, HAROLD WEBSTER
Educator. **Personal:** Born Jun 6, 1949, Little Rock, AR; son of Tracie Moses and Bishop Moses; children: Harold, Corye, Joshua. **Educ:** University of Arkansas, Little Rock, AR, BA, 1973, MPA, 1984; Southern Illinois University, Carbondale, IL, PhD, 1995. **Career:** Arkansas International Languages Program, Russellville, AR, French tutor, 1985-88; Illinois Legislative Research Unit, Springfield, IL, Research Assistant, 1985-86; Southern Illinois University, Carbondale, IL, graduate administrative assistant to Illinois Minority Fellowships, 1990, instructor, 1991-92, Bethne Cookman Coll, Daytona Beach FL, asst prof of Political Science. **Orgs:** Secretary, Graduate Assistantship Program, National Conference of Black Political Scientists, 1989-91; Graduate Political Science Committee; chair, Awards Committee, Southern Illinois University Political Science Dept, 1985-91; member, National Conference of Black Political Scientists, member, African Studies Association, 1991-. **Honors/Awds:** Merit Scholarship for the Study of Chinese Beloit College, 1991; Illinois Consortium of Educational Opportunity Award, Illinois Board of Higher Education, 1988-92; Graduate Deans Fellowship, Southern Illinois University, 1986, 1988; Rodney Higgins Award for Best Paper, National Conference of Black Political Scientists, 1987; Sammy Younge Award for Best Paper National Conference of Black Political Scientists, 1986. **Home Addr:** PO Box 734, Daytona Beach, FL 32115-0734.

MOSES, HENRY A.
Educator, educational administrator. **Personal:** Born Sep 8, 1939, Gaston County, NC; son of Mary Moses and Roy Moses. **Educ:** Livingstone Coll, BS 1959; Purdue Univ, MS biochemistry 1962, PhD biochemistry 1964. **Career:** TN State Univ, vstg lecturer biochemistry 1966-70; Meharry Medical College, asst professor, Biochemistry, 1964-69; consultant clinical chemistry 1968-74, assoc prof of biochem and nutrition 1969-81, provost internal affairs 1976-83, dir of continuing educ 1981-, prof of biochem 1981-, asst vice pres for academic support 1983-95, dir of continuing educ for area health educ ctrs 1984-, Coll Relations, & Lit Lang Learning, asst vp, 1995-. **Orgs:** Mem AAAS, ACS, Alpha Chi Sigma Frat for Chemists, Amer Assoc of Univ Profs, Beta Kappa Chi Scientific Honor Soc 1972-; chmn, mem Honors and Awds Comm The School of Medicine 1976-; mem Alpha Omega Alpha Honor Med Soc 1980; advisor The Meharrian Student Yearbook 1980-; chmn Academic Policy Comm The School of Medicine 1985-; mem McKendree United Methodist Church and Administration Bd. **Honors/Awds:** Service Awd Meharry Medical Coll 1971; Harold D West Awd Meharry Med Coll 1972; Kaiser-Permanente Awd for Excellence in Teaching Meharry Medical Coll 1976; Alpha Omega Alpha Honor Medical Soc 1981; Meritorious Service Awd Los Angeles Chap Meharry Medical Coll Natl Alumni Assoc 1985; Beta Kappa Chi Scientific Honor Soc Special Recognition Awd 1986; Presidential Citation as Outstanding Alumnus NAFEO 1986; also 29 publications; Distinguished by Alumni Purdue Univ, 1985; Building dedicated, 1996. **Business Addr:** Dir of Continuing Educ, Meharry Medical College, Nashville, TN 37208.

MOSES, MACDONALD
Educational administartor. **Personal:** Born May 20, 1936, Bailey, NC; married Marie Biggs; children: Alvin, Jacqueline, Reginald, Kenneth. **Educ:** Westchester Comm Coll; Alexander Hamilton Brooklyn Tech; IBM Education Center; American Management Assoc. **Career:** Church of Christ, Disciples of Christ, general bishop. **Orgs:** Manager MIS Botway Media Associates; pastor Mt Hebron Church of Christ. **Honors/Awds:** Homoray Doctor of Divinity Goldsboro Disciple Institute 1978. **Home Addr:** 330 Warwick Ave, Mount Vernon, NY 10553.

MOSES, MILTON E.
Chief executive officer. **Personal:** Born Aug 5, 1939, Chicago, IL; son of Mary Moses and Jeffery Moses; married Shirley C; children: Timothy E, Melody L. **Educ:** DePaul Univ, 1965. **Career:** Supreme Life Insurance Co of Amer, agt 1963; The Robbins Ins Agency Inc, underwriter 1965; Community Insurance Ctr Inc, pres, CEO. **Orgs:** Mem Ind Insurance Agents of Amer 1980, Chicago Bd of Underwriters 1980, Insurance Inst of Amer 1980; pres Men for Provident Hosp 1971; chmn of bd Human Resources Devel Inst 1980; pres We Can Found Inc 1980. **Honors/Awds:** Outstanding Support Award Southtown YMCA 1974; Dedicated Serv Award Third Ward Dem Party 1976; Black Businessman of the Year Blackbook Bus & Ref Guide 1980. **Business Addr:** President, Community Ins Center Inc, 526 E 87th St, Chicago, IL 60619.

MOSES, YOLANDA T.
Educational administrator. **Educ:** California State Univ, San Bernardino, bachelor's degree; Univ of California, Riverside, master's degree, doctorate. **Career:** Anthropologist; California State Univ, Dominguez Hills, vice pres of academic affairs, until 1993; CUNY, City College, pres, 1993-. **Business Addr:** President, CUNY, City College, 138th St & Covent Ave, New York, NY 10031.

MOSLEY, BENITA FITZGERALD
Athletic director. **Personal:** Born Jul 6, 1961, Warrenton, VA; daughter of Roger & Fannie Fitzgerald; married Ron Mosley, May 1, 1996. **Educ:** University of Tennessee/Knoxville, BS, industrial engineering, 1984. **Career:** Professor athlete, 1980-88; Tracor, Inc & MHP Fu-Tech Inc, industrial, systems & software engineer, 1991-95; Special Olympics International Inc, regional director, 1991-92, sports mktg manager, 1992-93; Atlanta Centennial Olympic Properties, program director, 1993-95; Media Spokesperson, 1988-; ARCO Olympic Training Ctr, Chula Vista CA, director, 1995-97; dir of US Olympic Training Centers for U.S. Olympic Committee, 1997-. **Orgs:** Women's Sports Foundation, president, bd of trustees; United States Olympics Committee, athlete's advisory council; USA Track & Field, board of directors; Women in Sports and Events, mem. **Honors/Awds:** Olympic Gold Medalist, 100 Meter Hurdles, 1984; US Olympic Teams, Alternate, Member, 1980, 1984, 1988; Track & Field News, "Hurdler of the Decade," 1980's; Dedication of Benita Fitzgerald Drive, Dale City VA; US Sports Academy, Distinguished Svc Awd, 1996; 15-Time NCAA All-America; Commendations: Virginia Legislature, Texas Legislature, Tennessee Legislature, District of Columbia, Prince William County Board of Supervisors, Prince William County School Board; University of Tennessee, Hall of Fame, 1994.

MOSLEY, CAROLYN W.
Educator. **Personal:** Born Nov 2, 1952, New Orleans, LA; daughter of Lillie Lee Washington and Johnny Washington Sr; married Shantell Nicole Mosley (divorced). **Educ:** LSUMC School of Nursing, BSN, 1974, MN, 1980; Texas Woman's University, Houston, PhD, 1994. **Career:** Charity Hosp of New Orleans, staff nurse, 1974-75; Veterans Administration of New Orleans, head nurse, 1975-81; LSUMC Sch of Nursing, assistant professor, 1981-87; Charity Hosp, staff nurse, 1987-90; LSUMC Sch of Nursing, assistant professor, beginning 1989, assoc prof, currently; Charity Hosp, staff nurse, 1991-. **Orgs:** American Nurses Association, 1990-; New Orleans District Nurses Association, 1990-; National League for Nurses, 1990-; Louisiana League for Nurses, president-elect, 1990-; Sigma Theta Tau, Epsilon NU, president-elect, 1982-; Chi Eta Phi Sorority of Blacks, 1976-; Association of Black Nursing Faculty, 1990-; Cope-line, volunteer, 1992-; ANA Council for Nursing, Research Exec Comm. **Honors/Awds:** LSU Medical Center, Board of Regents Doctoral Fellowship, 1987-90; American Nurses Association, Minority Doctoral Fellowship, 1988-91; Texas Woman's University, Mary Gibbs Doctoral Fellowship, Doctoral Traineeship, 1988; Chi Eta Phi, Soror of the Year, 1992; City of New Orleans, Vigor Volunteer of the Year; Lederle Award; Rosalyn Carter Caregiving Award; Volunteer of Distinction. **Special Achievements:** A Call to Action: Health Care Reforms as a Priority, 1992; plenary session speaker, National Center for the Advancement of Blacks in the Health Professions; speaker at national conferences by Contemporary Forum. **Home Addr:** 711 S Dupre St, New Orleans, LA 70119, (504)822-5886.

MOSLEY, CHRISTOPHER D.
Financial services officer. **Personal:** Born Jul 12, 1960, Atlanta, GA; son of Annie B Mosley and Lamar T Mosley. **Educ:** West Georgia College, BS, 1983. **Career:** NationsBanc Securities Inc, investment specialist, 1986, margin specialist, 1986-89, retirement plan administrator, 1989-. **Orgs:** Toastmasters International; Rehabilatation Exposure, board of directors, treasurer; Volunteer Income Tax Assistance, volunteer. **Honors/Awds:** NationsBanc Securities Inc, External Client Services Award, 1992; Dollars and Sense Magazine, America's Best & Brightest Professional Men, 1992; US Jaycees, Outstanding Young Men of America, 1983. **Home Addr:** 3796 Benjamin Court, Atlanta, GA 30331.

MOSLEY, EDNA WILSON
Administrator, councilwoman. **Personal:** Born May 31, 1925, Helena, AR; married John W; children: Edna L. **Educ:** Univ of No CO, attended 1942-43; Adams State Coll, attended 1968-69; Met State Coll, BA 1969; Univ of CO, attended 1975-76. **Career:** Univ of Denver, affirmative action dir 1978-; CO State & Dept of Personnel, asst state affirmative action coordinator

1974-78; CO Civil Rights Commn, community relations coordinator 1970-74; Co Civil Rights Commn, civil rights specialist 1969-70; Women's Bank NA Denver, founder 1975; Aurora CO, councilwoman. **Orgs:** Co-chmn Denver/Nairobi Sister-/City Com 1976-80; bd of dir Women's Bank NA Denver 1978-80; commr Nat Social Action Commn Delta Sigma Theta Sorority 1979-81; mem Higher Educ Affirmative Action Dir; mem Nat Assn of Affirmative Action Officers; mem CO Black Women for Polit Action; mem Delta Sigma Theta Denver Alumnae Chpt; mem Women's Forum of CO Inc Best Sustaining Pub Affairs Prog CO Broadcasting Assn 1972. **Honors/Awds:** Lola M Parker Achievement Award Iota Phi Lambda Far Western Region 1977; Headliner Award Women in Communications Inc 1978; Appreciation Award Nat Assn of Black Accountants 1978; distinguished serv award Intl Student Orgn Univ of Denver 1979. **Business Addr:** 1470 South Havana St, Aurora, CO 80012.

MOSLEY, EDWARD R.
Physician. **Personal:** Born in Chicago, IL; married Marian Kummerfeld; children: Cary, Laura, Kia, Rennie, Christopher, Caroline. **Educ:** Meharry Med Coll, MD 1948. **Career:** Pvt Prac, Physician 1956-; Psychiatric Serv VA Hosp Tuskegee AL, med coord 1954-56; VA Hosp Tuskegee AL, residency 1949-52; Harlem Hosp, internship 1948-49; Reg Med Consult State Dept of Rehab. **Orgs:** Pres bd dir Westview Convalescent Hosp; John Hale Med Cntr; mem Nat Med Assn; AMA; Golden State Med Assn; CA Med Assn; Daniel Hale William Medical Forum; Fresno Co Med Soc; Am Soc of Internal Med; Fresno Co Soc of Internal Med; mem Alpha Phi Alpha; F & AM Prince Hall Shrine; 20th Century Elks; chmn Citizen's Resource Com State Cntr Comm Coll 1969; bd trustees State Cntr Comm Coll 1971-; pres 1975-; bd dir Sequoia Boy Scout Council; mem Co Parks & Recreation Comm 1958-68; Mayor's Biracial Com on Hum Rel 1966-68; bd dir Easter Seal Soc TB Assn. **Honors/Awds:** AUS med corp capt 1952-54.

MOSLEY, ELWOOD A.
Federal official. **Personal:** Born May 12, 1943, Philadelphia, PA; son of Ethel Glenn and John Mosley; married Eileen Carson, Jan 14, 1967; children: Danielle Mosley. **Educ:** St Joseph's Univ, Philadelphia PA, Business Admin, 1972; Harvard Univ, Cambridge MA, MA, 1989. **Career:** Chase Manhattan Bank, New York NY, asst treasurer, 1972-76; CIGNA Insurance, Philadelphia PA, vice pres, 1976-82; USF&G Insurance, Baltimore MD, vice pres, 1982-85; Huggins Financial, Philadelphia PA, vice pres, 1985-87; US Postal Service, Washington DC, asst postmaster general, training & devel, 1987-. **Honors/Awds:** National Diversity Award. **Military Serv:** US Marine Corp, corporal, 1964-70. **Home Addr:** 1684 Kingsbridge Court, Annapolis, MD 21401-6408, (410)849-2261. **Business Addr:** District Manager, Customer Svcs & Sales, South Jersey District, United States Postal Svc, 501 Benegno Blvd, Bellmawr, NJ 08031-9998.

MOSLEY, GERALDINE B.
Nursing educator (retired). **Personal:** Born Oct 22, 1920, Petersburg, VA; married Kelly (died 1996). **Educ:** Hunter Coll, NYC, BS 1945; Coll Columbia Univ NYC, MA psychology 1950; NYU, PhD 1970. **Career:** Div of Nursing Dominican Coll of Blauvelt, dir 1973-91; Dept of Psychiatry Harlem Hospital Center, asso dir of nursing 1971-73; Mayor's Org Task For Comprehensive Health Planning, health planner 1970-71; Columbia Univ, asst prof dept of nursing 1968-71; Queens Coll NYC, lecturer, nursing 1956-58/ 1961-68; VA, instructor/supvr 1952-56; Dept of Health NYC, public health nurse 1947-52. **Orgs:** Bd of dirs, So NY League, Natl League for Nursing, 1974-76; sec, NY State Nurses Assn, Amer Nurses Assn; vice pres, Metro Regional Task Force for Nursing, 1975-; mem Assn of Univ Profs 1973-80. **Honors/Awds:** Distinguished achievement in comprehensive health planning Chi Eta Phi 19 Outstanding professional leadership award Dept of Psychiatry Harlem Hospital Center 1973; Distinguished serv to the Co of Rockland Co Leg & of Rockland Co 1976; professional Award Westchester County Club Natl Assn of Negro Business & Professional Women's Clubs Inc 1977; Division of Nursing, New York University, The Estelle Osborn Certificate of Achievement, 1996.

MOSLEY, JAMES EARL, SR.
Law enforcement official. **Personal:** Born Jan 19, 1939, Hackensack, NJ; son of Charles & Hattie Mae Mosley; married JoAnn, Jan 9, 1960; children: Paulette, Beverly Allen, James Jr. **Educ:** Bergen Comm College, AAS, 1975. **Career:** City of Englewood, chief of police, currently. **Orgs:** National Organization Black Law Enforcement Executives, 1990-; New Jersey State Police Chief's Assn, 1994-; Shiloh Masonic Lodge #53-F&AM, dean of instruction, 1983-; Holy Royal Arch Masons, Joshua Chapter #15, 1994-; MT Zion Baptist Church, 1953-. **Honors/Awds:** City of Englewood, Honorable Mention Award, 1968, Dedicated Service Award, 1983, Outstanding Service Award, 1985, 30 Year Service Award, 1994; Bergen County, Executive Certificate of Commendation, 1993. **Special Achievements:** Presented a resolution from the New Jersey State General, Sept 1993; Assembly for receiving The Pastor's Award for Comunity Service from the First Baptist Church of Englewood, NJ. **Military Serv:** US Marine Corps, sgt, 1958-61; Good Conduct Medal, 1961. **Business Addr:** Chief, Englewood Police Dept, 75 S Van Brunt Street, Englewood, NJ 07631, (201)871-6405.

MOSLEY, JOHN WILLIAM
Government administrator (retired). **Personal:** Born Jun 21, Denver, CO; married Edna W Wilson; children: Edna Lorette Futrell, John Gregory, Brian Wilson, William Eric. **Educ:** CO State Univ, BS; Denver Univ, MSW; Tuskegee Inst; NC A&T Univ. **Career:** Fed Regional Council Dept HEW Region Vii, spl asst prin regional ofcl for 1978-; Mtn Plains Fed Regional Council, staff dir 1978; James Farmer Dept HEW, spl asst asst sec 1970; NC A&T U, prof of air sci 1956. **Orgs:** Mem Acad of Cert Social Workers/Nat Assn of Social Workers 1980; bd mem Mile High United Way 1975-; chmn Aurora Human Relations Commn 1975; bd mem Denver People-to-people 1978-; bd mem YMCA; bd mem Goodwill Ind of Denver 1979-. **Honors/Awds:** Award/command Pilot USAF; all conf football & wrestling CO State Univ 1944; hon mention All Am Football; staff various White House Welfare Confs 1970-80; pub various articles "Educ today"; merit scholarship CO State U; outstanding black in CO History Denver Pub Library. **Military Serv:** USAF lt col 21 yrs; Commercial Pilot, Tuskegee Airman. **Business Addr:** Fed Bldg, 1961 Stout, Denver, CO 80294.

MOSLEY, LAWRENCE EDWARD, SR. See Obituaries section.

MOSLEY, MARIE OLEATHA
Educator, nurse. **Personal:** Born Jul 14, 1941, Miami, FL; daughter of Bertha Lee Pitts and Jimmie Pitts; divorced; children: DaShawn Lynette Young. **Educ:** Hunter College Bellevue School of Nursing, BSN, 1976, MSN (cum laude), 1983; Columbia University Teachers College, EdM, 1986, EdD, 1992. **Career:** Jackson Memorial Hospital; Boone Municipal Hospital Center, head nurse, 1971-80; staff relief, Staff Builders, 1980-82; Hunter College Bellevue School of Nursing, assistant professor, 1983-; LaGuardia Community College, assistant professor, 1985-86; US Army Reserve, Army Nurse Corp, assistant medical officer, 1989-. **Orgs:** Nurses for Political Action, rep; New York State Nurses Association, administrative rep, education committee, 1988-; American Association for the History of Nursing, 1992-; National Black Nurses Association, 1991-; Civil Affairs Officers Association, New York/New Jersey Chapter, 1989-; Association for Black Nursing Faculty in Higher Education, program committee, 1987-; Sigma Theta Tau, Inc, Alpha Phi Chapter, chairperson, nominating committee, 1984-; NYSNA District 13, education committee. **Honors/Awds:** Bronx Community College, Certificate of Service, 1970, Merit Award, 1970, Commencement Award, 1971, Student Government Service Award, 1971; Columbia University Teachers College, Professional Nurse Traineeship, 1985-91, Minority Scholarship, 1990-91; Hunter College Bellevue School of Nursing, Professional Nurse Traineeship, 1982-83; Association of Black Nursing Faculty in Higher Education, Dissertation Award, 1990; Nurse Education Fund, M Elizabeth Carnegie Scholarship, Nurses Scholarship & Fellowship Award, Mead Johnson & Co. Scholarship, 1989. **Special Achievements:** A History of Black Leaders in Nursing: The Influences of Four Black Community Health Nurses on the Establishment Growth and Practice of Public Health Nursing in New York City 1900-1930, National Association of Colored Graduate Nurses, Dr Mary Elizabeth Osborne, Estelle Riddl Carnegie, 1992. **Military Serv:** US Army Reserve, Nurse Corp, major, 1978-. **Home Addr:** 2541 7th Ave, #17B, New York, NY 10039, (212)926-1647. **Business Addr:** Assistant Professor, Hunter College, Bellevue School of Nursing, Brookdale Campus, 425 E 25th St, Rm 430A, New York, NY 10010, (212)481-7574.

MOSLEY, MAURICE B.
Attorney. **Personal:** Born Jun 4, 1946, Waterbury, CT. **Educ:** SC St Coll, BS 1968; Cntrl CT St Coll, MS 1972; Univ of CT Sch of Law, JD 1975. **Career:** State of CT, Rep,Atty, pvt prac; CT, lgsltr 1976-; CT St Treas, exec asst 1975-77; Urban Leag, legis consult 1974; Tchr, 1968-72. **Orgs:** Adv bd Colonial Bank & Trust Co; chmn Legis Black Caucus; bd trustees Waterbury Hosp; exec bd NAACP 1974-77. **Honors/Awds:** SC St Dist Bus Awd 1968. **Business Addr:** Rep of 72nd Assembly Dist, State of Connecticut, Capitol Bldg, Hartford, CT 06106.

MOSLEY, ROOSEVELT CHARLES, JR.
Actuary. **Personal:** Born Jul 29, 1972, Saginaw, MI; son of Roosevelt & Evelyn Mosley; married Yashica Mosley, Aug 13, 1994; children: Tanisha, Bria. **Educ:** University of Michigan, BS, actuarial science, 1993, BS, statistics, 1993. **Career:** State Farm, sr asst actuary, 1994-. **Orgs:** Kappa Alpha Psi Fraternity, Inc, 1991-; American Academy of Actuaries, 1996-; Casualty Actuarial Society, assoc mem, 1996-. **Business Addr:** Senior Assistant Actuary, State Farm, 1 State Farm Plz, E-3, Bloomington, IL 61701, (309)766-9942.

MOSLEY, WALTER
Author. **Educ:** Goddard College; Johnson State College, bachelor's degree, political theory; City College of New York, graduate writing program. **Career:** Computer programmer, 15 years; author, currently; titles include: Devil in a Blue Dress, 1990, A Red Death, 1991, White Butterfly, 1992; Black Betty, Norton, 1994; RL's Dream; A Yellow Dog; Always Outnumbered, Always Outgunned, 1997. **Honors/Awds:** Edgar Award, nomination, for Devil in a Blue Dress. **Business Addr:** Author, c/o Publicity Department, WW Norton & Co Inc, 500 Fifth Ave, New York, NY 10110, (212)354-5500.

MOSS, ALFRED A., JR.
Educator, clergyman. **Personal:** Born Mar 2, 1943, Chicago, IL; son of Ruth Watson Moss and Alfred Alfonso Moss Sr; married Alice E Foster (divorced 1985); children: Daniel Clement. **Educ:** Lake Forest College, Lake Forest, IL, BA, with honors, 1961-65; Episcopal Divinity School, Cambridge, MA, MA, divinity, 1965-68; University of Chicago, Chicago, IL, MA, 1972, PhD, 1977. **Career:** Episcopal Church of the Holy Spirit, Lake Forest, IL, assistant minister for urban ministry, 1968-70; University of Chicago, Episcopal Chaplaincy, Chicago, IL, associate chaplain, 1970-75; Univ of Maryland, Dept of History, College Park, MD, lecturer, 1975-77, assistant professor, 1977-83, associate professor, 1983-. **Honors/Awds:** The American Negro Academy, Louisiana State Univ Press, 1981; Looking at History, People for the American Way, 1986; From Slavery to Freedom, Alfred A Knopf, 1988; The Facts of Reconstruction, Louisiana State Univ Press, 1991. **Business Addr:** Professor, Dept of History, University of Maryland, College Park, MD 20742-7315.

MOSS, ANNI R.
Actress, singer, model, mktg computer consultant. **Personal:** Born Nov 17, Notasulga, AL; daughter of Rebecca Clark Moss and Samuel David Moss. **Educ:** West Virginia State College, BS, education, math, French, 1966; Boston University, Theatre Institute, 1988; State University of New York, 1984, 1991. **Career:** NASA Lewis Research, math assistant, 1965; IBM Corp., systems engineer, 1966-74, instructor, 1974-75, product planner, 1976-81, systems requirements specialist, 1981-82; IBM Germany, consultant, writer, 1976; IBM Worldwide, IS auditor, 1983-84, systems engineering manager, 1984-89, hq market planner, administrator, 1989-92; actress, films include: Bed of Roses, The Last Good Time; Movin' Up, Boston Cable; Mountain Don't Move for Me; others; television appearances include: Law & Order; The Cosby Mysteries; NY Undercover; others; National & Regional TV commercials; President's Council on Physical Fitness PSA, corporate videos; Community Scene, WICZ-TV; Black History Vignettes, WBNG-TV; Black Women's Special, WSKG-TV; dreamUp with Anni, cable TV show, host producer; radio show dreamSounds, WRTN/WVOX, host producer; Gospel Renaissance Music, WENE/WMRV, host producer; theatrical appearances include: Joe Turner's Come and Gone, Huntington Theatre, Boston; Antigone, Boston University; Over the Damn, Playwright's Platform; concert soloist of gospel, jazz, and pop; Sabby Lewis Band, Charlie Bateman Band, jazz singer, 1991-92; published writer: Women's News, Mentor Magazine, numerous others. **Orgs:** Screen Actors Guild, 1992-; AFTRA, 1988-. **Honors/Awds:** Black Achievers Award, 1985; IBM Hundred Percent Club & Golden Circle, 1985-88. **Special Achievements:** Unex corporate video, spokesperson, 1992; National Fire Protection Association international magazine publication, first female and first African-American to appear on the cover, 1992; IBM's System 390, originator, planner, producer, and executor of worldwide photography and videos for the system, 1990, author of mktg publications for the system, 1990-92. **Business Addr:** Actress, Singer, Model, PO Box 1272, White Plains, NY 10602, (212)724-2800.

MOSS, CARLTON. See Obituaries section.

MOSS, ESTELLA MAE
County official (retired). **Personal:** Born Sep 15, 1928, Providence, KY; daughter of Odessa Jones and Eugene Jones; married Charles E Moss Sr; children: Phyllis Johnson, Ardell, Sheila Spencer, Deborah L Ray, Charles E Jr, Angie V. **Educ:** Indiana State University, Evansville, IN, School of Public & Environ Affairs, 1975. **Career:** Superior Court, clerk probate 8 yrs; Pigeon Twp Assessor; chief deputy appointed 1974-76; Vanderburgh Cty, recorder 1976-84. **Orgs:** Vp Community Action Program 1969-77; bd of dir Carver Comm Day Care 1970-76; NAACP Coalition 100 Black Women Political Black Caucus 1978-85; bd of dir Liberty Baptist Housing Auth; appointed superintendent, City Cemeteries, 1987-91. **Honors/Awds:** Community Leadership Awd YWCA 1976; Black Woman of the Year in Politics Black Women Task Force 1977; State of IN Black Expo 1978; Selected & Honored as one of 105 Outstanding Black Women of IN by Natl Council of Negro Women 1983; Special Recognition Community Service Award, Black Women Task Force, 1990. **Home Addr:** 804 Mulberry, Evansville, IN 47713.

MOSS, JAMES EDWARD
Law enforcement official (retired). **Personal:** Born Jan 8, 1949, Columbus, OH; son of Ernestine Coggins Moss and Frank P Moss; married Jan 23, 1970; children (previous marriage): Shondrika, Marquai, Jamarran; married Andria Felder Moss, Jun 27, 1992; children: Jamelah. **Educ:** Columbus Business Univ, associate degree, business admin, 1973; Ohio Dominican

Coll, BA, business admin, 1975; Capital Univ, 1977-78; Ohio State University, MA, black studies, 1989, MA, US history, 1993, PhD, candidate history, 1994. **Career:** Columbus Police Dept, Columbus, OH, sgt, 1970-94. **Orgs:** Pres, Police Officers for Equal Rights, 1988-; mem, American Historical Assn, 1990-; mem, Organization of American Historians, 1990-; bd mem, Columbus Police Athletic League; mem, OH Guardians, 1988-; pres, Natl Black Police Assn, 1993-; vice pres, NAACP, Columbus chapter, 1994-; Natl Council for Black Studies; Assn for the Study of Afro American Life and History. **Honors/Awds:** Jefferson Award, 1985; Coach of the Year, Police Athletic League, 1983; Service Award, Police Athletic League, 1986, 1987, 1990; Natl Black Police Assn, Police Officer of the Year, 1993. **Military Serv:** US Army, sgt, E-5, 1967-70; Vietnam War Veteran, Good Conduct Medal, Combat Infantry Badge; Vietnam Service Medal; Tet Offensive Medal; Two Unit Citation; Vietnam Campaign Medal; Parachute Medal-Jump Wings. **Business Addr:** Retired Sergeant, Columbus Police Dept, Burglary Squad Sergeant, 120 W Marconi Blvd, Columbus, OH 43215.

MOSS, OTIS, JR.
Cleric. **Personal:** Born Feb 26, 1935, LaGrange, GA; married Edwina Hudson; children: Kevin, Daphne, Otis III. **Educ:** Morehouse Coll, BA 1956, Morehouse School of Rel, BD 1959; Interdenominational Theol Ctr, spec studies 1960-61; Temple Bible Coll, DD, Morehouse Coll, DD 1977. **Career:** Raymond Walters Coll, instr; Old Mt Olive Bapt Church, La Grange, pastor, 1954-59; Providence Bapt Church, Atlanta, pastor, 1956-61; Mt Zion' Baptist Church, minister, 1961-74; Mt Olivet Institutional Church, Cleveland, pastor 1975-. **Orgs:** Bd of dirs, Morehouse Sch of Religion & Morehouse Coll; bd of dir ML King Jr Ctr; bd of dir, vchmn Oper PUSH; mem Alpha Phi Alpha; past vice pres NAACP of Atlanta; past pres & founder Cinti Chap SCLC; bd of trustees Leadership Cleveland Civil Right Activist; mem of review comm Harvard Divinity School Harvard Univ 1975-82; mem bd of trustees Morehouse Coll 1979-; former columnist for Atlanta Inquirer Atlanta GA 1970-75; delivered speeches, sermons & addresses, Atlanta Univ, Colgate Rochester Divinity School, Coll of Mt St Joseph, Dillard Univ, Eden Theol Ctr, Howard Univ, Kalamazoo Coll, Miami Univ, Fisk Univ, Univ of Cincinnati, Vanderbilt Univ, Wilberforce Univ, Wright State Univ, Morehouse Coll; keynote speaker March on Cincinnati 1963. **Honors/Awds:** Man of the Year in Religion Atlanta 1961; Consult with Pres Carter Camp David 1979; invited as part of clergy mission to Republic of China Taiwan 1984; consult with govt officials as part of clergy mission to Israel 1977-78; served as part of clergy mission to the Far East Hong Kong, Taiwan & Japan 1970; invited to act as delegate to World Bapt Conf in Beirut; visited W Africa 1963; Govs Awd in Civil Rights Gov Richard F Celeste; Black Professional of the Year Black Professional Assn Cleveland OH 1983; Spec Awd in Leadership Central State Univ 1982; Human Rels Awd Bethune Cookman Coll 1976; Ranked as one of Clevelands 10 Most Influential Ministers Cleveland Press 1981; 1 of Amers 15 Greatest Black Preachers EbonyMag 1984; twice honored by OH House of Reps Resolutions 1971,75; sermon ''Gg from Disgrace to Dignity'' Best Black Sermons 1972; essays ''Black Church Distinctives'', ''Black Church Revolution'' The Black Christian Experience; listed in Ebony Success Library. **Business Addr:** Pastor, Olivet Inst Bapt Church, 8712 Quincy Ave, Cleveland, OH 44106.

MOSS, ROBERT C., JR.
Motivation consultant. **Personal:** Born May 30, 1939, San Diego; son of La Verne Moss and Robert C Moss Sr; married Edna Jean, Mar 17, 1962; children: Anita Louise, Parry Donald. **Educ:** San Diego State U, BA 1961; US Intl Univ, teaching cred 1965; San Diego State U, MS 1975. **Career:** Phys Educ Dept Univ of CA San Diego, supervisor 1971-92; professional baseball umpire 1969-71; San Diego HS, black studies tchr, black student motivation counselor 1969-71; Mission Bay HS, biology instr, football, baseball coach 1966-69; Lincoln HS, biology tchr 1965-66; founder/director of Moss-Cess Unlimited, a motivation consulting firm 1973-. **Orgs:** Kappa Alpha Psi Fraternity; Amer Alliance for Health, Physical Educ, Recreation & Dance; Amer Counseling Association; CA Assn for Health, Physical Educ, Recreation and Dance; CA Assn for Counseling & Devel; CA & Amer Assn for Multicultural Counseling & Devel; San Diego County Baseball Umpires Association, vice pres. **Honors/Awds:** Ted Williams Award, 1960, leading hitter on San Diego State Univ baseball team; Byron Chase Memorial Award, 1960, most valuable lineman on SDSU football team; Most Outstanding SDSU Senior Athlete, 1961; Associated Students Man of the Month at SDSU, May, 1961; Blue Key Honorary Society, 1961; Ashanti Weusi Award for teaching services to the Southeast San Diego community; CAHPERD, San Diego Unit Meritorious Service Award, 1975; CAHPERD President's Citation, 1981; Oustanding Teacher Award, Univ of CA, San Diego African American graduates, 1985; CAHPERD Emmett Ashford Community Spirit Award, 1986; AACD President's Citation, 1986; CACD Black Caucus Service Award, 1986; CAHPERD Honor Award, 1987; Special Recognition Award, UC San Diego Athletics Program; Special Recognition Award, US Intl Univ basketball team, 1988; CACD Black Caucus Dedicated Service Award, 1989; CACD-CAMC President's Outstanding Professional Service Award, 1989; Camperd Multicultural Dynamics Section, Outstanding Service Award, 1991; CACD Human Rights Award, 1993; ACA-AMCD Professional Development Award, 1994; author, Laff 4 Rx (Health), booklet on positive uses of laughter. **Military Serv:** Served USMC 1961-65.

MOSS, SIMEON F.
Military officer (retired), consultant, educator. **Personal:** Born Apr 5, 1920, Princeton, NJ; son of Mary Benning Moss and Simeon C Moss; married Edith Ashby Moss, Apr 6, 1946; children: Simeon Jr, Deborah A. **Educ:** Rutgers U, BS 1941; Princeton, MA 1949; Rutgers, EdD 1967. **Career:** National Executive Service Corps, director, management consulting, currently; Metro-ed Serv Inc, vice pres 1980-; Educ Dept Co of Essex, 1977-80; Essex Co Coll, exec vice pres 1969-77; Essex Co NJ Dept Educ, supt schools; Newark Schools, elem supt; NJ Dept of Labor and Industry, asst commr 1960-64; NJ Pub Schs, tchr adminstr 1954-60; NJ Manual Training Sch, field Rep 1949-53. **Orgs:** Trustee Essex Co Coll 1969-75; Essex Co Vocational Bd 1969-75; dir Essex Co Bd Educ Empl Pension Fund; dir City Natl Bank of Newark; adv comm teacher Educ Seton Hall Univ; chmn bd Inst Trustees NJ State Prison Complex 1972-92; membership chmn Orange Mtn Coun BSA 1973-74; sec-treas cham NJ Consultation Ethnic Factors in Educ; legislative chair ECREA. **Honors/Awds:** Bancroft History Prize, Journal of Negro History 1949; White House Invitee Centennial of Emancipation Proclamation 1963; Distinguished Serv in Educ Award Alpha Phi Alpha 1965-69; Frontiers Community Serv Award 1970; Loyal Son of Rutgers Award 1987. **Military Serv:** US Army 1st lt 1942-46; capt 1951-52; Njarng 1956-73; USAR; col retired. **Home Addr:** 440 Page Terr, South Orange, NJ 07079, (201)763-0360.

MOSS, TANYA JILL
Government administrator. **Personal:** Born Dec 20, 1958, Chicago, IL; daughter of Arzelia and Hiawatha Moss. **Educ:** Univ of Chicago, IL, BS, 1983. **Career:** Carson Pirie Scott & Co, personnel assisant, 1980-83; Quaker Oats, account rep, 1983-84; City of Chicago, proj coordinator, 1985-. **Orgs:** Alpha Kappa Alpha Sorority Inc, 1979-; Natl Forum for Black Public Admins, 1985-; Order of the Eastern Star, 1982-; Natl Assn of Female Executives, 1984-; Bd Mem, ETA Creative Arts Foundation; Exec Bd Mem, Political Action League. **Honors/Awds:** Appraising Real Property, Society of Real Estate Appraisers, 1990. **Special Achievements:** Developed the City of Chicago's Indebtedness Program, Scofflaw Program, 1989; assisted in the development of the False Burglar Program, 1994. **Home Phone:** (773)721-5194. **Business Addr:** Project Coordinator, Dept of Revenue, City of Chicago, 333 S State St, Ste LL540, Chicago, IL 60604.

MOSS, THOMAS EDWARD, SR.
Deputy chief of police. **Personal:** Born Nov 2, 1934, Detroit, MI; son of Leola Lorraine Davis Moss (deceased) and Thomas Whitting Moss (deceased); married Pearl Bonham, Nov 22, 1986; children: Thomas, Tonia Gaddis, Monica, Marc. **Educ:** Wayne State Univ, BA 1967; Univ of MI, MA 1977; Northwestern Univ, Evanston, IL, MBA 1989. **Career:** Wayne Co Youth Home, boys supr 1964-65; Detroit Public School, teacher 1966-70; Royal Oak Twp MI, police officer 1963-65; Oak Park MI, public safety officer 1965-74; Wayne Co Comm Coll, dir of law enforcement programs 1970-73; Detroit Police Dept, deputy chief of police 1974-. **Orgs:** One of dir & coaches Detroit Jr Football League 1968-; pres Guardians of MI 1971-73; vice pres 1971; dir Three Day Conf on Black Problems in Law Enforcement 1972; 1st natl chmn Nat Black Police Assn 1973; mem MI Assn of Chiefs of Police; directed security operations during Mayor Coleman Young's First Campaign 1973; dir Detroit Police Dept Jr Police Cadet Program; created community service officer program & in school colleges program involving Low Income Youth; aid Mrs Martin L King & Rev Martin L King Sr; mem Univ of MI Maize & Blue Club; mem Greater Alumni Assn of Univ MI; bd of dirs Detroit YMCA; bd mem Westside Cubs Athletic Assn; mem Am Psychological Assn National Org Law Enfor Exec Secretary Detroit Chapter, 1989-90. **Honors/Awds:** Elected bd of govs Univ of MI Alumni Assn 1986; developed Jr Police Cadet Prog; 1 of 18 for natl recognition by the Police Foundation Washington DC; Community service officer program, pre-police officer training program, high school, jr/sr's, 1988-; Spirit of Detroit Award, Detroit City Council, 1978, 1984. **Military Serv:** AUS 1954-57.

MOSS, WAYNE B.
Recreation commissioner. **Personal:** Born Jul 28, 1960, Cleveland, OH; son of Earlene Hill Moss and Ceasar Moss. **Educ:** Howard University, Washington, DC, broadcast journalism, 1982; Ohio University, Athens, OH, sports administration, 1988. **Career:** Ohio Bureau of Employment Services, Maple Heights, OH, account executive, 1984-87; Cleveland Browns, Cleveland, OH, public relations asst, 1988; Baltimore Orioles, Baltimore, MD, asst dir of community relations, 1989; Detroit Lions, Pontiac, MI, asst dir of public relations, 1989-91; City of Cleveland, Cleveland, OH, commissioner of recreation, 1991-95; Dekalb County, deputy dir of recreation, currently. **Orgs:** Member, Career Beginnings, 1988; member, UNCF, 1989. **Business Addr:** Deputy Director of Recreation, Dekalb County Government, 1300 Commerce Dr, #200, Decatur, GA 30030, (404)371-2475.

MOSS, WILMAR BURNETT, JR.
Educator. **Personal:** Born Jul 13, 1928, Homer, LA; married Orean Sanders; children: Dwight, Victor, Gary, LaDonna. **Educ:** AR Bapt Coll, attended 1949; So State Coll, attended 1955-57; AM&N Coll Pine Bluff, BS Bus Admin 1960; Univ of AR Fayetteville, MEd Educ Admin1970. **Career:** McNeil Cleaners, cleaner spotter presser; McNeil Lumber Co, tractor truck driver lumber grader; Partee Lumber Co, tractor driver; Navel Ordnance Plant Camden, light mach oper; Stuttgard, teacher 1960; E Side Lincoln Elem Schools Stuttgart, head teacher 1961-63; E Side Lincoln Holman, prin 1964-69; Holman Northside Elem Schools, prin 1969-72; Walker School Dist #33, supt of schools 1972-. **Orgs:** Mem AR Sch Admin Assn, AR Educ Assn, So AR Admins Assn, Columbia Co Educ Assn, Natl Educ Assn, Amer Legion former commander & vice dist commander; mem NAACP helped form Columbis Co Br; mem Natl Alliance of Black Sch Supts; mem Phi Delta Kappa; active Mason; mem Bethany Bapt Ch McNeil; Golden Diadem Lodge No 41; McNeil Jaycees; bd mem Pres Johnson's Concentrated Employ Prog 1971-72; active BSA; mem Stuttgart Civic League; organized WalkerAlumni Assn 1974. **Honors/Awds:** Comm Serv Awd Stuttgart Civic League 1972; Outstanding Serv Awd Stuttgart Faculty Club 1970. **Military Serv:** AUS 1951-53. **Business Addr:** Supt of Schools, Walker Sch Dist #33, PO Box 1149, Magnolia, AR 71753.

MOSS, WINSTON
Writer. **Personal:** Born in Selma, AL. **Educ:** Bellarmine Coll KY, 1962-64; Western KY Univ, 1968. **Career:** The Flip Wilson Show, staff writer 1970; Laugh In, staff writer 1972; That's My Mama, story editor 1975-76; The Jackson-5 Show, staff writer 1977; Writers Guild of Amer/WST, freelance writer. **Orgs:** Staff writer The Clifton Davis Spec 1977, All in the Family 1977-79, Archie Bunkers Place 1979-80; vice chmn Black Writers Comm 1979-81; mem Hollywood Branch NAACP, Local Black Groups & Writers Groups. **Honors/Awds:** 1st Black Story Editor for Network TV 1975; Golden Globe Awd for Writing on ''All in the Family'' 1977; Universal Studios TV Pilot Scheduled for ABC-TV Sep 1985; Stage Play ''The Helping Hand'' currently in production. **Military Serv:** AUS spec 4 1965-67. **Home Addr:** 4714 Rodeo Ln #3, Los Angeles, CA 90016.

MOSS, WINSTON
Professional football player. **Personal:** Born Dec 24, 1965, Miami, FL; married Zoila; children: Winston Jr, Victoria. **Educ:** Miami (Fla.). **Career:** Tampa Bay Buccaneers, linebacker, 1987-90; Los Angeles Raiders, 1991-94; Seattle Seahawks, 1995-. **Business Addr:** Professional Football Player, Seattle Seahawks, 11220 NE 53rd St, Kirkland, WA 98033, (206)827-9777.

MOSS, ZEFROSS
Professional football player. **Personal:** Born Aug 17, 1966, Tuscaloosa, AL. **Educ:** Alabama State, attended. **Career:** Indianapolis Colts, tackle, 1989-94; Detroit Lions, 1995-96; New England Patriots, 1997-. **Business Addr:** Professional Football Player, New England Patriots, 60 Washington St, Foxboro Stadium, Foxboro, MA 02035, (508)543-7911.

MOTEN, CHAUNCEY DONALD
Educator. **Personal:** Born Jul 2, 1933, Kansas City, KS; married Barbara Jean; children: Allison, Dion. **Educ:** TX Coll, BA, 1955; Vandercook Coll, MA, 1959; Univ of MO, MA, 1969; Univ of MI, PhD, 1972. **Career:** KS City Public School, teacher 1965-68; Univ of MO, dir 1968-70, 1971-73; Metro Comm Coll, exec & asst 1974-77; Metro Comm Coll Kansas City MO, exec dean ofc of human devel 1977-79; Penn Valley Comm Coll Kansas City MO, asst dean comm serv/instructional serv 1979-. **Orgs:** Review panalist HEW 1977; consult IO Assn for Equal Emplymnt Oppor/Affirmtn Action Prof 1977; consult Univ Resrch Corp 1978; consult Nat Counc for Staff Prog & Organztnl Devel 1978; consult Mid-am Regnl Counc 1978; consult OR State Univ 1979; consult NW Coll Personnel Assn 1979; consult Am Assn for Affirmatv Action 1980; consult Thomas E Baker & Asso 1980; consult KCRCHE 1976; HEW 1976; Mott Found 1975; CBS 1974; Serengeti Res Inst 1972; KS & MO Bds of Educ pres MO Assn for Affirmatv Action 1980-81; exec bd mem Charlie Parker Mem Found 1978-80; mem MO Black Ldrshp Assn 1977-80; exec bd mem Kansas CitySpirit of Freedom Fountn Inc 1978-80; exec bd mem Yng Men's Christian Assn 1974-76; ofcr Natl Univ Ext Assn 1975-77; mem Am Affr Act Assn 1975-77; comm MO Affm Act Assn1976-80; exec bd mem Momm Educ Assn 1975-80; mem KCMO Serboma Club; NAACP; exec bd mem Black Archives of Mid-am 1974-80; bd mem AFRICARE KCMO 1975-80; mem Urban Leag; bd mem KS Assn for Blind 1977-80. **Honors/Awds:** Mott Fellowship 1970-71; VFW VIP 1972; Man of the Yr 1972; Rockefeller Fellow 1973-74; Recog for Outstndg Srvc MO Assn for Affirmtv Actn 1977; Award of Apprec Am Assn for Affirmtv Actn 1978; Valuable Serv Award Spirit of Freedom Found 1978; Citation of Excellnc TX Coll 1980; Jefferson Award Am Inst for Public Serv 1980. **Military Serv:** AUS bandsman 1955-57. **Business Addr:** Dean, Penn Valley Comm College, 3201 Southwest Trafficway, Kansas City, MO 64111.

MOTEN, EMMETT S., JR.
Company executive. **Personal:** Born Feb 6, 1944, Birmingham, AL; son of Marie Creighton Moten and Emmett S Moten Sr; married Loran Williams Moten, May 29, 1965; children: Eric, Alicia. **Educ:** Grambling Univ, Grambling, LA, BS; LA State Univ, New Orleans, LA, Masters Degree. **Career:** St Augustine High School, New Orleans, LA, athletic dir, football coach, 1966-70; City of New Orleans, New Orleans, LA, rec dept-deputy dir, 1970-73, dir of policy planning and analysis, 1973-75, asst chief administrative officer, 1975-78; Detroit Economic Growth Corp, Detroit, MI, exec vice pres, downtown dev authority, 1978-79; City of Detroit, Detroit, MI, dir, community & economic dev, 1979-88; Little Caesar Enterprises Inc, vice pres, currently. **Orgs:** Chmn, Boys Hope; bd mem, Orchard Childrens Service; bd mem, Institute of Business; bd mem, Detroit Downtown Dev Authority; bd mem, Detroit Economic Dev Authority; pres, Joint Fraternal Devt Corp; Kappa Alpha Psi, Detroit chapter. **Honors/Awds:** Inducted in Grambling State Univ Hall of Fame, 1983; Martin L King Award, 1991; Honorary Alumnus Univ of Detroit, 1988. **Business Addr:** Vice President, Little Caesar Enterprises, Inc, 2211 Woodward, Detroit, MI 48201-3400.

MOTEN, LAWRENCE EDWARD, III
Professional basketball player. **Personal:** Born Mar 25, 1972, Washington, DC. **Educ:** Syracuse. **Career:** Vancouver Grizzlies, 1995-. **Business Addr:** Professional Basketball Player, Vancouver Grizzlies, 788 Beatty St, Ste 311, Vancouver, BC, Canada V6B 2M1, (604)688-5867.

MOTHERSHED, SPAESIO W.
Librarian. **Personal:** Born Jun 30, 1925, Bloomburg, TX; married Juliene Craven; children: Spaesio, Jr, Willa Renee. **Educ:** Jarvis Christn Coll, BA 1952; Syracuse U, MS 1956; N TX State U, post-grad 1963. **Career:** TX So U, dir libraries 1966-; Jarvis Christn Coll, head librarian 1960-66; State Library MI, cataloger 1956-60; Syracuse Univ Library, grad asst 1954-56. **Orgs:** Mem TX & SW Library Assns; Houston Met Archives; mem COSATI Sub-com Negro Resrch Libraries 1970-73; editor News Notes 1968-72. **Honors/Awds:** 2 gold stars USN 1945; Engl award; Journalism award. **Military Serv:** USN 1943-46. **Business Addr:** 3201 Wheeler, Houston, TX 77004.

MOTLEY, CONSTANCE BAKER, SR.
Federal judge. **Personal:** Born Sep 14, 1921, New Haven; daughter of Rachel Baker and Willoughby Baker; married Joel Wilson Jr; children: Joel Wilson III. **Educ:** NYU, AB 1943; Columbia Univ, LLB 1946. **Career:** NAACP Legal Def & Educ Fund NYC, staff mem and associate counsel 1945-65; NY State, senator 1964-65; Borough Manhattan, pres 1965-66; US Dist Court judge 1966-82, chief judge 1982-86, sr judge 1986-. **Orgs:** NY State Adv Cncl Empl & Unempl Ins 1958-64; Assn Bar City NY, Natl Bar Assn. **Honors/Awds:** Elizabeth Blackwell Award, Hobart & William Smith Coll, 1965; DHL, Smith Coll, 1965; LLB Degree's: New York University School of Law, 1985; Colgate University, 1987; Yale University, 1987; LLD Degree's: Western Coll for Women, 1965; Morehouse Coll, 1965; VA State Coll, 1966; Howard Univ, 1966; Morgan State Coll, 1966; Brown Univ, 1971; Fordham Univ, 1970; Atlanta Univ, 1973; Iowa Wesleyan Coll, 1969; Univ of Hartford 1973; Albertus Magnus Coll, 1976; John Jay Inst of Criminology, 1979; Spelman Coll, 1979; Trinity Coll, 1979; Univ of Puget Sound 1980; NY Law School, 1982; Univ of Bridgeport Law School, 1984; George Washington Univ School of Law, 1989; Princeton Univ, 1989; Tulane Univ, 1990; Univ of Connecticut, 1990; Claremont University, 1991; Colby College, 1991; Middlebury Coll, 1994; Russell Sage Coll, 1997. **Business Addr:** Senior Judge, US District Court, US Courthouse, 500 Pearl St, New York, NY 10007.

MOTLEY, DAVID LYNN
Corporate investments director. **Personal:** Born Sep 11, 1958, Pittsburgh, PA; son of Lillie M. Law Motley and Thomas A. Motley; married Darlene Gambill, Aug 18, 1990. **Educ:** University of Pittsburgh, Pittsburgh, PA, BSME, 1976-80; Harvard Business School, Boston, MA, MBA, 1986-88. **Career:** PPG Industries Inc, Pittsburgh, PA, analyst, 1980-82, St. Louis, MO, sales representative, 1982-84, New York, NY, res sales representative, 1984-86; MB&A Developments, Washington, DC, consultant, 1988-89; PPG Industries Inc, Pittsburgh, PA, director of corporate investments, 1989-. **Orgs:** Board of directors, Urban League of Pittsburgh, 1990-; board of directors, East Liberty Development Corporation, 1989-; alumni steering committee, NEED, 1990-; chairperson, Langley High School Future Jobs, 1989-; treasurer, Harvard Business School Club Pittsburgh, 1990-.

MOTLEY, JOHN H.
Business executive. **Personal:** Born Sep 11, 1942, Chicago, IL; married Susan; children: Nicole Johnson, Michael Johnson. **Educ:** S IL Univ, BS 1964; DePaul Univ, JD 1972; John Marshall Law Sch. **Career:** Central N/B, credit analyst 1969-73, atty law dept 1973-75, atty & loan officer 1975; Chemical Bank, vice pres & mgr legal dept 1975-79, vice pres disthead 1979-82, sr vice pres div head 1982-. **Orgs:** Mem Urban Bankers Coalition; mem Natl Assn of Urban Bankers; mem Amer Bar, NY Bar, IL Bar Associations; bd mem & treas Tougaloo Coll; bd mem UnitedNeighborhood Ctrs 1984-. **Honors/Awds:** Banker of Year Urban Bankers Coalition 1983; Outstanding Banker Awd Natl Assn of Urban Bankers 1983. **Military Serv:** AUS 1st lt 3 yrs.

MOTLEY, RONALD CLARK
Physician. **Personal:** Born Jan 25, 1954, Dayton, OH; son of Birdella M Rhodes Motley Dunson and Claude L Dunson (stepfather); married Charlyn Coleman, May 6, 1983; children: Melissa Charon. **Educ:** Northwestern Univ, BA 1976; Howard Univ Coll of Medicine, MD 1983. **Career:** Northwestern Univ, lab tech 1972-74; Industrial Biotest Labs, toxicologist and group leader skin sensitization 1976-77; Avon Products Inc, process control chemist 1977-78; Southern Illinois Univ School of Medicine, vstg asst instructor 1978-79; Howard Univ Coll of Medicine, instructor and tutor 1980-81; Howard Univ Coll of Medicine Health Scis Acad, general coord 1981-83; Mayo Clinic, general surgery internship 1983-84, urology residency 1984-88. **Orgs:** Equal opportunity comm Mayo Clinci 1985-; assoc mem Minority Fellows Mayo Clinic 1985-; mem Natl Medical Assoc 1985-; educ comm Dept of Urology Mayo Clinic 1987-88; bd of dirs, Family Service Agency of San Bernardino, CA 1989-. **Honors/Awds:** Who's Who Among Students in Amer Univs & Colls 1983; Lang Book Awd, Health Scis Acad Awd, Outstanding Geriatrics Awd, Excellence in Psychiatry Awd, CV Mosby Surgery Awd Howard Univ Coll of Medicine all rec'd in 1983; also numerous presentations and articles. **Business Addr:** Urologist, San Bernardino Medical Group, Inc., 1700 North Waterman Avenue, San Bernardino, CA 92404.

MOTT, STOKES E., JR.
Attorney. **Personal:** Born Mar 11, 1947, Tifton, GA; son of Kathleen M Mott and Stokes E Mott Sr; married Neilda E Jackman; children: Ako K, Khari S. **Educ:** Long Island Univ, BS 1968; New York Univ, MS Urban Planning 1971; Seton Hall Law Sch, JD 1979. **Career:** Essex Co Comm Coll, instructor; Law Office of Stokes E Mott Jr, attorney. **Orgs:** Mem Alpha Phi Alpha, Pennsylvania Bar Assoc, Philadelphia Bar Assoc. **Business Addr:** Attorney, 117 S 17th St, Fl 910, Philadelphia, PA 19103.

MOULDS, ERIC SHANNON
Professional football player. **Personal:** Born Jul 17, 1973, Lucedale, MS. **Educ:** Mississippi State Univ. **Career:** Buffalo Bills, wide receiver, 1996-. **Orgs:** NAACP. **Honors/Awds:** All Rookie Team, 1996; Buffalo Bills, Rookie of the Year, 1996. **Business Addr:** Professional Football Player, Buffalo Bills, 1 Bills Dr, Orchard Park, NY 14127.

MOURNING, ALONZO
Professional basketball player. **Personal:** Born Feb 8, 1970, Chesapeake, VA. **Educ:** Georgetown University, bachelor's degree in sociology. **Career:** Charlotte Hornets, center, 1992-95; Miami Heat, 1995-. **Orgs:** The Children's Home Society; Zo's Summer Groove, founder. **Special Achievements:** NBA Draft, First round pick, #2, 1992. **Business Addr:** Professional Basketball Player, Miami Heat, 721 NW 1st Ave, Miami Arena, Miami, FL 33136, (305)577-4328.

MOUTON, JAMES RALEIGH
Professional baseball player. **Personal:** Born Dec 29, 1968, Denver, CO. **Educ:** St. Mary's College. **Career:** Houston Astros, outfielder, 1994-. **Business Addr:** Professional Baseball Player, Houston Astros, PO Box 288, Houston, TX 77001-0288, (713)799-9500.

MOUTOUSSAMY-ASHE, JEANNE
Photographer, foundation executive. **Personal:** Born 1951, Chicago, IL; married Arthur Ashe, 1977 (died 1993); children: Camera. **Educ:** Cooper Union, BFA, photography, 1975. **Career:** Professional photographer; Arthur Ashe Foundation for the Defeat of AIDS, chairwoman, currently. **Special Achievements:** Books: "Daddy and Me," Knopf, 1993; "Viewfinders: Black Women Photographers, 1839-1985," New York: Dodd, Mead and Company, 1986; "Daufuskie Island: A Photography Essay," Columbia, SC: University of South Carolina Press, 1982. Exhibitions: "America: Another Perspective," New York University, 1986; "Three Photographers," Black Gallery, Los Angeles, CA, 1985; "Art Against Apartheid: 3 Perspectives," Schomburg Center for Research in Black Culture, New York Public Library, 1984; "Image and Imagination," Jazzonia Gallery, Detroit, MI, 1982. **Business Addr:** Chair, Arthur Ashe Foundation, 100 Park Ave, 10th Fl., New York, NY 10017.

MOWATT, OSWALD VICTOR
Surgeon. **Personal:** Born Apr 5, Spanishtown, Jamaica; married Glenda; children: Cecilia, Oswald Jr, Cyril, Raoul, Enrico, Mario. **Educ:** Roosevelt U, BS 1959; Loyola Univ Med Sch, MD 1963. **Career:** Surgeon, self-emplyd; St Bernard Hosp, chmn Dept Surg 1976-, consult surg 1973-; Provident Hosp, sr atdng surg 1971-; Westside VA Hosp, 1969-76; instr surg 1969-76; Proficent Hosp, chf emer serv, dir med affairs 1972-74; St Bernard Hosp, atnd surg 1970-73; Westside VA, resd surg 1969-70; Univ IL, 1967-60, chf, resd surg; gen prac 1965-67; Michale Reese Hosp, resd surg 1964-65; Cook Co Hosp, intern 1963-64. **Orgs:** Mem AMA 1965-; IL State Med Soc 1965-; Chicago Med Soc 1965-; Nat Med Assn; Bylaws Com of Nat Med Assn 1975-; Judicial Cncl Nat Med Assn 1975-; nominating com Nat Med Assn 1977-; Hse of Del Nat Med Assn 1974-; Assn for Hosp Med Educ 1973-74; bd dir Martin Luther King Boys Club; chmn bd dir Martin L King Boys Club 1977; chmn Bylaws com Cook Co Physicians Assn 1974-76; pres Cook Co Physicians Assn 1977; diplomate Am Bd Surgery 1976;flw Am Coll Surgeons 1977. **Business Addr:** 747 W 77th St, Chicago, IL 60620.

MOWATT, ZEKE
Professional football player. **Personal:** Born Mar 5, 1961, Wauchula, FL. **Educ:** Florida State Univ, attended. **Career:** New England Patriots, tight end, 1983-84, 1986-. **Honors/Awds:** Post-season play, 1986: NFC Championship Game, NFL Championship Game. **Business Addr:** Professional Football Player, New England Patriots, Sullivan Stadium, Rt 1, Foxboro, MA 02035.

MOXLEY, FRANK O.
Human resources executive. **Personal:** Born Jun 29, 1908, Bowling Green, KY; son of Hester Moxley and James Moxley; married Pearlee Goodbar, Sep 21, 1946; children: Donald, Shirley, Mary. **Educ:** Wilberforce Univ, BS 1930; Western KY Univ, MA 1959; E Coast Univ, EdD 1973. **Career:** US Steel Gary Works, 1940-42; Blue Label Foods, 1946-56; State St Sch, tchr coach 1931-55; High St Sch, coach 1956-65; Bowling Green High, counselor 1965-66; Western KY Univ, 1967-72; Bowling Green Schs, elem guidance 1967-72; Human Resource Consult Inc, pres. **Orgs:** Mem Amer Personnel & Guidance Assn; Proj Indy 1977; KY Personnel & Guidance Assn; 3rd Dist Personnel & Guidance Assn; Elem Sch Counselor Assn; Natl, KY, 3rd Dist, Educ Assns; Phi Delta Kappa; Kappa Alpha Psi; St Health Facilities Comm; Girls Club Bd; TB Bd; exec bd, sec Model City; Whitehouse Conf for Children & Yth; pilot Secondary Guidance Prog 1958-59; past chmn seven county OEO prog; rules comm KHHSAA; Natl Negro Basketbl Assn; chmn 1986-, bd chairman 1988-90, Cumberland Trace Legal Service; NAACP, Basketball Coach, 1996. **Honors/Awds:** Hank Titino Award, Human Rights; NAACP, Merit Award; NAAP, Elizabeth Edmonds Award; Kiwanis, Leadership Award; Kentucky Client Council, Merit Award. City Recreation Ctr, named Coach F O Moxley Ctr; Cumberland Track Legal Svc; Taylor Chapel Ame Church, 50 year Award. **Military Serv:** ROTC AUS Reserve 2nd lt. **Home Addr:** 303 Chestnut St, Bowling Green, KY 42101.

MOYLER, FREEMAN WILLIAM, JR.
Manager. **Personal:** Born Dec 10, 1931, New York, NY; married Aline Veronica; children: Stephanie, Joy. **Career:** NY Times, assoc labor relations mgr 1971-75, dir genl serv 1979, bldg mgr 1975-79, asst dir genl serv 1979, mgr 1973-. **Orgs:** Mem NY Times Found Inc 1971; bd dir Capital Formation Inc 1977; mem bd dir Cncl of Concerned Black Exec 1968-75. **Honors/Awds:** Achievement Awd Natl Youth Movement 1973; Hon MLK 1977. **Military Serv:** USAF 1951-55. **Business Addr:** Manager, New York Times, 229 W 43 St, New York, NY 10036.

MOYO, YVETTE JACKSON
Publishing executive. **Personal:** Born Dec 8, 1953, Chicago, IL; daughter of Pauline Jackson and Rudolph Jackson; children: Rael Hashiem. **Educ:** Eastern IL Univ, BS 1974. **Career:** Black United Fund, local convention coord 1976-77; Natl Publ Sales Agency, account exec 1977-79, sales mgr 1979-81, vp, dir of sales 1981-84, sr vice pres director of sales 1984-88; Resource Associates International, president 1988-. **Orgs:** Life subscriber NAACP 1985; mem Oper PUSH 1987, League of Black Women 1987. **Honors/Awds:** Black Achievers Awd YMCA 1983; Kizzy Awd Black Women's Hall of Fame 1985.

MSHONAJI, BIBI. See BELLINGER, MARY ANNE.

MTOTO, PEPO. See PRIESTER, JULIAN ANTHONY.

MUCKELROY, WILLIAM LAWRENCE
Attorney. **Personal:** Born Dec 4, 1945, Los Angeles, CA; son of Josie Muckelroy and John Muckelroy; divorced; children: William II, Heather. **Educ:** Univ Texas, BA 1967; Amer Univ, MS 1970, JD 1974. **Career:** Prothon Cyber Ltd, dir/pres; Riggs Liquor, dir/pres; Iram Amer Investments Ltd, dir/pres/chmn of bd; Amer Univ, teaching asst; Harry Diamond Labs WA, patent adv; RCA Corp, patent counsel; Muckelroy & Assoc, patent atty; Litton Industries, div patent & licensing counsel, 1977-78; US Patent Soc Inc, patent counsel. **Orgs:** Past pres Intl Soc for Hybrid Microelectronics Capital Chapt; pres elect dir Natl Patent Law Assn; mem NJ, Amer Bar Assns; trustee Montclair State Coll; dir Trenton Bus Asst Corp. **Honors/Awds:** 7 patents granted; Fellowship Wash Coll Law Amer Univ; Teaching Fellowship Amer Univ; Honors Univ TX 1963-64; Alpha Phi Alpha Scholarship; NSSFNS Scholarship; Lawrence D Bell Scholarship; trustee, Montclair State College, Governor of NJ, 1982-88. **Business Addr:** Patent Counsel, US Patent Soc Inc, Ewing Professional Bldg, 1901 N Olden Ave, Ext, Trenton, NJ 08618.

MUDD, LOUIS L.
Marketing specialist. **Personal:** Born Jul 29, 1943, Louisville, KY; married Marcella; children: Latonya, Darron, Bryan. **Educ:** TN St U, BS. **Career:** KY Commerce Cabinet, sr bus devel off; Brown & Williamson Tobacco Corp Louisville KY, asst to prof planning mgr; Kool Cigarettes, former asst brand mgr. **Business Addr:** 1600 W Hill St, Louisville, KY 40201.

MUHAMMAD, ABDUL-RASHEED
Chaplain. **Personal:** Born Dec 23, 1952, Buffalo, NY; son of Josephine & Randy Maxwell; married Saleemah R, May 24, 1978; children: Hamzah, Halimah, Hasan, Husayn, Haneef, Hedayah, Haroon. **Educ:** SUC of NY at Brockport, BS, anthropology, 1977; San Diego St Univ, MS, counseling ed, 1979; Univ of MI, School of Social Work, MSW, 1990. **Career:** San Diego St Univ, academic counselor, 1977-79; County of San Diego, job devt/counselor, 1979-82; US Army, chaplin's asst, 1982-85; Catherine McCauley Hospital, mental health therapist, 1986-91; Beyer Hospital, chemical dep therapist, 1987-91; Dept of Corrections, State of NY, chaplain, 1992-93; US Army, chaplain, 1994-. **Orgs:** Umoja, vp, 1976-77; Aztec Club, 1977-79; Muslim Community Assn, sec, 1987-89; NASBSW, 1990-; EAPA, 1988-89. **Honors/Awds:** Huron Valley Correctional Facility for Women, Certificate of Appreciation, 1988; Albion Correctional facility for Women; Plaque of Appreciation, 1993; Newark Mosque of Al-Islam, Plaque of Appreciation, 1994. **Special Achievements:** Selected as the nation's first Islamic clergy in US Armed Forces, 1993. **Military Serv:** US Army, captain, 1982-85, 1993-; Good Conduct Medal. **Business Phone:** (910)396-6178.

MUHAMMAD, ASKIA
Journalist. **Personal:** Born Mar 28, 1945, Yazoo City, MS; married Alverda Ann Muhammad; children: Nadirah I, Raafi. **Educ:** San Jose State Univ, 1966-70; Los Angeles City Coll, 1965; Los Angeles State Univ, 1963. **Career:** Newsweek Mag, corr 1968; Multi-Cult Prog Foothill Coll, dir 1970-72; Muhammad Speaks News, edit-in-chief 1972-75; Chicago Daily Defender, WA corr 1977-78; Black Journalism Review, founder, Pacifica Radio Natl News Bureau, diplomatic corr 1978-79, reporter 1979-80; Natl Scene Mag, editor 1978-80; Natl Public Radio, commentator, 1980-93; The WPFW Paper, editor; WPFW, news director, 1991-93, program director, 1994; Christian Science Monitor Radio, 1993-; The Final Call Newspaper, White House correspondent & Washington bureau chief, 1996-. **Orgs:** Mem Natl Press Club, Sigma Delta Chi, Washington Automotive Press Association, Capital Press Club, Natl Assn of Black Journalists, Soc of Professional Jrnl. **Honors/Awds:** Fred Douglass Awd Howard Univ School of Comm 1973; Annual Awd Fred Hampton Comm Serv Awd 1975; Outstanding Journalism Achievement Awd Natl Conf Black Lawyers 1977, Univ DC 1979; DuPont-Columbia Journalism Award, 1990; President's Award, Washington Assn of Black Journalists, 1993; DC Mayor's Award for Excellence in Service to the Arts, 1994. **Military Serv:** USNR e-4 (ocs) 1963-70. **Business Addr:** Editor, Black Journalism Review, PO Box 570, Washington, DC 20044-0570.

MUHAMMAD, BENJAMIN CHAVIS
Talk show host, cleric, former association executive. **Personal:** Born Jan 22, 1948, Oxford, NC; children: six. **Educ:** Univ of NC, BA, 1969; Duke Univ Divinity School, master's; Howard Univ, PhD, theology. **Career:** United Church of Christ, Commission for Racial Justice, dir, beginning 1972 , minister, 1972-, deputy dir, exec dir, currently, so dir, Comm Org; political prisoner, NC, 1976-80; NAACP, executive director, 1993-94; WOL-AM, Washington, DC, talk show host, 1995-. **Orgs:** AFSCME, labor organizer, 1969; Southern Christian Leadership Conf, civil rights organizer, 1967-69; Natl Alliance Against Racism & Political Repression, co-chm, 1977-; So Organizing Comm for Econ and Social Justice, co-chm, 1977; Natl Council of Churches, VP, Prophetic Justice Unit, chairman; Southern Organizing Committee for Economic and Social Justice, chairperson; Angola Foundation, pres; Washington Office on Africa, pres of the bd. **Honors/Awds:** Author, Let My People Go-Psalms from Prison, 1977; George Collins Comm Service award, Congressional Black Caucus, 1977; William L Patterson Award, Patterson Foundation, 1977; Shalom Award, Eden Theological Seminary, 1977; Gertrude E Rush Distinguished Service Award, Natl Bar Assn; J E Walker Humanitarian Award, Natl Business League; Martin Luther King, Jr Freedom Award, Progressive Natl Baptist Convention. **Special Achievements:** Author, An American Political Prisoner, Appeals for Human Rights, United Church of Christ Commission on Racial Justice, 1979; Author, Psalms From Prison, Pilgrim Press, 1983. **Business Addr:** Top Aide, Nation of Islam, 7351 S. Stony Island Ave., Chicago, IL 60649.

MUHAMMAD, CONRAD
Speaker. **Career:** Nation of Islam, national student and youth spokesman, New York rep for Minister Louis Farrakhan; runs elementary school. **Business Addr:** National Youth Spokesman, Nation of Islam #7, 106-8 West 127th st., New York, NY 10029, (212)865-1200.

MUHAMMAD, M. AKBAR
Sports executive. **Personal:** Born Apr 16, 1951, Edenton, NC; son of Ida Mae Morris Perry and Collar Lee Perry; married Juana Hart-Muhammad, Dec 11, 1987; children: Akbar, Sabbiyah, Kelli, Mechele. **Educ:** Essex College of Business, Newark, NJ, 1970-72. **Career:** Shabazz Restaurant, Newark, NJ, co-owner, 1971-74; Cornerstone Enterpirses, Newark, NJ, co-owner, secretary-treasurer, 1975-79; Top Rank Inc, Las Vegas, NV, senior vice president, 1979-. **Orgs:** Board member, Project Pride, Newark, NJ, 1978-; member, American Muslim Mission, Las Vegas, NV, 1967-. **Honors/Awds:** Man of the Year, Ralph Grant Civic Assn, NJ, 1984; America's Best and Brightest, Dollars and Sense Magazine, 1989. **Home Addr:** 6718 Turina Rd, Las Vegas, NV 89102.

MUHAMMAD, MUHSIN, II
Professional football player. **Personal:** Born May 5, 1973, Lansing, MI; married Christa; children: Jordan Taylor. **Educ:** Michigan State. **Career:** Carolina Panthers, wide receiver, 1996-. **Business Addr:** Professional Football Player, Carolina Panthers, 800 Mint St, Ericsson Stadium, Charlotte, NC 28202, (704)358-7000.

MUHAMMAD, SHIRLEY M.
President. **Personal:** Born Apr 28, 1938, Chicago, IL; married Warith Deen Muhammad; children: Laila, Ngina, Warithdeen, Sadrud-Din. **Educ:** Attended, Cortez Peters Business Coll 1957, Wilson Jr Coll 1958. **Career:** Clara Muhammad Memorial Fund, pres 1976-. **Orgs:** Pres CMMEF 1976-; bd of dirs Parkway Comm House 1982, Provident Hosp 1983. **Honors/Awds:** Outstanding Woman of the Year Provident Women's Aux 1982-; Outstanding Business Woman Parkway Comm House 1982-83; Appreciation Awd Masjid Saahin Jr Youth 1984; Key to the City Newark NJ 1987. **Home Addr:** 8752 So Cornell, Chicago, IL 60617. **Business Addr:** President, Clara Muhammad Memorial, Education Foundation Inc, 634 E 79th St, Chicago, IL 60619.

MUHAMMAD, VALENCIA
Author. **Personal:** Born in Dennison, TX; married. **Career:** Author, currently. **Orgs:** Urban League; NAACP; DC Students Coalition Against Apartheid and Racism, board of directors; DC Board of Education, 1993-. **Honors/Awds:** African-American Women of Distinction Award, 1991. **Business Phone:** (202)387-0404.

MUHAMMAD, WALLACE D. (WARITH DEEN MUHAMMAD)
Chief minister, Muslim leader. **Personal:** Born Oct 30, 1933, Hamtramck, MI; married Shirley; children: Laila, N'Gina, Wallace II, Sadrud-Din. **Educ:** Muhammad Univ of Islam, vocational training in welding. **Career:** Son of Elijah Muhammad; Philadelphia Temple, minister; Arabic & Islamic studies; leader of the American Muslim Mission (formerly World Community of Al-Islam in the West, formerly Nation of Islam and the Black Muslims). **Orgs:** Made pilgrimage to Mecca 3 times. **Honors/Awds:** Recip four Freedom Awards; Pioneer Award from Black Press; Humanitarian Awards from many cities & groups. **Business Addr:** MACA Fund, PO Box 1061, Calumet City, IL 60409.

MUHAMMAD, WARITH DEEN. See MUHAMMAD, WALLACE D.

MULDROW, JAMES CHRISTOPHER
Librarian, educator. **Personal:** Born Dec 17, 1945, Washington, DC; son of Josephine Cain Muldrow and James Walter Muldrow. **Educ:** Institute of African Studies University of Ghana at Legon, Accra, GH, 1971; Federal City College, Washington, DC, BA, history, 1973, MLS, 1975; Harvard University Graduate School of Education, Cambridge, MA, 1987-88. **Career:** Department of Education Government of US Virgin Islands, St Croix, VI, librarian/media specialist, 1977-80; World Hunger Education Service, Washington, DC, cataloguer, 1984-86; Washington Metro Area Transit Authority, Facilities Maintenance Office, Washington, DC, technical librarian, 1980-83; Washington Metro Area Transit Authority, Public Affairs Office, Washington, DC, librarian/public info specialist, 1983-87; DC Public Schools, Washington, DC, program coordinator, 1990-, library media specialist, 1994-. **Orgs:** Member, American Library Association, 1980-; member, Society for Intercultural Education Training and Research, 1981-; member, Society for International Development, 1981-; board member, Washington Chapter of Americans for Democratic Action (ADA), 1990-. **Honors/Awds:** Harvard Grant, American Library Association, 1980-; Experiment in International Living, Semester in Ghana, 1971; The Contribution of the African-American Soldier in the US Military from the Colonial Period thru the Vietnam War Era: An Annotated bibliography, US Army Walter Reed Institute of Research, 1972; book review for The Information, Virgin Islands Bureau for Libraries, Museums and Archaeological Services, 1977-80.

MULEY, MIRIAM
Marketing executive. **Personal:** Born Oct 3, 1954, New York, NY; daughter of Margaret & Ramon; children: Jasmine Forbes, Khayyam Forbes, Destinee Forbes. **Educ:** Marymount Manhattan College, BA, 1972; Columbia Grad School of Business, MBA, 1978. **Career:** Frito-Lay; Johnson & Johnson; Nestle/Beechnut, brand manager; Uniworld Group, vice pres/acct supervisor; Clairol, product manager; AVON, general manager; Carson Inc, executive vice pres of mktg, currently. **Honors/Awds:** Kizzy Awd; Black Achiever Awd, Top 10 Women in Advertising/Mktg. **Business Addr:** Executive Vice Pres, Mktg, Carson Inc, 64 Ross Rd, Savannah, GA 31405.

MULLEN, RODERICK
Professional football player. **Personal:** Born Dec 5, 1972, Baton Rouge, LA; married Deneca; children: Meagan, Roderick II. **Educ:** Grambling State, BS in criminal justice. **Career:** Green Bay Packers, defensive back, 1995-. **Business Addr:** Professional Football Player, Green Bay Packers, 1265 Lombardi Ave, Green Bay, WI 54304, (414)494-2351.

MULLENS, DELBERT W.
Business executive. **Personal:** Born Nov 14, 1944, New York, NY; son of Edythe J Mullens; married Lula Sweat Mullens; children: Dorian, Mandy. **Educ:** TN State Univ, Nashville, TN, BS, 1968; Univ of NY, Buffalo, NY, MS, 1974. **Career:** Flint Coatings, Inc, Flint, MI, chief executive, 1983-. **Orgs:** Omega Psi Phi Fraternity, 1965-; pres, Natl Assn of Black Automotive Suppliers, 1990-; sr mem, Society of Manufacturing Engineers, 1984-. **Honors/Awds:** Business of the Year, Black Enterprise Magazine, 1991; Business of the Year, Natl Minority Business Devt Council, 1990; Business of the Year, MI Minority Business Devt Council, 1990. **Military Serv:** US Air Force, Lt, 1968. **Business Addr:** CEO/President, Wesley Industries Inc, 4221 James P Cole Blvd, Flint, MI 48505.

MULLETT, DONALD L.
Educational administrator. **Personal:** Born Apr 10, 1929, New York, NY; son of Josephine Reid Mullett; married Mildred James; children: Barbara L, Donna M King, David R James, Lisa J James. **Educ:** Lincoln Univ, AB 1951; New York Univ, MBA 1952; Univ of DE, PhD 1981. **Career:** United Mutual Life Insurance Co, vice pres & sec 1954-62; Equitable Life Assurance Soc, cost analyst 1962-63; Lincoln Univ, comptroller 1963-69, vice pres for finance 1969-89, interim pres 1985-87; Texas Southern University, Houston, TX, vice president finance, 1989-90; Jarvis Christian College, Hawkins, TX, vice president for fiscal affairs, 1990-93; Cheyney University of Pennsylvania, vice pres, business affairs, 1993-. **Orgs:** Mem Omega Psi Phi Frat Inc 1948; mem & trustee Rotary Intl 1969-; mem New York Univ Club 1981-; dir Pan African Develop Corp DC 1981-89; dir Urban Educ Foundation of Philadelphia 1983-89; dir & treas Lincoln Univ Foundation 1986-89; trustee, Oakwood College, 1984-; director, Unity National Bank, 1990-; director, Comunmity Music Center of Houston, 1989-90. **Honors/Awds:** Achievement Awd Omega Psi Phi Frat 1969; Distinguished Alumnus Award, Lincoln University, Pennsylvania, 1991. **Military Serv:** US Army Finance Corps, S/sgt, 1952-54. **Home Addr:** PO Box 1070, Pearland, TX 77588-1070. **Business Addr:** Vice President for Business Affairs, Cheyney University of Pennsylvania, Cheyney, PA 19319.

MULLINGS, PAUL
Financial company executive. **Career:** First Interstate Mortgage Co, pres, currently. **Business Addr:** President, First Interstate Mortgage Co, 1200 W 7th St, #MS-2-28, Los Angeles, CA 90017-2361, (818)356-7600.

MULLINS, JARRETT R.
Company executive. **Personal:** Born Nov 16, 1957, South Bend, IN; son of Ralph & Mary Mullins; married Kathy; children: Kevin, John. **Educ:** Auburn University, BS, 1980. **Career:** Federal Express Corp, senior manager, cust svc, 1984-88; US Sprint, group mgr sales, 1988-91; Purator Courier, managing dir, cust svc & sales, 1991-93; TLI, dir, cust svc, 1993-94; Zenith Electronics, vp/sales, 1994-. **Orgs:** Kappa Alpha Psi; National Assn of Minorities in Cable; CTAM. **Business Phone:** (708)391-7000.

MUMFORD, ESTHER HALL
Researcher, writer, publisher. **Personal:** Born Jan 20, 1941, Ruston, LA; daughter of Nona Mae Hall and Shellie O Hall; married Donald Emerson Mumford; children: Donald Toussaint, Zola Marie. **Educ:** Southern University, 1958-59; Univ of Washington, BA, 1963. **Career:** Washington State Archives, oral history interviewer; Ananse Press, co-publisher, writer/researcher, 1980-, managing editor; Office of Archaeology & History Preservation, researcher; King County Historic Preservation Office, oral history interviewer; Washington Commission for the Humanities, lecturer; Yesler Terrace Comm Council, outreach worker; associate curator, Museum of History & Industry; Douglass-Truth Library, African American Museum, Tacoma; project consultant, State Centennial Exhibitions; lecturer, African Americans in the Northwest. **Orgs:** Black Heritage Society of Washington State, founding member; Natl Trust for Historic Preservation; Assn of King Co Historical Organiza-

tions; Episcopal Women's History Project; Raven Chronicles, board of directors; Seattle Archdiocesan Historical Commission; Festvial Sundiata Program Committee. **Honors/Awds:** Aspasia Pulakis Award, Ethnic Heritage Council of the NW; Washington Living Treasure, Washington State Centennial Commission; Peace and Friendship Medal, Washington State Capital Museum; Award for Outstanding Scholarly Achievement in Black Studies, Natl Council For Black Studies, Pacific NW Region; Voices of Kuumba Award, NW African American Writers Workshop; Seattle Heritage Award, Museum of History & Industry; Certificate of Recognition for Preservation of King County, WA, History, Association of King County Historial Organizations. **Special Achievements:** Publications: Seattle's Black Victorians: 1852-1901; Seven Stars and Orion: Reflections of the Past, editor; The Man Who Founded A Town; Calabash: A Guide to the History, Culture & Art of African-Americans in Seattle and King County. **Business Addr:** Editor, Ananse Press, PO Box 22565, Seattle, WA 98122-0565, (206)325-8205.

MUMFORD, JEFFREY CARLTON
Composer, educator. **Personal:** Born Jun 22, 1955, Washington, DC; son of Thaddeus Q and Sylvia J Mumford; married Donna Coleman, Nov 16, 1985; children: Blythe Coleman-Mumford. **Educ:** Univ of California, Irvine, BA, 1977; Univ of California, San Diego, MA, 1981. **Career:** Settlement Music School, theory, comp instructor, 1985-89; Westchester Conservatory of Music, theory instructor, 1986-89; Washington Bach Consort, asst dir, 1989-90; Washington Conservatory of Music, theory, comp instructor, 1989-; Concert Society at Maryland, seminar coord, production supvr, 1990-95. **Orgs:** League of Composers, ISCM, US Chapter, bd of dirs, 1990-. **Honors/Awds:** Grants: Guggenheim Foundation, 1995-96; DC Commission on the Arts & Humanities, 1992-94; Meet the Composer/Arts Endowment Commissioning Music USA, 1996; DC Commission on the Arts & Humanities, Technical Assistance Program, The Minnesota Composers Forum, 1985-86; Martha Baird Rockefeller Fund for Music Inc, 1979, 1981; AASCAP Foundation, 1979; ASCAP Aaron Copland Scholarship, 1981; Natl Black Art Festival, Atlanta Symphony Orchestra Composition Competition, winner, 1994. **Special Achievements:** Commissions include: Reston Preludes Festival, 1997; Meet the Composer/Arts Endowment Commissioning, 1996; Natl Symphony Orchestra, 1995; Cincinnati radio station, WGUC, 1994; cellist, Joshua Gordon, 1994; Walter W Naumburg Foundation, 1991; Roanoke Symphony Orchestra, 1991; Fromm Music Foundation, 1990; Amphion Foundation for the Da Capo Chamber Players, 1989; McKim Fund in the Library of Congress, 1986; Works performed both in the US and abroad including: London's Purcell Rm; Finland's Helsinki Festival; Musica nel Nostro Tempo Festival; Atlanta Symphony Orchestra; St Paul Chamber Orchestra; American Composer's Orchestra; Group for Contemporary Music; recording included on Bang On A Can Live, Vol 2, the focus of blue light, and Dark Fires. **Business Addr:** Composer, c/o Jecklin Associates, 2717 Nichols Lane, Davenport, IA 52803, (319)359-0866.

MUMFORD, THADDEUS QUENTIN, JR.
Writer, producer. **Personal:** Born Feb 8, 1951, Washington, DC; son of Sylvia J Mumford and Dr Thaddeus Q Mumford. **Educ:** Hampton Univ, 1968-69; Fordham Univ, 1969-71. **Career:** 20th Century Fox, Los Angeles CA, writer, producer, "MASH," 1979-83; Alien Productions, Los Angeles CA, writer, supervising producer, "ALF," 1986-87; Carsey-Werner, Studio City CA, writer, supervising producer, "A Different World," 1987-88, head writer, co-executive producer, 1988-90; CBS Entertainment, "Bagdad Cafe," head writer, co-exec producer, 1990. **Orgs:** Writers Guild of Amer, 1971-; American Society of Composers, Artists & Performers, 1973-; Humanitas Committee, 1984; mem, NAACP, 1984; mem, Save the Children, 1986-; mem, Friends of the Friendless, 1986-; mem, Los Angeles Partnership for the Homeless, 1986-. **Honors/Awds:** Emmy Award, "The Electric Co," 1973; Writers Guild Award, "The Alan King Show," 1974, Writers Guild Award, "MASH," 1979.

MUMPHREY, JERRY WAYNE
Professional baseball player (retired). **Personal:** Born Sep 9, 1952, Tyler, TX; married Gloria; children: Tamara, Jerron. **Career:** St Louis Cardinals, outfielder 1974-79; San Diego Padres, outfielder 1980; New York Yankees, outfielder 1981-83; Houston Astros, outfielder 1983-85; Chicago Cubs, outfielder, 1986-88. **Honors/Awds:** Had a string of 27 consecutive stolen bases, 1980; National League All-Star Team, 1984.

MUNDAY, CHERYL CASSELBERRY
Clinical psychologist. **Personal:** Born Jan 20, 1950, Osaka, Japan; married Reuben Alexander Munday; children: Reuben Ahmed. **Educ:** Cornell Univ, BA 1972; Univ of MI, MA 1978, PhD 1985. **Career:** Detroit Psychology Institute, dir of psychology, private practice, Farmington Hills; Sinai Hospital, consultant/faculty; Univ of Detroit Mercy, asst prof, psychology. **Orgs:** Mem MI Soc for Psychoanalytic Psychology, American Psychological Association; Michigan Psychological Association. **Business Addr:** 37923 W 12 Mile Rd, Farmington Hills, MI 48331.

MUNDAY, REUBEN A.
Attorney. **Career:** Lewis, White, and Clay, attorney, partner, currently. **Business Addr:** Partner, Lewis, White & Clay Law Firm, 1300 First National Bldg, Detroit, MI 48226, (313)961-2550.

MUNOZ, ANTHONY (MICHAEL ANTHONY)
Professional football player. **Personal:** Born Aug 19, 1958, Ontario, CA; married DeDe; children: Michael, Michelle. **Educ:** University of Southern California, BS, public administration, 1980. **Career:** Cincinnati Bengals, tackle 1980-93; Tampa Bay Buccaneers, 1993-. **Orgs:** Crusade for Life; United Appeal. **Honors/Awds:** Cincinnati Bengals Man of the Year, 1981; All-Pro Offensive Tackle, 3 years; played in Pro Bowl, 1981, 1983-86; 1988; 1989; NFL Lineman of the Yr 1981. **Business Addr:** Professional Football Player, Tampa Bay Buccaneers, 1 Buccaneer Pl, Tampa, FL 33607, (813)870-2700.

MUNSON, CHERYL DENISE
Greeting card company executive. **Personal:** Born Aug 3, 1954, Milwaukee, WI; daughter of Mattie Waldon Munson and John Munson. **Educ:** University of Wisconsin, Madison, WI, BA, journalism, 1975. **Career:** Leo Burnett Advertising, Chicago, IL, intern, 1975; Kloppenberg, Switzer & Teich Advertising, Milwaukee, WI, writer/producer, 1976-80; Foote, Cone & Belding Advertising, San Francisco, CA, copywriter, 1980-84; Love Auntie Cheryl Greetings Inc, San Francisco, CA, CEO, founder, 1984-. **Orgs:** Member, Greeting Card Assn of America, 1985; member, Third Baptist Church, 1980-. **Honors/Awds:** Outstanding Business Woman, Governor, State of California, 1989; Outstanding Alumnus, University of Wisconsin, 1984. **Business Addr:** CEO, Love Auntie Cheryl Greetings Inc, PO Box 15000, Dept 314, San Francisco, CA 94115.

MUNSON, EDDIE RAY
Certified public accountant. **Personal:** Born Aug 4, 1950, Columbus, MS; son of Rosetta Moore Munson and Ray Munson; married Delores Butler, Jun 9, 1973; children: Eddie III, Derek. **Educ:** Jackson State Univ, BS 1972. **Career:** Peat Marwick Main & Co, partner 1972-, audit partner 1983-. **Orgs:** Mem, MS Soc of CPAs, 1977-, American Institute of CPAs, 1980-, MI Assn of CPAs, 1980-; bd dir, Accounting Aid Soc, 1984-, Black Family Development Inc, 1984-, Boys and Girls Clubs, 1989-; bd dir, YMCA, Detroit, MI; bd dir, Urban League, Detroit, MI; mem, Natl Assn of Black Accountants.

MUNSON, ROBERT H.
Engineer. **Personal:** Born Jan 15, 1931, Detroit, MI; married Shirley C Segars; children: Renee Angelique, Rochelle Alicia. **Educ:** Detroit Inst of Tech, BS 1966; MI State Univ, MBA 1977. **Career:** Ford Scientific Lab, metallurgical engr, 1956; Ford Motor Co, materials design engr, section supvr front end section, bumper section, body engineering office, dept mgr elec components lighting dept body and elec engrg ofc, exec engr paint corrosion and matls engrg body and elec engrg ofc, exec engr lighting bumpers and grills, exec engr advanced and preprog engrg, exec engr instrument panels and elec systems, chief engr North Amer design, chief plastics engr plastics products div, dir of automotive safety ofc environmental and safety engrg staff; Automotive Safety & Engrg Standards Ofc, executive director, currently. **Orgs:** Mem, Amer Soc of Body Eng; Amer Metals Soc; Ford Coll Recruiting Prog; Adv Bd Coll of Engr, Univ of Detroit; eng school sponsor, NC A&T State Univ; mem Engrg Soc of Detroit, Soc of Automotive Engrs; Motor Vehicle Safety Research, advisory committee. **Honors/Awds:** Recipt Blue Ribbon Award Amer Soc of Metals 1963; co-author tech paper A Modified Carbide Extraction Replica Technique in Transactions Qrtly 1963; co-author tech paper Metallographis Examination of the Corrosion Mechanism of Plated Plastics 1969 SAE Intl Automotive Engr Congress & Exposition in Detroit; life mem, NAACP. **Business Addr:** Executive Director, Automotive Safety Engrg Standards Office, Fairlane Plaza South, 330 Town Center Drive, Dearborn, MI 48126.

MURDOCK, ERIC LLOYD
Professional basketball player. **Personal:** Born Jun 14, 1968, Somerville, NJ. **Educ:** Providence. **Career:** Utah Jazz, 1991-92; Milwaukee Bucks, guard, 1992-97; Miami Heat, 1997-. **Business Addr:** Professional Basketball Player, Miami Heat, 721 NW 1st Ave, Miami Arena, Miami, FL 33136, (305)577-4328.

MURDOCK, NATHANIEL H.
Associations executive. **Career:** National Medical Association, pres, currently. **Business Addr:** President, National Medical Association, 1012 10th St. NW, Washington, DC 20001, (202)347-1895.

MURDOCK, PATRICIA GREEN
Educator, educational administrator. **Personal:** Born Dec 12, 1949, Richmond, VA; daughter of Josephine Evelyn Green and William Green; married Hugh Murdock Jr; children: Elwin Michael, Patrice Michelle Cotman. **Educ:** Virginia Union University, BA, 1972; Virginia Commonwealth University, MSW, 1974; The American University, Washington DC, MSPR, 1980. **Career:** Virginia Union University, Richmond Virginia, director of practicum, director of urban studies, 1974-76; Natl Council of Negro Women-Operation Sisters United, natl resource developer, national director, national program/volunteer coordinator, 1977-81; Women's Ctr & Shelter of Greater Pittsburgh, community outreach coordinator, 1983-87; Community College of Allegheny County, Pittsburgh, adjunct sociology professor, 1988-89; Partnerships in Education, coordinator, open doors, 1991; La Roche College, director of public relations, adjunct professor, 1992-; Duquesne University, adjunct professor, 1995-. **Orgs:** National Council of Negro Women, pres, Pittsburgh section, 1989-92; YWCA Nominating Committee, 1992; American Wind Symphony Orchestra, board of directors, 1992; Myasthenia Gravis Association of Western PA, board of directors, 1991-; Public Relations Society of America, 1996; Pennsylvania Black Conference on Higher Education, 1993; Beginning with Books, bd of directors, 1996. **Honors/Awds:** Pennsylvania Council on the Arts, FAME Fellowship in Arts Management, 1989; Women in Communications, First Place Matrix Award, Annual Report category, 1987. **Special Achievements:** Co-authored a domestic violence training manual for nurses, 1986; co-authored National Council of Negro Women juvenile prevention article for "Vital Issues," 1978; Western Regional Committee Chair, Dr Martin Luther King Jr Youth Assembly, 1993. **Business Addr:** Assistant to the President for Community Relations, La Roche College, 9000 Babcock Blvd, Academic Hall, Rm 221, Pittsburgh, PA 15237-5898, (412)367-9299.

MURPHY, ALVIN HUGH
Business executive. **Personal:** Born Feb 22, 1930, Boston, MA; married Bobby Joan Tolbert; children: Marguerite Joan, Bernadette Joan, Annette Joan. **Educ:** The Cath Univ of Amer, BME 1951; Univ Santa Clara, MBA 1964. **Career:** Lockheed Missiles & Space Co Inc, prog engr; DeAnza College, instr 1969-; Lockheed Aircraft, assc engr 1951-54; US Naval Surface Weapon Center White Oak Silver Spring MD, mech engr 1955-59. **Orgs:** Mem Amer Soc of Mech Engrs; secr Reliability Stress Analysis & Failure Prevention Comm; mem Amer Def Prepardness Assc; past chmn Reliability Tech Section; mem exec bd Quality & Reliability Div Amer Soc for Quality Control; fellow grade prog chmn Reliability Div; mem bd dir San Jose Symphony Assc; reg prof engr fellow election Amer Soc for Quality Controls. **Business Addr:** PO Box 504, Sunnyvale, CA 94088.

MURPHY, CALVIN JEROME
Professional basketball player (retired). **Personal:** Born May 9, 1948, Norwalk, CT. **Educ:** Niagara Univ, Niagara University, NY, attended. **Career:** Guard: San Diego Rockets, 1970-71, Houston Rockets, 1971-83. **Honors/Awds:** NBA All-Rookie Team, 1971; NBA All-Star Game, 1979.

MURPHY, CHARLES A.
Physician/surgeon. **Personal:** Born Dec 29, 1932, Detroit, MI; son of Hazel C Robinson Murphy and Charles L Murphy; married Sandra Marie Scott Murphy, Jul 17, 1971; children: Charles A III. **Educ:** Wayne State Univ, 1953; Coll of Osteopathic Med and Surgery, DO 1957; Flint Osteopathic Hospital, Internship 1958. **Career:** Martin Place Hospital chief of staff 1964-65; Art Center Hospital, chief of staff 1971-73; Wayne County Osteopathic Assn, past pres 1977-79; Detroit Police Dept, sr police surgeon 1977-79; CA Murphy DO PC, physician surgeon 1958-; president, Michigan Assn of Osteopathic Physicians and Surgeons, 1987. **Orgs:** Bd mem Michigan Osteopathic Assn 1981-89; Michigan Osteopathic Medical Center 1972-; Omnicare Health Plan Org 1978-; clinical prof Michigan State Univ Coll Osteopathic Med 1973-; bd mem Michigan Peer Review Org 1985; House of Delelgate Amer Osteopathic Assn 1975-89; Michigan Osteopathic Assn 1970-; Osteopathic Rep Central Peer Review Comm Michigan Dept Health. **Honors/Awds:** Cert Amer Osteopathic Bd of Gen Prac 1973; Fellow Award Amer Coll Gen Prac 1974; mem Psi Sigma Alpha (Schlst Hnry Frat) 1955. **Business Addr:** President, CA Murphy DO Professional Corp, 12634 E Jefferson, Detroit, MI 48215.

MURPHY, CHARLES WILLIAM
Insurance company executive. **Personal:** Born Dec 6, 1929, Kinston, NC; son of Blanche Burden Murphy and Edgar D Murphy, Sr; married Geneva McCoy, Aug 9, 1954; children: Charles Jr, Donald Seth, Deanna Faye, Bryan Keith. **Educ:** NC A&T State Univ, Greensboro, NC, BS, bio science/chemistry, 1954; Butler Univ, Indianapolis, IN, 1968-69. **Career:** City-County Govt, Indianapolis, IN, mgmt analyst, 1974-75; Indianapolis Life Insurance Co, Indianapolis, IN, vice pres office admin, 1975-89. **Orgs:** Personnel dir, Indianapolis Chapter Admin Mgmt Soc, 1975-80; subscribing life mem, Indianapolis Chapter NAACP, 1979-; basileus, Zeta Phi Chapter, Omega Psi Phi Fraternity, 1979-81; exec comm, Administrative Servs Comm Life Office Mgmt Assn, 1979-90; Econ Devel Comm, Indianapolis Chapter Urban League, 1984-87; bd of trustees, N United Methodist Church, 1985-89; mem, Indiana Minority Supplier Devel Council, 1985-90; volunteer action center, United Way Bd, 1988-; exec comm, Interfaith Housing Bd, 1988-92; Indianapolis Education Advisory Council, 1983-85; National Urban League Conference, Minority Vendors Showcase, chair, 1994. **Honors/Awds:** Achievement in Military, NC A&T State

Univ, 1974; Advancement of Minority Enterprises, Minority Supplier Devel Council, 1987, Achievement in Business, Center for Leadership Devel, 1988; Citizen of the Year, Indianapolis Chapter, Omega Psi Phi Fraternity, 1994. **Military Serv:** US Army, lt col, 1954-74. **Home Addr:** 412 Shallow Brook Dr, Columbia, SC 29223-8114.

MURPHY, CLYDE EVERETT
Attorney. **Personal:** Born Jun 26, 1948, Topeka, KS; son of Everett E Murphy; married G Monica Jacobs; children: Jamal Everett, Akua Edith, Naima Lorraine. **Educ:** Yale Coll New Haven, BA 1970; Columbia Univ Sch of Law NY, JD 1975. **Career:** Kings Co Addictive Disease Hosp, asst dir 1970-72; Vassar Coll, lectr 1981-84; NAACP Legal Defense & Educ Fund Inc, asst counsel 1975-90, deputy-dir counsel, 1990-95; Chicago Lawyers' Comm for Civil Rights Under Law, Inc., exec dir, 1995-. **Honors/Awds:** Charles Evans Hughes Fellow Columbia Univ Sch of Law 1973-75. **Business Addr:** Executive Director, Chicago Lawyers' Committee for Civil Rights Under Law, Inc., 100 N. LaSalle St., Ste. 600, Chicago, IL 60602.

MURPHY, DANIEL HOWARD
Marketing manager. **Personal:** Born Aug 13, 1944, Washington, DC; son of Alice Adeline Quivers Murphy and John Henry Murphy; married Bernadette Francine Brown Murphy, Feb 15, 1969; children: Brett Nicole, Lynn Teresa. **Educ:** Wharton School, University of Pennsylvania, Philadelphia, PA, BS, Economics, 1962-66. **Career:** McCormick Spice Co., Baltimore, MD, project supervisor of marketing research, 1966-70; General Foods, White Plains, NY, brand research supervisor, 1970-73; Hunt Wesson Foods, Fullerton, CA, product research manager, 1973-76; R.J. Reynolds Tobacco Company, Winston-Salem, NC, board research manager, 1976-80, brand manager, 1980-85, senior group marketing research manager, 1985-. **Orgs:** Board member, Winston Lake YMCA, 1988-; board of directors, Winston-Salem Tennis Inc, 1986-; member and grammateus, Sigma Pi Phi Fraternity, 1986-; member, Alpha Phi Alpha Fraternity, 1990-. **Business Addr:** Senior Manager of Communications Research, Business Information Dept., RJ Reynolds Tobacco Co, 401 N Main St, Winston-Salem, NC 27102.

MURPHY, DONALD RICHARD
Attorney. **Personal:** Born Aug 1, 1938, Johnstown, PA; married Carol Handy; children: Steven, Michael, Richard. **Educ:** Wilberforce Univ, BA Econ 1960; NY Law Schl, JD 1969. **Career:** IBM Corp, acct supr 1963-66; Chem Bank of NY, oper mgr 1966-69; Soc Natl Bank, vice pres 1969-73; Sherwin Williams Co, staff atty asst dir of labor rel 1973-83; atty at law. **Orgs:** Mem EEO Sub Comm Amer Bar Assn 1974-; bd dir Health Hill Hosp 1970-78; bd trustees United Way Srvs 1980-; Cleveland Comm OH Fnd for Independent Coll 1970-; adv mem United Negro Coll Fund 1974-82; Cuyahoga City Bar Assn 1972-. **Honors/Awds:** Distinguished Service Award, Outstanding Alumnus of Year Wilberforce Univ 1972; First Black recruited for IBM Mgmt and Training Course 1963. **Military Serv:** AUS 1st lt 1959-62; Grad Army Adj General Schl 1960. **Home Addr:** 2987 Ludlow Rd, Shaker Heights, OH 44120. **Business Addr:** Attorney, Forest City Enterprises, Inc, 10800 Brookpark Road, Cleveland, OH 44130-1199.

MURPHY, EDDIE (EDWARD REGAN)
Comedian, actor. **Personal:** Born Apr 3, 1961, Brooklyn, NY; son of Lillian Murphy and Charles Murphy; married Nicole Mitchell, Mar 18, 1993; children: Bria, Miles, Shayne Audra. **Career:** Stand-up comedian; Saturday Night Live, cast member, 1980-84; films: 48 Hours, 1982, Trading Places, 1983, Best Defense, 1984, Beverly Hills Cop, 1985, The Golden Child, 1986, Beverly Hills Cop II, 1987, Eddie Murphy Raw, 1987, Coming to America, 1988, Another 48 Hours, 1990, Harlem Nights, 1990; Boomerang, 1992; comedy albums: Eddie Murphy, 1982, Eddie Murphy:Comedian, 1983; music album, How Could It Be, 1984; appeared in Michael Jackson's video, Remember the Times, 1992. **Honors/Awds:** Emmy Award nomination for outstanding comedy performance and outstanding comedy writing, for "Saturday Night Live"; Grammy Award nomination for best comedy album, 1982; Image Award, NAACP, 1983; Golden Globe Foreign Press Award, 1983; Grammy Award for best comedy album, 1984; Golden Globe Award nomination for best actor, 1985; Star of the Year Award, 1985; People's Choice Award, 1985.

MURPHY, FRANCES L., II
Educator (retired), publisher. **Personal:** Born Oct 8, Baltimore, MD; daughter of Vashti Turley Murphy and Carl J Murphy; divorced; children: Frances Murphy Draper, Dr James E Wood Jr, Susan M Wood Barnes, David Campbell. **Educ:** Univ of WI Madison, BA 1944; Coppin State Coll, BS 1958; Johns Hopkins Univ, MEd 1963; Univ of Southampton England, Study Tour 1966. **Career:** Morgan State Coll, dir news bureau asst prof 1964-71; Afro Amer Newspapers, chmn bd, CEO 1971-74; Univ of MD Baltimore Cty, visiting prof 1974-75; State Univ Coll at Buffalo NY, lecturer to assc prof 1975-85; Howard Univ, visiting prof 1984-85; Washington Afro-Amer Newspaper, publisher 1986-; Howard Univ, assoc prof 1985-91. **Orgs:** Ex com mem bd dir Afro Amer Newspapers 1985-87; advisory bd Howard Univ Partnership Inst 1985-91; Crisis Magazine NAACP 1979-85; mem exec comm Md Study Comm on Structure and Governance of Educ 1973-75; natl bd dir NAACP 1983-85; bd trustees Spec Contribution Fund NAACP 1976-83, State Coll of MD 1973-75; mem MD Bicentennial Comm 1973-75; Capital Press Club; Sigma Delta Chi; Delta Sigma Theta; Links Inc. **Honors/Awds:** Ebony Mag 100 Most Influential Black Amer 1973-74; Fellowship Kiplinger Foundation 1980; SUC Buffalo Faculty Grant to write A Beginning Student's Guide to Word Star 1983; Ida Barnett Wells Award, Congressional Black Caucus, 1989; Distinguished Journalist, Imani Temple/AACC, 1991; Black Woman of Courage Award, National Federation of Black Women Business Owners, 1993; The Frances L Murphy II Communications Award, Fed City Alumnae Chap of Delta Sigma Theta Sorority, 1993; Black Awareness Achievement Award, Holy Redeemer Catholic Church, 1993; Outstanding Service Award, Capital Press Club, 1993; The Business of the Year Award, Bus & Prof Women's League, 1993; Black Conscious Comm Trophy, Unity Nation, 1993; Distinguished Service, Local Journalism Award, Washington, DC Chapter, Society of Prof Journalists, 1994; Women Communicators: Women of Strength Award, Natl Black Media Coalition, 1994; Outstanding Woman of the Year Award, Alpha Gamma Chapter, Iota Phi Lambda Sorority, 1994; The Art Ctr Award of Excellence, Capital Press Club, 1994. **Home Addr:** 5709 First Street NW, Washington, DC 20011, (202)291-7846. **Business Addr:** Publisher, Washington Afro-American Newspaper, 1612 14th St NW, Washington, DC 20009, (202)332-0080.

MURPHY, HARRIET LOUISE M.
Judge (retired). **Personal:** Born in Atlanta, GA; married Patrick H Murphy; children: Charles Wray. **Educ:** Spelman Coll, AB 1949; Atlanta Univ, Masters 1952; Johns Hopkins School, school of advanced int studies 1954; Univ of TX Law School, JD 1969; Univ of Gratz, Austria 1971. **Career:** Fulton Co, GA, hs tchr 1949-54; Southern Univ, tchr 1954-56; Prairie View A&M Univ, teacher 1956-60; Womack Sr High, high school teacher 1960-66; Houston-Tillotson Coll, prof of govt 1967-78; City of Austin, assoc judge 1978-88, presiding judge, 1988-94. **Orgs:** Mem Delta Sigma Theta Soror 1964-; bd mem Greater Austin Council on Alcoholism 1970-93; mem Links Inc 1982-; bd mem Judicial Council NBA; bd mem TX Municipal Courts Found; mem Natl Bar Assn, TX Bar Assn; bd-at-large Austin Black Lawyers Assn; mem J Travis Co Women Lawyers Assn; Travis County Bar Assn; financial sec, Judicial Council; fin sec, bd, Habitat for Humanity; Intl Hospital Council of Austin; appointed by chief judge of TX Supreme Ct, Gender Bias Implementation Task Force; former mem, Municipal Ct Foundation; charter mem, Austin Black Lawyers Assn. **Honors/Awds:** Appointed to two year term US State Dept Adv Council on African Affairs 1970; Outstanding Sorority Woman Delta Sigma Theta Sor 1974; first black woman to be appointed a permanent judge in TX 1974; first black woman democratic presidential elector for TX 1976; appointed Goodwill Ambassador State of TX 1976; most outstanding class member by class of Spelman Coll 1984; Thurgood Marshall Legal Socity, U T Award, 1986; Distinguished Service Chairman's Award, Greater Austin Council on Alcoholism, 1990; Judicial Council, 1987; DeWitty Award for Civil Rights, Austin NAACP, 1989; Spelman College Hall of Fame, 1993; Hall of Fame, Natl Women of Achievement, Austin Chap, 1996.

MURPHY, IRA H.
Attorney. **Personal:** Born Sep 8, 1928, Memphis; married Rubye L Meekins. **Educ:** TN State Univ, BS; City Clge of NY, atnd; NY Univ, grad sch bus; NY Univ Schl of Law, LLB, LLM. **Career:** Gen law prac 1956-; Riverside San & Hosp Nashville, acct; Geeter HS, commerce tchr. **Orgs:** State Rep 86, 87, 88, 89, 90, & 91st Gen Assem; chmn Labor Com House Rep 87th Gen Assem; chmn Jud Com House Rep 88, 89, 90 & 91st Gen Assem del Limited Constis Conv 1971; Mem Slpha Phi Alpha; Kappa Delta Pi; Elks; Masons; Shriners; past pres 26 Ward Civic Club; former legal adv Bluff City Coun Civic Clubs; legal adv IBPOE of W of TN. **Military Serv:** AUS.

MURPHY, JEANNE CLAIRE FULLER
Volunteer. **Personal:** Born Nov 7, 1929, Chicago, IL; daughter of Clarabelle Kellogg Fuller and Richard S Fuller; married Col Donald G Murphy (deceased); children: Judith C. **Educ:** Univ of Chicago, BA 1948; Eastern Michigan Univ, EdB 1949; Northwestern Univ, MA 1951; George Mason Univ, JD 1987-90. **Career:** Vol A Hy-Fairfax County VA, 1990-; Va/Fed Bars 1990-. **Orgs:** Bd dir Fairfax Red Cross; life mem GSCNC; life mem AKA Sor 1949-, OWL 1984-; bd of dirs Vol Action Ctr Fx Cty VA; mem BWUFA, NAACP, Urban League; mem Washington DC Metro Red Cross Consortium; mem ABA, VA State Bar, Fairfax County Bar Assn, 1990-. **Honors/Awds:** Thanks Badge/Adult Appreciation Pin GSUSA; Special Recognition Awd Red Cross; Volunteer Recognition Fairfax Cty VA; Gold Pin GS Assoc 54; American Jurisprudence Award, Lawyer's Cooperative Publishing, 1989. **Home Addr:** 8902 Queen Elizabeth Blvd, Annandale, VA 22003.

MURPHY, JOHN H., III
Business executive. **Personal:** Born Mar 2, 1916, Baltimore, MD; married Camay; children: Sharon, Daniel. **Educ:** Temple U, BS 1937; Collumia U, Press Inst, 1952, 1971. **Career:** Washington Tribune, mgr 1937-61; Washington Afro-Amer, purchasing agent, asst bus mgr, bus mgr, chmn bd of dir 1974-. **Orgs:** Mem Churchman's Club; standing comm Diocese of MD; vestryman St James Episcopal Church; adv bd Morgan State Univ; mem School of Business, Morgan State Univ Cluster Prog, Sigma Pi Phi, Omega Psi Phi; bd mem Amalgamated Publs Inc, Natl Newspaper Publs Assoc, Council on Equal Bus Oppty, Natl Aquarium at Baltimore, Provident Hospital, Baltimore School for the Arts, Baltimore City Literacy Commiss. **Honors/Awds:** City of Baltimore Citizen Awd 1977; Publisher of the Year Awd Univ of DC 1979; Father of the Year Awd Redeemer's Palace Baltimore MD 1980; Cert MD Comm on Sickle Cell Anemia 1980; US Dept of Commerce Awd 1980; Appreciation Awd Race Relations Inst Fisk Univ 1981; Disting Citizens Public Serv Awd Coppin State Coll 1983; Hon degree Doctor of Humane Letters Towson State Univ 1984. **Business Addr:** Chairman, Board of Dir, Afro-American Newspaper, 628 N Eutaw St, Baltimore, MD 21201.

MURPHY, JOHN MATTHEW, JR.
Dentist, president. **Personal:** Born Mar 12, 1935, Charlotte, NC; son of Elizabeth Benton Murphy and John Matthew Murphy Sr; married Claudette Owens Murphy, Jan 3, 1983; children: Alicia Williams, Snowden Williams, John Matthew III, Brian Keith. **Educ:** Morgan State Coll, BS 1959; MeHarry Med Coll School of Dentistry, DDS 1965; VA Hosp, Cert 1966. **Career:** Meharry Med Coll School of Dentistry, rsch assoc dept of orthodontics 1966; VA Center Dayton OH, staff dentist 1967-70; Charles Drew Health Ctr Dayton OH, clinical dir dentistry 1971-73; Metrolina Urban Health Initiative Charlotte NC, originator and co-founder 1979; Private practice, gen dentist 1973-. **Orgs:** Pres elect Dayton Hosp Mgmt Assoc 1970-73; mem Charlotte C of C 1975-; Charlotte Bus League 1979-; treas Martin Luther King Mem Comm 1976-; council comm chmn Boy Scouts of Amer 1978; mem Sigma Pi Phi 1980; member, board of trustees Little Rock AME Zion Church 1975-; member NC chapter Guardsmen 1983-; pres and founder A J Williams Dental Study Club 1985-; life member NAACP 1977-; life member Omega Psi Phi Fraternity 1978-. **Honors/Awds:** Scroll of Honor Omega Psi Phi 1970; Cert of Appreciation Boy Scouts of Amer 1972; Fellow Royal Soc of Health 1974-; Fellow Acad of Gen Dentistry 1980. **Military Serv:** AUS spec 4; 1959-61. **Business Addr:** Dentist, 700 E Stonewall St, Ste 325, Charlotte, NC 28202.

MURPHY, LAURA W.
Association executive. **Personal:** Born Oct 3, 1955, Baltimore, MD; daughter of Judge William H and Madeline Murphy; divorced; children: Bertram M Lee Jr. **Educ:** Wellesley Coll, AB, 1976. **Career:** Office of Congressman, Parren Mitchell, legislative asst, 1976-77; Office of Congresswoman, Shirley Chisholm, legislative asst, 1977-79; ACLU, legislativ rep, 1979-82, ACLU Foundation of Southern California, dir of devt & planning giving, 1983-84; Mixner Scott Inc, proj mgr, 1984-87; Assembly Speaker, Willie L Brown Jr, chief of staff, 1986-87; Jesse Jackson for President Campaign, natl finance dir, 1987-88; Fundraising consultant, 1988-90; Exec Office of Mayor Sharon Pratt Kelly, mayor's tourism consultant, 1990-92; DC Govt, Office of Tourism, dir, 1992-93; ACLU, Washington Office, dir, 1993-. **Orgs:** DC Committee to Promote Washington, acting chair, 1993-95; Leadership Conference on Civil Rights, executive committee, 1993-; Public Defenders Service of Washington, bd mem, 1993-95; numerous past memberships. **Honors/Awds:** Congressional Black Caucus, William L Dawson Award, 1997; Mayor Sharon Pratt Kelly, Distinguished Public Service Award, 1994; Capital Entertainment Services, Honorary Tour Guide for DC, 1992; NAACP Legal Defense and Educ Fund Inc, Black Women of Achievement Award, 1987; ACLU, Washington Office, Human Rights Award, 1982; State of Maryland, Citation for Public Service, 1980; numerous others. **Special Achievements:** First African American and first female director of ACLU. **Business Addr:** Director, American Civil Liberties Union, 122 Maryland Ave., NE, Washington, DC 20002, (202)675-2305.

MURPHY, MARGARET HUMPHRIES
Administrator, government official. **Personal:** Born in Baltimore, MD; married Arthur G Murphy (deceased); children: Terry M Bailey, Arthur G Jr, Lynn M Press. **Educ:** Coppin St Coll, BS 1952, ME; Morgan St Coll. **Career:** MD St, del 1978-95; Baltimore City Public School, educ assn 1978-, teacher 1952-78. **Orgs:** Public School Teachers Assn, 1952-; MD St Teachers Assn, 1952-; Natl Educ Assn; NAACP; Lambda Kappa Mu; Red Cross; sec, Leg Black Caucus; treas, Org of Women Legislators; Delta Sigma Theta; Forest Park Neighborhood Assn; chmn, Baltimore City Health Sub-Committee; bd mem, Threshold Inc. **Business Addr:** Delegate, Maryland General Assembly, 314 Lowe Bldg, Annapolis, MD 21401.

MURPHY, MICHAEL MCKAY
Recycling company executive. **Personal:** Born Aug 13, 1946, Fayetteville, NC; son of Eleanor McKay Murphy (deceased) and Charles L Murphy (deceased); married Gwendolyn Ferguson; children: L Mark. **Educ:** St Louis Univ, BS commerce 1964-68. **Career:** John Hancock Insurance Co, life underwriter 1968-71; Ford Motor Co, bus mgmt specialist 1971-75; Dunkin

Donuts, purchasing mgr 1975-79, dir of quality control beginning 1979-, director of consumer affairs; Renewal Inc, president, currently. **Orgs:** Canton, MA Board of Health, clerk, 1996; mem, Phi Beta Sigma Fraternity, Inc, Zeta Kappa Sigma Chapter, pres 1988-89; past pres, Blue Hill Civic Assn. **Honors/Awds:** Governor's Council, Republican, elected, 1990; Congressional Candidate, MA Dist 9, 1994. **Home Addr:** 8 Flintlocke Ln, Canton, MA 02021. **Business Addr:** President, Renewal, Inc, 100 Boylston St, No 300, Boston, MA 02116.

MURPHY, PAULA CHRISTINE
Librarian. **Personal:** Born Dec 15, 1950, Oberlin, OH; daughter of Vivian Chiquita Lane Murphy and Paul Onieal. **Educ:** Rosary College of Dominican Univ, River Forest, IL, BA, 1973, School of Library Science, MLS, 1975; Northern Illinois University, Dekalb, IL, MA, 1982. **Career:** Chicago Public Library, Chicago, IL, librarian I, 1974-76; Governor's Library State University, University Park, IL, circulation/media librarian, 1976-80; Columbia College Library, Chicago, IL, head of audiovisual services, 1980-89; Loyola University Libraries, Chicago, IL, head of audiovisual services; Dominican University, head of access services, currently. **Orgs:** Chair, Video Roundtable, Amer Lib Assn, 1997-98; chair, arts section, Association of College and Research Libraries of American Library Association, 1989-90; treasurer, Junior Members Roundtable of American Library Association, 1980-82; member, American Library Association Divisions & Roundtables, 1974-; member, Illinois Library Association, 1975-80; member, Black Caucus of American Library Assn, 1987-; chair, ACRL New Publications Advisory Bd, 1993-95; chair, ACRL Arts Dance Subcommittee on the Interlibrary Loan of Video, 1994-96; mem, ALA Elections Committee, 1994-96; exec bd mem, Amer Film & Video Assn, 1992-95. **Honors/Awds:** African-American Women's Achievement Award, African-American Alliance, 1989; Elected to Membership in Beta Phi Mu, 1973; 3M/JMRT Professional Development, 3M Company and JMRT; Grant, American Library Association, 1977; Speaker, Art Libraries Society NA and Consortium of College & University Media Centers, 1986, 1989; Judge, American Film Festival, 1989-92; Speaker, Charleston Conference on Book & Serial Acquisitions, 1991; Natl Conference of African Amer Librarians, 1994; Speaker 6th Biennial Symposium of Arts and Technology, 1997. **Special Achievements:** Author "Visual Literacy, Libraries & Community Development in Collection Building," March 1981; Films for the Black Music Researcher in Black Music Research Journal, Center for Black Music Research, 1987; "Documentation of Performance Art," Coll and Research Libraries News, Apr 1992; "Audio Visual Services for the Performing Arts Programs at Columbia Coll, Chicago," in Performing Arts Resources, Vol 15, 1990; Senior Advisory Viewing Race Project, 1997-. **Business Addr:** Head of Access Services, Dominican University, Loyola University Library, 25 E Pearson, Room 713, River Forest, IL 60305.

MURPHY, RAYMOND M.
State representative. **Personal:** Born Dec 13, 1927, St Louis, MO; married Lynette; children: Clinton, Krystal, Leslie, Raymond, Anita, James, Brandon, Alicia. **Educ:** Detroit Inst of Tech, Wayne State Univ, attended. **Career:** Michigan State House of Representatives, state representative, 1982-. **Orgs:** Mem Natl Black Caucus of State Legislators; lifetime mem NAACP; imperial grand cncl Ancient Arabic Orders; Nobles of the Mystic Shrine; mem MI Legislative Black Caucus; exec bd mem Detroit Transit Alternative; mem Metro Elks Lodge; mem Eureka Temple No 1. **Honors/Awds:** Legislator of the Year Minority Women Network 1987. **Home Addr:** 610 Chicago Blvd, Detroit, MI 48202. **Business Addr:** State Representative, Michigan State House of Representatives, State Capitol Bldg, Lansing, MI 48909.

MURPHY, RIC
Government official. **Personal:** Born Jul 17, 1951, Boston, MA; son of Joan Cornwall-Murphy and Robert H Murphy. **Educ:** Boston State Coll, BS 1973; Boston Univ Metro Coll, MBA 1976; Harvard Univ Kennedy School, Cert 1986. **Career:** City of Boston Public Schools, teacher 1973-76, team consult 1976-78, principal 1978-79, asst community supt 1979-82; Commonwealth of MA State Office of Affirmative Action, dir 1983-; Commonwealth of Massachusetts, Boston, MA, state purchasing agent 1987-; Commonwealth of Massachusetts, Boston, MA, dir state office of affirmative action 1983-87; Dept of Procurement & General Services, Boston, MA, commissioner, 1989-91; District of Columbia, dir, dept of administrative services, 1991-. **Orgs:** Bd mem NAACP Boston Chap 1978-; vice pres Fort Hill Civic Assoc 1983-; mem Piggy Bank 1984-; mem adv bd Gannett Publ WLVI Channel 56 1985-; mem bd dir New England Hosp 1985-. **Honors/Awds:** Outstanding Leadership Award MA House of Reps 1980; Outstanding Serv to Community Award NAACP 1980; Community Dist Adv Council Award 1981; Outstanding Community Service, Boston Chapter, National Conference of Christian and Jews 1987.

MURPHY, ROBERT L.
Educator. **Personal:** Born Dec 23, 1935, Kinston, NC; married Gloria Walters; children: Robyn Denise. **Educ:** NC Central Univ, 1962; NC Central Univ, addl study; E Carolina Univ, addl study. **Career:** Lenoir Co Bd of Educ, math lab coord; Phys Educ Coord; W Elm Jr HS Goldsboro, phys educ tchr & coach; Frederick Douglass HS Elm City; Lenoir Co Bd of Educ, Savannah Middle School, Grifton, NC, coach, math teacher, 1971-. **Orgs:** Mem NEA; NC Assc of Educators; AHPER; NC Athletic Officials Assc; mem Amer Leg; NC Central Univ Alumni Assc; Omega Psi Phi; Basilus Nu Alpha; trustee board, steward, chanel choir, men's club Emmanuel Hill Memorial FWB Church, 1980-; basilus Lambda Pi Chapter, Omega Psi Phi, 1988-90. **Honors/Awds:** Coach of the Year (basketball), Pitt-Greene-Lenoir Conference, 1987, 1988; Coach of the Year (basketball), Eastern Middle School Conference, 1989; Teacher of the Year, Savannah Middle School, 1990-91. **Military Serv:** AUS 1954-57. **Business Addr:** Coach, Math Teacher, Savannah Middle School, 2583 Cameron Langston Rd, Grifton, NC 28530.

MURPHY, ROMALLUS O.
Attorney, educator. **Personal:** Born Dec 18, 1928, Oakdale, LA; son of Mary Celeste Collins Murphy and Jimmy Murphy; married Gale L Bostic; children: Natalie, Kim, Romallus Jr, Lisa, Verna, Christian. **Educ:** Howard Univ, BA 1951; Univ NC, JD 1956. **Career:** Pvt law prac 1956-62; Erie Human Rel Commn, exec dir 1962-65; Mitchell & Murphy, 1965-70; Mayor's Comm Rel Committee, exec secr 1968; Shaw Univ, spec asst to pres 1968-70; Shaw Coll at Detroit, pres 1970-82; Gen Counsel NC State Conf of Branches NAACP; gen practice emphasis on civil rights; private practice, atty 1983-. **Orgs:** Mem Intermittent consult conciliator 1966-69; Amer Arbitration Assoc, Arbitrators & Community Dispute Settlement Panel, ACE, AAHE, NBL, NEA, Positive Futures Inc, Task Force Detroit Urban League Inc, NAACP; bd mem Metro Fund Inc; mem Central Governing Bd & Educ Com Model Neighborhood Agency; charter mem Regional Citizens Inc; mem Greensboro Task Force One; bd mem Good News Jail & Prison Ministry; trustee, sec trust bd Shiloh Baptist Church; pres Laymen's League Shiloh Baptist Church; mem Omega Psi Phi; bd mem Greensboro Br NAACP; mem Foreign Travel for Intl Commun Agency & other govt agencies in South Africa, Zambia, Nigeria & Kenya; partic Smithsonian InstTravel Seminar in India; mem NC Assn Amer Bar Assn, NC Black Lawyers Assn. **Honors/Awds:** Omega Man of the Year 1968; Detroit Howardite for Year Howard Univ Alumni 1974; Key to City Positive Futures Inc New Orleans 1974; Citizen of the Year Awd Omega Psi Phi 1977; Community Serv Awd Greensboro Br NAACP 1985; Tar Heel of the Week NC; Educator of the Year, Gamma Phi Delta Sorority, 1975; William Robert Ming Advocacy Award, NAACP, 1990. **Military Serv:** USAF 1st lt 1951-53. **Business Addr:** Attorney, PO Box 20383, Greensboro, NC 27420.

MURPHY, VANESSA
Ms Plus USA. **Career:** Model; Ms Plus USA, 1997. **Business Addr:** Ms Plus USA 1997, Ms Plus USA Beauty Pageant, c/o Dimensions Plus, 551 36th St NW, Canton, OH 44709, (330)649-9809.

MURRAIN, GODFREY H.
Attorney. **Personal:** Born Mar 14, 1927, New York, NY; son of Ellouise Pearl Jones Murrain and Walter Herbert Murrain; married Peggy Gray; children: Michelle Pearl. **Educ:** Howard Univ, attended 1948-49; NY Univ, BS 1951; Brooklyn Law Sch, LLB, JD 1955. **Career:** Treasury Dept, IRS agent 1953-58; Godfrey H Murrain Esq, atty counsellor at law tax consult advising & counseling indivudal corp estates 1958-. **Orgs:** Mem Amer Arbitration Assn, NY Co Lawyers Assn, Metropolitan Black Bar Assn, Natl Bar Assn; mem Amer Civil Liberties Union; elder Hollis Presbyterian Church; Task Force for Justice Presbytery of the City of NY; adv bd Borough of Manhattan Comm Coll 1970; mem sec gen counsel One Hundred Black Men Inc; bd trustees Great Neck Library; bd mem NAACP of Great Neck Manhasset Port Washington Br; mem Departmental Disciplinary Comm First Judicial Dept Supreme Court of the State of NY; New York Surrogate's Court Advisory Committee, until 1996. **Honors/Awds:** 100 Blackmen Inc, Honorary Member, Board of Directors. **Military Serv:** US Army, 1945-46. **Business Addr:** Counselor at Law, 225 Broadway, New York, NY 10007.

MURRAY, ALBERT L.
Educator, writer. **Personal:** Born May 12, 1916, Nokomis, AL; son of Mattie Murray and Hugh Murray; married Mozelle Menefee; children: Michele. **Educ:** Tuskegee Inst, BS 1939; NY Univ, MA 1948. **Career:** Tuskegee Inst, instr Engl 1940-43, 1946-51; Colgate Univ, O'Connor prof Engl 1970; Emory Univ, writer in res 1978; Colgate, prof humanities 1982; Barnard, adjunct prof writing 1981-83; Drew Univ, Woodrow Wilson Fellow 1983; author. **Honors/Awds:** Alumni Merit Award, Tuskegee, 1972; Doctor of Letters Colgate, 1975; The Lincoln Ctr, Directors Emeriti Award, 1991; Books, "Omni Americans," "South to A Very Old Place," "The Hero and the Blues," "Train Whistle Guitar," "Stomping the Blues," "The Spyglass Tree," 1991, "The Seven League Boots," "The Blue Devils of Nada," 1996; Lillian Smith Award for "Train Whistle Guitar," ASCAP Deems Taylor Award for "Stomping the Blues" 1977; "Good Morning Blues", The Autobiography of Count Basie as told by Albert Murray 1986; Spring Hill College, doctor of humane letters, 1996. **Military Serv:** USAF major. **Home Addr:** 45 W 132nd St, New York, NY 10037.

MURRAY, ALBERT R.
State corrections official. **Personal:** Born Jan 25, 1946, Ripley, TN; son of Pearl L Murray and Rossie G Murray; married Connie Graffread, Aug 31, 1969; children: Andrea, Camille. **Educ:** Tenn State University, Nashville, TN, BS, English, 1969; Middle Tenn State University, Murfreesboro, TN, MA, psychology, 1973; Tennessee Government Executive Institute, graduate, 1988. **Career:** Spencer Youth Center, Nashville, TN, counselor, 1970-76; Tennessee Youth Center, Nashville, TN, assistant supt, 1976-81, superintendent, 1981-; Tennessee Department of Children Svcs, Nashville, TN, assistant commissioner, 1989-. **Orgs:** Auditor, American Correctional Assn, 1988-; board of governors, Tennessee Correctional Assn, 1990; board of managers, YMCA, 1987-; member, Phi Beta Sigma Fraternity, 1968-; member, Governors Advisory Council on Voc Ed, 1984. **Business Addr:** Assistant Commissioner, Tennessee Department of Children Svcs, Cordell Hull Bldg, 7th Fl, 436 6th Ave, W, Nashville, TN 37243.

MURRAY, ANNA MARTIN
Educator. **Personal:** Born Oct 31, Birmingham, AL; married Willie Alca Murray (deceased). **Educ:** AL State Coll, BS 1952; Samford Univ, Cert Early Childhood Educ 1975; The CA Inst of Metaphysics, 1952; George Peabody Coll; A&M, post grad study towards Masters 1964. **Career:** St Clair Bd of Educ, teacher 1944-46; Birmingham City Bd of Educ, teacher 1947-72; Helping Hand Day Care, teacher 1976-77; Birmingham City Bd of Educ, substitute teacher 1977-87. **Orgs:** Vice pres Deaconess Bd Macedonia Baptist Church 1970-85; sec Alert Professional Club 1980-85; sec Tyree Chap 77 OES 1981-85; mem AL Retired Teachers Assoc Montgomery AL, Amer Assoc of Retired Persons Long Beach CA, Gamma Phi Delta Alpha Mu Chap 1968-, Natl Ed Assoc WA DC; mem Fraternal OES, Alert Twelve Profl, Alpha Mu Gamma Phi Delta Sor; mem Ultra Modern Club 1930-87. **Honors/Awds:** New verses in American Poetry Vantage Press NY 1976; Inspiration from a Save in Action Vantage Press NY 1977; Dipl The Inst of Mentalphysics; Meritorious Serv Award Birmingham Educ Assn 1973; Outstanding Serv Award by Supreme Chap of Zeta Phi Lambda Sor 1983; Meritorious Serv Award Field of Journalism 1980; AwardNatl Black Women's Polit Leadership Caucus 1978. **Home Addr:** 2112-18th St, Birmingham, AL 35218.

MURRAY, ARCHIBALD R.
Association executive, attorney. **Personal:** Born Aug 25, 1933; married Kay C. **Educ:** Howard U, BA 1954; Fordham U, LLB 1960. **Career:** NY County, asst DA 1960-62; Gov NY, asst counsel 1962-65; NYC, Priv law prac 1965-67; NY State Crime Control Council, counsel 1967-68; NY State Office of Crime Control Planning NYC, counsel 1968-71; NY State Div Criminal Justice NYC, adminstr 1971-72; NY State Div Criminal Justice Servs NYC, commr 1972-74; The Legal Aid Soc NYC, atty-in-chief, exec dir 1975-94, chair of the board, 1994-. **Orgs:** Consultant, NY Temporary State Commn on Preparation for Constitutional Conv NYC 1966-67; NY State Comm on Revision Penal Law & Criminal Code 1965-70; NY State Bar Assn, president, 1993-94; American Bar Association, House of Delegates; NY Co Lawyers Assn; vestryman St Philips Episcopal Ch 1970-93; chancellor Episcopal Diocese of NY 1975-87. **Honors/Awds:** William Nelson Cromwell Award 1977; Doctor of Humane Letters, College of New Rochelle, 1983; Doctor of Laws, NY Law School, 1988; Emory Buckner Award, Federal Bar Council, 1989; Johy Jay College, CUNY, LLD, 1990; Metropolitan Black Bar Association, Special Merit Award, 1991; Fordham University, LLD, 1992. **Special Achievements:** First African-American pres of the New York State Bar Assn, 1993. **Military Serv:** US Army 1954-56. **Business Addr:** Chair of the Board, The Legal Aid Society, 90 Church St, New York, NY 10007-2919, (212)577-3313.

MURRAY, CECIL LEONARD
Cleric. **Personal:** Born Sep 26, 1929, Lakeland, FL; son of Minnie Lee Murray and Edward W Murray; married Bernadine Cousin, Jun 25, 1958; children: Drew David. **Educ:** Florida A&M University, BA, 1951; School of Theology at Claremont, Doctor of Religion, 1964. **Career:** US Air Force, captain, Jet Radar interceptor and Navigator; First AME Church, minister; religious posts in Los Angeles, Seattle, Kansas City, Pomona. **Orgs:** African Methodist Episcopal Church, general board, 1972-92; National Council of Churches, general board, 1972-92; Alpha Phi Alpha Fraternity, 1948-; NAACP; SCLC; CORE; Urban League; United Nations Association of the USA; National Council on the Aging, general board, 1988-93. **Honors/Awds:** United Nations Association, Ralph Bunche Peace Prize Award, 1992; Alpha Phi Alpha, Alpha Man of the Year, 1951; African Methodist Epicopal Church, Daniel Alexander Payne Award, 1992; NAACP, Los Angeles, Community Achievement Award, 1986; National Association of University Women, Outstanding Role Model, 1992. **Special Achievements:** Sermon in "Dreams of Fire," compendium of sermons after Los Angeles riots; named by President George Bush: 177th Point of Light, First AME Church; Excerpts in Time Magazine, Wall Street Journal, BBC, CNN. **Military Serv:** US Air Force Reserves, major, 1951-61; Soliders Medal for Heroism, 1958. **Business Addr:** Senior Minister, First AME Church, 2270 S Harvard Blvd, Los Angeles, CA 90018, (213)735-1251.

MURRAY, EDDIE CLARENCE
Professional baseball player. **Personal:** Born Feb 24, 1956, Los Angeles, CA. **Educ:** California State Univ, Los Angeles, CA, attended. **Career:** Baltimore Orioles, infielder, 1977-88; Los Angeles Dodgers, infielder, 1989-91; New York Mets, infielder, 1991-93; Cleveland Indians, 1993-96; Baltimore Orioles, 1996-97; Anaheim Angels, 1997-. **Orgs:** Involved in charitable activities with United Cerebral Palsy, Sickle Cell Anemia, Amer Red Cross, United Way, Johns Hopkins Children's Ctr, New Holiness Refuge Church and Park Heights Acad which dedicated a classroom in his honor; for past 7 seasons sponsored "Project 33". **Honors/Awds:** American League Rookie of the Year, Baseball Writers' Assn of America, 1977; won 3 Golden Glove Awds; has more RBIs (733) than any other big leaguer in the 1980's; led the Orioles in home runs 7 times; named first baseman on The Sporting News Amer League All-Star fielding teams 1982-84; named first baseman on The Sporting News Amer League Silver Slugger teams 1983, 1984; American League All-Star Team, 1981-85. **Business Addr:** Professional Baseball Player, Anaheim Angels, PO Box 2000, Anaheim, CA 92803.

MURRAY, EDNA MCCLAIN
Educator, association manager. **Personal:** Born Jan 2, 1918, Idabel, OK; daughter of Ruberda Lenox Moore and Swingley Lee Moore; married Mar 31, 1938 (widowed); children: Ruby J McClain Ford, Jacquelyn McClain Crawford. **Educ:** Wilson Jr Coll, AA; Roosevelt Univ, BA; Chicago State Univ, MEd; over 60 additional hours in administration, counseling & human relations. **Career:** Ru-Jac Charm Center & Beauty Shop, Chicago IL, owned/operated, 1948-59; Chicago Bd of educ, school teacher, 1959-, Learning Disabilities, resource teacher, 1974-95, Teacher Corp unit leader, 1970-71; Chicago State Univ, guest lecturer; Phi Delta Kappa Natl Sorority, executive secretary, 1982-92; Short Stop Restaurant, co-owner. **Orgs:** Natl Sorority of Phi Delta Kappa, natl supreme grammateus of sorority, 1979-83, basileus, Local Chapter, 1968-72, board of directors, executive council, natl exec scy, 10 years; organizer, Chicago Chapter, Top Ladies of Distinction; served as several natl officer, local pres, TLOD; Chicago Psychological Club; NAACP; UNCF; NCNW; Urban League; board of directors, executive council: Chicago African-American Teachers Assn; Phidelka Foundation; Michigan Avenue Block Club; Michigan Ave Condo Board; served as voting delegate of the Chicago Teachers Union over 20 yrs. **Honors/Awds:** Woman of the Year, Chicago Daily Defender, 1966; Outstanding 100 Black Women, Copin Church, 1986; Woman of the Year, Top Ladies of Distinction, 1981; Inducted into Chicago Senior Citizens Hall of Fame, Mayor Washington, 1987; Special Honor and Recognition by members of her school, Women's History Month, 1988; Outstanding Achievements, Chicago Asst Principal's Assn, 1990; Educator of the Year Award, Phi Delta Kappa, Chicago State Univ, Chapter Ed-320, 1991. **Special Achievements:** Pioneer in the field of modeling for African-American women as owner/operator, Ru-Jac Charm Center & Beauty Shop, 1948-59. **Home Addr:** 58844 Ash Rd, Three Rivers, MI 49093.

MURRAY, GARY S.
Computer systems and engineering company executive. **Career:** Sylvest Management Systems Corp, vp, currently. **Special Achievements:** Company is #74 on Black Enterprise magazine's list of top 100 industrial/service companies, 1992. **Business Addr:** VP, Sylvest Management Systems Corp, 10001 Derekwood Ln, Ste 225, Lanham, MD 20706, (301)459-2700.

MURRAY, J. RALPH
Business executive. **Personal:** Born Oct 4, 1931, Manatee, FL; married Alaine; children: James, Janmarie, Jodi. **Educ:** BS 1960. **Career:** Am Cyanamid Co Research Labs, employed; Travelers Ins Co, 1967; life Iis agency. **Orgs:** Mem bd finance City Stamford dir Liberty Nat Bank 1970; mem SW CT Life Underwriters Assn; bd dirs St Lukes Infant Child Care; former ch bd trustees, 1st Congregational Ch. **Honors/Awds:** Travelers Inner Circle Award 1970; Outstanding Political Serv Award Afro-am Club 1972; Civic Award Planning Bd City Stamford 1970. **Military Serv:** AUS 1952-54. **Business Addr:** 832 Bedford St, Stamford, CT 06901.

MURRAY, JAMES HAMILTON
Educator, dentist (retired). **Personal:** Born Nov 22, 1933, Washington, DC; married Joan; children: Christina, Michelle. **Educ:** Howard U, BS 1956; Meharry Med Coll, DDS 1960; Jersey City Med Cntr , rotating dental internship 1960-61; Johns Hopkins School of Hygiene and Public Health, MPH 1969. **Career:** Virginia Pub Health Dept, clinical dentist 1964-68; Howard Univ Coll of Dentistry Dept of Prosthodontics, asst prof 1964-68; Howard Univ Coll of Dentistry Dept of Community Dentistry, asst prof, 1968-69; Shaw Community Health Project Nat Med Assn Found, dental dir 1969-70; Matthew Walker Health Cntr Meharry Med Coll, project dir; Dept of Family & Community Health, prof 1970-71; Dept Health Educ & Welfare Family Health Serv Rockville MD, health adminstrn 1972-74; Dept of Human Resour Comm Hlth & Hosp Admintr Wash DC, 1974-75; Howard Univ College of Dentistry, Dept of Clinical Dentisty, assoc prof, 1975-92. **Orgs:** Mem Nat Dental Assn; Am Soc of Dentistry for Children; Am Acad of Gen Dentistry; Am Pub Health Assn; Am Dental Assn; Urban League; membership com Amer Public Health Assn, Sec Am Pub Health Assn 1974-75. **Honors/Awds:** Published articles for dental journals; Am Soc of Dentistry for Children Award 1960; US Pub Health Traineeship Grant 1968-69; Dental Alumnus of the Yr Meharry Med Coll 1970-71; DC Dental Soc Award 1969; Nashville Dental Supply Co Award for Clinical Dentistry 1960; Omicron Kappa Upsilon, Honorary Dental Society, 1960; Fellow of Amer College of Dentists; Fellow of the Academy of General Dentistry; Fellow of the Academy of Dentistry International; Psi Chi, Honorary Society, Psychology. **Military Serv:** Captain, USAF 1961-63. **Home Addr:** 1433 Locust Rd NW, Washington, DC 20012.

MURRAY, JAMES P.
Youth agency executive. **Personal:** Born Oct 16, 1946, Bronx, NY; son of Helena Murray and Eddie Murray; married Mary; children: Sean Edward, Sherron Anita, Angela Dawn. **Educ:** Syracuse Univ, BA 1968. **Career:** White Plains Reporter Dispatch, copy editor 1968; ABC-TV News, news trainee 1968-71; Western Electric Co, pub relations asso 1971-72; freelance writer 1972-73; NY Amsterdam News, arts & entertainment editor 1973-75; Nat Broadcasting Co, press rep 1975-83; Black Creation Mag, editor in chief 1972-74; freelancewriter 1983-85; USA Network, mgr public relations 1985-90, dir corporate relations 1990-91, freelance publicist, 1991-93; The Terrie Williams Agency, account supervisor, 1993, publicity consultant, 1993-94; The Valley Youth Agency, deputy dir, fund dev and public relations, 1994-. **Orgs:** 1st Black Member Fairview Engine Co #1 Greenburgh NY Volunteer Fire Company 1968; judge Newspaper Guild Page One Awd 1976-86; cont ed The Afro-Amer Almanac 1976,89; pres Fairview Engine Co #1 1980; judge Gabriel Awds 1986. **Honors/Awds:** Man of the Year Fairview Engine Co #1 1971; 1st Black elected to NY Film Critics Circle 1972; author book "To Find An Image" 1974; Humanitarian Achievement Awd MLK Players 1975; ordained elder Christs Temple White Plains NY 1978. **Military Serv:** AUS 1st lt 1968-70. **Business Addr:** Dep Director, Fund Dev and Public Relations, The Valley, Inc, 1047 Amsterdam Ave, New York, NY 10025.

MURRAY, J-GLENN
Educator, cleric. **Personal:** Born Apr 22, 1950, Philadelphia, PA; son of Lillian Marie Hilton Murray and James Albert Murray. **Educ:** St Louis University, BA, 1974; Jesuit School of Theology at Berkeley, MDiv, 1979; Aquinas Institute, MA, 1996; Catholic Theological Union of Chicago, DMin, 1996. **Career:** St Frances Academy, asst principal, 1981-88; Office for Pastoral Liturgy, asst dir, 1989-; St Mary Seminary, homiletics professor, 1992-. **Orgs:** National Black Catholic Clergy Caucus, 1979-; Catholic Assn of Teachers of Homiletics, 1992-; Academy of Homiletics, 1992-; North American Academy of Liturgy, 1993-; Black Catholic Theological Symposium, 1994-. **Honors/Awds:** Archdiocese of Baltimore, Youth Ministry Medal of Honor, 1988. **Business Addr:** Assistant Director, Office for Pastoral Liturgy, 1031 Superior Ave., Ste 361, Cleveland, OH 44114, (216)696-6525.

MURRAY, JOHN W.
Broadcasting executive. **Personal:** Born Jul 6, 1921, Washington, DC; children: John Jr. **Educ:** Syracuse & Lincoln Univ, AB 1947; New York Univ, St Johns Univ Law School, Grad Studies. **Career:** NY Time, staff-writer, sch prom 1952-54; NY Mirror, circulation promo writer 1954-55; WNBC-TV & Radio, reporter, asst prod 1955; Tex McCrary Inc, acct exec 1955-57; Harold L Oram Inc, acct exec 1957-58; Natl TB Assoc, dir publ & promo 1959-63; WCBS-TV, publ rel cons, writer & prod 1963-65, mgr ofspecial proj 1965-66, dir publ info & advtsg 1966-67, dir comm rel 1967-68; NY Urban Coalition, vp, comm 1968-70; WOR-TV, dir publ affairs 1970-71, vice pres publ affairs 1971-73; RKO Gen TV Inc, vice pres publ affairs 1973-79, sr vice pres 1979-. **Orgs:** Mem Natl Acad of TV Arts & Sci, Intl Radio & TV; founder & dir Assoc of Black Broadcast Exec; past dir Community News Svc; consult CUNY; dir, past pres Urban League of Greater NY; mem exec adv comm Journalism Resources Inst Rutgers Univ. **Honors/Awds:** Black Achievers Awd Harlem YMCA 1973; Citation of Merit NJ Conf of Mayors; Media Awd Natl Conf of Christians & Jews for Outstanding Editorials; Outstanding Comm Serv awd Massive Econ Neighborhood Devel Corp; Gold Key Awd Publ Rel News. **Military Serv:** AUS sgt 1943-46.

MURRAY, KAY L.
Government official. **Personal:** Born Sep 8, 1938, Greenville, MS; daughter of Ann De Jackson Lance and Preston Mike Lance; married Otis Murray, Aug 1, 1981; children: Gary Michael. **Educ:** Roosevelt Univ, Chicago IL, BA Public Admin, 1976; Northeastern Illinois, Chicago IL, MA, Urban Studies, 1993. **Career:** City Council, Chicago IL, sec to pres pro-tempore, 1960-74; City Dept of Public Works, Chicago IL, equal employment officer, 1974; Dept of Streets and Sanitation Commissioner's Office, Chicago IL, staff assistant commissioner, 1974-82; Bureau of Rodent Control, Chicago IL, asst commissioner, 1983-84; Dept of Streets and Sanitation Rodent Control, Chicago IL, deputy commissioner, 1984-; Illinois Dept of Professional Regulation, Chief of Staff, 1991-. **Orgs:** Mem, Natl Assn of Women Executives; mem, Hyde Park Community Organization; associate, Howard Univ School of Business, Management for Minority Women; mem, Amer Public Works Assn; community developer, John Marshall Law School; mem, NAACP, 1977; mem, 21st District Steering Committee, Chicago Police Dept, 1979; mem, Intl Toastmistress of Amer/Sirrah Branch, 1980; mem, Chicago Urban League, 1986; vice pres, Jackson Park Hospital, 1987-89; vice pres, Business and Professional Women, 1988-89; co-founder, Women in Government, 1984-89; vice pres, Genesis House Executive Board; treasurer, North Washington Park Community Corp. **Honors/Awds:** Outstanding Community Efforts Award, 1986; WGRT Great Guy Award; Dedication and Loyalty to Fellow Man Award; Outstanding Contributions to Departments of Health, Police, Fire, and Citizens of Chicago; Certificate of Achievement, Mid-Southside Health Planning Organization. **Business Addr:** Chief of Staff, Illinois Department of Professional Regulation, 100 W Randolph 9-300, Chicago, IL 60601.

MURRAY, LAMOND MAURICE
Professional basketball player. **Personal:** Born Apr 20, 1973, Pasadena, CA; married Carmen; children: Lamond Jr, Ashley. **Educ:** University of California. **Career:** Los Angeles Clippers, forward, 1994-. **Business Addr:** Professional Basketball Player, Los Angeles Clippers, Los Angeles Sports Arena, 3939 S Figuerua St, Los Angeles, CA 90037, (213)748-8000.

MURRAY, MABEL LAKE
Educator. **Personal:** Born Feb 24, 1935, Baltimore, MD; daughter of Iantha Alexander Lake and Moses Oliver Lake; married Elmer R Murray, Dec 16, 1968; children: Mark Alfonso Butler, Sarita Murray. **Educ:** Coppin State Teachers Coll, Baltimore MD, BS, 1956; Loyola Coll, Baltimore MD, MED, 1969; Virginia Polytechnic Institute, Blacksburg VA, Case, 1978-81, EdD, 1982. **Career:** Baltimore City Public Schools, teacher, 1956-68; Prince Georges County Public Schools, reading specialist, 1968-70; Project KAPS, Baltimore MD, reading coordinator, 1970-72; Univ of MD, reading coordinator, 1972-76; Johns Hopkins Univ, adjunct professor, 1972-76; Carroll County Public Schools, supervisor, 1976-87; Sojourner Douglass Coll, Baltimore MD, professor, beginning 1987-, supervisor, Student Teaching, currently; NAACP Education Dept, natl coordinator NTE; Sojourner-Douglass Coll, Human Growth Dev, coord, currently. **Orgs:** Mem, Delta Sigma Theta Sorority, 1972-; Baltimore County Alumnae Chapter, Delta Sigma Theta; advisor, Lambda Kappa and Mu Psi Chapters, Delta Sigma Theta; consultant, Piney Woods School, 1984-89; commission chair-instruction, Natl Alliance of Black School Educators, 1987-96; executive board, Natl Alliance of Black School Educators, 1987-; consultant, AIDS Project MSDE, 1988; consultant, Dunbar Middle School, 1989; consultant, Des Moines Iowa Schools; Natl Council on Educating Black Children; pres, Maryland Council of Deltas; natl pres, Pinochle Bugs Social and Civic Club; natl treas, The Societas Doctas; Baho Chap, The Society. **Honors/Awds:** Designed curriculum material for two school systems, 1968-72; Conducted numerous workshops, 1969-89; Guest speaker at variety of educ/human relations activities, 1969-89; Outstanding Educator, State of MD Intl Reading Assn, 1979; Guest Lecturer, Baltimore City Schools Special Educ, 1979; Developed reading program for state mental hospital, 1981; Mayor's Citation, 1982; Service Award, Baltimore City Chapter, Delta Sigma Theta, 1983; Mem of Congressman Louis Stokes Committee on Black Health Issues, 1989. **Home Addr:** 3 Kittridge Court, Randallstown, MD 21133.

MURRAY, SPENCER J., III
Software engineer. **Personal:** Born Jan 21, 1964, Seattle, WA; son of Peggy Murray and S Jack Murray Jr. **Educ:** Univ of WA, Seattle, WA, BS, electrical engineering, 1989. **Career:** Honeywell, Marine Systems Div, software engr; Jet Propulsion Laboratory, Pasadena, CA, microwave engr; IBM, Advanced Workstations Div, Palo Alto, CA, software engr; Silicon Graphics Inc, Mountain View, CA, software engr, currently. **Orgs:** Mem, Natl Society of Black Engineers, 1982-85.

MURRAY, SYLVESTER
Educational administrator. **Personal:** Born Aug 15, 1941, Miami, FL; son of Annie Anderson Murray and Tommy Lee Murray; children: Kimberly, Joshua. **Educ:** Lincoln Univ PA, AB 1963; Univ of PA Phila, MGA 1967; Eastern MI Univ, MA 1976; Lincoln Univ PA, LlD 1984. **Career:** City of Inkster MI, city mgr 1970-73; City of Ann Arbor MI, city admin 1973-79; City of Cincinnati OH, city mgr 1979-85; City of San Diego CA, city manager, 1985-87; Cleveland State University, educational administrator, currently. **Orgs:** Pres Intl City Mgmt Assn 1984; president, American Society of Public Administration, 1987. **Honors/Awds:** Publ Srv Award, Amer Soc of Publ Admin 1984. **Military Serv:** AUS sp5 1965-67. **Business Addr:** Cleveland State University, Public Management Program, College of Urban Affairs, Cleveland, OH 44115, (216)687-2139.

MURRAY, THOMAS AZEL, SR.
Consultant. **Personal:** Born Jan 15, 1929, Chicago, IL. **Educ:** OH State Univ, BA, awarded by CLEP, 1974; Sangamon State Univ, MA, counseling, 1976, MA, communication, 1977; Southern IL Univ, PhD, 1982. **Career:** Univ of IL Chicago, proj coord 1959-72; IL Natl Guard, equal opport spec 1973-75;

Fed Hwy Admin, civil rights ofc 1975-78; IL State Bd of Educ, affirmative action ofc 1978-84; Chicago Baptist Assc, dir Chicago Bapt Association 1971-72; IL Affirmative Action Ofc Assc, parliamentarian 1979-84, 1994-96; Sangamon State Univ Alumni Assc, dir 1979-85; US Dept of HUD Region V, director of compliance, Office of Civil Rights, deputy director, 1984-85, Office of Civil Rights, program operations division, director, 1985-87; US Office of Personnel Management, retired 1987; Illinois State Board of Education, consultant; Professional Service Corps, IL State Bd of Educ, 1989-; Chicago Administrator's Academy Educational Service Center VI, presenter, currently. **Orgs:** Dir Springfield Sangamon Cty Youth Svs Bureau 1974-75; adv comm mem Land of Lincoln Legal Acct Fnd 1978-80; adv council mem Region IV Career Guid Ctr Springfield IL 1982-83; Professional Svcs Corps, Illinois State Bd of Education, 1989-96; Chicago Bd of Education, Admin Acad, 1989-96; Educational Svc Ctr VI, presenter, 1989-96. **Honors/Awds:** Blk Aff Council Awd of Merit SIU, 1981; Phi Kappa Phi HE Honor Society SIU chapter. **Military Serv:** USAF; USAFR; USAR, first sgt, retired 1989; US Army; USANG. **Home Addr:** PO Box 430, Ramah, NM 87321, (505)775-3634.

MURRAY, THOMAS W., JR.
Clergyman. **Personal:** Born Mar 11, 1935, Wilmington, NC; married Mable; children: Thomas R, Dean W, Darrell L. **Educ:** BS, Ed 1968; ThM 1969; MEd 1973; DD 1973. **Career:** Shawtown HS, educator 1968-69; Community Coll, educator 1969-70; Bolivia HS, educator 1969-70; Philadelphia Sch Sys, educator 1970-74; Univ Bapt Ch, pastor. **Orgs:** Mem Black Economic Devel Self Help Prog Founder & Dir Operation Shout; Positive Self Image & Metaphysical Inst Cited Chapel 4 Chaplains 1974. **Military Serv:** USAF E5 1955-64. **Business Addr:** U Bapt Ch, 2041 E Chelten Ave, Philadelphia, PA 19138.

MURRAY, TRACY LAMONTE
Professional basketball player. **Personal:** Born Jun 25, 1971, Los Angeles, CA. **Educ:** UCLA. **Career:** Portland Trail Blazers, forward, 1992-95; Houston Rockets, 1995; Toronto Raptors, 1995-96; Washington Wizards, 1996-. **Special Achievements:** NBA Draft, first round pick, #18, 1992; Led NBA in Three-Point Field Goal Precentage, with .459 in 1993-94 season. **Business Addr:** Professional Basketball Player, Washington Wizards, MCI Center, 601 F St NW, Washington, DC 20071, (202)661-5000.

MURRAY, VIRGIE W.
Editor. **Personal:** Born Sep 4, 1931, Birmingham, AL; daughter of Martha Miller Reese (deceased) and Virgus Williams; married McKinley C Murray, Jun 1, 1949 (divorced); children: Charles Murray. **Educ:** Miles Coll; Booker T Washington Business Coll. **Career:** Dr John W Nixon, bookkeeper/recpt 1954-58; Thomas Floorwaxing Serv, bookkeeper 1954-64; Birmingham World, clerk/reporter 1958-64; First Baptist Church Graymont, sec 1960-64; religion editor, Los Angeles Sentinel 1964-. **Orgs:** West Coast PR Dr Frederick Eikerenkoetter (Rev Ike) 1974-; pr & consul NBC, USA, INC, AMES & CME's Genl Confs; first African-American sec Religion Newswriters Assn 1971; bd mem Inst of Sacred Music 1979-; bd mem Ecumenical Black Campus Ministry UCLA 1982-; mem Trinity Baptist Ch, NAACP, Urban League, Angeles Mesa YWCA, Aux Cncl RSVP; former den mother Boy Scouts of Amer; former mem LA Chap Business & Professional Women's Club Inc; spec task force of United Nations Assn of USA's Ralph Bunche Awds; mem LA chapter Lane College & Mileans & Parker High School Alumni; serving on Awards Committee, Religious Heritage of Amer 1989-90; Los Angeles Sentinel, Inc, board of directors. **Honors/Awds:** Tribute Awd Good Shepherd Bapt Ch 1983; City County State Councilman Supervisors & Assemblymen 1983; Awd of Merit Crenshaw Christian Center 1980; Christian Example First Church of God 1982; 22 other awds; Woman of the Year, Women At Work, auxilary of Southwestern CC 1989; Southern Conf of CME Church, special award and honors 1988; Coverage of the 81st Annual Convocation of Church of God in Christ, Memphis, TN 1988; The AME Gen Conf in Ft Worth Texas 1988; National Newspapers Publishers Assn, Best Church category, second place, 1997. **Special Achievements:** Journalist: participated and covered the Friendship Tour of Seoul, Korea, Oct 1992; covered the Church of God in Christ 85th Holy Convocation, Nov 1992; covered the dedication of the Civil Rights Institute and the dedication of Rev Fred Shuttlesworth, Birmingham, AL, Nov 1992; Covered the African American tour of the Holy Land in 1993 and the CME General Conference in Memphis, TN, in 1994; covered West Angeles COGIC retreat, 1995, Mexican Riviera Cruise retreat, 1996; covered AME General Conference, 1996; covered CME General Conference, 1998; World Pentecostal Conference, Seoul, Korea, 1998. **Business Addr:** Religion Editor, Los Angeles Sentinel, 3800 Crenshaw Blvd, Los Angeles, CA 90008.

MURRELL, ADRIAN BRYAN
Professional football player. **Personal:** Born Oct 16, 1970, Lafayette, LA; married Tanya; children: Tylan. **Educ:** West Virginia. **Career:** New York Jets, running back, 1993-. **Honors/Awds:** Marty Lyons Award, 1995. **Business Addr:** Professional Football Player, New York Jets, 1000 Fulton Ave, Hempstead, NY 11550, (516)560-8100.

MURRELL, BARBARA CURRY
Educational administrator. **Personal:** Born Jan 12, 1938, Starksville, MS; married Robert N Murrell. **Educ:** TN State Univ, BS 1960, MS 1963; Univ of IL, Post Grad Cert 1970. **Career:** TN State Univ, dir student activities 1965-75, asst vice pres student affairs 1975-81, vice pres student affairs 1981-. **Orgs:** State coord Natl Assn for Student Personnel Admins 1973; Task Force of Human Resources Assn of College Unions Intl 1968-79; Harvard Univ Inst for EducMgrs Program 1984; consul Prof Development Workshop Assn of College Unions Intl; bd of dirs Bordeaux YMCA; Assn of College Unions Intl; Natl Entertainment and Campus Activities Assn; Beta Kappa Chi Natl Honor Soc; Delta Sigma Theta Sor Inc. **Honors/Awds:** Omega Psi Phi Frat Sweetheart 1958-59; Miss TN State Univ 1960; Kappa Alpha Psi Frat Perpetual Sweetheart 1960-. **Business Addr:** VP for Student Affairs, Tennessee State Univ, 3500 John A Merritt Blvd, Nashville, TN 37203.

MURRELL, PETER C.
Dentist (retired). **Personal:** Born May 14, 1920, Glasgow, KY; son of Nellie Murrell and Samuel Murrell; married Eva Ruth Greenlee; children: Peggy, Peter Jr, Linda, James. **Educ:** KY State Coll, BS (Cum Laude) 1943; Marquette Univ, DDS 1947. **Career:** Howard Univ Coll Dentistry, instr 1947-48; Private practice, 1948-51, 1953-92. **Orgs:** Mem Amer WI & Gr Milwaukee Dental Assoc; pres Gr Milwaukee Dental Assoc; mem Amer Soc Preventive Dentistry, Amer Acad Gen Practice; treas, bd mem Childrens Serv Soc 1962-77, Garfield Found; former mem Frontiers Intl; co-founder, 1st pres Milwaukee Chap Frontiers Intl; past pres Delta Chi Lambda; fellow Intl Coll of Dentists 1978, Academy of General Dentistry 1981; trustee, WI Dental Assoc 7th Dist 1983-84; WI State Medical Assistance Advisory Comm; exec comm WI Dental Assoc; mem, Pierre Fauchard Academy 1989; fellow, American College of Dentists 1989; advisory council, Marquette Univ School of Dentistry 1988. **Honors/Awds:** Distinguished Serv Awd Opportunity Industrialization Ctr 1971; Service to Dentistry, Greater Milwaukee Dental Assn 1987; Lifetime Achievement Award, Wisconsin Dental Assn, 1993; Founders Plaque, Frontiers International, 1995. **Military Serv:** US Army 1942-44; USAF Dental Corps capt 1951-53. **Home Addr:** 1302 W Capitol Dr, Milwaukee, WI 53206.

MURRELL, SYLVIA MARILYN (MARILYN)
Business center administrator. **Personal:** Born Sep 7, 1947, Arcadia, OK; daughter of Inez Traylor Parks and Ebbie Parks, Jr; divorced; children: Monica A, Alfred H, Cypreanna V. **Educ:** Central State Univ, Edmond OK, 1964-66; Rose State Coll, Midwest City OK, 1981-82; Langston Univ, Oklahoma OK, 1986-87. **Career:** OK Business Devel Center, Oklahoma City, OK, variety of positions, 1975-, executive dir, 1985-; Town of Arcadia, mayor, 1989; M & M Business Consultants, president/owner, currently. **Orgs:** OK City Chamber of Commerce, 1977-; sec & chairman Economic Devel Committee, Conference Black Mayors, 1986-; bd mem, Youth Services OK County, 1986-; bd mem, OK City Chp Assault on Illiteracy, 1986-; steering committee, OK City Crime Prevention Task Force, 1988-; Central OK economic Devel Task Force, 1988-; Teamwork OK, 1988-; vice chair, OK Consortium for Minority Business Devel, 1988-89. **Honors/Awds:** Creative Christian Award, Forrest Hill AME Church, 1987. **Business Addr:** President/Owner, M & M Business Consultants, 1301 N Martin Luther King Ave, Oklahoma City, OK 73007.

MUSE, WILLIAM BROWN, JR.
Banking executive. **Personal:** Born Jul 18, 1918, Danville, VA; son of Maude S Muse and William B Muse Sr; married Naomi Hodge-Muse, Nov 19, 1988 (deceased); children: William K, Michael A, Eric V. **Educ:** Hampton Inst, BS Bus 1940. **Career:** Wm B Muse Agency Real Estate Gen Ins & Property Mgmt, owner 1940-73; Imperial Savings & Loan Assn, pres managing officer 1973-. **Orgs:** Dir First State Bank 1950-; pres Martinsville Branch NAACP 1951-57; 1st vice pres NAREB 1954-59; pres VA Assoc of Real Estate Brokers 1963-; mem VA Adv Comm to US Civil Rights Commn 1968-80; trustee St Paul's Coll 1968-78 & 1981-89; chmn Amer League Fin Inst 1983-84; dir Amer League of Fin; vice chmn bd NAREB; mem Federal Savings and Loan Adv Cncl 1985-86; mem bd of dir Martinsville County C of C 1986-90; mem bd of governors VA League of Savings Institutions 1986-89; mem exec comm Martinsville Democratic Party; treas Martinsville-Henry County Voters League. **Military Serv:** Field Artillery chief warrant officer 1942-46; ETO. **Home Addr:** 611 First St, P O Box 391, Martinsville, VA 24112. **Business Addr:** President, Managing Officer, Imperial Savings & Loan Assn, 211 Fayette St, P O Box 391, Martinsville, VA 24112.

MUSE, WILLIE L.
Educational administrator. **Educ:** Selma Univ, ThB; Alabama State Univ, BE; Interdenominational Theological Ctr, MDiv. **Career:** Selma Univ, professor of religion, pres, currently. **Special Achievements:** Received honorary doctorate from Selma Univ.

MUSGROVE, MARGARET WYNKOOP
Teacher, author. **Personal:** Born Nov 19, 1943, New Britain, CT; daughter of Margaret Holden Wynkoop and John T Wynkoop; married George Gilbert, Aug 28, 1971; children: Taura Johnene, George Derek. **Educ:** Univ of Connecticut, BA, 1966; Central Connecticut State Univ, MS, 1970; Univ of Massachusetts, EdD, 1979. **Career:** High school English teacher in Hartford, Ct, 1967-69 and 1970; teacher at various community colleges including W Bershireshire Comm Coll in Pittsfield, MA; Comm Coll of Baltimore, MD, english teacher, dir of developmental studies, coordinator for ctr for educ development, coord of early childhood educ, 1981-91; Loyola Coll, writing, media dept, writing teacher, 1991-. **Orgs:** Society of Children's Book Writers, Maryland Writer's Project & International Women's Writers Guild. **Honors/Awds:** Author of Ashanti to Zulu: African Traditions, Dial, 1976 (on Horn Book honor list and a Caldecott Award Winner, 1977).

MUTCHERSON, JAMES ALBERTUS, JR.
Physician. **Personal:** Born Mar 22, 1941, Tampa, FL; married Katherine; children: Rovenia, Kimberly. **Educ:** FAMU, 1960-62; Am Intl Coll, BA 1965; Howard Univ Coll of Med, 1967-71. **Career:** Clinical Allergy & Immunology, self emp; Howard Univ Hosp, clinical instr 1975-; Howard Univ Hosp, pediatric allergy fellow 1973-75; Childrens Hosp of DC, pediatric resd 1971-73. **Orgs:** DC Med Soc; DC Social Asthma & Allergy, American Accd of Asthma Allergy & Immunology; Pediatric Allergy Fellowship 1973-75. **Business Addr:** 1140 Varnum St, Ste 030, Washington, DC 20017.

MUTOMBO, DIKEMBE
Professional basketball player. **Personal:** Born Jun 25, 1966, Kinshasa, Zaire; married Rose; children: Carrie Biamba. **Educ:** Georgetown. **Career:** Denver Nuggets, center, 1991-96; Atlanta Hawks, 1996-. **Honors/Awds:** NBA All-Rookie first team, 1992; NBA Defensive Player of the Year Award, 1995, 1997; NBA All-Star, 1997, 1998. **Special Achievements:** NBA Draft, First round pick, #4, 1991. **Business Addr:** Professional Basketball Player, Atlanta Hawks, One CNN Center, Ste 405, Atlanta, GA 30335, (404)827-3800.

MUWAKKIL, SALIM (ALONZO JAMES CANNADY)
Writer. **Personal:** Born Jan 20, 1947, New York, NY; son of Bertha and Alonzo; married Karimah; children: Salimah, Rasheeda. **Educ:** Rutgers Univ; Newark Coll Arts & Science 1973. **Career:** Bilalian News, mng editor 1975-77; Muhammad Speaks, news editor 1974-75; Copy Editor 1974; AP, bur newsman 1972-74; Addiction Planning & Coordinator Agency of Newark, rsch specialist 1972; Livingston Nghbrhd Educ Ctr, co-founder educ 1971; Black Journalism Rev, consult editorial bd; Columbia College, Chicago, IL, journalism lecturer, 1986-90; Associated Colleges of the Midwest, Chicago, IL, part-time faculty, 1990-; In These Times Magazine, Chicago, IL, senior editor, 1990-. **Orgs:** Pres Black Students Union 1970-72; consult Livingston Coll Nghbrhd Educ Ctr 1972-74; bd Gov S Shore Comm Ctr Several Publ; Spl Observer Orgn of African Unity 1975. **Honors/Awds:** International Reggae Music Awards, Outstanding Music Criticism, 1983-84; Article of the Year, International Black Writers Conference, 1984; Outstanding Service Award, African-American Alliance of Columbia College, Chicago, 1990. **Military Serv:** USAF 1964-69. **Business Addr:** Senior Editor, In These Times Magazine, 2040 N Milwaukee Ave, Chicago, IL 60647.

MUYUMBA, FRANCOIS N. (MUYUMBA WA NKONGOLA)
Educator. **Personal:** Born Dec 29, 1939, Luputa Kasai-orien, Zaire; married Valentine Kanyinda; children: Walton M N, Muuka M K. **Educ:** David & Elkins Coll Elkins WV, BA 1963-67; Portland State U, MS 1969-70; IN Univ Boomington, MA & PhD 1977. **Career:** IN State Univ, asst prof 1977-; Univ Libre duCongo, asst prof/adminstrn asst 1968-69; Usaid-Kinshasa, asst training officer 1967-68; Youth Center (Carrefour deJeunes) Kinshasa Zaire, dir 1967. **Orgs:** Mem Tchrs of Engl as Second Lang 1973-80; mem Intl Peace Research Assn 1975-80; consult Inst for World Order's Sch Progs 1975-78; mem World Council for Curriculum & Instr 1974-80; mem Peache Educ Council 1978-80; mem Nat Council for Black Studies 1976-80. **Honors/Awds:** Soccer Letters & Trophies Davis & Elkins Coll Elkins WV 1963-67; Travel Grant Intl Peace Research Assn 1975; Consult Grant Gilmore Sloane Presbyterian Center 1975. **Business Addr:** Asst Professor, Afro-American Studies Dept, Indiana State Univ, Terre Haute, IN 47809.

MWAMBA, ZUBERI I.
Educator. **Personal:** Born Jan 3, 1937, Tanzania. **Educ:** Univ WI, BS 1968; Univ Pitts, MA 1968; Howard U, PhD 1972. **Career:** Govt Tanzania, radio announcer, court clerk, interpreter, information asst 1957-62; Howard U, instr 1968-72; US State Dept 1969-70; African Studies TX So U, prof dir 1982-. **Orgs:** Mem Am Political Sci Assn 1971-; Nat Council Black Political Scientists 1971-; Educator to Africa Assn 1972-; pres Pan African Students Orgn 1965-67; Tanzania Students Union 1968-70 1971-72; exec com East African Students Orgn 1968-70; adv TX So Univ Student Gov Assn 1974-75; faculty sponsor TSU YoungDemo 1974-75. **Honors/Awds:** Fellows Fulbright 1965-68; WI Legislature 1965-67; Howard Univ Trust 1969-70; International Election Observer at the general elections in South

Africa, 1994; TX Southern Univ, Distinguished Service of the Year Award, 1997. **Business Addr:** Texas Southern Univ, 3100 Cleburne Ave, Houston, TX 77004.

MYATT, GORDON J.
Administrative judge. **Personal:** Born Jan 2, 1928, Brooklyn, NY; son of Frances Simons and Carlton O Myatt Sr; married Evelyne E Hutchings; children: Gordon, Jr, Kevin, Craig. **Educ:** NY U, BS 1950; NY Univ Sch of Law, LLB 1956. **Career:** Pvt Practice, atty 1956-60; Natl Labor Relations Bd Chicago, trial atty 1960-62, supv atty 1962-64, legal advisor, administrative law judge, currently. **Orgs:** Member, National Bar Assn; member, National Bar Judicial Council; member, American Bar Assn; member, Alpha Phi Alpha, 1945-; member, Alpha Gamma Boule of Sigma Pi Phi 1989-. **Business Addr:** Administrative Law Judge, National Labor Relations Board, Div of Judges, 901 Market St, Suite 300, San Francisco, CA 94103.

MYERS, ANDRE
Insurance executive. **Personal:** Born Aug 2, 1959, Philadelphia, PA; son of George & Pauline Myers; married Linda Myers, Mar 24, 1962. **Educ:** Community College, retail mktg management, 1984; Eastern College, organizational management, 1996. **Career:** North American Co for Life & Health Ins, underwriting support, 1990-91, policy issue assistant, 1991-94, new business specialist, 1994-96, policy issue analyst, 1996-. **Orgs:** Janes United Methodist Church; Young Democrats of PA, vice pres, 1992-94; NAACP, subscripting life member; Church Mentoring Network, coord, 1996. **Honors/Awds:** Northwest District United Methodist Church, Southeastern PA, Certificate of Recognition, 1992. **Home Addr:** 710 Bullock Ave, Yeadon, PA 19050, (610)623-8468.

MYERS, BERNARD SAMUEL
Veterinarian. **Personal:** Born Jun 2, 1949, Moultrie, GA. **Educ:** Rollins Coll, BA 1970; Cornell U, DVM 1974. **Career:** Lynn Animal Hosp, vet 1985; Needham Animal Hosp, asso vet 1977-80; Stoneham Animal Hosp, asso vet 1975-77; Bruce Animal Hosp, asso vet 1974-75; Harvard Sch of Pub Health, res asst 1973. **Orgs:** Mem Am Vet Med Assn 1974-80; mem MA Vet Med Assn 1974-80; asst moderator Shiloh Bapt Ch 1980. **Honors/Awds:** Academic Scholarship Rollins Coll 1966-70; Algernon Sidney Sullivan Award Rollins Coll 1969; Health Professions Scholarship Cornell Univ 1970-74. **Business Addr:** Lynn Animal Hospital, 110 Weber St, Orlando, FL.

MYERS, DEBRA J.
Physician. **Personal:** Born Aug 3, 1952, Waynesville, NC; married Woodrow Myers Jr; children: Kimberly L Myers, Zachary A Myers. **Educ:** Stanford Univ, Stanford CA, BS, 1973; Harvard Univ, Boston MA, MD, 1977. **Career:** Pulmonary Assocs, physician, currently. **Business Phone:** (313)745-8471.

MYERS, EARL T.
Engineer, manager. **Personal:** Born Jul 26, 1930, Daytona Beach; married Clara Mills; children: Lesli, Linda. **Educ:** Walden U, PhD 1973; Worcester Polytechnic Inst, MSME; Northeastern U, MS 1965; Claflin U, BS 1952. **Career:** Xerox Corp, prog mgr; Application Engineering Gen Elec Co, mgr 1973-77; Freedom Tool & Die Inc, gen mgr 1970-73; Raytheon Co, sr scientist 1966-67; AVCO Corp, sr consulting scientist 1956-66. **Orgs:** Mem Ordnance Soc 1958-60; Am Ins of Aeronautics & Astronautics; Am Astronautical Soc Pres Montachusett Br NAACP 1974-; mem Bd Corp Emerson Hosp 1974-; Minority Sci Study Consult 1970-. **Honors/Awds:** Recip Outstanding Aurthors Award Raytheon Co 1967; Raytheon's Adv Study Fellowship 1967-70. **Military Serv:** Served AUS pfc 1952-54. **Business Addr:** 595 Swallow Ln, Spring Hill, FL 34606-5859.

MYERS, EMMA MCGRAW
Association executive. **Personal:** Born Nov 15, 1953, Hartsville, SC; married Kenneth E Myers. **Educ:** FL State Univ, BA 1974, MSoc Wk 1975. **Career:** United Way of Amer, united way intern 1976-77, consul planning & allocations div 1979-80; United Way of Tarrant Co, mang vol training 1977-78, campaign divdir 1978-79; UWA, assoc dir natl ag relations 1980-83; United Way of the Midlands, dir planning & allocations div. **Orgs:** Parlimentarian Episcopal Church Women 1985; treas FSU Black Alumin Assn; bd mem Natl Assn of Black Social Workers 1985-; pres Dutch Fork Citivans 1985-; pres Alpha Kappa Alpha 1985-; corresp sec Columbia Chap NABSW. **Honors/Awds:** Nominee Outstanding young Women of Amer 1983; NCNW Living the Legacy Awrd 1986; Civitan of the Year 1986. **Business Addr:** Dir Planning & Allocations, United Way of the Midlands, PO Box 152, Columbia, SC 29202.

MYERS, ERNEST RAY
Author, educator, management consultant, psychotherapist. **Personal:** Born in Middletown, OH; son of Alma Harper Myers and David Myers; married Carole E Ferguson. **Educ:** Howard Univ, BA 1962, MSW 1964; Amer Univ, PhD candidate 1974; The Union Institute Grad Sch, PhD 1976. **Career:** VISTA, prog ofcr proj develop div 1964-66, sr eval officer 1964-66, proj devel officer 1966-67, program plans & policy develop ofcr 1967; Dept of Housing & Urban Develop, neighborhood serv prog ofcr & coord 1967-68; Natl Urban League, asst dir 1968; Westinghouse Learning Corp, mgr of prog develop 1968-69; Fed City Coll, dir coll comm evaluation office 1969-71; Bureau of Higher Educ US Office of Educ, dir servicemen's early educ counseling prog 1971; Federal City Coll, asst prof 1972-77; Univ of DC, assoc prof 1977-86, chmn dept of human resource dev 1986-94; prof, Dept of Psych & Counseling, 1994-. **Orgs:** Editorial board, USA-Africa, 1990-92; trustee Woodley House (Rehab) 1982-88; mem advisor, Zest Inc, 1990-; mem Amer Psychological Assn 1975-; APA Fellow, 1995-; chmn DC Govt Mental Health Admin Adv Bd 1984-86; mem, Association of Black Psychologists, 1972-; chmn DC Mental Health Assn Professional Adv Comm 1984-86; chmn Howard Univ Alumni Sch of Social Work Fund Raising Comm 1984-86; mem Kiwanis Club GA Br1985-86; mem greivance comm Natl Assoc of Social Workers 1984-86; president, ERM Consulting Corp 1980-; Academy of Certified Social Workers, NASW, 1974-; mem, NASW, 1968-. **Honors/Awds:** Outstanding Alumni, The Union Institute, 1996;Outstanding Alumni Howard Univ Sch of Soc Wk 1982; Image Awd & Faculty Awd, University of DC 1996; Outstanding Serv Mental Health Assn (Natl) 1982; Outstanding Leadership Univ of DC Coll of Educ & Human Ecology 1981; Outstanding Scholar Assn of Black Psychologists 1981; numerous publs; Outstanding Leadership Awd Univ of DC 1985; Outstanding Scholar Awd Univ of DC 1986; textbook, The Community Psychology Concept 1977; book, Race and Culture in the Mental Health Service Delivery System 1981; book, Challenges of a Changing America, 1994; Outstanding Services Plaque, Grad, SGA Univ of DC, 1994; NAACP, Service Recognition Plaque, 1993. **Military Serv:** USAF Tech Sch Flight Commander, Personnel Specialist, 1956-60; 2 Good Conduct Medals. **Home Phone:** (202)882-8124. **Business Addr:** Professor, Department of Psychology & Counseling, University, District of Columbia, 4200 Connecticut Ave, NW, Washington, DC 20008, (202)274-6447.

MYERS, JACQUALINE DESMONA
Educator. **Personal:** Born Jan 5, 1951, Charleston, SC; daughter of Daisy Elouise Brown Myers (deceased) and William Nicholas Myers (deceased). **Educ:** Benedict College, Columbia, SC, BS 1971; Indiana Univ, Bloomington, MS 1972; Univ of Wisconsin, Madison, PhD 1980. **Career:** Benedict College, work study secretary 1968-71; Medical Univ of SC, clinic accountant 1971; Indiana Univ, asst instructor 1971-72; Alabama State Univ, asst prof 1973-86, assoc prof 1986-. **Orgs:** Mem Natl Bus Ed Assoc 1971-, Amer Vocational Ed Assoc 1977-, Amer Ed Rsch Assoc 1980-, Natl Council of Negro Women 1983-, asst correspondence sec Delta Sigma Theta Montgomery Alumnae 1983-84, NAACP 1984-, AL Assoc of Teacher Ed, Delta Pi Epsilon, AL Council of Computer Ed, Phi Delta Kappa, AL Assoc of Univ Professors, Assoc of Suprv & Curriculum Devel, Southern Reg Assoc of Teacher Eds, AL Vocational Assoc, Southern Bus Ed Assoc, AAUP; correspondence sec Delta Sigma Theta 1986; Southern Business Education Assn, 1989-91; secretary, Alabama State University Faculty Senate. **Honors/Awds:** Cum Laude Benedict College 1971; Outstanding Young Women of Amer 1977, 1980, 1984; published article in SBEA Bulletin 1980; Consortium of Doctors, 1991-97. **Home Addr:** 501 Deerfield Dr, Montgomery, AL 36109-3312.

MYERS, L. LEONARD
Business executive. **Personal:** Born Jan 25, 1933, Aliquippa, PA; son of Eddie Mae Ham Myers and Joseph Myers; married R Elizabeth; children: Linda Ann, Larry Leonard. **Educ:** Univ of Pittsburgh, BA; Life Underwriter Training Council LUTC; Chartered Life Underwriters, CLU; Amer Coll Amer Inst for Property & Liability Underwriter, CPCU. **Career:** First Summit Agency Inc, pres & CEO. **Orgs:** 1st black pres Long Island Chapter CPCU, Long Island Chap CLU, Hempstead Chamber of Commerce; past pres Natl Ins Ind Assoc, Lakeview Lions Club. **Military Serv:** AUS spec 4 2 yrs. **Home Addr:** 19 Surrey Lane, Hempstead, NY 11550. **Business Addr:** President & CEO, First Summit Agency, Inc, 126 North Franklin St, Hempstead, NY 11550.

MYERS, LENA WRIGHT
Educator. **Personal:** marrIed Dr Julius Myers Jr (deceased); children: Stanley. **Educ:** Tougaloo Coll, BA Sociology; MI State Univ, MA Sociology & Anthropology 1964, PhD Sociology & Social Psychology 1973. **Career:** Utica Jr Coll, instructor of soc & psych 1962-68; Washtenaw Comm Coll, asst prof of psychology 1968; Center for Urban Affairs MI State Univ, urban rsch 1970-73; Jackson State Univ, prof of sociology 1973-. **Orgs:** Mem of comm on status of women in sociology Amer Sociol Assoc 1974-77; rsch/consul TIDE 1975-78; pres Assn of Social/Behavioral Scientists Inc 1976-77; rsch/consul KOBA 1979-80; mem bd of dirs Soc for the Study of Social Problems 1980-83; rsch/consul Natl Sci Foundation 1983; pres Assn of Black Sociologists 1983-84. **Honors/Awds:** State of MS House of Rep Concurrent Resolution No 70 Commendation 1981; Disting Amer Awd 1981. **Home Addr:** 2320 Queensroad Ave, Jackson, MS 39213.

MYERS, LEWIS HORACE
Business executive. **Personal:** Born Apr 28, 1946, Carlisle, PA; married Cheryl; children: Donnell L, Marrielle, Lewis H III. **Educ:** UNC, Cert Basic Ind Dev Course 1979; UNC, MBA 1974; Franklin & Marshall Coll, BA 1968; Govt Exec Inst, 1981. **Career:** Off of Spec Progs Franklin & Marshall Coll, assoc dir 1968-69; Upward Bound Prog Harvard Univ, exec dir 1969-71; Soul City Found Inc, assoc dir 1971-75; Soul City Co, vice pres 1976-79; NC Minority Bus Dev Agency, dir 1980-82; NC Dept of Commerce Small Bus Devel Div, asst sec 1982-. **Orgs:** Mem Assn of MBA Execs 1975, NC Ind Dev Assn 1979-, So Ind Dev Cncl 1979-; founder, mem NC Assoc of Minority Bus. **Honors/Awds:** Series of 15 articles on Important Black People in Am Hist Lancaster Sun News 1968.

MYERS, PETER E.
Professional basketball player. **Personal:** Born Sep 15, 1963, Mobile, AL. **Educ:** Faulkner State Junior Coll; Arkansas-Little Rock. **Career:** NBA career: Chicago Bulls, 1986-87; San Antonio Spurs, 1988; Philadelphia 76ers, 1988; New York Knicks, 1988-90; New Jersey Nets, 1990; San Antonio Spurs, 1990; Washington Bullets, 1992; Chicago Bulls, 1993-97; New York Knicks, 1997-; CBA career: Rockford Lightning, 1987-88; Italian League career: Mang Bologna, 1991-92; Scavolini Pesaro, 1992-93. **Business Addr:** Professional Basketball Player, New York Knicks, 2 Pennsylvania Plaza, New York, NY 10121, (212)465-5867.

MYERS, RODNEY
Professional baseball player. **Personal:** Born Jun 26, 1969, Rockford, IL. **Educ:** Univ of Wisconsin, attended. **Career:** Chicago Cubs, pitcher, 1996-. **Business Addr:** Professional Baseball Player, Chicago Cubs, Wrigley Field, 1060 W Addison St, Chicago, IL 60613, (312)404-2827.

MYERS, RODNEY DEMOND
Professional baseball player. **Personal:** Born Jan 14, 1973, Conroe, TX. **Career:** Kansas City Royals, outfielder, 1996-. **Business Addr:** Professional Baseball Player, Kansas City Royals, PO Box 419969, Kansas City, MO 64141-6969, (816)921-2200.

MYERS, SAMUEL L.
Educator, association executive. **Personal:** Born Apr 18, 1919, Baltimore, MD; son of Edith Myers and David Myers; married Marion R Rieras; children: Yvette M , Tama M Clark, Samuel L Jr. **Educ:** Morgan State Coll, AB 1940; Boston Univ, MA 1942; Harvard Univ, MA 1948, PhD 1949; Morgan State Coll, LLD 1968; Univ of MD, LLD 1983; Sojourner/Douglass College, DH, literature, 1992. **Career:** Harvard Univ, rsch assoc 1949; Bureau Statistics US Dept of Labor, economist 1950; Morgan State Coll, prof, div chmn soc sci 1950-63; Inter-Amer Affairs US Dept State, adv 1963-67; Bowie State Coll, pres 1967-77, pres emeritus 1977-; Natl Assn for Equal Opportunity in Higher Educ (NAFEO), president, 1977-. **Orgs:** Mem MD Tax Study Comm 1958, Gov Comm on Prevailing Wage Law in MD 1962; vice chmn MD Comm for Humanities & Publ Policy; mem Alpha Kappa Mu, State Scholarship Bd 1968-77; vice chmn Gov Comm on Aide to Educ 1969-70; pres MD Assn Higher Educ 1971-72; chmn Comm Intl Prog, Amer Assn State Coll & Univ; rep Natl Adv Council for Intl Teacher Exchange; mem Steering Comm, Comm on Future Intl Studies; vice pres, bd of dir Natl Assn Equal Oppty in Higher Educ; mem Pres Comm on Foreign Lang & Intl Studies 1978-80; mem bd of dir Rassias Found 1980; mem Baltimore Urban League; rsch fellow Rosenwald Fellow Harvard Univ. **Honors/Awds:** Commandeur de L'Ordre National, Cote d Ivoire, 1991; Doctor of Humane Letters, Shaw Univ, 1994; National Economic Assn, Samuel Z Westerfield Award, 1995. **Military Serv:** US Army, capt 1942-46. **Business Addr:** Pres, Natl Assn for Equal Opportunity in Higher Educ, 400 12th St NE, #207, Washington, DC 20002.

MYERS, SAMUEL L., JR.
Economist. **Personal:** Born Mar 9, 1949, Boston, MA. **Educ:** Morgan State Coll, BA 1971; MIT, PhD 1976. **Career:** Univ of Minnesota, Roy Wilkins Chair prof, 1992-; Univ of Maryland, prof; Univ of Texas at Austin, asst prof of economics; Boston Coll, instr 1973; Bowie State Coll, visiting instr 1972. **Orgs:** Amer Economics Assn; Natl Economics Assn; Amer Acad of Political & Social Science; Amer Assn for the Advancement of Science; Alpha Phi Alpha; co-coordinator, Black Grad Economics Assn 1973. **Honors/Awds:** Alpha Kappa Mu Merit Award, 1970; Inst Fellow, MIT, 1971-73; Natl Fellowship Fund Fellow, 1973-75; Fulbright Lecturer in Economics, Cuttington Coll, Liberia, 1975-76; Fulbright Scholar, Univ of South Australia, Faculty of Aboriginal and Islander Studies, 1997. **Special Achievements:** Co-author: Bittersweet Success: Faculty of Color in Academe; Persistent Disparity: Race & Economic Inequality in the US; The Black Underclass: Critical Essays on Race and Unwantedness, 1994; Editor: Civil Rights and Race Relations in the Post Reagan-Bush Era; Co-editor: Economics of Race and Crime, Transaction Press, 1988; author, editor, and contributor of articles, chapters, and reviews to newspaper, periodicals, books, and journals. **Business Addr:** Roy Wilkins Chair Professor, University of Minnesota, H H Humphrey Institute of Public Affairs, 301 19th Ave, S, 257 Humphrey Center, Minneapolis, MN 55455.

MYERS, SERE SPAULDING
Dentist. **Personal:** Born Feb 8, 1930, Oklahoma City, OK; married MaryJane Barbara Stewart; children: Dr Serese Si C'Annon, Dr Sere S Jr, Robin Lynn, Stewart, Sheryll. **Educ:** Morehouse Clge, BS 1950; Univ of MO Kansas City, MS 1951; Howard Univ, DDS 1958; Queens Hosp, Cert in Oral Surgery 1959. **Career:** Forbes AFB, chief of oral surgery 1959-61; private practice, currently. **Orgs:** Pres Kansas City Howard Univ Alumni 1972-73, Natl Howard Univ Dental Assn 1983-85; Kansas City Dist Dental Soc; MO Dental Assn; Amer Dental Assn. **Honors/Awds:** Black Chamber of Commerce, Legacy Award, 1994. **Special Achievements:** One of the 100 Most Influential Blacks of Kansas City, 1993. **Military Serv:** USAF capt 1959-61. **Business Addr:** Dentist, 5240 Prospect, Kansas City, MO 64130.

MYERS, STEPHANIE E.
Business owner. **Personal:** Born Mar 7, 1950, Los Angeles, CA; daughter of Estelle E Lee and Robert W Lee (deceased); married Roy J Myers, 1991. **Educ:** CA St Coll Dominguez Hills, BA 1971; Coro Fellowship Prog, cert of comp 1973; Occidental Coll, MA 1975. **Career:** US Dept of Transportation, Washington DC, director of office of commercial space transportation, 1989-; US Dept of Health and Human Services, Washington DC, asst secretary for public affairs, 1983-89; US Dept of Commerce, Washington DC, special asst of public affairs, 1981-83; Contact California, Beverly Hills CA, owner, partner, 1979-81; Coro Found, fellow in public affairs, 1972-73, dir of comm prgm 1974-79; Cent City Men Hlth Centr, comm wkr 1971-72; Cmpgn to Elect Congresswoman Burke Cons, off mgr; Laison Cit Training Prgm, cons; LA Comm Coll Dist, cons; Now Wow Prod, pt owner; freelance songwriter, scriptwriter; vp, co-owner, RJ Myers Publishing Co, 1992-. **Orgs:** Cand LA City Council 1975; member, Natl Council of Negro Women; Soroptimist Intl; Delta Sigma Theta Pub Serv Sor; member, Council of 100 Black Republicans; mem Nat Coun Negro Women; member, Links, Inc; member, Woman in Aerospace. **Honors/Awds:** Ach award Soroptimist Intl, 1977; Coro Found Felshp 1972; del Rep Nat Conv 1977; del Rep Conv 1980; outstanding performance certificate, Secretary of Commerce, 1983; US delegate, Intl Women's Conference, 1985; Scroll of Merit, Natl Medical Assn, 1988; Secretarial Award, US Dept of Transportation; Outstanding Leader in Government, Delta Sigma Theta Public Service Sorority, 1994. **Business Addr:** VP & Co-Owner, The RJ Myers Publishing Co, 116 G St, SW, Washington, DC 20024, (202)863-0056.

MYERS, VICTORIA CHRISTINA
Corrections official. **Personal:** Born Nov 23, 1943, Indianapolis, IN; daughter of Victoria Knox Porter and Stanley Louis Porter; married Albert Louis Myers, Sep 4, 1965; children: David, John, Matthew. **Educ:** Indiana University, Bloomington, IN, AB, sociology, 1961-66; Webster University, Webster Groves, MO, MA, corrections, 1973-75. **Career:** Marion County Juv Court, Indianapolis, IN, juvenile probation officer, 1967-69; Missouri Board Probation and Parole, St Louis, MO, probation and parole officer, 1970-73; Missouri Board Probation and Parole, St Louis, MO, supervisor, 1973-84; Missouri Board Probation and Parole, Jefferson City, MO, board member, 1984-96, probation & parole administrator, 1996-. **Orgs:** President, Missouri Corrections Assn, 1978-79; board member, American Probation and Parole Assn, 1982-88; board member, 1982-88, natl sec, 1983-88, natl program chair, 1989-, National Assn of Blacks in Criminal Justice, chairman; Ethics Comm, 1990-92; program chair, 1994-96, vice pres, 1996-, bd of gov, delegate assembly, American Correctional Assn; commissioner, 1982-94, executive committee, 1988-92, Commission on Accreditation for Corrections; Grace Episcopal Church, vestry, 1992-95, sr warden, 1993-95; Episcopal Diocese of Missouri, diocesan council, 1995-2000. **Honors/Awds:** E R Cass Correctional Achievement Award, Amer Correctional Assn, 1994; Chairman's Award, National Assn of Blacks in Criminal Justice, 1987; Dedicated Service Award, National Assn of Blacks in Criminal Justice, St Louis Chapter, 1985; Outstanding Employee, Missouri Board of Probation and Parole, 1975. **Home Addr:** 2408 Parkcrest Dr, Jefferson City, MO 65101. **Business Addr:** Member, Missouri Board of Probation & Parole, Department of Corrections, 1511 Christy Dr, Jefferson City, MO 65101.

MYERS, WALTER DEAN
Writer. **Personal:** Born Aug 12, 1937, Martinsburg, WV; son of Mary Green Myers and George Ambrose Myers; children (previous marriage): Karen, Michael Dean, Christopher. **Educ:** State College of the City Univ of New York; Empire State College, BA. **Career:** New York State Dept of Labor, Brooklyn, employment supervisor, 1966-69; Bobbs-Merrill Co, Inc, New York City, senior trade book editor, 1970-77; writer, 1977-. **Orgs:** PEN, Harlem Writers Guild. **Honors/Awds:** Newbery Honor Book Award, two-time winner; Coretta Scott King Award, four-time winner; Margaret A. Edwards Award, 1994. **Special Achievements:** Author: Fallen Angels, 1988; Scorpions, 1988; It Ain't All For Nothin', 1978, The Young Landlords, 1979, Hoops, 1981; Motown and Didi, 1984; Now Is Your Time, The African American Struggle for Freedom, 1992; Brown Angels, HarperCollins, 1993; The Glory Field, 1994; New Jersey State Council of the Arts Fellowship, 1981, Natl Endowment for the Arts Grant, 1982. **Military Serv:** US Army, 1954-57. **Home Addr:** 2543 Kennedy Blvd, Jersey City, NJ 07304.

MYERS, WOODROW AUGUSTUS, JR.
Health services administrator. **Personal:** Born Feb 14, 1954, Indianapolis, IN; son of Charlotte Myers and Woodrow Myers; married Debra Jackson Myers; children: Kimberly Leilani, Zachary Augustus. **Educ:** Stanford Univ, BS (w/honors), biological sciences, 1973; Harvard Medical School, MD, 1977; Stanford Univ Grad School of Business, MBA, primary sector/hlth care mgt, 1982. **Career:** US Senate Cmte on Labor & Human Resources, physician hlth advisor 1984; Univ of CA, asst prof 1982-84; San Francisco General Hospital Med Center, quality assurance program chairman 1982-84, cost containment task force chrm, quality assurance/dept of med-computer system manager, dept of medicine/general internal medicine divattending physician, medical/surgical intensive care unit-assoc director; Univ of CA Institute of Hlth Policy Studies, affiliated faculty; IN Univ Med Center, asst prof of medicine; Stanford Univ Med Center, physician specialist in surgery, attending physician; State of IN, state hlth cmsnr; City of New York, hlth cmsnr; The Associated Group, senior vp, corporate medical dir, currently. **Orgs:** Amer Coll of Physicians; Amer Medical Assn; Natl Medical Assn; Society for Critical Care Medicine; IN State Medical Assn; Marion County Medical Society; diplomat Amer Board of Internal Medicine 1980; advisor US Senate Comm on Labor and Human Resources 1984; bd of trustees of Stanford Univ 1987-92. **Honors/Awds:** Hoosier Minority Chamber of Commerce, Living Legend Award, 1992; Governor Evan Bayh, Indiana, Spirit of the Heartland Award, 1990; Mayor William Hudnut, Key to the City of Indianapolis, Indiana, 1990; Indiana State Senator Carolyn B Mosby, Above and Beyond Award, Indiana Black Expo, 1990; Governor Evan Bayh, Sagamore of the Wabash, 1990; Student Natl Medical Assn, Region V, Distinguished Mentor Award, 1990; United States Surgeon General C Everett Koop, US Public Health Service Award, 1989; Indiana Trial Lawyers Assn, Hoosier Freedom Award, 1986; Governor Robert D Orr, Sagamore of the Wabash, 1986; The Sickle Cell Foundation of Northwest Indiana, Dr Charles F Whitten Award, 1985. **Special Achievements:** Author, works include: Problems of Minorities at Majority Institutions: A Student's Perspective; 23 articles; medical licenses in states of Indiana, California, and DC; appointed by President Reagan to 13 member cmte to find a strategy for battling AIDS 1987. **Business Addr:** Senior VP, Corporate Medical Director, The Associated Group, 120 Mounument Circle, Indianapolis, IN 46204-4903.

MYLES, ERNESTINE
Educator. **Personal:** Born Apr 19, 1921, Livingston, AL; son of Sophia Mae Abrams Jones and Lilart Jeff Jones; married Ernestine Jones (Long) Myles (divorced); children: Willie Long Jr. **Educ:** Miles Coll, BA; Alabama State Univ, MEd; Univ Amherst; Auburn Univ; Troy State Univ; Sanford Univ; Alabama State Univ, AA, 1978; Howard Univ, Humanities, 1986. **Career:** Butler County Bd of Educ, teacher 1950-86; Dept Physical Educ, vice pres 1968-69. **Orgs:** Mem VISTA 1965; chmn Physical Educ Dept Dist Mtg Leader; consultant, dir Camp Bonnie Brae; Organized Classroom Teachers 1967; dir Dist VIII 1975; dir Dist VI 1972-77; League Advancement Educ 1967; chairperson Uni Serv District XIV 1976-77; mem AEA Bd 1977-80; mem Assn of Classroom Teachers; mem S Central Alabama Girl Scout Council USA; mem League for the Advancement of Educ, pres Alabama Assn of Classroom Teachers 1979-80; pres Butler County Educ Assn 1976; sec Butler County Civic League Alabama Democratic Conf 1972-; sec Secondary Congressional Dist Alabama Democratic Conf 1976-; sec Alabama Democratic Conf Bd 1973-77; sec S Regional Assn of Classroom Teachers1974-76; Girl Scout Troops 1971; S Central Alabama Girl Scout Council Inc Bd Mem 1977; Sunday SchoolTeacher Friendship Baptist rch 1964-; dir BTU Friendship Baptist Church 1966-; US Award Sgt Shriver 1966; VISTA Pin Vice Pres; deputy registrar Butler County Alabama; Notary Public. Hubert Humphrey 1967. **Honors/Awds:** Outstanding Educ Serv Plaque Alabama State Teachers Assn 1969; Con Serv Citation Natl Educ Assn 1971.

MYLES, HERBERT JOHN
City official, educational administrator (retired). **Personal:** Born Jul 31, 1923, Abbeville, LA; son of Wilda A Myles (deceased) and Alexander Myles (deceased). **Educ:** USL-Lafayette, BA 1962; UNO-New Orleans, Med 1970; Nicholls St Univ, 30 plus 1971-72. **Career:** Vermilion Parish School System, teacher 1963-80; Herod Elem School, asst principal 1980-84; City of Abbeville, city councilman 1978-82, second term 1982-86; third term 1986-90, 4th term 1990-94. **Orgs:** Member KPC Council #77 Knights Peter Claver 1965-85; member KPC Fourth Degree 3rd Assembly 1975-85. **Military Serv:** USN aviation machinist 2nd class 6 yrs; American Campaign Medal-WW II Victory Medal 1943-49. **Home Addr:** 1629 13th St., Port Arthur, TX 77640-4463. **Business Addr:** Councilmember, City of Abbeville, City Hall, 101 N State St, Abbeville, LA 70510-5184.

MYLES, STAN, JR.
Host, producer. **Personal:** Born May 2, 1943, Los Angeles; divorced. **Educ:** CA State U, BA 1966. **Career:** KABC-TV LA, host-producer; manpower develop specialist 1969-71; MI Mining Mfg Co, sales rep 1968-69; LA Hair Co, pub rel rep 1968-69; AL Locke HS LA, tchr 1968-June 1968. **Orgs:** Dir pub info Westminister Neighborhood Assn LA 1965-68; Nat Assn of Marketing Developers; Am Fed of TV & Radio Artists; Kappa Alpha Psi; YMCA; life-time mem NAACP; Urban League. **Honors/Awds:** John Sweat Award CA Tchrs Assn; Urban Affairs Comm Rel Award LA City Schs; Man of Yr Award Bahai Faith.

MYLES, WILBERT
Business executive. **Personal:** Born Aug 28, 1935, Winnsboro, LA; son of Armeather Myles and John Myles; married Geraldine C Pinkney; children: Wilbert Anthony Jr, Nicole Denise. **Educ:** American Inst of Banking, attended; Pace University. **Career:** Corp Trust Dept Nat Bank of North Am, asst vice pres 1973-; Asst Cashier 1968-73; Supvr 1964-68; Clerk Typist 1962-64; Mail Clerk Home Ins Co 1961-62; Baltman & Co, nyc porter 1961. **Orgs:** Stock Transfer Assn 1968; Reorgn Group, Securities Industries Assn 1975; bd of mgrs, Harlem Br YMCA 1975; elected to the Nat Task Force Steering Comon YMCA in Black Comm 1975; BANWY's Black & Non-white YMCA's in Black Comm; Black Achiever's Com of Harlem YMCA of Gr NY 1974-. **Honors/Awds:** Recip Plaque Harlem Br of YMCA of Gr NY 1974; A Salute to Black Achievers in Industry; Plaque Honor of Bank from Harlem Br of YMCA of Gr NY in Appreciation of Banks Support of 1975 Black Achievers Proj. **Military Serv:** US Air Force, a/2c, 1956-61. **Business Addr:** Harris Trust Co of New York, 77 Water St, 4th Fl, New York, NY 10005.

MYLES, WILLIAM
Associate athletic director. **Personal:** Born Nov 21, 1936, Kansas City, MO; son of Vera L Phillips Myles and William Myles Sr; married Lorita Thompson, Jun 30, 1957; children: Debbie, Billy. **Educ:** Drake Univ, Des Moines, IA, BS, 1962; Central MO State, MS, 1967. **Career:** Manual HS, Kansas City, MO, assistant football/basketball coach, 1962-63; Lincoln HS, Kansas City, MO, assistant football/basketball coach, head football coach, 1963-69; Southeast HS, Kansas City, MO, head football coach, 1969-72; Univ of NE, Lincoln, NE, assistant football coach, 1972-77; OH State Univ, Columbus, OH, assistant football coach, 1977-85, associate dir of athletics, 1985—. **Orgs:** Mem Christian Science Church, Fellowship of Christian Athletes, 1964-, american Football Coaches Association, 1972-, Natl Association of College Directors of Athletics, 1985-; Boy Scouts of America. **Honors/Awds:** Kansas City Area Man of Year, Fellowship of Christian Athletes, 1970; Greater Kansas City Coach of Year, 1971; Double D Award, Drake Univ, 1981; Drake Natl Distinguished Alumni Award, Drake Univ, 1988. **Business Addr:** Associate Director of Athletics, Ohio State University, 410 Woody Hayes Dr, St John Arena #227, Columbus, OH 43210.

MYRICK, CLARISSA
Associate producer. **Personal:** Born May 24, 1954, Atlanta, GA. **Educ:** Morris Brown Coll, BA 1976; OH St U, MA cand 1977. **Career:** WOSU-TV, asso prod "Inquiry" 1977; Lovely Atlanta Mag, contrib editor 1976; Atlanta Daily World Newspaper, gen assignment reporter 1975; Nat Endowment for the Arts Scriptwriters Contest, prod asst during taping of prize-winning teleplay "The Tie That Binds" 1974-75; WCLK-RADIO, newscaster, reporter 1974; Morris Brown Literay Mag, editor "Visions"; WXIA-TV, recited original poems; co-author "Hungry Souls". **Orgs:** 1st v chpsn Nat Coop Educ Assn 1975. **Honors/Awds:** Dau of Am Revolution Medals 1967, 1972; Media Women Scholarship Awd Atlanta Chap 1974; 1st place Nat Endowment for the Arts Scriptwriters Prgm; Female Coop Educ Stud of Yr Awd Alpha Kappa Mu Honor Soc; OH St MA Fellowship 1976. **Business Addr:** Curator, Collections of Life & Heritage, 135 Auburn Ave NE, Atlanta, GA 30308.

MYRICK, HOWARD A., JR.
Educational administrator, educator. **Personal:** Born Jun 22, 1934, Dawson, GA; son of Lenora Pratt Myrick and Howard Myrick; married Roberta Bowens Myrick, Oct 8, 1955; children: Kyl V, Keris J. **Educ:** Florida A&M University, Tallahassee, FL, BS, 1955; University of Southern California, Los Angeles, CA, MA, 1966, PhD, 1967. **Career:** Corp for Public Broadcasting, Washington, DC, director of research, 1977-82; Clark-Atlanta University, Atlanta, GA, professor, 1982-83; Howard University, Washington, DC, chairman, radio/tv/film dept, 1983-89. **Orgs:** Editorial board, National Academy of Television Arts & Sciences, 1989-91; chairman, commission on minorities, Broadcast Education Association, 1988-90; board of directors, International Association of Knowledge Engineers, 1988-91; consultant, National Telecom and Info Agency, 1986-90; board of experts, National Endowment for the Arts, 1988-91. **Honors/Awds:** Legion of Merit, Dept of Defense, 1977; Distinguished Graduate, Florida A&M University, 1989; Soldier's Medal, Republic of China, 1969. **Military Serv:** US Army, Lt. Colonel, 1955-77; Legion of Merit, 1977, Joint Service Commendation Medal, 1973, Vietnam Combat Service Medal, 1969. **Business Addr:** Chairman, Dept of Radio, Television and Film, Temple University School of Communication, #15 Annenberg Hall, Philadelphia, PA 19122.

MYRICKS, NOEL
Educator, attorney. **Personal:** Born Dec 22, 1935, Chicago, IL; son of Mollie Palmer and Wyman Myricks; married Sherralyn Myricks; children: Toussaint L, Mollie. **Educ:** San Francisco State Univ, BA 1965, MS 1967; Howard Univ, JD 1970; The

American Univ, EdD 1974. **Career:** Howard Univ, prof 1967-69; Univ of Dist of Columbia, educ administrator 1969-72; Private Practice, attorney 1973-; (admitted to practice before US Supreme Court); Univ of Maryland, prof beginning 1972, associate professor, currently. **Orgs:** Certified agent NFL Players Assn 1984-; assoc editor Family Relations Journal 1978-82; mem, Kappa Upsilon Lambda, Alpha Phi Alpha, Reston, MD, 1984-; mem, American Bar Assn; mem, Groves Assn; educator, attorney coach, National Intercollegiate Mock Trial Champions, UMCP, 1992; Omicron Delta Kappa Honor Society, 1992. **Honors/Awds:** Appointed by Pres Jimmy Carter Natl Adv Council on Extension and Cont Educ 1978-81; Outstanding & Dedicated Serv to Youth & Community Easton, PA NAACP 1984; Outstanding Citizen of the Year Omega Psi Phi Frat Columbia, MD 1979; Faculty Minority Achievement Award, President's Commission on Ethnic Minority Issues, Univ of Maryland, 1990; Outstanding Advisor for a Student Organization, Campus Activities Office of Maryland, 1990; Superior Teaching Award, Office of the Dean for Undergraduate Studies, Univ of Maryland, 1990; Outstanding Mentor, UMCP, 1992; Outstanding Teacher of the Year, UMCP, 1992. **Military Serv:** USN Musician 3rd Class served 4 yrs.

N

NABORS, JESSE LEE, SR.
Educator. **Personal:** Born May 17, 1940, Columbus, MS; married Rebecca Gibson; children: Sherri, Tejia, Jesse Jr, Marcellus III. **Educ:** Tuskegee Inst, BS 1965; MEd 1968. **Career:** Stockton Unified Sch Dist, child welfare attendance 1971-; Tuskegee Inst, coord 1966; SUSD, tchr 1968; Tuskegee Inst, residence hall counselor 1967-68; City of Stockton, vice-mayor 1975. **Orgs:** Pres Stockton Br NAACP 1971-73; pres BTA 1972-73; polemarch Kappa Alpha Psi Frat; Stockton Alumni Chap 1975-77. **Honors/Awds:** Outst serv NAACP 1973; outst serv BTA 1973; outst serv City of Stockton 1976. **Business Addr:** 701 N Madison, Stockton, CA 95202.

NABRIT, JAMES M., JR. See Obituaries section.

NABRIT, JAMES M., III
Attorney (retired). **Personal:** Born Jun 11, 1932, Houston, TX; married Roberta Jacquelynn Harlan. **Educ:** Bates Coll, AB 1952; Yale Law Sch, JD 1955. **Career:** NAACP Legal Def & Educ Fund Inc, director, Executive Committee, mem, atty 1959-89. **Orgs:** Dir Lawyers Comm for Civil Rights; secretary, NAACP Legal Defense & Educational Fund Inc. **Military Serv:** AUS corpl 1956-58. **Home Addr:** 215 Park Row, New York, NY 10038.

NABRIT, SAMUEL M.
Association, executive (retired). **Personal:** Born Feb 21, 1905, Macon, GA; son of Augusta G West and James M Nabrit; married Constance Crocker, Aug 8, 1927. **Educ:** Morehouse Coll, BA 1925; Brown Univ, MS 1928, PhD 1932. **Career:** Morehouse Coll, prof of biology 1925-27; Atlanta Univ, instr chmn dept of biology dean of grad sch of arts & sci 1932-55; VI Educ Experimental Prog,prof of biology 1955; TX Southern Univ Houston, pres 1955-66; Atomic Energy Commn, appointed 1966-69; Southern & Natl Fellowships Fund, retired exec dir 1967-; interim executive director, Atlanta Univ Center. **Orgs:** Apptd to Natl Sci Bd 1956-61; bd dir Amer Council on Educ 1961; mgmt comm US So Africa Leader Exchange Prog; mem Natl Conf Christians & Jews Inc; chmn bd dirs Inst for Serv to Educ; chmn Natl Academy of Sci Panel on Hlth Svcs; served on several comms for depts of state & HEW; bd of dirof many colls & univs; pres Con Mortgage Co Atlanta; mem bd dir Afro-Am Life Ins Co Jacksonville; vice pres Standard Savings & Loan Houston; mem 1965 Houston Charter Review Commn; published several papers & articles; mem Amer Soc of Zoologists, Sigma Xi, Beta Kappa Chi, Pi Delta Phi, Omega Psi Phi, Sigma Pi Phi, Phi Beta Kappa, Institute of Medicine of Natl Acad of Sciences. **Honors/Awds:** Received many study & rsch grants; 2nd winner, J. William Rogers, Brown Univ 1987; Distinguished Award Achievement Medal, 1982; science bldgs named in honor, Texas Southern Univ and Morehouse College. **Home Addr:** 686 Beckwith St, Atlanta, GA 30314.

NAEOLE, CHRIS
Professional football player. **Personal:** Born Dec 25, 1974; married Tara; children: Azure Ke'alohilani. **Educ:** Univ of Colorado, bachelor's degree in sociology. **Career:** New Orleans Saints, guard, 1997-. **Business Addr:** Professional Football Player, New Orleans Saints, 5800 Airline Hwy, Metairie, LA 70003, (504)733-0255.

NAGAN, WINSTON PERCIVAL
Educator. **Personal:** Born Jun 23, 1941, Port Elizabeth, Republic of South Africa; married Judith Mattox; children: Jean, Catherine. **Educ:** Univ of Ft Hare, BA 1964; Oxford U, BA1966; Oxford U, MA 1971; Kuke U, LLM, MCL 1970; Yale U, JSD 1977. **Career:** Univ of FL Coll of Law, prof 1975-; Monash Univ School of Law Australia, visiting prof 1979; Yale Coll, lectr 1974-75; CLEO Inst, asso prof; 1974; De PaulU Coll of Law, asso prof, asst prof 1972-75; Expedited Arbitration Proc, arbitrator 1972-74; Valparaiso Univ Sch of Law, asst prof 1971-72; VA Polytech Inst St U, asst prof 1968-71; AALS Law Tchrs Clinic, 1971; Duke Law Sch, rsch asst 1968; Ross Arnold atty-at-law, law clerk 1967. **Orgs:** Am Soc of Intl Law; African Stud Assn; Assn of Am Law Sch; Am Bar Assn; Ctr for Study of Dem Instn; Am Soc for Social Philosophy & Philosophy of Law; Arts & Civil Sem Univ of FL; Am Civil Sem Univ of FL; sec Intl Campaign vs Racism in Sports 1972-74; consult Am Bar Assn 1976; trust Intl Def Aid Fund 1971-74; Minority Com; Prom Tenure Com; Curr Com; Library Com; Fac Recruit Com; chmn Adm of Fgn Lawyers Com Univ Senate; edit Soviet Pub Intl Law 1970; exec com; Intl Def & Aid Fund for So Africa 1972-74; test UN 1968-73. **Honors/Awds:** Faculty of Law prize Ft Hare 1963; Brasenose Oxford Overseas Scholar 1964-67; African-Am Inst Fellowship 1967-68; James B Warburg Fellow 1974-75; num appear on radio & TV; num publ papers & speeches; Senior Fulbright Scholar Monash Univ Australia 1979.

NAILS, JAMIE
Professional football player. **Personal:** Born Jun 3, 1975. **Educ:** Florida A&M. **Career:** Buffalo Bills, tackle, 1997-. **Business Addr:** Professional Football Player, Buffalo Bills, One Bills Dr, Orchard Park, NY 14127, (716)648-1800.

NAILS, JOHN WALKER
Attorney. **Personal:** Born Sep 5, 1947, Florence, AL; son of Mary Ester Nails and Rudolph Nails Jr; married Phyllis Johnson, Mar 9, 1974; children: Tanique Yvette, Rudolph IV. **Educ:** Howard University, BA, 1969; Villanova Law School, JD, 1972. **Career:** Community Assistance Project, legal representative, 1972-75; City of Chester, assistant city solicitor, 1978-87, city solicitor, 1988-91; self-employed attorney, 1975-. **Orgs:** Pennsylvania Bar Association, 1972-; Delaware County Bar Association, 1975-; National Bar Association, 1985-; Calvary Baptist Church, trustee, 1987-. **Honors/Awds:** Chester Scholarship Fund, Outstanding Community Service, 1983. **Special Achievements:** Villanova Law School, Co-winner of the Riemel Moot Court Competition, 1972; City of Chester, first black city solicitor, 1988. **Business Addr:** Attorney-at-Law, 19 W Fifth St, Chester, PA 19013, (215)876-0306.

NAJEE (JEROME NAJEE RASHEED)
Musician. **Personal:** Born Nov 4, 1957, New York, NY; son of Mary and Frank; married Regina Jackson, May 27, 1989; children: Noah Howard, Jamal Fareed. **Educ:** Bronx Community College, 1977-78; New England Conservatory of Music, 1978-82. **Career:** Recordings include: Najee's Theme, 1987; Day By Day, 1988; Tokyo Blue, 1990; Share My World, 1995; has performed with Ray Goodman and Brown. **Honors/Awds:** Just My Illusion, 1994; Tokyo Blue, 1992; Soul Train Music Awards, Best Jazz Album, 1991, 1993; Recording Industry Assn, Gold Album, 1987, Najee's Theme "Day by Day," 1989. **Special Achievements:** Plays soprano, alto and tenor sax and flute. **Business Addr:** Jazz Artist, c/o Walter Lee, 16133 Ventura Blvd, Ste 955, Encino, CA 91436.

NALL, ALVIN JAMES, JR.
Photojournalist. **Personal:** Born Nov 27, 1960, New York, NY; son of Emma Nall and Alvin J Nall. **Educ:** Cayuga Community College, AAS, 1995; Ithaca College, BS, 1997. **Career:** New York Air National Guard, media specialist, 1979-; Portrait Photographer, 1981-82; WTVH-TV, photojournalist/editor, 1982-93, production tech, tech sgt, 1993, 1995. **Orgs:** National Press Photographer's Association, 1988-94; Natl Assn of Black Journalists, 1989-; Syracuse Association of Black Journalists, 1991-; NAACP, ACT-So Program, mentor/coach, 1989-. **Honors/Awds:** National Academy of TV, Arts & Sciences, New York Emmy Award, 1988-89; The Associated Press, Spot News Award, 1985; National Press Photographer's Association, Clips Awards, 1989, 1992; Syracuse Press Club, 5 Professional Recognition Awards, 1985-90. **Military Serv:** US Air Force, technical sgt, 1990-91; SW Asia Service Medal w/3 Devices, Kuwait Liberation Medal, AF Commendation Medal; Air Force Achievement Medal. **Business Phone:** (315)454-6408.

NANCE, BOOKER JOE, SR.
Elected city official. **Personal:** Born Apr 10, 1933, Crockett Cty, TN; married Everlena Lucas; children: Alice Eison, Booker J Jr, Mary, Phyllis, Gladys, Marvin. **Career:** Nance's Construction & Contracting, pres 1984-; Town of Gates, town board, alderman 1973-. **Orgs:** Chmn Parents Advisory Committee Halls Elementary. **Military Serv:** AUS pfc 1953-55; Natl Defense Serv Medal. **Home Addr:** PO Box 97, Gates, TN 38037.

NANCE, HERBERT CHARLES, SR.
Government counselor. **Personal:** Born Dec 30, 1946, Taylor, TX; son of Alice Lavern Sanford Nance and Henry Nance Jr; married Linda Lee Brown; children: Charlinda Audlice, Herbert Jr. **Educ:** Huston Tillotson College, BA 1969; University of Texas at San Antonio, MA 1979. **Career:** Ross Jr High School, teacher/coach 1974-76; Kitty Hawk Jr High School, teacher/coach 1976-80; Vietnam Era Veterans Outreach Prog, counselor 1980-81; BASE Educ Serv Office, guidance counselor 1981-; Base Education Services SA-ALC/DPE Kelly AFB Texas Education Services Specialist 1987-. **Orgs:** Amer Assn Counseling 1981-; bd of trustees, Lackland Indep Sch Dist 1986-; adv counsel, Comm Coll of the Air Force 1986; asst keeper of records, Omega Psi Phi Frat, San Antonio Chap 1986; bd mem, Bexar County Sickle Cell Anemia 1988-; Vice Basileus, Psi Alpha Chapter, Omega Psi Phi Fraternity Inc 1987-. **Military Serv:** US Army, sp-5, 3 1/2 yrs; Army Commendation/Expert M-14. **Home Addr:** 2942 Lakeland Dr, San Antonio, TX 78222. **Business Addr:** Education Services Specialist, BASE Education Services, SA-ALC/HRE, San Antonio, TX 78241-5000.

NANCE, JESSE J., JR.
Educator. **Personal:** Born Aug 2, 1939, Alamo, TN; son of Lillie L Nunn Nance and Jesse J Nance. **Educ:** TN State Univ, Nashville, BS, 1961; Univ of WI Madison, MS 1971; Univ of TN, additional graduate studies. **Career:** TN High School, teacher 1961-67; Oak Ridge Assoc Univ, special training in atomic energy 1967, instructor nuclear science 1967-69; Atlantic Comm Coll, asst prof of biology 1971-76; Univ of TN Med Units Memphis, special training 1972; Jackson State Comm Coll, instructor, Biology 1976-78; Vol Comm Coll, assoc prof of biology 1978-. **Orgs:** Mem Phi Beta Sigma 1959; Intl Wildlife Fed 1972; church choir mem, dir male chorus, minister of educ, church school teacher. **Honors/Awds:** Serv Key Award Baptist Student Union, 1961; Danforth Fellowship Award, Danforth Found, 1969; Acad Grant, NSF & Atomic Energy Commn 1972; Teacher of the Year, 1984-85; Martin Luther King Brotherhood Award, 1988. **Home Addr:** 37 Nolan Dr., Gates, TN 38037-4115. **Business Addr:** Associate Professor of Biology, Volunteer State Comm College, Nashville Pike, Gallatin, TN 37066.

NANCE, LARRY DONELL
Former professional basketball player. **Personal:** Born Feb 12, 1959, Anderson, SC; divorced. **Educ:** Clemson Univ, 1981. **Career:** Phoenix Suns, 1981-88, Cleveland Cavaliers, 1988-94. **Honors/Awds:** NBA slam dunk champ; named NBA Player of Week; honorable mention on 1980-81 Assoc Press All-Am team; NBA All-Star Player. **Business Addr:** Former Professional Basketball Player, Cleveland Cavaliers, Gund Arena, One Center Ct, Cleveland, OH 44115.

NANCE, M. MACEO, JR.
Educational administrator. **Personal:** Born Mar 28, 1925, Columbia, SC; married Julie E Washington; children: Maceo, Robert Milton. **Educ:** SC State Coll, AB 1949; NY Univ, MA 1953; Morris Brown Coll, LLD 1968; Francis Marion Coll, LHD 1975; Clemson Univ, 1983; Citadel Mil Coll, 1983; Univ SC, LlD 1976. **Career:** SC State Coll Orangeburg, mil property custodian 1950-54, dir student union 1954-57, asst to bus mgr 1957-58, bus mgr 1958-67, vice pres bus fin 1967, acting pres 1967-68, pres 1968-1986; 1986 President Emeritus. **Orgs:** Dir Bankers Trust of SC; mem comm fed rel Amer Council Ed; mem Council of Pres of State Supported Insts Higher Ed SC; mem adv comm Natl Assoc Advancement of Public Negro Colls; chmn council pres Mid-Eastern Athletic Conf; mem SC State Council Boy Scouts Amer; bd dirs Coll Placement Svc, Blue Cross-Blue Shield SC; bd dir, mem exec comm United Way SC; mem Gov Comm on Police & Commun Relations; mem Natl Assoc State Univs, Land Grant Colls, NAACP; dir, treas Natl Assoc Equal Oppty in Higher Ed; mem NY Univ Alumni Assoc, Omega Psi Phi; past pres Sigma Pi Phi; mem Kiwanis, Masons. **Honors/Awds:** Coveted Outstanding Civilian Serv Medal by the Dept of the Army; State of SC Order of the Palmetto; City of Orangeburg Citizen of the Year. **Military Serv:** USN 1943-46. **Business Addr:** President, South Carolina State College, Orangeburg, SC 29117.

NANULA, RICHARD D.
Company executive. **Educ:** University of California; Harvard Business School. **Career:** Walt Disney Co, senior vp and cfo, 1991-94, Disney Stores, pres, 1994-96, sr exec vp/cfo, 1996-. **Business Addr:** Sr Exec Vice President/CFO, The Walt Disney Co, 500 S Buena Vista St, Burbank, CA 91521, (818)560-1000.

NAPHIER, JOE L.
Company executive. **Personal:** Born May 22, 1940, Florence, AL; son of Vera Lee Martin Naphier and Thomas James Naphier; married Mary Frances Scott, Aug 8, 1961; children: Jacquelyn Jo'von. **Educ:** George Washington University, Washington, DC, AS, 1975; Pepperdine University, Malibu, CA, BA, 1979, MA, HRM, 1981; National University, San Diego, CA, MBA, 1983. **Career:** MDAC, Long Beach, CA, branch manager human resources, 1980-87; MDC Space Systems Co, Huntington Beach, CA, director human resources, 1987-90; McDonnell-Douglas, Long Beach, CA, general manager, human resources, twin jet, 1990-92, workforce diversity, ombudsman, currently. **Orgs:** Member, consultant, Coleman-McNair, 1990-; member, NAACP, 1985-; member, Amer Management Association, 1984-; member, Black MBA Society, 1987-; 100 Black Men of Los Angeles. **Honors/Awds:** Coleman-McNair Leadership Award, 1992. **Military Serv:** US Navy, Senior Chief, 1956-75; Vietnam Medal, an array of military service awards. **Business Addr:** General Manager, Workforce Diversity, Ombudsman, McDonnell-Douglas Aircraft Co, 138-14, 3855 Lakewood Blvd, Long Beach, CA 90846.

NAPHTALI, ASHIRAH SHOLOMIS

Attorney, finance consultant. **Personal:** Born Apr 6, 1950, Kingston, Jamaica. **Educ:** New York Medical & Dental School, physician assistant certificate, 1974; New York Univ, BA 1979; Hofstra Univ, JD-MBA 1984. **Career:** Urban Devel, consultant/rsch asst, 1978-80; MAKKA Productions, mgmt consultant, 1980-82; Nassau County Office of Employment, legal asst, 1982-83; Colin A Moore Esquire, legal asst 1983; South Brooklyn Legal Svcs, law asst 1983-84; Michael M Laufer Esquire, assoc 1984; Helen Gregory Law Office, assoc 1987-; NACA Inc, pres 1984-; Law Office of Barbara Emmanuel, Queens, NY, associate 1989-; Law Office of Alarid, Alexander Al, law assistant/associate, 1989-90; Ashirah Naphtali Laurelton, NY, attorney/finance counsultant, 1990-. **Orgs:** WIBO; Natl Bar Assn; Intl Soc of Financiers, 1986-; Amer Consultant League, 1986-; Kiwanis Club of Cambria Heights, 1990-97; Macon B Allen Bar Association, 1991-92; BESLA, 1991-92; Queens Bar Association, 1990-95; New York State Bar Association, 1990-91. **Honors/Awds:** Cambria Heights Kiwanis Club, Inc, Certificate of Recognition, 1996; NYC Office of Vet Affairs, Cert of Recognition, 1995; National Library of Poetry, editors choice award, 1996; Beth Elohim Ethiopian Hebrew Congregation, Inc., Merit Award, 1996. **Military Serv:** USAF sgt 1969-74; USAR sgt 1980-83. **Business Addr:** Law Office of Ashirah Scholomis Naphtali, 130-33-217 St, Ste B, Jamaica, NY 11413-1230.

NAPOLEON, BENNY NELSON

Law Enforcement official. **Personal:** Born Sep 10, 1955, Detroit, MI; son of Betty Lee Currie Napoleon and Rev Harry Napoleon; children: Tiffani Chanel. **Educ:** Mercy College of Detroit, Detroit, MI, AA, cum laude, 1980, BA, cum laude, 1982; Detroit College of Law, Detroit, MI, JD, 1986. **Career:** Detroit Police Dept, inspector, 1975-93, deputy police chief, 1993-; Michigan Civil Rights Commission, commissioner, 1984-91; self-employed, attorney, beginning 1987. **Orgs:** Board of directors, GDIRT, NCCJ, 1990-; secretary, Coalition for DEMH, 1990-91; NOBLE, 1985-; FBI NAA, 1987-; IAATI, 1990-; State Bar of Michigan, 1986-; American Bar Association, 1986-. **Honors/Awds:** Trustee Scholarship, DCL, 1982; Dean's Award for Outstanding Scholarship, DCL, 1983; Distinguished Alumni Award, MCD, 1988; Police Community Serv Award, Greater Detroit Chamber of Commerce, 1990; Wolverine Student Bar Association, Detroit College of Law, Distinguished Alumni Award, 1991. **Business Addr:** Deputy Chief, Detroit Police Department, 1300 Beaubien, Detroit, MI 48226.

NAPOLEON, HARRY NELSON

Cleric. **Personal:** Born Nov 12, 1922, Brownsville, TN; son of Geneva Estes Napoleon and Harry Napoleon; married Betty Lee Currie Napoleon, Apr 17, 1951; children: Geneva Smitherman, Bobbie Napoleon Rearton, Anita Napoleon Taylor, Hilton, Benny N, Kathryn Napoleon Brogdon, Sharon Napoleon Seaton. **Career:** Tennessee Missionary Baptist Church, pastor, currently. **Orgs:** Council of Baptist Pastors of Detroit, MI. **Business Addr:** Pastor, Tennessee Missionary Baptist Church, 2100 Fischer, Detroit, MI 48214, (313)823-4850.

NAPPER, BERENICE NORWOOD

Musician. **Personal:** Born Dec 10, 1916, S Norwalk, CT; divorced; children: Patricia Knudsen, Alver Woodward Jr. **Educ:** Howard Univ Washington DC, MusB 1935-40; Westport Famous Writer's School Westport CT, diploma 1950. **Career:** Concert artist 1940-; Am Cyanamid Co, librarian foreign div 1964; Napwood Asso, owner, dir 1953-; Natl NAACP NY, field sec, troubleshooter 1951; CT Labor Dept, unemployment comp supvr 1946-53; CT Welfare Dept, social worker 1945-. **Orgs:** Exec dir Urban League White Plains 1942-; Dist 12 RTM Greenwich CT Town Gov 1960-68; commr CT State Bd of Parole 1971-75; bd mem Sigma Gamma Rho Sorority 1940; bd mem State & Nat LWV/PPLI Social Serv 1940-; bd mem Norwalk Comm Coll 1973-. **Honors/Awds:** 1st Negro woman cand Reb Nomination CT US Sen 1970; 1st Negro woman cand GOP Greenwich Nom 2nd Selectman 1979; 1st Negro vol nurse's aide Greenwich Chap ARC 1942-; Distinguished Alumni Award Howard Univ Alumni NY Chapter, 1970; Humanitarian Award Nigeria 1975; Outstanding Negro Woman CT Bicentennial Commn, 1976; Distinguished Black Women Greenwich YWCA 1977.

NAPPER, HYACINTHE T.

Government employee (retired). **Personal:** Born Feb 26, 1928, New York, NY; daughter of Georgiana Bergen Tatem and Charles A Tatem; divorced; children: Cynthia, Guy, Geoffrey. **Educ:** Fisk Univ, attended 1945-47; Howard Univ, AB 1951. **Career:** US Dept of Labor, sec Thomasina Norford Minority Groups consult 1951-53; Hon John Conyers Jr, admin asst retired 1988; After retired 1988; self employed as Financial Manager. **Orgs:** Mem Alpha Kappa Alpha Sor; interest in bringing greater polit awareness to Black comm improve voter turnout; US Figure Skating Assn; Ft Dupont Skating Club; Congressional Staff Club; Washington Figure Skating Club, board of governors; DC Special Olympics, ice skating coach; DC Police Boys and Girls Club; editor, The Blade, Washington Figure Skating Club newsletter. **Honors/Awds:** DC Special Olympics Figure Skating Coach Award. **Home Addr:** 13901 Amberfield Ter, Upper Marlboro, MD 20772.

NAPPER, JAMES WILBUR

Educator (retired). **Personal:** Born Feb 25, 1917, Institute, WV; son of Zanphra D Robinson and Walter J Napper; married Cassie McKenzie, Dec 23, 1950; children: Gregory S, David M. **Educ:** WV State Coll, BS 1937; WV Univ, MS 1949; Univ of CA Berkeley, Credential 1964. **Career:** Boyd School Charleston WV, teacher, coach 1950; Alameda Cty Oakland CA, dep probation officer 1954; DeAnza HS Richmond, teacher 1958; Richmond Unified School Dist, guidance consult 1965; Santa Rose Jr Coll, counselor 1969-82. **Orgs:** Mem California Teacher Assoc 1958-, NEA 1969, Phi Delta Kappa Ed Group 1976-; ed adv Alpha Phi Alpha; exec bd, NAACP; vice pres, Kiwanis; bd of dirs, AGAPE. **Honors/Awds:** 2 Letters of Commendation Santa Rose City School 1969-70; Cert of Appreciation Dept of California Youth Auth 1974. **Military Serv:** AUS staff sgt 1944-46; ETO 5 Battle Stars. **Home Addr:** 230 Frosti Way, Eustis, FL 32726.

NASH, BOB J.

Government official. **Personal:** Born in Texarkana, AR; children: Creshelle, Eric. **Educ:** Univ of Arkansas at Pine Bluff, BA, sociology, 1969; Howard Univ, MA, urban studies, 1972. **Career:** City of Washington, DC, asst to the deputy mayor; City of Fairfax Virginia, asst to the city manager; Natl Training and Development Serv, administrative officer; Arkansas State Dept of Planning, dir of community and regional aff; Winthrop Rockefeller Foundation, vp; Office of Former Arkansas Governor Bill Clinton, senior exec asst for economic development; Arkansas State Development Finance Authority, pres; White House Personnel, assoc dir; US Department of Agriculture, undersecretary of agriculture, 1993. **Business Addr:** Undersecretary, US Dept of Agriculture, 14th & Independence, SW, Washington, DC 20250.

NASH, CURTIS

Attorney. **Personal:** Born Jul 11, 1946, Tallulah, LA; married Betty Jean Gordon. **Educ:** So Univ Baton Rouge LA, BA 1969; Univ of IL Coll of Law, JD 1972. **Career:** Tax Div Dept of Justice Washington DC, trial atty 1975-; Corp Tax Br IRS Nat Office, tax law spec 1972-75; Vermillion Co Legal Aid Soc Danville IL, law clk 1972; Firm of Kidd & McLeod Monroe LA, law clk 1971. **Orgs:** Vp Fairfax Co Wide Black Citizens Assn 1980; mem Pi Gamma Mu; mem Omega Psi Phi Frat. **Honors/Awds:** Equal Oppor Fellowship Univ of IL Coll of Law. **Business Addr:** Department of Justice, Tax Division, 9th & Pennsylvania Ave, Washington, DC 20530.

NASH, DANIEL ALPHONZA, JR.

Physician. **Personal:** Born Jul 15, 1942, Washington, DC; son of Ruby I Nash and Daniel A Nash Sr; married Bettie Louise Taylor; children: Cheryl L, Daniel E. **Educ:** Syracuse Univ, BS 1964; Howard Univ, MD 1968. **Career:** Georgetown Med Serv DC Gen Hosp, internship 1st yr resd 1968-70; Brooke Army Med Ctr, resd nephrology fellow 1970-73, asst chf 1973-76; Walter Reed Army Med Ctr, asst chf 1976-77, chf nephrology serv 1977-83; Private Practice Washington DC, physician 1983-. **Orgs:** Mem Amer Colls of Physicians 1974, fellow 1976; mem Natl Med Assn 1974; mem AMA 1975; mem Amer Soc of Nephrology 1975; mem Intl Soc of Nephrology 1975; med licensure Washington DC 1969; MD 1977; assoc prof med Howard Univ Col Med 1978; diplomat Amer Bd of Intl Med 1973; subspecialty Bd in Nephrology 1974. **Honors/Awds:** 10 major medical publs; 12 publ abstracts; 4 sci presentations. **Military Serv:** US Army col MC 1970-83; USAR 1983-92. **Business Addr:** Physician, 6196 Oxon Hill Rd, Ste 300, Oxon Hill, MD 20745.

NASH, EVA L.

Government association executive. **Personal:** Born Jul 25, 1925, Atlantic City, NJ; widowed; children: Michele, Sharon. **Educ:** Howard Univ, AB (magna cum laude) 1945; Univ of Chicago, Sch of Soc Serv Admin 1945-46; Univ of Pgh Sch of Soc Work, MSW (summa cum laude) 1959. **Career:** Hubbard Hosp, med soc worker 1947-49; Atlantic City NJ, sub tchr 1954-55; City of Pgh, market surveyor 1956-57; Travelers Aid, 1957; Freedman's Hosp, 1961-64; Child Guid Clinic, clinical soc worker 1964-67; DC Developmental Svc, chief soc worker 1967-69; DC Model Cities Prog, health planner 1969; HUD, comm serv officer 1969-72, asst to dir admin on aging 1972-. **Orgs:** Mem Natl Assn for Soc Workers 1947-; Academy of Certified Soc Workers 1962-; Amer Orthopsychiatric Assn 1965; Northwest Settlement House Aux 1972-, pres 1972-73; Budget Comm Washington Council of Planned Parenthood 1973-; Mental Health Sub-Comm Urban League 1963-64; Howard Univ & Interdisciplinary Faculty Seminar 1963-64; Bunker Hill Sch PTA 1959-64, chmn nominating comm 1960; chmn Sch Fair 1961; Western HS PTA 1965-66; DC Citizens for Better Pub Sch Educ 1966-, co-chmn spec serv comm 1968-70; Natl Comm for Support of Pub Sch 1968-; consult Group Counseling Prog Model Sch Div Sec Sch 1967-68; DC Public Sch Model Sch Div sum staff 1968; Educ Working Party of Mental Retardation Planning Comm for DC 1968; workshop ldr Howard Univ Sch of Soc WorkSch Agency Inst 1967; NASW Regnl Conf Buffal968; cnsltng seminar ldr Wash Sch of Psychiatry 1968-69; Comm Chest Area Capt Nashville 1951; World & Polit Disc Grp Pgh 1955-57, ldr 1956; bd dir DC Planned Parenthood 1968; Marriage Prep Inst Bd 1963-64; V St Proj Com 1963-64; NAACP; Nat Cncl Negro Women. **Honors/Awds:** Urban League Vol Serv Awd 1967. **Business Addr:** Dir Info & Referral, Administration on Aging/HHS, Chief Educ & Career Prep Br, 200 Independence Ave SW, Washington, DC 20201.

NASH, HELEN E.

Physician. **Personal:** Born Aug 8, 1921, Atlanta, GA; daughter of Marie Graves Nash and Homer E. Nash; married James B Abernathy Sr (deceased). **Educ:** Spelman Coll Atlanta, AB 1942; Meharry Med Coll Nashville, MD 1945. **Career:** WA Univ School of Med, clinical instr 1949-71; St Louis Childrens Hosp, vstg prof 1949; St Louis Maternity & McMillan Hosp, asst pediatrician 1949; Homer G Phillips Hosp, pediatric supr, assoc dir of pediatrics 1950-64; St Lukes Hosp St Louis, vstg prof 1962; Jewish Hosp of St Louis, vstg prof 1963; Washington Univ George Waring Brown Sch of Soc Work, lectuer 1969-71; WA Univ School of Med, assoc prof clinical peds 1974, prof clinical peds 1984; St Louis Childrens Hosp, pres staff assoc 1977-79; private practice, physician 1949-. **Orgs:** Mem Amer Acad of Pediatrics 1953, Health & Welfare Council of Met St Louis, Comm of the State Welfare Dept of MO, St Louis Childrens Hosp Staff Soc, St Louis Med Soc; various committees St Louis Childrens Hosp 1948-79. **Honors/Awds:** Honor mem St Louis Med Soc 1975, Medical Woman's Society, 1991.

NASH, HENRY GARY

Engineering company executive. **Personal:** Born May 3, 1952, Macon, GA; son of Elizabeth Cason and Henry Nash; children: David, Gary Alton. **Educ:** Univ of Southern California, Los Angeles, MS, 1977-79; Savannah State College, Savannah, GA, BSEE, 1974. **Career:** Automation Industries, Silver Spring, MD, systems engineer, 1974-77; Raytheon Company, Burlington, MA, senior project engineer, 1977-81; General Electric Co, Arlington, VA, senior systems engineer, 1981-85; Tracor Applied Sciences Inc, Arlington, VA, program manager, 1985-87; General Scientific Corp, Arlington, VA, president, 1987-. **Orgs:** Member, Kappa Alpha Psi Fraternity, 1972; member, Arlington County Chamber of Commerce, 1987.

NASH, LEON ALBERT

Dentist (retired). **Personal:** Born Mar 19, 1912, Canton, MS; son of Estelle Nash and Leon Nash Sr; married Nora; children: Leon Jr, Anita. **Educ:** Tongaloo Coll, 1934; Meharry Dental Sch, 1947. **Career:** Hathesbury MS, 1947-51; Detroit MI, dentist 1951-80. **Orgs:** Omicron Kappa Epsilon Dental Soc; past pres Wolvermeed Dental Soc. **Military Serv:** AUS 1941-44.

NASH, ROBERT JOHNSON

Architect, urban planner. **Personal:** Born Jan 21, 1929, Memphis, TN; son of Vernon Nash and Andrew Nash; married Barbara Swan, Jan 1, 1983; children: Robyn, Carolyn, Steven, Terry. **Educ:** Howard University, BArch, 1952. **Career:** Johnson and Boutin Architects, chief of design, 1956-62; B-2 Ltd, president, 1984-93; B and N Developers, president, 1990-93; Robert J Nash FAIA & Associates PC, president, 1970-. **Orgs:** American Institute of Architects, vice pres, 1972-73; National Capital Planning Commission, vice-chair, 1979-92; National Organization of Minority Architects, president, 1983-84. **Honors/Awds:** National Organization of Minority Architects, Service Award, 1989; American Institute of Architects, Whitney M Young Citation, 1972, College of Fellows, 1973, Historic Preservation Award, 1981; DC Housing Industry Corp, Community Devt Award, 1983. **Special Achievements:** Chaired task force and consultant panel for the re-design of the nations capital monumental core for the next 100 yrs, the most prestigious urban planning task in America. **Military Serv:** US Army, sp-3, 1954-56. **Business Addr:** President, Robert J. Nash FAIA and Associates, P.C., 6448 Bock Rd, Oxon Hill, MD 20745, (301)839-7600.

NASH, THOMAS

Publisher. **Personal:** Born Oct 5, 1919, Muskogee, OK; married Betty Jean (deceased); children: Charlotte Ann, Thomas Jr, Susan Carol, Stephen Charles. **Educ:** Langston Univ, attended 1938-41, BA 1948. **Career:** The Post Newspaper Group, asst publisher. **Orgs:** Foreman pro-tem Monterey Co Grand Jury 1983-84; chmn of minority comm Monterey Co Affirmative Action Plan; state pres United Black Fund of CA. **Honors/Awds:** Certificate of Appreciation Seaside Chamber of Commerce 1985, Monterey County Legal Aid Soc, Concerned Citizens of Monterey; Proclamation City of Seaside 1986. **Military Serv:** AUS 1st sgt 1941-49; USAF 1st lt 1949-54. **Business Addr:** Assistant Publisher, The Post Newspaper Group, 630 20th St, Oakland, CA 94612.

NATHAN, TONY CURTIS

Professional football assistant coach. **Personal:** Born Dec 14, 1956, Birmingham, AL; son of Louise Nathan and William Nathan; married Johnnie F Wilson; children: Nichole, Natalie, Nadia. **Educ:** Univ of Alabama, attended. **Career:** Miami Dolphins, running back, 1979-87, assistant coach, 1988-95; Tampa Bay Buccaneers, assistant coach, 1996-. **Honors/Awds:** Named All-NFL Kick Returner, AP; All-AFC Punt Returner, Sporting News; played in Senior Bowl and Hula Bowl. **Business Addr:** Assistant Coach, Tampa Bay Buccaneers, One Buccaneer Place, Tampa, FL 33607.

NATTA, CLAYTON LYLE
Physician, educator. **Personal:** Born Nov 17, 1932, San Fernando, Trinidad and Tobago; son of Leonora and Samuel; married Stephenie Lukowich, Jul 4, 1964; children: Laura, Andrea. **Educ:** McMaster University, BA, 1957; University of Toronto, MD, 1961; Royal College of Physicians of Canada, FRCP, 1972; Royal College of Pathologists, FRC, pathology, 1990. **Career:** Ottawa Civic Hospital, 1965-66; New York University Medical Center, fellow in clinical hematology, 1966-68; Columbia University, instructor/associate, 1970-73, assistant professor of medicine & pathology, 1973-81, associate professor, clinical medicine, 1981-. **Orgs:** American Association for Advancement of Science, 1969-; American Society of Hematology, 1969-; New York Academy of Sciences, 1973-; New York State Society of Internal Medicine, 1974-; International Society of Hematology, 1983-; Biochemical Society of London, 1983-; Nutrition Society of London, 1985-; American Society of Clinical Nutrition, 1987-; Society for the Study of Blood, membership chairman, 1977. **Honors/Awds:** World Health Organization, Travel Fellowship, 1974; American College of Nutrition, Fellow, 1980; Meharry Medical College, 2nd Annual George M Howard Jr Memorial Lecture, 1987; National Heart, Lung, and Blood Institute, consultant, site visit, 1992; Royal College of Physicians of Canada, Fellow, 1972; Royal College of Pathologists of London, Fellow, 1992. **Special Achievements:** Co-author, Erythrocyte Polyamines of Normal Individuals and Patients with Sickle Cell Anemia, 1988; Co-author, Alteration in IgG Subclass Distribution in AIDS, 1989; Co-author, Antisickling Properties of Pyridoxine Derivatives: Cellular and Clinical Studies, 1990; Co-author, Selenium and Glutathione Peroxidase Levels in Sickle Cell Anemia, 1990; Co-author, Antioxidant status and free radical-induced oxidative damage of Sickle Erythrocytes, 1992. **Home Addr:** 300 W 55th St, Apt 14B, New York, NY 10019, (212)245-7607. **Business Addr:** Professor, Columbia University, College of Physicians and Surgeons, Department of Medicine, 630 W 168th St, New York, NY 10032, (212)305-2645.

NATTIEL, RICKY RENNARD
Professional football player. **Personal:** Born Jan 25, 1966, Gainesville, FL. **Educ:** Univ of Florida, received rehabilitation counseling degree, 1987. **Career:** Denver Broncos, wide receiver, 1987-. **Honors/Awds:** Post-season play, 1987, 1989: AFC Championship Game, NFL Championship Game.

NAVES, LARRY J.
Judge. **Career:** Denver District Court, judge, currently. **Business Addr:** Judge, Denver District Court, City & County Bldg, 1437 Bannock, Denver, CO 80202, (303)640-2309.

NAYLOR, GLORIA
Writer, film producer. **Personal:** Born Jan 25, 1950, New York, NY; daughter of Alberta McAlpin Naylor and Roosevelt Naylor. **Educ:** Brooklyn College, BA, English, 1981; Yale University, MA, Afro-American Studies, 1983. **Career:** George Washington University, visiting lecturer, 1983-84; New York University, visiting professor, 1986; Princeton University, visiting lecturer, 1986; Boston University, visiting professor, 1987; Cornell University, Society for the Humanities, senior fellow, 1988; One Way Productions, New York, NY, pres 1990-. **Orgs:** Book of the Month Club, executive board member, 1989-94. **Honors/Awds:** American Book Award 1983; NEA Fellowship Natl Endowment for the Arts 1985; Guggenheim Fellowship 1988; Lillian Smith Award, 1989. **Special Achievements:** Author, novels: The Women of Brewster Place, 1982; Linden Hills, 1985; Mama Day, 1988; Bailey's Cafe, 1992; The Best Short Stories by Black Writers, volume II, editor, Sept 1995; The Men of Brewster Place, 1998; World Premiere of ''Bailey's Cafe,'' the play, at the Hartford Stage Company, April 1994. **Business Addr:** One Way Productions, 638 2nd St, Brooklyn, NY 11215, (718)965-1031.

NAYLOR, LAURETTA. **See THOMPSON, LAURETTA PETERSON.**

NAYMAN, ROBBIE L.
Psychologist. **Personal:** Born Oct 7, 1937, Dallas, TX; married Dr Oguz B. **Educ:** BS 1960; MS 1962; PhD 1973. **Career:** CO St U, sr cnslr Univ Cnslng Ctr, dir Univ Lrng Lab 1970-; WI St Dept of Hlth & Soc Svcs, affirm act coord 1969-70; Univ of WI, tchng asst 1964-69; St Univ Coll, asst dean of stds 1962-64; So IL U, cnslr 1960-62. **Orgs:** Mem Am Personnel & Guidance Assn; Am Psychol Assn; Pi Lambda Theta; mem Urban Leag NAACP. **Business Addr:** Director of Student Services, California State University, Fullerton, 800 N State College, Fullerton, CA 92631-3599.

NEAL, ALIMAM BUTLER
Physician, anesthesiologist, pain consultant. **Personal:** Born Mar 29, 1947, Tuskegee, AL; son of Gladys Neal and Odis Neal; married Ruth Elizabeth Reid; children: Michael, Alimam Jr, Alaina, Angela. **Educ:** Howard Univ, BS 1968; Howard Univ Coll of Medicine, MD 1973. **Career:** Walter Reed Army Medical Ctr, intern 1973-74, resident anesthesiology 1974-77; Eisenhower Army Medical Ctr, chief dept anesthesiology 1978-80; Medical Coll of Georgia, asst prof anesthesiology 1980-81; Univ Hosp Augusta GA, private anesthesiologist 1981-; Augusta Diagnostic Pain Center, pres; A B Neal and Assoc, pres; ABNA Realty, pres, CEO. **Orgs:** Stoney Medical/Dental/Pharm Soc; life mem Alpha Phi Alpha; Natl Medical Assn; GA State Medical Assn; Amer Soc Anesthesiology; NAACP; trustee, Bethel AME Church. **Honors/Awds:** Diplomate Amer Bd Anesthesiology 1979; Fellow Amer Coll Anesthesiology 1977; Spinal Cord Stimulation Workshop Phoenix, AZ, 1989; Amer Academy of Pain Management, Fellow/Diplomate, 1992. **Military Serv:** US Army, major, 11 yrs; Army Commendation Awd 1978. **Home Addr:** 3731 Pebble Beach Dr, Augusta, GA 30907.

NEAL, BRENDA JEAN
Manager. **Personal:** Born Jan 3, 1952, Greenville, SC; children: Damon Yusef. **Educ:** New Mexico State Univ; Onondaga Community College, AA Social Work 1976; Le Moyne College, BA Sociology 1978. **Career:** Lincoln First Bank, teller 1974; Syracuse City School District, school social worker 1982-83; Xerox Corp, internal control mgr, customer service mgr 1983-. **Honors/Awds:** Black Achievers Award 1490 Enterprise Buffalo 1983; Special Merit Award Xerox Corp 1984. **Military Serv:** AUS Specialist 4; Outstanding Trainee Award (ranked 1st out of 34 men) 1971. **Home Addr:** 114 - Kay St, Buffalo, NY 14215. **Business Addr:** Customer Service Manager, Xerox Corporation, 450 Corporate Pky, Buffalo, NY 14226-1204.

NEAL, CHARLIE
Sports broadcaster. **Personal:** Born Oct 28, 1944, Philadelphia, PA; son of Elizabeth Neal and Robert Parrish. **Educ:** Villanova University, 1966. **Career:** CBS TV, sports broadcaster, 1982-85; TBS TV, sports broadcaster, 1986-88; Greyhound Lines Inc, safety instructor, 1971-; BET TV , sports broadcaster, 1980-. **Orgs:** Blue Knights, safety committee, 1985-; Arlington County Police, special operations section, 1986-; AFTRA, 1982-. **Honors/Awds:** 100% Wrong Club, Sportcaster of the Year, 1989; Arlington County VA, Outstanding Volunteer, 1991. **Home Addr:** 15105 Jennings Lane, Bowie, MD 20721. **Business Phone:** (202)636-2838.

NEAL, CURLY. **See NEAL, FREDERIC DOUGLAS.**

NEAL, CURTIS EMERSON, JR.
Consulting engineer. **Personal:** Born Feb 20, 1931, Yoakum, TX; son of Ellie Neal and Curtis Emerson Neal Sr; married Evelyn V Spears, Sep 21, 1963. **Educ:** Prairie View A&M University, BS, architectural engineering, 1958. **Career:** St Philip's College, instructor, 1958-63; WA Moore Engineering Co, vice pres, 1963-71, vice pres, 1973-75; GW Adams Manufacturing Co, president, 1971-73; Curtis Neal & Associates, president, 1975-. **Orgs:** Texas Society of Professional Engineers; National Society of Professional Engineers; Professional Engineers in Private Practice; National Association of Black Consulting Engineers; Alamo City Chamber of Commerce, board member; San Antonio Water Service Board, board member. **Honors/Awds:** The United Negro College Fund, Leadership in the Minority Community, 1980; The Alamo Chamber of Commerce, Business Vanguard Award, 1988; City of San Antonio, Outstanding Service to the Community, 1983; Legislative Black Caucas, State of Texas, Outstanding Contribution to the Business Field, 1983. **Military Serv:** US Army, staff sgt, 1952-54. **Business Phone:** (210)226-2772.

NEAL, EARL LANGDON
Attorney, chief executive officer. **Personal:** Born Apr 16, 1928, Chicago, IL; son of Evelyn S Neal and Earl J Neal; married Isobel, Sep 24, 1955; children: Langdon D Neal. **Educ:** Univ of IL, BA, 1949; Univ of MI, JD, 1952. **Career:** City of Chicago, Chicago, IL, attourney, Chicago Land Clearance Commission, 1955-61, assistant corporation counsel, 1961-68, special assistant corporation counsel, 1969—; Earl L Neal & Associates, proprietor, 1968—. **Orgs:** Trustee emeritus, Univ of IL; director, Chicago Title & Trust, Chicago Title Ins Co, Peoples Energy Corp, Lincoln Natl Corp, First Chicago Corp, First Natl Bank, Chicago Central Area Committee; life member, NAACP. **Honors/Awds:** Outstanding Leader Award, Little Flowers, 1977; outstanding service award, Univ of IL Black Alumni, 1982; Man of the Year, Boys and Girls Clubs of Chicago, 1985; distinguished service award, Univ of IL Alumni Association, 1988. **Military Serv:** US Army, cpl, 1953-54; served in Europe. **Business Addr:** Earl L Neal & Associates, 111 W Washington St, Suite 1010, Chicago, IL 60602.

NEAL, EDDIE
Engineer. **Personal:** Born Dec 18, 1943, Reidsville, NC; son of Gertrude Farrish Neal and Charlie H Neal; married Dianne Tyrance, Jun 28, 1986; children: Ayoka Z Neal, Damali C G Neal. **Educ:** Howard Univ, BS, 1966; Catholic Univ, MA, 1971, PhD, 1986; Graduate Studies, Univ of MI; Univ Coll (London, UK) Webb Institute; Teesside Polytechnic Institute (UK). **Career:** US Dept of Transportation, research engineer, 1966-67; US Navy, research scientist, 1967-76; Chi Associates, vice pres, 1976-79; The Scientex Corporation, pres/CEO, 1979-. **Orgs:** Mem, Sigma Xi, 1973-; mem, Society of Naval Architects, 1975-; mem, Touchdown Club, 1985-; mem, NAACP, 1986-; mem, Kappa Alpha Psi, 1987-; mem, Honorary Committee, Charles R Drew World Medical Prize, 1989; dir, Assn of Small Research, Engineering and Technical Services Companies, 1989-. **Honors/Awds:** Invited author, 8th and 10th International Symposia on Naval Hydrodynamics, 1970, 1974; invited speaker, ASCE Conference, Highway Safety: At The Crossroads, 1988.

NEAL, EDNA D.
Educational administrator. **Personal:** Born Jan 19, 1943, Pine Bluff, AR; daughter of Florell W Devoe and Jewell L Devoe, Sr; divorced; children: Yolande Aileen. **Educ:** AM&N Coll, AB 1965; Univ of AR, MEd 1973; IN Univ, EdD 1978. **Career:** Employment Security Div, career counselor 1961-69; Univ of AR at Pine Bluff, asst dir counseling ctr 1969-79; Youngstown State Univ, exec asst student svcs 1979-88; Sinclair Community College Dayton Ohio vice pres student serv 1988-. **Orgs:** Amer Assn of Higher Education; Natl Assn for Student Services Personnel Assn; Ohio Council on Student Development, pres; Otterbein Homes, bd mem; Mary Scott Nursing Ctr, pres, bd of trustees; Dayton Montgomery County Scholarship Committee; Red Cross, bd of trustees. **Honors/Awds:** Awd nominee YWCA Tribute to Black Women 1983; Prof Woman Natl Assn of Negro Bus & Prof Women's Clubs 1983. **Home Addr:** 131 Folsom Drive, Dayton, OH 45405.

NEAL, FREDERIC DOUGLAS (CURLY NEAL)
Public relations executive, professional basketball player. **Personal:** Born May 19, 1942, Greensboro, NC; son of Katie C Carter Neal and Alfonza Lowdermilk; married Rose Allen Neal, Sep 8, 1976; children: Lavern, Frederic Jr, Pamela, Toi, RoCurl. **Educ:** Johnson C Smith University, 1959-63, BS, 1975. **Career:** Harlem Globetrotters, Los Angeles, CA, basketball player, coach, public relations executive, 1963-85; Cernitin America, Yellow Springs, OH, public relations executive, 1985; Orlando Magic, Orlando, FL, ticket chairman, director of special projects, 1986-; Celebrity Golf Association (PGA), professional golfer, 1990-; has also appeared in numerous television shows, including Harlem Globetrotters Popcorn Machine, Wide World of Sports, Donnie and Marie Osmond Show, The Mandrell Sisters, The Love Boat, BBC TV Special, MTV, Don't Just Sit There, Comedy hour, Johnny Carson, Dick Cavett, David Frost, Good Morning America; spokesperson for Boeing, McDonalds, Coca Cola, Sherwin Williams Paint, and others. **Orgs:** Screen Actors Guild; American Federation of Television and Radio Artists. **Honors/Awds:** Outstanding Athlete, All State Basketball (NC), 1958-59; Best Athlete, CIAA, 1960-63; Best Five Award, GIT, 1961; Hall of Fame, CIAA, 1985, 1986; Just Say No, Apopka Police Department and Public Schools; J.C. Smith 100 Club Sports Hall of Fame, 1989; Outstanding Contribution to Youth, Special Olymipics, 1988-89; Contribution to Youth, Youth Basketball of America, 1988; Outstanding Contributor to the Youths of Greensboro, Greensboro Recreation Department, 1970; Superior Performance as a Dribbler, Harlem Globetrotters, 1970; Dedication to Youth, United Way, United Youths Sports League, 1988; sponsors basketball clinics and summer camps; participates in numerous speaking engagements for charities. **Business Addr:** c/o C & R Associates, Inc, PO Box 915415, Longwood, FL 32791.

NEAL, GREEN BELTON
Physician. **Personal:** Born Sep 4, 1946, Hopkins, SC; married Linda Mattison; children: Green II, Tiffany, Marcus. **Educ:** Benedict Coll, BS 1966; Meharry Medical Coll, MD 1971; GW Hubbard Hospital, resident, 1972-73; Vanderbilt Univ Med Sch, fellow, 1973-75. **Career:** Self-empl, physician; Providence Hosp, med staff; Columbia; SC Richland Memorial Hosp; Meharry Med Coll, asst prof med; GW Hubbard Hosp, dir cardiac catherization lab 1975-76. **Orgs:** GA St Med Assn 1975; LA St Med Assn 1975; consult Physician Tuskegee Inst; Mem Nat Med Assn; AMA; bd mem Boy's Club of Grtr Columbia; Columbia Med Assn; mem Am Heart Assn; Congaree Med Dental & Pharm Assn. **Honors/Awds:** Flwsp Grant in Cardiology NIH. **Business Addr:** Physician, 1415 Barnwell, Columbia, SC 29201.

NEAL, HERMAN JOSEPH
Physician. **Personal:** Born Dec 31, 1923, Alexandria, LA; son of Catherine Johnson Neal and Herman Joseph Neal; married Caridad Antiqueno Neal, 1980; children: Ronald, Antoinette, Renee, Eric John. **Educ:** Wilson Jr Coll, AA 1943; Howard Univ 1943-45; Northwestern Univ, pre-med 1945-48; Univ of IL Med School, 1952. **Career:** Cook County Hosp Chicago, phys (intern) 1952-53; Provident Hosp Chicago, physician 1953-67; Cook County Hosp, phys/pediatrician 1955-57; Walther Meml Hosp, 1967-80; St Mary of Nazareth Hosp, physician 1976-. **Honors/Awds:** ''Paratyphoid - Osteomyelitis in Sickle Cell Anemia'' Cook Co Hosp Phys Bulletin 1957. **Military Serv:** US Army Quartermaster, private first class, 1943-45; Overseas Serv Award 1945; European Service Award, 1943-45. **Business Addr:** Physician, 946 W 79th St, Chicago, IL 60620.

NEAL, HOMER ALFRED
Scientist, educator. **Personal:** Born Jun 13, 1942, Franklin, KY; married Donna Daniels; children: Sharon; Homer Jr. **Educ:** Indiana Univ, BS Physics 1961; Univ of Michigan, MS Physics 1963, PhD Physics 1966; Indiana Univ, DSc Hon Degree 1984.

Career: Indiana Univ, asst prof physics 1967-70, asso prof physics 1970-72, prof physics 1972-81, dean research & grad dev 1977-81; Suny Stony Brook, provost 1981-86, prof of physics; University of Michigan, vice pres for research, currently. **Orgs:** Fellow Amer Physical Society 1972-; mem Natl Sci Bd 1980-86; mem NY Seagrant Inst Bd of Directors 1982-86; fellow Amer Assoc for Adv of Sci 1983-; trustee Universities Research Assoc Bd of Trustees 1983-; mem SUNY Research Foundation Bd of Directors 1983-86; mem Scientist's Inst for Public Info Bd of Trustees 1985-87. **Honors/Awds:** Fellow Natl Sci Found, Washington, DC 1966-67; fellow Sloan Found 1968; chrmn Argonne Zero Gradient Synchrotron Users Group 1970-72; trustee Argonne Univ Assoc 1971-74; mem Physics Advisory Panel Natl Sci Found 1976-79; mem High Energy Physics Advisory Panel US Dept of Energy 1977-81; fellow JS Guggenheim Found 1980-81; chmn Natl Science Foundation Physics Adv Panel 1986. **Business Addr:** Interim President/Physics Professor, University of Michigan, President's Office, 503 Thompson, Ann Arbor, MI 48109-1340.

NEAL, IRA TINSLEY
Educational administrator. **Personal:** Born Nov 14, 1931, Memphis, TN; son of Ogie Neal and James Neal; married Jacqueline Elaine Wiley. **Educ:** Evansville Coll IN, BA 1960; IN Univ Bloomington, MS 1964. **Career:** Evansville-Vanderburgh School Corp, dir of fed projs 1977-, supr 1970-77; Comm Act Prog Evansville, exec dir 1966-70; Neighborhood Youth Corps, dir 1965-66; Evansville-Vanderburgh School Corp, teacher 1960-65. **Orgs:** Pres Pride Inc 1968-78; sec-treas New Hope Housing Inc 1979-80; ctr asso IL /IN Race Desegregation Assistance Ctr 1979-80; mem Kappa Alpha Psi Frat 1966-80; bd mem Vanderburgh Co Judiciary Nominating Com 1971-80; bd mem Inner City Cultural Ctr 1977-80. **Honors/Awds:** Nominated NEA's Carter G Woodson Award Local Black Tchrs 1978; Black Comm Award Black Comm of Evansville 1978; plaque for Srv Rendered Head Start of Evansville IN 1979. **Military Serv:** US Amry, SFC, 1947-56. **Home Phone:** (812)435-8459. **Business Addr:** 1 SE Ninth St, Evansville, IN 47708.

NEAL, JAMES P., SR. See Obituaries section.

NEAL, JAMES S.
Association executive. **Personal:** Born Sep 7, 1922, Washington, KY; married Manie; children: Patricia, Angela, John, Michael. **Educ:** Xavier U, BS, BA; Xavier Eveining Coll; Chase Coll of Commerce; LaSalle Ext U. **Career:** Urban Leag of Cincinnati Inc, proj dir 1973-; Am Agr Chem Co, supr 1942-67. **Orgs:** Pres Chief Contract Neg Local Union of Intrntl Un Dist 50 United Mine Wrkrs 22 yrs; past pres Cincinnati Chap Ohio Black Pol Assembly; past pres 13th Ward Avondale Dem Club; past mem Hamilton Co Dem Exec Com; precienct exec 8 yrs; past mem bd Seven Hills Neighborhood Houses Inc; past chmn Hlth & Safety Com Avondale Comm Cncl Inc; mem bd trustees, exec com Negro Sightless Soc; labor rep Handicaps United for Betterment Inc; 3rd Deg KC; cand for OH St Gen Assembly.

NEAL, JOSEPH C., JR.
Investment/insurance agent. **Personal:** Born Mar 23, 1941, Memphis, TN; son of Hattie Counts Owens and Joseph C Neal, Sr; children: Lisa M, Thomas Joseph. **Educ:** Trade Tech Coll LA, AA 1960; CA State Coll LA, BA 1973. **Career:** Phoenix Home Life Ins Co & Phoenix Equity Planning Corp, 1969-; Christian Method Episcopal Church, gen sec fin dept. **Orgs:** Mem NAACP 1965-; 32nd degree mason Prince Hall Grand Lodge 1966-; fin counselor Various businesses in CA 1969-; mem Los Angeles Life Underwriters Assoc 1969-; mem LA Kiwanis Club 1972-; licensed rep Natl Assoc of Securities Dealers 1974-. **Honors/Awds:** Outstanding Sales Phoenix Mutual Life Ins Co; Blue Vase Winner, presidents club mem; Honorary Dr of Laws Lane College 1989. **Business Addr:** General Secretary Fin Dept, Christian Meth Episcopal Ch, PO Box 75085, Los Angeles, CA 90075.

NEAL, LANGDON D.
Attorney. **Career:** Earl L Neal and Associates, managing partner, currently. **Orgs:** Chicago Board of Election Commissioners, chairman, currently. **Special Achievements:** Only the second African American to be elected to the Chicago Board of Election Commissioners. **Business Addr:** Managing Partner, Earl L Neal & Associates, 111 Washington St, Chicago, IL 60602, (312)641-7144.

NEAL, LAVELLE E., III
Sports writer. **Personal:** Born Sep 28, 1965, Chicago, IL; son of Lillian E Neal and La Velle E Neal Jr. **Educ:** Univ of Illinois, Champaign, 1983-86; University of Illinois, Chicago, BA, communication, 1989. **Career:** Chicago Illini, sports editor, 1986-89; Southtown Economist, Chicago, IL, sports writer, 1988-89; Kansas City Star, Kansas City, MO, sports writer, 1989-. **Orgs:** Kansas City Association of Black Journalists, secretary, 1989-; Natl Assn of Black Journalists, 1987-. **Honors/Awds:** Chancellor's Student Service Award, University of Illinois, 1989; Kansas City Assn of Black Journalists, President's Award, 1992. **Business Addr:** Sports Writer, Kansas City Star, 1729 Grand Ave, Kansas City, MO 64108, (816)234-4706.

NEAL, LORENZO LAVON
Professional football player. **Personal:** Born Dec 27, 1970, Hanford, CA. **Educ:** Fresno State. **Career:** New Orleans Saints, running back, 1993-96; New York Jets, 1997-. **Business Addr:** Professional Football Player, New York Jets, 1000 Fulton Ave, Hempstead, NY 11550, (516)560-8100.

NEAL, MARIO LANZA
Banking executive. **Personal:** Born Aug 3, 1951, Haines City, FL; son of Mary E Wolfe and Warren Neal Jr; married Emma L Woodward Neal, Dec 23, 1973; children: Warren Keith, Jennifer Woodard. **Educ:** Florida State University, double BS, finance/management, 1973; University of Delaware, Stonier Graduate School of Banking, 1989. **Career:** First Union Corporation, area president/Florida panhandle, 1973-. **Orgs:** Center for Drug-Free Living, Inc, board member, 1992-; Hi-Tech Learning Center, Inc, board member, 1992-; YMCA Black Achievers, Inc, 1992; INROADS of Tampa Bay, Inc, board member, 1989-; Family Housing Services, Inc, president, 1974-76; Energy Committed to Ex-Offenders, Inc, treasurer, 1978-83; Mecklenburg County Personnel Commission, 1980-85; chair-elect, United Way of the Big Bend Tallahassee, FL; chair-elect, Economic Development Council; board of directors, Tallahassee Area Chamber of Commerce; board of directors, March of Dimes; board of directors, Regional 5 Workforce Development Board; board of directors, Florida State University Alumni; mem, FSU College of Business Advisory Board; committee mem, Davis Productivity Awards, Florida TaxWatch; board of directors, Capital Cultural Center, Tallahassee. **Honors/Awds:** Central Florida YMCA Black Achievers, Inc, 1992. **Special Achievements:** Editor, Charlotte Citizen, publication of Charlotte Jaycees, 1975-76; Recognized as One of Two areas within First Union Corp for top performance, 1995. **Business Addr:** Area President, Florida Panhandle, First Union National Bank of Florida, 1201 N Monroe St, Tallahassee, FL 32303.

NEAL, RICHARD
Law enforcement official. **Career:** Philadelphia Police Dept, patrolman, 12th district, beginning 1962, community relations, Internal Affairs division, head, Housing Police, interim chief, Patrol Bureau, chief inspector, until, 1992, commissioner, 1992-. **Business Addr:** Commissioner, Philadelphia Police Department, Franklin Square, Philadelphia, PA 19106, (215)592-5753.

NEAL, SYLVESTER
State fire marshal (retired). **Personal:** Born Sep 21, 1943, Austin, TX; son of Ima L Jenkins Neal and Willis Neal; married Doris Marie (Mims) Neal; children: Sylvia, Sylvester L, Keith, Todd, Angela Williams. **Educ:** Univ of Alaska, Fairbanks, degree in criminal justice (magna cum laude), 1983. **Career:** City of Austin, Austin TX, firefighter, 1965-68; US Army, Fort Wainwright AK, firefighter, crew chief, 1968-70; State of Alaska, Dept of Transportation, Fairbanks AK, firefighter, security police, 1970-79, fire/security chief, 1979-83; Dept of Public Safety, Anchorage AK, state fire marshal, beginning 1983 (retired); Anchorage Daily News, safety director, 1994-. **Orgs:** Mem, bd (2 years), Alaska Fire Chiefs Assn, 1976-, Alaska Peace Officers Assn, 1979-; sec, Fairbanks Kiwanis Club, 1982-83; mem, Intl Fire Chiefs Assn, 1983-, Fire Marshals Assn of North Amer, 1984-; mem, consultant, Alaska Assn of Public Fire Educ, 1985-; pres, Anchorage Kiwanis Club, 1987-88; bd of dir, Community Action for Drug Free Youth, 1988-; lieutenant governor-elect, Kiwanis/Alaska-Yukon Div, 1989-90. **Honors/Awds:** Student of the Year Justice Dept, Univ of Alaska Fairbanks, 1982; Kiwanian of the Year, Fairbanks Kiwanis Club, 1983; Outstanding President, Kiwanis/Pacific Northwest Dist, 1989. **Military Serv:** US Army, Sgt, 1968-70. **Home Addr:** 4812 Hunter Dr, Anchorage, AK 99502.

NEALE, CHINYERE
Association executive. **Personal:** Born May 3, 1953, Detroit, MI; daughter of Josephine Robinson and Harold Lloyd Neal; married Heshimu Jaramogi, Aug 15, 1977; children: Anwar M Jaramogi. **Educ:** Wayne State Univ, Detroit, MI BA, 1981; Univ of Chicago, Chicago, IL, MA, 1982. **Career:** WDET, Detroit, MI, producer, host, 1983-85; Northeast Guidance Center, Detroit, MI, dir of PR and Marketing, 1982-85; US Postal Service, Detroit, MI public affairs officer, gen supervisor, 1985-91; Natl Assn of Women Business Owners, Detroit, MI, exec dir, 1991-94. **Orgs:** Mem, Women in Communication, 1983-; WSU Alumni Assn, 1989-; U of Chicago Club; bd of dirs, Legal Aid Defender's Assn of Detroit. **Home Addr:** 649 Gladstone, Detroit, MI 48202-1730.

NEALS, FELIX
Judge. **Personal:** Born Jan 5, 1929, Jacksonville, FL; married Betty Harris; children: Felice, Felix, Julien. **Educ:** ID State Univ, BS; Washburn Univ, LLB, JD 1958. **Career:** Appellate Law NY, private practice 1960-64; ITT & RCA, mgmt positions 1965-69; NY Dept of State, supervising admin law judge; Private Practice, corporate law. **Orgs:** Arbitrator Comm Dispute Serv Amer Arbitration Assn NY; founder ''Psycho-Systematics'' (course of mental control); authority and collector of matls on Black Magic; bd mem State Council of Societies for Prevention of Cruelty to Children Inc 1988-; exec vice president, New York State Administrative Law Judges Association; member, National Association of Administrative Law Judges. **Honors/Awds:** US Natl Intercoll Oratorical Champion 1954-55. **Military Serv:** AUS corpl 1946-49. **Business Addr:** Supervising Administrative Law Judge, NY State Department of State, 270 Broadway, New York, NY 10007.

NEALS, HUERTA C.
Physician (retired). **Personal:** Born Oct 23, 1914, Fernandina, FL; son of Hattie Brown Neals and Julius Neals; married Antoinette Johnson, Jun 8, 1967; children: Neal Byron, Huerta Johnson. **Educ:** Edward Waters Jr College, 1932-34; Morehouse College, Atlanta GA, BS 1936; Howard Univ Medical School, Washington DC, MD 1942; Grad Fellow Cardiovascular Dis Harvard Univ Med Sch, 1957-58. **Career:** JC Med Center, intern 1942-43; Am Bd of Internal Med, diplomate 1962; Amer College of Physicians, fellow 1963-; JC Med Center, attend phys med 64-94; Univ Med Dentistry of NJ, clinical assoc prof med 1967-; Med Center Jersey City, NJ, private phys attend phys med. **Orgs:** Life Mem NAACP 1962; pres Hudson County Heart Association, 1968-70; mem Hudson Health Sys 1983-; mem NJ Medical Soc Exec Council, 1984; past pres Alpha Phi Alpha Frat Beta; pres NJ Soc of Internal Med 1986-; president, New Jersey Society of Internal Medicine, 1986-88; president, New Jersey Guardsmen, 1986-88; founding member Assoc of Black Cardiologists, 1974-; life member, ABC, 1991. **Honors/Awds:** International attention & awards, The Pioneer in Motor Medical Outreach Care for the Disabled & Aged, 1970—; recognition of years of exemplary service NJ Soc Internal Med 1979; Whitney M Young Jr Award Urban League of Hudson County 1981; Medical Dental Staff Service Award 1981; Stanton HS Class of 1932 for Dedicated Compassionate Humanitarian Service 1982; special recognition award Am Soc Internal Med 1983; tribute from Afro-American Historical & Cultural Soc, 1987; governor's award, 1988, for outstanding senior citizen of Hudson County; Dr Wm G Wilkerson, Award Action for Sickle Cell Anemia, 1989; Liberty Healthcare System, Inc., Liberty Achievement Award. **Military Serv:** AUS captain 1943-45; first black officer assigned to a General Hosp in Italy during WW II 1945. **Business Addr:** Private Practice, Medical Cntr, 130 Atlantic St, Jersey City, NJ 07304.

NEARN, ARNOLD DORSEY, JR.
Fire safety equipment company executive. **Personal:** Born Jun 7, 1949, Philadelphia, PA; son of Isabelle Lawrence Nearn and Arnold Dorsey Nearn Sr; married Sharon Anderson Nearn, Oct 22, 1983. **Educ:** Delaware State College, BS, business administration, 1971; Temple University Law School, 1971-72; Rutgers University, Graduate Business School, 1974-76; Fairleigh Dickinson University, 1979-81. **Career:** Allstate Insurance Co, casualty claims adjuster, 1971-82; Ethicon Inc, head production supervisor, 1972-76; Monsanto Co, manufacturing foreperson, 1976-77; Calgon Corp, prime production foreperson, 1977-78, assistant manager, 1978-81; Schering-Plough Corp, Warehouse Operations, manager, 1981-82, manager, 1983; Belle-Sue Associates, president, 1983-87; Fire Defense Centers, president & CEO, 1987-. **Orgs:** Dania Chamber of Commerce, board of directors, 1988-; Broward County Boys & Girls Clubs, board of directors, 1989-; Council for Black Economic Development, board, 1985-; Florida Regional Minority Purchasing Council. **Honors/Awds:** Price Waterhouse ''Up & Comer's Award'' Outstanding Entrepreneur, 1989; Dania Chamber of Commerce, Small Business of the Year Award, 1989; Council for Black Economic Development ''Top 50 Business Awards,'' 1988-91; Distinguished Alumni Award, Del State Univ, 1990. **Special Achievements:** Publications: Plant Environmental Protection Program; Operational Training Guide; Preventive Maintenance Program; Warehouse Operations Employee Safety Manual; Warehouse Operations Policy Manual; spotlighted on television on 3 separate occasions by the Visual Communications Groups and Channel 17 (Miami, FL) on a program entitled The Black Entrepreneur on Location; received numerous community service awards from the Broward County Boys & Girls Clubs. **Home Addr:** 425 SE 6th St, Dania, FL 33004. **Business Addr:** President & CEO, Fire Defense Centers Inc, 1496-1502 Dixie Hwy, Dania, FL 33004, (954)922-9136.

NEAVON, JOSEPH ROY
Clergyman. **Personal:** Born Dec 4, 1928, New York, NY. **Educ:** Manhattan Coll NY, BA 1950; Gregorian Univ Rome Italy, STD 1973. **Career:** Blessed Sacrament Fathers, rev, dr, prof 1985. **Orgs:** Parliamentarian Cath Theol Soc of Am 1970-; mem Black Cath Clergy Caucus 1978-; Faculty Flwshp John Carroll Univ Cleveland OH 1980-81. **Business Addr:** 5384 Wilson Mills Rd, Highland Heights, OH 44143.

NEBLETT, RICHARD F.
Manager (retired). **Personal:** Born Mar 3, 1925, Cincinnati, OH; son of Haidee Greer Neblett and Nicholas Neblett; married Barbara Kibble; children: Elizabeth. **Educ:** Univ of Cincinnati, BS 1949, MS 1951, PhD 1953. **Career:** Exxon Corp, mgr 1973-86; Govt Rsch Lab, dir 1970; Agr Prod Lab, dir 1966; asst div dir 1965; Natl Action Council for Minorities in Engrg, pres 1986-89. **Orgs:** Mem Amer Chemical Soc; mem, pres Bd of Educ Plainfield 1963-74; board of governors Union Coll; mem Council on Foundations 1981-87; Liberty Science Center, Non Profit Facilities Fund; Chemists' Club. **Honors/Awds:** Phi Beta Kappa. **Military Serv:** AUS 1st lt 1943-46.

NEDD, JOHNNIE COLEMON. See COLEMON, JOHNNIE.

NEELY, DAVID E.
Educational administrator. **Personal:** Born in Chicago, IL. **Educ:** Fayetteville State Univ, BA Sociology 1975; Univ of ID, MA Sociology 1978; Univ of IA School of Law, JD 1981; Univ of IL at Chicago, PhD in Education, 1997. **Career:** Univ of IA, univ ombudsman 1979-81; IL State Univ, assoc prof pol sci 1981-83, dir of affirm action 1981-83; Natl Bar Assoc, reg dir; John Marshall Law School, asst dean; John Marshall Law School, practicing atty, prof of law, consultant, K-12, colleges and universities. **Orgs:** Legal counsel IL Affirm Action Officer Assoc, IL Human Relations Assoc, IL Comm on Black Concern in Higher Ed, Chicago Southside Branch NAACP. **Honors/Awds:** Capital punishment discrimination An Indicator of Inst Western Jrnl of Black Studies 1979; innovative approach to recruiting minority employees in higher ed EEO Today 1982; Blacks in IL Higher Ed A Status Report Jrnl for the Soc of Soc & Ethnic Studies 1983; The Social Reality of Blacks Underrepresentation in Legal Ed Approach Toward Racial Parity 1985. **Special Achievements:** Author of articles, "Pedagogy of Culturally Biased Curriculm in Public Education," 1994; "Social Reality of African American Street Gangs," 1997. **Business Addr:** Assistant Dean, The John Marshall Law School, 315 S Plymouth Ct, Chicago, IL 60604.

NEELY, HENRY MASON
Attorney. **Personal:** Born Jan 13, 1942, Washington, DC; married Elsie T; children: Allen, Frank. **Educ:** Morgan St Coll, BA 1963; Howard Univ Sch of Law, LlB 1966. **Career:** DC, spl US dep marshal 1964; Met Police Dept DC, mem 1965; Armstrong Adult Ed Ctr, bus law & polit sci instr 1966-70; Clinton W Chapman Firm, asso atty 1967-71; pvt prac of law; Pub Serv Commn DC, v-chmn 1971-. **Orgs:** Mem Washington Bar Assn; mem Jud Br DC Bar Assn; Grt Lks Conf of Utility Commr; Nat Assn of Regulatory Utility Commr; mem Gamma Theta Upsilon Frat; Nat Soc of Pershing Rifles; Intrntl Moot Ct Team; Sigma Delta Tau Legal Frat; active in Howard Univ Child Dev Ctr; past mem Wash Bar Assn Leg Com; former vol, supr, atty Howard Univ Legal Interns; trustee DC Inst of Mntl Hygiene. **Honors/Awds:** Recip Assn of AUS Medal 1962; Am Jurisprudence Prize, Joint Publ of Annotated Reports Sys, for Outstndng Academic Achiev in Commercial Law 1985. **Military Serv:** AUS. **Business Addr:** 1625 I St NW, Washington, DC 20006.

NEIGHBORS, DOLORES MARIA
Cleric. **Personal:** Born Aug 21, Chicago, IL; daughter of Ruth Smith and Roscoe Cokiegee; divorced; children: Deborah Ann, Eric Chanlyn, Lori Dee. **Educ:** Seabury Western Theological Seminary, MDiv, 1988; advanced seminar, psychiatry and pastorial counseling, 1992; Claret Center, internship, spiritual direction, 1997. **Career:** University of Chicago, National Opinion Research Center, area supervisor, 1967-78; Illinois Department of Human Rights, human rights investigator, 1978-86; Seabury Western Theological Seminary, seminarian, 1985-88; St George & Matthias Episcopal Church, seminarian assistant, 1988; Church of the Epiphany, associate priest, 1988-90; St Edmund Episcopal Church, assistant priest, 1990-96; St James Episcopal Cathedral, associate priest, 1997-. **Orgs:** Union of Black Episcopalians, 1985-; National Alliance for the Mentally Ill, 1981-; Alliance for the Mentally Ill, 1981-; Episcopal Diocese of Chicago, commission on ministry, 1990-97; Clergy Family Project Committee, 1993-96-. **Special Achievements:** Ordained to the Diaconate, Deacon, June 1988; Ordained to the Sacred Order of Priests, Dec 1988. **Home Addr:** 5555 S Everett Ave, #C4, Chicago, IL 60637-1968, (773)493-3429. **Business Phone:** (312)751-4200.

NEIZER, MEREDITH ANN
Transportation executive. **Personal:** Born Jul 24, 1956, Chateauroux, France; daughter of Roberta Marie Faulcon Neizer and Donald Neizer. **Educ:** US Merchant Marine Acad, Kings Point NY, BS, (honors), 1978, USCG Third Mate License, 1978; Stanford Graduate School of Business, Stanford CA, MBA, 1982. **Career:** Arco Marine, Long Beach CA, third mate, 1978-80; Exxon Intl, Florham Park NJ, sr analyst, 1982-86; US Dept of Defense, Washington DC, special asst, 1986-87; New York/New Jersey Port Authority, New York NY, business mgr, 1987-. **Orgs:** Kings Point information representative, Kings Point Alumni Assn, 1979-91; minority representative, Stanford Graduate School of Business Admissions, 1982-89; corporate liason comm, New Jersey Black MBA Assn 1983-89; consultant, Morris County Business Volunteers for the Arts, 1986; chair subcommittee #1; Defense Advisory Comm on Women in the Services, 1987-90; mem, Navy League, 1988-89; young exec fellow, Fund For Corporate Initiatives, 1989; member, Transportation Research Forum, 1989-; member, Leadership New Jersey, 1991-. **Honors/Awds:** Partner, Creative Renovations Assoc, 1984-85; White House Fellow, President's Commn on White House Fellowships, 1986, 1987; Leadership Award, New Jersey Black MBA Assn, 1986; Woman Pioneer, Kings Point Assn, 1988; Secretary of Defense Medal for Outstanding Public Service, 1990. **Business Addr:** Business Manager, Port Department, Port Authority of New York and New Jersey, New Jersey Marine Terminals, 260 Kellogg St, Newark, NJ 07114.

NELLUM, ALBERT L.
Management consulting executive. **Personal:** Born Apr 1, 1932, Greenville, MS; son of Thurma B Moore Nellum and Daniel F Nellum; married Velma Love Nellum, May 26, 1984; children: Brian, Judith Rebecca, Daniel. **Educ:** Loyola University, Chicago, IL, BS, 1955. **Career:** Catholic Interracial Council, Chicago, IL, assistant director, 1957-60; Chicago Comm on Youth Welfare, Chicago, IL, director, 1960-62; Natl Assn of Intergroup Relations, Special & Emergency Service, Chicago IL, asst director, 1962-63; Bureau of Labor Statistics, Chicago, IL, regional youth consultant, 1963-65; A L Nellum and Associates, Washington, DC, president, 1964-. **Orgs:** Vice president, member, Congressional Black Caucus Foundation, 1973-; member, Martin Luther King, Jr Federal Holiday Commission, 1985-90; trustee, board member, Martin Luther King Jr Center for Nonviolent Social Change, 1978-90; member, Democratic National Committee Site Selection, 1986. **Military Serv:** Army, Specialist 3rd Class, 1955-57. **Business Addr:** President, A L Nellum and Associates Inc, PO Box 19450, Washington, DC 20036-9450.

NELLUMS, MICHAEL WAYNE
Educational administrator, entertaiment productions company owner. **Personal:** Born Aug 6, 1962, England, AR; son of Shirley Nellums and Silas Nellums; married Brenda Kay Clipper, Sep 5, 1987; children: Michael Brandon. **Educ:** University of Central Arkansas, BSE, 1985, MSE, 1991. **Career:** City of Little Rock, pool mgr, 1983-; Pulaski Co Special School Dist, teacher/administrator, 1985-; Power 92-Radio, on-air announcer, 1990-; Sigma One Productions, owner, 1985-. **Orgs:** Teachers of Tomorrow Academy, director, 1992-; Phi Beta Fraternity, Mu Beta Sigma, education committee, 1983-; Arkansas Education Association, 1985-; National Education Association, 1985-; ASSCD, curriculum development, 1989-. **Honors/Awds:** Phi Beta Sigma Leadership Award, local chapter, 1989; North Hills Jaycee, Distinguished Service Award, 1992. **Business Addr:** President, Sigma One Productions, 35 Berkshire, Little Rock, AR 72204.

NELMS, OMMIE LEE
Association executive. **Personal:** Born Jul 4, 1942, Houston, TX; son of Thelma O Nelms and Wiley H Nelms; married Donna Marie Ashley. **Educ:** Dillard U; Univ of MO KC, BA 1965, Grad Study; St Paul School of Theology, Kansas City, MO, Master of Divinity, 1980. **Career:** MO Dept of Ins, Wstrn Div, asst mgr 1975-; Allstate Ins Co, KC Reg Off, undrwrtng div mgr 1969-75; Jr HS, tchr; United Methodist Church, West Conference, MO, minister, currently. **Orgs:** Mem Nat Undrwrtrs Soc 1970-75; yth coord KC Br NAACP; dist lay ldr MO W Conf of United Meth Ch 1974; del S Cen Jurisdictional Conf of United Meth Ch 1972; lay ldr Centennial United Meth Ch KC 1967-75; Delegate World Methodist Conf, 1985, 1991. **Honors/Awds:** Recip Paragon Award for Undrwrtng Excell 1971; Arch Bow Award for Reg Achiev in Undrwrtng 1973; elected to General Conf of United Methodist Church. **Business Addr:** Asst Mgr, Missouri Dept of Insurance, 609 N Quincy #293, Smithville, MO 64089.

NELOMS, HENRY
Distributing company executive. **Career:** Premium Distributors Inc, president, currently. **Special Achievements:** Company ranked #45 on BE's Top 100 Industrial/Service Companies, 1992. **Business Addr:** President, Premium Distributors Inc, 3350 New York Ave NE, Washington, DC 20002, (202)526-3900.

NELSON, A'LELIA
Business executive. **Personal:** Born Aug 14, 1918, Indianapolis, IN; divorced; children: Lynn, Jill, Stanley, Ralph. **Educ:** Talladega Coll, AB 1938; Columbia Univ, MS 1940. **Career:** Library of Congress, supr acquisitions dept 1942-47; Mme CJ Walker Mfg Co, vice pres 1947-53, pres 1953-. **Orgs:** Mem NAACP, Delta Sigma Theta; bd dir N Side Ctr for Child Devel; bd dir ICBO New York City Chapt; bd dir Vander Zee Inst; bd dir Studio Mus.

NELSON, ARTIE CORTEZ
Physician. **Personal:** Born Oct 6, 1955, Baltimore, MD; son of Maxine H Manning Nelson and Arthur W Nelson; married Stacy Haynes-Nelson; children: Kamaria Nicole. **Educ:** Comm Coll of Baltimore, AA 1975; Towson State Univ, BS 1979; Meharry Med Coll, MD 1984. **Career:** Sinai Hosp, pediatric res 1984-85; King Drew Hosp, pediatric res 1985-86; pvt practice 1986; pvt practice, creative psychiatry 1987; King/Drew Med Ctr, resident psychiatry. **Orgs:** Amer Med Association, 1979; Natl Med Student Association, 1979; Amer Psych Association, 1986. **Honors/Awds:** Fellowship, Cedars-Sinai Medical Center, 1988-90. **Special Achievements:** Workshops on racism, specializing in cross-cultural issues. **Home Addr:** 5149 Willow Way, Birmingham, AL 35242. **Business Addr:** Child Adolescent and Family Psychiatrist, 2 Inverness Pkwy, Ste 202, Birmingham, AL 35242.

NELSON, CHARLES J.
Government Official. **Personal:** Born Mar 5, 1920, Battle Creek, MI; son of Dayse Nelson and Schuyler A Nelson; married Maureen Tinsley. **Educ:** Lincoln Univ, AB 1942; NY Univ, MPA 1948. **Career:** Rsch assoc state govt 1949-52, program asst MSA Manila 1942-53, public admin analyst FOA 1953-54, public admin specialist 1954-55, deputy special asst for community devel ICA 1955-57, chief commun devel advisor Tehran 1958, commun devel adv dept of state 1960, chief Africa-Latin Amer branch 1960-61, detailed African branch 1961; Office Program Devel & Coord PC Washington, assoc dir 1961-63; Office Devel Resources AID, dir 1963-64; No African Affairs, dir 1964-66, dep dir Addis Ababa 1966-68, dir Dar es Salaam 1968-71; Botswana, Lesotho, Swaziland, Garborone, ambassador 1971-74, dir aid Nairobi, 1974-78; Howard University Sch Human Ecol, admin 1978-81, international consultant 1981-. **Orgs:** Chmn mayors Intl Adv Council; bd dir Girl Scouts; Council Nation's Capital; Georgetown Citizens Assn; Voice of Informed Community Expression; Smithsonian Inst; Amer Political Sci Assoc; Soc Intl Devel Clubs; Fed City Club WA; Natl Bd of Dir Sister Cities Intl 1986-, vp, bd of dirs, 1990; co chair Africa Round Table SID; Beijing Friendship Council, DC Dakar Friendship Council Bangkok; Council of the Overseas Development Council. **Honors/Awds:** Council of Amer Ambassadors; Assoc of Black Amer Ambassadors; Lincoln Univ Hall of Fame. **Military Serv:** US Army, captain, 1942-47. **Home Addr:** 1401 35th St NW, Washington, DC 20007.

NELSON, CLEOPATRA MCCLELLAN
Educator (retired). **Personal:** Born Sep 26, 1914, Norriston, PA; daughter of Maggie Del McClellan and James W McClellan; married Russell L Nelson. **Educ:** Attended, Cheyney Training Sch for Teachers; Cheyney State Coll, BS 1950; Temple Univ, Moore Inst, Dale Carnegie Inst, further study. **Career:** Kiddy Culture, 1938-40; Norriston Youth Center, teacher counselor 1940; aircraft mech oper aircraft riveter 1st class, 1942-45; Frankfud Arsenal, clerk 1945-46; W Side Day Care Center, teacher 1951-52; Bd of Educ Child Care Centres, teacher 1952-59; Blankenbury School Philadelphia, teacher 1965-72; Wm Dick School, teacher 1960-83; Philadelphia Bd of Educ, teacher 1975-83. **Orgs:** V chair Lower Merion-Boro of Narberth Dem Comm; cmtwmn Montgomery Co Dem 1946-84, ward ldr 1970-81; past officer Zeta Phi Beta Sor Beta Delta Zeta Chap 1951-84; mem Main Line Mercy Douglass Hosp Club; sec Ardmore Comm Dev Corp; fund raising chmn ACDC; mem parlimentarian Main Line Charities; sec MainLine Br NAACP 1967-84; sec, charter mem, Mary E Gould Assembly #61 OGC; sec Labor & Indus Com NAACP; sec Golden Circle #61; vice pres Main Line Assn of Bus & Professional Women 1978-80; appte Christian Ed Bd of Dirs Zion Bapt Ch Ardmore PA 1980; pres Dem Party Lower Merion & Narberth 1981-84, v chair 1984-85, cmtwmn 1984-86; mem Main Line Ind Dem; mem Bd Dirs Merion Dem Women; mem League of Women Voters; chmn Main Line Br NAACP Golden Anniv Marriott Hotel Philadelphia1976-80; banquet chair M E Gould #61 OGC 1986; exec bd mem, Main Line Branch NAACP, 1950-91, life mem. **Honors/Awds:** Exhibition for Delta Sigma Theta Sor at Drexel Inst Philadelphia 1978, Haverford Coll, Martin Luther King Celebration, Zion Bapt Church Ardmore PA; NAACP Most Outstanding Serv Awd Isabel Strickland Awd; Comm Serv Awd Calvary Baptist Ch Ardmore PA 1978; Dem Comm Lower Merion Narberth Awd at Haverford Coll; exhibition of personal artifacts collection Merion Tribute House for Philadelphia Arts Soc 1980; Mary E Gould #61 Serv Awd 1983; Mary E Gould OGC Serv Awd 1986; Women's Literary Guild Golden Anniversary Chair 1987; Honoree & Recipient of Outstanding Service Award as Secretary for Many Years, NAACP, 1989; "Sojourner Truth Award," NANBPWC, Inc, 1964; Elected to receive Assembly #61, OGC, OGC Charter Mem Recognition Award, 1991.

NELSON, DARRIN MILO
Professional football player. **Personal:** Born Jan 2, 1959, Sacramento, CA; married Camilla; children: Jordan. **Educ:** Stanford Univ, BS, urban and environmental planning, 1981. **Career:** Minnesota Vikings, running back, 1982-. **Honors/Awds:** Miller NFL Man of Year Award in 1984; played in NFC Championship Game, post-1987 season.

NELSON, DAVID S.
Judge, educator. **Personal:** Born Dec 2, 1933, Boston, MA; son of Enid Nelson and Maston Nelson. **Educ:** Boston Coll, BS 1957, JD 1960. **Career:** Crane Inker & Oteri, assoc 1960-73; US Commissioner, 1968-69; State of Massachusetts, asst atty general 1971-73; Superior Court, Boston MA, justice 1973-79; US Dist Court Massachusetts, judge 1979-91, sr status, 1991-. **Orgs:** Fellow Amer Bar Found; mem Amer Law Inst. **Honors/Awds:** Natl Award Christians & Jews, 1970; Thomas More Award, Boston College, 1973; Hon JD 1974-75. **Business Addr:** United States District Court, Federation Court, 1805 Post Office & Courthouse, Boston, MA 02109.

NELSON, DEBRA J.
Media relations director. **Personal:** Born Nov 12, 1957, Birmingham, AL; daughter of James Nelson. **Educ:** The University of Alabama, Tuscaloosa, BA, communications, 1980. **Career:** WSGN Radio, Birmingham, AL, director of public affairs, 1980-84; WBRC-TV, Birmingham, AL, director of community affairs, 1984-88, news anchor, noon show, 1987-88; University of Alabama at Birmingham, Birmingham, AL, special studies instructor, 1988-; University of Alabama System,

Tuscaloosa, AL, director of media relations, 1988-. **Orgs:** Convener, Birmingham Literacy Task Force, 1987-88; member, US Library Literacy Review Panel, 1988-91; director, American Heart Association, Alabama Affiliate, 1986-; communications chairman, American Heart Association, 1986-; member, Alabama-Japan Leadership Program, 1988-89; member, Military Academy Review Committee, 6th Congressional District, 1988. **Honors/Awds:** Distinguished Leadership Award, United Negro College Fund, 1985, 1987, 1988; Award of Distinction, International Assn of Business Communicators, 1985; Nominee, Career Woman of the Year, Birmingham Business and Professional Women's Club, 1987; Honorary Lieutenant Colonel, AL Militia Governor's Office, 1987; Woman of Distinction, Iota Phi Lambda Service Sorority, 1985; Outstanding Leadership Award, American Heart Association, 1987-89; Outstanding Volunteer Service Award, American Red Cross, 1985. **Business Addr:** Director, Media Relations, The University of Alabama System, 416 Medical Towers Building, Birmingham, AL 35294.

NELSON, DEBRA PONDER
Association executive. **Personal:** Born Jun 8, 1957, Midwest City, OK; daughter of Beulah Jacobs Ponder and Alonzo L Ponder; married; children: Kristen, Karmen. **Educ:** Oklahoma State University, BS, 1979. **Career:** Oklahoma City Limousine Service, owner, 1979-81; B & P Maintenance, general manager, 1981-83; General Mills, Inc, territory manager, 1983-89; Oklahoma Minority Supplier Development, executive director, 1990-. **Orgs:** Oklahoma City Chamber of Commerce Small Business Committee, board of directors; Appointed to the Central Oklahoma Private Industry Council; KOCO-TV, minority advisory board, board of directors; United States Department of Interior, Bureau of Indian Affairs Economic Development Committee, board; Oklahoma State Alumni Association; Society of Women in Business; Infant Crisis Center, volunteer; Delta Sigma Theta Sorority; Jack & Jill of America; Oklahoma Consortium for Minority Business Devt, program committee chair. **Honors/Awds:** Minority Business News USA, America's Women Who Mean Business; The Oklahoma Ebony Tribune Newspaper, Keepers of the Dream Award, Outstanding Achievement, 1993; General Mills Salesperson of the Year, 1986-87, District 600, 1987; Oklahoma State University Dean's Honor Roll of Distinguished Students, 1979; Oklahoma State University Resident Hall Academic Achievement Award, 1976-77; National Honor Society; Ralph Ellison Library Circulation Drive Community Appreciation Award, 1986. **Special Achievements:** United States Senate, internship, 1978; B & P Maintenance, Delegate to the White House Conference on Small Business, 1980. **Business Addr:** Executive Director, Oklahoma MSDC, Central Park One, 525 Central Park, Ste 106, Oklahoma City, OK 73105, (405)528-6732.

NELSON, DOEG M.
Police official. **Personal:** Born Sep 25, 1931, Daddridge, AR; married Rose Junior. **Educ:** St Mary's Coll, BA 1977; AZ St U, 1953-54; Phoenix Coll, 1955-66. **Career:** Phoenix Police Dept, asst police chief 1973-; maj 1972-73; capt 1969-72; lt 1967-69; sgt 1960-67; patrolman 1954-60. **Orgs:** Vp, treas Progress Assn for C Dev Grand Master, Prince Hall Masons; Elks; Frat Order of Police; comm rel ofcr Nat Assn of Police; IACP; Nat Assn of Soc Serv Wrkrs. **Honors/Awds:** Outst Serv Award Manpower Ctr 1969; Outst Cit Award Urban Leag 1971; Man of Yr Prince Hall Masonic Shriners 1970; Man of Yr Phoenix OIC 1972; Sup Serv Award Am Soc for Pub Adm 1973; Outst Serv Award LEAP 1974. **Military Serv:** AUS corpl 3 yrs. **Business Addr:** 620 W Washington, Phoenix, AZ 85003.

NELSON, EDWARD O.
Test engineer (retired). **Personal:** Born Feb 2, 1925, Johnsonville, TN; son of Lucille Nelson and Edgar Nelson; married Pauline; children: Stanley, Michael, Michelle, Cozetta, Richard, Viola. **Educ:** St Louis U; Rankin Tech Inst; Washington University, St. Louis, MO, BS, Engineering 1975. **Career:** Rockwell Insternat Envrnmntl Monitrng Serv Ctr, tech staff; US Envrnmntl Prtctn Agency St Louis, engr tech. **Orgs:** Mem Am Radio Relay Leag; AARP; IBEW-LU #4; American Legion; Disabled American Veterans. **Honors/Awds:** First black admitted to the Intl Brotherhood of Elec Workers, LU #4. **Military Serv:** US Army, WWII, tech 5th grade, 1943-45; Phillipine Island Liberation Medal, Asiatic Pacific Theater.

NELSON, EILEEN F.
Artist/designer. **Personal:** Born in Chicago, IL; daughter of Frances Irons Anderson and Summers Anderson; married Alphonzo George Nelson, Dec 7, 1975; children: Maisha Eileen Nelson. **Educ:** Attended, IL Inst of Tech 1966-69, Art Institute of Chicago 1959-64, Los Angeles City Coll 1970-74, Indian Valley Coll 1975-79. **Career:** Permanent Dimensional Art Mural Chatworth CA 1975; Permanent Art Mural San Francisco CA 1978; Novato Library, solo showing 1984; Fairfax Library, solo showing 1984; The San Francisco African Amer Historical & Cultural Soc, solo showing 1985; Crown Zellerbach Gallery, solo showing 1985; Utilitarian Church Martin Luther King Jr Room, solo showing 1986; The San Francisco African Amer Historical and Cultural Soc, solo showing 1986; work appears on several album covers, films and TV graphic designs; Soft Sculpture, "Children of Planet Earth" "Impressions of Sao Paulo Brazil" 1986-87; Studio F, artist/designer; self employed artist/designer, currently; mural, "San Francisco in Transition"; designed a bas relief mural for a new building in Chatworth, CA. **Honors/Awds:** Received awd for painting displayed at Henry Horner Boys Club of Chicago, IL; helped design the Afro-Amer Pavilion at the World's Fair in Spokane, WA; work included in an art showing at Los Angeles County Museum of Art; solo art show, San Francisco, l989; solo art show, Chicago, IL l989. **Home Addr:** 7 Regent Court, Novato, CA 94947.

NELSON, FLORA SUE
Public administrator (retired). **Personal:** Born Dec 14, 1930, Chicago, IL; daughter of Clara Payne Martin (deceased) and William Jarrett Martin (deceased); married Herman Nelson, Jul 6, 1962 (died 1981); children: Lisa, Tracey. **Educ:** Univ of Wisconsin, Madison WI, 1947-49; Roosevelt Univ, Chicago, BA, 1951; Univ of Chicago, Chicago, IL, MA, 1957. **Career:** Cook County Juvenile Ct, Chicago, IL, 1951-58; Dept of Housing, Chicago, IL, specialist, 1958-67, asst of relocation, 1967-76, dir of relocation, 1976-80, deputy commissioner, 1980-92. **Orgs:** Delta Sigma Theta Sorority, 1951-. **Home Addr:** 6707 Bennett, Chicago, IL 60649.

NELSON, GILBERT L.
Consultant. **Personal:** Born Oct 5, 1942, Princeton, NJ; son of Lillian Nelson and Gilbert Nelson; married J Mary Jacobs; children: Christine E Cave, Jessica L. **Educ:** Trinity College Ct, BA 1964; Georgetown Law School, JD 1967. **Career:** State of NJ, deputy public defender 1968-70; Middlesex Cty, NJ, assistant prosecuter 1970-72; New Brunswick, NJ, city atty 1975-86; self employed atty at law 1968-87; consultant, currently. **Orgs:** Dir Urban League of Greater NB 1968-70; dir Damon House 1975-81; mem Ntl Bar Assoc 1968-87; mem New Jersey Bar Assoc 1968-87. **Honors/Awds:** Mayor New Brunswick, NJ 1978; archon Mu Boule-Sigma Pi Phi 1984-. **Military Serv:** Army Reserve sgt 1968-74. **Home Addr:** 29 Goodale Cir, New Brunswick, NJ 08901. **Business Addr:** Consultant, PO Box 1292, New Brunswick, NJ 08903.

NELSON, H. VISCOUNT, JR.
Educator. **Personal:** Born Jul 10, 1939, Oxford, PA; son of Leanna Nelson and H Viscount Sr; married Joan K Ricks; children: Christer V, Berk William. **Educ:** West Chester State Coll, BS 1961; Univ of PA, MA 1962, PhD 1969. **Career:** The Center for Student Programming, Univ of CA, Los Angeles, dir, currently; Dartmouth Coll, assoc prof 1975-, asst prof 1972-75; UCLA, asst prof 1969-72; Univ of PA, teaching fellow, head teaching asst 1966-69; Abington High School, teacher, 1964-66; Oxford HS, public school teacher 1962-64. **Orgs:** Amer History Assn; Org of Amer Historians; former mem examining com Advance Placement in US History Educ Testing Serv; Danforth Assn unofficial part-time track & field coach. **Honors/Awds:** Author, "The Philadelphia NAACP Race vs Class Consciousness During the Thirties", Journal of Black Studies 1975; "Black Philadelphia & the Great Depression" in press. **Business Addr:** Director, Center for Student Programming, University of California at Los Angeles, 405 Hilgard Ave, Los Angeles, CA 90024.

NELSON, HAROLD E.
Law enforcement official. **Career:** Illinois State Police, 32 years of service, Cairo outpost, district commander, 1979-87; Cairo Police Department, asst chief, three months, 1992, chief, 1992-94. **Special Achievements:** First African-American police chief, Cairo, IL, 1992. **Business Addr:** Police Chief, Cairo Police Department, 1501 Washington, Cairo, IL 62914, (618)734-2131.

NELSON, IVORY VANCE
Educator. **Personal:** Born Jun 11, 1934, Curtiss, LA; son of Mattie Nelson and Elijah Nelson; married Patricia; children: Karyn R, Cherlyn Y Kirk, Eric R, Kimberlee A. **Educ:** Grambling State Univ, BS Chemistry (Magna Cum Laude) 1959; Univ of KS, PhD Analytical Chem (Summa Cum Laude) 1963. **Career:** Grambling State Univ, chem tchr 1961; Amer Oil Co, research chem 1962; Southern Univ Baton Rouge LA, assc prof dept chem 1963-67; Universidad Autonomous de Guadalajara Fulbright Lectureship, visiting prof dept chem 1966; Loyola Univ, visiting prof 1967; Southern Univ Shreveport LA, chrmn div natural sci 1967-68; Prairie View A&M Univ, prof asst acad dean univ 1968-71; Union Carbide, sr research chem 1969; Prairie View A&M Univ, prof vice pres Research & Spec Prog 1971-82, acting pres 1982-83; TX A&M Univ Syst, exec asst to chancellor; Alamo Community College District San Antonio TX, chancellor 1986-. **Orgs:** Pres council 1984-, pub rel adv comm 1984-, chancellor's student adv bd 1984-, System Long-Range Plan Comm 1984-, System Research Council 1983-, TX A&M Univ System; reorg of TX A&M Univ System 1980, System-Wide Study of Marine & Marine-Related Sciences 1980, Energy & Minerals Adv Council 1977-81, Mining & Minerals Flwshp & Research Council 1980, Pres Council 1975-78 Prairie View A&M Univ; Amer Assn for Adv of Science 1963-; Amer Chem Soc 1963-; TX Acad Science 1968-; TX Coastal & Marine Council 1983-; Agr Research Inst 1980-83; Natl Assn of State Univ & Land Grant Colleges Exec Comm 1980-82; NY Acad of Science 1976-83; Phi Delta Kappa Educ Prof Frat; S East Consortiumfor Intl Development Bd of Dir 1976-83; cnsl Oak Ridge Assn Univ; consult Natl Science Foundation; cnsl Natl Council forcreditation of Teachers Educ; bd of dirs San Antonio Chamber of Commerce; bd of visitors Defense Equal Opportunity Management Institute; bd of dirs United Way San Antonio TX; bd of dirs United Way of San Antonio, Boy Scouts, Symphony of San Antonio, Southwest Research Institute, American Institute of Character Educ. **Honors/Awds:** Omega Psi Phi Highest Freshman Schlst Award Grambling Univ 1956; TH Harris Schlrshp Grambling State Univ 1959; DuPont Tchng Flwshp Univ of KS 1962; Flwshp Natl Urban League 1969; Fulbright Lectureship; Phi Beta Kappa; Phi Lambda Upsilon; Sigma Xi; Beta Kappa Chi; Alpha Mu Gamma; Kappa Delta Pi; Sigma Pi Sigma; NAACP; Optimist Club of America Prairie View; Omega Psi Phi Frat. **Military Serv:** USAF staff sgt 1951-55; Top Secret Cryptographic Clearance 1952-55. **Business Addr:** Chancellor, Alamo Comm College District, 811 West Houston, PO Box 3800, San Antonio, TX 78284.

NELSON, JILL
Author, journalist. **Career:** Freelancer; Washington Post, journalist, begin 1986; author, currently; USA Today, columnist; USA Weekend, contrib editor. **Honors/Awds:** Washington DC, Journalist of the Year Award; American Book Award. **Special Achievements:** Written Volunteer Slavery: My Authentic Negro Experience, Noble Press, 1993; Straight, No Chaser: How I Become a Grown-up Black Woman, Putnam Books, 1997; written articles for: Essence; The Nation; Ms.; The New York Times; Village Voice.

NELSON, JONATHAN P.
Business executive. **Personal:** Born Jun 5, 1939, New York; married Dorothy Higgins. **Educ:** St John's U, MBA 1974; Howard U, BSEE 1963. **Career:** Pfizer Inc, mgr oral prod pkg dept 1968-94; EG&G Inc, electronics engr 1967-68; ACF Ind Inc, electronics design engr 1963-67; Nat Bur of Standards, std trainee 1961-63; The Haagen Dazs Company, engineering mgr, 1994-; Strategic Manufacturing Initiatives Inc, project director, 1995-. **Orgs:** Mem Nat Black MBA Assn 1974-; Am Fin Assn 1973-; IEEE 1963-; Nat Mgmt Assn 1968-; mem exec bd Brooklyn BSA; Omega Psi Phi. **Honors/Awds:** Recip Achiev Award Nat Assn of Negro Bus & Professional Women 1969; Black Achiever in Ind Harlem YMCA 1972, 1974. **Business Addr:** Project Director, Stategic Manufacturing Initiatives Inc, 242 Old New Burnswick Rd, Ste 100, Piscataway, NJ 08854.

NELSON, LEON T.
Company executive, publisher. **Personal:** Born Mar 25, 1938, New Haven, CT; married Charlotte M Nelson, Apr 1970; children: Lori D. **Educ:** Colby College, BA, 1960; Northeastern University, MA, 1964; Boston University, post grad studies. **Career:** Lolech Enterprises, president, currently; The Nelson Group, president; Lolech Enterprises, president, currently. **Orgs:** Greater Roxbury Chamber of Commerce, president; Greater Roxbury Economic Dev Corp, president; Mount Zion Lodge #15, F&AM; Syria Temple #31, AEONMS; Eta Phi Chapter, Omega Psi Phi Fraternity; Kiwanis Club of Roxbury; Boston Economic Development and Industrial Corp, director; Colby College, board of overseers; Bunker Hill Community College, board of visitors; Northeastern University, alumni executive forum. **Special Achievements:** Author: Minority Business in Boston. **Business Addr:** President, Greater Roxbury Chamber of Commerce, PO Box 116, Boston, MA 02121, (617)445-1077.

NELSON, MARIO
Marketing manager. **Personal:** Born Jan 19, 1955, Los Angeles, CA; son of George & Martha; married Cheryl, Nov 20, 1971; children: Mario Umjamo, Ahree Kashawn. **Educ:** Riverside City College, Associates of Art, 1981; California State College, San Bernardino, BA, 1983; California State University, San Bernardino, MBA, 1986. **Career:** Brown-Forman Beverages Worldwide: merchandiser, sales rep, regional mgr, chain channel mgr, convenient store mgr, regional sales mgr, division mktg mgr. **Orgs:** National Black MBA Association, mem. **Honors/Awds:** Top Sales Team, 1991; Fleet Owner Graphics Award, 1997. **Military Serv:** Army, E-5, 1974-77. **Business Addr:** Division Mktg Manager, Brown-Forman Beverages Worldwide, North American Group, 2001 Spring Rd, Ste 450, Oak Brook, IL 60521, (630)954-2122.

NELSON, MARY ELIZABETH
Attorney. **Personal:** Born Feb 6, 1955, St Louis, MO; daughter of Kathryn E Nelson and Clyde H Nelson; divorced. **Educ:** Princeton University, BA, 1977; University of Missouri, Columbia School of Law, JD, 1980. **Career:** Wilson Smith & McCullin, associate, 1981-82; Office of Business Development, minority business development director, 1982-86; Vickers Moore & Wiest, PC, associate, 1986-88; Lashley & Baer, PC, associate, 1988-92, partner, 1992-. **Orgs:** Mound City Bar Association, vice pres, 1988, corresponding secretary, 1985-87; Bar Association of Metropolitan St Louis, long-range planning committee, 1989-; Bar Foundation of St Louis, board of directors, 1990-; People's Health Center, board of directors, 1991-; Regional Arts Commission, board of commissioners, 1991-; Opera Theatre of St Louis, board of directors, 1992-; National

Bar Association, entertainment law committee, 1992; Black Entertainment & Sports Lawyers Association, 1992. **Business Phone:** (314)621-2939.

NELSON, NATHANIEL W.
Podiatrist. **Personal:** Born Nov 28, 1921, Birmingham, AL; married Lee E; children: Altamease, Beth, Nolita, Stanley, Pierre, Milford. **Educ:** Wayne Univ of Detroit, attended; Detroit Inst of Tech, 3 yrs; doctor degree in podiatry. **Career:** Podiatrist, foot and ankle surgery; foot surgeon license in podiatric & medicine AL, MI, MS, TN; constructed a med bldg in Detroit to practice foot corrections & treatments; podiatrist admitted hosp surgical staff; Old Kirwood Hosp, chief of podiatry svc. **Orgs:** MI Podiatry Assn; Am Podiatry Assn; Nat Podiatry Assn; OH Coll of Podiatric Med Alumni Assn; Bethal AME Ch BTA. **Honors/Awds:** Political work on bill in Lansing MI that helped include podiatrist work in the Blue Shield Act & the law that calls a podiatrist a physician & surgeon 1962; first black podiatrist to be aptd as examiner & consult in Detroit area of Aetna Life & Casalty Ins Co for foot & ankle disabilities Quarter Master Serv & Corp 1943-46. **Business Addr:** 16451 Schoolcraft Rd, Detroit, MI 48227.

NELSON, NOVELLA C.
Actress, singer, director, producer. **Personal:** Born Dec 17, 1939, Brooklyn, NY; daughter of Evelyn Hines and James Nelson; children: Alesa Novella Blanchard-Nelson. **Educ:** Brooklyn Coll. **Career:** J Papp, consult 6 yrs; Sundance Theatre Prog, dir; Lincoln Ctr Directors prog, dir; Hartford Stage, dir; KY Humana Fest, dir; Eugene O'Neill Ctr, dir; MTC, dir; public Theatre, dir; Negro Ensemble Co, dir; New Federal Theatre, dir; Seattle Rep, actress; ACT, actress; Alliance, actress; Mark Taper Forum, actress; Long Wharf Theatre, actress; Caucasian Chalk Circle, actress; singer, currently. **Orgs:** Mem ACT; Alliance Theatre; Seattle Rep; founder of "Creative Space" Argus School; mem Natl Council Negro Women; Delta Sigma Theta; mem bd DST Comm of Arts & Letters; Harlem Childrens Theatre; New Heritage Theatre; bd mem Studio WIS. **Honors/Awds:** Mary M Bethune Lifetime Achievement Award, National Council of Negro Women; NY State Council of The Arts Theatre Panelist, Young Playwrights Festival Selection Committee; Image Award, Theatre, NAACP. **Special Achievements:** Director, Hunana Festival, ATL; Appeared in: Hawk; Law & Order; The Littlest Victim; He's Hired She's Fired; Chiefs; The Doctor's Story; One Life to Live; You Are There; All My Children; As The World Turns; The Equalizer; Orphans; The Cotton Club; The Flamingo Kid; An Unmarried Woman, The Seduction of Joe Tynan; Green Card; The Devil's Advocate; A Perfect Murder; Clockers; Girl Six; Performed in: "Purlie;" "Hello Dolly;" "The Little Foxes;" "Caesar & Cleopatra;" "Having Our Say;" "Passing Game;" "Division Street;" "A Piece of My Heart;" "Trio;" "The Skin of Our Teeth;" "In New England Winter;" "South Pacific;" "Widows;" "Mecuba;" Directed: "Black Visions;" "Les Femme Noire;" "Sister Sonjii;" "Perfection In Black;" "Bailey's Cafe;" "Where We At;" "Nigger Nitemare;" "Sweet Talk;" "MuleBone," asst dir; album, Novella Nelson; numerous singing engagements. **Business Addr:** c/o DBA, 10 E 44th St, New York, NY 10012.

NELSON, OTHA CURTIS, SR. (CURTIS NELSON, SR.)
Attorney, notary public. **Personal:** Born Feb 28, 1947, Marion, LA; son of Wilma Pearson Nelson and Jeremiah Nelson; married Vernita Moore, Sep 1, 1968; children: Nelson, Otha Curtis Jr. **Educ:** Southern University, Agriculture and Mechanical College, BA, 1969; Southern University, School of Law, JD, 1972. **Career:** Capital Area Legal Service Corporation, law clerk, 1971-72, staff attorney, 1973-74; Southwest Louisiana Legal Service Corporation, staff attorney; Office of General Counsel, staff attorney, state of Louisiana, 1974-82; Simmons & Nelson Law Firm, founding partner, 1974-80; Otha Curtis Nelson, Sr, attorney-at-Law, notary public, 1980-. **Orgs:** Louis A Martinet Society, chaplain, 1972-92; Pentecostal Assembly of Christ, co-pastor, 1975-78; Holy Ghost Temple Church of God in Christ, Sunday School superintendent,1979-91, assistant pastor, 1985-; Southern University Law School Alumni, co-chaplain, 1992-; Martinet Financial Services, Inc, chairman of the board of directors, 1991-, Christians Basketball Teams, founder, sponsor, coach, 1982-87; Pentecostal Assemblies of the World Louisiana State Choir, president, 1975-76. **Honors/Awds:** Louis A Martinet Society, Valuable Services Rendered, 1991; Honorary Secretary of the State of Louisiana Award, 1980. **Special Achievements:** Coach, basketball champion teams, 1st place, 1985-86. **Business Addr:** Chairman of the Board of Directors, Martinet Financial Services, Inc, 1606 Scenic Hwy, Baton Rouge, LA 70802, (504)383-3675.

NELSON, PATRICIA ANN
Association executive. **Personal:** Born Aug 20, 1955, Brooklyn, NY; daughter of Doretha Smith Nelson and Herbert Lee Nelson. **Educ:** Long Island Univ Brooklyn Campus, AAS Bus Admin 1977, BS Mgmt 1978, MS Comm Health 1985. **Career:** Tri-State Health Svcs, office mgr 1978; Aspen Systems Corp, sr document analyst 1979; SUNY Health Science Center at Brooklyn, teaching hospital admin asst 1980; Kings Co Addictive Disease Hosp SUNY Health Science Center at Brooklyn, asst for univ financial analysis 1982-85; Wyckoff Heights Hospital, asst dir admitting 1985-86; Long Island Univ Brooklyn Campus, learning specialist in writing; 1986-89; Dime Savings Bank of NY, sales/management instructor, 1987-89; Girl Scout Council of NY, membership development director, 1989-90; Girl Scout Council of Greater New York, director of borough services, 1990-91; NY Department of Labor, training specialist, 1991-. **Orgs:** Serv volunteer WNET Channel 13 1980-; treasurer Long Island Univ Alumni Assn Brooklyn Campus 1983-85; pres bd of dirs Innervisions A Group of Young Performers Inc 1984-86; vice pres Long Island Univ Alumni Assn Brooklyn Campus 1985-86; bd mem Arnold & Marie Schwartz Coll of Pharmacy and Health Sciences Long Island Univ 1986-89; mem, American Society of Notaries, 1989-; member, African-American Wimmin United for Societal Change, 1990-91; Kaleidoscope Productions, 1992-; Girl Scout Council, Greater NY, trainer, 1985-. **Honors/Awds:** Outstanding Volunteer, Girl Scout Council of NY, 1989; Certificate of Appreciation, American Society of Notaries, 1990; Girl Scouts of the USA, Lifetime Member, 1991.

NELSON, RAMONA M.
Property management company executive. **Personal:** Born Mar 23, 1950, Pittsburgh, PA; daughter of Ramona L Collie and Pronty L Ford (deceased); divorced; children: Tawana R Cook, John Nelson. **Educ:** Knoxville College, psychology, 1972; University of Pennsylvania, MGA, governmental administration, 1984. **Career:** Pennsylvania Housing Finance Agency, housing management representative, 1979-84; Remanco, Inc, regional mgr, 1985-87; Nelson & Associates, Inc, president, CEO, 1987-. **Orgs:** Greater Cincinnati Chapter of IREM, past president, 1991; National Association of Realtors; National Association of Real Estates Brokers; Greater Cincinnati Chamber of Commerce; Delta Sigma Theta Sorority. **Honors/Awds:** YMCA, Black Achiever, 1992. **Special Achievements:** Licensed Real Estate Broker; Certified Property Mgr, 1984. **Business Addr:** President, Nelson & Associates, Inc, 2516 Park Avenue, Cincinnati, OH 45206, (513)961-6011.

NELSON, REX
Sports administrator. **Career:** Detroit Pistons, vice pres of community development and player programs, currently. **Orgs:** Pistons Palace Foundation, executive director. **Business Addr:** Detroit Pistons, 2 Championship Dr, Auburn Hills, MI 48326, (248)377-0100.

NELSON, RICHARD Y., JR.
Executive director. **Personal:** Born Aug 27, 1939, Atlantic City, NJ; married Nancy Allen; children: Michael, Michele, Cherie, Gregg, Nancy. **Educ:** San Fran State Coll, BA 1961; Temple Univ Law Sch, JD 1969. **Career:** Nat Assn of Housing & Redevel Ofcls, dep exec dir 1970-; Philadelphia Regional Ofc Dept of Housing & Urban Devel, area coord 1965-70; Def Support Agency Phila, purchasing agt 1961-65; NJ Bar, admitted 1969. **Orgs:** Mem Am Soc of Assn Exec; mem Alpha Phi Alpha Frat; NAACP; officer Local PTA. **Business Addr:** 2600 Virginia Ave NW, Washington, DC 20037.

NELSON, RICKY LEE
Corrections officer, professional baseball player (retired). **Personal:** Born May 8, 1959, Eloy, AZ; son of Willie Pearl Whitehead Nelson and Ebb Corelius Nelson; married Deanna Christina Perez Nelson, Sep 25, 1982; children: Alexis, Ashley, Austin. **Educ:** Arizona State Univ, Tempe, AZ, bachelors degree, 1991. **Career:** Seattle Mariners, oufielder 1981-86; New York Mets, outfielder, 1987; Cleveland Indians, outfielder, 1987; A L Williams Financial Services, Phoenix, AZ, regional manager, 1985-91; Durango Juvenile Court, youth supervisor/probations officer, currently. **Honors/Awds:** Attended AZ St Univ winning All-Pac 10 honors while playing for the 1981 Coll World Series champions; member of California All-Star Team, 1982.

NELSON, ROBERT WALES, SR.
Physician. **Personal:** Born Mar 26, 1925, Red Bank, NJ; married Pamela Diana Fields; children: Debra C, Renae V, Desiree M, Jason D, Roxanne W, Robert W. **Educ:** Howard U, 1947-51; Howard Med Sch, 1952-56; USC Med Ctr, 1956-57. **Career:** Gardena Med Ctr, phys; W Adams Emergency Med & Grp, emergency physician 1967-80; LA Co, hlth dept 1965-66, bd educ 1959-60; Private Pract, 1957-65. **Orgs:** Am Coll of Emergency Physicians; mem Am Arabian Horse Assn 1974-77; Intl Arabian Horse Assn 1974-77; breeder of Arabian Horses 1974-; breeder of Black Angus 1975-. **Military Serv:** USMCR corpl 1943-46. **Business Addr:** 1849 Royal Oaks Dr, Bradbury, CA 91010.

NELSON, RONALD DUNCAN
Police chief. **Personal:** Born Jun 17, 1931, Pasadena, CA; son of Zenobia D Nelson and Harold O Nelson; married Barbara Dorsey, Jul 3, 1954; children: Rhonda, Harold. **Educ:** Drake Univ, Des Moines IA, BA, 1956; California State Coll, Los Angeles CA, attended, 1961-66; Pepperdine Univ, Malibu CA, MA, 1977. **Career:** Los Angeles Police Dept, Los Angeles CA, police lieutenant, 1956-77; Compton Police Dept, Compton CA, police commander, 1977-79; China Lake Police Dept, China Lake CA, police chief, 1979-80; City of Compton, Compton CA, city mgr, 1980-82; Berkeley Police Dept, Berkeley CA, police chief, 1982-90; University of California, San Francisco Police Department, police chief, 1990-. **Orgs:** Mem, Kappa Alpha Psi Frat, 1955-, Pasadena Planning Commn, 1976-79, Kiwanis Intl, 1978-88, Berkeley Boosters Assn, 1983-, Berkeley Breakfast Club, 1984-, National Forum for Black Public Admin, 1987-; natl pres, Natl Org of Black Law Enforcement Exec, 1988-89; pres, Alameda County Chief of Police and Sheriffs Assn, 1989; member, Berkeley Booster Assn; member, National League of Cities; member, Commission on Accreditation for Law Enforcement Agencies; member, Black Men United for Change; member, United Black Clergy of Berkeley. **Honors/Awds:** Community Serv Awards, City of Berkeley; Natl League of Cities; Natl Organization for Black Law Enforcement Agencies; Natl Forum for Black Public Admin, 1988. **Military Serv:** US Army, Sergeant, 1951-53; Good Conduct Award, 1953. **Home Addr:** 1460 Lincoln St, Berkeley, CA 94702.

NELSON, RONALD J.
Automobile dealership executive. **Career:** Bill Nelson Chevrolet Inc, chief executive officer, currently. **Special Achievements:** Company ranked #85 on BE's Top 100 Auto Dealers, 1990, #81, 1992. **Business Addr:** Chief Executive Officer, Bill Nelson Chevrolet Inc, 3233 Auto Plaza, Richmond, CA 94806, (510)222-2070.

NELSON, WANDA JEAN
Association executive. **Personal:** Born Jul 5, 1938, Kingfisher, OK; married Earl Lee Nelson Sr; children: Marie, Stephen A, Earl Lee Jr. **Educ:** Madam CJ Walker's Beauty Coll, Graduated 1958; Natl Inst of Cosmetology Washington DC, Bachelors, 1966, Masters, 1968, Doctorate, 1973; Penn Valley Comm Coll in Science, A 1973; Univ of Ottawa, Ottawa, KS, BS, 1979. **Career:** Le Cont'e Cosmetics, tech hairstylist & instructor; Air Cargo TWA, supervisor; USDA, keypunch & verifier; US Postal Svcs, guard 1979-80; Ms Marie Cosmetics, owner; Associated Hairdresser Cosmetologist of MO, pres, currently. **Orgs:** Founder and 1st pres Young Progressors Beauty & Barbers; mem MO State Assoc of Cosmetology, Natl Beauty Culturist League Inc, Women's Political Caucus; 1st vice pres, Natl Beauty Culturist League, 1988-; parliamentarian, Black Chamber of Commerce, 1987-. **Honors/Awds:** Certificates for Volunteer Serv in the Comm; Certificate from Jackson County State Sch for Retarded Children; elected Alpha Beta Sor Woman of the Year 1985; Top 100 Influential Black Amers in Greater Kansas City 1985; Theta Nu Sigma Natl Sor Woman of the Year 1986; Alpha Beta Local Chap Woman of the Year 1986.

NELSON, WANDA LEE
Educational administrator. **Personal:** Born Nov 16, 1952, Franklin, LA; daughter of Geraldine Minor Green (deceased) and James Green (deceased); married Elridge Nelson; children: Michael, James. **Educ:** Grambling State Univ, BA 1973; Ball State Univ, MA 1975; Natl Cert Counselor 1984; Louisiana State Univ, Ed S 1985; Northern Illinois Univ DeKalb Il Ed.D 1989. **Career:** Bicester Amer Elem School, England, learning specialist 1974-76; Summer Enrichment Program LSUE, music teacher 1984; LSUE, counselor; Northern Illinois Univ, counselor & minority programs coordinator, 1985-89; Univ of Texas, Austin TX, asst dean of students 1989-92; aaoc dean of students, 1992-95, executive director university outreach centers, 1995-. **Orgs:** Advisor Awareness of Culture, Ed & Soc Student Club 1978-85; Anti-Grammateus Epsilon Alpha Sigma Chap, 1979-80; organized Mu Upsilon Chap, 1992; Basileus Alpha Kappa Sigma, Chapter 1994-; life mem, Sigma Gamma Rho Sorority, Inc; Jack and Jill of America Inc, 1996-; advisor, Innervisions Gospel Choir, Univ of Texas, 1993-95; advisor, Zeta Nu Chap, 1984-89; life member Grambling State Univ Alumni Assn; member Amer Assn for Counseling & Dev; American Assn of Higher Education; Amer college Personnel Assn. **Honors/Awds:** Magna Cum Laude Grambling State Univ 1973; President's Award Little Zion BC Matrons, Opelousas, LA 1985; Alpha Kappa Mu Honor Society, Grambling State Univ; Kappa Delta Pi Honor Society, Northern Illinois Univ 1988; Best Advisor of the Year, 1989; Alpha Golden Image Award, Northern ILL Univ; Outstanding Educator, Texas Employees Retirement System, 1991; African-American Faculty/Staff of the Year, 1995; Pan-Hellenic Image Award, Univ of Texas; Leadership Austin Class, 1997-98. **Business Addr:** Executive Director, University Outreach Centers, The University of Texas at Austin, 600 W 24th St, Austin, TX 78705, (512)472-3984.

NELSON, WILLIAM EDWARD, JR.
Educator. **Personal:** Born Mar 19, 1941, Memphis, TN; married Della Jackson; children: Nicholas. **Educ:** AM & N College Pine Bluff, Ark, BA 1962; Atlanta, Univ, MA 1964; Univ of Ill, PhD 1971. **Career:** Southern Univ, instr 1963-65; Univ of Ill, research assoc 1966-69; OH State Univ, prof 1969-. **Orgs:** Regl dir Alpha Phi Alpha Frat 1976-82; proclamation Ohio Senate 1977; proclamation Columbus City Cncl 1977; pres Natl Conf of Black Pol Scientists 1978-79; pres Black Political Assembly 1979-81; chrmn Natl Cncl for Black Studies 1980-82; pres, African Heritage Studies Association, 1991-96; vice pres, Ameri-

can Political Science Association, 1996-97. **Honors/Awds:** Outstanding adminstr Black Stdnt Caucus 1976; mem exec bd African Heritage Studies Assn 1980-; NAACP; Urban League. **Business Addr:** Prof Political Sci Chairman, Ohio State Univ, 230 N Oval Mall, Columbus, OH 43210.

NELSON-HOLGATE, GAIL EVANGELYN
Singer, actress, educator. **Personal:** Born Mar 29, 1944, Durham, NC; daughter of Jane Avant Nelson (deceased) and Reverend William Tycer Nelson (deceased); married Daniel A Holgate, Sep 27, 1987. **Educ:** Oberlin Coll, MMus 1965; New England Conserv of Music, Boston MA, MMus 1967; Mozarteum Conserv, Salzburg Austria, 1963-64; Metropolitan Opera Studio, 1970-72; Amer Inst of Musical Studies, Graz Austria, 1972. **Career:** Henry Street Music Settlement, private vocal teacher, 1986-87; New York City College, adjunct professor of contemporary pop-vocal music, 1986-89; D & G Productions Inc, vice pres, professional vocalist, currently. **Orgs:** AEA 1968; AGMA 1967; AFTRA 1968; SAG 1968; BWIT 1984; Oberlin Alumnae; New England Conserv Alumnae; Amer Cancer Soc 1975-; Mu Phi Epsilon 1967-; Black Women in Theatre 1985-87. **Honors/Awds:** Lucretia Bori Awd, NY Metro Opera Studio Performance Scholarship 1970-72; Humanitarian Plaque, Oakwood Coll 1977; In Recog of Your Valuable Contrib to Human Life & Dignity and to Black Cultural Enrichment in Particular United Student Movement 1977; Stone Soul Festival "7", Springfield, MA, 1995. **Special Achievements:** Films: The Way We Live Now, I Never Sang for My Father, Cotton Comes to Harlem; Recordings: Gail Nelson Sings! (on cassette), That Healin' Feelin' & Phase III from the US of Mind w/Horace Silver, Blue Note Label, the original broadway cast album of Tap Dance Kid; Lady Day at Emerson's Bar & Grill (Cast Recording Starring Gail Nelson as Billie Holiday); many television & radio commercials, voice overs, indust films & shows; numerous operas; orchs: The Maggio Musicale Orch Florence Italy, The Ball of the Silver Rose Deutsches Theatre, Munich, Germ, The Madame Mag Ball Baden Baden, Detroit Symph Gala, Buffalo Philharm, Philadelphia Pops, St Louis, Hartford, Tulsa, Chicago Ravinia Fest, Wmsburg Fest; Omaha, Oklahoma City Philhrm, Edmonton, Calgary Philh, Indianapolis; One Life to Live (ABC); Another World (CBS), Guiding Light (NBC); Maya Angelou's "King", as Coretta Scott King, Jan, 1997; broadway theatre, Hello Dolly, Applause, On The Town, Music Music, Eubie; Tap Dance Kid; Porgy and Bess as Bess with Houston Grand Opera, tour 1977; Bubbling Brown Sugar; (as Irene Page) 1986; Lady Day at Emerson's Bar & Grill, on four 1994-98; American Symphony at Carnegie Hall, debut, London Philharmonic, debut, guest artist Queen Elizabeth II Cruise Ship, Holland America Cruise Lines; New Jersey Symphony, debut, Buffalo Philharmonic New York, soloist; Indianapolis Symphony, debut, 1992; "Lady Day at Emerson's Bar & Grill," An Evening of the Life and Music of Billie Holiday (as Billie Holliday), Seabourn Spirit Cruise Ship thru Asia, guest artist, Soloist: Connecticut Symphony; New Jersey Symphony; Portland Maine Symphony; Indianapolis Symphony; "Funny, You Don't Look Like A Grandma", by Strouse 1995 "Talking Books," narrator for the American Foundation for the Blind, NY. **Home Addr:** 819 Putnam Ave, Brooklyn, NY 11221-2817.

NENGUDI, SENGA. **See FITTZ, SENGA NENGUDI.**

NESBITT, PREXY-ROZELL WILLIAM
Government official, consultant and teacher. **Personal:** Born Feb 23, 1944, Chicago, IL. **Educ:** Antioch Coll, BA 1967; Columbia Univ, Certificate in African Studies 1968; Northwestern Univ, MA 1974. **Career:** World Council of Churches, dir 1979-83; District 65 United Auto Workers Union, administrator 1983-86; School of the Art Inst of Chicago, lecturer african literature 1983-90; City of Chicago Mayor's Office, asst dir comm relations 1986-88. **Orgs:** Mem NAACP 1970-, Assoc of Concerned African Scholars 1980-; bd of dirs CA Newsreel 1980-; consultant Amer Comm on Africa 1980-; bd of dirs TransAfrica 1981-86, Crossroads Fund 1983-86; Nelson Mandela Freedom Fund, 1990-93; Institute for Food and Devel Policy, 1994-; Development Fund for a Free South Africa, 1989-; Anti-Racism Institute, Chicago, consultant, 1994-; John D and Catherine T MacArthur Foundation Program on Peace and International Cooperation, senior program officer, 1993-95, consultant, 1995-. **Honors/Awds:** Faculty Fellow Columbia Univ 1967; Steve Biko Awd Chicago TransAfrica 1987; Drylongso Award, Boston, 1994-, Order of Friendship and Peace, Mozambique Govt, 1989; 15 publications including "Beyond the Divestment Movement," The Black Scholar 1986; "Apartheid in Our Living Rooms, US Foreign Policy on South Africa," Midwest Research 1987; "Desbin Straight: A Reflection on Basil Davidson" Race and Class, 1994.

NESBITT, ROBIN ANTHONY
Attorney. **Personal:** Born May 17, 1956, New York, NY; son of Vivian Nimmo Nesbitt and Robert Nesbitt; married Michelle Ponds, Dec 19, 1987; children: Robin Anthony Jr, Christine Michelle. **Educ:** Morehouse College, BA, economics, 1977; Atlanta University School of Business, MBA, 1980; Southern University School of Law, JD, 1984. **Career:** First Federal Savings and Loan, managing attorney, 1984-87; Southern University, assistant professor, 1984-89; Nesbitt and Simmons, attorney, partner, 1984-. **Orgs:** Kappa Alpha Psi, 1974; Phi Alta Delta, 1982; Toastmasters, 1977; Community Association for the Welfare of School Age Children, 1989; O'Brien House, 1990. **Special Achievements:** Licensed registered representative, series #6, with National Association of Securities Dealers. **Home Addr:** 7928 Wimbledon Ave, Baton Rouge, LA 70810, (504)767-3107. **Business Addr:** Partner, Nesbitt & Simmons, Attorneys at Law, 118 S 19th St, Baton Rouge, LA 70806, (504)336-1296.

NESBY, DONALD RAY, SR.
Law enforcement official. **Personal:** Born Feb 16, 1937, Austin, TX; married Ruby J Thomas; children: Donald R Jr, Alex L. **Educ:** San Diego City Coll, 1964; Austin Comm Coll, 1975. **Career:** Travis Cty Sheriff Dept, deputy sheriff 1973-76; Constable Pct #1, constable 1976-. **Orgs:** Mem TX Peace Officer Assn 1978-; pres WH Passon Historical Soc 1983-85. **Honors/Awds:** Outstanding Comm Serv Alpha Kappa Zeta Chap 1977; Outstanding Serv Awd St Mary's Comm 1978; Recog Awd MW Mt Carmel Grand Lodge 1982. **Military Serv:** USN ao3 6 yrs. **Business Addr:** Constable, Travis Co Pct #1, 1811 Springdale Rd. #120, Austin, TX 78721-1354.

NETTERS, TYRONE HOMER
Legislative assistant. **Personal:** Born Oct 11, 1954, Clarksdale, MS; married Beverly Bracy; children: Malik, Toure. **Educ:** CA State Univ Sacramento, BS 1976. **Career:** Office of Majority Consultants, campaign specialist 1979-82; Assembly Ways & Means, consultant 1982-83; Office of Assemblywoman Moore, legislative assistant 1983-. **Orgs:** Bd of dirs Magalink Corp 1984-; mem A Philip Randolph Inst 1985-; founding mem Fannie Lou Hamer Demo Club 1985-. **Honors/Awds:** SABC Comm Serv Awd 1980; Natl Black Child Development Merit Awd 1981. **Home Addr:** 8720 Cord Way, Sacramento, CA 95829. **Business Addr:** Legislative Assistant, CA State Assembly, State Capitol Bldg Rm 2117, Sacramento, CA 95814.

NETTERVILLE, GEORGE LEON, JR.
Educational administrator. **Personal:** Born Jul 16, 1907, Dutchtown, LA; married Rebecca Franklin. **Educ:** So U, BS 1928; Columbia U, MA 1950; Wiley Coll, LittD 1968. **Career:** Natl Benefits Life Ins Co Baton Rouge, dist mgr 1928-32; LA Sausage Co, mgr 1934-38; So Univ Baton Rouge, former pres/acting pres/bus mgr 1938-80, dir of planning 1980-. **Orgs:** Mem Exec Cncl World Serv & Finance United Meth Ch 1964; mem Commn to Study Financing Meth Schs Theology 1964-68; Baton Rouge Civic Cntr Com 1970; LA Cncl Chs 1967; pres E Baton Rouge Parish Anti-Poverty Prog; Comm Assn Welfare Sch Chldrn; vice pres E Baton Rouge Parish Biracial Commn; LA Interch Cncl; sec Scotland Fire Prot Dist; mem/exec com LA Regl Med Planning Cncl; bd dirs Cerebral Palsy Ctr; Baranco-Clark YMCA; United Givers Fund Blundon Home; trustee Gammon Theol Sem; mem/past pres Am Assn Coll & Univ Bus Officers; past treas Nat Assn for Equal Opport in Higher Edn; Nat Alliance Bus Men; Phi Beta Sigma; Kappa Phi Kappa.

NETTLEFORD, REX MILTON (RALSTON)
Educator, dancer/choreographer. **Personal:** Born Feb 3, 1933; son of Lebertha Palmer and Charles Nettleford. **Educ:** UCWI London, BA 1956; Oxon, BPhil 1959. **Career:** Jamaica, Trinidad & Tobago, resident tutor 1956-57, 1959-61, staff tutor in political educ 1961-63; Trade Union Ed Inst, dir of studies, 1963-; UWI Dept of Govt, tutor, lecturer, political thought; Extra-Mural Studies, deputy dir, 1969-71, dir 1971, prof 1975-; Univ of West Indies, Kingston, Jamaica, pro-vice chancellor, 1990-; professor/deputy vice chancellor of School of Continuing Studies, 1996; professor/director of school of continuing studies, 1990-96; professor/deputy vice chancellor, 1996, chairman, Commission on National Symbols and National Observances (J'ca), 1996; member Caricom Commission on Culture, 1997; UNESCO Steering Committee on Culture and Development, 1993-. **Orgs:** Associate fellow, Centre for African & African-American Studies, Atlanta Univ; Intl Soc for the History of Ideas, acad counselor Latin Amer Studies, Wilson Center, Washington DC; trustee, AFS Intl, New York; chmn, Commonwealth Arts Organization, 1980; chmn, Inst of Jamaica, 1978-80; cultural advisor to Prime Minister of Jamaica, 1972-80; founder, artistic dir, Jamaica Natl Dance Theatre Co, 1962-; chmn, Tourism Product Devel Co, Jamaica, 1976-78; gov, Intl Devel Rsch Center, 1970-; CIDEC, Org of Amer States; Comm of Experts on Open Learning and Distance Educ, Commonwealth Secretariat, London UK 1986-87; board of directors, Natl Commercial Bank of Jamaica, 1987-; board of directors, Jamaica Mutual Life Assurance Society, 1989-; cultural advisor, Prime Minister of Jamaica, 1989-; board of directors, Panos Institute, 1990-; AFS International, international trustee, 1980-89; Group orperts Monitoring Sanctions Against Apartheid, ILO, 1989-; Committee of Advisors on Government Structure, Jamaica, chairman, 1992; West Indian Commission, 1990-92; UNESCO, executive bd, 1991-92; UNESCO, International Scientific Committee for the "Slave Route" Project, rappateur, 1994; Natl Council on Education, Jamaica, chairman, 1992; UNESCO Steering Committee on a Culture and Development, 1993-; chmn, Commission on Natl Symbols and Natl Observances, 1996; mem, Caricom Commission on Culture, 1997. **Honors/Awds:** Order of Merit Award, Govt of Jamaica, 1975; Gold Musgrave Medal, Inst of Jamaica, 1981; UCWI Exhibition Scholar, 1953: Issa Scholar, 1956; Rhodes Scholar 1957; ILO Fellow 1967; Jamaica Inst of Mgmt, Fellow, 1988-89; Patton lecturer, Indiana Univ, 1989; Pelican Award, University of West Indies Alumni, 1990; Fellow, Institute of Jamaica, 1990, 1991; Living Legend Award, National Black Arts Festival, USA, 1990; 1991; Zora Neale Hurston-Paul Robeson Award, 1994; Hon Doctor of Letters, St Johns University of Hartford, 1995; Presidential Medal, Brooklyn College, CUNY, 1995; Man of the Year Award, American Biographical Institute, 1995; Fellow, Institute of Jamaica, 1990; Honorary Doctorates: Doctor Humane Letters, CUNY, 1996; Hon Doctor of Letters, Univ of CT, 1997; Hon Doctor of Laws, Illinois-Wesleyan Univ, 1997. **Special Achievements:** Choreographer, over 50 major works for the National Dance Theatre Co of Jamaica, 1962-; author of many books and articles on Caribbean cultural development; editor, principal dancer, author, choreographer: leader of Cultural Missions to the USA, Canada, Latin American, Australia, and the USSR. **Business Addr:** Professor, Continuing Studies, University of the West Indies, Mona Campus, PO Box 42, Kingston 7, Jamaica, (876)977-0237.

NETTLES, JOHN SPRATT
Clergyman, civil rights leader, social worker. **Personal:** Born Jun 1, 1943, Darlington, SC; son of Townsend Nettles, Jr; married Gertrude Kidd, Oct 15, 1960; children: Madrica, John, Ralph. **Educ:** Kittrell Coll, AA, 1963; Bluefield State Coll, BA, 1965; Morehouse School of Religion of ITC, Atlanta GA, hours towards MD, 1965-68. **Career:** Community Action Agency, Anniston AL, director, 1970; Mt Olive Baptist Church, Anniston Al, pastor 1968-. **Orgs:** Director, Producing Ambitious Youth, 1970-; state pres, Alabama Southern Cristian Leadership Conf, 1978-; Natl Board of Dir, SCLC, 1978-; founding dir, Educ Par Excellence, 1983-; chairman, Alabama New South Coalition 3rd district, 1985-; commissioner, Alabama Education Study Commission, 1988-; founding chairman, Project DEED, 1988-; Pardon & Parole Bd, 1991-. **Honors/Awds:** Rosa Parks SCLC, National; Young Man of the Year, Anniston Community; MLK Humanitarian Award, SCLC; Frederick Douglass Christian Study Center of Alabama; Man of the Year; Education Award, AKA Sorority; The Ten Commandments for Becoming Productive Youth; The Beatitudes for Becoming Youth Employees; Crossing the Rubicon, Movement for A Just Society in South Africa; The Mirage of Racial Equity in Alabama (in process). **Business Addr:** Reverend, Director of Education Par Excellence, Mt Olive Baptist Church Community Action Agency, 1300 Moore Avenue, Anniston, AL 36201.

NETTLES, WILLARD, JR.
Fencing company executive, educator. **Personal:** Born Jan 17, 1944, Hooks, TX; son of Gladys Hammick Nettles and Willard Nettles; married Rosemary. **Educ:** Lewis & Clark Coll, BA 1967; Lewis & Clark College, Portland, OR, MAT, 1973. **Career:** Vancouver, WA, former city councilman; Portland School Dist, teacher; Crown Zellerbach Corp, prod planner 1967-70; VanCouver Public Schools, Vancouver, WA, Teacher Math/Spanish, 1978-91; Trailblazer Fence Co, Vancouver, WA, owner, 1982-91. **Orgs:** NAACP. **Honors/Awds:** 1st Black & Youngest Cnclmn Vancouver, WA. **Business Addr:** 210 E 13 St, Vancouver, WA 98661.

NEUFVILLE, MORTIMER H.
Educational administrator, educator. **Personal:** Born Dec 10, 1939, Portland, Jamaica; married Masie Brown; children: Sonetta, Nadine, Tisha. **Educ:** Jamaica School of Ag, Diploma 1961; Tuskegee Inst, BSc 1970; Univ of FL, MSc 1971, PhD 1974. **Career:** Univ of FL, grad asst 1971-74; Prairie View A&M, head dept of animal sci 1974-78; Lincoln Univ School of Appl Sci MO, assoc dean 1978-83; Univ of MD Eastern Shore, dean of agriculture, research dir 1983-91, assoc vp, 1991-93, Academic Affairs, vp, 1994-96; Natl Assn of State Universities and Land-Grant Colleges, 1997-. **Orgs:** Agr rsch asst Ministry of Agri-Jamaica 1961-68; mem Gamma Sigma Delta Hon Soc 1970, Alpha Zeta Hon Soc 1971, Bd of Dir North Central R&D Ctr 1982-83; mem Sigma Pi Phi 1984, Natl Higher Ed Comm 1985; mem North East Regional Council 1986; Governor's Commn on Education in Agriculture 1987; mem International Science and Education Council 1987; Assn of Research Directors, vice chairman, chairman, 1989-90; JCARD-CSRP Review Committee, chair, 1990; ACOP 1993, Budget Committee, chair, 1992; Northeast Regional Center for Rural Development, 1990. **Honors/Awds:** Most Outstanding Jr Agr Tuskegee Inst 1969; Most Outstanding Grad Sr Tuskegee Inst 1970; Review of Animal Sci Rsch at 1890 Univ Devel of Rsch at Historically Black Land Grant Inst 1-75. **Business Addr:** Director, Federal Relations - Food, Environment and International Affairs, National Association Of State Universities and Land-Grant Colleges, 1 Dupont Circle NW, Ste 710, Washington, DC 20036-1191, (202)778-0858.

NEUSOM, THOMAS G.
Attorney. **Personal:** Born Mar 7, 1922, Detroit; divorced. **Educ:** Detroit Inst Tech, BA 1947; Detroit Coll Law, LLB, JD 1949. **Career:** Private Practice, law 24 yrs. **Orgs:** Pres NAACP 1954-56; NAACP Legal Com 1956-60; bd mem Welfare Planning Cncl 1960-70; treas Comm Rel Conf 1966-67; mem CA Hosp & Hlth Facilities Planning Com 1962-72; MC Mars Post

Am Legion 1965; commander/mem LA Co Tax Assessment Appeals Bd 1962-69; bd mem Am Bar Assn 1960-; CA State-Bar Assn 1949-; pres bd So CA Rapid Transit Dist 1973-, mem bd 1969-. **Military Serv:** AUS lt 1943-46. **Business Addr:** 1485 W Adams Blvd, Los Angeles, CA 90007.

NEVILLE, AARON
Vocalist. **Career:** Singles and albums include: Tell it Like it is, 1966, 1991, Orchid in the Storm, 1990, The Classic: My Greatest Hits, 1990, Warm Your Heart, 1991, Dont' Know Much, with Linda Ronstadt, 1990; Warm Your Heart, 1991; with the Neville Brothers: Treacherous: A History of the Neville Brothers, 1987, Brother's Keeper, 1990, Fiyo On the Bayou, Nevilleization, Uptown, Yellow Moon, Treacherous Too, 1991; To Make Me Who I Am, 1997; A&M Records Inc, singer, currently. **Honors/Awds:** Grammy Award for Don't Know Much with Linda Ronstadt, 1990; Recipient, Down Beat Blues, Soul, R&B Group Award, 1990. **Business Addr:** Vocalist, Musician, A&M Records Inc, 1416 N LaBrea Ave, Hollywood, CA 90028, (213)856-2755.

NEWBERN, CAPTOLIA DENT
Educator, cleric (retired). **Personal:** Born Sep 22, 1902, Dublin, GA; daughter of Arnetta E Rozier Dent and John West Dent; married Rev Samuel H Newbern, Dec 2, 1939 (deceased). **Educ:** Paine Coll, Augusta, GA, Certificate Teacher Tgn 1923, BSEd (cum laude), 1925, 1931-32; Hampton Inst, 1926; Northwestern Univ Graduate School, English, 1928; Case Western Reserve Univ, 1931-32; Talladega Coll, MusB, 1937, 1937-38; School of Social Work, Columbia Univ, MSSW 1942; Teachers Coll, Columbia Univ, EdD 1954; United Theological Seminary, MDiv 1980, D Min 1982. **Career:** Lane Coll, chmn, prof, dir 1962-75; US Dept of HEW, Atlanta, liaison consultant devel in black inst project 1971-72; Lane-Lambuth Social Welfare Consortium with Dir of Dept of Sociology & Family Devel Lambuth Coll, co-dir 1972-75; Lincoln Meml Univ Harrogate TN, prof social work 1975-80; Ministry of Ecumenical Education & Action, volunteer, 1982 until retirement. **Orgs:** Am Assn of Univ Prof 1968-; Religious Educ Assn 1968; Natl Council of Black Social Workers Inc 1974-76; life mem NAACP 1974; natl adv bd Am Security Council 1976-77; dir ecumenics CME Church Seventh Episcopal Dist 1980-83; assoc minister Russell Tabernacle Church Philadelphia 1982-85; International Association of Women Ministers, 1985; Afro-American Historical and Cultural Museum; American Red Cross, 1989. **Honors/Awds:** Book Cert/Cert of Appreciation Russell Tabernacle CME Ch 1967; Lane Coll Plaque Lane Coll 1967-78; Ruth Pippert Core Meml Award United Theol Sem 1980; World Inst of Achievement, Chartered Life Membership 1985; Russell Tabernacle CME Church Christian Woman of the Year Plaque Awd, 1986; CME Church, Plaque Award, 1987; Talladega Clg, Golden Plaque Diploma, 1990, Research Advisor of the Year Plaque Award, 1990; American Biographical Institute, Woman of the Year Plaque Award, 1990; numerous other plaques, awards, and recognitions of service. **Special Achievements:** First African-American female appointed by War Department as employee counselor, The Pentagon Bldg, 1942.

NEWBERRY, CEDRIC CHARLES
Business executive. **Personal:** Born Aug 10, 1953, Perry, GA; son of Rubye L Allen-Newberry and Charlie C Newberry; married Lillie Ruth Brown; children: Carnice, Candice, Clayton. **Educ:** Fort Valley State Coll, BS 1975; Univ of WI-Madison, MS 1977; Southern IL Univ Edwardsville, MBA 1982. **Career:** Monsanto Co, sr rsch biologist 1977-83; Meineke Discount Mufflers/CC Newberry Automotive Corp, pres/general mgr 1983-. **Orgs:** Mem Amer Soc of Agronomy 1977-83; mem Comm to Support Black Business & Professionals 1983-; chmn educ comm Natl Black MBA Assoc 1986-87. **Honors/Awds:** Honors Convocation Fort Valley State Coll; Fellow Shion Univ of WI 1975-77. **Business Addr:** President/General Manager, CC Newberry Automotive Corp, 7760 Reading Rd, Cincinnati, OH 45237.

NEWBERRY, TRUDELL MCCLELLAND
Educational administrator. **Personal:** Born Jan 30, 1939, Junction City, AR; daughter of Margaret Knighten McClelland and Roosevelt McClelland; divorced; children: Fe Lesia Michelle, Thomas Walter III. **Educ:** Univ of AR Pine Bluff, BA 1962; Roosevelt Univ Chicago, MA 1980; Governors State, Post-Grad Work 1982-84; Northern Illinois Univ post graduate work 1988-89. **Career:** Almyra Public School System, teacher 1962-65; Franklin-Wright Settlement, social worker 1965-69; North Chicago Grade School, teacher 1970-90; Foss Park Dist North Chicago, recreational suprv 1982-83; City Council North Chicago IL, alderwoman 5th ward 1983-87; North Chicago Unit School District, North Chicago, IL, dean of students, 1990-92; Neal Elementary School, teacher, 1992-93. **Orgs:** Eureka Temple #1172, 1972-, North Chicago Library Bd 1986-87, UAPB Alumni Assoc 1982-, North Chicago HS PTO 1984-88, North Chicago Booster Club 1984-88; North Chicago Teachers Assn 1982-87; building representative for NCTA 1985-87; North Chicago Elementary Council of Federated Teachers, 1987-90, president, 1989-90; CNL Representative to Lake County Federation of Teachers Executive Bd, 1987-89; Committee of Ten Unification of North Chicago School System, 1988-89; North Chicago Unit Dist Council, 1992-. **Honors/Awds:** Arkansas Travelers Award as Ambassador of Goodwill, signed by Governor Bill Clinton, 1992. **Home Addr:** 2111 S Lewis Ave, North Chicago, IL 60064-2544.

NEWBILL, IVANO MIGUEL
Professional basketball player. **Personal:** Born Dec 12, 1970. **Educ:** Georgia Tech. **Career:** Detroit Pistons, center, 1994-95; Atlanta Hawks, 1996-97; Vancouver Grizzlies, 1997-. **Business Addr:** Professional Basketball Player, Vancouver Grizzlies, 718 Beatty St, Ste 311, Vancouver, BC, Canada V6B 2M1, (604)688-5867.

NEWBILLE, CYNTHIA
Association executive. **Career:** Charles Drew University of Medicine and Science, Head Start, program director; National Black Women's Health Project, executive director, currently. **Orgs:** Parent Policy Council, founder. **Business Phone:** (404)758-9590.

NEWBOLD, SIMEON EUGENE, SR.
Cleric. **Personal:** Born Sep 4, 1954, Miami, FL; son of Catherine Melvina Armbrister and David Jerome Newbold Sr; married Audrea Stitt, Aug 21, 1982; children: Simon Eugene Jr. **Educ:** Tuskegee Institute, BS, social work, 1977, MEd, personnel administration, 1979; Seabury-Western Theological Seminary, MDiv, 1989. **Career:** Barnett Bank, credit analyst; Operation PUSH (National), financial analyst; Messiah-St Bartholomew Episcopal Church, assistant; St Simon's Episcopal Church, rector, currently. **Orgs:** Union of Black Episcopalians; Omega Psi Phi Fraternity Inc. **Business Addr:** Rector, St Simon the Cyrenian Episcopal Church, 1700 Ave E, PO Box 1147, Fort Pierce, FL 34950, (407)461-2519.

NEWBORN, ODIE VERNON, JR.
Physician. **Personal:** Born Nov 5, 1947, Nashville, TN; married Trina. **Educ:** Tennessee State University, BS; Meharry Medical College, MD; Flint MI, Intern, Residency. **Career:** Physician, family practitioner, currently. **Orgs:** Natl Medical Assn; Georgia State Medical Society; Colquitt Co Medical Society; NAACP.

NEWBORN, PHINEAS LAJETTE, JR.
Pianist, recording artist, group leader. **Personal:** Born Dec 14, 1931, Whiteville, TN; son of Rosie Lee Murphy Newborn and Phineas Newborn; married Alelasta (divorced); children: Phineas III. **Educ:** Tennessee State College, Nashville, TN, music. **Career:** Willard Alexander Booking Agency, pianist, recording artist, currently. **Honors/Awds:** Harlem Blues, Gold Seal Million seller in Japan. **Military Serv:** Army.

NEWELL, KATHLEEN W.
Former judge, financial consultant. **Personal:** Born Aug 30, 1943, Alexandria, LA; daughter of Larry J Williams and Juanita Mandebourgh Williams; married; children: Oliver Joseph. **Educ:** UCLA; Wayne State Univ School of Law, JD, 1972. **Career:** MI Dept. of Treasury, administrative law judge, 1979-97; Ernst & Young, LLP, sr tax manager-SAL, 1997-. **Orgs:** State Bar Michigan, council mem, taxation section, 1985-88, chair, sr justice/elder law, 1996-97; New Home Community Development and Non-Profit Housing, president, 1995-96; Derby Home/Salvation Army Advisory Council, 1995-. **Business Addr:** Sr. Tax Manager-SAL, Ernst & Young, LLP, 500 Woodward Ave., Ste. 1700, Detroit, MI 48226-3426.

NEWELL, MATTHIAS GREGORY
Librarian. **Personal:** Born Jun 26, 1927, Colon, Panama. **Educ:** Univ of Dayton, BS 1951; Catholic Univ, MA 1960; Vatican Library School, diploma 1963; Vatican Archives School, diploma 1964; Catholic Univ, MSLS 1968; Simmons Coll, DA 1977; Latin Amer Tchng, fellow 1976. **Career:** Univ Centro-Americana, dir of library; Univ of Rhode Island, librarian 1973-; St Francis De Sales School, principal 1972-73; Eastern Michigan Univ, teacher 1971-72; Morgan State Univ, 1970-71; St Mary's Univ, librarian 1968-70; St Louis Milwaukee, teacher 1960-67; Rep of Peru, teacher 1951-58. **Orgs:** Mem, St Louis Province Soc of Mary, 1949-; mem, Black Caucus, Amer Library Assn; mem, Catholic Library Assn; mem, Common Cause; dir, Baltimore Black Catholic Lay Caucus, 1971; Patron de la Promocion Colegia San Antonio Callao, Peru, 1957; Latin Amer Teaching Fellowship, Tufts Univ, 1976-. **Honors/Awds:** Published articles in Catholic Library World & Rila Bulletin. **Business Addr:** Apartado 69, Managua, Nicaragua.

NEWELL, VIRGINIA K.
Educator (retired). **Personal:** Born Oct 7, Advance, NC; daughter of Dinah Kimbrough and William S Kimbrough (deceased); married George (deceased); children: Virginia D Newell Banks, Glenda Newell-Harris. **Educ:** Talladega Coll, AB 1940; NYU, 1956; Univ Chicago, ASF fellow 1958-59; Univ of Sarasota, EdD 1976. **Career:** Winston-Salem State Univ, asso prof, ch math/computer science. **Orgs:** Links Inc, Winston-Salem Chapter; former pres NC Cncl Tchrs Math; life mem NEA; editor newsletter Nat Assn Math; AMS; MAA; NCTM; life mem NAACP; State Cmsr Nat Cncl Negro Women; Alpa Kappa Alpha Sorority, Phi Omega Chapter; bd of dirs, Chamber of Commerce; bd of dirs, Arts Council; bd of dirs, Winston-Salem Symphony. **Honors/Awds:** Zeta Phi Beta's Woman of Yr 1964; Outstand Tchr Award 1960; Winston-Salem Chronicle, Woman of the Year, 1983, Citizen of the Year, 1987; Winston-Salem State University, Doctor of Humane Letters, 1989; east ward, elected to alderman, 1977-, re-elected to 3 terms. **Home Addr:** 2429 Pickford Ct NE, Winston-Salem, NC 27101.

NEWELL, WILLIAM
Social worker. **Personal:** Born Dec 28, 1938, Utica, MS; married Marie Bow; children: Raynard, Renee, Roseanne. **Educ:** Riverside Comm Coll, AA 1970; Cal State Coll San Bernardino, BA 1972; Univ of CA Los Angeles, MSW 1974. **Career:** San Bernardino County Mental Health, psychotherapist. **Orgs:** Mem Soc for Clinical Social Work 1972-, North Amer Soc Adlerian Psy 1980-; past pres Inland Assoc Black Social Worker 1976-, Toastmasters #797 1980-; adv bd Hard to Place Black ADoption Children Insland Area Urban League 1981-83; founder/pres Family Adolescent Child and Elderly Serv 1984-; mem Omage Psi Phi Inc 1983-, Natl Assoc of Social Work 1985-. **Business Addr:** Psychotherapist, San Bernardino Co Mental Hlth, 1777 W Baseline, San Bernardino, CA 92411.

NEWFIELD, MARC ALEXANDER
Professional baseball player. **Personal:** Born Oct 19, 1972, Sacramento, CA. **Career:** Seattle Mariners, outfielder, 1993-95; San Diego Padres, 1995-96; Milwaukee Brewers, 1996-. **Business Addr:** Professional Baseball Player, Milwaukee Brewers, County Stadium, 201 S 46th St, Milwaukee, WI 53214, (414)933-1818.

NEWHOUSE, MILLICENT DELAINE
Attorney. **Personal:** Born May 28, 1964, Detroit, MI; daughter of Janette Newhouse and Benjamin Newhouse. **Educ:** University of Michigan, BA, 1986; Howard University, JD, 1989. **Career:** State Attorney General's Office, assistant attorney general, 1989-; National Academy for Paralegal Studies, teacher, 1992-. **Orgs:** Loren Miller Bar Association, secretary, 1992-93; Neighborhood Legal Clinic, volunteer, attorney coordinator, 1992-; Equality in Practice Committee, 1992-; Boys & Girls Club, mentor, 1990-91; Maddona Presbyterian Church, tutor, 1990-92; Municipal League Candidate Committee, 1992; Howard University Alumni Association, 1989-. **Business Addr:** Assistant Attorney General, State Attorney General's Office, 900 Forth Ave, Ste 2000, Seattle, WA 98164, (206)389-2099.

NEWHOUSE, QUENTIN, JR.
Social psychologist, educator, researcher. **Personal:** Born Oct 20, 1949, Washington, DC; son of Berlene Byrd Newhouse and Quentin Newhouse Sr (deceased); married Debra Carter, Jul 7, 1984; children: Alyse Elizabeth Belinda. **Educ:** Marietta College, BA, psychology, 1971; Howard University, MS, psychology, 1974, PhD, psychology, 1980. **Career:** Antioch University, assistant professor, social sciences, 1976-79; Quentin Newhouse Jr and Associates, president, 1981-84; Howard University, assistant professor, social sciences, 1982-88; US Army, computer systems analyst, 1984, 85; University of District of Columbia, adjunct professor, psychology, 1984, 1991-; US Census Bureau, 21th Century Staff, computer specialist, 1988-91, Center for Survey Methods Research, statistician, 1991-93; Market Research Analyst, 1994; Job Developer, PG Private Industry Council, 1994; asst prof, Dept of Behavioral Sciences and Human Services, Bowie State Univ, Bowie MD, 1995-, interim chair, 1996-. **Orgs:** American Psychological Association, 1981, 1993-; American Statistical Association, 1993; Association of Black Psychologists, 1994-; Social Science Computing Association, affiliate, 1990-94; CENSUG, Census SAS User's Group, co-chairman, 1992-; Tau Epsilon Phi, life member, 1980-; Appointed bd of dirs, Mental Health Assn of PG County, 1994-95; Appointed Regional Advisory Board, United Way of PG County, 1994-; Appointed, bd of dirs, Metropolitan Police Boys and Girls Clubs, 1994-. **Honors/Awds:** US Army, Letter of Commendation for Outstanding Performance, 1988; University of District of Columbia, Community Service Award, 1982, 1984; Certificate of Appreciation, PG County Executive, 1995, 1996; Governor's Certificate of Achievement State of MD, 1995. **Special Achievements:** Appointed P G County Representative, State Advisory Commission for Children, Youth, and Families, 1992-95; appointed, P.G. County Children's Commission for Children and Families, 1992-95; appointed, P.G. County Commission for Children and Youth, 1991-92; Bureautots Inc, advisory board, vice pres, 1990-91; Prepare Our Youth Inc, advisory board, 1990-94. **Business Addr:** Interm Chair & Assistant Professor, Department of Behavioral Sciences & Human Svcs, Bowie State University, MLK, Rm 0201, Bowie, MD 20715, (301)464-7550.

NEWHOUSE, RICHARD H.
Senator (retired). **Personal:** Born Jan 24, 1924, Louisville, KY; married Kathi; children: Suzanne, Richard, Holly. **Educ:** Boston U, BS 1949, MS 1951; Univ of Chgo, JD 1961. **Career:** Illinois State Senate 13th Dist, senator, until 1991. **Orgs:** Pres/founder Black Legislators Assn; dir Black Legislative Clearing House in Chgo; fellow Adlai Stevenson Inst; practicing atty; chairman comm on Commerce and Economic Development, State Senate 1989-; board member, Joint Center for Political & Economic Studies 1990-. **Honors/Awds:** Named Best Legisla-

tor by both Independent Voters of IL & Am Legion; Outstand Pub Servant Cook Co Bar Assn; Senator of the Yr Bapt Ministers Conf of Chgo; Excellence Award, Illinois Leadership Council for Agricultural Education, 1990.

NEWHOUSE, ROBERT F.
Business executive. **Personal:** Born Jan 9, 1950, Gregg County, TX; married Nancy; children: Roddrick, Dawnyel, Shauntel, Reginald. **Educ:** Univ of Houston, MTH 1973; Univ of Dallas, MBA 1984. **Career:** Dallas Cowboys, player 1972-83; Tymeshare, computer oper; TX Bank & Trust, loan ofc; Trans Global Airlines, pres 1984; Dallas TX, real estate broker; Lone Star Delivery, pres; R Newhouse Enterprises Inc, pres; Dallas Cowboys, dir of community affairs, currently. **Orgs:** YMCA; United Way; Boys Club; Northern District Dallas Division, panel trustee. **Honors/Awds:** Sport Hall of Fame Univ of Houston. **Business Addr:** President, R Newhouse Enterprises Inc, 6847 Truxton, Dallas, TX 75231, (214)343-9064.

NEWKIRK, GWENDOLYN
Educator, educational administrator. **Personal:** Born Aug 14, Washington, DC; daughter of Rachel Cornelia Polk Jones and William Henry Jones. **Educ:** Tillotson College, Austin, TX, BS, 1945; Teachers College Columbia University, New York, NY, MA, 1946; Cornell University, Ithaca, NY, EdD, 1961. **Career:** Cornell University, Ithaca, NY, grad teaching & rest ass, 1960-61; Bennet College, Greensboro, NC, instructor, 1946-50; Lincoln University, Jefferson City, MO, professor, 1950-62; North Carolina College, Durham, NC, professor, 1962-69; Univ of Minnesota, Minneapolis, MN, associate professor, 1969-71; Univ of Nebraska, Lincoln, NE, dept chairman & professor, 1971-. **Orgs:** Life member, American Home Economics Assn (held several offices); member, Nebraska Home Economics Assn (held comm chair resp); life member, American Vocational Assn (held comm chair resp); member, Nebraska Vocational Assn, 1971-; member, Nebraska Education Association. **Honors/Awds:** Dr of Humane Letters, Tillotson College, 1990; Recognized by Optimists Club of Lincoln, 1986; Visiting Scholar, Indiana Univ in PA, 1982; Visiting Scholar, Home Ecomonics Women's Scolars Program, University of Oklahoma, 1976; Women Helping Women Recognition, Soroptimist International Lincoln Chapter, 1975. **Business Addr:** Department Chairman, Consumer Science & Education, University of Nebraska-Lincoln, 123 Home Economics Building, Lincoln, NE 68583-0801.

NEWKIRK, THOMAS H.
Educational administrator. **Personal:** Born in New York City, NY; son of Esther Newkirk and Climith J Newkirk Sr; divorced; children: Kori, Kisan, Kamila. **Educ:** Univ of MA at Amherst, MEd 1974, EdD 1985. **Career:** Pres, consult Newkirk Assoc Tax & Bus 1958-; education consult 1958-; ins broker 1959-63; Haryou-Act NYC, coord training testing youth div, dir mgmt training 6 yrs; SUNY Corland, dir emeritus spec ed prog. **Orgs:** Founding mem Holcombe Rucker Scholarship Fund 1967; consult State Ed Dept 1967-72; vice pres United Black Ed 1969; founding mem NYS Spec Prog Personnel Assoc 1973; chmn Spec Progs Inst on Teaching & Counseling 1979; mem Mayors Adv Comm at Cortland; swimming instr Cortland; lecturer Social Found Ed; past vice pres Spec Progs Pers Assoc State of NY. **Honors/Awds:** Publ ''Some Objective Considerations'' 1974, ''The New Disadvantaged'' 1975, ''Prob & Promises-Former Inmates on Coll Campuses'' 1976, ''History of Ed Oppty at Cortland Coll'' 1968-73; Superlative Comm Serv Awd, Intl Key Women 1974; SUNY Chancellors Awd for Excellence in Professional Serv, 1979; Arthur Eve Award, Outstanding Public Service, 1991. **Military Serv:** NY Natl Guard 1946-48. **Business Addr:** Dir Emeritus Special Ed Program, State Univ of NY, Cortland, NY 13045.

NEWLAND, ZACHARY JONAS
Podiatrist. **Personal:** Born Dec 15, 1954, Ft Lee, VA; son of Adeline M Newland and Archie J Newland; married Camillia Sutton; children: Yolanda. **Educ:** SC State Coll, BS Chemistry 1975; Medical Univ of SC, BS Pharmacy 1978; PA College of Podiatric Medicine, DPM 1984. **Career:** Thrift Drugs, asst mgr pharmacist 1978-80; SC Army Natl Guard, medical platoon leader 1978-80; Laurel Pharmacy, pharmacist 1982-84; Lindell Hosp, resident poliatric surgery 1984-85; Lindell Hosp, chief resident podiatric surgery 1985-86, resident teaching staff & lecturer 1986-; Metro Community Health Ctr, dir of podiatric medicine & surgery 1986-88; People's Health Center, staff podiatrist, 1988-; private medical practice, 1990-. **Orgs:** Mem SC Pharmaceutical Assoc 1978-, Natl Health Serv Corps 1980-, Amer Podiatric Medical Assoc, Omega Psi Phi Frat. **Honors/Awds:** Article published in Journal of Foot Surgery 1984. **Military Serv:** AMSC Reserves capt 1978-. **Business Addr:** Podiatrist, 8780 Manchester Rd, Brentwood, MO 63144.

NEWLIN, RUFUS K.
Educational administrator. **Career:** Morristown College, Morristown, TN, pres, currently.

NEWMAN, ANTHONY
Professional football player. **Personal:** Born Nov 21, 1965, Bellingham, WA; married Teri; children: Baylee, Anthony Jr. **Educ:** Univ of Oregon, attended. **Career:** Los Angeles Rams, defensive back, 1988-94; New Orleans Saints, 1995-. **Business Addr:** Professional Football Player, New Orleans Saints, 5800 Airline Hwy, Metairie, LA 70003, (504)733-0255.

NEWMAN, CONSTANCE BERRY
Government administrator. **Personal:** Born Jul 8, 1935, Chicago, IL; daughter of Ernestine Siggers Berry and Joseph Alonzo Berry; married Theodore Newman (divorced 1980). **Educ:** Bates College, Lewiston, ME, AB, 1956; University of Minnesota, School of Law, Minneapolis, MN, BSL, 1959. **Career:** Volunteers in Service of America, Washington DC, director, 1971-73; Consumer Product Safety Commission, Washington, DC, commissioner, 1973-76; US Dept of Housing & Urban Development, Washington, DC, asst secretary, 1976-77; Newman & Hermanson Co, Washington, DC, president, 1977-82; Government of Lesotho, Ministry of Interior, consultant, 1987-88; Bush-Quayle 1988 Campaign, Washington, DC, dep director, national voter coalitions, 1988; Presidential Transition Team, Washington, DC, co-director of outreach, 1988-89; US Office of Personnel Management, Washington, DC, director, 1989-92; Smithsonian Institution, Washington, DC, undersecretary, 1992-. **Orgs:** Bd of trustees, The Brookings Institution: mem, bd of trustees, Bates College; mem, District of Columbia Financial Responsibility & Management Assistant Authority. **Honors/Awds:** Honorary Doctors of Laws, Amherst College, 1980; Honorary Doctors of Laws, Bates College, 1972; Secretary of Defense Medal for Outstanding Public Service, 1985; Secretary's Award for Excellence, US Dept of Housing & Urban Development, 1977. **Business Addr:** Under Secretary, Smithsonian Institution, 1000 Jefferson Dr SW, Rm 219, Washington, DC 20560.

NEWMAN, DAVID, JR.
Musician. **Personal:** Born Feb 24, 1933, Dallas, TX; married Karen Newman; children: Terry, Andr, Cadino, Benji. **Educ:** Jarvis Christian Coll. **Career:** Newmanism, leader 1980; Muse Records, rec artist 1980; Fantasy Rec Co, rec artist 1978-80; Warner Bros, rec artist 1975-77; Atlantic Rec Inc, rec artist 1959-74; Herbie Mann & The Family of Mann, sideman 1970-71; Ray Charles Enterprises, sideman 1954-64; BMI, writer, publisher; Recording Artist, Koko Pelli Records, Inc. **Orgs:** NARAS, Rhythm & Blues Society; David ''Fat Head'' Newman & Newmanism. **Honors/Awds:** Down Beat Nomination 1968-70; Outstand Musicianship TX Jazz 1970; Grammy Nomination, 1990; Pioneer Award, BMI, 1990; Rhythm & Blues Foundation, Pioneer Award, 1998. **Business Addr:** Head Publishing Co, 168A Tanglewood Dr, West Hurley, NY 12491.

NEWMAN, ERNEST WILBUR
Minister. **Personal:** Born Apr 9, 1928, Kingstree, SC; son of Serena Hamilton Newman and Meloncy Newman; married Thelma Heard, Aug 12, 1955; children: Kathy Newman McCoy, Ernest Wilbur, Jr. **Educ:** Claflin Coll, Orangeburg SC, AB, 1948; Gammon Theological Seminary, Atlanta GA, master's degree, 1956. **Career:** Minister, Summerville Charge, Summerville SC, 1950-52; Rockmill Charge, Anderson SC, 1952-53; Kelley Chapel, Miami FL, 1953; Talladega Charge, Talladega AL, 1954-55; St. Joseph Methodist Church, Jacksonville FL, 1955-57; Zion Methodist Church, Ocala FL, 1957-64; Ebenezer United Methodist Church, Jacksonville FL, 1964-72; Florida Conference, Melbourne Dist, dist superintendent, 1972 -77; Plantation United Methodist Church, Plantation FL, 1977-82; Florida Conference, assoc coucil dir, 1982-83, dist superintendent, Deland Dist, 1983; elected bishop, 1984. **Orgs:** Mem, bd of dirs, Broward County Red Cross, Broward County Safety Council; mem, bd of trustees, Florida Conference; pres, Bishop's Cabinet, 1966-67; mem, Gen Commn on Religion and Race; pres, College of Bishops, southeastern jurisdiction, 1989. **Honors/Awds:** Honorary doctorates from Bethune Cookman Coll, 1974, Lambuth Coll, 1987.

NEWMAN, GEOFFREY W.
Educator. **Personal:** Born Aug 29, 1946, Oberlin, OH; son of Bertha Battle Newman and Arthur Eugene Newman. **Educ:** Howard Univ, Washington DC, BFA, 1968; Wayne State Univ, Detroit MI, MA, 1970; Howard Univ, Washington DC, PhD, 1978. **Career:** Actor, educator, consultant, theorist and director in theatre; Howard Univ, Wabash College, Drama Dept, chmn; Montclair State Coll, dean of School of the Arts, 1988-. **Orgs:** Mem, grant screening panels, District of Columbia Commn on the Arts and Humanities, Pennsylvania State Council for the Arts, and Illinois State Arts Council; artistic dir and cofounder, Takoma Players, Takoma Theatre, Washington DC; artistic dir, Ira Aldridge Theatre, Howard Univ, Washington DC; artistic dir, Park Place Productions, Washington DC; artistic dir, Young Audiences of District of Columbia. **Honors/Awds:** Directed world premiere of Owen Dodson's Sound of Soul and European premiere of Robert Nemiroff's Raisin; received Amoco Award for Theatrical Excellence, by John F Kennedy Center for the Permorming Arts in conjunction with Amer Theatre Assn; received special commendations from Mayor Marion Barry Jr, Washington DC, Mayor Pat Screen, Baton Rouge LA, and Gov Harry Hughes, State of Maryland; published articles in professional journals; served as nominator for Washington DC Awards Society's Helen Hayes Awards. **Business Addr:** Dean, School of the Arts, Montclair State College, 1 Normal Ave, Montclair, NJ 07043-1624.

NEWMAN, JOHN SYLVESTER, JR.
Professional basketball player. **Personal:** Born Nov 28, 1963, Danville, VA; married Tina. **Educ:** Univ of Richmond, Richmond, VA, 1982-86. **Career:** Cleveland Cavaliers, forward, 1986-87; New York Knicks, 1987-90; Charlotte Hornets, 1990-93; New Jersey Nets, 1993-94; Milwaukee Bucks, 1994-97; Denver Nuggets, 1997-. **Orgs:** Kappa Alpha Psi Fraternity. **Business Addr:** Professional Basketball Player, Denver Nuggets, 1635 Clay St, Denver, CO 80204-1743, (303)893-6700.

NEWMAN, KENNETH J.
Accountant/auditor. **Personal:** Born Nov 7, 1944, Vallijo; married Barbara B; children: Kenneth J Jr, Eric J. **Educ:** Gramblin Coll, BS 1967; Vet Adminstrn Data Processing Austin, TX, prgm instruction courses 1968; SACUBO & NACUBO, cont educ workshops 1969-; Univ NE atOmaha, course for bus mgrs 1977. **Career:** Grambling Coll, asst dir of computer ctr 1967; Veteran Admin Data Processing Ctr, acct trainee 1967-68, data processor 1968-69, asst auditor 1969-70; Grambling State Univ, bus mgr 1970-73; Mary Holmes Coll, bus mgr 1974-79; City of Monroe, prgms auditor 1979-81, dir of planning & urban develop. **Orgs:** Adv bd mem Special Serv Mary Holmes Coll; adv bd Gourmet Svcs; mem visiting com S Assn of Coll & Schs Atlanta 1976; mem Alpha Phi Alpha Frat 1979; mem bd of trustees Zion Travelor Bapt Church 1979-; bd mem Tri Dist Boys Club; mem United Way 1981-; PIC mem for JTPA 1984-90; mem Industrial Develop Bd 1986-92; mem Monroe Chamber of Commerce; pres Carroll HS PTA 1986. **Honors/Awds:** Outstanding Young Man of Am 1978-79. **Business Addr:** Dir of Planning & Urban Dev, City of Monroe, PO Box 7324, Monroe, LA 71201.

NEWMAN, MILLER MAURICE
Stock clerk. **Personal:** Born Oct 31, 1941, Terrell, TX; son of Lillie Vee Coleman Whestone and Miller Newman; married Alice Faye Keith, Feb 10, 1963; children: Keith, Donald, Mark. **Educ:** Eastern OK State Coll, 1968-71. **Career:** Hunt's Dept Store, Shipping & Receiving, 1960-66; Rockwell International, machine operator, 1966-83, stock clerk, 1983-; Teen's Vill USA, co-owner; B&B Skelly Station, 1968-76; Eastside Exxon, owner, 1970-75; Eastside Supperette, owner, 1976-81. **Orgs:** Keddo, 1972-; Model Cities, 1971-76; pres, Pitts Co NAACP, 1972-; scoutmaster, Boy Scouts of Amer, 1971-73; pres, UAW Local #1558, 1985-91; chairman, McAlster Housing Auth, 1989-92; recording secretary, Oklahoma State Capitol, 1990-; Pitts County Holiday Commission, 1985-. **Honors/Awds:** Martin Luther King Jr, Pitts Co Holiday Commission, 1985, Natl Alliance Against Racism, 1984. **Military Serv:** OK Natl Guard, Msg, ARCOM, Award for Valor, 1959-82; USAR School, 1982-91. **Business Addr:** PO Box 13, McAlester, OK 74502.

NEWMAN, NATHANIEL
County official, clergyman. **Personal:** Born Aug 6, 1942, Altheimer, AR; son of Marguerite Ruth Gordon Newman and Abraham Henry Newman; children: Mia Ruth Newman Williams, Angelique Marie. **Educ:** Merritt, Coll, Oakland, CA, AA, 1971; San Jose State Univ, BS, 1974, MS, 1976; Spring Valley Bible Coll, Alameda, CA, BA, 1983; Fuller Theological Seminary, Pasadena, CA, certificate in religious studies, 1985. **Career:** City of Oakland, Oakland, CA, patrolman, 1968-74; Santa Clara County, San Jose, CA, inspector, 1974-; Antioch Baptist, San Jose, CA, assoc minister, 1981-86; Concord Missionary Baptist, San Francisco, CA, youth minister, 1986-90; Santa Clara County District Attorney's Office, 1990-; Good News Missionary Baptist Church, pastor, 1991-; Santa Clara County District Attorney's Office, asst chief bureau of investigation, currently. **Orgs:** Mem, chaplain, Alpha Phi Alpha, 1973-; life member, Alpha Phi Alpha Fraternity, 1975-; pres, Black Peace Officers Assn, 1980-88; vice-chmn, mem, Minority Citizens Advisory Council, Metro Transportation Commission, 1980-; pres, District Attorney's Investigators Assn, 1982-84; pres/CEO, Frank Sypert Afro-Amer Community Service Agency, 1982-88; chaplain, Natl Black Police Assn, 1982-; chmn, Pack Committee, Boy Scouts of Amer, 1986-; board member, Santa Clara County District Attorney's Investigators Assn, 1990-; NAACP, San Jose Branch, president, 1991-92, executive committee member, 1993-; San Jose Traffic Appeals Commissioner, vice chair, 1991-; Mayor's Citizens Advisory Group, 1992-. **Honors/Awds:** Doctor of Divinity, School of Gospel Ministry, 1982; Peace Officer of the Year, Santa Clara County Black Peace Officers, 1983, 1985, and 1988; community recognition, Omega Psi Phi, 1985; Community Service Award, San Jose Black Chamber of Commerce, 1986; Humanitarian Award, Ministers Alliance of San Jose, 1986; organized workshops and agencies for community blacks and students; Brother of the Year, Alpha Phi Alpha Fraternity, Western Region, 1990; California District Attorney Investigators Association, Certificate of Appreciation, 1992; Martin Luther King Jr Association of Santa Clara County, Good Neighbor Award, 1993. **Home Addr:** 3208 Lyter Way, San Jose, CA 95135.

NEWMAN, PAUL DEAN
Automotive executive (retired). **Personal:** Born Dec 15, 1938, Zanesville, OH; son of Margaret Newman and Delbert Newman; married Norma Jean Guy; children: Vicki, Paula, Valerie, Paul II, Scott, Sharri. **Educ:** Tri State Univ, BS 1966; Univ of VA Exec Devel Prog, Diploma 1985; Univ of MI Exec Devel

Prog, Diploma 1986. **Career:** General Motors Corp, dir of urban affairs. **Orgs:** Michigan League for Human Services, exec leadership council; Genesee Intermediate School District Board of Education; Business Policy Review Council, Insight bd mem. **Honors/Awds:** Disting Serv Awd Tri State Univ 1986. **Home Addr:** 3020 Westwood Pky, Flint, MI 48503.

NEWMAN, THEODORE ROOSEVELT, JR.
Judge. **Personal:** Born Jul 5, 1934, Birmingham, AL; son of Ruth O Newman and Theodore R Newman. **Educ:** Brown Univ, AB 1955; Harvard Law Sch, JD 1958. **Career:** DC Superior Court, assoc judge 1970-76; Brown Univ, trustee 1979-83; DC Court of Appeals, chief judge 1976-84, judge 1984-91; senior judge, 1991-. **Orgs:** Pres Natl Ctr for State Courts 1981-82; fellow Amer Bar Foundation; mem Natl Bar Assn; past pres Judicial Council. **Honors/Awds:** C Francis Stradford Awd 1984; Natl Bar Assn; Brown Univ LLD 1980; William H Hastie Award Judicial Council Nalt Bar Assn 1988. **Business Addr:** Judge, DC Ct of Appeals, 500 Indiana Ave NW, Washington, DC 20001.

NEWMAN, WILLIAM THOMAS, JR.
Attorney, elected official. **Personal:** Born Sep 11, 1950, Richmond, VA; son of Geraldine Nunn Newman and William T Newman. **Educ:** Ohio Univ, Athens OH, BA, 1972; Catholic Univ School of Law, Washington DC, JD, 1977. **Career:** US Dept of Commerce, Washington DC, attorney, 1977-80; Self-Employed, Arlington VA, attorney, 1980-; Arlington County Bd, 1988-, chairman, 1991-, judge, 1993-. **Orgs:** Mem, Virginia State Bar Assn, 1977-, District of Columbia Bar Assn, 1978-; bd of dir, Northern Virginia Black Attorney's Assn, 1984-88; chmn, Arlington County Fire Trial Bd, 1985-87; trustees council, Natl Capital Area YMCA, 1985-; bd of dir, Arlington County United Way, 1985-86; mem, Arlington Comm of PO, 1985-, Northern Virginia Urban League Advisory Comm, 1985-; vice pres, Old Dominion Bar Assn, 1986; mem, Virginia Medical Malpractice Review Panel, 1986-; commn in chancery, Arlington County Circuit Court, 1986-; vice chmn, Arlington Civic Coalition for Minority Affairs, 1986-88. **Honors/Awds:** Corpus Juris Secundum, Catholic Univ School of Law, 1977; SAA, US Dept of Commerce, 1979; Community Serv, Alpha Phi Alpha, Theta Rho Lambda, 1990; Community Serv, Alpha Kappa Alpha, Zeta Chi Omega, 1988. **Business Addr:** Judge, Arlington County Circuit Court, 1425 N Courthouse Rd, Circuit Court Chambers, Arlington, VA 22201.

NEWSOME, BURNELL
Clergyman. **Personal:** Born Apr 13, 1938, Wesson, MS; son of Rev & Mrs James Newsome; married Gloria J Wilson; children: Burnell Jr, Kenneth. **Educ:** Marion Coll of Comm, Cert Business Admin 1962; Copiah Lincoln Jr Coll Wesson MS, Cert Carpentry 1977; MS Baptist Seminary Jackson MS, BTh. **Career:** Towne Shoes, store mgr, 1965; Commercial Credit Corp, dist rep, 1968; St Regis Paper Co, accountant 1973; BF Goodrich, budget control mgr; St Mary's United Methodist Church & Mt Salem United Methodist, pastor, currently. **Orgs:** Trustee, Hazlehurst MS Separate School Dist 1982; advisory committee Southwest MS Elect Power Assn 1983; bd mem MS Dept of Ed Comm on Accreditation 1984; chmn of steering committee "Copiah County Crusade for Christ" 1985; sec Copiah County Interdenominational Ministerial Alliance. **Honors/Awds:** FHA Farm Family of the Year USDA Farmers Home Admin 1977. **Business Addr:** Pastor, St Mary's United Methodist Church, PO Box 1003, Crystal Springs, MS 39059.

NEWSOME, CLARENCE GENO
Educator. **Personal:** Born Mar 22, 1950, Ahoskie, NC; son of Annie Butler Lewis Newsome and Clarence Shaw Newsome; married Lynne DaNean Platt, Jul 29, 1972; children: Gina Lynn, Brittany Ann Byuarm. **Educ:** Duke Univ, BA 1971; Duke Divinity School, M Div 1975; Duke U, PhD 1982. **Career:** Duke U, asst pro & dean of minority affairs 1973-74; Mt Level Baptist Church, Durham, NC Dem Nat'l Comm, asst staff dir demo charter comm 1974-75; Duke Divinity School, instructor 1978-82, asst prof 1982; Mt Level Baptist Church, Durham, NC Democratic Nat'l Comm 1974-75; Duke Univ, asst prof of Amer religious thought; Howard Univ DC Assistant Dean School of Divinity 1986-89, assoc dean, School of Divinity, 1989-. **Orgs:** Mem American Society of Church History 1980-; mem of finance comm Creative Ministries Assoc 1981; chrmn of the brd NC Gen Baptist Found, Inc 1982; mem of comm on educ Durham Comm on the Affairsof Black People 1983; co-chairman of comm on educ Durham Interdenominational Ministerial Alliance 1983-84; Planning Coordinator, Euro-American Theology Consultation Group, American Academy of Religion 1987-; pres Society for the Study of Black Religion 1989-. **Honors/Awds:** 1st Black to receive Athletic Grant-in-Aid (Scholarship) Duke Univ 1968-72; 1st Black to be named to the All Atlantic Coast Conf Acad Team Duke Univ 1970-71; 1st Black stud Comm Speaker Walter Cronkite was the Keynote Duke Univ 1972; Rockfellow Doct Fellowship, Natl Fellowship, James B Duke Dissertation Fellowship, 1975-78; published number of articles and completed book length manuscript on Mary McLeod Bethund, A Religious Biography. **Home Addr:** 6761 Sewells Orchard Dr, Columbia, MD 21045. **Business Addr:** Dean of Theology, Howard Univ, 2400 6th St, NW, Washington, DC 20059-0001.

NEWSOME, COLA KING
Physician. **Personal:** Born Sep 23, 1925, Ahoskie, NC; married Gerdine Hardin; children: Lars, Jon, Autumn, Ann, Peter. **Educ:** WV State Coll, BS 1949; Meharry Med Coll, MS 1952; MD 1956. **Career:** Evansville, IN, Physician 1957-; St Mary's Hosp, staff mem; Deaconess Hosp; Hubbard Hosp, intern 1956-57. **Orgs:** Mem Evansville Rec Com 1970-; Evansville & Sch Bd 1964-; sec 1970-; IN Med Assn; AMA; Govtl Affairs Com 1969; Alpha; Dem; New Hope Bapt Ch; PlazaYacht Club Spl. **Honors/Awds:** Recognition Black Expo 1977; bd dir Child Guidance Ctr; Housing Com; SW IN Adult Ctr; Deaconess Med Records Utilization Com; dir Central Comm Clinic USMCR 1943-46. **Business Addr:** 415 E Mulberry St, Evansville, IN 47713.

NEWSOME, CRAIG
Professional football player. **Personal:** Born Aug 10, 1971, San Bernardino, CA; married Debra; children: Garrett, Alexis. **Educ:** Arizona State University. **Career:** Green Bay Packers, defensive back, 1995-. **Special Achievements:** Selected in the 1st round/32nd overall pick in the 1995 NFL Draft. **Business Addr:** Professional Football Player, Green Bay Packers, 1265 Lombardi Ave, Green Bay, WI 54304, (414)494-2351.

NEWSOME, ELISA C.
Journalist. **Personal:** Born Jul 6, 1964, Detroit, MI; daughter of Gwendolyn Newsome and William York; children: Andrew I Lee. **Educ:** Miami Dade Community College, Miami, FL, AA & AS, 1986; University of Miami, Coral Glades, FL, BS, 1988. **Career:** Palm Beach Post, West Palm Beach, FL, reporter, 1989-. **Orgs:** Member, National Association of Black Journalists, 1987-. **Business Addr:** Reporter, Palm Beach Post, 900 Linton Blvd, Suite 201, Delray Beach, FL 33444.

NEWSOME, EMANUEL T.
Educator. **Personal:** Born Mar 21, 1942, Gary, IN; married Nellie Smith; children: Kim, Eric, Erika. **Educ:** BS 1964; MA 1965; PhD counseling guidance & Psycho Service 1976. **Career:** Univ of Toledo 1976-; dir of student activities 1976-; IN State Univ, asst dean of student life for stud activities; dir coordinator state educ talent search prog 1966-68; financial aid couns & field rep 1965-66; grad asst in physical educ 1964-65; head scout & asst basketball coach 1964-65. **Orgs:** Mem Midwest Stud Financial Aid Assn 1965-68; mem Nat Assn of Student Personnel Assn 1969-; mem bd dir Hyte Comm Center 1973-; mem bd dir Big Brother Orgn Kalamazoo MI 1965-66; basketball coach Terre Haute Boys Club 1973-; NAACP 1960-; Urban League 1967-; Gov Steering Com on Volunteerism 1975; adv bd Toledo March of Dimes; Western MI Univ Athletic Hall of & Fame 1974. **Honors/Awds:** All American in basketball 1964; 2nd leading scorer in nation major colleges1964; All Mid-american Conf in basketball for 3 yrs 1961-64; participant Olympic Trials in basketball; IN All-star Basketball Team 1960. **Business Addr:** Dean of Student Affairs, University of Toledo, 2801 W Bancroft St, University of Toledo, Toledo, OH 43606.

NEWSOME, MOSES, JR.
Educational administrator. **Personal:** Born Sep 6, 1944, Charleston, WV; son of Ruth G Bass Newsome and Rev Moses Newsome; married Barbara Newsome, Jun 8, 1968; children: Ayanna, Mariana. **Educ:** Univ of Toledo, BA 1966; Univ of MI, MSW 1970; Univ of WI, PhD 1976. **Career:** Howard Univ Human Serv Eval Design Div, asst dir 1977-78; Howard Univ School of Social Work, asst dean 1979-80, assoc dean 1980-84; Norfolk State Univ School of Social Work, dean, prof 1984-. **Orgs:** Rsch consult Assoc consult Inc 1975-77; lecturer Upward Mobility Prog Univ of DC, 1977-78; Natl Steering Comm Natl Assoc of Black Soc Workers, 1979; Delegate Assembly Natl Assoc of Soc Workers 1983-84; Natl Steering Comm Group for the Advancement of Doctoral Ed 1983-85; chairman VA Social Work Educ Consortium; district chmn, Va. Chapter Natl Assn of Social Workers, 1989-90; chmn, Norfolk City Council Task Force on Children in Need of Services, 1988-89; vice chmn, Norfolk Area Health Study, Advisory Bd, 1987-88; Bd of Accreditation Council on Social Work Educ, 1988-90; State Bd Virginia Council on Social Welfare, 1989-91; Planning Council, Norfolk, VA, board of directors, 1987-90. **Honors/Awds:** Outstanding Young Man in Amer US Jaycees 1977; Outstanding Macro Faculty Mem Howard Univ School of Soc Work 1978; "Frequency and Distribution of Disabilities Among Blacks," in Equal to the Challenge, Bureau of Educ Research, Washington, DC 1986; "Job Satisfaction and Work Relationships of Social Service Workers," Dept of Human Resources, Norfolk, VA, 1987. **Military Serv:** USAF. **Business Addr:** Dean, Professor, Norfolk State Univ, School of Social Work, 2401 Corprew Ave, Norfolk, VA 23504.

NEWSOME, OZZIE
Professional football player (retired). **Personal:** Born Mar 16, 1956, Muscle Shoals, AL; son of Ethel Newsome and Ozzie Newsome Sr; married Gloria Jenkins. **Educ:** Univ of Alabama, BS, recreation and park management. **Career:** Cleveland Browns, tight end, 1978-90. **Orgs:** Active in Fellowship of Christian Athletes, Big Brothers, Athletes in Action; bd of dirs, Police Athletic League. **Honors/Awds:** Voted Alabama Amateur Athlete of Year, Alabama Sportswriters Assn, 1977; AFC Pro-Squad, 1981; Teams Outstanding Player, 1981; All Pro, Pro-Football Writers Assn & Sporting News, 1979; Browns All-Time Leading Receiver; MVP on Offense, Cleveland TD Club (three times); ranked among NFL's top 10 in receptions; became 14th player in NFL history to make over 500 receptions; became the all-time leading tight end in NFL history; leading receiver in AFC, 1984. **Business Addr:** Cleveland Browns, 200 Saint Paul St, Ste 24, Baltimore, MD 21202-2004.

NEWSOME, PAULA RENEE
Optometrist. **Personal:** Born Jul 3, 1955, Wilmington, NC; daughter of Mercedes Newsome and Carter Newsome; divorced; children: Ayana Renee. **Educ:** Univ of NC-Chapel Hill, BA 1977; Univ of AL-Birmingham Med Center, OD, 1981, MS, 1981. **Career:** The Eye Institute Philadelphia, residency 1982; Univ of MO-St Louis School of Optometry; asst prof 1982-84; VA Hospital St Louis, optometric consultant 1983-84; Private Practice, optometrist 1984-. **Orgs:** Delta Sigma Theta Sorority Inc 1974-, Amer Optometric Assn, 1981-; treasurer Region III Natl Optometric Assn, 1981-; NC State Optometric Soc 1982-; Mecklenburg Co Optometric Soc 1984-; Charlotte Medical Soc 1984-; state legislative affairs advisory comm Scope of Practice AOA 1984-; Young Professional Network Mecklenburg Co 1984-; free visual screening for area churches 1984-; speaker Role Model Series Charlotte-Mecklenburg School System 1985-; advisory bd Total Care Comprehensive Home Health Serv Charlotte 1985-87; urban optometry Amer Optometric Assoc 1986-; board member Charlotte Women Business Owners 1986-87; charter mem Doctors with a Heart 1986-90; free visual screenings for Mecklenburg Co Parks and Recreation 1986; pres board of directors Focus on Leadership 1986-90; Mecklenburg Co, YWCA, 1988-90; Coalition for Literacy,88-90; Leadership Charlotte, 1986-90; Governor Morehead School for the Blind, 1988-; Charlotte Civic Index, 1988-89; Charlotte Chamber of Commerce, board of directors 1990-; Mint Museum of Art, board of directors 1991-; Central Piedmont Community College Foundation, board of directors, 1991-. **Honors/Awds:** Irv Borish Award for Outstanding Clinical Rsch 1981; The Las Amigas Outstanding Serv in Business Award 1985; 3 publications; numerous lectures. **Business Addr:** President/Optometrist, 107 W Morehead St, Charlotte, NC 28202.

NEWSOME, RONALD WRIGHT
Commercial banker. **Personal:** Born Jan 21, 1949, Charleston, WV; son of Ruth Newsome and Rev Moses Newsome; married Toni, Jun 21, 1973; children: Nicole, Kristine. **Educ:** Philander Smith College, BA, 1971; Clark/Atlanta University, MBA, 1973. **Career:** National Bank of Detroit, assistant branch mgr, credit officer, commerical loan officer, 1973-81; Bank One, Columbus, NA, commercial loan officer, senior loan officer, assistant vice pres, 1981-85, assistant vice pres, unit mgr, vp, 1988-; Huntington National Bank, assistant vice pres/commercial lender, 1985-88; Franklin University, adjunct professor, 1986-. **Orgs:** University Club of Columbus, 1983-; Columbus Urban League, board of directors, executive committee member & secretary, 1989-; The Private Industry Council of Columbus and Franklin County, Inc, board member/vice chairman, 1991-; Columbus Metropolitan Area Community Action Organization, board member/second vice pres, 1990-; Mark D Philmore Urban Bankers Forum of Central Ohio Inc, pres, 1994-. **Home Addr:** 1020 Zodiac Ave, Gahanna, OH 43230, (614)855-0120. **Business Addr:** VP, Bank One, Columbus, NA, 100 E Broad St, Columbus, OH 43215-0115, (614)248-5148.

NEWSOME, STEVEN CAMERON
Museum administrator. **Personal:** Born Sep 11, 1952, Norfolk, VA; divorced; children: Sanya. **Educ:** Trinity Coll, BA 1974; Emory Univ, MLS 1975. **Career:** Northwestern Univ Library, Afro-Amer studies librarian 1975-78; Univ of IL Chicago Univ Library, asst ref librarian 1980-82, head of reference 1982-83; Vivian Harsh Collection of Afro-Amer Hist & Lit The Chicago Public Library, curator 1983-86; MD Commn on Afro-Amer History and Culture, exec dir, beginning 1986; State of Maryland Dept of Housing and Community Development, Office of Cultural and Educational Services, chief, until 1991; Anacostia Museum, dir, 1991-. **Orgs:** Mid Atlantic Assoc of Museums, vp, 1994-, bd of governors, 1991-94; Maryland Humanities Council, bd of dirs, 1991-; Cultural Alliance of Greater Washington, bd of dirs, 1992-; John F Kennedy Ctr for the Performing Arts, comm & firends bd, 1993-. **Business Addr:** Director, Anacostia Museum, 1901 Fort Pl SE, Washington, DC 20020-3298.

NEWSOME, VINCENT KARL
Professional football player (retired). **Personal:** Born Jan 22, 1961, Braintree, England; married Tasha; children: Candace, Emerald. **Educ:** Univ of Washington. **Career:** Safety: Los Angeles Rams, 1983-90; Cleveland Browns, 1991-93; Baltimore Ravens, currently. **Honors/Awds:** Post season play: member of Los Angeles Rams for NFC Championship Game, 1989, NFC Championship Game, 1985; Ed Block Courage Award, 1988. **Business Addr:** Former Professional Football Player, Baltimore Ravens, 11001 Owings Mills Blvd, Owings Mills, MD 21117.

NEWSON, ROOSEVELT, JR.
Concert pianist, educator. **Personal:** Born Aug 30, 1946, Monroe, LA; son of Zipporah Newson and Roosevelt Newson; married Ethel Rae Whitaker; children: Erin, Meredith, Keirsten, Morgan. **Educ:** Southern Univ Baton Rouge, LA, BM 1968; Peabody Conserv of Music Baltimore, MD, MM 1971, DMA 1976; Juilliard Sch of Music NCY, professional studies 1982. **Career:** Appearances and performances with, York Symphony, Northeastern PA Philharmonic, Charlotte Symphony Orch, sev perf with Baltimore Symphony Orch; completed European tour incl perf in Salzburg, Vienna, Brussels, The Hague and a Wigmore Hall perf in London, 1978; numerous concerts on radio & TV; Western MI Univ, music faculty 1977-81; Wilkes Coll, chmn music dept/artist tchr, Bloomsburg University, associate dean of College of Arts and Sciences 1988-93; Georgia Southern Univ, dean of College of Liberal Arts and Soc Science, 1993-; Cleveland Philharmonic Orchestra; DeKalb Symphony Orchestra. **Orgs:** Mgmt Affiliate Artists Inc 1970-78; mgmt Perrotta Mgmt New York City 1981-83; mem Peabody Conservatory Alumni Council. **Honors/Awds:** Ford Found Grant Peabody Conserv 1972-75; Ford Found Grant Juilliard 1982-83; Premier Performances at Kennedy Center Wash, DC 1980, Charlotte Symphony Orch 1983; Amerian Council on Education (ACE) Fellow, 1987-88. **Military Serv:** AUS Natl Guard Spec 4 1969-75. **Home Addr:** 706 Anna Way, Statesboro, GA 30458. **Business Addr:** Dean, College of Liberal Arts and Social Sciences, Georgia Southern Univ, Statesboro, GA 30460.

NEWTON, ANDREW E., JR.
Attorney, photographer. **Personal:** Born Mar 9, 1943, Boston; married Joan Ambrose. **Educ:** Dartmouth Coll, AB 1965; Columbia U, JD 1969. **Career:** Winston A Burnett Constr Co, asst gen counsel 1969-70; Amos Tuch Sch of Bus Adminstrn, Dartmouth Coll, 1970-71; Burnett Intl Dev Corp, gen counsel 1971-72; Honeywell Information Systems Inc, operations counsel 1972-74, staff counsel 1974-75, regnl counsel, Western Region 1975-77; Amdahl Corp, dir mkt oper cnsl 1977-; Digital Research Inc, gen counsel. **Orgs:** Mem Am, Boston, Fed, MA, Nat Bar Assns; mem NY & MA Bars; mem Peninsula Assn of Gen Counsel; Computer Lawyers Assn; Nat Contract Mgmt Assn. **Business Addr:** Digital Research, Inc, 2180 Fortune Dr., San Jose, CA 95131-1815.

NEWTON, DEMETRIUS C.
Attorney. **Personal:** Born Mar 15, 1928, Fairfield, AL; son of Eola Williams Newton and Caiphus Newton; married Beatryce Thomas, Jun 19, 1954; children: Deirdre Cheryl, Demetrius C, Jr. **Educ:** Wilberforce U, BA 1949; Boston U, JD 1952. **Career:** Law firm of Newton & May; City of Brightond city atty 1973-; city of brownsville, city judge 1975-. **Orgs:** Pres Tittisville & Powderly Br NAACP; forner natl pres Wilberforce Univ Alumni Assn 1958-60; former pres Fairfield Voters League UMDCA; national president, Phi Beta Sigma, 1981-85. **Honors/Awds:** Man of Yr; Man of Yr So Beauty Congress; Man of Yr Phi Beta Sigma; counelor 82nd airborne div 1952-54; Honorary Doctor of Letters; Wilberforce University, 1984; Outstanding Alabama Lawyer's Association, 1982. **Business Addr:** City Attorney, City of Birmingham, 600 City Hall, Birmingham, AL 35203.

NEWTON, ERIC CHRISTOPHER
Software developer, consultant. **Personal:** Born Apr 5, 1965, Detroit, MI; son of Willie Bell Duncan and John Henry Newton; married Kimberly Brenner-Newton, Nov 28, 1992; children: Brittany Delamere, Haley Christine, Naomi Annabelle, & Gabrielle Leigh. **Educ:** Michigan State University, BS, 1988. **Career:** General Motors Corp., claims processor, 1983-84; Unisys Corp., programmer, analyst, 1984-85; Stroh Brewery Corp., programmer, analyst, 1987; Alpha II, systems director, 1988-93; InfoServices, Inc, pre, owner, div mgr; Gilbar Engineering, info systems mgr, currently. **Orgs:** Phi Beta Sigma Fraternity Inc, 1985-; Detroit Public Schools, Mentor Program, 1983-; Apple Programmers and Developers Association, 1988-; IBM Developer Assistance Program, 1991-; Michigan Association for Computer Users in Learning, 1989-. **Home Addr:** 6566 Horncliffe Dr, Clarkston, MI 48346, (810)625-5498. **Business Addr:** Information Systems Manager, Gilbar Engineering, 6570 19 Mile Rd, Sterling Heights, MI 48314, (810)254-7154.

NEWTON, ERNEST E., II
Elected official, business executive. **Personal:** Born Feb 21, 1956, Fort Belvoir, VA; married Pamela A; children: Ernest E III, Chad J Newton. **Educ:** Winston-Salem State Univ, BA 1978; Univ Bridgeport, grad prog 1980. **Career:** Bridgeport Bd of Educ, music teacher 1980-84; CT Natl Bank, personal banking rep 1984-; Peoples Bank, admin supv 1986-. **Orgs:** Former pres, former alderman, mem Bd of Aldermen 139th Dist; me Alpha Phi Alpha Frat; bdof mgrs YMCA; policy council Head Start; adv bd Greater Bridgeport Regional Narcotics Prog; comm Sikorsky Mem Airport; counsel of pres Red Cross; vice chmn 150th Anniversary of Bridgeport; pres of Bd of Alderman 139th Dist; mem Alpha Phi Alpha, James Wilkins Lodge #9 PHA afiliated FAMA. **Honors/Awds:** Outstanding Merit Awd Natl Blk Teachers Assn 1974; Scholarship Awd Alpha Phi Alpha Grad Chap 1976; Outstanding Young Men of Amer Awd Natl Jaycees 1983; Comm Serv Awd Bus & Prof Women Youth Dept; Heritage Awd Alpha Kappa Alpha Sor 1983; City Govt Awd Omega Psi Phi Frat Inc 1983; Outstanding Achievement Awd Natl Assn of Negro Bus & Prof Women 1983.

NEWTON, JACQUELINE L.
Athletic academic counselor. **Personal:** Born in Oklahoma City, OK; daughter of Josephine Jefferson and Jack Jefferson; divorced; children: Jeffrey, Richard. **Educ:** So Univ Lab Sch, Grad; Univ of OK, BBA, MEd 1974. **Career:** Univ Coll The Univ of OK, Norman, OK, acad adv, 1972-78; OK Univ, finan aids couns; Apco Oil Corp, Oklahoma City, OK, various positions from clerk to accountant; OK City Law Firm, bookkeeper; OK Univ, Mobil Oil Co adminstrv physical research coun, equal empl opp Com; Univ of NV, Las Vegas, NV, athletic academic counselor, 1978-. **Orgs:** Chrd empl orgn reprsntng all non-tchng empl at univ 1972-73; active OK Univ Professional Empl Grp; pres OK Univ Assn of Blk Prsnl 1975-76; NAACP Legal Def Fund conjnctn with st deseg plans for hghr edn; supr training sem in Jan 1974; mem Alpha Kappa Alpha Sor; chmn Com of OK Blk Coaltn for Edn; chair, Student Athlete Recognition Comm, Natl Assn of Academic Adv for Athletics, 1988-93; sec, UNLV Alliance of Black Professionals, 1984-. **Honors/Awds:** Voted outst achvmnt awd recip by fellow professional empl at OK Univ 1973. **Business Addr:** Academic Advisor for Athletics, Student Devel Center, University of Nevada at Las Vegas, 4505 Maryland Parkway, Box 452001, Las Vegas, NV 89154-2001.

NEWTON, JAMES DOUGLAS, JR.
Elected official, nurse (retired). **Personal:** Born Sep 3, 1929, Malakoff, TX; daughter of Mary Glenn Cook and Hillary Cook; widowed; children: Carolyn Andrenia Barron, Audry Laverne. **Educ:** Henderson Cty Jr Coll, LVN 1962-63; Navarro Coll, 1975; El Centro Coll 1975. **Career:** Lakeland Med Ctr, licensed vocational nurse, 1979-93. **Orgs:** Youth counselor, Cedar Forks Baptist Church, 1970; counselor, Galilee Griggs mem Dist Youth Conf 1975-; nursing faculty Lakeland Med Ctr 1979-87. **Honors/Awds:** Mem East TX Council of Governments 1980-, Trinidad Chamber of Comm 1980; appt mem State Task Force on Indigent Health Care 1984; Outstanding Black Henderson Countian Award; Black History Committee, 1989; attended and participated in the inauguration of President George Bush, 1989. **Home Addr:** 830 Pinoak, Trinidad, TX 75163.

NEWTON, JAMES DOUGLAS, JR.
Former city official. **Personal:** Born Jun 11, 1949, New Haven, CT; children: Bonita, Melissa, Tomeka, James D Newton III, Allen W Newton II. **Educ:** New Hampshire Coll, BS, Human Serv Admin, 1979; attended Yale Univ, school of public health and hospital admin, 1979-80; Southern Connecticut State Univ, MS, 1991. **Career:** City of New Haven Personnel Dept, records systems cnsultant, 1979-82; New Haven Board of Aldermen, chmn, 1983-87; City of New Haven, mayoral candidate, 1993; Connecticut Natl Bank, mgt trainee, 1984-85, branch mgr, Temple St, 1984-85, branch mgr, Church St, 1986-87; Greater New Haven Chamber of Commerce, Jobs Compact Program, assoc dir for educational programs, 1987-88; City of New Haven Bd of Education, assoc dir, 1988-90; YMCA Youth & Fitness Center, general mgr, 1990-91; N & N Construction Co, chmn, 1987-; City of New Haven Job Center, executive director and mgr, 1991-. **Orgs:** Yale Univ, City of New Haven, Science Park Dev Corp, chmn, 1992-. **Honors/Awds:** Rotary Club Intl, Community Services Award, 1990.

NEWTON, JAMES E.
Professor, educational administrator. **Personal:** Born Jul 3, 1941, Bridgeton, NJ; son of Hilda H Newton and Charles C Newton, Sr; married LaWanda Williams Newton, Dec 1967; children: Regina, Walidah, KaWansi. **Educ:** NC Central Univ, BA 1966; Univ of NC, MFA 1968; IL State Univ, PhD 1972. **Career:** Univ of NC, art instr 1967-68; W Chester State Coll PA, asst prof art 1968-69; IL State Univ Normal, asst prof art 1969-71; Western IL Univ Macomb, asst prof art 1971-72; Univ of DE Newark, asst prof ed 1972-73; Univ of DE Newark, prof, dir black amer studies 1973-. **Orgs:** Mem edit bd, Natl Art Ed Assoc; Editorial board Education 1974-; mem exec counselor Assoc Study Afro-Amer Life & History 1976-77; bd mem Western Journal of Black Studies 1983-; bd mem past chairman Walnut St YMCA Delaware 1983-; State Dir Assn for the Study of Afro-American Life & History 1988-. **Honors/Awds:** Publ, College Student Jrnl, Jrnl of Negro Ed, Negro History Bulletin, Crisis, Education, Clearing House; books, A Curriculum Eval of Black Amer Studies in Relation to Student Knowledge of Afro-Amer History & Culture R&E Assoc Inc 1976, Roots of Black Amer; aduio-tapes Slave Aritsans & Craftsmen, ContemporaryAfro-Amer Art Miami-Dade Comm Coll 1976; exhibitions, Natl Print & Drawing Show 11th Midwest Bienniel Exhib 1972; 1st prize Sculpture & Graphics 19th Annual Exhib of Afro-Amer Artists 1972; 23rd Annual Mid-States Art Exhibit 1972; Purchase Awd 13th Reg Art Exhibit Univ of DE 1974; DE Afro-Amer Art Exhib 1980; Exhibited Lincoln Univ, West Chester State Coll, FL A&M Univ, DE State Coll, Dover DE; Excellence in Teaching Award Univ of Delaware 1988; EasternRegion Citation Award Phi Deltappa National Sorority 1989; Wilmington News Journal, Hometown Hero Award 1990; Jefferson Award, Amer Inst for Public Service. **Military Serv:** US Army spec 4th class 1959-62. **Business Addr:** Professor & Senior Fellow, College of Urban Affairs & Public Policy & Professor of Black American Studies, University of Delaware, 417 Ewing Bldg, Newark, DE 19711.

NEWTON, LLOYD W.
Military official. **Educ:** Tennessee State University. **Career:** US Air Force, asst vice chief of staff, 1995-, US Special Operations Command, MacDill AFB, dir of operations; US House of Representatives, congressional liaison officer; TSU Air Force Reserve Officer Training Corp, group wing commander. **Orgs:** HQ Air Education & Training Command. **Special Achievements:** First African American to fly with US Air Force Aerial Demonstration Squadron, the Thunderbirds; 1 of 12 Four Star Generals in the US Air Force. **Military Serv:** US Air Force. **Business Addr:** Commander, Air, Education & Training Command, Randolph A F B, TX 78150, (210)652-5512.

NEWTON, NATE
Professional football player. **Personal:** Born Dec 20, 1961, Orlando, FL; married Dorothy; children: Nathaniel III. **Educ:** Florida A&M, attended. **Career:** Tampa Bay Bandits (USFL), 1984-85; Dallas Cowboys, guard, 1986-. **Honors/Awds:** Pro Bowl, 1992, 1993, 1994, 1995, 1996, 1997; NFL Alumni Assn, NFL Offensive Lineman of the Year, 1994. **Business Addr:** Professional Football Player, Dallas Cowboys, One Cowboys Pkwy, Irving, TX 75063, (214)556-9900.

NEWTON, OLIVER A., JR.
Educator (retired). **Personal:** Born Jan 31, 1925, Long Branch, NJ; married Eleanor M Simmons; children: Martha Louise. **Educ:** Howard Univ, BS 1949, MS 1950. **Career:** Inter-Amer Inst of Agr Sci Turrialba Costa Rica, rschr 1950-52; Univ of So CA, lab assoc 1952-56; Howard Univ, instr of botany 1956-58; William Paterson Coll of NJ, assoc prof 1958-90 (retired). **Orgs:** Mem AAAS, AAUP, AIBS, Botanical Soc of Amer, Alpha Phi Alpha, Ridgewood Glen Rock Council Boy Scouts of Amer, Soc for Econ Botany, Glen Rock Adult School Council, Glen Rock Civic Assoc; dir Glen Rock Human Relations Council, Cits Comm on Sch Plant & Classroom Eval; local asst bd Glen Rock 1966-74; Glen Rock Bd of Ed 1969-75; State Comm to Study Student Activism & Involvement in Ed Progs 1970; Community Relations Board of Ridgewood and Glen Rock, 1991. **Honors/Awds:** Pan Amer Union Fellowship 1950-52; Natl Sci Found Coll Faculty Fellowship Rutgers Univ 1964. **Military Serv:** USAF sgt 1943-46; USAFR maj retired. **Business Addr:** Associate Professor, William Paterson College, 300 Pompton Rd, Wayne, NJ 07470.

NEWTON, PYNKERTON DION
Physician. **Personal:** Born Nov 9, 1960, Marion, IN; son of John W Newton and Olivia McNair. **Educ:** Ball State Univ, BA, 1983, MA, 1986; Logan Coll of Chiropractic, DC, 1992. **Career:** Operation Crossroads Africa, group leader, 1986; Ball State Univ, asst director, 1986; Marine Midland Bank, corporate analyst, 1986-87, manager, 1987-89; Logan Coll of Chiropractic, coordinator, admissions dept, 1989-92, consultant, 1992-; Pynkerton Chiropractic Group, PC, director, 1992-. **Orgs:** American Black Chiropractic Assn, exec director, 1995-; American Chiropractic Assn, 1989-; National Assn of Medical Minority Educators, 1990-; Indiana State Chiropractic Assn, 1989-. **Honors/Awds:** Logan Coll of Chiropractic, meritorious award, 1992. **Special Achievements:** Proficient in Spanish. **Business Addr:** Chiropractor, Pynkerton Chiropractic Group, 2102 E 52nd St, Ste E, Indianapolis, IN 46205, (317)257-7463.

NEWTON, ROBERT
Attorney. **Personal:** Born Nov 13, 1944, Fairfield, AL; married Ruth Ann Boles; children: Robert Wade, Reginald Alan. **Educ:** Lincoln Univ Jeff City MO, BS 1968; Howard Univ Sch of Law, JD 1971; Yale U; Harvard-Yale-Columbia, intensive summer studeis certificate summer 1966. **Career:** MO Comm on Human Rights, spec field rep 1968; Economic & Opportunity Wash, legal asst ofc 1969; US Atomic Energy Comm, staff atty 1971-74; Newton Coar Newton & Tucker Law Firm, atty. **Orgs:** Mem Am Bar Assn AL Bar Assn NAACP Legal Defense Fund Earl Warren Fellow; mem Jeff C Ity MO Com on Fiar Housing 1966-67; Omega Psi Phi Frat Inc;pres Lincoln Univ Student Govt Assn 1966-67; Law Journal Howard Univ Law Sch 1969-70. **Honors/Awds:** Lincoln Univ Man of Yr 1966-67; Cobb-trustee Scholarship Howard Law 1969-70; 70-71; NAACP Earl Warren Legal Fellowship 1974-75. **Military Serv:** AUSR 1st lt. **Business Addr:** 2121 Bldg Ste 1722, 2121 Eighth Ave N, Birmingham, AL.

NEWTON, ROBIN CAPRICE
Physician. **Personal:** Born Jan 31, 1957, Washington, DC. **Educ:** Univ of WI-Milwaukee, BA 1979; Howard Univ Coll of Medicine, MD 1983. **Career:** DC General Hospital, chief resident internal medicine. **Orgs:** Mem Amer Medical Assoc 1980-, Amer Medical Women's Assoc, Alpha Omega Alpha Medical Honor Soc 1983-; mem DC Youth Chorale Alumni Chorus 1985-; assoc Amer Coll of Physicians 1985-; mem Medical Soc of the District of Columbia 1986-. **Honors/Awds:** Raymond P Jackson Awd for Tutorial Serv 1983; Emile C Nash Awd for Scholastic Achievement 1983; Citation of Scholastic Achievement Amer Medical Women's Assoc 1983; Outstanding Young Woman of Amer 1985; American Bd of Internal Medicine Certification 1986. **Business Addr:** Chief Resident Internal Med, DC General Hospital, 19th & E Sts SE, Washington, DC 20003.

NEYLAND, LEEDELL WALLACE
Educational administrator (retired), educator. **Personal:** Born Aug 4, 1921, Gloster, MS; son of Estella McGehee Neyland and Sam Matthew Neyland; married Della Louise Adams; children: Beverly Ann, Keith Wallace, Katrina Denise. **Educ:** Virginia State College, AB, 1949; New York University, MA, 1950, PhD, 1959. **Career:** Leland Coll Baker LA, professor of social science, dean of college, 1950-52; Grambling Coll, associate professor of social sciences, 1952-58; Elizabeth City Coll, dean, 1958-59; Florida A&M University, professor of history, dean of humanities/social science, 1959-84, College of Arts and Sciences, dean, 1968-82, vice pres for academic affairs, 1982-85; consultant, lecturer on Black history and education, currently. **Orgs:** Co-chairman, Governor's Dr Martin Luther King Jr Commemorative Celebration Commission, 1985-87; member, board of directors, Leon County/Tallahassee Chamber of Commerce, 1984-86; vice chairman, Tallahassee Preservation Board, 1984-88; member, Presbyterian National Committee on the Self-Development of People, currently; member, Florida Historial Records Advisory Board, currently; member, Phi Beta Sigma; member, Sigma Pi Phi; member, 32 Degree Mason, Modern Free and Accepted Masons of the World. **Honors/Awds:** Co-author: History of Florida A&M University, 1963; Twelve Black Floridians, 1970; History of the Florida State Teachers Assn, 1977; History of the Florida Interscholastic Assn, 1982; Florida A&M University: A Centennial History, 1887-1987, 1987; Historical Black Land-Grant Institutions and the Development of Agriculture and Home Economics, 1890-1990, 1990; author of numerous articles appearing in professional publications; Carnegie Grant, 1965. **Special Achievements:** Author, Unquenchable Black Fires, Leney Educational and Publishing Inc, 1994. **Military Serv:** USNR 1941-46. **Business Addr:** Former Vice Pres for Academic Affairs, Florida A&M Univ, Tallahassee, FL 32307.

NIBBS, ALPHONSE, SR.
Business executive, appointed official. **Personal:** Born Nov 10, 1947, Charlotte Amalie, Virgin Islands of the United States; son of Elenora Charles-Nibbs and Ernest Albert Nibbs; married Paulette E Shelford Nibbs, Oct 30, 1967; children: Berecia Nibbs-Cartwright, Alphonse Jr, Antoninette Nibbs, Annette Garces, Anthony, Alyssa. **Educ:** Coll of the VI 1980; Cert Labor Relations, Publ Admin, Personnel Mgmt 1980; Inst for Professional & Econ Devel 1981; Georgia Institute of Technology Atlanta GA Contract Administration, 1986. **Career:** Water & Power Authority, distribution engr 1967-76; Nibbs Brothers Inc, sec, treas 1974-; Dept of Housing, asst commiss 1977-84; Lt Governors Office, temp housing off hd-gar team, terr coord off 1979-86; VI Housing Authority, exec dir 1985-87; Legislature of VI, exec dir 1991-93; VI Cong Offc, dist chf of staff, 1995-97. **Orgs:** Mem Commiss on Aging 1977-87, Bd of Elections, elected 1978-87, VI Soc on Public Admin 1980-87. **Honors/Awds:** Lt Col/AIDE DeCamp, State of Georgia National Guard, Civilian Appointment. **Business Addr:** Secretary/Treasurer, Nibbs Bros Inc, PO Box 7245, 4A Estate Thomas, Charlotte Amalie, St Thomas, Virgin Islands of the United States 00801.

NICCO-ANNAN, LIONEL
Chief executive. **Career:** Clipper International Corp, Detroit, MI, chief executive, 1963-. **Business Addr:** Clipper International Corp, 8651 E Seven Mile Rd, Detroit, MI 48234.

NICHOLAS, BRENDA L.
Gospel vocalist/songwriter. **Personal:** Born Dec 16, 1953, Salem, NJ; daughter of Janette Coleman and John H Watson; married Philip Nicholas, Feb 18, 1978; children: Jennifer, Philip Jr. **Educ:** Career Educational Institute, AS, 1974. **Career:** Command Records, Nicholas Ministries, gospel vocalist, currently. **Honors/Awds:** Gospel Music Workshops of America, Excellence Awards, 1983, Dove Award, nomination, 1987; ARAS, Grammy Award, nomination, 1986; Southern California Motion Picture, Golden Eagle Award, 1986; Canada, Halo Award, Best Foreign Recording, 1988. **Business Addr:** Command Records, PO Box 1869, Los Angeles, CA 90078-1869, (818)995-6363.

NICHOLAS, DENISE
Actress. **Personal:** Born 1944, Detroit, MI; married Gilbert Moses (divorced). **Educ:** Univ of MI, 1962-65; Univ of Southern CA, Professional Writer's Prog 1985. **Career:** Negro Ensemble Co, actress 1967-69; TV series: Room 222, 1969-74; Baby I'm Back, 1978; Films: The Soul of Nigger Charley, 1973; Blacula; Let's Do It Again, 1975; Mr Ricco, 1975; A Piece of the Action, 1977; Ghost Dad, 1990. **Orgs:** Mem Neighbors of Watts, Inc 1976-; producer The Media Forum, Inc 1980-; bd of dir Communications Bridge Video School 1983-; mem & fund raiser Artists & Athletes Against Apartheid; mem Museum of African American Art LA; mem Museum of Afro-American History & Culture. **Honors/Awds:** 2 LA Emmy Awards producer/actress Voices of our People in Celebration of Black Poetry 1981; 2 CEBA Awds Excellence for Advertising & Communications to Black Comm 1981, 1982; 3 Emmy nominations Room 222; author, The Denise Nicholas Beauty Book, 1971; Black Filmmakers Hall of Fame, 1992.

NICHOLAS, FAYARD ANTONIO
Actor, entertainer. **Personal:** Born Oct 20, 1914, Mobile, AL; son of Viola Harden Nicholas and Ulysses Domonick Nicholas; married Barbara January Nicholas, Sep 17, 1967; children: Anthony, Paul Didier, Nina. **Career:** Dancer, with brother Harold, in ''Nicholas Brothers''; performer, radio shows, vaudeville; film actor, singer, dancer, musician works include: The Big Broadcast, 1936, Down Argentina Way, 1940, Tin Pan Alley, 1940, The Great American Broadcast, 1941, Sun Valley Serenade, 1941, Orchestra Wives, 1942, Stormy Weather, 1943, The Pirate, 1948, The Liberation of L B Jones, 1970; Broadway performer, shows include: Ziegfeld Follies, 1936, Babes in Arms, 1937, St Louis Woman, 1946; television performer in Las Vegas; toured around US, Mexico, South America, Africa, Europe ; private dance instructor; performer at numerous charitable events; Broadweay choreographer, Black and Blue, 1989; guest lecturer, USC, UCLA, San Francisco State University. **Orgs:** San Fernando Valley Art Council; Dance Gallery; Friars Club; Academy of Arts and Science. **Honors/Awds:** Black American Life Achievement Award; Royal Command Performance, King of England, London Palladium, 1948; performances at the White House, 1942, 1955, 1987; Honorary Chairman for Month of May, Arthritic Foundation Telethon, 1986; Tony Award, best choreography in a Braodway musical, Black and Blue, 1989. **Military Serv:** US Army Special Services, T5, 1943-44. **Home Addr:** 23388 Mulholland Dr, Woodland Hills, CA 91364.

NICHOLAS, GWENDOLYN SMITH
Transportation analyst. **Personal:** Born Jan 27, 1951, San Francisco, CA; divorced. **Educ:** Univ of San Francisco, BA 1972; Atlanta Univ, MSW 1974. **Career:** Fireman's Fund Ins Co, business systems analyst 1976-77; W Oak Mental Health Dept, psychiatric social worker 1977-78; State of CA Dept of Mental Health, psychiatric social worker 1978-81, mental health prog specialist 1981-83, State of CA, Department of Social Services, licensing program analyst II 1984-91; CA Public Utilities Commission, 1991-. **Orgs:** Area pub info officer, chap rec sec, National Nominating Committee SF Chap of Links Inc 1975-; mem Bay Area Assoc of Black Social Workers 1977-; contributor United Negro CollFund 1978-; contributor Bay Area Black United Fund 1980-; mem Soroptimist Intl Oak Founder Club 1986-91; Alpha Kappa Alpha 1972; mem Black Advocates in State Serv, Bay Area Heath Consortium. **Honors/Awds:** Outsanding Young Women of Amer 1983. **Business Addr:** Transportation Analyst, Tariff & License Branch, State of CA Public Utilities Commission, 505 Van Ness Ave, Second Fl, San Francisco, CA 94102.

NICHOLAS, MARY BURKE
Government official. **Personal:** Born in Tuskegee, AL; children: Tracy Nicholas Bledsoe, Scott Cardozo. **Educ:** Univ of WI Madison, BA High Hnrs 1948. **Career:** Housing Mayors Office NYC, exec asst 1960-66; US Dept of Housing & Urban Dev Reg II, congressional liaison 1966-70; Temporary Comm Local Govt NY State, deputy dir 1970-73; Public Affairs Cons1983-; Regional Econ Housing 1973-75; dir Women's Div Govt Office NY State 1975-82. **Orgs:** Fndr NY Coalition of 100 Black Women 1970-; mem Women's Forum of NY City 1974-82; board member NY State Comm Aid Assc 1980-; NYC Civilian Complaint Review Board, chairperson, 1987-92; Baynard Rustin Fund, board member; Resources for Mid-Life and Older Women, board member, 1980-. **Honors/Awds:** Pres Natl Assc of Commissions of Women 1980-82; mayoral appointee New York City Charter Revision Comm 1982-83; dir Fed Home Loan Bank Bd Reg II 1980-84; adv bd NY Univ Grad Schl of Public Admin.

NICHOLAS, PHILIP, SR.
Record company executive, gospel vocalist/songwriter. **Personal:** Born Feb 18, 1954, Chester, PA; son of Julia B Shade and Ross B Nicholas; married Brenda L Watson, Feb 18, 1978; children: Jennifer, Phil Jr. **Educ:** Drexel University, BS, 1977. **Career:** Command Records, Nicholas Ministries, president, gospel vocalist, currently. **Honors/Awds:** Gospel Music Workshops of America, Excellence Awards, 1983, Dove Award, nomination, 1987; ARAS, Grammy Award, nomination, 1986; Southern California Motion Picture, Golden Eagle Award, 1986; Canada, Halo Award, Best Foreign Recording, 1988. **Business Addr:** President, Command Records, PO Box 1869, Los Angeles, CA 90078-1869, (818)995-6363.

NICHOLS, ALFRED GLEN
Commercial printing. **Personal:** Born Mar 20, 1952, Jackson, MS; married Sylvia Lauree Robinson; children: Derek Allen, Shaunte Latrice. **Educ:** Purdue Univ, BS 1975; Univ of Chicago, MBA 1985. **Career:** RR Donnelley & Sons Co, price admin estimator 1975-78, industrial engr 1978-80, project engr 1980-86, supervisor plng & facil engr 1986-. **Orgs:** Dir Hazel Crest Jaycees 1982-85. **Honors/Awds:** Outstanding Young Men in Amer 1985; Black Achiever of Industry Chicago YMCA 1986. **Home Addr:** PO Box 315, 2918 Greenwood Rd, Hazel Crest, IL 60429. **Business Addr:** Supervisor Plng/Facil Engr, RR Donnelley and Sons Co, 750 Warrenville Rd, Lisle, IL 60532.

NICHOLS, CHARLES HAROLD
Educator (retired). **Personal:** Born Jul 6, 1919, Brooklyn, NY; son of Julia King Nichols and Charles F Nichols; married Mildred Thompson Nichols, Aug 19, 1950; children: David G, Keith F, Brian A. **Educ:** Brooklyn Coll, BA 1942; Brown Univ, PhD 1948. **Career:** Morgan State Coll, assoc prof, English, 1948-49; Hampton Inst, prof of English, 1949-59; Free Univ, Berlin, GE, prof, Amer lit, 1959-69; Brown Univ, Providence RI, prof of English, 1969-. **Orgs:** Mem Modern Lang Assn; Amer Studies Assn; Soc for Multi-Ethnic Lit of the US. **Honors/Awds:** Author, ''Many Thousand Gone,'' ''The Ex-Slaves Account of their Bondage & Freedom'' Brill, Leiden 1963, IN Univ Press, 1969, ''Black Men in Chains'' 1971, Instr Manual for Cavalcade, Houghton, Mifflin, 1971, ''African Nights, Black Erotic Folk Tales'' 1971, ''Arna Bontemps - Langston Hughes Letters 1925-67,'' Dodd Mead, 1980; sr fellow Natl Endowment for Humanities 1973-74; O'Connor Disting Vstg Prof Colgate Univ 1977. **Business Addr:** Professor of English, Brown University, Box 1852, Providence, RI 02912.

NICHOLS, DIMAGGIO
Company executive. **Personal:** Born May 8, 1951, Byhalia, MS; son of Lucille Bougard Nichols and Emmitt Nichols, Jr; married Lizzie Emma Shelton Nichols, Mar 16, 1974; children: Dimeka W, Dondra O. **Educ:** Rust Coll, Holly Spring MS, BS 1973; General Motor Institution, Flint MI, Dealer Development 1983. **Career:** Buick Motor Division, Flint MI, dist sales manager 1974-1983; General Motor Institution, Flint MI, trainee 1983-84; Sentry Buick, Omaha NE, salesperson 1984-85; Noble Ford-Mercury, Indianola IA, pres 1985-. **Orgs:** Bd mem Chamber of Commerce Indianola IA 1987-; board member Black Ford Lincoln Mercury Assn 1988-. **Honors/Awds:** Iowa Up and Comers Des Moines Register 1986; Quality Care Program Award for Excellence Ford Motor Company 1987; Top Return on Investment Ford Motor Company 1988. **Business Addr:** President, Noble Ford-Mercury Inc, 947 Hwy 65-69 North, Box I, Indianola, IA 50125.

NICHOLS, EDWARD K., JR.
Clergyman, attorney. **Personal:** Born Aug 10, 1918, Atlanta; son of Laura Ella Drake Nichols and Rev Edward K Nichols; married Ethel Williams; children: Charlotte A, Carolyn H, Eloise M, Lavra L. **Educ:** Lincoln U, AB 1941; Howard Univ Law Sch, LLB 1950; PA Law Sch, grad study 1951; Temple Univ Sch of Theo, grad study 1957. **Career:** Atty 1951-; City of Philadelphia, asst dist atty 1952-53; Private Practice, 1954-58; ordained Minister Meth 1956; Norris Green Harris Higginbotham, assoc1958-63; Nichols & Nichols, partner; Greater St Matthew Independent Church, pastor emeritus. **Orgs:** Mem Fellowship Commn; life mem NAACP; 1st vice pres Black Clergy of Philadelphia. **Military Serv:** KSM, Tuskegee Airmen, Airforce, 1942-46.

NICHOLS, EDWIN J.
Clinical/industrial psychologist. **Personal:** Born Jun 23, 1931, Detroit, MI; married Sandra; children: Lisa, Edwin. **Educ:** Assumption Coll CAN, attended 1952-55; Eberhardt Karls Universitat, Tubingen, Germany, 1955-57; Leopoline-franciscea Universitat, Innsbruck, Austria, on Fellow by Austrian Ministry of Edn, PhD 1961. **Career:** Natl Inst of Mental Health, Rockville, MD, chief Applied & Social Proj Review Branch; KS Neurological Inst Cleveland Job Corps Center for Women Meharry Med Coll & Fisk Univ, psychologist; Univ of Ibadan Nigeria, dir Childs Clinic 1974-77; Centre for Mgmt Devel Lagos Nigeria, mgmt consult 1974-77. **Orgs:** Veteran, Korean War. **Business Addr:** 1523 Underwood St NW, Washington, DC 20012.

NICHOLS, ELAINE
Archaeologist. **Personal:** Born Oct 5, 1952, Charlotte, NC. **Educ:** Univ of NC Charlotte, BA 1974; Case Western Reserve Univ, MSSA 1980; Univ of SC, MA, public service archaeology, 1988. **Career:** Planned Parenthood Charlotte, crisis intervention counselor 1974-75; Big Brothers/Big Sisters, social caseworker 1975-78; City of Cleveland, neighborhood planner 1980-81, asst mgr of planners 1981-82; Univ North Carolina Charlotte, lecturer 1982-85; Univ of South Carolina, graduate student dept of anthropology, 1985-88; South Carolina State Museum, curator of African-American culture & history, 1987-. **Orgs:** Charter mem Afro-Amer Serv Centtr 1974; mem Delta Sigma Theta Sor 1977-; Co-chairperson Afro-Amer Historical Soc Charlotte 1982-83; bd mem Metrolina Assoc for the Blind 1983-85; researcher Amer Heart Assoc Charlotte 1985. **Honors/Awds:** ''Pulse of Black Charlotte'' Urban Inst Grant UNCC 1984; Research Assistantship Dept of Anthropology USC 1985-; Service Award Alpha Kappa Alpha Sor 1986; Sigma Xi Science Award 1987. **Home Addr:** PO Box 3536, Columbia, SC 29230.

NICHOLS, GEORGE, III
State official. **Personal:** Born May 25, 1960, Bowling Green, KY; son of Vera & George Nichols Jr; married Cynthia J, Jul 14, 1984; children: Courtney, Jessica, George IV. **Educ:** Alice Lloyd College, AA, 1980; Western KY University, BA, 1983; University of Louisville, MA, 1985. **Career:** KY Dept for Mental Health, Mental Retardation Svcs, exec dir, 1984-89; Central State Hosp, CEO, 1989-92; Southeastern Group, Inc, BCBS of

KY, exec dir, 1993; Athena of North Amer, Inc, vp of mktg, 1993-95; KY Health Policy Bd, exec dir, 1995-96; KY Dept of Insurance, commissioner, 1996-. **Orgs:** Republic Bank & Trust Co, bd of dirs, 1993-96; 100 Black Men of Louisville, youth mentor, chair of youth prog, 1992-94; United Way of KY, bd of dirs, vice chair, 1993-96; Actors Theatre of Louisville, bd of dirs, 1993-95; Louisville Zoo Society, bd of dirs, 1993-95; Lincoln Foundation, bd of dirs, 1993-95; Big Brothers/Big Sisters, bd of dirs, 1992-94; NAIC, exec comm, 1996-; SE Zone, vice chair, 1997; Banking & Ins, chair, 1997-, scy, treas, 1998-. **Honors/Awds:** Alice Lloyd Coll, Social Sci Student of the Year, 1980; Sporting News, Top 200 Basketball Players in Jr Coll, Natl, 1980; Louisville YMCA, Adult Black Achiever, 1993; Bowling Green Sr High, Hall of Fame, 1994; Metro Louisville Business, First 40 Under 40 Foremost Young Business Leader, 1996; Shelby Ministrial Coalition, Wm E Summers Awd, Outstanding Bus Person, 1994; Central State Hosp, 1st African-American State Hosp Dir, Youngest, 1989; NAIC, 1st African-American Ins Commissioner, 1996, 1st African-American Officer in 126 Year History, 1998. **Home Addr:** 333 Comanche Rd, Shelbyville, KY 40065, (502)633-3259. **Business Addr:** Commissioner, Kentucky Department of Insurance, 215 W Main St, Frankfort, KY 40601, (502)564-6026.

NICHOLS, LEROY. See Obituaries section.

NICHOLS, NICHELLE
Actress, singer. **Personal:** Born Dec 28, Chicago, IL; daughter of Lishia Parks Nichols and Samuel Earl Nichols; married Foster Johnson (divorced); children: Kyle Johnson. **Educ:** Chicago Ballet Academy, Chicago, IL, 1950-56; Columbia Law School, New York, NY. **Career:** Actress, singer, dancer; began career with Duke Ellington; Women In Motion, pres; NASA, minority recruitment officer; Star Trek, played Lt Uhura; A-R Way Productions, pres, 1979-; Book, Beyond Uhura: Star Trek and Other Memories, G P Putnam's Sons, 1994. **Orgs:** Founding member, Kwanza Foundation, 1973-; board of governors, National Space Society; national board of advisors, SEDS-MIT (Students for Exploration and Development of Space), currently. **Honors/Awds:** Work as actress includes: Star Trek (Lt Uhura), 1966-69; Star Trek I, The Motion Picture; Star Trek II, The Wrath of Khan; Star Trek III, The Search for Spock; Star Trek IV, The Voyage Home; Star Trek V, The Final Frontier; Star Trek VI; Reflections, A One Woman Show; Cleopatra; Horowitz and Mrs. Washington; The Blacks; Kicks and Company; Porgy and Bess; The Lieutenant; albums include Uhura Sings and Hauntingly; nominated twice, Sarah Siddons Award for Best Actress for the Blacks and Kicks and Company; played prominent role in the recruitment of minorities and women by NASA for which she received Distinguished Public Service Award from the Agency, 1989; Women of the Year, National Education Association, 1978; ACTSO Award for Performing Arts, Academic Olympics, 1991. **Business Addr:** President, AR-Way Productions, 22647 Ventura Blvd, Suite 121, Woodland Hills, CA 91364.

NICHOLS, NICK
Engineer. **Personal:** Born Mar 26, 1944, Mobile, AL; son of Mamie Nichols and Charlie Nichols. **Educ:** Tuskegee Univ, BSEE 1967; Southern Methodist Univ, MBA 1975. **Career:** IBM Corp, systems engr 1966-67; Ford Motor Co, financial analyst 1976-79; Boise Cascade Corp, div staff engr mgr. **Orgs:** Life mem Kappa Alpha Psi Fraternity 1963-. **Military Serv:** USAF major 1967-76; Air Medal (6); Air Force Commendation (2); Meritorious Service; Joint Service Commendation Medal; Vietnam Service Medal; Selective Service Meritorious Service Medal; USAFR Colonel, 1976-.

NICHOLS, OWEN D.
Educator. **Personal:** Born Apr 8, 1929, Raleigh, NC; son of Pearl Nichols and William Nichols; married Delores Tucker; children: Bryan K, Diane Maria. **Educ:** Shaw Univ, BS 1955; Howard Univ, MS 1958; HIghland Univ, EdD 1975. **Career:** SC State Coll, assoc prof 1958-59; US Naval Res Lab Washington DC, res chemist 1959-62; Dept Defense Alexandria VA, physical science analyst 1962-66; Air Pollution Tech Info Center, Natl Air Pollution Control Admin Washington DC, deputy dir 1966-68; Office of Tech Info & Publs Natl Air Polllution Control Admin Washington DC, dir 1968-69; Howard Univ Washington DC, exec asst to pres 1969-71; Howard Univ, vice pres admins & sec 1971-88 (retired). **Orgs:** Alpha Kappa Mu Soc; Beta Kappa Chi Science Soc; Amer Chem Soc; Air Pollution Control Assn; Soc of Sigma XI; Intl Platform Assn; Amer Mgmt Assn; Amer Assn High Educ; Amer Assn Univ Admin; Commn on Educ Statis & Admin Affairs, Amer Council on Educ MD Congress; PTA; Adv Con on Hospital Constructionn MD; town councilman, Seat Pleasant MD; Prince Georges County Housing Authority; legislative chmn, 2nd vice pres Prince Georges Co Council, PTA; Lay Speaker United Methodist Church. **Honors/Awds:** Commin On Campus Ministry & Higher Educ; Baltimore Washington Conf United Methodist Church. **Military Serv:** AUS Corps of Engrs 1st lt 1950-53.

NICHOLS, RONALD AUGUSTUS
Hospital administrator. **Personal:** Born Jun 4, 1956, Louvain, Belgium; son of Janet Watson Nichols and Rufus Nichols; married Sati Harris Nichols, Jun 21, 1986; children: Aaron. **Educ:** Boston University, Boston, MA, BA, 1974-78; Brown University, Providence, RI, MD, 1978-82; Harvard University, Boston, MA, MPH, 1981-82. **Career:** Mt Sinai Hospital, New York, NY, residency in OB/GYN, 1982-86; University of Cincinnati, Cincinnati, OH, director, university obstetrics practice, 1987-88; Michigan State University/Sparrow Hospital, Lansing, MI, director, perinatal center, 1988-. **Orgs:** Board member, Michigan Board of Medicine, 1990-94; board member, Michigan Hospital Association, 1989-91; board member, Perinatal Association of Michigan, 1989-92; board member, Boy Scouts of America, Michigan, 1989-; board member, Lansing Urban League, 1989-. **Honors/Awds:** University of Cincinnati, Cincinnati, OH, fellowship in maternal-fetal medicine; Sigma Xi Honor Society for Research, 1980-81. **Home Addr:** 4250 Marmoor Dr, Lansing, MI 48917. **Business Addr:** Director of Perinatology, Sparrow Hospital, 1215 East Michigan Avenue, Lansing, MI 48909.

NICHOLS, ROY CALVIN
Clergyman. **Personal:** Born Mar 19, 1918, Hurlock, MD; son of Mamie and Roy; married Ruth Richardson, Jul 23, 1944; children: Melisande, Allegra, Nathan. **Educ:** Lincoln U, BA 1941; Pacific, DD 1959; Univ. **Career:** Bishop; S Berkeley Comm Ch, minister 1943-47; Meth Ch, ordained 1949; Downs Meml Meth Ch, Oakland, pastor 1949-64; Salem Meth Ch, NYC, 1964-68; United Methodist, emeritus bishop 1968-. **Orgs:** Pres Berkeley Bd Educ 1963-64; mem exec comm World Council of Churches 1968-75. **Honors/Awds:** Pacific Sch Religion, MDiv 1947, DD (hon) 1964; OH No U, D Pub Serv (hon) 1969; Allegheny Coll, DD (hon) 1969; Morningside College, Iowa, West Virginia, Wesleyan (hon); Doquesne U, (hon). **Special Achievements:** Author: Footprints in The Sea, 1980; The Greening of The Gospel, 1985; Doing The Gospel, 1990. **Home Addr:** 53 Ironwood, Oakland, CA 94605.

NICHOLS, SYLVIA A.
Public information specialist (retired). **Personal:** Born Nov 15, 1925, Washington, DC; daughter of Nellie Perry and Charles Perry; married Herb Nichols; children: Cynthia, Louie, Albert Blalock-Bruce, Carl, Donna. **Educ:** Univ of The DC, Washington, MA. **Career:** Dept of Labor, Occupational Safety and Health Admin, public affairs specialist 1971-87; US Dept of Labor, public affairs specialist, 1987 (retired). **Orgs:** Delegate Central Labor Council, DC 1972-85; founding member Washington Womens Forum 1977-; exec board Natl Assoc (BIG) DOL Chapter Blacks In Govt DC 1979-; pres Local #12, AFGE, Dept Labor 1982; dir Fed Credit Union, Dept Labor 1982-87; delegate Natl AFGE Convention 1984; delegate Natl AFGE Convention 1986; second vice pres #12 AFGE 1986-87; mem, Black Democratic Council Inc PG MD 1986-87; member, supervisory committee, Federal Credit Union Department, 1988; member, social activities committee, Greater Southeast Healthcare System, Iverson Mall Walkers, 1990-; Natl Political Conference of Black Women, delegate, 1993; Natl Political Conference of Black Women, 1992-95; Prince George's County Chapter, Iverson Mall Walker's Choral Group, PG County, MD, 1990-95, Activities Committee, 1990-95; Election Judge, 26th District, PG County, Maryland, 1994. **Honors/Awds:** Special serv Comm Award, The PG County Chapter of the Natl Hook Up of Black Women, Dept of Labor, 1982; Fed Serv Award for thirty years of honorable serv to the Dept of Labor. **Special Achievements:** Seabrook Elementary School, Career Day Speaker, Maryland, 1995. **Business Addr:** Public Affairs Specialist, US Department of Labor, 3rd & Constitution Ave, Washington, DC 20210.

NICHOLS, WALTER LAPLORA
Educator. **Personal:** Born Aug 31, 1938, Bolton, MS; married Louise Faye Harris; children: Anthony, Kala Faye. **Educ:** MS Valley State Univ, BS 1964; Northern IL Univ, MS 1978; Independence Univ, DEd 1979. **Career:** Sheridan Ind for Boys, teacher 1965-67; Fairmont Jr HS, teacher/coach 1967-71; Argo Comm HS, teacher/coach 1971-. **Orgs:** Vp Dist 86 School Bd 1981-; mem Natl School Bd Assoc 1981-, IL School Bd Assoc 1981-; consult Joliet Job Corp 1982-83; bd mem PUSH 1983-; 1st lt Marquette Joliet Consistory 1983; shriner 1984. **Honors/Awds:** Article "You Either Move Up or Move Out" Chicago Tribune 1967, "Title Triumph by Charger Something Special, Walt" 1967, "Remember Walter Nichols Offensive Tackle" Joliet Herald newspaper 1964-67, "Stand by Valley State Alumni Urge Official" Clarion Ledger Paper 1983. **Home Addr:** 701 Spencer St, Joliet, IL 60433.

NICHOLSON, ALEATHIA DOLORES
Educator, cleric. **Personal:** Born Apr 10, 1937, Salisbury, NC; daughter of Leathia Williams Nicholson and John Wadsworth Nicholson. **Educ:** Hampton University, BS, 1959; University of Connecticut, MA, 1965; George Peabody College/Vanderbilt University, educational specialist, 1968; Episcopal Theological Seminary in Kentucky, licentiate, 1989. **Career:** Public-Private Schools, music specialist, 1959-78; Meharry Medical College, student affairs director/nursing education, 1978-81; Tennessee State University, student affairs director/school of nursing, 1981-85; Fisk University, director of teacher education programs, 1985-92; Episcopal Diocese of Tennessee, vocational deacon, 1989-; Teach for America, curriculum consultant, 1990-92; Metro Board of Education, music specialist, 1992-. **Orgs:** North American Association for the Diaconate, 1989-; Deacon's Assembly, Diocese of Tennessee, 1989-; Neighborhood Education Project, board member, 1989-91; American Red Cross, Project Safety, Nashville Chapter, founding member, 1989; Nashville Association of Rabbis, Priests, and Ministers, 1990; National Education Association and Affiliates; Zeta Phi Beta Sorority, Inc, 1960-. **Honors/Awds:** Fisk University, Social Sciences Division, Outstanding Teacher, 1992; Governor of Tennessee, Award for JTPA Exceptional Youth Sub-Contracting, 1989; Peabody College, Experienced Teacher Fellowship in the Humanities, 1968. **Special Achievements:** Epic Lives, Visible Ink, contributor, two profiles, 1992; Notable Black American Woman, Gale, contributor, five biographies, 1992; Instructional Approaches to Classroom Management, TFA, editor/author, 1992; Black Nursing Pioneers, Leaders and Organizers, 1770-1980 ASALH, co-author, 1980; An Afro-Anglican Mass Setting, St Anselm's Episcopal Church, composer, 1980; Contributed nineteen biographies to Notable Black American Women; contributed twenty-five biographies to Notable Black American Men. **Home Addr:** 3729 Creekland Ct, Nashville, TN 37218-1803, (615)876-7914.

NICHOLSON, ALFRED
Educator. **Personal:** Born Jun 3, 1936, Edgefield, SC; children: Sharon Michell, Althea Gail. **Educ:** Comm Coll of Philadelphia, AAS 1968; LaSalle Univ, BS 1974. **Career:** AAA Refinishing Company, tanner/inspector 1956-59; Strick Corp, elec wireman 1961-68, personnel asst 1968-69; Comm Coll of Philadelphia, personnel officer/aa dir 1974-. **Orgs:** Treas Coll & Univ Personnel Assoc 1972-74; bd of trustees United Way of Southeastern PA 1986-. **Military Serv:** AUS corpl 2 yrs; Good Conduct Medal; Honorable Discharge. **Business Addr:** Personnel Officer/AA Dir, Community College of Philadelphia, 1700 Spring Garden St, Philadelphia, PA 19130.

NICHOLSON, JESSIE R.
Attorney. **Personal:** Born in Waterloo, IA; married Charles E Nicholson, Jul 22, 1972; children: Ephraim Nicholson. **Educ:** University of Northern Iowa, BA, 1974, MA, 1975; William Mitchell College of Law, JD, 1985. **Career:** Southern Minnesota Regional Legal Services, Deputy Exec dir, practicing in civil rights and immigration law areas. **Orgs:** American Bar Association, 1985-90; Minnesota State Bar Association, International Bar Rel Committee, 1989-; Ramsey & Washington Co Bar Association, 1989-; Minnesota Minority Lawers Association, 1989-; Conciliator Minneapolis-St Paul Archidocese, conciliator, Due Process Board, 1988-; Housing Trust Advisory Committee, board member, 1989-91. **Honors/Awds:** Minnesota State Housing Finance Agency, Service Recognition Award, 1991. **Military Serv:** US Navy Reserve, 3rd class, 1975-77. **Business Addr:** Deputy Executive Director, Southern Minnesota Regional Legal Services Inc, 46 E 4th St, Ste 700, St Paul, MN 55101, (612)228-9823.

NICHOLSON, LAWRENCE E.
Educator. **Personal:** Born Jul 10, 1915, St Louis. **Educ:** Lincoln Univ MO, BA 1938; Chicago U, MA 1942; Columbia U, MA, Doctorate. **Career:** Soc Caseworker, 1939-41; VA Couns Center, chief 1946-47; HS, teacher 1948-49; Harris Teachers Coll, prof Children Psych Dept 1950-. **Orgs:** Chmn Nat Schlrshp Comm Omega Psi Phi Frat 1950-60; Nat Bd ADA 1968-70; pres St Louis Dist MO St Tchrs Assn 1970-72; chmn bd Adult Wlfr SvcSt Louis 1968-; commnr chmn St Louis Hous Auth 1972-; bd St Louis Coun on Hum Relat 1972-F St Louis Sch Bd 1977; mem Bond Issue Supr Comm St Louis 1968-; bd St Louis Urban Leag 1972-; bd Chrctr Rsrch Assn 1965-69; bd NAACP 1963-65; bd Dept Chmn Relat Episcopal 1953-55; bd St Louis VocCouns Serv 1960-64; W End Comm Conf 1958-63; St Louis Opera Theatre 1963-65; Child Wlfr Comm MO Dept Wlfr 1968-70. **Honors/Awds:** Dist serv to comm medal Univ Chicago 1971; dist serv Nat Frat Omega Psi Phi 1972; man of yr awd St Louis ADA 1972; "Success Story" St Louis Globe DemNov 15, 1968; comm serv awd Sigma Gamma Rho 1972. **Military Serv:** USN 1942-45. **Business Addr:** Professor of Psychology, Harris Teachers College, 3026 Laclede, St Louis, MO 63103.

NICHOLSON, TINA
Professional basketball player. **Personal:** Born Sep 27, 1973. **Educ:** Penn State, bachelor's degree in exercise and sports management, 1996. **Career:** Cleveland Rockers, guard, 1997-. **Business Addr:** Professional Basketball Player, Cleveland Rockers, One Center Ct, Cleveland, OH 44115, (216)263-7625.

NICKERSON, DON CARLOS
Attorney. **Personal:** Born Aug 24, 1951, Wilmington, DE; son of Floretta W Nickerson and David B Nickerson; married Aug 24, 1989 (divorced); children: Christen, J D. **Educ:** Iowa State University, BS, sociology, journalism, 1974; Drake University Law School, JD, 1977. **Career:** WHO Radio & Television, news reporter, 1972-74; Parrish & Del Gallo, associate attorney, 1977-78; Des Moines, Iowa, assistant US attorney, 1978-80; Babich & Nickerson, partner, attorney; US attorney, Southern District of Iowa, currently. **Orgs:** Blackstone Inn of Court, barrister, 1989-; Iowa State Bar Association, Criminal Law Section, council member, 1991-; Natl Bar Assn, 1991-; Iowa Natl Bar Assn, president, 1991-92; National Association of Criminal

Defense Lawyers, 1991-; Drake University Law School Board of Counselors, 1989-92; Iowa Commission of the Aging, 1983-85; United Way of Central Iowa, Executive Committee, 1985-88. **Honors/Awds:** Martindale-Hubbell, AV (top lawyer rating), 1992; Amnesty International, Certificate of Recognition, 1991; Des Moines Register, Up & Comer, 1989; Iowa Governor's Volunteer Award, 1984, 1985, 1992. **Special Achievements:** Conference presenter, first annual state conference on the Black Male: Criminal Justice, 1992. **Business Addr:** US Attorney, Southern District of Iowa, United States Courthouse Annex, 2nd Fl, 110 East Court Ave, Des Moines, IA 50309.

NICKERSON, HARDY OTTO
Professional football player. **Personal:** Born Sep 1, 1965, Los Angeles, CA; married Amy; children: Ashleigh, Hardy, Haleigh. **Educ:** California, BA in sociology. **Career:** Pittsburgh Steelers, linebacker, 1987-93; Tampa Bay Buccaneers, 1993-. **Honors/Awds:** Pro Bowl, 1993, 1996. **Business Addr:** Professional Football Player, Tampa Bay Buccaneers, 1 Buccaneer Pl, Tampa, FL 33607, (813)870-2700.

NICKERSON, WILLIE CURTIS
Religious administrator. **Personal:** Born Apr 26, 1926, Macon Co, AL; married Sadie M Walker; children: Conway, Vernon, Christopher. **Educ:** Tuskegee Inst, attended 1950; Columbia Coll, BA 1957. **Career:** Calvary Bapt Ch;; minister of Social Concerns 1974-; Calvary Bapt Comm Educ Prog, exec dir 1974; Calvary Bapt Ch Center, dir Vocational Exploration 1972; Quaker City IN, serv mgr 1964; Evans Fur Co;; mdse mgr L1954; Calvary Bapt Ch;; chmn deacon bd 1969; Calvary Bapt Ch, councilman 1970; Calvary Housing Corp, chmn 1973. **Orgs:** Am Mgmt Assn 1974; vice pres NW Clubster Am Bapt Ch of NJ 1974; mem Visions & Dreams Com Am Bapt Ch NJ 1979; Boys State Chmn, Am Legion Post #268 1970; mem Paterson Rotary Club #70 1975; mem NAACP 1979. **Honors/Awds:** Nat Pub Speaking Awd NFA So Univ Baton Rouge 1950; Korean Serv Awds AUS 1952; Roberta Johnson Guild, Calvary Bapt Ch 1971; Faithful Witness & Serv Calvary Bapt Ch 1979. **Military Serv:** AUS corpl 1951-53. **Business Addr:** 575 E 18th & St, Paterson, NJ 07501.

NICKS, WILLIAM JAMES, SR.
Football coach (retired). **Personal:** Born Aug 2, 1905, Griffin, GA; son of Elnora Nicks and W M Nicks; married Lillie Bell, Aug 20, 1931; children: William James Jr, Fredric Nicks. **Educ:** Morris Brown Coll, AB 1928; Columbia Univ NY, MS 1941. **Career:** Morris Brown Coll, head football coach 1930-44; Prairie View A&M Coll, heal physical educ dept, athletic dir and head football coach 1945-66. **Orgs:** Phi Beta Sigma Frat; Sigma Pi Phi Frat. **Honors/Awds:** The Physical Educ Intramural Complex at Prairie View A&M Univ was named ''The WJ 'Billy' Nicks Physical Education and Intramural Complex'' in his honor; Hallof Fame inductee Natl Assoc of Intercollegiate Athletics 1964, Morris Brown Coll 1964, Extra Point Club Atlanta Univ Colls 1981; Coach of the Year 5 yrs. **Home Addr:** 3320 Rosedale, Houston, TX 77004.

NICKSON, SHEILA JOAN
Educational administrator (retired). **Personal:** Born May 20, 1936, Buffalo, NY; daughter of Genevieve Martha Briggs Harris and William Harris; children: Stephen Dwight, Roderick Matthew. **Educ:** Attended, Buffalo State Coll 1953-54, 1966-70, Erie County Coll 1963-66. **Career:** SUNY, asst to chancellor coord of compus programs 1980-83; Buffalo State Coll, asst to chair dept of chemistry 1966-74, asst to pres dir of affirmative action begin 1974, retired. **Orgs:** Exec bd SUNY Black Faculty & Staff Assoc 1980-; educ adv comm Natl Urban League 1983-; bd dirs YWCA Buffalo 1983-; vice chair NY State Human Rights Adv Council 1984-; past pres Natl Org Amer Assoc of Affirmative Action; bd mem, past vice pres Girl Scouts of Amer; bd mem Sheehan Memorial Hospital 1988-; NAACP 1987-. **Honors/Awds:** Citation for Serv to State Governor Carey NY State 1982; Citation of Appreciation Natl Alliance of Black Sch Educators 1984; Citation for Serv to Nation Commonwealth of VA 1986; Women Involved in Gloval Issues Alpha Kappa Alpha Awd 1987; Sojourner Truth Meritorious Service Award 1989; City of Buffalo Common Council Coalition 1988. **Business Addr:** Asst to Pres/Dir Affirm Action, Buffalo State College, 1300 Elmwood Ave, Buffalo, NY 14222.

NIGHTINGALE-HAWKINS, MONICA R.
Marketing executive. **Personal:** Born Feb 6, 1960, Topeka, KS; daughter of Carol Lawton and Floyd Nightingale; married Thomas Hawkins, Apr 9, 1989. **Career:** Office of the Mayor, on-the-job training program manager, 1982-83; KSNT-TV 27(NBC), operations engineering, 1984-85; KSNW-TV 3(NBC), news producer, 1985-87; KPRS/KPRT Radio FM, music director, 1987-89; A A Productions, marketing and promotions vice pres, 1989-; Church of The Ascension, youth minister, 1989-; The Wyandotte City Community Project, executive director, 1989-. **Orgs:** Episcopal Church Women, president, 1989-91; Turner House Episcopal Social Services, board member, 1987-90; State of Kansas, Commission on AIDS in the Black Community, 1988-89; Governors Artist in Residence, artist in education, 1988-. **Honors/Awds:** Mayor Richard Berkey, Key to The City, 1989; American Businesswomen, Salute to Women, 1988; A & M Records, Outstanding Female Broadcaster, 1989; State of Kansas, $32k grant to train inner-city youth. **Special Achievements:** Appeared on ''Mass Communications Project for Youth Intervention and Training,'' NBC television, Aug 1992; appeared in local, state, and national A A music trades magazines for community involvement and work in the inner-city, 1989-92; ''President's Glass Ceiling Commission,'' Witness, Dec 1992. **Business Phone:** (913)281-3094.

NILES, ALBAN I.
Judge. **Personal:** Born Jun 10, 1933, St Vincent, West Indies; son of Elsie Niles and Isaac Niles; children: Maria, Gloria, Angela. **Educ:** UCLA, BS 1959, JD 1963. **Career:** Ernst & Ernst, auditor 1963-64; Private practice, attny 1964-82; Kedren Comm Health Ctr Inc, pres 1968-79; LA Cty Civil Serv Comm, president commiss 1980; LA Municipal Court, judge, beginning 1982; LA Superior Court, judge, currently. **Orgs:** Mem Natl Bar Assn, Langston Bar Assn; chmn of bd Bus Devel Ctr of S CA, 1978-91; mem NAACP, Urban League; Parliamentarian 100 Black Men Inc of Los Angeles; Commander Post 116 American Legion; chair, Municipal Court Judges Association, 1992-93; treasurer, Judicial Division, Natl Bar Assn, 1991-93; 33 degree Mason and Honorary Past Potentate Shriners with rank of Ambassador at Large. **Honors/Awds:** Selected as person of Caribbean birth to make signif contrib 1976; Carnegie Found Fellowship in Urban Exec Leadership; UCLA Law Review; Passed the CPA examination 1960; appointed to the bench Feb 3, 1982; Honored by the State Legislature, The County Board of Supervisors, and The Los Angeles City Council, 1996. **Military Serv:** USAF a/2c 1951-55. **Business Addr:** Judge, Los Angeles Superior Court, 111 N Hill St, Los Angeles, CA 90012-3014.

NILES, LYNDREY ARNAUD
Educator. **Personal:** Born May 9, 1936; married Patricia Aqui; children: Kathryn Arlene, Ian Arnaud. **Educ:** Columbia Union Coll, BA 1963; Univ of MD, mA 1965; Temple U, phD 1973. **Career:** School of Communications Howard Univ, chmn Comm Arts & Sci Dept 1979-; Howard Univ, prof & asso dean 1975-79; Univ of MD, lectr 1971-75; Univ of DC, asst prof 1968-74, instr 1965-68; Columbia Union Coll, lectr 1964-65; Leadership Resources Inc, mgmt consult 1974-75. **Orgs:** Mem Speech Commn Assn/InternatrA Commn Assn/Am Soc for Training & Devel/NAACP; pres Met Wash Commn Assn 1974-75; pub article ''Listening & Note TakingMethods'' 1965; pub dissertation ''The Defel of Speech Educ Problems at Predominately Black Colls 1973; ''black rhetoric five yrs of growth, Encoder 1974; ''Communication ind Dental Office'', article in Encoder 1 979. **Business Addr:** Howard University, School of Communications, 24 6th Street, NW, Washington, DC 20059.

NILON, CHARLES HAMPTON
Educator. **Personal:** Born Jun 2, 1916, Maplesville, AL; son of Vesta Brewer Nilon and Elbert Nilon; married Nancy Mildred Harper, Aug 19, 1956; children: Charles H Jr. **Educ:** TN State Coll, BS (Cum Laude) 1936; Univ of KS, MA 1946; Univ of WI, PhD 1951. **Career:** Birmingham, AL Public Schools, Washington School & Parker HS, English teacher 1936-43; Wayne State Univ, asst prof of English 1951-56; Univ of CO, prof of English 1956-85; Univ of CO prof of English Emeritus l985-. **Orgs:** Mem Modern Language Assn 1952-, Boulder Housing Commission 1965-69; dir black studies Univ of CO 1969-73; chair, bd of dir HELP Inc 1969-73; chair, English dept Howard Univ 1974-76; language consultant School of Engrg at Stonybrook, 1976; mem Popular Culture Assn of Amer 1978-; treas Modern Humanities Rsch Assn; Coll Language Assn l956-; MELUS l978-. **Honors/Awds:** Editor MHRA Annual Bibliography of Language & Literature 1958-66; Citadell Faulkner & the Negro 1965; Bibliography of Bibliographies in Amer Lit 1970; Danforth Found Fellow 1972; Thomas Jefferson Awd 1973; Stearns Award, Univ of Colorado, l986; Award named in his honor, the Charles H and N Mildred Nilon Excellence in Minority Fiction Award, Univ of Colorado at Boulder, l989; ''The Science Fiction of Samuel R. Delany and the Limits of Technology'' Black Amer Literature Forum l984; ''The Ending of Huckleberry Finn: Freeing the Free Negro'' Mark Twain Journal l984. **Military Serv:** AUS corpl 1943-45. **Home Addr:** 702 Pine St, Boulder, CO 80302. **Business Addr:** Professor Emeritus of English, Univ of Colorado-Boulder, Boulder, CO 80309.

NIMMONS, JULIUS F., JR.
Educational administrator. **Career:** Jarvis Christian College, Hawkins, TX, president; Univ of DC, provost & vp for academic affairs, 1993-96; Univ of DC, acting president, 1996-. **Orgs:** Mem, United Negro College Fund; board of directors, NAFEO, Washington, DC. **Honors/Awds:** Outstanding Leadership & Service Award, Alpha Phi Alpha Fraternity; Dept of the Army, Camp All American Certificate of Achievement, Fort Bragg, NC. **Business Addr:** Acting President, University of DC, 4200 Connecticut Ave, NW, Washington, DC 20008.

NIMS, THEODORE, JR.
Appliance distribution company executive. **Personal:** Born Jun 6, 1942, Tallahassee, FL; son of Terri Courtney Nims (deceased) and Theodore Nims, Sr; married Gloria Lee; children: Chandra, Marjorie. **Educ:** Florida A&M Univ, BS 1964; various GE, AMA & Wharton management courses. **Career:** General Electric Co, various sales & mktg positions 1964-76, mgr compliance 1976-78, mgr retail parts 1978-79, zone mgr 1979-82, region manager 1982-86, mgr natl property mgmt sales 1986-89; pres Nims Distribution Inc Clearwater FL 1989-. **Orgs:** Roundtable mem Natl Minority Entre Devel Ment Ctr; co-founder/former chmn MN Black Networking Sys; mem Black Exec Exchange Program Natl Urgan League; mem Black MBA Assoc. **Honors/Awds:** Many civic, community and company awards.

NIPSON, HERBERT
Journalist. **Personal:** Born Jul 26, 1916, Asheville, NC; married E Velin Campbell; children: Herbert, Maria. **Educ:** Writers Workshop Univ of IA, MFA; Penn State, Journalism degree 1940. **Career:** Cedar Rapids Gazette, corres; Ebony Magazine, assoc editor 1949-51, co-managing editor 1951-64, managing editor 1964-67, exec editor. **Orgs:** Chmn bd dir South Side Comm Art Ctr; mem IL Arts Cncl, Joseph Jefferson Comm; bd of govs Urban Gateways. **Honors/Awds:** IA Press Photographers Assoc Awds; Capital Press Clubs Awd as Outstanding Journalist 1965; Disting Alumnus of Penn State 1973; named to Phi Eta Sigma and Sigma Delta Chi Frats. **Military Serv:** Armed Serv m/sgt 1941-45. **Business Addr:** Johnson Publishing, 820 S Michigan Ave, Chicago, IL 60605.

NIVENS, BEATRYCE THOMASINIA
Author, lecturer. **Personal:** Born Apr 1, 1948, New York, NY; daughter of Surluta Bell Nivens (deceased) and Thomas J Nivens (deceased). **Educ:** Fisk Univ, Nashville TN, BA 1969; Univ of Ghana Legon, Ghana W Africa, Summer School Certificate, 1970; Hofstra Univ, Hempstead NY, MS in Ed, 1971. **Career:** Denison Univ, Granville OH, asst dean of women, 1969-71; Hosftra Univ, Hemptead NY, pre-law counselor, 1971-73; Queens Coll, Flushing NY, counselor 1974-79; District Council 37, New York NY, part-time counselor, 1979-87; columnist, Essence Magazine, 1977-90; US Department of Health & Human Serv, Bronx NY, expert, 1980-83; Career Marketing Int, New York NY, pres, lecturer, writer, 1985-; lecturer for colls, univs, corporations and civic women's and black groups, currently. **Orgs:** Delta Sigma Theta Sorority, 1987-. **Honors/Awds:** Public Service Award US Dept of Labor 1982; author: Fellow, Virginia Center for the Creative Arts 1985; lecturer for Chevrolet's Natl Career Seminar to ten cities ''Strategies for Success'', 1985-86; Winthrop Rockefeller Distinguished Lecturer, Univ of AK, 1986; Careers for Women Without College Degrees, 1988; author: The Black Woman's Career Guide, 1982, 1987; How to Change Careers, 1990; How to Choose a Career, 1992; How to Re-Enter the Work Force, 1992; Success Strategies for African Americans, 1998.

NIX, RICK (JAIME RICARDO)
Catholic church administrator. **Personal:** Born Jan 6, 1950, Toledo, OH; son of Viola Crain Nix and Ulysesses S. Nix; children: Noel. **Educ:** St Joseph's College, Rensselaer, IN, BS, philosophy, 1972. **Career:** Ohio Civil Rights Commission, Toledo, OH, field representative, 1973; City of Flint, MI, management intern, 1974, community development, 1975; Genesee County, Flint, MI, community coordinating specialist, 1974-75; General Motors Corp, Flint, MI, inspector, 1976-82; Catholic Diocese of Saginaw, MI, Office for Black Concerns, director, associate director, Mission Office, 1982-. **Orgs:** Member, 1964-, communications committee, 1981-, NAACP; vice chairman, City-wide Advisory Committee Community Development, 1974-; Knights of St. Peter Claver, 1989-; founder and chairman, Black Fathers Day March Against Drugs and Crime, 1989-; National Association for Black Catholic Administrators, Communications Committee, 1982-; president & founder, Ministry to Black Catholic Men, 1995-; co-chairman & co-founder, The First Annual Bridge Walk (Bridging the Gap); United Saginaw Against Crime, 1993. **Honors/Awds:** Human Rights Award, City of Flint, MI Human Relations Committee, 1990; Voluntary Action Award, President George Bush, 1990; Community Service Award, Phi Delta Kappa Sorority, Saginaw Chapter, 1991; Community Service Award, Frontiers Intl Saginaw Chap, 1993; Community Service Award, The Diocese of Saginaw, St Joseph's Parish, Black History Month Award, 1993; Dr Martin Luther King Jr Unity Award, Iota Chi Lambda Chap, Alpha Phi Alpha Fraternity, Inc, 1994. **Special Achievements:** Manual: ''How to Drive Drug Dealers Out of Your Neighborhood'', 1989. **Business Addr:** Director, Office for Black Concerns, Associate Director, Mission Office, Catholic Diocese of Saginaw, 5800 Weiss St, Saginaw, MI 48603.

NIX, ROBERT N. C., JR.
State supreme court justice (retired). **Personal:** Born Jul 13, 1928, Philadelphia, PA; son of Ethel Lanier Nix and Robert N C Nix, Sr; married Dorothy Lewis (deceased); children: Robert Nelson Cornelius III, Michael, Anthony, Stephan. **Educ:** Villanova Univ, AB 1952; Univ of PA, JD 1955; Temple Univ, postgrad bus admin & econs; Bar PA 1956. **Career:** State of PA, deputy atty general 1956-58; Nix Rhodes & Nix Phila, partner 1958-68; Common Pleas Court Philadelphia County, judge 1968-71; State of PA, justice supreme court, 1972-84, chief justice, 1984-96. **Orgs:** Bd of dirs Germantown Boys Club 1968-; mem cncl pres assoc La Salle Coll 1971-; adv bd LaSalle Coll HS; bd consultors Villanova Univ Sch Law 1973-; mem Omega

Psi Phi; president-elect, Conference of Chief Justices, 1990-92, pres, beginning 1992. **Honors/Awds:** First PA Awd Guardian Civic League Achievement Awd; honoree, achievements as Chief Justice of PA Supreme Ct, pioneering accomplishments as the highest ranking Black official in history of PA; first justice from Pennsylvania supreme court to hold pres-elect post, Conf of Chief Justices. **Military Serv:** US Army, 1953-55.

NIX, ROSCOE RUSSA
Federal official, civil rights activist (retired). **Personal:** Born Jun 22, 1921, Greenville, AL; son of Jimmie Mae Nix and Comer Payton Nix; married Emma Coble; children: Veretta Tranice, Susan Lynette. **Educ:** Howard Univ, AB; Amer Univ, Grad Work 1950-52. **Career:** Labor Lodge #12 Civil Rights Comm US Dept of Labor, chmn 1964-66; US Dept of Labor Comm Rel Svc, field rep 1966-68; MD Comm Hum Rel, exec dir 1968-69; US Dept Justice Comm Rel Svc, chief state & local agencies sect 1969-73, chief tech support 1973-; Office of Technical Assistance, Community Relations Service, US Dept of Justice, assoc dir, 1980-86; Weekly political analyst, ''Twenty-One This Week''; columnist, The Montgomery Times. **Orgs:** Mem bd of trustees Stillman Coll, NAACP, Urban League 1964, Amer Civil Liberties Union 1969; mem Comm Church, Union Presbyterian Church; vice pres 1979, pres 1980-, Montgomery Cty NAACP; mem Comm on Assembly Oper Presbyterian Church 1979-; exec bd Montgomery Cty Chap Natl Conf of Christians & Jews 1979; mem Alpha Phi Alpha, United Way of Montgomery County; mem Montgomery County School Board 1974-78; founder, The African-American Family Festival for Academic Excellence, 1990. **Honors/Awds:** Montgomery County Government, Martin Luther King Jr Award, 1990; Washington Lawyer's Committee for Civil Rights Under Law, Wiley Branton Award, 1991. **Special Achievements:** Publ, ''When the Sword is Upon the Land,'' ''What Color Are Good Neighbors?,'' ''If We Must Die,'' ''The Ghost of Exec Order 10966,'' ''Wanted Missionaries to the Suburbs'', ''God Is White,'' ''Wanted, A Radical Black Church''. **Military Serv:** AUS T/4 1943-46. **Home Addr:** 11601 Le Baron Terr, Silver Spring, MD 20902.

NIX, THEOPHILUS RICHARD
Attorney. **Personal:** Born Jul 21, 1925, Chicago, IL; married Dr Lulu Mae Hill; children: Theophilus R. **Educ:** Lincoln U, PA, BA 1950; Howard Univ Law Sch Wash DC, LLD 1954. **Career:** Private Practice, atty 1954-; EEOC Phila, supr trial atty 1974-75; City of Wilmington, asst city solicitor 1955-56. **Orgs:** Mem DE Bar Assn 1956-; mem Bar St of MI 1957-; mem Nat Bar Assn 1970-; mem Bar MA 1975-; mem NAACP 1946-; legal coun DE Adolescent Prog Inc 1966-79; mem Correct Comm DE Bar Assn 1973-76; bd mem Martin Luther King Cntr Inc 1976-76; ETO/EUROPEAN Bandsmen/Drummajor, AUS 1943-46; Meretorfious Serv, DE PTA 1959; publ ''How To Operate a School of Business'' 1959; publ ''St Tutorial & Job Training Program'' 1962; publ ''Statistical Analysis NCC Sup Court Drug Sentencing'' 1972; Meretorious Commnty Serv DE Martin Luther Com 1978. **Honors/Awds:** Dist Serv Awd DE Adolescent Prog Inc 1979. **Military Serv:** AUS t/5 Bandsmen 1943-46. **Business Addr:** 914 French St, Wilmington, DE 19801.

NIX, THEOPHILUS RICHARD, JR.
Construction/contract lawyer. **Personal:** Born Oct 12, 1953, Washington, DC; son of Lula Mae Nix and Theophilus R Nix; married Myrtice Servance. **Educ:** Cincinnati Coll of Mortuary Sci, 1975; Ithaca Coll, BFA 1979; Howard Univ Sch of Law, JD 1982. **Career:** Bechtel Corp, construction/contract attorney, currently. **Orgs:** Mem Philadelphia Minority Contractors Assoc 1984-87, Philadelphia MBA Soc 1985-87, Philadelphia Barristers Assoc 1986-87; bd of dirs Bd of DE Contractors Assoc 1985-86. **Honors/Awds:** Written up in alumni bulletin Ithaca Coll Alumni Dir 1986. **Home Addr:** PO Box 2298, Oak Bluffs, MA 02557.

NIXON, FELIX NATHANIEL
Clergyman. **Personal:** Born May 27, 1918, York, AL; son of Savannah Carlisle Nixon and Nathan Nixon; married Callie Cotton Nixon, 1944; children: Felix Jr, Donald Roland, Charles, Samuel, Joe Rome, Josiah, John K, Jewel, Katie, Jeanette, Mildred, Joyce, Savannah, Zeala, John. **Educ:** Meridian Baptist Seminary, Meridian, MS, BTH, 1959; Union Baptist Seminary, Birmingham, AL, BD, 1972; Selma University, Selma, AL, DD, 1988. **Career:** Mt Hermon Baptist Church, pastor, 1948-64; Morningstar Baptist Church, pastor, 1963-65; Sumter Co Day Care Cntr, owner 1974-75; Nixon Ready to Wear Shop, owner 1974-75; Elim Baptist Church, pastor, 1976-. **Orgs:** Mem Sumter County Movement for Human Rights 1960-67; Sumter Co Br NAACP 1964-75; dir Sumter Econ Devel Corp Inc 1970-75; Ensley Pratt City Br NAACP 1968-75; chmn Sumter Co Dem Conf 1967-75; chmn Sumter Co Bd Educ 1978-80; president, NAACP, 1964-91; board member, Sumter County Board of Education, 1976-91; bd mem, National Baptist Convention; pres , Alabama Baptist Convention. **Honors/Awds:** Relcip The Most Dedicated Leader in West AL 1971; city of York, AL, Felix Nixon Day, Sept 1990. **Home Addr:** 510 Lincoln St, York, AL 36925.

NIXON, GEORGE W.
Airline pilot (retired). **Personal:** Born Mar 13, 1935, Pittsburgh, PA; son of Annie Nixon and James Nixon; married Heather Mary White; children: Lynnora, Rhonda, Nannette, George II, Vanessa. **Educ:** Univ of Pittsburgh School of Engrg, 1953-54; USAF Aviation Cadet School, 1955-56; USAF Navigator Engrg School, 1956-57; USAF Aerial Bombardment School, 1958-59; USAF Pilot School, 1961-62. **Career:** USAF, mil combat Korea Loas & Vietnam, comdr Boeing 707, B-47 Bombardier, B-36 engr; United Airlines, pilot 1966-87, captain, 1987-95. **Orgs:** Mem United Airlines Pilot Speakers Panel, Arline Pilots Assoc, United Airlines Black Professional Org; Organization of Black Airline Pilots; Alpha Phi Alpha. **Honors/Awds:** Won recognition & acclaim, filmed interview, Emmy Awd winning Realities in Black 1974; Nominee Cty Grand Jury. **Special Achievements:** Featured on United Airlines Safety Video, 1989-95. **Military Serv:** USAF capt 1954-66; Natl Defense Serv Medal; AF Expeditionary Medal; AF Reserve Medal; AF Outstanding Unit Awd; Vietnam Serv Medal; AF Longevity Serv Awd.

NIXON, HAROLD L.
Educator. **Personal:** Born May 31, 1939, Smithfield, NC; son of Lizzie O Nixon and Mark A Nixon; married Brenda Flint, Jun 8, 1962; children: Eric F, Leah. **Educ:** Fisk University, BA, 1962; North Carolina Central University, MA, 1976; University of North Carolina, Chapel Hill, PhD, 1988. **Career:** Food and Drug Administration, research biologist, 1963-64; National Institute of Health, research biologist, 1966-69; Fayetteville State University, director of financial aid, 1969-80, associate dean for special programs and student life, 1980-83, vice chancellor for student development, 1983-88; Wright State University, vice pres for student affairs, professor of education, 1988-. **Orgs:** National Association of Studet Personnel Administrators, 1983-; Ohio Association of Student Personnel Administrators, 1988-; Ohio College Personnel Association, 1988-; Mid-Western Research Association, 1990-; North Carolina Association of Financial Aid Administrators, president, 1976, chairman, legislative committee, 1975; Southern Association of Financial Aid Administrators, executive board, 1976; National Association of Financial Aid Administrators, national mamber-at-large, 1977. **Honors/Awds:** Wright State University, Student Government Association, Rookie Administrator of the Year, 1989; Fayetteville State University, Outstanding Service Award, 1983-88; North Carolina Association of Financial Aid Administrators, Outstanding Leadership Award, 1976; Alpha Phi Alpha Fraternity, Inc, 1989. **Special Achievements:** Factors Associated with Enrollment Decisions of Black Students and White Students in Colleges Where They Are in the Minority, Thoughts for Administrators, 1990; White Students at the Black University, A Report on Their Experiences Regarding Acts of Intolerance, 1992; The Adult Learner, A Comparison of Counseling Needs Between African-American and Caucasusian University Students, 1992; African-Americans in the 21st Century, The Agony and Promise of Higher Education, 1993. **Business Addr:** Vice Pres for Student Affairs, Wright State University, 3640 Colonel Glenn Hwy, Dayton, OH 45415, (513)873-2808.

NIXON, JAMES I., JR.
Automotive components manufacturing company executive. **Personal:** Born Jun 21, 1933, Pittsburgh, PA; son of Annie Forest Nixon and James I Nixon Sr; married Lea Young Nixon, Aug 5, 1988; children: James I Nixon III, Danita H Brown, James E Hair Jr, Janette S Dent. **Educ:** Carnegie-Mellon University, BSME, 1956; University of Cincinnati, 1958-59; Union College, Schenectady, NY, 1963-64. **Career:** General Electric Corp, district sales manager, 1956-74; ITT Corp., vp, Equal Opportunity Operations, dir, 1974-87; North America Venture Development Group, mng director, 1987-89; Metropolitan Transportation Authority, director-AA, 1989-91; Inline Brake Manufacturing Corp., president/chief executive officer, 1991-97; Beacon Partners Inc, managing dir, 1997-. **Orgs:** National Urban Affairs Council, chairman of the board, 1980-81; Equal Employment Advisory Council, chairman of the board, 1981-82; Associated Black Charities, Inc, board member and chairman, policy committee, 1984-96; Federal Reserve Bank of NY, small bus advisory coun, 1995-97; Bank of Boston/Connecticut, regional advisory bd, 1997-. **Honors/Awds:** Jr Chamber of Commerce, Outstanding Public Service Award, 1965, 1966, 1968; General Electric Co, Gerald L Phillipps Service Award, 1970; NAACP of New York, 1983; Harlem YMCA, Black Achievers in Industry Award, 1972, 1982. **Military Serv:** Army Corps of Engineers, sgt first class, 1950-52; achieved the rank of sgt at age 17 yrs old; sgt first class at age 18 yrs old. **Home Addr:** 337 Mayapple Rd, Stamford, CT 06903-1310, (203)329-3515. **Business Addr:** Managing Director, Beacon Partners, Inc, 6 Landmark Sq, 4th Fl, Stamford, CT 06901-2792, (203)359-5776.

NIXON, JAMES MELVIN
Association executive. **Career:** C of C, assoc exec professional dir. **Orgs:** Nat Cntr Youth Outreach Workers; mem Omega Psi Phi. **Business Addr:** Effingham St Br YMCA, 1013 Effingham, Portsmouth, VA 23704.

NIXON, JOHN WILLIAM
Dentist. **Personal:** Born Mar 2, 1922, Homeland, FL; married Ethyl Commons; children: John W, Jr, Karl H, Melba H. **Educ:** Union Academy, Bartow Fl, 1939; Bethune Cookman College, 1939-42; Fisk University, 1946-47; Meharry Medical College, DDS 1951. **Career:** Dentist, currently; community activist, currently. **Orgs:** Volunteer leader, Alabama Negro Comm; pres NAACP; Mayor's Community Affairs Committee; organizer, Jefferson County Employers Council; aptd chmn, Bi-Racial Jefferson County Manpower Coord Committee; spearheaded negotiation procedures betweel Local Labor Independent & Natl Equal Employment Opportunity Commission ; spokesman, Negro Comm & City Race Relations; org, bd dirs, Cits Fed Savings & Loan Assn; chmn, Birmingham Anti-TB Assn, Annual Christmas Seal Drive; University of Alabama Medical Center Expansion Committee; appointed member, Southeast Regional Manpower Advisory Council; appointedBirmingham Manpower Area Planning Council; appointed natl chairman, 21 member Natl Private Resources Advisory Committee, US Office of Economic Opportunity. **Honors/Awds:** Outstanding Service Award, Distinguished Service Award, Iota Phi Lambda; Man of Year Award, Omega Psi Phi, Alpha Phi Chapter; Outstanding Community Service Award, Miles College; Citation of Merit, Phi Lambda; Outstanding Community Service Award, Birmingham Area Chapter ARC; Outstanding Service Award, Lawson State Junior College; Honorary LLD, D Payne College; appointed Associate Clinical Instructor, UAB School of Dentistry 1974; Advisory Bd, School of Social Work, University of Alabama 1973; Birmingham Committee on Foreign Relations 1973-74. **Military Serv:** US Arny, 1st sergeant, 1942-45. **Business Addr:** Dentist, 840 Miami Pl, Birmingham, AL 35214.

NIXON, NORM ELLARD
Restauranteur, business executive, professional basketball player (retired). **Personal:** Born Oct 11, 1955, Macoun, GA; married Debbie Allen; children: Vivian. **Educ:** Duquesne, 1977. **Career:** Los Angeles Lakers, 1978-83, San Diego Clippers, 1984, Los Angeles Clippers, 1985-86, 1989; Nixon-Katz Assocs, personal manager/sports agents; Georgia Restaurant, owner, currently. **Honors/Awds:** 2nd best assist man in 6 seasons with Lakers; Laker's all time leader in steals; was named to the NBA All-Rookie Team in 1978. **Business Addr:** Owner, Georgia Restaurant, 345 N Maple Dr, Ste 205, Beverly Hills, CA 90210, (310)273-6122.

NIXON, OTIS JUNIOR
Professional baseball player. **Personal:** Born Jan 9, 1959, Evergreen, NC; married Juanita Leonard, Dec 24, 1992. **Educ:** Louisburg College. **Career:** New York Yankees, 1983; Cleveland Indians, 1984-87; Montreal Expos, 1988-90; Atlanta Braves, 1991-93; Boston Red Sox, 1994; Texas Rangers, 1994-96; Toronto Blue Jays, 1996-97; Minnesota Twins, 1997-. **Business Addr:** Professional Baseball Player, Minnesota Twins, 501 Chicago Ave S, Minneapolis, MN 55415, (612)375-1366.

NJOROGE, MBUGUA J.
Management consultant. **Personal:** Born Jun 15, 1944, Banana Hill, Kenya; son of Wanjigi Njoroge and Wanjiku Njoroge; married Josephine; children: Wanjiku Felicia Mbugua, Njoroge Mbugua. **Educ:** Baker Univ, Baldwin City KS, BA 1966; KS State Univ, Hayes KS, MS 1969; Univ of MO, Kansas City MO, masters of Public Admin 1972. **Career:** Edward D Jones & Company, stockbroker/investment banker; MCI Ltd/Mackenzie Consult Intl Ltd, managing dir 1978-; African Pavilion Ltd, Kansas City MO, pres 1973-78; Colum Union Natl Bank, Kansas City MO, marketing account exec 1969-70; Jones Store Co Kansas City, asst account dept 1969; KS State Univ, Hays KS, asst dept of Biology 1967-68; Woodlawn Jr High School Baltimore, science teacher 1966-67; Mackenzie Consultants Intl Ltd, intl Mgmt consultant 1970; Community Devel Corp, Kansas City MO, marketing analyst 1979. **Orgs:** Second vice pres Devel Corp 1977-80. **Honors/Awds:** Honorary Youth of Honor, United Methodist Women, United Methodist Church, Everest KS 1963; Certificate of Leadership, Community Devel Corp, Kansas City MO 1977-78; Outstanding Leadership Award, Black Economic Union, Kansas City MO 1979. **Business Addr:** 2450 Grand, PO Box 19842, Kansas City, MO 64141.

NKONGOLA, MUYUMBA WA. **See MUYUMBA, FRANCOIS N.**

NKONYANSA, OSAFUHIN KWAKU. **See PRESTON, GEORGE NELSON.**

NNAJI, BARTHOLOMEW O. (BART)
Professor of engineering. **Personal:** Born Jul 13, 1956, Oruku Enugu, Nigeria; son of Emmanuel & Nev; married Patricia, Aug 16, 1980; children: Chik & Nev. **Educ:** St John's Univ, NY, BS, 1980; VA Polytechnic & State Univ, MS, 1982, PhD, 1983. **Career:** Univ of Massachusetts, asst professor, 1983-91, prof, 1991-; Federal Republic of Nigeria, honorable minister, 1993. **Orgs:** Inst of Industrial Engineering, sr mem; Society of Manufacturing Engineers, sr mem; Robotics International; Amer Inst of Physics. **Honors/Awds:** M Eugene Merchant Best Textbook Award, 1994; Inducted in St John's Univ Sports Hall

of Fame, 1994; Appointed the Federal Minister of Science & Technology for Nigeria, 1993; International Society for Productivity Enhancement, Fellow, 1994; United Technology Corp, Outstanding Teaching Award, 1992; numerours others. **Special Achievements:** International Journal of Design & Manufacturing, Chapman-Hall Publishers, editor in chief, 1990-; Design & Manufacturing book series, Chapman-Hall Publishers, series editor, 1990-; Modern Manufacturing Planning & Control, Prentice Hall, co-author, 1995; SME Transactions on Robotics Research, Society of Manufacturing Engineers Publications, editor, 1992; Design by Product Modelling, Chapman and Hall, co-author; numerous others. **Business Addr:** Professor of Engineering, University of Massachusetts at Amherst, 114 Marston Hall, Amherst, MA 01003, (413)545-1652.

N'NAMDI, CARMEN ANN
Educator. **Personal:** Born May 13, 1949, Cincinnati, OH; daughter of Dorothy Jenkins Kiner and Carl Kiner; married George N'Namdi, Aug 14, 1971; children: Kemba, Nataki (deceased), Jumaane, Izegbe. **Educ:** Ohio State University, Columbus, OH, BS, education, 1971; Wayne State University, Detroit, MI, MA, education, 1978. **Career:** Nataki Talibah Schoolhouse, Detroit, MI, founder/headmistress, 1978-. **Orgs:** Board member, Detroit Children's Museum Friends, 1988-; executive board, Detroit Chapter Jack & Jill, 1987-; member, Greater Wayne County Links, 1990-. **Honors/Awds:** Professional Best Award, Learning Magazine, Michigan State University, College of Education, 1990; Michigan House of Representatives Resolution, Michigan House of Representatives, 1990; Salute to Black Women Who Make It Happen, National Council of Negro Women, 1989; Michigan State Resolution, Michigan Senate, 1989; Black Women of Michigan Exhibition, 1785-1985, Detroit Historical Museum, 1985; Headliners Award, Women of Wayne State Alumni Association, 1985; Spirit of Detroit Award, Detroit City Council, 1985; Maharishi Award, World Government of the Age of Enlightenment, 1983. **Business Addr:** Headmistress, Nataki Talibah Schoolhouse, 19176 Northrop, Detroit, MI 48219.

N'NAMDI, GEORGE RICHARD
Art gallery director. **Personal:** Born Sep 12, 1946, Columbus, OH; son of Ima Jo Winson Watson and George Richard Johnson; married Carmen Ann Kiner N'Namdi, Aug 14, 1971; children: Kemba, Nataki (deceased), Jumaane, Izegbe. **Educ:** Ohio State University, Columbus, OH, BS, 1970, MS, 1972; University of Michigan, Ann Arbor, MI, 1974, PhD, 1978. **Career:** University of Cincinnati, Cincinnati, OH, director of head start training, 1970,72; University of Michigan, Ann Arbor, MI, instructor, 1973-76; Wayne State University, Detroit, MI, asst professor, 1976-86; Wayne County Health Dept, Detroit, Mi, psychologist, 1978-82; Jazzonia Gallery, Detroit, MI, dir, 1981-84; G R N'Namdi Gallery, Birmingham, MI, director, 1984-. **Orgs:** Chairman of the board, Cass Food Co-op, 1983-86; treasurer, Nataki Talibah Schoolhouse, 1989-; member, Birmingham Bloomfield Cultural Council, 1990-; member, Paradigm Dance Co, 1986-88. **Honors/Awds:** Spirit of Detroit Award, City of Detroit, 1981, 1985; Art Achievement Award, Delta Sigma Theta Sorority, 1982. **Business Addr:** Director, G R N'Namdi Gallery, 161 Townsend, Birmingham, MI 48009, (810)642-2700.

NNOLIM, CHARLES E.
Educator. **Personal:** Born May 10, 1939, Umuchu, Nigeria; son of Lolo Ezelibe Nnolim and Nnolim Obidegwu; married Virginia Onwugigbo Nnolim, Oct 26, 1966; children: Emeka, Chinyere, Amaeze, Azuka. **Educ:** Benedictine College, Atchison, KS, BA (honors), 1966; Bemidji State Univ, Bemidji, MN, MA, English, 1968; Catholic Univ of America, Washington, DC, PhD, 1975. **Career:** Ferris State College, Big Rapids, MI, asst prof of English, 1969-70; Babson College, Wellesley, MA, asst prof of English, 1970-76; Univ of Port Harcourt, Port Harcourt, Nigeria, professor of English, 1980-. **Orgs:** Mem, African Studies Assn; mem, Modern Lang Assn of Amer; mem, Natl Soc of Literature & the Arts; pres, Literary Society of Nigeria, 1986-; member, African Literature Assn, 1974-; member, West African Assn of Commonwealth Literature & Language Studies, 1988-. **Honors/Awds:** Recipient, Doctoral Fellowship, Catholic Univ of Amer, 1968-72; author, Melville's Benito Cereno: A Study in Mng of Name-Symbolism, 1974; author, Pessimism in Conrad's Heart of Darkness, 1980; author, critical essays on African literature published in US and British journals. **Business Addr:** Professor, Department of English, University of Port Harcourt, Port Harcourt, Rivers, Nigeria.

NOAH, LEROY EDWARD
Elected official (retired). **Personal:** Born Jul 25, 1934, Clarksdale, MS; son of Lilliam Mae White Noah and Jesse Noah; married Grace Fulghum Noah, Dec 7, 1952; children: Sharon Davis, Carolyn Mann, Brenda. **Educ:** Forest Park Community College, AAS 1975; Natl Inst of Cosmetology, PhD 1987. **Career:** City of Kinloch, pres, bd of aldermen, retired. **Orgs:** Member/president School Board 1963-75; financial sec, Associated Hairdresser, Cosmetologist of MO 1980-94; United Beautician 1991-; 1st vp, Sigma Nu Theta Fraternity. **Honors/Awds:** Citizen of the Year Ward Chapel AME Church 1981, man of year Associated Hairdresser, Cosmetologist of MO 1988-; Natl King, Natl Beauty Culturist League, 1987-88; Dr John Bryant Memorial Award, 1988. **Military Serv:** USAF Sergeant; Korean Defense, Presidential Unit, Good Conduct, Korean Medal. **Home Addr:** 11849 Northport Dr, Florissant, MO 63033-6736.

NOBLE, JEFFREY V.
Company executive. **Personal:** Born in New York, NY; son of Bernice Harrall Noble and James Noble; children: Jeffrey Jr, Ranah. **Educ:** New York City Community College, New York, NY, AAS, 1974; Rochester Institute of Technology, Rochester, NY, BS, 1976. **Career:** Lithotronics Inc, White Plains, NY, sales executive, 1976-79; Quavice Press Inc, New York, NY, CEO/owner, 1979-. **Orgs:** Member, Community Board #10, 1989-; member, Board of Directors, CHAMP, 1988-.

NOBLE, JOHN CHARLES
Educational administrator. **Personal:** Born Sep 21, 1941, Port Gibson, MS; married Colleen L; children: Michaelle, Leketha, Carlos, Tracy, Stephanie. **Educ:** Claiborne Co Training Sch, 1959; Alcorn St U, bS 1962; TN A&I St U, MA 1971; Jackson St U. **Career:** Claiborne Co Schools, supt of educ, present; MS Chicago, teacher; Chicago, juvenile probation officer; Medgar Evers Comprehensive Health Center, dir research & evaluation; Opportunity Industrialization Center, instructor. **Orgs:** Omega Psi Phi; Am Assn of Sch Adminstgrs; fellow Inst of Politics; Rising Sun MB; chmn Bd trustees Hinds Jr Coll; bd trustee Utica Jr Coll; advanced ind instr Dr Thomas Gordons Parent Effectiveness Training & Tchr E Ffective Tng; Claiborn Co Chap NAACP; Port Gibson Masonic Lodge #21; bd dir MS Action for Progress; bd dir Urban League LEAP Prgm. **Business Addr:** Superintendent, Claiborne County Public School, PO Box 337, Port Gibson, MS 39150.

NOBLE, JOHN PRITCHARD
Administrator. **Personal:** Born May 31, 1931, West Palm Beach, FL; son of Aurelia Pritchard Noble and Floyd Grafton Noble; married Barbara Norwood, Aug 30, 1958; children: John Jr, Michael. **Educ:** FL A&M Univ, BS 1959; Columbia Univ NYC, MA Hosp Admin 1963; Cornell Univ Ithaca, attended 1969. **Career:** Arabian Amer Oil Co Dhahran Saudi Arabia, hosp admin 1962-69; Winston-Salem NC Hosp Authority, pres/chief exec officer 1969-71; Forsyth Hosp Authority Winston-Salem, vice pres planning & devel 1971-73; Homer G Phillips Hosp St Louis, admin 1973-78; Acute Care Hosp City of St Louis, dir 1978-79; Dept of Health & Hosp City of St Louis, hosp commr; Lambert-St Louis Intl Airport, asst dir. **Orgs:** Mem Amer Coll of Hosp Admins 1965-; mem Amer Pub Health Assn 1976-; chmn Natl Assn of Health Serv Exec 1978-80; bd mem Family & Children Serv 1977-; bd mem King Fanon Mental Health 1978-; life mem Alpha Phi Alpha Frat; bd mem Tower Village Nursing Home 1978-. **Honors/Awds:** Meritom Citation. **Military Serv:** USAF A/2C 1951-53. **Home Phone:** (314)367-6324. **Business Addr:** Assistant Dir, Lambert-St Louis Intl Airport, P O Box 10212, St Louis, MO 63145, (314)426-8034.

NOBLE, RONALD K.
Educator. **Personal:** Born in Fort Dix, NJ. **Educ:** University of New Hampshire; Stanford University law school. **Career:** US Dept of the Treasury, asst secretary, enforcement, undersecretary, enforcement, until 1996; New York University Law School, teacher, currently. **Special Achievements:** Highest ranking African American in the history of federal law enforcement, 1994. **Business Addr:** Professor, New York University School of Law, 40 Washington Square S, Rm 314, New York, NY 10012.

NOBLES, PATRICIA JOYCE
Attorney. **Personal:** Born Jun 16, 1955, St Louis, MO; daughter of Gwendolyn Bell Stovall and Henry Stovall. **Educ:** Southwest Baptist Coll, BA, 1976; Univ of AK, JD, 1981. **Career:** US District Judge, law clerk, 1981-83; Southwestern Bell Telephone Co, attorney, 1983-. **Orgs:** Mem of the executive bd, Urban League 1981-84; mem Amer Assoc of Trial Attorneys 1983-87; mem AK Bar Assn 1983-87; pres AK Assn of Women Lawyers 1985-86; mem of bd KLRE Public Radio Station 1986-87; mem NAACP 1989-; mem, Missouri Bar Assn, 1981-. **Honors/Awds:** Mem of UALR Law Review 1980-81; mem of 1988 Class of Leadership America; author with Alexander C. Larson, Calvin Manson, ''Competitive Necessity and Pricing In Telecommunications Regulation,'' Federal Communications Law Journal, 1989. **Business Addr:** Sr Attorney, Southwestern Bell Telephone Co, 1 Bell Plz, 201 S Arkard, Rm 2925, Dallas, TX 75202.

NOEL, GERALD T., SR.
Research physicist. **Personal:** Born Oct 10, 1934, Westchester, PA; son of Helen Madelyn Thomas Noel and Charles F Noel; married R Gail Walker, Mar 28, 1992; children: Gerald T Jr, Charles F, Owen R, Brandan J Walker. **Educ:** Drexel University, BS, physics, 1962; Temple University, MS, physics, 1965, PhD, course work solid state physics, 1966-68. **Career:** David Sarnoff Research Center, technical staff member, 1962-70; RCA Astro Electronics Division, engineering staff member, 1970-72; University of Pennsylvania, research staff member, 1972-77; Battelle Memorial Institute, senior research scientist, 1977-85, research leader, 1985-. **Orgs:** American Institute of Physics; Materials Research Society, 1985-; American Vacuum Society, 1984-; National Technical Association, board of directors, conference chairman, 1978-; Institute of Environmental Sciences, senior member, 1980-88; National Association of Blacks in Energy, 1989-; International Society for Hybrid Microelectronics, 1991-; IEEE Photovoltaic Specialists Conference Committee, 1976-89. **Honors/Awds:** National Technical Association, National Conference Chairman Award, 1990; Battelle Memorial Institute, Technolgy Commercialization Award, 1989. **Special Achievements:** Numerous publications in the fields of solar energy, microelectronic circuits, thin film materials and devices. **Military Serv:** US Navy, electronic tech 3, 1952-55. **Business Addr:** Research Leader, Battelle Memorial Institute, 505 King Ave, Columbus, OH 43201, (614)424-5862.

NOEL, PATRICK ADOLPHUS
Physician. **Personal:** Born Nov 9, 1940; married Evelyn Sebro; children: Carlita, Patrick Jr, John. **Educ:** Howard U, BS 1960-64; Howard U, MD 1964-68; Johns Hopking U, flwsp 1972; Howard U, resd 1969-73. **Career:** Pvt Prac, physician 1973-; Bowie State Coll, coll physician 1973-; Ortho Surgery Howard U, instr 1973-; Univ MD Coll Pk, consult 1973-76; Bowie State Coll Ftbl Team, orth consult 1973-76; Howard Univ Hosp, atdng surg; Leland Hosp; SSE Comm Hosp; Laurel Hosp. **Orgs:** Treas Soc of Hlth Profls of PG Co 1977; Flw of Intl Coll Surgeons 1974; Meritorious Serv Bowie State Coll 1976; mem Am Bd Orthopedic Surgery1974; flw Am Acad Ortho Surgery 1976. **Business Addr:** 8601 Martin Luther King Hwy, Lanham, MD 20706.

NOGUERA, PEDRO ANTONIO
Sociologist, educator. **Personal:** Born Aug 7, 1959, New York, NY; son of Millicent Yvonne Brooks Noguera and Felipe Carl Noguera; married Patricia Vattuone Noguera, Jul 6, 1982; children: Joaquin, Amaya, Antonio, Naima. **Educ:** Brown University, BA in sociology/American history, 1981, MA in sociology, 1982; University of California-Berkeley, PhD in sociology, 1989. **Career:** UC Berkeley, Course Instructor Dept, Ethnic Studies, 1983-84, Course Instructor, Dept of Sociology 1984-85; Goldberg & Assoc, Oakland CA, consultant, 1985; South Berkeley Youth Project, director, 1985-86; UC Berkeley, research specialist 1985-86; City of Berkeley, executive asst & mayor 1986-88; University of California-Berkeley, Berkeley, CA, assistant to the vice chancellor, 1988-89, coordinator of multicultural action team, 1989-90, assistant professor, 1990-. **Orgs:** Vice pres Berkeley Black Caucus 1985-; bd mem, Daily California Newpaper 1985-88; mem congressman Dellums Executive Committee, 1986-; pres Black Men United for Change, 1987-90; bd mem Berkeley YMCA, 1988-; board of directors, Berkeley Unified School District, 1990-; American Sociological Association; South African Education Fund, board of directors; South Berkeley Neighborhood Development Corporation, board of directors; Caribbean Studies Association; Berkeley Community Foundation, board of directors. **Honors/Awds:** Brown University, Teaching Assistant Prize, 1981; Samuel P Lambert Prize for Advanced International Understanding in Sociology, 1981; Rhodes Scholar Finalist, Rhode Island 1981; Elected Chairman Graduate Assembly UC Berkeley 1984-85; Elected President Associated Student UC Berkeley 1985-86; Fulbright Fellowship Recipient 1987-88; San Francisco Foundation School Improvement Research Award, 1992; Eisenhower Mathematics, Engineering and Science Award, 1993. **Special Achievements:** ''Tracking as a Form of Second Generation Discrimination and Its Impact on the Education of Latino Students,'' La Raza Law Journal, Spring 1995; ''Taking Chances, Taking Charge: A Report on a Drug Abuse Intervention Strategy Conceived, Created and Controlled by a Community,'' International Quarterly of Community Health Education, Spring 1995; ''Education and Popular Culture in the Caribbean: Youth Resistance in a Period of Economic Uncertainty,'' in Cultures in Transition: Latin America the Caribbean and Canada, Carleton University Press, 1995; ''Ties That Bind, Forces That Divide: Confronting the Challenge of Integration Forty Years After Brown,'' University of San Francisco Law Review, Spring 1995; ''Preventing Violence in Schools,'' Harvard Educational Review, 1995. Author, The Imperatives of Power: Regime Survival and the Sound Basis of Political Support in Grenada, 1951-1991. Pettier Lang Publisher, 1997. **Business Addr:** Assistant Professor, 4513 Tolman Hall, University of California-Berkeley, Berkeley, CA 94720, (510)642-1493.

NOISETTE, RUFFIN N.
Association representative. **Personal:** Born Mar 20, 1923, Summerville, SC; son of Louise Noisette and Joseph Noisette; married Thelma Anderson; children: Shelley, Karin, Robin, Louis. **Educ:** Howard U, AB 1946; Howard U, BD 1949. **Career:** Fisk Univ Nashville, asst to dean of chapel 1949-50; Ebenezer African Meth Episcopal Ch Rahway NJ, pastor 1950-51; Bethel African Meth Episcopal Ch Wilmington DE, pastor 1951-65; Delaware OEO, dep dir 1965; EI Dupont De Nemours & Co, professional staffing consultant 1965-85; Emily P Bissell Hosp Wilmington DE, chaplain 1986-92. **Orgs:** Mem Eastern Coll Personnel Officers 1970-; mem DE Personnel & Guidance Assn 1968; mem bd dir YMCA Wilmington DE; Boys Club of Wilmington; Opportunity Center Inc; Golden Beacon Coll; DE Council on Crime & Justice Inc; mem New Castle County Bd of Elections; mem bd of trustees DE State Coll Dover DE. **Hon-**

ors/Awds: Citizenship Award Alpha Phi Alpha 1959; Meritorious Serv Award YMCA 1964; Recruiter of Year Award LaSalle Coll 1973; Black Heritage Disting Serv Awd 1981; Delaware State Univ Div of Student Affairs, Outstanding Services Award, 1984; Wilberforce University of Ohio, Honorary Doctorate Degree; Delaware State University Trustee, Meritorious Service Award, 1997. **Home Addr:** 2659 Amesbury Rd, Winston-Salem, NC 27103.

NOLES, EVA M.
Nurse, educator (retired). **Personal:** Born Apr 5, 1919, Cleveland, OH; daughter of Ola Neal Bateman (deceased) and Charles Bateman (deceased); married Douglas Noles; children: Tyrone M. **Educ:** EJ Meyer Memorial Hosp Sch of Nursing, RN 1940; Nursing Univ of Buffalo, BS 1962; State Univ of NY at Buffalo, MEd 1967. **Career:** Roswell Pk Meml Inst, staff nurse & head nurse 1945-63, instr of nsg & asst dir of nsg 1963-68; State Univ of NY at Buffalo, clin assoc prof of nsg 1970-77; Roswell Pk Meml Inst, ret chief of nsg servs & training 1971-74; EJ Meyer Meml Hosp, coord fam planning nrs practitioner prog 1974-77; MedPersonnel Pool Inc, home care super/staff development 1977-84 (retired). **Orgs:** Mem NY State Nrs Assn, Amer Nrs Assn 1941-; mem (charter) External Deg in Nrsg NY State 1971-75; mem NY State Bd for Nrsg 1972-92; comm adv council State Univ of NY at Buffalo 1975-; chmn Nsg & Health Serv ARC Gtr Buffalo Chap 1978-84; bd of govs Comm Mental Health Ctr Buffalo NY 1979-; bd of dirs ARC; bd of trustees Buffalo General Hosp; bd of dirs Boys & Girls Clubs of Buffalo and Erie Co 1985; board of directors, American Cancer Society, 1965-. **Honors/Awds:** First African-American nurse educated in Buffalo NY EJ Meyer Meml Hosp 1936-40; Disting Service Awd for Outstanding Achievement in Public Health NY 1972; Disting Awd AAUW 1972; publ "Six Decades of Nursing 1914-1974"; Roswell Park Meml Inst 1975; Certificate of Merit ARC Greater Buffalo Chapt; Community Awds for Display "Buffalo Blacks-Talking Proud" 1986; published Buffalo's Blacks "Talking Proud" 1987; published Black History-A Different Approach; author, The Church Builder: The Life of Bishop Charles N McCoy, 1990. **Home Addr:** 780 Maryvale Dr, Buffalo, NY 14225.

NOONAN, ALLAN S.
Physician, state government official. **Career:** New York State Health Department, associate commissioner; Commonwealth of Pennsylvania, secretary of health, currently. **Business Addr:** Secretary of Health, Commonwealth of Pennsylvania, Health & Welfare Bldg, Room 802, Box 90, Harrisburg, PA 17120, (717)787-6436.

NOR, GENGHIS
Musician, educator. **Personal:** Born Jan 31, 1946, Brooklyn, NY; son of Esperanza V Strong and Thomas C Strong; married Laksmi Abdullah Nor; children: Selim Tahir, Amira Sakinah, Jibrail I'svar, Muhaimin Jaleel, Nisreen Ihsaan, Laila Saudah. **Educ:** State Univ of NY, BA 1971; Wesleyan Univ, MA 1978; various studies in trumpet, music theory & composition. **Career:** Genghis Nor & MAGIC, musician/composer/leader; Strong-Light Incorp, prdcr promoter; New York City Board of Education, Brooklyn, NY, music teacher, 1984-; Charli Persip's Supersound, New York, NY, featured soloist, 1985-; "Eric Frazier Sextet," New York, featured soloist, 1996-. **Orgs:** Mem past v chmn pres & pres adv State Univ Freedom Cncl; member, International Trumpet Guild, 1990-; board of directors, Bedford-Stuyvesant Carter Cadets Alumni Assn, 1990-; member, Local 802, American Federation of Musicians, 1988-; United Federation of Teachers, 1985-. **Home Addr:** 1240 Pacific St, Brooklyn, NY 11216, (718)756-3284.

NORFLEET, JANET
Postmaster (retired). **Personal:** Born Aug 14, 1933, Chicago, IL; daughter of Blanche Gilbert Richards and Willis Richards; married Junious Norfleet; children: Cedric Williams. **Educ:** Olive Harvey Coll, AA 1977. **Career:** US Postal Service, supt of customer serv reps, public affairs officer, mgr of retail sales and svcs, mgr of delivery and collection, mgr North Suburban IL mgmt sect ctr, field div mgr/postmaster South Suburban IL div, field div gen mgr; postmaster Chicago Illinois Div, retired. **Orgs:** Mem bd of dir Carson Pirie Scott & Co 1988-; board member, Red Cross; board member, Federal Executive. **Honors/Awds:** First Woman Postmaster of the US Postal Serv Chicago Div; Partnership For Progress Awd Postmaster General TISCH 1986; Appointment Congressional Records by Congressman Savage 1987; Proclamation by Mayor Washington Janet Norfleet Day in Chicago 1987; American Black Achievement Award for Business and Professions, Johnson Publications, 1987; African-American Award for Business and Professional Women, Dollars & Sense Magazine, 1989; Women's Hall of Fame, City of Chicago, 1990. **Home Addr:** 8217 S Evans Ave, Chicago, IL 60619-5305.

NORMAN, ALEX JAMES
Educator. **Personal:** Born Jul 2, 1931, Atlanta, GA; married Margaret Lawrence; children: Alex III, Keri Casady, Wendi Casady. **Educ:** Morris Brown College, AB 1957; Atlanta Univ, MSW 1959; Univ Of CLA School of Social Welfare, DSW 1974. **Career:** USEEOc, investigations supervisor 1967-69; Univ of CLA Extention, dir urban affairs 1969-73; Univ of CLA, acting assoc prof 1975-79; Univ of CLA, assoc prof 1979-. **Orgs:** Charter member Academy of Certified Social Workers 1960-; founder/dir Jenesse Ctr Inc 1980-83; dir Crittenton Center, Inc 1983; dir Future Homemakers of Amer 1984; charter member Cert Consultants Intrnl 1984; mem Assn of Black Social Workers. **Honors/Awds:** Distinguished Educ Assn of Black Social Workers 1981. **Military Serv:** USAF sgt 1949-52; Good Conduct, Presidential Unit Citation, Korean Medal, Dist Serv 1950-52.

NORMAN, BOBBY DON
Artist, tectonic analyst. **Personal:** Born Jun 5, 1933, Dallas, TX; son of Bessie Taylor Gregory and Ruben Norman; divorced; children: Parette Michelle Barnes. **Educ:** San Francisco City Coll, 1950-51; USAF, Radio Electronics Tech 1951-55; SW Sch Bus Admin, Certificate 1956-59. **Career:** Mile High Club Restaurant & Cabins, gen mgr, 1955-57; D H Byrd Properties, property mgr, 1957-65; US Post Office, distribution clerk, 1957-67; Univ Chicago-Dallas, National Opinion Research Center, field evaluation researcher 1969-70; AAAW, Inc Cultural Gallery, dir 1972; SCLC Dallas, TX, co-founder ofc mgr, co-dir 1970-72; PPANET, Inc, comm liaison developer 1974-76; Davis Norman Zanders Inc, vice pres & gen mgr 1976-77; free-lance artist & inventor anti-collision car; self-employed tectonic analyst, 1988-. **Orgs:** Pres, Forest Lakes Sportsmans Club; hunter safety instructor, NRA, 1963; pres & founder, Assn Advancing Artists & Writers 1969-74; commissioner Greater Dallas Community Relations Cmsn 1970-73; organizer & tech consult Greater DFW Coalition FFI 1971-74; alumnus Chi Rho Intrnl Business Frat; committeeman Block Partnership Comm of the Greater Dallas Council of Churches 1971-72; public speaking mem Intl Platform Assoc 1977-78. **Honors/Awds:** Citizenship training SCLC 1969; service GDCRC 1973; fine arts Dallas Black Chamber of Commerce 1973; leadership service Assoc Advancing Artists & Writers 1973. **Military Serv:** USAF corpl 1951-55; Korean Service Mdl, UN Service Mdl Good Conduct Mdl Nat Defense Mdl. **Business Addr:** Artist & Inventor, 914 62nd St, Oakland, CA 94608.

NORMAN, CALVIN HAINES
Physician. **Personal:** Born Sep 14, 1923, Jamaica, NY; married Ruth Elizabeth Gordon; children: Calvin H III, Robert Gregory, Wendy Beth. **Educ:** NC Coll, BS 1952; Howard Univ, MD 1956; Columbia Univ, MPH 1961, FACR 1980. **Career:** Downstate Med Ctr, instr 1964; VA Hosp, attending radiologist 1964; Kate Bitting Reynolds Hosp, attending radiologist 1965-69; Bowman Grey Sch of Med, instr 1968; St Mary's Hosp, attending radiologist dir radiology 1969-84; Medical Comprehensive Health Prog, 1969; Downstate Medical Ctr, asst prof 1970-;MIH, attending radiologist 1984-. **Orgs:** Pres, vice pres, sec-treas, exec com mem Brooklyn Radiol Soc 1971-75; pres med bd St Mary's Hosp 1975-76; treas med bd Cath Med Ctr 1975; pres elect med bd St Mary's Hosp 1978; mem Kings Co, NY State Medical Soc; mem AMA. **Honors/Awds:** Natl Medical Assn Fellow Columbia Univ 1960; Alpha Kappa Mu Natl Honor Soc 1952; Beta Kappa Chi Honor Sci Soc 1951; articles published Nephrocalcinosis; Pycnodysostosis; Chronic Subdural Hematoma; Retroperitoneal Mesenteric Cyst; Multiple Ureteral Diverticula. **Military Serv:** AUS sgt 1940-43; USAF, USAFR maj 1957-64.

NORMAN, CLIFFORD P.
Business executive. **Personal:** Born Mar 22, 1943, Detroit, MI; son of Claudia Cloud Norman and Leavi Norman; married Pauline C Johnson; children: Jays S, Rebecca L. **Educ:** Wayne State Univ, BA 1974, MA 1980. **Career:** Fisher Body Div GM, engr test 1967-71, sr analyst qc 1971-72, sr srv & tool spec 1972-74, div process engr 1974-76; Ford Motor Co, div staff engr 1976-80; Glasurit Amer Inc, acct exec; BASF Corp, account executive, currently. **Orgs:** Mem ESD 1975-; mem Soc of Engr & Applied Sciences 1975-82; exec comm BB/BSA 1981-; mem Budget & Allocation Comm UCS Detroit, 1981-84, 1995-; chr Nominating comm BB/BS Detroit 1980-; u-f Speakers Bureau 1985-. **Honors/Awds:** One In A Million WDME Radio Detroit 1976. **Military Serv:** USAF a/2c, 1963. **Business Addr:** BASF, 26701 Telegraph Rd, Southfield, MI 48034-2442, (248)304-5771.

NORMAN, GEORGETTE M.
Educator, consultant. **Personal:** Born Jan 27, 1946, Montgomery, AL; daughter of Thelma Juliette Graham Norman and George J Norman. **Educ:** Fisk University, Nashville, TN, BA, 1967; Hampton Institute, Hampton VA, MA, 1970. **Career:** Virgin Islands Library, St Croix, VI, program planner, NEH project, 1980-81; College of Virgin Islands, St Croix, VI, adjunct professor, 1980-85; Southern Poverty Law Center, Montgomery, AL, information analyst, data processor, 1987-89; Auburn University of Montgomery, AL, adjunct professor drama dept, 1987-; Federation of Child Care Centers of Alabama, Montgomery, AL, special consultant, coordinating black women's project, 1990-; The Eight-Thirty House, currently. **Orgs:** Board of directors, secretary, Springtree/Snowhill Institute for Performing Arts, 1989-; board of directors, Alabama Jazz Federation, 1991; board of directors, chair, Homeowner Assn Montgomery Habitat for Humanity, 19871-; panel mem, Literature & Rural Initiative Alabama State Council on Arts, 1988-; advisory board, multicultural chair, Armory Learning Center for Performing Arts, 1991; member, Leadership Montgomery Alumni Assn, 1987-; American Arts Allicance, 1992-. **Honors/Awds:** Citizen of Year St Croix, Rotary Club West, 1984; Teacher of the Year, St Joseph the Worker Catholic High, 1982; Regional Grant for Theater Productions Womanrise: Her Story/Her Self, American Assn University Women, 1981; Teacher of Year, Claude O Markoe Jr High, 1974. **Business Addr:** The Eight-Thirty House, 830 S Court St, Montgomery, AL 36104, (334)263-2787.

NORMAN, JAMES H.
Public administrator. **Personal:** Born Aug 14, 1948, Augusta, GA; son of Janie M King Norman (deceased) and Silas Norman, Sr (deceased); children: James H Jr. **Educ:** Mercer Univ Macon GA, AB Psych 1970; Western MI Univ Kalamazoo, MSW 1972. **Career:** Douglass Comm Assc Kalamazoo MI, coord job dev & placement 1972-74; Klamazoo MI Publ Schls, parent consult 1974-75; Oakland Livingston Human Srvs, Pontiac MI div mgr comm dev 1975-78; MI Dept of Labor, dir bureau of comm srv 1978-87; MI Dept of Labor, deputy dir, 1987-92; Action For a Better Community, executive director. **Orgs:** Chrmn & leg comm chr Natl Assc for State Comm Srv Prog 1981-82, 1985-87; exec secr MI Econ & Social Opp Commission 1983-87; life mem NAACP; mem Assc of Black Soc Workers; mem Phi Mu Alpha Natl Music Frat; mem amer Soc for Public Admin 1984-; mem Assoc of State Govt Execs 1986-92; mem Omega Psi Phi Frat Inc; life mem Western Michigan Univ Alumni Assoc; mem Natl Council of State Building Code Officials 1988-90; mem International Assn of Personnel in Employment Security 1988-90; bd mem MI Assn of Black Organizations 1988-92; mem Greater Lansing Urgan League 1989-92; advisory council member, EOC, SUNY, 1993-; advisory council, Leadership Rochester, 1993-. **Honors/Awds:** Outstanding Young Man of Amer US Jaycees Publ 1978, 1979; Comm Srv Award Natl Alliance of Businessmen 1973, 1974; Full Univ Grad Flwshp Western MI Univ 1970-72; srv award Natl Assc for State Comm Srv Prog 1983; Wall of Distinction Western MI Univ 1980. **Business Addr:** Executive Director, Action For a Better Community, 244 S Plymouth, Rochester, NY 14608.

NORMAN, JESSYE
Singer. **Personal:** Born Sep 15, 1945, Augusta, GA; daughter of Janie King Norman and Silas Norman Sr. **Educ:** Howard Univ, BM (Cum Laude) 1967; Peabody Conservatory Music, 1967; Univ MI, MMus 1968. **Career:** Deutsch Opera Berlin, debut 1969; Deutsch Opera Italy 1970; appeared in operas Die Walkure, Idomeneo, L'Africaine, Marriage of Figaro, Aida, Don Giovanni, Tannhauser, Gotterdammerung, Ariadne auf Naxos, Les Troyens, Dido and Aeneas, Oedipus Rex; La Scala Milan, Italy, 1972; Salzburg Festival 1977; Hollywood Bowl, US debut 1972; appeared with Tanglewood Festival MA, Edinburgh, Scotland Festival; Covent Garden, 1972; appeared in 1st Great Performers Recital Lincoln Center New York City 1973; guest performances incl, Los Angeles Philharmonic Orch, Boston Symphony Orch, Amer Symphony Orch, Chicago Symphony Orch, San Fran Symphony Orch, Cleve Orch, Detroit Symphony, NY Philharmonic Orch, London Symphony Orch, London Philharmonic Orch, BBC Orch, Israel Philharmonic Orch, Orchestre de Paris, ional Symphony Orch Australia. **Orgs:** Mem Gamma Sigma Sigma, Sigma Alpha Iota, Pi Kappa Lambda. **Honors/Awds:** Numerous recordings Columbia, EMI, Philips Records; recip 1st Prize Bavarian Radio Corp Intl Music Competitor; Grand Prix du Disque Deutsch Schallplatten; Preis Alumniat MI 1982; Outstanding Musician of the Yr Award, Musical Am, 1982; 5 Grand Prix du Disque, Acad du Disque Francais; Grand Prix du Disque, Academie Charles Cros 1983; Honorary Doctor of Music, Howard Univ, 1982; Honorary Doctor of Humane Letters, Amer Univ of Paris, 1989; Honorary Doctor of Music, Cambridge Univ, 1989; Honorary Fellow, Newnham Coll, Cambridge, 1989; Honorary Fellow, Jesus Coll, Cambridge, 1989; Musician of the Year, High Fidelity Musical/America, 1982; Grammy Awards, 1984, 1988; Council of Fashion Designers of America, Women of the Arts Award, 1992. **Business Addr:** Soprano Concert & Opera Singer, Shaw Concerts Inc, 130 W 57th St Apt 8-G, New York, NY 10019-3311.

NORMAN, KENNETH DARNEL (SNAKE)
Professional basketball player. **Personal:** Born Sep 5, 1964, Chicago, IL. **Educ:** Wabash Valley College, Mt Carmel, IL, 1982-83; Univ of Illinois, Champaign, IL, 1984-87. **Career:** Los Angeles Clippers, 1987-93; Milwaukee Bucks, 1993-94; Atlanta Hawks, 1994-. **Business Addr:** Professional Basketball Player, Atlanta Hawks, 1 CNN Center NW S Tower, Ste 405, Atlanta, GA 30335.

NORMAN, MAIDIE RUTH. **See Obituaries section.**

NORMAN, MOSES C.
Association executive. **Career:** Omega Psi Phi, Washington DC, grand basileus. **Business Addr:** Omega Psi Phi, 3951 Snapfinger Pky, Decatur, GA 30035-3203.

NORMAN, P. ROOSEVELT
Dentist. **Personal:** Born Sep 8, 1933, Mound Bayou, MS; married DeLois Williams; children: Philippa J, David W. **Educ:** Tougaloo Clg, BS 1955; Meharry Med Clg, DDS 1959. **Career:** Pvt Prac, dentist; Babe Ruth Leag Baseball Coach; Mound Bayou Comm Hosp, dental cons; Frances Nelson Hlth Ctr, adv cons; Union Med Cntr Dental Serv, formerly co-dir; Gen Dentistry Malcom Grow Reg Med Cntr USAF, ofcr in charge; Sheppard AFB TX, preventive dentistry ofcr; Misawa AFB Japan, air base oral surgeon; VA Hosp Tuskeegee, rotating dental internship. **Orgs:** Mem Natl Dental Assc; Am Dental Assc; Acad of Gen Diewntistry; Am Soc Of Preventive Dentistry; Am Endodontic Soc; Military Surgeons Assc; LicensedPrac in IL, TX, DC, MD, NH, PA, MS; mem Omega Psi Phi Frat; Champaign Co C of C; Neighborhood Commnr Boy Scouts of Am; Career Cnslg HS; bd dir Boys Clb of Am Champaign Co; Univ Dental Rsrch Team. **Honors/Awds:** Recip music schlrshp; Athletic Schlrshp; mosby schlrshp awrd for Scholastic Excellance. **Military Serv:** USAF; presently serving USAFR maj. **Business Addr:** P O Box 2808 Station A, Champaign, IL 61820.

NORMAN, PATRICIA
Business executive. **Personal:** Born Sep 3, 1947, New York, NY. **Educ:** St John's Univ Jr College, AAS 1964-66; St John's Univ College of Business Admin, BS 1968-75. **Career:** North General Hospital, Asst Dir of Finance, Comptroller. **Orgs:** Advanced member Healthcare Financial Management Assoc. **Business Addr:** Hospital Comptroller, North General Hospital, 1919 Madison Ave, New York, NY 10035.

NORMAN, WALLACE
Controller. **Personal:** Born 1961, Atlanta, GA. **Educ:** Univ of Georgia, political science degree, MBA (finance); Georgia State Univ, master's program, accounting. **Career:** Federal Express, associate financial analyst; Atlanta Falcons, controller, 1989-. **Honors/Awds:** First minority controller in NFL. **Business Addr:** Controller, Atlanta Falcons, Suwanee Rd & I-85, Suwanee, GA 30174.

NORMAN, WILLIAM H.
Psychologist. **Personal:** Born Dec 14, 1946, Sharon, PA; married Belinda Ann Johnson; children: Monica, Michael. **Educ:** Youngstown State Univ, BA 1968; Howard Univ, MS 1971; Duke Univ Medical Center, psychology internship, 1974-75; Pennsylvania State Univ PhD 1975. **Career:** Butler Hospital, dir of psychological consultation program 1976-93, dir of psychology 1982-91, coord, eating disorders program, 1987-; Brown Univ Internship Consortium, coord adult clinical psychology track comm 1983-92; Brown Univ Medical School, associate prof of psychiatry and human behavior, 1986-. **Orgs:** Mem, Amer Psychological Assn 1975-, Assn for the Advancement of Behavior Therapy 1975-, Soc for Psychotherapy Rsch 1986-. **Honors/Awds:** Reviewer for several journals including Journal of Abnormal Psychology and Journal of Consulting and Clinical Psychology; Master of Arts ad eundem Brown Univ 1987; recipient/co-recipient of Natl Inst of Health grants, 1979, 1981, 1983, 1990, 1992. **Business Addr:** Coordinator, Eating Disorders Program, Butler Hospital, 345 Blackstone Blvd, Providence, RI 02906.

NORMAN, WILLIAM S.
Travel and tourism official. **Personal:** Born Apr 27, 1938, Roper, NC; son of Josephine Cleo Woods Norman and James Colbitt Norman; married Elizabeth Patricia Patterson, May 31, 1969; children: Lisa Renee, William Stanley, II. **Educ:** West Virginia Wesleyan University, BS, 1960; American University, MA, 1967; Stanford University, executive program, 1976. **Career:** Washington High School, Norfolk, VA, teacher, 1961; Cummins Engine Co, Inc, Columbus, IN, director of corporate action, 1973-74, exec director of corporate responsibility, 1974-76, executive director of distribution and marketing, 1976-78, vp of eastern division, 1978-79; Amtrak, Washington, DC, vp of sales and marketing, 1979-81, group vp, 1981-84, exec vp, 1984-94; Travel Industry Assn of Amer, Washington DC, pres and CEO, 1994-; CPC International Inc, bd of dirs, 1993-; Logistics Management Inst, bd of trustees, 1993-; Amer Univ Kogod Coll of Bus Admin, bd of advisors, 1990-. **Orgs:** Board of directors, US Navy Memorial Foundation, 1980-; board of directors, Travelers Aid International, 1988-; board of governors, United Nations Association of the United States, 1983-; board of directors, Travel and Tourism Government Affairs Council, 1987-; chairman of the board, Travel Industry Foundation, 1989-; Travel Industry Association of America, board of directors, 1987. **Military Serv:** US Navy, Lt Cmdr, 1962-73; US Navy Reserves, Capt, currently. **Business Addr:** President & CEO, Travel Industry Assn of America, 1100 New York Ave, NW, Washington, DC 20005-3934.

NORMENT, HANLEY. **See Obituaries section.**

NORRELL-NANCE, ROSALIND ELIZABETH
City official. **Personal:** Born May 17, 1950, Atlantic City, NJ; daughter of Vivian M Rhoades-Norrell and Albert V Norrell, Jr; married Nelson W. Nance; children: Kimberly, Alisha, Nelson Jr., Antonio, Noel, Patrick. **Educ:** Hampton Inst 1967-69; Atlantic Comm Coll, AS, 1974-76; Glassboro State Coll, BA, 1976-78. **Career:** Pleasantville Sch Dist, educator 1976-84; City of Atlantic City, mayoral aide, 1984-90; Atlantic City, councilwoman, 1992-, 1994-97, president; Atlantic City Public Schools, Drug & Weapon Free Schools Program, 1991-96; Atlanticare Family Center, director, 1997. **Orgs:** Exec bd/youth advisor Atlantic City NAACP 1969-95; bd of dirs Atlantic Human Resources Inc 1981-97; mem natl Sor of Phi Delta Kappa Delta Lambda Chap 1982-; govtl affairs chairperson 101 Women Plus 1982-85; bd of dirs Minority Entrepreneur Develop Co 1984-85; bd of dirs United Way of S Jersey 1984-85 bd of dirs Black United Fund of NJ 1987; vice pres, bd of dir, Institute for Human Development; bd of dirs Atlantic City Coastal Museum 1985-89; mem NJ State Business & Professional Women; bd dir Atlantic Human Resources; chairperson Atlantic Co Comprehensive Network Task Force on Homeless Svcs; Atlantic City Publ Rel Adv Bd; mem Natl Cncl of Colored Women's Clubs; bd dir Atlantic Community Concerts 1984-87; mem Ruth Newman Shapiro Cancer Fund; bd of dir Atlantic City Local Assistance; mem Healthy Mothers/Healthy Babies Coalition of Atlantic City Hampton Alumni Assoc; president mayor's youth adv bd, chair educ task force Congressional Black Caucus; mem NJ State Division of Youth & Family Services Advisory bd 1985-; bd of dir Coalition of 100 Black Women 1987-; Atlantic County Red Cross 1988-92; founder Atlantic County Welfare Mothers Support Group 1992-; mem, Atlantic County Human Serv Advisory Bd; Atlantic City Drug Alliance, 1990-; Atlantic County Transportation Authority, board of directors, 1986-92; Atlantic City Inc, 1994-; Links Inc, 1995-. **Honors/Awds:** Comm Serv Awd West Side Parent Adv Council 1976; Outstanding Leadership Black Atlantic City Magazine 1983; NJ Div. of Youth & Family Service, Phi Delta Kappa-Leadership, 1995. **Home Addr:** 1105 Adriatic Ave, Atlantic City, NJ 08401. **Business Addr:** Council President, City of Atlantic City, 1301 Bacharach Blvd, Suite 311, Atlantic City, NJ 08401.

NORRELL-THOMAS, SONDRA
Educational administrator. **Personal:** Born May 31, 1941, Richmond, VA; daughter of Faith M Norrell and Edinboro A Norrell; married Chauncey S Thomas, Jun 1, 1978. **Educ:** Hampton Inst, BS 1961; Howard Univ, MS 1973. **Career:** Charlottesville Schools, teacher 1961-63; Richmond Public Schools, teacher 1963-64; Howard Univ, teacher 1964-77, assoc dir of athletics 1977-86, exec asst to vice pres for student affairs 1986-. **Orgs:** Mem Special Comm on Women's Interest NCAA 1983-85; council Natl Collegiate Athletic Assoc 1983-87; Division I Steering Comm (1st Black) NCAA 1983-87; special liasion Mid-Eastern Athletic Conference 1983-; past pres, Capital City Chapter, The Links Inc 1987-89; mem Alpha Kappa Alpha Sor, HUAA, NCNW, NAACP; NCAA Council (1995-1999) representing Division I; United Way of the District of Columbia Board; Consultant, Council of President/ Chancellors of the MEAC. **Honors/Awds:** Resolution for Outstanding Contribution to Athletic and Community as a Woman in Male-Dominated field DC City Council 1983. **Special Achievements:** First female inducted into the Mid-Eastern Athletic Conference (MEAC) Hall of Fame, 1993. **Business Addr:** Executive Assistant to Vice President of Student Affairs, Howard University, 2400 6th St NW Room 201, Washington, DC 20059, (202)806-2100.

NORRIS, ARTHUR MAE
Educator (retired). **Personal:** Born Oct 7, 1911, Montgomery, AL; married Albert. **Educ:** AL St U, BA, MEd; Gould Acad, Post Grad; Tuskegee Inst; Univ of AL. **Career:** Teacher, principal (retired). **Orgs:** Natl pres Sup Basileus; Natl Sor of Phi Delta Kappa Inc; 1st vice pres AL Fed of Womens Clbs; chmn Juvenile Prot Com; AL Cong of Parents & Tchrs; E Montgomery Dist Dir of Christ Ed; chmn Deserving Yth Com; Cleveland Ave YMCA; bd dir Com Action; mem Crim Just; bd Am Red Cross Bd; St Adv Com for Child & Yth; bd of dir Tumbling Waters Flay Mus; bd of dir Montgomery Area on Aging; bd of dir Black Caucus on Aging; Citizens Part Grp for Montgomery. **Honors/Awds:** Achievement Award Phi Delta Kappa Sor Inc; Achievement Award AL Assc of Womens Clbs; Distinguished Service Award Alpha Delta PDK; Unit Appeal Award Cent Anniv Award; AL St U; Certificate of Merit & Apprec Emancip Proc Celebrat Com.

NORRIS, CHARLES L., SR.
Cleric. **Personal:** Born Aug 14, 1926, Williston, SC; married Ruby Dent; children: Keith, Charles Jr. **Educ:** National Theological Seminary, BS, 1979, MDiv, 1984; Blanton Peale Institute, certificate in counseling. **Career:** Kitchen Modernization, prod mgr 1950-69; Bethesda Missionary Baptist Church, pastor, 1973-. **Orgs:** The City of New York Commission on Human Rights, 1993-; Eastern Baptist Association of Long Island Inc, vice moderator; Concerned Citizens of South Queens, co-chair, 1986-; United Negro College Fund Clergy Consortium of Queens County, 1985-; New York City Mission Society Urban Ministries, 1981-. **Honors/Awds:** Inwood-Nassau Community Health Committee, Leadership & Dedication Award, 1981; National Association of Negro Business & Professional Women Queensborough Club, Outstanding Clergy Award, 1983; United Negro College Fund, Meritorious Service Award, 1985, Outstanding Leadership and Dedicated Service, 1986. **Business Addr:** 179 09 Jamaica Ave, Jamaica, NY 11432, (718)297-5908.

NORRIS, CYNTHIA CLARICE
Educational administrator. **Personal:** Born Nov 16, 1956, Baltimore, MD; daughter of Clarice Gee Norris-Barnes and Robert John Norris, Sr; divorced. **Educ:** Coll of Notre Dame, BA French Religious Studies, 1978; St Mary's Ecumenical Institute, MA Theology, 1986; Leadership Greater Chicago, Fellowship Program, 1989. **Career:** St Bernardine Church, dir of religious educ, 1978-85; Natl Office of Black Catholics, consultant, 1981-85; Silver Burdett Publishing Co, religion consultant, 1984-; Archdiocese of Chicago, executive dir, 1985-90; Montay College, transfer center director, 1990-. **Orgs:** Mem, Regional Coordinator, 1984-; Natl Assn Black Admin, ex committee 1987-; mem League of Black Women 1986-; mem, Natl Assn Female Executives, 1986-. **Honors/Awds:** Evangelization in the Black Community, profile; Unraveling the Evangelical Cord, filmstrip; Search for Black Catholic Identity: If Rivers Could Speak, filmstrip; Contributing Columnist, In A Word (monthly newsletter), The Chicago Catholic (weekly newspaper).

NORRIS, DONNA M.
Psychiatrist. **Personal:** Born May 28, 1943, Columbus, OH; married Dr Lonnie H Norris; children: Marlaina, Michael. **Educ:** Fisk Univ Nashville TN, BA 1964; OH State Univ Clge of Medicine, MD 1969; Mt Carmel Medical Ctr Columbus OH, internship 1970; Boston Univ Med Ctr, residency 1972; Childrens Hosp Judge Baker Guidance Ctr 1974. **Career:** MA Rehab Comm Roxbury & Quincy MA, psych consult 1974-79; Boston Juvenile Court Clinic, sr psych 1974-88; Harvard Med Schl, instr psych 1974-; asst psych 1974-83; Family Srv Assc of Greater Boston, med dir 1981-89; Children's Hosp Med Ctr & Judge Baker Guidance Ctr, assc in psych 1983-. **Orgs:** Amer Acad of Child Psych 1974-; American Psych Association, fellow, 1985-; Black Psych of Amer; Soroptomist Assn 1985-89; Links Inc, Middle Clearwater Chapter, 1988-; Jack & Jill of Amer 1978-; staff consult Levison Inst 1981-; Falk Flwshp 1973-75; Exec Comm & Steering Comm to plan Conf on Psych Educ 1974-75; Task Force of Films 1975-77; edit bd Psych Educ, Prologue to the 1980s 1976-; Committee on Women 1976-79; edit newsletter Comm on Women 1977-79; Spouses Sub-comm 1977-78; Minority Deputy Rep to Leg Assembly of Amer Psych Assc 1981-83; Minority Rep to Leg Assembly of Amer Psych Assn 1983-; Task Force on Membership Non-participation 1983-85; Comm of Black Psych Amer Psych Assn 1984-; Site Visitor Ach Awards Bd 1984; MA Psych Society Boston 1973-; Ethic Committee, 1978-88; American Academy of Child Psych, 1974-; Rep to MA CoMrthopsychiatric Assn Inc 1983-; senior Massachusetts representative, legislative Assembly for the Amer Psychiatric Assn, 1986-; chp, membership committee, Amer Psychiatric Assn, 1990-91; Massachusetts Board of Registration in Medicine, 1988-91; Board of Trustees, University of Lowell, 1987-88. **Honors/Awds:** Falk Fnd Amer Psych Assc 1973-75; Amer Bds of Psych & Neurology 1978. **Business Addr:** Children's Hospital Medical Center, 300 Longwood Ave, Boston, MA 02115.

NORRIS, ETHEL MAUREEN
Educator. **Personal:** Born Mar 3, 1956, Petersburg, VA; daughter of Marie Perry Norris and Dr Granville M Norris. **Educ:** East Carolina Univ, B Mus 1977; OH State Univ, MA 1978; summer study, Westminster Choir Coll 1985-86; Ohio State Univ, doctoral study in music history 1987-; Ohio State Univ, PhD, 1994. **Career:** St Pauls Coll, instructor of music; Virginia State Univ, asst prof of music, currently. **Orgs:** Instr Piano Lessons 1979-; mem Sigma Alpha Iota, Coll Music Soc, Amer Guild of Organists, Phi Kappa Phi; Sonneck Society. **Honors/Awds:** Finalist Natl Achievement Scholarship Program for Outstanding Negro Students 1973; One-Year Minority Fellowship OH State Univ 1977-78; Graduate Teaching Assistantship OH State Univ 1987-88; Grant, UNCF, 1987-88; Grant, National Endowment for the Humanities, 1989-90; OSU Presidential Fellowship, 1993-94. **Home Addr:** 506 Byrne St, Petersburg, VA 23803.

NORRIS, FRED ARTHUR, JR.
Labor administrator. **Personal:** Born Nov 25, 1945, Ecorse, MI; son of Annie B Davis Norris and Fred Arthur Norris; married Betty Sue Graves, Nov 26, 1982; children: Tracy M Graves, Shawna L Norris. **Educ:** Attended, Wayne Cty Comm Coll, Wayne State Univ, IN Univ, Univ of WI, MI State Univ, George Meany School of Labor. **Career:** City of Ecorse, councilmember 1974-87; Local 616 Allied Ind Workers, pres 1977-. **Orgs:** Mem United Black Trade Unionist 1976; SPIDER 1979; bd mem MI Downriver Comm Conv 1979-; bd mem Metro Detroit Chap A Philip Randolph Inst 1984, Allied Indust Workers Human Rights; pres Independence Alliance; mem Natl Black Elected Officials; sec, tres New Center Med CLinic; personal ministry dir Ecorse Seventh Day Adventist Church; Elder Ecorse Seventh Day Adventist Church 1989. **Honors/Awds:** Community Serv Community Serv Awd Ecorse 1981, Wayne Cty 1982; Little League Awd Ecorse Little League 1982.

NORRIS, JAMES ELLSWORTH CHILES
Plastic surgeon. **Personal:** Born May 12, 1932, Kilmarnock, VA; son of Theresita Chiles Norris and Morgan E Norris, Sr; married Motoko Endo, Jun 21, 67 ; children: Ernest Takashi. **Educ:** Hampton Inst VA, BS 1949-53; Case Western Reserve

Cleveland OH, MD 1953-57; Grasslands Hosp, internship 1957-58; Queens Hosp Ctr Jamaica, gen surgery resd 1962-66; Univ of MI Med Ctr, plastic surgery resd 1972-74. **Career:** Kilmarnock VA & Melbourne Fl, gen practitioner 1958-62; VA Hosp Tuskegee Al, chief of surgical serv & dir surgical resd prog 1969-72; Burn Unit Div of Plastic Surgery Harlem Hosp Ctr NY, chief 1974-77; Hosp for Joint Diseases & Med Ctr NY, assoc attending plastic surgery 1975-88; Jamaica Hosp Jamaica NY, attending & chief plastic surgery 1975-88, Consultant in plastic surgery 1988-90; Coll of Physicians & Surgeons Columbia Univ NY, asst prof, clinical surgery, 1976-87; Div of Plastic Surgery Harlem Hosp Ctr NY, attending 1977-87; St Lukes-Roosevelt Hosp Ctr Manhattan, associate attending plastic surgery 1981-97; Private practice, physician, until 1997; founded Jamtak International Inc, consultant. **Orgs:** Reed O Dingman Society 1974; Mem Amer Burn Assoc 1975-94, New York County Medical Society 1975, New York State Medical Society 1975, Amer Soc of Plastic & Reconstr Surgeons 1975, New York Regional Socitey ASPRS 1976, Lipoplasty Society of North America 1987, Amer Cleft Palate Assn 1988-94, Amer Society for Laser & Medicine and Surgery Inc 1987; life member NAACP; NY Academy of Medicine, 1992-. **Honors/Awds:** Numerous med articles in various med jrnls; licensed OH, FL, VA, NY, AL 1957-70; Cert Natl Bd of Med Examiners 1958; Cert Amer Bd of Surgery 1967; Cert Amer Bd of Plastic Surgery 1975; Vol Surgeon Albert Schweitzer Hosp Haiti 1965; Volunteer Surgeon Christian Mission Pignon Haiti 1986, 1987. **Military Serv:** USNR comdr 1967-69. **Business Addr:** President, Jamtak International, Inc., 137 Fifth Ave, 9th Floor, New York, NY 10010, (212)358-9418.

NORRIS, LAVENA M.
Real estate broker. **Personal:** Born Sep 2, Chicago, IL; daughter of Annie M Collins and Robert W Collins; married Alvin Norris, Sep 6, 1970. **Educ:** De Paul University, BS, 1981. **Career:** LaVena Norris Real Estate, president, 1986-; US Bureau of the Census, Minority Business Opportunity Committee, executive director, 1991-. **Orgs:** Dearborn Real Estate Board, president, 1991-; National Association of Real Estate Brokers, Investment Division, 1991-; Children & Adolescents Forum, 1984-; Chicago Gray Panthers, board of directors, 1992-; Health & Medicine Research Group, advisory board member, 1992-; Physicians for a National Healthcare Program, 1991-; Rho Epsilon, Professional Real Estate Fraternity, 1980-. **Honors/Awds:** WK Kellogg Foundation, Kellogg National Fellowship, 1991; National Association of Real Estate Brokers Region IX, Fair Housing Advocate Award, 1988; National Association of Real Estate Brokers Inc, Presidential Service Award, 1989; Dearborn Real Estate Board, Dedicated Service Award, 1985; NAACP, Unsung Herione Award, 1983. **Special Achievements:** Author, "House Hunting," Black Family Magazine, 1982. **Home Addr:** 2772 E 75th St, Chicago, IL 60649, (312)978-0550. **Business Addr:** President, LaVena Norris Real Estate, 27 E Monroe St, 11th fl, Chicago, IL 60603, (312)641-0084.

NORRIS, LONNIE H.
Educational administrator. **Personal:** Born in Houston, TX; married Dr Donna M. Norris. **Educ:** Fisk Univ, BS; Harvard, MA, public health, MPH, dental medicine, DMD; Tufts Univ, residency. **Career:** Tufts Univ Dental School, tenured professor in oral and maxillofacial surgery, interim dean, 1995-96, dean, 1996-. **Orgs:** American Bd of Oral and Maxillofacial Surgery; Phi Beta Kappa; Diplomate. **Honors/Awds:** American Academy of Dental Science, Fellow; American College of Dentists, Fellow; International College of Dentists, Fellow. **Special Achievements:** First African American dean of Tufts' dental school. **Business Addr:** Dean, Dental School, Tufts University, Dental School, 1 Kneeland St, Boston, MA 02111.

NORRIS, WALTER, JR.
City official. **Personal:** Born Jan 9, 1945, Jackson, MI; son of Willie Mae Glaspie-Neely and Walter Norris Sr; married Rosie Hill, Aug 7, 1963; children: Gloria J, Anthony W, Vernon D, Shannon D. **Educ:** Spring Arbor Coll, Spring Arbor MI, BS 1970; Michigan State Univ, E Lansing MI, Graduate Study Educ Admin, 1979. **Career:** Jackson Community Coll, Jackson MI, financial aid dir 1968-70; Norris Real Estate, Jackson MI, owner & broker 1970-76; Jackson Public Schools, Jackson MI, dir minority affairs 1970-76; Jackson Housing Comm, Jackson MI, exec dir 1976-79; Lansing Housing Comm, Lansing MI, exec dir 1978-88; Housing Authority, Galveston TX, exec dir 1988-. **Orgs:** Natl Assn of Housing & Redevelopment Officials (NAHRO); Michigan Chapter of NAHRO; chmn, bd dir Legislative Comm; certification trainer HAHRO Public Housing Mgmt; Public Housing Authority Directors Assn; Texas Housing Assn; assoc mem Galveston Historical Found 1988-, Galveston Chapter NAACP 1988-; bd mem Galveston Boys' Club 1988-, Galveston Chamber of Commerce 1988-, Rotary Club of Galveston 1988-. **Honors/Awds:** Men's Union Award, Most Outstanding Young Man of the Year, Jackson Community Coll 1965; Sophomore Class President, Jackson Junior Coll 1965; Outstanding Young Man of the Year, Jackson Jaycees 1968; Service Award, Outstanding Service & Contributions, HUD Program 1982; NAHRO Public Housing Mgmt Certification (PHM). **Business Addr:** Executive Director, Galveston Housing Authority, 920-53rd St, Galveston, TX 77551.

NORRIS, WILLIAM E.
Automobile dealership executive. **Career:** Utica Chrysler-Plymouth Inc, CEO, currently. **Business Addr:** Chief Executive Officer, Utica Chrysler-Plymouth Inc, PO Box 214, Yorkville, NY 13495, (315)736-0831.

NORTHCROSS, DAVID C.
Physician. **Personal:** Born Jan 29, 1917, Montgomery, AL; son of Daisy Hill Northcross and David C Northcross; children: David, Michael, Gale, Gloria, Derrick, Grace. **Educ:** Univ Detroit; Meharry Med Coll, 1944; Univ of Pennsylvania, 1957. **Career:** Gen practice, physician; Mercy Gen Hospital, admin 1956-74. **Orgs:** Mem Detroit Medical Soc; Wayne County Medical Soc; Natl Medical Assn; Amer Medical Assn; Meharry Alumni Assn; Wolverine Medical Assnc; Michigan State Medical Assn; mem Booker T Washington Business Assn; Detroit C of C; UNA-USA; ACLU; Alpha Phi Alpha. **Military Serv:** US Army, 1943-45, 1953-55.

NORTHCROSS, DEBORAH AMETRA
Educational administrator. **Personal:** Born Jun 27, 1951, Nashville, TN; daughter of Nell Northcross and Theron Northcross. **Educ:** Mt Holyoke Coll, BA French 1969-73; Memphis State Univ, MEd Spec Educ 1973-75. **Career:** Shelby State Comm Coll, counselor 1973-76, dir/spec serv prog 1976-79, coord/fed affairs 1979-81, asst dir/stud develop 1981-83, dir/stud retention1982-83, grants officer 1983-84, dir of develop 1984-. **Orgs:** Field reader US Dept of Educ; pres TN Asso of Special Programs 1977-79; bd mem Southeastern Assn of Educ Oppor Program Personnel 1978-79; tutor Memphis Literacy Council 1983-87; chairperson Christian Educ Comm MS Blvd Christian Church 1984-; YWCA chair/nominating comm 1985, bd of dir 1986-, 2nd Vice Pres 1987; US Dept of Educ Special Programs Training Grant, evaluation consultant 1986-; Leadership Memphis, Vice Pres of alumni assoc 1987-88, bd mem 1987-89, vice chair bd of trustees 1989-; chair YWCA Financial Development committee 1988-. **Honors/Awds:** Kate Gooch Leadership Award leadership Memphis 1989. **Business Addr:** Dir of Development, Shelby State Community College, PO Box 40568, Memphis, TN 38174-0568.

NORTHCROSS, WILSON HILL, JR.
Attorney. **Personal:** Born Dec 8, 1946, Detroit, MI; son of Gwendolyn Pinkney and Wilson H Northcross, Sr; married Winifred C Wheelock; children: Jill Inez, Christopher Wilson. **Educ:** Wayne State Univ, BS 1969; Harvard Univ Law School, JSD 1972. **Career:** Canfield, Paddock & Stone, atty 1975-77; MI Supreme Court, assoc commissioner 1977-78; private law practice, 1975-77, 1981-83, 1987-; Senior Citizens Law Program, dir 1983-87. **Honors/Awds:** Publication "The Limits on Employment Testing," University of Detroit Journal of Urban Law, Vol 50, Issue 3 1973. **Military Serv:** USAF 1st lt 1969-73. **Home Addr:** 801 Sunrise Ct, Ann Arbor, MI 48103.

NORTHERN, CHRISTINA ANN
Attorney. **Personal:** Born May 21, 1956, Kansas City, KS; daughter of Emanuel & Christine Northern. **Educ:** Washington University, BA, 1978; Antioch School of Law, JD, 1981. **Career:** Self-employed, attorney, 1987-90. **Orgs:** New Columbia Community Land Trust, bd mem, chair of fund raising, asst treas, 1990-; Natl Bar Assn, 1981-; Amer Friends of the London of Economics, 1989-. **Business Addr:** 9039 Sligo Creek Pkwy, Ste 707, Silver Spring, MD 20901, (301)587-6409.

NORTHERN, GABRIEL O'KARA
Professional football player. **Personal:** Born Jun 8, 1974, Baton Rouge, LA. **Educ:** Louisiana State. **Career:** Buffalo Bills, linebacker, 1996-. **Business Addr:** Professional Football Player, Buffalo Bills, One Bills Dr, Orchard Park, NY 14127, (716)648-1800.

NORTHERN, ROBERT A. (BROTHER AH)
Musician, educator, lecturer. **Personal:** Born May 21, 1934, Kinston, NC; son of Madie and Ralph. **Educ:** Manhattan Sch of Music NYC, 1952-53; Vienna State Acad of Music Vienna Austria, 1957-58; Howard University graduate. **Career:** Brown Univ Afro Amer Studies Prg, lectr 1973-82; Artist in Res Dartmouth Coll Music Dept, lectr 1970-73; Brass Instrmnts Pub School Syst NYC, Instr 1964-67; Metro Opera NYC, 1958-59; Stage Band Symphony of the Air Orchestra NYC, 1958-70; Broadway Theatre Orchestra NYC, 1969-71; Jazz Composer Orchestra NYC, 1969-71; World Music Ensemble, founder/director; Smithsonian Institution, lecturer, currently; Umoja Music Publishing Co, owner, founder, 1973-; Divine Records, owner, 1975-; founder and producer of radio series, "The Jazz Collectors" on WPFW-FM, Washington, DC, 1993; produced CD "Celebration" with the World Music Ensemble for Mapleshade Records, 1993. **Orgs:** Performed as sideman & recorded with following artists, Thelonious Monk, Miles Davis, Gil Evans, Freddie Hubbard, Quincy Jones, Peggy Lee, Tony Bennett, Sun Ra, Ella Fitzgerald, numerous others; composer dir of following productions, Forces of Nature Brown Univ 1974, Symbols Dartmouth Clg 1972, Confrontation & Communication Dartmouth Clg 1971, Magical Mode Dartmouth Clg 1971, Ode to Creation Dartmouth Clg 1970, Ti-Jean Dartmouth Clg 1971, Child Woman Brown Univ 1973; chrtr mem Soc of Black Composers 1965; fndr Sound Awareness Ensemble 1968; fndr Radio Series Dimensions in Black Sounds WBAI-FM New York City 1970; fndr NY Wind Octet 1966; mus dir Black Fire Performing Arts Co Birmingham; Producers First Album for Black Chorus of Brown Univ Sound Awareness Vol I 1973; Sound Awareness Vol Move Ever Onward III 1975; The New World Vol III 1980; recordings: Meditation, Light from Womb, Open Sky. **Honors/Awds:** Mayor's Arts Award for Artistic Excellence, Washington DC. **Military Serv:** USAF a/1c 1953-57. **Business Addr:** Musician, Divine Records, PO Box 56481, Washington, DC 20011.

NORTHOVER, VERNON KEITH
Salesman. **Personal:** Born Jan 3, 1934, New York, NY; married Lyn Brown; children: Vivia, Vernon, Paul, Fran, Orville. **Educ:** London Sch of Econ, BS 1959. **Career:** GAF Corp, sales rep 1971-; British RR London, admstr 1960-71. **Orgs:** Bd of dir The Mus of Afro-Am Ethno History Inc 1977; pres Clb GAF Corp 1977.

NORTON, AURELIA EVANGELINE
Clinical psychologist. **Personal:** Born Feb 14, 1932, Dayton, OH; daughter of Aurelia DeMar Turner and Joseph Turner; divorced. **Educ:** Wayne State, BA Distinction MA PhD 1961; Cntrl State Univ of Dayton, Undergrad. **Career:** Wayne State, res psychologist; Childrens & Emergency Psychiat Clinic Detroit Gen Hosp, stf psychologist; Oak Pk Sch Sys, psychologist; Chrysler Corp, psychologist; Childrens Hosp Consulting Psychologist, res psychologist; Univ of Cincinnati Multi Ethnic Branch Psychological Svcs, assoc prof of psychology; Psychological Services Ctr, Univ of Cincinnati, dir of training. **Orgs:** Numerous Orgns & Industries; Police Selec Cincinnati; mem Psychologist Examination Bd State of OH; term mem Amer Psychological Assc; Assc of Black Psychologists; NAACP; Mt Zion Baptist Church. **Business Addr:** Assoc Prof of Psychology, Univ of Cincinnati, 316 Dyer Hall, Cincinnati, OH 45210.

NORTON, EDWARD WORTHINGTON
Government official. **Personal:** Born Apr 10, 1938, New York, NY; married Eleanor K Holmes; children: Katherine Felicia, John Holmes. **Educ:** Yale U, BA 1959; Columbia U, LlB 1966. **Career:** Dept of Housing & Urban Dev, dep gen cnsl; New York City Housing Authority, gen cnsl 1973-77; New York City Hlth Serv Admn, spl asst to admnstr 1970-73; NY Univ Law Sch;; adj asst proj 1971-73; Legal Serv Pgm NE Region OEO, dep dir 1968-70; Paul, Weiss, Rifkind, Wharton & Garrison, assc 1966-68; Lawyers Constitution Def Com 1966. **Orgs:** Tres Columbia Law Sch Alumni Assc 1970-74; bd dir 1969-; 100 Black Men Inc 1974-; Harlem Lawyers Assc 1976-; Equality Com Am Civil Liberties Union 1967-73; bd dir NY Civil Liberties Union 1971-74; vice pres Schlrshp Ed & Def Fund for Racial Equality 1972-; bd dir 1968-; bd dir Save The Children Fed 1975-. **Military Serv:** USN lt 1959-63. **Business Addr:** 451 7th St SW Rm 10214, Washington, DC 20410.

NORTON, ELEANOR HOLMES
Educator, government official. **Personal:** Born Jun 13, 1937, Washington, DC; daughter of Vela Holmes and Coleman Holmes; divorced; children: Katherine, John. **Educ:** Antioch Coll, attended; Yale Univ, MA 1963; Yale Law School, JD 1964. **Career:** American Civil Liberties Union, assistant legal director, 1965-70; New York University Law School, adjunct assistant professor of law, 1970-71; New York City Commission on Human Rights, chair, 1970-77; US Equal Employment Opportunity Commission, chair, 1977-81; The Urban Institute, senior fellow, 1981-82; Georgetown University Law Center, professor of law beginning 1982; US House of Representatives, Washington, DC, nonvoting member, currently. **Honors/Awds:** One Hundred Most Important Women, Ladies Home Journal, 1988; One Hundred Most Powerful Women in Washington, The Washingtonian Magazine, 1989; Distinguished Public Service Award, Center for National Policy, 1985; 60 honorary doctorates; articles: "Equal Employment Law: Crisis in Interpretation, Survival against the Odds," Tulane Law Review, v. 62, 1988; "The Private Bar and Public Confusion: A New Civil Rights Challenge," Howard Law Journal, 1984; "Public Assistance, Post New-Deal Bureaucracy, and the Law: Learning from Negative Models," Yale Law Journal, 1983; author, Sex Discrimination and the Law: Causes and Remedies. **Business Addr:** US House of Representatives, 1424 Longworth House Office Bldg, Washington, DC 20515.

NORTON, KENNETH HOWARD, JR.
Professional football player. **Personal:** Born Sep 29, 1966, Jacksonville, FL; son of Ken Norton Sr; married Angela; children: Brittney, Sabrina Brooke, Ken III. **Educ:** UCLA, attended. **Career:** Dallas Cowboys, linebacker, 1988-93; San Francisco 49ers, 1994-. **Honors/Awds:** Linebacker, Sporting News College All-America Team, 1987; involved with: Entertainers and Athletes (for kids in Los Angeles), Big Brothers; Pro Bowl appearances, 1993, 1995; Only player in NFL history to win three consecutive Super Bowl rings, 1992-94. **Business Addr:** Professional Football Player, San Francisco 49ers, 4949 Centennial Blvd, Santa Clara, CA 95054, (415)562-4949.

NORVEL, WILLIAM LEONARD
Clergyman. **Personal:** Born Oct 1, 1935, Pascagoula, MS; son of Velma H Norvel and William L Norvel, Sr. **Educ:** Epiphany Apostolic Coll, 1956; St Joseph's Seminary, BA 1959; St Michael's Coll, 1960-61; St Bonaventure Coll 1963; Marquette Univ, 1967. **Career:** Holy Family, asst pastor 1965; St Augustine HS, teacher 1965; Josephite Training Center, dir 1968; St Joseph's Seminary, staff asst 1970; St Benedict the Moor, pastor 1971; St Brigid, pastor 1979-83; consultant to Black Catholic Parishes in USA, 1983-; Josephite Soc, consultor-general 1983-; Most Pure Heart of Mary Church, pastor, 1987-. **Orgs:** Bd mem Lithurgical Conf 1978-82; bd mem SCLC/LA 1979/83; mem NAACP 1983-85; pres Black Catholic Clergy Caucus 1985-87; trustee bd Natl Black Catholic Congress 1987. **Honors/Awds:** Comm Action Awd Secretariat for Black Catholics 1978; Ecumenical Fellowship Awd by Baptists, Muslims, AME, CME 1983; Church of God in Christ & Holiness Churches of LA Achievement Awd SCLC/LA 1983; Serv Awd Loyola Marymount Univ 1983. **Business Addr:** Pastor, Most Pure Heart of Mary Church, 304 Sengstak St, PO Box 994, Mobile, AL 36601.

NORVELL, MERRITT J., JR.
Athletic director. **Career:** Michigan State Univ, athletic dir, 1995-; IBM, executive; Norvell Group marketing firm, founder. **Special Achievements:** Rose Bowl, Wisconsin, 1963. **Business Addr:** Athletic Director, Michigan State University, 218 Jenison Fieldhouse, East Lansing, MI 48824, (517)355-1855.

NORWOOD, BERNICE N.
Social worker. **Personal:** Born Oct 2, 1917, Guilford County, NC; widowed. **Educ:** Bennett Coll, BA 1938; Atlanta Univ School Soc Work, professional cert 1946. **Career:** Caldwell County NC Welfare Dept, case Worker 1945-50; Guilford Cnty NC Dept Soc Serv, case worker 1953-63, case work supr 1963-. **Orgs:** Mem, Natl Assn Social Workers; mem Acad Cert Soc Workers; mem NC Assn; Soc Workers; past program chmn pres Greensboro Branch Natl Council Negro Women; charter mem United Day Care Serv Bd, first sec exec com former chmn Admissions Metro Day Care Ctr; mem Greensboro, NC Mental Health Assn. **Honors/Awds:** Directory of Professional Social Workers, 1972. **Business Addr:** Guilford Co Dept of Social Serv, PO Box 3388, Greensboro, NC.

NORWOOD, BRANDY RAYANA. **See BRANDY.**

NORWOOD, CALVIN COOLIDGE
State official. **Personal:** Born Apr 1, 1927, Tunica, MS; son of Hester Norwood and Willie Norwood; married Ida Williams Norwood, Feb 14, 1946; children: Doris Norwood Jernigan, Deloris Norwood Sanders, Demetrice Norwood Burnette, Regina. **Educ:** Coahoma Jr Clg, GED 1979. **Career:** Co Rd Dept in Co Turstee Bd Rosa Fort Sch, foreman; Mississippi State Highway Dept, Tunica County, 1st black jury commiss supervisor, currently. **Orgs:** Pres NAACP 1966-; mem EDA Bd; mem Co Dem Party; mem Legal Aide Bd Joint Communication Activity & Job Care; mem State Bd NAACP; mem VFW. **Honors/Awds:** Job Core Cert Job Core 1979; Politician Action Awrd NAACP 1980; Ed Awrd NAACP 1980; Programmatic Award, NAACP, 1985-86, 1990; Recognition of Appreciation, Mississippi State Highway Dept, 1989. **Military Serv:** US Navy std 3rd class 1944-46; served overseas Island of Guam 18 mo's.

NORWOOD, JOHN F.
Clergyman (retired). **Personal:** Born Nov 28, 1927, Darlington, SC; son of Benzena Norwood and J R Norwood; married Zanthia Bush; children: John F Jr, Iris R, Lydia I. **Educ:** BA 1951; BD 1957; MDiv 1969; Wiley Coll, DD 1976. **Career:** Council on Finance & Adminstrs United Meth Ch, assoc gen sec; Camden SC, prin elem sch; Health & Welfare United Meth Ch, asst gen sec; Gammon Theo Sem Atlanta, pres 1967-68; Huntsville, dist supt 1962-66; Mt Zion M Baptist Church, Evanston, IL, pastor, currently. **Orgs:** Mem Nat Assn of Health & Welfare; Nat Alliance of Black Clergyman; delegate, jurisdoctoral conf mem Dist 65 Sch Bd Evanston IL 1972-75; re-elected 1975-; pres protem, bd dirs NAACP Evanston Br; Rotary Club Evanston; United Chris Ministry Bd; chaplain, Evanston Police Department, 1997; Family Focus, Inc, pres, 1995-. **Honors/Awds:** Recip hon cit Huntsville 1968; Key to City of Huntsville 1968; Outstanding Leadership Citation Evanston NAACP 1974; Key to City of Sparta TN 1974; NAACP Humanitarian Award 1989; Pastor of the Year, 1993, NAACP; Outstanding Pastor, Ushers League of US, 1994. **Military Serv:** AUS pvt 1945. **Business Addr:** 1200 Davis St, Evanston, IL 60201.

NORWOOD, KIMBERLY JADE
Educator. **Personal:** Born Aug 18, 1960, New York, NY; daughter of Marietta Holt & Ahmad Akbar; married Ronald Alan, Jul 2, 1988; children: Candice Jade, Ellis Grant, Donnell Bussey. **Educ:** Fordham Univ, BA, 1982; Univ of Missouri-Columbia, JD, 1985. **Career:** Hon. Clifford Scott Green, law clerk, 1985-86; Bryan Cave et al, litigation assoc, 1986-90; Univ of MO-Columbia, visiting lecturer, Cleo Program, 1990; Washington Univ School of Law, prof of law, 1990-. **Orgs:** Greeley Comm Assn, bd mem, 1993-94; St Louis Women Lawyers Assn, bd mem, 1993-94; Mound City Bar Assn, 1986-; Jack & Jill of America, 1994-96; Girls, Inc, bd mem, 1994; Bar Assn of Metro St Louis, 1986-; Illinois Bar Assn, 1987-; American Bar Assn, 1986-; American Assn of Law Schools, 1993-. **Honors/Awds:** American Jurisprudence Award, 1983; Bernard T Hurwitz Prize, 1984; Judge Shepard Barclay Prize, 1984-85. **Special Achievements:** ''Shopping for a Venue: The Need for More Limits on Choice,'' Miami Law Review, v 50, p 267, 1996. **Business Addr:** Prof of Law, Washington University Sch of Law, 1 Brookings Drive, Campus Box 1120, St Louis, MO 63130, (314)935-6416.

NORWOOD, RONALD EUGENE
Real estate examiner. **Personal:** Born Dec 24, 1952, Cresent, OK; son of Charlene L Norwood and Jimmie L Norwood (deceased); married Cathy Reed, Nov 20, 1971 (divorced); children: Katrina, LaFrances, Portia, Ronald II. **Educ:** Enid Business College, AS, accounting, 1974; Phillips University, BS, accounting, 1979. **Career:** Phillips Petroleum Co, junior accountant, 1974-75; Operation Uplift Inc, finance director, 1976-79; Nash & Associates, accountant, 1979-81; Mitchell Companies, accou ntant, 1981-83; De'Zanella by J Scott, consultant, 1983; Colorado Real Estate Commission, senior financial examiner, 1984-95; Guest Lecturer, real estate escrow accounting, Colorado Univ, 1987-95. **Orgs:** National Association of Black Accountants, 1984-. **Honors/Awds:** National Association Real Estate License Law Officials, Investigator of the Year, 1991. **Special Achievements:** Certification as fraud examiner, 1993; certification as real estate investigator, 1989; Qualified as Expert in Real Estate Accounting, Fifth Judicial District of Colorado, 1992. **Military Serv:** Army, sgt, 1970-73. **Business Phone:** (601)329-8923.

NORWOOD, TOM
Educational administrator, educator. **Personal:** Born Jul 19, 1943, Baton Rouge, LA; son of Corinne Burrell Norwood and Edward A Norwood, Sr; married Marjorie Marshall; children: Teri Lynn, Tony. **Educ:** Southern Univ & A&M Clge, BS Art/English 1964, MEd Educ Admin 1969; Univ of NE Lincoln, PhD Ed Adm 1975. **Career:** Omaha Publ Schl, traveling art tchr 1964-65, jr high art tchr 1965-68, jr high cnsl 1968-70; Clge of Educ Univ of NE Omaha, asst dean 1970-83, assc prof 1983-88; asst dean and prof, Univ Wisconsin, River Falls. **Orgs:** Pres 1981-83, vice pres NE Council on Tchr Educ; wrkshp dir Joslyn Art Museum ''Forever Free Exhibit'' 1981; wrkshp dir Sioux Falls SD City Dept Heads, ''Racism & Sexism'' 1979; vice pres Greater Omaha Comm Action 1975; mem Appointed by US Dist Court Judge Albert Schatz 1976; mem Urban League of NE 1983-84; consultant to Omaha Public School re Implementing Discipline Based Art Educ Prog 1987-87. **Honors/Awds:** Phi Delta Kappa Southern Univ & A&M Clge 1964; hnrbl mention Watercolor Council Bluffs IA Art Fair 1972; book ''Contemporary Nebr Art & Artists'' Univ of NE at Omaha 1978; article ''Facilitating Multicultural Educ Via the Visual Arts'' NE Humanist 1980; 1st pl award NE Art Educ Competition 1982; paintings selected natl & intl juried competitions, Natl Miniature Competition 1983, Natl Exhibition of Contemporary Realism 1983, Montana Intl Miniature Competition 1983, Intl Small Fine Art Exhibit 1984, Intl Miniature Competition 1984, Biennial Juried Competition (Natl) 1984, Tenth Intl Miniature Competition 1985; commissioned by St of NE to create poster design for first state observance of Martin Luther King, Jr holiday 1986; First Annual Natl NC Miniature PaintingShow Cert of Merit 1985; SecoAnnual NC Natl Miniature Painting Show Second Place Watercolor 1986; Arts West juried Competition, Eau Claire, WI, 1993-94; participated in 17 exhibition 1985-1987; commissioned by Chancellor of UW-RF to produce painting ''Celebration of Diversity,'' 1990; Greater St Paul YMCA Black Achievers Program, Achiever of the Year, 1991. **Business Addr:** Asst Dean, Coll of Educ, Univ of Wisconsin at River Falls, Ames Teacher Ed Center, 410 S 3rd St., River Falls, WI 54022.

NORWOOD, WILLIAM R.
Pilot (retired). **Personal:** Born Feb 14, 1936, Centralia, IL; son of Allingal (Humble) Norwood and Sam Norwood; married Molly F Cross; children: William R, George A. **Educ:** S IL U, BA 1959; Univ of Chicago, MBA 1974. **Career:** United Air Lines, captain 1983-96; airline pilot 1st ofcr 1968-83; 2nd ofcr 1965-68. **Orgs:** Air Line Pilots Assn; United Air Lines Speakers Panel; charter mem, Org of Black Air Line Pilots; Trust S IL Univ at Carbondale-Edwardsville 1974-; bd of dirs, Suburban Chap, SCLC; life mem, NAACP, 1985-; president, board of trustees, State Universities Retirement System. **Honors/Awds:** First African-American pilot with United Air Lines; Chem News All Am Football at SIU 1958; 1st African-American quarterback SIU; commencement speaker Shawnee Comm Coll 1975; an exhibition in Smithsonian Inst ''Black Wings''; United Airlines Corporate Community Relations Award, 1991, flight operations Div Special Achievement Aaward; Southern Illinois University, Carbondale ROTC Hall of Fame; Southern Illinois Univ, Carbondale Athletic Hall of Fame; The Museum of Science & Industry, Chicago Illinois, Boeing 727 Aircraft Named in Honor of Capt William R Norwood; United Airlines, O'Hare Captain of the Year, 1995; Chicagoan of the Year, 1995; Southern Illinois Reunion Councils Founders Award, 1996; United Airlines Black Professional Organization's Outstanding Achievement & Leadership Award, 1996; AKA Monary Award Winner, 1997; Destiny Church Community Service Award, 1997. **Military Serv:** AUS pilot B-52 capt 1959-65. **Business Addr:** Retired Captain, United Airlines, O'Hare International Airport, PO Box 66140, AMF OHare, IL 60666.

NOTICE, GUY SYMOUR
Clergyman, educator. **Personal:** Born Dec 6, 1929; son of Eugena Amanda Young Notice and Daniel Ezekiel Notice; married Azelma Matilda Notice, Nov 9, 1955; children: Donald Hylton, Sandra Simone. **Educ:** Bethel Bible Coll, certificate 1954; Amer Divinity School, BTh 1972; Fordham Univ & Goddard Coll, BA 1974; Luther Rice Seminary, MA, 1991. **Career:** Tutorial Coll, vice chmn, 1965-69; conv speaker, England, Canada, Dallas TX, Mexico, Eastern Caribbean, US Virgin Islands, 1968-81; Bethel Bible Coll, dir of educ 1973-77; Jamaica Theological Seminary, bd mem; New Testament Church of God, supt, 1982; justice of the peace, 1985. **Orgs:** Bd mem Jamaica Theological Seminary; chmn, Natl Chest Clinic, 1982; guest speaker, Conf Puerto Rico, 1985; chmn, Hope Inst; chmn of bd, Bethel Bible Coll. **Honors/Awds:** Certificate of merit for books published (They Shall See Visions, If We Could Begin Again, Beyond the Veil), Opa Locka City, 1982; author of book, Prison Life: The Jamaican Experience, 1991. **Business Addr:** PO Box 680205, Orlando, FL 32818.

NOWLIN, BETTYE J. ISOM
Nutrition educator, public affairs manager. **Personal:** Born in Knoxville, TN; daughter of Elizabeth & Jettie Isom; married Thomas A Nowlin III, Mar 12, 1957; children: Thomas IV, Mark, Brett. **Educ:** Tennessee A&I State Univ, BS, 1956; St Lukes Hospital & Medical Ctr, Dietetic Intership, RD, 1957; Univ of CA at Los Angeles, UCLA, MPH, 1971. **Career:** Cook County Hospital, therapeutic dietitian, 1957-59; Michael Reese Hospital, admini dietitian, 1959-61; Chicago Bd of Educ, teacher, 1961-63; Chicago Bd of Health, public health nutritionist, 1962-68; Delta Sigma Theta, Head Start, nutritionist, 1968-70; Dairy Council of CA, mgr, adult nutrition prog, 1970-90, public affairs, 1990-. **Orgs:** American Dietetic Assn, delegate, 1994-, mem, 1957-, media spokesperson, 1982-; Amer Public Health Assn, 1972-; Society for Nutrition Educ, 1971-; Amer School Food Service Assn, 1993-; CA Dietetic Assn, delegate, 1968-; CA Nutrition Council, 1970-; Natl Assn for Female Executives, 1995-; AM Dietetic Assn, Practice Groups, dietitians in business & comm, public health; Nutrition Educ for the Public, 1980-; Alpha Kappa Alpha Sorority, 1952-56. **Honors/Awds:** Amer Dietetic Assn, Medallion Award, 1994; CA Dietetic Assn, Excellence in Community Nutrition, 1994, Distinguished Service Award, 1990; Kroger Food Chain, Academic Scholarship, 1952; Alpha Kappa, Honor Society, 1955. **Special Achievements:** Publications, Development of a Nutrition Educ Program for Homemakers; Society for Nutrition Educ Journal; Leader-Led and Self Instruction Work Site Programs; Keep It Short & Simple, Journal of American Dietetic Assn; Marketing Social Programs, The Competetive Edge, ADA Mkting Manuel, 2nd Editon. **Business Phone:** (310)412-6488.

NOWLIN, FRANKIE L.
Foundation executive. **Career:** Borden Inc, director of social responsibility, currently; Borden Foundation Inc, pres, currently. **Business Addr:** President, Borden Foundation, Inc, 180 E Broad St, Columbus, OH 43215-3707, (614)225-4000.

NUNERY, GLADYS CANNON
Educator. **Personal:** Born Sep 7, 1904, Jersey City; divorced. **Educ:** Jersey City State Tchrs Coll, BS1951; NY Univ, MA 1957. **Career:** Jersey City Public Schools, taught elem grades 1924-64; Bergen Study Center, dir 1964-69; Luth Parochial School, teacher 1969-71. **Orgs:** Volunteer ch & community work 1971-74; mem Nat Educ Assn; NJ Educ Assn; Nat Retired Tchrs Assn; NJ Retired Tchrs Assn; Hudson Co Retired Tchrs Assn; Local YWCA; mem Claremont-Lafayette Presbnyn Ch; supt Ch Sch 25 yrs 1930-55; ch treas 1962-75; life mem NAACP; serving 3rd term of 3 yrs Jersey City Bd Edn; rep out of town meetings; organized natl sorority Phi Delta Kappa 1923; held various natl & local offices; speaker woman's orgns & chs. **Honors/Awds:** 1st woman elected trustee 1942; 1st woman elected an elder 1964; Outstanding Woman in City Jersey Journal 1965; Outstanding Soror Eastern Region 1966; Hon degree Dr of Humane Letters Jersey City State College 1986.

NUNERY, LEROY DAVID
Professional sports administrator. **Personal:** Born Dec 22, 1955, Jersey City, NJ; son of Thelma Jones Nunery and Leroy C Nunery; married Carolyn Thomas Nunery, Apr 24, 1982; children: Leroy David Nunery III. **Educ:** Lafayette College, BA (with honors), history 1977; Washington Univ, MBA, finance 1979. **Career:** Leroy Nunery & Sons Inc, vp, beginning 1973; Edward D Jones & Co, res analyst 1978-79; Northern Trust Co, comm banking officer 1979-83; First Natl Bank of Chicago, vice pres 1983-87; Swiss Bank Corp, director, 1987-93; Natl Basketball Assn, vp of human & info resources, 1993-. **Orgs:** Natl pres, Natl Black MBA Assn Inc 1986-89; dir Family Resource Coalition Inc 1988-90; trustee, Lafayette Coll 1988-; national conf chairperson, Natl Black MBA Assn, 1991; board of directors, Pitney Bowes Inc, 1991-94; Nu Beta Beta Chapter, Omega Psi Phi Fraternity, Inc. **Honors/Awds:** Black and Hispanic Achievers YMCA, 1983, 1986; Outstanding MBA of the

Year Natl Black MBA Assn 1984; Amer Best & Brightest, Dollars & Sense Magazine 1987; Alumni Recognition Award, Washington Univ Business Minority Council 1987; frequent speaker to graduate, undergraduate, high school and elementary school students. **Business Addr:** VP, Human & Info Resources, Natl Basketball Assn, 645 Fifth Ave, New York, NY 10022.

NUNEZ, MIGUEL A.
Actor. **Career:** Appearance in the television show ''Sparks.''. **Business Addr:** Actor, ''Sparks'', c/o Abrams Artists & Associates, Inc, 9200 Sunset Blvd, Ste 625, Los Angeles, CA 90069, (310)859-0625.

NUNN, BOBBIE B.
Educational administrator (retired). **Personal:** Born in Muskogee, OK; married Josiah; children: Darla, Joe Darryl. **Educ:** Portland State U, BS 1959; Univ of Portland, MEd 1970; Houston-Tillotson Coll; Prairie View Coll. **Career:** Portland Public School, teachers 1959-70; Paraprofl Devel System Portland Public School, dir; Career Oppor Program Portland Public School, dir; Portland State Univ, demonstration teacher summer 1960-66; Environmental Educ Program Boise Elem School, dir 1968-70. **Orgs:** Mem Am Assn of Sch Personnel Admin; Natl Council of Admin women in Education; Cascade Adv Bd; Nat Alliance of Black Sch Educators; Child Devel Learning Cntr-Bd; bd mem Model Cities Citizens Planning Bd; mem Metro Hum Rel Comm; chairperson Hum Rel Comm Oregon State Bd of Edn; NAACP; Alpha Kappa Alpha; Delta Kappa Gamma. **Honors/Awds:** Albina Lions Club Award for comm ser 1974; award for comm serv in educ Nat Conf of Christians & Jews 1975. **Business Addr:** 631 NE Clackamas St, Portland, OR 97208.

NUNN, JOHN, JR.
Company executive. **Personal:** Born Sep 19, 1953, Berkeley, CA; son of Yvonne Hunter Nunn and John Nunn; married Valmere Fischer, Jul 3, 1977; children: Arianna M, Julian G, Micheala Y. **Educ:** St Mary's Coll, Moraga CA, BS Biology 1971-76; Univ of California at Berkeley 1975. **Career:** World Savings, Alamo CA, asst vice pres branch manager, 1976-78; American Savings, Oakland CA, asst vice pres branch manager, 1979-80, El Cerrito CA, vice pres regional manager, 1980-85, Stockton CA, senior vice pres office chief admin officer, 1985-87, Stockton CA, senior vice president, North California Area Manager, 1987-89; senior vice pres dir, Sacramento, CA, Community Outreach & Urban Development, 1989. **Orgs:** Mem Alumni Board, Bishop O'Dowd HS Prep, 1980-85; pres, 1985-87; mem Stockton Chamber of Commerce, 1987-; mem Stockton Black Chamber of Commerce, 1987-; mem Sacramento Chamber of Commerce, 1987-; mem California League of Savings Institutions, 1988-; mem Business School Adv Board, California State Univ, 1988-. **Business Addr:** Sr Vice President, Dir, Community Outreach & Urban Devt, American Savings Bank, FA, 343 E Main, Suite 610, Stockton, CA 95202.

NUNN, ROBINSON S.
Judge. **Personal:** Born Sep 29, 1944, Blytheville, AR; married Glanetta Miller. **Educ:** MI State U, BA 1966; Am Univ Law Sch, JD 1969. **Career:** Admitted to Supreme Ct Bar 1976; US Tax Ct Wash DC, legal asst 1969; Little Rock AR, gen prac of law 1976. **Orgs:** Am Bar Assn; Nat Bar Assn; AR Bar Assn; NAACP; Kappa Alpha Psi Frat. **Military Serv:** USMC captain 1976-. **Business Addr:** Quarters 2947 D MCB, Quantico, VA 22134.

NUNN, RONNIE
Professional sports official. **Career:** NBA, referee, currently. **Orgs:** Concerned Black Men for Youth; Hord Foundation; Natl Basketball Referee Association. **Honors/Awds:** George Washington University, Hall of Fame; Basketball Player of the Decade, Leon Mexico. **Business Addr:** Referee, National Basketball Association, 645 5th Ave, 15th Fl, New York, NY 10022-5986.

NUNN, WILLIAM GOLDWIN, JR.
Asst dir player personnel. **Personal:** Born in Pittsburgh, PA; married Frances; children: Lynell Stanton, William III. **Educ:** West Virginia State, graduate 1948. **Career:** Pittsburgh Courier, sports editor; Pittsburgh Steelers, training camp director/personnel scout 1968, asst dir of player personnel.

NUNNALLY, DAVID H., SR.
Educator. **Personal:** Born Oct 16, 1929, Athens Clarke Co, GA; married Ileane I Nesbit. **Educ:** Union Bapt Inst; Tuskegee Inst; Atlanta U; Univ of GA; Gov State U, mS; Loyal Univ of Chicago, PhD. **Career:** Kennedy-Ing Coll, counselor; teacher; Jr HS counselor; HS counselor; residential counselor; Sutdent Personnel Ser, dir; Comm Adult HS, asst dir; athletic coach; employment counselor; camp counselor; Georgia Dome, personnel asst. **Orgs:** Mem PTA; AFT; NEA; Phi Delta Kappa; VFW; APGA; IGPA; ICPA; GAE; past dir Dist IX Assn of Educators; past mem Assn of Educ Bd of Dir; Chicago Hghts Ldrshp Forum; founder Athens Chap Ita Iota Lambda; mem Lions Intl Club; Alpha Phi Alpha; Masonic Lodge; sponsor Comm Ser Club; troop scout master. **Honors/Awds:** BSA Outstanding Male Tchr Am Tchr Assn 1964; Martin Luther King Hum Rel Award Eta Iota Lambda Chap 1970; Man of Yr Eta Iota Lambda Chap & GA Alpha Phi Alpha 1970. **Military Serv:** AUS sp 2 1951-53. **Business Addr:** 3394 Charlemagne Drive, Decatur, GA 30034.

NUNNALLY, JONATHAN KEITH
Professional baseball player. **Personal:** Born Nov 9, 1971, Pelham, NC. **Educ:** Miami-Dade (South) Community College. **Career:** Kansas City Royals, outfielder, 1995-97; Cincinnati Reds, 1997-. **Business Addr:** Professional Baseball Player, Cincinnati Reds, 100 Riverfront Stadium, Cincinnati, OH 45202, (513)421-4510.

NUNNERY, WILLIE JAMES
Deputy secretary for energy, attorney. **Personal:** Born Jul 28, 1948, Chicago, IL. **Educ:** Univ of KS Lawrence, KS, BS, CE 1971; Univ of WI Sch of Law, JD 1975. **Career:** State of WI, dep sec energy 1975-; Univ of WI Coll of Engrng, asst to dean 1972-75; Atlantic Richfield, legal intern 1972; Energy Research Ctr Univ of WI Coll of Engrng, asso dir; Atlantic Richfield, jr analytical engr, 1971. **Orgs:** Mem WI State Bar 1976-; Midwestern Gov Energy Task Force; scoutmaster, exec dir Four Lk Area Boy Scout Council WI; bd dir YMCA; mem Downtown KiwanisClub of Madison & Greenfield; mem Bapt Ch. **Business Addr:** 101 S Webster St, Madison, WI 53702.

NURSE, RICHARD A.
Educational administrator. **Personal:** Born Sep 1, 1939, New York, NY; son of Bernice Lawless and Reginald Nurse; married Laura Chapman Nurse, May 7, 1962; children: Allison, Richard C. **Educ:** Brown University, Providence, RI, BA, 1961; New York University, New York, NY, 1966-68; University of Rhode Island, Kingston, RI, MPA, 1973. **Career:** US Army, France & Germany, counterintelligence, 1962-64; Prudential Ins Co, Newark, NY, actuarial correspondent, 1964-66; US Army Electronics Command, Fort Monmouth, NJ, contract specialist, 1966-68; Brown University, Providence, RI, assoc director of admissions, 1968-73; Stockbridge School, Stockbridge, MA, headmaster, 1973-76; Rutgers University, New Brunswick, NJ, asst vice president for academic affairs, 1976-. **Orgs:** Member, board of trustees, Princeton Friends School, 1986-94; council member, New Jersey Basic Skills Council, 1978-90; state chairman, New Jersey Alumni of Brown Univ, 1986-90; member, board of directors, Planned Parenthood League of Middlesex County, 1989-94; co-chairman, Dance Power, 1988-; bd of trustees, Princeton Ballet. **Honors/Awds:** President, Brown Univ, 1961 class; Alumni Service Award, Brown University, 1990; Alumni Trustee Nominee, Brown University, 1976, 1978, 1988, Administrative Service Award, New Jersey Assn of Veterans Program Administrators, 1985. **Military Serv:** US Army, Spec 4th Class, 1962-64, Received 513th Intelligence Group Award, 1964. **Business Addr:** Assistant VP for Undergraduate Education, Rutgers University, Van Nest Hall, Room 302, New Brunswick, NJ 08903.

NURSE, ROBERT EARL
Business executive. **Personal:** Born May 25, 1942, New York, NY; son of Miriam Nurse and Earl Nurse; married Ann Marie Jameson (divorced); children: Douglas Jamal, India Marie. **Educ:** Univ VT, BA 1964; Fordham Univ, grad work. **Career:** Xerox Corp, sales rep, consultant, employee relations mgr, sales mgr, personnel operations mgr 1966-77; ITT, staffing mgr 1977-79; Citicorp, personnel mgr 1979-80; Pepsi-Cola, mgr of staffing 1980-81; Robert E Nurse Assoc Inc, pres 1981-88; J B Gilbert Assoc, vice pres, 1988-92; Hall's Security Analysts, Inc, vp, 1992-94; Independent Management, consultant, 1994-96; The Johnson Group, Unlimited, Chicago Branch, vp, gen mgr, 1996-. **Orgs:** Mem CCBE; mem 100 Black Men; mem NAACP. **Business Addr:** Vice Pres/General Manager, The Johnson Group, Unlimited, 125 S Wacker Dr, Ste 300, Chicago, IL 60606.

NUTT, AMBROSE BENJAMIN
Engineering consultant. **Personal:** Born Mar 16, 1920, Milwaukee, WI; son of Willette Nutt and Ambrose Nutt; married Viola Elaine Henderson; children: Jacqueline Nutt Teepen, Sandra. **Educ:** Univ of MI, BSc 1940; OH State Univ, MSc 1950; Air Force Command & Staff Coll, Graduate 1955; Industrial Coll of the Armed Forces, Graduate 1960. **Career:** Air Force Aircraft Lab, project engr 1941-43, 1946-56; Air Force Flight Dynamics Lab, chief mech & sp proj branches 1956-64, chief plans office 1964-69, chief tech operations office 1969-73, chief mgmt opns ofc 1973-76, dir vehicle equip div 1976-81; Wilberforce Univ, dir engrg & computer science 1981-88; Tractell Corp, Dayton, OH, member, tech staff, 1988-. **Orgs:** Pres bd of trustees SCOPE (5 county anti-poverty program) 1967-79; pres Yellow Springs (OH) School Bd 1968-74; mem bd of trustees Dayton (OH) Honor Seminars 1974-; member advisory board Dayton (OH) Math Collaborative 1989-. **Honors/Awds:** Assoc Fellow AIAA 1964; Literary Awd Armed Forces Mgmt Assoc 1971; Meritorious Civilian Serv Medal USAF 1977; Exceptional Civilian Serv Medal USAF 1981. **Military Serv:** USAF maj 1944-46 reserves 1950-60. **Home Addr:** 8379 Adams Rd, Dayton, OH 45424.

NUTT, MAURICE JOSEPH
Clergyman. **Personal:** Born Dec 20, 1962, St Louis, MO; son of Beatrice Lucille Duvall Nutt and Haller Levi Nutt. **Educ:** Holy Redeemer Coll, BA Philosophy, 1985; Catholic Theological Union, Master of Divinity, 1989; Xavier Univ of LA, Master of Theology, 1989; Aquinas Inst of Theology, Doctrinal Student, 1997-. **Career:** St Alphonsus Rock Church, St Louis Mo, associate pastor, 1989-; St. Louis University, Adjunct Professor of Theology, 1990-91; St Alphonsus Rock Church, Pastor, 1993-. **Orgs:** Pres, Natl Black Catholic Seminarians Assn 1986-87; mem bd of dir, Natl Black Catholic Clergy Caucus 1986-87; 1988-89; president, board of directors, Better Family Life Inc., 1990; board of directors, St. Charles Lwanga Center, 1990; St Louis Civil Rights Commission, 1994; NAACP, exec comm, St Louis Branch, 1994; Portfolio Art Gallery, 1993; Natl Council on Drug and Alcohol Abuse, St Louis Chapter, vice pres, board of directors, 1995. **Honors/Awds:** Man of the Year Award, St Joseph Preparatory Coll, 1980; preacher of the 1st Chicago Archdiocesan Black Catholic Youth Revival 1986; publication: Black Vocations: The Responsibility and Challenge 1987; keynote speaker Chicago Archdiocesan Youth Congress 1988; The Fr Clarence Williams Award, Natl Black Catholic Seminarians Assn 1988; organizer and speaker of the Redemptorist Conference on Black Ministry, 1989; Rodel Model Award, St. Louis Public Schools, 1990; ''Forty Under Forty Award'', St. Louis Magazine, 1990; Institute for Peace and Justice, Trumpet of Justice Award, 1994; Young Democrats of St Louis, 1994; Greater Preacher Award, Finalist, Aquinas Inst of Theology, 1995; Steller Performer Award, St Louis American Newspaper, 1996; The John Simon Civic Service Award, Maryville Univ, 1997. **Home Addr:** St Alphonsus Rock Church, 1118 N Grand Blvd, St Louis, MO 63106.

NWA, WILLIA L. DEADWYLER
Educator. **Personal:** Born Jul 20, Cleveland, OH; daughter of Josephine Deadwyler and Thurman Deadwyler; married Umoh Nwa, Sep 4, 1971; children: Idara Umoh, Jakitoro Deadwyler, Ayama Nseabasi, Ifiok Odudu, Uko Obong. **Educ:** Cleveland Institute of Music, 1965-66; Ohio State University, BS, 1971; Wittenberg University, 1973-74; University of Akron, MS, 1975, PhD, 1992. **Career:** 7th Avenue Community Baptist Church, pianist, organist, 1970-71; Northeastern Local Schools, educator, 1971-74; Canton City Schools, educator, 1975-; University of Akron, supervisor, 1989; Malone College, adjunct prof, 1997-. **Orgs:** Council for Exceptional Children, Chapter 464, executive committee; National Education Association; Ohio Education Association; Canton Professional Educators' Association; Ohio Teachers of Exceptional Children; Association for Supervision and Curriculum Development; American Educational Research Association; Kappa Delta Pi, Alpha Theta Chapter; Pi Lambda Theta, Beta Lambda Chap, exec committee; National Alliance of Black School Educators; Leila Green Alliance of Black School Educators; National Congress of Parents and Teachers Association; Sunday School; Deaconess Board, former assistant secretary; Missionary Society; East Central Ohio Education Assn. **Honors/Awds:** Forest City Foundaries, Charles F Seelback Scholarship, 1966; Ohio State University, Alice A White Scholarship, 1970; Canton City Schools, grant, co-author, ''Reading for Survival,'' 1988; University of Akron, University Scholarship, 1989; Recognition by Council for Exceptional Children, 1993. **Special Achievements:** Presentation at the 38th Biennial Convocation, Memphis, TN, Kappa Delta Pi, theme: Excellence in Education, 1992; dissertation, ''The Extent of Participation in Extracurricular Activities at the Secondary Level of Students with Different Exceptionalities in an Urban School District,'' 1992; Presentation at the 13th Annual Intl Conference of Critical Thinking and Educational Reform, Sonoma State Univ, 1993. **Business Addr:** Educator, Canton City Schools, 2800 13th St SW, Canton, OH 44710.

NWAGBARAOCHA, JOEL O.
Educational administrator. **Personal:** Born Nov 21, 1942; son of Christiana Nwagbaraocha and John Oluigbo Nwagbaraocha; married Patsy Coleman; children: Eric, Jason, John, Jonathan. **Educ:** Norfolk State University, BS, 1969; Harvard University, MEd, 1970, EdD, 1972. **Career:** Institute for Services, Division of Academic Planning & Fac Development, director, 1972-74; Morgan State University, vice pres, plan & operations anal, 1978-84; Technical Systems, president, 1982-86; Voorhees College, vice pres, academic affairs, 1985-90; Barber-Scotia College, president, 1990-. **Orgs:** Harvard University Cooperative Society, board of directors; Harvard University Phi Delta Kappa Chapter, board of directors; Children's Institute, board of directors; Higher Education Support Services, board of directors; African Relief Fund, Inc, board of directors; Higher Education Group of Washington, DC; American Council of Education; The National Council for the Social Studies; American Humanist Association. **Honors/Awds:** Training Teachers of Teachers, Harvard Teaching Fellow; Beta Kappa Chi; Phi Delta Kappa. **Business Addr:** President, Barber-Scotia College, 145 Cabarrus Ave W, Concord, NC 28025, (704)786-5171.

NWANNA, GLADSON I. N.
Educator. **Personal:** Born May 12, 1954, Mbonge, Cameroon. **Educ:** Essex Cty Coll, AS acct 1977, AA 1978; Rutgers State Univ, BA acct 1979; St Johns Univ, MBA fin 1980; Fordham Univ, PhD econ 1984; Amer Inst of Banking, banking for prof

cert 1985. **Career:** NJ Blood Center, distrib clerk 1978-79; St Benedict HS, math teacher 1979-80; Essex Cty Coll, adj prof of math & bus 1981-84; Kean Coll of NJ, asstprof fin & econ 1983-85; Rutgers State Univ, adj prof of math 1984; Morgan State Univ, asst prof fin, econ & acct 1985-. **Orgs:** Mem Rutgers State Univ Intl Student Org 1978-79, Amer Econ Assoc 1983-, Eastern Fin Assoc 1985-, World Acad of Devel & Coop 1986-; chief cons, founder African Rsch & Consult Serv 1985-; pres CAMA Trans Inc 1986-; mem NAACP 1986-, Natl Urban League 1986-, World Acad of Devel & Coop 1986-, Soc for Intl Devel 1986-. **Honors/Awds:** Student of the Month Essex Cty Coll 1978; Who's Who in Amer Jr Coll Essex Cty Coll 1978; Alpha Epsilon Beta Essex Cty Coll 1979; Omicron Delta Epsilon1980; Beta Gamma Sigma St Johns Univ 1981; author; publ several articles in prof jrnls. **Home Phone:** (410)377-4749. **Business Addr:** Professor, Dept of Accounting and Finance, Morgan State Univ, 1700 E Cold Spring, Baltimore, MD 21239-4001.

O

OAKLEY, CHARLES
Professional basketball player. **Personal:** Born Dec 18, 1963, Cleveland, OH. **Educ:** Virginia Union Univ, Richmond, 1981-85. **Career:** Chicago Bulls, forward, 1985-88, New York Knicks, 1989-; Oaktree Entertainment, founder. **Honors/Awds:** Led NCAA Division II in rebounding 1985; named to NBA All-Rookie Team 1986; NBA All-Defensive Team, 1994; NBA All-Star, 1994. **Business Addr:** Professional Basketball Player, New York Knicks, 2 Pennsylvania Plaza, New York, NY 10121, (212)465-5867.

OATES, CALEB E.
Cleric. **Personal:** Born Apr 5, 1917, Shelby, NC; married Authella Walker; children: Bernard D, David C. **Educ:** Union Sem, attended; Jewish Theol Sem, attended. **Career:** Baptist Church, ordained minister 1947; Bethany Baptist Church, pastor 1947-. **Orgs:** Mem Local, State, Fed Bapt Church Orgs, pres, chmn Howell-Farmingdale Juvenile Bd 1965-; pres Howell-Farmingdale Council Chs 1968-72; mem bd of dirHowell Rotary Club 1973-. **Honors/Awds:** Pastor of the Year in NJ 1953; Cert of Merit Comm Act Jewish War Vets 1961. **Military Serv:** AUS, ETO, chaplain 1943-45; Bronze Star; 5 Battle Stars. **Business Addr:** Pastor, Bethany Baptist Church, RFD 1 W Farms Rd, Farmingdale, NJ 07727.

OATES, GISELE CASANOVA
Psychologist, educator. **Personal:** Born Apr 27, 1960, Chicago, IL; daughter of Marguerite Boudreaux Casanova and Isidro Casanova; married Roger V Oates; children: Tatiyana Noelle. **Educ:** Illinois Wesleyan University, BA, 1982; Northern Illinois University, MA, 1986, PhD, 1989. **Career:** Institute for Stress Management, clinical associate, 1989-90, consultant, 1990-92; Purdue University, Calumet, assistant professor of psychology, 1990-94; associate professor of psychology, 1995-; Purdue Univ, Calumet, acting coordinator of the Ethnic Studies Program, 1994-. **Orgs:** Alpha Kappa Alpha, president, Xi Nu Omega Chapter, 1995, 1996, mem, 1981-. **Honors/Awds:** Purdue University, Calumet, Scholarly Research Award, 1992, 1993. **Special Achievements:** Co-author, Effects of Impaired Hearing and Favorable vs Unfavorable Personal Feedback on Negative Emotional Reactions, Journal of Clinical Psychology, p 982-987, 1988; Co-author, Physiological Responses to Non-Child-Related Stressors in Mothers at Risk of Child Abuse, Child Abuse and Neglect, p 31-44, 1992; Co-author, Physiological Repsonses to Child Stimuli in Mothers with/without a childhood history of physical abuse, XXV International Congress of Psychology Abstracts, p 15, 1992; Child Abuse & Neglect, p 995-1004, 1994; Co-editor, Intimate Violence, currently in preparation. **Business Addr:** Associate Professor of Psychology, Purdue University, Calumet, Department of Behavioral Sciences, Hammond, IN 46323, (219)989-2781.

OATES, WANDA ANITA
Athletic director. **Personal:** Born Sep 11, 1942, Washington, DC; daughter of Ruth Richards Oates and Robert L Oates Sr. **Educ:** Howard Univ, Washington DC, BS, 1965; George Washington Univ, Washington DC, MA, 1967. **Career:** F W Ballou High School, Washington DC, athletic coach, 1967-, athletic director, 1980-. **Orgs:** Delta Sigma Theta Sorority. **Honors/Awds:** Twice named Coach of the Year by Eastern Bd of Athletic Officials; Natl Honorary Basketball Official Rating, Washington DC Bd of Women Officials; Outstanding Achievement Award, Howard Univ Alumni Club; One of Washington's 100 Most Powerful Women, Washington Magazine; Coach of the Year, Interhigh East, Washington Post, 1991; Presented Key to the City, By Mayor of Washington, DC; DCPS & DCIAA Service Award, 1997. **Home Addr:** 5700 Fourth St NW, Washington, DC 20011.

O'BANNER-OWENS, JEANETTE
Judge. **Personal:** Born in Detroit, MI. **Educ:** Wayne State Law School, Detroit, MI. **Career:** 36th District Court, Detroit, MI, judge, currently. **Orgs:** Michigan District Judges Assn, pres; Assn of Black Judges, 1997; Fed Bar Assn; Amer Bar Assn; State Bar of MI; Amer Judges Assn, pres, immediate past pres, bd mem; Detroit Bar Assn; Wolverine Bar Assn; Judicial Conference, treas, bd mem; Natl Bar Assn; Natl Assn of Women Judges; Natl Judicial Coll, faculty advisor; Supreme Court Update; Harvard Law School; Wayne State Univ Law School; Friends of Wayne Medical School; 36th District Court, Law Day, organizer; Wayne County Criminal Advocacy Prog; Phi Alpha Delta Fraternity; Detroit Inst of Arts, founders society; Downtown Detroit Lion's Club; Elks, Beaulahland Temple No 569. **Business Addr:** Judge, 36th District Court, 421 Madison, Detroit, MI 48226.

O'BANNON, CHARLES
Professional basketball player. **Personal:** Born Feb 22, 1975. **Educ:** UCLA. **Career:** Detroit Pistons, guard-forward, 1997-. **Business Addr:** Professional Basketball Player, Detroit Pistons, 2 Championship Dr, Auburn Hills, MI 48326, (248)377-0100.

O'BANNON, DONNA EDWARDS (DONNA MARIA)
Attorney. **Personal:** Born Jun 26, 1957, New York, NY; daughter of Ione Dunkley Edwards and Theodore U Edwards (deceased); divorced; children: Danielle Salone, Dionne Teddie. **Educ:** Wellesley College, BA, graduated with honors, 1979; University of Virginia Law School, JD, 1982. **Career:** Exxon Co USA, tax attorney, 1982-85; Harris County DA, assistant DA, 1985-87; EEOC, attorney 1987-88; sr attorney, 1988-89; FDIC, Consolidated Office, staff attorney, 1989-90, Litigation Department, head, 1990-92, sr regional attorney, 1992-94; EEOC, administrative judge, 1994-. **Orgs:** 100 Black Women, 1989-94; Links, Inc, international trends chair, 1992-94, historian, 1994-96, corresponding scy, 1996-; Thurgood Marshall Recreation Ctr, advisory council, 1996-, vp, 1994-96, pres, 1996-; Jack & Jill of America, Inc. **Honors/Awds:** Mooreland YMCA, Pinkston Camp Award, 1991; The Dallas Chapter of Links; Dallas Chapter of Bench & Bar Spouses. **Special Achievements:** Tax article, UVA Tax Review, 1982. **Business Addr:** Administrative Judge, EEOC, 207 S Houston St, Dallas, TX 75202, (214)655-3341.

O'BANNON, EDWARD CHARLES, JR.
Professional basketball player. **Personal:** Born Aug 14, 1972, Los Angeles, CA. **Educ:** UCLA. **Career:** New Jersey Nets, professional basketball player, 1995-96; Dallas Mavericks, 1996-. **Special Achievements:** NBA, First Round Draft Pick, #9 Pick, 1995. **Business Addr:** Professional Basketball Player, Dallas Mavericks, Reunion Arena, 777 Sports St, Dallas, TX 75207, (214)988-0117.

OBAYUWANA, ALPHONSUS OSAROBO
Physician. **Personal:** Born Jul 26, 1948, Benin City, Nigeria; son of Irene Osemwegie Obayuwana and William Obayuwana; married Ann Louise Carter, Jun 11, 1977; children: Alphonsus, Anson. **Educ:** High Point Univ, BS (Summa Cum Laude) 1973; Howard Univ, MS 1977; Howard Univ Coll of Medicine, MD 1981. **Career:** South Baltimore General Hospital, intern 1981-82, resident 1982-85; The Johns Hopkins Univ Sch of Medicine, instructor 1985-86; Group Health Assoc, obstetrician/gynecologist 1986-93; Univ of Maryland Coll of Med, dept of obsterics & gynecology, clinical faculty position; Mitchell-Trotman Medical Group, 1993-97; Kaiser-Permanente Medical Group, 1997-. **Orgs:** Principal investigator Institute of Hope 1982-; mem Amer Medical Assoc, Natl Medical Assoc, Amer Soc of Psychosomatic Obstetrics and Gynecology; Consultant The Female Care Center Silver Spring MD 1985-. **Honors/Awds:** Amer College of Obsterics & Gynecology, fellow; Diplomate, Natl Bd of Med Examiners; Diplomate, Amer Bd of Obstetrics & Gynecology; Co-author "The Hope Index Scale," 1982; Natl Resident Research Paper Awd; "Psychosocial Distress and Pregnancy Outcome" 1984. **Business Addr:** Ob/Gyn, Kaise-Permanente Medical Group, 611 Executive Blvd, Rockville, MD 20852.

OBEN, ROMAN
Professional football player. **Personal:** Born Oct 9, 1972; son of Marie Oben. **Educ:** Louisville, bachelor's degree in economics. **Career:** New York Giants, tackle, 1996-. **Orgs:** Alpha Phi Alpha Fraternity. **Business Addr:** Professional Football Player, New York Giants, Giants Stadium, East Rutherford, NJ 07073, (201)935-8111.

OBERA, MARION L.
Government official. **Personal:** Born Sep 19, 1947, Chester, PA; daughter of Lavinia C Staton and Jesse Harper; children: James R Norwood. **Educ:** Prince George Community College, AAS, 1983; Bowie State University, 1985-86; University of Maryland, BS, 1987; Washington College of Law, JD, 1990; The American University, MS, 1992. **Career:** (PMC College) Widenere University, Administrative Assistant, 1966-68; Veterans Administration, Personnel Speciaist, 1975-80; Veterans Administration, Senior Personnel Spec, 1980-90; Department of Veterans Affairs, Chief Recruitment & Examing Division, 1990-. **Orgs:** American Bar Association, 1987-; National Bar Association, 1987-; Black Law Students Associate, vice chairman/AU Chapter, 1988-89; National Black Law Students Association, coordinator, mid-eastern region, F Douglass Moor Court, 1989-89; The American University Student/Facuty Committee, 1987-88; Pennsylvania Bar Association, 1992; Federation Bar Association, 1992; Phi Delta Phi Legal Frat, 1988-; Public Employees Roundtable, VA Coordinator PSRW, 1991-; American Society of Law & Medicine, mem, 1992. **Honors/Awds:** Prince George Comm College, Phi Theta Phi Honor Fraternity, 1983; Veterans Administration Medical Center, Philadelphia, Director Commendation, 1980; Veterans Administration, Word Master Award, 1981; Black Law Students Associate, Appreciation Plaque, 1989; Department of Veterans Affairs, Leadership VA Alumni Associate, 1992. **Business Addr:** Chief, Recruitment & Examining Division, Department of Veterans Affairs, 810 Vermont Ave, Tech World Blgd, Room, Washington, DC 20420, (202)535-8221.

OBI, JAMES E.
Manager. **Personal:** Born Sep 2, 1942, Lagos, Nigeria; married Olubosede Cecilia; children: Funke, Femi, Siji, Uche. **Educ:** St Peter's Coll Oxford England, BA 1963; Amer Coll of Life Underwriters, CLU 1973. **Career:** Equit Life Assurance Soc of the US, agent 1967-68, dist mgr 1968-72, agency mgr 1972-. **Orgs:** Bd mem Nigerian-Amer Friendship Soc 1979. **Business Addr:** President, Nigerian American Alliance, 2 Penn Plaza, Suite 1700, New York, NY 10121.

OBINNA, ELEAZU S.
Educator. **Personal:** Born Jun 4, 1934, Ogbeke-Obibi, Imo, Nigeria; married Carol Jean Miles; children: Iheanyi, Obageri, Marvin. **Educ:** BA 1969; Inst of Bookkeepers London , FCBI 1972; Loyola Univ of Los Angeles, MEd 1973; Univ of CA UCLA, EdD 1978; Univ of Hull England, post doc. **Career:** Redman Western Corp, acct controller 1968-69; Sec Pacific Bank, fin planning spec 1970-71; Pan African, prof bus econ educ 1971; CA State Univ Northridge, studies dept. **Orgs:** Vp Natl Alliance of Bus for youth motivation Wash DC 1984-; chrmn Pan African Studies Dept 1971-75; prof Bus Econ Educ Pan African Studies Dept 1971-; dir of fac & students affairs Pan African SD 1984-86; life mem NAACP 1972; bd dir NAACP San Fernando Valley 1973-74; pres United Crusade Fnd 1982-. **Honors/Awds:** Phelp Stokes Flw 1966-69; Phi Delta Kappa Prof Org 1977-; Black Educ Commissioner LAUSD 1972-82; Black Urban & Ethnic Dir 1972-; African Studies Assc 1971-. **Business Addr:** Prof of Business Econ Educ, CA State Univ Northridge, 18111 Nordhoff St, 18111 Nordhoff St, Northridge, CA 91330.

O'BRYANT, BEVERLY J.
Educator. **Personal:** Born Aug 21, 1947, Washington, DC; daughter of Gertrude Robb Jones and James C Jones; married Michael T O'Bryant II, Jun 7; children: Kimberly Michelle, Michael Tilmon II. **Educ:** Dunbarton College, BA (cum laude), 1969; University of Maryland, MA, 1972, PhD candidate, currently. **Career:** James C. Jones Builders Inc, assistant estimator, 1965-80; Mazima Corp., technical writer, editor, research analyst, 1979-80; District of Columbia Public Schools, counselor, 1978-88, 1990-92, regional counselor, 1986-88, Elementary Division, pupil personnel team coordinator, 1988-90, executive assistant to the superintendent, 1992-94, dir community service/service learning programs, 1994-. **Orgs:** American Counseling Association, president, 1993-94, Governing Council, 1989-94, Ethics Committee, chairperson, 1988-90, Counselor/Counseling Image Task Force, 1985-86, North Atlantic Region, vice pres, 1985-87; American School Counselor Association, president, 1990-91, Leadership Development Conference, chairperson, 1986, Interprofessional Relations, chairperson, 1983-85; Alpha Kappa Alpha Sorority Inc; Barrister's Wives of the District of Columbia; Jack and Jill Inc of America; Kiwanis Wives of the District of Columbia. **Honors/Awds:** Parents of District of Columbia, City-Wide Parent Conference Appreciation Award, 1992; Superintendent of DC Public Schools, Exemplary National Leadership Award, 1992; American Counseling Association, Carl D Perkins Government Relations Award, 1992; Arkansas School Counselor Association, Governor Bill Clinton, Arkansas Traveler Award, 1990; DC Counseling Association, J Harold McCully Recognition Award, 1991. **Special Achievements:** Author: Marketing Your School Counseling Program, A Monograph, ERIC/CAPS, 1992; presentations: Facelift for the 90's: Enhancing Counselor Image through Creative Partnerships, Nebraska School Counselor Association; Empowering the Positive Human Potential in Ourselves, Idaho School Counselors; A New Human Vision for Guidance, PBS Education Series. **Business Addr:** Dir, Comm Serv/Serv Learning Programs, American Counseling Assn, Rabaut Administration Bldg, 2nd and Peabody Sts, Washington, DC 20011, (202)541-5928.

O'BRYANT, CONSTANCE TAYLOR
Judge. **Personal:** Born Apr 12, 1946, Meherrin, VA; daughter of Mattie Naomi Taylor and Joseph E Taylor; divorced; children: Taylora Laurece, Kristal Cherrie. **Educ:** Howard University, College of Liberal Arts, BA, 1968, School of Law, JD, 1971. **Career:** DC Public Defender Service, sr staff attorney, 1971-81; Department of Health & Human Services, Social Security Adm, administrative law judge, 1981-83, administrative appeals judge, 1983-90, Departmental Appeals Board, administrative law judge, 1991, Social Security Adm, deputy chief ad-

ministrative law judge, 1991-94; Dept of Housing & Urban Development, administrative law judge, 1994-. **Orgs:** Natl Bar Assn; Judicial Council of NBA; National Association of Women Judges; DC Public Defender Service, board of trustees, 1992-, board of directors; Joint Educational Facilities, advisory board; Banneker School Council, secretary, 1989-91; Friends of DC Youth Orchestra, secretary, 1987-89; NAACP, mem; National Urban League, 1992; Office of Hearings & Appeals, SSA Law Journal, executive board, 1991-; SSA Strategic Planning Comm, 1991-; Project Champ, volunteer, 1996; Federal Administrative Law Judge Conference, executive board, 1995-; DC Public School-Reading and Math, tutor, 1995; Harvard Law Trial Advocacy Workshop, visiting faculty, 1996, 1997; John Marshall Univ, School of Law, visiting faculty, 1997, 1998. **Honors/Awds:** Social Security Adm, Deputy Commissioner Citation, 1992, Associate Commissioner Citations, 1984, 1985, 1986; Greater Washington Area Chapter, Women Lawyer's Division of NBA, outstanding leadership & service as jurist & lawyer, 1982. **Special Achievements:** First Woman and First African Amer Deputy Chief ALJ, Social Security Admin; First Woman & African Amer, ALJ, Dept of Housing & Urban Development; Annual Panelist, Natl Bar Assn, Convention on Social Security Law & Procedures, 1984-, How to Become an ALJ, 1990-95; Moderator, National Judicial Council's seminar on administrative law issues, 1992. **Business Addr:** Office of Administrative Law Judges, Dept of HUD, Ste 320, 409 3rd Street, SW, Washington, DC 20024, (202)708-5004.

O'BRYANT, TILMON BUNCHE. See Obituaries section.

O'CONNOR, RODNEY EARL
Dentist. **Personal:** Born Jun 25, 1950, Sharon, PA; son of Helena B McBride O'Connor (deceased) and Dr Lauriston E O'Connor; married Andrea; children: Elena Moi O'Connor. **Educ:** Kentucky State Univ, Frankfort, KY, 1968-71; Univ of Kentucky, Lexington, KY, College of Dentistry, DMD, 1975; Eastman Dental Center, Rochester, NY, 1975-76; Rochester Institute of Technology, 1983. **Career:** Rushville Clinic, dental consult 1976; Rochester Health Network, dental consult 1978-87; LE O'Connor DDS, PC, vice pres, currently. **Orgs:** Treas, Operation Big Vote, 1983; member, Acad of General Dentistry 1984-, Amer Dental Assoc, Natl Dental Assoc, Northeast Regional Dental Board; mentor, Urban League Mentorship Program, 1990-91; The Dental Society of the State of New York; 7th District Dental Society. **Honors/Awds:** Strong Hospital Dental Research fellowship, 1972; abstract/patent search, "Method of Ultrasonic Pyrogenic Root Canal Therapy," 1976; Urban League, Salute to Black Scholars, 1989, Distinguished Service, 1991, Distinguished Chefs, 1991, 1992. **Home Addr:** 311 Aberdeen St, Rochester, NY 14619. **Business Addr:** Vice President, L E O'Connor DDS PC, 503 Arnett Blvd, Rochester, NY 14619, (716)436-1640.

O'CONNOR, THOMAS F., JR.
Attorney. **Personal:** Born Mar 16, 1947, New Bedford, MA; married Donna L Dias; children: Jolon Thomas, Justin Kahil, Quinton Kolby. **Educ:** Roger Williams Coll Bristol, RI, AA, BA 1975; New England School of Law, Boston, MA, JD, 1993. **Career:** War II Providence, city councilman, sch committeeman, 1973-79; City Council, 1979-89; Dept of Planning, 1989-90; Port Commission, assoc dir project management & construction, 1990-94; Dept of Planning & Development, special assoc dir, currently. **Orgs:** Mem ILA Local 1329; bd dir Afro Arts Cntr; bd dir S Providence Tutorial; Omni Dev Corp, pres; RI Black Lawyers Assn, treasurer. **Honors/Awds:** Recip 2 Purple Hearts, Vietnam; Biography, Leaders of Black Am, Harco Press 1973. **Military Serv:** USMC 1966-70.

ODEN, GLORIA
Educator, poet. **Personal:** Born Oct 30, 1923, Yonkers, NY; married John Price Bell. **Educ:** Howard Univ, BA 1944, JD 1948; NY Univ, grad study. **Career:** Amer Inst of Physics, editor 1961-66; Inst of Electric & Electronic Engrs, sr editor 1966-67; Appleton-Century-Crofts, supr 1967-68; Holt Rinehart & Winston, proj dir for science and language arts books 1968-71; Univ of MD Baltimore County, assistant prof, assoc prof, prof of English. **Orgs:** PEN; The Poetry Soc of Amer; The Society for the Study of the Multi-Ethnic Literature of the United States. **Honors/Awds:** Creative Writing Fellowships John Hay Whitney Found 1955-57; Fellowship to Yaddo Saratoga Springs NY 1956; Breadloaf Writers Scholarship Middlebury College 1960; interviewed for Black Oral History Prog Fisk Univ Library 1973; Living Black American Authors 1973; Black Writers Past & Present 1975; Distinguished Black Women's Award, Towson University, 1984; William H Hastie Symposium Award, 1981; numerous others. **Business Addr:** Professor of English, Univ of MD Baltimore County, University of Maryland, Baltimore, MD 21228, (410)455-2384.

ODEN, WALTER EUGENE
Educator. **Personal:** Born Feb 26, 1935, Stuart, FL; married Edith; children: Walter II, Darin. **Educ:** Bethune-Cookman Coll, BS 1956; FL Atlantic Univ, MEd 1966; FL Atlantic, EdD 1975. **Career:** Brownsville Jr HS, principal 1955-68; Radio Station WSTU, ancr, dj; Univ of Miami, teacher 1956-63, dir 1963-66, principal 1966-67, consult 1967, guidance consult 1968-69, asst principal 1969; FL Atlantic Univ, asst prof 1971; FL Atlantic Univ, adj prof 1971-76; Jan Mann Oppty School North, principal 1982-. **Orgs:** Mem Phi Delta Kappa, 2nd Baptist Church, Omega Psi Phi, Bethune-Cookman Coll Alumni Assoc, Dade Cty Secondary School Principal Assoc. **Honors/Awds:** Natl Assn Secondary School Principal Plaque; Disting Serv Recruiting Students Bethune-Cookman Coll 1968; Outstanding Leadership CEEB Club Martin Co 1969; Outstanding Serv Plaque 1973; Dep Prin Amer School; Outstanding Serv Young Mens Prog Org 1975. **Business Addr:** Principal, Jan Mann Oppty School North, 4899 NW 24th Ave, Miami, FL 33142.

ODOM, CAROLYN
Communications executive. **Personal:** Born Aug 31, 1944, Augusta, GA; daughter of Marjorie Odom and P C Odom. **Educ:** Spelman Coll, BA (Hon roll) 1966; Amer Univ, MA Comm 1970. **Career:** Coll of Medicine & Dentistry of New Jersey, materials developer 1970; Minority Economic Devel Corp, admin asst, Educ 1971; New York City Addiction Serv Agency, deputy dir, public relations, community info 1972-76; Natl Health Council, asst dir, communications coordinator 1976-77; Earl G Graves Ltd, dir, public affairs 1977-83; Corporate Communications, vice pres 1983-, sr vice pres 1987-. **Orgs:** Bd of dirs Natl Black Child Devel Inst; co-chair Corporate Women's Roundtable, Spelman Coll; The EDGES Group; Women in Communications; board member, National Coalition of 100 Black Women. **Honors/Awds:** Natl French Hon Soc Pi Delta Phi 1963; YWCA Acad of Women Achievers 1984; publications: "Talking with the Inner City" Public Relations Journal 1969, "The Enigma of Drug Abuse" Journal of Practical Nursing 1974. **Business Addr:** Senior Vice President, Earl G Graves, Ltd, 130 Fifth Ave, New York, NY 10011.

ODOM, CLIFTON LEWIS
Professional football player. **Personal:** Born Sep 15, 1958, Beaumont, TX. **Educ:** Univ of Texas at Arlington, BA, business admin. **Career:** Cleveland Browns, 1980-81; Baltimore Colts, 1982-84; Indianapolis Colts, linebacker, 1984-90; Miami Dolphins, linebacker, 1990-94; Blockbuster Video Franchisee, currently. **Orgs:** Athlete in Action; Optimist Club of Arlington. **Business Addr:** Professional Football Player, Miami Dolphins, 2269 NW 199th St, Miami, FL 33056.

ODOM, DARRYL EUGENE
Human service administrator. **Personal:** Born Mar 14, 1955, Houston, TX; son of Elizia Amboree Odom and Cleveland Odom; children: Matthew, Crystal, Russell. **Educ:** Morgan State Univ, Baltimore, MD, BA, 1977; TX Southern Univ, Houston, TX, Masters of Public Administration, 1985; Rice Univ, Houston, TX, 1986. **Career:** City of Houston, Houston, TX, center administrator, asst multi-service, ctr, admin, program mgr. **Orgs:** Committee, American Red Cross, 1986-91; bd mem, Boy Scouts, 1989-91; literacy advance, Literacy Advance, 1989-91; mem, Family to Family, 1990-91. **Honors/Awds:** Outstanding Young Man of America, US Jaycees, 1979; Mayor's Appreciation Award, City of Houston, 1980; Community Service Award, YWCA, 1989; Young Black Achievers. **Home Addr:** 4306 Morris Ct, Pearland, TX 77584.

ODOM, STONEWALL, II
Public policy organization executive. **Personal:** Born Nov 1, 1940, Petersburg, VA; son of Flossie Odom and Stonewall Faison; married Marlena Hines Odom, Jan 29, 1989; children: Terrance, Jacqueline, Latisha, Nicole, Stonewall III, Marlena, Marcus, Malcolm, Mandela, Muhammad, Malik, Myles. **Educ:** John Jay Coll of Criminal Law. **Career:** Metropolitan Life, sales representative; City of New York, NY, police officer, 1965-73; CORE, chief coordinator and interim chairman, 1989-; Black Men Opposed to Drugs & Violence, Yonkers NY, chairman, currently; Odom & Sons Vending Co, principal owner. **Orgs:** Mem, Sammuel H Dow Amer Legion Post #1017; master mason, James H Farrell Lodge; mem, Vietnam Veterans of Amer; coordinating mem, The Yonkers Crack Task Force; founder, chmn, Tower Soc Citizens for Responsible Govt, 1985-89; legislative chmn, Sammuel H Dow Post #1017 Amer Legion, chmn, Veterans Comm for the Yonkers Branch of the NAACP, 1986. **Honors/Awds:** Two Meritorious Awards, New York Police Dept, 1969-72; Chairman of Veterans; Ethiopian Orthodox Church Public Award, 1988; ran for The New York State Assembly on the Conservative Line and Right to Life (received 7,000) votes, 1988; African American Association Community Service Award, 1996. **Military Serv:** US Army, Sp4, Airborne, 1961-64. **Home Addr:** 79 Oak St, Yonkers, NY 10701.

ODOMES, NATHANIEL BERNARD
Professional football player. **Personal:** Born Aug 25, 1965, Columbus, GA. **Educ:** Univ of Wisconsin, attended. **Career:** Buffalo Bills, cornerback, 1987-. **Honors/Awds:** Played in AFC Championship Game, post-1988 season. **Business Addr:** Professional Football Player, Buffalo Bills, One Bills Dr, Orchard Park, NY 14127-2296.

ODOMS, WILLIE O.
Data processing consultant. **Personal:** Born Mar 3, 1950, Eatonton, GA; son of Helen Reid Odoms and Willie Cleve Odoms; married Paulette Copel, Jul 25, 1987; children: Antoinette, Cristy Helena, A'seem Evans. **Educ:** Clayton State Coll, Morrow GA, AA, 1974; Dekalb Community Coll, Clarkston GA, AS, 1981; Brenau Professional Coll, Gainesville GA, BS, 1989. **Career:** State of Georgia, Atlanta GA, planner, 1981-84; Information Systems of Amer, Atlanta GA, product specialist, 1984-86; Equifax Inc, Atlanta GA, sr planner, 1986-89; Odoms Contracting Serv Inc, Ellenwood GA, consultant, 1989-. **Orgs:** Pres, Black Data Processing Assoc Inc, Atlanta Chapter, 1988-. **Honors/Awds:** DOAs Commissioner's Award, State of Georgia, 1983. **Military Serv:** US Army, sergeant first class, 1968-71; Vietnam Campaign Medal, 1971; Arcom, 1970-71. **Home Addr:** 3693 Windmill Rd, Ellenwood, GA 30049.

O'DONNELL, LORENA MAE
Educational administrator, clergyman. **Personal:** Born May 1, 1929, Cincinnati, OH; daughter of Charity Elizabeth O'Donnell and Charles Richard O'Donnell; children: Alena. **Educ:** Univ of Cincinnati, BS Ed 1951; Miami Univ, ME 1960; Yale Univ, Post Grad 1972; Nova Univ, EdD 1976. **Career:** Cincinnati Publ Schools, teacher 1951-61, personnel assoc 1961-65, suprv 1965-69; North Avondale School, principal 1969-72; Cincinnati Public Schools, dir of staff devel 1972-81; Hillcrest School, chaplain 1982-; University of Cincinnati, Cincinnati, OH, assoc dean, 1989; educ consultant, 1990; Wyoming Baptist Church, Wyoming, OH, dir of Christian educ, 1987-; Northern Kentucky University, coordinator of alternative teacher certification prog, 1993-. **Orgs:** Ed consult 1960-; dir Hamilton Cty State Bank 1976-; 1st black female mem Cincinnati Bd of Ed 1980-; dir Franchise Devel Inc 1980-; partner Loram Entr 1981-83; dir Red Cross Adv Bd 1981-; mem Juvenile Court Review Bd 1981-86; director, Ham County State Bank, 1976-86; director, Red Cross, 1981-87; president, Church Women United, Cincinnati Chapter, 1995-97. **Honors/Awds:** God in the Inner City Juv Religious Book 1970; God is Soul Juv Religious Book 1971; Kellogg Found Grant Yale Univ 1972; Grand Deputy Dist 6 State of OH, OES Amaranth Grand Chap 1985; One of Ten 1986 Enquirer's Women of the Year; author, Joy In Contemplation, Published 1991. **Business Addr:** Educational Consultant, Northern Kentucky University, Nunn Dr, Bep 282, Newport, KY 41076, (606)572-5235.

O'FERRALL, ANNE F.
Educator. **Personal:** Born Jun 28, 1906, Marshall, TX; daughter of Ardella Dawson Flowers (deceased) and Mack Flowers (deceased); married Ernest B O'Ferrall, Sep 3, 1938. **Educ:** Bishop Coll, BS; Univ of So CA, BS Ed, MS Math 1962, MS Ed 1963; FL A&M Univ, USC Educ of Mentally Retarded. **Career:** LA Unified Sch District, math teacher, teacher of trainable mentally retarded; Dade Co Miami, FL, math & sci tchr; English Enterprises, bookkeeper/accountant, 1944-; LA City School System, teacher, 1958-81. **Orgs:** Natl Council of Negro Women; past sec & vice pres United Nation Assn, LA; mem LA World Affairs Council; NAACP Legal Defense & Educ Fund; mem Freedom from Hunger Com; mem Comm Relations Conf of So CA; sec CA State Council UN Assn; mem, Phi Delta Gamma, Omicron Chap Univ So CA; UNA, Pasadena, 1st vice pres; bd mem, Community Relations Conf, Southern California. **Honors/Awds:** Cit of outstdng serv LA Co Conf on Comm Relations 1954; Outstanding Women of Yr in Intl Relations, LA Sentinel 1958; Certificate of Merit, Zeta Phi Beta 1956; UNICEF chmn/del to Biennial Conv UNA-USA 1977; Cert of Merit, appreciation, outstanding serv & devotion to volunteer duty, Vet Admin 1951, 1953, 1955, 1958.

OFFICER, CARL EDWARD
Mayor. **Personal:** Born Apr 3, 1952, St Louis, MO. **Educ:** Western Coll of Miami, Univ Oxford OH, BA, political science, philosophy, 1974; So Illinois Univ, Carbondale, mortuary science, 1975. **Career:** St Clair County, Illinois, deputy coroner 1975-77; State of Illinois, Drivers Services, deputy director 1977-79; Officer Funeral Home, East St Louis IL, vice pres 1970-; City of East St Louis IL, mayor 1979-. **Orgs:** Member, US Conference of Mayors; member, National Conference of Black Mayors; member, Urban League; member, Jaycees; member, NAACP; mem Sigma Phi Sigma; life mem Kappa Alpha Psi. **Honors/Awds:** Cert of Commendation, Top Ladies of Distinction 1980; Humanitarian Awd, Campbell Chapel AME Church 1980. **Military Serv:** Illinois National Guard, Second Lieutenant, 2 yrs.

O'FLYNN-THOMAS, PATRICIA
Business executive. **Personal:** Born Jul 28, 1940, E St Louis, IL; daughter of Margarette Matthews O'Flynn and James E O'Flynn; divorced; children: Terence, Todd. **Educ:** Southern IL Univ, BS 1963; Univ of WI Milwaukee, MA 1973; St Martins Acad, Hon Doct 1983. **Career:** Natl Newspaper Publishers Assn, pres 1987-, 2nd vice pres secy 1983-86; Milwaukee Minority C of C, dir 1986; Milwaukee NAACP; dir 1983; Milwaukee Community Journal Inc, newspaper publisher; PPP Inc, president; Speech of the singing group, Arrested Development, agent, currently. **Orgs:** Founder Eta Phi Beta Milwaukee Chap 1976; founder Milwaukee Comm Pride Expo 1976; mayoral appt Lakefront Design Comm 1979; founder Milwaukee Chap

Squaws1980; gov appt Comm of Small Business 1980; dir Milwaukee Chap of PUSH 1980; del White House Comm 1980. **Honors/Awds:** Publisher of the Year NNPA 1986. **Business Addr:** Publisher, Milwaukee Community Journal, 3612 N Martin L King Dr, Milwaukee, WI 53212.

OFODILE, FERDINAND AZIKIWE
Plastic surgeon. **Personal:** Born Oct 20, 1941, Nnobi, Anambra State, Nigeria; son of Regina Eruchalu Ofodile and Julius Ofodile; married Caroline Okafor Ofodile, Jul 5, 1969; children: Uchenna, Ikechukwu, Nnaemeka, Nnamdi. **Educ:** Northwestern University, Evanston, IL, BS, 1964; Northwestern Medical School, Chicago, IL, MD, 1968. **Career:** St Lukes/Roosevelt Hospital, New York, NY, assoc attending surgeon, 1982-; Columbia University, New York, NY, clinical prof of surgery, 1982-; Harlem Hospital Center, New York, NY, dir of plastic surgery, 1982-. **Orgs:** Member, American Society of Plastic & Recon Surgeon, 1986; fellow, American College of Surgeons, 1986; member, International programs Committee ASPRS, 1992; member, New York County Medical Society, 1988-; member, chairman of plastic surgery, American Assn Academic. **Honors/Awds:** Author of many scientific articles; lecturer in many international symposiums; Fellow, American Assn of Plastic and Reconstructive Surgeons. **Business Addr:** Director of Plastic Surgery Service, Harlem Hospital Medical Center, 506 Lenox Ave, New York, NY 10037.

OGDEN, JONATHAN PHILLIP
Professional football player. **Personal:** Born Jul 31, 1974, Washington, DC; son of Shirrel and Cassandra. **Educ:** UCLA. **Career:** Baltimore Ravens, offensive tackle, 1996-. **Honors/Awds:** Outland Trophy winner, 1995; The Sporting News, All-America first team, 1995; USA Today, All-Rookie Team, 1996. **Business Addr:** Professional Football Player, Baltimore Ravens, 11001 Owings Mills Blvd, Owings Mills, MD 21117, (410)654-6200.

OGLESBY, JAMES ROBERT
Educational administrator. **Personal:** Born May 30, 1941; married Barbara; children: James R Jr, Regina, David. **Educ:** SC State Coll, BS 1966; Univ of Missouri-Columbia, MEd 1969, PhD 1972. **Career:** Jefferson Jr High School, classroom teacher; Univ of Missouri-Columbia, graduate research asst 1969-70, graduate teaching asst 1970-71, coord of space & facilities and asst prof of educ 1972-74, asst prof of educ and asst provost for admin 1974-80, asst prof of educ and dir facilities utilization, beginning 1980, asst to the chancellor, currently. **Orgs:** Guest lecturer for educ courses Univ of MO-Columbia 1972-; bd dirs Columbia Day Care Corp 1973-; mem Bd of Educ Columbia MO 1974-; mem MO State Teacher's Assn 1974-; mem, 1976-, pres, 1989, Natl Sch Bds Assn; MO School Bd Assn 1977- (holding various positions and serving on numerous bds in both assocs); sec Bd of Trustees Columbia Coll 1978-; mem Ambassador Club 1982-; comm develop consultant on Educ and Politics for Minneapolis MN; consultant Task Force on Governance-Natl Sci Foundation; consultant site visitor Secondary Sch Recognition Program US Dept of Educ. **Honors/Awds:** Published material includes "Education for the Twenty First Century," Natl Science Foundation Comm on Public Educ 1983; grant received, Boone County Comm Serv Council (to partially fund a building addition for Columbia Day Care Corp), City of Columbia (to fund a summer youth employment prog titled CARE). **Military Serv:** AUS 2nd Lt 2 yrs. **Home Addr:** 1441 N Countryshire Dr, Columbia, MO 65202. **Business Addr:** Assistant to Chancellor, Univ of Missouri, 105 Jesse Hall, Columbia, MO 65211.

OGLESBY, JOE
Newspaper editor. **Personal:** Born Aug 1, 1947, Tampa, FL; son of Terrie Del Benniefield Yarde and Northern Oglesby; married Bloneva McKenzie (divorced 1984); children: Joy Denise; children: Lee Erin. **Educ:** Florida A&M University, Tallahassee, FL, BA, English, 1970. **Career:** The Miami Herald, Miami, FL, day city editor, editorial writer, reporter, 1972-87; The Philadelphia Inquirer, suburban editor, 1987-90; The Miami Herald, Miami, FL, assistant managing editor, 1990-. **Orgs:** Member, National Association of Black Journalists, 1977-. **Honors/Awds:** Pulitzer Prize, Editorial Writing, Columbia University, 1983. **Business Addr:** Associate Editor, The Miami Herald, One Herald Plaza, Miami, FL 33101.

OGLESBY, TONY B.
Banking executive. **Personal:** Born Jan 4, 1954, Atlanta, GA; son of Bunice Oglesby Sanders; married Cheryl Smith Oglesby, Apr 7, 1984; children: Jessica Lauren. **Educ:** Oglethorpe University, Atlanta, GA, BS, 1976. **Career:** Trust Company Bank, Atlanta, GA, operations supervisor, 1972-78, group vice pres, 1982-; First Georgia Bank, Atlanta, GA, operations officer, 1978-80; Federal Home Loan Bank, Atlanta, GA, operations mgr, 1980-82. **Orgs:** Chairman, Atlanta Exchange, 1989-90; president, National Assn of Urban Bankers, 1990-91; president, Atlanta Urban Bankers, 1986-87. **Honors/Awds:** Banker of the Year, 1987-88, Member of the Year, 1989, National Urban Bankers.

OGLETREE, CHARLES J., JR.
Educator, attorney. **Personal:** Born Dec 31, 1952, Merced, CA; son of WillieMae Reed Ogletree and Charles J Ogletree, Sr.; married Pamela Barnes Ogletree, Aug 9, 1975; children: Charles J III, Rashida Jamila. **Educ:** Stanford University, Stanford, CA, BA, 1974, MA, 1975; Harvard Law School, Cambridge, MA, JD, 1978. **Career:** District of Columbia Public Defender Service, Washington, DC, staff attorney, 1978-82, director of staff training, 1982-83; American University/Washington College of Law, Washington, DC, adjunct professor, 1982-84; Antioch Law School, Washington, DC, adjunct professor, 1983-84; District of Columbia Public Defender Service, Washington, DC, deputy director, 1984-85; Jessamy, Fort & Ogletree, Washington, DC, partner, 1985-89; Harvard Law School, Cambridge, MA, visiting professor, 1985-89, director, introduction to trial advocacy workshop, 1986-, assistant professor, 1989-93, professor of law, 1993-; Jessamy, Fort & Botts, Washington, DC, of counsel, 1989-; Harvard Law School, Criminal Justice Institute, Cambridge, MA, director, 1990-. **Orgs:** Member, American Bar Association; member, National Conference of Black Lawyers; member, National Bar Association; member, American Civil Liberties Union; member, Bar Association of DC; member, Washington Bar Association; defender committee member, National Legal Aid and Defender Association; Assn of American Law Schools; DC Bar; Southern Ctr for Human Rights Committee, chairperson. **Honors/Awds:** Hall of Fame, California School Boards Foundation, 1990; Nelson Mandela Service Award, National Black Law Students Association, 1991; Richard S Jacobsen Certificate of Excellence in Teaching Trial Advocacy, 1990; Honoree, Charles Hamilton Houston Institute, 1990; Award of Merit, Public Defender Service Associaton, 1990; Personal Achievement Award, NAACP and The Black Network, 1990; "Supreme Court Jury Discrimination Cases and State Court Compliance, Resistance and Innovation," Toward a Usable Past, 1990; "Justice Marshall's Criminal Justice Jurisprudence: The Right Thing to Do, the Right Time to Do It, The Right Man and the Right Place," The Harvard Blackletter Journal, Spring 1989; Boston Museum of Afro-American History, Man of Vision Award, 1992; Harvard Law School, Albert M Sacks-Paul A Freund Award for Excellence in Teaching, 1993; Criminal Practice Inst, A Champion of Liberty Award, 1994; NY State Bar Assn-Criminal Justice Sect, honoree, Award for Outstanding Contribution in Criminal Law Education, 1992; Transafrica-Boston Chapter, Outstanding Service Award, 1992; co-author: Beyond the Rodney King Story; "Just Say No! A Proposal to Eliminate Racially Discriminatory Uses of Peremptory Challenges," 31 American Criminal Law Review 1099, 1994; "The Quiet Storm: The Rebellious Influence of Cesar Chavez," Harvard Latino Review, vol 1, 1995. **Special Achievements:** Moderator of television programs including: "Surviving the Odds: To Be a Young Black Male in America," Public Broadcasting System, 1994; "Political Correctness and the Media," C-Span, 1994; "Don't Say What You Think!; Limits to Free Speech," C-Span, 1994. **Business Addr:** Professor, Harvard Law School, Hauser Hall, Room 320, 1575 Massachusetts Ave., Cambridge, MA 02138.

OGLETREE, JOHN D., JR.
Attorney, cleric. **Personal:** Born Mar 1, 1952, Dallas, TX; son of Marion Deckard and John D Ogletree Sr; married Evelyn Horn, Apr 14, 1973; children: Johnny, Lambrini, Joseph, Jordan. **Educ:** University of Texas at Arlington, BA, 1973; South Texas College of Law, JD, 1979. **Career:** Fulbright & Jaworski Law Firm, messenger, 1976-77; Harris County Sheriff Department, baliff, 1977-79; Caggins, Hartsfield & Ogletree Law Firm, partner, 1979-93; Antioch Missionary Baptist Church, minister of Christian development, 1985-86; First Metropolitan Baptist Church, pastor, 1986-. **Orgs:** Natl Bar Assn, 1979-; State Bar of Texas, 1979-; National Baptist Convention USA, 1986-; Urban Alternative, 1987-; Eastern Progressive Baptist Missonary Dist Association, instructor, 1987-; Baptist Missionary & Education State Convention, 1987-. **Special Achievements:** Evangelist for Gulf Coast Association, 1989; keynote speaker for Gulf Coast Keswick, 1990; teacher, Workshop for Cooperative Baptist Fellowship, 1992.

OGLIVIE, BENJAMIN A.
Professional baseball player (retired). **Personal:** Born Feb 11, 1949, Colon, Panama; married Tami; children: Trianni, Benjamin. **Educ:** Attended: Bronx Community College, Northeastern Univ, Wayne State Univ. **Career:** Boston Red Sox, outfielder 1971-73; Detroit Tigers, outfielder 1974-77; Milwaukee Brewers, outfielder 1978-86. **Honors/Awds:** Harvey Kuenn Award 1978; named to several post-season All-Star Teams 1980; Silver Slugger Team The Sporting News 1980; ranks in every Brewer category on the all-time top ten hitting list 1983. **Business Addr:** Outfielder, Milwaukee Brewers, Milwaukee County Stadium, Milwaukee, WI 53214.

O'GUINN, JO LYNN
Educator, nurse. **Personal:** Born Dec 13, 1954, Texarkana, AR; widowed. **Educ:** University of Arkansas, Fayetteville, 1976, Little Rock, BSN, 1979; University of Central Arkansas, nursing, 1981; Southern Arkansas University, education, 1989; Northwestern State University, MSN, 1990. **Career:** University Hospital, staff RN, 1979-80; Pulaski County, staff RN, 1980-81; Baptist Medical Center System, instructor of nursing, 1981-82; Warner Brown Hospital, social worker, patient care coordinator for home health, 1982-84; Department of Nursing, Associate Degree Nursing Program, Magnolia, AK, clinical nursing instructor, 1984; Red River Vocational Technical School, LPN Program, instructor of nursing; Ouachita County Hospital, Utilization Review Department, diagnostic related grouping staff, One Day Surgery Department, developer, coordinator, 1984-87; North Monroe Hospital, Skilled Nursing Facility; University of Arkansas at Monticello, Department of Nursing, assistant professor of nursing, 1987-91; Grambling State University, School of Nursing, assistant professor, 1991-94; Southern Arkansas Univ, asst professor, 1994-. **Orgs:** American Nurses Assn; Arkansas Nurses Assn; Little Rock Black Nurses' Assn; Assn of Black Nursing Faculty in Higher Education, state coordinator; Sigma Theta Tau, Gamma Xi Chapter. **Honors/Awds:** Little Rock Black Nurses' Assn, Award for Top Contribution, 1981. **Special Achievements:** Guest speaker: Graduating class, Red River Vocational Technical School of Licensed Practical Nursing, 1984, 1988; publications: abstract on diskette, Nursing Research Alerting Network, 1990; abstract, "Nursing Research on Aging: Insights and Innovations," Seventh Annual Phyllis J Verhonick Nursing Research Conference, 1992; numerous others. **Business Addr:** Assistant Professor, Southern Arkansas University, Dept of Nursing, Magnolia, AR 71753.

OGUNIESI, ADEBAYO O.
Investment banker, attorney. **Personal:** childRen: one son. **Educ:** Oxford University, Oxford, England; Harvard University, JD, MBA. **Career:** Harvard Law Review, editor; District of Columbia, US Court of Appeals, staff; Supreme Court Justice Thurgood Marshall, staff; Cravath, Swaine & Moore, attorney; First Boston Inc, director, currently. **Special Achievements:** One of the top 25 "Hottest Blacks on Wall Street" listed in Black Enterprise, October, 1992. **Business Addr:** Director, First Boston, Inc, 55 E 52nd, New York, NY 10055, (212)909-2000.

O'HARA, LEON P.
Clergyman, oral surgeon. **Personal:** Born May 13, 1920, Atlanta; married Geraldine Gore; children: Scarlett, Leon, Michael, Jeri, Mark, Miriam. **Educ:** Talladega Coll, AL, BA, BS 1942; Meharry Med Col, DDS 1945; Washington U, first Negro, postgrad Sch 1952; Providential Theol Sem, DD. **Career:** Oral surgeon, St Louis 1945-; Holy Metro Bapt Ch, fdr, pastor 1955-; City of St Louis, pub health oral surg. **Orgs:** Vp, pres Mound City Dental Soc 1952-56; pres Midwestern States Dental Soc; staff mem St Mary's Hosp, Peoples Hosp, Faith Hosp, Christian Hosp; mem, commr St Louis Mayor's Council on Human Relations; chmn Way Out Drug Abuse Prgm; parole adv Penal Adoption Prgm; bd dirs Urban League, St Louis; bishop Indep Peng Assemblies Chs; Omega Psi Phi; West Urban Renewal Dirs 1968-70; life mem NAACP; former mem CORE; former mem Ecumenical Coun of Chs. **Honors/Awds:** Pub Serv Award, 25 yrs svc, Pres Johnson; 8-state shotgun skeet shooting champ 1966; ETO Tennis Champ 1947; Ft Monmouth Tennis Champ (singles & doubles) 1945. **Military Serv:** AUS maj Dental Corps 1943-48. **Business Addr:** Mound City Med Center, 2715 Union Blvd, St Louis, MO 63113.

OHENE-FREMPRONG, KWAKU
Association executive, physician. **Career:** Natl Assn for Sickle Cell Disease Inc, national president, currently. **Business Phone:** (213)736-5455.

O'KAIN, MARIE JEANETTE
Educator. **Personal:** Born in Magnolia, AR; married Roosevelt O'Kain; children: Gregory L. **Educ:** Univ of AR Pine Bluff, BS (cum laude) 1953-59; Univ of MO St Louis, MEd 1968-71, Specialist 1981-82; St Louis Univ, Advanced Graduate Study toward Doctorate. **Career:** St Louis Co Elem Public School, teacher 1960-75, principal 1975-81; MINACI Inc/Job Corps, consultant 1982; St Louis Co Public School, unified studies lecturing and curriculum develop 1982-. **Orgs:** Mem Assn of Elem Sch Principals 1975-84; Alternate Prof Liability Review Bd 1978-80; alderwoman 3rd wd city of Pine Lawn MO 1979-; mem Welfare Bd 1979-; mem Parks & Recreation Comm 1979-; mem Streets & Lights Comm 1979-; mem Re-districting Comm 1979-; mem Norhill Neighborhood Adv Council 1979-; dir Budget & Finance 1979-; dir Public Relations 1979-; mem Conf of Educ; mem St Louis Univ Metro Coll Scholarship Selection Comm; mem St Louis Univ Metro College Upward Bound Adv Bd 1983-; mem Performance Based Teacher Eval Task Force, Human Rel Comm & Spec Activities; public speaker, pianist Church; pres Margaretta Block Unit #1; mem, Republican presidential task force comm, President Bush Task Force, 1990. **Honors/Awds:** Certificate three consecutive yrs Natl Guild of Piano Teachers 1967-69; Disting Serv Awd Teachers Assn St Louis 1970; Key Principal Awd Elem Principals Assn 1975-81; Cert of Appreciation 1st Congressional District 1980; Meritorious Cert Chap 9 OES Eastern Star 1980; Certificate of Recognition, President Bush, Republican Task Force, 1990; Medal of Merit & Republican Presidential Task Force Lapel Pin, 1990; Certificate for Distinction and Achievement in Who's Who in the Republican Party, 1991.

O'KAIN, ROOSEVELT
City official. **Personal:** Born Aug 21, 1933, Clarendon, AR; married Marie J Haymon; children: Gregory Lynn. **Educ:** For-

est Park Comm Coll, A 1973; Harris Teachers Coll, BS Educ 1978. **Career:** US Post Office, carrier 1965; City of Pine Lawn, alderman 1973-79; Pine Lawn MO, mayor. **Orgs:** Mem Bd of Jail Visitors St Louis Co 1977; mem Cit Adv Bd Job Corp Ctr 1978; mem bd of dir Normandy Council 1980. **Honors/Awds:** Awd of Appreciation St Louis Job Corps Ctr 1980. **Military Serv:** AUS pfc 1953-55; Good Conduct Medal & Natl Def Ribbon. **Business Addr:** Mayor, City of Pine Lawn, 6250 Forest Ave, Pine Lawn, MO 63120.

OKHAMAFE, IMAFEDIA
Educator. **Personal:** son Of Olayemi Okhamafe and Obokhe Okhamafe. **Educ:** Purdue Univ, PhD, Philosophy and English, 1984. **Career:** Univ of NE at Omaha, prof of philosophy & English 1993-. **Orgs:** Humanities consultant; member, Modern Language Association of America, member, American Philosophical Association. **Honors/Awds:** Purdue Univ David Ross Fellow 1983; Natl Endowment for the Humanities Summer Fellow 1985; Humanities Grant from Andrew W Mellon Foundation 1985; Natl Endowment for the Humanities summer grant 1987 for workshop on humanities for non-traditional students; and University of California-Berkeley 1996 Summer Research Fellowship to Study the Philosophy of Cognitive Neuroscience; articles have appeared in periodicals such as Black Scholar, Journal of the British Soc for Phenomenology, UMOJA, Intl Journal of Social Educ, Auslegung, Rsch in African Literatures, Soundings, Philosophy Today, and Africa Today; presented papers at such institutions as Univ of TX at Austin, Ohio Univ, Miami (of Ohio) Univ, and MI State Univ. **Business Addr:** Prof of Philosophy & English, University of Nebraska-Omaha, Annex 39, Omaha, NE 68182-0208.

OKINO, ELIZABETH ANNA (BETTY)
Gymnast. **Personal:** Born Jun 4, 1975, Entebbe, Uganda; daughter of Aurelia Okino and Francis C Okino. **Career:** Gymnast, currently. **Orgs:** 1992 Olympic Team, gymnast, 1992. **Honors/Awds:** World Championships, Indianapolis, Silver Team Medal, Bronze on Bean, 1991; American Cancer Society Bikethon, chairperson, 1992; Chicago State University, Special Sports Award, 1992; Illinois State House of Representatives Resolution #2583, 1992. **Special Achievements:** Women Gymnastics Team, Barcelona Olympics, 1992; Olympics, Bronze Medalist, 1992; World Championships, Indianapolis, Silver Team Medal, Bronze on Beam, 1991; World Championships Paris, Silver Medal Bars, 1992; Champion, American Cup, 1991. **Business Addr:** Athlete, US Women's Gymnastic Team, US Olympic Committee, 1750 E Boulder St, Colorado Springs, CO 80909.

OKORE, CYNTHIA ANN
Social worker. **Personal:** Born Nov 15, 1945, Philadelphia, PA; daughter of Jessie M Reed and William Reed (deceased); married Caleb J Okore; children: Elizabeth A. **Educ:** Cheyney Univ, BA 1974; Rutgers Univ, MSW, 1981. **Career:** Presbyterian University of Pennsylvania Hospital, Philadelphia, PA, social worker, 1977-79; John F Kennedy Community Mental Health/Mental Retardation Center, Philadelphia, PA, social worker, 1981-84; Philadelphia Veterans Affairs Medical Center, social worker, 1984-. **Orgs:** Member, National Black Women's Health Project, 1990-, National Council on Negro Women, 1989-, National Black Alcoholism Council, 1989-, National Association of Social Workers, 1980-, Pennsylvania Chapter of Social Workers, 1980-, Philadelphia Chapter of Social Workers, 1980-. **Honors/Awds:** Author, "The Nurse Practitioner," The Journal of Primary Health Care, July 1990; author, The Cocaine Epidemic: A Comprehensive Review of Use, Abuse, and Dependence. Technical Art and Publications Competition Award of Excellence, Society for Technical Communication, Puget Sound Chapter, 1990-91. **Home Addr:** 5543 Windsor Ave, Philadelphia, PA 19143. **Business Addr:** Social Worker/Family Therapist, Philadelphia Veterans Affairs Medical Center, 39th & Woodland Ave, Philadelphia, PA 19104.

OKOYE, CHRISTIAN E.
Professional football player. **Personal:** Born Aug 16, 1961, Enugu, Nigeria. **Educ:** Azusa Pacific Univ, received physical educ degree, 1987. **Career:** Kansas City Chiefs, running back, 1987-. **Honors/Awds:** Sporting News All-Star Team, 1989; played in Pro Bowl, post-1989 season. **Business Addr:** Professional Football Player, Kansas City Chiefs, One Arrowhead Dr, Kansas City, MO 64129-1651.

OKPARA, MZEE LASANA. **See HORD, FREDERICK LEE.**

OKUNOR, SHIAME
Educator, educational administrator. **Personal:** Born Jun 2, 1937, Accra, Ghana; son of Dorothea Okunor and Benjamin Okunor; divorced; children: Dorothy Ometse. **Educ:** New York Univ, Certificate 1968; Grahm Jr College, AAS 1971; The Univ of NM, BA Speech Communications 1973, MPA 1975, PhD 1981. **Career:** The University of NM, Afro-Amer studies 1981-82, dir academic affairs Afro-Amer studies 1982-, acting dean univ coll 1985-86, dean general coll 1986-87, asst prof educ found, Acting Assoc Dean Graduate Studies 1988-89. **Orgs:** Mem exec bd NAACP 1975-86; mem Affirmative Action Policy Comm; bd of dirs, pres NM Sickle Cell 1981-91; secretary, treasurer, New Mexico Endowment for the Humanities, 1987-92; member, New Mexico Jazz Workshop, 1991-92. **Honors/Awds:** Outstanding Sr Awd 1971; Outstanding Intl Awd 1971; Pres Recognition Awd Univ of NM 1981-85; AP Appreciation Awd Albuquerque Public Schools 1981; Comm Serv Awd NAACP 1982; WM Civitan Merit Awd 1984; Black Communication Serv Awd 1984; Presidency Awd Schomburg Ctr New York City 1985-86; NM Sec of State Cert of Apprec 1985; NM Assoc of Bilingual Teachers Awd 1986; US Military Airlift Command Cert of Recognition 1987; Cert of Apprec US Corps of Engrs 1987; Yvonne Ochillo, Southern Conference on African American Studies, 1990. **Home Addr:** 239 Yucca NW, Albuquerque, NM 87105. **Business Addr:** Director, African-American Studies, University of New Mexico, 1816 Las Lomas NE, Albuquerque, NM 87131.

OLAJUWON, HAKEEM ABDUL
Professional basketball player. **Personal:** Born Jan 21, 1963, Lagos, Nigeria; married Dalia Asafi. **Educ:** Univ Houston, 1981-84. **Career:** Houston Rockets, center 1984-; Barakaat Holdings Limited. **Orgs:** Played on the Nigerian Natl team in the All-African games as a 17-year-old. **Honors/Awds:** Voted Top Player of the 1983 Final Four; mem 2nd Team All-NBA; mem 36th & 37th NBA All Star Teams; Most Valuable Player Award, 1994; mem of NBA World Champion Houston Rockets Basketball Team, 1994; Olympics "Dream Team", gold medal, 1996. **Home Addr:** Barakaat Holdings Ltd, 5847 San Felipe, Ste 220, Houston, TX 77057. **Business Addr:** Professional Basketball Player, Houston Rockets, PO Box 272349, Houston, TX 77277, (713)627-0600.

OLAPO, OLAITAN
Consulting engineer. **Personal:** Born Apr 20, 1956, Lagos, Nigeria; son of F A Osidele and J O Osidele; married Oluwayimika Aduloju, Dec 23, 1989; children: Olabamigbe, Ayoola. **Educ:** Virginia Community College, AAS, 1980; Milwaukee School of Engineering, BSc, 1982; Marquette University, MSc, 1986. **Career:** Wisconsin Department of Transportation, 1983-90; Toki & Associates, Inc, vice pres, 1987-. **Orgs:** International Institute of Wisconsin, board of directors, 1991-; American Society of Civil Engineers,; Concrete Reinforcing Steel Institute. **Honors/Awds:** Wisconsin Department of Transportation, Secretary's Award, 1992. **Business Addr:** VP, Toki & Associates, Inc, 7100 N Fond du lac, Ste 201, Milwaukee, WI 53218, (414)463-2700.

OLAWUMI, BERTHA ANN
Employment counselor. **Personal:** Born Dec 19, 1945, Chicago, IL; married Aina M; children: Tracy, Tanya. **Educ:** Thronton Comm Coll, AAS 1979; John Marshall Law School, Cert 1980; Governors State Univ, BA Human Justice 1981-. **Career:** Tinley Park Mental Health Ctr, mental health tech 1979; Robbins Juvenile Advocacy, juvenile advocate 1979-83; John Howard Assoc Prison Watch Group, intern student 1984; Minority Econ Resources Corp, employment spec/instr. **Orgs:** Mem chairperson Thornton Comm Coll Mental Health Club 1978-79; mem bd of dir Worth Twp Youth Serv 1981; mem 1981-83, pres 1982 Amer Criminal Justice Assoc; mem Blue Island Recreation Commiss 1982-84; bd mem School Dist 143 1/2. **Honors/Awds:** Student Found Scholarship Awd Thornton Comm Coll 1979; Cert Cook Cty Sheriffs Youth Serv 1980; Cert Citizens Info Serv 1980; Cert Morraine Valley Comm Coll 1980; Cert St Xavier Coll 1981. **Home Addr:** 3032 West 140 St, Blue Island, IL 60406.

OLDHAM, ALGIE SIDNEY, JR.
Educator (retired). **Personal:** Born May 18, 1927, Dyersburg, TN; married Sarah Mae Graham; children: Roslynn Denise, Bryan Sidney. **Educ:** TN State Univ Nashville, BA 1949; Univ of Notre Dame, MA 1954. **Career:** South Bend Comm School, elem principal 1966-75, asst high school principal 1975-83, principal 1975-; Riley High School, principal 1983-89, retired. **Orgs:** Mem Phi Delta Kappa Educ Frat, Natl Assoc of Secondary School and IN Principal's Assoc; adv bd Vocational/Special Educ Handicapped for South Bend Comm Schools; life mem NAACP; bd mem South Bend Police Merit Bd; life mem Kappa Alpha Psi Frat; Most Worshipful Grand Master Prince Hall Grand Lodge Jurisdiction of Indiana 1981-83; Deputy Orient of Indiana, Ancient Accepted Scottish Rite Prince Hall Grand Lodge IN 1986; grand minister of state, United Supreme Council, Ancient Accepted Scottish Rite of Freemasonry, Prince Hall Affiliated, northern jursidiction, 1992, 1995. **Honors/Awds:** Invited to the White House during President Carter's administration for conference on Energy 1980; Sovereign Grand Inspector General Ancient Accepted Scottish Rite Prince Hall Northern Jurisdiction 1980; first Black High School Principal South Bend IN 1983; elevated to 33 degree United Supreme Council AASR, PHA, NJ, 1971. **Military Serv:** AUS supply sgt 1950-52.

OLDHAM, CHRISTOPHER MARTIN
Professional football player. **Personal:** Born Oct 26, 1968, Sacramento, CA. **Educ:** Univ of Oregon, attended. **Career:** Detroit Lions, defensive back, 1990; Buffalo Bills, 1991; Arizona Cardinals, 1994; Pittsburgh Steelers, 1995-. **Business Addr:** Professional Football Player, Pittsburgh Steelers, Three Rivers Stadium, 300 Stadium Circle, Pittsburgh, PA 15212, (412)323-1200.

OLDHAM, JAWANN
Professional basketball player. **Personal:** Born Jul 4, 1957, Seattle, WA. **Educ:** Seattle Univ. **Career:** Denver Nuggets, center 1980-81; Houston Rockets, center 1981-82; Chicago Bulls, center 1982-86; New York Nets, 1986-87; Sacramento Kings, 1987-88; Orlando Magic, 1989; Los Angeles Lakers, 1990; Indiana Pacers, 1991. **Honors/Awds:** One of three Bulls to shoot 500 or better from the field.

O'LEARY, HAZEL
Former government official. **Personal:** Born 1937, Newport News, VA. **Educ:** Fisk Univ; studied law at Rutgers Univ. **Career:** State of New Jersey, state and county prosecutor; Coopers and Lybrand, partner; US Community Services Adm, general counsel; Ford Administration, federal energy post; Carter Administration, federal energy post; Northern States Power Co, Minneapolis, MN, executive vice president; Clinton Administration, US Dept of Energy, Washington, DC, energy secretary; O'Leary and Associates, pres, currently. **Orgs:** Africare, bd of trustees; AES Corp, bd of trustees; The Center for Democracy, bd of trustees; The Keystone Center, bd of trustees; ICF Kaiser, Inc, bd of trustees; Morehouse College, bd of trustees, 1998-. **Honors/Awds:** Trumpet Award, 1997. **Business Addr:** Energy Secretary, US Department of Energy, 1000 Independence Ave SW, Washington, DC 20585-0001, (202)586-0000.

O'LEARY, TROY FRANKLIN
Professional baseball player. **Personal:** Born Aug 4, 1969, Compton, CA. **Career:** Milwaukee Brewers, outfielder, 1993-94; Boston Red Sox, 1995-. **Business Addr:** Professional Baseball Player, Boston Red Sox, Fenway Park, 24 Yawkey Way, Boston, MA 02215, (617)267-9440.

OLINGER, DAVID Y., JR.
Attorney. **Personal:** Born Jan 8, 1948, Hazard, KY; son of Zetta M Olinger and David Y Olinger Sr; married Betty Hyatt, Jun 2, 1969; children: Joslyn Hyatt. **Educ:** Berea College, BA, 1969; University of Kentucky, JD, 1976. **Career:** Kentucky Department of Transportation, staff attorney; Eastern District of Kentucky, assistant US attorney, currently. **Orgs:** Kiwanis Club of Berea, president, 1987; Kiwanis Club, Kentucky-Tennessee Division Nine, lt governor, 1992-93; Ashler Lodge #49 F & AM, past master. **Military Serv:** US Navy, sm3, 1969-73; Ameriman Spirit, 1970. **Home Addr:** 307 Brown St, Berea, KY 40403.

OLIVER, AL, JR.
Professional baseball player (retired). **Personal:** Born Oct 14, 1946, Portsmouth, OH; married Donna; children: Felisa, Aaron. **Educ:** Kent State Univ, attended. **Career:** Pittsburgh Pirates, outfielder/infielder, 1968-77; Texas Rangers, outfielder/infielder, 1978-81; Montreal Expos, infielder/outfielder, 1982-83; San Francisco Giants, infielder/outfielder, 1984; Philadelphia Phillies, infielder/outfielder, 1984; Los Angeles Dodgers, outfielder, 1985; Toronto Blue Jays, infielder, 1985. **Honors/Awds:** National League batting title winner, 1982; first player in history to have 200 hits & 100 RBI in same season in both leagues (1980, Texas, 1982, Montreal); named to The Sporting News National League All-Star team, 1975, 1982; National League All-Star Team, 1972, 1975, 1976, 1982, 1983; American League All-Star Team, 1980, 1981; collected the 2,500 hit of his career, 1983; played 2,000 major league game, 1983.

OLIVER, BRIAN DARNELL
Professional basketball player. **Personal:** Born Jun 1, 1968, Chicago, IL. **Educ:** Georgia Institute of Technology, Atlanta, GA, 1986-90. **Career:** Philadelphia 76ers, 1990-.

OLIVER, DAILY E.
Educator. **Personal:** Born Aug 5, 1942, Ft Devons, MA; married Mary E McConaughy; children: Brennen, Mona, Elizabeth. **Educ:** Univ of Utah, BS 1965; Univ of Utah, MEd 1973; Univ of Utah, PhD 1978. **Career:** Utah Board of Pardons, member 1979-83; Weber State College, dir Ethnic Studies 1985. **Orgs:** Member, Prof Ski Instructors of America, 1964-. **Honors/Awds:** Skiing Magazine, The Skiing 100, Sept 1996. **Military Serv:** UT Natl Guard, staff sgt, 1959-69. **Business Addr:** Dir Ethnic Studies, Weber State College, 3750 Harrison Blvd, Ogden, UT 84408.

OLIVER, DARREN CHRISTOPHER
Professional baseball player. **Personal:** Born Oct 6, 1970, Kansas City, MO. **Career:** Texas Rangers, pitcher, 1993-. **Business Addr:** Professional Baseball Player, Texas Rangers, 1000 Ballpark Way, Arlington, TX 76011, (817)273-5222.

OLIVER, EVERETT AHMAD
Brewing company executive. **Personal:** Born Nov 22, 1961, Memphis, TN; son of Evelyn Minor and George Oliver Sr; married Kim Manning Oliver, Aug 17, 1985; children: Trevor, Shane. **Educ:** University of Northern Colorado, BA, criminal justice, 1985. **Career:** Coors, security representative, 1985-, mgr of investment recovery, currently. **Orgs:** Coors African-American Association, board member, currently, Systems Monitoring, chairperson, currently; Colorado State Juvenile and De-

linquency Prevention Advisory Council, board member, 1989-92; Colorado Uplift, currently. **Honors/Awds:** Dollars and Sense Magazine, Americas Best and Brightest Business and Professional Men, 1992. **Special Achievements:** Developed, implemented, and managed the Coors Office Watch Program, 1992-; featured in Professional Security Training Network video on corporate security, 1992; featured in Security Management magazine, 1992. **Business Addr:** Manager, Investment Recovery, Coors Brewing Co, Golden, IR764, Golden, CO 80401, (303)277-2796.

OLIVER, JAMES L.
Automobile dealer. **Personal:** Born Oct 2, 1934, Little Rock, AR; son of Jessie M McKinley and Willie Oliver; married Doreatha, Jun 1952; children: Cornell, Patricia, Cheryl, Barbra. **Career:** Faust Polishing, Chicago IL, foreman, 1952-65; United Saving Life Insurance, regional mgr, 1970-75; Self-Employed in Ice Cream Business, 1975-80; Bonnie Brook Ford, mgr, 1982-84; Willow Brook Ford, mgr, 1984-85; University Ford, owner, CEO, 1985-. **Business Addr:** University Ford, 2100 W Pioneer Pky, Peoria, IL 61615-1830.

OLIVER, JERRY ALTON, SR.
Law enforcement official. **Personal:** Born Mar 2, 1947, Phoenix, AZ; son of Florine Goodman Oliver and Fred A Oliver; children: Jerry II, Hope. **Educ:** Phoenix College, Phoenix, AZ, associate, 1972; Arizona State University, Tempe, AZ, BA, 1976, MA, 1988. **Career:** Phoenix Police Dept, Phoenix, AZ, assistant police chief, 1970-90; City of Memphis, Memphis, TN, director, office of drug policy, 1990-91; City of Pasadena, chief of police; City of Richmond, chief of police, currently. **Orgs:** NOBLE, 1985-; past board president, Valley Leadership, 1985-86; Kappa Alpha Psi Fraternity; National 100 Black Men Inc, 1990; national steering committee, Urban Youth Education, Office of Substance Abuse Prevention, 1991. **Honors/Awds:** Veterans of Foreign Wars J, VFW, 1989; Hoover Award Hall of Fame Inductee, ASU Public Programs, 1988; Distinguished Alumni, Alumni Association Phoenix College, 1985; Distinguished Leadership Award, National Committee Leadership Organization, 1990; NAACP, Phoenix Chapter, Image Award, NAACP, 1990. **Military Serv:** Navy, E-4, 1966-68. **Business Addr:** Chief of Police, City of Richmond, 501 N 9th St, Richmond, VA 23219, (804)780-6489.

OLIVER, JESSE DEAN
Elected official. **Personal:** Born Oct 11, 1944, Gladewater, TX; married Gwendolyn Lee. **Educ:** Dallas Baptist Univ, B Career Arts Mgmt 1976; Univ of TX Sch of Law, JD 1981. **Career:** Sanger Harris Dept Stores, asst dept mgr 1971-72, dept mgr 1972-73; Intl Bus Machines Corp, admin spec 1973-78; Univ of TX Sch of Law, student asst to assoc dean Byron Fullerton 1979-80; Mahomes Biscoe & Haywood, assoc atty 1981-83; Attorney at Law, practicing attorney 1983-; TX House of Reps, mem of 68th & 69th TX Legislature 1983-. **Orgs:** Adv comm mem Licensed Voc Nurses Assn; participant Information Seminar for Amer Opinion Leaders Hamburg & Berlin Germany 1983; participant Natl Forum on Excellence in Educ 1983; planning comm mem Secretarial Initiative on Teenage Alcohol Abuse Youth Treatment Regional Conf 1983; exec comm Mayor's Task Force on Housing & Economic Development in S Dallas 1983-84; participant 19th Annual Women's Symposium The Politics of Power & conscience 1984; mem Natl Ctr for Health Serv Rsch User Liaison Prog 1984; speaker TX Public Health Assn Conf 1984; speaker Natl Conf of State Legislators Conf on Indigent Health Care 1984; speaker TX Public Health Assn Conf. **Honors/Awds:** "The Jesse Dean Oliver-Student Bar Assn Student Loan Fund" Honored by the Univ of Texas; Perigrinus Award for Outstanding Leadership TX Sch Student Bar Assn, Bd of Govs; Student Bar Assn Bd of Govs Awd Texas School of Law; Consul Award for Outstanding Serv to TX Sch of Law; Gene Woodfin Award, Univ of Texas School of Law; J L Ward Disting Alumnus Awd Dallas Baptist Coll 1984; Certificates of Appreciation, East Garland Neighborhood Serv Ctr 1974, 1975; Dallas Plans for Progress Youth Motivation Comm 1976 & 1977; Natl Fed of the Blind Progressive Chap 1983; TX State Council Natl Organ of Women 1983; Good St Baptist Church 1983; Harry Stone Middle Sch 1984; South Oak Cliff HS 1984; Dallas Independent Sch Dist Bus & Mgmt Ctr 1983, 1984. **Business Addr:** Representative, Texas House of Representatives, P O Box 2910, Austin, TX 78769.

OLIVER, JOHN J., JR.
Publishing company executive. **Personal:** Born Jul 20, 1945, Baltimore, MD. **Educ:** Fisk U, BA 1969; Columbia Univ Sch of Law, JD 1972. **Career:** Afro American Newspapers, chmn, publisher, CEO, currently; GE Information Serv Co, couns asst sec beginning 1980; Assigned Components GE Co, couns 1978-80; Davis Polk & Wardwell, corp atty 1972-78. **Orgs:** Bd of dirs 1972-; chmn bd of trust Afro-Am Newspapers; Kappa Alpha Psi; asso mem Musm of Natl Hist; Columbia Law Sch Alum Assn. **Business Addr:** Publisher, CEO, Afro American Newspapers, 2519 N Charles St, Baltimore, MD 21218.

OLIVER, KENNETH NATHANIEL
Business executive. **Personal:** Born Mar 6, 1945, Montgomery, AL; married Thelma G Hawkins; children: Tracey, Karen, Kellie. **Educ:** Univ of Baltimore, BS 1973; Morgan State Univ, MBA 1980. **Career:** Equitable Bank NA, sr banking officer 1973-83; Coppin State Coll, asst prof; Devel Credit Fund Inc, vp, senior vice pres, currently. **Orgs:** President, Baltimore Mktg Assoc; mem Baltimore Cty Private Ind Council, St of MD Advisory Bd, Walter P Carter Ctr; Baltimore County Planning Board; Investing in Baltimore, treasure; John Hopkins University, advisory council. **Military Serv:** AUS E-5 4 yrs. **Home Addr:** 8818 Greens Ln, Randallstown, MD 21133. **Business Addr:** Senior Vice President, Development Credit Fund Inc, 2550 N Charles St, Ste 20, Baltimore, MD 21218.

OLIVER, LOUIS, III
Professional football player. **Personal:** Born Mar 9, 1966, Belle Glade, FL. **Educ:** Florida, BS, criminology, law, 1989. **Career:** Miami Dolphins, safety, 1989-. **Honors/Awds:** Sporting News, college All-America team, defensive back, 1987. **Business Addr:** Professional Football Player, Miami Dolphins, 2269 NW 199th St, Miami, FL 33056, (305)620-5000.

OLIVER, MELVIN L.
Educator. **Personal:** Born Aug 17, 1950, Pittsburgh, PA; son of Ruby Oliver and Rev Loman Oliver. **Educ:** William Penn Coll, BA 1968-72; Washington Univ, MA 1972-74, Ph D 1975-77; Univ of MI, postdoctoral 1979. **Career:** Univ of MO, visiting asst prof 1977-78; UCLA, asst prof 1978-85, assoc prof 1985-. **Orgs:** UCLA Center for Afro-American Studies, faculty assoc 1978-; Resource Allocation Committee, mem 1981-86, chair 1986-. **Honors/Awds:** Nat'l Fellowship Fund, dissertation fellow 1975-77; Ford Foundation, post doctoral fellowship 1982-83; Rockefeller Foundation, research fellow 1984-85; Natl Science Foundation Research, Initiation Planning Grant, 1988; Social Science Research Council Grant on the Black Underclass, 1989. **Business Addr:** Assoc Professor, Dept of Sociology, UCLA, 405 Hilgard Ave, Los Angeles, CA 90024-1301.

OLIVER, PAM
Sportscaster. **Personal:** Born Mar 10, 1961. **Educ:** Florida A&M University, BS in broadcast journalism, 1984. **Career:** WFSU-TV, reporter/producer, 1984-85; WALB-TV, political/news reporter, 1985-86; WAAY-TV, science/military reporter, 1986-88; WIVB-TV, news reporter/anchor, 1988-90; WTVT-TV, news reporter/anchor, 1990-91, sports reporter/anchor, 1991-92; KHOU-TV, sports anchor/reporter, 1992-93; ESPN, sportscaster, 1993-. **Special Achievements:** Earned All-America honors six times as a member of Florida A&M University's women's track and field team and holds the school's mark in the 400 meters. **Business Addr:** Sportscaster, Sports Center, ESPN Inc, 935 Middle St, ESPN Plaza, Bristol, CT 06010, (203)585-2000.

OLIVER, ROBERT LEE
Attorney. **Personal:** Born Nov 14, 1949, Winnfield, LA; son of Alice P Oliver and Frank Oliver Sr; married Cynthia Marie Vessel Oliver; children: Robert Lee II. **Educ:** Southern University, BS, 1971; Southern University Law School, JD, 1974. **Career:** Louisiana Department of Transportation, sr attorney; attorney, notary public, currently. **Orgs:** Delta Theta Psi Law Fraternity, charter member. **Business Addr:** Attorney at Law, Notary Public, 1986 Dallas Dr, Ste 14, Baton Rouge, LA 70806, (504)924-7220.

OLIVER, RONALD
Medical technologist, author, electro-physiologist, educator. **Personal:** Born Jul 16, 1949, New Orleans, LA; son of Everlina Oliver Thompson and Wilbert Oliver; married Barbara Simpson Oliver, Nov 9, 1985; children: Nannette Marie, Joseph Byron. **Educ:** Southern University, BS, biology ed, 1980, BS, chemistry, 1983; Southwest University, MA, 1986, PhD, 1987; Columbia State University, PhD, 1992; Kennedy-Western University, PhD, health administration, 1993; Kensington Univ, PhD, environmental engineering, 1995; Summit Univ, PhD, electrophysiology, 1995. **Career:** Charity Hospital, medical technical assistant II, 1975-78; Tulane University School of Public Health, Tropical Med, faculty, staff, 1975-80; Charity Hospital, medical technologist, 1978-80, medical technologist supervisor I, 1980-; Delgado Community College, instructor, 1990; Pacific Western University, professor, allied health services, 1991-. **Orgs:** American Medical Technologist, medical technologist, 1983-, medical lab technician, 1977-83; American College of Healthcare Executives, nominee member, 1988-; National Society for Cardiovascular/Pulmonary Technologist, 1974-; Louisiana Environmental Health Association, Inc, 1976-; American Association of University Professors, 1992; American Association of Professional Consultants, 1992; Professional & Technical Consultants Association, 1992; Management Standards Committee, American Society of Cardiovascular Professionals, chairman. **Honors/Awds:** American Medical Technologist/Scientific Products, Highest Scholastic Achievement Award, 1978; Charity Hospital at NO, Outstanding Service Award, 1972; McDonogh Elementary Schools #19, Guest Speaker Award, 1992; The Nobel Foundation (Sweden), acknowledgement letter of committee protocol, 1992. **Special Achievements:** A Primer in Electrocardiography, 1st ed, Vantage Press, 1991, 3rd ed, 4th ed, Library of Congress, 1992; "The Anterior-Septal Reciprocity Theory;" "The Electrocardiographogenic Review;" "The Oliver's Theory: A New Bio-electrical Theoretic Addition;" "The Oliver's Tri-Pathway Conductivity Theory;" "The Human Heart, an Theoretical Approach". **Home Phone:** (504)241-9437.

OLIVER, RONALD DANIEL
Law enforcement officer. **Personal:** Born Dec 16, 1946, Philadelphia, PA; son of Anna Maude Frazier Oliver and Nero Oliver; married Phyllis Renee Diamond Oliver, Aug 26, 1988; children: Michael R, Chrystal K. **Educ:** Philadelphia College of Textiles Science, Philadelphia, PA, BS, criminal justice administration, associate science police operations, 1979. **Career:** US Army Security Agency E-S, comsec-analyst, 1965-68; Philadelphia Police Dept, Philadelphia, PA, 1969-. **Orgs:** President, GLC, 1987-; vice president, Alfonso Deal Community Development Corporation, member, American Civil Liberties Union of Pennsylvania. **Honors/Awds:** Alfonso Deal Courage Award, GCL, 1984. **Military Serv:** US Army, E-5, 1965-68; NDS Vietnam Service Campaign Medal 4 Stars, Good Conduct. **Business Addr:** Detective, HQS Investigation Unit, Philadelphia Police Department, 8th and Race, Philadelphia, PA 19104.

OLIVER, WINSLOW PAUL
Professional football player. **Personal:** Born Mar 3, 1973, Houston, TX; married Julie; children: Christopher, Steven. **Educ:** New Mexico. **Career:** Carolina Panthers, running back, 1996-. **Business Addr:** Professional Football Player, Carolina Panthers, 800 Mint St, Ericsson Stadium, Charlotte, NC 28202, (704)358-7000.

OLIVERA, HERBERT ERNEST
Educational administrator, educator. **Personal:** Born Apr 6, 1923, New York, NY; son of Francella Haylett-Olivera and James Phillip Olivera; divorced; children: Herbert E Jr, Angela. **Educ:** Kentucky State University, BS, 1950; New York University, MA, 1953; University of Arizona, master's, accounting, 1969, PhD, 1975. **Career:** University of Arizona, School of Business & Pub Adm, instructor, 1968-70; Pima College, School of Business, chair, 1970-73; Governors State University, School of Business, professor, 1973-78; Alabama A&M University, School of Business, dean, 1978-81; Morgan State University, School of Business & Management, dean, 1981-88; Towson State University, School of Business, professor of acctg, 1988-92, Department of Acct, chair, 1992-. **Orgs:** American Institute of CPAs, 1971-; American Acct Association, 1965-; American Taxation Assn, 1973-; Small Business Institute Directors Assn, 1978-; International Council on Small Business, 1983-; Maryland Banking Commission, 1987; Maryland Chamber of Commerce, 1983-88; Baltimore Engineering Society, 1984-89. **Honors/Awds:** Alpha Kappa Mu Honor Society, General Academic Honor, 1949; Beta Gamma Sigma, Business Adm Honory Award, 1975; Beta Alpha Psi, Accounting Honor Society, 1968; Kentucky State University, Outstanding Teachers Award, 1965. **Military Serv:** US Marine Corps, pfc, 1944-47. **Home Addr:** 1200 Griffith Place, Riverside, MD 21017-1324, (410)575-7155. **Business Addr:** Chair, Department of Accounting, School of Business & Economics, Towson State University, Stephens Hall, Room 102, Towson, MD 21204-7097, (410)830-3226.

OLIVER-SIMON, GLORIA CRAIG
Government official. **Personal:** Born Sep 19, 1947, Chester, PA; daughter of Lavinia C Staton and Jesse Harper; married Joseph M Simon; children: James R Norwood. **Educ:** Prince George Community College, AAS, 1983; Bowie State University, 1985-86; University of Maryland, BS, 1987; Washington College of Law, JD, 1990; The American University, MS, 1992. **Career:** PMC College, Widener University, administrative assistant, 1966-68; Veterans Administration, Medical Center, personnel specialist, 1975-80, senior personnel specialist, 1980-90; Department of Veterans Affairs, Recruitment & Examining Division, chief, 1990-96; human resources advisor and consultant, 1996-. **Orgs:** American Bar Association, 1987-; National Bar Assn, 1987-; Black Law Students Association, AU Chapter, vice chair, 1988-89; National Black Law Students Association, Mid-Eastern Region, coordinator, Frederick Douglass Moot Court Annual Competition, 1989; The American University, Student/Faculty Committee, 1987-88; Pennsylvania Bar Association, 1991-; Federal Bar Association, 1992; Phi Delta Phi Legal Fraternity, 1988-; Public Employees Roundtable, VA, coordinator, PSRW, 1991-92; American Society of Law, Medicine, and Ethics 1992-94; Federal Circuit Bar Assn, 1993; DC Bar, 1997; DAV Auxiliary, 1993-; AKA Sorority, Inc, 1995; AAUW, 1994. **Honors/Awds:** Prince George Community College, Phi Theta Kappa Honor Fraternity, 1983; Veterans Administration, Word Master Award, 1981, Medical Center, Philadelphia, Director's Commendation, 1980; Black Law Students Association, Appreciation Plaque, 1989; Department of Veterans Affairs, Leadership VA Alumni Association, 1992. **Business Addr:** Human Resources Advisor, Headquarters and Executive Resources (052), Department of Veterans Affairs, 810 Vermont Ave NW Room 240, Washington, DC 20420, (202)273-9737.

OLLEE, MILDRED W.
Educational administrator. **Personal:** Born Jun 24, 1936, Alexandria, LA; daughter of Pearl Herbert Wilkerson and Robert L Wilkerson; married Henry P Ollee Jr, Dec 21, 1957; children: David Michael, Darrell Jacques. **Educ:** Xavier Univ of LA, BA 1956; Univ of SW LA, Grad Courses 1960; Walla Walla Coll, Masters 1967; Univ of WA, Grad Work 1977-78; Seattle Univ, Seattle, WA, EdD, 1988. **Career:** Various cities in LA & WA

schools, hs teacher 1956-62; George Washington Carver HS LA, soc sci lead teacher 1960-61; WA Assn of Retarded Children Walla Walla Lillie Rice Activ Ctr for Youths & Adults, dir 1964-66; Walla Walla Cty Sup Ct, marriage counselor, therapist 1967; Walla Walla Comm Coll, instr faculty 1968-70; Birdseye Frozen Foods Div of Gen Foods Walla Walla WA, consult 1968; Seattle Central Comm Coll dist VI, counselor faculty 1970-73, dir spec serv to disadv students 1973-; AIDP SSDE FIPSE Dept of HEW Office of Ed, consult 1977-80; Seattle Comm Coll Dist VI, assoc dean of students 1976-, dean of student devt services, 1988-, Student Services, vice pres, 1992-. **Orgs:** Bd mem Amer Red Cross Walla Walla 1962-64, Puget Sound Black Ed Assoc Seattle 1970-72; chmn pres search comm Seattle Central Comm Coll 1979; pres elect NASP, NW Assoc of Spec Prog Reg X 1979-81; mem Delta Sigma Theta, Citizens Transit Adv Comm, METRO Council 1979-80; area rep Fed Way Comm Council 1979-80; financial sec, Links, Inc, 1983-90; exec bd, Leadership in Synthesis, 1989-91. **Honors/Awds:** Most Outstanding Young Coll Woman Awd, Xavier Univ 1956; Workshop Leader Compensatory Ed for the New Learner Univ of WA 1975; Co-author SSDS-TRIO Project Dir Manual Dept of HEW Office of Ed 1978; Presented paper "3 R's for Black Students, Recruitment Requirements & Retention" 4th Annual Conf of Council on Black Affairs. **Business Addr:** Dean/Vice Pres of Student Development Services, Seattle Community College, 1701 Broadway (BF4180), Seattle, WA 98122.

OLLISON, RUTH ALLEN
Journalist. **Personal:** Born Apr 1, 1954, Mount Pleasant, TX; daughter of Vera Allen Lewis; married Quincy L Ollison, Dec 28, 1980; children: Jacob Waelder Allen. **Educ:** University of Texas at Arlington, business courses; The American University, business courses; University of North Texas, BA, radio-tv-film, 1975; Wesley Theological Seminary, pursuing masters of theological studies. **Career:** KKDA-FM, news director, 1975-1978; KRLD Radio, reporter, 1978-80; KXAS TV, news manager, 1980-84; KDAF TV, news director/assistant news director, 1984-86; KETK TV, news director, anchor, 1986-87; Fox Television, assistant news director, 1987-; KEGG Radio Station, co-owner, manager, 1990-. **Orgs:** National Association of Black Journalists; Shiloh Baptist Church. **Honors/Awds:** Radio Television News Directors Association, 1989 Regional Overall Excellence Award; Associated Press, 1988 Outstanding News Operation; United Press International, 1987 Best Newscast. **Business Addr:** Asst News Director, Fox Television, WTTG-TV, 5151 Wisconsin Ave NE, Washington, DC 20016, (202)895-3004.

OLUGEBEFOLA, ADEMOLA
Artist, art director, educator. **Personal:** Born Oct 2, 1941, Charlotte Amalie, St Thomas, Virgin Islands of the United States; son of Golda Matthias Thomas and Harold Thomas II; children: Mona, Monica, Rahim, Ale, Tanyeni, Solar, Khari, Denise. **Career:** Artist lectr works include hundreds of vibrant cover designs & illustrations for leading authors pub by Doubleday, Broadside, William Morrow, Harper & Row, Am Museum of Natrl History and others; has been in numerous major exhibitions over 30 yr period; had over 50 one man exhibitions; work is in collections throughout US, S Am, Africa, Caribbean; Gumbs & Thomas Publishers, vp, currently. **Orgs:** Vice Pres, International Communications Association; vp, Harlem Artists & Scholars Interests Consortium; chmn Educ Dept of Weusi Acad of Arts & Studies; served as consultant to Mtro Museum of Art, NY Urban Coalition and is co-dir of Grinnell Fine Art Collection. **Honors/Awds:** Won critical acclaim for innovative set designs for Lew Lafayette Theatre, NY Shakespeare Fest, Nat Black Theatre; design comm, NY Urban Coalition, 1990; design comm, Literary Assistance Ctr, 1989; design comm, Chase Bank, 1997; Banco Popular de Puerto Rico, 1996. **Business Addr:** 800 Riverside Dr, #5E, New York, NY 10032.

OMOLADE, BARBARA
Educator. **Personal:** Born Oct 29, 1942, Brooklyn, NY; daughter of Mamie Taylor Jones (deceased) and Hugh Jones (deceased); children: Kipchamba, Ngina, Eskimo, Krishna. **Educ:** Queens Coll, BA 1964; Goddard Coll, MA 1980; City University of New York, New York, NY, PhD, Sociology, 1997. **Career:** Ctr for the Elimination of Violence in the Family, co-dir 1977-78; Women's Action Alliance, 1979-81; Empire State Coll Ctr for Labor Studies, instructor 1980-81; WBAI Radio, producer/commentator 1981-83; CCNY-CWE, higher educ officer/adjunct faculty 1981-; freelance writer 1979-; City University of New York, New York, NY, coordinator curriculum change faculty development seminars, 1988-. **Orgs:** Bd mem Sisterhood of Black Single Mothers 1983-, co-founder CUNY Friends of Women Studies 1984-; Career Faculty Member CCNY-CWE. **Honors/Awds:** Unit Awds in Media Lincoln Univ of MO 1981; Malcolm X Awd The East 1982; Susan B Anthony Awd New York City Natl Org of Women 1987. **Special Achievements:** Author, The Rising Song of African American Women. **Home Addr:** 231 Ocean Ave #4B, Brooklyn, NY 11225.

O'NEAL, CONNIE MURRY
Government official. **Personal:** Born Oct 9, 1951, Detroit, MI; married Booker L. **Educ:** MI State U, BS 1973, MA 1976. **Career:** MI Dept of Transportation, Bur of Urban & Mass Pub Trans, admisntr govtl relations & consumer affairs; Gov Milliken's Ofc, policy/legisltv liaison to MI Hs of Reps 1979; MI Hs of Reps, legisltv analyst rep caucus of MI 1977-79; Gov Milliken, dir vol for gubernatorial candidacy 1978; Greater Lansing Urban League, dir of comm devel 1976-77; Cath Orgn, community orgr 1973-74. **Orgs:** Pres Ctr of Urban Affairs MI State Univ 1976-77; bd of trustees Fam & Child Serv 1976-; del at lg Nat Women Polit Caucus 1979-; bd mem Am Soc for Pub Adminstrn 1980; mem Urban League Guild 1978-; life mem NAACP 1978-; co-chmn MI ERAmerica 1979; v-chmn Ingham Co Rep Party 1979. **Business Addr:** State Capitol, Lansing, MI 48909.

O'NEAL, EDDIE S.
Clergyman. **Personal:** Born Mar 28, 1935, Meridian, MS; son of Sara Lenora O'Neal and Eddie S. O'Neal; married Onita; children: Vallerie, Eddie III, Nancy, Michael. **Educ:** Tougaloo So Christian Coll, AB 1963; Andover Newton Theol Sch, BD 1967, STM cum laude 1969, DMin 1972. **Career:** Peoples Bapt Church, assoc minister; Clinton Ave Bapt, co-pastor; Myrtle Bapt, pastor; St Mark Congrtnl, assoc pastor; Mt Olive Bapt Ch, pastor; Pine Grv Bapt Ch, pastor; Andover Newton Theol Sch, prof. **Orgs:** Chmn Black Studies Comm of the Boston Theol Inst 1970-76; ministries to Blks in Higher Edn; Interfaith Coun on Ministry & Aging; Rockefeller Protestant Flwshp Prgm; trustee Andover Newton Theol Sch; auditor/parl United Bapt Conv of MA & RI; mem Nat Com of Blk Chmen; mem Soc for the Study of Blk Relgn; mem City Missionary Soc of Boston; mem Am Bapt Conv; mem NAACP; mem Omega Psi Phi Frat; consult Women's Serv Club. **Honors/Awds:** Rockefeller Protestant Fellowship 1962-66; Woodrow Wilson Flwshp 1963; Key to the City of Newton, MA 1969; articles Christian Century 1971; Andover Newton Quar 1970. **Business Addr:** Prof, Andover Newton Theol School, 210 Herrick Rd, Newton, MA 02159.

O'NEAL, FREDRICK WILLIAM, JR.
Government official, engineer, consultant. **Personal:** Born Dec 8, 1948, Chicago, IL; son of Essie M Reed O'Neal and Fredrick W O'Neal. **Educ:** Roosevelt Univ, Chicago IL, BS, 1985; Keller Graduate School of Management, Chicago IL, MBA, 1987. **Career:** Commonwealth Edison Co, Chicago IL, efficiency technician, 1966-71; Western Union Telegraph Co, Chicago IL, computer technician, 1972-88; City of Chicago, Department of Fleet Management, principal systems engineer, 1988-96; City of Chicago, Department of Fleet Management, director of data processing, 1996-. **Orgs:** Telecommunications Professionals. **Business Addr:** City of Chicago, Department of Fleet Management, 1685 N Throop St, Chicago, IL 60622.

O'NEAL, JERMAINE
Professional basketball player. **Personal:** Born Oct 13, 1978; son of Angela Ocean. **Career:** Portland TrailBlazers, forward, 1996-. **Special Achievements:** NBA Draft, First round pick, #17, 1996. **Business Addr:** Professional Basketball Player, Portland TrailBlazers, 1 Center Court, Ste 200, Portland, OR 97227, (503)234-9291.

O'NEAL, LESLIE CORNELIUS
Professional football player. **Personal:** Born May 7, 1964, Pulaski County, AR. **Educ:** Oklahoma State, attended. **Career:** San Diego Chargers, defensive back, 1986-95; St Louis Rams, 1996-. **Honors/Awds:** Associated Press, NFL Defensive Rookie of the Year, 1986; Pro Bowl appearances, 1989, 1990, 1992, 1993, 1994, 1995. **Business Addr:** Professional Football Player, St Louis Rams, One Rams Way, St Louis, MO 63045, (314)982-7267.

O'NEAL, MALINDA KING
Printing company executive. **Personal:** Born Jan 1, 1929, Cartersville, GA; daughter of Mr & Mrs Dan King; married Sheppard Dickerson Sr; children: Sheppard D Jr, Sherod Lynn. **Educ:** Morris Brown College, BA (cum laude), 1965; Atlanta Univ, MA, 1970; Alumni Admn Am Alumni Counc, Wash, DC, Cert; Skillings Bus College, Kilmarnock, Scotland, Professional Cert. **Career:** Radio Station WERD, record librarian/disc jockey/continuity writer 1949-50; Mammy's Shanty Restaurant Atlanta, sec bookeeper (with firm for 11 years prior to integration), 1951-53; Natl Congress of Colored Parents & Teachers Atlanta, ofc dir; Emory Univ Center for Res in Soc Change, field supervisor for special projects; Morris Brown College, former dir alumni affairs/gov rel/ dir of admissions, dean of students; Owner/President MKO Graphics and Printers, Atlanta GA 1987-. **Orgs:** Editor "The Alumni Mag" Morris Brown Coll 8 years; editor "The Ebenezer Newsletter"; writings, "How to Rear a Blind Child" 1959; United Negro Coll Fund; NAACP; YWCA; Kappa Omega chapter, Alpha Kappa Alpha; vol, Atlanta Counc of Intl Visitors; trustee bd, Ebenezer Baptist Church; Better Business Bureau 1988; Atlanta Business League 1988. **Honors/Awds:** Recipient, Morris Brown Coll Natl Alumni Assn, WA Fountain & JH Lewis Status Achievement Award 1975, Outstanding Dedicated Serv as Dir of Alumni Affairs 1974; Hon by Natl Congress of Colored Parents & Teachers on 2 occasions for outstanding & dedicated svcs; cited on 2 occasions for outstanding serv as Adv to the Undergrad Chapter of Alpha Kappa Alpha; Distinguished Alumni, NAFEO 1991; Business of the Year Award, 1992. **Home Addr:** 215 Piedmony Ave NE, Apt 306, Atlanta, GA 30308-3319, (404)523-0845. **Business Addr:** Owner, President, MKO Graphics & Printers, 846 M L King Jr Dr SW, Atlanta, GA 30314, (404)523-1560.

O'NEAL, RAYMOND W., SR.
Attorney. **Personal:** Born Feb 22, 1940, Dayton, OH; son of Carrie B O'Neal and Henry L O'Neal; married Brenda, Jun 22, 1963; children: Raymond Jr, Terisa. **Educ:** Ohio University, BA, 1968; Howard University, MA, 1968, JD, 1973. **Career:** US Department of Treasury, financial analyst, 1971-74; Wilberforce University, political science associate professor, 1977-79; Miami University, economics instructor, 1978-84; Attorney at Law, sole practitioner, 1981-. **Orgs:** Montgomery County Arthritis Foundation, board member, 1990-92; Dayton NAACP, board member, education/legal commission chairperson, 1987-92; Dayton-Miami Valley Minority Chamber of Commerce, founder, 1987-; Alpha Phi Alpha Fraternity Inc, 1970-; American Bar Association, 1982-; Ohio Bar Association, 1981-; Montgomery County Republican Party, 2nd vice pres, central steering committee, 1981-. **Honors/Awds:** City of Dayton, Citizens Volunteer Award, 1992; Middletown Ohio, Business Leadership Award, 1984; Dayton Bar Association, Assistance To Indigent Clients Award, 1992; Omicron Delta Epsilon, Economics Honorary, 1968. **Special Achievements:** The Black Labor Force in the USA: Critical Analysis (master's thesis), 1968; 39th House District candidate to Ohio Legislative, 1992. **Business Addr:** President, Dayton Miami Valley Minority Chamber of Commerce, c/o 7700 N Main St, Upper level, Dayton, OH 45415, (513)898-3278.

O'NEAL, RODNEY
Auto executive. **Personal:** Born Aug 27, 1953, Dayton, OH; son of James H & Ida B O'Neal; married Pamela Estell O'Neal, Aug 20, 1983; children: Heather Marie, Damien Cain. **Educ:** General Motors Institute, Bachelor of Industrial Administration, 1976; Stanford University, MBA, 1991. **Career:** General Motors, co-op student, gen dir of warehousing & distribution, vice pres & gen mgr, 1971-. **Orgs:** Kappa Alpha Psi Fraternity, mem, 1977-; General Motors Institute, Black Unity Congress, advisor, 1987-88; Windsor, Ontario, Canada Chamber of Commerce, mem, 1987-90; Industrial Mutual Association of Flint, MI, mem, 1995-96; One Hundred Club of Flint, MI, mem, 1995-. **Honors/Awds:** Dollars & Sense Magazine, America's Best & Brightest Young Businessmen, 1990; Consortium for Graduate Study in MGT, Distinguished Service Award, 1993. **Special Achievements:** Presenter at the Annual Trumpet Awards, Aired on TBS, 1995-. **Business Addr:** Vice Pres/General Manager, General Motors Corp., Delphi Interior & Lighting Systems, 6600 E 12 Mile Rd, Warren, MI 48092-5905, (810)578-3230.

O'NEAL, SHAQUILLE RASHAUN
Professional basketball player. **Personal:** Born Mar 6, 1972, Newark, NJ; children: Taahirah. **Educ:** Louisiana State, three years. **Career:** Orlando Magic, center, 1992-96; Los Angeles Lakers, 1996-; albums: Shaq Diesel; Shaq Fu: Da Return; You Can't Stop the Reign; movies: Blue Chips; Kazaam; T.W.id. record label, founder, 1997-. **Honors/Awds:** Eddie Gottlieb Award, NBA Rookie of the Year, 1993; NBA All-Rookie First Team, 1993; won a gold medal with the US Olympic Basketball Team, 1996; selected as one of the 50 Greatest Players in NBA History, 1996; NBA All-Star, 1993-98. **Special Achievements:** First pick, overall, NBA draft, first round, 1992. **Business Addr:** Professional Basketball Player, Los Angeles Lakers, PO Box 10, Inglewood, CA 90306, (310)419-3100.

O'NEAL, STANLEY
Financial services company executive. **Personal:** marrIed Nancy; children: two. **Career:** General Motors Corp, analyst, 1978-80, director, 1980-82, Spanish subsidiary, treasurer, 1982-84, asst treasurer, New York City, 1984-87; Merrill Lynch & Co, Inc, 1987-, high-yield finance group, managing director, exec vice pres, co-head, currently. **Business Addr:** Managing Director, Merrill Lynch & Co, Inc, World Financial Center, North Tower, 29th Fl, New York, NY 10281, (212)449-8320.

O'NEALE, SONDRA
Educational administrator. **Educ:** Asbury College, bachelor's degree in English literature; University of Kentucky, master's degree in American literature, doctorate degree in American literature. **Career:** Taught at the University of Kentucky, Emory University and the University of California at San Diego; University of Wisconsin-La Crosse, chair, Department of Women's Studies; Wayne State University, dean, College of Liberal Arts, 1994-. **Orgs:** Phi Beta Kappa. **Special Achievements:** Has published twenty articles since 1981; Author: Jupiter Hammon and the Biblical Beginnings of African-American Literature; Editor: Call & Response: An Anthology of African-American Literature. **Business Addr:** Dean, College of Liberal Arts, Wayne State University, 656 Kirby Ave, Detroit, MI 48202, (313)577-2545.

ONLI, TURTEL
Artist, art therapist, publisher. **Personal:** Born Jan 25, 1952, Chicago, IL. **Educ:** Olive-Harvey College, AA 1972; L'Academie De Port-Royal, 1977; School of the Art Institute of Chicago, BFA 1978; Art Institute of Chicago, MAAT, 1989. **Career:** Columbia Coll Chicago, instructor 1978-81; Dysfunctioning Child Center, art therapist 1978-82; Black on Black Love Fine Arts Center, acting dir 1984-85; Ada S McKinley Developmental Sch, art therapist; Onli-Wear Studio, master artist 1978-85, director/producer. **Orgs:** Founder BAG (Black Arts Guild) 1971-76; USA rep, FESTAC, Second World Festival of African Art and Culture 1976; inventor of rhythmistic style of art. **Honors/Awds:** Certificate of award Natl Conference of Artists 1972 & 1974; founder of Rhythmistic School of Art 1976; premiere prix aux foyer internatl D'Accueil De Paris 1978; Award Of Excellence Artist Guild of Chicago 1979. **Special Achievements:** Publisher, NOG Protector of the Pyramides and Future Funk News, the only black-owned & published comic characters; curator, Bag Retrospective Exhibition, 1991; publisher, Malcolm-10 Spawning The Black Age of Comics, 1992; Organizer & promoter of the Black Age of Comics National Convention, Chicago. **Business Addr:** Director, Producer, Onli Studios, 5121 S Ellis, Chicago, IL 60615.

ONWUDIWE, EBERE
Educational administrator. **Personal:** Born Oct 10, 1952, Isu-Njaba, Imo, Nigeria; son of Nwamgbede Onyegbule Achigaonye and Onwudiwe Simon Achigaonye; married Mamle, Jul 11, 1992; children: Chinwe, Mbamemme. **Educ:** Florida State University, Tallahassee, FL, MA, international rel, 1981, MSc, economics, 1983, PhD, political science, 1986. **Career:** Central State Univ, Wilberforce, OH, associate professor, 1986-; Antioch College, Yellow Spring, OH, adjunct professor; Central State Univ, director of National Resource Center for African Studies, currently. **Orgs:** Member, African Studies Association, member, Academy of International Business, member, National Association of Black Political Scientists, member, World Academy of Development & Cooperation. **Honors/Awds:** Congressional Citation of Published Editorial, US Senate, Congressional Record, 1990. **Business Addr:** Professor, Central State University, National Resource Center for African Studies, Wilberforce, OH 45384.

ONYEJEKWE, CHIKE ONYEKACHI
Physician. **Personal:** Born Jun 8, 1960, Okigwe; son of Engr E Onyejekwe. **Educ:** Western KY Univ, BS Biology, BS Chemistry 1981; Howard Univ, MD 1986. **Career:** DC General Hospital, medical officer, currently. **Orgs:** Sec Intl Red Cross 1976-78; mem Intl Forum WKU 1978-81; capt WKU Soccer Club 1980-81. **Honors/Awds:** Alpha Epsilon Delta Premed Honor Society; Chief Resident, Howard Medical Service, DC General Hospital. **Business Addr:** Medical Officer, DC General Hospital, 19th & Mass Ave, SE, Washington, DC 20003.

OPOKU, EVELYN
Physician. **Personal:** Born Jun 14, 1946, Accra, Ghana; daughter of Barbara Opoku and Ebenezer Opoku; divorced; children: James Boye-Doe. **Educ:** University of Ghana Medical School, West Africa, MD, 1971; Columbia University, MPH, 1990. **Career:** Korle Bu Teaching Hospital, house officer, 1971-72, medical officer, 1972-75; Health & Hospital Corp, Harlem Hospital, pediatric resident, 1976-79; Southern Medical Group, pediatrician, 1979-82; Hunts Point Multiservice, pediatrician, 1982-85; City of New York, Department of Health, senior medical specialist, 1986-91; Graham Windham, director, health services, 1991-. **Orgs:** American Academy of Pediatrics, fellow, 1990-; American Public Health Association, 1987-; New York Task Force on Immigrant Health, 1991-. **Business Addr:** Director, Health Services, Graham Windham, 33 Irving Place, New York, NY 10003, (212)529-6445.

O'REE, WILLIE
Sports management exeuctive. **Career:** Boston Bruins, professional hockey player, 1957-58, 1960-61; National Hockey League, director of youth development, currently. **Special Achievements:** First African American player in the National Hockey League. **Business Addr:** Director of Youth Development, National Hockey League, 1251 Ave of the Americas, New York, NY 10020, (212)789-2000.

ORMSBY, WILLIAM M.
Judge. **Career:** Los Angeles Municipal Court, judge, currently. **Business Addr:** Judge, Los Angeles Municipal Court, One Regent St, Rm 310, Inglewood, CA 90301, (310)419-5105.

ORR, CLYDE HUGH
Human resources executive. **Personal:** Born Mar 25, 1931, Whitewright, TX; son of Melissa Orr and Hugh Orr; married Maizie Helen Stell; children: 3. **Educ:** Army Command General Staff Coll, Grad, 1965; Prairie View A&M Coll, BA Political Sci 1953; Masters in Public Admin Univ of Oklahoma 1974. **Career:** US Army Fort Ord, CA, mgr 1968-70; US Army, mil advisor/Ethiopia-Haile Salassie Body Guard Division 1970-72; Lincoln Univ, administrator ROTC 1973-75; Metropolitan St Louis Sewer District, dir human resources 1976-. **Orgs:** St Louis Bi-state Red Cross; mem of corp YMCA Bd; mem Amer Cancer soc Bd of City Unit; member, Parkway School District Affirmative Action Committee. **Honors/Awds:** Lay Participant Awd St Louis School System; Boy Scouts of Amer Awd St Louis Chap 1984; Chairman of YMCA Bd Awd Monsanto 1985; Lay Participant Awd, Volunteer of the Year Awd, American Cancer Society 1992. **Military Serv:** US Army lt col 22 yrs; Legion of Merit; Bronze Star and Air Medal 1975. **Home Addr:** 12866 Topping Manor Dr, St Louis, MO 63131.

ORR, DOROTHY
Insurance company executive. **Educ:** Atlanta Univ, M; Columbia Univ, Accelerated Grad study. **Career:** Fordham Univ School of Social Work, assoc prof (first female); Equitable Life Assurance Soc, vice pres (first black woman officer of a major insurance co); Orr DaCosta Balthazar & Orr, pres/sr partner; vice pres, Equitable Life Financial Co. **Orgs:** Former commr NY State Commn on Human Rights.

ORR, JANICE
Attorney at law. **Personal:** Born Aug 10, 1944, St Louis, MO; daughter of Alma and William Cable. **Educ:** Roosevelt Univ, BA, 1966; Boston Univ School of Law, JD, 1972. **Career:** Chicago Bd of Educ, teacher, 1966-69; US Dept of Labor, law clerk, 1972-73; US Dept of Housing & Urban Development, attorney, 1973-74; International Communication Group, general counsel, 1974-75; Natl labor Relations Bd, attorney, 1975-76; Equal Employment Opportunity Commission, 1976-83; US Dept Health & Human Services, 1983-; Self Employed, attorney, entertainment, visual arts law, 1975-. **Orgs:** Natl Bar Assn, bd of dirs, 1973-79, 1986-, chair, Legislation Comm, 1994-, chair, International Law Section, 1989-94, chair, Committee on Southern Africa, 1986-89; Emarrons, general counsel, 1989-; DC Music Ctr, general counsel, 1982-90; Ctr for Independent Living, bd mem, 1995-; GWAC Women Lawyers Assn, NBA, bd mem, 1990-92. **Honors/Awds:** Natl Bar Assn, Best Section, 1993, Outstanding Achievement, 1987, 1991; US Dept Health & Human Services, Outstanding Achievement, 1993, 1995. **Business Addr:** Attorney at Law, Orr & Associates, 1815 E Street, NE, Washington, DC 20002, (202)965-4201.

ORR, LOUIS M.
Professional basketball player. **Personal:** Born 1958; married Amerine Lowry. **Educ:** Syracuse Univ. **Career:** Indiana Pacers, 1981-82, New York Knicks, 1983-88. **Honors/Awds:** Named First Team All-East by the Baketball Writers and Basketball Weekly.

ORR, MARLETT JENNIFER
Educator. **Personal:** Born Sep 30, 1970, Detroit, MI; daughter of Remal Orr. **Educ:** MI State Univ, BA, 1992; Univ of MI-Dearborn, MA, 1994. **Career:** Detroit Bd of Educ, educator, 1993-. **Orgs:** Council for Exceptional Students, 1990-. **Honors/Awds:** Detroit Bd of Ed, Young Educators Society, 1993. **Business Addr:** Educator, Detroit Public Schools/Noble Middle School, 28545 Thorn Apple Dr, Southfield, MI 48034, (313)873-0379.

ORR, RAY
Mailing service executive. **Personal:** Born Feb 13, 1953, Marks, MS; son of Ella Kuykendall; married Patrice Ann Clayton; children: Jacqueline Denise, Ray Jr, Reuben Patrick. **Educ:** Memphis State Univ, B Bus Admin 1978. **Career:** US Post Office Memphis, clerk/loader/sorter 1975-77; Methodist Hosp, distribution agent 1977-78; Federal Express Corp, cargo handler, sales trainee, sales rep sr sales rep 1978-82; Big "D" Mailing Service Inc, pres/CEO 1983-. **Orgs:** Chmn of bd Big "D" Mailing Serv Inc. **Honors/Awds:** Outstanding Sales Performance Federal Express Corp 1980; Letters of Praise from Vice Pres of Sales, Sr Vice Pres of Marketing, District Dir, Dist Sales Mgr Federal Express Corp 1980; Businessman of the Day KKDA Radio Dallas 1985; Entrepreneur of the Week Dallas Morning News 1986; Quest for Success Awd Dallas Black Chamber 1987. **Business Addr:** President & CEO, Big "D" Mailing Services, Inc, PO Box 565841, Dallas, TX 75356.

ORRIDGE, JEFFREY LYNDON
Olympic sports executive, attorney. **Personal:** Born Apr 11, 1960, New York, NY; son of Jacynth Paterson Orridge and Egbert Lyndon Orridge; married Avian Marie Trammell, Aug 31, 1991. **Educ:** Wesleyan University, exchange student, 1980; Amherst College, BA (magna cum laude), 1982; Harvard Law School, JD, 1986. **Career:** Rogers & Wells Law Firm, corporate law associate, 1986-88; Beekman Street Bakery, legal, business affairs consultant, 1988-89; North General Home Attendant Corp., executive director, general counsel, 1989-91; USA Basketball, assistant executive director, general counsel, 1991-. **Orgs:** American Cancer Society, New York Chapter, board of directors, 1989-91; Sports Lawyer Association, 1989-; American Bar Association, 1989-. **Honors/Awds:** Wesleyan University, Dean's List, 1980. **Business Phone:** (719)632-7687.

ORTICKE, LESLIE ANN
Consultant. **Career:** United Negro College Fund, assistant to the area dir; HIV Educator/Job Trainer, YWCA of Los Angeles, adolescent pregnancy childwatch, consultant. **Orgs:** United Negro College Fund, Delta Sigma Theta; Congregational Church of Christian Fellowship, United Church of Christ; YWCA; Junior League of Los Angeles; National Committee Member, chapter pres, Delta Sigma Theta Sorority; Congregational Church of Christian Fellowship, UCC; Jr League of Los Angeles; Lullaby Guild of the Children's Home Society; National Assn of Female Execs; LA Bruin Club. **Honors/Awds:** Recipient of several awards and certificates for volunteer services; Outstanding Young Woman, Delta Sigma Theta Sorority; Women's History Month Honoree, Los Angeles Black Employees Assn; numerous awards and certificates for volunteer service. **Business Addr:** Director of Volunteers, United Negro College Fund, City Court Plaza, 725 S Figueroa, Ste 800, Los Angeles, CA 90017, (213)689-0168.

ORTIQUE, REVIUS OLIVER, JR.
Justice (retired). **Personal:** Born Jun 14, 1924, New Orleans, LA; son of Lillie Long (deceased) and Revius Oliver Ortique (deceased); married Miriam Marie Victorianne; children: Rhesa Marie McDonald. **Educ:** Dillard Univ, AB 1947; IN Univ, MA 1949; So Univ, JD 1956; Campbell Coll, LLD; Ithaca Coll, LHD; Univ of Indiana, LLD; Morris Brown College, LLD; Loyola University, LLD; Dillard University, LLD. **Career:** Full-time practicing attorney New Orleans, LA, 1956-78; Civil Dist Court, judge 1979-92; Louisiana Supreme Court, justice, 1992-94. **Orgs:** US Dist Ct Eastern Dist LA; US 5th Circuit Ct Appeals; US Supreme Ct; former pres Natl Legal Aid & Defender Assn; mem Amer Lung Assn; Natl bd dir; Antioch Coll Law bd dir; Natl Bar Assn exec bd; exec bd Natl Bar Found; Former member bd Natl Sr Citizens Law Center, LA; exec com Amer Bar Assn; Amer Bar Assn Comm Legal Aid & Indigent Defenders; Amer Bar Assn House of Dels; LA State Bar Assn House of Dels; sr vice pres Metro Area Comm MAC Affiliate Urban Coalition; bd trustees Dillard Univ; exec com Criminal Just Coord Com; former bd mem LEAA; former bd mgmt Flint Goodridge Hosp; former bd City Trusts City of New Orleans; former exec com Indus Devel New Orleans Metro Area; adv bd League Women Voters Greater New Orleans; bd New Orleans Legal Assist Corp; former bd dir United Fed Savings & Loan Assn; former bd dir Comm Relations Cncl; men's bd YWCA; LA State Bar Assn; Ad Hoc Com Devel Central Business Dist New Orleans; general counsel eight dist AME Ch LA/MS; former mem Pres' Commn on Campus Unrest/Scranton Commn; past pres Amer Lung Assn LA; chart mem World Peace Through Law; Chairman of the New Orleans Aviation Board. **Honors/Awds:** Alpha Kappa Delta Honor Soc; Blue Key Honor Soc; Arthur von Briesen Medal of Distinguished Serv to Disadvantaged Americans 1971; Brotherhood Award Natl Conf of Christians and Jews Lifetime Achievement Award LA State Bar Assn, 1976; Outstanding Person in LA (one of ten persons cited by the Institute of Human Understanding) 1976; Gertrude Rush Award, Natl Bar Assn; many other citations, awards and plaques. **Special Achievements:** One of only a few Americans appointed to four boards and/or commissions, by four different presidents of the United States; First African American, elected to LA Supreme Court, 1992-94; Cited by government of Japan as "World Opinion Maker.". **Military Serv:** US Army 1st Lt, company commander. **Home Addr:** 10 Park Island Dr, New Orleans, LA 70122.

ORTIZ, DELIA
School board official. **Personal:** Born Nov 25, 1924; married Steve Oritz; children: Rosie, Vickie, Steven Jr, Clara, Sandra, Beinaldo. **Educ:** Columbia, 2 yrs. **Career:** PS 43-PS125, pres; Fama Film Prod, pres; Knickerbocker Hosp Ambulatory Care, pres; Drug Referral, pres; Community School Bd, pres 1973-75, sec 1982-. **Honors/Awds:** Tenant of the year Grant Housing Project 1966; Community Awd Salinas Socia Club 1970; School Service Awd President's council District 5 1972. **Business Addr:** Secretary School Board, Community Sch Dist 5, 433 W 123rd St, New York, NY 10027.

ORTIZ, VICTOR
Municipal judge. **Personal:** Born Dec 12, 1946, New York, NY; son of Manda Mays and Wendell Ortiz. **Educ:** BBA, marketing, 1970; JD, 1973. **Career:** Private practice, civil & criminal law, 1977-78, 1981-85; Office of District Attorney, Dallas County, TX, asst district attorney, 1978-81; Dallas County Mental Health Center, hearing officer, 1984-85; City of Dallas, TX, asst city attorney, 1974-77, associate municipal judge, 1977-78, 1984-85, municipal judge, 1985-. **Orgs:** Dallas Minority Repertory Theatre, board of directors, 1976-81; Committee of 100, vice pres, membership director, 1976-82; Dallas Black Chamber of Commerce, board of directors, 1979-81; Park South YMCA, board of directors, 1978-81; Progressive Voters League, 1975-86; Natl Bar Assn, 1982-; J L Turner Legal Assn, 1974-; St Paul AME Church, stewards board, 1978-. **Honors/Awds:** Natl Council of Negro Women, Man of the Year, 1986; Bancroft Witney Co., American Jurisprudence Award/Trusts, 1972; St Paul AME Church, Usher Board #2, Extra Mile Award, 1985; United Negro College Fund, Community Service Award, 1975; Natl Council of Negro Women, Man of the Year; St Paul AME Church, Man of the Year, 1997. **Business Addr:** Municipal Judge, City of Dallas, 2014 Main St, Suite 210, Dallas, TX 75201, (214)670-5573.

OSAKWE, CHRISTOPHER
Educator. **Personal:** Born May 8, 1942, Lagos, Nigeria; married Maria Elena Amador; children: Rebecca Eugenia. **Educ:** Moscow State Univ School of Law, LL B (First Class Hons) 1966, LL M 1967, Ph D (Law) 1970; Univ of IL College of Law, JSD 1974. **Career:** Univ of Notre Dame Law School, prof of law 1971-72; Tulane Univ School of Law, prof of law 1972-81; Univ of MI Sch of Law, vis prof of law 1981; Univ of PA sch of law, vis prof of law 1978; St Anthony's Coll, Oxford Univ, visiting fellow 1978; Washington & Lee Univ Sch of Law, visiting professor of law 1986; Tulane Univ School of Law, prof of comparative law 1981-. **Orgs:** Carnegie doctoral fellow Hague Academy of Int'l Law 1969; member Am Law Inst (since 1982), ABA (since 1970), Am Soc Int'l L 1970; research Fellow Russian Research Cntr, Harvard Univ 1972; dir Eason-Weinmann Cntr for Comparative Law 1978-86; dir bd of dir Am Assoc for the Comparative Study of Law 1978;visiting fellow Cntr for Russian and East Europ Studies Univ of MI 1981; scholar Sr US-Soviet Exchange Moscow State Univ Law Sch 1982; dir, bd of review and dvlpt, American Soc of Int'l Law 1982-87. **Honors/Awds:** Author The Participation of the Soviet Union in Universal International Organizations 1972; co-author Comparative Legal Traditions in a Nutshell 1982; co-author Comparative Legal Traditions-Text, Materials, Cases 1985. **Business Addr:** Prof Comparative Law & Dir, Tulane Univ Sch of Law, Tulane Univ Sch Of Law, New Orleans, LA 70118.

OSBORNE, ALFRED E., JR.
Educator, educational administrator. **Personal:** Born Dec 7, 1944; son of Ditta Osborne and Alfred Osborne. **Educ:** Stanford Univ, BSEE, 1968, MA, economics, 1971, MBA, finance, 1971, PhD, business, economics, 1974. **Career:** Western Development Labs, elec engr 1968; Sec & Exchange Commission, economic fellow, 1977-80; UCLA Grad School of Mgmt, asst prof 1972-78, associate prof 1979-, asst dean, MBA Prog, director, 1979-83, associate dean 1984-87, Entrepreneurial Studies Center, director, 1987-. **Orgs:** Dir, The Times Mirror Co, 1980-; past pres, Natl Economic Assn, 1980-81; dir, chair, Municipal Financial Advisory Comm City of Los Angeles, 1981-; bd of economists, Black Enterprise Magazine, 1982-85; dir, Nordstrom Inc, 1987-; dir, Industrial Bank, 1983-93; co-chair, Natl Conf of Christians & Jews, 1985-94; dir, First Interstate bank of CA, 1993-; dir, US Filter Corp, 1990-; dir, Greyhound Lines, Inc, 1994-; governor, Natl Assn of Securities Dealers Inc, 1994-; Council of Economic Advisors for CA, 1993-. **Honors/Awds:** Outstanding Faculty Award, UCLA Grad School of Mgmt, 1975-76; Fellow, Brookings Inst Economic Policy, 1977-78. **Special Achievements:** Author: Several scholarly articles in economics and finance. **Business Addr:** Director, Entrepreneurial Studies Center, UCLA Graduate School of Management, 405 Hilgard Ave, Los Angeles, CA 90024-1481.

OSBORNE, CLAYTON HENRIQUEZ
Business executive. **Personal:** Born Aug 16, 1945, Canal Zone, Panama; son of Hilda Rogers Osborne and Clayton F Osborne; married Dorelis Agnes Osborne, Jul 1975; children: Clayton C, Sheldon R. **Educ:** Ohio Northern University, Ada, OH, 1964-65; State University of New York at Albany, Albany, NY, BA, 1968, School of Social Welfare, MSW, 1972; University of Massachusetts at Amherst, ABD. **Career:** Rochester Institute of Technology, Rochester, NY, asst prof, 1974-75; NYS Division for Youth, Rochester, NY, district supervisor, 1976-79, regional dir, 1979-88; Monroe County, Rochester, NY, dir of operations, 1988-92; Bausch & Lomb, corporate director of employee rel, workforce diversity 1992-. **Orgs:** Chairman, drug abuse, NYS Assn of Counties, 1988-92; Monroe County Board of Ethics, Monroe County, 1988-92; board member, Monroe Co Employer Credit Union, 1988-92; board member, Urban League of Rochester, 1986-; board member, NYS Disabilities Council, 1989-93; Assoc for Battered Women, board member, 1992-; Rochester Business Opportunities Inc, board member, 1992-93; Mayor Commission Against Violence, chairman, 1992-93; St Marys Hospital, board of trustees; Career Development Service Board; Assn for Battered Women; United Way of Rochester; Black Business Assn. **Honors/Awds:** Distinguished Alumni, Gov Rockefeller School of Public Affairs, 1987; Father of the Year, Bethel AME Church, 1988; Distinguished Service, Urban League of Rochester, 1985; Distinguished Service, City of Rochester, 1979. **Home Addr:** 208 Cheney Pkwy, Pittsford, NY 14534. **Business Phone:** (716)338-6103.

OSBORNE, ERNEST L.
Government official. **Personal:** Born Nov 15, 1932, New York, NY; married Elizabeth; children: Mrs. **Educ:** Long Islan Du, 1953. **Career:** Travelers Corp, dir of natl & comm affairs; Dept of Hlth & Human Svcs, dep under sec for intergovtl affairs; Dept of Hlth Educ & Welfare Wash, DC, commnr APS/OHDS 1978-80, dir OSCA/OHDS 1977-80; Sachem Fund New Haven, CT, exec dir 1972-77; Yale Counc on Com Affs Yale U, exec dir 1968-71. **Orgs:** Bd mem Coop Assis Fund Wash 1972-75 & 80; bd mem Howard Univ Press Wash, DC 1979-80; bd mem Counc on Found Wash, DC 1980-81; mem NAACP 1963-. **Honors/Awds:** Dist Serv Awd Dept of Hlth Educ & Welfare Wash, DC 1980.

OSBORNE, GWENDOLYN EUNICE
Journalist, arts advocate. **Personal:** Born May 19, 1949, Detroit, MI; daughter of George William Osborne and Ida Juanita Jackson Osborne; married Harry Kaye Rye, Feb 12, 1977; children: Kenneth Anthony Osborne Rye. **Educ:** Detroit Conservatory of Music, AA 1966; MI State U, BA, English educ, 1971; Medill School of Journalism, NW U, MSJ 1976; Roosevelt Univ, litigation cert, 1986. **Career:** The Crisis/NAACP, contributing editor 1973-78; Players Magazine, book editor 1974-78; Unique Magazine, arts book & entertainment writer 1976-78; Scott-Foresman & Co, asst editor permissions asst 1978-79; Pioneer Press Newspapers, Inc, lively arts editor 1978-80; Rand McNally, production editor 1979; News Election Service, Chicago regnl personnel mgr 1980; Amer Bar Assoc, publishing specialist 1980-82; Southeastern MI Transp Authority, publications specialist 1982-84; Debbie's Sch of Beauty Culture/ Debbie Howell Cosmetics, spec asst to the pres 1985-86; 21st Century Woman, assoc editor 1986; ABA Commission on Opportunities for Minorities in the Legal Profession, communications consultant, 1988-89; American Civil Liberties Union of Illinois, public information director, 1989-91; University of Illinois at Chicago, arts & culture editor, 1991-95; Illinois Institute of Technology, Chicago-Kent College of Law, public affairs director, 1995-. **Orgs:** Natl board of directors, Michigan State University Black Alumni Assn; Second Baptist Church; Delta Sigma Theta; Evanston Arts Council; assoc member, American Bar Assn; Chicago Assn of Black Journalists; Natl Assn of Black Journalists; Soc of Professional Journalists; Natl Conference of Artists; Urban Professional Partners Program, Art Institute of Chicago; board of directors, Black Public Relations Soc of Chicago; Publicity Club of Chicago; Illinois Arts Alliance; Evanston Historical Society. **Honors/Awds:** Nominee, Governor's Award for Arts, IL Arts Council, 1979-81; Fellow, National Endowment for the Humanities Summer Seminar for journalists at UC Berkeley, 1979; Fellow, National Endowment for the Arts Office for Partnership, Washington, DC, 1980; Editorial Award, Arts Category, Pioneer Press Newspaper, 1980; Certificate of Merit, Family Law Section, American Bar Association, 1981-82; Proclamation, Office of the Mayor, City of Detroit, 1983; Certificate of Appreciation, Office of the Governor, State of IL, 1983; Editorial Award, Arts Category, Pioneer Press Newspapers, 1980, Leadership Evanston Program, 1992-93. **Home Addr:** Penguin, Inc., 635 Chicago Avenue, Ste. 218, Evanston, IL 60202-2365.

OSBORNE, HUGH STANCILL
City official. **Personal:** Born Jul 18, 1918, Birmingham, AL; married Ruby Jewel Williams; children: Sidney, Cheryl. **Educ:** Kentucky State Univ, BA, 1939; Loyola Univ, MA, 1977. **Career:** City of Chicago, Housing Authority, deputy director, 1946-65; City of Chicago Police Department, deputy director, 1969-75, acting commissioner, 1975-77, 1st deputy commissioner, 1977-. **Orgs:** Commr, Chicago Cook County Criminal Justice Commn; mem, Nat Council on Crime & Delinquency; Comm Devel & Housing Coord Chicago; Chicago Manpower Planning Council; Municipal Financial Officers Assn; Amer Society for Public Adminstrn; mem, Citizens Commission Juvenile Court of Cook County; Natl Assn for Comm Devel; Committee for Full Employment; Chicago Assn for Collaborative Effort; Kappa Alpha Psi; Conf on Minority Public Adminstrs. **Honors/Awds:** Brotherhood Award Chicago Conf of Brotherhood, 1976; Certificate of Appreciation, Lincoln Center, 1976. **Military Serv:** US Army, 1st Sgt, 1941-45. **Business Addr:** 640 N LaSalle St, Chicago, IL 60610.

OSBORNE, JEFFREY LINTON
Singer. **Personal:** Born Mar 9, 1948, Providence, RI; married Sheri; children: Tiffany, Dawn, Jeanine. **Career:** LTD, producer, singer 10 yrs; solo performer, currently. **Honors/Awds:** Albums include: The Last Time I Made Love; Stay With Me Tonight; Don't You Get So Mad; On The Wings of Love; Only Human; hit singles include: On the Wings of Love; I Really Don't Need No Light; She's On the Left. **Business Addr:** Recording Artist, Almo-Irving Publishing Co, 1358 N LaBrea, Hollywood, CA 90028.

OSBORNE, OLIVER HILTON
Educator. **Personal:** Born Feb 17, 1931, Brooklyn, NY; son of Mildred Branch Osborne and Deighton Hamilton Osborne; married Julianne Nason, Aug 25, 1985; children: Martin, Mary Ann, Michael, Michelle, Mathew. **Educ:** Hunter Coll NY, BS Nursing 1958; NY Univ, MA Psychiatric/Mental Healkh Nursing 1960; MI State Univ, PhD 1968. **Career:** Wayne State Univ, assoc prof nursing/adj prof anthropology 1960; McGill Univ Montreal, mental health consult 1969; Univ of WA Dept of Psychosocial Nursing, assoc prof & chmn 1969-74; Univ of Botswana So Africa, assoc rsch fellow 1976-78; Univ of WA Dept Anthropology, adj prof 1979-; Univ of WA Dept of Psychosocial Nursing, prof 1974-. **Orgs:** Mem Amer Anthropological Assn, Amer Nurses' Assn, Soc for Applied Anthropology, Soc for Med Anthropology (sec/treas 1970-73), Council on Nursing and Anthropology; numerous consultations including, East Model Cities Health Task Force Seattle, WA 1971; Rockefeller Foundation Univ del Valle Cali, Columbia 1973; Mental Health Clinic Group Hlth Coop Seattle, WA 1974; ANA Fellowship Pgm for Doctoral Training of Racial/Ethnic Minorities in Clin Mental Hlth Serv 1977-82; mem Interdiv Cncl on Certification Amer Nurses Assn 1976-80; Natl Adv Comm Center for Health Care and Research Sch of Nursing Univ of TX at Austin 1979-80; Psychiatric Nursing Educ Review Comm NIMH 1980-83; Natl Comm on Devel of Minority Curric in Psychiatric and Mental Health Disciplines HowardUniv NIMH 1980-; lay mem Judiciacreening Comm Seattle-King County Bar Assn; 1982-; member, Ogboni Society Ibara Abeokuta Nigeria; member, Northwest Assn of Clinical Specialists in Psychosocial Nursing; member, American Academy of Practice. **Honors/Awds:** Visit Prof Sch of Nursing Yale Univ 1979; Visit Prof Afro-Amer Studies Dept School of Nursing Univ of WI Milwaukee, WI 1979; Disting Lectr Sch of Nursing East Carolina Univ 1979; numerous papers including, "Violence and the Human Condition, A Mental Health Perspective" Univ of WI Milwaukee, WI 1979; "Psychosocial Nursing Research, The State of the Art" presented at the Conference, "Perspectives in Psychiatric Care," 1980 Phila, PA; Research Approaches to the Social Ecology of Health Sch of Nursing Columbia Univ New York, NY 1982; Occasioning Factors of Urban Violence, African-American Studies Ctr Madison, WI; "Point PrevalenceStudy of Alcoholism and Mental Illness among Downtown Migrants" (with Whitley, Marilyn P and Godfrey, M) Social Science & Medicine, an Intl Journal in 1985; FelloAmerican Academy of Practice, 1985; Frederick Douglass Scholar's Award, Natl Conference of Black Scholars, 1988; Chief Adila of Ibara, Ibara Abeokuta Nigeria, 1972. **Business Addr:** Professor, Department of Psychological Nursing, University of Washington, SC-76, Seattle, WA 98112.

OSBORNE, WILLIAM REGINALD, JR.
Health services administrator. **Personal:** Born May 10, 1957, Worcester, MA; son of Dolores Everett Osborne and William Reginald Osborne, Sr; married Cheryl Lowery, Jun 1980; children: Justin, Blake. **Educ:** Morehouse Coll, BS (Cum Laude) 1979; Howard Univ Coll of Medicine, MD 1983; Emory Univ Sch of Medicine, Dept of Internal Medicine. **Career:** Morehouse Coll, asst instructor of anatomy & physiology 1979-80, summer careers prog instructor of physics 1980; Morehouse Coll of Medicine Dept of Internal Medicine, clinical instructor 1986-; Health South, internist 1986-89; Southside Healthcare Inc, medical director 1989-. **Orgs:** Mem Omega Psi Phi Frat 1976-; mem Southern Christian Leadership Conf 1978-; mem Amer Coll of Physicians 1986; mem Natl Medical Assn; mem Georgia State Medical Assn 1989-. **Honors/Awds:** Scholastic Awd Omega Psi Phi Frat 1978,79; mem Atlanta Univ Center Biology Honor Soc; Fraternity 7th District Scholar Awd Omega Psi Phi Frat 1978; Beta Kappa Chi Scientific Honor Soc; Board Certified in Internal Medicine. **Business Addr:** Medical Director, Southside Healthcare, Inc, 1039 Ridge Ave, Atlanta, GA 30315.

OSBY, GREGORY THOMAS
Saxophonist, composer. **Personal:** Born Aug 3, 1960, St Louis, MO; son of Georgia Osby; married Kay Vaughn. **Educ:** Howard University, 1978-80; Berklee College of Music, 1980-83. **Career:** Oztone Productions, CEO, currently. **Business Addr:** CEO, Oztone Productions, PO Box 3174, Riverton, NJ 08077, (609)786-0927.

OSBY, PARICO GREEN
Educator, licensed dietician. **Personal:** Born Feb 7, 1945, Selma, AL; daughter of Rosetta Wilson Green and Marion L Green Sr; married Porter Osby Jr, Sep 12, 1965; children: Patrick, Phyllis, Portia. **Educ:** Tuskegee University, BS, 1968; Baptist Hospital, dietetic traineeship, ADA diploma, 1973; Central Michigan University, MA, 1977. **Career:** University of Nevada Las Vegas, student foodservice manager, 1968-70; Baptist Hospital, dietetic trainee, 1970-73; St Francis Xavier Hospital, clin & adm dietician, 1973-75; St Elizabeth Hospital, Dept of Nutrition, director, 1976-87; Tuskegee University, instructor, 1989-92, Hospitality Management Program, acting coordinator, instructor, 1992-93. **Orgs:** American Dietetic Association, 1973-; Alabama Dietetic Association, Scholarship Committee, 1988-; American Hotel/Motel Association, 1991-; NAACP, 1975-. **Honors/Awds:** Tuskegee University, Faculty Service, 1990, School of Agriculture & Home Economics, Teacher of the Year, 1991; Alabama Dietetics Association, granted licensure for practice of dietetics, 1990; Graduate of Leadership Dayton Program for promising community leaders, 1985; Supervising Agent, Extension System, with Expanded Fd & Nutri Ed Program, Auburn University. **Business Addr:** Montgomery County Extension System, 125 Washington Avenue - Courthouse Annex II, First Floor, Montgomery, AL 36104-4247.

OSBY, SIMEON B., JR.
Journalist. **Personal:** Born May 15, 1909, Springfield, IL; married Annabel Marie Anderson. **Educ:** Univ of IL, 1929-32. **Career:** Fed Transient Bur, caseworker 1934-36; Natl Youth Admin, field rep 1936-43; Capitol City News, publ weekly paper 1947-51; Chicago Daily Defender, legislative corr 1953-86; Capitol City News Serv, editor & publisher 1980-. **Orgs:** Organizer IL State NAACP; sec IL State NAACP 1933-36; past pres Springfield NAACP 1939-43; mem Omega Psi Phi Frat 1940-; mem IL Legislative Corr Assn 1953-; Comdr Col Otis B Duncan Post 809 Amer Legion 1962-63; exec dir IL Legislative Com Minority Group Employment 1969-73; Soc Prof Journalist Sigma Delta Chi 1972-; bd trustees Lincoln Library

Springfield 1980-. **Honors/Awds:** Appointed to Press Comm of IL State Senate 1975. **Military Serv:** AUS 1st lt 1943-46; AUSR 1947-52. **Business Addr:** Editor & Publisher, Capitol City News Service, Press Rm Mezzanine Floor, State Capitol, Springfield, IL 62706.

OSHIYOYE, ADEKUNLE

Physician. **Personal:** Born Jan 5, 1951, Lagos, Nigeria; son of Grace Apena Oshiyoye and Alfred Oshiyoye; married Oluwatoyin Oshiyoye, Dec 28, 1991. **Educ:** Howard Univ, Washington, DC, 1972-73; Univ State of NY, Albany, NY, BS, 1975; Columbia Univ, New York, NY, 1974-78; American Univ, Montserrat, WI, MD, 1979. **Career:** South Chicago Comm Hosp, Chicago, IL, physician, 1980-81; Cook County Hosp, Chicago, IL, resident physician, 1981-85, executive chief resident, ob-gyn, 1984-85; Mercy Hosp, Chicago, Il, attending physician, 1987-89; Chicago Osteopathic Hosp Medical School, Chicago, IL, asst prof, 1988-; City of Chicago, Dept of Health, Chicago, IL, consulting physician, 1989-. **Orgs:** Urban League; life mem, Alpha Phi Alpha Fraternity, 1988-, black & gold comm, 1989, 1991, labor day comm, 1991, director of education program; Investigating Comm Eureka #64, 1987-; Pan-Hellenic Action Council, chairman publicity committee; Ancient Arabic Order Shrine, 1988-; American Med Assn, 1983-; chmn, Health Comm, Nig-American Forum, 1989-; American Coll Obstetrics-Gynecology, 1983-; Cook County Physician Assn, 1983-; Mayor's Comm on Human Relations, 1990-; founding mem, Harold Washington Health Coalition, 1983-; founding member, Obstetrics-Gynecology Video Journa 1989-; 32 degree mason, Scottish Rite, Knights of Rose Crux, 1988-; Chicago Urban League, 1990-; Operation Push, 1988-; Chicago Med Society, 1983-; IL Med Assn, 1983-. **Honors/Awds:** Physician Recognition Award, American Medical Assn, 1986-88; Medical Editor, African Connections, 1980-; Chief Resident, Ob-Gyn, Cook County Hosp, 1984-85; Beta Kappa Chi Honor Society, Howard Univ, 1974; Cerebral Palsy Research Grant, Cerebral Palsy, 1975; Federal Govt Scholarship Award, Federal Govt, 1972; Federal Govt Post-Graduate Scholarship Award, Federal Govt, 1976; Pharmacology Honors, Columbia Univ, 1977; Alpha Phi Alpha, Recognition Award, 1991; Chicago Police Department, Recognition Award, 1991-92; Chicago Board of Education, Role Model Award, 1991-92.

OSIBIN, WILLARD S.

Physician. **Personal:** Born Feb 2, 1925, Oakland, CA; married Shirley M Wilson; children: Willard S. **Educ:** Univ of CA Berkeley, 1946-49; Meharry Med Coll Nashville, TN, MD 1953. **Career:** Physician & surg, pvt prac 1656-80. **Orgs:** Mem CA Med Assn Com on Collective Bargaining 1980; mem CA Med Assn Com on Evolving Trends in Soc Affecting Life 1978-80; v-chmn CA Med Com on Emergency Med Care 1978-80; alternate del CA Med Assn, AMA 1976-80; hs of del CA Med Assn 1973-80; past diplomate/mem Am Bd Family Practice 1971-; trustee San Luis Obispo/Santo Barbara Med Care Found 1973-80; exec com sec & fdg dir Area XVI PSRO 1974-80; mem CA State MQRC #8 Bd of Med Quality Assurance 1975-80; med ofcr Composite Squadron #103 Civil Air Patrol; past pres & current dir San Luis Obispo CA Fair Bd; past pres San Luis Obispo Co Civil Serv Commn 1970-78; past cmdr W States Assn of Sheriffs Aero Squadron; past pres Atascadero Lions Club; past pres San Luis Obispo Co Alcoholic Adv Com 1975; appointed trustee, CUESTA COMMUNITY COLLEGE, San Luis Obispo, CA; exec comm & chief pacific regional dir, Physicians For Social Responsibility, Washington, DC; dir & founding mem, Santa Lucia Natl Bank, Atascadero, CA; trustee, Comm Church of Atascadero, CA. **Honors/Awds:** M Airman Award & others, AUS 1943-45; Bronze & Silver Medallions, Am Heart Assn 1973 & 1977; Lion of the Yr, Lions Intl 1975; Citizen of the Month, Atascadero Businessmen's Assn 1976; Citizen of the Yr, Atascadero C of C 1977. **Military Serv:** AUS corpl 1943-45; AF Aux 1979. **Business Addr:** 1050 Las Tablas Rd, Ste 6, Templeton, CA 93465.

OTIENO-AYIM, LARBAN ALLAN

Dentist. **Personal:** Born Sep 15, 1940; son of Dorcas Ayim and Jonathan Ayim; married Agness Auko; children: Peter, Paul, James, Anna. **Educ:** Univ of WI, 1969; Meharry Med Coll Nashville, TN, DDS 1973; Univ of MN Sch of Public Health, MPH 1975. **Career:** Dentist, private practice 1977-; State of MN Dept of Public Welfare, staff dentist 1975-77; Pilot City Health Ctr Minneapolis, clinical dentist 1974-75. **Orgs:** Mem Am Dental Assn; mem Minneapolis Dist Dental Soc; mem MN Dental Assn; mem Am Public Health Assn; mem MN Public Health Assn; mem Masons. **Business Addr:** 2126 West Broadway, Minneapolis, MN 55411.

OTIS, AMOS JOSEPH

Professional baseball player. **Personal:** Born Apr 26, 1947, Mobile, AL. **Career:** New York Mets, outfielder, third baseman 1967-69; Kansas City Royals, outfielder 1970-83; Pittsburgh Pirates, outfielder, 1984. **Honors/Awds:** Sporting News Am League All-Star Team 1973; Sporting News Am League All-Star Fielding Teams 1971, 72 & 74; mem Am League All-Star Team 1970-71, 1973-76; tied major league records for fewest times caught stealing one season, 50 or more stolen bases (8) 1971; set league records for highest stolen base percentage lifetime 300 or more attempts (799) 1975; most stolen bases 2 consec games (7) 1975; led Am League in stolen bases (52) 1971; played in 3 Championship Series 1976-78; tied series record most stolen bases one series (4) & total series (6) 1978.

OTIS-LEWIS, ALEXIS D.

Judge. **Educ:** Washington University School of Law, JD. **Career:** St Clair County, IL, assistant state's attorney; private practice, East St Louis, IL, 1989-92; St Clair County 20th Judicial Circuit, associate judge, currently. **Orgs:** Alpha Kappa Alpha Sorority. **Special Achievements:** First African-American woman judge elected to serve in the 20th judicial circuit Which includes St Clair, Monroe, Perry, Washington and Randolph Counties; First African American federal law clerk, Southern District of IL. **Business Addr:** Associate Judge, St Clair County Circuit Court, 10 Public Square, Belleville, IL 62220, (618)277-7325.

OTTLEY, AUSTIN H.

Association executive. **Personal:** Born Jun 17, 1918, NYC; married Willie Lee; children: Federic Wayne, Dennis. **Educ:** Empire State Coll, BS. **Career:** Mayors Com Exploitation Workers NY, sr rep 1965-67; IBEW Local 3, shop steward 1959-65; New York City Central Labor Council ALF-CIO, asso dir. **Orgs:** Mem Local 3 IBEW; F Div Adv Bd, Local 3 IBEW 1954-; Lewis Howard Latimer Progressor Assn 1958-; Independent United Order of Scottish Mechanics 1936-; Chap 80 St Geo Assn 1972; mem Labor Com Jamaica NAACP 1962-66; Negro Am Labor Council 1962. **Military Serv:** USAF sgt 1942-46; USAFR s/sgt 1948-52, active duty 1951-52. **Business Addr:** 386 Park Ave S, New York, NY 10016.

OTTLEY, NEVILLE

Physician, surgeon. **Personal:** Born Dec 18, 1926; married Esther; children: Russell Mark, Melanie Dawn. **Educ:** Andrew U, BA 1953; Howard Univ Coll of Med, MD 1957; DC Gen Hosp, intern 1957-58; Howard Univ Freedmen's Hosp, resident, gen sergery 1958-62. **Career:** St Elizabeth's Hosp, chf dept of surgery 1965-, med ofcr & gen surgeon 1962-65. **Orgs:** Diplomate Am Bd of Surgery 1963; fellow Am Coll of Surgeons; fellow Intl Coll of Surgeons; fellow Am Geriatrics Soc; diplomate mem Pan Am Med Assn; mem DC Med Soc; St Elizabeth's Med Soc; mem Credentials Com, Res Review Bd, Environ & Infection Control Com, St Elizabeth's Hosp. **Honors/Awds:** Monographs the effect of adrenalectomy on electrolye balance in rats; carcinoma of the esophagus treated with right & left colon transplant. **Business Addr:** 2642 12 St NE, Washington, DC 20018.

OUBRE, HAYWARD LOUIS

Artist. **Personal:** Born Sep 17, New Orleans, LA; son of Amelie Marie Keys Oubre and Hayward Louis Oubre Sr; married Juanita B Hurel Oubre, Jan 2, 1945 (deceased); children: Amelie Geneva. **Educ:** Dillard U, BA 1939; Univ of IA, MFA 1948. **Career:** FL A&M College, assoc prof of art 1949-50; AL State College, prof of art chrmn 1950-65; Winston-Salem State U, prof of art chrmn 1965-81, curator Selma Burke Art Gallery 1984-90; researcher in color. **Honors/Awds:** 1st prize oils IA State Fair, IA 1947; 8 prizes Atlanta U, Atlanta, GA 1947-68; 3rd prize sculpture Emancipation Proclamation Centennial 1963; author of directors in modern art Art Review Magazine Natl Art Exhibit New Orleans 1966; corrected color triangle Devised by Johann Wolfgang Von Goethe 1976; four intensity color band wheel (in color), 1977. **Special Achievements:** Auctioned Paintings: ''Pensive Family,'' ''Cotton Picker,'' 1992, pictured in Art and Auction Magazine. **Military Serv:** Engineer, sergeant, 1941-43; American Defense Ribbon, 1942; North American Service Ribbon, 1943; Asiatic Pacific Ribbon, 1943; Alcan Highway Citation, 1943; Sharp Shooter Medal (Rifle). **Home Addr:** 2422 Pickford Ct, Winston-Salem, NC 27101.

OURLICHT, DAVID E.

Investment banker. **Personal:** Born Oct 22, 1957, Detroit, MI; son of Borus & Myrtle; married Marybeth, Aug 21, 1983; children: David E II, Christine F. **Educ:** State University of New York, College at Buffalo, BS, 1979. **Career:** National Association of Securities Dealers, senior examiner, 1981-84; Daniels & Bell, vice president, 1984-87; Marine Midland Bank, vice president, 1987-88; Drexel Burnham Lambert, vice president, 1988-90; Chase Manhattan, consultant, 1990-91; State of New York, executive director, Council on Fiscal & Economic Priorities, 1991-93; Dillon Read & Co Inc, vice president, 1993-. **Orgs:** South Street Seaport Museum, trustee, 1992-; University Settlement Society, board member, 1992-. **Honors/Awds:** YMCA of Harlem, Black Achiever in Industry, 1989. **Business Phone:** (212)906-7240.

OUSLEY, HAROLD LOMAX

Educator, music producer/publisher. **Personal:** Born Jan 23, 1929, Chicago; son of Nellie Ousley Farabee; married Alice Inman; children: Sheronda, Saundra Hepburn, Renee Watson. **Career:** Jamaica Art Center, music dir, coord, 1982-; Queens Council on The Arts, jazz music coord, 1982-85; Jazz Interactions, music coord, 1980-85; Broadcast Music Inc, composer, music publisher, 1967-; Mountain Neighborhood Network, jazz cable show producer, 1992; Time, NY, NY, 1998; A Jazz Circle of Friends, OPTV, 1990; Time Flushing, NY, ''Harold Ousley Presents,'' cable jazz producer; Leader Muse Records, Bethlehem Records, J's Why Records, recording artist. **Orgs:** Therapeutic music coord Key Sch York Manor Branch Key Women of Amer 1970-85; National Jazz Organization, 1991-; Jazz Bureau, 1991-. **Honors/Awds:** Comm serv Key Women of America 1981; jazz achievement Jazz at Home Club 1972; Jazz Pioneer Award Broadcast Music Inc 1984; wrote movie theme, 'Not Just Another Woman,' 1974; Greater Jamaica Development Corp, Award, 1997. **Business Addr:** Music Coord & Dir, Jamaica Art Center, GPO Box 1119, New York, NY 10116.

OUTLAW, CHARLES (BO)

Professional basketball player. **Personal:** Born Apr 13, 1971, San Antonio, TX. **Educ:** Houston. **Career:** Los Angeles Clippers, forward-center, 1993-97; Orlando Magic, 1997-. **Business Addr:** Professional Basketball Player, Orlando Magic, 1 Magic Pl, Orlando, FL 32801, (407)649-3200.

OUTLAW, PATRICIA ANNE

Psychologist. **Educ:** Mt Providence Jr College, AA 1966; Towson State U, BA 1968, MA 1971; Univ of MD College Park; Ph D 1977; St Mary's Seminary & U, MA Th 1985. **Career:** Baltimore City Sch, school psychologist, 1970-71; Towson State U, dir of study skills center, 1971-77, assoc dean of students, 1977-79; Cheltenham Ctr, staff psychologist, 1979-83; Walter P Carter Ctr, senior psychologist, 1985-94; Spring Grove Hosp, staff psychologist, 1994-; Outlaw and Associates, pres, 1993-; Accessible Health Associates Inc, vp, 1995. **Orgs:** St John AME Church, associate minister, 1984-87; Hemingway Temple AME Church, associate minister, 1987-88; Mt Joy AME Church, pastor, 1988-92; Payne Memorial AME Church, associate minister, 1992-. **Honors/Awds:** Strong Blacks in Health, 1995. **Business Addr:** Pres, Outlaw & Associates, 2300 N Calvert St, Ste 219, Baltimore, MD 21218.

OUTLAW, SITNOTRA

Airline captain. **Personal:** Born Feb 25, 1957, Detroit, MI; son of Erma Outlaw and Jack Outlaw; children: Sitnotra Jr. **Educ:** Spartan School of Aeronautics, commercial flight instructor, commercial instrument instructor, 1979. **Career:** Fayetteville Flying Serv, chief flight instructor; Schedule Sky Ways, captain; USAir Lines, captain, currently. **Orgs:** Organization of Black Airline Pilots; USAir Lines, ambassador; National Brotherhood of Skiers. **Honors/Awds:** Outstanding Father Awards, 1991. **Military Serv:** US Air Force, e-4, 1974-78. **Home Addr:** 218 Briar Path, Imperial, PA 15126, (412)695-1898.

OUTLAW, WARREN GREGORY

Counselor. **Personal:** Born Mar 25, 1951, South Bend, IN; married Iris L Hardiman; children: Lauren, Gregory. **Educ:** Lincoln Univ, BS 1974; IN Univ-South Bend, MS Educ 1980. **Career:** South Bend School Corp, substitute teacher 1974-75; YMCA Comm Service Branch, asst dir 1975-80; Educ Talent Search, assoc dir 1980-83, dir 1983-. **Orgs:** Chmn scholarship comm NAACP 1984-; chmn financial dev comm IN Mid-Amer Assoc Educ Oppor Prog Pers 1985-; chmn Black Comm Sch Comm 1986-. **Honors/Awds:** Service Citation YMCA 1980; IN Black Achievers IN Black Expo 1984; Youth Leadership & Service John Adams High School 1985. **Home Addr:** 2902 Bonds Ave, South Bend, IN 46628. **Business Addr:** Director, Educ Talent Search, Univ of Notre Dame, PO Box 458, Notre Dame, IN 46556.

OUTTERBRIDGE, JOHN WILFRED

Artist. **Personal:** Born Mar 12, 1933, Greenville, NC; son of Olivia Outterbridge and John Outterbridge; divorced; children: Tami Lyn. **Educ:** A&T Univ, 1952-53; Amer Acad of Art, 1957-59, 1960-61; State of CA Teaching Credential, 1970. **Career:** Traid Corp, artist/designer 1964-68; Communicative Arts Acad, co-founder, artistic dir, 1969-75; CA State Univ, lecturer African Amer art history 1970-73; Pasadena Museum of Art , art instructor & installation 1968-72; Watts Towers Arts Center, Cultural Aff Dept, City of Los Angeles, dir, 1976-92. **Orgs:** County of Los Angeles Art Ed Dept, Aesthetic Eye Proj, 1974; Natl Endowment of the Arts, Expansion Arts panelist, 1977-79, Crafts Div Task Force, research committee member, 1980-81; California Arts Council, grants panelist, 1978-82; J Paul Getty, Discipline Based Art Ed for the Visual Arts, advisory bd member, 1980-82; Watts Towers Community Trust, bd mem, 1985-88. **Honors/Awds:** Watts Summer Festival, 1974; KNX Newsradio, Citizen of the Week, 1977; 15th Councilmanic District, City of Los Angeles, 1980; Los Angeles Unified School District, Cultural Awareness, 1981; California State Univ Los Angeles, Paul Robeson Black Leadership, 1982; Pasadena, California, Cultural History, 1985; Watts Health Foundation, 1985; Central Cities Gifted Children's Assn, 1988; State of California, Distinguished Artist, 1988; California State Univ, Dominguez Hills, Miriam Matthews Achievement Award, 1988; New Afrikan People's Org, Malcolm X Freedom Award, 1990; 1st Annual King Blvd Memorial Project, Lifetime Achievement Award, 1990; Western Region NAACP, 14th Annual Act-So Award, 1993; State of California Legislature Assembly, 13th Dist, 1993; County of Los Angeles, 2nd Supervisory Dist Award, 1993; Fullbright Visiting Artist Fellowship, New Zealand, 1986; J Paul Getty Visual Arts Fellowship, 1994; Natl Endowment of the Arts, Visual Arts Fellowship, 1994; Otis Coll of Art and Design, honorary degree, doctor of fine arts, 1994; JR Hyde Visiting Artist Fellowship, 1994; National Conference of Art Educators, 1987. **Military Serv:** US Army corpl 1953-56. **Home Addr:** 5838 S Woodlawn Ave, Los Angeles, CA 90003.

OVERALL, MANARD
Marketing/engineering development manager. **Personal:** Born Sep 20, 1939, St Louis, MO; son of Emma Overall (deceased) and Walter Overall (deceased); married Arclethia Ann Abbott (divorced). **Educ:** Hampton Univ Hampton, VA, BS 1973; Fairleigh Dickinson Univ NJ, MBA, management, 1977; City Univ, currently. **Career:** Aerospace Group Tracor Inc, mrktng mgr 1979-82; TX Inst Inc, computer sys mrkt engr mgr 1978-79; TX Inst Inc, prodr eng mgr 1977-78; St Edward's U, instr 1978; Austin Comm Coll, instr 1978-; Mgmt Objectives Co Bus Consultant, managing dir/owner; Modular Power Systems Director Mktg and programs 1981-86; Eldec Corporation engineering manager 1986-. **Orgs:** Coach youth sports teams 1960-80; vice pres Pond Springs Sch PTA 1977-78; CO rep TX Alliance for Minority Engrs 1977-78; President Puget Sound Black Professional Engineers 1988-90; Advisory bd Seattle WA, MESA; adv bd, Seattle B lacks in Science. **Honors/Awds:** Scholastic honors Hampton Univ Engineering 1973. **Military Serv:** US Coast Guard CPO 1957-77; Legion of Merit (Plus 12); US Army chief warrant ofcr 1967-77.

OVERBEA, LUIX VIRGIL
Staff writer. **Personal:** Born Feb 15, 1923, Chicago, IL; married Elexie Culp. **Educ:** NWU, PhB 1948; MS 1951. **Career:** Assoc Negro Press, chf copy desk 1948-54; OK Eagle Tulsa, cty editor 1954-55; The Winston-Salem Journal, staff writer 1955-68; The St Louis Sentinel, mng edtr 1968-70; the St Louis Globe-Dem, asst mkup editor staff & reporter 1970-71; The Christian Sci Monitor, staff writer 1971-; Winston-Salem State Coll, tchr 1965-68. **Orgs:** Mem Sigma Delta Cig; mng edtr The Black Ch Mag 1974; commentary Black News TV Show 1973-; mem NAACP; Kappa Alpha Psi; Prnts Counc; Metco; 2nd Ch of Christ. **Honors/Awds:** Sci NNPA Aws St Louis Sentinel. **Military Serv:** AUS ASTP corpl 1943-46. **Business Addr:** 1 Norway St, Boston, MA 02115.

OVERSTREET, EVERETT LOUIS (LOUIE)
Civil engineer. **Personal:** Born Oct 9, Dekalb, MS; son of Myrtha Crawford Overstreet and Pervis Overstreet; married JoAnn Gregory Overstreet, Jun 28, 1970; children: Lorie Danielle, Piper Sabrina. **Educ:** Ohio University, Athens, OH, BSCE, 1967; Carnegie Mellon University, Pittsburgh, PA, MSCE, 1973; California Coast University, Santa Ana, CA, PhD, 1988. **Career:** Contra Tech Inc, Anchorage, AK, partner, 1978-85; Anchorage Times, editorial columnist, 1980-86; Tundra Times, editorial columnist, 1986-88; Anchorage School District, Anchorage, AK, exec director, 1986-92; Trigen-Peoples District Energy Company, general manager, currently. **Orgs:** Board of Trustees, Alaska Pacific University, 1985-92; board of directors, Alaska Black Caucus, 1980-92; life member, Golden Heritage; life mem, NAACP, 1994-. **Honors/Awds:** Author, Black on a Background of White, 1988; Cited for Volunteer Service, Alaska Legislature, 1988. **Home Addr:** 8321 W Sahara Ave #2122, Las Vegas, NV 89117-1874.

OVERSTREET, HARRY L.
Architect. **Personal:** Born Jun 30, 1938, Conehatta, MS; son of Cleo Huddleston-Overstreet and Joe Overstreet; divorced; children: Anthony, Harry II, Nile. **Educ:** Attended CCAC, Oakland CA, 1956-57; Contra Costa Coll, San Pablo, CA, 1955-56. **Career:** Gerson/ Overstreet, San Francisco CA, vice pres, partner, 1968-85, pres, 1985-. **Orgs:** Past pres, mem, Berkeley Planning Comm, 1967-73; bd mem, Hunter Point Boys Club 1975-; pres, Natl Org of Minority Architects, 1988-90; co-founder, Northern CA Chapter of NOMA, 1972; American Institute of Architects, San Francisco Chapter; board member, CCAIA, 1992-93; co-chair, San Francisco Ho Chi Minh City Sister City committee, 1997-98. **Honors/Awds:** Award of Merit, Palace of Fine Arts, 1975; Serv for Engineering Career Day, U C Davis, 1979; Career Workshop, City of Berkeley, 1979. **Military Serv:** US Army, 1957-60. **Business Addr:** President, Gerson/Overstreet, Architects, 25 Kearny/Maiden Lane, 6th Floor, San Francisco, CA 94108-5524, (415)989-3830.

OVERSTREET, MORRIS L
Judge. **Career:** Texas Court of Criminal Appeals, judge, currently. **Orgs:** Phi Beta Sigma Fraternity Inc, life member; NAACP, life member. **Special Achievements:** First African-American to be elected to Statewide Office in Texas. **Business Addr:** Judge, Texas Court of Criminal Appeals, Box 12308, Capitol Station, Austin, TX 78711-2548.

OVERTON, DOUGLAS M.
Professional basketball player. **Personal:** Born Aug 3, 1969, Philadelphia, PA; married Chanel; children: Miles Randall. **Educ:** LaSalle University. **Career:** Rockford Lighting (CBA), 1991-92; Washington Bullets, guard, 1992-95; Denver Nuggets, 1995-96; Philadelphia 76ers, 1996-. **Business Addr:** Professional Basketball Player, Philadelphia 76ers, One Corestates Complex, Philadelphia, PA 19148, (215)339-7676.

OVERTON, VOLMA ROBERT
Association executive (retired). **Personal:** Born Sep 26, 1924, Travis County, TX; married Warneta. **Educ:** Huston-Tillotson College, BS 1950. **Career:** Pres, Austin Branch NAACP, 1962-82, sec/treas; Credit Union, founder 1969; Federal Credit Union, scoutmaster 1954-65. **Orgs:** Texas State Conference NAACP, first vice pres, 1970-72; PTA, president. **Honors/Awds:** Arthur Dewitty Award 1967; Scoutmaster Award 1960; Zeta Phi Beta Civic Award 1970; Sakarroh Temple #1 Award, Outstanding Community Service 1973. **Military Serv:** US Marine Corps 1943-46; US Army Reserve, lt colonel, 1947-77. **Business Addr:** President, NAACP, Austin Branch, 1704 E 12th St, Austin, TX 78721.

OVERTON-ADKINS, BETTY JEAN
Educational administrator. **Personal:** Born Oct 10, 1949, Jacksonville, FL; daughter of Miriam Crawford and Henry Crawford; married Eugene Adkins; children: Joseph A, Jermaine L. **Educ:** TN State Univ, BS 1970, MA 1973; George Peabody of Vanderbilt Univ, PhD 1980. **Career:** Metropolitan Nashville School Bd, teacher 1970-72; TN State Univ, teacher, program dir 1972-76; Univ of TN at Nashville, instructor 1973-78; Nashville State Tech Inst, asst prof 1976-78; Fisk Univ, asst prof, asst dean 1978-83; Univ of Arkansas, assoc dean, dean 1983-91; W K Kellogg Foundation, coordinator, higher education, program dir, assistant director, 1991-. **Orgs:** Race Relations Information Center, reporter 1970-71; Nashville Panel of American Women, bd mem 1973-83; Natl Council of Teachers of English 1979-; ACE, admin fellow 1980; Arkansas Women's History Inst, bd mem 1983-; Teak Reportory Theatre, bd mem 1983-; Women of Color United Against Domestic Violence, bd mem, founding mem 1985; Scarritt Coll, consultant; YMCA, counsultant. **Honors/Awds:** Alpha Kappa Alpha, Outstanding Leadership Award 1981; articles published in: Southern Quarterly 1985; The Race Relations Reporter 1971; Tennessee Developmental Studies Notes 1977; Calloloo Magazine 1981; W K Kellogg Natl Leadership Development Fellowship, W K Kellogg Foundation 1988-91; Award for Meritorious Achievement, Office of Research and Sponsored Programs, Univ of Arkansas at Little Rock 1989. **Home Addr:** 223 Berkley Avenue, Battle Creek, MI 49017. **Business Addr:** Coordinator, Higher Education & Program Director, W K Kellogg Foundation, One Michigan Ave E, Battle Creek, MI 49017.

OWENS, ANDI
Educator. **Personal:** Born Jul 21, 1934, Minneapolis, MN. **Educ:** Columbia Univ, BA 1962; NY School for Social Work, graduate work 1963. **Career:** Genesis II Museum of Intl Black Culture, dir 1980-; Brooklyn Museum, museum prep 6 curatorial depts work proj 1978-80; Afro-Amer Cultural Found Westchester Co, coordinator, 1976-77; Black History Museum of Nassau Co, museum curator 1974-75; The Met Museum of Art, Rockefeller fellow 1973-74; Genesis II Gallery of African Art, co-fdr 1972; Indus Home for the Blind, asst dir recreation 1965-72; Church of St Edward the Martyr, dir recreation 1962-65. **Orgs:** Fdr experimental drama group The Queens Revels Columbia Univ 1958-62; orkshopws Documentation & Exhbn for Mus Educators 1974; Fedn of Prot Welfare Agys "Creative Comm Involvement" 1974; Met Mus of Art "Art Discovery Workshop for Comm Grps" 1974; Met Mus rep designer for YM-YWHA 1974; chmn Visual Arts Discipline for Mid-West Regn; 2nd World Festival of Black & African Arts & Culture 1975; panelist Blacks & Mus; Am Assn of Mus 1974; bd advr Bronx Comm Bd 7 Cultural Arts Ctr 1974; NY State chmn of exhbns Nat Conf of Artists 1974; part NY State Cncl on the Arts 1975; Smithsonian Inst Mus Prgm 1975; panel chmn Mus & Visual Art Instns for Rgnl Nat Conf of Artists 1976. **Honors/Awds:** Grant recipient NY State Cncl on Arts for Genesis II Traveling Exhbn Prgm 1973. **Military Serv:** USAF sgt 1953-57. **Business Addr:** 509 Cathedral Pkwy, New York, NY 10025.

OWENS, ANGLE B., JR.
Superintendent. **Personal:** Born Sep 17, 1922, Wilmington, NC; married Mattie L Bagby. **Educ:** Hampton Inst, BS; VA Polytechnic Inst; State U; Univ of NE at Omaha; GA Tech; Univ of Cincinatti; Lasalle U. **Career:** AUS, horticulturist 1951-52; Hampton Inst, asst grounds supt 1952-55; Hampton Inst, grounds supt 1955-59; Hampton Inst, asst supt maint 1959-66; Building & Grounds Hampton Inst, supt 1966-. **Orgs:** Mem Peninsula C of C 1965-71; mem Assn Physical Plant Adminstr %For Coll & Univ; Nat Safety Council Coll Div; Hampton Inst Alumni Assn; consult various Penninsular Garden Clubs; Pioneer Lodge #315 Free & Accepted Masons PM; Hampton Inst Commn 1970-71; past v chmn Hampton Dem Com 1959-60; mem Am Numismatic Assn; Nat Negro Commerative Soc; NAACP; Wythe Southampton Action Com; consult Moton Found; consult FL Meml Coll; served on Review Com Handbook for Physical Plant Operations for Small Coll; served on Transportation Policy Review Com Hampto Pub Sch. **Military Serv:** AUS 1944-46; USAR 2nd lt 1946-53. **Business Addr:** Hampton Inst, Hampton, VA.

OWENS, ARLEY E., JR.
State government official. **Personal:** Born Oct 14, 1948, Lima, OH; son of Loretta J Owens and Arley E Owens Sr; married Audrey M Bankston, Nov 9, 1968; children: Scott, Kevin. **Educ:** Ohio State University, BA, communications, 1977. **Career:** CONSOC, housing consultant, 1976-78; Ball Realty, property manager, 1978-79; Lane Realty, sales manager, 1979-80; Ohio Department of Natural Resources, project supervisor, 1980-81, employee relations coordinator, 1981-85, communications administrator, 1985-. **Orgs:** National Organization of Minorities in Recycling and Waste Management, vice pres, 1991-, communication committee chairperson; National Recycling Coalition, 1991-, bd of dirs, 1993-, chairperson, NRC Communication and Education Committee, 1993-, NRC Minority Council, 1993-, chairperson, 1994-95; Public Relations Society of America, membership committee, 1994. **Honors/Awds:** US Department of Interior, Take Pride in America, National Winner, 1991, 1992; Ohio Department of Natural Resources, Outstanding Professional Employee Award, 1988, Employee of the Month, 1985; Keep America Beautiful Inc, National Recycling Award, 1989; The Black Communicator, Citizen of the Week Award, 1990. **Special Achievements:** Creator: nation's first Pride in Public Housing Campaign, Ohio's Public Housing Authorities, 1990, state-wide Recycling Awareness Campaign involving Ohio's five major zoos, 1989. **Military Serv:** US Air Force, sgt, 1967-70; Vietnam Service Campaign Medal, Distinguished Unit Citation. **Home Addr:** 7954 Slate Ridge Blvd, Reynoldsburg, OH 43068. **Business Addr:** Admin, Div of Litter Recycling & Prevention, Ohio Department of Natural Resources, 1889 Fountain Square, Bldg F-2, Ste 203, Columbus, OH 43224, (614)265-6333.

OWENS, BILLY EUGENE
Professional basketball player. **Personal:** Born May 1, 1969, Carlisle, PA. **Educ:** Syracuse. **Career:** Golden State Warriors, forward/guard, 1991-94; Miami Heat, 1994-96; Sacramento Kings, 1996-. **Honors/Awds:** NBA All-Rookie first team, 1992. **Special Achievements:** NBA Draft, First round pick, #3, 1991. **Business Addr:** Professional Basketball Player, Sacramento Kings, One Sports Pkwy, Sacramento, CA 95834, (916)928-6900.

OWENS, BRIGMAN
Business executive. **Personal:** Born Feb 16, 1943, Linden, TX; son of Roxie Love Owens and Alfred L Owens; married Patricia Ann; children: Robin, Tracey Lynn. **Educ:** Univ of Cincinnati, BA 1965; Potomac Sch of Law, JD 1980. **Career:** Dallas Cowboys, prof athlete 1965-66; Washington Redskins, prof athlete 1966-78; NFL Players Assn, asst exec dir 1978-84; Brig Owens & Assocs, pres, currently. **Orgs:** Exec bd Boy Scouts of Amer 1974; vice pres Mondale's Task Force on Youth Employment 1978; mem Comm on Caribbean for Governor of FL 1978; bd of dirs USA Telecomm Inc 1985; bd of dirs Natl Bank of Commerce 1985; bd of dirs Big Bros of America 1985; vice pres Leukemia Soc 1985; president's board, University of Cincinnati, 1990. **Honors/Awds:** All American Univ of Cincinnati 1965; author "Over the Hill to the Superbowl" 1971; Distinguished Alumni Fullerton Jr Coll 1974; Washingtonian of the Year Washington magazine 1978; Washingtonian of the Year Maryland Jaycees 1978; Hall of Stars Washington Redskins; Hall of Fame Univ of Cint; Hall of Fame Orange Co CA, NCAA Silver Anniversary Award Winner, 1990. **Military Serv:** ANG 1965-70. **Business Addr:** President, Brig Owens & Assocs, 3524 K St NW, Washington, DC 20007-3503.

OWENS, CHANDLER D.
Clergyman. **Career:** Church of God in Christ Inc, presiding bishop, currently. **Business Addr:** Presiding Bishop, Church of God In Christ Inc, World Headquarters, 938 Mason St, Memphis, TN 38106, (901)578-3838.

OWENS, CHARLES CLINTON
Dentist. **Personal:** Born Sep 3, 1942, Smithville, TX; son of Dr & Mrs E A Owens; married Dianne Burdel Banks; children: Euau Cha, Chelsi Dion. **Educ:** Prairie View A&M Univ, BS 1965; Howard Univ Sch of Dentistry, DDS 1970. **Career:** Model Cities Lawton, dentist 1971-72; OK State Health Dept, dentist 1972-79; dentist. **Orgs:** Consult OK State Health Dept 1972-79; 2nd vice pres PIC Invest Corp 1978-; treas Northside C of C 1979; treas PIC Invest Corp; mem OK Health Planning Com 1973; member, Alpha Phi Alpha Fraternity; board member, Selective Services; board member, United Way; board member, Lawton Chapter Red Cross. **Honors/Awds:** Outstanding Young Man of the Year Lawton Jaycees 1972; Appreciation Award Great Plains Vo Tech 1979; Appreciation Award Eisenhower Sr High Sch 1979. **Business Addr:** 1316 Ferris, Lawton, OK 73501.

OWENS, CHARLES EDWARD
Educator. **Personal:** Born Mar 7, 1938, Bogue Chitto, MS; married Otis Beatrice Holloway; children: Chris Edward, Charles Douglas, Bryant Holloway. **Educ:** WV State Coll, BA 1961; WV U, MA 1965; Univ of NM, EdD 1971. **Career:** Psychology Dept Univ of AL, assoc prof 1973-; VA Commonwealth Univ Richmond, counselor 1971-73; Univ of WI Madison, counselor 1969-71; Albuquerque Job Corps Center for Women NM, counselor 1967-68; Charleston Job Corps Center for Women WV, coordinator of testing & referals 1966-67; Wheeling WV, teacher 1965-66. **Orgs:** Mem Am Psychol Assn; mem Nat Assn of Black Psychol; mem Nat Assn of Blacks in Crimnl Just; mem NAACP; mem Tuscaloosa Mental

Health Assn; Plemarch Kappa Alpha Psi WV State Coll 1960-61; Phi Delta Kappa WV Univ 1965. **Honors/Awds:** US Office of Educ Fellowship Univ of NM 1968-69; book publ ''Blacks & Criminal Justice'' 1977; book publ ''Mental Health & Black Offenders'' 1980. **Military Serv:** AUS 1st lt 1961-64. **Business Addr:** Box 2968, Tuscaloosa, AL 35486.

OWENS, CURTIS
Business executive. **Personal:** Born Oct 18, 1938, Philadelphia, PA; children: Curtis Derek. **Educ:** Central State Univ Wilberforce, OH, BS 1962; Temple Univ, MPA 1970; California Coast Univ Santa Ana, CA, working towards PhD. **Career:** Mercy Douglass Hosp PA, asst adminstr; Gen Elect PA, operations & rsch analyst; Philco Ford Corp, sr instr; Neighborhood Health Svc, cntr admin; Temple Univ Comprehensive Health Svcs, prog adminstr, director; African American Unity Center, pres, currently. **Orgs:** Mem Polit Sci Soc; mem Natl Health Consumer's Orgn; past pres Natl Assn of Neighborhood Health Centers Inc; mem Health Task Force Philadelphia Urban League; bd dirs Regional Comprehensive Health Planning Cncl. **Honors/Awds:** Congressman's Medal of Merit 1975; Key to City of San Francisco 1975; MLK Jr Social Justice Award, California State Univ, Dominguez Hills. **Military Serv:** AUS 1st Lt Med Serv Corp. **Business Addr:** President, African American Unity Center, 5300 South Vermont Ave., Los Angeles, CA 90037.

OWENS, DAVID KENNETH
Engineer, business executive. **Personal:** Born Jun 14, 1948, Philadelphia; son of Grace Owens and Erwin D Owens; married Karen P, Nov 20, 1971; children: Pharis, Phyllis, Kenneth. **Educ:** BS elec engr 1969; Howard U, MSEE 1977; Geo Wash U, MSEA 1977. **Career:** Securities & Exchange Commn, chief engr, 1974-80; Fed Power Commn, 1970-74; Gen Elec Co, 1969-70; Philadelphia Elec Co, 1968; Edison Electric Inst, sr vice pres, 1980-. **Orgs:** Mem Inst of Elec & Electronics Engrs; Kappa Alpha Psi Frat; mem Nativity BVM Ch; mem, Blacks in Energy; mem, Natl Black Engineer's Assn. **Honors/Awds:** Kappa Alpha Psi Frat Schroller of Yr Award, 1969; Superior Perf Award 1972; Outstanding Award 1974; Outstanding Employee of the Year Award, EEI, 1987; Most Distinguished Professional, EEI, 1988; Special Rec Award, EEI, 1990. **Business Addr:** Senior Vice President, Edison Electric Inst, 701 Pennsylvania Ave NW, Washington, DC 20004-2696.

OWENS, DEBBIE A.
Journalist. **Personal:** Born Jan 23, 1956, Brooklyn, NY. **Educ:** Brooklyn Coll CUNY, BA (Cum Laude) 1977; Univ of IL Urbana-Champaign, MS 1982. **Career:** Chicago Tribune Newspaper, reporter 1976; NY Amsterdam Newspaper, reporter 1977; New York City Bd of Educ, hs English teacher 1978-79; JC Penney Co NY, catalog copywriter 1979-81; WPGU-FM ''Black Notes'', public affairs reporter 1981-82; WCIA-TV, news reporter/minority affairs prog prod 1982-85; Edward Waters Coll, radioTV broadcast instr 1982-85; Edward Waters Coll, radio/tv broadcast instr 1985-. **Orgs:** Mem Mayor's Vol Action Ctr of NY 1980; mem NY Vol Urban Consulting Group 1980; mem Radio-TV News Dir Assn 1982-; writer for grad newsletter Univ of IL 1981-82; mem IL News Broadcasters Assoc 1983-85. **Honors/Awds:** Scholars Program Brooklyn Coll of CUNY 1975-77; Scholarship/Intern Newspaper Fund Prog 1976; Book Reviewer Freedomways Magazine NY 1980; Scholarship Scripps-Howard Found 1981; Grad Fellowship Univ of IL at Urbana-Champaign 1981-82. **Business Addr:** Radio/TV Broadcast Instructor, Edward Waters College, 1658 Kings Rd, Jacksonville, FL 32209.

OWENS, GEOFFREY
Actor. **Personal:** son Of Major Owens. **Career:** ''The Cosby Show,'' until 1992; ''Built To Last,'' NBC. **Orgs:** New York City Church of Christ. **Honors/Awds:** Danny Kaye Award; BACA Brooklyn Bridge Award. **Business Addr:** Actor, 50 W 96th St, #4C, New York, NY 10025.

OWENS, GEORGE A.
Educational administrator. **Personal:** Born Feb 9, 1919, Hinds Co, MS; son of Robbie Henry Owens and Charlie Owens; married Ruth B Douglas, Apr 22, 1944; children: Paul Douglas Owens, Gail Patrice Owens Baity. **Educ:** Jackson State Coll MS; Tougaloo Coll, AB 1941; Columbia U, MBA 1950. **Career:** Security Life Ins Co, clk 1946; Jersey City, bookkeeper hardware store 1947-48; Talladega Coll, bus mgr chief financial officer 1949-55; Tougaloo Coll, chief financial officer 1955-64, acting pres 1964, pres 1965-84; LeMoyne Owen Coll, interim pres 1986-87. **Orgs:** Mem Alpha Phi Alpha Frat Incor; United Negro Coll Fund; life mem NAACP; Boy Scouts of Amer; Sigma Pi Phi Fraternity. **Honors/Awds:** Recipient honorary LLD degrees from Bethany Coll 1967, Huston-Tillotson Coll 1967, Brown Univ 1967; LHD Wilberforce Univ 1970; 1st black pres of Tougaloo Coll; Hon LLD Tougaloo Coll 1984; president emeritus Tougaloo Coll, 1986; Silver Beaver Award Boy Scouts of America, 1988; The Silver Order of the de Fleury Medal, US Army Engineering Association; Recognized as the first Black American to earn an MBA Degree, Columbia University Business School. **Military Serv:** AUS Corps of Engrs Captain 1941-46 Honorable Discharge. **Home Addr:** 815 Winthrop Circle, Jackson, MS 39206.

OWENS, GRADY D., SR.
Hotel owner. **Personal:** Born Jul 20, 1938, New York, NY; son of Bridget Owens and Grady Owens; married Judith Joyinens Owens; children: Keith, Erin, Grady Jr. **Educ:** Mount St Mary College, 1963-64; Orange County Community College, AA. **Career:** New York State Department of Social Services, child careworker; Burlington Ind, market research; King Lodge, partner/owner, currently. **Orgs:** Horton Hospital, board of directors, chairman of the investment committee; Orange County Community College, board of directors; Orange County Chamber of Commerce, board of directors; NAACP Western Orange County, president, 4 yrs. **Honors/Awds:** Burlington Ind, Kepner-Trago Award, 1976. **Military Serv:** US Marine Corps, cpl, 1961-68; Expert-Rifle. **Business Addr:** President, Owner, Kings Lodge, Rd 1, Shoddy Hollow Rd, Otisville, NY 10963, (914)386-2106.

OWENS, HUGO ARMSTRONG, SR.
Dentist (retired). **Personal:** Born Jan 21, 1916, Chesapeake, VA; son of Grace M Owens and James E Owens; married Helen West Owens, Sep 2, 1941; children: Paula C Parker, D Patrice, Hugo A Jr. **Educ:** Virginia State University, BS, general science and science education, 1939; Howard University Coll of Dentistry (cum laude), DDS, 1947. **Career:** Crisfield MD Public Schools, science and math teacher, asst principal; private practice, dentistry; Chesapeake City Council, vice mayor, 1970-80; Norfolk State Univ, bd of visitors; Virginia State Univ, rector, bd of visitors, 1982-86; Howard Univ, professor; Medical College of Virginia, professor; Old Dominion Univ, rector, 1993-. **Orgs:** John L McGriff Dental Society, founder; American Society for Preventive Dentistry, founding member, 1969; Committee of Concerned Citizens; NAACP. **Honors/Awds:** Norfolk-Virginian-Pilot, Citizen of the Decade, 1980; Norfolk Ledger Dispatch, Citizen of the Decade, 1980; City of Chesapeake, First Citizen, 1988; Howard Univ, Distinguished Alumni; Virginia State Univ, Distinguished Alumni, honorary doctorate degree; Ebony, Most Influential African Americans. **Special Achievements:** First African American elected to Chesapeake, VA, city council, 1970; Author, articles in Journal of the American Society for Preventive Dentistry; The National Dental Association; American Dental Assn; Natl Medical Assn; Virginia Teacher Assn; Journal of Prosthetic Dentistry. **Military Serv:** US Army, personnel officer. **Home Addr:** 4405 Airline Blvd, Chesapeake, VA 23321.

OWENS, ISAIAH H.
Educator, business executive. **Personal:** Born Jan 8, 1920, Columbus, GA; son of Mary D Owens and Isaiah H Owens; married Nell Craig; children: Whitlynn, Isaiah Jr, Bert, Barrington. **Educ:** Univ of IL, BFA 1948; IN U, BS 1959. **Career:** Roosevelt HS Gary, teacher; Owens & Craig's Inc, pres; Standard Oil, industrial distributor 1950-58; Owens' Gift & Toy Shoppe, owner 1949-65; Chicago Rockets, pro football 1948. **Orgs:** Vp Midtown Businessmen Assn 1970-73; mem Residence Com Model Cities; chmn Economic Task Force; mem Gary Alumni Chap Kappa Alpha Psi; NAACP; Roosevelt HS Alumni Assn. **Honors/Awds:** Big Ten Football 1941, 1945, 1947; All American 1947; Most Valuable to Team 1947; All Big Ten 1947; All Midwest 1947. **Military Serv:** AUS sgt 1941-45. **Business Addr:** 1638 Broadway, Gary, IN 46404.

OWENS, JAMES E.
President. **Personal:** Born Sep 7, 1937, Stonewall, MS; married Evelyn Robinson; children: James, III. **Career:** Chicago Metro Mutual Ins Co, mgr 1959-71; Supreme Life Ins Co, sr vice pres 1971-82, mem bd of dir 1976-82; American Investors Life Ins Co, regional dir1983-; Owens Enterprises, president 1983-. **Orgs:** Bd of dir Chicago Ins Assn; asst dean Cosmopolitan CC Free Sch of Bus; sect Natl Ins Assn; instr Chicago Ins Assn; mem Southend Jaycees; mem NAACP; Boy Scouts of Amer; Amer Assn of Comm & Indus; Chicago Ins Assn 1975-76; mem Natl Assn of Life Underwriters. **Honors/Awds:** Chicago Merit Chicago Assn of Life Underwriters 1968-69; Outstanding Man of the Year Chicago Southend Jaycees 1973; Golden Scepter Award 1974. **Military Serv:** AUS E4 1960-62. **Business Addr:** President, Owens Enterprises, 523 E 67th St, Chicago, IL 60637.

OWENS, JAY R.
Dentist. **Personal:** Born Feb 17, 1944, Pine Bluff, AR; married Staggie Darnelle Gordon; children: Kevin, Jay II, Latitia. **Educ:** Howard Univ, BS 1967; Meharry Medical Coll, DDS 1971. **Career:** Private Practice, dentist. **Orgs:** Pres AR Medical Dental Pharmaceutical Assoc 1982-83; vice speaker of house Natl Dental Assoc 1984-85; bd of dirs Urban League of AR 1984. **Military Serv:** AUS capt 2 yrs. **Business Addr:** Ste 714 University Tower Bl, Little Rock, AR 72204.

OWENS, JEFFERSON PLEAS
Educator (retired). **Personal:** Born Jul 10, 1917, Wharton, TX; son of Manola Struber Owens and Isaac Owens; married Addye B Leroy, Oct 26, 1943; children: Sharynn. **Educ:** Prairie View State Coll, Prof, Shoemaking Certificate, 1933-35; Boy Scout Exec School 89th, Exec Certificate 1943; Knoxville Coll; BA 1961; Univ of TN, MS, Educ 1977; Intl Univ Found of Europe, PhD 1985. **Career:** Knoxville Coll, coordinator of Alumni Affairs 1962-70; Knoxville Recreation Dept, recreation supvr 1957-62; Knoxville City Schools, classroom teacher 1971-84; TN Dept of Educ, teacher evaluator 1984-; Vine Middle School Knoxville, language arts teacher, 1985-87; Urban Ministries, Chicago, Il, Christian education consultant, currently. **Orgs:** Field scout exec, Boys Scouts of Amer 1943-53; charter pres Y's Men's Club (YMCA) 1960; bd of mgmnt YMCA 1964-70; sec-treasurer educ Carpetbag Theatre 1970-80; minister of christian Ed Mount Zion Baptist Church 1980-87; life mem, Alpha Phi Alpha Fraternity; Vice Moderator of Educ, Knoxville Dist Baptist Assn, 1987-88; Deputy Governor, Amer Biographical Inst, Rsch Assn, 1989. **Honors/Awds:** Knoxville Sponsored Negro Man of the Year 1945; Religious Service Award NCCJ 1974; Outstanding Homeroom Teacher Park Jr HS 1980; Golden Apple Award by Knoxville News-Sentinel 1985. **Home Addr:** 310 Ben Hur Ave SE, Knoxville, TN 37915.

OWENS, JERRY SUE
Educational administrator. **Personal:** Born Jan 16, 1947, Kentucky; married Ronald L Owens. **Educ:** Murray St Univ, BA 1969, MA 1970; Univ of TX, PhD 1983. **Career:** Earlington Elem Sch, 6th grade educator 1970; Murray High School, Jr/Sr english 1970-71; Triton Coll, instructor 1971-77, asst/ assoc/ & dean of arts & sciences 1978-85; Lakewood Comm Coll, president 1985-. **Orgs:** Mem Natl Cncl of Teachers of English, Amer Assoc of Comm & Jr Colls, Amer Assoc of Higher Educ, Women in Higher Educ; vice pres bd YWCA St Paul MN; bd mem United Way St Paul; mem Urban League, NAACP. **Business Addr:** President, Lakewood Community College, 3401 Century Ave, White Bear Lake, MN 55110.

OWENS, JIMMY
Musician, trumpeter, composer, educator. **Personal:** Born Dec 9, 1943, New York, NY; children: Milan, Ayan. **Educ:** Univ of MA, MEd 1976. **Career:** The Collctv Blk Artsts Inc, co-fndr 1969-; Atlantic Records, recs ''You Had Better Listen'' 1967; Polydor Records, ''No Escapin' It'' 1970; A&M Records, ''Jimmy Owens'' 1976; ''Headin' Home'' 1978; recorded over 150 albums with other jazz artists; performed at the concerts & workshops USA & Eur 1973-97; Teaching Positions, Queens Borough Comm Coll 1985-86, SUNY-Old Westbury 1981-86; Jazzmobile Jazz Workshop, dir, 1985-91; Jay-Oh Music Co, composer/musician/educator; faculty, New School Jazz and Contemporary Music Program; guest visiting professor at Oberlin Conservatory of Music; City Univ of New York, conducting Workshops in Career development in the music industry. **Orgs:** Amer Fed Mscns; Brdcst Music Inc;Awards Dowbeat Critic's Poll; mem bands led by Lionel Hampton, Slide Hampton, Hank Crawford, Herbie Mann, Charles Mingus, Duke Ellington, Count Basie, Thad Jones, Mel Lewis, Billy Taylor, May Roach, Peter LaRoca Sims, NY Jazz Sextet; concerts in Europe Senegal Morocco Tunisia Algeria Egypt Pakistan South America with band ''Jimmy Owens Plus''; mem Intl Assoc of Jazz Educators 1974-; mem Natl Jazz Serv Org 1985, board of dirs, Jazz Foundation of America, chairman, Jazz Musician Emergency Fund of JFA. **Honors/Awds:** Pres Citation for Excellence in Advancement of the Contributions of Black AmS ot Music in Am 1978; major articles written on Jimmy Owens NY Times, Downbeat Mag, Jazz Mag, Arts Midwest Jazz Letter, Jazz Journal; cited in Black Enterprise Magazine ''New Leaders for the 80's''; Intl Success Awd Marabu Club (Italy); Borough President of Manhattan Awd for Excellence in the Arts 1986; Natl Endowment for the Arts, 1980, 1993. **Business Addr:** Composer, Jay-Oh Productions, Inc, 236 Park Avenue South, New York, NY 10003.

OWENS, JOAN MURRELL
Educator (retired), paleontologist. **Personal:** Born Jun 30, 1933, Miami, FL; daughter of Leola Peterson Murrell and William Henry Murrell; married Frank A Owens; children: Adrienne Johnson-Lewis, Angela. **Educ:** Fisk Univ, BA (Magna Cum Laude) 1954; Univ of MI, MA (Pi Lambda Theta) 1956; George Washington Univ, BS 1973, M Phil 1976, PhD 1984. **Career:** Children's Psych Hosp Univ of MI, reading therapist 1955-57; Howard Univ Dept of Eng, reading specialist 1957-64; Inst for Services to Educ DC & MA, curriculum Spec 1964-71; Smithsonian Inst DC, museum technician 1972-73; Howard Univ Washington, DC, 1976-95, assoc prof of Geology, 1976-91; assoc prof Biology, 1991-95. **Orgs:** Speaker 4th Intl Symposium Fossil Cnidaria 1983; mem, Minority Affairs Committee, Natl Assn of Geology Teacher, 1988-90; geology councilor, Council on Undergraduate Research, 1990-91. **Honors/Awds:** College Reading Skills (Co-author), Alfred J Knopf 1966; Ford Fellowship Nat'l Fellowships Fund, Atlanta 1973-76; ''Microstructural Changes in the Micrabaciidae and their Taxonomic & Ecologic Implications,'' Palaeontographica Americana, 1984; 1st Black American Woman Geologist with PhD in the field; mem Delta Sigma Theta; ''Evolutionary Trends in the Micrabaciidae, An Argument in Favor of Pre-Adaptation,'' 1984 Geologos Vol II No 1; ''Rhombopsammia: A New Genus of the Family Micrabaciidae,'' 1986 Proceedings of the Biological Soc of Washington Vol 99 No 2; ''On the Elevation of the Stephanophyllia Subgenus Letepsammia to Generic Rank,'' Proceedings of the Biological Soc of Washington Vol 99 No 3; Scientist, Black Achievers in Science, Exhibit Chicago's Museum of Science & Indus, 1988; ''Letepsammia Franki, A New Species of Deep-Sea Coral,'' 1994; Proceedings of the Biological Society of Washington, Vol 107, No 4. **Home Addr:** 1824 Upshur St NE, Washington, DC 20018.

OWENS, JUDITH MYOLI
Educator (retired). **Personal:** Born Jun 18, 1940, Carlisle, PA; daughter of Estella Pickens Owens and Benjamin Myoli Owens. **Educ:** Shippensburg Univ, BS Educ 1962; Monmouth Univ, MS Educ 1975; Nova University, Ed.D, 1990. **Career:** NJ Educ Assc, pres 1975-77; Asbury Park Bd Educ, elem tchr, math resource room tchr, chrprsn spec educ, affirmative action ofcr, supr, vice principal; Asbury Park Bd Educ Bradley School Asbury Park NJ principal 1987-91; Educational Testing Svcs, consultant, 1989-; The College of New Jersey, asst prof, 1991-95. **Orgs:** Natl Educ Assoc; NJ Ed Assoc; Order of Kentucky Colonels; Delta Kappa Gamma; Central Jersey Club NANB PWC Inc; member, Mensa International, 1990-. **Honors/Awds:** Natl Ach Award Natl Assc of Negro Bus & Prof Women's Clubs; Mini-grant Prog NJ State Dept of Educ; Educ Ach Award Central Jersey Club NANBPW Inc; Educ Ach Award Asbury Park Study NJ Org of Tchrs; Educ Ach Award Psi Upsilon Chptr Omega Psi Phi Frat; Educ Ach Award Monmouth Cty Bus & Prof Women's Council; Woman of Year 1976 Camden Area Club NANBPW Inc; Gold Award The United Way; Womon of the Year, Educ; Monmouth Cnty Advisory Committee on The Status of Women 1986. **Home Addr:** 64 Kathy Ct, Brick, NJ 08724.

OWENS, KEITH ALAN
Journalist. **Personal:** Born May 1, 1958, Denver, CO; son of Geneva M Owens and Sebastian C Owens. **Educ:** Colorado College, BA, 1980. **Career:** Littleton Independent, intern, 1984; Denver Post, intern, 1984-85; Los Angeles Times, journalism trainee, 1985-86; Ann Arbor News, reporter, 1986-89; Fort Lauderdale Sun-Sentinel, editorial writer, reporter, 1989-93; Detroit Free Press, editorial writer, columnist, 1993-. **Orgs:** Natl Assn of Black Journalists, 1984-; Mid-Michigan Association of Black Journalists, president, 1988-89; Palm Beach Association of Black Journalists, secretary, 1991, parlimentarian, 1992; Phillips Exeter Academy Committee on Excellence thru Diversity, chairman, 1988-89. **Honors/Awds:** Phillips-Exeter Academy, President's Award, 1990, Class of 1976, Service to PEA Award, 1991. **Home Addr:** 2900 Jefferson Ave, #D-500, Detroit, MI 48207.

OWENS, KENNETH, JR.
Architect. **Personal:** Born May 23, 1939, Chattanooga, TN; son of Lydia A Owens and Kenneth Owens Sr; married Dannetta Kennon, Nov 24, 1989; children: Kevin L, Keith L. **Educ:** Tennessee State University, BS, 1963; Birmingham Southern College, MA, 1989. **Career:** US Corps of Engineers, draftsman, 1963-65; Rust Engineers, draftsman, 1966-68; CH McCauley, architect, 1969-73; The Owens and Woods Partnership, PC, architect/president, 1974-. **Orgs:** Birmingham Jefferson Metro Chamber of Commerce, chairman/president, 1992; Operation New Birmingham, vice pres, board, 1987-90; Metropolitan Development Board, board member, 1988; Omega Psi Phi Fraternity, 1957; Leadership Birmingham, 1985; Sixth Avenue Baptist Church, deacon, 1989; Vulcan Kiwanis Club, past president, 1987; Newcomer Club, 1989. **Honors/Awds:** UNCF Birmingham, Father of the Year, 1978; Boy Scouts of America, Silver Beaver, 1982; Tennessee State University, Outstanding Engineer Alumni, 1985; Engineers for Professional Development, Outstanding Engineer Award, 1985. **Business Addr:** Architect/President, The Owens and Woods Partnership, PC, 214 N 24th St, Birmingham, AL 35203, (205)251-8426.

OWENS, LYNDA GAYLE
Family consultant, educator. **Personal:** Born Jun 16, 1956, Elizabethtown, NC; daughter of Eunice Bryant Owens Houston and David P Owens; children: LaTisha, Larry, Solomon, Aljawanna. **Educ:** Rutledge College, Richmond, VA, 1981; ICC Career Center, Richmond, VA, nurses aide, certificate; Richmond Virginia Seminary, J Sargeant Reynolds College. **Career:** Richmond Public Library, Richmond, VA, pager, library asst, 1979-81; Henrico Co Jail, Richmond, VA, supervisor, 1982-85; City of Richmond Recreation and Parks, Richmond, VA, volunteer, 1985-; Richmond Public School, Richmond, VA, instructional asst, 1985-; HEAL, Richmond, VA, AIDS health educator, 1991-; self-employed parental & family consultant, Richmond, VA, 1989-; The Carver Promise, exec dir, 1992-96; Virginia Dept of Juvenile Justice, coord of youth svcs, currently. **Orgs:** Exec Secretary, RAAC, 1991; vice pres, Mosby PTA, 1989-; member, Shared Decision Making Committee, 1990-91; member, Richmond Education Assn, 1985-; member, Speaker's Bureau, 1989-; Greater Mt. Moriah Baptist Church, assoc minister; NAACP; Eastern Star; Crusade for Voters; Sistercare; N-Pac. **Honors/Awds:** America's Award, Positive Thinking Foundation, 1990; Proclamation, Mayor, City of Richmond, 1990; Resolution, Richmond City Council, 1990; Outstanding Employee and Parent, Richmond Public School Board, 1990; Outstanding Citizen and Role Model, Board of Commissioners of Richmond Redevelopment & Housing Authority; first woman ever recognized nationally as a National Unsung Hero who personified the American Dream for sacrificing and devoting her life to children in oppressed communities; Governor's Commission on Citizen Empowerment of the Commonwealth of VA, 1994; Richmond Times Dispatch, Community Service Award, 1992; Ascended Woman Award, 1992; Lynda G Owen Day, Dec 10, 1990; ABC Nightly News, Person of the Week; ABC-Family Values Special; ABC Special-Real Kids, Real Solution; numerous speeches, articles, and documentaries. **Home Phone:** (804)323-7720. **Business Addr:** Consultant, Single Parenting & Empowerment, PO Box 7937, Richmond, VA 23223, (804)257-0407.

OWENS, MAJOR R.
Congressman. **Personal:** Born Jun 28, 1936, Memphis, TN; son of Edna Davis Owens and Ezekiel Owens; children: Christopher, Geoffrey, Millard. **Educ:** Morehouse Coll, BA 1956; Atlanta Univ, MLS 1957. **Career:** Brooklyn Public Library, comm coord 1964-66; Brownsville Comm Council, exec dir 1966-68; NYC, commr 1968-73; Columbia Univ, instr 1973-; Communovation Assoc, pres cons; State of New York, senator 1974-82; NY State Senate Albany NY Senator 1975-82; NY City Deputy Administrator Community Development Agency; US House of Representatives, member, 1983-. **Orgs:** Commn on XVI Intl Conf Hague Netherlands 1972; mem 100 Black Men; mem NY State Black & Puerto Rican Caucus; mem Beta Phi Mu; mem Central Brooklyn Mobilization for Polit Action; NY chmn Brooklyn Congress Racial Equality; Lifetime member NAACP. **Honors/Awds:** Awds in Black Found for Rsch & Educ in Sickle Cell Disease 1973; Honoree Awd Fed of Negro Civil Serv Orgn 1973; Achievement Awd Widow Sons' Lodge #11 Prince Hall Masons 1973; Major R Owens Day Sept 10, 1971 Pres of Borough of Brooklyn; pub author and lecturer on library sci; keynote speaker White House Conf on Libraries 1979; Honorary Doctorate of Law Degree Atlanta Univ 1986; Appointed Chairman House Subcommittee on Select Education 1987-. **Business Addr:** Congressman, US House of Representatives, 114 Cannon House Ofc Bldg, Washington, DC 20515.

OWENS, MERCY P.
Bank officer. **Personal:** Born Sep 30, 1947, Jenkinsville, SC; daughter of Unita Pearson and Fred Pearson Sr (deceased); divorced; children: Tia and Trey. **Educ:** St Augustines Coll; Cannon Trust School. **Career:** FNB/SCN, floater, customer svc operations officer; SCN/Wachovia Bank of SC, C/D IRA coordinator, trust officer, asset mgt account officer; Wachovia Bank of SC, corporate compliance officer, CRA administrator, vice president. **Orgs:** Richland Memorial Hospital Center for Cancer Treatment, trumpeter gala; Eboni Dance Theatre, board member; SC Bankers Assn, compliance comm; SC Low Income Housing Coalition, advisory board; United Way of the Midlands, project blueprint; NAACP; James R Clark Sickle Cell Foundation, executive comm; SC Assn of Urban Bankers. **Honors/Awds:** United Black Fund/Eboni Keys, Eboni Keys Award, Women Opening Doors, 1991; Minority Business Devel Center, Minority Bankers of the Year, 1994; Pee Dee Times and Carolina Tribune, Positive Image Award, 1995. **Business Addr:** VP, Wachovia Bank of South Carolina, 1401 Main St, Ste 402, Columbia, SC 29226.

OWENS, NATHANIEL DAVIS
Judge. **Personal:** Born Feb 17, 1948, Hartsville, TN; married Barbara Catlin; children: Marsha. **Educ:** Univ of South Sewanee TN, BA (with Honors) 1970; Emory Univ Law School, JD 1973; Northwestern Univ School of Law, Grad Prosecutors Course 1976; Univ of NV at Reno, Grad Natl Judicial Coll 1979. **Career:** Atlanta GA, rsch 1971-72; USMC Asst Defense Counsel, spec prog 1972; Atlanta Legal Aid Soc 1972; Thelma Wyatt Atty, 1972-73; Kennedy Bussey Sampson Attnys 1973-74; Huie Brown & Ide Attnys, 1974- US Army AGO Basic Course AGOBC, 1974, Ft McClellan 1974-76; Jacksonville State Univ, adj prof 1975-; 7th Judicial Circuit, asst dist attny 1976-79; Distric Court of Cleburne & Calhoun Counties, dist court judge 1979-. **Orgs:** Mem Mt Olive Baptist Church 1975-; 32nd Degree Master Mason 1976-; Royal Arch Mason Chap 47; Hartsville Commandry No 5 TN 1976-; 1st vice pres Assoc of US Army 1978-; former mem bd of dir Anniston Area Chamber of Commerce 1978-79; pres Club of AL State Demo Party 1978-; Omega Psi Phi Theta Tau Chap 1978-; chmnState & Local Govt Comm Chamber of Comm 1978-80; co-chmn Citizens Org for Better Ed 1979-82; Beta Kappa Boule Sigma Pi Phi 1981-. **Honors/Awds:** Omega Man of the Year Awd Theta Tau Chap 1979; Outstanding Serv Awd Alpha Kappa Alpha Sor 1980; Case Club Awd Appellate Arguments; Case Club Judge; Moot Court Competition Awd Emory Univ School of Law. **Military Serv:** AG/FA/CML capt 1974-; commander 496 chem detachment. **Home Addr:** PO Box 2641, Anniston, AL 36202-2641.

OWENS, RICH
Professional football player. **Personal:** Born May 22, 1972, Philadelphia, PA. **Educ:** Lehigh, attended. **Career:** Washington Redskins, defensive end, 1995-. **Business Addr:** Professional Football Player, Washington Redskins, 13832 Redskin Dr, Herndon, VA 22071, (703)471-9100.

OWENS, ROBERT LEON, III
Educator. **Personal:** Born Nov 3, 1925, Arcadia, FL; married Nancy Gray; children: Raymond, Ronald, Nancy. **Educ:** Tuskegee Inst, BS summa cum laude, class valedictorian 1949; State Univ of IA, MA 1950; State Univ of IA, PhD 1953; N Park Coll, LHD 1968; New York U, 1954; Columbia U, 1957; Inst for the Study of Acad Leadership, 1961; Harvard U, 1965; PA State U, 1967; Univ of MI, 1970. **Career:** Coll of Liberal Arts Howard U, dean 1971-; Univ of TN, v prof educ psychol 1969-71; Knoxville Coll, pres, prof of psychol 1966-71; Coll of Arts & Sci, dean; So Univ Baton Rouge, prof of psychol & educ 1962-66; So Univ Baton Rouge, dean grad sch, prof of psychol & educ 1958-62; So U, prof psychol & educ 1957; So U, asso prof psychol 1956; So U, asst prof psychol 1953-55; State Univ of IA, instr psychol of reading 1953. **Orgs:** Mem exec com Land Grant Assn of Deans of Grad Schs 1959-71; mem Exec Com of Deans of Arts & Sci Land Grant Univs 1963-65; symposium participant Am Psychol Assn 1959, 1962, 1964; panelist Assn for Higher Educ 1959, 1963, 1972; mem exec com Am Soc for Curriculum Devel 1970; duscussant Am Conf ofAcad Deans 1973; group leader Am Conf of Acad Deans 1977; chmn, nominating com Am Conf of Acad Deans 1976; mem, bd of dir Am Conf of Acad Deans1977-80; Mem Exec Com of the Cncl on Religion & Higher Educ Research Assbn 1974-77; symposium leader Annual Conf of Inst for Intl Educ 1971-76; lectr convocation & commencement addresses at various instutions of higher educ 1975-; life mem Phi Delta Kappa. **Business Addr:** Howard Univ, Coll of Liberal Arts, Washington, DC 20059.

OWENS, RONALD
Attorney. **Personal:** Born Feb 4, 1930, Newark; married Louise Redding; children: Randall, Pamela. **Educ:** Seton Hall Law, LLB 1959. **Career:** Asso Newk Muni, Judge Charles A Stanziale Jr ofcs in Newark, atty; NJ, acting governor 1976; Pro-Tempore, assembly speaker; Dist 29 Essex Co, assemblyman 1965-; NJ Gen Assembly, asst dem ldr 1972-73; City of Newark, asst corp counsel 1968-70; served in following, Assembly Educ Com; Assemblee Tax PolicyStudy Commn; Assembly Welfare Commn; Assembly Criminal Law Revision Study Commn; Assembly Sex Educ Commn; Assembly Ins Revision Commn; Assembly Child Abuse Study Commn; Assembly Permanent Commn on Sch Aid; Assembly Bateman Commn; NJ Hist Commn. **Orgs:** Mem Nat Bar Assn; Am Bar Assn; NJ Bar Assn; Essex Co Bar Assn; Commerical Law League Of Am; trustee Anna Whittington Scholarship Fund; trustee NewarkPub Library; commr Newark Wathershed Commn; BSA; Robt Treat Council; Weequahic Comm Council; YMCA Newar Br; NAACP. **Military Serv:** US Signal Corp 1953-55. **Business Addr:** 50 Park Pl, Newark, NJ 07102.

OWENS, RONALD C.
Attorney. **Personal:** Born May 1, 1936, Conway, AR; married Lois Adamson; children: Ronald, Alan, Veronica. **Educ:** Morehouse Coll, 1952-54; Univ of AR at Pine Bluff, BS 1957; Univ of Baltimore Law Sch, JD 1973. **Career:** Baltimore City, former asst states atty; asst city solicitor; att pvt prac; Johns Hopkins U, pre-law advisor 1975-; Johns Hopkins U, former asst dir of admissions 1969-73; Ft Howard Am Bar Assn, corrective therapist. **Orgs:** Monumental City Bar Assn; Phi Beta Gamma Legal Frat; steward Douglas Memorial Ch. **Honors/Awds:** Recip Ford Found Scholarship Morehouse Coll; Law Review of Univ of Baltimore Sch of Law 1972-73; Outstandin Advocate for 1972-73; Univ of Balt Sch of Law. **Military Serv:** AUS. **Business Addr:** 3705 Dorchester Rd, Baltimore, MD 21215.

OWENS, TERRELL ELDORADO
Professional football player. **Personal:** Born Dec 7, 1973, Alexander City, AL. **Educ:** Tennessee-Chattanooga, attended. **Career:** San Francisco 49ers, wide receiver, 1996-. **Business Addr:** Professional Football Player, San Francisco 49ers, 4949 Centennial Blvd, Santa Clara, CA 95054, (415)562-4949.

OWENS, THOMAS C., JR.
Educational administrator (retired), florist. **Personal:** Born May 11, 1922, Dillion County, SC; married Dorothy Stevens; children: Jacquelyn Hillman, Thomas C III, Brenda Hamlett, Linda Cooper, Darwin. **Educ:** SC State Coll, BS 1948; SC State Coll, MA 1957; Atlantic Univ, Fellowship to study the middle school concept 1969; University of Georgia; USC, Col, SC. **Career:** Amer Legion Post 222, 1st post commander 1950-70; Kappa Alpha Psi, historian 1975-80; Johnston city councilman, 1977-; Charleston/Columbia Dist, district lay leader 1978-81; NC & SC Conf of the Methodist CME Churches, vice pres 1981-84; Riverside School, principal, 1955-87. **Orgs:** Advisor to registrant Bd of Registration 1972-; mem NAACP, SCEA, SC Assn of School Admin. **Honors/Awds:** Achievement Award Outstanding Serv to School & Community 1980, SC Admin Leadership Acad 1982; Outstanding & Dedicated Service Awd, Child Devel Class 1985; Loyal and Dedicated Service 12 year Award, Town Council 1985; Award in Appreciation for Developing ''Little Minds of the Future'' 1986. **Military Serv:** AUS sgt 3 years; Purple Heart, Five Battle Stars, Good Conduct Medal, Medal of Honor 1944.

OWENS, TREKA ELAINE
Accountant. **Personal:** Born Dec 6, 1953, Chicago, IL; daughter of Pauline Berry and Alfred Berry; married Johnny C Owens; children: Kellie. **Educ:** DePaul Univ, BSC Acctg 1975; DePaul University, College of Law, Chicago, IL, JD, 1990. **Career:** Arthur Young & Co, auditor 1975-77; Avon Products, staff accountant 1977-78; Borg-Warner Corp, corporate acct 1978-80; Johnson Publishing Co, chief accountant 1980-86, vice pres finance 1986-. **Orgs:** Mem Amer Inst of CPA's 1982-, IL Soc of CPA's 1982-; member, American Bar Association, 1991; member, Illinois Bar Association, 1991; member, Chica-

go Bar Association, 1991. **Business Addr:** Vice President Finance, Johnson Publishing Co, 820 So Michigan Ave, Chicago, IL 60605.

OWENS, VICTOR ALLEN
Telecommunications executive. **Personal:** Born Sep 30, 1945, Bronx, NY; married Ruth Morrison; children: Malcolm. **Educ:** Wilberforce Univ, BA 1967; Univ of Dayton, MA 1971. **Career:** Ohio Bell Telephone, mgr 1967-71; YWCA, business mgr 1971-76; Colonial Penn Group, mgr 1976-79; The Equitable, vice-pres 1979-. **Orgs:** Chmn Minority Interchange; assoc mem Big Brothers; mem Intl Communications Assoc. **Home Addr:** 169 Rutland Rd, Brooklyn, NY 11225. **Business Addr:** Vice President, The Equitable, 787 7th Ave, New York, NY 10019.

OWENS, WALLACE, JR.
Educator (retired). **Personal:** Born in Muskogee, OK; son of Sarah Owens and Wallace Owens. **Educ:** Langston Univ, BA Art Educ 1959; Univ of Central OK, 1965; Instituto Allende-Mexico, MFA Painting 1966; Univ Rome, Italy, Fulbright Scholor 1970; N TX State Univ, Doctoral Studies 1970-71. **Career:** Sterling HS Greenville SC, art instructor, 1969-71; Lockheed Missile Co Sunnyvale, CA, electronics tech 1971-74; Langston Univ, prof art 1966-80; Central State Univ, prof art 1980-87, retired. **Orgs:** Member Lions Intl 1976; Natl Conference of Artists. **Honors/Awds:** Educators to Africans, African Amer Inst Study Tour W Africa 1973; painting owned by State Arts Collection OK. **Special Achievements:** Executed Centennial Sculpture for Langston University, 1997. **Military Serv:** AUS cpl. **Home Addr:** Rt 6, Box 782, Guthrie, OK 73044.

OWENS, WILLIAM
State senator. **Personal:** Born Jul 6, 1937, Demopolis, AL; son of Mary A Clemons Owens and Jonathan Owens; married Cindy Edwards; children: Laurel, Curtis, William Jr, Adam, Sharra, Brenda. **Educ:** Harvard U, MEd 1971; Boston U, 1970; Univ MA, doc cand. **Career:** State of Massachusetts, state senator 1975-; MA, state rep 1973-75; Proj Jesi-Jobs Univ MA, local proj dir 1971-72; State Dept Edn, dir career oppt prgm 1970; Urban League Grtr Boston, proj coord 1968-70; Sunrise Dry Cleaners, owner, mgr 1960-68. **Orgs:** Mem MA Leg Black Caucus; MA Black Polit Assembly; Nat Black Polit Assembly; Dept Corrections Adv Task Force on Voc Edn; bd dir Roxbury Defenders; Resthaven Corp; Boston Black Repertory Co; S End Neighborhood Action Prgm; mem Harvard Club of Boston; Caribbean Am Carnival Day Assn; New Hope Bapt Ch; member, Urban League of Greater Boston; member, Boston Black United Front; member, National Assn of School Administrators; member, NAACP; member, National Educators Assn. **Honors/Awds:** Man of Yr Award; Black Big Bros Award of Excellence; Houston Urban League Plaque; Ft Devens Black Hist Mth Plaque; Big Black Brother Alliance Award. **Business Phone:** (617)296-8568.

OWENS-HICKS, SHIRLEY
State official. **Personal:** Born Apr 22, 1942, Demopolis, AL; daughter of Mary Owens and Johnathan Owens; children: Dawn Deirdre, Stephanie Alicia. **Educ:** Chandler School for Women, Certificate 1961; Boston Univ School of Educ, 1969-71; Harvard Univ Graduate School of Educ, EdM 1972. **Career:** Massachusetts Senate, chief aide to senator 1975-80; Urban League of Eastern Mass, Inc, deputy dir 1980-81, president/exec dir 1981-83; Boston School Committee, vice president 1984-88; Univ of Massachusetts at Boston, advocacy counselor 1984-86; Commonwealth of Massachusetts, state rep 1987-. **Orgs:** Mem Delta Sigma Theta Sorority, Harvard Univ Alumni Assn, Urban League, NAACP, Massachusetts Black Legislative Caucus, chair Joint (House & Senate) Comm on Educ, 1995-97; Nat'l Black Caucus of State Legislators; Brookview House honorary board member; Safe Futures, Mattapan goverance bd; Boston State Citizens Advisory Committee. **Honors/Awds:** Certificate of Appreciation Simmons College 1978; Achievement Plaque Urban League Guild of Eastern Massachusetts 1983; Woman of the Year Zeta Phi Beta Sorority 1984; Certificate of Appreciation Boston Students Advisory Council 1985, 1987; Promoting Excellence in Educ Award Freedom House Inst on Schools and Educ 1986; Educ Award Black Educators Alliance of MA 1986; Bilingual Master Parents Advisory Council Award 1986; Woman of the Year Univ of MA at Boston Black Students Org 1987; Central Boston Elder Services Distinguished Service to Older Bostonians, 1989; Berea 7th Day Adventist, Womans Ministry Outstanding Leadership Award, 1993; City of Boston, African American Achievement Award in Public Service, 1995; Network for Women in Politics & Government, 1996 Woman of the Year Award; Black Educators Alliance of MA, Distinguished Service to Education Award, 1997. **Home Addr:** 15 Outlook Rd., Mattapan, MA 02126. **Business Addr:** State Representative, Commonwealth of Massachusetts, State House Room 167, Boston, MA 02133.

OWENS-SMITH, JOYCE LATRELL
Association executive, administrator. **Personal:** Born Jul 21, 1949, Leland, MS; divorced; children: Kevin, Kelli. **Educ:** Seattle Pacific Univ, BA Sociology 1973-77; Univ of Washington Seattle, MSW 1977-79. **Career:** Highest High Inc, prog coord 1973-76; New Careers Inc OJSD, career counselor 1976-; Seattle Counseling Svc, exec dir 1976-78; CA State Office of Econ Devel, field rep 1978-79; Human Resources Bureau Train & Employ, planner III 1979-80; Urban League of Portland, comm svcdir 1981-83, vice pres prog 1983-84; Orange Cty Urban League, pres. **Orgs:** Suprv bd mem WA State Fed Feminist Credit Union 1977; newsletter ed grant writing Assoc of WA Comm Youth Serv 1977; grant writer/resource devel Sacramento Women's Ctr 1978-79; past pres, vice pres Multnomah Cty Comm Health Council 1980-84; chap sponsor Parent's Anonymous 1982; mem Delta Sigma Theta 1983-. **Honors/Awds:** Acad Scholarship WA State Black Soc Workers 1977; nominee CA State Assembly Fellowship 1979; Cert Labor Market Info & CETA Planning US Dept of Labor Training 1980; Cert Contemporary Issues for the Black Family Howard Univ School of Continuing Ed Washington DC 1981.

OWES, RAY
Professional basketball player. **Personal:** Born Dec 12, 1972. **Educ:** Arizona. **Career:** Golden State Warriors, 1996-. **Business Addr:** Professional Basketball Player, Golden State Warriors, 1221 Broadway, 20th Floor, Oakland, CA 94612, (415)638-6300.

OWSLEY, BETTY JOAN
Educator, librarian. **Personal:** Born Mar 15, Chicago, IL; daughter of Willa Hyde Owsley and Holsey C Owsley. **Educ:** Fisk University, Nashville, TN, BA; Howard University, Washington, DC, MA, Indiana University, Bloomington, IN, MLS, Butler University, Indianapolis, IN. **Career:** Indianapolis Public Schools, Indianapolis, IN, teacher, currently; Howard University, Allen M Daniel Law Library, Washington, DC. **Orgs:** Board member, Indianapolis Council of International Visitors, 1984-90; American Library Assn; ALA Intl Relations Round Table; Black Caucus of American Library Assn; Delta Sigma Theta Sorority, Indianapolis Alumnae Chapter; librarian, founder, Willa H Owsley Institute; member, advisory committee and Host Family Committee, Council of Intl Programs, Indiana University; International Center of Indpls; NAACP; Natl Council of Negro Women; Indiana International Council Inc; Corinthian Baptist Church. **Honors/Awds:** Participated in Quaker summer work camps in Finland & Mexico; (AFSC); attened IFLA Paris, 1989, Stockholm, 1990, Moscow, 1991, Cuba, 1994, Beijing, 1996; Women In Africa and the African Diaspora Conference, Nigeria, 1992; NAACP delegate to observe South African election, 1994; Co-organizer of International Conference for Early Childhood Educators in Southern Africa, Maseru, Lesotho. **Home Addr:** 505 W 40th St, Indianapolis, IN 46208, (317)283-7883.

OXENDINE, JOHN EDWARD
Company executive. **Personal:** Born Jan 20, 1943, New York, NY. **Educ:** Hunter Coll City Univ of NY, AB 1965; Harvard Univ Grad Sch of Bus, MBA 1971. **Career:** Blackstar Communications, chair/CEO, currently; FAD FSLIC Fed Home Loan Bank Bd, acting chief 1979-; First Nat Bank of Chicago Mexico, asst rep 1977-79; First Nat Bank of Chicago, asst mgr 1974-77; Korn & Ferry Internat, sr asso consulting 1973-74; Fry Consultants, mgmt consultant 1971-73; Bedford Stuyvestant Restoration Corp, mgmt adv 1968-70; Bd of Educ NY City, tchr 1965-68; Univ of Redlands Redlands CA, lectured 1974. **Orgs:** Bd of trustees mem Nat Urban League 1972-78. **Honors/Awds:** Award of Excellence in Russian Language & Studies USMCR 1968; "Importance of Profit Motivation & Mgmt Assistance in Develop Programs" Duke Univ Law Review 1970; JH Whitney Grad Fellowship Grant JH Whitney Found 1970. **Military Serv:** USMCR staff sgt 1967-73.

OXLEY, LEO LIONEL
Psychiatrist. **Personal:** Born Jul 9, 1934, Raleigh, NC; children: Keith Charles, Claire Elaine. **Educ:** St Augustine Coll, Raleigh NC, BS 1955; Meharry Med Coll, MD 1959. **Career:** William Beaumont General Hosp, internship; Walter Reed General Hosp, chief resident 1960-63; Brooklyn-Staten Island Mental Health Serv of Hlth Insurance Plan of Greater NY, dir 1971-73; Natchaug Hospital, staff psychiatrist 1973-74; Newington Veterans Admin Hosp, chief psychiatry serv 1974-78; GA Mental HealthInst, supt 1978-80; The Institute of Living, sr staff psychiatrist 1980-82; VA Medical Ctr Chillicothe OH, chief psychiatry serv 1982-83; VA Medical Ctr Leavenworth KS, chief psychiatry serv 1983-84; Brecksville VA Med Ctr Natl Ctr for Stress Recovery, assoc clinical dir 1984-85; VA Med Ctr, chief mental hygiene clinic 1985-86; VA Med Ctr Cleveland, staff psychiatrist; VA Outpatient Clinic, chief medical officer, 1991-. **Orgs:** Life mem Alpha Phi Alpha Frat; Amer Psychiatric Assoc, DAV, ROA, licensed to practice medicine in MO, GA. **Honors/Awds:** Mem Alpha Omega Alpha Honor Medical Soc; publication "Issues and Attitudes Concerning Combat Experienced Black Vietnam Veterans," Journal Natl Medical Assoc Vol 79 No 1 1987 pp 25-32. **Military Serv:** US Army col 1958-67; USAR 1977-.

OYALOWO, TUNDE O.
Senior corporate consultant. **Personal:** Born Oct 16, 1953, Lagos, Nigeria; married Marie Bongjoh; children: Akin. **Educ:** State Univ of NY Brockport, BS 1979; Atlanta Univ, MBA 1980. **Career:** APC Skills Co FL, project mgr 1981-86; APC Mgmt Serv Brussels, project mgr 1983-84; Mellon Bank Corp NA, sr corporate consultant. **Orgs:** Mem Amer Mgmt Assoc 1980-84, Amer Soc for Quality Control, Natl Assoc of Black MBA's, 100 Black Men of Western PA, Toastmaster Intl; volunteer United Way; dir Kolet Construction. **Honors/Awds:** Beta Gamma Sigma Atlanta Univ 1980. **Business Addr:** Senior Corporate Consultant, Mellon Bank Corporation NA, One Mellon Bank Ctr, Pittsburgh, PA 15258.

OYESHIKU, PATRICIA DELORES WORTHY
Educator. **Personal:** Born Nov 3, 1944, Miami, FL; daughter of Inez Brantley; married Anthony A Oyeshiksu, May 25, 1968; children: Kama Charmange Titilola, Chaundrissa Morenike. **Educ:** Knoxville Coll, Knoxville TN, BS English, 1964; San Diego State Univ, San Diego CA, MA Curriculum, 1971; US Intl, San Diego CA, PhD Educational Leadership, 1980. **Career:** Peace Corps, Brazil, volunteer, 1964-66; Peace Corps, San Francisco CA, recruiter, 1966-67; Peace Corps, Boston MA, deputy dir recruiter, 1967-68; San Diego City Schools, San Diego CA, teacher, 1970-. **Orgs:** Volunteer, Homeless Shelter, San Diego CA. **Honors/Awds:** Outstanding Peace Corps Volunteer, presented by Hubert Humphrey, 1966; California Teacher of the Year, 1980-81; Natl Teacher of the Year Finalist, 1980-81; Press Club Award, San Diego CA; Outstanding Alumni in Education, San Diego State Univ; doctoral dissertation "The Effect of the Race of the Teacher on the Student.". **Home Addr:** 7985 Hillandale Dr, San Diego, CA 92120.

OYEWOLE, SAUNDRA HERNDON
Educator. **Personal:** Born Apr 26, 1943, Washington, DC; daughter of Helen Kirkland Herndon and Laurence Homer Herndon; married Godwin G Oyewole, Mar 21, 1970; children: Ayodeji Babatunde, Monisola Aramide, Kolade Olufayo. **Educ:** Howard Univ, BS (Magna Cum Laude, Phi Beta Kappa, Beta Kappa Chi) 1965; Univ of Chicago, MS 1967; Univ of MA Amherst, PhD, microbiology, 1973. **Career:** Electron microscopist; Hampshire Coll, asst prof of Microbiology 1973-79, assoc prof of Microbiology 1979-81; Trinity Coll, Washington, DC, assoc prof of biology 1981-87, chair, health professions advisory committee, 1982-, prof of biology, 1988-, chair, biology dept, 1990-; Division of Undergraduate Education, Natl Science Foundation, program dir, 1994-96. **Orgs:** Mem Amer Soc for Microbiology; member, 1984-, treasurer, 1989-, Comm on the Status of Minority Microbiologists of the Amer Soc for Microbiology 1984-; exec comm Northeast Assoc of Advisors for the Health Profs 1984-87; chair Health Professions Adv Comm Trinity Coll; coord Pre-Nursing Prog Trinity Coll; mem, advisory council of North East Assn of Advisors for the Health Professions, 1987-; Natl Assn of Advisors for the Health Professions, bd of dirs, 1993-95, sec of the bd, 1994-96; pres-elect, 1996-98; Wye Faculty Seminar, vice chair governing council, 1997; Minority Education Committee, American Society for microbiology, chair, 1997-; Post-Baccalaureate Premed Prog at Trinity College, dir, 1993-. **Honors/Awds:** Danforth Associate 1979; pres Epsilon Chap of Phi Beta Kappa 1983-85; Clare Boothe Luce Professor of Biology, 1990-93. **Business Addr:** Professor of Biology, Trinity College, 125 Michigan Ave NE, Washington, DC 20017.

OZANNE, DOMINIC L.
Construction company executive. **Personal:** Born Apr 10, 1953, Cleveland, OH; son of Betty Peyton Ozanne and Leroy Ozanne; married Gaile Cooper Ozanne, Jun 30, 1984; children: Dominic, Monique. **Educ:** Boston University, Boston, MA, BS, BA (magna cum laude), 1975; Harvard Law School, Cambridge, MA, JD, 1978. **Career:** Thompson, Hine, Flory, Cleveland, OH, associate, 1978-80; Ozanne Construction Co, Cleveland, OH, president, 1980-. **Orgs:** President, National Assn of Minority Contractors, 1989-90. **Honors/Awds:** Top Black Student, Black Enterprise Magazine, 1975; 1990 Marksman, Engineering News Magazine, 1990. **Business Addr:** President, Ozanne Construction Co, Inc, 1635 E 25th St, Cleveland, OH 44114.

OZANNE, LEROY
Construction company executive. **Career:** Ozanne Construction Co Inc, CEO, currently. **Honors/Awds:** Listed #88 of 100 top industrial service companies, Black Enterprise, 1992. **Business Addr:** CEO, Ozanne Construction Co Inc, 1635 E 25th St, Cleveland, OH 44114, (216)696-2876.

OZIM, FRANCIS TAIINO
General surgeon. **Personal:** Born Oct 1, 1946, Lagos, Nigeria; married Margaret Fay Taylor; children: Brion Olufemi, Frances Adetola, Melissa Funmilayo. **Educ:** St Finbarr's Coll Lagos Nigeria, WASC 1965; St Gregory's Coll Lagos Nigeria, HSC 1967; Howard Univ Medical Sch, MD 1976; University of Albuquerque, NM, 1969-72. **Career:** Georgetown Univ Med Ctr, intern 1976-77; Howard Univ Hosp, resident surgery 1977-81; District of Columbia General Hosp, attending in surgery 1981-82; Charlotte Memorial Hosp & Medical Ctr, active staff 1982-86; Norfolk Comm Hosp, active staff 1987-; Sufnor Surgical Group, general surgeon. **Orgs:** Active staff Louise Obici Memorial Hosp Suffolk 1987-, Norfolk Comm Hosp 1987-, Norfolk General Hosp 1987. **Honors/Awds:** Fellow Southeastern Surgical Congress 1982-, Amer Coll of Surgeons 1986-. **Business Addr:** 142 W York St, Ste 312, Norfolk, VA 23510.

P

PACE, ORLANDO
Professional football player. **Personal:** Born Nov 4, 1975. **Educ:** Ohio State. **Career:** St. Louis Rams, tackle, 1997-. **Special Achievements:** NFL Draft, First round pick, #1, 1997; Football News, National Offensive Player of the Year, 1996; Outland Trophy, 1996. **Business Addr:** Professional Football Player, St Louis Rams, One Rams Way, St Louis, MO 63045, (314)982-7267.

PACE-HINTON, LANITA
Journalist. **Personal:** Born Sep 3, 1958, New Orleans, LA; daughter of Addie Benjamin Pace and Orea Pace; married Keith Allen Hinton, Apr 27, 1988; children: Mark-Lewis. **Educ:** Howard University, School of Communications, BA, 1986. **Career:** Gannett News Service, feature writer, 1984-85; The Press-Enterprise, assistant to the managing editor, 1987-. **Orgs:** Inland Association of Black Media Professionals, founding president, 1991-; National Association of Black Journalists, 1988-. **Honors/Awds:** California Association of School Administrators, Media Excellence Award, 1992. **Business Addr:** Assistant to the Managing Editor, The Press-Enterprise Newspaper, 3512 14th St, News Department, Riverside, CA 92501, (909)782-7563.

PACK, ROBERT JOHN, JR.
Professional basketball player. **Personal:** Born Feb 3, 1969, New Orleans, LA. **Educ:** Tyler Junior College; University of Southern California, bachelor's degree in sociology, 1991. **Career:** Portland Trail Blazers, guard, 1991-92; Denver Nuggets, 1992-95; Washington Bullets, 1995-96; Dallas Mavericks, 1996-. **Business Addr:** Professional Basketball Player, Dallas Mavericks, Reunion Arena, 777 Sports St, Dallas, TX 75207, (214)748-1808.

PACKER, DANIEL FREDRIC, JR.
Utilities company manager. **Personal:** Born Dec 8, 1947, Mobile, AL; son of Algie V Ervin Packer and Daniel F Packer; married Catherine August Packer, Jul 7, 1983; children: Randall Ross, Reginald Ross, Maria Ross, Timothy Packer, Vanice Packer. **Educ:** Tuskegee Univ, Tuskegee, AL, 1965-68; Middlesex Community Coll, Middletown, CT, AS, 1978; Charter Oak Coll, Hartford, CT, BS, 1980. **Career:** CT Yankee Atomic Power, Haddam, CT, sr reactor operator, 1975-81; General Physics Corp, Columbia, MD, sr engr, 1981-82; LA Power & light, Tact, LA, training mgr, 1982-1990; Entergy Operations, Inc, training mgr/plant mgr of o&m, 1990-. **Orgs:** Mem, Amer Assn Blacks in Energy, 1982-; mem, Amer Nuclear Society, 1982-. **Honors/Awds:** Black Achievement Award, YMCA, 1988; Sr Nuclear Plant Mgr Course, Institute for Nuclear Power Operations, 1990. **Military Serv:** US Navy, e-6, 1969-75. **Business Addr:** General Manager, Plant Operations, Louisiana Power and Light Co, Waterford 3 Nuclear Generating Unit, Hwy 18, Killona, LA 70066.

PACKER, LAWRENCE FRANK
Dentist. **Personal:** married Erma Hill. **Educ:** Tougaloo Coll; Megarry Med Coll, DDS 1927. **Career:** Rollins United Meth Ch, lay pastor; Beasley United Meth Ch; Meharry, 50 yrs dental serv 1927-77. **Orgs:** Mem OBE; IBPOE. **Business Addr:** 634 E Harrison, Ruleville, MS 38771.

PADDIO, GERALD
Former professional basketball player. **Career:** Cleveland Cavaliers, beginning 1990; Indiana Pacers, until 1993. **Business Addr:** Former Professional Basketball Player, Indiana Pacers, 300 E Market St, Indianapolis, IN 46204.

PADDIO-JOHNSON, EUNICE ALICE
Educational administrator, cleric. **Personal:** Born Jun 25, 1928, Crowley, LA; daughter of Cécile Artris Cheslé and Henry Paddio; married John David Johnson Sr; children: Deidre Reed Dyson (deceased), Clarence III, Henry P, Bertrand J, Cecile A Reed. **Educ:** Leland Coll Baker, LA Grmblg State Univ Grambling LA, BS 1949; UCLA, MA 1960; LA State Univ Baton Rouge, 1966, 1975; Univ MN St Paul, 1975; State Univ NY Albany, 1980; Cornell Univ, Ithaca, MS, 1988; Progressive Univ, PhD, 1993. **Career:** St Helena Parish Shls (LA), tchr/cous, 1949-72; St Helena Smr Hd Start (LA), asso dir 1965-69; St Helena Assis Resou Est (LA), pres/dir 1972-73; Cornell Univ (NY), admin 1973-85; St Helena Head Start, dir 1986-87; Paddio-Johnson Enterprises Inc, pres, 1987-; Gaines Chapel AME Church, pastor, currently. **Orgs:** Am Assn Univ Wmn 1980-; edt jour exec comm hee mem LA Ed Assn 1964-69; schl brd mem St Helena Parish Schl (LA) 1972-73, and Ithaca City Schl NY 1975-82; pres Paddio Ent Hmn Relat Consu 1980-; brd dir Fmly & Childs Serv, Plnd Parenthd of Tompkins Co; Ithaca Nbhd Hsg Svcs; P-R Foundation; Atlanta Child 1975-; pres emeritus Martin Luther King Jr Schlshp Fund of Ithaca Inc 1982-86; Delta Sigma Theta Sorority; NAACP. **Honors/Awds:** Grd assoc Matron for LA Esther Grand Chptr OES 1963-74; outstdng cit City of New Orleans 1973; blk & gold awd Grambling State Univ 1973; Creat Career Exp Prog 1975; author Gene Wng Behvr Skills 1976-77; hnr Eunice Paddio-Johnson Foundt Inc 1972-; Citizen of the Year, 1974; Outstanding Humanitarian and Trailblazer Award. **Home Addr:** PO Box 245, Greensburg, LA 70441.

PADGETT, JAMES A.
Educator, artist. **Personal:** Born Nov 24, 1948, Washington, DC; son of Pauline C Flournoy and James Padgett; married Joan M Jemison; children: Anthony A. **Educ:** Corcoran Sch of Art, WW; Howard U, BFA, 1972; Howard Univ Grad Sch, MFA, 1974. **Career:** Wilberforce Univ Dept of Art, instructor. **Orgs:** Howard Univ Mural Proj Com, 1968-; DC Comm on the Arts Mural Proj Comm, 1968-72; murals erected & various sites Howard U, Anacostia Museum, Smithsonian Inst, Sch of Soc Work, Howard U; traveling mural touring 30 states; Shaw Com Comp Health Cntr Nat Med Assn Found Howard Univ Hosp Coll of Med; co-dir Martin Luther King Jr Arts Festival; many gallery exhibitions. **Honors/Awds:** Selected to participate in touring art exhib ''Paintings from Am U''; recip Cert of Appreciation Univ Neighborhood Coun, 1964; Cert of Accom Summer Enrich Prog Art Dir, 1965; Wash Rel Arts Exhib Am Savings & Loan Assn DC; first prize Collage & Painting, 1966; Cert of Commen Upward Bound Coll Prog Howard Univ, 1966; Corcoran Schlship Award W W Corcoran Sch of Art, 1967; Cert of Art DC Rec Dept Art & Splst Instr, 1967-68; scnd prize The Town Square Art Show Inc Collage & Painting, 1969; thrd prize Outdoor Art Exhib Painting, 1969; thrd prize Artists Unlmtd Painting, 1969; first & scnd prize Artists Unlmtd Painting, 1970; Monitor Asst Grant Howard Univ Coll of Fine Arts 1970; first prize Hon Mention Ch of the Brethren Arts Exhib Painting, 1971.Schlrshp Award Howard Univ Coll of Fine Arts, 1-72; Schlrshp Award Howard Univ Grad Sch of Fine Arts, 1972-73; Schlrshp Award Skowhegan Sch of Painting & Sculp summer, 1971; Afro-Am Artist a bio-bibliog directory; Images of Change-1 Art Society in Transition; Chrmn 4th International Conference on Art, in honor of her majesty Queen Elizabeth II, 1977; K Miller Galleries LTD, the Old Bank Gallery, 1979; Galerie Des Deux Mondes Gallery of Art, 1980. **Business Addr:** Humanities, Wilberforce University, Wilberforce, OH 45384.

PADULO, LOUIS
Educational administrator. **Personal:** Born Dec 14, 1936, Athens, AL; son of Helen Margaret Yarbrough Padulo and Louis Padulo; married Katharine Seamans; children: Robert, Joseph. **Educ:** Fairleigh Dickinson Univ, BS 1959; Stanford Univ, MS 1962; GA Inst Tech, PhD 1966. **Career:** RCA, systems analyst 1959-60; San Jose State Coll, asst prof 1962-63; GA State Coll, asst prof 1966-67; GA Tech Eng Experiment Station, consult 1966-69; Morehouse Coll, assoc prof chmn of math dept 1967-69; Stanford Univ, assoc prof 1969-75; Columbia Univ, 1969; Harvard Univ, visiting prof 1970; Atlanta Univ Center & GA Tech, founder & dir dual degree prog; Boston Univ, dean coll of engrg prof of math & engrg 1975-88, assoc vice pres, 1986-87; Massachusetts Institute of Technology, Cambridge, MA, visiting prof, 1987-88, visiting scientist, 1991-92; University of Alabama in Huntsville, Huntsville, AL, pres, 1988-90; University City Science Center, president and chief executive officer, 1991-. **Orgs:** Chmn planning commn Expanding Minority Oppors Engrg 1973-; mem Natl Acad Engrg Com Minorities Engrg; Congress of Higher Education, president, 1992-; Fairleigh Dickinson University, trustee, 1992-. **Honors/Awds:** Awd for Excellence in Sci & Engrg Educ Natl Consortium for Black Professional Devel 1977; W Elec Fund Awd 1973; Walter J Gores Awd Stanford Univ 1971; Vincent Bendix Awd 1984; Reginald H Jones Awd of NACME 1983; Fellow, American Society for Engineering Education, 1988; Pinnacle Award, Fairleigh Dickinson University, 1989; Fellow, Institute of Electrical and Electronic Engineers, 1991. **Business Addr:** President, CEO, University City Science Center, Office of the President, 3624 Market St, Philadelphia, PA 19104.

PAGE, ALAN CEDRIC
Attorney. **Personal:** Born Aug 7, 1945, Canton, OH; son of Georgianna Umbles and Howard Felix Page; married Diane Sims, Jun 5, 1973; children: Nina, Georgianna, Justin, Khamsin. **Educ:** Univ of Notre Dame, BA 1967; Univ of MN Law Sch, JD 1978. **Career:** Minnesota Vikings, professional football player 1967-78; Chicago Bears, professional football player 1978-81; Lindquist & Vennum, associate 1979-84; State of MN, spec asst atty gen 1985-87, asst atty general 1987-92; Minnesota Supreme Court, associate justice, 1993-. **Orgs:** Amer Lung Assn Run for Your Life 1978; exec com Artists & Athletes Against Apartheid 1984; Mixed Blood Theatre Adv Bd 1984; Fedn for Progress ad hoc comm to keep S Africa out of Olympics 1984; search com Univ of MN football coach 1983; adv bd League of Women Voters 1984; comm mem Honeywell Literacy Task Force 1984; hon co-chair Child Care Works 1984; concert sponsor Natl Multiple Sclerosis Soc 1985; player rep Natl Football League Player's Assn 1970-74 and 1976-77; mem NFLPA's exec com 1972-75; weekly commentary for Morning Edition on Natl Pub Radio 1982; Color commentary work for TBS Sports -Coll Football Game of the Week 1982; speaker to minority youth on the importance of education; MN State Bar Assn; Natl Bar Assn; Amer Bar Assn; HennepinCnty Bar Assn; bd mem Chicago Assn Retarded Citizens; Chicago MS Read-A-Thon 1979; chmn United Negro Coll Fund 1972; chmn MN Cncl on Physical Fitness 1972; Minneapolis Urban League, bd mem 1987-91; bd of regents, Univ of Minnesota 1989-92; member, Minnesota Minority Lawyers Assn. **Honors/Awds:** First defensive player in hist of NFL to rec Most Valuable Player Award 1971; NFL's Marathon Man First NFL player to complete a full 26.2 mile marathon; inducted into NFL Hall of Fame, 1988; completed Edmund Fitzgerald Ultra-Marathon (62 miles) 1987; established Page Education Foundation to assist minority youth in post secondary education 1988; Nike Walk of Fame, 1990; established Page/Kodak Challenge encouraging urban youth to recognize the importance of an education, 1989-92; National Education Association, Friend of Education Award, 1991; Notre Dame Alumni, Reverend Edward Frederick Sorin CSC Award, 1992; NCAA, Silver Anniversary Award, 1992; East-West Game, Babe Hollinsberry Award, 1992. **Business Addr:** Associate Justice, Minnesota Supreme Court, Minnesota Judicial Center, 25 Constitution Ave, St Paul, MN 55155.

PAGE, CLARENCE
Journalist. **Career:** Chicago Tribune, columnist, currently. **Special Achievements:** Author: The Jaws of Success; Showing My Color: Impolite Essays on Race and Identity. **Business Addr:** Columnist, Chicago Tribune, Tribune Company, 1325 G St, NW, Washington, DC 20005.

PAGE, GREGORY OLIVER
Dentist. **Personal:** Born Feb 26, 1950, Philadelphia, PA; son of Bernice and William; children: Dylan Mikkel, Erin Leah. **Educ:** Howard Univ, BS 1972; Univ of Pennsylvania, DMD 1976. **Career:** North Central Bronx Hosp, attending dentist,1978-80; Health Insurance Prog of New York, Bronx, dir of dentistry, 1978-82; private practice, dentist, 1982-; Hostos Community Coll, CCNY, asst adjunct prof, 1978-87. **Orgs:** Mem, Howard Univ Alumni Club of New York City, 1976-; mem, Acad of Gen Dentistry, 1976-; mem, Amer Dental Assn, 1976-; mem, Amer Dentists for Foreign Serv, 1983-; mem, St Phillip's Church of New York City, 1986-; mem, 100 Black Men of New York City, 1987-; American Cancer Society, 1991. **Honors/Awds:** Fellowship in Restorative Dentistry, Albert Einstein Coll of Medicine, 1976; author of ''Some Wisdom About Teeth,'' Ebony magazine, 1987. **Business Addr:** Asst Adjunct Professor/Dentist, Hostos Community College, 10 W 135th St, #1-E, New York, NY 10037.

PAGE, HARRISON EUGENE
Actor, director, writer, producer. **Personal:** Born Aug 27, 1941, Atlanta, GA; son of Roberta Fambro Hunter and Harry Page; married Christina Giles Page, Dec 30, 1989; children: Delisa Hutcheson, Terry Lynn. **Career:** NBC Television, Los Angeles, CA, actor, 1975-83; ABC television, Los Angeles, CA, actor, 1984-85; New World Television, Los Angeles, CA, actor, 1985-87, actor, 1989; Universal Pictures and Imperials Pictures, Los Angeles, CA; actor, 1989; Orion Pictures, Los Angeles, CA, actor, 1991; Universal Pictures, Off Balance Producer, Los Angeles, CA, 1991. **Orgs:** Buddhist, NSA, 1985-91.

PAGE, JAMES ALLEN
Librarian, author (retired). **Personal:** Born Jan 31, 1918, Lexington, KY; son of Margaret Frances DePrad Porter and James Henry Page; married Ethel Stene Ross Page, Jan 29, 1949; children: Ramona Jean Page, Anita Maria Page Assemian. **Educ:** Roosevelt University, Chicago, IL, BA, 1950; University of Southern California, Los Angeles, CA, MSLS, 1957; Indiana University, Bloomington, IN, MA, 1967. **Career:** Los Angeles County Public Library, Los Angeles, CA, regional reference librarian, 1961-64; Hampton Institute, Hampton, VA, college librarian, 1964-65; Gary Public Library, Gary, IN, coord of adult education, 1966-68; Mid Hudson Libraries, Poughkeepsie, NY, adult services consultant, 1968-71; Los Angeles Public Library, Los Angeles, CA, senior librarian, 1971-83; El Camino College, Torrance, CA, reference librarian (part-time), 1987-. **Orgs:** Basileus, Sigma Epsilon Chapter, Omega Psi Phi Fraternity, 1946-50; chair, Lake County (Ind) Adult Education Coord Council, 1966-68; member, American Library Assn, 1964-71; member, California Librarians Black Caucus, 1974-87; member, Nationals Assn for Advancement of Colored People, 1980-. **Honors/Awds:** Fellowship, School of Adult Education, Indiana University, 1966; California State Senate Resolution, 1978, 1983; Vassie D Wright Author's Award, 1977, 1984. **Special Achievements:** Author, Selected Black American Authors, G K Hall, 1977; Selected Black American, African & Caribbean Authors, Libraries Unlimited, 1985; author, Black Olympian Medalists, Libraries Unlimited, 1991. **Military Serv:** US Army, Technician 4th Gr, 1941-45. **Home Addr:** 1205 S Spaulding Ave, Los Angeles, CA 90019.

PAGE, JOHN SHERIDAN, JR.
Librarian. **Personal:** Born Dec 29, 1942, Pace, MS; son of Mary Lee Page and John Sheridan Page Sr. **Educ:** Tougaloo College, Tougaloo, MS, BA, 1964; Long Island University, Greenvale, NY, MS, 1967. **Career:** Oceanside Free Library, Oceanside, NY, young adult librarian, 1966-68; Stone-Brandel Center, Chicago, IL, librarian, 1968-69; Federal City College, Washington, DC, senior media specialist, 1969-76; University of DC, Washington, DC, assoc dir, tech services, 1976-84, asst dir, learning resources, 1984-. **Orgs:** ALA; DC Library Association; Black Caucus of ALA; member 1988-90, chair, 1990-92,

standards and accreditation committee, ACRL of ALA. **Honors/Awds:** Mellon ACRL Intern, University of California-Berkeley, 1974-75. **Home Addr:** 3003 Van Ness St NW, W522, Washington, DC 20008, (202)363-4990. **Business Addr:** Assistant Director, Learning Resources Division, University of the District of Columbia, 4200 Connecticut Ave NW, MB4101, Washington, DC 20008, (202)274-6030.

PAGE, MARGUERITE A.

Educator. **Personal:** Born in Savannah, GA; married Charles D (deceased); children: Carrie, Gregory Allen, Charles, Jr, Linda. **Educ:** Howard U, BS 1944; NY Inst of Dietetics, 1945; NY U, MS 1951. **Career:** St Francis Hosp Trenton NJ, dietitian 1946-47; NYC, nursery sch tchr 1947-49; helped organize Guidance Guild Nursery 1949; Guidance Guild Nursery, tchr, dietitian 1949-51; Paterson Pub Sch, tchr 1951-54; Newark NJ, tchr of trainable mentally retarded 1954-; Headstart, tchr summer 1966; Passaic Summer Headstart, asst dir 1967; Passaic Summer Headstart, dir 1968-69. **Orgs:** Former mem Fair Housing Commn; mem Passaic Human Relations Commn; mem NAACP; sec Passaic Rub Orgn; v chmn Passaic Rep Orgn; League of Women Voters; Cit Action Com; Black Women's Council; bd dir Guidance Guild Nursery Sch; mem Alpha Kappa Alpha Sor; mem Roger Williams Bapt Ch; supt of Sunday Sch; mem Passaic Bd of Educ 1971-77; Passaic; Commissioner NJ Advisory Commission Status of Women 1985-. **Honors/Awds:** Bd of trustees St Mary's Hosp Passaic 1st bld so honored; received GOP nom for Passaic Co freeholder 1st black woman to receive legis nom for either party in Passaic Co; testimonial dinner Black Women's Council 1975; 1st black woman elected official in Passaic; Comm Involmt Award Nat Counc of Negro Women 1975; outstanding community service Pi Xi Omega Chapter Alpha Kappa Alpha Sorority 1989.

PAGE, ROSEMARY SAXTON

Attorney (retired). **Personal:** Born Jan 29, 1927, New York, NY; daughter of Earle Day Saxton (deceased) and Oliver W Saxton (deceased); divorced; children: Marjorie, Christopher. **Educ:** Fisk Univ, BS 1948; Howard Univ Sch of Law, 1959. **Career:** Legal Aid Soc of NYC, assoc coun 1967-70; Nassau Co Law Svcs, atty 1970-72; Fordham Univ Sch of Law, adjunct prof 1983-95; Amer Arbitration Assn, assoc gen counsel, 1973-95; Touro Law Sch, adjunct 1986. **Orgs:** Editor Digest of Ct Decisions 1973-76; Arbitration Com Bar Assn of New York City 1974-77; Labor & Employment Com Bar Assn of New York City 1981-85; Natl Bar Assn 1977-; NBA Bd of Govs & chmn NBA Arbitration Sect 1981-95; NY State Ba 1961-; USDC, SDNY 1969; USDC, EDNY 1969; USDC, NDNY 1984; US Ct of Appeals 1969; US Supreme Ct 1973; bd of dir Huntington Youth Bd 1972-77, vice chmn of bd 1976-77; published numerous articles.

PAGE, WILLIE F.

Educator. **Personal:** Born Jan 2, 1929, Dothan, AL; married Gracie Tucker. **Educ:** Wayne State University, BSME, 1961; Adelphi University, MBA, 1970; NY University, PhD, 1975. **Career:** Brooklyn Coll, CUNY, asso prof, 1979-; Dept of Africana Studies, Brooklyn Coll, chmn, asso prof, 1974-79; Nassau-Suffolk CHES, exec dir, 1972-74; Glen Cove Coop Coll Center, SUNY, dir, lectr, 1971-72; Grumman Aerospace, asst to dir prodn, 1967-70; The Boeing Co, engr, 1961-63; New York City Head Start Regional Training Office, consult, 1975-79; Natl Endowment for the Humanities, consult, 1977-78; NY State Educ Dept, consult, 1977-79. **Orgs:** African Heritage Studies Assn, 1974-80; Am Educ Research Assn, 1974-80; Weeksville Soc Brooklyn, board member, 1979-80. **Honors/Awds:** EPDA Fellowship, USOE, NYU, 1973; Dissertation Year Fellowship Nat Fellowships Fund Atlanta, 1975; Henry Meissner Research Award, Phi Delta Kappa, NYU, 1975; NEH, Fellowship Seminar on Slavery, Harvard Univ, 1978. **Military Serv:** AUS 1st lt 1950-53. **Business Addr:** Afro-American Studies, C U N Y, Brooklyn College, 2901 Bedford Ave, Brooklyn, NY 11210-2813.

PAIGE, ALVIN

Education administrator, artist. **Personal:** Born Jul 13, 1934, LaGrange, GA; son of Dora Jane McGee Paign and Edward Paige; married Susan Lee, Feb 29, 1988; children: Monica L, Paige, Gaila R Paige, Alvin Jr, Shaneane Paige Foster. **Educ:** American International College, BA Political Sci 1980; Antioc Coll, MA Administ 1981; advanced graduate studies, Harvard Univ. **Career:** The Beeches Resort Rome, NY, art dir 1965-67; Display workshop Hartford, CT, chief designer 1967-68, dir of art 1968-69; Paige Innovations Enterprise, managing dir 1970-75; American Intl Coll, resident artist/designer & dir of cultural and perf arts center 1978-. **Orgs:** Bd dirs Natl Collegiate Conf Assn 1979; chmn Symphony Hall Promotion Comm; mem Inst of Urban Design Architectural League of NY; mem Natl Sculptors Soc; mem British Sculptors Soc; mem Free Painters and Sculptors of London, England; bd of directors Berkshire Ballet 1987-89; bd of directors Springfield Mayors Office of Cultural Affairs 1988-89; bd of directors Springfield Neighborhood Housing Services 1988-89; cooperator: Stage West Theatre Company 1988-89. **Honors/Awds:** "The Gift" public art Springfield, MA 1978 largest indoor public art installation 20,000 sq ft Springfield, MA 1980; Produced sculpture "Dignity" for year ofHandicapped at United Nations NY, NY 1981; Largest outdoor conceptual art installation 6 ton limestone "Stage of Dionysus" 1984 Springfield, MA; Rome, NY largest statue of Christ in US 1959; 1960-61 two 55 foot conceptual kinetic art install Rome, NY; Natl One man sculptors exhibit tour 1984-85; Acad Polit Sci Achvmnt American Intl College 1980; US Steel Cost Incentive Award 1982; Alvin Paige Day LaGrange, GA 1983; Council for Advance Support to Education "ExceptAchvmnt" Award 1982; Outstanding Amer Spirits of Honor Medal 1957; Governor TX Citizenship Award 1958; 3 Intl Art ExhibitsPeople's Republic of China 1989; Invitational Intlxhibit Royal Hibernian Academy Dublin Ireland 1988. **Military Serv:** USAF 8 years; Maj; Non-Commissioned Officers Award (4-times). **Business Addr:** Resident Artist/Designer, American International College, 1000 State St, Springfield, MA 01109.

PAIGE, EMMETT, JR.

Military officer. **Personal:** Born Feb 20, 1931, Jacksonville, FL; son of Elizabeth Core Paige and Emmet Paige; married Gloria Mc Clary, Mar 1, 1953; children: Michael, Sandra, Anthony. **Educ:** Univ of MD, BA 1972; Penn State, MA 1974; Army War Coll, 1974. **Career:** 361st Signal Brigade US Army Vietnam, comdr 1969; 11th Signal Brigade US Army Ft Huachuca, AZ, comdr 1975; US Army Comm Elec Engr & Install Agy, comdr1976-79; US Army Comm & Syst Agy, comdr 1976-79; US Army Inform Sys Command, commanding gen; US Army Communicat Rsrch & Devel Command, comdr 1979-; advanced through grades to Lieutenant General on July 1, 1984. **Orgs:** Bd of dir Armed Forces Comm Elect Assn 1980 mem Am Leg Post 224 1976-; mem Amer Radio Relay League. **Honors/Awds:** Legion of Merit with three oak leaf clusters 3 times AUS; only blck signal corps ofcr ever promoted to Grade of Gen AUS 1976; Major Gen AUS 1979; Army Commendation Medal; Bronze Star; Meritorious Service Medal. **Military Serv:** US Army, gen, 33 yrs.

PAIGE, RODERICK

Educational administrator. **Personal:** Born Jun 17, 1935, Brookhaven, MS; divorced; children: Rod Paige Jr. **Educ:** Jackson State Univ, BS, 1955; Indiana Univ, MS, 1964, DPEd, 1969. **Career:** Utica Jr Coll, head football coach, 1957-67; Jackson State Univ, head football coach, 1962-69; Texas Southern Univ, asst/head football coach, asst prof, dean, athletic dir, beginning 1971; Houston Independent School District, superintendent, 1994-. **Orgs:** Pres Hirma Clarke Civic Club; sec Houston Job Training Partnership Council; adv bd mem Professional United Leadership League; mem of dirs Tri-Civic Assoc; former commnr Natl Commn for Employment Policy; coord Harris Co Explorer Olympics for the Boy Scouts of Amer. **Honors/Awds:** Brentwood Dolphins Comm Serv Awd; Natl Assoc of Health PE and Recreation; "An Employment Policy for America's Future" Natl Commn for Employment Policy; "Grading in Physical Education" MS Teachers Journal. **Military Serv:** USN hospital corpsman 2 yrs. **Business Addr:** Superintendent, Houston Independent School District, 3830 Richmond St, Houston, TX 77027.

PAIGE, STEPHONE

Professional football player. **Personal:** Born Oct 15, 1961, Long Beach, CA. **Educ:** Attended: Saddleback College, Fresno State Univ. **Career:** Kansas City Chiefs, wide receiver, 1983-. **Business Addr:** Professional Football Player, Kansas City Chiefs, One Arrowhead Dr, Kansas City, MO 64129-1651.

PAIGE, WINDELL

Consultant. **Personal:** Born Oct 25, 1950, Dade City, FL; son of Bertha and Hezikiah; married Pia Tuff Paige, Dec 3, 1983; children: Sonya, Zabronda Akins, Felicia. **Educ:** Florida A&M University, BS, 1975. **Career:** Xerox Corporation, salesman, 1975-77; BellSouth Corporation, manager, minority business, 1977-91; Tem Associates, Inc, associate vice pres, 1989-91; WP and Associates Inc, president, 1991-. **Orgs:** Governor's Advisory Board, Small & Minority Business, chairman, 1993-; Broward County Salvation Army, advisory board member, 1990-; Broward City Urban League, board member, 1988-; Boy Scout Executive Board, board member, 1990-; Florida Road Fund Committee, 1992-; Leadership Broward, alumni, 1988-; Consumer Protection Board, 1990-; Kappa Alpha Psi Fraternity, 1973-. **Honors/Awds:** Broward County Black Leadership, Community Servant of the Year, 1989; State of Florida, Service Award, 1991; Boy Scout of America, Service Award, 1991; NAACP Youth Council, Distinguished Service, 1990. **Military Serv:** US Army, sgt, 1970-72; Good Conduct Medal, 1972, Vietnam Era Veteran, 1972. **Home Phone:** (305)486-6313. **Business Addr:** President, WP and Associates, 3680 NW 26th St, Ste 4, Lauderdale Lakes, FL 33311, (305)485-8191.

PAILEN, DONALD

Attorney. **Personal:** Born Mar 25, 1941, Washington, DC; son of Cora Johnson Pailen and William Pailen; married Wendy Boody Pailen, Jun 10, 1967; children: Donald Jr, William. **Educ:** Howard University, Washington, DC, BA, 1968, JD, 1971. **Career:** US Dept of Justice, Civil Rights Division, Washington, DC, attorney, 1971-82; City of Detroit, Detroit, MI, corporation counsel, 1982-. **Orgs:** Member, Michigan State Bar Association, 1982-; member, Nebraska State Bar Association, 1972-; member, National Bar Association, 1971-. **Honors/Awds:** Special Commendation, US Justice Dept, 1981; Exceptional Performance Awards, US Justice Detp, 1975-1982; Award of Appreciation, Guardians Police Organization, Chicago, 1977. **Military Serv:** US Army, E-5, 1960-63. **Business Addr:** Corporation Counsel, Law Department, City of Detroit, 1010 City-County Building, Detroit, MI 48226.

PAINTER, NELL IRVIN

Educator. **Personal:** Born Aug 2, 1942, Houston, TX; daughter of Dona Donato McGruder Irvin and Frank Edward Irvin; married Glenn R Shafer, Oct 14, 1989. **Educ:** Univ of CA Berkeley, BA 1964; Univ of CA Los Angeles, MA 1967; Harvard Univ, PhD 1974. **Career:** Harvard Univ, teaching fellow 1969-70, 1972-74; Univ of PA, asst prof 1974-77, assoc prof 1977-80; Univ of NC Chapel Hill, prof of history 1980-88; Princeton Univ, professor of history, 1988-91, edwards professor of American history, 1991-. **Orgs:** Natl dir Association Black Women Historians 1982-84; amer studies comm Amer Council of Learned Societies 1982-; exec bd Organization of Amer Historians 1984-87; mem NOW, The Nation Assocs; mem Harvard and Radcliffe Alumni/ae Against Apartheid; national council, American Historical Association, 1990-94; national council, American Studies Association, 1989-92; Southern Historical Association, Syndor prize committee, chair, 1991-92. **Honors/Awds:** Fellow Natl Humanities Ctr NC 1978-79; Fellow John Simon Guggenheim Foundation 1982-83; Candace Awd Natl Coalition of 100 Black Women 1986; Fellow, Center for Advanced Study in the Behavioral Science, 1988-89; 1989 Alumnus of the Year, Black Alumni Club, Univ of California, Berkeley, 1989; Peterson Fellowship, American Antiquarian Society, 1991; National Endowment for the Humanities, Fellow, 1992-93; Wesleyan Univ, hon doctorate, 1996; Dartmouth Coll, hon doctorate, 1997. **Special Achievements:** Author, 30 publications, 18 reveiws and review essays. **Business Addr:** Edwards Professor of American History, Princeton University, History Dept, 129 Dickinson Hall, Princeton, NJ 08544-1017.

PAJAUD, WILLIAM E.

Business executive. **Personal:** Born Aug 3, 1925, New Orleans, LA; married Donlaply. **Educ:** Xavier Univ, BFA, 1946; Chouinard Art Inst. **Career:** Golden St Mutual Life Ins Co, pub rels. **Orgs:** Mem Life Ins Advertisers Assn; Pub Rels Soc Am; Graphic Designers Assn; Nat Watercolor Soc; pres Art Ed Found. **Business Addr:** 1999 W Adams Blvd, Los Angeles, CA 90018.

PALCY, EUZHAN

Film director. **Personal:** Born in Fort de France, Martinique; daughter of Romauld Palcy and Leon Palcy. **Educ:** Sorbonne, Paris, France, BA, French literature; Vaugirard, Paris, France, degree in filmmaking. **Career:** Film director. **Honors/Awds:** Writer/director, The Messenger; director of: Sugar Cane Alley, 1984; A Dry White Season, 1989; The Ruby Bridges Story, Disney, 1998; Candace Award, National Coalition of 100 Black Women, 1990.

PALMER, DARLENE TOLBERT

Government broadcasting administrator. **Personal:** Born Jul 4, 1946, Chicago, IL; married Mickey A; children: Terri, Jonathan, Tobi. **Educ:** St Univ of NY Albany, BA 1973, MA 1974; Harvard Grad Sch of Bus Admin, Cert of Broadcasting Mgmt 1978-79. **Career:** Minority Telecomm Dev Nat Telecomm & Info Admin, prog mgr 1979-; Nat Assn of Brdcstrs Wash DC, asst dir brdcst mgmt 1977-79; Litt Enterprises Wash DC div pres 1975-77; WTEN-TV Albany, prod 1973-75; Palmer Media Asso Schenectady, prtnr 1970-75. **Orgs:** Media rels dir Nat Hookup of Black Women 1976-78; rec sec Am Women in Radio & TV 1980; chmn Affirm Act Am Women in Radio & TV 1980; co-chmn MinorityOwnrshp Cong Black Caucus Communications Brain Trust DC 1977-78; mem Com on Media & Natural Disaster Nat Acad Sci DC 1979; bd dirs Am Nat Metric Cncl Wash DC 1979. **Honors/Awds:** Prod "Black English" WTEN-TV Albany; Nat Med Assn. **Business Addr:** Nat Telecommunications & Info, Washington, DC 20230.

PALMER, DAVID

Professional football player. **Personal:** Born Nov 19, 1972, Birmingham, AL; children: David, Davin, Davida. **Educ:** Univ of Alabama, attended. **Career:** Minnesota Vikings, running back, 1994-. **Business Addr:** Professional Football Player, Minnesota Vikings, 9520 Viking Dr, Eden Prairie, MN 55344, (612)828-6500.

PALMER, DENNIS, III

Educator (retired). **Personal:** Born Jan 23, 1914, Steubenville, OH; son of Ruth Merriman Palmer and Dennis Palmer II; married Soundra Lee Palmer, Feb 23, 1979; children: Denise Evans Dickerson, Jeffrey, Mark. **Educ:** WV St Coll; Coll of Steubenville. **Career:** Steubenville Post Office, OH, employee 1937-67; Washington Hdqs, reg post office 1968-71; Coll Steubenville, dir finan aid 1971-85. **Orgs:** Mem Nat Assn Student Finan Aid Asminstrsn; Midwest & OH Adminstrs Assn; 1st African-American jury commr Equal Opport Com Fed; exec bd mem Rotary Club; 1st African-American bd advs Coll Steubenville; life mem NAACP; trust Quinn AME Ch; past grand lctr Prince Hall Grand Lodge of OH; past jury commn Equal Employment

Oppr Commn; past vice pres Dollars ofr Scholars; past pres Jefferson Co OEO; Prince Hall Mason. **Honors/Awds:** Outstnd citz Elks Club; outstnd citz OH 1974; 1st black elected Sch Bd Steubenville; first African-American sur Steubenville PO; host of weekly TV talk show, "The Dennis Palmer Show," 1974-; Community Award, Quinn Church, 1989. **Special Achievements:** First African-American supervisor, Steubenville, OH Post Office. **Home Addr:** 802 Lawson Ave, Steubenville, OH 43952.

PALMER, DOREEN P.
Physician. **Personal:** Born Jun 1, 1949, Kingston, Jamaica; daughter of Icilola Dunbar and Granville Palmer. **Educ:** Herbert H Lehman Coll, Bronx NY, BA, 1972; Downstate Medical School, Brooklyn NY, MD, 1976; Johns Hopkins Univ, Baltimore City Hospital, fellow gastroenterologist, 1981. **Career:** New York Medical Coll, Valhalla NY, asst prof, 1981-86; Metropolitan Hospital, New York City, asst chief GI, 1981-88, chief GI, 1983-86; Lenox Hill Hospital, New York City, adjunct physician, 1986-; Cabrini Hospital, New York City, atteding physician, 1986-; Doctors Hospital, New York City, attending physician, 1986-.

PALMER, DOUGLAS HAROLD
Elected official. **Personal:** Born Oct 19, 1951, Trenton, NJ; son of Dorothy Palmer and George Palmer. **Educ:** Hampton Inst, BS 1973. **Career:** Trenton Bd of Educ, sr accountant, 1976-78, coord of comm educ, 1981-82, asst sec of purchasing, beginning 1982; Mercer County Legislator, freeholder; City of Trenton, NJ, mayor, currently. **Orgs:** Pres mgr West End Little League; treas Trenton Branch of the NAACP; bd of dirs Amer Red Cross; mem Forum Project, Boy Scouts, WE Inc, Carver Center, Urban League Guild of Metro Trenton, Project Help; pres Freeholder Bd; served on Memorial Comm, Comm on the Status of Women, TRADE Adv Bd, Disabled Adv Bd, Mercer Co Bd of Social Svcs, Cultural & Heritage Comm. **Honors/Awds:** Comm Serv Awds: Fai-Ho-Cha Club, Twig Mothers, Hub City Distributors, Voice Publications, NJ Assn of Black Social Workers; Outstanding Chmn, DE Valley United Way, 1977; Man of the Year, Omega Psi Phi Frat, 1984; Community Serv Awd, Lifeline Energy Shelter. **Business Addr:** Mayor, City of Trenton, 319 E State St, Trenton, NJ 08608.

PALMER, EDGAR BERNARD
Counselor, educator. **Personal:** Born Aug 12, 1953, Hartford, CT; son of Emma Frances Ragins Palmer and Clitus Vitelius Palmer; married Carie Lyn Treske, May 25, 1985; children: Rachel Erin, Jordan Michael, Andrew David. **Educ:** Gallaudet University, BA, history, 1977; Western Maryland College, MEd, 1980; Gallaudet University, part-time doctoral student, supervision & administration, 1990-. **Career:** Maryland School for the Deaf, Columbia Campus, instructional counselor, 1980-81, Frederick Campus, instructional counselor, 1981-82; Maryland State Department of Educ, vocational rehabilitation counselor, 1982-88; Model Secondary School for the Deaf, guidance counselor, 1988-; Gallaudet Univ, Honors Program, programs corrd, 1993-. **Orgs:** Black Deaf Advocates, Inc, board member, 1989-92; American Deafness and Rehabilitation Association, Metro-Washington Chapter, board member, 1988-90; Telecommunications Exchange for the Deaf, Inc, advisory board member, 1985-87; People Encouraging People, Inc, board member, 1992-94; National Association of the Deaf, 1983-85; Black Deaf Advocates, Inc, 10th Anniversary Celebration, co-chair, 1991; Model Secondary School for the Deaf, Microcosm planning committee; Penn Visions, bd of dirs, 1994-. **Honors/Awds:** Maryland State Department of Education, Counselor of the Year, 1986; American Deafness and Rehabilitation Association, Metro Washington Chapter, Outstanding Achievement Award, 1991; Cross Country Girls Potomac Valley Athletic Conference Champions, Model Secondary School for the Deaf Coaching Award, 1990; Maryland State Department of Education, Certificate of Achievement, 1985. **Special Achievements:** Preview Magazine, Pre-College Programs, Gallaudet University, Special Edition: Communication and Cultural Issues, fall 1990; Montgomery County Journal, write-up related to multicultural program sponsored by A G Bell, Associate & Gallaudet University, spring 1992. **Home Addr:** 4412 Stockbridge Court, Bowie, MD 20720, (301)464-4184.

PALMER, EDWARD
Educator. **Personal:** Born Jul 26, 1928, Williamsburg, VA; divorced; children: Karen, Brian. **Educ:** VA Coll, 1946-48, 1954-56; AB 1962; City Coll, City Univ of NY; Columbia U, MS 1967; EdD Cand 1975. **Career:** Coll Ent Exam Bd, asso dir 1973-; US St Dept, ofcr; CEEB, asst dir 1970-73; CUNY, asst ofcr; New York City Bd of Ed, tchr, vo cnsl 1960-68; Yth House for Boys, cnsl, supr 1959-60; VA St Coll Variety Show WXEX-TV, MC 1954-55. **Orgs:** Distrib UNRA & Brethern Serv Ctr 1946; ldr Operation Crossroads Africa; consult EPDA Summer Inst New York City Comm Coll; cons, com mem UFT Coll Schlrshp Fund; mem bd of dir Urban Leag for Bergen Co 1979-; NY St Regents Adv Bd on Tchr ed, Cert & Prac 1966-69; NAACP Labor & Ind Com 1960-61; New York City Bd of Ed tchr consult 1964-68; curr dev com New York City Bd of Ed 1966; APGA; NYSPGA; NAFSA; NY Assn of Std Fin Aid Admin; bd of dir Harlem Coll Asst Proj; LOGOS Drug Rehab Ctr; New York City Coll Bound Prog; Operations Crossroads Africa Screen & Sel Com 1969-76; pres Nu Psi Chpt, Omega Psi Phi 1955-56; pres Radio-TV Grp 1954-55; vice pres VA St Vet Assn. **Honors/Awds:** Outst Achiev Award VA St Plyrs Guild 1954-55; 1st Prize Frgn Lang Declamation VA St 1956; compiled resource book Serv for Disadvtg Stds 1970; num publ. **Military Serv:** AUS 1950-53. **Business Addr:** 3440 Market St, Philadelphia, PA 19104.

PALMER, EDWARD
Physician. **Personal:** Born Jul 25, 1937, New York, NY; son of Thelma Lester Palmer and Edward Palmer Sr; married Maria Palmer; children: Neeco. **Educ:** Adelphi Univ, 1960; Meharry Med Coll, 1964; Kings Co Hosp Cen, 1964-65. **Career:** Elmhurst Hosp Cen, staff attending; Mt Sinai Sch of Med, lectr; Hosp of the Albert Einstein Coll of Med, staff attending; Montefiore Hosp & Med Ctr, staff attending; State University of New York, assoc prof; University Hospital and Kings County Hospital Center, dir eye service, currently. **Orgs:** Mem Cen NY State Ophthalmologic Soc; Amer Acad of Ophthalmology & Otolaryngology; fellow Amer Coll of Surgeons; NY Clinical Soc; Intl Eye Found The Soc of Surgeons; Amer Assn of Ophthalmology; rsch to prevent blindness; diplomate, associate examiner, American Bd of Ophthalmology. **Honors/Awds:** Founding editor Journal of Cataract; numerous publs; listed as one of best black physicians in America, Black Enterprise Magazine, 1988. **Military Serv:** USN lt 1965-67. **Business Addr:** Director, Eye Service, University Hospital of Brooklyn and Kings County Hospital Ctr, 100 Casals Pl, Bronx, NY 10475.

PALMER, ELLIOTT B., SR.
Associate executive secretary (retired). **Personal:** Born Mar 7, 1933, Durham, NC; son of Ada Brown Palmer (deceased) and Clarence Palmer (deceased); married Juanita Brooks; children: Elliot, Douglas, Ruth, Tonya. **Educ:** NCCU, AB 1955, MA 1961; Duke U, post grad; Bemidji State Univ, MN; UNC, Chapel Hill, NC, post grad. **Career:** Little River HS Durham Co, tchr 1956-60; Lakeview Elem Sch Durham Co, prin 1960-64; NC Tchrs Assn Raleigh, exec sec 1964-70; NC Assn of Educators, asso exec sec 1970-82; African Amer Culture Complex Museum, founder & curator, 1984-. **Orgs:** Mem Nat Ed Assn; chmn Nat Cncl Off of St Tchrs Assn 1969-71; mem Pi Gamma Mu Nat Soc Sci Honor Soc; pres Std Gov 1954; found Diversified Invest Spec Org 1960; mem NAACP; Hunter Lodge FM & AM; Mayor's Comm on Plan & Dev Raleigh 1974; pres Comm on Urban Redev of Durham 1958; gov comm Study of NC Pub Schls 1972; natl pres Official Black Caucus of Nat Ed Assn 1985; 1st Black chrprsn Nat Comm of Ed for Hum Rights; exec dir Hammocks Beach Corp; co-chmn NEA Joint Comm Publ & Textbook Comm 1972-73; Boy Scouts Raleigh 1974; initiated Leg Def for Educrs by any education assn in the country, 1965. **Honors/Awds:** Rec H Cncl & Trenholm Award NEA for protection of educ rights, Outstanding Alumni Award Hillside HS Durham 1974; inv to White House Conf on Ed 1964; cited by two Govs for Outstndg Cont to Fld of Ed 1972-73; consultant for minority artifacts, NC State Museum of History, 1990; Outstanding Contributions Towards The Advancement of Human Rights and Fundlemental Freedoms, by the United Nations/NEA Education Committee, 1978. **Home Addr:** 119 Sunnybrook Rd, Raleigh, NC 27610.

PALMER, JAMES D.
Physician. **Personal:** Born Oct 10, 1928, Sumter, SC; son of Ellie Dibble Palmer and Edmund Palmer; married Rose Martin; children: James Jr. **Educ:** Fisk Univ 1949; Meharry Med Coll 1954. **Career:** Atlanta Life Ins Co, sr vice pres & med dir 1968-; private practice, physician, internal med 1961-, senior vp, currently. **Orgs:** Bd dir Atlanta Life; trustee AF & NB Herndon Found; trustee Clark-Atlanta Univ and Gammon theological Seminary; past pres Atlanta Med Assn; mem GA State Med Assn; Natl Med Assn; Med Assn of Atlanta; Med Assn of GA; Amer Med Assn; mem Med Assn of Med Directors; life mem NAACP; mem Omega Psi Phi Frat; Kappa Boule of Sigma Pi Phi Frat; Warren United Meth Church Lay Leader; Atl Guardsmen. **Military Serv:** USAF Ret Maj. **Home Addr:** 1350 Niskey Lake Trail, Atlanta, GA 30331.

PALMER, JAMES E.
Educator, minister. **Personal:** Born Jul 6, 1938, Butler, AL; married; children: two. **Educ:** Selma U, BTh; State Univ Montgomery, AL, BS; Appalachian State Boone, NC, addl study; NC State U; Birmingham Bapt Coll, DD. **Career:** Univ Park Bapt Church Charlotte, past 3 yrs; Iredell Co Public Schools Statesville, NC, teacher 5 yrs; Jones Chapel Bapt Church Mooresville, NC, past 5 yrs; Catawba Coll & Catawba Co Public School, teacher & counselor, 7 yrs. **Orgs:** Moderator Mt Catawba Assn which incl 39 Chs with app 5000 membrs 3 yrs; mem Jaycees; mem Mayor's Counc; ex bd mem Gen State Bd Conv NC Inc; mem Nat Educ Assn; BSA; ex bd mem YMCA; mem Black Pol Caucus; mem NAACP. **Honors/Awds:** NDEA Grant for stud in Asia; Sst Tchrs grant for stud in Communism. **Business Addr:** Senior Pastor, University Memorial Baptist Church, PO Box 667944, Charlotte, NC 28266-7944.

PALMER, LAURA OLIVIA
Public relations executive. **Personal:** Born Nov 19, 1955, Queens, NY; daughter of Elizabeth Duckworth Scott and Oliver Clark Palmer. **Educ:** Howard University, Washington, DC, 1973-74; Fisk University, Nashville, TN, 1975-76; University of Massachusetts, Amherst, MA, BA, communication/journalism, 1977. **Career:** Record World Magazine, Los Angeles, CA, assistant editor, 1978-80; Solar Records, Inc, Los Angeles, CA, account executive/public relations, 1981-82; House of Representatives, Commonwealth of Massachusetts, Boston, MA, legislative aide, 1983-84; Metropolitan District Commission, Boston, MA, public relations director, 1984-86; Cultural Exchange, Inc, Springfield, MA, president, 1984-91; Action for Boston Community Development, Boston, MA, director of public relations and publications, 1989-. **Orgs:** Secretary, Boston Association of Black Journalists, 1989-; member, National Association of Black Journalists, 1988-; member, Twelfth Baptist Church, 1985-; member, Urban League of Eastern Massachusetts, currently; member, Cultural Exchange, Inc, 1986-; publisher/editor, The Eye-Monthly Calendar of Events, 1984-90. **Honors/Awds:** Magazine Publishing Procedures Course Scholarship, Howard University, Continuing Education Dept, 1990. **Business Addr:** Director of Public Information, Action for Boston Community Development, Inc, 178 Tremont St, 9th Fl, Boston, MA 02111.

PALMER, NOEL
Educational administrator. **Personal:** Born Nov 14, 1926, Jamaica, WI; son of Ruth Palmer and Septimus Palmer; married Daisy Mae; children: Janet, John, Jules. **Educ:** Union Theological Coll, 1951-54; William Penn Coll, BA 1956; Columbia Univ Teachers College, BSc 1977, MA 1959. **Career:** SUNY Farmingdale, assist to president 1968-70, vice pres Urban Center 1970-73, vice pres Educational Opportunity Center 1973-80, vice pres student affairs 1980-. **Orgs:** Superintendent Swift Purscell Boys Home 1964-66; dir on-the-job training Five Towns Community House 1966-68; part-time teacher Lawrence Public School 1967-69; president Advisory Council-BOCES 1978-82; president Half Hollow Hills Rotary 1980-81; vice chairman WLIW Educational TV 1982-84; Religious Society of Friends (Quakers); president, Westbury Friends School Board. **Honors/Awds:** Appeared "Outstanding Educators in America" 1972-74; member Friends World Committee for Consulation; President Central Westbury Civic Assn; Education Committee Westbury Branch NAACP. **Home Addr:** 609 Oxford St, Westbury, NY 11590. **Business Addr:** Vice President Student Affairs, State Univ of NY-Farmingdale, Administration Bldg, Melville Rd, Farmingdale, NY 11735.

PALMER, ROBERT L., II
Educational administrator. **Personal:** Born Mar 1, 1943, Tuscaloosa, AL; son of Arnetta Greene Palmer and Robert L Palmer; married Beverly Spencer Palmer, Feb 10, 1990; children: Anthony, Tracie, Monifa, Reginald, Robert. **Educ:** Indiana University, Bloomington, IN, BS, 1969, MS, 1973; State University of New York at Buffalo, Buffalo, NY, PhD, 1979. **Career:** State University College at Buffalo, Buffalo, NY, counselor education opportunity program, 1972-74, assistant director educational opportunity program, 1973-74; State University of New York at Buffalo, Buffalo, NY, assistant vice president of student affairs, 1974-82, associate provost, 1982-87, provost for student affairs, 1987-. **Orgs:** Co-chair, United Negro College Fund, Buffalo & Western New York Campaign, 1989-; board of directors, Coordinated Care, 1989-; chairman, board of directors, Buffalo Urban League, 1987-90; member, board of directors, Buffalo Area Engineering Awareness, 1982-; member, The Western New York Health Science Consortium Minority Manpower Task Force for Minorities, 1989-. **Honors/Awds:** Outstanding Service Award, Buffalo Urban League, 1989; Buffalo Black Achievers Award, Buffalo 1840 Enterprise Inc, 1985; Outstanding Leadership Award, University at Buffalo Campus Ministry, 1985; Award of Excellence, United Way of Buffalo & Erie County, 1989; Human Relations Award, Buffalo NAACP, 1988. **Military Serv:** US Air Force. **Business Addr:** Vice President, State University of New York at Buffalo, Student Affairs, 542 Capen Hall, Buffalo, NY 14260.

PALMER, RONALD DEWAYNE
Educator, consultant, diplomat (retired). **Personal:** Born May 22, 1932, Uniontown, PA; son of Ethel Roberts and Wilbur Fortune Palmer; married Tengku Intan Badariah Abubakar, Jul 25, 1987; children: Derek R, Alyson C, Natasha E Aziz, Nadiah R Aziz. **Educ:** Howard University, BA (magna cum laude) 1954; Inst de'Etudes Politiques Univ of Bordeaux France, 1954-55; School of Advanced Intl Studies, Johns Hopkins University, MA 1957. **Career:** US State Dept, foreign service officer, 1957-89, faculty member, USMA, West Point, 1967-69, Togo, ambassador 1976-78; foreign service dep dir gen 1979-81, Malaysia, ambassador 1981-83, foreign service officer on detail to CSIS/Georgetown 1983-86, Mauritius, ambassador, 1986-89; George Washington University, professor, 1990-. **Orgs:** Kappa Alpha Psi, 1952-; American Foreign Service Assn, 1957-; Council on Foreign Relations, 1979-; Africare; Washington Institute of Foreign Affairs; Malaysian-American Society; Royal Asia Society; Institute of Intl Studies, United Nations Association, DC Council on the Humanities; Friends of the Chapel, Howard University. **Honors/Awds:** Knight Commander, Order of Mono, Republic of Togo 1978; commander Setia Mahkota Johor, Malaysia 1984; NAFEO & NAACP Awardee, 1988; publication: Building ASEAN: 20 Years of Southeast Asian Cooperation, Praeger, 1987; Write on local history and genealogy for Journal of the African-American Historical and

Geneological Society. **Business Addr:** Professor, Elliott School of Intl Affairs, The George Washington University, Stuart 201A, 2013 G St NW, Washington, DC 20052, (202)994-0563.

PALMER, TERRY WAYNE
Financial analyst. **Personal:** Born Sep 19, 1962, Sanford, NC; son of Betty L Palmer. **Educ:** North Carolina Central University, BA, 1985. **Career:** Department of Air Force, budget analyst, 1985-89, Keesler Air Force Base, financial analyst, 1992-. **Orgs:** American Society of Military Comptrollers, 1985-. **Honors/Awds:** Air Training Command Civilian of the Quarter, 1990; Dollars and Sense Magazine, Best and Brightest Business and Professional Men, 1991. **Business Addr:** Financial Analyst, Department of Air Force, Keesler Air Force Base, 500 I St, Ste 211, Sablich Center, Rm 212-A, Biloxi, MS 39531, (601)377-4642.

PALMER, VIOLET
Sports official. **Personal:** Born in Compton, CA. **Educ:** Cal Poly-Pomona. **Career:** NBA, referee, currently. **Special Achievements:** First African American female to officiate games in the NBA; one of two women officials to referee in any men's pro sports league. **Business Addr:** Referee, NBA, 645 5th Ave, New York, NY 10022.

PALMER, WENDY
Professional basketball player. **Personal:** Born Aug 12, 1974. **Educ:** Univ of Virginia, attended. **Career:** Utah Starzz, forward, 1997-. **Honors/Awds:** All-WNBA Second Team, 1997. **Business Addr:** Professional Basketball Player, Utah Starzz, 301 West South Temple, Salt Lake City, UT 84101, (801)355-3865.

PALMER-HILDRETH, BARBARA JEAN
Educator. **Personal:** Born Jan 10, 1941, Jackson, MS; daughter of Thelma Palmer and John Palmer; married Truman A Hildreth, Aug 15, 1970. **Educ:** Jackson State Univ, BS 1964; Natl Coll of Educ, MS 1986. **Career:** Canton Public Schools, teacher 1964-67; Rockford Bd of Educ, teacher 1967-, head-teacher 1984-. **Orgs:** 2nd vice pres/life mem Natl Council of Negro Women 1984; mem Legislative Comm IEA 1986-87; Big Sisters Inc, 1975-89. **Honors/Awds:** Mary McLeod Bethune Serv Awd Natl Council of Negro Women 1976; service award Rockford Memorial Hospital 1989. **Home Addr:** 2228 Pierce Ave, Rockford, IL 61103.

PALMORE, LYNNE A. JANIFER
Advertising, public relations executive. **Personal:** Born Oct 3, 1952, Newark, NJ; married Roderick Palmore; children: Jordan, Adam. **Educ:** Yale Univ, BA 1974. **Career:** J Walter Thompson, media trainee 1975-76, media planner 1976-78; Creamer Inc, media super 1978-80; Needham Harper Worldwide Inc, vice pres assoc media dir. **Orgs:** Mem Northshore Chapter Jack & Jill. **Business Addr:** Vice Pres & Assoc Media Dir, DDB Needham Worldwide, 303 E Wacker Drive, Chicago, IL 60601.

PALMORE, RODERICK A.
Consumer products company executive. **Personal:** Born Feb 14, 1952, Pittsburgh, PA; son of Jefferson & Sophie Palmore; married Lynne Palmore, Jun 3, 1978; children: Jordan, Adam. **Educ:** Yale University, BA, 1974; University of Chicago Law School, JD, 1977. **Career:** Berkman Ruslander, assoc, 1977-79; US Attorney, asst US attorney, 1979-82; Wildman Harrold Allen & Dixon, partner, 1982-93; Sonnenschein Nath & Rosenthal, partner, 1993-96; Sara Lee Corp, vp & deputy general counsel, 1996-. **Orgs:** Chicago Bar Association, bd of mgrs, 1992-94; Chicago Bar Foundation, bd of dirs, 1993-94; Illinois Judicial Ethics Comm, 1996-; Legal Assistance Foundation of Chicago, bd of dirs, 1994-97; Public Interest Law Initiative, bd of dirs, 1993-96; Boys & Girls Clubs of Chicago, bd of dirs, 1997-; Centers for New Horizons, bd of dirs, 1997-; The Village Foundation, bd of dirs, 1997-. **Honors/Awds:** Dollars & Sense Magazine, Best & Brightest African American Business People, 1991. **Business Addr:** Vice Pres & Deputy General Counsel, Sara Lee Corp, 3 First National Plz, 70 W Madison St, Chicago, IL 60602, (312)558-8536.

PANDYA, HARISH C. (H. CHRISTIAN POST)
Business executive. **Personal:** Born Oct 22, 1945, Zanzibar, United Republic of Tanzania. **Educ:** Univ IN, MA 1971; NE MO St U, BS 1968; Univ Cambridge, 1966; Univ London, 1964. **Career:** Essence Mag, mid-west dir of Advertising 1977-; Tuesday Publs, dir of mrktng 1971-76; Johnson Pub Co, mrktng-editorial rsrchr 1970-71; Westinghouse Corp, 1969-70; Clopton HS, cnslr, tchr 1969. **Orgs:** MO Hist Soc; Wrtrs & Edtrs Guild; Nat Assn of Mrkt Dvlprs; Chicago Advertising Club; Chicago Press Club; Am Mrktng Assn; bd mem Pullen Sch for Exceptional Children, 1973; bd of dirs, Coalition of Concerned Women in War on Crime 1977; Pro & Con Screening Bd 1975. **Honors/Awds:** 10 Outst Young Citizens Jr C &Of C 1976; Spl Achiev US Citizen 1976. **Business Addr:** Essence, C/O 919 N Michigan Ave Ste #1, Chicago, IL 60611.

PANNELL, PATRICK WELDON
Artist. **Personal:** Born Apr 13, 1936, New York, NY; son of Gwendolyn Pannell and Patrick S Pannell; children: Duffman Pannell. **Educ:** Morgan State Coll, BA; Coll Univ & New Sch Social Rsch, attended. **Career:** Public & Private Art Projects, dir 1962-64; Profiles in Cultural Revolution, 1964-66; S Bronx Comm Arts Prog, dir 1967-69; Marcus Garvey Ctr, dir; New Experience Gallery, co-owner, co-founder; Rhino Arts Inc, head of co 1980-; co-founder of Panox Inc Silk Art Co; NY City, dir special progs, currently. **Orgs:** Artist Professional Rec Union; Artists Coalition; charter mem The Committee of Concerned Artist and Profls. **Honors/Awds:** Special Awd for Work with Youth in New York City Wham-O Mfg Co 1978. **Military Serv:** US Army, specialist, 4th class, 1957-59.

PANNELL, WILLIAM E.
Director, associate professor. **Personal:** Born Jun 24, 1929; married Hazel Lee Scott; children: 2 sons. **Educ:** Wayne State Univ, BA, black history; Univ of So CA, MA, social ethics; Malone Coll, honorary doctorate. **Career:** Brethren Assemblies, asst pastor, youth dir; Christian Assemblies, pastor; School of Theol, Fuller Theol Sem, dir black ministries, assoc prof evangelism. **Orgs:** Tom Skinner Assn, vp; Staley Found, lecturer George Fox Coll, Newburg, OR; speaker at many conferences including consultation on the Gospel & Culture of Lausanne Comm, 1978; US Consultation on Simple Lifestyle, Ventnor, NJ, 1979; Church and Peacemaking in a Nuclear Age Conf, speaker, Pasadena, CA, 1983; Youth for Christ USA, chairman, 1980; Acad for Evangelism, president, 1983-84. **Honors/Awds:** Author, "My Friend My Enemy", 1968; Div Malone Coll, 1975; Delta Epsilon Chi Honor Soc of the Accrediting Assoc of Bible Colls; numerous articles in: Eternity, The Other Side, Sojourners, The Amer Scientific Affiliation, The Herald, The Gospel Herald, Theology, News & Notes, Christianity Today, Leadership Magazine, etc. **Business Addr:** Dir Black Min/Assoc Prof Evang, Fuller Theological Seminary, 135 N Oakland Ave, Pasadena, CA 91101-3397.

PAPPILLION, GLENDA M.
Government official. **Personal:** Born Nov 28, 1951, Lake Charles, LA; daughter of Viola Pappillion and John Pappillion; divorced. **Educ:** McNeese State University, BS, accounting, 1973. **Career:** Internal Revenue Service, criminal investigator, Houston, 1976-81, CI coordinator, Washington, DC, 1981-82, criminal investigator, Chicago, 1982-84, group supervisor, CI division,Chicago, 1984-86, branch chief, CI division, Chicago, 1986-88, chief, criminal investigation, Houston, 1988-91, assistant district director, 1991-93, asst regional commissioner of criminal investigations, 1993-. **Orgs:** Alpha Kappa Alpha, 1971-; Big Sister/Big Brother, 1978-90; National Organization of Black Law Enforcement Executives, 1988-. **Honors/Awds:** Internal Revenue Service Distinguished Performance Award, 1986, 1987, 1988, 1989. **Special Achievements:** First female chief in history of IRS, Criminal Investigation Division, 1988. **Business Addr:** Assistant Regional Commissioner, Internal Revenue Service, 915 2nd Ave, Rm 2498, M/S 600, Seattle, WA 98174, (206)220-6011.

PARHAM, BRENDA JOYCE
Nursing administration. **Personal:** Born Jun 3, 1944, Ft Lauderdale, FL; daughter of Mr & Mrs Clarence Ray Sr; divorced; children: Grant III, Valorie, Stephanie, Deidra. **Educ:** FL A&M Univ, BS 1966; Memphis State Univ, MEd 1972; Univ of TN Ctr for the Health Sci, MSN 1981. **Career:** Holy Cross Hosp, staff nurse 1966-67; Plantation Gen Hosp, staff nurse 1967; US Air Force, staff nurse 1967-68; Methodist Hosp, charge nurse 1966-69, instr 1969-71; Shelby State Comm Coll, dept head of nursing; Liaison nurse & suprv Baptist Mem Hosp, 1971-72; asst Prof Memphis State University, 1972-80; staff nurse, suprv, asst director, Reg Med Ctr, 1973-81; staff devel coord, Methodist Hosp, 1982; assoc professor, instr Shelby State Comm College, 1982-83; dept head, nursing Shelby State Comm College, 1984-87; mem TN Nurses Association, 1984-; National League of Nurses, 1985. **Honors/Awds:** Pastor - Temple of Joy Deliverance Ctr Church, 1983; Advisory Bd Mem Amer Home Health Agency 1984. **Military Serv:** USAF 1st lt 1 1/2 yrs. **Business Addr:** Department Head of Nursing, Shelby State Community College, 737 Union Ave, Memphis, TN 38174.

PARHAM, DASHTON DANIEL
Art director. **Personal:** Born Jan 22, 1956, Brunswick Co, VA; son of John and Sarah Parham; divorced; children: Erin, Sarah. **Educ:** Virginia Commonwealth Univ, BFA, Communication Art & Design, 1978. **Career:** Finnegan & Agee Advertising, asst art director, 1978; Central Fidelity Bank, designer, pr dept, 1979; Kell and Assoc, art director, 1980; Designer's Folio, art director, illustrator, 1980-83; USA Today, illustrator, 1983-85; USA Weekend, art director, 1985-86; USA Today, art director, 1986-96, director of graphic, 1996-. **Orgs:** National Assn of Black Journalist, 1994; Society of Newspaper Design, 1983-86; Art Directors Club of Metropolitan Washington, 1980-86. **Honors/Awds:** Society of Newspaper Design, 3 awards of excellence, 1984-86; Art Directors Club of Metro Washington, 8 awards of excellence, 1980-85. **Special Achievements:** Designer of publication entitled Information Illustration, Dale Glasgow in 4 languages, 1994, Addison-Wesley Publishing; Howard University School of Journalism, adjunct prof, publication design. **Business Addr:** Director of Graphics, USA Today, 1000 Wilson Blvd., Tower 1, 16th floor, Arlington, VA 22229.

PARHAM, DEBORAH L.
Government official, registered nurse. **Personal:** Born Apr 20, 1955, Glouster, OH; daughter of Rose L Parham and William M Parham Jr. **Educ:** University of Cincinnati, BSN, 1977; University of North Carolina at Chapel Hill, MSPH, 1979, PhD, 1990. **Career:** Department of Health & Human Services, presidential management intern, 1979-81; Institute of Medicine, research associate, 1981-83; National Health Service Corps, public health analyst & chief nurse, 1983-86; Bureau of Health Care Delivery & Assistance, perinatal coordinator, 1988-89; Office of the Surgeon General, deputy staff director/special asst, 1989-91; Bureau of Health Care Delivery & Assistance, public health analyst, 1990-91; Bureau of Primary Health Care, DHHS, branch chief, 1991-97; HIV/AIDS Bureau, DHHS, division director, 1997-. **Orgs:** American Public Health Association; 1977-; National Minority Health Association, 1992-94; Academy of Management, 1988-95; American Nurses Association, 1984-95; National Black Nurses Association, 1985-95; Coalition of 100 Black Women, parliamentarian, 1992-94, 2nd vice president, 1995-97; Urban League, 1992-94; NCNW, 1988-. **Honors/Awds:** University of Cincinnati, Sigma Theta Tau, 1977; University of North Carolina, Delta Omega Service Award, 1979; HRSA, Administrator's Citation, 1984. **Military Serv:** US Public Health Service, captain, 1984-; USPHS: Citation, 1986, 1990, 1991; Chief Nurse Officer Award, 1991; Emergency Preparedness Ribbon, 1989; Commendation Medal, 1986; Director's Award, 1986; Achievement Medal, 1985; Unit Commendation, 1984, 1988, 1992, 1994, 1995; Outstanding Unit Citation, 1996; Outstanding Service Medal, 1997. **Business Addr:** Division Director, Division of Community-Based Programs, HIV/AIDS Bureau- DHHS, 4350 East West Highway, Bethesda, MD 20814, (301)594-4444.

PARHAM, FREDERICK RUSSELL
Senior electrical engineer. **Personal:** Born Aug 13, 1953, Columbus, OH; son of Madeline Inez Holland Parham and E A Parham; married Barbara Ann Kimble Parham, Dec 31, 1979; children: Jonathan. **Educ:** Northwestern Univ, Evanston, IL, BA, biomed engineering, 1976, MA, biomed engineering, 1977. **Career:** Batelle Memorial Institute, Columbus, OH, senior lab technican, 1972; G D Searle, Skokie, IL, research associate, 1973-76; 3M, Maplewood, MN, senior electrical engineer, 1977-. **Orgs:** Director, Region 1, National Technical Association, 1979-80; director, Music Dept, Jubilee Christian Church, 1982-; director, IBM Special Interest Group, 3M, 1982-. **Honors/Awds:** Genesis Grant Recipient, 3M, 1987; Golden Step Award, 3M, 1989. **Home Addr:** 8185 Ivywood, Cottage Grove, MN 55016.

PARHAM, JAMES B.
Educational Administrator. **Personal:** Born Dec 6, 1942, Chattanooga, TN; son of James W & Pearl Parham; married Loretta O'Brien Parham, Apr 9, 1997; children: Francia Greer, Scott, Trace, Quantrell, Perry O'Brien, Leah O'Brien, Aaron Walton. **Educ:** Central State Univ, BS, 1964; Eastern Kentucky Univ, MS, 1973; Natl Univ, MBA, 1983; Univ of MI, Ann Arbor, PhD, bus admin, 1992. **Career:** Department of the Army, proj mgr, computer assisted trng, 1977-80; Readiness group, dir, sr consultant, 1980-83; Department of the Army Trng Prog, deputy dir, 1983-85; Central State Univ, dept chair, military sci, 1985-88; Univ of Pittsburgh, asst prof, 1972-96; Hampton Univ, dean, school of business, 1996-. **Orgs:** Academy of Management; American Management Association; Strategic Management Society; The International Society of Strategic Management and Planning. **Honors/Awds:** Univ of MI, Rackman Grad School, Rackman Merit Awd, Academic Excellence, Academic Fellowship; Inst for Social Research, Research Fellowship, Summer 1990-91; Univ of MI, Thomas W Leabow Fellowship, Excellence in Teaching, Teaching Awd, Fellowship, 1991; Univ of Pitt, Coll of General Studies, Teaching Awd, 1993, Intl Business Ctr, Instructional Devel Grant, 1995. **Special Achievements:** Consulting experience, executive trng prog, Hurgdga, Egypt, contracted by Dallah-Albarka Group to provide instructor to senior executives going through leadership trng program, summer 1996; Czechoslovak Management Ctr, Celakovice, Czech Republic, contracted by US AID to provide instruction and evaluate the instruction being provided to Czech citizens attending a US sponsored school of management, provided consultations with the center's dean and selected faculty members, summer 1994. **Military Serv:** US Army, lt colonel, 1964-99; BS 3, AM 4, MSM 3. **Home Addr:** 3808 Chesapeake Ave, Hampton, VA 23669. **Business Addr:** Dean, School of Business, Hampton University, Buckman Hall, Hampton, VA 23668, (757)727-5361.

PARHAM, JOHNNY EUGENE, JR.
Fund-raiser. **Personal:** Born Jan 22, 1937, Atlanta, GA; son of Carolyn Anderson Parham and Johnny Eugene Parham; married Ann Cox Parham, Jun 24, 1961; children: Johnny Eugene III. **Educ:** Morehouse College, Atlanta, GA, BA, 1958; Atlanta University, Atlanta, GA, MSW, 1960; Woodrow Wilson College of Law, Atlanta, GA, JD, 1978. **Career:** New York Urban League, Brooklyn, NY, branch director, 1962-65; Training Resources for Youth, Brooklyn, NY, dupty director, 1965-66; Opportunities Industrialization Center, Brooklyn, NY, executive director, 1966-67; Curber Assoicates, New York, NY, executive vice president, 1967-70; Social Dimensional Associates, New York, NY, president, 1970-75; United Negro College

Fund, New York, NY, vice president, 1979-94; Thurgood Marshall Scholarship Fund, executive director, 1994-. **Orgs:** Board member, Community League for Retarded Children, 1991; board member, Big Brothers of New York, 1970-75; bd mem, Nat Soc of Fund Raising Executives, New York Chap, 1995-. **Honors/Awds:** 30th Anniversary of Student Movement, Clark Atlanta University, 1990. **Business Addr:** Executive Director, Thurgood Marshall Scholarship Fund, 100 Park Ave, 10th Fl, New York, NY 10017.

PARHAM, MARJORIE B.
Publisher, editor. **Personal:** Born in Batavia, OH; married Hartwell (deceased); children: William M Spillers Jr. **Educ:** Wilberforce Univ; Univ of Cincinnati; Chase School of Business. **Career:** Cincinnati Herald, publisher, president, 1963-. **Orgs:** Bd mem Comm Chest & Council United Appeal; Hamilton County YMCA; Natl Newspaper Publishers Assn; former trustee Univ of Cincinnati; former bd mem Cincinnati OIC; Hamilton County Amer Red Cross; Greater Cincinnati Urban League; former chmn of bd Cincinnati Tech Coll; Women in Communications Inc; Iota Phi Lambda Business Women's Sor; St Andrew's Episcopal Church. **Honors/Awds:** Iota Phi Lambda Business Woman of the Year 1970; Outstanding Woman in Communications 1973; named 1 of 12 most influential to the Queen City 1974; Outstanding Citizen Award, Omega Psi Phi 1975; Community Serv Media Award, Natl Conf of Christians & Jews 1977; Hon DTL, Cincinnati Tech Coll 1977. **Business Addr:** President/Publisher, Cincinnati Herald, 354 Hearne Ave, Cincinnati, OH 45229-2818.

PARHAM, SAMUEL LEVENUS
Educator. **Personal:** Born Oct 3, 1905, Henderson, NC; married Erma Price; children: Marcia, Morma Lowe. **Educ:** Shaw U, AB 1929; Columbia U, MA 1932. **Career:** Retired 1985; cosmetic mfr, exporter 1943-71; Lincoln Acad, prin 1934-43; Tillotson Coll, prof hist, acting dean 1933-34; Jr Coll Palmer Meml Inst, teacher, acting dean 1930-33; Afro-Amer Hist, lectr. **Orgs:** Former mem, bd of trustees Westchester Comm Coll; v-pres Urban Leag of W; former chrm Hum Rels Com, Bd of Ed; former pres NAACP Greenburgh & White Plains; mem Steering Com Urban Renewal of White Plains; mem, resolution com NY St Sch Bd Assn; mem Bd of Ed White Plains; pres White Plains Housing Auth. **Honors/Awds:** Recip Annual Brotherhood Award Interchurch Cncl of White Plains 1964.

PARHAM, THOMAS DAVID, JR.
Clergyman. **Personal:** Born Mar 21, 1920, Newport News, VA; son of Edith Seabrook Parham and Thomas David Parham Sr; married Marion Cordice, Jun 1, 1951; children: Edith Evangeline Greene, Mae Marian, Thomas David III. **Educ:** NC Central Univ, BA (magna cum laude) 1941; Pittsburgh Theol Seminary, STB, STM (summa cum laude) 1944; Amer Univ Washington, MA 1972, PhD 1973. **Career:** Butler Memorial Presby Church, pastor 1941-50; Duke Univ Medical Ctr, chaplain 1982-84; Duke Divinity Sch, asst for black church affairs 1984-86; NC Central Univ, campus minister 1985-86; Messiah Presby Church, senior minister, currently. **Orgs:** Life mem Kappa Alpha Psi; mem NAACP; life mem Military Chaplains Assn; executive committee, Chaplaincy, Full Gospel Churches 1985-88; corporate, Presbyterian Ministers Fund. **Honors/Awds:** Alumnus of the Year Pittsburgh Seminary 1983; Doctor of Divinity, Ursinus College, 1970. **Military Serv:** US Navy, 1944-82; Meritorious Serv Medal 1972, Legion of Merit 1982. **Business Addr:** Senior Minister, Messiah Presbyterian Church, 1485 Johnston's Road, Norfolk, VA 23513.

PARIS, BUBBA (WILLIAM)
Professional football player. **Personal:** Born Oct 6, 1960, Louisville, KY. **Educ:** Univ of Michigan, received degree, 1982. **Career:** San Francisco 49ers, offensive tackle, 1983-91; Indianapolis Colts, 1991; Detroit Lions, 1991-92. **Honors/Awds:** Post-season play: NFC Championship Game, 1983, 1984, 1988, 1989, NFL Championship Game, 1984, 1988, 1989.

PARIS, CALVIN RUDOLPH
Inventor, entrepreneur, developer, philanthropist (retired). **Personal:** Born Sep 5, 1932, New Haven, CT; son of Nellie Belle Baker Paris and Samuel Felix Paris; divorced 1990; children (previous marriage): Calvin Jr, Priscilla Naomi, Theodore Thurgood, April Nell, Samuel Felix Paris; married Claudette, 1992; children: Calvin Jr (adopted), Pricilla Noami, Theodore Thurgood, April Nell, samuel Joshua. **Educ:** Howard Univ, BS 1956; Meharry Medical College Dental School, 1957-58. **Career:** Fld Enterprises Educ Corp, asst vp, gen mgr sales 1958-81 (retired); Paris Health Systems Mgmt Inc dba Nutri/Systems Weight Loss Centers, pres & treas; Baskin Robbins 31 Flavors Chicago IL, franchiser, retired 1990; Mango de Paris Estates, developer, 1993-. **Orgs:** Life mem NAACP. **Honors/Awds:** Superior Srv Key; 17 yr mbrshp 100 Order Club; winner (2) Top Mgmt Award; Flying Circus 1969, 1973; runner-up 1974; pres & major stockholder in largest black owned chain of weight loss centers in world; 30 Honors and Awards, Field Enterprises Edl Corp, 1957-81; William H Douglass Citizen of the Year Award, Dixwell Community House Alumni Assn, 1984. **Home Addr:** 600 NW 13th St, Delray Beach, FL 33444.

PARISH, ROBERT
Professional basketball player (retired). **Personal:** Born Aug 30, 1953, Shreveport, LA; married Nancy; children: Justin. **Educ:** Attended, Centenary Coll. **Career:** Golden State Warriors, center 1976-80; Boston Celtics, center 1980-94; Charlotte Hornets, 1994-96; Chicago Bulls, 1996-97. **Honors/Awds:** Named to The Sporting News All-Amer First Team 1976; Gold Medalist World University Games 1975; named to the All-NBA Second team 1982; scored the 10,000th point of career on 2/26/84 in Phoenix; number retired, Boston Celtics, 1998. **Special Achievements:** NBA, Championship, 1981, 1984, 1986; NBA, All-Star game, 1981-87, 1990-91. **Business Addr:** Retired Professional Basketball Player, Chicago Bulls, 1901 W Madison St, Chicago, IL 60612-2459, (312)943-5800.

PARKER, ANTHONY
Professional football player. **Personal:** Born Feb 11, 1966, Sylacauga, AL. **Educ:** Arizona State. **Career:** Indianapolis Colts, defensive back, 1989; Kansas City Chiefs, 1991; Minnesota Vikings, 1992-94; St Louis Rams, 1995-96; Tampa Bay Buccaneers, 1997-. **Business Addr:** Professional Football Player, Tampa Bay Buccaneers, One Buccaneer Place, Tampa, FL 33607, (813)870-2700.

PARKER, ANTHONY
Professional basketball player. **Personal:** Born Jun 19, 1975. **Educ:** Bradley. **Career:** Philadelphia 76ers, guard, 1997-. **Business Addr:** Professional Basketball Player, Philadelphia 76ers, 1 Corestates Complex, Philadelphia, PA 19148, (215)339-7676.

PARKER, AVERETTE MHOON
Physician. **Personal:** Born Jan 27, 1939, Memphis, TN; divorced; children: Rosalind. **Educ:** Hillsdale Coll, BS 1960; Howard U, MD 1964. **Career:** Children & Family Mntl Hlth & Mntl Retardation Unit of N Cntrl Philadelphia Comm Mntl Hlth & Mntl Retardation Ctr, dir 1974-; Corinthian Guidance Ctr forSrvs to Children, aso dir 1973-74; Woodburn Ctr for Comm Mntl Hlth, dir 1973; N Cnty Ctr Fairfax Falls Ch Mntl Hlth Ctr, dir 1972-73; Com Mntl Hlth Ctr, dir adult outpatient dept 1970-71; Area B to DC Pub Sch, consult 1969-70; Hillcrest Children's Ctr to DC Headstart Prog, consult 1968; WNVT TV Natl Instrnl TV, consult 1973-74. **Orgs:** Gen mem Am Psychiatric Assn 1969-; mem PA Psychiatric Soc 1974-; professional adv com Soc Ctr 1973-75; adv cncl N VA Hot Line 1973; appearance in WKBSTV DE Vly Today Mntl Hlth Srvcs 1975; SPVI TV Woman's Perspective & Perspective on Yth "The Black Family" 1975; "Hostility in the Black Male" 1976; "Aggression in Children & Adolescents" 1976; "Crisis Intervention-effects on Women & their Family" 1976; panel mem Blk Hlth Consumer Conf N Cntrl Philadelphia Comm Mntl Hlth & Mntl Retardation Ctr 1975; panel mem PA Assn of Mntl Hlth Providers-Annual Meeting 1975; panel mem Orthopsychiatry Annual Meeting Primary Prevention & Early Intervention Progs 1976; panel mem, lectr "Hostility in the Blk Male-Fact or Fiction" N Cntrl Philadelphia Comm Mntl Hlth& Mntl Retardation Ctr 1976; lects Blk Famil Roles Swarthmore Coll Upward Bound Parents 1976; selected for externship Obstet & Gynecol 1963. **Honors/Awds:** Rec Neuro-Psychiatry Dept Award for Achiev 1964. **Business Addr:** Adult & Child Psychiatry, 3645 Veazey St, NW, Washington, DC 20008.

PARKER, BARRINGTON D., JR.
Judge. **Personal:** Born Aug 21, 1944; son of Barrington D Parker Sr (deceased). **Educ:** Yale University, BA, 1965; Yale University Law School, LLB, 1969. **Career:** Honorable Aubrey E Robinson Jr, law clerk, 1969-70; Sullivan & Cromwell, attorney, 1970-77; Parker Auspitz Neesemann & Delehanty, partner, 1977-87; Morrison & Foerster, partner, 1987-94; US District Court, judge, 1994-. **Orgs:** Federal Bar Council; American Bar Association; New York State Bar Association; Association of the Bar of the City of New York, vp; New School for Social Research, board of trustees; St Paul's School, board of trustees; Council on Foreign Relations; South Africa Legal Services & Legal Education Project Inc; Governance Institute, bd of trustees. **Business Addr:** Judge, US District Court, 300 Quorropas St, White Plains, NY 10601, (914)390-4177.

PARKER, BERNARD F., JR.
County official. **Personal:** Born Dec 16, 1949, Detroit, MI; married Sandra Bomar; children: Bernard III, Bukika, Bunia, Damon Bomar, Deric Bomar. **Educ:** Univ of Michigan, BA 1973. **Career:** Operation Get Down, exec dir 1973-; Wayne County, Detroit, MI commissioner, 1991-. **Orgs:** Vice pres Universal Variable Staffing 1979; bd mem Southeast Michigan Food Coalition 1979; vice pres Midwest Group Mgmt 1980; bd mem Governors Task Force Infant Mortality 1985, Michigan Bell Citizen Adv Group 1986; comm mem Detroit Strategic Planning Commn 1987; pres CAD Cable 1987-. **Honors/Awds:** Natl Community Serv Awd United Community Serv 1979; Detroit City Council Community Awd 1984; Michelob Comm Serv Awd 1985. **Business Addr:** Executive Dir, Operation Get Down, 9980 Gratiot, Detroit, MI 48213.

PARKER, CHARLES MCCRAE
Biological science technician (retired), histotechnologist. **Personal:** Born Aug 13, 1930, Farmville, NC. **Educ:** NC A&T State Univ, BS 1951, BS 1958; Natl Inst of Health. **Career:** Natl Inst Health, messenger-clerk 1961-65; USDA, biol sci tech 1965-67, biol sci tech path 1967-80, sr biol sci tech 1980-87, FSIS, until 1990; Armed Forces Inst of Pathology, histotechnologist, 1990-; Federation of Amer Societies for Experimental Biology, currently. **Orgs:** Mem Phi Beta Sigma. **Honors/Awds:** Quality Increase APHIS USDA 1975; Letter of Achievement FSIS USDA 1983; Special Achievement FSIS USDA 1985. **Military Serv:** AUS sp3 1954-57; Honor Graduate NCO School 1956. **Home Addr:** 7131 8th St NW, Washington, DC 20012.

PARKER, CHARLES THOMAS
Law enforcement officer. **Personal:** Born Oct 26, 1918, Cleveland, TN; son of Ida Westfield Parker and Bud Parker; married Zilla Goldston Parker, Feb 2, 1942; children: Garland E Parker. **Educ:** College Hill School. **Career:** Charleston Police Dept, patrolman 1954, sgt of police 1956, asst chief 1974, chief of police 1979. **Orgs:** Mem Blue Lodge 1960, Shriner's Org 1974; adv capacity North East Advisory Bd 1981. **Honors/Awds:** Awd for Outstanding Serv to Comm Amer Legion 1970; Future Farmer of Amer Charleston FFA Chap 1978; Ordained Elder Green's Chapel Cumberland Presbyterian Church 1979; 2nd Chief of Police City of Charleston TN 1979; Citizen of the Year Hiwassee Mental Health Ctr 1981; 1st Black Chief of Police for State of TN. **Military Serv:** AUS corpl 1942-46; Battle Star Awd, Good Conduct Medal 1942-46. **Home Addr:** PO Box 154, Bates St, Charleston, TN 37310.

PARKER, CHARLIE
Professional basketball assistant coach. **Educ:** Findlay. **Career:** Dallas Mavericks, asst coach, 1996-. **Business Addr:** Assistant Coach, Dallas Mavericks, Reunion Arena, 777 Sports St, Dallas, TX 75207, (214)988-0117.

PARKER, CLARENCE E.
Automobile dealer. **Career:** Gresham Chrysler-Plymouth Inc, chief executive officer, currently. **Business Addr:** CEO, Gresham Chrysler-Plymouth Inc., PO Box 1947, Gresham, OR 97030, (503)665-7121.

PARKER, CLAUDE A.
Quality control manager. **Personal:** Born Oct 24, 1938, Branchville, VA; son of Alma Virginia Wyche and Claude A Parker Sr; married Constance Yvonne; children: Ryan. **Educ:** Comm Coll of Baltimore, AA 1960; Morgan State Univ, BS 1964. **Career:** Joseph E Seagram & Sons Inc, chemist 1965-66, supr quality control 1966, distiller 1967-70, quality control mgr 1970-. **Orgs:** Mem Amer Mgmt Assn 1971, Applied Mgmt Sci Inc 1972, Wine Adv Bd of CA 1972; mem Meritocrats Inc, YMCA. **Honors/Awds:** Listed in 1975 Ebony Success Library. **Business Addr:** Quality Control Manager, Joseph E Seagram & Sons Inc, PO Box 357, Baltimore, MD 21203.

PARKER, DARWIN CAREY
Electrical engineer. **Personal:** Born Feb 22, 1956, Detroit, MI; son of Melvina Theresa Parker and Arthur Parker; children: Kenyota, Aisha, Omega, Alpha. **Educ:** OH Institute of Tech, EET 1976; Highland Park Comm Coll, AAEE 1980; Siena Hieghts Coll, BAS 1982; Wayne State Univ MI Graduate Student 1987-89. **Career:** Lanier Business Products, customer serv eng 1976-78; WGPR Radio & TV, radio engr 1977-79; Howe-Richardson Scale Co, electronic field engr 1978-81; Shining-Star Intl, owner/producer 1980-83; FAC Enterprises, vice pres sales & public relations 1981-82; Omega Star, owner/engineer 1983-90; Detroit Engrg SSI, cons/prog coord, elect engr, author 1985-88; Wayne State Univ MI Lab, Research Technician 1987-90; Star International, Detroit, MI, executive consultant/engineer, 1990-. **Orgs:** Dir Young Democrats 13th District 1980-87; mem NAACP 1981-; mem Operation PUSH 1982, 1983; sr mem Soc of Mfg Engrs 1986-; mem Soc Auto Eng 1986-; Steward UAW Local 2071 1988-89. **Honors/Awds:** First completely full service black owned ad agency in Detroit Shining Star Intl 1980-83; Outstanding Community Leader Budd Local 306 1984; publication "Electronic Troubleshooting, Art & Science," DEI 1986; publ "A Day In The Life of The Civil Rights Movement, The Story of Dr William V Banks" 1987; Distinguished Service UAW Local 2071 1988. **Military Serv:** ARNG pfc 1984-85. **Business Addr:** Electronic Engineer, Author, Detroit Engineering/SSI, 4420 Townsend, Detroit, MI 48214.

PARKER, DAVID GENE
Professional baseball player. **Personal:** Born Jun 9, 1951, Jackson, MS; son of Dannie M Parker and Richard Parker; married Kellye Crockett; children: Danielle, David II, Dorian. **Career:** Pittsburgh Pirates, outfielder 1973-83; Cincinnati Reds, outfielder 1984-87; Oakland Athletics, outfielder, 1988-89; Milwaukee Brewers, outfielder, 1990-91; California Angels, outfielder, 1991-. **Honors/Awds:** National League All-Star Team, 1977-81, 1985, 1986, 1990; three-time Gold Glove Awd 1977-79; National League Most Valuable Player, Baseball Writers Assn of America, 1978; All-Star game MVP in 1979; Cincin-

nati Reds MVP 3 yrs 1984, 1985, 1986; voted by managers and coaches to the Silver Slugger team; picked by The Sporting News for its post-season All Star team; MVP, Milwaukee Brewers, 1990; Designated Hitters Award, 1989-90. **Business Addr:** Professional Baseball Player, California Angels, PO Box 2000, Anaheim, CA 92803-2000.

PARKER, DORIS S.

Foundation administrator. **Personal:** Born Aug 23, 1931, Marvel, AR; daughter of Earlie Mae Sims Watson (deceased) and Percy L Watson (deceased); divorced; children: Karen Parker Stewart, Terri L. **Educ:** Indiana Central College, BA, 1959. **Career:** US Army, Finance Center, military pay clerk, 1952-66; Veterans Administration Regional Office, adjudicator veteran claims examiner, 1966-73; Indiana Vocational Tech College, asst director of student services, 1973-75, regional relations coordinator, 1975-82; YWCA, executive director, 1982-85; independent consultant, 1985; Alpha Kappa Alpha Educational Advancement Foundation, Chicago, IL, executive secretary, 1987-. **Orgs:** Member, Fund for Hoosier Excellence, 1983-; member, Blacks in Development, 1990-; US Commission for Civil Rights, Indiana advisory commission, currently; Saint Mary of the Woods College, bd of trustees, 1985-94, trustee emeritus, 1994-; Assn of Black Foundation Executives, 1993-; Saint Felicitas Roman Catholic Church; Natl Committee Campaign for Human Development, US Catholic Conference, 1973-77, chmn, 1976-77; president, Hoosier Capital Girl Scout Council, 1978-82. **Honors/Awds:** Brotherhood Award, Indiana Chapter, National Conference of Christians & Jews, 1975; Human Relations Award, Indianapolis Education Assn 1976; Achievement Plus Public Service, Center for Leadership Development, 1985; Harriet Tubman Award, Community Action Against Poverty, 1982; Thanks Badge, Hoosier Capital Girl Scouts Council, 1982. **Business Addr:** Executive Secretary, Alpha Kappa Alpha Educational Advancement Foundation, 5656 S Stony Island Ave, Chicago, IL 60637, (312)947-0026.

PARKER, E. CHARMAINE ROBERTS

Editor, journalist. **Personal:** Born May 30, 1956, Salisbury, NC; daughter of Elizabeth Caldwell Roberts and James Deotis Roberts; married Ricardo Parker, Sep 10, 1988; children: Jazmin Monet, Tangela. **Educ:** Howard University, BFA, 1977; American University, graduate studies, journalism, 1978; University of Southern California, MA, print journalism, 1983. **Career:** The Washington Times, editor, copy editor, reporter, 1984-. **Orgs:** Natl Assn of Black Journalists, 1991. **Honors/Awds:** Society of Newspaper Design, Feature Section/Lifestyle, 1991-92, Arts Section & Metropolitan Times Section, 1994-95, Design & Layout Awards, 1995-96. **Business Addr:** Editor, The Washington Times, 3600 New York Ave NE, Washington, DC 20002.

PARKER, FRED LEE CECIL

Educator, clergyman (retired). **Personal:** Born Jun 16, 1923, Calvert, TX; married Elsie Evans; children: Patricia Ann, Willard Dean. **Educ:** Southwestern Baptist Theological Seminary, Ft Worth, Diploma 1956; Bishop Coll Dallas, BA 1968; E TX State Univ Commerce, MEd 1975; S Bible Sem Burnwsick GA, ThD 1978. **Career:** Geochem Surveys, lab tech 1944-70; Dallas Independent Sch Dist, tchr 1969-84; Goodwill Baptist Ch, assoc minister, 1977-94; D Edwin Johnson Baptist Inst, seminary & ext teacher 1979-91, administrative dean 1984-91; Tabernacle of Praise Baptist Church, pastor's asst, 1994-. **Orgs:** Mem GT Dallas Math Tchrs TSTA NEA 1970-; mem Classroom Tchrs of Dallas 1970-84; local & state chaplain Phi Beta Sigma Frat Inc 1970-84; Elem Math Tchrs Dev, US Off of Ed Bishop Coll Dallas 1971; Nat Sci Found, Math Bishop Coll Dallas 1972-73; Professional Growth in Ed Dallas Independent Sch Dist 1973-74; regvp, natl dean Universal Bible Inst Inc 1978-79; reg dir, dean S Bible Sem Inc 1978-79; fld rep, cnslr World-Wide Bible Inst Inc 1979-84. **Honors/Awds:** Panalist Radio Sta KNOK Dallas-Ft Worth 1954-71; hon DD Universal Bible Inst Inc Brunswick GA 1977; cert Pastoral Cnsl Birmingham AL 1977. **Home Addr:** 2023 Cedar Crest Blvd, Dallas, TX 75203.

PARKER, G. JOHN, SR.

Fire chief. **Personal:** Born Dec 29, 1941, Drew, MS; son of Anna Mae Tyler Parker (deceased) and Loys Parker; married Eva M Semien Parker, Sep 1, 1990; children: Jannie Lynn, G John Jr, Dannette Shaton, Toni Michelle, Stephanie A. **Educ:** Illinois Central College, East Peoria, IL, AA, 1975, AAS, 1979. **Career:** Caterpillar, Peoria, IL, machine operator, 1964-65; Peoria Fire Dept, Peoria, IL, 1965-91, fire chief, 1988; City of Pomona, Pomona, CA, fire chief, 1991-. **Orgs:** Board member, Peoria Urban League, 1989-; International Assn of Fire Chiefs, 1988-; International Assn of Black Professional Firefighters, 1975-; American Society of Public Administrators, 1988-; board member, Afro-American Hall of Fame, 1989-; Greater Pomona Kiwanis, 1992; Pomona Valley Red Cross, board member, 1991; National Forum of Black Public Administrators, 1991. **Honors/Awds:** Outstanding Alumni, Illinois Central College, American Council on Education, 1989; Outstanding Service Arson Investigator, Governor of Illinois, 1982; Dr Martin Luther King Leadership Award, South Side Pastors Assn, 1990; Sigma Image Award, Sigma Gamma Rho, 1990; Applaud Peoria-Outstanding Service, Peoria Chamber Achievers, 1990. **Military Serv:** US Marines, Master Sergeant, 1960-64; Outstanding Commissioned Officer, 1989; 182nd Illinois Air National Guard, 1976-, Deputy Fire Chief. **Business Addr:** Fire Chief, Pomona Fire Department, 590 S Park Ave, Pomona, CA 91766.

PARKER, GEORGE ANTHONY

Financial executive, leasing company executive. **Personal:** Born Jan 29, 1952, Norfolk, VA; son of Lillian B Carr and Milton A Parker; married Michele Annette Fleuranges; children: Jenifer Ann. **Educ:** Wake Forest Univ, BS 1974; Univ of NC Chapel Hill, MBA 1976. **Career:** Continental IL Natl Bank, banking assoc 1976-78, banking officer 1979-80, 2nd vice pres 1980-82; DPF Computer Leasing Corp, vice pres & treas 1982-84; Atlantic Computer Funding Corp, chmn of bd & pres 1984-; CT Bancorp Inc, dir 1986-88; The Norwalk Bank, dir 1986-88; Leasing Tech Intl Inc, dir/vice pres/chief financial officer 1984-95, executive vice pres, CFO/CMO, 1996-. **Orgs:** Vice pres Urban Bankers Forum Chicago 1981-82; mem Glenwood Lake Comm Assn 1983-, Natl Black MBA Assn 1986-, YMCA 1986; mem Wake Forest Univ Alumni Letterman Club 1986-; director, treasurer, St Bernard's Ctr for Learning, Inc. **Honors/Awds:** Western Electric Scholarship Awd 1971-73; Consortium for Grad Studies in Mgmt Fellowship Awd 1974-76. **Business Addr:** Director, Exec VP, CFO, Leasing Tech Intl Inc, 221 Danbury Rd, Wilton, CT 06897.

PARKER, H. WALLACE

Attorney. **Personal:** Born Dec 8, 1941, North Carolina; married Patricia W; children: Meriel S Parker. **Educ:** Winston-Salem State Univ BS, 1967; NCC Univ JD, 1970. **Career:** Reg Herb Smith Lwyr Fellow Prog, 1970-72; Legal Dept, City of Pontiac, Deputy City Atty 1971-75; pres, Bloomfield Law Center, 1975-; pres/owner, Check Mate Transportation System 1974-; v pres/atty, V-Tech Corp 1976-. **Orgs:** Mem Am St Nat, Oakland Co Wolverine Bar Assns; chief legal counselor, NAACP 1984-; atty/bd of dirs, OAR Program 1987-. **Honors/Awds:** First black deputy city atty, City of Pontiac,1971; Norcroff Award, NAACP 1986; Outstanding Service Award, 0AR 1987; modified jury selection system and statue for state of MI, 1987; judgement to remove discrimination, Pontiac Police Dept, 1988. **Military Serv:** USMC, Sgt 1960-63; Outstanding Soldier Award, 1962. **Business Addr:** Attorney, Bloomfield Law Center, 1275 S Woodward Ave #200, Bloomfield Hills, MI 48302.

PARKER, HENRY ELLSWORTH

Elected official. **Personal:** Born Feb 14, 1928, Baltimore, MD; married Janette; children: Curtis, Janet. **Educ:** Hampton Inst, BS 1956; Southern CT State Univ, MS 1965; Sacred Heart Univ, JD (Hon) 1983. **Career:** State of CT Hartford, treasurer 1975-86; Atlanta Sosnoff, senior vp, public fund sector, 1986-. **Orgs:** Pres Natl Assoc of State Treasurers 1985; pres Kappa Alpha Psi Found, 1981-86; mem Fed Natl Mortgages Assoc Advisory Comm, 1982-84; Past Grant Exalted Ruler of the Elks; 33 Degree Mason; trustee Instnl Responsibility Rsch Corp; bd dirs Inst Living. **Honors/Awds:** Prince Hall Masons Bicentennial Awd 1975; Civil Rights Awd CT NAACP 1976; One of Ebony Mag 100 most influential Black Amers 1976-86; Lovejoy Awd Elks 1984. **Military Serv:** AUS 1951-53. **Business Addr:** Treasurer, State of Connecticut, 20 Trinity St, Hartford, CT 06115.

PARKER, HENRY H.

Educator. **Personal:** Born Sep 11, 1933, Memphis, TN; son of Mr & Mrs Ben Parker. **Educ:** St Thomas Coll, BA 1956; Univ of MN, MA 1959; Univ of IL, PhD 1975. **Career:** Univ of MN, asst prof 1961-65; Univ of N Iowa, asst prof 1965-68, Univ of IL, asst prof 1968-71; Univ of N Iowa, asst prof 1971-84, full prof 1984-; Univ of Tennessee, Martin, professor, Dept of Psychology, Philosophy & Religion, 1990-. **Orgs:** Pres the Off-Campus Univ consulting firm; founder & principal Waterloo-Pre-Sch Acad; pres The Parker Reading Co; pub The Parker Reader Elem Sch Newspaper;producer & star the Hank Parker Show Ch 7; co-dir with Marilyn Crist of CP Collegians Gifted Children's Prog; National Director of Curriculum, Jesse Jackson's PUSH-Excel. **Honors/Awds:** NDEA Lecturer in Rhetoric 1965; Danforth Assoc Danforth Found; Iowa's Most Outstanding Prof Awd 1972; Geo Wash Carver Disting Lecturer Awd 1975; Ford Foundation Fellow, 1969. **Business Addr:** Prof, Univ of Tenn at Martin, Dept of Psychology, Philosophy & Religion, Martin, TN 38237.

PARKER, HERBERT GERALD

Educational administrator. **Personal:** Born May 13, 1929, Fayetteville, AR; son of Anna Fisher Parker and Otis James Parker; married Florida Fisher; children: Christie Lynne. **Educ:** Univ of NE, BS 1962; NC A&T State Univ, MS 1971; FL State Univ, PhD 1982. **Career:** Rep of China, Taipei, Taiwan, adv ministry of natl defense 1962-65; NC A&T State Univ, prof of mil sci 1965-68; AUS Spec Forces The Delta of Vietnam, commander 1968-69; US Army Civil Affairs Sch Fort Bragg, dir 1969-73; FL A&M Univ, prof of mil sci 1973-77; State of FL Bureau of Crimes Compensation 1979-87; Florida Dept of Education, Tallahassee, FL, chief internal auditor, 1987-91, director of administrative services, 1991-94. **Orgs:** Kappa Alpha Psi; Sigma Pi Phi Fraternity; Bd dir Civil Affairs Assn 1970-73; mem Natl Assn of Soc Scientist 1973-; bd of dir Three C's Corp 1974-79; bd of dirs Tallahassee Urban League 1981-; Board Chrmn 1986-88; Tallahassee Area C of C 1974-82; Bd of Dirs Oppor, Indus Ctrs 1975-78; bd dirs, United Way of Leon Co 1978-82; pres Natl assn of Crime Victim Compensation Bd 1984-87; bd dirs FL Victim & Witness Network 1984; mem Tallahassee NAACP. **Honors/Awds:** Distinguished Serv Awd Boy Scouts of Amer 1968; Distinguished Serv Awd Civil Affairs Assn 1974; Outstanding Serv Awd Coll of Humanities & Soc Sciences, FL A&M Univ 1977; Phi Kappa Phi Hon Soc 1979; Distinguished Service Awd, Natl Assn Crime Victim Compensation Brds, 1986; FL Network of Victim Witness Services; James Fogarty Distinguished Service Award 1988; Tallahassee NAACP, Distinguished Black Achiever Award, 1991. **Special Achievements:** Youngest African-American promoted to Col, US Army, 1969. **Military Serv:** US Army col 1947-77; 2 Legion of Merit; Silver Star; 3 Bronze Stars; Purple Heart; Meritorious Serv Awd; 12 other awds Airborne Ranger & Spec Forces Qualified; Joint Service Commendation Medal; 3 Air Medals; 2 Army Commendation Medals; United Nations Ribbon; Korean Campaign Awd; Vietnamese Cross of Gallantry with Palm; Reserve Forces Award with 10 year device, Good Conduct Medal. **Business Addr:** Director of Administrative Services, Florida Department of Education, 325 W Gaines St, Tallahassee, FL 32399.

PARKER, IRVIN

Engineering executive. **Personal:** Born Aug 21, 1946, Pittsburgh, PA; son of Irvin & Sara; married Caroline, Oct 14, 1988; children: Bryan, Aaron, Zachary. **Educ:** University of Pittsburgh, BS, 1979. **Career:** Mackintosh-Hemphill Co, design engineer; Koppers Co, Inc, sr design engineer; North Star Steel Co, melt shop engineer/gen supervisor of Casting; Gladwin Corp, Mini-Mill Div, gen mgr; New Jersey Steel Co, chief engineer; D&L, vp of operations. **Orgs:** Association of Iron & Steel Engineers; Iron & Steel Society; Engineers Society of Western Pennsylvania. **Special Achievements:** Holder of several US patents. **Business Addr:** Vice Pres, Operations, D&L, Inc, A Philip Services Co, 4 Gateway Ctr, 12th Fl, Pittsburgh, PA 15222, (412)765-3643.

PARKER, JACQUELYN HEATH

Organization executive. **Personal:** Born Dec 29, Memphis, TN; daughter of Nezzie Heath and Fred Heath; married William A Parker; children: Kimberly, Shane. **Educ:** Southern IL Univ, BS 1963, MS 1967; Univ of Illinois, post graduate. **Career:** Olive-Harvey Community College, reading specialist/adm 1996-; Top Ladies of Distinction Inc, natl pres 1987-91, program coordinator, 1996-. **Orgs:** Scholarship chmn Build Inc 1983-90; sponsor NIA Club 1985-95; pres Theta Rho Omega Chap of Alpha Kappa Alpha Sor 1987-89; Jack & Jill, Inc; Links, Inc; Ten Community Builders Award South Suburban Chicago AKA 1990; Jacquelyn Parker's Day 1990; Mayor Cincinnati, OH, 1990; A Woman of Distinction Award Chicago, Top Ladies of Distinction 1991; Natl Council of Negro Women, exec bd, 1991-95. **Honors/Awds:** Soror of the Year Theta Rho Omega Chap of Alpha Kappa Alpha Sorority; Lady of the Year Top Ladies of Distinction Chicago 1985; Top 40 Finest Women of Community Women Together of South Suburban Chicago 1988; Nominee-Top Women of Chicago Midwest Center of Chicago 1989; Orchid Award Top Ladies of Distinction, Inc. 1989; Illinois State Board of Education, "Those Who Excel," Winner, 1991; Univ of Chicago, Outstanding Teacher Award, 1994. **Home Addr:** 254 E Denell Dr, Crete, IL 60417.

PARKER, JAMES L.

Contract administrator (retired), accountant. **Personal:** Born Oct 29, 1923, Salina, KS; son of Classie (Meadows) Parker and John Henry Parker; married Berma Jeane (Wells) Parker, Jan 16, 1946 (deceased); children: Cheri D Ware, Jami L, Kathleen L Sullivan, Beryl J, Rosalind A Crutcher, Donna J, Janice E, Gloria J Shelton. **Educ:** Kansas Wesleyan Univ, 1949-50; Brown-Makie School of Business, BA, 1950. **Career:** Salina Recreation Dept, Carver Rec Ctr Salina KS, asst rec dir 1946-50; E Side Rec Ctr Freeport IL, exec dir 1951-66; Sundstrand Advanced Tech Div, contract adminstr 1967-87; tax accountant, currently. **Orgs:** Mem Gov Commn on Minority Entrepreneurship; Gov Commn on Emancipation Centennial; Freeport Hum Rels Commn; IL Law Enforcement Commn; Freeport Adult Ed Cncl Freeport Nrthwstrn IL Comm Act Prog Bd; Intrntl Toastmasters Club; adv bd Freeport Jr Coll; ML King Jr Comm Ctr Bd N IL Constr Affirm Act Prog; steward, St James CME Church. **Honors/Awds:** Recip Yth Award Freeport C of C 1956. **Military Serv:** US Army, Sgt maj 1943-45; NATO & ETO Battle Clusters. **Home Addr:** 632 E Iroquois St, Freeport, IL 61032.

PARKER, JAMES THOMAS

Business executive, professional football player (retired). **Personal:** Born Apr 3, 1934, Macon, GA; married Esther Mae; children: Pamela, Sheri, James Jr, Diane, David, Maisha, Anwar, Christian. **Educ:** Ohio State Univ. **Career:** Baltimore Colts, offensive tackle, guard, 1957-67; Jim Parker Publs, owner, 1985-. **Orgs:** Board of governors, Goodwill Ind. **Honors/Awds:** Inducted into the Pro Football Hall of Fame, 1973; Inducted into the Georgia Hall of Fame Toledo Hall of Fame, College Hall of Fame, Baltimore Hall of Fame, and Ohio State Univ Hall of Fame; All American, Ohio State Univ, 1955-56;

Outland Trophy, 1956; All Pro Eight Consec Seasons, 1958-65. **Business Addr:** Owner, Jim Parker Publishing, 333 Garrison Blvd, Baltimore, MD 21215.

PARKER, JEAN L.
Educator. **Personal:** Born Feb 22, 1923, Cincinnati, OH; widowed; children: Anthony. **Educ:** H&PE Wilberforce U, BS 1942; Wayne U, MA 1949; Columbia U; MI St. **Career:** Detroit Bd of Ed, conselor, consult 1962-72; H&PE Ft Vly St Coll, dept head 1942-43; City Detroit Highland Pk, rec lead 1944-48; H&PE Detorit Bd Ed, special educ teacher 1944-70; Joy Cleaning & Pressing Srv, co-owner 1965-76; Detroit Bd of Ed, pres, voc special 1970-76; Parke Lanie Jewelry, distrib 1970-75; Parker's Party & Bridal Consult Service, founder, owner 1954-. **Orgs:** Dir N Reg Eta Phi Beta Sor 1975-; past grand dir, Ed 1962-66; past grand Jour 1968-70; past Nat Pres Cntrl St Univ Nat Alumni Assn 1967-69; past bd dir Lucy Thurman YWCA; past bd mem Detroit Fed Tchrs Local #231; past mem, bd Delta Hm for Girls; past mem, bd dir Wayne St Univ Alumni Assn; Coll Ed Cur; pres Shay Ladies Aux; mem NAACP; NCNW; Narcerima Wives. **Honors/Awds:** Town Sq Coop Schlrshp CO Univ Detroit Roundtable Ch 1951; 25 yr Award for Srv Am Fed Tchrs 1973; Recog Award Detroit City Cncl 1977; Spl Award USO; YWCA; Grt Cities; Detroit Fed Tchr; Delta Sigma Theta; Detroit Bd of Ed. **Business Addr:** PO Box 32159, Detroit, MI 48232.

PARKER, JEFF, SR.
Physician. **Personal:** Born Aug 19, 1927, Big Cane, LA; son of Stella Parker and Edmond Parker; married Patricia O; children: Jeff Jr, Jacqueline, James, Janice. **Educ:** Howard Univ, BS 1962, MD 1966; Union Meml Hosp Baltimore, MD, rotating internship 1966-67; Sinai Hosp of Baltimore, MD, asst resid internal med 1967-69; Univ of MD Hosp, fellowship in cardiology 1969-70. **Career:** Private Practice, internist/cardiology. **Orgs:** Mem Black Cardiologists Assn 1974-; active staff Maryland General Hosp, Union Memorial Hosp; pres Medical Foundation Baltimore Inc; pres Reliable Medical rental and Serv Inc. **Honors/Awds:** Phi Beta Kappa Howard Univ 1962; Presidential Medallion/Recognition of Medical Arts by Church of God in Christ Bishop JO Patterson 1984; Alan Locke Meml Plaque Howard Univ 1958; Dean's Honor Roll Under-Grad Howard Univ 1962; Natl Honor Soc Psychol Psi Chi Howard Univ 1962; Magna Cum Laude Coll Liberal Arts Howard Univ; Honors Coll of Med Ped & Psych Howard Univ 1966; author: A christian Guide to the War on Drugs; A Christian Child's Guide to the War on Drugs. **Military Serv:** AUS Sgt 1st Class 1947-58; Good Conduct Medal. **Home Addr:** 1012 Argonne Dr, Baltimore, MD 21218. **Business Addr:** Internist, 2300 Garrison Blvd, Baltimore, MD 21216.

PARKER, JERRY P.
Attorney. **Personal:** Born Mar 1, 1943, West Blocton, AL; married Patricia Wall; children: Jerry, Jennifer. **Educ:** Bowling Green St U, BS, BA 1965; Cleveland Marshall Sch of Law, JD 1970. **Career:** Sears Roebuck & Co, tax atty 1973-; Ernst & Ernst Cleveland, tax supr 1968-73; E OH Gas Co, syst analyst 1965-68. **Orgs:** Am Bar Assn; Nat Bar Assn; Cook Co Bar Assn; Chicago Bar Assn; iL bar assn; mem iL & oH st bar bd of trust consult prot assn; bd of trust, exec com Child Srv; bd of trust Friendly Inn Settle House. **Business Addr:** Tax Dept #568, Sears Roebuck & Co Sears Tower, Chicago, IL 60684.

PARKER, JOSEPH CAIAPHAS, JR.
Attorney, educator. **Personal:** Born Sep 25, 1952, Anniston, AL; son of Addie Ruth Fox Parker and Rev Dr Joseph C Parker Sr (deceased); married J LaVerne Morris, Aug 14, 1976; children: Jessica, Jennifer. **Educ:** Morehouse Coll, BA 1974; Univ of Georgia, M Public Admin 1976; Univ of TX at Austin, JD 1982. **Career:** City of Dallas, admin asst mgmt serv 1976-77, admin asst office of the city mgr 1977-79, mgr summer youth employment program 1979; Travis Co Attorney Office, trial attorney 1983-84, chief trial div 1985-86; David Chapel Missionary Baptist Church, assoc pastor 1984-; Long, Burner, Parks & Sealy PC, attorney, dir, vice pres, 1986-; Univ of TX at Austin, instructor in trial advocacy, 1991-. **Orgs:** Mem Natl Conf of Minority Public Administrators 1974-80; mem Amer Soc for Public Admin; bd dirs Morehouse Coll Natl Alumni Assn; bd dirs Austin Child Guidance and Evaluation Ctr; mem Conference of Christians and Jews; mem Black Austin Democrats; mem Urban League, NAACP, Austin Jaycees; mem Travis County Public Defender Task Force; mem State Bar of TX, TX and Austin Young Lawyers Assns, Natl Bar Assns; mem Austin Black Lawyers Assn and Federal Bar Assn; mem Association of Trial Lawyers of America. **Honors/Awds:** Man of the Year Spelman College Student Govt Assn 1973-74; Univ of GA Fellowship 1974-76; Pi Sigma Alpha Honor Soc 1976; Dallas Jaycees Rookie of the Yr 1978-79, Presidential Awd 1978-79; Outstanding Achievement Awd Natl Conf of Minority Public Administrators 1979; Gene Woodfin Awd Univ of TX 1982; Leadership Austin 1984-85; Distinguished Morehouse Coll Alumni Citation of the Year 1986; Baptist General Convention of TX Theological Scholarship 1986-87; Benjamin E Mays Fellowship in Ministry, Fund for Theological Studies; publication "Prosecuting the DWI", True Bill Vol 6 No 4 TX Prosecutor Council. **Business Addr:** Trial Attorney, Long, Burner, Parks and Sealy, PC, PO Box 2212, Austin, TX 78768.

PARKER, JOYCE LINDA
Educator, educational administrator. **Personal:** Born Aug 16, 1944, New Orleans, LA; children: Cynthia Lorraine. **Educ:** Santa Ana Coll, AA psychology 1977; Chapman Coll, BA Social Work/Personnel 1979; Univ of LaVerne, MS Business Mgmt 1986. **Career:** Univ of CA-Irvine, admin asst, 1970-78; North Orange County Comm Coll, business instructor 1981-85 (part time); AME Johnson Chapel, assoc minister 1984-; Rockwell Intl, coord educ prog 1978-84, EEO Rep, 1984-. **Orgs:** Mem Natl Womens Assoc of Orange County 1978-; speaker Youth Motivation Task Force of Orange Co 1979-; mem Santa Ana Comm Coll APL Adv Bd 1981-83; sec bd dirs Youth Motivation Task Force 1985-; mem Governor's Comm for Employment of the Handicapped 1985-. **Honors/Awds:** Personnel Administration Fellowship, Chapman Coll, 1979; Special Recognition Award, Orange Coast Comm Coll, 1982-83; Outstanding Achievement Award, EEO, 1983; Gold & Bronze Key Award O C Youth Motivation Task Force 1985-86. **Business Addr:** EEO Representative, Rockwell International, 3370 Miraloma Ave, Anaheim, CA 92806.

PARKER, KAI J.
Appointed official, business executive. **Personal:** chilDren: Darren, Darnel. **Educ:** Compton Coll, AA Social Welfare 1965; Loyola Marymount Univ, grad studies in Psychology & Guidance Counseling 1979, the Human Construction of Sexuality 1980, Alcohol & Drug Studies 1982; Univ of Redlands, BA Management 1981. **Career:** Amer Telegraph & Tele, customer serv rep 1966-68; LA Co Dept of Social Svcs, eligibilty worker 1968-70; LA Co Dept of Public Social Svcs, eligibility super 1970-79; Aide Sanitary & Supply Co, mgmt consultant 1979-80; LA Co Assessment Appeals Bd, comm 1980-82; Group W Cable, public affairs & govtl relations coord 1982-91; LA County, Dept of Children Services, special programs coordinator, 1991-. **Orgs:** 20 memberships including NAACP; Asian-Pacific legal Defense & Educ bd of dir; United Negro Coll Fund; Gardena Local Manpower Adv Bd; Gardena Interagency Health Comm; Gardena Martin Luther King Cultural Comm; Asian Amer Drug Abuse Prog; CA Afro-Amer Museum Art Council; Museum of African Amer Art; vice pres, S Bay Coalition on Alcoholism; adv bd, LA Co Child Health Disease Prevention; vp, Gardenia Valley Lions. **Honors/Awds:** Outstanding Leadership Award City of Gardena; Recognition Awd Gardena Elks Leadership; Outstanding Serv Award AFL-CIO; Community Involvement Award Soroptimist Intl; Comm Involvement Award, Gardena Sorptomist; Comm Serv Awd CA Black Comm on Alcoholism; Commendations, LA Co; Outstanding Serv Bd of Supvr, Dept of Public Soc Serv, 1982; Zeta Phi Beta, Political Award; Founder, Gardenia African Centered Saturday School; Natl Assn of Counties Award, 1992-96; U.S. Congress House of Representatives, 35th District, Women of the Year, 1996. **Business Addr:** Coordinator, Special Programs, LA County Dept of Children Services, 425 Shato Pl, Rm 604, Los Angeles, CA 90020.

PARKER, KAREN LYNN
Journalist. **Personal:** Born Dec 21, 1943, Salisbury, NC; daughter of Fred and Clarice Parker; married Barry J Lambert, 1996; children: Jonah Evan Kuttner. **Educ:** Univ of North Carolina, BA, 1965. **Career:** Winston-Salem Journal, 1962-65; Grand Rapids, MI, Press, 1965-67; Rochester Democrat and Chronicle, 1967; Los Angeles Times, sunday news editor, 1978-93; Salt Lake Tribune, asst natl editor, 1994-96; Winston-Salem Journal, 1997-. **Orgs:** National Assn of Black Journalists, 1997; American Copy Editors Society, 1997. **Special Achievements:** First African American woman to graduate from University of NC, Chapel Hill, 1965. **Business Addr:** 416 N Marshall St, Winston-Salem, NC 27101, (336)727-7469.

PARKER, KEITH DWIGHT
Educator. **Personal:** Born Oct 15, 1954, Philadelphia, MS; married Emery D Woodruff; children: Narroyl, Malcolm. **Educ:** Delta State Univ, BA 1978; Miss State Univ, MA 1981, PhD 1986. **Career:** Delta State Univ, assistant to the dean 1979-82; Mississippi State Univ, resident asst 1982-85, teaching assistant 1982-86; Auburn Univ, asst prof 1986-89; Univ of Nebraska-Lincoln 1989-94, assoc prof, 1994-. **Honors/Awds:** Pres Graduate Black Student Org 1983; advisor Black Student Org 1982; Minority Fellowship Mississippi State 1982; Alpha Kappa Delta MS State 1983, Outstanding Student 1986; Outstanding Minority Faculty, Auburn Univ, 1989; Afrikan People's Union, University of Nebraska, advisor, 1990-94; Big 8 Conference Black Student Government, Barbara Jordan Award, 1991-94. **Business Addr:** Assoc Professor, Sociology, University of Nebraska, 730 Oldfather Hall, Lincoln, NE 68588-0324, (402)472-7973.

PARKER, KELLIS E.
Educator, attorney. **Personal:** Born Jan 13, 1942, Kinston, NC; children: Kellis, Kimberly, Emily. **Educ:** University of North Carolina, BA, 1960; Howard Univ School of Law, JD, cum laude, 1968. **Career:** Columbia University, law professor, 1975-; Columbia University, associate professor of law, 1972-75; Univ of California, acting professor of law, 1969-72; Judge Spottswood W Robinson III, law clerk, 1968-69. **Orgs:** NAACP, Legal Def Fund, consultant; New World Found; Comm Action Legal Serv, chairperson, 1977-79; Nat Conf on Black Lawyers; Minority Groups Com, chairperson; Assn of Am Law Schs, 1976-77; Nat Com on Legal & Ethical Implications of Sickle Cell Anemia; Comm Action for Legal Svcs, board member. **Honors/Awds:** Publ, "Modern Judicial Remedies", Little Brown & Co, 1975; editor in chf, Howard Law Journal, 1967-68. **Business Addr:** Columbia University, School of Law, 435 W 116th St, New York, NY 10027-7279.

PARKER, LEE
Educator, business consultant. **Personal:** Born May 31, 1949; married; children: 2. **Educ:** LeMoyne Owen College, BS, BBA (magna cum laude), 1979; Trevecca Nazarene College, MEd, 1990. **Career:** US Treasury, assoc natl bank examiner 1979-83; Natl Bank of Commerce Memphis, vice pres 1983-84; Gospel TV Network Inc, business consultant 1984-; Memphis City Schools, teacher, BASIC programming and mathematics, 1985-. **Orgs:** Co-chmn Memphis Housing Comm; registered with Securities and Exchange Commission; elected to LeMoyne Owen Coll Religious Life Comm; apptd naval advisor NAUS-UPPACT forces. **Honors/Awds:** Natl Science Award, Eastman Kodak Co; Distinguished Alumnus, Natl Assn for Equal Opportunity in Higher Educ; UNCF Awd. **Military Serv:** USN petty officer 1966-76; Naval Commendation Medal.

PARKER, MARYLAND MIKE
Journalist. **Personal:** Born Feb 5, 1926, Oklahoma City, OK; married John Harrison Parker (deceased); children: Norma Jean Brown, Janice Kay Shelby, Joyce Lynn, John H Jr, Cherie D Hite, Patrick Scott, Charles Roger, John H III. **Educ:** Univ of AR Pine Bluff, 1970-71; Marymount Coll Salina KS, 1974-77. **Career:** MD House of Beauty Salina KS, beautician 1964-69; NAACP Salina, youth adviser 1970-72; BACOS Newsletter, newspaper reporter 1971-77; KINA BACOS Report, radio announcer 1973-84; Kansas State Globe, reporter & photographer, currently. **Orgs:** Mem YWCA 1958-, Saline Cty Democratic Women 1960-, VFW Aus 1971-, Amer Leg Aux 1973-, Natl Fed of Press Women 1973-, KS Press Women 1973-; bd of dir Salina Chilc Care Assoc 1973; part time volunteer Salvation Army 1979-; mem Intl Platform Assoc 1983-; bd of dir Gospel Mission 1984; American Business Women Assn, 1991-. **Honors/Awds:** Lifetime member NAACP 1980; Good Citizenship Award from VFW 1432 Salina KS 1982; Award of Merit, Salina Human Relations, 1986; American Business Association, Woman of the Year, 1997. **Home Addr:** 920 Birch Dr, Salina, KS 67402.

PARKER, MATTHEW
Business executive. **Personal:** Born Nov 14, 1945, Cincinnati, OH; son of Ruth Spann (deceased) and Matt Parker (deceased); married Karon Lanier Parker, Aug 8, 1981; children: Matthew Lloyd Jr, Tiffany Barbara, Michael Jones, Kelly Betsy. **Educ:** Grand Rapids School of Bible & Music, diploma Bible 1970; Wheaton Coll, BA Sociology 1976; Univ of Detroit, MA Educ Admin 1981. **Career:** Campus Crusade for Christ, black campus staff 1971-72; Wheaton Coll, minority student adv 1973-77; Great Commiss Comm Ch, founder, pastor 1978-83; Detroit Afro-Amer Mission Inc, consultant 1979-80; J Allen Caldwell Schs, admin 1981-83; William Tyndale Coll, faculty mem 1982-87, assoc vice pres urban academic affairs; Institute for Black Family Development, pres, currently. **Orgs:** Mem, Natl Religious Broadcasters; mem, Christian Management Assn. **Honors/Awds:** MVP Grand Rapids School of Bible & Music Basketball team 1969; MVP MI Christian coll Conf 1969; Achievement Awd Minority Student Organ at Wheaton Coll 1974; publ, "God Sent Him" 1984, "Black Church Development" 1985; Mission Leadership; Destiny Movement Inc, 1987; Leadership Development Natl Black Evangelical Assn, 1988; The Black American Family: A Christian Legacy (film).

PARKER, MICHAEL WAYNE
Automobile dealer. **Personal:** Born Jan 23, 1947, Washington, DC; son of Webster H & Laverne C Parker; married Monika L Lewis, Apr 4, 1970; children: Genell S, Tia T. **Educ:** Hampton University, BS, 1970. **Career:** Sheehy Ford Inc, general sales manager, 1971-80; Rosenthal Toyota Inc, general manager, 1980-85; Conn Ave Nissan, general manager, 1985-87; Stolhman Nissan-Saab, general sales manager, 1987-88; Lexington Park Chrysler Plymouth Dodge, general manager, 1988-89; MP Chrysler Plymouth Dodge Inc, president/owner, 1989-. **Orgs:** Rotary Intl, president, 1993-; Minority Dealers Association (Chrysler), 1989-; NADA, 1989-. **Honors/Awds:** Toyota of America, Admiral Club, 1983, 1984; Ford Motor Co., Marketing Achievement Winner, 1978, 1979; Chrysler Corp., Best of the Best, 1990, 1994, 5 Star Award, 1991, 1992, 1995, 1996, 1997; Pacesetter, 1994. **Business Addr:** Owner/President, M P Chrysler/Plymouth/Dodge Inc, Rte 6, Box 224, Lexington, VA 24450, (540)463-9111.

PARKER, PAUL E.
Educational administrator. **Personal:** Born Oct 23, 1935, Jenkins Bridge, VA; son of E Alma Logan Parker and Edward L. Parker; married Ann Withers; children: Paul Jr, Kenneth. **Educ:** North Carolina A&T State Univ, BSME, 1961; State Univ of NY Buffalo, MSME, 1969. **Career:** Bell Aerosystems, stress analyst, 1961-67; North Carolina A&T State Univ, asst prof mech engrg, 1967-73, asst to dean engrg, 1971-73; Univ of IL, asst dean of engrg, currently. **Orgs:** Engrg coop dir, North Car-

olina A&T State Univ, 1970-73; pres, Natl Assn of Minority Engrg Prog Administrators, 1985; consul Battelle Lab 1984; bd dirs Urban League of Champaign Co 1983-90; bd of trustees Mt Olive Bapt Church 1980-; chmn adv comm Unit 4 Schools 1975-78; bd dir GEM 1986-; ASEE/CIP newsletter editor, 1989-. **Honors/Awds:** Pi Tau Sigma Hon Soc; Tau Beta Pi Hon Soc; Promotion of Higher Education, Black Engineer of the Year, US Black Eng, 1991; Vincent Bendix Minorities in Engineering, American Society for Engineering Educ, 1990. **Military Serv:** AUS sp3 instr engrs school, 1955-57. **Business Addr:** Asst Dean, Engineering, University of Illinois, 1308 W Green St, #207, Urbana, IL 61801.

PARKER, PERCY SPURLARK
Author, salesman. **Personal:** Born Apr 6, 1940, Chicago, IL; son of Percy & Ponce Parker; married Shirley, Aug 2, 1958; children: Sheila Parker-Hill, Sherri Parker, Percy III. **Career:** Osco Drug Co, store manager, 1965-75; Quitable Insurance Co, salesman, 1975-76; Swain Drug Co, store manager, 1976-77; Dekoven-Perry Drug, store mgr, 1977-87; Highland Appliance Store, appliance salesman, 1987-92; Montgomery Ward, appliance salesman, 1992-. **Orgs:** Mystery Writers of America, treasurer, director, Midwest Chapter; Private Eye Writers of America; Mystery Writers of America, pres, Midwest Chapter, 1987-88. **Special Achievements:** 22 short stories in various mystery magazines, 1972-; Novel, Good Girls Don't Get Murdered, Scribners, 1973. **Business Addr:** Senior Sales Assoc, Montgomery Ward, 7503 W Cermak Rd, North Riverside, IL 60546.

PARKER, RAY, JR.
Singer, songwriter, producer. **Personal:** Born 1954, Detroit, MI. **Career:** Songwriter: Herbie Hancock ''Keep on Doin It'', Chaka Kahn & Rufus ''You got The Love'', Stevie Wonder, Barry White, Temptations, Gladys Knight & The Pips, Spinners; Singles: A Woman Needs Love, Ghostbuster; Albums: I Love You Like You Are, 1991. **Honors/Awds:** 5 gold albums; Grammy nom ''Keep on Doin' It''; Academy Award Nomination Best Orig Song from ''GhostBusters'' 1984. **Business Addr:** c/o Geffin Record Label, 9130 Sunset Blvd, Los Angeles, CA 90069.

PARKER, RIDDICK
Professional football player. **Personal:** Born Nov 20, 1972. **Educ:** Univ of North Carolina, history major. **Career:** Seattle Seahawks, defensive tackle, 1997-. **Business Addr:** Professional Football Player, Seattle Seahawks, 11220 NE 53rd St, Kirkland, WA 98033, (206)827-9777.

PARKER, SIDNEY BAYNES
Clergyman, educator. **Personal:** Born Jul 13, 1922, Jamaica, West Indies; son of Rachael E Parker and Luther A Parker; married Carolyn Bardine, Oct 26, 1978; children: Philip, Cynthia, Israel, Lisa, Alfred, Keith. **Educ:** Mico Teachers' College, attended, 1941-43; Howard University, BS, MA, 1949, MDiv, 1953; Geneva Theological College, EdD, 1970; LaSalle University, LLB, 1970. **Career:** Excelsior High School, teacher, 1944-45; St Michael's Episcopal Church, vicar, 1953-57; Leland College, instructor, 1953-57; Trinity Episcopal Church, rector, 1957-70; Newark Public School System, instructor, 1960-70; St Mary's Anglican Church, interim rector, 1967; St Philip's Episcopal Church, rector, 1970-78; St Gabriel's Episcopal Church, vicar, 1970-; Edward Waters College, professor, 1976-. **Orgs:** Montclair Mayor's Committee, president, 1969-70; Diocese of Florida Standing Committee, 1976-79; Jacksonville Library, bd of trustees, 1987-. **Honors/Awds:** Howard University, Homiletic Award, 1952; City of Jacksonville, Mayor's Award, 1979; University of North Florida, Achievement Award, 1990.

PARKER, STAFFORD W.
Government official. **Personal:** Born Sep 12, 1935, Kansas City, MO; son of Erma Thurston Freeman and Cato Parker; married Anita McBride Parker, Aug 17, 1963; children: Monique V. Parker, Dana V. Parker. **Educ:** University of Kansas, Lawrence, KS, BA, 1958, LLB, 1963. **Career:** City of Lawrence, KS, probation officer, 1962; Travelers Insurance Co Agency, Cleveland, OH and Oakland, CA, claims examiner, adjuster, 1963-66; San Francisco Redevelopment Agency, San Francisco, CA, administrative assistant to project director, 1966-67, assistant business relocation supervisor, 1967-68, salvage section coordinator, 1967-68, community services supervisor, 1968; Fresno Redevelopment Agency, Fresno, CA, project manager of general neighborhood renewal area, 1968-70, assistant director, 1970-77; City of Fresno, assistant director of Housing and Community Development Dept, 1977-82, assistant director of Development Dept, 1982-88, director of Housing and Community Development Dept, 1988-. **Orgs:** Member, National Association of Housing and Redevelopment Officials, 1975-; member, NAACP, 1968-; member, 1976-, president, 1986-89, Black Lawyers Assn of Fresno; president, Boys Club, West Fresno Chapter, 1979-81. **Honors/Awds:** Honoree of Year, Government Category, NAACP, 1988; Recognition Award for Work With Youth, Boys Club of America, 1981. **Military Serv:** US Army, Spc 4, 1958-60; received Good Conduct Medal. **Business Addr:** Director, Housing and Community Development Dept, City of Fresno, 2326 Fresno St, Fresno, CA 93721.

PARKER, STEPHEN A.
Psychologist, educator and consultant. **Personal:** Born in Chicago, IL; son of Ilena Parker; married Diana Louise; children: Stephen A II, Daniel Edmond. **Educ:** IL Teacher Coll S, BS 1965; Chicago State Coll, MS 1970; Northwestern Univ Evanston IL, PhD 1974. **Career:** Chicago Board of Education, teacher, 1965-70, recreational instructor, 1966-70; Chicago State Univ, instr of psychology 1970-74, asst to dir of financial aid 1970-74, assistant to associate professor of psychology 1978-83, prof of psychology 1983-, and dean of admissions & records 1983-86, full professor of psychology 1983-. **Orgs:** Affiliate Henry Horner Chicago Boys Club, 1957-; Amer Psychological Assn, 1974-; Phi Delta Kappa, 1975-; Natl Rsch Cncl, Ford Foundation; panel mem doctoral fellowships, 1987; International Council on the Education of Teachers, 1987-. **Honors/Awds:** Special Teaching Recognition Award, Chicago State Univ 1977; Chicago Urban League Achievement Award 1976; Black Students Psychological Assn 1975; Natl Assn of Bahamian Cosmetologists 1979; Appreciation Award Business Educ Student Assn CSU 1982; Distinguished Alumni Award Crane HS Hall of Fame 1985; Special Guest Speaker Award 1986; Distinguished Serv Award Henry Horner Boys & Girls Club 1987; Distinguished Westsider Award, Westside Organization, 1988; Appreciation Award, Crane High School, 1990; Volunteer Award, Tougaloo Alumni Assn, Chicago Chapter, 1990; Boys and Girls Clubs of America, Alumni of the Year, 1991; Chicago State University, Faculty Excellence Award, 1992; Natl Council of Negro Women, Recognition Award, 1997; Certificate of Appreciation, Black Student Psychological Association, 1996. **Business Addr:** Professor of Psychology, Chicago State Univ, 9501 S King Dr, Chicago, IL 60628, (312)995-2394.

PARKER, TED N., JR.
Marketing executive. **Personal:** Born May 7, 1967, New York, NY; son of Ted Parker Sr & Constance Benjamin. **Educ:** St John's Univ, BS, marketing, 1991. **Career:** Xerox, territory mktg rep, 1991-93, mktg rep, 1993-95, account mgr commercial print, 1995-97, document production marketing exec, 1997-. **Orgs:** Xerox, advisory comm mem, 1994-. **Honors/Awds:** Xerox President's Club, 1994-95; Xerox, Par Club.

PARKER, THOMAS EDWIN, III
Public & government affairs advisor. **Personal:** Born Dec 11, 1944. **Educ:** Princeton U, MPA 1971; Howard U, BA 1967; Woodrow Wilson Sch of Pub & Intrntl Affairs. **Career:** Standard Oil Co, prog coord, pub & govt aff 1985; Am Soc for Pub Admin Wash, dir of progs 1974-76; City Cncl of DC, legis asst 1971-74; Wash Concentrated Empl Prog, prog coord 1967-69. **Orgs:** Admin prog dev consult Ghana W Africa; OIC Rsrch Asso NJ St Landlord; Tenant Relationship Study Commn Pub Defenders Off NJ Am Soc for Pub Admin; Intrntl City Mgmt Assn; Urban Leag; NAACP. **Honors/Awds:** Woodrow Wilson Flwshp; Pub Affairs Intrnshp; Outstdng Young Men of Am 1972. **Business Addr:** Amoco Oil Co, 6 Executive Park Dr NE, Atlanta, GA 30329.

PARKER, VAUGHN ANTOINE
Professional football player. **Personal:** Born Jun 5, 1971, Buffalo, NY. **Educ:** UCLA, majored in sociology. **Career:** San Diego Chargers, tackle, 1994-. **Honors/Awds:** Played in Super Bowl XXIX. **Business Addr:** Professional Football Player, San Diego Chargers, 9449 Friars Rd, Qualcomm Stadium, San Diego, CA 92108, (619)280-2111.

PARKER, VERNON B.
Attorney. **Personal:** Born Nov 16, 1959, Houston, TX; son of Lillie Mae Parker; married Lisa Farringer Parker, Apr 27, 1991; children: Sonya Zepeda, Ian Bernard. **Educ:** Bilingual and Cultural Institute of Cuernavaca, Mexico, 1980; California State Univ at Long Beach, BS, 1980-83; Georgetown Univ, JD, 1988. **Career:** Rockwell International, financial analyst, 1983-85; US Office of Personnel Management, counselor to the dir/dir of policy, 1989-91, general counsel, 1992; White House, special asst to the pres, 1992-93; Kenny Rogers Roasters of Chicago, vice pres, 1993-94; Multinational Legal Services, partner, 1994-; Parian International, president & CEO; Parker, Farringer, Parker, attorney, currently. **Orgs:** National Bar Association, 1991-; District of Columbia Bar, 1989-; Virginia Bar Association, 1995; Student Bar Association, Georgetown Univ Law Center, vice pres, 1986-87. **Honors/Awds:** Georgetown Univ Law Center, Outstanding Leader, 1988; Georgetown Univ Law Center, Outstanding Tutor, 1988, Foreign Language Scholarship recipient, 1980. **Special Achievements:** Editor-in-chief, Georgetown American Criminal Law Review; Author, ''Annual Survey of White-Collar Crime Attorney Client Privilege,'' American Criminal Law Review, Winter 1986-1987; Selected by President to represent US at swearing in of President of Ghana, 1993. **Home Addr:** 5729 E Indian Bend Rd, Paradise Valley, AZ 85253.

PARKER, WALTER GEE
Physician. **Personal:** Born Feb 11, 1933, Branchville, VA; son of Theresa Parker and Roosevelt Parker; married Henri Mae Smith; children: Jennifer L, Walter G Jr, Brian K. **Educ:** Hampton Inst, BS 1955; Meharry Medical Coll, MD 1962; University of MI, MPH 1967. **Career:** Univ of MI, Ann Arbor, MI, instructor in pediatrics, 1966-69; Univ of MI Sch of Public Health, rsch assoc 1967-69; Wayne County Health Dept, public health phys 1969-75; Univ of MI, Ann Arbor, MI, clinical instructor in pediatrics, 1969-; Southwest Detroit Hospital, vice pres of medical affairs 1975-86; W Wayne Correctional Facility, State of MI Dept of Corr, medical dir 1986-. **Orgs:** Mem Amer Public Health Assoc 1967-, Amer Acad of Pediatrics 1973-, Detroit Medical Soc 1975-, Wayne Co Medical Soc 1975-. **Honors/Awds:** Mem Delta Omega Public Health Honorary Society 1967-; Bd Certified Amer Bd of Pediatrics 1971; article ''Michigan Rheumatic Fever Study,'' in Michigan Med 1969. **Military Serv:** AUS sp-3 1956-58; Good Conduct Medal. **Business Addr:** Medical Dir, W Wayne Correctional Facility, 48401 Five Mile Rd, Plymouth, MI 48170.

PARKER, WILLIAM C., JR.
Real estate developer. **Personal:** Born Apr 16, 1939, Mt Gilead, NC; son of Vallie Simon Parker and William Carter Parker Sr; married Markethia Baldwin; children: Kamala O, Keisha D. **Educ:** North Carolina A&T State Univ, MS 1965, BS 1961; Univ NC-Chapel Hill, Med, 1967; Indiana Univ, doctorate 1971. **Career:** Shepargib Foods Inc Burger King Franchise in Greensboro & Winston-Salem, founder/pres/CEO 1976-84; Wilpar Develop Corp, founder/pres/CEO 1977-; Wilpar Construction Co, founder/pres/CEO 1977-; Parker Brothers Restaurant, founder/pres/CEO 1980-; Wilpar Corp, founder/pres/CEO 1983-; Southeastern Develop Group, founder 1985; Joint Ctr for Economic Develop, founder 1985-; Piedmont Develop Corp, founder/pres/CEO 1974-. **Orgs:** Mem Omega Psi Phi Frat 1963-, Phylaxis Soc 1975-, Natl Restaurant Assoc 1976-; life mem Univ of NC at Chapel Hill Alumni Assoc 1977-; mem Natl Bd of Realtors 1979-; mem adv bd Carolina Peacemaker Newspaper 1980-; mem Greensboro Bd of Realtors 1979-; deputy grand master Prince Hall Grand Lodge of NC and its Jurisdictions 1980-; sec A&T Univ Foundation Inc 1982-; bd of dirs Foundation of Greater Greensboro 1983-; mem The Greensboro Conversation Club 1985-, Greensboro Men's Club 1985-; past chmn NC A&T State Univ Bd of Trustees 1985-; mem Beta Epsilon Boule Sigma Pi Phi Frat 1986-, Greensboro Natl Bank Adv Bd 1986-; vice pres NC Black Leadership Caucus 1986; mem bd of trustees, chmn long range plng comm Shiloh Bapt Church 1986; life mem NAACP; mem Greensboro Merchants Assoc; Grand Master, Prince Hall Grand Lodge, 1987-94. **Honors/Awds:** James T Isler Comm Serv Awd Family Children Serv of Greater Greensboro 1982; presented the ''Order of the Long Leaf Pine'' by Gov James B Hunt 1985; Economic Develop Awd NAACP 1985; Outstanding Alumnus Awd Natl Assoc on Higher Educ 1985; Levi Coffin Awd for Leadership and Human Serv Greensboro Area Chamberof Commerce 1986. **Military Serv:** US Army 2 yrs. **Business Addr:** President & Chief Executive Officer, Wilpar Corporation, 1616 East Market St, Suite 104, Greensboro, NC 27401, (910)379-1880.

PARKER, WILLIAM HARTLEY
Company executive. **Personal:** Born Nov 7, 1947, Pittsburgh, PA; son of Gwendolyn T Dodson and William H Parker; divorced; children: William, Gregory. **Educ:** Fashion Institute of Technology, 1971; Empire State/SUNY, New York, NY, BBA, 1972. **Career:** Parkview Gem, New York, NY, buyer, 1970-74; Macy's, Newark, NJ, buyer, 1974-77; May Co, Cleveland, OH, DMM, 1977-80; Dayton-Hudson, Detroit, MI, general manager, 1980-85; Carson Pirie Scott, Chicago, IL, senior vice president, 1985-89; K-Mart, vice pres, 1989-91, pres of Reader's Market Div, 1991-. **Orgs:** President, Black Retail Action Group, 1972-74; board of trustees, Music Hall, 1989-; vice president, Black Retail Action Group, 1971-76. **Honors/Awds:** Hall of Fame Fashion, Fashion Institute of Technology, 1986; YMCA Outstanding Black Achiever, 1983. **Military Serv:** Marine Corps, Sgt, 1965-70; Meritorious Mast, 1969, Outstanding Marine, Boot Camp.

PARKER, WILLIAM HAYES, JR.
Director/producer. **Personal:** Born May 2, 1947, Mt Vernon, NY; married Yvonne Kelly; children: Eric Hayes, Steven Lee, Stella Cailan. **Educ:** Univ of Cincinnati, 1965-66; Macomb Co Coll, 1967-69; Los Angeles City Coll, 1973-75. **Career:** EUE Screen Gems, prod mgr 1977-78; New Genesis Prods, producer 1978-79; BAV Inc, producer/LD 1980-82; BPP, director/producer 1982-. **Orgs:** Children's Fund Defense. **Military Serv:** USAF sgt 1966-70. **Business Addr:** Director-Producer, B Parker Prods/ Renge Films, 8400 DeLongpre Ave, Los Angeles, CA 90069.

PARKER-ROBINSON, D. LAVERNE
Software development company executive. **Personal:** Born Jan 14, 1949, New York, NY; daughter of Emma Smith Parker and Tommie B Parker (deceased); married Guy Robinson, Aug 28, 1990. **Educ:** Bernard M Baruch Coll CUNY, BA 1974; Fordham Univ, MSW 1978. **Career:** Harlem Dowling Children's Svcs, caseworker 1974-77; Greater NY Fund/Tri-State United Way, tech asst intern 1977-78; Abraham & Straus Dept Stores, coord of public affairs 1978-79, asst mgr/computer opers 1979-81, internal consultant/special projects mgrs 1981-82, data processing financial controller 1982-85; Strategic Intelligence, Inc, vice pres, CFO, product rsch, 1985-. **Orgs:** Mem Randolph Evans Scholarship Awds Dinner Comm 1979-; bd mem Strategic Intelligence, Inc, 1985-; mem Mgmt Assistance Comm Greater NY Fund/United Way 1985-87; pres Brooklyn Mgmt

Club 1986-87; New York Ubran League, Manhattan Branch, board member, 1991-94; school volunteer NY City School Volunteer Prog 1986-87; mem Natl Assoc of Social Workers. **Honors/Awds:** Disting Service Awd Salvation Army Brownsville Corps 1979. **Business Addr:** Vice President, CFO, Product Research, Strategic Intelligence, Inc, 60 East 42nd Street, Suite 2238, New York, NY 10165, (212)687-1378.

PARKER-SAWYERS, PAULA
Deputy mayor. **Personal:** Born Oct 5, Indianapolis, IN; daughter of Dorthea Shelton Parker and Thomas Parker; married James Sawyers, Oct 9, 1982; children: Elizabeth, Parker, Patrick. **Educ:** Ball State University, Muncie, IN, 1969-71; George Washington University, Washington, DC, 1971-72; Indiana University-Purdue University at Indianapolis, Indianapolis, IN, BA, Political Science, 1980. **Career:** LS Ayres & Co, Indianapolis, IN, 1974-78; AT&T, Indiana Bell, Indianapolis, IN, 1978-85; Browning Investments, Indianapolis, IN, 1985-86; Blue Cross/Blue Shield, 1986-89; City of Indianapolis, Indianapolis, IN, deputy mayor, currently. **Orgs:** Indianapolis Museum of Art; Coalition of 100 Black Women; National Council of Negro Women; Indianapolis Campaign for Healthy Babies. **Honors/Awds:** Madame CJ Walker Women of the Year, Center for Leadership Development, 1989. **Business Addr:** Deputy Mayor, City of Indianapolis, 2501 City-County Building, Indianapolis, IN 46204.

PARKINSON, NIGEL MORGAN
Construction company executive. **Personal:** Born Aug 26, 1953, Freetown, Sierra Leone; married; children: Nigel Jr, Malcolm. **Educ:** Florida A & M, BS, 1974; Florida State University, MSPA, 1975; Leadership Washington, 1992; MIT, Center for Real Estate, 1993. **Career:** Davis Foundation, junior executive, 1975-78; Management Support Services, 1978-83; Parkinson Construction, president, 1983-. **Orgs:** US Chamber of Commerce; Masonry Institute; US General Service Administration, advisory board, 1991; District of Columbia Contractors Association, board member/treasurer, 1988-93; National Assn of Minority Contractors, treasurer, 1992-94, president, 1994-. **Honors/Awds:** US General Service, Public Service Award, 1993; Natl Assn of Minority Contractors, Contractor of the Year Award, 1992; District of Columbia Contractors Assn, Excellence Award, 1991. **Business Addr:** President, Parkinson Construction, 3905 Perry St., Brentwood, MD 20722, (301)985-6080.

PARKS, ALFRED G., JR.
Radio station administrator. **Personal:** Born Jan 20, 1951, Atlanta, GA; son of Marion B Parks and Alfred G Parks Sr; married Juanita W Parks, Jun 4, 1978; children: Johnaton Richard. **Career:** WQIM, program director, 1980; WVEE, V-103, assistant program director/music director, 1980-85, sales, 1985-87; WAOK, assistant program director/music director, 1983-89; WIGO Radio, general mgr, 1990-95; WMPZ, Chattanooga, TN, general manager, currently. **Honors/Awds:** Radio Advertising Bureau, Certified Radio Marketing Consultant, 1987. **Special Achievements:** Largest Exclusive Cume Exclusive, 1985; nominated as Jock of the Year, Radio & Records, 1985. **Home Addr:** 4289 Loveless Pl, Ellenwood, GA 30049, (404)241-2894.

PARKS, ARNOLD GRANT
Educator, educational administrator. **Personal:** Born Nov 19, 1939, St Louis, MO; married Lennette Bogee; children: LaShawn Michelle, Anna Louise, Alicia Victoria. **Educ:** Harris Teachers Coll, AA, 1959; Washington Univ, BS, 1962; St Louis Univ, MA, 1964, PhD, 1970. **Career:** St Louis Univ, instructor, 1964-66; Delta Educ Corp, deputy dir, 1966-69; Malone & Hyde Inc, training dir, 1969-71; Memphis State Univ, associate professor, 1971-76; Lincoln Univ, professor of sociology, exec dir, advancement and external affairs, 1976-; Second Christian church, Jefferson City, MO, co-pastor, currently. **Orgs:** Mid-Amer Congress on Aging, board of directors, life mem; National Society of Fundraising Executives; Alpha Phi Alpha, life member; United Methodist Church; Benefits 2000 Task Force, gen bd of Pension Health Benefits, MO East Conf Listening Team; Black Methodists for Church Renewal; Amer Diabetes Assn; Mid-Amer Regional Bd; MO River Regional Library, bd of trustees. **Honors/Awds:** National Science Foundation, faculty fellowships, 1976-79; Ethel Percy Andrus Gerontology Center, post-doctoral fellowship, 1979; Natl White House Conf on Aging, delegate, 1995; numerous other federal and state grants. **Special Achievements:** Author: Urban Education: An Annotated Bibliography, Century 21 Publishing Co, 1981; Black Elderly in Rural America: A Comprehensive Study, Wyndham Hall Press, 1988; Aging and Mental Health: Aging in the Heartland, Kendall-Hunt Publishing Co, 1996; published numerous articles in journals. **Home Addr:** 1521 Timber Trail, Jefferson City, MO 65109, (573)635-0725. **Business Addr:** Professor of Sociology/Executive Director of Advancement & External Affairs, Lincoln University, 820 Chestnut St, Jefferson City, MO 65101-0029, (573)681-5580.

PARKS, BERNARD
Attorney. **Personal:** Born Jun 10, 1944, Atlanta; married Joyce Williams; children: Bernard Jr. **Educ:** Morehouse Coll, BA 1966; Emory Univ Sch of Law, JD 1969. **Career:** Patterson Parks Jackson & Howell, ptr 1973-; Jackson Patterson Parks & Franklin, ptr 1970-73; Jackson & Handler, Asso 1970; Jud Elbert Parr Tuttle United Cir Ct of Appeals, law clk 1969-70; Atla Leg Aid Soc Inc, law asst 1968-69; Sen Horace Ward Atla, leg intern 1968; Aldmn Q V Williamson Atla City, gov intern 1967 Cts admitted to prac Fulton Co GA Sup Ct, GA Ct of Appeals, GA Sup Ct, US Dis Ct, US Ct of Appeals, US Sup Ct. **Orgs:** Co-chmn Men Hlth Com Yng Law Sect; Am Bar Assn; Atla Bar Assn; bd of dir Atla Coun Yng Law; co-chmn Ment Hlth Com GA Bar Assn; vice pres GA Leg Serv Prog Inc; Gate Cty Bar Assn; Nat Bar Assn; Law Com Civ Rights under Law; Chmn bd of dir Opp Ind Cent of Atla; bd dir Opp Ind Cent of Am ; chmn bd of mgrs E Cent Br Butler St YMCA; bd dir Butler St YMCA Assn; Gov Ment Hlth Com Task Force; Met Atla Coun on Crime & Juv Del; chmn Pri Alloc Com Uni Way Allo Com for Comm Sec; Local Govt Task Force Com Atla C of C; Atla Crim Just Coord Com; bd of dir Big Bros Assn; Atla Bus League; Atla Urban League; NAACP; Am Civ Lib Un; SE Region Bd YMCA; Atla Coal on Curr Comm Aff; Omega Psi Phi Frat; Phi Alpha Delta Frat; Y'S Men Int. **Honors/Awds:** Omega Chap Outstndg Young Man of Year in Prof; Mr Psi 1967f Omega Psi Phi Frat Psi Chap Morehouse Coll; WSB Nesmaker Award 1972; five Outstndg Young Men In 1974. **Business Addr:** 101 Marietta Towers, Atlanta, GA 30303.

PARKS, DONALD B.
Physician. **Personal:** Born Nov 2, 1950, Philadelphia, PA; son of Dewitt and Bertha Parks; married Sharon, Jun 20, 1976; children: Laurie, Drew, Sharon-Candace. **Educ:** Temple Univ, 1968; Jefferson Medical Coll of the Thomas Jefferson Univ, 1973; Mercy Catholic Medical Center-Phila, PA, residency, 1978. **Career:** SmithKline-French, group dir of clinical investigation, 1981-85; Parkstone Medical Assoc, physician/medical dir, 1985-. **Orgs:** PA Blue Shield, board member, 1994-97; Philadelphia Police and Fire Dept, consultant, 1983; Dept Health Education and Welfare, consultant, 1979-82; Health Policy and Manpower Comm, consultant, 1980. **Honors/Awds:** NAACP, Exemplar Award, 1992; President James F Carter, Education and Commun Involvement, 1980; Alpha Beta Alpha Sorority, Commun Involvement and Svcs to the Afro-American Historical and Cultural Museum, 1980; Chairman, Development Comm/Morehouse School of Medicine, 1994-; Exec Excellence Prog/National Urban League, board member 1989-92; American Found for Negro Affairs, board member, 1988-. **Business Addr:** President, Parkston Medical Assocs, 2305 N. Broad St., Philadelphia, PA 19132, (215)229-2022.

PARKS, EDWARD Y.
Attorney. **Personal:** Born Feb 5, 1951, Thomson, GA; son of Roy L Parks Sr; married Sequoyah, May 25, 1975; children: Akil-Dabe T, Alkebu S. **Educ:** Otterbein College, BA, 1973; Howard Univ, JD, 1979. **Career:** Ohio Public Interest campaign, assoc dir, 1979-81; Legal Aid Society, attorney, 1981-83; Public Utilities Commission, attorney examiner, 1983-86; Ohio Dept Health, legal counsel, 1986-89; Law Office, Edward YA Parks, president, 1989-. **Orgs:** Assoc Juvenile Attorneys, presiding officer, 1989-; NAACP, 1979-; Urban League, 1991-; Columbus Bar Assoc, 1980-; Natl Conference Black Lawyers, 1980-; Shiloh Baptist Church, trustee, 1993; Legal Aid Society Lawyer Referral, 1989-; Natl Bar Assn, 1993-. **Honors/Awds:** Welfare Rights, Outstanding Legal Advocate, 1983; NAACP, Community Service Award, 1985; Shiloh Baptist Church, Outstanding Service-Softball Program, 1987 & 1988. **Special Achievements:** Shiloh Baptist Church Plan, 1990; Book of Poems-In Progress. **Business Addr:** President & CEO, Law Office, Edward Y A Parks, 8 E Long St, Ste 225, Columbus, OH 43215, (614)228-6535.

PARKS, GEORGE B.
Educator, attorney, consultant. **Personal:** Born in Lebanon, KY; son of Eleanor Parks and George W. Parks; children: Paula Lynn, William Earle. **Educ:** Howard Univ Sch of Law, LLB 1948; George Washington Univ Sch of Law, LLM 1951. **Career:** Coleman Parks & Washington law firm, atty 1948-60; professional consul to title companies 1963-73; LA City Councilman David Cunningham, spl asst 1973-74; Glendale Univ Sch of Law, asst dean/prof of law 1979-80; Summa Corp, consult 1979-84; land use and polit procedure, consul 1984-. **Orgs:** KY Bar Assn; DC Bar Assn; Amer Bar Assn; educ consul to consol Realty Bd; CA Real Estate Advancement Adv Comm; life mem SW Music Symphony Assn; consol Realty Bd; Mid-City C of C; Luth Housing Corp; LA Co Dist Atty Adv Comm; Soc of Amer Law Tchrs; founding dir CA Timeshare Owners Found; consul Timeshare Mgmt Corp; owner/pres Parks Course in Continuing Real Estate Educ 1979-; City of Los Angeles Productivity Commission, president, currently. **Honors/Awds:** Spl Serv Awd Law Enforcement Council Wash 1959; Man of Yr Natl council Bus & Professional Women 1968; Spl Citizens Testimonial Awd LA 1969; Human Rel Awd LA 1970; Man of Yr Crenshaw C of C 1972; LA City Council Awd 1969; Disting Alumni Awd from Howard Univ Alumni Club of Southern CA 1982; Natl Soc of Real Estate Appraisers Educ Awd 1981; Lutheran Housing Corp Awd for Outstanding Leadership 1980; CA State Assoc of Real Estate Brokers Awd 1980; numerous city/county/state awards and citations.

PARKS, GILBERT R.
Psychiatrist. **Personal:** Born May 14, 1944, Arcadia, OK; married Jenice L; children: Garmez, Melanese, Ronee. **Educ:** Cntrl St, BS 1967; Thomas Jefferson Med Coll, MD 1973. **Career:** Topeka St Hosp, psychiatrist; Menninger Found, Topeka, present; Priv Prac, part-time; HEW, 3 yr res Psychiatry complete 1976. **Orgs:** Chmn bd Student Nat Med Assn 1972-73; dir Health Career Progs Philadelphia 1970-72; OK St Dept of Pub Hlth, Environ Hlth Div of Water Quality Control 1967-69; psychiatry asst Hosp of Univ of oK 1965-67; rancher 1960-69; adminstrv consult adv Student Nat Med Assn; mem KS Dist Br of Am Psychiatric Assn; consult Ofc of Hlth Resources Opp, Hlth Resources Adminstrn Dept of HEW; sec Nat Assn of Post Grad Physicians; bd dirs Boys Club Topeka. **Honors/Awds:** Recip Outstanding Ldrshp Awd Stdnt Nat Med Assn; Outstanding Stdnt Awd Med Com Concerned with Civil Rights 1970; Solomon Fuller Fellowship 1975. **Business Addr:** 629 Quincy, #205, Topeka, KS.

PARKS, GORDON ROGER ALEXANDER BUCHANNAN
Film director, author, photographer, composer. **Personal:** Born Nov 30, 1912, Fort Scott, KS; son of Jackson and Sarah Ross Parks; married Genevieve Young, Aug 26, 1973 (divorced 1979); children: Gordon Jr (deceased), David, Toni, Leslie; married Elizabeth Campbell, 1962 (divorced 1973); married Sally Alvis, 1933 (divorced 1961). **Career:** Freelance fashion photographer, 1937-42; Farm Security Admin, correspondent 1942-43; OWI, correspondent 1944; Standard Oil of NJ, correspondent 1945-48; Life, photo-journalist 1948-68; Essence Magazine, founder/editorial director, 1970-73; independent photographer, filmmaker, 1954-. **Orgs:** Schomburg Center for Research in Black Culture, board of directors; NY Urban League; ASCAP; Writer's Guild; NAACP; Academy of Motion Pictures Arts and Sciences; AFTRA; International Mark Twain Society; Newspaper Guild Association; Directors Guild, national director; American Society of Magazine Photographers; National Association for American Composers and Conductors; Stylus Society; US Tennis Association; American Film Institute. **Honors/Awds:** American Society of Magazine Photographers, Photographer of the Year, 1960, 1985; American Library Association, Notable Book Award for A Choice of Weapons, 1966; Emmy Award for Diary of a Harlem Family, 1968; Ohio University, Carr Van Anda Journalism Award, 1970; NAACP, Springarn Medal, 1972, Hall of Fame, 1984; Sons and Daughters of Kansas, Kansan of the Year, 1985; Commonwealth of Massachusetts Communications, National Medal Arts Award, 1988; World Press Photo Award, 1988; NY Mayor's Award, 1989; Artist of Merit Josef Sudek Medal, 1989. **Special Achievements:** Wrote, produced, and directed the films The Learning Tree, 1969; Shaft, 1972; Shaft's Big Score, 1972; The Super Cops, 1974; Leadbelly, 1976; Odyssey of Solomon Northrup, 1984; Moments Without Proper Names, 1986; author: Flash Photography, 1947; Camera Portraits: The Techniques and Principals of Documentary Portraiture, 1948; The Learning Tree, 1963; A Choice of Weapons, 1966; A Poet and His Camera, 1968; Whispers of Intimate Things, 1971; Born Black, 1971; Moments Without Proper Names, 1975; Flavio, 1977; To Smile in Autumn, 1979; Shannon, 1981; Voices in the Mirror, 1990; Arias in Silence, 1994; composed Piano Concerto, 1953; Tree Symphony, 1967; composed film scores for The Learning Tree, Shaft's Big Score, The Odyssey of Solomon Northrup, Moments Without Proper Names, Ballet for Martin Luther King; Glimpses Toward Infinity, 1996; Half Past Autumn, 1997.

PARKS, JAMES CLINTON, JR.
Marketing manager. **Personal:** Born May 12, 1944, Kannapolis, NC; married Corine Musgrave; children: Crystal Westray, James III, Shawnda M. **Educ:** Livingstone Coll, BS 1965. **Career:** EI Du Pont, employment supv 1965-77; US Army, 1st lt 1967-69; Miller Brewing Co, mgr spec mktg prog 1977-. **Orgs:** Mem Phi Beta Sigma 1963-; bd of dir Milwaukee Min Chamber of Comm 1983-86, Waukesha County WI NAACP 1984-86; mem Frontiers Intl 1987-; bd mem Fayetteville State Univ Foundation; bd mem Cal-Pac Corp Advisory Bd. **Honors/Awds:** Order of Long Leaf Pine St of NC 1984; Distinguished Alumnus, Livingstone Coll 1989. **Military Serv:** AUS 1st lt 1966-69. **Business Addr:** Manager-Spec Mkt Programs, Miller Brewing Co, 3939 W Highland, Milwaukee, WI 53201.

PARKS, JAMES DALLAS
Educator. **Personal:** Born Aug 25, 1906, St Louis, MO; married Florence Wright; children: James Peter. **Educ:** Bradley U, BS 1927; St Univ of IA;; MS 1943; Academyy Italia Delle Artiedellavorse Parma Italy, Dliploma of Academician of Italy 1980. **Career:** Lincoln U, emeritus prof of art 1976-, head art dept 1927-76; Sphinx Mag Alpha Phi Alpha, art ed 1956-50. **Orgs:** Past pres Natl Conf of Artists 1961-62; past pres MO Coll Art Conf 1955-56; past commr MO Negro Inter-sch Ath Assn 1943-54; ''Juan Paraja the Man in 5 1/2 Million Dollar Painting'', St Louis Post-dispatch 1970; Co-author Comprehensive Exam for Undergrad; Majors in Asrt History, Educ Testing Serv Princeton NJ 1970. **Honors/Awds:** Spl Honored Alumnus, Bradley Univ 1973; ''Robert Scott Duncanson-19th Cent Black Painter'', Assn for study of Negro Life & History 1980.

PARKS, JAMES EDWARD
Attorney. **Personal:** Born Mar 22, 1946, Pine Bluff, AR; son of Cora Parks and James Parks; married Gwendolyn Jean Fane, Sep 4, 1965; children: James Jr, Latina, Lisa. **Educ:** CA St Univ at Fresno, BS 1972; Harvard Law Sch, JD 1975. **Career:** Dawson & Ninnis Fresno CA; atty 1977-82; San Fernando Val Neighborhood Legal Serv Van Nuys CA, atty 1975-77; Parks & Smith, Fresno, CA, 1982-89; Law Offices of James E Parks, attorney, 1989-. **Orgs:** Mem Fresno Co Bar Assn present; mem CA St Bar & Assn, present; mem Assn of Defense Counsel, present; bd of dirs Fresno Co Legal Servs Legan Advis, Black Polit Council of Fresno 1980; member, Fresno City Bar Assn; member, Fresno Trial Lawyer's Assn; member, United Black Men; member, Black Lawyers Assn of Fresno; member, NAACP; board member, Fresno Tomorrow. **Business Addr:** Attorney, Law Offices of James E Parks, 4944 E Clinton Way, Suite 101, Fresno, CA 93727.

PARKS, PAUL
Corporate executive. **Personal:** Born May 7, 1923, Indianapolis, IN; son of Hazel Parks and Cleab Parks; married Virginia Loftman; children: Paul, Pamela, Stacey. **Educ:** Purdue Univ, BS 1949; MA Inst of Tech, postgrad 1958; University of Massachusetts, Amherst, MA, DEd (ABD), 1985; Northeastern University, Doctor of Engineering, 1994. **Career:** Paul Parks & Associates, Inc, pres, 1979-; Tufts University, School of Engineering, Medford, MA, professor, 1976-90; Commonwealth of MA, sec Educ Affairs 1975-; Boston Model City Admin, admin 1968-75; Architecture & Engineering Firm, Boston, partner 1957-67; Pratt & Whitney Aircraft, nuclear engr 1953-57; Chance Vought Aircraft; missile designer 1952-53; Fahy Spofford & Thorndike, Boston; Stone & Webster Engring, designer 1951; IN St Hwy Commn Indianapolis, 1949-51; Mayors Com for Admin of Justice, consult gen accounting office. **Orgs:** Mem Atty Gen Adv Com on Civil Rights 1961-71; mem Hlth Task Force, Boston Fed Exec Bd; adv Boston Mothers for Adequate Welfare 1966-68; speech therapist, Vets Lang Clinic 1964-66; mem MA Ad Council on Educ 1968-71; MA Commn on Children & Youth 1962-67; chmn MA Adv Com to US Civil Rights Commn 1961-73; chmn Urban Affairs com, MA Fedn of Fair Housing & Equal Rights 1961-67; mem Comm Educ & Council 1961-73; pres com for Comm Educ Devel Inc 1968-74; adult leader Youth Prgms Roxbury UMCA; trustee Peter Bent Brigham Hosp; bd dir MA Planned Parenthood Assn; MA Mental Hlth Assn; MA Soc for Prevention of Blindness; Boston Coll, Upward Bound Prog; registered professional engr; Am Soc of Civil Engrs; Nat Soc of Professional Engrs; Nat Acad of Pub Adminstrn; NAACP; Nat Bd of the Ams for Dem Action 1-74; St Bd of the Am for Dem Action 1970-74; Steering Com, Educ Commn of the States Books; ''Racism'', ''Elitism'', ''Professionalism Barriers to Comm Mental Hlth'' 1976; pres, Board of Librarys, City of Boston, MA; member, educator, Commonwealth of the States, 1976-80; member, Zoning Board of Appeals, City of Boston, 1983-; Boston School Committee, chmn, 1992-95. **Honors/Awds:** Goodwill Industries, Outstanding Service Award; Franconia College, Honorary Degree. **Military Serv:** AUS 1st sgt 1942-46. **Business Addr:** 1 Ashburton Pl, Boston, MA 02108.

PARKS, ROSA
Civil rights activist. **Personal:** Born Feb 4, 1913, Tuskegee, AL; daughter of Leona Edwards McCauley and James McCauley; married Raymond Parks, 1932 (died 1977). **Educ:** Alabama State Coll. **Career:** Dressmaker; life insurance agent; housekeeper; Congressman John Conyers Jr, staff assistant, 1965-88. **Orgs:** Secretary & former youth advisor, Montgomery NAACP, 1943-56; active with SCLC, Detroit & Women's Public Affairs Comm; Women's Public Affairs Committee of 100; deaconess, St Matthew AME Church, Detroit; founder, Rosa & Raymond Parks Institute for Self-Development, 1987. **Honors/Awds:** Refused to give up her bus seat to a white passenger & triggered a bus boycott, which resulted in the outlawing of segregation on city buses in Montgomery, 1955; known as the Mother of the Civil Rights Movement; SCLC sponsors an annual Rosa Parks Freedom Awd; honored by Women's Missionary Soc, AME Church at Quadrennial Conventions, Los Angeles 1971; 10 Honorary Degrees including Shaw Coll in Detroit; Spingarn Medal, NAACP, 1979; Martin Luther King Jr Award, 1980; Service Award, Ebony, 1980; Martin Luther King Jr Nonviolent Peace Prize, 1980; The Eleanor Roosevelt Women of Courage Award, Wonder Women Foundation, 1984; Medal of Honor, awarded during the 100th birthday celebration of the Statue of Liberty, 1986; Martin Luther King Jr Leadership Award, 1987; Adam Clayton Powell Jr Legislat Achievement Award, 1990; Rosa Parks Peace Prize. **Special Achievements:** Co-author w/Jim Haskins, Rosa Parks, My Story, 1992; Quiet Strength; co-produced, Verity Records Presents A Tribute To Rosa Parks.

PARKS, SHERMAN A.
Judge. **Personal:** Born May 15, 1924, Topeka, KS; married Alberta Lewis; children: Sherman Jr. **Educ:** Washburn U, Bba 1949; Washburn Univ Sch of Law, Llb 1955, JD 1970. **Career:** KS Ct of Appeals, judge 1977-; Sec of St, dep asst 1971-76; Atty Gen KS, asst 1968-71; KS Alcoholic Beverage Control, atty 1966-68; Co Atty, 1st asst 1961-66; Pvt Law Prac, 1955-61; KS Supreme Ct; US Dist Ct for KS; 10th Judicial Circuit; US Supreme Ct; Washburn Univ Sch of Law, lectr 1969. **Orgs:** Mem Omega Psi Phi Frat; Chmn pro tem Steward Bd of St John AME Ch 1972-76; chmn bd of regents Washburn Univ 1968-76; mem Selective Serv Bd #71 1967-76; bd dir Topeka UMCA 1966-76; bd trustee Topeka YMCA 1976; bd of gov Washburn Law Sch Assn 1964-72; pres Topeka Council of PTA 1962 st francis hosp adv bd 1962-65; first black to serve on appellate-level ct kS; first black to serve on washburn u bd of regents; first black to serve on the Selective Serv Bd, KS. **Military Serv:** USN yhoeman 1st class 1943-46. **Business Addr:** Judge, Court of Appeals State House, Topeka, KS 66612.

PARKS, THELMA REECE
Educator, city offical. **Personal:** Born Apr 4, Muskogee, OK. **Educ:** Langston U, BS 1945; Univ of OK, M 1955; Central St U, professional cert 1963 additional study 1980-81. **Career:** Oklahoma City Housing Authority, commr 1977-84; US Grant High School; counselor/dept head 1973; Douglass High School, counselor 1970-71, English teacher/dept head 1961-70; Dunbar & Truman Elem Schools, teacher 1951-61; Oklahoma City Board of Education, president, 1990-. **Orgs:** OK City Guidance Assn, president, 1976-77; life mem, NEA; OEA COA; McFarland Br YWCA 1973-; adv, Capitol Improvement Plan OK City 1975-; Adv Com Black Family; NE YMCA; Alpha Kappa Alpha Sor; NAACP; Urban League; board of directors, Urban League Guild; Womens Day speaker, Tabernacle Baptist Church, 1992, Wildwood Christian Ch 1978; chmn, Blue Ribbon Comm Fund Raising 1982-86; bd dir YWCA 1983-86; sec OK City Langston Alumni 1986-88; panelist, OK State Dept of Ed Conf on Educ 1987; board member, Langston Univ Alumni Assoc 1987-90; task force comm, OEA improving schools in OK 1987-; Natl Sor of Phi Delta Kappa; Oklahoma School Board Association, board of directors, 1992; Black Caucus, board of directors, 1992; Urban League Equal Opportunity Day, panelist, 1991; Oklahoma City Education Round Table, founding member, 1991-; Natl Sorority Phi Delta Kappa, gamma Epsilon Chap, OK, pres, 1997; Black Caucus, Natl School Bds Assn, bd of dirs. **Honors/Awds:** National Black College Alumni, Hall of Fame, inductee, Atlanta, GA, 1991; Nu Vista Club, Lady of Distinction, 1991; Oklahoma Achiever's Award, 1989; Alpha Kappa Alpha Sorority, Soror of the Year, 1990; Phi Delta Kappa, Soror of the Year, 1990; Urban League of Oklahoma City, Volunteer of the Year Award, 1990; Langston University, Distinguished Alumni, 1990; Men of Distinction, Outstanding Citizen, 1991; Oklahoma Black Public Administrator Award, 1992; Top Ladies of Distinction, Outstanding Achievement Award, 1997. **Special Achievements:** Elementary School named in her honor, Oklahoma City, 1997; First African-American female trustee, Faith Meml Bapt Ch 1975; first African-American female member, Kappa Delta Pi, Gamma Chap, University of OK 1955. **Business Addr:** Member Representing District #5, Oklahoma City Bd of Education, 900 North Klein St, Oklahoma City, OK 73119.

PARKS-DUNCANSON, LOUISE
Entertainer. **Personal:** Born Mar 19, 1929, Raleigh, NC; married David. **Educ:** Emerson Coll, BA 1951. **Career:** Lu Parks Jazz & Soul Dance Ensemble, dir/leader 1951; prog initiated by Gov Rockefeller & Bd of Educ, dance drama specialist, taught in underprivileged area of NYC; performer in several Broadway plays; appeared w/ensemble on all major TV networks throughout country; concert tour of US colleges & universities.

PARMALEE, BERNIE
Professional football player. **Personal:** Born Sep 16, 1967, Jersey City, NJ; married Angela; children: Nakia Marie, Tre Bernard. **Educ:** Ball State. **Career:** Miami Dolphins, running back, 1992-. **Business Addr:** Professional Football Player, Miami Dolphins, 2269 NW 199th St, Miami, FL 33056, (305)620-5000.

PARMS, EDWIN L.
Attorney. **Personal:** Born Jun 18, 1937; son of Ophelia Parms and Johnson Parms; married Margaret; children: Stephanie, Deborah. **Educ:** Univ of Akron, BA 1960, JD 1965. **Career:** Parms, Purnell & Gilbert, atty 1965-; Akron Pub Schs, tchr 1960-65; St Univ of Akron, co-counsel. **Orgs:** Mem Local, State & Am Bar Assn; mem Black & Barristers Club; legal counsel Akron NAACP, past br pres; Salvation Army Bd; United Way Bd; Visiting Nurses Bd; Local Urban League Bd; Fair Housing Bd; Co Legal Aid Bd; co-author Akron Plan, plan to get more blacks in Akron construction industry; mem Akron Rew Devel Bd; mem Eta Tau Lambda Chpt, Alpha Phi Alpha Frat; chmn spl library proj working to improve reading abilities minority youth; mem States Citizens Task Force on Higher Edn; pres Akron Frontiers Inc; Wesley Temple AME Zion Ch; sec of Akron Bar Assoc. **Honors/Awds:** First black chosen Young Man of Yr, Akron Jr C of C. **Military Serv:** AUS 1st Lt.

PARNELL, ARNOLD W.
Business executive. **Personal:** Born Jan 21, 1936, Philadelphia, PA; son of Eva Parnell and Jesie Parnell; married Thelma; children: Steven, Paula, Michael. **Educ:** Villanova Univ, BSCE 1957; USC, MSCE 1962; USC & UCLA, postgraduate. **Career:** Nellson Candies, original owner & founder 1962-68; N Amer Aviation, sr research engineer 1957-62; P&L Mgmt Systems, corporate dir 1972-; TRW Systems Group, div staff mgr 1962-82, dir indus research center 1982-86; ELI Mgmt Corp, general mgr 1986-. **Orgs:** Professional license Mechanical Engineering; mem Small Business Devel Advisory Bd; Amer Inst of Aeronautics & Astronautics 1967-; assoc fellow AIAA 1970. **Business Addr:** General Manager, ELI Management Corporation, 15201 So Broadway, Gardena, CA 90248.

PARNELL, JOHN V., III
Business executive. **Personal:** Born Oct 4, 1944, Boston, MA; married Patricia Meehan; children: Elizabeth, Monica, Andrea. **Educ:** Univ MA, BS 1966. **Career:** General Foods Corp, sr food tech 1966-72; Latouraine Bickford's, new prod devel mgr 1972; Miralin Co, prod devel mgr 1972-74; General Foods Corp, lab mgr, sr lab mgr, 1974-90; Kraft General Foods, group director, 1990-95; Kraft Foods, group director, currently. **Orgs:** Pres AEPI Frat 1965, vice pres Class 66; mem Inst of Food Technologist; pres Univ MA Alumni Assn 1975-77, vice pres 1973-75; bd of dir Univ MA Alumni Assn 1970-80; Univ MA Found Inc 1977-80; past mem Sportsmens Club of Greater Boston. **Honors/Awds:** Outstanding Sr Awd 1966; Distinguished Serv to Univ Awd Univ MA 1977; Black Achievers in Industry Awd YMCA of Greater NY Harlem Br 1979. **Business Addr:** Group Director-Technical Research, Kraft General Foods, 250 North St, White Plains, NY 10625.

PARNELL, WILLIAM CORNELLUS, JR.
Accountant. **Personal:** Born Feb 10, 1940, Burton, SC; married Carolyn E Howard; children: Wanda, Debra, Monique. **Educ:** Univ Detroit, MBA 1974; Howard U, BA 1962; Mil Comptrollership; honor cert 1969; Walsh Coll Bus. **Career:** Independent Fin Serv Inc, pres, chief fin dir; Vickers Inc, bus analyst 1974-86; Ford Mtr Co Birmingham MI, financial analyst 1968-74; Citizens Crusade Against Poverty, Washington, comptroller 1966-68; Defense Contract Audit Agy, Alexandria VA, auditor 1965-66; practicing accountant & tax practitioner; US Treasury Card Holder #04857. **Orgs:** MI Ind Accounts Assn; Nat Assn Accountants; Inst Mgmt Accountants; Nat Black MBA Assn; Assn of MBA Exec; Nat Assn of Black Accountants; Nat Soc Enrolled Fed Tax Agents; treas, vice pres Howard U; Alumni Club Detroit; Omega Psi Phi Frat; Luth Intl Mens League; panelist Detroit Ind Adv Group; life mem NAACP 1980; treasurer, Hope United Methodist Church, 1990-93; vice chair, finance, Hope UM Church, 1994-95. **Honors/Awds:** City of Detroit, Community Award for Business Leadership, 1990; Howard Univ, Alumni Award for Outstanding Commitment, 1992; Hope United Methodist Church, Outstanding Leadership, 1993. **Military Serv:** US Army 1st lt 1962-64; USAR capt 1964-75; Mil Hon Ribbon 1961; Army QM Theater Operations Ft Lee VA 1967; Letter of Commendation Command Post Exercise; Finance and Accounting Officer, US Army Reserve, Detroit, Michigan. **Business Addr:** President, Chief Fin Dir, Independent Financial Serv Inc, 19750 James Couzens Dr, Detroit, MI 48235.

PARRIS, ALVIN, III
Clergyman, music minister. **Personal:** Born Sep 23, 1951, Washington, DC; son of L Edith Simmons Parris and Alvin Parris Jr; married Debra Bryant Parris, Jul 16, 1976; children: Benjamin James, Christopher Alvin, Jonathan Gregory, Cherise Danielle. **Educ:** Eastman School of Music, Rochester, NY, Bachelor of Music Education, 1973. **Career:** Rochester City School District (John Marshall High School), Rochester, NY, orchestra dir, 1973-79; Parris Community School for the Performing Arts, Rochester, NY, dir, 1975-; University of Rochester, Rochester, NY, gospel choir dir, music instructor, 1976-; Golden Heights Christian Center, Brockport, NY, music pastor, 1987-90; Syracuse Symphony Orchestra, Syracuse, NY, dir, Project 2000 program, composer, conductor, 1990-; New Life Fellowship, Rochester, NY, assoc pastor, music minister, 1990-. **Orgs:** Member, Rochester Rotary Club, 1987-89; music dir, Greater-Rochester Martin Luther King Festival Commission, 1986-. **Honors/Awds:** Artistic Achievement Award, Colgate-Rochester Divinity School, 1987; Community Service Award, Saint Monica School, 1986. **Business Addr:** Associate Pastor, New Life Fellowship, 362 Columbia Ave, Rochester, NY 14611.

PARRISH, CLARENCE R.
Circuit court judge. **Personal:** Born Oct 22, 1921, Louisburg, NC; married Mildred; children: Sheila, Sharon. **Educ:** St Johns Univ, LLB; Univ WI, LLM. **Career:** Private Practice, Milwaukee attorney; Circuit Court Milwaukee, judge. **Orgs:** Mem Am WI & Milwaukee Bar Assns, Natl Bar Assn; mem bd State Bar Commrs; appeal counsel Local Draft Bd #44; past pres Milwaukee NAACP; past pres Chaplaincy Ct Serv; mem adv bd trustees Gr Milwaukee YWCA; lectured 3 yrs Milwaukee Area Teach Coll evening sch part time lecturer 2 yrs on law politics& religion; mem Amer Bd Arbitration; writer short stories & essays; Univ WI Law Sch Charter mem Omega Frat Milwaukee; Ct Commr for Milwaukee Courts; magistrate Milwaukee Co; trustee & deacon Calvary Baptist Ch; author novel; contrib literary pubs. **Honors/Awds:** Honors & awds, from Omega Phi Psi, YMCA; former gen counsel Central City Dev Corp. **Military Serv:** Veterab WW II overseas. **Business Addr:** Judge, Circuit Court, 901 N 9th St, Milwaukee, WI 53233.

PARRISH, JAMES NATHANIEL
Insurance company executive. **Personal:** Born Feb 3, 1939, Winter Park, FL; son of Celeste Colston Parrish and Amos L Parrish; married Carolyn Portia Payne, Feb 24, 1962 (divorced 1984); children: Bethany C, James N Jr. **Educ:** Fisk University, BA, 1958; University of Wisconsin, MS, 1960. **Career:** Western & Southern Life Insurance Co, assistant actuary, 1960-67; Inter-Ocean Insurance Co, vice pres, actuary, 1967-74; Sun Life Insurance Co of America, second vice president, New Business, 1974-75; Towers, Perrin, Foster & Crosby, consultant, 1975-79; Fidelity Mutual Life Insurance Co, vice president, actuary, 1979-86; NC Mutual Life Insurance Co, senior vice president, actuary, 1986-90; NC Mutual Life Insurance Co, executive vice pres, 1990-. **Orgs:** Society of Actuaries, fellow, 1971-; American Academy of Actuaries, 1969-. **Business Addr:** Executive Vice President, North Carolina Mutual Life Insurance Co, 411 W Chapel Hill St, Durham, NC 27701, (919)682-9201.

PARRISH, JOHN HENRY
Clergyman. **Personal:** Born Dec 14, 1924, Clarkdale, AR; married Marie Jones; children: John Jr, Roland. **Educ:** Manassas High School, diploma 1942. **Career:** Hammond Branch NAACP, pres 1959/1972; 3rd Dist Hammond, councilman 1972-91; First Tabernacle Baptist Church, pastor 1977-. **Military Serv:** USN seaman 1st class 3 yrs. **Home Addr:** 1108 Cleveland St, Hammond, IN 46320. **Business Addr:** Pastor, First Tabernacle Baptist Church, 643 W 41st St, Gary, IN 46408.

PARRISH, MAURICE DRUE
Museum administrator. **Personal:** Born Mar 5, 1950, Chicago, IL; son of Ione Yvonne Culumns Parrish and Maurice Parrish; married Gail Marie Sims Parrish, Sep 2, 1978; children: Theodore, Andrew, Brandon, Cara. **Educ:** University of Pennsylvania, Philadelphia, PA, BA, 1972; Yale University, New Haven, CT, Masters, Architecture, 1975. **Career:** City of Chicago, city planner, 1975-81, John D Hiltscher & Assoc Architects, Chicago, IL, vice pres, 1981-83; Barnett, Jones, Smith Architects, Chicago, IL, principal, 1983-84; City of Chicago, zoning administrator, 1984-87, building commissioner, 1987-89; Detroit Institute of Arts, Detroit, MI, deputy dir, 1989-. **Orgs:** Member, Lambda Alpha Land Use Society, 1985; member, Chicago Economic Dev Commission, 1987-89; chairman, St Philip Neri School Board, 1982-85; president, South Shore Commission, 1983-85. **Honors/Awds:** State and Local Government Program, Harvard University, 1988; King/Chavez/Parks, Visiting Prof, University of Michigan, 1991; H I Feldman Fellow, 1974-75, Franklin W Gregory Scholar, 1973-74, Yale University; National Achievement Scholarship Corporation (NMSC), 1968-72. **Business Addr:** Deputy Director, Detroit Institute of Arts, 5200 Woodward Ave, Detroit, MI 48202.

PARRISH, RUFUS H.
Physician (retired). **Personal:** Born in Donora, PA; son of Mary E Wright Parrish and Rufus Parrish; married Alma Marion, Nov 24, 1957. **Educ:** St Augustine's Coll, BS (magna cum laude) 1938; Meharry Med Coll, MD (honors) 1944. **Career:** Wayne Co Genl Hosp, staff psychiatrist 1964-68, asst dir psych serv 1969-73; Wayne Co Mentl Health Clinic, dir 1973-76; Kirwood Mental Health Ctr; consultant; Highland Park Mental Health Ctr, consultant; Wayne State Univ Coll of Medicine, instructor 1969-; Walter P Reuther Psychiatric Hosp Westland MI, dir of psychiatric serv 1979-91. **Orgs:** Courtesy staff Psychiatric Div Harper-Grace Hosp 1977-; mem NAACP, Mason (Prince Hall Affil) 32nd degree Shriner; Detroit Chap of Natl Guardsmen Inc; mem Kappa Alpha Psi, St Matthew-St Joseph Episcopal Church; diplomate of Amer Bd Psychia and Neurology 1967; diplomate Amer Bd of Quality Assurance and Utilization Review Physicians 1985.

PARRON, DELORES L.
Government official. **Personal:** Born Jan 14, 1944, Red Bank, NJ; daughter of Ruth Parron and James W Parron (deceased). **Educ:** Georgian Court Coll, BA 1966; Cath Univ Amer, MSW 1968, PhD 1977. **Career:** Dept Human Resources, soc worker 1968-69; Childrens Hosp Natl Med Ctr, psychiat soc worker 1969-71; Coll Med Howard Univ, asst prof 1971-78; Fed City Coll, lecturer 1973-75; Pres's Comm on Mental Health White House, soc sci analy 1977-78; Inst Med Acad Scis, prin staff ofcr 1978-83; Natl Inst of Mental Health, assoc dir. **Orgs:** Bd mem Assoc Catholic Charities; bd dir Bur of Rehab 1977; bd mem Pacifica WPFW-FM 1976-78, Area A Comm Mental Health Ctr 1977-79; mem Acad of Certified Soc Workers 1975-, Natl Assoc of Soc Workers; bd dir Phyllis Wheatley YWCA 1974. **Honors/Awds:** Kappa Gamma Phi Acheivement Awd Georgian Ct Coll 1966; Fellowship Grad Study Cath Univ of Amer; mem Sigma Phi Sigma Natl Hon Soc 1964; parron Soc &psychol Dimensions of Behavior; A Reader for Student Physicians 1974; parron Mental Health Serv in Gen Health Care 1980, Health & Behavior 1982. **Business Addr:** Associate Dir, Natl Inst of Mental Health, 5600 Fishers Lane, Rockville, MD 20857.

PARROTT-FONSECA, JOAN
Government official. **Educ:** Georgetown University Law School. **Career:** US General Services Administration, Office of Enterprise Development, assoc administrator, until 1995; Minority Business Development Agency, Dept of Commerce, dir, 1995-. **Special Achievements:** First woman named director of Minority Business Development Agency. **Business Addr:** Director, Minority Business Development Agency, US Dept. of Commerce, 14 St. Const. Ave. E St., Washington, DC 20230, (202)482-2000.

PARSON, WILLIE L.
Educator. **Personal:** Born Apr 25, 1942, Newellton, LA; married Sylvia Sanders. **Educ:** So Univ Baton Rouge, BS Biol 1963; Washington State Univ, MS Microbiology 1967, PhD Microbiology 1971. **Career:** So Univ Baton Rouge, instructor biology dept 1963-65; WA State Univ, teaching asst 1965-67, rsch asst 1965-67; The Evergreen State Coll, mem of the faculty 1971-74, sr acad dean 1974-78, mem of the faculty-microbiology 1978-. **Orgs:** Panelist for grants review Natl Sci Found 1977-80; mem Amer Soc for Microbiology; mem Amer Assn for the Advancement of Scis; mem Phi Delta Kappa Educ Soc; mem Alpha Phi Alpha Frat. **Honors/Awds:** Outstanding Young Man of Amer-Outstanding Young Men of Amer Inc 1977. **Business Addr:** Faculty-Microbiology, The Evergreen State Coll, Lab II 2249, Olympia, WA 98505.

PARSONS, KARYN
Actress. **Personal:** Born in Hollywood, CA. **Career:** NBC-TV, "The Fresh Prince of Bel Air," actress, until 1996; film appearance, Class Act, 1992, Major Payne, 1995; appearances on television series "Bronx Zoo," "Hunter," "Capitol News" and "Rough House.". **Business Addr:** Actress, Fresh Prince of Bel-Air, c/o NBC-TV, 3000 W Alameda Blvd, Burbank, CA 91523-0001, (818)840-4444.

PARSONS, PHILIP I.
Financial services executive. **Personal:** Born Nov 18, 1941, Cherry Hill, NJ; son of Kathyrn M Beverly-Brooks Parsons and Nathaniel I Banks Parsons; children: Andrea LaVerne. **Educ:** Gettysburg Coll, BA 1964; Harvard Business School, MBA 1972; IL Inst of Tech, MPA 1988. **Career:** Scott Paper Co, sales mgr 1964-70; Quaker Oats Co, market mgmt 1973-78; AT&T, staff mgr 1979-82; Perfect Pinch Inc, Soft Sheen Products, general mgr 1982-90; Equitable Financial Services, manager, beginning 1991; Ubia Financial Services, president, chief executive officer, currently. **Orgs:** Bd mem Hyde Park Neighborhood Club 1978; pres 3100 S King Dr Condo Assn 1984-87; trustee Gettysburg Coll 1986-91; mem East Bank Club 1987; bd mem, Chicago Youth Center, Robbins, IL, 1992. **Honors/Awds:** Trainee of the Cycle Fort Dix NJ 1964; Outstanding Salesman Scott Paper Co 1968; Regional Representative Tau Kappa Epsilon 1975; Article on Minority Business Grocery Marketing 1986; Calvary Youth Council Award, Calvary Baptist Church, 1982; Chicago Boys Club Award, 1989. **Military Serv:** US Army lt. **Business Addr:** President, CEO, Ubia Financial Services, 401 N Michigan Ave, Ste 1450, Chicago, IL 60611.

PARSONS, RICHARD
Company executive. **Personal:** Born 1949, Queens, NY; married Laura; children: Gregory, Leslie, Rebecca. **Educ:** University of Hawaii; Union University's Albany Law School, 1971. **Career:** Patterson, Belknap, Webb and Tyler, New York, former attorney/partner; counsel to Nelson A. Rockefeller and former Pres Gerald R Ford; chief executive officer, Dime Savings Bank, New York, beginning 1988; New York City, Economic Devt Corp, chairman, currently; Time Warner Inc, pres, 1995-. **Business Addr:** President, Time Warner Inc., 75 Rockefeller Plaza, New York, NY 10019, (212)484-8000.

PASCHAL, ELOISE RICHARDSON
Educator (retired). **Personal:** Born Feb 7, 1936, Hartsville, SC; married Willie Lee Paschal; children: William. **Educ:** Benedict Coll, AB 1954-58; Atlanta Univ, MSLS 1967. **Career:** Tooms Cty GA Public Schools, teacher 1958-60; Americus Public Schools, teacher 1960-65, career media spec, beginning 1965. **Orgs:** Mem Sumter Cty Mental Health Assoc 1971-, Flint River Girl Scout Council 1982-; chmn Sumter Cty Mental Health Mental Retardation Bd of Dir 1982-84; mem Amer Library Assoc, Amer Assoc of School Librarians, Natl Ed Assoc, GA Assoc of Educ, GA Library Assoc, Third Dist Dept; pres GA Library Media; Georgia Southwestern State Univ Foundation; advisory council, Rosalynn Carter Carenet; elected, Americas City Council; Delta Sigma Theta Sorority. **Honors/Awds:** Woman of the Year Boy Scout Units #226 1980; Disting Serv Awd Sumter Cty Mental Health Assoc 1982. **Home Addr:** 310 Vista Drive, Americus, GA 31709. **Business Addr:** Career Media Specialist, Staley Middle School, 915 North Lee St, Americus, GA 31709.

PASCHAL, WILLIE L.
Educational administration. **Personal:** Born May 9, 1926, Americus Sumter, GA; married Eloise Richardson; children: William Stanley. **Educ:** Morehouse Coll, BA Bus Admin 1949; Atlanta Univ, MA Educ & Admin 1957; GA State Univ Atlanta GA, EdS EAS 1978. **Career:** Webster Cty Bd of Educ Preston GA, principal/teacher 1949-52; Twiggs Cty Bd of Educ, teacher 1952-53; Sumter Cty Bd of Educ, principal/teacher 1953-72; Amer Bd of Public Ed, principal 1972-; Eastview Elementary School, principal. **Orgs:** Life mem Alpha Phi Alpha Frat Inc 1949-; asst sec Amer/Sumter Cty Payroll Dev Auth 1980-; sr vice comm Amer Legion Dept of GA 1984-85; mem NAESP,GAESP 3rd Dist 1984-85, Phi Delta Kappa 1984-85, GAEL 1984-85; mem team chmn Chamber of Comm 1985. **Honors/Awds:** Distinguished Citizen Mental Health Assoc of Sumter Cty 1982; Disting Serv Mental Health Assoc of Sumter Cty 1982. **Military Serv:** AUS corpl 1 yr 4 mo's. **Home Addr:** 310 Vista Dr, Americus, GA 31709.

PASCHALL, EVITA ARNEDA
Attorney, editor, publisher. **Personal:** Born May 18, 1951, Augusta, GA; daughter of Lucille T Paschall and Marion R Paschall; married Felix Bryan Andrews, May 5, 1990; children: Felix Bryan, Jr., Evita Lucille Young. **Educ:** Howard Univ, BA, 1973; Univ of Georgia, JD, 1976. **Career:** Augusta Judicial Circuit, asst district attorney, 1976-79; Brown & Paschall Attorneys at Law, attorney, 1979-81; State Court of Georgia, Augusta, assistant solicitor, 1982-84; Magistrate Court, Augusta, GA, assistant solicitor, 1984-86, solicitor, 1986-94; Augusta Today Magazine, editor, publisher, currently; Evita A Paschall PC, attorney, begin 1981; Municipal Court, judge, 1994-. **Orgs:** Augusta Conference of African-American Attorneys, president, 1992-93; Augusta Jaycees; Leadership Augusta; Natl Bar Assn, 1983-; Bethlehem Community Center, bd of dirs, 1984-95. **Honors/Awds:** WHAM, Woman of the Year, 1973; Outstanding Young Women of America, 1979. **Home Addr:** 3835 Villa Ln, Martinez, GA 30907. **Business Addr:** Attorney, Evita A Paschall, PC, 137 Broad St, PO Box 2201, Augusta, GA 30901, (706)722-0174.

PASSMORE, JUANITA CARTER
Marketing executive. **Personal:** Born Mar 4, 1926, Chicago, IL; married Maymon Passmore. **Educ:** Long Beach City College; Columbia College. **Career:** Johnson Prod Co, director of special promotions; Totaly Beauty You, TV Program host. **Orgs:** Founder, 69 Choppi Block Club; chmn, Natl Media Women; parliamentarian, Chicago Chapter, Women's Board, Operation PUSH; chmn, Fashion Therapy Mental & Health; mem, Operation Snowball. **Honors/Awds:** Media Woman of Yr Awd Chicago Chap 1974; Outstng Woman of Yr, Chicago S End Jaycees Women Assn 1977; Comm Wrkr Debutante Master AME Ch 1977.

PASSMORE, WILLIAM A.
Job developer. **Personal:** Born Apr 4, 1929, E Chicago, IN. **Educ:** Calumet Coll, BS; Wayne St U; E Chicago Bus Coll IN U. **Career:** Red Top Cab Co, dispatcher 1951-63; Vetold Photo, ofc mgr 1950-51; IN Univ Spl Services, adminstrv asst 1970-73; Chicago Daily Defender, columnist 1954; Neighborhood Youth Corps, work coord 1965-73; E Chicago Fed Prog, manpower splst 1973; Com on Emp of Handicapped, pres 1969, gov 1970. **Orgs:** Mem Nat Rehab Assn 1970; vice pres E Chicago Lib Trustees; mem Am Lib Trustees Assn; del White House Conf on Handicapped Indvls 1977; adv council IN St; Civil Rights Commn 1 975; adv bd mem E Chgo Salvation Army 1976; Urban League for Veterans 1976; adv bd St Catherines Hosp for Accessibility 1977; bd dir E Chicago Exchange Club; Com on New Central HS; bd dir Consumer Credit Cnslng Serv of NW IN; mem Mid Am Educ Oppty Personnel Prgm; Natl Parpalegic Found 1972; past pres E Chicago Exchange Club; bd dir Camp Fire Girls; bd dir Tri-city Mental Hlth; past bd dir Natl Easter Seal Soc; past pres E Chicago Jaycees; past sec Anselm Forum; bd dir Referral Emerg Serv NW IN; past bd dir Twin City Comm Serv; past asst supt St Mark AME Ch; memPirate Trade Winds; co-chmn Wheel Chair Bsktbl & JCI InSenate 5817; exec bd Trade Winds Rehabv Ctr; gov St Youth Counc; gov St Commn on Handicapped. **Honors/Awds:** Recipient EC Cit of Month, Book of Golden Deeds E Chicago Exchange; Outstndng New Jaycees; Evelyn Davis Eastern Star Awd for Achvmnt; Hoosier Handicapped Awd for 1968; Handicapped Am 1969 Duble Amputee; hon mem cert for IN St Prison; St Catherine Visitor of Yr Awd; IN Mason Outstndng Man of Yr Awd; E Chicago Mason Otstndng Achvmnt Awd; St Mark AME Zion Ch Handicapped Awd 1968; Rotary Club Good Cit Awd 1971. **Business Addr:** 3522 1/2 Main St, East Chicago, IN 46312.

PASTEUR, ALFRED BERNARD
Educator. **Personal:** Born Apr 14, 1947, Ocala, FL. **Educ:** FL A&M Univ, AB; IN Univ, MS; Northwestern Univ, PhD. **Career:** Temple Univ, asst prof; Chicago Bd of Educ, counselor admins; Hunter Coll, prof, currently. **Orgs:** Mem Dayton OH Model Cities, Morgan State Coll, Bethune Cookman Coll, MN State Dept of Educ, Kennedy Found, Atlanta Univ, Chicago Career Oppor Prog, Southern Univ, Savannah State Coll, OIC Phila, Princeton Univ, Univ of Delaware, Univ of TX Austin, Virgin Islands Univ; mem Amer Personnel & Guidance Assn, Amer Psychol Assn, Assn of Black Psychol, Phi Delta Kappa, Assn for Non-White Concerns in Personnel & Guidance; devel stages of Black Self-Discovery Journal of Negro Educ 1972; soul music technique for therapeutic intervention Journal of Non-White Concerns 1972; Therapeutic Dimensions of the Black Aesthetic Journal of Non-White Concerns 1976; publication "Roots of Soul, A Psychology of Black Expressiveness" Doubleday Press 1982; "Black Academic &Cultural Excellence" Alliance for Black SEducators 1984; rsch travel to Nigeria, W Africa, Senegal, Ghana, Haiti, Trinidad, Barbados, Brazil, Jamaica, Virgin Islands.

PATE, JOHN W., SR. (JOHNNY)
Musician, composer, conductor (retired), arranger. **Personal:** Born Dec 5, 1923, Chicago Heights, IL; son of Nora R Pate and Charles H Pate Sr; married Carolyn; children: John Jr, Yvonne, Donald, Brett. **Educ:** Midwestern Conservatory of Music Chicago 1950; UCLA Elec Music, Script Writ, Act-Dir workshop. **Career:** Professional bass player, composer, producer, arranger, Chicago, 1946-; Johnny Pate Trio, Chicago, founder, musician, 1957-62; ABC Records, Chicago, midwest director of A&R, 1963-65; MGM-Verve Records, NY, east coast director of artists & repetoire, 1966-68. **Orgs:** Pres of Yvonne Publ & Nod-Jon Mus pub cons. **Special Achievements:** First African-American to become president of Local NARAS Recording Academy, Chicago Chapter; member of BMI 25yrs; composer of musical scores for following films: Shaft in Africa, 1973; Satan's Triangle, 1975; Bucktown, 1975; Dr Black & Mr. Hyde, 1976; Sudden Death, 1976; Every Girl Must Have One, 1978; musical director for the following TV productions: "The Lou Rawls Special," 1979; "Future Stars," 1979; "The Richard Pryor Show," 1977; produced and/or arranged albums for numerous artists including: Wes Montgomery, Kenny Burrell, Peabo Bryson, The Bee Gees, Natalie Cole, Gladys Knight & The Pips, BB King, Stan Getz, Ruth Brown, Curtis Mayfield, Ahmad Jamal, Joe Williams, Jimmy Smith, the late Minnie Riperton, and the late Donny Hathaway. **Military Serv:** US Army, 1943-46. **Home Addr:** 7463 Trudy Lane, Las Vegas, NV 89123.

PATERSON, BASIL ALEXANDER
Attorney. **Personal:** Born Apr 27, 1926, New York, NY; son of Evangeline Rondon and Leonard J Paterson; married Portia Hairston; children: David, Daniel. **Educ:** St John's Coll, BS 1948; St John's Univ, JD 1951. **Career:** Paterson Michael Jones & Cherot Esqs, partner 1956-77; Inst for Mediation & Conflict Resolution, pres & chief exec officer 1972-77; City of NY, dep mayor for labor relations 1978; State of NY, sec of state 1979-82; Meyer, Suozzi, English & Klein, PC, partner. **Orgs:** Mem NY State Senate 1965-70; mem NY State Temp Commn for Revision of New York City Charter; v chmn Dem Nat Com 1972-78; Judicial Screening Comm for Second Dept chair 1985-95; NYS Judicial Nominations Commission mem 1986-; chairman, Mayor's Committee on the Judiciary, 1990-93; commissioner, The Port Authority of New York and New Jersey, 1989-95. **Honors/Awds:** Eagleton Inst of Politics Award Excellence in Politics 1967; Black Expo Award f1973; Interracial Justice Cath Interracial Counc 1978; Humanitarian Award Coalition of Black Trade Unionists 1980; St John's Univ Medal of Excellence; City Univ of NY Kibbee Awd for Outstanding Public Serv & Achievement, 1987; PSC Friend of CUNY Award, 1989. **Home Addr:** 40 W 135th St, New York, NY 10037.

PATES, HAROLD
Educational administrator. **Career:** Kennedy-King College, Chicago IL, president. **Business Addr:** Kennedy-King College, Chicago, IL 60621.

PATIN, JOSEPH PATRICK
Physician. **Personal:** Born Jan 10, 1937, Baton Rouge, LA; son of Harriet D Patin and Henry W Patin; married Rose; children: Joseph, Karla. **Educ:** Univ MI, BS Meharry Med Coll, MD 1964. **Career:** Pvt Prac, physician; 85th Evac Hosp, chf surgery 1970-71; Raymond W Bliss Army Hosp, 1969; St Elizabeth Hosp, res 1964-69; LA St U, asso prof. **Orgs:** Mem Baton Rouge Parish Bd Hlth; Kappa Alpha Psi; Cancer So of Grtr Baton Rouge; Operation Upgrade Baton Rouge; Baton Rouge Med Soc; So Med Assn; Nat Med Assn Diplomate Bd Surgeons 1970; director, Burn Unit, assistant director, Trauma Unit, currently; Diplomat, bd of surgical critical care, 1992. **Honors/Awds:** Fellow, Amer Coll Surgeons. **Military Serv:** AUS, MAJ, Bronze Star, Dist Med. **Business Addr:** 7777 Hennessy Blvd, Ste 306, Suite 100, Baton Rouge, LA 70806.

PATIN, JUDE W. P.
Military officer. **Personal:** Born Jan 25, 1940, Baton Rouge, LA; son of Mary Harriett Domingue Patin and Henry Wilmot Patin; married Rose Marie Darensbourg Patin, Aug 22, 1964; children: Michelle, Steve. **Educ:** Southern Univ, Baton Rouge, LA, BS, architectural engineering, 1962; Arizona State Univ, Tempe, AZ, MA, industrial engineering, 1971; Harvard Univ, Cambridge, MA, John F Kennedy School of Govt & Public Management Senior Executive Course, 1990; US Army Engineer Officer Advanced Course; US Army Command & General Staff College; Natl Security Mgmt Course, Industrial Coll of the Armed Forces; US Army War Coll. **Career:** US Army, 1962-; brigadier general, currently. **Orgs:** Alpha Phi Mu Industrial Engineering Honor Society; US co-chair on four intl joint commissions dealing w/elements of water resource mgmt on the Great Lakes; vice pres, Soc of Amer Military Engineers, 1991; mem, American Public Works Assn; mem, Assn of the US Army. **Honors/Awds:** Alpha Phi Mu Industrial Engineering Honor Society; Black Engineer of the Year, 1991; numerous public presentations involving engineering & military defense concerns, including speeches, briefings, articles and public letters; registered professional engineer in Wisconsin. **Military Serv:** Legion of Merit w/Oak Leaf Cluster; Bronze Star Medal w/Oak Leaf Cluster; Meritorious Service Medal, w/Oak Leaf Cluster; Air Medal (second award); Army Commendation Medal (second Oak Leaf Cluster); Natl Defense Service Medal (second Oak Leaf Cluster); Army Service Ribbon w/Oak Leaf Cluster; Overseas Service Ribbon w/Oak Leaf Cluster; Republic of Vietnam Campaign Medal; Republic of Vietnam Cross of Gallantry w/Palm; Meritorious Unit Citation; Republic of Vietnam Civil Actions Meritorious Unit Citation; US Army Parachutist Badge. **Business Addr:** Commanding General/Div Engineer, US Army Corps of Engineers, North Central Div, 111 N Canal St, 12th Fl, HQ NCD Command Suite, Chicago, IL 60604.

PATNETT, JOHN HENRY
Business executive. **Personal:** Born Nov 21, 1948, New Orleans, LA; son of Mary Patnett and Melvin Patnett; married Lynn J Patnett. **Educ:** Southern Univ of New Orleans, BA 1971; Southern Univ Baton Rouge LA, Cert Furn Upholstery 1980. **Career:** LA Black Republican Council, director of public relations, 1983-85; Mel & Son Upholstery Inc, pres. **Orgs:** Bd mem US Selective Service 1980. **Honors/Awds:** Certificate of Merit Outstanding Comm Serv 1974; apptd to Orleans Parish Republican Exec Comm 1985. **Business Addr:** President, Mel & Son Upholstery, Inc, 2001 Touro, New Orleans, LA 70116.

PATRICK, CHARLES NAMON, JR.
Business executive. **Personal:** Born Feb 5, 1949, Birmingham, AL; son of Rutha Mae Robbins Patrick and Charles Patrick; married Gwendolyn Stephanie Batiste Patrick, Apr 13, 1975; children: Gentry Namon Patrick, Jessica Sherrie Patrick, Charles Stephan Patrick III, Hope Naomi Patrick, John Paul Patrick. **Educ:** Coll of Data Processing, Los Angeles CA; Life Underwriters Training Council, certificate of completion, 1979. **Career:** VIP Manufacturing, North Hollywood CA, sales dist, 1970-76; Prudential Insurance Co, Los Angeles CA, sales agent/manager, 1976-82; Pioneer Capital & Associates, Dallas TX, western reg vice pres, 1982-83, owner, 1982-84; Patrick, Patrick & Associates, Lawndale CA, pres, 1984; Austin Diversified Products, Ingelwood CA, corp sales mgr, 1985-88; PPA Industries, Compton CA, owner, 1988-. **Orgs:** Admin/asst, The Way Church at Ingelwood, 1981, block club president, Action Block Club, 1982-85; mem, Greater LA Visitors & Convention Bureau, 1984, program coordinator, Black Amer Response to the African Community (BARAC), 1987-88; counselor, Fellowship West Youth Ministries, 1987-88. **Honors/Awds:** Business Man of the Year, ACC News, 1985. **Business Addr:** Owner, PPA Industries/Pioneer Patrick & Associates Industries, PO Box 5365, Compton, CA 90224-5365.

PATRICK, DEVAL L.
Government official. **Personal:** Born Jul 31, 1956, Chicago, IL; son of Laurdine Kenneth Patrick and Emily Mae Wintersmith; married Diane Louise Bemus Patrick; children: Sarah Baker, Katherine Wintersmith. **Educ:** Milton Academy, English and American literature; Harvard Coll, BA, 1978; Harvard Law School, JD, 1982. **Career:** US Court of Appeals, law clerk; NAACP Legal Defense and Education Fund, litigator; Hill and Barlow, partner, beginning 1986; Dept of Justice, assistant attorney general for Civil Rights, currently. **Orgs:** Massachusetts Bar Assn; Black Lawyers Assn; Boston Bar Assn; Harvard Club of Boston; Harvard Alumni Assn, director, 1993-96. **Honors/Awds:** Harvard Law School, George Leisure Award, 1981; Rockefeller fellowship, United Nations in Sudan and Nigeria, 1978. **Business Addr:** Assistant Attorney General for Civil Rights, US Department of Justice, 950 Pennsylvania Ave, NW, Washington, DC 20531, (202)514-2151.

PATRICK, ISADORE W., JR.
Judge. **Personal:** Born Mar 27, 1951, Jackson, MS; son of Esterline Patrick and Isadore W Patrick Sr; married Deborah Williams, Dec 18, 1971. **Educ:** Jackson State Univ, Jackson, MS, BS, 1973; Univ of MS, Oxford, MS, JD; Natl Judicial Coll, Reno, NV, Judicial Certificate. **Career:** IBM, Manassas, VA, computer programmer, 1973-78; Hinds Co Public Defender Office, Jackson, MS, public defense attorney; Ninth Judicial Circuit Court, Vicksburg, MS, asst district attorney, 1981-89, circuit court judge, 1989-. **Orgs:** Mem, Natl Judges Assn; mem, MS Conference of Judges; mem, MS State Bar; mem, Magnolia State Bar; mem, Warren Co Bar; mem, bd of dir, Salvation Army; mem, Jackson State Alumni Assn; American Bar Association; American Trial Lawyers Association; Natl Bar Assn. **Honors/Awds:** Recipient of the NAACP Legal Award, 1989. **Business Addr:** Circuit Court Judge, PO Box 351, Warren County Courthouse, 10001 Grove St, Vicksburg, MS 39180, (601)636-8042.

PATRICK, JAMES L.
Business executive. **Personal:** Born Nov 11, 1919, Prairie View, TX; married Gladys A Holloway; children: Charles, James, Harold, Wayne, Sheldon. **Educ:** TX Coll, AB 1941; Loyola Univ Chgo, MSA 1949. **Career:** N Central Region, Cook Co, IL Dept of Pub Aid, dir 1949-. **Orgs:** Vp chmn budget United Comm Serv of Evanston; registered social worker; mem Am Mgmt Assn; mem NAACP; mem Urban League; mem Alpha Phi Alpha Frat; mem Teelan Coll of Loyola Univ Alumni Assn; mem APWA; mem IWA Sr warden, ch sec, St Andrews Episicopal Ch; sec Mens Club, St Andrews Episicopal Ch; mem Phi Delta Psi Hon Soc; Supply Officer 1941-46. **Honors/Awds:** Made Deans List. **Business Addr:** 624 S Michigan, Chicago, IL 60605.

PATRICK, JENNIE R.
Engineer. **Personal:** Born Jan 1, 1949, Gadsden, AL; daughter of Elizabeth Patrick (deceased) and James Patrick; married. **Educ:** Tuskegee Inst, 1967-70; Univ of CA Berkeley, BS 1973; MIT, ScD 1979. **Career:** Dow Chem Co, asst engr 1972; Stauffer Chem Co, asst engr 1973; MIT, rsch assoc 1973-79; Chevron Rsch, engr 1974; Arthur D Little Inc, engr 1975; Gen Elect Co, rsch engr 1979-83; Phillip Morris Inc, sr engr 1983-85; Rohm and Haas Co, rsch section mgr 1985-90; Southern Company Services, Inc, asst to exec vice pres, 1990-92; Tuskegee University, Chemical Engineering Department, 1993-. **Orgs:** Mem Sigma Xi, AIChE, NOBCChE. **Honors/Awds:** First African-American female in the US to earn doctorate in chem engrg 1979; NOBCChE Outstanding Women in Science & Engrg Awd 1980; a subject in Exceptional Black Scientists Poster Prog CIBA-GEIGY 1983; Tuskegee Inst, Hon PhD, 1984. **Home Addr:** PO Box 530734, Birmingham, AL 35253-0734.

PATRICK, JULIUS, JR.
Educational administrator, mayor. **Personal:** Born May 16, 1938, Natchitoches, LA; married Beatrice M Jackson; children: Ronald, Karen, DiAnthia, Riqui. **Educ:** Dillard Univ, BA 1966; Tuskegee Inst, MS Ed 1970. **Career:** Rapide Parish School Bd, teacher 1966-69, vice prin 1972-75, Town of Boyce LA, mayor; Rapides Parish School Bd, principal 1975-. **Orgs:** Pres Boyce Civic Improvement League Inc; v chmn Police Jury's Rehab Com 1977-80; mem Parish's Housing Auth Bd 1978; chmn Natl Conf of Black Mayors;pres boyce Civic Improvement League Inc; mem Rapides Parish Housing Auth, Rapides Area Planning Commission, Trade Mission to People's Republic of China, UMTA Rural Transportation Mission to Peurto Rico; pres Rapides Assoc of Principals and Asst Principals. **Honors/Awds:** Hon Ambassador of Goodwill Exec Branch State of LA 1980. **Military Serv:** AUS sp/4 1961-64. **Business Addr:** Principal, Rapides Parish Sch Bd, PO Box 1052, Alexandria, LA 71301.

PATRICK, LAWRENCE CLARENCE, JR.
Attorney. **Personal:** Born Feb 8, 1945, Detroit, MI; son of Ada D Patrick and Bishop Lawrence C Patrick; married Raynona P Fuller, Jun 23, 1973; children: Lawrence C Patrick III, Joseph E Patrick, Ayana B Patrick, Goldie E Patrick. **Educ:** Wayne State Univ, Detroit MI, BA, 1972; Harvard Univ, JD, 1975. **Career:** Honigman Miller Schwartz & Cohn, Detroit MI, assoc, 1975-77; Patrick, Fields & Preston-Cooper, Detroit MI, partner, 1977-93; Jaffe, Raitt, Hever & Weiss, partner; Detroit Board of Education, president, 1989-92, chair, Detroit 2000, Visiting Fellow, Hudson Institute, 1992-. **Orgs:** Mem, bd of dir, Wolverine Bar Assn, 1978-81; corp dir and bd chmn, Black United Fund, 1978-88; mem, Michgan Transportation Commn, 1979-84, vice chmn, 1981-84; chmn of bd, Black United Fund, 1985-88; chmn of bd, Wayne County Social Services Bd, 1986-88. **Honors/Awds:** Michigan Senate Resolution, Michigan Senate, 1981; Trio, Wayne State Univ, 1988; Founder's Award, Student Motivational Program, 1989, Outstanding Service, Church of God in Christ, 1989. **Business Addr:** Attorney, Jaffe, Raitt, Heuer and Weiss, Detroit, MI 48226.

PATRICK, ODESSA R.
Educator. **Personal:** Born Oct 22, 1933, Mt Gilead, NC; married Joe L; children: Krystal, Joseph, Jasmine. **Educ:** NC A&T St U, BS 1956; Univ of NC, MA 1969. **Career:** Univ of NC Greensboro, instr Biology Dept 1969-, lab techn 1958-69. **Orgs:** Mem Am Assn of Univ Women; Girl Scout Ldr; Delta Sigma Theta; Scientific paper published in Journal of Elisha Mitchell Scientific Soc 1969. **Business Addr:** Prof, Biology, Univ of North Carolina, 312 Eberhart Blvd, Greensboro, NC 27412-5001.

PATRICK, OPAL LEE YOUNG
Educator. **Personal:** Born Jul 16, 1929, Tatums, OK; daughter of Connie V Mitchell Young and L P Young Jr; married Charles Patrick; children: Langston Univ, BA 1951; Univ of NM, MA 1963; Univ of UT, PhD 1974. **Career:** Public School OK, teacher 1951-56; Bur Ind Affairs, inst counselor 1956-63; Univ of MD Educ Centers Deptnd School, 1963-66; USAFE W Germany, instr lecturer teacher; Clearfield Job Corp, inst counselor adminstr 1966-70; Univ of UT, inst of educ 1971-74, asst prof of educ 1974-77; guest lecturer, coordinator, consultant, tutor, 1979-91. **Orgs:** Presenter various conf; participant presenter Natl Organ; guest lectr coord of various projects & research activities; mem State Mental Health Assn, 1973-; UT Acad of Sci 1974-; Natl Coll of Soc Studies 1976-; Assn of Teach Educ 1974-; Natl Cncl Tchrs of Eng 1973-; vice pres Natl Cncl Tchrs of Eng 1973; Assn of Sch & Currs Develop 1975-; pres Davis Co NAACP 1978. **Honors/Awds:** Doctoral dissertation "An Effective Teacher Profile" 1976; article "A Recipe for Effective Teaching" 1977; speech "The Culturally Unique" 1973; speech "Mental Health & the Cultural Differ" 1975; speech "Blacks in Edn" 1976; article, "Ethnic Student's Perceptions of Effective Teachers," Educational Research Quarterly, Vol. 3, No. 2, Summer 1978.

PATRICK, VINCENT JEROME
Marketing executive. **Personal:** Born Oct 21, 1959, Delray Beach, FL; son of Mattie Hough Patrick and Freddie W Patrick. **Educ:** University of Florida, Gainesville, FL, BS, Journalism,

1977-81. **Career:** Jordan Marsh, Miami, FL, assoc buyer, 1981-85; The Rouse Co, Miami, FL, asst mktg mgr, 1985-88; The Rouse Co, Atlanta, GA, mgr, sales and mktg, 1988-. **Orgs:** Board of directors, Atlanta Downtown Partnership; board of directors, Travel Georgia, Inc; member, Downtown Public Relations Council; member, Fernbank Museum of Natural History Communications Advisory Committee. **Honors/Awds:** MAXI/Marketing, Underground Atlanta Grand Opening, 1990, MAXI/Marketing Excellence, Bayside Marketplace Grand Opening, 1989, Intl Council of Shopping Centers; Paper Clip Award/Advertising, Underground Atlanta Advertising Campaign, Atlanta Journal Constitution, 1990; Silver Anvil/Public Relations, 1989, Phoenix Award, Public Relations, 1989, Underground Atlanta. **Business Addr:** Manager, Sales and Marketing, Rouse-Atlanta/Underground Atlanta, 50 Upper Alabama St, Ste 007, Atlanta, GA 30303.

PATTEN, EDWARD ROY (COUSIN EDS)
Entertainer. **Personal:** Born Aug 22, 1939, Atlanta, GA; married Renee Brown; children: Stephanie, Steve, Sonya, Edward II, Elliott. **Career:** Gladys Knight & the Pips, entertainer 1956-; Lagoons, sing group 1955; Cashmere, sing group 1954; Overalls, performer 1952; travelled through GA doing plays & dances 1950; Barber Shop Quartet, 1949. **Orgs:** Exec pres, Patten & Guest Production Co Inc; NAACP. **Honors/Awds:** Recognition Mayors M Jackson & Coleman Young helping in their campaign; Grammy award best R&B Group 1969, 1971, 1972; Am Music Award 1973; Grammies, Record World, Cash Box, Billboard, Rolling Stone, Bobby Pop's Pop, Soul Magazine Awards; rock music award Radio CLIO 1975; Entertainer of the Year, 1974. **Business Addr:** 1414 Avenue of the Americas, New York, NY 10019.

PATTERSON, ALONZO B.
Clergyman. **Personal:** Born Nov 5, 1937, New Orleans, LA; married Shirley May Smith; children: Edna, Mitchell, Norris, Janet, Kim. **Educ:** Am Bible Inst, ThD 1977; Univ AK, BA 1974; AA 1974; Univ AK, AA 1973. **Career:** Shilo Misionary Bapt Ch, pastor; Anchorage Sch Dist, person spl 1976; Shilo Bapt Ch, religious adminstr 1970-75; MHE, supr 1966-70; AUS, food serv supr 1956-66. **Orgs:** NAACP; Comm Action; Human Rel Commn; Anchorage OIC; Ministerial Alliance; Civilian & Mil Cncl; Anchorage Comm Hlthl Ctr; Minority Culture Assn; vice pres March of Dimes. **Military Serv:** AUS 1956-66. **Business Addr:** 855 E 20th, PO Box 3156 ECB, Anchorage, AK 99501.

PATTERSON, BARBARA ANN
Association executive. **Personal:** Born in Pennsylvania; married Billy W Patterson; children: Gwendolyn Patterson-Cobbs, Kimberly, Damali. **Educ:** Trinity Coll, BA Ed 1984, MA counseling, 1993. **Career:** Independent & Public Schools, teacher; private practice in Cross-Racial Communications and Personal Growth Counseling for Professionals; Black Student Fund, pres, currently. **Orgs:** Project Match, advisory bd; Friends for Community Future; Trinity Coll, bd of governors. **Honors/Awds:** Washington Woman of the Year WA Women Mag; Chapter Contributor ''Promoting Independent School Enrollment'', Visible Now Blacks in Private School by Slaughter & Johnson 1989; researcher & resource for a History Deferred, A Guide for Teachers; ''Pioneering Multiracial Education,'' Independent School, vol 53, 1993. **Business Addr:** President, Black Student Fund, 3636 16th St NW, Suite AG15, Washington, DC 20010.

PATTERSON, CECIL BOOKER, JR.
Judge. **Personal:** Born May 15, 1941, Newport News, VA; son of Marie E Patterson and Cecil B Patterson Sr; married Wilma M Hall; children: Angela D, Cecil M. **Educ:** Hampton Univ VA, BA 1963; AZ State Univ, JD 1971. **Career:** Maricopa Cnty Legal Aid Soc, staff atty 1971-72; Bursh & Patterson, private law practice 1972-73; Phoenix Urban League, house counsel 1973-75; Maricopa Cnty Publ Defend Office, trial atty 1975-80; Maricopa Cnty Superior Ct, judge, 1980-91; Atty General's Office, Human Services Div, AZ, chief counsel, 1991-95; AZ Court of Appeals, 1995-. **Orgs:** Mem rep Amer Bar Assn House of Del 1978-80; mem bd governors AZ State Bar 1977-79; pres AZ Black Lawyers Assn 1979-80; mem Natl Conf of Christians & Jews 1981-; mem Valley of the Sun, AZ United Way bd 1984-; mem bd Maricopa Cnty Red Cross 1978; mem AZ Academy 1975 & 1978. **Honors/Awds:** Law Fellowship Reginald Heber Smith Program 1971; Law Scholarship Scholarship Educ & Defense Fund 1970; Grant Martin L King Jr Woodrow Wilson Found 1969. **Military Serv:** USAF Captain 1963-68; Outstanding Weapons Controller Officer 27th Air Div Luke AFB 1968; Good Conduct Ribbon; Marksmanship Ribbon 1967. **Business Addr:** Judge, Arizona Court of Appeals, Div I, State Courts Bldg, 1501 W Washington St, Phoenix, AZ 85007.

PATTERSON, CECIL LLOYD
Educational administrator (retired). **Personal:** Born Jun 10, 1917, Edna, TX; married Vivian Rogers. **Educ:** Samuel Huston Coll, BA Eng 1941; Univ of PA, MA English 1947, PhD English 1961. **Career:** Ft Valley State Coll GA, instructor 1947-48; NC Central Univ, instructor-prof 1950-68, dean-undergrad sch 1968-78, vice chancellor for acad affairs, 1978-86. **Orgs:** Mem So Conf of Deans & Acad Vice Pres 1970-; chmn NC Com on Coll Transfer Students 1974-78; chaplain Gen Bd of Examining Chaplains of the Epis Church 1976-. **Honors/Awds:** Professor Emeritus of English, North Carolina Central University, 1986. **Military Serv:** US Army engrs col 1941-74; Southwest Pacific Theater; Misc Battle Stars; Campaign Medals. **Home Addr:** 409 Lawson St, Durham, NC 27707.

PATTERSON, CHARLES JERRY
Business executive. **Personal:** Born Jan 8, 1925, Ft Wayne, IN; married Dorothy Smith; children: Mark Watson, Tracy Jacqueline. **Educ:** Antioch Coll, BA 1951; Case Western Res U, Ma 1956; Univ CA, post grad 1958063. **Career:** World Airways Inc, dir; Wold Am Investment Co, dir; World Airways Inc, sr vice pres asst to pres of bd; US Dept of Commerce Econ Devel Adminstrn, spec asst to dir 1966-68; Peace Corps, asso dir for prgm devel & operations 1965-66; Inst of Current World Affaris New York City & Africa, fellow 1961-64. **Orgs:** Dir Herrick Hlth Care Found; trst Antioch Coll; dir KQED TV Inc9; dir San Francisco Found; manower adv bd City of Oakland; dir African Student Aid Fund; dir New Oakland Com; past dir SF Unitarian Ch; Intl Hse Barkeley; United Bar Area Crusade; Unitarian Universalist Serv Com; Friends of LangleyPorter Neuropsychiat Inst; Yth for Understanding; Art Commn Berkeley; life mem NAACP; mem Coun of Fgn Rels; mem ACLU. **Business Addr:** Oakland Intl Airport, Oakland, CA 94614.

PATTERSON, CHERYL ANN
Accountant. **Personal:** Born Jul 5, 1957, Columbus, OH; daughter of Geraldine Williams and John B Williams; married Dale Patterson, May 31, 1981. **Educ:** Columbus State Community College, AS, optometric technology, 1979; Franklin University, BS, accounting, 1984. **Career:** Ohio State University, College of Optometry, optometric technican; Ohio Department of Taxation, tax agent; Columbus Convention Center, junior accountant, senior accountant, vp/treasurer, currently. **Business Addr:** VP/Treasurer, Greater Columbus Convention Center, 400 N High St, Columbus, OH 43224, (614)645-5032.

PATTERSON, CHRISTINE ANN
Educational administrator. **Personal:** Born Sep 9, 1949, Wilkes-Barre, PA; daughter of Stella Bienwski Patterson and James Samuel Patterson; married Walter DeFrantz, Feb 15, 1968 (divorced 1983); children: Waltrina, Felicia, Amanda. **Educ:** Wilkes University, Wilkes-Barre, PA, BA, communications, 1983-86, MS, education, 1987-89; The Pennsylvania State University, University Park, PA, PhD, currently. **Career:** The Pennsylvania State University, Media, PA, coordinator of minority advanced placement program, 1986; The Pennsylvania State University, Hazleton, PA, minority student counselor/coordinator, 1986-88; The National Multiple Sclerosis Society, branch coordinator, 1987-88; The Pennsylvania State University, Scranton, PA, extension agent/4-H urban youth, 1988-89; The Pennsylvania State University, University Park, PA, director, multi-cultural affairs, 1989-. **Orgs:** Chair of women, Color Winter Ball, 1990; chair, Forum on Black Affairs, 1990; member, President's Council Undergraduate Recruitment & Retention, Pennsylvania State University, 1989-; membership coordinator, Wilkes-Barre chapter, NAACP, 1986-88; member, Martin Luther King Committee for Social Justice, 1983-. **Honors/Awds:** Recognition Award, Forum on Black Affairs, 1990; Special Friend Award, Luzerne County Head Start, 1987; Publicity Award, NAACP Press, 1987; Scholarship Award, College and University Public Relations Association of Pennsylvania Minorities in Communication, 1986; author of ''The Black Experience in Wyoming Valley''. **Home Addr:** 1652 Oxford Circle, State College, PA 16803. **Business Addr:** Director of Multicultural Affairs, School of Communications, The Pennsylvania State University, 205 Carnegie Bldg, University Park, PA 16802.

PATTERSON, CLARENCE J.
Business executive. **Personal:** Born Feb 23, 1925, Bogalusa, LA; married; children: Clarence, Robert. **Educ:** SF State U, BA 1949; Univ of CA, MA 1951. **Career:** CJ Patterson Co, pres; Oakland CA, real dev ins broker 19 yrs; Focus Cable TV Oakland, org chmn of bd of dir. **Orgs:** Mem bd of dir Oakland RE Bd; pres chmn bd of dir Golden St Bus Leag Oakland; mem exec com natl bd of dir Nat Bus Leag; vice pres Reg 11 Nat Bus Leag; pres Nat Mortgage Co; chmn of bd Cty Cen Econ Dev Corp; mem Civic & Leg Com of Oakland RE Bd; mem US dept of Comm Nat Min PurcCoun; mem bd of dir Peralta Coll Dist Found; mem bd of dir Northwestern Title Co Inc; mem bd fo dir New Oakland Com; mem bd of dir Manpower Area Plan Coun; mem Bd of dir East Bay Bus & Prof Org; mem bd of dir Plan & Red Com & Educ Com Oakland C of C; chmn bd of dir Asso Real Prop Brok Inc; consult Dept Parks & Rec CA on Lnad Acq; also form mem of many org bd o Fdir NAACP; ex bd NAACP Oakland Br; mem SF Bay Area Coun Boy Scouts; co-found chmn E Oakland Ad-Hoc Com for Hsg & Econ Dev; mem bdof dir Uplift Corp Oakland;m Cooper AME Zion Ch; mem of trst bd; also mem of many polit org. **Honors/Awds:** Horace Sudduth Aws Nat Bus Leag 1974; mer awd City of Oakland 1972; CA awd Nat Asso RE Bd 1970; cong awd for cont toward econo dev City of Oakland 1966. **Business Addr:** Golden State Business League, 333 Hegenberger Rd Ste 203, Oakland, CA 94621.

PATTERSON, CLINTON DAVID
Clergyman, staff manager. **Personal:** Born Nov 11, 1936, Uniontown, AL; son of Mattie Mason Patterson and David Patterson; married Lillie Young, Dec 24, 1961; children: Michael, Florencia, Donnetta, Clintonia, Edshena, Bernita. **Educ:** Birmingham Bapt Coll, 1963; Liamia, 1969; Elba Sys, 1970; Liamia, 1973. **Career:** Second Ave Beulah Baptist Church, pastor; Booker T Washington Inc Co, mgr; New Morning Star Baptist Church, pastor 1965-72; Demopolis Fed Credit Union, former vice pres; Fed Credit Union, loan off teller; asst trea manager, BBM Federal Credit Union, currently. **Orgs:** Pres Demopolis Ministeral Fellow, 1966-72; bd dirs Together Inc Demopolis AL; bd dirs BBM Fed Credit Union; Prof Bus Men's Assn 1964-75; mem bd dirs BBM Birmingham, AL; mem Demopolis Fed Credit Union; mem AL Cntrl Credit Union; mem AL Bapt State Conv & Congress; Nat Bapt Sunday Sch & Training Union Congress; Nat Bapt Conv Inc; Birmingham Bapt Min Conf; Jeff Co Dist Assn; NW Dist Conv; lectr Jeff Co Dist Sun Sch & BTU Congress; hon mem AL Sheriff Assn 1974; AL Motorist Assn 1974; past pres S Pratt City Civic Leag 1967; mem AL Fed Civic Leag; mem trst bd Peace Bapt Ch 1957; Geometry Lodge 410; NAACP; AL Chris Movement for Human Rights; mem Tuxedo Height Civic Leag; moderator, Jefferson County Assn; pres, Northwest District Convention. **Honors/Awds:** Cit Fed Savings & Loan Assn; recip C J McNear Awd 1963; Com Serv Awd Pratt City 1971; Com Serv Awd Demopolis AL 1972; NIA Awd for Outsnd Salesmanhip 1974. **Business Addr:** 1022 Second Ave N, Bessemer, AL 35020.

PATTERSON, CURTIS RAY
Educator. **Personal:** Born Nov 11, 1944, Shreveport, LA; married Gloria M Morris; children: Curtis R. **Educ:** Grambling State U, BS educ 1967; GA State U, MVA 1975. **Career:** Atlanta Coll of Art Atlanta GA, art instr 1976-; Atlanta Pub School, art instr chpsn 1970-76; Caddo Parish School Bd Shreveport LA, art instr 1968-70; Muscogee Co School Columbus GA, art instr 1967-68; Gov Hon Prog, instr 1973; Atlanta Life Ins Co, adv com art 1979-80; Piedmont Arts Festival, juror 1980. **Orgs:** Mem Black Artist of Atlanta 1974-80; mem 13 Minus One Sculpture Group 1975-80; adv bd mem Atlanta Bur of Cutlural Affairs 1975-80; sculpture commn Met Atlanta Rapid Transity Authority 1978. **Honors/Awds:** Rep in Visueal Arts Festival of Arts & Cultur Lagos Nigeria 1977; ''Sculpture in the Park'' Commn Atlanta Bur of Cultural Affairs 1977; bronze jubilee awd visual arts WETV Network Channel 30 1979; Atlant Ainternat Airport Sculpture Commn Atlanta Bur of Cultural Affaris 1980. **Business Addr:** Atlanta Coll of Art, 1280 Peachtree St NE, Atlanta, GA.

PATTERSON, DAVID
Government official. **Career:** State of New York, state senator, currently. **Business Addr:** State Senator, 29th Senatorial District Bronx County, 163 West 125th St., 9th Fl., State Office, New York, NY 10027, (212)870-8500.

PATTERSON, DESSIE LEE
City official. **Personal:** Born Jul 6, 1919, Grand Cane, LA; daughter of CarLee Guice Jackson (deceased) and Clinton Jackson, Sr.; widowed; children: Willie Leroy, Betty Marie P Smith, Corrie Jean P Reed. **Educ:** Attained 9th grade. **Career:** Mansfield Desoto LA NAACP, secretary since 1971; City of So Mansfield, mayor 1971-. **Orgs:** Mem Desoto Parish Chamber of Commerce 1979-; library bd of controls; member, Desoto Parish School Board Advisory Council. **Honors/Awds:** First Black female Mayor of the State of LA; first Black female Mayor in the US. **Business Addr:** Mayor, City of So Mansfield, PO Box 995, Town Hall, Mansfield, LA 71052.

PATTERSON, ELIZABETH ANN
Radiologist, educator. **Personal:** Born Feb 2, 1936, Wilkes-Barre, PA; daughter of Edythe Enty Patterson and Benjamin A Patterson; divorced; children: Tonya L Henry. **Educ:** Univ of MI, BS 1957; Howard Univ Coll of Medicine, MD 1961. **Career:** Mercy Hospital, radiology 1972-80; Univ of Pgh/Magee Women's Hosp, asst prof of radiology 1981-85; Central Medical Ctr & Hosp, diagnostic radiologist 1985-88; assistant professor of radiology, Hospital of Univ of Pennsylvania, 1988-. **Orgs:** Pres Pittsburgh Roentger Soc 1982-83; pres Gateway Medical Soc 1983-88; councilor Amer Coll of Radiology 1985-91; secty/program chair Radiology Section of Natl Medical Assoc 1985-87, vice chariman 1987-90; bd of dirs Amer Cancer Soc, Pittsburgh Division 1986-88, Philadelphia Division, 1992-; mem Amer Assoc of Women in Radiology, Alpha Kappa Alpha; chairman, Radiology Section of the Natl Med Assn, 1989-91; Philadelphia Roentgen Ray Society, pres, 1994-95; Society of Breast Imaging; Natl Mammography Quality Assurance Advisory Comm, chairman; Pennsylvania Radiological Society, pres, 1996-97. **Honors/Awds:** American College of Radiology, Fellow. **Home Addr:** 232 Berwind Rd, Radnor, PA 19087. **Business Phone:** (215)662-6726.

PATTERSON, ELIZABETH HAYES
Attorney, educational administrator. **Personal:** Born Jun 25, 1945, Boston, MA; daughter of Lucille Hayes Young and Alan L Young; married Jerome Alexander; children: Sala Elise, Malcolm Atiim. **Educ:** Sorbonne Univ of Paris, diploma with hon-

ors 1966; Emmanuel Coll, AB with distinction in French 1967; Stanford U, 1967-68; Columbus Sch of Law Cath Univ of Am, JD 1973. **Career:** Georgetown Ul Law Cntr, assoc dean JD & graduate programs, 1993-97, asso prof 1980-; DC Pub Sev Commn, chmn 1978-80; DC Pub Serv Commn, commr 1977-80 Columbus Sch of Law Cath U, adj prof 1976; Hogan & Hartson Law Firm, asso 1974-77; Hon Ruggero Aldisert US Ct of Appeals, law clk 1973-74. **Orgs:** National Florence Crittenton Mission Foundation Board, trustee, 1995-; bd of dirs, Child Welfare League of America, 1997; Amer Law Institute, 1995-; Trst Family & Child Sev Wash DC 1977-; bd of dirs, Frederick B Abramson Foundation, 1992-; trst, Emmanuel Coll, 1994-; ACLU Litigation Screening Com 1977-80; DC Bar Div I Steering Com 1980-82, DC Bar Screening Comm 1985-86; bd editors Washington Lawyer 1986-91; Sec of State's Adv Comm on Private Intl Law; study group on the Law Applicable to the Intl Sale of Goods 1983-85; adv comm Procedures Judicial Council of the DC Circuit 1981-84; DC Law Revision Comm, 1990-93; treas, District of Columbia Bar, 1987-88. **Honors/Awds:** Woodrow Wilson Fellow Woodrow Wilson Soc 1967; A Salute to Black Women in Gov Iota Phi Lambda Sor Gamma Cht 1978; "UCC 2-612(3): Breach of an Installment Contract and a Hobson's Choice for the Aggrieved Party," 48 Ohio State Law Journal 227, 1987; "UN Convention on Contracts for the Intl Sale of Goods: Unification and the Tension Between Compromise and Domination," 22 Stanford Journal of Intl Law 263, 1986. **Business Addr:** Assoc Professor of Law, Georgetown Univ Law Center, 600 New Jersey Ave NW, Washington, DC 20001.

PATTERSON, EVELYNNE
Educational administrator. **Personal:** Born Feb 28, 1930, Meadville, PA; married Herman; children: Alice, Patricia. **Educ:** NY U, BS 1962; NY U, post grad. **Career:** NY Univ, exec asst to pres dir office for affirmative action dir office for comm rel asso prof 1975-; asst dep chancellor dir asso prof 1972-75; NY Univ, dir asso 1968-72. **Orgs:** Mem adv bvd Harvard Univ 1974-77; mem Comm Bd #2 Borough of Manhattan 1977-; bd of dir WA Sq Assn 1977-. **Business Addr:** 70 Washington Sq s, New York, NY 10012.

PATTERSON, FLOYD
Professional boxer (retired), business owner. **Personal:** married Janet; children: Janene, Jennifer, Tracy. **Career:** Professional Heavyweight Boxer, 1952-72; Huguenot Boxing Club New Paltz NY, owner. **Orgs:** Mem New York State Athletic Commn; presently working on behalf of a variety of charitable orgs including New York City's Inner-City Scholarship Fund. **Honors/Awds:** Middleweight Gold Medal winner 1952 Olympic Games in Helsinki; World Heavyweight Champion 1956-59, 1960-62; first man to win the heavyweight title twice and youngest man to ever capture the heavyweight crown.

PATTERSON, GERALD WILLIAM
Business executive. **Personal:** Born May 9, 1953, Cleveland, OH; son of Willa Mae Patterson and William Robert Johnson; married Diana Crump-Patterson; children: Monique Camille Patterson. **Educ:** Michigan State Univ, BA, l975; Wayne State Univ, specialist, 1977; Central Michigan Univ, MA, l978; Univ of Wisconsin, transportation certificate, l987. **Career:** Ford Motor Co, sr transportation agent, 1978-80; Amway Corp, traffic coordinator, 1980-82, traffic supvr, 1982-83; Kellogg Co, truck pricing mgr, 1984-87, mgr logistics services, 1988, mgr outside warehouses & dist centers, 1988-91, logistics mgr, 1992-. **Orgs:** Phi Beta Sigma, 1975-; Delta Nu Alpha, 1982-89; Southwest Michigan Traffic Club, 1984-; Battle Creek Area Urban League, 1985-; advisor, Jr Achievement, 1986-88; 60NR Committee, 1987-88; NAACP, 1988-; advisor, Upward Bound, 1989-; Council of Logistics Mgmt, 1989. **Honors/Awds:** Transportation Negotiation Strategies, 1987; Service Award, Governor of Tennessee, 1989. **Home Addr:** PO Box 923449, Norcross, GA 30092.

PATTERSON, GRACE LIMERICK
Library director. **Personal:** Born Nov 21, 1938, New York, NY; daughter of Frieda Sajac Limerick and Robert Limerick; married Joseph Nathaniel Patterson, Oct 30, 1956 (deceased); children: Lorrayne, Joseph Jr. **Educ:** City College of New York, New York, NY, BA, 1971; Columbia University, New York, NY, MLS, 1975; College of New Rochelle, New Rochelle, NY, MS, 1989. **Career:** Paterson Public Library, Paterson, NJ, outreach coordinator, 1975-79; Passaic County College, Paterson, NJ, media specialist, 1979-81; Irvington Public Library, Irvington, NJ, branch coordinator, 1981-84; Rockland Community College, Suffern, NY, assoc prof, 1984-89; Hudson County College, director, 1989-. **Orgs:** Chair, public relations committee, Black Caucus of the American Library Assn, 1988-90; chair, outreach services committee, New Jersey Library Assn, 1981-85; member, Arts Council of Rockland County, 1987-89; member, American Library Assn, 1978-; delegate, member, State University of New York Library Assn, 1984-89; chair, ALA Louise Giles Scholarship Committee, 1985-87; secretary, treasurer, International Federation of Library Associations, Cipert, 1996-97; Instructional Resources Committee, HCCC, chair, 1995-. **Honors/Awds:** Title IIB Fellowship, Department of Education, 1974-75; Public Relations Award, New Jersey Library Assn, 1979, 1996; basic tutor, Literacy Volunteers of America, 1978; Professional Librarian Certification, Education Department, New Jersey, 1981; Community Development Associate, Mott Foundation, Flint, MI, 1983. **Business Addr:** Director, Library, Hudson County Community College, 25 Journal Sq, Jersey City, NJ 07306, (201)714-7109.

PATTERSON, JAMES
Business executive. **Personal:** Born May 10, 1935, Augusta, GA; married Phyllis Black; children: Katy, Jacqueline, Jennifer. **Educ:** State Clge, MD 1957. **Career:** Mutual of NY, field underwriter 1966-; Supreme Life Phila, debit & staff mgr 1960-66 business unlimited inc, pres 1975-. **Orgs:** Mem Million Dollar Round Table; Mutual of New York Hall of Fame; mutual of NY Pres's Council; Natl Assc of Life Underwriters; past mem Philadelphia Jaycees; mem Philadelphia chap Natl Bus League, vice pres 1972. **Honors/Awds:** Rec'd Mutual of New York's highest hnr Hall of Fame 1974; agcy Man of yr 1967. **Military Serv:** Mil srv 1958-60. **Business Addr:** 146 Montgomery Ave, Bala Cynwyd, PA 19004.

PATTERSON, JOAN DELORES
Education specialist. **Personal:** Born Mar 17, 1944, Columbia, SC; daughter of David Creech (deceased); divorced; children: Torrey. **Educ:** City Colleges of Chicago, AA 1976; Chicago State Univ, BA 1979; Univ of North FL, MEd 1982. **Career:** US Navy, dir of personal serv 1982-83, educ tech 1983-84, personnel clerk 1984; US Air Force, guidance counselor 1984-88, education specialist, 1988-. **Orgs:** Mem Amer Soc for Training and Devel 1982-85; chief counselor Equal Employment Opportunity 1984-85; mgr Federal Women's Program 1984; mem American Counseling Assoc, 1985-; mem Military Educators & Counselors Assn 1985-; mem Assn for Multicultural Counseling & Devel 1985-; bd of dir, Military Educators Counseling Assn, 1989-94; secretary, Tuskegee Airman Institute, 1990-. **Honors/Awds:** Outstanding Performance Award, US Air Force, 1992, US Navy, 1983; Letters of Commendation (5), US Air Force 1986. **Military Serv:** US Army Reserves, staff sgt 1977-85. **Business Addr:** Education Specialist, US Air Force, 45 MSSQ/DPE, Patrick AFB, FL 32925-6505.

PATTERSON, JOAN LETHIA
Labor union administrator. **Personal:** Born Apr 9, 1940, Detroit, MI; daughter of Thelma Warfield and Clarence Warfield; widowed; children: three sons. **Educ:** University of Detroit, attended, 1968-73; Wayne County Community College, attended, 1972-73; Wayne State University, attended, 1975-77; Mercy College, attended, 1982-84. **Career:** UAW, Local 1248, various positions, 1966-74; UAW, Region 1, education director, 1974-79, Chrysler Department, international representative, 1979-82; International Union, arbitration coordinator, 1982-86; UAW-Chrysler National Training Center, executive codirector, 1986-; UAW-Chrysler Department, administrative assistant, 1990-. **Orgs:** Secretaries Commission for Achieving Necessary Skills of US Labor Department, committee mem, 1990-92; Trade Union Leadership Council, 1979-; National Council of Negro Women, 1990-; March of Dimes, board of directors, 1990-; North American Auto-Steel Curriculum Research Foundation, board of directors, 1990-; American Society for Training & Development, board of governors, 1991-; Michigan Job Training Coordinating Council, 1988-; Oakland Area Labor-Management Committee, advisory board, 1989-. **Honors/Awds:** UAW Region 1 Women's Council, Service Award, 1990; March of Dimes, Volunteer Award, 1992; Cody High School Compact Program, Volunteer Service Award, 1991. **Special Achievements:** Initiated the first on-site child care center for workers in the American automotive industry; administered work and family life regional training centers for 7 states, 1986-89. **Business Addr:** Executive Co-Director, UAW-Chrysler National Training Center, 2211 E Jefferson, Detroit, MI 48207, (313)567-3016.

PATTERSON, JOHN T., JR.
Business executive (retired). **Personal:** Born Apr 4, 1928, New York, NY; son of Mildred Clemens and John T Clemens Sr; married Jane Slaughter; children: Linda, Sherri; children: Ramona Jamelle, Jodie Miishee. **Educ:** Lincoln Univ PA, AB 1950; Brooklyn Law Sch, LLB 1954, JD 1967. **Career:** Patterson & Co, owner, 1957-61; Bache & Co, investment broker, 1961-65; Interracial Council for Business Opportunity, natl exec dir, 1965-68; econ devel consultant, 1968-72; South Bronx Overall Econ, president, beginning in 1972, retired. **Orgs:** Exec com Assn for Better NY 1980-; trustee Herbert H Lehman Coll Foundation 1983-87; mem Bronx C of C; Terence Cardinal Cooke Health Care Center, vice chairman, 1991-. **Honors/Awds:** The Frederick Douglass Award New York Urban League 1986; Honorary Doctor of Laws, Lehman College, The City of New York, 1992.

PATTERSON, KAY
State Senator. **Personal:** Born Jan 11, 1931, Darlington County, SC; married Jean James; children: Eric Horace, Pamela Maria. **Educ:** Allen Univ, AB 1956; SC State Coll, MEd 1971. **Career:** WA Perry Middle School, teacher 1956-70; Benedict Coll, teacher 1966; SC Educ Assn, uniserv rep 1970-86; SC House of Representatives, rep 1975-85; SC Senate, senator, 1985-. **Orgs:** Life mbr Natl Educ Assn; life mbr NAACP; Educ Comm of the States 1978-84; former mbr Southern Regional Educ Bd 1985; Univ of SC Trustee, former mbr 1985. **Military Serv:** USMC Sgt 1951-53. **Business Addr:** Senator, South Carolina Senate, PO Box 142, Columbia, SC 29202.

PATTERSON, LLOYD
Law enforcement consultant. **Personal:** Born Feb 2, 1931, Cleveland, OH; son of Willa Byrd Patterson and Ambrose Patterson; married Lena Burgan Patterson, Dec 31, 1975. **Educ:** Cuyahoga Comm Coll, attended 1965-66; FBI Natl Acad, grad 1975; Natl Training Ctr of Polygraph Science NYC, graduate; Attended, Dignitary Protection School, US Treasury Dept, OPOTA Hypnosis School. **Career:** Cleveland PD, police officer patrolman thru lieut 1957-82, deputy chief of police 1982-83; CWRU Law Medicine Ctr, staff instructor 1978-83; L & L Patterson Consultants Las Vegas, exec dir, currently. **Orgs:** Past potentate El Hasa Temple #28 Shriners 1961-; 32nd Degree Bezaleel Consistory AASR 1961-; Eureka Lodge #52 Prince Hall Masons 1961-; disting fellow Acad of Certified Polygraphists 1976; pres Black Shield Police Assoc 1980-; trustee Cleveland Police Hist Soc 1982-; co-owner Bar 2 L Ranch 1983-; parliamentarian Las Vegas Appaloosa Club 1985; imperial dir NAACP; charter member: Natl Organization of Black Law Enforcement Execs; NBPA; FOP; Intl Assn of Chiefs of Police; Black Shield Police Assn; NV Black Police Officers Association; FBINAA; Ohio Police & Fire Retirees, 1983-; life mem, Natl Rifle Assn, 1951-; chmn, Project PRIMES, Cleveland Urban League, 1982-83; Clark County Counseling Center, past board of directors; Las Vegas Valley Water District, public information officer, 1989-96. **Special Achievements:** Appeared in Disney Movie: "You Ruined My Life," 1987; HBO Special: "VIVA-SHAF," 1987; movie: Crime Story, 1988; movie: Midnight Run, 1988; author: Chicken Every Sunday (cookbook), Pet Peeves Etc (humor), 1989; Profiles of Blacks in Blue (history). **Military Serv:** US Army, sgt, 1952-53; Good Conduct Medal 1952-53, Natl Service Defense Medal, Presidential Unit Citation, Solider of the Month 2 times. **Business Addr:** Executive Dir, L & L Patterson Consultants, 5654 Smithsonian Way, Las Vegas, NV 89130.

PATTERSON, LYDIA R.
Consultant, educator. **Personal:** Born Sep 3, 1936, Carrabelle, FL; daughter of Johnnie Mae Thomas Ross and Richard D Ross; married Berman W Patterson; children: Derek, Kelley, Corley. **Educ:** Hunter Coll, BA 1958. **Career:** US Energy Dept, industrial rel specialist 1966-68; NY State Div Human Rights, regional dir/mgr 1962-66, 1969-76; Extend Consultant Serv, pres/CEO 1982-; Bankers Trust Co, vice pres 1976-87; Merrill Lynch & Co, vice pres, mgr corp EEO serv dept 1987-90; Borough of Manhattan Community College, New York, NY, adjunct lecturer, 1991-. **Orgs:** Govt affairs commn Fin Women Assn/Natl Assn Blk Women 1978-; prof devel comm Urban Bankers Coalition 1978-; mem Society for Human Resources Mgmt, 1979-,Natl Urban League 1979-; exec bd NY Women Employment Center 1985; exec bd, mem EDGES 1985-; member, City University of New York Vocational & Technical Education Advisory Council, 1990-; member, Women's Forum (National & International), 1988-. **Honors/Awds:** Women in Industry Natl Council of Negro Women 1978; Women Who Make A Difference, Minorities and Women in Business Magazine 1989; Corporate/Community Partnership Award, Greater New York Chapter Links 1989; Economic Justice Award, Judicial Council, Natl Bar Assn. **Special Achievements:** Seminar speaker: Columbia University; Wharton School of Harvard University; Duke University; Cornell School of Industrial Relations, 1976-; article, Columbia School of Industrial Social Welfare Journal, 1981. **Home Addr:** 12689 Coral Breeze Dr, West Palm Beach, FL 33414-8070.

PATTERSON, MICHAEL DUANE
Attorney, managing partner. **Personal:** Born Jul 27, 1949, Detroit, MI; son of Myra Howard Patterson and Harry B Patterson Dr; children: Lisa Marie. **Educ:** Ferris State Coll, Big Rapids MI, attended, 1967-68; Western Michigan Univ, Kalamazoo MI, BS, 1970; The Natl Law Center, George Washington Univ, Washington DC, JD, 1974. **Career:** Mayor Robert B Blackwell, Highland Park MI, special asst to mayor, 1971; US Senator Birch Bayh, Washington DC, legal intern, 1971-72; US Senator Philip A Hart, Washington DC, staff asst, 1972-74; Herman J Anderson PC, Detroit MI, law clerk, 1974; Wayne County Community Coll, Detroit MI, instructor, 1974-81; Community Youth Serv Program, Detroit MI, legal coord, 1975; Michigan and US Dist Court, Eastern Dist of Michigan, 1976; US Court of Appeals, Sixth Circuit, 1977; Stone, Richardson, Grier & Allen PC, Detroit MI, assoc, 1975-80, partner, 1978-80; District of Columbia, 1980; US Supreme Court, 1982. **Orgs:** Mem, Wolverine Bar Assn, Natl Bar Assn, NAACP, Amer Bar Assn, New York State Bar Assn, Joint Center for Political Studies, 1971-72; chmn of bd of trustees, Renaissance Baptist Church of Detroit, 1984-86, 1987-89; vice chmn, Committee on Property Insurance Law, Tort and Insurance Practice Section, 1986-88, vice chmn, Committee on Membership Involvement, 1987-88, chair elect, Membership Committee, 1988-, New York State and American Bar Assns; mem, State Bar of Michigan; mem, The District of Columbia Bar; mem, National Bar Assn. **Honors/Awds:** Spirit of Detroit Award, Mayor's Certificate of Merit Award. **Business Addr:** Patterson, Phifer & Phillips, PC, 1274 Library St, L B King Bldg, Suite 500, Detroit, MI 48226.

PATTERSON, ORLANDO HORACE
Educator. **Personal:** Born Jun 5, 1940; married Nerys (divorced 1994); children: Rhiannon, Barbara; married Anita, 1995. **Educ:** London Univ, BS, economics, 1962; London School of Economics, PhD, 1965. **Career:** Harvard University, professor, Department of Sociology, 1971-; Allston Burr Sr, tutor, 1971-73; Univ West Indies, lecturer, 1967-70; London School of Economics, assistant lecturer, 1965-67. **Orgs:** Tech Adv Com to Prime Minister & Govt of Jamaica, 1972-; Jamaica Govt Exhbn; American Sociological Assn. **Honors/Awds:** National Book Award, 1991; American Academy of Arts and Sciences, Fellow; Honorary Degrees: Harvard University, AM, 1971; Trinity College, LHD, 1992; The American Sociological Association, Distinguished Contribution to Scholarship Award, 1983; Best Book on Phisolism-American Political Science Association, Ralph Bunche Award, 1983; UCLA, Medal of Merit, 1992. **Special Achievements:** Author: The Sociology of Slavery, 1967; The Children of Sisyphys, 1964; An Absence of Ruins, 1967; Die the Long Day, 1972; Freedom, Vol 1, Basic Books, 1991; "The Crisis of Gender Relations Among African-American," Anita Hill & Emma Jordan, eds, Race Gender & Power in America, Oxford vp, 1985; Ethnic Chauvinism: The Reactionary Impulse, Stein & Day, 1977; Slavery & Social Death, Harvard University Press, 1982; The Ordeal of Integration: Progress & Resentment in America's "Racial" Crisis, Civitas-Counterpoint Books, 1997; "Rituals of Blood: God, Sex and Violence in Black & White Culture," Civitas-Counterpoint, 1998. **Business Addr:** Professor, Harvard University, Department of Sociology, 520 James Hall, Cambridge, MA 02138.

PATTERSON, PAUL
Supervisor, director. **Personal:** Born Aug 6, 1926, Aurora, IL; married Shirley Glenn; children: Charles, Carrie. **Educ:** Univ IL, 1950. **Career:** Chicago Bears, dir player rels; Anheuser-Busch Inc, sales supr; Chicago Bears, traveling sec 1973, scout dir of player rel 1967; Anheuser-Busch, sales rep 1965; owned & oper food & liquor store 1965; Capitol Dairy 1950. **Orgs:** Bd dir IL Athl Assc at Univ IL 1974; State of IL Athl Bd 1974; bd chmn Athletic Bd of State of IL 1975; Rose Bowl 1947; Jr Mens Hon Soc SACHEH; Mawanda Sr Men Hon Soc; Kappa Alpha Psi. **Military Serv:** USN 1945-46. **Business Addr:** Anheuser Busch, 4841 S California, Chicago, IL 60632.

PATTERSON, PAUL A.
Business executive. **Personal:** Born Mar 5, 1929, Richmond, IN; divorced; children: 3. **Educ:** Earlham Coll, BS 1951; IN Mortuary Coll, 1964. **Career:** Patterson's Funeral Home, mortician, owner, currently; Wayne Co, coroner 1984-93, 1997-2000. **Orgs:** Lions Club; Townsend Comm Ctr; pres Wayne Co Fed Welfare Adv Bd; bd Amer Red Cross; bd Boys Club; bd Jr Achievement; past pres IN Voc Tech Coll; bd Salvation Army; Richmond Funeral Dirs Assn; IFDA & NFDA; Buckeye State Funeral Dir Assoc of OH; past pres Richmond Comm Sch Bd 1966-77;Mayor's Select Group 1972-73; past exalted ruler IBPOEW #479; 32 deg Malta-Consistory #34 shriner; Quinn Lodge #28 F&AM; Tyre Temple #129 Trustee Bethel AME Church; National Disaster Team, REG V FEMA. **Honors/Awds:** Gov Evan Bayh, Sagamore of the Wabash, 1992. **Business Addr:** 110 S 8th St, Richmond, IN 47374, (765)962-0335.

PATTERSON, POLA NOAH
Librarian. **Personal:** Born Aug 7, 1935, Jennings, LA. **Educ:** Univ of IL, BA French 1970, MS Libr Sci 1971. **Career:** Calcasieu Parish Sch Bd LA, sub elem tchr 1956; Univ of IL Library, Afro-American biblio librn 1971-78; CA State Univ at San Bernardino, John M Pfau Library, reference librarian, online database coordinator, 1979-. **Orgs:** Amer Libr Assn; Black Caucus of Amer Libr Assn; CA Libr Assn; Amer Fed of Tchrs; life mem Zeta Phi Beta Sor Inc; CA Black Faculty & Staff Assn. **Honors/Awds:** Cert Internship in Black Studies Librnshp Fisk Univ 1972; Hon Soc Chi Gamma Iota, Pi Delta Phi, Beta Phi Mu. **Military Serv:** USAF capt 1958-69; USAFR retired major. **Business Addr:** Online Database Coordinator, California State University, John M Pfau Library, 5500 University Pkwy, San Bernardino, CA 92407.

PATTERSON, RAYMOND R.
Educator (retired). **Personal:** Born Dec 14, 1929, New York, NY; son of Mildred Lena Mae Clemens Patterson (deceased) and John Tollie Patterson (deceased); married Boydie Alice Cooke; children: Ama. **Educ:** Lincoln Univ, AB 1951; NY Univ, MA 1956. **Career:** Youth House for Boys NY, children's super 1956-58; Benedict Coll, instructor 1958-59; New York City Public Schs, teacher 1959-68; City Coll CUNY, professor emeritus, 1991-. **Orgs:** Dir author Black Poets Reading, Inc; dir City College Langston Hughes Festival; mem Poetry Society of Amer; trustee Walt Whitman Birthplace Assoc; bd of dirs, 1989-; mem, PEN American Center. **Honors/Awds:** Borestone Mountain Poetry Awds 1950; Natl Endowment for the Arts Awd 1970; Creative Artists Pub Serv Fellowship 1977; City Coll Langston Hughes Awd 1986; honorary mem Golden Key National Honor Society - The City College, 1989; author, poems, Elemental Blues, 1983; author, poems, 26 Ways of Looking at a Black Man, 1969; opera libretto - David Walker, 1989; Collaborative Grant, National Endowment of the Arts, 1989-91; Three Patterson Lyrics for Soprano and Piano, Hale Smith, 1986; Opera Libretto - Goree, 1996. **Military Serv:** US Army corpl 1951-53. **Business Addr:** Professor Emeritus, City Coll CUNY, English Dept, 138 St at Convent Ave, New York, NY 10031.

PATTERSON, ROBERT L.
Judge. **Personal:** Born Aug 2, 1945, Detroit, MI; son of Florence & Clarence Patterson (deceased); married Joyce Hurst Patterson; children: Kevin, Robert II. **Educ:** Colorado State Univ, BS, 1968; Univ of Colorado, Boulder, JD, 1974. **Career:** Univ of Colorado, dir, black educ program, 1969; Colorado State Univ, asst dir project go, 1970-71; Legal Aid Society, staff attorney, 1974-76; Colorado Public Defender, attorney, 1976-80; Federal Public Defender, asst fed defender, 1980-81; Colorado Attorney General, asst attorney general, 1981-85; Denver County Court, judge, 1985-. **Orgs:** Natl Bar Assn, 1980-95; Sigma Pi Phi, Delta Eta Boule, pres, 1991-. **Honors/Awds:** Lane College Alumni Assn, Man of Distinction, 1990. **Business Addr:** Judge, Denver Cnty Court, Presiding Judge, 1457 Bannock, Courtroom 108, Denver, CO 80202.

PATTERSON, RONALD E.
Bank executive. **Career:** Commonwealth National Bank, Mobile AL, chief executive. **Business Addr:** Commonwealth National Bank, 2214 St Stephens Rd, Mobile, AL 36617.

PATTERSON, WILLIAM BENJAMIN
Recreation administrator (retired). **Personal:** Born May 19, 1931, Little Rock, AR; son of Perrish Childress Patterson and William Benjamin Patterson Sr; married Euradell Logan; children: William, David. **Educ:** California State Univ San Francisco, BS Recreation 1956, MS Recreation Admin 1963. **Career:** City of Oakland Office of Parks & Recreation, recreation dir 1952-56, head recreation dir 1956-62, district supervisor 1962-74, admin supervisor 1964-74, visitor services mgr 1974-87, recreation serv mgr 1987-89; City of Oakland, Office of Mayor Lionel J Wilson, special consultant 1989; Growth Opportunities Inc, pres/CEO 1988-. **Orgs:** Foreman Alameda County Grand Jury 1982-83; mem Oakland Baseball Athletics Advisory Bd 1982-; mem Natl Life Mem Comm NAACP 1982-87; treasurer, bd of dirs Joe Morgan Youth Foundation 1983-; vice pres/dir Mitre Business Org Inc 1983-88, pres/CEO 1988-; past pres 1984, chairperson of bd New Oakland Comm Inc 1985-; pres bd chair Greater Acorn Community Improvement Assn Inc 1985-87; mem California Parks and Recreation Soc East Bay Recreation Exec Assn, Amer Assn of Zoological Parks and Aquariums; life mem Kappa Alpha Psi Frat 1982-; mem Sigma Pi Phi Frat 1984-. **Honors/Awds:** Outstanding Contributions Award, California Youth Authority 1977; Outstanding Serv Award, Alameda County Bd of Supervisors 1977; Comm Testimonial, McClymonds Alumni Assn 1982; Commendation for Community Serv, Oakland City Council 1983; Christian Leadership Award, Downs mem Methodist Church, Oakland, 1990; Outstanding Community Service, Congress of the United States, 1988; California Assembly, Senate Resolution Recognition of Public Service, 1988; Resolution, Commendation for Outstanding Public Service, Alameda County, bd of supervisors, 1988; management, Oakland City Council, 1988; Outstanding Constributors Award, National Parks Service, 1988. **Military Serv:** AUS pfc EII 1951. **Business Addr:** Community Consultant, Mayor Lionel J Wilson-City of Oakland, One City Hall Plaza, City Hall, Oakland, CA 94612.

PATTERSON, WILLIS CHARLES
Educator, performer. **Personal:** Born Nov 27, 1930, Ann Arbor, MI; married Frankie Bouyer; children: Sharon, Kevin, Shelia, Jamal. **Educ:** University of Michigan, MusB, M Mus; PhD, Higher Education. **Career:** Southern Univ, Baton Rouge, LA, 1959-61; Virginia State College, associate professor, 1962-68; Univ of Michigan, professor, 1977; Univ of Michigan, School of Music, associate dean, 1979; Major, Our Own Thing Inc, performer; Univ of Michigan School of Music, associate dean/prof of voice. **Orgs:** National Opera Assn; National Assn Teachers Singing; Alpha Phi Alpha; NAACP; Natl Assn of Negro Musicians; Natl Black Music Caucus. **Honors/Awds:** Compiled "Anthology of Art Songs by Black Amer Composers", Edward B Marks Music Corp, 1977; Recorded with: RCA Victor, Philips Records, NBC, BBC. **Military Serv:** USAF staff sgt 1949-52. **Business Addr:** University of Michigan, Ann Arbor, 3028 Moore - Music Bldg, North Campus, Ann Arbor, MI 48109-2085.

PATTERSON-TOWNSEND, MARGARET M.
Health care administrator, polysomnographic technologist. **Personal:** Born Jul 4, 1951, Flint, MI; daughter of Zelma V Stewart & Albert Patterson; divorced; children: Marc A Patterson, Sommer C Green. **Educ:** Bakers Bus College, bus admin, 1987; Univ of MI, health care admin, 1992; Univ of MI Med Ctr, polysomnography, 1992. **Career:** Flint Gen Hosp, admin assistant, 1978-86; HealthPlus of MI, assistant to dir of special accts, 1986-89; Manpower Inc, admin troubleshooter, 1990-91; Sleep Disorders Inst of MI, assistant coordinator, 1991-92; Genesee Co Substance Abuse, assistant to dir of development, 1991-92; MI Sleep Consultants, dir, 1992-. **Orgs:** Flint Chamber of Commerce, ambassador; National Assn of Female Execs, dir; Amer Bus Women's Assn; Flint Women's Forum, business; Mid Michigan's Coordinator for National Narcoleptic Foundation, dir. **Honors/Awds:** Flint Area Chambers of Commerce, Nomination for Athena Award. **Special Achievements:** First minority female to successfully own & operate sleep disorders in US. **Business Addr:** Exec Dir, Michigan Sleep Consultants & Research Center, G-3237 Beecher Road, Ste M, Flint, MI 48532, (810)733-8338.

PATTILLO, JOYCE M.
Human resources executive, diversity consultant. **Personal:** Born Apr 28, 1951, Little Rock, AR; daughter of Johnnie C and Mable Stubblefield; married Conrad S Pattillo, Dec 24, 1977; children: Conrad Peyton. **Educ:** Univ of Arkansas Pine Bluff, BA, sociology and history, 1969-72; Webster Univ, MA, pursing human resources. **Career:** Social Security Admin, claims rep, 1973-80; US Dept of Labor, investigator, 1980-82; US Dept of Army, chief technical services, 1982-87; EEOC, investigator, 1987-90; Alltel Information Svcs, mgr affirmative action/diversity, 1990-. **Orgs:** Arkansas ABIE, board member, 1992-; Lions World Services for the Blind, advisory council, 1990-; Toastmasters, CTM, 1992-; United Way, allocations comm, 1993-; Urban League, board member, 1992; Alpha Kappa Alpha Sorority, 1970-; Greater Little Rock Chamber of Commerce, education comm, 1992-; Arkansas Human Resources Association; Society for Human Resources Management; Leadership Greater Little Rock, Class IX; Help Individuals Receive Employment (HIRE) Inc, board member; Lions World Svcs, advisory council; Ourtown 1; bd mem, Arkansas Children's Museum. **Honors/Awds:** Univ of Arkansas, Cum Laude Graduate, 1972, Means McClellan Award, history dept, 1972; Alpha Kappa Alpha Sorority, Professional Achievement, 1986; NAACP, Black Corporate Executive, 1994. **Special Achievements:** 1991 SBA Region IV Natl Award, Systematics Information Services, Inc, 1991; Agency Leader for Partners in Education, Superintendents Award, 1994; Author, Diversity, 1994; Dept of Army, Special Act Award, 1986; Graduate Leadership Greater Little Rock Class IX, 1994.

PATTILLO, ROLAND A.
Physician, educator. **Personal:** Born Jun 12, 1933, DeQuincy, LA; son of Rhena Pattillo and James Pattillo; divorced; children: Catherine, Michael, Patrick, Sheri, Mary. **Educ:** Xavier Univ, BS 1955; St Louis Univ, MD; Johns Hopkins Univ, post-doc flwsp 1965-67. **Career:** Med Coll WI, prof; WHO, consult 1977, prof dir cancer research & research sci; Med Coll WI, physician 1968-; Harvard Univ, fellow, resd 1960-64; Marquette Univ; Morehouse School of Medicine, interim chmn, 1996, dir residency prog, OBGYN dept. **Orgs:** Bd dir Amer Cancer Soc; mem Milwaukee Div Sci Jour Reviewer; Jour of Natl Cancer Inst Sci; Cancer Rsrch; Amer Jour OB-GYN; OB-GYN Jour NIH flwsp 1965-67. **Honors/Awds:** Rscrh award Amer Clge OB-GYN 1963; Found Thesis Award Amer Assc OB-GYN 1975; author publ; Physician of the Year, Cream City Medical Society, 1990; Medical College of Wisc, Distinguished Service Award, 1994. **Business Addr:** 720 Westview Dr, SW, Atlanta, GA 30310-1495.

PATTMAN, VIRGIL THOMAS, SR.
Electronic engineer. **Personal:** Born Nov 29, 1940, Detroit, MI; children: Virgil Thomas Jr, Randall H, Tiffaney Lynn. **Educ:** Lawrence Inst of Tech, BS 1969; Detroit Inst of Tech, BS 1981; Central MI Univ, MA 1983. **Career:** General Electric Co, electronic tech 1964-67; GM Corp Proving Ground, elec engr 1967-78; GM Corp Tech Ctr Mfg Div, safety engr 1978-82; GM Corp Tech Ctr Adv Eng Staff, sr safety engr 1983-. **Orgs:** Bd of trustees 1968-84, church treas & finance sec asst 1972-84, audio engr 1984-, church school tchr 1985-, bd of christian educ 1986- Peace Bapt Church Detroit; mem Amer Soc of Safety Engrs 1980-. **Honors/Awds:** Appeared in Ebony Magazine Who's Who 1982; First black senior safety engr at the GM Tech Ctr responsible for staff of 1500 persons. **Military Serv:** AUS Reserves sgt 1963-69; instructor of chemical biological & radiological warfare. **Home Addr:** 15015 Glastonbury St, Detroit, MI 48223. **Business Addr:** Senior Safety Engineer, GM Tech Center, Advanced Engrg Staff, 30300 Mound Rd, Warren, MI 48090.

PATTON, CURTIS LEVERNE
Scientist, educator. **Personal:** Born Jun 13, 1935, Birmingham, AL; married Barbara Beth Battle, 1963; children: Lynne Martine. **Educ:** Fisk Univ, BA, 1956; Michigan State Univ, MS, 1961, PhD, microbiology, 1966. **Career:** Michigan State University, assistant microbiologist, 1960-63, assistant instructor to instructor, 1963-67; Rockefeller University, guest investigator, 1967-70; Yale University, School of Medicine, assistant professor microbiology, 1970-74, director of graduate studies, 1972-74, assistant professor of epidemiology, public health & microbiology, 1974-76, associate professor of epidemiology, public health & microbiology, 1976-. **Orgs:** Interdisciplinary Parasitol Training Program, director; Minority Access Research Careers & National Institute of General Medical Sciences, 1978-82; National Research Council Community Human Resources Evaluation Panel, 1979-81; US Army Medical Research & Development Command, consultant, 1979-82; AAAS; American Society of Parasitologists; Society of Protozoologists. **Honors/Awds:** Biomedical Science Support Grant, 1966-67; Rockefeller University, Parasitology Fellowship, 1967-70; USPHS, Training Grant, 1967-69, Research Grants, 1972-77, 1978-86.

Military Serv: AUS spec 6th class 1956-59. **Business Addr:** Professor, Yale University, School of Medicine, New Haven, CT 06510.

PATTON, GERALD WILSON
Educator, educational administrator. **Personal:** Born Nov 13, 1947, Chattanooga, TN; son of Ruby Griffin Patton and William Patton II (deceased); married Linda S Williams; children: Germond Che'. **Educ:** Kentucky State Univ, BA 1969; Western Illinois Univ, MA 1973; Univ of Iowa, PhD 1978. **Career:** North Carolina State Univ, asst prof history 1978; Washington Univ, asst dean of graduate school of arts & science 1978-81; North Central Assn of Colleges & Schools, assoc dir, commission on institutions of higher eduction, currently. **Orgs:** Coordinator "St Louis A Policy Framework for Racial Justice, an Agenda for the 80's" sponsored by the Danforth Found 1984-85; chmn Educ Comm 100 Black Men of St Louis 1983-; chmn MO Comm of Black Studies 1984-. **Honors/Awds:** "War and Race, Black Officer in the Amer Military" 1981; Congressional Black Caucus Found Scholars lecturer 1984.

PATTON, JEAN E.
Color consultant, educator, business executive. **Personal:** Born Mar 14, 1947, Bronx, NY; daughter of Estelle Witherspoon Patton and John Henry Patton. **Educ:** City University of the City of New York, BA, psychology, 1971. **Career:** Training for Living Institute, group facilitator, 1971-73; Harlem Confrontation Drug Rehabilitation Ctr, dir of educ, 1973-75; National Westminster Bank, asst vice pres, corp training & devt mgr, 1975-83; Second Skin Cosmetics, founder, pres, 1983-; Color Education Resources, founder, president, 1986-. **Orgs:** Association of Image Consultants Intl, local & national boards, various committees. **Honors/Awds:** Harlem YMCA, Black Achievers in Industry Award, 1983; Assn of Image Consultants Intl, Image Makers Merit & Industry Excellence Award, 1992. **Special Achievements:** Introduced the first personal color analysis course at Parsons School of Design, School of Continuing Education, 1986; author of numerous articles on color analysis, image and color psychology; created the first skin tone analysis system that makes it easy to accurately select complexion flattering colors for ethnic skin tones; Author, Color to Color, The Black Woman's Guide to a Rainbow of Fashion and Beauty, Simon & Schuster, 1991. **Business Addr:** President, Color Education Resources, PO Box 7704, New York, NY 10016-6432, (212)564-3082.

PATTON, JOSEPH
Professional football player. **Personal:** Born Jan 5, 1972, Birmingham, AL. **Educ:** Alabama A&M, attended. **Career:** Washington Redskins, guard, 1994-. **Business Addr:** Professional Football Player, Washington Redskins, 13832 Redskin Dr, Herndon, VA 22071, (703)471-9100.

PATTON, JOYCE BRADFORD
Educational Administrator, educator. **Personal:** Born May 31, 1947, Shreveport, LA; married Jerry A Patton (deceased); children: Blythe. **Educ:** Grambling State Univ, BA 1969; SUNY Teacher Coll at Buffalo, MS 1972; LA State Univ at Shreveport, 1983. **Career:** Caddo Parish Schools, teacher of earth science, assistant principal of curriculum and instruction, currently. **Orgs:** Mem Prog Scholarship Comm Alpha Kappa Alpha Inc 1966-; mem Natl Educ Assn 1972-, YWCA 1983-, Natl Science Teachers Assn 1984-; local school chmn Substance Abuse Prevention Educ 1984-; local board 1st vice pres Parent Teacher Student Assn 1984-85; mem Natl Earth Sci Teachers Assn 1986-; youth Sunday school supt Mt Canaan Baptist Church 1986-; member Phi Delta Kappa 1987-; president, Northwest Louisiana Science Teachers Assn, 1991-92; exec board member, Louisiana Science Teacher Assn, 1990-93; Alpha Kappa Alpha Sorority Inc, Ebony Fashion Fair, chair, 1993-94. **Honors/Awds:** Presidential Awds for Excellence in Science & Math Teaching LA State winner 1986, natl winner 1986; Teacher Enhancement Program Evaluator Natl Science Foundation 1987; Educator of Distinction Louisiana PTA 1987; Middle School Teacher of the Year Caddo Parish School Bd 1988; Selected for the National Science Foundation Sposored "Operation Physics," 1988; Teacher Enhancement Program Evaluator, National Science Foundation 1988-94; Louisiana Middle School Association, Educator of the Year, 1992-93. **Special Achievements:** Louisiana's teacher representative to the first Japan/America Grassroot Summit in Tokyo and Kyoto, Nov 1991. **Home Addr:** 6306 Kenwood Lane, Shreveport, LA 71119. **Business Addr:** Assistant Principal of Curriculum and Instruction, Caddo Parish Schools, 7635 Cornelious Dr, Shreveport, LA 71106.

PATTON, LEROY
Cinematographer. **Personal:** Born Apr 14, 1944, Alabama; son of Neuria Patton and Charles H Patton; married Jessie Maple Patton; children: Mark A, Edward L, Audrey Maple. **Educ:** IN Central Coll; IN Univ, 1967; CA Film Inst for Filmmakers, 1971. **Career:** LJ Film Prod, pres/dir of photography; "Ft Apache, The Bronx" Time Life Prod Inc, cameraman; "Fame" MGM Prod Inc, stand-by dir of photography 1979; "Will" LJ Film Prod Inc, dir of photography 1978; "Black Econ Power - Realty or Fantasy", dir of photography; "Up Against the Wall," African-American Images Production, Chicago, IL, dir of photography, 1990. **Orgs:** Pres Concerned Black Filmmakers of NYC; mem 100 Black Men Inc mem found for independent video & film; mem cameraman union iatse local 644. **Honors/Awds:** Publ "How to Become a Union Camerawoman Film-Videotape" 1977; 1st & 2nd prize NY Black Film Festival 1977; Freedoms Found Award WCBS-TV spec "My Seeds Are Gone" 1979. **Business Addr:** President, Concerned Black Filmmakers, 1270 Fifth Ave, Ste 10C, New York, NY 10029.

PATTON, MARVCUS RAYMOND
Professional football player. **Personal:** Born May 1, 1967, Los Angeles, CA; son of Raymond (deceased) and Barbara; married Brigitte. **Educ:** University of California, Los Angeles, BS, political science, 1990. **Career:** Buffalo Bills, linebacker, 1990-94; Washington Redskins, 1995-. **Special Achievements:** Played in Super Bowls with the Buffalo Bills, 1991-94. **Business Addr:** Professional Football Player, Washington Redskins, 13832 Redskin Dr, Herndon, VA 22071, (703)471-9100.

PATTON, PRINCESS E.
Journalist, editor. **Personal:** Born Jan 1, 1954, Nashville, TN; daughter of Mary Frances Corder Gordon (deceased) and Gill H Gordon Sr; married Alexander Patton Jr, Aug 25, 1990; children: Keisha RaNese Simmons Clopton, Ayesha Patrice Patton, H Eric Simmons. **Educ:** Fisk University, BA, 1978. **Career:** United Methodist Publishing House, Abington Press, copy editor; Vanderbilt University, staff reporter, calendar editor, 1984-86; The Tennessean, forum editor, columnist, editorial writer, 1986-92; Meharry Medical Coll, publications editor, 1994-. **Orgs:** National Association of Black Journalists, 1986-; Nashville Association of Minority Communicators, 1986-; Minority Journalism Workshop, executive committee member, 1991-92; Parents for Public Education, steering committee member, 1990-91; Parents Against Paddling, advisory committee member, 1989-. **Honors/Awds:** Domestic Violence Program, Peace and Justice Award, 1990. **Home Addr:** PO Box 22698, Nashville, TN 37202.

PATTON, RICARDO
Basketball coach. **Personal:** marrIed Jennifer. **Career:** Univ of Colorado at Boulder, head basketball coach, 1996-. **Business Addr:** Head Coach, Basketball, University of Colorado-Boulder, Campus Box 378, Boulder, CO 80309-0001.

PATTON, ROBERT
Educator. **Personal:** Born Jun 29, 1947, Clarksdale, MS; married Dorothy J Johnson; children: Kamela. **Educ:** Jackson State Univ, atnd 1968; Delta State Univ, mA 1976. **Career:** Bolivar Co School Dist 3, teacher; Bolivar Co, city alderman. **Orgs:** Mem Jackson State Alumni Assc; mem St Andrews Bapt Ch; vice pres PTA Broad St Sch; St Andrews Bapt Church, trustee. **Honors/Awds:** Recip Outst Comm Ldr 1974-75.

PATTON, ROSEZELIA L.
Consultant. **Personal:** Born Sep 25, 1934, Cincinnati, OH; daughter of Rosezelia Bradshaw Leahr (deceased) and Robert L Leahr; married Walter B Patton, Sep 6, 1958 (deceased); children: Councill M Harris III, Rebecca Leah Harris-Ragland. **Educ:** Miami Univ 1975-1984; Western College 1970-72. **Career:** DuBois Bookstore Oxford OH, trade buyer 1962-69; The Western Coll Oxford OH, registrar 1969-74; Miami Univ Sch of Ed & Allied Prof, prog consul 1974-82; Miami Univ Roudebush Hall Oxford, asst to dir aff act 1982-84; Sears Roebuck & Co, sales rep 1987-88; Acme Wrecking, Cincinnati, OH, consultant, 1990-. **Orgs:** Housemother Alpha Phi Alpha Miami Univ 1959-62; bd dirs Butler Co Mental Health/Retardation 1966-69; volunteer Planned Parenthood 1965-70; treas Church Women United Oxford 1962-63; vice pres treas Oxford Bus & Professional Women 1973-74 1974-75; Minister of Music Bethel AME Oxford 1962-72 1977-; chair of budget & financial estimates Conf Branch of the Women's Missionary Soc 1978-86; pres Women's Missionary Soc 1977-84; bd of dir Oxford Crisis and Referral Center 1984-91; citizens advisory committee, Butler County Children's Services Board, 1990-92, 1993-. **Home Addr:** 520 S Main St, Oxford, OH 45056-2363.

PAUL, ALVIN, III
Educator, educational administrator. **Personal:** Born Feb 17, 1941, New Roads, LA; son of Pearl H Paul and Alvin Paul; married Vera; children: Alvin Jerome, Calvin James, Douglas Fairbanks. **Educ:** Southern Univ, Baton Rouge LA, BS 1961; Northeastern Illinois Univ, MEd 1970; Nova Univ Ft Lauderdale, EdD, 1979. **Career:** Pointe Coupee Parish Schools, New Roads LA, math & science teacher 1961-62; Gary Public Schools, math teacher 1962-71, team leader & asst principal 1967-69; Prairie State Coll, math & educ teacher 1971-90; Marcy Newberry Center Chicago, acting exec dir & dir 1971; Our Lady of Solace Catholic School Chicago, principal 1974-75; Triton Coll, River Grove IL, math teacher 1979-; Prairie State Coll, professor, Math department, 1990-. **Orgs:** Mem St Dorothy Parish Council 1976-79; pres St Dorothy School Bd 1976-79; mem Personalized Learning Program Advisory Bd Prairie State Coll 1976-87; mem Human Serv Advisory Bd Prairie State Coll 1977-90; mem Archdiocese of Chicago Bd of Educ 1979-84; chmn Human Serv Dept Prairie State Coll 1980-83; mem metric adv bd Prairie State Coll 1980-82; Keeper of Records 1982; Kappa Alpha Psi Chapter Guide Right Comm 1982, 1985, 1987; chmn Academic Program Review Comm PSC 1983-85; vice polemarch Kappa Alpha Psi Frat 1985-87; deputy grand knight, Knights of Peter Claver Council #158 1987-89; chmn Academic Program Review Comm Prairie State Coll; former chmn Financial Comm St Dorothy School Bd; treasurer PSC Fed of Teacher Union; mem Curriculum Comm & Faculty Senate (PSC); chmn Teacher Aide Advisory Bd Prairie Coll; former business mgr Our Lady of Peace Home Sch Assn; former mem, Our Lady of Peace Parish Council; polemarch, Chicago Hts Alumni, Kappa Alpha Psi Frat, 1987-88; keeper of records, Chicago Alumni, Kappa Alpha Psi 1993-; bd mem, Chicago Heights, BRCEDA, 1983-; president, Association Black Personnel, PSC; chairman, Spiritual Life Commission; prayer group, coordinator, promise keepers at St Dorothy Catholic Church, 1996-; chair, NCAAAE Committee, PSC. **Honors/Awds:** Dissertation, Perceived Satisfaction of Traditional Students with Traditional Coll Programs, Nova Univ, 1979; PSC, Faculty of the Year; 1981, 1996, Polemarch Award; Distintuished Alumni Award, N Central Province, KAY, 1996. **Business Addr:** Professor, Math Department, Prairie State Coll, Illinois Jr Coll Dist 515, Chicago Heights, IL 60411.

PAUL, BEATRICE
Business executive. **Personal:** Born Mar 13, 1943, Portsmouth, VA; divorced; children: Kellene, Keith Jr, Kerrith. **Educ:** Empire State Clge, BA 1973. **Career:** 19th Ward Youth Proj, dir; SUC Brockport, adj prof; Early Childhood Devel Ctr, exec dir; Early Childhood Learning Ctr Rochester Assc for Educ of Young Child, dir 1973-75. **Orgs:** Chmn Staff Devel & Training Task Force 1973-75; Rochester Chap Natl Assc of Black Social Workers; bd dir Western NY Child Care Council 1974-75; Natl Caucus of Black Sch Bd mems; Rochester Sub-region N Eastern Black Polit Caucus; Black Ldrshp studies grp; adv bd Comm Educ Ctr 1971-72; FIGHT Inc vice pres bd of educ 1977-78; pres Rochester Bd of Educ 1978-79. **Honors/Awds:** Comm Involvement Award Comm Schl Council 1976; Oustst Comm Serv Award Nghbrhd St Acad; Comm Serv Award Wilson Jr High 1975-76; Comm Srv Award CommSch Council 1977; Comm Srv Award Title I 1978; Outst Citizen Award Genesee Settlement House 1978; Political Srv Award Eureka Lodge 1979; Political Srv Award Electric City Lodge 1979; Comm Srv Award Marcus Garvey Meml 1979; Appreciation Award Franklin High 1979; Spec Recog Class of '79 Franklin 1979; Meritorious Srv Award Title I 1979; Outst Citizen Award Comm Sch Council 1980. **Business Addr:** 447 Genesee St, Rochester, NY 14611.

PAUL, JOHN F.
Business executive. **Personal:** Born Sep 13, 1934, Miami, FL; married Betty; children: Dana, Derek, Darryl, Darin. **Educ:** BA 1964; MPA 1970; Cert Mgmt Devel Inst, 1970; Cert Inst for Ct Mgmt, 1971; Cert Inst of Labor & Industrial Rel 1972; Cert Natl Inst of Corrections, 1973-74. **Career:** CEA Dept of Human Resources Devel Los Angeles CA, mgr 1969-71; State Serv Ctr Los Angeles, asst mgr 1968-69, supr cnslr 1967-68; CA Youth & Corrections Agy, parole ofcr 1964-67; CA Youth & Corrections Agency Norwalk CA, sr grp supr 1960-64; Circuit Ct Probation Dept, dir. **Orgs:** Consult US Dept of Justice Comm Rel Ofc 1974; consult Univ of So CA Cntr for Adm of Justice 1974; mem Amer Soc for Pub Admin; mem Natl Council onCrime & Delinquency; mem MI Correctional Assc; mem Acad of Ct Admin; mem NAACP; Trade Unionist Ldrshp Conf; MI Black Caucus. **Honors/Awds:** Recip Flwshp Univ of Denver Inst of Ct Mgmt; China Serv Award. **Military Serv:** USN petty ofcr 3rd class 1952-56; Good Conduct Award. **Business Addr:** 3600 Cadillac Tower, Detroit, MI 48226.

PAUL, TITO
Professional football player. **Personal:** Born May 24, 1972, Kissimmee, FL. **Educ:** Ohio State Univ, attended. **Career:** Arizona Cardinals, defensive back, 1995-97; Cincinnati Bengals, 1997-. **Business Addr:** Professional Football Player, Cincinnati Bengals, One Bengals Dr, Cincinnati, OH 45202, (513)621-3550.

PAUL, VERA MAXINE
Educator. **Personal:** Born Dec 14, 1940, Mansfield, LA; daughter of Virginia Elzania Smith Hall and Clifton Hall; married Dr Alvin James Paul III, Jun 14, 1964; children: Alvin Jerome, Calvin James, Douglas Fairbanks. **Educ:** Southern Univ, Baton Rouge LA, BS, 1962; Chicago State Univ, Chicago IL, 1968-69; Roosevelt Univ, Chicago IL, MA, 1975. **Career:** Union Street High School, Shreveport LA, teacher, 1962-64; South Bend Community School System, South Bend IN, 1967-68; Chicago Bd of Educ, Chicago IL, teacher, asst principal, 1964-67, 1968-. **Orgs:** Mem, Chicago Teacher Union, 1964-; mem, Natl Assn for the Advancement of Colored People, 1965-; mem, Illinois Teacher Union, 1968-; mem, Natl Mathematics Assn, 1969-88; mem, Illinois Mathematics Assn, 1975-88; mem, Operation Push, 1975-88; mem, Amer Federation of Teachers, 1978-; mem, Urban League, 1980-88; mem, Chicago Area Alliance of Black School Educators, 1982-87; life mem and Great Lakes regional dir, Zeta Phi Beta Sorority, Inc, 1986-90. **Honors/Awds:** Distinguished Volunteer Leadership, March of Dimes, 1982; Mayoral Tribute from City of Pontiac MI, 1987; Zeta of Year, Zeta Phi Beta Sorority, Inc, 1988; Distinguished Service Award,

City Council of Detroit, 1988; Award Excellence in Education, New School Administrator, 1988; Outstanding Leadership & Direction, Chicago Women Connecting The UIC Ctr for Research on Women & Gender, 1997; Outstanding Leadership Award, Zeta Phi Beta Sorority, Inc, 1996; Distinguished Service Award, Program Director, Zeta Phi Beta Sorority, Inc, 1992. **Home Addr:** 8505 S Phillips Ave, Chicago, IL 60617.

PAUL, WANDA D.
Hospitality industry executive. **Personal:** Born May 3, 1957, Philadelphia, PA; daughter of Henry and Maude Daniels; married. **Educ:** Temple Univ, BBA, 1979. **Career:** Deloitte Haskins & Sells, auditor, 1980-82; Goode for Mayor Campaign, dir commun fundraising, 1983-84; Philadelphia Convention Bureau, vp finance and admin, 1985-. **Orgs:** Urban League of Philadelphia, chairperson-board of dir, 1980, chair, 1993-95; American Institute of CPA's, 1990-; Pennsylvania Institute of CPA's, 1990-; National Assn of Black Accountants, 1980-; Intl Assn Convention & Visitors Bureau, 1989-; Intl Assn Hospitality Accountants, 1990-. **Honors/Awds:** Toastmasters Intl, Communication Award, 1992; Commonwealth of PA, Certified Public Accountant, 1990; NABA's Pro, Professional Achievement Award, 1990; Urban League of Philadelphia, Whitney Young Community Service Award, 1989; United Negro College Fund, Service Award Alumni Council Conf, 1993; Urban League Guild, Service Award, 1993. **Business Addr:** VP, Finance & Admin, Philadelphia Convention & Visitors Bureau, 1515 Market St, Ste 2020, Philadelphia, PA 19102, (215)636-3325.

PAWLEY, THOMAS D., III
Professor (retired). **Personal:** Born Aug 5, 1917, Jackson, MS; son of Ethel John Woolfolk and Thomas D Pawley; married Ethel Louise Mc Peters; children: Thomas IV, Lawrence. **Educ:** VA State Coll, AB (with distinction) 1937; Univ of IA, AM 1939, PhD 1949. **Career:** Prairie View A&M State Coll, instr 1939-40; Lincoln Univ of MO, div chmn 1967-77, dean of arts & scis 1977-83, instr/asst prof/assoc prof/prof 1940-, writer in residence, head dept of communications 1983-85, curators disting prof of speech and theatre, head dept of communications 1985-88, curators' distinguished prof emeritus, speech and theatre, 1988-. **Orgs:** Visit prof at: Univ of CA Santa Barbara 1968; Northern IL Univ 1971; Univ of IA 1976; Univ of MO 1980, 1988, 1990; pres Natl Assn of Dramat and Speech Arts 1953-55; adv com Am Educ Theatre Assn 1953-55; comm on Theatre Educ Am Theatre Assn 1977-79; pres Speech & Theatre Assn of MO 1977-78; Theatre Adv Comm of the MO Arts Cncl 1979-87; Exec Com Black Theatre Prgm Am theatre Assn 1980-; delegate to the Episcopal Diocesan Conv St Louis 1963; treas Jefferson Reg Libr Bd 1974; pres J C Library board 1970-72; v chmn Mayor's Comm on Resid Standards; mem organiz comm Jefferson City Cncl on Race and Religion; delegate Governor's Conf on Libr Services 1978, 1990; bd of dirs Mid Amer Arts Alliance 1981-, MO Arts Council 1981-87; Natl Endowment for the Arts Theatre Panel 1986-88; National Conference on African-American Thre, president, 1987-90; Missouri Humanities Council, 1989-95; delegate, White House Conf on Library & Information Services, 1991; midwestern vice pres, Alpha Phi Alpha Frat, 1975-79; Historian Alpha Phi Alpha Fraternity, Inc, 1993-96; Vestry, Grace Episcopal Church, 1994-97. **Honors/Awds:** Contemporary Authors 1971; Living Black Authors 1973; Shields-Howard Creative Writing Award VA State Coll 1934; Natl Theatre Conf Fellowship 1947-48; Winner of 1st Prize Jamestown, VA Corp Playwriting Contest 1954 for play "Messiah"; Outstanding Teacher Award Speech and Theatre Assn of MO 1977; Elected to Coll of Fellows Amer Theatre Assn 1978; Author of numerous books/articles/plays and poetry incl, "The Black Teacher and the Dramatic Arts" with Wm Reardon Negro Univ Press 1970; "The Black Theatre Audience" Players Mag Aug-Sep 1971; "FFV" Full-length drama 1963 First production by Stagecrafters Lincoln Univ 1963;"The Tumult and the Shouting" Drama in Two Acts 1969 First production by Inst in Dramatic Arts Lincoln Univ 1969 Publ in Hatch and Shine 1974; Natl Assoc of Dramatic & Speech s Outstanding Serv Awd 1984; Natl Conf on African Amer Theatre Mister Brown Awd 1986; Distinguished Alumnus NAFEO Virginia State Univ 1988; American Theatre Fellow, 1989; Distinguished Alumnus Achievement Award, Univ of Iowa Alumni Assn, 1990. **Home Addr:** 1014 Lafayette, Jefferson City, MO 65101. **Business Addr:** Professor Emeritus, Lincoln University Box 212, Jefferson City, MO 65101.

PAXTON, GERTRUDE GARNES
Dentist. **Personal:** Born Oct 9, 1931, Raleigh, NC; married Lawrence Paxton; children: Lynn, Lori, Lawrence Jr. **Educ:** Univ CA, 1966; DDS 1956; Howard Univ Clge Dentistry, flw; Howard Univ, BS 1956. **Career:** Dentist pvt prac; Pub Hlth, 1966-71, 1956-58; Howard Univ Clge Dentistry, instr 1956-58. **Orgs:** Mem Dental Adv Bd S Cntrl Multi-Srv & Child Devel Ctr; Alain Lock HS 1976-; Adv Cncl Reachout Com Cncl; Performing Arts Music Ctr; mem Omicron Kappa Upsilon Natl Dental Hon Soc; Beta Kappa Chi Sci Hon Soc; Links Inc; Angel City Chpt; Jack & Jill of Amer; pres Circle-Lets 1973-75; Med Dental & Pharm Aux 1968-70; Alva C Garrott Dental Aux 1966-68; mem Natl Dental Assc; Amer Dental Assc. **Honors/Awds:** Outst Black Women in Dentistry Alpha Kappa Alpha Heritage Series; cited Natl Arthritis Found; bd dir YWCA LA. **Business Addr:** 3310 W Slauson Ave, Los Angeles, CA 90043.

PAXTON, PHYLLIS ANN
Health services administrator. **Personal:** Born May 5, 1942, Birmingham, AL; daughter of Neida Mae Perry and Dan Roland Perry; married Herbert W Laffoon, Apr 2, 1979; children: Terella. **Educ:** Grady Memorial Hospital School of Nursing, certificate, 1963; The Atlanta Center of Medical College of GA, BS, nursing, 1968; Emory Univ, MN, maternal & child health educ, 1970. **Career:** Univ of AL Birmingham, asst prof nursing; UCLA Extension-Continuing Educ in Health Sci Div of Nursing, proj dir Family Planning Nurse Practitioner Prog 1975-77; LA Regional Family Planning Cncl, training assc 1973-75; UCLA, asst prof of nursing 1970-73; L A Regional Family Planning Council, principal assoc 1978-85; JWCH Institute Inc, manager 1985-89, exec dir 1989-. **Orgs:** Consult Western Interstate Commn on Higher Educ Proj, Models Intro Cultural Diversity in Nursing Curricula 1974-; consult list Amer Pub Health Assn 1974-76; CA Nurses Assn Minority Grp Task Force 1971-73; field rep Proj Breakthrough recruitment of Blacks, Amer Indians, Chicanos, Puerto Ricans & Males into Nursing Schl leading to RN licensure 1972-73; devel 1st Summer Pre-entry Retention Prog for Ethnic Students of Color at UCLA Sch of Nursing 1972; sec Redeemer Alternative School Board 1988-; mem bd of dirs, California Reproductive Health Assn, 1989-; member, Community Coalition for Prevention of Substance Abuse, 1991; bd California's Women & Children's Health Coalition (CALWACHO), 1997; bd Mother Voices, Los Angeles Chap, 1997. **Honors/Awds:** Outst Nurse Award Nursing Fund Inc of LA 1973; Natl Med Assn Fnd Award Commitment to action in increasing number of minorities in Health Careers 1972; publ "Providing Safe Nursing Care to Ethnic People of Color" 1976; "Continuing Educ Needs of Nurses Serving Minorities & The Poor" Jour of Continuing Educ in Nursing 1974; National Association of County Organizations Award 1987; developed a comprehensive perinatal services program which served as a model for the Lost Angeles County Dept of Health Services programs in 1985; LA Women's Foundation Mercedes Mentor Award, 1996. **Business Addr:** Executive Director, JWCH Institute Inc, 1910 Sunset Blvd Suite 650, Los Angeles, CA 90026, (213)484-1186.

PAYDEN, HENRY J., SR.
Clergyman. **Personal:** Born Apr 3, 1923, Columbus; married Phyllis M Smith; children: Garnet, William B, Linda, Henry J. **Educ:** Capital Univ; Cleveland Bible Clge Westminster; Western Res Univ; Cert in Clin Psychology & Pastoral Counseling, Ashland Theological Seminary, 1971. **Career:** Holy Trinity Bapt Ch, organizer & pastor 1961-; St Paul Bapt Ch New Castle PA, former pastor; Macedonia Bapt Ch Toledo; Gr Abyssinia Bapt Ch Cleveland. **Orgs:** Featured soloist with "Wings Over Jordan"; Cleveland Women's Sym Orch; Chpln of Amvets; Mem Mt Pleasant Comm Ctr; mem Pub Bd & Tchr Prog Natl Bapt Conv Inc. **Honors/Awds:** Hnrd as Pastor of Year 1956; awarded automobile as Soloist in Burts Hour Cleveland 1947. **Military Serv:** US 9 Cav sgt. **Business Addr:** Pastor, Holy Trinity Baptist Church, 3808 14 E 131 St, Cleveland, OH 44120.

PAYNE, ALLEN
Actor. **Career:** Actor, appearances in the films: "Rooftops," "New Jack City," "CB4," "Jason's Lyric," and "The Walking Dead"; "The Tuskegee Airmen," HBO Movie, 1995. **Business Addr:** Actor, c/o Bragman Nyman Cafarelli, 9171 Wilshire Blvd., Penthouse, Beverly Hills, CA 90210.

PAYNE, ALLISON GRIFFIN
Broadcast journalist. **Personal:** Born Feb 12, 1964, Richmond, VA; daughter of Kathryn Griffin Payne and Dana Payne. **Educ:** University of Detroit, BA, 1985; Bowling Green State, MA, 1992. **Career:** WNWO-TV, Toledo, OH, reporter, 1987-88; WNEM-TV, Saginaw, MI, anchor, 1988-90; WGN-TV, Chicago, IL, anchor/reporter, 1990-. **Orgs:** Delta Sigma Theta, member. **Honors/Awds:** Best Documentary Series, Regional Award, Radio Television News Directors, 1991; Emmy recipient, 1991-92; Chicago Association of Black Journalists, Mark of Excellence Award, 1992; Society of Professional Journalists, Peter Lisage Award, 1991; Illinois Broadcasters Association, Silver Dome Award, 1991-92. **Business Addr:** News Reporter/Co-Anchor, WGN-TV, Channel 9, 2501 W Bradley Place, Chicago, IL 60618-4767.

PAYNE, CECILIA
Graphic design & advertising company executive. **Personal:** Born Dec 5, 1962, Bronx, NY; daughter of Patricia McKinney & Noah Blount; married George T Payne, Jul 24, 1988; children: George M. **Educ:** School of Visual Arts, BFA, 1984. **Career:** Juvenile Diabetes Magazine, assoc art dir/production, 1987-88; Philip Morris Magazine, assoc art dir/production, 1987-88; Signs & Unique Designs, partner/ceo, 1991-. **Business Addr:** CEO, Signs & Unique Designs, 18 Fairview Street, West Hartford, CT 06119-1808, (203)233-6694.

PAYNE, CYNTHIA PAULETTE
Childcare worker/purchasing secretary. **Personal:** Born Jun 9, 1958, Cleveland, OH; daughter of Zella Rae Ivey (deceased) and Bert William Jackson; divorced; children: Quentin Burkes, Altovise Wilcox, Gregory Jr. **Educ:** Cleveland State University; Dyke College. **Career:** Elyria Police Department, Service Division, secretary, 1978-; Lorain County Detention Home, child care worker, 1990-. **Orgs:** Negro Business and Professional Women's Club, secretary, 1990-; NAACP, 1992-; Lorain County, Ohio, 13th District Congressional Caucus, 1992; Lorain, Ohio, Democratic Women's Club, 1993-; Friendship Baptist Church, usher board, 1992-, youth choir booster club, 1991-. **Honors/Awds:** Chairperson for Ebony Fashion Fair, 1991-. **Home Phone:** (216)277-5869.

PAYNE, DONALD M.
Congressman. **Personal:** Born Jul 16, 1934, Newark, NJ; son of Norma Garrett Payne and William Evander Payne; married Hazel Johnson Payne, Jun 18, 1958 (died 1963); children: Donald Milford, Wanda. **Educ:** Seton Hall University, BA, social studies, 1957, grad study, 1957-63. **Career:** South Side High School, Newark, NJ, teacher, 1957; Robert Treat Junior High School, Newark, NJ, teacher, 1957-59; Pulaski Elementary School, Passaic, NJ, teacher, 1959-64; Prudential Insurance Company, Newark, NJ, affiliated with, 1964-69, manager, beginning 1969; Urban Data Systems, Newark, NJ; Atlantic Western Insurance Co, Hamilton, Bermuda, director, president; Essex County Board of Chosen Freeholders, Newark, NJ, member, 1972-77, director, 1977-82; Newark Municipal Council, councilmember, 1982-88; US House of Representatives, member, 1988-. **Orgs:** President, Natl Council of YMCA's, beginning 1970. **Honors/Awds:** First Black president of the YMCA. **Business Addr:** Congressman, 417 Cannon, Washington, DC 20515-3010.

PAYNE, FREDA
Vocalist. **Personal:** Born 1944, Detroit, MI; married Gregory Abbott; children: Gregory Jr. **Career:** Invictus Record Co, artist. **Special Achievements:** Appeared in Hallelujah Baby; on tour with Quincy Jones, Duke Ellington Orchs; worked with Billy Eckstine/Bob Crosby; num nightclubs TV shows; Broadway play, Jelly's Last Jam, with Maurice Hines. **Business Addr:** 10160 Cielo Dr, Beverly Hills, CA 90210.

PAYNE, GARY D.
Judge. **Personal:** Born Jan 30, 1948, Paducah, KY; son of Sara Cooper Payne and William J Payne; married M Diane Pullen Payne, Sep 16, 1972; children: Lucretia Marie, Cynthia Anne, J Elliot. **Educ:** Pepperdine University, Malibu, CA, BA, 1976; University of Kentucky, Lexington, KY, JD, 1978. **Career:** Kentucky Supreme Court, Frankfort, KY, law clerk, 1979; Kentucky Revenue Cabinet, Frankfort, KY, attorney, 1979; Internal Revenue Service, Louisville, KY, estate attorney, 1980; Crenshaw and Payne, Lexington, KY, partner, 1981-85; University of Kentucky, Lexington, KY, adjunct professor, 1981-; Fayette County Attorney, Lexington, KY, assistant county attorney, 1985-88; Kentucky Corrections Cabinet, Frankfort, KY, staff attorney, 1988; Fayette District Court, Lexington, KY, district judge, 1988-. **Orgs:** Member, Martin Luther King Jr. State Commission, 1988-91; member, Kentucky Crime Commission, 1989-91; member, Child Abuse and Sexual Exploitation Prevention Board, 1989-91; member, Lexington Chapter, National Conference of Christians and Jews, 1990-; member, Big Brothers/Big Sisters of Bluegrass, 1991-; director, Syncopated Inc, 1990-92; adjunct professor, University of Kentucky, 1981-; major, Kentucky Army National Guard, 1981-; Kentucky Council on Child Abuse, 1991-. **Military Serv:** US Marine Corps, E-6; 1970-76; Kentucky National Guard, major, JAG, 1981-.

PAYNE, JACQUELINE LAVERNE
Attorney. **Personal:** Born Dec 15, 1957, Atlanta, GA; daughter of Amos Jr & Doris Hanson Payne; married Timothy Beckum, May 21, 1994; children: Alexis Payne-Scott, Brooke Payne-Scott, Jordan T Beckum. **Educ:** Spelman College, BA (cum laude), 1977; Univ of Georgia, JD, 1980. **Career:** Atlanta Legal Aid Society, staff attorney, 1980-85; managing attorney, 1985-86; Hyatt Legal Services, managing attorney, 1986-88; Atlanta Legal Aid Society, managing attorney, 1988-. **Orgs:** State Bar of Georgia, 1982-; Georgia Assn of Black Women Attorneys; Atlanta Bar Assn; Atlanta Fulton County Commission on Children & Youth, executive committee, 1992-; Northwest Georgia Girl Scout Council, troop leader, 1991-. **Honors/Awds:** Reginald Heber Smith Community Lawyer Fellowship, 1980-82. **Home Addr:** 1268 Brandl Dr, Marietta, GA 30060. **Business Addr:** Managing Atty, Atlanta Legal Aid Society, Inc, 151 Spring St, NW, Atlanta, GA 30303-2097, (404)614-3938.

PAYNE, JAMES EDWARD
Managing attorney. **Personal:** Born Jul 7, 1944, Cleveland, OH; son of Booker T and Vito Payne; married Margaret Ralston Payne, Dec 5, 1976; children: Maya Renee. **Educ:** Cleveland State University, BBA, 1973; University of Akron School of Law, JD, 1977. **Career:** Cleveland Trust Company, staff assistant, 1975-77; Ford Motor Company, labor relations representative, 1977-82, industrial relations analyst, 1982-83; Western Reserve Legal Services, staff attorney, 1983-84; Parms, Purnell & Gilbert, associate attorney, 1984-87; City of Akron, assistant director of law, 1984-87, deputy director of law, 1987-. **Orgs:** Ohio State Bar Assn, council of delegates, 1979-; Akron Bar Assn, board of trustees, 1983-; Alpha Phi Alpha Fraternity Inc, 1986-; Akron Branch NAACP, subscribing life member, 1988-; Planned Partnerhood, president of board, 1989-; Goodwill In-

dustries of Akron, 2nd vice chairman of board, 1990-; Leadership Akron Alumni Assn, 1990-; Salvation Army Advisory Board, 1993-. **Honors/Awds:** Akron Urban League, Service Award, 1988; University of Akron Black Law Students Assn Service Award, 1992; St Paul AME Church, Harold K Stubbs Humanitarian Award, 1994. **Military Serv:** United States Army, 1st lt, 1965-68. **Business Addr:** Deputy Director of Law, City of Akron Dept. of Law, 161 S High St., Ste. 202, Akron, OH 44308-1655, (216)375-2030.

PAYNE, JAMES FLOYD
Higher education administrator. **Personal:** Born Jul 19, 1943, Boonville, IN; married Madelyn Brown; children: Detra, Niambi. **Educ:** Los Angeles City Coll, AA 1968; CA State Univ-Los Angeles, BA 1970; Harvard Univ, MEd 1971; Univ of CA-Irvine, PhD 1975. **Career:** California State Univ-Los Angeles, coordinator of advanced educ and occupational services 1968-70; Harvard Univ and Educational Development Center, rsch assoc 1970-71; California State- Univ Los Angeles, asst prof 1971-82; Oregon State System of Higher Educ, asst in academic and student affairs 1984-86, asst vice chancellor for curricular affairs 1986-. **Orgs:** Mem, Natl Council for Black Studies, 1976-84; bd dirs, California Black Faculty & Staff Assn, 1979-81. **Honors/Awds:** Regents Fellowship, Univ of California-Irvine, 1974. **Military Serv:** USMC cpl-E4, 1961-65.

PAYNE, JERRY OSCAR
Educational administrator. **Personal:** Born Jul 31, 1953, Madera, CA; son of Sallie Ophelia Smiley-Payne and Oscar Payne, Jr (deceased); divorced; children: Deidre Avery, Jonathan. **Educ:** San Jose State Univ, San Jose CA, BA, 1975; Arizona State Univ, Tempe AZ, MA, 1978; Lewis and Clark Coll, Portland OR, education administration certification, 1984; California Schools Leadership Academy, 1987-90; University of Michigan, Ann Arbor, MI, Horace Rackham doctorate fellow, 1990; Harvard Principal's Center, 1992; UC Davis/CSU Fresno Joint Doctoral Program, 1992-. **Career:** Fremont Unified School District, Sunnyvale, CA, Title VII, instructor, 1974-76; Phoenix Union High School, Phoenix, AZ, special educ, Arizona history instructor, 1976-78; El Dorado High School, Las Vegas NV, special education instructor, 1978-80; Clark County Classroom Teachers Assn, Las Vegas, negotiations chairman, 1978-80; Grant High School, Portland OR, special education instructor, 1980-82; Benson Polytechnic High School, Portland, integration counselor, 1982-84, admin asst to principal, 1984-87; Lincoln Summer High School, Portland, principal, 1985-87; Martin Luther King, Jr, Junior High School, Sacramento CA, principal, 1987-90; Parker Elementary School (K-6), Oakland, CA, principal, 1990-96; Hayward Unified District, Hayward, CA, dir of pupil services and health services, 1996-. **Orgs:** Association for California Administrators; Association for Supervision and Curriculum Development; American Association of School Administrators; mem Commission of District Administrators; bd of dir, treas, foundation Bd mem, and life member, National Alliance of Black School Educators; American Vocational Association; National Council of Local Administrators of Vocational, Technical and Practical Arts Education; Hugh O'Brian Alumni Assn; California League of Middle Schools; National Assn of Elementary School Principals; Arizona State University Alumni Assn; Kiwanis International; Toastmasters International; Harvard Principal's Center Alumni; NAACP, life mem; mem NAACP Legal Redress Committee. **Special Achievements:** Author, Turning Around an Urban School: The Vision Versus the Reality, Far West Regional Lab, San Francisco, CA, 1989; author, Effects of Low Expectations on Minority and Low Socio-Economic Students, Educational Research Project, 1985; author, Do Children Whose Parents Have Less Than a High School Diploma Impact Their Child's Academic Achievements?, Arizona State University Graduate School, 1978; co-author, Administrators and Choice, UC Davis CSU, Fresno, 1992; State of California Commission on Teacher Credentialing, admin advisory panel, 1990-96. **Business Addr:** Director of Pupil Services and Health Services, Hayward Unified School District, PO Box 5000, Hayward, CA 94540-5000, (510)784-2625.

PAYNE, JESSE JAMES
Association executive, clergyman. **Personal:** Born Apr 26, 1947, Fayette, AL; son of Lydia R Payne and R P Payne; married Regina Ann Payne, Apr 13, 1989; children: Robert, Yolanda, Jesse III, Jarred. **Educ:** Univ of Nebraska, Lincoln NE, BS, 1973, MS, 1977, attended, 1981-84. **Career:** Lincoln Public Schools, Lincoln Ne, teacher, 1973-75; Lincoln Action Program, Lincoln NE, exec dir, 1975-78; Nebraska Dept of Educ, Lincoln NE, program dir, 1980-81; Kansas State Univ, Manhattan KS, assoc prof, 1981; Lincoln OIC, Lincoln NE, exec dir, 1982-84; Newman Methodist Church, Lincoln NE, pastor, 1982-84; Urban League of Broward County, Ft Lauderdale FL, pres/CEO, 1986-; Bay Area Urban League Inc, Oakland, CA, pres/CEO, currently. **Orgs:** Mem, Council of Chief Exec, Natl Urban League, Council of Exec, United Way of Broward County, Vision ''94'' Comm, City of Ft Lauderdale, BETA Indus Council, City of Ft Lauderdale, Health Access Comm, Broward County Bd Comm, NAACP, 1980-, Natl Urban League, 1986-, Leadership Broward Alumni Assn, 1987-. **Honors/Awds:** Graduated with Honors, Univ of Nebraska-Lincoln, 1973. **Business Addr:** President and Chief Executive Officer, Bay Area Urban League Inc, 344 Twentieth St, Kaiser Center Mall, Suite 211, Oakland, CA 94612.

PAYNE, JUNE EVELYN
Psychologist. **Personal:** Born Jun 11, 1948, Charlottesville, VA; daughter of Theola Reaves Payne and Walter A. Payne; married Charles R Payne EdD; children: Lauren R, Gregory A. **Educ:** VA State Univ, BA 1970; Ball State Univ, MA 1974, PhD 1980. **Career:** Charlottesville Dept of Public Welfare, social worker 1970-72; The Cambridge House Inc, counselor 1974-75, dir of treatment 1976-78; Comprehensive Mental Health Serv of East Central IN, psych 1980-83; Ball State Univ Counseling and Psychological Serv Ctr, counseling psychologist 1983-. **Orgs:** Pres, mem, sec 1984-85 IN Assoc of Black Psych; mem bd of dir Wapahani Girl Scout Council; mem NAACP, Riley-Jones Womens Organization, Delta Sigma Theta Sor. **Home Addr:** 2905 W Woodbridge, Muncie, IN 47304. **Business Addr:** Counseling Psychologist, Ball State Univ, Counseling & Psychological Serv, Muncie, IN 47306.

PAYNE, KENNETH VICTOR
Professional basketball player. **Personal:** Born Nov 25, 1966, Laurel, MS. **Educ:** Univ of Louisville, Louisville, KY, 1985-89. **Career:** Philadelphia 76ers, 1989-.

PAYNE, LESLIE
Journalist. **Personal:** Born Jul 12, 1941, Tuscaloosa, AL; married Violet S Cameron; children: Tamara Olympia, Jamal Kenyatta, Haile Kipchoge. **Educ:** Univ of Connecticut, BA Eng 1964. **Career:** Newsday, natl correspondent/columnist 1980-85, assistant managing, editor, 1985-, investigative reporter 1972-80, minor affairs specialist, 1973-78, editor, writer 1971, asst editor 1970, Babylon Town Beat reporter 1969. **Orgs:** International Press Institute; Natl Assn of Black Journalists 1978; NY Assn of Black Journalists, 1977-80. **Honors/Awds:** Pulitzer Prize Cable TV Ace Award, 1990; Headliner Awd 1974; Sigma Delta Chi Awd 1974; $10,000 United Nations Hunger Award, 1983; Tobenkin Awd Columbia Univ 1978; Man of the Year Award, Natl Assn Black Business & Professional Women 1978; Frederick Douglass Prize, Natl Assn of Black Journalists 1978; AP & UPI Commentary Awards, 1983, 1984; Journalism Prize, 100 Black Men; 2 Unity Awards Lincoln Univ; Pulitzer Prize Selection for Foreign Reporting 1978. **Special Achievements:** Author: The Heroin Trail; Life and Death of the Symbionese Liberation Army. **Military Serv:** US Army, capt, 6 yrs; Bronze Star, 2 Commendation Medals. **Business Addr:** Asst Managing Editor, Newsday, 235 Pinelawn Rd, Melville, NY 11747.

PAYNE, LISA R.
Public relations officer. **Personal:** Born Apr 2, 1962, Bronx, NY; daughter of Florence Grant Payne and Harold Payne Sr. **Educ:** University of Dayton, Dayton, OH, BA, 1984; Fordham University, Bronx, NY, MA, 1989. **Career:** Girls Club of NY, Bronx, NY, dir of youth employment services, 1984-86; Monroe Business College, Bronx, NY, community liaison, 1986-87; Union Theological Seminary, New York, NY, dir of housing, 1987-89; Bronx Museum of the Arts, Bronx, NY, dir of public affairs, 1989-92; Governor Mario Cuomo, regional representative, 1992-95; Offices of Bronx District Attorney, Robert T Johnson, director of community affairs, currently. **Orgs:** Founder, network director, NIA: A Minority Women's Professional Network, Inc, 1984-; president and founder, The Bronx Assn of African American Professionals; board of trustees, Bronx Museum of the Arts, 1994-95; board of dirs, Edenwald Community Center; network dir, National Assn for Female Executives, 1983-. **Honors/Awds:** Humanitarian Award, NIA: A Minority Women's Professional Network, 1988; Woman of the Year, All Saints Roman Catholic Church of Harlem, 1990; Community Service Award, Bronx Center for Progressive Services, 1992; Achievement Award, Natl Council of Negro Women, 1995. **Business Addr:** Director of Community Affairs, Office of the Bronx District Attorney, 198 E 161st St, Bronx, NY 10451, (718)590-2272.

PAYNE, MARGARET RALSTON
Educator, educational administrator. **Personal:** Born Jan 31, 1946, Louisville, KY; daughter of Rena Owens Ralston and Henry Morris Ralston; married James Edward Payne, Dec 11, 1976; children: Maya Renee. **Educ:** Kalamazoo Coll, BA 1968; Fourah Bay Coll Univ of Sierra Leone, attended 1966-67; Kent State Univ, MA 1972, PhD in progress. **Career:** Kent State Univ, asst prof psychology 1972-78, adjunct asst prof psychology 1978-, asst dean prof for developmental services 1973-89, special asst to vice provost for student affairs, 1989-92, Corporate and Foundation Relations, director, 1992-96; Board of Trustees, executive assistant to the president and secretary, 1996-. **Orgs:** President, Kathryn Sisson Phillips Trust, 1994-96; Mem OH & Natl Assn for Women in Education, 1979-; The Links Foundation, Inc, director, 1992-94; pres Kent Area Chap The Links Inc 1984-88; past board member Western Reserve Girl Scout Council; bd mem Portage Co Comm Action Council 1979-85; dist advisor Natl Alpha Lambda Delta 1985-87; mem National Council Alpha Lambda Delta 1985-88; mem Natl Advisory Committee, SAGE: a scholarly journal on black women 1985-95; bd mem Akron Urban League 1988-91; trustee, Summa Health System Foundation, 1995-; board member, Women's Endowment Fund, Akron Community Foundation, 1995-. **Honors/Awds:** Fellow Natl Educ Policy Fellowship Prog 1979-80; Grants OH Rehabilitation Serv Commn 1974, 1975, Lilly Endowment (for NAWDAC) 1982, Fed Dept Health Educ & Welfare Dept of Educ 1974, 1978-; Service Certificate, Assn on Handicapped Student Service Programs in Post Secondary Education 1987; national finalist, White House Fellowship Program 1979; Leadership Award, Kent State University Upward Bound 1989; NAWE, Hilda A Davis Award for Educational Leadership, 1992. **Home Addr:** 797 Cliffside Drive, Akron, OH 44313-5609. **Business Addr:** Executive Assistant to the President & SCY to the Board of Trustees, Executive Offices, Kent State University, PO Box 5190, Kent, OH 44242-0001, (330)672-2210.

PAYNE, MITCHELL HOWARD
Educational administrator. **Personal:** Born Feb 2, 1950, Shelbyville, KY; son of Hattie Cohrell and Llewellyn Payne; married Karen W Bearden, Jul 11, 1987; children: Janell Mitchet, William Mitchell. **Educ:** Western Kentucky Univ, BA, 1972, MPA, 1973; Univ of Louisville, JD, 1978. **Career:** Univ of Louisville, dir minority affairs; Commonwealth of Kentucky, Frankfort KY, exec asst to sec of finance comm for admin; University of Louisville, assoc vice pres, administration, 1990-. **Orgs:** Natl Bar Assn; Amer Soc for Public Admin; Natl Assn of State Dir of Admin & Gen Serv, 1987-; Kappa Alpha Psi Frat; bd mem, Prichard Comm on Academic Excellence, 1987-; advisory council, Kentucky State Univ School of Public Affairs, 1987-; Natl Forum for Black Public Admin, 1988-; steering comm, YMCA Black Achievers Program, 1989-; Sigma Pi Phi Frat, 1989-; NACUBO, 1990; Kentucky Chamber of Commerce, Minority Business, business advisory board, 1992; Kentucky Heritage Council, African-American heritage task force, 1992; 100 Black Men of Louisville, founding member. **Honors/Awds:** Kappa Alpha Psi Frat Alumni Achievement Award, 1985; Dr Martin Luther King Appreciation Award, Western Kentucky Univ, 1986; Alpha Kappa Alpha Sorority, ''Men Who Cook,'' 1988; Volunteer of the Year, Louisville YMCA Black Achievers, 1989; Shelbyville KY, Black Achiever of the Year Award, NAACP, 1989; Sigma Pi Phi, Man of the Year Award, 1991. **Business Addr:** Associate Vice Pres, Administration, University of Louisville, Office of the Vice Pres for Administration, Louisville, KY 40292, (502)852-5155.

PAYNE, N. JOYCE
Educational administrator. **Personal:** Born Jan 29, 1941, Washington, DC; daughter of Eunice Brown Johnson Tyson and Jesse Maryland Tyson; married Charles Harrington (divorced 1984); children: April A, Wynton K. **Educ:** DC Teachers College, Washington, DC, BS, 1971; Atlanta University, Atlanta, GA, MS, 1976, EdD, 1976. **Career:** Presidential Council on Women's Educational Programs, DC specialist, 1977-79; President's Advisory Council on Women, DC, educational specialist, 1979-81; National Association of State Universities & Land-Grant Colleges, DC director, Office for the Advancement of Public Black Colleges, 1979-. **Honors/Awds:** Spencer Research Grant, Spencer Foundation, 1975; Ford Fellowship, Ford Foundation, 1971; Founder of the Thurgood Marshall Scholarship Fund, 1984. **Business Addr:** Dir, Office for the Advancement of Public Black Colleges, 1 Dupont Circle, NW, Suite 710, Washington, DC 20036.

PAYNE, OSBORNE ALLEN
Consultant. **Personal:** Born May 26, 1925, Bedford, VA; married Famebridge Cunningham; children: Andrea Kyles, Famebridge S, Sarita S. **Educ:** VA Union Univ, BS 1950, VA State Univ MS 1955; Univ of VA, 1961; Univ of MD, 1974. **Career:** Richmond, VA, tchr 1950-57, principal 1957-62; Cuttington Coll Liberia, W Africa, act dean of instr 1963-65; TAP Roanoke, VA, field dir 1965-66, educ dir 1966-68; NEA Search, dir 1968-70; NEA Special Svcs, field coord 1970-73; Natl Educ Assn, consumer adv 1974-75; Baltimore-Specialty Tours, pres; Broadway-Payne Inc, president, currently. **Orgs:** Bd of dir VA Union Univ 1980; bd of associate St Paul's Coll 1983; past president Pres's Roundtable; Greater Baltimore Committee 1984-. **Honors/Awds:** Golden Arch Elite McDonald's 1976-77; Governor's Citation for Outstanding Serv MD 1982; Presidential Citation Natl Assn for Equal Oppty in Higher Educ 1983; Senator's Citation for Many Years of Dedicated Serv to the Community 1984; President's Citation, Baltimore City Cncl 1985; Citations MD Senate, Governors MD, Citizens by Mayor WD Schaefer, MD Black Caucus 1985; Honorary Degree Dr of Intl Law, 1985; Citations Md House of Delegates, 41st Dist Baltimore, Congressional Merit, US Senate, 1985; Businessman of the Year Intl Assn of Negro & Professional Women; ''An Evening With'' honoree Project Survival 1985; Ronald McDonald Awd for community involvement 1985; small business awd by Mayor of Baltimore 1985; Baltimore Mktg Assoc Man of the Year 1985. **Military Serv:** USN 3rd Class Petty Officer 1943-46. **Business Addr:** President, Broadway-Payne, Inc, 10 East Lee Street, Baltimore, MD 21202.

PAYNE, RICHELLE DENISE
Media executive. **Personal:** Born Dec 8, 1967, Charleston, WV; daughter of Richard H & Barbara B Payne. **Educ:** Hampton Univ, BA, 1989; Duquesne Univ, MA, 1991. **Career:** Renaissance Publications, editorial staff assistant, 1989; Kaufmann's Dept Store, advertising intern, 1990; Duquesne Univ, grad research assistant, 1991; Innerlink Publications, assoc document specialist, 1993; Hampton Univ, news bureau dir, 1993,

university relations directory, currently. **Orgs:** Hampton Roads Black Media Professionals, 1993-; International Platform Assn, 1993-; Natl Assn Black Journalists, 1993; International Assn of Bus Communicators, 1993; College News Assn, 1993; Public Relations Society of America, 1993. **Honors/Awds:** Dalton Pen Award, Excellence in Feature Writing, 1997. **Business Addr:** News Bureau Director, Hampton University, PO Box 6446, Hampton, VA 23668.

PAYNE, ROD
Professional football player. **Personal:** Born Jun 14, 1974. **Educ:** Univ of Michigan, attended. **Career:** Cincinnati Bengals, center, 1997-. **Business Addr:** Professional Football Player, Cincinnati Bengals, One Bengals Dr, Cincinnati, OH 45202, (513)621-3550.

PAYNE, RONNIE E.
Consultant, company executive. **Personal:** Born Jun 12, 1940, Palmersville, TN; son of Thelma Williams-Payne and Noel Payne; married Jerry Miller-Payne, 1959 (died 1983); children: Angela, Sherri Williams, Anita, Antoinette Benford. **Educ:** Tennessee State University, BS, 1961; Georgia State, attended, 1967-68. **Career:** Lockheed, Missiles & Space, subcontract coordinator, 1961-64, GA, div purchasing supervisor, 1965-67; IBM, senior buyer, 1968-70, central purchasing procurement manager, 1971-76; Digital Equipment Corp., Springfield plant manager, 1978-83, corporate purchasing manager, 1983-88, corporate purchasing vp, strategic resources group staff manager and vp, 1988-93; Excel Partners Inc, general partner, managing dir, 1993-95; Purchasing Services, Inc, founder, CEO, 1995-. **Orgs:** National Minority Supplier Development Council, board of directors, 1987-; Shawmut Middlesex Bank, board of directors, 1986-; Boston University, School of Theology, board of visitors, 1990-; Digital's African Heritage Alliance, advisor, 1990-; Digital's NAACP/ACT-SO, steering committee co-chair, 1987-92. **Honors/Awds:** "A Blueprint for Success," Leadership Council Study of Black Executives, subject of study. **Special Achievements:** First African-American Chief Executive Officer of the Greater Springfield Chamber of Commerce, 1981-82; Rocky Mountain Adoption Exchange Conference, keynote speaker, 1992; "Synergies, Alliances, & New Ventures," Rosabeth Moss Kanter, Harvard Video Series (HBS), 1990; Association of Corporate Travel Executives International, Amsterdam, Holland, presenter, 1990; The Planning Forum, Washington, DC, presenter, 1990. **Home Phone:** (508)651-0105. **Business Addr:** President/CEO, Purchasing Services, Inc, PO Box 5338, Cochituate, MA 01778-6338.

PAYNE, SAMUEL, SR.
Government official. **Personal:** Born Jun 16, 1919, Zion, IL; son of Dora Smith and Samuel Lincoln Payne; married Pearl V Darnell; children: Richard, Robert, Irene, Samuel Jr. **Educ:** Lake Forest Coll, attnd. **Career:** Mem of bd Lke Co Dist #3 1972-; US Steel Wire Co 37 yrs. **Orgs:** Mem Zion Boy Scouts 1949-55; mem Zion Pub Library Bd 1958-62; Spl Zion Police 1958-68; mem Zion Christian Bus Men Com; mem bd of adv Zion Bento Hosp; found mem Mt Zion Missionary Bapt Ch. **Honors/Awds:** 1st Black elem sch bd mem 1970; 1st Black mem bd Lake Co Bd 1972. Special Citizen Award, City of Zion, 1975; Special Citizen Award Mt Lebannon Lodge #715 1985; instrumental in making the first Lake County documentary for the preservation of Lake County's Natural Resources, 1988.

PAYNE, VERNON
Educational administrator. **Personal:** Born Apr 20, 1945, Michigan City, IN; married Dorphine; children: Linda, David, Arthur. **Educ:** Indiana State University, BS, speech pathology and audiology, 1968, MS, guidance and counseling, 1972; George Washington University, Juran Institute, total quality management. **Career:** IBM Corp., research intern, Summer 1967; City of Michigan City, Office of Economic Opportunity, assistant executive director, 1968-70; Western Michigan University, Office of Admissions and Orientation, assistant director, 1989-92, University Recreation Programs and Facilities, director, 1992-. **Orgs:** Lakeside Home, board of directors, 1990-; Kalamazoo County Walk for Warmth, advisory board, 1990-; Resource Development Committee, chairman, 1991-; American Cancer Society of Kalamazoo County, board of directors, 1990-91; Western Michigan University, Fund for the Advancement of Minorities in Education, scholarship committee, 1989-, diversity committee, 1989-; Detroit Edison School Community, Personnel Committee, chairman, 1977-79; numerous others. **Honors/Awds:** Michigan Volunteer of the Year, Outstanding Service to the Detroit Public School System, 1990; Indiana Basketball Hall of Fame, Silver Anniversary Team, Inductee, 1989; National Association of Basketball Coaches of the United States, Merit Award for Distinguished Coaching, 1988; Omega Psi Phi, Man of the Year, 1987; Western Michigan University's National Pan-Hellenic Conference, Faculty Member of the Year, 1992; numerous others. **Home Addr:** 1412 W Kilgore Rd, Kalamazoo, MI 49008. **Business Addr:** Director, University Recreation Programs and Facility, Western Michigan University, 120 Gary Center, Kalamazoo, MI 49008.

PAYNE, WILFORD ALEXANDER
Chief executive officer. **Personal:** Born Jan 4, 1945, Youngstown, OH. **Educ:** Blufton Coll Blufton OH, attnd 1963-65; Youngstown State Univ OH, bA Soc 1973; OH State U, MHA 1975. **Career:** Primary Care Hlth Serv Inc Alma Illery Med Ctr Pittsburgh, proj dir 1977-; Monongahela Valley Assn of Hlth Cntrs Inc Fairmont WV, admin asst 1976-77; Monongahela Valley Assn of Hlth Cntrs Inc, hlth main coord 1976-77; OH State Univ Hosp Columbus, admin asst 1975; St Joseph's Riverside Hosp Warren OH, admin resident 1974. **Orgs:** Bd of dir Eastern Allegheny Co Hlth Corp 1977-; bd of dir Family Plng Counc of Southwestern PA 1977-; instr Tri Reg Cluster Training Cntr NY 1979-; mem Nat Assn of Comm Hlth Cntrs Inc 1977-; com mem Untd Way Review Com of Plng & Allocations Com present. **Honors/Awds:** Scholar Hlth & Welfare Assn 1973-75. **Military Serv:** USAF sgt 1966-70. **Business Addr:** Primary Care & Health Services, 7227 Hamilton Ave, Pittsburgh, PA 15208.

PAYNE, WILLIAM D.
Elected official. **Educ:** Rutgers Univ, BA, political science. **Career:** NJ General Assembly, assemblyman, 1998-. **Orgs:** NJ General Assembly, appropriations comm. **Business Addr:** Assemblyman, 29th Assembly dist, 40 Clinton St, Ste 200, Newark, NJ 07102, (973)621-1400.

PAYTON, ALBERT LEVERN
Organic chemist. **Personal:** Born Feb 8, 1944, Hattiesburg, MS; married Maggie Belle Smith, 1965; children: Al Michaelis, Andriae Monique. **Educ:** Alcorn State Univ, BS, 1965; Southern Univ, Baton Rouge, LA, MS, 1969; Univ of So MS, PhD, chemistry, 1976. **Career:** Hattiesburg Public High School, teacher of chemistry, physics, & math, 1965-67; Southern Univ, asst teacher of chemistry, 1967-69; Dillard Univ, instructor of chemistry and math, 1969-71; Univ Southern Miss, teaching assistant, chemistry, 1971-74; Mississippi Valley State Univ, associate professor, chemistry, 1974-. **Orgs:** Am Chem Soc; Nat Inst Sci. **Honors/Awds:** Southern Fel Fund, Atlanta, 1972-73; Outstanding Young Men of America, 1979; research article, Lithium-Amine Reduction, Journal of Org Chem Acs, 1979; research grant, Acetylenic Acid Syntheses, Nat Sci Found, 1978-81.

PAYTON, BENJAMIN FRANKLIN
Educator. **Personal:** Born Dec 27, 1932, Orangeburg, SC; son of Leroy R & Sarah M Payton; married Thelma Plane; children: Mark Steven, Deborah Elizabeth. **Educ:** SC State Coll, BA (honors) 1955; Harvard Univ, BD 1958; Columbia Univ, MA 1960; Yale Univ, PhD 1963. **Career:** Howard Univ, asst prof 1963-65; Commn on Religion & Race & Dept of Social Justices; Natl Cncl of Churches in USA; Benedict Coll, pres 1967-72; The Ford Found, prog officer 1972-81; Tuskegee Univ, pres 1981-. **Orgs:** Dir Am South Bancorporation; mem Business-Higher Education Forum; mem Amer Soc of Scholars; mem Exec Bd of the Nat'l Consortium for Educ Access; mem Leadership Alabama; dir, AmSouth Bank; dir, ITT Corp, 1987-; dir, Liberty Corp; dir, SONAT, Inc; dir, PRAXAIR, Inc; dir, Ruby Tuesday, Inc; dir, Morrison HealthCare, Inc. **Honors/Awds:** Phi Beta Kappa Delta of Morehouse College Atlanta; Alpha Kappa Mu Honor Soc, SC State Coll; Hon Degrees, Eastern MI, Morris Brown, Benedict, Morgan State University of MD, Lehigh University; Fellowship, Danforth Graduate Fellowship 1955-63; Napoleon Hill Foundation Gold Medal Award 1987; Benjamin E Mays Award, South Carolina State College 1988; Team Leader, Presidential Task Force on Agricultural Development in Zaire, 1984; Educational Advisor to VP George Bush, Seven Nation Tour of Africa, 1982. **Home Addr:** 399 Montgomery Rd, Tuskegee, AL 36083. **Business Addr:** President, Tuskegee University, Kresge Center, Tuskegee Institute, AL 36088.

PAYTON, CAROLYN ROBERTSON
Educator (retired). **Personal:** Born May 13, 1925, Norfolk, VA; daughter of Bertha Flanagan Robertson and LeRoy Solomon Robertson; married Raymond Rudolph (divorced). **Educ:** Bennett Coll, BS 1945; Univ WI Madison, MS 1948; Columbia Univ Tchrs Coll, EdD 1962. **Career:** Howard Univ, asst psych prof 1959-64; US Peace Corps, chief field selection ofcr 1964-66, Peace Corps Eastern Caribbean, dep dir to dir 1966-71; Howard Univ Counseling Svcs, dir 1970-78; US Peace Corps, dir 1978-79; Howard Univ Counseling Svcs, dean 1980-95. **Orgs:** Dir Ctr for Multicultural Awareness 1979; sec DC Psychologist's Examiners Bd 1980-83; mem DC Commn on Homelessness 1984-87; chair & mem Comm on Scientific & Professional Ethnics & Conduct APA 1972-77. **Honors/Awds:** Apptd by Pres of USA to Bd of Dirs of the Inter-American Found 1978-82; Disting Professional Contributions to Public Serv Awd APA 1982; publ "Who Must Do the Hard Things?" Amer Psychologist 39 391-397 1984; Lake Erie Coll for Women, LLD, 1978; Bennett College, LLD, 1995. **Business Addr:** Retired Dean, Counseling & Career Devt, Howard Univ, 6th & Bryant St NW, Washington, DC 20059.

PAYTON, GARY DWAYNE
Professional basketball player. **Personal:** Born Jul 23, 1968, Oakland, CA. **Educ:** Oregon State Univ, Corvallis, OR, 1986-90. **Career:** Seattle Supersonics, guard, 1990-. **Honors/Awds:** NBA All-Star, 1995, 1996, 1997, 1998. **Business Addr:** Professioanl Basketball Player, Seattle Supersonics, PO Box 900911, Seattle, WA 98109, (206)281-5850.

PAYTON, JEFF
Attorney. **Personal:** Born Sep 11, 1946, Canton, MS; married Carol E Rooks. **Educ:** Ashland Coll, BS 1969; John Carroll U, attnd; John Marshall Coll of Law-Cleveland State U, JD 1975. **Career:** Mansfield Municipal Court, judge, 1987-; Richland Co Legal Serv, dir 1977-; Cleveland Legal Aid Soc, atty staff 1975-77; US Dept of Just, legal intern 1972-73; Cleveland HS OH, biology instr 1969-71. **Orgs:** Mem OH State Bar Assn; mem Richland Co Bar Assn; bd of trustees Ashland Alumni Assn; bd of trustees Planned Parenthood Assn 1979-; bd of trustees Heritage Trls Girl Scouts Counc 1979-; bd of trustees Richland Co Juvenile Just Commn 1980; mem exec com Mansfield Chap NAACP; chmn NAACP Legal Redress Commn. **Business Addr:** Judge, Mansfield Municipal Court, Municipal Bldg, 2 N Diamond St, Mansfield, OH 44907.

PAYTON, LAWRENCE. **See Obituaries section.**

PAYTON, NICHOLAS
Musician. **Personal:** Born 1973, New Orleans, LA; son of Walter Payton and Maria Payton. **Educ:** Univ of New Orleans. **Career:** Trumpeteer, currently; Albums: From This Moment, 1994; Gumbo Nouveau, 1995; Peyton's Place, 1997; Toured with Marcus Roberts, 1992, Jazz Futures II, 1994, and Elvin Jones, 1994. **Business Addr:** Musician, c/o Verve, 825 Eighth Ave, New York, NY 10019, (212)333-8000.

PAYTON, NOLAN H.
Attorney. **Personal:** Born Dec 23, 1919; married; children: 1. **Educ:** AZ St, BA; USC, MA 1940; Am Clg Life Undrwrtrs, CLU 1954, LLB 1962; Certificates for attending legal seminars in London, England; Oxford, England; Moscow, Russia; Bombay, Deli, India; Madrid, Spain; The Holyland. **Career:** Golden St Mut Life Ins, agnt 1938-42, mgmt 1942-49; Priv Prac, atty 1969-. **Orgs:** Mem Twn Ha; Am Bar Assc; Bvrly Hills Bar Assc; Langston Law Assc; LA Cnty Bar Assc; Lwyrs Clb of LA; SW Bar Assc; Am Arbrtn Assc; NAACP; Sigma Lambda Sigma; Alpha Phi Alphi; mem Alpha Mu Gamma; Desert Bar Assn; life member, Sigma Pi Phi Fraternity; USC Alumni Assn; Legion Lex; Arizona State Alumni Assn. **Business Addr:** Payton Law Center, 1728 W King Blvd, Los Angeles, CA 90062.

PAYTON, VICTOR EMMANUEL
Physician. **Personal:** Born Jun 3, 1948, Savannah, GA; married Gwendolyn Middleton Payton; children: Khary, Kurlen, Kurtis, Kalere. **Educ:** Mercer Univ Macon, GA, BS Chem 1971; Med Clg of GA Augusta, MD 1975. **Career:** Noble Army Hosp Ft McClellan, AL, pediatrician 1978-; Tripler Army Med Ctr Honolulu, residency (pediatrics) 1977-78; Med Clg of GA Augusta, residency (pediatrics) 1976-77, intrnshp (pediatrics) 1975-76; Dept of Human Resources, Georgia Retardation Center, Athens, GA, medical director 1981-. **Orgs:** President Advisory Committee, Head Start 1987-. **Honors/Awds:** Diplomate, American of of Pediatrics, 1984; diplomate, Natl Bd of Med Examiners, 1976. **Military Serv:** AUS capt 1978-81; Army Commendation Medal, 1980.

PAYTON, WALTER JERRY
Business executive. **Personal:** Born Jul 25, 1954, Columbia, MS; married Connie; children: Jarrett, Brittney. **Educ:** Jackson State Univ, BA, communications and special education. **Career:** Chicago Bears, running back, 1975-86; Walter Payton Inc, owner 1979-; Walter Payton ower Equipment, maj owner, currently; CART racing team, co-owner, currently. **Orgs:** Hon chmn, Illinois Mental Health Assn, 1978-80; assists Boy Scouts of America, March of Dimes, Piccolo Research Fund, United Way, Peace Corps; hon chmn, Heart Assn Jump Rope for Heart, 1983; hon chmn, Ben Wilson Memorial Dinner, 1985; George Halas/Walter Payton Foundation, board of directors. **Honors/Awds:** Youngest player to be voted NFL MVP, 1977; NFC Player of the Year, Sporting News, 1976-77; NFC Player of Year, UPI, 1977; NFL MVP, 1978; selected All-Pro by TSN, PFW, Football Digest, AP, NEA, UPI, PFWA; broke club record for career receptions; holds NFL records for the following: most rushing yards, career (16,193); most rushing attempts, career (3,692); most combined yards, career (21,053); most combined attempts, career (4,189); most consecutive combined 2,000 yards seans (three), 1983-85; most games, 100 yards rushing, career (77); most seasons, 1,000 yards rushing (10); Chicago Red Cloud Athlete of the Year; UPI Athlete of the Year; NEA Thorpe Trophy, Mutual Radio, AP, Football Digest,Sport Mag NFL Player of the Year, AP NFL MVP; Pro Football Weekly Offensive Player of the Year; Sram's "Oscar" Award for Football; Wisconsin Pro Football Lombardi Dedication Award, 1983; Black Athlete of the Year, voted on by black media members nationwide, 1984; played in Pro Bowl, 1976-80, 1983-86 seasons; biography, Sweetness, 1978 by Contemporary Books; inductee into the Pro Football Hall of Fame. **Business Addr:** Owner, President, Walter Payton Inc, 5407 Trillium Blvd, Ste 270, Hoffman Estates, IL 60192.

PAYTON, WILLIS CONWELL
Attorney. **Personal:** Born Feb 9, 1923, Grifton, NC; son of Lillian Payton and Sidney Payton; married Mary E; children: Paula. **Educ:** NC Cntrl Univ, 3 yrs; Terrell Law Sch, LLB 1950. **Career:** Cortez Peters Bus Coll, prof 1950-52; Pvt Practice,

atty 1952-; Payton & Vance, attorney. **Orgs:** Mem Natl Bar Assn; Washington Bar Assn DC Bar Assn; VA Bar Assn; Old Dominion Bar Assn 1952; mem Sigma Delta Tau Legal 1947-; Univ S Supreme Ct Bar & Virginia Bar. **Honors/Awds:** Juvenile ct award 1960.

PAYTON-NOBLE, JOMARIE
Actress. **Personal:** Born Aug 3; married Rodney Noble; children: Chanele. **Career:** ABC-TV, ''Family Matters,'' actress, currently. **Business Addr:** Actress, Family Matters, The Irv Schechter Co, 9300 Wilshire Blvd, Ste 410, Beverly Hills, CA 90212, (213)278-8070.

PEACE, EULA H.
Educator. **Personal:** Born Jul 22, 1920, Norfolk, VA; children: Wesley H III. **Educ:** VA Union U, VA St Coll & NJ St Tchr Coll, grad. **Career:** City of Playground, teacher; World Book, mgr. **Orgs:** Norfolk Chap Assn of Coll Women; pres former bd mem League Women Voters & Demo Women's Club; pres Norfolk Club Assn of Negro Bus & Prof Women ; mem Phi Delta Kappa; city-wide Girls' Week 1948-68; bd mem Hunterville Heighborhood Cntr 1974; adv bd mem Area III Model City Prog 1974; Demo Committeewoman 1968-77; City Dem Com 1972-74; build rep Educ Assn of Norfolk 1973-80; del VA Educ Assn 1974-80; mem VA Educ Assn Women in Educ 1977-78; del Nat Educ Assn 1978-80; sec/treas Dist 19 Yr of the Child 1978-80; part Gov Conf on Edn; bd mem Educ Assn of Norfolk; chrprsn Women in Edn-Educ Assnof Norfolk; mem Legisltr & Polit Action Commn/Women Abuse Com/Mental Retard Assn/ Children in Need Com/Les Gemmes Civic & Soc Club. **Honors/Awds:** City coord for Gov's campaign.

PEACE, G. EARL, JR.
Educator, scientist. **Personal:** Born Feb 4, 1945, Norfolk, VA; son of Margaret Douthit Peace and George Earl Peace; married Renee Marie Filas; children: Trevor D, Nicole K. **Educ:** Lafayette Coll, BS Chem 1966; Univ of IL at Urbana-Champaign, MS Chem 1968, PhD Analyt Chem 1971. **Career:** Lafayette Coll, asst prof of chem 1971-78, assoc prof of chem 1978-79; CO State Univ, vstg assoc prof chem 1985-86; Coll of the Holy Cross, assoc prof of chem 1979-92; University of Wisconsin System, Office of Academic Affairs, academic planner; Univ of Wisconsin-Madison, faculty assoc/lecturer in chemistry, currently. **Orgs:** Mem of exec com NE Assn of Advisors to the Health Prof 1974-79; mem Citizen Adv Council to the PA Dept of Environ Resources 1976-79; mem American Chemical Society 1967-92; mem American Assoc for the Advancement of Science 1979-92; mem Shrewsbury (MA) Conservation Commission 1989-92. **Honors/Awds:** Rsch Grants Natl Sci Found 1972, 1974; Student Govt Superior Teaching Awd Lafayette Coll Student Govt 1974; Citizens Adv Council PA Dept of Env Res(named by Gov Milton Shapp) 1976-79; AAAS/EPA Environmental Sci & Engrg Fellow 1981; Summer Faculty Rsch Fellowship; Amer Cyanamid Corp CEEOP Rsch Grant 1986-87; ACE Fellow, American Council on Education, 1990-91. **Business Addr:** Faculty Associate, University of Wisconsin-Madison, Department of Chemistry, 1101 University Avenue, Madison, WI 53706.

PEACOCK, EULACE. See Obituaries section.

PEACOCK, NICOLE
Government official. **Career:** US State Dept, public affairs specialist, currently. **Special Achievements:** Led the effort to have the main library at the US State Dept named in honor of Ralph Bunche. **Business Addr:** Public Affairs Specialist, US State Department, 2201 C St, NW, Washington, DC 20520, (202)647-4000.

PEAGLER, FREDERICK DOUGLASS
Educator. **Personal:** Born Mar 23, 1922, New Milford, CT; married Dr Joyce Reese; children: Douglass Frederick Jr. **Educ:** Wilberforce Univ, 1940-43; Howard Univ, DDS 1948; Univ of MN, MSD 1965. **Career:** Private Practice, 1953-59; Howard Univ, prof 1960-73; Univ of MN, visiting prof 1973-74; Job Corps, consul lab dept; Natl Cancer Inst, consul; St Elizabeth Hosp, consul; Howard Univ, dent educ prof 1974-. **Orgs:** Mem pres Amer Assn for Cancer Educ; fellow Amer Acad of Oral Pathology, ADA, Amer Cancer Soc, Amer Coll of Dentists, Amer Acad of Oral Pathology; mem Sigma Xi, Omicron Kappa Upsilon. **Honors/Awds:** Harold Krogh Awd Amer Cancer Soc. **Military Serv:** USAF capt 1949-53. **Business Addr:** Dental Education Professor, Howard University, 600 W State NW, Washington, DC 20059.

PEAGLER, OWEN F.
Educator. **Personal:** Born Nov 28, 1935, New Milford, CT; son of Myrtle E Gary and Robert J Peagler; married Teresa Balough; children: Catherine Ann, Robert G, Kirin E. **Educ:** Western CT State Univ, BS 1956; New York Univ, MA 1958, Prof diploma 1962. **Career:** NY State Office of Economics, deputy director; New York City Metro Area Director 1966-69; Pace Univ, dean school of continuing educ 1969-78; Dept of Comm Affairs Delaware, sec 1982-83; Eastern CT State Univ, School of Continuing Education, dean, currently. **Orgs:** Pres 70001 Development Foundation 1976-88; bd dirs 70001 Training & Employment Inst 1975-; chmn President's Adv Council on Disadvantaged Children 1973-80; chairman, bd of dir, WAVE Inc 1988-96; pres, Connecticut Assn for Continuing Education, 1985-86. **Honors/Awds:** Young Man of the Yr NY State Jr Chamber of Commerce 1964; Distinguished Serv Awd White Plains NY JCC 1964; Science Fellowship Weslyan Univ 1956; CT Natl Guard, Outstanding Educator, 1988. **Business Addr:** Eastern Connecticut State University, Dean, School of Continuing Education, State of Connecticut, Willimantic, CT 06226.

PEAKE, EDWARD JAMES, JR.
Union official (retired). **Personal:** Born Jan 19, 1933, Akron, OH; son of Minnie L Peake (deceased) and Edward J Peake Sr (deceased); married Louise; children: Teresa E, Linda K, Kenneth T. **Educ:** Akron Univ, Fin 1965-69. **Career:** Goodyear Tire & Rubber Co, rubber worker-tirebuilder 1950-; US Dept of Labor, team mgr 1967-68; United Rubber Workers Intl, field rep, spec rep 1969-75, dir fair practices dept 1975-78, dir pension & ins dept 1978-80, asst to pres 1980, dir, education, 1980, dir, fair practices beginning 1983, international representative, until 1996. **Orgs:** Bd mem Natl Urban League Akron, AIA Homes Inc; life mem Alpha Phi Alpha Frat Eta Tau Chap Akron; mem Natl Labor Comm NAACP, Natl Oper Comm, A Philip Randolph Inst; URW rep Leadership Conf on Civil Rights; bd mem Akron Comm Serv Ctr & Urban League; natl bd A Philip Randolph; state and local bd of APRI. **Military Serv:** US Army,pfc 1954-56. **Business Addr:** International Representative, United Rubber Workers Intl, 811 Euclid Ave, Akron, OH 44307.

PEARCE, RICHARD ALLEN
City government official. **Personal:** Born Oct 4, 1951, New York, NY; son of Edith Burwell Pearce and Marvin Pearce; married Lois A Mayo; children: Alysia Daphine, Ryki Desiree, Zuri Damita. **Educ:** Hampton Inst, BS 1973; Univ Bridgeport, MBA; Williams Sch of Banking, 1978; Stonier Graduate School of Banking, 1986. **Career:** Carver Federal Savings and Loan Assn, New York, NY, administrative assistant, 1973; Carteret Savings and Loan Assn, Newark, NJ, assistant manager, New Jersey Office, 1973-75; Union Trust Company of Connecticut, assistant treasurer, Branford Office, 1975-77; State National Bank of Connecticut, branch manager, 1977-80; Colonial Bank of Connecticut, assistant vice president, corporate banking, 1980-84; Connecticut Savings Bank, vice president/ regional manager, commercial banking, 1984-88; First Constitution Bank, vice president of commercial banking, 1988-89; City of West Haven, director of finance and comptroller, 1989-. **Orgs:** Bd dir Hampton Alumni Fed Credit Union 1973-74; Alpha Phi Alpha; Dean of Mens Stf Concert Clg Chapel Choirs; Karate Clb; 1969 Track Team; Bus Clb; MensAssc; Hampton Inst Concert Master; Hampton Concert Choir 1972; Dean of Pledges Gamma Iota Chap Alpha Phi Alpha 1973; board of directors, New Haven Community Investment Corp; board of directors, West Haven Community House; board of directors, Childrens Center of Harlem; board of directors, Connecticut Afro-American Historical Society; board of directors, The Greater New Haven Business & Professional Assn.

PEARMAN, RAVEN-SYMONE CHRISTINA (RAVEN-SYMONE)
Entertainer, actress. **Personal:** Born Dec 10, 1985, Atlanta, GA; daughter of Lydia Gaulden Pearman and Christopher Barnard Pearman. **Career:** Actress, television series include: ''The Cosby Show,'' 1989-92; guest-starred on ''A Different World,'' 1990; Appeared in TV movie ''Queen, The Roots Sequel,'' 1993; guest appearance on ''Fresh Prince of Bel-Air,''; ''Hangin' With Mr. Cooper'', currently. **Orgs:** American Federation of Television & Radio Artists, 1989-; Screen Actors Guild, 1989-. **Honors/Awds:** Presenter at numerous award shows including: The People's Choice Awards, NAACP Image Awards, New York Music Awards, Intl Emmy Awards; participant in various fundraising events including: Comic Relief 3, Night of 100 Stars 3, Intl Earth Day Celebration, Pediatric AIDS Foundation; Youth in Film Award, Outstanding Young Actress, 1990, 1991; nominated, People's Choice Award, Outstanding Young Television Performer, 1991; nominated, NAACP Image Award, Outstanding Young Actress in a Series, 1991, 1992; SCLC, Junior Achievement Award for Excellence in Television Series; guest apppearances include: ''Live with Regis and Kathie Lee,'' 1989, 1990, 1991; ''The Oprah Winfrey Show,'' 1991; ''The Arsenio Hall Show,'' 1990, 1991; ''The Tonight Show,'' 1991; ''The Today Show''. **Special Achievements:** Signed solo artist recording contract with MCA Records at the age of 5 years old.

PEARSON, CLIFTON
Educator, educational administrator, consultant. **Personal:** Born Jun 24, 1948, Birmingham, AL; married Clementene Hodge; children: Monica Denise, Clifton Anderson. **Educ:** AL A&M Univ Normal AL, BS in Art 1970; IL State U, MS 1971, EdD in Art 1974. **Career:** AL A&M Univ, chmn/assc prof, 1974-, acting chmn, 1973-74; art education consultant, 1973-; IL State Univ, grad teaching asst 1971-73. **Honors/Awds:** Ford fellowship, Ford Found NY; southern fellowship, Southern fellowship Fund; Acad fellowship, IL State Univ; acad scholarship, AL A&M Univ; creator, For Arts Sake. **Business Addr:** Chairman/Professor of Art, Alabama A&M University, Normal, AL 35762.

PEARSON, DREW
Business executive, professional football player (retired). **Personal:** Born Jan 12, 1951, South River, NJ; children: Tori, Britni. **Educ:** Tulsa Univ, grad, 1973. **Career:** Dallas Cowboys, wide receiver, 1973-83; CBS Sports, color commentator; Smokey's Express Barbecue Restaurant, partner; Drew Pearson Mktg, chairman/shareholder, currently. **Orgs:** Past chairman, March of Dimes Crusade; national spokesman, Distilled Spirits Council. **Honors/Awds:** Played in Pro Bowl, 1974, 1976, 1977; All-Pro, 1974-77. **Business Addr:** Chairman, Drew Pearson Mktg, Inc, 15006 Beltway, Addison, TX 75001, (214)702-8055.

PEARSON, HERMAN B.
City contract coordinator. **Personal:** Born Mar 2, 1947, Omaha; divorced; children: Nicole, Carmen, Selina, Quatica. **Educ:** Univ of NE, BS 1972. **Career:** Minister 1973-; Mayor's Ofc City of Omaha, contract coord. **Orgs:** Evaluator Mental Retardation Pgm; Comm Ldr Among Young Adults; Professional Ftbl Plyr Washington Redskins 1972; professional dj cofounder First Black Owned Radio Station Omaha Area 1969; asst pastor Tabernacle Bapt Ch Council Bluff, IA; Recreational Activities Ldr; mem NATRA. **Business Addr:** 723 N 18 St, Omaha, NE 68111.

PEARSON, JAMES A.
Judge. **Personal:** Born Apr 25, 1925, Cincinnati, OH; son of Ethel Martin Pearson and William Arthur Pearson; married Julia Carter; children: 4. **Educ:** OH State Univ, BS 1951, LLB 1953, JD 1969. **Career:** Private practice, 1953-55; Franklin Cty Probate Court, chief dep 1955-61, asst pros 1961-69, judge 1969-. **Orgs:** Mem OH & Columbus Bar Assoc, OH Mun Judges Assoc, Amer Judicature Soc, Robert B Elliott Law Club; bd trustees Maryhaven Inc; bd govs Columbus Bar Assoc; mem Columbus Area Leadership Lab; mem bd trustees Cath Social Svcs, J Ashburn Jr Youth Ctr, Franklin Cty Com Criminal Justice. **Military Serv:** USN 1943-46. **Business Addr:** Judge, Franklin Cty Municipal Court, 375 S High St, 14th Floor Courtroom 14D, Columbus, OH 43215.

PEARSON, JESSE S.
Church official (retired). **Personal:** Born Apr 24, 1923, Gasden, AL; son of Donia and Jesse; married Mary Lee; children: Milbrun, Eric Hart, Peter Hart, Kelli Hart. **Educ:** Wayne State Univ, BS bus admin 1969. **Career:** Highland Park Genl Hosp, deputy dir 1971; Bon Secours Hosp, asst controller 1967-71, controller 1971-86; Hartford Baptist Church, administrator, begin 1986. **Orgs:** Dir Homemaker's Agency MI 1982-83; dir Agape House Hartford Ch 1985; natl bd mem Health Care Financial Mgmt Assn 1978-80; pres Eastern MI Chap HFMA 1976-77; pres Detroit Set, 1985-94; Le Chateau Condominium, dir, 1991. **Honors/Awds:** William G Follmer Awd HFMA Eastern MI 1974; Robert Reeves Awd HFMA Eastern MI 1978; Frederick C Muncie Awd HFFMA Eastern MI 1981; Ernest C Laetz Awd HFMA 5 MI Chapts 1978. **Military Serv:** AUS sgt, 2 yrs; South Pacific Combat Ribbon.

PEARSON, MARILYN RUTH
Financial consultant. **Personal:** Born Nov 12, 1955, Saginaw, MI; daughter of Bernice Richard Townsend and Hollis Townsend; married Tommie L Pearson Sr, Aug 9, 1975; children: Tamara Bernice, Tommie L Jr. **Educ:** Saginaw Valley State Univ, University Center MI, BA, 1978. **Career:** Ford Motor Credit Co, Saginaw MI, credit investigator, 1977-80; Merrill Lynch, Saginaw MI, financial consultant, 1980-84, New York NY, sr training consultant, 1984-87, Princeton NJ, AVP mgr sel & devel, 1987-. **Orgs:** First vice pres, Zeta Phi Beta Sorority Epsilon XI Zeta, 1980-; Executive Club Merrill Lynch, 1981-82; mem, President's Club, Merrill Lynch, 1983; Natl Assn Securities Professionals, 1987-; bd mem, Jr Achievement of Mercer County, 1987-; bd mem, Literacy Volunteers of Amer State NJ, 1988-; bd mem, YWCA, Trenton, 1989-; mem, NAACP; mem, Shiloh Baptist Church. **Honors/Awds:** Achievement Award Natl Assn of Negro Business & Prof Women, 1982; designed, developed and implemented Auditors Training Program, 1984; creative director for Black FC ads; nominated for 1988 CEBA Award; Zeta of the Year Epsilon Xi Zeta Zeta Phi Beta Sorority, 1988; Faith, Hope & Charity Award, FAI HO CHA, Trenton NJ, 1988; featured in Merrill Lynch ad in Black Enterprise, Essence, Ebony, 1988-89; Intl Business & Professional Women Dolars & Sense, 1989; Black Achievers in the Industry Award, Harlem Branch YMCA, 1989; special tributes from State of Michigan and Mercer County NJ. **Business Addr:** AVP Financial Consultant Training, Merrill Lynch, PO Box 9032, Princeton, NJ 08543-9032.

PEARSON, MICHAEL NOVEL
Banker. **Personal:** Born Feb 12, 1956, Memphis, TN. **Educ:** Fisk Univ, BS 1978; Pepperdine Univ, MBA 1980; Coll for Financial Planning, CFP 1984. **Career:** Ford Motor Credit Co, cust acct rep 1978-79; M-Bank Houston NA, energy loan officer 1981-83; Pearson Assoc, financial planner 1982-; First City

Bank Corp, sr loan review officer 1984-89, Healthcare Group Wholesake Banking Division, vice pres, 1989-. **Orgs:** Series 7 Registered Rep Lowry Financial Serv Corp 1986; Life Health Disability Ins license State of TX 1986; Registered Investment Adviser US Securities & Exchange Commn 1986; treas Natl Black MBA Assoc Houston Chap 1987; mem Alpha Phi Alpha Frat; mem Inst of Certified Financial Planners, Intl Assoc of Financial Planners, Urban Bankers Assoc; adjunct instr Amer Inst of Banking Houston Chapt. **Honors/Awds:** Young Achiever Awd Riverside General Hosp 1986; Human Enrichment Awd Human Enrichment of Life Progs Inc 1987. **Home Addr:** POB 55708, Houston, TX 77255.

PEARSON, PRESTON JAMES
Company executive, professional football player (retired). **Personal:** Born Jan 17, 1945, Freeport, IL; married Linda; children: Gregory, Matthew. **Educ:** Univ of Illinois. **Career:** Running back: Baltimore Colts, 1967-69; Pittsburgh Steelers, 1970-74; Dallas Cowboys, 1975-80; Preston Pearson Inc, owner; Time Inc & Am Tel Communication, marketing executive. **Orgs:** Fndr tres Consult Mgmt Enterpises. **Honors/Awds:** Broke his own record 47 Catches 1978; only player to appear in Super Bowl with three different teams (Colts, Steelers, Cowboys); led NFL in kickoff returns and kickoff returns for touchdowns; set Cowboy record for running back with 46 receptions, 1977.

PEARSON, RAMONA HENDERSON (RAMONA ESTELLE HENDERSON)
County official. **Personal:** Born Oct 3, 1952, Baltimore, MD; daughter of Doris Green Henderson and Robert Henderson; married Edward Pearson, Nov 20, 1989; children: Leora. **Educ:** Morgan State U, BS 1975; Morgan State U, candidate MBA 1982. **Career:** Arthur Young & Co, sr auditor; Linwood Jennings PA CPA's, asso 1977-79; Constant Care Comm Health Center Inc, controller 1976-77; Ernst & Ernst, auditor 1975-76; Wayne State Univ, director internal audit, 1985-87; Wayne County Govt, auditor general, 1987-. **Orgs:** Mem Am Inst of CPA's 1976-; president Nat Assn of Black Accountants; mem NAACP; mem Big Brothers & Sisters of Am; member, Michigan Assn of CPA's, 1981-; member, Institute of Internal Auditors, 1985-; member, Government Accountants Assn, 1988-; member, Government Finance Officers Assn, 1988-; member, Local Government Auditors Assn, 1988-. **Honors/Awds:** "How to Start a Small Business" Afro-Am Newspaper 1977; Outstanding mem, Natl Assn Black Accountants 1983. **Home Addr:** 4690 W Outer Drive, Detroit, MI 48235-1221.

PEARSON, STANLEY E.
Physician. **Personal:** Born Oct 21, 1949, Quitman, GA; son of Mattie A. Bowles and Rev Oliver Pearson, Jr. **Educ:** Univ of FL Gainesville, attended 1967-71; Meharry Medical Coll, MD 1975. **Career:** Providence Hospital, residency 1975-78; Fitzsimons Army Medical Ctr, fellowship 1978-80; Landstahl Army Regional Medical Ctr West Germany, chief cardiology serv 1981-83; United States Army Europe 7th Medical Command, cardiology consultant 1982-83; Madigan Army Medical Ctr, staff cardiologist 1983-84; CIGNA Health Plan of Arizona; dir cardiac rehab 1984-, chief of staff 1986-88; chmn, department of internal medicine 1988-. **Orgs:** Mem Alpha Omega Alpha Honor Med Soc; fellow Amer College of Cardiology; mem Colorado Medical Soc, Tau Epsilon Phi Frat. **Honors/Awds:** Diplomate Amer Bd of Internal Medicine 1978, Amer Bd of Internal Medicine Cardiovascular Disease 1981. **Military Serv:** US Army, active duty, major, 6 years, active reserves, col; Army Commendation Medal 2nd Oak Leaf Cluster. **Business Addr:** Chairman, Department of Internal Medicine, CIGNA Healthcare of Arizona, Phoenix Div, McDowell Health Care Facility, 755 E McDowell Rd, Phoenix, AZ 85006.

PEASE, DENISE LOUISE
State official. **Personal:** Born Mar 15, 1953, Bronx, NY; daughter of Louise Marion Caswell Pease and William Henry Pease, Jr. **Educ:** Columbia Univ, New York NY, BA, 1980; Columbia Univ Graduate School of Business, Special Certificate, 1982; Bernard Barauch Graduate School of Public Administration, 1982-83. **Career:** Elmcor Youth & Adult Activities, dir of community services, 1980-82; Essex County, Newark NJ, special asst to county exec, 1982-83; New York State Department of Banks, urban analyst III, 1983-86, exec asst to supt 1986-87; deputy supt, 1987-. **Orgs:** Bd mem, Handier, 1974-; mem, Governor's Economic Devel Sub-Cabinet, 1985-; bd mem, Cornell Univ Cooperative Extention Advisory Comm, 1986-; bd mem, Elcor Youth & Adult Activities, 1986-87; mem, Coalition of 100 Black Women, 1988-; life mem, Natl Council of Negro Women, 1988-; representative, Governor's, Housing Policy Cabinet, 1989; mem, Financial Women's Assn, 1989; member, Society of Consumer Affairs Professionals in Business; life member, National Council of Negro Women; life member, NAACP; member, Coalition of 100 Black Women; board of directors, Financial Womens Association of New York. **Honors/Awds:** Professional Achievement Award, Natl Assn of Negro Business and Professional Women, 1980; Charles H Revson Fellow on the Future of New York, Columbia Univ, 1981; Natl Urban Fellow, Natl Urban Fellows Org, 1982; Citation of Merit, New York State Assembly, 1989; Salute to Outstanding African American Business and Professional Women, Dollar & Sense Magazine, 1990; Citation of Merit, New York State Assembly, 1988; Governor's Citation, 1993; New York State Black And Puerto Rican Legislators Assn, Community Service Award, 1993. **Business Addr:** Deputy Supt, New York State Dept of Banking, 2 Rector St, 18th Floor, New York, NY 10006.

PEAVY, JOHN W., JR.
Judge. **Personal:** Born Apr 28, 1943, Houston, TX; married Diane Massey; children: 4. **Educ:** Howard Univ, AB 1964; Howard Univ School of Law, postgraduate 1964-67. **Career:** Natl Aero & Space Council, The White House, Washington DC, acct, 1961-64, admin asst 1964-67; Berry Lott Peavy & Williams, practice law 1967-72; Harris Cty Comm Action Assoc, assoc field coordinator, 1967-68; County Judge Bill Elliott, exec asst 1968-70; Home Pilot Program, Amer Bar Assn, Houston Bar Assn funded by Ford Found HUD Houston, assoc counsel for projects 1970-71; Harris County Court Precinct 7, judge, justice of the peace position 1973-77; 246th Dist Judicial Dist Ct Harris County Houston, judge. **Orgs:** Chmn WL Davis Div Sam Houston Boy Scouts 1976; mem Alpha Phi Alpha, Urban League, Harris Cty Council of Orgs; life mem NAACP; mem nom comm Houston Bus & Professional Men's Club, YMCA Century Club; former dem precinct chmn Precinct 292 Houston TX; mem adv bd KYOK Radio Sta; legal adv Riverside Lion's Club; mem bd of dir Mercy Hosp; mem steering comm A Phillip Randolph Inst; mem bd of dir Houston Citizens Chamber of Commerce, Project Pull, Eliza Johnson Ctr for the Aged, So Ctr Br YMCA, United Negro Coll Fund, Julia C Hester House, St Elizabeth Hosp, Houston Council of Human Rel, Volunteers of Amer; appt mem Housing Asst Tech Adv Group 1974; hon co-chmn Citizens for Better Transit 1978; mem Downtown Rotary Club of Houston, Urban Policy Task Force for the City ofHouston 1978; mem Pol ActiComm Houston Lawyers Assoc; mem bd of dir Natl Bar Found, Houston Bar Assoc, Natl Bar Assoc, Amer Bar Assoc, State Bar of TX, Jr Bar Assoc of Houston, St Jr Bar Small Claims Court Handbook Comm 1977, State Bar TX Ct Reorg Comm, Judicial Council. **Honors/Awds:** Outstanding Military Student Chicago Tribune Award; Contributor, Most to the Comm YMCA; Acad Scholarship to Howard Univ School of Law; Eagle Scout & mem Order of the Arrow of Boy Scouts of Amer 1960; Distinguished Achievers Award YMCA 1973, 1977; YMCA Award for Outstanding Serv to the Community 1974, Certificate of Citation by the State of TX House of Reps 1975; Natl Judicial Intl Achievement Award; Houston Lawyers Assn Achievement Award, 1980; Outstanding Young Business & Professional Man, Houston Young Adult Club, 1979; Appreciation Award, Exploring Div, Sam Houston Area BSA, 1979. **Business Addr:** Judge, State District Court, 246th Dist, 1115 Congress, Houston, TX 77002.

PEAY, FRANCIS
Professional football coach. **Personal:** Born in Pittsburgh, PA; married Patricia; children: Aryca, Aisha. **Career:** Professional football player with New York Giants, Green Bay Packers, Kansas City Chiefs; Univ Sr HS in St Louis, defensive coord; Notre Dame, jr varsity and offensive line coach; Univ of CA, outside linebacker coach; Northwestern Univ, defensive coordinator, head coach; Indianapolis Colts, defensive line coach, currently.

PEAY, ISAAC CHARLES, SR.
Clergyman. **Personal:** Born Jun 3, 1910, Stone Co, MS; married Velma L Bluitt; children: Minnie Lee Purnell, Isaac Charles Jr, Mary Nell, Robert James, Sylvia Hennings, James Hennings. **Educ:** MS Bapt Sem, BTh 1948, MCT 1949, ThM 1951, ThD 1953; Jackson Clg, BS 1953; MS Bapt Sem, DD 1960; MO Bapt Clg, LlD 1979. **Career:** Galilee Bapt Ch St Louis, MO, pastor 1954-80; MO Bapt Clg St Louis, tchr 1975-80; MO Bapt Messenger, edtr 1968-74; Mt Zion Bapt Ch Hattiesburg, MS, pastor 1950; Friendship Bapt Ch Laurel, MS, pastor 1943. **Orgs:** Dir fndr Beautification Youth Corps Inc 1968; vice moderator Berean Dist Assc 1973; vice pres Missionary Bapt State Convention of MO 1979; vice pres Conf on Religion & Race 1966; pres Bapt Ministers Union 1967, 77; mem Mayor's Commn on Human Relations 1968. **Honors/Awds:** "Stewardship Made Simple" Copyrighted 1969; minister of yr awrd St Louis Argus Nwspr 1972; 50 yr pastorate & awrd MO Bapt State Conv of MO 1979; 20 yr awrd St Louis Bapt Missionary Flwshp 1979. **Business Addr:** Galilee Baptist Church, 4300 Delmar Blvd, St Louis, MO 63108.

PEAY, SAMUEL
Judge. **Personal:** Born Jun 2, 1939, Ridgeway, SC; son of Geneva Peay and English Peay; married Lillian Bernice Chavis; children: Clifton Delmineo, Ira Aloysius. **Educ:** Basic Law Enforcement Training, certificate; Univ of Nevada Nat'l Judicial Acad 1985, 1986. **Career:** Richland Co Sheriff's Dept Cola SC, dep sheriff 1964, 1st Black sgt in law enforcement 1969, juvenile/arson/criminal invest 1971-78; Magistrate's Court, judge. **Orgs:** Nat Sheriff's Assn, SC Law Enforcement Assn, SC Summary Court Judges Assn, life mem; Richland Cnty Summary Court Judges Assn, pres 1986-88; Nat'l Judges Assn, vice chairman, bd of deacons, chairman; Zion Canaan Baptist Church, Columbia SC, family activities cmte. **Honors/Awds:** Nat'l Council of Negro Women, honored as outstanding South Carolinian 1980; honored by Capital City Lodge #47 Columbia SC 1985; Optimist Club of Columbia, "Respect for Law" Awd 1986; Dept of Military Sci Army ROTC, Benedict Coll, Serv Awd 1986; Honored by Columbia, SC Branch of NAACP, 1991; honored by Columbia Lawyers Assn, 1996; honored by SC Black Lawyers Assn, 1996. **Business Addr:** Judge, Magistrare's Court, 4919 Rhett St, Columbia, SC 29203.

PEBBLES. **See MCKISSACK, PERRI.**

PECK, CAROLYN
Head basketball coach. **Educ:** Vanderbilt Univ. **Career:** Nippondenso Corp, professional basketball player; Purdue Univ, asst coach, recruiting coordinator, head basketball coach, currently. **Business Addr:** Head Coach, Women's Basketball, Purdue University, Intercollegiate Athletic Administration, 1790 Madkey, West Lafayette, IN 47907-1790.

PECK, LEONTYNE CLAY
Educator. **Personal:** Born Nov 14, 1958, Keyser, WV; daughter of Suellen Gaiter Clay and Russell Clay Sr; married Lyle, Jun 2, 1990; children: Whitney. **Educ:** American University, Washington, DC, BA, political science; West Virginia University, Morgantown, WV, MA, education administation; American Univ of Rome, Rome, Italy, certificate in Italian studies. **Career:** US Department of Housing & Urban Dev, Washington, DC, consumer affairs specialist, 1978-81; Congressman Cleve Benedict, LB Johnson legislative intern, 1981-82; US Conference of Mayors, Washington, DC, public affairs officer, 1984-88; Center for Black Culture, Morgantown, WV, program manager, 1989-91; West Virginia Univ, program mgr, Potomac State College of West Virginia; Whitney Management Group, currently. **Orgs:** Founder/pres, Project Heritage, 1990-; founder, Club Noir, 1989-; sponsor, HAL Jackson's Talented Teens International, 1991-; founder, Leontyne Peck Productions, 1989-; state chair, ACTSO/NAACP, 1991. **Honors/Awds:** Ford Foundation Grant, National Council for Black Studies, 1990; Outstanding West Virginian for Public Service, Common Cause, 1989; Commissioner on African American History & Culture for Maryland, 1997. **Home Addr:** 804 Buckingham Rd, Cumberland, MD 21502-2717.

PEEBLES, ALLIE MUSE
Educator. **Personal:** Born Apr 12, 1926, Danville, VA; daughter of Maude B Smith Muse and William Brown Muse Sr; married Millard R Peebles Sr, Aug 16, 1947 (deceased); children: Martha Elaine Peebles Brown, Brenda LaVerne, Millard R Jr. **Educ:** Hampton Univ, Hampton VA, BS, 1943-47; St. Augustine's Coll, Raleigh NC, certificate renewal; attended North Carolina Central Univ, Durham NC, 1965-69; North Carolina State Univ, Raleigh NC, certificate renewal. **Career:** Prince Edward County School System, Farmville VA, English teacher, 1947-48; Raleigh-Wake County School System, Raleigh NC, English teacher, 1963-78; M. R. Peebles and Son Masonry Contractors, Raleigh, owner and pres, 1978-82; Telamon Corp, Smithfield NC, job counselor, 1983-86; The Carolinian (newspaper), Raleigh, columnist, 1984-; St. Augustine's Coll, Raleigh, English instructor, 1987-. **Orgs:** Mem, Martin St Baptist Church Choir, 1955-; pres 1962-64, 1984-86, vice pres, 1979-84, Raleigh Hampton Univ Alumn Assn; treas, Jack and Jill of America, 1966-68; mem 1969-, sec, 1972-74, chmn of publicity and public relations 1985-89, Delta Sigma Theta-Raleigh Alumnae Chapter; chmn of nat recruitment 1978-82, 2nd vice pres of NC region 1983-89, Nat Hampton Alumni Assn; life mem and chmn, Raleigh-Apex NAACP, 1978-; mem, Wake County Private Industry Council, 1980-82; mem, Raleigh Civil Service Commision, 1980-82; board mem, YWCA of Wake County, 1980-86; consultant, Women in Communication Workshop, 1987; mem, Delta's Nat Comm on Neritage and Archives; solicitor for several fundraising drives; volunteer for voter registration and political candidates; secretary, finance committee, Martin Saptist Church, Raleigh, NC, 1989-93; public relations dir, Delta Sigma Theta, Raleigh Chapter, 1990-93. **Honors/Awds:** NC Hamptonian of the Year Award, Hampton Univ, 1974; mem, Million Dollar Club, NAACP, 1981-89; recognition of service from nat office of NAACP; writes column, "Raleigh's Social Scene," for local black paper; editor-in-chief, "Tar-Heel Hamptonian," NC newsletter of Nat Hampton Alumni Assn. **Home Addr:** 721 Calloway Dr, Raleigh, NC 27610. **Business Addr:** Instructor, St Augustine's College, 1315 Oakwood Ave, Raleigh, NC 27610.

PEEBLES, DANIEL PERCY, III
Professional football player. **Personal:** Born Apr 30, 1966, Raleigh, NC. **Educ:** North Carolina State Univ, received accounting and business management degrees. **Career:** Tampa Bay Buccaneers, wide receiver, 1989-. **Business Addr:** Professional Football Player, Tampa Bay Buccaneers, One Buccaneer Pl, Tampa, FL 33607-5797.

PEEBLES-MEYERS, HELEN MARJORIE
Physician (retired). **Personal:** Born Oct 6, 1915, New York, NY; daughter of Elizabeth Peebles and James Peebles; married Frederic Ricksford Meyers, Dec 27, 1939 (deceased); children: Joy V Lilly. **Educ:** Hunter Coll, BA 1937; Columbia Univ, MA 1938; Howard Univ Med Sch, 1938-40; Wayne State Univ Sch of Med, MD 1943. **Career:** Detroit Receiving Hosp, intern 1943, asst resident, resident & chief 1945-47; private practice

1947-77; Ford Motor Credit Co, physician in charge, 1977-85; Hutzel Hosp, sr attending physician; Evang Deaconess Hosp courtesy staff; Alexander Blain Hosp, cons; Wayne State Univ, clinical assoc prof; Ford Motor Co World Headquarters, chief physician retired 1985. **Orgs:** Bd mem MI Heart Assn 1966-71; treas Detroit Adventure 1969-71; past bd of govs Wayne State Univ Med Sch Alumni Assn 1970-72; mem Nat Med Assn; del to MI State Med Soc from Wayne Co Med Soc; AMA; Wayne Co Med Assn; Am Diabetes Assn on Com on Prgm & Planning; MI Diabetes Assn; Fdrs Soc of Detroit Inst of Arts; Oakland Univ Arts Soc; Detroit Symphony Orch; bd dir Amer Diabetes Assn; United Found; Detroit Urban League; Nghbrhd Serv Organizations; exec bd Mt Carmel Hosp Community Bd; United Com on Negro History. **Honors/Awds:** Hall of Fame Hunter Coll 1977; YWCA Metro Detroit 1978; Alpha Kappa Alpha Patron of the Arts Awd 1982; Mercy Medallion Mercy Coll of Detroit 1983; DowntownYWCA 1984; Focus and Impact Awd Black Awareness Month Comm Oakland Univ 1984; Summit Awd Greater Detroit C of C 1984; Detroit Urban Center Awd 1985; President's Cabinet Awd Univ of Detroit 1985; Heritage Awd in Med Little Rock Baptish Church 1985; Union of Black Episcopalians 1985; Disting Warrior Awd Detroit Urban League 1986; MI Women's Hall of Fame 1992; Spirit of Detroit Awd 1986; One of Amer Top 100 Citizens Newsweek Mag 1986.

PEEBLES-WILKINS, WILMA CECELIA
Educator. **Personal:** Born Apr 21, 1945, Raleigh, NC; daughter of Mary Myatt Peebles and Millard Peebles. **Educ:** NC State Univ, BA, 1967; Case Western Reserve Univ, MSSA, 1971; Univ of NC at Chapel Hill, PhD 1984. **Career:** Cuyahoga Co Div of Child Welfare, social worker 1967-72; Mental Develop Ctr, dir of intake 1972-76; Eastern KY Univ, asst prof 1976-77; NC Memorial Hosp, chief pediatric social worker 1977-78; NC State Univ, assoc prof and director of social work 1978-91; Boston University, associate dean, 1991-93, acting dean, 1993-94, dean, 1994-. **Orgs:** Mem Natl Assoc of Black Social Workers 1976-; consultant Wake Co Council on Aging 1979, Raleigh Housing Authority 1979; vice chairperson NC Certification Bd for Social Work 1984-; competence certification bd Natl Assoc of Social Workers 1984-; commn on minority group concerns Council on Social Work Education 1985-87; serves on several editorial boards; past chairperson, New England Assoc of Deans and Directors of Schools of Social Work. **Honors/Awds:** Irene Sogg Gross Serv Awd 1971; Swedish Intl Fellowship for Youth Leaders/Social Workers 1980; articles in Encyclopedia of Social Work, Journal of Social Work; Black Caucus Journal, Children and Youth Services Review, Journal of Education for Social Work; Black Women in American History and Black Women in American: An Historical Encylopedia. **Business Addr:** Dean, Boston University, School of Social Work, 264 Bay State Rd, Boston, MA 02215.

PEEK, BOOKER C.
Educator. **Personal:** Born May 22, 1940, Jacksonville, FL; son of Estella Peek (deceased) and Oscar Peek (deceased); married Annette Jones, Jun 29, 1958; children: Cheryl, Joseph, Angela. **Educ:** FL A&M U, BA; Oberlin Coll, MAT; Univ FL, further study. **Career:** Hampton Jr Coll, teacher; Matthew W Gilbert HS; Ribault Sr High; Albany State Coll; Oberlin Coll, assoc prof, currently. **Orgs:** Mem Am Assn Univ & Professions; NAACP; former mem Intl Longshoremen Assn; mem Oberlin Comm Welfare Council; pres Toward Am Togetherness Comm Orgn 1968; FL Star Tchr 1968; So Fellow 1969-70. **Honors/Awds:** Scholarship Jacksonville Univ 1969. **Business Addr:** Associate Professor, Oberlin College, African American Studies Department, Oberlin, OH 44074.

PEEK, GAIL LENORE
Attorney. **Personal:** married. **Educ:** The City College of New York, BA, 1972; Princeton University, MA, 1974, PhD, 1978; University of Chicago, Law School, JD, 1984. **Career:** Williams College, assistant professor, 1976-80; Kirkland & Ellis, associate, 1984-87; Premark International, Inc, senior attorney, 1987-90, corporate counsel, 1990-91, general counsel, 1991-93; Ralph Wilson Plastics Co, vice pres, general counsel, 1993-. **Orgs:** American Bar Association; Illinois State Bar Association; Association of Corporate Counsel of America; Illinois State Bar, 1984. **Honors/Awds:** Ford Foundation, Black American Fellow, 1972-76. **Business Addr:** Vice Pres, General Counsel, Ralph Wilson Plastics Co, 600 General Bruce Dr, Temple, TX 76504, (817)778-2711.

PEELE, JOHN E., JR.
Patent attorney. **Personal:** Born May 19, 1934, Durham, NC; married Lucia F; children: John III, Steven, Beverly. **Educ:** NC Central U, BS 1955; Georgetown Univ Law Cntr, JD 1962. **Career:** Northrop Corp Hawthorne CA, pat couns 1980-; Vivitar Corp Santa Monica CA, pat couns 1977-79; Bell & Howell Co Chicago, pat atty 1963-77; US Patent & Trademark Off DC, pat & exam 1955-63. **Orgs:** Mem Omega Psi Phi; mem Photograph Soc of Am; mem Am Bar Assn; mem Nat Bar Assn; mem Nat Patent Law Assn. **Business Addr:** Northrop Corp, 3901 W Broadway, Hawthorne, CA 90250.

PEELER, ANTHONY EUGENE
Professional basketball player. **Personal:** Born Nov 25, 1969, Kansas City, MO; children: Marcus Anthony, Chynna. **Educ:** Missouri, 1992. **Career:** Los Angeles Lakers, guard, 1992-96; Vancouver Grizzlies, 1996-. **Special Achievements:** NBA Draft, First round pick, #15, 1992. **Business Addr:** Professional Basketball Player, Vancouver Grizzlies, 788 Beatty St, Ste 311, Vancouver, BC, Canada V6B 2M1, (604)688-5867.

PEELER, DIANE FAUSTINA
Instructor/orthopedically handicapped. **Personal:** Born Mar 14, 1959, Greeneville, TN; daughter of Marilyn and Segeet. **Educ:** Univ of TN Knoxville, BS 1982; Attended, Southern Univ of New Orleans, Xavier Univ. **Career:** Orleans Parish Comm Schools, modern dance teacher 1983-85; Office of Employment & Develop, summer youth counselor 1986; Orleans Parish School Bd, instructor 1982-. **Orgs:** Vice pres Delta Sigma Theta Sor Inc 1980-81; physical therapy volunteer Meadowcreast Hosp 1985-86. **Business Addr:** Instructor, Orleans Parish School Bd, 3411 Broadway, New Orleans, LA 70125.

PEEPLES, AUDREY RONE
Association executive. **Personal:** Born May 22, 1939, Chicago, IL; daughter of Thelma Shepherd Rone and John Drayton Rone; married Anthony Peeples; children: Jennifer Lynn, Michael Anthony. **Educ:** Univ of IL, BA; Northwestern Univ, MBA. **Career:** Continental Bank, trust admin 1961-72; Girls Scouts of USA, asst reg dir 1972-76; GS of Chicago, assoc exec dir 1976-83, exec dir 1983-87; YWCA of Metropolitan Chicago, CEO, 1987-. **Orgs:** Natl bd GS of USA 1971-73; Jack & Jill of Chicago 1973-; Jr Govt Bd Chicago Symphony Orchestra 1976-83; bd mem, Women in Charge 1983-95, Chicago Network 1988-; Economic Club of Chicago 1988; bd mem, United Way of Chicago, 1988-92; Chicago Network, board member, 1991-; First Non Profit Trust, trustee, 1992-; Chicago Foundation for Women, board member, treasurer, 1992-97; CACE (Chicago Alliance for Collaborative Effort), chair; Governors Commission on Women, commissioner, 1997. **Honors/Awds:** Kizzy Award; Outstanding Achievement Award, Girl Scouts of Chicago; Merit Award, National Council of Negro Women, Cosmopolitan Section. **Business Addr:** CEO, YWCA of Metropolitan Chicago, 180 N Wabash, Chicago, IL 60601.

PEEPLES, DARRYL
Designer. **Personal:** Born Mar 20, 1943, Detroit, MI. **Educ:** Steelcase Mfg Co, 1974; Soc of Arts & Crafts, MA 1970; Tapahagen Sch of Design, cert 1967; NY Phoenix Sch of Design, MA 1967; Pratt Inst, BA 1965; Sch of Interior Design, AA 1963. **Career:** Inter Internat, design admin; James Hill & Co, contract specif int design sales rep; Larwin Homes Ctr, int design 1973; Sofas Inc, sr design 1969; House of Living Rooms, design consult 1968; Decors Unlimited, inter Design 1967; United Nations NYC, master design 1965; Professional Rendering Serv, design consult 1977; Environ Design of San Francisco, design adv 1977. **Orgs:** Mem Victorian All; Native Sons of San Francisco; 3rd World Tours House Beautiful 1969; house Restor & Remldg Show 1977; Presidio Mall 1977; Interior InterShowrooms 1977. **Business Addr:** 1451 McAllister St, San Francisco, CA 94115.

PEER, WILBUR TYRONE
Educator. **Personal:** Born Apr 28, 1951, Lee County, AR; married Patricia Nelson; children: Andre B, Yolanda, Wilbur T II. **Educ:** AM&N College, BA History & Govt 1973. **Career:** Phillips College, vet counselor 1974-76; Lee County Coop clinic, project mgr 1976-81; Phillips County Comm Coll, voc counselor 1982-. **Orgs:** Owner/oper Wilbur Peer Farm 1977-; justice of the peace Lee County quorum Court 1980-; owner/broker Wilbur T Peer Realty Co 1982-; exec dir Delta Improvement 1982-; PIC mem East AR Private Industry Council 1983-. **Honors/Awds:** Mem Phi Beta Sigma 1972. **Military Serv:** USAR 1lt transportation 8 yrs. **Home Addr:** P O Box 34, La Grange, AR 72352. **Business Addr:** Justice of the Peace, 33 N Poplar St, Marianna, AR 72360.

PEERMAN-PLEDGER, VERNESE DIANNE
Foundation executive. **Personal:** Born Jan 1, 1958, Pinehurst, NC; daughter of Otelia Cooke Peerman and William Donald Peerman; married Vincent Lewis Pledger, Oct 4, 1988. **Educ:** North Carolina Central University, BA, journalism, 1979. **Career:** Eunice Advertising, sr account executive, business manager; Carrington & Carrington Advertising, partner, business manager; Dudley Products Company Inc, national advertising manager; Western Career College, PR director, high school coordinator; Chapel Hill/Carrboro Downtown Commission, director of special projects; St Joseph's Historic Foundation, Inc, COO, exec director, currently. **Orgs:** North Carolina Cultural Network, president, 1992-; The Scrap Exchange, board of directors; Delta Sigma Theta Sorority Inc, Chapel Hill Carrboro Alumnae Chapter; South Orange Black Caucus; American Cancer Society, volunteer; St Paul AME Church, Steward Bd, choir member; Chapel Hill Women's Ctr, bd; Arts Advocates, bd. **Business Addr:** Chief Operating Officer/Exec Director, St Joseph's Historic Foundation, Inc, 804 Old Fayetteville St, PO Box 543, Durham, NC 27702, (919)683-1709.

PEERY, BENJAMIN FRANKLIN, JR.
Astronomer. **Personal:** Born Mar 4, 1922, St Joseph, MO; married Darnelle; children: Yvany. **Educ:** Univ of Minnesota, bachelor's degree in physics 1949; Fisk Univ, MA 1955; Univ of Michigan, PhD 1962. **Career:** Howard Univ, prof 1977-; Indiana Univ, prof 1959-76; Univ of Michigan, instr 1958; Agricultural & Techical Coll of North Carolina, instr 1951-53; California Inst of Tech, visiting assoc 1969-70; Harvard Univ, visiting assoc prof 1971; Kitt Peak Natl Observer, visiting research astronomist 1975-76. **Orgs:** Mem US Natl Comm Intl Astron Union 1972-77; mem Amer Astron Soc; chmn Comm on Manpower & Employment 1977; mem Astron Adv Panel Natl Sci Found 1974-78; consultant NSF NASA Ind Syst of Sci Instr Florida State Univ; writ Elem Sch Sci Prgm 1961-66; participant Visiting Prof AAS 1964-; trustee Adler Planetarium; mem Astron Soc of The Pac; fellow Amer Assn for the Adv of Sci Rec; NSF Res. **Honors/Awds:** Grants; published numerous articles in Astrophysical Journal of the Astron Soc and in Japan Astron & Astrophysics Journal. **Military Serv:** AUS 1942-45. **Business Addr:** Dept of Physics & Astron, Howard Univ, Washington, DC 20059.

PEETE, CALVIN
Professional golfer. **Personal:** Born Jul 18, 1943, Detroit, MI; son of Irenia Bridgeford Peete and Dennis Peete; married Elaine Bolden, Dec 31, 1992; children: Calvin, Rickie, Dennis, Kalvanetta, Nicole, Aisha, Aleya. **Career:** Farm laborer, Florida, 1957-60; itinerant peddler, 1961-71; professional golfer, 1971-; real estate investor, currently. **Orgs:** Professional Golfers Association. **Honors/Awds:** Eleven PGA victories, including Greater Milwaukee Open, 1979, Anheuser-Busch Classic, 1982, Phoenix Open, 1985; member, US Ryder Cup team; honorary degree, Wayne State University, 1983; Ben Hogan Award, 1983; Jackie Robinson Award, 1983; two-time winner of Vardon Award for lowest stroke average on PGA Tour; winner of awards for driving accuracy and hitting most greens in regulation number of strokes; over $1 million in career earnings. **Business Addr:** Peete Management, PO Box 2645, Ponte Vedra Beach, FL 32004.

PEETE, RODNEY
Professional football player. **Personal:** Born Mar 16, 1966, Mesa, AZ; son of Willie Peete; married Holly Robinson, 1995; children: two. **Educ:** Univ of Southern California, BS, communications, 1989. **Career:** Detroit Lions, quarterback, 1989-93; Dallas Cowboys, 1994; Philadelphia Eagles, 1995-. **Special Achievements:** Appearance on ABC's ''Hangin' With Mr. Cooper''; one of nine African-American quarterbacks, largest number in NFL history, 1997. **Business Addr:** Professional Football Player, Philadelphia Eagles', 3501 S Broad St, Philadelphia, PA 19148, (215)463-2500.

PEGRAM, ERRIC DEMONT
Professional football player. **Personal:** Born Jan 7, 1969, Dallas, TX. **Educ:** North Texas State, attended. **Career:** Atlanta Falcons, running back, 1991-94; Pittsburgh Steelers, 1995-96; San Diego Chargers, 1997; New York Giants, 1997-. **Business Addr:** Professional Football Player, New York Giants, Giants Stadium, East Rutherford, NJ 07073, (201)935-8111.

PEGUES, ROBERT L., JR.
Educational administrator. **Personal:** Born Mar 6, 1936, Youngstown, OH; children: Tamara Pegues Brooks, Robert L III. **Educ:** Youngstown State Univ, BS 1958; Westminster Coll PA, MS 1963; Kent State Univ OH, Doctoral Prog. **Career:** Youngstown City Schools, teacher/admin 1959-72; Educ Research Council of Amer Cleveland, OH, dir urban education 1969-70; Youngstown City Schools, superintendent 1972-78; Youngstown State Univ, dir/instr 1978-79; Warren City School Dist, supt of schools. **Orgs:** Bd of trustees St Elizabeth's Med Cntr Youngstown, OH; bd dir Warren Redevel & Planning Corp Warren, OH; bd dir Warren-Trumbull Urban League. **Honors/Awds:** Humanitarian Award Trumbull Co Br NAACP 1984; Outstanding Educator Warren-Trumbull Urban League 1981; Finis E Engleman Scholarship Amer Assn of Sch Admin 1981; Bowman Fellowship Kent State Univ 1979. **Military Serv:** AUS Capt (active & reserves) 1954-68. **Business Addr:** Superintendent of Schools, Warren City School District, 261 Monroe NW, Warren, OH 44483.

PEGUES, WENNETTE WEST
City administrator. **Personal:** Born Nov 25, 1936, Pittsburgh, PA; married Julius Pegues; children: Mary Pamela, Michael David, Angela Suzette. **Educ:** Carlow Coll Pittsburgh, BSN 1958; Univ of Tulsa, CCS 1974; Univ of Tulsa, EdD 1978. **Career:** Langston Univ Urban Center, assoc acad dean 1979-80; Univ of Tulsa, asst dean 1978-79; asst dean 1976-78; Univ of Tulsa, grad Research fellow 1975-76; Univ of Tulsa, grad asst 1974-75; RN adminstr teacher & staff position 1958-74. **Orgs:** Mem AAUW; mem Am Personnel & Guid Assn; mem Nat Conf on Acad Advising; mem Pub Welfare Assn Sch Bd; mem Osage Co Dept Dist #55 Acad Cent Sch 1979-80; commr OK State Dept of Human Serv 1979; mem Delta Sigm Theta 1980; sch bd pres Osage Co Dept Dist #55 Acad Cent Sch 1980-81; mem bd of dir Tulsa Sr Citizens Inc 1980. **Honors/Awds:** Educ Honor Soc Kappa Delta Outstndg Wom in the comm N Tulsa B & P Wom; Disting Alumni Serv awd in the Educ Calow Coll

1979. **Military Serv:** ANC 2 lt 1956-59. **Business Addr:** Div Mgr - Human Development, City of Tulsa, 200 Civic Center, Tulsa, OK 74103.

PEGUESE, CHARLES R.
Librarian, educational administrator. **Personal:** Born Aug 3, 1938, Philadelphia, PA. **Educ:** LaSalle Coll Phila, BS 1960; Drexel Univ Phila, MLS 1962-65. **Career:** NE Area Young Adult Free Library of Phila, coordinator 1960-69; Action Library Learning Ctr Philadelphia Sch Dist, dir 1970-74; State Library of PA, coordinator networking & academic libraries 1974-78; Harrisburg Area Community College, director, McCormick Library, assistant dean, instructional resources, 1988-. **Orgs:** Omega Psi Phi, 1957-; president, board of directors, N City Cong of Philadelphia, 1966-74; committee member, PA Library Association, 1970-; committee chairman, American Library Association, 1971; adv bd, Philadelp hia United Way, 1972-74; chair, Harrisburg Historical Architectural Review Bd, 1980-90; Historic Harrisburg Association, 1980-; City of Harrisburg, Redevelopment Authority Board, 1989-; Leadership Harrisburg Area, Class of 1993. **Honors/Awds:** American Library Association, Association of College and Research Libraries, National Leadership Award, 1990. **Special Achievements:** Writer, articles in PA Library Association Bulletin, Library Journal. **Military Serv:** US Army, sgt, 1961-66. **Business Addr:** Assistant Dean, Instructional Resources, Harrisburg Area Community College, One HACC Dr, Harrisburg, PA 17110-2999.

PELOTE, DOROTHY B.
County official, educator (retired). **Personal:** Born Dec 30, 1929, Lancaster, SC; daughter of Ethel Green and Abraham Barnes; married Maceo R Pelote (deceased); children: Deborah Pelote Allen, Miriam Pelote Heyward. **Educ:** Allen Univ, BS 1953; Savannah State College, attended. **Career:** Chatham Co Bd of Educ, teacher 1956-85; Chatham Co GA, county commissioner. **Orgs:** Mem Legislative Study Comm for Memorial Med Ctr; pres Carver Height Organ; mem Adv Comm on Local Govt; mem Water & Sewer Auth of Chatham Co; mem Chatham Assn of Educ; mem Phi Delta Kappa Educ Frat 1978; pres Savannah Fed of Teachers 1982-83; mem Coastal Comm Food Bank; mem bd dir YMCA; bd mem United Way; mem Business and Professional Women's Club; board member, Phoenix Project; member, National Council of Negro Women Inc; member, NAACP. **Honors/Awds:** Carver Heights Comm Serv Awd 1981-82; Rep Roy Allen Awd for Excellence 1982; Zeta Phi Beta nomination for Minority Women of the Yr 1984; Dorothy Pelote Day City of Savannah & Chatham Co 1985; First Female elected Co Commission Chmn Pro Tem; mem State Bd of Postsecondary Vocational Educ by appointment of the Gov of GA; Mem of the Chatham Co Employees Retirement Bd; Mem of Coastal Area Planning & Devel Commn for Seminar Agendas; electec vice pres of the Black Caucus of the Assoc of County Commissioners of GA; Testimonial Banquet by Constituents of Eighth Commission District; one of the first Black females to be elected to the Chatham County Commission. **Business Addr:** County Commissioner, Chatham County Commission, 133 Montgomery St, Savannah, GA 31401.

PELTIER, ARMA MARTIN
Physician. **Personal:** Born Apr 22, 1938, New York, NY; married Maria Virginia Gonzalez; children: Coulissa, Michelle. **Educ:** Fordham U, BS 1965; Long Island U; Meharry Med Coll, MD 1973. **Career:** Hunter Found, intrnst 1977-; Prospect Hosp, phys 1976-77; Harlem Hosp Ctr, intrn, res 1973-76; Exlay, chemist 1965-69; Brooklyn Coll of Pharm, chem instr 1962-65; Good Samaritan, atdng phys; St Joseph; Cntrl Bapt Hosp. **Orgs:** Mem Nat Assn of Intrns & Rsdnts; asso Am Coll of Phys. **Business Addr:** 212 N Upper, Lexington, KY 40507.

PEMBERTON, DAVID MELBERT
Insurance broker. **Personal:** Born Apr 24, 1926, Chicago, IL; son of Cleo Davis Ward and David M Pemberton Jr; married Masseline Gibson Pemberton, Jun 26, 1949; children: Dianna, Debra, Denise, Kim. **Career:** Midwest Nat Life Ins Co, reg mgr 1965-. **Orgs:** Mem Life Underwriters Assn Miami; elder Bethany SDA Ch; NAACP; treas Locka Br; chmn Commun Act Nghbrhd Counc. **Honors/Awds:** Civic awd 1969; natl qual Awd; natl & sales achvemnt awd 1974; 51st All-Star Honor Roll 1973; Urban League, Father of the Year, 1993. **Home Addr:** 2520 NW 156th St, Opa Locka, FL 33054.

PEMBERTON, GAYLE R.
Educator. **Personal:** Born Jun 29, 1948, St Paul, MN; daughter of Muriel E Wigington Pemberton and Lounneer Pemberton. **Educ:** Lake Forest College, attended, 1966-68; University of Michigan, BA, 1969; Harvard University, MA, 1971, PhD, 1981. **Career:** Columbia University, lecturer, 1974-77; Middlebury College, instructor, 1977-80; Northwestern University, assistant professor, 1980-83; Reed College, visiting associate professor, 1983-84; Bowdoin College, African-American Studies, visiting associate professor, acting director, 1986-88, Minority Affairs, director, 1988-90; Princeton University, African-American Studies, associate director, 1990-. **Orgs:** Modern Language Assn. **Honors/Awds:** W E B DuBois Foundation, 1975; Ford Foundation, Doctoral Fellowship, 1969-74; Southwest Review, Margaret Hartley Memorial Award, 1992. **Special Achievements:** Author: ''A Sentimental Journey,'' Race-ing Justice En-Gendering Power, 1992; The Hottest Water in Chicago, 1992; ''It's The Thing That Counts,'' State of Black America, 1991; John Simon Guggenheim Fellow, 1993; New Jersey Committee for the Humanities, Book of the Year Award, for Hottest Water. **Business Addr:** Associate Director, African-American Studies, Princeton University, 112 Dickinson Hall, Princeton, NJ 08544-1017.

PEMBERTON, HILDA RAMONA
County official. **Personal:** Born Jun 29, 1940, Norman, NC; daughter of Judy Pearl Bostic and Archie C Bostic (deceased); divorced; children: Eugenia, Charles. **Educ:** North Carolina Central University, BS, 1961; Southeastern University, masters, 1981. **Career:** Prince Georges County government: psychiatric social worker, chief of employee relations division, office of personnel, deputy director of personnel, councilmember, currently. **Orgs:** National Association of Counties, board of directors; National Association of Black County Officials, past president; Prince George's County Economic Development Corporation, board member; Council of Governments, chair of board; Washington Sanitary Transit Authority, board of directors; National Council of Negro Women; Alpha Kappa Alpha; First Baptist of Highland Park. **Honors/Awds:** American City & County Magazine, County Leader of the Year, 1991; Washingtonian Magazine, One of 100 Most Influential Women, 1989; Presidential Citation for outstanding dedication to the career development of our nation's youth; Governor's Award for dedicated service to the homeless. **Home Addr:** 7608 Swan Terrace, Landover, MD 20785.

PEMBERTON, PRISCILLA ELIZABETH
Educator. **Personal:** Born Jan 4, 1919, New York; married William. **Educ:** Brooklyn Coll, BA, 1952; Bank Street College of Education, MS, 1960. **Career:** Non-Matric Study, Bank Street College of Education, NYC, director 1966-; NY City Pre-schs, teacher, 1944-48; Intl Nurs Sch & Kinder, NY, director, 1949-65; mis cler pos 1937-43; Ministry Educ British Guyana, education consultant, 1962-63; One Summer's Tchr Training, Barbados, 1969; Pub & Ind Schs, Various States, consultant, 1967-. **Orgs:** Early Childhood Educ Council, New York City, 1961-; New Lincoln School, New York City, on board of trustees, 1971-74; Clinton Pre-sch Head Start, board of trustees mem, 1972-; Allen AME Ch, Jamaica, 1935-; NAACP 1939-50; Bus & Professional Women's Clubs, 1959-64. **Honors/Awds:** Achievement Educ Awarded by Bus & Professional Women's Clubs 1963. **Business Addr:** Child Study, Boro of Manhattan C C, 199 Chambers St, New York, NY 10007-1006.

PEMBERTON-HEARD, DANIELLE MARIE
Attorney. **Personal:** Born Nov 29, 1964, New York, NY; daughter of Dennis & Andrea Pemberton; married Gregory McQuade Heard, Aug 26, 1995. **Educ:** Tufts University, BA, 1986; Case Western Reserve University, School of Law, JD, 1989. **Career:** Time Life Inc, vice pres of business affairs, 1986-; Cowan Luiebowitz & Latman, attorney associate, 1991-93; Wiggin & Dana, attorney associate, 1989-91; Discovery Communications, director, sr counsel legal & business affairs, 1993-96. **Orgs:** Delta Sigma Theta Sorority Inc, 1984-; Habitat for Humanity, N Virginia, community mem, 1996-; Professional Alliance, vice pres of programming, 1994-. **Special Achievements:** Recent Developments in Copyright, 1992; Contributing Author, Journal of The Copyright Society, 1992; 1991 Letter Updates, Trademark & Unfair Conpetion Law, Cases and Materials, The Michie Co., 1990. **Business Addr:** Vice Pres, Legal & Business Affairs, The Life Inc, 2000 Duke St, Alexandria, VA 22314, (703)838-5630.

PENA, ROBERT BUBBA
Professional football player (retired), actor, business executive. **Personal:** Born Aug 8, 1949, Wareham, MA. **Educ:** Dean Junior College, AA; Univ of Massachusetts. **Career:** Offensive guard: Cleveland Browns; actor: Love of Life, Dogs of War, Ft Apache, The Four Seasons, TV pilot; Street, various commercials; business ventures, Domingo's Chowder House Restaurant, W Falmoreth Fish Market, Health Club Enterprises; Robert Pena and Associates, president; Mortgage Security, Inc, president/CEO, currently. **Orgs:** Founder and co-chairman, Roche Pires Scholarship Fund; mem, Cape Verdean Club of Falmouth MA; mem, Lambda Chi Alpha Frat; volunteer work, Northampton Jail in MA; worked with Black students at Barnstable HS MA Jr Coll. **Honors/Awds:** All-Amer 2 yrs; All-East 2 times; All New England 2 times; MVP 3 yrs in coll; Special Athletic Awd for Jr Coll; played in Coll All-Star Game in Lubbock TX 1971; Awd from Falmouth MA Local Real Estate Beautification Comm for restoring a piece of historically zoned real estate. **Business Addr:** President/CEO, Mortgage Security, Inc, 31 Teaticket Highway, East Falmouth, MA 02536.

PENA, TONY (ANTONIO FRANCESCO)
Professional baseball player. **Personal:** Born Jun 4, 1957, Montecristi, Dominican Republic; married Amaris; children: Tony Jr, Jennifer Amaris. **Career:** Pittsburgh Pirates, infielder, 1980-86; St Louis Cardinals, infielder, 1987-89; Boston Red Sox, infielder, 1990-. **Honors/Awds:** Led all league catchers in double plays 1979; Gold Glove Awd winner 3 times; led NL catchers in putouts, assists, total chances, & double plays; selected starting catcher on The Sporting News 1983 post-season NL All-Star team, led all NL catchers in putouts, & total chances 1983; TOPPS Rookie All-Star; fourth major league catcher in 40 years to reach the 100 mark in assists 1985; named to Sporting News first Latin Amer All-Star Team; mem major league All-Star Team that toured Japan; National League All-Star Team, 1982, 1984, 1985, 1986, 1989. **Business Addr:** Professional Baseball Player, Boston Red Sox, 24 Yawkey Way, Fenway Park, Boston, MA 02215-3496.

PENCEAL, BERNADETTE WHITLEY
Educator. **Personal:** Born Dec 16, 1944, Lenoir, NC; daughter of Thelma Simmons Whitley and Walter Andrew Whitley; married Sam Penceal, Apr 29, 1967. **Educ:** Syracuse Univ, Syracuse NY, BS, 1966; The City Coll, New York NY, MA, 1973, Letter of Completion, 1974; Fordham Univ, New York NY, PhD, 1989. **Career:** Fashion Inst of Technology, New York NY, instructor of English, 1973-74; Green Haven Maximum Security Prison, Stormville NY, instructor of English, 1974-76; Malcolm-King Coll, New York NY, instructor of English, 1974-78; Hunter Coll, New York NY, instructor of reading, 1974-79; Coll of New Rochelle, New Rochelle NY, instructor of English, 1977-89; New York Univ, New York NY, mentor of English, 1980-. **Orgs:** Mem, Assn of Black Faculty & Admin, New York Univ, 1981-, Phi Delta Kappa, 1981-; pres, Assn of Black Women in Higher Educ Inc, 1985-87, J & B Whitley's Inc, 1985-; bd mem, Urban Women's Shelter, 1985-87; mem, New York Urban League, 1987-, Amer Assn of Univ Women, 1989-. **Honors/Awds:** ''Bernadette Penceal Day,'' Office of the President of the Borough of Manhattan, City of New York, 1987; ''Non-Intellective Factors as Predictions of Academic Performance of Non-Traditional Adult College Freshmen,'' 1989. **Business Addr:** English Mentor, New York University, 239 Green St, 8th Floor, New York, NY 10039.

PENDER, MEL
Athletics executive. **Educ:** Adelphi Coll, BS, social science. **Career:** National Assn of Homebuilders, southeast regional coordinator; Atlanta Hawks, director of community affairs, currently. **Orgs:** Atlanta Hawks Foundation, president. **Special Achievements:** Olympic Games, 1964; Olympic Games, gold medal, 4x100-meter relay, 1968. **Military Serv:** Vietnam War, Bronze Star. **Business Addr:** Dir, Community Affairs, Atlanta Hawks, 1 CNN Center NW, S. Tower, Ste. 405, Atlanta, GA 30335, (404)827-3800.

PENDERGRAFT, MICHELE M.
Banking executive. **Personal:** Born Sep 6, 1954, Trenton, NJ; daughter of Lena Mae Kelly Meekins and Leon Edward Meekins Sr; married James William Pendergraft Sr, May 17, 1980; children: James William Jr. **Educ:** Mercer County Community College, Trenton, NJ, 1977; American Institution of Banking, Anchorage, AK, 1983. **Career:** Mercer Street Friends Center, Trenton, NJ, dance instructor, 1970-78; Ginger Bread House, Anchorage, AK, asst mgr, 1978-79; First National Bank of Anchorage, Anchorage, AK, customer service rep, 1979-80, asst vice pres, branch mgr, currently. **Orgs:** Member, Business Professional Women Club, 1990. **Home Addr:** 7041 Scalero Circle, Anchorage, AK 99507. **Business Addr:** Assistant Vice President/Branch Manager, Parkway Branch, Operati, First National Bank of Anchorage, 5305 E Northern Lights Blvd, Anchorage, AK 99507.

PENDERGRASS, EMMA H.
Attorney. **Personal:** Born Jun 1, Orangeburg, SC; daughter of Catherine Humphrey and W W Humphrey; children: Bailey III, Gary W. **Educ:** Howard U, BS; Westfield State Coll, MEd 1964; Armstrong Law Sch, JD 1976; CA Western Univ, PhD 1976. **Career:** Law Office of Emma H Pendergrass, atty of law 1976-; Hayward Unified Sch Dist, career educ counselor 1971-76; Hayward Unified Sch Dist, sci tchr 1967-71; Chicopee High Sch, sci tchr 1960-67; US Govt, chemist 1955-56. **Orgs:** Past pres Charles Houston Bar; bd of dirs YWCA Oakland; Natl Bar Assn; Delta Sigma Theta Sorority Inc; Alameda Co Bar Assn 1977-; Pro Bono Serv Judicare Program Charles Houston Bar Assn 1977-80; past pres, California Assn of Black Lawyers; Links, Inc. **Business Addr:** Attorney, Members Link, Inc, One Kaiser Plaza, Ste 1015, Oakland, CA 94612.

PENDERGRASS, MARGARET E.
Librarian (retired). **Personal:** Born Aug 9, 1912, Springfield, IL; daughter of Susie K Huston Pendergrass and Ulysses Grant Pendergrass. **Educ:** Hampton Inst, BS 1934; Extra Mural Courses in Lib Sci 1967-68; LaSalle U, certificate in computer programming 1972. **Career:** Phyllis Wheatley Br, br libr 1934-41; War Dept Ft Custer, army libr 1941-43; Camp Ellis 1943-45; Camp Miles Standish 1945-46; Camp Joyce Kilmer 1946-49; IL State Libr, cataloger 1950-57; head juvenile unit 1957-70; Head Children's Book Reviewing Ctr, asst ref libr 1970-73; Order Libr, Juvenile cataloger 1973-79; Adult Books & Spcl Proj Fed Doc Switching Proj, cataloguer 1979-; IL State Library, librarian. **Orgs:** Am Libr Assn 1942-44, 1950-; past pres & sec Springfield Lib Club 1953-; board member Springfield Chap NAACP 1954-; v chmn Children's Sect IL Libr Assn 1956-57; chmn Educ Com James Weldon Johnson Study Guild 1962-; Belleville Springfield Chap Cath Lib Assn; asst sec Order of Golden Circle 1973-; Zion Bapt Ch; pres Missionary

Soc; bd mem World Federalists 1980-. **Honors/Awds:** Citizens Award NAACP 1974; Citation Award Am Bicentennial Research Inst 1974; Certificate of Appreciation Historical Project Black Women in the Middle West 1985; Davis Cup, Children's Section, Illinois Library Association, 1976. **Home Addr:** 2001 S 11 St, Springfield, IL 62703.

PENDERGRASS, THEODORE D. (TEDDY)
Singer. **Personal:** Born Mar 26, 1950, Philadelphia, PA; married Karin Still, Jun 1987; children: Theodore Jr, Tisha Lazette, LaDonna, Tamon. **Career:** Played the drums in James Browns' band; Harold Melvin & the Blue Notes, drummer, 1968, lead singer, 1970-77; solo performer, 1977-; Solo LPs include: "Life is a Song Worth Singing," 1978; "Teddy," 1979; "TP," 1980; "Live Coast to Coast," 1980; "It's Time for Teddy," 1981; "Teddy Pendergrass," 1982; "This One's For You," 1982; "Heaven Only Knows," 1983; "Greatest Hits," 1984; "Love Language," 1984; "Workin' It Back," 1985; "Joy," 1988; "Truly Blessed," 1991. **Honors/Awds:** Recipient of numerous civic and public service awards; Image Award, NAACP, 1973, 1980; Black Achievement Award, Ebony Magazine, 1979; Keys to Cities: Detroit, Savannah, Lakeland, FL, Memphis. **Special Achievements:** 12 gold and 7 platinum albums.

PENDLETON, BERTHA MAE OUSLEY
Educational administrator. **Personal:** Born Oct 15, 1933, Troy, AL; married Oscar Pendleton; children: Gregory. **Educ:** Knoxville College, bachelor's degree (with honors); United States International University, master's degree; University of San Diego, doctorate, educational leadership. **Career:** Tennessee Valley Authority, cartographic engineering aide, 1954-55; Chattanooga Public Schools, 1956-57; Memorial Junior High School, teacher/counselor, 1957-68; Morse High School, parent counselor, 1968-70; Compensatory Education Unit, coordinator, 1970-72; Crawford High School, vice principal, 1972-74; Lincoln High School, principal, 1974-76; Programs Division, director of compensatory education, 1976-83; School Operations Division, assistant superintendent, 1983-85; Superintendent's Office, special assistant to superintendent, 1985-86; Deputy Superintendent's Office, deputy superintendent, 1986-93; San Diego Unified School District, superintendent, 1993-; Point Loma Nazarene College, adjunct professor, currently. **Orgs:** United Way of San Diego County; Natural History Museum; The National Center for Education and the Economy; Danforth Foundation Advisory Committee; Association of California School Administrators; Alpha Kappa Mu Honor Society; Elementary Institute of Science; YMCA; US Dept of Defense, advisory council; Alpha Kappa Alpha Sorority; Institute for Educational Inquiry. **Honors/Awds:** San Diego Urban League, George Edmund Haynes Award; Senator David Kelley, Legislative Woman of the Year; Point Loma College, Woman of Change, 1994; Salvation Army, Woman of Distinction; San Diego Chamber of Commerce, Chairman's Award; Phi Delta Kappa, Educator of the Decade, 1993; National Council of Negro Women, Woman of Distinction; selected as one of 100 role models in the "Songs of My People" exhibit at the San Diego Museum of Art; United Negro College Fund, Frederick D. Patterson Award, 1996; Univ of San Diego, Author E. Hughes Career Achievement Award, 1996. **Business Addr:** Superintendent, San Diego Unified School District, 4100 Normal St., San Diego, CA 92103-2682, (619)293-8686.

PENDLETON, FLORENCE HOWARD
District representative, educational administrator. **Personal:** Born Jan 28, Columbus, GA; daughter of Elease Brooks Howard and John Milton Howard; married Oscar Henry Pendleton Sr, 1943; children: Oscar Henry Jr, Howard Thompson. **Educ:** Howard University, BS, 1949, MS, 1957; American University, SScD, 1976; Catholic University, SScD, 1970. **Career:** District of Columbia Public Schools, teacher, 1958-70, assistant principal, 1970-80, principal, 1980-; Ward Five Democratic Committee, chairperson, 1979-82, member, 1979-; Ward Five CO7, Adv Neighborhood Committee, comissioner, currently; District of Columbia, shadow senator, currently. **Orgs:** Alpha Kappa Alpha; District of Columbia Assn of Secondary School Principals, secretary, 1980-; Natl Assn of Secondary School Principals. **Honors/Awds:** Hine Junior High School, Student Government Assn, Outstanding Principal, 1981; Ward Five, Berean Baptist Church, Outstanding Community Leader, 1981. **Business Addr:** Shadow Senator, District of Columbia, 147 S St NW, Washington, DC 20001.

PENDLETON, TERRY LEE
Professional baseball player. **Personal:** Born Jul 16, 1960, Los Angeles, CA; son of Ella Pendleton and Alfred Pendleton. **Career:** St Louis Cardinals, 3rd baseman, 1982-90; Atlanta Braves, 1991-. **Orgs:** 5th player to Steal 20 Bases 1984; selected Texas League All-Star Team 1983. **Business Addr:** Professional Baseball Player, Atlanta Braves, 521 Capitol Ave SW, Atlanta, GA 30312-2803.

PENELTON, BARBARA SPENCER
Educator. **Personal:** Born Apr 8, 1937, Chicago, IL; married Richard; children: Kim, Lisa. **Educ:** Univ of IL, BS Elem Educ 1958; Univ of IL, MS Guidance/Counseling 1961; Univ of IN, edD Higher Educ 1977. **Career:** Bradley Univ Peoria IL, dir student teaching 1978-, asso prof of educ 1969-; Tri-County Urban League Peoria, dir of educ programs 1966-69; McCosh Elementary School Chicago, teacher 1958-66; Ten-year Review Team IL State Board of Educ, evaluation team Consult 1979; IL Council of Right to Read, adv/cons 1980; Rockefeller-Kellogg Found Leadership Training Project, consult 1980. **Orgs:** Bd of trustees Nat Urban League 1980; bd of trustees Proctor Hosp Peoria 1980; pres bd of dirs Tri County Urban League 1980. **Honors/Awds:** Outstanding Educator Young Women's Christian Assn 1973; Outstanding Grad Adv Central Region Alpha Kappa Alpha Sorority 1975. **Business Addr:** Bradley University, 1501 W Bradley Ave, Peoria, IL 61604.

PENISTON, CECE
Vocalist. **Personal:** Born in Dayton, OH. **Career:** Albums: featured on Overweight Pooch's Female Preacher; Finally, 1992; Thought 'Ya Knew; singles include: "Finally," "We Got a Love Thang.". **Honors/Awds:** Miss Black Arizona; Miss Galaxy. **Special Achievements:** "Finally," topped Billboard magazine's dance chart. **Business Addr:** Singer, c/o A&M Records, Inc, 1416 N LaBrea Ave, Hollywood, CA 90028, (213)856-2755.

PENN, CHARLES E.
Association executive (retired). **Personal:** Born Oct 10, 1928, Pittsburgh; son of Matilda Peace Lawson and William Donald Penn; married Mavis V (deceased); children: Robert E, Ronald L. **Educ:** Bluefield State Coll WV, BS, 1951; Univ MI School of Social Work, 1957-58. **Career:** Todd-Phillips Children's Home Detroit, exec dir 1965-84; MI Dept Soc Servs, child welfare wrkr 1956-59; Wayne Co Juv Ct, prob officer & counselor 1959-65; Detroit Bar Assn, legal services mgr, 1985-89. **Orgs:** Founder & dir Boy's Club of Inkster MI 1957-; pres MI Assn Children's Agencies 1974; bd dirs MI Council on Crime & Delinquency 1973-; bd dirs Boys Work Council 1962-64; pres People's Action Com of Inkster & Dearborn Hts MI 1971-; community resources coord Inkster Br NAACP 1973-; exec bd mem 2nd Dist Rep Nat Assn of Homes for Boys, First Black to Hold Membership & Office in Hist of Orgn; v-chmn Soc Dev Com City of Inkster 1974; 50 Anniv Medallion Services to Humanity 1970; Jaycees (Name Enshrined at Nat Jaycee Hq Tulsa, OK); Sigma Rho Sigma Honoary Soc of the Soc Scis; Alpha Phi Alpha; bd of dirs, Natl Assn of Homes for Children, 1981-84; pres, MI Federation of Private Children's Agencies, 1979-81; consultant apointee, pro bono comm, State Bar Assn, 1987-90. **Honors/Awds:** Lafayette Allen Sr Dist Serv Award 1971; Dist Serv To Youth Wayne Co Sheriffs Assn 1972; Cert Merit Plymouth United Ch Christ 1972; Outstanding Achievement Award, Delta Sigma Theta Sorority, 1984; Concurrent Resolution, MI State Senate & House of Representatives, 1984; Honorary Resolution, County of Wayne, 1984. **Military Serv:** USAF 1951-55.

PENN, CHRISTOPHER ANTHONY
Professional football player. **Personal:** Born Apr 20, 1971, Lenapah, OK. **Educ:** Northeastern Oklahoma A&M; Tulsa. **Career:** Kansas City Chiefs, wide receiver, 1994-96; Chicago Bears, 1997-. **Business Addr:** Professional Football Player, Chicago Bears, 1000 Football Dr, Halas Hall at Conway Park, Lake Forest, IL 60045-4829, (847)295-6600.

PENN, JOHN GARRETT
Judge. **Personal:** Born Mar 19, 1932, Pittsfield, MA; son of Eugenie Heyliger Penn and John Penn; married Ann Elizabeth Rollison; children: John II, Karen, David. **Educ:** Univ of MA, BA 1954; Boston Univ School of Law, LLB 1957; Princeton Univ, attended; Woodrow Wilson School of Intl & Public Affairs; Natl Coll of St Judicial. **Career:** AUS, judge, advocate general corps 1958-61, trial attorney 1961-65, rev 1965-68, asst chief 1968-70; US Dept of Justice, general litigation section 1961-70; Court of General Sessions, judge 1970-71; Superior Court of DC, assoc judge 1970-79; US District Court for Washington DC, district judge 1979-. **Orgs:** DC Bar Assn, MA Bar Assn, Amer Judicial Assn, Boston Univ School of Law Alumni Assoc; fellow Princeton Univ 1967-68; honorary bd mem District of Columbia Dept of Recreation Day Care Program; boule Sigma Pi Phi. **Honors/Awds:** Natl Inst of Public Affairs Fellow, Princeton Univ 1967-68; Outstanding Jurist, District of Columbia Bar Assn; Fort Lewis Certificate of Achievement, US Army 1960; Silver Shingle Award, Boston Univ School of Law, 1987. **Military Serv:** US Army, Judge Advocate Judges Corp, 1st lieutenant 1957-61. **Business Addr:** US District Judge, US District Court of the District of Columbia, Third and Constitution Ave, NW, Suite 6600, Washington, DC 20001.

PENN, MINDELL LEWIS
Small business affairs coordinator. **Personal:** Born Mar 27, 1944, Detroit, MI; daughter of Mamie Underwood and Artis Underwood; married Leon Penn, Feb 3, 1974; children: Michael Artis, Courtney Leon. **Educ:** Wayne State University, Detroit, MI BS, business administration, 1964. **Career:** Michigan Consolidated Gas Co, Detroit, MI, tele-type operator, 1961-64; San Diego Gas & Electric Co, San Diego, CA, credit rep, 1964-67; Pacific Gas & Electric Co, Sacramento, CA, small business affairs administrator, 1967-. **Orgs:** Chair, Sacramento Girl Scout Advisory Board; chair, board of directors, Sacramento Urban League; board member, St Hope Academy; member, Sacramento Metropolitan Arts Commission's County Cultural Awards Committee. **Business Addr:** Small Business Affairs Administrator, General Services, Pacific Gas and Electric, 2740 Gateway Oaks Dr, Sacramento, CA 95833.

PENN, NOLAN E.
Educator. **Personal:** Born Dec 1, 1928, Shreveport, LA; son of Bessie Penn and Henry Penn; married Barbara Pigford; children: Joyce, Carol. **Educ:** CA State Univ, AB 1949; Univ of So CA, MS 1952; Metro State Hosp, psych intern 1955; Univ of Denver, PhD 1958; Univ of WI School of Med, Postdoctoral fellow 1959-61; Harvard Med School, Cert in Comm Mental Health 1969. **Career:** Larue Carter mem Hosp Indianpolis, staff psychologist 1958-59; Mendota State Hosp, staff psychologist 1961-63; Univ of WI Madison, asst prof to prof 1963-70; Univ of CA San Diego School of Med, prof of psychiatry 1970-, reg dir area health ed ctr office of the dean 1982; Univ of Cal-San Diego, assoc chancellor, 1988-. **Orgs:** Pres WI State Psychological Assoc 1967-68; mem WI Leg Comm to recodify the Mental Health & Mental Retardation Codes 1967-70; founder & chmn Afro-Amer Studies Dept Univ of WI Madison 1969-70, Urban & Rural Studies Univ of CA San Diego 1970-73; dir Comm & Forensic Psych Trg UCSD 1974-88; mem Amer Psych Assoc,Inter-Amer Soc of Psych, Sigma Xi; ed bd Jrnl of Consulting & Clinical Psych, Amer Jrnl of Publ Health. **Military Serv:** AUS corpl 1952-54. **Business Addr:** Assoc Chancellor, Univ of California-San Diego, La Jolla, CA 92093-0001.

PENN, ROBERT CLARENCE
Public policy administrator. **Personal:** Born Mar 6, 1943, Buffalo, NY; son of Jeanette Robinson Penn and William C Penn; married Barbara Bowman; children: Robert C Jr. **Educ:** Morgan State Univ, BS 1965; Howard Univ 1967; MIT 1976. **Career:** US Dept of Justice, asst 1967; Manhattan, spec asst borough pres 1967-68; Sen Robert Kennedy campaign staff, mem 1968; Model Cities Agy, dir 1971-73; City of Buffalo, commr of parks 1973-75, commr human resources 1975-78; Manpower Demonstration Rsch Corp, senior vice pres 1978-85; New York Works Inc, pres 1985-86; Universal Management Consulting Grp, pres 1986-. **Orgs:** V chmn United Way of Buffalo & Erie Co; Natl League of Cities/US Conf of Mayors Vet Educ Trng; prog chmn NY State NAACP Legisl Comm; vice pres Catholic Diocese Timon Towers Hous Corp; dir Natl Child Labor Comm; NY Statewide Adv Council on Youth; Alpha Phi Alpha; Bd of dir Natl Child Labor Comm; mem MDC Inc; bd of dir and exec comm New York City Vietnam Veterans Memorial Commn; vice pres, African Amer Men of Westchester Inc, 1987-; sec/treasurer, MDC Inc, 1989-. **Honors/Awds:** Ford Found Scholarship. **Military Serv:** AUS 1968-71; numerous military awards.

PENN, SHELTON C.
Judge, attorney (retired). **Personal:** Born Dec 9, 1925, Winston Salem, NC; married Sadie W. **Educ:** Morehouse Coll, BA 1948; Univ of Mich Law School, JD 1951. **Career:** Attorney pvt practice 1951-75; chief asst pros attorney 1963-66; asst pros attorney Calhoun County, MI 1957-66; practicing attorney & civil rights hearing referee 1973-75; appointed judge Tenth Dist Ct Calhoun County. **Orgs:** Member Calhoun Co Bar Assn; MI Bar Assn; Amer Bar Assn; Natl Bar Assn; Natl Conf of Black Lawyers; past bd of dir Cripple Childrens' Soc; YMCA, Urban League, ARC; Humane Soc; Battle Creek Human Rel Comm; past pres Battle Creek NAACP; Legal Aid Soc; bd of dir South Central MI Planning Cnc of MI Crime Comm; bd of dir Big Brothers & Big Sisters of S Central MI. **Military Serv:** AUS WWII.

PENN-ATKINS, BARBARA A.
Business executive. **Personal:** Born Nov 11, 1935, Gary, VA; married Will E Atkins; children: Lawrence Nichols, Cheryl Nichols Smith, Brian L Nichols. **Educ:** MI State Univ 1954-55; Wayne State Univ 1962-64; Oakland Comm Coll, 1979; Wayne Co Comm Coll, 1977-79. **Career:** Univ of Detroit, adm asst; Wayne Co Comm Coll, accts rec super 1968-72; BPA Enterprises, Inc, vice pres 1972-; Pica Systems Inc, pres 1980-. **Orgs:** Past pres Amer Business Women's Assn/MCCC 1981; gen co-chair/MI United Negro College Fund 1983,84,85; mem allocations/review United Foundations 1983,84,85; 2nd vice pres/bd of dirs Minority Tech Council MI 1985; bd dir Detroit C of C. **Honors/Awds:** Woman of the Year Motor City Charter Chap of Amer Bus Women's Assn 1979; Spirit of Detroit Detroit Convention Bureau 1980; Founders Awd United Negro Coll Fund 1984; Minority Business Awd MI Dept of Commerce 1984; Pioneering Business Award Natl Assn of Women Business Owners MI Chapter 1985. **Business Addr:** President, Pica Systems, Inc, 19980 James Couzens Hwy, Detroit, MI 48235.

PENNICK, AURIE ALMA
Attorney, civil rights activist. **Personal:** Born Dec 22, 1947, Chicago, IL; daughter of Aurie A Watts; children: Faith, Keidra. **Educ:** Univ of IL, BA 1971, MA 1981; John Marshall Law Sch, JD 1986. **Career:** Coalition of Concerned Women Inc, exec dir 1976-78; Chicago Abused Women Coalition, exec dir 1978-81; Citizens Alert, exec dir 1981-82; Chicago Comm Trust Fellowship, staff assoc 1982-84; John D & Catherine T MacArthur Foundation, asst dir spec grant; Chicago Transit Authority Chief Adminstrative Atty; managing attorney/

administration; Leadership Council for Metropolitan Open Communities, president, chief executive officer, currently. **Orgs:** Part time trainer Vista/Action Region V 1980-81; part time faculty Roosevelt Univ 1986-; mem Chicago Police Bd, Chicago Women in Philanthropy, Chicago Blacks in Philanthropy, Phi Alpha Delta Legal Frat; mem Cook County Bar Assoc 1988-; mem American Bar Assoc 1988-. **Honors/Awds:** Ten Outstanding Young Citizens Chicago Jr Assoc of Commerce & Industry 1984; Kizzy Image & Achievement Awd 1985; Natl Council of Negro Women, Chicago Midwest Section, Ida B Wells Education Award, 1992. **Business Addr:** President, CEO, Leadership Council for Metropolitan Open Communities, 401 S State St, Ste 860, Chicago, IL 60605.

PENNICK, JANET
Law enforcement official. **Personal:** Born Feb 6, 1946, Philadelphia, PA; daughter of Roosevelt Matthews & Ella Matthews; married Frank Nelson Pennick, Jan 27, 1966 (divorced); children: Kelly Lynn. **Career:** Philadelphia Sheriff's Office, lieutenant, 1996-. **Orgs:** Philadelphia Guardians for Peace, pres, 1997-. **Military Serv:** US Army Reserves, master sgt, 1977-; Bronze Star Metal, Desert Storm, 1991. **Business Phone:** (215)686-3550.

PENNIMAN, RICHARD WAYNE (LITTLE RICHARD)
Entertainer. **Personal:** Born Dec 5, 1932, Macon, GA; son of Leva Mae Penniman and Bud Penniman; married Ernestine Campbell, 1959 (divorced 1961). **Educ:** Oakwood College, Huntsville, AL, attended. **Career:** Performing and recording artist, 1948-57, 1960-76, 1986-; albums: Here's Little Richard, 1958; The Fabulous Little Richard, 1959; Little Richard Sings Freedom Songs, 1964; King of Gospel Songs, 1965; Little Richard's Greatest Hits, 1972; Shut Up!: A Collection of Rare Tracks, 1951-64, 1988; Little Richard: Specialty Sessions, 1990; TV appearances: Merv Griffin; The Tonight Show; Midnight Special, Rock 'n' Roll Revival, 1975; Night Dreams, 1975; Dinah, 1976; Tomorrow, 1976; Mother Goose Rock 'n' Rhyme, 1990; Arsenio Hall Show; appeared at Radio City Music Hall, 1975; church soloist; Black Heritage Bible, salesman, 1977; Universal Remnant Church of God, minister; performer in traveling medicine show; film appearances: Rock Around the Clock, 1956; The Girl Can't Help It, 1956; Mr Rock 'n'll, 1974; Down & Out in Beverly Hills, 1986. **Honors/Awds:** Hit Singles include ''Tutti-Frutti,'' 1955; ''Long Tall Sally,'' 1956; ''Slippin' and Slidin','' 1956; ''Rip It Up,'' 1956; ''The Girl Can't Help It,'' 1957; ''Lucille,'' 1957; ''Jenny, Jenny,'' 1957; ''Keep a Knockin','' 1957; ''Good Golly, Miss Molly,'' 1958; Rock and Roll Hall Of Fame, charter mem; received star on Hollywood Walk of Fame, 1990; Little Richard Day recognition from Mayor Tom Bradley, Los Angeles, 1990. **Business Addr:** Entertainer, c/o William Morris Agency, 151 E. El Camino Dr., Beverly Hills, CA 90212.

PENNINGTON, JESSE C.
Attorney. **Personal:** Born Jul 1, 1938, Percy, MS; married Roberta; children: Bradford, Johnny. **Educ:** Howard Univ, BA 1964, JD 1969; Wright Jr Coll, AA 1969; Central YMCA Real Estate Inst, certificates; Natl Coll Criminal Lawyers & Public Defenders, 1974; Reginald Heber Smith Fellow, 1969-71. **Career:** US Postal Serv, clerk 1957-60; Seyfarth, Shaw, Fairweather & Geraldson Law Firm, office boy 1957-60; Travis Realty Co, real estate broker 1960-61; Sen Paul H Douglas, legislative asst 1964-67; Natl Labor Relations Bd, legal asst 1967-68; Fed Home Loan Bank Bd, 1968-69; Mary Holmes Coll, instr 1970-71; Northern Mississippi Rural Legal Serv, managing staff atty 1969-72; Pennington Walker & Turner, sr partner 1973-; Micronesian Legal Serv Corp, directing atty. **Orgs:** Mem, Mississippi Bar Assn, Iowa Bar Assn, Natl Bar Assn; Natl Conf Black Lawyers; pres, Mississippi Assn Attys Inc, 1974-; Natl Defense Lawyers Assn; bd dirs, Northern Mississippi Rural Legal Serv, 1973-; Black Appalachian Commn; Clay County Community Devel Prog Inc; mem, Trust Terr of the Pacific Bar, 1976-. **Business Addr:** Special Asst Attorney General, Attorney General's Office, State of Mississippi, 120 N Congress St, Suite 1100, Jackson, MS 39201.

PENNINGTON, LEENETTE MORSE
Educator. **Personal:** Born May 10, 1936, Webster, FL; married Bernard; children: Bernadette, Brigette. **Educ:** Morgan State Coll, BS 1956; Univ of Miami, EdM 1970; Univ of FL 1974-76. **Career:** Elem Basic Skills Project Dade Co Public Schools Miami, project mgr 1973-; Dade Co, admin asst 1970-72; Inst Dade Co Div of Staff Dev, coord 1971; curriculum writer 1969-70; educator 1963-69; FL State Welfare, caseworker 1958-63. **Orgs:** Mem Adv Coun of Elem Educ FL Intl U; mem Assn of Supervision & Curriculum Dev; mem Intl Reading Assn; past pres Nat Coun of Negro Women; Sigma Gamma Rho; consult Desegration Ctr Univ of Miami; mem Dade Co Comm on Status of Women; African Meth Epis Ch. **Honors/Awds:** Recipient Outstanding Educ Achievement Award Sigma Gamma Rho 1972; Outstanding Religious Serv AME Ch 1970; Cited by Bishop Hatcher as Outstanding Young AME Churchwoman 11 Epis Dist. **Business Addr:** 7100 NW 17 Ave, Miami, FL 33147.

PENNINGTON, RICHARD
Law enforcement official. **Career:** New Orleans Police Dept, police chief. **Business Addr:** Chief, New Orleans Police Dept., 715 South Board St., New Orleans, LA 70119, (504)826-2727.

PENNY, ROBERT
Physician. **Personal:** Born Jun 6, 1935, Cincinnati, OH; son of Marie Penny and Ralph Penny; married Joselyn E; children: Angeline E Penny. **Educ:** University of Cincinnati, BS, 1959; Ohio State University, MD, 1963. **Career:** Children's Hospital, Columbus, internship pediatrics, 1963-64; Children's Hospital, Cincinnati, residency pediatrics, 1964-66; Loma Linda Univ, instructor pediatrics, 1967-68; Johns Hopkins Hospital, Baltimore, fellow ped endocrinology, 1968-71; Univ of Southern California, assistant professor ped, 1971-75, associate professor ped, 1975-81, professor of pediatrics, 1981-; Univ of Southern California Medical Center, director, div of pediatric endocrinology, 1985-91, professor, research medicine, 1991-, director, Core Molecular Biology Laboratory, General Clinic Research Center, 1991-. **Orgs:** The Endocrine Soc; The Lawson Wilkins Ped Endocrine Soc; Soc for Pediatric Research; American Pediatric Soc; editorial board of AJDC, 1988; The American Board of Pediatrics, associate member, 1989-91; American Pediatric Society, adolescent medicine section, chairperson, 1990-. **Honors/Awds:** 53 articles in peer review journals; 9 chapters; 48 abstracts; chairperson, Endocrinology Sect Western Soc for Ped Rsch, 1983; question writer, Pediatric Endocrinology Examination, 1984, 1989, 1991; Rho Chi Soc Beta Nu Chap, Cincinnati, 1959; reviewer, J Endo & Metabolism, AJDC, and pediatric research. **Military Serv:** USAF Med Corps capt 1966-68. **Business Addr:** Professor of Pediatrics, Professor of Research Medicine, University of Southern California School of Medicine, 1975 Zonal Ave, Room HMR-701, Los Angeles, CA 90033-1039.

PENNY, ROBERT L.
Educator, writer. **Personal:** Born Aug 6, 1940, Opelika, AL; son of Lillie Penny and J D Penny; married Betty Jean Johnson; children: John, Robert Jr, Kadumu Jua. **Educ:** Central Dist Catholic High School, 1958. **Career:** US Post Office, clerk 1965-67; Opportunities Indust Ctr, counselor 1967-69; Univ of Pittsburgh/Black Studies Dept, teacher 1969-, chairperson 1978-84, assoc prof, currently. **Orgs:** Coord/co-founder Kuntu Writers Workshop 1976-; playwright-in-residence Pittsburgh Public Theatre 1976-77; sec Pittsburgh Front for Black Unity 1980. **Honors/Awds:** National Association of Negro Business and Professional Women's Club Inc, Business and Professional Award, 1979. **Special Achievements:** Poetry: Black Tones of Truth, poetry collection, Oduduwa Prod, 1970; plays: ''Little Willie Armstrong Jones,'' Kuntu Repertory Theatre, 1974; ''Who Loves the Dancer,'' The New Fed Theatre, 1982; ''Good Black,'' ETA, Chicago, 1990; ''Good Black Don't Crack,'' Billie Holiday Theatre, NY, 1992; ''Boppin' With the Ancestors,'' Kuntu Repertory Theatre, 1995, ETA, Chicago, 1997. **Home Addr:** 1845 Bedford Ave, Pittsburgh, PA 15219. **Business Addr:** Associate Professor, University of Pittsburgh, 230 S Bouquet St 3T01 FQ, Pittsburgh, PA 15260.

PENNYWELL, PHILLIP, JR.
Educational administrator, psychologist. **Personal:** Born Aug 1, 1941, Shreveport, LA; son of Rosa Pennywell and Phillip Pennywell Sr; married Janet E M; children: Phyllis, Twanda, Pamela, Phillip Wayne. **Educ:** Southern Univ, BS 1972, MEd 1974; N TX State Univ, PhD 1980. **Career:** Caddo Parish Sch Bd, teacher 1972-74; Parish Govt, police juror 1984-85; Southern Univ, chmn div Behavioral/sci educ. **Orgs:** Mem Phi Delta Kappa 1976; mem Kappa Alpha Psi Frat 1983; bd of dirs Shreveport Leadership sponsored through the Shreveport Chamber of Commerce; chmn bd of dirs Socialization Serv Inc funded through the State of Louisiana (Gerontology); SSI Drug Alcohol Abuse Educ Prog, executive director; Democratic State Central Committee; City of Shreveport River Front Development, citizens advisory committee, Shreve Square; Caddo-Bossier Port Commission Advisory Board, board of directors; Louisiana Association for The Blind, board of directors. **Home Addr:** 7412 McArthur Dr, Shreveport, LA 71106. **Business Addr:** Chmn Div of Social Sci/Educ, Southern Univ, 3050 Dr ML King Jr Dr, Shreveport, LA 71107.

PENTECOSTE, JOSEPH C.
Educator, psychologist (retired). **Personal:** Born Jul 30, 1918, Selma, AL; son of Georgia Alvastine Watson Pentecoste and Clarence Joseph Pentecoste; divorced; children: Joseph, Maria, Tai. **Educ:** Roosevelt Univ, BA 1954; Northeastern IL Univ, MA; Purdue Univ, PhD. **Career:** United Farm Equipment Workers, P&E dir, 1941-52; Hall & Brock Accts, 1952-63; Better Boys Found, rsch dir 1965-70; Northeastern IL Univ, grad faculty 1969-72; IN Univ Northwest, chmn Afro-Amer studies 1972-81, minority studies 1981-; assoc prof emeritus, 1989-. **Orgs:** Am Psychol Assn; Assn Black Psychologists; Am Educ Rsrch Assn; Kappa Alpha Psi Frat; editorial bd of Coll Student Jr. **Honors/Awds:** 20 articles published in scholarly publs Psi Chi Phi Delta Kappa ''Systems of Poverty'' 1977, ''Rats, Roaches & Extension Cords'' 1977.

PEOPLES, DOTTIE
Vocalist. **Personal:** Born in Dayton, OH. **Career:** Gospel singer, currently; producer. **Honors/Awds:** Stellar Awards, Female Vocalist (Traditional), Choir of the Year (Traditional), Album of the Year, Song of the Year, 1995; Bobby Jones Gospel Show, Vision Award, 1995; Atlanta Gospel Choice Award, Song of the Year; Soul Train Music Awards, Best Gospel Album nominee; Dove Awards, Traditional Gospel Album nominee. **Special Achievements:** Albums include: Live, 1993; On Time God, 1994; Christmas With Dottie, 1995; Testify, 1997; Collection-songs of Faith and Love, 1998; Count On God; produced self, Rev. Dreyfus Smith and The Wings of Faith Mass Choir, Rev. Andrew Cheairs and The Songbirds of Byhalia, MS. **Business Addr:** Gospel Singer, Atlanta International Record Company (AIR), 881 Memorial Dr, Atlanta, GA 30316, (404)524-6835.

PEOPLES, EARL F., SR.
Association executive. **Personal:** Born Oct 12, 1930, Bastrop, LA; son of Fannie Williams Peoples and Fate Peoples; married Lillie Jefferson; children: Earl F Jr, Vincent Edward. **Educ:** Southern University, 1948-50; Grambling University, BS, 1954; Cleveland State University, grad work, 1967. **Career:** Galion Elem Sch, Galion, LA, teacher 1954-55; Our Lady of Christian HS, Bastrop, LA, teacher 1954-55; OH Bur Unemployment, stenographer 1958-61; Sun Finance & Loan Co, supr multilith dept 1961-69; Cleveland Urban League, employer relations rep 1969-72; Action Against Addiction Job Devel Comm, dir 1972-73; Cleveland Vocational Educ Proj, supr 1973-76; Fed Govt Emp Opportunity Commn, Detroit, investigator 1976; OH Commn on Aging, asst coord 1976-77; County Employment & Training, account exec 1977-85; NCMD, Inc, Cleveland, OH, community relations dir, 1989-93; Ohio Citizen Action, 1990-93; Network of Small Businessmen/Women, chairman, 1989-. **Orgs:** Exec bd mem 21st Cong Dist Caucus 1972-; chmn memb com 21st Cong Dist Caucus 1972-; chmn Sr Citizen Com 21st Cong Dist Caucus; 2nd vice pres Cleveland Heights Lions Club 1980; memb chmn Cleveland Hts Lions Club 1980; bd of dir The Triangle Indsl & Econ Soc Inc of Shaker Heights Comm Ch 1980; chmn, Econ Com, vice pres, membership serv, bd of dir, Job Serv Empl Comm for Richard Celeste; Fndr 5% Cash Refund Pilot Prgm for Senior Citizens 1987; founder Mr Sirloin Prgm, 1990. **Honors/Awds:** 21st Caucus Achievement Award, 21st Congressional Dist Caucus, 1979; 21st Caucus Small Businessmen/women Award, 1989; Businessmen/women Economics Development Award, 1989; established Willie Jackson Transportation Program for East Surburban Montessori school; established National Coalition Business Enterprise, 1988; Cleveland Black Beautiful Award, Explorer 12 Club, United Labor Agncy; Intl Platform Speaker Ladder Awd, 1986; Appointment to Advsory Bd, Job Serv Empl Comm, by John R Tasin, Chpsn for Governor Richard Celeste. **Home Addr:** 3452 E 116th St, Cleveland, OH 44120.

PEOPLES, ERSKINE L.
Salesman. **Personal:** Born Oct 16, 1931, Gadsden, AL; married Dorothy Thompson; children: E Ladell Jr, Tamatha M. **Educ:** Mus Educ TN A&I State U, bS 1953; TN A&I State U, Addl Studies; Chattanooga Assn of Life Underwriters. **Career:** Mutual Benefit Life Ins Co, salesman 1966-; BT Washington HS Chattanooga, band dir 12 yrs; Security Fed Savings & Loan Assn Chattanooga, vice pres & dir 1971-. **Orgs:** Chmn Hamilton Co Sch Bd Chattanooga 1973-75; mem bd Greater Chattanooga C of C; Goodwill Industries Inc; Meth Neighbrohood Ctrs; deacon Mt Calvery Bapt Ch; mem Alpha Phi Alpha; Chattanooga Underwriters; pres Club Mutual Benefit Life; Man of Yr Psi Lambda 1968. **Military Serv:** AUS spl/4 1956-58. **Business Addr:** The Mutual Benefit Life Ins Co, Ste 500 Pioneer Bldg, Chattanooga, TN 37402.

PEOPLES, FLORENCE W.
Hospital supervisor. **Personal:** Born Jul 21, 1940, Charleston, SC; married Earl Calvin Peoples; children: Patricia Peoples Lowe, Jonelle Elaine Washington, Deborah Simmons Jones, Sheyla Simmons, Pamela, Calvin. **Educ:** Roper Hosp School of Practical Nursing, Diploma 1963; Northeastern Univ, BSN 1977. **Career:** New England Reg Black Nurses, bd dir 1982-85; H McCall Nurses Unit/Grant AME Church, pres 1986-87; Amer Cancer Soc William Price Unit, bd of dir, co-chairperson 1987; MA Mental Health Ctr, hospital supv. **Orgs:** Mem Natl Black Nurses 1978-, New England Regional Black Nurses 1978-, Amer Nurses Assoc 1978-, MA Nurses Assoc 1978-, NAACP 1982-, Eastern MA Urban League1983-. **Honors/Awds:** Public Serv Awd NERBNA Inc 1982; 5 Yrs Membership Natl Black Nurses 1986; Committee of the Year NERBNA Inc 1987. **Home Addr:** 70 Nelson St, Boston, MA 02124. **Business Addr:** Hospital Supervisor, Massachusettes Mental Health, 74 Fenwood Rd, Boston, MA 02115.

PEOPLES, GERALD
Educational administrator. **Career:** City of Grambling, city councilman; Southern Univ at Baton Rouge, vice chancellor for student affairs; Southern Univ at New Orleans, chancellor, currently. **Business Addr:** Chancellor, Southern University, 6400 Press Dr, New Orleans, LA 70126, (504)286-5000.

PEOPLES, GREGORY ALLAN
Educational administrator. **Personal:** Born May 17, 1951, Ravenna, OH; married Alice Leigh; children: Allaina Terice, Ashleigh Gail, Angela Marie. **Educ:** Allegheny Coll, BA 1973; Kent State Univ, MEd 1977. **Career:** Allegheny Coll, asst dir of admissions 1973-75; Kent State Univ, resident hall dir 1975-77; Center-Eastern MI Univ, coord of campus info 1978-80; Eastern MI Univ, asst dir of admiss 1980-82, assoc dir of admiss 1982-83; GMI Engrg & Mgmt Inst, admiss, corp spec 1983-84, dir of admiss; Washtenaw Community College, director of enrollment management, 1985-91; Eastern Michigan University, associate dean of students, 1991-. **Orgs:** Mem Delta Tau Delta 1973-; treas Black Faculty & Staff Assn 1978-82, 1991-95; mem Delta Sigma Pi 1980; mem bd of dir Natl Orientation Dir Assn 1981-; advisor Delta Sigma Pi 1981-83, Delta Tau Delta 1984-. **Honors/Awds:** Outstanding Young Men of Amer 1984. **Home Addr:** 5445 Scott Court, Ypsilanti, MI 48197.

PEOPLES, HARRISON PROMIS, JR.
Organizational development executive. **Personal:** Born Mar 23, 1940, Anawalt, WV; son of Harrison P Peoples; married Aug 6, 1966 (divorced); children: Jacqueline Phaedra, Nikki-Nicole. **Educ:** Chapman Coll, Orange CA, BA, 1976; Pepperdine Univ, Malibu CA, MS, 1986. **Career:** Motorola, Cupertino CA, manager, 1980-85; Transition Strategies, Los Altos CA, vice pres, 1985-88; Natl Traffic Safety Institute, San Jose CA, instructor, 1988-89; US Census Bureau, San Jose CA, mgr, 1989-; Natl Traffic Safety Institute, regional director, 1989-96; Lighthouse Worldwide Solutions, Inc, vice-pres, 1996-97; Peoples and Associates, owner, consultant, 1997-. **Orgs:** Mem, Penninsula Assoc Black Personnel Admin, 1981-88; recorder, Human Resources Planning Soc, 1983; mem, Org Devel Network, 1984-86; NAACP, pres, state, 1987-89, vice pres, 1989. **Honors/Awds:** Recognition, Salinas NAACP, 1983; Service Award, Palo Alto NAACP, 1988; DEA Appreciation, Drug Enforcement Admin, 1988; Omega Man of the Year, Omega Psi Phi. **Military Serv:** US Army, major, 1959-80. **Home Addr:** 1065 Rankin Dr, Milpitas, CA 95035.

PEOPLES, JOHN ARTHUR, JR.
Educational administrator (retired). **Personal:** Born Aug 26, 1926, Starkville, MS; son of Maggie Rose Peoples and John A Peoples Sr (deceased); married Mary E Galloway; children: Dr Kathleen Peoples-Sedlak, Mark. **Educ:** Jackson State Univ, BS 1950; Univ of Chicago, MA 1951, PhD 1961. **Career:** Gary IN Pub Sch System, principal 1951-64; Jackson State Univ, asst to pres 1964-65; State Univ of NY at Binghamton, asst to pres 1965-66; Jackson State Univ, vice pres 1966-67, pres 1967-84, president emeritus, currently. **Orgs:** Bd of trustees Amer Coll Test Corp 1973-79; bd of control Southern Regional Educ Bd 1974-86; chair American Council on Education; consul Kellogg Foundation 1981-84; consul Killy Endowment Fund, 1976-77; mem Noon Optimist Club Jackson 1981-; life mem NAACP; bd of dirs MS Ballet Intl Inc 1980-; board of directors Piney Woods Cty Life School; board of directors Jackson Hinds Comprehensive Health Ctr; board of directors Smith Robertson Museum & Cultural Ctr; board of directors, Jackson State Natl Alumni Assn; Jackson Civil Svc Comm; deacon Farish St Bapt Ch; Omega Psi Phi; Sigma Pi Phi; 33rd degree Mason. **Honors/Awds:** Fellow Amer Council on Education 1965-66; Education Specialist US State Dept 1977; Man of Yr Alpha Chi Chap 1962; elected Jackson State Univ, Sports Hall of Fame; elected Southwestern Athletic Conf, Hall of Fame; Natl Black Coll, Hall of Fame Lifetime Achievement Award, 1993; NAFEO, Distinguished Alumni Award, 1993. **Special Achievements:** First African American to chair ACE; wrote book ''To Survive and Thrive.''. **Military Serv:** USMC sgt 1944-47.

PEOPLES, JOHN DERRICK, JR.
Sports reporter. **Personal:** Born Jul 23, 1951, Seattle, WA; son of Gertrude Johnson Peoples and J D Peoples Sr; married Julie Selman, Jun 1989. **Educ:** University of Montana, Missoula, MT, 1969-71; Texas Southern, Houston, TX, 1978-79; University of Washington, Seattle, WA, BA, communication, 1984. **Career:** The Times Seattle, Seattle, WA, sports reporter, currently. **Orgs:** Member, NABJ, 1984. **Business Addr:** Sports Reporter, The Seattle Times, Fairview Ave N and John St, PO Box 70, Seattle, WA 98111.

PEOPLES, JOYCE P.
Educator. **Personal:** Born Aug 27, 1937, Huntsville, AL; divorced; children: Alycia Peoples-Behling. **Educ:** AL A&M Univ, BS (Cum Laude) 1957, MS 1965; The Amer Univ, PhD (with Distinction) 1977. **Career:** AL A&M Univ, asst prof 1967-76; Voorhees Coll, dir interdisciplinary studies 1976-77; Univ of MD-ES, asst vice chancellor 1977-78; Inst for Serv to Educ, special asst to pres 1978-83; Southern Univ, vice chancellor academic affairs 1983-. **Orgs:** Regional dir Black Women Academicians 1982-83; consultant Amer Council on Educ 1982-86; parliamentarian NAUW 1985-87; pres Top Ladies of Distinction Inc 1985-87; bd mem Natl Assoc of Univ Women 1986-87. **Honors/Awds:** Listed in Intl Dictionary of Biography London, England 1973; Natl Citation for Assault on Illiteracy AOIP 1985-86; selected Woman of the Year Natl Assoc of Univ Women 1986-87; Natl Top Lady of the Year TLOD Inc 1986-87; listed in Who's Who of Amer Women 1986-87. **Business Addr:** V Chancellor, Academic Affairs, Southern University, 3050 ML King Jr Dr, Shreveport, LA 71107.

PEOPLES, L. KIMBERLY
Educational administrator. **Career:** Golightly Career and Technical Center, principal, currently. **Honors/Awds:** Michigan Assn of Secondary School Principals, MetLife/NASSP Michigan Principal of the Year, 1997. **Business Addr:** Principal, Golightly Career & Technical Ctr, 900 Dickerson St, Detroit, MI 48215, (313)822-8820.

PEOPLES, SESSER R.
Educator. **Personal:** Born Dec 7, 1934, Newark; married Irma; children: 4. **Educ:** Jersey City State Coll, BA 1963; Kean Coll, MA. **Career:** Mentally Retarded Plainfield Public School, teacher; Urban Processes Coordinated, coor 1971-; Black Studies Jersey City State Coll, dir 1969-73; Jersey City State Coll, affirmative action officer 1973-. **Orgs:** Mem Phi Delta Kappa 1972-; Nat Assn Black & Urban Ethnic Dirs 1971-72; African-Am Studies Assn 1970-73; African Heritage Studies Assn; Urban Processes Coordinated Consulting Firm 1971-; Third World Enterprises 1968-; mem bd dirs Leaguers Inc. **Military Serv:** AUS 1957-59. **Business Addr:** Jersey City State Coll, Jersey City, NJ 07305.

PEOPLES, VEO, JR.
Attorney. **Personal:** Born Sep 13, 1947, St Louis, MO; married Linda Sing; children: Nicole, Nissa. **Educ:** Univ of MO Rolla, BS Chem Engr 1970; St Louis Univ School of Law, JD 1975. **Career:** Ralston Purina Co, patent agent 1973-75; Ralston Purina Co, patent attny 1975-78; Monsanto's Patent Dept, patent trainee; Monsanto Co's Cntrl Engrg Dept, process design engr; Monsanto Co, engrg intern; Anheuser-Busch, assoc gen council 1978-84; private practice, patent attorney. **Orgs:** Mem Ralston Purina Corp Devel Bd 1977; spec task force MO Bar Assoc 1976-77; entertainment chmn Mound City Bar Assoc 1976-77; sec exec comm bd of dir Legal Serv of Eastern MO Inc; dist commiss Western Dist of St Louis for Boy Scouts of Amer; bd of dir W Co Amer Cancer Soc; dist exec Mark Twain BSA 1976-; mem Optimist Club of St Louis; circuite comm 22nd Judicial Bar 1984-92; chmn patent section BAMSL; pres, founder CADRE 19 Inc; bd of dirs, Federal Reserve Bank of St Louis, 1994-99. **Honors/Awds:** Achievement Awd Urban League 1975; Rosalie Tilles Scholarship 1966-70; Univ of MO Curators Scholarship 1966; Student Chap Awd of Excellence AIChE 1970; Univ Scholar Awd Univ of MO 1976; Undergrad Rsch Fellowship 1970. **Home Addr:** 342 Jamboree Dr, Manchester, MO 63011.

PEOPLES, VERJANIS ANDREWS
Educator. **Personal:** Born Aug 8, 1955, Monroe, LA; daughter of Willie & Vernita Andrews; married Gerald C Peoples, Aug 9, 1975; children: Takiyah, Nicholas. **Educ:** Grambling St University, BS, 1976, MS, 1978; Kansas St University, PhD, 1990. **Career:** Bienville Parish School System, teacher, 1976-79; Grambling St University, lab school, teacher, 1979-88, College of Education, professor, 1989-90; Southern University, College of EDU, professor, 1991-92, assistant dean, 1992-95, interim dean, 1995-. **Orgs:** LA Association of Teacher Educators, 1996; Association of Teacher Educators, 1996; Association for Supervision & Curriculum Dev, 1996; LA Alliance for Education Reform, 1996; LA Council for Teacher Education, 1996; American Association of Colleges for Teacher Education, 1996. **Honors/Awds:** Teacher of the Year, Grambling Lab School, 1989. **Special Achievements:** Created proposal for Teachers Alumni As-Partners Program (TAAP); Instituted ''First Class Teachers Program;'' Dev Partnership programs with surrounding parishes; Published article, ''Restoring Human Dignity: A Model for Prevention & Intervention;'' Published chapter, ''Teacher Preparation Programs at Historically Black Colleges.''. **Business Addr:** Interim Dean, College of Education, Southern University, PO Box 9983, Stewart Hall, Rm 242, Baton Rouge, LA 70813, (504)771-2290.

PERARA, MITCHELL MEBANE
Physician. **Personal:** Born Feb 11, 1924, Tulsa, OK; married Jean Wolfe; children: Susan, Mark, Georgianna. **Educ:** VA Union Univ, BS 1944; Howard Univ, MD 1948. **Career:** Amer Coll of Surgeons, diplomate 1955-85; Private Practice, physician 1955-85. **Honors/Awds:** Fellow Amer Cancer Society 1955.

PERDREAU, CORNELIA WHITENER (CONNIE)
Educator. **Personal:** Born Nov 7, Beacon, NY; daughter of Mazie Martin and Henry Whitener; married Michael Perdreau, Jun 14, 1969; children: Maurice. **Educ:** Potsdam Coll, Potsdam, NY, BA, 1969; OH Univ, Athens, OH, MA, 1971, MA, 1972. **Career:** OH Univ, Athens, OH, lecturer & study abroad coordinator, 1976-. **Orgs:** Chair, Administrators & Teachers in English as a Second Language; pres, OH Univ African-Amer Faculty, Administrators and Staff Caucus, 1990-91; pres, OH Teachers of English to Speakers of Other Languages, 1987-88; mem, Black Professionals in Intl Affairs, 1989-; Fulbright Enrichment Center Committee, 1991-96; Cooperative Grants Committee, 1990-95; Ohioana Library Association, trustee, 1988-96; Black Professionals in Teachers of English to Speakers of other Languages, founder, chair, 1992-; USIA English Language Programs, advisory bd, 1995-98; NAFSA: Assn of International Educators, team mem, 1988-90, 1991-93, pres elect, 1995-96, pres, 1996-97. **Business Addr:** Prof, Study Abroad Office, Ohio University, 201 Gordy Hall, Athens, OH 45701.

PERDUE, FRANKLIN ROOSEVELT
Psychologist, author. **Personal:** Born Jan 30, 1944, Birmingham, AL; married Carolyn Jean Walton; children: Stephannie Denise, Francis Renee. **Educ:** Miles Coll, BS 1974; AL State Univ, MEd 1979; Century Univ, PhD 1984; UCLA Marriage Family Child Counsel Sem, Post Doct 1984; LA Hypnotism Training Inst, post doct hypnotist; Coastview Memorial Hosp-Long Beach CA, marriage family child counsel alcohol & drug abuse internship 1985-86; Kaizer Permanente Hosp, hospice intern. **Career:** Los Angeles Comm Coll, college instructor 1980; US Naval Sea Cadet Corp, commanding officer 1980-; Vantage Pres, author 1980-; Lincensed hypnotist 1985; LA & State of CA chapters, psychologist, MFCC, internist 1984-87. **Orgs:** Mem Phi Beta Sigma Frat 1970-73; cadet USAF Res Officer Training Samford Univ 1970-74; teacher, educator Birmingham Bd of Ed 1973-80; mem Retired Military Officers Assoc 1981-; postal carrier/clerk Los Angeles Postal Serv 1963-67, 1980-; Los Angeles Chapter, internist-marriage, family, child counseling 1984-; CA marriage, family, child counseling chapter, mem 1987. **Honors/Awds:** Authored reports on The Privite Life of Petty Officer FDR Perdue, Segregation & Integration 1983. **Military Serv:** USNR lt 26 years. **Home Addr:** 575 West Cocoa St, Compton, CA 90220.

PERDUE, GEORGE
State representative. **Personal:** marrIed Delores; children: Cindy, Joy. **Educ:** Morehouse College, BS; Atlanta University, MS. **Career:** University of Alabama, Human Resources System, project coordinator, currently; Alabama House of Representatives, state representative, 1985-. **Orgs:** NAACP; YMCA; bd dirs, Birmingham Girl's Club. **Business Addr:** State Representative, Alabama Legislative Black Caucus, 11 Union Street, Montgomery, AL 36130.

PERDUE, JOHN F.
Educational administrator (retired). **Personal:** Born Dec 14, 1912, Ypsilanti, MI; son of Maggie B Saxon Perdue and John Wesley Perdue; married Trunetta V Perdue, Dec 29, 1954. **Educ:** Toledo Univ, BED; Univ of MI, MA; Oakland Univ, MI State Univ, attended. **Career:** Union Mutual Health, Life, & Accident Ins Co, Philadelphia, salesman/agency dir, 1934-42; Toledo Urban League, indus rel sec 1946-50; MI Sch Dist, teacher, 1950-56; Bagley & Whittier Elementary Schools, Jefferson Jr High School, Pontiac MI, principal, 1956-66; Sch Com Rel of Pontiac School Dist, dir, 1966-retirement; Wayne State Univ Desegregation Inst, on staff summer 1966; School Com & Rel Pontiac School Dist, dir; Emergency Sch Aid Act, dir, retired. **Orgs:** Mem DESP reg, state & natl; ASCD; MASSP; NSPRA; PTA Coun of Pontiac; Pi Gamma Mu; Natl Soc Sci Hon Soc; past vice pres, AFT, Ferndale MI Chapter; life mem, Alpha Phi Alpha Frat; mem Hum Rel Com of St Dept of Educ of MI; mem Assn for Study of Afro-Am Life & Hist; mem Natl Assn of Sch Pub Rel Assn; mem Natl Alliance of Black Sch Edu; organ W Philadelphia Youth Civic League 1936; worked with Armstrong 1935-40. **Honors/Awds:** Outstanding Achievement Award, Natl Alliance of Black School Educators, 1975; spec tribute, State of MI Legislature, 1976, 1977; Res of Commend from City Commis of City of Pontiac 1976; mem, bd of dirs, Pontiac Urban League past sec vp; past mem Detroit Presb Comm on Religion & Race; testified for NAACP in Desegregation Case Davis vs Sch Dist of City of Pontiac 1970; rec Dabney Awd outstndg civic contri for yr 1937; Prin of Yr 1961; Arthur Croft Pub Co Annual Pontiac Urban League Awd 1961; citznshp awd St Stephens Ch 1962; awd of merit Jefferson Jr HS PTA & Whittier Elem Sch PTA 1966; Lakeside Tenants Org Awd 1970; Oakland Co Br of NAACP 1971; Cert of Mer; 761st Tank Batalion Allied Vets Assn 1974; cit of yr MI Chronicle Newspaper 1968; Retirement testimonial dinner atSilverdome, 1977;ciety of Afro-American Police, 1977; Oakland County Afro-American Bar Assn, 1977-; Pontiac Jaycees Award, 1978; Award, US Office of Education, 1978; Award, Omicron Mu Foundation, Chapter of Alpha Phi Alpha, 1986. **Military Serv:** 1st sgt 1942-46. **Home Addr:** Presbyterian Vlg, #113, 2000 East-West Connector, Austell, GA 30001-1123.

PERDUE, WILEY A.
Educational administrator. **Educ:** Morehouse College, graduated 1957; Atlanta University, MBA; Indiana University-Bloomington, advanced studies. **Career:** Savannah State College, registrar; Morehouse College, bursar, business manager, vice president for fiscal affairs, acting president. **Business Addr:** Acting President, Morehouse College, 830 West View Drive, Atlanta, GA 30314, (404)215-2645.

PEREIRA, SARAH MARTIN
Educator. **Personal:** Born Dec 12, 1909, Cleveland, OH; daughter of Mary B Martin and Alexander H Martin; widowed; children: Carlos Martin. **Educ:** OH State Univ, AB (with honors & distinction in French) 1931; Western Reserve Univ

Cleveland, MS French 1935; OSU, PhD Romance Langs 1942. **Career:** Shaw Univ Raleigh, instr spanish/french 1931-41; Miner Teachers Coll, instr spanish/french 1941-46; Howard Univ Grad Sch, part-time assoc prof french 1942-46; Cleveland Coll, part-time lectr in spanish 1946-50; Fenn Coll, part time lectr in spanish 1946-52; WV State Coll Inst WV, prof & chair of dept1952-58; DC Tchrs Coll Washington, prof & chair dept of for langs 1971-76; Univ of Dist Col, acting academic dean Harvard Campus 1976-78, prof of spanish & portuguese 1978-70; Johnson C Smith Univ, visiting prof of spanish. **Orgs:** Mem Natl Spiritual Assembly Baha'i Faith 1961-73; mem Continental Bd of Counsellors Americas Baha'i World Faith 1973-85; mem Spiritual Assembly of Baha'is of Charlotte, NC 1986-. **Honors/Awds:** Phi Beta Kappa OH State Univ Epsilon Chap 1931; Kappa Delta Pi DCTC Washington DC 1965; Delta Sigma Pi (Spanish Honors); Phi Delta Kappa (French Honor Soc); Phi Lambda Beta (Portuguese Honor Soc); honored in formal ceremony as Disting Alumna OH State Univ Cols 1972 first Black so honored at OSU.

PEREZ, ALTAGRACIA
Youth ministries coordinator. **Personal:** Born Sep 19, 1961, New York, NY; daughter of Esther Zoraida Maceira-Ortiz and Ramon Eduardo Perez. **Educ:** New York University, SEHNAP, BS, 1982; Union Theological Seminary, MDiv, 1985, STM, 1986. **Career:** Astor Mental Health Center, special education teacher, 1982; Church of the Living Hope, day camp director, 1984; Union Theological Seminary, co-coordinator, Women's Center, 1984-85; Mision San Juan Bautista, youth leader/minister, 1985-86; Pilsen Catholic Youth Center, associate director, 1986-89; Diocese of Chicago, coordinator youth ministries, 1990-; Episcopal Church Center, National, provincial youth coordinator, 1991-. **Orgs:** Hispanic AIDS Network, president, board of directors, 1992-, founding member of board, 1986-; Hispanic Designers Inc, education leadership council, 1990-; Commission to End Racism, Episcopal Diocese of Chicago, 1990-92; AIDS Task Force, Episcopal Diocese of Chicago, staff liaison, 1990-; Chicago Women's AIDS Project, advisory council, 1991-; General Convention Joint Commission on AIDS, Episcopal, secretary, 1992-; Chicago Area AIDS Care-Givers Retreat, co-chair, 1991-92. **Honors/Awds:** New York University Higher Education Opportunity Program, Bertha Dixon Memorial Award, 1982. **Special Achievements:** A Faith of One's Own, "Este Es Mi Cuerpo," Crossing Press article in anthology, 1987; "The Spiritual Cost of Abuse," Prevention Resource Services: Journal on Abuse, 1992. **Business Addr:** Coordinator of Youth Ministries, Episcopal Diocese of Chicago, 65 E Huron St, Episcopal Church Center, Chicago, IL 60611, (312)751-4214.

PEREZ, ANNA
Company executive. **Personal:** Born 1952, New York, NY; married Ted Sims; children: 3. **Educ:** Hunter College. **Career:** Tacoma Facts, Tacoma, WA, publisher; Senator Slade Gordon, press secretary; Representative John Miller, press secretary; Barbara Bush, Washington, DC, press secretary, 1989-93; Creative Artists, head of media relations and external affairs, 1993-. **Honors/Awds:** First Black press secretary to a First Lady. **Business Addr:** Head, Media Relations and External Affairs, Creative Artists, 9830 Wilshire Blvd, Beverly Hills, CA 90212.

PERINE, JAMES L.
Educator. **Personal:** Born Jun 23, 1943, St Louis; married B Rosalie Hicks; children: Lori, Keith, Kelly. **Educ:** NE MO State U, BA 1964; Univ MD, MA 1967; PA State U, PhD 1979. **Career:** Washington, research psychol 1964-68; Univ MD, oeo grad & teaching asst 1965-67; Coll Human Devel PA State Univ, presently asst to dean. **Orgs:** Mem Phi Delta Kappa; Nat Educ Hon Frat; Am Vocational Assn; Am Personnel & Guidance Assn; Am Psychological Assn; St Paul's United Meth Ch State College; NAACP; adv bd Lewisburg Prison; bd dirs State Coll Comm Theatre; Comm Vol to Mountainview Unit Centre Comm Hosp. **Honors/Awds:** Blue Key; State Coll Kiwanis Club; Spl Citation Optimists Club 1970. **Business Addr:** PO Box 654, Centreville, MD 21617.

PERINE, MARTHA LEVINGSTON
Business executive. **Personal:** Born Jun 27, 1948, Mobile, AL; married David Andrew; children: David Jr, Alissa, Alison. **Educ:** Bus Adminstr Clark Coll Atlanta GA, BA 1965-69; Washington Univ St Louis, MA Econ 1969-71. **Career:** Fed Reserve Bank of St Louis, asst vice pres 1971-. **Orgs:** Mem Nat Assn of Bank Women 1985; mem Am Inst of Banking 1985; financial sec Gamma Omega Chap Alpha Kappa Alpha Sor Inc 1985; fin sec Holy Metro Missionary Bapt Ch 1985. **Honors/Awds:** Outstanding Yng Woman in Am Outstanding Yng Am's 1970; Achievement Nominee St Louis Jaycee Wives 1978; Outstanding Young Women in Am, Outstanding Yng Am's 1979. **Business Addr:** Federal Reserve Bank of St Lou, 411 Locust St, St Louis, MO 63102.

PERKINS, CHARLES WINDELL
Business executive. **Personal:** Born Mar 12, 1946, New Orleans, LA; children: Evany Joy. **Educ:** Univ of CA Berkeley, BA 1968; Southwestern Grad Sch of Banking SMU Dallas, grad degree banking 1978. **Career:** Security Pac Nat Bank, vp; San Leandro, vice pres & mgr 1978. **Orgs:** Asst vice pres San Mateo & SF; mgr Foster City 1974; asst mgr Hayward Fremont; asst cashier SF; supr SF & Berkeley; mgmt trainee Security Pacific Bank 1968; bd mem Hunters Point Boys' Club of SF 1972; treas Foster City C of C 1974; co-founder Black Officers Group Sec Pac Bank 1980; mem Univ of CA Alumni Assn. **Honors/Awds:** All-conf basketball Univ CA Berkeley 1967; $1,000,000 trust award Security Pacific Bank 1979.

PERKINS, EDWARD JOSEPH
Federal official. **Personal:** Born 1928, Sterlington, LA; son of Tiny Estella Noble Holmes and Edward Joseph Perkins Sr; married Lucy Chien-mei Liu, Sep 9, 1962; children: Katherine Karla Shih-Tzu, Sarah Elizabeth Shih-Yin. **Educ:** Univ of MD, BA 1968; Univ of Southern CA, MPA 1972, PhD 1978. **Career:** AID Far East Bureau Washington, asst general serv officer; US Operations Mission to Thailand Bangkok, asst genl serv officer 1967-69, mgmt analyst 1969-70, deputy asst dir for mgmt 1970-72; Office of the Dir General of the Foreign Serv Washington, staff assistant 1972, personnel officer; Bureau of Near Eastern & South Asian Affairs, admin officer 1974-75; Office of Mgmt & Opers, mgmt analysis officer 1975-78; Accra, counselor for polit affairs 1978-81; Monrovia, deputy chief of mission 1981-83; Bureau Of African Affairs Office of West African Affairs, dir 1983-85; Dept of State, ambassador to Liberia 1985-86, ambassador to South Africa 1986-89, dir general The Foreign Service 1989-92; United Nations and UN Security Council, ambassador, 1992-93; US ambassador to Australia, 1993-96; The Univ of Oklahoma, International Programs Center, William J Crowe chair professor of geopolitics, 1996-. **Orgs:** Epsilon Boule of Sigma Pi Phi Fraternity; Kappa Alpha Psi Fraternity; Navy League; Honor Society of Phi Kappa Phi; American Society for Public Administration, 1971-; Veterans of Foreign Wars, Chevy Chase Chapter; American Academy of Diplomacy; American Foreign Service Assn; American Political Science Assn; World Affairs Councils of Central OK and Washington, DC; Cranlana Programme, bd; Asia Society, bd of trustees; Joint Center for Political and Economic Studies, bd of govs; numerous other organizations, councils, and boards. **Honors/Awds:** Univ of Southern California, Distinguished Alumni Award, 1991; Southern Univ, Achievement Award, 1991; Kappa Alpha Psi, C Rodger Wilson Leadership Conference Award, 1990; The Links, Inc, Living Legend Award, 1989; Eastern Province, Kappa Alpha Psi, Award for Distinguished Service as US Ambassador to South Africa, 1989; Presidential Distinguished Service Award, 1989; Una Chapman Cox Foundation Award, 1989; Presidential Meritorious Service Award, 1987; Kappa Alpha Psi Fraternity Award for Outstanding Achievement in the Foreign Service, 1986; Dept of State, Superior Honor Award, 1983; Agency for Intl Development, Meritorious Honor Award, 1967; National Academy of Public Administration, fellow; Statesman of the Year, George Washington Univ, 1992; Distinguished Honor Award, Department of State, 1992; St Augustine College, Doctor of Humane Laws, Honoris Causa, 1993; Beloit College, Doctor of Humanities, 1990; and numerous other honorary degrees. **Special Achievements:** Author, "New Dimensions in Foreign Affairs: Public Administration Theory in Practice," Public Administration Review, July-August 1990; "Divsersity in US Diplomacy," The Bureaucrat, Vol 20, No 4, 1991-92; "The United States and the UN", Yale Univ Law Journal, 1993; "Global Institutions (Action for the Future)," U.S. Catholic Conference, 1995; "Resolution of Conflict, the Attainment of Peace", University of Sydney, Centre for Peace and Conflict Studies, 1996; "An International Agenda for Change," American Behavorial Scientist, Vol 40, Number 3, Sage Publishers, 1997; Distinguished Jerry Collins Lecturer in Public Administration, Florida State Univ; presidential appointment to the Presidential/Congressional Commission on Public Service, 1992-93. **Military Serv:** USMC 1954-58; US Army 1951-54. **Business Addr:** Executive Director, International Programs Center, The University of Oklahoma, 339 West Boyd Street, Room 400, Norman, OK 73019-5144.

PERKINS, FRANCES J.
Educator, social worker. **Personal:** Born Dec 14, 1919, Boston, MA; married W Wentworth; children: Joseph W. **Educ:** Boston State, BSE 1941; Tufts Univ, EdM 1957; Boston Univ, EdM counseling 1981. **Career:** Tufts Univ, summer faculty Eliot-Pearson Dept of Child Study 1960-65, lecturer; Garland Jr College, instructor summer inst 1965-66; Head Start Training Prog Wheelock Coll sum, dir 1966-67; Peace Corps, Tunisia, project director, Training Prog Wheelock Coll 1966-67; EPDA Inst Garland Jr Coll, asst dir 1969; Wheelock Coll, instr psychology 1970-73, associate professor psychology, 1973-85; evaluator of Head Start programs, 1970-85; consultant, Center for Individual & Family Services, Family Mediation Prog and Head Start programs; founder, dir, St Mark Nursery School, Boston, MA, 1941-53; dir, Parent COOP, NS Belmont, MA 1953-61; dir Lemberg Lab Preschool, Brandeis University, 1961-73; consultant, Jackson-Mann Early Childhood Program, Horace Mann School for the Deaf, 1974-75. **Orgs:** Natl Assn for Educ of Young Children; Amer Assn of Univ Women; past pres bd dir Freedom House Inc; mem Parents & Children's Serv; MA Com for Children & Youth; Professional Adv Com Ft Hill Mental Health Assn; life mem Delta Sigma Theta; bd mem Urban League of Eastern MA; bd mem NAUSET Workshop, Center for Individual & Family Services, Cape Cod, MA. **Honors/Awds:** One of team of 3 to create Head Start Program for Boston for Action for Boston Community Development, 1965.

PERKINS, GLADYS PATRICIA
Engineering specialist (retired). **Personal:** Born Oct 30, 1921, Crenshaw, MS; daughter of Zula Crenshaw Franklin and Douglas Franklin. **Educ:** LeMoyne Coll, BS Math 1943; Univ of MI, Math; Hughes Aircraft, ATEP; UCLA Ext. **Career:** Amer Missionary Assoc Athens AL, teacher 1943-44; Natl Advisory Comm for Aeronautics, 1944-49; Natl Bureau of Standards, mathematician 1950-53; Aberdeen Bombing Mission, mathematician 1953-55; Lockheed Missle Systems, assoc engr math analyst 1955-57; Hughes Aircraft Co, staff engr 1957-80; Rockwell Intl, engrg specialist 1980-87 (retired). **Orgs:** Mem Alpha Kappa Alpha Sor 1941-, LeMoyne-Owen Coll Alumni Assoc 1943-, Assoc of Computing Machinery 1964-, Soc of Women Engrs 1981-, NAFEO 1983. **Honors/Awds:** LeMoyne Owen College, Alumnus of the Year Award, 1982, Golden Parade Gallery of Outstanding Alumni, 1982; National Association for Equal Opportunity in Higher Education, 1983. **Special Achievements:** Author, works include: Lunar Trajectory Program (surveyor), Three Dimensional Boost-Coast Trajectory, High Speed Trajectory Simulator Hughes Aircraft Co; Program to Determine a Satellite Ground Trace Hughes Aircraft 1978; Users Guide to Ascent, Insertion, Orbit, Deorbit Program, Space Shuttle Rockwell Intl, 1987.

PERKINS, HUEL D.
Educator. **Personal:** Born Dec 27, 1924, Baton Rouge, LA; married Thelma O Smith; children: Huel Alfred. **Educ:** Southern U, BS highest honors 1947; Northwestern U, MusM 1951, PhD 1958. **Career:** So U, dean coll of arts & humanities 1968-78; Nat Endowment for Humanities, dep dir educ prog 1978-79; Acad Affairs LA St U, asst vice chancellor 1979-, executive assistant to chancellor, 1990-; So U, asso prof music 1951-60; Lincoln U, instr music 1948-50; Huel D Perkins and Associates, president, currently. **Orgs:** Mem visiting fac prog Harvard Univ 1968; part Caribbean-Am Scholars Exchange Prog 1974; part So Assembly 1973; visiting prof LA State Univ 1972, 1974; mem Mayor's Commn of Youth Activities 1969; Nat Bd of Consult Nat Endowment for the Humanities; bd of dir LA Arts & Sci Ctr; mem Alpha Phi Alpha; Pi Kappa Lambda; Phi Mu Alpha; Pi Gamma Mu; Alpha Kappa Mu; Sigma Pi Phi; Omicron Delta Kappa; Phi Kappa Phi; Golden Key Honor Society; Rotary Club of Baton Rouge; Sunburst Bank, board of directors, Federation of State Humanities Councils, board of directors; ASCAP; mem bd dirs Blundon Orphanage 1970-71; bd dirs Baton Rouge Symphony Orchestra 1971-; pres bd dir Capital Area United Way 1986; bd mem Baton Rouge Opera, New Orleans Museum of Art, Salvation Army; mem Rotary Club of Baton Rouge, Baton Rouge Chamber of Commerce, Omicron Delta Kappa Leadership; Baton Rouge Area Foundation; Louisiana Public Broadcasting Corp; Commerce Bank Community Development Corporation; director, Union Planters Bank; trustee, Mt Zion First Baptist Church. **Honors/Awds:** Recip Outstdg Prof Student Govt Assn 1970, 1974; Danforth Tchr Grant 1957-58; flwshp Nat Endowment for Humanities 1972; chmn Dean's Sec of Conf of LA Coll & Univ 1974; recip Brotherhood Awd Natl Conf of Christians & Jews 1987; Humanist of the Year, 1988; Educator of the Year, 1988; Volunteer Activist, 1990; Service Award, 1990; Humanitarian Award, 1990; Distinguished Citizen Award, 1991. **Military Serv:** US Navy, musician 1st class, 1943-46. **Business Addr:** President, Huel D Perkins & Associates, Inc, Consulting Firm and Speakers' Bureau, 1923 79th Ave, Baton Rouge, LA 70807-5528, (504)357-3751.

PERKINS, JAMES CONNELLE
Clergyman. **Personal:** Born Mar 14, 1951, Williamson, WV; son of Chaddy B Perkins (deceased) and Cecil Perkins; married Linda Carol Adkins, Mar 2, 1979; children: Tamaria Yvette, Lindsey Camille. **Educ:** Wiley College, BA, 1972; Andover-Newton Theological School, MDiv, 1974; United Theological Seminary, DMin, 1990. **Career:** St Paul Baptist Church, St Albans, WV, pastor, 1974-80; Greater Christ Baptist Church, pastor, 1981-. **Orgs:** Nat Association for Leaders of Black Church Youth Groups; Detroit Baptist Pastors Council; Progressive National Baptist Convention Inc, American Baptist Convention; Founder, Benjamin E Mays Male Academy, 1993; Founder, Fellowship non-profit Housing Corporation, 1992; President, Detroit East side Coalition of Churches, Inc, 1994-. **Honors/Awds:** Virginia Seminary, DD, 1982; United Seminary, Samuel DeWitt Procter Fellow, 1990. **Special Achievements:** Writer for The Worker, a mission periodical for the Progressive National Baptist Convention. **Home Addr:** 3510 Iroquois St, Detroit, MI 48214. **Business Addr:** Pastor, Greater Christ Baptist Church, 3544 Iroquois St, Detroit, MI 48214, (313)924-6900.

PERKINS, JOHN M.
Business executive. **Personal:** Born in New Hebron, MS; married Vera Mae; children: Spencer, Phillip, Joan, Derek, Debbie, DeWayne, Priscilla, Betty. **Career:** Voice of Calvary Ministries, pres; num lecuring posts travelled over US as Ford Found 1972-73; through Israel to study cooperatives 1968; through Caribbean to study econs of disad 1966; through Germany on NEA 1972; through Germany to speak to servicemen 1976; to Gr Britain 1977; Fed of S Cooper, co-fdr; S Cooper Devel Fund, co-fdr; Voice of Calvare Ministries; Voice of Calvary Cooper Hlth Clinic; People Devel Inc; several other coopers; Gen Session spkerUrbana 1976; MS Billy Graham Crusade, steering com 1975; Tom Skinner MS Mgmt Sem, sponsor 1975. **Orgs:** Pres Voice of Calvary Ministries; bd mem Bread for the World;

Nat Black Evangelical Assn; Convenant Coll; S Devel Found; Koinonio Partners. **Honors/Awds:** Author, Let Justice Roll Down; A Quiet Revolution; contrib editor Sojourners mag The Other Side mag, Radix mag; Decision mag; several other periodicals. **Military Serv:** AUS 1951-53. **Business Addr:** 1655 St Charles St, Jackson, MS 39209.

PERKINS, LINDA MARIE
Educator. **Personal:** Born Nov 22, 1950, Mobile, AL; married Vincent Lee Wimbush. **Educ:** Kentucky State University, BS, 1971; Univ of Illinois, C-U, MS, 1973, PhD, 1978. **Career:** Univ of Ill-Champaign Urbana, Asst Dir of Minority Affrs, 1973-75; William Paterson Coll Dir of Affirmative Action, 1978-79; Radcliffe College, The Mary Bunting Institute, Research Fellow, Asst Dir, 1979-83; The Claremont Coll, asst vice pres, 1983-86; Center for Afro-Amer Studies, UCLA, visiting scholar, 1986-. **Orgs:** Big Sisters of Boston, 1981-83; Pomona Valley YWCA, Board Member, 1984-; Los Angeles United Way, Allocation Team, 1984-86. **Honors/Awds:** Research Grant, Natl Inst of Educ, 1979-81; Natl Endowment for the Humanities, 1984; Spencer Foundation, 1986- .

PERKINS, LOUVENIA BLACK (KITTY)
Fashion doll designer. **Personal:** Born Feb 13, 1948, Spartanburg, SC; daughter of Helen Goode Black and Luther Black; married Gary Perkins, May 1, 1981; children: Erika Nicole. **Educ:** Los Angeles Trade Tech College, AA, 1971. **Career:** Mattel Toys, El Segundo CA, principal designer, 1976-. **Honors/Awds:** President's Award, 1985; Employee of the Month, 1986; President's Award, 1987; Subject of Several Articles: Essence; Ebony; LA Times; Woman's Day; Los Angeles Magazine; Fox TV's Personalities; The Tim & Daphne Show. **Business Addr:** Principal Designer, Girls Preliminary Design Dept, Mattel Toy Co, 333 Continental Blvd, Mail Stop DI-0130, El Segundo, CA 90245-5012.

PERKINS, MYLA LEVY
Educator. **Personal:** Born Feb 25, 1939, Pueblo, CO; daughter of Naomi Levy and Addison Levy; married Edgar L Perkins; children: Julie, Steven, Todd, Susan. **Educ:** Wayne State Univ, BS 1960. **Career:** Detroit Public Schools, teacher, 1960-66; Sugar N Spice Nursery School, co-owner, 1966-; Pyramid Elementary School, co-owner 1976-92. **Orgs:** Mem Alpha Kappa Alpha Sor 1957-; mem Tots & Teens of Amer 1967-. **Special Achievements:** Author, Black Dolls, 1820-1991, An Identification and Value Guide, Collector Books; NAACP, life member; Author, Black Dolls Book II. **Business Addr:** Sugar N Spice Nur, 16555 Wyoming Ave, Detroit, MI 48221.

PERKINS, ROBERT E. L.
Oral/maxillofacial surgeon. **Personal:** Born May 17, 1925, Carthage, TX. **Educ:** Wiley College, BS 1945; Howard University, DDS 1948; Tufts University, MSD 1956. **Career:** Childrens' Hospital of Michigan, courtesy staff, 1960-87; Metro Hospital of Detroit, 1965-87; Hutzel Hospital, junior staff member, 1983-87; oral/maxillofacial surgeon, currently. **Orgs:** American Dental Assn 1949-87; Natl Dental Assn 1963-87; pres/founder, DSACE 1964-87; Michigan and American Assn of Oral and Maxillofacial Surgeons 1970-87; bd of dir, treas, Your Heritage House 1977-87; bd of dirs, Detroit Symphony Orchestra 1980-87; life mem, NAACP; Natl Urban League; United Negro College Fund; Alpha Kappa Alpha. **Honors/Awds:** Key to the City of Detroit; Patron of the Arts Award, Detroit Musicians Assn; Alumni Awards, College of Dentistry; Howard University Alumni Award 1983. **Military Serv:** US Air Force, major, 1949-54. **Business Addr:** Oral Maxillofacial Surgeon, 2673 W Grand Blvd, Detroit, MI 48208.

PERKINS, SAM BRUCE
Professional basketball player. **Personal:** Born Jun 14, 1961, Brooklyn, NY. **Educ:** North Carolina, BA, 1984. **Career:** Dallas Mavericks, forward-center, 1984-90, Los Angeles Lakers, 1990-93; Seattle SuperSonics, 1993-. **Honors/Awds:** Won a gold medal with the US Olympic Basketball team, 1984; NBA All-Rookie Team, 1985. **Business Addr:** Professional Basketball Player, Seattle SuperSonics, PO Box 900911, Seattle, WA 98109, (206)281-5850.

PERKINS, THOMAS P.
Church executive. **Personal:** Born Jan 12, 1940, Jersey City, NY; married; children: Thomas Jr, Susan, Stephen. **Educ:** Univ IA, BA 1965; Seton Hall U, JD 1968. **Career:** Pvt Prac, atty 1970-; former state assemblyman; Judiciary Law & Pub Safety Com, atty pvt prac chmn house; State NJ Affirmative Action Com. **Orgs:** Bd tst Jersey & State Coll. **Honors/Awds:** Human Rights Awd State NJ. **Business Addr:** 7887 Walmsley Ave, New Orleans, LA 70125.

PERKINS, WILLIAM O., JR.
Government official. **Personal:** Born Jun 5, 1926, Gregory, NC; married Arthur; children: 4. **Educ:** Elizabeth City State U, BS 1949; Atlanta U, addtl study; Univ of GA. **Career:** Atlanta Pub Schs, tchr 1957-76; Turner Co Schs, tchr 1952-53; Morgan Co Schs, tchr 1949-51, 53-56. **Orgs:** Mem bd of dir Atlanta Asn of Educ 1973-75; GA Assn of Educ 1976-77; mem bd of dirs GA Assn of Classroom Tchrs; mem NEA 1957-77; mem Metro Atlanta Counc Intl Reading Assn mem bd of dir Metro Atlanta Girls Club 1972-75; YWCA 1957-77; NAACP; sec Atlanta Dist Bapt Missionary Soc 1976-77; Beulah Bapt Ch; Gate City Tchrs Assn 1957-70; mem Alpha Kappa Mu Nat Hon Soc Article Four Tchrs Sound Off About Class Size Today's Educ 1976. **Honors/Awds:** Nom Bronzew Woman 1976; Atlanta Classroom Tchr of Yr 1976-77; GA Tchr Classroom of Yr 1976-77. **Business Addr:** Attorney at Law, 921 Bergen Ave, Jersey City, NJ 07306.

PERRIMAN, BRETT
Professional football player. **Personal:** Born Oct 10, 1965, Miami, FL; married Laundria. **Educ:** Univ of Miami (FL), attended. **Career:** New Orleans Saints, wide receiver, 1988-90; Detroit Lions, 1991-96; Kansas City Chiefs, 1997; Miami Dolphins, 1997-. **Business Addr:** Professional Football Player, Miami Dolphins, 2269 NW 199th St, Miami, FL 33056, (305)620-5000.

PERRIMON, VIVIAN SPENCE
Educator. **Personal:** Born Jun 5, 1926, Gregory, NC; daughter of Hallard Dozier Spence (deceased) and Edmund Clay Spence (deceased); married Arthur Perrimon (deceased); children: Petronia P Martin, Geraldine P Thomas. **Educ:** Elizabeth City State Univ, Elizabeth City, NC, BS, 1949; Atlanta Univ, Atlanta, GA, 1956-57; Univ of GA, Athens, GA, 1960s. **Career:** Turner Co Schools, Ashburn, GA, teacher, 1952-53; Morgan Co Schools, Madison, GA, teacher, 1949-51, 1953-56; Atlanta Public Schools, Atlanta, GA, teacher, 1957-76 (retired). **Orgs:** Charter pres, Atlanta Metro Alumni Chapter, 1978-91; life mem, ECSU General Alumni Assn, 1978-91, 2nd vice pres, 1986-90; Lambda Epsilon Omega Chapter, Alpha Kappa Alpha Sorority, 1991-97; program coordinator, 5th district, General Missionary Baptist Convention of GA, Inc, 1991; bd of dirs, Metro Atlanta Girls Club, 1980-83; bd of dirs, Metro Atlanta YWCA, 1979-85, finance comm; bd of dirs, DeKalb Co EOA, 1979-85, chairperson, Head Start Comm; bd of dirs, North Central GA Health Systems Agency, review comm; meals on wheels volunteer, DeKalb County Community Council on Aging, 1978-86; volunteer tutor, School/Partnership Program, Atlanta Chamber of Commerce, 1982-; Natl Bapt Conv, hosting comm sec, 1992; 5th Dist, Gen Missionary Batp Conv, GA, hosting comm sec, 1997. **Honors/Awds:** ECSU General Alumni Association, Alumni Community Service Award, 1979, VIP Membership Award for Membership Campaign, 1992; Natl Assn for Equal Opportunity in Higher Educ Pres Citation, Washington, DC, 1981; Atlanta Metro Alumni Service Award, 1982; Georgia Classroom Teacher of the Year, 1976, 1977; Outstanding Alumni Service Award, Atlanta Metro Chapter, ECSU, 1992. **Home Addr:** 2930 Edna Ln, Decatur, GA 30032.

PERRIN, DAVID THOMAS PERRY
Cleric. **Personal:** Born May 16, 1951, Cleveland, OH; married Elizabeth Ann Jackson (deceased); children: Caleb Karamo, Quianne Shapearl, MiLeah Niambi. **Educ:** Hamilton Coll, 1969-71; Carnegie Mellon Univ, BFA 1975; Gordon-Conwell Theological Seminary, MTS 1978; Andersonville Baptist Seminary, PhD. **Career:** Corning Comm Coll, instr 1981-83; Friendship Baptist Church, pastor 1981-83; Elmira Correctional Inst, vstg lecturer 1982-83; TDX Systems Inc, sales analyst 1984-85; Parkway Baptist Church, pastor. **Orgs:** Campus ministry dir Howard Univ 1978-80; ed consult Perrin & Perrin 1978-; computer coord The Alliance of Interdenominational Ministers 1983; mem Natl Speakers Assoc 1983, Amer Soc for Training & Dev 1983; vstg lecturer Elmira Correctional Inst 1983. **Honors/Awds:** Article "Making Senses of the Sixties" in Hawken Review 1983; Hosted TV Spec Dr ML King Birthday Elmira NY 1983; Hosted Mayoral Political Forum, 1983; Alliance of Ministers 183. **Home Addr:** 12902 St Edmund Way, Mitchellville, MD 20721. **Business Addr:** Sr Pastor, Church of the Great Commission, 5055 Allentown Rd, Camp Springs, MD 20746.

PERROT, KIM
Professional basketball player. **Personal:** Born Jan 18, 1967. **Educ:** Southwestern Louisiana, attended. **Career:** Vasby (Sweden), guard, 1990-91; Bramen Wuppertal (Germany), 1991-92; Maccabbi Tel Aviv (Israel), 1994-95; Racing Strasbourg (France), 1996-97; Houston Comets, 1997-. **Business Addr:** Professional Basketball Player, Houston Comets, Two Greenway Plaza, Ste 400, Houston, TX 77046, (713)627-9622.

PERRY, ALEXIS E.
Corporate executive. **Personal:** Born Feb 9, 1944, New York, NY; daughter of Eliza McBurnett Perry and Elex W. Perry; children: Ronald Earl Arlington Kirby. **Educ:** Nancy Taylor Secretarial School, NY, degree, 1965; attended Borough of Manhattan Community Coll, 1972-78, received associates degree; attended Queens Coll, Flushing NY, 1982-83. **Career:** Norton Simon Inc, New York NY, legal sec, 1973-76, equal employment coord, 1976-78, equal employment analyst, 1978-81, worked in charitable contributions, 1978-81, mgr of corp progams, 1981-84; RKO General, New York NY, corp mgr of equal employment opportunity, 1984-87, corp dir of affirmative action and equal employment opportunity, 1987-. **Orgs:** Mem 1983-, sec 1988-, Natl Urban Affairs Council; mem of advisory comm 1985-87, Comm Associates Devel Corp; mem 1985-, Coalition of 100 Black Women (NY); mem 1987-, Harlem YMCA Black Achiever Comm; mem 1988-, EDGES Group Inc. **Honors/Awds:** Black Achiever in Industry, Harlem YMCA, 1980.

PERRY, AUBREY M.
Psychologist, educator. **Personal:** Born Jan 14, 1937, Petersburg, VA; married Clarie; children: Vanessa, Aubrey Jr, Kenneth. **Educ:** Virginia State College, AB, 1958, MS, 1960; Indiana University Medical Center, Diploma, 1972; Florida State University, PhD, 1972. **Career:** Crownsville Hospital, psychologist intern, 1959; Central State Hospital, staff psychologist, 1960; FAMU, assistant professor psychology, 1961-68; Indiana Medical Center, psychologist intern, 1971; Apalachee Comm Mental Health Services, clinical psychologist, 1972-; Florida A&M University, associate professor psychology, 1969-, College of Arts & Science, dean, 1972-. **Orgs:** Association Black Psychologists, Psi Chi, Southeastern Psychol Association, Florida Psychol Assn, Assn Social & Behavioral Scientists, Phi Delta Kappa, Pi Gamma Mu, Leon Co Mental Health Assn, Omega Psi Phi. **Honors/Awds:** Florida A&M University, Teacher of the Year, 1961-62; NSF Summer Fellow, 1964; Carnegie Fellow, 1968; Florida A&M University, Psychology Teacher of the Year, 1974-75. **Business Addr:** Dean, Coll of Arts & Sciences, Florida A&M University, 208 Tucks Halls, Tallahassee, FL 32307-9515.

PERRY, BENJAMIN
Fire chief. **Personal:** Born Feb 12, 1939, Gary, IN; son of Mary Ellen Horton Childress (deceased) and Bennie Perry; married Kathryn A Gillespie, Nov 17, 1978; children: Sharlan Renee, Lonydea Marie, Gina Dyan. **Educ:** Indiana Univ, 1957-58; Ocean Side Carlsbad CA, 1958-59; Marine Inst, 1959-60/. **Career:** Inland Steel Co, E Chicago IN, headleader, 1961-65; Gary Fire Dept, Gary IN, firefighter, 1965-68, lieutenant, 1968-71, captain, 1971-78, battalion chief, 18-80, asst chief, 1980-86. **Orgs:** Mem, Intl Assn of Firefighters, 1965-, Intl Fire Chiefs, 1978-, Indiana Fire Chief's Assn, 1978-, Marine Corp Assn, 1980-, Natl Fire Protection Assn, 1981-;mem, advisory bd, Ivy Technical Coll, 1988-. **Honors/Awds:** Developed Large Diameter Hose Conception, Gary IN, Tactics Manual for Gary IN Fire Dept; Developed the Drivers Training Program for Gary Fire Dept. **Military Serv:** US Marine Corps, Sergeant E-5, Good Conduct, Indo-China Medal, 1961; Expert, rifle, piston, machine gun, automatic rifle, 1958-61.

PERRY, BENJAMIN L., JR.
Educational administrator, consultant. **Personal:** Born Feb 27, 1918, Tallahassee, FL; son of Annie Louise Gordon and Benjamin Luther Perry Sr; married Helen N Harrison Perry; children: Kimberley Victoria Perry Williams. **Educ:** FL A&M Coll, BS 1940; IA State Coll, MS 1942; Cornell U, PhD 1954; Claremont Coll CA, adv study 1955. **Career:** Florida A&M University, pres emeritus, 1986-, dean admn, 1986, pres, 1968-80; MGT Inc, consult 1980-; Kellogg Found, consult 1980-; Intl Educ Assn Workshop, 1970; US Dept Treas Wash, consult 1970; Higher Educ Columbia Sch Bus NY, mgmt planning instr 1971; So Assn Land-Grant Coll & U, pres 1972-73; FL Assn Colls & U, pres 1972-73. **Orgs:** Pres Tallahassee Urban Leage 1972; Phi Delta Kappa; C of C; Fronties Intl Club BSA; Pythian Knights of City State & Tallahasse, FL; Tiger Bay Club; Alpha Kappa Mu; adv com Ofc of Adv Pub Negro Colls 1972. **Honors/Awds:** Danforth Flwshp Grant for Travel & Study Abroad on Promotion for Human Understanding 1972-73; Phi Delta Kappa Man of Yr 1970; Outstdg Civilian Serv Medal Dept of Army 1973; Disgshd Leader of Educ Awd Lily White Assn 1969; Awd of Excellence Tallahassee Urban League 1973; Distinguished Alumni Award, Florida A&M University, 1990; Distinguished 1890 President, NALCU, 1990. **Military Serv:** US Army Corps of Engineers, 1st Lt, 1942-46.

PERRY, BRENDA L.
Educator. **Personal:** Born Nov 8, 1948, New Bedford, MA; daughter of Mary Mendes and Frank Andrade; married Clyde L Perry; children: Lisa Marie, Scott Anthony. **Educ:** Middlesex Comm Coll, AS 1975; Goddard Coll, MA 1977; Stonehill Coll, BA 1981. **Career:** Roxbury Multi Svcs, asst dir of female residential serv 1976-78; Commonwealth of MA Dept of Youth Svcs, dir of female serv 1978-81; Commonwealth of MA Dept of Social Svcs, program evaluator & monitor 1981-83; Rollins Coll, asst dir of admissions 1983-. **Orgs:** Mem Theosophical Soc; natl mem The Smithsonian Assocs; voting mem Natl Assoc of College Admissions 1983-; voting mem Southern Assoc of College Admissions 1983-; mem Natl Assoc of Foreign Student Serv 1984-; mem bd dirs Seminole Co Mental Health Serv 1985-; mem Natl Assoc of Black School Educators 1986; mem Natl Arbor Day Foundation 1988-90; mem Natl Wildlife Assn 1989-. **Honors/Awds:** Certificate of Appreciation Seminole Co Bd of Mental Health; Certificate in Drug Abuse Counseling Simmons Sch of Social Work 1975; poetry publication, American Poetry Anthology 1988.

PERRY, CARRIE SAXON
City official. **Educ:** Howard Univ. **Career:** Amistad House Inc, exec dir; Community Renewal Team of Greater Hartford Inc, administrator; Ambulatory Health Care Planning Inc of Hart-

ford, administrator; Hartford Comm Trainers, administrator; CT Welfare Dept, administrator; CT General Assembly, state rep; City of Hartford, CT, mayor, 1987-. **Orgs:** Life mem NAACP; pres Hartford Chap of 100 Black Women; exec bd mem Greater Hartford Black Democrats; exec bd mem Organized North Easterners; delegate Fed eration of Democrat Clubs; mem CT Caucus of Black Women for Political Action; mem Hartford Federation of Democratic Women; nominating chmn Permanent Commn on the Status of Hartford Women; corporator Oak Hill Sch for the Blind, Hartford Public Library, CT Black and Hispanic Urban Inst Inc; regional dir Natl Org of Black Elected Women Legislators, Nat Black Caucus of State Legislators; pres Order of Women Legislators; chairperson NBCSL 1987 Conference; apptd Natl Conf of State Legislatures; treasurer National Conference of Black Mayors; comptroller Connecticut Convention Center Authority. **Honors/Awds:** WKND's & CT Mutual's Leader of the Month Awd; Black People's Union, Univ of Hartford Outstanding Comm Serv Awd; Greater Hartford YWCA's Woman of the Year Award; Certificate of Merit for Distinguished Achievement; Ancient and Accepted Scottish Rite of Free Masonry Certificate of Merit; CT Minority Business Assn Salute; Special Award, National Conference of Christians and Jews Connecticut Chapter. **Business Addr:** Mayor, City of Hartford, PO Box 3989, Old State House Station, Hartford, CT 06103.

PERRY, CLIFFORD, III
Banking executive. **Personal:** Born Feb 8, 1945, Chicago, IL; son of Gloria Dixon Perry and Clifford Perry Jr; married Mattie Pointer Perry; children: Michele Walton, Renee Scott, Clifford R, Michael S. **Educ:** Governor State University, BA, marketing, 1991. **Career:** Harris Bank, bank department vice pres, 20 yrs; Northwest Bank, president, 1 1/2 yrs. **Orgs:** YMCA, investment committee board member, 1992-; Boys Club, board member, 1992-; Boy Scouts, board member, 1992-; Omaha Small Business Network, board member, 1992-; Noth Omaha Business Development Corp., board member, 1992-; Greater Omaha Private Industry Council, council member, 1992-; SBA Region VII, Omaha Advisory Council, advisory council member, 1992-; National Bankers Association, associate member, 1975-.

PERRY, DARREN
Professional football player. **Personal:** Born Dec 29, 1968, Chesapeake, VA; married Errika; children: Danielle. **Educ:** Penn State Univ, degree in business administration/management, 1992. **Career:** Pittsburgh Steelers, defensive back, 1992-. **Business Addr:** Professional Football Player, Pittsburgh Steelers, Three Rivers Stadium, 300 Stadium Circle, Pittsburgh, PA 15212, (412)323-1200.

PERRY, ED
Professional football player. **Personal:** Born Sep 1, 1974. **Educ:** James Madison. **Career:** Miami Dolphins, tight end, 1997-. **Business Addr:** Professional Football Player, Miami Dolphins, 2269 NW 199th St, Miami, FL 33056, (305)620-5000.

PERRY, ELLIOTT
Professional basketball player. **Personal:** Born Mar 28, 1969, Memphis, TN. **Educ:** Memphis State. **Career:** Los Angeles Clippers, guard, 1991; Charlotte Hornets, 1991-92; Portland TrailBlazers, 1992, 1993; Phoenix Suns, 1994-96; Milwaukee Bucks, 1996-. **Honors/Awds:** NBA Most Improved Player Award, 1995. **Business Addr:** Professional Basketball Player, Milwaukee Bucks, 1001 N 4th St, Bradley Ctr, Milwaukee, WI 53203, (414)227-0500.

PERRY, EMMA BRADFORD
Library dean. **Personal:** Born Dec 25, Hodge, LA; daughter of Mattie Stringfellow Bradford and Ibe Bradford; married Huey L Perry, Aug 26, 1972; children: David Omari, Jeffrey Donovan. **Educ:** Grambling State University, Grambling, LA, BS; Atlanta University, Atlanta, GA, MLS, Western Michigan University, Kalamazoo, MI, EdS. **Career:** Battle Creek Public Schools, Battle Creek, MI, librarian, 1971-72; Evanston Public Library, Evanston, IL, branch head, 1972-76; Texas A & M University, College Station, TX, assistant professor, 1977-83; State Library of Louisiana, Baton Rouge, LA, library consultant, 1985-87; Harvard University Business School, Cambridge, MA, associate library director, 1987-89; Dillard University, New Orleans, LA, director, university library, 1989-92; Southern University, dean of libraries, currently. **Orgs:** American Library Association, 1973-; Louisiana Library Association, 1985-; Texas Library Association, 1977-87; Association of College & Research Libraries, 1988-; Solinet, bd of dirs, chair, 1995-96; LLA, vp. **Honors/Awds:** Editorial Board, College & Research Libraries, ALA; SACS, Accreditation Team, ALA. **Business Addr:** Dean of Libraries, Southern University, Baton Rouge, LA 70813, (504)771-4991.

PERRY, EUGENE CALVIN, JR.
Sports management executive. **Personal:** Born Feb 8, 1953, Charlottesville, VA; son of Elizabeth Blair Perry and Eugene C Perry, Sr; married Shelia Herndon, Sep 1, 1978; children: Shannon Janine Xavier Perry, Eugene Calvin Perry III. **Educ:** Washington & Lee Univ, BA History 1975, JD 1978. **Career:** Justice Dept FBI, special agent 1978-86; Wilkinson & Perry Ltd, pres 1986-; Perry Group Intl Inc, pres 1987-89; Visions Video Ltd, Inc, partner, currently. **Orgs:** Phi Alpha Delta Legal Fraternity 1977-; parliamentarian Jr Chamber of Commerce 1979-; Amer Mgmt Assoc 1983-, Washington & Lee Alumni Council 1985-, Washington & Lee Univ Alumni Bd of Dirs 1987-; Special Olympics, Philadelphia Adopt-A-School Program, Omega Psi Phi Inc; NAACP, 1991-; First Baptist Church of Lincoln Gardens; Pop Warner Football, coach, currently; Wash and Lee Univ Alumni, bd of dirs, 1987-91; First Baptist Community Devel Corporation, bd of dirs, 1994-; Omega Psi Phi Fraternity, Inc, life member. **Honors/Awds:** Honor Award, Norfolk Jaycees 1980; Omega Man of the Year, 1993, Ma Gamma Gamma Chapter.

PERRY, FELTON
Actor, playwright. **Personal:** Born Oct 11, Evanston, IL. **Educ:** Wilson Junior College; Roosevelt University, BA, Spanish/French; University of Chicago, graduate study. **Career:** Theater appearances include: Nobody, 1996; The Meeting, 1987; MacBird, 1968; Chemin de Fer, 1969; Tiger, Tiger Burning Bright; No Place to Be Somebody; Second City Touring Company; film appearances include: Magnum Force, 1973; Walking Tall, 1973; The Towering Inferno, 1974; Mean Dog Blues, 1978; Down and Out in Beverly Hills, 1986; Robocop, 1987; Weeds, 1987; Checking Out, 1989; television appearances include: Matt Lincoln, 1970-71; Hooperman, 1987-; Hill Street Blues, 1985; LA Law, 1986-87; Harry, 1987; Stingray, 1987; numerous television movies; YAY Production Compnay, founder; actor in various tv commercials; writings include: by the bi and bye, 1979; Or; Sleep No More; Theatre Appearances: Ritual, 1989-90; Killing Time, 1990; Hamlet, 1995; Television: NYPD Blue, 1994; Living Single, 1995; Films: Dumb and Dumber, 1995; Red Snow, 1996. **Orgs:** American Federation of Television & Radio Artists; Actors' Equity Assn; Screen Actors Guild. **Honors/Awds:** NAACP Image Award for Playwrighting. **Special Achievements:** Performances: "Murphy Brown," "Fresh Prince of Bel-Aire," "Hanging With Mr. Cooper," "Civil Wars," Robocop II, 1989; Robocop III, 1991; Talent For The Game; author: The Reverend's Good Wife, 1992; Author: Buy the Bi and Bye, 1976; Author: Ironsides, 1973. **Military Serv:** US Marine Corps, sgt, 4 years. **Business Addr:** YAY Productions, 8205 Santa Monica Blvd, #261, West Hollywood, CA 90046.

PERRY, FRANK ANTHONY
Surgeon, educator (retired). **Personal:** Born Dec 16, 1921, Lake Charles, LA; married Helena, 1948; children: Clara, Frank Jr, Robert, David. **Educ:** Meharry Medical College, MD, 1945; American Board of Surgery, diploma, 1953. **Career:** Meharry Medical College, intern, 1945-46, resident surgeon, associate professor, 1956, 1958-68, director of resident surgery, 1958-88, professor of surgery, 1968-88. **Orgs:** Sloan Kettering Institute, consulting surgeon, 1955-56; Regional Medical Program, coordinator, 1967-72; Learning Resources Center Program, director, 1973-81; American Society of Head and Neck Surgery; American College of Surgeons. **Military Serv:** US Navy, lt comdr, 1956. **Home Addr:** 4223 Drake Hill Dr, Nashville, TN 37218.

PERRY, GARY W.
Automotive executive. **Personal:** Born Jun 3, 1952, Roanoke, VA; son of Rosetta Perry and Leroy Perry Sr; married Carlleena Herring, Oct 15, 1977. **Educ:** Winston-Salem State University, BA, 1975; Northwood Institute, Certificate, 1978-79; Wharton School of Business, Certificate, 1990; University of Michigan, Business, Certificate, 1990. **Career:** General Motors, Oldsmobile Division, assistant office mgr, 1976-77; Oldsmobile Division, Boston Zone, district mgr, sales, 1977-80; Oldsmobile Division, Washington Zone, district mgr, sales, 1980-83, car distributor, 1983-86; Oldsmobile Division, Detroit Zone, area fleet mgr, 1986-89, assistant zone mgr sales, 1989-. **Orgs:** Tau Phi Tau Fraternity, president, 1972; Appointed by General Sales Mgr to Business Process Reengineering Team-Oldsmobile. **Honors/Awds:** General Motors, Oldsmobile Division, District Mgr of the Year, 1978, 1982, 1983; General Motors, Robert Stempel, Highest Achievement, 1991; Dale Carnegie, Highest Achievement Award, 1991, Highest Award, Human Relations 1991, Highest Award, Reporting, 1991; General Motors, John F Smith President's Council Exceptional Performance Award, 1992, 1993, 1994, 1995; Appointed by Vice Pres of General Motors-Oldsmobile to Executive Leadership Team. **Home Addr:** 27166 Pierce, Southfield, MI 48076-7407, (313)569-6178. **Business Addr:** Director Oldsmobile Dealer Business Center, Oldsmobile Division, General Motors Corp., 400 Renaissance Center, PO Box 400, Detroit, MI 48265-4000.

PERRY, GERALD
Professional baseball player. **Personal:** Born Oct 30, 1960, Savannah, GA. **Career:** Atlanta Braves, infielder/outfielder, 1983-89; Kansas City Royals, infielder, 1990; St Louis Cardinals, infielder, 1991-. **Honors/Awds:** Bill Lucas Minor League Player of the Year Award, Atlanta Braves, 1982; National League All-Star Team, 1988. **Business Addr:** Professional Baseball Player, St Louis Cardinals, 250 Stadium Plaza, Busch Memorial Stadium, St Louis, MO 63102.

PERRY, HAROLD
Physician. **Personal:** Born Jun 26, 1924, Hamtramck, MI; son of Ida Barcelona Perry and James Arthur; married Agnes; children: Harold, Karen, Michael. **Educ:** Wayne State Univ, 1941-43; Cornell Univ, 1944; Howard Univ Coll of Medicine, MD 1948; Diploma Amer Bd Radiology 1955; Kress Fellow in Radiation Therapy, Memorial Hospital & Dept of Biophysics, Sloan-Kettering Inst, New York 1956-57. **Career:** Cincinnati General Hospital, attending rad therapy 1957-66, assoc dir rad 1957-66; VA Center, attending rad 1961-66, consultant 1965-66; Sinai Hospital, sr assoc attending physician 1966-73; Abraham & Anna Srere Radiation Oncology Center, dir radiation therapy 1966-81; Detroit General Hospital, sr assoc 1968-; VA Hospital, consultant radiotherapist 1972-; Sinai Hospital of Detroit, attending physician 1973-; Detroit-Macomb Hospital Assn, consultant 1976; Wayne State Univ School of Medicine, clinical prof dept of radiation oncology 1982-; Sinai Hospital of Detroit, Department of Radiation Oncology, chmn 1981-93, physician 1966-94. **Orgs:** AMA; Hospital Advisory Council SE MI Reg Med Program 1969-; MI State Medical Soc Com on Cancer 1971; chmn Radiation Therapy Advisory Panel Comp Health Plan Council of SE MI 1978-; Radiology Section Natl Med Assn 84th Annual Convention & Science Assembly 1979; Wayne County to MI State Med, del, 1982-83; chairman of the board NSTR 1983-84; reg rep council for Affiliated Radiation Oncology Soc; MI State Med Soc; Wayne County Med Soc; pres, Alumni Assn, Dept of Radiation Oncology Memorial Sloan Kettering Cancer Ctr, 1987-88, chmn of the bd, 1988-89, councilor, 1989-; alternate councilor, American Coll of Radiology, 1986-89, councilor, 1990-94; MI Soc of Therapeutic Radiology, pres elect 1981-82, chmn of the bd 1990-91, pres, 1989-90. **Honors/Awds:** Licensure DC 1950, OH 1957, MI 1966; mem Kappa Pi Hon Med Soc; Hon mention A Cressy Morrison Award 1963; Alumni Hall of Hon Hamtramck HS 1970; Fellowship Amer Coll of Radiology 1976; Alpha Omega Alpha, Honor Medical Society, 1993; numerous rsch projects presentations bibliographies. **Military Serv:** US Army, pfc, 1942-46; US Air Force, capt, 1953-55. **Home Addr:** 3220 Red Scott Cir, Las Vegas, NV 89117-3200.

PERRY, JEAN B.
Educator. **Personal:** Born Aug 31, 1946, New York City. **Educ:** Fashion Inst of Tech, AA 1968; NY Univ, BS 1970; NY city Tech Coll, AA 1980; Teacher Coll Columbia Univ, MA 1986. **Career:** NY Daily News "Good Living" section, feature writer; NY Daily News, reporter 1970; Black Enterprise Mag, wrote "Black Bus in Profile" column on free lance basis 1973-74; Daily News Conf for HS Editors, speaker 1974 & 75; Essence Mag, health & fitness editor 1982-84; Ethical Culture School, asst teacher 1985-87; Los Angeles Unified School Dist, teacher 1987-. **Orgs:** Mem Kappa Tau Alpha 1970-, Kappa Delta Pi 1986-. **Honors/Awds:** Recip Martin Luther King Alumni Assn Awd for Print Journalism NY Univ 1978; Media Awd for an Invest Feature Story for NY Daily News on Childhood Obesity NY Heart Assn 1979; Conceived and edited story on hypertention for Essence which received a William Harvey Awd from the Squibb Corp and the Amer Med Writers Assoc 1984; Conceived and edited story on Diabetes for Essence which received the Media Awd from the Amer Diabetes Assoc 1984. **Business Addr:** Educator, Los Angeles Unified School, 315 Holmby Ave, Los Angeles, CA 90024.

PERRY, JERALD ISAAC, SR.
Clergyman & consultant. **Personal:** Born Jun 3, 1950, Edenton, NC; son of Evelyn Jones Perry and John Isaac Perry; married Deborah Mayo, Mar 19, 1989; children: Jerald I Jr, Davin E, Felicia Shantique Mayo. **Educ:** Automation Machine Training Center, diploma 1968; Elizabeth City State Univ, BA matriculating; Shaw Divinity School, MA matriculating; Aviation Storekeeper "A" School Meridian MS. **Career:** Edenton Housing Auth, be member 1979-86; Amer Heart Fund Assoc, bd member 1980-86; bd member Edenton Chowan Bd of Education 1982-86; Elizabeth City State Univ, computer oper, programmer. **Orgs:** Bd mem Church of God in Christ Trustee Bd; mem NC Corsortium Comm 1972; gospel disc jockey/acct mgr WZBO-AM 1975-; mem NC State School Bd Assn 1982-;mem Natl School Bd Assn 1982-; mem NC Humanities Comm 1982-; bd mem State Employees Assoc of NC 1985; mem Black State Ministers Coalition; bd mem EdentonChowan Civic League; disc jockey/acct mgr WBXB-Love 100 FM Station; Sunday school supt Eastern NC Greater NC Diocese of Church of God in Christ Inc; mem Meridian Lodge #18; JW Hood Consistory #155 United Supremem Council; 33 degree AASR of Freemasonry Prince Hall Affiliation. **Honors/Awds:** Outstanding Young Man of America 1979;1983; Kappa Delta Phi Honor Soc Eliz City State Univ 1982-83; Letter of Accomodation Commanding General for ExpeditingH1 Priority Documents; Letter of Accomodation for Serving as Wing NCO of Barracks when received Barracks of Quarter Selection; Bluejacket of the Month and Bluejacket of the Quarter MCAS Cherry Point, NC. **Military Serv:** USN. **Home Addr:** PO Box 1211, Edenton, NC 27932. **Business Addr:** Computer Operator/Programmer, Elizabeth City State Univ, Information Systems Div, Elizabeth City, NC 27909.

PERRY, JOHN B.
Transportation services manager. **Personal:** Born Jan 14, 1945, Americus, GA; married Yvonne P Halback; children: Monique,

Keith. **Educ:** Stony Brook Univ Stony Brook, NY, 1973-74; Miami Dade Community Coll Miami, FL, 1978-79. **Career:** Eastern Airlines, senior instructor Miami, FL 1977-80; operating manager Atlanta, GA 1980-83; manager sales & services Daytona Beach, FL 1983-85; manager ramp services Atlanta, GA 1985-86; Newark Intl Airport NJ, dir sales & serv 1986-. **Orgs:** Member Black Caucus of Eastern Airlines 1977-; member Amer Soc of Travel Agents 1983; co-chairman United Negro College Fund Drive Volusia County 1984-85; chairman business ed & youth comm Rotary Intl 1984-85; board of directors Richard V Moore Comm Center Daytona Beach, FL 1984-85. **Honors/Awds:** Salute to Leadership Award United Negro College Fund Daytona Beach, FL 1984; Carter G Woodson Award Westside Business & Prof Assn Daytona Beach, FL 1984. **Home Addr:** 151 Country Club Dr #8, Union, NJ 07083. **Business Addr:** Dir Sales & Service, Eastern Airlines, Newark International Airport, Newark, NJ 07114.

PERRY, JOSEPH JAMES
Cleric. **Personal:** Born Oct 8, 1936, Sprott, AL; son of Ola Mae Ford Perry and Calloway Alphonso Perry; married Dorothy M Cutts Perry, Sep 22, 1957; children: Sherron, Joseph Jr, Kenneth, Keith, Andrea Perry Davis. **Educ:** Union Baptist Seminary, BTh, 1974; Southern Bible Seminary, MTh, 1975; University of Seattle, BA, 1976; New Era Baptist Seminary, DTh, 1977. **Career:** Little Rock Missionary Baptist Church, pastor, 1957-62; Good Hope Missionary Baptist Church, pastor, 1960-62; Holly Grove Missionary Baptist Church, pastor, 1962-65; Exodus Missionary Baptist Church, pastor, 1971-. **Orgs:** Baptist Missionary & Educational Convention of Michigan, president, 1991-96; Wayne County Sheriff's Department, Chaplin, 1988-; Plight of the Black Doctor, 1992-; One Church One Child of Michigan, treasurer, 1989-; SCLC, Michigan Chapter, executive director, 1989-; National Baptist Convention USA Inc, vice pres, 1960-; Detroit Commission for Fair Banking, 1992-; NAACP, 1957-. **Honors/Awds:** State of Michigan, Distinguished Service Award, 1990; Mobile Alabama, Honorary Citizen, 1988; SCLC, Outstanding Citizen, 1991; Detroit Rescue Mission, Martin Luther King Jr Award, 1993. **Business Addr:** Pastor, Exodus Missionary Baptist Church, 8173 Kenney, Detroit, MI 48234.

PERRY, JUNE CARTER
Foreign service officer. **Personal:** Born Nov 13, 1943, Texarkana, AR; daughter of Louise E Pendleton Carter and Bishop W Carter; married Frederick M; children: Chad Douglass, Andre Frederick. **Educ:** Loyola University, fine arts scholarship; Loyola Univ, BA (cum laude), 1965; Univ of Chicago, Woodrow Wilson fellow, MA, 1967; Hamline Coll, St Paul MN, faculty fellowship at Middle East Inst, Certificate, 1968. **Career:** College instr & high school teacher, 1967-70; WGTS-FM & WTOP-AM, producer/ commentator, 1973-74; WGMS-AM/FM, dir of public affairs, 1974-77; US Community Serv Admin, special asst for public affairs, 1977-79; ACTION Peace Corps, dir of public affairs, 1979-83; American Embassy, Lusaka, 1983-85, Harare, 1986-87; Dept of State, political officer, desk officer for Botswana, 1987-89; Secretary of State, special asst, 1989-90; American Embassy, Paris, first secretary, political affairs, 1990-93; Pol Mil Policy, State Dept, a dir, 1993-95; American Embassy Bang, deputy chief of mission, 1996-. **Orgs:** Amer Assn of Univ Women, 1973-76; AFTRA, 1974-78; former vice pres, advisory council, Women's Inst, Washington, DC, 1975-; bd mem, Greater Washington Boys & Girls Club, 1975-79; Finance Comm Natl Capital YMCA, 1975-79; vice pres, Friends for the Advancement of African Civilization, 1979; American Foreign Service Association, 1985-. **Honors/Awds:** Blacks in Industry Award, Harlem Y & Time Magazine, 1975; Sup Achiever Award, RKO General Broadcasting, 1976; Human Rights Award, UN Natl Capital Chapter, 1977; Distinguished Alumna Award, Mundelein Coll, 1980; Special Achievement Award, Action Agency, 1980; Outstanding Performance Award, Action Agency, 1982; Meritorious Service Award, Dept of State, 1985, 1987; Meritorious Honor Award, Dept of State, 1990; Superior Honor Award, Dept of State, 1995. **Special Achievements:** Author: "Ancient African Heroines," Washington Post, 1983. **Business Addr:** Deputy Chief of Mission, US Embassy Bangui, Dept of State, Washington, DC 20521-2060.

PERRY, JUNE MARTIN
Association executive. **Personal:** Born Jun 10, 1947, Columbia, SC; daughter of Junie Alberta Martin and Mark Anthony Martin; divorced; children: Kevin Martin Perry, Krystle Martin Perry. **Educ:** North Carolina Central Univ, Durham NC, BS Psychology, 1969; Univ of Wisconsin, Milwaukee WI, MSSW Social Welfare, 1971; Univ of Wisconsin, PhD candidate. **Career:** Milwaukee Co DSS, Milwaukee WI, social worker, 1971-73, purchase of service coord, 1973-75; New Concept Self Devel Center, Milwaukee WI, co-founder exec dir, 1975-. **Orgs:** Mem, Delta Sigma Theta Sorority, 1969; mem, NASW, 1971; mem, Natl Black Child Devel Inst, 1986; mem, bd of dir, Girl Scouts of Amer, 1986-88; mem, bd of dir, Wisconsin Council on Human Concerns, 1986; mem, bd of dir, Wisconsin Advocacy Coalition, 1987; mem, bd of dir, Milwaukee Mgmt Support Org, 1987; mem, Natl Forum for Black Public Admin, 1988. **Honors/Awds:** Sojourner Truth Award, Eta Phi Beta, 1986; Trailblazer of the Year, Black Women's Network, 1986; Toast & Boast Award, Natl Women's Political Caucus, 1986; author of "Parents As Teachers of Human Sexuality," 1986; Top Ladies of Distinction Comm Service Award, 1987; Social Worker of the Year, Health Service Professionals of Wisconsin, 1988; Wisconsin's Unsung Hero, Newsweek, 1988; Woman of the Year, Calvary Baptist Church, 1990; Leadership America Alumnae, 1990; UWM School of Social Work, Alumni of the Year, 1993; Milwaukee NOW, Woman of the Year, 1994. **Business Addr:** Exec Dir, New Concept Self Devel Center, Inc, 4828 W Ford de Loc Ave, Milwaukee, WI 53216, (414)444-1952.

PERRY, LAVAL
Automobile dealership executive. **Career:** All American Ford, president, currently. **Orgs:** Michigan Ford Dealers Advertisers Fund, bd of dir; Ford Lincoln-Mercury Minority Dealers Association, vice pres, bd mem; OIC Industrial Council, bd mem. **Special Achievements:** Co. is ranked #68 on Black Enterprise magazine's list of top 100 auto dealers, 1995. **Business Addr:** President, All American Ford, 4201 Bay Rd, Saginaw, MI 48603, (517)792-1700.

PERRY, LEE CHARLES, JR.
Company executive. **Personal:** Born Feb 22, 1955, St Louis, MO; married Rena Armstrong; children: Raimon, Jonathan. **Educ:** Forest Park Comm Coll, AS Elec Engrg Tech 1974; Comm Coll of the Air Force, Electronics Honor Grad 1975; Eastern KY Univ, BS 1980; Industrial Tech, grad with recognition. **Career:** IBM St Louis, customer engr 1980-83, program support rep 1983-85; IBM Regional Office Kansas City, sr nsd specialist 1985-87; IBM, availability services mgr, 1987-. **Orgs:** Minister United Pentecostal Church 1984-. **Honors/Awds:** IBM Means Service Award. **Military Serv:** USAF e-5 staff sgt equipt chief 4 yrs; Good Conduct Medal, Certificate of Recognition for Outstanding Performance as Peer Instructor USAF. **Business Addr:** Availability Services Manager, IBM Corporation, 860 Ridge Lake Blvd, Ste 200, Memphis, TN 38120.

PERRY, LEONARD DOUGLAS, JR.
Educational administrator. **Personal:** Born Mar 14, 1952, Philadelphia, PA. **Educ:** Temple Univ, BS, MEd; Purdue Univ, EdS. **Career:** Temple Univ, resident coord 1976-77, assoc to dean of students 1977-80; Purdue Univ, asst dean of students 1980-85; FL State Univ, assoc dean of students, 1985-92; Brown Univ, assoc dean of student life, 1992-. **Orgs:** Member, NAACP; Urban League; American Society for Training and Development; member, National Assn of Student Personnel Administrators; member, Southern Assn for College Student Affairs; member, National Society for Performance and Instruction; board of directors, Black Families of America, Inc; bd, CHOICES, Rhode Island, Inc. **Honors/Awds:** Martin Luther King Award, Florida State University, 1987; Advisor of the Year Award, Black Student Union, Florida State University, 1987; NAACP Chapter Award, 1992. **Home Addr:** PO Box 2533, Providence, RI 02906-0533. **Business Addr:** Associate Dean, Brown Univ, 26 Benovolent St, Box P, Providence, RI 02912.

PERRY, LOWELL W.
State government official. **Personal:** Born Dec 5, 1931, Ypsilanti, MI; son of Lillian Bass Perry and Lawrence C Perry; married Maxine Lewis; children: Lowell Jr, Scott, Merrideth. **Educ:** Univ MI, BA 1953; Detroit Coll of Law, JD 1960. **Career:** Pittsburgh Steelers Football Club NFL, player 1956, asst coach 1957, scout 1958-60; Frank A Picard, law clrk 1960-61; Chev Motr Div GM Detrt, personnel rep 1961-62; Nat Lbr Rel Bd 7th Reg Dtrt, atty 1962-63; Chrysler Corp, dir of personnel 1963-79; LIP Inc, pres 1979-83; Michigan Bell Telephone Co, dir of government affairs 1983-; chrmn US Equal Opportunity Commission (EEOC) 1975-76; Michigan Bell Telephone Co, director of Government Affairs, beginning 1976; Michigan Department of Labor, director, 1991-96; State of Michigan Office of Urban Programs, director, currently. **Orgs:** Mem, Michigan State Bar Assn; dir, Sky-pac Entrprs Inc, mem, bd dir, NFL Charities, NY; bd dir, Untd Found Met Dist; bd dir, Boys Clubs Met Dist; bd Gov, Univ MI Club of Detroit; bd dir, Black Child and Family Inst, Lansing; bd of dirs, Detroit College of Law; bd of dirs, Starr Commonwealth Schools. **Honors/Awds:** Nat Hnr Soc Ypsilanit High Sch; Sr Hopn Univ MI; All-Amer Ftbl Hon Univ MI; NCAA Silver Anniversary Athlete Scholar Awd 1978; Honorary Doctorates of Laws, Ferris State Univ, 1976, Wilberforce Univ, 1976, Eastern Michigan Univ, 1996. **Military Serv:** US Air Force, 1st Lt. **Business Addr:** Director, State of Michigan Office of Urban Programs, 1200 6th St, 11th Fl, Detroit, MI 48226.

PERRY, LOWELL WESLEY, JR.
Business executive. **Personal:** Born May 10, 1956, Ypsilanti, MI; son of Maxine Lewis Perry and Lowell Wesley Perry Sr; married Kathleen Tucker Perry, Mar 21, 1987; children: Lowell Wesley III, Tucker Nichol, Trenton Lewis. **Educ:** Yale Univ, BA Admin Sciences 1978; graduate work marketing, Seattle Univ 1987. **Career:** Nutone Div Scovill, sales rep 1978-81; Seattle Seahawks, dir sales & mktg 1981-88; Access Plus Communications, field sales manager, 1988-89; Seattle Mariners, account executive, 1989-90; Perry Marketing Group, Inc, president, 1990-94; Hiram Walker & Sons Inc, integrated marketing mgr, 1994-; commercials, industrial training films, print ads, actor & model. **Orgs:** Bd mem Kirkland C of C 1984-; bd Kidsplace-Action Agenda Taskforce 1985; corresp sec Zeta Pi Lambda Chap of Alpha Phi Alpha 1983-84; 1st vice pres Zeta Pi Lambda of Alpha Phi Alpha 1984-; bd East Madison YMCA 1985-; pub rel comm Eastside Mental Health Cntr 1983-84; bd Cooperative Charities; bd Washington Generals; life member, NAACP. **Honors/Awds:** Rookie of the Year Nutone Div Scovill 1978-79; Chairman Sustaining Membership Drive East Madison YMCA 1984-85; Project Developer & Coord of "Blow the Whistle on Drugs" a statewide family substance abuse prog; speaker of the house Seattle Marketing Executives. **Business Addr:** Integrated Marketing Mgr, Hiram Walker & Sons Inc, 3000 Town Center, Ste 3200, Southfield, MI 48075, (810)948-6500.

PERRY, MARC AUBREY
Marketing company executive. **Personal:** Born in Michigan; son of Lawrence C & Carrie O Perry; married Pamela E, Mar 23, 1995; children: Aubrey Mariah. **Educ:** Eastern Michigan University, mktg, 1978. **Career:** Chevrolet, mktg special, 1978-90; Donald Coleman, acct supervision, 1990-94; Perry Mktg Group Inc, president, CEO, 1994-. **Orgs:** Black United Fund, bd mem; Blacks In Advertising, Radio & Television, founder; Eastern Michigan Almuni, comm chair. **Business Addr:** President, Perry Marketing Group, Inc, 16250 Northland Dr, Ste 318, Southfield, MI 48075, (248)443-0382.

PERRY, MARGARET
Library director (retired), writer. **Personal:** Born Nov 15, 1933, Cincinnati, OH; daughter of Elizabeth Munford Anthony and Rufus Patterson Perry. **Educ:** Western MI Univ, AB 1954; Cath Univ of Amer, MSLS 1959; Universite de Paris, Certificat d'Etudes Sum 1956; NY City Coll, 1957-58. **Career:** New York Publ Library, young adult/reference librarian 1954-55, 1957-58; US Army Europe, post librarian 1959-67; US Military Acad West Point, circulation librarian 1967-70; Univ Rochester, head educ library 1970-75, assoc prof 1975-82, joint appt asst prof English dept 1973-75, head reader serv div acting dir of libraries; asst dir of libraries for reader serv 1975-82; Valparaiso Univ, dir of libraries 1982-93; author, currently. **Orgs:** Life mem Amer Library Assn; assoc editor Univ Rochester Library Bulletin 1970-73; chair education comm, 19th Ward Community Assn Rochester 1972-73; 2nd vice pres Urban League of Rochester 1978-80; pres Northern IN Area Libraries 1986-88. **Honors/Awds:** Scholarship to Seminar of American Writing and Publishing, Schloss Leopoldskron Salzburg, Austria, 1956; Armed Forces Writers League, Short Story Contest, Honorable Mention, 1965, First Prize, 1966; Frances Steloff Armed Forces League Short Story Contest, Second Prize, 1968; Directory of Librarians in the US and Canada, bibliography listing; Arts Alive, Short Story Contest, First Prize, 1990; Willow Review, Short Story Contest, Second Prize, 1990. **Special Achievements:** Author, works include: A Bio-Bibliography of Countee P Cullen, Greenwood Press 1971; Silence to the Drums: A Survey of the Literature of the Harlem Renaissance, Greenwood Press 1976; Harlem Renaissance: An Annotated Bibliography and Commentary, Garland 1982; Short Fiction of Rudolph Fisher, Greenwood Press 1987; "An Interview Margaret Perry," Cobblestone Magazine, 1991; "Gwendolyn Brooks," Notable Black American Women, ed by Jessie Carney Smith, Gale Publishing, 1992; Freelance writing, 1993-; Contributor to Michigan Land Use Insitute, 1994-; "Carol Moseley Braun," Notable Black Amer Women, ed by Jessie Carney Smith, Gale Pub, 1995. **Home Addr:** 15050 Roaring Brook Rd, Thompsonville, MI 49683.

PERRY, MARLO
Professional football player. **Personal:** Born Aug 25, 1972, Forest, MS. **Educ:** Jackson State. **Career:** Buffalo Bills, linebacker, 1994-. **Business Addr:** Professional Football Player, Buffalo Bills, One Bills Dr, Orchard Park, NY 14127, (716)648-1800.

PERRY, MICHAEL DEAN
Professional football player. **Personal:** Born Aug 27, 1965, Aiken, SC; married Trini; children: Taylor Denise, Amber, Tyrah. **Educ:** Clemson Univ, attended. **Career:** Cleveland Browns, defensive tackle, 1988-94; Denver Broncos, 1995-97; Kansas City Chiefs, 1997-. **Honors/Awds:** Sporting News, NFL All-Star Team, 1989; United Press International, Defensive Player of the Year, 1989; Cleveland Touchdown Club, Defensive Player of the Year, 1991; Pro Bowl, 1989, 1990, 1991, 1993, 1994, 1996. **Business Addr:** Professional Football Player, Kansas City Chiefs, One Arrowhead Dr, Kansas City, MO 64129, (816)924-9300.

PERRY, PATSY BREWINGTON
Educator. **Personal:** Born Jul 17, 1933, Greensboro, NC; daughter of Rosa Kirby Brewington and James C Brewington; married Wade Wayne Perry, Dec 23, 1955; children: Wade Wayne Perry, Jr. **Educ:** North Carolina Coll, Durham, NC, BA (magna cum laude), 1950-54; North Carolina Coll, Durham, NC, MA, 1954-55; Univ of North Carolina, Chapel Hill, NC, PhD, 1968-72. **Career:** Georgetown High School, Jacksonville, NC, teacher, 1955-56; Duke University, visiting professor, 1975; North Carolina Central Univ, Durham, NC, reserve book

librarian, 1956-58, instructor, 1959-63, asst prof, 1964-71, assoc prof, 1972-74, prof, 1974-, English dept chmn, 1979-90, special asst to the chancellor, currently. **Orgs:** Mem, YWCA, 1976-; mem The Links Inc, 1976-; life mem, Coll Language Assn; mem, senator 1986-, Philological Assn of the Carolinas; mem, South Atlantic Modern Language Assn; mem, Assn of Departments of English; mem, The Langston Hughes Soc; reader, College Board English Composition Test (ETS), 1985-; board member, Women in Action for the Prevention of Violence, 1990-. **Honors/Awds:** Alpha Kappa Mu Honorary Soc, 1953; Danforth Scholarship Grant, Summer, 1967; Career Teaching Fellowship, Univ of North Carolina, 1968-69; Faculty Fellow, North Carolina Central Univ, 1968-71; nominee, ACE Fellow Program in Academic Admin, Amer Council on Educ, 1977; Ford Foundation Writing Fellow, Recognition for Excellence in Teaching Writing, 1989; author of "The Literary Content of Frederick Douglass' Paper Through 1860," CLA Journal 1973, "One Day When I Was Lost: Baldwin's Unfulfilled Obligation," chapter in James Baldwin: A Critical Evaluation, edited by Therman B O'Daniel, Howard Univ Press 1977, and biographical essays in Southern Writers-Biographical Dictionary, Louisiana State Univ Press 1979, The Dictionary of Literary Biography, 1986; Notable BlackAmerican Women, edited by Jessi Smith, 1991, Southern Writers of the Second Renascence—Poets, Dramatists, Essayists, and others, edited by Joseph Flora and Robert Bain, 1992; Silver Medallion Award for Excellence in Education, YWCA of Durham, 1991; Research Award, North Carolina Central University, 1991. **Business Addr:** Professor, Special Assistant to the Chancellor, Dept of English, North Carolina Central Univ, Communications Bldg, Rm 327, Durham, NC 27707.

PERRY, RICHARD
Novelist, educator. **Personal:** Born Jan 13, 1944, New York, NY; son of Bessie Draines Perry and Henry Perry; divorced; children: Malcolm David, Alison Wright. **Educ:** City College of the City University of New York, BA, 1970; Columbia University, MFA, 1972. **Career:** Pratt Institute, Brooklyn NY, professor of English, 1972-, dean of liberal arts and sciences, 1993-. **Orgs:** PEN, Teachers and Writers Collaborative, National Council of Teachers of English. **Honors/Awds:** New Jersey State Council on the Arts Award, 1980; New Jersey Writers Conference Citation, 1985; author of Changes, Bobbs-Merrill, 1974; author of Montgomery's Children, Harcourt, 1984; author of No Other Tale to Tell, William Morrow, 1994; New Jersey Council on the Arts Award for Fiction, 1983, 1985, 1990; Black History Month Award, The Association for Study of Afro-American Life and History, 1986; Fellowship in Writing, National Endowment of the Arts, 1989; author of The Broken Land, St. Martin's Press, 1996. **Military Serv:** US Army, 1968-70. **Business Addr:** School of Liberal Arts & Sciences, Pratt Institute, 200 Willoughby Ave, Brooklyn, NY 11205.

PERRY, RITA EGGLETON
Publisher, writer, photographer. **Personal:** Born Jul 24, 1943, Atlantic City, NJ; daughter of Christine Archer Luffborough & Jesse B Eggleton Jr; divorced; children: Sylvia Rosella Eggleton Carter-Perry. **Educ:** University of Detroit; Norfolk State University. **Career:** Jacksonville Free Press, publisher/owner, 1985-; Mel-Lin, Pres-Jas Broadcasting Companies, vice pres of sales, 1973-85; Florida Star Newspaper, assistant to publisher, 1971-73; Macon Times Newspaper, managing editor, 1968-71; Muziki Publishing Co, administrator, 1965-68. **Orgs:** Bold City Chapter the Links Inc, public relations officer, 1993-; A L Lewis YWCA Board; One Church/One Child Board; Jacksonville Negro Business & Professional Women, former president; Southeast Black Publishers Association, former secretary; Southeast African-American Publishers Association, former secretary; Jacksonville Coalition of Community Clubs, former president; National AAssault of Illiteracy Program Board (AOIP); Edward Waters College, board of visitors. **Honors/Awds:** Martin Luther King Foundation, Community Svc, 1990, 1996; Alpha Kappa Alpha Sorority, Community Svc, 1992, 1994, Academy Awd, 1995; Sickle Cell Foundation, Partner for Caring, 1991; and many others. **Special Achievements:** One of 14 publishers called by President Bush for consultation, 1991; State of Florida Commendation for Voter Education Projects, 1993; Jacksonville Urban League Awd, 1988; Awd for Dedication to Black History Education by Florida Jr College, 1990; Visions of Jacksonville, 1990; Edward Waters College, 1987; many other awards and citations.

PERRY, ROBERT CEPHAS
Government official. **Personal:** Born Mar 1, 1946, Durham, NC; married Blossom N Sanborn; children: Jessica Lahela, Benjamin Lono. **Educ:** Wittenberg Univ, BA Political Sci; American Univ, MA International Relations, 1969; National Defense Univ, 1990; Department of State, Senior Seminar, 1995. **Career:** Dept of State, foreign serv officer Vietnam 1969-70, foreign serv officer Santiago Chile 1971-72, foreign serv officer Asmara Ethiopia 1973-75; foreign serv officer 1975-77; foreign serv officer Mexico City Mexico 1977-80; foreign serv officer 1980-84; deputy chief of mission, Port Louis, Mauritius, 1986-89; foreign service officer, 1990-94; deputy chief of mission, La Paz, Bolivia, 1995-97. **Honors/Awds:** Meritorious Honor Awd Dept of State 1975. **Business Addr:** Dept of State, Washington, DC 20520.

PERRY, ROBERT LEE
Educational administrator. **Personal:** Born Dec 6, 1932, Toledo, OH; son of Katherine Bogan Perry (deceased) and Rudolph R Perry; married Dorothy Larouth Smith; children: Baye' Kito, Kai Marlene, Ravi Kumar. **Educ:** Bowling Green St Univ, BA sociology 1959, MA sociology 1965; Wayne St Univ, PhD sociology 1978. **Career:** Lucas Cnty Juv Ct Toledo, OH, probation counselor 1960-64, juvenile ct referee 1964-67; Detroit Inst Techn, asst prof 1967-70; Department of Ethnic Studies, Bowling Green State Univ chmn, 1970-; licensed professional counselor, 1988; Ohio certified prevention consultant, 1989-. **Orgs:** Consult Natl Inst of Law Enf and Crimin Just 1978-82; consult Div Soc Law and Econ Scis Natl Sci Found 1980; consult Children's Def Fund Task Force on Adoption Assist 1980; chair Status of Women & Minorities Comm N Cent Sociol Soc 1983-85; bd mem Citizens Review Bd Lucas Cnty Juv Ct Toledo, OH 1979-91; bd mem Inst for Child Advocacy Cleveland, OH 1981-85. **Honors/Awds:** Sigma Delta Pi natl Spanish Hon Soc 1958; Alpha Kappa Delta Natl Soc Honor Soc 1976; $37,000 Grant, Dept HEW 1979; Post Doct Fellowship Amer Social Soc Inst for Soc Research UCLA 1980; Charles C Irby National Association of Ethnic Studies (NAES), Distinguished Service Award, 1994. **Military Serv:** USAF A/IC Air Man First Class 1953-57. **Business Addr:** Department Head, African American Studies, Eastern Michigan University, 620 Pray Harrold, Ypsilanti, MI 48197.

PERRY, TIMOTHY D.
Professional basketball player. **Personal:** Born Jun 4, 1965, Freehold, NJ. **Educ:** Temple Univ, Philadelphia, PA, 1984-88. **Career:** Forward: Phoenix Suns, 1988-92, Philadelphia 76ers, 1992-95; New Jersey Nets, 1995-.

PERRY, WAYNE D.
Research economist. **Personal:** Born Oct 14, 1944, Denton, TX; married Linda Jackson; children: LaNitha, Chelese, Wayne. **Educ:** Tuskegee Inst, BS 1967; B NM, MS 1969; Carnegie Mellon U, PhD 1975. **Career:** Ford Motor Co, co-op student mfg eng 1964-67; Tuskegee Inst, resrch & tchng asst 1963-67; Sandia Lab, mech engr dir adv computer aided design proj1967-71; Manpower Studies Proj Carnegie Mellon U, instr mgr rsrch coor 1971-75; Housing Studies Defense Manpwr & Energy Pol Studies The RAND Corp, econ pol proj dir 1975-. **Orgs:** Mem Am Statis Assn; The Inst of Mgmt Sci; Econometric Soc N Am; Am Soc Mech Engr; pub many rsrch papers mem Omega Psi Phi; NAACP; co-fndr Concerned Black Employees Sandia Lab; Black Coalition Albuquerque & Pitts; LA Yth Motivat Task Force; dir LA Carnegie-Mellon Univ Alum Assn; dir Ladera Heights Civic Assn. **Honors/Awds:** Rsrch grnts from US Dept of Labor; Dept of Energy; Dept of Defense; HUD; HEW; Sandia Lab & Serv Awd Nuclear Weapons Devel Atomic Energy Comm 1969; edit reviewer "Policy Analysis" Univ of CA Berkeley 1978-; Resrch Paper Winner Am Soc Mech Engr 1967; Adad Schlshp Tuskegee Inst 1962-67; grad flwhp Carnegie-Mellon Univ 1971-75. **Business Addr:** 1700 Main St, Santa Monica, CA 90406.

PERRY, WILLIAM RODWELL, III
Government official, sports administrator. **Personal:** Born May 19, 1959, Baltimore, MD; son of Charlotte Marshall Perry and William R Perry Jr; married Dynise Williamson Perry, Dec 9, 1989. **Educ:** Morgan State University, BS, Psychology, 1981, MBA, Business, 1983. **Career:** United Parcel Service, Baltimore, MD, primary supervisor, 1981-85; Perkins & Partners, Miami, FL, marketing mgr, 1985-86; City of Miami Commission Office, Miami, FL, sr adm asst, 1986-90; Miami Space & Exhibition Authority, Miami, FL, exec dir, 1990-. **Orgs:** Board member, YMCA, 1987-, Community Dev Corp, 1989-, Health Clinic, 1989-, One-Church/One-Child, 1988-89, Hotel/Motel Assn, 1990-. **Honors/Awds:** Golden Coconut Award, Coconut Grove Chamber, 1990; Outstanding Citizen Award Nominee, Bna'i Brith Assn, 1991.

PERRY-HOLSTON, WALTINA D.
Economist. **Personal:** Born Jan 6, 1959, Augusta, GA; daughter of Mabel Wingfield Perry and James W Perry; married Kevin Holston, Jun 22, 1991. **Educ:** Spelman College, BA, 1980; Georgia State University, attended, 1982. **Career:** General Services Administration, technical support clerk, 1980-82; US Department of Education, Litigation Unit, legal technician, 1982-83; US Department of Labor, economist, 1983-. **Orgs:** Spelman College Alumni Association, 1980-; National Association for Female Executives Inc, 1980-; American Economic Association. **Honors/Awds:** US Department of Labor, Performance Management System Award, 1992, 91, Combined Federal Campaign Coordinator, 1991, Savings Bond Canvasser, 1990; Women's Executive Leadership Program, 1994-95. **Business Addr:** Economist, US Department of Labor, Bureau of Labor Statistics, 1371 Peachtree St NE, Ste 500, Atlanta, GA 30367, (404)347-7575.

PERRYMAN, LAVONIA LAUREN
Company executive. **Personal:** Born in Detroit, MI. **Educ:** Wayne State U, BA 1971; Ferris Coll, 1969; Howard U, MA 1978. **Career:** Soc Res Applic Corp, comm dir; owner opr 1st girls bskbl clinic; Pizazzz Corp, pres; Afbony Modeling & Talent Agy, professional model instr; Teai & Record, pub rel dir; WCAR Radio, reprt 1973-76; WTVS-56, black journal reprt; Smith, Sanders & Perryman, vp, currently. **Orgs:** Vp Nat Assn of Media Women; mem NAACP; Negro Counc of Women; Black Commctrs; All Star Bsktbl Player; Congressman John Conyers Women Orgn; Stud Non-violents Orgn; Congress of Black Women; Natl Coalition of 100 Black Women. **Honors/Awds:** Athletic awd Ferris State Coll 1969; Ms Soul of MI & Ms Autorama 1972; speech awd VFW 1973-74; Ms Black MI; Ms Black Detroit; Ms Elks; Ms Swimsuit; Ms Congeniality; Ms Misty of MI 1974-75; Media Woman of the Yr; Spirit of Det Awd City of Detroit; Citz Awd Booker T Wash Bus Assn; Most Unique Dresser Detroit News 1976-77; Citz Awd Detroit City Counc; Detroiter's Awd Detroit Experience; Disco Martin Citz Awd; Washington DC's 10 Most Admired Women Award.

PERRYMAN, ROBERT
Professional football player. **Personal:** Born Oct 16, 1964, Raleigh, NC. **Educ:** Univ of Michigan, received degree, 1987. **Career:** New England Patriots, running back, 1987-. **Business Addr:** Professional Football Player, New England Patriots, Sullivan Stadium, Rt One, Foxboro, MA 02035.

PERRY-MASON, GAIL F.
Banker. **Personal:** Born Dec 4, 1962, Detroit, MI; daughter of Clarence and Frankie Perry; married Lance W Mason, Aug 3, 1985; children: Brandon, Dexter, Scott. **Career:** Wayne County Commun Coll, instructor; Henry Ford Commun Coll, instructor; Marygrove Coll, instructor; Native Detroiter Magazine, writer of financial section; Barden Cablevision, host of "Detroit Business Exchange"; First of Michigan, Corp, vp of investments, currently. **Orgs:** Michigan Assn of Pension Plan Professionals; Women's Economic Club, finance comm; Women's Exec Golf League; That's What Friends Are For, board of directors; National Assn of Female Execs; NAACP; Detroit Institute of Arts, founder's society; National Urban League, Blue Monday Network. **Honors/Awds:** Gentleman of Wall Street, Community Achievement Award; WJLB Radio, Super Achiever's Award. **Business Addr:** VP, Investments, First of Michigan Corp., 100 Renaissance Ctr., 26th Fl., Ste 2600, Detroit, MI 48243, (313)259-2600.

PERSAUD, INDER
Business executive. **Personal:** Born Oct 23, 1926, Georgetown, Guyana; married Nalini Singh; children: 4. **Educ:** London Engl, prof degree in hosp admin Inst Hosp Admin 1956. **Career:** Berbice Group Guyana, hosp admin 1958-60; Georgetown Hosp, 1960-67; Morrisania Hosp Bronx, acting admin 1967-68; Cumberland Hosp Brooklyn, asso exec dir 1968-73, exec dir 1973-. **Orgs:** Mem Hlth Com Nat Urban League; New York City chap Nat Assn Hlth Serv Exec pres 1972; founder mem Consumers Accreditation Counc; fdr vch Ft Greene Coop. **Business Addr:** 39 Auburn Pl, Brooklyn, NY.

PERSON, CHUCK CONNORS
Professional basketball player. **Personal:** Born Jun 27, 1964, Brantley, AL. **Educ:** Auburn Univ, Auburn, AL, 1982-86. **Career:** Indiana Pacers, forward, 1986-92, Minnesota Timberwolves, 1992-94; San Antonio Spurs, 1994-. **Honors/Awds:** NBA Rookie of the Year, 1987; NBA All-Rookie Team, 1987. **Business Addr:** Professional Basketball Player, San Antonio Spurs, 600 E Market St, San Antonio, TX 78205, (210)554-7773.

PERSON, DAWN RENEE
Professor. **Personal:** Born Dec 10, 1956, Sewickley, PA; daughter of Fannie Mae Thomas Person (deceased) and Conrad Person Sr; married Harold Eugene Hampton, Aug 2, 1986; children: Bryson Thomas Person-Hampton, Amara Renee Person-Hampton. **Educ:** Slippery Rock Univ, BS Educ 1977, M Educ 1979; Teachers College, Columbia Univ, EdD, 1990. **Career:** Slippery Rock Univ, human relations counselor 1978-79, minority affairs coord 1979-80, advisor to black & intl students 1980-81; CO State Univ, dir black student services 1981-85; Lafayette College, asst dean of academic services, 1985-90; Teachers College, Columbia Univ, asst prof of higher educ, 1990-97; Student Development in Higher Education, assoc prof. **Orgs:** Workshop facilitator Male/Female Relation 1978-; mem ACPA; mem NAACP Easton PA Chap 1985-87; mem Black Conference-Higher Educ PA 1986-87; NASPA; Leadership Lehigh Valley 1989-90. **Honors/Awds:** Outstanding Black Achiever in Pennsylvania, Black Opinions, 1989; Service Award, Lafayette College Alumni Chapter of Black Collegians, 1988; Excellence in Higher Education, Lafayette College Minority Students, 1990; Publication & Research in Minority Student Retention, Student Cultures, & Multicultural Issues in Higher Educ. **Business Addr:** Associate Professor, Student Devt in Higher Education, California State University, Department of Educational Psychology, Administration & Counseling, Bellflower Blvd, Ed Bu II, #214, Long Beach, CA 90840.

PERSON, EARLE G.
Dental surgeon. **Personal:** Born Apr 28, 1928, Mt Vernon, IL; married Estelle Mccraty. **Educ:** Univ IL, BS 1950; Creighton Univ Omaha, DDS 1958. **Career:** Pvt Pract dentistry 1958-; Creighton U, faculty 1960-62. **Orgs:** Mem IL Soc Microbiologists; Amer & NE Dent Assc; surg staff Archbishop Bergan

Mercy Hosp & Doctor's Hosp Omaha; state chmn NDA Council Dental Care Prog 1974-; pres NE Soc Clin Hypnosis 1973; mem Creighton Univ Adv Council 1972-; bd dir KOWH AM/FM Radio; Acad Gen Dentistry 1972-; pres bd dir Comprehensive Health Assc Omaha 1973-; pres Urban League 1965-68; assemblyman Natl Black Pol Assembly 1972-; del Natl Black Conv Gary 1972; Little Rock1974; natl Dem Conv 1972; mem Alpha Sigma Nu, Omicron Kappa Upsilon. **Honors/Awds:** Owler's Award dist srv dent & civic affairs 1968; Intl Platform Assn 1974-75. **Military Serv:** AUS 2nd lt 1950-52, 1st lt 1952-53. **Business Addr:** PO Box 11628, Omaha, NE 68111-0628.

PERSON, LESLIE ROBIN
Deputy ATC operations officer. **Personal:** Born Nov 14, 1962, St Louis, MO; married Kyro Jonathan Carter. **Educ:** Attended, Nichols State Univ 1979-80, Kent State Univ 1980-81; Univ of Cincinnati, BA 1982. **Career:** US Air Force, 2012 communications squadron atc officer trainee 1984-85, 1903 communications squadron deputy atc ops officer 1985-86, 2146 communications group deputy atc ops officer 1986-. **Orgs:** Mem 2012 CS Unit Adv Council 1984-85; assoc mem Pima Country Special Olympics Group 1985; sec Davis-Monthan Company Grade Officer GP 1985-86; founding mem Davis-Monthan Special Olympics GP 1985-86; mem Santas in Blue 1985-86; base chairperson Combined Federal Campaign 1985. **Military Serv:** USAF 1st lt 3 1/2 yrs; Air Force Commendation Medal 1985-86. **Home Addr:** 11991 Hitchcock Dr, Cincinnati, OH 45240.

PERSON, ROBERT ALAN
Professional baseball player. **Personal:** Born Oct 6, 1969, Lowell, MA. **Educ:** Seminole Junior College. **Career:** New York Mets, pitcher, 1995-96; Toronto Blue Jays, 1997-. **Business Addr:** Professional Baseball Player, Toronto Blue Jays, 300 Bremmer Blvd, Ste 3200, Toronto, ON, Canada M5V 3B3, (416)341-1000.

PERSON, WAVERLY J.
Geophysicist. **Personal:** Born May 1, 1926, Blackridge, VA; son of Bessie Butts Person and Santee Person; married Sarah Walker Person, Nov 6, 1954. **Educ:** St Paul's Coll, Lawrenceville VA, BS, 1949; American Univ, Washington DC, attended, 1959-60; George Washington Univ, Washington DC, attended, 1960-63. **Career:** Dept of Commerce, NOAA, Boulder CO, geophysicist, 1958-73; US Geological Survey, Denver & Golden CO, geophysicist, 1973-94, Natl Earthquake Information Ctr, director, 1994-. **Orgs:** Seismological Soc of Amer, 1965-, treasurer, Eastern Section, 1968-; past pres, Flatirons Kiwanis, 1972-; Amer Geophysical Union, 1975-; bd of dir, Boulder County Crimestoppers, 1986-. **Honors/Awds:** Honorary Doctorate, St Paul's Coll, 1988; Outstanding Govt Communicator, Natl Assn of Govt Communicators, 1988; Distinguished Alumni: Citation of the Year Award, Natl Assn for Equal Opportunity in Higher Educ, 1989; Meritorious Serv Award, USGS, 1989; many publications on earthquakes in scientific journals and contribution to a number of text books in the Earth Sciences. **Military Serv:** US Army, 1st Sergeant, 1944-46, 1951-52; Good Conduct Medals, Asian Pacific Medal. **Home Addr:** 5489 Seneca Place, Boulder, CO 80303.

PERSON, WESLEY LAVON
Professional basketball player. **Personal:** Born Mar 28, 1971, Crenshaw, AL; married Lillian; children: Nykera, Wesley Jr. **Educ:** Auburn University. **Career:** Phoenix Suns, forward-guard, 1994-97; Cleveland Cavaliers, 1997-. **Honors/Awds:** NBA All-Rookie Second Team, 1995. **Business Addr:** Professional Basketball Player, Cleveland Cavaliers, One Center Ct, Cleveland, OH 44115-4001, (216)659-9100.

PERSON, WILLIAM ALFRED
Educator. **Personal:** Born Aug 29, 1945, Henderson, NC; married Juanita Dunn; children: William Alfred II; Wilton Antoine. **Educ:** Johnson C Smith University, BA, 1963-67; University of Georgia, MEd, 1972-73, EdD, 1973-77. **Career:** Wilkes City Board of Education, teacher, 1967-72; University of Georgia, Grad Asst/Admin Asst, 1973-77; Mississippi State Univ, asst prof, 1977-80, assoc professor, 1980-. **Orgs:** Treasurer, Phi Delta Kappa, 1982-83; vice pres, Phi Beta Sigma, 1982-83; president, Phi Beta Sigma, 1983-; bd of directors, Starkville Kiwanis Breakfast Club, 1984-. **Honors/Awds:** Two academic scholarships, 1963-65; Sigma Man of the Year, Phi Beta Sigma, 1979. **Home Addr:** PO Box 424, Starkville, MS 39759. **Business Addr:** Associate Professor, Mississippi State University, P O Box 6331, Mississippi State, MS 39762-6331.

PERSONS, W. RAY
Attorney, state official, educator. **Personal:** Born Jul 22, 1953, Talbottan, GA; son of Frances Crowell Persons and William Persons; married Wendy-Joy Mottley Persons, Sep 24, 1977; children: Conrad Ashley, April Maureen. **Educ:** OH State Univ, 1971-72; Armstrong State Coll, BS 1975; OH State Univ, JD 1978. **Career:** Armstrong State Coll, coll prof 1979-80; Natl Labor Rel Bd, attny 1980-82; Wells Braun Persons Law Firm, partner/owner 1982-; Cong Lindsay Thomas, legislative counsel; Arrington & Hollowell, PC, attorney l986-; Georgia State Univ College of Law, adjunct professor of litigation, 1989-; State of Georgia, special asst attorney general, 1989-. **Orgs:** State Bar of GA 1979-; treas Riceboro Comm Improvement Found 1982-83; gen counsel Congressional Black Assoc 1984-85; Fed Bar Assoc 1984-85, Leadership GA Foundation 1985-; Legal Advisor to Brook Glen Neighborhood Assn 1986-; Ohio State Univ Alumni Assn 1981-; Georgia Defense Lawyers Association; Lawyers Club of Atlanta; American Bar Association; Emory University Law School, Master Lamar Inn of Court; State Bar Disciplinary Board. **Honors/Awds:** Regents Scholar Armstrong State Coll 1973-75; Silver ''A'' Awd Armstrong State College 1975. **Special Achievements:** Co-author, Ohio Civil Rules Supplement, 1978. **Home Addr:** 5615 Silver Ridge Dr, Stone Mountain, GA 30087. **Business Addr:** Partner, Attorney, Arrington & Hollowell, PC, 191 Peachtree St NE, Ste 3550, Atlanta, GA 30303-1735.

PETERMAN, LEOTIS
Educational administration. **Personal:** Born Sep 19, 1934, Abbeville, AL; married Lucy Bell; children: Karen Yvette, Sharron Yvonne. **Educ:** AL State Univ, BS 1955; IN Univ, MS 1959; Univ of AL, Doctorate in Ed 1982. **Career:** Lemoyne-Owen Coll, registrar, bus mgr 1955-62; AL State Univ, asst to pres, bus mgr 1962-67, vice pres for admin 1967-75, budget dir, controller 1975-84, vice pres for bus & finance 1984-85; Fisk Univ, chief financial officer 1986-. **Orgs:** Pres Pan-Hellenic Council 1977-85; state dir Alpha Phi Alpha 1979-85; mem Phi Delta Kappa, Delta Pi Epsilon, Kappa Delta Pi, Montgomery United Way, YMCA, The Comm Council; past pres Alpha Phi Alpha; trustee bd mem & deacon First Baptist Church; mem Assoc of Supervision & Curriculum Develop, Natl Assoc of Coll & Univ Business Officers, First Baptist Capitol Hill Church. **Honors/Awds:** Dir of the Year Alpha Phi Alpha 1980. **Business Addr:** Chief Financial Officer, Fisk University, 1000 17th Avenue North, Nashville, TN 37208.

PETERMAN, PEGGY M.
Newspaper columnist, educator. **Personal:** Born Oct 6, 1936, Bessemer, AL; daughter of Annie M Townsend Mitchell and William P Mitchell; divorced; children: Frank W, John M. **Educ:** Howard Univ Sch of Lib Arts, BA 1958; Howard Univ of Law, LLB 1961. **Career:** White, Peterman & Sanderlin, legal secretary, 1963; St Petersburg Times, columnist/editorial writer, women's department, 1968-70, news/features dept, 1970-; St Petersburg Junior College, adjunct professor, intro to African-American history; St Petersburg Times, columnist/editorial writer, currently. **Orgs:** Delta Sigma Theta Sor, St Petersburg Chapter; Natl Assn of Black Journalists, 1980-. **Honors/Awds:** Comm Serv Award African People's Socialist Party; Meritorious Achievement Award 1988, Florida A & M Univ; Gwen Cherry Freedom Fighters Award, Heritage Foundation 1988; Woman of Achievement Award, St. Petersburg Links; fellow Multicultural Management Program, Univ of Missouri 1988; Speakers Bureau, Florida Endowment for the Humanities 1987-88; Lifetime Achievement Award, Natl Assn of Black Journalists 1989; Liberty Bell Award, St Petersburg Bar Assn, 1993; Humanitarian Award by the ML King Commemorative Committee and St Petersburg Links. **Home Addr:** 1015 28th Ave S, St Petersburg, FL 33705.

PETERS, AULANA LOUISE
Attorney. **Personal:** Born Nov 30, 1941, Shreveport, LA; married Bruce Franklin Peters. **Educ:** Notre Dame School for Girls, diploma 1959; College of New Rochelle, BA Philosophy 1963; Univ of S CA, JD 1973. **Career:** Publimondial Spa, secty/English corres 1963; Fibramianto Spa, secty/English corres 1963-64; Turkish Delegation to Org for Economic Coop and Develop, English corres 1965; Cabinet Braconnier AAA Translation Agency, translator/interpreter 1966; Organ for Economic Coop and Develop Scientific Rsch Div, admin asst 1966-67; Gibson Dunn & Crutcher, attorney 1973-84; US Securities and Exchange Comm, comm 1984-88; Gibson, Dunn & Crutcher, partner, 1988-. **Orgs:** Los Angeles Co Bar Assn, State of CA Bar Assn, Langston Hughes Assn; Black Women Lawyers Assn, Amer Bar Assoc; mem Univ of S CA Law Sch Law Alumni Assn; Council on Foreign Relations Inc NY; panelist Los Angeles Co Bar Assoc Law & Motion Bd 1980; panelist Los Angeles Co Bar Assoc sponsored prog entitled ''Bridging the Gap'' 1980; lecturer Rutter Group Prog entitled ''Successful Discovery in the Los Angeles Superior Court'' 1981; panelist Assoc of Bus Trial Lawyers Seminar on Unfair Competition Los Angeles 1982; Bd of Dirs: Mobil, Merrill Lynch, 3M, Northrop Grumman Corp. **Honors/Awds:** Natl Assoc of Bank Women Inc Washington Achiever Awd 1986. **Business Addr:** Partner, Gibson, Dunn & Crutcher, 333 S Grand Ave, Los Angeles, CA 90071-1504.

PETERS, BROCK G.
Actor, singer, producer. **Personal:** Born Jul 2, 1927, New York, NY; son of Alma A Norford Fisher and Sonny Peters; married Dolores Daniels, Jul 29, 1961; children: Lise. **Educ:** Univ of Chgo, 1944-46; City Coll NY, 1946-47; student of acting with various individuals. **Career:** Theatrical appearances include: Porgy & Bess 1943, South Pacific 1943, Anna Lucasta 1944-45, My Darlin' Aida 1952, Great White Hope 1970, Lost in the Stars 1974, numerous stock engagements; DePaur Inf Chorus, bass soloist 1947-50; films include: Carmen Jones 1954, Porgy & Bess 1959, To Kill a Mockingbird 1962, The L-Shaped Room 1963, The Daring Game, 1966, The Pawnbroker 1968, The Incident 1969, Black Girl, 1972, Slaughter II, 1976, Lost in the Stars 1975, Soylent Green 1977, Huckleberry Finn 1981; Star Trek IV, Abe Lincoln: Freedom Fighter, Ace High; producer, Five on the Black Hand Side 1973, This Far by Faith 1975; actor Roots II Next Gen, num TV guest appearances; PBS Network ''Voices of Our People'' actor & supervising producer. **Orgs:** Mem Actor's Equity, AFTRA, Screen Actors Guild, Amer Guild Variety Artists; chairman, Dance Theatre of Harlem; member, Writers Guild of America; member, National Academy of TV Arts and Sciences; founder and chmn Dance Theatre of Harlem, Free So Theatre, Third World Cinema, Media Forum; former chmn CA State Arts Comm; bd of trustees Dance Gallery of LA; founder/chmn Maga Link Inc and Communications Bridge Inst; commnr CA State Film Commn. **Honors/Awds:** All Amer Press Assn Awd; Box Office Blue Ribbon Awd; Allen & AME Awd; Amer Soc African Culture Emancipation Awd 1962; Man of the Year Douglas Jr HS 1964; Golden Globe Awd 1970; Drama Desk Awd 1972; Outer Circle Critics Awd 1972; Tony Nomination 1973; Best Actor Mar del Plata Film Fest 1974; Neil Smith Awd S Afr Film Fest 1974; Hon Docts Sienna Hgts Fine Arts Coll Univ of MI, Otter Beia Coll 1975, 1978; inducted Black Filmmakers Hall of Fame 1976; Life Achievement Awd Natl Film Soc 1977; Image Awd NAACP 1979, 1982, 1987; Emmy Awd 1982; Life Achievement Award, Screen Actors Guild, 1990; Distinguished Achievement, LA Drama Critics Circle, 1990; Theater Award, NAACP, 1990.

PETERS, CHARLES L., JR.
Real estate developer, business executive. **Personal:** Born Sep 20, 1935, New Orleans; married Doris Jackson; children: Leslie Jean, Cheryl Lynne. **Educ:** So Univ, BS (cum laude) 1955; USC, MS 1959, grad study. **Career:** Natl Housing Consult Inc, pres ch bd 1973-; NHC Data Services, President/CEO. **Orgs:** Mem Omega Psi Phi; LA Urban League; YMCA; Natl Assn of Housing & Redev Officials, Omega Life Membership Foundation, comptroller. **Honors/Awds:** Natl Assn of Homebuilders Man of Yr Omega Psi Phi 1964, 1974, 1983; Outstanding Educator LA City Cncl 1970. **Military Serv:** US Army, capt 1955-67. **Business Addr:** President, Natl Housing Consult Inc, 4640 Lankershim Blvd, Ste 202, North Hollywood, CA 91602.

PETERS, ERSKINE ALVIN
Educator. **Personal:** Born Mar 16, 1948, Augusta, GA; son of Marie Johnson Peters and George Raymond Peters Sr. **Educ:** Yale Univ, summer study 1968; Paine Coll, BA English 1969; Oberlin Coll, Post-baccalaureate study 1969-70; Princeton Univ, PhD English 1976; Sorbonne Paris, summer study 1984. **Career:** Morristown Coll, tutor 1970-72; Univ of CA Berkeley, assoc prof of Afro-Amer Literature; Univ of Notre Dame, prof of English, currently. **Orgs:** Advisor Oakland Scholar Achiever Program 1980-82; discussion leader SATE Program at San Quentin Prison 1980-83. **Honors/Awds:** First Recipient of Frank J Henry Award, Univ of GA 1968; Rockefeller Fellowship in Afro-Amer Studies 1972-76; Books, William Faulkner, The Yoknapatawpha World and Black Being 1983, African Openings to the Tree of Life 1983, Fundamentals of Essay Writing 1983. **Business Addr:** Professor of English, Univ of Notre Dame, Notre Dame, IN 46556.

PETERS, FENTON
Educational administrator. **Personal:** Born Jul 10, 1935, Starkville, MS; son of Cora Gandy Peters and Pellum Peters; married Maggie Teresa Malone; children: Avis Campbell Wilcox, Pellum, Alton. **Educ:** Rust Coll, AB 1958; MS State Univ, MEd 1969, Ed D 1983. **Career:** Henderson HS, principal 1968-70; Henderson Jr HS, principal 1970-76; Starkville HS, principal 1976-81; Starkville Public Schools, chap 1 coord 1981-84, admin asst to supt; Holly Springs Public Schools, superintendent, 1986-92; Christ Missionary and Industrial School, principal, currently. **Orgs:** Presenter Student Teaching MS St Univ 1978; presenter Continuing Educ MS St Univ 1979; bd of dirs Starkville Chamber of Comm 1983-84; bd of trustees Oktibbeha Co Hosp 1984-; state choir dir, Church of Christ, 1983; bd of dir Holly Springs Chamber of Commerce 1988-89; State Supts Comm of 12, State Superintendent of Education, 1987-88; Arts in Education Task Force, MS Arts Comm, 1991; Phi Delta Kappa. **Honors/Awds:** Natl Science Found science fellowship 1962, 1962-63, 1967; Public Serv Awd United Way 1985; Presidential Citation, Natl Assn for Equal Opportunity in Educ, 1987. **Home Addr:** Route 6, Box 82, Starkville, MS 39759.

PETERS, JAMES SEDALIA, II
Educator, psychologist. **Personal:** Born in Ashdown, AR; son of Ardell Duckett Merritt and Walter Lee Jack Peters; married Marie Ferguson Peters, Jun 25, 1942 (deceased); children: James S III, Donna Marie, Kimberly C Bourne-Vanneck. **Educ:** Southern Univ Baton Rouge, BS; Hartford Seminary Found, MA; IL Inst of Tech, MS; Purdue Univ, PhD. **Career:** US Naval Training Ctr Great Lakes IL, tchr psychologist 1942-45; Veterans Adminstration, clinical & counseling psychologist 1946-55; Springfield Coll, dir asst prof of psychology 1955-56; Div of Vocational Rehab CT, administrator 1956-81; Univ of Hartford, adjunct prof; private practice, psychologist. **Orgs:** Dir New England Bank & Trust Co 1968-; dir Amer Automobile

Assn 1970-; mem Alpha Phi Alpha Frat, Society for Sigma Xi, Sigma Pi Phi Frat, Episcopal Church. **Honors/Awds:** TH Harris Fellowship Southern Univ; Genl Educ Atlanta Univ; Veterans Admin Fellow Purdue Univ; Dept of Health Educ & Welfare Harvard Univ. **Military Serv:** USN specialist tchr 1st class 1942-45. **Home Addr:** PO Box 431, Storrs, CT 06268.

PETERS, KENNETH DARRYL, SR.
Government official. **Personal:** Born Jan 27, 1949, Englewood, NJ; son of Lena Jones Peters and John C Peters, Jr; married Katie Coleman, Nov 27, 1976; children: Kenneth Jr, Kevin. **Educ:** Fisk Univ, BA 1967-71; Univ of KS, MSW 1971-73; Univ of CA, Cert 1973; Acad of Health Sci Ft Sam Houston, Cert 1981. **Career:** Catholic Social Svc, school consult 1973-78; State of CA Stockton, psychiatric soc worker 1978-80; State of CA Sacramento, soc serv consult 1980-84, program analyst 1984, soc serv admin; California Department of Transportation, district contracts officer; California Dept of Health Services, health trainer, currently. **Orgs:** Bd of dir Fisk Student Enterprises 1968; vice pres NAACP-Collegiate Chapter Nashville 1968-69; minority recruitment comm Univ of KS 1971-72; mem San Joaquin Mental Health Advisory Bd 1978-88; bd of dir Maternal & Child Health Disability Prevention Bd 1979-86; sec Alpha Phi Alpha Frat Inc 1980; mem Natl Conf on Social Welfare 1982-88, CA Respiratory Examining Bd 1983-92. **Honors/Awds:** Dean's List Univ of KS 1972-73; Acad Honors Spanish Fisk Univ 1968; Eligible Bachelor Ebony Mag 1975; Commendation CA Assemblyman Pat Johnston 1983, CA Senator John Garamendi 1983. **Military Serv:** US Army Reserves, lt col, 1979-; Appt Asst Detach Cmdr 1982; Commend for Combat Environ Transition Training 1983; Appt Annual Training Module Officer in Charge 1985, participated in Team Spirit '86 in Republic of Korea; Mobilization Officer for 6253d US Army Hospital, Santa Rosa, CA, 1994-. **Home Addr:** 2911 Sleepy Hollow Dr, Stockton, CA 95209, (209)475-0199. **Business Addr:** California Department of Health Services, 830 S St, Sacramento, CA 95814, (916)327-3245.

PETERS, PAMELA JOAN
Business owner. **Personal:** Born Feb 3, 1947, York, PA; daughter of Maurice E & Ruth V Peters. **Educ:** Tennessee State Univ, BA, 1969; Southern Illinois Univ, MSCED, 1975; Walden Univ, PhD, 1992. **Career:** Pan American World Airlines, airline stewardess, 1969-70; Delaware State Coll, director of student activities, 1970-74; Johnson & Johnson Corp, compensation admin, supv of traffic, 1974-76; Xerox Corp, personnel rep, 1976-78; ICI Americas, Inc, recruiter, eeo analyst, 1979-84; Univ of Delaware, dir of cooperative ed, 1984-86; Center for Stress, Pain, and Wellness, Mgmt, Inc, president, 1986-. **Orgs:** Founding member, Brandywine Professional Assoc, chair, program, nomination committees, 1981; Wilmington Women in Business, 1980; Mental Health Assoc, board member, 1988; Delaware Guidance Assoc, 1986-87; Civil Rights Commission, 1985-86; Girl Scouts of America, board of dir, 1984-86; YMCA, board of dir, exec, comm, chair personnel comm, search comm, 1982-84; Forum for Minority Engineers, chairperson, 1981-83; Delta Sigma Theta, lifetime member. **Honors/Awds:** Brandywine Professional Org, outstanding service, 1990; Sigma Rho Sigma Honor Society, national sec, 1968-69; West York Area High School, outstanding athlete of the year, 1965. **Special Achievements:** Dissertations, Lifestyle Changes of Selected Therapeutic Touch Practitioners, an Oral History; Papers, copyright, Prevention & Treatment Using Alternative Therapies for Injuries and Stress, Sports and Socialization of Youth into Health and Wellness; Published Article, Pregnancy/Childbirth, Therapeutic Insight; Author: My Hands: My Feet: standing out, My Heart: Loving Enough to Let Go, 1996. **Home Addr:** 315 W 36th street, Wilmington, DE 19802. **Business Phone:** (302)654-1840.

PETERS, ROSCOE HOFFMAN, JR.
Automobile dealer. **Personal:** Born Mar 3, 1945, Charleston, WV; son of Elenora Victoria Lindsay-Peters and Roscoe Hoffman Peters; married Sandra L Phillips-Peters, Jul 16, 1994; children: Roscoe H III, Carrie Jeaninne. **Educ:** General Motors Inst, attended 1973. **Career:** IBM Corp, customer engr 1968-72; Chevrolet Motor Div, zone serv mgr 1972-82; RH Peters Chevrolet, pres 1982-. **Orgs:** Owner Peters Fuel 1976-; president Peters Realty 1980-; Peters Broadcasting, dir of eng, 1984-94. **Military Serv:** USAF staff sgt 4 yrs active, 3 yrs reserves; Airman Medal for Valor, 1967. **Home Addr:** 100 Brierwood Estates, Hurricane, WV 25526. **Business Addr:** President, RH Peters Chevrolet, Inc, 102 Orchard Park Rd, Hurricane, WV 25526.

PETERS, SAMUEL A.
Attorney. **Personal:** Born Oct 25, 1934, New York, NY; son of Amy Matterson and Clyde Peters; married Ruby M Mitchell; children: Robert, Samuel Jr, Bernard. **Educ:** New York Univ, BA 1955; Fordham Univ Sch of Law, LLB 1961. **Career:** Federal Communications Comm, law clerk 1961; Lawyer's Comm for Civil Rights Under Law, staff atty 1968-69; US Dept of Justice, trial atty 1961-68; Atlantic Richfield Co, employee relations counsel 1970-85, sr counsel public affairs; Rio Hondo Coll, professor of law; private practice, attorney, 1986-. **Orgs:** National Bar Assn; American Bar Assn; Fordham Law Review Alumni Assn; CA Museum of Afro-American History & Culture; NAACP OC Chapt; bd of dirs Weingart Ctr Assoc; Central City East (Los Angeles) Task Force; Alpha Phi Alpha Fraternity, Nu Tau Lambda Chapter, treas; Toastmasters International Club #1391; board of directors, Women's Transitional Living Center. **Military Serv:** US Army, sp-2, 3 yrs. **Home Addr:** 11471 Kensington Rd, Los Alamitos, CA 90720. **Business Addr:** Attorney, 11471 Kensington Rd, Los Alamitos, CA 90720.

PETERS, SHEILA RENEE
Psychologist. **Personal:** Born Jun 27, 1959, Columbus, MS; daughter of Anne Glover Peters and Dr James Calvin Peters Sr; divorced. **Educ:** Univ of NC at Chapel Hill, BA (w/Honors in Psychology) 1981; Vanderbilt Univ, MS 1985, PhD, 1989. **Career:** Luton Community Mental Health Ctr, dept of psychology/human develop doctoral candidate in clinical psychology prog, clinical therapist; coordinator, community services, Meharry Medical Coll, "I Have A Future" teenage pregnancy prevention program, partner; Greene, Peters & Assoc, clinial & consulting psychology program, partner, currently. **Orgs:** Pres Org of Black Grad & Professional Students 1982-85; steering comm 1983 Eco-Psychology Conf 1982-83; dir of youth ministries Key-Stewart UM Church 1983-87; treas Assoc of Black Psychologists 1984-85; mem Div of Psychology of Women 1984-87, Div of Comm Psychology 1984-87, Southeastern Psychological Assoc 1986-87, Nashville Alum Chap of Delta Sigma Theta 1986-87; tres, Nashville Assn of Black Psychologist, 1989-; nominations chairperson, TN Conference of United Methodist Women, 1989; dir, Youth Ministries Ernest Newman UM Church, 1988-91; bd mem, Wesley Foundation, district trustee, UM Church. **Honors/Awds:** Outstanding Young Woman of Amer 1981; Peabody Minority Fellowship Vanderbilt 1981-84; Crusade Scholarship Bd of Global Ministries 1982-85; NIMH Traineeship 1984-85. **Home Addr:** 4224 Kings Ct, Nashville, TN 37218.

PETERS, WILLIAM ALFRED
Manager. **Personal:** Born Mar 1, 1940, Atlantic City, NJ. **Educ:** Temple Univ, BS 1963; Pace Univ, MBA 1978. **Career:** Fortune Circulation Time Inc, natl sales dir 1979-; Fortune Mag Time Inc, asst circulation dir 1978-79; Time Inc, dir of edn; Emerson Hall Pub, vpof mrkt 1970-72; Harper & Row Pub, editor 1968-70, mrkt & rep 1976-80. **Honors/Awds:** Recipt Black Achgievers in Industry Award Harlem Br YMCA 1978. **Business Addr:** Time Inc, 1271 Sixth Ave, New York, NY 10020.

PETERSEN, ALLAN ERNEST
Manager (retired). **Personal:** Born Dec 13, 1918, New York, NY; married Florence Ridley; children: Robert. **Educ:** W Hervey Bus Coll, AD 1952; City Coll of NY, 1954. **Career:** NY State Div of Unemployment Ins, supv 1946-52; Our World Mag, bus mgr 1952-54; Distilled Brands, sales rep, sales mgr 1954-78; Gotham Merchants Div of Peerless Importers, general sales mgr 1987. **Orgs:** Mem NAACP; Urban Leg; Bottle & Cork Sales Club; Nat Negro Golf Assn. **Honors/Awds:** AUS 1st lt 1941-45.

PETERSEN, ARTHUR EVERETT, JR.
Business development consultant. **Personal:** Born Feb 5, 1949, Baltimore, MD; son of Marguerite Petersen and Arthur E. Petersen, Sr. **Educ:** Comm Coll of Baltimore, AA 1971; Morgan State Univ, BA 1973; Atlanta Univ, MBA 1975. **Career:** Transportation Inst NC A&T State Univ, rsch assoc 1975-77; Exec Office of Transportation & Construction, sr planner 1977-79; Simpson & Curtin, Inc, consultant 1979-80; Lawrence Johnson & Assoc, rsch assoc 1980-82; Ctr for Transportation Studies, Morgan State Univ, project dir 1982-83; Public Tech projectmgr 1983-88; Baltimore Minority Business Develop Ctr, procurement specialist 1986-86; Associated Enterprises, Inc Consultant 1988-89; Boone, Young & Assoc Inc, Baltimore Minority Business Development Center, Management Services, director 1989-91, 1991-92, executive director; John Milligan & Associates, PC, Baltimore Minority Business Development Center, executive director, 1992-93; David J. Burgos and Associates, Washington, DC, Minority Business Development Center, business development specialist, 1994-96; Council for Economic and Business Opportunity Inc, director, contract procurement services, 1996-. **Orgs:** Mem Conf of Minority Transp Officials Transp Rsch Board, Natl Forum for Black Public Admin, Baltimore Marketing Assoc. **Business Addr:** Director, Contract Procurement Services, Council for Economic and Business Opportunity Inc, 800 N Charles St, Ste 300, Baltimore, MD 21201.

PETERSEN, EILEEN RAMONA
Judge. **Personal:** Born Apr 18, 1937, Christiansted, St Croix, Virgin Islands of the United States; daughter of Anna Leevy and Hugo R Petersen. **Educ:** Hampton Inst, BS 1958, MA 1959; Howard Univ, JD 1966; Geo Wash Univ, Advanced Studies MA 1970. **Career:** Territorial Court of the VI, judge, currently. **Orgs:** Mem VI, Natl, Wash DC, Amer Bar Assocs 1967-; Natl Assoc of Women Judges, mem; Amer Judges Assoc, mem; World Assoc of Judges of the World Through Peace Law Ctr, mem; League of Womens Voters & Bus and Professional Women's Club, mem; VI Cncl of Boy Scouts of Amer, cncl mem; VI Girl Scouts of Amer, board mem 1982-85. **Honors/Awds:** William Hastie Awd Natl Bar Assoc 1982; Women of the Yr Business & Professional Women's Club 1976; Outstanding Woman of the Yr Howard Univ 1970; Alpha Kappa Alpha Sorority, Inc 1970. **Business Addr:** Judge, Territorial Court of the VI, RFD 2 Box 9000, Kingshill, St Croix, Virgin Islands of the United States 00850.

PETERSEN, FRANK EMMANUEL, JR.
Corporate executive. **Personal:** Born Mar 2, 1932, Topeka, KS; son of Edith Sutthard Petersen and Frank Emmanuel Petersen; divorced; children: Gayle, Dana, Frank III, Lindsey, Monique. **Educ:** George Washington University, BS, 1967, MS, 1973. **Career:** US Navy, 1950-52, US Marine Corps, 1952-88, senior ranking pilot, US Navy & US Marine Corps, 1985-88, US Armed Forces, senior pilot, 1986-88; Du Pont, vp, 1989-. **Orgs:** Tuskegee Airmen, 1960-; National Bone Marrow Foundation, vice chair, board of directors, 1988-; Higher Education Assistance Foundation, board of directors, 1989-; Opportunity Skyway, vp, 1990-; Institute for the Study of American Wars, board of directors, 1990-93; National Aviation Research and Education Foundation, board of directors, 1990-92; Montford Pt Marines, 1960-; Business Executives for National Security, 1991-. **Honors/Awds:** Virginia Union University, Honorary Doctorate of Law, 1987; George Washington University, Distinguished Graduate, 1986; NAACP, Man of the Year. **Special Achievements:** First African-American pilot in US Marine Corps, 1952; first African-American general in US Marine Corps, 1978. **Military Serv:** US Navy, 1950-52, US Marine Corps, 1952-88, lt gen, US Marine Corps, 1986-88; 20 individual medals for Combat Valor. **Business Addr:** VP, Du Pont, New Castle County Airport, 199 N DuPont Hwy, New Castle, DE 19720, (302)996-8025.

PETERSON, ALAN HERBERT
Association executive. **Personal:** Born Jul 9, 1948, East Orange, NJ; son of Evelyn Lucretia Hughes Peterson and William Willis Peterson (deceased); married Michelle Monica Morrison Peterson, Sep 27, 1986. **Educ:** Central TX Coll, Criminal Invest Cert 1970; LaSalle Law School, Cert 1971; Essex Co Police Acad, 1971-72; Bergen Co Police Acad, Cert 1978; Law Enforcement Officers Training Sch, Cert 1979; Doctor of Divinity 1985; Natl Inst for the Study of Satanology, Las Vegas, NV, certificate, 1990. **Career:** Rutgers Univ Police Dept, police officer 1971-72; East Orange NJ Aux Police, patrolman 1972-; Essex Co Sheriff's Dept NJ, spec deputy 1972-75; Modern Carpet Serv NJ, vice pres 1972-75; Conrail Police Dept, police officer/investigator 1975-85; Survival Assn, pres, ceo 1975-; Masters of Philanthropy, CEO 1982-; Suicide Prevention Group PA, exec dir, suicidologist 1985-; ordained minister 1985-; Law Enforcement Special Agent, Law Enforcement Div, NJ Soc for the Prevention of Cruelty to Animals 1988-; USCCCN National Clearinghouse on Satanic Crime in America, natl executive dir, 1988-; Montgomery County Constable's Office, Precinct 2, ritual crime investigator, 1990-. **Orgs:** NJ Narcotic Enf Officers Assn NJ 1976-; 1st black So NJ Police Invest for Conrail Police Cmtr Div 1978; Amer Criminal Justice Assn 1979-, Police Benev Assn NJ #304 1982-, Natl Disabled Law Officers Assn NJ 1983-; 1st black bd mem, vp, chmn of the bd Make A Wish Found NJ 1983-86; Candlelighters Fnd DC 1984-; 1st blk sec 1984, 1st blk pres 1985 NJ Law Enf Lions Club; Texas Narcotic Officers Assn, 1991-; Texas Ritualistic Crime Information Network, 1991-; Natl Assn of Black Achievers, 1990-; natl pres, Natl Police Officers' Assn of America, 1991-; Intl Narcotic Enforcement Officers Assn, 1990-; Natl Organization of Black Law Enforcement Executives, 1991-. **Honors/Awds:** First black Heroism Commendation Recipient from Conrail Police Dept for heroic actions during Jan 7, 1983 Texaco Oil Co explosion 1984; Citation for Bravery Natl Police Ofcrs Assn of Am, Louisville, KY 1985; Veterans Admin, Leadership Award 1985, Voluntary Serv Award 1985; Jerseyan of the Week, Newark, NJ Star Ledger, as result of receipt of Citation for Bravery; Cert of Appreciation Southern NJ Region of Hadassah; Outstanding Community Service Award, Intl Youth Org, 1988; author: American Focus on Satanic Crime - Volume 1, 1988, Volume 2, 1990, Volume 3, 1991; Satanic Crime and the SPCA, 1988; Certificate of Merit, Natl Police Officers' Assn of America, 1989; coproducer, Satanism in Prisons - Video Volume 1; coproducer, Exorcism - Video Volume 1; foreword contributor, The Christian Apach to Spiritual Warfare by Rev Frank M Brim. **Military Serv:** US Army, 1967-70; Vietnam Campaign Medal, Vietnam Service Medal; Good Conduct Medal. **Home Addr:** PO Box 403, Chatham Road, Short Hills, NJ 07078. **Business Addr:** National Executive Director, USCCCN National Clearinghouse on Satanic Crime in America, PO Box 1092 - National Headquarters, South Orange, NJ 07079.

PETERSON, ALPHONSE
Dentist, dental educator. **Personal:** Born Sep 9, 1926, St Louis, MO; son of Pearl Peterson and Alphonse H Peterson; married Jessie Clark; children: Alphonse Jr, Alan, Alex. **Educ:** Howard Univ, Washington DC, BS 1948; Meharry Med Coll, School of Dentistry, Nashville TN, DDS 1954; Royal Soc of Health, England, DDS 1954; postgraduate study, Northwestern Univ Dental School 1961, State Univ of Iowa 1963, St Louis Univ 1965, Washington Univ School of Dentistry 1969, Univ of Nebraska Medical Center 1971, Harvard Univ 1971, Armed Forces Inst of Pathology 1972. **Career:** Gen practice dentist, 1957-; Washington Univ School of Dental Medicine, St Louis MO, assoc prof of oral diagnosis and radiology, 1972-84; Homer G Phillips

Hospital and Ambulatory Center, St Louis MO, asst chief, dept of oral surgery, and dir of cardiopulmonary resuscitation educ, 1973-85; Meharry Medical College, School of Dentistry, Nashville TN, assoc prof, adjunct prof, 1981-. **Orgs:** Sec-treas, Guam Dental Soc, 1956-57; pres, Amer Acad Dental Electrosurgery, 1977; mem, pres 1983, Downtown St Louis Lions Club; mem, Kappa Alpha Psi Frat; mem, Pleasant Green Missionary Baptist Church; mem, Chi Delta Mu Medical-Dental Fraternity; mem, 33rd Degree Prince Hall Free Masons; mem Medinah Temple #39 AEAONMS; bd dir, Ferrier Harris Home for the Aged; bd dir St Louis Branch of the Opportunities Industrialization Center. **Honors/Awds:** Selected to represent the US at the Third Kenyan-Amer Dental Seminar, Nairobi, Kenya, 1973; elected Fellow, Royal Soc of Health, England, 1972; published ''Diagnostic Electrosurgery, To Rule In or Out Malignacy of Oral Tissues,'' Quintessence Intl-Dental Digest, 1977, and ''The Use of Electrosurgery in Reconstructive and Cosmetic Maxillofacial Surgery,'' Dental Clinics of North Amer, 1982; mem Kappa Sigma Pi Scholastic Hon Frat; mem Gamma Chap, Omicron Kappa Upsilon Natl Dental Hon Soc; lectr ''The Use of Electrosurgery in Reconstructive Surgery of the Tongue, Lip, Ear and Nose,'' 66th Annual World Dental Congress of Federation Dentaire Internationale, Madrid Spain, 1978; author, Electrosurgical Correction of Maxillary Double Lip, Dental Digest, 1972; Fellow, Royal Society of Health, England, 1972; Fellow, American Academy of Dental Electrosurgery, 1989; lecture, The Use of Electrosurgery in Diagnostic & Reconstructive of the Lip, First International Dental Congress of the Egyptian Clinical Dental Society, Cairo, 1984; Inducted, Hall of Fame, Charles Summer High School, 1995. **Special Achievements:** Elected Fellow, American Academy of Dental Rlectrosurgery, 1989; Elected Fellow, American College of Dentists, 1991. **Military Serv:** US Air Force, oral surgery resident, capt, 1955-57, chief of oral surgery, major, 1970-72. **Business Addr:** 3737 N Kingshighway Blvd, Saint Louis, MO 63115.

PETERSON, AUDREY CLINTON
Government official (retired). **Personal:** Born Feb 16, 1917, Lancaster, SC; daughter of Emily Jackson Clinton and John J Clinton; married James C Peterson, Jan 1952 (died 1958); children: Sushila J. **Educ:** South Carolina State College, Orangeburg, SC, BS Ed, 1939; Atlanta University, Atlanta, GA, MA, 1943; Chicago University, Chicago, IL, 1945. **Career:** DC Public School System, Washington, DC, teacher/school attendance officer, 1948-52, 1958-69; US State Dept, Washington, DC, diplomatic wife, 1952-58; Walter Reed Army Medical Center, Washington, DC, EEO officer, 1969-74. **Orgs:** Member, American Wives Club, 1952-58; member, American University Women's Club, 1952-; member, Alpha Kappa Alpha Sorority, 1982-; member, National Teachers Association, 1948-52; member, National Association of Federal Retired Employees, 1974-; member, American Association of Retired People, 1974-. **Home Addr:** 3816 Eighth Street, NW, Washington, DC 20011.

PETERSON, CARL M.
Surgeon. **Personal:** Born Jun 5, 1914, Opelika, AL; son of Carrie Belle Prince Peterson (deceased) and William L Peterson Sr (deceased); married Hulda P Hayward, Aug 3, 1942; children: Carl M, Louis H. **Educ:** Morehouse Coll, AB 1937; Meharry Med Coll, MD 1941; KC Gen Hosp, resident 1946-49. **Career:** The Doctors Clinic KC MO, founding partner, surgeon. **Orgs:** Diplomate Am Bd Surgery 1953; fellow Am Coll of Surgeons 1956; fellow Intl Coll of Surgeons 1956; fellow SW Surgical Congr 1968; pres Jackson Co Med Soc 1972; pres KC Surgical Soc 1973-74; pres Truman Med Ctr West Med Dentl Stf 1975; bd Trustees KC Blue Shld 1975; life NAACP 1963; curator Lincoln Univ 1960-66; commr Urban Renewal Bd of KC 1967-72; Urban Leg Bd KC 1960; chmn Citizens Assn 1968; elder United Presby Ch USA. **Military Serv:** US Army Medical Corps, maj med corps 1942-46. **Home Addr:** 5200 Spruce Ave, Kansas City, MO 64130.

PETERSON, CLARENCE JOSEPHUS
Labor representative. **Personal:** Born Sep 18, 1932, Stubenville, OH; married Diane Gladys Johnson; children: Robin Whitaker, Dana W Scott, Phillip P Scott, Marla J Peterson. **Educ:** Findlay HS, grad 1951. **Career:** City of Jamestown, council at large 1971-75; Cty of Chautauqua 1976-79; Jamestown Com Coll, bd of trustees 1981-; IAMAW Dist 65, bus rep. **Orgs:** Mem United Way Planning Council Chautaugua Cty 1982-, Full Gospel Bus Men's Org 1983-. **Home Addr:** 33 W 18th St, Jamestown, NY 14701.

PETERSON, COLEMAN HOLLIS
Company executive. **Personal:** Born Apr 6, 1948, Birmingham, AL; son of George and Doris; married Shirley, May 31, 1975; children: Rana, Collin. **Educ:** Loyola University, BA, 1972, MS, 1977. **Career:** Venture Stores, district personnel manager, 1978-79, regional personnel manager, 1979-82, vice president, Organizational Development, 1982-84, senior vice president, Human Resources, 1984-94; Wal-Mart Stores Inc, senior vice president, people division, 1994-. **Orgs:** Kappa Alpha Psi Fraternity; Sigma Pi Phi Fraternity; mem advisory boards, Univ of Fl, Florida A & M Univ. **Honors/Awds:** Natl Academy of Human Resources, Fellow. **Business Addr:** Sr Vice Pres, People Division, Wal-Mart Stores Inc, 702 Southwest 8th St, Bentonville, AR 72716-9032.

PETERSON, GERARD M.
City official. **Personal:** Born Sep 10, 1932, Hartford, CT; son of Edythe Peterson and Rufus Peterson; divorced; children: Brian, Bradford. **Educ:** Univ CT, BA 1957; Cert Data Processing 1965. **Career:** Aetna Life & Casualty, adm roles 1957-69, dir mktg 1974-83; OUR Corp, pres 1969-72; Natl Alliance Businessmen, exec vice pres 1969-70; Stanford U, asst dean grad sch bus 1970-73; Star Lite Industries, dir 1970-71; Hartford Civic Center, CEO, exec dir 1983-93; Johnson Controls Inc, project mgr, 1995-. **Orgs:** Mem Alpha Phi Alpha, NAACP, Urban League, Intl Assoc of Auditorium Mgrs; vchmn Greater Hartford Red Cross; dir, trustee Hartford Club, Hartford Hospital, St Francis Hospital, Kaisen Permanente, St Joseph Coll; Bay Bank Connecticut. **Honors/Awds:** Arena and Mgr of the Year Performance Mag Readers Poll 1986. **Military Serv:** AUS corpl 1953-55. **Business Addr:** Project Mgr, Johnson Controls, 150 Trumbull Street, Hartford, CT 06103.

PETERSON, HARRY W.
Business executive. **Personal:** Born May 13, 1923, Chanute, KS; son of Bertha Peterson and Harry Peterson; married Kathryn Elizabeth Boggs (divorced); children: Donna (Waller), Jerry Ronnell. **Career:** Lincoln Police Dept, 1956-66; King's Food Host USA Inc, 1966; dir, Motor Vehicles, NE, 1979-83. **Orgs:** Mem bd dir Lincoln General Hospital; chmn Human Rights Comm Lincoln 1962; Advisory Comm Head Start 1967; St Selection Comm Natl ROTC Scholrships 1970; dir Nebraska Red Cross bd; mem City Council 1969-73; v chmn 1971-73; mem Volunteers in Probation; NE Citizens Advisory Alcoholism Chcl; pres mem bd trustees NE Human Resources 1973; mem Chamber of Commerce; mason; Kiwanis; squires; Methodist Church. **Honors/Awds:** Outstanding Public Serv Award 1970, Kiwanis Club; Good Govt Award 1972, Lincoln JC'S. **Military Serv:** AUS 1943-46. **Home Addr:** 8601 NE Highway 6, Lincoln, NE 68507.

PETERSON, LLOYD, JR.
Educational administrator. **Personal:** Born Jul 20, 1958, San Antonio, TX. **Educ:** CO State Univ, BA English 1980, M Higher Educ 1982. **Career:** CO State Univ, admissions counselor 1982-83; CO College, asst dir/admissions; Yale University, assoc dir/admissions; Vassar College, director of admissions, currently. **Orgs:** Bd dirs Jolly Jills Civic and Social Club 1983-; 1st vice pres El Paso County Black Caucus 1984-86; bd dirs Urban League of Colorado Springs 1984-. **Honors/Awds:** Mem Outstanding Young Men of America 1983; guest instructor College Board Summer Admission Inst 1986. **Business Addr:** Director, Admissions, Vassar College, Poughkeepsie, NY 12601.

PETERSON, LORNA INGRID
Librarian. **Personal:** Born Jul 22, 1956, Buffalo, NY; daughter of Sybil Odette Lythcott Peterson and Raymond George Peterson. **Educ:** Dickinson College, Carlisle, PA, BA, 1977; Case Western Reserve Univ, Cleveland, OH, MS library science, 1980; Iowa State University, PhD, 1992. **Career:** Wright State University, Dayton, OH, humanities reference librarian/special college cataloger, 1980-81; Ohio University, Athens, OH, special college cataloger, 1982-82; Iowa State University, Ames, IA, cataloger, 1983-85, bibliographic instructor, 1985-91; SUNY-Buffalo, Buffalo, NY, assistant professor, assoc, prof, currently. **Orgs:** Board member, Ames, ISU YWCA, 1984-89; chair communications committee, Iowa Library Assn/ACRL, 1984-86; chair membership committee, Iowa Library Assn/ACRL, 1987-88; representative to ALA/RTSD Org & Bylaws, American Library Assn, 1984-86; member, Black Caucus of ALA, 1980, 1988-; African American Librarian Assn of Western New York, 1990-; ALA-Lirt Research Committee, 1994-96; ALA-ACRL/BIS, Education for Bibliographic Instruction, 1994-96; ALA-RASD/MOPSS, Catalog Use Committee, 1992-96; Committee on Accreditation, 1997-2001. **Business Addr:** Associate Professor, School of Information and Library Studies, State University of New York at Buffalo, 534 Baldy Hall, Buffalo, NY 14260.

PETERSON, MARCELLA TANDY
Educator. **Personal:** Born in Detroit, MI; married Harvey Hughes Peterson. **Educ:** Wayne St Univ, BS 1949, DEd 1973; Univ of MI, MA 1955; Univ of Chicago; MI State Univ; Merrill-Palmer; Univ of Detroit; Trinity Coll; George Washington Univ, Paralegal certificate 1983. **Career:** Detroit Bd of Educ, reg asst supt; Detroit Public School, teacher; Miller Jr HS, counselor; Condon Jr HS, asst principal; Noble Jr HS, principal; Delta Sigma Theta Sorority Inc, exec dir. **Orgs:** Mem, Detroit Home Econ Assn 1949-57; et Guidance Assn 1957-61, Detroit Counselors' Assn 1957-61; chmn bd Delta Home for Girls 1957-58; mem Detroit Asst Principals' Assn 1961-63; Negotiating Team Org of School Admin & Supvr 1969, 1971, 1973; Detroit Women Admins; Phi Upsilon Omicron Fraternity, 1949-57; Delta Kappa Gamme Soc; Beta Sigma Phi Fellow; MI Assn for Supvr & Curriculum Devel; Amer Assn of Univ Women; Natl Council of Admin; Women in Educ; pres Detroit Principals' Assn 1965-66; Defense Advisory Comm on Women in the Serv 1967-70; sec Org of School Admins & Supvrs 1972-75; chmn Residence Com YMCA Bd of Mgmt Downtown Branch 1972-73; mem bd of dirs St Mary Cou 1985-86; mem bd of governors Women's Natl Democratic Comm 1987-; mem Washington Comm ABetter Chance; mem, Governing Bd Women-Natl Democratic Club, 1987-89.

PETERSON, MICHELLE MONICA
Association executive. **Personal:** Born Oct 21, 1959, Newark, NJ; daughter of Christine Hall Morrison and Alvin Morrison; married Alan H Peterson, Sep 27, 1986. **Career:** Ward Baking Company, CRT operator, 1977-80; First Natl State Bank, direct deposit administrator, 1980-81; Schering-Plough Corp, lead terminal operator, 1981-. **Orgs:** Supporter, Make-A-Wish Found of New Jersey, 1983-; consultant, Natl Police Reserve Officers Assn (New Jersey State), 1987-; bd mem, Heath Center Black History Comm, 1987-; exec dir, New Jersey State Chapter, Natl Police Officers Assn of America, 1987-; Pride In Excellence, 1988-, US Citizens' Commission on Crime & Narcotics, 1988-; bd mem, Masters of Philanthropy, 1988-. **Home Addr:** PO Box 350, East Orange, NJ 07019. **Business Addr:** Lead Terminal Operator, Lead Terminal Operations-Computerized Hi-Rise Div, Schering-Plough Corporation, Galloping Hill Rd, K-2-1, Kenilworth, NJ 07033.

PETERSON, ROCKY LEE
Attorney. **Personal:** Born Apr 29, 1952, New York, NY; son of Natalia Lee Peterson; married Paulette Sapp, Dec 21, 1985; children: Malik, Danita, Corrie. **Educ:** Cornell Univ, AB, 1974, JD, 1977. **Career:** Administrative Office of Courts, clerk-civil practice, 1977-78; NJ Div of Criminal Justice, deputy attorney genl, 1978-83; City of Trenton, city attorney, 1990-; Hill Wallack, partner, 1983-. **Orgs:** Kappa Alpha Psi, 1993-; NAACP, bd of trustees, 1988-89; YMCA, bd of dirs, 1988-89; Granville Academy, bd of trustees, 1988-89; Crossroads Theatre Co, bd of trustees, 1988-94; Disciplinary Review Board of NJ Supreme Court, 1991-; NJ Bar Assn Minorities in the Profession, 1988-; Mercer Cty Bar Assn, 1989-. **Honors/Awds:** NJ Bar Minorities in the Profession, Service Award, 1995; Crossroads Theatre Co, Service Award, 1994. **Business Addr:** Attorney, Hill Wallack, 202 Carnegie Ctr, Princeton, NJ 08543, (609)924-0808.

PETERSON, SUSHILA JANE-CLINTON
Dentist. **Personal:** Born Jun 4, 1952, New Delhi, India; daughter of Audrey Clinton Peterson and James C Peterson (deceased). **Educ:** Howard Univ, BS 1974; Howard Univ Dental School, DDS 1979. **Career:** Private practice, dentist 1984-. **Orgs:** Mem Amer Dental Assoc 1980-, Alpha Kappa Alpha Sor 1982-, Amer Assoc of Univ Women 1982-, District of Columbia Dental Soc 1984-, MD State Dental Assoc 1984-, Howard Univ Dental Alumni Assoc 1984-; US Chamber of Commerce 1987-88; Robert T Freeman Dental Society; Association for Study of Afro-American Life and History. **Military Serv:** US Army capt 4 yrs active 2 yrs reserves, Servicemen's Merit Awd 1983. **Home Addr:** 3816 8th St NW, Washington, DC 20011.

PETETT, FREDDYE WEBB
Association executive. **Personal:** Born Dec 27, 1943, Monroe, LA; daughter of Barbara Mansfield; divorced; children: Andre. **Educ:** Portland State Univ, BS 1969-73; Portland Comm Coll, AS 1968-69; Southern Univ, 1961-62; Portland State Univ; Union Institute, PhD Candiate. **Career:** W K Kellogg Foundation, Battle Creek, MI, associate program director, 1990-92, program coordinator, 1992-93, dir of international leadership program, currently; State of Oregon, public welfare administrator, 1987-90; Portland Urban League, executive director 1979-86; mayor's Office City Portland, asst to mayor 1976-79; Crime & Prevention Bureau, dir 1974-76; Office of Emergency Servcs, coordinator 1973-74; Nero & Assoc, project dir 1971-73; Portland Model Cities, syst coordinator 1970-71; Portland Comm Coll, programmer analyst 1969-70. **Orgs:** Past board of directors Housing Authority Portland; Delta Sigma Theta Sorority; mem, World Affairs Council; past bd mem, Federal Home Loan Bank of Seattle; member, Battle Creek Urban League; past board member United Arts Council. **Honors/Awds:** WK Kellogg Natl Fellowship, Kellogg Found, 1983; Woman of Excellence, Delta Sigma Theta Sorority, 1985. **Special Achievements:** Published: ''My Life's Journey'' in Voices of Women Moving Forward with Dignity & Wholeness, 1995. **Business Addr:** Director, International Leadership Program, W K Kellogg Foundation, One Michigan Ave E, Battle Creek, MI 49017.

PETIONI, MURIEL M.
Physician, educator. **Personal:** Born Jan 1, 1914; children: Charles M Woolfolk. **Educ:** New York U, 1930-32; Howard U, BS 1934, MD 1937; Harlem Hosp Internship, 1937-39. **Career:** New York City Dept Hlth, sch phys 1950-80; prvt practice 1950-; NY Hlth & Hosp Corp Harlem Hosp, med stf 1960-80; New York City Dept Hlth, spvr/sch phys 1980-84; Harlem Hosp Dept Peds, spvsing phys & cnsltnt 1982-; Dept of Peds Columbia U, asst clncl prof 1982-. **Orgs:** Natl Med Assn; Empire State Med Assn; tres Manhattan Cntr Med Assn; flw Am Acad Fmly Phys; Howard Univ Med Alumni Assn; founder pres Susan SmithMcKinney Steward Med Assn 1974-84; fndr 1st chrprsn Med Women of NMA 1977-83; tres Doctors Cncl of City of NY 1980-84; Doctors Cncl City NY 1950-80; pres Trinidade & Tobago Gyap Orgn; Delta Sigma Theta Soc; Coalition of 100 Black Women; New York City Dept Hlth Child Hlth Forum; NAACP; NY Urban League. **Honors/Awds:** Woman of yr Morrisania Youth & Comm Serv Ctr Inc 1969; awrds in black Found Rsrch & Ed Sickle Cell Disease 1973; first harlem humanitarian awrd NY Cncl Smlr Chrchs 1975; Martin Luther King, Jr Democrates Salute 1975; harlem brnch ymca world

serv awrd Harlem YMCA 1978; women of yr Everybody's Mag 1979; practitioner of yr Natl Med Assc 1979; ed dept awrd City Tabernacle SDA Chrch 1979; dstngshd serv awrd Lehman HS Bio-Med Inst 1981; profsnl ed awrd Harlem Unit/Am Cancer Soc 1982; black achvmnt awrd Comm Church NY 1983; cert aprctn Pioneer in Treatment of Drug Abuse Edward I Koch Mayor of City of NY 1983; spec rcgntn Muriel Petioni MD Fndr of NMA Women in Medicine Task Force on Conserns of Women Phys; harlem wk 83 hlth serv awrd Harlem Week Inc 1983; harlem hospmeritorious serv awrd Harleospt Ctr & NY Hlth & Hosp Corp 1983; Whitney M Young Jr Comm Rltns Awrd Annual African-American Heroes & Heroines Day 1984; distngshd serv awrd Doctors Cncl 1984; city of ny Proclamation Ofc of City Clrk David N Dinkins City of NY 1984; outstndg serv to chldrn harlem awrd Med Stf & Med Bd Harlem Hosp 1984; numerous others. **Business Addr:** 114 West 131st, New York, NY 10027.

PETTAWAY, CHARLES, JR.
Pianist, educator. **Personal:** Born Jun 7, 1949, Philadelphia, PA; son of Lorraine Thornton Pettaway and Charles Henry Pettaway; divorced; children: Ashley. **Educ:** Philadelphia Mus Acad, BM 1971; Temple Univ, MM 1976; Fontainbleau Acad France, 1973; Ravel Acad France, Cert 1974. **Career:** Performed throughout the US and Europe making European debut in 1974; musical performances incl: Tour of Switzerland summer 1981; Great Hall of Moscow Conserv Russia; Carnegie Hall NY; Acad of Music Phila; Philharmonic Hall NY; Yacht Club of Chicago; Boston Univ; Music Hall at Ciboure; Palais de Fontainebleau France; Center Coll KY; Windsor Sch NC; Tanglewood Music Fest Recanti Auditorium Tel Aviv, Israel; Kennedy Center Wash, DC; Orchestra Hall Chicago; Settlement Sch of Music, concert pianist/tchr; Lincoln Univ Lincoln PA, tenured professor of music, 1988-. **Orgs:** Performing artist-piano, arranger, choir director, board member, Manyunk Council of the Arts, 1990-; board member, Philadelphia Gospel Seminars, 1996. **Honors/Awds:** Robert Casadesus International Piano Competition, France, First Place Winner, 1974; selected as De Bose Artist, Southern Univ, Baton Rouge, LA, 1997. **Special Achievements:** Article publ in Society Newsletter (musical publ) "The American Audience" 1984; 1st commercial recording released "Charles Pettaway Performs Music by Russian Composers" 1985. **Home Phone:** (215)706-0617. **Business Addr:** Lincoln University, Lincoln University, PA 19352.

PETTERWAY, JACKIE WILLIS (JACKIE O OF HOUSTON)
Fashion designer. **Personal:** Born in Galveston, TX; married Arthur L Petterway; children: Chiquita. **Educ:** Prairie View A&M Univ, BS clothing and textiles 1970; Magnolia Business Ctr Inc, Small Business Certificate of Merit 1972; Natl Sch of Dress Design, attended 1973; Univ of Houston, M Retailing 1979. **Career:** Jackie O Designs Inc Houston, designer/proprietor 1970-80, designer/chairperson of the bd 1980-. **Honors/Awds:** Developed, produced and directed several fashion shows for charitable orgs; presented Jackie O's 1982 holiday collections during 2nd annual fashion extravaganza benefitting the Sickle Cell Anemia Foundation 1982; presented 3rd annual fashion extravaganza benefitting The Greater Houston Civic Ballet Co 1983; Ebony Fashion Fair featured Jackie O designs in their Yearly Fashion Extravaganza (internationally) 1982-83, 1983-84, 1984-85, 1985-86; YWCA Woman of the Yr Awd 1983; Designer of the Yr Awd and Key to the City from Cincinnati OH 1986; Beefeater Fashion and Jazz Competition Grand Awd 1986; Natl Awd Natl Best Dressed Awd, Civic Org Inc of Chicago.

PETTIFORD, QUENTIN H.
City official. **Personal:** Born Dec 6, 1929, Marion, IN; married Betty I. **Educ:** IN Univ Kokomo, ABA Banking 1978. **Career:** Marion Police Dept, asst chief police 1975-75; Amer Bank & Trust, asst vice pres 1975-; Grant County, councilman. **Orgs:** Pres bd dir Marion Urban League 1980-81, 1984-; bd dir Grant Cty Economic Growth Council 1981-, Grant Cty Convention Bureau 1982-; mem Grant Cty Tax Council 1983-84; Grant Blackford Opportunities Ind 1984-. **Honors/Awds:** Serv Awd Marion Pal Club 1972; Serv Awd United Way 1979-84. **Home Addr:** 1819 S Selby, Marion, IN 46953.

PETTIFORD, REUBEN J., JR.
Health services administrator. **Personal:** Born Jun 30, 1960, Bronx, NY; son of Georgiana Cameron Pettiford and Reuben J Pettiford; married Lisa Farmer Pettiford, Jun 18, 1988; children: Robert Anthony. **Educ:** University of Buffalo, Buffalo, NY, BA, 1983; Baruch College, New York, NY, MPA, 1990. **Career:** Bellevue Hospital Center, New York, NY, health care analyst, 1983-86; North General Hospital, emergency services manager, 1986-89; New York City Department of Health, area manager, 1989-90; North General Hospital, New York, NY, Paul Robeson family medical center, executive director, 1990-. **Orgs:** Board member, East Harlem Council for Human Services, 1990-. **Business Addr:** Executive Director, Paul Robeson Family Medical Center, 140 West 125th Street, New York, NY 10027.

PETTIFORD, STEVEN DOUGLAS
Automotive executive. **Personal:** Born Aug 24, 1948, Dayton, OH; son of Martha E Streaty Pettiford and Edwin E Pettiford; married Donna F McKeever Pettiford, Aug 17, 1970; children: Yvonne Michelle, Yvette Rene. **Educ:** General Motors Inst, Flint MI, bachelor mechanical engineering, 1972; Massachusetts Inst of Technology, Cambridge MA, masters mgmt, 1978. **Career:** General Motors, Dayton OH, production engineer, 1972-75, asst supt prod engineering, 1975-76, asst supt mfg, 1976-77, plant mgr mfg, 1977-82; Warren MI, dir ind engineering, 1982-85, Lansing MI, mgr product assurance, 1985-87, Kalamazoo MI, plant mgr, 1987-. **Orgs:** Mem, GMI Alumni Assn, 1972-; mem, Tau Beta Pi Inc, 1972-; mem, Engineering Soc of Detroit, 1985-; mem, Engineering Bd of Visitors, Western Michigan Univ, 1987-; trustee, Nazareth Coll, 1987-91; bd mem, Forum, 1987-91; mem, NAACP, 1988-; bd mem, CEO of Kalamazoo, 1989-; mem, exec bd, Chamber of Commerce, 1989-91; sec exec bd, United Way, Kalamazoo, 1989-91. **Honors/Awds:** Honoree, Tau Beta Pi, 1972; instructor and developer of pre-apprentice training course, 1973-77; Alumnus for a Day, GMI-EMI, 1986; America's Best and Brightest, Dollars and Sense, 1988; GMI-EMI, distinguished alumnus, 1992. **Business Addr:** Plant Mgr, General Motors Corp, 5200 E Cork St, Kalamazoo, MI 49001.

PETTIGREW, GRADY L., JR.
Judge. **Personal:** Born Jun 21, 1943, Forrest City, AR; married Carolyn Landers; children: Dawn Karima, Grady Landers. **Educ:** OH State Univ, BA 1965; Howard Univ School of Law Wash DC, 1968-69; OH State Univ, JD 1971. **Career:** Columbus State Hosp, activities therapist 1965; Huntington Natl Bank Columbus, mgr trainee 1968; Legal Aid Agency DC, investigator law clerk 1969; Vorys Sater Seymour & Pease, assoc atty 1971-77; US Bankruptcy Court, judge 1977-86; Arter & Hadden, partner. **Orgs:** Mem Columbus & OH State Bar Assoc, ABA; corr sec Robert B Elliott Law Club 1977-, Natl Conf of Bankruptcy Judges Adj Prof of Law Capital Univ 1979, OH State Univ 1980; bd of trustees chmn Comm Devel Com Ctrl Comm House 1972-75; bd of trustees Ecco Manor 1973, United Way of Franklin Cty 1974-75; solicitor Village of Urbancrest OH 1975-76. **Honors/Awds:** Natl Moot Ct Championship Young Lawyers Comm NY Bar Assoc 1971; Outstanding Young Men of Amer Chicago 1972. **Military Serv:** AUS 1st lt 2 yrs. **Business Addr:** Partner, Arter & Hadden, 1 Columbus, 10 W Broad St, Columbus, OH 43215.

PETTIGREW, L. EUDORA
Educator, educational administrator. **Personal:** Born Mar 1, 1928, Hopkinsville, KY; daughter of Corrye L Newell Williams and Warren C Williams; children: Peter W Woodard. **Educ:** West Virginia State College, BMus, 1950; Southern Illinois University, MA, counseling, 1964, PhD, ed psych, 1966. **Career:** Southern Illinois University, instructor, 1964-66; University of Bridgeport, associate professor, 1966-70; Michigan State University, professor, chair, 1970-80; University of Delaware, associate provost, 1981-86; SUNY College at Old Westbury, president, 1986-. **Orgs:** American Association of State Colleges and Universities, 1991-94; North American Council of IAUP, executive board, 1992-; Long Island Forum for Technology, 1987-; Long Island Regional Advisory Council on Higher Education, 1986-, chair, 1988-91; Economists Allied for Arms Reduction, advisory committee, 1996; Intl Assn of Univ Presidents (IAUP/UN), Comm on Disarmament Educ, Conflict Resolution and Peace, chair, 1996-; Commission on the Univ of Peace in Costa Rica, 1997; Univ of Pretoria Foundation, South Africa, board of directors, 1997. **Honors/Awds:** Black Women's Agenda Inc, BWA Achievement Award, 1988; Nassau/Suffolk (NY) Council of Administrative Women in Education, Woman of the Year, 1989; Long Island Women's Council for Equal Education, Training and Employment, Distinguished Educational Leadership Award, 1989; National Association for Equal Opportunity in Higher Education, Distinguished Alumna Award, 1990; Long Island Business News, Long Island Distinguished Leadership Award, 1990; Natl Council of Negro Women Inc, New York City, Distinguished Black Woman in Education Award (highest award), 1991; Southern IL Univ, Distinguished Alumna, 1997. **Special Achievements:** Papers, "Old Westbury: Access and Excellence for All," Campus Commentary: SUNY Research '88, Albany, NY, Jan-Feb 1988; "Business, Industry and Universities: Partners for Multicultural Education," guest column, Economic Times of Long Island, Mineola, NY, Feb 1990; Intl Conf on the New Role of Higher Educ in the Context of an Independent Palestinian State, An-Najah Natl Unit, Nablus, Palestine, guest speaker, Nov 1996; conducted wkshp "Conflict Resolution the Woman's Role in Our World," UN Conference on Women, China, 1995; numerous guest lectures. **Business Addr:** President, SUNY College at Old Westbury, PO Box 210, Campus Center, Rm 400, Old Westbury, NY 11568, (516)876-3160.

PETTIS, BRIDGET
Professional basketball player. **Personal:** Born Jan 1, 1971. **Educ:** Univ of Florida, attended. **Career:** Fenerbache, guard, 1993-95; Anatalya Koleji (Turkey), 1995-96; Faenza (Italy), 1996-97; Phoenix Mercury, 1997-. **Honors/Awds:** Turkish League MVP, 1995. **Business Addr:** Professional Basketball Player, Phoenix Mercury, 201 E Jefferson St, Phoenix, AZ 85004, (602)252-9622.

PETTIS, GARY GEORGE
Professional baseball player. **Personal:** Born Apr 3, 1958, Oakland, CA. **Educ:** Laney College, Oakland, CA, attended. **Career:** California Angels, 1982-87, Detroit Tigers, 1988-89, 1992-, Texas Rangers, 1989-92; Oakland Athletics, 1993-.

PETTIS, JOYCE OWENS
Educator. **Personal:** Born Mar 14, 1946, Columbia, NC; daughter of Victoria Hill Owens and Howard Owens; married Bobby Pettis (deceased); children: Darryl; married Enoch Charles Temple. **Educ:** Winston Salem State Univ, BA 1968; East Carolina Univ, MA 1974; Univ of NC-Chapel Hill, PhD 1983. **Career:** NC Public Schools, teacher 1968-71; Pitt Tech Inst, teacher 1972-74; East Carolina Univ, asst professor of Eng 1974-; NC State Univ, asst prof of English 1985-. **Orgs:** Alpha Kappa Alpha; Popular Culture Assn; College Language Assn; teacher North Carolina History Summer Inst 1984; teacher Summer Institutes Incorp the New Scholarship on Women 1984. **Honors/Awds:** Minority Presence Fellowship Univ of NC - CH 1978-80; UNC Board of Gov Doctoral Award Univ of NC - CH 1981; Danforth Associate 1981; Natl Humanities Faculty Mem 1984; College Language Association, Scholarship Award for Publication: Toward Wholeness in Paule Marshall's Fiction, 1995. **Home Addr:** 1108 Cedarhurst Dr, Raleigh, NC 27609. **Business Addr:** Associate Professor of English, North Carolina State University, PO Box 8105, Raleigh, NC 27695.

PETTRESS, ANDREW WILLIAM
Printing company director. **Personal:** Born Jul 11, 1937, Steubenville, OH; son of Bessie Louise Pettress and Andrew Pettress; divorced; children: Andrews W Pettress IV, Andrew W Pettress Jr. **Educ:** Xavier Univ, Cincinnati OH, BA, 1966; Univ of Cincinnati, Cincinnati OH, Master/Labor Relations, 1977. **Career:** City of Pontiac, Pontiac MI, exec asst to mayor, 1982-86; Dan T Murphy for Governor, State of Michigan, deputy finance dir, 1986; Amer Speedy Printing, Bloomfield Hills MI, dir/special market devel, 1986-; Metro Substance Abatement Center, Detroit MI, self-employed; affiliated with Amer Football League, San Diego CA; Pettress & Associates, Detroit MI, self-employed. **Orgs:** Mem, Amer Society for Training and Devel; mem, Intl Assoc for Inter-Group Relations officials; mem, Intl Personnel Mgmt Assn; mem, Amer Mgmt Assn; president (3 terms) Alpha Phi Alpha Fraternity (Oakland County Graduate Chapter); mem, Natl Black Republican Council, MI; mem, Kiwanis Club Intl, Detroit MI; bd mem, Pontiac Creative Art Center of Pontiac, MI; mem, Michigan Comm for Honest Elections; mem, President's Commission, Oakland Univ, Rochester MI; vice-chmn, Minority Enterprise Comm, Intl Franchise Assn Conf of Black Mayor's Economic Devel Task Force. **Honors/Awds:** Money Mgmt of Methadone Clinics (State of Michigan), 1979; George E Baker Foundation fellow at Harvard Univ, 1980; Amer Speedy Printing Co, Midwest Devel Dir Mgr of the Year for Outstanding Sales Performance, 1987, Team Player of the Month, 1988; Broadcaster of the year, WCIN, Cincinnati OH. **Military Serv:** US Marine Corps, staff sgt, 1958-60, Sec to Admiral of the Fleet.

PETTUS-BELLAMY, BRENDA KAREN
Pediatrician. **Personal:** Born May 7, 1957, Washington, DC; married K Daniel Bellamy; children: Daniel K Jr. **Educ:** GA Southern Coll, BS Biology 1979; Howard Univ, MD 1983. **Career:** Howard Univ Hosp, intern/resident 1983-86; West Baltimore Health Ctr, pediatrician 1986-. **Honors/Awds:** Ruth E Moore Serv Awd Howard Univ 1982. **Home Addr:** 340 Taylor St NE, Washington, DC 20017.

PETTWAY, JO CELESTE
Judge. **Personal:** Born Mar 18, 1952, Consul, AL; daughter of Menda G Pettway and Joseph Pettway. **Educ:** Auburn Univ, BA 1973; The Univ of AL, BSW 1976, MSW 1978, JD 1982. **Career:** Children's Aid Soc, social worker 1975-77; Jefferson Co Dept of Pensions and Security, social worker 1977; Miles Coll, instructor of social work 1978-79; Legal Serv Corp of AL, summer clerk 1980; England and Bivens PC, assoc 1982-84; Jo Celeste Pettway Attorney at Law, solo practitioner 1984; Wilcox County, district judge 1984-. **Orgs:** Mem Natl Bar Assn, Amer Bar Assn, Natl Assn of Women Judges, Natl Assn of Juvenile and Family Court Judges, AL Lawyers Assn; president, Zeta Eta Omega Chap of Alpha Kappa Alpha Sor Inc; bd of dirs Health Improvement Project; Natl Council of Negro Women; Past Basileus - Zeta Eta Omega Chapter of Alpha Kappa Alpha Sor Inc. **Honors/Awds:** Outstanding Achievement Awd BLSA Univ of AL; Humanitarian Award Concordia College 1988; Outstanding Alumni Black Law Students Assn of Univ of Alabama 1987; Soror of the Year, South Eastern Region, 1989. **Home Addr:** PO Box 86, Alberta, AL 36720. **Business Addr:** District Judge, Wilcox Co, PO Box 549, Camden, AL 36726.

PETTY, BOB
Reporter, anchorman. **Personal:** Born Nov 26, 1940, Memphis; married Cora; children: Bobby, Cory. **Educ:** AZ State U, BS 1969. **Career:** KAET TV Tempe AZ, 1968; KPHO TV News, 1969; KOOL TV News 1969-70; WLS TV News 1970-; with the exception of KAET TV all experience is in news as film cameraman, soundman, lightingman, asst editor, writer, producer & reporter-anchorman reporter, producer; "Your Comment", community affairs program dirested at black communi-

ty. **Orgs:** Mem fun raising com Hyde Park YMCA; mem Provident St Mel Cath HS only black cath HS on Chicago's Westside. **Honors/Awds:** Univ of Chicago, Urban Journalism Fellowship Program, 1970; One of several black broadcasters honores by Club Date Magazine of Chicago 1974; Emmy Local News Coverage, 1985; Univ of Chicago, William Benton Fellowship Program, 1986. **Business Addr:** c/o WLS-TV, 190 N State St, Chicago, IL 60601.

PETTY, BRUCE ANTHONY
Company executive. **Personal:** Born Nov 15, 1938, East St Louis, IL; son of Helen Smith Petty and Bruce Petty; married Madeline McCollough Petty (divorced); children: Tanya, Avril Petty Weathers, Anthony. **Educ:** Southern IL Univ, BA 1960; Howard Univ, MPA 1973. **Career:** AL Nellum & Assoc, exec vice pres 1973-77; Univ Rsch Corp, vice pres 1978-81; AL Nellum & Assoc, exec vice pres 1981-83; Pettsons Inc, pres 1984-. **Orgs:** Former assoc dir Natl Civil Service League. **Home Addr:** 5700 16th St NW, Washington, DC 20011. **Business Addr:** President, Pettsons Inc, 545 8th St SE, Washington, DC 20003.

PETTY, RACHEL MONTEITH
Educator/psychologist. **Personal:** Born Jun 21, 1943, Columbia, SC; daughter of Susie E Monteith and Frank H Monteith Sr (deceased); married LaSalle Petty Jr, Sep 3, 1966; children: Adrienne, Erin. **Educ:** Univ of Maryland, PhD, 1980; Howard Univ, MS 1968, BS 1964. **Career:** Howard Univ, lecturer 1968-71; Prince Geo Pub Sch, sch psych 1968-72; DC Pub Sch, sch psych 1967-68; Univ of the District of Columbia, chairperson, and asst prof of psych, assoc prof of Psychology 1971-. **Orgs:** Assc Black Psychologists; Amer Assc Advancement Sci; MD Assc Sch Psychologists; research on Black Child; consultant DC Dept Human Services 1987-88; consulting psych St Ann's Infant Home Hyattsville, MD 1974-; bd mem Lutheran Social Services of the Natl Capital Area 1989-. **Home Addr:** 2124 Sudbury Place, NW, Washington, DC 20012. **Business Addr:** Chairperson, Department of Psychology, University of the District of Columbia, 4200 Connecticut Ave NW, Washington, DC 20008.

PETTY, REGINALD E.
Executive director, educational publisher. **Personal:** Born Oct 7, 1935, St Louis, MO; son of Helen Smith Petty and Bruce Petty; married Lucy Klaus; children: Joel, Amina. **Educ:** Southern IL Univ, BS 1956; MS Educ 1966. **Career:** Educ Resources Intl Inc, pres, 1986-; Your World Intl Newspaper for Students, publisher; Peace Corps, Kenya 1979-82, Swaziland, dir 1977-79; Natl Advisory Council Vocational Educ, deputy dir 1974-, dir rsch, 1971-74; General Learning Corp, assoc dir, Educ, 1970-71; Peace Corps W Africa Upper Volta, dir, 1969-70, deputy dir 1967-69; St Clair County IL Community Action Program, community relations consultant, 1966-67; Training Corp Amer, asst dir 1965-66; Breckenridge Job Corps Ctr, 1964-65; S IL, graduate rsch asst, 1962-64; IL State Dept Welfare, Child Welfare Div, 1961-62. **Orgs:** Amer Vocational Assn; Natl Sociological Soc Mid-Western Sociological Soc; Natl Educ Assc; Natl Alliance Black School Educators; Natl Assn of Black Adult Educators; Educ consultant, Gary IN, Newark NJ, E St Louis IL; Africare on West African Famine Relief Program, 1973; Corp Public Broadcasting, 1973-74; mem NEA, Kappa Alpha Psi, Urban League, NAACP, Natl Alliance of Black School Educators; TransAfrica; African Natl Congress. **Honors/Awds:** Published "Minorities & Career Education," 1973; chmn, 1st minority conf career educ, 1973; Outstanding Dir, Peace Corps, 1979, 1980, 1982.

PETTY-EDWARDS, LULA EVELYN
Educational administrator. **Personal:** Born Mar 10, 1945, Cedar Bluff, MS; daughter of William Jr and Omy A Deans Petty; married Ozzie L Edwards; children: Brett Tirrell Edwards, Daryl Westfield Edwards, Omy Lela Edwards. **Educ:** Mary Holmes Coll, associates degree, 1965; Knoxville Coll, bachelor's degree, 1968; Illinois State Univ, master's degree, 1973. **Career:** Univ of MI, lecturer, 1974-78; Mary Holmes Coll, faculty, Dir of Reading Ctr, Director Alumni, 1980-81; Univ of Louisville, part-time faculty, 1982-85; Northeastern Univ, coord, reading, writing, study skills, 1985-93, asst dir, Academic & Cultrual Programs, 1989-93, assoc dean, dir, currently. **Orgs:** Natl Council of Teachers of English; Natl Assn of Student Personnel Administrators; Black Educator's Alliance of MA; Natl Political Congress of Black Women Inc. **Honors/Awds:** Natl Assn for Equal Opportunity in Higher Educ, Distinguished Alumni Award, 1995; African Methodist Episcopal Women, New England Area, Black Women Achievers Award, 1991; Northeastern Univ, Black Student Assn, Positive Force Award, 1986-88. **Special Achievements:** Cofounder, Imani Inst, private elementary school in Roxbury, MA. **Business Addr:** Assoc Dean, Director, Northeastern University, John D O'Bryant African-American Institute, 40 Leon St, Boston, MA 02115, (617)373-3143.

PEYTON, JASPER E.
Assistant educational director. **Personal:** Born Dec 30, 1926, Richmond; widowed; children: Rose La Verne Abernathy. **Educ:** Univ Philippines, attended 1946; City Coll NY, 1952. **Career:** Local 66 Intl Ladies Garment Workers, trade unionists, shop steward 1952-64; Civil Rights Comm Dir Educ, exec bd mem dir 1965-69, asst dir educ. **Orgs:** Mem Council Chs Brooklyn Div 1971-; Assc minister Bethany Bapt Ch; bd dir CLICK-COMMERCE Labor Industry Corp of Kings for Brooklyn Navy Yard; bd memFulton Art Fair. **Honors/Awds:** Award Pub Rel Dir Bethany Bapt Ch. **Military Serv:** AUS sgt. **Business Addr:** 1710 Broadway, New York, NY 10019.

PHEARS, WILLIAM D.
Association executive. **Personal:** Born Sep 3, 1917, Arkansas; married; children: William D, Jr, Jo Alison. **Educ:** Long Island Univ, BS, MS 1967. **Career:** Brevard Engr Co Cape Canaveral FL, consult 1975; Water Hempstead NY, commr 1972-, dep commr pub wks 1966-72; real est broker; clge instr. **Orgs:** Trustee Uniondale Pub Lib 1963-64. **Honors/Awds:** APWA Top Ten Engr Award 1969. **Military Serv:** USAF lt col 1941-64. **Business Addr:** 1995 Prospect Ave E, Hempstead, NY 11554.

PHELPS, C. KERMIT
Clinical psychologist. **Personal:** Born Dec 4, 1908, Newton, KS; son of Eva Bradshaw Phelps and Clifford Phelps; married Lucille Mallory, Sep 11, 1936; children: Patricia Ann Phelps Evans, Sr Constance Kay Phelps. **Educ:** Univ of KS, Lawrence KS, AB, 1933, MA, 1949, PhD, 1953. **Career:** Veteran's Admin, Topeka KS, psychologist, 1949-52, Kansas City MO, psychologist, 1952-55, chief psych service, 1955-75, assoc chief of staff-educ, 1975-78; Avila Coll, evening div, Kansas City MO, prof psych, 1955-72; Kansas City MO, private practice, 1955-81; KU Medical Center, Kansas City, KS, assoc prof psych, 1961-69; Univ of Kansas, Lawrence KS, asst prof psych, 1962-64; Shepherds Center, Kansas City MO, dir life enrichment, 1974-. **Orgs:** Bd of Regents Rockhurst Coll, 1962-; cochmn, Natl Conf of Christians & Jews, 1965-67; chmn, Jackson County Civil Rights Comm, 1967-72; Rotary Club 13 Kansas City, 1972-; Red Cross, bd of dirs, 1977-79; bd mbr, 1981, chmn natl bd, 1986, AARP; Geriatric Center, bd of directors, secy. **Honors/Awds:** Civil Servant of the Year, VA, 1964; Man of the Year, Ivanhoe Club, 1966; Knight of Holy Sepulchre, Pope Paul VI, Rome, 1966; Getting Ready for Retirement, Intl Gerontololical Congress, paper presented in Vienna, 1966; Aging in Youth Oriented World, Spain, 1970; Life Enrichment, Hew, 1975; Honorary PhD, St Mary's Coll, 1976; Counseling the Elderly, MO Counsel of Churches, 1980; Honorary PhD, Avila Coll, 1991. **Home Addr:** 3437 Quincy St, Kansas City, MO 64128.

PHELPS, CONSTANCE KAY
Educational administrator. **Personal:** Born Sep 16, 1940, Topeka, KS; daughter of Lucille Mallory Phelps and C Kermit Phelps. **Educ:** St Marys Coll, BA 1962; Wash Univ St Louis, AM 1970, PhD 1977; Center for Concern, Washington DC, 1986; Bryn Mawr, 1991. **Career:** St Mary Clge, prof of soc 1970-; Denver Parochial Sch System, tchr 1962-68; Harvard MIT, research asst 1970; Comm Crisis Intervention Ctr research asst 1974-75; HEW, grant reviewer 1979; St Mary Coll, dean of students 1986-95, vp for student life, 1995-, interim president, 1997. **Orgs:** Mem, Sisters of Charity of Leavenworth, 1959-; Mem Amer Soc Assc 1969-; proj mgr Long Range Planning proj St Mary 1977-78; on campus coord small clge consortium Wash DC 1977-80; consult Natl Consult Network 1977-; asst w/documentsGhana Mission to UN 1981; coord Social Justice Network Sisters of Charity of Leavenworth 1985; bd dir Leavenworth City-County Alcohol & Drug Abuse Council 1985; Civilian Based Defense, 1986; bd of dirs, St Vincent Clinic, 1988-94; Catholic Social Services, 1988-93; consultant/evaluator, N Central Assn of Colleges & Schools, 1988-; mem, Natl Assn of Student Personnel Admin; chair, Leavenworth County Human Relations Commission, 1990-; bd of dirs, Providence/Saint John Hospital 1997-; bd of dirs, Leavenworth Catholic Schools 1997-. **Honors/Awds:** Natl Delta Epsilon Sigma Acad Honor Soc, 1970-; fellowship, Hamline Univ, 1973; fellowship, Washington Univ, 1973-75; Fulbright Hays Fellowship, Ghana, W Africa, 1975-76; assoc mem, Danforth Assn, 1980. **Business Addr:** VP of Student Life, St Mary College, 4100 S 4th St TFWY, Leavenworth, KS 66048.

PHELPS, DONALD GAYTON
Educational administrator. **Personal:** Born Jul 22, 1929, Seattle, WA; son of Louise E Gayton Adams and Donald G Phelps; married Pamela, Jul 4, 1981; children: Richard W, Michael K, Dawn S. **Educ:** Cornish School of Allied Arts, Seattle WA, Music Major 1948-51; Seattle Univ, Bachelor of Educ 1959, Master of Educ 1963; Univ of Washington, Doctor of Educ 1983; Harvard Graduate School of Educ, Inst for the Mgmt of Lifelong Educ, 1987. **Career:** Bellevue Community Coll, Bellevue WA, exec asst to the pres and dir of personnel 1969-72; Natl Inst on Alcohol Abuse and Alcoholism, dir 1972-76; Lake Washington School Dist, interim supt 1976-77; King County WA, dir of exec admin 1977-80; Seattle Central Community Coll, Seattle WA, pres 1980-84; Seattle Community Coll Dist VI, Seattle WA, chancellor 1984-88; Los Angeles Community Colleges, Los Angeles CA, chancellor 1988-. **Orgs:** Natl Council on Black American Affairs, AACJA; bd of dirs, Amer Council on Educ; Amer Council on Educ, Commission on Minorities in Higher Educ; bd of advisors, Inst for the Mgmt of Lifelong Educ, Harvard Univ; Sigma Pi Phi Fraternity, Phi Delta Kappa; bd of trustees, Seattle Univ; life mem, NAACP; mem, Seattle Urban League, Los Angeles Chamber of Commerce Educ Committee; director, Federal Res Bank of San Francisco, Los Angeles Branch, 1991-94; director, Metropolitan YMCA; director, Los Angeles Area Chamber of Commerce. **Honors/Awds:** Author of Measuring the Human Factor of Classroom Teaching 1978, The Progress of Developmental Students at Seattle Central Community Coll 1981-83; author of articles "What Can Be Done to Enhance the Status of the Associate Degree?" AACJC Journal 1985, "A Nation Comfortable With Its Prejudices," article taken from speech delivered to the Girl Scout Leaders of Amer 1987, "The Legacy of Martin Luther King Jr and Its Continuing Effect on Today's Society" 1987; Natl Business League President's Washington State Award 1987; selected in The Univ of Washington's first group of Alumni Legends 1987; President's Award, Natl Business League, Washington State Affiliate 1988; Frederick Douglass Award, Black Faculty Staff Assn, Los Angeles Harbor Coll 1989. **Military Serv:** US Army 1951-53. **Business Addr:** Chancellor, Los Angeles Community Colleges District, 617 W Seventh St, Los Angeles, CA 90017.

PHELPS, WILLIAM ANTHONY
Entrepreneur. **Personal:** Born May 19, 1964, Detroit, MI; son of Terry Dean Hodges and James Mize Phelps. **Educ:** National Institute of Technology, technical certificate; Redford High School, Night School, cosmetology certificate. **Career:** Men at Work Power Salon, owner, 1989-; Club Network, owner, 1991-. **Orgs:** First Friday's Organization of Detroit, organizer, 1993-; Will Phelps Promotional Services; Upfront Promotional Organization; Gables Promotional Organization; Charivari Promotional Organization. **Honors/Awds:** Spirit of Detroit Award, 1988. **Business Addr:** Owner, Men At Work Power Salon, 18928 W McNichols, Detroit, MI 48219, (313)534-3655.

PHELPS-PATTERSON, LUCY
Company executive. **Personal:** Born Jun 21, 1931, Dallas, TX; daughter of Florence Louise Harllee Phelps and John Clarence Phelps Jr; married Albert S Patterson; children: Albert H. **Educ:** Howard Univ, BA 1950; Univ Denver, MSW 1963. **Career:** OIT Inter-Continental Marketing Group Inc, president and vice pres Dallas Roadway Products, currently; National Alliance of Senior Citizens, pres, CEO, 1990-92; Educ Transformation Inc, pres/CEO, 1988-90; Bishop Clge, Ethel Carter Branham prof & dir soc work prog 1978-88; N TX State Univ, asst prof 1974-78; Dallas Co Child Care Coun, exec dir 1971-74; Grtr Dallas, plng dir Comm Coun 1971-72; Inter-Agency Proj, dir 1968-71; Dallas Co Dept Pub Welfare, casework supr 1963-68. **Orgs:** Chrtr mem N TX Assc Black Social Workers; Natl Assc Social Workers; Acad Cert Social Workers; publs in field; city councilwoman Dallas 1973; pres TX Mun League Region 13 1974-; chrwmn Human Devel Com Dallas; Mun Ct Com & Inter-govtmntl Affairs Com; Natl League of Cities Comm Devel Policy Com 1973-76; Human Resources Com Policy Com 1976; mem Coun on Social Work Educ; ldrshp com E Oak Cliff Sch Dist Cert of Recog House of Reps State of TX 1973, 1975; pres NASC elected, 1989; chairwoman, National Afro-American History and Culture Commission, 1985; National Association of Female Executives, 1991-; Dallas Area Rapid Transit Art and Design Committee; Diamite. **Honors/Awds:** Woman of Year Zeta Phi Beta Soc 1975; Social Worker of Year; NASW Dallas 1975; Civil Rights Worker of Year; Phi Delta Kappa 1975; Gold Plate Award Alpha Kappa Alpha Sor; Outst Educ of Amer NTSU 1975; Com of 100 Award Outst Contrib in Politics 1975; Achvmt Award Henry J Longfellow Sch 1976; Citizens Award TSABCL 1976; Mother of Year John Neely Bryan Elem Sch 1976; awarded Endowed Chair in Social Work Bishop Clge; Fair Housing Award 1979; City of Dallas 1980; Ldrshp Dallas Cert of Award 1979-80; Recognition of Dedicated Service to Citizens of Dallas County, Appraisal Review Board 1988; Appreciation, 1st African-American Pioneer as 1st City Councilwoman of Dallas, Mastid Ansar Allah, 1988; Faculty Making a Difference in Higher Education, American Assn of Higher Education, 1986; Junior BlaAcademy, Living Legend, 1993; Afro-American Postal League United for Success, Woman Who Moved Mountains; Mastio Ansar Allah, 1st African-American Pioneer of Civil Rights, Dallas, TX. **Home Addr:** 2779 Almeda Dr, Dallas, TX 75216. **Business Addr:** President, OIT Inter-Continental Marketing Group, Inc, 3939 Beltline Rd, Dallas, TX 75244.

PHIFER, B. JANELLE BUTLER
Attorney. **Personal:** Born Jul 26, 1949, Springfield, MA. **Educ:** Howard Univ Sch of Business, BA 1971; Howard Univ Sch of Law, JD 1975; Admitted to Ohio State Bar 1975. **Career:** State of OH, asst atty gen 1975-78; Toledo Legal Aid Soc, exec dir 1978-; Toledo Legal Aid Society, staff attorney, 1990-. **Orgs:** Toledo Bar Assn; pres Thurgood Marshall Law Assn; Toledo Chapter, The Links Inc; Delta Sigma Theta Sorority, Toledo Alumnae Chapter; Jack and Jill Inc, Toledo Chapter; Maumee Valley Girl Scout Council, co-leader troop 1077; St Paul Baptist Church. **Honors/Awds:** Outstanding Young Women of Amer; Delta Sigma Theta Sor Toledo Alumnal Chpt; Outstanding Professional Devel, Toledo Legal Aid, 1982, 1992; 1983, Woman of the Year in Law, Model Neighborhood Development Assn; Certificate of Appreciation, Supreme Court of Ohio Continuing Legal Education Commission, 1989, 1990; ProBono Public-Toledo Bar Assn, 1990. **Business Addr:** Attorney, Toledo Legal Aid Society, 1 Stranahan Sq, Ste 342, Toledo, OH 43604.

PHIFER, MEKHI
Actor, rapper. **Career:** Appearances in films and television shows: The Tuskegee Airmen, 1995; Clockers, 1995; High School High, 1996; Soul Food, 1997; New York Undercover; Homicide. album: New York Related: The HF Project. **Business Addr:** Actor, William Morris Agency, 151 El Camino Dr, Beverly Hills, CA 90212, (310)859-4000.

PHIFER, ROMAN ZUBINSKY
Professional football player. **Personal:** Born Mar 5, 1968, Plattsburgh, NY; married Alexis; children: Jordan. **Educ:** UCLA, attended. **Career:** Los Angeles Rams, linebacker, 1991-94; St Louis Rams, 1995-. **Honors/Awds:** Ed Block Courage Award, 1994. **Business Addr:** Professional Football Player, St Louis Rams, One Rams Way, St Louis, MO 63045, (314)982-7267.

PHIL. See LASLEY, PHELBERT QUINCY, III.

PHILANDER, S. GEORGE H.
Scientist. **Personal:** Born Jul 25, 1942; son of Alice E Philander and Peter J Philander; married Hilda Storari; children: Rodrigo. **Educ:** Univ Cape Town, BS 1963; Harvard Univ, PhD 1970. **Career:** MA Inst Tech, rsch assoc 1970-71; NOAA/Dept of Commerce, sr rsch oceanographer 1978; Princeton Univ, rsch assoc 1971-78; Princeton University, full prof, Department of Geological and Geophysical Sciences, 1990, Atmospheric and Oceanic Sciences Program, director, 1990-, Department of Geological & Geophysical Sciences, chmn, 1994-. **Orgs:** Consultant World Metrology Organization 1973-; numerous articles in oceanographic rsch journal; contributor "The Sea" 1977; mem, Natl Academy of Sciences Gate Comm, 1977-79; chmn, EPOCS Steering Comm, 1978-85; mem, SEQUAL Steering Comm, 1981-87; chmn, CCCO Atlantic Panel, 1981-; mem, Mass Inst of Tech Visiting Comm; mem, Natl Acad of Sciences TOGA Panel, 1985-; mem, Dynamics of Atmospheres and Oceans; mem, Geofisica Intl; mem Oceanographie Tropicale; lecturer with rank of professor in geological and geophysical sciences, Princeton Univ, 1980-; University Consortium for Atmospheric Research, board member, 1991-. **Honors/Awds:** NOAA Environmental Rsch Labs, 1979; Distinguished Authorship Award, 1979; NOAA Environmental Rsch Labs, 1983; Distinguished Authorship Award, 1983; Awarded Sverdrup Gold Medal by Amer Meteorological Soc, 1985; Dept of Commerce Gold Medal, 1985; Elected Fellow of the Amer Meterological Soc, 1985. **Special Achievements:** Author: Is The Temperature Rising? The Uncertain Science of Global Warming, Princeton Univ Press, 1998; El Nino, La Nina & The Southern Oscillations, Acad Press, 1989. **Business Addr:** Director, Atmospheric & Oceanic Science Program, Princeton University, Guyot Hall, Princeton, NJ 08544.

PHILLIP, MICHAEL JOHN
Educator. **Personal:** Born May 27, 1929, Port-of-Spain, Trinidad and Tobago; married Germaine Victor; children: Roger, Brian. **Educ:** Univ of Toronto, BSc 1960, MSc 1962; MI State Univ, PhD 1964. **Career:** John Carroll Univ Cleveland, assoc prof biology 1969-72; Univ of Detroit, prof microbiology 1977-, dir genetics 1982; Univ of Florida, dean of grad minority prog, currently. **Orgs:** Mem bd trustees St Mary's Hosp 1983-; vice chmn bd of dirs Alexandrine House Detroit 1979-. **Honors/Awds:** Distinguished Faculty Awd Univ of Detroit Black Alumni 1983; Outstanding Foreign Student MI State Univ 1963. **Business Addr:** Dean, Graduate Minority Programs, University of Florida, 238 Grinter Hall, Gainesville, FL 32611-2037.

PHILLIPS, ACEN L.
Clergyman, business executive. **Personal:** Born May 10, 1935, Hillhouse, MS; married E La Quilla Gaiter; children: Acen Jr, Gregory, Delford, Vicky Lynn, Aaron La Bracc, Carole Knight. **Educ:** Denver Univ, BA, MA; Conservative Baptist Theol Seminary, BD; Iliff Sch of Theology, MRC; Amer Baptist Theology Seminary, DD. **Career:** Denver Public Schs, educator; Ace Enterprises, pres; Mt Gilead Bapt Ch, minister. **Orgs:** Pres WSBC; state vice pres NBC USA Inc; pres East Denver Ministers Alliance; organizer of Denver OIC; organizer/founder first chmn of bd & pres Productions Inc; organizer/founder pres & bd chmn Ace Enterprises Inc; pres Natl Amer Church Union Inc; chmn Intl Interdenominational Ministers Alliance; bd chmn DTP Ministers Inc. **Honors/Awds:** Brought opening prayer for US Congress 1976; listed in Congressional Record; Man of the Yr. **Business Addr:** Minister, Mt Gilead Bapt Church, 195 S Monaco, Denver, CO 80224.

PHILLIPS, BARBARA
Educator (retired). **Personal:** Born Sep 5, 1936, Winston-Salem, NC; married Garret Elroy Phillips Jr; children: Eleanor. **Educ:** WSSU, BS 1957; IN Univ, MS 1958; UNC, EdS 1975, EdD 1979. **Career:** Winston-Salem Forsyth Co School, principal; teacher; guidance counselor; librarian; psychometrist, asst superintendent. **Orgs:** Dir Continuing Educ; coord Model Cities Natl Pres Alpha Kappa Alpha; trustee Winston-Salem State Univ 1974-79; former bd mem YWCA; former bd mem GSA; former bd mem Robert Vaughn Agcy; bd dir Big Bros-Big Sisters; trustee 1st Bapt church; Winston-Salem Foundation Community Fund, president; Links Inc, NAACP. **Honors/Awds:** Jessie Smith Noyes Flwshp to grad student 1957; Ldrshp Award NC/VA Alpha Kappa Alpha Sor 1977.

PHILLIPS, BASIL OLIPHANT
Administrator. **Personal:** Born Feb 19, 1930, Kansas City, MO. **Educ:** Roosevelt Univ & Inst of Design at IL Inst of Tech, atnd. **Career:** Johnson Pub Co Inc, photo editor; JPC Book Div, dir spec mrkts & promo & former sales mgr 1950-; Abraham Lincoln Bookstore, former employee. **Business Addr:** 820 S Michigan Ave, Chicago, IL 60605.

PHILLIPS, COLETTE ALICE-MAUDE
Public relations executive, communications executive. **Personal:** Born Sep 20, 1954, St John's, Antigua-Barbuda; daughter of Ionie Phillips and Douglas Phillips. **Educ:** Emerson Coll, BS Speech Communications 1976, M Business & Org Communications 1979. **Career:** Press sec to prime minister of Antigua, 1976-78; Patriots' Trial Coun, public relations dir 1980-84; Cablevision of Boston, public relations dir 1984-85; Royal Sonesta Hotel, public relations dir 1985-86; Colette Phillips Communications, pres, currently. **Orgs:** Mem bd of dirs Urban League Eastern MA 1980-85; bd mem Women in Communication Boston Chap 1984-86; vice pres Financial Develop MA Assoc of Mental Health 1984-87; vice pres Horizons for Youth 1986-; bd mem Boston AIDS Action Comm 1986-87; mem Amer Cancer Soc Public Information Comm, Public Relations Soc of Amer, Develop Comm of Spaulding Rehab Hosp; bd mem Museum of Fine Arts Council 1988-; bd mem Freedom House 1989-93; trustee Friends of Boston Ballet, 1986-90; bd mem, Advertising Club of Boston, 1991-93; bd mem, Betty Taymore Fund, 1991-; founding mem, Coalition of 100 Black Women, Boston Chapter, 1991. **Honors/Awds:** United Way Communications Awd 1981; Certificate of Appreciation Boston Univ PRSA Student Chap 1982; Outstanding Alumni Awd Emerson Coll 1983; 100 Most Influential Blacks in Boston 1986-89; One of Ten Outstanding Young Leaders in Boston, Boston Jaycees, 1988; Distinguished Alumnae Award, Emerson College, 1990.

PHILLIPS, CONSTANCE ANN
Sales manager. **Personal:** Born Jun 19, 1941, Hamilton, OH; married Lloyd Garrison Phillips Jr; children: Allan Lloyd, Garrison Loren. **Educ:** Miami Univ of OH, BA 1964; St Elizabeth Hosp Sch of Med, ASCP Registered Med Tech 1962. **Career:** St Elizabeth Hosp Dayton, medical tech 1962-64; Miami Valley Hosp Dayton, medical tech chemistry 1964-66; Univ of MN Hosp, medical tech supv pulmonaryfunction lab 1966-69; Mary Kay Cosmetics, beauty consultant 1974-, sales dir 1976-. **Orgs:** Mem Alpha Kappa Alpha Sor; sec Gem City Medical Dental & Pharm Aux 1982-83; mem Natl Assoc for Female Execs 1982-, Black Career Women 1983-84; editor, newsletter Jack & Jill of Amer 1983-85; pres Twentig Inc 1985-; mem hospitality comm Dayton Philharmonic Womens Assoc; mem Montgomery County Medical Assoc Aux. **Honors/Awds:** Miss Go Give Awd Mary Kay Cosmetics Inc 1980; Jill Business Woman of Year Jack & Jill of Amer 1983; 6 Pink Cars Mary Kay Cosmetics 1986.

PHILLIPS, DANIEL P.
Business executive. **Personal:** Born Feb 20, 1917, Sharon, PA; married Dorothy Weston; children: Dana Jean Johnson, Robin Dale. **Educ:** Lincoln U, BA 1939. **Career:** Chem Proc Fed Tool & Plstcs Co, plnt mgr div of ethyl corp; Cyrus Realtors Inc, realtor, currently. **Orgs:** Pres Evnstn Pk & Rec Bd 1953-73; vice pres Evanston YMCA Bd 1959-76; mem 1964-89, pres Evnstn HS Bd of Educ 1969-73, 1987,88; mem dir Evanston Rotary Club 1969-; mem bd of dirs IL Assoc of School Bds 1983-89; pres Evanston Rotary Club 1989-1990. **Honors/Awds:** Recip Outstanding Sch Bd Mem St of IL 1974; Disting Comm Contrib NAACP 1974; St Awd Otstndng Rehab Empl 1973. **Business Addr:** Sales Associate, Cyrus Realtors, Inc, 2929 Central St, Evanston, IL 60201.

PHILLIPS, DILCIA R.
Educator. **Personal:** Born Nov 30, 1949, Colon, Panama; children: Melbourne Alexander Hewitt Jr. **Educ:** Kingsborough Comm Coll, AA 1977; Brooklyn Coll, BA Educ 1979, MS Educ 1982; Brooklyn Coll, advanced degree Guidance/Couns 1982. **Career:** Maternal Infant Care Family Planning Project, counselor 1978-81; Women's Medical Serv at Kingsbrook Hosp, counselor 1981-83; Women Medical Serv at Kingsbrook Hosp, dir of public relations and agency afrs 1983; New York City Bd of Educ, bilingual teacher 1983-90, district monitor, 1990-. **Orgs:** Dept coord STEP Prog/Columbia Univ 1986-; chairperson Comprehensive School Improvement Prog 1986-; mem, Puerto Rican Educ Assn, 1987; chairperson, Corridor Program Bd of Ed, 1989-90. **Honors/Awds:** Outstanding Serv to the Grad Students of Brooklyn Coll 1982. **Home Addr:** 111 Dehaven Dr, Yonkers, NY 10703-1267. **Business Addr:** District Monitor, Comprehensive Program Services, Board of Education, District 23, 2240 Dean St, Brooklyn, NY 11212.

PHILLIPS, EARL W.
Educator (retired). **Personal:** Born Sep 20, 1917, Teague, TX; son of Arnetta Phillips and Austin Phillips; married Dorothy S Reid; children: Eart, Jr, Betty, Carol. **Educ:** Huston Tillotson, BA 1940; Boston Univ, MBA 1947; NC Central Univ, JD 1953; Univ NC, MA 1960; Univ CO, PhD 1965. **Career:** Met State Coll, prof; CO Dept Educ, cons; US Dept State & US Dept Commerce, economist; Univ CO, prof; NC Central Univ, asst prof (retired). **Orgs:** Mem Presbyterian Mens Assn; elder Peoples Presbyterian Church; mem W Reg Sic Assn; Amer Economic Assn; Indus Relations Rsch Assn; Natl Business Law Assn; Soc Intl Devel; mem bd dir Home Neighborly Serv; trustee Wasatch Acad & Westminster Coll; chmn Personnel Com Gen Council; mem Urban League CO. **Honors/Awds:** Fellowship Univ Oslo Norway 1956; Certificate of Merit CO Dept Educ 1970; Human Relations Awd CO Educ Assn 1975. **Military Serv:** USN 1942-45. **Home Addr:** 3085 Fairfax, Denver, CO 80207-2714.

PHILLIPS, EDWARD ALEXANDER
Utility manager. **Personal:** Born Jul 27, 1942, Cordele, GA; son of Eloise Moore Phillips and Sylvester Phillips; married Maxine Broussard Phillips, Feb 15, 1986; children: Kimberly L. **Educ:** Tuskegee University, Tuskegee, AL, BSME, 1965; University of Idaho, Moscow, ID, 1981. **Career:** Pacific Gas Transmission Co, Bend, OR, various engineering, 1966-73; Pacific Gas & Electric Co, Oakland, CA, senior dsbn enginer, 1973-74; Pacific Gas & Electric Co, San Rafael, CA, supt of opers/engr, 1974-79; Pacific Gas & Electric Co, Oakland, CA, district gas supt, 1979-81; Pacific Gas & Electric Co, San Francisco, GA, gas engineer, 1981-82; Pacific Gas & Electric Co, Salinas, CA, division gas supt, 1982-85; Pacific Gas & Electric Co, Sacramento, CA, region gas manager, 1982-90, region general services manager, 1990-. **Orgs:** President, chairman, Sacramento Black Chamber of Commerce, 1989-; board member, Sacramento Black Employees Assn, 1986-; board member, NAACP, 1990-; Sacramento Urban League, 1989-; awards committee, Pacific Coast Gas Assn, 1970-; Pacific Coast Electric Assn, 1970-. **Honors/Awds:** Community Service Award, Pacific Gas & Electric Co, 1989, 1990. **Business Addr:** Manager, Region General Services, Pacific Gas & Electric Co, 2740 Gateway Oaks Dr, Sacramento, CA 95833.

PHILLIPS, EDWARD MARTIN
Chemical engineer, educator, consultant. **Personal:** Born Dec 23, 1935, Philadelphia, PA; son of Sylvia D Phillips and Edward M Phillips; married Audrey Henrietta Longley. **Educ:** Lafayette Coll, BS ChE 1958; Northwestern Univ, MS ChE 1959; Univ of Pittsburgh, PhD ChE 1969. **Career:** Arco Rsch & Engrg, engr 1959-64; Exxon Engrg Co, project engr 1968-72; Tufts Univ, assoc prof 1972-74; Air Products & Chemicals Inc, engrg assoc, 1974-86; Rutgers Univ, professor, 1987-. **Orgs:** Mem Amer Inst of Chemical Engrg 1958-; mem Amer Chem Soc 1969-; dir Lehigh Valley Child Care 1977-. **Honors/Awds:** NASA Predoctoral Fellow Univ of Pittsburgh 1964-68; Fellow of Amer Institute of Chemical Engineers. **Home Addr:** Beacon Hill at Somerset, 43 Sapphire Lane, Franklin Park, NJ 08823. **Business Addr:** Professor & Associate Director, Center for Packaging Science & Engineering, Rutgers Univ, Bldg 3529, Busch Campus, Piscataway, NJ 08855.

PHILLIPS, ERIC MCLAREN, JR.
Supervisor. **Personal:** Born Oct 19, 1952, Georgetown, Guyana; married Angela; children: Takeisha Sherrill, Eric McLaran, Ashley Nicole. **Educ:** McMaster Univ, BS Engrg 1976; New York Univ, MBA 1983; Stevens Inst of Tech & Bell Laboratories, Certificate in Telecommunication Engrg 1985. **Career:** Apollo Technologies, test engr 1977-78, project engr 1978-79, sr project engr 1979-80, r&d product development leader 1980-82; AT&T Communications, staff mgr local area networks 1983-84, 1984-85, staff mgr network planning 1985-86; AT&T Bell Laboratories, supervisor mem tech staff 1986-; AT&T Central Europe Ltd (Belgium), managing dir, 1993; AT&T Africa & The Middle East, managing dir, 1994; AT&T Subsaharan Africa, sales vp, 1994; ACTCL (African Continental Telecommunications Ltd), COO of ACTCL, dir, 1995; Matrix Cellular Inc, pres, 1995. **Orgs:** Pres Phillips Smith & Assocs Inc 1982; exec dir The Caribbean Theatre of the Performing Arts New York City 1983; program dir 1986, pres 1985 NYU Black Alumni Assoc. **Honors/Awds:** Top Engineer 6 consecutive Quarters Apollo Technologies Inc 1979,80; R&D Scientific Achievement of the Year Awd Apollo Technologies Inc 1981; Merit Awd Grad Sch of Business Admin New York Univ 1983; AT&T Management Succession Roster 1983-86. **Business Addr:** Matrix Cellular Inc, 544 Irvington Avenue, Maplewood, NJ 07040.

PHILLIPS, EUGENIE ELVIRA
Physician. **Personal:** Born Jan 4, 1918, New York, NY; widowed; children: Eugenie, Randolph. **Educ:** Hunter Coll, BA 1940; Meharry Med Coll, MD 1944. **Career:** Harlem Hosp, intern 1944-45; Provident Hosp, ob/gyn 1945-47; Maternity Hosp, ob/gyn 1945-47; Mrgrt Hague, ob/gyn res 1945-47; Coppin State Teachers Coll, assoc sch phy 1959-74; Morgan State Univ, medical dir health svcs; Private Practice, ob/gyn physician 1947-. **Orgs:** Mem Nat Med Assn; Mnmntl Med Soc; MD St Med Soc; Bltmr City Med Soc; Med & Chrrgcl Fac of MD; Ob-Gyn Soc of MD; Am Med Wmns Assn; So Med Soc; Am Frtlty Soc; Am Soc for Clpscpy & Clpmcrscpy; NAACP. **Business Addr:** Gynecologist, 1612 Edmondson Ave, Baltimore, MD 21223.

PHILLIPS, F. ALLISON
Clergyman. **Personal:** Born Jan 5, 1937, Brooklyn, NY; married Velma Carr; children: Denise Mitchell, Alyson. **Educ:** Virginia Union Univ, BA 1958; Colgate Rochester Divinity

School, BD 1967; New York Theological Seminary, STM 1975, DMin 1981. **Career:** YMCA, assoc dir 1958-64; Garrison Blvd Comm Ctr, dir 1967-71; North Congregational Church, pastor 1971-82; Mt Zion Congregational Church, pastor 1982-. **Orgs:** Mem Alpha Phi Alpha 1955-; bd mem Amer Red Cross 1983-87; pres Inner City Renewal Soc 1984-; moderator African Amer Family Congress 1986-; bd mem Greater Cleveland Roundtable 1986-, Leadership Cleveland 1986-. **Honors/Awds:** Service Awds YMCA 1966, Council of Churches 1971, UCC Clergy Black Caucus 1981; Leadership Awd ISTEM 1982. **Business Addr:** Pastor, Mt Zion Congregational Church, 10723 Magnolia Dr, Cleveland, OH 44106.

PHILLIPS, FRANCES CALDWELL
Educator (retired). **Personal:** Born Feb 13, 1923, Concord, NC; daughter of Cora Louise Caldwell and Robert Caldwell; married Jonas H Phillips, Nov 15, 1986; children: Deborah Waddell Williams. **Educ:** Barber-Scotia Jr College, attended; Winston-Salem State University, BS, 1942; A&T State University, Greensboro, NC, MS, 1955. **Career:** Martin County School System; Stanley County School System; Charlotte Mecklenburg School System; Barber-Scotia College Upward Bound Program. **Orgs:** Albemarle City Schools Accredations, Steering Committee; Phi Delta Kappa Inc, Basileus; YWCA, Charlotte, NC, board of directors; Delta Sigma Theta Sorority, golden life member; First United Presbyterian Church, Charlotte, NC, elder; NAACP Legal Defence Fund, steering committee; Urban League; Urban League Guild; Barber-Scotia College, board of trustees; First Baptist Church West, deaconess. **Home Addr:** 1632 Patton Ave, Charlotte, NC 28216.

PHILLIPS, FRANK EDWARD
Government official, attorney (retired). **Personal:** Born Mar 3, 1930, Pittsburgh, PA; son of Annie Evans Phillips and Emanuel Phillips; married Mary E Britt-Phillips, Jun 10, 1989 (deceased); children: Nancy Phillips-Perry, Judith Lynne Phillips, Yvette Jacobs Davis; married Thelma Harrison Phillips (divorced); children: Jay Clark; married Saundra T Mitchell, Nov 29, 1997; children: Michael, Michelle. **Educ:** Shaw Univ, AB 1952; Howard Univ, LLB 1955. **Career:** IRS, Washington DC, rev officer 1955-62; IRS Los Angeles, CA, off chief counsel tax atty 1962-66, sr tax atty 1966-69, staff asst to regional counsel, general litigation, 1969-72, assistant district counsel, tax court litigation, 1972-86. **Orgs:** Natl Bar Assn; Fed Bar Assn; VA St Bar; bd dir Crenshaw YMCA; mem Chrstn Dcsn Dept Episcopal Church; board of directors, Crenshaw Neighbors; member, Alpha Kappa Mu Honor Society; member, Omega Psi Phi; bd of dirs, African American Unity Ctr. **Honors/Awds:** 1st Chief Counsel, EEO Award, IRS, 1980; 3 Outstanding Award, IRS, 1980; Gallatin Award, 1986; Treasury Dept, Outstanding Award. **Business Addr:** Attorney, Law Firm of Phillips & Phillips, 110 S LaBrea Ave, #220, Inglewood, CA 90301.

PHILLIPS, FREDERICK BRIAN
Psychologist. **Personal:** Born Sep 2, 1946, Philadelphia, PA; married Vicki Altemus, May 25, 1986; children: Jamali, Jasmine. **Educ:** Penn State Univ, BA 1968; Univ of PA, MSW 1970; The Fielding Inst, PsyD 1978. **Career:** Dist of Columbia Govt, psychologist 1978-81; Institute for Life Enrichment, assoc dir 1981-83; Progressive Life Inst, director/pres. **Orgs:** Mem Assoc of Black Psychologists 1978-85; mem Kappa Alpha Psi 1965-85. **Military Serv:** AUS capt 3 yrs. **Business Addr:** Director/President, Progressive Life Center, 1123 11th St, NW, Washington, DC 20001.

PHILLIPS, GLENN OWEN
Educator. **Personal:** Born Sep 26, 1946, Bridgetown, Barbados; son of Dorothy E Phillips and E Owen Phillips; married Ingrid Denise Tom, Aug 27, 1972; children: Mariette. **Educ:** Atlantic Union College, BA 1967; Andrews Univ, MA 1969; Howard Univ, PhD 1976. **Career:** Caribbean Union Coll, lecturer 1969-71, Howard Univ, asst prof history 1981-82, Morgan State Univ, asst prof history 1978-, asst dir Univ Honors Program 1981-82, research assoc 1982-92, acting dir of Institute for Urban Research 1986-89, asst prof 1989-90; Morgan State Univ, Baltimore, MD, acting chair, dept of history, 1989-90, 1995-96, assoc prof, 1990-. **Orgs:** MSU Liaison Officer to NAFEO, DC 1985-94; president, Barbados National Association of Washington District of Columbia, 1985-89; Comm Council of Caribbean Organizations, DC 1985-89; School Bd Chair, 1991-94; G E Peters Elementary School 1987-; bd of trustees, Caribbean Union Coll, 1989-94; Assn of Amer Univ Professors, 1995-97. **Honors/Awds:** HBCU Faculty Fellshp United Negro Coll Fund/US Dept of Lab 1980; Morgan State Univ Honorary Member (Promethean Kappa Tau) 1982; Cited Nat'l Dir Latin Americans; Assoc Editor Afro- Hispanic Rev, 1982-84; Books, The Making of Christian College, 1988; "The Caribbean Basin Initiative" co-editor 1987; Over a Century of Adventism, 1991, Fulbright Summer Scholar, Cairo, Egypt, 1994. **Business Addr:** Assoc Professor, Department of History, Morgan State Univ, Cold Spring Ln & Hillen Rd, Baltimore, MD 21239, (410)319-3004.

PHILLIPS, HELEN M.
Educator (retired). **Personal:** Born May 29, 1926, Norfolk, VA; daughter of Rosa Battle (deceased) and Thomas Battle (deceased); children: Marcia Anita Baynes, Brian O D. **Educ:** VA State Univ, Petersburg VA, BS 1954; Suffolk Univ, Boston MA, MEd 1983; studied at Univ of MD, Fairleigh Dickinson Univ, Salem State Coll, Catholic Univ of Amer & Boston Univ; University of Mass, certified in gerontology, 1994; advanced certificate, 1997. **Career:** Carnegie Inst, dir of prog for medical sec & assistants; Staff Norfolk State Coll 1951, East Boston HS, Boston Sch of Business, Brighton HS; Malden Public Sch System, Malden MA, teacher of typewriting, word processing, money and banking. **Orgs:** Former mem Natl Business Education Association; Natl Educ Assn; MA Teachers Assn; Malden Teachers Assn, Eastern Business Teachers Assn, The Resolutions Comm of the MA Teachers Assn; VA State University Alumni Assn; board of directors, charter mem, Cynthia Sickle Cell Anemia Fund; Concord Baptist Church, Boston MA; charter mem, Concord Optimist Club of Boston; former project dir of Women in Community Serv Boston; founder of Black Student Union at MHS; AKA Sor, 40 yrs; former columnist for the Boston Graphic and the Boston Sun newspapers; served on Ad Hoc Comm responsible for incorporating black studies into the Malden School System; natl bd dir, representing the 17th Dist, VA State Univ Alumni Assn, 1982-85, 1986-87; mem of task force comm, Restructuring Malden High School, 1988-89. **Honors/Awds:** Selected to serve on Evaluation Team New England Assn for Accreditation of Coll & Secondary Schs 1972; selected by MA Teachers Assn to represent MA in Cadre Training Session Univ of NH 1973; selected to attend MIP Conf at Cheyney State Coll by MA Teachers Assn; Responsible for starting MIP Conf in MA; First Place Dist Representative Awd, VA State Univ Alumni Assn, 1986; one of five educators in Malden School System selected as a mem of Needs Assessment Comm for Students at Risk-Dropouts, Prevention Program Junior High Schools in Malden to Middle Schools, 1987. **Special Achievements:** Recognized for positive image and involvement in the Malden community at the Martin L. King Luncheon, "Involvement Makes A Difference"; first black female teacher at Malden High School; teaching English as a second lang. **Home Addr:** 41 Acorn St, Malden, MA 02148.

PHILLIPS, JAMES LAWRENCE
Physician, educator, educational administrator. **Personal:** Born Mar 1, 1932, Sharon, PA; son of Roxie B Phillips and Daniel S Phillips; married Barbara A Eiserman; children: James Jr, Jeffrey, Steven. **Educ:** Washington & Jefferson Coll, BA 1954; Case Western Reserve Univ School of Medicine, MD 1958; Harvard Univ, advanced mgmt program 1979. **Career:** Kaiser Found Hospital Parma 1970-; Case Western Reserve Univ School of Medicine, asst clinical prof in pediatrics 1972-87; Cleveland Cavaliers Basketball Team, asst team physician 1973-79; West OH Permanente Med Group Inc, physician-in-chief 1968-86; Rocky River Med Off, physician in charge 1986-87; Case Western Reserve Univ School of Med, associate dean for student affairs and minority programs, currently. **Orgs:** Mem Acad of Medicine of Cleveland; mem OH State Med Assn; mem N OH Pediatric Soc; pres Case Western Reserve Univ School of Med Alumni Assn 1980-81; bd trustees Washington & Jefferson Coll 1982-; mem Case Western Reserve Univ School of Med Comm on Students 1982-87; bd trustees Mt Pleasant Church of God 1976-82; chmn United Way Serv New Programs Comm 1985; pres Northern OH Pediatric Soc 1988-89; bd of trustees, Washington & Jefferson College, 1988-94; pres, Northern Ohio Pediatric Society, 1988-89; mem, Cleveland Medical Association, 1988-. **Honors/Awds:** Bd Certified Amer Bd of Pediatrics 1963; Birch Scholarship Award Washington & Jefferson Coll 1954; Jessie Smith Noyes Found Med School Scholarship 1954-55; Leadership Cleveland, 1989-90. **Military Serv:** USNR lt comdr 2 yrs; Commendation from Commanding Officer. **Business Addr:** Associate Dean for Student Affairs and Minority Programs, School of Medicine, Case Western Reserve University, 10900 Euclid Ave, Cleveland, OH 44106.

PHILLIPS, JERRY P.
Electronics company executive. **Personal:** Born Jul 24, 1939, Lyons, GA; son of Ase Lue Phillips and P T Phillips; married Maxine Glass, Jun 20, 1964; children: Damon J, Dyelan J. **Educ:** Savannah State College, 1958-59; Rollins College, BS, 1985. **Career:** US Air Force, administrative superintendent, 1976-80; Harris Corporation, receiving & shipping supervisor, senior material administrator, 1980-89; Alphatech Systems, Inc, president, 1989-. **Orgs:** Historical Underutilized Business Counsil (HUB); Palm Bay FL, Citizen Saturday Committee, 1994-; Macedonia Baptist Church Trustee, board member, 1991-; NAACP, 1975-; Macedonia Baptist Church, Building Committee, chairman, 1991-; United Negro College Fund, Men Who Cook, honorary chairman, 1991-; Palm Bay Chamber of Commerce, 1990-; Palm Bay FL, Citizen Assistance Committee, 1994-96; Melbourne/Palm Bay Area Chamber of Commerce, trea, 1996-; Brevard County Workforce Development Board, mgr, 1996-; Natl Minority Supplier Development Council, 1990-. **Honors/Awds:** Governor of Florida, Governor's Award for Excellence in Manufacturing, 1991; Harris Corporation, Minority Business Enterprise of the Year, 1991; Sun Bank, NA, Minority Business Enterprise of the Year, 1990, 1991; Florida High Tech & Industry Council, One of the top 20 Small Disadvantaged Businesses in Florida, 1991; Greater Florida Development Council, Minority Business Enterprise of the Year, 1990; Macedonia Baptist Church, Man of the Year, 1994; Small Business Person of the Year Nominee, Melbourne/Palm Bay Chamber of Commerce, 1996; Community Business Award, Outstanding Services, 1996; Natl Minority Supplier Development Council of Florida, Business of the Year, 1995; Economic Development Commission Industry Appreciation, 1996. **Special Achievements:** Quality Work on Change Perception, Florida Today Paper, 1992; The US Air Force F-22/F119 Mentor-Protect Program, participation with Pratt & Whitney, 1995-. **Military Serv:** US Air Force, Master Sgt, 1960-80; Air Force Commendation Medals, 1966, 1970, 1973, 1977; Vietnam Service Medal with 2 Devices. **Business Addr:** President, Alphatech Systems, Inc, 2530 Kirby Ave NE, Ste 305, Palm Bay, FL 32905, (407)729-0419.

PHILLIPS, JOHN JASON, II
Corporate manager. **Personal:** Born Jul 10, 1938, Cincinnati, OH; son of Mary Chenault Phillips and John Jason Phillips; married Norma J Phillips, Sep 8, 1963 (divorced 1984); children: Nina J, Dyan R. **Educ:** Central State University, BS, 1960. **Career:** US Army, infantry officer, 1960-70; McCormick Schilling, safety/training supvr, 1970-79; Miller Brewing Co, safety/security mgr, 1979-81; Carrier Corp, safety/security mgr, 1981-85; Hughes Aircraft Co, sr safety engr, 1985-87; Lockheed Corp, corp safety mgr, 1987-93; Lockheed Environmental Systems and Technologies Co., corporate safety manager, currently. **Orgs:** Pres, American Society of Safety Engineers, Los Angeles Chapter, 1991-92; Natl Assn of Black Military Officers, 1985-; Alpha Phi Alpha Fraternity, 1958-; Reserve Officers Assn, 1973-; NAACP, Las Vegas Chapter, 1970-. **Military Serv:** US Army, lt colonel, 1960-88.

PHILLIPS, JULIAN MARTIN
Television journalist. **Personal:** Born Dec 5, 1955, New York, NY; son of Cecil & Enola Phillips; married Barbara King-Phillips, Dec 3, 1983. **Educ:** Purdue Univ, BA, 1977. **Career:** ABC-TV, desk assistant, 1977; Black Enterprise Magazine, 1980; WNEW-TV, Channel 5, production assistant, 1981; WNBC-TV, Channel 4, mgr of comm relations, 1984, anchor/journalist, 1993-. **Orgs:** NY Coalition on Adoptable Children, bd of dir, 1992-; Crohns & Colitis Foundation of Amer, advisory bd mem, 1989-92; National Puerto Rican Forum, advisory bd mem, 1984-90; National Assn of Black Law Enforcement Execs, 1994-; NYC Dept for Aging, sr employment advisory bd, 1985-89; National Broadcast Assn for Community Affairs, region vp, 1985-89. **Honors/Awds:** NY Academy of TV Arts & Sciences, Emmy Award, 1986; Radio & TV News Director Assn, Edward R Murrow Award, Best Natl Newscast/Best Spot News, 1994; Purdue Univ, Distinguished Alumni Award, 1988; Associated Press, First Place News Award, 1996; NYS Broadcasters Award, Outstanding Public Affairs Series; Nominated for 4 Emmy Awards, 1994-96. **Business Addr:** Reporter/Anchor, WPIX-TV, Host "Best Talk", Tribune Broadcasting, 220 E 42nd St, 10th Fl, New York, NY 10017, (212)210-2469.

PHILLIPS, JUNE M. J.
Educator, writer. **Personal:** Born May 31, 1941, Ashdown, AR; married A W Phillips; children: Roderick, Calandra Camille. **Educ:** Philander Smith College, BA, English (Magna Cum Laude), 1963; Louisiana State University, MA, English, 1971; Northwestern State University, doctoral candidate; Bakers Prof Real Estate College, license, 1977. **Career:** Port Arthur Texas Schools, teacher, 1963-65; Caddo Parish Schools, Shreveport, teacher, 1965-68; Board of Louisiana Colleges & Universities, trustee, 1983-; consultant on education for minorities; orator and poet; Southern University, Shreveport, asst prof english, 1968-. **Orgs:** Sales associate, Century 21, 1977-79; sales assoc, Lester Realty, 1979-83; sales assoc, Ferdinand Realty, 1984-; consultant, Lynell's Cosmetics, 1984-; bd mem, United Way of NW, LA, 1979-; secty-treas, Caddo Parish Charter Study Com, 1981-82; delegate, Democratic Natl Conv, 1984; NAUW; OEO #175; Shreveport Chap of Links; Zeta Phi Beta Sor; pres elect, Louisiana Philosophy of Educ Soc; vice pres, CODAC; mem bd of trustees, Louisiana Colleges and Universities, gubernatorial apptmt; chairs academic affairs comm for 9 LA colls; First black woman to serve on state bd. **Honors/Awds:** Woman of the Year, Zeta Phi Beta Sor, Inc, 1975; Caddo Parish School Board, 1976-77; Fellowship NDEA, Texas So & So Univ; editor/critic, Holbrook Press, NY & Roxbury Press, CA; selected by City of Shreveport as "Woman Who Has Made a Difference". **Business Addr:** Assistant Professor of English, Southern University, 3050 Martin Luther King Drive, Shreveport, LA 71107-4795.

PHILLIPS, LAWRENCE LAMOND
Professional football player. **Personal:** Born May 12, 1975, Little Rock, AR. **Educ:** Nebraska. **Career:** St Louis Rams, running back, 1996-97; Miami Dolphins, 1997-. **Special Achievements:** NFL Draft, first round pick, #6, 1996. **Business Addr:** Professional Football Player, Miami Dolphins, 2269 NW 199th St, Miami, FL 33056, (305)620-5000.

PHILLIPS, LEO AUGUSTUS
Molecular biologist, biophysical chemist. **Personal:** Born Feb 21, 1931, Nashville, AR; married Hattie M, 1957; children: Philip, Phyllis, Pebbles, Phil. **Educ:** Univ of Southern CA, BS, 1954; Arizona State Univ, MS, 1963; Univ of KS, PhD, microbiology, 1967. **Career:** Natl Cancer Inst-NIH, Pub Health Res Inst, City of New York, fel molecular biophys, 1967-69, staff

fel, 1969-71, sr staff fel, 1971-73, scientist, 1973-. **Orgs:** Fellow American Academy of Microbiology; American Soc of Microbiol; Sigma Xi; Biophys Soc; American Assn Cancer Res. **Special Achievements:** Numerous contributions to the research of leukemia, sarcoma viruses, and studies on the nucleic acids of normal, benign, and malignant tissues. **Military Serv:** AUS 1955-57. **Business Addr:** Bldg 41, Suite 300, 9000 Rockville Pike, Bethesda, MD 20814.

PHILLIPS, LEROY DANIEL
Consultant. **Personal:** Born Jul 10, 1935, Texarkana, TX; son of Jessie Mae Phillips and L D Phillips; married Mary A; children: Kevin V. **Educ:** Los Angeles City Coll, AA 1967; California State Univ Los Angeles, BA 1972; Century Univ Los Angeles, MBA 1979. **Career:** Los Angeles County, various positions including pharmacy storekeeper, pharmaceuticals supply mgmt for med center, div chief supply & transportation mechanical dept, building crafts mgr 1956-85; Business Mgmt Consulting, commodities broker 1986-. **Orgs:** Apptd Interview Bds Dept of Personnel LA County 1977-83, 1979-81; chmn Coastal Mental Health Governing Bd 1980-83; president Diane Watson Semi-Professional Sports Assoc 1986-; volunteer role player LA County Sheriff Dept 1986-; trustee Intergroup Trust 1987-; lifetime mem LA County Employees Assoc. **Honors/Awds:** Special Citation Serv Employees Intl Union 1985; United Way Award 1985; Leadership Award Brotherhood Crusade 1986; Leadership Award United Negro College Fund 1986.

PHILLIPS, LIONEL GARY
Media executive. **Personal:** Born May 1, 1950, New York, NY; son of Oscar & Johnetta; divorced. **Educ:** City Coll of New York, BA, English, 1973. **Career:** CBS News, Crisis in Black America, field producer, CBS reports, 1985, CBS Morning News, producer, 1986-87; New Jersey Network Mews, exec prod, 1987-88; WCBS TV News, segment prod, 1988-91, prod, Sunday Edition, 1990-91, exec prod, 1991-, news mgr, 1991-. **Orgs:** Natl Assn of Black Journalists; Writers Guild of America. **Honors/Awds:** Natl Academy of TV Arts & Sciences, Emmy, 1978, 1989; Harlem YMCA, Black Achievers in Industry, 1976. **Special Achievements:** Instructor, NABJ Journalism Short Course, Temple Univ, 1995. **Business Addr:** News Manager, WCBS - TV News, 524 W 57th St, New York, NY 10019, (212)975-5589.

PHILLIPS, LLOYD GARRISON, JR.
Thoracic/cardiovascular surgeon. **Personal:** Born May 23, 1941, Dayton, OH; son of Mary Phillips and Lloyd Phillips; married Connie Cunningham; children: Allan, Garrison. **Educ:** Miami Univ Oxford OH, BA 1962; Meharry Medical Coll, MD 1966; Univ of Minnesota, PhD 1973. **Career:** Univ of Minnesota, grad stud anat 1966-73, resident genl surgery 1966-74; OH State Univ, resident thoracic & Cardiovascular surg 1974-76; Dayton VA Medical Ctr, chief thoracic & cardiovascular surgery 1978-. **Orgs:** Medical advisor Concerned Citizens for Cancer 1982-; mem bd dirs Otterbein Home Lebanon OH 1983-; founding mem Amer Assoc of Clinical Anatomists 1983-; mem Alpha Phi Alpha, Alpha Omega Alpha. **Honors/Awds:** Published papers, monographs, book chapter. **Home Addr:** 9572 Bridlewood Tr, Spring Valley, OH 45370.

PHILLIPS, RALPH LEONARD
Senior planning analyst. **Personal:** Born May 11, 1925, Sacramento, CA; son of Bessie Wundus Phillips and Harry Wendall Phillips, Jr; married Alice Hall Phillips, Dec 1, 1990. **Educ:** Univ of CA Berkeley, AB (Cum Laude) 1949, MA; Institute of African Studies Northwestern Univ, Special Studies. **Career:** Bureau of Intl Relations Univ of CA, rsch assoc 1950; Univ of CA, teaching fellow political science 1952-55; USIA, information officer/cultural attache 1956-68, Arabic language training, 1959-61 (Beirut, Lebannon), special asst to the dir Near East & Southeast Asia Washington Headquarters 1963-64; Mobil Oil Community & Public Affairs Tripoli Libya, 1969-71, International Gov Rels New York and Fairfax, Virginia, sr planning analyst, Intl Division, 1971-. **Orgs:** Dir of Planning Educ Task Force Council of Econ Develop New York City as Mobil rep 1971-72; bd of dirs DPF Inc (NYSE) 1972-74; mem Mayor's Adv Council on Housing Princeton 1973-75; bd of dir Council on Intl Programs 1975; mem Campanille Soc Univ of CA 1976-; mem Zoning Bd Princeton 1977-79; vice pres Princeton Republican Assoc 1978-80; mem Princeton Regional Planning Bd 1981-86; mem bd of trustees St Paul's Coll Lawrence VA 1983-; mem Prince Hall F&A Masons Aaron #9 Princeton NJ; 32nd Degree Ophir Consistory, Trenton NJ; Shriner Prince Hall Masons Kufu, Princeton NJ; American Legion Post #218 Princeton NJ. **Honors/Awds:** Hon Students Soc Univ of CA Merit Awd Dept of St 1956; Merit Awd Dept of St 1967; Pi Sigma Alpha Natl Polit Sci Hon Soc; Delta Sigma Rho Natl Forensic Hon Soc. **Military Serv:** US Army T/4 Med & Phil Islands; US Army Ready Reserve Presidio of San Francisco Military Intelligence 1957-61. **Home Addr:** 156 13th St, SE, Washington, DC 20003.

PHILLIPS, ROBERT HANSBURY
Personnel manager (retired). **Personal:** Born Nov 19, 1924, Detroit, MI; son of Bertha Hansbury Phillips and William Phillips; married Rose Mary Franklin Phillips, Sep 4, 1946; children: Hilanius Hansbury. **Educ:** Wayne State University, Detroit, MI, BS, 1952, MPA, 1967, PhD, 1987. **Career:** City of Detroit Personnel Department, Detroit, MI, personnel manager, 1953-88. **Orgs:** Member, International Personnel Management Association, 1953-; past director, Personnel Management Association, Michigan Chapter, 1953-; member, Public Personnel Administration; member, American Political Science Association, 1983-88; member, Detroit Personnel Council, 1953-88. **Honors/Awds:** Equal Employment Opportunity, Affirmative Action, Mayoral Initiatives and Bureaucratic Responses: The Case of Detroit, Dissertation, 1987; Author, A Peek Through the Curtain: A Trilogy; Men Are Like A Puff of Wind, unpublished; Lives of Tears, unpublished; Up Jumped the Canaille, unpublished, 1991. **Military Serv:** US Army, Sergeant, 1943-46; Victory Medal, American Theatre Ribbon, Asiatic Pacific Theatre Ribbon with 2 Bronze Battle Stars, Philippine Liberation Ribbon with 1 Bronze Star, 3 Overseas Service Bars, Good Conduct Medal. **Home Addr:** 6054 Oakman Blvd, Detroit, MI 48228.

PHILLIPS, ROMEO ELDRIDGE
Educator. **Personal:** Born Mar 11, 1928, Chicago, IL; son of Sissieretta Lewis Phillips and James M Phillips Sr; married Deloris R Jordan; children: Pamela Marlene, Arthur JH. **Educ:** Chicago Conservatory Coll, MusB 1949; Chicago Musical Coll, MusM 1951; Eastern MI Univ, MA 1963; Wayne State Univ, PhD 1966. **Career:** Chicago IL Public Schools, teacher 1949-55; Detroit MI Public Schools, teacher 1955-57; Inkster MI Public Schools, teacher 1957-66; Kalamazoo Coll, chmn dept of educ 1974-86, tenured prof of educ/music 1968-93, prof emeritus, 1993-; Portage MI, city councilman, 1991-. **Orgs:** Mem Amer Assoc of Coll for Teacher Educ, Music Educators Natl Conf, MI Sch Vocal Assoc, Assoc for Supervison & Curriculum Develop, MI Assoc for Supervision & Curriculum Develop, MI Assoc for Improvement of Sch Legislation, Natl Alliance of Black School Educators, Natl Assoc of Negro Musicians, Phi Delta Kappa, Kappa Alpha Psi; conductor AfraAmerican Chorale. **Honors/Awds:** Invited by the govt of the Republic of Nigeria West Africa to be a guest to the World Festival of Black and African Art 1977; Omega Psi Phi Leadership Awd 1982; Committee of Scholars for the Accreditation of MI Colls 1982-84; Kalamazoo NAACP Appreciation Awd 1982; Fulbright Scholar to Liberia West Africa 1984-85; 13 journal publications; 1 magazine article; 2 book reviews; chapters contributed to or credit given in 6 books. **Military Serv:** AUS sgt 1951-53. **Home Addr:** 6841 Welbury, Portage, MI 49081. **Business Addr:** Prof Emeritus, Kalamazoo College, 1200 Academy, Kalamazoo, MI 49006.

PHILLIPS, ROSEMARYE L.
Retired educator. **Personal:** Born Jun 21, 1926, McNary, AZ; daughter of Octavia McNealy Howard and William LeForbes; married David Phillips, Nov 1949 (divorced); children: Pamela Phillips, Margaret McCalla, Darryl A Phillips. **Educ:** Arizona State Univ, Tempe AZ, AB, l947; Univ of Southern California, Los Angeles CA, MS, l956, MEd, l958; Brigham Young Univ, Provo, UT, Ed, l974. **Career:** Phoenix Dist #1, Phoenix AZ, teacher, 1947-50; Los Angeles City Schools, Los Angeles CA, teacher K-6, reading and math coordinator, supervising training teacher for USC, UCLA, Mt St Marys Coll, Los Angeles CA, asst principal, l952-86; prof educ, Mt St Mary's Coll, Pepperdine Univ, California State Univ, Los Angeles, Dominguez Hill. **Orgs:** Mem and recording sec, Natl Allance of Black School Educators (NABSE); mem, Health and Educ Groups, Congressional Black Caucus; past pres, Delta Sigma Theta, Beta Theta Chapter; l945-46; past pres, Council of Black Admin, Los Angeles, , l981-82; mem and sec, UNCF advisory bd, Los Angeles CA; trustee, First AME Church, Los Angeles CA; telephone coordinator, floor mgr, Lou Rawls Parade of Stars production, Los Angeles CA, l982-. **Honors/Awds:** Scholarship, Delta Sigma Theta to Arizona State Univ, l943-47; scholarship, Minister of Educ, Korea, l983.

PHILLIPS, TARI LYNN
Professional basketball player. **Personal:** Born Mar 6, 1969, Winter Park, FL; daughter of John and Doris Phillips. **Educ:** Univ of Georgia, 1987-88; Central Florida, bachelor's degree in communications, 1992. **Career:** Colorado Xplosion, forward, 1996-. **Business Addr:** Professional Basketball Player, Colorado Xplosion, 800 Grant St, Ste 410, Denver, CO 80203, (303)832-2225.

PHILLIPS, TONY (KEITH ANTHONY PHILLIPS)
Professional baseball player. **Personal:** Born Apr 25, 1959, Atlanta, GA. **Career:** Oakland A's, infielder, outfielder, 1982-89; Detroit Tigers, infielder, outfielder, 1990-95; California Angels, 1995-. **Honors/Awds:** World Series games with Oakland, 1988, 1989. **Business Phone:** (312)924-1000.

PHILLIPS, W. THOMAS
Business executive. **Personal:** Born Aug 2, 1943, Charleston, MS; son of Jessie Phillips and Walter Phillips; married Carline Bradford; children: Craig, Lee, Ernest. **Educ:** Univ Northern IA, Bus Admin 1966; Northeastern Univ Boston MA, Mgmt Devel 1978; Harvard University Graduate School of Business, advanced management program, 1988. **Career:** General Foods, sales rep dist mgr 1966-72; Quaker, sales planning zone mgr 1973-77, mgr sales devel 1978-79, mgr dir corp prog 1980-84, vice pres corp prog. **Orgs:** Mem Loaned Exec Assoc United Way of Chicago 1979-; bd mem Chicago Hearing Soc 1979-82, Donors Forum of Chicago, Natl Charities Info Bureau 1984-; mem Assn of Black Foundation Executives. **Honors/Awds:** 1st Black Vice Pres & Corp Officer elected by Quaker. **Home Addr:** 2415 N Douglas Ave, Arlington Heights, IL 60004. **Business Addr:** Vice President Corp Programs, The Quaker Oats Company, PO Box 9001, Chicago, IL 60604.

PHILLIPS, WILBURN R.
Bank executive. **Career:** Home Federal Savings Bank, Detroit MI, chief executive. **Business Addr:** Home Federal Savings Bank, 9108 Woodward Ave, Detroit, MI 48202.

PHILLS, BOBBY RAY, II
Professional basketball player. **Personal:** Born Dec 20, 1969, Baton Rouge, LA. **Educ:** Southern University, 1991. **Career:** Cleveland Cavaliers, guard, 1992-. **Business Addr:** Professional Basketball Player, Cleveland Cavaliers, Gund Arena, One Center Ct, Cleveland, OH 44115, (216)659-9100.

PICKARD, WILLIAM FRANK
Plastics company executive. **Personal:** Born Jan 28, 1941, La Grangee, GA; son of Victoria Woodyard Pickard and Willie H Pickard. **Educ:** Flint Mott College, Flint, MI, AS 1962; Western Michigan Univ, Kalamazoo, MI, BS 1964; Univ of Michigan, Ann Arbor, MI, MSW 1965; Ohio State Univ, Columbus, OH, PhD 1971. **Career:** Cleveland Urban League, dir educ 1965-67; NAACP, exec dir 1967-69; Wayne State Univ, prof 1971-74; McDonalds Res, owner 1971-; Cleveland State Univ, Cleveland, OH, associate director of urban studies, 1971-72; Wayne State Univ, Detroit, MI, associate professor, 1972-74; Regal Plastics Company, Roseville, MI, chairman/CEO, 1985-. **Orgs:** Board of directors, Michigan National Corporation, 1989-; board of directors, National Association of Black Automotive Suppliers, 1986-; board of directors, Federal Home Loan Bank, Indianapolis, IN, 1990-. **Honors/Awds:** Mental health NIMH Fellowship 1964; Haynes Fellowship Natl Urban League 1965; Honorary Doctorate in Business Administration, Cleary College, 1980. **Business Addr:** Chairman/CEO, Regal Plastics Company, 15700 Common Rd, PO Box 246, Roseville, MI 48066.

PICKENS, CARL MCNALLY
Professional football player. **Personal:** Born Mar 23, 1970, Murphy, NC. **Educ:** Univ of Tennessee, attended. **Career:** Cincinnati Bengals, wide receiver, 1992-. **Honors/Awds:** Pro Bowl, 1995. **Business Addr:** Professional Football Player, Cincinnati Bengals, One Bengals Dr, Cincinnati, OH 45202, (513)621-3550.

PICKENS, ERNESTINE W. MCCOY
Educator. **Personal:** Born Dec 21, 1936, Braden, TN; daughter of Rhobelia Alexander Williams and Ernest W Williams; married William G Pickens, Sep 30, 1977; children: Marcus Christopher McCoy, Leslie, Reese, Todd. **Educ:** Tennessee State University, BS, 1958; Atlanta University, MA, 1975; Emory University, PhD, 1986. **Career:** Shelby County Board of Education, Barret's Chapel High School, teacher, 1958-60; Cassopolis High School, teacher, 1961-62; Weaver High School, teacher, 1964-71; John Overton High School, teacher, 1971-73; Atlanta University, communications skills instructor, 1973; Clark College, assistant professor of English, 1975-86; Clark-Atlanta University, professor of English, 1987-. **Orgs:** College Language Association Standing Committee: English Curriculum; American Studies Association; National Council of Teachers of English; Toni Morrison Society; Langston Hughes Society. **Honors/Awds:** United Negro College Fund, Lilly Grant, 1982, Dana Award, 1981; US Labor Department, Appreciation Award, 1992; National Council of Teacher's of English, Appreciation Award, 1990; Clark College, Outstanding Teacher Award, 1978. **Special Achievements:** Author: Charles W Chesnutt and the Progressive Movement, 1994; Charles W Chesnutt's ''The Conjure Woman,'' Masterpieces African-American Literature, Harper and Collins Publishing, 1992; Charles W Chesnutt's ''The House Behind the Cedars in Master Plots,'' Salem Press, 1993; Scholar in Residence, New York Univ, 1996; founding pres, Charles Waddell Chessnutt Assn. **Business Addr:** Professor of English, Department of English, Clark Atlanta University, James P Brawley Dr & Fair St, Atlanta, GA 30314.

PICKENS, WILLIAM GARFIELD
Educator, author. **Personal:** Born Dec 27, 1927, Atlanta, GA; son of Eula Reese Pickens and William Garfield Pickens; married Theresa Smith, Aug 20, 1950; children: Leslie Rochelle, Kelsey Reese, Peter Todd, Marcus McCoy; married Ernestine McCoy, Sep 30, 1977. **Educ:** Morehouse College, BA (magna cum laude), 1948; Atlanta University, MA, 1950; University of Hartford, 1953-54, 1964-65; Trinity College, Summers, 1954-59; University of Connecticut, PhD, 1969. **Career:** Hillside High School, Durham NC, teacher, 1950; Chandler Evans, W Hartford CT, clerk, 1952-54; Hartford Board of Education, Hartford CT, teacher & dept head, 1954-70; US Post Office, Hartford CT, clerk, 1954-56; Pickens Realty, Hartford CT, pres, 1956-71; Morehouse College, Atlanta GA, professor/dept

chmn, 1970-84; prof, 1970-; Emory Univ, Atlanta, visiting prof of humanities, 1992-93. **Orgs:** College Language Assn, 1970-; Natl Council of Teachers of English, 1971-; Conference of College Composition & Communication, 1972-; American Dialect Society, 1975-; Friendship Baptist Church, 1977-; Peyton Woods Chalet Community Organization, 1978-; Langston Hughes Society, 1983-; Toni Morrison Society, 1992-; Phi Beta Kappa. **Honors/Awds:** Service plaque, Realty Bd of Greater Hartford, 1964; Author, Trends in Southern Sociolinguistics, 1975; Benj E Mays & Margaret Mitchell, A Unique Legacy in Medicine, 1996; Phi Beta Kappa, Delta of Georgia, 1984; Social Dialectology in Chesnutt's House behind Cedars, 1987; Distinguished Faculty Scholar, UNCF, 1984-85; Dana Faculty Fellowship, Dana Foundation, 1992-93. **Military Serv:** US Army, SFC, 1950-52. **Home Addr:** 2617 Peyton Woods Trail, Atlanta, GA 30311. **Business Addr:** Professor, Dept of English, Morehouse College, 830 Westview Dr SW, Brawley Hall 224, Atlanta, GA 30314.

PICKERING, ROBERT PERRY
Government administrator. **Personal:** Born Oct 23, 1950, Charleston, SC; married Deborah DeLaine; children: Robert, Richard, Russell, Randall. **Educ:** Voorhees Coll, BS 1972. **Career:** Chas Co Health Dept, environ tech 1976; SC Swine Flu Prog Cola, state coord 1979; DHEC SC State, epidemiologic Asst 1978-80; Health Dept Chas Co SC, prog dir 1980-81; Congressman T H Harnett, spec asst. **Orgs:** Treas Mitchell Elem Sch PTA 1978-85; pres St Patrick Parish Council 1979-82; chmn Mitchell Elem Sch Adv Council 1979-83; bd mem Charleston OIC 1980-83; bd mem Morris Coll Indus Bd 1983-86; adv SC Natl Black Republican Council 1984-. **Honors/Awds:** Comm Serv Omega Psi Phi Frat Mu Alpha Chas SC 1978; OYMOA US Jaycees 1981 & 1982. **Home Addr:** 179 Line St, Charleston, SC 29403. **Business Addr:** Special Assistant, Congressman TH Hartnett, Rm 640 334 Meeting St, Charleston, SC 29403.

PICKETT, ALVIN L.
Business executive (retired). **Personal:** Born May 22, 1930, Mt Morris, MI; married Patricia L Lett; children: Rocky, George, Tricia. **Career:** MI Dept of Lbr, chf dept dir; MI St Empl Assn, lgsltv agnt-adm asst 1965-72; MI St Senate, chf snt dcmnts rm 1957-65; Boys Training Sch, super 1955-57. **Orgs:** Mem Intl Assn of Govt Lbr Ofcls IAGLO; Am Soc for Training & Devel ASTD; Intl Assn of Indus Accid Bds & Commns IAIABC; pres Lnsng Urban Leag 1971-73; pres Lnsng Old Nwsbys 1970-71; bd of dir Mid-MI Chap Am Red Cr 1968-73; bd of dir Lnsng NAACP 1960-62; Cub Mstr 1960-64; Sct Mstr 1964-66; Cptl Ldg No 8 Pnnslr Cnsstry No 44; Shrine Tmpl No 167 Prince Hall Affil; Dlgt Nat Rep Cov 1972; Rep St Cntrl 1971-; DAV Am Leg. **Military Serv:** USMC sgt 1950-53.

PICKETT, DONNA A.
Public affairs executive. **Personal:** Born Jun 11, 1949, Lexington, VA; daughter of Gladys Jones Harris and Mallory Wayne Harris; married Edward E. Pickett; children: Monica, Aaron. **Educ:** Virginia Commonwealth University, Richmond, VA, BA, English. **Career:** Virginia Power, Richmond, VA, office supervisor, supervisor personnel services, supervisor of records management, directors of minority affairs, currently, with company since 1969. **Orgs:** Chairperson, Virginia Council on Status of Women, 1991-94; board member, Virginia Black History Museum and Cultural Center, 1989-; chairperson, Business Advisory Council, Organization of Chinese Americans; vice president, external relations, Virginia/North Carolina AABE Chapter. **Honors/Awds:** Performance Award, 1985, Achievement Award, 1984, 1985, Suggestion Patent Award, 1984, Virginia Power; Mentorship Program Award, Virginia Commonwealth University, 1987; Award, Bennett College Board of Trustees, Black Executive Exchange Program, 1989, 1991, 1992. **Home Addr:** 7805 Kahlua Dr, Richmond, VA 23227. **Business Addr:** Director, Minority Affairs, Public Affairs Dept, Virginia Power, PO Box 26666, 20th Fl, Richmond, VA 23261.

PICKETT, DOVIE T.
District chairperson. **Personal:** Born Nov 22, 1921, Hinze, MS; widowed; children: Fosterson Eddie Lee Brown. **Educ:** Lewis Bus Coll, 1952; Int Data Proc Inst, 1956; Univ of MI Cntr for Adlt Std, 1969; Wayne Co Comm Coll. **Career:** 13th Cong Dist Repub Com, pct del/chrprsn 1954-, 13th dist coord, elected 13th dist repub com chrprsn 1969-, exec sec 1963-66; MI Chmn Com & MI State Repub Com, v chrprsn; Eisenhower/Nixon for Pres & VP, dist cam chrprsn 1954; 13th Cong Dist Hdqtrs, apptd exec sec 1962-67; 13th DistRep Women Club, pres 1963-67; Rep Women's Fed of MI, elected sec; 13th Dist Cam for Pres Nixon & Sen Robert P Griffin, coord 1972. **Orgs:** Mem Elec Coll MI 1972; co-chrprsn MI Nat Black Com for Re-elect of Pres Nixon 1972; del Repub Nat Conv 1972; 1st vice-chrprsn Nat Black Repub Coun MI Chpt; mem Black Coun for Rep Pol Inc; mem Intl Platform Assn; bd of dir United Rep of MI; mem Wayne Co Rep Educ Coun; mem Rep Women's Fed of MI; bd mem Wayne Co Juvenile Fac Network; mem Friends of Equal Justice Com; Cit Governing Bd Model Neighborhood Agency; chrprsn Economic Devel Loan Group; mem Economic Devel Com; Trans & Comm Com 1971-73; life mem NAACP; mem Order of Estrn Star; mem Star of Bethlehem Chap III; mem People's Comm Ch; mem Sigma Gamma Rho; vol GM Red Cross Open Heart Surgery Prog; adv bd The Optometric Inst & Clinic of Detroit Inc; mem Citizen's Adv Counc Wayne Co Comm Coll; pres stdnt govt WayneCo Comm Coll; chrprsn BalThomas Comm Counc 1976-78; Nat Black Women's Caucus. **Honors/Awds:** Cert of Accomplishment Div of Bus Admin Univ of MI 1971; Serv Award Black Nat Voters Div for Re-Elect of the Pres & Vice Pres 1972 & 1976; Cert as Mem of Elec Coll 1972 Election; delegate to Repub Nat Conv 1972 & 1976; Citation Pres Richard Nixon 1972; Citation Sen Robert P Griffin 1972; Elected to Serve on Com on Orgn Repub Nat Conv 1976; Spl Tribute MI Repub House of Rep 1977; Outstand Serv Award MI Repub Party 1977; Cert of Apprec Wayne Co Repub Educ Counc 1977; Cert of Recog Detroit Pub Sch Reg I 1977; Outstand Serv Award Gov Wm G Milliken 1977. **Business Addr:** c/o Office of Student Act, Wayne Co Community Coll 4612 W, Detroit, MI 48201.

PICKETT, HENRY B., JR.
Cleric, educator (retired). **Personal:** Born Mar 21, 1938, Morehead City, NC; married Mary Louise Hoffler; children: Marquis DeLafayette, Sherry Louise. **Educ:** Elizabeth City State Univ, BS 1961; NC Central Univ, MA 1973; Shaw Divinity Sch, Shaw Divinity Sch, MDiv, 1977. **Career:** Raleigh City, elem tchr 1963-72; St Augustine's Coll, counselor foreign student adv 1972-73; Fuguay Varina, counselor 1973-76; Oberlin Bapt Ch, pastor 1977-80; Wendell First Baptist Ch, pastor 1982-85; East Millbrook Middle Sch, counselor 1976-91. **Orgs:** Bapt minister Wake Co Bd Edn; Amer Personnel & Guidance Assn; Amer Sch Counselor Assn; NEA; NCPGA; NC Assn Educators; Phi Delta Kappa; NAACP; Kingwood Forest Comm Assn Inc; pres Black Dem Caucus; Wake Co chmn 1974; Omega Psi Phi Frat Inc. **Honors/Awds:** Man of Yr Oberlin Bapt Ch 1968; Phi Delta Kappa 1975; Omega Achievement Award; Citizen of Yr 1974; Iota Iota Chpt; Boy Scout Dist Award Merit 1971; Elizabeth City State Univ, Outstanding Alumni Service Award, 1995; Downtown Housing Improvement Award, 1995; Sertoma Club Service to Mankind Award, 1997; NC Conference of Brances, NAACP, President's Award, 1997. **Military Serv:** US Army, cpl, 1961-63. **Home Addr:** 824 Cross Link Rd, Raleigh, NC 27610.

PICKETT, ROBERT E.
Educator. **Personal:** Born Sep 8, 1936, Brookhaven, MS; married Dorothy Owens; children: Deborah Denise, Ritchie Elyot. **Educ:** Alcorn State U, BS 1957; MS Jackson State U, 1969; MS State U; Atlanta U; Jackson State U. **Career:** Vicksburg Jr High School, prin, 1977-80; Vicksburg High School, admin prin 1973-77; Randolph High School Passchristian, MS, teacher/coach 1957-59; Weathers High School Rolling Park, MS, teacher 1959-60; Temple High School Vicksburg, MS, teacher/coach/adm asst 1960-64; McIntyre Elem Jr High School Vicksburg, MS, prin 1964-66; Jefferson Jr High School Vicksburg, MS, prin 1966-73; Vicksburg Warren School District, superintendent, 1994-, deputy superintendent, 1987-94; Vicksburg High School, principal, 1980-87. **Orgs:** Mem Vicksburg Tchr Assn; Nat Ed Assn; Am Assn of Sch Admin; mem/2 yr vice-chmn Elks Fidelity Lodge #507; ETA TAU Chap Omega Psi Phi Frat Basileus 1969-71; pres Warren Co United Fund 1973; bd mem mgmt/5 yrs as chmn Jackson St YMCA 1966-70; mem Vicksburg Park Comm 1970-80; pres Port City Kiwanis Club 1975-76; bd dirs Communications Improvement Inc WLBT-TV 3; bd of dirs, Vicksburg Warren Cty Chamber of Commerce; bd of dirs, Merchant Bank. **Honors/Awds:** YMCA Serv Award 1969; UGF Serv Award 1973; Golden Lamp Award, MS Assn, 1997. **Business Addr:** Superintent, Vicksburg Warren School District, 1500 Mission 66, Vicksburg, MS 39180, (601)638-5122.

PIERCE, AARON
Professional football player. **Personal:** Born Sep 6, 1969, Seattle, WA; son of Samuel. **Educ:** Univ of Washington, attended. **Career:** New York Giants, tight end, 1992-. **Business Addr:** Professional Football Player, New York Giants, Giants Stadium, East Rutherford, NJ 07073, (201)935-8111.

PIERCE, AARONETTA HAMILTON
Association executive. **Personal:** Born Jan 8, 1943, Somerville, TN; daughter of Clementine Lofties Hamilton and David A Hamilton; married Joseph A Pierce Jr, Mar 1, 1964; children: Joseph Aaron, Michael Arthur. **Educ:** Tennessee State University, Nashville, TN, 1959-61; State University of Iowa, Iowa City, IA, BA, 1961-63. **Career:** San Antonio Independent School District, San Antonio, TX, teacher, 1964-67. **Orgs:** Bd of trustees, Fisk University, 1992-; Commissioner, Texas Commission on the Arts, 1985-91; chairperson, Mayor's Blue Ribbon Committee on the Arts for San Antonio, 1988-89; chairperson, first Martin Luther King Jr. Commission and Celebration for San Antonio, Natl Arts dir, The Links Inc, 1994-98, 1986-87; chairperson, Texas Arts Award, Texas Arts Alliance, 1988; regional arts committee chairperson, Alpha Kappa Alpha Sorority, 1991; executive committee, United Way of San Antonio, 1988-94. **Honors/Awds:** San Antonio Women's Hall of Fame, City of San Antonio, 1984; Texas Black Women's Hall of Fame, 1986; Nominee, Inductee into Texas Women's Hall of Fame, 1993; Headliner Award, Women in Communications, 1989; JC Penney Golden Rule Award, Cultural Category, 1984. **Business Phone:** (210)490-4084.

PIERCE, ABE, III
Mayor. **Career:** Mayor, Monroe (LA), 1996-; Ouachita Parish school system, asst superintendent, until 1996. **Orgs:** Ouachita Parish police jury. **Special Achievements:** First African American mayor of Monroe (LA) since Reconstruction. **Business Addr:** Mayor, City of Monroe, City Hall of Monroe, P O Box 123, Monroe, LA 71210-0123, (318)329-2310.

PIERCE, CHESTER MIDDLEBROOK
Educator. **Personal:** Born Mar 4, 1927, Glen Cove, NY; son of Hettie Pierce and Samuel Pierce; married Jocelyn Patricia Blanchet, Jun 15, 1949; children: Diane Blanchet Williams; Deirdre Anona. **Educ:** Harvard Coll, AB 1948; Harvard Med Sch, MD 1952. **Career:** Univ of Cincinnati, instructor 1957-60; Univ of OK, asst prof, prof 1960-69; Harvard Univ, prof 1969-. **Orgs:** Pres Amer Bd of Psychiatry & Neurology 1978; pres Amer Orthopsychiatric Assn 1983; founding natl chmn Black Psychiatrists of Amer 1969; advisor Children's TV Workshop (Sesame Street) 1969-; sr consul Peace Corps 1965-69; natl consult to the surgeon genl USAF 1976-82; director, NASA's Life Sciences & Microgravity Sciences Research Advisory Committee, 1996. **Honors/Awds:** Pierce Peak (in Antartica for biomedical rsch) 1968; Special Recog Awd Natl Med Assn 1974; Honorary Fellow Royal Australian & New Zealand Coll of Psychiatrists 1978; mem Inst of Medicine at the Natl Acad of Sciences; Solomon Carter Fuller Awd, American Psychiatric Assn 1986; Chester M Pierce Annual Research Seminar Natl Medical Assn 1988-; Honorary ScD degree, Westfield State, 1977, Tufts Univ, 1984; World Psychiatric Assoc, Masserman Award, 1989; Honorary Fellow, Royal College of Psychiatrists, 1995. **Military Serv:** USNR comdr. **Home Addr:** 17 Prince St, Jamaica Plain, MA 02130. **Business Addr:** Prof, Educ Psych Public Health, Harvard Univ, Nichols House Appian Way, Cambridge, MA 02138.

PIERCE, CYNTHIA STRAKER
Educator. **Personal:** Born Jul 20, Brooklyn, NY; daughter of Enid Bayley Straker and Milton Straker; married Lawrence W. **Educ:** Hunter Coll, AB 1950; Brooklyn Law Sch, LLB 1953, LLM 1956. **Career:** Private Practice, atty 1954-56; Howard Univ, faculty 1956-62; FAA, atty, advisor 1962-69; US Dept of Transp, atty Ofc of Sec 1969-82; St John's School of Law, assoc prof 1983-. **Orgs:** NY, WA & DC Bar Assn; US Supreme Ct Nat Bar Assn; Fed Bar Assn; NAACP; Nat Urban League. **Honors/Awds:** Fed Women's Award Dept of Transp 1979; Hunter Coll Hall of Fame 1983. **Special Achievements:** Author, DC Lawyer's Handbook. **Business Addr:** Associate Professor, St Johns Univ School of Law, Grand Central & Utopia Pkwy, Jamaica, NY 11439.

PIERCE, EARL S.
Clergyman. **Personal:** Born Nov 29, 1942, Bridgeton, NJ; married Joyce; children: Amy. **Educ:** Glassboro State Coll, AB 1965; Philadelphia Div Sch, MDiv 1970. **Career:** Dicoese of NJ, episcopal priest; A & A Frat Rho Chap Phila, chaplain; Migrant Laborers in NJ, chaplain 1966-74; St Cyprians Glassboro, NJ, seminarin in charge 1969-70. **Orgs:** Mem Inter & Borough Ministerium; pres Lawnside Bd of Educ 1974-; chaplaing US Army Nat Guard of NJ; Black Elected Ofcls of NJ; trustee Lawnside Five Co; Lawnside Dem Club. **Honors/Awds:** Recip Chapel of Four Chaplains Award.

PIERCE, FRANK POWELL
City official, attorney. **Personal:** Born Dec 28, 1953, San Antonio, TX; son of Marie Pierce and Arnold L Pierce Sr; married Ernestine Marlbrough, Jun 20, 1989; children: Stephen. **Educ:** University of Houston, BA, politcal science, 1977; Thurgood Marshall School of Law, JD, 1980. **Career:** City of San Antonio, staff attorney, legal aid associate, 1980-83, municiple court prosecutor, 1983-84, assistant city attorney, 1984-87, Bexar County Court at Law #2, state judge, 1987-88, private law practice, 1988-; Incarnate Word College, adjunct professor, 1989-; City of San Antonio, city council member, 1991-. **Orgs:** Martin Luther King Commission, multi-cultural chairman, 1988-89; College of Texas State Bar, 1989-; Texas State Judicial Council, 1987-88; admitted to practice in US District Court, 1982, US Court of Appeals Circuit, 1982, US Supreme Court, 1984. **Honors/Awds:** Omega Psi Phi Fraternity Inc, Citizen of the Year, 1987; The Judicial Council of the National Bar Association, Outstanding Service Award, 1989, Certificate of Ordination, Baptist deacon, 1987. **Special Achievements:** Chairman, City Council Affirmative Action Committee, 1991; chairman, City Council Small Business Committee, 1991; chairman, City Council Neighborhoods & Business Sub-Committee, 1991.

PIERCE, GREGORY W.
Physician. **Personal:** Born Sep 25, 1957, Vallejo, CA; son of Geraldine Brunridge Pierce and Raymond O Pierce Jr; married Eurica Hill Pierce, Aug 4, 1990. **Educ:** Wabash Coll, BA 1979; Meharry Medical Coll, MD 1983. **Career:** Univ of TN Jackson-Madison Co General Hospital, intern & resident 1983-86; Family Health Assocs, staff physician 1986-. **Orgs:** Chmn Journal Comm Malcolm X Inst of Black Studies Wabash Coll; jr class pres, sr class pres Meharry Medical Coll; term trustee Meharry Medical Coll Bd of Trustees; certified instructor Advanced Cardiac Life Support; mem Amer and TN Medical Assocs; mem Amer and TN Acad of Family Physicians; mem Southern Medi-

cal Assoc, Natl Medical Assoc; chmn, Dept of Medicine, Middle TN Med Ctr, 1990-91. **Honors/Awds:** Honor Scholarship & Dean's List Wabash Coll; Alvin P Hall Scholarship; Mosby Scholarship Book Award; Upjohn Award for Excellence in Clinical and Academic Obstetrics and Gynecology; Pre-Alumni Assoc Annual Senior Recognition Award; Alpha Omega Alpha Honor Medical Soc; Board Certified Amer Bd of Family Practice 1986-99. **Business Addr:** Staff Physician, Patient First, 5000 Cox Rd, Glen Allen, VA 23060-9200.

PIERCE, LAWRENCE WARREN
Judge. **Personal:** Born Dec 31, 1924, Philadelphia, PA; son of Leora Bellinger Pierce and Harold E Pierce; married Wilma Taylor, Sep 1948 (died 1978); children: Warren Wood, Michael Lawrence, Mark Taylor. **Educ:** St Joseph Univ, BS 1948; Fordham Univ, JD 1951. **Career:** Gen law practice New York City 1951-61; Kings Co NY, asst dist atty 1954-61; NYC, dep police comm 1961-63; NYS Div Youth Albany, dir 1963-66; NYS Narc Addiction Cont Comm, chmn 1966-70; SUNYA Grad Sch Crim Justice, vis prof 1970-71; S Dist NY, US dist judge 1971-81; US Foreign Intelligence Surveillance Ct, judge 1979-81; US Court of Appeals, judge 1981-91; senior judge, 1991-95; Cambodian Court Training Project of Intl Human Rights Law Group, 1995-. **Orgs:** Pres Cath Inter Council 1957-63; trustee Fordham Univ, 1985-91; mem NBA, ABA; Former board member, Lincoln Hall for Boys, 1972-92; bd mgrs, Havens Relief Fund Soc; Amer Law Inst, CARE USA; member of board, St Joseph's University, Phil, PA, practising law inst; bd of trustees Practising Law Inst; formerly mem Amer Law Inst; mem of delegations to Africa, Sweden, England, Japan, Vietnam, Korea, West Germany, and People's Republic of China to study legal, judicial and correctional systems; member; Council on Foreign Relations. **Honors/Awds:** Fordham Univ Sch of Law BALSA's Ruth Whitehead Whaley Awd for Distinguished Legal Achievement; Judicial Friends' Judge Jane Bolin Awd; Honorary degrees: St Joseph Univ, DHL, 1967; Fairfield Univ, LLD, 1972; Fordham Univ, LLD, 1982; Hamilton College, LLD, 1987; St John's Univ, LLD, 1990. **Military Serv:** US Army, Sgt, 1943-46. **Business Addr:** Circuit Judge, US Court of Appeals, US Courthouse, Foley Sq, New York, NY 10007.

PIERCE, PONCHITTA A.
Magazine/television journalist. **Personal:** Born Aug 5, 1942, Chicago, IL; daughter of Nora Pierce and Alfred Pierce. **Educ:** Univ of Southern CA, BA 1964; Cambridge Univ, attended summer 1962. **Career:** Ebony Magazine, asst editor 1964-65, assoc editor 1965-67; Johnson Publishing Co, NY editorial bureau chief 1967-68; CBS News, special correspondent 1968-71; McCall's Magazine, contributing editor 1973-76; Reader's Digest, staff writer 1975-77, roving editor 1977-80; WNBC-TV, magazine writer/TV host, currently; Parade Magazine, contributing editor, 1994. **Orgs:** Mem Theta Sigma Phi NY Chapter, Amer Fedn of TV & Radio Artists, Amer Women in Radio & TV, Natl Acad of TV Arts & Sciences, NY Chapter dir African Student Aid Fund; mem Women's Forum, mem Manhattan advisory comm NY Urban League. **Honors/Awds:** Penney-Mo Magazine Award 1967; Headliner Award Natl Theta Sigma Phi 1970. **Business Addr:** WNBC-TV, 30 Rockefeller Cntr, #315 W, New York, NY 10020.

PIERCE, RAYMOND O., JR.
Educator, physician. **Personal:** Born May 17, 1931, Monroe, LA; married Geraldine Brundidge; children: Raymond III, Gregory, Leannette, Geralyn, Lori. **Educ:** Fisk Univ Nashville, TN, BA 1951; Meharry Med Clg Nashville, TN, MD 1955; VA Hosp Des Moines, IA Univ of IA, Residency 1963. **Career:** Self-employed physician, 1963-69; Methodist Hospital, courtesy staff, 1969-; Winona Hospital, hon staff, 1969-; IN Univ Med Ctr, asst prof, 1970-76; consulting staff, US Army Hospital Ft Benjamin Harrison, 1976-79; IN Univ Med Ctr, assoc prof, 1976-80, prof of ortho, 1981-. **Orgs:** Bd dir Martin Ctr 1970-; bd dir St Elizabeth's Home 1980-83; bd dir Flanner House 1980-; pres Aesculapian Med Soc 1972-75; Am Acad Ortho Surg; Am Assc Advncmnt Sci; Am Assc Surg Trauma; exmnr cert Am Bd Ortho Surg 1976-84; credentials com Am Clg Surgeons 1983-84; Am Fracture Assn; Am Soc Sports Medicine; chrtr mem Am Trauma Soc; chrmn bd Group Practice Inc 1973-79; sec pres Hoosier State Med Assn 1968-75; pres sec/Tres IN Bone & Joint Clb 1980-; chrmn cont med ed com IN Ortho Soc 1970-80; Intrl Clg Surgeons; bd trustee MDDS 1968-74; house delegates co-chrmn ortho sect exec com ortho sec Natl Med Assn 1963-76; Pan-Pacific Surg Soc; Sigma XI-Rsrch Soc. **Honors/Awds:** One of 50 black distngshd blck ldrs Honoree FAC Clb Indianpolis, IN 1973; summer furness award Outstndg Comm Serv 1977; phys rcgntn award AMA 1977-83; Phys Recognition Award NMA 1981-83; third place scntfc award "Treatment of Osteonecrosis of the Hip" IN State Med Assc Meeting 1980; first place scntfc award "The Assessment of Bone Healing in Bone Impedance" IN State Med Assn Meeting 1982; third pl scntfc award "The Effect of Alcohol on the Skeletal System" IN State Med Assc Meeting 1984; Govnr Award Cncl of the Sagamore of Wabash 1984; publctns including Alcohol, Underlying Cause of Many Skeletal Lesions Ortho News Vol 6 2 Mar/Apr 1984 p3, The Effect of Alcohol on Skeletal System Ortho Review Vol XIV 1 Jan 1985 pp45-49, Treatment of Subtroc hanteric Fractures with a FlexibleIntramedulla-Rod Ortho Transctns Vol 8 3 Fall 1984 441, The Effect of Alcohol on Skeletal System IN State Med Assc Scntfc Award Third Pl Indpls, IN Oct 1984, Immediate Intrnl Fixation of Gunshot Fracturs Am Acad Ortho Surgeons Las Vegas, NV Jan 1985. **Military Serv:** USAF capt 1956-58. **Business Addr:** Professor of Orthopaedic Surg, Indiana Univ Medical Center, 960 Locke St, Indianapolis, IN 46202.

PIERCE, REUBEN G.
Educator. **Personal:** Born Nov 30, 1926, Omaha, NE; married Leslie Ann Hazur; children: 5. **Educ:** Univ Omaha, BA 1949; Univ Omaha, MS 1952; Columbia U, Grad Work 1957-60; Univ MA, EdD 1974. **Career:** Johnson C Smith Univ, instr 1953-54; VA State, 1954-60; VA State Coll, asst prof 1960-61; asso prof 1961-65; Bennett Coll, asso prof 1965-67; Dept Science DC Schools, asst dir 1967-69; Dept Science DC Public Schools, supr dir 1969-74; Washington DC HS, prin; Natl Science Found Coop Coll School Science Program Amer Univ Cath Univ, asso dir 1968-70; Fed Funded Projects DC, dir 1971-73. **Orgs:** Chmn Assn Central Office of School Ofcrs 1969-; Nat Sci Tchrs Assn; chmn NSTA Black Caucus 1971-72. **Honors/Awds:** Ford Found Fellow 1972-73; Phi Delta Kappa Hon Frat; Kappa Delta Pi Hon Soc; Beta Kappa Chi Hon Soc; Sigma Pi Sigma Hon Soc. **Military Serv:** USAAF sgt 1945-46. **Business Addr:** Ballou Sr HS, 4 & Trenton Sts, Washington, DC 20032.

PIERCE, RICKY CHARLES
Professional basketball player. **Personal:** Born Aug 19, 1959, Dallas, TX. **Educ:** Rice Univ Houston, TX, 1979-83. **Career:** Detroit Pistons, 1983, San Diego Clippers, 1984, Milwaukee Bucks, 1985-91; Seattle SuperSonics, 1991-94; Golden State Warriors, 1994-95; Indiana Pacers, 1995-96; Charlotte Hornets, 1996-. **Honors/Awds:** NBA, Sixth Man Award, 1987, 1990. **Special Achievements:** NBA Draft, First round pick, #18, 1982; NBA, All-Star game, 1991. **Business Addr:** Professional Basketball Player, Charlotte Hornets, One Hive Dr, Charlotte, NC 28217, (704)357-0252.

PIERCE, RUDOLPH F.
Attorney. **Personal:** Born Aug 12, 1942, Boston, MA; married Carneice T; children: Kristen, Khari. **Educ:** Hampton Inst, BA 1967; Harvard Law Sch, JD 1970. **Career:** Goulston & Storrs, attorney, 1991-; Superior Ct of MA, judge; Magistrate US Dist Ct, judge; Keating Perretta & Pierce, ptnr 1975-76; Crane Inker & Oteri, ptnr 1974-75; Crane Inker & Oteri, asso 1972-74; Roxbury Multi-Svc Ctr, dir legal serv 1971-72; Mayor's Safe St Act Com, legal adminstr 1970-72; Atty David S Nelson, asso; Harbridge House Inc, 1970; Boston Legal Asstnc Proj, legal intern 1968-69. **Orgs:** Pres, Boston Bar Assn, 1989-90. **Honors/Awds:** First black pres, Boston Bar Assn. **Military Serv:** AUS Sp-4 1960-63. **Business Addr:** Attorney, Goulston & Storrs, 400 Atlantic Ave, Boston, MA 02110.

PIERCE, SAMUEL R., JR.
Government official (retired), attorney. **Personal:** Born Sep 8, 1922, Glen Cove, NY; son of Hettie E and Samuel R; married Barbara Wright; children: Victoria Pierce. **Educ:** Cornell Univ, AB (Hon) 1947, JD 1949; NY Univ, LLM Taxation 1952; NY Univ, LLD 1972; Hon Degrees incl, LLD, LHD, DCL, D. Litt. **Career:** New York City, asst dist atty 1949-52; S Dist NY; asst U.S. attny 1952-54; Undersecretary of Labor, asst 1954-56; US House of Rep, Subcom Antitrust of Jud Comm, counsel 1956-57; private practice, attny 1957-59, 1961-70, 1973-81, 1989-; NY Court Gen Sess, judge 1959-60; Battle Fowler Stokes & Kheel, partner 1961-70; US Treas, gen couns 1970-73; Battle Fowler Jaffin Pierce Kheel partner 1973-81; Sec, Housing & Urban Devel, 1981-1989; The Turner Corp, consultant, 1989-. **Orgs:** Dir Prudential Ins Co of Amer 1964-70, 1973-81, US Industries 1964-70, 1973-79, Intl Paper Co 1973-81, 1989-, Gen Elect Co 1974-81, Intl Basic Econ Corp 1973-80; adj prof NY Univ School of Law 1957-70; trustee Mt Holyoke Coll 1964-80, Hampton Inst 1964-, Inst Intl Ed 1967-, Cornell Univ 1973; mem bd Overseers Visiting Comm for Psych & Soc Rel Harvard Univ 1969-74; mem, natl exec bd Boy Scouts of Amer 1969-; mem Alpha Phi Alpha, Alpha Phi Omega, Ford Found Fellow Yale Law School 1957-58; chmn impartial disciplinary rev bd New York City Transit System 1968-81; mem natl adv com Comptroller of Currency 1975-80; mem Natl Wiretapping Comm 1973-76; dir NY Worlds Fair Corp 1964-65; gov Amer Stock Exchange 1977-80; contrib articles to professional journals,1976-81; mem panel arbitrators Amer Arration Assn; Fed Mediation & Conciliation Serv, 1957-. **Honors/Awds:** Alexander Hamilton Awd US Treas Dept 1973; New York City Jr C of C Ann Distinguished Serv Awd 1958; Fellow Amer Coll Trial Lawyers; Martin Luther King, Jr. Center Salute to Greatness Award l989; Reagan Revolution Medal of Honor l989; The Presidential Citizens Medal l989.

PIERCE, WALTER J.
Educator. **Personal:** Born Jan 16, 1941, Minden, LA; married Iopha Douglas; children: Gay, Gwenevera, Iopha Anita. **Educ:** BS, 1964; graduate study. **Career:** Kiwanis Club, counselor, 1968-70; Atascadero State Hospital, recreation therapist, 1964-69; Tulare View, dir rehabilitation, 1969-70; Northside Hospital, dir activities, 1970-71; California State University, affirmative action coordinator, 1972-74, assistant coordination advising & testing services, 1974-. **Orgs:** Kiwanis Club, 1968-70; NAACP; Black Educator, Fresno, CA; Fresno Housing Affirmative Com; Bapt Sun Sch Supt; Plan Variation; chairman, Man Power & Econ Area 6. **Honors/Awds:** Outstanding Young Men America, 1970. **Business Addr:** Counselor, California State University, Fresno, Adivising Services, 5150 N Maple, Fresno, CA 93740-0066.

PIERCE, WILLIAM DALLAS
Psychologist. **Personal:** Born Nov 16, 1940, Sunbury, NC. **Educ:** Univ of Pitts, BS 1962; OH State U, MA 1965; OH State U, PhD 1967. **Career:** Priv Prac San Francisco CA, clinical psychologist 1969-; Dept of Psychology Univ of CA at Berkeley, lectr 1970-; Dept of Mentl Hlth Commn of MA, regional serv admin 1979-80; Westside Coimm Mental Hlth Cntr San Francisco, exec dir 1973-77; Westside Comm Mental Health Cntr, dir of clinical serv 1971-73. **Orgs:** Founding mem Assn of Black Psychologists 1968; chmn com on mental hlth Assn of Black Psychologists 1971-73; pres Bay Area Assn of Black Psychologists 1978-79. **Honors/Awds:** Apprec aw Assn of Black Psychologists 1970; Blacks in the West Hall of Fame San Francisco Africam Hist Cultural Soc 1976; annual aw for ldrshp & serv Assn of Black Psychologisgts 1980. **Business Addr:** 361 Upper Terr, San Francisco, CA 94117.

PIERRE, DALLAS
Dentist. **Personal:** Born Jun 9, 1933, Charenton, LA; son of Mr & Mrs Russell Pierre Sr; married Carol Ann Yates; children: James Darian. **Educ:** Prairie View A&M Coll, BS 1955; TX So Univ, MS 1963; Univ of TX Dental Br, DDS 1968; Trinity Univ, adv study. **Career:** Private practice, dentist, currently. **Orgs:** E TX Area BSA; Natl Platform Assn; Phi Beta Sigma; Univ of TX Alumni Assn; Citizens C of C Angelina Co; deacon, finance com chmn, Baptist Church; Piney Woods Kiwanis Club; past pres, Gulf State Dental Association; secretary, East TX Med Dent Phar Association; life mem, NAACP; E TX Minority Business Development Foundation Inc 1974-; Lufkin Daily News Editors' Roundtable; American Dental Association; National Dental Association, house of delegates, Academy of General Dentistry; Texas Dental Association; East Texas Dental Society; former member, Lufkin ISD School Board; Intl Platform Assn; Academy of General Dentistry. **Honors/Awds:** Colgate Dental Health Education Advisory Board, Honoree; Top Ladies of Distinction, Honoree for Support; Professional Activities Club of Nacogdoches and Angelina Counties, Citizen of the Year; NAACP, Golden Heritage Member; Notable Americans of the Bicentennial Era, Honoree; Community Leaders and Noteworthy Americans, Honoree. **Military Serv:** USAF airman 1st class 1956-60. **Business Addr:** Dentist, PO Box 1236, 809 Kurth Dr, Lufkin, TX 75901.

PIERRE, GERALD P.
Physician. **Personal:** Born Oct 14, 1951, Cayes, Haiti; divorced; children: Jeanette C. **Educ:** Bard Coll, AB 1975; Meharry Medical Coll, MD 1980. **Career:** Physician in Practice, ob/gyn 1980-. **Orgs:** Mem Amer Coll of Obstetrics & Gynecology 1980, Hartford Co & CT State Medical Assns 1984; diplomate Amer Bd of Ob/Gyn 1986. **Honors/Awds:** Teacher of the Year Ob/Gyn Dept Mt Sinai Hosp 1985; Plaque Hartford Police Dept 1986.

PIERRE, JENNIFER CASEY
Tobacco company executive. **Personal:** Born Aug 25, 1953, Baltimore, MD; daughter of Mary L Murreld and Johnny Casey; married Clifford Marston Pierre, May 9, 1987; children: Marianne Alicia Pierre, Marissa Janelle Pierre. **Educ:** Carnegie-Mellon University, Pittsburgh, PA, BS, Math, 1975; Columbia Business School, New York, NY, MBA, 1977. **Career:** General Foods Corp, White Plains, NY, asst brand mgr, 1977-79; American Can Co, Greenwich, CT, assoc brand mgr, 1979-81; RJ Reynolds Tobacco Co, Winston-Salem, NC, mgr of fulfillment, 1981-. **Orgs:** Visiting professor, Natl Urban League BEEP, 1986-; board member, Baldwin School, 1985; volunteer, Forsyth Court Volunteers, 1981-84. **Honors/Awds:** Scholarship for Boarding School, A Better Chance, 1968-71; Graduate Fellowship/Internship, General Foods Corp, 1975-77. **Business Addr:** Manager, Fulfillment, RJ Reynolds Tobacco Co, 401 N Main St, Winston-Salem, NC 27102, (910)741-7548.

PIERRE, PERCY ANTHONY
Educational administrator. **Personal:** Born Jan 3, 1939, St James, LA; son of Rosa Villavaso Pierre and Percy Pierre; married Olga A Markham, Aug 7, 1965; children: Kristin Clare, Allison Celeste. **Educ:** Univ Notre Dame, BS Elec Engrg 1961, MS 1963; Johns Hopkins Univ, PhD Elec Engrg 1967; Univ of MI, postdoc 1968. **Career:** So Univ, asst prof elec engrg 1963; Johns Hopkins Univ, instr elec engrg 1963-64; Morgan State Coll, instr physics 1964-66; Univ MI, intr info & control engrg 1967-68; UCLA, instr systems engrg 1968-69; RAND Corp, rsch engr in communications 1968-71; Office of Pres, White House fellow spl asst 1969-70; Howard Univ, dean sch engrg 1971-77; Alfred P Sloan Found, prog officer for engrg educ 1973-75; US Dept of Army, asst sec for rsch Devel & acquisition 1977-81; engrg mgmt consul 1981-83; Prairie View A&M Univ, pres 1983-89, Honeywell, professor of electrical engineering, 1989-90; MI State Univ, vice pres, research & grad studies, 1990-95, prof elec engineering, currently. **Orgs:** Aerospace Corp, director, 1991-; CMS Energy Corp, director, 1990-; Center for Naval Analysis, 1987-94; Dual Inc, director, 1992-;

Hitachi Foundation, director, 1988-; Industrial Technology Institute, director, 1992-94; Michigan Biotechnology Institute, 1990-; Old Kent Financial Corp, director, 1992-; University of Notre Dame, trustee, 1974-. **Honors/Awds:** Distinguished Civilian Serv Awd Dept Army 1981; Awd of Merit from Sen Proxmire 1979; mem IEEE (sr mem Edison Awd Comm 1978-80); Sigma Xi; Tau Beta Pi; honorary degrees: Univ of Notre Dame, Rensselaer Polytechnic Institute; author of over thirty articles on engineering research, engineering education, systems analysis and military research and development. **Business Addr:** Professor, Elec Engineering, Michigan State University, Department of Electrial Engineering, East Lansing, MI 48824.

PIERRE-LOUIS, CONSTANT
Physician. **Personal:** Born Feb 11, 1939; married Jeany; children: Marilyn, Pascale, Carolyn. **Educ:** State Univ Port-au-Prince Med Sch, MD 1963. **Career:** Columbis Univ, 1971-75; Downstate Univ, clinic asst prof of urology 1975-; Adelphi Med ARt Assn, fndg mem partner 1975-; staff mem Brookdale Hosp, St John's Epis Hosp, Unity Hosp; Private Practice, urologist 1971-. **Orgs:** Mem Amer Bd Urology; fellow Amer Coll Surgery; mem NY State Med Soc, Natl Med Assn; bd mem pres Assn of Haitian Drs Abroad 1975-76; publications "Lymphoma of the Urethra Masquerading as a Caruncle" 1972; "Morphologic Appearance of Leydig Cells in Patients with Prostatic Cancer & Benign Prostatic Hypertrophy" NY Acad Med Urol Resd; "Delayed Subcapsular Renal Hematoma" Urology 1977. **Honors/Awds:** Essay Contest 3rd prize 1969. **Business Addr:** Urologist, 2832 Linden Blvd, Brooklyn, NY 11208.

PIERSON, DERRON
Construction company executive. **Career:** Solo Construction Corp, vice president, currently. **Business Addr:** Vice President, Solo Construction Corp., 15251 NE 18th Ave, North Miami Beach, FL 33162, (305)944-3922.

PIERSON, KATHRYN A.
Attorney. **Personal:** Born May 27, 1956, Chicago, IL; daughter of Edward & Myrtle Pierson; married Cedric Hendricks, Jul 17, 1982; children: Malcolm, Marcus, Nikki Henricks. **Educ:** George Washington Univ, BA, journalism/political sci, 1979; Howard Univ, JD, 1985. **Career:** US Dept of Justice, Antitrust Div, honors grad, 1985-86; Pierson & Archibald, managing partners, 1987-93; Minority Asset Recovery Contractors Assn, exec dir, 1993-95; Tradewinds International, dir of bus devt, 1995; Airport Finance Enterprises, CEO, 1996. **Orgs:** District Curators, chair, bd of dir, 1991-; Pacifica Foundation Corp Secy, chair, Devt Committee, 1984-90; WPFW-FM, chair, bd of dirs, 1982-84; Marshall Heights Comm Devt Organization, bd member, 1989-91; Rhythm & Blues Foundation, bd of trustees, 1990-. **Business Addr:** CEO, Airport Finance Enterprises, Inc, 601 Madison St, Alexandria, VA 22314, (703)299-9078.

PIERSON, RANDY
Construction company executive. **Career:** Solo Construction Corp, chief executive officer, currently. **Business Addr:** CEO, Solo Construction Corp., 15251 NE 18th Ave, North Miami Beach, FL 33162, (305)944-3922.

PILE, MICHAEL DAVID MC KENZIE
Health care administrator. **Personal:** Born Jan 28, 1954, New York, NY; son of Ulalie Mc Kenzie Pile and Ernest S Pile; married May 20, 1989. **Educ:** Colgate University, Hamilton, NY, BA, 1976; New York University, New York, NY, MPA, 1983. **Career:** Queens Hospital Center, Queens, NY, assistant director, 1978-86; Long Island Jewish Hillside Medical Center, Queens, NY, 1984-86; Syracuse University, Syracuse, NY, health service administrator, 1983-89; California State Univ, Sacramento, Sacramento, CA, director univ health center, 1989-. **Orgs:** Chair, Constitution & Bylaws, Pacific Coast College Health Assn, 1990-92; member, American College Health Assn, 1984-; member, American Public Health Assn, 1981. **Business Addr:** Director of Health & Psychological Services, California State University, Sacramento, 6000 J St, Health Center, Sacramento, CA 95819-6045.

PILLOW, VANITA J.
Sales representative. **Personal:** Born Dec 16, 1949, Nashville. **Educ:** BS 1971; MS 1985. **Career:** Fayette Co Bd Edn, secondary instr & Beta Honor Soc sponsor 1973; Experimental Theatre sponsor; Electric Dance Workshop Sponser 1972; des Moines Main PO Supply & Procurement Asst; TN State U, part time istrn 1971; speech dramatics arts grad asst; S Central Bell Bus Office, sales rep teller. **Orgs:** Mem NAACP; Minority Consumer Communications Theatre Nashville 1974; mem USO Tour Germany, Holland, Belgium 1970; mem Women's Bowling League 1971; Theta Alpha Phi 1969; Univ Couns; pres TN State Plyrs Guild. **Honors/Awds:** Miss TN State Plyrs Guild; best female actress 1971; Children's Theatre Chicago Grad top 10 percent class.

PILOT, ANN HOBSON
Musician. **Personal:** Born Nov 6, 1943, Philadelphia, PA; daughter of Grace Stevens Hobson Smith and Harrison Hobson; married R Prentice; children: Lynn, Prentice. **Educ:** Cleveland Inst, BM 1966. **Career:** Pittsburgh Symphony Orchestra, 2nd harpist 1965-66; Washington Natl Symphony, principal harpist 1966-69; Ambler Music Festival, faculty 1968-69; New England Conservatory of Music, Boston, MA, harp teacher, 1971-; Boston Symphony Orchestra, asst principal harpist, principal harpist 1980-; Tanglewood Music Ctr, Lenox, MA, harp faculty, 1989-. **Orgs:** Participant Marlboro Music Festival; faculty New England Conservatory of Music, Berkshire Music Center; soloist Boston Symphony Orchestra; founder mem New England Harp Trio 1971-; mem Contemporary Music Ensemble, College performances in Europe, Japan, China and Haiti; bd of dir, Holy Trinity School of Haiti; Longy School of Music, bd of trustees, 1993-96; Boston Music Education Collaborative, bd of dirs. **Honors/Awds:** Honored by the Professional Arts Soc of Philadelphia 1987; Honorary Doctorate of Fine Arts, Bridgewater State College, 1988. **Special Achievements:** Recordings for Boston Records, Ann Hobson Pilot, solo harp; Contrasts, music for flute and harp with Leone Buyse; for Koch Intl, Ginastera and Mathias Concerti with the English Chamber Orchestra; Dello-Joie harp concerto with the New Zealand Symphony; Chamber Music of William Mathias and Arnold Bax. **Business Addr:** Principal Harpist, Boston Symphony Orchestra, 117 Mason Ter #2, Brookline, MA 02146-2651.

PINADO, ALAN E., SR.
Educator. **Personal:** Born Dec 15, 1931, New York, NY; son of Agnes Steber Pinado and Herman E Pinado; married Patricia LaCour; children: Alan E Jr, Jeanne M Pinado-Getter, Anthony M, Steven L. **Educ:** Fordham Univ, Coll of Bus Admin, BS Mktg 1953; Univ of Notre Dame, MBA, 1958. **Career:** Wm R Morris Agency South Bend IN, real estate sales, devel 1960-61; Allied Fed Savings & Loan Jamaica NY, exec vp, mortgage loan officer 1961-67; IBM Corp NY, mktg rep 1967-68; NY LIfe Ins Co NY, vice pres re fin 1968-84, vp, mgmt coord/trng 1984-85; Real Estate Inst of Clark Atlanta Univ/Morehouse Coll, dir 1986-. **Orgs:** Dir Oppty Funding Corp 1979-90, Urban Home Ownership Corp 1980-92, NY Life Pac 1983-85; Wilton CT United Way 1983-85; dir emeritus Minority Interchange Inc 1975-; United Mutual Insurance Co 1985-87; director, University Community Development Corp., 1996; advisory committee, mem, The Prudential bank, 1995-97; director, National Housing Council, 1994-. **Honors/Awds:** Dr of Literary Letters Mary Holmes Coll 1976; Horace Sudduth Awd Natl Bus League 1978; James J & Jane Hoey Awd Catholic Interracial Council of NY 1972. **Military Serv:** AUS 1st lt 1953-55; Commendation Medal 1954. **Business Addr:** Dir, Real Estate Inst, Clark Atlanta Univ, Sch of Business, Atlanta, GA 30314, (404)880-8477.

PINCHAM, R. EUGENE, SR.
Judge (retired). **Personal:** Born Jun 28, 1925, Chicago, IL; married Alzata Cudalia Henry; children: 3. **Educ:** Tennessee State Univ, BS 1947; Northwestern Univ School of Law, Juris Dr Deg 1951; admitted to the bar of Illinois, 1951. **Career:** Circuit Ct of Cook Co, judge 1976-84; Attorneys T Lee Boyd Jr & Isaiah S Gant, assoc 1974-76; Atty Charles B Evins, assoc 1955-76; Atty Joseph E Clayton Jr, assoc 1951-55; criminal trial lawyer appellate litigation; Lecturer/instructor, Notre Dame Univ School of Law; Northwestern Univ School of Law; Univ of Illinois School of Law; Univ of Houston Bates Coll of Law; Natl College of Criminal Defense Lawyers & Public Defenders; Univ of Colorado-Boulder College of Law; Natl Inst of Trial Advocacy, Univ of Nevada. **Orgs:** Mem Chicago Bar; Cook County Bar; Illinois Bar; Natl Bar; Amer Bar Assn; The Chicago Council of Lawyers; life mem NAACP; life mem Amer Civil Liberties Union; Kappa Alpha Psi Frat; the Amer Judicature Soc; mem, former trustee Faith United Methodist Church. **Honors/Awds:** Award of merit, the Northwestern Univ Alumni Assn, 1975; certificate of appreciation, Chicago Bar Assn, 1974; Richard E Westbrook Award for Outstanding Contrib to the Legal Profession, Cook County Bar Assn; certificate of serv, the Lawyers Constitutional Def Comm of the Amer Civil Liberties Union, 1965.

PINCKNEY, ANDREW MORGAN, JR.
Administrator. **Personal:** Born Jul 2, 1933, Georgetown, SC; married Brenda Cox; children: Meika, Margo. **Educ:** Morris Brown Coll Atlanta, BS 1960; Lasalle Coll Phila, Bus Adminstrn 1967-68; Univ of PA Phila, Wharton Mgmt 1974-76. **Career:** Merck Sharp & Dohme West Point PA, adminstsr 1973-; Merck Sharp & Dohme, rsrch Biol 1963-73; Skin & Cancer Hosp Phila, rsrch asso 1962-63; Frnaklin Inst Lab Phila, rsrch chemist 1961-62. **Orgs:** Mem Am Mgmt Assn 1975-; mem Black Univ Liasion Com Merck & Co 1977-; mem of steering com United Way Campaign Merck Sharp & Co 1976-79; pres Philadelphia Alumni Chap of Morris Brown 1970-; pres Club Noble Gents 1971-; finan sec Black Polit Forum 1975. **Honors/Awds:** Medal of Merits; good conduct; marksman USAF 1951-55; taste & odors Jour of Water Pollu Franklin Inst Philadelphia 1961; Morris Brown Coll Athletic Hall of Fame TAY Club Atlanta 1975; Purple & Black Serv Award Morris Brown Coll Nat Alumni Atlanta 1979; racquetball trophy North Penn Racquetball Club N Wales PA 1980. **Military Serv:** USAF a/1c 1951-55. **Business Addr:** Sumneytown Pike, West Point, PA 19486.

PINCKNEY, CLEMENTA
Government Official. **Career:** State Representative, South Carolina, currently. **Business Addr:** State Representative, State of South Carolina, Blatt Bldg, PO Box 11867, Columbia, SC 29211.

PINCKNEY, EDWARD LEWIS
Professional basketball player. **Personal:** Born Mar 27, 1963, Bronx, NY. **Educ:** Villanova Univ, Villanova, PA, 1981-85. **Career:** Phoenix Suns, 1985-87; Sacramento Kings, 1987-88; Boston Celtics, 1989-94; Milwaukee Bucks, 1994-95; Toronto Raptors, 1995; Philadelphia 76ers, 1996; Miami Heat, 1996-. **Special Achievements:** NBA Draft, First round pick, #10, 1985. **Business Addr:** Professional Basketball Player, Miami Heat, 721 NW 1st Ave, Miami Arena, Miami, FL 33136, (305)577-4328.

PINCKNEY, JAMES
Elected official. **Personal:** Born Jun 24, 1942, Fairfax, SC; married Gladys M Simmons; children: Janet, Jerome, Zachary, Lorraine. **Educ:** Allen Univ, BS Phys Ed 1964. **Career:** Lower Saunnal Council of Govts, bd mem 1984-; Allendale Co, co councilman 1985-. **Orgs:** Bd mem Allendale-Fairfax HS Advisory Council 1982-84. **Business Addr:** Councilmember, Allendale County, PO Box 677, Allendale, SC 29810.

PINCKNEY, LEWIS, JR.
Hospital administrator. **Personal:** Born Dec 25, 1932, Columbia, SC; son of Channie Hopkins Pinckney and Louis Pinckney Sr; married Johnnye Caver; children: Lewis III, Johnette V. **Educ:** DePaul U, 1975; Benedict Coll, 1952-53; Cook Co Grad Sch of Med, ARRT 1956-57. **Career:** Cook County Hosp, staff tech 1957-64, qual control supv 1964-68, chief x-ray tech educ dir 1968-69, admin asst to chmn 1969-73, admin; St Bernard Hosp, dir radiological svcs. **Orgs:** John Jones Lodge #7 F&AM IL 1963-; IL State Soc of Radiologic Tech 1971-74; Lions Assn 1971-73; Amer Soc of Radiologic Tech 1973; Amer Hosp Radiology Admin 1973-76; WA Park YMCA 1974; conf ledr Inst for Graphic Communication 1974; evaluating quality control Cook Co Grad School of Med 1977. **Military Serv:** AUS sgt 1953-56. **Business Addr:** Dir, St Bernard Hospital, 64th & Dan Ryan Expressway, Chicago, IL 60612.

PINCKNEY, STANLEY
Artist, educator. **Personal:** Born Sep 30, 1940, Boston, MA. **Educ:** Famous Artist School, Westport CT, commercial art, 1960; Music School Fine Arts Boston MA, Diploma 1967; Music School Fine Arts Boston MA, Certificate, Graduate Program, 1969. **Career:** Music School Fine Arts, teacher, 1972-; Coll Art, guest-artist 1979; Boston Univ Program In-Artisanry, guest-artist 1967. **Orgs:** Mem, African-Amer Artists-in-Residency Northeastern Univ Boston MA 1978. **Honors/Awds:** Blanche E Colman Fellowship Blanche E Colman Found Boston 1978; Ford Found Grant Music School, Fine Arts Boston 1978; Albert H Whitin Fellowship Music School, Fine Arts, Boston 1978. **Business Addr:** c/o Music School of Fine Arts, 230 Fenway, Boston, MA 02115.

PINDELL, HOWARDENA D.
Painter, curator, educator. **Personal:** Born Apr 14, 1943, Philadelphia, PA; daughter of Mildred Lewis and Howard Douglas Pindell. **Educ:** Boston University, BFA, 1965; Yale University, MFA, 1967. **Career:** Pratt Inst, guest lecturer 1972; Hunter Coll, 1972; Morivian Coll, 1973; Queens Coll, 1973; Sch Visual Arts, 1973, 1975; Montclair State Coll, 1974; Brooklyn Mus, 1976; SUNY at Stony Brook, prof; Yale Univ, fall semesters, visiting prof, 1995-97. **Orgs:** Intl Art Critics Association; Intl House of Japan; College Art Assn; ACASA. **Honors/Awds:** Afro-Amer Artists 1973; Natl Endowment for the Arts Grant 1983-84; Boston University, Alumni Awd for Disting Serv to the Profession, 1983; Ariana Foundation Grant 1984-85; Guggeneheim Fellowship 1987-88; US/Japan Friendship Commn Creative Arts to Fellowship; College Art Association Award for Best Exhibitor 1990; Studio Museum in Harlem Award, 1994; Joan Mitchell Fellowship, 1994; Women Caucus for Art Distinguished Contribution to the Profession Award, 1996; Massachusetts College of Art, Hon Doc of Fine Arts, 1997. **Business Addr:** Professor, SUNY at Stony Brook, Art Department, Stony Brook, NY 11794.

PINDER, FRANK E.
Foreign service officer. **Personal:** Born Feb 24, 1911, Key West, FL; children: Terrecita E, Frank E III, Dorothea I. **Educ:** FL A&M Coll, BS 1933; Cornell Univ, Dept State Fellow 1951-52; Monrovia Coll Liberia, LLD 1955; Campbell Coll, LHD 1956; Morris Brown Coll, attended 1973. **Career:** Alachua Co, co agr asst 1933-41; US Dept of Agr Wash, asst coop specialist 1941, agriculturist 1942, agr econ 1943; US Econ Mission Dept State Liberia, head agriculturist 1944-48; TCA Liberia, agr adv 1949-51; FOA & successor agency, chief agricul 1952-57; ICA Ghana, food & agr officer 1958-64; UN Econ Comm for Africa, cons; US Aid Mission to Ghana, dep dir 1964, dir 1964-68; UN Econ Comm for Africa, spl adviser to exec sec 1968-. **Orgs:** Mem Amer Acad Pol & Social Scis, Amer Pub Health Assn, Assn for Advancement of Agr Scis in Africa, Amer Fgn Serv Assn; life mem Soc for IntlDevel; mem Alpha Phi Alpha, Urban

League, NAACP; Protestant Episcopal Mason. **Honors/Awds:** Meritorious Serv Awd Dept of State 1951; ICA 1955; Citation Govt Liberia 1957; Govt Chana 1961; Disting Serv Awd AID 1967; The Mary McCleod Bethune Medallion 1973; appointed Pres Comm on Liberia-US Relations 1980.

PINDER, NELSON W.
Clergyman. **Personal:** Born Jul 27, 1932, Miami; son of Coleen Saunders Pinder and George Pinder; married Marian Grant; children: Gail, Squire. **Educ:** Bethune-Cookman Coll, BA 1956; Nashotah House Sem, BD 1959; Inst IN U, Adult Educ 1959; Urban Training Cntr, 1964; FL A&M, MEd 1974; Bethune-Cookman Coll Daytona Beach FL, DD (honoris causa) 1979. **Career:** St John the Bapt Epis Ch Orlando, priest 1974-; Diocese of Cntrl FL, staff mem 1971-; Awareness Cntr Orlando, dir 1969-71f St John the Bapt Epis Ch, vicar 1959-69. **Orgs:** Chmn Recruitment & Equal Employ Oppor Com Province VI Epis Ch 1972-; mem bd dir Union of Black Episcopalians 1973-74; mem Joint Commn on Ch in Small Comm 1970-; assoc trst Bethune-Cookman Coll; mem bd of trsts Bethune-Cookman Coll; mem Orlando C of C; Dept of Urban Affairs; mem Phi Delta Kappa; Walt Disney World Awards Com 1973; past Pres Delta Ix Lambda; mem Natl Commn on Social & Specialized Ministry 1989-; trustee Univ of the South, Sewanee, TN 1983-. **Honors/Awds:** Knights of Columbus Citznshp Award 1974; US Congress Chaplains' Award 1973; 1st Annual Disney World Comm Serv Award 1972f black comm Award 1972; United Negro Coll Fund Award 1971f Alpha Kappa Alpha Comm Award 1972; Bethune-Cookman medallion 1975. **Military Serv:** AUS 1953-55. **Business Addr:** St John the Baptist, 1000 Bethune Drive, Episcopal Church, Orlando, FL 32805-3480.

PINDERHUGHES, CHARLES ALFRED
Psychiatrist (retired). **Personal:** Born Jan 28, 1919, Baltimore, MD; married Elaine Brazier; children: Charles Jr, Robert, Ellen, Richard, Howard. **Educ:** Dartmouth, AB 1940; Howard Univ Sch Med, MD 1943; Boston Psychoanalytic Soc & Inst 1955. **Career:** Boston VA Hosp, chief psychiatry 1960-65; E N Rogers Memorial Veterans Hosp, asst chief psychiatry serv for clinical training 1975-; Boston Univ Sch of Med, psychiatrist psychoanalyst 1950-72, prof 1971-. **Orgs:** Mem Surgeon Gen Sci Adv Com on TV & Soc Behavior 1970-74; chmn Task Force on Aggression & Violence 1972-75; mem Amer Psychiat Assn, bd trustees 1974-77; numerous articles. **Honors/Awds:** Amer Psychiatric Assn, Fuller Award and Vestermark Awards. **Military Serv:** AUS med corps capt 1944-46.

PINKARD, BEDFORD L.
City official. **Personal:** Born Oct 9, 1931, Jacksonville, TX; son of Adela Pinkard and Dee Pinkard; married Dr Irene Stephens, Aug 1, 1987; children: Derek Louis, Keven D. **Educ:** LA State Coll 1956-58, California Polytechnic Coll 1950-51; Ventural Coll, AA 1953; Cal State Univ Northridge, BS 1973. **Career:** City of Oxnard, Community Youth Project, dir, 1979-80, recreation supervisor 1959-91, councilman, currently. **Orgs:** Oxnard Noontimers Lions Club 1964-; pres Bd of Educ Oxnard Union High School Dist, 1972-92. **Honors/Awds:** PTA Hon Serv Awd; Esquire Social Club Citizen of the Yr Awd; Resolution of the Oxnard City Council for Dedicated Svcs; 22 Years Perfect Attendance Oxnard Noontimers Lions Club. **Military Serv:** US Army pfc 2 yrs. **Home Addr:** 2047 Spyglass Tr E, Oxnard, CA 93030.

PINKARD, DELORIS ELAINE
Educational administrator. **Personal:** Born Oct 22, 1944, Kansas City, KS; daughter of Ella Mae Williams Jackson and Andrew D Jackson; widowed; children: Karisse W Grigsby, Robert C Edwards. **Educ:** Emporia State Univ, BS (cum laude), elementary educ, 1966, MS, educ admin, 1984; Univ of Kansas, MS, educ psychology & research, 1980; Univ of Kansas, doctorate of education, 1995. **Career:** Washington Dist Schools, Kansas City KS, teacher, 1966-69; Kansas City KS Catholic Diocese, Kansas City KS, teacher, 1970-72; Kansas City KS Public Schools, Kansas City KS, teacher, 1972-82, admin intern, 1982-83, principal, 1983-86, personnel dir, 1986-92; KS Kansas Comm Coll, dean of human resources, 1992-94, vp for exec services, currently. **Orgs:** Past bd mem, Yates Branch YWCA, 1969; bd of dir, Wyandotte County Mental Health Commn, 1971; mem, Missouri Valley School Personnel Admin Assn, 1986-, Assn for School, Coll & Univ Staffing, 1986-, Amer Assn of School Personnel Admin, 1986-, Kansas City KS Women's Chamber of Commerce, 1987-; sec, Kansas-Natl Alliance of Black School Educ, 1988-; bd of dir, Martin Luther King Urban Center, 1988-; interim sec, NAACP, 1989; Kansas City KS coord, United Negro Coll Fund Drive, 1989. **Honors/Awds:** Kappa Delta Pi, Honors Soc in Educ, 1966; research thesis, Teacher Attitudes as Related to the Differences in Achievements of Reflective and Impulsive Children, 1980; Phi Delta Kappa, Emporia State Univ, 1982; conf presenter, Networking for Women in Educ Admin, 1984; Admin-in-Residence, Emporia State Univ, 1985; induction speaker, Lyons County Phi Delta Kappa, Fighting Teacher Burnout, 1985; Woman of Distinction for Community Serv, Friends of Yates, 1986; keynote speaker, Sorority Founders Recognition, Equity With Excellence, 1986; conf presenter, Kansas Black Legislative Conf, The Direction of Educ for Minority Students and Legislative Alternatives, 1987; Dissertation: School Reform Success: Critical Issues for Teachers/Determining Teacher's Concerns During the Process of Planned Change in Schools, 1995. **Business Addr:** Vice President for Executive Services, Kansas City Kansas Community College, 7250 State Ave, Kansas City, KS 66112, (913)334-1100.

PINKARD, NORMAN THOMAS
Financial consultant. **Personal:** Born Feb 26, 1941, Orange, NJ; married Betty Holmes; children: Anthony, Gail, Cathy, Lisa. **Educ:** Syracuse U, BS, political science, 1969, MA, public administration 1970. **Career:** Indus & Corp Devel NYS Dept of Commerce, dep commr; NYS Div for Youth, exec dep dir 1975-77; Human Rights Commn Syracuse & Onondaga Co, exec dir 1970-75; State Assemblyman Mortimer Gallivan, legis aide 1967-69; Syracuse U, urban econ devel spec 1968-70. **Orgs:** Host Straight to the Sourc Pub Affairs Prgm 1973-75; host PULSE Pub Serv Prgm 1976-; NY State Bd of Regents; rep NY State Adv Coun for Voc Edn; appointed by Gov Ofc to Bny State Aprenticeship & Training Coun; 1st vice chmn NY State Black Polit Caucus. **Honors/Awds:** HUD Flwshp 1967-68; outstndg comm serv Award Careerco. **Military Serv:** AUS s/sgt 1959-67.

PINKETT, ALLEN JEROME
Professional football player. **Personal:** Born Jan 25, 1964, Washington, DC. **Educ:** Univ of Notre Dame, BBA, marketing, 1986. **Career:** Running back: Houston Oilers, running back, 1986-92, New Orleans Saints, 1992-. **Business Addr:** Professional Football Player, New Orleans Saints, 1500 Poydras St, New Orleans, LA 70112.

PINKETT, HAROLD THOMAS
Consultant. **Personal:** Born Apr 7, 1914, Salisbury, MD; son of Catherine Richardson Pinkett and Rev Wilson Pinkett; married Lucille Cannady, Apr 24, 1943. **Educ:** Morgan Coll, AB; Univ of PA, AM; Columbia Univ, Grad Study; Amer Univ, PhD. **Career:** Natl Archives, staff archivist, 1942-59, suprv archivist 1959-79; Livingstone Coll, prof of history 1938-39, 1941-42; Howard Univ, adjunct prof of history and archival admin 1970-76; American Univ, 1976-77; Private practice, archival & historial consult 1980-, archival consultant; Howard Univ, 1980; The Links Inc, 1986; Natl Bus League, 1982-84; United Negro Coll Fund, 1983-84; Cheyney Univ, 1984-85; North Carolina Central University 1992-93; Clark Atlanta University, 1992; Eugene and Agnes Meyer Foundation, 1993-94. **Orgs:** Editor Soc of Amer Archivist 1968-71; bd of dirs US Capitol Historical Soc 1972-1992; adv bd District of Columbia Historical Records 1978-; National Advisory Board of the African Methodist Episcopal Zion Historical Society, 1990-; Soc of Amer Archivists; Org of Amer Historians; Assn for Study of Afro-American Life and History; Agricultural History Soc pres 1982-83; Forest History Soc pres 1976-78; Southern Historical Assn; Omega Psi Phi Frat; Sigma Pi Phi Fraternity; Cosmos Club, Washington, DC. **Honors/Awds:** Fellow Soc of Amer Archivists 1962-; Fellowship Grant Council on Library Resources 1972-73; Book Awd Agricultural History Soc; Carroll Lecturer in History, Mary Baldwin Coll 1986; author of many historical and archival publications, including Gifford Pinchot (1970), Research in the Administration of Public Policy (1975), and National Church of Zion Methodism 1989. **Military Serv:** AUS t/sgt 1943-46; European & Asiatic-Pacific Serv Awds. **Home Addr:** 5741 27th St NW, Washington, DC 20015-1101.

PINKETT, JADA
Actress. **Personal:** Born 1971; married Will Smith, Dec 31, 1997; children: one. **Career:** Actress, appeared on television series "A Different World"; roles in Moe's World, 21 Jump Street, Doogie Howser, the Trials of Rosie O'Neil, and True Colors; appeared in the films: Menace II Society, Demon Night, The Inkwell, A Low Down Dirty Shame, Jason's Lyric, The Nutty Professor, Set It Off; theater roles: August's Wilson's Joe Turner's Come and Gone, the Nutcracker. **Business Addr:** Actress, c/o United Talent Agency, c/o Nick Stevens, Agent, 9560 Wilshire Blvd, Ste 500, Beverly Hills, CA 90212.

PINKINS, TONYA
Actress, singer. **Personal:** Born May 30, Chicago, IL; daughter of Anita Pinkins and Thomas Swoope; children: Maxx Brawer, Myles Brawer. **Educ:** Carnegie Mellon University, 1980-81. **Career:** Movie appearances include: See No Evil, Hear No Evil; Beat Street; American Dream; television appearances include: "All My Children," 1991; theatre appearances include: Death and the Kings Horseman, 1979-80; Merrily We Roll Along, 1981-82; Five Points, 1982; Just Say No, 1988; Joe Turner's Come and Gone, 1989-90; Jelly's Last Jam, Broadway, 1992-. **Orgs:** Nontraditional Casting Project, board of directors; Carousel Theatre, board of directors. **Honors/Awds:** American Theater Wing, Tony Award, featured actress, musical, 1992; Social Council Actors Equity, Clarence Derwent Award, 1992; New York Drama Critics, Drama Desk, 1992; NCAA, Monarch Award, 1992; NAACP, Best Actress, Daytime Drama, nominated, 1992.

PINKNEY, ALPHONSO
Educator. **Personal:** Born Dec 15, 1930, Tampa, FL; son of G Johnson Pinkney and A Pinkney; divorced. **Educ:** Cornell Univ, PhD 1961. **Career:** Univ of Chicago, prof of sociology 1969-71; Howard Univ, prof of sociology 1972-73; Univ of CA-Berkeley, prof of criminology 1973-75; Hunter Coll CUNY, prof of sociology 1961-69, beginning 1975, prof emeritus, currently. **Orgs:** Contributor to all major civil rights and civil liberties orgs; member, Assn of Black Sociologists. **Honors/Awds:** Ford Foundation Fellowships; published eight books including: The Myth of Black Progress, 1984; Lest We Forget: Howard Beach and Other Racial Atrocities, Third World Press, 1994. **Business Addr:** Professor Emeritus of Sociology, Hunter College CUNY, 695 Park Ave, New York, NY 10021.

PINKNEY, ARNOLD R.
Educator. **Personal:** Born Jan 6, 1931, Youngstown, OH; married Betty; children: Traci. **Educ:** Albion Coll MI, BA. **Career:** Cleveland Bd of Edn, pres; Pinkney-Perry Ins Agency Cleveland, bd Chmn. **Orgs:** Mem OH Nat Life Underwriters Assn; exec com Grtr Cleveland Growth Assn; Cleveland Bus League; orgn dir The First Nat Bank Assn; mem vice pres & pres Cleveland Bd of Educ 1967-; bd of tst Albion Coll; pres bd of tst Central State U; chmn Devel & Goals Com; Com on Black Phys; bd of tst Cncl on Human Rel; Phyllis Wheatley Found; mem Urban League of Grtr Cleveland; bd mem Metro Hlth Planning Corp; past treas Black Econ Union; bd of tst The Citz League; life mem NAACP; candidate Mayor of Cleveland 1971, 75; dir Nat Deputy Campaign Senator Humphrey's 1972; exec com v chmn Cuyahoga Co Dem Party 1973; chmn Dem Party's Vice-pres Selection Com 1973; co-chmn Dem Nat Cpgn Com 1974; bd of elections Cuyahoga Co 1974; steering com Nat Caucus of Black Dem 1974; del Dem &Mini-conv Kansas Cty 1974; Dem Conv 1976; adv Local State & Nat Dem Officials 1976; state chmn OH State Voter Registrtn Drive 1976; headed crive Get Out The Vote 1976; mem Olivet Int Bapt Ch. **Honors/Awds:** 1000 Successful Black in Ebony Mag; apt Exec Order of the OH Commodore; num lctr. **Military Serv:** US Army, 1952-54. **Business Addr:** 2131 Fairhill Rd, Cleveland, OH 44106.

PINKNEY, BETTY KATHRYN
Attorney, educational administrator. **Personal:** Born Aug 27, Cleveland, OH; daughter of Naomi Inez Yates Butts and Emmett Maceo; married Charles E Pinkney; children: Jacqueline Pinkney-Royster, Pamela, Merle. **Educ:** Central State University, BA, 1956; Western Reserve University, MA, 1961; Cleveland State University, JD, 1976. **Career:** Cleveland Public Schools, teacher, administrator, 1961-77; Carl J Character Law Firm, associate, 1977-79; EEOC, Cleveland, trial attorney, 1979-81; East Ohio Gas Co., attorney, beginning 1981. **Orgs:** Cleveland Public School System, advisory committee, superintendent, 1987-; Judge Lloyd O Brown Scholarship Fund, board of trustees, supertintendent, 1984-; ABA; Ohio State Bar Association; Natl Bar Assn; Cleveland Bar Association, volunteer, 1984-; Delta Sigma Theta; Central State University Board of Trustees, 1987-, chairperson, currently. **Special Achievements:** Admitted to: Ohio Bar, 1977; US District Court, Ohio, 1977; US Court of Appeals, DC Circuit, 1979; US Court of Appeals, 6th circuit, 1981; US Supreme Court, 1981; areas of specilization: public utilities, civil litigation, workers' compensation. **Business Addr:** Chairperson, Board of Trustees, Central State University, Wilberforce, OH 45384, (513)376-6011.

PINKNEY, DOVE SAVAGE
Government affairs coordinator (retired). **Personal:** Born May 18, 1932, Macon, GA; daughter of Mildred Goodwin Savage and Edward Warren Savage Sr; divorced; children: Rhonda Michelle Pinkney Washington, Roderick Stephen. **Educ:** Talladega Coll, 1954; Inst of Pathology Case-Western Reserve Univ, Cleveland OH, Certificate Medical Techn 1955; Univ of Denver, post grad course; UCLA, post grad courses. **Career:** Univ Hospital Cleveland, technologist and supervisor 1955-59; Children's Hospital Los Angeles, technologist in charge of outpatient clinic lab 1960-73, hematology clinical lab supervisor 1973-94, government affairs coordinator, 1994-95. **Orgs:** Chairperson Children's Hospital Los Angeles Employee Recognition Comm 1973-89; campaign chairperson Children's Hospital Los Angeles United Way Campaign 1975; treasurer 1978-80, mem 1981-, chair 1988-90, Bd of Mgrs Crenshaw/28th St YMCA; pres CA Assn for Medical Laboratory Technology, Los Angeles Chpt, 1982-83, treas, 1978-80; mem, trustee and exec bd mem 1978-95; New Frontier Democratic Club, treas, 1989-90, pres, 1992-93; dir, CA Soc for Medical Technology, 1981-83, 1983-85; coord CSMT Student Bowl 1983; delegate to over 15 state conventions; delegate to 20 natl conventions; chairperson ASMT Forum for Concerns of Minorities By-Laws Com, 1979-86; natl pres Talladega College Alumni 1984-87; regional advisor 1997-98, bd mem and fund raiser, United Negro College Fund, 1984-; life mem Natl Council of Negro Women; life mem Delta Sigma Theta Sorority; life mem, Urban League, NOW, PUSH, NAACP; member, Comm Relations Council of Southern CA; member, Black Women's Forum, African-American Museum, Museum of Afro-Amer History and Culture, Trinity Baptist Church; Delta Sigma Theta Head Start Board, 1970-76; board of directors, Delta Sigma Theta Life Devel (senior citizens program), 1982-92; member

1988-, fin secretary 1989-93, Coalition of 100 Black Woman; LA Cty Commissioner, 1994-. **Honors/Awds:** Awards received from Delta Sigma Theta Los Angeles Chapter, Talladega Coll Local Alumni Assoc, Talladega Coll Natl Alumni Assoc, Crenshaw YMCA, UNCF, Amer Soc of Medical Technology, New Frontier Democratic Club, Children's Hospital Los Angeles Employees, Federal Credit Union; co-author of two professional (scientific) papers; CA Assembly; CA State Senate; LA Care. **Home Addr:** 5601 Coliseum St, Los Angeles, CA 90016, (213)295-3437.

PINKNEY, JERRY
Illustrator, educator. **Personal:** Born Dec 22, 1939, Philadelphia, PA; son of Willie Mae Landers Pinkney and James H Pinkney; married Gloria Jean Maultsby Pinkney; children: Troy Bernardette Pinkney Johnson, Jerry Brian, Scott Cannon, Myles Carter. **Educ:** Univ of the Arts, Philadelphia PA, 1957-59. **Career:** Rustcraft Publishing Co, Dedham MA, designer, 1960-62; Barker-Black Studio, Boston MA, designer-illustrator, 1962-64; Kaleiodoscope Studio, Boston MA, designer-illustrator, 1964-66; Jerry Pinkney Studio, Boston MA, designer-illustrator, 1966-70; Rhode Island School of Design, visiting critic, 1969-70; Jerry Pinkney Inc, Croton-on-Hudson NY, pres, 1970-; Pratt Inst, Brooklyn NY, assoc prof, 1986-87; Univ of Delaware, distinguished visiting prof, 1986-88, assoc prof of art, 1988-92; US Military Academy, West Point NY, lecturer; Univ of Buffalo, Buffalo, NY, visiting prof of art, 1991-. **Orgs:** Mem, Society of Illustrators; mem, US Postal Service Citizens Stamp Advisory Comm, 1982; mem, Artist Team NASA, Space Shuttle Columbia, 1982; mem, US Postal Service Quality Assurance Comm, 1986-92. **Honors/Awds:** Annual Show, NY Soc of Illustrators, 1965-83, 1986-95; Caldecott Honor Book, Amer Library Assn, 1989; CEBA Award, World Inst of Black Communications, Inc, 1989; Amer Visions Magazine, 1989; designer of eleven commerative postage stamps, US Postal Service; Randolph Caldecott Medal-Honor Book, Amer Library Assn, 1990; The YearsBest Illustrated Books for Children, New YoTimes, 1989; First Place, New York Book Show, 1989; Retrospective, Schomburg Center for Research, NY, 1990, University at Buffalo, NY, 1991; One Man Show, The Art Institute of Chicago, 1993; One Man Show, Univ of Arts, Phila, PA, 1994; Society of Children's Book Writers, 1990 Golden Kite Award, 1991; State of CO, CO Children's Book Award, 1991; NY Book Show, NY Honor Book, 1991; 34th Society of Illustrators Annual Show, Gold Medal, 1992; Phila School of Art & Design, Univ of Arts, Alumni Award, 1992; Drexel Univ, Phil PA, Drexel Citation for Children's Literature, 1992; Farmington State Coll, Framingham, MA, David McCord Award, 1992; Nebraska Lib Assn, Nebraska Children's Book Award, 1992; Society of Illustrators Annual 35, Gold Medal, 1993, Silver Medal, 1993, Hamilton King Award, 1993; Amer Inst of Graphic Arts, NY, Fifty Best Books, 1993; Book Binders Annual, NY, Second Place, Book Jackets, 1993; M Dobbins Voc High School, PA, Alumni Award, 1993; Orig Art Show, Society of Illustrators, Gold Medal, 1994; New York Times, Year's Best Illustrated Books for Children, 1994; Parents Choice "John Henry," Parents Choice Award for Story Book, 1994; Parents Choice "The Sunday Outing," Parents Choice Award for Story Book, 1994; Honor Book "John Henry," Randolph Caldecott Medal, 1994. **Business Addr:** Associate Professor of Art, University of Delaware, Dept. of Art, Newark, DE 19716.

PINKNEY, JOHN EDWARD
Consumer products manager. **Personal:** Born May 6, 1948, Landover, MD; married Gloristine Wilkins; children: Nikole, John, April. **Educ:** Prince George Comm Coll, AA 1973; Bowie State Coll, BS 1976. **Career:** Dept of Agriculture, computer operations 1970-71; Shadyside Barber & Beauty Salon, hair stylist/co-owner 1971-77; Philip Morris USA, sales rep 1977-79, miliary mgr 1979-80, division mgr, 1980-88; An Answer 4 U Telecommunications Co, owner, chief executive officer, 1991-. **Orgs:** Natl Business League of Southern MD pres 1981-83, bd dirs 1984-; youth task force participant Natl Alliance of Business 1981-83. **Honors/Awds:** Community Serv Award, Dist of Columbia; Presidential Citation Natl Assoc for Equal Opportunity in Higher Educ. **Military Serv:** US Army, Sgt, 3 yrs; Bronze Star; Vietnam Serv Medal; Vietnam Campaign Medal; Natl Defense Serv Medal. **Home Addr:** 6110 Joyce Dr, Camp Springs, MD 20748. **Business Addr:** Owner/CEO, An Answer 4 U, 5000 Pennsylvania Ave, Suitland, MD 20746.

PINKNEY, ROSE CATHERINE
Television executive. **Educ:** Princeton Univ; Univ of California in Los Angeles, MBA. **Career:** Twentieth Century Fox Television, director of programming; Uptown Entertainment, vice president of television; Paramount Network Television Division, vice president of comedy development, currently; Def Jams How to be A Player, co-producer. **Orgs:** Women in Film, bd mem; The New Leaders, trea. **Business Addr:** Vice Pres, Comedy Development, Network Television Div, Paramount Television Group, 5555 Melrose Ave, Los Angeles, CA 90038.

PINKNEY, WILLIAM D.
Business executive. **Personal:** Born Sep 15, 1935, Chicago, IL; married Ina Brody; children: Angela Walton. **Educ:** NY City Comm Coll; Adelphi Univ. **Career:** Astarte, natl sales mgr 1971-72; Cleopatra Creations, vice pres 1972-73; Revlon, mktg mgr 1973-77; Johnson Products Co, dir of mktg 1977-80; Dept of Human Serv City of Chicago, dir of family serv 1980-84; Combined Construction Co, vice pres; The Dessert Kitchen Ltd, dir. **Orgs:** Mem Natl Assoc Broadcast Engrg & Tech 1970-, Lake Michigan Yacht Racing Assoc 1974-; past commodore Belmont Yacht Club; life mem Lake Michigan Singlehanded Soc; Royal Yacht Club of Tasmania, Australia; Chicago Yacht Club. **Honors/Awds:** Guest Lecturer Worton School of Business Univ of PA 1978; Contrib Writer Great Lakes Boating Mag 1982-83; LMYA, Chicago Yachting Association; Yachtsman of the Year, 1992; Martin Luther King, Jr Legacy; Boy's and Girls Clubs of Chicago; Monarch Award, Alpha Kappa Alpha Sorority; Founders Award; Cosmopolitan Chamber of Commerce. **Special Achievements:** First African-American to Solo Circumavigate The World Via Cape Horn. **Military Serv:** US Navy hm2 1953-60, US Coast Guard licensed capt 1990-92; 2 Good Conduct Medals 1953-57.

PINKSTON, MOSES SAMUEL
Clergyman (retired). **Personal:** Born Jan 14, 1923, Camden, NJ; son of Rev & Mrs William L Pinkston; married Esther Miller; children: M Samuel Jr, Steven A. **Educ:** VA Union Univ Richmond, VA; Howard Univ Washington DC; Gordon Coll Boston MA, BA 1949; Temple Univ Sch of Theology, MDiv 1952; Rutgers Univ School of Social Work New Brunswick NJ, MSW 1969; CA Grad School of Theology, PhD 1977. **Career:** Pastor Mt Olivet Bapt Ch Newport RI 1953-57; pastor Mt Pisgah Bapt Temple Asbury Park NJ 1957-65; pastor Faith Bapt Tabernacle Asbury Park NJ 1965-69;organized & Dir of Shore Comm Child Care Center & Nursery Sch Asbury Park NJ 1966-69; social worker Monmouth Co Welfare Dept 1966-69; dir Public Ministries & East Bay Area Minister Am Bapt Churches of West Oakland, CA 1970-75; pastor Antioch Bapt Ch San Jose CA 1974-88, pastor emeritus, currently. **Orgs:** Past pres Ministerial Alliance San Jose & Vic 1978-80; prof - lecturer San Jose St Univ San Jose CA 1977-83; former mem commr Santa Clara Co Comm of Human Relations 1975-77; mem San Jose Downtown Redvlpmnt Comm under Mayor Janet Gray Hayes 1981-82; mem Mayors Comm on Minority Affairs for San Jose CA 1984-; hold Permanent Life Time St of CA Tchng Crdntls in Cnslng Psych, Pub Serv, Rel & Soc Studies, Soc Welfare & Hist; NAACP; Free & Accepted Masons, R C Marshall Lodge #15-San Jose; Natl Assn of Soc Welfare; Natl Assn of Social Workers (Golden Gate Chapter); Acad of Certificate, Social Workers (ACSW). **Honors/Awds:** Travelled extensively in Europe, Middle East & Holy Land directed Organized tour groups to Hawaiian Islands, Caribbean Islands, Greek Islands, South Africa and Far East. **Military Serv:** US Army, 1943-46. **Business Addr:** Pastor Emeritus, Antioch Baptist Church, 268 E Julian St, San Jose, CA 95112.

PINN, SAMUEL J., JR.
Educator. **Personal:** Born May 25, 1935, Brooklyn, NY; married Cynthia; children: Samuel III, Gregory, Charles. **Educ:** Morgan State University, BA, 1959; Rutgers University, MSW, 1970. **Career:** Ramapo College, associate professor; SJP Cons, president, 1968-; Wiltwick School, director, 1971-72; Mayors Action Task Force, director, 1968-71. **Orgs:** Consultant, Nassau & Co Equal Oppty Commin, 1976; College for Human Service, 1973-75; National Conference on Penal Reform, 1975-76; president, Bedford Study Institute of Afro-American Studies & Cont Edn; chmn & fdr, Ft Greene Sr Citzn Ctr; chairman, Brooklyn Core; sr citzn colmnst, NY Amsterdam News; Human Resource Dist #11; Omega Psi Phi; Assn of Black Social Workers; chairman, Comm School Board Dist 196. **Honors/Awds:** Community Service Award, John Jay College; Civic Leadership, Brooklyn Civic Assn; Comm Educ, JHS 117; Youth Leadership Recreation Teacher Assn; author "Comm Organizing for Small Groups", 1970. **Military Serv:** Military Serv first lt 1959.

PINSON, HERMINE DOLOREZ
Associate professor of English. **Personal:** Born Jul 20, 1953, Beaumont, TX; daughter of Robert B & Enid Davis Harris; married Donald E Pinson, Sep 10, 1976; children: Leah Courtney. **Educ:** Fisk University, BA, 1975; Southern Methodist University, MA, 1979; Rice University, PhD, 1991. **Career:** Houston, Community Coll, 1977-79; Texas Southern Universitys, asst prof, 1979-92; The College of William & Mary, assoc prof of English, 1992-. **Orgs:** Modern Language Assn; Southern Conference on African-American Studies, Inc; American Literature Assn; Southern Modern Language Assn. **Honors/Awds:** Vermont Studio Ctr, fellowship, 1997; Macdowell Colony, fellow, 1996; Yaddo Colony, fellow, 1996; Ford Postdoctoral, fellow, 1991; National Endowment for the Humanities fellow, 1988. **Special Achievements:** Author: "Ashe," collection of poems, 1992; Mama Yetta and Other Poems, 1988; work published in anthologies: Common Bonds, 1986; Loss of Ground Note, Callaloo and African-American Review, 1989. **Business Addr:** Associate Prof, Dept of English, Coll of William & Mary, PO Box 8795, Williamsburg, VA 23187-8795.

PINSON, MARGO DEAN
Alumni administrator. **Personal:** Born Oct 29, 1937, Washington, DC; daughter of Irene F C Dean and Dr Millard R Dean; married Dr Thomas J Pinson, Aug 21, 1969; children: Wendie F Barbee. **Educ:** Howard University, certificate, dental hygiene, 1959, BS, 1977; Catholic University, summer session, 1973, 1974. **Career:** Michael Reece Hospital, clinical dental hygienist, 1959-61; Jewish Memorial Hospital, clinical dental hygienist, 1961-62; DC Government, clinical dental hygienist, 1966-68, dental hygiene counselor, 1968-77; Howard University, special events officer, beginning 1977; Southeastern University, exec asst to the pres, currently. **Orgs:** Sigma Phi Alpha Dental Hygiene Honor Society, president, 1963-64; Howard University Alumni Association, 1977-; Howard University Dental Hygiene Alumni Association, 1960-; NAACP Montgomery County Branch, 1991-, fund raising dinner committee, 1992, 1993 Westover School, board of governors, 1986-92, board of governors, chairman of the annual fund, 1990-92; Northeasterners, Inc, Washington Chapter, president, 1988-90, national vice pres, 1990-92, national president, 1992-; Town of Highland Beach, board of commissioners, town treasurer, 1984-, appointed commissioner of finance, 1992-; National Coalition of 100 Black Women, 1990-. **Home Addr:** 3316 Brooklawn Terrace, Chevy Chase, MD 20815, (301)656-3284. **Business Addr:** Executive Assistant to the President, Public Relations, Southeastern University, 501 I St, SW, Washington, DC 20024-2788, (202)488-8162.

PINSON, THOMAS J. See Obituaries section.

PINSON, VALERIE F.
Legislative representative. **Personal:** Born Apr 30, 1930, Newburgh, NY; divorced; children: Tracey. **Educ:** Howard U, 1948-50; Bus Sch, 1950-51. **Career:** Sen Thomas J Dodd, asst 1960-64; White House Hon Hobart Taylor, exec asst 1965-66; Ofc Econ Opp, 1966-71; Comm Action Spec 1971-72; Congresswmn Yvonne B Burke Dem CA, admin asst; The White House, spec asst; Nat Assn of Counties, leg repr. **Orgs:** Bd mem Wash Urban League; bd Family & Child Serv; Com Minority Fellow Prgm Am Univ. **Business Addr:** The White House, 1600 Pennsylvania Ave NW, Washington, DC 20500.

PIPER, ADRIAN MARGARET SMITH
Educator, artist. **Personal:** Born Sep 20, 1948, New York, NY; daughter of Olive Xavier Smith Piper and Daniel Robert Piper. **Educ:** School of Visual Arts, New York, NY, AA, fine arts, 1969; City College of New York, New York, NY, BA, philosophy, 1974; Harvard University, Cambridge, MA, philosophy, 1977, PhD, philosophy, 1981. **Career:** Harvard University, graduate teaching assistant, 1976-77; University of Michigan, assistant professor, 1979-86; Georgetown University, associate professor, 1986-88; University of California, San Diego, associate professor, 1988-90; Wellesley College, professor, 1990-. **Orgs:** American Philosophical Association, 1979-; AAUP, 1979-; Association for Legal and Political Philosophy, 1979-; College Art Association, 1983-; North American Kant Society, 1979-. **Honors/Awds:** Sperling Prize for Excellence in Philosophy, 1974, Phi Beta Kappa Medal for the Best Honors Essay in the Social Sciences, 1974, Research Honors in Philosophy, 1974, City College of New York; First Prize in Drawing, Annual Student Exhibition, 1968, School of the Visual Arts; Stanford University, Mellon Post-Doctoral Research Fellowship, 1982-84; Woodrow Wilson International Scholars' Fellowship, 1989-90; NEA, Visual Artists' Fellowship, 1979, 1982; Guggenheim Fellowship, 1988-89; Awards in the Visual Arts Fellowship, 1990; California Institute of the Arts, Honorary Doctorate of Arts, 1991; NEH Coll Teacher's Research, Fellowship, 1998; Getty Research Inst, Distinguished Scholar, 1998-99. **Business Addr:** Professor of Philosophy, Wellesley College, 106 Central St, Founders Hall, Wellesley, MA 02181-8249.

PIPER, ELWOOD A.
Educator (retired). **Personal:** Born Apr 13, 1934, Bastrop, TX; son of Ruby and John H Piper; married Ora Lean Williams; children: Malcom, Karen, Adrian, Kenneth. **Educ:** Wiley Coll, BA 1956; TX So U, MA 1965. **Career:** Houston Independent School District, teacher/coach, 1958-65, assistant principal, 1965-70, principal, 1970-85. **Orgs:** Mem Pleasantville Civ Club; mem bd of dir Riverside Meth Ch; mem Rotary of Houston; Phi Delta Kappa; Natl Assoc of Sec Prin; Boy Scouts of Amer; Big Broth of Amer; TXJ Prin Assn. **Honors/Awds:** Man of the Yr, Civ Club 1965; serv awrd in Negro Hist 1968; cit of the wk KNUZ-Radio 1973; Silver Beaver Awrd, Boy Scouts of Amer 1976; Outstanding Administrator, 1980; COTC Award, 1984. **Business Addr:** Owner, Piper's Automotive Service Center, 2004 N Main, Baytown, TX 77520.

PIPER, PAUL J.
Physician. **Personal:** Born Jun 19, 1935, Detroit; married Mary K Harris; children: Paul, Michael. **Educ:** Univ MI, BS 1962; MS 1967; Wayne State U, MD 1973. **Career:** MI Dept of Corrections, physician; Pvt Pract, Phys; HS, Tchr; coach track & cross country. **Orgs:** Mem Detroit Med Soc, Sigma Phi Pi; Detroit Surg Soc; Nat Med Assn. **Military Serv:** USAF 1955-58.

PIPER, W. ARCHIBALD
Physician. **Personal:** Born Apr 13, 1935. **Educ:** Mt Allison U, BSc 1961; Dalhousie U, MD 1966; McGill Univ Can, MSc 1969; FRCS 1972; FACS 1976. **Career:** W Archibald Piper PC, plastic surgeon; MI St U, asst prof surgery. **Orgs:** AMA;

MI St Med Soc; Am Coll of Surgeons; Am Soc of Plastic Recons Surgeons; Flint Acad of Surgeons; MI Acad of Plastics Surgeons; Rotary Club; pvtpilot; mem Intl Coll of Surgeons. **Honors/Awds:** Bd cert Am Bd of Plastic Surgery; MSc thesis "The Fibrolast in Wound Healing". **Business Addr:** Plastic Surgeon, 2313 Stone Bridge Drive, Flint, MI 48504.

PIPKINS, ROBERT ERIK
Athlete, engineer. **Personal:** Born Feb 23, 1973, Buffalo, NY; son of Joan E Pipkins and Robert E Pipkins. **Educ:** Drexel Univ, BS, architectural engineering & civil engineering, 1995. **Career:** Luge, Men's Singles, US, junior development team mbr, 1987-88, junior candidate team mbr, 1988-89, junior national team mbr, 1989-92, Olympic team mbr, 1992, senior national team mbr, 1992-94; Olympic team mem, 1994. **Honors/Awds:** US National Champion, 1993-95; US Olympic Team Mbr, 1992, 1994; Junior World Champion, 1992; Lake Placid Track Record Holder, 1992-. **Home Addr:** 13 Bailey Place, Staten Island, NY 10303.

PIPPEN, SCOTTIE
Professional basketball player. **Personal:** Born Sep 25, 1965, Hamburg, AR; married Larsa Younan, 1997. **Educ:** Univ of Central Arkansas, Conway, AR, 1983-87. **Career:** Chicago Bulls, forward-guard, 1987-. **Honors/Awds:** All-NBA First Team, 1994-96; All-NBA Second Team, 1992, 1997; NBA All-Defensive First Team, 1992-97; NBA All-Star, 1990, 1992-97; NBA All-Star Game Most Valuable Player, 1994; won gold medals with the US Olympic Basketball Team, 1992, 1996; selected as one of the 50 Greatest Players in NBA History, 1996. **Special Achievements:** Personality behind the Scottie Candy Bar, 1993; author, Reach Higher, 1997. **Business Addr:** Professional Basketball Player, Chicago Bulls, 1901 W Madison St, Chicago, IL 60612, (312)455-4000.

PIRTLE, RONALD M.
Automobile company executive. **Personal:** Born Jun 19, 1954, Jackson, TN; son of Ida Pirtle; married Brenda Moore-Pirtle, Aug 30, 1980; children: Crystal, Kelli, Kimberly. **Educ:** General Motors Institute, Flint, MI, BSIA, 1977; Harvard Graduate School of Business Administration, Boston, MA, MBA, 1980. **Career:** Chevrolet Motor Div, Flint, MI, industrial engr, 1977-78; GM Corporate Fin Staff, Detroit, MI, dir, operations analysis, 1984, dir, cost analysis, 1985, dir, budget analysis, 1986; B-O-C Flint Automotive, Flint, MI, mgr, fin & business planning, 1987-88; Pontiac Motor Div, Pontiac, MI, comptroller, 1989-90; GM Corporate Strategic Planning Group, Detroit, MI, exec in charge, 1990-92; GM Corp, AC Rochester East Division, finance director, 1992-. **Orgs:** Mem, Trinity Baptist Church in Pontiac; mem, Harvard Business Club of Detroit; life mem, Kappa Alpha Psi Fraternity, Inc. **Honors/Awds:** America's Best & Brightest Young Business & Professional Men, Dollars & Sense, 1990. **Business Addr:** Finance Director, GM Corp, AC Rochester Division, 1300 N Dort Hwy, Flint, MI 48556, (810)236-5000.

PITCHER, FREDERICK M. A.
Airline captain, pilot. **Personal:** Born Mar 9, 1932, Washington, DC; son of Sylvia Saunders Hardy; divorced; children: Frederick II, Riccardo, Tia Pitcher Clarke, Mikela, Ericka, Elliott. **Educ:** DeVry Tech Inst, Diploma 1953; Northrop Univ, Cert, License A&P 1965; Fowler Aeronautical, Diploma 1966; LA Trade Tech Coll , AS Dean's List 1969; UCLA, Teaching Credential 1977; Natl Radio Inst, Diploma 1977; KIIS Radio Broadcasting, Diploma 1979. **Career:** US Naval Model Basin, engrg aide 1955; Burroughs Corp Computers, electronic tech 1955-59, electronics engr 1959-64; Tech Enterpries, owner, oper 1961-; Electronic Memories Inc, quality control 1964; Rose Aviation, flight instr 1975-85; Western Airlines, airline pilot, 1966-87; Delta Airlines, airline pilot, 1987-. **Orgs:** Mem/restorer, March Air Force Base Museum, California, 1988-89; founder, Soc for Preservation of Antique Technical Equipment, 1989; industry resource person, Los Angeles School Distict, 1986-; mem/builder, Experimental Aircraft Assn, 1965-; pilot/instructor, Civil Air Patrol, 1948-; Pres Mktg Intl Ltd 1983-; exec vice pres Worldwide Tax & Bus Consult Inc 1984-85; ceo Tech Enterprises 1966-; chief fin officer the DW Ford Corp Inc 1982-85; dir DW Ford Seminar Assoc 1983-85; mem LA Urban Bankers Assoc 1984-85; cert flight instr Worldwide 1961-85; station engr KFAR-TV 1962-63; west reg vice pres Org of Black Airline Pilots 1984-86; dir mem Northrop Univ Alumni 1979-; reading tutor CA Literacy Prog 1984-87; comm rel officer AirlinePilots Assoc 1983-85; guestlecturer LA School Dist 1968-85; Educare USC Alumni 1977. **Honors/Awds:** Certificate of Recognition, State Senator Bill Greene, California, 1989; Professional Recog Edges Group Inc of Fortune 500 1984; Commendation CA State Senator Green Comm Asst 1980; Disting Alumni Northrop Univ 1976; Good Samaritan Awd Church of Jesus Christ of Latter Day Saints 1976; Community Serv LA School Dist 1971; Scholarship Sci Bosch & Lomb 1950; People & Choices Harcourt BraceJovonovich Publ Co 1971. **Military Serv:** USNR-R atr-2 10 yrs. **Home Addr:** PO Box 73CN, Broadway-Manchester Station, Los Angeles, CA 90003.

PITCHFORD, GERARD SPENCER
Business executive. **Personal:** Born Dec 8, 1953, Jersey City, NJ; son of Gloria Oliver Pitchford and Gordon Pitchford; married Janet F Hardy, Nov 25, 1987; children: Uonisha, Paris. **Educ:** Rutgers Univ, 1970. **Career:** Dynamic Service Unlimited, sales mgr 1976; Time to Order Corp, pres 1984-86; Communications Equipment Repair, pres 1977-; Corporate Promotions International, president, currently. **Orgs:** Bd mem treasuer Chicago Regional Purchasing Council 1980-; bd mem Chicago State Univ Found 1982-; bd mem Private Industry Council 1984-; bd mem Push International Trade Bureau; commissioner City of Chicago Dept of Human Rights; chairman Chicago Reg Purchasing Council Comm on Certification; Deacon, Chicago United 1987. **Honors/Awds:** Vendor of the month, state of Illinois 1986.

PITT, CLIFFORD SINCLAIR
Educational administrator. **Personal:** Born in Georgetown, St Vincent, West Indies; son of Carmen and Alphonso; divorced; children: Amanda, Carolyn. **Educ:** Newbold College, BA, 1971; Andrews University, MA, 1972; University of London, PhD, 1976. **Career:** British Union of Seventh-Day Adventists, minister; Oakwood College, associate professor; Miles College, dean of academic affairs, currently. **Honors/Awds:** Newbold College, Valedictorian/President of the Senior Class, 1971. **Special Achievements:** Author, Church, Ministry and Sacraments: A Critical Evaluation of the Thought of Peter Taylor Forsyth, University Press of America, 1983. **Business Addr:** Dean of Academic Affairs, Miles College, PO Box 3800, Birmingham, AL 35208, (205)923-2771.

PITTMAN, AUDREY BULLOCK
Educator. **Personal:** Born Dec 16, 1916, Philadelphia, PA; daughter of Annie Beaden Bullock and Oscar Wyle Bullock; married James Pittman, Jan 17, 1942 (died 1989); children: Joyce Ann. **Educ:** Morgan State Univ, BA 1948; Univ of Pennsylvania, MSW; Waldon Univ, PhD 1984. **Career:** Philadelphia Dept Welfare, supervisor 1951-57; Pennsylvania State Dept Welfare, day care dir 1964-69; Children's Aid Soc, adoption super & consultant 1957-64; Temple Univ, assoc prof 1969-84, prof emeritus. **Orgs:** Founding mem Philadelphia Assoc Black Social Workers 1969-; board president, Christian Educ AME Church 1971-; trustee Cheyney Univ 1977-; adv bd Philadelphia Dept Welfare 1981-88; board member/vice president, Black Family Serv 1984-; bd mem Women's Christian Alliance 1986-89; member, Philadelphia County Board of Assistance, 1990-; trustee, Valentine Foundation, 1990; Phila Child Guidance Clinic, bd mem, vp, 1994-. **Honors/Awds:** Linback Awd Excellence in Teaching Temple Univ 1981; Service Awd Natl Alliance Black Social Workers 1984; Alumni of Year Awd William Penn High School 1985; AME Womens Missionary Society, Meritorius Christian Service, 1992; Dorothy M Jenkins, Christian Educ Award, Outstanding Christian Service, 1993; Morgan State Univ, Phil Alumnu Chapter, Distinguished Service Award, 1994; Blacks Networking for Progress Inc, African Amer Community Award, Enhancing and improving the quality of life for African-American families, 1994; Rho Chapter Alpha Phi Alpha Fraternity, The Alpha African Amer Heritage Award, Achievement in the Field of Educ, 1995. **Business Addr:** Professor Emeritus, Temple University, Ritter Hall Annex, 13th & Columbia Ave, Philadelphia, PA 19107.

PITTMAN, DARRYL E.
Government official. **Personal:** Born Jul 11, 1948, Pittsburgh, PA; son of Eunice W Pittman and J Ronald Pittman; married Deborah Durham, Aug 8, 1980; children: Darryl M, Sholah, Jordan, Cassi, Nolan. **Educ:** Columbia Coll, New York NY, AB, 1970; Columbia Univ School of Law, New York NY, JD, 1973. **Career:** Hardiman, Alexander, Pittman & Howland, Cleveland OH, partner; Hahn Loeser, Freedheim, Dean & Wellman, Cleveland, OH, assoc; City of East Cleveland OH, mayor. **Orgs:** Pres, Software Specialist; mem, Norman Minor Bar Assn; former pres, Ohio Chapter of Black Mayors; mem, 21st District Congressional Caucus, bd mem, Cleveland Branch NAACP. **Home Addr:** 16119 Oakhill Rd, East Cleveland, OH 44112.

PITTMAN, KAVIKA
Professional football player. **Personal:** Born Oct 9, 1974, Leesville, LA. **Educ:** McNeese State, attended. **Career:** Dallas Cowboys, defensive end, 1996-. **Business Addr:** Professional Football Player, Dallas Cowboys, One Cowboys Pkwy, Irving, TX 75063, (214)556-9900.

PITTMAN, KEITH B.
City official. **Personal:** Born 1971. **Career:** New Orleans Metropolitan Convention and Visitors Bureau, Inc., director of governmental affairs, 1997-. **Special Achievements:** First African American director at the Visitor's Bureau, as well as the youngest director. **Business Addr:** Director, Governmental Affairs, New Orleans Metro Convention & Visitors Bureau, Inc, 1520 Sugarbowl Dr, New Orleans, LA 70112, (504)566-5011.

PITTMAN, MARVIN B.
Dentist. **Personal:** Born May 31, 1931, Blakely, GA; son of Lucile Brewster Pittman and Johnnie Will Pittman; married Amanda B Nelson; children: Marvin B Jr. **Educ:** Savannah State Coll, BS (Hon) 1953; Univ of MI, MS 1957; Howard Univ, DDS (Hon) 1966. **Career:** VA Center Los Angeles, rsch biochemist 1957-62; AUS, dental officer 1966-70; Private practice Los Angeles, dentist 1970-. **Orgs:** Mem, Amer Dental Assn, CA Dental Assn, Angel City Cental Soc, Century Club Univ SC, Holman Meth Church, Urban League, NAACP, Alpha Phi Alpha, YMCA, Reserve Officers Assn; bd of dirs, pres, JW Ross Med Ctr Los Angeles; bd of dir Omicron Kappa Upsilon, Beta Kappa Chi; bd of dirs, Los Angeles Free Clinic. **Military Serv:** US Army, NCO, 1953-56; US Navy Reserve, 1964-66; US Army Reserves Col 1971; Bronze Star, Army Commendation, Good Conduct, Army Achievement. **Business Addr:** Dentist, JW Ross Medical Center, 1828 S Western Ave #18, Los Angeles, CA 90006.

PITTMAN, SAMPLE NOEL
Educator. **Personal:** Born Apr 22, 1927, Texas; married Vivian Jo Byars; children: Sample Jr, Ava, Nicholas. **Educ:** NYU, PhD, 1974; TX Southern Univ, MA 1952; Samuel Huston Coll, BA 1949. **Career:** Borough of Manhattan Comm Coll City Univ of NY, dean of admin 1970-, asso dean of students 1971; Corp Consortium-Harlem Inst for Teachers NYC, dir teacher 1970; Poverty Program, Training Resources for Youth Educ Dept, dir 1969; Inst of Strategic Study United Presbyterian Church, New York City rsch assoc 1967; New York City Housing & Redevel Bd Hudson Consev Project, asst dir 1966; Dillard Univ, dean of students 1964; Chicago Comm Coll, instructor 1962; Chicago Commn on Race Relations; asst dir; Mayors Com on New Residents, 1959; IL Youth Commn, juvenile parole officer 1957; St Charles St Training School. **Orgs:** Mem bd dir, Chicago Halfway House 1962; consulting lecturer, Natl Conf of Chrstns & Jews Chicago 1962; Chicago City Comm Coll Faculty Rep United Natl Inst 1962; vice pres Parents Teachers Students Assn 1962; vice pres Greenview Comm Council, Chicago 1962; Chicago City Comm Coll Faculty Rep Intercollegiate Counc 1961; panelist, DePaul Univ & Natl Conf of Christians & Jews, Chicago 1962; treasurer, Comm Bd #9 Manhattan NY. **Honors/Awds:** Diploma de hon Borough of Manhattan Comm Coll 1975; Outstanding Educ of Amer Award 1975; adminstr of yr award Borough of Manhattan Comm Coll 1974; founders day award NYU, 1974; Phi Delta Kappa mem 1966; Alpha Phi Alpha mem 1948; Bertha Lockett achievement award Brownwood TX 1975. **Military Serv:** AUS. **Business Addr:** Borough Manhattan Comm Coll, 199 Chambers St, New York, NY 10031.

PITTS, BRENDA S.
Corporate responsibility executive. **Personal:** Born Aug 29, 1950, Madison, IN; daughter of Theola I Hunter and Kenneth W Hunter; married Joseph David; children: Nichole, Christopher. **Educ:** IN Univ, BS Educ 1972. **Career:** Knox Co News, writer 1972-73; Cummins Engine Co Inc, communication spec 1974, couns 1975, personnel admin 1975-78, mgr EEO 1978-82, mgr personnel 1982-83, director of personnel, 1983-88, executive director of personnel 1988-92, vice pres, human resources, 1992-97; vp, diversity & corporate responsibility, 1997-. **Orgs:** Alpha Kappa Alpha Sorority 1970-72; scholarship chmn Laws Found 1975-79; commr Columbus Human Rights Commn 1978-79; Columbus NAACP, vice pres. **Honors/Awds:** Freshman Hon Soc IN Univ 1968-69; Dean's List IN Univ 1968-72. **Business Addr:** VP, Diversity & Corporate Responsibility, Cummnis Engine Co, mail code 60911, PO Box 3005, Columbus, IN 47202.

PITTS, CORNELIUS
Attorney. **Personal:** Born Aug 3, 1933, Detroit, MI; son of Zenolia O'Rear Pitts and Percy James Pitts; married Mildred D Johnson, Aug 2, 1956; children: Byron Horace. **Educ:** Wayne State University, BA, 1959, LLB, 1964. **Career:** Self-employed, attorney, 1965-. **Orgs:** Wolverine Bar Association, 1965-; National Bar Association, 1965-; Detroit Bar Association, 1965-; Michigan Bar Association, 1965-. **Military Serv:** US Army, Cpl, 1953-55. **Home Phone:** (313)393-3333. **Business Addr:** Attorney, 3650 Penobscot Bldg, Detroit, MI 48226, (313)964-0066.

PITTS, DONALD FRANKLIN
Judge. **Personal:** Born Aug 30, 1933, Pontiac, MI; married Patricia Florence Washington; children: Gregory Leroy, Gail Lynn, Kimberly Marie Thomas, Mark Robert Brown, Donald F Jr, Maureen Alyce. **Educ:** East Los Angeles Coll, AA 1952; CA State Univ, BA 1954; Southwestern Univ, JD 1962. **Career:** LA CA, probation officer 1955-63, attny at law 1963-71; CA State Univ Long Beach, assoc prof 1972-75; Superior Court, referee 1969-71, commissioner 1971-84, judge 1984- (Court of Appeals State of CA 2nd District, justice pro tem Dec 1985 & Jan 1986). **Orgs:** Mem State Bar of CA, Natl Bar Assoc, John M Langston Bar Assoc, LA Cty Bar Assoc, Long Beach Bar Assoc, YMCA, NAACP; bd dir Comm Devel Inc of Long Beach. **Business Addr:** Judge, Superior Court, 825 Maple Ave, Torrance, CA 90503.

PITTS, DOROTHY LOUISE WALLER
Social worker (retired). **Personal:** Born Jun 29, 1913, Memphis, TN; daughter of Corinne Aline Walton Waller and Oscar Rand Waller; married Walter Lee Pitts (died 1991); children:

Edolia Pitts Goudeau. **Educ:** LeMoyne Coll, AB 1935; Howard Univ, MA 1940; Univ of CA, Cert Soc Welfare 1957. **Career:** deFremery Rec Ctr, rsd dir 1947-48, head dir 1948-56; San Francisco State College Summer Workshop in Ed for Human Rel, staff teacher 1952; Oakland Rec Dept, suprv 1956-62, trng-cons 1962-63, suprv of rec 1964; Richmond comm Devel Demo Proj, suprv new careers 1965-66; Advance Negro Council for Comm Improvement, exec dir 1966; Social Plng Dept Berkeley, neighborhood cons, soc plng analyst 1966-73; Div on Aging City of Berkeley CA, chief 1973-78, dir. **Orgs:** Mem Western Gerontological Soc; CA Spec on Aging; National Council of Sr Cit Inc, CA Association for Health & Welfare; National Council on Aging; Howard Univ Alumni Association; NAACP El Cerrito Br; Natl Council of Negro Women Inc; charter mem, vp 1985, natl bd dir The Older Women's League 1980-; org sponsor & 1st pres Rainbow Sign; pres Progressive Black BPW Inc 1974-85, Sojourner Truth Housing Inc 1974-85; adv bd Univ of CA; chrpsn of board of directors YWCA 1974-75; 1st vice pres Berkeley Bar Area Alumnae Chap Delta Sigma Theta 1978-79; founder, 1989, mem task force Constitution & By-Laws Comm, Ntl Assn of Negro & Prof Women's Clubs; member, LeMoyne-Owen College Alumni Assn, 1991; LeMoyne-Owen Task Force on Planned Giving, 1991-, chair, currently; Tennessee Commission on Aging, appointed by Governor Ned McWherter, 1993-98; President's Advisory Council of Le-Moyne-Owen College; Memphis Metro Club ofNPWC Inc, founder, advisor, currently; Delta Sigma Theta, Memphis Alumnae Chapter, currently. **Honors/Awds:** Author of article Rec Mag Sep 1966; CA Park & Rec Assoc Awd for Exceptional Achievement in Field of Parks & Rec 1963; Delta Women of Achievement Delta Sigma Theta 1965; Cal-Pal Awd for Outstanding Serv to Community 1974; Woman of the Year Sun Reporter Merit Awd 1973; Disting Alumna Awd Bay Area Howard Univ Alumni Assoc 1975; WAVE Awd Women of Achievement Vision & Excellence Alumnae Resources 1984; Awd for Outstanding Community Serv Natl Inst for Minority Women of Color 1984; Community Service Awd Alameda Contra Costa Links Inc 1985; Ella Hill Hutch Award, Black Women Organized for Political Action 1986.

PITTS, GEORGE EDWARD, JR.
Picture editor, artist, painter. **Personal:** Born Sep 10, 1951, Pennsylvania; son of Phyllis and George Pitts Sr; married Janis Pitts, Dec 25, 1978. **Educ:** Howard University, 1969-70; Skowhegan School of Painting and Sculpture, 1971; Bennington College, BA, 1973. **Career:** Phillips Exeter Academy, art teacher, Summer 1972; Time Inc Picture Collection, picture researcher, 1979-90; Sports Illustrated Picture Collection, picture reseacher, 1982; Entertainment Weekly Magazine, assistant picture editor, 1990-93; Vibe Magazine, picture editor, 1993-. **Orgs:** Society of Publication Design, 1994-. **Honors/Awds:** Skowhegan School of Painting and Sculpture, 1st Prize Painting, 1971; Communication Arts, Photography Award, 1991-93; ASME Nomination, Best Photography, Vibe Magazine, 1994; Festival De La Mode, Louvre Museum, Paris, Exhibition of Vibe Fashion Photography, 1994; American Photography, Certificate of Merit, 1995. **Special Achievements:** Group Art Exhibition: Social Studies: Truth, Justice, and the Afro-American Way, Illinois State University, 1989; Men, Myth, and Masculinities, Ledisflam Gallery, NYC, 1993; The Return of the Cadaure Exquis, The Drawing Center, NYC, 1993; Go Back and Fetch It (It means Sankofa), Gallery Annex I & II, 1994, 1995. **Business Addr:** Picture Editor, VIBE Magazine, 215 Lexington Avenue, 6th Fl, New York, NY 10016, (212)448-7437.

PITTS, JACK NELSON EVANGELISTA
Insurance company executive. **Personal:** Born Apr 27, 1948, Decatur, GA; son of Lillie Mae Seals Pitts and Jack Nelson Pitts; married Greta Ann Coleman Pitts, Apr 20, 1980; children: Jack N E Jr, Jean Coleman Pitts. **Educ:** Michigan State Univ, East Lansing, MI, BS, MBA, PhD candidate. **Career:** Lansing Community College, Lansing, MI, instructor, 1983-88; Blue Cross Blue Shield of Michigan, Detroit, MI, professional consultant, 1984-88, assistant vice president, 1988-. **Orgs:** Bd of directors, YMCA of Metropolitan Detroit, 1989-; board of trustees, Jr Achievement of SE Michigan, 1990-; board of directors, Black Caucus Foundation of Michigan, 1990-; board of directors, Detroit Urban League, 1990-; board of directors, Black Family Development Inc, 1990-. **Business Addr:** Assistant Vice President, Community Relations, Blue Cross and Blue Shield of Michigan, 600 E Lafayette, #2025, Detroit, MI 48226.

PITTS, JAMES DONALD, JR.
Natural gas utility company executive. **Personal:** Born Aug 7, 1938, Chicago, IL; son of Jewell Johnson Richmond-Anderson and James Donald Pitts, Sr. **Educ:** Illinois Inst of Technology, Chicago IL, BS, 1968; Univ of Chicago, Chicago IL, MBA; 1979; Northwestern University, executive management program, 1990. **Career:** The Peoples Gas Light & Coke Co, Chicago IL, 1956-. **Orgs:** Mem, Amer Gas Assn; dir, Amer Assn of Blacks in Energy; mem, Chicago Urban League; mem, Executive Program Club-Graduate School of Business, Univ of Chicago; dir Centers for New Horizons; Guardianship and Advocacy Comm; dir, Greater State St council, treasurer, pres, Mental Health Association of Greater Chicago. **Military Serv:** US Army, SP4 E4, 1962-64, Army Commendation Award, 1964.

PITTS, LEE H.
Banking executive, swimming coach. **Personal:** Born Jul 7, 1960, Birmingham, AL; son of Johnnie and Lee Pitts. **Educ:** Talladega Coll, BBA, 1982; Atlanta Univ, MA, economics, 1985. **Career:** A G Gaston Boys Club, smim instructor, 1979; Collegeville Pool, head swim instructor, 1981; Norwood Pool, head swim team coach, 1982; Adams Park Pool, head swim instructor, 1984; Star Complex of Fort Myers, FL, head swim instructor, currently; Dr Martin Luther King Pool, head swim team coach, 1992; WEVU-TV Talk Show, producer/host, ''Lee Pitts Live,'' currently; First Union Bank of FL, vice pres, currently. **Orgs:** The Lee Pitts Swim School, founder; Natl Assn of Black Scuba Divers, 1992; Natl Assn of Swim Instructors, 1993; American Red Cross, bd of dirs, 1990; Natl Assn of Urban Bankers, 1988; Intl Swim Hall of Fame; Phi Beta Sigma Fraternity; United States Swim; Quality Life Ctr, SW Florida; numerous others. **Honors/Awds:** NAACP, Distinguished Service, 1993; Lee County Black History Soc, Induction, 1995; American Red Cross, Outstanding Contribution to Swimming, 1991; State of Florida, Crime Prevention Among Black Youths, 1994; Edison Community Coll, Outstanding Youth Devt Award, 1991; Talladega College Alumni Spotlight Award, 1991; NAACP, Outstanding Community Involvement Award, 1984; numerous others. **Special Achievements:** First African-American to produce, direct, write, and star in a swim lesson video, 1993; First African-American to be a spokesman on swim instruction commercials for NBC-TV, 1992; author of 25 published swimming-related articles; Keynote speaker at numerous elementary/high schools and colleges around the country; Inducted into the SW Florida Black History Museum, 1995; spokesman for WFLA, Channel 8, NBC, pool safety commercials in Tampa Bay; numerous other achievements. **Business Addr:** President, Pitts Swim School, PO Box 2662, Fort Myers, FL 33902-2662, (941)656-3446.

PITTS, RONALD JAMES, SR.
Attorney. **Personal:** Born Nov 2, 1942, Wheeling, WV; married Nellie M Price; children: Ronnelle, Rhonda; Ronald J II. **Educ:** BS 1966; LLB 1969; JD 1970. **Career:** Atty, pvt prac; IRS Estate & Gift Tax Reg Analyst Cincinnati, est tax grp mgr; IRS, Atty; Greensboro Dist Greensboro NC, quality & productivity coord, currently; technical reviewer, 1997-. **Orgs:** Vp NAACP Huntington WV; Huntington URA Commr; Legal Counc Bluefield St Alumni; sec NAACP 1973-74; chmn C-H Hum Rights Counc 1970-73; mem WV Black Caucus; supvs C/UNIDN chmn; pres Chap 64 Nat Treas Empl Union; mem Mtn St Bar Assn, sec 1972-73, histrn; mem WV St Bar Assn; Am Bar Assn 1969; mem Pres Cncl of Wheeling Coll; EEO Consult RJP Consult Fdr Fed Bsktbll Leag 1970; cmmr 1970-75; bd mem Tri-St Tax Inst 1975; mem St Legisl Interim Com; quality instr Regional 1987; natl exec bd AIM-IRS 1986-87, natl parliamentarian, 1986-; OD, consultant. **Honors/Awds:** Distingushed Performer 1986, 1987.

PITTS, VERA L.
Educator, educational administrator. **Personal:** Born Jan 23, 1931, Wichita, KS; daughter of Maggie Johnson and Wade Johnson; widowed. **Educ:** Mills Coll, AA 1950; NC Berkeley, BA 1953; Sacramento State Univ, MA 1962; MI State Univ, PhD 1969. **Career:** Stockton Unified School Dist, teacher, counselor, admin 1954-65; City Coll NY, asst prof 1967-69; Palmer Handwriting Co, consult 1975-; CA State Univ Hayward, prof, dept chair ed admin 1969-; program mgr, Dept of Educ, 1986-87; assoc supt, Oakland Unified School District l987-88; Oakland Public Schools, Oakland, CA, interim supt, 1989; Natl Hispanic Univ, San Jose, CA, provost, 1990-91. **Orgs:** Mem bd dir League of Women Voters 1975-; mem Western Assoc Accrediting Teams 1975-; pres San Mateo Br Amer Assoc Univ Women 1976-77; vice pres CA State Div Amer Assoc Univ Women 1978-82; mem Foster City Ed Facilities Comm 1983; counselor Univ of CA Alumni Assoc 1979-83; Natl Urban League Ed Adv Comm 1979-; dir-at-large Natl Council Admin Women in Ed 1982-; Phi Delta Kappa 1982-85; Pacific School of Religion Bd of Trustees, l989-; Rotary Intl, l988-. **Honors/Awds:** Mott Fellowship Natl Awd MI 1965-67; Danforth Assoc Found 1974-; Vstg Professorships Univ Houston, Univ MI, Pepperdine Univ 1974-; Rockefeller Postdoctoral Fellowship 1978-80; Natl Faculty Exchange to US Dept of Ed 1986-87. **Home Addr:** 1557 Beach Park Blvd., Foster City, CA 94404-1437. **Business Addr:** Professor, Dept Chair, California State Univ, 25800 Carlos Bee Blvd, Hayward, CA 94542.

PITTS, WILLIAM HENRY
Dentist. **Personal:** Born Sep 19, 1914, New Haven, CT; son of Lillian Cambridge Pitts and William Henry Pitts; married Eleanor Mable Eaton; children: William H III, James J, Clarence E. **Educ:** Lincoln Univ, AB 1937; Meharry Medical Coll Sch of Dentistry, DDS 1942; NYU, post grad 1946; New Orgn Sch for Grad Dentist, attended 1946; State of CT, post grad work 1965. **Career:** Yale New Haven Hosp, staff 1955; PA Dental Soc of Anesthesiology, post grad course pain control & patient mgmt; State of CT Correction Dept, dentist 1982; private practice, dentist. **Orgs:** Mem Amer Dental Assoc 1942-, New Haven Dental Assoc 1947-, CT State Dental Assoc 1947-; mem Intl Acad of Anesthesiology 1951, Natl Dental Assoc 1955-; PGER of IBPO Elks of the World; Prince Hall Mason 32nd degree. **Honors/Awds:** 1st Black Sch Dentist New Haven 1952-57; Certificate of Qualifications Natl Bd of Dental Examiners; Fellow Royal Soc of Health. **Military Serv:** AUS Dental Corps capt 1942-46. **Business Addr:** Dentist, 206 Dixwell Ave, New Haven, CT 06511.

PLATT, RICHARD A.
Construction executive. **Career:** Platt Construction Inc, Franklin WI, chief executive. **Orgs:** ACC; WUCA; MWCA; TCCA. **Honors/Awds:** Regional V, 8A Graduate of the Year Award, 1992; Department of Transportation, Secretary's Award, 1988; SBA, National Graduate of the Year Award, presented at the White House, Washington, DC, 1992.

PLAYER, WILLA B.
Educational consultant, educational administrator (retired). **Personal:** Born Aug 9, 1909, Jackson, MS; daughter of Beatrice D Player and C C Player. **Educ:** OH Wesleyan Univ, BA; Oberlin Coll, MA; Univ Grenoble France, Cert d'Etudes; Univ of Chicago & Univ of WI, grad student; Columbia Univ, DEduc 1948; OH Wesleyan Univ, LD 1953; Lycoming Coll, LD 1962; Morehouse Coll, LD 1963; Albion Coll, LD 1963; Keuka Coll, DH Litt 1967; Univ NC Greensboro,HD Litt 1969; Prairie View A&M Coll, DPS 1971; Bennett Coll, HD Litt 1976. **Career:** Bennett Coll, French & Latin instr, dir admissions, coord of instr, vp, pres 1955-66; Bureau of Postsecondary Educ Wash, DC, dir div institut devel 1966-77; consultant in higher edn; Bennett Coll, pres Emerita, currently. **Orgs:** Mem bd trustees Charles Stewart Mott Found; mem adv comm on Black Higher Educ Mott Found; mem bd dir United Negro Coll Fund NYC; mem Univ Senate United Meth Ch Nashville, TN 1976-84; mem Comm on Funding Black Colls Nashville, TN 1976-84; mem Ford Found Study of Black Coll CAEL Baltimore, MD; mem steering comm ISATIM ACE/UNCF/Kellogg Found Study; mem First United Meth ChAkron, OH. **Honors/Awds:** Superior Serv Award & Disting Serv Award Dept HEW 1970 & 1972; Disting Achievement Citation OH Wesleyan Univ 1980; Gen Educ Bd Fellowships 1945 & 1947; Frank Ross Chambers Fellow Columbia Univ 1948; Ford Fellow on study tour of 12 colleges and universities in US; study made possible by grant from Fund for Educational Advancement; Presidential Ldrshp Grant to Japan Carnegie Corp of NY; travel to England, France, Italy, Switzerland, East and West Africa, Japan, Israel and Egypt.

PLEAS, JOHN ROLAND
Psychologist. **Personal:** Born Nov 11, 1938, East St Louis, IL; son of Daisy Walton Pleas and Henry Pleas; married Katherine Pleas, Dec 26, 1985; children: Chandra. **Educ:** McKendree Coll, BA 1960; Univ of IL Urbana, MEd 1967; Vanderbilt Univ Nashville TN, PhD 1980. **Career:** Univ of Chicago Billings Hosp, res tech 1963-67; St Leonards House, dir com devel 1967-71; Competence Inc, pres 1975-; Vanderbilt Univ Weight Mgmt Prog, co-dir 1977-84; Columbia Coll, asst prof, 1984-85; Middle Tennessee State Univ, assoc prof 1985-. **Honors/Awds:** Danforth Fellowship, Vanderbilt Univ, 1971-73; Recognition Award, Natl Medical Assn of Northwest Indiana, Inc, 1988; Amer Soc for Engineering Education, Certificate of Recognition Award, Naval Health Res Ctr, San Diego, CA, 1990. **Military Serv:** US Army, spec 5th class, 1960-63; Good Conduct Medal. **Business Addr:** Associate Professor, Dept of Psychology, Middle Tennessee State University, Murfreesboro, TN 37132.

PLEASANT, ALBERT E., III
Administrator. **Personal:** Born May 22, 1944, Cincinnati, OH; son of Margaret Nesbitt Pleasant and Albert E Pleasant Jr; married Barbara Greene Pleasant, Apr 28, 1989; children: Albert E IV, Dennis R Green Sr. **Educ:** Univ of Cincinnati, BS 1973. **Career:** University of Cincinnati, dean's office, College of Medicine, fiscal asst, 1969-74; Children's Hospital Medical Ctr, Div of Neonatology, business mgr 1974-89; University of Cincinnati, Dept of Peds, bus affairs asst 1974-79, sr business admin 1979-89; Howard University, dir office research adm, 1989-90; University of Cincinnati Medl Ctr, Dept of Environmental Health, assoc dir adm & bus services, executive director, 1990-. **Orgs:** Mem Natl Council of Univ Rsch Adminis 1974-; mem Soc of Rsch Administrators 1974-; lay delegate 51st Reg Conv of the Lutheran Church Missouri Synod 1975; mem Assn of Amer Medical Colls Group on Business Affairs 1982-; assoc mem Natl Health Lawyers Assn 1984-; Business Mgmt Consultant NICHHD, PHS, DHHS 1985-; mem OH Dist Bd for Parish Serv 1985-87. **Honors/Awds:** Elected mem Republican Central Comm Hamilton Co Cincinnati OH 1982-86. **Military Serv:** AUS specialist 5th class 1967-69; Vietnam Serv Medal; Good Conduct Medal; Army Commendation Medal. **Business Addr:** Associate Director, Admin & Business Services, Univ of Cincinnati Medical Ctr, Department of Environmental Health, 3223 Eden Ave, Cincinnati, OH 45267-0056.

PLEASANT, ANTHONY DEVON
Professional football player. **Personal:** Born Jan 27, 1968, Century, FL; married Renita; children: Hannah Denette. **Educ:** Tennessee State, attended. **Career:** Cleveland Browns, defensive end, 1990-95; Baltimore Ravens, 1996; Atlanta Falcons, 1997-. **Business Addr:** Professional Football Player, Atlanta Falcons, Two Falcon Place, Suwanee, GA 30174, (404)945-1111.

PLEASANT, MAE BARBEE BOONE
Educational administrator (retired). **Personal:** Born Jul 8, 1919, Kentucky; daughter of Minnie Mae Burks and Zelma Clarence Barbee; married Noel J (deceased); children: Eugene Jr. **Educ:** Tennessee State Univ, BS 1941; Hampton Inst, MA 1962; George Washington Univ. **Career:** Hampton Inst, admin asst to pres, sec of corp 1973-, faculty mem 1968-71, admin asst to pres 1957-63, business mgr 1946-53; African Amer Affairs, assoc dir 1971-73; OEO, educ specialist 1966-68; Univ MD, dean of women 1963-66; Clark Coll, past exec sec pres 1953-57; Virginia State, past sec supt 1944. **Orgs:** Mem Alpha Kappa Mu; Girl Scout Leader; area chmn UNCF; chmn Human Relations Comm, League of Women Voters; pres Peninsula Pan Hellenic Council; state chmn Assn for Study of Negro Life & History 1973-75; bd dir YWCA 1953-57; vice-chmn Professional Sec 1955-57; mem Vestry & Register, St Cyprian's Episcopal Church 1974, 1984, 1989; basileus, Alpha Kappa Alpha, Gamma Upsilon Omega 1977-79; Quarter Century Club of Hampton Univ; bd of dir, Children's Home Society, Richmond VA; former vice chairman, King Street Community Center; trustee, VA Theological Seminary; first black lay person, 1979-89; tres, bd mem, Downtown Day Care Ctr; treasurer, St Anne Chapter, Daughters of the King of St Cyprian's Episcopal Church; Peninsula Pastoral Counseling, bd Finance Comm and Retreat Comm, Nominating Comm; secretary and member, Executive and Program Co, MS of Peninsula Chapter of Natl Conference of Christians and Jews. **Honors/Awds:** Citation HEW 1967; citation TN St Univ 1962; Woman of Yr Hampton Inst 1957, 1963; editor, History of Mid-Atlantic Region of Alpha Kappa Alpha Sorority, 1981; editor, Hampton University: Our Home by the Sea, 1992; editor, Hampton's Pictorial History published in 1962; cited as Outstanding Soror (AKA), 1978; Delta Sigma Theta Sorority, Community Woman of the Year, 1994; Peninsula Pan-Hellenic Council, Outstanding Contributions to the Community, 1994; Eula Edmonds Glover Volunteer Community Service Award, Alpha Kappa Alpha Sorority, Inc, 1994. **Home Addr:** 11 Mimos Crescent, Hampton, VA 23661.

PLEASANTS, CHARLES WRENN
Educational administrator. **Personal:** Born Feb 28, 1937, Newport News, VA; children: Charles W Jr, Michael L, Linda Y. **Educ:** Norfolk State Univ, BA 1961, MA 1973; The Coll of William and Mary, advanced study. **Career:** Carver HS, instr 1962-69; VA Sch for Deaf & Blind, dir student serv 1969-73; Norfolk State Univ, dir intensive recruitment 1978-81, alumni dir 1973-81, asst dir admissions 1981-84, assoc dir admissions 1984-. **Orgs:** Past dist treas Cncl for Advancement & Support of Educ 1981-83; mem Natl Educ Assn; mem Natl Assn of Coll Admiss Couns; mem VA Assn of Coll Admiss Officers; pres Natl Alumni Assn Norfolk State Univ 1973; mem Omega Psi Phi Frat; mem Norfolk State Athletic Found. **Honors/Awds:** Case III Southeastern Dist Chair Citation Southeastern Dist 1981; Outstanding Leadership and Serv Award Norfolk State Univ Natl Alumni Assn 1981; Cert of Merit Inter-Collegiate Press 1983.

PLEDGER, VERLINE S.
Educator. **Personal:** Born May 11, 1927, Macon, GA; married Charles L Pledger; children: Charles III, Bever Lyne. **Educ:** Morris Brown Coll, BS with Hon 1957. **Career:** Atlanta Bd Educ, teacher execp children (EMR) 1957-; Atlanta Girls Club, teacher 1946-48; Pilgrim Health & Life Ins Co, bookkeeper 1950-51. **Orgs:** Mem exec bd NAACP chmn voter reg Atlanta Br; mem AAE; NEA; CEC; past pres Atlanta Chap Las Amigas 1969-71; mem Wheat St Bapt Ch; secy Deacon's Wives' Cir; treas Adamsville Garden Club 1972-74; parliamentarian Atlanta Chap The Cont Socs Inc 1972-; vice pres Loyal Friends Birthday Club 1972-; mem AltantaChldrns Theatre Guild 1969-; mem 5 yr breast cancer screening proj. **Honors/Awds:** Award of merit Gov of GA for Civic Work 1971; most dist exhib award Conclave Las Amigas 1970; merit outst work CF Harper 1965; yrly cert Voter Reg Fulton Co 1968-; asst chmn Procedure Book CF Harper 5 yrs, Blue Ribbon ea yr; chmn cultural prgm chmn Girl Scout Prgm. **Business Addr:** 200 Casanova SE, Atlanta, GA 30315.

PLESS, WILLIE
Professional football player. **Personal:** Born Feb 21, 1964. **Educ:** Kansas. **Career:** Edmonton Eskimos, linebacker, currently. **Honors/Awds:** Canadian Football League, Outstanding Defensive Player, 1995. **Business Addr:** Professional Football Player, Edmonton Eskimos, 9021 111th Ave, Edmonton, AB, Canada T5C 05B, (403)448-3757.

PLINTON, JAMES O., JR.
Business executive. **Personal:** Born Jul 22, 1914, Westfield, NJ; son of Mary Williams Plinton and James O Plinton, Sr; married Kathryn Hancock, May 14, 1952; children: James Norman, Kathryn Ann Breen. **Educ:** Lincoln Univ, PA, BS, 1935; Univ of Newark, Newark NJ, received commercial pilots certificate and flight instructors rating, 1942. **Career:** Haitian-American Drycleaners and Laundry Inc, president, 1947-57; Quisqueya Airways Ltd, Port-au-Prince, Haiti, co-owner and chief pilot, 1947-49; Trans World Airlines (TWA), New York NY, exec asst to sr dir of mktg, 1957-71; Eastern Airlines Inc, Miami FL, corp vice pres, 1971-79; Metropolitan Fellowship of Churches, Miami, exec dir, 1980-; Tacolcy Economic Development Corp, Miami, chmn of bd, 1983-. **Orgs:** Charter member, Negro Airmen Intl, 1958-; dir, Caribbean Tourism Assn, 1972-79; pres, vice chmn of bd, comm chmn, YMCA of the United States, 1973-81; mem of bd dir, South Florida Jail Ministry, 1975-; trustee, Embry-Riddle Aeronautical Univ, 1976-; sec to bd of dir, P L Dodge Found, 1977-; trustee, South Florida Center for Theological Studies, 1985-; mem of advisory comm, Urban Coalition of Miami, 1985-; mem of bd of dir, Miami Museum of Science and Space Transit, 1988-. **Honors/Awds:** First African-Amer to complete the Army Air Corps' Central Instructors School, 1944; first African-Amer to co-organize and operate a passenger/cargo airline outside the USA, Quisqueya Ltd, Port-au-Prince, Haiti, 1948; first African-Amer corp exec for major US airline, 1957; received doctor of laws degree, Fisk Univ; doctorate in aeronautical science, Embry Riddle Aeronautical Univ; National Order of Honour and National Order of Labor from three different presidents of Haiti; distinguished serv award, Lincoln Univ; Outstanding Man of the Year Award in intl mktg, Long Island Univ; award for outstanding achievement in aviation, Negro Airmen Intl; President Kenneth David Kaunda Award for Humanism; CHIEF Award, Assn of Pres of Ind Coll and Univ of Florida,1980; first of 15 Americans and firAfrican-Amer to be elected to YMCA of the USA Natl Treasure body (Hall of Fame) out of 11 million members; numerous other honors. **Military Serv:** US Army Air Corps, flight officer, 1944-46; Army Air Corps flight instructor at Central Instructors School, Tuskegee Institute, Tuskegee AL, 1944. **Business Addr:** Chairman of the Board, Tacolcy Economic Development Corporation, 645 NW 62nd St, Miami, FL 33150.

PLUMMER, GLENN
Actor. **Career:** Actor, currently. **Special Achievements:** Films include: South Central, Menace II Society, Who's That Girl?, Showgirls, Strange Days, Speed, Up Close and Personal; TV include: ''ER''. **Business Addr:** Actor, c/o ''ER'', 1999 Ave of Stars, Ste 2850, Los Angeles, CA 90067, (310)553-5200.

PLUMMER, MATTHEW W., SR.
Attorney. **Personal:** Born Apr 14, 1920, Bexar Co, TX; son of Minnie and M William; married Christine J; children: 4. **Educ:** Tuskegee Institute, Trade Diploma 1939, BA 1947; TX So Univ, LLB 1951. **Career:** Atty, pvt prac; former district judge. **Orgs:** Pres Tuskegee Civic Club 1945-46; 2nd pres of TCV; chmn TX Del to Nat Black Polit Conv; pres Harris Counc of Orgns 1962; fdr past pres Bronze Eagles Flying Club; past pres Houston Lawyers Assn; District Judge 133rd Court of Harris County. **Honors/Awds:** Org 1st Flying Club Tuskegee forerunner of Aviation Airbase & Schs; org Tuskegee Br NAACP 1947; 1st class at TSU Law Sch; 1st Invstgtr Harris Co Dist Attys Ofc; org TX Counc of Voters; outst stdnt interested in Govt Affairs 1947. **Military Serv:** US Army, flight instr, 1941-45; USAAF Res, WW II. **Business Addr:** Attorney at Law, 1010 Lamar St, Ste 1510, Houston, TX 77002.

PLUMMER, MICHAEL JUSTIN
Sociologist, teacher. **Personal:** Born Apr 15, 1947, Cambridge, MA; son of Kathleen Plummer and Justin Plummer. **Educ:** Trinity Coll, BA Religion 1970; Harvard Univ Grad Sch of Educ, MEd 1972; Brandeis Univ Florence Heller Sch, MMHS 1986; Boston College, MA, 1993, ABD, Sociology, 1994, PhD, Sociology, 1998. **Career:** Adjunct prof, sociology, UMass/Boston and Lesley College, Cambridge, MA, 1994-; esl instructor, Bunsai Gakuen Intercultural School, Lincoln, MA, 1994-95; teaching fellow, adjunct prof, Sociology, Boston College, Chestnut Hill, MA, 1990-; visiting lecturer, Sociology, Northeastern University, Boston, MA, 1989-90; Integrated Systems Information Serv Co, founder/principal 1986-. **Orgs:** Chmn Proposal Review Comm (1983) and bd mem Cambridge/Somerville MA Council for Children 1983-84; mem Cambridge MA, Human Svcs Commission, 1995-96. **Honors/Awds:** Lifetime certification from Commonwealth of MA as Teacher of Secondary Sch Social Studies; Certificate of Accomplishment MA Governor Dukakis 1986; Winner, Boston College, Men's Intermediate Tennis Intraminrals, 1996. **Home Addr:** 156 Fayerweather St, Cambridge, MA 02138, (617)661-7897. **Business Addr:** 410 B McGivan Hall, Boston College, Chestnut Hill, MA 02167-3407.

PLUMMER, MILTON
Bank executive. **Career:** City National Bank of New Jersey, Newark NJ, chief executive. **Business Addr:** City National Bank of New Jersey, 900 Brood, Newark, NJ 07102.

PLUMMER, ORA B.
Educator. **Personal:** Born May 25, 1940, Mexia, TX; daughter of Macie I Echols; children: Kimberly, Kevin, Cheryl. **Educ:** Univ NM Coll Nursing, BS, 1961; UCLA, MS, 1966; Faculty Practitioner Nursing Course, 1973; Univ of CO, postgraduate; variety of continuing educ courses, 1973-92. **Career:** Staff Nurse, 1961-62, 1962-64, 1967-68; Staff Nurse & Relief Super, 1962-64; USPHS, nurse traineeship 1964-66; NM Coll Nursing Albuquerque, instructor 1968-69; Univ of CO School of Nursing, sr instructor 1971-74, asst prof 1974-76; West Interstate Comm for Higher Educ, staff assoc III 1976-78; Garden Manor, dir of nursing service 1978-79; CO Dept of Health, nursing consultant 1979-87, long term care process trainer 1986-, training coordinator, 1987-. **Orgs:** Amer & CO Nurses' Assn; Alpha Tau Delta; Phi Delta Kappa; CO Black Nurses Council, master ceremonies recruitment day; Black Educ Day Boulder 1971; Navy Orientation trip for educators & admins 1971; Air Force Orientation Trip 1971; faculty devel comm School of Nursing 1974-; Interdisciplinary AMSA Proj 1975-76; rsch The Effects of Nursing Reassurance on Patients Vocal Stress Levels 1976; coordinator Comm for Bacc Program postgraduate drug therapy for elderly; Minority Affairs Comm 1971-74; WICHE Project Faculty Devel to Meet Minority Group Needs 1971-73; coordinator & implementation pre-nursing program Univ of CO School of Nursing 1972; Natl Black Nurses Assn 1976-; advisory bd of Sickle Cell Anemia 1976-; advisory committee, Metropolitan State College, 1989-94, bd of trustees, Colorado Academy, 1990-96; State Institutional Child Abuse & Neglect, 1983-92; American Society for Training and Development, 1990-; National Assn for Female Executives, 1990-. **Honors/Awds:** Scholarships, NM Med Soc Women's Aux, 1960; Keynote Speaker ID Nurses Assn Conv ''Patient Educ-The Politics & The Nurse,'' 1979; Amer Business Women's Assn, Scholarship, 1958-60; Confederated Art Club, Scholarship, 1958-59; Certificate of Appreciation for 15 years of dedicated service to the citizens of Colorado, Colo, Dept of Public Health and Environment, 1994. **Special Achievements:** Author: Long Term Care, Implications of Medical Practice, 1988; co-author: ''A Demonstration Model for Patient Education, A Final Report,'' WICHE, 1978; ''Improvement of Rehabilitative Nursing Service to the Elderly in Long Term Care Facilities in Colorado, A Final Report,'' 1989; Co-author, ''Nursing Reassurance, Patient Denial and Vocal Distress, Nursing Research,'' 1976. **Business Addr:** Trainer, Surveyor, Complaint Investigator, Colorado Department of Health, 4300 Cherry Creek Dr S, Aurora, CO 80013.

PLUMMER-TALLEY, OLGA ANN
Educational administrator. **Personal:** Born Dec 2, 1934, Kansas City, KS; daughter of Bernadette Brummell and Ulysses Grant Plummer Jr; married Benjamin F Talley Jr, Nov 9, 1957; children: Karla, Stephanie, Benita Lynn Gilliard, Deanna, Benjamin F III (deceased). **Educ:** Univ of Portland, BA Elementary Educ 1970; Portland State Univ, MS 1973, Standard Admin Certificate 1985; US Dept of Health & Human Serv Natl Mgmt Training School, attended 1989. **Career:** Portland Public Schools, teacher 1970-72; St Vincent de Paul Child Development Center, child devel coordinator 1973-78; Portland State Univ/Div Continuing Educ, child development specialist 1978-79; Portland Public Schools, supervisor of early childhood educ 1979-90, elementary principal, 1990-; principal, Head Start/Chap I Pre K Prog. **Orgs:** Mem Delta Sigma Theta Sorority 1954-; mem Natl State & Local Assn for the Educ of Young Children 1973-; mem Portland Chapter of Links Inc 1974-; bd mem Parent Child Serv Inc 1982-; mem Natl & Local Assns of Black School Educ 1982-; mem Natl Black Child Development Inst 1985-; chp Natl Head Start Assn Training Conf 1986; mem early childhood advisory comm Oregon Dept of Educ 1987; mem Natl Assn of Female Execs 1987-; mem Urban League of Portland, NAACP; Assn for Area & Central Admin Personnel 1985-; Assn for Supervision & Curriculum Devel 1988-; Natl & Local Alliance of Black School Educator 1982-; Natl & State Head Start Assn 1979-; Intl Montessori Soc 1986-; member, Confederation of Oregon School Administrators, 1990-; member, National, State and LocalAssn of Elementary School Principa 1990-; Portland, Oregon, Future Focus Educ Task Force. **Honors/Awds:** Fellowship Grant Portland State Univ Dept of Special Educ 1972; Certificate Portland Public Schools Career & Vocational Advisory Council 1984; Certificate District Chapter I Parent Advisory Council 1985; Kindergarten Guide Oregon Dept of Educ Participant and Review 1988; Oregon Mathematics Guild, k-12 Reviewer & Writer 1978; Headstart Staff Policy & Personnel Handbook 1980-. **Home Addr:** 6933 NE 15th Ave., Portland, OR 97211-4733.

PLUMPP, STERLING DOMINIC
Educator. **Personal:** Born Jan 30, 1940, Clinton, MS; son of Mary Emmanuel and Cyrus H Plumpp; divorced; children: Harriet Nzinga. **Educ:** St Benedict's College, Atchison, KS, 1960-62; Roosevelt University, Chicago, IL, BA, 1966-68, further study, 1969-71. **Career:** US Postal Service, Chicago, IL, distribution clerk, 1962-69; North Park College, Chicago, counselor, 1969-71; Univ of Illinois at Chicago, African-American Studies Department, associate professor, 1971-. **Orgs:** Black American Literature Forum, 1980-89. **Honors/Awds:** Illinois Arts Council Literary Awards, 1975, 1980, 1986; Carl Sandburg Literary Award for Poetry, 1983. **Military Serv:** US Army, spec 4, 1964-65.

PLUNKETT, RAPHAEL HILDAN
Customer support manager. **Personal:** Born Feb 11, 1966, Chicago, IL; daughter of Hettie Perry Mahan and Ralph B Marrs, Sr; children: Tabitha Talai Marrs. **Educ:** De Paul Coll, liberal arts. **Career:** Helene Curtis, Chicago, IL, customer support specialist, 1987-. **Orgs:** Editor, Helene Curtis Newsletter, 1989-92; United Way/Crusade of Mercy Volunteer, 1987-93. **Honors/Awds:** Crusade of Mercy Rep, 1992-93.

POCKNETT, LAWRENCE WENDELL
Insurance executive (retired). **Personal:** Born Sep 23, 1934, Boston, MA; married Mary Seiter, May 6, 1977; children: Law-

rence Jr, Lorraine. **Educ:** Boston University School of Liberal Arts, BA, 1962. **Career:** Liberty Mutual, chief underwriter, 1971-73; Aetna Insurance, underwriting manager, 1973-76; Hartford Insurance Group, division vice pres. **Honors/Awds:** ITT, Black Achiever's Award, 1979. **Military Serv:** US Army, spc4, 1955-58.

POE, ALFRED

Food company executive. **Personal:** marrIed Carol; children: two. **Educ:** Polytechnic Inst of Brooklyn, BS, 1971; Harvard University, MBA, 1975. **Career:** General Foods, numerous marketing positions; M&M/Mars, Kal Kan Foods, dir of dog-care, 1982, vice pres of brands, 1983-86, purchasing dir, marketing dir, Pedigree Petfoods, United Kingdom, 1986-88, vice pres of brands, 1988-91; Campbell Soup Co, vice pres/general mgr, condiments & sauces, 1991-93, pres, Meal Enhancement Group, 1993-. **Business Addr:** Pres, Meal Enhancement Group, Campbell Soup Co, Campbell Place, Camden, NJ 08103-1799, (609)342-6378.

POE, BOOKER

Physician. **Personal:** Born Jul 9, 1936, Eustis, FL; son of Janie Jackson Poe (deceased) and Rev William Poe (deceased); married Gloria Reeves Poe, Aug 15, 1959; children: Janita L, Brian D. **Educ:** Tennessee State University, BS, (with honors) 1957; McHarry Medl Coll, MD, 1963. **Career:** Private practice, pediatrician, currently. **Orgs:** Chrmn medl legs GA State Medl Assoc 1976; breakfast prog chmn Atlanta Medl Assoc 1970-76; chmn awds GA State Medl Assoc 1977; comm advisor Min-Dent/Physns GA 1980; pblc rels Atlanta Medl Assoc 1980-; chmn bd dir GA Medical Assoc 1973-; bd dir prec Morehouse Sch Med 1980-; ex brd Atlanta Branch NAACP 1982-; assoc clin prof of Peds GA Univ 1974-; leglt GA Am Acad Peds 1982-; mem of Chmn's Council Scholarship Fund, Morehouse School of Medicine l987-; bd of dir/treasurer, Health lst (HMO) l979-89. **Honors/Awds:** Young Physician of the Year Atlanta Med Assn 1974; Physician of the Year Atlanta Med Assn 1980; Doctor of the Year GA House Rep 1980; Pres Awd GA Medl Assoc 1982; publ, "EPSDT and the Black Medical Community in Georgia" Natl Med Assoc Jrnl 1979, "Why Attend a Legislative Breakfast?" The Microscope Newsletter 1980; President's Awd GA State Med Assoc 1982, 1986; 25 years of Service Award, Atlanta Medical Assn 1989; President's Award, 25 years of service McHarry Medical Coll 1989; Distinguished Service Medallion, Georgia State Medical Association, 1990; Nash Carter Honoree, Atlanta Medical Association, 1992. **Military Serv:** USAF capt 1965-69. **Home Addr:** 3518 Lynfield Dr SW, Atlanta, GA 30311. **Business Addr:** Physician, 2600 Martin Luther King Jr Dr, Suite 202, Atlanta, GA 30311.

POELLNITZ, FRED DOUGLAS

Educational administrator. **Personal:** Born Aug 3, 1944, Philadelphia, PA; married Stephanie Snead MD; children: Andrew, Michelle. **Educ:** Univ of Pittsburgh, BSEE 1966; NY Univ, MSEE 1970; Harvard Univ, MBA 1972. **Career:** Bendix Corp, project engr 1967-70; Touche Ross & Co, consult 1972-76; Sorbus Inc, dir of acctg 1976-80; Smith Kline Beckman, asstmgr 1980-81; Meharry Medical Coll, vp. **Orgs:** Mem Alpha Phi Alpha Frat 1963-; bd of dir Electronic Typesetting Corp 1972-76; mem Natl Assoc of Accountants 1974-; mem Financial Exec Inst 1983-; bd of advisors TN State Univ Business School 1983-. **Honors/Awds:** Cogme Fellow Harvard Univ 1970-72. **Business Addr:** Vice Pres for Finance & Business, Meharry Medical College, 1005 D B Todd Blvd, Nashville, TN 37208.

POGUE, BRENT DARYL

Nuclear engineering executive. **Personal:** Born Sep 3, 1954, Sumter, SC; son of Arnetta McCain Ellison and Clarence W Pogue. **Educ:** Cornell Univ, Ithaca, NY, BS, 1976, Master of Engineering, 1977. **Career:** Polaroid Corp, Cambridge, MA, technical supervisor, 1977-80; Bechtel Power Corp, San Francisco, CA, sr engr, 1980-85; Impell Corp, Walnut Creek, CA, lead sr engr, 1985-88; Pacific Gas & Electric, San Francisco, CA, nuclear generation engr, 1988-95, individual consultant, currently. **Orgs:** Cornell Univ Society of Engineers, 1980-; Amer Society of Mechanical Engineers, 1980-; Amer Assn of Blacks in Energy, 1989-; Amer Nuclear Society, 1984; Urban Service Project of San Francisco, 1995; San Francisco Proj Inform, 1996-; Commonwealth Club of California, 1997-. **Honors/Awds:** Representative, CA Commission of Environmental & Economic Balance, 1980-81; College Recruiter, Polaroid Corp, 1977-79; various volunteer awards. **Home Addr:** 1958 Greenwich St, San Francisco, CA 94123, (415)775-2309.

POGUE, D. ERIC

Personnel executive. **Personal:** Born Feb 12, 1949, Southampton, NY; son of Virginia Mines Pogue and Isaiah P Pogue (deceased); married J Marie, Aug 21, 1982; children: Eric Spencer. **Educ:** Heidelberg Coll, BS Psych 1970; Bowling Green State Univ, MA Personnel 1971. **Career:** Case Western Reserve Univ, asst dir acad support, 1971-72; Cleveland State Univ, staff devel trainer, 1972-76; Diamond Shamrock Corp, mgr human resources, 1976-82; Cuyahoga Comm Coll, adj prof 1978-79; Reichhold Chem Inc, White Plains NY, vice pres human resources, 1982-87, senior vice president, 1987-88; Philip Morris Co Inc, New York NY, vice pres employee relations, 1988-. **Orgs:** Mem Soc of Human Resource Management, 1980-, Westchester/Ct Personnel Round Table 1983-88; coord-annual dr United Way of Greater Cleveland 1982; board of directors, National Alliance to End Homelessness; board of advisors, Cornell University School of Industrial and Labor Relations, 1990-; member, Human Resources Council, American Management Assn, 1987-.

POGUE, FRANK G., JR.

Educator, educational administrator. **Personal:** Born Nov 3, 1939, Mobile, AL; son of Annie B Pogue; married Dorothy Dexter; children: Constance L. **Educ:** Bishop Jr Coll, 1958-59; Alabama State Univ, BA, sociology, 1961; Atlanta Univ, MA, sociology, 1966; Univ of Pittsburgh, Ph D, sociology, 1973. **Career:** Philander Smith College, Little Rock, AR, assistant professor, 1962-66; Chatham College, Pittsburgh, PA, instructor, 1969-71; Meharry Medical College, Nashville, TN, assistant professor, 1971-73; State University of New York at Albany, Albany, NY, associate professor, 1973-, chair, department of African and Afro-American Studies, 1973-83, associate vice president for research and educational development, 1982-83, vice president for student affairs, 1983-86, vice chancellor for student affairs and special programs, 1986-. **Orgs:** Member, National Assn of Student Personnel Administrators; member, National Assn for the Study of Afro-American Life and History; member, College Student Personnel Assn of New York State; member, Chief Student Affairs Administrators for the State University of New York; member, Sigma Pi Phi Fraternity; member, National Council for Black Studies; member, Delta Sigma Pi Professional Business Fraternity. **Honors/Awds:** Alpha Kappa Mu Hon Soc Most Outst Yng Men of Am 1968-69. **Business Addr:** Vice Pres for Student Affairs, State University of New York, at Albany, 1400 Washington Ave, Albany, NY 12222.

POGUE, RICHARD JAMES

Civil service. **Personal:** Born May 25, 1943, Cortelyou, AL; married Birdie Raine; children: Tiffany Denise, Karen Lanise. **Educ:** Alabama State Univ, BS (high honors), 1971; Pepperdine Univ, 1977; Intl Seminary. **Career:** Robins Air Force Base, personnel mgmt specialist, 1971-73; Air Force Reserves, personnel mgmt specialist, 1973-75; Keesler Air Force Base, chief employment & staffing, 1975-76; Randolph Air Force Base, personnel mgmt specialist, 1976-79; Headquarters USAF Pentagon Washington DC, deputy EEO, 1979-80; Robins AFB, GA, equal oppor/affirmative action officer, 1980-86, chief employee devt & training section, 1986-91, chief of Employment and Staffing, Classifications, 1992-; Friendship Memorial Baptist Church, pastor, currently. **Orgs:** Mem NAACP 1980-; pres K&R Shoes Inc 1983-85; pres Intl Personnel Mgmt Assoc 1984-85; mem Better Mgmt Assoc 1985-; bd of career advisors Atlanta Univ 1986; historian Alpha Phi Alpha Frat Inc 1986-87; bd dirs Middle Georgia Educ Talent Search 1986-; bd dirs Air Force Assoc 1986-; Blacks in Govt, 1985-; bd of dirs, Combined Federal Campaign. **Honors/Awds:** Outstanding Young Men of Amer Awd 1971; Key to the City of New Orleans 1975; Affirmative Action of the Year Robins AFB 1981. **Military Serv:** USN third class petty officer 1963-67; Natl Defense. **Home Addr:** 139 Stewart Dr, Warner Robins, GA 31093. **Business Addr:** Chief, Classification & Wage Administration, Robins Air Force Base GA, STGP/DPCC, Civilian Personnel, Warner Robins, GA 31098.

POINDEXTER, CHARLES L. L.

Cleric. **Personal:** Born Apr 11, 1932, Richmond, VA; son of Pearl Maria Robinson and Walter E Poindexter; married Judith L Owens, Feb 24, 1962; children: Maria, Byroh, Evangeline. **Educ:** West Virginia State College, BA, 1954; Philadelphia Divinity School, MDiv, 1958. **Career:** St Ausgustine's Church, vicar, 1958-65; St Monica's Church, rector, 1963-65; St Barnabas Church, rector, 1965-68; St Luke's Church, rector, 1968-. **Orgs:** Phi Beta Sigma, national jr vice pres, 1953-54; The Brahaman Society, 1955-; Union of Black Episcopalians, national vice pres, 1986-92, Aids Task Force, president, 1987-92; All Saints Hospital, board, 1975-81; Springside School, board, 1974-80; Sigma Pi Phi Boule, 1980-; Home for the Homeless Fund, president, 1985-. **Honors/Awds:** St Augustine's College, Doctor of Humane Letters, 1988; College of Four Chaplins, Achievement, 1988; St Barnaba's Founders, Achievement Award, 1989; Union of Black Episcopalians, Achievement Award, 1991. **Special Achievements:** St Barnabas Episcopal School, headmaster, 1969-75, founder; Wissahickon Deanery, dean, 1975-81; Pamphlet, Aids in the Black Church, 1990; Book, History of St Luke's Church, 1991. **Business Addr:** Episcopal Priest, St Luke's Episcopal Church, Germantown, 5421 Germantown Ave, Philadelphia, PA 19144.

POINDEXTER, GAMMIEL GRAY

Attorney. **Personal:** Born Sep 22, 1944, Baton Rouge, LA; daughter of Lee Ethel Gray and James Gray; married Geral G; children: John L R, Christopher R. **Educ:** Univ of IN, AB Government 1965; LA State Univ, JD 1969. **Career:** Office of Solicitor US Dept of Labor, staff attorney 1968-70; Richmond Legal Aid Soc, dept dir 1971-73; Poindexter & Poindexter, partner 1973-; Surry Co VA, commonwealth's atty 1976-. **Orgs:** Past pres Old Dominion Bar Assn 1980-82; bd of visitors, Old Dominion University, 1982-; chmn, Surry Co Democratic Party, 1983-; bd of dirs, VA Assn of Black Elected Officers; Virginia State Bar Council; Virginia State Community College System, board member. **Business Addr:** Commonwealth Attorney, Surry Co, PO Box 358, Surry, VA 23883.

POINDEXTER, MALCOLM P.

Newscaster, program host producer. **Personal:** Born Apr 3, 1925, Philadelphia, PA; son of Alda F Palmer Poindexter and Malcolm Poindexter Sr; children: David, Lynne E Poindexter, Malcolm III. **Educ:** Several private and military schools, 1943-47; Temple Univ, 1953. **Career:** The Philadelphia Tribune, reporter/columnist/business mgr/controller 1949-60; The Evening Bulletin, reporter 1960-65; KYW-TV, editorial spokesman/reporter/producer/program host 1965-89, host, producer, Eyewitness Newsmakers, 1990-. **Orgs:** Honorary bd Norris Square Neighborhood Project 1990-; board member, Mann Music Center. **Honors/Awds:** Received more than 300 awards for professional and civic achievement. **Military Serv:** US Army, t-sgt, 4 years. **Business Addr:** Host/Producer/Journalist, KYW-TV/News 3, PO Box KYW3, Philadelphia, PA 19105.

POINDEXTER, ROBERT L.

Educator. **Personal:** Born Mar 12, 1912, Philadelphia, PA; married Josephine. **Educ:** Temple U, BSE 1942, ME 1944, PdM 1972. **Career:** Educator, Elem Prin; Jr HS Prin; Dist Supr; Dep Supr; Exec Dep Supr. **Orgs:** Vp Philadelphia Tchrs Credit Union; mem Philadelphia Bicentennial Comm; YMCA; Exec Bd; BSA; March of Dimes; McKee Schlrshp Com; bd trustees Messiah Coll.

POINDEXTER, ZEB F.

Dentist. **Personal:** Born Apr 5, 1929, Fort Worth, TX; son of Leonra Camilla Wilburn (deceased) and Zeb F Poindexter, Sr (deceased); married Ruby Revis, Oct 30, 1953; children: Merlene, Patricia, Zeb III. **Educ:** Wiley Coll, BS 1945; TX So U, MS 1952; Univ of TX Dental Br, DS 1956. **Career:** Gulf St Dental Assn, pres 1966-67; Nat Dental Assn, local conv chmn 1968; Univ of TX, asso prof of Comm dentistry 1973, dentist, Dental Br. **Orgs:** Mem NAACP; bd mem Negro Coll; treas Charles A George Dental Soc; bd mem Baker-Jones Invest Co; Houston Dist Dental Soc; Nat Dental Assn; mem Alpha Phi Alpha Frat 1947; YMCA Century Club 12 yrs; Eldorado Soc Club; Gulf St Dental Assn; Am Dental Assn; trustee NDA 1973; del NDA 1971 & 73; del TX Dental Assn 1968; member, Minority Faculty Assn, 1987-; chairperson, Multicultured Faculty Committee, 1986-88. **Honors/Awds:** YMCA Century Man 10 yrs 1972; elected to OK Univ Hon Soc Zeb F Poindexter Chap Stdnt Nat Dental Assn 1980; 1st African-American to finish Univ of Texas as Dentist 1956; Outstanding Alumnus, Univ of Texas Dental School, 1990; Texas Academy of General Dentistry, Outstanding Dentist of the Year, 1991; International College of Dentists, Fellow, 1992. **Military Serv:** USAF capt. **Business Addr:** Dentist, 7703 Cullen Blvd, Houston, TX 77051.

POINSETT, ALEXANDER C.

Journalist. **Personal:** Born Jan 27, 1926, Chicago, IL; son of Adele Leola Prindle Poinsett and Alexander A Poinsett (deceased); married Norma Ruth Miller, Aug 25, 1951; children: Pierrette M, Alexis Pierre. **Educ:** Univ IL, BS (Journlism) 1952, MA (Phlsphy) 1953; Univ Chicago, completed all work execpt Thesis for MA in Lbry Sci 1956. **Career:** Johnson Publ Co, contributing editor 1959-, sr staff edt 1956-82; Grumman Corp, mgr edtl serv 1982-83; Johnson Prod Co, mgr corp commu 1983-85; The Ford Found, cons. **Orgs:** Const US Off Ed; spch wrtr Mayor Richard G Hatcher (Gary IN) 1969-75; guest lectr More Then 50 US Coll/U 1969-81; past pres, Chicago Prairie Tennis Club. **Honors/Awds:** Atr Blk Power Gary Style 1970; PUSH awd Optn PUSH 1977; outstdng person awd Univ IL Blk Alumni Assn 1980; CEBA awd CEBA 1982; J C Penney Award, Univ of Missouri 1967; Author of "Black Power Gary Style", 1970. **Military Serv:** US Navy, yeoman 3rd class 1944-1947.

POINTER, RICHARD H.

Scientist/educator. **Personal:** Born Jun 4, 1944, Covington, GA; son of Sarah Eunice Weaver Pointer and H B Pointer; married Rosie Lee Davis, Apr 30, 1966; children: Richard Hamilton Jr., Rawlinson Lee, Robert Lewis. **Educ:** Morehouse Atlanta Ga, BS 1968; Brown U, ScM 1973; Brown Univ Providence RI, PhD 1975. **Career:** Research assoc Vanderbilt Univ 1975-77; research biochemist Massachusetts General Hosp 1977-78; Harvard Univ Instructor 1977-80; assistant professor Howard Univ 1980-87; assoc professor Howard Univ 1987-, visiting scientist, membrane regulat sect, LCDB, NIDDK, NIH, 1992. **Orgs:** Mem Sigma Xi 1973; Am Assn Advancement Sci 1972-; rec sec exec bd PACE 1973-74; research papers pub biochem & pharmacol jrnls; American Physiological Society 1975-; American Diabetes Assn 1979-; Adult Leader Boy Scouts of America 1979-; science fair judge Southern MD School Area 1988-; bd of dir PG County Chapter American Diabetes Assn 1988-89; vice pres PG County Chapter American Diabetes Assn 1989-90; president, PG Chapter ADA, 1990-92; American Society for Biochemistry and Molecular Biology, 1995-. **Honors/Awds:** Publications in Biochemical Journals 1973-; research grants from NSF and NIH 1976-; research fellow Howard Hughes Medical Institute 1978-80; Commissioners Award Boy Scouts of America 1988; American Diabetes Association,

Meritorious Service Award, 1992; Johnetta Davis Mentorship Award, Graduate School of Arts and Sciences, 1996. **Home Addr:** 7501 Epping Ave, Fort Washington, MD 20744. **Business Addr:** Professor of Biochemistry and Molecular Biology, Howard University College of Medicine, 520 W St, NW, Adams Bldg, Washington, DC 20059.

POITIER, SIDNEY
Actor, director, producer, government official. **Personal:** Born Feb 20, 1927, Miami, FL; son of Evelyn Outten Poitier and Reginald Poitier; married Joanna Shimkus, 1969; children: Beverly, Pamela, Sherri, Gina, Anika, Sydney. **Career:** Acted & starred in over 38 motion pictures; made film debut in ''No Way Out'' 1950; others include ''Cry the Beloved Country'' 1952, ''Go Man Go'' 1954; ''Blackboard Jungle'' 1956; ''Edge of the City'' 1957; ''Something of Value'' 1957; ''Porgy & Bess'' 1959; ''Lillies of the Field'' 1963; ''In the Heat of the Night'' 1967; ''Guess Who's Coming to Dinner'' 1968; ''They Call Me Mister Tibbs'' 1971; ''The Wilby Conspiracy'' 1975; ''Little Nikita'' 1987; ''In the Hall of the Mountain King'' 1987; ''Hard Knox'' 1987; ''Deadly Pursuits'' 1988; ''The Jackal,'' 1998; directed and starred in ''Buck & the Preacher'', ''A Warm December'', ''Uptown Saturday Night'', ''Let's Do it Again'', ''A Piece of the Action'' 1977; starred in Broadway production of ''Raisin in the Sun'' 1959; directed Richard Pryor & Gene Wilder in ''Stir Crazy'' 1980; directed Gene Wilder & Gilda Radner in ''Hanky Panky'' 1982, Sneakers, 1992; directed youth musical ''Fast Forward'' 1985; US Ambassador to the Bahamas. **Orgs:** Walt Disney Co, bd of dirs, 1994-. **Honors/Awds:** First black actor nominated for Academy Award for ''The Defiant Ones''; first Black actor to record footprints in concrete of Grauman's Chinese Theater 1967; first black actor to win an Oscar ''Lilies of the Field'' 1963; autobiography published ''This Life'' by Alfred Knopf Pubs 1980. **Military Serv:** US Army, WWII. **Business Addr:** Ambassador to Japan, Bahamas Foreign Ministry, East Hill St, PO Box N-3746, Nassau, Bahamas.

POLITE, CARLENE HATCHER
Dancer. **Personal:** Born Aug 28, 1932, Detroit, MI. **Educ:** Sarah Lawrence Coll NY, attended; Martha Graham School of Contemporary Dance, attended. **Career:** Concert Dance Theatre of NYC, dancer 1955-59; Vanguard Playhouse, dancer 1960-62; The King & I, The Boy Friend, Dark of the Moon, dancer 1963; Wayne State Univ, visiting instructor; SUNY Buffalo, assoc prof, English. **Orgs:** Guest instr Detroit YWCA 1960-62; org No Negro Leadership Conf; mem Detroit Council for Human Rights. **Honors/Awds:** Author The Flagellants, Sister X & The Victims of Foul Play 1975. **Business Addr:** Farrar, Straus & Giroux, Publicity Department, 19 Union Square West, New York, NY 10003.

POLITE, CRAIG K.
Educator, psychologist. **Personal:** Born Aug 29, 1947, New York, NY; married Cheryl Yvonne Bradford; children: Kimberly L, Craig K II, Adam. **Educ:** Univ of Toledo, BA 1969; Michigan State Univ, MA 1971, PhD 1972; NY Univ, Certificate, psychoanalysis 1983. **Career:** Michigan State Univ, research asst center urban affairs 1970-72; Economic Opportunity Planning Assn of Greater Toledo, employee 1968-69; industrial & clinical psychologist; State Univ of NY at Stony Brook, asst prof 1972-76; Private Practice, clinical psychologist 1976-; Midtown Psychological Serv Inc, president, currently. **Orgs:** Teaching fellow Michigan State Univ 1971-72; consultant School Dental Med SUNY Stonybrook 1974-; Metro Comm Mental Health Center NY 1974-; New York City Head Start 1973; mem Amer Psychology Assn; Assn of Black Psychologists; Omega Psi Phi. **Honors/Awds:** Dean's List Univ Toledo 1968. **Special Achievements:** Children of the Dream: The Psychology of Black Success, coauthor with Audrey Edwards, 1992. **Military Serv:** AUS capt 1969-77. **Business Addr:** President, Midtown Psychological Service Inc, 340 East 52nd St, Suite 4C, New York, NY 10022.

POLITE, MARIE ANN
Educator, educational administrator. **Personal:** Born Jan 26, 1954, Savannah, GA; daughter of Leola Denegall Levett and Lucius Levett, Sr; married Alan Polite, Sep 1, 1972; children: Sharmona, Nakisha. **Educ:** Armstrong State Coll, BS (cum laude) 1976; GA Southern Coll, MEd 1980, MPA 1987; Georgia Southern Coll Statesboro GA EdS 1989; University of Georgia, Athens, GA, EdD, 1991. **Career:** Savannah-Chatham Bd of Educ, learning disabilities specialist 1976-; MAP to Success, consultant, 1985; Georgia Employers Assn, consultant, 1986; Savannah-Chatham Bd of Educ, Bartlett Middle School, asst principal, 1988-90, Beach High School, asst principal, 1990-92, Savannah High School, pricipal, 1992-. **Orgs:** Bd of dirs Savannah Police Athletic League 1975-; mem Phi Delta Kappa, Chapter 1219 1982-; state vice pres GA Federation of Teachers 1983-87; Deputy Vote Registrar 1984-85; bd of dirs GA HEAT Prog 1984-85; pres MAP to Success Consulting Agency 1985-; dist vice dir 1986-87; mem Zonta Club of Savannah 1986-; dist dir 1987-88 GA Fed of Business & Professional Women; bd of commissioners Savannah Housing Auth 1987-92; mem, Education's Leadership Georgia, 1988-92; Site Visitor, US Dept of Educ Secondary School's Recognition Program, 1989-93; Close Up Foundation Publishers Advisory Bd, 1991-92; Delta Sigma Theta Sorority; Rape Crisis Center, board of directors, 1993-95; Girl Scout Council of Savannah, board of directors, 1993-95. **Honors/Awds:** Outstanding Serv Savannah Police Dept 1982; Outstanding Serv Port City BPW Inc 1984, 1986; GA Regents Scholarship GA Southern Coll 1985-86; Georgia Regent's Scholarship, GA Southern Coll, 1989; Pi Alpha Alpha Honor Society, GA Southern Coll, 1989; participant/selected to Harvard Univ Graduate School's Principalship Seminar, 1989; Leadership Savannah, Savannah Chamber of Commerce, 1990-92; Kappa Delta Pi, Georgia Southern College, 1989; Leadership Program, Vanderbilt University, 1990; Site Visitor, Review Panelist, US Dept of Education's School of Recognition Program, 1990-91; Georgia Woman of Achievement, 1992; Education Boss of the Year, 1992. **Business Addr:** Principal, Savannah-Chatham Bd of Educ, Savannah High School, 500 Washington Ave, Savannah, GA 31405.

POLK, ANTHONY JOSEPH
Military officer. **Personal:** Born Mar 8, 1941, New Orleans, LA; son of Edolia Stephens (deceased) and Middleton Brooks Polk (deceased); married Maxine Polk (divorced 1986); children: Patricia, Michael, Stephen. **Educ:** McNeese State Univ, Lake Charles, LA, BS, 1966; Bowling Green State Univ, Bowling Green, OH, MS, 1974. **Career:** US Army, Washington, DC, colonel, 1967-91, dir, Armed Services blood program office, 1984-91. **Orgs:** Clinical laboratory manager, Fort Rucker, AL, 1967-68; joint blood program officer, CP Zama, Japan, 1968-72; laboratory manager/blood bank manage, Fort Hood, TX, 1974-78; commander blood bank, Landstuhl, Germany, 1978-81; joint blood program officer, Stuttgart, Germany, 1981-83; NATO blood program officer, Shapie BE, 1983-84; director DVD Armed Serices blood program, Pentagon, Washington, DC, 1984-91. **Honors/Awds:** Numerous military awards; Publication in military journal. **Military Serv:** US Army, Colonel, 1967-91; Defense Meritorous Medal, 1, Meritorious Sevice Medals, 3. **Home Addr:** 12047 Bridle Post Pl., Manassas, VA 22111-5515.

POLK, EUGENE STEVEN, SR.
Personnel administrator. **Personal:** Born Oct 24, 1939, Detroit, MI; son of Josephine and Wardell; married Barbara Jean Edwards; children: Camille, Kent, Eugene Jr, Chris. **Educ:** Shaw Coll at Detroit, BA 1971. **Career:** Ford Motor Co, employment coord 1966-69; Pontiac General Hosp, asst dir personnel 1970-74; Comprehensive Hlth Serv of Detroit, personnel dir 1975-79; Kelly Services Inc, mgr headquarters personnel 1980-87; Mazda Manufacturing, Professional, personnel administrator, beginning 1987-, employee relations, leader, currently. **Orgs:** Bd mem Metro Detroit Youth Foundation 1983-87; polemarch Detroit Alumni Chap Kappa Alpha Psi Frat 1984-88; bd mem Northside Family YMCA 1985-88; pres Industrial Relations Assoc of Detroit 1985-86; chmn bd of dir South Oakland Family YMCA 1986-87; bd mem Don Bosco Hall 1986-89; mem NAACP, Detroit Urban League. **Honors/Awds:** Minority Achiever Kelly Serv Inc Metro Detroit YMCA 1987.

POLK, GENE-ANN (GENE-ANN P. HORNE)
Physician, educator (retired). **Personal:** Born Oct 3, 1926, Roselle, NJ; daughter of Olive Bond Polk (deceased) and Charles C Polk (deceased); married Edwin C Horne, Aug 23, 1952; children: Carol Anne Horne Penn, Edwin Christian Horne. **Educ:** Oberlin Coll, BA 1948; Wmn's Medl Coll PA, MD 1952; Columbia U, MPH 1968. **Career:** Englewood NJ, prv prac 1959-68; Columbia University, Harlem Hospital Center, Pediatrics Clinic, chief, 1968-75, acting director pediatrics, 1975-77, Ambulator Care Services, director, 1977-1988; Dept of Pediatrics, attending physician, 1988-93, professor of clinical pediatrics, 1990-93; Columbia University, professor Emerita of clinical pediatrics, 1994. **Orgs:** Fellow American Bd of Medical Examiners 1952; Fellow Intl Coll of Ped, 1978; Fellow American Academy of Pediatrics 1958; Schl phys City Englewood, NJ 1960-67; Basileus Alpha Kappa Alpha Sorority Iota Epsilon Omega Chapter 1971-73; bd mem Grtr Harlem Nrsng Hme 1982-84; UNCF, 1970-; bd member Bergen County Girl Scouts; bd mem, Bergen Youth Orchestra; bd mem, Englewood Adult School; member, The Links, Inc. **Honors/Awds:** Proclamation: Dr Gene-Ann Polk Day, by President of the Borough of Manhattan, 1987; Proclamation by Mayor of the City of New York, Dr Gene Ann Polk Day, 1993; Child Advocacy Award, Barristers' Wives of New York, Inc, 1985; UNCF NJ Volunteer Recognition Award for Outstanding Service, 1990; Leadership in Medicine, Susan Smith McKinney Steward Medical Society (NMA), 1980; Outstanding Professional Achievement, Englewood-Teaneck B&P, 1980; Service Award, Harlem Hospital Center Auxiliary, 1993; Friends of Harlem Hospital Center, 1997. **Home Addr:** 374 Miller Ave, Englewood, NJ 07631, (201)567-4767.

POLK, GEORGE DOUGLAS
Business executive. **Personal:** Born Oct 6, 1919, St Louis, MO; married Mary Attyberry; children: Mary Olivia MD. **Educ:** Lincoln Univ Of MO, BA Mod Lang 1940; St Louis Univ Inst Tech, BSEE 1949;; St Louis Univ Grad Schl, MS in Eng Res 1960. **Career:** UniDynamics St Louis, sr elec engr 1953-, mgr prod supt. **Orgs:** Brd mem Ctl Inst Deaf St Louis MO 1984-; past polemarch St Louis Alumni Kappa Alpha Psi 1958-60; past kpr recds and exchequer mdl western prov KappaAlpha Psi 1955-67. **Military Serv:** USN radarman 2/c 1943-45. **Home Addr:** 5160 Norwood Ct, St Louis, MO 63115. **Business Addr:** Manager of Product Support, UniDynamics St Louis, 472 Paul Ave, 472 Paul Ave, Ferguson, MO 63135.

POLK, LORNA MARIE
Educational Administrator. **Personal:** Born Aug 3, 1948, St Louis, MO; daughter of Louise Polk and Ora Polk. **Educ:** Fisk Univ Nashville TN BA Psychology 1968; George Washington Univ DC MA Human Resource Development 1973; Catholic Univ of Amer EdD Educational Admin 1982. **Career:** US Dept of Educ, ed prog spec, Ed Personnel Development 1968-69; Career Opp Program 1969-73; Postsecondary Ed 1973-75; Migrant Education 1975-83; White House Initiative on Historically Black Coll & Univ, educational administrator 1983-95; Federal Trio Programs, 1994-97; US Dept of Education, Higher Education Prog, Chicago, IL, area rep, 1997-. **Orgs:** Mem American Assoc of Public Admin; mem American Soc of Prof and Exec Women; mem Phi Delta Kappa; mem Natl Alliance of Black Sch Educators; mem Blacks in Govt; mem Ed Joint Dissemination Review Panel, Educ, 1981-88; vp for Personnel, Flair Promotions Inc 1985-89; vp Southwest DC Neighborhood Assembly 1986-87; vice pres River Park Members Council 1987-88; executive bd, East Coast Chapter, Tuskegee Airmen, Inc; mem, Zonta Intl, Inc; bd of advisors, African-American Studies Program; executive bd, Organization of Black Airline Pilots; Natl Council of Negro Women; American Society for Training and Development. **Honors/Awds:** Department of Education, Quality Service Award, 1992, 1988, 1982. **Special Achievements:** Published ''The Effects of Migrant Educ Centers in the State of FL'' 1981; article presented in the Natl Society of Black Engineers Journal Annual Commemorative Issues 1986-87; honored as ''Black Female in Aviation Award,'' Atlanta, GA, 1996. **Home Addr:** 87 E Elm St, Chicago, IL 60611.

POLK, RICHARD A.
Association executive. **Personal:** Born Jun 4, 1936, Moss Point, MS; married Mary Dennis; children: Clay, Phyllis, Beverly, Richard. **Educ:** Alcorn St Univ Lorman MS, BS 1957; TN A&I Univ Nashville, MS 1965. **Career:** Fed Equal Empl Opport Comm, invstgtn supr; Newton & Carthage MS, tchr, ath coach 1957-66; STAR Inc, 1966-70; Mound Bayou Comm Hosp, dir 1970; Hosp & Hlth Ctr, dir 1972. **Orgs:** Mem NAACP; Jackson Urban Leag 1968-70; STAR Inc 1971-; Delta Ministry 1975-; S Legal Rights Corp 1975-; Leake Co Voters Leag 1975-; Delta Found Greenville MS 1975-; MS Cncl Hum Rels 1970; MS ACLU 1974; MS Cath Found 1975; pres Parish Cnsl St Anne Cath Ch Carthage MS; MS Cath Blue Ribbon Com to make Cath Ch more relevant to needs of Blacks & other minorities. **Honors/Awds:** Applicant for opertnl rights for a Jackson MS TV sta OEO Award 1969; MS Inst of Politics Fellow 1971. **Business Addr:** 203 W Capitol St, 203 Bldg, Jackson, MS 39201.

POLK, ROBERT L.
Clergyman, educational administrator. **Personal:** Born May 8, 1928, Chicago, IL; son of Lillie Bell Polk and Tillman Polk; divorced; children: George R. **Educ:** Doane Coll, BA 1952; Hartford Theol Sem, MDiv 1955; Doane Coll, Hon Dr of Div 1971; Huston-Tillotson, Hon Dr of Div 1984. **Career:** 1st Congregational Church Berthold ND, pastor 1955-57; YMCA Minot ND, youth prog coord 1957-60; Riverside Church, minister to youth 1960-66; Dillard Univ New Orleans, dean of chapel & dean of students 1966-68; Riverside Church, minister of urban affairs 1969-76; Edwin Gould Serv for Children, exec dir 1976-80; Council of Churches City of NY, exec dir, 1980-88; City Coll of New York, City Univ of New York, acting vice pres External Relations & Community Affairs, 1988-. **Orgs:** Chmn CUNY Constr Fund; Mayor's Comm of Religious Leaders, Assoc Black Charities, Hole-in-the-Wall-Gang Camp Inc; New York City Bd of Educ, Capital Task Force on Construction & Renovation of Public Schools; New York State Dept of Educ Interfaith Educ Advisory Council to the Commr of Educ; Governor's Comm on Scholastic Achievement; Health Watch Advisory Bd. **Honors/Awds:** Distinguished Service Award, Black Christian Caucus Riverside Church 1983; Sam Levinson Memorial Award, Jewish Community Relations Council, New York City 1984.

POLK, WILLIAM C.
Educator. **Personal:** Born Aug 2, 1935, Philadelphia; son of Ruby Polk and William Polk Sr; married Aundria Willis; children: Catherine Collette, William David. **Educ:** West Chester St Coll, BS 1958; Columbia U, MA 1961; PA St U, DEd 1970. **Career:** Neshaminy Sch Dist, tchr 1958-68; PA St U, grad asst 1968-70; asso prof; Slippery Rock, prof ed 1974-. **Orgs:** Mem Nat Cncl for Soc Studies; coms for Tchr Certifications, & Rural Ed; sec Mdwstrn PA Cncl for Soc Studies 1973-; guest lectr Intrntl Studies Inst, Westminster Coll 1974-75; consult Commodore Perry Schs 1976; mem Nat Geographic Soc; mem Alpha Tau Chpt; Phi Delta Kappa 1968-; Rho Chap Alpha PhiAlpha; bd dirs EL Cunningham Comm Ctr 1963-70; faculty sponsor Black Action Soc, Slippery Rock St Coll 1972, 1975-77. **Honors/Awds:** Nat Sci Found Grant 1966; Outstndng Educator 1972. **Business Addr:** Professor, Slippery Rock University, McKay Educ Bldg, Slippery Rock, PA 16057.

POLLARD, ALFONSO MCINHAM
Labor leader, conductor, educator. **Personal:** Born Jun 13, 1952, Washington, DC; son of June Reynolds Brice and Alfonso Pollard; married Lynda Lea Harrod Pollard, Sep 1, 1973; children: Prentice Odell, Lauren Jamille. **Educ:** Boston University, 1970-72; Juilliard School, bachelor of music, 1975; Catholic University, master of music, 1978. **Career:** Washington DC Youth Orchestra, 1970-92; US Air Force Band, Washington, DC, bandsman, tech sgt, 1975-79; Howard University, assoc prof of music, 1979-91; Metropolitan Cultural Productions, president, 1986-; Orchestra Foundation of Metro Washington DC, CEO, 1989-92; American Federation of Musicians, Local 161-710 (AFL-CIO), director; Conductor In Residence, The American University, 1994-96; American Federation of Musicians, national legislative director, 1995-. **Orgs:** American Symphony Orchestra League, 1988-; American Federation of Musicians, 1968-; Filene Center Orchestra at Wolf Trap, principal timpanist, 1986-; Baltimore Opera Orchestra, principal timpanist, 1989-; Annapolis Symphony Orchestra, principal timpanist, 1976-87. **Honors/Awds:** Washington, DC Brd of Education, Resolution for Outstanding Service to Education, 1992; Washington, DC, City Council, Maestro Alfonso Pollard Day, 1991; US Information Agency, teaching/conducting grant, 1990; DC Comm Arts & Humanities, Individual Fellowship Performance Award, 1986; Partners of the Americas, Travel Award to Brazil, 1990; Music Assistance Fund, NY Phil, academic fellowships, 1972-75; Young Artist Program at Tanglewood, Performance Fellowship, 1968. **Military Serv:** US Air Force, tech sgt, 1975-79; BMT Distinguished Honor Graduate, 1975, Good Conduct Medal, 1978. **Home Addr:** 3013 Memory Lane, Silver Spring, MD 20904, (301)890-1941. **Business Phone:** (202)338-0469.

POLLARD, ALTON BROOKS, III
Educator. **Personal:** Born May 5, 1956, St Paul, MN; son of Lena Laverne Evans Pollard and Alton Brooks Pollard, Jr; married Jessica Bryant; children: Alton Brooks IV, Asha Elise. **Educ:** Fisk Univ, BA 1978; Harvard Univ Divinity School, MDiv 1981; Duke Univ, PhD 1987. **Career:** John St Baptist Church, pastor 1979-82; Clark Univ, dir 1981-82; New Red Mountain Baptist Church, pastor 1984-86; St Olaf Coll, asst prof 1987-88; Wake Forest Univ, asst prof, beginning 1988, assoc prof, currently. **Orgs:** Mem Soc for the Scientific Study of Religion 1984-, Assoc for the Sociology of Religion 1985-; mem (clergy) Amer Baptist Convention; mem NAACP, Amer Acad of Religion 1987; Religious Research Assn 1988-; member, Society for the Study of Black Religion, 1989-. **Honors/Awds:** Thomas J Watson Fellowship Fisk Univ 1978; Fund for Theological Educ Fellowships Princeton NJ 1978-81, 1983-86; Andrew Mellon Fellowship Duke Univ 1986-87; article ''Religion, Rock, & Eroticism,'' The Journal of Black Sacred Music 1987; ''The Last Soul Singer in Amer,'' Black Sacred Music 1989; review of ''The Color of God'' and ''Black Theology in Dialogue,'' Perspectives in Religious Studies 1989; ''Howard Thurman and the Experience of Encounter,'' Journal of Religious Thought, 1990; ''Of Movements and Motivations,'' AME Zion Quarterly Review, 1991; ''The Promise and Peril of Common Ground,'' BRIDGES, 1991. **Home Addr:** 2026 Storm Canyon Rd, Winston-Salem, NC 27106. **Business Addr:** Associate Professor of Religion, Wake Forest Univ, Dept of Religion, Box 7212, Winston-Salem, NC 27109.

POLLARD, DIANE S.
Educator. **Personal:** Born Oct 31, 1944, Richmond, VA; daughter of Clara Bayton Stewart and Elric Stewart; married Scott; children: Amina, Almasi. **Educ:** Wellesley Coll, BA 1966; Univ of Chicago, MA 1967, PhD 1972. **Career:** Roosevelt Univ, instructor 1969-72; Univ of WI, asst prof 1972-76, assoc prof 1976-, assoc prof of educ psychology & dir ctr for study of minorities & disadvantaged 1979-85; prof, 1993-. **Orgs:** Mem Amer Educ Rsch Assn 1972-; mem Assn of Black Psychologists 1973-; mem Eta Phi Beta Inc 1978-; mem Soc for the Psychological Study of Social Issues; mem Alpha Kappa Alpha, Inc. **Honors/Awds:** AERA/SIG Research on Women & Education, Willystine Goodsell Awd, 1996; Faculty Distinguished Public Service Award, 1993. **Special Achievements:** Author: ''A Profile of Black Professional Women in Educ, Psychology and Sociology''; ''Perceptions of Black Parents Regarding the Socialization of their Children''; ''Against the Odds: A Profile of Academic Achievers from the Urban Underclass,'' Journal of Negro Education, 1989; ''Patterns of Coping in Black School Children;'' Motivational Factors Underlying Achievement; book chapter, Black Women, Interpersonal Support and Institutional Change in Changing Education: Woman as Radicals and Conservators; ''Reducing the Impact of Racism on Students,'' in Educational Leadership, 1990; ''Toward a Pluralistic Perspective on Equity,'' WEEA Digest, 1992; co-author, book, Gender and Achievement, 1993; ''Perspectives on Gender & Race,'' Educational Leadership, 1996; ''Race, Gender & Educational Leadership,'' Educational Policy, 1997. **Business Addr:** Prof of Educ Psych, Univ of Wisconsin-Milwaukee, Milwaukee, WI 53201.

POLLARD, EMILY FRANCES
Physician. **Personal:** Born Oct 19, Milwaukee, WI. **Educ:** Smith Coll, attended 1975-77; Univ of WI Madison, BS 1980; Meharry Medical Coll, MD 1984. **Career:** Georgetown Univ Hosp, general surgery resident. **Orgs:** Mem Alpha Kappa Alpha sor 1978-. **Honors/Awds:** Alpha Omega Alpha Medical Honor Soc 1983. **Business Addr:** General Surgery Resident, Georgetown Univ Hospital, 3800 Reservoir Rd, Washington, DC 20007.

POLLARD, FREEMAN WALLACE
Educational administrator. **Personal:** Born Aug 8, 1922, Mobile, AL; married Helen Louise. **Educ:** Univ of South Alabama, AB 1973; Indiana Univ, MA 1978, PhD 1981. **Career:** Mobile Cty Voter Educ Proj, dir 1962-69; St Ambrose Coll, prof of political sci 1978-, dir public admin. **Orgs:** Dir of black student union Promotion & Amplification of (Negro) Black Culture 1980-; chmn, consultant, Davenport Civil Rights Comm 1981-84; co-organized & dir Freedom Road Found St Ambrose Coll 1983-84; commissioner Scott Cty Alcohol & Drug Abuse Rehab Bd 1984-; mem of bd of dir Scott Cty Comm Univ 1984-. **Honors/Awds:** Black Scholar & Fellow Amer Assoc Pol Sci 1973; Outstanding Accomplishment in Pol Sci & Philosophy & Cert for 37 GPA in a double major Univ of South AL 1973. **Military Serv:** USMC Sgt 1943-46, 1950-52; Pres Citation 1945. **Home Addr:** 4023 N Lillie Ave, Davenport, IA 52806. **Business Addr:** Dir Public Admin Prog, St Ambrose College, 518 W Locust St, Davenport, IA 52803.

POLLARD, MARCUS LAJUAN
Professional football player. **Personal:** Born Feb 8, 1972, Lanett, AL. **Educ:** Bradley. **Career:** Indianapolis Colts, tight end, 1995-. **Business Addr:** Professional Football Player, Indianapolis Colts, PO Box 535000, Indianapolis, IN 46253, (317)297-2658.

POLLARD, MURIEL RANSOM
Engineer. **Personal:** Born Nov 5, 1953, Isola, MS; daughter of Mr & Mrs Arthur Ransom; divorced; children: Kendra, Eyphra, Elverna. **Educ:** Meharry Medical Coll, attended biomedical science summer program 1972-74; Dillard Univ New Orleans, BA Chem 1975. **Career:** South Central Bell Telephone Co, engr supervisor 1977-. **Orgs:** Mem Delta Sigma Theta Sorority 1973-, Telephone Pioneers of Amer 1981-; consultant religious speech writing & delivery 1984-; mem admin comm MS Political Action Comm for South Central Bell 1986-. **Honors/Awds:** President's Award, Mississippi Head Start Parents Assn, 1989; Recognition of Service, Mississippi Delta Community College, 1989; BellSouth Area Operations Council Recognition Award, 1990; BellSouth Department Head Award, 1996; BellSouth PRIDE Award, 1996; BellSouth, Vice Pres's GALAXY Award, 1997. **Home Addr:** PO Box 1484, Indianola, MS 38751. **Business Addr:** Engineering Supervisor, BellSouth, 268 N Raceway Rd, Greenville, MS 38701, (601)378-5000.

POLLARD, PERCY EDWARD, SR.
Company manager (retired). **Personal:** Born Jun 3, 1943, King & Queen, VA; son of Hattie Bell Taylor Pollard (deceased) and George T Pollard (deceased); married Annie Randolph, May 22, 1965; children: Tracie Anita, Percy Jr. **Educ:** VA State Univ, BS 1966; Emory Univ, Certificate Mgmt Dev Program 1985; VA State Univ, MS, 1997. **Career:** IBM Corporation, jr instructor 1966, sr educ specialist 1969, equal oppor admin 1970, mgr of equal oppor 1972, mgr equal oppor & comm progs Gaithersburg 1973, district personnel programs mgr Office Products Div 1976, regional personnel mgr Washington/Baltimore Metro area 1977, personnel planning mgr Office Products Div Franklin Lakes, NJ 1979, corporate mgr equal oppor prog 1981, admin asst to the vice pres of personnel 1982, personnel mgr Rsch Div Yorktown, NY 1984, mgr staff services White Plains, NY 1986-, Special Asst for Employee Charitable Contributions 1988, IBM Corporate Headquarters Personnel Manager beginning 1989, dir, Cultural & Human Services Program, 1991-93; IBM Faculty Loan, 1993-95; Pollard Consulting Services, 1997. **Orgs:** Mem Bergen Co Urban League; trustee Franklin Lakes United Methodist Church; mem President's Exec Exchange Assoc; steering comm Organizational Resource Counselors; mem VA State Univ Alumni Assoc No NJ Chapt; mem Kappa Theta Lambda Chap Alpha Phi Alpha Frat; founder/chmn VA State Univ Special Action Team; Deacon, First Mt Olive Baptist Church; chm bd Evironmental Careers Org; chm, advisory council, Richmond Technical Ctr. **Honors/Awds:** Certificate of Merit, Broome Co NY NAACP 1972; Family and Children's Soc Special Recognition Certificate 1973; Kiwanis Club President's Awd 1975; Alpha Phi Alpha Outstanding Tenure Awd 1976, Sustained Serv Awd 1977, President's Impact Awd 1978; IBM Office Products Div People Management Awd 1979; Division Excellence Award, IBM, 1988; Lead IBM's Charitable Contribution Program ($31.8 million raised), 1988; Presidential Exec Exchange 1980-81; Sr Management Citation Dept of Health and Human Serv 1981; Outstanding Natl Achievement Awd 1981; Alpha Phi Alpha Iota Theta Lambda Chap Awd 1983; SES Candidates Certificates of Recognition Dept of Health & Human Serv 1983; Alpha Phi Alpha New York/New Jersey Archives Awd 1983; NAFEO Presidential Citation Awd 1986;Alumnus of the Year, Virginia State v, 1989; President's Special Recognition Award, Alpha Phi Alpha, 1990; editor, Sphinx Magazine, Alpha Phi Alpha. **Home Addr:** PO Box 280, St Stephens Church, VA 23148.

POLLARD, RAYMOND J.
Educational administrator (retired). **Personal:** Born Mar 31, 1932, Lamar, SC; son of Ethel Pollard and Gussie Pollard; married Eloise Wilson. **Educ:** FSU, EdB 1953; Univ of PA, M Equivalent 1957; Antioch Coll, MS 1977. **Career:** Internal Revenue, mail clerk 1953-54; AUS, communication coding clerk 1954-56; Kenderton Sch, spl educ tchr 1957-58; McIntyre Sch, tchr 1958-61; CPA, caseworker male clerk 1961-62; LP Hill Sch, 1962-64; Levering Sch, 1966-67; LPHill Sch, 1967-71; Turner Middle Sch, phys educ tchr 1971-73; PA Fedn of Tchrs, staff rep 1973, general vice president retired. **Orgs:** Finan sec mem usher bd chsch schlshp com co-dir rec Met Bapt Ch; past pres bus mgr chmn hospitality com Fayetteville State Univ Alumni; mem exec bd co-chmn Progressive Philadelphia Fedn of Tchrs; bldg rep LP Hill Sch & JP Turnr Sch; mem NAACP; PUSH; CORE; SCLC; APHI; treas BSA; vice pres Negro Trade Unoin Ldrshp Coun 1971; 1st v,chmn A Phillip Randolph Inst 1972. **Military Serv:** AUS 1954-56.

POLLARD, WILLIAM E.
Association executive. **Personal:** Born Sep 14, 1915, Pensacola, FL; married Josephine Mays; children: Constance Lagness, Barbara Ann LaCarra. **Educ:** UCLA; LA City Coll. **Career:** Dining Car Employees #582, sec treas 1941-45; Dining Car Employees #456 & #582, gen chmn 1945-; LA Co Fedn Labor, vice pres 1959-64; AFL-CIO Dept Civil Rights, staff rep 1964-74; Dept Civil Rights AFL-CIO, dir 1974-86; NAACP, deputy exec dir 1986-retirement, special asst to exec dir, currently. **Orgs:** Pres Joint Counc Dining Car Employees 1954-68; former orgn LA Joint Exec Bd Hotel & Restaurant Employees & Bartenders Intl Union; mem natl exec bd NAACP; natl exec bd Ldrshp Conf on Civil Rights; natl labor adv com Nt Urban Leag; natl exec bd A Philip Randolph Inst; Mason. **Honors/Awds:** Serv Awds Natl Urban League, NAACP, Metrop Red Yth Adv Coun, Metrop Police Dept, Cath Labor Inst 1974; Public Serv Awd Dept of Justice 1978; Scroll of Merit Natl Medical Assoc 1983. **Business Addr:** Special Asst to Executive Director, NAACP, 4805 Mt Hope Dr, Baltimore, MD 21215.

POLLARD, WILLIAM LAWRENCE
Educator. **Personal:** Born Nov 27, 1944, Raleigh, NC; son of Bettie Pollard and Linwood Pollard; married Merriette Maude Chance; children: William Lawrence, Frederick Touissaint. **Educ:** Shaw Univ, AB 1967; Univ of NC Chapel Hill, MSW 1969; Univ of Chicago, PhD 1976. **Career:** Livingstone Coll, instr 1969-71, asst prof & dir social welfare prog 1973-76; Univ of Pittsburgh, asso prof & chairperson of comm orgn skill set school of social work 1976-82; Grambling State Univ, assoc prof & dir of undergrad social work 1984-; Syracuse University, Syracuse, NY, dean, 1989-. **Orgs:** House of dels Council on Social Work Educ 1974-77, 1979-82; bd of dir Friendship House Salisbury NC 1974-76; sec bd of dir Dial Help Salisbury 1974-76; bd of dir YMCA Salisbury 1975-76; bd of dirs Council on Social Work Educ; adv comm Citizen Educ Action Group for Criminal Justice; board of directors, Natl Assn of Deans & Directors of Schools of Social Work, 1991-; Salvation Army, board of directors; Elmcrest Children's Center, board of directorss. **Honors/Awds:** Fellowship Grant Met Applied Rsch Corp 1974; A Study of Black Self Help R&E Rsch Assocs 1978; ''The Black Child'' in proceedings of New Concepts in Human Serv for the Developing Child 1978; Distinguished Graduate, Shaw University, 1991; First Annual, NY Governor's Award for African-Americans of Distinction, Awardee. **Special Achievements:** Co-Author, ''How Do We Get There: Strategic Planning for Schools of Social Work,'' Journal of Social Work Education, 1992. **Business Addr:** Dean, Syracuse University, School of Social Work, Sims Hall, Syracuse, NY 13244-1230.

POLLEY, WILLIAM EMORY
Physician. **Personal:** Born Feb 16, 1921, Huntington, WV; married Revella Justice; children: William, Aaron, Sharon Nott, John, Brenda, Susan, Leslie, Douglass. **Educ:** WV State Coll, BS 1943; OJ Coll of podiatry 1953. **Career:** Podiatrists 22 yrs. **Orgs:** Treas WV State Alumni Assn 11 yrs; chaplain 9 yrs; 33rd degree Mason; mem Forest City Hosp; Royal Craft & Grand Lodge; sec 20 yrs; past pres Credit Union; Holy Trinity Bapt Ch9; pres of trst bd Mt Olive Bapt Ch 1962-69; life mem Alpha Phi Alpha Frat; NAACP; Phyliss Wheatley Assn; Northeastern OH Podiatry Assn 22 yrs; Am Podiatry Assn 22 yrs; PTA 10 yrs; Boy Scouts; Cub Scouts Com 1957-67. **Honors/Awds:** Awd plaque from WV Alumni Assn for 21 yrs of serv 1975. **Military Serv:** AUS sgt 1943-46. **Business Addr:** 14011 Kinsman Rd, Cleveland, OH 44120.

POLYNICE, OLDEN
Professional basketball player. **Personal:** Born Nov 21, 1964, Port-au-Prince, Haiti; children: Nikolas Justin, Tiara Alysha. **Educ:** Univ of Virginia, Charlottesville, VA, 1983-86. **Career:** Played in Italy, 1986-87, Seattle SuperSonics, center, 1987-91, Los Angeles Clippers, 1991-92, Detroit Pistons, 1992-94; Sacramento Kings, 1994-. **Business Addr:** Professional Basketball Player, Sacramento Kings, One Sports Pkwy, Sacramento, CA 95834, (916)928-6900.

POMARE, ELEO
Artistic director. **Personal:** Born Oct 20, 1937. **Educ:** Studied with, USA: Louis Horst, Curtis James, Jose Limon, Asadafa

Dafara; Germany: Kurt Jooss; Switzerland: Harold Kreutzberg. **Career:** Eleo Pomare Dance Co, artistic director; first co., American, 1958-62, second co., European, toured Germany, Holland, Sweden, and Norway, 1962-64, Revival and expansion of first co., toured throughout the US, Canada, Puerto Rico, the West Indies, Australia, and Italy, 1964-; has choreographed works for: Alvin Ailey Dance Co.; Maryland Ballet Co.; Dayton Contemporary Dance Co.; Cleo Parker-Robinson Dance Co.; Alpha and Omega Dance Co.; National Ballet of Holland; Balletinstituttet, Oslo, Norway; Australian Contemporary Dance Co.; Ballet Palacio das Artes, Belo Horizonte, Brazil. **Honors/Awds:** John Hay Whitney European Fellowship, 1962-64; Guggenheim Fellowship Grant, 1973; TOR, Superior Artistry Award, 1983, Award for Direction and Choreography; National Endownment for the Arts, Choreographer's Grants, 1975, 1982, 1988, 1989. **Special Achievements:** Contributor: "The Black Tradition in American Modern Dance," project of the American Dance Festival, reconstructing three choreographed works documented as classics: "Las Desenamoradas," "Blues for the Jungle," "Missa Luba"; yearly supporters/sponsors include: National Endowment for the Arts; New York State Council on the Arts; Avon Corp.; McGraw Hill Co.; NY State Black and Puerto Rican Legislative Caucus/Natural Heritage Trust; participant: Nationwide Artist-in-the-Schools Projects; numerous lectures and presentations on modern dance, African-American artist and their artistic heritage and contributions. **Business Addr:** Artistic Director, Eleo Pomare Dance Co., 325 W 16th St, New York, NY 10011.

POMPEY, CHARLES SPENCER
Educator (retired). **Personal:** Born Jul 31, 1915, McClenny, FL; married Hattie Ruth Keys; children: Cheryl Zaneta. **Educ:** FL Meml Coll, AA 1935; Bethune Ckmn Coll, AA 1936; Johnson C Smith U, AB 1939; Univ MN, MA 1947. **Career:** Pinemount Elem School, prin 1936-37; Washington Jr/Boynton Elem, prin 1939-45; Carver High School, teacher coach 1946-64; Carver H/Seacrest H, asst prin 1964-69; Jr H Atlantic H Carver Middle School, prin 1969-80; Delray Beach Planning/Zoning/Cty Land Use Adv Com, 1968-82; Palm Beach Community Coll, assoc ed, Like A Mighty Banyan, 1982. **Orgs:** Author "A sch & its cmnty-prtnr's in Soc Engrng" 1956; Negro Jrnl of Higher Ed "An Analysis of The Wash-DuBois Contrvrsy" The Bulletin, Mn Cncl for Social Studies 1957; "More Rivers to Cross" Copyright 1984; co-fndr & 1st pres Palm Bch Co Tchrs Assn 1941; chmn FL State Tchrs Assn Pgm Action Com 1966-67; chmn mem Budget Comm Exec Com-FL Ed Assn 1968-71; pres Phi Delta Kappa Ed Frat; Palm Beach County Black Historical Soc, dir, 1986; South Florida Museum of African-American Heritage, Inc, board, 1992; South County Mental Health Board, charter director, 1973-. **Honors/Awds:** First Annual hmn relt awd FL Tchg Prof 1977; coach yr EE FL Athl Conf 1949-50, 1954, 1961-64; First Martin Luther King ctzn awd Palm Beach Cty 1977 "Pompey Pk/Rec Ctr," Cty Delray Beach 1976; "Black FL Hall Fame," Univ FL 1984; Palm Beach Comm Coll, hon dir of Black Hist Archives, 1988; documented research for Official Dedicaton of "Five Historical Sites in Black Sector by the Delray Historic Preservation Bd," 1990-; Founder's Day "Humanitarian Award," Florida Memorial Col, 1990; "Black Migrations into Florida-1865-1990-An Untold Story," presented to the Historical Society of Palm Beach County, 1989; inducted into Johnson C Smith Univ Hall of Fame by JCSU 100 Club, 1991; Urban League of Palm Beach County Inc, The Martin Luther King Jr Award, 1992. **Home Addr:** P O Box 1533, Delray Beach, FL 33447. **Business Addr:** PO Box 1533, Delray Beach, FL 33447.

PONDER, EUNICE WILSON
Educator. **Personal:** Born Sep 4, 1929, Oklahoma; daughter of Kate Wilson and Austin Wilson; married Dr Henry; children: Cheryl, Anna. **Educ:** Langston U, BS 1951; OK State U, MS 1958; Univ of SC, EdD 1977. **Career:** Planning Research & Mgmt Benedict Coll, institutional researcher 1977-84; Benedict Coll, tchr 1977-84; Millie Lewis Agency Columbia SC, model; OK, tchr pub schs 1951-58. **Orgs:** Mem Nat Delta Pi Epsilon Bus Frat 1958-; mem Nat Assn of Institutional Researchers 1977; vol worker Red Cross; mem NCATE Self-Study Team HEW 1978-80; reader tite IV HEW 1979-80; life mem Delta Sigma Theta Sor; mem Jack & Jill of Am Inc; mem Links Inc. **Honors/Awds:** Dissertation "A Study of Selected Characteristics Affecting the Survival Rate of Black & White Students at the Univ of SC" 1977. **Business Addr:** 400 12th St NE, Washington, DC 20002.

PONDER, HENRY
Educational administrator. **Personal:** Born Mar 28, 1928, Wewoka, OK; son of Lillie Ponder and Frank Ponder; married Eunice Wilson Ponder, Nov 22, 1952; children: Cheryl, Anna. **Educ:** Langston Univ, BS 1951; OK State Univ, MS 1958; OH State Univ, PhD 1963. **Career:** OK State Univ, rsch asst 1961-63; VA State Coll, asst prof 1958-61; OH State Univ, rsch asst 1961-63; VA State Coll, chmn dept agri/business 1963-64; Fort Valley State Coll, chmn dept business & econs 1964-66; Irving Trust Co, econ consult 1968; AL A&M Univ, dean 1966-69, vice pres academic affairs 1969-73; Benedict Coll, pres 1973-84; Fisk Univ, pres 1984-96. **Orgs:** Mem Amer Econ Assoc; mem Amer Farm Econ Assoc; Mason 32nd Deg C of C; gen pres Alpha Phi Alpha; National Association for Equal Opportunity in Higher Education. **Honors/Awds:** OK State Univ, distinguished alumnus award 1986; 100 Most Effective College Presidents in US 1986. **Military Serv:** AUS chief computer fdc sgt 1953-55. **Business Addr:** President, Nat Assn for Equal Opportunity in Higher Education, 400 12th St NE, Washington, DC 20002.

POOL, VERA C.
Correctional facility commander. **Personal:** Born Jul 27, 1946, Greenwood, MS; daughter of Alberta Lofton Corbin and Rayfield Corbin; married John Pool, Jul 26, 1969; children: Sheina Karia. **Educ:** Portland Community College, Portland, OR, AA, 1969; University of Portland, Portland, OR, BA, Psychology, 1972, MA, Education, 1974, MS, Criminal Justice, 1978. **Career:** Veterans Administration, Portland, OR, food services, 1965-70; Multnomah County Sheriff's Dept, Portland, OR, 1970-. **Orgs:** Founder & former chapter president, National Assn of Black Correctional Justice, 1984-91; sgt-at-arms, Delta Sigma Theta Sorority, 1989; appointed to national board, NABCJ, 1979-86, 1989-, elected national assistant secretary, Board on Police Standards and Training, 1981-89; member, Governor Steering Committee on Sex Offenders, 1990. **Honors/Awds:** Award for Dedicated Services in Corrections/Prison, Albina Ministrial Alliance, 1990; The Chairman Emeritus Award 1989, Service to the Community 1987, National Assn of Black Correctional Justice; Professional Achievement, Delta Sigma Theta Sorority, 1988; Woman of the Year, American Business Women's Assn Chapter (Mt Hood), 1979. **Business Addr:** Lieutenant Commander, Corrections, Multnomah County Correctional Facility, 1115 SW 11th Ave, Portland, OR 97205.

POOLE, CECIL F. See Obituaries section.

POOLE, DILLARD M.
Educator. **Personal:** Born Sep 15, 1939, Birmingham, AL. **Educ:** BA 1971; MA 1977. **Career:** State OH, clerk; Warner & Swasey Machine Tool Co, tool supply worker; Cleveland State Univ, asst to dean for student life 1971-72; Afro-Amer Cultural Center Cleveland State Univ, dir. **Orgs:** Nat Conf Artists 1973-74; trst Parkwood CME Ch 1974-. **Honors/Awds:** Mem dean's list Cleveland State Univ 1970. **Military Serv:** USAF airman 2nd class 1959-63. **Business Addr:** 2121 Euclid Ave, Cleveland, OH 44115.

POOLE, JAMES F.
Investment counselor. **Personal:** Born Apr 12, 1936, Laurens, SC; married Martha; children: Stephanie, Heather. **Educ:** Benedict Coll, 1959; Univ of PA, Univ of CO & CO Coll, grad work. **Career:** Central HS Pueblo, tchr math 1962-67; Amer Capital Financial Serv Inc, investment couns div mgr 1967-. **Orgs:** Mem Est Planning Coun of Colorado Springs; Sale & Mrkt Exec Club; mem Alpha Phi Alpha Frat; Pueblo Country Club; apptd CO Centennial-Bicentennial Commn 1975; bd trst Benedict Coll Columbia SC; mem Millionaires Club of Amer Capital Financial Serv Inc. **Military Serv:** AUS e-5 1959-62. **Business Addr:** Certified Financial Planner, 119 W 8th, Pueblo, CO 81003.

POOLE, MARION L.
Reading instructor. **Personal:** Born May 25, 1921, Sumter, SC; son of Rena Poole and Edward Poole; married Dr Rachel Johnson; children: M Brevard El, Andrea, Adriene. **Educ:** BS 1959; MEd 1964; EdD 1972. **Career:** Pennsylvania Welfare Dept, sr visitor; Pittsburgh Public Schools, teacher, admin; Univ of Pittsburgh, consultant & faculty 1968-84 retired; teacher corps dir 1969-72; Univ Pittsburgh & General Assembly Center School Desegregation & Conflict, principal research asst lecturer staff specialist; Comm Coll, Alleghany County, part-time instructor, 1984-. **Orgs:** Natl Training Labs 1970; current ed Center Communicator 1973-; Phi Delta Kappa Doctoral Assn Educ 1973-; AERA; pres current bd dirs Promethenas Inc 1972-74; vice pres Emanons; mem NAACP. **Honors/Awds:** Astp Howard Univ; 92nd INF Div Hq 1944-45; co-author, Comprehensive Affirmative Action for Equal Educational Opportunity in the Racially isolated school district, 1981; Bronze Medallion, Outstanding Service to Students in DE, 1984; Merit Plaque, Service to Students. **Home Addr:** 137 Kilmer St, Pittsburgh, PA 15221.

POOLE, RACHEL IRENE
Nurse (retired), advisor, counselor. **Personal:** Born Dec 2, 1924, Uniontown, PA; married Dr Marion L Poole; children: Andrea Lynell, Adriene Charisse Dilworth. **Educ:** Univ of Pittsburgh PA, BS nursing 1947; Univ of Pittsburgh, ML nursing educ 1952; Univ Pittsburgh, PhD 1977. **Career:** Allegheny Campus Community Coll of Allegheny Co Pittsburgh PA, retired asst dean of life sci and dir of nursing prog 1979-84; Community Coll of Allegheny Co, adminstrv intern/Adminstrv asst to pres 1977-79; Inst for Higher Educ Sch of Educ Univ of Pittsburgh, lectr/adminstrv asst 1974-77; Western Psychiatric Inst and Clinics, dir of Nursing; Dept of Psychiatric Mental Hlth Nursing Sch of Nursing Univ of Pittsburgh, asso prof and asso chmn 1967-72; Dept of Psychiatric Mental Hlth Nursing Sch of Nursing Univ of Pittsburgh, asso prof 1972-73; hlth integrator 1972; Homewood-Brushton Branch Allegheny Comm Coll, part-time advisor, counselor 1984-. **Orgs:** Amer Nurses Assn; Amer Assn of Higher Educ, 1975-76; Ille Elegba, bd of dirs, 1968-74; Black Women's Forum, org/treasurer, 1969-71; Visions: Women's Art Collective, adv bd mem, 1989-; Univ of Pittsburgh African Amer Alumni Scholarship Committee, 1989-. **Honors/Awds:** Interviewee "Racism" WIIC's TV Prog Face to Face 1968; Sigma Theta Tau 1953; selected PA Nurses Assn "Brain Trust" 1965-67; author of many writings; "Proposal for a Plan of Action" Com on Recruitment of Minorities into Nursing Dept of Hlth Commonwealth of PA 1973; Panelist Nursing Programs WTAE's TV Prog Pgh Today 1982; Panelist Minorities and Nursing WQED's TV Prog Black Horizons 1981; Black Achiever of Year, NIP Magazine 1986; Special Recognition Award, Community Coll of Alleg County 1986; frequent speaker to many groups such as Bus/Prof Women; Penn Bar Assn, legal assistants, paralegals, single mothers, sec, nurses, ex-convicts, fed women employees, & women in military on the subject of "Assertiveness" 1979-88, 1988-90; Outstanding/Dedicated ServicesAward, Student Advisory Bd, CommuniColl of Allegheny County Allegheny Campus 1990; Distinguished Alumnus Award, Univ of Pittsburgh School of Nursing 1990; Outstanding Black Nurse Citation, City Council, Pittsburgh, PA. **Business Addr:** Advisor, Counselor, Comm Coll of Allegheny Cty, 701 N Homewood Ave, Pittsburgh, PA 15221.

POOLE, TYRONE
Professional football player. **Personal:** Born Feb 3, 1972, LaGrange, GA. **Educ:** Fort Valley State University. **Career:** Carolina Panthers, defensive back, 1995-. **Special Achievements:** Selected in the 1st round/22nd overall pick in the 1995 NFL Draft. **Business Addr:** Professional Football Player, Carolina Panthers, 800 Mint St, Ericsson Stadium, Charlotte, NC 28202, (704)358-7000.

POOL-ECKERT, MARQUITA JONES
Journalist. **Personal:** Born Feb 19, 1945, Aurora, IL; daughter of Jeanne Boger Jones and Mark E Jones; married Knut Eckert, May 21, 1988. **Educ:** Boston Univ, BS 1966; Columbia Univ, MA, Journalism, 1969. **Career:** WABC-TV New York, producer 1970-74; WNET/13 Public TV, producer 1974-75; CBS News, assoc prod 1975-84, producer 1984-90, senior producer, Sunday Morning, 1990-. **Orgs:** Bd of dirs Nzingha Soc Inc 1976-89, pres 1976-85; mem NY Assoc Black Journalists 1985-, Womens Media Group 1986-; board of directors, NY Women in Film, 1994-; board of directors Frederick Douglas Creative Arts Ctr, 1994-; mem Council on Foreign Relations; mem Friends of Museum of Modern Art, NY, 1995-. **Honors/Awds:** Emmy Awd Producer "The Bombing of Beirut" 1983; Emmy Awd Producer "The Black Family - A Dream Deferred" 1983; Dollars and Sense Magazine Awd 100 Top Professional Black Women 1986; Natl Monitor Award 1988; Emmy Award Producer "Racism" 1986; Emmy Award Producer "Pan Am 103 Crash" 1988; International Monitor Award for "80's Remembered" 1990; Norfolk State University, Career Achievement Awd, 1996. **Business Addr:** Senior Producer, CBS News, 524 W 57th St, New York, NY 10019.

POPE, COURTNEY A.
Cleric. **Personal:** Born Mar 29, 1964, Philadelphia, PA; son of Gloria J Pope & Cromwell Pope; married Audrey D Pope, Aug 1, 1987; children: Jazmine, Chaz. **Educ:** Temple University, BA, communications, 1988. **Career:** Eastern Atlantic Diocese Youth Congress, pres, 1984-97; Church of the Living God, Natl HYPBC, vp, 1985-87; Holy Temple Church, pastor, 1995-; Eastern Atlantic Diocese, district elder, 1996-. **Orgs:** Philadelphia Music Alliance, affiliated, 1992; Bishop L Colene Williams Comm Ctr, bd of dirs, 1998-; Jhazzi Music Publishing, pres, 1997-; Fresh Harvest Ministries, bd of dirs, 1998-. **Honors/Awds:** Holy Temple Church, Youth of the Year, 1990, 15 Years in the Gospel Ministry, 1991; American Family Inst, Gift of Time, 1995; Borough of Penns Grove, NJ, Mayor's Award, 1996. **Special Achievements:** Performed and recorded "Make A Joyful Noise," 1984; wrote & performed musical score for drama, "Practical Spirits," 1985; performed & recorded, "All My Help," 1986; performed on "Spirit of Philadelphia," cruise, 1994; performed & recorded, "Living to Live Again," 1996. **Business Addr:** Pastor, Holy Temple Church, Willis & Cumberland Sts, PO Box 541, Penns Grove, NJ 08069.

POPE, DERRICK ALEXANDER
Attorney, educator. **Personal:** Born Dec 7, 1964, Atlanta, GA; son of Sallie Pope Howard. **Educ:** Morris Brown College, BA, political science, 1987; Loyola University School of Law, JD, 1992. **Career:** Morris Brown College, adjunct professor of law, 1992-; Special Judiciary Committee, lawyer, 1992-93; Georgia House of Representatives; Georgia General Assembly, lawyer/assistant legislative counsel, 1993-94; Medical Assn of Georgia, lawyer, legislative counsel, currently. **Orgs:** Atlanta Inner Circle (Democratic Party of Georgia), general counsel, 1993-; State Bar of Georgia, 1992-; American Bar Assn, 1993-; Alpha Phi Alpha Fraternity Inc, 1984-. **Honors/Awds:** Loyola University School of Law, Foti Criminal Advocacy Award, 1992; NCCU School of Law, American Jurisprudence Award, 1989; Council on Legal Education Opportunity, Sterling Performance Award, 1987; National Intercollegiate Mock-Trial, Top Attorney Award, 1987. **Special Achievements:** A Constitutional Gem of Interpretive Reason: Or in Other Words..The Ninth

Amendment, 37 Hon LJ, 201, 1994. **Home Addr:** 416 Carriage Place Ct, Decatur, GA 30033. **Business Addr:** Legislative Counsel, Medical Assn of Georgia, 938 Peachtree St, NE, Atlanta, GA 30309-3990, (404)876-7535.

POPE, HENRY
Psychiatrist. **Personal:** Born May 1, 1922, Athens, GA; married; children: 4. **Educ:** Howard U, BS 1949; Meharry Med Coll, MD 1958. **Career:** Provident Hosp, intern 1958; St Elizabeth's Hosp, 1960; St Elizabeths Hosp, staff physician 1960-65; Self-employed, 1960-; Crownsville Hosp Cntr, res psychiat staff psychiat 1970-. **Orgs:** Mem Nat Med Assn 1960-; DC Med Soc 1970. **Military Serv:** Sgt 1943-45. **Business Addr:** 5502 Colorado Ave NW, Washington, DC 20011.

POPE, ISAAC S.
Physician. **Personal:** Born Mar 6, 1939, S Pittsburgh, TN; married Joan Darby; children: David, Stephen, Theresa. **Educ:** Gonaaga Univ, Spokane WA, BS 1965; Univ WA Seattle, MPA 1970; Univ WA Seattle, MD 1974. **Career:** Peace Corps in Sierra Leone, volunteer 1965-67; Peace Corps Training Program Gambia dir 1969; model cities program Seattle, asst dir employee economic devel 1969-70; US Army Ft Leonard Wood MO, staff pediatrician, 1977-79; private practice, pediatrician, 1979-. **Orgs:** Regional dir Student Natl Med Assn 1972-73; WA State Med Assn Lewis Co Med Socty; WA State Soc of Pediatrics; Kiwanis, 1979-, president, 1985; bd mem Lewis County Work Opportunity, 1981-86; bd mem St Helen Hospital Chehalis WA 1982-; bd mem Lewis County Special Olympic, 1983-86; Twin Cities Chamber of Commerce, 1985-, president, 1987; pres The Center Foundation, president, 1986-; Chehalis City Council, 1988-. **Honors/Awds:** Conc patient care Ft Leonard Wood Army Hospital 1978; Army Commendation Medal, AVS, 1979; Daily Chronicle, Businessmen of the Year, 1988; Sertoma Club, Service to Mankind Award, 1989; Gonzaga University, Distinguished Alumni Merit Award, 1990; Elks, Distinguished Citizenship Award, 1991. **Military Serv:** USAF airman 1/c 1956-59; US Army, major 1974-79. **Business Addr:** Pediatrician, 370 S Market Blvd, Chehalis, WA 98532.

POPE, JAMES M.
Government official (Retired). **Personal:** Born Apr 17, 1927, Sharon, PA; son of Mattie Pope Wells and Matthew Pope; married Cora Silver Pope, Jun 23, 1956; children: Anthony V, Michael R. **Educ:** OH Wesleyan U, BA 1950; Boston U, MA 1951; Harvard U, 1955. **Career:** Bureau of African Aff State Dept, publ aff adv 1971-77, US Arms Contl/Disarm Agen, deputy publ aff adviser 1977-82; US Information Agency, Foreign Press Ctr, Washington, DC, dir, 1983-92. **Orgs:** Pi Delta Epsilon 1950; Omicron Delta Kappa 1950; vice pres Cpt Press Club 1971; Natl Press Club, 1989-; Capital Press Club. **Honors/Awds:** Meritorious Hnr Awd US Infor Agency 1964; Meritorious Hnr Awd Dept of State 1974; Meritorious Hnr Awd Arms Ctrl/Disarm Agency 1980. **Military Serv:** AUS corpl 1945-46; Pacific Theater, Japanese Occupation Ribbon, Good Conduct Medal. **Home Addr:** 1402 Sheridan St NW, Washington, DC 20011.

POPE, MARQUEZ PHILLIPS
Professional football player. **Personal:** Born Oct 2, 1970, Nashville, TN. **Educ:** Fresno State, attended. **Career:** San Diego Chargers, defensive back, 1992-93; Los Angeles Rams, 1994; San Francisco 49ers, 1995-. **Business Addr:** Professional Football Player, San Francisco 49ers, 4949 Centennial Blvd, Santa Clara, CA 95054, (415)562-4949.

POPE, MARY MAUDE
Clergyman. **Personal:** Born Jan 27, 1916, Wake Co, NC; widowed. **Educ:** Amer Sch of Chicago; Univ NC; NC St U. **Career:** Mt Sinai Saints of God Holy Chs & Mt Sinai Chs Worldwide, bishop. **Orgs:** Past fndr Mt Sinai Chs 1946. **Business Addr:** Mt Sinai Ch, 301 S Swain St PO Box J27411, Raleigh, NC 27611.

POPE, MIRIAN ARTIS
Business executive. **Personal:** Born Nov 3, 1952, Franklin, VA; married Johnnie Lee Pope Jr; children: Ebonee Johndrea, Courtney LaVerne. **Educ:** Norfolk State University, BS 1975; Old Dominion University, graduate school. **Career:** United Virginia Bank, branch manager 1975-81; Community Federal S/L Assn, managing officer 1981-. **Orgs:** Adv bd of banking & fin comm Norfolk State Univ 1977-81; mem Natl Assn of Bank Women, Inc 1977-81; dir Norfolk C of C 1980; dir Amer Red Cross Tidewater Chap 1979-81; dir United Way 1981-82; mem, sec Order of Eastern Star of VA, PHA 1979-; adv to Jr Achievement of Tidewater 1976. **Honors/Awds:** Scholarship Norfolk State University 1971; appreciation Junior Achievement of Tidewater 1976; appreciation Norfolk Chamber of Commerce 1980; appreciation American Red Cross 1981. **Home Addr:** 387 Brock Circle, Norfolk, VA 23502. **Business Addr:** Chief Executive Officer, Community Fed S & L Assn, 1512 27th St, Newport News, VA 23607.

POPE, RUBEN EDWARD, III
Personnel administrator. **Personal:** Born Jun 28, 1948, Cleveland, OH; married Cheryl Ann Jones; children: Walter, Yolanda, Yvonne. **Educ:** Kenyon Coll, BA 1970; Boston Coll Law Sch, JD 1973. **Career:** Wyman-Gordon Co, dev benefits mgr 1975-; Arthur Andersen & Co, auditor 1973-75. **Orgs:** Mem OH Bar 1978; mem Am Bar Assn 1978; bd of dir Untied Way of Central MA 1979-; treas Yth Guid Assn Inc 1979-; bd of dir Prospect Hse Inc 1980; finan sec Quinsigamond Lodge #173 IBPOE OFW Elks; sec Belmont St AME Zion Ch. **Business Addr:** 244 Worcester St N, North Grafton, MA 01536.

PORCHE-BURKE, LISA
Educational administrator. **Personal:** Born Nov 9, 1954, Los Angeles, CA; daughter of June Porche and Ralph Porche; married Peter Burke, Oct 27, 1984; children: Mallory, Dominique, Lauren. **Educ:** University of Southern California, BA, 1976; University of Nortre Dame, MA, 1981, PhD, 1983. **Career:** California School of Professional Psychology, assistant professor, professional training faculty, 1985-87, assistant professor, 1987-90, Ethnic Minority Mental Health Proficiency, coordinator, 1987-90, associate professor, 1990-91, Multicultural Community Clinical Proficiency, coordinator, 1990-92, acting provost, 1991-92, chancellor, 1992-. **Orgs:** Assn of Black Psychologists, 1980-; National Council of Schools of Professional Psychology, executive cmte, 1990-92, membership chair, 1992-; California Psychological Assn Foundation, board member, 1992-; American Psychological Assn, Division 45, Society for the Study of Ethnic Minority Issues, executive cmte, 1985-, secretary-treasurer, 1991-, Division of Psychotherapy, executive bd, 1991-; American Assn of Higher Education, 1993-. **Honors/Awds:** California School of Professional Psychology, Distinguished faculty Contribution Award; Division 29, American Psychological Association, Jack B Krasner Award; Association of Black Psychologists, Exemplary Professional Service Award; Honorary Doctor of Letters, 1994. **Special Achievements:** Author: "Minority Student Recruitment and Retention: Is There a Secret to Success?" Towards Ethnic Diversification in Psychology Education and Training, Stricker, 1990; "The Particularly Insidious Effects of Stress on Women of Color," w/Funk, 1991; "Recommendations From the Working Group on Predoctoral Training," 1991, "Ethnic Minority Issues in Clinical Training at CSPP-LA," 1991, Ethnic Minority Perspectives on Clinical Training and Service in Psychology, Myers; "The Insidious Impact of Gang Violence: Strategies for Prevention and Intervention," Substance Abuse and Gang Violence, Cervantes, 1992. **Business Addr:** Chancellor, California School of Professional Psychology, 1000 S Fremont Ave, Alhambra, CA 91803, (818)284-2777.

PORCHER, ROBERT, III
Professional football player. **Personal:** Born Jul 30, 1969, Wando, SC; married Kimberly; children: Morgan Latreese. **Educ:** South Carolina State University, bachelor's degree in criminal justice. **Career:** Detroit Lions, defensive tackle, 1992-. **Honors/Awds:** First-round draft pick, 1992. **Business Addr:** Professional Football Player, Detroit Lions, 1200 Featherstone Rd, Pontiac, MI 48342, (248)335-4131.

PORTEE, FRANK, III
Pastor. **Personal:** Born Jun 16, 1955, York, SC; son of Alvon Pendergrass Portee and Frank Portee Jr (deceased); married Yvonne Fersner, Sep 10, 1983; children: Alyssa Shanee. **Educ:** Carson-Newman Coll, BA 1977; Interdenominational Theological Seminary, MDiv 1980. **Career:** New Light UM Church, pastor 1980-83; United Methodist Church SC, coord of youth ministry 1980-83; Coll of Charleston, campus minister 1983-; Old Bethel UM Church, pastor 1983-. **Orgs:** pres Greater Charleston Community Development, Inc 1988-; chrmn Avery Research Bd. 1988-; Vice pres Natl Kidney Foundation 1984-; bd mem Action Council Comm Mental Health 1984-; columnist Charleston Chronicle 1985-; bd mem Comm Relations Council 1985-, Florence Crittenton Homes 1986; consultant General Bd of Global Ministries 1987; chrmn First Congressional District Rainbow Coalition, 1988. **Honors/Awds:** Rsch Fellow Emory Sch of Theology 1982-83; Disting Serv Prince Hall Lodge #46 F&AM 1986; Disting Serv Chas Air Force Base 1987; Social Action, Phi Beta Sigma 1989; Delegate - Democratic National Convention 1988. **Home Addr:** 513 Huger St, Charleston, SC 29403. **Business Addr:** Senior Minister, Old Bethel United Meth Church, 222 Calhoun St, Charleston, SC 29401.

PORTER, BLANCHE TROULLIER
Educator. **Personal:** Born Nov 22, 1933, New Orleans; divorced; children: Louis Porter, II. **Educ:** Dillard U, BA 1955; Univ of So CA; Xavier U; So U. **Career:** Elementary school teacher, 15 years prior to becoming resource teacher. **Orgs:** Mem United Tchr of New Orleans; Nat Educ Assn; Am Fedn of Tchr; LA Educ Assn; Parent Tchr Assn Andrew Jackson Ele Sch; McDonogh #35 High; mem Nat PTA Grammeteus Alpha Kappa Sor 1954; Grace United Meth Ch Adm Bd; sec United Meth Women; sec Coun on Ministries mem Parents Aux Club BSA Troop 155. **Honors/Awds:** Granted key to city of Louisville KY 1968. **Business Addr:** 703 Carondelet St, New Orleans, LA.

PORTER, CAROL DENISE
Graphic designer. **Personal:** Born Mar 4, 1948, Washington, DC; daughter of Alma Dodson Porter and Wiley Waverly Porter. **Educ:** Howard Univ, attended 1966-67; Independent Study Tour European Capitals, 1970; Moore College of Art, BFA 1971; Sterling Institute, attended 1975; Hartford Graduate Ctr, attended 1976; Poynter Inst of Media Studies, attended 1986. **Career:** WJLA-TV7 Washington, graphic artist 1971-73; WBBM-TV2 Chicago, graphic artist 1973-75; WFSB-TV3 Hartford, art dir 1975-77; WDVM-TV9, asst art dir/graphic designer 1977-79; Needham Harper and Steers Advertising Falls Church, art dir/graphic designer 1979-80; Ketchum Advertising, art dir 1984-85; WashingtonPost, graphic designer 1980-84, 1985-. **Orgs:** Mem Alpha Kappa Alpha Sor; sec Natl Academy of TV Arts & Sciences; mem Capital Press Club; volunteer Family Place; freelance design/art director; mem Speakers Bureau Washington Post; mem Broadcast Designers Assoc; mem Soc of Newspaper Design; 2nd vice pres, Capital Press Club 1987-89; moderator/participant, Howard Univ Comm Conference: workshop on careers in newspaper communication 1988. **Honors/Awds:** Washington Art Directors Club Awds of Merit 1973, 79, 81, 83 (two); Emmy Awd Outstanding Individual Achievement in Scenic Design 1972; Awds of Excellence Chicago '75 Communications Collaborative Show for TV Spots 1975; bd of govs Washington Chap Natl Acad of TV Arts and Scis 1979; Awd of Merit Soc of Newspaper Design 1986; Award of Excellence "Page Design", Print Magazine 1988; Award of Excellence "Portfolio of 6 Page Designs", Society of Newspaper Design 1989; Award of Excellence "Page Design" Washington Art Directors Club 1989; Award of Excellence "Portfolio Page Design", Society of Newspaper Design, 1990; Award of Excellence "Page Design", Washington Metro Art Directors Club, 1990; Society of Newspaper Design, 2 Awards of Excellence: "Portfolio of 6 Business News Pages" and "Page Front Show Section," Bronze Award: "One Page Front," ("Summer"), Print Magazine Award: Award of Excellence for "Food" page for locally brewed beer ("Brewed Near Here"); Society of Newspaper Design Competition, National Design Contest, judge, 1993; Moore College of Art & Design, board of managers (appointed alumna), 1990-93, 1993-96. **Special Achievements:** Turner Elementary School Newspaper, DC, volunteer/community sponsor, 1993-94; Ellinston High School of Arts, DC, guest instructor, Design Class, 1994. **Home Addr:** 2242 Washington Ave, Silver Spring, MD 20910.

PORTER, CHARLES WILLIAM
Editor, publisher. **Personal:** Born Oct 6, 1939, Mobile, AL; son of Rosie Porter (deceased) and Quillie Porter (deceased); married Joyce A Wallace; children: Nikki, Terri, Michael, Stanley. **Educ:** Bishop State Jr Coll, AS 1960; AL State Univ, BS 1962; Univ of AL, MA 1970; Chicago City Coll, 1993; Alabama Interdenominational Seminary, Masters of Divinity, 1972. **Career:** Public school teacher 1962-68; Mobile Press Register, news reporter, 1968-69; Tougaloo College, Tougaloo, MS, dir of public relations, 1970-71; Northwestern Univ, sr publications editor 1971-74; Mobile Beacon, editor 1974-76; Inner City Printers, owner, 1977-; Bishop State Jr Coll, dir of public relations 1982-86; Inner City News, editor & publisher 1976-; Bishop State Jr Coll, instructor of Journalism 1984-87; Inner City Public Relations, relations consultant 1986-; past exec dir, Human Relations Comm; exec dir, Minority Tech & Entrepreneural Ctr, Bishop State Comm Coll, currently. **Orgs:** Founder & pres Media Coalition 1976-; chmn of bd OIC Mobile Area 1980-81; mem Sigma Delta Chi; Natl Assn of Black Journalist; Amer Coll Public Relations Assn, Educ Writers Assn; Natl Council of Coll Public Advisors; NAACP; Sickle Cell Rsch Found, Omega Psi Phi Fraternity Inc; Concerned Citizens for Police Reform, Chicago, Southern Christian Leadership Conf: YWCA (honorary); YMCA; Urban League. **Honors/Awds:** Natl, regional & local honors for establishing the Southern AL Task Force on Illiteracy; Numerous honors for community serv. **Business Addr:** Editor & Publisher, Inner City News & Printers, PO Box 1545, Mobile, AL 36633-1545.

PORTER, CLARENCE A.
Educator. **Personal:** Born Mar 19, 1939, McAlester, OK; son of Myrtle Porter; children: Richard, Cory. **Educ:** Portland State Univ, BS 1962; OR State Univ, MS 1964, PhD 1966. **Career:** OR State Univ, grad asst 1961-64, asst vet med 1964-66; Portland State Univ, asst prof 1966-70, exec asst to pres & assoc prof 1970-72; Univ of NH, asst v provost acad affairs 1972-76; State Univ of MN, assoc v chancellor acad affairs 1976-78; Phyllis Wheatley Comm Cntr, exec dir 1979-83; Cheyney Univ of PA, vice pres for acad affairs 1983-84; Montgomery Coll Takoma Park, MD, instructional dean 1985-. **Orgs:** Mem Sigma Xi; Helminthological Soc of Wash; National Council of Instructional Administrators; Natl Council of Black African American Affairs; Coll Management Programs, Carnegie Mellon, 1988; League of Innovation in the Comm Coll, Exec Leadership Inst, 1997. **Honors/Awds:** Summer Fellow LA State Univ 1968. **Business Addr:** Instructional Dean, Montgomery College, Takoma Park Campus, Takoma Park, MD 20912.

PORTER, CURTISS E.
Educator. **Personal:** Born Dec 29, 1939, Braddock, PA; divorced; children: Dennis, Janice, Natiata, Tajudeen, Lelle, Omar, Jolan. **Educ:** Univ Pgh, BA; Univ Pgh, PhD cand. **Career:** Univ Pittsburgh, chmn dept of black comm educ research

& devel; DBCERD/PITT, asso dir 1969-72; DBCERD-PITT, dir program devel 1972-74. **Orgs:** Chmn Reg 3 Nat Counc of Black Studies; consult Def Race Rels Inst; spl guest 6th Pan African Congress; mem Commn on Educ & Rsrch African Heritage Studies Assn; exec bd Nat Coun of Black Studies; mem Assn for the Study of Afro-Am Life & Hist; part Kuntu Writers Workshop; fdr Black Horizons Theatre; fdr Black Action Soc; mem Adv EST; mem EST Hunger Proj Com. **Military Serv:** USAF a/1c 1958-63.

PORTER, E. MELVIN
Attorney, businessman. **Personal:** Born May 22, 1930, Okmulgee, OK; son of Mary Cole Porter and Victor E. Porter; married Jewel, 1955; children: E Melvin II, Joel Anthony. **Educ:** Tennessee State Univ, BS, 1956; Vanderbilt Univ, LLB, 1959. **Career:** Oklahoma State Senate, senator; attorney and businessman, currently. **Orgs:** Oklahoma County Bar Assn; Oklahoma Bar Assn; American Bar Assn; American Judicature Society; life mem, NAACP; YMCA; Oklahoma City Chamber of Commerce; Sigma Rho Sigma; Kappa Alpha Psi. **Honors/Awds:** Honorary LLD, Shorter College, AR; Kappa of the Month. first black to serve in State Senate of Oklahoma. **Military Serv:** US Army, Cpl, 1948-52. **Business Addr:** Attorney, 2116 NE 23 St, Oklahoma City, OK 73111.

PORTER, ELLIS NATHANIEL
Clergyman. **Personal:** Born Apr 26, 1931, Sumter, SC; son of Frances Jenkins Porter and Nathaniel Porter. **Educ:** South Carolina State College, Orangeburg, SC, BS, 1958; Philadelphia Divinity School, Philadelphia, PA, STB, 1963; Howard Univ School of Divinity, Washington, DC, D Min, 1985. **Career:** Episcopal Diocese of North Carolina, Durham, NC, vicar/director of urban crisis program, 1966-72; Episcopal Diocese of Washington, Washington, DC, university chaplain, 1972-87; St Edward the Martyr Church, priest-in-residence, 1988-; Episcopal Church Center, New York, NY, coordinator/ministry in higher education, 1988-92; Episcopal Church Ctr, NYC; Staff Officer for Africa, 1992-94; Interim Rector of Church of St Mark, Head Master of St Mark's Day School, 1994-95; Canon at Trinity & St Philips Catheral, Newark, NJ, 1995-. **Orgs:** Afro-Anglican Steering Committee, 1991-; Bd mem Union Black & Epis; Angus Dun Fellowship Comm; Citz Comm on Adoption 1965-66; exec bd Citz antiPoverty Comm 1956-66; exec bd Better Hlth Found 1968-72; Black Sol Comm 1968-72; Smithsonian Inst Copr 1952-55; convenor, Council for Ecumenical Student Christian Ministry, 1990-. **Honors/Awds:** Appreciation Award, The Advisory Jones Student Ass, Howard Univ, 1978; EFMM Unit Award, Chateau De Bossey, Celigny, Switzerland, 1988; Union of Black Episcopalians Recognition Award, 1996. **Military Serv:** US Army, specialist 2, 1953-55. **Business Addr:** Clergyman, Canon Trinity & St Philips Catherdal, 24 Rector St, Newark, NJ 07102.

PORTER, GLORIA JEAN
Business administrator. **Personal:** Born Apr 15, 1951, Baltimore, MD; daughter of Lillian Porter and Percy Porter. **Educ:** Adelphi Univ, BSW (Summa Cum Laude) 1973; Univ of Illinois, MSW (Summa Cum Laude) 1974. **Career:** Univ of Mass Mental Health Service, therapist 1975-78; Univ of Southern Cal Counseling Serv, psychotherapist, asst dir, dir 1978-84; Univ of Southern Cal; Dataproducts Corp, employee assist mgr 1984-90; Los Angeles County, Employee Assistance Program, dir 1991-. **Orgs:** Mem bd of dir, Ebonics, Alcohol Info Ctr San Fernando Valley Council on Alcoholism, NAACP, Black Women's Forum, Black Women's Network, Black Agenda, Women in Mgmt, Amer Personnel & Guidance Assoc, NASW Reg of Clinical Soc Workers, Natl Assoc of Soc Workers, Assoc of Black Soc Workers; Natl Health Attitudes Research Project; Amer Personnel and Guidance Assn; NASW Register of Clinical Social Workers. **Business Addr:** Director, Employee Assistance Program, 2615 S Grand Ave, Room 502, Los Angeles, CA 90007.

PORTER, GRADY J.
Law enforcement official. **Personal:** Born Sep 1, 1918, Carrollton, GA; son of Amandie Porter and James Porter; married Marcella M Larriere; children: Liliane, J Anthony, Sylviane, Patricia. **Career:** Dem Ward Chairman, 4 yrs; State Convention, delegate 30 yrs; Oldsmobile Gen Motors Corp, retired employee; Ingham Co, commr 1967-; Law & Cts Comm, chmn protem; Ingham County, bd of commr chairperson; City of Lansing, police commissioner, currently. **Orgs:** Chmn Fair Prac Anti-Discrim Com Local 652 UAW 17 yrs; Unit chmn Local 652 UAW 1952-54; transportation officer US Zone Germany UNRRA & ORT 1945-48; mem MI Assn Co; NACO; Capitol Lodge AF & AM Prince Hall; life mem NAACP; attended & participated in all the NAACP Natl Conv for the last 17 yrs; mem Union Baptist Ch; Boy Scouts; Urban League; mem Lansing Human Relations Comm 1952-53; spl comm on Sch Needs & Sights 1953; NABCO; chairperson Laymen League Union Baptist Church; mall advisory bd Mayor committee; life member NAACP; Michigan State Conference, branches treasurer, 6 years, 3rd vp, 4 years; bd mem, RSVP Lansing; mem, 7 Block Devel Comm, Capital Area, West Lansing; VAW; PTA; KDP. **Honors/Awds:** Nominated Outstanding Man of Yr 1966; 1st Black elected official in history of Ingham Co; Fredrick Douglass Awd 1986; special recognition to Black History Ingham County housing; Outstanding Community Serv Awd NAACP; Ingham County Democratic Party, 20 year elected county commr 1988, 1990; Ingham County Bd Commrs Service Award 1988; National Association of Black County Officials Distinguished Service Award 1990. **Special Achievements:** Ingham County Bldg, Lansing, MI, renamed in honor for outstanding contributions to community by Ingham County Board of Commissioners, 1992; 1st Black Unit Chairperson, Local 652 UAW Oldsmobile, Fair Practice Comm; Graduation Class Speaker, Sexton High School Breslin Center MSU, 1995. **Military Serv:** US Army S/Sgt, four invasions, five battle stars, 1941-45. **Home Addr:** 745 W Lenawee, Lansing, MI 48915.

PORTER, HENRY LEE
Clergyman. **Personal:** Born Jan 2, 1948, Sarasota, FL; son of Hazel Elkins Porter and Lee Ernest Porter; married Cynthia Elayne Johnson, Oct 23, 1976; children: Henry II, Etienne, Tsadok, Zacchur. **Educ:** Florida A&M University, BS, 1969; Yale University, doctoral studies, 1969-71. **Career:** Florida A&M University, professor, mathematics, 1973-75; Henry L Porter Evangelistic Assn, president, founder, 1971-; Westcoast School for Human Development, principal, founder, 1981-; Trinity College of Ministerial Arts, visiting professor, 1985-; Black Action Magazine, publisher, 1986-; Henry L. Porter Nursery Primary School, Takum, Nigeria, West Africa, 1990-; Westcoast Theological Seminary, president, 1989-; HL Porter School of music, president, currently. **Orgs:** Kappa Alpha Psi Fraternity, life mem, 1967-, president, 1968-69; Alpha Kappa Mu, president, 1968-69; American Assn of University Professors, 1973-; Math Assn of America, 1973-; Yale Club, 1989-; Bobby Jones Gospel, board member, 1989-; Advisory Bd on Education for Country of Nigeria, board member, 1993; Westcoast Gospel Chorus of Florida, founder, 1969. **Honors/Awds:** Harvard University, Harvard Prize Book, 1964; Alpha Kappa Mu, Scholar of the Year, 1968; Ford Foundation, Doctoral Fellowship in Mathematics, 1969; Intl Conference of Upcoming Christian Leaders, US Delegate to Singapore, 1988; Sarasota Magazine, one of The 100 Most Popular People in Sarasota, 1993; Ebony Man Magazine, Men Give Back to the Community, 1993; Honorary Degrees: United Bible College, DLit, 1986; Trinity College of Ministerial Arts, Nigeria, DDr, 1989. **Special Achievements:** Author, publications include: Word of the Lord, 1979; First Steps in Christ, 1987; Healing, A Gift from God, 1988; Child of the Thought, 1989; Higher Thoughts and Peaceful Ways, 1990; Faces of Love, 1990; Therapy, 1990; Forgiveness Manual, 1990; Duties of an Assistant, 1991; How to Start a Prayer Group, 1991; Africa Alive, 1993; featured: Westcoast School, "Street Stories with Ed Bradley," CBS-TV, 1993. **Business Addr:** Founder, President, Henry L Porter Evangelistic Assn, Westcoast Center, 403 N Washington Blvd, Sarasota, FL 34236, (813)365-7543.

PORTER, JAMES H.
Educator. **Personal:** Born Nov 11, 1933, Portchester, NY; divorced; children: Michael Brandon, Adrienne Michelle, Lynn Sharon. **Educ:** Renselaer Polytechnic Inst, BChE 1955; MIT, ScD 1963. **Career:** UV Technologies Inc, chmn/ceo, 1994-; Energy and Environmental Engineering Inc, chmn/ceo, 1994-96, pres, 1979-94; Energy Resources Co Inc, vice pres, energy division, 1976-79; MIT, assoc prof, chem engineering; Energy Resources Inc, consultant 1974-; MA Inst Tech, assoc prof 1971-76; Abcor, mgr computer application design 1967-72; Cornell Univ, visiting lecturer 1970; Chevron, sr research engineer 1963-67. **Orgs:** Visiting staff mem Elect Systems Lab 1966-67; engr Exxn 1955-58; mem Am Inst Chem Engrs; United Comm Devel; MIT Alumnit Adv Coun; vchmn SocProfessional Advancement Black Chemists & Chem Engrs; science advisory board, USEPA, 1976-81; science advisory committee, Great Lakes-Mid Atlantic Hazardous Waste Research Consortium, 1993-; science advisory committee, Ohio Univ Consortium on Coal Research, 1991-; consult NIH; Num Publs Patent on Gas Well Sulfur Removal by Diffusion through Polymeric Membranes 1970. **Honors/Awds:** Jesse Smith Noyes found fellowship 1953,54; Chevron Research Fellowship 1962; outstanding professor award MIT 1974,75. **Business Addr:** c/o AICE, 345 E 47th St, Attn: Member Records, New York, NY 10017.

PORTER, JOHN T.
Business executive. **Personal:** Born Feb 21, 1941, Brady, TX; children: John Jr, Christian (deceased). **Educ:** IL Coll, BA 1968; Sangamon State U, MA 1971. **Career:** IL Bell Telephone Co, various 1968-79, dist mgr training 1979-80, dist mgr AA/EEO 1980-90, dir, human resources, 1990-91; Power Process Engineering Inc, vice pres, general manager, currently. **Orgs:** Chairperson, Illinois Planning Council on Developmental Disabilities, 1984-; brd mem IL State Assn Retd Citiz 1984-; pres Hope Schl 1975-81; mem Disbl Am Vet's 1963-; board member, Illinois Self Sufficiency Trust, 1989-; board member, The Hope School Trust, 1989-; Natl Assn of Developmental Disability Councils, 1994. **Military Serv:** US Army, Sgt, 3 yrs, 7 mos. **Home Addr:** 190 S Wood Dale Rd, Unit 905, Wood Dale, IL 60191. **Business Addr:** Vice Pres/General Manager, Process Power Engineering, Inc, 18003 Skypark S, Ste J, Irvine, CA 92714.

PORTER, JOHN W.
Educational administrator. **Personal:** Born Aug 13, 1931, Ft Wayne, IN; son of Ola Mae Porter and James Porter; widowed. **Educ:** Albion Coll, Albion MI, BA, 1953; Michigan State Univ, East Lansing MI, MA, 1957, PhD, 1962. **Career:** Lansing Public Schools, Lansing MI, counselor 1953-58; Michigan Dept Public Instruction, consultant, 1958-61; Michigan Dept HE Asst Auth, dir, 1961-66; Michigan Dept of HE, assoc supt, 1966-69, state supt, 1969-79; Eastern Michigan Univ, Ypsilanti MI, pres, 1979-89; Detroit Publ Schools, gen supt 1989-91; Urban Educ Alliance, Inc, chief exec officer 1989-. **Orgs:** Chmn Natl Sel Comm for Outstanding HS Seniors sponsored by NASSP/Cent III 1981; chmn AASCU Task Force on Excellence in Educ 1983; chmn Coll Ent Exam Bd NY 1984; apptd by Sec of HEW Jos Califano to the Natl Adv Cncl on Soc Svcs; chmn Amer Assoc of State Colls & Univs Task Force on Excellence in Educ 1984-86; mem MI Council for the Humanities; mem holiday commn MI Martin Luther King 1986; mem Natl Commn for Coop Educ 1986, Governor's Blue Ribbon Commn on Welfare Reform 1986-87; vice chmn Natl Commn on the Future of State Colls & Univs 1986. **Honors/Awds:** Marcus Foster Distinguished Educator Award Natl Alliance of Black Sch Educators' Conv 1979; Cert of Recog Alpha Kappa Alpha Sorority Eastern MI Univ 1979; State Admin Bd Ten-Year Serv Resolu State Cap Lansing, MI 1979; Educator of the Decade Award MI Assn of State and Fed Program Spec 1979; MI Pub Sch Cert of Award Pontiac Pub Sch 1979; Res of Serv as Supt of Pub Instr Metro Detroit Alliance of Black Sch Educators 1979; Anthony Wayne Award Coll of Educ Wayne State Univ 1979; Distinguished Alumni Award MI State Univ 1979; Recong Award for Contrib to Educ Wayne Cnty Comm Coll 1979; Momento for Serv as Supt of Pub Inst Coll of Educ Alumni Assn Wayne St Univ 1979; Cert of Commendation Educ Serv Award MI Cong of Parents Teachers and Students 1979; President's Award as Disting Educator Natl Alliance of Black School Educators 1977. **Special Achievements:** Numerous publications include: "The Counselor as Educationalist," The Personnel and Guidance Journal, 1982; "Why Minimum Competency Now?" JC Penney Forum, 1980; "Education, The Challenging Frontier," Colorado Journal of Educ Research, 1976; "Better Education Through Accountability, Research, Program Budgeting," Michigan Challenge, 1973. **Business Addr:** Chief Executive Officer, Urban Education Alliance, 2000 Huron River Dr, Ypsilanti, MI 48197.

PORTER, KARL HAMPTON
Musician, conductor, educator. **Personal:** Born Apr 25, 1939, Pittsburgh, PA; son of Naomi Mitchell Givens and Reginald Porter; divorced; children: Marc, Turin, Nadia, Kenneth, Michael, Kelly, Kevin. **Educ:** Carnegie-Mellon; Peabody Conservatory; Juilliard Sch of Music; Domaine Sch of Conductors; Fordham Univ; State Univ of New York, New York, NY, 1986-87. **Career:** Baltimore Symphony, conductor 1971-72; Massapequa Symphony, conductor 1975-78; Park West Symphony, conductor; Harlem Philharmonic, conductor; NYCTC/CUNY, instructor; Josephine Baker - Musical Director/Cond, 1974; St Thomas the Apostle, choir dir, 1988-91; NY State Council on the Arts, consultant, 1990; Harlem Music Society, New York, NY, dir, 1990-91. **Orgs:** Pres Finale Productions 1978-87; Sickle Cell 1970-; Arts & Letters 1974-; Dance Theatre of Harlem 1971-78; coach, NAACP, Act-So, 1988-91. **Honors/Awds:** Natl Endowment Grant. **Home Addr:** 425 Central Park West, New York, NY 10025. **Business Addr:** PO Box 445, New York, NY 10025.

PORTER, KEVIN
Professional basketball player (retired). **Personal:** Born Apr 17, 1950, Chicago, IL; married Cleota; children: Kevin, Kandace, Kelly. **Career:** Baltimore Bullets, 1973, Capital Bullets, 1974, Washington Bullets, 1975, 1980-81, 1983, Detroit Pistons, 1976-78, New Jersey Nets, 1978, Detroit Pistons, 1979. **Honors/Awds:** Led NBA in assists three times; holds leag record for assists in one Game (29) 1978; holds NBA assist record 1099 in a season 1978-79; Bullets assist record 650 in one seasn & 80 average 1974-75; holds Bullets career record 59 average during playoffs.

PORTER, KWAME JOHN R.
Clergyman. **Personal:** Born Apr 2, 1932, Mineral Springs, AR; married June Carol McIntosh; children: John Thomas, Joseph Dubois, Julia Magdilene, Jessica Retha, Jorja Angela, Jerrianne Carol. **Educ:** IO Wesleyan Coll, BA 1959; Garrett Evan Theol Sem, MDiv 1962; Union Grad Sch, PhD 1975. **Career:** Christ United Meth Ch, pastor 1962-71 & 1979-95; Urban Young Life, vice pres 1974-79; Chicago Cntr Black Religious Studies, dir 1971-74; Sch of Human Dignity, dir, 1967-70; Fellowship United Methodist Church, pastor, 1996-; National Urban Black Church Growth Institute, Chicago, dean. **Orgs:** Adj prof Garrett Theol Sem; mem Intl Black Writers 1980; pres Student Assn Garrett Theol Sem 1961; community trainer, JCPT/CAPS, Chicago Alliance for Neighborhood Safety, 1995-96; founding mem, Operation Breadbasket PUSH, 1966. **Honors/Awds:** Pub book "Dating Habits of Young Black Ams" 1979; pub articles best black sermons Vol II Judson Press 1979; pub articles Metro Ministry David C Cook Pub 1979; Three awards for work in 7th District's CAPS projects; Alumnus of the year, 1996 Iowa Wesleyan College, 1994-95. **Special Achievements:** Research writer, proposal developer, chair, Englewood's New Village, EZEC

project, 1994-95; author, "The Dating Habits of Young Black Americans," 1979; Pending publications "Black Male Violence," 1997; "How Blackfolk and Others Die," 1997; "Basic Training Manual for 21st Century Christians.". **Military Serv:** AUS sgt 1954-57. **Business Addr:** Pastor, Fellowship United Methodist Church, 447 W 120th St, Chicago, IL 60628.

PORTER, LINSEY
Mayor. **Personal:** Born 1954; married Patricia. **Career:** Colonial Life and Accidnet Insurance Co, sales dir; City of Highland Park, councilman, 1983-87, council pres, 1987-91, mayor, 1991-. **Business Addr:** Mayor, City of Highland Park, 30 Gerald Ave, Highland Park, MI 48203, (313)252-0022.

PORTER, LIONEL
Business executive. **Personal:** Born Jan 26, 1943, Canton, MS. **Educ:** IN State Univ, BA 1966; Univ of CT, MA, ABD 1975, JD 1985. **Career:** Arsenal Tech HS, english teacher 1966-68; Aetna Life & Casualty, mgmt trainee 1968-69; Hartford Public HS; english teacher 1969-70; Univ of Hartford, instr/am lit 1975-78; Univ Conn Health Ctr, title XX cons, training dir 1978-. **Orgs:** Vp Blue Hills Civic Assoc 1978-80; participant Leadership Greater Hartford 1980-81; bd mem Community Council of Capitol Reg 1981-82, Amer Heart Assoc 1984-. **Honors/Awds:** Outstanding Young Men in Amer Awd; EPDA Fellowship Univ of CT 1970-75.

PORTER, MIA LACHONE
Client computing analyst. **Personal:** Born Jan 21, 1965, Birmingham, AL; daughter of Dorothy Rogers Porter and John T Porter. **Educ:** University of Alabama-Birmingham, 1982-85; Alabama State University, BS, 1988; Samford University, 1991-. **Career:** Southern Co. Services, client computing analyst I, currently. **Orgs:** Alpha Kappa Psi Professional business Fraternity, 1988; Alpha Kappa Alpha Sorority Inc, 1987-; Natl Management Association, 1989-; financial secretary, American Association of Blacks in Energy, 1990-91. **Business Addr:** Client Computing Analyst, Southern Company Services, 64 Perimeter Center E, Atlanta, GA 30346.

PORTER, MICHAEL ANTHONY
Product design engineer. **Personal:** Born Sep 4, 1968, Bronx, NY; son of Ryland & Delrose Porter; married Tanya Porter, Jul 28, 1990. **Educ:** Howard Univ, BSME, 1993. **Career:** Ford Motor Co, production engineer, 1987-91; Environmental Protection Agency, envr engineer, 1992-93; Martin Marietta, product design engr, 1993-. **Orgs:** National Society of Black Engineers, professional advisor, 1992-; Engineering Explorer Post, chairman, 1993-. **Business Addr:** Product Design Engineer, Martin Marietta Control Systems, 600 Main Street, MD R29, Johnson City, NY 13790-1888, (607)770-2100.

PORTER, MICHAEL LEROY
Archives administrator. **Personal:** Born Nov 23, 1947, Newport News, VA; son of Doretha Bradley Porter and Leroy Porter. **Educ:** VA State Univ, BA, (hon) sociology 1969; Atlanta Univ, MA, hist 1972; Leonardo DaVinci Acad, Rome, Italy, MCP Contem 1983-84; Emory Univ, PhD hist/Amer studies 1974; Thomas Nelson Community Coll, cert crim justice 1981; US Armed Forces Staff Coll, Norfolk VA, US Pres Appt, 1987. **Career:** WA State Univ, asst prof of history, black studies prog 1974-75; Mohegan Comm Coll, Dept History lectr 1975-76; Newport News VA, asst education coord, education comp, target proj prog 1977; Hampton Univ, asst prof history 1977-80; NC Mutual Ins Co, life ins underwriter 1980-81; Mullins Prot Serv VA Bch, private investigator, 1981-83; Amer Biographical Inst Raleigh, media free-lancer 1984-85, publications dir/deputy governor 1985-; Old Dominion Univ, Norfolk VA, consultant 1985; Michael Porter Enterprises International, president, founder, 1985-88; Intl Biographical Ctr, Cambridge England, deputy dir gen 1986-. **Orgs:** Life patron World Inst of Achievement 1985; curator "Michael L Porter Historical & Literary Collection"; World Literary Acad 1984-85; World Biographical Hall of Fame 1985; Federal Braintrust, 1990; Intl Advisory Council, 1989-; African American Hall of Fame, 1994; Elite International, 1992; Phi Beta Kappa; Intl Academy of Intellectuals, 1993; Famous Poet's Society, 1996; chairman, US Selective Service Bd #32, 1986-92; chief delegate, Intl Congress on Arts & Communications, Nairdgi, Kenya, 1990. **Honors/Awds:** 1st Black Concert Pianist to play Carnegie Hall, 1963; Lyon Dissertation Prize, 1974; Ebony Magazine, Eligible Bachelor, 1975; Outstanding Black, 1992; Hero, 1992; International Honors Cup, 1992; Abira Genius Grant, 1992; World Greetings, 1992; Pioneer Award, 1992; Great American, 1991; World Intellectual, 1993; Golden Academy Award, 1991; One of 500 Leaders of Influence in the 20th Century; Intl Hall of Leaders, Amer Biographical Inst, 1988; participant (exhibit), DuSable Museum of Black History, 1988; honoree, Intl Exhibit, Singapore, Malaysia, 1988; Outstanding Man of the World, Ormiston Palace, Tasmania, Australia, 1989; Exhibit, Intl Music Museum, London, ENG, 1989; Michael Porter Poetry Exhibit, Internet Intl Poetry Hall of Fame, 1997-2002; Lecture, Oxford Univ, Oxford, ENG, 1997; 20th Century Award for Achievement, 1990; Black History Maker, 1992; International Man of the Year, 1992; Most Admired Person of the Decade, 1990-99; US Congress, Certificate of Appreciation, 1991; Honorary US Congressman, 1993; Hampton History Center, Historical Marker, 1992; Appearances before US President's Council of Economic Advisors & Senate Finance Committee, 1992; US Presidential Medal of Freedom, 1993. **Special Achievements:** Television Programs: Cited On World News Tonight; Hard Copy; 60 Minutes; Current Affairs; Entertainment Tonight; CBS Evening News; NBC Nightly News; Film: The Making of Black Atlanta, 1974; 1st Black Elected to Intl Academy of Intellectuals, Paris, France, 1993; Radio: Empire State Bldg Broadcasting Ctr, WRIN, 1997; Publications: Ebony, Jet, Intl, Digest, Tacent. **Military Serv:** US Army pfc, 1969-71; Natl Defense Medal, 1971; Certificate of Appreciation Vietnam Vets Natl Medal, 1986; Good Conduct Medal, 1971. **Home Addr:** 3 Adrian Cir, Hampton, VA 23669-3814.

PORTER, OTHA L.
Educator, city official (retired). **Personal:** Born Apr 2, 1928, Indianapolis, IN; son of Addie J Porter and Theodore Porter; married Ruth; children: Theodore C, Otha Jr, Lola Geneva. **Educ:** IN Univ, BS 1949, MS 1950, EdD 1970. **Career:** Langston HS, teacher 1950-51; Ft Valley State Coll, teacher 1951; Carver Elem School, instr 1954-57; Pulaski Jr HS, asst princ 1957-58, 1968-69; Drew Elem School, prin 1958-66; Horace Mann HS, asst prin 1966-67; Edison HS, prin 1967-68; IN Univ, admin asst 1969-70; Gary Publ Schools, suprv 1970-71, dist supt 1971-72; E Orange NJ Publ Schools, supt 1972-82; Plainfield NJ HS, science suprv, 1982-84, vice principal 1984-88; Hubbard Middle School, principal, 1988-; Plainfield Bd of Ed, NJ, director of buildings & grounds, 1990-94. **Orgs:** Commissioner Northwest Div IN State Teachers Association; Northwest IN Association Elem School Princ; Association Gary Elem Princ; IN State Teachers Association; NJ Ed Consortium, Title I State Adv Council; E Orange Publ Library Bd Trustees; NJ Schoolmasters Club; Phi Delta Kappa; Kappa Kappa Psi; NEA; Association of Childhood Ed; Intl Reading Association; life mem IN Univ Alumni Association; bd treasurer Gary Legal Aid Society; bd sec St Timothy Community Ch; Alpha Phi Alpha Frat; NAACP; bd pres Gary Sanitary Dist; elder Elmwood Presbyterian Church East Orange NJ 1988-; elder, member of session, Elmwood Presbyterian Church 1989-; consultant: President Johnson's National Advisory Council on the Education of Disadvantaged Youth, HEW; Bureau of Educational Personnel Devt, USOE; Rockefeller Foundation's Superintendents Training Program; Essex County Division of Corrections, NJ. **Special Achievements:** Author: "The Need for Minimum State Standards," The Sunday Star Ledger, Mar 14, 1976; "Contracted School: An Instrument of Educational Change," The Journal of Negro Education, Vol XXXX, Num 3, p 233-239, Summer 1971, numerous others. **Military Serv:** Instructor SE Signal Sch Camp Gordon GA 1951-53.

PORTER, ROY LEE
Musician (retired), composer, author. **Personal:** Born Jul 30, 1923, Walsenburg, CO; son of Charlotte Chapell Porter and William Nelson Porter; married Ernestine Cecilia Collins, Jan 1957 (divorced); children: Daryl Roy. **Educ:** Wiley College, attended, 2 years. **Career:** Drummer, band leader with Howard McGhee, Charlie Parker, Dexter Gordon, Perez Prado, Louis Jordan, Earl Bostic, numerous others, 1945-49; Roy Porter Big Band, 1948-50; Rotine Music Co, composer, owner, currently. **Orgs:** AFM, Local 47. **Honors/Awds:** Black Music History of Los Angeles, by Mayor Tury Bradley; Certificate of Appreciation, International Assn of Jazz Educators, 1995; Certificate, Advancement of African American Music Culture, Service Employees Intl Union Locals 660 and 347. **Special Achievements:** Recording with Charlie Parker: Ornithology/A Night in Tunisia, Dial; author, with David Keller, There and Back, the Roy Porter Story, Louisiana State University Press, 1988; composed "Lonesome Mood," million seller hit for Friends of Distinction, 1969. **Military Serv:** US Air Force, pvt, 1941-44. **Home Addr:** 2931 Ridgeley Dr, Los Angeles, CA 90016, (213)938-9200.

PORTER, RUFUS
Professional football player. **Personal:** Born May 18, 1965, Amite, LA; married Anita; children: Atina, Rufus Jr. **Educ:** Southern University, attended. **Career:** Seattle Seahawks, linebacker, 1988-94; New Orleans Saints, 1995-96; Tampa Bay Buccaneers, 1997-. **Honors/Awds:** Pro Bowl, 1988, 1989. **Business Addr:** Professional Football Player, Tampa Bay Buccaneers, One Buccaneer Place, Tampa, FL 33607, (813)870-2700.

PORTER, SCOTT E.
Dentist. **Personal:** Born Nov 15, 1924, Humboldt, TN. **Educ:** Univ of Toledo Coll of Arts & Sci, BS 1949; OH State U, BS Scndry Educ 1952; OH State Univ Coll of Dentistry, DDS 1957. **Career:** Dentist, pvt prac; Toledo Health Dept, asst to dir of Dental Serv 1960-66. **Orgs:** Mem Bd Mgrs YMCA 1958-; life mem NAACP; mem Am & OH Dental Assn; Toledo Dental Soc; OH State Univ Alumnae Assn; Univ of Toledo Alumnae Assn; life mem Kappa Alpha Psi Frat; Rep Party; Mason; Shriner; mem Worldwide Sportsmen's Club. **Honors/Awds:** Recip Spl Award for Support of YMCA Serv 1974, 75, 76, 77. **Home Addr:** 1023 Lincoln Ave, Toledo, OH 43607.

PORTER, TERRY
Professional basketball player. **Personal:** Born Apr 8, 1963, Milwaukee, WI. **Educ:** Univ of Wisconsin at Stevens Point, Stevens Point, WI, 1981-85. **Career:** Portland Trail Blazers, guard, 1985-95; Minnesota Timberwolves, 1995-. **Honors/Awds:** J Walter Kennedy Citizenship Award, 1993. **Business Addr:** Professional Basketball Player, Minnesota Timberwolves, 600 1st Ave N, Minneapolis, MN 55403, (612)337-3865.

PORTIS, KATTIE HARMON (JESSIE KATE HARMON)
Organization executive. **Personal:** Born Oct 28, 1942, Kinterbish, AL; married Jesse; children: Dawn, Luther, Torris, James, Faye, Raymond. **Educ:** Franconia Coll, BA 1976; Antioch Coll, MA, Human Service Mgmt. **Career:** Women Inc Dorchester MA, founder/exec dir; Concilio Drug Program, counselor 1974; Stamford Outreach Proj Turnabout, 1973; 1st Residental Drug-Free Program for Women & Children Who are Abusing Alcohol or Drugs, founder, 1973; Community Coordinator/founder, Boston Women and Aids Risk Network, 1987-present. **Orgs:** Consultant, Women & Health 1975; Northeastern Univ 1974; Research & Demonstratn Project, 1975; Treatmnt conf for Women 1976; mem 3rd World Womens Caucus 1974; mem Policy Advisory Bd; chmn Boston Univ Screening Bd; mem Mayor Coordinating Council on Drug Abuse; MA Comm Children & Youth Advisory Bd. **Honors/Awds:** Certificate Yale Univ 1973; Testimony US House of Reps Select Comm on Narcotics Abuse & Control Task Force on Women & Drug Abuse 1980; presentation "Lack of Serv for Women" Sec of State Patricia Harris 1980; Hero Award, Boston Parents Paper; Abigal Adams Award; Metro Boston Alive Leadership Award; Dept of Public Health Leadership Award; Office for Children, Outstanding Service for Children. **Business Addr:** New England Medical Center, 750 Washington Street, Box 790 Social Work Services, Boston, MA 02111.

PORTLOCK, CARVER A.
Educational administrator. **Personal:** Born Jun 8, 1934, Muskogee, OK. **Educ:** Bethune Cookman Coll, BA, religion/philosophy 1955; Syracuse U, grad study, 1956-57. **Career:** Bethune Cookman Coll, asst instr speech & drama 1955-56; Dade Cty Jvnl Ct/Miami, cnslr of dlnqnt boys 1959-61; CME Church Paine Coll, admin asst/bdlay actvts 1960-62; Natl Alumni Assoc/Bethune Cookman Coll, exec sec 1962-66; SmithKline Corp, information services coord, 1966-68, mgr community rels, 1968-88; Bethune-Cookman College, Northeast Regional Office, director, 1988-. **Orgs:** Pres Natl Alumni Assoc/Bethune Cookman Coll 1982-84; mem bd of dirs Big Brother/Big Sister Assoc 1981-. **Honors/Awds:** United Negro Coll Fund Achvmnt Awrd 1984; Cmnty Serv Awd Berean Inst 1983; Professional Serv Awd Crisis Intrvntn Network 1981; Hon LLD Bethune-Cookman Coll 1986; Orthodox Catholic Archdiocese of Philadelphia, Honorary LHD, 1985. **Military Serv:** US Army, 1957-59. **Business Addr:** Director, Northeast Regional Office, Bethune-Cookman College, Philadelphia, PA 19144.

POSEY, ADA
Government official. **Career:** The White House, deputy assistant and director of general services, currently. **Business Addr:** Deputy Asst, Director of Office Admin-General Services, The White House, 1600 Pennsylvania Ave, NW, Washington, DC 20500, (202)456-1414.

POSEY, BRUCE KEITH
Regulatory counsel. **Personal:** Born Mar 22, 1952, Baton Rouge, LA. **Educ:** Univ of OR, BS 1970-74; Univ of MI, JD 1974-77. **Career:** US West Communications; Pacific Northwest Bell; Stoel Rives Boley Fraser & Wyse, attorney 1977-; Urban League of Portland, dir 1979-; Martin Luther King Jr Scholarship Fund of OR, pres 1979-. **Orgs:** Mem ACLU 1978-; sec OR State Bar Affirmative Action Steering Com 1979-; mem Assn of OR Black Lawyers 1979-. **Business Addr:** US West Communications, 1801 California St #5100, Denver, CO 80202.

POSEY, DEBORAH
Communications executive. **Personal:** Born Dec 16, 1949, Detroit, MI; daughter of James & Kathleen Parker; divorced; children: Kelly M McGee, Raymond Posey Jr. **Educ:** Wayne State University, BA, 1975. **Career:** Business Communications, sales mgr, 1982-83; Frontier, supervisor customer service, 1984-90, supervisor credit collection, 1990-94, senior mgr of credit collections, 1994-96, vp credit and collections, rev protection, 1996-. **Orgs:** NACM, 1990-; WTDE; National Association of Toll Fraud Managers. **Business Addr:** Frontier Communications, 20 Oak Hollow, Ste 210, Southfield, MI 48034, (810)386-8603.

POSEY, EDWARD W.
Psychiatrist. **Personal:** Born May 29, 1927, Youngstown, OH; son of Margie King Posey and Alex Posey; married Fanny Berryman; children: Bruce, Ada, Michael. **Educ:** Ohio State Univ, 1944-48; Meharry Medical Coll, MD 1952; Univ of Minnesota, Psychiatry 1965. **Career:** Minneapolis VA Medical Center, dir

day hospital 1965-71, chief psychiatry serv 1971-79, chief outpatient psychiatry 1979-; Univ of Minnesota, psychiatrist, asst prof 1965-. **Orgs:** Const Pilot City Health Center 1969-; chmn minority studies program comm Univ of Minnesota Medical School 1971-; Sigma Pi Phi; Natl Medical Assn. **Honors/Awds:** Fellow Amer Psychiatric Assn 1972; diploma Amer Bd of Psychiatry/Neurology 1968; examiner Amer Bd of Psychiatry/Neurology. **Military Serv:** USNR lieutenant 1953-55. **Home Addr:** 2808 W Highland Dr, Burnsville, MN 55337. **Business Addr:** Chief, Outpatient Psychiatry, Minneapolis VA Medical Center, Minneapolis, MN 55417.

POSEY, RONALD ANTHONY
Architect. **Personal:** Born Feb 19, 1953, San Diego, CA. **Educ:** Southern Univ, BA (magna cum laude) 1976; Univ of CA-Berkeley, MA (with highest honors) 1978. **Career:** Pacific Gas & Elec, summer inst 1974; Perkins & James, internship 1975-76; Burns & McDonnell, project architect 1978-83, project mgr 1983-. **Orgs:** Career awareness Urban League 1979-82; educ comm Amer Inst of Arch 1980; program comm of architects 1982; pres Southern Univ Alumni Assoc KCMO 1982-87; bd of dirs Clymer Comm Ctr 1983-87; mem Urban League 1986, Legislative Action 1987; cultural arts presentor KCMO; bd of dirs Euphrates Art Gallery; mem Alpha Kappa Mu Natl Honor Soc. **Honors/Awds:** Amer Inst of Architects Medal of Excellence 1976; cultural and artistic production presentations Gentlemen of Distinction 1981-87; Black Achiever in Business& Industry Southern Christian Leadership Conf 1982; Centurion Leadership Develop Kansas City Chamber of Commerce 1983; Urban Design Publication Baton Rouge LA; Man of the Yr Gentlemen of Distinction Civic Inc Kansas City 1986. **Business Addr:** Architectural Project Manager, Burns & McDonnell, 4800 East 63rd St, Kansas City, MO 64141.

POST, H. CHRISTIAN. **See PANDYA, HARISH C.**

POSTEN, WILLIAM S.
Judge. **Personal:** Born Mar 10, 1931, E Moline, IL; son of Aquilla Teague and Vernie Teague; married Pauline Ann; children: Karen, Scott, David, Elaine, Melissa. **Educ:** Minneapolis Coll Law, BSL 1953; Wm Mitchell Coll Law, JD 1959. **Career:** US Govt SS Admin, 1960-61, asst cty attny 1961-73; Hennepin Cty, mun ct judge 1973-76; Minneapolis Dist Court, judge 1976-. **Orgs:** Past mem, adv bd Turning Point; adv bd Genesis II; adv bd Salvation Army; mrm Amer, MN & Hennepin Cty Bar Assoc, Amer Assoc Black Lawyers, NAACP, Amer Leg; former Comm Health & Welfare Cty; mem Met Minneapolis March of Dimes. **Military Serv:** Mil Serv 1953-55. **Business Addr:** Judge, District Court of Minneapolis, Hennepin Co Gvt Cntr, 18 Fl Courts Tower, Minneapolis, MN 55487.

POSTON, CARL
Attorney, sports agent. **Personal:** Born in Detroit, MI. **Educ:** Fisk University, BS degrees in mathematics and business (with honors), 1977; Wayne State University, JD. **Career:** McKenzie & Poston, managing partner; Professional Sports Planning, Inc, currently. **Honors/Awds:** NCAA All-America tennis player. **Special Achievements:** Negotiated an unprecedented thirteen-year, $68 million dollar contract for Orlando Magic star Anfernee Hardaway. **Business Addr:** Sports Agent, Professional Sports Planning, Inc, 909 Fannin, Ste 2090, Houston, TX 77010, (713)659-2255.

POSTON, CARL C., JR.
Attorney. **Personal:** Born Oct 13, 1921, Memphis; married Thelma Kirkland; children: Carl, Keith, Kevin, Craig. **Educ:** LeMoyne Coll, BA 1942; Univ Training Ctr Florence Italy, 1945; Wayne St U, Law Degree 1950. **Career:** Attorney, self-emplyd; Saginaw City Cncl, 1970-73; Mayor Pro Tem, 1971-73; Asst Co Prosecutor, 1966-68; Human Relatns, 1961-68; Civil Rights Referee, 1967-70. **Orgs:** Mem Fraternities; Press Club; MI St Bar Grievnc Referee 1972; St Bar Econ Com 1969; Workmens Compenstn Sec 1960; Negligence Sec 1960-; St Bar Legisltv Com 1972-73; mem & past pres Saginaw Co Youth Protectn Cncl 1962-; vice pres Big Brothers 1966-67; treas & mem OIC Metropolitan Saginaw 1968-; mem Alpha Phi Alpha Frat; city rep Saginaw Co Bd of Supervis 1960-66, 68-70; past pres Frontiers 1963. **Honors/Awds:** Outstndg Servc as mem chrmn NAACP; award C of C civic respnsblty; Frontiersman of Yr 1968. **Military Serv:** US Army, sgt tech, 1943-46. **Business Addr:** PO Box 1749, Saginaw, MI 48605.

POSTON, KEVIN
Attorney, sports agent. **Personal:** Born in Saginaw, MI. **Educ:** Fisk University, BA in business administration (magna cum laude), 1981; Thurgood Marshall School of Law, Texas Southern University, JD. **Career:** Attorney; Professional Sports Planning, Inc, currently. **Special Achievements:** Negotiated an unprecedented thirteen-year, $68 million dollar contract for Orlando Magic star Anfernee Hardaway. **Business Addr:** Sports Agent, Professional Sports Planning, Inc, 909 Fannin, Ste 2090, Houston, TX 77010, (713)659-2255.

POTTER, JUDITH DIGGS
Educator. **Personal:** Born Jul 23, 1941, Norwood, MA; divorced; children: Wende Beth, Kimberly Ann. **Educ:** Lesley Coll, BS Educ 1964; Wheelock Coll, MS Educ 1977. **Career:** Boston Public Schools, teacher 1964-65; Medway Public Schools, teacher 1965-66; Brookline Headstart, teacher 1968; Boston Public Schools, teacher 1968-. **Orgs:** Delegate MA Federation of Teachers, Amer Federation of Teachers 1977-85; delegate Boston Labor Council, Building Rep-Boston T Union 1977-87; founder secty/treas Black Caucus Boston Teachers Union #66 1978-83; coord Try Arts & Chap 188 Boston Public Sch 1978-86; grad advisor Delta Sigma Theta Inc Boston Alumnae 1980-81; co-author Boston Public School Kindergarten Exam 1981; panelist Natl Endowment for the Arts 1984. **Honors/Awds:** Teacher of the Year Boston Public Schools 1983; featured in Christian Science Monitor and Albuquerque Journal 1986. **Home Addr:** One Brook St, Brookline, MA 02146.

POTTER, MYRTLE STEPHENS
Pharmaceutical company executive. **Personal:** Born Sep 28, 1958, Las Cruces, NM; daughter of Allene Baker Stephens and Albert Stephens; married James Potter; children: Jamison, Lauren Elizabeth. **Educ:** University of Chicago, Chicago, IL, BA, 1980. **Career:** IBM, Chicago, IL, marketing intern, 1979-80; Procter & Gamble, Cincinnati, OH, sales representative, 1980-81, district sales training manager, 1981-82; Merck Sharp & Dohme, West Pointe, PA, sales representative, 1982-84, marketing analyst, 1984-85, training & planning manager, 1985-86, field meeting services manager, 1986-87, district sales manager, 1987-89, product manager, 1989-90, director, Astra/Merck affairs, 1990-92, senior director sales planning, 1992-, senior director marketing planning, 1992-. **Orgs:** Philadelphia Urban League, 1988-. **Honors/Awds:** Merck Chairman's Award Nomination. **Home Addr:** 5963 Shetland Dr, Doylestown, PA 18901. **Business Addr:** Senior Director, Marketing Planning, Merck and Co, USHH, Sumneytown Pike, WP 37-B3, West Point, PA 19486.

POTTINGER, ALBERT A.
Attorney. **Personal:** Born Apr 24, 1928, Topeka, KS; married Delores Johnson. **Educ:** Washburn Munic U, BBA 1951; Cleveland St Law Sch, LLB 1959. **Career:** Atty, self; City Cleveland, cnclmn 1968-69, relocator, property mgr 1968-69, 1st asst prosecutor 1964-65. **Orgs:** Bd tsts Children Serv; Cath Big Bros; Cath Charities; Harvard-Lee Comm Serv. **Business Addr:** 33 Pub Sq, Cleveland, OH 44113.

POTTS, HAROLD E.
Educator. **Personal:** Born Jun 26, 1921, Youngstown, OH; married Audrey; children: Stephen, Stephanie, Christopher. **Educ:** Springfield Coll, Doctoral Study 1962, MS 1961; NY U, MA 1954, Certf 1951; Springfield Coll, BS 1950. **Career:** Quinnipiac Coll, prof, dir physical Therapy 1969-; Springfield Coll, bd of Trustee; Quinnipiac Coll, bd of trustee; US Dept Health Educ & Welfare, prog specialist 1966-69; Gaylord Hosp, admin asst 1962-66; Springfield Coll, research asst 1961-62; Neuromuscular Diagnostic Serv Hospital Center, W Orange NJ, chief physical therapist, research asst, conselor, asst 1960-61; St CT Veterans Hospital Rocky Hill, research asst, supr, clincal instr 1958-60; Kessler Inst Rehabilitaion Physically Handicapped, W Orange NJ, dir physical therapy 1956-58, asst dir physical therapy, supr clinical exprnc for student therapists 1955-56. **Orgs:** Numrs publs speakg expernc 1951-75; bd of dir New Haven Easter Seal Goodwl Ind Rehab Ctr; Am Phys Therapy Assn; CT Chap APTA bd dir; Nat Rehab Assn; Nat Athltc Trnrs Assn; Am Coll Sports Medicine; Intl Soc Electromyogrphc Kinesiology; NE Phys Therapy Eductrs; Rotary Club Wallingford CT bd dirs, schlrchp awards com, vocatnl serv com; Comm Devel Action Prog N Branford Hlth Com; N Branford Schlrshp Assn Inc bd dir; New Haven Schlrshp Assn; Greater New Haven Area Rehab Cncl; Wallingford YMCA bd dirs Bldg Com; Springfield Coll Alumni Assn; Springfield Coll Corp Academic Affrs Com; Zoning Bd Appeals N Branford. **Honors/Awds:** Nat Found Phys Therapy Schlrshp 1950; Offc Vocatnl Rehab Traineeship 1957; Am Phys Therapy Assn Traineeship 1961; Rotarian of Yr 1973. **Military Serv:** USCG signal man 2nd class. **Business Addr:** Co-Chm of Physical Therapy, Quinnipiac College, Mt Carmel Ave, Hamden, CT 06518.

POTTS, ROBERT LESTER
Cleric, educator. **Personal:** Born Jan 28, 1923, Muskogee, OK; son of Beatrice Onque Potts and Howard William Potts; married Ethel Kudrna, Jun 29, 1979; children: Robert Onque, Randolph G, Ronald Kjell, Clayton Lewis, Susan Sherman. **Educ:** Lane College, AB, 1945; Garrett Theological Seminary, MDiv, 1952; University of Chicago, Human Relations Institute, 1956; University of Michigan, EdD, 1975. **Career:** CME Church, minister, 1948-63; Lane College, professional chaplain, 1951-55; Texas College, president, 1961-63; Episcopal Church, priest, 1963-; Ann Arbor Public Schools, assistant superintendent/ombudsman, 1970-86; Diocese of Michigan, Region IV, archdeacon, 1988-90; Cathedral Church of St Paul, clergy staff, 1991-92. **Orgs:** Virginia Park Citizens Rehabilitation Commission, one of founders/president, 1963-68; New Detroit, Inc, founding member/trustee, 1967-69; City Planning Commission, 1971-76; Comprehensive Employment & Training Program, CETA, chairman, 1975-83; Cleary College, board of trustees, 1984-88; A2 Public Library Advisory Committee, 1987-; United Ministries in Higher Education, chairman of board, 1989-; Avalon Non-Profit Hsg Corp, 1991-. **Honors/Awds:** Lane College, Doctor of Divinity, 1962. **Special Achievements:** Administration Perceiver Specialist Award, 1981; Harvard University, Institute on Psychological Development, Certificate, 1985; Ombudsmanship in Public Elementary and Secondary Schools, a doctoral dissertation, 1975. **Military Serv:** US Air Force, 2nd lt, 1945-47. **Home Addr:** 1014 Elder Blvd, Ann Arbor, MI 48103.

POTTS, ROOSEVELT BERNARD
Professional football player. **Personal:** Born Jan 8, 1971, Rayville, LA. **Educ:** Northeast Louisiana. **Career:** Indianapolis Colts, running back, 1993-97; Miami Dolphins, 1997-. **Business Addr:** Professional Football Player, Miami Dolphins, 2269 NW 199th St, Miami, FL 33056, (305)620-5000.

POTTS, SAMMIE
Educational administrator. **Career:** Mary Holmes College, West Point MS, president. **Business Addr:** President, Mary Holmes College, PO Box 1257, West Point, MS 39773.

POUNDER, C. C. H.
Actress. **Personal:** Born Dec 25, 1952, Georgetown, Guyana; daughter of Betsy Enid Arnella James Pounder and Ronald Urlington Pounder. **Educ:** Ithaca Coll, BFA 1975. **Career:** Actress, currently. **Orgs:** Artists for a New South Africa, 1989-. **Honors/Awds:** Nominated for NAACP Image Awd for Best Actress in TV Drama 1986, 1987, 1988, 1989, 1990; Cesar (French Oscars), Best Foreign Film, "Bagdad Cafe"; nominated for an Emmy; nominated for Grammy for best spoken word category; Nominated for "Best Supporting Actress" for ER; Museum of Contemporary & Traditional Art, Senegal West Africa, 1998; NAACP nominations/wins, Best Actress Category, 1997, nominated for 1998; Honored by Institute of Caribbean Studies, Contributions to the Arts, 1997.

POUNDS, AUGUSTINE WRIGHT
Educator, educational administrator (retired), executive consultant. **Personal:** Born Jul 20, 1936, Wadley, AL; daughter of Flossie Wilkes Busbee (deceased) and Cortelyou Busbee (deceased); married Russell G Pounds, Jul 4, 1981; children: Karen Williams, Georgina Young. **Educ:** Pontiac Business Inst, attended 1958-60; Oakland Comm Coll, attended 1965; Oakland Univ, BA 1973, MA 1975; IA State Univ, PhD 1980. **Career:** Oakland Univ, consultant black cultural ctr 1966-68, admin asst to vice pres for urban affairs 1968-71, asst dir of commuter serv 1971-73; Oakland Univ, asst dir student ctr 1973-75; Univ of Zambia, vstg prof 1984; IA State Univ, asst dir minority student affairs 1975-76, asst dean of student life 1976-80, assoc dean of student life 1980-84, dean of students 1984-88; Murray State Univ, vice pres of student devel, 1988-90; Anne Arundel Community College, college development and intercollegiate athletics, vice pres for student services, 1990-95. **Orgs:** Mem White House Conf on Families Des Moines IA 1980; consultant evaluator North Central Assoc of Colls and Schools 1987; mem Ames Human Relations Commn; bd mem United Way of Ames, Amer Coll Personnel Assoc; mem Oakland Univ; adv bd Fine Arts Inst for Region V US Office of Educ; staff adv Assoc of Black Students; mem City Human Relat Commn; bd mem Family Serv of Oakland Co; first vice pres Oakland Co NAACP; bd mem New Horizons of Oakland Co; mem Amer Cncl on Educ, Natl Identification Prog, IA Student Personnel Assoc, Natl Assoc of Student Personnel Administrators; admin bd All Univ Comm Cncl; founding co-chair, ISU birthday celebration comm Martin Luther King Jr; mem Natl Assoc of Women Deans Adminis and Counselors; vice pres of assn relations, pres, 1993-94, NAWDAC; chair exec comm, ACPA/CMA, 1988-89; bd mem, Iowa Student Personnel Journal, 1987-; mem and vice pres, AAUW Legal Advocacy Committee. **Honors/Awds:** Citizen of Yr Oakland Co Ministerial Assn 1970; Cert of Appreciation Cit Finance Study Com City of Pontiac Sch Dist 1968; Serv Awd OU Credit Union Adv Council 1973; Matilda Wilson Awd 1974; Outstanding Contribution to Quality of Life of all Students Oakland Univ 1977; Woman of the Year Story Co Women's Polit Caucus 1983; Martin Luther King Service Award, MLK Inc, State of Iowa; author of 2 publications on black students; ISU Educ Leadership Award, 1994, Advisory Fundraising Committee, 1994-; MLK Zeitgeist Award, 1996. **Home Addr:** 8210 Woburn Abbey Rd, Glenn Dale, MD 20769-2023.

POUNDS, DARRYL
Professional football player. **Personal:** Born Jul 21, 1972, Fort Worth, TX. **Educ:** Nicholls State, attended. **Career:** Washington Redskins, defensive back, 1995-. **Business Addr:** Professional Football Player, Washington Redskins, 13832 Redskin Dr, Herndon, VA 22071, (703)471-9100.

POUNDS, ELAINE
Public relations consultant. **Personal:** Born Dec 31, 1946, Detroit, MI; daughter of Ethel Loyd Pounds and George Pounds; divorced; children: Adrian Molett, Allen Parks. **Educ:** Los Angeles Southwest Coll, 1971; California State Univ, Los Ange-

les, BA, 1978; Los Angeles City Coll and Santa Monica City Coll, 1979-80. **Career:** Former production asst, KNBC-TV; former producer, KACE-Radio; former programming asst, Theta Cable Television; former promotions coord and traffic mgr, Group W Cable/Westinghouse Broadcasting Co; former asst traffic mgr, KTTV/Metromedia Television; KCET-TV, Los Angeles CA, former corp mktg asst; Los Angeles Black Media Coalition, executive director, currently. **Orgs:** Natl Assn of Media Women; Alliance of Black Entertainment Technicians; Women in Show Business; NAACP; REEL Black Women; Southern Christian Leadership Conference; Los Angeles City Cultural Affairs, commissioner.

POUNDS, KENNETH RAY
Business executive. **Personal:** Born Jan 2, 1942, Herminie, PA; married Patricia Dore; children: Kenneth Troy. **Educ:** Univ of Wash, BA 1971, MA/Urban Planning 1975. **Career:** PACE Property Mgmt Co Inc, pres 1980-; city of Seattle, asst supt of bldg 1979-80; Security Pacific Inc, vice pres 1976-78; Fed Energy Adminstrn, spl asst 1974-76; Dept of HUD, housing mgmt offcr 1971-74; city of Seattle-Dept of Comm Devel, loan offcr 1970-71. **Orgs:** Vp Central Area Fed Credit Union 1975-76; treas NW Conf of Black Pub Officials 1979; first vice pres Nat Bus League-Seattle chap 1979; mem Seattle KingCo Bd of Realtors 1978-80; mem Hercules Lodge No 17 1979; mem Central Area Kiwanis 1980. **Honors/Awds:** Employee of yr Fed Reg Adminstrn Region X 1974; Potential Black Ldr NW Conf of Black Pub Officials 1979. **Military Serv:** AUS e-5 1967-69. **Business Addr:** 1801 E Yesler Way, Seattle, WA 98122.

POUNDS, MOSES B.
Public health services researcher. **Personal:** Born Feb 18, 1947, Baltimore, MD; son of Katherine McCutcheon Pounds and Moses B Pounds, Sr; married Ann P McCauley, Dec 28, 1981; children: M Andrew. **Educ:** Univ of CA Santa Cruz, AB Anthrop 1974; Univ of CA Berkeley, MA Anthrop 1975; Univ of CA Berkeley and San Francisco, PhD Med Anthrop 1982. **Career:** The Johns Hopkins Univ, School of Hygiene and Public Health, Department of Behavioral Sciences and Health Education, asst professor, 1982-88; Univ of Maryland at Baltimore, asst to the pres, Mid-Atlantic AIDS Regional Education and Training Center, project director, principal investigator, 1988-91; US Public Health Service, Health Resources Services Administration, Bureau of Health Resources Development, Office of Science and Epidemiology, senior staff fellow, 1991-94, medical anthropologist, 1994-. **Orgs:** American Anthropological Assn; Assn for Asian Studies; Society for Med Anthrop; Kroeber Anthropological Society; American Public Health Assn. **Honors/Awds:** Biolog Sci Rsch Grant NIH The Johns Hopkins Univ 1982-84, 1984-85; Fellow Grad Minority Fellowship Univ of CA Berkeley 1979-81; Trainee Natl Inst of Gen Medical Serv NIH Grant 1977-79; Fellow Natl Sci Found Pre-doctoral Fellowship 1974-77; Amer Found for AIDS Rsch Grant 1987-88; Natl Cancer Inst Grant 1988; Health Resources and Services Admin Grant 1988-91. **Military Serv:** US Army, admin asst, Sgt, 1966-70. **Business Addr:** Medical Anthropologist, Office of Science and Epidemiology, US Public Health Service, Health Resources Services Administration, HAB, 5600 Fishers Ln, Rm 7A-07, Rockville, MD 20857.

POURCIAU, KERRY L.
Business executive. **Personal:** Born Sep 4, 1951, Baton Rouge. **Educ:** LA State U, 1973. **Career:** Bauerlein Inc New Orleans, acct exec; Sen Russell B Long , spl asst;Sst. **Orgs:** Wash chap LSU Alumni Assn; vice pres So Univ Sigma Delta Chi; Theta Alpha Phi; mem Pendulum Club Capit Hill; Capit Hill Dem; Smith Asso 1974-. **Honors/Awds:** 1st blck stud bdy pres LA State Univ 1972-73.

POUSSAINT, ALVIN FRANCIS
Educator. **Personal:** Born May 15, 1934, East Harlem, NY; son of Harriet and Christopher; married Tina Young; children: Alan. **Educ:** Columbia Coll, BA 1956; Cornell Univ Medical Coll, MD 1960; Univ CA Los Angeles, MS 1964. **Career:** Tufts Univ Medical School, sr clinical instructor 1965-66; Med Com Human Rights, so field dir 1965-66; Tufts Univ Medical School, asst prof 1967-69; Columbia Pt Health Center, dir psychiatry 1968-69; MA Mental Health School, assoc psychiatrist 1969-78; Harvard Medical School, assoc dean students 1969-; Judge Baker Children's Center, senior assoc psychiatrist 1978-; Harvard Medical School, clinical prof, psychiatry, currently. **Orgs:** Mem bd trustees Wesleyan Coll 1968-69; mem bd trustees Natl Afro Amer Artists 1968; chmn bd Solomon Fuller Inst 1975-81; mem bd dirs Operation PUSH 1971-85; fellow Amer Psychiat Assn 1972-; mem Natl Medical Assn 1968-; natl treasurer Med Com Human Rights 1968-69; fellow, Amer Assn for the Advancement of Science, 1981-; Amer Academy of Child Psychiatry, 1985-; fellow, Amer Orthopsychiatric Assn, 1987-; UCLA Medical Alumni Association. **Honors/Awds:** Honorary degrees, Dr Humanities Wilberforce Univ 1972; Human Letter Govs State Univ 1982; Amer Black Achievement Award in Business and the Professions, Johnson Publishing 1986; John Jay Award for Distinguished Professional Achievement, 1987; Medgar Evers Medal of Honor, Beverly Hills/Hollywood, chapter of NAACP, 1988; Award of Professional Achievement—UCLA Housestaff, 1990. **Business Addr:** Clinical Professor of Psychiatry, Judge Baker Children's Center, 3 Blackfan Circle, Boston, MA 02115.

POUSSAINT, RENEE FRANCINE
Journalist. **Personal:** Born Aug 12, 1944, New York, NY; married Henry J Richardson. **Educ:** Sorbonne Paris France/Yale Law Sch, attended 1965-67; Sarah Lawrence Coll Bronxville NY, BA 1966; UCLA, MA 1971; IN U, PhD studies 1972; Columbia USch of Jornalism, attended 1973. **Career:** WJLA-TV, anchor/reporter 1978-; CBS Network News Chicago Wash DC, reporter 1977-79; WBBM-TV Chicago, reporter/anchor/show host 1973-77; IN Univ Bloomington, lectr/doctoral candidate 1972-73; African Arts Mag Los Angeles, editor 1969-73. **Orgs:** Program dir AIESEC New York 1967-69; dancer Jean Leon Destine Haitian Daznce 1967; translator UC Press 1970; peaker various pvt & govt orgn 1977-; mem Sigma Delta Chi; lifetime mem NAACP; mem Women in Communications Awards TV Reporting Nat Assn of Media Women 1975; Illinois Mental Health Assn 1975; Young Achiever YMCA Chicago 1976; Am Firefighters Assn 1977; Am Assn Univ Women 1979. **Honors/Awds:** Outstanding serv US Dept of Labor Ed Women 1979; emmy Nat Acad of TV Arts & Scis 1980; religiton in Media 1980. **Business Addr:** News Anchor, WJLA-TV, 4461 Connecticut Ave NW, Washington, DC 20008.

POUSSAINT-HUDSON, ANN ASHMORE
Psychologist. **Personal:** Born Jun 23, 1942, Atlanta, GA; married James L Hudson Esq; children: Alan Machel Poussaint. **Educ:** Spelman Coll Atlanta, BA 1963; Simmons Coll Sch of Social Work, MS 1965; Univ of CA Berkeley, MA 1976, PhD 1979. **Career:** San Mateo Co CA Child Guidance Clinic, psychiatric social worker 1965-68; Roxbury Multi-Serv Center, social work supr 1968-69; PHP NY Hosp, patient coord 1969-70; Pacific Psychotherapy Assn, consult clinician 1970-73; Pacific Training Assn State Univ of CA at San Francisco, consult 1970-73; Private Practice, clinical psychologist 1974-81; Min Training Prog for Psychol BU & City Hosp, supr 1978-80; Urban Psychological Associates, founder & dir 1981-93. **Orgs:** Consult Howard Univ Press 1980; mem pub rel com Amer Psychol Assn; mem Assn of Black Psychologists; mem Links Inc. **Honors/Awds:** Lectr & Contributor of articles in field to mags; Outstanding Young Women of Amer Spelman Coll 1969; Fellowship US Pub Health Scholar 1971-73; Cert of Appreciation Precedent Setting in Jury Selection Assn of Black Psychologists 1974.

POWE, JOSEPH S.
Engineer. **Personal:** Born Jul 26, 1946, Bremerton, WA. **Educ:** Univ of WA, BS 1968; MS Physics 1971; MS Aero & Astro Engineering 1972. **Career:** Hughes Aircraft Co, senior scientist. **Orgs:** Mem Mensa. **Business Addr:** Senior Scientist, Hughes Aircraft Co, 1950 E Imperial Hwy, BS41/MSA315, El Segundo, CA 90245.

POWELL, ADAM CLAYTON, III
Broadcasting executive. **Personal:** Born Jul 17, 1946, New York, NY; son of Hazel Dorothy Scott Powell and Adam Clayton Powell Jr; divorced; children: Adam Clayton IV, Sherman Scott. **Career:** CBS News, New York, NY, manager & producer, 1976-81; Gannett Center for Media Studies, Columbia Univ, New York, NY, fellow lecturer & consultant, 1985-; National Public Radio, Washington, DC, news vice president, 1987-90; Quincy Jones Entertainment, producer, currently. **Orgs:** Academy of Political Science; American Academy of Political and Social Science; American Association for the Advancement of Science; Florida A&M University Board of Visitors, vice chairman, 1991-92; International Media Consortium: board of directors; National Association of Black Journalists; Radio Television News Directors Foundation: advisory council; Society of Professional Journalists; Songwriters Guild of America; University of Texas at Austin: College of Communication Advisory Board, executive committee, 1990-92. **Honors/Awds:** Overseas Press Club Award for Best Reporting of International News.

POWELL, ADDIE SCOTT
Community organization founder and volunteer coordinator. **Personal:** Born Nov 14, 1922, Augusta, GA; daughter of Tillie Lyons Scott and Matthew Marion Scott; divorced; children: Frances Powell Harris. **Educ:** Paine Coll, AB 1943; Univ of IA, MA; Atlanta U, MA 1949. **Career:** Brooklyn Public Library, dist supv of adult svcs, 1970-74 (retired); Branch Lib Augusta GA, 1961-62; librarian various posts 1949-74; freelance writer resrchr & lecturer. **Orgs:** Mem Am Lib Assn; mem Round Table Coll Res Libraries; mem So Cncl on Human Relatns 1960-62; YMCA; Sickle Cell Anemia Assn; TV appearance ''Voices of Bklyn'' (intercultrl series Brooklyn Coll); Leadership Augusta l986; bd of directors Fund for Southern Communities l984-87; bd of directors Georgia Housing Coalition l983-. **Honors/Awds:** Carnegie Fellow 1951-52; author various works, tech publicatns; Community Service, Seventh-day Adventist Church 1982; Citizen of the Year, Augusta Unit, Natl Assn Social Workers l983; Citizen's Participation Study of Black Residents of Bethlehem l980-8l; Economic Devel Study: Marketable Skills Among Low Income Residents of Bethlehem; Land Use Study of Low Income Community of Bethlehem 1985-86. **Business Addr:** Coordinator, Bethlehem Area Community Assn, Inc (BACA, Inc), 1634 Milledgeville Rd, Augusta, GA 30901.

POWELL, ARCHIE JAMES
Educator. **Personal:** Born Jun 1, 1950, Lakeland, FL; children: Kevin J. **Educ:** Univ of Nantes, France, certificate 1971; Morehouse Coll, BA 1972; Brown Univ, MA 1974, PhD 1984. **Career:** RI Dept of Educ, planning specialist 1978-81; Brown Univ, minority affairs office 1981-85; Albany Medical Coll, asst professor 1985-, asst dean for minority affairs 1985-. **Orgs:** New England Assoc of Black Educators, mem; Organization of Amer Historians, mem; American Historical Society, mem; Assoc for the Study of Afro-American Life and History, mem; Rhode Island Black Heritage Society, mem; Natl Assoc of Medical Minority Educators, Inc, mem, northeast regional coord, 1987 conference co-chair; Albany Symphony Orchestra, bd of directors 1986-; Albany Boys Club, bd of directors 1986-; Black Dimensions in Art, Inc, bd of directors 1986-; Israel African Methodist Episcopal Church, trustee 1986-. **Honors/Awds:** Morehouse Coll, merrill overseas travel-study grant 1970-71; The Ford Foundation, doctoral fellowship 1972-75; Phi Beta Sigma, distinguished service as as reg dir 1985; Mt Hope Day Care Center, Inc, distinguished service as board pres 1985; Outstanding Young Men of America 1986. **Home Addr:** 285 Hudson Ave, Albany, NY 12210. **Business Addr:** Asst Dean for Minority Affair, Albany Medical College, 47 New Scotland Ave, Albany, NY 12208.

POWELL, ASTON WESLEY
Educator. **Personal:** Born May 21, 1909, Santa Cruz, St Elizabeth, Jamaica; married Cynthia Marguerite; children: Leighton, Marilyn Yvonne Robinson, Douglas. **Educ:** Columbia Univ, BSc 1945, MA 1946. **Career:** Blackman (daily newspaper), reporter 1929; Excelsior School, founder/headmaster 1931; Excelsior Educ Centre, founder/dir 1971, consultant/fund-raiser 1981-; North St Excelsior, dir, currently. **Orgs:** Chmn, Amer Univ Grad Assn, 1954-57; pres, YMCA, 1972-77; pres, Jamaica Tchrs Assn, 1964-66; chmn, JTA Prof and Dev Comm, 1970-83; mem, Inst Bd of Tchr Educ (Univ of West Indies), 1970-76; dir, Kingston Rotary Club, 1972-83; mem, Jamaica Club, 1973-75; mem, Ministry of Educ Working Party on Post-Secondary Educ, 1973-74; mem, Coun Coll of Arts Science and Tech (CAST), 1975-79; mem, Jamaica Natl Reserve Coun, 1976-77; mem, Jamaica Honour Awards Comm, 1976-83; mem, Western New York/Jamaica Partners and mem of its Personal Comm, 1978-83; bd mem, Inst of Jamaica, 1980-83; mem, Jamaica/New York Concerned Citizens Christian Educ, 1981-83; mem, The Victoria League for Commonwealth Friendship, 1982-85. **Honors/Awds:** Order of the British Empire; Outstanding Contrib to Jamaica in the Field of Educ, Jamaica Progressive League of New York Inc, 1970; Norman Manley Awd of Excellence, 1971; Catholic Tchrs Assn Jamaica, Special Awd, 1972; Dictionary of Intl Biography Certificate of Merit Distinguished Serv, 1973; Order of Jamaica, 1976; Jamaica Teachers' Assn Natl Roll of Honour, 1977; pres emeritus, YMCA, 1979; Outstanding & Unequalled Contrib to the Prov & Advancement of Educ for all Jamaicans, Rotary Club of Kingston, 1979; Recognition of Excellent & Dedicated Serv in Field of Educ, Jaycees of Jamaica, 1980; Daily Gleaner Certificate of Merit, 1980; Long Service Awd, Excelsior Old Students' Assn, 1981; Jamaica Distinguished Methodist Church Recog Outstanding Serv Field ofEduc 1981; Plaque Contribution the Devel of Higher Educ for the Blind in Jamaica, 1982; pres emeritus, Jamaica Tchrs Assn, 1983; chmn, Leila Tomlinson Wareika Basic Sch Bd, 1983; LLD Hon Dr of Laws, Univ of the West Indies, 1983; Outstanding Service to Independent Schools in Jamaica, 1983; Jamaica Geog Soc, Pioneer Geographer of Jamaica Awd, 1985; Nova Univ Citation of Merit, 1986; Foundation for International Self-Help, board of directors. **Home Addr:** 8 Ottawa Ave, PO Box 209, Kingston 7, Jamaica. **Business Addr:** Director, North St Excelsior, 16 North St, Kingston, Jamaica.

POWELL, BERNICE JACKSON
Association executive. **Career:** United Church of Christ, exec associate to the pres; United Church of Christ Commission for Racial Justice, exec dir, 1993-. **Business Addr:** Executive Director, United Church of Christ, Commission for Racial Justice, 700 Prospect Ave, Cleveland, OH 44115-1110, (216)736-2100.

POWELL, BETTYE BOONE (B. J)
Banking officer. **Personal:** Born Apr 10, 1947, Garysburg, NC; daughter of Mr & Mrs James W Boone Jr; married Carlie W Powell, Mar 28, 1970; children: Carlton G. **Educ:** NC Central Univ, BA, 1969. **Career:** Hibernia National Bank, employee relations coord, 1981-84; asst personnel office, benefits coord, 1984-88; AVP, sr compensation analyst, 1988-90; vp, EEO/AA officer, 1990-. **Orgs:** Human Relations, advisory committee, 1994-; Children's Bureau, bd of dirs, 1992-; YMCA of Greater New Orleans, bd of dirs, 1992-; Southern Univ of New Orleans, foundation bd, 1990-; New Orleans Chapter of the Links, Inc, 1975-. **Honors/Awds:** Inroads/New Orleans Inc, Business Coordinator of the Year, 1990-91; Oryades YMCA, Black Achiever In Business, 1989. **Business Addr:** VP, EEO Affirmative Action Officer, Hibernia National Bank, PO Box 61540, New Orleans, LA 70161, (504)533-3262.

POWELL, C. CLAYTON
Eye care specialist. **Personal:** Born Apr 11, 1927, Dothan, AL; son of Evelyn Powell and Willie Powell; married Romae Tur-

ner, Mar 11, 1954 (deceased); children: C Clayton, Jr, Rometta E; married Deborah S Goodlett, Jul 30, 1994. **Educ:** Morehouse Coll, AB; IL Coll of Optometry, BSc; Coll Optometry, OD; Univ of MI, graduate study MPH Program; Atlanta Univ, MEd; Illinois Coll of Optometry, Honorary DOS 1987. **Career:** Metro-Atlanta Child Devel Center & Health & Vision Clinic, devel vision specialist/exec dir; Atlanta Southside Comprehensive Health Center, exec dir 1973-76, chief of Optometry Dept 1968-73; Private Practice, 1953-; AL, jr high school teacher/asst prin; PA Coll of Optometry, Sou Coll of Optemetry. **Orgs:** Mem Natl Eye Inst, NH; adv com State Univ, NY; Natl Assn Neighborhood Health Centers; Amer Public Health Assn; legis com NANHC; mem 5th Dist, GOA, Amer & Natl Optometric Assns; mem GA Vision Serv Inc; organizer, chmn Metro-Atlanta OEP Study Group; Ad Hoc Com Group Practice by pres Amer Optometric Assn; mem, offcr, coms, numerous other orgs; mem Beta Kappa Chi Natl Science Hon Soc/Tomb & Key Natl Hon Optom Soc/Beta Sigma Kappa Intl Hon Optom Soc/ Mu Sigma Pi Professional Fraternity; Omega Psi Phi Fraternity; Development Authority of Fulton County, chairman of the authority, 1973. **Honors/Awds:** Recipient Outstanding Man of the Year Clark Coll, Morehouse Coll, Morris Brown Coll; Atlanta Graduate Chapter Omega Psi Phi Fraternity; Outstanding Achievement Award Fulton Co Rep Club, Atlanta Postal Acad, Pine Acres Town & Country Club; Optometrist of the Year, Natl Optometry Assn 1984; Honorary Degree, Doctor of Ocular Science, Illinois Coll 1987; Founders Award, NOA; The Kaufman Award, NAACP; St Peter Missionary Bapt Church, Outstanding Leadership Award. **Home Addr:** 403 Fielding Ln SW, Atlanta, GA 30311. **Business Addr:** The Health and Vision Clinic, 2039 Stewart Ave, SW, Suite A, Atlanta, GA 30315.

POWELL, CARL
Professional football player. **Personal:** Born Jan 4, 1974, Detroit, MI. **Educ:** Louisville. **Career:** Indianapolis Colts, defensive end, 1997-. **Business Addr:** Professional Football Player, Indianapolis Colts, PO Box 535000, Indianapolis, IN 46253, (317)297-2658.

POWELL, CHARLES P.
Physician (retired). **Personal:** Born Sep 20, 1923; son of Rev & Mrs C P Powell; married Margaret (deceased); children: Patricia, Leslie, Sylvia. **Educ:** Howard Univ, 1941-44; MD 1948; Harlem Hosp, intern 1948-49; New Britain Gen Hosp, resident 1953-54; post-grad Yale, Harvard, Boston Univ, Tufts, Oak Ridge Inst Nuclear Med, Princeton. **Career:** Univ of Colorado Med Ctr & Western Res, post-grad atomic energy commission rsch fellow 1949-51; Connecticut VA Hosp, 1954-59; VA Ctr, Dayton, OH, sr physician 1959-65; Prudential Ins Co, asst med dir 1965-75; Samuel Shattuck Hosp, consul 1966-67; clincial asst OH State Sch Med 1961-65, Tufts Sch Med, clinical asst 1967-70; Dreyfus Consumer Life Ins Co, med dir 1984-85; Hartford Ins Grp, med dir 1975-85; Internal Med Consultant, Hartford Insurance Group, 1986; Commissioner of Health, US Virgin Islands, consultant, 1987; State of Connecticut, Dept of Corrections, VISTA volunteer, 1989-90. **Orgs:** Certified Amer Bd Intl Med; past mem Soc Nuclear Med; past mem Exec Council Assn of Life Ins Med Dirs of Amer; Fellow Amer Coll Physicians; past bd mem Roxbury MA Fed of Neighborhood Ctr; Vis Nurses Assn of Boston; stadium phys in charge New England Patriots 1971, 1974. **Military Serv:** USAF mc capt 1951-53. **Home Addr:** 2569 7th Ave. 19-G, New York, NY 10039-3224.

POWELL, CLARENCE DEAN, JR.
Airline pilot. **Personal:** Born Aug 26, 1939, Kansas City, MO; son of Capitola Powell and Clarence Powell Sr; children: Pamela Diane. **Educ:** Univ of Kansas City, 1957-60; Troy State University, Montgomery, AL, 1965-66. **Career:** Darben Clifton & Gordon Construction Co, proj engr 1968-69; Hadden Investment & Devel Co, proj engr & cons 1971-72; Afro Air Inc, pres & ceo 1974-77; Organ of Black Airline Pilots, eastern region vice pres 1979-; Prof Photographer; TWA Inc, first officer beginning 1966, captain, currently. **Orgs:** Mem Negro Airmen Intl 1967-; mem NAACP 1967-; consult Natl Urban League 1967-77; member, Tuskegee Airman, Inc, 1990-. **Honors/Awds:** Honor grad AUS Basic Training & Warrant Officer Training 1962-63; Awd of Excellence TWA Airlines 1979. **Military Serv:** US Army, WO, 1962-66; Vietnamese Cross of Gallantry; Gold Leaf Air Medal w/4 Silver Leaf Clusters & v for Valor; Commendation Medal w/V for Valor. **Home Addr:** 2986 Balearic Dr, Marietta, GA 30067.

POWELL, COLIN L.
Military officer (retired). **Personal:** Born Apr 5, 1937, New York, NY; son of Maud Powell and Luther Powell; married Alma Vivian Johnson; children: Michael, Linda, Anne Marie. **Educ:** City Coll of NY, BS 1958; George Washington Univ, MBA 1971; Nat War Coll, attended 1976. **Career:** AUS, career army infantry officer 1958-, brig comdr 101st airborne div 1976-77, asst div comdr 4th inf div Ft Carson, CO 1981-82, mil asst Dep Sec of Def 1982-86; The White House, dep asst to the pres for Natl Security Affairs, National Security Council; Joint Chiefs of Staff, chairman, 1989-93. **Honors/Awds:** White House Fellow; Living Legend Award. **Special Achievements:** Harvard University, Commencement speaker, 1993. **Military Serv:** Purple Heart 1963, Bronze Star 1963, Legion of Merit awds 1969 & 71, Dist Serv Medal, AUS lt.

POWELL, CRAIG
Professional football player. **Educ:** Ohio State University. **Career:** Cleveland Browns, 1995-. **Special Achievements:** Selected in the 1st round/30th overall pick in the 1995 NFL Draft. **Business Addr:** Professional Football Player, Cleveland Browns, 80 First Ave, Berea, OH 44017, (216)891-5000.

POWELL, DANTE (LEJON DANTE)
Professional baseball player. **Personal:** Born Aug 25, 1973, Long Beach, CA. **Educ:** Cal State Fullerton. **Career:** San Francisco Giants, outfielder, 1997-. **Business Addr:** Professional Baseball Player, San Francisco Giants, 3 Com Park, San Francisco, CA 94124, (415)468-3700.

POWELL, DARLENE WRIGHT
Attorney. **Personal:** Born Dec 1, 1960, Brooklyn, NY; daughter of Elaine Wright and Franklin P Wright, III; married Clayton J Powell Jr, Jul 28, 1984; children: Jessica Marie Powell. **Educ:** Cornell University, Ithaca, NY, BS, 1981; University of Maryland School of Law, Baltimore, MD, JD, 1985. **Career:** Frank, Berstein, Conaway, and Goldman, law clerk, 1983-84; Burke, Gerber, Wilen, Francomano, and Radding, law clerk, Summer 1984; The Fidelity and Deposit Company of Maryland, attorney, 1986; Maryland-National Capital Park and Planning Commission, associate general counsel, 1986-87; Kaiser Permanente, associate regional counsel, 1987-88; Maryland Office of the Public Defender, part-time attorney, 1989-90; Powell and Powell PC, principal attorney, 1990-92; Powell and Powell, PA, principal attorney, 1992-. **Orgs:** District of Columbia Bar Association; Board of Trustees, State of Maryland Public Defender System, 1990-92; board member, University of Maryland Prince George's County Alumni Club, 1990-91; past member, Prince George's County Bar Association Committee on Committees, Continuing Legal Education Committee; past member, Bar Association of Baltimore City; past member, Public Service Committee of the Maryland State Bar Association's Young Lawyers' Section. **Honors/Awds:** Participant, Harvard Law School's Program of Instruction for Lawyers, June 1987; Young Careerist, Business and Professional Women's Clubs, Bowie-Crofton Chapter, 1987-88; Finalist Award, Young Career Woman Competition, Maryland Federation of Business and Professional Women's Clubs, 1987-88; staff writer, The Daily Record, 1983-84. **Business Addr:** Principal Attorney, Powell and Powell, PA, 7307 Hanover Pkwy, 2nd fl, Greenbelt, MD 20770.

POWELL, DARRELL LEE
Television reporter. **Personal:** Born Mar 20, 1959, Cumberland, MD; son of Gloria Louise Powell; married Jacqueline Lavern Barnes-Powell. **Educ:** Frostburg State University, Frostburg, MD, BS, sociology, 1983. **Career:** Frostburg State University, Frostburg, MD, librarian aid, 1978-83; Western MD Consortium, Cumberland, MD, counselor, 1983; Allegany County School Board, Cubmerland, MD, teacher, 1985-1987; TCI Cable Vision, Cumberland, MD, photographer/writer, 1984-87; WTBO/WKGO Radio,Cumberland, MD, disc jockey, 1987; WHAG-TV 25, Hagerstown, MD, reporter, 1987-. **Orgs:** Treasurer, NAACP, 1980-; member, Human Resource Development Commission Board, 1990-; member, Vocational Education Advisory Council, 1990-; Cumberland, Theatre bd, 1993-. **Business Addr:** Reporter, News, WHAG-TV (Ch 25), 111 S George St, Cumberland, MD 21502.

POWELL, DAVID L.
Dentist. **Personal:** Born Apr 9, 1938, Tuskegee, AL; son of Emma Henderson Powell and David L Powell; married Carol June Gandy; children: Paul, Mark, Melanie, Peter. **Educ:** St Michael's Coll, AB 1959; Howard Univ Coll of Dentistry, DDS 1963; OH State Univ, MS 1971. **Career:** USAF, lt col 1963-75; prv practice, dental specialist endodontics 1975-. **Orgs:** Assoc bd mem Dayton Art Inst 1979-84; pres OH Assoc of Endodontist 1982-83; bd trust Miami Valley School 1982-; mem Centerville Optomist 1984-; bd dir Superior Dental Care 1986; pres Dayton Dental Soc 1987-88. **Honors/Awds:** Amer Bd of Endodontics, Diplomate; International College of Dentists, Fellow. **Military Serv:** US Air Force, lt col, 1963-75. **Business Addr:** Dentist, 529 E Stroop Rd, Dayton, OH 45429.

POWELL, DUDLEY VINCENT
Business executive, pharmacist, physician. **Personal:** Born Jul 23, 1917; married Beryl Mae Prettigar Henry; children: Dudley Vincent Jr, Hubert Barrington, Tyrone Anthony. **Educ:** Syracuse Univ Hosp, internship; Met Hosp Cleveland, residency Ob-Gyn 3 yrs; Univ of Rochester Sch of Medicine & Dentistry NY, MD 1950. **Career:** Western Reserve U, instr ob-gyn 1 yr; Ft Carson CO, chief ob-gyn 2 yrs; Dallas, pvt prac ob-gyn 1958-; Ob-Gyn Hlth Sci Cntr Univ of TX, clinical prof; St Paul Presb Med Arts Hosp. **Orgs:** Dir Planned Parenthd of NE TX 1960-76; mem Nat Planned Parenthd Bd 1968-72; life mem NAACP. **Honors/Awds:** Margaret Sanger Award; Man of the Yr Omega Psi Phi; Merit Award AUS Reserve; Legion of Merit AUS Reserve. **Military Serv:** AUS Reserve col 1958-77. **Business Addr:** St Paul Professional Bldg, 1906 Peabody Ave, Dallas, TX 75215.

POWELL, ELAINE
Professional basketball player. **Personal:** Born Aug 9, 1975; daughter of James and Merlene Powell. **Educ:** Louisiana State Univ. **Career:** Portland Power, guard, 1997-. **Business Addr:** Professional Basketball Player, Portland Power, 439 N Broadway, Portland, OR 97227, (503)249-1130.

POWELL, GAYLE LETT
Consultant, business executive, furrier. **Personal:** Born Dec 18, 1943, Manhattan, NY; daughter of Claire G & Robert A Lett. **Educ:** Central Univ, BSE 1966. **Career:** Newark Bd of Educ, teacher 1966-72; She Creations Inc, corp pres 1969-80; Essex Coll of Bus, teacher, 1980-81; The Fur Vault, fur sales 1981-82; Antonovich Furs Inc, fur sales 1982-84; Fur You Inc Outside Fur Sales, corp off 1984-; The Fur Mart Inc, retail furs & service manufacturer, CEO, 1985-. **Orgs:** Mem Alpha Kappa Alpha Sorority, Master Furriers Guild, Amer Bridge Assn; Natl Assn of Female Executives; Fur Info Council of America. **Business Addr:** CEO, Fur Mart Inc, 1220 Rt 46, Parsippany, NJ 07054, (201)335-3378.

POWELL, GEORGETTE SEABROOKE
Artist, art therapist. **Personal:** Born Aug 2, 1916, Charleston, SC; married Dr George W (deceased); children: George W III, Phyllis A Manson, Richard V. **Educ:** Harlem Art Workshop NYC; Cooper Union Art School NYC; Fordham Univ NYC; Turtle Bay Music Sch NYC; Dept Agr Grad School Washington, DC; DC Teachers Coll; WA School Psychiatry, Howard Univ, BFA; grad Metro Mental Health Skills Center. **Career:** Artist, art therapist. Numerous exhibits and collections including, Carnegie Inst; Natl Exhibit Hall Gallery; Harmon Found; Waltha Daniels Libr; ''Forever Free'' a traveling art exhibit of Amer Black Women Artists; Charleston Black Arts Festival; Ormond Beach Art League; Palm Coast, FL Art Festival; 18th Art Festival of Capital City Artists; Numerous art positions including, DC Gen Hosp, art therapist 1963-66; Art in Action, inceptor/cons 1967-68; Comm Art Happening Annual Art Show, inceptor/dir 1967-; George Wash Univ Grad Sch Art & Sci, art therapy program 1972-; Flagler County Bunnell FL, minority arts coord 1982-; Tomorrow's World Art Center, dir/fdr 1975-. **Orgs:** Amer Art Therapy Assn; Amer Art League; DC Art Assn; bd mem Howard Theatre Found; mem Natl Conf of Artists; consult bd Createadrama Educ Centre of IN; Women in the Arts WI/NYC/Wash,DC; mem DC Mental Health Assn; DC Commn on the Arts & Humanities; Natl Endowment of the Arts; des cover & illustrator, Black Arts Calendar Josephite Pastoral Center, 1976-80; designed brochure cover Sidwell Friends Summ Program; booklet of drawings of Black Artists Natl Afro-Amer Hist Kit 1977; exhibited ''Forever Free'' Black Women's Natl Traveling Art Show; exhibits Intl NCA Natl Conf of Artists Dakar Senegal 1984; guest Comm Folk Art Gallery 1986; panelist WPA & the Harlem Artists Guild New York. **Honors/Awds:** 1st Prize Cooper Union Art Sch, Dillard Univ, Amer Art League 1967; Outstanding Perf Awd DC Publ Hlth Art Therapy Acute Psychiatry 1964; Quality Perf Awd DC Dept Rec 1974; Natl Achvmnt Awd Natl Conf of Artists 1975; Natl Exhbn of Minority Artists of Amer 1976; DC Art Assn Awd 1977; Festac Ptcpt Awd 1977; select particip 2nd World Black & African Fest of Arts & Culture Lagos, Nigeria 1977; Listed in, Ebony, Jet Mag, WA Artists Dir 1972, Artists USA1973, WA Post, Evening Star News, Afro-Am Newspapers, Intl Artist Dir 1974-75; Panelist Amer Art Therapy Conv 1972, 1974; Merit Award Howard Univ Comm Action Prog DC 1978; Comm Serv Award Neighborhood Plng Cncl 1979; Jos Parks Spl Award Natl Conf of Artists 1979; Juris Art Citation Plaque WA Bar Assn 1980;Humanities Awd Black History Month Peos Congregational Church 1985; Outstanding Comm Serv in the Arts Awd St Patrick's Episcopal Church Sr Ctr 1986 and Honoree Salute to Georgette Seabrooke Powell 1986; Comm Serv Plaque DC Art Assoc; Art Serv Plaque NCA Conf Los Angeles CA 1987. **Business Addr:** Dir, Tomorrow's World Art Cntr Inc, 410 8th St, NW, Washington, DC 20004.

POWELL, GRADY WILSON
Clergyman. **Personal:** Born Aug 6, 1932, Brunswick Co, VA; son of Lillie T Powell and Herbert V Powell; married Dr Bertie J; children: Sandra Z, Dorthula H, Grady W Jr, Herbert C, Eric C. **Educ:** St Paul's Coll, BS 1954; VA Union Univ Sch of Theol, MDiv 1959. **Career:** Amity Bapt Church S Hill VA, pastor 1953-58; Greensville Co Pub Schools Emporia VA, teacher 1954-56; Quioccasin Bapt Church Richmond, pastor 1958-61; Richmond Pub Schools, teacher 1959-60; Gillfield Bapt Church, pastor 1961-. **Orgs:** Treas/bd member Children's Home of VA Bapt Inc 1959-70; sec/governing bd VA Council of Churches 1960-66; Petersburg Biracial Comm City of Petersburg VA 1961-62; bd member/sec, State Bd of Corrections of VA 1974-78; governing bd Natl Council of Church of Christ 1979-; advisory board, NationsBank, 1988-; corporate board, WCVE-TV, 1990-; advisory board, Energy Share, Virginia Power, 1989-; advisory board, United Way, Petersburg, VA, 1989-; Hospital Authority of Southside Regional Medical Center, 1991-. **Honors/Awds:** Distinguished Serv NAACP 1961; Man of the Year Omega Psi Phi Frat Petersburg 1963; Honorary Degree St Paul's Coll 1976; Presidential Citation Nat Assn Equal Opportunity in Higher Educ 1979. **Business Addr:** Pastor, Gillfield Baptist Church, Perry & Farmer Sts, Petersburg, VA 23803.

POWELL, JOSEPH T.
Clergyman. **Personal:** Born Nov 11, 1923, Baltimore; married Alice Pettiford; children: Cynthia R, Jo Anne M. **Educ:** Oakwood Coll Huntsville AL, BA 1946; Andrews Univ Berring Spgs MI, MA 1951. **Career:** AUS Ft Ord CA, chaplain 1960-; Academy Ch, pastor 1948-52; AUS chpln 1952-57; Immanuel Temple Seventh Day Adv Ch Durham NC, chpln 1957-60. **Orgs:** Mem NAACP Durham Interden Minis Assn 1957-60; Durham Com Negro Affairs 1957-60. **Honors/Awds:** Merit serv awd Durham Com Negro Affairs 1960; achievement awd Oakwood Coll 1974; Col AUS Res; numerous medals & commendatiosn Korea, Viet Nam, Armed Forces.

POWELL, JUAN HERSCHEL
Construction company manager. **Personal:** Born Aug 11, 1960, Roanoke, VA; son of Shirley Oliver Powell and John Henry Powell; married Eugenia Toliver Powell; children: Jamaal Khari Powell. **Educ:** Howard Univ, BSCE, 1982; Univ of MD, MBA, 1988. **Career:** The CECO Corp, construction engr, 1983-85; The George Hyman Construction Co, project engr 1985-89, project manager, 1990-; Buildtech Construction Co, Principal, 1989-. **Orgs:** Mem Amer Soc of Civil Engrs 1979-, Alpha Phi Alpha Frat Inc 1980-, Tau Beta Pi Natl Engrg Honor Soc 1982-, Natl Black MBA Assoc 1986-; pres, George Hyman Chapter, Toastmasters Inc, 1988; DC Contractors Assn, 1989; Howard University Engineering Alumni Association, president, 1989-92. **Honors/Awds:** Leadership Awd ASCE Howard Univ 1982; Certificate of Appreciation Alpha Phi Alpha Beta Chap 1983. **Business Addr:** Project Manager, George Hyman Construction Co, 7500 Old Georgetown Rd, Bethesda, MD 20814.

POWELL, JULIE
Public relations representative. **Personal:** Born Feb 21, 1957, Oakland, CA; daughter of Margaret Y Walker Wright and Sandy W Wright Jr. **Educ:** Scripps College, BA, classics, 1980; Boston University, MS, journalism, 1983, MA, Afro-American studies, 1983. **Career:** State House News Service, Boston, MA, reporter, 1983; United Press Intl, San Francisco, CA, reporter, 198-85; The Dallas Morning News, Dallas, TX, reporter, 1985-87; Fort Worth Star-Telegram, Fort Worth, TX, asst editor, 1987-91; The Seattle Times, Seattle, WA, asst city editor, 1991-92; EDS, Dallas, TX, PR representative, 1992-. **Orgs:** Natl Assn Black Journalists, 1983-; PRSA, 1992-. **Business Addr:** Public Relations Rep, EDS, 5400 Legacy H3-6F-47, Plano, TX 75024.

POWELL, KENNETH ALASANDRO
Consultant. **Personal:** Born Nov 26, 1945, Mobile, AL; son of Myrtle E Powell (deceased) and William O Powell Sr. **Educ:** Howard Univ, BS Mathematics 1967; Harvard Business School, MBA Finance 1974. **Career:** McKinsey & Co, associate mgmt consulting 1974-77; Chase Manhattan Bank, 2nd vice pres vice pres strategic mgmt 1977-83; Marine Midland Bank, vice pres and manager, mgt info sys, 1983-90; Powell Consulting Corp pres, strategy, mktg, real estate, finance, 1990-. **Orgs:** Pres 1989 Harvard Business School Assoc (all alumni); pres 1983-86, bd member, 1986-; Harvard Business School Club of NY; pres, Harvard Business School African American Alumni Assoc, 1997-; mem Harvard Club bd mem Foundation for Dance Promotion 1987; bd mem Victim Services/Travelers Aid, 1989-; mem American Society for Training and Development (ASTD), 1988-90; bd mem New York American Institute of Banking 1990; bd mem Foundation for Leadership Quality & Ethics Practice 1991-94, bd chrmn, 1995-; vice chairman, trea and bd mem, Jobs for Youth, 1991-; bd member, chair, investment committee, Inwood House, 1993-; advisory bd, Harvard Business School African American Student Union, 1995-. **Honors/Awds:** COGME Fellowship (Honorarium) Cncl of Grad Mgmt Educ Boston 1972-74; Martin Luther King Fellowship Woodrow Wilson Foundation 1972-74; Howard Univ Disting Alumnus Natl Assoc for Educ Oppor 1984; Harvard Business School, Bert King Service Award for Alumni Distinction, 1997. **Military Serv:** AUS and Reserves lieutenant colonel (retired) 5 yrs active, 23 yrs reserves; Bronze Star; Vietnam Cross of Gallantry 1969, Ranger Qualified. **Home Addr:** 245 E 87th St, Apt 11E, New York, NY 10128, (212)289-3525.

POWELL, KEVIN
Writer, actor. **Personal:** Born Apr 24, 1966, Jersey City, NJ; son of Shirley Mae Powell. **Educ:** Rutgers University, State University of New Jersey, 1984-88. **Career:** New York University, instructor, English, 1990-92; MTV, "Real World," writer, host, cast member, 1992-; Vibe Magazine, staff writer, 1993-. **Special Achievements:** Editor, In The Tradition: An Anthology of Young Black Writers, Harlem Writers Press, 1993; MTV, "Straight From the Hood," writer, host, 1993; Keeping it Real, 1997. **Business Phone:** (312)321-7908.

POWELL, LEOLA P.
Educator. **Personal:** Born Oct 9, 1932, Dawson, GA; married Benjamin; children: Gwendolyn, Benita, Benjamin Jr. **Educ:** Edward Waters Coll, BS 1962; FL A&M U, MA 1966. **Career:** School Psychology Services, Duval County School Bd, acting supr, psychologist 1967-74; School Psychology Services, Duval County, coordinator; teacher 1963-67; bookkeeper 1960-63; sec 1955-60. **Orgs:** Phi Delta Kappa 1975; mem St Pius Cath Ch; am Black FL NE FL Psychologist Assn; FL & Duval Co Prsnl Guidance Assn; treas Wmn's Political Caucus;Black Coalition; Charmettes Inc; mem Delta Kappa Gamma Soc Intrntl; mem St Bernadette Guild; mem Minority Womens Coalition. **Honors/Awds:** Am Heritage Tchng Accomps 1966; Academic Hons 1962. **Business Addr:** Counselor, Duval County School Board, 1701 Prudential Drive, Jacksonville, FL 32202.

POWELL, MARVIN
Professional football player (retired). **Personal:** Born Aug 30, 1955, Fort Bragg, NC; married Kristen; children: Amerique, Beronique. **Educ:** Univ of Southern California, BA, speech and political science, 1977; New York Univ Law School. **Career:** Tight end: New York Jets, 1977-85; Tampa Bay Buccaneers, 1986. **Orgs:** Vice pres NFL Players Assn; player rep NY Jets. **Honors/Awds:** Forrest Gregg Offensive Lineman of the Year, 1982; MVP 1979; honored by Women's Natl Republican Club NY; named to NFL All-Rookie Team, UPI, 1977; played in Pro Bowl, 1979-82; played in 3 Rose Bowls and 1 Liberty Bowl.

POWELL, MICHAEL K.
Government official. **Personal:** son Of Colin & Alma; married Jane Knott Powell; children: Jeffrey, Bryan. **Educ:** College of William and Mary, degree, government, 1985; Georgetown Univ Law Center, JD, 1993. **Career:** US Army, cav off, 1985-88; Dept of Defense, asst to secretary, 1988-90; US Court of Appeals, judicial clerk for chief judge, 1993-94; O'Melveny & Myers LLP, assoc, 1994-96; Dept of Justice, Antitrust Div, chief of staff, 1996-97; Federal Communications Commission, commissioner, 1997-. **Military Serv:** US Army, 3/2 Armored Calvary Regiment, cavalry platoon leader, troop exec off, 1985-88. **Business Addr:** Commissioner, Federal Communications Commission, 1919 M Street NW, Washington, DC 20554, (202)418-2200.

POWELL, MIKE
Olympic athlete. **Personal:** Born Nov 20, 1963, Philadelphia, PA; son of Carolyn Carroll. **Educ:** University of California, Irvine; UCLA, BA, sociology, 1986. **Career:** US Olympics, long jumper, 1988, 1992. **Orgs:** Alpha Phi Alpha. **Honors/Awds:** Olympic Games, Seoul, Korea, Silver Medal, 1988; Foot Locker SlamFest Champion, 1990, 1993; Amateur Athletics Foundation, Southern California Athlete of the Year, 1991; World Championships, Tokyo, world record jump, 1991; BBC TV Sports, Overseas Personality of the Year, 1991; James E. Sullivan Memorial Award, Outstanding Amateur Athlete, 1991; Jeep Superstars Champion, 1992; Jim Thorpe Pro Sports Award, Special Achievement, 1992; Olympic Games, Barcelona, Spain, Silver Medal, 1992. **Special Achievements:** World recordholder in the long jump since 1990.

POWELL, MYRTIS H.
Educator. **Personal:** Born Feb 6, 1939, Evergreen, AL; daughter of Lula B Jones Hall and Arthur Lee Hall; married Lavatus Powell; children: Kimberly, Robin, Judy, Lavatus III. **Educ:** Univ of Cincinnati, AS 1968, BS 1969, MA 1974, PhD 1978; Harvard Univ, certificate higher educ mgmt 1975; Salzburg Seminar in Amer Studies Salzburg Austria, certificate 1980. **Career:** Univ of Cincinnati, teacher asst 1969-71, asst to dean, lecturer 1971-73, assoc dean, adjunct, asst prof 1973-78; Edna McConnell Clark Found, program dir 1978-81; Miami Univ Oxford Campus, exec asst to the pres, adjunct asst prof of psychology, vice pres of student affairs 1989-. **Orgs:** Mem Leadership Cincinnati Alumni Assn; Chair, Mayerson Academy for Human Resource Devel; Univ of Cincinnati Clinical Center of the Women's Health Initiative; Pres, Natl Network of Runaway and Youth Services, Inc, Washington; vice pres, bd mem Seven Hills Neighborhood Houses Inc Cincinnati; bd mem, Natl Child Labor Comm NY; bd pres, Hamilton County Alcohol and Drug Addiction Svcs; Univ of Cincinnati, CLG of Medicine, Community Gerontology Program, board member. **Honors/Awds:** Univ of Cincinnati United Black Faculty Association Black Excellence Award 1973, 1978; Leadership Education & Service Award 1976, 1978; New Hope Baptist Church Outstanding Black American Recognition Award 1983; Cincinnati Urban League Guild Leadership Award 1977; National Council of Urban League Guilds Leadership Award 1978; Salute to Outstanding Volunteer 1978; Community Serv Award 1978; Cincinnati Community Chest & Council Outstanding Leadership Award Allocations Div 1979; National Association of Minority Women in Business 1980; Carver Community Center Leadership Award Peoria IL 1981; YWCA Career Woman of Achievement 1984; Leadership Cincinnati Graduate Class VIII 1984-85; Brotherhood Award, National Conference of Christians and Jews, 1988; Cincinnati YMCA, Black Achiever Award, 1991; Cincinnati Enquirer, Woman of the Year Award, 1991; Lighthouse Youth Services, Beacon of Light Award, 1996; United Way & Community Chest, Joseph A Hall Award, 1996; University of Cincinnati Alumni Achievement Award by Class of 1966; University of Cincinnati African American Alumni Assn, Sankofa Award for Excellence in Higher Education, 1997. **Business Addr:** Vice Pres for Student Affairs, Miami University, 113 Warfield Hall, Oxford, OH 45056.

POWELL, PATRICIA
Educator. **Personal:** Born May 4, 1966, Spanish Town, Japan; daughter of Winifred Powell and Philip Powell. **Educ:** Wellesley College, BA, 1988; Brown University, MFA, 1991. **Career:** South Boston High School, lecturer, 1987-88; University of Massachusetts, Boston, lecturer, Summers 1990, 1991; Brown University, teaching asst, 1990-91; University of Massachusetts, Boston, creative writing assistant professor, 1991-. **Orgs:** Wellesley College Academic Advisory, academic advisor, 1987-88; Boston Public Schools, peer advisor, 1987-88; Elerestory, Brown/RISD Journal of Arts, editor, 1990-91; Boston Public Schools, Caribbean literature course consultant, 1991; African Writers Conference, coordinator, 1991; Independent Black Filmmakers Series, coordinator, 1991; Search Comm Chair of Black Studies, 1992. **Honors/Awds:** MacDowell Writers Colony, MacDowell Fellow, 1992; Poets, Essayists, Novelists, PEN, New England Award, 1991; Brown University, Graduate Fellowship, 1989. **Special Achievements:** Author: "Repercussions," Ethos Woman, 1985; "Me Dying Trial," novel excerpt, The Boston Phoenix Literary Supplement, Dec 1987; "Me Dying Trial," novel excerpt, The Caribbean Writer, 1990; "A Small Gathering of Bones," novel excerpt, Art and Understanding, 1992; Me Dying Trial, novel, Heinemann Press, London, Nov 1993. **Business Addr:** Assistant Professor, English Dept, University of Massachusetts, 100 Morrisey Blvd, Wheatley Hall, Dorchester, MA 02125, (617)287-6701.

POWELL, PHILIP MELANCTHON, JR.
Educator. **Personal:** Born Jan 30, 1941, Greenwood, MS; son of Mamie Lee McCain Powell and Philip Melancthon Powell, Sr; married Sharon; children: David, Aaron, Robert, Kirby. **Educ:** Roosevelt Univ, BA 1964; Univ of Chgo, MA 1970, PhD 1971. **Career:** St Xavier Coll, instr 1971; Univ of Chicago Vocational Counseling Inst, instr 1971; Yale Univ, asst prof psych 1971-76; Univ of TX, assoc prof ed psych 1984-. **Orgs:** Contrib ed Roeper Review 1980-85; mem Natl Assoc of Gifted Children; mem The Natl Assoc of Black Psychologists; mem adv bd Umoja Family 1975-; caseworker Cook Cty Dept of Publ Aid 1964; co-investigator Yale Criterion Study 1971; former policy com mem Yale Dept of Afro-Amer Studies; speaker Columbia Univ 1974, Mensa Natl Conv 1974, Conf on Empirical Rsch in Black Psychology 1974-; chmn Devel Soc Personality Area of Dept Ed Psych Univ TX Austin 1984-85. **Honors/Awds:** Postdoctoral fellow Ford Found/NRC 1980-81; Teaching Execllence Award, College of Education, 1984. **Business Addr:** Associate Professor, Univ of Texas, Martin Luther King & Speedway, Ed Bldg 506F, Austin, TX 78712.

POWELL, RICHARD MAURICE
Corporate banking officer. **Personal:** Born Jan 8, 1951, Baltimore, MD; son of Peggy A Powell and John J Powell; married Debra S Powell, Jun 28, 1990; children: Richard Jr, Hakim, Qiana. **Educ:** Temple University, Philadelphia, PA, BS, 1974. **Career:** First Pennsylvania Bank, Philadelphia, PA, commercial loan officer, 1974-79; Crocker National Bank, San Diego, CA, assistant vice president, 1979-81; San Diego Trust & Savings Bank, San Diego, CA, vice president & manager, 1981-89; First Interstate Bank, San Diego, CA, vice president, 1989-. **Orgs:** Member, Healthcare Financial Management Assn, 1982-85; treasurer, Southeast San Diego Rotary Club, 1981-87; member, Door of Hope Salvation Army, 1981-83; member, Lay Advisory Committee, Mercy Hospital and Medical Center, 1988-89. **Home Addr:** 3654 Avocado Village Ct, #59, La Mesa, CA 91941.

POWELL, ROBERT E. **See Obituaries section.**

POWELL, ROBERT JOHN
Human resources executive. **Personal:** Born May 20, 1961, New York, NY; married Carlotta, Jun 1987; children: Selene, Jonathan, Courtney. **Educ:** Florida State University, attended, 1979-81; University of Central Florida, BA, 1990. **Career:** Walt Disney World, prof musician, personnel rep, sr personnel rep, HRD rep, 1983-94; Carlson Companies, mgr employee relations, dir employee relations, vp human resources, 1994-. **Orgs:** American Heart Association, human resources advisory bd, 1997-; Kappa Kappa Psi, regional member at large, vp. **Honors/Awds:** Outstanding Young Man of America, 1984. **Business Addr:** Vice Pres, Human Resources, Carlson Wagonlit Travel, Carlson Companies, Inc, PO Box 59159, Carlson Parking, Minneapolis, MN 55459-8206.

POWELL, ROBERT MEAKER
Clergyman. **Personal:** Born Apr 23, 1930, Cumberland, MD. **Educ:** Morgan St U, AB 1954; VA Theol Sem, MDiv 1957; NY Sch of Soc Wrk, 1958-61. **Career:** St Philip's Epis Ch, vicar 1971-; Chapel of the Holy Trinity, vicar 1964-67; St James' Ch, asso rector 1963-64; Lafayette Sq Comm Ctr, exec dir 1958-63; diocesan, missionary 1957-63. **Orgs:** Sec Stndng Com 1969-; pres Stndng Com 1976-77; mem Ecclesiastical Ct 1965-69; mem Yth Commn 1963-70; dir Summer Yth Conf 1959-71; mem Christian Soc Relat Commn of the Diocese; supr Mid-Atlantic Parish Training Inst 1966-69; epis chaplain Morgan St Univ 1962-71; instr Lay Sch of Theol; vice pres MD Clericus 1965; num Ad Hoc Com of thebishop; supr Deacon Training Prog 1969; nom Suffragan Bishop of Diocese of MD 1972; Ch Mission of Help; Florence Crittenton Svcs; Citizens Plng & Housing Assn; Citizens Sch Adv Bd; Urban Leag Bd; MD St Interracial Commn 1963-67; MD Cncl of Chs; Harlem Pk Urban Renewal Bd; ABCD Adoption Agy; consult Clifton T

Perkins St Hosp, Criminally Insane; Girl Scouts of Ctrl MD; Camp Fire Girls of MD; Literacy Cncl of MD; trustee Balt CommChest; Prisons Aid Soc; Balt-Cl MD Leag for Crippled Children & Adults; Planned Prnthd Assn of AA Co; Anne Arundel Co EOC Bd; chaplain Clifton T Perkins St Hosp; consult Anne Arundel Co Bd of Ed; num other orgs. **Honors/Awds:** Awards Balt Urban Leag; Anne Arundel Co Comm Svcs; Balt-Cntrl MD Leag for Crippled Children & Adults; NAACP; nom Outstndng Men of Yr, MD Jaycees; Afro-Am Hon Roll Plaque, Afro-Am Nwspr 1961, 1967; nom Caroline Brady Humanitarian Award, Anne Arundel Cncl of Comm Svcs; num comm & orgs awards. **Business Addr:** Vicar, St Phillip's Episcopal Church, Bestgate & Severn Grove Rds, Annapolis, MD 21401.

POWELL, THOMAS FRANCIS A.
Physician. **Personal:** Born Feb 13, 1925, Philadelphia, PA; married Mary Elizabeth Holloway; children: Thomas Jr, Allyson, Linda, Tracy, Earl Patrick. **Educ:** Univ PA, 1952; Philadelphia Coll Osteo Med, 1956. **Career:** Met Hosp, chf of staff, co-chmn gen surg; Philadelphia Coll Osteo Med Des Moines Coll, asst prof surg; Philadelphia Coll Podiatric Med, adj faculty; Am Coll, osteo Surgs. **Orgs:** AOA; POMA; Am Assn of Univ Profs Inner City Cncl; SE PA Heart Assn; past bd Houston Comm Ctr, Med Com Concerned Civil Rights; AFNA. **Honors/Awds:** Publ several med articles on Surg. **Military Serv:** USAF 1943-46. **Business Addr:** 5725 Lansdowne, Philadelphia, PA 19131.

POWELL, WAYNE HUGH
Financial administrator. **Personal:** Born Jul 29, 1946, Petersburg, VA; son of Lena Powell and Willie Powell; married Leslie J; children: Farrah, Brandi, Kristin. **Educ:** Lincoln Univ, BS Bus Admin 1970; Rockhurst Coll, MBA Fin 1979. **Career:** General Mills, reg office mgr 1975-79, reg credit mgr 1980-81, mgr gp fin analysis 1981-82, mgr of admin 1982-85. **Home Addr:** 18440 Beaverwood, Minnetonka, MN 55345-3110. **Business Addr:** Manager of Administration, General Mills Inc, 1701 Technology Drive, San Jose, CA 95110.

POWELL, WILLIAM
Sports executive. **Personal:** married Marcella (deceased); children: Renee, Lawrence. **Career:** Clearview Golf Club, owner; Timken Bearing and Steel Company, security guard. **Military Serv:** US Army, WWII. **Business Addr:** Owner, Clearview Golf Club, 8410 Lincoln St., East Canton, OH 44730-9443, (330)488-0404.

POWELL, WILLIAM
Dentist. **Personal:** Born Mar 6, 1935, Greenville, MS; married Carolyn M. **Educ:** Xavier Univ New Orleans, 1957; Meharry Med Coll Sch of Dent, 1963. **Career:** DDS Inc Bakersfield CA, pvt prac dent 1965-. **Orgs:** Mem Am Dent Assn; CA Dent Assn; Kern Co Dent Soc; Am Endodontic Soc; Aca Gen Dent; Pierre Favehard Acad; Assn Military Surg; Nat Dent Assn; pres Kern Co Dent Soc 1974; sec 1972; treas 1971; Kappa Alpha Psi Frat; NAACP. **Military Serv:** USAF capt 1963-65.

POWELL, WILLIAM J.
Clergyman. **Personal:** Born Nov 2, 1908, Crenshaw County, AL; married Bessie Ford Powell. **Educ:** Livingston Coll Salisbury NC, AB 1947, Doc Div Deg 1980; Hood Theol Sem Salisbury, MDiv 1950. **Career:** YMCA Birmingham, sec 1927-43; William's Chpl AME Zion Ch, pstr 1974-78; Oak St AME Zion Ch, 1978-; Birmingham & Montgomery AL, pastor; Cherryville Charlotte & E Spencer NC, pastor; Ridgewood & Asbury Pk NJ, pastor. **Orgs:** Mem Bd of dirl Montgomery Multi-Co Chpt, AL Caucus on Black Aging; del Wrld Meth Conf London 1966; del Denver 1971; bd dir YMCA Ridgewood NJ; memBd Mgnt Ridgewood Comm Chest; pres Wmancptn Procl Com Montgomery AL; sec, 1st vice pres Montgomery Impvmnt Assn; mem exec com Fair Hsng Com Ridgewood; mem Vlg Com on Yth; Kiwanis Club Ridgewoos & Asbury Pk; Mayor's Adv Com Asbury Pk; pres Shore Area Cncl Chs; led the Cong of St Stephen AME ZionCh, Asbury Pk NJ, in bldng a 90-unit, $1,501,000 hsng proj as means of identifying the ch with a real comm need; led same cong in estb a credit union. **Honors/Awds:** Spl cit 1956 Nat Bible Guild Inc Montgomery; Minister of Yr Award Asbury Pk Yth Cdts 1973; Award AME Zion Mnstrs All of NJ 1974. **Business Addr:** 2816 Tremont St, Montgomery, AL 36110.

POWELL, WILLIAM O., JR.
Dentist. **Personal:** Born Sep 19, 1934, Andalusia, AL; son of Myrtle Estelle Powell and William O Powell Sr; married Anna D Thompson; children: Rosalyn F, Michelle R. **Educ:** Talladega Coll, AB 1955; Howard Univ Coll of Dentistry, DDS 1967. **Career:** Ft Detrick Dept of Defense, histopath tech 1958-61; Mt Sinai Hosp, internship 1968; Walter Reed Army Medical Ctr, rsch biologist 1961-63; Howard Univ Coll of Dentistry, asst prof 1968-69, dir dental therapist training 1969-75; Private Practice, dentist 1968-. **Orgs:** Omega Psi Phi Frat; Amer Dental Assn; Natl Dental Association; Maryland State Dental Association; Southern Maryland Dental Society; Robert T Freeman Dental Society; Kiwanis Intl; Montgomery County Maryland Drug Abuse Advisory Council; NNGA; Nomads Golf Assn; Pro Duffers Golf Club; Sigma Pi Phi Frat. **Honors/Awds:** Published paper on "Comparison of Dental Therapists Trainee and Dental Students'' Journal of Dental Education; Fellow, American College of Dentists, 1989. **Home Addr:** 14801 Waterway Dr, Rockville, MD 20853. **Business Addr:** 809 Viers Mill Rd, Ste 213, Rockville, MD 20851.

POWELL, YVONNE MACON (YVONNE MACON COOK)
Corrections administrator (retired). **Personal:** Born Dec 8, 1936, Harlem, NY; daughter of Eugenia Wright Jackson and James Macon; married Alfred J Powell Jr, Sep 2, 1962; children: Richard L Cook III, Stacy D Powell, Alfred Edward Powell, Natasha N Powell, Ronald L Gardner, Towano Y Pittman, Terrence L Gardner, Sharon M Gardner. **Educ:** Tennessee State Univ, Nashville TN, 1955-57; Mercy Coll, Dobbs Ferry NY, BS criminal justice, 1980; Natl Academy of Corrections, Denver CO, 3 certificates, 1981, 1982; Long Island Univ, Dobbs Ferry NY, 1981. **Career:** Dept Public Safety, White Plains NY, parking enforcement, 1962-65; Westchester County Sheriff's Dept, White Plains NY, deputy sheriff, 1967-; West County Dept of Correction, Valhalla NY, correction officer, 1969-71, sergeant, 1971-82, captain, 1982-84, asst warden, 1984-88; assoc warden, 1988-91. **Orgs:** NAACP; Urban League of Westchester; Daughter of Elks-Rosebud Temple; Alpha Kappa Alpha; Alpha Psi Epsilon. **Honors/Awds:** Commissioner's Award, Westchester County Dept of Correction, 1981, 1983; Community Service, Central 7, Greenburgh NY, 1982; Mem of the Year, Northeast Region Natl Black Police Assn, 1983; Guardian of the Year, Westchester Rockland Guardians Assn, 1984; Contribution to Law Enforcement, Tri-County Federation of Police, 1984; Community Service, Westchester Co-op, 1985; Coach of the Year, Kenisco Little League, 1986; Achievement Award, Natl Negro Business and Professional Women, 1989; Honorary Doctrate Deg, Dr of Humane Letters, Coll of New Rochelle, New Rochelle NY, 1994; Inductee, Wesichester Women's Hall of Fame, 1994.

POWELL-JACKSON, BERNICE
Church administrator. **Personal:** Born Mar 9, 1949, Washington, DC; daughter of Bernice Fletcher and Otis Fletcher; married Robert C S (deceased); married Dr Franklin Jackson, 1991. **Educ:** Wilson Coll, BA 1971; Columbia Univ Grad Sch of Journalism, MS 1975; Union Theological Seminary, MDiv, 1991. **Career:** United Church of Christ, exec assoc to the pres, 1989-93, exec dir, commission for racial justice, currently; Women's Div Gov Offc NY, spl asst for pub info 1979-; Equitable Life Assur Soc, asso mgr pub relations 1977-79; Natl Urban Leag, communctns spec 1975-77; Renewal Mag, asst managing editor 1974-75; Nat Cncl of Ch, Africa dept asst 1972-74; Wash DC Sch System, tchr 1971-72. **Orgs:** Bd mem Manhattan Br NY Urban Leag 1978-; chrprsn Riverside Ch Video Project 1979-; vice pres Coalition of 100 Black Women 1980-81; pres, NY Coalition of 100 Black Women, 1981-85. **Honors/Awds:** Honorable Doctorate in Humane Letters, Defiance College, 1994. **Business Addr:** Executive Director, Commission for Racial Justice, United Church of Christ, 700 Prospect Ave, Cleveland, OH 44115.

POWERS, CLYDE J.
Sports administrator. **Personal:** Born Aug 19, 1951, Pascagoula, MS. **Educ:** Oklahoma University. **Career:** New York Giants, defensive back, 1974-78; Kansas City Chiefs, defensive back, 1978, 1979; Indianapolis Colts, assistant coach for special assignments, 1980-82, college scout, 1982-85, 1988-91, director of pro personnel, 1985-87, 1992-. **Special Achievements:** Earned All-Big Eight honors at cornerback as a senior at Oklahoma; Coaches All America "Ernie Davis" Award Winner. **Business Addr:** Dir of Pro Personnel, Indianapolis Colts, POB 535000, Indianapolis, IN 46253, (317)297-2658.

POWERS, GEORGIA M.
Government official (retired). **Personal:** Born Oct 29, Springfield, KY; daughter of Frances Walker Montgomery and Ben Montgomery; married James L (deceased); children: William F Davis (deceased), Cheryl Campbell, Deborah Rattle. **Educ:** Lou Munic Coll, 1940-43. **Career:** KY State Senate, senator (retired). **Orgs:** Chmn Senate Lbr & Indstry Com; mem Jeff Co Dem Exec Comm 1964-66; mem Lbr & Indstry Comm; Cities Comm; YWCA; NAACP; Urban League; frmr Bd of ovrsrs Univ of Louisville; 1st wmn & 1st blck elected to KY Sen; mem bd of dir Fund for Women, Inc. **Honors/Awds:** Kennedy King awd Young Dem KY 1968; Ky Cong of Barb & Beau Ach Awd 1968; AKA Recg Awd 1970; Zeta Phi Beta; Sor outsdng serv awd 1971; Merit awd Zion Bapt Ch 1969; Honorary Doctor of Laws, Univ of Kentucky; Doctor of Humane Letters, Univ of Louisville, 1988. **Special Achievements:** Author: "I Shared the Dream" (New Horizon Press) 1995. **Home Addr:** 800 S 4th St, Apt 2705, Louisville, KY 40203.

POWERS, MAMON, SR.
Construction company executive. **Career:** Means Developers, apprentice carpenter, 1946, journeyman carpenter to vice president, 1949-58; Winters-Powers Construction Company, Inc, secretary/treasurer, 1958-67; Powers & Sons Construction Company, Inc, president, 1967-. **Orgs:** Board of directors, Northern Indiana Home Builders Assn; member, Chamber of Commerce of Greater Gary; member, Gary Rotary Club; member, Calumet Builders Assn; member, Associated General Contractors of America; board of directors, State Chamber of Commerce; chairman, Lake County Community Development Committee; life member, NAACP. **Business Addr:** President, Powers & Sons Construction Co Inc, 2636 W 15th Ave, Gary, IN 46404.

POWERS, MAMON M., JR.
Business executive. **Personal:** Born Mar 10, 1948, Gary, IN; son of Leolean Powers and Mamon Powers; married Cynthia R Berry, Jul 23, 1972; children: Kelly, Mamon. **Educ:** Purdue Univ, BS, civil engineering, 1970. **Career:** Am Oil Co Whiting IN, design engr 1970-71; Powers & Sons Const Co, sec-treas, 1971-88, pres 1988-. **Orgs:** Former pres Calumet Chap IN Soc of Professional Engrs; bd of dirs Constr Advance Found; Assn Gen Contrs; former chrm Const Advancement Foundation 1983-85; former pres Calumet Builders Assn 1985-87; National Assn of Minority Contractors; Black Contractors United; Young Presidents Organization; trustee, Purdue University. **Honors/Awds:** 60th largest African-American owned business (industrial & service) 1995; NAACP, Benjamin Hooks Award for Achievement. **Business Addr:** President, Powers & Sons Construction Co Inc, 2636 W 15th Ave, Gary, IN 46404.

POWERS, RUNAS, JR.
Physician. **Personal:** Born Dec 11, 1938, Jackson's Gap, AL; son of Geneva Powers and Runas Powers Sr; married Mary Alice; children: Tiffany, Trina, Runas III. **Educ:** TN State, BS 1961; Meharry Med Coll, MD 1966. **Career:** Private Practice, physician. **Orgs:** Mem Arthritis Foundation, Amer Rheumatism Assn, Natl Med Assn, Amer Fed Clinical Rsch; American College of Rheumatology; American Medical Assn. **Honors/Awds:** Alexander City Chamber of Commerce, Man of the Year, 1991. **Military Serv:** USN Reserve lt cmdr 1967-69. **Business Addr:** Physician, 3368 Hwy 280 Bypass, Ste 108, Alexander City, AL 35010.

PRATER, OSCAR L.
Educational administrator. **Personal:** Born in Sylacauga, AL; married Jacqueline P; children: Lamar, Marcus. **Educ:** Talladega College, BA 1961; Hampton University, MA 1967; The College of William and Mary, MS 1968, EdD 1977. **Career:** Middlesex Co Public Schools, mathematics teacher 1961-62; Wmsbg-James City Public Schools, mathematics teacher 1962-72; Rappahanock Community College, chairman, division of mathematics 1972-79; Hampton University, vice-president for administrative services, 1979-90; Fort Valley State College, pres, 1990-. **Orgs:** Member Human Services Board, Hampton Roads Cultural Action Committee, trustee, chairman First Baptist Church 1980-84; institutional representative American Council Teacher Education 1980-; management consultant HU Administrative Leadership Team 1982-83-84; member Board of Visitors/VA State Univ 1982-. **Honors/Awds:** Citizen of the Year Chamber of Commerce 1970; publication Faculty Perceptions of Selected Student Characteristics 1978; Outstanding Man of the Year Omega Psi Phi Fraternity 1982. **Business Addr:** President, Fort Valley State College, Fort Valley, GA 31030.

PRATER-HARVEY, PEGGY. See Obituaries section.

PRATHER, JEFFREY LYNN
Administrator. **Personal:** Born May 14, 1941, New York, NY; son of Mary Jane Dickerson Prather and James Basil Prather. **Educ:** Howard Univ Washington DC, 1959-60; Queens Coll CUNY Flushing NY, BA 1965; CA State Univ Northridge CA, MS Equiv 1967. **Career:** Operation Head Start Brooklyn NY, consultant psychologist 1967-71; MDTP Bd of Ed of City of NY, asst in guidance 1968-72, counseling suprv 1969-72, admin asst adult training ctr 1969-72; Sacramento City Coll, instr 1978; Malcoln-King Harlem Coll Ext NYC, instr, interim chmn psych 1979-80; Dept of State USA, escort/interpreter 1979-; Sacramento CA, consult juristic psych 1982-; Pratherian Enterprises, director, 1972-. **Orgs:** Action Co-op Volunteer, Attica Correctional Facility, Literacy Vol of Amer 1975-76; corr proj dir NY, CA Literacy Vol of Amer 1976-77; consult CA State Dept of Ed, Migrant Ed 1977-79; mem Intl Assoc of GP Psychotherapy, Intl Council of Psych, Assoc of Black Psych. **Honors/Awds:** Author, "A Mere Reflection, The Psychodynamics of Black & Hispanic Psychology," Dorrance & Co, 1977; author, "400 Days at Attica," Dorrance & Co, 1983. Honorary doctorate, Rockdale College, Toronto, Canada, 1971. **Business Addr:** Director, Pratherian Enterprises, 21031 Woodfield Rd, Laytonsville, MD 20882-1204, (301)963-1370.

PRATHER, THOMAS L., JR.
Military officer. **Personal:** Born Jun 25, 1940, Washington, DC; son of Jestina Jones Stewart and Thomas L Prather Sr (deceased); married Beulah Sullivan Prather, Nov 3, 1962; children: Delia, Marcia, Thomas III. **Educ:** Morgan State University, Baltimore, MD, BS, 1962; Command General Staff College, Fort Leavenworth, KS, 1972; Florida Institute of Technology, Melborne, FL, MS, 1974; US Army War College, Carlisle, PA, 1982. **Career:** United States Army, US Army Troop Support Command, St Louis, MO, commanding general, currently. **Orgs:** Member, The Ordnance Corps Association, 1988-; member, Association of the US Army, 1978-; honorary member,

Non-Commissioned Officer Association, 1990. **Honors/Awds:** Distinguished Alumni of the Year Citation, National Association for Equal Opportunity in Higher Education, NAFEO, 1991. **Military Serv:** US Army, Brigadier General, 1962-; Army Commendation Medal, 1964-65; Army Commendation Medal, 1966-67; Bronze Star Medal, 1968-68; Army Commendation Medal, 1969-70; Meritorious Service Medal, 1974-75; Meritorious Service Medal, 1975-76; General Staff Identification Badge, 1976; Meritorious Service Medal, 1982-85; The Legend of Merit, 1985-87; Defense Superior Service Medal, 1987-90. **Business Addr:** Commanding General, US Army Troop Support Command, 4300 Goodfellow Blvd, Bldg 101, St Louis, MO 63120-1798.

PRATT, A. MICHAEL
Attorney. **Personal:** Born Apr 1, 1959, Grindstone, PA; son of Joan A Richardson and Brady Pratt; children: Jeanine. **Educ:** Washington and Jefferson College, BA, 1981; University of Stockholm, International Graduate School, 1983-84; Harvard Law School, JD, 1985. **Career:** Hon Nathaniel R Jones, Sixth Circuit Court of Appeals, law clerk, 1985-86; City of Philadelphia Law Department, chief deputy city solicitor, 1992-94; Pepper Hamilton & Scheetz, attorney/partner, 1986-92, 1994-. **Orgs:** National Bar Assn, board of governors, 1992-; Barrister Assn of Phila Inc, president, 1991-92; Philadelphia Bar Assn, chair, Young Lawyers Section, 1991, board of governors, 1991, 1993-95; Omega Psi Phi Fraternity; City of Philadelphia Activities Fund Inc, board of directors, 1995; Foundation for Education Excellence, Inc, chair of board of directors; Community Legal Services of Philadelphia, Inc, chair of board of trustees. **Honors/Awds:** Community Legal Services Inc, Equal Justice Award, 1993; National Black Law Students Assn, Nelson Mandela Service Award, 1992; Philadelphia Business Journal, "40 Under 40" Business Award, 1991; National Bar Association, Presidential Award, 1994; Delaware Valley Counselor, Ten Fresh Faces for the 90's, 1989. **Home Addr:** 2124 N 50th Street, Philadelphia, PA 19131. **Business Addr:** Attorney, Pepper, Hamilton & Scheetz, 3000 Two Logan, Sq., Philadelphia, PA 19103-2799, (215)981-4386.

PRATT, ALEXANDER THOMAS
Educational administrator. **Personal:** Born Sep 18, 1938, St Martinville, LA; son of Oliver Thompson and Louise Thompson; married Mable Agnes Lee; children: Thomas, Thaddeus. **Educ:** Prairie View A&M, BA 1961, MA 1963. **Career:** Prairie View A&M, asst circulation librarian 1962-63; La Marque Ind School, teacher & head of history dept 1963-70; Coll of the Mainland, instructor 1970-76, chairman Social Science Division 1976-. **Orgs:** mayor pro tem City of La Marque 1974-; Galveston Co Hist Commn 1975-; Galveston Co Mayors Assn 1979-80; TX State Comm onUrban Needs 1980-; member Phi Alpha Theta; Galveston Historical Foundation. **Honors/Awds:** HK "Griz" Eckert Award Coll of the Mainland 1975; Jaycee of the Year The La Marque Jaycee 1975-76; Disting Serv Award La Marque Jaycee 1978; Outstanding Comm Serv Delta Sigma Theta 1980. **Business Addr:** Chm, Social Science Div, College of the Mainland, 8001 Palmer Hwy, Texas City, TX 77591.

PRATT, J. C.
Educator, author, clergyman. **Personal:** Born Nov 15, 1927, Selina, TX; son of Annie and Jack; children: Cardelia Marie, John Curtis. **Educ:** Langston U, BS 1961. **Career:** Kiamichi Area VO-TECH Sch E Star Bapt Ch Mcalester OK, educ bapt min civ ldr 1974-; US Civil Svc, 1947-52, 1962-72; BTU & Bible Inst Centralwayland Bapt Dist, 1962-65; Bethlehem Bapt Ch, past 1959-66; E Star Bapt Ch, assoc min 1967. **Orgs:** Not pub OK 1962-64; chmn Soc Ser Task Force for Moc Cit 1970-73; chmn bd dir Eastsde Comm Ctr 1972-; chmn Voc Serv Prog 1974-; mem Pitts CoYth Shelt Bd 1971-; assn exec NAACP OK 1965-67; assn exec Pitts Co CORE 1967-; most worship mstr Prince Hall Mason Ldge Eufaula OK 1962-; OK Dept of Agric for the state of OK 1976; comm Amer Leg Post 293 1959-. **Honors/Awds:** Nat def arm forces med 1954; cert for dist serv in hum rhts 1969; pub "The blck Ldrs in Indus" The Blck Voices 1973; list Men of Achieve Intnl Biograph Cambrid Eng 1977-79. **Military Serv:** AUS E-5 1952-57.

PRATT, JOAN M.
City official. **Career:** City of Baltimore, comptroller, 1995-. **Special Achievements:** Second African American female city comptroller in the history of Baltimore. **Business Addr:** City of Baltimore, Office of Comptroller, Room 204 City Hall, 100 N Holliday, Baltimore, MD 21202, (410)396-4755.

PRATT, LOUIS HILL
Educational Administrator. **Personal:** Born Aug 11, 1937, Savannah, GA; married Darnell Myrtice Dixon; children: Karen Lynnette, Kenneth Dwayne. **Educ:** Savannah State College, BS (cum Laude), 1958; Columbia Univ Teacher Coll, MA, 1967; Florida State University, Tallahassee, PhD, 1974. **Career:** Public School State of Georgia, teacher, 1958-62, 1964-69; US Army Air Def Command, operations assistant, 1962-64; Florida A&M University, Language Dept, instr, 1969-74; Florida A&M University, Freshman Comp Dept of Language & Lit, asst professor & director, 1974-75; Florida A&M University, Department of English, professor of English, 1975-. **Orgs:** Life member, College Language Association; Alpha Phi Alpha; pres, Middle Atlantic Writers Assn, 1994-96; charter member, Seven Hills Toastmasters Club. **Honors/Awds:** Recipient NDEA Fellowship, Florida State University, 1972-74; J Russell Reaver Award, Florida State University, best creative scholarship in American Literature in dissertation, 1974-75; National Endowment for the Humanities Stipend to attend Afro-Amer Culture Inst, Univ of Iowa, 1977; Man of the Year Award, Alpha Phi Alpha, 1979; Presidential Medallion, Excellence from the Savannah State Univ Natl Alumni Assn, 1990; Teacher of the Year, 1994; Advanced Teacher of the Year, Florida A&M University, 1995. **Business Addr:** Professor of English, Florida A&M University, Rm 414, Tucker Hall, Tallahassee, FL 32307-4800.

PRATT, MABLE
Elected official, educator. **Personal:** Born May 27, 1943, Houston, TX; married Alexander Pratt; children: Thomas, Thaddeus. **Educ:** Prairie View A&M, BS Home Econ Ed 1967; Univ of Houston, MS Ed Mgmt 1978, starting in doctoral program summer 1985. **Career:** Queen of Peace School Lamarque, second teacher 1969-70; Sacred Heart School Galveston, third grade teacher 1970-71; Rosenberg Elem Galveston, fifth grad teacher 1971-77; Rosenberg Elem Galveston, title I reading/math teacher 1977-82; Alamo Elem Galveston, fifth grade teacher 1982-; LaMarque School Dist, bd mem. **Orgs:** Mem Assoc of Childhood Ed, TX Classroom Assoc, TX professional Ed, Alpha Kappa Alpha Sor, Amer Business Women's Assoc, Amer School Bd Assoc, Gulf Coast Area Assoc of School Bds, Lamarque Gifted and Talented, School Home Adv Panel of Ed, Amer Bus Women Assoc, Alpha Kappa Alpha Sor of LaMarque; dir LaMarque Youth Aid Proj, United Way of the Mainland; LaMarque School Bd; Queen of Peace Instr of Interior Decorating COM; LaMarque Parent Teachers Assoc; Helped toorganize Non-Graded Reading Program in GISD; served on Teacher Adv Council, Policy Revision Comm, Pres & several other offices of ACE, state vice pres of Assoc of Childhood Ed; hospitality chmn at Rosenberg; served as Admin Designee for ARD Meetings; attended many seminars on HB 246, HB 72, Chap 75. **Honors/Awds:** Jaycee-ette of the Year 1974,75; TX Hon Life Mem Jaycee-ettes 1978; TX Hon Life Mem PTA 1980; Serv Above Self-Rotary Intl Awd 1978; Outstanding Young Woman of Amer 1979. **Home Addr:** 2616 Lake Park Dr, La Marque, TX 77568.

PRATT, MELVIN LEMAR
City official. **Personal:** Born Mar 16, 1946, Jackson, MS; son of Lula B Hamilton Pratt and Alvin Pratt Sr; married Mary Frances Buchanan, Apr 30, 1964; children: Kim Evette, Yuvette Patriece, Eric Marlowe, Justin Lavelle, Aaron Antion. **Career:** Maywood Concerned Citizens Org, second in command 1976-85; Village Bd, 3rd dist trustee, currently. **Orgs:** Mem NBC-LEO 1983-; parent helper Boy Scouts of Amer 1978-80; usher St James Catholic Church 1977-84. **Honors/Awds:** Image Awd; Fred Hampton Scholarship Awd 1982. **Home Addr:** 214 So 7th Ave, Maywood, IL 60153. **Business Addr:** Trustee Dist 3, Village Board, 115 So 5th Ave, Maywood, IL 60153.

PRATT, RUTH JONES (RUTH J. KING)
Educator. **Personal:** Born Aug 2, 1923, Baltimore, MD; married James; children: Karl. **Educ:** Coppin State Tchrs Coll, BS 1943; Howard U, MA 1948; Johns Hopkins U, attnd; Univ of MD; Towson State U; Morgan State U. **Career:** Baltimore City Public Schools, sr educ officer to supt of public instr present; elem prin 1968-75; asst prin elem school 1963-68; curriculum specialist elem school 1961-63; sr teacher master teacher 1959-61; supr teacher 1952-55; demo teacher 1945-49; teacher 1943; Morgan State Univ, asst prof reading devel & educ psychology 1969-73; Reading Workshops, consultant 1968-71; Human Relations Inst Towson State Univ, consultant 1968-70; Youth Summer Human Relations Workshop Natl Conf of Christians & Jews 1969-70; cosmetics consultant wig stylist 1968-77. **Orgs:** Chmn Miss Untd Negro Coll Fund Contest 1972-76; vice pres Provident Hosp Aux 1974-75; exec com dir search for talent 1969-76; chmn Untd Fund CICHA Campaign Baltimore City Pub Schs 1975-77; allocation panel Untd Fund 1976-77; bd dir Untd Way 1976-79; chmn Baltimore Employ Adv Com 1976-77; pres Professional Untd in Serv to Cherry Hill Comm 1970-75; long range plng com Girl Scouts of Central MD 1976-79; bd dir YWCA Central MD 1977; com for Preserv of OrchardSt Ch 1977; pres Baltimore Alumnae Chap Delta Sigma Theta Sor 1974-76; Mayor's Bicent Ball Com 1976; Afro Am Expo Steering Com 1976-77; mem Sharon Bapt Ch; organ dir Sunday Sch Choir; chrpsn annl mus Schlrshp Benefit; chmn 85th Anniv of Sharon 1970; Comm Leaders of Am 1971. **Honors/Awds:** Serv plaque Untd Negro Coll Fund 1974; serv cert SE Br Kiwanis Club 1975; cert awds plaque Delta Sigma Theta Sor; sincere ded serv plaque PUSH 1975; outstnd woman panelist St John's Bapt Ch 1977; comm serv awd Untd Fund-CICHA Campaign 1975-76. **Business Addr:** Principal, Baltimore City Public Schools, 5025 Dickey Hill Rd, Baltimore, MD 21207.

PRATTIS, LAWRENCE
Judge. **Personal:** Born Jun 16, 1926, Philadelphia, PA; married Marie; children: Susan, David. **Educ:** Howard Univ, AB 1946; Temple Univ School of Law, JD 1951. **Career:** Maple Corp, sec 1967-69; HAAS Comm Fund, sec 1969-72; Eastern Dist of PA, asst city solicitor; private practice 1953-73; Court of Common Pleas, judge 1973-. **Orgs:** Mem Distrib Com Philadelphia Found 1971-73; Lectr in Law Sch Villanova Univ 1976-80; mem Exec Com PA Conf of State Trial Judges. **Military Serv:** USMC 1951-53. **Business Addr:** City Hall, 1400 Market St, Philadelphia, PA 19107.

PREISKEL, BARBARA SCOTT
Attorney. **Personal:** Born Jul 6, 1924, Washington, DC; daughter of B Beatrix and James Scott; married Robert H Preiskel; children: John S, Richard A. **Educ:** Wellesley Coll, BA 1945; Yale Univ, LLB 1947. **Career:** Hon Charles E Wyzanski Boston, law clerk 1948-49; Dwight Royall Harris Koegel & Caskey, assoc free lance 1950-59; Motion Picture Assn of Amer, dep atty/vp 1959-77, sr vice pres & general counsel 1977-83; self-employed attorney, 1983-. **Orgs:** Trustee, American Museum of the Moving Image, 1986-94; trustee, Wellesley College, 1988-; director, Tougaloo College Economic Development Corporation, 1991-; dir, American Women's Economic Development Co, 1982-93; trustee, Ford Foundation, 1982-94; chairman, New York Community Trust, 1990-; distribution com, New York Community Trust, 1978-89; director, New York Philharmonic, 1971-94; director, American Stores Company, 1985-; director, General Electric Co., 1982-; director, MassMutual, 1983-; director, Textron Inc, 1975-; director, The Washington Post Company, 1985-. **Honors/Awds:** Meritorious Award Natl Assn of Theatre Owners 1970, 1972; Theatre Owners of New England Award 1971; Wellesley Coll Alumni Achievement Award 1975; Catalyst Award for Women of Outstanding Achievement 1979; YWCA Elizabeth Morrow Achievement Awd 1985; Award for Outstanding Contributions to Women's Economic Development, AWED, 1985; Tribute to Women in International Industry Honoree, YWCA, 1984; Director's Choice Award, National Women's Economic Alliance Foundation, 1989, Keystone Award, Federation of Protestant Welfare Angencies, Inc, 1991. **Business Addr:** Attorney, 60 E 42nd, New York, NY 10165.

PREJEAN, RUBY D.
Educator. **Personal:** Born Feb 20, 1925, Terrell, TX; married Wilbur. **Educ:** BS 1958; Southwestern Christian Coll, teaching fellow. **Career:** Quinlan Schools, teacher 1942; NV Public Schools, 1948; Southwestern Christian Coll Terrell, 1958; Hardin-Jefferson Ind School Dist Sourlake, presently. **Orgs:** Hardin-Jefferson Educ Assn; TX State Tchrs Assn; Hardin Jefferson Classroom Tchrs Assn; TX State Classroom Tchrs Assn; Nat Educ Assn YMCA; pres Zeta Phi Beta Sor Inc Pub Relations 1966-68; spl liason com Welfare Dept Beaumont 1975. **Honors/Awds:** Classroom tchr awd outstndg serv Hardin-Jefferson 1969-70; Outstndg Tchrs Am Elem 1972. **Business Addr:** PO Box 398, China, TX.

PRELOW, ARLEIGH
Filmmaker, writer, graphic designer. **Personal:** Born Feb 1, 1953, Los Angeles, CA; daughter of Leona Kern Prelow and Clifford Nathaniel Prelow; children: Alison Guillory, Kara Guillory. **Educ:** Univ of California, Berkeley, BA, 1974; attended Laney Coll, Oakland CA, 1984-86; Univ of California, Los Angeles, 1986-89. **Career:** KQIV-Radio, Portland OR, program producer, host, writer, and spot announcer, 1975; KPIX-TV, San Francisco CA, segment producer and writer, researcher, production asst, sec, 1975-77; WTBS-TV, Atlanta GA, producer, writer, researcher, on-air dir, 1977-78; WSB-TV, Atlanta, segment writer and researcher, 1977; WETA-TV, Washington DC, associate producer, 1978-80; Scott Hall Productions, San Anselmo CA, administrator, 1980-81; Moti-Vision, Richmond CA, exec dir and producer, 1981-84; Arleigh Prelow Design, Los Angeles, owner and graphic designer, 1984-90; ROJA Productions, Boston, MA, filmmaker, administrator, 1990-; freelance writer, Boston, MA. **Orgs:** Sec and mem, Natl Assn of Negro Business and Professional Women's Clubs, 1986-89; mem, Worship '89 Conference Planning Comm, Synod of Southern California and Hawaii Presbyterian Church USA, 1988-89; treas and mem, Presbyterian Women, Redeemer Presbyterian Church, Los Angeles, 1988-. **Honors/Awds:** Feature editor and writer, Black Thoughts Newspaper, Berkeley CA, 1973-74; writer, Portland Observer, Portland OR, 1975; writer, Soul Newsmagazine, 1978; Emmy Award for producer of cultural affairs prog, Acad of Television Arts and Sciences, Atlanta, 1978; third place in publication design California, Cappy Awards, California Public Information Officers Assn, 1988; gold winner in magazine design intl, Mercury Awards, 1988; grand prize, best publication US and Canada, City Hall Digest Awards, 1988. **Business Addr:** Filmmaker, Administrator, ROJA Productions, 486 Shawmut Ave, Boston, MA 02118.

PRESLEY, CALVIN ALONZO
Educator. **Personal:** Born Jun 11, 1914, Statesboro, GA; married Viola Brown. **Educ:** Savannah State Coll, BS 1940; Tuskegee Inst, MAgrEd; Univ WI, addl study; Univ of GA; Auburn U; GA So. **Career:** Randolph Co Comprehensive HS, teacher vocational agriculture; Randolph Co Sys, teacher vocational agriculture 1942-75; Jeffersonville GA, teacher 1940-42. **Orgs:** Mem Duroc Breeding Assn; Farm Bureau; Randolph Co Assn Educators; GA Assn of Educators; GA Voc Agr Assn; NEA; Am Voc Asso; master mason S T Thomas #70 Cuthbert GA;

Eta Omicron. **Honors/Awds:** Serv awd GA Voc Educ Agr 10 yr cert 1950, 20 yr cert 1960, 30 yr plaque 1970; letter of rec from Pres F D Roosevelt.

PRESLEY, OSCAR GLEN
Veterinarian. **Personal:** Born Dec 19, 1942, Kosciusko, MS; married Ethel Rita Scott; children: Wanda, Glen Jr, Corey. **Educ:** Rust Coll, BS 1966; TX Southern Univ, MS 1971; Tuskegee Inst, DVM 1974. **Career:** Meridian Public School, teacher 1967-69, dir independent study 1968-69; Tuskegee Sch of Vet Med Freshman Class, president 1969-70; Lexington Animal Clinic, pres. **Orgs:** Bd mem Jackson Chap Natl Bus League 1977-; bd mem K & S Chemical 1979-; bd mem New Hope Church 1980-84; vice pres MS Vet Med Assn 1983; natl chmn Fund Raising Rust Coll 1983; Phi Beta Sigma 1985; pres Lexington & hanging Moss Clinics. **Honors/Awds:** Outstanding Young Man of Amer 1972; Outstanding Service Awd Jackson State Univ Minority Student 1985, 86. **Military Serv:** AUS capt 2 yrs. **Home Addr:** 571 Woodson Dr, Jackson, MS 39206. **Business Addr:** President, Lexington Animal Clinic, 1250 Forest Ave, Jackson, MS 39206.

PRESS, HARRY CODY, JR.
Educator. **Personal:** Born Aug 22, 1931, Chesapeake, VA; son of Vianna Press and Harry Press; married Francella Jane Teele; children: H Cody III, Lillian Jan. **Educ:** VA Union U, BS 1952; Medl Coll VA, MD 1957; Am Brd Radiology, Diplomate 1965; Am Coll Radiology, Flw 1980. **Career:** Howard U, chmn dept radiology 1966-79, prof radiology 1978-. **Orgs:** Advy brd Washington Inst Techlgy 1970-78; const radlgy Commty Grp Found 1969-; commt grants James Picker Found 1972-74; brd dir Silver Spring Boys Club 1971-74; sr warden Trinity Epis Chrh 1972-74; tm phys Bethesda Chevy Chase Ftbl Tm 1984. **Honors/Awds:** Spel serv awd Howard Univ Const 1975; medl tm Urban Leag Trk Run 1981-82; invested foreign bds Am Jourl Roentlgy 1976. **Military Serv:** USN lt med Ofc 2 yrs. **Home Addr:** 6745 Newbold Dr, Bethesda, MD 20817. **Business Addr:** Professor of Radiology, Howard Univ, 2041 Georgia Ave NW, Washington, DC 20060.

PRESSEY, JUNIUS BATTEN, JR.
Business executive. **Personal:** Born Apr 6, 1947, Hampton, VA; married Elaine F Jenkins. **Educ:** Central State Univ Bus Adminstrn, 1971-72; IN Univ, BS 1975; Attending, Coll for Financial Planning. **Career:** Magnavox Corp, account intern 1972-73; City Util of Ft Wayne IN, acct trainee 1974; Natl Life & Acc Ins Co, life ins agent 1975-76; Metropolitan Life Ins Co, sales rep 1976-79; Lincoln Natl Sales Corp, tax deferred prog mgr 1979-; Lincoln Natl Life Employee Benefits Div, pensions mktg 1984-86; The Pressey Financial Planning Group Inc, pres/chairman; Communications consultant, currently. **Orgs:** Mem Ft Wayne Nat Life Underwriters Assn 1976-; bus consult Proj Bus of Jr Achievement 1978; bd mem Ft Wayne Opport Indsl Cntr Inc 1975-; bd mem Ft Wayne Sickle Cell Found 1978-; pres Ft Wayne NAACP 1978-; chmn econ task force Ft Wayne Future Inc C of C 1978-79; chmn Ft Wayne Affirmative Action Adv Cncl 1980-86; mem Comm Harvest Food Bank 1983-87; chmn Ft Wayne NBE/WBE Cncl 1984-86; mem Ft Wayne Anti-Apartheid Action Comm 1985; pres Ft Wayne/Allen Cty Martin Luther King Jr Memorial Inc 1985-87; bd mem Ft Wayne Business Cncl 1986; mem Intl Financial Planners Assoc 1986. **Honors/Awds:** Metropolitan's Ldrs Club Met Life Ins Co 1976; Natl Sales Achievement Awd Natl Life Underwriter-sAssoc 1977-79; IN Life Ins Ldrs Club Nat Life Underwriters Assn 1977; Pres Con Awd Met Life Ins Co 1978; Agent of the Yr Awd Gen Agent & Mgmt Assn 1978; The Cosmopolitan Outstanding Leadership Awd 1981; FWES Black Heritage Achievement Awd 1982; The Frederick Douglass Awd 1982; IN Grand Lodge Prince Hall Freedom Awd 1983; The NAACP Marjorie D Wickliffe Awd 1983. **Military Serv:** USAF a/1c 1966-70; Natl Defense Awd. **Business Addr:** Communications Consultant, 371 Rupp Dr, Fort Wayne, IN 46815.

PRESSEY, PAUL MATTHEW
Professional basketball coach. **Personal:** Born Dec 24, 1958, Richmond, VA; married Elizabeth; children: Ashley. **Educ:** Univ of Tulsa, BS 1982. **Career:** Milwaukee Bucks, 1983-90, San Antonio Spurs, 1990-92; Golden State Warriors, asst coach; San Antonio Spurs, asst coach, currently. **Business Addr:** Assistant Coach, San Antonio Spurs, 600 E Market St, San Antonio, TX 78205.

PRESSLEY, DELORES
Pageant founder. **Career:** Ms Plus USA Beauty pageant, founder, currently; Dimensions Plus Modeling Agency, head, currently. **Business Addr:** Founder, Ms Plus USA Beauty Pageant, Dimensions Plus, 551 36th St NW, Canton, OH 44709, (330)649-9809.

PRESSLEY, STEPHEN, JR.
Administrator social work. **Personal:** Born Feb 1, 1947, Canton, OH; children: Lance E, Akima M, Stephen III. **Educ:** Kent State Univ, AS 1975, BA 1977. **Career:** Stark Co CAP, dir of manpower 1971-73; Canton Urban League, dir of employment 1973-78; Lorain Co Urban League, exec dir 1978-80; Pittsburgh Urban League,dir of employment 1980-83; Urban League of Muskegon, exec dir 1983-. **Orgs:** Mem Alpha Phi Alpha; pres Civil Serv Commn Muskegon. **Home Addr:** 1274 5th St, Muskegon, MI 49440. **Business Addr:** President/CEO, Urban League of Muskegon, 1823 Commerce St., Muskegon, MI 49441.

PRESTAGE, JAMES J.
Educator (retired). **Personal:** Born Apr 29, 1926, Deweyville, TX; son of Mona Wilkins Prestage and James Prestage; married Jewel Limar Prestage, Aug 12, 1953; children: Terri, James Grady, Eric, Karen, Jay. **Educ:** Southern Univ, Baton Rouge, LA, BS, biology, 1950; Univ of IA, Iowa City, Iowa, MS, zoology, 1955, PhD, zoology, 1959. **Career:** Prairie View A&M Univ, Prairie View, TX, instructor, biology, 1955-56; Southern Univ, Baton Rouge, LA, asst prof, assoc prof, biology, 1959-68, dir of computer ctr, chair, computer science, 1968-73; LA Coordinating Council for Higher Education, asst dir, 1972-73; Southern Univ, Baton Rouge, LA, dean of academic affairs, 1973-, vice pres, 1973-82, chancellor, 1982-86; Dillard Univ, distinguished prof of biology, 1987-97, chair, div of Nat Sci, 1991-97. **Orgs:** Mem, bd of trustees, American Coll Testing, 1983-88; vice pres, Conference of LA Colleges & Universities, 1974-75; mem, comm of scholars, State of IL Bd of Higher Education; pres, Beta Iota Lambda Chapter, Alpha Phi Alpha Fraternity, 1975; exec bd, Istrouma Council, Boy Scouts of America. **Honors/Awds:** Journal of Morphology; Journal of Parasitology; Cum Laude, Southern Univ, 1950; Sigma Xi Scientific Honors Society, 1958; Distinguished Professor, Southern Univ, 1985; Alpha Kappa Mu Honor Society, Southern Univ, 1949; Fellow, Natl Medical Fellowships, Inc, 1956-59; Outstanding Faculty Mem, Southern Univ, 1966-67. **Military Serv:** US Navy, 1944-46, 1950-52. **Home Addr:** 2145 77th Ave, Baton Rouge, LA 70807.

PRESTAGE, JEWEL LIMAR
Educator, educational administrator. **Personal:** Born Aug 12, 1931, Hutton, LA; daughter of Sallie Bell Johnson Limar and Brudis L Limar; married Dr James J Prestage; children: Terri, J Grady, Eric, Karen, Jay. **Educ:** Southern Univ & A&M Coll, BA 1951; Univ of Iowa, MA 1952, PhD 1954. **Career:** Prairie View A&M Coll, assoc prof Political Science 1954-56; Southern Univ, assoc prof Political Science 1956-62, prof Political Science 1965-, chairperson dept of Political Science 1965-83, dean school of Public Policy & Urban Affairs 1983-89; Prairie View A&M Univ, Benjamin Banneker Honor College, interim dean & honors professor of political science, 1989-, dean, 1990-. **Orgs:** Pres SW Soc Science Assn Scientists 1973-74; pres Natl Conf Black Political Scientist, 1976-77; pres Southern Political Science Assn 1975-76; vice pres Amer Political Science Assn 1974-75; mem bd Voter Educ Project, Atlanta GA 1978-; state chmn mem Louisiana State Advisory Committee US Commission on Civil Rights 1974-81; mem bd Louisiana Common Cause 1983-; mem of bd Louisiana Capital Area Chapter Amer Red Cross 1985-; mem Alpha Kappa Alpha Sor Inc, Jack & Jill of Amer Inc; Links, Inc; president, National Assn of African American Honors Programs, 1993-94. **Honors/Awds:** Citizen of the Year, Alpha Kappa Alpha Sorority S Central 1971; Honor, Women's Pavillion 1984; World's Fair 1984; postdoctoral research Fellow Ford Found 1969-70; Honored Contributer Prof Amer Political Science Assn 1984; co-author A Port Marginality The Political Behavior Of Amer Women 1977; Distinguished Alumni Award, Natl Assn for Equal Opportunity in Higher Educ 1981; Baton Rouge Women of Achievement Award 1983; Distinguished Alumni Achievement Award Univ of Iowa 1986; Hancher-Finkbine Medallion, Univ of Iowa, 1989; Fannie Lou Hamer Award, Natl Conf of Black Political Scientists, 1989; University of District of Columbia, LHD, 1994. **Home Addr:** 2145 77th Ave, Baton Rouge, LA 70807. **Business Addr:** Dean, Prairie View A&M University, Benjamin Banneker Honors College, PO Box 125, Prairie View, TX 77446.

PRESTON, EDWARD LEE
Musician. **Personal:** Born May 9, 1925, Dallas, TX; son of Beulah Mae Williams Downs and Swanee Preston Sr; divorced. **Educ:** UCLA, 1945-47; Wiley Coll, 1941-42. **Career:** Count Basie Orchestra, trumpet player 1963; Charles Mingus Sextex, trmpt plyr 1963-66; NY Committee Young Audiences, bnd ldr musician 1975-; Jazzmobile Inc, lectr instr 1974-87; Jazzmobile Inc 1974-. **Orgs:** Trumpet plyr Duke Ellington Orchestra, 1963, 1971-72, Archie Shepp Band 1979, Hamptons Band 1955-56; mem Mscn Local 802 1962-; mason Thomas Waller Masonic Lodge 1947; mem Musicians Local 47 1945-; made rcrdngs with all bands except "All Am Brass Band". **Honors/Awds:** Russian Tour Duke Ellington Orch 1971; Japan tour Chas Mingus Combo 1970; Afrn tour All Am Brass Bnd 1964; Israel & European Tour Lionel Hampton Bnd 1955. **Home Addr:** 100-16 32nd Ave, East Elmhurst, NY 11369.

PRESTON, EUGENE ANTHONY
Business executive. **Personal:** Born Jan 10, 1952, Zanesville, OH; married Karen Y Booker. **Educ:** Central State Univ Wilberforce OH, 1969-71; Franklin Univ Columbus OH, AS Bus Mgmt, BS Employee Assistance Counseling; Eastern Union Bible Coll Columbus OH, attended; MA Candidate, Ashland Theological Seminary. **Career:** Perry Cty Drug Abuse Council, pres 1973-80; Rendville, mayor 1975-80; Rendville Housing Auth, vice pres 1976-80; Perry Cty Plng Comm, chairman 1976-80; Arvin Systems Inc, former asst serv mgr; Amer Electric Power, contract administrator, currently. **Orgs:** Mem Rendville Village Cncl 1973-75; pres, Lancaster-Fairfield Co NAACP 1980-84; mem & deacon New Salem Bapt Ch; past pres OH Bapt Gen Conf Laymens Aux, 1978-82; former vice pres Providence Baptist Assoc, BTU; former treas Providence Baptist Assoc Laymen's Aux; N Amer Baptist Men's Fellowship; spec projects comm Natl Baptist Convention USA Laymens Aux; committeeman Dem Central 1971-79; Omega Psi Phi Fraternity; exec dir Perry Cty Plng Commiss 1976-78. **Honors/Awds:** Listed in Natl Jaycee's Outstanding Young Men of Amer 1983. **Home Addr:** 348 Kendall Pl, Columbus, OH 43205.

PRESTON, FRANKLIN DEJUANETTE
Automobile company executive. **Personal:** Born Nov 28, 1947, Kansas City, KS; son of Vivian A Wilson Preston and Beryl L Preston Sr; married Alpha Theresa Johnson, Oct 8, 1972; children: Kameron DeJon, Ashley Terese, Christopher Franklin. **Educ:** General Motors Institute, BSME, 1970; University of Missouri, industrial engineering program, 1971-77; GMI Engineering & Management Institute, MS, manufacturing management, 1991. **Career:** GMAD, Fairfax, engineer, supervisor, 1970-76, Headquarters, sr project engineer, 1977-79, Doraville, quality control superintendent, 1979; GM, Fisher Body, divisional/plant engineer, 1982-85; GM BOC, FAD, Facilities Engineering, director, 1985-92; GM, CLCD, Manufacturing Technical Staff, manager, 1992-94; NAO Metal Fabricating Div, Pontiac Site Operations, mgr, 1994-. **Orgs:** Jack & Jill of America, Oakland County Chapter, 1978-; Metro Housing Partnership of Flint & Genesse County, board of directors, 1992-95; ASPIRE, advisory board, 1986-88; Trinity Baptist Church, choir, member, Men's Fellowship, 1977-, Sunday School teacher, 1983-, Board of Deacons, secretary, 1985-89, vice chairman, 1989-. **Business Addr:** Mgr, Pontiac Site Operations, GM NAO Metal Fabricating Division & Tech Ctr, One Pontiac Plaza, Mail Drop 483-012-101, Pontiac, MI 48340, (810)857-5393.

PRESTON, GEORGE NELSON (OSAFUHIN KWAKU NKONYANSA)
Educator. **Personal:** Born Dec 14, 1938, New York City, NY; married Adele Regina; children: Matthew, Afua-Magdalena, John. **Educ:** City College of New York, BA, 1962; Columbia University, MA, 1967, PhD, 1973. **Career:** Dept of art, City Coll, City Univ, NY, assoc prof, art & art hist, 1980-, asst prof art & art history, 1973-80; dept of art, Livingston College, Rutgers University, asst prof, art & art hist, 1970-73. **Orgs:** Special consultant, New York State Commn on the Arts, 1967-68; special consultant, New World Cultures, Brooklyn Museum, 1968; associate, Columbia Univ Seminar on Primitive & Precolumbian Art, 1973-80; bd of dir, Bd of Adult Educ, Museum of African Art, Washington, DC, 1972-80; Roger Morris-Jumel Hist Soc, 1973-80; bd of dir, Cinque Gallery, New York, NY, 1977-79. **Honors/Awds:** Foreign area fellow, Joint Comm of the American Council of Learned Soc & the Soc Science Rsch Council, 1968-70, 1972; numerous publications. **Business Addr:** Art Department, C U N Y, City College, 160 Convent Ave, New York, NY 10031-9101.

PRESTON, JOSEPH, JR.
State official. **Personal:** Born May 28, 1947, New Kensington, PA; son of Therese Mae Buckner Preston and Joseph Preston; married Odelfa Smith; children: Joseph III, Diana. **Educ:** Wilberforce Univ, attended; Univ of Pittsburgh, BA, 1979. **Career:** Pennsylvania House of Reps, representative, 1983-. **Orgs:** Bd mem, Homewood Revit Devel Corp, Allegheny Academy, Pittsburgh Water & Sewer Authority; member, National Organization of Women; member, National Conference of Black State Legislators; member, NAACP. **Business Addr:** Representative Dist 24, PA House of Representatives, PO Box 153 Main Capitol, Harrisburg, PA 17120.

PRESTON, LEONARD
Automobile dealer. **Personal:** Born Sep 8, 1948, LaGrange, TX; son of Lula Gates Preston and Verge Preston; married Cleo Jacko, Sep 26, 1970; children: LaTrondria, Byron, Germain. **Educ:** Prairie View A&M Univ, Prairie View, TX, Industrial Ed, l971. **Career:** Ford Motor Co, Memphis, TN, field zone sur mgr, l971-78, Lansing, MI, owner relations mgr, l979-85; All American Ford-Lincoln Mercury, Covington TN, owner. **Orgs:** Mem, Covington Rotary Club, l985; mem, Chamber of Commerce, l985; coach, Dixie Youth Baseball, l987, sponsor, l988.

PRESTON, MICHAEL B.
Professor, educational administrator. **Personal:** Born Aug 20, 1933, Tyler, TX; son of Marie B Preston Bicknell and Dwight M Preston; married Mary E; children: Sherry, Sonja, Adrienne, Rymicha. **Educ:** Wiley College, Marshall, TX, BA, 1954; University of California, Berkeley, CA, MA, 1971, PhD, 1974. **Career:** Univ of California, Berkeley, CA, lecturer, 1968-73, supervisor of Social Science, professor, 1968-73; University of Illinois, Urbana, IL, asst prof, associate professor, professor 1973-86; University of Chicago, Chicago, IL, visiting associate professor, 1983-84; USC, Los Angeles, CA professor and chair, political science, 1986-95; Western Political Science Assn,

pres, 1995-96. **Orgs:** Member, Executive Council, Western Political Science Assn, 1988-90; president, National Conference of Black Political Scientists, 1985-86; vice president, Midwest Political Science Association, 1985-87; vice president, American Political Science Association, 1989-90; member, National Advisory Committee, Institute of Government and Public Affairs, University of Illinois, 1986-. **Honors/Awds:** Distinguished Scholar Award, American Political Science Association, 1990; Leadership Award, Champaign County Urban League, 1982; Author, The New Black Politics, 2nd Edition, Longman Press, 1987, The Politics of Bureaucratic Reform: the Case of California State Employment Service, Univ of Illinois Press, 1984; Co-editor, Race, Sex, and Policy Problems, Lexington Books, 1979; Racial and Ethnic Politics in California, 2d ed, 1998. **Military Serv:** US Army, 1955-57. **Business Addr:** Director, Center for Multiethnic & Transnational Studies, University of Southern California, GFS, Rm 344, Los Angeles, CA 90089-1694.

PRESTON, SWANEE H. T., JR.
Physician (retired). **Personal:** Born Mar 10, 1924, Dallas, TX; son of Beulah M Williams-Preston and Swanee Preston; married Hazel Elizabeth Bjorge; children: Dorrlyn Jean, Tyrone Hudson, Wayne Raynard. **Educ:** Great Lakes Coll Clvlnd OH, MM 1948, DM 1952; Am T Univ Arcade MO, ND 1953; Wiley Coll Marshall TX, BS 1943; Univ Cincinnati CT, Counseling 1981 . **Career:** Hair Weev Inc, administrator, 1957-72; City Cleveland, EMT para medic, 1973-79; Operation Newstart, soc wrkr, drug counseling specialist, 1976-80; Salvation Army (Adult Rehab Ctr), supr stores, 1980-83; Dept Inmate Svcs, actng unit dir soc serv 1982-92; private practice, beginning 1952. **Orgs:** Past vice pres NY Naturapathic Soc; founder Phys Medl Soc; Am Techlgy Assn; 1st aid/emrgcy care instructor, Am Red Cross; CPR instructor, Am Heart Assn; board of directors, YMCA. **Honors/Awds:** ausn Man yr Hair Inc 1964; Busn Man Day Radio Sta WDOK; mem Myr Cncl City Cleve Carl Stokes Mayor; LA soc intl Who's Who (work in Liberia, Africa 1969). **Military Serv:** USCG lt 1/c 3 yrs 5 Battle Stars & Medals & Theater Ribbons 1943-46. **Home Addr:** 9378 SE 174 Loop, Summerfield, FL 34491.

PRESTWIDGE-BELLINGER, BARBARA ELIZABETH
Banker. **Personal:** Born Dec 5, 1945, Baltimore, MD; daughter of Gladys Thompson Prestwidge (deceased) and Algernon A Prestwidge; married George M Bellinger, Oct 7, 1989; children: Monique A Jackson, Melanie K Jackson. **Educ:** Howard Univ, BA 1967; Southern CT State Univ, MS Ed 1972; CT Sch of Broadcasting, graduate 1979. **Career:** Essex Co Coll, adjunct instructor 1972-77; South End Community Day Care Center, executive director, 1972-74; Kean Coll, adjunct instructor 1974-77; Farleigh Dickinson Univ, adjunct instructor 1975-77; Messiah Luthern Day Care Ctr, dir 1976-77; Child Care Gtr Bpt, exec dir 1977-78; Sacred Heart Univ, adjunct instructor, 1980; Peoples Bank Bridgeport, branch mgr, 1984, asst treasurer, 1984-86, asst vice pres, mgr, Boston Ave Office, 1986, vice pres, 1987-. **Orgs:** Vice chairman 1982, chairman 1982-87, Action for Bridgeport Comm Dev, Inc; allocation comm, 1980-, loaned exec, 1983, United Way of Fairfield Co 1983; mem Coalition of 100 Black Women 1986-; moderator "Today's Woman" radio talk show WICC Radio Bridgeport 1979; advisory board member, Bridgeport Public Education Fund, 1984-; board member, Discovery Museum, 1989-; board member, American Festival Theatre, 1989-; board member, Greater Bridgeport Symphony, 1989-. **Honors/Awds:** Glamour Magazine 10 Best Dressed Coll Girls Contest 1 of 25 Natl runners up 1965; Alpha Phi Alpha Sweetheart 1965; Pi Sigma Alpha Pol Sci Honor Soc 1967; Chairman's Awd People's Bank 1984; Hawley Award for Public Service, People's Bank Bridgeport, 1987. **Business Addr:** Vice President/Branch Manager, People's Bank, 58 Boston Ave, Bridgeport, CT 06610.

PRETTYMAN, QUANDRA
Educator. **Personal:** Born Jan 19, 1933, Baltimore, MD. **Educ:** Antioch Coll, BA 1954; Univ of MI, graduate study 1955-57. **Career:** Barnard Coll, senior assoc in English, currently; Coll of Ins, instr 1962-67; New School for Social Research, lectr 1959-62; Scholastic Book Serv NY, editor The Open Boat & other short stories by Stephen Crane 1968. **Honors/Awds:** Out Of Our Lives: A Selection of Contemporary Black Fiction, Howard Univ Press 1975; poems in many anthologies Most Notable Arnold Adoff, The Poetry of Black Amer, Black World Barnard Publ. **Business Addr:** Associate in English, Barnard College, 3009 Broadway, New York, NY 10027.

PREWITT, AL BERT
Educator, elected official. **Personal:** Born Feb 17, 1907, Tuscaloosa, AL; married Audrey Monroe; children: Jean, AB, Jr, Juan, Maryann Davis, Gloria P Cooke, Jessee D. **Educ:** Langston University, BSA 1935. **Career:** Langston Univ, instructor 1934-47; Langston High School, teacher 1947-57; Boley High School, teacher 1958-65; City of Langston, chairman-trustee board. **Business Addr:** Chairman, Board of Trustees, City of Langston, PO Box 116, Langston, OK 73050.

PREWITT, LENA VONCILLE BURRELL
Educator. **Personal:** Born Feb 17, 1932, Wilcox, AL; daughter of Cornelia Burrell and Leo Burrell; married Moses K Prewitt; children: Kenneth Burrell Prewitt. **Educ:** Stillman Coll, BS in Business Educ, 1954; Indiana Univ, MA in Business Educ, 1955, EdD in Business Educ, 1961, postdoctoral study, 1965; Indiana University, 1965; postdoctoral study in France, Czechoslovakia, and Germany, 1968-69; postdoctoral study, Texas Southern Univ 1969, Univ of California at Los Angeles 1978, Georgia Tech Univ 1980, Harvard Univ 1987, Univ of South Carolina 1987, Univ of Bocconi, Milan Italy, 1988. **Career:** Pacific Telephone & Telegraph, Los Angeles CA, special mgmt consultant 1968; Marshall Space Flight Ctr, Huntsville AL, employee devel officer 1964; Stillman Coll, asst prof, assoc prof, prof 1955-67; Texas Southern Univ, assoc prof, dept chmn 1967-69; Florence State Univ, assoc prof 1969-70; Univ of Alabama, assoc prof 1970-74, prof 1974-; IBM, consultant; USAF, consultant; US Fire College, Charlespfizer, NY, consultant; US Congress, advisor. **Orgs:** Special rsch consultant, TTT Proj, Texas Southern Univ, 1969; mem, Acad of Mgmt; mem, European Found for Mgmt Devel, 1968-; mem, Southern Mgmt Assn; mem, Amer Assn for Univ Women; mem, Natl Business Educ Assn; mem Delta Pi Epsilon; mem gen exec bd, Presbyterian Church US, 1973-; vice pres, FOCUS on Sr Citizens; mem, Century Club YMCA; chair, US Selective Service Appeals Bd, 1980-; bd dir, AMI-West Alabama Hospital, 1986-. **Honors/Awds:** Urban League Fellowship 1966; Ford Found Fellow 1965; Presbyterian Church US Fellow 1958-60; Maritime Admin Fellowship 1965; published numerous articles incl "The Role of Human Resources Mgmt in Econ Devel" 1982, "Selling Cable TV as Career Opportunity for Coll Students" 1979, "Black Capitalism: A Way or a Myth?" Journal of Small Business, 1973, "Facing the Realities of Executive Burnout and the Need to Manage Stress," Intl Mgmt Devel, 1982; participated in numerous lectures including Human Resources Mgmt & Motivation 1982, Preventing Discrimination Complaints, a Guide for Line Managers 1980, The Black Experience in Higher Educ; numerous seminars & workshops; TV appearances in "Work and the Modern Family," program taped for NBC-TV for the Natl Endowment for the Humanities. **Special Achievements:** Author, "Merit Pay in Academia: Perceptions From the School of Business," Public Personnel Management, Vol.20, No.4, Winter, 1991. **Business Addr:** Prof of Management, Univ of Alabama, PO Box 865237, Tuscaloosa, AL 35486.

PREZEAU, LOUIS E.
Banking executive. **Personal:** Born Mar 4, 1943, Port-au-Prince, Haiti; son of Yia Roy and Emile Prezeau; married Ramona A Prezeau, Apr 4, 1964; children: Jasmine, Louis Jr, Rodney. **Educ:** Bernard M Baruch, New York NY, BBA, 1970. **Career:** Freedom Natl Bank of New York, New York NY, chief operating officer, 1975-, acting pres, 1987-88; City Natl Bank of New Jersey, Newark NJ, pres/CEO, 1989-. **Orgs:** New York State Soc of Certified Public Accountants, 1973-; treasurer, trustee, Community Serv Soc, 1985-; trustee, Newark Chamber of Commerce, 1991; investment comm, Natl Council of Churches, 1988-; NJ Bankers Association, executive committee. **Business Addr:** President & Chief Executive Officer, City National Bank of New Jersey, 900 Broad St, Newark, NJ 07102.

PREZEAU, MARYSE
Educational administrator. **Personal:** Born Feb 20, 1942, Port-au-Prince, Haiti. **Educ:** Hunter College, BA (cum laude), 1970, MA, 1971; CUNY, PhD, 1976. **Career:** Hunter Coll, adj lecturer 1970-76; York Coll, adj asst prof 1973-77; Barnard Coll, lecturer 1977-78; NY Inst of Tech, asst provost, 1978-87; LaGuardia Community College, CUNY, dean of institutional advancement, 1987-90; New York Institute of Technology, vice pres for student affairs, 1990-. **Orgs:** Bd mem Nassau Cty Med Ctr 1978-88; mem & NYIT Corp rep Amer Assoc of Univ Women 1982-87; member, Council of Graduate Schools, 1990. **Honors/Awds:** New York Institute of Technology, President's Service Award, 1992; VIDCAPT Caribbean Cultural Heritage Festival, Education Award, 1991. **Business Addr:** Vice Pres, Student Affairs, New York Institute of Technology, NYIT Old Westbury, Old Westbury, NY 11568.

PRICE, ALBERT H.
Business executive. **Personal:** Born Jun 21, 1922, Somerville, MA; married A Terry; children: Glenn, Kendal, Byron. **Educ:** Howard Univ, BA 1942; cum laude, Grad Sch of Bus Adminstrn NYU, MBA, 1948; Grad Sch Pub Adminstrn NYU, MPA 1955. **Career:** Ronson Corp, vice pres & asst treas 1968-81; controller 1965; chief accountant 1954; jr accountant 1948. **Orgs:** Dir First Nat Bank of Princeton 1972-76; dir UJB Central, NA, 1976-87; dir Princeton YMCA 1967-74; trustee Middlesex Co Coll Scholar Fund 1971; dir Interracial Counc for Bus Oppor of NJ 1968-78; mem Nat Alliance of Bus 1972; srvd on various sch study com 1970-72; Dir Easter Seal Soc of NJ 1986-; trustee, Medical Center at Princeton, 1978-. **Military Serv:** AUS infantry capt 1942-46. **Home Addr:** 38 Magnolia Ln, Princeton, NJ 08540.

PRICE, ALFRED DOUGLAS
Educator. **Personal:** Born Jul 6, 1947, Buffalo, NY; son of Virginia M Allen and Alfred D Price; married; children: A Douglas V. **Educ:** Princeton Univ, M Arch & Urban Plan'g 1975; Princeton Univ, AB-Sociology 1969. **Career:** Harvard Univ, co-dir AAEO 1969-71; Schl of Arch-NJ Inst of Tech, asst dean 1975-77; School of Architecture and Planning, SUNY at Buffalo, assoc dean 1977-84, assoc prof of planning, currently. **Orgs:** Mem exec coun, Episcopal Church of the USA; mem US Assn for Club of Rome 1980-; mem & chair of selection Bflo City Arts Comm 1980-; chrm architectural comm Episcopal Diocese of Western NY 1980-; bd of dir Buffalo Convtn Cntr 1981-84; chrmn City of Buffalo Urban Design Task Group 1980-; bd of dir Seventy-Eight Restoration Corp 1979-. **Honors/Awds:** Jamaican Ambassador to the US, Marcus Garvey Medal of Distinction, 1991; Grants Exceeding 1/4 Million Dollars Harvard 1969-71; Butler Travelling Flwshp Princeton Univ 1973; Jury Member, 1975 Honor Awards, Amer Inst of Architects 1975. **Home Addr:** 77 Huntington Ave, Buffalo, NY 14214. **Business Addr:** Associate Professor of Planning, Sch of Architecture and Planning, State Univ of NY at Buffalo, Buffalo, NY 14214.

PRICE, ANDREA R.
Hospital administrator. **Personal:** Born Jun 16, 1959, Flint, MI; daughter of Clara Jones Price; married Edward Johnson. **Educ:** University of Michigan, Ann Arbor, MI, BA, 1977-81; Tulane University School of Public Health, New Orleans, LA, MHA, 1981-83. **Career:** DC Hospital Association, administrative resident, 1983-84; DataCom Systems Corp, manager, ambulatory care services, 1984-85; Children's National Medical Center, administrative fellow, 1985-86, assistant vice pres, administrative services, 1988-89, vice pres, professional services, 1989-. **Orgs:** President, American College Health Care Executive Women's Forum, 1988-89; president, Association of Health Care Administrators of DC, 1991-92; national board member/membership chairman, National Association of Health Services Executives, 1986-91; vice president/secretary, DC chapter, National Association of Health Services Executives. **Honors/Awds:** Excellence in Health Care Industry, International Business Network, 1987; Young Health Services Executive Award, 1992; American College of Health Care Executives, Early Career Award, 1992. **Business Addr:** Vice President of Professional Services, Children's National Medical Center, 111 Michigan Ave NW, Washington, DC 20010.

PRICE, BRENDA G.
Health insurance executive. **Educ:** Oakland Univ, BA, political sci, 1979; Wayne State Univ, MEd, 1993. **Career:** Blue Cross/Blue Shield of Michigan, local government liaison, currently. **Business Addr:** Local Government Liaison, Blue Cross/Blue Shield of Michigan, 600 E Lafayette Blvd, MC 241, Detroit, MI 48226.

PRICE, CHARLES
Judge. **Personal:** Born May 9, 1940, Montgomery, AL; married Bernice B; children: Susan Y, Charles II. **Educ:** VA Union Univ, BS 1969; Natl Law Ctr; George Washington Univ, JD (Honors) 1972. **Career:** US Dept of Justice Washington DC, intern 1972-73; State of AL, asst atty gen 1973-75; Escambia Cty AL, acting dist atty 1974; Montgomery Cty AL, dep dist atty 1975-78, asst municipal judge, 1978-83; private law practice, 1978-83; State of AL, circuit judge, 1983-. **Orgs:** Natl Bar Assn; asst municipal judge, Montgomery, 1978-83; pres, Montgomery Cty Trial Lawyers Assn, 1982-83. **Military Serv:** USAR Judge Advocate Corps, ltc, (retired); Active Duty-3 years 82nd Airborne; 3 years 8th Special Forces (Green Beret). **Home Addr:** 501 Wiltshire Dr, Montgomery, AL 36117. **Business Addr:** Judge Circuit Court, State of Alabama, 251 S Lawrence St, Montgomery, AL 36104.

PRICE, CHARLES EUGENE
Attorney. **Personal:** Born in Apalachicola, FL; married Mrs Lennie B; children: Charles E Jr (deceased). **Educ:** Johnson C Smith U, BA 1946; Howard U, AM 1949; Johns Hopkins U, further study 1951-52; Boston U, further study 1956; John Marshall Law Sch JD, 1967; Harvard Law Sch, CS, 1980. **Career:** NC Mutual Life Ins, ins mgr 1949-50; Butler Coll, dean of coll 1950-53; FL Mem Coll, dean of coll 1953-55; NAACP (assgnd to GA), field dir 1955-57; Livingstone Coll, asst prof 1957-59; Morris Brown Coll, assoc prof/atty. **Orgs:** Bd dir Hemphill Food Serv 1982-; cnsltnt Thomas & Russell 1979-; atty at law State Bar of GA Fed Bars 1968-; bd dir Dekalb, GA EOA 1965-70; pres Dekalb, GA NAACP Chptr 1962-70; adv bd Sm Bsns Adm GA 1968-82. **Honors/Awds:** Ldrshp Awrd GA NAACP 1965-66; schlrshp Alpha Kappa Mu 1954; artcls pub Atlanta Daily Wrld & Pittsbrgh Courier 1955-57; Tchr of Yr Morris Brown Coll 1972, 1980-81. **Home Addr:** 1480 Austin Rd SW, Atlanta, GA 30331. **Business Addr:** Associate Prof/Attorney, Morris Brown Coll, 643 MLK Dr NW, Atlanta, GA 30314.

PRICE, DARYL
Professional football player. **Personal:** Born Oct 23, 1972, Galveston, TX; married Audra; children: Jeremiah Kingdom. **Educ:** University of Colorado, attended. **Career:** San Francisco 49ers, defensive end, 1996-. **Business Addr:** Professional Football Player, San Francisco 49ers, 4949 Centennial Blvd, Santa Clara, CA 95054, (415)562-4949.

PRICE, DAVID B., JR.
Chemical company executive. **Personal:** Born Nov 9, 1945, St Louis, MO; son of Ethel L Armstrong Price and D Birdet Price; married Joyce A Jacobs, Dec 3, 1966; children: Danyale A Price, Jason J Price. **Educ:** Univ of Missouri, Rolla MO, BS, 1968; Harvard Business School, Boston MA, MBA, 1974-76. **Career:** Laclede Gas Co, St Louis MO, project engineer, 1968-72; Monsanto Co, St Louis MO, sr engineer, 1972-74, various managerial jobs, 1976-81, mgr, commercial devel, 1981-83, dir, investor relations, 1983-86, dir, commercial devel, 1986-87, vice pres & gen mgr, begin 1987, pres, performance materials; BFGoodrich Specialty Chemicals, exec vp, currently. **Orgs:** Harvard Business Club of St Louis, 1976-; bd mem, Young Men's Christian Assn of St Louis, 1988-; bd mem, St Louis Urban League; bd mem, Boatmen's National Bank of St Louis; board member, Urban League; board member, WKENS. **Military Serv:** US Army, ssgt, 1969-71. **Business Addr:** President, Performance Materials, Monsanto Co., 800 N Lindbergh Blvd, G5NV, St Louis, MO 63141, (314)694-2984.

PRICE, DAVID LEE, SR.
Educator. **Personal:** Born Jan 11, 1934, Greenville, NC; married Eva W Price; children: David L Jr, Scott A. **Educ:** North Carolina A&T State Univ, BS, 1959; Univ of Virginia, MEd, 1971, post-masters work, 1973; Univ of Maryland, post-masters work, 1973. **Career:** Fairfax Co VA Public Schools, adminstrative aide 1978-89; Fairfax Co VA Public Schools, reading specialist 1968-78; Newport News Public Schools, reading specialist 1966-68; Newport News VA Public Schools, teacher 1961-66. **Orgs:** Spl police ofcr Hampton VA Police Dept 1961-68; ldr-supr Fairfax Co VA Rec Dept 1968-; lib asst Fairfax Co Pub Lib VA 1968-72; mem Fairfax Educ Assn; VA Educ Assn; Fairfax Co Reading Assn; various others; mem Mt Vernon Civic Assn 1975-; coach-mgr Mt Vernon Youth Ath Assn 1975-; mem Woodley Hills Sch PTA 1975-; mem H&T State Univ Alumni Chpt; Univ of VA Alumni Chpt; Big Brothers of Am; Toastmasters Intl 1971-; National Education Assn; Kappa Alpha Psi National Social Fraternity; Big Brothers of America; Order of the Knights of Pythagoras; Lee-Mount Vernon Youth Assn; New Bethel Baptist Church, 1968-. **Honors/Awds:** John Marshall Elementary School, Outstanding Teacher of the Year, 1965; New Bethel Baptist Church, Father of the Year, 1975, Perennial Man of the Year, 1996; Fairfax County School, Office of Human Relations, 1981; Fairfax County Recreation Dept, Community Service Certificate of Appreciation, 1992; Kool Achiever Awards Nominee Certificate, 1993; Tennessee School of Religion, Doctor of Humanities, 1994; Eastern North Carolina Theological Institute, Doctor of Humane Letters, 1996. **Military Serv:** AUS corpl 1953-55. **Business Addr:** Fairfax Co VA Pub Sch, 10700 Page Ave, Fairfax, VA 22030.

PRICE, FAYE HUGHES
Mental health administrator. **Personal:** Born in Indianapolis, IN; married Frank Price Jr; children: Faye Michele. **Educ:** WV State Coll, AB (honors scholarship) 1943; IN Univ Sch of Social Work, scholarship 1943-44; Jane Addams Sch of Social Work Univ IL, MSW 1951; Univof Chicago, summer institutes 1960-65; IL MH Inst Abra Lincoln Sch of Med; Fam Inst of Chicago; Inst of Psych Northwestern Meml Hosp; Northwestern Medical Sch. **Career:** Flanner House, supv youth activities 1945-47; Parkway Comm House, prog dir 1947-56; Parway Comm House, dir 1957-58; Bureau Mental Health Chicago Dept ofHealth, dir social work 1958-61; Chicago Dept Health, asst dir bureau of mental health. **Orgs:** Consul various health welfare & youth agencies; field instr Univ IL- Univ Chicago-Atlanta Univ-George Williams Univ; lecturer Chicago State Univ- Univ ILother professional workshops seminars and confs; mem Art Inst Chicago; mem Chicago Lyric Opera; mem Chicago Urban League; mem Southside Comm Art Ctr mem Chicago YWCA; mem Parnell Ave Block Club; mem DuSable Mus; mem Psychotherapy Assn; mem Amer Public Health Assn; mem IL Public Health Assn; mem Alpha Gamma Phi; mem Alpha Kappa Alpha; mem NAACP; mem natl Council Negro Women; life mem WV State Coll; life mem Univ of IL; Jack and Jill Assn; The Chums Inc; Chicago Chap The Links Inc; Natl parliamentarian Natl Assn of Parliamentarians; Zonta Intl; Les Cameos Social Club; Assn of Retarded Citizens of IL; Natl Assn of SocWkrs; Acad of Cert Sokrs; Certified Soc Wkrs of IL; Assn of Clin Soc Wkrs; Natl Conf Soc Wel; Natl Assn Black Soc Wkrs; IL Grp Psych Assn. **Honors/Awds:** Mother of the Yr Award Chi State Univ; Natl Outstanding Serv Award Links Inc; Outstanding Serv Award Links So Suburban Chpt. **Home Addr:** 9815 S Parnell Ave, Chicago, IL 60628. **Business Addr:** Assistant Dir, Chicago Dept of Health, Richard J Daley Center LL139, Bureau of Mental Health, Chicago, IL 60602.

PRICE, GEORGE BAKER
Brigadier general (retired), business executive. **Personal:** Born Aug 28, 1929, Laurel, MS; son of Mrs James A Price and Mr James A Price; married Georgianna Hunter; children: Katherine, James, William, Robert. **Educ:** SC State Coll, BS 1947-51; US Army Command & Genl Staff Coll, certificate 1964-65; US Army War College, certificate 1970-71; Shippensburg State Coll, MS 1970-71. **Career:** US Army, platoon leader 3rd Bn, 30 Inf Rgt, 1951, platoon leader L Company 179 Inf Rgt, 1952, company commander specialist training regiment 1953-57, opers officer 1957-61, personnel mgr 1961-62, adv 1st Vietnamese infantry div 1964-65, dept of army staff 1965-68, battalion commander 1968-70, brigade commander 1971-73, chief of staff 1973-74, asst div commander 1974-76, chief of staff 1976-78; Techdyn Systems Corp, dir govt operations 1978-81; Unified Industries, special asst to pres 1981-82; Southern Brand Snack Inc, exec vice pres 1978-81; Price Enterprises, personal mgr Leontyne Price, currently. **Orgs:** Mem Kappa Alpha Psi Frat; mem Military & Veterans Adv Comm Natl Urban League; mem Vietnam Veterans Memorial Fund 1980-85; bd of visitors US Military Academy, West Point; bd of Advisors Womans Vietnam Veterans Memorial. **Honors/Awds:** Distinguished Patriot Awd Natl Womens Republican Club; Distinguished Serv Awd SC State Coll 1975; distinguished Vietnam Veteran National Association Paramedics 1989-. **Military Serv:** US Army brigadier gen 1951-78; Legion of Merit; Bronze Star; Meritorious Serv Medal; Commendation Medal; Air Medal; Purple Heart; Combat Infantryman Badge, airborne, ranger. **Business Addr:** Personal Manager, Price Enterprises, 1133 Broadway, New York, NY 10010.

PRICE, GLENDA DELORES
Educational administrator, educator. **Personal:** Born Oct 10, 1939, York, PA; daughter of Zelma E McGeary and William B Price. **Educ:** Temple University, BS, 1961, MEd, 1969, PhD, 1979. **Career:** Temple University, clinical laboratory science professor, 1969-79, College of Allied Health, assistant dean, 1979-86; University of Connecticut, School of Allied Health Professions, dean, 1986-92; Spelman College, provost, 1992-97; Marygrove College, Detroit, president, 1998-. **Orgs:** American Society for Medical Technology, past president; Alpha Kappa Alpha Sorority Inc, 1959-; American Association of Higher Education. **Honors/Awds:** Association of Fellow Schools of Allied Health Professions, 1988; SUNY-Buffalo, Warren Perry Allied Health Leadership Award, 1982; Temple University, Alumni Fellow, 1992; University of Connecticut, Medallion Award, 1992; Pennsylvania Society for Medical Technology, Member of the Year Award, 1979. **Special Achievements:** Author: ''Ethics in Research,'' Clinical Laboratory Science, July/Aug 1979; ''Health Care Technologies: Political & Ethical Considerations,'' Healing Technology: Female Perspectives, 1989; The Role of Professional Associations in the Education Process in Allied Health Education, 1989; ''Consulting as a Professional Role,'' Textbook of Clinical Laboratory Science, 1988; ''Reimbursement Mechanisms: Their Link with Professional Organizations,'' Interpersonal Skills and Health Professional Issues. **Business Addr:** President, Marygrove College, 8425 W McNichols, Detroit, MI 48221.

PRICE, HUBERT, JR.
State representative. **Career:** Oakland County Board of Commissioners, commissioner; MI House of Representatives, state representative, currently. **Orgs:** NAACP; Pontiac Area Urban League; OIC Oakland County. **Honors/Awds:** Pontiac Area Achievers Awd, Boy Scouts of America, 1996; Outstanding Legislator, Honorary Lay Membership Michigan Association, Osteopathic Physicians & Surgeons, Inc, 1995. **Business Addr:** State Representative, Michigan House of Representatives, State Capitol Bldg, Lansing, MI 48913, (517)373-0475.

PRICE, HUGH BERNARD
Association executive. **Personal:** Born Nov 22, 1941, Washington, DC; son of Charlotte Schuster Price and Kline Armond Price Sr; married Marilyn Lloyd; children: Traer, Janeen, Lauren. **Educ:** Yale Law Sch, LLB 1966; Amherst Coll, BA 1963. **Career:** City of New Haven Human Resources, adminstrn; Cogen Holt & Asso, partner; The Black Coalition of New Haven, exec dir; Urban Renewal Agency New Haven Redevel Agy, asst couns; New Haven Legal Asst Assn, neighbrhd atty; New York Times, New York, NY, editorial bd, 1978-82; WNET/Thirteen, New York, NY, sr vice pres, 1982-88; Rockefeller Foundation, New York, NY, vice pres, 1988-94; National Urban League, president, 1994-. **Orgs:** Mem bd dir Cntr for Comm Change Washington DC; mem bd dir exec com real estate com New Haven Water Co; past mem Distrib Com New Haven Found; past mem bd dir past vice pres for planning United Way of Grtr New Haven; mem Nat Bus Leag; mem NAACP; mem Alpha Phi Alpha Frat; mem Proj Planning Com Grtr New Haven Black Soc Civic Orgn Higher Educ Fund; past mem bd dir New Haven Legal Asst Assn Daytop Inc; Polly T McCabe Cntr; Grtr New Haven UMCA; Lewis Latimer Found; trustee, NAACP, Legal Defense & Education Fund, NYC, 1988; trustee, Public Devt Corp, NYC, 1991-; trustee, Municipal Art Society, NYC, 1990-; trustee, Rochefeller Brothers Fund, NYC, 1987-88. **Honors/Awds:** Co-authored several art. **Business Addr:** President/CEO, National Urban League Inc, 500 E 62nd St, New York, NY 10021, (212)310-9000.

PRICE, JAMES ROGERS
Personnel administrator. **Personal:** Born Sep 19, 1942, Atlanta, GA; married Jean Wade; children: Roderick. **Educ:** Morris Brown Coll Atlanta, BS 1964. **Career:** Dobbs House Inc, reg personnel mgr 1972-76; EEO Affairs Dobbs-Live Savers Inc, mgr 1976-78; Metro Atlanta Rapid Transit Auth, dir of personnel 1978-81;M&M Products Co, employment serv mgr 1981-. **Orgs:** Bd mem TAY Morris Brown Coll 1983; mem Amer Soc of Personnel Admin, Morris Brown Coll Natl Alumni Assoc; mem Alpha Phi Alpha 1977; chmn Indust Adv Council Atlanta Job Corps Ctr 1983-; mem Adv Comm on Vocational Ed; past mem Leadership Fort Worth; deacon Union Bapt Church, Soloist Union Bapt Church Choirs. **Honors/Awds:** Outstanding Alumnus Morris Brown Coll 1975; Employee of the Month Lockheed- GA Co 1969. **Business Addr:** Employment Services Manager, M&M Products Co, PO Box 16549, Atlanta, GA 30321.

PRICE, JOHN ELWOOD
Musician, educator. **Personal:** Born Jun 21, 1935, Tulsa, OK; son of Irma Verila and Carter Elwood. **Educ:** Lincoln Univ, BMus 1957; Univ of Tulsa, MM 1963; attended Washington Univ 1967-68. **Career:** Karamu Theatre Cleveland, staff composer/pianist/vocal c 1957-59; FL Meml Coll Miami, chmn Music/Fine Arts, composer-in-residence 1967-74; Tuskegee Univ, composition/history 1980; Portia, Washington-Pittman Fellow 1981-82; Eastern IL Univ, mem music dept 1970-71, 1974-80; Tuskegee Univ, mem music dept 1982-. **Orgs:** Life mem Alpha Phi Alpha 1954-, Phi Mu Alpha Sinfonia 1954-; ASCAP 1970-; Assn for the Study of Afro-Amer Life & History 1970; Amer Music Soc 1970-; mem Natl Black Music Caucus; Soc for Ethnomusicology 1974; Medieval Acad of Amer 1975; Spirituals for the Young Pianist Book I Belwin Mills NY 1979; pub: Invention I for Piano 1952, Blues & Dance I Clarinet & Piano 1955, Scherzo I Clarinet & Orch 1952 & 1955; Two Typed Lines 1959; The Lamp FMC 1969; The Lamp FL Memorial Coll; Prayer, Martin Luther King Baritone Solo SSAATT-BB a cappella 1971; Barely Time to Study Jesus 3rd Version Solo Gospel Choir 7 speakers percussion ensemble 1977; pub A Ptah Hymn UnaccompaniedCello 1978; Menes, The Uniter Unaccompanied C Bass 1979; Natl Assn Composers USA 1982; Slave Ship Press Tuskegee Inst AL 1983; Moomery Symphony Bd, Alabama Council on the Arts. **Honors/Awds:** Black Musician as Artist & Entrepreneur Awd Phelps-Stokes Fund Scholarship Exchange 1974-; Disting Faculty Awd Eastern IL Univ Charleston 1979-80; 2nd Disting Faculty Awd Black Student Union E IL Univ 1980; listed in: ''Fifteen Black American Composers,'' by Alice Tischler, 1981, Black American Music Vol II, by Hildred Roach, 1985; Biographies of Black Composers and Songwriters, Ellistine Holly, 1990; Woodwind Music by Black Composers and Piano Music by Black Composers, Arron Horne; Fellowship Grant AL Arts Council 1986; Rural Arts Coord State of AL apptd 1986; featured Alabama Adver Journal Feb 1987; Composers of the Americas Pan Amer Un Vol 19 1977 Washington DC; The Sphinx mag of Alpha Phi Alpha Frat 1976; photographic posters of the Tuskegee City Dance Theatre in 8 rest areas for the St of AL; honored as one of the musical ''gems'' of Oklahoma Musical History during American music week 1988; ASCAP Award, 1990-91; Most Outstanding Composition, Black Arts Festival, Atlanta, 1991; Isis and Osiris premiered ballet, Auburn University, 1992; ASCAP Award, 1993-94; John E Price: His Life and Analysis of two(2) works for Sting Bass, Jackie Pickett, PhD, 1995; Links (Tuskegee Chapt) Arts Award, 1994. **Military Serv:** AUS sp4 1959-61. **Business Addr:** Professor, Tuskegee Univ, The Chapel, Tuskegee Institute, AL 36088.

PRICE, JOSEPH L.
Clergyman. **Personal:** Born Dec 25, 1931, Gary, IN; married Edria Faye; children: 6. **Educ:** East Los Angeles Jr Coll; Moody Bible Inst; Chicago Bapt Bile Inst; Indiana Christian Theol Sem, 1969. **Career:** St Jude Deliverance Ctrs of Amer, pastor Evangelist minister organ & fndr 1971-; Church of God in Christ, bishop dist supr & pastor 1963-71; photo, welder, owner, furniture & appliance store; real estate & ins broker. **Honors/Awds:** Award for community serv & leadership Mayor Richard Lugar; hon DDiv Natl Inst of Relig Sci & Arts. **Military Serv:** AUS airborne spl/4c 1951-56. **Business Addr:** 975 N Delaware, Indianapolis, IN.

PRICE, JUDITH
Business executive. **Personal:** Born Feb 10, 1937, New York, NY; married; children: Toni, Marc. **Educ:** City Coll of NY, attnd; Bernard Baruch Sch of Bus Adminstrn. **Career:** James B Beam Import Corp subsidiary of James B Beam Distilling Co NY, vice pres dir 1972-, former adminstrv dir & asst sec. **Orgs:** Mem Traffic Assn of the Liquor Industry. **Business Addr:** 5800 Arlington Ave, Riverdale, NY 10471.

PRICE, LEONTYNE
Opera diva, humanitarian. **Personal:** Born Feb 10, 1927, Laurel, MS; daughter of Kate Baker Price and James A Price; married William C Warfield, Aug 31, 1952 (divorced 1973). **Educ:** Central State Coll, BA, 1949; Juilliard School of Music, 1949-52; Florence Page Kimball, private study. **Career:** Actress, Porgy & Bess, Europe, 1952-54; recitalist, soloist with symphonies in US, Canada, Australia, Europe, 1954; performed in Tosca, NBC Opera Theater, 1954; appeared in concert, India, 1956-64; soloist, Hollywood Bowl, 1955-59, 1966; Berlin Festival, 1960; San Francisco Opera, 1957-59, 1960-61, 1963, 1965, 1967, 1968, 1971; Vienna Staatsopera, 1958-59, 1960-61; opened new Metropolitan Opera House Lincoln Center, 1968; six performances at the White House; performed Live from Lincoln Center; performed at 2 presidential inaugrations and for the Pope; RCA recording artist, 1958-. **Orgs:** Honorary bd mem, Campfire Girls; co-chairperson, Rust College Upward Thrust Campaign; trustee, Intl House; honorary vice chmn, US

Comm UNESCO; AFTRA; American Guild Mus Artists; Actors Equity Assn; Sigma Alpha Iota; Delta Sigma Theta; Natl Inst of Music Theater; NAACP; Whitney Young Foundation; New York Univ, bd of trustees. **Honors/Awds:** 20 Grammy Awards; Spirit of Achievement Award, Albert Einstein College of Med, 1962; Silver Medal of San Francisco Oper Italy's Order of Merit; Presidential Medal of Freedom, 1964; Spingarn Medal, NAACP, 1965; Schwann Catalog Award, 1968; Kennedy Center Honors for lifetime achievement in the arts, 1985; Natl Medal of Arts, 1985; Handel Medallion New York City; Associated Black Charities Grammy Lifetime Achievement Award; 26 honorary doctorates. **Business Addr:** c/o Columbia Artists Mgmt Inc, 165 W 57th St, New York, NY 10019.

PRICE, PAMELA ANITA
Librarian. **Personal:** Born Nov 30, 1952, Washington, DC; daughter of Gwendolyn Elizabeth Moses Price and John Robert Price. **Educ:** North Carolina Agricultural and Technical State University, Greensboro, NC, BS, 1974; University of Wisconsin, Madison, WI, MS, 1975. **Career:** University of Maryland, College Park, MD, serials cataloger, 1975-76; Delaware State College, Dover, DE, coord of evening reader services, 1976-81; Mercer County Community College, Trenton, NJ, dir of library services, 1981-. **Orgs:** Member, American Library Assn, 1974-; member, membership committee, YWCA, Trenton, NJ, 1987-; member, United Way, Princeton Area Community, 1987-; member, Kappa Delta Pi, 1974-; member, Delta Sigma Theta Sorority, Inc, 1977-. **Honors/Awds:** Certificate of Advanced Study, Drexel University, 1985. **Business Addr:** Director of Library Services, Mercer County Community College, 1200 Old Trenton Rd, Trenton, NJ 08690.

PRICE, PAUL SANFORD
Librarian. **Personal:** Born Mar 30, 1942, Coffeyville, KS; son of Anna Belle Price (deceased) and Ovie Price (deceased). **Educ:** University of Connecticut, Storrs, CT, BA, 1971, MA, 1974, PhD, 1982; University of Denver, Denver, CO, MA, 1985. **Career:** University of Connecticut Library, Storrs, CT, department mgr, 1972-84; The Quinoco Companies, Denver, CO, records administrator, 1985-87; Three Rivers Community Technical College, director, Learning Resources, 1987-. **Orgs:** Member, Southeastern CT Library Assn, 1987-; member, Connecticut Library Assn, 1987-; member, New England Library Assn, 1987-; member, American library Assn, 1987-; member, Mountain/Plains Library Assn, 1984-87. **Honors/Awds:** Delegate to White House Conference on Library and Information Services, Governor's Conference on Libraries, Connecticut, 1991; Governor's Blue Ribbon Commission on the Future of Libraries in Connecticut. **Military Serv:** US Army, Sgt, E-5, 1964-70; Commendation Medal, Air Medal, Vietnam Medal, Bronze Star with OLC, Good Conduct Medal, National Defense Service Medal, 1964-66. **Home Addr:** PO Box 282, Norwich, CT 06360-0282. **Business Addr:** Director, Learning Resources Center, Three Rivers Community Technical College, Thames Valley Cam, 574 New London Turnpike, Norwich, CT 06360.

PRICE, PHILLIP G.
Automobile dealership owner. **Career:** Red Bluff Ford-Lincoln-Mercury Inc, owner, currently. **Special Achievements:** Ranked 55 of 100 auto dealers, Black Enterprise, 1992. **Business Addr:** Owner, Red Bluff Ford, PO Box 1050, Red Bluff, CA 96080, (916)527-2816.

PRICE, RAMON B.
Educator. **Personal:** Born 1933, Chicago, IL. **Educ:** Art Inst of Chicago, BFAE 1958. **Career:** Du Sable High School, teacher 1959-72; South Side Community Art Center, dir 1960-68; George Williams College, dept chmn 1969-73; Indiana Univ, presently assoc instructor; DuSable Museum of African American Hi story, chief curator, currently. **Orgs:** Liason vol Blacks in Chicago auspicies; mem Natl Conf of Christians and Jews 1960-73; visual art consultant and instructor Urban Gateways 1971-74; visual art dir Amer Friends Serv Comm 1963-66; youth dir Natl Conf of Artists 1972-74; bd dirs South Side Community Art Ctr; advisor Du Sable Museum of African-Amer Art and Hist. **Honors/Awds:** Numerous awards, prizes, comm in sculpture & painting. **Military Serv:** USMC 1952-54. **Business Addr:** Chief Curator, DuSable Museum of African American History, 740 E 56th Place, Chicago, IL 60637.

PRICE, RAY ANTHONY
Educator, television producer. **Personal:** Born Jun 21, 1957, High Point, NC; son of Johnny and Carrie Price; married Gayle Lynnette Price, Sep 3, 1977; children: Samuel Ray, Rajeanna Lynn, Michael Terrell. **Educ:** Yuba College, AS, 1984; California State University, BA, 1986; Regent University, MA, 1993. **Career:** KVIE, Channel 6 (PBS), production assistant, 1990-91; Yuba Community College, TV instructor, 1990-91; Continental Cablevision, Channel 5, producer, 1984-91; Portmouth Public Schools, Channel 28, associate producer, 1992-; Portmouth City Channel 29, video technician, 1992-; Newport News Public Schools, assistant supervisor, telecommunications, 1992-. **Orgs:** Hampton Roads Black Media Professionals, 1994-; Big Brother/Big Sister, board member, 1988-91; Yuba-Sutter Regional Arts Council, board member, 1990-91; Marysville Chamber of Commerce, board member, 1987-91; Marysville Kiwanis Club, 3rd vice president, 1990-91. **Honors/Awds:** Citys of Yuba City and Marysville CA, Outstanding Service, 1989. **Special Achievements:** Music Video "Believe In Yourself," 1993; Developer of "The Classified Channel," 1984. **Military Serv:** US Air Force, staff sgt, 1976-; Distinguish Honor, Graduate School of Aerospace Medicine, 1981. **Home Addr:** 70 Park Avenue, Newport News, VA 23607. **Business Addr:** Assistant Supervisor, Telecommunications Education, Newport News Public Schools, Channel 6, 4 Minton Drive, Newport News, VA 23606.

PRICE, SUZANNE DAVIS
Educator (retired). **Personal:** Born Aug 19, 1921, Baltimore, MD; married Charles K Price. **Educ:** Howard Univ, BA, MA. **Career:** Div of Prog Devel Bureau of Elementary & Secondary Educ US Dept of Educ, dir 1973-81; USOE, chief analyst res & mat staff 1968-73; Div of Equal Educ Opportunity USOE, educ program specialist 1965-68; HEW, asst rev officer 1964-65; Coll of Liberal Arts Howard Univ, instructor 1960-64; US Dept of State, intell rsch specialist 1961. **Orgs:** Mem Phi Alpha Theta Natl Hist Hon Soc; mem Kappa Delta Pi Natl Educ Hon Soc; mem Amer Hist Assn; mem Amer Assn of Univ Women; mem Delta Sigma Theta Inc; mem The Links Inc Columbia MD Chapter; mem Natl Council of Negro Women Howard Co MD Chapter. **Honors/Awds:** Cash Award for Super Performance US Office of Educ 1968; Letter of Commendation US Commr of Educ Harold Howe 1968; Group Award F Div of Equal Educ Opportunity 1970; Cash Award for Super Performance US Office of Educ 1973; Super Serv Award US Office of Educ 1974. **Home Addr:** 4202 Bright Bay Way, Ellicott City, MD 21042, (410)461-3353.

PRICE, WALLACE WALTER
Business executive. **Personal:** Born Mar 10, 1921, East St Louis, IL; son of Pennie Johnson Price (deceased) and Samuel P Price (deceased); married Adrienne Walton, Jun 5, 1982; children: Sandra D, Wallace W II, Catherine A Counts. **Educ:** So IL Univ Carbondale, BE 1942; E Univ Sch of Commerce & Law Baltimore MD, attnd 1947-48; Univ of MD Aberdeen Coll Pk MD, attnd 1948-49; master of science, VA State Coll Petersburg, 1952-53; Univ of PA Grad Sch, post grad work 1958-61; Seton Hall Univ Sch of Law Newark NJ, attnd 1977-79; tchng permits IL/NJ/VA; 8th US Army Central Exchange School, Kobe, Japan, certificate, 1949. **Career:** VA State Coll, commandant of cadets 1951-53; MS&T VA State Coll, assoc prof 1951-53; OLIN Corp Stamford CT, mgr proc finance chem gr 1964-72; Seatrain Shipbuilding Corp Brooklyn, asst vice pres 1972; Pan Am World Airways NY, corp dir 1972-75; Becton Dickinson Co Rutherford NJ, corp mgr affirm prog 1976-77; United Cerebral Palsy Assoc of NJ, exec dir 1978-82; Consultants Admin Mgmt, consultant, currently. **Orgs:** Bd of dir Comm Chest Englewood NJ 1968-87; treas former pres & co-founder The Edges Gr Inc NY-NJ-CT 1979-; former pres & treas Alpha Phi Alpha Frat IL & Germany; mem Fair Hous Counc of Bergen Co Hackensack; mem bd of dir Untd Way of Bergen Co NJ 1972-85; pres emeritus Urban League of Bergen Co NJ; vice pres, European Congress of American Parents & Teachers, West Germany, 1962-63. **Honors/Awds:** Collegiate Professional Tchng Permit Commonwealth of VA 1953; Annl Awd of Mer E Reg Alpha Phi Alpha Frat Inc 1960; Life mem European Cong of Am Parents & Tchrs Germany 1963; 1 of the 10 Great Men of Bergen Co NJ 1970; Master Mason Prince Hall F&A Masons DE 1970; Urban League of Bergen Co Outstndg Achiev Awd Englewood NJ 1972; AUS awd for Outstndg Support of Northeastern Reg Comman 1975; v chmn Black Am Law Students Assn Seton Hall Law Sch 1978-79. **Military Serv:** US Army, Lt Col, 1943-64. **Business Addr:** Consultant, Consultants Admin Management, 585 W Englewood Ave, Teaneck, NJ 07666.

PRICE, WILLIAM S., III
Judge. **Personal:** Born Sep 30, 1923, Hennessey, OK; married Dilys A. **Educ:** Washburn U, AB JD 1950. **Career:** Genesee County, atty asst pros 1951-72; asst pros 1956-59; 68th Dist Ct Flint MI, presently presiding judge. **Orgs:** Pres Genesee County Bar Assn 1970-71; Genesee County Legal Aid 1956-57; pres Flint Civil Serv Commn 1969-72; mem & jud counc Nat Bar Assn. **Honors/Awds:** Achieve awd No Province Kappa Alpha Psi. **Military Serv:** Capt A&M Soc Corps ETO 1944-45; ETO 1942-46. **Business Addr:** Judge, 68th District Court, 630 S Saginaw St, Flint, MI 48502-1526.

PRICE-CURTIS, WILLIAM
Educator. **Personal:** Born Nov 10, 1944, Oklahoma City, OK; son of Algie Price Curtis and Jonathan Curtis. **Educ:** OK State U, BA 1966, MS 1970; OK U, PhD 1976. **Career:** Hoffmann Laroche Inc, mktg spl 1971; Oscar Rose Coll, prof 1972-79; Youth Career Devel Nat Urban League, natl dir 1979-86; Okla City Public Schools, Equity Officer, l987-. **Orgs:** Mem OK Psycholosical Assn, Am Assn for Cnslng & Dev, Am & Personnel & Guidance Assn, Am Psychological Assn, Councial Black Am Affairs, OK City Urban League Dept Health Ed & Welfare, Rehabilitation Couselor Fellowship 1969, Alpha Phi Alpha; bd dir US Youth Council 1983-86; gov bd Intl Youth Year Commission 1983-85; bd of directors, Urban League of Okla City l989-. **Honors/Awds:** Publs "Black Amer Progress in the Attainment of Educational Equity" Educ Leadership 1981, "An Examination of the Variables Related to Minority Youth Employment" Jrnl of Employment Counseling 1982.

PRIDE, CHARLEY
Singer. **Personal:** Born Mar 18, 1938, Sledge, MS; son of Mack Pride; married Rozene Pride, Dec 28, 1956; children: Kraig, Dion, Angela. **Career:** Detroit, Birmingham Black Barons, Memphis Red Sox, Los Angeles Angels, baseball player; Anaconda Mining; RCA Victor, solo recording artist, currently. **Honors/Awds:** Sold more than 35 million albums & five million singles; twelve of his 40 LP's have gone gold in the US Market; 31 gold & four platinum LP's; awarded the first Golden Opal Awd in Australia for album sales in excess of one and a half million; listed in Book of Lists as one of the top fifteen all-time world-wide record sellers; won three Grammy Awds-Best Country Vocal Performance Male "Charley Pride Sings Heart Songs" 1972, Best Gospel Performance "Let Me Live" 1971, Best Sacred Performance "Did You Think to Pray" 1971; Entertainer of the Year Awd 1971; Best Male Vocalists Awd CMA; Amer Music Awd Favorite Male Vocalist in Country Music 1976. **Military Serv:** US Army, 1956-58. **Business Addr:** Recording Artist, CECCA Productions Inc, PO Box 670507, Dallas, TX 75367.

PRIDE, CURTIS JOHN
Professional baseball player. **Personal:** Born Dec 17, 1968, Washington, DC. **Educ:** William & Mary, bachelor's degree. **Career:** Montreal Expos, outfielder, 1993, 1995; Detroit Tigers, 1996-97; Boston Red Sox, 1997; Atlanta Braves, 1998-. **Business Addr:** Professional Baseball Player, Atlanta Braves, 521 Capitol Ave SW, Atlanta, GA 30312, (404)522-7630.

PRIDE, HEMPHILL P., II
Attorney. **Personal:** Born May 19, 1936, Columbia, SC; son of Maud Pendergrass Pride and Hemphill P Pride; divorced; children: Hemphill III, Elliott Caldwell. **Educ:** SC State Coll; Johnson C Smith U; FL A&M U. **Career:** Self Emp, atty; NAACP, cola br 1964-; SC Housing Auth, vchmn 1972-77; Nat Bar Assn, adv bd 1972-76; Gov's Bi-Centennial Com, 1976; SC Taxpayers Assn, atty 1973; Cty of Columbia, asst pros 1973; 1st black to construc 55 unit high-rise 236 housing proj 1970; Jenkins Perry & Pride, prtnr 1965. **Orgs:** Mem SC Bar 1963; Nat Bar Assn 1964; admitted to practice US Supreme Ct 1968; State Dem Com of 100 1970; gen counsel allen Univ 1977; legal counsel NAACP1977. **Business Addr:** Attorney at Law, 1401 Gregg St, Columbia, SC 29201.

PRIDE, J. THOMAS
Company executive. **Personal:** Born Jan 18, 1940, Highland Park, MI; married Vernester Green; children: Leslie, Thomas, Alesia. **Educ:** Highland Park Jr Coll, 1958-59, 1962; Wayne State U, 1962-64. **Career:** Ross Roy Inc, vice pres; J Walter Thompson Co Detroit, media buyer 1964-69; Campbell Ewald Co, acct exec 1969-72; Amer Assn Advertising Agys, tchr; Health Alliance Plan, dir of communications, assoc vice pres, currently. **Orgs:** Adcraft Club of Detroit Nat Assn of Market Devel; Black Applied Res Cent; Detroit Boat Club; spkr Black Applied Res Cntr 1972; mem Blacks Against Racism 1969; trustee Kirkwood Gen Hosp Club. **Business Addr:** Associate Vice President, Health Alliance Plan, 2850 W Grand Blvd, Detroit, MI 48202.

PRIDE, JOHN L.
Association executive. **Personal:** Born Nov 4, 1940, Youngstown, OH; married Sallie Curtis; children: Jacqueline, Curtis. **Educ:** Capital Univ Columbus, BA 1963; Howard Univ, grad work in Psy. **Career:** US Office of Educ, chief SE oper Bran 1970-72, deputy asst dir for oper 1972-74; US Dept HEW, spec asst to dep asst sec for human dev 1974-. **Orgs:** Consult to White House Conf on Food Health & Nutrition 1969; US Senate Select Comm on Human Needs 1968; Natl Adv Com on Civil Disorders 1968; mem Adv Comm on Special Educ Montgomery Co MD Pub Schls; mem Adv Comm on Family Life & Human Dev Mont Co MD Pub Schls; pres Mont Co Assn for Language Handicapped Children; mem Big Brothers of the Natl Capital Area. **Honors/Awds:** 4 yr coll Athletic Scholarship; MVP Coll Track Team 1963; 5 ltrs basketball & track in coll. **Business Addr:** Spec Asst to Dep Asst, U S Department HEW, 330 Independence Ave SW, Ste 5717, Washington, DC 20202.

PRIDE, WALTER LAVON
Attorney. **Personal:** Born Apr 4, 1922, Birmingham, AL; son of Althea Pride and George Thomas Pride; divorced; children: Karen, Pamela. **Educ:** Roosevelt Univ, BS; John Marshall Law Sch, JD; Univ of Michigan, Roosevelt Univ, grad study. **Career:** Chicago Assn of Defense Lawyers, former pres 1967-69; Pride Leaner Stewart & Elston Chicago, attorney-at-law. **Orgs:** Mem Chicago Bar Assn, IL State Bar Assn; attended Legal Seminars Northwestern Univ, Univs of MI IL WI; mem Alpha Phi Alpha; Il State Bar Assn; mem bd of dir Stuart Townhomes Corp; mem Chicago Conf on Brotherhood; mem Cook Co Bar Assn; mem Natl Bar Assn; mem Natl Assn Defense Lawyers; life mem NAACP. **Honors/Awds:** Cook County Bar Association, Senior Counselor of the Year, 1995. **Military Serv:** AUS s/sgt WW II. **Business Addr:** Attorney, Pride Leaner Stewart & Elston, 180 N La Salle St, Chicago, IL 60602.

PRIEST, MARLON L.
Physician, educational administrator. **Personal:** Born Jan 31, Moulton, AL; son of Odra McKelvy Priest and Charlie W. Priest, Sr. **Educ:** University of North Alabama, Florence, AL, BS, 1974; University of Alabama at Birmingham School of Medicine, Birmingham, AL, 1974-77. **Career:** Baptist Medical Center, Birmingham, AL, dir of outpatient medicine, 1980-81; University of Alabama at Birmingham, deputy medical dir, Emergency Dept, 1982-85, medical dir/univ hospital emergency dept, 1985-89, asst prof of surgery, 1985-86, assoc prof of surgery, 1986-94, professor, 1994, asst vice pres for health affairs, 1988-92, div dir/emergency services, 1989-90, dir of emergency medical residency program, 1989-90; Univ of Alabama, School of Medicine, assoc dean, 1992-. **Orgs:** Natl councilor, 1990-93, Alabama Chapter, president, 1988-90, bd of dirs, 1982-, American College of Emergency Physicians; president, Mineral District Medical Society, 1988-90; bd of dirs, American Heart Assn Jefferson/Shelby, 1984-; Alabama Affiliate American Heart, president, 1994-95; undergraduate curriculum committee, Soc for Academic Emergency Medicine, 1984-86; president, Beta Beta Beta, 1973; admissions committee, University of Alabama Sch of Medicine, 1983-86; bd of dirs, University of Alabama at Birmingham National Alumni Assn, 1989-93; president's advisory council member, University of Alabama at Birmingham, 1982-. **Honors/Awds:** Executive Management Fellowship, PEW Foundation, 1988; Outstanding Contribution, American Heart Assn, 1985; Leadership Development, Birmingham Area Chamber of Commerce, 1990; Outstanding Contribution, Student Natl Medical Assn, 1986; Honor Graduate, University of North Alabama, 1974, Alumus of the Year, 1989; ''Advanced Systemic Effect of Ocular Drug Therapy,'' Clinical Ocular Pharmacology, 2nd Ed, 1988-94; ''The Trauma Cardiorespiratory Arrest,'' Basic Trauma Life Support, 2nd Ed, 1987-94; ''Injury: A New Perspective on an Old Problem,'' Natl Medical Assn, 1991; Student National Medical Assn Mentor of the Year Award, 1992; Assn of Academic Medical Centers, Scholar in Academic Admin & Health Policy, 1994. **Business Addr:** Associate Vice President for Health Affairs, University of Alabama at Birmingham, 701 20th St South, AB 720E, Birmingham, AL 35294-0107.

PRIESTER, JULIAN ANTHONY (PEPO MTOTO)
Jazz musician, composer, educator. **Personal:** Born Jun 29, 1935, Chicago, IL; son of Colelia Smith-Priester and Lucius Harper Priester; married Jaymi Goodenough; children: Julia Antoinette, Claudette Ann Campbell, Adebayo Goodenough, Atuanya Goodenough. **Educ:** Sherwood School of Music, Chicago, IL, attended. **Career:** ECM Records, Riverside Records, trombonist/bandleader 1954-91; Sun Ra Arkestra, trombonist, soloist, 1954-56, 1990-; Max Roach Quintette, trombonist/soloist 1959-61, 1964-65; Art Blakey's Jazz Messingers, trombonist/soloist 1968; Duke Ellington Orchestra, lead trombonist 1970; Herbie Hancock Sextet, trombonist/soloist 1971-73; Dave Holland Quintet, trombonist/soloist, 1984-87; Cornish College of the Arts, Music Department, administration/faculty, 1979-. **Orgs:** Adj to the faculty Lone Mountain Coll 1976-77; program dir/faculty Cazadero Music Camp 1978-80; mem Music Adv Council 1979-80; faculty Naropa Inst 1981-83; faculty Banff Center for the Arts 1984-87; bd of dirs Pacific Jazz Inst 1987; commr Seattle Arts Commn 1988-91. **Honors/Awds:** Commemorative Plaque Msingi Workshop 1972; Grant NEA 1975; Best Horn Player Award Bay Area Music Magazine 1978; Commemorative Plaque San Francisco Jazz Comm 1979; King County Arts Commn Grant 1987; Seafirst Faculty Award, 1990. **Military Serv:** Fifth Army Reserves, Corpl 1955-63. **Business Addr:** Music Department Faculty, Cornish College of the Arts, 710 E Roy St, Seattle, WA 98102.

PRIMM, BENY JENE
Physician, business executive. **Personal:** Born May 21, 1928, Williamson, WV; married Annie Delphine Evans (deceased); children: Annelle Benne, Martine Armande, Jeanine Bari, Eraka. **Educ:** WV State Coll, BS, 1950, postgraduate work, 1994; Univ of Geneva Switzerland, MS 1959. **Career:** Interfaith Hosp, Medical Aff, dir, 1965-66; Harlem Hosp, Ctr, assoc anesthesiologist, 1966-68; Harlem Hosp Ctr, Narcotics Control Hosp Orientation Ctr, founder/dir, 1968-69; Control Hosp Orientation Ctr, Columbia Univ, founder/dir, 1968-69; Addiction Research and Treatment Corp, exec dir, 1969-; Natl Ctr for Substance Abuse Treatment, 1989-93. **Orgs:** Urban Resource Inst, pres, 1983-; U S Info Agency, East and West Africa, U S speaker, 1989; World Summit on Substance Abuse and AIDS, US rep, 1990; Presidential Commn on HIV, presidential appointee, 1987-88; Meharry Medical Coll, bd of dirs, 1988-; West Virginia State Coll Foundation, bd of dirs, 1993-; Natl Med Assn, Minority AIDS Council, bd of dirs, 1994; Black Leadership Commn on AIDS, bd of dirs, 1989. **Honors/Awds:** HHS, Cert of Appreciation, 1988; J Michael Morrison Award for Science Adm, 1993; West Virginia State Coll, Honorary Doctor of Science, 1994. **Military Serv:** US Army, 1st lt 1950-52. **Business Addr:** Executive Dir, Addiction Research & Treatment Corp, 22 Chapel St, Brooklyn, NY 11201.

PRIMO, QUINTIN E., JR. **See Obituaries section.**

PRIMOUS, EMMA M.
Educator. **Personal:** Born Oct 5, 1942, Olive Branch, MS; married Commodore Cantrell; children: Commodore, Christopher. **Educ:** Memphis State Univ, BS 1964, EdM 1971. **Career:** Memphis Public Schools, teacher 27 years; MSU Reading Workshop Elem School Teachers, cons; WKNO-TV County Schools Program, panel mem; Open-Space Schools Benoit, cons; MSU TN State Univ LeMoyne-Owen Coll, supr teacher & student teachers; Program on Problem-solving Skills Memphis City Bd Educ, staff teacher; night adminstrator, Adult High School; Instructional Facilitator, Memphis City Schools, currently. **Orgs:** Ant Educ Assn; TN Educ Assn; Memphis Educ Assn; past vice pres Rubaiyats Inc; Les Casuale Bridge Club; Cherokee Civic Club; NAACP; Delta Sigma Theta Sor; Kappa Delta Pi; International Reading Association. **Honors/Awds:** Outstanding Young Educator of the Year, Parkway Village Jaycees, 1974; Outstanding Teacher Award, Phi Delta Kappa, 1990. **Home Addr:** 1575 Galveston St, Memphis, TN 38114.

PRIMUS-COTTON, BOBBIE J.
Educator, researcher. **Personal:** Born Jul 20, 1934, Daytona Beach, FL; daughter of Lillie Rose Primus (deceased) and William Primus (deceased); married Rev Jesse Cotton; children: Robyn, Jonathan R. **Educ:** Florida A&M University, Tallahassee, FL, BS, 1952; University of North Carolina, Chapel Hill, NC, MPH, 1972; Virginia Polytechnic Institute and State University, Blacksburg, VA, Certificate Public Policy EdD, 1984; UCLA-Berkeley, Berkeley, CA, Post-doctorate, 1986. **Career:** American Assn of State Colleges and Universities, Washington, DC, associate coordinator of allied health project, 1980-82; Howard University College of Allied Health, Washington, DC, associate coordinator of allied health project, 1982-84; National Cancer Institute, Cancer Prevention Awareness Program for Black Americans, Co-Authored with J Hatch, L Monroe, 1985; associate coordinator, cancer prevention awareness, 1984-86; National Institutes of Health, Bethesda, MD, American Red Cross, Washington, DC, associate coordinator, Black Elderly Project, 1984-86; Morris Brown College, Atlanta, GA, chair, dept of nursing, 1986-88; University of Central Florida, Orlando, FL, associate professor of nursing, coordinator of special projects, 1988-93; Bethune Cookman Coll, currently. **Orgs:** Dir, Project SUCCEDS, 1987-; first vice president and chairman, National Black Nurses Assn, 1990-; president, Professional Images International, Inc, 1984-; minority grantsmanship chairman, National Institutes of Health, 1988-90; trustee, board of trustees, Daytona Beach Community College, 1988-93. **Honors/Awds:** Merit Award, Outstanding Contribution to Education, University of Central Florida, nominated to Hall of Fame, Nursing FL A&M Univ, Tallahasse, FL, 1990; author, The SEEED Report: A Cultural Diversity Workshop, 1990; author, Developing Intuition in Youth Through Empowerment: A Step Toward Professionalism Through Mentoring, 1990; author with M. Lenaghan and W. Primus, Making Cultural Diversity a Reality Within the College of Health and Professional Studies at the University of Central Florida, 1990; co-author, Introduction to the Preceptor Role in the BS Program, 1989; Cancer Prevention Awareness Program for Black Americans, 1985; author, Mentor/Protege Relationships Among Black Professionals in Allied Health: Professional Development (dissertation), 1984. **Home Phone:** (904)672-7148. **Business Addr:** Bethune-Cookman College, 640 Dr Mary McLeod Bethune Blvd, Daytona Beach, FL 32114.

PRINCE, ANDREW LEE
Basketball coach. **Personal:** Born Dec 14, 1952, Victoria, TX; son of Hazel Lewis Prince and Andrew Prince. **Educ:** Abilene Christian Univ, BSEd 1975, MEd 1980. **Career:** Barcelona, Spain, pro basketball 1975; Graz, Austria, pro basketball 1979; Gottingen, Germany, pro basketball 1981; Abilene Christian Univ, asst coach 1983-. **Orgs:** Black Coaches Association; National Association of Basketball Coaches. **Honors/Awds:** Inducted into the Abilene Christian University Sports Hall of Fame, 1994. **Business Addr:** Basketball Coach, Stephen F Austin State University, PO Box 13037 SFA, Nacogdoches, TX 75962, (409)468-4329.

PRINCE, EDGAR OLIVER
Elected official. **Personal:** Born Sep 13, 1947, Brooklyn, NY. **Educ:** CUNY at NYCCC, AA Liberal Arts 1968; SUNY at Stony Brook, BA Sociology 1971, MA Sociology 1974; CW Post Center of LIU, MPA Public Admin 1980; NY Univ, PhD candidate in Publ Admin 1981-. **Career:** Mission of Immaculate Virgin 1968, St Agatha's Home for Children 1969, St Vincent Hall Inc 1970-71, sr residential child care counselor; Suffolk Co SummerIntern Prog Youth Bd, rsch analyst 1972; SUNY at Stony Brook, dept of sociology grad teaching assistantship 1971-73; CW Post Ctr of LIU Dept of Criminal Justice, adjunct asst prof 1974-79; Suffolk Co Criminal Just Coord Cncl, co exec offices sr rsch analyst 1974-75; Suffolk Co Dept Health Svcs, sr rsch analyst 1975-. **Orgs:** Mem Amer Public Health Assn 1975-; mem Amer Soc for Public Admin 1976-; mem Intl Soc for System Sci in Health Care 1980-; mem Natl Forum for Black Public Admins 1983-; official sponsor GOP Victory Fund 1984-; charter mem Statue of Liberty Ellis Island Found Inc 1984-; mem Congressional Black Caucus Health Brain Trust chaired by Louis Stokes 1984-; charter mem and trustee Republican Presidential Task Force 1984-. **Honors/Awds:** Grad Teaching Assistantship SUNY at Stony Brook Dept of Sociology 1971-73; Honorarium Columbia Univ 1976; Pi Alpha Alpha CW Post Ctr Chap NASPAA 1981; Presidential Medal of Merit, 1985, Presidential Honor Roll, 1985, Pres Reagan; Cert of Merit, Presidential Commn Republican Presidential Task Force 1986; several publications & presentations including ''Welfare Status, Illness and Subjective Health Definition,'' Amer Journal of Public Health 1978 presented at 103rd annual meeting of the Amer Public Health Assn Chicago 1975, ''Productivity Monitoring & Improvement, Managing Primary Care Svcs'' System Science in Health Care 1984 presented at the Third Intl Conf on System Sci inHealth Care Germany 1984; ''Needs Assessment Through Analysis of Social Indicators'' Systems Sci in Health & Social Servr the Elderly & the Disabled presented at the 1st Intl Conf on Systems Sci in Health and Social Serv for the Elderly & Disabled Canada 1983; Cert of Recognition Natl Republican Congressional Comm signed by Congressman Guy Vander Jagt 1985. **Military Serv:** Commissioned 2nd lt US Army Reserves Medical Serv Corp 1981-. **Home Addr:** 22 E 29th St Apt 214, New York, NY 10016.

PRINCE, JOAN MARIE
Hematologist. **Personal:** Born Jan 14, 1954, Milwaukee, WI. **Educ:** Univ of WI-Milwaukee, BA 1977, BS 1981, MS, 1992. **Career:** St Joseph's Hosp, hematologist 1981-; Medical Science Labs, supervisor, hemotology, beginning 1988; University of Wisconsin Med School, manager of health professions partnership initiative, currently. **Orgs:** Assoc mem Amer Soc of Clinical Pathologists 1981-; mem Delta Sigma Theta Sor 1974-; Black Women's Network, pres; mem Cancer & The Black Amer Comm 1982-; task force mem Black Women's Health Project 1983-; speakers bureau Ronald McDonald House 1984-86; bd of dirs Amer Cancer Soc 1985-; assoc mem Amer Soc of Medical Technologists; bd of dir UW Milwaukee Alumni Assoc 1985-86; mem Citizens Review Bd 1987; mem Future Milwaukee 1988-. **Honors/Awds:** Published article ''Black Women & Health,'' 1984; 1989 Black Role Model Milwaukee Public Library 1989; 12 articles in The Business Journal magazine, topic: ''Instilling Entrepreneurial Spirit In Youth'' 1989; Future Milwaukee Community Service Award, 1992; Women of Color Recognition Award, 1991; Future Milwaukee Community Svc Awd, 1993; WITI-TV 6 & The Milwaukee Times, Black Excellence Awd for Community Svc, 1994; First Annual Executive Committee Awd for Volunteerism-Community Brain Storming Conference, 1996. **Home Addr:** 8712 W Spokane, Milwaukee, WI 53224. **Business Addr:** Manager, Health Professions Partnership Initiative, University of Wisconsin Med School, 945 N 12th St, OHC, 3rd Fl, PO Box 342, Milwaukee, WI 53201, (414)219-7720.

PRINCE, RICHARD EVERETT
Journalist. **Personal:** Born Jul 26, 1947, New York, NY; son of Audrey White Prince and Jonathan Prince. **Educ:** New York Univ, BS 1968. **Career:** Newark Star Ledger, reporter 1967-68; Washington Post, reporter 1968-77; Democrat and Chronicle, asst metro editor 1979-81, asst news editor 1981-85, editorial writer/columnist 1985-93, op-ed editor, 1993-94; Gannett News Service, columnist 1988-93; Communities In Schools Inc, publications editor, 1994-. **Orgs:** Mem Natl Assoc of Black Journalists 1984-; pres Rochester Assoc of Black Communicators 1986-87; bd mem Writers & Books 1988-94; mem National Conference of Editorial Writers, 1993-; mem National Society of Newspaper Columnists 1989-; NABJ Journal, editor, 1990-93, associate editor, 1994-97. **Honors/Awds:** 2nd place writing competition, National Society of Newspaper Columnists 1989; 3rd place writing competition, commentary, National Assn of Black Journalists 1987, 1988, 1989. **Military Serv:** USAF Reserve, sgt, 1968-73. **Home Addr:** 11 E Oxford Ave, Alexandria, VA 22301. **Business Addr:** Communities In Schools, Inc, 1199 N Fairfax St, Ste 300, Alexandria, VA 22314.

PRINGLE, MIKE
Professional football player. **Personal:** Born Jan 10, 1967. **Educ:** Washington State; California State Fullerton. **Career:** Edmonton Eskimos, running back, 1992; Sacramento Gold Miners, 1993; Baltimore Stallions, 1994-95; Montreal Alouettes, 1996-. **Honors/Awds:** Canadian Football League, Most Outstanding Player, 1995. **Business Addr:** Professional Football Player, Montreal Alouettes, 4545 Pierre de Coubertin, PO Box 65, Station M, Montreal, PQ, Canada H1V 3L6, (514)254-1818.

PRINGLE, NELL RENE
Academic counselor. **Personal:** Born Jun 21, 1952, Baytown, TX; daughter of Elsie M Fontenot and Earlest Fontenot Sr; married Danny C Pringle Sr, Aug 23, 1983; children: Danny Jr, Courtney Tenille, Jaime Reshaude. **Educ:** Lee College, AA, 1971; Lamar University, BS, 1973; Texas Southern University, MEd, 1976, EdD, 1991. **Career:** Crosby Independent School District, educator, 1975-89; San Jacinto College, dir of counseling, 1989-. **Orgs:** Texas Junior College Teachers Assn. **Honors/Awds:** Ford Foundation, scholarship, 1971; Lee College, Most Representative Student Award, 1971; Texas A&M University, Fellows Award, 1990; Kellogg Fellow, 1997. **Home Phone:** (713)451-6233.

PRIOLEAU, PETER SYLVESTER
Private banker. **Personal:** Born Dec 10, 1949, Hopkins, SC; son of Ruth Byrd Prioleau and Jessie Prioleau; married Brenda Mickens, Nov 24, 1984. **Educ:** Midland Technical Coll, AA Retail Mgmt 1974; Benedict Coll, BS Business 1975. **Career:** Davision-Macy's Dept Store, assoc mgr 1972-75; Nations Bank of South Carolina, vice pres 1975-. **Orgs:** SC Bankers Assoc 1975-; Greater Columbia Chamber of Commerce 1975-; NAACP 1978-; SC Assn of Urban Bankers, 1993-; Committee of 100 Black Men. **Honors/Awds:** Awd of Appreciation United Negro Coll Fund 1983-85; Appreciation Awd United Way of the Midlands SC 1983; Natl Assoc for Equal Oppor in Higher Educ 1986. **Military Serv:** US Army specialist sgt 2 yrs; SC Air Natl Guard; US Air Forces Reserves msgt 1975-. **Home Addr:** P O Box 1823, Columbia, SC 29202. **Business Addr:** Vice President, Nations Bank of South Carolina, P O Box 448, Columbia, SC 29202.

PRIOLEAU, SARA NELLIENE
Dental services director. **Personal:** Born Apr 10, 1940, Hopkins, SC; daughter of Wilhelmina Prioleau and Willie Ore Prioleau; married William R Montgomery; children: Kara I, William P. **Educ:** SC State Coll, BS 1960, MS 1965; Univ of PA, DMD 1970. **Career:** Comph Grp Hlth Svcs, pbl hlth dent 1971-72; Hamilton Hlth Ctr, dir dental serv 1972-; Commu Dental Assco PC, pres 1976-. **Orgs:** Nat'l Dntl Assn 1970-; Am Dental Assn 1970-; Harrisburg Dental Assn 1972-; member, 1976-, pres, 1979-81, Links Inc Hbg Chap 1976-; Exec Women Intl Hbg Chap 1984-; vchmn The Status of Women, 1986-, chairman for Health, 1988-, Soroptomist Intl North Atlantic Reg; vice pres Soroptomist Intl Hbg 1986-; bd dir Mental Health Assoc Tri County Inc 1986-88; pres Soroptomist International of Harrisburg 1987-89; Dental Sub Committee State of PA, medical assistance; Harrisburg Area Community College, board of trustees. **Honors/Awds:** Working Woman of the Year, Health Service Pomecoys, 1982; Woman of the Year, Black Women's Caucus; Cumberland Co Mental Retardation Award 1987, 1995; Koser Award, Athena Recepient, 1995; Fellow, International College of Dentist, 1996. **Business Addr:** Dir of Dental Services, Hamilton Hlth Ctr, 2451 N 3rd St, Harrisburg, PA 17110.

PRIOR, ANTHONY
Professional football player. **Personal:** Born Mar 27, 1970, Lowell, MA; children: Anthony Jordan. **Educ:** Washington State, attended. **Career:** New York Jets, defensive back, 1993-95; Minnesota Vikings, 1996-. **Business Addr:** Professional Football Player, Minnesota Vikings, 9520 Viking Dr, Eden Prairie, MN 55344, (612)828-6500.

PRITCHARD, DARON
Elected official. **Personal:** Born Aug 26, 1954, Vicksburg, MS; married Juanita Hill; children: LaTonzia, LaToya, LaKeita, Daron Jamaal. **Educ:** Utica Jr Coll, attended; Alcorn State Univ Lormaums, BA 1977. **Career:** Eastern Foods Inc, branch mgr; Town of Edwards, mayor. **Orgs:** Deacon Friendship MB Church. **Home Addr:** 104 McCurtis Lane, Edwards, MS 39066. **Business Addr:** Mayor, Town of Edwards, PO Box 215, Edwards, MS 39066.

PRITCHARD, MICHAEL ROBERT
Professional football player. **Personal:** Born Oct 25, 1969, Shaw A.F.B., SC. **Educ:** Colorado. **Career:** Atlanta Falcons, 1991-93; Denver Broncos, 1994-95; Seattle Seahawks, 1996-. **Business Addr:** Professional Football Player, Seattle Seahawks, 11220 NE 53rd St, Kirkland, WA 98033, (206)827-9777.

PRITCHARD, ROBERT STARLING, II
Concert pianist, composer, educator, foundation executive, publisher. **Personal:** Born Jun 13, 1929, Winston-Salem, NC; son of Lucille Pickard Pritchard and R Starling Pritchard, Sr. **Educ:** Syracuse Univ, Syracuse NY, BS, 1948, MM, 1950; private piano study with Edwin Fischer, Arturo Benedetti Michelangeli, Carl Friedberg, Hans Neumann, and Robert Goldsand, 1948-59. **Career:** Touring concert pianist, 1951-; Conservatoire Nationale D'Haiti, Port-au-Prince, Haiti, artist-in-residence, 1958; Univ of Liberia, Monrovia, artist-in-residence, 1959; New School for Social Research, New York NY, faculty member, 1962; Black History Month, founder, 1965; Panamerican/Panafrican Assn, Baldwinsville NY, cofounder and chairman, 1968-; Kahre-Richardes Family Found, Baldwinsville, cofounder and chairman, 1972-; Impartial Citizen Newspaper, Syracuse NY, publisher, 1980-; Lincoln University, Lincoln University PA, artist-in-residence, 1988-. **Honors/Awds:** Doctorate honoris causa, Nat Univ of Haiti, 1968; citation, Org of Amer States, 1969; founder and organizer, Louis Moreau Gottschalk Intl Pianists and Composers Competition, Dillard Univ, 1970; artistic dir, Gala Concert on Peace and Reconsiliation DAR Constitution Hall, Washington DC, 1970; artistic dir, United Nations General Assembly Concert Gala for US Bicentennial and 13th Anniv of Org of African Unity, 1976; artistic dir, Martin Luther King Concerts, Riverside Church and Cathedral of St. John the Divine, 1978; Black History Month Founder's Citation, Governor of New York, 1987; Bayard Rustin Human Rights Award, A. Philip Randolph Inst, 1988; President's Centennial Medal, Lincoln Univ, 1988; artistic dir, Black History Month Concert Gala, Lincoln Univ, 1989. **Business Addr:** Chairman, Two Foundations at "Applecrest", Panamerican/Panafrica Association Inc, P O Box 143, Baldwinsville, NY 13027.

PRITCHETT, KELVIN BRATODD
Professional football player. **Personal:** Born Oct 24, 1969, Atlanta, GA. **Educ:** Univ of Mississippi, attended. **Career:** Detroit Lions, defensive tackle, 1991-94; Jacksonville Jaguars, 1995-. **Business Addr:** Professional Football Player, Jacksonville Jaguars, One Stadium Place, Jacksonville, FL 32202, (904)633-6000.

PRITCHETT, STANLEY
Professional football player. **Personal:** Born Dec 12, 1973, Atlanta, GA. **Educ:** Univ of South Carolina, BA in history. **Career:** Miami Dolphins, running back, 1996-. **Business Addr:** Professional Football Player, Miami Dolphins, 2269 NW 199th St, Miami, FL 33056, (305)620-5000.

PROBASCO, JEANETTA
Counselor, educator (retired). **Personal:** Born Aug 30, Needville, TX; married James A; children: Wardell. **Educ:** Prairie View A&M U, BS 1941; MEduc 1950; Univ of TX, completed couns certif work 1965. **Career:** Kilfore Jr HS, counselor; CB Dansby HS, counselor teacher math 1953-59; Fredonia School, teacher homemaking 1953-59; Fredonia School, teacher homemaking math 1942-53. **Orgs:** Asst chmn Texarkana Dist of New Homemakers of Am 1958-59; served on stud activities Com Kilgore Jr HS; served as sec PTA; elected chmn TEPS 1974-75;bd mem Kilgore Br TSTA; bd mem Kilgore Br TX State Tchrs Assn 1973-74; mem NEA; Piney Woods Pers & Guid Assn; TX Am Pers & Guid Assn; CntrlSteering Com Kilgore Indpt Sch Dist 1972-73; organized co-sponsored a chap of Future Tchrs of Am Dansby HS 1969; organ currently Spons FTA Kilgore Jr HS; mem co & dist adult 4-H ldrs Assn; organized 3 new 4-H Clubs active particip in num 4-H Functions; clk Fedonia Bapt Ch Kilgore; mem Heroniesof Jerioch; Am Assn of Univ Women; Gregg Co Home Economics Assn; Marquis Library Soc. **Honors/Awds:** Recip State 4-H Alumni Award 1967; State 4-H Adult Ldrs Award 1969; WD McQueen 4-H Award 1971; Nat 4-H Alumni Recog Award 1975; selected outstndng FTA sponsor Dist VIII TSTA 1974. **Home Addr:** 304 Gum St, Longview, TX 75601.

PROCOPE, JOHN LEVY
Insurance company executive. **Personal:** Born Jun 19, 1925, New York, NY; married Ernesta G Procope, Jul 3, 1954. **Educ:** Morgan State Coll, BS 1949; New York Univ Grad School of Business, 1955. **Career:** Tuesday Publ Inc, vice pres 1965-66; Slant Fin corp, dir mktg 1969-70; NY Amsterdam News, vp, gen mgr 1966, 1970, pres & publisher; NY Amsterdam News, editor & publshr 1974-; EG Bowman Co Inc, chmn; Batton, Durstein & Osborn, Marketing Specialist; Advertising Representative, Associated Publishers, Inc; Advertising Prepresentative, the Afro-American Newspapers. **Orgs:** Dir Apple Savings Bank, Shopwll Inc, YMCA, 100 Black men Inc, Siloam Presbyterian Church; chmn Task Force on Minority Bus Devel for White House Conf on Small Bus; pres, bd mem Natl Assoc of Newspaper Publs 1980-84; trustee Springfield Coll; mem United Way of Tri-State; bd dir New York City Indust & Commercial Incentive Bd; gov's appointee States Council on Intl bus; trustee Grad School of Bus NY Univ; bd mem Howard Univ; pres, Harlem Business Alliance, 1986-. **Honors/Awds:** Hon commiss, "Civic Affairs & Public Events", "Cultural Affairs" NYC; Doctor of Humanities, Universal Orthodox College-Nigeria. **Military Serv:** Vetern USA Corp of Engineers, private. **Business Addr:** Chairman of the Board, EG Bowman Co Inc, 97 Wall St, New York, NY 10005.

PROCTER, HARVEY THORNTON, JR.
Automobile company executive. **Personal:** Born Dec 29, 1945, Monongahela, PA; son of Charlene McPherson Procter (deceased) and Harvey T Procter Sr (deceased); divorced; children: Karyn Michele. **Educ:** Southern IL Univ, BA 1967; Roosevelt Univ, MA 1970; Wayne State Univ, JD 1976. **Career:** Chicago Comm on Youth Welfare, asst zone dir 1966, dir special events 1967; Ford Motor Company, various human res 1968-; University of Michigan, School of Business, LEAD Program, lecturer, 1986-; National Urban League, Black Executive Exchange Program, visiting professor, 1988-. **Orgs:** Mem Amer, MI State, Detroit Bar Assocs, Assoc of Trial Lawyers of Amer; mem Amer Mgmt Assoc; Society of Human Resource Management; Midwest Co-op Educ Assoc, Employer Management Assoc; life mem Alpha Phi Alpha Inc, NAACP; parish council St Thomas the Apostle Church; assy & comm chmn Midwest Coll Placement Assoc 1983-; pres bd of dirs Earhart Village Homes; pres, exec bd, Midwest College Placement Assoc 1988-; mem Business Advisory Council Univ of MI Comprehensive Studies Program 1989-; mem Business Advisory Council Clark-Atlanta University Center 1988-89; mem Business Advisory Council GMI Mgt Instit 1987-90; president, National Association of Colleges & Employers, 1997-; vp, employer relations, board of governors, College Placement Council, 1991-; task force mem, National Governor's Assn, 1990-. **Honors/Awds:** Univ of IL Law Fellowship; IL General Assembly Scholarship; Vice President's Award - Youth Motivation, Vice President of the United States, 1970; Citation of Merit, City of Detroit Police Dept, 1990, 1991; Award of Merit, Jarvis Christian College, 1990, 1992. **Business Addr:** Union Relations Manager, Abritration & Wage Administration, Ford Automotive Operations, Ford Motor Co., The American Rd, Rm 367, Dearborn, MI 48121.

PROCTOR, BARBARA GARDNER
Business executive. **Personal:** Born Nov 30, Black Mountain, NC; divorced; children: Morgan. **Educ:** Talledega Coll, BA Psych Sociol, BA Engl Ed. **Career:** Downbeat mag, contrib ed; Vee Jay Records Intl, intl dir 1961-64; Post-Keyes-Gardner Advt, 1965-68; Gene Taylor Assoc, 1968-69; North Advertising Agency, copy suprv 1969-70; Proctor & Gardner Advertising Inc, pres. **Orgs:** Mem contg ed Down Beat Mag 1958-; mem Chicago Econ Devel Corp, Chicago Media Women, Natl Radio Arts & Sci, Chicago Advertising Club, Chicago Womens Advertising Club, Female Exec Assoc; mem bd dir Better Bus Bur, Cosmopolitan C of C; chmn WTTW TV Auction; mem Chicago Econ Devel Corp, Chicago Urban League, NAACP, Smithsonian Inst, Chicago Symphony; bd dir Seaway Natl Bank, Mt Sinai Hosp, IL State C of C, Council of Univ of IL. **Honors/Awds:** Listed in Blue Book of London; 20 Industry Awds incl Clio-Amer TV Commercial Festival; 2 CFAC Awds; Frederick Douglass Humanitarian Awd 1975; Amer TV Commercial Awds, 1st Pl TV, 1st Pl Print 1972; Blackbook Businesswoman of the Year; Chicago Advertising Woman of the Year 1974-75; Small Bus of Year 1978; Headline Awd 1978; Charles A Stevens Intl Org of Women Exec Achievers Awd 1978.

PROCTOR, EARL D.
Business executive. **Personal:** Born May 20, 1941, Philadelphia, PA; son of Louise Culbreath Proctor and Earl M Proctor; married Jean E Matlock, Sep 27, 1978; children: Denise, Eric, Monica. **Educ:** Temple Univ, BS 1963; Temple Univ, Grad 1965; NY Univ, Grad Courses 1966-69; Harvard Business Schl, MBA 1975. **Career:** Ford Motor Co, 1968-73; Cummins Engine Co, mktg dir; Rockwell Internatl, mktg dir 1977-79; Ferguson/Bryan Assoc, partner 1979-80; DOT/MBRC, exec dir 1980-81, Commission on the Bicentennial of the United States Constitution dep dir mktg; Hidden Creek Industries, vice pres; TGP Inc, Virginia, president/CEO, currently. **Orgs:** Mem Amer Acad of Political & Soc Sci; mem PA Soc World Affairs Cncl; life mem NAACP; PA Society, Natl Urban League-Beep Visiting Professor. **Honors/Awds:** Honorary Citizen New Orleans; US Small Business Natl Award of Excellence 1983. **Home Addr:** 3102 Spinnaker Pt, Forest, VA 24551-1936.

PROCTOR, LEONARD D.
Auditor (retired). **Personal:** Born Jun 9, 1919, Jackson, MS; married Dell; children: 1. **Educ:** Tougaloo Coll, BA 1941; Wayne State U, MEd 1961. **Career:** Detroit Pub Sch, tchr 1946-66; 1st black cty assessor 1966; Elected Wayne Co Bd of Auditors, 1972-82; 1st black chmn 1971-72; Appointed by Governor Blanchard & Governor Engler to Michigan Tax Tribunal, retired, 1995. **Orgs:** Mem Municipal Finance Ofcrs Asso; Nat'l Assoc Counties; exec bd SE MI Counc Govts; mem Exec counc Trade Union Ldrshp Counc; trea Detroit Chap Coal of Black Trade Unionists; bd trsts Wayne Co Gen Hosp; Detroit Econ Club; past pres Detroit Counc Polit Ed; past pres Cotillion Club; life mem NAACP & various Frats. **Honors/Awds:** Man of yr Cotillion Club 1959; citation aw Nat'l Med Assoc for work on hosp-med probs 1960; cited for ldrshp in prep of hosp discrimination ordinances adopted Cotillion Club 1964; cert of apprec for contrib in Negro Hist 1968. **Military Serv:** USAC 1942.

PROCTOR, SAMUEL DEWITT. See Obituaries section.

PROCTOR, SONYA T.
Law enforcement official. **Career:** DC Metropolitan Police Dept, asst chief of police, acting chief of police, currently. **Special Achievements:** First female to head the Washington DC police force. **Business Addr:** Acting Chief, DC Metropolitan Police Dept, Municipal Center, 300 Indiana Ave NW, Washington, DC 20001, (202)727-4220.

PROCTOR, TIMOTHY DEWITT
Attorney. **Personal:** Born Dec 15, 1949, Fredericksburg, VA; son of B T Proctor and S D; married Karen L McNulty, Dec 1977; children: T David, Kathryn A. **Educ:** Yale University; University of WI, 1968-71; University of Chicago, MBA, JD, 1975. **Career:** Union Carbide Corp, attorney 1975-80; Merck & Co Inc, sr attorney 1980-83, secretary, new products comm 1984-85, assoc intl counsel 1985-88, counsel, Merck Sharp & Dohme Div, 1988-91, assoc general counsel 1991-93, vice pres & assoc general counsel, 1993-. **Orgs:** Abyssinian Baptist Church; American Bar Assn 1975, New York Bar 1976; US Supreme Court Bar 1979; NJ Bar 1980; bd of trustees, Edwin Gould Service for Children 1978-80; PA Bar 1981; Natl Bar Assn 1984-; American Corporate Counsel Association, 1986-; life member Kappa Alpha Psi 1969; American Mensa Ltd 1982; Sigma Pi Phi, Mu Boule 1985; merit selection panel, Federal Magistrate US Dist Court (NJ) 1985; Dept of Health & Human Services, Advisory Comm on Childhood Vaccines 1989-91; bd

of trustees, St Benedict's Preparatory School 1989-; bd of trustees, Princeton Day School 1990-91; Food & Drug Law Institute, board of trustees, 1992-. **Honors/Awds:** Black Achievers in Industry Award, YMCA Harlem Branch, 1979, 1983; Merck & Co Inc, Special Chairman's Award, 1990. **Business Addr:** Vice Pres & Associate General Counsel, Merck & Co, Inc, PO Box 100, WS 2A-57, Whitehouse Station, NJ 08889-0100.

PROCTOR, WILLIAM H.
Educator. **Personal:** Born Jan 15, 1945, Baltimore, MD. **Educ:** PA St U, BS 1967; NC Cent Univ Law Sch, JD 1970; Univ PA, MBA 1973. **Career:** Fed Trade Comm, examiner mgmt mktg 1970-71; Pagan & Morgan, consultant 1973; Morgan St Univ, asst prof business & management. **Orgs:** Mem US Supreme Ct 1976; mem Kappa Alpha Psi Frat 1963; ptnr Harris & Proctor 1973-; pres CBH Invstmt Corp 1966-; mem Phi Alpha Delta Law Frat 1971;US Supreme Ct 1976; Phi Alpha Delta; Kappa Alpha Psi; Am Bar Assn; mem Rapid Transit Coal Balt 1973-; Proctor Enterprises 1974-; mem PA Bar Assn; mem York Co Bar; mem US Dist Crt. **Military Serv:** US Army Res capt. **Business Addr:** Morgan State Univ, Baltimore, MD 21239.

PROPES, VICTOR LEE
Foundation director. **Personal:** Born Dec 22, 1938, Fort Worth, TX; son of Verlene V Reeves and Arthur L Propes; married Beverly P Galloway, May 25, 1966 (divorced); children: Pashell, Tarik Yusef, Hakim Malik. **Educ:** CA State Univ-Los Angeles, BA Bus Ed 1970; Univ of MN, MA Bus Ed 1981. **Career:** Minneapolis Dept of Civil Rights, exec dir 1974-76, 1978-80; Comm Dvlpmnt Agency of LA, equal employment officer 1976-78; Propes & Assoc, consultant 1980-83; State of MN Council on Black Minnesota, exec dir 1983-; Metropolitan Univ, history instructor 1989-; Minneapolis Community College, Minneapolis, MN, prof, 1989; Lakewood Community College, White Bear, MN, prof, 1989-90; W Harry Davis Foundation, Minneapolis, MN, exec dir, 1990-. **Orgs:** Pres NAACP-ST Paul, MN Branch 1985-87; fndr MN State Affirmative Action Assn 1974-84; corp fndr Neighborhood Housing Servcs N Minneapolis 1981-85; exec producer Focus-On; exec producer The Grand Lizard and the Kute Little Koulored Kids; mem National Forum of Black Public Administrators 1987-; mem MN Adult Literacy Campaign 1987-; bd mem U of MN Black Learning Resource Center 1988-. **Honors/Awds:** Fellow, Woodrow Wilson Foundation 1972-74. **Military Serv:** US Army, PFC, 1962-65; Honorable Discharge. **Business Addr:** Executive Director, WH Davis Foundation, 1015 Olson Memorial Hwy, Minneapolis, MN 55405.

PROPHET, RICHARD L., JR.
Automobile dealer. **Personal:** son Of Richard L Prophet Sr. **Career:** Gulf Freeway Dodge, Inc, Houston TX, chief executive, currently. **Business Addr:** Chief Executive Officer, Gulf Freeway Dodge Inc, 7250 Gulf Freeway, Houston, TX 77017.

PROPHETE, BEAUMANOIR
Physician. **Personal:** Born Sep 6, 1920, Cap Haitien, Haiti; married Anne-Marie Charles; children: Maud, Yve Robert, Mary Kathleen, Jo Anne, Myrtha, John Pierre. **Educ:** Faculte de Medecin D'Haiti Port-Au-prince Haiti, Grad 1948; Freedman Hosp Howard Univ Wash DC, Fellwoship In Urology; Homer G Phillips Hos Wash U, Residency 1949-50; Am Bd of Urology, Cert 1954. **Career:** Pvt Prac, phys 1954-; Dept of Urology Homer G Phillips Hosp, supr; Dept of Urology St Louis Univ Med Sch, asst. **Orgs:** Pres Mound Cty Med Forum 1970-72; exec sec Homer G Phillips Hosp Interns Alumni 1973-; treas W End Comm Conf 1970-71; chmn Bd of Educ St Rose of Lima Sch 1973-75. **Honors/Awds:** Recip Fulbright Grant Fellowship in Urology Howard Univ Wash DC. **Business Addr:** 3737 N Kingshighway, St Louis, MO 63112.

PROTHRO, GERALD DENNIS
Computer company executive. **Personal:** Born Sep 27, 1942, Atlanta, GA; son of Esther Jones Prothro and Charles Emery Prothro; married Brenda Jean Bell, Feb 14, 1976; children: Gerald Dennis. **Educ:** Howard University, Washington, DC, BS, 1966, MS, 1969; Harvard Graduate School of Business, postgraduate studies, 1975. **Career:** Goddard Space Flight Center, Green Belt, MD, physicist, 1965-69; IBM, Burlington, VT, associate systems analyst, 1969, senior systems anaylst, 1969-71, mgr of process line central engineering systems, 1971, mgr for process line central anaylsis systems, 1971-73, project mgr for systems facilities and support, 1973-74, Systems Products Div (IBM), White Plains, NY, mgr, information systems strategy, 1974-75, director of system assurance and data processing product group, 1975-78, Poughkeepsie Development Lab, Data Systems Div (IBM), Poughkeepsie, NY, mgr of processors systems, 1978-79, mgr of site resources and business planning, 1979-81, quality assurance mgr, beginning 1981, vice president and site general mgr, until 1989, secretary of management board, 1989-. **Orgs:** NAACP; Urban League; American Institute of Physics; AAAS; Automatic Computing Machines Assn. **Honors/Awds:** Black Achievers Award, YMCA, 1976; numerous awards for IBM; NDEA Fellow, 1967-69; author of numerous articles on computer science.

PROTHRO, JOHNNIE WATTS
Educator. **Personal:** Born Feb 26, 1922, Atlanta, GA; son of Theresa Louise Young and John Devine Hines; married Charles E Prothro Jr; children: 1. **Educ:** Spelman Coll, BS 1941; Columbia Univ, MS 1946; Univ of Chicago, PhD 1952. **Career:** Tuskegee Inst, asst prof 1952-63; Univ of CT, assoc prof 1963-68; Emory Univ, prof 1975-79; GA State Univ, prof 1979-. **Orgs:** Bd mem Intl Food & Agr Devel 1978-81; mem Geo Washington Carver Rsch Fdn 1979-85; mem Intl Union of Nutritional Scientists 1982-85. **Honors/Awds:** Borden Award Amer Home Ec Assoc 1950-51; Special Fellow Natl Inst of Health 1958-59; OEEC Fellow Natl Sci Fdn 1961; Fellow March of Dimes 1984. **Business Addr:** Professor, Georgia State University, PO Box 873, Atlanta, GA 30303.

PROTHROW-STITH, DEBORAH BOUTIN
Educational administrator, physician. **Personal:** Born Feb 6, 1954, Marshall, TX; daughter of Mildred Prothrow and PW Prothrow Jr; married Charles Stith, Aug 30, 1975; children: Percy, Mary. **Educ:** Spelman College, BA, 1975; Harvard University Medical School, MD, 1979. **Career:** Boston City Hospital, senior resident in charge of medical/surgical unit, 1982, staff physician, 1982-87; co-principal investigator, numerous adolescent violence projects, 1984-87; City of Boston, Dept of Health and Hospitals, Health Promotion Center for Urban Youth, co-director, 1985-87; Harvard Street Neighborhood Health Center, clinical chief, 1986-87; Commonwealth of Massachusetts, commission of public health, 1987-89; Community Care Systems Inc, vice pres, medical director, 1989-90; Harvard Univ, School of Public Health, assistant dean for government and community programs, 1990-; Harvard School of Public Health, professor of public health practice, 1994-. **Orgs:** Spelman College, trustee, 1989-; Hyams Foundation, trustee, 1990-. **Honors/Awds:** Black Caucus of Health Workers, Hildrus A Poindexter Distinguished Service Award, 1992; American Assn for World Health, World Health Day Award, 1993; Secretary Louis Sullivan, Exceptional Achievement in Public Service, 1989; Massachusetts Department of Public Health, Rebecca Lee Award, 1990; Honorary Degrees: Wheelok College, EdD, 1992; North Adams State College, PSD, 1988; numerous others. **Special Achievements:** Author, numerous works include: Violence Prevention Curriculum for Adolescents, 1987; Deadly Consequences: How Violence is Destroying Our Teenage Population, 1991; Health Skills for Wellness, Prentice Hall, 1994. **Business Addr:** Assistant Dean, Government & Community Programs, Harvard University, School of Public Health, 677 Huntington Ave, 718E, Boston, MA 02115, (617)432-0814.

PROUT, PATRICK M.
Banker. **Personal:** Born Jul 8, 1941, Port-of-Spain, Trinidad and Tobago; son of Iris Smith Prout and Rupert Prout; married Faye Whitfield Prout, Apr 17, 1976; children: Nicole, Danielle, Dominique. **Educ:** US Naval Academy, Annapolis, MD, BS, Engineering, 1964; Harvard Univ Grad School of Business, Cambridge, MA, MBA, 1973. **Career:** IBM, Washington, DC, marketing rep, 1968-71; Miller Brewing Co, Milwaukee, WI, product mgr, 1973-75; Chase Manhattan Bank, New York, NY, vice pres, 1975-82; Ranier Bank, Seattle, WA, vice pres, 1982-84; Seafirst Bank, Seattle, WA, sr vice pres, 1984-90; Bank of America, San Francisco, CA, exec vice pres, beginning 1990; Bank One Cleveland, pres/COO, currently. **Orgs:** Executive Leadership Council; HBS Alumni Assn, Cleveland Chapter; USNA Alumni Assn; NAUB. **Military Serv:** US Marine Corp, captain, 1964-68; Bronze Star with Combat "V", Vietnam Campaign, Vietnam Operations. **Business Addr:** Pres, COO, Bank One Cleveland, Banc One Corp, 600 Superior, Cleveland, OH 44114.

PROVOST, MARSHA PARKS
Educational administrator. **Personal:** Born Feb 6, 1947, Lynchburg, VA; married George H Provost; children: Geoffrey. **Educ:** Hampton Inst, BA 1969; Univ of TN Chattanooga, MEd 1976; Univ of TN Knoxville, working toward EdD 1982-; Univ of MI, C3 Experience, counselors computers & creative change 1984; Univ of TN, Inst of Leadership Effectiveness 1983-84. **Career:** Guilford Co Dept of Social Svcs, counselor-intern 1968; City of Hampton, juvenile probation officer 1969-71; Guilford Co Dept of Social Svcs, social worker II 1971-75; Counseling & Career Planning Ctr UTC, counselor 1977-81, asst dir 1981-. **Orgs:** Mem Amer Assn for Counseling & Develop 1975-; mem Amer Coll Personnel Assoc 1977-; mem Chattanooga Area Psychological Assn 1977-; mem vice pres Women in Higher Educ in TN 1981-82; pres mem Chattanooga Alumnae Chap Delta Sigma Theta Inc 1977-; mem New Dimensions Club of Toastmistress Inc 1982-; Chattanooga Bus & Prof Women's Club 1982-83; mem Chattanooga Chap Amer Soc for Training & Develop 1982-84. **Honors/Awds:** Outstanding Young Woman of Amer-Outstanding Young Women of Amer Inc 1981; Woman of the Yr Chattanooga Bus & Prof Women's Clubs 1981-82; Natl Certified Counselor Natl Bd of Certified Counselors 1984; mem Leadership Chattanooga 1984-85. **Home Addr:** 2441 Leann Circle, Chattanooga, TN 37406. **Business Addr:** Asst Dir Cnslng/Career Ctr, Univ of TN at Chattanooga, 231 University Ctr, Chattanooga, TN 37403.

PRUDHOMME, NELLIE ROSE
Educator. **Personal:** Born Aug 28, 1948, Lafayette, LA; daughter of Mary August and Richard August (deceased); married Hilton James Prudhomme (divorced); children: Eunisha, Shannon. **Educ:** Univ of Southwestern LA, BS Nursing 1970; Tulane Univ School of Public Health, M Publ Health 1974; Univ of Southern MS, 9 cr hrs 1974-77; Univ of Southwestern LA, 15 cr hrs 1981-84; LA State Univ Medical Ctr, doctorate in nursing science, 1997. **Career:** Lafayette Charity Hosp, staff nurse 1970; Vermilion Parish School Bd, health nurse 1971-72; Touro Infirmary City Health Dept, staff nurse 1972-73; Univ of Southern MS Nursing School, asst prof 1973-78; Family Health Found, staff nurse summer 1973; Univ of Southwestern LA Nursing School, asst prof 1978-81; Univ Medical Ctr, staff nurse II 1981-82; TH Harris Vo-Tech School, instr 1983-84; Univ Med Center at Lafayette, RN iv nurse consult 1986-; LA State Univ, asst prof; Univ of Southwestern LA, asst prof, 1988-; Pennington Biomedical Research, faculty scholar, 1997-98. **Orgs:** Mem Sigma Theta Tau 1978-, USL Nursing Hon Soc 1981-; Reserve Officers Assoc 1983-85; mem Southern Nursing Research Society, Amer Nurses Assoc; mem Zeta Phi Beta Sorority Inc 1988; bd mem March of Dimes Birth Defects Foundation 1989-; mem Mayor's Human Services Commission 1989-; bd mem, SW LA Health Education Council, 1997. **Honors/Awds:** Aaron Fellowship Tulane Univ School of Publ Health 1972-73; USPHS Traineeship Univ School of Publ Health 1972-73; Outstanding District RN or, 1989; Career Achievement Award, 1994; Fellowship- American Nurses Association's Ethnic Minority Fellow, 1994-97. **Military Serv:** US Army Reserve, lieutenant colonel, 20 years; 4 yrs Achievement 1983; Army Commendation, Meritorious Service, 1990; Army Nurse Corps, Lt Colonel, 1989-; active duty Desert Storm, 1991. **Home Addr:** 157 S Richter Dr, Lafayette, LA 70501. **Business Addr:** Assistant Professor, McNeese State University, Ryan St, Lake Charles, LA 70609.

PRUITT, ALONZO CLEMONS
Episcopal priest. **Personal:** Born Feb 20, 1951, Chicago, IL; son of Louise Clemons Hodges and Alonzo Pruitt; married Doris Brown Pruitt, Aug 28, 1983; children: Alexander, Nicholas. **Educ:** Roosevelt University, Chicago, IL, BA, public administration, 1975; University of Illinois at Chicago, Chicago, IL, MSW, 1978; Seabury-Western Theological Seminary, Evanston, IL, master of divinity, 1984. **Career:** Chicago Urban League, Chicago, IL, community organizer, 1971-73; Lake Bluff Homes for Children, Park Ridge, IL, 1973-79; Mary Bartelme Homes, Chicago, IL, director, social worker, 1979-84; St. George and St. Matthias Church, Chicago, IL, pastor, 1984-; Seabury-Western Theological Seminary, Evanston, IL, adjunct professor, 1989-; The Episcopal Church Center, New York, NY, interim national staff officer for black ministries, 1990-. **Orgs:** Member, Ministers for Mayor Washington, 1982-87; member, past president, Chicago Chapter, Union of Black Episcopalians, 1979-; board vice president, Chicago Work Ethic Corp, 1987-; diocesan council member, The Episcopal Diocese of Chicago, 1987-; member, former convenor, The Society of St. Francis, 1982-; dean, Chicago South Episcopal Deanery, 1989-. **Honors/Awds:** Community Service Award, Village of Oak, Community Relations Commission, 1974; Field Prize for Preaching, Seabury-Western Theological Seminary, 1984; Cotton Award for Oral Reading of the Bible, Seabury-Western Theological Seminary, 1984. **Military Serv:** US Army Reserve, Chaplain, First Lieutenant, 1990-. **Business Addr:** Dean, Vicar, St George and St Matthias Church, 164 E 111th St, Chicago, IL 60628.

PRUITT, ANNE SMITH
Educational administrator. **Personal:** Born in Bainbridge, GA; daughter of Anne Ward Smith and Loring Smith; married Harold G Logan; children: Leslie, Dianne Newbold, Pamela Green, Sharon, Ralph Pruitt Jr., Harold J, Minda, Andrew Logan. **Educ:** Howard Univ, BS (cum laude), 1949; Teachers Coll Columbia Univ, MA 1950, EdD 1964. **Career:** Howard Univ, counselor 1950-52; Hutto HS, dir of guidance 1952-55; Albany State Coll, dean of students 1955-59; Fisk Univ, dean of students 1959-61; Case Western Reserve Univ, prof of educ 1963-79; OH State Univ, assoc dean grad school 1979-84, assoc provost 1984-86, dir Center for Teaching Excellence 1986-94, prof of Educ Policy and Leadership 1979-95; Council of Graduate Schools, dean in residence, 1994-96, scholar in residence, 1996-. **Orgs:** Mem Alpha Kappa Alpha Sor; mem Links Inc; consultant Women's Job Corps creation Pres Lyndon Johnson's War on Poverty 1964; mem bd of trustees Cleveland Urban League 1965-71; consultant Southern Regional Educ Bd 1968-81; mem Bd of Trustees Central State Univ 1973-82; moderator Mt Zion Congregational Church 1975-78; Research Task Force Southern Educ Found 1978-87; mem Adv Comm US Coast Guard Acad 1980-83; Amer Assn for Counseling and Devel; sec, Journal bd mem, pres-elect, pres 1976-77, 1st Black Amer Coll Personnel Assn; Amer Educ Research Assn; Amer Assn for Higher Educ; Amer Assn of Univ Professors; mem Columbus, OH, Mayor's Task Force on Private Sector Initiatives 1986-88, bd of trustees, Case Western Reserve Univ 1987-; member, board of directors, Columbus Area Leadership Program, 1988-92; member, Columbus 1992 Education Committee, 1988-92; co-chairperson, Ohio State Univ United Way Campaign, 1990-91; member, National Science Foundation, Committee on Equal Opportunities in Science and Engineering,

1989-95; coordinator, CIC Alliance for Success Planning Committee, 1989-90. **Honors/Awds:** Outstanding Alumnus Howard Univ 1975; Amer Council on Educ Fellow 1977-78; honorary degree DHum Central State Univ 1982; Named one of America's Top 100 Black Business & Professional Women, Dollars & Sense Magazine 1986; Ohio State Univ Distinguished Affirmative Action Award 1988; Amer Coll Personnel Assn Senior Scholar Award 1989, Dipolmate, 1996; Phi Beta Delta Honor Soc for Intl Scholars 1989. **Business Addr:** Scholar in Residence, Council of Graduate Schools, One Dupont Circle NW, Ste 430, Washington, DC 20036-1173.

PRUITT, FRED RODERIC
Physician. **Personal:** Born Dec 17, 1938, Birmingham, AL; married Joan Simmons; children: Christopher, Lisa. **Educ:** TN State U, BS 1961; Howard U, MS 1963; Meharry Med Coll, MD 1967. **Career:** Phys splst internal med 1973-; St Elizabeth Hosp, resd 1971-73; St Elizabeth Hosp, intern 1967-68. **Orgs:** Med dir Mahoning Co Drug Prgm Inc; mem Lions Internat; pres Boardman Lions Club; mem Nat Med Assn; Boh State Med Assn; Alpha Phi Alpha Frat; Mahoning Co Med Soc. **Military Serv:** USAF mc maj 1968-71. **Business Addr:** 407 Belmont Ave, Youngstown, OH 44502.

PRUITT, GEORGE ALBERT
Educational administrator, educator. **Personal:** Born Jul 9, 1946, Canton, MS; children: Shayla Nicole. **Educ:** IL State Univ, BS 1968, MS 1970; The Union Grad School, PhD 1974. **Career:** Illinois State Univ, asst to vice pres for acad affairs 1968-70; Towson State Univ, dean of students 1970-72; Morgan State Univ, vp/exec asst to pres 1972-75; TN State Univ, vice pres 1975-81; Council for the Advancement of Experiential Learning, exec vice pres 1981-82; Thomas Edison State Coll, pres 1982-. **Orgs:** Bd of trustees CAEL 1983-87; chairman, Committee on Alternatives and Innovation in Higher Education, AASCU 1985-87; ACE, Labor/Higher Education Council, 1982-, Commission of Educational Credit & Credentials, 1991-; Commission on Higher Education and the Adult Learner, ACE 1982-88; board of trustees, The Union Institute, 1988-; board of directors, Mercer County Chamber of Commerce, 1988-; board of directors, Mercer Medical Center, 1989-; board of directors, New Jersey Assn of Colleges and Universities, 1989-; United States Department of Education, National Advisory Committee on Accreditation and Institutional Eligibility, 1989-92, National Advisory Committee on Institutional Quality and Integrity, 1993-; Trenton Savings Bank, board of managers, 1991-; American Cancer Society, New Jersey Division, board of directors, 1992-; Kellogg National Fellowship Program, Group XII, advisor, 1990-; SEEDCO, board of directors, 1990-. **Honors/Awds:** Governor's Citation for Outstanding Serv Gov Alexander St of TN 1981; Outstanding Serv to Educ Award TN State Univ 1981; Honorary Mem House of Representatives TN Gen Assembly 1981; Honorary Mem of Congress US House of Representatives 1981; Recip of Resolution of Commend Bd of Trustees Morgan St Univ 1975; named one of the most effective college presidents in the United States by EXXon Education Foundation Study 1986; Outstanding Alumni Achievement Award, Illinois State Univ 1984; Achievement in Education Award, Natl Assn of Negro Business and Professional Clubs Inc, New Jersey 1987; Doctor of Public Service, Bridgewater State College, MA 1990. **Business Addr:** President, Thomas Edison State College, 101 W State St, Trenton, NJ 08608-1176.

PRUITT, GREGORY DONALD
Professional football player (retired). **Personal:** Born Aug 18, 1951, Houston, TX. **Educ:** Univ of Oklahoma, BA, journalism. **Career:** Running back: Cleveland Browns, 1973-81; Los Angeles Raiders, 1982-84. **Honors/Awds:** Two yearr consensus All-American, 1972-73; second to Heisman Trophy, 1973, third, 1972; All Professional, 1973-74, 1976; Offensive Player of the Year, Cleveland Browns, 1974; led Browns Rushing 1974-79; established NFL record for most punt return yards (666), 1983; played in Pro Bowl, 1973-77, 1983.

PRUITT, JAMES BOUBIAS
Professional football player. **Personal:** Born Jan 29, 1964, Los Angeles, CA. **Educ:** California State Univ at Fullerton, attended. **Career:** Wide receiver: Miami Dolphins, 1986-88; Indianapolis Colts, 1988-93; Cleveland Browns, 1993-. **Business Addr:** Professional Football Player, Cleveland Browns, 80 First Ave, Berea, OH 44017.

PRUITT, MICHAEL
Automobile dealership executive. **Career:** Lima Ford, owner, currently. **Special Achievements:** Co. is ranked #75 on Black Enterprise magazine's list of top 100 auto dealers, 1992. **Business Addr:** Owner, Lima Ford, 2045 N West St, Lima, OH 45801, (419)224-3673.

PRUITT, MIKE
Business executive, professional football player (retired). **Personal:** Born Apr 3, 1954, Chicago, IL; married Karen Boulware; children: Aaron Michael. **Educ:** Purdue Univ, BA, business administration. **Career:** Fullback: Cleveland Browns, 1976-84; Buffalo Bills, 1985; Kansas City Chiefs, 1985-86; Pruitt & Grace Develop Corp, president. **Honors/Awds:** 22nd NFL Player to pass 6000 yards rushing; Cleveland's Player of the Year, Akron Booster Club, 1981; Best Offensive Player, TD Club Cleveland, 1980; Miller Man of the Year, 1980; played in Pro Bowl, 1979, 1980.

PRUNTY, HOWARD EDWARD
Social worker. **Personal:** Born in Maybeury, WV; son of Ruth Eleanor Carter and Leon C Prunty; married. **Educ:** Bluefield State Coll, Bluefield WV, BS, l953; Univ of West Virginia, Morgantown WV, MSW, l955; Univ of Pittsburgh, Pittsburgh PA, MPHA, l976. **Career:** Univ of Pittsburgh MH/MRC, Pittsburg PA, director, 1974-76; Project Hope MH/MRC, Detroit MI, dir, l976-78; Center for Advocacy, Family Service of Greater Boston, Boston MA, dir, currently. **Orgs:** Chmn, Natl Black Admin in Child Welfare, l969-; chmn, Brookline Human Relations Commn, l988-. **Military Serv:** US Army, Cpl, 1950-52. **Business Addr:** Dir, Center for Advocacy, Family Service of Greater Boston, 34 l/2 Beacon St, Boston, MA 02108.

PRYCE, EDWARD L.
Sculptor, painter. **Personal:** Born May 26, 1914, Lake Charles, LA; son of Dora C Pryce and George S Pryce; married Woodia Smith; children: Marilyn Alim, Joellen G Elbashir. **Educ:** Tuskegee Institute, BS Agric, 1937; Ohio State University, BLA, 1948; University of California at Berkeley, MS, 1953. **Career:** Ornamental Horticulture, Tuskegee Inst, head dept 1948-55, supt of bldgs grds 1955-69; Dept of Architecture, prfsr 1969-77; private practice landscape architect 1948-. **Orgs:** Chmn AL State Brd of Examiners of Landscape Architects 1981-83; mem Tuskegee City Plng Comm 1970-76; mem Tuskegee Model Cities Comm 1968-72; mem ALState Outdoor Rec Plng Bd 1978-. **Honors/Awds:** Fellow Am Soc of Landscape Archts 1979; fellow Phelps-Stoke African Fac Exch Prog 1976; Tuskegee Institute, Alumni Merit Award, 1977; Ohio State University, Distinguished Alumnus Award, 1980.

PRYCE, TREVOR
Professional football player. **Personal:** Born Aug 3, 1975. **Educ:** Clemson. **Career:** Denver Broncos, defensive tackle, 1997-. **Special Achievements:** NFL Draft, First round pick, #28, 1997. **Business Addr:** Professional Football Player, Denver Broncos, 13655 Broncos Pkwy, Englewood, CO 80112, (303)649-9000.

PRYDE, ARTHUR EDWARD
Mechanical designer. **Personal:** Born Jul 8, 1946, Providence, RI; married Lydia. **Educ:** RI School of Design, BA 1968-72. **Career:** AVID Corp E Prov RI, designer 1971-74; General Motors Corp, designer 1974-85. **Orgs:** Owner LPA Design 1983-85; design consult to Different Drummer; crew tech C Little Racing 1983-85; racing 2 liter Can-Am Championship Car 1984. **Home Addr:** 17249 Melrose, Southfield, MI 48075. **Business Addr:** Assistant Chief Designer, General Motors Corp, G M Technical Center, 3100 Mound Rd, Warren, MI 48090.

PRYOR, CALVIN CAFFEY
Attorney. **Personal:** Born Oct 16, 1928, Montgomery, AL; divorced; children: Linda Pryor Elmore, Debra E. **Educ:** AL State Univ, BS 1950; Howard Univ, LLB 1957. **Career:** Sole prac, atty 1958-70; US Dept Justice, asst atty 1971-94. **Honors/Awds:** Spec Ach Award Dept of Justice 1975; Spec Alumni Award AL State Univ. **Business Addr:** PO Box 1213, Montgomery, AL 36102.

PRYOR, CHESTER CORNELIUS, II
Ophthalmologist. **Personal:** Born Jan 2, 1930, Cincinnati, OH; married Audrey; children: Marcus. **Educ:** Cntrl State Univ, BS 1951; Howard Univ Coll of Medicine, MD 1955. **Career:** Boston City Hospital, resident 1957-58; MA Eye & Ear Infir, heed fellow 1959; Univ of Cincinnati Coll of Med, asst prof; Deaconess & Christ Good Samaritan Hosp, assoc; Jewish Bethesda & Children's Clermont Co Hosp, staff; Private Practice, ophthal 1961-. **Orgs:** Pres Cinn Ophthal Soc 1976; treas Cinn Acad of Med 1969; chmn sec opthal Natl Med Assn 1970-71; dir Unity State Bank 1970-76; mem bd of dir Cinn Assn for the Blind 1968-; mem Counc on Aging 1962-68; life mem Alpha Phi Alpha Frat; treas Delta Gamma Lambda Chap 1963-77; charter mem Delta Xi; life mem NAACP; mem Argus Club; mem True Am Ldg #2; mem FA&M 1962; mem Worshipful Master 1972; mem Noble of Sinai Temple #59; mem King Solomon Consis #20 1962; comdr in chief King Solomon Consis #20 1972-73; mem GIG 1975; Beta Kappa Chi 1950; Alpha Kappa Mu 1950; mem Amer Chem Soc 1951; fellow Amer Coll of Surgeons 1971-; diplomat Amer Bd of Ophthal 1960; Eye & Ear Infir. **Military Serv:** AUS capt 1959-61. **Business Addr:** 2828 Highland Ave, Cincinnati, OH 45219.

PRYOR, JULIUS, JR.
Physician. **Personal:** Born Jul 19, 1924, Montgomery, AL; son of Lucille Pryor and Julius Pryor Sr; married Joan Scales; children: Julius III, Pamela, Jonathan. **Educ:** Lincoln Univ, AB 1947; Meharry Dental Sch, DDS 1952; Meharry Med Coll, MD 1957. **Career:** Montgomery County Detention Facility, Montgomery, AL, staff denist, 1990-; Jackson Hospital, Montgomery, AL, courtesy staff surgeon, 1976-; Memorial Hospital for Cancer and Allied Diseases, Neww York, NY; John A Andrew Hosp, surgeon 1968-; St Margaret's Hosp, 1968-; Firview Med Ctr, 1964-; VA Hosp, consult surg 1968-; Meharry Med Coll, surg instr 1963-64; Hubbard Hosp, attending surgeon, 1963-64; Hubbard Hospital, Nashville, TN, gen surgery residency, 1959-64; Bridgeport Hospital, Bridgeport, CT, gen rotating internship, 1957-58. **Orgs:** Mem Montgomery Area Chamber of Commerce; bd mem YMCA; Omega Psi Frat Inc; Am Coll of Surgeons; diplomate Natl Bd Dentistry; Am Bd Surgery; bd trustees, Old Ship AME Zion Church; member, physician, Medical Retirement System Board of Montgomery County, 1981; chairman, dept of surgery, Humana Hospital Montgomery, 1990-92. **Honors/Awds:** Omega Man of the Year, Sigma Phi Chapter, Omega Psi Phi Fraternity, 1973, 1990. **Military Serv:** USN phm 3/c. **Business Addr:** Pryor-Winston Ctr, 1156 Oak St, Montgomery, AL 36108.

PRYOR, LILLIAN W.
Educator. **Personal:** Born Dec 13, 1917, New Orleans, LA; divorced; children: Mignon M Schooler. **Educ:** Univ of CA Berkeley, BA 1942; Roosevelt U, MA 1966; Loyola Univ Sch of Soc Work. **Career:** Chicago Bd of Educ, teacher physically handicapped children 1963-; elem teacher 1948-53; Cook Co Hospital, medical social worker 1948-53; Dept Public Asst, social worker 1943-48. **Orgs:** IL State co-chmn educ NAACP; women's bd Am Cancer Soc; mem Mus of Contemporary Art; Art Inst; bd mem Chicago S Side NAACP; bd mem Counc for ExcepChildren; bd mem S Side Comm Art Cntr; mem Women's Benefit Board Operation PUSH; Bravo Chap Lyric Opera; com mem Harris "Y"; life mem NAACP; mem Urban League Women's Counc Proj 75. **Honors/Awds:** Serv aw Women's Aux NAACP; top tagger NAACP. **Business Addr:** Bd of Educ, 228 N La Salle St, Chicago, IL 60601.

PRYOR, MALCOLM D.
Bank executive. **Educ:** Howard University, graduate; Wharton School of Business, MBA. **Career:** Goldman Sachs and Co, salesman, until 1979; formed investment partnership, 1979; Pryor, Govan, Counts & Co, founder, 1981; Pryor, McClendon, Counts and Co, formed by merger of Pryor, Govan, Counts & Co and R J McClendon Capital Corp, chairman, 1989-. **Special Achievements:** Co. is largest African-American-owned investment bank in the United States; Black Enterprise magazine, 25 Hottest Blacks on Wall Street, Oct 1992; Co. is ranked #2 on Black Enterprise's list of top 12 Black-owned investment banks, Oct 1992, #7 in 1997. **Business Addr:** Chairman, Pryor, McClendon, Counts & Co Inc, #3 Penn Center, 1515 Market St, Ste 819, Philadelphia, PA 19102, (215)569-4544.

PRYOR, RICHARD (AARON RICHARD)
Comedian, actor, writer, producer. **Personal:** Born Dec 1, 1940, Peoria, IL; son of Gertrude Thomas Pryor and Leroy Pryor; divorced; children: Rain, Richard Jr, Elizabeth Ann, Steven, Kelsey, Franklin. **Career:** Comedian, actor; Indigo Productions, owner; Richard Pryor Enterprises Inc, owner, 1975-; films include: Bustin' Loose; Blue Collar; California Suite; Harlem Nights; See No Evil, Hear No Evil; Which Way Is Up?; The Wiz; The Toy; Richard Pryor Live in Concert; Some Kind of Hero; Superman III; Lady Sings the Blues; Silver Streak; Stir Crazy; Moving; Critical Condition; Another You; Car Wash; The Mack; White Lightning; Jo Jo Dancer: Your Life Is Calling; Harlem Nights; writer, director, producer, actor; writer: "Sanford & Son," "The Flip Wilson Show"; co-writer: Blazing Saddles; television apperances include: "Rowan & Martin's Laugh In," NBC-TV; "Saturday Night Live," NBC-TV; "The Richard Pryor Show," NBC-TV, 1977; "Martin," Fox-TV; recordings include: That Nigger's Crazy; Bicentennial Niggels It Something I Said?; Richard Pryor Live from The Sunset Strip. **Orgs:** Supporter, charities & human rights organizations; National Academy of Recording Arts & Sciences; Writers Guild Am. **Honors/Awds:** 4 Grammys for comedy albums; 5 Emmys for screenplays; 4 certified gold albums; 1 certified platinum; two American Academy Humor awards; American Writers Guild award; Academy Award nomination, Lady Sings the Blues, 1972. **Special Achievements:** Pryor Convictions and Other Life Sentences, Pantheon Books, 1995. **Military Serv:** US Army Airbone Division, 1958-60.

PRYSOCK, ARTHUR. See Obituaries section.

PUALANI, GLORIA
Business development manager. **Personal:** Born Nov 30, 1950, San Augustine, TX; daughter of Mary Lee Phelps and R C Phelps; married Jeffrey Ortiz, Apr 14, 1984; children: Ronald Bree. **Educ:** California State, BA, 1976; UCLA, purchasing certificate, 1981; National University, MBA, 1989. **Career:** ABC Television, script supervisor, production assistant, 1976-80; Pacific Aircraft, buyer, 1980-81; Northrop Corporation, administrator, 1981-. **Orgs:** Southern California Regional Purchasing Council, vice pres, external affairs, 1989-; Orange County Regional Purchasing Council, 1991-; Black Business Association Advisory Board, 1988-; Department of Commerce Minority Enterprise Development, 1988; National Association of Women Business Owners, 1989-; Association of Black Women Entrepreneurs Advisory Board, 1990-. **Honors/Awds:** Ebony Magazine, 100 Most Priomising Black Women in Cor-

porate America, 1991; Dollars and Sense Magazine, America's Best & Brightest, 1991; Georgia Association of Minority Entrepreneurs, Service Award, 1992; MENTOR NETWORK, Business Development Award, 1992; Mayor Tom Bradley Recognition Award for Business Development, 1992. **Special Achievements:** Museum of African-American Art, 1991. **Business Addr:** Manager, Northrop Corp, 1 Northrop Ave, Organ 123-99, Bldg 202, Hawthorne, CA 90250, (310)331-4784.

PUCKETT, KIRBY
Professional baseball player (retired). **Personal:** Born Mar 14, 1961, Chicago, IL; married Tonya Hudson; children: Catherine Margaret. **Educ:** Bradley Univ, Peoria, IL; Triton College, River Grove, IL. **Career:** Minnesota Twins, outfielder, 1984-96. **Honors/Awds:** Topps Major League All Rookie Team, 1984; voted to Amer League Silver Slugger Team 1986; Gold Glove Awd 1986; Most Valuable Player, Twins Cities Chapter, Baseball Writers Assn of America, 1986; American League All-Star Team, 1986-91. **Business Addr:** Retired Professional Baseball Player, Minnesota Twins, 501 Chicago Ave S, Metrodome Stadium, Minneapolis, MN 55415-1596.

PUCKREIN, GARY ALEXANDER
Publisher. **Personal:** Born Aug 18, 1949, New York, NY; married Joanne Harris; children: 1. **Educ:** CA State Univ, BA 1971; Brown Univ, MA 1974, PhD 1978. **Career:** Rutgers Univ, asst prof 1978-82, assoc prof 1982-; The Visions Foundation, exec dir; American Visions Magazine, publisher. **Orgs:** Assn of American Historians; Assn of Caribbean Historians. **Honors/Awds:** Free to Die (monograph) RI, Black Heritage Soc 1978; Fellow Vstg Scholar Smithsonian Inst 1982-84; Little England NY Univ Press 1984.

PUGH, CLEMENTINE A.
Educator. **Personal:** Born in Raleigh, NC; daughter of Alberta Harris High and Otho High; married George Douglas Pugh; children: Douglas, Janet. **Educ:** Shaw Univ, BA 1945; Columbia Univ, MSW 1948; Univ of MA Amherst, EdD 1982. **Career:** Hunter Coll, soc worker, rsch assoc educ clinic; Comm Serv Soc Family, psych soc; Herbert H Lehman Coll, prof of educ 1970-90; Lehman Coll, prof emeritus, 1991-. **Orgs:** Fellow Amer Orthopsychiatric Assc 1975-, prog fac 1980-; mem Natl Assc of Black Social Wrkrs 1980-; bd dir Homes for the Homeless; mem Assoc of Black Women in Higher Educ, Natl Women's Studies Assoc; lifetime mem NAACP; bd of trustees, Bank Street Coll, 1990-94. **Honors/Awds:** Book Publ "Those Children" Wadsworth Publ 1970; Article "Multi-Ethnic Collaboration to Combat Racism" Journal of Applied Behaviorial Sci 1977; numerous articles & publ 1980-85; book chapter: collaboration through validation of difference: an interracial model for change 1988. **Business Addr:** Prof Dept of Education, Herbert H Lehman Coll, Bronx, NY 10468.

PUGH, G. DOUGLAS
Government official. **Personal:** Born Dec 14, 1923, New York, NY; married Clementine A; children: Douglas E, Janet A. **Educ:** Columbia Univ, BS 1951, MBA 1957. **Career:** Urban League of Greater NY, ind rel dir 1955-60; Trafalgar Hosp, personnel dir 1960-62; Fed Mediation & Conciliation Svc, commiss 1962-67; Haryou-Act Inc, assoc exec dir; Ford Found, prog adv on urban affairs 1966-69; Dormitory Auth NY, dir labor rel & urban affairs 1970-75; Unemployment Inst Appeal Bd, commiss, mem of bd 1976-87, chmn, 1987-. **Orgs:** AFSCME AFL-CIO officer, 1958—. **Honors/Awds:** Publ "Black Economic Development" 1969.

PUGH, ROBERT WILLIAM, SR.
Business executive. **Personal:** Born May 10, 1926, New York, NY; son of Vennette I Pugh and William R Pugh; married Barbara Johnson; children: Robert Jr, Lori. **Educ:** Newark Sch of Fine Indsl Art, 1946-49; Mus of Moder Art, 1946; NY U, 1947-48. **Career:** Wynson Inc, designer 1945-46; Desagnet Hsng Corp, 1946; Nowland & Schladermundt, designer 1949-51; Assn Granite Craftsman's Guild Inc, pres 1975; Keystone Monument Co Inc, founder/pres; pres, Edward M Blesser Co, currently. **Orgs:** Mem Indusl Designer's Inst; Design Guild of NJ bd of mgrs Harlem YMCA; bd of trsts Youth Consult Serv; pres Asso Granite Craftmen's Guild Inc 1976-77& 1979-80; bd mem NY State Monument Bldrs Assn Inc; mem Monument Bldrs of N Amer; bd dirs New York State Monument Builders Assn Inc; mem Frank Silvera Workshop. **Honors/Awds:** Disting Serv Awd Assn Granite Craftsman's Guild 1976; designed and erected a public monument to Dr Martin Luther King in Harlem 1976; Man of the Yr Harlem YMCA 1977; First place awd design contest Monument Builders of North Amer 1977; only Black owner of monument co NY; spkr Tri-State Funeral Dirs Conv Granit NY 1979; guest AUS War Coll Nat Security Seminar 1979; Unity Award Assoc Granite Craftsman's Guild & Met Meml Indust Inc 1979; first Black man to serve as pres of Assoc Granite Craftsman Guild of NY (served 5 terms); Archie L Green Awd for Excellence 1982 and 83; donated and designed memorial dedicated to the slain children of Atlanta; Excellent Achievement Award, Nancy R Cherry Association 1989; Archie L Green Award for Excellence, Monument Builders ofNorth America, 1990. **Military Serv:** US Army, pvt 1944-45. **Business Addr:** President, Edward M Bleser Co, 37 Conway St, Brooklyn, NY 11207.

PUGH, RODERICK W.
Clinical psychologist, educator. **Personal:** Born Jun 1, 1919, Richmond, KY; son of Lena B White Pugh and George W Pugh; divorced. **Educ:** Fisk Univ Nashville TN, BA (cum laude), 1940; OH State Univ, MA 1941; Univ of Chgo, PhD Clinical Psych 1949. **Career:** Hines VA Medical Center Chgo, staff psych 1950-54, asst chief clin psych for psychotherapy 1954-58, chief clin psych sect 1958-60, suprv psych & coord psych internship training 1960-66; Private practice, clin psych 1958-; Loyola Univ of Chgo, assoc prof psych 1966-73, prof of psych 1973-89, prof emeritus, psychology, 1989-. **Orgs:** Illinois Div Voc Rehab 1965-; Chicago VA Reg Psych Training Prog 1966-, Amer Psych Assn & Natl Inst Mental Health Vis Psych Prog 1968-; National Institute Mental Health Juvenile Problems, research review committee, 1970-74; professional adv com Div of Mental Health City of Chicago 1979-; mem Natl Adv Panel Civilian Health & Med Prog of the Uniformed Serv Amer Psych Assn 1980-83; civilian adv comm US Army Command & Genl Staff Coll 1981-83; Joint Council on Professional Education in Psychology, 1987-90; fellow Amer Psych Assn, Amer Psych Soc, Soc for Psych Study of Soc Issues; Assn of Behavior Analysis; IL Psych Assn; Alpha Phi Alpha; visiting scholar/professor psych, Fisk Univ, 1966, 1994; mem 1968-78, sec 1970-77, Fisk Univ Bd Trustees; mem, Psi Chi, Sigma Xi, Univ of Chicago 1948; diplomate clin psych Amer Bd Prof Psych 1975. **Honors/Awds:** Author, "Psychology & The Black Experience" 1972, "Psychological Aspects of the Black Revolution"; Distinguished Serv Awd Amer Bd of Professional Psychology 1986; Illinois Psychological Assn, Distinguished Psychologist Award (top annual IL State Award) 1988; Assn Black Psychologists, Chicago Chapter, Award for Distinguished Service to Black Community 1984 & 1988; Natl Assn Black Psychologists Guiding Light Award for Pioneering Service 1979. **Military Serv:** US Army 1943-46; Battlefield Commn as 2nd lt, Patton's 3rd US Army, Alsfeld Germany 1945. **Business Addr:** Clinical Psychologist, 30 N Michigan Ave, Suite 1515, Chicago, IL 60602.

PUGH, THOMAS JEFFERSON
Educator. **Personal:** Born Oct 25, 1917, Lewiston, NC; married Lillian Ruth; children: John. **Educ:** Clark Coll, AB 1940; Gammon Theo Sem, MDiv 1942; Atlanta U, MA 1947; Boston U, PhD 1955. **Career:** Theol Center, vice pres acad servs interdenominat 1979-, exec vice pres 1980; Acad Affairs, acting vice pres 1978-79; Theol Center, prof interdenom 1958-78; Albany State Coll, chap 1948-58; Bryant Theo Sem, tchr 1944-47; Bethesda Bapt Ch, pastor 1943-46; Tri-Comm Consol HS, prin 1942-44; Jas Andrews Farm, dir religion educ to migrants 1942. **Orgs:** Contrib YMCA; life mem Alpha Phi Alpha Frat; ldr Career Devel Inst for AF; indiv grp marriage therapy to alcoholic patients GA Clinic; Psychol Eval ofCand for Ministry; Marriage & Family Enrich Workshops; mem Friendship Bapt Ch, Amer Psych Assn, GA Psych Assn, Soc for Sci Study of Rel; supr AAMFt; AAUP; GA AMFt; Atlanta MHA; bd of dirs GA Assn for Past Care; bd trust ITC; faculty rep; pastoral therapist GA Clinic for Alcoholics elected mem Intl Soc of Theta Phi. **Honors/Awds:** NIMH Fellow; grant Lilly Endowment Couns Educ Prgm; cit Judge Baker's Ct; ldr 2 CDI Missions to Air Force Chaplains etc overseas 1973; Fellow The Case-Study Inst 1975; Fellow Ecumenical Cultural Inst 1975; num publ in professional & ch journals; Fellow in Gerontology GSU 1986-87; Morehouse School of Medicine, institutional review board, 1987. **Business Addr:** Professor, Interdenominational Theological Center, Psy of Relig & Pastoral Care, 671 Beckwith St SW, Atlanta, GA 30314.

PULLEN-BROWN, STEPHANIE D.
Attorney. **Personal:** Born Dec 11, 1949, Baltimore, MD; married Gerald O Brown; children: Margot. **Educ:** MD Inst of Art, BFA 1970; Coppin State Coll, MEd 1973; Loyola Coll, MEd 1979; Univ of Maryland, JD 1991. **Career:** Baltimore City Public Schools, teacher 1970-74, admin specialist 1974-80; Univ of MD, coop extn serv city dir 1980-86, asst to vice president/dean 1986-91; attorney, currently. **Orgs:** Commissioner Baltimore City Commn for Women 1984-86; mem Johnson Foundation Bd Baltimore Museum of Art 1985-; mem Bd YMCA 1985-. **Honors/Awds:** Search for Professional Excellence Natl Assoc of County Agricultural Agents 1983; Woman Manager of the Year, Conf of Women in MD State Serv 1984.

PULLEY, CLYDE WILSON
Educator (retired). **Personal:** Born Sep 21, 1934, Spring Hope, NC; son of Madge Pulley and Zollie Pulley; children: Mary A, Jessie F. **Educ:** Culver-Stockton Clge Canton MO, BS 1973; Xavier Univ Cincinnati OH, MS 1978. **Career:** USAF, police admin 1952-74; OH Dept Rehabilitation & Correction, correction admin 1974-77; NC Dept of Correction, correction dir 1977-79; Wilson Co Tech Inst, instructor correction and social services 1979-81; Metro State Coll, professor criminal justice & criminology 1981-87; Ashland University, professor, criminal justice and sociology. **Orgs:** Consult Amer Corr Assn 1979-81; spec correspondent Afro-American Newspapers, Balto, MD 1979-81; mem bd dir Comitis Crisis Cntr 1983-84, CO Prison Assn 1984-87; Williams St Ctr; Natl Assn of Blacks in Criminal Justice; Natl Assn Human Service Workers; Ohio Council Criminal Justice Education. **Honors/Awds:** Natl Assn of Blacks in Criminal Justice, 1982-91, Amer Correctional Assn, 1977-89; Outstanding Educ Award, Goldsboro, NC, 1980; candidate, Lt Gov NC Demo Primary, 1980. **Military Serv:** US Army, USAF, master sgt, 1952-74; AFCM NDSM KSM VSM GCM UNSM 1952-74. **Home Addr:** 111 Meadow Trail Dr, San Antonio, TX 78227-1638, (210)675-4144. **Business Addr:** Retired, Prof of Criminal Justice and Sociology, Ashland University, 401 College Ave, Ashland, OH 44805.

PULLIAM, BETTY E.
Government official, business executive. **Personal:** Born Jun 4, 1941, Woodruff, SC; daughter of Gertrude Greene Ferguson and Shewerl Douglas Ferguson; married Herman; children: Trudy, Vanessa, Herman Jr. **Educ:** Wayne State University; National Judicial College, Reno, NV, 1989. **Career:** St Mark's Comm Ch, sec 1958-64; Mayor's Youth Employment Prog Comm for Human Resources Devel, 1965-69; Robert Johnson Asso Training Inst, office mgmnt 1971-73; Payne-Pulliam School of Trade & Commerce, pres, co-owner, 1973-; Michigan (State) Liquor Control Commission, commissioner, 1989-. **Orgs:** 1st female pres & chairwoman of the board 1990-, Booker T Washington Business Assoc; mem of the Detroit Stategic Planning Cncls (Jobs & Economic Devel Task Force); Designated Educ Planning Entity for Job Training Partnership Act, bd mem; Mich Dept of Educ Adult Exte Learning Adv Bd mem; Commerce High School Alumni bd mem; Mich Org of Private Schools mem; Greater New Mt Moriah Bapt Church choir mem; Women's Economic Club; board member, Greater Detroit Chamber of Commerce, 1987-89; board member, National Alcohol Beverage Control, 1989-. **Honors/Awds:** Business Woman of the Month; Pinch Cert of Ach 1978; Spirit of Detroit Awd 1983; Golden Heritage Awd for Educ Exc 1984; Detroit City Cncl Cmty Awd 1983; Black History Month Recog Awd 1985; Wayne Cnty Exec Office Ach Awd 1986; Proclamation from the Mayor Detroit 1983; Cert of Appr for Natl Business Week 1985; Cert of Recog City of Highland Park 1987; Cert of Rec from the Mayor 1987; Outstanding Ach for Historical Accomplishment 1987; Community Service Award, Councilwoman Barbara R Collins 1988; appointment to Michigan Liquor Control Commission, by Governor James Blanchard, 1989. **Home Addr:** 18945 Woodingham, Detroit, MI 48221. **Business Addr:** President, Payne-Pulliam Sch of Trade/Com, 2345 Cass Ave, Detroit, MI 48201.

PULLIAM, HARVEY JEROME, JR.
Professional baseball player. **Personal:** Born Oct 20, 1967, San Francisco, CA. **Career:** Kansas City Royals, outfielder, 1991-93; Colorado Rockies, 1995-97; Arizona Diamondbacks, 1998-. **Business Addr:** Professional Baseball Player, Arizona Diamondbacks, BankOne Ballpark, 401 E Jefferson, Phoenix, AZ 85004.

PURCE, THOMAS LES
Chief operating engineer. **Personal:** Born Nov 13, 1946, Pocatello, ID. **Educ:** BA Psychology 1969; MEd 1970; EdD 1975. **Career:** Washington State Univ, counsel psychologist 1970-72; ID State Univ, dir coop educ 1974-75, asst prof of counselor ed 1975-77; Pocatello, ID, mayor 1976-77; State of ID Dept of Adminstrn, adminstr div of gen serv 1977-79, dir 1979-81; State of ID Dept of Health & Welfare, dir 1981-83; POWER Engineers Inc, chief operating engineer 1983-. **Orgs:** Mem Assn Univ Prof; Assn of Counselor Educ & Supr; Assn of ID Cities; Assn of Black Psychologists; v chmn City Council; mem ID Water & Sewage Cert Bd; NAACP; Urban League Task Force; SE ID Cncl of Govt; ID Housing Agency; Kappa Alpha Psi; City Councilman. **Honors/Awds:** Outstanding Young Men of Amer; mem State Exec Com Dem Party. **Business Addr:** Chief Operating Engineer, Power Engineers Inc, 805 SW Crestview St, Pullman, WA 99163.

PURDEE, NATHAN
Actor, artist. **Personal:** Born Aug 6, 1950, Tampa, FL; son of Anna Beatrice Alston and Emmanuel Purdee Johnson; married Roberta Morris, Nov 9, 1991; children: Taylor Armstrong. **Educ:** Metro State, AA, mental health; Linfield College, attended, theatre arts, criminolgy. **Career:** CBS-TV, The Young and the Restless, actor 1984-91; NBC-TV, Santa Barbara, actor, 1989; Littoral Productions, Return of Superfly, actor, 1989; ABC-TV, One Life to Live, actor, 1992-. **Orgs:** Installations Art Gallery, charter member, 1988-93; Art Students League, artist, 1993; NATAS/ATAS, 1985-93. **Honors/Awds:** NATAS, Emmy Honors, Best Drama (Young & Restless), 1985, 1986; Hollywood Tribute to Soaps, Favorite Newcomer, 1985; Soap Opera Digest, Top Ten TVQ, 1990, 1991, 1992. **Special Achievements:** Featured artist, American Dream Art Festival, 1988; "I Will Not Be Denied," performance art, 1990; "The Other Side of Daytime," variety show, 1990, 1991; "Stars Behind Bars," self-motivational seminar, 1987-88; subject of articles which have appeared in various issues of Ebony Magazine, Soap Opera Digest, Episodes, and Soap Opera Magazine. **Business Addr:** Actor, Artist, Feldman Public Relations, 9220 Sunset Blvd, Ste 230, Los Angeles, CA 90069, (310)859-9062.

PURIFOY, NOAH SYLVESTER
Assemblage artist. **Personal:** Born Aug 17, 1917, Snowhill, AL; son of Georgia & Henry Purifoy. **Educ:** Alabama State Teachers College, BS, 1943; Atlanta Univ, MSW, 1948; Chounard Art Inst, BFA, 1956. **Career:** Alabama State Bd of Education, teacher, 1939-42; Cuyahaga Cty, Child Welfare Bd,

Cleveland OH, social worker, 1948-50; Los Angeles Cty General Hosp, social worker, 1950-52; Broadway Dept Store, LA CA, commercial artist, 1956-64; Watts Tower Art Ctr, Los Angeles, CA, founder, dir, 1964-66; Central City Com Mental Health Facility, vp, 1970-76; University of CA, artist in resident; Cowel College, Santa Cruz, dir of social service, 1977-81; assemblege artist, currently. **Orgs:** Los Angeles Culture Affairs, deputy, mem, 1970-74; CA State Arts Council, Sacramento CA, 1976-87, chmn, Art-In-Education sub-committee. **Honors/Awds:** Richard Florshine Art Foundation, grant, 1995-96; Pollach-Krasner Foundation, Inc, grant, 1996; Adolph and Ester Gohlieb Foundation, grant, 1996; Flintridge Foundation, Visual Artists Award, grant, 1997-98. **Special Achievements:** Cofounder of the Watts Summer Festival, 1964-66; created ''66 Signs of Neon,'' (66 pieces of sculpture made from the debris of the Watts riot), 1966-70; created Art-in-Education Programs, CA Arts Council, 1976-87; retrospective, ''Outside and In the Open,'' an exhibition, 1997-98. **Military Serv:** Navy Cee Bees, petty officer 1st class, 1942-46.

PURNELL, CAROLYN J.
Attorney. **Personal:** Born Aug 16, 1939, Memphis, TN; married; children: Monica, Mardine. **Educ:** Univ of WA, BA 1961; Univ of WA School of Law, JD 1971. **Career:** Pros Attny Office, sr legal intern 1971, civil dep 1972-74; City of Seattle, legal couns to mayor; Weyerhaeuser Co Fed Way Wash, corp attny, dir of corp matls; Washington Round Table, exec, chief counsel, 1989-93, deputy director, 1993; executive director, 1994-96, management consultant, 1996-. **Orgs:** Vp Housing Corp Devel of Washington; panelist Human Rights Comm Tribunal; past exec bd sec March of Dimes; bd of trustees Epiphany School; mem Phi Alpha Delta Legal Frat; sec Delta Sigma Theta Sor; former mem Providence Hosp Found; mem WA State Bd of Bar Examiners, City of Seattle Bd of Adjustments, Scholastic Honor Soc; mem Pacific Med Ctr Bd, Mayors Centennial Parks Commiss, Mayors Zoo Commiss. **Honors/Awds:** Outstanding Young Women Dir for US 1976; 1 of 100 Lawyers in US to attend Amer Assembly on Law; Selected 1st Class of Leadership for Tomorrow Seattle C of C. **Business Addr:** Executive, Washington Round Table, 16 W Harrison, Washington Round Table, Seattle, WA 98119.

PURNELL, LOVETT
Professional football player. **Personal:** Born Apr 17, 1972, Seaford, DE; son of Ronald and Betty Harmon. **Educ:** Univ of West Virginia, attended. **Career:** New England Patriots, tight end, 1996-. **Business Addr:** Professional Football Player, New England Patriots, 60 Washington St, Foxboro Stadium, Foxboro, MA 02035, (508)543-7911.

PURNELL, MARK W., CIMA
Investment consultant. **Personal:** Born Oct 23, 1957, Wilmington, DE; son of Yolanda V Purnell and Ernest W Purnell Sr; married Brenda Dillard Purnell, Jun 28, 1980; children: Devon, Faith, Brandon. **Educ:** Delaware State College, BS (high honors), accounting, 1979; University of Wisconsin Madison, MBA, finance/investments, 1982. **Career:** Peat Marwick Mitchell, senior accountant; Arthur Andersen & Co, consultant; Offerman & Co Inc, divisional manager; Kemper Securities Inc, senior vp, investments, currently. **Orgs:** National Association of Black Accountants Inc, 1995 Natl Convention, chair; Univ of Wisconsin Alumni Association; Milwaukee Athletic Club. **Honors/Awds:** Consortium for Graduate Study in Management, Distinguished Service Award, 1991; Investment Management Cosnultants Association, CIMA Designation. **Special Achievements:** ''Managed Money: The Dynamics of Personalized Investing,'' Research Magazine, June 1992. **Business Addr:** Senior VP, Investments, Everen Securities Inc, 815 N Water St, 2nd Fl, Milwaukee, WI 53202, (414)347-3357.

PURNELL, MARSHALL E.
Architect. **Personal:** Born Jun 8, 1950, Grand Rapids, MI; son of Lelia Givens Purnell and Curtis Purnell; married Tawana Cook Purnell; children: Justin, Tara, Austin. **Educ:** University of Michigan, Ann Arbor, MI, BS, architecture, 1973, MA, architecture, 1973. **Career:** University of Maryland, Washington, DC, lecturer teaching 2nd yr studio, 1973-74; Fry & Welch Architects, Washington, DC, architect, 1973-74; The American Institute of Architects, Washington, DC, administrator, 1974-78; Devrouax & Purnell, Washington, DC, principal, 1978-. **Orgs:** Past president, National Organization of Minority Architects, 1975; DC chairman, United Way, 1999. **Honors/Awds:** University of Michigan Alumni Scholarship, University of Michigan. **Business Addr:** Principal, Devrouax & Purnell, Architects-Planners, PC, 717 D St, NW, 5th Fl, Washington, DC 20004.

PURVIS, ANDRE
Professional football player. **Personal:** Born Jul 14, 1973. **Educ:** Univ of North Carolina, attended. **Career:** Cincinnati Bengals, defensive tackle, 1997-. **Business Addr:** Professional Football Player, Cincinnati Bengals, One Bengals Dr, Cincinnati, OH 45202, (513)621-3550.

PURVIS, ARCHIE C., JR.
Business executive, consultant. **Personal:** Born May 24, 1939, New York, NY; son of Millicent Purvis and Archibald Purvis Sr; married Candace H Caldwell; children: Christian. **Educ:** Univ of Munich, 1960; City Coll of NY Sch of Business, BS 1969; Stanford Executive Program 1989. **Career:** Gen Foods Corp, account manager 1963-66; Polaroid Corp, natl sales mgr 1966-74; Lear Purvis Walker & Co, exec vice pres 1974-75; MCA Inc Univ Studios, vp ind mktg 1975-79; Amer Broadcasting Co, vp, general mgr video sales div; ABC Distribution Co, pres; Capital ABC Inc, Ambroco Media Group, pres, 1980-95; Purvis Enterprises Inc, pres, 1995-. **Orgs:** Mem Amer Mktg Assn; mem Amer Mgmt Assn, mem Sales Exec of NY; dir San Fernand Fair Housing, 1979; dir Intl Children's Sch; dir Corporation for Public Broadcasting 1987; Academy of Motion Picture Arts & Sciences, Hollywood Radio & TV Society; bd of dirs, GTE California, 1988-; GTE West, dir; YMCA Metropolitan, Los Angeles, dir; Keep California Beautiful, dir; Los Angeles Community Colleges, advisor. **Honors/Awds:** Adopt-A-Hwy Volunteer of 1997. **Military Serv:** AUS Sp-5; Advanced Commendation Award. **Business Addr:** Purvis Enterprises, Inc, 2040 Ave of the Stars, Ste 400, Los Angeles, CA 90067.

PURYEAR, ALVIN N.
Educator. **Personal:** Born Apr 6, 1937, Fayetteville, NC; married Catherine; children: 3. **Educ:** Yale Univ, BA 1960; Columbia Univ, MBA 1962, PhD 1966. **Career:** Mobil Oil Corp, employee relations advisor 1965-66, financial analyst 1966-67; Allied Chem Corp, computer systems specialist 1967-68; Rutgers Univ, assoc prof 1968-70; Baruch Coll, associate prof, 1970-72, dean 1972-75, prof of mgmt 1972-; The Ford Foundation, vice pres organiz & mgmt 1980-82; City of NY, first deputy comptroller 1983-85. **Orgs:** Yale Univ, trustee, 1994-; GP Financial Corp, director, 1994-; Green Point Savings Bank, trustee, 1992-; Smithsonian National Board, 1989-. **Business Addr:** Professor, Baruch Coll City Univ of NY, 17 Lexington, New York, NY 10010.

PUTNAM, GLENDORA M.
Attorney. **Personal:** Born Jul 25, 1923, Lugoff, SC; daughter of Katherine Stewart McIlwain (deceased) and Simon P McIlwain (deceased). **Educ:** Barber Scotia Jr Clge, Cert 1943; Bennett Clge, AB 1945; Boston Univ, JD 1948. **Career:** Dept of HUD, deputy asst secr 1975-77; MA Office of Atty Gen, asst atty gen 1963-69; MA Comm Against Discrimination, chair 1969-75; MA Housing Finance Agcy, equal opport ofcr, 1977-88. **Orgs:** Mem MA Bar 1949-, Federal Bar 1st Dist 1956-, US Supreme Court Bar 1964-, MA Bar Assc 1971-; bd trustee Boston Conservatory, 1972-; pres YWCA of the USA 1985-91; bd NAACP Legal & Educational Defense Fund; Boston Bar Assoc; Boston Lawyers Committee for Civil Rights Under Law; life mem Exec Committee BU Law School Alumni Assn. **Honors/Awds:** Women of the Year Greater Boston Bus & Prof Club 1969; Humanitarian Award Boston Branch NAACP 1973; Academy of Distinguished Bostonians, Greater Boston Chamber of Commerce 1988; Doctor of Laws (hon), Southeastern Mass Univ 1986; Woman of Achievement, Boston Big Sisters 1985; Silver Shingle for Distinguished Public Service, Boston Univ Law School 1988; Bennett College, LLD, honorary, 1991. **Home Addr:** 790 Boylston St, Boston, MA 02199.

PYKE, WILLIE ORANDA
Educator. **Personal:** Born May 6, 1930, Plymouth, NC. **Educ:** NC A&T State Univ Greensboro, BS 1953; Columbia Univ NY, MA 1965f No IL U, EdD 1972. **Career:** Dept of Bus Educ & Adminstrv Services So IL Univ, prof and chairperson 1972-; Hampton Inst VA, assoc prof of business 1971-72; Langston Univ OK, asst of business 1967-69; Albany State & Coll GA, asst prof of business 1965-67; Teachers Coll Columbia Univ NY, TC fund officer 1963-65; St Augustine's Coll Raleigh NC, execsec 1960-63. **Orgs:** Mem lgislative com IL Bus Educ Assn 1979-80; mem bd of dir SW IL Intern'l Word Processing Assn 1979-80; mem State of IL Adv Com for Bus Mkt & Mgmt Occupations; sec bd of dir E St Louis Met Ministry 1978-81; mem Commn of Ministry So IL. **Honors/Awds:** Award for Doctoral study Ford Found 1969-71; oman of achievement award Edwardsville Bus & Professional Women's Club; author of several articles in Nat Professional MagS and Yearbooks; numerous service awards Bus Orgns. **Business Addr:** Southern Illinois University, PO Box 106, Edwardsville, IL 62026.

PYLES, J. A.
Educational administrator. **Personal:** Born Feb 23, 1949, Sanford, FL. **Educ:** Bethune-Cookman Coll, BA 1971; Roosevelt Univ MA 1975. **Career:** United Negro Coll Fund, asst area dir; Alpha Kappa Alpha Sorority Inc, program specialist; Social Security Admin St Petersburg, 1970; Bethune Cookman Coll, vice pres for development, special asst to the pres, 1990-. **Orgs:** Soc of Fund-Raising Execs; Natl Soc of Fund-Raising Execs; Bethune-Cookman Coll Alumni Assn; Roosevelt Univ Alumni Assn; Gamma Mu Omega Chat, Alpha Kappa Alpha Sorority, Inc; consultant, AGAPE Ministries; Mount Carmel Baptist Church. **Honors/Awds:** Recipient United Negro Coll Fund Alumni Achievement Award 1980; Salute to Leadership Award, United Negro College Fund Inc; Recognition Award, Black College Fund; Council for the Advancement & Support of Education, Intern Honors Program, 1982, 1983. **Business Addr:** Special Assistant to the President, Bethune-Cookman College, 640 Dr Mary McLeod Bethune Blvd, Daytona Beach, FL 32114, (904)255-1401.

PYLES, JOHN E.
Attorney, judge. **Personal:** Born Jan 11, 1927, Memphis, TN; married Deborah; children: 8. **Educ:** BCL 1951; JD 1968. **Career:** Office of John E Pyles, attorney 1968-; municipal judge 1979-81. **Orgs:** Mem Wichita Bar Assn; Sedgwick County Bar Assn; Wichita Bd of Realtors 1960-; Multilist Serv of Wichita 1967-; MS Trial Lawyer Assn 1967-. **Military Serv:** USAF Signal Corp Sgt 1945-47. **Business Addr:** Judge, 2703 E 13th, Wichita, KS 67214.

Q

QAMAR, NADI ABU
Musician, composer. **Personal:** Born Jul 6, 1917, Cincinnati, OH; son of Alberta Bennett Givens and William Givens; married Rose Ann Dolski; children: Fabian Billie, Alberta Edith. **Educ:** Attended Intl Univ Foundation Independence MO. **Career:** Jazz Pianist, Composer and Arranger, 1934-65; Inaugural History of Jazz series 1965; composer, musician, 1965-77; Bedford Study Youth in Action, oratorio composer/mus dir; Countee Cullen, concerts 1965-68; New Lafayette Theatre, artist in residence 1970-72; Nina Simone World Tours 1972-74; ''Wy Mbony Sita,'' ballet, New York City 1973; Museum of Natural History NY, perf series 1976; Bennington Coll, prof of voice, piano and orchestra 1978-85; lecturer, leader of workshops at various universities and study centers, 1977-89; Nuru Taa African Idiom and Nuru Taa Music, afromusicologist, director. **Orgs:** Broadcast Music, 1958-; American Federation of Musicians; member, National Music Publisher's Assn, Inc. **Honors/Awds:** Drummer & singer with Zulu Singers & Dancers at World's Fair African Pavillion, Flushing Meadows, NY, 1965; composer/scorer/director, premiere performance of Likembican Panorama, 1969; asst mus dir of ''Black Picture Show'' at Jos Papp Shakespeare Festival 1974; Likembi/mbira Performance Workshop Series Dir Museum of Natural History Dr Barbara Jackson Coord 1976; Certificate of Recognition for Exemplary Representation of African Amer Artistic and Cultural Expression at FESTAC 1977; records Nuru Taa African Idiom, The Mama Likembi Instruction Manual CRB 14, The Likembi Songbook Manual of Annotated Songs & Recorded Compositions CRB 15 Folkway Records; citation for concerts at FESTAC 1977; performed at Detroit Inst of Art Inaugural Nok Igbo Sculpture Show1980; Folkways recording artist; Debut Fantasy recording of strings & keys duo w/Charles Mingus, Max Roach original composition, Blue Tide Art, Music and Publishers 1989; Wisconsin Public Television, Prime Time Wisconsin, 1990-91. **Business Addr:** Director, Nuru Taa Arts/Music/Publishers, Route 1, Box 274, Kewaunee, WI 54216.

QUANDER, ROHULAMIN
Attorney. **Personal:** Born Dec 4, 1943, Washington, DC; son of Joheora Rohualamin Quander and James W Quander; married Carmen Torruella; children: Iliana Amparo, Rohulamin Darius, Fatima de los Santos. **Educ:** Howard Univ, BA 1966, JD 1969. **Career:** Neighborhood Legal Serv, 1969-71; Geo Wash Univ, 1970-72; Intl Investors, Inc, market cons, attorney, state dir 1973-; private practice 1975-; Office of Adjudication DC Govt 1986-; geneological hist and researcher for private groups; attorney examiner under consulting contract to various DC Govt agencies. **Orgs:** Mem Superior Ct of DC 1975; US dist Ct of DC 1976; mem Amer Bar Assn; Natl Bar Assn; DC Bar Assn; Bar of Supreme Ct of PA; US Dist Ct for Eastern PA; Ct of Appeals DC; Phi Alpha Delta Law Frat 1967; Phi Alpha Theta His Soc; founder Howard Univ Chap of Black Amer Law Students Assn 1968; mem Omega Psi Phi Frat 1964-; pres Student Bar Assn 1968-69, vice pres 1967-68; mem bd of dir The Wash DC Parent & Child Center 1977-81; chief archivist Quander Family History 1977-; reg chmn Howard Univ Alumni 1979-87; chmn Educ Inst Licensure Commn of DC 1979-; bd dir Wash Urban League 1969-70; pres Howard Univ Alumni Club for Wash DC 1970-71; guest lecturer on the geneology hist & contributions of the Quander Family (America's oldest documntd black fam); member, MLK Holiday Commission for DC, 1987-89;s Quanders United, Inc 1983-; mem of, Columbia Hist Soc, Int'l Platform Speakers Assoc 1985-, Republican Party of DC; bd of dir Pigskin Club 1986-; pres, founder, Quanders Historical Society, Inc, 1985-; co-chair, founder, Benjamin Banneker Memorial Comm, Inc, 1991; dir and vp, Torruella-Quander Gallery, Ltd, 1988-; founder and pres, IliRo-Fa International, Inc, 1991-. **Honors/Awds:** Man of Yr Award Omega Psi Phi Frat 1965 & 1968; Spl Award Howard Univ Outstdg Serv to Law Sch, the Community and the Univ 1969; Dean's List Howard Univ 1964, 1965, 1968; Travel Fellowship to 13 foreign countries 1964; Outstanding Service Award, Quanders United, Inc, 1991; author, The History of the Quander Family, 1984; have published numerous articles for Howard Univ Alumni newspaper. **Business Addr:** Attorney, 1703 Lawrence St NE, Washington, DC 20018.

QUANSAH-DANKWA, JULIANA ABA
Dentist. **Personal:** Born Aug 11, 1955, Apam, Ghana; daughter of Elizabeth Quansah and S T Quansah; married Joseph Ofori-Dankwa. **Educ:** Univ of Michigan Dental School, Zoology 1974-76, DDS 1980. **Career:** Lawrence D Crawford DDS PC, assoc dentist 1980-83; Comm Action Comm, dental dir 1981-85; Riverfront Dental Ctr, dentist 1982-83; Private Practice, dentist 1984-. **Orgs:** Mem, NAACP 1984; chmn, Intl Trends & Serv Tri City Links Inc 1984-; mem, African of Greater Flint Inc 1984-; mem, Saginaw Chamber of Commerce 1985; bd mem, Headstart Saginaw 1985-. **Honors/Awds:** Commendation Award, Ross Medical Educ Center, 1986; Appreciation Award, Averill Career Opportunities, 1986.

QUARLES, GEORGE R.
Educational administrator (retired). **Personal:** Born Jul 14, 1927, Morgantown, WV; son of Mabel and George; married Barbara; children: Karen, Niama. **Educ:** Hampton Inst, BS 1951; NY U, MA 1956. **Career:** Ctr for Career & Occup Edn, chief admin; NYC, bd of edn; City Univ of NY, dir regional oppor cntr; Sam Harris Asso Ltd Washington, DC, exec vp; NJ State Educ Dept, dir voc educ dept; Newark Skills Cntr, dir; New Rochelle HS New Rochelle, NY, tchr; deputy assistant secretary, US Dept of Educ, Washington DC, Office of Vocational and Adult Ed, 1980-81; Sewanhaka Central High School District, Floral Park, NY, dir of occupational educ, 1985-90; Southern Westchester Board of Cooperative Educational Services, Richard Lerer Center for Technical and Occupational Education, assistant director 1991-. **Orgs:** Mem Am Vocational Assn; former mem NY State Adv Counc for Vocat Edn; adjunct staff New Sch for Soc Research; consult Vocat Educ mem Omega Psi Phi Frat; mem tech review panel Nat Inst of Edn's Study of Vocat Edn; former mem Nat Faculty for the Nat Center for Research in Vocat Educ OH State U; consultant, US Aid African Bureau, 1983-84; consultant, Academy for Educational Devel, 1984-91; consultant, Mitshita Educational Foundation 1988-89. **Honors/Awds:** NY State Sidney Platt Award for Outstanding Administrator of Vocational Education; Winged Trophy Newark Anti-Poverty Agency; Omega Man of the Year, Omicron Iota Chapter; numerous radio & TV appearances articles for various newspapers on vocational education; major paper on Equity in Vocational Education, Natl Center for Research in Vocational Education; numerous articles & studies on vocational education & youth employment; Education Secretary's Special Achievement Pin. **Military Serv:** 1st lt field artillery; Bronz Star for Valor; Purple Heart with Oak Leaf Cluster.

QUARLES, HERBERT DUBOIS
Educator (retired). **Personal:** Born Feb 24, 1929, Charlottesville, VA; son of Mattie Virginia Davis Quarles and John Benjamin Quarles. **Educ:** James Millikin University, Decatur, IL, BA, music education, 1952; Howard University, Washington, DC, BA, Music, 1962; Catholic University of America, Washington, DC, MA, music, 1965. **Career:** Federal government, Washington, DC, clerk typist, 1955-61; Public Schools, Washington, DC, music teacher, 1959-60, Public Schools, Alexandria, VA, music teacher, 1961-62; Public Schools, Washington, DC, music teacher, 1962-80; Public Schools, PT evening, Washington, DC, teacher, 1967-; Afro American Newspaper, Washington, DC, columnist/reporter, 1972-. **Orgs:** Vice president, Phi Mu Alpha Fraternity, 1950-52; president, Washington Bridge Unit, 1977-83; vice president, Mid-Atlantic Section American Bridge Assn, 1983-88, 1994-95; member, several church groups. **Honors/Awds:** Service Award, Francis Junior High School, 1980; American Bridge Association, Life Membership. **Military Serv:** Army reserves, Sergeant Major E-9, 1952-79; several letters of commendation. **Home Addr:** 5616 13th St, NW #109, Washington, DC 20011-3529.

QUARLES, JOSEPH JAMES
Physician (retired). **Personal:** Born Aug 10, 1911, Norfolk, VA; divorced. **Educ:** West Virginia State College, BA, 1934; Meharry Medical College, MD, 1941. **Career:** Retired physician. **Orgs:** Retired dir, Berkley Citizens Mutual Savings and Loan 1951; pres, chrmn of board, CEO, 1974, v chrmn, Community Facilities Comm City of Norfolk, VA 1975. **Military Serv:** US Army, Medical Corps, captain.

QUARLES, NORMA R.
Journalist. **Personal:** Born Nov 11, 1936, New York; divorced; children: Lawrence, Susan. **Educ:** Hunter Coll; City Coll of NY. **Career:** CNN, correspondent, 1990-, daytime anchor, 1988-90; NBC-TV, news reporter, beginnning 1970; WKYC-TV, Cleveland, OH, news reporter/anchorwoman 1967-70; NBC News Training Prog, 1966-67; WSDM-FM, Chicago, IL, news reporter, 1965-66; Katherine King Associates, Chicago, IL, real estate broker 1957-65. **Orgs:** Nat Academy of TV Arts & Sci, bd of gov; Sigma Delta Chi; Natl Assn of Black Journalists. **Honors/Awds:** Front Page Award, WNBC-TV, 1973; Deadline Club Award, Sigma Delta Chi, 1973; inducted into NABJ Hall of Fame, 1990. **Special Achievements:** Selected as a panelist, The League of Women Voters Vice Presidential Debate. **Business Addr:** Reporter, CNN, 5 Penn Plaza, New York, NY 10001.

QUARLES, RUTH BRETT
Educator (retired). **Personal:** Born Nov 23, 1914, Murfreesboro, NC; daughter of Julia Pierce Brett and Arthur Brett; married Benjamin Quarles (deceased); children: Roberta Knowles, Pamela. **Educ:** Shaw Univ Raleigh, NC, AB 1935; Hartford Seminary Foundation, MA 1936; Teachers College, Columbia Univ, EdD 1945. **Career:** Spelman College, Atlanta, assistant to dean 1936-38; Dillard Univ, New Orleans, dean of women 1938-42; Bennett Coll Greensboro, dean of students 1942-44; Tuskegee Inst, assoc personnel dir 1945-49; Univ of Munich Student Ctr Munich, Germany, asisstant in student ctr 1949-51; Fisk Univ, dean of students, 1951-53; Morgan State Univ, dir of counseling ctr 1956-80. **Orgs:** Pres Assoc of Deans of Women and Advisers to Girls 1944-46; fellow Natl Cncl Religion in Higher Education 1944-; consultant Amer Cncl Ed 1953-57; member Comm on Ed of Women Amer Cncl on Ed 1953-57; member Brd of Dir of YWCA on US 1956-60; mem Bd of Trustees of Morgan Christian Ctr 1960-; life member of NAACP; mem MD Intl Women's Year Coord Comm 1977; mem Exec Bd of Dir and Dir of Coll Sect of Natl Assoc for Women Deans, Counselors and Admin 1977-80; published article Journal of the NAWDAC 1984-86 on "Our Living History, Reminiscences of Black Participation in NAWDAC"; prgm participant in annual conf of NAWDAC 1984, 1986. **Honors/Awds:** Member Kappa Delta Pi Honor Soc 1944-; member Pi Lambda Theta Honor Soc 1944-; citee Outstanding Achvmnt NAWDAC 1980; symposium set up by NAWDAC in her honor on Counseling for Minorities 1982; Promethean honor soc at Morgan St named for one of founders and advisor for 23 yrs, Grant-Brett Kappa Tau honor soc. **Home Addr:** 10450 Lottsford Road, # 2115, Mitchellville, MD 20721-2748.

QUARRELLES, JAMES IVAN
Association executive. **Personal:** Born Apr 2, 1926, Morgantown, WV; son of Elsie Quarrelles and John H Quarrelles; married Gladys; children: Tracy Marie, Jamie C. **Educ:** Hilltop Radio & Electronic Inst, 1947. **Career:** Martha Table nonprofit corp, chmn 1984-; NAC of NDC #1 UPO, pres 1982-. **Orgs:** Mem Mayor's Task Force on Ambulatory Health Care for the Metro Area 1975; mem Childrens Hosp Comprehensive Health Care Prog 1978; mem Childrens Hosp Natl Health Ctr task force comm 1978; mem Childrens Hosp Natl Health Ctr Spec Comm 1978; mem Notre Dame Acad PTA Assn 1980; mem 3rd Dist Adv Council 1980. **Honors/Awds:** Certificate of Appreciation US Dept of Commerce 1970; Certificate of Appreciation United Planning Organ 1984. **Military Serv:** USN petty officer 2nd class 3 yrs; Amer Theater Ribbon. **Home Addr:** 2101 New Hampshire Ave NW, Washington, DC 20009. **Business Addr:** President, NAC of NDC #1 UPO, 1336 8th St NW, Washington, DC 20001.

QUASH, RHONDA
City official. **Personal:** Born in Greensboro, NC. **Educ:** City Univ of New York. **Career:** Trans World Airlines, corporate staff manager; City of New Rochelle, city councilwoman, currently. **Orgs:** New Rochelle Democratic City Committee, district leader; Black Democrats of Westchester County; League of Women Voters, Coalition of Mutual Respect; Jack and Jill of America. **Special Achievements:** First African American woman elected to the City Council of New Rochelle. **Business Addr:** City Councilwoman, City of New Rochelle, 515 North Ave, New Rochelle, NY 10801, (914)654-2161.

QUEEN, EVELYN E. CRAWFORD
Judge. **Personal:** Born Apr 6, 1945, Albany, NY; daughter of Iris Crawford and Richard Carter; married Charles A Queen, Mar 6, 1971; children: George Y. **Educ:** Howard University, BS, 1963-68, JD, 1972-75. **Career:** National Institute of Health, support staff, 1968-75; Metropolitan Life Insurance Co, attorney, 1975-77; United States Department of Commerce, Maritime Adm, attorney-advisor, 1977-79; United States Attorneys Office, assistant United States attorney, 1979-81; DC Superior Court, commissioner, 1981-86; judge, 1986-; DC School of Law, adjunct professor, 1991-92. **Orgs:** ABA, 1975-; NBA, 1975-. **Honors/Awds:** Hudson Valley Girl Scout, Trefoil Award, 1988; Director of Distinguished Americans, Achievement in Law, 1985; Personalities of America, Contributions to Government and Justice, 1986; Department of Justice, Special Achievement Award, 1981; Department of HEW, Special Achievement Award, 1975. **Business Addr:** Judge, DC Superior Court, 500 Indiana Ave NW, H Carl Moultne I Courthouse, Ste 1510, Washington, DC 20001, (202)879-4886.

QUEEN, ROBERT CALVIN
Editor. **Personal:** Born Jun 10, 1912, Newark, NJ; divorced; children: Delores H Fields, Roberta L Burroughs, Robert C Jr. **Career:** NJ Guardian, reporter 1938-40; NJ Herald News, reporter city editor 1941-49; Philadelphia Independent, managing editor 1950-57; Philadelphia Edition Pittsburgh Courier, managing editor 1957-63; Philadelphia Afro-Amer, managing editor 1963-67; NJ Afro-Amer, editor 1968-. **Orgs:** Mem Philadelphia Citizens Comm City Planning 1954-67; mem Sigma Delta Chi Journalistic Soc 1964; pr comm Philadelphia Child Devel Prog; panelist "Ben Hur" Centennial Crawfordsville IN 1980. **Honors/Awds:** Disting Serv Free & Accepted Mason 1961; Philadelphia Cotillion Soc Plaque 1964; Journalism Awd Temple Univ School of Journalism 1968; WEB Dubois Awd Newark Branch NAACP 1982; Awd NJ Assoc of Black Journalists 1984; Assoc in Arts Liberta Arts Humanitis Honoris Causa Essex Co Coll Newark NJ 1986. **Business Addr:** Editor, New Jersey Afro-American, 439 Central Ave, East Orange, NJ 07018.

QUEEN LATIFAH (DANA OWENS)
Rap singer, actress. **Personal:** Born Mar 18, 1970, New Jersey; daughter of Rita Owens and Lance Owens. **Educ:** Borough of Manhattan Community College, broadcasting. **Career:** Flavor Unit Entertainment, CEO, currently; Actress, currently starring in Fox sitcom Living Single; other television appearances include: Fresh Prince of Bel Air. In Living Color, The Arsenio Hall Show; films include: Jungle Fever, 1991; Juice, 1992; House Party 2, 1992, My Life, Set It Off, 1996, Hoodlum, 1997; solo artist, rapper, albums include: All Hail the Queen, 1990; The Nature of a Sista, 1991; X-tra Naked, 1992; Black Reign, 1994. **Honors/Awds:** New Music Seminar, Best New Artist, 1990; Rolling Stone Readers' Poll, Best Female Rapper, 1990; Grammy Award nominee, 1990; Soul Train Music Awards, Sammy Davis Jr Award, Entertainer of the Year, 1995. **Business Addr:** CEO, c/o Flavor Unit Entertainment, 155 Morgan St., Jersey City, NJ 07302.

QUICK, CHARLES E.
Clergyman. **Personal:** Born Oct 29, 1933, Raeford, NC; married Ruby Lee Williams; children: Charliss Quinae. **Educ:** Clinton Jr Coll, 1958; Livingstone Coll, BA 1960; UCLA, further studies 1974; Temple U, 1976; Rutgers U; Hood Theo Sem, MDiv 1963; Univ of MD; Univ of NC; VA Chpln Sch, 1971. **Career:** VA Hosp, v chmn hire the handicap com, chpln; Coatesville, PA VA Med Center, chpln 1975-; Clinton Jr Coll Rock Hill, SC, tchr 1964-71; Western NC Conf Charlotte, NC, pastor 1960-71; AME Zion Ch Pee Dee Conf SC, pastor 1958-60; NC, TN, VA AME Zion Ch, Christ educ dir 1969-71. **Orgs:** Mem bd dirs NC Coun of Chs 1968-71; mem NAACP Charlotte Augusta 1951-; SC Educ Assn 1964-71; mem Legion 505 Augusta 1971-; mem bd dirs Prog Assn for Econ Devel 1968-71; mem Elks 1966; chmn Chpln Serv VA Hosp Augusta 1974; mem Charlotte-mecklenburg Sch Bd Com 1965-69; Com of Equal Empl OppVA Hosp 1972-; Vietnam ERA Com VA Hosp 1971-; originator & coor Annual Dr Martin L King Jr Meml Day Celebration at Coatesville VA Med Cntr; mem Black History Com Coatesville VA Med Cntr; instr Assaultive Behavior & Suicide Prevention Class Coatesville VA Med Cntr; chmn 50th Anniversary Com Coatesville VA Med Cntr. **Honors/Awds:** Recip Oratorical first place winner Clintor Jr Coll Rock Hill, SC 1958; Hon DD Teamers Sch of Religion Charlotte 1968; Humanitarian Awd Charlotte 1971; Outstdg Serv Awd AME Zion Ch Communion 1971; comm awd Coatesville 1976; Augusta, GA 1974; recip Good Citizenship Awd.

QUICK, GEORGE KENNETH
Banking executive. **Personal:** Born Apr 14, 1947, Orangeburg, SC; son of Geneva Shokes Quick and Oscar Quick; married Gloria Grainger Quick, Jun 10, 1972; children: Jeffrey George, Erica Camille. **Educ:** South Carolina State Univ, Orangeburg, SC, BS, 1968; Atlanta University, Atlanta, GA, MBA, 1975; The School of Banking of the South Louisiana State Univ, Baton Rouge, LA, certificate, 1984-86. **Career:** US Army, various, captain, 1968-74; First Union Natl Bank, Charlotte, NC, assistant vice president, 1975-86; Mutual Savings & Loan Association, Durham, NC, executive vice president, COO, 1986-; Mutual Community Saving Bank, Inc, pres, 1994. **Orgs:** Chairman of the board, UDI/CDC, 1987-; board of directors, Chamber of Commerce, 1991-; chairman, Private Industry Council, 1989-; board of trustee/member, St Joseph AME Church, 1990-; board of directors, North Carolina Museum of Life & Science, 1989-; Board of Trustees, Durham County Hospital Corp. **Honors/Awds:** NAFEO, Distinguished Alumnus of the Year, 1990; Distinguished Business Alumnus, South Carolina State Univ, 1992. **Military Serv:** Army, Captain, 1968-74; Bronze Star, Air Metal, Vietnam Service Medal. **Business Addr:** President/CEO, Mutual Community Savings & Bank Inc SSB, 315 E Chapel Hill St, PO Box 3827, Durham, NC 27702.

QUICK, MIKE
Professional athlete. **Personal:** Born May 14, 1959, Hamlet, NC; son of Mary Quick and James Quick. **Educ:** Attended, NC State. **Career:** Philadelphia Eagles, wide receiver 1982-. **Orgs:** Active in community affairs especially Big Brothers/Big Sisters; madeTV announcements for KYW-TV's Project Homeless Fund, WCAU-TV's School Vote Program, the Franklin Inst, 7-Eleven/Coca Cola Freedom Run for Sickle Cell; co-owner All Pro Fitness and Racquet Club in Maple Shade NJ. **Honors/Awds:** Played in the Blue-Gray Game and Olympia Gold Bowl; became first Eagle in history to surpass 1,000 yards receiving in 3 straight seasons; first team all-pro selections by AP, Newspaper Enterprises Assoc, College and Pro Football Newsweekly, The Sporting News, Sports Illustrated and NFL Films 1985; named first team All-NFC by UPI; led NFC with 11 TD receptions 1985; honored in 1985 with a special night "The Pride of Hamlet-The Fantastic Four"; mem Pro Bowl teams 1986,87. **Business Addr:** Philadelphia Eagles, Veterans Stadium, Broad St & Pattison Ave, Philadelphia, PA 19148.

QUICK, R. EDWARD
Travel agent. **Personal:** Born Jan 22, 1927, Youngstown, OH; son of Loretta Quick and William Quick; married Constance D; children: Cheryl Quick Pope, Renee C Quick-Fountain. **Educ:** OH State Univ, 1944-45, 1947-49; Howard Univ, LLB 1952. **Career:** Rural Electrification Adm US Dept of Agriculture, special asst to administrator 1968-69; Federal Hwy Admin US Dept of Transportation, chief contract compliance Div 1969-76, acting deputy dir 1976-77, dir office of civil rights 1977-86; pres El Dorado Travel Service, Washington, DC, 1982-. **Orgs:** Mem Natl Assn of Human Rights Workers 1970-; bd of dirs El Dorado Travel Service 1982-; mem MD Assoc of Affirmative Action Officers 1984-; mem NAACP, Urban League, Pacific Area Travel Assoc, South American Travel Assoc, Africa Travel Assoc, Interamerican Travel Agents Society; board member, Central Atlantic Chapter, American Society of Travel Agents. **Honors/Awds:** Administrator's Special Achievement Awd Federal Hwy Admin 1977; Sr Executive Service Bonus Awd Federal Hwy Admin 1980; Vice President Washington Sub Chapter Amer Society of Travel Agents 1988-89. **Military Serv:** USAF sgt 18 months. **Business Addr:** President, El Dorado Travel Service, 2446 Reedie Dr, Wheaton, MD 20906.

QUIGLESS, MILTON DOUGLAS, SR. See Obituaries section.

QUIGLESS, MILTON DOUGLAS, JR.
General surgeon. **Personal:** Born Oct 15, 1945, Durham, NC; son of Helen Gordon Quigless and Milton Douglas Quigless, Sr; divorced; children: Leslie, Matthew, Christine, Ashley, Maryanna. **Educ:** Morehouse College, BS 1970; Meharry Medical Coll, MD 1971. **Career:** Meharry Medical Coll, instructor in surgery 1976-77; UNC Chapel Hill, clinical assoc prof of surgery 1986-; Wake County Med Ctr, president/medical staff, 1986-87. **Orgs:** St Augustine College Bd 1985-88. **Honors/Awds:** Doctor of the Year Old North State Medical Soc 1984. **Business Addr:** 3362 Six Forks Rd, PO Box 20127, Raleigh, NC 27609, (919)571-1170.

QUINCE, KEVIN
Government official. **Personal:** Born Jul 4, 1950, Atlantic City, NJ; son of Doris Pratt Griffith and Remer Quince; married Regina Gumby, Jan 8, 1972; children: Gyasi, Khary. **Educ:** Hampton Univ, BA, sociology, 1972; Rutgers Univ, Masters of City & Regional Planning, 1974; Univ of Pennsylvania, The Wharton School, CEC real estate investment analysis, 1980; Harvard Univ, program for sr execs, 1990. **Career:** New Jersey Housing and Mortgage Finance Agency, Trenton, NJ, sr development officer, 1974-80, syndication officer, 1980-84, asst dir of research and development, 1984-86, dir of research and development, 1986-88, asst exec dir, 1988-90, exec dir, 1990-; Quince Associates Inc, Real Estate Development Consultants, president, currently. **Orgs:** Vice pres, secretary, Housing Assistance Corp, 1988-; board member, Council on Affordable Housing, 1990-; board of directors, Police Athletic League, 1989; chairman, Mercer County Housing Advisory Board, 1987-89; vice pres, East Windsor Planning Board, 1982-83. **Honors/Awds:** Achievements in Affordable Housing, NJ Black Housing Administrators, 1990; Achievements in Affordable Housing, NJ Chapter of Housing and Redevelopment Officials, 1989. **Business Addr:** President, Quince Associates, Inc, Real Estate Development Consultants, PO Box 1135, Hightstown, NJ 08520-0035.

QUINCY, RONALD LEE
Association exective. **Personal:** Born Sep 8, 1950, Detroit, MI. **Educ:** Univ of Detroit, BA, MA; Michigan State Univ, PhD; John F Kennedy Sch of Govt Harvard Univ, completed Senior Managers in Govt Program. **Career:** State of MI Contractual Program for Minority and Woman-Owned Businesses, chief administrator; Michigan Equal Employment Opp Council, exec dir; Office of Human Resource Policy and Spec Projects, director; former Governor William G Milliken, spec asst; US State Dept, foreign affairs advisor; US Dept Housing andUrban Develop, special asst to the secty; Michigan Dept of Civil Rights, dir; Harvard Univ, assoc vice pres, asst to the pres; Martin Luther King Jr Center for Nonviolent Social Change, exec dir; Congressional Black Caucus Foundation, executive director, currently. **Orgs:** Bd mem MI State Univ Natl Criminal Justice Alumni Assn; past co-chair of the Governor's 1980 US Census Special Population Comm; mem State Criminal Justice Comm. **Honors/Awds:** SWhite House Fellowship 1985-86. **Business Addr:** Executive Director, Congressional Black Caucus Foundation, 1004 Pennsylvania Ave SE, Washington, DC 20003.

QUINN, ALFRED THOMAS
Educational administrator (retired). **Personal:** Born Sep 21, 1922, Omaha, NE; married Sylvia Price. **Educ:** Univ of CA Los Angeles, BA 1950, MEd 1956, EdD 1964. **Career:** USAF, 1942-45; Vet Admin, emp relation off 1946-48; Santa Monica Sch Dist, teacher 1951-63; Santa Monica Coll, prof 1963-73. **Orgs:** Phi Delta Kappa Ed UCLA 1955; Santa Monica Parks Recreation Comm 1958-63; Santa Monica Charter Review Comm 1962; Santa Monica Housing Comm 1980-84; bd of dirs Natl Conf of Christians & Jews; NAACP; Rotary Intl; Santa Monica Community College, district member, board of trustees, chair. **Honors/Awds:** Outstanding teacher Awd Santa Monica Sch Dist 1956; Awd League United Latin Amer Citizens 1970; NCCJ Brotherhood Awd 1973; NAACP, Beverly Hills Branch, Humanitarian Award, 1988; Low Income Elderly United, Community Assistance Program, Community Service Award, 1990; Santa Monica High School, Distinguished Alumni Award, 1992; Santa Monica Comm College, prof emeritus. **Special Achievements:** Author: Persistent Patterns and Problems Peculiar to Schools and Communities in Racial Transistion, 1964; Race Relations and Public Schools in the Latter 20th Century, 1980. **Military Serv:** USAF psnl sgt/major 3 yrs.

QUINN, DIANE C.
City government official. **Personal:** Born May 9, 1942, Chicago, IL; children: Caren Clift. **Educ:** American University. **Career:** Illinois Bell Telephone Co, sales mgr 1974-79; C&P Telephone Co, industry mgr 1978-79; AT&T, market mgr 1979-83, mgr mgmt employment 1983-84, mgr univ relations 1984-87; Dept of Public & Assisted Housing, regional manager, 1989-94; executive assistant to the director, DC Dept of Recreation and Parks, 1994-. **Orgs:** AT&T rep Natl Urban League 1972-; lecturer Natl Alliance of Business 1972-74; consultant Wilberforce Univ 1979; consultant R Burton & Co Inc 1986; lecturer College Bd Conference on Industrial Partnerships 1986. **Honors/Awds:** Black Achiever YMCA 1973, 74; AT&T Loaned Executive Univ of MD 1987. **Home Addr:** 1708 15th St NW, Washington, DC 20009. **Business Addr:** Executive Asst to the Director, DC Dept of Recreation & Parks, Washington, DC 20009.

QUINTON, BARBARA A.
Educator. **Personal:** Born Jul 1, 1941, Sharptown, MD; children: Keith F Nichols, Kyle B Nichols. **Educ:** Morgan State University, BS, 1963; Meharry Medical College, MD, 1967. **Career:** Hubbard Hospital, intern, 1967-68; St Louis Children's Hospital, resident, 1968-69, fellowship, 1969-71; Howard University, fellowship, 1971-74, assistant professor, 1974-76, associate professor, 1976-. **Orgs:** Church rep, NAACP, 1985-. **Honors/Awds:** Outstanding Teacher Award, Howard University, 1975, 1978; Honorary Mem, Intern/Resident Association, Howard University, 1983. **Business Addr:** Associate Professor of Pediatrics, Howard University College of Medicine, 520 W St NW, Washington, DC 20001-2337.

QUINTYNE, IRWIN SINCLAIR
Organization executive (retired). **Personal:** Born Jul 25, 1926, New York, NY; married Delores; children: 7. **Educ:** Stony Brook Univ NY. **Career:** Women's wear cutter, patternmaker, marker, prod mgr 1949-69; Suffolk County Econ Oppor Counc, vocational couns 1969-70; Wyandanch Coll Cntr, part-time faculty 1971-72; Stony Brook Coll, dir field serv EEO 1970-77; Congress of Racial Equality Suffolk Cnty, dir 1966-; Suffolk Cnty Core, co-founder 1964, dir 1967-89; Nassau/Suffolk Minority Coalition, chmn 1971; Alba-Neck Halfway House Drug Prog, co-founder, bd chmn 1970-84. **Orgs:** Bd mem Alliance of Minority Group 1970-; co-founder bd mem Black Students Assistance Fund Stony Brook Univ 1972-; mem Central LI Br NAACP; 100 Black Men Nassau/Suffolk Counties 1975; North Amityville Community Economic Council, coordinator, 1992-95. **Honors/Awds:** Numerous awards. **Military Serv:** USN 1944-46.

QUIVERS, ERIC STANLEY
Physician. **Personal:** Born Oct 27, 1955, Winston-Salem, NC; married Mara Williams; children: Micah Stanley, Lucas Sorrell. **Educ:** Morehouse Coll, BS (magna cum laude) 1979; Howard Univ Coll of Medicine, MD 1983; Pediatric Cardiology, pediatrics, Board Certified. **Career:** Howard Univ Hosp Dist of Columbia, pediatric resident 1983-86; Park West Medical Center, staff pediatrician, 1986-; Sinai Hospital, provisional medical staff, 1986-88; Mayo Clinic, pediatric cardiology fellowship, 1988-91; Children's National Medical Center, Department of Cardiology, staff cardiologist, Preventative Cardiology and Exercise Laboratory, director, currently. **Orgs:** Natl Medical Assn 1983-; American Academy of Pediatrics, junior fellow, 1986-; District of Columbia Hunger Project, 1992-; Mayor's Commission for Food, Health and Nutrition, 1993-; Association of Black Cardiologists, 1990-. **Honors/Awds:** Phi Beta Kappa 1977; Beta Kappa Chi 1977; Certificate of Appreciation Howard Univ Coll of Med SGA 1983; Roland B Scott Departmental Awd in Pediatrics 1983. **Special Achievements:** Co-author: ''Hepatic Cyst Associated with Ventricular Peritoneal Shunt in a Child with Brain Tumor,'' Child's Nervous System, 1985; ''Variability in Response to a Low-fat, Low-cholesterol Diet in Children with Elevated Low-density Lipoprotein Cholesterol Levels,'' Pediatrics, 1992. **Home Addr:** 14 Foxlair Ct, Gaithersburg, MD 20882. **Business Addr:** Director, Preventive Cardiology and Exercise Laboratory, Department of Cardiology, Children's National Medical Center, 111 Michigan Ave NW, Washington, DC 20010.

QUIVERS, WILLIAM WYATT, SR.
Physician (retired). **Personal:** Born Sep 14, 1919, Phoebus, VA; son of Irma Robinson Branch and Robert McKinley Quivers; married Evelyn C Seace; children: William Jr, Eric, Celia. **Educ:** Hampton Inst, BS 1942; Atlanta Univ, 1946-47; Meharry Medical Coll, MD 1953; Pediatric Cardiology Fellowship USPH grant at Univ Los Angeles 1962-63, 1964-65. **Career:** KB Reynolds Meml Hosp, internship and pediatric residency 1953-55; Meharry Medical Coll Hubbard Hosp, pediatric resident 1959-63; Meharry Medical Coll, assistant professor of pediatrics, 1963-64, associate professor of pediatrics, 1965-68, med dir child & youth project 1967-68; Reynolds Memorial Hosp, dir of pediatrics 1968-72; Bowman-Gray Sch of Med, assoc prof of ped 1968-72; Provident Hosp Inc, dir of ped 1972-85; Univ of MD Sch of Med, assoc prof of ped 1972-85; Liberty Medical Ctr, acting chief of pediatrics 1986-91; Total Health Care, consultant/provider. **Orgs:** Fellow Amer Academy of Pediatrics, Natl Medical Assn; diplomate Amer Bd of Pediatrics, Royal Soc of Health, Amer Heart Assn, People to People Intl, Chinese Amer Scientific Soc, East Coast Ch Tuskegee Airmen; bd of dirs Homewood School and Baer School; Assn of Black Cardiologists; Central MD Heart Assn. **Honors/Awds:** First Annual Physician Appreciation Award, 1990; Liberty Medical Center, Medical Staff Award for Outstanding Contributions in Ambulatory Services, 1990; Hampton University/Alumni Association, 14th Annual National Conference on The Black Family, Honored Black Family, 1992. **Special Achievements:** Author: ''Rhematic Heart Disease: A Review,'' Volunteer State Journal, 1962; co-author: ''Use of Isoproterenol in the Evaluation of Aortic and Pulmonic Stenosis,'' American Journal of Cardiology, 1963, ''The Electrocardiogram and Vectorcardiogram in Children with Severe Asthma,'' American Journal of Cardiology, 1964, ''Congenital Duplication of the Stomach,'' Journal of Abdominal Surgery, 1982; ''My Activities During WWII,'' Maryland Medical Journal, December, 1995. **Military Serv:** USAF 1st lt 1942-46. **Home Addr:** 6110 Benhurst Rd, Baltimore, MD 21209.

R

RAAB, MADELINE MURPHY
Business executive. **Personal:** Born Jan 27, 1945, Wilmington, DE; married Dr Maurice F Rabb Jr; children: Maurice F III, Christopher. **Educ:** Univ of MD, 1961-63; MD Inst Coll of Art, BFA 1966; IL Inst of Tech, MS 1975. **Career:** Tuesday Publ, asst dir of art & prod 1966-68; Myra Everett Design, vice pres bus mgr 1977-78; Corp Concierge, acct exec 1978-79; Rabb Studio & Gallery, artist 1978-83; Chicago Office of Fine Arts, exec dir 1983-. **Orgs:** Bd mem The Hyde Park Arts Ctr 1981-83, Univ of Chicago Women's Bd 1980-85, Afro-Amer Newspaper Co Baltimore MD 1981-84; adv Folk Art Exhibition Field Museum of Natl History 1984; treas US Urban Arts Fed 1984-86; adv Black Creativity Celebration Museum of Science & Industry 1985-86, Arts Culture & Entertainment Comm 1992 Chicago World's Fair 1985; bd mem Channel 20 WYCC-TV 1985-86, IL Arts Alliance 1986-88; co-chair Special Interest Areas Natl Assembly of Local Arts Agencies 1986-88; panelist Natl Assembly of Local Arts Agencies Convention Wash DC 1986; moderator IL Arts Alliance Annual Conf 1986; panelist Local Arts Agencies IL Arts Council; panelist Natl Assembly of Local Arts Agencies Annual Conv Portladn OR 1987; panelist Local Programs NatlEndowment for the Arts 1987-88. **Honors/Awds:** Paintings drawings & prints ''The Chicago Exchange Group'' Chicago State Univ Gallery 1981, ''Emma Amos & Madeline Rabb'' Jazzonia Gallery Detroit MI 1983, ''A Portfolio of Prints by Madeline Murphy Rabb'' Fells Point Gallery Baltimore MD 1987; publ, ''Removing Cultural Viaducts, Initiative for Traditionally Underserved Audiences'' Connections Quarterly 1986, ''Chicago, An Artistic Renaissance Under Way'' Amer Visions Afro-Amer Art 1986; permanent collections, Standard Oil Co Chicago IL, Johnson Publish Co Chicago IL, IL Inst of Tech, Inst of Design Chicago IL, The Chicago Community Health Ctr Chicago IL, The Evans-Tibbs CollectionWash DC. **Business Addr:** Executive Dir, Chicago Office of Fine Arts, 78 E Washington, 2nd Floor, Chicago, IL 60602.

RABOUIN, E. MICHELLE
Educator, attorney. **Personal:** Born Nov 7, 1956, Denver, CO; daughter of Eva M Thomas Smith and John V Smith; divorced; children: Dion Malik. **Educ:** University of Colorado, BS, 1977; University of Denver, MBA, 1984, JD, 1984. **Career:** Coal Employment Project, assistant director, 1983-85; Colorado Office of Attorney General, assistant attorney general, 1986-89; Colorado Education Association, legal counsel, 1989-90; Community College of Denver, management chair, faculty, 1991-94; Texas Southern Univ, visiting prof of law, 1994-95; Washburn Univ School of Law, assoc prof of law, 1994-. **Orgs:** Colorado Coalition of Mediators & Mediation Organization. 1990-; Colorado Bar Association, 1984-; Colorado Women's Bar Association, 1988-;Colorado Chapter, National Association of Black Women Attorney, Founding Member, 1987-; American Civil Liberties Union, board member, 1991-92; Junior League of Denver, 1988-1991; Northeast Women's Center, board member, 1980-82; Colorado Black Women for Political Action, board member, editor, 1979-. **Honors/Awds:** Colorado Energy Research Fellow, 1983; Colorado Black Women for Political Action, Community Service Award, 1981; University of Colorado, President's Academic Scholarship, 1974-77. **Special Achievements:** Co-author with Anthony Leo, ''1992 Tenth Circuit Court of Appeals Survey of Corporate and Commercial Law'', Denver University Law Review, 1601; author, Valuing Diversity: Train the Trainer Manual, Mahogany Mountain Press, 1992; author, ''The Legal Dimensions of Diversity: the

Civil Rights Act of 1991, and the ADA,'' City of Boulder, Department of Social Services, 1992; lecturer, ''Pro Bono: Enforceable Duty of Voluntary Obligation,'' ''Intersection of Race and Poverty, Common Issues,'' Statewide Legal Services Conference, 1992. **Home Addr:** 4986 Worchester St, Denver, CO 80239.

RABY, CLYDE T.
Government official. **Personal:** Born Sep 14, 1934, Baton Rouge, LA; married Elaine Miller; children: Dwight Tillman, Iris R Locure, Wayne A, Eric C, Trudi E. **Educ:** Southern Univ, BS 1960; Tuskegee Inst, DVM 1964. **Career:** Southern Univ, asst prof 1964-70; Plant Road & Port Allen Animal Hosps, owner 1970-; LA Dept of Agriculture, asst commissioner 1980-. **Orgs:** Mem AVMA 1963-; mem Beta Beta Beta Siol Soc 1970-; chmn LA Veterinary Med Assoc 1982; bd of dirs Reddy Cultural Ctr 1985. **Honors/Awds:** Veterinarian of the Year LA Vet Med Assoc 1982; Bigger and Better Business Awd Phi Beta Sigma Frat 1986; article published Journal of Dairy Science, Journal of Animal Science, Amer Journal of Vet Research. **Military Serv:** USAF airman 2st class 1954-57. **Home Addr:** 2737 Brandywine Dr, Baton Rouge, LA 70808. **Business Addr:** Assistant Commissioner, LA Dept of Agricultura, PO Box 1951, Baton Rouge, LA 70821.

RACKLEY, LURMA M.
Writer. **Personal:** Born Apr 24, 1949, Orangeburg, SC; daughter of Gloria Blackwell and L G Rackley; children: Rumal Blackwell Rackley. **Educ:** Clark Atlanta Univ, BA with honors, 1970; Columbia Univ School of Journalism Special Masters, 1970. **Career:** Washington Star, reporter and editor, 1970-79, freelance writer, 1970-; District of Columbia Government, 1979-90; Office of Planning, Deputy Press Scy, Deputy Communications Dir, Press Scy to the Mayor; Hill and Knowlton Public Affaris Worldwide, vp, media realtions, 1993-95; Amnesty Intl USA, Deputy Exec Dir for Communications, 1995-. **Orgs:** Alpha Kappa Alpha; DC Clark Atlanta Univ Club; Capital Press Club; Black Public Relations Society; DC Hampton Univ Parents Club. **Honors/Awds:** Commitment to Excellence Awd Dep Mayor for Economic Devel, 1985; Outstanding Women in DC Government, 1989-90. **Home Addr:** 8103 Pinelake Court, Alexandria, VA 22309.

RADCLIFFE, AUBREY
Educator. **Personal:** Born Aug 27, 1941, NY, NY; married Katherine; children: Rick, Deborah. **Educ:** Mich State Univ, BA 1968, MA 1972, PhD 1975. **Career:** White Plaines Public School, counselor 1962-63; Lansing Public School, counselor 1966-74; Univ of MI, prof 1974-75. **Orgs:** Mem assn of Governing Bds; Assn of Admin & Higher Ed; Amer Guidance & Personnel Assn; program dir Am Legion Boys' State; Lansing Jaycees; Phi Delta Kappa; Greater Lansing Urban League; former young rep natl committman, MI 1966; former state dir & adv MI Teenage Rep 1967; former ad hoc rep chmn Human Relations 1968; mem MI Veteran Trust Fund 1980; mem E Lansing Lions' Club 1980; v comdr E Lansing Amer Legion Post 205 1980; bd of trustees MI State Univ 1980; rep candidate US Congress 1980. **Honors/Awds:** Outstanding Teacher of the Year Award 1965; MI Republican's Youth Award 1966; Outstanding Young Man in Amer 1973. **Business Addr:** PO Box 806, East Lansing, MI 48823.

RADDEN, THELMA GIBSON
Nurse, association executive (retired). **Personal:** Born Feb 18, 1903, Oakland, CA; daughter of Maude Esther Johnson Gibson (deceased) and Charles Nelson Gibson (deceased); married Karl Angel Radden, Aug 12, 1942 (deceased). **Educ:** BA nursing educ 1952; Wayne State Coll of Nursing, 1952; HS & KC Gen Hosp Sch of Nursing, 1933; UC Hosp, post grad 1934. **Career:** Sacramento Area Long Term Care Ombudsmen Inc Advocacy Orgn, coor; Continuing Patient Care Met Hosp Detroit, coor; Norfolk Com Hosp, adminstr 1936-40; Trinity Hosp Detroit, supr & dir of nurses 1940; Homer G Phillips Hosp St Louis, surgical supr instr surical nursing; Grace Hosp Detroit, surgical wards 1942; Detroit Chap ARC, asst dir nursing serv 1955-78; Detroit Dist MI State Nurses Assn, past prog chmn. **Orgs:** Detroit League for Nursing; mem Gerontological Sect Detroit Dist MI State Nurses Assn past pres Urban League Guild; pres Detroit Br AAUW; mem Detroit Chap KC Hosp Alumni Assn; mem Delta Sigma Theta; Chi Eta Phi; Detroit Intl Inst; vice pres Citizens for Better Care; past Matron Dorician Chap #32 OES-PHA & Daus of Isis Marracci Ct; mem E Bay CA Negro Hist Soc; state legislative chairman, California Federation of Women's Clubs, 1986-88; mem, Northern Area California State American Red Cross Retirees Assn, 1986-. **Home Addr:** Pioneer Towers Apt 604, 515 P St, Sacramento, CA 95814.

RAGLAND, MICHAEL STEVEN
Obstetrician, gynecologist. **Personal:** Born Aug 23, 1958, Brooklyn, NY; son of Violet B Ragland and Fountain W Ragland; married Laurena Moore, Aug 10, 1985. **Educ:** Fisk Univ, BS 1980; Meharry Medical Coll, MD 1984. **Career:** Physician obstetrics/gynecology. **Orgs:** Mem Student Natl Medical Assoc 1980-84, Amer Medical Assoc 1980-; junior fellow Amer Coll of Obstetrics/Gynecology 1986-; Bay Area Medical Society 1988; Southern Medical Assn, 1988-. **Honors/Awds:** Beta Kappa Chi Natl Scientific Honor Society; Alpha Omega Alpha Honor Medical Soc; Diplomate of American Coll of Obstetrics & Gynecology, 1990.

RAGLAND, SHERMAN LEON, II
Real estate developer. **Personal:** Born Jul 4, 1962, Stuttgart; son of G Anita Atkinson Ragland and Lt Col Sherman L Ragland; married Chevelle Loreen Calloway, Jun 15, 1986. **Educ:** Towson State Univ, Towson MD, BS Mass Communications, 1984; The Wharton School of the Univ of Pennsylvania, MBA Finance/Real Estate; The University of Virginia, MUEP, 1992. **Career:** Xerox Realty Corp, Stamford CT, financial analyst, 1986-87, Leesburg VA, assoc devel dir, 1987-88; The Oliver Carr Co, Washington DC, devel mgr, 1988-89; Tradewinds Realty Advisors, president, 1989-. **Orgs:** Pres, Natl Assn of Black Real Estate Professionals, 1988-; bd of dir, Christmas in April USA, 1988-, Christmas in April Alexandria, 1988-; bd of advisors (alumni), Wharton Real Estate Center, 1988-; bd of dir, Towson State Univ Alumni Assn, 1989; commr, Alexandria Human Rights Commn, 1989, Alexandria Equal Opportunities Commn, 1989; pres, The Wharton Alumni Club of Washington, 1989-; Alexandria Board of Zoning Appeals, 1990-93; vice chairman, Alexandria Board of Zoning Appeals, 1990-93; Alexandria Planning Commission, 1993-. **Honors/Awds:** Johnson & Johnson Leadership Award, Johnson & Johnson, 1984; Wharton Public Policy Fellow, The Wharton School, 1985; Black Alumni of the Year, Towson State Univ, 1989; author of 2 publications, Motivation, 1985, and Lease vs Purchase of Real Estate, 1989; ''50 Future Leaders,'' Ebony Magazine, Nov 1992.

RAGLAND, WYLHEME HAROLD
Clergyman. **Personal:** Born Dec 19, 1946, Anniston, AL; son of Viola Pearson Ragland and Howard Ragland; children: Seth H III, Frederick D. **Educ:** Jacksonville State Univ, BA 1972, attended grad school 1972-73; Emory Univ, MDiv (Cum Laude) 1975; Vanderbilt Univ, DMin 1978. **Career:** Center Grove United Methodist Church, pastor 1975-77; King's Memorial United Methodist Church, sr pastor 1977-; North Alabama Regional Hospital, Decatur, AL, dir of religious service/coordinator of employee assistance program, 1984-, patient rights implementer, 1989-; staff development officer, currently. **Orgs:** Charter mem The Employee Assistance Soc of North Amer 1985; mem Phi Alpha Theta, Pi Gamma Mu, Sigma Tau Delta, The North AL Study Club, The Morgan County Historical Soc, The Mental Health Assn of Morgan Co; chairperson The Rights Protection Advocacy Committee 1987-89; mem The Needs Assessment Committee, The Decatur City Bd of Educ, The Advisory Committee The Albany Clinic 1989; member, Quest Advisory Board, 1990-; member, North West Counseling Center Board, 1991; member, The Ministerial Alliance of Decatur, 1989; Key Communicator, Decatur Board of Education. **Honors/Awds:** Pierce Pettis, Guitar Man Speaking Out newspaper Decatur AL 1984; editor, Patient Rights Handbook, North Alabama Regional Hospital, 1991. **Military Serv:** USNR communication yeoman 3rd class 3 yrs; Highest Honor and 1st in Class CYN School. **Home Addr:** 511 Walnut St NE, Decatur, AL 35601. **Business Addr:** Dir of Religious Studies/Staff Development Officer, North AL Regional Hospital, PO Box 2221, Decatur, AL 35602.

RAGSDALE, CHARLES LEA CHESTER
Manager. **Personal:** Born Aug 7, 1929, Coweta, OK; married Joyce E Phillips; children: Theresa (Chappelle), Sylvia, Angela, Tammy, Tamara. **Educ:** Langston U, BS; OK St U, grad studies. **Career:** Wagoner Sch, tchr July 1949, Sept 1950, 1951-55; Beggs Sch, tchr 1955-56; Mcdonnell Douglas Tulsa, OK, sr employ repr 1956-, pres (currently $5 million in asset); Tulsa Urban Leag Found, pres; Mcdonnell Douglas Tulsa Man Club, past 1st vP; Ex Comm So Cal Pro Eng Assn, past chmn; Tulsa Urban League, past pres & vp. **Orgs:** Mem Tulsa Pub Sch Bd of Edn; past chmn CPAC; mem Tulsa Co Sch & Tulsa Met CC Speaker's Bureau; Tulsa Econ Oppor Task Force Bd Dir; Mcdonnel Douglas Coor Youth Motivation Prog mem Christ Emple Christian Meth Epis Ch; past supt ch Sch; chmn steward bd. **Honors/Awds:** Plaque from Mcdonnell Douglas for Contr of Comm Rel. **Business Addr:** Mc Donnell Douglas Tulsa, 2000 N Memorial Dr, Tulsa, OK 74115.

RAGSDALE, LINCOLN JOHNSON. See Obituaries section.

RAGSDALE, PAUL B.
Government official. **Personal:** Born Jan 14, 1945, Jacksonville, TX. **Educ:** Univ TX, BA. **Career:** State rep 1972-; chf planner Dallas 1968-72. **Orgs:** Bd mem Black C of C; numerous others. **Honors/Awds:** Numerous awards. **Business Addr:** 1209 E Red Bird Ln, Dallas, TX 75241.

RAHMAN, MAHDI ABDUL. See HAZZARD, WALTER R.

RAIFORD, ROGER LEE
Orthopedic surgeon. **Personal:** Born Nov 1, 1942, Greensboro, NC; son of Ernest L Raiford & Blanche Reynolds Raiford; married Pamela Gladden; children: Gregory, Brian. **Educ:** Howard Univ, BS 1964; Howard Medical School, MD 1968. **Career:** Bowie State College, team physician, 1974-75; Leland Hospital chief of orthopedic surgery, 1992-93; Howard Univ, asst prof orthopedic surgery. **Orgs:** Mem Amer Bd of Orthopedic Surgery, Amer Acad of Orthopedic Surgery, DC Medical Soc. **Honors/Awds:** Howard University, Medical School, Oath & Honors Day, 1968; National Board of Medical Examiners, Diplomate, 1969. **Business Addr:** Asst Prof Orthopedic Surgery, Howard University, 8601 Martin Luther King Hwy, Lanham, MD 20706.

RAINBOW-EARHART, KATHRYN ADELINE
Psychiatrist (retired). **Personal:** Born Mar 21, 1921, Wheeling, WV; daughter of Addaline Holly Rainbow and John Henry Rainbow; married William Earhart, Jul 29, 1966; children: Frederic B Jr, Holly R Bryant. **Educ:** Ft Valley State Coll, BS 1942; Meharry Med Coll, MD 1948; Menninger Sch of Psychiatry, 1965. **Career:** Rocky Mount, private pediatric practice 1952-54; Lakin State Hosp, staff physician 1954-59, clinical dir 1959-60, supt 1960-62; Topeka State Hosp, staff psychiatrist 1965-79; Shawnee Comm Mental Health Center Inc, staff psychiatrist 1979-81; Kansas Reception and Diagnostic Center, staff psychiatrist 1981-83. **Orgs:** Shawnee County Med Soc; past pres WV Med Soc; KS Med Soc; American Medical Assn; American Med Women's Assn; Am Psychiatric Assn; Black Psychiatrists of Amer; Natl Med Assn; emeritus courtesy staff, Stormont-Vail & St Francis Hosps; Alpha Kappa Alpha Soc; past pres Topeka Chap Links, Inc; past pres Quota Intl of Topeka; life member NAACP; St John AME Church; board of directors, The Villages; board of directors, Topeka Assn for Retarded Citizens, 1972-78, 1983-87; National Council of Negro Women; Stormont-Vail Hopsital Foundation, board of directors, 1993-. **Honors/Awds:** Meharry Medical College, Plaque, 25-Year Service to Humanity; National Med Fellowship Inc, Pediatric Fellowship, 1950-52; NIMH Fellowship, 1962-65; Delta Kappa Gamma Society International, Honorary Membership; Honoree of the Consortium of Doctors, 1993; Certificate of Recognition, An outstanding Woman of African Decent, 5th Episcopal District of the AME Church, 1994. **Home Addr:** 2916 Kentucky Ave, Topeka, KS 66605-1466.

RAINE, CHARLES HERBERT, III
Physician. **Personal:** Born Oct 31, 1937, Selma, AL; married Martha A Lewis; children: Charles IV, Christopher, Shani. **Educ:** Attended, Miles Memorial Coll 1953-55, TN A&I State Univ 1955-57; Meharry Medical Coll, MD 1961. **Career:** GW Hubbard Hosp, internship 1961-62, resident 1962-65; Smith Clinic Glasgow MT, physician/partner 1970-72; Kurten Medical Group Racine, physician/partner 1972-89. **Orgs:** Human subjects rsch committeeman Univ of WI Parkside 1983-; assoc clinical prof of allied health Univ of WI Parkside 1984-; medical dir Area 19 Wisconsin Div Amer Cancer Soc 1985-; editorial bd mem State Medical Soc of WI Medical Journal 1985; chmn dept of medicine St Mary's Medical Ctr 1986-87. **Special Achievements:** Published: Contemporary Health Journal, health newsletter, 1983-86. **Military Serv:** USAF lt col 1965-70.

RAINES, COLDEN DOUGLAS
Dentist. **Personal:** Born Oct 17, 1915, Apex, NC; married Frances Johnson; children: Tajuana Raines Turner, Colden Jr, Romley H. **Educ:** Shaw Univ, BS 1940; Howard Univ, DDS 1946. **Career:** Mary C Leonie Guggenheim Dental Clinic, intern 1948. **Orgs:** Mem Bergen Co Dental Soc; Amer Dental Assn; Natl Dental Assn; Essex Co Dental Soc; Commonwelath Dental Assn; past pres Dental Sect Acad of Med; Acad of Gen Dentistry; Soc of Oral Physiology & Occlusion; trustee Acad of Med of NJ; pres Howard Univ Dental Alumni 1977; past pres Bergen Passaic Howard Univ Alumni Club; Alpha Phi Alpha Frat; Chi Delta Mu Frat; fellow Acad of Med NJ. **Honors/Awds:** Alumni Award Howard Univ Coll of Dentistry 1975; Fellow Acad of Gen Dentistry 1979; Fellow Amer Coll of Dentists 1979; Fellow Amer Soc for Advancement of Anesthesia in Dentistry 1982; Howard Univ Alumni Achievement Awd 1984. **Military Serv:** AUS Maj 1957. **Business Addr:** 603 Clinton Ave, Newark, NJ 07108.

RAINES, FRANKLIN D.
Federal official. **Personal:** marrIed Wendy; children: Sarah. **Educ:** Harvard Law School; Rhodes Scholar. **Career:** Lazard Freres & Co, general partner; Federal National Mortgage Association (Fannie Mae), vice chairman, 1991-96; Office of Management and Budget, director, 1996-98; Fannie Mae, CEO, chair of the board, 1998-. **Special Achievements:** Instrumental in creating ''Access,'' a program designed to increase minority participation in Fannie Mae's $380 billion-plus securities business; Created ''Fannie Neighbors,'' a program that helps low-income homebuyers qualify for mortgages; First African American White budget chief. **Business Addr:** CEO/Chair of the Board, Fannie Mae, 3900 Wisconsin Ave NW, Washington, DC 20016, (202)752-7000.

RAINES, TIMOTHY
Professional baseball player. **Personal:** Born Sep 16, 1959, Sanford, FL; married Virginia. **Career:** Montreal Expos, outfielder 1980-90; Chicago White Sox, outfielder, 1991-96; New York Yankees, 1996-. **Orgs:** Works with youngsters at baseball camps during off-season. **Honors/Awds:** Led the Natl League in stolen bases with 75; led the league in steals each of his first four seasons; all-time leader in stolen base percentage; Rookie of the Year, Sporting News, 1981; The Sporting News Gold

Shoe Awd 1984; National League All-Star Team, 1981-87. **Business Addr:** Professional Baseball Player, New York Yankees, Yankee Stadium, Bronx, NY 10451, (212)293-6000.

RAINES, WALTER R.
Choreographer. **Personal:** Born Aug 16, 1940, Braddock, PA; son of Alberta Mason Raines and Roosevelt Raines. **Educ:** Pittsburgh Playhouse School of Theatre & Dance, 1955-58; Carnegie-Mellon Univ, 1958-59; School of Amer Ballet, 1959-63. **Career:** Dance Theatre of Harlem, res choreographer/faculty, dir of the school, 1989-; The Ice Break Royal Opera London, choreographed & staged; Peter & The Wolf, Haiku, After Corinth, Dance Theatre of Harlem, choreographed; Tenessee Williams, Lady of the Larkspur Lotion, Birmingham, directed; Syrinx, Chamber Ballet & Summerset, Panamanian Ballet, choreographed; New York City Ballet Munich Opera Ballet, guest artist; Arthur Mitchell Ballets, created leading male roles; City College of New York, New York, NY, co-chairman of dept of theatre & dance, 1978-89; Alvin Ailey American Dance Center, New York, NY, chairman of ballet dept, 1981-89, scholarship dir/choreographer. **Orgs:** Mem Stuttgart Ballet 1963-67; choreographed opera Carmen, Regansburg Opera; in fashion field staged the Von Furstenberg Collection; designed costumes for Ballet, Opera, Drama & Burlesque; member of the Dance Panel for New York State Council on the Arts; New York State Council on the Arts for Am Jewish Congress; Choreo styles with Harriett Pitt; artist in residence for Co of City of NY; taught & lectured for 1st congress of Black & Dance in Am; lectured at State U; discussed music of Sir Michael Tippett & genius of Arthur Mitchell, BBC London; student of Japanese Philosophy; 1st black to choreograph for Royal Opera 1977; ballet "After Corinth" included in Balanchine's Complete Stories of the Great Ballets. **Honors/Awds:** 1st black to teach classic ballet for AL Dance Conf 1976; 1st black to become permanent mem of Suttgart Ballet 1963-67; Internationale Sommer Akademie Des Tanzes, Cologne Germany, 1981-. **Business Addr:** Director of the School, Dance Theatre of Harlem, Inc, 466 W 152nd St, New York, NY 10031.

RAINEY, BESSYE COLEMAN
Educator (Retired). **Personal:** Born Jul 15, 1929, Boydton, VA; daughter of Rosa Jones Coleman and John W Coleman; married Bob; children: Martin, Karl. **Educ:** Saint Paul's Coll, BS 1962; Union Coll, MS 1965; Univ of VA, EdD 1977. **Career:** East End High School, Sci & Math teacher 1961-69; Saint Paul's Coll, dean of women 1969-74, acting chmn dept Sci & Math 1977-79, dir acad comp & inst rsch 1984-87, prof of education 1987-96. **Orgs:** Adjunct prof Univ of VA 1982; consultant Brunswick Co Public Sch 1984-85, Chase City Elementary School 1986; mem Phi Delta Kappa. **Honors/Awds:** Membership Awd Lychnos Soc of Univ of VA 1976; Natl Science Found Fellowship.

RAINEY, SYLVIA VALENTINE
Marketing communications consultant. **Personal:** Born in Chicago, IL; children: Meredith Terzol. **Educ:** Univ of IL Champ Urbana, BA 1967; Univ of IL Circle Campus, MBA Uncompleted. **Career:** Compton Adv Agy, cpywtr 1973-75; Am Hosp Sply Corp, mgr of mktg comm 1975; Nalco Chl Co, dir of mktg comm 1978-84. **Orgs:** Consult AT & T Infor Syst 1984-; consult William A Robinson Mktg 1984-; consult Paul Simon for Str Agency Camp 1984; Alpha Kappa Alpha Sorority; pres of brd SJnrl Truth Child Care Ctr; Am Mktg Assoc. **Honors/Awds:** Advertising Awds. **Business Addr:** ATTN: Vanessa, University of Illinois-Chicago Alumni Association, 412 S Peoria, Chicago, IL 60607.

RAINEY, TIMOTHY MARK
Editor. **Personal:** Born Jul 27, 1956, Mobile, AL; son of Rev W D Rainey (deceased) & E S Rainey; married Gloria Johnson Rainey, Apr 7, 1979; children: Tiria, Mark. **Educ:** Troy State Univ, BS, 1977; Huntsville Bapt Institute, bachelor of Theology, 1994. **Career:** The Mobile Press Register, reporter, 1977-78; Alabama A&M Univ, publication & news specialist, 1978-82; The Huntsville Times, editor, 1982-; The Mobile Press Register, reporter, 1977-78; Mt Lebman, P B Church, pastor, 1991-96; Indian Creek PB Church, pastor, 1996-. **Orgs:** Huntsville Ministerial Alliance; School of Religion; Tri-State PB Convention, assistant dean of religion; Huntsville Baptist Institute, bd of trustees and school registar. **Honors/Awds:** Douglas L Cannon, Medical Journalism Award, 1990; Alabama Press Assn Award, Honorable Mention, 1987; Associated Press Newswriting Award, Second Place, 1984; Sigma Delta Chi, Excellence in Journalism, 1974. **Home Addr:** 3704 Frost Street, Huntsville, AL 35810.

RAINS, HORACE
Physician. **Personal:** Born Jan 13, 1912, Atlanta, GA; married Frances Mary Mchie; children: Anthony, Kimberly. **Educ:** Wilberforce U, BS 1937; OH State U, MA 1938; Meharry Med Coll, MD 1953. **Career:** LA Co Gen Hosp, intern 1953-54; Atlanta Life Ins Co, ins salesman 1938-40; Lincoln U, instr hlth & phys educ 1940; Wilberforce, OH, recreation dir natl youth admin 1941; Wilberforce U, asst prof, mil sci & tactics 1941-44; Long Beach, CA, prac of med 1954-. **Orgs:** Mem staff St Mary's Long Beach Hosp 1954-, bd dir 1971-; Long Beach Meml Hosp Med Cntr 1954-; Comm Hosp 1954-; Long Beach Hosp 1964; chmn Med Educ Sub-com CA Rsrch Med Educ Fund 1970-71; chmn Long Beach Human Relations Commn 1972-; mem Am Acad Gen Prac; Am Geriatrics Soc; TB & Respiratory Disease Assn CA bd dir 1966-, pres Long Beach chap 1964-65; chmn United Civil Rights Com 1963-65; bd dir Family Serv Long Beach 1966-; Fair Housing Found 1965-; Wilberforce Univ Aluni Assn & pres So CA chap 1969-. **Honors/Awds:** Recip Man of Yr Awd Bernard & Milton Sahl Post Am Legion 1965. **Military Serv:** AUS 1944-45. **Business Addr:** 1533 Alamitos Ave, Long Beach, CA 90813.

RAINSFORD, GRETA M.
Pediatrician. **Personal:** Born Dec 28, 1936, New York, NY; daughter of Gertrude Eleanor Edwards Rainsford and George Maurice Rainsford; married Samuel K Anderson. **Educ:** AB 1958; MD 1962; Internship 1962-63; Pediatric Res 1963-65; Dipl Bd of Ped 1967. **Career:** Mercy Hosp, Assoc Attending Pediatrician 1965-; NCMC, Asst Attending Pediatrician 1965-; Sickle Cell Clinic, dir 1971-85; Planned Parenthood of Nassau County, med adv bd, 1971-; Roosevelt School Dist, school physician 1975-; Hempstead Sch Dist, school pediatrician 1975-77; Old Westbury Campus State Univ of NY, clinic phys 1976-; Private Practice, physician/pediatrician 1965-; Hofstra Univ, Hempstead, NY, exec dir, community services ctr, 1990-. **Orgs:** Comm Health & Ed 1971-; Nassau Pediatrician Soc Me; bd dir Roosevelt Ment Health Ctr 1976-85; bd of trustees Hofstra Univ 1978-90; pres bd of dirs Long Island Gate 1979-81; SUNY Stony Brook Council 1981-95; mem Nassau Co Med Soc; NY Med Soc; bd mem, Planned Parenthood, Nassau County, 1986-91; Nassau Chpt American Red Cross, mem, med adv bd, 1971-, chair, 1997-2000. **Honors/Awds:** Plaque for Service to Sickle Cell Anemia 1972; Plaque for Service to Youth & Mankind 1974; Commendation for Service to Youth Hempstead C of C 1974; Disting Serv Award HCTA 1974; Comm Serv Award Natl Assn of NBPWC Inc 1974; Comm Serv Award Black Hist Museum 1977; Med Serv Award LI Sickle Cell Proj 1977; MLK, JR Birth Celebration Award, 1988; Equal Award Nass NOW, 1991; FSA Comm Lead Award, 1991; Women of Dist, March of Dimes, 1992; Comm Serv AMWA, 1994. **Business Addr:** Pediatrician, 756 Front, Hempstead, NY 11550, (516)481-6633.

RAKESTRAW, KYLE DAMON
Company executive, engineer. **Personal:** Born Apr 9, 1961, Dayton, OH; son of Delores Robinson Rakestraw. **Educ:** Univ of Cincinnati, BSIM 1984; Xavier Univ Cincinnati, MBA 1988. **Career:** General Motors Corp, professional practice 1982-84; General Motors Co, Delco Moraine Division, Dayton, OH, purchasing agent, 1986-89, sr project engineer, 1990-92; Pepsi Cola Co, Indianapolis, IN, warehouse operations manager, 1989-90; ITT Automotive Electrical Systems, North America, business planner and pricing administrator, 1994-96; Allied Signal Inc, pricing manager, 1996-. **Orgs:** Mem Natl Black MBA Assn 1987. **Honors/Awds:** Voorheis Coll Scholarship Univ of Cincinnati 1979; Dorothy Gradison Memorial Scholarship Univ of Cincinnati 1983. **Home Addr:** 11528 Floyd Dr, #2405, Overland Park, KS 66210. **Business Addr:** Pricing Manager, Allied Signal Inc, 11300 Corporate Ave, PO Box 15995, Shawnee Mission, KS 66285-1804.

RALPH, SHERYL LEE
Actress, singer, writer. **Personal:** Born Dec 30, 1956, Waterbury, CT; daughter of Ivy Ralph and Stanley Ralph; married Eric George Maurice; children: Etienne Maurice, Ivy Victoria. **Educ:** Rutgers University, BA, theater arts and English literature. **Career:** Actress, Television: It's a Living, 1986-89; New Attitude; Designing Women; George; Moesha; Films: The Mighty Quinn; To Sleep With Anger; Distinguished Gentlemen; Sister Act 2; Bogus; Mistress; children's-wear designer; Broadway: Dreamgirls, 1992; Director/Actress, Secrets; Island Girls Productions, owner. **Orgs:** Screen Actors Guild; Actor's Equity; American Federation of Television and Radio Artists; Diva, AIDS fundraiser. **Honors/Awds:** Stage appearances include: Reggae, 1980, Identical Twins from Baltimore, 1987; Divas: Simply Singing; film appearances include: A Piece of the Action, 1977, Finding Maubee, 1988, voice of Rita in Oliver, 1988, television appearances in Codename, Foxfire, Good Times, The Jeffersons, LA Law, Sister Margaret and the Saturday Night Ladies; host of video and author of book: Sheryl Lee Ralph's Beauty Basics, 1987; recorded album, In the Evening, 1984; Tony Award nomination and Drama Desk nomination for Dreamgirls, 1982. **Business Addr:** Actress, c/o Michael Schlessinger, Michael Schlessinger & Associates, 8730 Sunset Blvd, Ste 220, Los Angeles, CA 90069.

RALSTON, EDWARD J.
Director. **Personal:** Born Jun 4, 1938, St Louis, MO; married. **Educ:** Univ of Mo, BA 1973. **Career:** Malcolm Bliss Hosp St Louis Hosp, co-dir of drug prog 1974-, drug couns 1972-74; Archway House, dir legal dept 1971-72. **Orgs:** Mem Drug Abuse Dist Agencies; mem Drug & Sub Counc; mem Drug Abuse Coord Counc; mem Phi Thetta Kappa Forest Pk Comm Coll; consult Parole & Probation Bd on Drug Abuse Detection & Prevention.

RAMBO, BETTYE R.
Educator. **Personal:** Born Sep 2, 1936, Jasper, CO; married Leon Taylor, Jan 1, 1980; children: Valencia A, Sherryle B. **Educ:** Stillman Coll, BA 1959; IN Univ, MA 1968; Postgrad study at Univs of IL, Laverne Coll, Moray House Coll Edinburgh Scotland 1974; Illinois State Univ, attending. **Career:** Educator various positions since 1959; Bd of Educ Springfield, educator 1968-. **Orgs:** Mem Jasper Co Tchrs Assoc 1959-68; life mem Natl Educ Assoc 1959-74; mem MS Teachers Assoc 1959-68, IL Educ Assoc 1968-74; human relations coord REgion #32; mem Hum Rel Comm for IL Educ Assoc 1974 & 75; local minority caucus; mem Zion Missionary Baptist Church; bd dir Stillman Coll Alumni Assoc; participant NDEA Inst for Culturally Disadvantaged Youth; delegate to NEA Conventions; mem NAACP, The Smithsonian Assoc, NRTA; sec PDK 1985-87; education chair ABWA 1986; worthy matron Order of Eastern Star (Estella Chapter) 1989; life mem Springfield Civic Garden Club 1988; mem, Washington St Missions Bd; scy, St Patrick's School Bd, 1992-94. **Honors/Awds:** Airline Passengers Assoc; Teacher of Excellence, Iota Phi Lambda Sorority 1986; Education Award, NAACP (Springfield Branch) 1983; NCATE Evaluation Team Member 1982-87; Spotlight Feature, Springfield Public Schools 1986; Women's Day Speaker 1981, 1983, 1988. **Home Addr:** 2025 Gregory Ct, Springfield, IL 62703.

RAMEY, ADELE MARIE
Attorney, government official. **Personal:** Born Jun 30, 1954, New York, NY; daughter of Delphenia A Taylor and Wilburn Taylor Sr; married Martin G Ramey, Nov 2, 1991. **Educ:** Ohio Wesleyan University, BA, 1976; Indiana University, Purdue University at Indianapolis, Paralegal Certificate, 1985, JD, 1989. **Career:** Sears, Roebuck & Co., manager trainee, 1976-77; Churches Chicken, manager, 1977-79; Red Lobster, assistant manager, 1979-81; Lucky Steer Restaurant, executive assistant manager, 1981-82; McDonalds, assistant manager, 1982-84; Marion County Public Defender's Office, paralegal, 1984-89; Public Defender of Indiana, deputy public defender, 1989-. **Orgs:** American Bar Association, 1989-; Indiana Bar Association, 1989-; Indiana Bar, 1989-; National Bar Association, 1989-. **Business Addr:** Deputy Public Defender, Office Defender of Indiana, 1 N Capitol Ave, Ste 800, Indianapolis, IN 46204, (317)232-2475.

RAMEY, FELICENNE H.
Educator, educational administrator. **Personal:** Born in Philadelphia, PA; daughter of Bertha A Houston and George A Houston; married Melvin R Ramey, Sep 5, 1964; children: David A, Daina L. **Educ:** Pennsylvania State University, PA, BS, 1961; Duquesne University, MS, 1967; University of California, JD, 1972; California State University, MA, 1978. **Career:** Self-employed attorney, Davis, CA, 1975-84; City and County of Sacramento, dir of litigation, 1975-76; California State University, Sacramento, CA, prof of business law, 1975-, asst to the pres, 1984-86, dept chair, 1986-88, assoc dean, prof, 1988-94; Office of the Chancellor, University of California, Davis, CA, executive officer, beginning 1994; California State Univ, Sacramento, School of Business Administration, prof and dean, currently. **Orgs:** Board of directors, chair, Education Committee, Sacramento Black Chamber of Commerce, Sacramento, CA, 1990-; board of directors, Cal Aggie Alumni Assn, 1989-; pres, Western Business Law Assn, 1975-; member, National Assn of Women Deans, Administrators, and Counselors, 1990-; member, California Bar Assn, 1973-; National Association of Women in Education, 1989-; University of California, American Council on Education, fellow, 1992-93. **Honors/Awds:** Citation for Excellence, October 1994, Cal Aggie Alumni Assn; Woman of Color Achievement Award, March 1994, California State Univ, Sacramento, CA. **Business Addr:** Professor, California State University, Sacramento, School of Business Administration, Sacramento, CA 95819-6088, (916)278-6578.

RAMEY, MELVIN R.
Educator. **Personal:** Born Sep 13, 1938, Pittsburgh, PA; son of Eleanor & Ethrem; married Felicenne, Jun 1964; children: David, Daina. **Educ:** Pennsylvania State Univ, BS, 1960; Carnegie Mellon Univ, MS, 1965, PhD, 1967. **Career:** Pennsylvanis Dept of Highways, bridge design engr, 1960-63; Georgia Inst of Tech, visiting prof, 1980; Mass Inst of Tech, visiting prof, 1988; Univ of CA, prof, 1967-; prof & chairperson, 1991-96. **Orgs:** Amer Society of Biomechanics; Amer Society of Civil Engineers; Amer Concrete Inst; Amer Assn for Higher Education. **Honors/Awds:** Student Chapter of Am Soc of Civil Engrs, Outstanding Teacher, 1974; Assoc Students of the Univ of CA, Maynor Ronning Award for Teaching Excellence, 1985; Golden Key Natl Honor Society, Honarary Mem, 1992; Council of Engineering, Deans of the Historically Black Colleges and Universities, Black Engineer of the Year, 1993. **Special Achievements:** Over 50 published articles & reports. **Business Addr:** Professor, Dept of Civil & Environmental Engineering, University of California Davis, Davis, CA 95616.

RAMIREZ, GILBERT
Justice. **Personal:** Born Jun 24, 1921, Vega Alta, Puerto Rico; son of Paulita Hernandez and Virgilio Ramirez; married Marla Ramirez. **Educ:** Univ of PR, BA edn; NYU Grad Sch; Colum-

bia Univ Tchrs Coll; Brooklyn Law Sch, JD 1956. **Career:** New York State Supreme Court, justice, 1975-; Family Ct of State of NY, judge, 1968-75; NY State Constitutional Conv, delegate, 1967; NY State Assembly, assemblyman, 1965; private law practice, 1957-68. **Orgs:** Vice chmn of bd Bedford-Stuyvesant Lawyes Assn; life mem Natl Bar Assn; dir, Brooklyn Law Sch Alumni Assn; mem Bedford-Stuyvesant Beautification Assn; mem Natl Fedn of Blind; vp Guiding Eyes for Blind; member, Assn of Justices of the Supreme Court of the State of New York; member, Supreme Court Justices' Assn of the City of New York; member, New York Puerto Rican Bar Assn; member, Brooklyn Bar Assn; board of directors, Brooklyn Society for the Prevention of Cruelty to Children, Bedford-Stuyvesant Community Legal Services Corp, Vacations and Community Services for the Blind. **Honors/Awds:** Had a senior citizens apartment complex named in his honor, 1984; Distinguished Service Award, Borough of Manhattan Community College; Presidential Medal, Brooklyn College, 1984; Award of the Hispanic Law Students Assn of Brooklyn Law School, 1990; Emilo Nunez Judiciary Award, Puerto Rican Bar Assn, 1989; Honorary Doctor of Laws Degree, Long Island Univ, 1991. **Business Addr:** Justice, New York State Supreme Court, 360 Adams St, Brooklyn, NY 11201.

RAMIREZ, RICHARD M.
Financial executive. **Career:** Apex Securities Inc, CEO, currently. **Special Achievements:** Company is ranked #9 on Black Enterprises's list of top investment banks, 1994. **Business Addr:** CEO, Apex Securities Inc, 333 Clay St, Ste 1310, Houston, TX 77002, (713)650-1122.

RAMPERSAD, ARNOLD
Educator. **Personal:** Born Nov 13, 1941, Port of Spain, Trinidad and Tobago; married. **Educ:** Bowling Green State Univ, Bowling Green, OH, BA, 1967, MA, 1968; Harvard Univ, Cambridge, MA, MA, 1969, PhD, 1973. **Career:** Univ of VA, Charlotteville, VA, asst prof, 1973-74; Stanford Univ, Stanford, CA, prof, 1974-83; Rutgers Univ, New Brunswick, NJ, prof, 1983-88; Columbia Univ, New York, NY, prof, 1988-90; Princeton Univ, Princeton, NJ, Woodrow Wilson prof of literature, 1990-, dir, Program in Afro-American Studies, 1994-. **Orgs:** Dir, Program in American Studies, Princeton Univ, 1990-95. **Honors/Awds:** Art & Imagination of W E B DuBois, Harvard Univ Press, 1976; Life of Langston Hughes (2 Vols), Oxford Univ Press, 1986, 1988. **Special Achievements:** The Collected Poems of Langston Hughes, editor, 1994; Jackie Robinson: A Biography, author, Knopf, 1998. **Business Addr:** Professor, Princeton University, McCosh 22, Princeton, NJ 08544.

RAMSEUR, ANDRE WILLIAM
Poet, employee development specialist. **Personal:** Born Jan 15, 1949, Manhattan, NY; son of Creola Howard and Otho William Ramseur, Jr. **Educ:** St Augustines Coll Raleigh, BA Eng 1971; Miami Univ Oxford OH, futher study, 1972; George Washington Univ DC, further study 1980; VA Polytechnic Institute & State Univ, MS, Education; Emphasis in Adult Education, 1992. **Career:** Adjunct/Professor-Strayer College-Washington, D.C, 1992 Miami Univ Oxford OH, grad asst 1971-72; St Augustines Coll, instr of eng 1972-74; Equitable Life Assurance Soc of US, agency sec Wash DC, asst suprv New Bus Indianapolis, admin trainee Washington DC 1974-77; Eton Towers Tenants Assoc, legal coord 1975; Pres Comm on White House Fellowships, staff asst 1977-79; Office of Personnel Mgmt Washing DC, ed specialist 1979-86; Defense Info Systems Agency, supervisory employee devel specialist 1986-92; Strayer College, adjunct prof, 1992-. **Orgs:** Co-founder Station to Station Performance Poets & Writers Collective 1980; bd mem, 1990-92, mem, Federal Educations and Technology Assoc (FETA). **Honors/Awds:** Outstanding Young Man Dees & Fuller Org 1975; finalist Clover Intl Poetry Contest Wash DC 1975; Notable Amer Awd Notable Historian Soc Raleigh 1976-77; Spec Achievement Awd Pres Comm on White House Fellowship 1979; poetry publ "You Never Tried" Clover Publ 1976, "After the Fact" Young Publ 1978, "Greenhouse Poetry" Collection of Love Poems Triton Press 1977-78, "Greenhouse Poetry" Vol 2 1979-80; annual 1 man poetry performance 1982-; group performances with Station to Station 1980-85; special achievement OPM Director's Award 1984; special act or service Info Systems Agency 1986; poetry collection inprogress "It's About Time" 1989; outstanding Act or service, Def Info Systems Agcy 1990; Spec Achievement, DISA 1987-88; Letter of Appreciation, DISA Inspector General for Participation & Performance, Organization Assessment Audit Team, (1996). **Home Addr:** 5745 Independence Cir, Alexandria, VA 22312-2628.

RAMSEUR, DONALD E.
Judge (retired). **Personal:** Born Dec 17, 1919, Cleveland County, NC; son of Annis B Ramseur and Charlie J Ramseur; married Prince Alma Whitworth; children: 3. **Educ:** Johnson C Smith Univ, BS 1941; NC Coll Sch of Law, LLB 1954. **Career:** 27th Judicial Dist, dist judge (retired 1985). **Orgs:** Past pres, founder, Gaston Boys' Club; bd of trustees Gaston Mem Hosp; former memb Gastonia City Bd of Ed; mem Mayor's Comm on Human Relations; past pres, mem, Gaston County Bar Assn; mem NC Bar Assn; NC Black Lawyers' Assn; NC conf Dist Ct Judges; bd of trustees, First Congregational United Church of Chirst. **Honors/Awds:** Man & Boy Award Boys' Clubs of Amer 1968; Omega Man of the Year; Citizen of the Year. **Military Serv:** US Army, T/Sgt.

RAMSEUR, ISABELLE R.
Councilwoman. **Personal:** Born Feb 21, 1906, North Carolina; married Charles; children: Harold D, Albertine. **Career:** Philadelphia Gen Hosp, nursing vol work; Mercy Douglas Hosp; Nursery Sch Fernwood, tchrs asst; Boro Darby, councilwoman. **Orgs:** Mem Needlework Guild Am 1933; Ladies Aux to WMCA Phila; Blessed Virgin Mary Ch; mem NAACP; past matron Order E Star; chrtrd mem Rose of Sharon Chap #80. **Honors/Awds:** 1st prize ARC Talent Rally Rose of Sharon.

RAMSEY, DAVID P.
Actor. **Educ:** Wayne State Univ, graduated. **Career:** Actor. Films: The Line, 1980; The Nutty Professor, 1996; A Very Brady Sequel, 1996; Con Air, 1997. TV appearances: Lovers and Friends/For Richer, For Poorer, 1977; Sanctuary of Fear, 1979; Deutschlandlied, 1996; The Good News, 1997-. **Business Addr:** Actor, c/o UPN, 5555 Melrose, Hollywood, CA 90038, (213)956-5000.

RAMSEY, DONNA ELAINE
Librarian. **Personal:** Born Oct 10, 1941, Charlotte, NC; daughter of Mabel Brown Tatum and William A Epps; married Reginald E Ramsey, Apr 9, 1979 (died 1985); children: Gina M Clark (deceased), Ona B, Reginald E II. **Educ:** Johnson C Smith Univ, BA, 1969; Atlanta Univ, MSLS, 1971; Univ of North Carolina, 1973, 1976-77; Kent State Univ, 1976. **Career:** Barber-Scotia College, Concord, NC, reference/circulation librarian, 1971-73; Friendship Junior College, Rock Hill, SC, chief librarian, 1973-77; New Mexico State Univ, Las Cruces, NM, assistant serials librarian, 1977-81; Cochise College, Fort Bliss, TX, librarian, 1984-85; US Army Air Defense Artillery School Library, Fort Bliss, TX, supervisory librarian, 1985-89, librarian, 1989-92; US Army Sergeants Major Academy, Fort Bliss, TX, librarian, 1992-97; US Army Air Def Art School, Mickelsen Library, librarian, 1997-. **Orgs:** American Library Assn, 1976-, Staff Organizations Roundtable, chair, 1991-93; Black Caucus American Library Assn, 1978-; life member, NAACP, 1989-; golden life member, Delta Sigma Theta Sorority, Inc, 1989-; Links, Inc, 1986-, chair, intl trends, 1992-; chair, program planning, Fort Bliss Black Employment Program Committee, 1989-90; den leader, Boy Scouts of America, 1989-93; assistant den leader, Girl Scouts of America, 1988-95; parents advisory council, Socorro Independent School District, 1996-; mem, American Platform Association, 1995-; mem, research bd of dirs, American Biographical Institute, 1994-; ALA President's San Francisco Conference Program Committee, 1991-92; Program Format Chair, 1990-92; Staff Organization Roundtable, ALA, 1979-; Constitution and Bylaws Chair, 1993; chair-elect, 1990-91; chair, 1991-93; Annual Program Chair, 1991-93. **Honors/Awds:** Civic Achievement Award, United Way, Las Cruces, 1981; Certificate of Achievement, Dept of the Army, 1990, 1991; "Librarians: Starring in the Information Age," Monitor, 1990; "Woodson: Father of Black History, Revisited," Monitor, 1990; "Black History and Studies Reveal the Story," Massinga, 1978; Black Caucus, ALA, National Conference of African-American Librarians, Certificate of Achievement Award, 1992; American Library Association, Certificate of Achievement, 1992; American Biographical Institute, Certificate of Appreciation, 1995; Kent State University Graduate Assistanceship; Certificate of Recognition, Association of College and Research Libraries (ACRL); US Army, Certificate of Achievement, 1997. **Home Addr:** PO Box 6769, El Paso, TX 79906, (915)857-8462. **Business Phone:** (915)568-1491.

RAMSEY, FREEMAN, JR.
Photographer. **Personal:** Born Oct 8, 1943, Nashville, TN; son of Rosetta Scott (deceased) and Freeman Ramsey (deceased); married Doretha Pipkin Ramsey, Apr 20, 1968; children: Freeman Ramsey III, Ronald Ramsey, Christine Renee. **Educ:** Tennessee State University, Nashville, TN, BS, business, 1970; Nashville Technical Institute, Nashville, TN, diploma communications & photography, 1983. **Career:** CBS Records, Nashville, TN, recording engineer, 1969-82; Ramsey's Photography, Nashville, TN, self-employed, photographer, 1982-85; Metro Bd of Education, Nashville, TN, transportation, 1984-90; The Tennessean, Nashville, TN, staff photographer, 1989-. **Orgs:** Member, National Press Photographers Association, 1989-; member, Tennessee Press Association, 1989-; member, National Association of Black Journalists, 1989-. **Honors/Awds:** Photographic Achievement, The Tennessean, 1965; Photographic Achievement, The Tennessean, 1966; Gordon Parks Photography Competition, second place, 1994; NABJ Photography Competition, Third Place, 1994; AP Awards, First and Second Place, 1994; Southern Short Course in News Photography, Second Place, 1992, Honorable Mention, 1993, Second Place, 1994; Atlanta Seminar in Photojournalism, Honorable Mention, 1993; TN Press Assn, Best News Picture, 1994; Tennessean, Outstanding Achievement Award, 1993; Gannett Well Done Awards, 1991, 1994; AP, Feature Picture Award, 1991; NPPA Awards, First Place, News, 1991, 1993; 3rd Place, Sports Feature Photo, AP, 1991; 1st Place, News Picture, Penn Press Association, 1995; Best News Picture Story, AP, 1995; Best of Gannett, 2nd Place, Color Photography, 1994; 1st Place, Feature Picture, AP, 1994; 3rd Place, Feature Picture, NPPA, 1991; 2nd Place & 3rd Place, New Picture, AP, 1992. **Military Serv:** US Air Force, A 3/c, 1966. **Business Addr:** Staff Photographer, Photo Dept, The Tennessean, 1100 Broadway St, Nashville, TN 37203.

RAMSEY, HENRY, JR.
Educational administrator, judge. **Personal:** Born Jan 22, 1934, Florence, SC; married Eleanor Anne Mason; children: Charles, Githaiga, Robert, Ismail, Yetunde, Abeni. **Educ:** Univ of California, Riverside CA, AB 1960; Univ of California, School of Law, Berkeley CA, LLB 1963; Harvard University Institute for Educational Management, 1992. **Career:** Contra Costa County, CA, dep dist atty 1964-65; Ramsey & Rosenthal, Richmond CA, partner 1965-71; Univ of California Sch of Law, Berkeley CA, prof of law 1971-80; Univ of Texas, Austin TX, visiting prof of law 1971-77; Univ of Colorado, Boulder CO, visiting prof of law 1977-78; Univ of New Mexico School of Law, Special Scholarship Prog for Amer Indians, Albuquerque NM, visiting prof of law 1980; State of California, County Co of Alameda, superior ct judge 1980-90; Howard Univ School of Law, Washington, DC, dean, 1990-96, vp for legal affairs and acting general counsel of Howard University, 1994-95. **Orgs:** Past mem Curriculum Devel & Supplemental Materials Comm of State of CA; mem CA Bar Assn, 1964-80; mem CA Judges Assn; past mem Human Rel Comm City of Richmond; past mem bd dir Redevelopment Agency; United Bay Area Crusade; bd dir Amer Civil Liberties Union of Northern CA; past mem Berkeley City Council; past mem exec comm Assn of Amer Law Sch; past mem Council on Legal Educ Oppor; mem 1987-, pres Council on Legal Educ Oppor; mem Council of the Sect on Legal Educ and Admission to the Bar of the Amer Bar Assn, 1982-; mem Amer Law Inst; past mem Accreditation Comm of the Sect of Legal Educ & Admissions to the Bar Amer Bar Assn; mem Commn on Trial Court Performance Standards, Natl Center for State Courts, 1987-95; mem Blue Ribbon Commn on Inmate Population Mgmt, 1987-90; mem Judicial Council of California, 1988-; chairperson, Judicial Council Advisory Comm on Change of Venue, Judicial Council of California, 1988-89; Natl Commn on Trial Court Performance Standards; life mem NAACP; life mem Amer Civil Liberties Union; mem Amnesty Intl; chair, Council of the Sect on Legal Education and Admissions to the Bar of the ABA, 1991-92; Appointed Trustee of Fibreboard Asbestos Compensation Trust. **Honors/Awds:** Author, "Affirmative Action at Amer Bar Assn Approved Law School: 1979-1980," Journal of Legal Educ, 1980; author, "California Continuing Education of the Bar," chapter in California Criminal Law Procedure and Practice, 1986; Fellow, Amer Bar Foundation; mem Amer Law Inst; Distinguished Alumnus Award, Univ of California (Riverside) Alumni Assn, 1987; Distinguished Service Award, The National Center for State Courts, 1990; Fifth Annual Distinguished Service Award, The Wiley Manuel Law Foundation, 1987; Bernard S Jefferson Jurist Award, California Assn of Black Lawyers, 1986; American Bar Association Law Student Div, Henry Ramsey Jr Awd, 1996; Honorary Doctor of Laws, William Mitchell College of Law, 1996. **Military Serv:** USAF 1951-55. **Business Addr:** Dean, Howard University School of Law, 2900 Van Ness St NW, Washington, DC 20008.

RAMSEY, JAMES H.
Educational administrator (retired). **Personal:** Born Apr 20, 1931, Memphis, TN; son of Hilda Ophelia DuPree Ramsey and John Alvin Ramsey; married Gertrude McKlin, Aug 6, 1988; children: Patricia Joyce, Karin Joy. **Educ:** Tennessee A & I State University, Nashville, TN, BS, 1952; Fisk University, Nashville, TN, 1959-60; Brown University, Providence, RI, MAT, 1961; New Jersey Institute of Technology, Newark, NJ, 1962-63; Montclair State College, Montclair, NJ, 1963-64. **Career:** Cedar Grove Board of Education, Cedar Grove, NJ, biology teacher, 1961-69; Rutgers, The State University, Newark NJ, director EOF, 1969-83, associate provost, 1983-93; Barber Soctia Coll, special asst to pres, 1996-97. **Orgs:** Member, Newark Education Council, Academic Task Force Committee/Steering Committee; president, Newark Day Center; chairman, Dr Martin Luther King Scholarship Fund; member, Kessler Institute Board of Trustees; member, Mountainside Hospital Board of Trustees; Board of Education, president; Montclair Savings Bank, board of directors; Montclair Township Council; Mayor of Montclair Township; In Roads of No New Jersey; 100 Black Men of Charlotte, NC; Charlotte Mecklenburg Education Foundation. **Honors/Awds:** Fellowship Award, National Science Foundation; Man of the Year, Omega Psi Phi Fraternity, 1978; Achievement Award, Kappa Alpha Psi; Outstanding Service Award, Newark Board of Education, 1984; Layman of the Year Award, New Jersey Council of Churches, 1985; Dr Martin Luther King Service Award, Essex County Freeholders, 1989. **Military Serv:** US Army, Corporal, 1952-54. **Home Addr:** 4131 Hyde Park Dr, Charlotte, NC 28216.

RAMSEY, JEROME CAPISTRANO
Attorney, business executive. **Personal:** Born Mar 28, 1953, San Bernardino, CA. **Educ:** Univ of CA, BA honors 1975, JD 1978. **Career:** Holland and Hart, attorney 1978-80; US Dept of Justice, asst US attorney 1980-82; Mile Hi Cablevision, vp/genl counsel 1982-86; Paragon Communications, regional vice president, 1986-90; American Telecommunications, New England

Division, president, 1990-. **Orgs:** Mem Amer Bar Assn 1978-; mem CO & Denver Bar Assn 1978-; board member, 1990, chairman, Maine executive committee, 1991, New England Cable Television Assn. **Honors/Awds:** Distinguished Service US Dept of Justice 1982; Executive Excel the Minority Prof Directory 1984. **Business Addr:** President, American TV & Communications, New England Division, 118 Johnson Rd, Portland, ME 04102.

RAMSEY, WALTER S.
Business executive. **Personal:** marrIed Grace E Walker; children: Dr Walter S Jr. **Educ:** Coll of City of NY, BS. **Career:** Sylvania Electric, proj engr 1946-53; Raytheon Mfg Co, proj engr 1945-46; Standard Eletronics, physicist 1943-45; US Signal Corps, physicist 1942-43; Ramsey Electronics, owner mgr consult 1953-. **Orgs:** Mem adv com August Martin HS Jamaica NY; mem bd Queens Child Guidance; bd chmn NAACP Jamaica; Montauk Day Care Cntr; educ chmn Queensboro Fed of Parents Clubs; pres Jamaica Br NAACP. **Business Addr:** 114-74 176 St, Jamaica, NY 11434.

RAND, A. BARRY
Corporate vice president. **Personal:** Born 1945, Washington, DC; son of Helen Matthews Rand and Addison Penrod Rand; divorced. **Educ:** Rutgers University, Camden, NJ; American University, Washington, DC, BS; Stanford University, Stanford, CA, MBA, MS. **Career:** Xerox Corp, Rochester, NY, sales representative, 1968-70, regional sales representative, 1970-80, corporate director of marketing, 1980-84, vice president of eastern operations, 1984-86; Xerox Corp, Stamford, CT, corporate vice president, president of US Marketing Group, begin 1986, exec vice pres, operations, currently. **Business Addr:** Exec VP, Xerox Corp, 800 Long Ridge Rd, Stamford, CT 06902.

RAND, CYNTHIA
Government official. **Educ:** Hampton Univ, bachelors, mathematics; Fairleigh Dickinson Univ, MS, computer science. **Career:** Transportation Dept, IRM dir, begin 1991; US Dept of Defense, principal dir for info mgmt, currently. **Business Addr:** Principal Director for Information Management, US Dept of Defense, Rm E 160, Pentagon (OSD), Arlington, VA 20301, (703)614-0548.

RANDALL, ANN KNIGHT
Educator, librarian. **Personal:** Born in NYC; married Julius T; children: Christine Renee. **Educ:** Barnard Coll, BA 1963; NY U, post grad study 1967; Columbia U, DLS 1977. **Career:** US Social Security Admin NYC, claims adjuster 1963-64; AUS Bamberg Germany, lib asst 1964-65; Brooklyn public library, library adult trainee 1965-67; City Univ of NY Queens Coll, instr 1967-69; Brookyn Coll, adjunct lectr 1976-; Columbia Univ, Pratt Inst, Queens Coll, Rutgers Univ, teacher part-time 1970-73; Univ S Educ Resources Info Center ERIC, indexer 1967-68; Urban Center Columbia Univ, library consultant 1970-; Urban Resources Sys Univ of MI, 1973; RR Booker, public consultant 1973. **Orgs:** Mem YWCA Brooklyn; Acad of Pol Sci; Am Lib Assn 1966-; Assn for Study of African Am Life & History 1968-; exec bd Spl Lib Assn NY Group 1969-71;pres NU chap Columbia Univ Beta Phi Mu 1971-72. **Honors/Awds:** Publ review & art in jour and book chpt; recip NDEA Fellowship Awd for doctoral studies.

RANDALL, DUDLEY FELKER
Librarian, publisher, poet. **Personal:** Born Jan 14, 1914, Washington, DC; son of Ada Viola Bradley Randall and Arthur George Clyde Randall; married Ruby Hands, May 27, 1935; children: Phyllis Ada. **Educ:** Wayne Univ, Detroit MI, BA, 1949; Univ of Michigan, Ann Arbor, MALS, 1951; Univ of Ghana, 1970. **Career:** Lincoln Univ, Jefferson City MO, librarian, 1951-54; Morgan St Coll, Baltimore MD, assoc librarian, 1954-56; Wayne Co Federated Library Sys, Wayne MI, branch librarian, 1956-63, head of ref, 1963-69; Univ of Detroit, MI, ref librarian & poet-in-res, 1969-75. Visiting lecr, Univ of MI, 1969; fndr, gen editor, Broadside Pr, 1965-77; fndr, Broadside Poets Theatre, Broadside Poetry Wkshp, 1980; consultant, 1977—. **Orgs:** Mem, New Detroit Inc com on arts, 1970—; MI Coun Arts Adv Panel on Lit, 1970—; Detroit Coun Arts, 1975-76; mem, Intl Afro-Amer Museum, NAACP, Amer Libr Assoc, MI Libr Assoc, MI Poetry Soc, Detroit Soc for Advncmt of Culture & Educ. **Honors/Awds:** Tompkins Awd, Wayne St Univ, 1962, 1966; Kuumba Libn Awd, 1973; Arts Awd in Lit, MI Found for Arts, 1975; Creative Artist Awd in Lit, MI coun for Arts, 1981; NEA fellowshps, 1981, 1986; appt 1st Poet Laureate of Detroit by Mayor Coleman A. Young, 1981. Author num poems; author of books A Capsule Course in Black Poetry Writing (with others), Broadside Pr, 1975, Broadside Memories: Poets I Have Known, Broadside Pr, 1975, A Litany of Friends: New & Selected Poems, Lotus Press, 1981, Homage To Hoyt Fuller, Broadside Pr, 1984; ed, contr to anthologies. **Military Serv:** US Army, signal corps, 1942-46. **Home Addr:** 12651 Old Mill Pl, Detroit, MI 48238.

RANDALL, QUEEN F.
Educational administrator. **Personal:** Born Jan 28, 1935, Pine Bluff, AR; children: Barbara J. **Educ:** Lincoln Univ, BS Ed 1956; Indiana Univ, AM 1961; Nova Univ, EdD 1975. **Career:** Lincoln Univ, math instructor 1956-58; American River Coll, math instructor 1962-70, math & engineering dept chair 1970-72, assoc dean of instr 1972-76; Pioneer Comm Coll, dean, instructional systems & student development 1976-78, president 1978-80; Metropolitan Comm Coll, asst to chancellor 1980-81; El Centro Coll, president 1981-84; American River Coll, president 1984-93; Los Rios Community College District, chancellor, 1993-. **Orgs:** Pres Delta Kappa Gamma; mem Alpha Kappa Alpha 1953-; pres Soroptimist Club Kansas City MO 1981; bd of dirs Industrial Develop Corp 1982-85; adv bd Treescape Dallas, Contact Dallas; Crocker Art Museum; bd of dirs, Mercy Healthcare Sacramento; bd of dirs, Methodist Hospital Sacramento; bd of dirs, The Sacramento Theatre Co. **Honors/Awds:** Fellow John Hay Whitney Foundation 1961; Fellow Delta Kappa Gamma 1974; Trailblazer So Dallas Business & Professional Club 1982; Outstanding Educator YWCA 1985; Outstanding Alumni Nova Univ 1985; Women of Distinction Award Soroptimist Intl of Sacramento North 1986; Dollars and Sense Magazine's Second Annual Salute to America's Top 100 Business and Professional Women 1986.

RANDLE, BERDINE CARONELL
Business executive. **Personal:** Born Mar 18, 1929, Lufkin, TX; married Lucious; children: Lydia. **Educ:** Prairie View A&M U, BA 1949; Prairie Vew A&M U, Ms 1955; Univ of Houston, post grad. **Career:** Miss Lucy's Acad & Early Chldhd Educ Cntr, exec dir 1969-; Friendship Rlty Co, owner 1970-; HI SD Houston, 1957-72; Marlin ISD, phys educ tchr1951-57; tchr elem sch 1951-55; phys educ tchr 1946, 48, 49, 51; YMCA Waco, dance instr. **Orgs:** Adv bd consult Clanthe Hse of Bees Halfway Hse 1973-77; vice pres North Forest Sh Bd 1974-76; vice pres Fontaine Scenic Woods Civic Club 1976-; golden life mem Delta Sigma Theta Sor 1972; life mem YWCA 1975; Nat State & Houston Area Assn for the Educ of Young Children 1976-; ACEI 1974-77; SACUS 1973-; NAESP 1973-; AAHPER 1955-; mem chrpsn NFTFO 1976-; AUCW 1974-77; HALBPWC 1973-; NALBPWC 1973-; mem chrpsn F SWCC 1976; Alpha Tau chptr Theta Nu Sigma Nat Sor; charter member, Diamond Jubilee; Delta Sigma Theta Sorority, Inc, life member; Natl Council of Negro Women; NAACP; bd of dirs, Habitat for Humanity, and Delta's Education Foundation; Nominated to Prairie View A&M Univ, Sports Hall of Fame, 1994. **Honors/Awds:** Comm serv awd 1974; natl coun of negro women's awd 1973; outstdng comm serv awd 1973; TX Assn of Sch Bd Awd 1975; Kashmere Gdns HS Comm Srev Awd 1975; Fontaine Scenic Woods Civic Club's Civic Minded Awd 1973, 74; Pres Coun on Phys Fitness Awd 1966; Bd of Educ North Forest Sch Dist Awd 1976;Miss Lucy's Acad Outstdng Serv & PTO Awd 1977; ded serv awd Houston Ind SchDist 1977; Gulf Coast Comm Serv Awd 1977; ded serv awd Calanthe Hse of Bees 1977; cert of merit serv Mayor of Houston Gov of TX Hse Spkr Bill Clayton 1977; achiev awd for excell in educ & comm serv Houston Leag of Bus & Prof Women's Club. **Business Addr:** 10620 Homestead Rd, Houston, TX 77016.

RANDLE, CARVER A.
Attorney. **Personal:** Born Jan 12, 1942, Indianola, MS; married Rosie Knox; children: Regina, Carver Jr, Rosalyn. **Educ:** MS Valley State U, BS 1965; Univ MS, JD 1973. **Career:** Pattonlane HS, tchr coach 1965-67; Washington Co Schs, tchr 1967-68; Quitman Co, spl proj dir 1968-69; N MS Rural Legal Svcs, staff atty 1973-. **Orgs:** Mem Nat Conf Black Lawyers; MS Nat Bar Assn; cand Mayor City Indianola 1968; cand state rep MS 1971; mem bd dirs Indianola Fed Credit Unoin 1969-; ACSC 1967-70; pres Sunflower Co MS Br NAACP 1967-; mem MS Coun on Human Rel 197-. **Honors/Awds:** Coach of yr N Central Athletic Conf 1965-66; awd for outstdng achvmnts & ldgrshp Indianola 1973. **Business Addr:** PO Box 546, Indianola, MS 38751.

RANDLE, JOHN
Professional football player. **Personal:** Born Dec 12, 1967, Hearne, TX; children: Brittany. **Educ:** Texas A&M-Kingsville, attended. **Career:** Minnesota Vikings, defensive tackle, 1990-. **Honors/Awds:** Pro Bowl, 1993, 1994, 1995, 1996. **Business Addr:** Professional Football Player, Minnesota Vikings, 9520 Viking Dr, Eden Prairie, MN 55344, (612)828-6500.

RANDLE, LUCIOUS A.
Educator. **Personal:** Born Aug 15, 1927, Mcgregor, TX; married Berdine C Reese; children: Lydia Louise. **Educ:** BS 1949; MEd 1953; Univ of TX, post grad work. **Career:** Robert E Lee Sr HS Houston Indendent School Dist, vice prin 1970-; Attucks Jr HS, teacher part-time prin 1962-70; Worthing HS, science teacher 1958-62; Charlie Brown HS, 1957-58; OJ Thomas HS 1949-57; Friednship Realty Co, owner-broker 1970-; Homestead Rd School of Dance, owner 1971-; Miss Lucy's Acad & Early Childhood Educ Center, owner-dir 1969-; Homefinders Real Estate Inc, co broker 1965-70. **Orgs:** Mem NEA; TSTA Houston Prin Assn; Nat Assn Real Est Brokers; Houston Realtors Assn; TX Realtors Assn; N Forst Task Force Orgn; Fontaine-Scenic Woods Civic Club; Masonic Lodge; Lions' Club. **Honors/Awds:** Tchr of Yr 1954-55; Real est Salesman of Yr 1964-65; comm serv awd Nat Coun of Negro Women 1974; hon mem FFA awd 1973. **Military Serv:** AUS signal corps med br oc classification 1951-53. **Business Addr:** 10620 Homestead Rd, Houston, TX 77016.

RANDLE, THERESA
Actress. **Career:** Actress, currently. **Special Achievements:** Films include: Space Jam, Girl 6, Bad Boys, Beverly Hills Cop III, Sugar Hill, The Five Heartbeats, CB4, Malcolm X, Jungle Fever, The King of New York. **Business Addr:** Actress, c/o ICM, 8942 Wilshire Blvd, Beverly Hills, CA 90211, (310)550-4000.

RANDLE, WILMA JEAN-ELIZABETH EMANUEL
Journalist. **Personal:** Born Apr 20, 1955, Chicago, IL; daughter of Ruth Helen Emanuel Randle. **Educ:** Rosary College, River Forest, IL, BA, history, communication arts, 1977; University of Southern California, MA, international journalism, 1991. **Career:** Chicago Independent Bulletin, news editor, 1977-78; Muskegon Chronicle, reporter; St Paul Pioneer Press Dispatch, reporter/columnist, 1984-88; Chicago Tribune, business reporter, 1988-. **Orgs:** National Association of Black Journalists; International Woman's Media Foundation. **Honors/Awds:** International Women's Media Foundation International Conference, delegate, 1990; University of Southern California, Center for International Journalism Fellowship, 1990; Davenport Business and Economics Reporting Fellowship, 1984. **Business Addr:** Business Reporter, Chicago Tribune, 142 E Golf Rd, Schaumburg, IL 60173, (847)843-6131.

RANDOLPH, BERNARD CLYDE
Physician. **Personal:** Born May 22, 1922, New York, NY; son of Jessie K Briggs Randolph and William F Randolph; married Bille Jean Coleman; children: Dana Grace, Bernard C Jr, MD, Paul Allen Esq. **Educ:** City Coll of New York, BS 1943; Howard Univ Coll of Med, MD 1947. **Career:** Mound City Medl Forum, pres 1963-65; MO Pan-Medical Assoc, pres 1966-67; Talent Rec Council of Natl Med Assoc, chmn 1972-81. **Orgs:** Founder and pres St Louis Council Env Health and Safety 1975-; past pres Gamma Chapter Chi Deltu Mu Frat; mem Phi Beta Signa Frat; life mem and golden heritage mem NAACP; chair, Health & Hospital Comm; former chmn Hlth Comm of 5th Senatorial Dist Corporate and Professional Round Table; Selection Comm, Dorothy I Height Lifetime Achievement Award of the 5th Biennial Symposium on Minorities, the Medically Underserved & Cancer, 1995. **Honors/Awds:** Mem Mission to W Africa Natl Med Assoc, 1961; mem NMA delegate Conference on Hosp Discrimination Pres John F Kennedy 1963; Practitioner of the Year, National Medical Assn 1988; Community Service Award, Legal Services of Eastern Missouri 1989. **Military Serv:** USAF capt 1952-54. **Business Addr:** 3737 N Kinshighway, St Louis, MO 63115.

RANDOLPH, BERNARD P.
Air Force commander. **Personal:** Born Jul 10, 1933, New Orleans, LA; son of Claudia Randolph and Philip Randolph; married Lucille Robinson; children: Michelle, Julie, Michael, John, Liane, Mark. **Educ:** Xavier Univ LA, BS Chem (cum laude) 1954; Air Force Inst Tech, BS (magna cum laude) 1964; Univ of N Dakota, MS Electrical Engineering 1965; Auburn Univ, MS Business Admin 1969. **Career:** 834th Air Div Tan Son Nhut Air Base Vietnam, airlift ops officer Chu Lai, airlift coord 1969-70; Hdqrs Air Force Systems Command Andres AFB MD, chief command plans br office dep, chief staff ops 1970-72, exec officer to dep chief staff ops 1972-73; Space & Missile Systems Orgn Los Angeles Air Force Sta, dir space systems plnng 1974-75; Air Force Satellite Commun System Space & Missile Systems Orgn, system program dir 1975-78, prog dir space defense systems 1978-80; Warner Robins Air Logistics Ctr Robins AFB CO, vice comdr; 1980-81; US Air Force, Washington DC, dir, space systems/CCC, 1981-84; Air Force Systems Command Adrews AFB, vice comdr 1984-85; USAF Washington, chief staff for R&D & acquisition hdqrs 1985-87; Air Force Systems Command, Andrews AFB, dir, 1987-. **Honors/Awds:** Disting Grad Air War Coll 1974; second Black named a Four-Star General in Air Force; third Black Four-Star General to be named in US. **Military Serv:** US Air Force, general, 1964-; Decorated Disting Serv Medal, Legion of Merit w/oak leaf cluster, Bronze Star Medal, Meritorious Serv Medal, Presidential Unit Citation.

RANDOLPH, ELIZABETH
Educator (retired). **Personal:** Born Mar 18, 1917, Farmville, NC; daughter of Pearl Schmoke and John Schmoke; married John D Randolph (deceased). **Educ:** Shaw Univ, AB 1936; Univ of MI, MA 1945; Univ of NC, Certificate School Admin 1964; Shaw Univ, Hon DHL 1979. **Career:** NC Public School, teacher 1936-58; Charlotte Mecklenburg School, principal 1958-67; ESEA Title I, dir 1967-73; Charlotte Mecklenburg Bd of Educ, admin asst 1973-76, asst supt 1976-77, assoc supt 1977-82 (retired). **Orgs:** Mem bd of mgrs Charlotte Mem Mecklenburg Hospital 1971-; mem Charlotte Mecklenburg Human Relations Comm 1972-75; supreme parliamentarian Alpha Kappa Alpha Sorority Inc 1974-78; pres ASCD 1977; bd of dirs Mecklenburg Boy Scout Council 1978-; mem Charter Review Comm 1979-80; mem Phi Delta Kappa Educ Fraternity; bd oftrustees Shaw Univ; bd of trustees NC A&T State Univ; bd of trustees Public Library of Charlotte and Mecklenburg Co; co-chmn Friends of Johnson C Smith Univ; bd of commissioners Charlotte-Mecklenburg Hospital Authority; mem bd of trustees Davidson Coll 1987-, Queen's Coll 1988-; University of North Carolina at Charlotte, honorary DHL, 1991; Museum

of the New South, 1992; Association of Black Women in Higher Education, public service award, 1991. **Honors/Awds:** Citation Local Press Civic Educ Org 1958-77; Citation Alpha Kappa Alpha Sor 1977; Citation ASCD 1977; Citation Public Library of Charlotte and Mecklenburg County; Citation Mecklenburg County Commissioners; Citation Charlotte-Mecklenburg Bd of Educ; Citation Mecklenburg General Baptist Convention; The National Conference of Christians and Jews, Humanitarian/Silver Medallion Award 1996; Charlotte-Mecklenburg Urban League Whitney M Young Award 1996-.

RANDOLPH, JAMES B.
Educator. **Personal:** Born Jul 23, 1923, Richland, LA; married Gloria D Jackson; children: Gina Lynne, Cecily Karen, James Bolton. **Educ:** FL A&M U, BA 1950; Western Reserve U, MA 1951; KARAMU Theatre, spec stud; Univ of Miami Barry Coll , addl Stud. **Career:** Westveiw Jr HS, prin 1973-; Carol City Jr HS, asst prin admin 1970-73; Educ Testing Serv, writer 1969-71; Units on Negro History & Culture Dade County School, 1969; Dade County School, teacher drama 1958-69; Prairie View A&M Coll, asst prof of speech 1956-58; Comm Youth Center Springfield, dir 1954-56; FL A&M Univ instructor asst prof of drama 1951-54. **Orgs:** Mem Phi Delta Kappa; Nat Educ Assn; 1st vice pres FL Interscholastic Speech & Drama Assn; bd of dir Sec Sch Theatre Conf; pres Dade Co Speech Tchr Assn; mem FL Assn Sec Sch Prin; Nat Assn Sec Sch Prin; chmn; Ch Coun Ch of the Open Door; chmn Scholarship Com Miami Edison PTSA; Omega Psi Phi; exec bd Sigma Alpha Chap Miami. **Honors/Awds:** Distngd ser to N Dade HS honor soc 1962-63; outs serv Dramatic Arts Deerfield Bch Elem Sch 1963; awd of exec ser to N Dade HS Faculty & Students 1958-66; cover DRAMATICS Mag 1962. **Military Serv:** AUS. **Business Addr:** Westview Jr HS, 1901 NW 127 St, Miami, FL 33167.

RANDOLPH, LAURA B.
Publishing company executive. **Personal:** Born Aug 1, 1957, Washington, DC; daughter of Horace & Anna Randolph. **Educ:** George Washington Univ, BA, 1979; Georgetown Univ Law Center, JD, 1987. **Career:** US Dept of Health & Human Services, regulations analyst, 1980-82, health policy specialist, 1982-84, program analyst, 1984-85, legal assistance specialist, 1985-87; Johnson Publishing Co Inc, editor, 1987-. **Orgs:** White House Correspondents Assn, 1992-; US Senate/House Press Gallery, 1987. **Honors/Awds:** US Dept of Health & Human Services, secretary of HHS, Superior Achievement Award, 1982. **Business Addr:** Senior Editor, Ebony Magazine, Johnson Publishing Co, Inc, 1750 Pennsylvania Avenue, NW, Ste 1301, Washington, DC 20011, (202)393-5860.

RANDOLPH, LEONARD WASHINGTON, JR.
Corrections official. **Personal:** Born Oct 15, 1954, Newark, NJ; son of LaVera Conover Randolph and Leonard Randolph Sr. **Educ:** Correction Officers Training Academy, Trenton, NJ, 1981; New Jersey State Police Academy, Sea Girt, NJ, drug enforcement, 1981; Correction Officers Training Academy, Trenton, NJ, hostage negotiations hostage trainer, 1983-85; Division of Criminal Justice, Lawrenceville, NJ, co & state investigator, 1991. **Career:** New Jersey Dept of Corrections, East Jersey State Prison, correctional officer, 1979-90, internal affairs inc, 1990-. **Orgs:** 1st vice pres, National Board of Men & Women for Justice, 1989-; president, Men & Women for Justice, New Jersey Chapter, 1989-; chapter delegate, Men & Women for Justice to New Jersey Council of Charter Member of the National Black Police Assn, 1988-; chapter delegate, Men & Women for Justice, to National Black Police Assn, 1988-. **Business Addr:** Senior Investigator, East Jersey State Prison, Dept of Corrections Internal Affairs Unit, Lock Bag ''R'', Rahway, NJ 07065.

RANDOLPH, LONNIE MARCUS
State senator, attorney. **Personal:** Born Aug 7, 1949, Auburn, AL; son of Gertha Mae French and Charles Boyd French; married Linda Diane Johnson Randolph, Aug 25, 1973; children: Lakesha, Lonnie Marcus II. **Educ:** Northern Illinois University, BS, 1973; John Marshall Law School, JD, 1978. **Career:** State of Illinois, assistant state's attorney, 1978-79; State of Indiana, deputy prosecutor, 1979-81; self employed, attorney, 1981-; State of Indiana, state senator, 1992-. **Orgs:** NAACP, board mem, 1983-; Lions Club, 1983-; Exchange Club, 1983-; Boys Club, advisory board mem. **Honors/Awds:** Northern Illinois University, Talent Award, 1972; East Chicago, John Marshall Law School Service Award, 1991; NAACP, Recognition Award; Indiana State Senate, Freshman Legislator of the Year, 1991; Black Law Student Association, Spark Plug Award, 1978; Fred Hampton Scholarship Fund, Image Award, 1983. **Business Addr:** Attorney, Lonnie M Randolph & Associates, 1919 E Columbus Dr, East Chicago, IN 46312, (219)397-5531.

RANDOLPH, LOUIS T.
Business executive. **Personal:** Born May 5, 1928, Washington, NC; married Betty Jean Barr; children: Naomi Ann. **Educ:** NC Central U, BS 1951. **Career:** Randolph Funeral Home, owner funeral serv dir; Wash NC, mayor pro-tem; VA Washongton, educator 1951-52. **Orgs:** Chmn bd of trst Beaufort Co Tech Inst; mem Human Rel Coun; bd dir Nat Funeral Dir & Morticians Assn Inc; Odd Fellow Lodge; IBPOE of W; Masonic Lodge; NC Assn of Educators; NEA; Elite Club; life mem Kappa Alpha Psi; sec bd of gov Univ of NC; mem United Supreme Cncl Ancient & Accepted Scottish Rite of Freemasonry So Jurisdiction Prince Hall Aff 32nd degree; life mem NAACP; bd dir Grtr Washington C of C. **Honors/Awds:** Oustndg ldrshp awd Funeral Dir & Morticians Assoc of NC Inc 1971, 1972; man of yr E Dist Funeral Dir & Morticians Assn 1971-72; Nat Mortician of Yr 1975-76; distngd serv awd Princee Hall Free & Accepted Masons of NC; man of yr Kappa Alpha Psi Frat 1976; outsdng citz of Beauford Co & Wash NC 1976; distgsd serv awd Funeral Dir & Morticians Assn 1977. **Business Addr:** 208 W 4 St, Washington, NC 27889.

RANDOLPH, ROBERT LEE
Educator/economist. **Personal:** Born Jan 2, 1926, East St Louis, IL; children: Heather. **Educ:** DePauw Univ, AB 1948; Univ IL Urbana, MS 1954, PhD 1958; Case Western Reserve Univ 1960, Univ of MI 1962, Postdoctoral study. **Career:** Springfield Coll MA, from instructor to assoc prof 1958-65, chmn dept 1960-63, dir evening and summer schs 1960-64; Job Corps, deputy assoc dir 1965-67; Equal Employment Oppor Commn Washington, dep exec dir 1967-68; Chicago State Univ, exec vice pres 1969-73; Westfield Coll MA, pres 1973-79; MA State Coll System, vice chancellor 1979-81; Alabama State Univ, pres 1981-83; Univ Montevallo AL, prof economics 1983-. **Orgs:** Vice pres Springfield Urban League 1962-66; pres Randolph Assocs Birmingham AL, Boston 1983-; consultant to industry; mem Amer Assoc State Colls & Univs, Amer Assoc Polit and Social Scis, Amer Economic Assoc, Phi Delta Kappa, Alpha Phi Omega, Kappa Alpha Psi. **Honors/Awds:** Danforth Foundation Awd 1943; State of IL Scholar 1952-56; Bailey Fellow 1957-58; Carnegie Fellow 1962; Vice President's Awd Excellence Pub Serv US Govt 1967; Outstanding Alumni Awd Lincoln HS East St Louis 1973.

RANDOLPH, THOMAS
Professional football player. **Personal:** Born Oct 5, 1970, Norfolk, VA. **Educ:** Kansas State, attended. **Career:** New York Giants, defensive back, 1994-. **Business Addr:** Professional Football Player, New York Giants, Giants Stadium, East Rutherford, NJ 07073, (201)935-8111.

RANDOLPH, TONI REGINA
News director. **Personal:** Born Nov 20, 1962, Buffalo, NY; daughter of Sarah Lee Randolph. **Educ:** State University College at Buffalo, Buffalo, MY, BA, 1984; Columbia University Graduate Schools of Journalism, New York, NY, MS, 1988. **Career:** WBLK-FM, Buffalo, NY, news director, 1986; WYRK-FM, Buffalo, NY, news assistant, 1987; WBFO-FM, Buffalo, NY, news director, 1988-. **Orgs:** Member, National Association of Black Journalists, 1987-; member, Society of Professional Journalists, 1987. **Honors/Awds:** Residency-Report for NPR, National Public Radio, 1989. **Business Addr:** News Director, WBFO-FM, 3435 Main St, Allen Hall, Buffalo, NY 14214.

RANDOLPH, WILLIE LARRY, JR.
Professional baseball assistant general manager. **Personal:** Born Jul 6, 1954, Holly Hill, SC; married Gretchen Foster; children: Daniesha, Chantre, Andre, Ciara. **Career:** Pittsburgh Pirates, infielder, 1975; New York Yankees, infielder, 1976-88; Los Angeles Dodgers, infielder, 1989-90; Oakland Athletics, infielder, 1990; Milwaukee Brewers, infielder, 1991-92; New York Mets, 1992-93; New York Yankees, asst general mgr, 1993-. **Honors/Awds:** James P Dawson Award, 1976; Topps All-Rookie team, 1976; named to AP, UPI and TSN All-Star Teams, 1977; tied a major league record for most assists by a second baseman in extra-inning game since 1900 with 13, August 25, 1976; American League All-Star Team, 1977, 1980, 1981, 1987; National League All-Star Team, 1989. **Business Addr:** Professional Baseball Player, New York Yankees, Yankee Stadium, Bronx, NY 10451.

RANDOLPH-JASMINE, CAROL DAVIS
Television anchor, lawyer. **Personal:** Born in St Louis, MO; daughter of Clarice and John Davis; married Frank Jasmine, Jan 1, 1980. **Educ:** Catholic Univ, Law Degree; Washington Univ, St Louis, Masters; Fisk Univ, BA. **Career:** Washington Times, columnist, 1987-88; WUSA Television, talk show host, 1987-90; Gold, Farb, Kaufman, lawyer, 1987-90; O'Toole and Rothwell, lawyer, 1990-93; Court TV, anchor, 1993-. **Orgs:** DC Commission on the Arts, commissioner, 1987-; Women's Museum, advisory board; AFTRA, 1970-; Zonta, 1992-; Links Inc, president, vice president, 1984-; ACLU, nomination committee, 1988-93. **Honors/Awds:** Bowie, doctorate. **Business Addr:** Anchor, Court TV, 600 3rd Ave. Btw. 39th & 40th, 2nd Fl., New York, NY 10016, (212)692-7851.

RANGEL, CHARLES B.
Congressman. **Personal:** Born Jun 11, 1930, New York, NY; married Alma Carter Rangel; children: Steven, Alicia. **Educ:** NY Univ, BS Bus Admin 1957; St Johns Univ Law School, LLB 1960, JD 1968. **Career:** Weaver Evans Wingate & Wright, attny 1960; US Attny So Dist of NY, asst attny 1961; NY State Assembly, mem 1967-70; US House of Rep, congressman 1970-. **Orgs:** Mem House Judiciary Comm 1973-74; chmn Congressional Black Caucus 1974-75; mem House Comm on Ways and Means 1975-; mem House Select Comm on Narcotics Abuse & Control 1976-82; chmn House Select Comm on Narcotics Abuse & Control 1983-93; dean, NY State Congressional Delegation, 1993-; Joint Committee on Taxation, 1995-; Congressional Advisory to the US Trade Representative, 1995-; President's Export Council, 1995-; mem New York Bar Assn; mem 369th Vet Assn. **Military Serv:** AUS Sgt 1948-52; Bronze Star, Purple Heart, US Korean Presidential Citations, Four Battle Stars. **Business Addr:** Representative, US House of Representatives, 2354 Rayburn Office Building, Washington, DC 20515.

RANKIN, EDWARD ANTHONY
Surgeon. **Personal:** Born Jul 6, 1940, Holly Springs, MS; son of Robbie Lee Rankin and Edgar E Rankin Jr; married Dr Frances Espy; children: Tony Jr, Marc. **Educ:** Lincoln Univ (MO), BS 1961; Meharry Med Coll (TN), MD 1965. **Career:** Howard Univ School of Med, asst prof 1973-78, assoc prof 1978-89, professor 1989-; Georgetown Univ School of Med, assoc prof 1982-; Providence Hospital, chief of orthopaedic surgery. **Orgs:** Pres Washington Ortho Soc 1982; sec tres 1983, pres 1989-; Washington Soc for Surgery Hand 1983-; delegate bd coun Am Acad Ortho Surgery 1982-; comm mem Regl Advisors Am Acad Ortho Surgery 1984-; comm mem Regl Advisors Am Coll Surgeons 1980-; oral examiner Am Bd Ortho Surgery 1980-84, 1993-; editorial Bd, Sports Medicine Today; Chief Orthopedics, Providence Hosp; pres, Metro Washington Society for Surgery of the Hand 1989; vice pres, Metro Washington Chapter, American College of Surgery 1989, president 1991; program chmn, Liberia Project, Ortho Overseas 1989; American Ortho Assn 1988; Washington Academy of Surgery 1989-, pres 1998; Am Acad Ortho Surgeons, bd of dir, member-at-large, 1996-98. **Honors/Awds:** Bronze Star USNA (Vietnam) 1971; army comm medical USNA 1973; public works 2 Chptr. **Military Serv:** US Army, major 1965-73. **Business Addr:** 1160 Varnum St NE, Suite 312, Washington, DC 20017.

RANKIN, MARLENE OWENS
Foundation executive. **Personal:** Born Apr 19, 1939, Cleveland, OH; daughter of Minnie Ruth Solomon Owens and James Cleveland (Jesse) Owens; married Stuart McLean Rankin, Nov 19, 1961; children: Stuart Owen. **Educ:** Ohio State University, Columbus, OH, BSW, 1961; University of Chicago, IL, MSW, 1978. **Career:** Cook County Department of Public Aid, Children's Division, Chicago, IL, social worker, 1961-66; Chicago Youth Centers/Project Learn, Chicago, IL, social worker, 1968-69; Chicago Committee on Urban Opportunity/Model Cities, Chicago, IL, planning unit coordinator, 1969-74; Governor's Office of Human Resources, social service planner, 1974-75; United Charities of Chicago, IL, clinical social worker, personnel associate, director of personnel, 1978-90; Museum of Science and Industry, Chicago, IL, director of human resource management, 1990-91; The Jesse Owens Foundation, Chicago, IL, executive director, 1991-. **Orgs:** Member, board of directors, University of Chicago School of Social Service Administration, 1990-93; member, Academy of Certified Social Workers, 1980-; sustaining member, board of directors, Hyde Park Neighborhood Club, 1985-; member, board of directors, City of Chicago Board of Ethics, 1987-92; member, board of directors, The Jesse Owens Foundation, 1980-; chairman, OSU Annual Fund, 1991-95; board of directors, OSU Alumni Association, 1985-90; board of directors, Sporting Chance Foundation, 1995-. **Honors/Awds:** OSU Distinguished Service Award, 1993; Annual Orchid Award, Top Ladies of Distinction, 1992; 100 Women Making A Difference, *Today's Chicago Woman*, 1992. **Business Addr:** Executive Director, The Jesse Owens Foundation, 401 N Michigan Ave, Suite 290, Chicago, IL 60611, (312)527-3311.

RANKIN, MICHAEL L.
Judge. **Personal:** marrIed Zinora M. Mitchell; children: Lee, John-Michael, Michael Joseph, Everette. **Educ:** Howard University School of Law, JD. **Career:** United States Attorney's Office Felony Trial Division, Washington, DC, deputy chief; Superior Court of the District of Columbia, Washington, DC, judge, 1985-, Criminal Div, dep presiding judge, currently. **Orgs:** Charlotte E Ray America Inn of Court, Master. **Business Addr:** Judge, Superior Court of Washington, DC, 500 Indiana Ave NW, Chamber Room 2620, Washington, DC 20001.

RANN, EMERY LOUVELLE
Physician (retired). **Personal:** Born Mar 9, 1914, Keyestone, WV; son of Vicie Froe and Emery Rann Sr; married Flossie Aurelia Fox; children: Judith Rann Thompson, Emery L III, J D, Lara Diane, Jonathan Cheshire, Flossie Aurelia. **Educ:** JC Smith U, BS (cum laude) 1934; Univ MI, MS 1936; Meharry Med Coll, MD 1948; Johnson C Smith U, ScD (Hon) 1981. **Career:** Old N State Med Soc, pres 1959; Mecklenburg Co Med Soc, v pres 1958; NC Acad Fmly Pract, dist dir 1981; Imhotep Conf (For Hosp Integ), chrmn 1961-63. **Orgs:** Pres Natl Med Assn 1973-74; fellow Amer Acad Family Practice 1975; mem past chmn bd of trustees, Johnson C Smith Univ 1966-; boule sire archon Sigma Pi Phi Fraternity 1968; Alpha Phi Alpha (Life Mem) 1931-. **Honors/Awds:** Award of Merit, Johnson C Smith Univ 1954, 1968; Doctor of the Year Old N State 1961; Charlotte Med Soc 1972; ZOB mert ZOB Sor 1981; mer scs awd

Family Practice Div NMA 1984; initiated into Alpha Omega Alpha Meharry Chapter, 1991; Southeast Regional Sire Archon, Sigma Pi Phi, 1989-91. **Military Serv:** USNA capt 1955-57. **Home Addr:** 4301 Hamilton Cir, Charlotte, NC 28216.

RANSBURG, FRANK S.
Educator. **Personal:** Born Jan 29, 1943, Keatchie, LA; married Ivory Bowie; children: Ursula. **Educ:** So U, BA 1965; LA State U, MA 1970; Loyala University-New Orleans, Graduate Institute of Politics, 1994. **Career:** Southern Univ, counselor 1965-69, asst dean men 1969, instructor 1969-; Jr Div LA State Univ, counselor 1969-73; HS Rel LA State Univ, named asst dir 1975; Southern Univ, dean of student act 1969-81, director of international student affairs, 1981-87, director of planning, 1987-91, assistant to chancellor, 1991-97; vice chancellor for student affairs, 1997-; Cleo Fields for Governor, state campaign manager. **Orgs:** Adminstr asst Lt Gov's Office summers 1973, 1974; mem LA Commn on Campaign Prac 1974; mem Am Polit Sci Assn; So Polit Sci Assn; AAUP; NAACP; Am Personnel & Guid Assn; Nat Assn Personnel Workers. **Honors/Awds:** Faculty Awd So Univ 1970; hon mem LA State Senate 1974.

RANSBY, BARBARA
Historian, professor, writer, community activist. **Personal:** Born May 12, 1957, Detroit, MI; married. **Educ:** Columbia Univ, BA, 1984; Univ of MI, MA, 1987, PhD, 1996. **Career:** Institute for African Affairs and Department of History, Columbia University, research asst, 1982-84; Univ of MI, instructor, 1986-87, 1989, teaching asst, 1987, research asst, 1988; Museum of African American History, curator of Nineteenth and Twentieth Century special projects, 1989-90; Chicago Clergy and Laity Concerned, group trainer, 1992; Crossroads Foundation, group trainer, 1992; DePaul Univ, instructor, 1992-95, director, asst prof, 1995-96; Ancona School, consultant, group facilitator, 1993; Chicago Historical Society, consultant, panelist, 1993; Mac Arthur Foundation, consultant, 1994; American College Testing, consultant, 1996; Univ of IL at Chicago, asst prof, 1996-; Northwestern University, manuscript reviewer, 1997. **Orgs:** Anti-Racism Institute, Clergy and Laity Concerned, bd mem; Chicago Coalition in Solidarity with Southern Africa, bd mem; Univ of MI, History Dept Search Committee, student mem; Editorial Board of the Journal Race and Class; Ella Baker-Nelson Mandela Center for Anti-Racist Education, Univ of MI, bd mem; Association for the Study of Afro-American Life and History; Association of Black Women Historians; Coordinating Committee for Women in the Historical Profession; Organization of American Historians; United Coalition Against Racism, co-founder; Free South Africa Coordinating Committee, co-founder, co-chair. **Honors/Awds:** Univ of MI, Student Recognition Award for Leadership, 1987; Women's Action for Nuclear Disarmament, Annual Peace Award, 1988; Columbia University, Herman Ausubel Student Award for Achievement in History, 1983; Univ of MI, Women Studies Program fellow, 1986; Univ of MI, Student Essay Competition Award, 1986; Woodrow Wilson Fellowships Foundation, National Mellon Fellowship, 1984-86; Univ of MI Rackham Graduate School Fellowships, Michigan Minority Merit Fellowship, 1986-90; Ford Foundation and Center for Afro-American and African Studies, Grad Student Research grant, 1990; DePaul Univ School of Liberal Arts and Sciences, Summer Faculty Research Award, 1993; Univ of IL at Chicago, Office of Social Science Research Seed Fund Initiative, grant, 1996. **Special Achievements:** Annual Anheiser Bush Martin Luther King Jr Essay Contest, reader judge; African American Women in Defense of Ourselves, an ad campaign, one of the founders; Author, works include: "Ella Baker and the Black Radical Tradition," U of NC Press, 1999; "Black Women and the Black Freedom Movement: Following Ella Baker's Path", 1998; "US: The Black Poor and the Politics of Expendability", Race and Class, 1996; numerous articles and essays. **Business Addr:** Asst Professor of African American Studies and History, University of Illinois at Chicago, 601 S Morgan, M/C 069, Chicago, IL 60607, (312)996-2961.

RANSIER, FREDERICK L., III
Attorney. **Personal:** Born Dec 3, 1949, Brooklyn, NY; son of Doris A Ransier and Frederick L Ransier Jr; married Kathleen Hayes, Nov 16, 1973; children: Bradley, Charles, Frederick IV. **Educ:** Central State University, BA, 1971; Ohio State University College of Law, JD, 1974. **Career:** Ohio Attorney General, assistant attorney general, 1974-76; Ransier & Ransier, partner, 1976-. **Orgs:** Columbus Bar Association, 1974-; National Bar Association; Ohio State Bar Association; American Bar Association; Office of the United States Trustee, panel trustee, 1988-; Columbus Municipal Civil Service Commission, commissioner, 1987-, president 1994-; Village of Urbancrest, Ohio, law dir, 1978-; Central State Univ Bd of Trustees, chair. **Honors/Awds:** Columbus Bar Association, Community Service Award. **Business Addr:** Partner, Ransier & Ransier, 66 Thurman Ave, Columbus, OH 43206, (614)443-7429.

RANSOM, BURNELLA JACKSON. See JACKSON-RANSOM, BUNNIE.

RANSOM, GARY ELLIOTT
Judge. **Personal:** Born Dec 23, 1941, New Brunswick, NJ; married Gloria P. **Educ:** Rutgers Univ BA Econ 1965; Univ of the Pacific-McGeorge School of Law, JD 1974. **Career:** Sacramento Cty Publ Defenders Office, asst publ defender 1974-81; Court of Appeals-Third Appellate Dist, justice pro tem 1983; NJ Div on Civil Rights, field rep 1965-66; Sacramento Municipal Cty Dist, judge 1981-88; California Superior Court, judge 1988-. **Orgs:** Bd of dir Planned Parenthood Assn of Sacramento 1978-81; pres Wiley Manuel Bar Assn 1981; bd of dir Family Serv Agency of Greater Sacramento 1981-; mem CA Judges Assn 1981-; mem Sigma Pi Phi, Gamma Epsilon Boule, Prince Hall F&AM 33rd Deg; life mem Kappa Alpha Psi; bd dir Easter Seals Soc of Gr Sacramento 1978-; life mem No CA Peace Officers Assn; vice pres CA Assoc of Black lawyers 1981; mem Intl Platform Assn; pres, bd of dirs Greater Sacramento Easter Seals Society 1988-. **Honors/Awds:** Phi Nu Pi Awd from Kappa Alpha Psi Frat 1981; Sacramento Wardens & Masters Achievement Awd 1982; Earnest E Robinson Jr Awd Black Law Students Assoc of Univ of the Pacific 1982; Justice Pro Tem Court of Appeals Third Appellate Dist 1983; Bernard S Jefferson Jurist Award, California Assn of Black Lawyers 1989; Friends Outside, McKusick Award, 1994. **Military Serv:** USAF capt 1966-71. **Home Addr:** 1406 Commons Dr, Sacramento, CA 95825. **Business Addr:** Judge, Superior Court of the State of California, County Courthouse, 720 9th St, Sacramento, CA 95814, (916)874-5243.

RANSOM, LILLIE
Educational administrator. **Career:** Maryland School for the Deaf, pres, currently. **Orgs:** Maryland School for the Deaf, bd of trustees, vice chair. **Business Phone:** (301)662-4159.

RANSOM, NORMAN
Clergyman. **Personal:** Born Aug 23, 1923, St Stephen, SC; married Martha Cole; children: Helen, Alice, Norman Jr, Melvin. **Educ:** SC State Coll, BS 1948, PE 1951, Masters 1951; AL A&M Coll, Chem 1955; MI Tech Univ, PhD & BS physics 1966; Duke Univ, DD 1970. **Career:** Orangeburg SC, athlete 1946-51; Cainhoy HS, teacher/coach 1949-54, admin 1957-69; Alston HS, teacher/coach 1969-79; St Stephen SC, councilmember 1974-85; Cainhoy HS, admin 1979-84; United Methodist Church, minister 1960-85. **Orgs:** Commissioned notary public SC 1950-85; athletic dir SC League 1953-77; mgr McGowan Corp 1967-71; sec Snack Land Corp 1973-74; ordained minister SC Conf 1974-85; sec United Supreme Council 1975-84; dir St Stephen Play Ground 1975-80. **Honors/Awds:** Most Valuable SC State Coll 1946-48; Pass Tryouts Pittsburgh Pirates, St Louis Cardinals 1946; All Amer SC State Coll 1947-48; Athletic Awd & Achievement SC League 1976; many trophies and plaques in high school and college. **Military Serv:** USN warren officer 3 yrs 8 mos; Pass Examination Officers Training 1944. **Home Addr:** PO Box 295, St Stephen, SC 29479.

RANSOM, PRESTON L.
Educator, educational administrator. **Personal:** Born Jan 2, 1936, Peoria, IL; son of Spezzie and James; married Mildred D Murphy; children: Patricia Lynn, Michael Murphy. **Educ:** Univ of IL at Urbana-Champaign, BS 1962, MS 1965, PhD 1969. **Career:** Raytheon Co Bedford MA, electrical engr 1962-63; Univ of IL, grad rsch asst 1963-67, instr 1967-70, asst prof electrical engr dept 1970-72, assoc prof electrical engr l972-88, prof elec engr, l988-; asst dean and dir cont engineer educ, l988-. **Orgs:** Sr mem Inst of Elec & Electronic Engrs 1970-; mem Amer Soc of Engrg Educ 1972-; mem Optical Soc of Amer 1972-. **Honors/Awds:** Paul V Golvin Teaching Fellow Univ of IL 1967-68; Hon Rsch Fellow Univ Coll London 1976; Ete Kappa Nu Honorary Soc. **Business Addr:** Asst Dean, Prof, Univ of Illinois at Urbana-Champaign, 422 Engineering Hall, 1308 W Green St, Urbana, IL 61801.

RAO, KODURU V. S.
College administrator. **Personal:** Born Mar 1, 1940, Vigayawada, IN; married Beverlye Taylor; children: Kishore, Kristina. **Educ:** Andhra Univ India, BA 1959, MA 1962, LLB 1965; Atlanta Univ, MBA 1967. **Career:** FL Memorial Coll, vice pres for business & fiscal affairs. **Orgs:** Mem Natl Assoc of Coll and Univ Business Officers 1975-; consultant Robert R Moton Memorial Inst 1975-86; consultant Business Mgmt 1975-; mem Alpha Phi Alpha Frat 1977-; consultant ISATIM Amer Council on Educ 1983-; mem Natl Assoc of Black Accountants 1985-; mem Small Colls and Minority Institutions Comm 1986-. **Honors/Awds:** Grantsmanship US Education Dept 1977. **Home Addr:** 20049 NW 65 Ct, Miami, FL 33015.

RAPHAEL, BERNARD JOSEPH
Educational administrator. **Personal:** Born May 4, 1935, Rock Castle, VA; married Lynne Keyes. **Educ:** Xavier Univ of LA, BA 1959; St Thomas Coll, MA 1968; Univ of No CO, EdD 1976. **Career:** MN Public Schools, teacher/writer coord 1966-67; Hopkins Public Schools, teacher 1967-68; Normandale Comm Coll, chmn div eng 1968-71, dir coop ed 1971-75, assoc dean/instruction 1975-. **Orgs:** Consult Twin Cities OIC 1966-72; mem Affairs Natl Coun Teachers of English 1971-73, Commiss of Curriculum & Intercultural; pres MN Council Teacher of English1973-74; consult US Dept of Ed 1973-; pres Phi Delta Kappa 1975-76. **Honors/Awds:** Excellence in English Xavier Univ New Orleans 1959; Bush Summer Fellow Bush Found St Paul 1975; Harvard Univ Mgmt Lifelong Ed 1984; Publication, Cooperative Education in Higher Ed Univ of No CO; Fulbright Fellow to West Germany, administrator's prgm spring 1986. **Business Addr:** Associate Dean of Instruction, Normandale Community College, 9700 France Ave S, Bloomington, MN 55431.

RASBERRY, ROBERT EUGENE
Clergyman, educatar. **Personal:** Born in Philadelphia, PA; married Gloria E Hooper; children: Roslyn, Robert, John, Denise. **Educ:** Morgan State Coll, AB 1955; Howard U, sch of soc work 1956; NY U, MA 1958; Andover-Newton Theol Sch, BD 1966. **Career:** Bethany Baptist Church Syracuse NY, pastor; Mt Calvary Baptist Church Springfield MA, pastor 1965-73; Episcopal Church of Atonement Westerfield MA, asst to rector 1970-72; Messiah Bapt, pastor 1962-65; Friendship Bapt, pastor 1959-62; First Bapt, pastor 1957-59; Springfield Tech Comm Coll, asst prof 1969-73; Bureau of Child Welfare NYC, social investigator 1956-57; Big Bros of Baltimore, social case worker 1954-56. **Orgs:** Exec com Am Assn of Univ Prof; Urban Leag; Human Righst Commn; Protestant Comm Ministries; bd dir Syracuse Univ Hill Corp Syracuse Chap OIC's of Am; coun of rep NY State Counc of Chs; past exec com TABCOM; assn moderatr Pioneer Valley Am Bapt Chs of MA. **Honors/Awds:** Host producer WSYR Words & Music for a Sunday Morning Syracuse; ten most watchable men Post-Standard Newspaper Syracuse 1977; Nat Forsensic Coun; natl hon soc Philosophy. **Business Addr:** 601 Irving Ave, Syracuse, NY 13210.

RASBY, WALTER HERBERT
Professional football player. **Personal:** Born Sep 7, 1972, Washington, DC; married Cortney. **Educ:** Wake Forest. **Career:** Pittsburgh Steelers, tight end, 1994; Carolina Panthers, 1995-. **Business Addr:** Professional Football Player, Carolina Panthers, 800 Mint St, Ericsson Stadium, Charlotte, NC 28202, (704)358-7000.

RASHAD, AHMAD (BOBBY MOORE)
Sportscaster. **Personal:** Born Nov 19, 1949, Portland, OR; married Phylicia Allen, 1986; children: Keva, Maiysha, Ahmad Jr, Condola Phylea. **Educ:** Univ of Oregon, degree in education. **Career:** Wide receiver: St Louis Cardinals, 1972-73, Buffalo Bills, 1974-76, Seattle Seahawks, 1976, Minnesota Vikings, 1976-82; KMSP-TV, Minneapolis, MN, host monday night football preview show; WCCO-TV, Minneapolis, MN, sports reporter; NBC Sports, host, 1982-. **Honors/Awds:** Played NFL Champ Game 1976; set NFL record for longest non-scoring play from scrimmage when he caught a 98 yd pass from Jim Hart 1972; caught more passes (250) as wide receiver in four years with Vikings than any other wide receiver in NFL during that time; All Am Running Back; All Conf 3 Times; Pro Bowl 1979; author, Vikes, Mikes and Something on the Backside, 1988. **Business Addr:** NBC, 30 Rockefeller Plaza, New York, NY 10020.

RASHAD, JOHARI MAHASIN
Government official, freelance writer. **Personal:** Born Mar 13, 1951, Washington, DC; daughter of Millie Lucerita Adams & Henry Jones; children: Chekesha Wajeehah Rashad. **Educ:** Howard Univ, BA, 1976; Univ of the Dist of Columbia, MBA, 1981. **Career:** US Customs Service, GS-4, clerk typist, 1976; US Civil Service Comm, standardization specialist, 1976; Office of Personal Management, instructor, 1980; US Coast Guard, employee devt specialist, 1986; Bureau of Land Management, employee devt specialist, currently. **Orgs:** American Assn of Univ Women; Amer Society for Training & Devt; International Communication Assn; National Assn of Female Execs; National Careet Devt Assn. **Honors/Awds:** Bureau of Land Management, Special Achievement Award, 1992; Downtown Jaycees, Exceptional Service Award, 1984. **Business Addr:** Employment Devt Specialist, US Dept of the Interior/Bureau of Land Management, 1849 C Street, NW (WO-510), Washington, DC 20240, (202)208-6551.

RASHAD, PHYLICIA
Performing artist. **Personal:** Born Jun 19, 1948, Houston, TX; daughter of Vivian Ayers Allen and Andrew A Allen; married William Lancelot Bowles Jr (divorced 1975); children: William Lancelot III; married Victor Willis, 1978 (divorced 1980); married Ahmad Rashad, Dec 1986; children: Condola Phylea, 3 stepchildren. **Educ:** Howard University, BFA (magna cum laude), 1970. **Career:** Off-Broadway and Broadway actress, including: Into the Woods; Dreamgirls; The Whiz; Ain't Supposed to Die a Natural Death; television shows include: soap opera, "One Life to Live"; situation comedy, "The Cosby Show", 1984-92; "Cosby", currently; television films include: "Uncle Tom's Cabin", 1987; "False Witness", 1989; "Polly", 1989; "Polly Once Again", 1990; "Jailbirds", 1990. **Orgs:** Board of directors, Recruiting New Teachers, 1990-; spokesperson, Cancer Information Service, 1990-91; spokesperson, Save the Children, 1989-91. **Honors/Awds:** 2 Emmy nominations for "The Cosby Show"; 2 People's Choice Awards for most popular actress on network television; NAACP Image Award as the best actress in a comedy series for 3 consecutive seasons; Ace Award nomination for best supporting actress in television film "Uncle Tom's Cabin"; Outstanding Achievement Award, Women in Film, 1991; Honoree of the Year, Harvard Foundation, 1991; Honorary Doctorate, Providence College, Providence, RI, 1991; Honorary Doctorate of Humanities, Barber-Scotia College, Concord, NC, 1989.

RASHEED, FRED
Association executive. **Career:** NAACP, past co-interim executive director, director of economic development, currently. **Business Addr:** Director of Economic Development, NAACP, 586 Central Ave, Ste 10, East Orange, NJ 07018, (201)672-0211.

RASHEED, HOWARD S.
Financial executive. **Personal:** Born Feb 3, 1953, Chicago, IL; son of Kathlene P. Lee and Howard L. Lee, Sr.; married Barbara; children: Candace, Derick, Hassan, Mikal. **Educ:** Univ of West FL, BS Marketing 1978, MBA Finance 1979. **Career:** FSC Business Development, financial analyst 1973-74; AMM Journal, purchasing mgr 1974-75; Southern Bell, account exec 1978-83; Ver Val Enterprises, dir of finance 1983-87. **Orgs:** Dir Pensacola Private Industry Council 1982-85; mem Assoc of MBA Execs 1983-87; commissioner Pensacola-Escambia Develop Commn 1984; dir Ft Walton Beach Comm of 100 1986-; mem Natl Black MBA Assoc 1987. **Home Addr:** 16 Neptune Dr, Mary Esther, FL 32569.

RASHEED, JEROME NAJEE. See NAJEE.

RASHFORD, JOHN HARVEY
Educator, anthropologist. **Personal:** Born May 10, 1947, Port Antonio Jamaica, West Indies; son of Winifred Jacobs Rashford and Hector G Rashford; married Grace Maynard. **Educ:** Friends World Coll, BA 1969; CUNY Grad Center, MA, PhD 1982. **Career:** Crossroads Africa, group leader 1971; CUNY, adjunct lecturer: Brooklyn Coll, 1974-75, Queens Coll, 1977-80, Lehman Coll, 1977-82; Rutgers Univ, visiting lecturer 1980-82; Coll of Charleston, associate prof anthropology, currently. **Orgs:** Mem Soc for Econ Botany 1979-, SC Acad of Science 1982-; clerk, Charleston Friends Quaker Meeting 1984-; mem, editorial bd, SC Historical Soc, 1989-. **Honors/Awds:** Distinguished Service Award, Omicron Delta Kappa, 1989; Phi Kappa Phi, Coll of Charleston, 1989. **Business Addr:** Associate Professor of Anthropology, College of Charleston, Department of Sociology/Anthropolgy, 66 George St, Charleston, SC 29401, (803)953-5738.

RASPBERRY, WILLIAM J.
Columnist. **Personal:** Born Oct 12, 1935, Okolona, MS; married Sondra Dodson; children: Patricia D, Angela D, Mark J. **Educ:** Indiana Central Coll, BS 1958; Indiana Univ, additional study; George Washington Univ. **Career:** The Indianapolis Recorder, reporter, editor 1956-60; WTTG Washington, TV commentator 1973; Howard Univ, instr journalism 1971-; Washington Post, columnist 1962-; Duke University School of Public Policy, professor, 1995-. **Orgs:** Mem Grid Iron Club; National Press Club; Capitol Press Club; National Association of Black Journalists; Wash Assoc of Black Journalists, Kappa Alpha Psi. **Honors/Awds:** Winner of several awds for interpretive & reporting; served on Pulitzer Prize Jury 1975-79; mem Pulitzer Prize Bd 1980-86; winner of Pulitzer Prize, 1994. **Military Serv:** AUS 1960-62. **Business Addr:** Columnist, Washington Post, 1150 15th St, NW, Washington, DC 20071.

RATCLIFF, WESLEY D.
Computer services executive. **Career:** Advanced Technological Solutions Inc, CEO, currently. **Special Achievements:** Company is ranked #99 on Black Enterprise magazine's 1997 list of Top 100 Black businesses. **Business Addr:** CEO, Advanced Technological Solutions Inc, 585 DeKalb Ave, Brooklyn, NY 11205, (718)780-2100.

RATCLIFFE, ALFONSO F. (RICK)
Educational administrator. **Personal:** Born Oct 21, 1928, St Louis, MO; son of Alice Elizabeth Carter Ratcliffe and William Morgan Ratcliffe; married Dolores Corita Potter Ratcliffe, Jan 16, 1969. **Educ:** UCLA, BA, physics, 1951, MS, engineering, 1963, PhD, engineering, 1970. **Career:** Ogden Technology, Monterey Park, CA, dir, special projects, 1955-69; Audio Magnetics Corp, Gardena, CA, mgr, special projects, 1973-74; Mattel, Inc, Hawthorne, CA, staff engineer, 1969-73, 1974-75; California State University, Northridge, CA, professor of engineering, 1975-80, assoc dean of engineering, 1980-81, dean of engineering, beginning 1981, dean emeritus, currently. **Orgs:** Board member 1984-86, 1987-88, chair 1986-87, Pacific Southwest Section of American Society for Engineering Education; chairman 1988-90, board member 1990-91, San Fernando Valley Engineers' Council. **Honors/Awds:** Senior Member, Institute of Electrical and Electronic Engineers, 1978; Fellow, Institute for Advancement of Engineering, 1983; Distinguished Engineer, Tau Beta Pi Engineering Honorary Society, 1981; Educator of the Year, Society of Manufacturing Engineers, Region VII, 1982; Distinguished Professional Engineering Education Achievements Award, National Society of Professional Engineers, 1987. **Military Serv:** US Army, Corporal, 1946-48. **Business Addr:** Dean Emeritus, Engineering and Computer Science, California State University at Northridge, 18111 Nordhoff St, EN IOI, Northridge, CA 91330.

RATES, NORMAN M.
Clergyman. **Personal:** Born Jan 1, 1924, Owensboro, KY; married Laura Lynem; children: Sondra, Shari. **Educ:** KY State Coll, AB 1947; Lincoln Univ, BD 1950; Oberlin Coll, MDiv 1952; Yale Univ, MAR 1961; Vanderbilt Univ, DMin 1974; Oberlin Coll, STM 1953; Harvard Univ, independent study 1968-69. **Career:** Camac Comm Ctr Phila, student counselor 1947-48; Philadelphia Gen Hosp, asst to protestant chaplain 1948-49; St Paul Bapt Ch W Chester PA, asst to pastor 1949-50; Div of Home Missions Natl Council for Ch of Christ in USA NY FL DE, missionary to agricultural migrants 1948-56; Morris Coll, minister dean of men tchr 1953-54; Morehouse Spelman Coll Pre-Coll Prog summers, counselor & minister 1966-67; Central Brooklyn Model Cities Summer Acad Spelman Coll summer, couns 1972; Interdenom Theol Ctr, guest lectr & part-time tchr 1971; Westhills Presb Ch GA summer, interim pastor 1963; Spelman Coll GA Dept of Religion, coll minister & chmn 1954-. **Orgs:** Mem Natl Assn of Coll & Univ Chaplains; mem Ministry to Blacks in Higher Educ; mem Amer Assn of Univ Profs; mem Natl Assn of Biblical Instr; mem Univ Ctr in GA Div of Tchr of Religion; Petit Juror Fulton Co Superior Ct 1971, 1973; grand juror Fulton Co Superior Ct 1972; ministerial standing The United Ch of Christ; Fellow Conf on African & African-Amer Studies Atlanta Univ Campus; bd mem Camping Unlimited Blue Star Camps Inc; bd dir Planned Parenthood Assn of Atlanta; chmn Religious Affairs Com Planned Parenthood Assn of Atlanta; mem Com on the Ministry The United Ch of Christ; mem The Metro Atlanta Christian Council; mem GA-SC Assn of the United Ch of Christ SE Conf; mem Alpha Phi Alpha Frat. **Honors/Awds:** C Morris Cain Prize in Bible Lincoln Univ 1949; Samuel Dickey Prize in New Testament Lincoln Univ 1949; Campus Christian Worker Grant Danforth Found 1960-61; Atlanta Univ Ctr Non-Western Studies Prog Grant for Travel & Study Ford Found 1968-69. **Business Addr:** College Minister/Chmn, Dept Religion, Spelman College, 350 Spelman Lane SW, Atlanta, GA 30314.

RATHMAN, THOMAS DEAN
Professional football player. **Personal:** Born Oct 7, 1962, Grand Island, NE. **Educ:** Univ of Nebraska, attended. **Career:** San Francisco 49ers, fullback, 1986-. **Honors/Awds:** Postseason play, 1988, 1989: NFC Championship Game, NFL Championship Game.

RATLIFF, JOE SAMUEL
Minister. **Personal:** Born Jul 24, 1950, Lumberton, NC; married Doris Gardner. **Educ:** Morehouse Coll, BA 1972; Interdenominational Theol Ctr Atlanta, MDiv 1975, DMin 1976. **Career:** Cobb Memorial Church Atlanta, pastor 1971-78; Morehouse Coll, prof 1974-77; Brentwood Bapt Church Atlanta, pastor 1980-. **Orgs:** Mem bd of trustees, Morehouse School of Religion; mem bd of trustees Interdenominational Theol Ctr Atlanta 1986-. **Honors/Awds:** 1986 Minister of the Year Natl Conf of Christians and Jews. **Home Addr:** 8202 Frontenac Dr, Houston, TX 77071, (713)270-7743. **Business Addr:** Pastor, Brentwood Baptist Church, 13033 Landmark St, Houston, TX 77045, (713)729-5933.

RATLIFF, THEO CURTIS
Professional basketball player. **Personal:** Born Apr 17, 1973, Demopolis, AL. **Educ:** Wyoming. **Career:** Detroit Pistons, forward-center, 1995-97; Philadelphia 76ers, 1997-. **Special Achievements:** NBA, First Round Draft Pick, #18 Pick, 1995. **Business Addr:** Professional Basketball Player, Philadelphia 76ers, One Corestates Complex, Philadelphia, PA 19148, (215)339-7676.

RATTLEY, JESSIE M.
Educator, former city official. **Personal:** Born May 4, 1929, Birmingham, AL; daughter of Mr. and Mrs. Alonzo Menifield (deceased); widowed; children: Florence, Robin. **Educ:** Hampton Inst, BS 1951; grad courses; IBM Data Processing School; LaSalle Extension Univ. **Career:** Huntington HS Newport News, established Business Dept (the first Black High School in Newport News to offer business training to its students); Newport News City Council, 1st Black & 1st woman councilman elected 1970-86; City of Newport News, vice-mayor 1976; 1st black & 1st woman mayor 1986-90; Peninsula Bus Coll, dir; Newport News General Hospital, Newport News, VA, administrator; Harvard University, Cambridge, MA, fellow, institute of politics, 1990; Hampton University, Hampton, VA, senior lecturer, 1991-. **Orgs:** Pres Peninsula Coord Comm; mem Carver Memorial Presb Ch; hon mem Natl Assn of Negro Bus & Professional Women's Clubs;former basileus Lambda Omega Chap Alpha Kappa Alpha; mem Mental Health Bd; mem VA Peninsula Chaplaincy Svc; mem Southeastern Business Coll Assn; life mem NAACP; sponsor Delta Mu; chmn Revenue Sharing Task Force; mem City Policy Leadership Issues Task Force; mem Women in Municipal Govt Steering Comm; mem Infrastructure Task Force; appt by Gov to Criminal Justice & Crime Prevention Task Force; comm on Volunteerism; mem Special Task Force to study VA Jails; mem bd dir Public Admin Adv; vice pres bd of dir Whittaker Meml Hosp; mem bd of dir Natl Inst of Publ Mgmt; mem adv comm Inst of Govt VA; appt by Gov to Commiss on Future of Virginia; mem, Board of Trustees, St Paul's College, 199 chairman, Virginia Civil RIghts Commission, 1992-. **Honors/Awds:** Sojourner Truth Awd Natl Assn of Negro Business & Professional Women's Clubs 1978; Intl Woman of the Year Radio Sta WRAP-Norfolk VA 1979; Unique Achiev Awd for Polit Serv by Dubois Circle of Baltimore MD 1981; second annual Martin Luther King Jr Meml Awd Old Dominion Univ in recognition of lendership in social justice 1986; Presidential Award for Outstanding Citizenship, Hampton Institute; Fitz Turner Award, Virginia Minority Caucus of the Virginia Education Association; Plaque for Outstanding and Dedicated Service, Zeta Lambda Chapter, Alpha Phi Alpha Fraternity; Annie L Harvey Achievement Award, Mid-Atlantic Region Alpha Kappa Alpha Sorority, Inc; Certificate of Appreciation, Newport News Branch, NAACP.

RAUCH, DOREEN E.
University administrator. **Personal:** Born Jul 17, 1947, Port of Spain, Trinidad and Tobago; daughter of Stella M B Estrada & Joseph Fernandes (both deceased); married Terry M Rauch, Sep 2, 1969; children: Camille M Welch, J Roxanne, Jeanne M, Terry Michael. **Educ:** Univ of Cincinnati, BA, 1976; Howard Univ School of Law, JD, 1984. **Career:** Emerson Law School, faculty, 1984-89; Univ of Massachusetts-Boston, instructor, 1985-86; Massachusetts Bay Comm College, instructor, 1985-86; Murray State Univ, dir of equal opportunity & affirm action, 1991-93; Northern Michigan Univ, afirmative action officer, 1993-. **Orgs:** Natl Organization of Women, 1990-; Amer Assn of Univ Women, 1990-; Amer Assn of Univ administrators, 1995; Amer Assn of Affirmative Action, 1990-. **Honors/Awds:** Howard Univ, Amer Jurisprudence Award in Commercial Paper, 1983; Amer Jurisprudence Award in Criminal Law, 1982; Amer Jurisprudence Award in Contracts, 1983; Amer Jurisprudence Award in Municipal Law, 1982; Univ of Cincinnati, Dean's List, 1974-76. **Business Addr:** Affirmative Action Officer, Northern Michigan University, 1401 Presque Isle Avenue, Marquette, MI 49855, (906)227-2420.

RAULLERSON, CALVIN HENRY
Association executive. **Personal:** Born Dec 18, 1920, Utica, NY; son of Cora White Raullerson and Calvin T Raullerson; married Olive Lewis; children: Cheryl G, Earl Henry, Kevin Greer. **Educ:** Lincoln Univ, AB 1943; Harvard Univ, post grad 1947; NY Univ, MPA 1949. **Career:** Asst to executive dir, director, Div Educ Services, United Negro Coll Fund 1952-61; Amer Soc African Culture Lagos Nigeria, dir 1961-64; Amer Soc African Culture, exec dir 1964-66; E & So African Peace Corps, chief 1966-69; Kenya Peace Corps, dir 1969-71; Africa Peace Corps, reg dir 1971-73; Intl Ctr for Arid & Semi-Arid Land TX Tech Univ, exec asst to dean, asst prof Health Org Mgmt 1973-78; Bur Pvt Devel Coop, asst admin Agency for Intl Devel 1978-81; African Amer Inst, vice pres 1981-85; Keene Monk Assocs, assoc 1985-86; One America Inc, dir intl programs 1987-88; Labat-Anderson, Inc, pres, Intl Div, 1988-94, global business, senior proj manager, currently. **Orgs:** Rockefeller travel grantee E & Central Africa 1960; del Intl Conf on African Hist Univ Ibadan Nigeria 1962; del Intl Conf on African Affairs Univ Ghana 1963; Treasurer US Planning Comm 1st World Festival Negro Art Dakar 1965-66; mem inform resources con group on business affairs Assn Amer Med Colls; mem adv com on desentification AAAS 1976-78; clubs, Harvard, Washington ; African Wildlife Foundation, board of trustees, strategic planning committee chairman. **Honors/Awds:** Del UN Conf on Desertification Nairobi 1977; mem Career Ministers Selection Bd Dept of State 1980; asst ed & dir of rsch, Who's Who in Colored Amer; assoc ed, Who's Who in the UN; contributor Negro Yearbook; Woodrow Wilson Scholar 1978-80; head of US delegation Comm on Food Aid and Policy World Food Program Rome Italy 1980. **Military Serv:** US Army 1942-44. **Business Addr:** Sr Project Manager, Global Business, Labat-Anderson Inc, 8000 Westpark Dr, Mc Lean, VA 22102.

RAVELING, GEORGE HENRY
College basketball coach. **Personal:** Born Jun 27, 1937, Washington, DC; married Vivian James; children: Mark. **Educ:** Villanova U, BS 1960. **Career:** University of Southern California, head basketball coach, currently; University of Iowa, head basketball coach; WA State U, head basketball coach; Villanova Univ, asst basketball coach; Sun Oil Co, marketing analysis/sales rep; Converse Rubber Co, promotions rep; former syndicated newspaper columnist in Pacific Northwest; conducts annual basketball coaches clinic. **Orgs:** Mem, Natl Speakers Assn; Sports Illustrated Speakers Bur; mem, Natl Assn of Basketball Coaches; Amer Humor Studies Assn; adv bd, Uniroyal Corp, Spaulding Corp, Joseph P Kennedy Found for Mentally Retarded, Letterman Coach & Athl Mags. **Honors/Awds:** Inductee, Black Hall of Fame, Natl Black Sports Foundation; Honorary Certificate Citizenship, Kansas City & New Orleans; voted Pac-8 Coach of Year 1975; voted UPI West Coast Coach of the Year, 1975; voted National College Coach of the Year, 1977; Distinguished Alumnus and Humanitarian Awards, Villanova Univ; Certificate of Merit for Outstanding Sales, Public Relations, and Marketing, Philadelphia Tribune Newspaper.

RAVENELL, JOSEPH PHILLIP
Clergyman. **Personal:** Born Jan 20, 1940, Pinesville, SC; married Mary Jane Frazier; children: Joseph, Phillip, Byron. **Educ:** St Peters Coll, BS Hist 1973; Princeton Theol Sem, MDiv 1976. **Career:** NJ St Prison, institutional chpln; Samaritan Bapt Ch,

pastor 1979-; Trenton St Coll, coll chpln 1975-78; US Postal Svc, letter carrier 1966-75. **Orgs:** Pres of NJ Chap St Chpln Orgn 1978-; dir Com Network Proj 1979-; mem AUS Nat Guard Assn 1978-; mem Mil Chplns Assn 1978-; mem Am Correctnl Chplns Assn 1978-. **Honors/Awds:** Good Conduct Medal AUS 1963. **Military Serv:** AUS qsp/4 served 2 yrs. **Business Addr:** New Jersey State Prison, Third Federal St, Trenton, NJ 08625.

RAVENELL, MILDRED
Educator. **Personal:** Born Dec 1, 1944, Charleston, SC; married William Ravenell; children: William Samuel, Teressa Emlynne. **Educ:** Fisk Univ, BA 1965; Howard Univ, JD 1968; Harvard Univ, LLM 1971. **Career:** IBM, systems engr 1968-70, marketing rep 1970; Boston Univ, asst dean for admissions & financial aid 1971-72; FL State Univ, assoc prof of law 1976-84; Univ of VA, visiting assoc prof of law 1984-85. **Orgs:** Mem Phi Beta Kappa; mem Amer Bar Assn; mem MA Bar Assn; mem Bethel AME Church; mem Delta Sigma Theta Sor; mem Jack & Jill of Amer Inc; former mem bd of dirs Terrell House at Tallahassee; mem bd of trustees Law Sch Admission council; former mem Bd of Bus Regulation FL.

RAVENELL, WILLIAM HUDSON
Attorney, educator. **Personal:** Born May 31, 1942, Boston, MA; son of Isabella T Ravenell and William S Ravenell; children: William Samuel, Teressa Emlynne. **Educ:** Lincoln Univ PA, BA 1963; State Coll at Boston, MEd 1965; Howard Univ Sch of Law, JD 1968. **Career:** John Hancock Ins Co, analyst 1968-71; Housing Inspection Dept, admin 1971-72; State Dept of Comm Affairs, dep sec 1972-75; FL Dept of Comm Affairs, sec 1975-79; FL A&M Univ, prof 1979; FL Office of the Atty Gen, special asst 1979-80; US Dept of Transportation Fed Hwy Admin, chief counsel 1980-81; State of FL, asst attorney general 1982-85; Florida A&M Univ, attorney, professor 1985-. **Orgs:** Chmn FL Commn on Human Relations 1975-77; chmn FL Manpower Serv Council 1975-80; FL, DC, VA, Natl, Amer Bar Assns; mem Phi Alpha Delta, Omega Psi Phi, FL Council of 100; First Union Bank, board of directors, 1990-; NAACP, life member. **Business Addr:** Attorney/Professor, Florida A&M University, Tallahassee, FL 32303.

RAVEN-SYMONE. See **PEARMAN, RAVEN-SYMONE CHRISTINA.**

RAWLINGS, MARILYN MANUELA
Electronics company executive. **Personal:** Born Feb 29, 1956, Baltimore, MD; daughter of Marion Edwina Simon Rawlings (deceased) and Prince Henderson Rawlings. **Educ:** Frostburg State Univ, Frostburg MD, BS, 1977. **Career:** Walper, Smullien & Blumenthal, Towson MD, tax acct, 1978-80; Lincoln Natl Life, Baltimore MD, exec sec for sales, 1980-81; Cameo Electronics Co Inc, Owings Mills MD, pres, 1981-. **Orgs:** Senior advisory committee chairman of Minority Input Committee, MD/DC Minority Purchasing Council; member, National Association of Female Executives; executive board member, Maryland TEN, currently. **Honors/Awds:** One of 50 Outstanding Business Leaders in MD, Baltimore Sun, 1988-91; Product/Supplier of the Year, MD/DC Minority Purchaing Council, 1987; Outstanding Achievement Award, MD/DC Minority Purchasing Council, 1988; Certificate of Appreciation, Minority Business Committee/Federal Exec Board, 1985; Speaker to the Black Student Body of Frostburg State Univ, 1987; Speaker for Elementary School System, Baltimore MD; Listed in Black Enterprise Magazine as One of Top Black Businessmen, 1988-91; Recognized for Generous Service & Committment to Business Education, Baltimore Co Public Schools.

RAWLINS, ELIZABETH B.
Educational administrator (retired). **Personal:** Born Nov 25, 1927, Cambridge, MA; married Keith W Jr; children: Paul, Pattie E. **Educ:** Salem St Coll, BS 1950; Simmons Coll, MS 1967; Tufts U, grad study; Harvard U, grad study; Univ of MA, Amherst, MA, EdD, 1991. **Career:** Dorman School, teacher 1950-52; Narimasu Elem School Japan, 1953-54; Buckingham School, 1952-62; Hingham MA Public Schools, 1964-67; Simmons Coll, instr lectr 1967-75, asst prof 1975-79, assoc prof of educ 1979; Simmons Coll, assoc dean 1976-79, assoc dean of coll, prof of educ, 1984-92. **Orgs:** Exec com pres MA Assoc for Mental Health 1970-; rsch com Legis Task Force Natl Assoc Mental Health; exec comm Natl Mental Health Assoc; gov task force Determination of Need; chmn Children's Adv Com MA Dept Mental Health; bd of regents for Higher Educ MA 1980-82, reapptd 1983-88; mem Educ Commn of the States 1982, reapptd 1985-. **Honors/Awds:** Disting Alumna Awd Salem State Coll 1982; Educ Awd Boston Branch NAACP 1986; M L King Award, St Cyprian's Episcopal Church & Union United Methodist Church, Boston, 1989.

RAWLINS, SEDRICK JOHN
Dentist. **Personal:** Born May 29, 1927, NYC, NY; married Alyce Taliaferro; children: Wayne, Mark. **Educ:** Lincoln U, AB 1950; Meharry Med Coll, DDS 1954. **Career:** E Hartford CT Dentist, pvt prac 1956-; CT Savs & Loan, incorporator 1969-70; Manchester Meml Hosp, 1969-72. **Orgs:** Mem Manchester Hum Relat Com 1959-; CT St Bd Parole 1959-, chmn 1966-68; CT Govt Plng Com Crmnl Adminstrn, chmn correction com 1967-69; mem CT House of Del 1970; mem Nat Dental Assn st vice pres 1968-70; Am & CT Dental Assn; CT Counc on Nat Paroling Authorities; mem Phi Beta Sigma; NAACP pres 1959-60; Dem; Bapt; mem High Noon Club Hartford CT. **Honors/Awds:** Recip hum relat award E Hartford 1970; serv award NAACP 1960. **Military Serv:** USAAF Dental Corps 1944-46; AUS 1954-56. **Business Addr:** 183 Burnside Ave E, Hartford, CT 06108.

RAWLS, GEORGE H.
Surgeon. **Personal:** Born Jun 2, 1928, Gainesville, FL; son of Lona Rawls and Nicholas Rawls; married Lula; children: Yvonne, Bettye Jo, Sherrie. **Educ:** FL A&M Univ, 1948; Howard Univ Sch Med, MD, 1952. **Career:** VA Hosp Dayton, surg resd 1955-59; OH State Univ, clinical instr surgeon 1957-59; Am Bd Surgery, diplomate 1961; private surgical practice, 1959-93; IL School of Medicine, asst dean, currently. **Orgs:** Fellow Amer Coll Surgeons 1963; guest examiner Amer Bd Surgery 1977; co-chmn life mem NAACP; life mem bd Natl NAACP, 1961-91; prs Marion Co Med Soc; mem Alpha Phi Alpha; bd of dirs Urban League; Children's Mus; past bd dir Flanner House clinical asst prof surg IN Sch Med; IN State Med Assn, 1979. **Honors/Awds:** Citizen of the Yr Omega Psi Phi 1971; Citizen of the Yr Federated Clubs 1976; several articles publ in surgical journals; Sagamore of Wabash, Governor Bayh, 1990; Alpha Phi Alpha Man of the Year, Alpha Phi Alpha, Indianapolis, 1970. **Military Serv:** AUS 1st lt 1953-55. **Business Addr:** IN University School of Medicine, 535 Barnhill Dr, Indianapolis, IN 46202.

RAWLS, LOU
Singer. **Personal:** Born Dec 1, 1936, Chicago, IL. **Career:** Lou Rawls & The Golddiggers, performer 1969; 77 Sunset Strip, Bourbon St Beat, The Big Valley, Mannix Fall Guy, Fantasy Island, actor; Stormy Monday, Lou Rawls & Strings, Tobacco Rd, Black & Blue, Nobody But Lou, singer; Dick Clark Show, Tonight Show, Steve Allen Show, performer; Uptown A Tribute to Apollo Theatre, singer 1980; Sam Cooke Pilgrim Travelers, singer 1962-; TV Program, Rhythm and Rawls 1982; vocals in two animated Garfield specials; featured on the Garfield soundtrack album; classic song hits ''You'll Never Find'', ''Natural Man'', ''Lady Love'', ''Deadend Street'', ''Love is a Hurtin' Thing'', ''Love Your Blues Away','' ''At Last'', 1989, ''It's Supposed to Be Fun,'' 1990; appeared in HBO's Don King: Only In America, 1997. **Orgs:** Natl spokesman Anheuser-Busch 1976; hon chmn United Negro Coll Fund 1979; organized The Lou Rawls Parade of Stars Telethon to benefit UNCF, 1980-; 1983 Christmas tour of military bases in Korea, Japan and the Phillipines. **Honors/Awds:** Grammy Awards, 1967, 1971, 1977, 1978; 1 Platinum album ''All Things In Time'', 5 Gold Albums ''All Things In Time'', ''Lou Rawls Live'', ''Soulin''', ''Unmistakably Lou'', ''When You Hear Lou''; Gold single ''You'll Never Find''; Chicago Street named in his honor, 1989; Raised well olver $70 for black colleges; Organizer, Lou Rawls' Celebrity Golf Tournament, Los Angeles. **Military Serv:** US Army, 82nd Airborne Division, 1956-58. **Business Addr:** Singer, The Brokaw Co, 9255 Sunset Blvd, Los Angeles, CA 90069.

RAWLS, LOUIS
Cleric. **Personal:** Born Jul 16, 1905, Johns, MS; married Willia J Lowe; children: Lou, Samuel B, Julius. **Educ:** Moody Bibile Inst, Grad 1932; Rodger Williams U, BS 1932; No Bapt Theol Sem, BTh 1938; Northwestern Univ Garrett Biblical Isnt, BD 1945, MD 1961; MS Coll, 1954; Geo Williams Coll, MS 1961; Universal Bible Inst, PhD 1977. **Career:** Tabernacle Missionary Bapt Ch, pastor, 1941-; founder; Caanan Bapt Ch, 10 yrs; various businesses; funeral, real est, car wash, ins, printing, finance since 1932; Cook Co Jail, 1st black chpln; Chicago Bapt Inc, tchr 38 yrs; notary 48 years; founder, Atlas Real Estate & Mortgage Corporation. **Orgs:** Organized Tabernacle Bapt Ch; fdr Tbrncl Comm Hosp & Hlth Ctr; helped rgn Progsv Nat Baptist Convention; only surviving organizer Chicago Bapt Inst; past pres Bapt St Conv 4 yrs; Arabic Temple; pres Bapt St Conv of IL; trustee Chicago Bapt Inst; Chicago C of C; Chicago Conf of Brotherhd; Met C of C; trustee Moorehouse Sch of Rel; trustee NAACP; Operation PUSH; SCLC; pres Tbrncl Bapt Ch Found; Tabernacle Bapt Ch Comm Ctr; United Bd Coll Devel for the 70 Predominately Black Coll in USA; Urban Leag; Wash Park YMCA; Wisdom Lodge; founder 7 bd EB Devel 1934, Community Hosp 1971, PHB Comm 1968; erected the Willa Rawls Senior Citizens Complex 1981; Board of Directors: Morehouse College, National Board of Higher Education Church Federation, State of Illinois Battered Men and Women, National Religious Broadcasters of NAACP, Chicago Chamber of Commerce, National Association of Eveangelicals, founder, Illinois Baptist State Convention; founder, Tabernacle Community Hospital & Health Center; founder, Deluxe Printers and Publishers; founder, Tabernacle Nursery School. **Honors/Awds:** Recip award of merit Men Benevolent Serv Club 1958; cert of merit Bapt St Conv 1960; cert of commndtn Chicago Area Counc 1967; brthrhd award Chicago Conf for Brthrhd 1967; testimnl award Dr CO Cartlstrom Comm 1973; cert of recog Chicago Bapt Inst Alumni Assn 1973; Prog Nat Bapt Cong of Chris Educ 1973; apprctn award Pilgrim Bapt Mission 1973; humanitrn award Nat Sor Mu Chap 1975; industrl comm award Spiegel Inc; Central State University, LLD, Hon DD, 1957; Ideal Bible Coll, Hon DD, 1968; Natchez Coll Hon HHD, 1975. **Special Achievements:** Assisted in the construction or finance of over sixty centers and churches including St Paul Church of God in Christ, Israel Tabernacle Baptist Church, Greater Canaan Missionary Baptist Church, Willa Rawls Senior Citizens Complex, 1981; called first meeting that resulted in formation of Chicago Baptist Institute, 1934; organized the first headstart program, 1946. **Business Addr:** Pastor, Tabernacle Missionary Baptist Church, 4120 S Indiana Ave, Chicago, IL 60653.

RAWLS, RALEIGH RICHARD
Attorney. **Personal:** Born Jun 12, 1925, Gainesville, FL; married Annie R Robinson; children: Regina D, Rene N, Renard A, Rodney P. **Educ:** Howard U, BA 1950, LLB 1956. **Career:** City of Ft Lauderdale, pub defender 1973-; Atty, pvt prac 1957-. **Orgs:** Mem Braward Co Bar Assn; Nat Bar Assn; life mem Alpha Phi Alpha; NAACP. **Military Serv:** UUSN 1943-46. **Business Addr:** 1018 1/2 NW 6 St, Fort Lauderdale, FL.

RAWLS, WILLIAM D., SR.
Insurance executive. **Career:** Golden Circle Life Insurance Co, Brownsville TN, chief executive. **Business Addr:** Golden Circle Life Insurance Co, PO Box 293, Brownsville, TN 38012-0293.

RAWLS BOND, CHARLES CYNTHIA
Life insurance executive. **Personal:** Born Feb 10, 1934, Brownsville, TN; daughter of Maude E Rawls and C A Rawls; married Maltimore Bond, Aug 27, 1961; children: Jo Zanice, Alan R, Andrea C Bond Johnson, Maude Y. **Educ:** Fisk University, 1955; New York University, 1956. **Career:** Riverside Hospital, psychometrist, vocational rehabilitation counselor, 1956-57; Golden Circle Life Insurance Co, personnel director, 1957-60, assistant secretary, treasurer, 1960-87, president, 1987-. **Orgs:** Brownsville Bank, board of directors, 1987-; Methodist Haywood Park Hospital, board of directors, 1987-; Lane College, board of trustees, 1988-; Delta Sigma Theta Sorority, 1954-; National Insurance Association, board of directors, 1987-; Haywood County NAACP Branch, life member, chairperson, 1980-. **Business Addr:** President, Golden Circle Life Insurance Co, 39 S Jackson Ave, PO Box 293, Brownsville, TN 38012, (901)772-9283.

RAY, ANDREW
Educator. **Personal:** Born Feb 4, 1948, Centreville, MS; son of Ruby Ray and Perry Ray. **Educ:** Southern Univ, BS Economics 1969; State Univ of NY, MS Educ 1970; Univ of Buffalo MS Admin 1982; Univ of Buffalo, PhD, administration & policy, 1994. **Career:** Dept of State, intern 1968; US Congress, intern 1974; Urban League, career educator 1983; Adolescent Vocational Exploration Prog NY, dir; CSD, instructor/dean 1985-; admin vice pres 1988-. **Orgs:** Chair of brd Baden Federal Credit Union 1978-; comm mem YMCA 1979-; first vice dist rep Omega Psi Phi 1984, dist rep 1986; founder Black Educators Assoc; bd of dirs, Omega Scholarship Foundation, 1991. **Honors/Awds:** Foreign Affairs Scholar Dept of State Wash DC; Presidential Fellow Wash DC; Teacher of the Year city of Rochester 1974; Distinguished Citizen Urban League 1980; Administrator of the Year 1989; Outstanding Mentor, 1991; New York State, Outstanding Educator of the Year, 1991; The Urban League, Charles Lunsford Distinguish Community Service Award, 1997. **Business Addr:** Principal, CSD, 131 W. Broad Street, Rochester, NY 14614.

RAY, AUSTIN H.
Copier/electronic printing company executive. **Personal:** Born Aug 23, 1943, Lexington, MO; son of Auline A Ray and Artice H Ray; married Geneva Green; children: Keith, Krista. **Educ:** Pittsburg State Univ, BA 1965; Western Michigan Univ, MBA 1973. **Career:** Case Western Reserve Univ, rsch assoc 1967-70; General Foods Corp, buyer/distribution supr 1970-73; Xerox Corp, dist plnr/mktg & prog mgmt 1973-83, plng mgr/quality mgr 1983-87, mgr future product marketing 1987-90, world wide quality launch manager, 1990-92, Multinational Program, Dist MICR Printers, bus mgr, 1993-. **Orgs:** Life mem Kappa Alpha Psi Frat (polemarch/bd dir Roch Alumni, 1973-84), LA Alumni, 1986-90; adv bd Finger Lakes Health Systems Agency 1976-78, Baden St Settlement (Rochester) 1978-83; dir for Junior Achievement Xerox Mgmt Assoc 1978-81; prog chmn Boys and Girls Club of Rochester 1980-83; mem Rochester Chamber of Commerce 1981-83; moderator, Community Congregational Church, 1995-97, member/board of directors, endowment and finance committees; member, Sigma Pi Phi Fraternity, 1985-; board of directors 100 Black Men, Orange County CA, 1994-. **Honors/Awds:** Disting Serv Kappa Alpha Psi Roch Alumni 1974-83; Disting Svc/Leadership Xerox Mgmt Assoc for Junior Achievement 1978-81; Outstanding Young Men in Amer US Jaycees; Outstanding Serv Urban League Rochester; Leadership/Disting Serv CARI Inc Rochester NY; Community Congregation Service Appreciation. **Military Serv:** AUS 1st lt 2 yrs; Army Commendation Medal, Vietnam Serv Awd 1967. **Home Addr:** 4888 Elder Ave, Seal Beach, CA 90740. **Business Addr:** Business Operations Manager, MidRange Printing Systems, Xerox Corp, 701 Aviation Blvd, ESAE 380, El Segundo, CA 90245, (213)333-3601.

RAY, FRANCIS
Writer, school nurse practitioner. **Personal:** Born Jul 20, 1944, Richland, TX; daughter of Mc & Venora Radford, Sr; married William H Ray, Jul 28, 1967; children: Carolyn Michelle. **Educ:** Texas Woman's Univ, BS, nursing, 1967; Amer Nursing Assn, School Nurse Practitioner, 1992. **Career:** Parkland Memorial Hosp, staff nurse, 1967-68; Chester Clinic/Hosp, LVN Prog, teacher, 1968-71; Dallas Cty Health Dept, nursing super, 1971-82; Dallas Public Schools, school nurse practitioner, 1982-. **Orgs:** Romance Writers of Amer, 1984-; Women Writers of Color, 1992-; Amer Nurses Assn, 1992-. **Honors/Awds:** Dallas Public Library, Polk Wisdom Branch, Outstanding Achievement, 1996; Texas Black Women's Writers, Appreciation Award, 1996; Romantic Times Magazine, Multicultural Career Achievement Award, 1995-96; Blackboard/Essence Magazine, Best Sellers List, 5 Titles, 1994-98; North Texas Romance Writers, for Service, Yellow Rose Award, 1990. **Special Achievements:** Fallen Angel, book, Odyssey Pub Co, 1992; Forever Yours, book, Kensington Pub Co, 1994; Spirit of the Season, anthology, Kensington Pub Co, 1994; Undeniable, book, Kensington Pub Co, 1995; The Bargain, book, Kensington Pub Co, translated Taiwan/Italian, 1995; Only Hers, book, Kensington Pub Co, 1996; Romantic Times Magazine, p 53, April, 1996; Incognito, book, Kensington Pub Co, 1997; Today's Black Woman, excerpt of Incognito, p 94, fall 1997; Silken Betrayal, book, Kensington Pub Co, 1997; Heart of the Falcon, book, Kensington Pub Co, 1998; Heart of the Falcon, alternate for Doubleday/Literary Book Club, 1998; Forever Yours, 2nd ed for TV movie, Chuck Fries Prod, 1998. **Home Phone:** (214)375-5419. **Business Addr:** Author of "Hear of the Falcon", Kensington Publishing Corp., PO Box 764423, Dallas, TX 75376.

RAY, GREG ALAN
Attorney. **Personal:** Born Jul 22, 1963, Harrisburg, PA; son of Geraldine V Roach-Ray and Warren Wesley Ray. **Educ:** University of Pittsburgh, BA, 1986, School of Law, JD, 1989. **Career:** Pennsylvania Superior Court, Judge Justin Johnson, law clerk, 1989-90; Allegheny County District Attorney, assistant district attorney, 1990-92; self-employed, attorney, 1992-94, Assoc counsel, 1993-. **Orgs:** Omega Psi Phi, 1983; Homer S Brown Law Society, president-elect, 1994; National Football League Players Association, contact advisor, 1992; National Bar Association, 1989; Prince Hall Free & Accepted Masons, 1990. **Business Phone:** (303)292-3212.

RAY, JACQUELINE WALKER
Educator. **Personal:** Born May 14, 1944, Buffalo, NY; married Lacy Ray Jr. **Educ:** SUNY at Buffalo, BA, 1965, MSW, 1967; New York University, PhD, 1975. **Career:** Columbia Univ Coler Project, social worker, 1967-68; New York City Housing Authority Model Cities Prog, field supervisor, 1968-70; Jersey City State College, assistant professor of psychology, 1970-71; York College of CUNY, associate professor of psychology. **Orgs:** American Psychological Association; bd of dir, Comm Mediation Servs; Queens City Mental Health Soc; Alpha Kappa Alpha; League of Women Voters, Region II, Mental Health Consultant, Job Corps. **Honors/Awds:** Articles published: Jrnl of Gen Ed, 1979-, Jrnl of Intergroup Tensions, 1983, Jrnl of Coll Student Personnel; Urban Ed Rsch Trainee, CUNY, Fellowship, 1982-83; Ford Found Study Grant, 1980, CUNY, Faculty Fellow, 1989-90. **Business Addr:** Associate Professor of Psychology, York College of CUNY, ATTN: DACOTA STEWART-DICK, 94-20 Guy Brewer Blvd, Jamaica, NY 11451.

RAY, JAMES R., III
Consultant. **Personal:** Born Feb 10, 1963, Brooklyn, NY. **Educ:** John Jay College, New York, NY, BA, 1988; Long Island Univ, MBA. **Career:** New York City Police Dept, Brooklyn, NY, police officer, 1987-88; BEST Advisory Group, New York, NY, CEO, 1988-. **Orgs:** Basilieus 1986-87, member 1987-, Omega Psi Phi Fraternity. **Honors/Awds:** Excellence in International Business, 1996; Black Achievers in Industry Award, Harlem YMCA, 1991; National Sales Quality Award. **Military Serv:** US Marine Corps, Corporal, 1981-85; Good Conduct Ribbon, Sea Service Ribbbon. **Business Addr:** CEO, BEST Advisory Group, 26 Broadway, Ste 400, New York, NY 10004.

RAY, JOHNNY
Professional baseball player. **Personal:** Born Mar 1, 1957, Chouteau, OK; married Tammy; children: Jasmine, Johnny Jr. **Educ:** Northeastern Oklahoma A&M, Miami, OK, attended; Univ of Arkansas, Fayetteville, AR, attended. **Career:** Pittsburgh Pirates, infielder, 1981-87; California Angels, infielder, 1987-90; Yakult Swallows, Japanese Baseball League, 1991-. **Honors/Awds:** 6th Pirate 2nd baseman in history to reach .300 level in a single season, 1984; National League Silver Slugger Award, 1983; Rookie Player of the Year, The Sporting News 1982; American League All-Star Team, 1988. **Home Addr:** RR 1, Box 64-A, Chouteau, OK 74337.

RAY, JUDITH DIANA
Educator. **Personal:** Born Sep 14, 1946, St Louis, MO; daughter of Pauline Malloyd Ray and Arthur Charles Ray Sr. **Educ:** Harris Stowe Teachers Coll St Mo, ABEd 1968; WA Univ MO, MAEd 1972; WA State Univ Pullman WA, MS 1979; Univ of Minnesota, PhD, 1996. **Career:** St Louis Bd of Ed, teacher 1968-72; WA Univ, St Louis, WA State, Univ Pullman, grad teaching, rsch asst 1970-79; ARC Milwaukee Pierre Marquette Div, natl field rep 1972-73; York Coll CUNY Jamaica Queens, lectr 1973-75; WA State Univ Sch of Vet med, equine rschr; West Chester Univ, asst prof 1977-. **Orgs:** Life mem Amer Alli of Health PE & Rec & Dance 1968-80; vol & mem Amer Soc of Testing & Matls 1978-89; Intl & Amer Soc of Biomechs 1978-89; vol teacher ARC 1960-80; faculty adv Gamma Sigma Sigma Natl Serv Sor 1978-80; Phi Delta Kappa W Chester 1978; Intl Soc of Biomechanic in Sport; Alpha Kappa Alpha; US Fencing Coaches Assn; life mem US Tennis Assn; US Prof Tennis Assn; EUSPTR, Registry. **Honors/Awds:** Common Ground Consortium, Bush Grant, Univ of Minnesota. **Special Achievements:** Co-author: "EEG Analysis of Equine Joint Lameness," 1977; The Effects of Different Ground Surfaces of Equine Joint, 1980; Motion As Analyzed by EEG, Journal of Biomechanics, vol 13, p 191-200, 1980. **Business Addr:** Assistant Professor, West Chester University, 307 South Campus, West Chester, PA 19383.

RAY, MARY E.
Organization chairman. **Personal:** Born Jul 6, 1911, Toones, TN; children: Janice Marie White, Mary Alice Crowder. **Career:** Macon Co Policy Bd Sr Cit IL, chmn 1975-. **Orgs:** Mem sec NAACP Mounds IL 1952-56; pres PTA Madison IL 1955-56; instituted nutrition prgm Sr Cit Macon Co 1974-; chmn Family Plng Adv Coun 1970-74;mem Planned Parenthood; mem New Salem Bapt Ch; mem vol outreach wrkr Ofc Aging Decatur IL; pres Mother's Bd of New Salem MBC Brother Dr SW BywarmCharlotte NC.

RAY, MERCER Z.
Retired insurance executive. **Personal:** Born Feb 28, 1911, Roxboro, NC; son of Alberta Ray and James Ray; married Grace Mauney; children: Alice, Mercedes, Consuelo, John. **Educ:** A&T State Univ, BS 1939. **Career:** NC Mutual Life Ins Co, agent 1939-40; Golden State Mutual Life Insurance Co, business exec 1941-76 (retired). **Orgs:** Mem NAACP, Urban League, Alpha Phi Alpha Frat, BSA; elder Presbyterian Church. **Honors/Awds:** Order of Merit BSA 1959.

RAY, MOSES ALEXANDER
Dentist. **Personal:** Born Sep 25, 1920, Clinton, NC; married Helen Bettina Jones; children: Shelia Anne, Ernest Alexander. **Educ:** Shaw U, BS 1941; Howard U, DDS 1945. **Career:** Dentistry, Tarboro, pvt prac 1946-; Edgecombe Gen Hosp, mem staff. **Orgs:** Mem NC Dental Soc; Am Dental Assn; pres fdr Ranola Hgts Housing Devel Corp Inc 1970-; dir Nash Edgecombe Econ Devel Corp Tarboro; pres E Tarboro Citizens Leag 1965; councilman Tarboro 1967-; mem NC Govs Counc Occupational Hlth 1968-71; trustee Edgecombe Econ Devel Corp; mem Omega Psi Phi. **Military Serv:** USAF 1951-53. **Business Addr:** 409 Panola St, Tarboro, NC 27886.

RAY, RICHARD REX
Military officer. **Personal:** Born Apr 10, 1942, Dover, OH; married Vernell Lynette Cain; children: Richard Rex Jr, Rolland. **Educ:** Kent State Univ, BBA 1967; Univ of MO Kansas City, MPA 1974. **Career:** Maxwell AFB AL, air force reserve, officers training corps headquarters, chief western resource branch 1976, student air command and staff coll 1979-80; Personnel Ctr Randolph AFB TX, resource mgr 1980-82, chief special assignments branch 1982-83, commander squadron sect 1983-85; USAF Recruiting Squadron St Louis, commander 1985-88; US Air Force Scott AFB IL, director, personnel programs 1988-89; US Air Force Randolph AFB TX, deputy chief, colonels' group 1989-91; US Air Force Mather AFB CA, commander, 323rd airbase group 1991-. **Orgs:** Coach/manager, Little League/Amateur Baseball 1973-84; adjunct faculty, Troy State Univ, Montgomery AL 1977-80; life mem, Air Force Association. **Honors/Awds:** Publ "The Headquarters Squadron, The Junior Officer as Leader" Air Univ Review 1975; speaker, NAACP Freedom Fund Banquet, Dover OH 1978; George Washington Medal of Honor, for essay Peace with Freedom, Freedom's Foundation at Valley Forge 1988; Role Model, Black Americans in Defense of Our Nation, Department of Defense Publication. **Military Serv:** US Air Force, col, 1989-91; Meritorious Serv Medal, 4 Oak Leaf Clusters, Air Force Commendation Medal, Outstanding Unit Awd, Air Force Organizational Excellence Awd.

RAY, ROSALIND ROSEMARY
Attorney. **Personal:** Born Jun 29, 1956, Washington, DC; daughter of Rosemary W Ray and Walter I Ray Jr. **Educ:** Georgetown University; Harvard University, 1976; Boston University, BA, 1978; Howard University, School of Law, JD, 1990. **Career:** DC Superior Court, law clerk, 1990-91; Law Office of Idus J Daniel, Jr, attorney, 1991-; Law Office of Leonard L Long, Jr, attorney, 1991-93; Entertainment Resources, assistant general counsel, 1992; DC Housing, hearing officer, 1994-. **Orgs:** National Bar Association, asst editor, 1987-; American Bar Association, 1987-; Alpha Kappa Alpha Sorority, 1977-; Phi Delta Phi Legal Fraternity, 1987-; Howard University Law Alumni Association, 1990-. **Honors/Awds:** Law Offices of Jack Olender & Howard University, Earl B Davis Trial Advocacy, 1988; Howard University, Merit Scholarship for High Academic Achievement, 1988-90. **Special Achievements:** NBA Magazine, 1992. **Home Addr:** 1205 Morningside Dr, Silver Spring, MD 20904, (301)384-9155. **Business Addr:** Christina Northern & Associates, 9039 Sligo Creek Pkwy, Ste 707, Silver Spring, MD 20901.

RAY, WALTER I., JR.
Business executive. **Personal:** Born Sep 2, 1923, Newburgh, NY; son of Mary Bingham R Robinson and Walter I Ray Sr; married Rosemary White; children: Rosalind R, Walter I III. **Educ:** WV State Coll, 1941-43; Howard U, BS 1949. **Career:** Anheuser Busch, Inc, sales/sales supr 1958-70, branch mgr 1971-81; Esoray Publ/Business & Mkt, consultant 1983-85; Game Prod Inc (DC Lottery) vice pres 1982-83; John N Miller Assoc, assoc vice pres 1983-; Esoray Publ Co, pres 1983-. **Orgs:** Writer, Broadcast Music Inc; consultant, DC Gov; life mem NAACP; mem Masons Shriners Consi; mem Omega Psi Phi. **Honors/Awds:** Black Achievers of Industry 1972; Natl Capital Parks 1973; Leadership Mem BSA 1979; United Black Fund 1979; Walter I Ray Jr Day proclaimed in District of Columbia 1981. **Military Serv:** AUS s/sgt 3 Yrs; USA. **Home Addr:** 1205 Morningside Dr, Silver Spring, MD 20904.

RAY, WILLIAM BENJAMIN
Educator, opera singer. **Personal:** Born in Lexington, KY; son of Beatric Clifton Smith and Mason Ray; married Carrie Walls Kellogg, Sep 1, 1949; children: Alexander Pierre, William Benjamin Jr. **Educ:** Attended Acad of Music Vienna Austria; KY State Coll, attended 1946-47; Oberlin Coll, BA 1952; Western Reserve Univ, attended 1953; Univ of Heidelberg Heidelberg, Germany, attended 1980-81; Boston Univ, MEd 1982. **Career:** De Paur's Infantry Chorus, featured soloist 1953-54; Karamu Theater, opera singer 1954-56; Cleveland Playhouse, opera singer 1954-56; Frankfurt Opera Frankfurt, Germany, opera singer 1957; actor/singer appeared in 14 different roles in Germany and Austrian Film and Television, in the German language; Decca, Intercord, Marcato, BBC, CBS, recording artist 1960-78; Concert Tour of Europe, concert/opera singer 1983-; Peabody Conservatory of Music, professor of voice 1982-94; Howard Univ, professor of voice. **Orgs:** Founder/pres Black Theater Productions 1974-82; mem Alpha Phi Alpha Frat 1947-; appointed exclusive Amer rep to select operatic talent for the Kaleidoscope Production Co Munich Germany; National Association of Negro Musicians; Gamma Boyle Sigma Pi Phi Frat, 1993; Board member Annapolis Opera, Inc. **Honors/Awds:** Recip Gold Medal Lions Club of Italy 1978; listed in Blacks in Opera by Eileen Southern; Berlin Opera Yearbook by Walter Felsenstein; Black Americans in Cleveland by Russell Davis. **Military Serv:** Engr Sgt 1942-44; Bronze Medal, Purple Heart, Good Conduct, Excellent Marksmanship, ETO Medal, PTO Medal. **Business Addr:** Professor of Voice, Howard Univ, Dept of Music, Sixth & Fairmont Streets, NW, Washington, DC 20059.

RAYBURN, WENDELL GILBERT
Educational administrator. **Personal:** Born May 20, 1929, Detroit, MI; son of Grace Victoria Winston Rayburn (deceased) and Charles Jefferson Rayburn (deceased); married Gloria Ann Myers; children: Rhonda Renee, Wendell Gilbert, Mark K Williams. **Educ:** Eastern MI Univ, BA 1951; Univ of MI, MA 1952; Wayne State Univ Detroit, EdD 1972. **Career:** Detroit Public Schools, teacher, admin, 1954-68; Univ Detroit, asst dir to dir special projects 1968-72, assoc dean acad support programs 1972-74; Univ Coll Univ Louisville, dean 1974-80; Savannah State Coll GA, pres 1980-88; Lincoln Univ, pres 1988-. **Orgs:** Amer Assn Higher Educ; Natl Assn Equal Oppty in Higher Educ, Kappa Alpha Psi, Sigma Pi Phi; dir Jefferson City Area Chamber of Commerce, Jefferson City Rotary Club; board of directors, American Association of State Colleges and Universities; board of trustees, Stephens College; board of directors, Capital Region Medical Center; board of dir, United Way; exec board, Boy Scouts of America, Great Rivers Council; director of the Missouri Capital Punishment Resource Center; International Food and Agriculutural Development (BIFAD), board, 1988-. **Honors/Awds:** Recipient Whitney M Young Jr Award Lincoln Found 1980; Distinguished Citizens Award City of Louisville 1980; Communicator of the Year (Mid-Missouri Chapter), Public Relations Soc of Amer 1988; United Way of the Coastal Empire 1988; Savannah Port Authority, Savannah GA 1982-87; West Broad Street YMCA 1986; author, "Compensatory Education: Effective or Ineffective," Journal of Counseling Psychology, 1975; Executive of the Year, 1989-90, Ink & Quill Chapter of Professional Secretaries International; Jefferson City Rotary Club, Rotarian of the Year, 1990; Wayne State University (Detroit), Distinguished Alumni Award, 1993. **Military Serv:** AUS 1952-59. **Business Addr:** President, Lincoln University, 820 Chestnut St, Jefferson City, MO 65102-0029.

RAYE, JOHN. **See SMITH, JOHN RAYE.**

RAYE, VANCE WALLACE
Attorney, judge, state official. **Personal:** Born Sep 6, 1946, Hugo, OK; son of Lexie Marie Raye and Edgar Allen Raye; married Sandra Kay Wilson; children: Vanessa. **Educ:** Univ of OK, BA 1967, JD 1970. **Career:** Bulla and Horning, attorney;

US Air Force, asst staff judge advocate, Beale AFB chief of military justice, chief of civil law, judge advocate, 1970-74; CA Attorney General, civil division, deputy atty general 1974-80, sr asst atty general 1980-82, deputy legislative scty 1982-83; Governor of CA, legal affairs secretary, advisor, legal counsel, 1983-89; Sacramento County Superior Court, judge, 1989-90; California Court of Appeal, Third District, associate justice, 1991-; Lincoln Law School, professor. **Orgs:** State Bar of CA 1972-; vice chair CA Exec Emergency Council 1984-; CA Assn of Black Lawyers; NAACP; Urban League; CA State Bar Commn on Malpractice Insurance; chmn Staff Adv Council Natl Governors Assn Comm on Criminal Justice and Public Safety; Government's Emergency Operations Executive Council, vice chairman; National Institute of Justice, peer reviewer; Martin Luther King Holiday Commission, vice chairman; California Health Decisions; 100 Black Men of Sacramento; National Bar Association; Wiley Manuel Bar Association; California Judges Association; Judicial Council Committee on Family Law, chairman; Amer Bar Assn, criminal justice standards comm; CA Commission on the Future of the Courts, Family Relations Comm, chair; Judicial Council Appellate Standards Committee, chair legislative subcommittee; CA Commission on the Status of the African American Male; Univ of CA, Davis Med School Leadership Council. **Special Achievements:** Publications: Contributor, "California Public Contract Law;" co-author: California Family Law Litigation, 3 volumes. **Military Serv:** USAF capt 4 yrs; Air Force Commendation Medal. **Business Addr:** Associate Justice, California Court of Appeal, 3rd Appellate District, 914 Capitol Mall, Sacramento, CA 95814.

RAYFIELD, DENISE E.
Personnel manager. **Personal:** Born Jan 13, 1955, New York, NY; daughter of Laura Chandler Rayfield and Thomas Rayfield. **Educ:** Temple University, Philadelphia, PA, BA, 1976; Fordham University, New York, NY, MBA, 1981. **Career:** WR Grace & Co, New York, NY, benefits administration asst, 1977-81; Ziff-Davis Publishing Co, New York, NY, benefits mgr, 1981-83; The Hearst Corporation, New York, NY, asst mgr, employee benefits, 1983-90, mgr, employee benefits, 1990-94, senior manager, employee benefits, 1994-. **Business Addr:** Senior Manager, Employee Benefits, The Hearst Corporation, 227 W Trade St, Charlotte, NC 28202.

RAYFORD, BRENDA L.
Director, social worker. **Personal:** Born Apr 3, 1940, Dayton, OH; married Kent A; children: Blake Nyette, Valdez Kamau. **Educ:** Cntrl St U, BA 1962; Wayne St U, MSW 1971. **Career:** Detroit Black United Fund Inc, exec dir 1971-; Comp Hlth Svc, soc wkr 1969; Highland Park Pub Sch Spl Proj, soc work supr 1967-69; Travelers Aid Soc, soc wkr 1966-67; Montgomery Co Wlf Dept, soc wkr-intake 1962-66. **Orgs:** Consult Creative Strategies Inc 1970-; 3rd vice pres Nat Black United Fund Inc 1974-; field work supr Wayne St Univ Sch of Soc Work 1980-; chwm Fund Raising Com Bus & Professional Wmn Inc New Metro Chap 1975-; adv commn Detroit Pub Sch 1980-; co-author "The Guy Who Controls Your Future" 1970. **Honors/Awds:** Outst commun ldrshp St Rep Barbara Rose Collins 1978; wmn of yr Negro Bus & Professional Wmn-New Metro 1978; commun serv award World of Islam in W Commun 1978; St of MI tribute MI St Sen 1979. **Business Addr:** Executive Dir, Black United Fund of MI, 2187 W Grand Blvd, Detroit, MI 48208.

RAYFORD, FLOYD KINNARD
Professional baseball player (retired). **Personal:** Born Jul 27, 1957, Memphis, TN; married Mary Luvenia Hawkins. **Career:** Baltimore Orioles, infielder, 1980, 1982; St Louis Cardinals, infielder, 1983; Baltimore Orioles, infielder, 1984-87. **Business Addr:** Baltimore Orioles, Memorial Stadium, 333 W Camden St, Baltimore, MD 21201-2435.

RAYFORD, LEE EDWARD
Government official. **Personal:** Born Nov 17, 1935, Fordyce, AR; married La Neal Lucas; children: Vickie, Celese. **Educ:** Agr Mech & Normal Coll Pine Bluff AR, BS 1961; Univ of AR, M 1963; E TX St U, edD 1979. **Career:** St of NV Equal Rights Commn Las Vegas, exec dir 1979-80; Econ Oppor Bd Las Vegas, ESAA prgm dir 1974; Clark Co School Dist Las Vegas, research teacher 1973, adult educ teacher 1969-74; CCSA Las Vegas, site admin 1970-72. **Orgs:** Bd dir Westside Commun Devel; treas bd dir OIC/A; mem NAACP Las Vegas; mem SW Equal Employment Oppor Ofcrs (SWEEOA); mem Intl Assn of Hum Rghts Agy(IAOHRA); mem Prsnnl Adv Commn (Pac) St of NV; mem Kappa Alpha Psi Las Vegas; Phi Delta Kappa Las Vegas; Kappa Delta Psi Las Vegas. **Honors/Awds:** Publ "Criteria for the Selection of Pub Elemntry Sch Princ of the St of NV" 1979. **Military Serv:** USAF a/2c 1955-59. **Business Addr:** 1515 E Tropicana #590, Las Vegas, NV 89158.

RAYFORD, PHILLIP LEON
Educational administrator. **Personal:** Born Jul 25, 1927, Roanoke, VA; son of Eva E Rayford and Roosevelt T Rayford Sr; married Gloria Geraldine Kimber. **Educ:** A&T State Univ, BS 1949; Univ of MD, MS 1970, PhD 1973; USDA Grad Sch, chemistry & math. **Career:** NIH Bethesda MD, super biologist endocrinology branch 1955-62, super biol Ghana, W Africa radiobiol & biochem lab 1962-64, super biologist radioimmunoassayist endocrinology branch 1964-70, super biologist bio-radioimmunoassayist reproduction rsch branch 1970-73; Univ of TX Med Branch, asst prof dir surgical biochemistry lab dept of surgery 1973-76, assoc prof dir surgical biochemistry lab dept of surgery 1976-77, prof dir surgical biochemistry lab dept of surgery prof div of biochem human biological chem & genetics 1977-80, asst dean of medicine 1978-80; Univ of AR Coll of Medicine, prof & chmn dept of physiology and biophysics 1980-, associate dean of medicine, 1991-. **Orgs:** Mem F&AM Prince Hall 1977; editorial bd Peptides Soc for Exptl Biology & Med 1979-; site visitor NIH Bethesda MD various times; scientific reviewer Gastroentology Endocrinology Peptides various times; exec comm Univ of AR for Med Scis 1982-; deans adv comm Univ of AR for Medical Scis 1984-; study section General Med A NIH 1985-89, study section MARC NIH NIGMS, 1990-91; NIH NIDK, advisory council, 1990-; mem Amer Assn for the Advancement of Scis; mem Amer Assn of Univ Profs; mem Amer Federation for Clinical Rsch; mem Society of Sigma Xi; mem Amer Gastroenterology Assn; mem Natl Assn of Minority Medical Educators. **Honors/Awds:** Adelphi Club Man of the Yr Galveston TX 1978; Omega Psi Phi Award for 25 yrs of Outstanding Serv 1982; Omega Psi Phi, 9th District, Man of the Year, 1976, 1984; Cosmos Club Washington DC 1984; numerous publications including Rayford PL JA Jones and JC Thompson Gastrointestinal hormones In, Basic Clinical Endocrinology PO Kohler (ed) John Wiley, NY; Chowdhury P K Inoue and PL Rayford Effect of Nicotine on Basal and Bombesin Stimulated Canine Plasma Levels of Gastrin, Cholecystokinin and Gastrin in Rats Peptides; Baba N P Chowdhury K Inoue M Ami and PL Rayford Ileo-Caecal Resection Induced Pancreatic Growth in Rats Peptides; J C Thompson, GG Greely, PL Rayford and CW Townsend, "Gastrointestinal Endocrinology," McGraw Hill, 1986; SNMA Community Service Award, 1988; co-author, "Receptor mediatedbiologic actions of CCK in Gastrointestinal Endocrinoy," Academic Press, 1990; honorary doctorate, NC A&T State University, 1985; UAMS, Distinguished Faculty Award, 1994. **Military Serv:** AUS tech 5 1946-47. **Business Addr:** Chmn Dept Physiology, Coll of Medicine, Univ of Ark for Med Sci, 4301 W Markham, Little Rock, AR 72205.

RAYFORD, ZULA M.
Educator. **Personal:** Born Aug 5, 1941, Memphis, TN. **Educ:** Langston U, BA 1964; Univ WI, Grad Work 1969-71; MEd, Natl-Louis Coll, Evanston IL, 1984. **Career:** YWCA, program counselor 1964-68; Holy Angels Catholic School, teacher 1968-70; Milwaukee Public School, teacher 1970-. **Orgs:** Mem NEA; WI Educ Assn; United Milwaukee Edn; Milwaukee Tchrs Assn; United Tchrs; mem Northside Nghbrhd Action Grp; Recording Sec; Black Educators; International Masons & OES; North Central Service Club, bd mem; State Funded Kindergarten Day Care Program; Milw Public School Alternative Education, advisory mem. **Honors/Awds:** Rep NEA Minority Ldrshp Conf & WI St Delegate NEA Convntn. **Business Addr:** LaVarnway Alternative Middle School, 2479 N Sherman Blvd, Milwaukee, WI 53210.

RAY-GOINS, JEANETTE
Educational executive. **Personal:** Born Dec 8, 1933, St Louis, MO; daughter of Alma Payne Ray and Gene Ray; divorced; children: Denise Alma, Maria Josette. **Educ:** Bradley Univ, BA 1955; St Louis Univ, M of Urban Affairs 1972. **Career:** Chicago & St Louis Public Schools, teacher 1956-69; Yeatman Comm Corp, deputy executive dir 1970-79; R-G Group, Inc, businesswoman; CO Dept of Education, equity supervisor 1979-. **Orgs:** Pres/owner R-G Group, Inc 1981; mem CO Black Elected Officials 1981-85; vice-pres Aurora School Dist Bd of Ed 1981-85; pres/co-founder Western States Black Women and Business Enterprises, Inc 1984; natl consultant Educational Institutions, Natl Black Women Groups 1983-; owner Black Women West Products 1985; mem Delta Sigma Theta; Natl Coalition of Black School Board Members; exec adv bd CO Network; member, Black Women in Government Services, 1990-; member, The Order of the Eastern Star, Electra Chapter 16, 1986-. **Honors/Awds:** Danforth Fellowship Danforth Found 1978-79; Tribute to Outstanding Woman in Politics Award by Co Black Women for Political Action Organization 1982-83; Consultant Award AWARE West Phoenix AZ 1983; Award, Womens Bank of Denver, 1988. Developed: Reducing Sexual Harassment in the Workplace Training Model, 1985-; Beyond Racism-A Training Model, 1988-; Empowering Minority Parents to School Leadership. **Business Addr:** Educational Equity Programs Supervisor, Colorado Dept of Education, 201 E Colfax Ave, Rm 206, Denver, CO 80203.

RAYMOND, HENRY JAMES, II
State official. **Personal:** Born Apr 29, 1957, Fort Meade, MD; son of Dr & Mrs Henry J Raymond Sr; married Cauldia Ann Murray. **Educ:** NC A&T State Univ, BA 1979; Univ of Baltimore, MPA 1980; Bowie State Univ, MBA 1986. **Career:** MD Dept of Natural Resources, admin specialist 1981-84, admin officer 1984-87; MD Dept of Budget & Fiscal Planning, Annapolis, MD, mgmt analyst, 1987-90; Office of the Governor, Annapolis, MD, deputy chief of finance, 1990-. **Orgs:** Mem Omega Psi Phi Frat 1976-, Natl Black MBA Assoc 1985-, Amer Soc of Public Admin 1986-; mem NAACP, Natl Urban League. **Home Addr:** 4920 Lindsay Rd, Baltimore, MD 21229. **Business Addr:** Deputy chief of Finance, Office of the Governor, Executive Department, State House, Annapolis, MD 21401.

RAYMOND, PHILLIP GREGORY
Designer. **Personal:** Born Jul 31, 1957, Berkeley, CA. **Educ:** Univ of CA Berkeley, AB Arch 1975-80; Cambridge Univ England, 1979. **Career:** Lawrence Berkeley Lab, engr asst 1978-; Chem Dept Univ CA Berk, illustrator 197-78; Free Lance Designer, self employeed 1975-. **Orgs:** Mem Stdt Chap AIA 1975-; mem No CA Solar Enrgy Assn 1978-; mem Am Assn of Blacks in Enrgy 1979-; pres No Area NAACP Yth Counc 1979-; del Statehouse Conf on Chldrn & Yth 1980. **Honors/Awds:** Artist of tomorrow award Gamma Phi Delta Sor Inc 1977. **Business Addr:** Lawrence Berkley Lab, 1 Cyclotron Rd, Berkeley, CA 94720.

RAYMOND, USHER. **See USHER.**

RAYNOR, ROBERT G., JR.
Attorney. **Personal:** Born Jul 18, 1954, New Bern, NC; son of Cora P Raynor and Robert G Raynor Sr. **Educ:** North Carolina Central University, BA, 1977, School of Law, JD, 1981. **Career:** Harmon & Raynor, Attorneys At Law, lawyer, 1984-87; Attorney Robert G Raynor Jr, PC, private practice, 1987-. **Orgs:** Kappa Alpha Psi Fraternity Inc, 1973-; NAACP, 1985-; Craven County Voters League, 1985-; Neuse River Development Authority Inc, secretary, 1986-; New Bern-Craven County Library, trustee, 1987-; Big Brothers-Big Sisters of Lower Neuse, board of directors, 1984-86; North Carolina Association of Black Lawyers, 1984-; North Carolina Association of Black Elected Municipal Officials, 1986-; National Black Caucus of Local Elected Officials, 1988-. **Honors/Awds:** Craven County Voters League, Robert G Raynor Jr Day Honoree, 1985; NAACP, New Bern Chapter, Achievement Award, 1985; Zeta Phi Beta, Achievement Award, 1985. **Special Achievements:** Elected: Board of Alderman, City of New Bern, North Carolina, 1986; Mayor Pro-Tem, City of New Bern, North Carolina, 1987; Board of Alderman, 2nd Ward, New Bern, North Carolina, 1989. **Home Addr:** 1511 Spencer Ave, New Bern, NC 28560, (919)637-5276. **Business Addr:** Attorney at Law, 417-B Broad St, PO Box 446, New Bern, NC 28563, (919)633-5299.

RAYON, PAUL E., III
Real estate manager. **Personal:** Born Apr 15, 1950, Chicago, IL; married Freddie M Parr; children: Anjela N; Paul E IV. **Educ:** TN State Univ, BS Criminal Justice 1976. **Career:** Thornton Twp Youth Comm, family counselor 1976-78; Cook Cty Housing Authority, housing mgr 1978-; Robbins Park Dist, commiss. **Orgs:** Parlimentarian Robbins Comm Agency Council 1983-; mem United Way of Robbins 1984; chmn Mayor's Office of Community Affairs Village of Robbins 1984. **Honors/Awds:** Cert Natl Assoc of Housing & Re-Devel Officials 1979; Cert Robbins YMCA 1980; Cert Cook Cty Sheriff's Youth Serv 1983. **Home Addr:** 4107 W 127th St, #4W, BLDG2, Alsip, IL 60658.

READY, CATHERINE MURRAY
Educator. **Personal:** Born Apr 22, 1916, Richmond, VA; daughter of Etta Johnson Murray and George Murray; married Edward K Ready, Feb 3, 1941; children: Diane C. **Educ:** Hampton University, attended, 1936; Virginia Union University, attended, 1948. **Career:** Richmond City Schools, teacher. **Orgs:** Virginia Retired Teachers; YWCA, World Mutual Committee; Urban League Guild of Greater Richmond; Zeta Phi Beta; Black History and Cultural Center of Virginia. **Honors/Awds:** Urban League Guild, Service Award, 1986-88; Senior Golfers of Virginia, Volunteer Service Award, 1985; YWCA, Community Service Award, 1983, Appreciation Award, 1986; Martin Luther King "Community Learning Week," Volunteer Sponsor Award, 1992.

REAGON, BERNICE JOHNSON
Museum curator, historian, composer, singer, author. **Personal:** Born Oct 4, 1942, Albany, GA. **Educ:** Albany State College, Albany, GA, BA, 1959-; Spelman College, Atlanta, GA, BA, 1970; Howard University, Washington, DC, PhD, 1975. **Career:** Student Non-Violent Coordinating Comm, civil rights activist, 1961-62, field sec & freedom singer, 1962-64; African American Folklore, field researcher, 1965-; Sweet Honey in the Rock, Washington, DC, founder/artistic director, 1973-; Smithsonian Institution, Museum of American History, Program in Black American Culture, program director and cultural historian, 1976-88; Smithsonian Institution, Museum of American History, Division of Community Life, curator, 1988-; Amer Univ, distinguished prof of history, 1993-. **Honors/Awds:** MacArthur Fellowship, 1989; Charles E. Frankel Prize, 1995. **Special Achievements:** Publications: Voices of the Civil Rights Movement: Black American Freedom Songs, 1960-1966. **Business Addr:** Amer Univ, Coll of Arts & Sciences, Dept of History, Mccabe Hall, Rm 120, 4400 Massachusetts Avenue, NW, Washington, DC 20016, (202)885-1000.

REARDEN, SARA B.
Attorney. **Personal:** Born in Edgefield, SC; daughter of Mamie Lewis Rearden and Oacy Rearden; married Nigel Lauriston Haynes; children: Kai Nicole Haynes. **Educ:** Howard Law Sch, JD; NC St A&T U, BS Bus Adm with hons. **Career:** US Merit Systems Protection Bd, sr appellate atty 1979-; George Wash

Law Cntr Wash DC, part-time asst prof 1978-82; Equal Employ Opport Com, supr atty 1974-79; Equal Empl Opp Comm, atty adv 1973-74; Neighborhood Legal Serv Wash DC, mang atty 1971-73; Reginald H Smith Comm Law Fellow Prog; Fellow NLS, prog staff 1969-71. **Orgs:** Adm to the Bars sup ct of SC 1971, DC 1973, us dist ct for DC 1973, us ct of appeals for the DC 1973; co-chmn bd of dir Neighborhood Legal Serv Prog Wash DC; mem NBA, ABA; Nat Conf of Black Lawyrs; Natl Assn of Black Women Attys, past vice pres Howard Law Alumni Assn; Natl Couns of Negro Women; Howard Law Journ 1968-69; pres 1st & 2nd yr law class; NBA member, Counsel on Legal Education Opportunity, 1990- member/secretary, Baord Washington DC, Neighborhood Legal Service, 1980-; Admitted to Bar of the United States Supreme Court, 1983; Admitted to US Court of Appeals for the Federal Circuit. **Honors/Awds:** Wnr Constance Baker Motley Scholar 1968; MSPB Merit Awards, 1991, 1990, 1989, 1988, 1987, 1986; Chairman's Award for Extraordinary Performance, 1992.

REASON, JOSEPH HENRY
Librarian (retired). **Personal:** Born Mar 23, 1905, Franklin, LA; son of Bertha Peoples Reason (deceased) and Joseph Reason (deceased); married Bernice Chism, Jun 24, 1931; children: Barbara Butler, J Paul. **Educ:** New Orleans Univ, AB 1928; Howard Univ, AB 1932; Univ of PA, AM 1933; School of Library Serv Columbia Univ, BS 1936; Catholic Univ of Amer, PhD 1958. **Career:** Gilbert Acad New Orleans, language teacher 1928-29; FL A&M Coll, language teacher, l929-31, 1934-35, chief libarian l936-38; Howard Univ, reference librarian 1938-46, Univ librarian 1946-57, dir Univ library 1957-71; FL State Univ School of Library Sci, visiting prof 1972-73 (retired). **Orgs:** Library adv Univ of Rangoon Burma 1961-62; exec sec Assn of Coll & Rsch Librarians 1962-63; pres Assn of Coll & Rsch Librarians 1971-72; consultant Coll of the Sacred Heart 1972; trustee Eckerd Coll 1976-82; mem Sr Social Planning Council 1977; vice chmn Legislative Task Force State Library of FL 1977; mem bd of trustees Leon County Public Libr 1979-86; mem bd of dir Area Agency for Aging of Northern FL 1979-85, vice pres 1980-81. **Honors/Awds:** Author of "An Inquiry Into the Structure, Style & Originality of Crestien's Yvain"; Fellowship Gen Ed Bd 1935-36; published articles Library Professional Journal.

REAVES, BENJAMIN FRANKLIN
Educational administrator. **Personal:** Born Nov 22, 1932, New York, NY; son of Lella Brinson Reaves and Ernest McKinley Reaves; married Jean Manual, Sep 4, 1955; children: Terrilyn Reaves Jackson, Pamela, Benjamin. **Educ:** Oakwood Coll Huntsville AL, BA, 1955; Andrews Univ, MA, M Div; Chicago Theological Seminary. **Career:** MI Conference of Seventh-Day Adventist, pastor, 1956-68; Westside Hospital, Chicago IL, counselor, 1968-72; Andrews Univ, Berrien Springs MI, youth pastor, 1972-73, assoc prof, 1973-77; US Army, instr for homeletics, 1977-85; Oakwood Coll, Huntsville AL, pres, 1985-. **Orgs:** Mem, Advisory Board of Andrews Univ; mem, Advisory Board of Loma Linda Univ; mem, United Negro College Fund; mem, Natl Assn for Equal Opportunity in Higher Educ; mem, Council for the Advancement of Private Colleges in AL; mem, Huntsville Chamber of Commerce Board; mem, Vision 2000; mem, Rotary club; mem, Urban Ministries Program; board of directors, UNCF; Chicago Sunday Evening Club, speaker. **Honors/Awds:** Distinguished Alumnus Award, Oakwood Coll, 1973; Teacher of the Year, Oakwood Coll, 1983; Music Humanitarian Award, Oakwood Coll, 1984; Outstanding Leadership Award, Oakwood Coll, 1986; author of articles in numerous journals such as: Message, The Review and Herald, Ministry, The Adventist Laymen, Collegiate Quarterly, South African Signs of the Times. **Business Addr:** President, Oakwood College, Oakwood Road, Huntsville, AL 35896.

REAVES, E. FREDERICKA M.
Educator. **Personal:** Born Nov 7, 1938, Washington, DC; married Robert (deceased); children: Reginald, Ricardo. **Educ:** Morgan State U, BS 1960. **Career:** Sosa Jr High School, math teacher 1961; Goam Public Schools, math teacher 1964; San Diego City School, math teacher 1966; Alameda Unified School, math teacher 1967-83; Oakland Unified School Dist 1984-86. **Orgs:** Mem Natl Ed Assn 1967-; sec Alameda NAACP 1967-; brd mem Alamedans HOPE 1967-70; advisor Youth NAACP 1968-75; brd mem Am Red Cross 1970; chrpr Multicul Ins to Impl Article 33% CA Ed Code Training Grp 1970-74; mem Natl Coul Tchr Math 1970-82; mem Phi Delta Kapna 1973-. **Honors/Awds:** Article publ Math Tchr 1973; PTA schlshp Fairmont Hgts High 1956; Morgan state u Merit Schlshp 1957. **Home Addr:** 762 Santa Clara Ave, Alameda, CA 94501.

REAVES, FRANKLIN CARLWELL
Business executive. **Personal:** Born Aug 7, 1942, Mullins, SC; married Willie Dean White; children: Kathy Juanita, Jacquelyn C, Frankie Diana, Anthony "Kenny", Ron, Randy, Dexter, Branden. **Educ:** Fayetteville State Univ, BS 1968; A&T State Univ, MS 1974; LaSalle Ext Univ, LLB 1978; A&T State Univ, MS 1982; Allen Univ, Hon Dr of Humanity 1984; Univ NC Greensboro, candidate for PhD; Attended, Lutheran Theology Seminary. **Career:** Columbus Co Bd of Educ, teacher 1968-; Operation HELP, president/founder 1968-. **Orgs:** Pres Columbus Co Unit for NC Assn of Educators; pres NC Region V Leadership Prevocational Planning Council; pres Black Educators Leadership Council 1984-;pastor African Methodist Episcopal Church 1968-; pres & founder Help the Economic Linkage of the Poor 1971-; pres Marion Co Chap of NAACP 1973-76; pres SC Affiliate of ACLU 1979-82; mem Amer Friends Serv Comm 1978-84; mem Natl Bd of Directors of ACLU 1982-; mem Southern Regional Council; pres & organizerof The Store Inc 1984-. **Business Addr:** President, Operation HELP, PO Box 534, Mullins, SC 29574.

REAVES, GINEVERA N.
Educator. **Personal:** Born Jan 21, 1925, Greenwood, MS; married Henry Eugene Sr; children: Henry Eugene, Jr, Naomi Normene (dec). **Educ:** Rust Coll, BA 1951; Univ of Chgo, MA 1954; Univ of Tn; VA St; TX So; TN St; So Univ of New Orleans; Ball St IN. **Career:** MS Public School, teacher 1942-64; Rust Coll, asst prof 1964, dir of teacher educ. **Orgs:** Mem Phi Delta Kappa; Am Assn of Univ Wmn; MS Tchr Assn; Historian Phi Delta Kappa 1976-77; mem US Commin on Civil Rghts 1976-77; 3rd Vice Pres MS Assn of Higher Edn; Delta Sigma Theta Sor; mem Benton Co NAACP; chpn First Congrsnl Dist Dem Party MS 1972; alt del Dem Nat Mid-Term Conf 1974; st exec bd Dem Party of MS; mem MS Affirmative Action Com 1975. **Honors/Awds:** Runner-uo tchr of yr Rust Coll 1966; Sargent Shriver Award for alleviating poverty in rural Am 1966; Miss Finer Wmnhd award Zeta Phi Beta 1968; tchr of yr Rust Coll Zeta Phi Beta 1972; ginevera Reaves Day Benton Co NAACP 1975. **Business Addr:** Rust Coll, Holly Springs, MS 38635.

REAVIS, JOHN WILLIAM, JR.
Educator, social worker. **Personal:** Born Oct 30, 1935, Nyack, NY; son of Frances Reavis and John Reavis; married Catherine Smith (divorced); children: Dawn, John, III, Timothy; married Doris S Bailey, Aug 31, 1997. **Educ:** NYU, MA 1965; Fayetteville St NC U, BS (cum laude) 1959; Univ of Rochester, NDEA Inst for Guidance, 1965; SUNY-Albany Higher Ed. **Career:** Port Chester Carver Center, Port Chester, NY, executive director, 1990-; SUNY-Farmingdale, Educ Oportunity Center, dean 1981-86, prof, 1986-90; asst to pres for affirmative action 1980-81, dean; Central Admn State Univ of NY, asst dean 1972-80, coord special programs 1969-72; EDPA Grant Garnett Patterson Jr HS, consultant 1972-73; Montgomery St School, principal 1968-69, elem guidance counselor 1962-67; Grand St School, asst principal 1967-68, tchr 1959-61; Elem English Negro Hist, adult educ teacher 1961-62; Continental Can Co, machine tender, packer 1953-55, part-time 1956-59; minority youth groups sports counsultant; college dormitory asst; sports statistician; newspaper public relations writer; mgr of athletic teams. **Orgs:** Mem Natl Assn for Supervision & Curriculum Devel 1969-; life mem Omega Psi Phi Frat Inc; Phi Delta Kappa; Natl Alliance of Black School Educators; comm mem Natl Legislative Comm; NY State Teachers Assn; NY State Guidance Assn; Fayetteville St Coll Alumni Assn; NY Alumni Assn; pres bd dir Schenectady Carver Comm Ctr 1973-78; steward Schenectady's Duryee AMEZ Ch; life mem PTA; pres Grand-Montgomery St Schools; mem adv council Suffolk Co BOCES Dist III 1978-89; chairman draft bd US Selective Serv for Suffolk Cty 1983-89; Grumman Ski Club 1980-; vice chairman, Suffolk County Human Rights Commission, 1981-89; educ comm, life member, NAACP, 1981-; Port Chester/Town of Rye Council of Community Services, president; Port Chester Midget Football League, division coordinator; St Francis' AME Zion Church, stewart; Sno-Burners Ski Club of New York City, board member; Campaign for Kids in Westchester County, steering committee; National Brotherhood of Skiers, eastern regional racing coordinator, 1994-, national youth racing director, 1996-. **Honors/Awds:** Cited local Omega Man of Yr 1977; Notable Amer 1976-77; Presidential Citation to Distinguished Alumni NAFEO 1987; Dedicated Service, SUNY College at Farmingdale, 1986; Omega Man of The Year, 1978. **Business Addr:** Executive Director, Port Chester Carver Center, 35 Traverse Ave, Port Chester, NY 10573.

RECASNER, ELDRIDGE DAVID
Professional basketball player. **Personal:** Born Dec 14, 1967, New Orleans, LA; married Karen, Aug 14, 1993. **Educ:** Washington. **Career:** Played in Germany, 1990-91; Louisville Shooters (CBA), guard, 1991-92; Yakima Sun Kings (CBA), 1992-95; Denver Nuggets, 1995; Houston Rockets, 1995-96; Atlanta Hawks, 1996-. **Honors/Awds:** CBA, MVP, 1995; CBA, All-League first team, 1995. **Special Achievements:** CBA, Championship, 1995. **Business Addr:** Professional Basketball Player, Atlanta Hawks, One CNN Center, Ste 405, Atlanta, GA 30335, (404)827-3800.

REDD, ALBERT CARTER, SR.
Chaplain. **Personal:** Born Mar 13, 1917, Columbia, SC; son of Polly Carter Redd and Curtis Redd; married Georgia Harrison, Sep 29, 1952; children: Althea B, Albert C Jr. **Educ:** Benedict College, Columbus, SC, BA, 1948; Howard Theological Seminary and School, Washington, DC, social work/YMCA certificate, 1949, MA, 1951; Union Theological Seminary, New York, NY, 1954. **Career:** Turner Chapel CME Church, Mt. Clements, MI, pastor, 1958-61; Womack CME Church, Inkster, MI, pastor, 1961-63; Grace CME Church, Detroit, MI, pastor, 1963-67; Cleaves CME Church, Denver, CO, pastor, 1967-74; Veterans Administration Medical Center, Kansas City, MO, chaplain, 1974-75; Veterans Administration Medical Center, Augusta, GA, chaplain, 1975-. **Orgs:** Member, Board of Trustees, Penn Com Center, St Helena, SC, 1986; member, Board of Trustees, Eden Theatrical Workshop, 1979; board member, Society Concerns, Georgia Conference, CME Church, 1980; member, Augusta Black History Committee, 1981. **Honors/Awds:** Minister of the Year, Denver Area, 1974; Key to the City, Denver City Council, 1974; Public Service Award, Veterans Adminstration Hospital, 1978; Plaque, Alpha Chi Lambda, 1984; Superior Performance Award, 1979, 1982, 1984, 1989, Employee of the Year, 1989, Administrator's Hand and Heart Award, 1989, Veterans Administration Medical Center; Eden Award, Eden Theatrical Workshop, 1990; established scholarship for children in the Denver, CO area; Golden Rule Award, 1993. **Military Serv:** US Army, Spc 6, 1941-46; received Good Conduct Medal.

REDD, M. PAUL, SR.
Publishing executive. **Personal:** Born Aug 11, 1928, Martinsville, VA; son of Lucy Martin Redd and Peter Redd; married Orial Banks, Sep 4, 1954; children: M Paul, Jr, Paula A. **Educ:** A&T Coll Greensboro NC, 1953-55. **Career:** Owner of floor waxing company 1955-66; Wechsler Coffee Co, salesman, sales manager, 1966-69; MA Life Insurance Co, agent, 1972-74; Westchester-Putnam Affirmative Action Program Inc, president/chief operating officer, 1974-; Westchester County Press, president/publisher, 1986-. **Orgs:** Mem, 1964-, first vice pres, NY State Conference, 1966-70, legislative chmn, NY State Conference, 1977-, NAACP; founding mem, Black Democrats of Westchester, NY, 1966-; vice chmn, Rye City Democratic Comm, 1966-; vice chmn, Westchester County Democratic Comm, 1967-; mem, 1967-70, chmn Personnel Comm, 1968-70, Urban League of Westchester; mem of Task Force of the County Exec, Westchester Coalition, 1968-70; bd of dirs, United Way of Westchester, 1970-86; mem, 1970-, vice pres, 1972-, Council of Black Elected Democrats of NY State; chmn Region III, NY State Division of Human Rights, 1985-88; first vice chmn, 1987, chmn, 1988, Hudson Valley Economic Development District. **Honors/Awds:** Eugene T Reed Award NY St NAACP 1978. **Military Serv:** AUS m sgt 1950-52. **Business Addr:** President/Chief Operating Officer, Westchester-Putman Affirmative Action Program, Inc, 61 Mitchell Place, White Plains, NY 10601.

REDD, ORIAL ANNE
Government official (retired), newspaper executive. **Personal:** Born Apr 19, 1924, Rye, NY; daughter of Ethel Griffin Banks and William A Banks; married M Paul Redd Sr, Sep 4, 1954; children: Paula Redd Zeman, M Paul Jr. **Educ:** Bennett College, BA, 1946. **Career:** Urban League of Westchester, housing specialist, 1970-72, program director, 1972-74; County Human Services Dept, asst of county executive, 1974-83, Records and Archives, deputy county clerk, 1983-91; The Westchester County Press, vice president, executive editor, currently. **Orgs:** Black Democrats of Westchester, chair; Zeta Phi Beta; NAACP. **Honors/Awds:** Mercy College, Honorary Doctorate in Human Letters; New York State Black & Puerto Rican Caucus, Community Service Award; Natl Assn of Minority Bankers, Government Achievement Award; New York State Conf of NAACP Branches, Community Service Award; Westchester County Bd of Legislators, Government Achievement Award; United Hospital Medical Center, Community Service Award; Daughters of Isis, Woman of the Year; Black Democrats of Westchester, Ernest G Lindsay Award; Westchester Community Opportunity Program, Community Service Award; Operation PUSH Westchester, Community Service Award. **Home Addr:** Rye Colony Apartments, Rye, NY 10580.

REDD, THOMASINA A.
Educator. **Personal:** Born Aug 4, 1941, Montgomery, WV; daughter of Catherine Caves Atwater and Thomas Z Atwater; married Dr Bruce L Redd; children: Paul F, Stephen E. **Educ:** West Virginia Univ, AB 1963, MS 1969, PhD 1986. **Career:** West Virginia Univ, lab tech 1962-63; Alderson-Broaddus College, instructor 1969-71, asst prof 1962-85, chair, div of natural sci, 1985-, assoc prof 1985-91, professor of biology, 1991-. **Orgs:** Member Philippi Baptist Church 1964-; member WV Acad Science 1970-; trustee Barbour Library Board 1978-; trustee WV Foundation for Campus Ministry 1980-; member Allegheny Branch Amer Soc Microbiol 1983-; member Amer Soc of Microbiol 1983-; College Sci Teachers Assn 1982-; Amer Inst of Biological Sci 1982-; Southeastern Assn of Biology, 1989; adv council, WV Inst for School Success, 1989-; mentor & visiting scientist, Amer Soc for Microbiology, 1989-. **Honors/Awds:** Grant Educ DKG Intl Assn Women Educ 1981; Faculty Merit Foundation of WV, Professional Excellence Award, 1990; Sear Roebuck Foundation, Teaching Excellence Award, 1991. **Business Addr:** Professor of Biology, Aiderson-Broaddus College, PO Box 518 A-B College, Philippi, WV 26416, (304)457-6245.

REDD, WILLIAM L.
Attorney. **Personal:** Born Sep 3, 1950, Wilcoe, WV; married Marie E; children: Le Marquis, D'Ann. **Educ:** Marshall Univ, BA 1972; NC Central Univ Law Sch, JD 1976. **Career:** Mar-

shall Univ, instructor 1976; Henderson & Redd, attorney 1976-82; Law Office, sole practitioner attorney 1982-. **Orgs:** Mem Grad Chap Omega Psi 1971; past pres Black Alumni Inc 1978-81; past pres Mountain State Bar Assn 1980-82; former sec Cabell Co Commission on Crime & Delinquency 1982-83; chmn bd of dirs Green Acres Found 1982-84; mem Marshall Univ Memorial Tournament Comm 1984; Little League Baseball coach 1984-85; NAACP Legal Redress Officer Huntington Branch NAACP 1976-; Legal Redress Comm WV Conference 1976-; pres Cabell Co Deputy Sheriff's Civil Serv Comm 1981-; vice pres Green Acres Mental Retardation Center 1981-; trustee First Baptist Church Huntington 1981-; chmn Scottie Reese Scholarship Bd First Baptist Church 1982-; mem Big Green Scholarship Fund Marshall Univ 1982-; mem adv counsel Licensed Practical Nurses Cabell Co 1982-; chmn Minority Recruitment Comm for Faculty &Staff at Marshall UnNAACP 1984-. **Honors/Awds:** Prentice Hall Awd NCCU Sch of Law 1976; Omega Man of the Year Omega Psi Phi Nu Beta Chap 1978; Outstanding Black Alumni Black Alumni Inc Marshall 1979; Recognition Awd Adbul Temple 1981; Outstanding Leadership Mt State Bar Assn 1982. **Military Serv:** USAR sp-4 6 yrs. **Business Addr:** Attorney, 530 Fifth Ave, Huntington, WV 25701.

REDDEN, CAMILLE J.
Reference librarian. **Personal:** Born Oct 30, 1930, Paducah, KY; daughter of Susie Kevil Johnson and James R Johnson; married James M Redden, Feb 12, 1953; children: Enid, Rosland, Jane, Paula, Mona. **Educ:** Tennessee State University, Nashville, TN, BA, 1952. **Career:** Southern University-Shreveport, Shreveport, LA, reference librarian, 1970-. **Orgs:** Louisiana Library Assn, 1990-; American Library Assn, 1990-. **Business Addr:** Reference Librarian, Library, Southern University-Shreveport, 3050 Martin Luther King Dr, Shreveport, LA 71107.

REDDICK, ALZO JACKSON
Educator, elected official. **Personal:** Born Nov 15, 1937, Alturas, FL; married Elouise Williams; children: Nesper, Tausha, Alzo J Jr, Jason. **Educ:** Paul Quinn Coll, BS 1960; FL A&M, mEd 1971; Nova U, EdD 1977. **Career:** High School teacher; Valencia Comm, asst to vice pres of planning; Rollins Coll, asst dean, 1970-; State of Florida, state rep, currently. **Orgs:** Pres-elect SABAP; chmn, Florida Caucus Black Dems; consult Florida Drug Abuse Trust; adv Criminal Justice Task Force; bd dir Youth Programs Inc; bd dir, Additions Orange Co Inc; bd dir Mid-FL Ctr for Alcoholism; bd dir Channel #24 Pub TV; mem Florida Bureau of History Museum; youth comm, chmn dep majority leader Dem natl Comm 1984-86; chmn, Affirmative Action Comm FL Dem Party Orlando Single Mem Dist Task Force; mem, Amer Assoc of Higher Educ, Southern Coll Placement Assoc; bd dir Orange County Additions; bd dir Better Bus Bureau, Brookwood Comm Hosp, Guardian Care Nursing Home; mem Alpha Phi Alpha, Phi Delta Kappa; chmn Mercy Drive Neighbors in Action; exec comm 1976,82, chmn 1980-81 Orange County Dem; mem FL Police Standards Comm 1980-81; chmn United Negro Coll Fund. **Honors/Awds:** Comm Serv Award, Washington Shores Assn for Recreation; Cited for Historical Presentations of the Black Cowboys Orange County Dem Exec Comm Community Serv Award 1981; Cited for Community Contribs WASAR, The Additions Inc, Modern Majestic Club First Black Legislative Award 1982; Law Enforcement Most Effective Freshman 1983; Jones High School Serv & Leadership Award 1983; Natl Dem Comm Appreciation Awd 1983. **Military Serv:** AUS 1961-64. **Business Addr:** State Representative, State of Florida, 725 S Goldwyn, Orlando, FL 32805.

REDDICK, LINDA H.
Educator (retired). **Personal:** Born Dec 20, 1916, Bronwood, GA; daughter of Anna Harris and Morgan Harris; married Booker T (deceased). **Educ:** Spelman Coll; Wiley Coll, AB 1935; NY U; Stetson U. **Career:** Edgewater HS, tchr; Jones HS Orlando, head of English Dept. **Orgs:** 1st black to serve as pres Co of Orange Tchr of English 1965; Reader & Adjudicator of English Written Composition Natl Council Teachers of English 1965; mem FL Council Teachers of English; am Assn of Univ Wmn; past area chmn So Area Links Inc 1963-67; vice-chmn City's Minimum Standards Bd of Adjmts & Appeals; mem Delta Sigma Theta Sor Inc; mem Orange Co Bd of Comm Svc; mem adv bd Orange County Council of Sci & Arts; bd of directors, Florida Symphony Orchestra; bd of directors, Metropolitan Orlando Urban League; first committee, First Academy, A First Baptist of Orlando Ministry; immediate past pres, founder, National Chatterbox editor 1988-89; Orlando Chapter, Girl Friends Inc; mem, First Baptist/Orlando; teleton chm, UNCF 1990-. **Honors/Awds:** Greater Orlando Chamber of Commerce's Community Award 1988; Recipient of Summit Award for Outstanding Community Service, 1994; served on Disney's "Terrific Teacher" selection committee, 1995.

REDDICK, THOMAS J., JR.
Judge. **Personal:** Born Jan 4, 1919, Sarasota, FL; divorced; children: Conrad R, Cedrick J, Thomas J, III. **Educ:** FL A&M U, BS; Howard U, LLB. **Career:** St of FL, circuit judge, ct of record judge 1971-72, asst municipal judge 1970-71; Broward Co FL, pub defender 1965-67. **Orgs:** Mem Am Bar Assn; FL Bar Assn; Nat Bar Assn; fdr mem Judicial Counc of Nat Bar Assn; Broward Co Bar Assn; Alpha Kappa Mu Hon Soc; trustee Mt Hermon AME Ch; mem Elks; Omega Psi Phi Frat; Mason Sat on 4th Dist Ct of Appeals St of FL 1975. **Military Serv:** M sgt 4 yrs. **Business Addr:** 201 SE 6 St, Fort Lauderdale, FL 33301.

REDDING, LOUIS L.
Attorney. **Personal:** Born in Alexandria, VA; married Gwnedolyn Kiah; children: Ann Holmes, Rupa R Lallinger, Judith R. **Educ:** Brown Univ, AB, LLD Hon 1973; Harvard Law Sch, LLB 1928. **Career:** Fessenden Acad Ocala FL, vice principal 1923-24; Morehouse Coll, tchr 1924-25; State of DE, public defender 1965-84; Attorney at Law. **Orgs:** Mem Amer Bar Assn; mem Natl Bar Assn. **Home Addr:** 158 Locksley Rd, Glen Mills, PA 19342. **Business Addr:** Attorney, 1200 Mellon Bank Building, Wilmington, DE 19801.

REDDRICK, MARK A.
Oil company executive. **Career:** Phoenix Oil Co, chief executive officer, currently. **Special Achievements:** Company listed #99 on Black Enterprise's list of the top 100 industrial/service companies, 1994. **Business Addr:** CEO, Phoenix Oil Co., 1434 W 76th St, Chicago, IL 60620, (312)224-8809.

REDMON, ANN LOUISE. **See ALI, FATIMA.**

REDMON, ANTHONY
Professional football player. **Personal:** Born Apr 9, 1971, Brewton, AL. **Educ:** Auburn, attended. **Career:** Arizona Cardinals, guard, 1994-. **Business Addr:** Professional Football Player, Arizona Cardinals, 8701 S Hardy, Tempe, AZ 85284, (602)379-0101.

REDMOND, EUGENE B.
Poet, educator. **Personal:** Born Dec 1, 1937, East St Louis, IL; son of Emma Hutchinson Redmond and John Henry Redmond; children: Treasure. **Educ:** Southern Illinois University, BA, 1964; Washington University, St Louis MO, MA, 1966. **Career:** East St Louis Beacon, East St Louis IL, associate editor, 1961-62; Monitor, East St Louis IL, contributing editor, 1963-65, executive editor, 1965-67, editorial page and contributing editor, 1967-; Southern Illinois University at Edwardsville, East St Louis IL branch, teacher-counselor in Experiment in Higher Education, 1967-68, poet in residence and director of language workshops, 1968-69; Oberlin College, Oberlin OH, writer in residence and lecturer in Afro-American studies, 1969-70; California State University, Sacramento CA, professor of English and poet in residence in ethnic studies, 1970-85; Eugene B. Redmond Writers Club, East St Louis IL, founder and director, 1985-; East St Louis Public Schools, East St Louis IL, special asstsuperintendent for cultural and language arts, 1985 Wayne State University, Detroit MI, Martin Luther King Jr-Cesar Chavez-Rosa Parks Visiting Professor, 1989-90; founder and publisher, Black River Writers Press; coordinator, Annual Third World Writers and Thinkers Symposium, 1972-; director, Henry Dumas Creative Writing Workshop, 1974-; assoc pub, Litenati Int'l; prof of English, Southern IL U, 1990-. **Orgs:** Congress of Racial Equality; American Newspaper Guild; Natl Newspaper Publishers Assn; Natl Assn of African American Educators; African Assn of Black Studies; California Assn of Teachers of English; California Writers Club; Northern California Black English Teachers Assn. **Honors/Awds:** Washington Univ Annual Festival of the Arts first prize, 1965; Free Lance magazine first prize, 1966; Literary Achievement Award, Sacramento Regional Arts Council, 1974; Best of the Small Press Award, Pushcart Press, 1976; Poet Laureate of East St Louis IL, 1976; California State Univ, Sacramento, faculty research award, 1976; California Arts Council grant, 1977; Illinois Arts Council grant, 1977-78; National Endowment for the Arts fellowship, 1978; author of Sentry of the Four Golden Pillars, Black River Writers, 1971; author of In a Time of Rain and Desire: Love Poems, Black River Writers, 1973; author of Drumvoices: The Mission of Afro-American Poetry, A Critical History, Anchor, 1976; Pyramid Award from Pan African Movement USA, 1993; American Book Award, for collection of poems The Eye in the Ceiling, 1993-; Illinois Author of the Year (IL Assn of Teachers of English), 1989. **Military Serv:** US Marines, 1958-61. **Home Addr:** PO Box 6165, East St Louis, IL 62202.

REDMOND, JANE SMITH
Educational administrator. **Personal:** Born Jul 20, 1948, Cleveland, TN; daughter of Earnestine Smith and V. Campbell Smith; children: Gyasi. **Educ:** Knoxville Coll, BS 1970; Univ of TN, MS 1979; Ph.D. Student Ohio State Univ Columbus, Ohio; Ohio State University, PhD, 1991. **Career:** UTK Program Office, prog advisor; UTK Women's Ctr, dir; Office of Minority Student Affairs Univ TN, dir; Student Affairs, assistant vice chancellor, currently. **Orgs:** Mem officer Alpha Kappa Alpha Sor Inc; bd of dirs United Way of Knoxville 1984-; bd of dirs Knoxville Inst for the Arts 1985-. **Honors/Awds:** Knoxville's 10 Most Eligible Career Women 1983; Bronze Woman Candidate, 1996-97; Chancellors Citation, Extraordinary Community Service, 1994-. **Home Addr:** 8650 Eagle Pointe Dr, Knoxville, TN 37931. **Business Phone:** (615)974-6861.

REDON, LEONARD EUGENE
Service industry executive. **Personal:** Born Nov 4, 1951, St Louis, MO; son of Joyce Woodfox Redon (deceased) and Leonard Redon; married Denise Socquet Redon, Aug 26, 1972; children: Jason, Jennifer. **Educ:** Worchester Polytechnic Institute, Worchester, MA, BS, Chemical Engineering, 1973. **Career:** Eastman Kodak, Rochester, NY, district service mgr, 1984-86, product service mgr, 1986-87, market mgr copy product, 1987, corporate account exec, 1987-88, asst to the chairman and president, 1988-89, director of service parts management, 1989-. **Orgs:** Board chairman, Network North Star, Inc, 1989-; board director, Center for Youth Services, 1989-; member, Association Field Service Managers, 1984-; member, Urban League of Rochester, 1989-. **Business Addr:** Director, Service Parts Management, Customer Equipment Services Division, Eastman Kodak, 800 Lee Rd, Rochester, NY 14650-0803.

REDUS, GARY EUGENE
Professional baseball player. **Personal:** Born Nov 1, 1956, Athens, AL; married Minnie Diggs; children: Lakesha, Manesha, Nakosha. **Career:** Outfielder: Cincinnati Reds, 1982-85, Philadelphia Phillies, 1986, Chicago White Sox, 1987-88; Pittsburgh Pirates, infielder/outfielder, 1988-93; Texas Rangers, 1993-. **Honors/Awds:** Led all National League rookies in stolen bases, triples, runs and game-winning RBIs, 1983. **Business Addr:** Professional Baseball Player, Texas Rangers, 1250 Copeland Rd, Ste 1100, Arlington, TX 76011.

REECE, AVALON B.
Educator (retired). **Personal:** Born Oct 10, 1927, Muskogee, OK. **Educ:** Langston U, Bachelors Degree 1948; Univ Southern CA Los Angeles; M Music Ed 1954; Pepperdine Clg Los Angeles CA; Vander Cook Sch Music Chicago, IL; Northeastern OK State U, Standard Cert Phys Ed 1963, Standard Cert HS Cnslr 1967; Southwestern OK State U. **Career:** Manuel Training HS, band directress 1948-66, girls physical educ instructor 1953-67, activity dir 1967-70, counselor 1967-70; EASP, secondary activity coordinator 1971-73; Muskogee HS, counselor. **Orgs:** Life mem Natl Ed Assc; mem Am Prsnl & Guid Assc; mem Am Sch Cnslr Assc; mem Profsnl Recgntn Com Am Sch Cnslr Assc; mem Assc Non White Concern; mem OK Prsnl & Guid Assc; mem Midwest Reg Brnch Assbly OK Prnsl & Guid Assc; mem OK Ed Assc; mem Human Relations Cmsn OK Ed Assc; mem Eastern Dist Deans & Cnslr OK Ed Assc; mem Muskogee Ed Assc; mem Natl League of Cities; mem OK Muncipal League; mem Professional Standards Bd State Bd of Ed; mem Natl Black Caucus of Local Elected Ofcrs; mem Women in Municipal Govt; mem Area VI Rep Bd of Dir; mem Citizens Advsry Cncl on Goals for OK Higher Ed; mem OK UN Day Com IWY; mem Human Resource Com NLC; parlimentarian southwest region Natl Sorority of Phi Delta Kappa- Delta Omicron Chptr; mem Assc Governing Bd; mem Real Estate Sales Assc; mem Muskogee City Cncmem Mayor's City Chrtr Revison; mem bd dir Muskogee Cty Cncl of Youth Serv; Mayor's Cncl Drug Abuse; mem WIBC; mem Juvenile Prsnl Training Pgm; mem AAUW; mem Alpha Epsilon Omega Chap of Alpha Kappa Alpha Sor; Foundation for Excellence, Top Ladies of Distinction, selection committee, Inc. **Honors/Awds:** First black city cnclwmn State of OK; distgshd women Muskogee Serv League; Woman of the Year, Zeta Phi Beta Sorortity, 1975; demo presdtl elector 1976; Patriot of the Month, Muskogee Bicentennial Com, 1976; Key to the City, Gary, IN, 1976; Key to the City, Kansas City, MO, 1979; delegate to the Demo Natl Conv 1980; Honorable Order of Kentucky Colonel; Distinguished Public Service Award, OK Clg of Osteopatic Medicine & Surg 1985; Ambassador of Goodwill Award, Governor Nigh, 1982; Distinguished Public Service Award, The OK Coll of Osteopathic Medicine & Surgery 1985; Awd 35 yr Pin Muskogee Educ Assoc; apptd as Hon Atty General by OK State Atty Genl Michael C Turpen 1986.

REECE, GUY L., II
Judge. **Career:** Franklin County Municipal Court, judge, currently. **Business Addr:** Judge, Franklin County Municipal Court, 369 South High Street, Court Room 6B, Columbus, OH 43215, (614)462-3550.

REECE, STEVEN
Business executive. **Personal:** Born Sep 12, 1947, Cincinnati, OH; son of Claudia Reece and Edward Reece; married Barbara Howard, Sep 12, 1970; children: Alicia Michelle Reece, Steven Reece Jr, Tiffany Janelle Reece. **Educ:** Xavier Univ, BS communication 1970; Ohio Business Coll BA 1985; Amos Tuck/Dartmouth Coll, MBA 1987. **Career:** WCPO-TV, TV director; Motown Records, road mgr for Supremes, Temptations, Stevie Wonder; Cincinnati's 1st Black Mayor Theodore M Berry, exec asst; Communiplex Services, pres/founder; Reece & Reece Enterprise, Cincinnati OH, pres/founder, currently. **Orgs:** Pres Operation PUSH; co-chmn Rev Jesse Jackson's Presidential Campaign in Hamilton County; first Black elected to Cincinnati Advertising Club; radio program (WCIN-AM) "What Are the Issues?"; local chmn Operation PUSH Intl Trade Bureau; mktg chmn Greater Cincinnati Chamber of Commerce; jr grand warden Prince Hall Masons; promotion dir Prince Hall Shriner's Free & Accepted. **Honors/Awds:** Certificate of Honor Central State Univ; CEBA Awd; Feature stories Jet, Time, Cincinnati Magazine, Nip Magazine and Natl TV Stations; Local School

Chmn, Withrow High School; Cum Laude Honor Society, Withrow High School; America's Best and Brightest Young Business and Professional Men, Dollars & Sense Magazine, 1987; Chmn, Communiplex Natl Women's Hall of Fame.

REED, ADDISON W.
Educator. **Personal:** Born Apr 22, 1929, Steubenville, OH; married Sylvia A; children: 1. **Educ:** Kent St U, AB 1951; MA & BS 1953 & 1957; Univ NC Chapel Hill, PhD 1973. **Career:** St Augustine's Coll, Raleigh NC, chmn music dept, div humanities; Albany St Coll, dir choral activities 1965-69; St Augustine's Coll, asst prof 1961-65; Booker HS, Sarasota, FL, instr music (choral) 1958-61; Henderson Inst, Henderson NC, instr music (choral) 1953-54. **Orgs:** Mem Musicological Assn; Music Educators Nat Conf; Nat Assn of Tchrs of Singing; Raleigh Chamber Music Guild; Am Musicological Soc; bd of dir NC Symphony Orch; Mu Beta Psi Outstdg Educator of Am 1973. **Honors/Awds:** Dist Young Black American, 1973; Ford Dissertation Fellowship, 1972; Dissertation Topic the life and works of scott joplin; article on scott- joplin in VI edof Grove's Dict of Music and Musicians. **Military Serv:** Pfc 1954-56. **Business Addr:** Chrmn, Div of Hum & Mus Dept, St Augustines College, 1315 Oakwood Ave, Raleigh, NC 27611.

REED, ADOLPHUS REDOLPH
Expediter, law enforcement official. **Personal:** Born May 18, 1912, Pittsburg, TX; son of Mr & Mrs Frank Reed; married Ernestine; children: 1. **Career:** GD Convair, expediter 1975-; Betsy Ross School, Anaheim, California, security officer; San Diego County, special deputy sheriff. **Orgs:** Pres, United Comm Dem Club 1975-; elect Co Dem Dent Comm by popular vote, 8 terms (16 yrs), v chmn 4 times still serv; v chmn, Unit Comm Dem Club, 6 terms; chmn, United Comm Dem Club, nine 1 yr terms pres serv; apptd club chart chmn, Co Dem Cent Comm 5 terms; v chmn, NAACP, 2 terms; city commn to elim litter; State Dem Cent Com; cau chmn 79th Assem Dist; com pres Kenn & Pres Johnson visit to San Diego; deacon Mt Olive Church. **Honors/Awds:** Rec awds from Sen Pro-Tem of 4th Dist on 2 occasions; awds NAACP; Black Fed of San Diego; spon beauty contest, more than 50 girls received scholarships. **Business Addr:** Community Liaison, Senator Wadie P Deddeh, Fortieth Senatorial District, California Legislature, 430 Davidson St, Chula Vista, CA 91910.

REED, ALFONZO
Attorney. **Personal:** Born Jun 5, 1938, Bessemer, AL; son of Willie Mae Taylor Reed and Scieb C. Reed. **Educ:** Talladega Coll Talladega AL, BA 1958; Atlanta U, MS 1964; Howard Univ Washington DC, JD 1975. **Career:** Private Practice, atty 1976-; Wien Lane & Malkin NYC, legal asst 1975-76; Greenwich CT, tchr 1966-72; Atlanta GA, tchr 1965-66; Groton CT, tchr 1964-65; Calhoun AL, tchr 1959-63. **Orgs:** Parliament Delta Theta Phi Law Frat 1973-75; bd of dir Urban League SW Fairfield Co CT 1975; mem CT Bar Assn 1976; mem Greenwich Bar Assn; chmn Black Awareness Comm Grnwch 1968-69; chmn Org of Black Studies Grnwch 1968-69; pres Grnwch Educ Assn 1970-71; mem Alpha Phi Alpha Frat Inc. **Honors/Awds:** Man of the yr distinguished Serv awd Grnwch Jaycees 1971; Earl Warren scholarship NAACP Legal Def & Educ fund 1972-75; scholarship Howard Univ Sch of Law 1973; student of the yr Howard Univ Sch of Law 1975.

REED, ALLENE WALLACE
College administrator. **Personal:** Born in Harpersville, AL; daughter of Eula Bell Davis Wallace and Waymon Lether Wallace; married Jesse Reed Jr; children: Jesse III, Gwenderlyn Carol. **Educ:** Univ of Cincinnati, BS 1972, EdM 1975, PhD 1980. **Career:** Ben Siegel Realtor, real estate sales assoc 1956-72; Cincinnati Public Schools, teacher 1968-72; Univ of Cincinnati, assoc to the dean 1973-75; asst to the dean 1972-73; asst dean dir div of social science 1975-89; assistant dean, graduate studies and research, 1990-. **Orgs:** Mem Natl Assn for Women Deans, Administrators and Counselors; mem Ohio Assn for Women Deans, Administrators, and Counselors; The Assn for Continuing Higher Educ; Natl Univ Contining Educ Assn; The Ohio Conf on Issues Facing Women, Black Faculty and Administration in Higher Educ; Rainbow Coalition; Natl Political Congress of Black Women NAACP; The Southern Poverty Law Center; Citizen's Cable Communication Bd of Cincinnati; Citizen's Comm on Youth; Woman's City Club of Greater Cincinnati; former chair Univ of Cincinnati City of Cincinnati Police Consortium; vice pres Charter Committee of Greater Cincinnati, Ohio Psychological Assn; Delta Sigma Theta; Psi Chi; Natl Political Women's Caucus 1988-89; Black Forum; Operation Bootstrap; Council of Graduate Studies. **Honors/Awds:** Outstanding Woman's Awd NAACP Natl Office 1981; Outstanding Contribution to the Black Community UBAFAS 1981; Image Maker Radio Station WCIN 1984; Honorary Societies, Psi Chi; Alpha Sigma Kappa; Alpha Sigman Lambda; Citizen for the Day; 200 Univ of Cincinnati Alumni, Univ of Cincinnati 1988; Enquirer Woman of the Year, Cincinnati Enquirer 1986; 200 Greater Cincinnatians, Cincinnati Bicentennial Commn 1988; Portraits of Excellence: 100 Black Cincinnatians, Cincinnati Bicentennial Commn 1988. **Home Addr:** 3931 Wess Park Drive, Cincinnati, OH 45217. **Business Addr:** Asst Dean, Research & Advanced Studies, Univ of Cincinnati, 305 Braunstein, ML 627, Cincinnati, OH 45221.

REED, ANDRE DARNELL
Professional football player. **Personal:** Born Jan 29, 1964, Allentown, PA; married Cyndi; children: Auburn. **Educ:** Kutztown State College, attended. **Career:** Buffalo Bills, wide receiver, 1985-; Fitness Powerhouse Gym, owner. **Orgs:** Big Brothers/Big Sisters of Western New York, celebrity spokesperson. **Honors/Awds:** Post-season play: AFC Championship Game, 1988, 1990, 1991; Pro Bowl, 1988, 1989, 1990, 1991, 1992, 1993, 1994; Appearances in Super Bowl XXV, XXVI, XXVII, XXVIII; Hall of Fame Inductee, Kutztown University, 1991. **Business Addr:** Professional Football Player, Buffalo Bills, One Bills Dr, Orchard Park, NY 14127, (716)648-1800.

REED, BEATRICE M.
Real estate broker. **Personal:** Born Jan 5, 1916, St Georges, Grenada; children: 1 Daughter. **Educ:** Howard Univ Wash DC, BA 1967. **Career:** Beat M Reed RE Co, own brok 1951-; Unit Pub Wkrs of Am CIO, intnl rep 1946-48; DC Br NAACP, admin asst 1944-46; War & Product Bd USGovt, asst supr stat sec 1942-44; NC Mut Ins Co, ins agt 1940-42. **Orgs:** Cam mgr Camper for Congr 4th Congress Dist MD 1948; pres Bymarc Inc 1975-; past pres Wash R E Brok Assn 1975-76; chmn const & by-laws com Nat Assn of R E Brok 1979-; past pres Cent Club Nat Assn of Negro Bus & Professional Wom Clubs Inc 1968-71; chmn natl hous com Nat Assn of Neg Bus & Professional Wom Clubs Inc 1978-; bd of dir Sub MD Bd of Dir 1978-; pres Carib Am Intercul Orgn 1980. **Honors/Awds:** 1st Black Civ Serv employ to serve as civ serv exam US Civ Serv Commn 1943; 1st Black Wom to be Intnl Rep Labor Un Unit Pub Wrkrs of Am CIO 1946-48; feat in HUD Chal Mag Intnl Wom Yr iss Dept of Hous & Urb Devel 1975; pres of the yr awd Nat Assn of RE Est Brok Inc 1976; pion wom in RE Nat Wom Counc of Nat Assn of RE Brok Inc 1979; awd of recog Nat Assn of RE Brok Inc 1980. **Business Addr:** Beatrice M Reed Real Estate Co, 9320 Greyrock Road, Silver Spring, MD 20910.

REED, CHARLOTTE (CHARLOTTE REED PEEBLES)
Educator. **Personal:** Born Apr 27, 1948, New York, NY; daughter of Thomas L & Lillian M Reed; married Twain M Peebles, Sep 12, 1987; children: Mark D Peebles. **Educ:** Richmond College, CUNY, BA, 1972; Univ of Virginia, MEd, 1977, EdD, 1980. **Career:** New York City Public Schools, English teacher, 1972-76; Charlottesville Public Schools, behavior modification teacher, 1976-77; Univ of Virginia, project dir, 1977-81; Univ of Louisville, assistant prof, 1981-87; Alverno College, asst and assoc prof, 1987-90; Purdue Univ, Calument, assoc prof, 1990-92; Indiana Univ Northwest, dir/assoc prof, 1992-. **Orgs:** International Alliance for Invitational Education, advisory bd member, 1982-; American Education Research Assn, 1981-; Phi Delta Kappa, Chap 1029, 1993-96, exec bd mem, 1978-; National Assn for Multicultural Education, 1992-; National Council for Black Studies, 1992-94; Assn of Teacher of Educators, commission member, 1992-. **Honors/Awds:** National Academy of Education, Fellowship, 1983; State of Kentucky House of Representatives, Cert of Commendation for Comm Service, 1984; Governor of Kentucky, Kentucky Colonel Comm, 1984; Women Educators, Activism Award, 1993; College of Staten Island, Alumni Hall of Fame, 1994; Phi Delta Kappa, Outstanding Service, 1994-95. **Special Achievements:** Chapter in Advancing Invitational Thinking, Novak, J (Ed), 1992; "Invitational and Multicultural Perspectives: What Do They Have in Common?"; "Family Stress and Self-Esteem," Denver Univ Law Review, 1992; "Enhancing Self-Esteem in Multicultural Classrooms," Invitational Education Forum, 1992; "Teacher Invitations and Effectiveness," ERIC, 1981; "Overcoming Prejudices: An Invitational Approach," The Urban Review, 1996. **Business Addr:** Dir/Assoc Prof of Educ, Indiana University Northwest, Urban Teacher Education Program, 3400 Broadway, 301 Hawthorn Hall, Gary, IN 46408, (219)980-6887.

REED, CLARA TAYLOR
Health services administrator. **Career:** Mid-Delta Home Health Inc, chief executive officer, currently. **Special Achievements:** Company is ranked #83 on Black Enterprise's list of top 100 companies, 1994. **Business Addr:** CEO, Mid-Delta Home Health Inc., PO Box 373, ATTN: Mary Daniel, Belzoni, MS 39038, (601)247-1254.

REED, CLARENCE HAMMIT, III
Sales executive. **Personal:** Born Oct 25, 1957, Amite, LA; son of Eunice Paddio Johnson and Clarence Reed; married Sandra A Reed (divorced 1987); children: Doreal Hayes, Matthew David. **Educ:** Cornell University, Ithaca, NY, BS, 1979. **Career:** Eli Lilly & Co, Indianapolis, IN, sales, 1979-81; Solar Resources of American, Columbus, OH, sales manager, 1982-83; Xerox Corp, Columbus, OH, sales, 1983-86; Reed Enterprises & Development, Columbus, OH, owner, 1986-; Animed Computer Systems, Oshkosh, WI, sales, 1986-88; CMHC Systems, Dublin, OH, sales representative, 1988-. **Home Addr:** 2332 Vendome Dr, Columbus, OH 43219-1437, (614)258-7292. **Business Phone:** (614)764-0143.

REED, CORDELL
Vice president. **Personal:** Born Mar 26, 1938, Chicago, IL; married Ora Lee; children: Derrick, Brian, Steven, Michael. **Educ:** Univ of IL, BSME 1960. **Career:** Commonwealth Edison, vice pres nuclear operations; des op coal-fired generator Sta, 7 yrs; des construction oper nuclear power generator sta, 13 yrs. **Orgs:** Mem Amer Nuclear Soc; mem West Soc of Engineers; Natl Technical Assn; trustee Metropolitan Comm Church; trustee Abraham Lincoln Center; dir Independent Bank of Chicago. **Honors/Awds:** Black Achievers of Industry, recognition award, YMCA. **Business Addr:** One First Nat Plaza, Box 767, Chicago, IL 60690.

REED, DAISY FRYE
Educator. **Personal:** Born in Washington, DC; daughter of Alberta Ruth Edwards Frye and James Edward Frye Jr; divorced; children: James S Jr, Kristel M. **Educ:** DC Teachers Coll, BS 1953-56; George Washington Univ, MA 1957-61; Teachers Coll Columbia Univ, MEd, EdD 1973-75; Loyola Univ, MRE, 1992-94. **Career:** Washington DC Publ Schools, teacher 1956-73; Teachers Coll Columbia Univ, asst prof, dir of teacher corps proj 1975-76; Publ School Syst VA, consult; State Department of Education, consultant; School of Ed VA Commonwealth Univ, professor, 1976-. **Orgs:** President, Assn of Teacher Educators in Virginia, 1988-91; ATE, 1978-; Phi Delta Kappa; Zeta Phi Beta Sorority, 1955-. **Honors/Awds:** Innovation Awd DC Publ Schools Washington; Minority Student Scholarship Teachers Coll Columbia Univ; Reise-Melton Award for Promoting Cross-Cultural Understanding, Virginia Commonwealth University, 1990-91; Outstanding Service Award, 1991-92; Outstanding Teacher Award, 1994-95. **Special Achievements:** Co-Author: Classroom Management for the Realities of Today's Schools; Author of book chapter in J Wood's Mainstreaming; articles published in Action in Teacher Education; NASSP Journal; Middle School Journal; research studies: Resilient At-Risk Children; Teaching in Culturally Diverse Classrooms; African-American Women in Higher Education. **Business Addr:** Professor, Virginia Commonwealth University, School Of Education, Box 842020, Richmond, VA 23284-2020.

REED, DERRYL L.
Telecommunications executive. **Personal:** Born in Chicago, IL; son of Jesse A Reed Jr. **Educ:** Southern IL Univ, BS Math 1970; Univ of Chicago, MBA Marketing/Finance 1976. **Career:** Chicago Bd of Educ, substitute teacher 1970-77; American Can Co, sales rep 1970-73, account mgr, 1973-75, area mgr, 1975-77, assoc product mgr, napkins, 1977-78, asst product mgr, Aurora Bathroom Tissue, 1978-80; Tetley Inc, product mgr soluble tea products, 1980-83, product mgr tea bags, 1983-85, sr product mgr tea bags, 1985-86, sr product mgr tea products, 1986-87; Heublein Inc, dir of marketing prepared drinks, 1987-89; Teachers Insurance & Annuity Assn of Amer, asst vice pres of insurance services, 1989-94; Ameritech, dir of brand management, dir of market planning and development, 1994-95, dir of marketing, 1995-. **Orgs:** Mem bd of dirs Chicago NAACP 1975; consulting partner Reed & Reed Assocs; bd of dirs Natl Black MBA Assn, 1986-; assoc bd of dirs Tea Assoc of the USA Inc; past chmn NY Corp Matching Gift Fund for Lou Rawls Parade of Stars Telethon for United Negro Coll Fund; life mem Kappa Alpha Psi Frat; mem, Consumer Promotion Comm, Assn of Natl Advertisers; national president, National Black MBA Association; advisory bd mem, Southern Illinois Univ School of Business, 1992-. **Honors/Awds:** A Black Achiever in Industry Awd Amer Can Co; Outstanding Service & Achievement Awd Kappa Alpha Psi Frat; MBA of the Year, 1988; featured in Oct 1985 issue of Black Enterprise Magazine; participant in 2 TV programs hosted by Phil Donahue; guest speaker, Connecticut Public Television; guest lecturer at the Univ of CT and Atlanta Univ. **Home Addr:** 3297 Woodview Lake Drive, West Bloomfield, MI 48323.

REED, EDDIE
Educator. **Personal:** Born May 31, 1945, Jemison, AL; son of Ola Mae and Curtis; married Clarissia Smitherman. **Educ:** Daniel Puyne Coll, BS 1967; Auburn Univ, 1971; Univ of Montevallo, MEd 1973. **Career:** City of Jemison, councilman 1976-; Curtis-James Patio Furniture, pres 1987-. **Orgs:** Mem NEA & AEA 1967-; worshipful master F&AM of AL 1971-85; mem Park & Rec Bd Town of Jemison. **Honors/Awds:** Awd State of AL for Outstanding Achievement 1984; awd Chilton Improvement Assn Outstanding Services 1985; commissioner Election Law Comm State of AL 1980-. **Home Addr:** P O Box 267, Jemison, AL 35085. **Business Addr:** President, Curtis-James Patio furniture, R L Langston Dr, Jemison, AL 35085.

REED, FLORINE
Clergyman. **Personal:** Born Dec 11, 1905, Turlton, OK; married Eugene H. **Educ:** Boston, BTh 1959. **Career:** Non-Denom Ch, pastor; Temple Christ Chs Inc, overseer; Dorchest MA & San Anton TX Chs, pastor. **Business Addr:** 115 Connelly St, San Antonio, TX 78203.

REED, FLOYD T.
Clergyman. **Personal:** Born Feb 4, 1915, Leavenworth, KS; married Lorene B; children: 3. **Career:** Resurrection Church of God in Christ, Kansas City MO, founder and pastor 1975-. **Military Serv:** AUS 1st sgt 1941-49.

REED, GREGORY J.
Attorney. **Personal:** Born May 21, 1948, Michigan; son of Bertha Mae Reed and James Reed; married Verladia T; children: Arian Simone, Ashley Sierra. **Educ:** MI State Univ, BS 1970, MS 1971; Wayne State Univ, JD 1974, LLM 1978. **Career:** Gregory J Reed & Assocs PC, attorney specializing in corporate, taxation and entertainment law, currently; Wayne State Univ, Detroit MI, prof 1988-89; AHR Packaging Consultant Corp, Detroit MI, pres/developer 1987-. **Orgs:** Chairperson, Martin Luther King Statue Committee; bd of dirs MI Assn of Community Arts Agencies; mem Natl Bar Assn; MSU Foundation, board of directors; comm mem of entertainment sports, taxation, corp and real estate sects Amer Bar Assn; mem Amer Bar Assn; mem Accounting Aide Soc of Metro Detroit; bd comm New Detroit Inc; tax and corp advisor BUF; mem MI State Bar Taxation and Corporate Div; mem Amer Arbitration Assn; bd of dir BESLA Entertainment Law Assn; bd of dirs MI Assn of Community Arts Agencies; mem State Bar Law Media Comm; first black attorney adv bd mem US Internal Revenue Serv; founder Advancement Amateur Athletics Inc 1986; first black chmn in US State Bar of MI Arts Communication Sports and Entertainment Sect 1987; speaker, lecturer US & foreign countries; MSU Foundation, vice chairperson, 1996-97. **Honors/Awds:** Graduate Professional Scholarship 3 consecutive years; Distinguished Alumni of the Yr Awd MI State Univ 1980; Resolution for Achievement State of MI Senate, City of Detroit; one of the top ten blacks in the law profession, Detroit News 1985; implemented Gregory J Reed Scholarship Foundation 1986; Award for Contributions to the arts Black Music Month State of MI House of Rep 1987; govt appointment Martin Luther KingCommn of Michigan 1989-; 1992 Hall of Fame inductee by BESLA. **Special Achievements:** Author: Tax Planning and Contract Negotiating Techniques for Creative Persons; Professional Athletes and Entertainers (first book of its kind cited by American Bar Association); This Business of Boxing & Its Secrets, 1981; This Business of Entertainment and Its Secrets, 1985; Negotiations Behind Closed Doors, 1987; Economic Empowerment through the church, American Book Award, 1994; ''Quiet Strength,'' co-author with Rosa Parks; ''Dear Mrs Parks,'' co-author with Rosa Parks. **Business Addr:** Gregory J Reed & Associates, PC, 1201 Bagley, Detroit, MI 48226.

REED, JAKE
Professional football player. **Personal:** Born Sep 28, 1967, Covington, GA; married Vinita; children: Jake Rashann. **Educ:** Grambling State, bachelor's degree in criminal justice. **Career:** Minnesota Vikings, wide receiver, 1991-. **Business Addr:** Professional Football Player, Minnesota Vikings, 9520 Viking Dr, Eden Prairie, MN 55344, (612)828-6500.

REED, JAMES
Educational consultant. **Personal:** Born Oct 1, 1935. **Educ:** Grambling Coll, BS; Colum Univ Teachers Coll, MA; New York Univ Dir coll based second prep prog, additional study. **Career:** NY & LA HS & Elem School, teacher 1958-66; Hunter Coll, supr; NY Univ, curr supr consultant to fed funded program 1967-71; School of Educ Hofstra Univ, consultant early childhood 1971-. **Orgs:** Consultant, hosp hms for mentally retarded public school special educ prog; mem, NY Mayor's Task Force Rec for Hand; Phi Delta Kappa; Intern Read Assn; PTA Urban League NAACP. **Honors/Awds:** Author, ''Music is Fun for Children,'' Play School Assn; co-author, ''Play With A Difference,'' Play School Assn. **Business Addr:** Ed Consultant, PO Box 26, Lincolnton Station, New York, NY 10037.

REED, JAMES W.
Endocrinologist, author. **Personal:** Born Nov 1, 1935, Pahokee, FL; son of Chineater Gray Whitfield and Thomas Reed; married Edna; children: David M, Robert A, Mary I, Katherine E. **Educ:** WV State Coll, BS (summa cum laude) 1954; Howard Univ, MD 1963; resident/internal medicine Tacoma, WA 1966-69; post doctoral research fellowship Univ of California, San Francisco 1969-71. **Career:** Madigan Army Medical Ctr, resident/internal 1966-69; US Army Med Dept, chief of medicine 1978-81; Univ of TX at Dallas, dir of internal medical educ 1982-84; State of WA Med Asst Prog, int med consultant 1984-85; Morehouse School of Medicine, prof/chmn dept of medicine 1985-. **Orgs:** Cons-med Tuskegee VA Hospital 1982-; med dir MMA Inc 1982-; mem Amer Med Assoc, Amer Diabetic Assoc, Amer Endocrine Soc; mem bd of dir Intl Indisciplinary Soc of Hypertension in Blacks; pres Intl Society on Hypertension in Blacks 1987-; pres, Intl Society on Hypertension in Blacks; course director, 7th Intl Conf in Hypertension in Blacks, 1992. **Honors/Awds:** Fellow American College of Physicians; Natl Alumnus of the Year W.VA St Coll 1987; Distinguished Alumni Award NAFECO 1989; Course Director 2nd Intl Conf on Hypertension in Blacks 1987; Fellow American College of Endocrinology. **Special Achievements:** Co-author, The Black Man's Guide to Good Health, Perigee Books, 1994. **Military Serv:** US Army, col, 1962-81; Meritorious Service Medal, Legion of Merit. **Business Addr:** Prof/Chmn Dept of Medicine, Morehouse School of Medicine, 720 Westview Drive SW, Atlanta, GA 30310.

REED, JASPER PERCELL
Educator. **Personal:** Born Mar 2, 1929, Centenary, SC; married Sandra Lee; children: Rosalyn Jackson, Rene Jackson, Valerie Linette. **Educ:** South Carolina State College, BS, biology, 1957; Pennsylvania State University, MEd, bio sci, 1968, DEd, bio sci, 1977. **Career:** Community College of Philadelphia, prof of bio, 1965-; Temple University of Medicine, assisant instructor, 1957-65; City University System, New York, evalu, 1970; Education Testing Service, CLEP, test prod, 1970-73. **Orgs:** Kappa Alpha Psi, 1956-; Beta Kappa Chi, 1957; bd of deac, White Rock Bapt Church, 1962-; American Society Allied Health Profn, 1979. **Honors/Awds:** Recipient, Bronze Star Combat Medic Badge, Good Conduct, AUS, 1948-54; Annual Achievement Award, Philadelphia, Kappa Alpha Psi, 1974; Allied Health Admin Am Assn of State College & Universities, 1979. **Military Serv:** AUS sgt, 1948-54. **Business Addr:** Department of Biology, Community College of Philadelphia, 1700 Spring Garden St, Philadelphia, PA 19130-3936.

REED, JERRILDINE
Attorney. **Personal:** Born in Jersey City, NJ; daughter of Jesse Henry Reed & Della Mae Anderson-Reed; divorced; children: Steven M Adams. **Educ:** Temple Law School, JD, 1981. **Career:** Daniel Preminger, PC & Hugh Clark Esq, law clerk, 1981-83; Congressional Staff of Robert A Borski MC, 1983-86; Greater PA Chamber of Commerce, 1986-90; Rohm & Haas Co., in-house counsel, treasurer for political action committee, 1990-. **Orgs:** Delta Sigma Theta, 1961-96; NJ Bar Association, 1990-96; American Bar Association, 1990-96; National Bar Association, 1990-96; Barristers Association of Philadelphia, 1990-96; Community College of Philadelphia, trustee, 1980-92; Project Bar Association, homeless advocacy, 1990-96; Phildelphia Futures, mentor, 1990-96. **Honors/Awds:** Temple Law, Robt Kline Academic Achievement, 1981; Small Business Advocate, Chamber of Commerce, Appointment, 1989; Volunteer of the Year Awd, Rohm & Haas Co., 1995. **Special Achievements:** Author ''Budget Crisis, A Turning Point for the City,'' Urban League Leadership Institute, 1990; Presentation of ''How To Launch a Judicial campaign,'' Barristers' Association Conference, 1992; Completion of Public Affairs Council Institute Program for Senior Public Affairs Professionals, 1993-96. **Home Addr:** 520 General Patterson Dr, Glenside, PA 19038, (215)886-3077. **Business Addr:** Attorney, Rohm & Haas Co., Rte 413 & State Rd, Corporate Engineering Div, Bristol, PA 19007, (215)785-7451.

REED, JOANN
Educator. **Personal:** Born Mar 28, 1939, Flint, MI; daughter of Robin B Green Owens and Wendell A Owens; married Willie C Reed, Oct 22, 1960; children: Kim F, George, Troy M. **Educ:** Eastern MI Univ, BS 1960, MA 1982. **Career:** Carman-Ainsworth Schools, teacher of educable mentally impaired 1963-73; Bassett Sch Dist, inst for prog inst lab 1973-74, teen mother prog coord 1973-74; Metro Day Care Ctr, admin 1975-76; Ken MacGillivray Buick, salesperson 1976-77; Flint Community Schools, administrator, 1995-. **Orgs:** Mem Natl Assn of Negro Business & Prof Women's Club Inc; teach consultant 1977-, asst sec treas 1981, vice pres 1984, treasurer 1988-89, president 1985-86, 1989-, Flint Bd of Education; prog development Mott Comm Coll 1984; mem Alpha Kappa Alpha Sor; mem Adahi-Hon Soc; mem Carman Educ Assn; mem Natl Roster of Black Elected Officials; Greater Flint Afro-American Hall of Fame 1985-; board member, Urban Coalition, 1989-. **Honors/Awds:** Educators Awd Zeta Phi Beta Sorority Flint 1981; Appreciation Awd Natl Assn Negro Business & Professional Women 1982. **Business Addr:** Teacher Consultant, Carman-Ainsworth School Dist, 1591 S Graham, Flint, MI 48504.

REED, JOE LOUIS
Executive secretary. **Personal:** Born Sep 13, 1938, Evergreen, AL; married Mollie; children: Irva, Joe, Steven. **Educ:** AL State U, BS 1962; Case West Resv U, MA 1966. **Career:** AL Educ Assn Inc, asso sec 1969-; AL State Tchrs Assn, exec sec 1964-69; AL State U, stud act 1963; Trenholm HS, tchr 1962. **Orgs:** Mem loc st & natl professional assn; life mem NEA; mem exec bd NCSEA 1969-75; coord vice pres NCSEA 1975; pres NCSEA 1976-; consult AL Educ Assn Professional Rts & Resp Commn; chmn DuShane Com Tchrs Rights NEA 1971-; stf advsr Unit Tchng Prfsn; delg NEA Conv & Rep Assemb; pres AL Leag for the Advncment of Educ Chrm AL Dem Conf 1970-; mem AL Advsry Com on Civil Rts; v chrm Mnrty Afrs AL Dem Pty 1974-; chm NAACP Com on Ecn 1969-; del Dem-Nat Conv 1968; natl co-Chm Com of Edctrs for Humphrey-muskie pres tkt 1968; city cnclmn City Of Montgomery 1975-; mem Masons; mem Omega Psi Phi Frat. **Honors/Awds:** Received Abraham Lincoln Award, Natl Educ Assn; addressed Democratic Natl Conv, 1972; initial report, Alabama League for Advancement of Educ, ''The Slow Death of the Black Educator in Alabama''; pres, jr class, Alabama State Univ 1960-61; pres, student body, Alabama State Univ, 1961-62. **Military Serv:** AUS 1956-58. **Business Addr:** 422 Dexter Ave, Montgomery, AL 36101.

REED, KATHLEEN RAND
Sociologist. **Personal:** Born Feb 6, 1947, Chicago, IL; daughter of Johnie Viola Rand Cathey and Kirkland James Reed; divorced. **Educ:** San Francisco State Univ, BA. **Career:** IL Supreme Ct Comm on Character and Fitness/(IICLE) Chicago, IL, investigator/rsch consultant 1970; ETA Public Relations Chicago, IL, acct exec 1970-72; WTVS TV 56 (Public TV) Detroit, MI, public relations & promotion dir 1972; WJLB Radio Detroit, MI, public affairs dir 1972-74; KH Arnold (self-employed) San Francisco, CA, business resource and resource consult 1974-80; The Headquarters Co Subsidiary of United Techn, special proj coord 1980-81; Natl Alliance of Business San Francisco, CA, administration mgr 1981-83; Michael St Michael/Corp Leather (self-employed), manufacturing exec/pres 1983-; Necronomics/Ethnographics, Palo Alto, CA, pres, 1989-. **Orgs:** Pres, Amer Futurists for the Educ of Women; mem, World Future Soc, NOW, Women's Inst for Freedom of the Press, World Affairs Council, Bay Area Urban League, League of Women Voters, Natl Women Studies Assn, Natl Council of Negro Women, Commonwealth Club of CA 1977; Intl Aff Com;Women in Commn; aptd by Mayor of SF to Commn on Status of Women 1977-80; Media & Public Info Com; consult & contrib to ''Black Esthetics'' 1972; bd of dirs San Francisco Convention and Visitors Bureau 1987-90, Urban Coalition West, Phoenix AZ 1987-93; chmn, African American Donor Task Force, 1990-. **Honors/Awds:** National Association of Negro Business and Professional Women, Western Region Volunteer Award, 1977; San Mateo Co Women's Hall of Fame, 1993. **Special Achievements:** Publications/productions: ''Femininity'' Book Review Women's Review of Books 1984; ''San Francisco Government, The City, The Citizen and Technetronics'' 1978; Lectures/Speeches, Univ of CA Davis ''The Black Female in Contemporary Society'' Afro-American Studies and Women's Studies Combined Session 1984; Univ of San Francisco Lecturer ''Women and the Working World'' 1978. **Business Addr:** President, Principal, Necronomics, PO Box 75005, Washington, DC 20013-0005.

REED, KIMBERLEY DEL RIO
Chief legal counsel. **Personal:** Born Jan 7, 1957, Detroit, MI; daughter of William F Reed II & Charlie Reed Johnson; children: William Mandela Matthews. **Educ:** Kentucky State Univ, BS,1978; Howard Univ School of Law, JD, 1981; Wayne State Univ School of Law, LLM, 1995. **Career:** Am Inst Paralegal Studies, law instructor, 1986-87; MI Paralegal Inst, law instructor, 1988-89; US Dept of Labor, law clerk, 1980-81; UAW Legal Dept, law clerk, 1981-82; Legal Aid & Defender Assoc, deputy defender, 1982-92; Detroit Recorders Ct, State Judicial Council, Chief Legal Counsel-judicial asst, 1992-. **Orgs:** Oak Grove AME Church, Sunday school teacher,1992-; Oak Grove AME Church, chancel choir, 1982-; Delta Sigma Theta Sorority Inc, life member, 1975-; Detroit Alumnae Chap, const bylaws comm, 1990-; Jr Achievement, consultant, 1992-; African Amer Enrichment Assn, bd member, 1990-; KY State Unive Alum Assn, trea-Detroit chap, 1987-1990; Howard Univ Alum Assn, vp Detroit chap, 1987-88. **Honors/Awds:** Delta Sigma Theta Sorority Inc, Service Award Teenlift, 1993; KY State Univ Alum Assn, Service Award, 1991; Outstanding Alumnus Mumford High Achool, Outstanding Alumnus, 1984; Mumford Class of 1974, Service Award, 1994. **Special Achievements:** The Exclusionary Rule is There Life After Lean? Vol I Criminal Practice Law Rev 137, 1980; The Economic Impact of Colonialism on the Legal Systems of Cameroon, Cote D'Ivorie and Senegal; Wayne State Law Lib, Masters Essay, 1994; Admitted to the State Bar of MI, 1992. **Business Addr:** Chief Legal Counsel/Judicial Asst, Recorder's Court for the City of Detroit, 1441 St Antoine, Ste 1069, Detroit, MI 48226.

REED, LAMBERT S., II
Business executive. **Personal:** Born May 31, 1937, Denton, GA; son of Nilie Reed and Lambert Sylvester Reed; married Melvynne Joyce Clark (divorced); children: Lambert III, La Jean Rooszon, Lamont. **Educ:** Morris Brown Coll, BA 1959; FL A&M U, addl studies; Univ of Miami. **Career:** Morris Brown Coll, head football coach 1978; Univ of FL, 1st black coach 1975-77; Ax Handle Beer & Enterprises, owner; SEC, 1st black coach; Univ of Miami; 1st black coach 1972-74; miami killian sr hs, head varsity football coach, athletic dir, asst to prin 1966-72; mays hs, head football coach 1965; GW Carver HS, defensive football coach, head basketball coach 1962-65. **Orgs:** Mem exec com Greater Miami Athletic Conf 1971; Greater Miami Athletic Conf 1972; mem Alpha Phi Alpha; mem Citizens Rating Bd 1969-71; Big Bro & Sis of Greater Miami Adv Bd 1971-74; bd dir Greater Miami Boys Club; charter mem Miami Bapt Hosp Comm Liaison Comm. **Honors/Awds:** Coach of yr S Dade News Leader 1968; coach of yr Alpha Phi Alpha 1971; coach of yr S Dade News Lealder 1972; Miami Herald Athletic Hall of Fame 1973; 1st black coach in state of FL to be head coach in integrated sch 1966; SIAC Coach of the Year, Southern Intercollegiate Athletic Conf 1980-81; coach of confernce championship team, Morris Brown College 1980-81; All Amer Football Player Morris Brown College 1957-58. **Business Addr:** Owner, CEO, Ax Handle Reed Enterprises, Inc, 1839 A Hollywood Rd, NW, Atlanta, GA 30318.

REED, LLOYD H.
Corporate attorney. **Personal:** Born Jul 31, 1922, Washington, DC; married June E Moore; children: Rebecca C, Lloyd A. **Educ:** Howard Univ, BA 1943; Harvard Law School, LLB 1949; Columbia School of Bus, 1977. **Career:** Mutual of NY, attny, asst counsel, assoc counsel, counsel, asst gen counsel, assoc gen counsel, vice pres real estate investment counsel 1949-; Mony Financial Services, vice pres corporate relations. **Orgs:** Mem Amer Bar Assoc, The Assoc of Life Ins Counsel, INSCOLAW; life mem NAACP; former mem School Bd of Gr-

eenburgh NY; founder, dir Westchester Comm Oppty Prog; gen couns Black Lawyers of Westchester Inc; dir Minority Interchange Inc. **Business Addr:** Vice Pres Corporate Relations, Mony Financial Services, 1740 Broadway, New York, NY 10019.

REED, LOLA N.
Librarian. **Personal:** Born Nov 27, 1923, Sneads, FL; widowed; children: Emmitt Jr, Gwendolyn, Bettye, Reginald, Ronald, Michael. **Educ:** FL A&M Univ, BS Bus Ed 1946, BLS 1948; Rutgers State Univ, MLS 1960. **Career:** FL A&M Univ Dean of Ed, admin sec 1949-59; Mommouth Cty Library Freehold NJ, childrens librarian 1960-63; W Orange Free Publ Library, childrens librarian 1963-71, acting dir to dir 1971-. **Orgs:** Mem Amer Library Assoc, NJ Library Assoc, Essex Cty Directors Group, SW Essex Dir Council, FL A&M Univ Alumni Assoc, Rutgers Univ Alumni Assoc, Comm Serv Council of the Oranges & Maplewood, Natl Council of Univ Women. **Business Addr:** Dir, W Orange Free Publ Library, 46 Mt Pleasant Ave, West Orange, NJ 07052.

REED, MAURICE L.
Mathematician. **Personal:** Born Jan 3, 1924, Chgo; married Betty E; children: Verna O, Pamela C, Maureen R. **Career:** City of Sprngfld OH, data proc supr; Ops Res Analyst Sys Simu Br Wright Patter AFB, act br chief 1974-79; Sys Simu Br, math 1968-74; Adv Res & Techn Sec Plans & Mgmt Br, math 1966-68; Data Reduct Div Dir of Test Data Dep for Test & Support, math 1961-66. **Orgs:** Past pres OH Urban League Bd of Dir 1967; chmn resltns com Alpha Phi Alpha Frat 1969-74; educ counc Nat Urban League 1969-75; past v chmn bd of dir Clark Tech Coll 1971-74; mem Nat Assn of Parliam 1975; mem Am Inst of Parliamentarians 1977; bd Of dir Nat Counc of YMCAs of the US 1980; memnum other orgns. **Honors/Awds:** Outstdg reg alumni brot of yr Alpha Phi Alpha Frat 1974; natl outstdg alumnus of yr Alpha Phi Alpha Frat 1974; cit of yr awd Front Intnl 1975. **Military Serv:** USMC 1943-46. **Business Addr:** Police Dept, City of Springfield, Springfield, OH 45501.

REED, MICHAEL H.
Attorney. **Personal:** Born Jan 17, 1949, Philadelphia, PA; married Yalta Gilmore Reed, Aug 12, 1978; children: Alexandra, Michael Jr. **Educ:** Temple Univ, Philadelphia, PA, BA, 1969; Yale University, New Haven, CT, JD, 1972. **Career:** Pepper Hamilton & Scheetz, Philadelphia, PA, partner, 1972-. **Orgs:** Trustee, Episcopal Hospital, 1986-; trustee & corporate secretary, Academy of Natural Sciences, 1988-; member, Pennsylvania Judicial Inquiry & Review Board, 1990-93; chairman, Professional Guidance Committee, Philadelphia Bar Assn, 1986; chairman, Pennsylvania Bar Assn Minority Bar Committee, 1988-90; Pennsylvania Bar Association, board of governors, 1993-. **Honors/Awds:** Special Achievement Award, Pennsylvania Bar Assn, 1989; Outstanding Service Award, Philadelphia Bar Assn Young Lawyers Section, 1975; Certificate of Honor, Outstanding Alumnus, Temple Univ, College of Arts & Sciences, 1995. **Business Addr:** Partner, Pepper, Hamilton & Scheetz, 3000 Two Logan Square, 18th & Arch Sts, Philadelphia, PA 19103.

REED, RODNEY J.
Educational administrator, educator. **Personal:** Born May 16, 1932, New Orleans, LA; son of Ursul C Desvignes Reed (deceased) and Edgar J Reed (deceased); married Vernell M Auzenne, Aug 5, 1961; children: Karen, Ursula. **Educ:** Clark Coll, BA 1951; Univ of MI, MA 1956; Univ of CA, Berkeley, PhD 1971. **Career:** Southern Univ Baton Rouge LA, asst prof/asst cond bnds 1956-61; Oakland CA Unified Sch District high sch tchr/vice prin 1961-68; Univ CA Berkeley, asst, assoc prof and prof 1970-90; Univ CA Berkeley, faculty asst chancellor, affirmative action 1980-82; Pennsylvania State Univ, Coll of Education, prof, dean, 1990-. **Orgs:** Mem Am Ed Res Assoc 1970-; mem editorial bd Educ and Urban Soc 1972-86; pres Fornax, Inc Edtl Consult 1975-88; life mem NAACP 1975-; mem Assoc CA Schl Admin 1976-; mem editorial bd, Policy Studies Review Annual 1976-; mem Nat'l Conf Prof Edtl Admin 1977-; vice chair & mem brd Bay Area Urban Leag 1980-; chair Edtl Comm Bay Area Blk United Fund 1979-82; mem editorial bd, Educational Researcher 1982-; mem editorial bd, Natl Forum of Educ Admin & Supervisors 1983-; editorial board, Educational Administration Quarterly, 1993-; mem, Omega Psi Phi Fraternity; mem Sigma Pi Phi Frat 1983-; mem Amer Assoc of Sch Admin 1986-; mem, Phi Delta Kappa, 1971-; mem, Amer Educ Research Assn, 1974-; Cleveland Conference, 1991-; Omicron Tau Theta National Honary Society, 1990-; mem editorial advisory bd, Journal of African Amer Male Studies, 1990-; treasurer, mem, exec comm, Assn of Colleges & Schools of Educ in State Universities & Land Grant Colleges & Affiliated Private Universities, ACSESULGC/APU, 1992-95, pres, 1995-98; mem-at-large, bd of dirs, The Holmes Partnership, 1994-; mem-at-large, bd of dirs, Amer Assn of Colleges for Teacher Education, (AACTE), 1994-97; ACSESULGC/APU rep, bd of dirs, Amer Assn of Colleges for Teacher Education, 1996-; bd of dirs, Pennsylvania Goals 2000, 1994-96. **Honors/Awds:** Outstanding Man Yr, Omega Psi Phi Frat Sigma Iota, 1966; urban fellowship Univ CA Berkeley, 1968-70; Bronze Award, Bay Area Black United Fund, 1982; Order of the Golden Bear, Univ of CA Berkeley, 1985-; Golden Key Natl Honor Soc; author, School & College Competency Testing Programs; Perceptions of African-Amer Students in Louisiana & North Carolina, author, Expectation & Student Achievement; co-author, (James W Gutherie) Edtl Admin Policy Ldshp Am Ed, Second Edition, 1991; co-author, The Politics of Urban Educ in the US, 1992; co-author, Restructuring Public Schooling: Europe, Canada, America, 1997; Recipient CA State Legislatue Assembly & Senate Resolutions, 1989; Recipient CA, Assembly Speakers Player, 1989; Alumnus Year, Black Alumni Club, Univ of CA Berkeley, Alumni Club, 1992. **Military Serv:** AUS specialist 3 1953-55. **Business Addr:** Dean, College of Education, Penn State University, University Park, PA 16802.

REED, SHEILA A.
Journalist, editor. **Educ:** University of Florida, Gainesville, FL, BSJ, 1981. **Career:** Sarasota Herald Tribune, Sarasota, FL, copy editor, 1982-83; Gainesville Sun, Gainesville, FL, copy editor, 1984-86; Florida Times-Union, Jacksonville, FL, copy editor, 1986-87; St Petersburg Times, St Petersburg, FL, copy editor, 1987-91; Gannett Suburban Newspaper, White Plains, New York, special sections editor, 1991-94; Lexington Harold-Leader, Lexington, KY, assistant features editor, 1994-95, features editor, 1995-. **Orgs:** National Assn of Black Journalists, 1990-. **Home Addr:** 120 East Main St, Apt 2002, Lexington, KY 40507.

REED, THERESA GREENE
Physician, government official (retired). **Personal:** Born Dec 9, 1923, Baltimore, MD; daughter of Theresa Greene Evans and William James Greene; divorced. **Educ:** VA State Coll, BS 1945; Meharry Med Coll, MD 1949; The Johns Hopkins Univ, MPH 1967. **Career:** Homer G Phillips Hosp, staff physician, public health physician 1950-58; Private practice, physician 1950-65; Homer G Phillips Hosp, asst clinic dir 1958-66; Johns Hopkins Univ and Sinai Hosp, preventive med fellow 1966-68; FDA med epidemiology officer 1968-, lecturer clinical pharmacology 1983-; Howard Univ, assoc prof comm med 1972-; FDA, medical officer 1968-92, supervisory medical officer, 1977-80, 1988-92; National Medical Association, historian. **Orgs:** Amer Coll of Epidemiology; fellow Amer Coll of Preventive med; Soc for Epidemiological Rsch; Amer Soc for Microbiology; Amer Med Womens Assn; Amer Publ Health Assoc; vice pres of the medico Chirurgical Soc of DC; Assoc of Teachers of Preventive med, Amer VD Assoc; fellow Cty Med Soc; Intl Epidemiological Assoc; Alpha Kappa Alpha; sec, treas Daniel Hale Williams Med Reading Club; Natl Med Assn, chairman Committee on Admin & Financial Affairs, 1987-89, historian, chairperson, 4 yrs; Chi Delta Mu Fraternity; Delta Omega. **Honors/Awds:** Author of numerous papers in med jrnls; 1st pres Mound City Women Physicians; 1st Black Female Med Epidemiologist; Public Health Serv Special Recognition Award, 1985; Outstanding Serv Award, Natl Medical Assn, 1986-87; Food and Drug Administration, Commendable Serv Award, 1985; Devel directory of 1100 Black Physicians in the Metropolitan DC area; National Medical Assn Region II, Distinguished Service Award; American Medical Women's Association, Community Service Award, 1992. **Home Addr:** 11516 Patapsco Dr, Rockville, MD 20852.

REED, THOMAS J.
Legislator. **Personal:** Born Sep 17, 1927, Brookhaven, MS; married Sereeta; children: Thomas, Jr, Ava, Evelyn. **Educ:** MS Tuskegee Inst, BS. **Career:** Mem, AL Legislature. **Orgs:** Chmn, Black Elected & Appointed Officials of AL; state pres NAACP. **Honors/Awds:** First black to serve as rep in AL state legislature since Reconstruction; Instrumental in getting legislature to hire first black page; pres over public hearing on maltreat Of AL prison inmates; pres Dept of Public Safety to hire 350 blacks in various positions; filed charges against 17 fed agencies in the state demand that blacks be given 25% of all federal jobs in AL. **Business Addr:** Drawer EE, Tuskegee Institute, AL 36088.

REED, VINCENT EMORY
Educator, newspaper executive. **Personal:** Born Mar 1, 1928, St Louis, MO; son of Velma Reed and Artie Reed; married Frances Bullitt. **Educ:** WV State Coll Inst, BS Educ 1952; Howard Univ, MA 1965; Wharton School of Finance and Comm Univ of PA, completed inst on collective negotiations; VA State Coll, Guidance NDEA Scholarship; Iowa Univ. **Career:** WV State Coll, football coach 1955; Jefferson Jr HS, teacher 1956; Anacostia HS, Cardozo HS, Jefferson Jr HS, counselor 1963; Manpower Devel Training Program DC Public Schools, asst dir 1964; Dunbar HS, Wilson HS, asst principal; Woodrow Wilson Sr HS; DC Public School, asst supt personnel 1969-70; DC Public School, asst supt safety & security 1970, exec asst 1970-71, asst supt 1971-74, assoc supt office of state admin 1974-75, supt 1975-80; President of US, asst sec for elem and secondary educ 1981-82; The Washington Post, vice pres for communications 1982-. **Orgs:** Mem NAACP, mem Jr Achievement (bd dir) Washington, DC; bd dir Stonewall Athletic Club; bd dir YMCA; bd dir Natl Conf of Christians and Jews; bd trustees Univ of DC; bd trustees Southeastern Univ; bd trustees Gallaudet Coll; bd trustees Amer Univ; found trustee WV State Coll; exec comm Convention and Visitors Center; Howard Univ Charter Day Comm; bd dir Big Brothers Inc; chmn Sch and Summer Jobs Board of Trade Washington, DC; bd dir Girl Scouts; bd dir Boy Scouts; bd dir Boys' and Girls' Club DC Police Dept; Merit Select Panel for US Magistrates; DC chmn United Way; past mem Amer Assn of Sch Personnel Admin; Amer Personnel and Guidance Assn; past chmn Area Supts Study Seminar; past bd dir Goodwill Industries. **Honors/Awds:** Comm Serv Award SE Citizens Assn 1970; Superior Serv Award DC Bicentennial Assembly 1976; Outstanding Achievement Award WV State Coll 1976; Outstanding Comm Serv Award NAACP 1977; Distinguished Serv Award Phi Delta Kappa Intl George Washington Univ 1979; Keynote Speaker NY State Urban League Convention; Keynote Speaker Natl Head Start Conf; Keynote Speaker Seven-State Conf of the PTA; mem of a comm evaluation qualifications of private school to admin vocational training for DC public schools; Principal Speaker at Commencement Exercises of Univ of DC, Southeastern Univ, etc; Honorary degrees, WV State Coll, HHD; Southeastern Univ, Doctor of Public Admin; Georgetown Univ, Doct of Humane Letters; Univ of DC, Doctor of Laws; Strayer Coll, Doctor of HumaneLetters; Harris-Stowe Univ, Doctor Humane Letters. **Military Serv:** AUS 1st lt. **Business Addr:** VP for Communications, The Washington Post, 1150 15th St NW, Washington, DC 20071.

REED, WILBUR R.
Government official, real estate broker. **Personal:** Born Mar 13, 1936, St Louis, MO; son of Lurline Knighton Reed and Ike Reed; married Bettye Freeman; children: Delecia, LaDonica, Durleon. **Educ:** Univ of Toledo, BE 1960, MA 1968; School of Mediation Amer Arbitration Assn, Graduate 1974; Jones College of Real Estate, graduate, 1979. **Career:** Lott Day Sch, teacher 1960-61; Child Study Inst, probation counselor 1963-67; City of Toledo, dir delinquency div 1967-69; Univ of Toledo, lecturer 1967-69; Denver Juvenile Ct, probation officer 1969-, probation supervisor 1969-72; Comm Coll of Denver, instructor 1969-75; US Dept of Justice, mediator 1972-; real estate broker, 1979-. **Orgs:** Bd of dirs Urban League 1978; commissioner Aurora Civil Service Commn 1980-82; member, Kappa Alpha Psi Fraternity, 1957-; founder, Mountain States Coalition Against Malicious Harassment; founder, Institute of Urban Affairs, Loretta Heights College Special Projects; Mile High United Way, 1988-; Grand Boule, Sigma Pi Phi Fraternity, 1992. **Honors/Awds:** Special Appreciation Awd Denver Urban League 1982; publication "Crime and Delinquency, A Study of Toledo and Lucas County Ohio"; Outstanding Service Award, Dept of Justice, numerous times; Leadership Award, Colorado Black Chamber of Commerce, 1990; Blacks Who Make a Difference in Colorado, Urban Spectrum News, 1990; Special Commendation, The Development of the Minority Business and Professional Managers Committee, State of Utah, 1991; Milton D Lewis Award, Excellence in Mediation & Human Relations, US Justice Dept, 1976-94. **Military Serv:** AUS 1st lt 2 yrs. **Home Addr:** 2027 S Ironton Ct, Aurora, CO 80014. **Business Addr:** Mediator, US Dept of Justice, 333 W Colfax, Denver, CO 80204.

REED, WILLIS
Professional basketball player (retired), professional sports administrator. **Personal:** Born Jun 25, 1942, Bernice, LA; married Gale; children: Carl, Veronica. **Educ:** Grambling Coll, attended. **Career:** NY Knicks, center, forward, 1964-74, head coach, 1977-79; St John's Univ, asst basketball coach, one season; Creighton Univ, head basketball coach; Atlanta Hawks, assistant coach, 1985-87; Sacramento Kings, assistant basketball coach, until 1988; New Jersey Nets, head coach, 1988-89, vice pres, basketball and business development, 1989-90, senior vice president, basketball operations, 1990-, executive vice pres, general manager, currently. **Orgs:** NY Knicks, team's all-time leading rebounder (8,414) during 10-year playing career; Rookie of the Year, 1965; MVP, regular season, All-Star game, playoffs, 1970; MVP, playoffs, 1973; National Memorial Basketball Hall of Fame, elected, 1981; NAIA Basketball Hall of Fame, elected, 1970; All Star Team 1965-71, 1973; NBA World Championship Team 1970, 1973; coauthor, with Phil Pepe, The View from the Run, 1971. **Business Addr:** Executive VP, General Manager, New Jersey Nets, Brendan Byrne Arena, East Rutherford, NJ 07073.

REED-CLARK, LARITA D.
Financial administrator, convention center controller. **Personal:** Born Sep 26, 1960, Chicago, IL; daughter of Joyce Hinton Reed and Henry Reed; married Gregory A Clark, Jun 18, 1988. **Educ:** Loyola Univ, Chicago IL, BBA, 1982; Kellogg School of Business, Northwestern University, Masters degree in Management, 1993. **Career:** Peat Marwick Mitchell, Chicago IL, auditor, 1982-84; McCormick Place, Chicago IL, asst controller, 1982-84, controller, fiscal operations director, 1984-. **Orgs:** Mem, Natl Assn of Black Accountants, 1980-; mem, Amer Institute of CPA's, 1983-; mem, IL CPA Society, 1983-; mem, Family Christian Center Church, 1992-; mem, Government Finance Officers Assn, 1984-. **Honors/Awds:** Named among top black business & professional women, Dollars & Sense Magazine, 1988. **Business Addr:** Controller, Director Fiscal Operations, McCormick Place, 2301 S Lake Shore Drive, Chicago, IL 60616.

REED-HUMES, ROBI
Producer, director. **Personal:** married; children: two. **Educ:** Hampton University, BA, speech, drama. **Career:** Casting director for numerous films, including: The Falcon and the Snowman, production assistant; Best Seller, casting assistant; She's Gotta Have It, 1984; School Daze, 1988; Do the Right Thing, 1989; Mo' Better Blues, 1990; Jungle Fever, 1991; Malcolm X, 1993; I'm Gonna Git You Sucka, 1988; Harlem Nights, 1989; Soul Food, 1997; television casting includes: Roc, The Robert Guillaume Show, A Different World, In Living Color, and Good News; Michael Jackson's music video, ''Remember the Time,'' casting director, 1993; ''Woo,'' casting director, 1998; other experience includes: McClean and DiMeo, former casting assistant; To The Glory of God, founder, president; Robin Reed-Humes and Associates, president, currently. **Honors/Awds:** Emmy for casting ''The Tuskegee Airmen''; Black Hollywood Education and Resource Center, Emmy for casting. **Business Addr:** Casting Director, Raleigh Studios, 5300 Melrose Ave, Office Bldg East, 4th Fl, Los Angeles, CA 90038, (213)871-4440.

REED-MILLER, ROSEMARY E.
Businesswoman. **Personal:** Born Jun 22, 1939, Yeadon, PA; married Paul E Miller (deceased); children: Sabrina E, Paul D. **Educ:** Temple Univ, BA 1962. **Career:** US Dept Agriculture, information specialist 1966-67; jewelry design, crafts development, journalism, Jamaica, WI, & Washington, DC (Womens Wear Daily, Afro-American, et al); Toast & Strawberries Inc Boutique, owner & oper 1967-; Howard Univ, School of Fine Arts & Ecology Awards, adjunt teacher; TV Shows until 1993; Work Post Home Magazine, 1995. **Orgs:** Pres Task Force on Educ & Training for Minority Bus Enter 1973-74; bd mem Interracial Council on Bus Oppor 1973-; pres Howard Univ Faculty Wives Assn 1973-; mem founding group Assn Women Bus Owners 1974; del White House Conf on Small Bus 1980; mem Dupont Circle N Bus Assn; mem DC Barristers Wives Assn; DC Govt Economic Development Commission bd mem 1983-86; Woodley House bd mem 1986; TV shows, Eye on Washington, maternity fashions 1985, Black Dressmakers in History 1986, America's Black Forum, fashion business, 1986; radio show, Fashion Business, Capital Edition WUSA, News WJLA, Inaugural Dressup, Washington Post; bd mem, ACTCO Theatre Group, African Coalition; bd mem, Washington Ethical Society School, 1997-. **Honors/Awds:** Bus Awd Century Club Natl Assn Negro Bus & Prof Women's Clubs 1973; Bus Awd for Serv Washington Black Econ Devel Corp 1973; Businesswoman of Yr Natl Council for Small Bus Dev Eastern Region 1974; Black Academic Development Alpha Kappa Alpha Sor 1975; Appreciation Plaque Awd Bus & Prof Women's League 1980; Black Women in Sisterhood Calendar Honoree 1982; Bus Serv Awd Century Club Club 20 1983; bd mem Economic Develop Bd-Mayor's Office 1983; Serv Awd Howard Univ, Institute of Urban Affairs 1984; Bus Serv Awd Blacks Within Govt 1984; Comm Serv Awd RSVP Club 1984; delegate White House Conf on Sm Bus, delegate White House Commission on Entrepreneural Educ, 1973; Minority Women's Enterprise Fund, Business Accomplishment, 1995; DC Private Industry Corriel Award, 1996; National Theatre Supporter Award, 1996. **Business Addr:** Owner, Toast & Strawberries, 1608 20th St, NW, Washington, DC 20009.

REESE, ALBERT
Professional football player. **Personal:** Born Apr 29, 1973. **Educ:** Grambling State. **Career:** San Francisco 49ers, defensive tackle, 1997-. **Business Addr:** Professional Football Player, San Francisco 49ers, 4949 Centennial Blvd, Santa Clara, CA 95054, (415)562-4949.

REESE, DELLA (DELLAREESE PATRICIA EARLY)
Singer, actress, composer. **Personal:** Born Jul 6, 1931, Detroit, MI; daughter of Nellie Early and Richard Early; married Vermont Adolphus Bon Taliaferro; children: Della Jr. **Educ:** Wayne State Univ, attended. **Career:** Appeared on The Tonight Show, Merv Griffin Show, Ed Sullivan, McCloud, Police Woman, Twice in a Lifetime, Chico & the Man, Petrocelli, Mike Douglas Show, num game shows, TV spec; Mahalia Jackson Troupe, performed 1945-49; Sahara-Tahoe, Caesar's Palace, Coconut Grove, Mr Kelly's, Caribe Hilton, Flamingo, performer; Let's Rock 1958, The Last Minstrel Show 1978, actress; Jubilee, RCA, Victor Records, ABC Paramount, recording artist; Della Variety Show, hostess 1969-70; solo recording artist 1957-; recordings include Della, Special Delivery, I Like It Like Dat, Sure Like Lovin' You, Something Cool; Royal Family, 1991-92; minister, currently; ''Touched By An Angel'', currently. **Honors/Awds:** Num gold records; Most Promising Girl Singer 1957; NAACP, Image Award, TV Drama Actress, 1998. **Business Addr:** William Morris Agency, 151 El Camino, Beverly Hills, CA 90212.

REESE, FREDERICK D.
Pastor, educator. **Personal:** Born Nov 28, 1929, Dallas County, AL; married Alline Toulas Crossing; children: Frederick, Jr, Valerie, Marvin, Christa, Alan. **Educ:** Alabama State Univ, BS; Atlanta Bible Inst Clark Coll, adv study; Southern Univ; Selma Univ; Univ of Alabama; Livingston Univ, MEd. **Career:** Ebenezer Bapt Church, Selma AL, pastor; Eastside Jr High & Selma High School, principal; city councilman. **Orgs:** Mem Natl Educ Assn; Alabama Educ Assn; dist VI Educ Assn; Phi Beta Sigma; bd dir YMCA; pres Dallas County Voters League. **Honors/Awds:** Local leader in 1965 Voters Rights Movement, Selma; organized black teachers for the right to vote; led demonstrations against local newspaper; resp for black clerks and cashiers in stores and banks; organized black citizens for position on Dallas County Dem Exec Comm; Abraham Lincoln Award; outstanding leadership educ NEA Detroit 1971; Teacher of the Year Award, Selma City Teachers Assn; Good Guy Award chmn Unit Appeal; numerous plaques & certificates for outstanding leadership in education and civil rights. **Business Addr:** 300 Washington St, Selma, AL 36701.

REESE, GREGORY LAMARR
Library director. **Personal:** Born Jul 30, 1949, Cleveland, OH; son of Margaret Smith Reese and Jasper Reese; married Evangeline Bynum Reese, Dec 13, 1975; children: Michael. **Educ:** Morehouse College, Atlanta, GA, BA, history, 1975; Case Western Reserve University, Cleveland, OH, MLS, 1977. **Career:** Cuyahoga County Public Library, Cleveland, OH, librarian, 1975-80, branch manager, 1980-85; East Cleveland Public Library, East Cleveland, OH, assistant director, 1985-88, director, 1988-. **Orgs:** Member, Alpha Phi Alpha Fraternity, 1986-; past pres, East Cleveland Kiwanis; Cleveland, Area Metropolitan Library Srvice, 1980-; member, Cleveland Opera Multicultural Awareness Program, 1988-. **Honors/Awds:** Friend of Literacy Award, Project Learn, 1990; Alumni Fund Chairman, Case Western Reserve, 1981; Jazz Volunteer, Northeast Ohio, 1989; Martin Luther King Jr, Altruism Award, East Cleveland Citizens for Sound Government, currently; Librarian of the Year, Ohio, 1992. **Business Addr:** Director, East Cleveland Public Library, 14101 Euclid Ave, East Cleveland, OH 44112.

REESE, MAMIE BYNES
Educator. **Personal:** Born Sep 3, Gibson, GA. **Educ:** Spelman Coll, BS 1933; Drake U, MS 1948; OH State U, adv study; Univ So CA; Simmons Coll; Boston U. **Career:** Center HS, teacher; Des Moines Tech HS; Baker & Burke Counties, home demon agnt; Albany State Coll, asso prof dean women. **Orgs:** Mem GA State Bd Pardons & Pardons; past pres Nat Assn Colored Wom Club Inc; mem GA Assn Educat; NEA; Sigma Rho Sigma Honor Sor; aux GA Osteop Med Assn; Nat Health Assn, Delta Sigma Theta Sor; Assn Parol Author; Am Correct Assn; World Fedn Meth Wom; Hines Memorial Butler St Meth Episco Chs; Albany Urban League & Guide; Albnay C Of C; Govs Spl Counc on Fam Plan; bd dir; Semper Fidel Club; GA Div Am Canc Soc; com mem Girl Scouts Am; num off NAACP. **Honors/Awds:** Couple of yr Albany Chap Zeta Phi Beta Sor Inc 1958; cit Spelman Coll 1966; outstndg Citizen Albany State Coll Comm Relat Com 1966; women of conscience awd Nat Counc Wom USA 1969. **Business Addr:** 800 Peachtree St NE, Atlanta, GA 30309.

REESE, MILOUS J.
Chiropractor (retired). **Educ:** Midwestern Univ, BA; Amer Inst of Science, MS, Philosopher of Chiropractic Degree; Ohio Christian Coll, doctor of psychology; American Non-Allopathic Univ, doctor of chiropractic; Emory Univ, Postgrad Work in Internal Medicine; McCormick Medical Coll; Nei Ching Intrl Chinese Healing Arts, Doctor of Philosophy; Univ AL, Spec Study of Alphine Culture Art & Lang; TX Chiropractic Coll, post graduate studies, applied kinesiology, 1972, diagnostic roentgenology, 1976; Emerson Coll of Herbology, MA in Herbology, 1978. **Career:** Chiropractor in private practice. **Orgs:** AL State Chiropractic Assn; Jefferson County Chiropractic Soc; Acupuncture Soc AL; Acupuncture Soc Amer Kansas City, MO; Ctr Chinese Med Los Angeles, CA; US Acad Acupuncture; Traditional Acupuncture Found Columbia, MD; First African-American Appointed US Bd Acupuncture; Kappa Phi Sigma Med Frat; Amer Coll Chiropractic Orthopedist 1979; Council Nutrition to the Amer Chiropractic Assn Inc; Orthopedic Class 1979; cert mem Natl Chiropr actic Assn 1945; crt mem Amer Council on Chrpctc Orthopedics of the ACA 1979; Natl Psychiatric Assn 1978; mem, Big Brothers Club 1975; honorary mem, Beta Psi Accounting Honor Society, Booker T Washington Business College 1972; founder, Alabama College of Drugless Therapy (medicine) 1950; Academy of Holistic Practitioner, certified holistic practitioner, life mem; Natl Assn of Naturopathic Herbalists of American, 1945; Alabama Acupuncture Council, first black, 1993; American Federation of Physio-Therapists, 1943; NY State Chiropractic Society, associate member. **Honors/Awds:** Dinner & Plaque in Recogn for Exemplary Serv in Field of Med for Humanitarian Serv and Dedicated Professional Leadership from Univ of Montevallo 1985; Doctor of Humane Letters, Miles College 1989; Certificate of Membership Gold Lapel Pin-50 years, The National College of Chiropractic 1989; Certificate of Expression of Gratitude for Support of Columbia Institute of Chiropractic Diplomat Club, 1977; Plaque in Recognition of Continued Support of College Development, Palmer College of Chiropractic, Davenport, IA; Chiropractic Assn, Lifetime Achievement Plaque, 1993; Proclamation from Senator Earl Hilliard; Milous Reese Day, July 2, proclaimed by Birmingham Councilman, Roosevelt Bell; American Coll of Chiropractic Specialist, completed the required examination in physiology; Notary Public for Jefferson County, 1954; Alabama State Chiropractic Association, Certificate of Appreciation. **Business Addr:** 2117 18th St Ensley, Birmingham, AL 35218.

REESE, POKEY (CALVIN JR.)
Professional baseball player. **Personal:** Born Jun 10, 1973, Columbia, SC. **Career:** Cincinnati Reds, infielder, 1997-. **Business Addr:** Professional Baseball Player, Cincinnati Reds, 100 Riverfront Stadium, Cincinnati, OH 45202, (513)421-4510.

REESE, VIOLA KATHRYN
Social service administrator. **Personal:** Born Aug 23, 1953, Lexington, TN; daughter of Willie Mae Smith Dabbs and Rev Billy Frank Dabbs; married J Monroe Reese Jr; children: Idesha, James III. **Educ:** TN State Univ, BS 1975; Washington Univ, MSW, 1977. **Career:** Children's Ctr for Behavioral Devel, therapist 1977-80, satellite coord 1980-82, interim clinical dir 1982-83, family therapist/coordinator 1983-84; RDS Foundation Inc, exec dir 1986-. **Orgs:** Mem Natl Assoc of Social Workers 1972-, Natl Assoc Black Social Workers 1972-, IL Assoc Sch Social Workers 1976-; mem St Clair Co Comm on Difficult Children 1980-84; mem bd of dirs Council House 1981-84; sec bd of dirs 1980-83, pres bd of dirs 1983-84 Big Brothers/Big Sisters; private consultant 1981-; Optimist Intl Lexington Charter Board Member, 1989-; Caywood PTO, sec, 1988-90; bd mem, E-911, 1989-91; TENA, 1989-90; bd mem, LHCCN, 1990-; PADA, 1991-; SEC, 1992-95; Jonah, 1995. **Honors/Awds:** Outstanding Black College Female, Essence Magazine, 1975; TN State Alumni Assn, 1975-; University Scholar TN State Univ 1975; Washington Univ Alumni Assn 1977-; MADD, 1980-; League of Women Voters, deputy registar, 1980-84; Spanish Lake Democratic Party, 1980-86; Storman Stufflin PTA, 1981-86; Outstanding Achievement Big Brothers/Big Sisters 1982, 1984; Certificate of Achievement CCBD 1984; Montgomery High Alumni Assn, 1986-; Living Life on Wheels Par Limentarian, 1987-; Outstanding Parent Volunteer, Caywood PTO, 1989; Natl Spinal Cord Assn, 1989-; Henderson County Democratic Party, 1989-; Outstanding Parent Volunteer, Caywood PTO, 1990; Outstanding Parent Volunteer, 1991, 1992-95; Outstanding Volunteer, 1992; FKIX Community Award, 1991; Caywood School, Volunteer Award, 1992-93; Outstanding Parent Volunteer, 1993-94; School Bell Award, 1994-95; Outstanding Parent Volunteer, 1995-96. **Business Addr:** Executive Dir, RDS Foundation Inc, PO Box 1084, Lexington, TN 38351.

REEVES, ALAN M.
Automobile dealership executive. **Career:** Quality Ford Sales Inc, Columbus GA, chief executive; Spalding Ford-Lincoln-Mercury Inc, Griffin GA, chief executive. **Honors/Awds:** Auto 100, Spalding Ford-Lincoln-Mercury Inc, Black Enterprise, 1991. **Business Addr:** President, Spalding Ford-Lincoln-Mercury, Inc, 1710 N Expressway, Griffin, GA 30223.

REEVES, ALEXIS SCOTT
Media company executive, journalist. **Personal:** Born Feb 4, 1949, Atlanta, GA; daughter of Marian Willis Scott and William Alexander Scott III; married Marc Anthony Lewis (divorced 1973); children: Cinque Scott Reeves, David L Reeves Jr. **Educ:** Barnard College, 1966-68; Columbia University School of Journalism, Michelle Clark Fellowship, 1974; Spelman College, 1989-90; Leadersip Atlanta, 1991; Regional Leadership Institute, 1992. **Career:** Atlanta Constitution, Atlanta, GA, reporter, 1974-78, copy editor, 1978; Atlanta Journal-Constitution, Atlanta, GA, editor, Intown Extra, 1979-81, assistant city editor, 1982-84, editor/director, video edition, 1984-86, vice president of community affairs, 1986-93; Cox Enterprises, director of diversity, 1993-97; Atlanta Daily World, Inc, chmn, pres, 1997-; Atlanta Daily World Newspaper, publisher, 1997-. **Orgs:** Chair, Atlanta Children's Shelter, 1995-96; chair, Exodus/Cities in Schools, 1990-91; steering committee member, Georgia Partnership for Excellence in Education, 1990-91; ad-hoc committee chair, Multi-Cultural Audience Development, High Museum of Art, 1990-91; vice chair, board of directors, High Museum of Art, 1991-93; chair, NAACP Youth Achievement Academy, 1987-90; vice chair, Friends of Spelman, 1990, 1991; chair, Friends of Spelman, 1992-94; president, Atlanta Chapter, National Association of Media Women, 1985-87. **Honors/Awds:** Pioneer Black Journalist Award, Atlanta Assn of Black Journalists, 1998; named Among 20 Women Making A Mark on Atlanta, Atlanta Magazine, 1998; Academy of Women Achievers, YWCA, 1989; Top 100 Business and Professional Women, Dollars & Sense Magazine, 1986; National Media Woman of the Year, National Association of Media Women, 1983; Distinguished Urban Journalism Award, National Urban Coalition, 1980; School Bell for Excellence in Education Reporting, Georgia Association of Educators, 1977. **Business Addr:** Publisher, Atlanta Daily World, 145 Auburn Ave E, Atlanta, GA 30305.

REEVES, CARL
Professional football player. **Personal:** Born Dec 17, 1971; married Iris. **Educ:** North Carolina State, attended. **Career:** Chicago Bears, defensive end, 1996-. **Business Addr:** Professional Football Player, Chicago Bears, 1000 Football Dr, Halas Hall at Conway Park, Lake Forest, IL 60045-4829, (847)295-6600.

REEVES, DIANNE
Jazz vocalist. **Personal:** Born 1956, Detroit, MI. **Educ:** University of Colorado. **Career:** Accomplishments include: Clark

Terry Band, singer; Colorado Symphony Orchestra; Monterey Jazz Festival; worked with: Sergio Mendez, Harry Belafonte, George Duke, Herbie Hancock, numerous others; Albums: For Every Heart, Welcome To My Love, Dianne Reeves, 1987, Art and Survival. **Business Phone:** (310)659-1700.

REEVES, JOHN E.
City official. **Career:** Southfield (MI) City Council, councilman, 1996-. **Orgs:** Kappa Alpha Psi Fraternity; Cypriaw Ctr, chmn, bd of dirs. **Honors/Awds:** Leadership, Kappa Alpha Psi Fraternity. **Special Achievements:** First African American male elected to Southfield City Council. **Business Addr:** Councilman, Southfield City Council, PO Box 2055, Southfield, MI 48037-2055, (810)354-9380.

REEVES, JULIUS LEE
Engineer. **Personal:** Born Nov 10, 1961, Detroit, MI; son of Delores Johnson Reeves and Troy Reeves, Sr; married Jun 16, 1990. **Educ:** Wayne State Univ, Detroit, MI, BSIE, 1986; Univ of Michigan, Dearborn, MI, MSIE, 1992, Univ of Chicago, Chicago, IL, MBA, 1991. **Career:** Midwest Aluminum Corp, engrg asst 1983; Kelsey-Hayes, mfg engr 1984-85; Electronic Data Systems, systems engr 1985-86; General Motors, Warren, MI, engineer, 1986-89, business planner, 1989-92, sr engineer, 1992-97, strategic business planner, 1997-. **Orgs:** Mem Phi Delta Psi 1979-, Inst of Industrial Engrs 1983-, Engrg Soc of Detroit 1984-; chapter pres Phi Delta Psi Fraternity 1984-85; national president, Phi Delta Psi Fraternity, 1990-92; vice president, African-American MBA Assn, 1990-91. **Honors/Awds:** College of Engrg Deans List Wayne State Univ 1984-85; Natl Dean's List 1984-85; Fellowship, General Motors, 1989. **Home Addr:** 28170 Shenandoah, Southfield, MI 48076.

REEVES, KHALID
Professional basketball player. **Personal:** Born Jul 15, 1972, Queens, NY. **Educ:** Arizona. **Career:** Miami Heat, guard, 1994-95; Charlotte Hornets, 1995-96; New Jersey Nets, 1996; Dallas Mavericks, 1996-. **Special Achievements:** NBA Draft, First round pick, #12, 1994. **Business Addr:** Professional Basketball Player, Dallas Mavericks, Reunion Arena, 777 Sports St, Dallas, TX 75207, (214)748-1808.

REEVES, LOUISE
Government administrator. **Personal:** Born Aug 13, 1944, St Louis, MO; married Charles B Mitchell. **Educ:** St Louis U, BA Polit Sci 1976; Webster Coll, MA Pub Admin 1980. **Career:** St Louis Agency on Training & Employment, dep dir 1977-; St Louis Met YWCA, dir housing & counsel 1976-77; Consul Nghbrhd Serv Inc, asso dir 1965-76; MO State Housing Devel Commn , commr 1978-; Freedom of Res Inc, pres 1978-79; Women in Community Svcs, director, 1983-95; Grace Hill Neighborhood Svcs, associate executive director, 1995-. **Orgs:** Chmn Monsignour John Schocklee Scholarship Com 1979-; mem YMCA & YWCA; mem St Louis Wom Polit Caucas 1975-; Council Negro Women 1976. **Honors/Awds:** Fellowship SIU Edwardsville Il 1974; YWCA serv (vol) awd St Louis Met YWCA; 70001 support awd St Louis Chap 70001 Youth Orgn 1979. **Business Addr:** ECHO, 3033 N Euclid Ave, St Louis, MO 63115.

REEVES, MARTHA ROSE
Entertainer. **Personal:** Born Jul 18, 1941, Eufaula, AL. **Career:** The Vandellas, lead singer, 1963-71; Martha Motown Records, leader 10 yrs. **Orgs:** Mem AFTRA; mem AGUA; mem SAG; mem Negro Women's Assn; mem Mt Zion Bapt Ch. **Honors/Awds:** Recipient of 7 Gold Singles; numerous Grammy nominations; 12 albums.

REEVES, MICHAEL S.
Business executive. **Personal:** Born Oct 2, 1935, Memphis, TN; son of Grace Stanley Reeves (deceased) and William Reeves (deceased); married Patricia; children: Michael, Michelle. **Educ:** Roosevelt U, BA 1964; NW U, MBA 1972. **Career:** Peoples Gas, mktg mgr 1972-73, customer rel supt 1973-74, office of the pres admin asst 1974-75, customer relations dept genl supt 1975-77, vice pres 1977-87; exec vice pres 1987-. **Orgs:** Better Business Bureau, executive committee, director, 1978-; Exec Leadership Cnl; Shedd Aquarium, director; LISC (Local Initiatives Support Corp of Chicago), advisory committee; Abraham Lincoln Center, board member; Children's Memorial Hospital, board member; American Heart Association of Metropolitan Chicago, board member; American Association of Blacks in Energy; Better Business Bureau of Chicago and Northern Illinois, chairman, 1994. **Military Serv:** USNA Signal Corp speclt 1958-60.

REEVES, WILLIE LLOYD, JR.
Attorney, elected government official. **Personal:** Born Apr 17, 1949, Portsmouth, VA. **Educ:** Howard Univ, BA 1971, JD 1974. **Career:** Fed Communications Comm, trial atty 1976-; FCC Chap 209 NTEU Union, pres 1979-. **Orgs:** Chmn Adv Neighborhood Comm 2D 1981, 1982, 1984, 1985; vice chmn ANC-2D 1980,83,86,87; vice pres Labor Sect Natl Bar Assn 1984-85; mem Natl, American, Washington Bar Assns; mem Natl Conf of Black Elected Officials; mem Omega Psi Phi Frat; bd of dirs Southwest Neighborhood Assembly 1983-; MUSCLE 1980-; mem Phi Alpha Delta Legal Frat, NCBL; pres Southwest Neighborhood Assembly 1986. **Honors/Awds:** Spec Achievement Awd Capital South Improvement assn 1983, 1984, 1985.

REGISTER, JASPER C.
Educator. **Personal:** Born Jan 15, 1937, Valdosta, GA; son of Audra Mae Hall Register and Perry Register; divorced. **Educ:** Morehouse Coll, AB (with honors) 1959; Univ of KY, MA 1969, PhD 1974. **Career:** Stillman Coll, instr 1966-67; Baldwin-Wallace Coll, asst prof 1971-73; East Carolina Univ, assoc prof sociology. **Orgs:** Mem Amer Sociol Assoc 1974-, Southern Sociol Soc 1974-, Human Relations Council 1980-83; mem bd of dir Mental Health Assoc 1984-87, 1989-92. **Honors/Awds:** Research Awd Social Sci Rsch Council 1968; Assoc Danforth Found 1981-86. **Military Serv:** AUS capt 3 yrs; Occupation Medal 1962-65. **Home Addr:** 104 Fairwood Ln, Greenville, NC 27834. **Business Addr:** Associate Professor, Sociology, East Carolina Univ, Brewster Bldg, Greenville, NC 27858.

REID, ANTONIO (L. A)
Songwriter, producer. **Personal:** Born in Cincinnati, OH; married Perri McKissick (Pebbles) (divorced 1995); children: 1. **Career:** The Deele, R&B group, singer; albums include: Street Beat, Material Thanz, Eyes Of A Stranger; Producer, songwriter with Kenny Edmonds (Babyface) for: Bobby Brown, Karyn White, Sheena Easton, Pebbles, Paula Abdul, MAC Band, numerous others. **Special Achievements:** Grammy award nomination for song "Every Little Step," 1989; accomplished songwriters producing music which sold a double-platinum album for Bobby Brown, a Grammy nomination for Karyn White, and a Top-10 single for Paula Abdul. **Business Phone:** (404)416-6100.

REID, BENJAMIN F.
Clergyman, college administrator, author. **Personal:** Born Oct 5, 1937, New York City, NY; son of Viola Reid and Noah Reid; married Anna Pearl Batie; children: Benjamin Jr, Sylvia, Angela, Kathy, Judith, Stephanie. **Educ:** Univ of Pittsburgh, attended; No Bapt Theol Sem, attended; Amer Bible Inst, DD 1971; CA Western Univ, PhD 1975; Ctr for Pastoral Studies Anderson IN School of Theol, 1980; CA Grad School of Theol, LD 1981; Anderson Coll, DD 1982; Univ of So CA, Diploma Continuing Educ Ctr 1982-86; World University, DTheol 1988; DD Pacific Christian Coll, 1996. **Career:** Springfield IL, pastor 1958-59; Junction City KS, pastor 1959-63; Detroit MI, pastor 1963-70; LA 1st Church of God, pastor 1971-96. **Orgs:** Mem Natl Bd of Ch Ext & Home Missions of the Church of God 1968-80; police chpln Inglewood CA 1973-84; founder, pres So CA Assoc of Holiness Chs 1977-79; dir West Coast Effective Ministries Workshop 1975, 1977-84; vice-chmn General Assembly of the Ch of God 1977-79; pres Partners in Ecumenism SW USA Reg 1979; pres LA Council of Chs 1980; presiding bishop 1st Ch of God Nigerian Conf Africa 1980-95; mem bd of trustees Anderson College 1982-92; pres So CA School of Ministry LA 1984-; elected Sr Bishop The Interstate Assoc of the Ch of God 1985; chmn Ministerial Assembly of the So CA Assoc of the Ch of God 1986; mem Natl Black Evangelical Assoc 1988-; founding mem Black Ecumenical Task Force Los Angeles CA 1988-; mem bd dir LA Urban League; gen chmn Interstate WestCoast Assoc of the Ch of God;m Council of Churchmen School of Theol Azusa Pacific Univ; mem bd of trustees, Hope Intl Univ, 1997-; mem LA Council of Chs, So Christian Leadership Conf, LA Met Learning Ctr, Ecumenical Ctr for Black Ch Studies of LA, USC Comm Advs Bd; elected pres; Nat Assn of the Church of God, 1996-. **Honors/Awds:** Author "Confessions of a Happy Preacher" 1971, "Black Preacher Black Church" 1975, "Another Look at Glossalalia" 1977, "Another Look at Other Tongues" rev ed 1982, "Glory to the Spirit" 1989; "Glory to The Spirit" Pastor's Workbood ed, 1998; Mayor's Awd (LA) for community serv 1986, 1996; Outstanding Bishop's Awd LA Awds Dinner; "Excellence in Preaching Awd Disciples of Christ." Indianapolis IN 1986; Inglewood Mayor's Awd 1987, 1996; CA Senate Awd 1987, 1996; Los Angeles City Council Awd 1987, 1996; Compton Mayor's Awd 1987; Los Angeles County Supervisor's Awd 1987, 1996; named by Los Angeles Times as "One of Southern California's Twenty Outstanding Preachers"; Los Angeles Mayor's Award 1988, 1996; Honored Service Award City of Inglewood CA 1988; Ebony Mag, List of Great Black Preachers, 1997. **Business Addr:** Episcopal Office, LA 1st Church of God, 9550 S Crenshaw Blvd, Inglewood, CA 90305.

REID, CLARICE WILLS
Physician, government official. **Personal:** Born Nov 21, 1931, Birmingham, AL; daughter of Willie Mae Brown and Noah Edgar Wills Sr; married Arthur Joseph Reid Jr, Jun 11, 1955; children: Kevin, Sheila, Jill, Clarice. **Educ:** Talladega Coll, BS 1952; Meharry Med Coll, med tech 1954; Univ Cincinnati Sch Med, MD 1959. **Career:** US Natl Institutes of Health, Sickle Cell Program, natl coord, currently, acting dir, div of blood diseases & resources, 1988-89; Health Serv Admin, dep dir 1973-76; Dept of Health, Education, and Welfare, medical consultant, 1972-73; Pediatric Jewish Hospital, dir 1968-70; OH Dept Health, pediatric consultant 1964-70. **Orgs:** Mem Natl Med Assn; AAAS; asst clinical prof Univ Cinnati School of Medicine 1965-70; Amer Acad of Pediatrics; Amer Public Health Assn; mem Hamilton Co Adoption Agency 1966-69; Visiting Nurse Assn 1968-70; Amer Bridge Assn; mem NY Acad of Sci, Amer Soc of Hematology, Asst Clinical Prof Pediatrics, Howard Univ Coll of Medicine; Links, Inc. **Honors/Awds:** Co-author chapter "Family Care" Wms & Wilkins Co 1973; Outstanding Student Faculty Awd Meharry Med Coll 1954; NIH Dir Awd; NIH Merit Awd; co-author "Management & Therapy in Sickle Cell Disease"; PHS Special Recognition Award l989; PHS Superior Service Award, 1990; Presential Meritoroius Executive Award, 1991.

REID, DESIREE CHARESE
Company executive. **Personal:** Born Jan 13, 1964, Bronx, NY; daughter of Elsie McDaniels Reid & John Reid Jr; divorced. **Educ:** Seton Hall Univ, BA, 1984; The Paralegal Institute, 1987-88; Adelphi Univ, MBA, 1993; NY Restaurant School, Professor Management Dev Prog, 1997-98. **Career:** Jordache Enterprises, chargeback supervisor, 1985-86; H Cotler Co, exec acct mgr, 1986-92; John Kaldor, accts rec supervisor, 1992; Farberware, corp credit mgr, 1994-96. **Orgs:** NAACP, 1992-; Delta Sigma Theta Sorority Inc, 1983-; Mayor Dinkins Re-Election Camp, volunteer, 1993; Black Filmmaker Assn; Thruway Homeowners Assn; National Assn Female Execs; Black Students Union, co-chair, 1982-83; Drama Society, mem/actress; National Association of Credit Management. **Honors/Awds:** MLK Academic Scholarship, 1980-84; National Association Negro Business & Professional Women's Clubs Inc, Business Award, 1996. **Special Achievements:** Peter Kump Pastry, certificate prog, 1997; First & youngest African-American Corp Credit Mgr, 1994-96; Dean's List, Natl Honor Society, 1977-83; Founding Member, MLK Assn at Seton Hall Univ, 1981. **Home Addr:** 3118 Mickle Avenue, Bronx, NY 10469-3104. **Business Addr:** President, Ms Reid Enterprises, Baychester Station, PO Box 1061, Bronx, NY 10469.

REID, DON
Professional basketball player. **Personal:** Born Dec 30, 1973, Washington, DC. **Educ:** Georgetown, graduated. **Career:** Detroit Pistons, forward, 1995-. **Business Addr:** Professional Basketball Player, Detroit Pistons, 2 Championship Dr, Auburn Hills, MI 48326, (248)377-0100.

REID, EDITH C.
Cardiologist. **Personal:** Born in Atlantic City, NJ; married John L Edmonds. **Educ:** Hunter Coll, BA; Meharry Med Coll, MD. **Career:** St Albans NY, pvt practice; Flower & 5th Ave Monroe, clin asst; clinical instr & asst physician; New York City Dept Health, physician chest clinic Jamaica Hosp, asst visiting physician; assoc attend med; Carter Community Health Ctr, chief med. **Orgs:** Mem Queens Clinical Soc Inc; Natl Amer Med Assn; Med Soc Queens & NY State; NY Heart Assn; Empire State Soc; Ad Hoc Com; NY Trudeau Soc; Amer Geriatric Soc; Ethics Comm; Civic Assn; NAACP; Neighborhood Health Council; Med Adv Comm NY Univ Bd Regents. **Honors/Awds:** Quest hon wives club lunch 1973; achievement award Omega Psi Phi 1974; friends York Coll 1974; outstanding serv Delta Sigma Theta Sor. **Business Addr:** Carter Community Health Center, 97 04 Sutphin Blvd, Jamaica, NY.

REID, ELLIS EDMUND, III
Judge. **Personal:** Born May 19, 1934, Chicago, IL; son of Carrie Belle Graham Reid and Ellis Edmund Reid; married Barbara Alice Kline Reid, May 25, 1959 (divorced 1976); children: Ellis Edmund IV, David E, Noelle E; married Shella Janice Miller Reid, Jul 31, 1980. **Educ:** Univ of IL, BA 1956; Univ of Chicago, JD 1959. **Career:** IL Bar, admitted 1959; Circuit Court of Cook County, judge, 1985-; McCoy Ming & Black Chicago & Predecessor Firm, law practice 1959-, partner 1964-; Ofc Econ Opportunity Legal Serv Program, cons, 1961-69, real estate broker, 1963-85; Property/Casualty Insurance Broker, 1980-85; Cook County IL, states atty spl asst, 1970-72; Fair Employment Practices Commn, hearing examiner, 1968-76. **Orgs:** Cook County Bar Assn, pres, 1970-72; Bar Assn 7th Fed Circuit; mem Am Arbitration Assn; mem Nat Panel Arbitrators, 1968-85; mem Phi Delta Phi; Kappa Alpha Psi; bd dir Better Boys Found, 1966-80; dir Highland Comm Bank; vice pres Chatham Avalon Park Comm Council, 1963-65, 1967; life member, National Bar Assn; member, Illinois State Bar Assn; member, Illinois Judicial Council, chairman, 1990-91; member, Illinois Judges Assn; Chicago Inn of Court. **Honors/Awds:** Civil Rights Award, Cook County Bar Association, 1970; Civic Award, AME Ministerial Alliance, 1985; Grand Polemarch's Certificate of Appreciation for Service as General Counsel of Kappa Alpha Psi, 1985; Judicial Award, Cook County Bar Assn, 1985; Distinguished Humanitarian Award for Outstanding Community Service, 1986; Achievement Award for Contribution to Law, Chicago Alumni Chapter, Kappa Alpha Psi, 1988; Meritorious Service Award, Illinois Judicial Council, 1988; Monarch Award, Alpha Kappa Alpha, 1988; Kenneth E Wilson Memorial Award, Cook County Bar Association, 1991, and Illinois Judicial Council, 1996. **Military Serv:** US Army, Capt, 1957. **Business Addr:** Judge, Chancery Division, Circuit Court of Cook County, 2502 R J Daley Center, Chicago, IL 60602.

REID, F. THEODORE, JR.
Psychiatrist, educator. **Personal:** Born Nov 22, 1929, New York, NY; married Diane; children: Lynne, Frank. **Educ:** Columbia Coll Columbia U, BA 1950; McGill Univ Montreal, CAN, MD faculty of med 1954; King Co Hosp Brooklyn, intern 1955, psychiatry resident 1957; VA Rsch Hosp Chicago, chf resident psychiatry 1960. **Career:** Private Practice, psychiatry 1960-; Pritzker Sch of Med Univ of Chicago, clinical assoc prof psychiatry 1975-76; Camelback Hosp, assoc 1977-; Maricopa Co Hosp AZ State Hosp, instr; psych residency 1976; Scottsdale Memorial Hosp Family Practice Residency, instr 1977; Phoenix Indian Hosp, consultant 1977-80; Northwestern U, assoc dept of psych neurology 1966-72; Michael Reese Hosp, coor group therapy training 1969-76; Adult Outpatient Psychiatric Clinic 1967-69; Madden Zone Ctr, dir ct referral unit 1966-67; M Reese Hosp Serv ISPI, chf 1961-66; Mental Health Assoc, owner. **Orgs:** Mem Comm on Emerging Issues APA 1978-80; bd of dirs Camelback Hosp Found 1979; dir Amer Group Psychotherapy Assn 1979-82, 1983-; co-chmn Inst Comm Amer Group Psychotherapy Assn 1974-78; fellow Amer Orthopsych Assn 1974-80; mem exec comm Amer Group Psych Assn 1973-75, 1977-79, 1984-86. **Honors/Awds:** APA, Life Fellow; AGPA, Distinguished Fellow. **Military Serv:** USNR lt med corps 1957-59. **Business Addr:** Owner, Mental Health Associates, 6991 E Camelback Rd, C-310, Scottsdale, AZ 85251-2436.

REID, INEZ SMITH
Attorney. **Personal:** Born Apr 7, 1937, New Orleans, LA. **Educ:** Tufts Univ, BA 1959; Yale Univ Law Sch, LLB 1962; UCLA, MA 1963; Columbia Univ, PhD 1968. **Career:** Barnard Coll Columbia Univ, assoc prof 1969-76; NY State Div for Youth, genl counsel 1976-77; Dept of Health Educ & Welfare, deputy genl counsel 1977-79; Environmental Protection Agency, inspector genl 1979-80; Dist of Columbia Govt, corp counsel. **Orgs:** Past bds Antioch Univ Bd of Trustees, United Ch of Christ Bd for Homeland Ministries. **Honors/Awds:** Numerous articles published; numerous awds.

REID, IRVIN D.
Educational administrator. **Personal:** married Pamela Trotman Reid; children: Two. **Educ:** Howard Univ, BS, MS; University of Pennsylvania, MBA, PhD. **Career:** Pres, Montclair State Univ, 1989-97; pres, Wayne State Univ, 1997-. **Special Achievements:** First African American pres of Wayne State Univ. **Business Addr:** President, Wayne State University, Office of the President, 6050 Cass Ave, Detroit, MI 48202, (313)577-2424.

REID, J. R. (HERMAN)
Professional basketball player. **Personal:** Born Mar 31, 1968, Virginia Beach, VA. **Educ:** Univ of North Carolina, Chapel Hill, NC, 1986-89. **Career:** Charlotte Hornets, 1989-92; San Antonio Spurs, 1992-. **Honors/Awds:** NBA All-Rookie Second Team, 1990; US Olympic Team member, 1988. **Business Addr:** Professional Basketball Player, San Antonio Spurs, 600 E Market St, Ste 102, San Antonio, TX 78205.

REID, JANIE ELLEN
Administrator. **Personal:** Born Feb 15, 1950, Pelzer, SC. **Educ:** SC State Coll, BS Bus Admin (Honor Grad) 1972. **Career:** SC Assoc of Student Financial Aid Admin, mem 1973-87, sec/treas 1975-77; JE Sirrine Scholarship Advisory Bd, mem 1974-75, chmn 1980-82; SC Commiss on Higher Ed, adv bd mem 1975-78; US Dept of Ed Bureau of Student Financial Aid, inst appl review panel mem 1976; Greenville Tech Coll, fin aid dir. **Orgs:** Instr New Financial Aid Officer Workshop Southern Assoc of Student Fin Aid Admin 1978,79; charter mem Greenville Urban League's Early Leadership & Confidence Training 1978-79; advisory bd SC Student Loan Corp 1981-83; chmn adv bd Greenville Urban League's Ed Talent Search Prog 1982-84; minister of ed Shady Grove Baptist Church 1983-85; ed advisory comm SC Appalachian Council of Governments 1983-89; chmn Greenville Cty Human Relations Comm 1985. **Honors/Awds:** Citizenship Awd Greenville Civitan Club 1968; mem Iota Phi Lambda, Delta Eta Chap 1971-; Annual Pastor's Awd Shady Grove Baptist Church 1981,82,83. **Home Addr:** 405 Old Hundred Rd, Pelzer, SC 29669. **Business Addr:** Dir of Financial Aid, Greenville Technical College, PO Box 5616 Station B, Greenville, SC 29606.

REID, JOEL OTTO
Educator. **Personal:** Born May 17, 1936, Newark, NJ; children: Joel II, Nicol. **Educ:** New York University School of Education, BS, 1959; Montclair State College, MA, 1965; Claremont Graduate School, Claremont, CA, PhD, 1973. **Career:** Elizabeth Public School System, Elizabeth, NJ, teacher; White Plaines High School, counselor, teacher, 1962-65; White Plaines Board of Education, professional recruiter, 1965-67; National Teachers Corps, Migrant University, Southern California, teacher, leader, 1967-68; Claremont Graduate School, staff member, 1971-72; Social Science Department, professor, 1978; Pasadena City College, dean of continuing education, 1968-78, professor of social science, 1978-. **Orgs:** Pasadena Education Association; Pasadena City College Faculty Association; NEA; Los Angeles Co Adult Education Adminstrators Association; chairman, Eval Com for Western Associations Schools & Colleges, 1969, 1970, 1974; board of directors, Urban League Com for Educ Fund Dr; Fair Hsg Com of Westchester Co, New York; Am Friends Ser Com on Hsg, Pasadena; counseled Neighborhood Youth Center; worked with economically educationally deprived areas; lectured at educational, civic, & religious organizations; consultant to schools, pvt groups & Comm agencies. **Honors/Awds:** Two year Scholarship to College; Kiwanis Rotary Club Scholarship; Valley Settlement House Scholarship, West Orange, NJ; Womens Aux Scholarship, West Orange, NJ. **Military Serv:** AUS sp5, 1959-62. **Business Addr:** Professor of Social Science, Pasadena City College, 1570 E Colorado Blvd, Pasadena, CA 91106.

REID, LESLIE BANCROFT
Dentist educator. **Personal:** Born Nov 7, 1934, Clarendon, Jamaica; son of Walter B Reid; married Norma A Morris; children: Donovan, Diane. **Educ:** Howard Univ, BS 1968, DDS 1972. **Career:** Govt Bacteriological Lab Jamaica, med tech 1953-59; Tia Maria Ltd Jamaica, chemist 1959-64; Cafritz Hosp Washington DC, med tech 1966-72; Howard Univ Dental Sch, faculty mem 1972-. **Orgs:** Dir Reid-& Yip Young DDS PA 1973-; consult Ministry of Health Jamaica 1974; consult Ministry of Health Guyana 1976; partner Eastover Dental Serv 1979-; consultant Ministry of Health Belize Central Amer 1984; bd of trustees Hospice of Charles County 1985-; staff Greater Southeast Comm Hosp 1986-; clinician numerous dental conventions; bd of trustees, Charles County Comm Coll 1969-76; bd of trustees, Warner Pacific Coll 1989-. **Honors/Awds:** Co-author (paper) ''Adaptability of Several Amalgam to Enamel Surface'' Journal of Dental Rsch 1985; co-author A Manual of Fixed Prosthodontics Howard Univ 1986; Outstanding Faculty, Howard Univ Coll of Dentistry Student Council 1989; Laboratory Manual of Dental Anatomy and Occlusion 1988. **Business Addr:** Faculty Member, Howard Univ Coll of Dentistry, 600 W St NW, Washington, DC 20059.

REID, MALISSIE LAVERNE
Interior decorator, realtor. **Personal:** Born Aug 23, 1953, Orange, NJ; daughter of Malissie Elizabeth Reid and Joseph Wilbur Reid Sr. **Educ:** Rider College, BA, political science, 1971-75; Professional School of Business, insurance broker, 1978; New York School of Interior Design, 1980-82; Kovats School of Real Estate, 1987. **Career:** Union Camp Corporation, Tax Department, administrative assistant, 1975-76; Aetna Life & Casuality, commercial lines underwriter, 1976-78; Chubb Custom Market, speciality lines underwriter, 1978-81; Cigna Insurance Company, underwriting mgr, 1981-86; Home Insurance Company, underwriting mgr, 1986-87; Reid's Interior Decorators & Upholstery, exec vp, 1987-. **Orgs:** Town of Nutley, board of adjustments, 1991-; Community Mental Health, board of directors, 1991-. **Business Addr:** Exec VP, Reid's Interior Decorators & Upholstry, 573 Bloomfield Ave, Montclair, NJ 07042, (201)744-6644.

REID, MAUDE K.
Educational administrator (retired). **Personal:** Born in Georgetown, SC; daughter of Katye N Kennedy and William Kennedy; divorced; children: Kennedy. **Educ:** FL A&M Univ, BS 1936; Columbia Univ, MA; studied at Univ of Miami. **Career:** Negro Progs of FL Tuberculosis & Health Educ Agy, first field sec; Bethune-Cookman Coll & FL A&M Coll, summer workshop cons; Pittsburgh Courier, social columnist; FL State Dept of Educ, teacher trainer in home econ; Dade Co Public School System Miami, retired supr adult home educ 1965-. **Orgs:** Mem, Amer Vocational Assn; mem Natl Educ Assn; mem Amer Home Econ Assn; mem FL Educ Assn; mem Amer Assn of Univ Women; mem League of Women Voters; pres Council of United Fund Women; past pres Greater Miami Urban League Bd; mem Natl Council of Urban League Guilds; mem Links Inc; Greater Miami Urban League Guild; bd dir YMCA sr citizen; mem League of Women Voters; exec comm Natl Council of Jewish Women. **Honors/Awds:** Recipient Woman of the Yr Awd Links Inc; Meritorious Achievement Awd FL A&M Univ. **Home Addr:** 5121 High Pointe Drive, Pensacola, FL 32505.

REID, MILES ALVIN
Educational administrator (retired). **Personal:** Born Oct 23, 1931, West Point, VA; son of CeCelia Whiting Reid and William E Reid; married Alice Lee, Aug 14, 1966; children: Alicia Mia. **Educ:** Morgan State Coll, BA 1953; Hampton Inst, MA 1968. **Career:** King & Queen Central High School, tchr 1957-64; King & Queen Elem School Shanglai, VA, principal 1964-72; Hamilton Holmes Elem School King William VA, principal 1972-78; King William West Point Schools, dir federal prog 1978-83, assoc supt, 1980-91, school board clerk, 1980-97. **Orgs:** Mem VA Assn School Admin 1978-96; mem Assoc Supvn Curric Devel 1980-96; mem VA Assoc Federal Educ Prog 1978-91; mem West Point Bi-Racial Comm 1968-; mem West Point Bd Zoning Appeal 1971-80; gen supt Mt Nebo Baptist Church School 1964-84; prog chmn Pamunkey Baptist Literary Union 1970-85; trustee Pamunkey Baptist Assoc 1985-; teacher, Mt Nebo Baptist Church School 1985-. **Honors/Awds:** Appreciation Award Mt Nebo Baptist Church 1972; Area Appreciation Award VA Peninsula Clubs Negro Business and Professional Womens Clubs 1982; honored, State Farmers Degree, VA Future Farmers of Amer 1976; honored, Chapter Farmers Degree King William HS Chapter FFA; Man of the Year Third Union Baptist Church 1985; Man of the Year Awd VA Peninsular Clubs Negro Business & Professional Women's Clubs Inc 1985. **Home Addr:** 216 16th St Box 103, West Point, VA 23181. **Business Addr:** Clerk, King William School Board, PO Box 185, King William, VA 23086.

REID, MILTON A.
Minister, publisher, businessman. **Personal:** Born Jan 26, 1930, Chesapeake, VA; son of Mary M Reid (deceased) and Rev Moses Annias Reid (deceased); married Marian Elean Todd, Aug 18, 1952; children: Maravia Nse Ebong, Humphrey T, Michelle A Brown, Milton A Jr. **Educ:** Virginia Union Univ, AB 1958; Virginia Union Univ School of Religions, MDiv, 1960; Boston Univ School of Theology, DMin, 1980. **Career:** Minister, Gideon's Riverside Fellowship; Guide Publishing Co, publisher/pres, 1974-87, publisher emeritus, 1987-. **Orgs:** Former mem, STOIC Natl Newspaper Publishers Assn; life mem, SCLC; founder, organizer, & past pres, Virginia State Unit, SCLC; past moderator, Bethany Baptist Assn; life mem, Norfolk Branch, NAACP, 1982-; bd of dirs, Interreligious Found for Community Org, 1972-; chmn, bd of dirs, Gideon Family Life Center, 1985-; pres, Faith Village Corp. **Honors/Awds:** Doctor of Divinity Degree, Virginia Seminary & Coll, 1960; Distinguished Leadership Award, Virginia State Conf of NAACP, 1974; Meritorious Serv Award 1974-87 Journal & Guide Citizens Award; recipient of numerous other awards & citations; civil rights activist with Southern Christian Leadership Conf & mem of bd, 1963-70; dir, TRUST Inc; dir, NNPA, 1975-81. **Military Serv:** US Army 82nd Airborne Div, corporal, 1948-52; numerous awards. **Home Addr:** 1909 Arlington Ave, Norfolk, VA 23523, (757)545-4312. **Business Addr:** Minister, Gideon's Riverside Fellowship, 366 Campostella Rd, Norfolk, VA 23523.

REID, N. NEVILLE
Attorney. **Personal:** married. **Educ:** Harvard University, BA, magna cum laude, 1984; Harvard Law School, JD, 1987. **Career:** Mayer Brown & Platt, associate, 1987-96, partner, 1996-. **Orgs:** ABA Conference on Minority Partners in Majority/Corporate Law Firms, 1996-; Panel of Private Trustees, Northern District of Illinois, 1994-; Amer Bankruptcy Inst, 1994-; Leadership Greater Chicago, fellow, 1997-; Beverly Area Local Dev Corp, chmn, 1996-; Good Shepherd Community Svcs Organization, bd of dirs, 1995-. **Honors/Awds:** Harvard University, Harvard College Scholarship, 1981, John Harvard College Scholarship, 1982-84, Rhodes Scholarship Finalist, 1983. **Business Addr:** Partner, Mayer, Brown & Platt, 190 S LaSalle St, Chicago, IL 60603.

REID, ROBERT
Professional basketball player. **Personal:** Born Aug 30, 1955, Atlanta, GA; married Donna; children: Robert, Keva Rachel. **Educ:** St Mary's Univ, 1973-77. **Career:** Houston Rockets, 1978-82, 1984-88, Charlotte Hornets, 1989, 1990, Portland Trail Blazers, beginning 1990; Yakima Sun Kings, coach, currently. **Orgs:** Rec the NBA Humanitarian of the Year Awd in 1981; works with Spec Olympics, Big Brothers, hospital groups. **Honors/Awds:** Was a first team NAIA All-Amer st St Mary's of San Antonio which twice finished 4th place in the NAIA finals.

REID, ROBERT DENNIS
Educator (retired). **Personal:** Born Nov 9, 1924, Atlanta, GA. **Educ:** Clark Coll of Atlanta, 1941-43; Art Inst of Chicago 1946-48; Parson's School of Design, NY City 1948-50 diploma in illustration. **Career:** Lecturer Drew Univ, 1969; instructor of painting Summit Art Center, 1970-74; SUNY, instr painting 1975; Drew Univ, instr painting 1978; Dordogne Coll France, lecturer 1978; Parsons School of Design, instr of drawing 1978-83; Rhode Island School of Design, assoc prof of drawing 1970-89. **Honors/Awds:** Childe Hassam Purchase Amer Acad of Arts & Letters 1969; MacDowell Colony Fellow. **Military Serv:** USN pttm 3/c 3 yrs. **Home Addr:** 309 Mott St #2-C, New York, NY 10012.

REID, ROBERT EDWARD
Clergyman. **Personal:** Born Sep 13, 1903, Como, MS; married Clara A Humphress; children: Orien E. **Educ:** Lane Coll, BA 1941; Gammon Seminary, MDiv 1971; Univ of MO & Kansas Univ, additional studies. **Career:** Covington GA Murray Chapel, Lane Chapel, Holsey Temple, Phillip's Temple, Bower Memorial, pastor; CME Church, dir visual aid 1940; Paseo Leadership Training School, dean 1959; CME Church, presiding elder 1959-69, admin asst sr bishop. **Orgs:** Attended one week's seminar Hebrew Univ Jerusalem, Israel 1964; vice pres Council on Religion & Race Kansas City, MO; chmn com which drew up resolution to establish Kansas City Council on Religion & Race 1964. **Honors/Awds:** Cited by Kansas-Missouri Annual Conf for Civic Work in Kansas City, MO Area 1963; God & Man Award Council of Religion & Race 1969. **Home Addr:** 5201 Spruce, Kansas City, MO 64130.

REID, ROBERTO ELLIOTT
Educator. **Personal:** Born Nov 12, 1930, Panama, Panama; son of Ettie Reid and Exley Reid; married Joyce. **Educ:** NY U, AB 1954; Western Res Univ Sch Med, MD 1958; Philadelphia Gen

Hosp, 1958-59; Bronx Municipal Hosp. **Career:** Assoc prof urology 1973; asst prof urology 1965-73; Albert Einstein Coll Med, assoc prof of urology 1963-85, prof of urology, 1985-; Bronx Municipal Hosp, dir urology 1973. **Orgs:** Coun Amer Coll Surgeons 1975-77; mem NY sec rep AVAA 1976; mem Sigma Pi Phi. **Business Addr:** 1695 Eastchester Road, Ste 306, Bronx, NY 10461.

REID, RONDA EUNESE
Security specialist. **Personal:** Born May 1, 1955, Dayton, OH; married Washington Reid Jr, Sep 26, 1981; children: Darnell, Byron. **Educ:** Sinclair Community College, Dayton, OH, AS, law enforcement, 1974; University of Dayton, Dayton, OH, BS, criminal justice, 1976; Central Michigan University, Mount Pleasant, MI, MS, public administration, 1992. **Career:** US Air Force, civilian: Wright Patterson AFB, Dayton, OH, research and development, administrative support, 1977-84, security specialist, 1984-86, General Electric Co, Cincinnati, OH, security specialist, 1986-88, Johnson Space Center, Houston, TX, security specialist, 1988, The Pentagon, Washington, DC, security specialist, 1989-. **Orgs:** Member, National Classification Management Society, 1985-; member, 1981-86, vice president, 1984-85, president, 1985-86, American Business Women's Association, Gem City Chapter; holds one of six seats, USAF Security Career Program Training and Development Panel; Blacks in Government, Pentagon Chapter. **Honors/Awds:** Outstanding Performance Rating, 1979, Sustained Superior Performance Award, 1984, Superior Performance Award, 1985, Notable Achievement Award, 1986, Quality Step Increase, 1986, Performance Award, 1987, 1990-92, US Air Force. **Home Addr:** 6132 Surrey Sq Ln #203, Forestville, MD 20747. **Business Addr:** Security Specialist, US Air Force International Affairs Office, The Pentagon, Rm 4C1074, Washington, DC 20330-1010.

REID, RUBIN J.
Real estate agent. **Personal:** married; children: 2. **Educ:** VA, Grad Coll Bus 1963; BS Business Admnstrn. **Career:** Glenarden, mayor, vice mayor; Gitelson Neff Asso Inc, real estate agent. **Orgs:** Chmn Town Council. **Military Serv:** US Army, Sgt; Korean Service Medal; Good Conduct Medal; National Defense Serv Medal; Bronze Star; United Nations Service Medal; Republic of Korea Presidential Unit Citiation.

REID, SELWYN CHARLES
Attorney. **Personal:** Born Apr 19, 1944, Los Angeles, CA; married Beverly A Washington. **Educ:** LA City Coll, AA 1970; CA St U, BA 1970-71; Univ So CA, JD, MPA 1971-74. **Career:** LA Co Dist Atty, dep dist atty; Legal Aid Found of LA, atty 1975-76; LA Dist Attys Ofc, law Clk 1972; US Post Ofcx, 1966-69. **Orgs:** State & Bar CA; LA Co Bar Assn; Langston Law Clb; Phi Alpha Delta Law Frat; USC Alumni Assn. **Military Serv:** USMC corpl 1962-65. **Business Addr:** 417 S Hill St, Los Angeles, CA 90013.

REID, SINA M.
Business executive. **Personal:** Born Feb 8, 1944, Marion, NC; daughter of Hazel McGimpsey and Edward McGimpsey; married Harold G Reid; children: Derek, Deren. **Educ:** Univ of NC, BA 1965; Antioch Univ, MA 1978. **Career:** NTL Educ Assn, admin asst 1965-67; Hope Ctr for Retarded, dir of social serv 1967-70; NTL Educ Assn, admin mgr 1970-76; Broadway-Payne Inc, exec vice pres 1976-; SMR Ltd, pres 1980-. **Orgs:** Mem Natl Assoc of Bus & Professional Women; hon bd of dir mem, Natl Black McDonalds Opers; mem, Gr Baltimore Committee/Leadership Board; life mem, NAACP, Delta Sigma Theta, Continental Soc Inc; mem, President's Roundtable; bd of dirs, Boy Scouts of Amer; vice chairman/bd of dirs, Associated Black Charities; UNCG Excellence Foundation, Baltimore County Community College Board, Private Industry Council. **Honors/Awds:** Disting Serv VA Union Univ; Cert of Merit for Outstanding Serv Hope Ctr; Bus Woman of the Year Natl Assoc of Negro Bus & Professional Women Inc. **Home Addr:** 102 Charlesbrooke Rd, Baltimore, MD 21212.

REID, TIM
Actor, producer, writer, company executive. **Personal:** Born Dec 19, 1944, Norfolk, VA; son of Augustine Wilkins and William Lee Reid; married Daphne Maxwell, 1982; children: Tim II, Tori LeAnn, stepson: Christopher Tubbs. **Educ:** Norfolk State College, BS, Business Marketing 1968. **Career:** Dupont Corp, marketing representative, 1968-71; Tim and Tom Comedy Team, 1971-75; stand-up comedian; Timalove Enterprises, founder, 1979; United Image Entertainment Enterprises, cofounder, with BET, 1990, co-chairman; television appearances include: "The Richard Pryor Show," 1977; "WKRP in Cincinnati," 1978; "Teachers Only," 1982; "Simon & Simon," 1983; "Frank's Place," 1987; "Snoops," 1989; television movies include: "You Can't Take It With You," 1979; "Perry Mason Movie," 1990; Stephen King's "IT," 1991; "The Family Business," 1991; feature films include: Dead Bang, 1989; The Fourth War, 1990; creator, producer: Stop The Madness, nation's first anti-drug video, 1986; co-executive producer: Frank's Place, 1987; co-creator, executive producer: Snoops, 1989; creator, producer: The Tim and Daphne Show, talk show,1; Sitcom: Sister, Sister, 1994; TV series, "Save Our Streets"; produced and directed feature film, "Once Upon a

Time.. When We were Colored". **Orgs:** Writers Guild of America; Screen Actors Guild; Phoenix House of California, board of directors; Norfolk State University, Commonwealth of Virginia; National Academy of Cable Programming, board of directors; AFTRA; NAACP, life member. **Honors/Awds:** Critics Choice Award, Producer Best Comedy, 1988; NAACP, Image Award, Best Actor in a Comedy, 1988; Viewers For Quality Television Award, Best Actor in a Comedy, 1988; National Black College Alumni Hall of Fame, Entertainment Inductee, 1991; 2 Emmy Nominations, 1988. Ft. Lauderdale Int'l Film Festival, directional award; Houston Int'l Film Festival Best Producer; NAACP, Image Award Nominee for Producer. **Special Achievements:** Involved in efforts to provide scholarship funds for Minority students; organizer, sponsor: Annual Tim Reid Celebrity Tennis Tournament, Norfolk State University Campus; actively involved in anti-drug movement since 1969; testified many times before House and Senate Subcommittees. **Business Addr:** Co-Chairman, Tim Reid Productions, Inc, 1640 S Sepulveda Blvd, #311, Los Angeles, CA 90025-7510.

REID, VERNON H.
State employee (retired). **Personal:** Born Nov 6, 1904, Columbus, OH; daughter of Cora Jones and John Jones; divorced. **Educ:** BS Educ 1927; MA Spanish 1928. **Career:** Penn Transfer Co, mgr; semi-retired; St OH, deputy asst gov, retired asst to gov of OH. **Orgs:** Mem OH St Civl Svc.

REID, WILFRED
Cleric. **Personal:** Born Oct 9, 1923, Detroit, MI; married Loretta Adams; children: Paul Wilfred, Lorna Joyce, Stephen Wilfred, Patricia Lorene. **Educ:** Roosevelt Univ, BS; Northwestern University Garrett Theological Seminary, MA; Monrivia University, DDiv; Edwards Waters College, DHum; Payne Theological Seminary, DDiv, 1994. **Career:** Bethel AME Ch, pastor 1956-57; Allen & Chapel AME Ch, 1957-60; Bethel AME Ch, 1960-64; St Stephen AME Ch, 1964-85; 4th Dist African Meth Episcopal Ch, dir of evangelism 1969-71; Chicago Conf Arcn Meth Episcopal Ch, dir Christian educ 1969-74; Grant Memorial AME Ch, pastor, 1985-, 4th Dist African Meth Episcopal Ch, dir ministerial training. **Orgs:** Mayor's Comm Human Relations Galesburg IL 1958-60; chmn N Suburban Coord Council & Social Rights Group 1963-64; Chicago Urban Legislative Investigative Comm 1964-65; Midwest Comm Council Exec Bd 1964-74; organizer Control W Shng & Neighborhood Com 1965-74; exec comm Neighborhood 13th Dist Police Work shop 1968-74; adv council Malcolm X College 1971-72; exofficial, bd trustees Garrett Theol Seminary 1972; chmn Ft Dearborn BSA 1972; exec bd dir Church Federation Grtr Chicago 1972; adv council Evangelical Child Welfare 1973; pres Chicago Chapter Operation PUSH 1974; Chicago Com Black Churchmen 1974; pres St Stephens Terrace Corp Chicago IL; Chicago Bd of Educ; bd dir Du Sable Museum; adv comm Chicago City Colleges; Midwest Community Council; bd dir Mile Square Community Org and Medic Center; bd dir Martin Luther King Boy's Club; adv council Provident Hospital; bd dir South Shore YMCA; comm mem Chicago Urban League; chair of the Finance Committee of Fourth Episcopal District and Chicago Conference. **Honors/Awds:** Certif Appntmnt Bicentennial Celebrtn Afrcn Meth Epscpl Ch 1960; Pastor Yr Awd 1961; Chicago Com Urbn Opprtnty Certif Comm Srv 1967; Cert Merit Chicago Com Urbn Opprtnty 1968; Outstndng Srv Nghbrhd Yth Corp 1968; Christian Debutante 1972; BSA Ldrshp Awd 1972; edit Silver Beaver Awd BSA 1973; Humanitarian Awd St Matthew AME Ch Argo IL Man Dstnctn 1973; Chicago Area Almanac & Ref Book 1st edit 1973. **Military Serv:** AUS 1943-46. **Business Addr:** Grant Memorial AME Church, 4017 South Drexel Blvd, Chicago, IL 60653.

REIDE, JEROME L.
Attorney, educator. **Personal:** Born Apr 23, 1954, New York, NY; son of Leonora E Reide and St Clair E Reide Sr. **Educ:** SUNY, New Paltz, BA, 1977; Hofstra University Law School, JD, 1981; Columbia University Graduate Journalism School, MS, 1982; Michigan State University, PhD, 1991. **Career:** American Civil Liberties Union, Access to Justice, coordinator, 1986-87; Center for Labor Studies, SUNY, political science lecturer, 1986-87; Eastern Michigan University, African-American studies lecturer, 1987-88; Detroit City Council, special projects assistant, 1987-88; Michigan State University, Dean of Urban Studies, research assistant, 1988-90; Wayne State University, School of Education, lecturer, 1992-93; NAACP, Special Contribution Fund Midwest, development director, 1990-93; Wayne County Commission, Chair of Ways and Means, legislative aide, 1993-94; Wayne State Univ, Interdisciplinary Studies, asst prof, 1994-. **Orgs:** Urban League, Michigan, 1988-; Dispute Resolution Coordination Council, board of directors, 1991-95; NAACP, life member, 1975-; Boniface Community Action, board of directors, 1991-95; Urban Affairs Graduate Studies Association, president, 1989-90; National Conference of Black Lawyers, press secretary, 1986-87; Black Law Students Association, national press secretary, 1980-81; Sutton for Mayor, press aide, 1977; Global Economic Development Conf, pres, 1993; Wayne State Univ, Ctr for Peace & Conflict Studies, Exec Committee, 1994; State Bar of Michigan, 1996; American Bar Assn, 1997-; Wolverine Bar Assn, 1997-; Team Justice, 1997. **Honors/Awds:** NAACP, Religious Affairs, Back to School/Stay in School, 1992; Universi-

ty of Michigan, Flint, College Bound, Most Inspirational Teacher, 1992; Jackson Fair Housing Commission, Fair Housing Award, 1992; Governor of Kentucky, Order of the Kentucky Colonels, 1991; Committee on Institutional Cooperation, Social Science Fellow, 1988; State Legislature of Michigan, Special Tribute, 1994; Wayne State Univ, ISP, CLL Teaching Excellence Award, 1997. **Special Achievements:** Author, Justice Evicted, American Civil Liberties Union, 1987; executive producer/moderator, "The State of Black Michigan," 1989-; editor, Mulitcultural Education Resource Guide, Michigan State Board of Education, 1990; executive producer, "Human Rights and Civil Wrongs," Museum of African-American History, 1991; writer, "NAACP Community Economic Development," The Crisis Magazine, 1992. **Home Addr:** Brightmoor Station, PO Box 23384, Detroit, MI 48223, (313)535-1498. **Business Addr:** Asst Professor, Interdisciplinary Studies, Wayne State University, 2220 Academic/Administrative Bldg, Detroit, MI 48202, (313)577-6581.

REIDE, SAINT CLAIR EUGENE, JR.
Registered professional nurse. **Personal:** Born Aug 24, 1950, Brooklyn, NY; son of Saint Clair E Sr & Leonara E Reide; married Portia Gayle Reide, Dec 29, 1972; children: Saint Clair E, III, Nicole A. **Educ:** Morris High School, LPN, 1968; Boro Manhattan Comm Coll, AAS, 1971; Hunter College, Bellevue School of Nursing, BSN, 1974. **Career:** NY Univ Med Ctr, LPN, 1968-71, staff nurse sr, 1971-74; Dept of Health, Prison Health Nursing, psy staff nurse, 1974; Dept of Vet Affairs, nursing supervisor, 1974-. **Orgs:** Trinity Luthern Church, pastoral asst, 1970-, sunday school superintendent, 1993-; Reserve Officers Assn, life mem, 1975-. **Honors/Awds:** Manhattan Comm Coll, Dean List, 1971; Dept of Vet Affairs, St Albans, Employee of the Month, 1987. **Special Achievements:** Portrait Photographer, Owner Creative Photography by Saint studio; American Nurses Assn, certification in Nursing Administration, 1989-93, Gerontological Nurse, 1989-93; USA Goju, karate, Brown Belt, 1972; Radio License Novice, KB2CQA. **Military Serv:** US Army Reserve, army nurse corp, lt colonel, 1975-; Army Reserve Component Achievement Medal, 1991; Army Forces Reserve Medal 1985; Natl Defense Service Medal, 1991. **Home Addr:** 115-02 223 St, Cambria Heights, NY 11411, (718)527-7838. **Business Addr:** Nursing Supervisor, Evenings, St Albans VA - Extended Care Ctr - Dept of Vet Affairs, 179 Street & Linden Blvd, Nursing Office 1182, Jamaica, NY 11425, (718)526-1000.

REID-MCQUEEN, LYNNE MARGUERITE
Attorney, health ctr administrator. **Personal:** Born Jan 26, 1958, Great Lakes, IL; daughter of B Jacquelyne & F Theodore Reid; married Leigh E McQueen, Feb 9, 1985; children: Naima Marguerite, Jared Leigh. **Educ:** Mount Holyoke College, AB, 1980; University of Connecticut, School of Law, JD, 1983. **Career:** State of Connecticut, Judicial Department, Supreme Court, law clerk, 1983-85; NYC Commission on Human Rights, staff attorney, 1985-90; SUNY Health Science Center, deputy director for policy analysis, 1990-. **Orgs:** YWCA of Brooklyn, board of directors, 1991-, first vice pres, 1994-96, chair, nominating committee, 1993-; National Health Lawyers Association, 1990-; Brooklyn Mediation Ctr, pro bono mediator, 1996-. **Home Addr:** 102 Bainbridge St, Brooklyn, NY 11233.

REID-MERRITT, PATRICIA ANN (PATRICIA ANN REID-BOOKHART)
Educator. **Personal:** Born Oct 31, 1950, Philadelphia, PA; daughter of Etrulia Reid and Curtis Reid (deceased); married William Thomas Merritt; children: Christina, Brahim. **Educ:** Cabrini College, BA, 1973; Temple University, MA, social work, 1975; University of Pennsylvania, advanced certificate social work educ, 1979, PhD, social work, 1984. **Career:** Philadelphia General Hospital, psychiatric social worker, 1975-76; National Association of Black Social Workers, national interim executive, 1984-85; Lawnside Public Schools, school social work consultant, 1980-; Stockton State College, professor and coordinator of social work. **Orgs:** Founder/artistic director, Afro-One Dance Drama and Drun Theatre, 1975-; human services task force chair, New Jersey Black Issues Convention, 1984-; co-founder, president, Willingboro Black Business & Professional Association, 1985-89; co-founder/chair, Burlington County Interorganizational Black Leadership Council, 1986-; board of directors, Association of Black Women in Higher Education, 1986-88, Black United Fund of New Jersey, Burlington County, 1986-; founder/president, National Association of Black Social Workers, South Jersey; founding president, Association of Black Women in Higher Education, Greater Philadelphia, 1986-88. **Honors/Awds:** 100 Philadelphia Women, Philadelphia Publishing Group, 1983; Citizen of the Year, New Jersey State Council Black Social Workers, 1983; Youth Role Model Award, Lawnside Board of Education, 1984; Commitment to Black Youth Award, Board of Directors, Afro-One, 1984; Distinguished Alumni Achievement Award, Cabrini College, 1986; Certificate of Honor, Temple University General Alumni Association, 1987; Civic Award, Links, Inc, Eastern Area Conference, 1989; Outstanding Achievement Award, Council of Black Faculty and Staff, 1989; NAACP, South Burlington Branch, NAACP, 25th Anniversary Freedom Award, 1991. **Business Addr:** Prof/Coord Social Work, Stockton State College, Jimmy Leeds Rd, Pomona, NJ 08240.

REINHARDT, JOHN EDWARD
Educator. **Personal:** Born Mar 8, 1920, Glade Spring, VA; married Carolyn; children: Sharman, Alice, Carolyn. **Educ:** Knoxville Coll, AB 1939; Univ of WI, MS 1947, PhD 1950. **Career:** VA State Coll, prof eng 1950-56; USIS Manila Philippines, cultural affairs officer 1956-58; Amer Cultural Ctr Kyoto Japan, dir 1958-63; USIS Tehran Iran, cultural attache 1963-66; Office E Asia & Pacific USIA, dep asst 1966-68; Nigeria, ambassador 1971-75; Washington DC, asst sec state 1975; Intl Comm Agency, dir 1976-81; Smithsonian Inst, asst sec for history & art 1981-84; Smithsonian Inst, dir, directorate of intl activities 1984-87; professor, Political Science, University of Vermont, 1987-91, professor, emeritus, 1991-. **Orgs:** Mem, Amer Foreign Serv Assn, 1969-, Modern Language Assn, Intl Club, Cosmos Club. **Military Serv:** AUS officer 1942-46. **Home Addr:** 4200 Massachusetts Ave, NW #702, Washington, DC 20016.

REMBERT, EMMA WHITE
Educational administrator. **Personal:** Born in Quincy, FL; daughter of Jessie White and Zinerva White. **Educ:** FL A&M Coll, AB 1945; FL A&M Univ, MEd 1958; Syracuse Univ, EdD 1972. **Career:** Pinellas Co, supr & teacher 1954-67; Mobilization for Youth NYC, supr/clinician 1963-64; Charles E Merrill Pub, educ consul 1967-72; FL Intl Univ, prof 1972-, asst and dean, 1980-88; Bethune-Cookman College, chairperson of education, currently. **Orgs:** State organizer Natl Council of Negro Women; mem Phi Delta Kappa; mem Kappa Delta Pi; mem Pi Lambda Theta; consult & lecturer Ministry of Educ-Commonwealth of Bahamas 1973-; dir adult vet ed Okeechobee Schs Ed & prof consul Textbook Series C E Merrill Co 1975; pub com Intl Reading Assn 1976-; manuscript reviewer McGraw Hill & Allyn & Bacon Co 1977-; dir Hemispheric Women's Cong 1977-; chairperson Delta Sigma Theta FL Council 1978-80; member, Delta Sigma Theta Leadership Academy, 1988-92. **Honors/Awds:** Competence Awd State of FL 1965-66; Intl Scholarship-Leadership Awds Delta Sigma Theta 1967 1972 & 1977; EPDA Fellow Syracuse Univ 1970-72; "Alternative Strategies" Kendall Hunt Pub Co 1976; FL Outstanding Teacher/Educator 1981; CRA Service Award. **Business Addr:** Chairperson of Education, Bethune-Cookman College, Daytona Beach, FL 32114.

REMSON, ANTHONY TERENCE
Physician. **Personal:** Born Dec 17, 1952, Anniston, AL. **Educ:** KY State Univ, BS 1975; Meharry Medical Coll, MD 1980; MI State Univ, Int Med Specialization 1983. **Career:** Northwest Roanoke Physicians Assoc, president. **Orgs:** Mem North Central TX Independent Practice Assoc 1984; teaching faculty Roanoke Mem & Community Hospitals 1984-; bd dirs Roanoke Chap Amer Heart Assoc 1984-86; mem Salem Chap NAACP 1985; consultant Roanoke Div Amer Red Cross 1985; bd dirs Harrison Cultural Ctr 1985-86; bd dirs Hunton Livesaving Group1985; mem Amer, Natl Medical Assocs; mem Amer Coll of Physicians; bd dirs Natl Bus Coll. **Honors/Awds:** MI Medical Soc Resident Phys Section Delegate 1982-83; participant McNeil-Lehrer Report 1983; Outstanding Young Men of Amer 1984-85; Honors Convocation apeaker KY State Univ 1986; Leadership Honoree Roanoke Valley Chamber of Commerce 1986; NAFEO Disting Corporate Alumni of the Year 1986. **Military Serv:** USNR lt cmdr, mc 1981.

REMUS, EUGENE
Association executive. **Personal:** marrIed Gloria Benson; children: Marvin, Barbara, Billy, Eugene Jr, Tina Ray. **Career:** Fleetwood Mbl Homes MS, skilled carpenter engineer. **Orgs:** Pres Lexington MS Br NAACP. **Honors/Awds:** Spl achvmnt cmmndtns MS NAACP.

RENDER, ARLENE
Government official. **Personal:** Born Aug 16, 1943, Cleveland, OH; children: Jonathan Blake, Kiara Isabella. **Educ:** West VA State Coll, Institute, WV, BS, 1965; Univ of MI, Ann Arbor, MI, MPH. **Career:** US Diplomat, 1970-; US Ambassador to the Gambia, 1990-; US Ambassador to the Republic of Zambia, 1996. **Honors/Awds:** Two Dept of State Meritorious Honor Awards and one Superior Honor Award.

RENDER, WILLIAM H.
Physician. **Personal:** Born Feb 9, 1950, LaGrange, GA; son of Elizabeth Render; married Barbara Jean; children: Eric, Keyiana. **Educ:** Emory Univ, A Medicine 1974; GA State Univ, Premed; Meharry Medical Coll, MD 1984. **Career:** Dr James B Palmer Atlanta GA, physician asst 1975-80; Emory Univ Affiliated Hosp, medical resident 1984-87; private practice, Internal Medicine 1987-; Fulton County Jail, physician 1987-92, Med dir, 1992-. **Orgs:** Atlanta Medical Assn; Georgia State Medical Assn; Southern Medical Assn; American College of Physician. **Honors/Awds:** Honor Medical Soc Alpha Omega Alpha 1984. **Special Achievements:** Board Certified in Internal Medicine. **Military Serv:** USN E-3 4 yrs. **Business Addr:** Physician/Owner, Renders Primary Care Ctr, PC, 970 Martin Luther King Jr Dr, No 305, Atlanta, GA 30314, (404)524-1721.

RENFORD, EDWARD
Company executive. **Career:** Grady Health System, CEO, currently. **Business Addr:** CEO, Grady Health System, 80 Butler SE, Atlanta, GA 30335, (404)616-4250.

RENFRO, MEL
Professional football coach (retired). **Personal:** Born Dec 30, 1941, Houston, TX; children: 4. **Educ:** Attended, Univ of Oregon. **Career:** Dallas Cowboys, all pro defensive back, scout; Miller Beer Dallas, account mgr; Los Angeles Express, defensive secondary coach; St Louis Cardinals, defensive back coach. **Orgs:** Involed in various charitable activities. **Honors/Awds:** All-America running back in coll; All-Pro at both safety and cornerback; selected to the Pro Bowl 10 straight seasons; voted an All-Pro five times; inducted into Dallas' Ring of Honor at Texas Stadium 1981 (only one of six Cowboys to gain such distinction); inductee Football Hall of Fame; High School All-Amer Football & Track; MVP East/West Game 1960 HS OR; MVP Natl Golden West Track Meet HS 1960; MVP Pro-Bowl NFL 1971; 4 Super Bowls Dallas Cowboys.

RENFROE, EARL W.
Orthodontist, educator. **Personal:** Born Jan 9, 1907, Chicago, IL; son of Bertha and Eugene; married Hilda Forte; children: Earl Jr, Diane L, Stephen P. **Educ:** Univ IL, DDS 1931, MS 1942. **Career:** Univ of IL, prof emeritus orthodontics 1982-. **Orgs:** Life mem IL & Chicago Dental Socs; mem Amer Dental Assn; mem Amer & Chicago Assns Orthodontists; mem IL State Soc Orthodontists; author 2 textbooks "Ed H Angle Soc of Orth"; mem Chicago Coun Foreign Rel; Intl Visitors Ctr Chicago; Alpha Phi Alpha; Druids Soc Club; 1st black amer to receive Commercial Air License IL 1936; Fellowship Amer Coll Dentists; 1st Black person certified by Amer Bd Orthodontics; pres Chicago Assn of Orthodontists 1963-64; bd of dir Council on Foreign Rel 1963-68, vice pres 1968-69; Socio-honorario Sociadade Paulista de Ortodontia Sao Paulo Brazil. **Honors/Awds:** IL NG 1932-40; ORC 1940-41; Alumni Loyalty Awd Univ IL 1971; 1st black full prof Univ of IL Med Campus; 1st black dept head Univ of IL Med Campus; Distinguished Alumnus Award, Dental Alumni Assn Univ of IL 1988; Chicago Sr Citizens Hal of Fame, Mayor Daly & City Council 1990. **Military Serv:** AUS Col (first black col) 1941-46; AUS brigadier general 1984-.

RENFROE, IONA ANTOINETTE
Attorney. **Personal:** Born Feb 13, 1953, New Orleans, LA; daughter of Leona "Maude" Madison Renfroe and George Renfroe. **Educ:** Loyola Univ, New Orleans LA, BA, 1975; Loyola Law School, New Orleans LA, JD, 1978. **Career:** TANO Inc, New Orleans LA, technical writer, 1975; Chevron USA Inc, New Orleans LA, landman, 1979-81; LP&L/NOPSI, New Orleans LA, corporate counsel, 1981-. **Orgs:** Mem, Louisiana State Bar Assn, 1980-; mem, Louis Martinet Soc, 1980-; New Orleans Assn of Black Women Attorneys, 1984-; corporate dir, Sec Riverland Credit Union, 1985-; US Dist Court, Eastern Dist of Louisiana, 1986-; counsel to bd, Natl Forum for Black Public Admin, New Orleans Chapter, 1986-; mem, New Orleans Pro Bono Program, 1987-; mem, Louisiana State Bar Assn Continuing Legal Educ Theme Subcommittee 1988-; dir, New Orleans Children's Bureau, 1988-; counsel to bd, New Orleans Birthright Soc Inc, 1988-.

RENICK, JAMES C.
Educational administrator. **Personal:** Born Dec 8, 1948, Rockford, IL; son of Constance Carmachael Renick and James Renick; married Peggy Gadsden; children: Karinda. **Educ:** Central OH State Univ, BA 1970; KS Univ, MSW 1972; FL State Univ, 1980. **Career:** Univ of West FL, prof 1975-81; Univ of So FL, prof 1981-83, asst to pres 1983-85, asst dean & educ chmn 1985-88, department chair, 1988-89; George Mason Univ, Fairfax, VA, vice provost, 1989-93; University of Michigan-Dearborn, chancellor, 1993-. **Orgs:** Trustee Univ Psy Ctr 1984-; chmn Amer Assn for Higher Educ Black Caucus 1985-; mem FL Leadership Network, FL C of C 1985-; mem FL Inst of Govt Policy Council 1986-89; exec comm Council of Fellows Amer Council on Educ 1987-89. **Honors/Awds:** Leadership Florida FL C of C 1985; Vstg Prog Assoc Smithsonian Inst 1987; Up and Comers Awd Price Waterhouse 1987. **Business Addr:** Chancellor, Univ of Michigan-Dearborn, 4901 Evergreen, Dearborn, MI 48128.

RENTIE, FRIEDA
Actress. **Personal:** Born Dec 29, 1932, Chicago, IL. **Educ:** Attended Wayne Univ Detroit. **Career:** Free-lance actress beauty consult model NY & Detroit; actress various feature motion pictures network TV shows; Financial Mgmt Co, pres. **Orgs:** Bd mem New Frontier Democrats; mem NAACP; mem Urban League; treas exec bd NAACP Beverly Hills Hollywood Br. **Honors/Awds:** Outstanding Mem of Yr Awd New Frontier Democrats 1973.

RENWICK, LUCILLE CHRISTINE
Journalist. **Personal:** Born Dec 13, 1965, Bronx, NY; daughter of Evril Cummings Renwick and Septimus Renwick. **Educ:** Wesleyan University, Middletown, CT, BA, 1987. **Career:** Los Angeles Times, Los Angeles, CA, reporter, 1988-89, 1992-; The Hartford Courant, Hartford, CT, reporter, 1989-92. **Orgs:** National Assn of Black Journalists, 1988-. **Honors/Awds:** Hartford Courant's Award, 1991. **Business Addr:** Reporter, City Times, Times Mirror Square, Los Angeles, CA 90053.

RESPERT, SHAWN CHRISTOPHER
Professional basketball player. **Personal:** Born Feb 6, 1972, Detroit, MI. **Educ:** Michigan State University, graduated. **Career:** Milwaukee Bucks, guard, 1995-96; Toronto Raptors, 1996-98; Dallas Mavericks, 1998-. **Honors/Awds:** The Sporting News, NCAA Player of the Year, 1995; National Assn of Basketball Coaches, Player of the Year, 1995. **Special Achievements:** NBA, First Round Draft Pick, #8 Pick, 1995. **Business Addr:** Professional Basketball Player, Dallas Mavericks, 777 Sports St, Reunion Arena, Dallas, TX 75207, (214)748-1808.

RETTIG, FRANNIE M.
Nurse, educator. **Personal:** Born Mar 15, 1947, Henderson, TX; daughter of Mable Bradley Tenner and Donnie Bob Rettig; married Romaine Francis, May 30, 1987. **Educ:** Prairie View A & M University, Prairie View, TX, BSN, 1969; Texas Woman's University, Denton, TX MSN, 1977. **Career:** US Army Research Nurse, staff nurse, head nurse, 1969-80; US Army, Landshut, Germany, 2nd General Hospital, patient education coordinator, 1980-83; Boston University, Landshut, Germany, research instructor and clinical preceptor, 1982-83; US Army, El Paso TX, chief, head nurse, general medicine ward, 1983-84, chief, nursing administration evening/night, 1984-85; US Army, Fort Sill, OK, Reynolds Army Hospital, chief, nursing education, 1986-89; US Army, Fort Sam Houston, TX, William Beaumont Army Medical Center, director, US Army practical nurse program, 1989-. **Orgs:** Chairperson, Council on Practice, Oklahoma Nurses Association, 1988-89; vice president & chairperson, Program Committee, Oklahoma Nurses Association, District 11, 1987-89; Archivist, Pi Chapter of Sigma Theta Tau, 1979-80; chairperson, Nursing Research Committees, Reynolds Army Hospital, 1986-89; chairperson, Nursing Research Committees, William Beaumont Army Center, 1984-85; Pan Hellenic Council Representative, Alpha Kappa Alpha Sorority, 1988. **Honors/Awds:** Dr Anita Newcomb McGee Award, US Army Nurse of the Year, Daughters of American Revolution, Membership Award, Oklahoma Nurses Association, District 11, 1988. **Military Serv:** US Army, Colonel, 1969-, Bronze Star, 1971, Meritorious Service Medal with 4 Oak Leaf Clusters, 1975, 1983, 1985, 1989, Army Commendation Medal 1973, National Defense Service Medal, 1969, Vietnam Service Medal UN Overseas medal.

REUBEN, GLORIA
Actress. **Career:** ER, actress, currently. **Business Addr:** Actress, ER, Huvane, Baum, and Halls, 8383 Wilshire Blvd, Ste 444, Beverly Hills, CA 90211.

REUBEN, LUCY JEANETTE
Educator. **Personal:** Born Dec 15, 1949, Sumter, SC; married Dr John A Cole; children: Kwame Odell Oliver, John Akayomi Cole. **Educ:** Oberlin Coll, AB 1971; The Univ of MI, MBA 1974, PhD 1981. **Career:** Ford Motor Co, financial analyst 1974-75; Duke Univ, asst prof 1981-83; Bd of Governors Fed Res, vstg prof 1983-84; Financial Rsch Assoc Inc, vice pres, beginning 1984; George Mason Univ, assoc prof of finance; Florida A & M Univ, assoc prof of finance; South Carolina State Univ, dean and professor, currently. **Orgs:** Hayti Develop Corp, adv bd, 1982-84; Washington DC Urban Bankers Assn, 1984-; Washington DC Women Economists 1984-; Natl Bankers Assn, consultant, 1984-; US Dept of Commerce, consultant, 1984-; Metropolitan Washington Planning & Housing Assn, bd of dirs, 1986-; Amer Finance Assn; Eastern Finance Assn; Natl Black MBA Assn; Natl Economic Assn; Natl Assn for Female Execs; Natl Assn of Urban Bankers; Southern Finance Assn; Southwestern Finance Assn; Florida Black Business Investment Board, board of directors, vice-chair. **Honors/Awds:** Earhart Foundation Fellowship 1978; Ayres Fellow Stonier Grad Sch of Banking 1982; 12 publications including "Black Banks, A Survey and Analysis of the Literature" (with John A Cole, Alfred L Edwards, and Earl G Hamilton) Review of Black Political Economy Fall 1985. **Business Addr:** School of Business, South Carolina State Univ, 300 College St NE, Orangeburg, SC 29117, (803)536-8186.

REVELLE, ROBERT, SR.
City official. **Personal:** Born Jan 6, 1947, Harrellsville, NC; son of Carrie L Revelle and Hugh L Revelle (deceased); married Annie M (Adams) Revelle, Dec 9, 1969; children: Sharon Marie, Robert Jr. **Educ:** Goldey Beacom Business College, AA/Mgmt 1969-71; Natl Graduate University, Certificate 1973; Wilmington College, BBA 1973-78; Eastern Theological Seminary, Certificate 1989. **Career:** CDA, Wilmington, planner/consultant 1971-73, admin chief 1973-74; Community Affairs, dept dir 1974-75; Community Ctr, superintendent 1975-84; City of Wilmington, dir, minority bus prog 1984-87, deputy personnel dir, beginning 1987, personnel recruitment specialist, currently. **Orgs:** Member YMCA Resource Center 1983-84; pres vice-pres member Amer Cancer Society 1973-; pres vice-pres member Price Run Child Center 1976-; mem NAACP; mem 1984, president DE chap 1990-, Natl Forum for Black Public Administrators; mem Wilmington Small Business Develop Ctr; mem DE Minority Business Med Week/Trade Fair Comm 1984-87; Delaware Private Industry Council, 1988-; ambassador, YMCA Black Achievers Program, 1989-. **Honors/Awds:** US Army Personnel School of Personnel Mgmt 1967; honor certificate Freedom Foundation of Valley Forge 1970;

certificate of merit American Cancer Society 1975; certificate of appreciation West Center City Community Ctr 1980; member/chmn organ comm Police/Community Council Wilmington 1983-. **Military Serv:** AUS spec E-5 1966-69; Outstanding Soldier 1966. **Business Addr:** Deputy Personnel Director, City of Wilmington, DE, 800 French St, Wilmington, DE 19801.

REVELY, WILLIAM
Clergyman, social worker. **Personal:** Born Jan 20, 1941, Charlottesville, VA; son of Reaver E Carter Revely (deceased) and William Revely, Sr (deceased); children: Christana Re, Christopher. **Educ:** Howard Univ, BA 1964, M Div 1967, MSW 1971, D Min 1982. **Career:** Messiah Baptist Church, pastor, 1989-; Mt Gilead Baptist Church, pastor 1979; Union Baptist Church, pastor 1965-79; Nara II Aftercare Unit Bureau Rehabilitation, chf 1973-76; Shaw Residence III (Hlfway House) Bureau Rehabilitation, dir 1976-77; Howard Univ School of Social Work, 1977-79. **Orgs:** Mem NAACP; SCLC; ACA; NABSW; Natl Progressive Baptist Convention; Natl Baptist Convention USA Inc; bd of trustees, Shaw Divinity School; board chairman, GOIC, Detroit, 1991; board of directors, mortuary science, Univ of DC, 1989; Lott Carey Foreign Missions Convention, clergy support committee; International Foundation for Education & Self Help. **Honors/Awds:** Vernon Johns Preaching Award, School of Religion Howard Univ 1967; NIMH Fellowship 1967-71; author of Poetry From the Heart, Foster Publications, 1989. **Business Addr:** Pastor, Messiah Baptist Church, 8100 W Seven Mile Road, Detroit, MI 48221.

REVIS, NATHANIEL W.
Scientist. **Personal:** Born Jul 27, 1939, Glenridge, NJ; married Sheena. **Educ:** Fairleigh Dickinson Univ NJ, BS 1962; Univ of Louvain Belgium, MD 1968; Univ of Glasgow Scotland, PhD 1972. **Career:** Univ of TN, assoc prof 1980; Oak Ridg Nat Lab, sr sci 1977; Univ of TN, asst prof 1974-80; Univ of Glasgow Dept Cardiology, asst prof 1972-74; Oak Ridge Research Inst, Oak Ridge, TN, sr scientist, dir, 1981-. **Orgs:** Mem Intl Soc Biochemistry 1972; mem Am & Intl Soc of Cardiology 1975; advsr (brain trust) Congressional Black 1978; advsr (Grant review) NCI 1979. **Business Addr:** Dir, Oak Ridge Research Institute, 113 Union Valley Rd, Oak Ridge, TN 37830.

REVISH, JERRY
Broadcast journalist. **Personal:** Born Mar 15, 1949, Youngstown, OH; son of Estelle Revish and Dewey Revish; married Danielle Revish, Jun 22, 1974; children: Nicole, Jerome II. **Educ:** Youngstown State University, 1967-69; Chapman College, 1969-70. **Career:** WBBW Radio, anchor/reporter, 1972-74; WBNS Radio, assignment editor/reporter, 1974-80; WBNS-TV, anchor/reporter, 1980-. **Orgs:** Columbus Association of Black Journalists, president, 1991-92; United Way, Project Diversity, board member, 1991-; NAACP 1990-. **Honors/Awds:** National Academy of TV Arts & Sciences, Emmy, 1991, 2 Tours of Persian Gulf Operation Desert Shield Desert Storm, 1991, 4 Emmy Nominations, 1980-90; Associated Press, Best Spot, news, feature & documentary, 1980-90; UPI, Best Spot, news, feature & documentary, 1980-90; Sigma Delta Chi, Best Series, 1979. **Business Addr:** TV News Anchor/Reporter, WBNS-10-TV, 770 Twin Rivers Drive, Columbus, OH 43216, (614)460-3950.

REYNOLDS, ANDREW BUCHANAN
Executive consultant. **Personal:** Born Jun 29, 1939, Winston-Salem, NC; son of Florence Terry Reynolds and Andrew Buchanan Reynolds; divorced. **Educ:** Lincoln Univ PA, BA 1960; NC A&T Greensboro, BS 1962; Columbia Univ NY, Certificate of Journalism 1970. **Career:** Andy Reynolds & Assoc, owner, principal; Executive Diversity Services, owner/vp, currently; Washington State Lottery Commission, chair; King Broadcasting Co, TV news reporter; New Day Inc, prod, dir 1975; September & Assoc, prod, dir 1973-75; WCAU-TV, reporter, prod 1970-71; PA Advancement Sch, curriculum & devel specialist 1967-70; NC Advancement School, counselor, tchr 1966-67; AUS Madigan General Hospital Ft Lewis WA, radioisotope tech 1964-65; Bowman Gray Sch of Med Dept of Pharmacology, research asst 1962-63; CORE, dir 1963; City of Seattle, Seattle Dept of Parks & Recreation, Seattle, WA, mgr, marketing & public relations, 1987-93. **Orgs:** Board, Greater Seattle Chamber of Commerce; mem NAACP 1978; dir, co-chmn CORE 1963; pres, bd of trust Educ Opportunity Prog Univ of WA; chmn, editor, Leadership Tomorrow; former chmn WA State Lottery Commn; prog chmn UNCF Telethon Comm; former mem Public Defender Assn; mem Northwest Aids Foundation, Marketing Commn, Seattle/King Co Red Cross. **Honors/Awds:** Leadership Tomorrow, Outstanding Alumni Award, 1992; Honorable Mention Sigma Delta Chi Features 1973; first place Sigma Delta Chi Spot News 1975; third place Sigma Delta Chi Documentary 1977; Humbolt Award, first place for News Documentary 1978; Honorable Mention, Puget Sound Public Relations Society of America, 1983. **Military Serv:** AUS E-4 1963-65. **Home Addr:** 3315 37th Pl S, Seattle, WA 98144. **Business Phone:** (206)224-9293.

REYNOLDS, AUDREY LUCILE
Educator. **Personal:** Born Jul 19, Weatherford, OK; daughter of Josephine Barbee-Reynolds and John Reynolds; divorced. **Educ:** Wichita University, BA 1932; KS State University, USC, graduate studies; Langston University; City College of Los Angeles. **Career:** Los Angeles CA, elementary school teacher 1948; Booker T Washington High School, Sapulpa OK, prof English; Bennett College, Greensboro NC. **Orgs:** Iota Phi Lambda 1947, natl pres 1973-77. **Honors/Awds:** AME Church Certificate Outstanding Elementary Teacher 1973; Golden Bell Award 1970; 25 Year Award Iota Phi Lambda; nom Outstanding Teacher of the Year Main St School 1973-74; Life Mem PTA; Cit Gov dedicated serv Children & Com 1974; Life Membership NAACP; participated in First Vice President's Conference on Civil Rights under President Nixon, also under Vice President L B Johnson.

REYNOLDS, BARBARA A.
Editor, columnist. **Personal:** Born in Columbus, OH; daughter of Elizabeth Taylor and Harvey Reynolds; divorced; children: John Eric. **Educ:** OH State Univ, BA, 1967; Howard Univ, School of Divinity, MA, 1991. **Career:** Ebony Magazine, Chicago, IL, editor, 1968-69; Chicago Tribune, Chicago, IL, reporter, 1969-81; USA Today, Arlington, VA, ed, columnist, 1983-; Reynolds News Service, pres, currently. **Orgs:** Chmn, Women's Task Force; Natl Assn of Black Journalists, 1991-. **Honors/Awds:** Nieman Fellow, Harvard Univ, 1976-77; Outstanding Alumni, OH State Univ, 1990; Honorary Doctorate in Humane Letters, Ohio State Univ; Honorary Doctorate in Humane Letters, Shenandoah Univ, 1995. **Business Addr:** President, Reynolds News Service, 7124 Temple Hills Rd, Ste 176, Camp Springs, MD 20748.

REYNOLDS, BRUCE HOWARD
Dentist. **Personal:** Born Oct 7, 1935, Chicago, IL; married Ellen Barnes; children: Bruce Jr, Jana. **Educ:** Dillard U, BS 1959; Howard U, DDS 1963. **Career:** Dentist, pvt prac, currently. **Orgs:** Am Dntl Assn; Nat Dntl Assn; Am Endodontic Soc; Evanston Dntl Assn; Dntl Consult IL Dentl Srv NAACP; bd Op PUSH; The Cheesmen Inc. **Honors/Awds:** AUS, medic 1957-59; USAF DDS 1963-65. **Business Addr:** D.D.S., 1310 Hartrey Ave, Evanston, IL 60202.

REYNOLDS, CHARLES MCKINLEY, JR.
Business executive. **Personal:** Born Jan 11, 1937, Albany, GA; son of Johnnie Hadley Reynolds and Charles McKinley Reynolds; married Estella Henry Reynolds, Aug 19, 1956; children: Eric Charles, Gregory Preston. **Educ:** Morehouse Coll, BA 1954; Wayne State Univ, mortuary sci cert 1962; Albany State Coll, middle grades cert 1964. **Career:** Southside Jr HS, teacher & chmn dept of social studies 1962-65; US Treasury Dept, asst examiner 1965-69, natl bank examiner 1969-71; Citizen Trust Bank, vice pres 1971, pres 1971; Atlantic Natl Bank, pres and CEO 1975-88; Reynolds & Associates, president, 1988-. **Orgs:** Bd of dir Atlantic Natl Bank; bd dir Norfolk C of C; mem Jr Achievement of Tidewater Inc; mem Tidewater Area of Minority Contractors; exec comm Greater Norfolk Develop Corp; treas Norfolk Investment Co Inc; bd of visitors James Madison Univ; treas bd of dirs Norfolk State Univ Foundation; corp bd mem & chmn Audit Comm SCI Systems Inc; adv bd mem Norfolk State Univ Business and Social Work; gerontology adv cncl Hampton Inst; life mem Alpha Phi Alpha Frat; mem Sigma Pi Phi Frat, Guardsmen Inc, Rotary Club, Old Dominion Univ Exec Adv Cncl. **Honors/Awds:** Outstanding Achievement Awd Alpha Phi Alpha Gamma Omicron Lambda Chap 1966; Congress of Racial Equality 1975; CORE Publs & Camaro Publ Co; 100 Black Am A1/C 1956-60; Minority Advocacy of the Year Awd 1984; Natl Assoc of Minority Contractors 1984; US Presidential Citation White House Conf on Small Business; Metro Atlanta Rapid Transit Auth Commendation; Comm Serv Awd Madison Secondary Sch 1985; Disting Leadership Awd United Negro Coll Fund 1985; McDonald's Black Achievement Awd 1986; Old Dominion Univ First Black Student Awds Banquet 1986; Delicados Inc Awd for Blazing New Horizons in Banking 1986. **Military Serv:** US Air Force, A/lc, 1956-60. **Business Addr:** President, Reynolds & Associates, 5544 Greenwich Rd, Ste 300, Virginia Beach, VA 23462.

REYNOLDS, EDWARD
Educator. **Personal:** Born Jan 23, 1942; son of Elizabeth Reynolds; children: Joel. **Educ:** Wake Forest Univ, BA 1964; OH Univ, MA 1965; Yale Univ, MDiv 1968; London Univ PhD 1972. **Career:** Christ United Presby, assoc pastor 1982-; Univ of CA San Diego, asst prof 1971-74, assoc prof 1974-83, prof 1983-; City of San Diego, planning commissioner, 1989-93. **Honors/Awds:** Books-Trade and Economic Change on the Gold Coast 1974; Stand the Storm A History of the Atlantic Slave Trade 1985; Focus on Africa, 1994; vice moderator Presbytery of San Diego, 1993; Excellence in Teaching Award, University of California, San Diego, 1990-91; Moderator, Presbytery of San Diego, 1994; Director Univ of CA Study Center, 1994-96. **Business Addr:** Director, Study Center, Prof of History, Univ of California-San Diego, Dept of History 0104, 9500 Gilman Dr, La Jolla, CA 92093-0104.

REYNOLDS, GRANT
Attorney, educator, educational administrator (retired). **Personal:** Born Jul 29, 1908, Key West, FL; son of Emma Flowers (deceased) and Frank Reynolds; married Lillie Hobby. **Educ:** Eden Seminary, BD 1936; Fenn Coll, AB 1940; Columbia Univ Law Sch, JD 1948. **Career:** Atty private practice beginning 1951; Republican Natl Comm Chief of Minority Div, counsel to chmn 1962; US Dept Housing & Urban Develop, asst regional admin reg II 1970, dep reg admin region II 1972; Nova Univ Law Sch, prof of law & dir of minority affairs, retired. **Orgs:** Grace Congregational Church; White Plains, Westchester Cty, NY State, Amer Natl Bar Assns; Amer Trial Lawyers Assn, Amer Legion, Amer Vet Comm, NAACP, Urban League of Westchester, Omega Psi Phi, Masons Imperial Shrine 32nd Degree, US Power Squadron; asst grand legal adv IBPOEW; Westchester Club Men Inc, Lions Club; pres White Plains-Greenburgh NAACP; chmn Council Republican Organs; pres Natl Negro Republican Assembly; pres NY State Chap Natl Negro Republican Assembly; vice chmn Republicans for Progress; founder & co-leader of org that secured from Pres Truman the order banning segregation in the Armed Forces; past grand basileus, Omega Psi Fraternity, 1952-54; mem, Sigma Pi Phi Fraternity; mem, Tower Club. **Honors/Awds:** Doctor of Humane Letters, Hampton Univ, 1991. **Military Serv:** US Army, Capt. **Home Addr:** 7 Pine Ridge Rd, White Plains, NY 10603.

REYNOLDS, HAROLD CRAIG
Professional baseball player. **Personal:** Born Nov 26, 1960, Eugene, OR. **Educ:** San Diego State University; Canada College, California; Cal State University, Long Beach. **Career:** Seattle Mariners, 1983-92; Baltimore Orioles, 1992-94; California Angels, 1994-. **Orgs:** Harold Reynolds Children's Charities, founder, activist; Role Models Unlimited, founder; Harold's Helpers, sole sponsor; Partners in Public Education, honorary chairman; IBM Student Pennant Race, honorary chairman. **Honors/Awds:** 21st Roberto Clemente Award; American League, Gold Glove, 1988-90; President George Bush, Daily Point of Light honors, first professional athlete and only baseball player recipient; Seattle Post-Intelligencer, Publisher's Award, first recipient; Seattle Mayor Norman Rice, Martin Luther King Humanitarian Award, 1990; Mariner's Care Community Service Award, first recipient; American Legion, Graduate of the Year Award, 1990. **Special Achievements:** All-Star Game participant, American League, 1987, 1988. **Business Phone:** (714)937-7200.

REYNOLDS, HARRY G.
Educator. **Personal:** Born Nov 6, 1915, Baldwin, LA; son of Annie Bell Reynolds and JR Reynolds; married Ada Woodson; children: Harry Gjr. **Educ:** Rust Coll MS, BA 1935; Columbia U, MA Tchr Coll 1947; Univ of TX, Completed Course Work For EdD 1962. **Career:** Public School New Albany MS, math teacher, band dir 1936-39; Conroe TX, 1939-42; TX Southern Univ, educ psychology summer 1947-48; Wheatley HS, math teacher 1947-52; EO Smith Jr HS, 1952-57; Kashmere Jr & Sr HS, counselor 1957-69; Francis Scott Key Jr HS, 1969; Houston Independent School Dist, chmn guid dept. **Orgs:** Mem Houston Cnslrs Assn; bldg rep United Fund; United Negro Coll Fund; mem BSA; tchr Adult Bible Class, Trinity E Meth Ch; Trinity Grdns Cvl Leg. **Honors/Awds:** Contbd articles related to adolescent devel to TX St Tchr Journal, 1952-57; presently working on original tapes for cnslng Pupils on Secondary Level; srvd with 731 Military Police & Core Area. **Military Serv:** AUS 1942-46. **Business Addr:** 4000 N Loop, Houston, TX 77026.

REYNOLDS, IDA MANNING
Government official. **Personal:** Born Sep 8, 1946, Hines, FL; daughter of Catherine Mosley Manning and James Westley Manning; married Wilfred Reynolds Jr, Sep 8, 1984; children: Ronald Jr, Katrina, Joseph Hayes Rawls, Tina, Wilfred Reynolds III. **Educ:** Lincoln Technical Inst, Computer Science 1963-66. **Career:** Alachua Cty FL, benefit & payroll supvr 1963-73, personnel specialist 1973-79, personnel mgmt analysis 1979-81, dir of equal opportunity div, 1981-. **Orgs:** Sec Local Chapter Amer Soc Personnel Admin 1979; 1st vice pres Central FL Conf Women Missionary 1980-; state coord Amer Assoc Affirmative Action 1982; mem adv bd Santa Fe Comm Coll Human Serv 1982-; mem bd of dir, FL Assn Comm Professionals, 1983-; chairperson area XIV FL Church Women United 1984-; regional pres FL Assn Comm Relations 1984-; bd of dir, One Church One Child Black Adoption, 1986-; mem, 1st vp 1990-, Natl Forum of Black Public Administrators; chap chair, Natl Assn of Human Rights Workers, 1990-; Governor's Comm on Martin Luther King Commemorative Celebration 1986, Amer Assn of Public Admin and Conf of Minority Public Admins; bd of dirs Gainesville/Alachua Co Martin Luther King Fund Inc; bd of dirs, UnitedGainesville Comm Develop Corp, 1984-; mem Alachua County Black Adopt Bd; producer/host, annual locally televised Forum on Black Social & Economic Issues, 1989-; first vice pres, North Central Florida National Forum for Black Public Administrators, 1990-. **Honors/Awds:** Future Business Leaders of Amer 1981; Appreciation Awd Amer Cancer Soc 1981; Outstanding Contrib Reg IV Amer Assoc Affirm Action 1982; Outstanding Contrib Gainesville Job Corps 1984; Certificate of Recognition and Certificate of Appreciation Governor of the State of FL 1986; Distinguished Service Award Alachua County, 1989; Developed, implemented and coordinated private and public participation in Countywide Annual Conference on Human Rights and Equal Opportunity Law; Special Recognition Plaque, Mental Health Services of Central Florida, 1989; Distinguished Service Award, Gainesville/Alachua County Martin Luther King Jr Foundation, 1991. **Home Addr:** 2405 NE 65th Terrace, Gainesville, FL 32609.

Business Addr: Director, Equal Oppty Div, Alachua County Florida, 21 East University Ave, 3rd Floor, Gainesville, FL 32602.

REYNOLDS, JAMES F.
Director. **Personal:** Born Aug 29, 1914, Winston-Salem, NC; married Alice Gertrude Rausch; children: Lanell Rhone, Alice Owens, Micaela Jones, John. **Educ:** Univ of Denver, BA 1960-62, MA 1962-63; Met State Coll, D of PA 1980. **Career:** City & Co of Denver, race consult 1963; Univ of CO, tchr 1967-75; Univ of Denver, teacher 1970-74; United for Progress Head-start, pres 1967-; CO Civil Rights Comm, dir 1963-80. **Orgs:** Pres Black Dir Council 1980; pres People to People/Sister Cities Intl 1980. **Honors/Awds:** Man of the Yr Awd Delta Psi Lambda 1967; Whitehead Awd ACLU CO Chap 1978; Martin Luther King Awd Martin Luther King Found 1980; Awd Intl Assn of Ofcl Human Rights Agency 1980. **Military Serv:** USAF maj 24 yrs. **Business Addr:** CO Civil Rights Comm, 1525 Sherman St, Denver, CO 80203.

REYNOLDS, JAMES VAN
Actor, artistic director. **Personal:** Born Aug 10, 1950, Kansas City, MO; son of Dorothy J Cotton Reynolds and Leonard Reynolds; married Lissa Layng, Dec 21, 1985; children: Jed. **Educ:** Washburn Univ, Topeka KS, BFA, 1970. **Career:** Los Angeles Repertory Theater, managing artistic dir, 1975-82; LaFamille Enterprises, pres, 1987-; South Pasadena Repertory Theater, managing artistic dir, 1989-; La Famile Films, South Pasadena, CA, pres, 1990-; Generations, Burbank, CA, lead actor, 1990-91; Days of Our Lives, lead actor, NBC; Classics Unlimited, South Pasadena, vice pres; Free State Productions, CEO, 1996-. **Orgs:** Mem, advisory bd, Topeka Performing Arts Center, 1989-. **Honors/Awds:** Man of the Year, Natl Jewish Hospital, Natl Asthma Center, 1985, 1986, 1987; Volunteer of the Year, Dir of Volunteers in Amer, 1987; Honorary Citizen, Wichita KS, 1988; Honorary Citizen, Kansas City KS, 1988; I, Too, Am American (a one man play performed nationally), 1988-89; Time Express, Burbank CA, actor, 1979; ''Days of Our Lives,'' Burbank CA, actor, 1981-; other acting roles include, ''Highway to Heaven,'' ''Different Strokes,'' ''The Incredible Hulk,'' Hound of Hell, Nero Wolfe, Keeper of the Wild, The Magic of Lassie, Hotline, Mr Majestyk; Business Person of the Year, 1994. **Military Serv:** US Marine Corps, 1964-66.

REYNOLDS, JAMES W.
Government official. **Personal:** Born Jun 25, 1944, Florence, AL; son of Evelyn M Reynolds and Welton Reynolds; married Dianne Daniels, Jun 26, 1969; children: Rodney James. **Educ:** Talladega College, AB, 1966; Alabama A&M College, MBA, 1975; Florida Institute of Technology, MS, 1980. **Career:** Florence City Schools, math teacher, 1966; US Army Misslie Command, procurement intern, 1966-67, procurement agent, 1970-71; US Army Corps of Engineers, contract specialist, 1971-80, branch chief, acquisition mgt, 1980-86, deputy director of contracting, 1986-91, director of contracting, 1991-. **Orgs:** National Contract Management Association, chapter director, 1987-89, chapter president, 1984-85, chapt vice pres, 1983-84, chap program chairman, 1982-83; Huntsville High School PTA, treasurer, 1986-87; Talladega College Alumni, chairman for southern region meeting, 1989, chapter secretary, 1991-; Church Street Cumberland Presbyterian Church, deacon board secty, 1991-96; deacon board chairman, 1997-98. **Honors/Awds:** National Contract Management Association, certified professional contract mgr, 1975; Omega Psi Phi Fraternity, Chapter Man of the Year, 1986; Huntsville Boys Club, century club member, 1990-91; Natl Contract Mgmt Assn, fellow, 1987. **Special Achievements:** Graduate, US Army Logamp Program, 1992. **Military Serv:** US Army, sgt, 1967-70; Army Commendation Medal, 1968-69; US Army Corps of Engineers, Employee of the Year, 1979. **Home Addr:** 128 Heritage Ln, Madison, AL 35758, (205)461-4220. **Business Addr:** Director of Contracting, US Army Corps of Engineers, Huntsville, PO Box 1600, Attn: CEHND-CT, Huntsville, AL 35807, (205)895-1110.

REYNOLDS, JERRY
Professional basketball player. **Personal:** Born Dec 23, 1962, Brooklyn, NY. **Educ:** Madison Area Technical College, Madison, WI, 1981-82; Louisiana State Univ, Baton Rouge, LA, 1982-85. **Career:** Milwaukee Bucks, 1985-88; Seattle Supersonics, 1988-89; Orlando Magic, 1989-93.

REYNOLDS, MEL
Congressman. **Personal:** Born Jan 8, 1952. **Educ:** Oxford University, Rhodes Scholar, JDS. **Career:** College professor; US House of Representatives, Democratic congressman for Illinois, 1992-, House Ways and Means Committee, seat, currently. **Special Achievements:** First African-American Rhodes Scholar in Illinois. **Business Addr:** Congressman, US House of Representatives, 514 Canon HOB, Washington, DC 20515, (202)224-3121.

REYNOLDS, NANETTE LEE
State official. **Personal:** Born Feb 22, 1946, Oberlin, OH; married Murphy L Reynolds (deceased); children: Malika, Michon Imani. **Educ:** Howard Univ, BA, 1967; Southern IL Univ at Carbondale, MS, Educ, 1969; Harvard Univ, EdD, 1978. **Career:** MIT, asst dean for student affairs, 1970-72; Brown Univ, asst dean of academic affairs, 1972-74; RI Consortium for Continuing Educ in Human Serv & Comm Welfare, exec dir, 1977-78; The Reynolds Group Human Resources Consultants, managing dir, 1980-81; Federated Council of Domestic Violence Progs, exec dir, 1982-83; Office of MI's Governor, prog specialist in educ and civil rights, 1983-85; MI Dept of Civil Rights, exec asst to the dir, 1985-87, community services bureau director, 1987-93, director & member of the Governor's Cabinet, 1993-. **Orgs:** NAACP, Delta Sigma Theta Sor Inc, second vp, 1966-67; mem of sev natl comms, pres Boston Alumnae, 1970-72, pres Providence RI Alumnae, 1973-74; vp Lansing Assn of Black Organizations; Dev Comm of Ele's Place for grieving children; Food Bank Council of Michigan, bd mem; Student Advocacy Ctr, adv comm; Michigan Protection & Advocacy Services for Developmentally Disabled Citizens, bd mem; Jack & Jill of America. **Honors/Awds:** Ford Fellowship for Black Americans, 1975-78. **Special Achievements:** First African-American female to head Michigan's Civil Rights Department; 1994 NAFEO Honoree as a Distinguished Alumna of the Historically & Predominately Black Colleges and Universities; 1994 Honoree as a ''Delta Legacy: Women Making a Difference''; MI Dept of Civil Rts Director's Award, 1987; listings in ''Outstanding Young Women of America'' and ''Outstanding Black Americans''. **Business Addr:** Director, Michigan Dept of Civil Rights, 303 West Kalamazoo, 4th Floor, Lansing, MI 48913, (517)335-3164.

REYNOLDS, PAMELA TERESE
Journalist. **Personal:** Born Dec 10, 1963, Los Angeles, CA; daughter of Mr & Mrs Theodore Reynolds; married Philip G Roth, Feb 13, 1988 (deceased). **Educ:** Univ of MO Columbia School of Journalism, BJ (magna cum laude) 1985. **Career:** The Boston Globe, feature writer, reporter, national reporter, 1987-89, asst arts ed, 1990-91, asst living ed, 1991-. **Orgs:** Mem Sigma Delta Chi 1984, Boston Assoc of Black Journalists 1986, Young Black Journalists Under 30 1985; tutor Literacy Volunteers of MA 1987. **Honors/Awds:** Natl Achievement Scholar 1981; Reynolds Scholar Donald W Reynolds Found 1983; Kappa Tau Alpha Hon Journalism Soc 1985; Best Student Journalist New England Women's Press Assoc 1985. **Business Addr:** Asst Living Editor, The Boston Globe, 135 Morrissey Blvd, Boston, MA 02107.

REYNOLDS, R. J. (ROBERT JAMES)
Professional baseball player. **Personal:** Born Apr 19, 1960, Sacramento, CA; children: Fawn Rashelle, Robert IV. **Educ:** Sacramento City College, attended; Cosumnes River College, attended. **Career:** Outfielder: Los Angeles Dodgers, 1983-85, Pittsburgh Pirates, 1985-90, Yokohama Taiyo Whales, Japanese Baseball League, 1990-. **Honors/Awds:** First major league hit was a three-run home run.

REYNOLDS, RICKY SCOTT (DERRICK)
Professional football player. **Personal:** Born Jan 19, 1965, Sacramento, CA. **Educ:** Washington State Univ, attended. **Career:** Tampa Bay Buccaneers, defensive back, 1987-. **Business Addr:** Professional Football Player, Tampa Bay Buccaneers, One Buccaneer Pl, Tampa, FL 33607-5797.

REYNOLDS, VIOLA J.
Educator. **Personal:** Born Feb 4, 1925, Savannah; widowed; children: LaVerne, Freddie Mae, Fred Jr, Janice, Marcia, Felicia, Tonia. **Educ:** Nat Sch of Bus, 1946; Comm Devel Seminar, 1967-69. **Career:** US Dept of Labor, cost of living survey 1946; Univ of GA, nutrition Aide 1969-74; Univ of GA, nutrition Ldr aide & Coopertive extension serv 1974. **Orgs:** Chatham Cit Dem Clb 1946; mem PTA 1953-74; Girl Scout Ldr 1954-59; Y Teen Ldr 1961-63; YWCA Bd 1961-63; adv bd Savannah St Coll Emrgncy Sch Aid Act Prog 1974; crrspndng sec Chatham Co Coun PTA 1973-75. **Honors/Awds:** Mem, seminar on rural hlth, Am Med Assn 1971; honorary Life Mem PTA 1968; natl honors for wk Expanded Foods & Nutrition Educ Prog 1974; Cit Day, Savannah 1974. **Business Addr:** US PO Wright Sq Br, Savannah, GA.

RHAMES, VING (IRVING)
Actor. **Personal:** son of Ernest and Rather Rhames; married Valerie Scott. **Educ:** Juilliard, BFA, 1983. **Career:** Stage: The Boys of Winter, 1985; Television: Another World, The Guiding Light, The Equalizer, Suicide Squad, ER; Don King: Only in America, HBO, 1997; Film: Go Tell It on the Mountain, 1984, Patty Hearst, 1988, Jacob's Ladder, 1990, Dave, 1993, Pulp Fiction, 1994, Kiss of Death, 1995, Striptease, 1996, Mission: Impossible, 1996, Dangerous Ground, 1997, Rosewood, 1997. **Honors/Awds:** Golden Globe Awards, Best Actor, Miniseries or Movie Made For Television, 1998. **Business Addr:** Actor, William Morris Agency, 151 El Camino Dr, Beverly Hills, CA 90212, (310)274-7451.

RHEA, MICHAEL
Association executive. **Personal:** Born Oct 3, 1946. **Educ:** UCLA; UCLA, MBA; Memphis St U, Tokyo U, LA Wrtrs Wrkshp, Postgrad. **Career:** Met Manpwr Commn, Indianapolis, dept admnstr 1973; WLWI TV ''Here & Now'', host 1970-74; Econ Devel Corp , mgr 1970-73; Thomas Ryan Inc Mgmt Cons, reg mgr 1969-70. **Orgs:** Mem Gov's Commn Status & Women 1973; chmn bd dirs Yth Market Pl 1973; pres & chmn bd People Better Brdcstng 1973; Jaycees; adv Black Stdnt Union; adv Black Arts Wrkshp; Mayor's Task Force Improve City Govt; Indianapolis Cable Steering Com; Adult Educ Coun Central IN; New World Cmmnctns; bd City & State Black Caucus; CORE; Young Rep; Nat Assn Execs & Mgr; Professional Mgrs Clb; Artist Am; Midwst Poet's Orgn; adv Boys Clb Am. **Business Addr:** 2101 N College Ave, Indianapolis, IN 46202.

RHETT, ERRIC UNDRA
Professional football player. **Personal:** Born Dec 11, 1970, Pembroke Pines, FL. **Educ:** Univ of Florida, attended. **Career:** Tampa Bay Buccaneers, running back, 1994-97; Baltimore Ravens, 1998-. **Honors/Awds:** NFL Players Assn, NFL Offensive Rookie of the Year, 1994; Pro Bowl alternate, 1995. **Business Addr:** Professional Football Player, Baltimore Ravens, 11001 Owings Mills Blvd, Owings Mills, MD 21117, (410)654-6200.

RHETT, MICHAEL L.
Law enforcement official. **Personal:** Born Dec 1, 1954, Charlottesville, VA; son of Bernice N Rhett and Walter P Rhett Sr. **Educ:** Newberry College, 1973-74; Ohio State University, 1973-78. **Career:** State of Ohio, Natural Resources, park ranger, 1978-80; Standard Oil of Ohio, manager, 1980-82; City of Columbus, police officer, 1982-. **Orgs:** Fraternal Order of Police Conductor, newsletter editor, 1982-92; Crittenton Family Services, board member, 1983-, board chair, 1986-87, board chair elect, 1993-94; board chair, 1994-95, Central Community House, board member, 1992-; Fraternal Order of Police, vice pres, 1992-. **Special Achievements:** First black chair of largest United Way agency in Franklin County, Ohio, 1986-87; First black elected bd mem FOP CCL #9. **Home Addr:** 4194 Berry Ridge Ln, Gahanna, OH 43230, (614)785-7597. **Business Addr:** Police Officer, City of Columbus, 120 Marconi Blvd, Columbus, OH 43215, (614)645-4864.

RHETTA, HELEN L.
Physician. **Educ:** Univ MI, AB; Univ MI Med Sch, MD; Univ MI Sch of Pub Health US Dept HEW, MPH 1968-76. **Career:** Provident Hosp, intern & resident 1938-39; physician 1939-. **Orgs:** Mem IL State, Chicago, Med Soc; AMA; Amer Pub Health Soc; Delta Sigma Theta; Amer Physicians Art Assn. **Honors/Awds:** USPH Fellowship 1966-67; Superior Serv Awd US Dept HEW 1972; Natl Assn of Coll Women Awd; Amer Physicians Recognition Awd; Zeta Phi Beta Woman of the Year.

RHINEHART, JUNE ACIE
Publishing executive. **Personal:** Born Jul 1, 1934, McKeesport, PA; daughter of Gladys Cornelia Allen Acie and William Elmer Acie; married Vernon Morel Rhinehart, Apr 4, 1958 (divorced 1975). **Educ:** Wilson Jr Coll, AB 1962; Roosevelt Univ, Chicago, BA 1968; Northwestern Univ; Loyola Univ Chicago, Grad Sch of Bus 1972; Loyola Univ of Chicago Sch of Law, JD 1980. **Career:** Johnson Pub Co, Inc, Chicago, IL, secretary, 1955-60, administrative asst, 1960-71, vice pres, asst to pub, 1971-80, senior vice pres, general counsel, 1980-. **Orgs:** Mem adv bd exec prog Stanford U, 1976-78; mem Roosevelt Univ Alumni Bd; mem bd of trustees Chic St Univ Found; mem Alpha Kappa Alpha Sor; Chicago Network; Women's Div Oprtn PUSH; Chicago Focus. **Honors/Awds:** Achievement Awd Nat Counc of Negro Women 1973; 1,000 Successful Blacks. **Business Addr:** Sr Vice President/Genl Counsel, Johnson Publishing Co, Inc, 820 S Michigan Ave, Chicago, IL 60605.

RHINEHART, N. PETE
Company executive. **Career:** A T & T, vp, CFO, currently. **Business Addr:** VP, CFO, AT&T, 295 N Maple Ave, Basking Ridge, NJ 07920, (908)221-2000.

RHINEHART, VERNON MOREL
Attorney. **Personal:** Born Sep 27, 1935, Kansas City, KS; son of Anna P Pennyman-Rhinehart and Thomas A Rhinehart, Sr; married Carmen M Melendez-Rhinehart, Oct 1, 1983. **Educ:** Howard Univ, Schl Of Law, LLB/JD 1966; Boston Univ Coll of Lib Arts, BA 1958; Chicago Tchrs Coll; The Univ of Chgo. **Career:** Elliot Donnelley Youth Cntr, group worker 1959; Cook Cnty Dept of PA, social worker 1959; Internatl Hrvstr Co, indstrl rel emplyee Rel Staff 1967; Off of Economic Opprtnty, 1967; Brunswick Corp, mngr 1967-68; Comm on Human Rel, human rel ofcr 1968-69; First Natl Bank of Chicago , ofcr cand comm lending 1969-70; Rivers, Cousins, Lawrence & Clayter, assoc 1972-74; Herman, Glazer, Rhinehart, Waters & Kessler, partner 1974-79; Clayter, Wood & Rhinehart, partner 1979-82; Law Offices of Vernon Morel Rhinehart, princple 1982-. **Orgs:** Mem IL Trial Lawyers Assoc; Natl Bar Assoc; Amer Bar Assoc; Cook Cnty Bar Assoc; IL State Bar Assoc; Alpha Phi Alpha Frat Inc; Amer Judicature Soc; Boston Univ Alumni Club of Chicago; Howard Univ Chicago Alumni; City Club of Chicago; Chicago Urban Leaguel; NAACP; bd Woodlawn/ Yancey Units; Chicago Boys Club; Chicago Assoc of Black Journalists; Amer Arbitration Assoc; Natl Assoc of Health Services Execs; Amer Soc of Law & Med; Comprand (Compre-

hensive Research & Development). **Honors/Awds:** Bancroft-Whitney Company's Award; Amer Jurisprudence Prize for Excellence in Fed Jurisdiction; Commissioner City of Chicago Health Systems Agency (appointed by Harold Washington, Mayor of Chicago, 1985); Recognition Award, Alpha Phi Alpha Frat Inc, XI Lambda Chap, 1987; Alpha Phi Alpha, Charles F Lane Award, 1992. **Home Addr:** 9400 S Forest Ave, Chicago, IL 60615, (773)726-1177. **Business Addr:** Attorney & Commissioner, Law Office of Atty Vernon Rhinehart, Marmon Bldg, 39 S LaSalle St, Ste 825, Chicago, IL 60603.

RHINES, JESSE ALGERON
Educator. **Personal:** Born Jul 30, 1948, Washington, DC; son of Julia Marie Watson Barbour and Jacinto Rhines. **Educ:** Antioch Coll, BA, pol comm, 1974; NYU, film production certificate, 1983; Yale Univ, MA, Afro-American Studies, 1983; UCLA, MA, political science, 1986; Univ of California, Berkeley, PhD, ethnic studies, 1993. **Career:** YMCA World Ambassador to Hong Kong, Japan, South Korea, 1975; Congressman R on Dellums, leg intern, admin aide, 1975-76; Mayor, New Haven, leg affairs offi cer, 1978-890; U-Skate Rollerskates, founder, 1979-81; Operations Crossroads Africa Inc, Mali group leader, 1980; IBM Corp, systems eng, 1981-83; State of NY Mortgage Agency, computer systems analyst, 1989-90; Cineaste magazine, asst editor, co-editor, Race in Contemporary Cinema Section, 1992-; Eugene Lange Coll, instructor, 1993; Rutgers Univ, asst prof, 1993-. **Orgs:** Black Filmmaker Foundation; Independent Feature Project; NAACP; Soc for Cinema Studies; Natl Council of Black Political Scientists, fellow, 1976; Amer Political Science assn, fellow, 1976. **Honors/Awds:** Ideals of the Center Award, Yale Afro-Amer Cultural Center, 1981; Outstanding Young Man of Amer, Jaycees, 1982; exhibited photographs taken in Mali, West Africa, at Yale Univ; Distinguished Scholarship Award; Dona & Albert R Broccoli Foundation Scholarship, 1997. **Special Achievements:** Publications: Black Film, White Money: African American Entrepreneurship and Employment in the American Film Industry, dissertation, 1994; ''Integrating the Hollywod Craft Uniions,'' Cineaste, 1994; ''Stimulating a Dialogue Among African American Viewers: An Interview with Daresha Kyi,'' 1994; Black Film, White Money(book), Rutgers Univ Press, 1996; numerous others. **Home Addr:** 219 W 16th St, #1A, New York, NY 10011-6028.

RHOADES, SAMUEL THOMAS
Educational administrator. **Personal:** Born Aug 11, 1946, Raleigh, NC; children: Audria Michelle Humes. **Educ:** NC Central Univ, BA Psych 1967; NC Central Univ, JD 1973. **Career:** Durham Coll, counseling & cooperative ed 1973-77; St Paul's Coll, spec asst/fed programs 1977-. **Orgs:** Treas Phi Alpha Delta Law Frat 1975; parliamentarian Natl Assoc of Title III Admin 1978; mem Amer Legion, Omega Psi Phi Frat, Beauty of Dunn Lodge of F&A Masons. **Honors/Awds:** Law Jrnl NC Central Univ 1972; Honor Grad NC Central Univ 1972; Omega Man of the Year Omega Psi Phi Frat 1977. **Military Serv:** AUS sgt E-5 2 yrs. **Business Addr:** Special Asst to the President, St Pauls College, 406 Windsor Ave, Lawrenceville, VA 23868.

RHODEMAN, CLARE M.
Educator. **Personal:** Born Jul 21, 1932, Biloxi, MS; married Thomas Johan; children: Rennee Maria, Thomas Johan, Nichole Irene. **Educ:** Xavier U, New Orleans, BA 1953; Xavier U, MA 1957. **Career:** Elementary, Jr High & Sr High teacher & Sr High counselor; Nicholas Jr HS Biloxi Municipal Separate School System, Jr HS counselor; MTA BEA, coordinator 1973-74. **Orgs:** Mem MS Prsnl & Guid Assn; prof Stndrds Com; chmn guid Com 6th dist MS Tchr Assn; Nat Educ Assn; Cath 67, sec 67-71, vice pres 1971-72 Biloxi Interparochial Sch Bd; mem Our Mother Sorrows Cath Ch; Parish Cncl; MS Gulf Coast Alumnae Chpt, Delta Sigma Theta Sor; Biloxi NAACP; mem bd dir Harrison Co Devl Commn; Harrison Co Comm Action Prog; Harrison Co Untd Fnd; Dem Party; vol wrkr, Mothers March Birth Defects, Heart Fnd & PTA. **Business Addr:** 950 Bellman St, Biloxi, MS 39530.

RHODEN, RICHARD ALLAN
Health scientist. **Personal:** Born May 8, 1930, Coatesville, PA; son of Dorothy Rhoden; married Yvonne Latitia Mills; children: Richard A Jr. **Educ:** Lincoln Univ, AB 1951; Drexel Univ, MS 1967, PhD 1971. **Career:** Naval Air Devel Ctr, rsch chemist 1972; Environmental Protection Agency, environ scientist 1972-75; Natl Inst for Occupational Safety & Health, rsch pharmacologist 1975-82; Natl Insts of Health, health scientist administrator 1982-89; American Petroleum Institute, health scientist 1989-. **Orgs:** Exec sec subcomm on toxicology, exec comm, science adv bd US Environ Protection AGency 1979; sr policy analyst Office of Science & Tech Policy Exec Office of the President 1980-81; mem Environmental Studies Inst Adv Comm Drexel Univ 1980-84; rapporteur WHO Study Group on Recommended Health Based Limits in Occup Exposure to Pesticides Geneva Switzerland 1981; keeper of records & seal, Alpha Omega Chapter, Omega Psi Phi Frat Inc, 1992-; Amer Chemical Society; Amer Coll of Toxiology; Society of Toxicology; Amer Industrial Hygiene Assn; Amer Conf of Governmental Industrial Hygienists; Air & Waste Management Assn. **Honors/Awds:** Fellow, American Association for the Advancement of Science; Fellow, American Institute of Chemists; Omega Man of the Year, Alpha Omega Chapter, 1996-97. **Home Addr:** PO Box 34472, Washington, DC 20043-4472. **Business Addr:** Health Scientist, American Petroleum Institute, 1220 L Street NW, Washington, DC 20005, (202)682-8480.

RHODES, ANNE L.
City official (retired). **Personal:** Born Oct 9, 1935, Richmond, IN; daughter of Margaret Rhodes and George Rhodes. **Educ:** Whittier Coll, BA Polit Sci 1957; Fresno State Coll, Sch of Social Work, MSW 1968; CA Scholarship Fed. **Career:** San Bernardino Co Dept of Public Social Svcs, social worker 1959-62, social serv supvr I 1962-63, social serv super II 1963-68, social serv supr III 1968-71; Univ of CA Ext at Riverside, instr 1969; San Bernardino St Coll, lectr 1971-72; City of San Bernardino, mgmt analyst 1972-74; Chaffey Coll, instr 1973; City of San Bernardino, supt of comm serv dir human svcs; St Bernardine Med Cntr, medical social worker 1987. **Orgs:** Consult prog developer self employed; trained Head Start Staff of Econ Oppor Bd of Riverside Co 1970; served as trainer, consult Parents for Progress del agency of San Bernardino Co Dependency Prevention Commn; lifetime Comm Coll Teaching Cert; mem San Bernardino Co Affirmative Action Task Force 1972; City of San Bernardino EEOC 1973-; pres San Bernardino NAACP 1960-61; bd dirs San Bernardino Family Serv Agency 1971-74; Inland Empire Adolescent Clinic 1970-71; consult mem Local Welfare Rights Orgn; bd dirs Inland Area Urban League 1970-71; current mem NASW, ACSW, NOW, League of Women Voters, Urban League, Natl Cncl of Negro Women, NAACP; Zonta Intnl 1986-. **Honors/Awds:** Cert of Recog for Outstanding Support of San Bernardino Black Athletes Hall of Fame 1975; Cert Los Padrinos in recog for contrib to betterment of youth comm 1974; Cert in recognition San Bernardino Westside Comm Devel Corp 1974; first Black Dept Head in history of City of San Bernardino; German Minority Professional Exchange Prog 1979; mem State Com of Credentials 1980; commendation Common Council City of San Bernardino 1986.

RHODES, ARTHUR LEE, JR.
Professional baseball player. **Personal:** Born Oct 24, 1969, Waco, TX. **Career:** Baltimore Orioles, pitcher, 1991-. **Business Addr:** Professional Baseball Player, Baltimore Orioles, 333 W Camden St, Baltimore, MD 21201, (410)685-9800.

RHODES, AUDREY B.
Company president. **Career:** State project dir, HOPE for Kids; South Carolina Academy of Family Physicians, pres, 1996-. **Special Achievements:** First African American and second female to be installed as pres of South Carolina Academy of Family Physicians. **Business Addr:** President, South Carolina Academy of Family Physicians, PO Box 312, Laurens, SC 29360.

RHODES, C. ADRIENNE
Marketing chairman, communications director. **Personal:** Born Jul 16, 1961, Camden, NJ; daughter of Adele Clark Polk. **Educ:** Pratt Inst, School of Art & Design, 1978-80; State Univ of NY at FIT, AAS 1984, BS 1989; New York Univ, School of Film, Video and Broadcasting, 1993-94. **Career:** The New York Times Magazine Group, circ/prom serv asst, 1980-82; Diane Von Furstenberg Inc, public relations mgr, 1982-84; United Negro Coll Fund, mgr of media relations, 1984-86, asst dir of communications, 1986-89, dir of communications, 1989-93; New York Daily News, LP, dir of communications & media relations, 1993-. **Orgs:** Senator, Student Govt Assn, Pratt Inst, 1979-80; mem, PRSA Young Professionals Comm, NY Chap, 1983-84; assoc mem, NY Assn of Black Journalists, 1986; mem, Public Relations Soc of Amer, Natl Chap, 1987-89; marketing chmn, Natl Assn of Black Journalists, 1989; co-founder, Black Public Relations Society of Greater New York, 1990; Columbia Univ, OPOs, memntor, 1994-; Natl Black Women's Political Caucus, media and entertainment commission, 1993-; NY Urban League, advisory bd, 1993-; Publisher's Liasion, Harlem Y Steering Committee, 1994; US Commission on Minority Business Development, Media and Perception Task Force, 1991. **Honors/Awds:** CEBA Awd of Merit, World Inst of Black Comm, 1986; Certificate of Special Merit for an Outstanding Example of Graphic Arts, Assn of Graphic Arts, 1992; Art Directors' Club, Silver Medal Award for Outstanding Advertising, 1992; Advertising Women of New York, ADDY Award for Outstanding Television Advertising, 1992; Black Public Relations Society-Los Angeles Chapter, Outstanding Women in Public Relations, 1991; Advertising Club of New York, ANDY Award for Outstanding Television Advertising, 1991; Intl Film Festival, Gold Medal, 1991; World Inst of Communications, CEBA Award of Excellence, 1991.

RHODES, EDWARD THOMAS, SR.
Small business executive. **Personal:** Born Mar 20, 1933, Cumberland, MD; son of Ella Harrison Burgee Rhodes and John Henry Rhodes; married Ovetta Lyles Williams; children: Shari, Edward Jr. **Educ:** Kenyon Coll, BA 1955. **Career:** W-PAFB, contract negotiator 1958-61; GSFC, sr procurement analyst 1961-64; FWPCA Dept of the Int, dir div of general serv 1964-71; EPA, dir contract mgmt div 1971-75, dep asst administrator, 1975-78; HEW dep asst sec grants & procurement mgmt 1975, dep asst sec grants & procurement 1978-80, deputy assoc dir/admin group Office of Personnel Mgmt 1980-86; Office of Procurement, Washington Metro Area Transit Authority, director, 1986-92; Sektek, Inc, president, currently. **Orgs:** Mem Natl Bd of Advisors Natl Contract Mgmt Assn; past mem Bd of Regents Institute of Cost Analysis; past pres, Natl Assn of Black Procurement Professionals; past director, Procurement Roundtable. **Honors/Awds:** Meritorious Serv Award, Dept of Int, 1967; Distinguished Serv Award, Dept of Interior, 1967; Award for Achievement in Public Admin Wm A Jump Mem Found 1969; Silver Medal for Sup Service EPA 1972; Meritorious Serv Award OPM. **Military Serv:** AUS sp-4 1955-57. **Business Addr:** Sektek, Inc, 208 Elden St, Ste 201, Herndon, VA 22070, (703)834-0507.

RHODES, JACOB A.
Association executive. **Personal:** Born Nov 30, 1949, Brownsville, TN; son of Mary J Rhodes and Franklin A Rhodes; married; children: Jalena. **Career:** YMCA of Greater Rochester, president, chief executive officer, currently. **Special Achievements:** Author: ''Management Styles of 30 CEOs,'' Jun 1990; Managing in a Changing Environment, 1982. **Business Addr:** President/CEO, YMCA of Greater Rochester, Corporate Office, 444 E Main St, Rochester, NY 14604, (716)546-5500.

RHODES, JEANNE
Business executive. **Personal:** Born in Monongahela, PA; widowed; children: Joseph Simmons Scott, Margaret Herndon. **Educ:** Duffs Bus Sch; Univ Pitts; Duquesne U. **Career:** Philadelphia Tribune, vice pres pub rltns. **Orgs:** Bd mem Am Red Cross; life mem, exec com, Grad Hosp Aux; bd mem Inglis Hse Home for Incurables; bd mem Philadelphia Tribune Co; bd trustee Ruth W Hayre Schlrshp Fnd; mem Spnsrs Schlrshp Clb; La Cabaneetas Estrn Seabrd Dinner Clb; Finesse Brdg; DCR Birthday Clb; bd mem Philadelphia 76; bd trustee Dowingtown Agr & Indsl Sch; spec Dept of Labor; p pres, p sec, Pitts Br, NAACP; p chmn bd Lemington Home Aged; p natl pres Iota P Hi Lambda; mem bd Cvl Light Opera Pittsburgh; hon bd mem Tribune Charities; Adv com Afro-am Mus; bd mem YWCA Belmont Br; Philadelphia Bicentennial Commn; Cenntennial Com for Lucretia Mott 1980; mem Bethesda United Presbyterian Ch; adhoc com for Floyd Logan Archives Temple U; treas S St W Bus Assn 1979; lay mem Fee Disputes Com Philadelphia BarAssn 1979. **Honors/Awds:** Serv Awd Philadelphia Tribune Charities 1973; Decision Maker, Nat Assn of Media Women, 1974; Bi-centennial Achvmt Awd, AME Ch 1976; Nat Assn of Univ Women; Apprctn Awd Bicentennial Commn of PA; Police Athletic Leg, recog awd 1977; Serv Awd ARC 1978; Distngshd Serv Awd, Downingtown A&I Sch 1979; 50th Anniversary Ldrshp Awd Iota Phi Lambda Sor 1979. **Business Addr:** 520-26 16th St, Philadelphia, PA 19146.

RHODES, JOHN K.
Government official. **Personal:** Born Mar 18, 1965, San Francisco, CA; son of Gus and Lillian Rhodes. **Educ:** Univ of Nevada-Las Vegas, post graduate, 1989, BS, 1987; Univ of Nebraska-Lincoln, 1983-84. **Career:** Univ Medical Center, personnel, 1989; Clark County, agent, 1989-94; John K Rhodes Consulting, president, 1991-. **Orgs:** City of Las Vegas, task for children, 1992; Omega Psi Phi Fraternity, life member, 1988-; Committed 100 Men Helping Boys, founding member, 1991-; Lied Discovery Museum, board, 1992-93; DARE Inc, board, 1992-93; Board of Equalization, 1995-. **Honors/Awds:** NAACP, banquet awardee, 1993; MLK, give me the ballot award, 1994; US Senate, certificate of special recognition, 1994; US Congress, congressional recognition, 1992. **Business Addr:** President, John K Rhodes Consulting Inc, 1316 Walstone Road, North Las Vegas, NV 89031, (702)649-0860.

RHODES, KARL DERRICK
Professional baseball player. **Personal:** Born Aug 21, 1968, Cincinnati, OH. **Career:** Houston Astros, 1990-94; Chicago Cubs, 1994-. **Business Phone:** (312)924-1000.

RHODES, PAULA R.
Educator, attorney. **Personal:** Born Jul 18, 1949, New Orleans, LA; daughter of Marie Richard Rhodes and Leroy Rhodes. **Educ:** Amer Univ, BA 1971; Harvard Univ, JD 1974. **Career:** Legal Serv Corp, atty 1977-79; Mid Atlantic Legal Educ, prof 1980; Univ of San Diego Law School, visiting prof 1983-84; Howard Univ School of Law, assoc prof 1979-90; Univ of Bridgeport, adjunct prof 1985; Univ of Denver College of Law, Denver, CO, visiting prof, 1989-90, professor, 1990-. **Orgs:** Dist of Columbia Bas Assn; LA Bar Assn; American Bar Assn; Inter Wolsa; American Soc of Intl Law; Academic Council on United Nations Studies; American Friends Serv Committee; Afr Amer United Nations Comm; Transafrica; Natl Rainbow Coalition, Legal Comm; Educ Serv; Haverford Col Corp; Mountainview Friends Meetings, bd of trustees. **Honors/Awds:** Various conferences including Amer Friends Serv Committee Consultation on Korea, Los Angeles, CA 1983, Inst for Policy Studies/Transnatl Inst Intl Conf on ''Meeting the Corporate Challenge'' Washington DC 1984; Brown Univ, ACUNS/ASIL Summer Workshop on Intl Organization Studies, 1994; African American Leaders Meetings with Mexican Leaders, Mexico City, Mexico, delegation spokesperson, 1992; publications include ''Expanding NGO Participation in Intl Decision Making,'' World Debt and the Human Condition: Structural Adjustment and the Right to Development, 1993; ''Devel of New Business

Opportunities for Minorities in the Synthetic Fuels Program'', Rsch & Legislative Narrative 1981; ''Energy Security Act and its Implications for Economic Devel'', Howard Law Journal 1981, ''We the People and the Struggle for a New World,'' WSA Constitution on Human Rights 1987; Assoc Ed Fed Bar Assn Forum 1982-83; featured in Lisa Jones, The Path, Six Women Talk About Their Religious Faith Essence vol16 #9 Jan 1986; Phi Delta Phi Legal Fraternity; panelist, moderator, v of Denver Consortium on Rights Development, seminar, international debt, structural adjustment, development and human rights, 1990; panelist, Human Rights and the Underclass, CORD, 1990. **Business Addr:** Professor, University of Denver College of Law, 1900 Olive St, Denver, CO 80220, (303)871-6258.

RHODES, RAY
Professional football coach. **Personal:** Born Oct 20, 1950, Mexia, TX; married Carmen; children: Detra, Candra, Tynesha, Raven. **Educ:** Texas Christian Univ, attended. **Career:** NY Giants, wide receiver/defensive back; San Francisco 49ers, defensive back 1980, asst secondary coach, 1981-82, defensive backfield coach, 1982-91; Green Bay Packers, defensive coordinator, 1992-93; San Francisco 49ers, defensive coordinator, 1994; Philadelphia Eagles, head coach, 1995-. **Honors/Awds:** Named NFL Coach of the Year, 1996. **Special Achievements:** One of only a few African American NFL coaches, third in NFL history. **Business Addr:** Head Coach, Philadelphia Eagles, Broad St & Pattison Ave, Veterans Stadium, Philadelphia, PA 19148.

RHODES, ROBERT SHAW
Physician. **Personal:** Born Mar 3, 1936, Orangeburg, SC; son of Emma W Rhodes and John D Rhodes; married Gwendolyn M; children: Robin, Robert Jr, Nekole Smith, Candace Smith. **Educ:** Meharry Med Coll, MD 1962; Hubbard Hosp, Internship 1962-63; Meharry Med Coll, Resident 1963-67; Vanderbilt Univ School of Med, Fellowship 1967-70; Univ of MI School of Public Health, MPH 1981-83. **Career:** Meharry Med Coll, head div of hematology 1972-78; Multiphasic Screening Lab, dir 1973-78; Hubbard Hosp, med dir 1975-78; Hydra-matic Div of GMC, assoc med dir 1978-80, med dir 1980-82; Health Serv and Safety, div dir 1982-87; General Motors Corp, Detroit West Medical Region, regional med dir 1988-. **Orgs:** Mem ed comm Natl Sickle Cell Found 1981-; chairperson Sickle Cell Adv Comm 1977-81; pres elect 1984-, vice pres 1983-84 MI Occupational Med Assoc; chmn Med Audit Comm Beyer Hosp 1980-83; exec bd Wolverine Council BSA, house of delegates, 1988-90, board of directors, 1990-; American College of Occupational Medicine; president, ACOEM, 1997-98. **Military Serv:** USMC major 1967-70; US Army Commendation Medal 1970; AFIP Certificate of Meritorious Achievement 1970. **Business Addr:** Regional Medical Director, General Motors Corp, Powertrain, M/C 340, Ypsilanti, MI 48198.

RHODES, RODRICK
Professional basketball player. **Personal:** Born Sep 24, 1973; children: Ro'deira. **Educ:** University of Southern California. **Career:** Houston Rockets, guard/forward, 1997-. **Business Addr:** Professional Basketball Player, Houston Rockets, PO Box 272349, Houston, TX 77277, (713)627-0600.

RHONE, SYLVIA M.
Record company executive. **Personal:** Born Mar 11, 1952, Philadelphia, PA; daughter of Marie Christmas Rhone and James Rhone; married. **Educ:** University of Pennsylvania, Wharton School of Business and Commerce, MA, 1974. **Career:** Bankers Trust, 1974; Buddah Records, various positions, administrative asst through promotions coordinator; Atlantic Records, Natl Black Music Promotion, director, starting 1985, Black Music Operations, vice president/general manager, sr vice president, 1988, EastWest Records America, chairperson/CEO, 1991, Atco-EastWest label, chairperson/CEO, 1991-94; Elektra/East West Co, chair, 1994-. **Honors/Awds:** Jack the Rapper, 15th Annual Convention, honoree, 1991.

RIBBINS, GERTRUDE
Singer, writer. **Personal:** Born Dec 28, 1924, Memphis, TN; daughter of Annie W Pugh and James Pugh; married John W (deceased); children: Anne Sylvia, John, Mark. **Educ:** Lmyn Coll; Kent St. **Career:** Detroit SS Assn, guest soloist; Gr Chicago SS Assn, guest soloist; Wmn Alv Ont Can, conf soloist; Faith at Wrk Ont, conf slst; The Old Stn Ch Cleveland Lntn Srs, concerts 1973-74; E Stanley Jones St James AME Church, ashrm soloist; USA & Can, speaking & sngng tours. **Orgs:** Mem Adv Com Str for Hmn Serv 1974; bd mem, Wings Over Jordan, 1990-91; pres, Progressive District Women, Cleveland, 1977-81; bd of trustees, Sunny Acres Skilled Nursing Care Facility, Cleveland. **Honors/Awds:** Author of articles on Negro Mus & Dvtnls for Periodicals; Ftrd in The Gospel Herald; Union Gospel Press 1973; Clubdate Magazine 1988; Sojourner Truth Award, NANBPWC-Cleveland 1989; MTV Certificate of Commendation 1988; Cleveland Federation for Community Planning; Ebony Rose Tribute, 1990. **Special Achievements:** Soloist & Song Leader Women Alive. **Business Addr:** Ribbins Book Store, 3612 East 116th, Cleveland, OH 44120.

RIBBS, WILLIAM THEODORE, JR.
Race car driver. **Personal:** Born Jan 3, 1956, San Jose, CA; son of Geraldine Henderson-Ribbs and William T. Ribbs, Sr.; married Suzanne Hamilton-Ribbs, Nov 22, 1979; children: Sasha Wanjiku. **Educ:** San Jose City Coll San Jose, CA 1973-75. **Career:** Formula Ford Circuit, driver 1977; Formula Atlantic events; Sports 2000 events; Neil Deatley Trans-Am Team, driver 1983; Ford Motors Sports, 1984-85; Digard & Brooks Racing, 1986; racing driver Dan Gurneys All American Racers Santa Ana, CA, 1987. **Honors/Awds:** Dunlop Star of Tomorrow Champion Europe 1977; Intl Driver of the Yr Europe 1977; British Sports Writers Awd Europe 1977; Trans-Am Rookie of the Year 1983; winner of 45 percent of races entered since 1983; winner of 1985 Trans-Am series opener in Phoenix (10 victory in 25 Trans-Am starts); 17 victories in 39 Trans-Am starts; 5 Intl Motor Sports Assn victories; 3 time 1986 Norelco Driver Cupt Awd winner; Proclamation Willy T Ribbs Day City of Miami 1984, City of Atlanta 1984, City of St Petersburg 1987; Interamerican Western Hemisphere Driving Champion 1984; Motorsports Press Assoc All Amer Drivers Awd 1984-85; Phillips Business systems l987 Norelco GTO Driver of the Year, Phillips Business systems l988 Norelco GTO Driver of the Year; S.C.C.A. Trans Am AllTime Money Earner l988; first bl to compete in Indianapolis 500, 1991.

RIBEAU, SIDNEY
Educational administrator. **Career:** Bowling Green State University, pres, 1996-; California State Polytechnic University at Pomona, vp of academic affairs, until 1996. **Business Addr:** President, Bowling Green State University, President's Office, 220 Mcfall Center, Bowling Green, OH 43403, (419)372-2211.

RICANEK, CAROLYN WRIGHT
City official. **Personal:** Born Mar 10, 1939, Washington, DC; married Karl Ricanek; children: Lloyd O Taylor, Carooq M Taylor, Carmen T Harris, Demetrius A, Karl II. **Educ:** Federal City Coll, 1972-76; George Mason Univ 1976-79. **Career:** K&R Plumbing Heating Co, vice-pres 1969-87; ANC Commissioner 7C, 1st elected 1976-85, chairperson 1986-87; Phelp Career Center, chmn 1982-87; Marshall Heights Comm Devel Corp, asst treasurer 1983-85, financial sec 1983-87; Advisory Neighborhood Comm, vice-chmn. **Orgs:** Chmn HD Woodson Athletic Booster Cl 1976-79; mem Deanwood Civic Assn 1970-85; mem Metropolitan Women Democratic Club 1980-85; asst coord Garden Resource Org 1983-85; mem Majestic Eagles Minority Entrepreneur Inc. **Honors/Awds:** Cert of appreciation Houston Elem School 1979; Outstanding Citizen Coun Willie Hardy 1979-80; cert of award HD Woodson Sr High/Comm Services 1982; cert of appreciation Phelps Car Dev Cent 1983-84; First Elected Comm Mayor Marion Barry 1985. **Home Addr:** 1220 47th Place NE, Washington, DC 20019.

RICARD, JOHN H.
Auxiliary bishop. **Personal:** Born Feb 29, 1940, Baton Rouge, LA; son of Albanie St Amant Ricard and Maceo Ricard. **Educ:** Tulane Univ, New Orlenas, LA, M.A. l970-72; The Catholic Univ Washington, D C, PhD, 1985. **Career:** Archdiocese of Baltimore, auxiliary bishop 1984-. **Business Addr:** Bishop, Archdiocese of Pensacola-Tallahassee, P.O. Drawer 17329, Pensacola, FL 32522.

RICE, ALLEN TROY
Professional football player. **Personal:** Born Apr 5, 1962, Houston, TX. **Educ:** Attended: Wharton County Junior College, Ranger Junior College, Baylor Univ. **Career:** Minnesota Vikings, running back, 1984-. **Honors/Awds:** Played in NFC Championship Game, 1987. **Business Addr:** Professional Football Player, Minnesota Vikings, 9520 Viking Dr, Eden Prairie, MN 55344-3825.

RICE, CONDOLEEZZA
Educational administrator. **Personal:** Born Nov 14, 1954, Birmingham, AL; daughter of Angelena Ray Rice and John Wesley. **Educ:** University of Denver, BA (cum laude), 1974, PhD, 1981; Notre Dame University, MA, 1975. **Career:** US Department of State, intern, 1977; Rand Corp, Santa Monica, CA, intern, 1980; political science consultant, 1980-; Stanford University, assistant professor of political science, 1981-87, assoc professor, 1987-93; prof, provost, 1993-; assistant director of arms control program, 1981-89; National Security Council, from director to senior director of Soviet and East European Affairs, 1989-91. **Honors/Awds:** Fellow, Natl Fellowship Fund, Ford Fdn, Hoover Institute, Council on Foreign Relations; American Academy of Arts & Sciences; co-author, Germany Unified and Europe Transformed; author, The Gorbachev Era; author of numerous other books and articles. Award for Excellence in Teaching, Stanford University. **Special Achievements:** First African-American chief academic and budget officer, and second-ranking official behind the president, Stanford Univ, 1993-. **Business Addr:** Provost, Stanford University, Stanford, CA 94305, (650)723-6867.

RICE, CONSTANCE WILLIAMS
Business executive, educational administrator. **Personal:** Born Jun 23, 1945, Brooklyn, NY; daughter of Beulah Marshall Williams and Elliott Williams; married Norman Blann Rice, Feb 15, 1975; children: Mian A. **Educ:** Queens Coll, BA 1966; Univ of WA, Masters Public Admin 1970, PhD Higher Educ Admin 1975; Carnegie Mellon Univ, Sr Exec Mgmt 1983. **Career:** State Bd, prog asst; Shoreline Community Coll, chairperson; Corporate Comm METRO, mgr; US West, Seattle, WA, advisory board, 1981-; Public Relations/Management Firm, pres, 1984-89; Sec Pacific Bank, Seattle, WA, bd dir, 1985-; Community College District VI, vice chancellor; North Seattle Community College, president; Seattle Comm Coll, senior VP, currently. **Orgs:** Pres-Elect Seattle Chapter 101 Black Women 1984-85; trustee Seattle Fdn 1984-92; bd mem Amer Soc of Public Admin 1984; pres, Seattle Chap LINKS 1985-86; past vice pres Seattle King County United Way 1983-84; Links Inc 1986-; bd of governors Shoreline Comm Coll Foundation; past bd mem Fred Hutchinson Cancer Research Foundation; vice chair King County Open Space Commn 1989; bd mem King County Chamber of Commerce 1989-96; Rotary, Evergreen State Coll; asst exec dir, Washington Education Assn, 1987-88; Seafirst, board of directors, 1992-96; Bonneville Broadcast Group, brd, 1993-96. **Honors/Awds:** NY State Regents; Natl Sci Foundation Traineeship; Ed Professional Dir Award; Kellogg Grant; NW Outstanding Young Woman 1983-86; Women Entrepreneur of The Year runner-up 1985; White House Small Business delegate 1986; Top 25 Influential Women (Seattle) The Seattle Weekly 1986; Dorothy Bullitt Award, Women's Funding Alliance, 1991; Natl Council of Jewish Women's, Woman of Distinction Award; B'Nai B'rith, Torch of Liberty & Distinguished Comm Service Award; Njeri Temple, Special Individual Award; Seattle First Citizen Awd, 1994. **Business Addr:** Senior Vice Chancellor, Seattle Community College, 1500 Harvard, Seattle, WA 98122.

RICE, CORA LEE
Business executive. **Personal:** Born Jun 18, 1926, Edenton, NC; divorced; children: 5. **Educ:** Elizabeth City St Teachers, 1946; NYU, BA 1948. **Career:** Professional Answering Serv Inc, pres 1976-80; Commu Grfnckls, dir 1973-76; Ctrl Chrg Serv, training dir 1970-72. **Orgs:** Exec bd SCLC Metro Wash 1974-80; exec dir Prnc Grgs Untd Blk Fund 1976-80; pres Blk Wmns Assmbly 1978-80; exec bd NAACP MD 1969-80; pres PrncGrgs NAACP 1969. **Honors/Awds:** Outstanding leadership Pres L B Johnson 1964; hon awd Human Rights & Justice NAACP 1967; outstanding achievement Prsnlts of the S 1973; Human Rights SCLC 1979.

RICE, DAVID EUGENE, JR.
Association executive, attorney. **Personal:** Born Jul 1, 1916, Greenwood, SC; son of Mamye Elizabeth Johnson Rice and David Eugene Rice, Sr; married Beryl Lena Carter, Jun 5, 1971. **Educ:** Ohio State Univ, Columbus OH, BA, 1937; Northwestern Univ, Evanston IL, JD, 1941; Yale Law School, New Haven CT, Master of Law, 1950. **Career:** Lincoln Univ School of Law, St. Louis MO, assoc prof & editor Natl Bar Journal, 1946-48; Texas Southern Univ School of Law, Houston TX, dean, 1950-55; IL Federal Savings & Loan Assn, Chicago IL, savings officer, 1956-65; Chicago Small Business Opportunities Corp, Chicago IL, assoc dir, 1965-67; Natl Business League, Washington DC, dir Project Outreach, 1967-68, asst to the pres, 1969-83, dean of Certificate Institutes, 1977-87, resident historian, 1981-, vice pres for Const Aff, 1984-86, executive vice pres, 1987-. **Orgs:** Liaison, Natl Student Business League, 1975-87; chair, Rules Committee, DC Black Republican Council, 1985-; attorney, DC Black Republican Scholarship Fund, 1985-; mem, Screening Committee, KOOL Achiever Awards, 1987-; mem, Natl Bar Assn 1987-; mem, Coalition of Prof Organizations, 1988-; mem, Sub-Comm on Trade & Commerce; trustee bd, class leader, Metropolitan AME Church; mem, Fact Finding Committee, The Coalition to Protect Black Business; member, Pigskin Club. **Honors/Awds:** Published articles in Journal of Criminal Law & Criminology, 1939, Illinois Law Review, 1941; Award of Recognition, Natl Student Business League, 1978, 1981; composer of musical compositions, ''Night Songs,'' 1979-80; Presidental Citation, Natl Business League, 1985; 50 Year Certificate of Service, Kappa Alpha Psi Fraternity, 1986; Humanitarian Award, Natl Student Business League, 1988; Frederick Douglass Patterson Award, Natl Business League, 1988. **Military Serv:** Counter Intelligence Corps, agent, 1943-45; Corps of Military Police, 2nd Lieutenant, 1945-46. **Business Addr:** Executive Vice President, National Business League, 1629 K St NW, Suite 605, Washington, DC 20006.

RICE, EDWARD A.
Computer company executive. **Personal:** Born Apr 8, 1929, Richmond, VA; married Josie Wigfall; children: Patricia, Edward, Audrey. **Educ:** VA Union U, BS 1949; Columbia U, MA 1952; Univ CT, MBA 1963. **Career:** Central State Univ, Wilberforce OH, asst prof, chmn business admin 1967-89; USAF Nuclear Engineering Center, Wright-Patterson AFB, asst dir 1966-71; Aerospace Medical Div, Wright-Patterson AFB, rsch sci 1956-61; Air Force Units, admin 1951-56; Edward Rice Trust, Dayton, OH, CEO, 1989-; CAPCOM, president, 1989-. **Orgs:** Mem Rsch Faculty & School of Aerospace Medicine, San Antonio 1962-66; mem Ohio Business Teachers Assn; pres Green County Joint Vocational School Bd 1973-74; Miami Valley Consortium; Midwest Business Admin Assn; Amer Nuclear Soc; Alpha Phi Alpha 1948-; Amer Assn of Univ Professors; Yellow Springs Bd Educ 1972-. **Honors/Awds:** USAFR

Medal; Natl Defense Serv Medal; Krn Serv Medal; UN Serv Medal; AF Commendation Medal. **Military Serv:** USAF maj ret 1951-71. **Business Addr:** President, Computer Aided Protype Co, 678 Omar Cir, Yellow Springs, OH 45387.

RICE, EMMETT J.
Government official. **Personal:** Born in Florence, SC. **Educ:** CCNY, BBA 1941, MBA 1942; Univ of CA Berkeley, PhD 1955. **Career:** Univ of CA Berkeley, rsch asst in econs 1950-51, teaching asst 1953-54; Cornell Univ, asst prof econ 1954-60; Fed Reserve Bank, economist 1960-62; Central Bank of Nigeria Lagos, advisor 1962-64; Office Developing Nations Dept Treasury, dep dir, acting dir 1964-66; World Bank, exec dir 1966-70; Mayor's Econ Devel Comm Washington, 1970-71; Natl Bank Washington, sr vice pres 1972-79; Fed Reserve Bank Washington, gov 1979-. **Business Addr:** Governor, Federal Reserve Board, Fed Reserve Bldg, Room B-2064, Washington, DC 20551.

RICE, FRED
Superintendent police. **Personal:** Born Dec 24, 1926, Chicago, IL; married Thelma Martin; children: Lyle, Judith. **Educ:** Roosevelt Univ, BS 1970, MS Pub Admin 1977. **Career:** Chicago Police Dept, mem 1955 promoted to sgt 1961, lt 1968, capt 1973, dist comdr 1970-78, dep chief patrol Area Four 1978-79, chief patrol div 1979-83, supt police 1983-. **Honors/Awds:** Num awds for contribs to community. **Military Serv:** AUS 1950-52. **Business Addr:** Office of the Police Chief, Chicago Police Dept, 1121 S State St, Chicago, IL 60605.

RICE, FREDRICK LEROY
Attorney. **Personal:** Born Feb 26, 1950, Indianapolis, IN; son of Marion I & Willie B Rice; married Ellen M Rice, Aug 10, 1974; children: John F, Edward C. **Educ:** Beloit College, BA, 1972; Indiana University School of Law, JD, 1977. **Career:** Landmein & Beatty, associate attorney, 1977-82; UAW Legal Service Plan, staff attorney, 1982-83; Indianapolis Public School, general counsel, 1983-90; State of Indiana, general counsel, 1990; Indianapolis Public Schools, general counsel, 1990-96; Indiana Supreme Court Disciplinary Comm, staff attorney, 1996-. **Orgs:** ITC, board of directors, 1980-; Waycross, vice pres/mem, 1994-; Mental Health Association of Marion County, board member, 1986-90; Indianapolis Bar Association, bd of governors, 1984-85; NSBA Council of School Attorneys, board member, 1984-88. **Home Addr:** 4451 N Park Ave, Indianapolis, IN 46205. **Business Addr:** Staff Attorney, Indianapolis Supreme Court Disciplinary Commission, 115 W Washington St, Ste 1060, South Tower, Indianapolis, IN 46204.

RICE, GLEN A.
Professional basketball player. **Personal:** Born May 28, 1967, Jacksonville, AR. **Educ:** Univ of Michigan, Ann Arbor, MI, 1985-89. **Career:** Miami Heat, 1989-95; Charlotte Hornets, 1995-. **Honors/Awds:** NBA All-Rookie Second Team, 1990; MVP, All Star Game, 1997; Mr Basketball, 1985; NBA Second Team, 1997; 3 Point Champion, 1995. **Special Achievements:** NBA Draft, First round pick, #4, 1989. **Business Addr:** Professional Basketball Player, Charlotte Hornets, One Hive Dr, Charlotte, NC 28217, (704)357-0252.

RICE, HORACE WARREN
Law professor, arbitrator, mediator. **Personal:** Born Feb 14, 1944, Huntsville, AL; son of John W & Lucy E Rice; divorced; children: Tasha M. **Educ:** Chicago City College, AA, 1964; Alabama A&M University, BS, 1966; University of Toledo, JD, 1972. **Career:** Chicago Legal Assistance Foundation, attorney, 1972-75; University of Alabama-Huntsville, professor, 1976-82; self-employed, player representative, sports agent, 1977-84; Alabama A&M University, professor, 1976-; self-employed, arbitrator/mediator, 1977-. **Orgs:** American Arbitration Association; Academy for Legal Studies in Business; American Management Association; Society of Professionals in Dispute Resolution. **Honors/Awds:** Ohio State Impass Panel, appointed to Arbitration Panel, 1985; American Arbitration Association, National Panel, 1980; Federal Mediation & Conciliation Service, National Panel, 1982; United States Postal Service, National Panel, 1983; Citizens Ambassador Program, US State Department, educator, Europe, Russia, Africa, 1988-89. **Special Achievements:** "Zoning: A Substantive Analysis," AAMU Faculty Research Journal, 1978; "Labor Arbitration: A Viable Method of Dispute Resolution," American Business Law Assn Journal, 1983; "Class Actions Under the 1964 Civil Rights Act," AAMU Faculty Res Journal, 1989; "What Consumers Should Know About Installment Buying," Business Newsletter, 1980; published 23 arbitration cases in Bureau of National Affairs, Commerce Clearinghouse, Labor Relations Reporter, Labor Arbitration In Government.

RICE, JERRY LEE
Professional football player. **Personal:** Born Oct 13, 1962, Starkville, MS; married Jackie; children: Jaqui Bonet, Jerry Jr, Jada Symone. **Educ:** Mississippi Valley State University. **Career:** San Francisco 49ers, wide receiver, 1985-. **Honors/Awds:** NFC Rookie of the Year, UPI, 1985; NFLPA NFC Offensive Rookie of the Year, 1985; Sports Illustrated, NFL Player of the Year, 1986, 1987, 1990, 1993; Pro Bowl, 1986, 1987, 1988, 1989, 1990, 1991, 1992, 1993, 1994, 1995, 1996; wide receiver, Sporting News NFL All-Pro team, 1986-91; NFL Player of the Year, Sporting News, 1987, 1990; NFC Championship game, 1988-90; Super Bowl XXIII MVP, 1989; Pro Football Hall of Fame, NFL "Team of the 1980s", 1989; Super Bowl XXIV, 1990; Len Eshmont Award, 1993. **Special Achievements:** Career touchdowns record holder; most 100-yard games for a receiver. **Business Addr:** Professional Football Player, San Francisco 49ers, 4949 Centennial Blvd, Santa Clara, CA 95054, (415)562-4949.

RICE, JIM
Professional baseball player (retired). **Personal:** Born Mar 8, 1953, Anderson, SC; married Corine Gilliard; children: Chauncy Brandon, Carissa Jacinda. **Career:** Boston Red Sox, outfielder, 1974-89; So Bank & Trust Co, Greenville, SC, public relations representative. **Honors/Awds:** Only player to ever have 3 straight 35 home run-200 hit years 1977-79; AL Player of the Year, The Sporting News 1978; MVP Amer League 1978; co-winner Joe Cronin Awd 1978; American League All-Star Team 1977, 1978, 1979, 1983, 1984, 1985, 1986; co-winner Tucson Pro-Am Gold Tournament 1977; T A Yawkey Awd as Sox MVP, Boston Writers 1983; UPI & AL All-Star Team 1984; Sporting News Silver Bat Team. **Business Addr:** Boston Red Sox, 1989, Fenway Park, Boston, MA 02215.

RICE, JUDITH CAROL
City Official. **Personal:** Born Jul 30, 1957, Chicago, IL; daughter of Fred & Thelma Rice. **Educ:** Northern Illinois University, 1975-76; Loyola University, BA, 1981; John Marshall Law School, JD, 1988. **Career:** Cook County, staff assistant, 1982-88, assistant state's attorney, 1988-89; City of Chicago, dir of administrative adjudication, 1990-92, parking administrator, 1992-93, revenue dir, 1993-95, executive assistant to the Mayor, 1995-96, water commissioner, 1996-. **Orgs:** Chicago Bar Association, mem, 1988-; March of Dimes, associate bd mem, 1995-; STEP School, School for the Treatment of Children with Emotional Problems, bd mem, 1996-. **Business Addr:** Commissioner, City of Chicago Department of Water, 1000 E Ohio St, Jardine Water Purification Plant, Chicago, IL 60611, (312)744-7001.

RICE, LEWIS, JR.
Federal law enforcement official. **Educ:** St John's Univ, degree in criminal justice. **Career:** Drug Enforcement Task Force, New York, NY, assoc special agent in charge; Drug Enforcement Administration, Detroit, MI, special agent-in-charge, New York, NY, special agent-in-charge, currently. **Orgs:** National Organization of Black Law Enforcement (NOBLE). **Honors/Awds:** NOBLE Achievement Award, 1997; Sr Executive Svc Award, 1997; St John's Univ, Alumni of the Year Award, 1997. **Special Achievements:** One of two African Americans heading DEA field offices. **Business Addr:** Special Agent-In-Charge, Drug Enforcement Administration, 99 10th Ave, 8th Fl, New York, NY 10011.

RICE, LINDA JOHNSON
Publishing company executive. **Personal:** Born Mar 22, 1958, Chicago, IL; daughter of Eunice W Johnson and John H Johnson; married Andre Rice. **Educ:** Univ of So CA Los Angeles, BA Journalism 1980; Northwestern Univ Evanston, Mgmt 1988. **Career:** Johnson Publishing Co, vice pres, president/chief operating officer, currently. **Orgs:** Exec producer Ebony/Jet Showcase; bd trustees Museum of Contemporary Art; women's bd Boys & Girls Club of Chicago; mem Natl Assn of Black Journalists; bd of directors Continental Bank Corp; bd of dir of Magazine Publishers America; board of directors Bausch & Lomb. **Business Addr:** Pres, Chief Operating Officer, Johnson Publishing Company, 820 S Michigan Ave, Chicago, IL 60605.

RICE, LOIS DICKSON
Educator, former computer company executive. **Personal:** Born Feb 28, 1933, Portland, ME; married Alfred B Fitt (deceased); children: Susan E, Emmett John Jr. **Educ:** Radcliffe Coll, AB, 1954; Columbia U, Woodrow Wilson Fellow. **Career:** Natl Scholarship Serv Fund for Negro Students, dir 1955-58; Ford Foundation, educational specialist 1963-64; Coll Entrance Exam Bd, dir 1959-62, dir 1973-74, vice pres 1974-81; Control Data Corp, sr vice pres for govt affairs, beginning 1981-91; The Brookings Inst, guest scholar, currently. **Orgs:** Bd dir Beauvoir Sch 1970-76; bd dir Childrens TV Workshop 1970-73; bd dir Fund for Improvement of Post Sec Educ 1972-75; bd trustees Urban Inst Potomac Institute; mem Carnegie Council on Policy Studies in Higher Edn; mem Commn on Acad Afrs Am Council on Educ 1974-76; mem DC Commn On Postsec Educ 1974-76; mem, natl adv bd Inst for Study of Educ Policy 1974; chmn, vis com Afro-Am Studies Harvard Univ 1974-77; mem Gov Temporary State Commn on Future of Postsec Educ in NY 1976-77; trustee Stephens Coll 1976-78; corporate boards: Control Data Corporation, 1978-91; Bell Atlantic CDC, 1987-96; McGraw-Hill, 1988-; The Hartford Steam Boiler Inspection and Insurance Company, 1990-; Intl Multifoods Corp, 1991-; First Financial Group, 1995-; UNUM Corp, 1992-; President's Foreign Tubell Service, advisory board, 1993-. **Honors/Awds:** Distinguished Serv Award, HEW, 1977; Phi Beta Kappa; numerous publications. **Business Addr:** Guest Scholar, Brookings Iushhihu, 1775 Massachusetts Ave, NW, Washington, DC 20036.

RICE, LOUISE ALLEN
Educator. **Personal:** Born Nov 21, 1940, Augusta, GA; daughter of Elnora Allen and Willie Allen; married Wilson L Rice, Apr 4, 1965; children: Wilson L Jr, Robert Christopher. **Educ:** Tuskegee Univ, BS 1963; Columbia Univ Teachers Coll, MA 1969; Univ of GA, PhD 1979. **Career:** Washington High Sch, English teacher 1963-66; Lucy Laney High School, English Teacher 1966-68; Paine Coll, instructor/reading specialist 1968-71; Lansing School Dist, instructor/reading specialist 1971-72; Paine Coll, assoc prof/asst academic dean 1972-77, 1979-81; Lamar Elem Sch, instructional lead teacher 1981-84; Augusta Coll, assoc dir of admissions 1984-88, asst prof of educ and reading 1988-, asst prof of developmental reading 1989-. **Orgs:** Adv bd Richmond Co Bd of Educ 1982-; bd dirs CSRA Economic Opportunity Authority Inc 1984-; dir Southern Region Delta Sigma Theta Sor Inc 1986-91; Educ Comm Augusta Human Relations Comm, 1989-90. **Honors/Awds:** Black Womanhood Speaker's Awd Paine Coll 1983; Distinguished Serv Awd Augusta Pan-Hellenic Council 1984; Urban Builders Awd Augusta Black History Comm 1985; Outstanding Comm Svcs, Leadership and Achievement Certificate Amer Assoc of Univ Women 1986, Educ of the Year, Lincoln League, Augusta, 1988; Distinguished Leadership Award United Negro College Fund 1990; Woman of the Year Augusta Alumnae Ch Delta Sigma Theta Sorority 1991; National Secretary, Delta Sigma Theta Sorority, Inc., 1992-. **Business Addr:** Department of Developmental Studies, Augusta College, 2500 Walton Way, Augusta, GA 30904-2200.

RICE, MITCHELL F.
Educator. **Personal:** Born Sep 11, 1948, Columbus, GA; son of Clarice Mitchell Rice and Joseph M Rice; married Cecelia Hawkins Rice (divorced); children: Colin C Rice, Melissa E Rice, Van Artis, Michael Overton; married Donna Artis. **Educ:** LA City Coll, AA 1969; CA State Univ LA, BA 1970, MS 1973; Claremont Grad Sch, PhD 1976. **Career:** Bonita Unified Sch Dist, public sch teacher 1971-76; Prairie View A&M Univ, asst prof 1976-77; Southwest TX State Univ, assoc prof of pol sci 1977-85; LA State Univ, prof of publ admin, pol sci, 1985-97; Texas A&M Univ, prof Bush School of Govt, dir Race & Ethnic Studies Inst, currently. **Orgs:** Former pres, chair-elect, natl chair Conference of Minority Pub Admn; Mem Amer Political Sci Assn; mem Natl Conf of Black Pol Scientists; mem Amer Soc for Public Admin; pres/owner Mgmt Develop & Training Consulting Serv 1980-; mem Amer Public Health Assn. **Honors/Awds:** Amer Council on Educ Fellowship in Academic Admin 1983-84; Natl Rsch Council Ford Found Postdoctoral Fellowship for Minorities 1984-85; co-author of Contemporary Public Policy Perspectives and Black Amers Greenwood Press 1984; Rockefeller Found Postdoctoral Fellowship for Minorities 1985-86; co-author "Health Care Issues in Black America," Greenwood Press 1987; "Black Health Care, An Annotated Bibliography," Greenwood Press 1987; co-author, Blacks and American Government, Kendall Hunt 1987. **Business Addr:** Bush School of Govt, Texas A&M Univ, College Station, TX 77843-4220.

RICE, NORMAN BLANN
Banking executive. **Personal:** Born May 4, 1943, Denver, CO; son of Irene Johnson Powell and Otha Patrick Rice; married Constance Williams Rice, Feb 15, 1975; children: Mian A. **Educ:** Univ of Washington, BA, communications, 1972, MPA, 1974. **Career:** KOMO TV News, news asst, editor 1971-72; Seattle Urban League, asst dir, media action proj monitor 1972-74; Puget Sound Council of Govts, exec asst, dir of govt serv 1974-75; Rainier Natl Bank, mgr of corp contribs, soc policy coord 1976-78; City of Seattle, council mem 1978-83, pres 1983-90, mayor, 1990-97; Federal Home Loan Bank of Seattle, exec vp, 1997-. **Orgs:** Chap mem, pres NW Min Commun Assn; Amer Soc of Publ Admin; Natl Acad of TV Arts & Sci; Sigma Delta Chi; Municipal League of Seattle & King Cty; bd of dirs, Allied Arts; bd of dirs, Planned Parenthood, 1978; Human Serv Comm 1978; life mem, NAACP. **Honors/Awds:** Outstanding Public Citizen, National Assn of Social Workers, 1991. **Business Addr:** Executive Vice President, Federal Home Loan Bank of Seattle, 1501 4th Ave, Ste 1900, Seattle, WA 98101-1693, (206)340-2300.

RICE, PAMELA ANN
Educator, counselor. **Personal:** Born Jun 27, 1956, Baltimore, MD; daughter of Rev Shirley Carrington and Edward Rice. **Educ:** VA State Univ, BS 1977; Coppin State Coll, MEd 1980; The Johns Hopkins Univ, Advanced degree 1982; The Amer Univ, Washington, DC, Ed.D, 1982, 1988. **Career:** Baltimore City Govt, worksite supervisor 1978; State of MD, juvenile counselor, 1978-; Prince George's Community College, Largo, MD, adjunct instructor of psychology, 1989-; State of Maryland, Baltimore, MD, adjunct instructor of rehabilitation counseling, 1990-. **Orgs:** Mem VA State Alumni Assoc Baltimore Metro Chapter 1980-, Amer Assoc for Counseling & Develop 1980-, Alpha Kappa Alpha Sorority 1982-. **Honors/Awds:** Graduate Award, Coppin State College, 1980; Service Award for Post-Doctoral Work, Howard University, 1989; Research Fellow, Howard University, 1989. **Home Addr:** 3708 Campfield Road, Baltimore, MD 21207. **Business Addr:** Juvenile Counselor, State of Maryland, 242 So Hilton St, Baltimore, MD 21207.

RICE, ROBERT C.
Elected official. **Personal:** Born Aug 27, 1923, Birmingham, AL; married Susie Leon; children: Brenda Wright. **Educ:** Southern Univ, BS 1946; OH State Univ, MA 1949; Kent State Univ, Cert in Guid 1953. **Career:** Cleveland Public Schools, teacher 1955-60, supv voc educ 1960-83; Woodmere Village, mayor. **Orgs:** Life member Alpha Phi Alpha 1965-. **Home Addr:** 3707 Avondale Rd, Cleveland, OH 44121. **Business Addr:** Mayor, Woodmere Village, 27899 Chagrin Blvd, Cleveland, OH 44120.

RICE, RONALD
Professional football player. **Personal:** Born Nov 9, 1972. **Educ:** Eastern Michigan, bachelor's degree in communications. **Career:** Detroit Lions, defensive back, 1996-. **Business Addr:** Professional Football Player, Detroit Lions, 1200 Featherstone Rd, Pontiac, MI 48342, (248)335-4131.

RICE, SIMEON
Professional football player. **Personal:** Born Feb 24, 1974, Chicago, IL. **Educ:** Univ of Illinois, bachelor's degree in speech communications. **Career:** Arizona Cardinals, defensive end, 1996-. **Business Addr:** Professional Football Player, Arizona Cardinals, 8701 S Hardy, Tempe, AZ 85284, (602)379-0101.

RICE, SUSIE LEON
City councilwoman. **Personal:** Born Dec 28, 1922, Corona, AL; married Robert Calvin Rice; children: Brenda Sue Wright. **Educ:** OH State Univ, BS Education 1948; Western Reserve Univ, MA Education 1953; John Carroll Univ, Certificate Elem Admin & Guid 1968; Cleveland State Univ, continued studies 1975. **Career:** Cleveland Bd of Educ, elem teacher 1948-69, jr/sr high guidance counselor 1969-78; Woodmere OH, city councilwoman 1978-. **Orgs:** Bd of mgmt Glenville YWCA 1962-68; bd of dirs Valley YMCA-YWCA 1969-75; pres Lambda Phi Omega Chap Alpha Kappa Alpha Sor Inc 1980-81. **Honors/Awds:** Outstanding Volunteer Serv Valley YM-YWCA bd of dirs 1975; Professional Honors Achievements Pi Lambda Theta Cleveland State Univ 1977. **Home Addr:** 3707 Avondale Rd, Cleveland, OH 44121.

RICE, WILLIAM E.
Government employee. **Personal:** Born Dec 18, 1933, Huntsville, AL; married Delores; children: Duane, Donald, Marvin. **Educ:** AL U, BS 1955; DePaul U, Grad Stud 1971. **Career:** Bur Lbr Ststcs, regl commr 1971-, dep regl dir 1970-71, asst regl dir 1967-70, regl empl ana 1962-65; OEO Chgo, asst regl mgr admin 1965-67; MI Empl Sec Commn, prog coord 1955-62. **Orgs:** Mem Am Ststcl Assn; Am Soc for Pub Admin; Chicago Guid Assn; Indstrl Reltns Rsrch Assn; mem Exec Club of Chgo; chmn Adv Com Rsvlt Univ Sch ofPub Admin; chmn Ecnmc & Mnpwr Devel Adv Com Chicago Urban Leag; chmn Rsrch Com for Chicago Cnstrctn Coord Com; mem Adv Com Curr Devel; YMCA Coll. **Honors/Awds:** Recip otstndng vc awd Chicago US Dept of Lbr 1964; auth num artcls on regl lbr mkt ana. **Military Serv:** AUS 1956-58; USAR 1958-62. **Business Addr:** 230 S Dearborn, Chicago, IL 60604.

RICH, MATTY (MATTHEW STATISFIELD RICHARDSON)
Filmmaker. **Personal:** Born 1972. **Educ:** New York University, film school, attended. **Career:** Filmmaker, Straight Out of Brooklyn, released by Samuel Goldwyn, writer, producer, director, actor, 1991; director, The Inkwell, 1994; Blacks N Progress, film production company, founder/owner, currently. **Honors/Awds:** Special Award, Sundance Film Festival, 1991; author, Short-term and Long-term Thinking, 1991. **Business Addr:** Filmmaker, Straight Out of Brooklyn, ATTN: Michael Gruber or Beth Swofford, William Morris Agency, 151 S El Camino Dr, Beverly Hills, CA 90212.

RICH, STANLEY C.
Police official. **Personal:** Born Feb 25, 1920; married Coralie. **Educ:** Morris Brown Coll, AB; Wayne State U, MA. **Career:** Detroit, MI Police Dept, second dep commr; Detroit Hlth Dept, former pvt acctnt a jr acctnt 1947-50; Mayor's Com for Human Resources Devel, sr acctnt 1964-65; Small Bus Devel Center, adminstr 1965-67; Mayor's Com for Human Resources Devel 1967; chmn police trial bd equal employ officer small & minor bus enter ofcr for police dept. **Orgs:** Mem Kappa Alpha Psi Frat; United Comm Serv of Met Detroit; bd dir St Peter Claver Comm Cntr.

RICH, WILBUR C.
Educator. **Personal:** Born Sep 28, 1939, Montgomery, AL; son of Lydia Rich and Savage Rich; married Jean; children: Rachel, Alexandra. **Educ:** Tuskegee Inst, BS 1960; Univ IL, EdM 1964, PhD 1972. **Career:** Columbia Univ, asst prof of political science; Wayne State University, Univ IL Urbana, visiting asst prof; Wesleyan Univ Middletown CT, vis lecturer; vis associate, University of Michigan; vis professor, University of Wisconsin; Dept Mnt l Hlth St IL, cnslr asst admin 1965-67; Mntl Hlth CT, asst st dir 1969-72; Wellesley College, prof, currently. **Orgs:** Mem Am Soc Pub Admin; Nat Conf Blk Pol Sci; Am Pol Sci Assn; Alpha Phi Alpha; Chi Gamma Iota; Phi Delta Kappa. **Honors/Awds:** Career Devel Chair Award, Wayne State Univ, 1989; publications: The Politics of Urban Personnel Policy, 1982; Coleman Young & Detroit Politics, 1989; Black Mayors & School Politics, 1996; The Politics of Minority Coalitions, 1996. **Military Serv:** USAF 1961-65. **Business Addr:** Professor, Wellesley College, 106 Central St, Wellesley, MA 02181.

RICHARD, ALVIN J.
Educator. **Personal:** Born Oct 14, 1932, New Orleans, LA; married Arlene Lecesne; children: Terrence, Kent, Wendy. **Educ:** Univ of IL, EdD 1972; Xavier Univ of LA, MA 1967, BS 1955; Fellow Ford Found, 1972. **Career:** Orleans Preschool School Bd, teacher 1957-65; Xavier Univ, asst dean of men 1965-66, dean of men 1966-70, dir univ administration 1972-75, dir rcrtmnt prprtn for ald hlth cars pro 1972-, dean of admsns & fncl aid 1975-; Univ of IL, staff asst 1970-72; So Univ in New Orleans, asso prof 1973-. **Orgs:** Mem Am Assn of Collgt Reg & Admsns Ofcrs; So Assn of Collgt Regs & Admsns Ofcrs; LA Assn of Collgt Regs & Admsns Ofcrs; Nat Assn of Coll Deans Regs & Admsns Ofcrs; Am Soc of Ald Hlth Profs; bd mem Yng Adlts Sprts Assn; mem Met Area Com; mem Strng Com Am Found of Negro Afrs;cons Mtn Cnsrtm on Admsns & Fncl Aid 1974-; prtcptn as pnlst spkr conf chmn for num agency 1972-74. **Business Addr:** 7325 Palmetto St, New Orleans, LA 70125.

RICHARD, ARLENE CASTAIN
Physician. **Personal:** Born Mar 1, 1955, St Martinville, LA; daughter of Mary Luna Louis Castain and Joseph Soban Castain; married Donald Ray Richard, Apr 6, 1974; children: Dawnia, Donald Jr, Sterlyn, Arlen. **Educ:** Univ of Southwestern LA, BS, BA, accounting, (Cum Laude) 1977; Howard Univ Coll of Medicine, MD 1983. **Career:** Earl K Long Memorial Hosp, internship 1983-84; Univ Medical Ctr, LSU staff physician 1985; Howard Univ Hosp, family practice resident 1985-87. **Orgs:** Mem Alpha Kappa Alpha Sor 1974-, Amer Medical Assoc. **Business Addr:** Physician, Richard Medical Clinic, 511 N Market St, Opelousas, LA 70570, (318)948-1212.

RICHARD, FLOYD ANTHONY
Physician ob/gyn. **Personal:** Born May 5, 1952, Opelousas, LA; married Robin; children: Keiana, Floyd II, Jonathan. **Educ:** Southern Univ, BS 1973; Meharry Medical Coll, MD 1981. **Career:** Conoco Oil, process control chemist 1973-74; The Upjohn Co, asst rsch chemist 1976-77; Meharry Medical College, asst prof dept ob/gyn 1985; Central North Alabama Health Svcs, chief dept ob/gyn. **Orgs:** Chairman youth div Second Ward Voters League 1976. **Honors/Awds:** Uphohn Awd in Ob/Gyn 1981; Outstanding Young Men of America 1982; Gynecologic Laparoscopist Awd 1984; AOA Med Hon Soc. **Home Addr:** 6520 Willow Springs Blvd, Huntsville, AL 35806. **Business Addr:** Chief Dept Ob/Gyn, Central North AL Health Serv, PO Box 380, Madison, AL 35758.

RICHARD, HENRI-CLAUDE
Physician. **Personal:** Born Feb 12, 1944, Port-au-Prince, Haiti; son of Christiane and Theophile; children: Maurice. **Educ:** Howard Univ Coll of Liberal Arts, BS 1968; Howard Univ Coll of Medicine, MD 1972. **Career:** Ireland Army Hospital, radiologist 1977-87; Breckenridge Memorial Hospital, radiologist 1980-94; Park duValle Health Ctr, radiologist, 1992-; Private Practice, radiologist. **Orgs:** Amer Med Assn; Kentucky Med Assn; Hardin County Med Assn; Radiological Society of North America; Amer Coll of Radiology; Amer Inst of Ultrasound in Med; Falls City Med Soc; Inter-Amer Coll of Physicians & Surgeons. **Business Addr:** Physician, 650 W Lincoln Trail Blvd, Radcliff, KY 40160.

RICHARD, R. PAUL
Lawyer. **Personal:** Born Jul 24, 1950, Washington, DC; son of Adele Mitchell Richard and Robert James Richard. **Educ:** Brown Univ, AB 1972; Georgetown Univ Law Center, JD 1976. **Career:** Georgetown Univ Law Center, asst dean 1976-78; Assoc of Amer Law Schools, assoc dir 1979-82; Law School Admin Council/Law School Admin Services, dir of special projects 1983-84, deputy exec dir 1984-86, consultant 1986-87; Goldfarb & Lipman, associate 1986-88; Brobeck, Phlegler & Harrison, associate 1989. **Orgs:** Council mem Council on Legal Educ Opportunity 1984-88, member exec comm 1985-87; mem Bar Assn of San Francisco, Comm on Minority Hiring 1989-; mem bd of dirs, 1990-, co-chair, 1991-, AIDs Legal Referral Panel. **Honors/Awds:** Natl Merit Scholar 1968; Law Fellow Georgetown Univ Law Center 1974-75; mem Barristers' Council Georgetown Univ Law Center 1975-76.

RICHARD, STANLEY PALMER
Professional football player. **Personal:** Born Oct 21, 1967, Miniola, TX. **Educ:** Univ of Texas, attended. **Career:** San Diego Chargers, defensive back, 1991-94; Washington Redskins, 1995-. **Business Addr:** Professional Football Player, Washington Redskins, 13832 Redskin Dr, Herndon, VA 22071, (703)471-9100.

RICHARDS, BEAH
Actress. **Personal:** Born in Vicksburg, MS; married Hugh Harrell. **Educ:** Attended, Dillard University; stage training, San Diego Community Theatre. **Career:** Actress, off-Broadway and stage appearances: Take a Giant Step, 1956, A Raisin in the Sun, The Miracle Worker, 1959, Purlie Victorious, 1961, The Amen Corner, Arturo Ui, 1963, The Little Foxes, 1967, One Is a Crowd, 1970, A Black Woma Speaks, 1975, Iago, An Evening with Beah Richards, 1979; film: Mahogany, 1975, The Biscuit Eater, 1972, The Great White Hope, 1970, In the Heat of the Night, 1967, Inside Out, 1986, Big Shots, 1987; numerous television appearances. **Orgs:** Actors' Equity Assoc; Screen Actors Guild; Congress of Racial Equaliy; NAACP. **Honors/Awds:** Academy Award nomination for Best Supporting Actress in Guess Who's Coming to Dinner; recip All-Amer Press Assoc Awd 1968; Black Filmmakers Hall of Fame 1974; poetry published "A Black Woman Speaks and Other Poems". **Business Addr:** Actress, Gores/Fields Talent Agency, 10100 Santa Monica Blvd, Ste 700, Los Angeles, CA 90067.

RICHARDS, DELEON MARIE (DELEON)
Recording artist, actress. **Personal:** Born Sep 18, 1976, Lake Forest, IL; daughter of Deborah Y Richards Wallace and Robert Leon Richards Jr. **Educ:** Steve Scott, Goodman Theatre; Northwestern Univ, Music Dept; Sherwood Conservatory. **Career:** Film & Television: Brewster Place, Legends from the Land of Lincoln, Patti LaBelle Gospel Special, Ebony/Jet Showcase, March of Dimes Telethon, McDonald Gospel Fest, Kelly & Co; Theatre/Stage: Polly and the Dinosaurs, World Book Encyclopedia Musical; Albums: DeLeon, 1985, Don't Follow the Crowd, 1987, Christmas, 1988, We Need to Hear from You, 1989; latest recording "New Direction," 1992; Videos: DeLeon in Concert; latest concept video recording "When," 1993; has toured the far east with The Mighty Clouds of Joy; starred in and contributed musical input for Nancy Reagan's anti-drug film, "I Believe in Me," 1986. **Honors/Awds:** Grammy Nomination (youngest artist ever to be nominated), 1986; Stellar Nomination, 1991; GMWA Award, 1988; participated in the Chicago Gospel Fest at the age of 5, 1982; recently performed for over 4,000 military recruits at Great Lakes Naval Training Center. **Business Addr:** Gospel Singer, c/o Word Records, 4800 W Waco Dr, Waco, TX 76710.

RICHARDS, EDWARD A.
Military official (retired), security professional. **Personal:** Born Dec 15, 1930, Trenton, NJ; married Barbara; children: Edward Jr, Denise. **Educ:** Univ of California at Los Angeles; Washburn Univ; Bellvue Coll; Univ of Maryland; Management Schools; USAF Sr NCO Academy. **Career:** USAF, chief mgmt & prcdrs branch, enlisted, and with exception of seven months, remained on active serv 1950-80; Golden Nugget Hotel/Casino, security, beginning 1980; Grand Hotel/Casino, asst dir of security, currently. **Orgs:** Life mem AF Sgt Assn; Human Relations Council; Enlisted Adv Council; servd Cmplnts NCO; Disabled American Veterans, 1990; American Assn of Retired People (AARP). **Honors/Awds:** Has received numerous decorations most important AF Cmmndtn 1962; two Oak Leaf Clusters 1968, 1974. **Military Serv:** USAF chf m/sgt, beginning 1950. **Business Addr:** 26 Supply Squad, Box 1512 APO, New York, NY 09860.

RICHARDS, HILDA
Educational administrator. **Personal:** Born Feb 7, 1936, St Joseph, MO; daughter of Rose Avalynne Williams Young-Ballard and Togar Young-Ballard. **Educ:** St John's Sch of Nursing St Louis, diploma 1956; CUNY, BS cum laude, 1961; Tchrs Coll Columbia U, MEd 1965; NY U, MPA 1971; Tchrs Coll Columbia U, EdD 1976; Fellow in Acad Admin Amer Council on Educ 1976-77; Inst for Educ Mgmt Harvard Univ, Cert 1981. **Career:** Dept of Psych Harlem Rehab Center, coord clinical serv div of rehab serv 1965-69; Harlem Rehab Center Dept of Psych Harlem Hosp Center, dep chief 1969-71; Medgar Evers Coll, assoc prof, dir nursing prog 1971-73; Medgar Evers Coll, prof dir nursing prog 1973-76; CUNY, assoc dean acad affairs 1976-79; OH Univ Coll of Health & Human Svc, dean 1979-86; IN Univ of PA, provost, vice pres for acad affairs 1986-93; Indiana Univ NW, chancellor, president, 1993-. **Orgs:** Board Member, Big Brothers/Big Sisters, 1989-; board member, Indiana Co Community Action, 1986-91; Pennsylvania Nurses Assn, 1986-; Economic Development Commission, 1986-; Assn of Black Women Faculty, 1988-; Assn of Black Women in Higher Education Inc, 1988-; American Nurses Assn; American Assn for Higher Education; American Public Health Assn; National Assn of Allied Health Professions; member, National Women's Studies Assn; AVANTA Network, board member, 1984-; Pennsylvania Academy for the Profession of Teaching, board member, 1990-; Pennsylvania Black Conference on Higher Education, executive committee, 1988; National Black Nurses Association, board member, 1974-77, 1983-84, 1988-91, first vice pres, 1984-88, member, 1972-; American Council on Education, Administrative Fellows Alumni, executive committee, 1982-85; NAACP, Indiana Chapter, life mem, executive committee, 1988-; Citizen's Ambulance Service, Indiana County, board member, 1987-; American Association of University Administrators; American Association of University Women; Association of Bl Nursing Faculty in Higher Education; Association of Black Women Faculty; Pennsylvania Nurses Association; Phi Delta Kappa; Sigma Theta Tau; ACE Com-

mission on Minorities in Higher Education, Diversity and Social Change; Zonta Club of Ind County; bd of dirs, Sta 56-TV; active NW Satir Inst, Execs Coun, NW, Ind; Urban League, 1993; NW Ind Forum, 1993; Bank One Regional bd, Merrillville, IN, 1994; Meth Hosp Inc, Gary, 1994; Lake Area United Way, 1994; Boys and Girls Clubs, NW IN; NW Kiwanis. **Honors/Awds:** Black Achiever Award, Black Opinion Magazine, 1989; Outstanding Woman of Color, American Nurses Assn Inc, 1990; Distinguished African/American Nurse Educator, Queens County Black Nurses' Assn, Queensborough Community College, 1991; Athena Award, Business and Professional Women's Club of Indiana, 1991; Special Recognition Award, National Black Nurses Association, 1991; Martin Luther King Grantee, NYU, NYC, 1969-70; Grant Found Grantee, Harvard Inst Ednl Mgmt, Cambridge, MA, 1981; recipient, Rockefellow Found Award, Amer Coun Edu, WA, 1976-77. **Special Achievements:** Author (with others), "Curriculum Development and People of Color: Strategies and Change," 1983; editor, "Black Conf on Higher Education Jnl," 1989-93. **Business Addr:** Chancellor/President, Indiana University NW, 3400 Broadway, Gary, IN 46408-1101.

RICHARDS, JOHNETTA GLADYS
Educator. **Personal:** Born Jul 18, 1950, Bronx, NY; daughter of Nettie James and Leo Richards. **Educ:** Virginia State Coll, BA 1972; Univ of Cincinnati, MA 1974, PhD 1987. **Career:** Trinity Coll, asst prof of history 1979-84; Univ of California Santa Barbara, lecturer Afro-Amer history 1977-78; Univ of Cincinatti, lecturer Amer history 1976-77; Northeastern Univ, adjunct instructor Afro-Am history 1971; Women's Studies California State Univ at Fresno, assoc prof 1984-88; San Francisco State Univ, assoc prof Black Studies 1988-. **Orgs:** Mem Assn for the Study of Afro-Am Life & History 1978-; mem Phi Alpha Theta Natl Honorary Frat of Historians 1974-; mem NAACP Hartford CT 1979-80;life mem Assn of Black Women Historians, 1983-; chair Far Western Region of the Assn of Black Women Historians 1986-88; Amer Historical Assoc, Pacific Coast Branch; national director, Assn of Black Women Historians, 1990-92; African American Museum and Library, Oakland, life member. **Honors/Awds:** Doctoral Fellowship, Natl Fellowship Fund, Atlanta GA 1978-79; Dissertation Fellowship, Center for Black Studies Univ of California 1977-78; Graduate Research Grant, Univ of Grad 1977; Danforth Fellowship, Univ of Cincinnati 1972-73; Mellon Research Grant 1981. **Business Addr:** Assoc Prof, Black Studies Dept, San Francisco State University, 1600 Holloway Ave, Psychology Bldg, #103, San Francisco, CA 94132.

RICHARDS, LAVERNE W.
Educational administrator. **Personal:** Born Jun 19, 1947, Gaffney, SC; divorced; children: Brant, Jerrel. **Educ:** San Jose State Coll, BA 1969; Univ of CA Berkeley, Teach Certificate 1970; Univ of Houston TX, MEd 1974, Mid-Management Administrator 1981. **Career:** Oakland Unified Sch Dist, teacher 1969-72; Delta Sigma Theta Inc, prog asst 1972; El Paso ISD, teacher 1974-76; Houston ISD, teacher 1972-74, 1977-85, asst principal 1985-. **Orgs:** Fine arts chmn Delta Sigma Theta Ft Bend 1984; coord United Way Clifton Middle Sch 1985,86,87; coord United Negro Coll Fund 1985,86,87; finance comm Houston Assoc of School Administrators 1985-; mem TX Assoc of Secondary School Principals 1985-; mem Phi Delta Kappa, Assoc of Supervision & Curriculum 1985-;mem Urban League Guild 1986-; scholarship chmn Human Enrichment of Life Prog 1987; Human Enrichment of Life Prog 1986-. **Honors/Awds:** Exec bd mem Windsor Village Elem Vanguard Parents Assoc 1983-85; HISD Instructional Adv Comm Houston 1984; Young Black Achiever of Houston Human Enrichment of Life Programs Inc 1986. **Home Addr:** 12211 Preakness Way, Houston, TX 77071.

RICHARDS, LEON
Educator, educational administrator. **Personal:** Born Jun 7, 1945, Montgomery, AL; son of Carrie Mae Smith Richards and John Richards; married Pauline Sakai Richards, Dec 31, 1969; children: Kayin Takao, Kalera Toyoko. **Educ:** Alabama State University, BS (summa cum laude), 1968; University of Hawaii-Manoa, MA, 1970, PhD, 1974. **Career:** East-West Center, University of Hawaii, Honolulu, HI, research assistant, 1970-71, 1974-75; Leeward Community College, Pearl City, HI, staff development specialist, 1975-77; Kapiolani Community College, Honolulu, HI, assistant dean of instruction, 1977-81, acting provost, 1983-84, dean of instruction, 1983-. **Orgs:** Vice president, Hawaii Assn of Staff, Program & Organizational Development, 1978-90; member, National Committee of Black Political Scientist, 1979-; member, National Council of Resource Development, 1980-. **Honors/Awds:** Alpha Kappa Mu Scholastic Honorary Society, 1966-68; Sigma Rho Sigma Scholastic Honorary Society for History Majors, 1966-68; American Council on Education Fellow in Academic Administration, 1981-82; Summer In-Residence Fellowship at National Center for Research in Vocational Education, 1979; East-West Ctr Fellows, 1993-97; Field Study Fellows to Peking University; Fulbright Study Abroad, Korea Foundation, for Field Study in China and Korea; Field Study Fellow to Peking Univ. **Home Addr:** 98-363 Puaalii St, Aiea, HI 96701. **Business Addr:** Dean of Instruction, University of Hawaii, Kapiolani Community College, 4303 Diamond Head Road, Honolulu, HI 96816.

RICHARDS, LLOYD G.
Director, educator. **Personal:** Born in Ontario;married Barbara Davenport; children: Scott, Thomas. **Educ:** Wayne State Univ, BA 1944; Yale Univ, MFA 1980. **Career:** Yale Univ Sch of Drama, dean, 1979-91; Yale Repertory Theatre, artistic dir, 1979-91; Hunter Coll, prof dept of theatre & cinema; O'Neill Ctr Nat Playwrights Conf, artistic dir 1969-; Natl Theatre Inst, teacher 1970-. **Orgs:** Soc of Stage Dirs & Choreographers, past president, 1970-; charter fellow Black Acad Arts & letters; co-chmn Theatre Panel Natl Endowment Arts; pres bd dirs Theatre Dev Fund; Rockefeller Found Playwrights Selection Com; former adv bd VISIONS KCET-TV Los Angeles; dir, teacher, lecturer, actor, announcer, advisor, found mem, These Twenty People Co Detroit; Actor's Co Repertory Detroit; Greenwich Mews Theatre NY; consultant to various foundations; professional adv groups, task forces; Actors Equity Assn, AFTRA, Dirs Guild Amer. **Honors/Awds:** Yale School of Drama, Professor Emeritus; Helen Hayes Award, Best Director, "Two Trains Running," 1992; Beverly Hills/Hollywood NAACP, Best Director Award, "The Piano Lesson," 1991; Mayor of New York City, Award of Honor for Art and Culture, 1988; Writer's Guild of America, Evelyn F Burkey Award, 1986; Middlebury College, Arts Consultant; Honorary Degrees: Albert Magnus, Doctorate, 1990; University of Hartford, Doctorate, 1991; Webster College, LHD, 1992; National Medal of Arts, Presented by President Clinton, 1993; numerous other honors and honorary degrees. **Special Achievements:** Director: Broadway, "Two Trains Running," August Wilson, 1992; "The Piano Lesson," August Wilson, 1990; "Fences," August Wilson, Tony Award, Best Director, 1987; "A Raisin in the Sun," Lorraine Hansberry, 1959; OFF Broadway, "The Lion and the Jewel," Wole Soyinka, 1977; "The Great I Am," Phillip Hayes Dean, 1972; Television, "Medal of Honor Rag," Tom Cole, 1982; "Paul Robeson," Phillip Hayes Dean, 1970; numerous others. **Military Serv:** US Air Force, 1944-45. **Business Addr:** Artistic Director, National Playwrights Conference, O'Neill Theatre Center, 234 W 44th St, New York, NY 10036.

RICHARDS, SISTER LORETTA THERESA
Religious educator. **Personal:** Born Apr 8, 1929, New York, NY; daughter of Mary Cornelius Richards Edwards and David A Richards. **Educ:** College of Mt St Vincent, New York NY, BA, 1954; Catholic Univ, Washington DC, MA, 1960; Catechetical Institute, Yonkers NY, MRS, 1984. **Career:** St Aloysius School, New York NY, teacher, 1954-55, 1957-61; St Thomas School, Wilmington NC, teacher, 1955-57; Cathedral High School, New York NY, teacher, 1961-64; FHM, New York NY, supervisor of schools, 1964-74, president of congregation, 1974-82; St Aloysius Parish, New York NY, pastoral assoc, 1982-90, pres of congregation, 1990-. **Orgs:** President of National Black Sisters Conference, 1985-89; vice president of National Black Catholic Congress, 1989-91; mem, Natl Forum on the Catechumenate, 1990-; mem, Vicariate Council of Central Harlem. **Honors/Awds:** Doctor of Pedagogy, New York College of Podiatric Medicine, 1981; Doctor of Humane Letters, College of New Rochelle, 1997. **Home Addr:** 15 West 124th St, New York, NY 10027.

RICHARDS, WILLIAM EARL
Architectural design and engineering company executive. **Personal:** Born Oct 19, 1921, New York, NY; son of Camily Deravaine Richards and John Earl Richards Jr; married Ollun Sadler, Sep 16, 1949; children: William Jr. **Educ:** Washburn Univ, BA; NY Univ, Additional Study; Officer Cand School, attended; AF Spec Weapons School, attended. **Career:** Lipsett Steel Co, gen supt 1946-49; Progressive Life Insurance agent 1949-51; NAACP, staff dir, legislative agent 1972; KS Comm on Alcoholism 1972-73; KS Dept of Soc & Rehabilitation Svcs, commn income maintenance & med asst 1973-83 retired; Richards Et Cie, pres; Myers and Stauffer CPA's, sr consultant; pres Cottonwood Technology Corporation, Kansas City KS Dec. 1988-. **Orgs:** Mem Washburn Alumni Assn, Amer Public Welfare Assn, Retired Officers Assn, Amer Defense Preparedness Assn, Assn of AUS, Alpha Phi Alpha; Sigma Pi Phi, life mem NAACP, Euclid Lodge #2 F&AM, Kaw Valley Consistory #16, Oasis Temple #29; mem Topeka Knife & Fork Club. **Honors/Awds:** KS Governor Certificate for Meritorious Service. **Military Serv:** AUS lt col 27 yrs; Asiatic-Pacific Campaign Medal; Natl Defense Medal Oak Leaf Cluster; Korean Serv Medal; 2 Battle Ser Starr; AF Expeditionary Serv Medal; Vietnam Serv Medal; Battle Star; Armed Forces Res Medal 10 yr Device; United Nations Serv Medal; Legion of Merit, Army Commend Ribbon with Pendant; 1st Oak Leaf Cluster; Good Conduct Medal; Amer Campaign Medal; Battle Service Star. **Business Addr:** President, Cottonwood Technology Corporation, Sadler Bldg, 625 Western, Topeka, KS 66603.

RICHARDS, WINSTON ASHTON
Educator. **Personal:** Born Mar 7, 1935, Chaguanas, Trinidad and Tobago; son of Leanora Nimblett and Edward Ivan Richards; married Kathleen Marie Hoolihan Richards, Apr 4, 1964; children: Ashton, Winston, Marie, Michael, Bridgette, Mary, Patricia, Edward. **Educ:** Marquette Univ, Milwaukee, WI, BSc, 1959, MSc, 1961; Univ of Western Ontario, London, Ontario, MA, 1966, PhD, 1970. **Career:** Aquinas College, Grand Rapids, MI, instructor, 1961-62; Wayne State Univ, Detroit, MI, part-time lecturer, 1962-64; University of Western Ontario, graduate assistant, 1964-69; Univ of the West Indies, Trinidad, visiting senior lecturer, 1980-81, senior lecturer, 1981-82; Penn State Univ, The Capital College, Middletown, PA, associate professor of math and statistics, 1969-; Stanford University, Department of Statistics, visiting professor, summers of 1995-97. **Orgs:** Treasurer, 1987, president, 1989-90, 1992-93, Harrisburg Chapter, American Statistical Assn; Mathematical Assn of America; Inter American Statistical Institute; Institute of Statisticians; International Statistical Institute; Pennsylvania Black Conference on Higher Education. **Honors/Awds:** Recognition Award, Harrisburg Chapter, American Statistical Assn, 1990; Recognition Award, Philadelphia African American Alumni Assn of Penn State Univ, 1990; Appreciation Award, Black Students Union of Penn State Univ, 1989-90; Recognition Award, Harrisburg Chapter, Pennsylvania Society of Professional Engineers, 1987; Fellow of the Institute of Statisticians, 1985; Miembro Honorario, LA Sociedad Venezolana de Biometria y Estadistica, 1994; Fellow of the Amer Statistical Assn, FASA, 1997; Nat Mathematics Honor Fraternity, Pi Mu Epsilon, 1960; Excellence in Teaching Award, James A Jordan, Jr Award, 1997. **Home Addr:** 2100 Chestnut St, Harrisburg, PA 17104. **Business Addr:** Assoc Prof of Mathematics & Statistics, Math Sciences Dept, Penn State Univ, The Capital College, Route 230, Middletown, PA 17057.

RICHARDS-ALEXANDER, BILLIE J.
Consultant, company president. **Personal:** Born Mar 20, Austin, TX; daughter of Johnnie M Barber Bacon and Roy A Bacon; married Castomal Alexander Sr, Jun 6, 1987; children: Roy, Dianne, Reginal. **Educ:** Huston Tillotson Coll Austin, TX, BS 1962; Univ of TX Austin, attended 1963; Scarritt Coll Nashville, attended 1966; Univ of TX Arlington, MA 1974; London School of Business, London England, 1986. **Career:** Ebenezer Bapt Ch Austin, dir educ 1960-61; Dunbar High Sch Temple, TX, tchr 1961-64; Bethlehem Ctr, asst dir 1965-66, dir 1966-73; Fed Home Loan Bank Bd Center for Exec Devel, urban program coord 1962-73; Neighborhood Housing Serv of Dallas Inc, exec dir 1973-78; Dallas Fed Svngs & Loan Assn Urban Lending Dept, vice pres/dir 1978-80, sr vice pres 1980-87; Billie Richards Associates, pres, 1987-; Dallas County, housing administrator, 1988. **Honors/Awds:** Woman of the Year United for Action Women's Affiliate of the Dallas Black C of C 1978; Comm Affairs Award Com of 100 1978; Trailblazer Award S Dallas Bus & Professional Women's Orgn 1979; International Business Fellow 1986. **Special Achievements:** First Black Female Senior Vice President of a major financial institution in the Southwest, 1980. **Business Addr:** President, Billie Richards & Associates Inc, 1517 Bar Harbor Drive, Dallas, TX 75232.

RICHARDSON, ALBERT DION
Company executive. **Personal:** Born Dec 14, 1946, New York, NY; son of Onolda Jacquelyn McKinney and Robert L McKinney; married Beverly V A Richardson, Jan 15, 1984; children: Dara, Erika. **Educ:** Mercer County Community College, Trenton, NJ, 1973. **Career:** Richardson Environmental Contracting, pres, 1986-. **Orgs:** National Association of Minority Contractors, 1986-. **Military Serv:** USMC, E-5, 1965-71.

RICHARDSON, ALFRED LLOYD
Consulting geotechnical engineer. **Personal:** Born Jan 17, 1927, Kerens, TX; married Georgia E Murphy; children: Paul G, Yllona, Victor. **Educ:** Prairie View A&M U, 1950; Univ of So CA, 1952. **Career:** Pcfc Sls Engrng Inc, vice pres copr tech servs, dir fnd tech servs 1971-76, proj engr 1963-71; LACFCD, ce asso ce asst 1952-65; CA Div of Hwys, jr civil engr 1950-52. **Orgs:** Pres LA Cncl of Blk Professional Engrs 1969-71; Lic Professional Engr CA; Engrs Cncl for Professional Devel 1970-84; ASCE Nat Com on Mnrty Progs 1975-79; asso mem Strctrl Engrs Assn CA; mem Engrng Professional Adv Cncl CA St U; mem Intl Soc of Soil Mech & Fnd Engrs; chmn ASCE LA Sect Hmn Rsrcs Devel Com 1971-77; So CA Engrng Soc Com Mnpwr Training 1970-71; adv Nat Soc of Blk Engrng Stud 2nd Anl Nat Conf CA Poly Univ Pmn 1975-76. **Honors/Awds:** Fellow Am Soc of Civil Engrs; fellow Inst for Advnc of Engring. **Military Serv:** Mltry serv 1946-47; commd ofcr 1947-53. **Business Addr:** 1402 W 240th St, Harbor City, CA 90710.

RICHARDSON, ANDRA VIRGINIA
Magistrate. **Personal:** Born Apr 16, 1954, Detroit, MI; daughter of James and Odessa Law; married William Lee Richardson, Sep 22, 1984; children: Brittney Leigh, Chelsea Anne. **Educ:** Wayne State Univ, BS, 1984; Wayne State Univ Law School, JD, 1987. **Career:** Delta Airlines, reservation sales agent, 1977-86; Oakland County Prosecutor, asst prosecuting atty, 1988-90; 52nd-1st District Court, Magistrate, 1990-. **Orgs:** Top Ladies of Distinction, Inc, exec board, recording secretary, 1993-95; Top Ladies, president, 1995-97; Jack & Jill of America, Inc, exec board, parlimentarian, 1993-95; Oakland County Chap Child Abuse and Neglect Council, executive bd/chair, 1990-94; Girl Scouts of America, board of directors, 1991-94. **Honors/Awds:** Dollars and Sense Magazine, Outstanding Business and Professional Award, 1993; National Assn of Negro Business and Professional Women Club, Inc, Professional Woman of the Year, 1993. **Business Addr:** Magistrate Andra V Richardson, 52nd 1st District Court, 48150 Grand River Avenue, Novi, MI 48374.

RICHARDSON, ANTHONY W.
Dentist. **Personal:** Born Mar 15, 1957, New York, NY; son of Harriet Boyd Brooks and Archie Richardson; children: Solunda Yvette, Sherie Odetta, Toni Charisse. **Educ:** Bucknell Univ, BS 1979; Fairleigh Dickinson Univ School of Dental Medicine, DMD 1983. **Career:** Montefiore Hospital & Medical Center, general practice resident 1983-84; Fairleigh Dickinson Univ Sch of Dental Medicine, asst dir of minority affairs 1984-86, asst prof 1984-87, asst dir of admissions 1986-87, asst dir program for grads of nonapproved dental schools 1986-87, dir of minority affairs 1986-87; Con-Court Dental Associates, Bronx, NY, owner, 1989-. **Orgs:** Charter mem Phi Beta Sigma Fraternity Iota Gamma Chap 1977; mem Amer Assoc of Dental Schools 1981-88; Acad of General Dentistry 1982-; Natl Dental Assoc 1983-; NJ Commonwealth Dental Soc 1983-; advisory bd mem Health Careers Program Montclair State Coll 1983-90; chapter advisor Phi Beta Sigma Fraternity Xi Omicron Chap 1984, 1985; graduate mem Phi Beta Sigma Frat Epsilon Sigma Chap 1984-; Greater Metropolitan New York Dental Society, 1985-. **Honors/Awds:** New York State Governor's Citation 1975; New York State Regents Scholarship 1975; Women's League of Science and Medicine Scholarship 1980, 1981; Outstanding Service Certificate Student Natl Dental Assoc 1982, 1983; NJ Society of Dentistry for Children Award 1983; NJ Commonwealth Dental Soc Award 1983; bd of trustees, Natl Dental Assn, 1989-94. **Business Addr:** Owner, Con-Court Dental Associates, 840-11 Grand Concourse, Ste 1BB, Bronx, NY 10451, (718)585-1616.

RICHARDSON, CHARLES RONALD
University admissions director. **Personal:** Born Jun 8, 1949, Bartow, FL; married Karen Janine Hill; children: Ericka, Charles Jr, Elden. **Educ:** Univ of MD-Eastern Shore, 1967-70; Univ of MD-College Park, BGS 1976-77, MEd 1984. **Career:** Haven Connuty Ctr Inc, executive dir 1974-76; Univ of MD-College Park, program & resident dir 1977-78, academic advisor 1978-80, admissions counselor 1980-84; Minority Student Education, community liaison and info coord 1984-86; Drew Univ, asst dir of admissions 1986-. **Orgs:** Urban Resources Consultants, consultant 1980-86; Kappa Alpha Psi, keeper of records 1980-84; UMCP Black Alumni Assoc, president 1984-86; UMCP Black Faculty Staff Assoc, president 1984-86. **Honors/Awds:** Winter Haven, FL Boys Club, "Man of the Year" 1976; Univ of MD-College Park, other race fellowship 1977-80; Zeta Phi Beta, "Zodiac Man of the Year" 1978; Goddard Space Flight Center, NASA-SHARP humanitarian award 1983-86. **Home Addr:** 45 Lafayette Ave #D, Chatham, NJ 07928. **Business Addr:** Asst Dir of Admissions, Drew University, 36 Madison Ave, Madison, NJ 07940.

RICHARDSON, CLINT DEWITT
Professional basketball player. **Personal:** Born Aug 7, 1956, Seattle, WA; married Vicki; children: Tiffany Jade. **Educ:** Univ of Seattle, 1979. **Career:** Philadelphia 76er's, 1979-85, Indiana Pacers, 1986-87. **Honors/Awds:** Noted for his hard style of play and defensive prowess.

RICHARDSON, DAVID PRESTON, JR.
State official. **Personal:** Born Apr 23, 1948, Philadelphia, PA; son of Elaine A Robinson Richardson and David P Richardson Sr; children: Chryledine Jones, Nikki A. **Career:** Greater Germantown Youth Corporation, Philadelphia, PA, executive director, 1970-75; Pennsylvania House of Representatives, Harrisburg, PA, state legislator, 1975-. **Orgs:** Exec dir Greater Germantown Yth Corp 1968-73; bd dir Germantown Stlmnt; adv cncl E Germantown; cncl City-Wide Black Comm; urb studies bd LaSalle Coll; Germantown Br Yng Afro-Ams; mem Black Guard; Black People's Unity Mvmnt; mem RAM; board member, City of Goal Assn; board member, African American Heritage Corporation; board member, Mayor's Office of Community Services; board member, Urban League of Philadelphia; board member, East Germantown Organization; board member, Germantown Business Assn; board member, East Germantown Assn. **Honors/Awds:** Outstanding Service Award, Children's Hospital of Philadelphia, 1990; Outstanding Service Award, Disabled Persons in Pennsylvania, 1990; Outstanding Leadership Award, National Black Caucus of State Legislators, 1990; Outstanding Legislative Service for the Community, United Cerebral Palsy Association of Philadelphia, 1990; Political Achievement Award, First District Plaza, 1990; Unselfish, Devoted and Distinguished Service Award, Life Modeling Workshop, 1991; Outstanding Leadership Award, Janes United Methodist Church, 1991; Outstanding Leadership Award, Boy Scouts of America, Inc, 1991.

RICHARDSON, DELROY M. See Obituaries section.

RICHARDSON, DERUTHA GARDNER
Educator. **Personal:** Born May 3, 1941, Muskogee, OK; married Alfred; children: Allyn Christopher, Adrian Charles. **Educ:** Muskogee Jr Coll, Muskogee OK, AA 1960; NE State Coll, Thlqh OK, BS 1962, masters degree 1964. **Career:** Muskogee High School, first black business dept head and teacher coord 1967-; Taft St Children's Home Mtn School, exec sec ged teacher 1966-67; Central High School, first black secondary business teacher 1965-66; Mtn High School, secondary business teacher 1963-65; L'Ouverature High School, teacher sec 1962-63; Atty C P Kimble, part-time private legal sec 1955-70; Muskogee County Head Start, sec bookkeeper 1966-68; YWCA Cnnrs St Coll, adult business teacher 1975-77. **Orgs:** Natl Grmmts Zeta Phi Beta Sorority Inc WA 1973-74; treas Alpha Lambda Zeta Sorority 1975-80; pres Eastern Dist Oklahoma Educ Assn 1977-78. **Honors/Awds:** First black teacher of the year, Muskogee Educ Assn 1977; teacher of the year finalist, Oklahoma Educ Assn 1977; Black Heritage Hon, Mt Calvary Baptist Church Muskogee 1977; first black fourth place and second runner-up plaques, Oklahoma Teachers 1978-80; outstanding teachers plaque, DuBois School Reunion 1980; author Dear Teacher, Carlton Press NY 1980. **Business Addr:** Assistant Principal, West Junior High School, 6400 Mathew Dr, Muskogee, OK 74401.

RICHARDSON, EARL STANFORD
University president. **Personal:** Born Sep 25, 1943, Westover, MD; son of Mr and Mrs Phillip Richardson; married Sheila Bunting; children: Eric. **Educ:** Univ of MD Eastern Shore, BA 1965; Univ of PA, MS 1973, EdD 1976. **Career:** Univ of MD, Eastern Shore, dir of career planning & placement 1970-72, acting dir admiss & reg 1970-71; Univ of PA, grad asst sch study council 1973-74; Univ of MD, Eastern Shore, dir of career planning & placement 1974-75, exec asst to chancellor 1975-82; Univ of MD System, assistant to pres 1982-84; Morgan State Univ, pres 1984-. **Orgs:** Consult Coll Placement Serv 1979; pres, bd of dir, mem Somerset Cty Head Start Prog 1974-; chap pres Alpha Phi Alpha Frat Inc 1976-79; pres Panhellenic Council of the Eastern Shore 1977-79, Alpha Kappa Mu Honor Soc Intl 1964-65; Sigma Pi Phi Fraternity Gamma Boule; member, Maryland State Board of Higher Education, 1984-; member, Goldseker Foundation, 1985-. **Honors/Awds:** Fellowship Ford Found NY 1972-75; Phi Kappa Phi Hon Soc Intl 1979-; Fellow Kellogg Found NY 1980-83. **Military Serv:** USAF Capt 4 yrs; Commendation Medal 1970. **Business Addr:** President, Morgan State University, Cold Spring La & Hillen Rd, Baltimore, MD 21239.

RICHARDSON, EDDIE PRICE, JR.
Publisher, editor. **Personal:** Born Mar 29, 1936, Carrollton, MS; son of Helen Richardson and Eddie Price Richardson; married Katherine Etta Shorter, Apr 5, 1958; children: Karen Lorriane Munds, Angela Renea. **Educ:** University of Maryland, human relations, 1954-58; McNease State College, sociology, 1964-68; Lubbock Christian University, 1968-69. **Career:** US Air Force, 1954-64; E P Richardson & Associates, management consultant, 1970-; Lubbock Opportunities Industrialization Center, executive director, 1970-74; Wyatt's Cafeteria, assistant manager, 1974-76; Lubbock Black Chamber of Entrepreneurs, founder, president, 1977-91; Southwest Digest Newspaper, publisher, editor, 1977-. **Orgs:** June Tenth Celebration Committee, organizer, 1981; Martin Luther King Celebration, organizer, 1983; East Lubbock Development Association, organizer, 1987; West Texas Black Heritage and Cultural Center, founder, 1987; East Lubbock Central Core Development Project, founder, 1988; West Texas Farmers Center and Cultural Project, organizer, 1988; East Lubbock Affordable Home Research Project, 1991. **Honors/Awds:** NAACP, Journalism Award, 1992; Merit Award, National Newspaper Award, Advertisement Original, 1983, 1984, 1985; NBC KCBD TV, Electronic Media Associates, Best Talk Show Host, 1989. **Military Serv:** US Air Force, m sgt, 1954-58, 1958-64; Natl Defense, 1954; Good Conduct; various unit citations, 1958; Bronz Star, 1964. **Business Addr:** Publisher, Editor, Southwest Digest Newspaper, 902 E 28th St, Lubbock, TX 79404.

RICHARDSON, ELISHA R.
Dentist, educator. **Personal:** Born Aug 15, 1931, Monroe, LA; married Pattye Whyte; children: Scott, Jonathan, Mark. **Educ:** Sthrn U, BS 1951; Meharry Med Coll, DDS 1955; Univ of IL Med Ctr, MS 1963; Univ of MI, 1973; Harvard U, 1973; NY Acad of Sci; University of Michigan, PhD, 1988. **Career:** SOD, asso dean chmn dept orthdntc; Meharry Med Coll, dir of rsrch sch of dent 1969-78, pres med & dent staff hbrd hosp 1971-72, rsrchr lectr cons; Univ of Colorado, prof and chairman div of orthodontics 1985-; Meharry Med College, dean, School of Dentistry, 1988-92, Regional Research Center, director, 1992-. **Orgs:** Chrmn Orthodonitc Amer Assoc Dental Sch 1972-73; pres Craniofacial Biology 1978-79; pres elect chmn bd of tst Nat Dental Assn 1980; mem Am Assn Orthdntst; Nat Dental Assn; Am Dental Assn; Am Soc of Dent for Chldrn; Intl Assn for Dental Rsrch; Am Assn for Dental Schs; Am Assn for Advanc of Sci; Crnfcl Bio Grp; Meharry Almn Assn; Univ of IL Orthdntc Almn Assn; Am Pub Hlth Assn; Am Coll of Dntsts; mem Alpha Phi Alpha; NAACP; Nshvl Urban Leag; YMCA; Nshvl Symphny Assn; Civitan Internat; pres Natl Dental Assoc 1981; chrmn Council on Education American Assoc of Orthodontists 1987. **Honors/Awds:** Beta Kappa Chi 1950; Kappa Sigma Phi 1954; Physio Soc of Upper 1/10th 1955; Omicron Kappa Upsilon 1955; named one of the 100 Most Influential Black Americans by Ebony Mag 1981; Commissioned an Arkansas Traveler by Governor Frank White 1981. **Military Serv:** USAF capt 1955-60. **Business Addr:** Director, Regional Research Center, School of Dentistry, Meharry Medical College, 1005 DB Todd Blvd, Box 33-A, Nashville, TN 37208.

RICHARDSON, ERNEST A.
Consultant. **Personal:** Born Aug 2, 1925, NYC, NY; married Olive; children: Brenda. **Educ:** Columbia Univ NY city B.A. 1952; NY Univ NY City M.B.A. 1958. **Career:** Schnly Indst, accountant 1952-60; Intl Pearl Corp, controller 1960-66; St Regis Paper Co, mgr minority affairs. **Orgs:** Bd chmn New York City Task Force on Youth Motivation; natl chmn Nat Urban Afrs Cncl; indst chmn Fisk Univ Cluster; mem bd adv TN St Univ Cluster; mem adv com Nat Task Force Youth Motivation; mem Blk Corp Caucus; adv com Nat Urban Leag Skills Bank. **Honors/Awds:** Hon Jacksonville FL Urban League 1972; hon Fisk Univ 1973; hon TN St Univ 1972; Exec of the Year, Assn of Meeting Planners 1983; Crusade Award, Amer Cancer Soc 1985; Merit Award, St Regis 1985; Natl Urban Affairs Council Appreciation 1987. **Military Serv:** USMC staff sgt 1943-46, 1950-51. **Home Addr:** 186-30 Mangin Ave, Jamaica, NY 11412.

RICHARDSON, FRANK (FRANK)
Artist. **Personal:** Born Jan 14, 1950, Baltimore, MD. **Educ:** Comm Coll of Baltimore; MD Inst Coll Art, AA; Towson St Coll Baltimore, BFA. **Career:** News Amer, 1976-; Baltimore's Black Art's Museum, dir 1976; 3rd World Prep Sch of Art, headmaster, 1975; Enoch Pratt Free Library Branch 17, painted mural interior & Exterior; Phase's Gallery, 1977; Ebony Collective, 1977. **Orgs:** Black Cultural Endowment 1974; Artist Fellowsihp Program MD Arts Council, 1977; Natl Soc of Public Poets. **Honors/Awds:** African-Amer Day Parade, 1976; advertisement, United Fed of Black Comm Org; Art show, Univ of Ife Bookshop Ltd Nigeria; stroy Cape Herald & So Afrcn Newppr; reviews of work Colorful Mural Baltimore Sun 1967, Mr Richardsons Beautiful Wall Baltimore Afro-Amer, 1972, Mus Unit to Expand New Amer 1975, NY Times Intl Exp Imp Trd Opportunity Metro Magazine, 1977. **Business Addr:** 552 Baker St, Baltimore, MD 21217.

RICHARDSON, GEORGE C.
Legislator. **Personal:** Born Feb 19, 1929, Newark, NJ. **Educ:** USAF Adminstrv Sch, grad; Jersey City Tech. **Career:** NJ St Assembly, asst minority ldr 1961-. **Orgs:** Chmn NJ Black Legsl Caucus; served on NJ St Narcotics Div Com on Inst & Agy; Com on Transp & Pub Utilities Sub-com on Hwy & Com on Taxation; pres Periscope Asso. **Military Serv:** USAF Korean War.

RICHARDSON, GILDA FAYE
Elected government official. **Personal:** Born May 8, 1926, Wichita Falls, TX; married James Richardson; children: Linda Moore, Michael Cooper. **Educ:** Southern Univ, 1943-45; Lansing Bus Univ, 1945-46; MI State Univ, 1972. **Career:** Beurmann/Marshall Adv Agency, commercial photographer 1965-68. **Orgs:** Bd mem YWCA 1967-85; bd mem/guild chairperson Lansing Urban League 1968-77; mem bd Lansing Family Health Ctr 1972, Housing Asst Found 1973-74, Office of Econ Opportunity 1973-74, Capital Area United Way 1973-78; sec/bd United Negro Coll Fund 1974-77; mem/sec Lansing Bd of Ed 1975-85. **Honors/Awds:** Community Serv Natl Assn Negro Bus Professional Women 1967; Dedicated Serv Awd Lansing Urban League 1973; Dedicated Serv Awd Ingham Cty Commiss 1979; Diana Awd Comm Serv YWCA 1980; Multicultural Awd Lansing School Dist 1982. **Home Addr:** 3024 Colchester, Lansing, MI 48906. **Business Addr:** Elected Official Secretary, Lansing School Dist, 519 W Kalamazoo, Lansing, MI 48933.

RICHARDSON, GLOSTER V.
Sports adiministrator, professional athlete (retired). **Personal:** Born Jul 18, 1941, Clarksdale, MS; son of Mary Alice Tompkins and Rev. Willie Richardson, Sr.; married Bettye Neal, Dec 27, 1966; children: Glasetta, Maury. **Educ:** Jackson State Coll, 1965. **Career:** Kansas City Chiefs, Dallas Cowboys, Cleveland Browns, professional football player; instr phys ed; dir/organizer, touch football, Chicago Public Schools, 1990-. **Orgs:** Mem Better Boys Found Benefit; works with young boys & the handicapped in many areas; Team Up, NFL Retired Players Assn; Mt. Carmel H.S. Father's Assn; vice pres, Rainbow Bench, 1991-92; dir, organizer, Touch Football, Public School of Chicago, 1990-. **Honors/Awds:** Played in 3 Super Bowl Championships; Football Hall of Fame, Jackson State Univ; NFL Alumni Award, NFL Alumni Assn, 1990-91.

RICHARDSON, HAROLD EDWARD
City official (retired). **Personal:** Born Dec 14, 1922, Portland, ME; son of Edward Richardson; married Helen J; children: Haroldeane, Lura, Carol, Robert. **Career:** Portland Boys Club, dir 1982; ME Lions Sight & Hearing Assn, chmn 1981-84; Box 61 Inc, pres 1983-84; Grant Committee, dir 1985-90; Portland Water & Sewer Dist, trustee, currently. **Orgs:** Chmn Civic Serv Police & Fire 1982; treasurer Kippy Serv Inc 1985; Democratic Precinct, committeman, precinct 38; Derring Lion's Club, past president, 1969-70; Kissimmee Lion's Club, past president, 1990-91; Florida Antique Bucket Brigade; North Star Lodge; Holy Sepulcher Consistory #17. **Honors/Awds:** Certificate of Recognition the Jefferson Awards 1984, 1985.

RICHARDSON, HENRY J., III
Educator. **Personal:** Born Mar 24, 1941, Indianapolis, IN. **Educ:** Universite de Besancon, France, Cert en Histoire, 1962;

Antioch College, AB, 1963; Yale Law School, LLB, 1966; UCLA School of Law, LLM, 1971. **Career:** Temple University, professor of law; Govt of Malawi Central Africa, international legal advisor, 1966-68; African Studies Center, UCLA, faculty africanist in law, 1969-71; School of Law, Indiana University, assistant professor, 1971-74, associate professor, 1974-; Northwestern University School of Law, visiting associate professor of law, 1975-76. **Orgs:** Chairman, National Conference of Black Lawyers Task Force on International Affairs; former rep, UNNGO; executive council, American Society of International Law, 1975-; various panels, presentations, pro mtg including NCBL Annual Mtg & panels at Annual Mtg; Indiana Bar; National Conference of Black Lawyers; American Society of International Law; World Peace Through Law Ctr, Section of International Legal Ed; AID Research Team on Law & Social Change, 1971; World Peace Through Law Con, Abidjan Ivory Cst; chairman, International Legal Education in Africa, 1973; NCBL del to Cuba to study legal inst, 1974; advisory committee, ITT International Fellowship Program; American Society of International Law Working Group on Info Systems. **Honors/Awds:** Author of numerous publications in various legal journals on International Law, African Law, Legal Ed, Law & Black People; recipient, Maxwell Afro-Asian Fellowship, 1966-68; Maxwell Writing Fellowship, 1968-69; UCLA, Ford LLM Fellowship, 1969-71; Faculty Research Fellowship, Indiana University, 1973. **Business Addr:** School of Law, Temple University, 1719 North Broad Street, Philadelphia, PA 19122-2585.

RICHARDSON, JOHNNY L.
Company executive. **Personal:** Born Jul 14, 1952, Cleveland, MS; married Mary Goins; children: Teria D; Rapahelle K. **Educ:** Ripon Coll WI, BA Econ 1974. **Career:** Miller Brewing Co, pricing analyst 1974-75, merchandising rep 1975-77, area mgr 1977-82, reg merchandising mgr 1982-. **Orgs:** Mem Natl Urban League; vice pres 1981-82; mem Chicago Merchandiser Exec Club 1982-; grad instructor Dale Carnegie Inst 1984; dir Park Ridge Jaycees 1984-85,Ripon Coll Alumni Bd 1984-87. **Honors/Awds:** Dir of the Year Chicago South End Jaycees 1980; Pres Awd of Merit Chicago South-End Jaycees 1982. **Business Addr:** Regional Merchandising Manager, Miller Brewing Co, 500 Park Blvd, Itasca, IL 60143.

RICHARDSON, JOSEPH
Owner, president. **Personal:** Born Apr 23, 1940, Kansas City, MO; son of Genevieve and Joseph; married Jacquel. **Educ:** Lincoln U, BA sociology 1964; MA Leadership, Augsburg Coll, Minneapolis, MN l989. **Career:** JR & Assocs Inc, pres 1980; The Toro Co, dir employees relations mgr 1979-80, corp mgr manpower planning 1978-79, corp training mgr 1977-78, corp employment mgr 1976-77; Mgmt Recruiters, account exec 1973-76; John Tschohl & Assocs, VP 1972-73; Butler Mfg Co, div employee relations mgr 1970-72; Butler Mfg Co, copr employment rep 1968-70; Pan Hellenic Council, pres 1978-; MN Council of Ex-offender Employment, pres 1979-; Honeywell Inc, senior human resources rep 1984-. **Orgs:** Mem Twin City Personnel Assn Vietnam Serv; Gamma Xi Lambda Alpha Phi Alpha Frat, VP 1977. **Honors/Awds:** Medal-AUS Commedation Medal/Pres Citation/Oak Leaf Cluster AUS. **Military Serv:** AUS captain l964-68. **Business Addr:** Senior Human Resources Rep, Human Resources, Honeywell Inc, Honeywell Plz, Minneapolis, MN 55408.

RICHARDSON, LACY FRANKLIN
Human resources executive. **Personal:** Born Apr 8, 1937, Lynhurst, VA; son of Roxie E Richardson Burgess and Lacy Richardson; married Regina L Crick, Mar 1, 1980; children: Darnel, Tina, Dori, Alexander. **Educ:** OH Christian Coll, BTh (Summa Cum Laude) 1972; Univ of Pittsburgh, BA (Cum Laude) 1976, MSW 1977; Bible Philosophical Intl Seminary, PhD (Summa Cum Laude) 1984; Certified Licensed Social Worker, Commonwealth of PA. **Career:** United States Steel, laborer, 1955-64; Westinghouse Air Brake, tester, 1964; Auburn & Associates, design draftsman, 1964-68; Kaiser Engineers, design draftsman, 1968-72; Mon Yough Community Svcs, Inc, dir of consultation and education, 1972-85, Mon Yough Community Servics Inc, human resources dir, 1985-; Pastoral assignments include: Mount Zion Baptist Church, West Newton PA, 1971-74; The First Baptist Church, Donora PA, 1974-78; St John Baptist Church, Wilmerding PA, 1979-81; Metropolitan Baptist Church, Northside, Pittsburgh PA, 1981-; Department of State Bureau of Professor and Occupational Affairs. **Orgs:** Governor's Justice Commission, bd of dirs; Auberle Home for Boys, bd of dirs; Counseling and Tutoring Serv, bd of dirs; Title 1, McKeesport Area School District, Parents Advisory Counsel; Baptist Ministers Conf of Pittsburgh and vicinity; Northside Pastor's Alliances, vice pres; NAACP; Research and Planning Committee, Mon Valley Health Ctr, bd of dirs; Boy Scouts of America, Long Range Study Membership Committee. **Honors/Awds:** Humanitarian Award Parents for Adult Mentally Ill 1986, Mon-Yough Community Serv Inc, Humanitarian Awd for Outstanding Achievement, 1985; Outstanding Employee Award, Mon-Yough Community Serv Inc, 1986; Outstanding Service Award, Auberle Homes for Boys, 1987; Execulink Member. **Business Addr:** Human Resources Director, Mon-Yough Community Services Inc, 500 Walnut St, 3rd Floor, Equibank Bldg, Mc Keesport, PA 15132.

RICHARDSON, LEO
Government official. **Personal:** Born Dec 19, 1931, Marion, SC; son of Ethel Richardson and Isiah Richardson; married Mary Jane Frierson; children: Sandra Jane, Alfred Leo, Beverley Lynette:. **Educ:** Morris Coll, BS 1954; Tuskegee Univ, MA 1961; SUNY at Buffalo, PhD 1985. **Career:** Morris Coll, head football & basketball coach 1961-64; Savannah State Coll, head football & basketball coach 1964-71; SUNY at Buffalo, head basketball coach & administrator 1972-84; SC Dept of Social Services, asst to commissioner 1984-86; Deputy Commissioner, 1986-. **Orgs:** Natl Assoc of Basketball Coaches, mem 1971-78; Natl Assoc of Basketball Coaches Clinic Committee, mem 1974-76; Buffalo Urban Caucus, mem 1974-78; Black Educator Assoc of Buffalo, mem 1975-76; PUSH Inc, mem 1976; Natl Assoc of Basketball Coaches Research Comm, mem 1976-78; Committee Action Organization, educational task force committee 1977-84; Buffalo Public Schools, task force on discipline chairman 1979, sports advisory committee chairman 1979-80; NAACP, board of directors 1979-82; Board of Directors Housing Assistance Center of Niagara Frontier, Inc, pres 1979-82; Dept of Education, chairman - advisory comm for single parents/homemakers & sex equity prgms 1985; Francis Burns United Methodist Church, board of trustees 1985; Leadership Columbia, 1986;Alpha Phi Alpha Frat; Morris ColleBoard of Trustees; Leadership SC Board of Regents. **Honors/Awds:** University at Buffalo Community Advisory Council, Community Service Staff Award 1983; Black Educators of the Niagara Frontier, Community Service Award 1984-85; Man of the Year Award, Alpha Phi Alpha, 1987. **Military Serv:** US Army, specialist third class. **Home Addr:** 241 King Charles Rd, Columbia, SC 29209. **Business Addr:** Assistant to Commissioner, SC Dept of Social Services, PO Box 1520, Columbia, SC 29202.

RICHARDSON, LEROY
Professional sports official. **Career:** NBA, referee, currently. **Business Addr:** NBA Official, National Basketball Association, 645 5th Ave, 15th Fl, New York, NY 10022-5986.

RICHARDSON, LINDA WATERS
Consultant. **Personal:** Born Nov 21, 1946, Philadelphia, PA; daughter of Bertha Stovall and Lester Waters; married Albert J Pitts; children: Aissia, Tarik, Monifa, Mariama. **Educ:** Overbrook HS, Business 1964; New Hampshire College, MS, 1990. **Career:** BEDC Inc, asst dir 1971-73; Peoples Fund, coord 1973-74; Philadelphia Clearing House, dir 1974-81; Black United Fund, exec dir 1982-89, pres/CEO, 1989-. **Orgs:** Mem Natl Black United Fund 1983-89; mem Willingboro Home & Sch 1986; mem adv comm Episcopal Comm Svcs; mem Interfaith Revolving Loan Fund; mem, Women in Philanthropy, Assn of Black Foundation Executives. **Honors/Awds:** Merit Chapel of 4 Chaplains 1985; Comm Leadership Awd Comm Leadership Seminars 1985; Minority Mental Health Advocacy Task Force Award 1989.

RICHARDSON, LOUIS M.
Government official, minister. **Personal:** Born Nov 7, 1927, Johnstown, PA; married Allie; children: April, Louis III, Emmett, Alan T, Hope C, Peter, Holly A. **Educ:** Livingstone Coll, AB 1952-55; Hood Theological Seminary NC, bD 1958. **Career:** City of Paterson City Hall, affirmative action coordinator 1976-; Paterson CETA Program, dir 1973-76; Martin Luther King Comm Center, dir 1970-73; NJ StateEmployment Serv, counselor 1967-70; First AME Church, minister 1964-; OIC, pres 1970-71; Paterson Bd of Ed, vP 1969-74. **Orgs:** Mem Paterson Rotary #70 1970-74; pres Alpha Phi Alpha Frat. **Honors/Awds:** 1976-77; Citizenship Award Paterson Teachers Assn 1971. **Business Addr:** City of Paterson, City Hall Ellison, Paterson, NJ 07505.

RICHARDSON, LUNS C.
Educator. **Personal:** Born Apr 29, 1928, Hartsville, SC. **Educ:** Bendict Coll, AB 1949; Columbia Univ Teachers Coll, MA 1958. **Career:** Denmark Tech Educ Ctr, dean 1949-64; St Helena HS, prin 1964-66; Wilson HS, prin 1966-67; Benedict Coll, staff/acting pres 1967-73; Voorhees Coll,vice pres, 1973-74; Morris Coll, pres 1974-. **Orgs:** Chmn Com on Rsch & Special Proj, Southern Assoc of Colls & Schs; bd of dirs SC State C of C; mem bd of dir Sumter C of C; mem Wateree Comm Actions Bd; adv bd Citizens & Southern Bank of Sumter; mem Omega Psi Phi Frat, NAACP, NEA, AAHE, Amer Acad of Polit & Social Sci, SC Educ Assoc, Sumter Co Econ Develop Admin Com, Sumter Human Relations Cncl. **Honors/Awds:** Mem Alpha Kappa Mu Honor Soc, Phi Delta Kappa; Hon Ped D Benedict Coll; Hon LHD Morris Coll; Citation Links Inc 1973; Citation Voorheez Coll BD of Trustees 1974. **Business Addr:** President, Morris College, 100 W College Street, Sumter, SC 29150-3599.

RICHARDSON, MADISON FRANKLIN
Surgeon. **Personal:** Born Dec 26, 1943, Prairie View, TX; son of Dr & Mrs William Richardson; married Constance; children: Kelly, Kimberly, Karen. **Educ:** Howard Univ, BS 1965, MD 1969. **Career:** Walter Reed Hosp, chief, head & neck surgery 1974-76; Martin Luther King Hosp, chief head & neck surgery 1977-. **Orgs:** Bd chair Los Angeles Urban League 1984-87; pres Charles Drew Med Soc 1984-85; chief surg serv Daniel Freeman Hosp 1986-87; pres bd chair Natl Urban League 1986; mem CA Medical Bd 1987-; bd dir Charles Drew Medical School 1988; bd dir Salerni Collegium; Alpha Omega. **Honors/Awds:** Mem of Distinction Los Angeles AME Church 1982; Meritorious Awd LA NAACP 1983; dist alumnus Howard University 1987; Appointee of Governor to California Medical Board, 1988. **Military Serv:** USA, Lt col, 1968-77. **Business Addr:** Surgeon, 6200 Wilshire Blvd, Ste 908, Los Angeles, CA 90048.

RICHARDSON, MARY MARGARET
Educational adminstrator. **Personal:** Born Feb 19, 1932, Christian County, KY. **Educ:** KY Community College, Hopkinsville, AA, 1970; Valdosta State College, BSN, 1973; Medical College of GA, MSN, mental health/psych nursing, 1974. **Career:** Brooks Hosp, ofc nurse, 1952-72; Western KY State Mental Hosp, clin nurse, 1956-71; Jennie Stuart Memorial Hosp, private duty nurse, 1970-71; Col Manor Hosp, part time head nurse, 1974-75; School of Nursing, Univ of N AL Florence, asst prof, 1974-75; Grad School of Nursing, Med College of Augusta GA, asst prof, 1975; Valdosta State Coll, asst prof nursing, 1975-78, assoc prof nursing, 1978-80, asst dir nursing, 1980-, dept head, undergrad studies. **Orgs:** Natl League for Nursing; Amer Nursing Assn; GA League for Nursing; GA Nurses Assn; KY Fed of LPN; Amer Assn of Univ Prof; Amer Assn of Univ Women; task force leader, Faculty Devel Proj, SREB at Valdosta State; Sigma Theta Tau, Epsilon Pi Chap; PDK; ODK. **Honors/Awds:** Federal Traineeship Scholarship, 1973. **Business Addr:** Dept Head, Undergraduate Studies, Valdosta State College, Division of Nursing, Valdosta, GA 31601.

RICHARDSON, MATTHEW STATISFIELD. **See RICH, MATTY.**

RICHARDSON, NOLA MAE
Medical administrator, poet. **Personal:** Born Nov 12, 1936, Los Angeles, CA; daughter of Jessie Mae Anderson Smith and Oscar Smith; divorced 1969; children: Nolan, Virgil, Anthony, Julie, Dawn. **Educ:** Compton Junior College, Compton CA, certificate in management, 1973. **Career:** North American Rockwell, Downey CA, administrative secretary, 1954-70; Drew Postgraduate Medical School, Los Angeles CA, administrative assistant, 1970-73, 1974—; Central Medical Group, Los Angeles CA, executive secretary and supervisor, 1973-74; poet. **Honors/Awds:** Author of When One Loves: The Black Experience in America, Celestial Arts, 1974; author of Even in a Maze, Crescent, 1975. **Home Addr:** 10426 Crenshaw Blvd, #1, Inglewood, CA 90303. **Business Addr:** Drew Postgraduate Medical School, 12012 Compton Ave, Los Angeles, CA 90059.

RICHARDSON, NOLAN
College basketball coach. **Personal:** Born Dec 27, 1941, El Paso, TX; married Rose; children: Madalyn, Bradley, Nolan III, Yvonne (deceased), Sylvia. **Educ:** Univ of TX at El Paso, BA, 1964. **Career:** Univ of Arkansas, head basketball coach, 1986-. **Orgs:** American Red Cross, bd of dir; Easter Seal, chairman. **Special Achievements:** Second African-American coach to win the NCAA title, 1994; First college coach to win the NCAA Natl Invitational Tournament and community college natl championships. **Business Addr:** Head Basketball Coach, University of Arkansas, PO Box 7777, Fayetteville, AR 72701.

RICHARDSON, ODIS GENE
Educator, freelance writer. **Personal:** Born Nov 29, 1940, Lakes Charles, LA; son of Estella Scott Richardson and Lucky Sip Richardson; children: Ron Pressley, Odis G II. **Educ:** Univ of Tampa, BS 1965; Chicago State Univ, MA 1971; Roosevelt Univ, MS 1983; Northwestern Univ, post graduate studies. **Career:** Boy Scouts of Amer, executive 1965-66; Dept of Public Assistance, social caseworker 1966-67; Chicago Public Schools, teacher 1967-; free lance writer, currently. **Orgs:** Public relations chmn IL Speech & Theatre Assoc 1985-86; pres bd of dirs Maranatha Youth Ministries 1985-87; fellow Northwestern Univ 1986; mem IL Council on Exceptional Children; dir Richardson Special Educ Consultants; mem Phi Beta Sigma, Phi Delta Kappa, Chicago Urban League, NAACP; deacon South Shore Bible Baptist Church; mem Emergency Land Fund; bd of dirs Chicago Citizens Schools Committee 1987-89; fellow Foundation for Excellence in Teaching 1986-89; research linker Chicago Teacher's Union, Educational Research & Development; volunteer Project Image, Man-Boy Conference 1988-89; precinct captain, Fourth Ward Regional Democrats 1981-; teacher sponsor PAPPA Club, Pan African Pen Pal Assn 1988-89; writer/diarist, Catalyst Magazine-Chicago School Reform, 1990-91; Don Nash Community Center, board of dirs; Maranatha Youth Ministries Head Start, board of dirs. **Honors/Awds:** DuSable Man of the Year DuSable High School Chicago 1985; South Shore Outstanding Community Volunteer 1986; Golden Apple Awd 1986; Leadership, Illinois Council on Exceptional Children 1989; Volunteer, DuSable Museum of African-American History 1987; Volunteer Award, Pace Institute, Cook County (Jail) Dept of Corrections 1979; Educator of the Month-Jan 91, Coca Cola Bottling Co, 1991; Celebration of Excellence in Teaching-Organizer, 1991; Blum-Kolner Outstanding Teacher Award (Univ of Chicago). **Special Achievements:** Featured on the Home Show (Natl TV); Student Cultural Exchange Program; Proposal Writer School granted over 1 million dollars from proposals. **Military Serv:** USAF A/2C

admin spec 4 yrs; Distinguished Airman Award. **Business Addr:** Chicago Public Schools, DuSable High School, 4934 So Wabash, Chicago, IL 60609.

RICHARDSON, OTIS ALEXANDER
Health care company executive. **Personal:** Born Jan 16, 1943, Newport News, VA; son of Mildred C Richardson and Carey D Richardson; married Corrine Foots, Dec 4, 1965; children: Otis Alexander II, Shamagne Nicole. **Educ:** Hampton University, BS, accounting & finance, 1965; Pace University, MBA, executive management, 1978. **Career:** Johnson & Johnson, national sales mgr, 1979-80, director, sales planning & development, 1980-82, director, professional markets, 1982-83, director, new product development, 1983-85, group product director, 1985-86; Oral Health USA, Inc, president/chief executive officer, 1986-. **Orgs:** National Association of Accountants, 1965-72; National Association of Dental Laboratories, steering committee, 1985-86; National Dental Association, corporate sponsor, 1986-92; American Academ of Dental Group Practices, 1981-89; Dental Group Management Association, 1987-90. **Honors/Awds:** Pace University, GSB, National Honor Society, 1978; National Dental Association, Clinician Commerative Award, 1983; MAC Dental Technology, Clinician Commerative Award, 1985. **Special Achievements:** Clinical Presentation & Seminar, Use of Color in Dentistry, 1991, State of Art-Dental Restoratives, 1990; Marketing Techniques for Dental Labs, 1984-86; Practice Building for Dental Groups, 1980-84; "Make That Dental Center Your New Account," Dental Lab Review, 1986. **Military Serv:** US Army, captain, 1966-68. **Home Addr:** 32 Coventry Circle, Piscataway, NJ 08854, (908)572-4308. **Business Addr:** President/CEO, Oral Health USA, Inc, 255 Old New Bunswick Rd, Ste S-30, Piscataway, NJ 08854, (908)981-9440.

RICHARDSON, POOH (JEROME JR.)
Professional basketball player. **Personal:** Born May 14, 1966, Philadelphia, PA. **Educ:** Univ of California at Los Angeles, Los Angeles, CA, 1985-89. **Career:** Minnesota Timberwolves, guard, 1989-92, Indiana Pacers, 1992-94; Los Angeles Clippers, 1994-. **Honors/Awds:** NBA All-Rookie First Team, 1990. **Business Addr:** Professional Basketball Player, Los Angeles Clippers, Los Angeles Sports Arena, 3939 S Figueroa St, Los Angeles, CA 90037, (213)748-8000.

RICHARDSON, RALPH H.
Attorney. **Personal:** Born Oct 12, 1935, Detroit, MI; son of Lucinda Fluence Richardson (deceased) and Ralph Onazime Richardson (deceased); children: Traci, Theron (deceased), Cassandra Jo Williams, Arvie Lyn Williams, Tanya Elaine Hunter (divorced). **Educ:** Wayne St U, BA 1964; Wayne St Law Sch, JD 1970. **Career:** City of Detroit, clerk, public aid worker 1956-65; Ford Motor Co, sr labor rel rep 1965-70, wage admin 1966, labor rel rep 1967; Citizens Urban Opportunity Fund, dir 1970; Brown Grier & Richardson PC, sr partner 1970-71; Richardson & Grier PC, sr partner 1971-73; Stone & Richardson PC, labor arbitrator, sr partner 1973-. **Orgs:** Wolverine Bar Assns; Am Arbitration Assn; MI Trial Lawyers Assn; Am Judicial Soc; MI Criminal Defense Lawyers; Phi Alpha Delta, Kappa Alpha Psi; Smithsonian Inst; Natl Geographic Soc; Recorder's Ct Bar Assn; Labor Arbitrators; Am Arbitration Assn; Mason; Grtr Detroit Chamber of Commerce; Palmer Woods Assn; Econ Club of Detroit; Renaissance Club; Detroit Bar Assn, Natl Bar Assn, State Bar of MI, Amer Bar Assn, Amer Trial Lawyers Assn, MI Assn of the Professional, Boy Scouts of Amer, Jr Vice Polemarch Northern Reg; appointed by Gov to serve on bd of appeals for Hosp Bed Reduction in SE MI 1982; appointed special asst atty general by Frank J Kelley, Atty General for the State of MI 1984; exec bd, Detroit Golden Gloves Inc; bd of dir, Legal Aid& Defenders Assn 5; past master, Hiram Lodge #1 1986; commander-in-chief, Wolverine Consistory #6 1988; Marracci Temple #13, past potenate, past imperial potentate, imperial legal advisor, Shriners, 1988; David Leary Lodge #6, GEM, knight templar, 1989; Optomist Club, 1990-; Michigan State Bar Fellow, 1990-. **Honors/Awds:** Cert of Appreciation Native Amer Strategic Serv 1976; MI State Bar Young Lawyers Sect Prison Proj Serv Awd 1977; Awd of Merit Mother Waddles Perpetual Mission 1979; Distinguished Recognition Awd Detroit City Council 1981; Spirit of Detroit Awd 1981, Honored Citizen Awd Mayor Coleman Young, Distinguished Detroit Citizen Awd 1981; Office of the City Clerk James Bradley 1981; life membership NAACP 1983; contributing supporter Golden Heritage (NAACP) 1989; appointed to committee on Child Care Homes by City Council member Mehaffey 1988-89. **Military Serv:** AUS sp4 1958-60. **Business Addr:** Labor Arbitrator, Sr Partner, Stone & Richardson PC, 2910 East Jefferson, Detroit, MI 48207.

RICHARDSON, RHONDA KAREN
City official. **Personal:** Born Dec 8, 1956, Louisville, KY; daughter of Dorothy Bryant Richardson and Charles Robert Richardson. **Educ:** Fisk University, Nashville, TN, BA, psychology; University of Louisville, JD, 1987. **Career:** City of Louisville, alderman, 1990-. **Business Addr:** Alderman, Board of Louisville, 601 W Jefferson St, Third Floor, Louisville, KY 40202.

RICHARDSON, ROBERT EUGENE
Attorney. **Personal:** Born Jul 16, 1941, Kansas City, MO; son of Genevieve Richardson and Joseph Richardson; married Shirley Ann Durham; children: Kerri L, Patrick G. **Educ:** Rockhurst Coll, KC, MO, 1959-62; Georgetown Univ, Washington, DC, AB 1972; Georgetown Univ Law School, JD 1975. **Career:** US Dept of Justice, special asst to the asst atty gen 1978; Georgetown U, asst to the exec vice pres 1970-74; US General Service, asst legal policy coordinator 1975-76; US Dept of Justice, trial atty 1976-78; Civil Div US Dept of Justice, sr trial atty 1979-85; Howard Univ, exec asst to vice pres for legal affairs & general counsel 1985-86, private practice, atty, 1986-94; US Dept of Veteran Affairs, aty, currently. **Orgs:** Alpha Phi Alpha Fraternity. **Honors/Awds:** Academic Fellow Whitney M Young 1973-75. **Military Serv:** AUS captain 1963-70; USAR 1970-84. **Home Addr:** 1371 Underwood St NW, Washington, DC 20012, (202)726-3131.

RICHARDSON, ROGER GERALD
Educational administrator. **Personal:** Born Dec 23, 1953, Chicago, IL; son of Ella Brown Richardson and Eddie Richardson. **Educ:** University of Wisconsin-Stout, BA, psychology, 1976, MS, counseling and guidance, 1979; New York University, PhD candidate. **Career:** Univ of Wisconsin-Stout, coordinator, educ & culturals enrichment ctr, 1976-79, dir, black student services, 1979-80; Cornell Univ, admin mgr/counselor, College of Human Ecology, 1980-84, acting dir, counseling services, College of Human Ecology, 1983, assoc dir, minority educ affairs & state programs, 1984-85; Dartmouth College, asst dean of residential life, 1986-88; New York University, director, African-American Student Services, 1988-. **Orgs:** Chair, Affirmative Action Task Force; member, University Personnel Policy Committee, chair, Educational Opportunity Advisory Board, member, Alcohol Policy Committee, member, Academic Review Committee. **Honors/Awds:** Outstanding Alumni Award, 1992. **Business Addr:** Director, African American Student Services, New York University, 566 La Guardia, Loeb Student Center, Room 623, New York, NY 10012.

RICHARDSON, RUPERT FLORENCE
Government official (retired), consultant. **Personal:** Born Jan 14, 1930, Navasota, TX; daughter of Albert S Richardson (deceased) and Mary E Samuels Richardson; divorced; children: Gaynell V, Marilyn Joy, James A III, Marlon Richardson, Thomas Kennedy II, Tanya C, Jaquetta B, Todd Samuels. **Educ:** Southern Univ, BS, 1952; McNeese State Univ, MED, 1962. **Career:** Louisiana Dept of Labor, master counselor, 1965-74; Dept of Health & Hospitals, deputy asst secretary, 1974-94, planning consultant, 1997-; Office of Alcohol and Drug Abuse, deputy asst secretary to the state, 1992-94; Rupert Richardson & Associates, pres/CEO, 1994-. **Orgs:** Governor's Council for Drug Free Schools and Communities; National Assn of State Alcohol and Drug Abuse Directors; Alpha Kappa Alpha Sorority; Top Ladies of Distinction Inc; Coalition of 100 Black Women; Council For a Better Louisiana; Shiloh Baptist Church; NAACP, national pres, 1994-96, national life membership coalition, 1996-; US Commission on Civil Rights; Louisiana Commission on Human Rights, commissioner. **Honors/Awds:** Phi Beta Sigma Fraternity, Louisiana Citizen of the Year, 1984; Southern Univ, Outstanding Alumnus, 1984; Louisiana Capitale Links, Human Rights Award, 1993; Louisiana Women's Political Hall of Fame, 1995; Colorado Tech Univ, Honorary Doctorate, 1996. **Home Addr:** 10334 Sunny Cline Dr, Baton Rouge, LA 70814, (504)275-9059.

RICHARDSON, SALLI
Actress. **Career:** Actress; Roles include: I spy; How U Like Me Now; Sioux City; Posse; A Low Down Dirty Shame; Guest appearance, Roc; TV miniseries True Women, 1997.

RICHARDSON, SCOVEL
Judge. **Personal:** Born Feb 4, 1912, Nashville, TN; married Inez; children: Elaine Harrisingh, Alice Inez, Mary Louise Johnson, Marjorie Linda Forsythe. **Educ:** Univ of Illinois, BA, MA; Howard Univ, JD 1937. **Career:** US Customs Ct, judge beginning 1957; 3d Div, presiding judge 1966-70; US Bd of Parole Washington, chmn 1954-57; Office of Price Administration, Washington, sr atty 1943-44; dean prof law 1944-53; Lincoln Univ, asso prof law 1939-43; Lawrence Richardson, atty 1938-39. **Orgs:** Mem, American Law Inst, American Bar Assn, American Judicature Soc, Inst of Judicial Adminstrn, Nat Bar Assn, Federal Bar Assn, MO Bar Assn, Bar Assn of St Louis; judiciary mem Assn of Bar of the City of New York; 2nd vp Bd of Govs New Rochelle Hosp Med Center; trustee, Colgate Univ Howard Univ, Nat Council on Crime & Delinquency. **Honors/Awds:** Recip Cit Urban League St Louis 1953; Alumni Award Howard Univ 1958; Nat Bar Assn 1967; Wisdom Award of Honor 1970; Intl Trade Serv Award 1973; cert in Appreciation of Merit Serv Standing Com Customs Law of Am Bar Assn 1974. **Business Addr:** Judge, US Customs Court, One Federal Plaza, New York, NY 10007.

RICHARDSON, TIMOTHY L.
Organization executive. **Personal:** Born Jul 28, 1958, Los Angeles, CA; son of Christeale Dandridge and Irving Berlin Richardson; children: Camille, Charles, Bradley. **Educ:** West Los Angeles College, AA, 1980; Chapman Univ, Orange, CA, BS, marketing, 1986. **Career:** Boys & Girls Club of Tustin, CA, program director, 1980-85; Boys & Girls Clubs of America, North Hollywood, CA, coordinator, Olympic Sport Program, 1985-89, New York, NY, then Atlanta, GA, assistant director, National Program Services, 1989-94, National Prog Svcs, director, 1994-96, sr director, 1997-. **Orgs:** United States Olympic Committee, board of directors, 1989-, Athlete Identification and Development Committee, 1990-93, Education Committee, 1993-; United States Table Tennis Association, Executive Committee, 1986-91; US Olympic Academy XI, delegate, 1987; Intl Olympic Academy, Olympia Greece, head of US delegation, 1992; Centennial Olympic Games, assistant envoy, 1996; Women's Sports Foundation, bd of dirs, 1990-; Cultural Enrichment Foundation, associate; President's Council on Physical Fitness and Sports, Natl Strategic Planning Forum, panelist, 1993. **Honors/Awds:** New Zealand Symposium on Sports Psychology, University of Waikato, NZ, presenter, 1988; Sports Spirit Newspaper, founding editor, 1987-90; National Youth Sports Coaches Association, Coach of the Year, 1983; Escorted 1996 Olympic Team to the White House, 1996; Womens Sports Foundation, President's Awd, 1995. **Special Achievements:** Secured a $3 million congressional grant to serve children of Desert Storm war; author, Boys and Girls Club Guide to Military Outreach; negotiated with US Air Force, Marine Corps & Navy to convert on-base youth centers into Boys and Girls Clubs, 1995-96; US Olympic Congress, presenter, 1994; NIKE Kids Movement Summit, organizer, 1993; NIKE PLAY Daily, Natl Youth Fitness Program, co-creator/project manager; US Information Agency, Assn for Better Zambian Youth Project, consultant, 1993; Inkanta Freedom Party Youth Brigade, consultant; Nike Youth Sports Summit, organizer, 1996. **Business Addr:** Sr Assistant Director, Prog Svcs, Boys & Girls Clubs of America, 1230 W Peachtree St, Atlanta, GA 30309.

RICHARDSON, VALERIE K.
Market analyst, evaluation specialist. **Personal:** Born Aug 5, 1955, Oakland, CA; daughter of Clarice Reynolds and Clyde Reynolds Sr; married Victor E Richardson II, Feb 14, 1981; children: Whitney K, Victor E III. **Educ:** San Jose State University, BA, 1981. **Career:** Ketchum Communications, research assistant, 1978-81; McKesson Corp., project manager, 1982-86; Mervyn's Corp., media/market planner, 1986-87; Pacific Gas & Electric Co., market analyst, 1988-, evaluation/quaility control specialist, 1991-. **Orgs:** American Association of Blacks in Energy; American Marketing Association. **Business Phone:** (415)973-7000.

RICHARDSON, WALLACE HERMAN, JR.
Professional football player. **Personal:** Born Feb 11, 1974. **Educ:** Penn State Univ, bachelor's degree in administration and justice, 1996. **Career:** Baltimore Ravens, quarterback, 1997-. **Business Addr:** Professional Football Player, Baltimore Ravens, 11001 Owings Mills Blvd, Owings Mills, MD 21117, (410)654-6200.

RICHARDSON, WAYNE MICHAEL
Attorney. **Personal:** Born Sep 22, 1948, Philadelphia, PA. **Educ:** Cheyney State Coll, BA 1970; Temple Univ Law Sch, JD 1976. **Career:** PA Dept of Education, regional legal counsel 1976-83; PA State System of Higher Educ, chief legal counsel 1983-95; Rutgers Univ, Dept of General Services, asst counsel, 1995-96. **Orgs:** Mem Natl Assn of Coll & Univ Attys 1977-; mem Alpha Phi Alpha Frat 1968-. **Honors/Awds:** Distinguished Service Awd, United Cerebral Palsy Assn of the Capital Area, 1996; Distinguished Service Awd, Bd of Trustees, Pennsylvania Faculty Health and Welfare Trust Fund, 1995. **Business Addr:** Employment & Labor Counsel, Rutgers Univ, Winants Hall, 7 College Ave, New Brunswick, NJ 08901.

RICHARDSON, WILLIAM J.
Spirits & wine importer executive. **Personal:** Born Apr 30, 1933, Suffolk, VA; married Gertrude Flood; children: Traci L. **Educ:** VA State Coll, BS 1954. **Career:** Schieffelin & Co, metro sales mgr 1981-84, sales serv dir 1984-85, dir urban market develop 1985-87, vice pres urban market development 1987-. **Orgs:** Bd of dirs Prince Hall Day Care 1971-, United Mutual Insurance Co 1977-; mem Natl Assoc Mktg Developers, NY Sales Executive Club. **Honors/Awds:** NAACP Freedom Awd; Man of the Year Negro Business & Professional Women; Achievement Awd Amer Cancer Soc; Black Achievers Awd Harlem YMCA; Support to Youth Awd New York City. **Home Addr:** 144 Stuyvesant Rd, Teaneck, NJ 07666.

RICHIE, LEROY C.
Attorney. **Personal:** Born Sep 27, 1941, Buffalo, NY; son of Mattie Allen Richie and Leroy C Richie; married Julia C Thomas, Jun 10, 1972; children: Brooke, Darcy. **Educ:** City Coll of New York, BA 1970; New York Univ Sch of Law, JD 1973. **Career:** White & Case NY, attorney 1973-78; Federal Trade Commn, dir NY regional office 1978-83; Chrysler Corp, asst general counsel 1983-84, assoc general counsel 1984-86, vice pres/general counsel.; US Golf Assn, general counsel, currently. **Orgs:** Chmn, Visiting Nurse Association; chmn, Highland Park Development Corporation; bd mem, Marygrove College; bd mem, St Josephs Hospital, Pontiac; bd mem; Detroit Bar Foundation. **Honors/Awds:** Valedictorian, City College of New

York 1970; Arthur Garfield Hays Civil Liberties Fellowship, New York Univ Law School 1972. **Military Serv:** AUS sp4e4 4 yrs. **Home Addr:** 1900 West Lincoln, Birmingham, MI 48009.

RICHIE, LIONEL BROCKMAN, JR.
Singer/songwriter. **Personal:** Born Jun 20, 1950, Tuskegee, AL; son of Alberta Foster Richie and Lionel Brockman Richie, Sr; married Brenda Harvey, 1975 (divorced); children: Nicole; married Diane Alexander; children: Miles Brockman. **Educ:** Tuskegee Univ, graduated 1974. **Career:** Mem of musical group The Mystics (name later changed to The Commodores); Brockman Music, Los Angeles, CA, pres; songwriter, composer of theme song for movie "Endless Love,"; writer and producer of: "Lady," "All Night Long," "Truly," "Can't Slow Down," "Say You, Say Me," "Dancing on the Ceiling," "Easy," "Three Times a Lady," "Still," "Sail On.". **Orgs:** Mem UNCF, Amer Soc of Composers Authors and Publishers, Natl Acad of Recording Arts and Sciences, Amer Acad of Motion Picture Arts & Sciences, Natl Assn of Songwriters. **Honors/Awds:** 3 Platinum Albums; 4 Gold Albums; Grammy nominee 18 times; Amer Music Award, 1979, 1982(2), 1983(2), 1984, 1985(2), 1987(4); People's Choice Award for best song, 1979, 1980, 1982, 1983, 1986, and for best composer, 1981; Natl Music Publications award, 1980, 1981, 1984; Best Young Artist in Film, 1980; Grammy Award, 1982(2), 1985, 1986; Amer Movie Award, 1982; NAACP Image Award, 1983(2), NAACP Entertainer of Year Award, 1987; Black Gold Award, 1984(3); ASCAP Writer of Yr, 1984, 1985, 1986, ASCAP Publisher of Year, 1985, ASCAP Pop Award, 1987; Man of Yr, Children's Diabetes Foundation, 1984; Alumnus of Yr, United Negro Coll Fund, 1984; 1985 ABAA Music Awd for efforts in conceiving and giving leadership to USA and Africa, producing the album and video "We Are theWorld"; honorary DMus, Tusee Univ, 1986; Academy Awd (Say You, Say Me), 1986; Golden Globe Awd, 1986; American Music Academy Awd, 1987(2); Favorite Male Vocalist, Soul/R&B Award, American Music Academy, 1987.

RICHIE, SHARON IVEY
Military nurse. **Personal:** Born Dec 14, 1949, Philadelphia, PA; daughter of Helen L Oglesby Richie (deceased) and William Joseph Richie Sr; married Paul A Henri. **Educ:** Wagner Coll, BS Nursing 1971; Univ of TX Grad Sch of Nursing, MSN 1976; military educ, AMEDD Officer Basic Course 1971, Psychiatric Mental Health Clinician Course 1972, Clinical Head Nurse Course 1973, Alcoholism Orientation Course 1977, AMEDD Officer's Adv Course 1979, Combat Psychiatry Course 1980, Command and Genl Staff Coll 1982, Field Combat Nursing Course 1984; US Army War College, Carlisle PA, Diploma 1987-88; George Washington Univ, Washington, DC, PhD Candidate, 1986-, part-time. **Career:** Walter Reed Army Medical Ctr, clinical staff nurse 1971-72, clinical ICU staff nurse 1972, asst head nurse 1972-74; Brooke Army Med Ctr, asst head nurse 1974-75; 5th Gen Hosp Germany, hospital psychiatric nurse consul & head nurse 1976-77; Alcoholism Treatment Facility, psychiatric clinical nurse specialist 1977-79; The Pentagon Office of Drug & Alcohol Abuse Prevention, asst dir educ & rehab 1980-82; The White House, White House fellow office of intergovtl affairs 1982-83; 8th Evacuation Hosp, PROFIS chief nurse 1984-86; Letterman Army Med Ctr, chief ambulatory nursing serv 1984-86; Ft George G Meade Med Dept Activity, chief dept of nursing; Walter Reed Army Medical Center, Washington DC, Clinical Nursing Service, chief 1988-; Letterman Medical Ctr, San Francisco,CA, chief, dept of nung, 1990-. **Orgs:** Sec White House Fellows Assn; mem Sigma Theta Tau, Natl Black Nurses Assn, Amer Nurses Assn, Drug & Alcohol Nurses Assn, Assn of the US Army, Assn of Military Surgeons of the US; regional comm White House Fellowship Comm; vice pres The Rocks Inc; vice pres, White House Fellows Alumni Assn and Foundation Board 1989-90. **Honors/Awds:** 12 presentations including "Racism in Psychiatry" 1975; "Psychological & Emotional Aspects of the Rape Victim" 1976; "Alcoholism Workshop" 1977-78; "Combat Nursing Are You Ready?" 1984; Alumni of the Yr Awd Wagner Coll 1983; White House Fellowship 1983; Sec of Defense Meritorious Medal; Sec of Defense Identification Badge; Martin Luther King Memorial Awd Wagner Coll; publications "Drug Abuse in the Military, An Adolescent Misbehavior Problem" 1983; "Nurses and Policy Making, Washington Fellowships" Nursing Economics 1983; publication, Combat Nurses: You Won't Be Alone, Military Review Vol LXIX No 1 1989 p65-73. **Military Serv:** AUS Nurse Corps colonel 18 yrs; 4 Army Meritorious Serv Medals; Army Commendation Medal; Natl Defense Ribbon; Army Serv Ribbon; Overseas Ribbon; Secretary of Defense Meritorious Serv Medal.

RICHIE, WINSTON HENRY
Association executive, dentist (retired), real estate agent. **Personal:** Born Sep 18, 1925, Jersey City, NJ; son of Celeste Strode Richie and Dr William F Richie; married Beatrice, Sep 5, 1953; children: Winston, Jr, Beth E, Laurel L, Anne C. **Educ:** Adebert Coll Western Reserve Univ, BS 1948; Western Reserve Univ, DDS 1952. **Career:** East Suburban Council for Open Communities, exec dir 1984-90; self-employed dentist, 35 years (retired); Realty One, real estate agent, currently. **Orgs:** Mem American Dental Assn; Cleveland Dental Soc; Ohio State Dental Assn; Elder Fairmount Presbyterian Church 1972-75; pres Fair Housing Inc; Shaker Heights City Council 1972-; Shaker Heights City Council 1972-84, vice mayor 1977. **Honors/Awds:** Distinguished Service in Open Housing Award given by Cuyahoga Plan of Cleveland; invited to Australia to represent the Ford Foundation & Harvard Univ discussing racial integration in the USA. **Military Serv:** USN seaman 2nd cl 1944-46. **Home Addr:** 2741 Green Rd, Shaker Heights, OH 44122.

RICHMOND, DELORES RUTH
Real estate managing broker. **Personal:** Born May 28, 1951, Chicago, IL; daughter of Mamie Elizabeth McBride Freeman and Arthur Lee Freeman; married Larson Richmond, Oct 18, 1980; children: Tesha Elizabeth, Dwayne L, Nicole L'Nae. **Educ:** Chicago College of Commerce, Chicago, IL, 1975-76; Prairie State College, Chicago Heights, IL, 1980-81; Real Estate Education School, South Holland, IL, certificate, 1985; School of Ministry, licensed/ordained minister, 1985; Real Estate Education School, Homewood, IL, realator broker's certificate, 1989; US Fed Gov Courses, credited by state of IL, 28 hours. **Career:** Illinois Department of Insurance, agent & producer; US Federal Government, Chicago, IL, Administrator, 1970-79; Continental Bank, Matteson, IL, assistant supervisor, 1981-84; TV 38 Christian Station and Radio, Chicago, IL, studio audience coordinator, 1984-87; Century 21 Dabbs & Associates, Homewood, IL, broker, associate relocation director, 1985-. **Orgs:** Member, Homewood Full Gospel Church, 1981-; member, NAACP, 1982-; president, Today Is Your Day, 1984-, member of board of directors, Century 21 Dabbs & Associates, 1986-; member, Jack and Jill, 1988-; publicity director, Women's Council of Realators, 1988-; pres, Rich Star Inc, 1990. **Honors/Awds:** Bronze, Silver, and Gold medals, Illinois Association of Realtors, 1986-94; Centurian Award, National Century 21, 1986-91; Appreciation Award, Ford Motor Company, 1987, 1988, 1989; Kizzy Award, Kizzy Scholarship Fund Foundation, 1989; has received hundreds of other real estate awards; 17 Million Dollar Club, Century 21 International, 3 yrs; International Panelist, Century 21 International, 1991; UNCF, 1989-. **Special Achievements:** Stockbroker Series 6 & 22, Licensed 1992. **Business Addr:** Broker Associate-Relocation Director, Century 21 Dabbs & Associates, 17804 South Halsted, Washington Park Plaza, Homewood, IL 60430.

RICHMOND, MITCH (MITCHELL JAMES)
Professional basketball player. **Personal:** Born Jun 30, 1965, Fort Lauderdale, FL; son of Ernell O'Neal; married Juli; children: Phillip, Jerin. **Educ:** Moberly Area Junior College, attended; Kansas State Univ, attended. **Career:** Golden State Warriors, guard, 1988-91; Sacramento Kings, 1991-98; Washington Wizards, 1998-. **Honors/Awds:** NBA Rookie of the Year, 1989; US Olympic Team, 1988; NBA All-Rookie Team, 1989; NBA, All-Star Game Most Valuable Player, 1995; NBA All-Star, 1993-98; National Committee to Prevent Child Abuse, Special Friend Award. **Business Addr:** Professional Basketball Player, Washington Wizards, MCI Center, 601 F St NW, Washington, DC 20071, (202)661-5000.

RICHMOND, MYRIAN PATRICIA
City official. **Personal:** Born Sep 28, 1942, Birmingham, AL; divorced; children: Brian, Kevin. **Educ:** Lane Coll, BA 1965; Atlanta Univ, 1971-72. **Career:** Beauford Cty Schools, teacher 1967-69; WAOK Radio, writer/reporter 1973-76, news dir 1976-78; Fulton Cty Govt, info officer, beginning 1978, deputy director, dept of information and public affairs, currently. **Orgs:** Consult The Onyx Corp 1973-75; alumna Leadership Atlanta 1980-;TV show host GA Public TV 1981-84; consult Martin L King Ctr 1982-84; mem Atlanta Assoc of Black Journalists 1984-85; bd mem Neighborhood Arts Ctr 1984-85. **Honors/Awds:** Media Woman of the Year Natl Assn Media Women 1975; Essence Woman Essence Mag 1975; SCLC Achievement Awd Natl SCLC 1983; GA Black Women Honoree GA Coalition of Black Women 1984-85. **Business Addr:** Deputy Director, Department of Information & Public Affairs, Fulton County Government, 141 Pryor St SW, Atlanta, GA 30303.

RICHMOND, NORRIS L.
Educator, dentist. **Personal:** Born Jun 19, 1931, Gary, IN; son of Queenie Richmond and Norris Richmond; married Conden L Green; children: Taiyan, Tish. **Educ:** IN U, BS 1959, DDS 1963, MSD 1965. **Career:** IN Univ School of Dentistry, full prof 1963-; IN Girl's School, staff dentist 1964-; private practice, Indianapolis 1963-66. **Orgs:** Mem Psi Omega; IN Dental Assn; Am Dental Assn; Indianapolis Dist Dental Soc; IN Pub Health Dentists Orgn; Am Assn of Pub Health Dentists; Am Academy of Gold Foil Operators; mem Student Affairs Com IN U; consult IN Health Careers; mem Housing Oppor Multiplied Ecumenically; Amateur Organists Assn Internat; couns to dental students; mem Hygienist Adm Com; mem Omicron Kappa Upsilon Theta Theta Chpt. **Honors/Awds:** "Cool Breeze" award, IN Univ 1975; Golden Hatchet Award, IN Univ 1977; Certificate for Presenting Scientific Contribution, Natl Dental Assn 1982; Distinguished Award (role model for Black students), Center for Leadership Development 1985; Certificate of Appreciation Chi Eta Sorority Inc 1985. **Military Serv:** USAF ssgt 1952-56. **Business Addr:** 1121 W Michigan St, Indianapolis, IN 46202.

RICHMOND, RODNEY WELCH
Labor union official. **Personal:** Born Jul 25, 1940, Washington, DC; son of Ella Welch Richmond and Vernon Richmond; married Joyce Reeves, Jun 24, 1981; children: Inga, Anthony, Ronda. **Educ:** Howard University, Washington, DC, BA, 1977; American University, Washington, DC, 1984-85; University District of Columbia, Washington, DC, 1986. **Career:** Washington Metropolitan Transit Authority, Washington, DC, bus operator, 1962-86; Amalgamated Transit Union, Washington, DC, international vice pres, 1986-. **Orgs:** Reserve Civil Sheriff, Civil Sheriff's Office, 1989-. **Military Serv:** US Army, SP/4, 1958-61. **Business Addr:** International Vice President, Amalgamated Transit Union, 5025 Wisconsin Ave, NW, Washington, DC 20016.

RICHMOND, TYRONZA R.
Educator. **Personal:** Born Jan 27, 1940, Memphis, TN; son of Deulia Richmond and Basil Richmond; married Carol Kelly; children: Mark, Kelly. **Educ:** Fisk Univ, BA (Cum Laude) 1962; American Univ, MA 1967; Purdue Univ, PhD 1971. **Career:** US Naval Weapons Lab, math/oper rsch 1962-72; Howard Univ, assoc dean business 1972-77; NC Central Univ, dean sch of business 1977-86, chancellor 1986-. **Orgs:** Consultant Federal Insurance Admin 1974, Alcoa 1974-76, EPA 1979; mem bd of dirs INROADS, Amer Assembly Coll & Schs, NCAA Presidents Commission; commissioner, Colleges of the Southern Association of Colleges & Schools. **Business Addr:** Chancellor, North Carolina Central Univ, 1801 Fayetteville St, Durham, NC 27707.

RICKETTS, DAVID WILLIAM
Professional baseball coach. **Personal:** Born Jul 12, 1935, Pottstown, PA; son of Margaret Lewis Ricketts and Richard John Ricketts; married Barbara Boswell, Aug 17, 1957; children: Marie Candace Ricketts-Powell, David. **Educ:** Duquesne U, BA. **Career:** St Louis Cardinals, catcher 1967-69; Pittsburgh Pirates, catcher/bullpen coach 1970-73; John Fisher Coll, coached basketball; St Louis Cardinals, coach 1974-; Roving Minor League, catching instructor, currently. **Orgs:** World Series 1967 & 1968; coach, World Series 1971, 1982, 1985, 1987. **Honors/Awds:** Pennsylvania (Keystone) Hall of Fame; Duquesne Univ Hall of Fame. **Military Serv:** AUS 1st Lt. 1957-59. **Business Addr:** Coach, St Louis Cardinals, 250 Stadium Plaza, St Louis, MO 63102.

RICKMAN, LEWIS DANIEL, SR.
Business executive. **Personal:** Born Aug 20, 1900, Middleport, OH; married Odella McCoy; children: Duana Johnson, Lewis, Cassandra, Earl, Dellria, Eileen Ramsey, Marcel Alexander, James. **Educ:** Wilberforce Univ, BS (Cum Laude) 1944; Meharry Med Coll, MD 1947. **Career:** Wright-Patterson Air Force Base Allison Motor Parts, suprv 1941-43; Rickman Med Clinic, owner. **Orgs:** 1st black on med staff St Joseph Hosp Mt Clemens 1949; charter mem & bd dir Mt Clemens YMCA 1958-60, Macomb Clinic Guid Clinic 1964-66; pres Macomb Cty NAACP 1966-70; sec med staff St Joseph Hosp 1968-70; consult Camall Co 1968-76; bd of dir MI Cancer Soc 1968-76; med examiner Mt Clemons City 1970-73; exec comm St Joseph Hosp 1974-76; dep med examiner Macomb Cty 1974-79. **Honors/Awds:** Beta Kappa Chi Natl Hon Sci Frat 1943; 1st black professional Macomb Cty 1949; bd of trustees 1950, chairperson 1968-, treas 1968-71, Turmer Chapel; 1st blackelected official 1960, pres 1982-84, Mt Clemons Bd of Ed; 1st black mem 1970, chairperson 1972-76 Macomb Cty Selective Serv Bd #52; Most Outstanding Black Bicentennial Celebration Mt Clemons 1976; Brother & Sister Awd Macomb Cty Interfaith 1982; Pres Detroit Dist CME Church Bd of Trustees 1984-; Comm on Mortgages Abstracts & Deed MI-IN Conf CME Church 1984-; Alpha Phi Alpha; Master Mason 32 Degree; Shriner; Macomb Cty Med Soc; MI State Med Soc; Amer Med Soc; Natl Med Soc. **Military Serv:** ASTP ROTC pfc 18 mo. **Home Addr:** 158 Clemens St, Mount Clemens, MI 48043.

RICKMAN, RAY
State official. **Personal:** Born Nov 25, 1948, Galatin, TN; son of Betty Richards Rickman and James Bailey Rickman. **Educ:** Eastern Michigan Univ, Ypsilanti MI, attended 1967-68; Wayne State Univ, Detroit MI, BA 1971. **Career:** US Congressman John Conyers, Detroit MI, chief asst 1971-74; Jeff Chalmers Non-Profit Corp, exec dir 1974-77; Harmony Village Non-Profit Corp, exec dir 1977-79; MA Medicaid Handicapped Program, dir 1979; Police Abuse Housing Issues, lecturer; Providence Human Relations Commn, exec dir 1979-; Affirmative Action, cons; MA Housing Finance Agency, equal opportunity officer 1982-85; Cornerstone Books, owner 1985-; General Assembly of RI, state rep 1986-; Shades-Talk Show, host, producer 1986-. **Orgs:** Pres Friends of Belle Isle, Detroit MI, 1974-78; bd mem Langston Hughes Center 1986-89; bd mem ACLU of RI 1979-80; bd mem NAACP RI Chapter 1980-82; commr Providence Historic Dist Commn 1986-; bd mem Rhode Island Historical Soc 1989-. **Honors/Awds:** Numerous awards City of Detroit, County of Wayne, State of MI & Civ Org; City of Providence-Resolution 1987; Talk Show Host of the Year 1988; many op-ed articles in Detroit Free Press, Detroit News, Providence Journal, Maine Times 1971-. **Home Addr:** PO Box 2591, Providence, RI 02906-0591.

RICKS, GEORGE R.
Educator, administrator. **Personal:** Born Oct 9, 1924, Washington, DC; divorced; children: Lynne L, Jeanne M. **Educ:** Northwestern University, BMEd, 1948, MA, 1949, PhD, 1960; University of ME, grad studies, 1969; University Cape Coast, Ghana, 1970; University Ibadan, Nigeria, 1970; Howard University, University of CT, National College of Education, additional studies. **Career:** Chicago Public School, teacher 1953-59; Chicago City Coll, instr 1960-63; Northeastern IL State Coll, asst prof 1963-64; Chicago State Coll, asso prof 1964-65; Northwestern Univ NDEA Summer Inst for Advanced Study for Teachers of Disadvantaged Youth, appointed to faculty 1965; Northeastern IL State Coll, instr grad studies in disadvantagement 1966-69; Dept of Human Relations, Chicago Public School, dir human relations 1961-. **Orgs:** Mem Soc for Applied Anthropology; Am Anthropology Assn; Phi Delta Kappa; Am Soc for Training & Devel; Orgn Devel Network of NTL, Orgn Renewal Inc; Aesthetic Dynamics Inc; rsrch spl IL Comm on Human Rel; inst bilingual prgm Spanish Speaking Students, Chicago State Univ 1974; EEO planner spl IL Sch Dist; Samuel B Stratton Educ Assn; mem Am Red Cr; mem bd dir & chmn Youth Serv; jr warden vestry Trinity Epis Ch; hearing bd Univ Civil Serv Sys of IL; Nat Urban League; NAACP; Assn for Study of Negro Life & History; Afro-Am Music Opportunities Inc; Alpha Phi Alpha. **Honors/Awds:** Northwestern Univ Alumni Assn recip Rockefeller Fam/African Am Inst Study Grant 1970; author of numerous publs. **Military Serv:** AUS 1942-45. **Business Addr:** 228 N La Salle St, Chicago, IL 60601.

RICKSON, GARY AMES
Artist. **Personal:** Born Aug 12, 1942, Boston, MA; married; children: Kianga Akua, Tianee Rayna, Alea Sekua. **Educ:** Ministry Degree, 1964. **Career:** Boston African Amer Artist, pres 1964-68; Harvard Radio Brdcst Corp, artist-poet 1974-84. **Orgs:** Cultural advsr Roxbury YMCA 1984-85; pub reltns Boston African Amer Artists 1985-; mem Boston Urban Gardeners 1984-; Roxbury Boys Club 1970. **Honors/Awds:** Began Mural Mvmnt in Boston 1968; Outstanding Roxbury Cit Awd Black Bros Assoc 1970; Natl Endwmnt Grant 1970; Champ of Black Youth Award-Roxbury Boys Club 1970. **Special Achievements:** Author, ART, Artist Manifesto for the 13th Cnetury Artist, 1998. **Home Addr:** 107 Dewitt Dr, Roxbury, MA 02119.

RIDDICK, EUGENE E.
Engineer. **Personal:** Born Jan 23, 1938, Lee Hall, VA; son of Gertrude Burks Reid and James Wesley Riddick; married Evelyn G McNeese, Sep 8, 1962; children: Eric. **Educ:** Howard Univ, BSME 1961; State of NJ, Prof Engrs License 1970; State of Kentucky, PE license, 1989. **Career:** Gibbs & Cox, Inc, asst engr 1963-64; MW Kellogg, sr engr 1964-70; Badger Engrs, Inc, mgr, fired heaters 1970-74, mgr, piping engrg 1974-79, mgr engrg aux 1979-82, mgr heat transfer 1982-95; Kinetics Technology Intl Corp, mgr heat transfer group, 1995-. **Orgs:** Mbr ASME 1972-; chmn API Manuf & Contractors S/C on Fired Heaters 1984-94; treas First Parish Unitarian Church 1980-82, chrmn, Art Comm 1980-87. **Honors/Awds:** Black Achiever of 1989, Boston YMCA 1989; Raytheon Black Achievers Alumni, 1990-95; API, Certificate of Appreciation, 1994. **Military Serv:** AUS first lt 2 yrs. **Home Addr:** 14161 Heatherville Dr, Chino Hills, CA 91709-5902. **Business Addr:** Manager, Heat Transfer Group, Kinetics Technology Intl Corp, 650 Cienega Ave, San Dimas, CA 91773, (909)592-4455.

RIDEAU, WIBERT
Prison journalist/editor, photographer. **Personal:** Born Feb 13, 1942, Lawtell, LA. **Career:** The Angolite, editor, 1976-; ABC-TV, DayOne correspondent, 1993-94; Fresh Air, WHYY-FM, correspondent, 1994-95. **Honors/Awds:** Southern Illinois Univ School of Journalism, Charles C Clayton Award, 1977; RFK Foundation, Robert F Kennedy Journalism Award, 1979; American Bar Assn, Silver Gavel Award, 1979; Long Island Univ, The George Polk Award, 1980; Sidney Hillman Foundation, The Sidney Hillman Award, 1982; Council on International Non-Theatrical Events, Golden Eagle Award, 1995. **Special Achievements:** "The Wall Is Strong: Corrections In Louisiana", USL, 1989, Second Edition, 1991, Third Editon, 1996; "Life Sentences: Rage & Survival Behind Bars", Times Books, 1992. **Business Addr:** Editor, The Angolite Magazine, Louisiana State Penitentary, Angola, LA 70712, (504)655-4411.

RIDENHOUR, CARLTON. See CHUCK D.

RIDER, ISAIAH, JR. (J. R)
Professional basketball player. **Personal:** Born Mar 12, 1971, Oakland, CA. **Educ:** Univ of Nevada, Las Vegas. **Career:** Minnesota Timberwolves, guard, 1993-96; Portland TrailBlazers, 1996-. **Honors/Awds:** NBA All-Rookie First Team, 1994. **Special Achievements:** NBA Draft, first round, fifth pick, 1993. **Business Addr:** Professional Basketball Player, Portland TrailBlazers, 1 Center Court, Ste 200, Portland, OR 97227, (503)234-9291.

RIDGEL, GUS TOLVER
Educational administrator. **Personal:** Born Jul 1, 1926, Poplar Bluff; son of Lue Emma Davis Ridgel and Herford S Ridgel; married Gertrude Cain Ridgel; children: Betty Bolden. **Educ:** Lincoln Univ, BS, 1950; Univ of MO, Columbia, MO, MA, 1951; Univ of WI, Madison, PhD, 1956. **Career:** Fort Valley State Coll, Ft Valley, GA, head dept of business, 1952-58; Wiley Coll, Marshall, TX, dean academic affairs, 1958-60; Kentucky State Univ, Frankfort, KY, dean, School of Business, 1960-84; Central State Univ, Wilberforce, OH, vice pres, academic affairs, 1972-74; Southern Univ, Baton Rouge, vice pres of academic affairs, beginning 1985; Kentucky State Coll, vice pres of admin affairs, currently. **Orgs:** Advisory bd, Republic Savings Bank, 1983-86; mem of LA Univ, Marine Consortium Council, 1986-. **Honors/Awds:** Univ of Missouri-Columbia, The Gus T Ridgel Minority Graduate Fellowship, 1988. **Military Serv:** Army, CPL, 1945-46. **Home Addr:** 312 Cold Harbor Dr, Frankfort, KY 40601-3082.

RIDGES-HORTON, LEE ESTHER
Physician. **Personal:** Born Jan 27, 1951, Bennettsville, SC; married Michael Earl Horton; children: Steven Bernard Ridges. **Educ:** NIH Rsch Spelman Coll, trainee 1974-75; Spelman Coll, cum laude BS biology 1975; Meharry Med Coll, MD 1980. **Career:** GA Ave Southside Day Care, teacher's asst 1975-76; Martin Luther King Gen Hosp, pediatric intern 1980-81; USA, med officer 1981-86; Fed Civil Svc, med officer 1987-. **Orgs:** Mem Amer Med Assoc, Southern Med Assoc; youth instr Amer Red Cross 1987-, Amer Acad of Family Physicians. **Honors/Awds:** Listed in Who's Who in Amer Coll & Univ 1974-75; mem Beta Kappa Chi Scientific Honor Soc. **Military Serv:** USA capt 5 yrs; Army Serv Ribbon 1982. **Business Addr:** Medical Officer, US Government Europe, 536th Gen Dispensary, APO New York, NY 09177-3494.

RIDGEWAY, BILL TOM
Zoology educator. **Personal:** Born Aug 26, 1927, Columbia, MO; married Leta M Baker; children: Mark B, Myra Chesser, Beth A. **Educ:** Freidns Univ of Wichita KS, AB 1951; Wichita Univ KS, MS 1958; Univ of MO Columbia, PhD 1966. **Career:** Wichita State Univ Wichita, grad rsch asst 1956-58; SW Coll Winfield KS, asst prof of zoology 1958-66; Univ of MO Columbia, asst prof of zoology 1966; IL Dept of Conservation, contract rsch sci 1970-; Univ of MD, visiting prof 1976; E IL Univ, prof of zoology 1966-. **Orgs:** Regional dir Alpha Phi Alpha 1969-77; dir Afro-Amer Studies Prog Eastern IL Univ 1971-73; rsch assoc 1974, vstg prof 1975, Natural Resources Inst Univ of MD 1974; treas Concerned Citizens of Charleston Assoc NAACP 1975-; prog officer 1981, presiding officer 1985, Midwest Conf of Parasitologists; mem spec ministries commn 1982, soc concerns commn Episcopal Diocese of Springfield; pres Rotary Club of Charleston 1986. **Honors/Awds:** Graduate Fellowship in Zoology Wichita State Univ 1957; NSF Fellowship Univ of WA Marine Sta 1960; NSF Fellowship Univ of MI Biol Sta 1961-62; Rsch Fellowship in Zool Univ of MO Columbia 1963-66. **Military Serv:** AUS 1945-47. **Business Addr:** Professor of Zoology, Eastern Illinois University, Department of Zoology, Charleston, IL 61920.

RIDGEWAY, WILLIAM C.
Business executive. **Personal:** Born Sep 24, 1942, Selma, AL; married Charlotte A Nicholson; children: Traci L, Kristina L. **Educ:** TN St U, BSEE 1965. **Career:** Chevy Motor Div, auto engr 1965-67; IBM Corp, jr component eng 1967-68; IBM Corp assoc component eng 1968-69; IBM Corp, sr assoc component eng 1969-72; IBM Corp, staff component eng 1972-73; IBM Corp, proj eng 1973-76; proj mgr 1976-. **Orgs:** IBM Golf Club; mem IEEE; vice pres Sr Class TN St U. **Business Addr:** 555 Bailey Ave, PO Box 50020 Dept H83 Bldg G13, San Jose, CA 95150.

RIDLEY, ALFRED DENIS
Educator. **Personal:** Born Jun 23, 1948, Kingston, Jamaica; married Pamela; children: Andrew, Jon. **Educ:** Univ of the West Indies, MSc 1977; Clemson Univ, PhD 1982. **Career:** Jamaica Public Serv Co, mgr system planning 1970-79; Clemson Univ, lecturer 1979-82; George Mason Univ, prof 1982-84; Howard Univ, prof of information systems & analysis. **Orgs:** Pres Engineering Mgmt Consultants 1983-. **Honors/Awds:** Jamaica Ind Govt Scholarship 1965; JPS Co Scholarship 1974; Intl Atomic Energy Agency Fellowship 1977. **Special Achievements:** Publications: paper "Economic conductor size under load growth conditions, constrained by load limited life times" 1978; OAS Fellowship 1980; paper "A spectral analysis of the power market in South Carolina" 1981; monograph "Fourcast-multivariate spectral time series analysis & forecasting" 1984; review "Promoting Management Science" PBS TV course 1986; Moving Window-Spectral Method, p 192, Sept/Oct 1984; "Application of a Spectral Analysis algorithm (MWS) to time series analysis of automobile demand," Refereed Proceedings, Washington operations research management science annual symposium, p 139, 1987; "Competing with Global Quality Control," Journal of Business Strategies, Vol 7, No 2, p 125, Fall 1990; "Counterbalancing another approach to forecasting," Journal of Business Forecasting, Vol 10, No 3, p 8, Fall 1991; "Spectral Forecasting and the Financial Market," Technical Analysis of Stocks and Commodities, Vol 11, No 1, p 84, 1993; "Combining Negatively Correlated Forecasts," Technical of Analysis of Stocks, Commodities, Vol 11, No 5, p 66, 1993; "Variance Stabilization: A Direct yet Robust Method," Journal: Review of Business, Vol 15, No 1, p 28, Summer/Fall 1993; "Optimal Window Length for MWS Forecasting," Technical Analysis of Stocks and Commodities, Vol 12, No 3, p 70, March 1994; "Counterbalancing Using Unequal Weights," Production Planning and Control, Vol 5, No 2, March/April 1994; "A Model-free Power Transformation to Homoscedasticity," Intl Journal of Production Economics, 1994; Preprints: "The Global Univariate Moving Window Spectral Method," Supercomputer Computations Research Institute, Feb 1994; "Antithetic Forecasting from a Lognormal history," Supercomputer Computations Research Inst, 1994; "Combining Global Antithetic Forecasts," Intl Trans in Operational Research, 1995; "Optimal Weights for combining Antithetic Forecasts, Computers & Industial Eng, 1996; "Antithetic Log Normal/Normal Random Variables,: Proceeding of 21st conf on C&IE, Puerto Rico, 1997; "On the Sum of Weights: antithetic forecasting," Int Trans, 1998; "Internet Learning Ctr for Time Series Analysis & Forecasting," www.polaris.net/~fourcast/, 1996; "Color TV Industry Sales Forecasting," proceedings of 21st Decision SC Inst Conf, 1995. **Business Addr:** Prof of Management Science, Florida A&M University, Tallahassee, FL 32307.

RIDLEY, CHARLES ROBERT
Educator. **Personal:** Born Aug 6, 1948, Philadelphia, PA; married Iris Rochelle Smith; children: Charles, Charliss. **Educ:** Taylor Univ, BA 1970; Ball State Univ, MA 1971; Univ of MN, PhD 1978. **Career:** VA Hosp, psychology intern 1974-76; IN Univ, asst prof 1977-79; Univ of MD Coll Park, asst prof 1979-80; Personnel Decisions Inc, consult psych 1980-83; Fuller Theol Sem Grad School of Psych, asst prof of psych. **Orgs:** Bd mem Urban League Marion IN 1971-73; mem Amer Psych Assoc 1977-; consult Private Practice 1983-. **Honors/Awds:** Rsch Grant Spencer Found 1978; "Clinical Treatment of the Nondisclosing Black Client, A Therapeutic Paradox" Amer Psych 1984. **Business Addr:** Asst Prof of Psychology, Fuller Theological Seminary, 177 N Madison Ave, Grad Schl of Psychology FTS, Pasadena, CA 91101.

RIDLEY, HARRY JOSEPH
Educational administrator. **Personal:** Born Oct 8, 1923, Baton Rouge, LA; married Yvonne F Bozonier; children: Alexander J, Harry M. **Educ:** Spaulding Bus Coll, bus mgmt 1949-50; Southern U, BA Educ 1953; Souther Univ & LA State U, MaA Educ plus 30 hrs 1967. **Career:** E Baton Rouge Parish Comm School, adminstr supr 1970-; E Baton Rouge Parish Adult Educ Prog, intgr spl 1953-70; Wilbert Elem School, prin 1957-58; New Roads High Sch, athl coach 1953-57; Exxon USA Baton Rouge Refinery, supr testing 1975-80; EBR Parish Continuing Educ Prog, pub rel spl 1970-80; Head Start Prog, educ tech asst 1976-80. **Orgs:** Active mem Phi Delta Kappa LSU Chap 1975-80; active mem Nat Educ Assn 1953-80; active mem Nat Comm Educ Assn 1970-80; mem LA Assn for Pub Continuing Adult Edn; mem E Baton Rouge Parish Supr Assn. **Honors/Awds:** Outstnd personality awd Southern Univ 1953; outstnd tchr awd EBR Parish Educ Assn 1967; head start awd Comm Action Inc 1972-77; outstnd citz awd key to city City of Baton Rouge 1978; LUTC & CLU awd Ins Underwriters Assn 1979; 1st registered supr of comm sch in LA; plaques comm serv awds & letters ofappre from numerous orgn & Assn; 5 battle stars good conduct & army of occupation awd AUS. **Military Serv:** AUS sgt 1943-49. **Business Addr:** E Baton Rouge Parish Comm Schs, 2928 College Dr, Baton Rouge, LA 70808.

RIDLEY, MAY ALICE
Educational administrator. **Personal:** Born in Nashville, TN; widowed; children: Donald G Jr, Yvonda P. **Educ:** TN State Univ, BS 1959, MS 1967; Univ of Pittsburgh, PhD 1982. **Career:** Metro Public Schools, tchr 1962-84; Univ Pittsburgh, asst prof 1975-76; TN State Univ, adjunct prof 1982-; Dept of Ed, State, dir of staff dev, 1984; Tennessee Dept of Educ, exec admin asst to the commr of educ. **Orgs:** Mem TN State Bd of Ed 1981-; chr of special schls Comm TN State Bd of Ed 1982-83; mem Metro Nashville Human Rel Comm; mem St Vincent de Paul Church, Alpha Kappa Alpha Sor, Phi Delta Kappa Ed Frat; pres Parthenon Chapter of the Links Inc. **Honors/Awds:** Alumnus of Year, TN State Univ 1978-79, Phi Alpha Theta Honor Soc, TN Colonel State Honor, Award of Appreciation from Nashville Mayor 1979; Humanitarian Award, TN State Univ 1985. **Home Phone:** (615)244-4090. **Business Phone:** (615)532-4980.

RIDLEY, WALTER N. See Obituaries section.

RIER, JOHN PAUL, JR.
Educator. **Personal:** Born Apr 10, 1925, Boyce, VA; married Nadine Smith; children: John III, David. **Educ:** Virginia State College, BS, 1947; Howard University, MS, 1950; Harvard University, AM, 1958, PhD, 1960. **Career:** Graduate professor, 1974-; Graduate School, Howard University, professor, associate dean, 1971-74; Rutgers College, professor, 1968-71; Howard University, 1959-68. **Orgs:** American Bot Soc of Devel & Biologists; Science Advisory Board; Ecology Advisory Committee, Environmental Protection Agency, 1976-; Na-

tional Medical Fellowship for Graduate Study. **Honors/Awds:** 10 research articles; distinguished service award, University Without Walls; award of distinction, Howard Graduate School. **Business Addr:** Geography & Geology Department, Howard University, 2400 Sixth St NW, Washington, DC 20059-0002.

RIFE, ANITA
Doctoral student. **Personal:** Born Jan 10, 1946, Des Moines, IA; daughter of Mary C Finney (deceased) and Charles R Finney (deceased); married Donald Rife (divorced 1971); children: Donnyta, Donald, Charles. **Educ:** Metropolitan State College, Denver, CO, 1975-77; University of Northern Colorado, Greeley, CO, BA, 1979, MA, 1990; Southern Illinois University, Carbondale, IL, 1988-. **Career:** KARK-TV, Little Rock, AR, producer/researcher, 1982-86; University Northern Colorado, Greeley, CO, teaching assistant, 1986-88; Southern Illinois University, Carbondale, IL, teaching/research assistant, 1988-89. **Orgs:** Association Educators Journalism Mass Communication, 1989-; Alpha Kappa Alpha Sorority, Gamma Kappa Omega Chapter, 1991; past president, Black Graduate Student Association, 1989-90; past member, National Womens Studies Association, 1987-89; past member, Colorado Womens Studies Association, 1987-89. **Honors/Awds:** Illinois Consortium for Education Opportunity, Fellowship SIU, 1989-; Graduate Dean's Fellowship, declined, SIU, 1989; Fred L McDowell Award, Outstanding Scholar at SIU-C, 1990; Graduate Student Council Award, Study British Broadcast London, England, UNC, 1987; Marcus Garvey Cultural Center, UNC Greeley Co, study BBC in London, England, 1987.

RIGGINS, JEAN
Music company executive. **Career:** Arista Records, Black Music, sr vp, until 1996; Universal Records, Black Music, pres, 1996-. **Business Addr:** President, Black Music, Universal Records, 1755 Broadway, 7th Fl, New York, NY 10019, (212)373-0600.

RIGGINS, LESTER
Educator, administrator. **Personal:** Born Dec 8, 1928, Marshall, TX; son of Effie Riggins and John Riggins; married Marvell; children: 6. **Educ:** FSC, BA 1951, Indiana Univ, MBA 1962; Fed City, MA 1974; USC, DPA prog, 1984. **Career:** Advocate Newspaper, owner pres bd 1976; State of CA, dept of genl serv dir, 1977; counselor Grank Skill Center; Askia World Game System Inc, secty/treas KA2 prods, currently. **Orgs:** Mem Amer Personal & Guidance Assn 1971-75; senator CSUF 1971-75; coord Ethnic Studies CSUF 1971-76; mem Amer Legion Post 511; Bass-Black Advocates in State Serv 1977-83; Educators to Africa Assn; Reserve Officer Assn; Woodlin Lodge #30 Prince Hall Masons; mem Black Polit Council; mem Sacto Chap NAACP; central vice pres BAPAC 1979-; mem Victoria Consistory #25, Menelik Temple #36; mem CA Dem Council Black Caucus, Phi Gamma Mu; mem Fresno Dem Coalition; mem Affirmative Action Comm Sacto Unified Sch Dist; mem Affirmative Action Comm City of Sacto; pres Fannie Lou Hamer Democratic Club 1987-; mem AARP; Harry S Truman Democratic Club, president; Harold C Washington Democratic Club; pres, Civil Service Board, Sacramento City, 1994-. **Honors/Awds:** Outstanding ROTC Cadet 1951; Blue Key Honor Soc 1950-51; Troy Awd 1974; Advocates Awd 1977; LABBA Presidents Awd 1979-81; Alpha Man of the Year 1985; Outstanding Democratic Activist 1988; lifetime mem Urban League, Sacto 1987; nominee Community Award Human Rights, Fair Housing Commn of Sacramento CA. **Military Serv:** USAF lt col 1951-71. **Business Addr:** Secretary/Treasurer, Askia World Game System Inc, PO Box 38818, Sacramento, CA 95838.

RIGGS, ELIZABETH A.
Judge. **Personal:** Born Jan 2, 1942, Camden, NJ; children: Luke, Michael, Adam. **Educ:** Bennett Coll, BA 1963; Rutgers Univ Sch of Law, JD 1973. **Career:** San Diego Co District Attorney, dep dist atty; State of CA, deputy atty gen 1977-79; El Cajon Judicial Dist, judge municipal ct 1979-84, presiding judge 1984-86, judge, 1985-; California Judicial College, instructor, felony sentencing, 1986; Hastings Trial Advocacy Summer School, 1983-86. **Orgs:** Dir YWCA Greensboro NC 1964-65; Camden City OEO; Neighborhood Youth Corp, coordinator; dir Head Start 1966-68; Rutgers Univ Proj Talent Search 1968-70; Citizens Adv Bd Rutgers Univ 1970-73; CA State Bar 1974-; chmn Minority Affairs Comm San Diego City Bar 1978-79; bd of dirs Black Atty Assn; Legal Aid Soc Lawyers Club 1977-79; San Diego Co Black Atty's Assn 1974-; CA Assn of Black Lawyers 1976-; Dimensions 1977-; Speakers Bur San Diego Co Natl Conf of Negro Women; Mayors Comm on Status of Women; dimensions & charter 100 Professional Womens Associations; Natl Assn of Women Judges; CA Judges Assn; Co Women's Network; Soroptimist Intl; National Bar Assn; Earl B Gilliam Bar Assn; Urban League, board of directors, 1989-91. **Honors/Awds:** Woman of the Yr San Diego Tribune 1974; CA Women in Govt Law & Justice Awd; Earl B Gillian Bar Assn Comm Appreciation Awd 1984; Disting Service Awd 1982; Women's Criminal Defense Appreciation Awd 1983; Disting Serv Awd Black Student Union Grossmont Coll 1981; San Diego Superior Court Valuable Serv Awd 1983; Black Achievement Awd In Law 1980; Delta Epsilon Chap Kappa Alpha Psi Awd in Law 1980; NAWJ, Moderator; Na-

tional Women's Political Caucus, Alice Paul Award, 1986. **Special Achievements:** Only African American woman judge ever appointed or confirmed in the history of San Diego County. **Business Addr:** Judge, El Cajon Municipal Court, 250 E Main St, El Cajon, CA 92020-3990.

RIGGS, ENRIQUE A.
Dentist. **Personal:** Born Jun 3, 1943, Panama City, Panama; son of Winifred Riggs and Eric Riggs; married Carol S Morales DDS; children: Myra Christine. **Educ:** Central State Univ, BA Psychology 1968; State Univ of NY at Albany, MS Counseling 1971; Howard Univ Coll of Dentistry, DDS 1978; Sydenham Hosp NFCC, Certificate 1980; Iona College, MBA/Finance Cert International Business, 1997. **Career:** State Univ of NY Albany, EOP counselor 1968-71; Hudson Valley Comm Coll, EOP dir 1971-72; Private Practice, general dentist 1978-; New York City Health & Hosp Corp Sydenham Hosp, resident 1979-80; NYSA-ILA Medical Ctr, general dentist 1980-84; NYS Dept of Corrections, dental dir 1984-90; Council's Ambulatory Health Care Center, executive director, 1991-92; American Arbitration Assn, arbitrator, 1993-. **Orgs:** Mem Alpha Phi Alpha 1964-; mem Natl & Amer Dental Assocs 1973-; bd of dirs Uptown Chamber of Commerce 1978-; dir Central State Univ General Alumni Assoc 1978-91, bd of dirs, Health Systems Agency 1979-82; mem Acad of General Dentistry 1980-88; dir Save Amateur Sports 1981-82; mem, bd of gov Small Business Stock Exchange of America 1983-; mem 100 Black Men 1980-; vice pres C&E Assocs 1983-; nominating comm Howard Univ AA 1985; mem exec comm Howard Univ AA 1985; chmn Central State Univ Centennial Football Classic Comm 1987; dir NY Urban League 1986-88; mem NYUL Finance Comm 1986-88; pres Central State Univ Gen Alumni Assoc 1987-91; bd of dirs 100 Black Men; vice chairman, Small Business Stock Exchange of America; bd of dir, Small Business Stock Exchange Development Corp; bd of dirs Amer Assn of Securities Dealers; bd of dirs, American Cancer Society; bd of dirs, The New York Foundling Hospital; Zeta Boule Sigma Pi Phi; Prince Hall F&AM. **Honors/Awds:** Table Clinic Awd DC Dental Soc and Howard Univ Coll of Dentistry 1974; Oral Cancer Fellowship Memorial Sloan-Kettering Hosp 1976; Distinguished Alumni Award, NAFEO 1988; Alumnus of the Year, Central State Univ 1988. **Military Serv:** AUS Reserve LTC 18 yrs. **Home Addr:** 25 Kathwood Rd, White Plains, NY 10607. **Business Phone:** (212)281-5500.

RIGGS, GERALD ANTONIO
Professional football player. **Personal:** Born Nov 6, 1960, Tullos, LA. **Educ:** Arizona State Univ, attended. **Career:** Running back: Atlanta Falcons, 1982-88, Washington Redskins, 1989-92. **Honors/Awds:** Post-season play: Pro Bowl, 1985-87.

RIGSBY, ESTHER MARTIN
Educational administrator. **Personal:** Born in Port Gibson, MS; daughter of Annie M. Wilson Martin (deceased) and Rev. Alex L. Martin (deceased); married Dr John D Rigsby; children: Dr Reginald, Atty Delbert, Mark, Kenneth. **Educ:** Alcorn State Univ, BS 1954; IN Univ, MS 1959; MS State Univ, Doctoral study 1980-83; Univ of MS, additional study 1980; Univ of So MS, doctoral study 1985. **Career:** Jackson Public Schools, teacher 1960-; chmn, English & journalism teacher 1960-, Alcorn State Univ, adjunct instructor 1965. **Orgs:** MS Ed Assoc 1960-, NEA 1975-, mem NAACP 1975-, Natl Council of Negro Women 1977-, liaison coord Jackson Council & Natl Council of English Teachers 1979; Jackson Urban League 1980-; admin bd New Hope Bapt Church 1982-85; natl bd mem Alpha Kappa Alpha 1982-; supt adv council Jackson Public Schools 1984-85; mem YWCA 1985, Opera South Guild 1985; Links Inc, 1987. **Honors/Awds:** Awd Loyal Alumnae Alcorn State Univ 1977; Serv Awd Natl Council of Negro Women 1981; Serv Awd Women for Progress 1981; Serv Awd Alpha Kappa Alpha Sor Inc 1975-85. **Home Addr:** 5952 Hanging Moss Rd, Jackson, MS 39206-2147.

RIJO, JOSE ANTONIO
Professional baseball player. **Personal:** Born May 13, 1965, San Cristobal, Dominican Republic. **Career:** New York Yankees, pitcher, 1984; Oakland Athletics, pitcher, 1985-87; Cincinnati Reds, pitcher, 1988-. **Business Addr:** Professional Baseball Player, Cincinnati Reds, 100 Riverfront Stadium, Cincinnati, OH 45202.

RILES, WILSON CAMANZA
Business executive. **Personal:** Born Jun 27, 1917, Alexandria, LA; son of Susie Anna Jefferson and Wilson Roy Riles; married Mary Louise Phillips;; children: Michael, Narvia Bostick, Wilson Jr, Phillip. **Educ:** Northern AZ Univ, BA 1940, MA 1947. **Career:** Elementary school teacher, administrator, 1940-54; Fellowship of Reconciliation, executive secretary, 1954-58; California State Department of Education, consultant, chief, 1958-70; State of California, superintendent of public instruction, 1971-83; Wilson Riles & Associates, Inc, president, 1983-. **Orgs:** Director, Wells Fargo Bank and Wells Fargo Company, 1977-93; member, Cleveland Conference; member, NAACP; member, Phi Beta Kappa; member, National Advisory Council; member, Assn of California School Administrators; member, American Assn of School Administrators; member, National Committee on US-China Relations; member, Save the Red-

woods League. **Honors/Awds:** Berkeley Citation Distinguished Achievement and Notable Serv to the Univ of CA 1973; Spingarn Medal Natl Assn for the Advncmnt of Colored People 1973; dist Alumnus Award Amer Assoc of State Coll & Univ 1978; distinguished serv awd Harvard Club of San Francisco 1978; Robert Maynard Hutchins Awd 1978; medal for distinguished serv Columbia Univ 1979; distinguished alumnus awd American Assoc of State Coll & Univ 1979; 6 Honorary Doctor of Law Degrees; 3 Honorary Doctor of Humane Letters; African-American Critical Issues Network, Distinguished Svc Award. **Military Serv:** USAAC WWII. **Business Addr:** President, Wilson Riles & Associates Inc, 400 Capitol Mall, Ste 1540, Sacramento, CA 95814-4407.

RILEY, ANTONIO
State representative. **Personal:** Born Aug 22, 1963. **Educ:** Carroll College, BA. **Career:** Milwaukee Mayor's Office, staff assistant; Wisconsin State Assemblyman, District 18; Wisconsin State Capital, state representative, currently. **Orgs:** Midtown Neighborhood Association. **Business Phone:** (608)266-0645.

RILEY, AVIS MONICA
Business executive. **Personal:** Born Oct 10, 1953, Franklin, LA; daughter of Ora Molo Bolden and Arthur James Bolden; married Charles W Riley, May 28, 1983; children: Damonic, Charles, LaTara, Terrence. **Educ:** Southern University, Baton Rouge, LA, BS, accounting, 1976; Cardinal Stritch College, Milwaukee, WI, MS, management, 1985. **Career:** Miller Brewing Company, Milwaukee, WI, project control analyst, 1979-80, supervisor, construction accounts payable, 1980-81, supervisor, project control, 1981-84, manager, project control, 1985-84; Coors Brewing Company, Golden, CO, manager, accounts payable, 1985-87, manager, financial control, advertising, 1987-89, manager, financial, control, corporate affairs, 1989-. **Orgs:** Member, NAACP, 1989-; member, Jack-N-Jill of America, 1990-; member, Sippers-N-Sliders Ski Club, 1985-; member, National Association of Black Accountants, 1990-; member, Volunteers in the Community Enrichment Program, 1987-; past treasurer and vice president, Southern University Alumni-Milwaukee Chapter, 1979-85; Delta Sigma Theta Sorority Inc, Denver Alumnae Chapter; Natl Black MBA Assn Inc, Denver Chapter. **Honors/Awds:** Who's Who's in Beverage and Tobacco Industry, Dollars & Sense Magazine, 1990; America's Top Business and Professional Women for 1990, Dollars & Sense Magazine, 1990; Very Important Prestigious Women, Dollar & Sense Magazine, 1993.

RILEY, BARBARA P.
Librarian (retired). **Personal:** Born Nov 21, 1928, Roselle, NJ; daughter of Olive Bond Polk and Charles Carrington Polk; children (previous marriage): George Jr, Glenn, Karen; married William F Scott, Oct 6, 1990 (divorced). **Educ:** Howard Univ, AB 1950; NJ Coll Women, BS 1951; Columbia Univ, MS 1955; further study, Catholic Univ, Jersey City State Coll, Rutgers Univ, Kean Coll. **Career:** FL A&M Univ, asst librarian 1951-53; Morgan, asst librarian, 1955; US Dept of Defense, lib 1955-57; SC State Coll, asst librarian 1957-59, 1960; Univ WI, asst lib 1958-59; Atlanta Univ, circulation acquisitions librarian, 1960-68; Union Co Tech Inst, lib 1968-82; Union Co Coll, librarian, Scotch Plains campus 1982-92, Plainfield Campus, librarian, 1992-95. **Orgs:** Asst dir, Union Co Anti-Poverty Agency 1968; Just-A-Mere Literary Club; ALA Black Lib Caucus; mem Alpha Kappa Alpha Sor; mem Bd of Educ Roselle NJ 1976-78; bd dirs Union Co Psychiatric Clinic 1980-83; mem Urban League of Eastern Union Co; bd dirs Roselle NAACP 1984-88; bd of dirs Pinewood Sr Citizens Housing 1982-85; NJ Coalition 100 Black Women 1983-90; NJ Black Librarians Network 1983-, bd of dir 1986; bd of dir Black Womens History Conf 1986-89; Links Inc.

RILEY, BERYL ELISE
Mortgage banker. **Personal:** Born Sep 24, 1960, Boston, MA; daughter of Gwendolyn M Riley and Negail R Riley (deceased). **Educ:** Hampton University, BA, finance and theater arts, 1982; Webster University, MA, finance, 1985. **Career:** International Funding Corp., mortgage investment analyst, 1982-83; Brown Realty Inc, salesperson, 1983-85; Gateway Mortgage Corp., Post Closing Department, manager, 1985-86; Bear Stearns Inc, senior mortgage underwriter, 1986-87, Mortage Capital Corp., Legal Review Department, manager, 1987-89; Chase Community Development Corp., vice president/manager, Residential Lending 1989-94; Prudential Home Mortgage, marketing dir, currently. **Orgs:** African-American Professionals in Real Estate; FNMA-Southeast Region, advisory bd; Jamaica Business Resource Center, congressional appointee, vice chair; The Support Network, Latimer Woods Local Development Corp., vice chair board of directors. **Honors/Awds:** NE Brooklyn Housing Development, 1992; Women of Today, 1992. **Home Addr:** 115-46 174th St, Jamaica, NY 11434.

RILEY, CHARLES W., SR.
Brewing company executive. **Personal:** Born Dec 4, 1950, Bartow, FL; son of Flossie B Harvey Riley and James F Riley, Sr; married Avis Monica Bolden, May 21, 1983; children: Damonic Robertson, Charles Riley, Jr, LaTara Riley, Terrence Riley. **Educ:** Florida A&M Univ, Tallahassee, FL, BS-Accounting, 1968-72; Central MI Univ, Mt Pleasant, MI, MBA,

1977-79. **Career:** General Motors Co, Pontiac, MI, sr auditor, sr cost analyst, 1972, plant analyst, property accountant 1979; Miller Brewing Co, Milwaukee, WI, mgr of operations analysis, 1979-82, mgr of budgets & forecasting 1982-83; Adolph Coors Co, Golden, CO, mgr of plant operations finance, 1983-88, mgr of planning, 1989-. **Orgs:** Treasurer, Grandville Heights, Homeowners Assn, 1980-83; sec, bd of dir, Wisconsin Mesbic Finance Inst, 1981-83; treasurer & bd of dir, Colorado Business League, Business League, 1987-90; bd of dir, 1987-, chairman of trustee board, 1990-, Zion Baptist Church; Curtis Park Community Center, board of directors.

RILEY, CLAYTON
Writer, educator, journalist. **Personal:** Born May 23, 1935, Brooklyn, NY; married Nancy; children: Hagar Lowine, Grayson. **Career:** Ebony, NY Times, The Liberator, Chicago Sun-Times & other publications, free-lance journalist; Fordham Univ Grad Sch of Educ & Sarah Lawrence Coll, tchr; former performer tech theater film; Nothing But A Man, production asst. **Orgs:** Mem Drama Desk; Harlem Writers Guild. **Business Addr:** 523 W 112 St, New York, NY 10025.

RILEY, DOROTHY WINBUSH
Educational administrator (retired), writer. **Personal:** Born Jun 16, Detroit, MI; daughter of Odessa and Jack Winbush; married Robert Riley (divorced); children: Schiaui, Ted, Robert, Tiaudra, Martay. **Educ:** Wayne State Univ, BS, 1969, MSLS, 1972; MSGC, 1983; Eastern Michigan Univ, administration certification, 1986. **Career:** Detroit Board of Education, teacher, 1969-94, principal, 1987-94. **Orgs:** Delta Sigma Theta; NAACP; Hartford Missionary Bapt Church; Natl Assn of Black School Educators; Metropolitan Detroit; Natl Assn of Elem School Principals; Natl Council of Teachers of English; Assn of Curriculum and School Development. **Honors/Awds:** Milken Foundation, Educator Award, 1994. **Special Achievements:** Author, "My Soul Looks Back;" "'Less I Forget," 1993; "The Complete Kwanzaa," 1995. **Home Addr:** 16821 Muirland, Detroit, MI 48221, (313)861-6590. **Business Addr:** Principal, Higgins School, 9200 Olivet, Detroit, MI 48209, (313)849-2023.

RILEY, EMILE EDWARD
Physician. **Personal:** Born Jul 30, 1934, New Orleans, LA; son of Mercerdell Riley and Emile E Riley Sr; married Jacqueline; children: Wayne, Debra, Steven, Monique, Michelle. **Educ:** Univ of MI, BS, zoology, 1956; Meharry Medical Coll, MD, 1960. **Career:** Private practice, general surgery 1967-82; NASA, staff physician 1969-70; LSU School of Medicine, clinical instructor in general surgery, 1970-83; Flint-Goodridge Hospital, medical staff, 1972-79; Orleans Parish, asst coroner 1979-82; US Post Service, New Orleans, medical dir 1981-82; private practice, general surgery and medicine 1983-85; St Landry Parish LA, deputy coroner 1983-85; Burks-Farber Clinics, group practice, general surgery, 1988-; Tulane Univ School of Medicine, Department of Surgery, clinical instructor, 1990-; Orleans Parish Prison, surgical consultant, 1991-. **Orgs:** Bd mem Kingsley House 1973-; NAACP 1974-; exec comm New Orleans Drug Abuse Adv Council as apptd by Mayor 1979; founder New Orleans Sickle Cell Anemia Foundation; Southern Medical Assn; Soc of Abdominal Surgeons; LA State Medical Soc; St Landry Parish Medical Soc; John D Rives Surgical Soc; Prince Hall Mason; Knights of Peter Claver; Opelousas Chamber of Commerce; life mbr Alpha Phi Alpha Frat; life mbr Michigan Alumni Assn. **Honors/Awds:** Certificate of Achievement for Outstanding Work as Chief of Outpatient Clinic US Army; American Legion Awd Joseph S Clark Sr High School New Orleans. **Special Achievements:** Co-author: "Freezing of Blood Vessels and Bile Ducts without Excision," Surgical Forum, 1965; "Effects of Freezing of the Common Bile Ducts," American College of Surgeons, 1966; "Freezing Injury to Large Blood Vessels in Dogs," Surgery, 1967. **Home Addr:** 27 Shenandoah St, Kenner, LA 70065.

RILEY, EVE MONTGOMERY
Judge. **Personal:** Born Oct 8, 1955, Sedalia, MO; daughter of Neppie Elizabeth Gerhardt Montgomery and Ralph Montgomery; married Joel Younge Riley, Aug 6, 1988; children: Max Sebastian, Cruz Dylan. **Educ:** Fisk University, Nashville, TN, 1973-74; Carthage College, Kenosha, WI, 1975; Roosevelt University, Chicago, IL, BA, 1976; Valparaiso University School of Law, Valparaiso, IN, JD, 1978; Fontbonne College, Clayton, MO, MBA, 1995. **Career:** United States Office of the Special Counsel, Washington, DC, law clerk, 1979-80, staff attorney, 1980-82; United States Merit Systems Protection Board, Philadelphia, PA, administrative judge, 1982-87; Support Center for Child Advocates, Philadelphia, PA, executive director, 1987; St Louis University School of Law, St Louis, MO, instructor, 1988-89; self-employed, St Louis, MO, attorney at law, 1988-94; NAACP, St Louis Branch's Lawyer Referral Service, director, 1993-94; Social Security Adminstration, admin law judge, 1994-. **Orgs:** President, Federal Bar Association, St Louis Chapter, 1988-90; member, National Association of Women Business Owners, 1987-89; leader, Girl Scout Council of Greater St Louis, 1989-; Ladue Chapel Presbyterian Church, Children's Work Comm, 1997. **Honors/Awds:** Delta Mu Delta Honor Society, EOR Business Administration, 1994. **Business Addr:** Administrative Law Judge, Social Security Administration, St Louis Office of Hearings & Appeals, 815 Olive, Rm 220, St Louis, MO 63101, (314)539-2804.

RILEY, GLENN PLEASANTS
Television production specialist. **Personal:** Born Jan 17, 1960, Milwaukee, WI; son of Annie Pleasants Riley and Robert Riley; married Felice Ligon Riley, Jun 7, 1987. **Educ:** Milwaukee Area Technical College, Milwaukee, WI, AAS, 1977-80; University of Wisconsin-Milwaukee, Milwaukee, WI, 1982-86. **Career:** WITI TV6 Incorporated, Milwaukee, WI, traffic log keeper, 1980-81; WMVS/WMVT Television, Milwaukee, WI, production specialist, 1982-. **Orgs:** Member, National Association of Black Journalists, 1987-; member, Wisconsin Black Media Association, 1988-. **Business Addr:** Producation Specialist, WMVS/WMVT-TV, 1036 N 8th St, Fourth Floor, Milwaukee, WI 53233.

RILEY, KENNETH J.
College football coach. **Personal:** Born Aug 6, 1947, Bartow, FL; married Barbara Moore; children: Kimberly, Ken II, Kenisha. **Educ:** FL A&M Univ, BS Health & Phys Ed 1969; Univ of North FL, MEd Administration, 1974. **Career:** Cincinnati Bengals, def back 1969-83; Green Bay Packers, secondary coach, beginning 1984; Florida A&M University, football coach, athletic director, currently. **Orgs:** Bd dir Big Brothers of Polk County; mem Alpha Phi Alpha Frat; mem Mt Gilboa Bapt Church; consult FL A&M Natl Alumni; Florida Sports Hall of Fame, inducted 1991; Polk County Schools, Hall of Fame, 1992; FAMU Distinguish Alumni Award, 1988; NFL Advisory Board; mem NCAA Advisory Committee (football). **Honors/Awds:** Inducted FL A&M's Hall of Fame Tallahassee, FL 1982; NFL 4th All-time Interceptor NFL 1983; Ken Riley Day at Riverfront Stadium (retired #13 jersey) 1983; Inducted into Tallahassee Hall of Fame, Sept 1996. **Military Serv:** US Army Reserve, Sgt. **Business Addr:** Athletic Director, Florida A&M Univ, c/o Athletic Dept, Tallahassee, FL 32307.

RILEY, ROSETTA MARGUERITTE
Automobile company executive. **Personal:** Born Oct 25, 1940, Kansas City, MO; divorced; children: Courtney Elizabeth Riley. **Educ:** California State Univ, Los Angeles, BS, 1968; UCLA, MA, 1969. **Career:** Bendix Corporation, Detroit MI, manager of business planning, marketing manager; General Motors, Detroit MI, Product Team, manager quality, Rochester NY Products Division, quality improvement mgr, Buick Oldsmobile Cadillac Group, Detroit MI, manager operations planning, Cadillac Motor Car Division, Detroit MI, director. **Orgs:** Amer Society for Quality Control; General Motors Key Executive to Tennessee State Univ; life mem, NAACP, 1984-89; mem, Detroit Institute of Arts, 1987-; Zeta Phi Sorority, 1964-; mem, United Foundation, 1984-. **Business Addr:** Director of Customer Satisfaction, Cadillac Motor Car Division, General Motors Corporation, PO Box 9025, Warren, MI 48090.

RILEY, SUMPTER MARION, JR.
Clergyman. **Personal:** Born Jun 10, 1903, Greenwood, SC; married Varina Lone; children: Phyllis M. **Educ:** DePauw U, AB 1926; Garrett Theological Seminary, BD 1930; Boston Univ Sch Theology, STM 1938; Philander Smith Coll, DD 1952; OH Northern U, HHD 1974. **Career:** Princeton, preacher 1927; S Park, Chicago, asst pastor 1928-29; Negro Work, asst dir 1930-31; Akron Centenary, 1931-32; Denver, 1932-34; Des Moines, 1934-36; St Louis, 1936-37; Boston, 1937-42; Columbus, 1942-43; Detroit, 1943-45; Chicago, Gorham, 1945-51; Chicago Dist, district supt 1951-57; Cory, 1957-68; Lima District, 1968-74. **Orgs:** Pres NAACP Chicago Branch; past pres Interdenominational Ministers Alliance, Cleveland; active civic & youth groups; mem Gen Conf Union; mem World Meth Council; mem General & Uniting Conf; mem World Meth Conf.

RILEY, TEDDY
Producer, songwriter, musician. **Personal:** chilDren: three. **Career:** Member of the group Guy; recordings include: Guy, 1988; High Hat, 1989; The Future, 1990; Juice, 1992; Dangerous, 1992; Bobby, 1993; Eleven, 1993; recording appears on Heavy D's album Peaceful Journey; singles include: "D-O-G Me Out"; "Let's Chill"; "Long Gone"; "No Diggity"; has produced, written and played for: Bobby Brown, Stevie Wonder, Boy George, Kool Moe Dee, Michael Jackson; mem of BLACKSTREET, 1994-. **Honors/Awds:** Grammy, Award for Best Rhythm and Blues Performance by a Duo or Group, 1998. **Special Achievements:** Debut recording, Guy, sold over 2 million copies.

RILEY, WAYNE JOSEPH
Physician, health care official. **Personal:** Born May 3, 1959, New Orleans, LA; son of Jacqueline Cerf Riley and Emile E Riley Jr, M.D.; married Charlene Dewey, M.D. **Educ:** Yale Univ, BA 1981; Morehouse School of Medicine, MD 1993; Tulane Univ, New Orleans LA, MPH Health Mgmt 1988. **Career:** Dept of Medicine, Baylor College of Medicine, Houston, TX; City of New Orleans, Office of the Mayor, administrative asst to the mayor 1981-86, exec asst to the mayor 1986; State of Louisiana, Office of Public Health, health serv planner 1987-88; Morehouse School of Medicine, Minority AIDS Education Project, project assistant, consultant; Baylor College of Medicine, assistant professor, 1996-. **Orgs:** American Coll of Physicians, Natl Medical Assn; Mem Kingsley Trust Assoc Yale Univ 1981-, Yale Alumni Assoc of LA 1981-88; bd of dirs LA Youth Seminar 1984-86; mem NAACP, Amer Medical Student Assn, Amer Medical Assn, Student Natl Medical Assn; exec dir Louisiana Independent Fedn of Electors Inc 1985-88; sec, treasurer Yale Alumni Assn of Louisiana 1988; mem Eta Lambda Chapter, Alpha Phi Alpha Fraternity Inc; national coordinator, Standing Committee on Minority Affairs, AMSA, 1990-91; vice pres, Student Government Association, Morehouse School of Medicine, 1990-91; class president, Class of 1993, Morehouse School of Medicine; Boy Scouts of America Health Explorer's Post, advisor, 1990-93; AUC Student Leadership Forum, 1992-93. Forum, 1992-93. **Honors/Awds:** Hall of Fame Inductee, Louisiana Youth Seminar 1986; participant, Metropolitan Leadership Forum, New Orleans 1987; President, Tulane Univ Black Professional Student Assn 1987-88; Lecturer, Adolescent Health Concerns Project, Emory Univ 1989; 1991 Alpha Omega Alpha Student Research Fellowship, 1990 NMF/Prudential Foundation AIDS Education & Public Policy Fellow; Morehouse School of Medicine, president, Class of 1993; president, Student Government Association, MSM, 1992-93; St Vincent dePaul Scholarship, 1989-93; Diplomate, American Board of Internal Medicine, 1996. **Business Addr:** Assistant Professor, Department of Medicine, Baylor College of Medicine, 6550 Fannin Street, Suite 1207, Houston, TX 77030.

RILEY, WILLIAM SCOTT
Police officer. **Personal:** Born Sep 24, 1940, Chester, PA; son of Leanna Riley and Benjamin Riley; married Deloris L; children: Kimberly, Kelly, William S Jr. **Educ:** Eastern Carolina Coll, attended 1960-61; Lincoln Univ, Masters, human services. **Career:** City of Chester, Police Dept, police officer, liaison to mayor, 1989-. **Orgs:** Sec William Penn Lodge #19 FOP 1987; bd mem Delaware Co Selective Serv Bd 1987; bd mem (1st Black) Delaware Co Democratic Exec Bd 1987; political chm Cultural Development Cnl of Delaward County 1990-; bd mem Chester Community Prevention Coalition 1990-; pres, Chester Police Athletic League. **Honors/Awds:** Outstanding Comm Serv Awd Chester Scholarship Comm 1983; Eva Lou Winters Johnson Freedom Awds Chester Branch NAACP 1985. **Military Serv:** USMC corpl 3 yrs. **Home Addr:** 918 Lloyd St, Chester, PA 19013. **Business Addr:** Police Officer, City of Chester Police Dept, 4th & Welsh Sts, Chester, PA 19013.

RIMM, BYRON NEWTON
Plant manager. **Personal:** Born Apr 10, 1948, Norfolk County, VA; son of Audrey Olivia Rimm and Isaac Newton Rimm; married Gayle L Sword, Oct 30, 1971; children: Byron Newton II, Anicia Renee. **Educ:** Virginia Polytechnic Institute, BS, physics, 1970; Georgia State University, MEd, 1985. **Career:** Procter & Gamble, warehouse operations department manager, customer service operations group manager, Puff manufacturing brand manager, plant manager, currently. **Orgs:** Procter & Gamble, Albany, GA, Black Managers Work Team, prime mover, 1979-85; BASE Network Inc, founding charter member, 1983-85; Ebony Family, president, 1985-91; UNV of Wisconsin Minority Affairs, industrial advisory council president, 1991; Green Bay Wisconsin Area Strategic Planning Committee, 1990-91; Omega Psi Phi Fraternity Inc, 1986; Greenville, South Carolina Chamber of Commerce, board of directors, 1991-93; Greenville, South Carolina Urban League, board of directors, 1993-. **Honors/Awds:** Procter & Gamble Mehoopany Plant, Rosa Park Award for work in diversity, 1990. **Military Serv:** US Air Force, captain, 1970-79; Air Force Commedation Medal, Distinguished Service Medal. **Home Addr:** 2201 Broadmoor Ct, Oxnard, CA 93030-7706, (310)322-6271.

RINGGOLD, FAITH
Artist, author. **Personal:** Born Oct 8, 1930, New York, NY; daughter of Willi Jones and Andrew Jones; married; children (previous marriage): Michelle Wallace, Barbara Wallace. **Educ:** City Coll of NY, BS 1955; City Coll of NY Grad Sch, MA 1959. **Career:** Artist & writer; Univ of CA at San Diego, prof of art 1984-. **Honors/Awds:** Sculpture Fellowship Amer Assn of Univ Women 1976; Sculpture Fellowship Natl Endowment for the Arts 1978; Wonder Woman Foundation Awd 1983; 20 yr retrospective exhibition at Studio Museum in Harlem 1984; Warner Communications Candace Awd 100 Black Women 1984; Moore Coll of Fine Art, honorary doctor of fine art 1986; Wooster Coll, doctor of fine art 1987; John Simon Guggenheim Foundation Award 1987; La Napoule Foundation Award, 1990; Honorary Doctor of Fine Art, MA Coll of Art, 1991; Honorary Doctor of Fine Art, City Coll of New York, 1991; Parent's Choice, Gold Award for Illustration, 1991; ALA Notable Children's Book, Tar Beach, 1991; Aunt Harriet's Underground Railroad in The Sky, Crown Press, 1992; Honorary Doctor of Fine Arts, Brockport State College, 1992; Booklist Editor's Choice, Aunt Harriet's Underground Railroad in the Sky, 1993; Parenting Magazine, Reading Magazine Award, 1993; Jane Addams Peace Assn, Picture Book Award, 1993; Honorary Doctorate, California College of Arts and Crafts, 1993; Woman's Caucus for the Arts Honors Awd, Outstanding Achievement in the Visual Art, NY, 1994; Honorary Doctor of Fine Arts, Rhode Island School of Design, 1994; Women's Caucus for the Arts, Honors Award for Outstanding Achievement in the Visual Arts, 1994; Guggenheim Museum Children's Program, Art Start for Children Award, 1994; New York State Fibers Assn, Recognition Award, 1994; Townsend Harris Medal, City Coll, Alumni Assn, 1995; Lake Charles, LA, Key to the City, 1995; Parent's Choice Award, 1996; Honorary Doc-

tor of Fine Arts, Parsons School of Design, 1996; Honorary Doctor of Fine Arts, Russell Sage College, 1996; Honorary Degrees: Russel Sage, Troy, NY, 1996; Parsons Sch Dsgn, NYC, 1996; Wheelock Coll, Boston, 1997; Molloy Coll, NYC, 1997; New Jersey Artist of the Year Awd, New Jersey Ctr for the Visual Arts, 1997. **Special Achievements:** Author & illustrator, ''Tar Beach,'' published by Crown press, 1991; ''Dinner at Aunt Connie's House,'' 1993; ''Talking to Faith Ringgold,'' 1995; ''We Flew Over the Bridge: Memoirs of Faith Ringgold,'' 1995; ''Bonjour Lonnie,'' 1996; ''My Dream of Martin Luther King Jr,'' 1996; Solo exhibits include: ACA Gallery, NYC, 1998; Exhibition Dancing at the Louvre: Faith Ringgold's French Collection and Other Story Quilts, The New Mus of Contemp Art, NYC, 1998-2000; group exhibits: ''The Art of the American Negro,'' Harlem Cultural Council, NYC, 1966; ''Cairo Biennial,'' Aknaton Gallery, Egypt, Cairo, Alexandria, Arman, Jordon, 1994; Damascus, Syria, 1995; Doha & Gala, Bahrain, 1996; ''Sewing Comfort Out of Grief-OK Bombing,'' 1996-98; ''A Shared Experience: 100 yrs at the Mac Dowell Colony,'' NYC, 1997; collections: ARCO Chemical, Phila; Fort Wayne Mus of Fine Art, Ind; Harold Washington Libr Ctr, Chicago; Public Art For Public Schools, PS 22 Bklyn, NY; Spenser Mus, Lawr, Kansas. **Business Addr:** Author, c/o Marie Brown Associates, 625 Broadway, New York, NY 10012.

RINSLAND, ROLAND D.
University official (retired). **Personal:** Born Apr 11, 1933, Low Moor, VA; son of Lottie Parks and Charles Henry. **Educ:** VA State Univ, AB with Distinction 1954; Columbia Univ Tchrs Coll AM 1959, Professional Diploma 1960; Columbia Univ Tchrs Coll, EdD 1966; Co Officers Sch, diploma mil 1954; Post Graduate Study, Columbia Univ, Tchrs Coll 1982-83. **Career:** VA State Coll, student asst dean of men 1952-54; Glyco Products Co NYC, asst purchasing agt 1956-57; Columbia Univ, sec to sr clk registrar's office 1957-60, professional asst registrar's office 1960-66, registrar 1966-71, asst dean for student affairs & registrar & dir office of doctoral studies 1971-95. **Orgs:** Amer Acad of Polit & Social Sci; Amer Assn Advancement of Sci; Assn for Institutional Rsch; Amer Assn Collegiate Registrars & Admissions Officers; Amer Assn Higher Educ; Amer Educ Rsch Assn; Amer Coll Personnel Assn; Assn of Records Exec & Adminstr; Natl Educ Assn; Natl Soc of Scabbard & Blade; Natl Soc Study Edn; Middle State Assn of Collegiate Registrars & Officers of Admission; Soc for Applied Anthropology; NY State Personnel & Guidance Assn; Intl Soc of Applied Psychology; Kappa Delta Pi; Kappa Phi Kappa; Phi Delta Kappa; Tchrs Coll Columbia Univ Faculty Exec Com; Coll Policy Council ex officio 1972-82; Com on Instr & Rsch 1972-82; resource person to Com on Institutional Rsch 1968-95; subcom on Student Petitions for Exemptions from Degree Requirements, 1972-95; rep to New York City Selive Serv 1966-95; rep New York City Supt's Adv Com 1966-95; Affirmative Action Comm 1981-83; Metro New York City Chap Assn of Records & Exec & Adminstr; Tchrs Coll Century Club 1970-95; Tchrs Coll Devel Council 1974-76, 1992-95; Amer Assn of Counseling & Devel. **Honors/Awds:** Distinguished Military Student 1953; Disting Mil Grad 1954; Blanche B Carter Trophy & Key for Scholarship in ROTC VA State Coll 1954; charter mem & pres Beta Omicron Chap Kappa Phi Kappa 1953-54; Leah B Sykes Awd of Life mem NEA VA State Coll 1954; charter mem New York City Chap Assn Records Exec & Adminstr 1967; designated as an important and valuable Human Resource of USA by Amer Heritage Rsch Assn of First Amer Bicentenium; presenter of degrees, Teachers College in Japan, 1989, 1991, 1993, 1994. **Military Serv:** AUS 1st lt 1954-56; USAR 1956-62.

RIPPY, RODNEY ALLEN
Actor. **Personal:** Born Jul 29, 1968, Long Beach, CA; son of Flossie Hubbard Rippy and Fred Rippy. **Educ:** Cerritos Coll, Norwalk, CA, AA, Business Admin, 1991. **Career:** Actor: Jesus is the Answer, 1991; Personalities, Fox-TV, 1991; Memories, NBC-TV, 1991; appeared on the Oprah Winfrey Show, 1991; Live From LA with Tonya Hart, 1991; Black Etertainment Television (BET), Screen Scene, 1991.

RISBROOK, ARTHUR TIMOTHY
Physician, businessman, administrator. **Personal:** Born Dec 21, 1929, Brooklyn, NY; son of Ruby Isolene Wilkinson Risbrook and Belleville Timothy Risbrook; married Ida Marie Slaughter Risbrook, Jun 8, 1957; children: Donna Michelle, Deborah Nicole. **Educ:** City Coll of NY, BS 1955; Meharry Med Coll, MD 1961; Bank Dir's Sch Montreal, attended 1973; CW Post Coll, nursing/home admin course 1980. **Career:** Trida Travel Service, owner; Hempstead Sch Dist, chief physician; Nassau Co Drug Abuse & Addiction Center, founder dir med servs; Nassau Co Med Center, intern, resd; Physician: Mercy Hosp, A Holly Patterson Home for Aged, Hempstead Genl Hosp, Nassau Co Med Ctr 1965-; Chapin Nursing Home, medical director; A Holly Patterson Geriatric Center, medical director; P&R Advertising Co, founder 1974; Greater Harlem Nursing Homes, medical director, 1976-84; Marcus Garvey Nursing Homes, medical director, 1977-84. **Orgs:** AMA; Natl Med Assn; Empire State Med Assn; Nassau/Suffolk Clinical Assn; Clinical Soc NY Diabetes Assn; Amer Thoracic Soc; Nassau Co Med Soc; Amer Cancer Soc; fndr Topic House Drug Abuse Prog 1966; life mem NAACP; NY State Bd Profesional Med Conduct; NY Statewide Advisory Council; dep Soc Serv; board of directors Nassau Profesional Rev Orgn; chmn sub-comm Medicaid Serv NY Statewide Adv Comm Soc Svcs; Caduceus Med Hon Soc; mem at large, executive committee, Nassau County Medical Center; chairman of the board Vanguard National Bank 1972-74; president medical/dental staff Nassau County Medical Center 1972-74; American Medical Directors Association 1990-; New York Medical Directors Association 1990-; elder, Memorial Presbyterian Church, Roosevelt NY, 1995-. **Honors/Awds:** Mayor's Com, Trail Blazer Award for Founding Vanguard Natl Bank; Man of Yr Award, Westbury Business & Professional Women; Brooklyn Business & Professional Women, Achievement Award 1973; Meharry Medical College President's Award; Certified Medical Director, Long Term Care, AMDA 1992-; Dr Martin Luther King Award; Pioneer in Humanitarianism, New York State and Nassau County-Human Rights Commissions, 1993. **Military Serv:** US Army, artillery, capt, 1950-54; Purple Heart, 3 Battle Stars. **Home Addr:** 629 Oxford St, Westbury, NY 11590. **Business Addr:** Medical Director, A Holly Patterson Geriatric Center, Uniondale, NY 11553.

RISCOE, ROMONA A.
Organization executive. **Personal:** Born Sep 18, 1959, Brooklyn, NY; daughter of Alfonso Riscoe & Mary Crawford. **Educ:** Univ of Pittsburgh, 1977-81; Antioch Univ, BA, human service admin, 1986. **Career:** Abraxas Foundation, Abraxas Group, marketing liaison, facility dir, regional dir, vp; New Jersey state Aquarium, dir, visitor services & comm relations; Philadelphia Multicultural Affairs Congress, exec dir; pres, Riscoe & Associates, currently. **Orgs:** Amer Management Assn; Natl Coalition of Black Meeting Planners; African Amer Travel & Tourism Assn; Meeting Planners International; Hospitality Sales & Mktg International; Philadelphia Urban League; International Visitors Council; Afro-Amer Historical & Cultural Museum; Mayor's Hospitality Cabinet; Black Family Reunion Cultural Center, bd mem; Johnson House, advisory comm. **Honors/Awds:** Philadelphia Hotel Association, Hospitality Award, 1996; Share the Heritage Award, 1997; Hospitality Sales & Marketing Association Award, 1996. **Special Achievements:** Appointed to serve as delegate to the White House Conference on Travel & Tourism. **Business Addr:** President, Riscoe & Associates, 2707 Chestnut Street, Philadelphia, PA 19107.

RISHER, JOHN R., JR.
Attorney. **Personal:** Born Sep 23, 1938, Washington, DC; son of Yvonne G Jones Peniston and John R Risher; married Carol Adriane Seeger Risher; children: John David, Michael Temple, Mark Eliot, Conrad Zachary. **Educ:** Morgan State Univ, BA 1960; Univ of S CA, JD 1962; John F Kennedy Sch, Harvard U, postgrad 1977. **Career:** US Dept of Justice, staff attorney 1965-68; US Dept of Justice, special asst US attorney 1966-68; Dist of Columbia Govt, corp cnsl 1976-78; Arent, Fox, Kintner, Plotkin & Kahn, associate 1968-74; partner 1975-76, 1978-. **Orgs:** Mem exec comm Nat Capital Area Civil Liberties Union 1969-71; chmn Montgomery Co Civil Liberties Union 1970-71; chmn Nominating Comm DC Bd Elections & Ethics 1974-76; mem DC Jud Conf 1975-; bd dir DC Pub Defender Serv 1975-76; bd dir, chm DC Comm on Licensure to Practice Healing Arts 1976-78; mem Jud Conf DC Cir 1976-; mem Adv Comm on Rules & Evidence Superior Ct DC 1976; DC Law Revision Comm 1976-78; mem Jud Planning Comm 1976-81; dir & sec Jewish Social Serv Agncy 1979-85; mem DC Bar AD-Hoc Comm on Transfer of Felony Prosecutorial Jurisdiction 1979-81; dir Greater Washington Jewish Comm Ctr 1982-91; dir Amer Jewish Comm, DC Chptr 1981-90; pres DC Jewish Comm Ctr 1985-87; bd dir DC Jewish Community Center 1986-; bd dir United Jewish Appeal Fedn, 1988-; mem District of Columbia commn on Admissions 1986-92; trustee 2nd executive committee, Supreme Court Historical Society 1990-; bd of dirs, Washington Civic Symphony, 1992-; secretary-treasurer, DePriest Fifteen, 1994-; fellow, Amer Bar Assn, 1995-; bd of dirs, Frederick B Abramson Memorial Foundation, 1995-; bd of dirs, Smithsonian Institute Washington Council, 1997-. **Military Serv:** AUS capt 1963-65. **Business Addr:** Attorney, Arent Fox Kintner Plotkin/Kahn, 1050 Connecticut Ave NW, Washington, DC 20036-5339, (202)857-6452.

RISON, ANDRE PREVIN
Professional football player. **Personal:** Born Mar 18, 1967, Flint, MI. **Educ:** Michigan State Univ, attended. **Career:** Indianapolis Colts, 1989; Atlanta Falcons, wide receiver, 1990-95; Cleveland Browns, 1995; Green Bay Packers, 1996; Jacksonville Jaguars, 1996; Kansas City Chiefs, 1997-. **Honors/Awds:** Pro Bowl, 1990, 1991, 1992, 1993. **Business Addr:** Professional Football Player, Kansas City Chiefs, One Arrowhead Dr, Kansas City, MO 64129, (816)924-9300.

RISON, FAYE
Educator. **Personal:** Born Feb 25, 1942, Nacogdoches, TX; daughter of Rebecca Rison and Archie Rison; children: Sondra R Scott. **Educ:** Univ of CO, MA 1970, PhD 1984. **Career:** Univ of CO Med Ctr, psychiatric nurse 1965-67; NW Team Dept of Health Hosp Denver, CO, psychiatric nurse 1967-71; Metro State Coll, asst prof 1971-82, assoc prof 1982-, prof of human serv. **Orgs:** Natl Orgn of Human Serv, bd mem 1980-84; Amer Civil Liberties Union; Delta Sigma Theta; Black Womens Network; Denver Sister Cities; Black Women with Advanced Degrees. **Honors/Awds:** Doct Fellowship Univ of CO 1980-82; Outstanding Faculty Award Human Serv 1979-82. **Home Addr:** 8792 E Kent Pl, Denver, CO 80237. **Business Addr:** Professor of Human Services, Metro State Coll of Denver, PO Box 173363, Dept of Human Services WC 236, Denver, CO 80217-3362.

RIST, SUSAN E.
Attorney. **Personal:** Born in Chicago, IL; daughter of Irma Tatum Rist (deceased) and Seward Rist Sr (deceased); married Steve F Sbraccia, Sep 9, 1989. **Educ:** Principia College, Elsah, IL, BA; Boston University, Boston, MA, MS; Suffolk University, JD, 1995. **Career:** KAAY Radio, Little Rock, AR, news anchor, reporter, 1978-80; WHDH Radio, Boston, MA, news anchor, reporter, 1980-82; WLVI-TV, Boston, MA, news anchor, reporter, 1982-85; WBOS Radio, Boston, MA, news anchor, 1985-87; WHBQ-TV, Memphis, TN, news reporter, 1987; WBZ Radio, Boston, MA, news anchor, reporter, 1987-95; Emerson College, Boston, MA, broadcast journalism instructor, 1987-92; Suffolk County District Attorney's Office, asst district attorney, 1995-. **Orgs:** Natl Assn of Black Journalists, 1989-95; Society of Professional Journalists, 1990-95; Black Law Students Association, 1992-95; Massachusetts Bar Association, 1995-; American Trial Lawyers Association, 1994-. **Honors/Awds:** 11th Annual Suffolk University Mock Trial Winner, 1994; Harold Goodwin Best Trial Advocate Award, 1994. **Home Addr:** 29 Irving St, Newton, MA 02159-1611. **Business Phone:** (617)287-1195.

RITCHEY, MERCEDES B.
Educator. **Personal:** Born Sep 23, 1919, Washington, DC; married Alfred S. **Educ:** UCLA, AB 1941; LA City Coll, AA; USC Berkeley tchr cred 1943; U of So CA, grad studies; San Diego St U, MA 1963. **Career:** Douglas HS & Jr Coll El Centro CA, Teacher 1943-46; Gompers Jr HS San Diego, teacher 1955-59; O'Farrell Jr HS San Diego, teacher 1959-63; Jr HS Dist San Diego City School, resource teacher 1963-65; Lewis Jr HS San Diego, vice-prin 1965-68; Lincoln HS San Diego, vice-prin 1968-70, acting prin 1970-71, prin 1971-74; San Diego Unified School Dist, dir sec school div 1974-. **Orgs:** Mem San Diego Admin Assn; ACSCA; NASSP; past pres Delta Kappa Gamma Hon Ed Soc; mem Am Assn of Univ Wmn; Nat Cncl of Admin Wmn in Ed; mem, past pres Alphas Kappa Alpha Sor; Braille Trnscrbrs Guild; YWCA; Urb Leag; past pres Las Munecas; NAACP; SW Involvement Proj; adv com to Cnclmn; Pres Cncl; corr sec Lincoln Booster Club; proj adv com Comm Ctr for Std Dev; vice pres, pres Braille Transcribers Guild. **Honors/Awds:** Hon life mem PTA Lewis Jr HS; Tchr of Wk 1963; Begro Bus & Pro Women of SD Ed 1966; 10 yrs Srv Awd Childrens Hm Soc Las Munecas Aux 1966; Wmn of Dstnctn Ed Wmn Inc 1966; Black Fed Outst Contrib to Black Comm 1973; Nat Assn of Negro Bus & Pro Wmn's Club Nat Sojourner Truth Meritorious Srv Awd 1974; Pacific St Assn IBPOE of W Abners Awd of Valor 1974; Outst Edctrs of Am 1974-75; San Diego Comm Ldrshp Rsltn Awd CA St Asmbly; Wmn of Achiev 1975. **Business Addr:** San Diego City Schools, c/o Mrs Betty Ormsbee, 4100 Normal St, San Diego, CA 92103.

RITCHIE, JOE (JOSEPH EDWARD RITCHIE, II)
Educator, journalist. **Personal:** Born Jul 10, 1949, Oak Hill, WV; son of Dorothy Ritchie and Joseph E Ritchie Sr; married Louise Reid Ritchie, Jun 23, 1979; children: Jabari Russell, Akin Zachary. **Educ:** Calvin Coll, Grand Rapids, MI, AB, 1970; Ruprecht-Karl Universitat, Heidelberg, West Germany, 1971-72; OH State Univ, Columbus, OH, MA, German, 1973, MA, Journalism, 1975. **Career:** OH State Univ, Columbus, OH, graduate teaching asst, 1972-75; Washington Post, Washington, DC, reporter, 1975-77; Hampton Institute, Hampton, VA, visiting prof, acting chmn, dept of mass media arts, 1982-84; Washington Post, Washington, DC, asst foreign editor, 1977-86; Detroit Free Press, Detroit, MI, natl/foreign editor, 1986-92; Florida A&M University, Knight Chair in Journalism, 1992-. **Orgs:** Natl Assn of Black Journalists; Society of Professional Journalists, Sigma Delta Chi, 1882-86; mem, bd of dir, The American Council on Germany, 1984-; life mem, mem of rules & referees comm, US Team Handball Federation. **Honors/Awds:** Wilbur Award (co-winner as staff mem), Granted for Outstanding Coverage of Religion Issue, 1990; Woodrow Wilson Fellow, 1970; Duke University-Washington Post Fellowship, 1981. **Home Addr:** 1001 Lasswade Dr, Tallahassee, FL 32312-2862. **Business Addr:** Knight Chair in Journalism, Ste 305, Tucker Hall, Florida A&M University, Tallahassee, FL 32307.

RITCHIE, LOUISE REID
Newspaper executive. **Personal:** Born Jul 10, 1951, Niskayuna, NY; daughter of Antoinette Lyles Reid and Lester Frank Reid Sr; married Joseph E Ritchie II, Jun 23, 1979; children: Jabari Russell, Akin Zachary. **Educ:** Harvard University, Radcliffe College, Cambridge, MA, AB, government, 1973; George Washington University, Washington, DC, M Phil, psychology, 1982, PhD, 1986. **Career:** Associated Press, Atlanta, GA, Nashville, TN, reporter, 1974-76; The Washington Post, Washington, DC, reporter, 1976-77; Detroit Urban League, Detroit, MI, director, substance abuse prevention, 1987; Detroit Free Press, columnist, 1987-92; self-employed professional public speaker, 1987-; Wayne State University, instructor, 1988-92; Detroit Free Press, executive assistant to the publisher, 1990-

92; Knight-Ridder Inc, human resources consultant 1993-. **Orgs:** Vice chairman, community advisory board, WTVS-TV, Detroit, MI, 1989-90; member, National Speakers Association; member, Michigan Professional Speakers Association; member admissions committee, Harvard University, 1989-92; member, Samaritan Hospital Substance Abuse Committee, 1987; member, Childrens Center Perinatal Health Committee, 1988; Wayne County Juvenile Court Substance Abuse Committee, 1988, member board of directors, Radcliffe College Club, Washington DC, 1985-86; member, Delta Sigma Theta Sorority, 1984-; member, Sorosis Arts & Literacy Club, member, Hartford Memorial Baptist Church; Newspaper Association of America Diversity, subcommittee co-chair, 1992-. **Honors/Awds:** Woman Who Makes Things Happen Award, Detroit Chapter Natl Council of Negro Women, 1987; Navy Health Professionals Scholarship, 1979; Martin Luther King Community Service Award, Southfield, MI, 1990; Woman of the Year for Journalism, Hartford Memorial Baptist Church, 1991; first place, social issues articles, 1990, first place, personal columns, 1989, Michigan Press Women; first place, personal columns, 1989, honorable mention, social issues articles, 1990, Natl Federation of Press Women; Distinguished Graduate Award, Niskayuna High School, New York, 1990; Celebrate Literacy Award, Oakland County Reading Assn, 1989; Celebrate Literacy Award, Metropolitan Detroit Reading Council, 1988; Eastern Michigan University, Community Service, 1992; Knight-Ridder, Award of Excellence, 1992. **Military Serv:** USNR, O-3 (LT), 1979-86. **Business Addr:** Human Resources Consultant, Knight-Ridder Inc, 1 Herald Plaza, Miami, FL 33132.

RITTER, THOMAS J.
Business executive. **Personal:** Born Dec 24, 1922, Allendale, SC; married Betty Davis; children: Eva, Jephrey. **Educ:** E Bapt Coll, BS 1959; Morris Coll, DD honorary 1968; E Bapt Coll, DD 1969; Dr Humane Letters, Pentecostal Theol Sem 1970. **Career:** Ritter Bros Med Equip Sales Co, partner 1947-49; ins 1949-55; Second & Macedonia Bapt Ch, pastor 1958; Dept of Welfare, PA, caseworker 1959-60; N Philadelphia Youth Community & Employment Serv, exec dir 1960-63; Opportunities Industrialization Cntr Inc, exec dir 1963-. **Orgs:** Bd mem Franklin Inst; Philadelphia Nat Bank; E Bapt Coll; Albert Einstein Med Cntr; Pathway Sch; Area Manpower Planning Coun; PA Industrial Devel Auth; Contact Philadelphia; pres Coun of Am Inst of Mgmt; Acad for Career Educ Mem, Philadelphia Partnership; Mayor's Com of Twelve; Bapt Ministers Conf of Philadelphia & vincinity; Greater Philadelphia C of C; Governor's adv coun on Housing; Crime Commn of Philadelphia; adv Coun Vocational Educ Sch Dist of Philadelphia; Am Inst of Mgmt; Philadelphia Bapt Keystone Assn; Lower KY Environmental Cntr. **Honors/Awds:** Cit com No-fault Ins; recipient OIC, Decade of Progress Award 1974; distinguished cit award US Civil Serv Commn 1972; outstanding serv award BronzeAssn for Cultural Advancement 1971; humanitarian award World Alliance of Holiness 1970; award of achievement Philadelphia Tribune Charities 1967; outstanding alumni award E Bapt Coll 1964; Margaret Van Dyne Award for outstanding scholarship & christian devotion 1959. **Military Serv:** AUS 1942-45. **Business Addr:** 1231 N Broad St, Philadelphia, PA 19122.

RIVERA, EDDY
Attorney. **Personal:** Born Jul 23, 1938, St Croix, Virgin Islands of the United States; son of Margot M Rivera and Adelo Rivera; married Gloria Maria Rojas, Feb 26, 1967; children: Lisette M, Julia I, Eddy Jr, Vanessa M. **Educ:** Interam Univ San German PR, 1960; Univ of PR San Juan, BBA (cum laude) 1963, JD 1972. **Career:** VI Properties Inc, chief accountant 1966-69; Govt of VI, asst attny gen 1973-76; mem, VI Board of Education, 1976-78; Govt of VI, senator 1979-80; private practice, attny 1976-. **Orgs:** Mem Amer Bar Assn 1981-96; PR Bar Assoc 1973; VI Bar Assoc 1976; bd mem CAMP ARAWAK Youth Serv Org 1974-76; pres Hispanos Unidos VI Inc 1974-78, 1992-; bd of ed Govt of VI 1976-78; mem Assn of Trial Lawyers 1982-94; pres Full Gospel Business Men's Fellowship Intl 1981-86. **Military Serv:** AUS pfc 1963-65. **Business Addr:** Attorney, 1168 King St, Ste 2, Christiansted, St Croix, Virgin Islands of the United States 00820.

RIVERS, ALFRED J.
Business executive. **Personal:** Born Sep 18, 1925, Crisp Co, GA; married Vera Stripling; children: Gwendolyn Thrower, Gregory Rivers, Glenda. **Educ:** LUTC, 1976; Grad Sch, 1976; TN State U. **Career:** NC Mutual Ins Co, 1946-; Gillespie Selden Comm Devel Ctr, dir vice pres 1972-77; Middle Flint Planning APDC, dir 1973-77; Crisp Cordele & C of C, dir 1973-77; Cordele City Commn, v chmn 1972-77. **Orgs:** Mem NAACP; mem Local Am Legion; Cancer Soc. **Military Serv:** AUS capt 1943-46. **Business Addr:** PO Box 1077, Cordele, GA 31015.

RIVERS, CLARENCE JOSEPH
Priest. **Personal:** Born Sep 9, 1931, Selma, AL. **Educ:** BA 1952; MA 1956; St Mary's Sem, Cincinnati; English Lit Xavier U; Cath Univ of Am; Union Grad Sch, PhD; Institut Catholique, Paris. **Career:** Archdiocese of Cincinnati, priest 1956-; Purcell HS, tchr, English Lit 1956-66; St Joseph's & Assumption Parishes, asso pastor 1956-66; recorded publishes ''An Am Mass Prog,'' 1963; Dept of Culture & Worship Nat Ofc of Black Cath, founder first dir 1972, spl cons; Stimuli Inc, ''Newborn Again'', pres; authorbooks on worship; CBS Network, spripted/co-prod/starred ''Freeing the Spirit'' 1971; CBS Network Easter Special, prod cons/narrator/composer ''The Feast of Life''. **Orgs:** Mem bd dir Nat Liturgical Conf; N Am Academy of Liturgy; Martin Luther Kings Fellows; pub ''Turn Me Loose''; mem worship comm Archdiocese of Cincinnati. **Honors/Awds:** Recipient pub serv awards; 1966 Gold Medal of Cath Art Assn for ''An Am Mass Prog''. **Business Addr:** PO Box 20066, Cincinnati, OH 45220.

RIVERS, DENOVIOUS ADOLPHUS (D. ADOLPHUS RIVERS)
Judge. **Personal:** Born Feb 2, 1928, Chicago, IL; son of Irene and Denovious; married Loretta Faulkner; children: Donald Adolphus. **Educ:** Wilson Jr Coll, Cert 1948; John Marshall Law School, JD 1951. **Career:** IL Supreme Court, admitted IL Bar 1951; US Dist Court, Northern Dist IL, admitted 1958; US Dist Court, Northern Dist IN, admitted 1960; State of Illinois, licensed real estate broker, 1971-; Circuit Court Cook Cnty, IL, assoc judge 1984; US Supreme Court, admitted, 1991; Parentage Courts, supervising judge, 1991-94; Forciable Entry & Detainer Courts, supervising judge, 1994-96, 1998; Circuit Court, Cook County, IL, judge, 1995. **Orgs:** Cook Cnty Bar Assn, bd of dirs; Natl Bar Assn 1954-, bd of dirs, 1993-94; Chicago Bar Assn 1968-; IL State Bar Assn 1982-; IL Judges Assn 1984-; IL Judicial Cncl, asst sec 1984, sec 1985, chair-elect, 1991-92, chairperson, 1992-93, exec committee, 1993-95; trustee Abraham Lincoln Cntr, sec and chairman By-Laws, 1968-84; vstrymn & treas St Bartholomew Episcopal Church 1960-76; Messiah-St Bartholomew Episcopal Church 1976-; frmr treas Omega Psi Phi Frat, Iota Chap 1948-; governing bd, treas, vice pres, pres: The Chicago Asmbly, Chicago Steering Cmte, NAACP Legal Def & Ed Fund 1967-84; The Drids Club 1984-; bd mem Harvard St George Schl 1971-80. **Honors/Awds:** FBI Commendation 1971; Meritorious Serv, Big Buddies Youth Serv, Inc 1972; Natl Bar Assn, Hall of Fame; Judicial Awd Cook Cnty Bar Assn 1984; Outstanding Serv Award, Phoenix Park Dist 1984; IL Judicial Council, Distinguished Service Award, 1993; Kenneth E Wilson Memorial Award, 1996; Judicial Career Service Award, 1997. **Military Serv:** IL Nat Guard, Infantry 1st lt 20 yrs. **Home Addr:** 6947 Cregier Ave, Chicago, IL 60649. **Business Addr:** Judge, Circuit Court Cook County, Richard J Daley Center, Chicago, IL 60602.

RIVERS, DOROTHY
Administrator. **Personal:** Born Aug 14, 1933, Chicago, IL; divorced. **Educ:** John Marshall Law Sch, 1950-51; Nrthwstrn U, BA 1959. **Career:** Michael Reese Hosp & Med Ctr, exec adminstr, dept of psychtry; Nelson Prods Inc, vp. **Orgs:** Fndr, chrwmn Women's Div Chicago Ec Dev Corp; fndr, mem The XXI of Michael Reese Hosp; chrwmn 1st, 2nd & 3rd Mdwst Rgnl Conf on Bus Opport for Women; vp, bd dir Chicago Ec Dev Corp; bd dir Chicago Fin Dev Corp; chrprsn Vanguard of Chicago Urban Leag; chrprsn, exec adv bd Big Buddies Yth Serv 1964-; mem Bravo Chap Lyric Opera; bd dir Operation PUSH Found; wmns bd United Negro Coll Fund; mem Chicago Chap of Links. **Honors/Awds:** Recip Vol Serv Awd Chicago Ec Dev Corp 1973; Vol Serv Awd Gov of IL 1967; Lady of the Day Awd Radio Sta WAAF & WAIT; cert of ldrshp Met YMCA 1975;cert of merit Chicago Heart Assn 1975; M F Bynun Comm Serv Awd 1975.

RIVERS, GARY C.
Fundraiser. **Personal:** Born Jan 6, 1951, Hardeeville, SC. **Educ:** New York Univ, BA Biology 1973. **Career:** Boy Scouts of Amer, dist exec 1973-75; West Point Pepperell, institutional salesman 1975-78; Westvaco, fine papers salesman 1978-79; Boy Scouts of Amer, finance dir 1979-80; David M Winfield Foundation, exec dir. **Orgs:** Dir of develop Congressional Black Caucus Foundation 1980-85; bd mem Natl Coalition of Black Meeting Planners 1986; mem-at-large Natl Soc of Fund Raising Execs 1986-; mem 100 Black Men 1986-; bd mem Amer Cancer Soc.

RIVERS, GLENN ANTON (DOC)
Professional basketball player. **Personal:** Born Oct 13, 1961, Maywood, IL. **Educ:** Marquette Univ, Milwaukee, WI, 1980-83. **Career:** Guard: Atlanta Hawks, 1983-91, Los Angeles Clippers, 1991-92, New York Knicks, 1992-94. **Honors/Awds:** Shares NBA playoff-game record for most assists in one half, 1988.

RIVERS, JESSIE
Correctional facility administrator. **Educ:** Wayne State Univ, undergraduate and graduate degrees. **Career:** Camp Gilman, supvr; Michigan Reformatory, deputy warden; Michigan Parole Bd; Egeler Correctional Facility, warden; Ryan Regional Correctional Facility, warden, currently. **Business Addr:** Warden, Ryan Regional Correctional Facility, 17600 Ryan Rd, Detroit, MI 48212, (313)368-3200.

RIVERS, JOHNNY
Recording artist. **Personal:** Born Nov 7, 1942, New York, NY. **Career:** Rivers Music, pres; Imperial Records, rcrdng artst 1963-; Soul City Records, LA, owner 1967-; Soul City Prods, Johnny Rivers Mus. **Orgs:** Firsthit Record Memphis 1964. **Business Addr:** 3141 Coldwater Canyon Lane, Beverly Hills, CA 90210.

RIVERS, JOHNNY
Executive chef. **Personal:** Born Oct 5, 1949, Orlando, FL; married Shirley Capers; children: Johnny Jr, Djuan, Dwain, Tanya, Zina. **Career:** Flountainbleu Miami FL, chef 1968; Mission Inn Country Club, chef 1963-64; Palmer House Chicago IL, chef 1969; Walt Disney World Co, exec chef 1970-. **Orgs:** Pres Central FL Chef Assoc 1974-75; host World Chef Congress 1984; publ relations Amer Culinary Fed 1984-85; mem Orange Cty School Bd 1985. **Honors/Awds:** Acad of Chefs Amer Culinary Fed 1976-77; Award of Gratitude Brown Coll 1979; Chef of the Year Central FL Chef Assn 1980; American Culinary Federation Chef Professionalism Award, 1994. **Business Addr:** Executive Chef, Contemporary Resort Hotel, Walt Disney World Co, PO Box 10,000, Lake Buena Vista, FL 32830.

RIVERS, KENYATTA O.
Speech language pathologist. **Personal:** Born Nov 26, 1966, Washington, DC; son of Arthur C & Octovene M Rivers. **Educ:** Lake Sumter Comm Coll, AA, 1986; Univ of Central FL, BA, 1988, MA, 1990; Univ of FL, PhD, 1994. **Career:** Pinellas County School System, speech language pathologist, 1994-. **Orgs:** Amer Speech Language Hearing Assn, 1990-; Tyrone Elem School Advisory Council, 1994-; Bd of Dirs of the Family Worship Ctr & Academy, 1992-94; Beta Eta Sigma Honor Society, 1992-94; Univ of Fl, Office of Grad Minority Programs, advisory council, 1991-92; Black Grad Student Organization, 1990-94; McKnight Ctr of Excellence, Coll Reach-Out Advisory Council, 1989-90; Church of God in Christ, 1990-. **Honors/Awds:** FL Educ Fund, McKnight Doctoral Fellowship, 1990-94; Univ of Central FL, Delores Auzenne Fellowship, 1988-90; Black Grad Student Organization, Academic Excellence & Comm Service Award, 1993, Academic Achievement Award, 1994; Daily Commercial Newspaper, Black Role Model Award, 1990. **Special Achievements:** Publications: co-author, ''Language and Behavioral Concerns for Drug Exposed Infants and Toddlers,'' Infant-Toddler Intervention: The Transdisciplinary Journal, p 63-73, 1992 and Developmental Problems of Drug-Exposed Infants, p63-73, 1992; co-author,''Effects of Phonological Decoding Training on Children's Word Recognition of CVC,CV and VC Structures,'' American Journal of Speech Language Pathology.

RIVERS, LEN
Sports franchise executive. **Educ:** Springfield College, attended. **Career:** Franklin Township High School, head football coach; New Jersey Nets, director of community affairs, 1989-. **Orgs:** Sponsors clinics and programs from young people that promote the benefits of education and the dangers of drugs. **Business Addr:** Director of Community Affairs, New Jersey Nets, Brendan Byrne Arena, East Rutherford, NJ 07073.

RIVERS, LOUIS
Educator. **Personal:** Born Sep 18, 1922, Savannah, GA; married Ligia Sanchez; children: Luisa, Liana, Loria, Leigh. **Educ:** Savannah State Coll, BS 1946; New York Univ, MA 1951; Fordham Univ, PhD 1975. **Career:** WV State Coll, instructor 1951-52; Southern Univ, instructor 1952-53; Tougaloo Coll, asst prof 1953-58; New York City Tech Coll, professor 1970-. **Orgs:** Mem Natl Writers Club, Dramatist Guild, Speech Communication Assn, College Language Assn, Phi Delta Kappa, Kappa Delta Pi. **Honors/Awds:** John Hay Whitney Theater 1957; Outstanding Teacher Plaque from Kappa Delta Pi 1983; Andrew Mellon Creative Writing Fellowship 1984. **Military Serv:** US Corps of Engrs pvt 1942. **Business Addr:** Professor of Writing/Speech, New York City Tech College, 300 Jay St, Brooklyn, NY 11201.

RIVERS, MICKEY (JOHN MILTON)
Professional baseball player (retired). **Personal:** Born Oct 31, 1948, Miami, FL. **Educ:** Miami-Dade (North) Community College, Miami, FL, attended. **Career:** California Angels, outfielder, 1970-75; New York Yankees, outfielder, 1976-79; Texas Rangers, outfielder, 1979-85. **Honors/Awds:** Rangers Player of the Year, 1980; American League All-Star Team, 1976.

RIVERS, ROBERT JOSEPH, JR.
Physician. **Personal:** Born Nov 14, 1931, Princeton, NJ; married Ruth Lewis; children: Michael, Scott, Wendy, Robert D. **Educ:** Princeton Univ, AB (Cum Laude) 1953; Harvard Medical School, MD 1957. **Career:** Private practice, vascular surgery 1965-86; Univ of Rochester School of Medicine & Dentistry, prof of clinical surgery 1984-89; assoc dean for minority affairs 1984-89. **Orgs:** Trustee Princeton Univ 1969-77; bd of trustees Rochester Savings Bank, 1972-83; chief Div of Vascular Surgery The Genesee Hosp 1978-85. **Honors/Awds:** President's Citation Medical Soc of the State of NY 1971; Distinguished Alumni Service Award, Assn of Black Princeton Alumni, 1982; Outstanding Service Award, Natl Assn of Medical Minority Educators Inc, 1989. **Military Serv:** USN lt USNR 1959-61. **Home Addr:** 86 Great Oak Road, Orleans, MA 02653.

RIVERS, RONALD LEROY
Professional football player. **Personal:** Born Nov 13, 1971, Elizabeth City, NJ; married Myla; children: Malia. **Educ:** Fresno State, attended. **Career:** Detroit Lions, running back, 1995-. **Honors/Awds:** Detroit Lions, Special Teams MVP, 1995. **Business Addr:** Professional Football Player, Detroit Lions, 1200 Featherstone Rd, Pontiac, MI 48342, (248)335-4131.

RIVERS, VALERIE L.
Appointed official & attorney. **Personal:** Born Nov 25, 1952, Birmingham, AL; daughter of Eddie Rivers. **Educ:** Tuskegee Inst, BS 1975; Southern Univ School of Law, JD 1980. **Career:** Wayne County Community Coll, Asst Dir Human Resources 1976; Gov Office of Consumer Protection State of LA, investigator 1979-80; B'ham Area Legal Service, staff atty candidate 1981; City of Birmingham, city council admin-first Black and first female to hold this position. **Orgs:** Mem Phi Alpha Delta Law Frat Intl 1978-; big-sister 1981-, adv comm 1983-, minor recruit 1983-, bd of dir 1985-88 Big Bros/Big Sisters of Gr Birmingham; mem Amer Soc Public Admin 1981-; mem natl Forum Black Admin 1983-. **Honors/Awds:** First & past justice of AP Tureau Chapter of Phi Alpha Delta Law Frat intl & founding mem of Chapter 1978; Reginald Heber Smith Comm Lawyer Fellowship 1980-81; Hon Mayor of Pritchard, AL 1980; exec in residence Birmingham-Southern Coll 1983; Govt & Politics Black Women Business & Professional Assn 1984. **Home Addr:** 1908 Huntington Circle, Birmingham, AL 35214. **Business Addr:** Council Administrator, Birmingham City Council, 710 North Nineteenth St, Birmingham, AL 35203.

RIVERS, VERNON FREDERICK
Educational administrator (retired). **Personal:** Born Jul 25, 1933, Peekskill, NY; married Audrey Cherry; children: Gregory, Pamela, Karen. **Educ:** State Univ of NY, BS Ed 1955; Teachers Coll Columbia Univ NY, Grad Work 1960; City Coll of NY, Grad Work 1963; State Univ of NY New Paltz, MS Ed 1971. **Career:** Peekskill NY School Syst, teacher, 1957-61; Irvington NY School System, teacher, 1961-68; Elmsford NY School System, principal, 1968-72; Elmsford School System, fed funds coord, 1971-72; Ossining NY School Syst, teacher adult ed, 1975; Brewster School Syst, principal, 1972-88, director of professional services, 1988-91. **Orgs:** Kappa Alpha Psi Fraternity, Inc; AARP; Salisbury Wicomico Arts Council, bd of dirs; Deer's Head Hosp; Ward Museum of Wildfowl Art. **Honors/Awds:** Vanguard Awd Peekskill NAACP 1959; Cert of Apprec Elmsford Comm 1972; Cert of Apprec Lions Club of Yorktown & Rotary Club of Brewster NY 1974; Cert of Apprec Yorktown Area Jaycees 1978; Cert of Safety & Good Medal; first black teacher and principal in each school system employed. **Military Serv:** US Army, PFC, 1955-57.

ROACH, DELORIS
Public relations manager. **Personal:** Born Apr 15, 1944, Pine Bluff, AR; children: Yvette Guyton, Frank, Anthony, Monica. **Educ:** Univ of CA Berkeley, BA Journalism 1975; San Francisco State Univ, MA Radio/TV 1979. **Career:** KQED-TV Educ TV, admin asst 1979-81; KQED-TV Educ Films, rschr 1981-82; New Images Prod Inc, production coord 1982-84; Fleming Co Inc advertising coord; Emery Unified School Dist, mem, bd of trustees. **Orgs:** Consult CA Schools Bd Assoc 1979; mem CA School Bds Assoc, Alameda Cty School Bds Assoc 1979, CA Black School Bd Mem Assoc 1981. **Honors/Awds:** Outstanding Citizen Award Emeryville Neighborhood Assoc 1981; Disting Serv Awd Alameda Cty School Bds Assoc 1984. **Business Addr:** Emery Unified Sch Dist, 4727 San Pablo Ave, Emeryville, CA 94608.

ROACH, HILDRED ELIZABETH
Educator. **Personal:** Born Mar 14, 1937, Charlotte, NC; daughter of Pearl Caldwell Roach and Howard Roach. **Educ:** Fisk University, Nashville, TN, BA, 1957; Juilliard School of Music, New York, NY, 1958-59; Yale University, New Haven, CT, MM, 1962; University of Ghana, 1969. **Career:** Tuskegee Institute, Tuskegee, AL, 1957-60; Fayetteville State College, Fayetteville, NC, 1962-66; Howard University, Washington, DC, 1966-67; Virginia State College, Petersburg, VA, 1967-68; University of DC, Washington, DC, professor, 1968-. **Orgs:** Alpha Kappa Alpha; Music Educators; Natl Black Music Caucus; NAACP; NANM; Phi Beta Kappa. **Honors/Awds:** Author, Black American Music: Past & Present, Krieger, 1985, 1992; Ford Foundation Scholarship, 1953-57; scholarship, Omega Psi Phi, 1953-57; Theodore Presser Award, 1956; Yale Merit Award, 1982; Lockwood Concerto Competition, Yale, 1961. **Business Addr:** Professor, University of the District of Columbia, Department of Music, 4200 Connecticut Ave NW, #46, Washington, DC 20008.

ROACH, LEE
Association executive. **Personal:** Born Jan 3, 1937, Rock Hill, SC. **Educ:** Lincoln U, BA 1960; Bryn Mawr, MSW 1969; Cornell U. **Career:** Health Adminstr Program, 1972; Regional Comprehensive Health Planning Council Inc, sep asso dir 1969-; Grad Sch of Soc Work, Bryn Mawr, comm organization instr 1970-71; Health & Welfare Council, asst dir 1966-67; tchr, Math & Sci 1960-66; owner-mgr restaurant 1955-74; Equestrian Academy. **Business Addr:** Dir of Planning, The Graduate Hospital, One Graduate Plaza, Philadelphia, PA 19146.

ROACH, MAX
Musician, composer, educator. **Personal:** Born Jan 10, 1924, Elizabeth City, NC; married Mildred Wilkinson; children: Daryl, Maxine. **Educ:** Manhattan School of Music, composition. **Career:** Jazz clubs, drummer; University of Massachusetts, Dept of Music & Dance, faculty. **Orgs:** Jazz Artists Guild. **Honors/Awds:** Winner, Down Beat poll, 1955, 1957, 1958, 1959, 1960, 1984.

ROAF, WILLIAM LAYTON
Professional football player. **Personal:** Born Apr 18, 1970, Pine Bluff, AR. **Educ:** Louisiana Tech, attended. **Career:** New Orleans Saints, tackle, 1993-. **Honors/Awds:** Pro Bowl, 1994, 1995, 1996; NFLPA, NFC Offensive Lineman of the Year, 1994; NFL Alumni Assn, Offensive Lineman of the Year, 1995. **Business Addr:** Professional Football Player, New Orleans Saints, 5800 Airline Hwy, Metairie, LA 70003, (504)733-0255.

ROANE, GLENWOOD P.
Attorney. **Personal:** Born Jul 26, 1930, Virginia; married Lucie Porter; children: Karen, Glenwood Jr, Rosemary. **Educ:** VA State Coll, BS 1952; Howard Univ, JD 1957; Fletcher School of Law, Postgrad 1970-71. **Career:** Teacher 1957-59; USVA, adjudicator & attny rev 1960-62; USN, negotiator 1962-65; USAID/Liberia, officer 1966-68; USAID/Ghana, asst dir 1968-70; Reg Population Office, dir 1971-73; USAID/Vietnam, asst dir 1974-75; USAID Cairo, officer 1976; Agency for Intl Devel Office Equal Oppty Prog dir 1977-78; USAID Kenya, dir; VSU, diplomat in residence 1980-83; Peterson & Basha, PC Law Firm, of counsel atty. **Orgs:** Former pastor 1st Bapt Church Vienna VA 1977-; interim pastor, Shiloh Baptist; assoc pastor Purity Bapt Church 1976-; pres 1st Baptist, Warrenton, VA. **Honors/Awds:** Superior Performance Awd 1962; Merit Honor Awd EOE Efforts 1976; Fulbright Nom 1957; Farfax County Citizen of the Year, Human Rights Award, 1985. **Military Serv:** AUS 1st lt 1952-54. **Business Addr:** Attorney, 717 Marshall Rd, Vienna, VA 22180.

ROANE, PHILIP RANSOM, JR.
Educator, virologist. **Personal:** Born Nov 20, 1927, Baltimore, MD; son of Mattie Brown Roane and Philip Ransom Roane; married Vernice Haynes, Aug 1, 1981; children: Crystal Reed, Donald H Reed. **Educ:** Morgan State Coll, BS 1952; Johns Hopkins, ScM 1960; Univ MD, PhD 1970. **Career:** Johns Hopkins, asst Microbiology 1960-64; Microbiol Assocs Inc, virologist 1964-72, dir quality control 1967-72; Howard Univ, asst prof microbiology 1972-79, Howard Univ, asst prof oncology 1977-, graduate associate professor, 1979-, associate professor, college of medicine, 1979-. **Orgs:** Mem Amer Assn Immunologists; Virology Study Sect NIH; Amer Soc Microbiology; mem NIH Virology Study Sect 1976-80; mem Dept of Army Viral & Rickettseal Diseases Review Grp 1979-81; mem Sigma Xi; rsch publs in field of virology. **Honors/Awds:** Kaiser Permanente Award for Distinguished Teaching 1979; Inspirational Leadership Award, Pre-Clinical Professor 1982; Merit Award at the Outstanding Instructor in Microbiology, Howard Universtiy Graduate Student Council, 1982; Certificate of Appreciation, Medical College Class of 1987, 1985. **Military Serv:** USAAF 1946-47. **Business Addr:** Associate Professor, Howard University-College of Medicine, Department of Microbiology, Pre-Clinical Bldg, 520 W St, NW, Washington, DC 20059.

ROBBINS, ALFRED S.
Justice. **Personal:** Born Nov 9, 1925; married Louise; children: Daryl Lynn, Alfred. **Educ:** Brooklyn Coll, BA; Brooklyn Law Sch, JD. **Career:** Nassau Hosp, dir; Supreme Ct, State of NY, justice 1979-; Dist Ct Nassau County, admin judge 1974-78; Legal Aid Soc, trial atty NY State Liquor Authority; private practice; Dist Atty's Office of Nassau County, asst dist atty 1967; Dist Ct Nassau County, judge 1971, admin judge 1974. **Orgs:** Pres Bd Judges; mem Nassau County Bar Assn; NY State Dist Atty Assn; Natl Dist Atty Assn; former dir Sheltering Arms Children's Aid Serv; former New York City Protestant Placement & Adoption Agency; former arbitrator Amer Arbitration Assn; former mem chmn Council of the State Univ of NY at Old Westbury Elder Presbyterian Church; commr Commn on Religion & Race; mem Hempstead Lion's Club; NAACP; former Eagle Scout Review Bd; Nassau County Council BSA; mem exec bd Nassau County Council of Boy Scouts. **Military Serv:** US Navy. **Business Addr:** Justice, Supreme Court Bldg, Supreme Court Dr, Mineola, NY 11501.

ROBBINS, AUSTIN DION
Professional football player. **Personal:** Born Mar 1, 1971, Washington, DC. **Educ:** Univ of North Carolina, attended. **Career:** Oakland Raiders, defensive tackle, 1995; New Orleans Saints, 1996-. **Business Addr:** Professional Football Player, New Orleans Saints, 5800 Airline Hwy, Metairie, LA 70003, (504)733-0255.

ROBBINS, CARL GREGORY CUYJET
Human resources executive. **Personal:** Born Feb 2, 1948, Philadelphia, PA; son of Leon Wallace Robbins Sr & Agnes Cuyjet Robbins; married Sydney, Aug 20, 1977; children: Five. **Educ:** University of Pennsylvania, BA, 1970; University of Pennsylvania, The Wharton School, MBA, 1980. **Career:** The Vanguard Group Inc, institutional marketing, director of consultant relations, currently. **Honors/Awds:** National Achievement Scholar, 1966-70. **Business Addr:** Director of Consultant Relations, The Vanguard Group Inc, M32, PO Box 2900, Valley Forge, PA 19482, (610)669-2703.

ROBBINS, HERMAN C.
Educational administrator. **Personal:** Born Jul 23, 1928, Ft Gibson, OK; children: Kelly, Beverly, Carol, Jacquelyn Shirley, Gerald, Ronald, Herman Jr. **Educ:** Langston U, BS 1947-51; OK State U, MS 1951-52; Univ of Tulsa, post grad study 1968-69. **Career:** Tulsa Jr Coll, vice pres bus & aux svcs; Tulsa Jr Coll, asso dean evening programs 1974-75; Tulsa Jr Coll, chmn bus serv div 1971-74; Tulsa Jr Coll,mid-mgmt coordinator, bus instr 1970-71; Hanna Lumber Co, mgr 1965-70; Nanna Lumber Co, dept head gen hardware 1960-65; Hanna Lumber Co, floor salesman 1953-60; Hanna Lumber Co, bldg engr 1947-53; Hanna Lumber Co, dir 1965-70; Multi Fab Mfg Corp, dir 1968-71; Tulsa Jr Coll Found Inc, financial agt 1976-. **Orgs:** Turstee, treas First Bapt Ch 1965-; bd mem Hutcherson Br YMCA 1965-; exchequer Kappa Alpha Psi Frat 1970-; bd mem ARC 1976-; bd mem Childrens Med Center 1978-; mem Gov Council on Physical Fitness 1980-; mem Nat Conf of Christians & Jews 1980-. **Business Addr:** 909 S Boston, Tulsa, OK 74119.

ROBBINS, KEVIN F.
Attorney. **Personal:** Born Nov 17, 1958, Detroit, MI; son of Beryl E Claytor Robbins and Robert J Robbins. **Educ:** Univ of MI, Ann Arbor, MI, BA, 1980; Thomas M Cooley Law School, Lansing, MI, JD, 1984. **Career:** City of Detroit, Detroit, MI, asst corporation counsel, 1985-89; Kmart Corporation, Troy, MI, asst public liability counsel, 1989-. **Orgs:** Natl Minority Counsel Demonstration Program; Assn of Defense Trial Counsel; American Corporate Counsel Assn; Detroit Bar Assn; Wolverine Bar Assn; mediator, 36th District in Detroit; mediator, Michigan Mediation Assn for Wayne County. **Honors/Awds:** Faculty Commendation Award, American Inst for Paralegal Studies, 1990. **Business Addr:** Asst Public Liability Counsel, Legal Dept, Kmart Corporation, 3100 W Big Beaver Rd, Troy, MI 48084.

ROBBINS, LEONARD
Architect, builder. **Personal:** Born Nov 3, 1955, Okaloosa County, FL; son of Elizabeth Eady Robbins and Bonzie Robbins; married Celia King Robbins, May 26, 1985. **Educ:** Syracuse University, Syracuse, NY, Bachelors, Architecture, 1979; New York University, New York, NY, Diploma, Construction Management, 1987; Upsala College, East Orange, NJ, Small Business Management, 1989. **Career:** City of Syracuse, Dept of Buildings, Syracuse, NY, architect, 1979-81; Syracuse NHS, Syracuse, NY, rehabilitation specialist, 1981-82; NHS of East Flatbush, Brooklyn, NY, construction specialist, 1982-85; NHS of New York City, Inc, New York, NY, neighborhood dir, 1985-87; Creative Restoration Consultants, Inc, Maplewood, NJ, vice president, owner, 1984-91; Unified Vailsburg Services, Newark, NJ, housing dir, 1991-; LR Construction Management, Maplewood, NJ, sole owner, 1990-. **Orgs:** Member, Building Trades Association, 1988; member, National Association of Home Builders, 1989-90; member, Builders Association of Metropolitan New Jersey, 1989-90. **Honors/Awds:** Certificate, New York State, Construction Code, 1981; Certificate, HUD Default Counseling HUD, 1984; Safety Certificate, OSHA, New York Building and Construction Industry Council, 1986; Recognition, McCreary Report, WNEW-TV Channel 5, New York, 1988; Recognition, Entrepreneur Series, WWOR-TV Channel 9, New York, 1989. **Home Addr:** 90 Plymouth Ave, Maplewood, NJ 07040, (201)763-3677. **Business Phone:** (201)763-2453.

ROBBINS, MILLARD D.
Insurance broker. **Personal:** Born Oct 7, 1919, Columbus, OH; son of Martha and Millard; married Alma Williams; children: Elizabeth Jones, Millard M, Jean M Brown, John J. **Educ:** Roosevelt Univ, BA 1954. **Career:** Robbins Ins Agcy, Inc, pres 1947; Robbins Mortgage Co, pres 1962-72; BMJ Co, spres 1981; Robbins Ins Agcy, Inc, broker, currently. **Orgs:** Dir Peoples Energy Corp 1972; dir Independent Bank 1965; dir Chicago Met Mutual Assn Co 1980; dir TR Auto Handling Co 1981; trustee DePaul Unv 1981; bus adv comm Chicago Urban League 1970; co-chmn mem comm Chicago Econ Club 1970; mem Univ Club 1970. **Honors/Awds:** Am Mem Lloyds of London 1978. **Military Serv:** AUS 1st sgt 1943-46. **Business Addr:** Broker, Robbins Insurance Agency Inc, 8224 S King Dr, Chicago, IL 60619.

ROBBINS, WARREN
Museum director. **Personal:** Born Sep 4, 1923, Worcester, MA; son of Pauline Sharfman Robbins and Harry Leo Robbins. **Educ:** Univ of NH, BA, 1945; Univ of Michigan, MA, 1949; Lebanon Valley College, LLD, 1975. **Career:** Worcester Gazette, aviation editor, 1945; teacher, 1948-50; US Cultural Program, lecturer, 1950; US High Commission to Austria, editor, education advisor, 1951-55; consul for cultural and public affairs, Stuttgart, Germany, 1955-57; attache, chief of American cultural program, Bonn, Germany, 1958-60; US Adv Commission on Education and Cultural Relations, asst staff director, 1960-61, asst to dep asst sec of state for education and cultural and cultural relations, 1961-62, Foreign Service Institute, course chairman, 1962-63; Museum of African Art, Washington, DC, director, currently. **Orgs:** Member, Assn of Art Museum Directors; member, DC Comn Arts & Humanities. **Honors/Awds:** Order of Merit, Government of Cameroon, 1973; Int Human Rights Award, Rothko Chapel, 1981; Henry Medal, Smithsonian Institute, 1982; Washington DC Mayors Art Award, 1985; author: "African Art in American Collections," Praeger, Vol 1, 1966, "Art of Henry O Tanner," Smithsonian

Institute, 1969, "How to Approach Traditional African Sculpture," Smithsonian, 1972, "Traditional American Values in a World of Hostilities," Adult Education, 1975.

ROBERSON, DALTON ANTHONY
Judge. **Personal:** Born May 11, 1937, Mount Vernon, AL; son of Sarah Ann Williams-Roberson and Drue Roberson; married Pearl Janet Stephens; children: Portia, Dalton Jr. **Educ:** MI State Univ, BA, JD; Detroit Coll of Law, BA, JSD. **Career:** State of MI, soc worker 1964-68; Wayne Cty, asst prosecutor 1969-70; US Dist, atty 1970-71; Harrison Friedman Roberson, criminal defense lawyer 1970-74; City of Detroit Recorders Court, judge, executive chief judge, currently. **Orgs:** Mem MI State Bar Assn 1969, Wolverine Bar Assn 1969, Criminal Defense Lawyers Assn 1970-74, MI Civil Rts Commn 1972-73; chmn MI Civil Rts Commn 1973-74; mem MI Judges Assn 1974-; chmn Assn of Black Judges of MI; former bd mem Detroit Branch NAACP; mem exec comm Combines Wayne Circuit/Recorders Court; former mem exec comm MI Judges Assn; bd mem State of MI 1989-. **Honors/Awds:** Natl Conf of Black Lawyers, Judge of the Year Award, 1991. **Military Serv:** USAF a/1c 1954-58. **Business Addr:** Executive Chief Judge, City of Detroit, The Circuit Court, for the Third Judicial Circuit of Michigan and the, Recorder's Court of the City of Detroit, 1441 St Antoine, Rm 801, Detroit, MI 48226.

ROBERSON, EARL
College president. **Personal:** Born Dec 28, 1931, Troy, AL; son of Rebecca Skings Roberson and John Wesley Roberson; married Jessie Shears Roberson, Dec 23, 1956; children: Earl II, Katrina Lynn. **Educ:** AL A&M Univ, Normal, AL, BS, 1954, MS, 1962; Univ of South AL, Mobile, AL, 1971-72. **Career:** Shellhorn High School, Shellhorn, AL, teacher, asst principal, 1956-57; Academy State High School, Troy, AL, coordinator, diversified occupation, 1957-62; Tech Carver State Technical College, Mobile AL, asst dir, 1962-76, president, 1976-. **Orgs:** Bd of dirs, past pres, West Mobile Kiwanis Club, 1972-. **Honors/Awds:** Doctor of Humane Letters, AL Interdenominational Seminary, Inc, 1987. **Military Serv:** US Army, sp-4, 1954-56; Honorable Discharged, Good Conduct Medal, European Theater Service. **Business Addr:** President, Carver State Technical College, 414 Stanton St, Mobile, AL 36617.

ROBERSON, F. ALEXIS H.
Administrator. **Personal:** Born Sep 20, 1942, Aiken, SC; daughter of F M Gomillion Hammond and T A Hammond; divorced; children: Alan. **Educ:** Howard Univ, Washington DC, BA, 1963, Masters in Educ, 1974; Univ of the District of Columbia, Washington DC, Post Graduate. **Career:** Opportunities Industralization Center, Washington DC, dir remedial educ, 1967-70, curriculum specialist, 1970-73, deputy dir, 1973-80; Washington DC Government, Washington DC, Dept of Recreation, deputy dir, 1980-82, dir, 1983-86, Dept of Employment Serv, dir, 1987-. **Orgs:** Commr, Washington DC Bd of Appeals and Review, Commn of Post-Secondary Educ; chairperson, bd of dir, US Youth Games; mem, The Links Inc, The Girl Friends Inc, The Washington Chapter NAACP, Zion Baptist Church, Washington DC; Govt Representative, The Washington DC Wage-Hour Bd, The Private Industry Council; pres, Washington Metropolitan Area Chapter, Natl Forum for Black Public Admn, 1987-. **Honors/Awds:** Creator, Neighborhood Arts Acad Program, 1984; oraganizer, Ppotomac Riverfest, 1984; organizer, The Mayor's Amateur Boxing Tournament, 1985; The President's Award, Washington NAACP, 1986; Tribute from US House of Representatives, 1987; organizer, Project Success, Washington DC, 1987; Top 100 Black Business & Professional Women, Dollars & Sense Magazine, 1988; Public Serv, Natl Coalition of 100 Black Women, 1989; Public Serv, Washington Urban League, 1989; organizer, Design-A-Youth Program, 1989.

ROBERSON, GLORIA GRANT
Librarian, educator. **Personal:** Born in East Meadow, NY; daughter of Lillie Cofield Grant and William Grant; married Clifford Roberson, Oct 31, 1965; children: Gloriane, Cynthia, Clifford. **Educ:** Adelphi University, Garden City, NY, BS, 1980, MS, 1987; Long Island University, Brookville, NY, MLS, 1984. **Career:** Adelphi University, Garden City, NY, asst prof, 1975-; Hofstra University, Hemp, NY, adj asst prof, beginning 1980, assoc prof, currently. **Orgs:** Correspondence secretary, Academic and Special Libraries Nassau County Library Assn, 1989-90; American Assn of University Professors. **Honors/Awds:** Person of the Year Award, Third World Studen Assn, 1990. **Business Addr:** Associate Professor, Adelphi University, Swirbal Library, Garden City, NY 11530.

ROBERSON, LAWRENCE R.
Money manager, investment consultant. **Personal:** Born Aug 26, 1946, Birmingham, AL; son of Ressie Roberson and Mack Roberson. **Educ:** Alabama A&M Univ, BS 1967; Indiana Univ, MBA 1970; College for Financial Plng, CFP 1986. **Career:** IBM, systems engr 1967-68, financial analyst 1969; Ford Motor Co, supervisor financial analysis 1973-83; Wealth Management Group Inc, pres. **Orgs:** Mem Inst for Certified Financial Planners 1983-, Internatl Assoc for Financial Plng 1984-; dir Intl Exchange Cncl 1986-. **Honors/Awds:** White House Fellowship Prog Regional finalist 1983-84. **Business Addr:** President, Wealth Management Group Inc, PO Box 27666, Detroit, MI 48227, (313)835-6562.

ROBERSON, SANDRA SHORT. See SHAKOOR, WAHEEDAH AQUEELAH.

ROBERTS, ALFRED LLOYD, SR.
Educational administrator. **Personal:** Born Dec 18, 1942, Austin, TX; son of Ellen Woodfork Arnold and James Roberts; married Billie Kerl Roberts, Feb 17, 1968; children: Alfrelynn, Latasha, Alfred Jr. **Educ:** Prairie View A&M U, BS 1963; TX A&M U, MEd 1966, PhD 1973. **Career:** Dallas Independent Sch Dist, teacher, 1965-69, elem prin 1969-71, dir community relations 1971-75; E Oak Cliff Sub Dist, dep asst supt, administrator subdistrict III, executive director, 1975-89, assistant supt personnel, 1989-93, exec dir, alternative certification, 1993-. **Orgs:** Nat Educ Assn; Phi Delta Kappa; Dallas Sch Administrators Assn; mem Alpha Phi Alpha; mem St Luke Comm United Meth Ch; mem Historic Preservation League; mem Com of 100; YMCA; member, Texas Alliance of Black School Educators; member, past natl pres, National Alliance of Black School Educators; member, Dallas Regional Alliance of Black School Educators. **Honors/Awds:** Dallas Black C of C nominee; Ford Found Urban Educ Adminstr fellow nominee, 1970. **Business Addr:** Exec Director, Alternative Certification, Dallas ISD, 3434 S R L Thornton Fwy, Dallas, TX 75224.

ROBERTS, ANGELA DORREAN (PEOPLES)
Administrator. **Personal:** Born Nov 21, 1960, Chicago, IL; daughter of Betty Williams and Morris Peoples; married Marvin James Roberts, Oct 3, 1992; children: Anjai G Shields. **Educ:** California State University, BA, communications. **Career:** Weiss, Jones & Co., data processing manager, 1979-85; Associated Students of UCLA, computer operations manager, 1985-89; Housing Authority of the City of Los Angeles, MIS director, 1989-. **Honors/Awds:** City of Los Angeles, Outstanding Service Award, 1992. **Business Addr:** MIS Director, Housing Authority City of Los Angeles, 2600 Wilshire Blvd, Ste 5300, Los Angeles, CA 90057, (213)252-5365.

ROBERTS, BIP (LEON JOSEPH III)
Professional baseball player. **Personal:** Born Oct 27, 1963, Berkeley, CA. **Educ:** Chabot College. **Career:** San Diego Padres, infielder, 1986-91, 1994-95; Cincinnati Reds, 1992-93; Kansas City Royals, 1996-97; Cleveland Indians, 1997; Detroit Tigers, 1998-. **Business Addr:** Professional Baseball Player, Detroit Tigers, 2121 Trumbull St, Detroit, MI 48216, (313)962-4000.

ROBERTS, BLANCHE ELIZABETH
Bank executive. **Personal:** Born Apr 23, 1955, Chicago, IL; daughter of Alexandra Mary Hoover Johnson and Dr Leroy Edison Jones; married Charles Scott Roberts, Nov 23, 1985; children: Alexis Cleo. **Educ:** Univ of Iowa, Iowa City IA, attended, 1972; Dartmouth Coll, Hanover NH, BA, 1977; DePaul Univ, Chicago IL, MBA, 1983. **Career:** Universidad de Granada, Granada, Spain, Spanish teaching asst, 1978; Instituto Chileno Norte Am, Santiago, Chile, English instructor, 1978-79; Charles of the Ritz, Chicago IL, commn sales, 1979-80; Freedom Systems, Chicago IL, exec asst, 1980-82; Northern Trust Company, Chicago IL, intl officer, 1982-85; First Natl Bank of Chicago, Chicago IL, asst vice pres, 1985-87; Exchange Natl Bank, Chicago IL, vice pres, 1987-. **Orgs:** Volunteer, Recording for the Blind, 1980; mem, State Microscopical Soc of Illinois, 1971; jr mem, Soc of Cosmetic Chemists, 1976-78; mem, Beta Gamma Sigma, Natl Honor Soc, 1983, Natl Corporate Cash Mgmt Assn, 1985-; dir, Visiting Nurse Assn of Chicago, 1988-, VNA Ventures (for profit company), 1988-. **Honors/Awds:** First Place Winner (Outstanding), Chicago Science Fair, 1971, 1972, 1973; Semi-Finalist, Westinghouse Science Talent Search, 1973; First Place Winner (Outstanding), State Science Fair, 1973; Outstanding Sr in Science, Math Kenwood Acad, 1973; Vice President, Senior Class, 1973; Varsity Letter Winner, Dartmouth Coll, 1974, 1975, 1976; Willard Tostman Mmemorial Scholar, Dartmouth Coll, 1975; Chicago's Up and Coming, Dollars and Sense Magazine, 1988. **Home Addr:** 5448 South Cornell Ave, Chicago, IL 60615.

ROBERTS, BOBBY L.
Manufacturing executive (retired). **Personal:** Born Sep 19, 1938, Windom, TX; son of Mr & Mrs Dee Roberts. **Educ:** Prairie View A&M Univ, BS 1960; Fairleigh Dickinson Univ, MBA 1978. **Career:** Plantation Foods Corp, supervisor 1960-62; Houston Lighting-Power Co, aux engr 1965-70; Anheuser-Busch Inc, operations engr 1970-72; Johnson & Johnson, chief engr 1972-86; Wesley-Jessen, corporation director of operations engineering, 1988-89, director of manufacturing 1989-94. **Orgs:** Mem NB MBA Assn Inc 1982-; mem sec Assn for Faciliter Engineering 1984-. **Honors/Awds:** Chicago Metropolitan Black and Hispanic Achievers of Industry Recognition Awd YMCA 1980; Plant Engineer of the Year Assn for Faciliter Engineering Fox Valley Chap 1986. **Military Serv:** AUS specialist 4th class 2 yrs. **Home Addr:** 1609 Signal Dr, Naperville, IL 60565.

ROBERTS, BRETT
Professional baseball player. **Educ:** Morehead State University. **Career:** Minnesota Twins, 1993-. **Business Addr:** Professional Baseball Player, Minnesota Twins, 501 Chicago Ave S, Minneapolis, MN 55415, (612)375-7444.

ROBERTS, BRYNDIS WYNETTE
Educational administrator. **Personal:** Born Sep 4, 1957, Sylvania, GA; daughter of Josie Spencer Walls and Roy Heyward Roberts; children: Jennifer Yvonne, Jessica Kathleen. **Educ:** Wesleyan Coll, Macon, GA, AB (magna cum laude), 1978; Univ of GA, Athens, Ga, JD (cum laude), 1981. **Career:** State Law Dept, Atlanta, GA, asst attorney general, 1981-87; Univ of GA, Athens, GA, vice pres for legal affairs, 1987-. **Orgs:** Mem, Classic City Pilot Club, 1991-92, sec, School & College Law Section, State Bar, 1988-89; mem, National Association of College & University Attorney's, 1987-92, 1986-, chairman, 1986-87; mem, GA State Board of Accountancy, 1988-; Wesleyan Board of Trustees, 1991. **Honors/Awds:** Business & Professional Women Young Careerist, DeKalb Business & Professional Women, 1985; Outstanding Woman Law Student, GA Assn of Women Lawyers, 1981. **Business Addr:** Vice President, Legal Affairs, University of Georgia, 310 Old College, Athens, GA 30602, (706)542-0006.

ROBERTS, CECILIA
Insurance company executive. **Career:** Majestic Life Insurance Co, CEO, currently. **Special Achievements:** Company is ranked #14 on Black Enterprise's list of top insurance companies, 1994. **Business Addr:** CEO, Majestic Life Ins Co, 1833 Oretha C Haley Blvd, New Orleans, LA 70113, (504)525-0375.

ROBERTS, CHARLES L.
Executive director. **Personal:** Born May 25, 1943, Farmerville, LA; married Charlesetta Shoulders; children: Traci, Channa. **Educ:** KY State U, BS; Univ of Louisville, MS; Univ of GA. **Career:** City of Louisville, dir of sanitation; Met Parks & Recreation Bd, asst dir 1970-74; Louisville Sch Dist, tchr 1964-70. **Orgs:** Mem Am Pub Works Assn; Mgmt Planning Council; State Reg Crime Council; NAACP; Omega Psi Phi. **Honors/Awds:** Outstanding citizen award 1973. **Business Addr:** 400 S 6 St, Louisville, KY.

ROBERTS, CHERYL DORNITA LYNN
Educator. **Personal:** Born Jul 31, 1958, Martinsburg, WV; daughter of Dorothy J Davenport Roberts and Shelby L Roberts Sr (deceased). **Educ:** Shepherd Coll, BS 1980; Univ of DC, MA 1984. **Career:** Edgemeade of MD, recreation specialist 1980-81; Univ of DC, asst coach men's basketball 1981-85; Veterans Affairs Med Ctr, recreation therapist 1985-87, vocational rehabilitation specialist 1987-88, asst chief, Domiciliary Care Program, 1988-94; Education Specialist, 1994-97; 12th National Veterans Golden Age Games, coord, 1997-. **Orgs:** Focus, board of directors, 1991-96, treasurer, 1992; Delta Sigma Theta Sor Inc, 1984-, Shepherd College Alumni Assn, NAACP; Employees Assn, advisor, VAMC; Mandela Chapter of Blacks in Government. **Honors/Awds:** TV Appearances Good Morning Amer 1981, 1982; NY Times Feature Article Sports World Specials 1984; Outstanding Performance in Educational Civic & Professional Sports Accomplishments, Serenity 7th Day Adventist Church, 1990; VAMC, Team Excellence Award, 1992; Special Contribution Award, 1994. **Home Addr:** 329 W German St, PO Box 217, Shepherdstown, WV 25443, (304)876-2277. **Business Addr:** Coordinator, NVGAG, VA Medical Center, Martinsburg, WV 25401, (304)263-0811.

ROBERTS, DONALD LEE
General manager. **Personal:** Born Dec 20, 1929, South Orange, NJ; married Margaret Robinson. **Educ:** WV State Coll, BS 1952. **Career:** Amalgamated Publishers Inc, vice pres gen mgr 1975-, gen mgr 1966-75, bus mgr 1958-66; Internal Revenue, agt 1955-58; Friendly Fuld Neighbrhd Ctr, pres. **Orgs:** Life mem NAACP; interim aud of accts natl office Kappa Alpha Psi Frat; life mem Kappa Alpha Psi Frat; mem 100 Black Men; mem Essex Co Urban League; mem Civil Liberties Union; mem Nat Bus League; mem Nat Assn of Mkt Develrs. **Honors/Awds:** Kappa Alpha Psi Award, Northeastern Province 1977. **Military Serv:** AUS 1st lt 1952-54. **Business Addr:** 293 E Hazelwood Ave, Rahway, NJ 07065.

ROBERTS, EDGAR
Construction company executive. **Personal:** Born Aug 8, 1946, Valdosta, GA; son of Fannie Mae Davis Roberts and John Roberts; married Mary Catherine Gardner Roberts, Dec 12, 1965; children: Tia Charlotte, Sherri Latrell, Carla Maria. **Educ:** Temple Business School, Washington, DC, 1964-66; Central Business School, Valdosta, GA, 1969-70; Georgia Military College, Valdosta, GA, 1971-72. **Career:** Elcona Mobile Homes, Valdosta, GA, receiving clerk, 1969-71; self employed, Valdosta, GA, minit market manager, 1971-72; Elcona Mobile Home, Valdosta, GA, receiving clerk, 1972-73, purchasing manager, 1973-76; A-1 Construction Co Inc, Valdosta, GA, president/treasurer, 1976-. **Orgs:** Trustee, Valdosta State College Foundation, 1988-; chairman, Valdosta State College Minority Foundation, 1988-; vice president, Minority Business Group of Valdosta, 1989-; board of directors, First State Bank & Trust, 1989-; board of directors, Art Commission, 1990-; advisory board, Superintendent of Lowndes Co Schools, 1989-; board of directors, Leadership Lowndes, 1989-; president/owner, James Scott & Son Funeral Home Inc, 1989-; executive board, Valdosta-Lowndes Co Chamber of Commerce, 1990-; member, VSC School of Business, 1990-; member of the board, Governor's Commission on Economy and Efficiency in State Govern-

ment, 1990-; board of directors, GAME (Georgia Association of Minority Entrepreneurs), 1991-. **Honors/Awds:** Outstanding Business of the Year (Const), US Dept of Commerce, Minor Bus Dev Agency & Columbus Min Bus Dev Ctr, 1984; Minority Small Business of the Year, US Dept of Commerce, Minor Bus Dev Agency & Columbus Min Bus Dev Ctr, 1987; Appreciation Award for Distinguished Achievements & Performance in Const, US Dept of Commerce Minority Business Development Agency, 1990; Atlanta Region Minority Construction Firm of the Year, Minority Business Development Assn, 1990; Appreciation of Service in the Field of Business, Black History Action Committee, 1990; Appreciation for Dedicated & Outstanding Participation, Valdosta/Lowndes County Zoning Board of Appeals, 1984-90; Distinguished Service as President, National Assn of Home Builders of the US, 1983-84. **Military Serv:** US Marine Corps, E-5, 1966-68. **Home Addr:** PO Box 56, Valdosta, GA 31603-0056.

ROBERTS, EDWARD A.
Educational administrator. **Personal:** Born Jun 17, 1950, Brooklyn, NY; married Yuklin B John. **Educ:** City Coll of NY, BA 1979. **Career:** 902 Auto Inc, asst dir 1980-; City Univ of NY, bd of trustees 1976-80; Univ Student Senate City Univ of NY, chmn 1976-80; CCNY Office of the Dean of Students, asst higher educ officer 1975-76. **Orgs:** Exec mem Com for Pub Higher Educ 1977-79; mem NY State Higher Educ Servs Corp 1978; mem Gov's Task Force on Higher Educ 1979; mem City Coll Pres Policy Adv Com 1976-77; pres Carter's Action Review Commn 1977. **Honors/Awds:** Outstanding Enlisted Man Award AUS 1972; award of merit Bronx Comm Coll 1979, Queens Coll 1978, City Coll NY 1978. **Military Serv:** AUS E-5 1971-73. **Business Addr:** 535 E 80th St, New York, NY 10021.

ROBERTS, ELLA S.
Occupancy supervisor. **Personal:** Born Aug 30, 1927, New Castle, KY; widowed; children: 5. **Educ:** Lincoln Inst of Kentucky, 1945; Business School, 1946; Univ of Louisville, certificate. **Career:** Housing Authority of Louisville, Jefferson County School Dist Title I ESEA Parent Advisory Council, occupancy supervisor chmn; Louisiana Urban League, Housing Counseling and Information Program, program mgr, counselor, currently. **Orgs:** Citizens Team for Schools Eval; asst dir Central Dist Young People of WMU; financial sec Central Dist Sun School & BTU Conv; Louisville Urban League; Shelby Park Neighborhood Association, Inc, president; NAACP; Mt Olive Missionary Baptist Church Sunday School, general superintendent; City of Louisville Community Design Center; Metropolitan Housing Coalition, board of directors; SPARC, board of directors; Community Winterhelp, Inc, consultative committee; MHNA Steering Committee; Goals for Greater Louisville; School Task Force, Many People One Community. **Honors/Awds:** Rev J L Roberts Scholarship Award, 1990; Graduate Focus Louisville, 1991; Pride's Humanitarian Award, 1992. **Business Addr:** Program Manager, Counselor, Louisville Urban League, Housing, Counseling and Information Program, 1535 Broadway, Louisville, KY 40203.

ROBERTS, GRADY H., JR.
University educator, administrator. **Personal:** Born Feb 8, 1940, Pittsburgh. **Educ:** Central State Univ, Wilberforce OH, BS 1963; Univ of Pittsburgh, MSW 1965, MPH 1971, PhD 1974. **Career:** Univ of Pittsburgh School of Social Work, dir of admissions, asst prof 1969-; Western Psychiatric Inst & Clinic, psychiatric social worker 1967-69; Madigan Gen Hosp Tacoma WA, clinical social work officer, social work serv 1965-67. **Orgs:** Mem Assn of Black Soc wrkrs; Cncl on Soc wrk Ed; Nat Assn of Soc Wrkrs; mem Alpha Phi Alpha; NAACP. **Military Serv:** AUS capt 1965-67; AUSR maj 1985. **Business Addr:** University of Pittsburgh, School of Social Work, 2103 Cathedral of Learning, Pittsburgh, PA 15260.

ROBERTS, HARLAN WILLIAM, III
Systems engineer, consultant. **Personal:** Born Jan 12, 1931, Wilmington, DE; divorced; children: Teala Jeanne, Harlan David. **Educ:** Univ of PA, BS, MSW 1976. **Career:** United Methodist Action Program, suprv 1968-69; Family Serv Northern DE, counselor 1969-74; Univ of PA Family Maintance Org, coord 1975-76; Mental Health-Child Protective Serv of MD, clinical therapist. **Orgs:** Bd mem Delaware OIC 1970-74; bd mem Family Assoc of Amer 1971-74; exec bd Wilmington DE Chap NAACP 1971-82; 1st vice pres Wilmington United Neighborhood 1973-74; vice pres & pres Red Clay Consolidated Sch Bd 1981-85. **Honors/Awds:** Harriet Tubman DE Chapter Harriet Tubman 1984. **Military Serv:** AUS capt 8 yrs; US Ranger, Counted Intellegent Corp. **Home Addr:** 221 N Cleveland Ave, Wilmington, DE 19805.

ROBERTS, HERMAN
Business executive. **Personal:** Born Jan 21, 1924, Beggs, OK; married Sonja Williams; children: Stephan, Herman, Fredric, Ewan, Rodne. **Career:** Taxicab Co, owner; Roberts Show Club, 1954-61; Roberts Motels Inc, pres 1961-88. **Orgs:** Active in various comm endeavors; mem IL Citizens Found. **Honors/Awds:** Disting Publ Serv Awd; Spec Recognition Awd Washington Pk YMCA; Man of the Year FFAF & Amer Guild Variety Artists Awd; Cert of Appreciation BSA; Honoree Annual Brotherhood Banquet. **Business Addr:** President, Roberts Motels Inc, 301 E 63rd Dr, Chicago, IL 60637.

ROBERTS, HERMESE E.
Educator (retired). **Personal:** Born Sep 22, 1913, Panama Canal Zone, Panama; daughter of May Johnson and Jonathan Johnson; married Edward J Roberts Sr; children: Edward James Jr, Hermese Edwina. **Educ:** Hunter Coll of NY, BA 1934; Atlanta Univ Atlanta, GA, MA 1941; Nova Univ Ft Lauderdale, FL, EdD 1975; Columbia Univ, Univ of Chgo, Advanced Stds. **Career:** Atlanta Univ Lab Sch, tchr 1934-39; Peach Cty Tr Sch Ft Valley, prin 1939-45; Southern Univ, reading program dir, 1945-46; Univ of Chicago Reading Clinics, reading clinician, 1946-49; Chicago Pub Sch, clin psych 1949-54; Dartmouth Coll, reading specialist, 1964; Amer Book Co, consultant, 1965-71; Mayo Elem Sch Chgo, IL, prin 1955-83. **Orgs:** Mem, Natl Educ Assn 1957; mem Intl Reading Assn; mem Chicago Princpals Assn. **Honors/Awds:** Author, Dandy Dog Early Learning Program, Am Book Co 1966; co-author, Amer Book Co Basic Readers 1970; author, The Third Ear, English Language Inst 1970; "Don't Teach Them to Read" Elementary English NCTE 1970; editor, The Glories of Christ, by H J Heijkoop (translated from the German), Believers Bookshelf, Ontario, Canada, 1985.

ROBERTS, JACQUELINE JOHNSON
State representative. **Personal:** Born Apr 30, 1944, Dermott, AR; daughter of Gertrude Colen Johnson and Ocie Johnson; married Curley Roberts, Aug 16, 1964; children: Lisa LaVon, Curlee LaFayette, Dwyane Keith. **Educ:** Arkansas AM&N College, BS, 1967, elementary education teaching certificate, 1968, library science, 1970. **Career:** Bradley Elementary, Warren, AR, teacher, 1967-68; Arkansas AM&N College Library, shipping and receiving, 1969-74; B&W Tobacco Co, sales representative, 1979-83; Dancy Oil Co, office manager, 1983-85; St. John Apartments, manager, 1986-89; State of Arkansas, state representative, 1991-. **Orgs:** Pine Bluff Downtown Development, Special Events Committee, 1990-; secretary, Jefferson County Black Caucus, 1987-; Arkansas Democratic Party, Filing Fee Committee, 1988-90; member, National Committee to Preserve Social Security, 1988-90; board member, Association of Community Organizations for Reform Now (ACORN), 1986-; member, Urban League of Arkansas, 1991-; Pine Bluff Chamber of Commerce, Membership Committee, 1990-. **Honors/Awds:** Certificate of Honor for Community Service, Top Ladies of Distinction, 1990; Recognition of Outstanding Achievement, Arkansas State Press and Central Arkansas Association of Black Journalist, 1991; Certificate of Recognition, Female Black Action, Inc, 1991. **Home Addr:** PO Box 2075, Pine Bluff, AR 71613-2075.

ROBERTS, JAMES E.
Physician. **Personal:** Born Jul 27, 1903, Mt Pleasant, PA; married Sylvesta R; children: Karen, Lisa. **Educ:** Howard U, BS 1931, MS 1933, MD 1937. **Career:** Physician surgeon Ob-gyn; Howard Univ Med Sch, clinical instr, Obs-gyn 1941-75; MD Fair Housing Inc, Montgomery Co MD, founder vice pres 1961-; Montgomery Co Gynecological Soc, founder vice pres 1962-; Am Cancer Soc Metro Comm, Metropolitan Area Wash, pres 1974-75; Am Cancer Soc Div State of MD, pres elect 1976-77. **Orgs:** Mem Chi Delta Mu 1937-; chmn serv com Montgomery Co Unit Am Cancer Soc 1962-70, vice pres 1970-72, pres 1972-75; bd dir MD Div Am Cancer Soc 1964-. **Honors/Awds:** Certificate of appreciation Pres Harry S Truman 1953, Dwight Eisenhower 1958, Lyndon B Johnson 1963; volunteer of year Am Cancer Soc 1972; citation 21 yrs serv treas of Assoc of Former Interns & Residents of Freedman's Hosp, Wash, DC; outstanding serv award White Oak Civic Assn; Father of Yr, Jack & Jill of Am Inc 1973. **Business Addr:** 2328 Georgia Ave NW, Washington, DC 20001.

ROBERTS, JANICE L.
City official. **Personal:** Born Dec 31, 1959, Pine Bluff, AR; daughter of Deloris Diane Strivers Roberts and James C Roberts. **Educ:** University of Arkansas at Pine Bluff, Pine Bluff, AR, BA, economics, 1981; University of Southern California, Los Angeles, CA, MPA, 1989; New York University, Baruch College, New York, NY, MPA, 1991; National Urban Fellows, New York, NY, urban studies, 1991. **Career:** US Dept of Agriculture, Soil Conservation Service, economist, 1979-85; US Army Corps of Engineer, Los Angeles, CA, economist, 1985-90; World Port Los Angeles, Port of Los Angeles, Los Angeles, CA, executive director special assistant, 1990-. **Orgs:** Assistant chairperson, student advisory, Los Angeles Chapter, National Forum for Black Public Administrators, 1987-; member, National Association of Female Executive, 1982-; member, American Association of Port Authorities, 1990-; member, SRI International Association, 1990-; treasurer, Delta Sigma Theta Sorority, 1987-. **Honors/Awds:** Advisor, United States Congressional Advisory Board, US Congressional Office 1982; Outstanding Young Women of America, US Representative Dale Bumper, 1989; Federal Executive Board Fellowship, Univ of Southern California, 1987. **Business Addr:** Executive Director Special Assistant, Executive Office/CEO, Port Authority, 425 S Palos Veders, San Pedro, CA 90733.

ROBERTS, JOHN B.
Business executive. **Personal:** Born Mar 23, 1912, Dublin, GA; married Helen; children: John Jr. **Career:** Stunt bicycle rider 1930's; Cleveland Area Bicycle Dealers Assoc, org 1946; Roberts Enter, owner 1940-. **Orgs:** Bd mem Cleveland Bus League 25 yrs; mem Minority Econ Council, Comm Businessmen Credit Union, LERTA. **Honors/Awds:** Awd of Hon Cleveland Bus League 1948. **Military Serv:** AUS pvt 1943. **Business Addr:** Roberts Enterprise, 7703-5-7 Cedar Ave, Cleveland, OH 44103.

ROBERTS, JOHN CHRISTOPHER
Automobile dealer. **Personal:** Born Sep 12, 1944, Boston, MA; son of Lillian G Roberts and John Warren Roberts; married Joan Clarke, Dec 28, 1968; children: John Michael, Jason Martin, Kristen Renee. **Educ:** GMI Engineering and Management Institute, BSME, 1967; Xavier University, MBA, 1970. **Career:** Inland Division General Motors, various engineering and managerial positions, 1962-1979; Ford Motor Co, sr product planner, 1979-81; Hydramatic Division General Motors, mgr experimental, 1981-89, dealer development trainee, 1989-91; Roberts Buick Saab GMC Truck Inc, pres, 1991-. **Orgs:** Board of trustees GMI Alumni Foundation, treasurer, 1982-; Haverhill Chamber of Commerce, board of directors, 1992-; Bethany Home Board of Directors, director, 1992-; GMI Alumni Association, vice pres, treasurer, 1976-86; General Motor Minority Dealer Association, 1991-; Society of Automotive Engineers; Georgia Tech Minority Development Advisory Committee, 1986-89; Society of Plastics Engineers, board of directors, Miami Valley section president, 1972-76; Rotary Intern ational; National Assn of Minority Automobile Dealers; Merrimac Valley Red Cros s, board of directors; Northern Essex Community College Occupational Advisory C ouncil; ESRA Inc, board of directors; General Motors Youth Educational Systems National Advisory Board. **Special Achievements:** GMI Engineering & Management Institute Distinguished Alumni Award, 1986; Robot Society for Leadership in Student Affairs at GMI, 1965; Dayton Ohio Area General Motors, speakers bureau, 1971-76; Wolverine Council, Boy Scouts, membership drive, 1981-89; Massachusetts Black Caucus, Minority Business Award, 1995. **Business Addr:** President, Roberts Buick-Saab-GMC Truck, 901 S Main St, Haverhill, MA 01830, (508)373-3882.

ROBERTS, JONATHAN
Hospital administrator. **Career:** The Medical Center of Louisiana, CEO, currently.

ROBERTS, KAY GEORGE
Orchestra conductor. **Personal:** Born Sep 16, 1950, Nashville, TN. **Educ:** Fisk University, Nashville, TN, BA, 1972; Yale University, New Haven, CT, MM, 1975, MMA, 1976, DMA, 1986. **Career:** University of Massachusetts, Lowell, conductor-univ orchestra, professor of music, 1978-; Ensemble Americana, Stuttgart, Germany, music director/founder, 1989-; Artemis Ensemble, Stuttgart, Germany, conductor, 1990-; String Currents, music dir/founder, 1994-. **Orgs:** Guest Conductor: Chicago Symphony, Dallas Symphony, Cleveland Orchestra, Dayton Philharmonic, Detroit Symphony, Indianapolis Symphony, Nashville Symphony Orchestra, Chattanooga Symphony, Bangkok Symphony Orchestra (Thailand), Charlotte Symphony, Des Moines Symphony, Grant Park Symphony, New Haven Symphony, Savannah Symphony, New York City Housing Authority Symphony, National Symphony Orchestra, Louisville Orchestra, Shreveport Symphony Orchestra, Louisiana Philharmonic, Cincinnati Chamber Orchestra, Black Music Repertory Ensemble, Orchestra della Svizzera Italiana (Lugano, Switzerland); Masterclasses with: Leonard Bernstein, Seiji Ozawa, Andre Previn, Gustav Meier, Margaret Hillis. **Honors/Awds:** League of Black Women, Outstanding Achievement in the Performing Arts, 1991; Distinguished Alumna USN/PDS University School Nashville/Peabody Demonstration School, 1991; Research Grant, German Academic Exchange Service, 1990, 1992; Black Achievers Awards, Greater Boston YMCA, 1988; Cultural Specialist in Music (Egypt) US State Department, 1988; Distinguished Alumni of the Year Award, National Assn for Equal Opportunity in Higher Education, 1987; Natl Achievement Award from the National Black Music Caucus, 1993. **Business Addr:** Professor, Music Department, College of Fine Arts, University of Massachusetts, Lowell, 1 University Ave, Lowell, MA 01854.

ROBERTS, KIM A.
Executive labor organization. **Personal:** Born May 28, 1957, New York, NY; daughter of Doris Galiber Roberts and Howard A Roberts. **Educ:** Harvard University, BA, 1978; Georgetown University Law Center, JD, 1981. **Career:** American Federation of Television & Radio Artists, 1981-87, San Francisco executive director, 1987-92, national assistant executive director, 1992-. **Orgs:** Mayor's Film Advisory Council, San Francisco, 1990; San Francisco Labor Council, delegate, 1989-92; New York Central Labor Council, delegate, 1986-87; Natl Assn of Black Journalists, associate member, 1992-. **Business Addr:** Assistant National Executive Director, American Federation of Television & Radio Artists, 260 Madison Ave, 17th Fl, New York, NY 10016, (212)532-0800.

ROBERTS, LILLIAN
Business executive. **Personal:** Born Jan 2, 1928, Chicago, IL; daughter of Lillian Henry Davis and Henry Davis; divorced. **Educ:** Univ of IL, 1944-45; Roosevelt Univ, Labor School 1958-60. **Career:** Lyng-in-Hospital, nurse aide, operating room

technician, 1945-58; Chicago AFSCME, District Councils 19, 34, labor organizer, mental health employees, 1958-65; District Court 37, AFSCME Division Director, Hospital Division, New York City, 1965-67; Associate Director of District Council 37, AFSCME, AFL-CIO, New York City, 1967-81; New York State Commissioner of Labor, appointed, 1981-86; Total Health Systems, senior vp, 1987-90; Cigna, consultant, 1991-. **Orgs:** Mem of numerous soc welfare and cultural orgn; hon adv bd of Natl Medical Fellowships; natl exec bd, Jewish Labor Comm Amer Jewish Congr; adv bd of Resources for Children with Special Needs Inc, A Philip Randolph Inst; Coll of New Rochelle, board of directors; Amer for Democratic Action; NAACP NY Branch; Delta Sigma Theta Sorority, honorary member, NOW; AFSCME, New York City Clerical Employees Union, Local 1549, honorary member. **Honors/Awds:** Roy Wilkins Award NAACP; Benjamin Potoker Award NYS Employees' Brotherhood Comm; Westchester Minority Contr Assn Achievement Award for Industry; Histadrut Humanitarian Award the Amer Trade Council for Histadrut; Good Govt Award NYS Careerists; Adam Clayton Powell Govt Award the Opport Indust Center 1982; the Hispanic Women's Center (NYC) Honorary Award; Friends of Educ Award the Assn of Black Educators of NY 1983; Frederick Douglass Award NY Urban League; Labor Award for Leadership Adjunct Faculty Assn of Nassau Comm Coll 1984; A Salute to America's Top 100 Black Business and Professional Women 1985; Honorary Degree, Coll of New Rochelle, 1973; numerous others.

ROBERTS, LORRAINE MARIE
Consultant - NYSED (retired). **Personal:** Born May 12, 1930, Philadelphia, PA; daughter of Adele Pettie and Willie Pettie; children: Kevin M, Harlan K. **Educ:** Hampton University, BS 1952; Bucknell Univ, exchange student; Columbia Univ, MA 1954. **Career:** Bowling Green Bd of Educ VA, teacher 1952-53; Rochester City School Dist, teacher 1956-64; NYS Univ System State Educ Dept, adj prof; Poughkeepsie NY City School Dist, coordinator, Business Educ, teacher, chairperson, Occupational Education, 1966-96, SED Curriculum, Assess OE, Technical Studies Comm, co-chairperson, 1992-95; NYS, Resource Guide, consultant, 1996-97. **Orgs:** BTA; EBTA; NBEA; PPSTA; NYSUT; AFL-TA Bd of trustees YWCA, Dutchess Co 1970-75; board member, secretary, United Way of Dutchess County 1973-80; chrpn Central Alloc Div United Way of Dutchess Co 1979-80; basileus, Iota Alpha Omega Chapter, Alpha Kappa Alpha Sor 1969-; Bethel Missionary Baptist Church; AFS of Poughkeepsie Comm Serv Awards, Am Legion; United Way; NAACP; bd Dutchess County/Dominica Partnership of Amer 1984-92; bd Friends of Greater Poughkeepsie Library Dist 1988-94; Business Teachers of Mid-Hudson, president, 1989-92; Dutchess Co Historical Soc, president, 1996-; DC Girl Scouts, bd, treas, 1993-. **Honors/Awds:** Area 10 leader/consultant/regents com; mem Bus Educ Div NYS Educ Dept; Outstanding Occupational Educ (Reg 3) NYS Educ Dept 1989; co-author Invisible People , Stories: A Historical Overview of the Black Community in Poughkeepsie (Dutchess County Historical Society Yearbook), 1987; Outstanding Bus Teacher, NYS, 1994; Outstanding Education Dutchess Beulah Bapt Chr, 1992; Salute to Women, YWCA Award, 1993; Martin Luther King Honoree, 1997.

ROBERTS, LOUIS WRIGHT
Government transportation official (retired). **Personal:** Born Sep 1, 1913, Jamestown, NY; son of Dora Catherine Wright and Louis Lorenzo Roberts; married Mercedes Pearl McGavock, Jun 8, 1938; children: Louis M, Lawrence E. **Educ:** Fisk Univ, AB 1935; Univ of MI, MS 1937; MIT, PhD candidate, 1946. **Career:** Fisk Univ, teaching asst, physics dept, 1935-36; St Augustine's Coll, instructor, 1937-40, associate prof of physics & mathematics, 1941-42; Howard Univ, associate prof of physics, 1943-44; Sylvania Electric Products Inc, mgr, tube div, 1944-50; MIT Research Laboratory for Electronics, tube consultant, 1950-51; Microwave Associates Inc, founder & pres, 1950-55; Bomac Laboratories Inc, engineering specialist & consultant, 1955-59; METCOM Inc, founder, vice pres & dir, 1959-67, Elcon Laboratories, pres, 1962-66; Addison-Wesley Press, consultant, 1963-67; NASA Electronics Research Center, chief, microwave laboratory, 1967-68, chief, optics & microwave laboratory, 1968-70; MIT, visiting sr lecturer, 1979-80; US Dept of Transportation, Transportation System Center, deputy dir, office of technology, 1970-72, dir, office of technology, 1972, dir, office of energy & environment, 1977-79, deputy dir, 1979, dir, office of data systems and technology, 1980-82, dir, office of admin, 1982-83, assoc dir, office of operations engineering, 1983-84, acting deputy dir, 1984, acting dir, 1984-85, dir, 1985-89. **Orgs:** Mem Marine Electronics Comm Panel of the US-Japan Natural Resources Commn 1969-; mem adv bd Coll of Engrg Univ of MA 1972-; mem bd of trustees Univ Hosp Boston Univ 1973-; mem President's Adv Bd Bentley Coll 1974-90; corporator Wakefield Svgs Bank 1975-91; life fellow IEEE; mem AAAS, AAAA, Soc of Automotive Engrs. **Honors/Awds:** Life Fellow Inst of Electrical and Electronic Engrs 1964-; Apollo Achievement Awd NASA; Outstanding Achievement Awd Univ of MI 1978; Letter of Appreciation AGARD/NATO 1979; Certificate of Appreciation Chelsea Kiwanis Club 1979; Order of the Engr Awd Univ of MA 1980; Sr Exec Service Bonus Awd 1983; Presidential Rank Meritorious Exec 1984; Doctor of Laws Fisk Univ 1985; Sr Exec Serv Bonus Awds 1985, 1986, 1987, 1988; author of 15 journal articles & about 120 company, univ & govt reports; editor, author, Handbook of Microwave Measurements, McGraw-Hill; holder of 9 patents. **Home Addr:** 5 Michael Rd, Wakefield, MA 01880. **Business Addr:** Dir, Transportation Systems Ctr, 55 Broadway, Cambridge, MA 02142.

ROBERTS, MALKIA (LUCILLE E. DAVIS)
Educator. **Personal:** Born in Washington, DC; daughter of Jackson L Davis-Cicely; married Andrew. **Educ:** University of Michigan, MFA. **Career:** SUNY, prof, 1972; Smithsonian Institute, Museum of African Art, docent, 1987-97; Hirshorn Museum, docent, 1990-91; Howard Univ, prof, 1990; Natl Gallery of Art, docent, 1991-92; Elizabeth Town College, prof, 1991-92. **Orgs:** Black Academy of Arts & Letters, 1971. **Honors/Awds:** Elizabeth Town College, Hon Doctor of Fine Arts, 1992; Agnes Meyer Fellowship. **Special Achievements:** published "Review of Exhibit," in Art in America Magazine.

ROBERTS, MARGARET MILLS
Speech-language pathologist and audiologist. **Personal:** Born Dec 5, 1936, Pittsburgh, PA; daughter of Isabelle (deceased) and Everett (deceased); married Vernard T Roberts Sr; children: Vernard Jr, Sharon Renee. **Educ:** Fisk University, 1954-57; The Ohio State University, BA, 1962, MA, 1964, PhD, 1966. **Career:** Children's Hospital, founder/director of speech pathology and audiology, 1966-95; Ohio State University, adjunct assistant professor, 1972-94; MMR Consultants, 1995-. **Orgs:** Ohio Board of Speech Pathology and Audiology, chair, 1984-91; OSU Alumni Advisory Council, 1985-93; Crittenton Family Services Board, vice pres of various committees, 1976-85, 1987-; Association for Developmental Disabilities, board member, 1982-89; Ohio Speech and Hearing Association, president elect, 1993, executive board and various other chair positions, 1972-; American Speech-language-Hearing Association, elected legislative councilor, 1980-. **Honors/Awds:** American Speech-Language-Hearing Association, Fellow, 1991; The OSU Alumni Association, Outstanding Alumni Award, 1991; Ohio Speech and Hearing Association, Honors of the Association, 1990; Delta Sigma Theta, Community Service Award, 1986; Alpha Kappa Alpha, Community Service Award, 1972. **Home Addr:** 2365 Bellevue Ave, Columbus, OH 43207, (614)445-8714.

ROBERTS, MARGARET WARD
Educator (retired). **Personal:** Born Jul 18, 1934, Chapel Hill, NC; daughter of Margaret S Skinner and James S Ward. **Educ:** Virginia State College, BS, 1960; Old Dominion University, special education, 1975; reading certification, 1988. **Career:** Portsmouth School System, state remedial teacher, retired. **Orgs:** Program Development, Work Incentive Program; Alliance Concerned with School-Age Parents; Task Force on Teen-Age Pregnancy; Chesapeake Chapter Pinochle Bugs, Inc; Norfolk Chapter, Delicados Inc, vice pres; Portsmouth Reading Council, chairperson, literacy project, Teacher of the Year committee; Virginia Reading Association; Portsmouth Education Association; National Education Association; Democratic Women; Association for Supervision and Curriculum Development; Delta Sigma Theta; Grace Episcopal Church; Jack & Jill Mother, Chesapeake Chapter; Coalition of Black Women, Tidewater Chapter; Urban League of Hampton Roads; Boys and Girls Club of Hampton Roads, board member; Safety & Crime Prevention, Level Green Civic League, coordinator; Project (AIMS), Activities That Intergrate Math & Sccience. **Honors/Awds:** Honorary Citizen, City of Chesapeake, VA. **Special Achievements:** Dedicated Supporter of Reading & Mathematics Programs in Portsmouth Public Schools; Selected by Portsmouth Public School System to Participate in Workshop For Teachers of Upgraded Groups; Dedicated & Invaluable Services Rendered to Project Lead's Partnership Forum, Norfolk, VA. **Home Phone:** (804)424-3613.

ROBERTS, MICHAEL V.
Broadcast company executive. **Personal:** Born Oct 24, 1948, St Louis. **Educ:** Lindenwood Coll, BS; St Louis Univ Law Sch, JD; Hague Acad Intl Law, Hague Holland, cert; Intl Inst Human Rights, Strasbourg France, cert. **Career:** TV 46 WHSL, Roberts Broadcasting Co, owner, currently; Roberts-Roberts & Associates, president, chairman, currently. **Orgs:** Kappa Alpha Psi Frat; Phi Delta Phi Legal Frat; MO Athletic Club; St Louis Council on World Affairs; St Louis Arts & Education Council; Cert PADI Scuba Diver's Association; Better Family Life, board of directors; Home Shopping Network, board of directors; All Saints Epis Ch; tchr, leader Am Youth Found; alt commr St Louis Land Reutil Auth. **Honors/Awds:** JCCA tennis champ; Danforth Found Fellowship. **Business Addr:** President, Roberts & Roberts and Asiciates, 1408 N Kings Hwy, St Louis, MO 63113.

ROBERTS, PAQUITA HUDSON
Educator. **Personal:** Born Mar 2, 1938, Andrew, SC; children: Craig, Tali, Paquita. **Educ:** South Carolina State Coll, BA 1961; Newark State Coll, MA 1967. **Career:** Hospital Center of Orange, speech pathologist 1964-67; Newark Bd of Educ, 1968-69; Mt Carmel Guild, prog dir 1969-75; NJ Dept of Educ, educ program specialist 1979-. **Orgs:** Consultant Orange Head Start, Intercoastal Business Associates, Barnett Hosp Speech and Hearing Div, CH Aston Assocs; adv bd RAP NY Univ Council forExceptional Children 1979-; vice pres chairperson bd of educ Christian St Marks AME Church. **Honors/Awds:** Special Education Fellowship NJ Dept of Educ; Professional Recognition NJ Div for Early Childhood Awd 1986. **Home Addr:** 29 Burchard Ave, East Orange, NJ 07017. **Business Addr:** Education Program Specialist, NJ Department of Education, 225 West State St, Trenton, NJ 08625.

ROBERTS, RAY
Professional football player. **Personal:** Born Jun 3, 1969, Asheville, NC; married Beth, May 8, 1993. **Educ:** Virginia, bachelor's degree in communications, 1991. **Career:** Seattle Seahawks, tackle, 1992-95; Detroit Lions, 1996-. **Business Addr:** Professional Football Player, Detroit Lions, 1200 Featherstone Rd, Pontiac, MI 48342, (248)335-4131.

ROBERTS, ROBIN
Broadcast journalist. **Personal:** Born Nov 23, 1960, Pass Christian, MS; daughter of Lawrence and Lucimarian. **Career:** ESPN, anchor, currently; ABC Sports, "Wide World of Sports," host. **Orgs:** Arthur Ashe Athletic Assn; Women's Sports Foundation. **Honors/Awds:** 2 Emmy's; DAR Television Award for Merit. **Business Addr:** Anchor, ESPN, ESPN Plaza, Bristol, CT 06010, (203)585-2000.

ROBERTS, ROY J.
Educator. **Personal:** Born Jul 1, 1940, Carthage, TX; son of Thelma Hicks Roberts and Baker Roberts; married Barbara Brown Roberts; children: William, Ronan. **Educ:** Willey Coll, BS 1964; Yeshiva U, atnd 1967-69; State Univ of NY at Stony Brook, 1969-70; Adelphi, 1973-74. **Career:** Upward Bound Project Director, Dowling Coll, affirmative action comm chairperson 1973-77; Bellport NY, mathematics teacher 1967-70; E Islip NY, mathematics teacher 1966-67; John Marshall HS, physics instr 1964-66; Long Island Assn of Black Counselors, treas 1969. **Orgs:** Mem Minority Educators Assn of Long Island 1974-; Cits United for the Betterment of Educ 1967-; NEA 1968-; treas Assn fr Equality & Excellence in Educ 1979-; mem Bayshore Cntrl Islip NAACP 1966-; vol Bellport Ambulance Co 1968-; Bellport Fellowship 1968-. **Business Addr:** Proj Dir, Upward Bound, Dowling Coll, Oakdale, NY 11769.

ROBERTS, ROY S.
Automobile company executive. **Personal:** married. **Educ:** Western Michigan Univ, business grad; Harvard PMD Program, International Business, Venz Switzerland. **Career:** Navistar Intl, vice pres/general mgr, 1988-90; General Motors Corp, 1977-: GM Assembly Plant, North Tarrytown, NY, mgr; GM Flint Automotive Division, Flint, MI, vice pres of personnel, until 1988; Cadillac Motor Car, general mfg manager, 1990-91; Pontiac GMC Division, vice pres/general mgr, currently. **Orgs:** Board, National Urban League, National Boy Scout, executive committee; Western Michigan University, board of trustees; Morehouse School of Medicine, board of trustees. **Honors/Awds:** Honorary doctorate, Florida A&M University, Grand Valley State College; President Bush, American Success Award. **Business Addr:** Vice Pres & General Manager, Pontiac GMC Division, General Motors Corp., 100 Renaissance Ctr, MC: 482-A30-D10, Detroit, MI 48243.

ROBERTS, SALLY-ANN. See CRAFT, SALLY-ANN ROBERTS.

ROBERTS, SAMUEL KELTON
Educator. **Personal:** Born Sep 1, 1944, Muskogee, OK; married Valerie Hermoine Fisher; children: Samuel Kelton Jr, Franklin. **Educ:** Univ de Lyon France, Diplome 1966; Morehouse Coll, BA 1967; Union Theol Sem, MDiv 1970; Columbia Univ, PhD 1974. **Career:** New York City Mission Soc, summer proj dir 1967-70; S Hempstead Congregational Church, pastor 1972-73; Pittsburgh Theol Sem, asst prof 1973-76; Union Theol Sem, asst prof religion & soc 1976-80; VA Union Univ, dean 1980-. **Orgs:** Mem Amer Acad of Rel; mem Soc for the Scientific Study of Rel; mem Soc for the Study of Black Relition. **Honors/Awds:** Merril Overseas Study Award Morehouse Coll 1965-66; Protestant Fellow Fund for Theol Educ 1967-70; Fellow Columbia Univ 1970-72; author "George Edmund Haynes" 1978. **Business Addr:** Dean, VA Union University, 1500 N Lombardy St, Richmond, VA 23220.

ROBERTS, STANLEY CORVET
Professional basketball player. **Personal:** Born Feb 7, 1970, Hopkins, SC. **Educ:** Louisiana State, 1991. **Career:** Orlando Magic, center, 1991-92; Los Angeles Clippers, center, 1992-97; Minnesota Timberwolves, center, 1997-. **Business Addr:** Professional Basketball Player, Minnesota Timberwolves, 600 First Ave North, Minneapolis, MN 55403, (612)337-3865.

ROBERTS, TARA LYNETTE
Editor. **Personal:** Born Feb 5, 1970, Atlanta, GA; daughter of Lula Roberts & Melvin Murphy. **Educ:** Mount Holyoke College, BA, 1991; New York University, MA, 1994. **Career:** Scholastic Books, assistant editor, 1992-93; Essence Magazine, editorial assistant, 1993-94, lifestyle editor, 1994-. **Orgs:** National Association of Female Executives, 1996-; Mount Hol-

yoke College Alumnae Quarterly, committee mem, 1995-; Black Filmmaker Foundation, 1991-94; Alpha Kappa Alpha Sorority Inc, 1989-. **Honors/Awds:** New York University, NYU Publishing Fellowship, 1991-93; Council for International Educational Exchange, Travel Grant, 1991; Mount Holyoke College, Student Svc & Leadership Awd, 1991; Association for Education in Journalism & Mass Communications, Summer Fellow, 1990; Scripps Howard Foundation Scholarship, 1989. **Special Achievements:** Am I the Last Virgin? Ten African-American Reflections On Sex & Love, Editor. **Business Addr:** Lifestyle Editor, Essence Magazine, 1500 Broadway, 6th Fl, New York, NY 10036.

ROBERTS, TERRENCE JAMES
Psychologist, educator. **Personal:** Born Dec 3, 1941, Little Rock, AR; son of Margaret Gill Thomas and William Roberts; married Rita Anderson Roberts, Mar 8, 1962; children: Angela Rayschel, Rebecca Darlene. **Educ:** California State Univ at Los Angeles, Los Angeles, CA, BA, 1967; UCLA, Los Angeles, CA, MSW, 1970; Southern Illinois Univ, Carbondale, IL, PhD, 1976. **Career:** Southern Illinois Univ, Carbondale, IL, assistant professor, 1972-75; Pacific Union College, Angwin, CA, assistant professor, 1975-78; St Helena Hospital, Deer Park, CA, director, mental health, 1975-85; UCLA, Los Angeles CA, assistant dean, 1985-93; Chair, Masters in Psychology Program, Antioch University, 1993-. **Orgs:** Member, American Psychological Assn, 1980-; member, Assn of Black Psychologists, 1985-88; board member, African American Cultural Institute, 1988-; board member, Infina Technologies, Inc, 1990-; Eisenhower Institute for World Affairs, bd mem, 1991-; Economic Resources Corporation, bd member, 1995-. **Honors/Awds:** Civil Rights Award, NAACP Legal Defense & Education Fund, 1982; Spingarn Medal, NAACP, 1958; SCLC Women "Drum Major for Justice Award," 1995. **Business Addr:** Chair, Masters in Psych Prog, Antioch Univ, 13274 Fiji Way, Marina Del Rey, CA 90292, (310)578-1080.

ROBERTS, THOMAS L.
Educator (retired). **Personal:** Born Apr 17, 1932, Key West, FL; son of Learline E Roberts and James D Roberts Jr; children: Kevin D, Garrett L, Elizabeth A. **Educ:** Talladega Coll Talladega, AL, BS 1957; Trinity Univ San Antonio, TX, MS 1961 Clark Univ Worcester, MA, PhD 1965; Walden Univ Naples, FL, PhD 1977. **Career:** Univ TX Med Branch Galveston, rsch asst 1957-59; USAF Sch Aerospace Med, San Antonio, TX, microbiolgst 1959-63; MELPAR Inc, Falls Church, VA, scientist-microbiolgst 1963; Worcester State Coll, Worcester, MA, prof 1965-88; Univ MA Med Sch Worcester, prof nuclear med 1976-88. **Orgs:** Consultant Kane Med Labs Worcester, MA 1965-76; editoral bd Science of Biology Journal 1977-81; visiting prof Univ Liberia, WA 1972; bd dir Worcester Co-op Council Inc 1968-72; bd of dir Worcester Model Cities Inc 1967-70; pres Rehab Ctr of Worcester Inc 1978-81; chmn bd of trustees/dirs Rehab Ctr Worcester Inc 1979-81; mem Corp of Bermuda Biological Rsch Station. **Honors/Awds:** John Hay Whitney Foundation Fellow Clark Univ Worcester, MA 1964-65; Teaching Fellow Clark Univ, MA 1963-65; Post-Doc Fellow Clark Univ, MA 1965-68; 20 research articles & comm; Fellow Soc of Sigma XI; Fellow, Amer Inst of Chemists; Fellow New York Academy of Sciences. **Military Serv:** AUS cprl 1952-55; USNR cmdr 1964-83. **Business Addr:** Professor Emeritus of Biology, Worcester State College, 486 Chandler St, Worcester, MA 01602.

ROBERTS, TRISH
Professional basketball coach. **Personal:** Born in Monroe, GA. **Educ:** North Georgia College; Emporia State, KS; University of Tennessee; Central Michigan University, MA. **Career:** Central Michigan University, Women's Basketball, assistant coach; University of Maine, Women's Basketball; University of Michigan, Women's Basketball, coach, currently. **Special Achievements:** US Olympic Women's Basketball Team, 1976; USA National Women's Basketball Team, 1978. **Business Addr:** Head Coach, Atlanta Glory, 2100 Powers Ferry Road, Ste. 400, Atlanta, GA 30339, (770)541-9017.

ROBERTS, TROY
Journalist. **Personal:** Born Sep 9, 1962, Philadelphia, PA; son of Robert & Ellen. **Educ:** University of California-Berkeley, AB, 1984. **Career:** KPIX-TV, magazine show host; KATV-TV, correspondent; WCBS-TV, anchor, correspondent, 1990-93; CBS News, anchor "Up to the Minute," 1993-94, anchor Morning News, 1994-96, correspondent Evening News, 1996-. **Orgs:** National Association of Black Journalists; Harlem YMCA; Big Brothers of America. **Honors/Awds:** National Emmy Award, Olympic Park Bombing, 1997. **Business Addr:** Correspondent, CBS-TV, 524 West 57th St, New York, NY 10019, (212)975-4290.

ROBERTS, VIRGIL PATRICK
Record company executive. **Personal:** Born Jan 4, 1947, Ventura, CA; son of Emma Haley Roberts and Julius Roberts; married Brenda Cecelia Banks; children: Gisele Simone, Hayley Tasha. **Educ:** Ventura Coll, AA 1966; UCLA, BA 1968; Harvard Univ, JD 1972. **Career:** Pacht, Ross, Warne, Bernhard & Sears Law Firm, assoc 1972-76; Manning & Roberts Law Firm, sr partner 1976-81; Dick Griffey Prod/Solar Records, pres 1981-; pres, Hines Company, 1993. **Orgs:** Judge pro tem Beverly Hills & L A Municipal Courts 1979-; pres Beverly Hill Bar Scholarship Found 1980; bd mem LA Educ Partnership 1983-; bd mem CORO Found 1984-90; treas bd mem Museum of African-Amer Art LA 1982-86; commr State of CA Comm Tchr Cr 1981-84; treasurer, Los Angeles Private Industry Council, 1986-93; chairman, Los Angeles Educational Partnership, 1988-91; vice chairman, Public Education Fund Network, 1990-; board member, California Community Foundation, 1991-; board member, LEARN, 1991-; chairman of bd, Los Angeles Metropolitan Project (LAMP); bd member, Community Build, 1993-. **Honors/Awds:** Comm Serv Awrd LA Urban League 1978; Image Awrd Hollywood Beverly Hills NAACP 1980; Foreign Affairs Schlr Ford Found/Howard Univ 1968-69; "Discourage on Black Nationalism" Amer Behavorial Scientst 1969; "Minority Interest in Value & Power & Power Conflicts" Chapter of Book 1969; Law & Justice Award, NAACP Legal Defense and Education Fund, 1988.

ROBERTS, WESLEY A.
Educator, clergyman. **Personal:** Born Jan 3, 1938, Jamaica, WI; son of Rayness Wong Roberts and Ignatius Roberts; married Sylvia Y Forbes; children: Paul, Carolyn, Suzanne, Michael. **Educ:** Waterloo Lutheran Univ, BA 1965; Toronto Baptist Seminary, MDiv 1965; Westminster Theological Seminary, ThM 1967; Univ of Guelph, MA 1968, PhD 1972. **Career:** Gordon-Conwell Theological Seminary, asst prof of black studies 1972-73, asst prof of Christian Thought 1974-75, assoc prof of Church History, 1977-84, asst dean for acad prog 1980-84, prof of Church History 1984-85; Peoples Baptist Church of Boston, MA, interim pastor, 1980-82, pastor, 1982-; Gordon College, Wenham, MA, adjunct professor of History, 1974-. **Orgs:** Mem Soc for the Study of Black Religion, Amer Soc of Church History, Conf of Faith & History; mem exec comm The Assoc of Theological Schools in the US & Canada 1980-84; pres, Black Ministerial Alliance of Greater Boston 1994-. **Honors/Awds:** Articles published in Eerdman's Handbook of Amer Christianity, Eerdman's Handbook of the History of Christianity Fides et Historia; Ontario Grad Fellowship Government of Ontario 1968-70; Canada Council Doctoral Fellowship Government of Canada 1970-72; author, Chapter on Cornelius Vantil in Reformed Theology in America, Wm B Eerdman, 1985, in Dutch Reformed Theology, Baker Bookhouse, 1988; article, Martin Luther King Jr and the March on Washington, in Christian History Magazine, 1989; article, Rejecting the "Negro Pew," in Christian History Magazine, 1995. **Home Addr:** 1 Enon Rd, Wenham, MA 01984. **Business Addr:** Senior Pastor, Peoples Baptist Church of Boston, 134 Camden Street, Boston, MA 02118.

ROBERTS, WILLIAM HAROLD
Professional football player. **Personal:** Born Aug 5, 1962, Miami, FL. **Educ:** Ohio State. **Career:** New York Giants, guard, 1984-94; New England Patriots, 1995-96; New York Jets, 1997-. **Business Addr:** Professional Football Player, New York Jets, 1000 Fulton Ave, Hempstead, NY 11550, (516)560-8100.

ROBERTSON, ALAN D.
Banker. **Personal:** Born Sep 10, 1958, Chicago, IL; son of Gloria D Sadberry-Robertson and Carl T Robertson; married Julia M Southern, Jun 19, 1983; children: Jessica Marie, Gloria Lauren. **Educ:** DePaul Univ, BSC Accounting (Sum Cum Laude) 1980; Certified Public Accountant Univ of IL Urbana 1980; Northwestern Univ, MM Finance and Marketing 1983. **Career:** Arthur Andersen, auditor 1980-81; Continental Bank, banking officer 1983-87; First Chicago, vice president 1987-; DePaul Univ, Chicago IL, part-time faculty 1988-90. **Orgs:** Bd mem Inroads Inc 1980; mem ILCPA Soc 1980-; mem AICPA Soc 1981-; treas Inroads Alumni Assoc 1983; mem Urban Bankers Forum 1983-; mem Natl Black MBA Assoc, Natl Assoc of Black Accountants; bd of dir, Chicago Children's Chour 1988-89; mem Assn for Corporals Growth; mem Grand Rapids Econ Club. **Honors/Awds:** Beta Alpha Psi, Delta Mu Delta; Natl Dean's List 1980; Johnson & Johnson Leadership Awd 1981; Outstanding Young Man in Amer 1983. **Home Addr:** 17301 Bryant, Hazel Crest, IL 60429.

ROBERTSON, ALVIN CYRRALE
Professional basketball player. **Personal:** Born Jul 22, 1962, Barberton, OH. **Educ:** Arkansas, studied criminal justice, 1984. **Career:** San Antonio Spurs, 1984-89, Milwaukee Bucks, 1990-93; Detroit Pistons, 1993;Denver Nuggets, 1993-94. **Honors/Awds:** US Gold Medal-winning Olympic team; post-season Aloha and Hall of Fame classics; all-tournament & voted top defensive plyr in the Aloha; All-Plains by Bsktbl Weekley; MVP when Razorbacks won Southwest Conf tournmnt 1981-82. **Business Addr:** Former Professional Basketball Player, Denver Nuggets, 1635 Clay St, Denver, CO 80204.

ROBERTSON, ANDRE LEVETT
Professional baseball player (retired). **Personal:** Born Oct 2, 1957, Orange, TX; married Lanier Hebert; children: Ryan Andre, Chrystina Ulyssa, Jace Christian. **Educ:** Univ of Texas, BBA, management. **Career:** New York Yankees, shortstop 1981-85; Dupont DeNemours EI & Co, currently. **Business Addr:** Dupont DeNemours EI & Co, FM 1006, Orange, TX 77630.

ROBERTSON, BENJAMIN W.
Clergyman, educational administrator. **Personal:** Born Apr 6, 1931, Roanoke, VA; son of Anna Mary Holland Robertson (deceased) and Clarence Robertson (deceased); married Dolores Wallace; children: Benjamin W Jr. **Educ:** VA Theol Seminary, BTh 1951; VA Union Univ, AB 1954; VA Seminary & Coll MDiv 1956, DD 1959, DMin 1968; Union Baptist Seminary, LLD 1971; Richmond VA Seminary LLD 1982; VA Union Univ, HLD. **Career:** Cedar St Memorial Bapt Ch of God, pastor 1955-; Radio Station WLEE, radio preacher 1961-; Natl Progressive Bapt Cong, tchr 1962-; Radio Station WANT, 1965-; Robertson's Kiddie Coll, pres 1968-; First Union Bapt Ch Chesterfield, pastor; Piney Grove Bapt Ch, pastor; Richmond VA Seminary, pres, 1981-; Virginia Theological Seminary & College, Lynchburg, VA, pres, currently. **Orgs:** Bd dirs Commonwealth of VA Girl Scouts 1960-69, Brookland Branch YMCA 1963-75, Rich Met Blood Serv 1963-68, Rich Br NAACP 1964-68, vice pres Lott Carey Bapt Foreign Miss Conv 1976-83; treas Baptist Ministers Conf 1960-70; founder Progressive Natl Bapt Convention 1961; dean of preaching VA Theological Seminary 1965-75; pres VA Seminary & Coll 1980-81; Xi Delta Lambda Chap of Alpha Phi Alpha Frat Inc; tchr of leaders PNBC 1961-81; Founder and First Pres of Richmond VA Seminary 1981-State Board of Psychology, 1996-2000; mem VA State Board of Psychology. **Honors/Awds:** Afro-Amer Awd for Superior Public Serv without Thought of Gain 1981; Minister of Yr Hayes-Allen VTS&C 1975; Rich Com Hosps Humanitarian Awd 1975; Beta Gamma Lambda Chap Alpha Phi Alpha Frat Inc 1968; FOX Channel 35, television ministry. **Home Addr:** 8901 Strath Road, Richmond, VA 23231. **Business Addr:** President, Richmond Virginia Theological Seminary, 2318-20 Cedar St, Richmond, VA 23223.

ROBERTSON, CHARLES E., JR.
Parks and recreation administrator. **Personal:** marrIed Angela; children: Kendall. **Educ:** Southern University, BS, bus mgmt, 1986; Mountain State, mgmt development, 1987; Dale Carnegie Mgmt Seminar, 1990; American Hotel and Motel Assn, Certificate in Security and Loss Prev Mgmt, 1989-90. **Career:** Harmony Center, Baton Rouge, LA, counselor, 1982; Capitol House Hotel, Baton Rouge, LA, mgmt trainee program, 1984-1986; Copper Mountain Resort, Copper Mountain, Co, mgr, 1986-1994; Denver Parks and Recreation Department, deputy mgr for parks, 1994-. **Orgs:** Appointed by Colorado Governor to Utility Consumers Bd; Summit County Chamber of Commerce Statesmen Committee; Natl Coalition of Black Meeting Planners; Religious Conference Management Association; Society of Government Meeting Planners; Phi Beta Sigma Fraternity, Inc; National Brotherhood of Skiers; Young Adults for Positive Action. **Business Addr:** Deputy Manager for Parks, Danver Parks and Recreation Department, 2300 15th St, Ste 150, Denver, CO 80202, (303)964-2580.

ROBERTSON, DAWN SMITH. See SMITH, DAWN C. F.

ROBERTSON, EVELYN CRAWFORD, JR.
Educational administrator. **Personal:** Born Nov 19, 1941, Winchester, TN; son of Pearl Robertson and Evelyn Robertson; married Hugholene Ellison; children: Jeffrey Bernard, Sheila Yvette. **Educ:** TN State Univ, BS 1959-62, MA 1969; Southwest MO State Univ, NDEA Cert 1970. **Career:** Allen White HS, teacher/coach 1962-68; Allen White Elem Sch, principal 1969; Central HS, asst principal 1970-74; Western Mental Health Inst, asst super 1974-79; Nat T Winston Develop Center, supt 1979-83; Western Mental Health Inst, supt 1983-; Tennessee Department of Mental Health & Mental Retardation, former commissioner, beginning 1991-; Bank of Bolivar, director, 1991-; Southwest TN Development District, executive director, 1996-. **Orgs:** Pres Harden Co Teachers Assn 1973; chmn Whiteville Civic League 1976-79; chmn of bd Harden Co Developmental Service Ctr 1977-78; pres Bolivar Civitan Club 1981; vice-pres Whiteville Bus Enterprise, Inc 1982; chmn Admin Div SEAAMD 1983; consultant Hardeman Mental Health Assn 1983; bd mem Amer Heart Assn affiliate 1980-. **Honors/Awds:** Outstanding Young Educator Hardeman Co Jaycees 1976; EC Robertson Day given by citizens in my honor 1983. **Home Addr:** 2665 Newsom Rd, Whiteville, TN 38075.

ROBERTSON, GERTRUDE
Educator. **Personal:** Born Feb 11, 1924, Waskom, TX; daughter of Estella Spillman Harris and Chesley Harris; married Rev L E Robertson, Jan 25, 1947 (deceased); children: Elkins Renee. **Educ:** Bishop Coll, Dallas, TX, BS, 1949; N TX State Univ, Denton, TX, MS, 1967. **Career:** Dallas Independent School Dist, teacher, 1950-. **Orgs:** Southwestern regional dir, The Natl Sorority of Phi Delta Kappa; pres, The Baptist Ministers' Wives, Dallas, TX; teacher of Adults at D. Edwin Johnson Bible Inst Dallas. **Honors/Awds:** Teacher of the year, Thomas J. Rusk, Middle School and N Dallas, Chamber of Commerce; The Sorority of the year, The Natl Sorority of Phi Delta Kappa Inc. **Home Addr:** 3929 Kiest Meadow Dr, Dallas, TX 75233.

ROBERTSON, JAMES B.
Civil engineer. **Personal:** Born Sep 5, 1940, Roanoke, VA; married Marjorie N Morris; children: James II, Cheryl, Bradley. **Educ:** Howard U, BSCE 1963. **Career:** AZ Proj Office Water

& Power Resource Serv, chief operations div, 1978-; US Bur of Reclamation, supr hydraulic engr 1972-78; Channing Co Inc, registered rep 1970-72; US & Bur of Reclamation, civil engr 1966-70; Omega Psi Phi Frat 1960-. **Orgs:** Sec Ancient Free & Accepted Mason 1970-; budgetary panel United Way 1976-77. **Honors/Awds:** Meritorious serv awards Dept of Interior 1970&72; Mgrs Devel Prog Dept of Interior 1977. **Military Serv:** AUS capt 1963-66.

ROBERTSON, KAREN A.
Librarian. **Personal:** Born Oct 21, Montclair, NJ; daughter of H June Hawkins Robertson and Joesph C Robertson. **Educ:** Morgan State University, Baltimore, MD, BA, 1966; Atlanta University, Atlanta, GA ,MSLS, 1967; University of Baltimore, Baltimore, MD, MBA, 1983. **Career:** Prince George's County, Hyattsville, MD, reference librarian, 1967-68; Morgan State Univ, Baltimore, MD, chief reference librarian, 1968-80, director of library, 1980-. **Orgs:** Member, Maryland Library Assn, 1974-; member, American Library Assn, 1975-; member, Alpha Kappa Alpha Inc, 1964-. **Business Addr:** Director of Library Services, Soper Library, Morgan State University, Cold Spring Lane and Hillen Rd, Baltimore, MD 21239-4098.

ROBERTSON, LYNN E.
Clergyman. **Personal:** Born Jun 18, 1921, Franklin, TX; married Gertrude Harris. **Educ:** BA 1949. **Career:** Alta Mesa Mesa Pk Bapt Ch, Pastor; Inter-racial Bible Inst, instr; So Dallas Br NaAACP, pres. **Orgs:** Mem Bapt Min Union of Dallas; mem Interdenominational Ministerial All of Gr Dallas; mem Min All W Dallas. **Military Serv:** AUS sgt 1942-46. **Business Addr:** 2939 Palo Alto Dr, Dallas, TX 75241.

ROBERTSON, MARCUS AARON
Professional football player. **Personal:** Born Oct 2, 1969, Pasadena, CA; married Holly, Jun 27, 1992; children: Morgan Ashley. **Educ:** Iowa State Univ, attended. **Career:** Houston Oilers, defensive back, 1991-96; Tennessee Oilers, 1997-. **Honors/Awds:** Selected First-Team All-Pro by the Associated Press and the Sporting News, 1993; Ed Block Courage Award, 1994. **Business Addr:** Professional Football Player, Tennessee Oilers, c/o Baptist Sports Park, 7640 H 70-5, Nashville, TN 37221.

ROBERTSON, OSCAR PALMER
Chemical company executive. **Personal:** Born Nov 24, 1938, Indianapolis, IN; son of Mazell Bell Robertson and Henry Bailey Robertson; married Yvonne Crittenden, Jun 25, 1960; children: Shana Robertson Shaw, Tia, Mari. **Educ:** Cincinnati Univ, BBA 1960. **Career:** Cincinnati Royals NBA, guard 1960-70; Milwaukee Bucks NBA, player 1970-74; TV sports announcer; ORCHEM Inc, Cincinnati, OH, pres/CEO, 1981-; pres, Oscar Robertson & Assocs, 1983-. **Orgs:** Pres, Natl Basketball Players Assn, 1964-74; mem, NAACP Sports Bd, 1987; trustee, Indiana High School Hall of Fame, 1984-89; trustee, Basketball Hall of Fame, 1987-89; natl dir, Pepsi Cola Hot Shot Program; NBA Retired Players Assn, pres, 1993-. **Honors/Awds:** Mem State Dept Tour Africa 1971; High Sch All-Amer; set 14 major collegiate records at Univ of Cincinnati; Recip All Star Game's Most Val Player Award 1961; NBA Most Valuable Player Award 3 times; Rookie of the Yr Award 1961; co-capt US Olympic Gold Medal Team 1960; mem World Championship Team 1971; Ranked 2nd only to Wilt Chamberlain as All-Time NBA Scorer with 26,710 points 1980; 4th Infield Goals (9058); 5th Field Goals Attempted (19620); 3rd Most Minutes Played (43,886); 1st Most Free Throws (9,887); First Milwaukee Buck to be inducted into Basketball Hall of Fame 1979; widely recognized as one of the greatest all around players in game history; mem Basketball Hall of Fame, 1979; mem, Olympic Hall of Fame, 1984; Natl Award, Boys Clubs of Amer, 1987; developer, Avondale Town Center, Cincinnati, 1981; developer/owner, Oscar Terrace (affordable housing units), Indianapolis, IN, 1989; Univ of Cincinnati Campus, Statue in his Honor, 1994. **Military Serv:** US Army, private first class, 1960-67. **Business Addr:** Pres & CEO, ORCHEM Inc, 4293 Muhlhauser Rd, Fairfield, OH 45014, (513)874-9700.

ROBERTSON, PAUL FRANCIS
Computing professional. **Personal:** Born Aug 23, 1953, Galveston, TX; son of Gilfred & Wilda Robertson; divorced; children: Chiquita Monique, Paul Alexander, Andrea Celecte. **Educ:** University of Houston, 1971-72; Texas Southern University, BA, Math, 1972-75. **Career:** Union Carbide Corp process computer programmer, 1974-80; Lockheed Engineering & Management Co, computer programmer, 1980-81; System Software Inc, systems programmer, 1981; Houston Community College System, data processing instructor, 1981; Southwestern Bell, operator (telecommunications), 1982; County of Galveston, applications specialist, 1982-. **Orgs:** Society for Computer Simulation, 1981-83; Computer Professionals for Social Responsibility, 1984; Association for Computing Machines, 1985-86, 1994-95; Texas State Teachers Association, NEA, 1986-88; Texas Federation of Teachers, AFT, associate mem, 1995-; National Writers Union. **Honors/Awds:** Texas Southern University, magna cum laude, 1975, Honor Roll Status Achievement Certificate, 1975; Gulf Coast Big Brothers/Big Sisters, Outstanding Support Certificate, 1987, 1996; Galveston Ball High School (Communities in Schools), Certificate for Outstanding Svc, 1996. **Special Achievements:** FORTRAN IV Applications-Advanced Systems 3255 Assembly Language Programming, "Learning Assembly Language Programming Made Simple by a high-level Programming Language Correlation", (publication pending through National Writers Union UAW Local 1981/AFL-CIO), 1997. **Business Addr:** Applications Specialist, County of Galveston, Information Technology Department, 722 Moody St, Galveston County Courthouse, 2nd Fl, Galveston, TX 77550, (409)766-2220.

ROBERTSON, QUINCY L.
Educational administrator. **Personal:** Born Jul 30, 1934, Wedowee, AL; son of Viola Wilkes Robertson and Jessie Robertson; married Dollie Williams; children: Stephanie. **Educ:** TN State Univ, BA 1955, MA 1957. **Career:** Richmond County Bd of Ed, guidance counselor 1959-68; Paine Coll, dir of upward bound 1968-69, business mgr 1970-83, vice pres admin & fiscal affairs 1983-. **Orgs:** Bd of dir USO 1964-68; commiss Richmond Cty Personnel Bd 1973-78; chmn Thankful Baptist Church Trustee Bd 1977-85; vice pres Frontiersman 1984-85; bd of dir EIIA 1985-; bd of dir Univ Hosp; board of directors, Richmond County Hosp Authority; board of directors, treasurer, The Gertrude Herbert Art Institute; board of directors, Sun Trust National Bank; board of directors, Augusta Rescue Mission; mem Amer Assn for Affirmative Action, 1982-; mem Natl Assn of Black Public Admin, 1983-; mem Natl Assn of Human Rights Workers, 1986-; mem DeKalb County NAACP; den leader, Boy Scouts of America, 1992-. **Honors/Awds:** Man of the Year Thankful Baptist Church 1969; Admin of the Year Paine Coll 1973-74; Citizen of the Year Alpha Phi Alpha Frat 1984; Outstanding Young Men of America, 1984; Distinguished Service Award, Univ of Georgia, 1985; Community Service Award, Black Pages Magazine, 1990; Minority Business Advocate of the Year, 1991. **Military Serv:** AUS spec 4 1957-58; Good Conduct Medal, Expert Rifleman, Honorable Discharge. **Home Addr:** 3219 Tate Rd, Augusta, GA 30906. **Business Addr:** VP Admin & Fiscal Affairs, Paine College, 1235 15th St, Augusta, GA 30910.

ROBERTSON, QUINDONELL S.
Educator. **Personal:** Born Jan 28, Dallas, TX; married J William. **Educ:** BA 1954, MA 1970. **Career:** Dallas Independent School Dist & School Sec, educator 1957-58, education cluster coordinator 1984-. **Orgs:** Mem NEA, TX State Teacher Assoc, Classroom Teachers of Dallas, TX Classroom Teacher, TX Assoc Teacher Ed, Amigos, Sigma Gamma Rho, TX Coll, TX So Univ Alumni Assoc; life mem YWCA; charter mem Dallas Urban League Guild; pres Top Ladies of Distinction Inc; bd dir Dallas Pan Hellenic Council; mem Phi Delta Kappa; master educator, Amer Board of Master Educators, 1987; mem, Amer Assn of Univ Women, 1986. **Honors/Awds:** 9 plaques for leadership & svc; 1 silver tray for leadership & svc; Gavel for leadership; 2 trophies for leadership & svc, Medallion for YWCA Quota Buster; Gold Cup for chartering Arlington TX Sigma Gamma Rho 1983; Gold Charm for serving 3 yrs as pres of Sigma Gamma Rho, 1985-88; Teacher of The Year, 1990-91; Sigma Gamma Rho, Yellow Tea Rose Award, 1992; SW Reg Sigma Gamma Rho, Service Award, 1992, life member, 1992.

ROBESON, PAUL, JR.
Lecturer. **Personal:** Born Nov 2, 1927, Brooklyn, NY; son of Eslanda Goode Robeson and Paul Leroy Robeson; married Marilyn Paula Greenberg, Jun 19, 1949; children: David Paul, Susan. **Educ:** Cornell University, BSEE, 1949. **Career:** School of Industrial Technology, instructor, 1949-52; Othello Associates, CEO, 1953-56; International Physical Index, executive editor/partner, 1957-70, free-lance translator from Russian, 1971-89; Program Corp of America, lecturer, 1990-. **Orgs:** American Physical Society, 1980-; New York Academy of Sciences, 1991-. **Honors/Awds:** Cornell University, Tau Beta Pi Honor Society, 1949, Eta Kappa Nu Honor Society, 1949; Alpha Phi Alpha Fraternity; Founders Award of Excellence, 1991. **Special Achievements:** Producer/script writer, Celebration of Paul Robeson, Shubert Theater, 1988; producer, Odyssey of Paul Robeson, compact disc, Omega Record Group, 1992; author, Paul Robeson, Jr Speaks to America, Rutgers University Press, 1992. **Military Serv:** Army Air Force, corporal, 1946-47. **Business Addr:** Lecturer, Program Corp of America, 599 W Hartsdale Ave, White Plains, NY 10607, (914)428-5840.

ROBICHAUX, JOLYN H.
Business executive (retired). **Personal:** Born May 21, 1928, Cairo, IL; widowed; children: Sheila, Joseph. **Educ:** Chicago Teachr Coll, AB 1960; PA State Univ Ice Cream Tech, Cert. **Career:** State Dept Tour of Africa, spec nutritions consult 1956; Betty Crocker Home Serv Dept of Gen Mills, 1960-65; Cook Cty, jury comm 1971-72; Baldwin Ice Cream Co, owner 1971-92. **Orgs:** Bd of dir Chicago United Way 1984. **Honors/Awds:** Elected 1 of 10 Outstanding Black Bus Leaders Black Book 1973; Comm Serv Awd Chicago S End Jaycees 1973; Black Excellence Awd in Bus by PUSH 1974,75; Achievement Awd So IL Council 1974; Achievement in Bus World of Black Women, Iota Phi Lambda 1974; Bus Woman of the Year Cosmopolitan C of C 1976; Disting Alumna Awd Chicago State Univ 1984; Par Excellence Awd PUSH Bus Woman of the Year 1984; Natl Minority Entrepreneur of the Year Univ S Dept of Commerce presented by Vice Pres George Bush 1985.

ROBIE, CLARENCE W.
Electrical parts distributor. **Career:** B & S Electric Supply Co, Inc, Atlanta GA, chief executive, president, currently. **Orgs:** Greater Atlanta Electric League. **Business Addr:** Chief Executive Officer, President, B & S Electric Supply Co, Inc, 4505 Mills Place, SW, Atlanta, GA 30336.

ROBINET, HARRIETTE GILLEM
Author. **Personal:** Born Jul 14, 1931, Washington, DC; daughter of Martha Gray Gillem and Richard Avitus Gillem; married McLouis Joseph Robinet, Aug 6, 1960; children: Stephen, Philip, Rita, Jonathan, Marsha, Linda. **Educ:** College of New Rochelle, BS, 1953; Catholic University of America, MS, 1957, PhD, 1962. **Career:** Children's Hospital, Washington DC, bacteriologist, 1953-54; Walter Reed Army Medical Center, Washington DC, medical serologist, 1954-57, research bacteriologist, 1958-60; Xavier University, New Orleans LA, instructor in biology, 1957-58; US Army, Quartermaster Corps, civilian food bacteriologist, 1960-62; free-lance writer, 1962—. **Orgs:** Society of Childrens Book Writers and Illustrators; Children's Reading Roundtable. **Honors/Awds:** Carl Sandburg Children's Literature Award, Washington City is Burning, 1997; Children's Literature Award, Friends of American Writers, Children of the Fire, 1991; Notable Children's Trade Books in Social Studies: Mississippi Chariot, 1994; Children of the Fire, 1991; Books for the Teen Age, NYC Librarians: Mississippi Chariot. **Special Achievements:** Author of Jay and the Marigold, Childrens Press, 1976; author of Ride the Red Cycle, Houghton-Mifflin, 1980; Children of the Fire, Atheneum/Simon & Schuster, 1991; Mississippi Chariot, 1994; If You Please, President Lincoln, 1995; Washington City is Burning, 1996; The Twins, The Pirates & The Battle of New Orleans, 1997; Forty Acres and Maybe a Mule, 1998. **Home Addr:** 214 South Elmwood, Oak Park, IL 60302. **Business Addr:** 214 South Elmwood, Oak Park, IL 60302.

ROBINSON, ADELINE BLACK
Educator. **Personal:** Born Mar 7, 1915, Columbia, TN; married Phillip Edward Robinson. **Educ:** TN State Univ, BS Eng & Educ 1935; Fisk Univ, MA Educ 1950; Teachers Coll Columbia Univ, EMR Prof Diploma in Educ 1955; Peabody Coll, post grad study 1960-62. **Career:** Metropolitan Nashville School, teacher 39 yrs, 20 yrs teaching EMR Classes, 8 summer sessions as Demonstration Class teacher in coop with TSU & Kennedy Center. **Orgs:** Mem law enforcement com Citizen's Goals 2000 Com; rep Diocesan Ecumenical Commn; Coord Council on Legislative Concerns 1975-76; recorder for League of Women Voters Unit Mtgs; monitor TN Legislature; reporter & asst with mailing CCLC Legislative Newsletter 1975; life mem NEA, Council for Exceptional Children; mem NEA Black Caucus; bd of dir Grace M Eaton Day Home; mem NAACP, natl Council of Negro Women YWCA, Common Cause, League of Women Voters, Holy Trinity Episcopal Ch, Natl Sor of Phi Delta Kappa Alpha Beta Chap tamias for 1975-76; mem Federation of Colored Womens Clubs; Garden Lovers Club; bd dirs St Luke Comm Ctr; mem of Ecumenical Action Comm of Church Women United. **Honors/Awds:** Grad Cum Laude TSU; Awd of Merit Inst on Mental Retardation & Intellectual Devel; George Peabody for Tchr Nashville TN in recog of significant contributor behavioral sci by serving as an experimental tchr in EMR Lang Devel Proj 1965-67; Educ Fellowship Gift named in Honor of AAUW Nashville Br; Certificate of Recognition for Disting Leadership NCNW 1983; Woman of the Yr Natl Assn of Negro Bus & Professional Womens Clubs Inc 1984.

ROBINSON, ALBERT ARNOLD
Salesman. **Personal:** Born May 2, 1937, Lawrenceville, VA; married Mary Elizabeth Wright; children: Terence, Todd, Trent, Tevis, Lisa. **Educ:** VA State Univ, BS with distinction 1958; Central State Univ BS with distinction 1965-68; East Carolina Univ, 1976-77. **Career:** US Army, commissioned officer 1958-78; Ford Motor Co, manufacturing super 1978-80; Bechtel Power Corp, super fo reprographics 1980-84; Natl Reproductions Corp, sales rep 1984-85; Eastern MI Univ, mgr service operations 1985-. **Orgs:** Trustee Second Baptist Church 1979-; mem Ypsilanti/Willow Run Br NAACP 1980-; councilman Ypsilanti City Council 1981-; mem Ann Arbor/Ypsilanti Bus & Prof League 1982-; mem Emanon Club 1983-. **Honors/Awds:** Mem Beta Kappa Chi Honorary Scientific Frat 1958; mem Kappa Phi Kappa Hon Educational Frat 1958. **Military Serv:** AUS lt col 20 yrs; Legion of Merit, Bronze Star, Meritorious Serv Medal, Army Commendations, Parachutist Badge 1958-78. **Home Addr:** 918 Pleasant Dr, Ypsilanti, MI 48197. **Business Addr:** Manager of Sales Operations, Eastern MI University, Physical Plant EMU, Ypsilanti, MI 48197.

ROBINSON, ALBERT M.
Association executive. **Personal:** marrIed Jane B Carter; children: Albert Jr, Kimberly. **Educ:** VA State Coll, BS; Rutgers U; Rider Coll. **Career:** United Progress Inc, exec dir; Dept Comm Affairs NJ, relocation ofcr; Trenton Hous Auth, mgr; Lockerman High Sch Denton, tchr; Trenton Br NAACP, pres. **Honors/Awds:** Brotherhood award Jewish Fedn; outstanding & comm serv award 1970; Trenton Pub Serv Award 1968; outstanding achiev comm affairs NAACP 1971; pol action council award 1967. **Military Serv:** AUS 1942-46. **Business Addr:** 401 03 Pennington Ave, Trenton, NJ.

ROBINSON, ALCURTIS
Insurance company executive. **Personal:** son Of Corean Skinner Robinson and Eris Robinson Sr. **Educ:** Harris Teachers College, AA, 1960; Purdue University, Professional Management Institute, 1976. **Career:** Mutual of Omaha-United of Omaha, St Louis, MO, salesman, 1967-69, sales training instructor, 1969-70, district manager, 1970-73; Mutual of Omaha-United of Omaha, Omaha, NE, associate director of management training, 1973-75, assistant vice president in career development and management training, 1975-77, second vice president, 1977-82, vice president in career development and public affairs, 1982-85, vice president in public service and minority affairs, 1985-, vice president in minority and community affairs, 1988-; Insurance Industry Designation, register health underwriter, currently. **Orgs:** NAACP, Baltimore, MD; board member, National Association for Sickle Cell Disease Inc; Black Executive Exchange Program, National Urban League, Inc, New York, NY; Natl Alliance of Business; Career development advisory committee, National Urban League; development director, United Negro College Fund Drive; chmn, public employees retirement board, State of Nebraska; chmn, board of directors, Christian Urban Education Services; Urban League of Nebraska; president, Omaha School Foundation, 1990-91; board of directors, YMCA of Omaha. **Honors/Awds:** Harris-Stowe State College, Distinguished Alumni Award, 1992; National Eagle Leadership Inst, Distinguished Eagle Award, 1997; Western Heritage Museum, Omaha, African-American award, 1998. **Military Serv:** US Army, 1963-65. **Home Addr:** 1411 North 128th Circle, Omaha, NE 68154.

ROBINSON, ALFREDA P.
Educational administrator. **Personal:** Born May 7, 1932, Charlotte, NC. **Educ:** Upsala Coll, BA 1954; Rutgers Sch of Social Work, 1957; Union Graduate School, doctoral candidate. **Career:** Rutgers Graduate School of Mgmt, dean in charge of student servics; Rutgers Univ Graduate School of Bus & Adminstrn, asst dean in charge of student services; Financial Aid Douglass & Cook Coll of Rugers Univ, dir; Essex Co Probation Dept, sr probation officer; NJ Bureau of Children Serv Natl, case worker. **Orgs:** Proj com mem Delta Sigma Theta Inc; Nat Scholarship & Standards Com NJ Alumnae Chpt; corr sec, editor, Eastern Assn of Student Financial Aid Adminstr; councilman, Natl Council on Student Financial Aid; NJ Assn of Student Financial Aid Adminstrn; councilman, Coll Entrance Exam Bd; Middle States Regional Councilman Pub & Guidance Com; Upper Div Scholarship Review; mem, New Jersey Alumnae Chpt; vice pres bd trustees St Timothy House. **Honors/Awds:** Com serv award Sigma Gamma Rho 1979; serv award Rutgers Black MBA Assn 1979. **Business Addr:** Rutgers Grad Sch of Mgmt, 92 New St, Newark, NJ 07102.

ROBINSON, ANDREW
Educator. **Personal:** Born Feb 16, 1939, Chicago. **Educ:** Chicago State U, BA 1966; Roosevelt U, MA 1970; Northwestern U, PhD 1973. **Career:** Univ of KY, asst prof, asso dir Cntr for urban educ 1975-; Chicago City Colls, adminstr 1974-75; Urban & Ethnic Edn, Asst dir; Pub Inst Chicago, supt 1973-74; Chicago Urban League, educ dir 1970-73; Univ IL, visiting instr 1972-73; Chicago Pub Schs, tchr 1966-69. **Orgs:** Mem Phi Delta Kappa; Am Assn Sch Adminstrs; Am Assn of Tchr Edn; Nat Alliance Black Sch Educators; Prog Planning Comm Am Assoc of Coll Tchr Edn. **Military Serv:** Mil serv 1962-63.

ROBINSON, ANGELA YVONNE
Broadcast journalist. **Personal:** Born Jul 14, 1956, Atlanta, GA; daughter of Ann Roberts Robinson and Johnny Robinson (deceased). **Educ:** Syracuse Univ, Syracuse, NY, BS, public communications, television/radio broadcasting, 1974-78. **Career:** WAGA-TV, Atlanta, GA, production assistant, 1978-83; WTTG-TV, Washington, DC, general assignment reporter, talk show host, news anchor, news editor & reporter, 1983-94; WXIA, co-anchor, 1994-97. **Orgs:** Member, National Assn of Black Journalists; member, Washington Assn of Black Journalists, 1984-; executive board member, National Academy of Television Arts and Sciences, 1985-; member, Washington Chapter, National Council of Negro Women, 1989-; executive board member, Washington Local, AFTRA, 1985-. **Honors/Awds:** Emmy Award, National Academy of Television Arts and Sciences, 1980; United Press International Award, 1980, Editing Award, 1981; Emmy Award Nominee, National Academy of Television Arts and Sciences, 1986, 1989, 1990; Outstanding Enterprise Reporting, Associated Press International; Award of Distinction, George Aman, 1989; National Association of Black Journalists Award, 1990; Associated Press Award, Sports Feature, 1990, Feature/Humor Interest, 1991; National Association of Black Journalists Award, 1991-92; Omega Psi Phi Fraternity Inc, Public Service Award, 1992; Atlanta Assn of Media Women; Chancellor's Citation, Syracuse Univ, Distinguished Achievement in Journalism; Angela Y Robinson, Student Scholarship, Syracuse Univ; Atlanta Business League: 100 Women of Vision; Several Awards of Excellence, National Assn of Black Journalists; Southern Regional Emmy Awards, News Anchor, 1995, Best Newscast & Olympic Special, 1996, Special Series, 1997; Atlanta Association of Black Journalists Pioneer Award, Special Reports, 1995, 1997. **Home Addr:** 3141 Gold Dr SW, Atlanta, GA 30311-3668.

ROBINSON, ANN GARRETT
Educator. **Personal:** Born Jun 8, 1934, Greenville, NC; married Charles Robinson; children: Angela Carol, George Carl. **Educ:** North Carolina Central University, BA, 1954; Wayne State University, MA, 1957; Nova University, EdD, 1975; Yale University, research fellow, 1986. **Career:** Robinson Behavioral Science Consultant, New Haven, co-owner; North Carolina Board of Corrections, 1956-57; Central State Hospital, LaRue Carter Hospital, Augusta State Hospital, clinical psychology, 1958-64; Yale University Child Study Center, research assisant, 1968-70; Trinity College, Hartford, assistant professor psychology, 1970-72; Co Central Community College, professor of psychology; freelance writer, 1983-; New Haven Register, newspaper columnist, 1985-; South Central Community College, professor of psychology, project coordinator, life review/life history analysis. **Orgs:** Board director, South Central Connecticut Mental Health Planning Reg, 1974-77; NEA, American Psychology Association; board of deaconnesses, Immanuel Baptist Church, Alpha Kappa Alpha, Black Educators Association, Afro-Amer History Board, Jack & Jill of America, Inc; regional vice president, North East Psi Beta, Inc; The National Honor Society in Psychology; pres-elect, National Council, Psi Beta, Inc; chairlady, Immanuel Baptist Church, board of deaconesses, 1985-. **Honors/Awds:** Nannie H Burroughs Award Outstanding Black Educator of New Haven, 1974; Presidential Citation Award, SCCC, 1977; Community Service Award, New Haven; author, "Clouds & Clowns of Destiny", "Behind Krome Detention Center Walls", "Are the Doors to Higher Education Starting to Close", "Heroic Women of the Past, The Three Wives of Booker T Washington"; Church of Christ National Youth Conference Award, 1986; SCCC, Most Scholarly Award, 1987; Most Influential Professor, SCCC Student Government Award, 1987; Professional Woman of the Year, Elm City Business and Professional Women. **Business Addr:** Professor of Psychology, South Central Community College, 60 Sargent Drive, New Haven, CT 06511.

ROBINSON, ANTHONY W.
Company executive. **Personal:** Born Dec 11, 1948, Clarksville, TN; son of Eva Mae Childs & Charles C Robinson; married Yvonne Davis Robinson, Aug 30, 1980; children: Charles Anthony, Camille A. **Educ:** Morgan State College, BS, 1970; Washington College of Law-American University, JD, 1973. **Career:** Equal Employment Opportunity Commission, legal counsel, 1973-75; Singleton, Dashill & Robinson, partner, 1975-84; Minority Business Enterprise Legal Defense & Education Fund, Inc, president/CEO, 1984-. **Honors/Awds:** NMSDC, Recognition Awd, 1996; Minority Business Report, Advocate of the Year, 1996; Minitory Human Business Enterprise, Advocate Recognition Awd, 1995; National Conference of Black Mayors, 1995; State of Maryland, Governor's Citation, 1996. **Special Achievements:** The Affirmative Action Debate edited by George E Curry, 1996. **Military Serv:** US Army, 1st lt, 1972-78. **Home Addr:** 8134 Scotts Level Rd, Baltimore, MD 21208. **Business Phone:** (202)289-1700.

ROBINSON, AUBREY EUGENE, JR.
Judge. **Personal:** Born Mar 30, 1922, Madison, NJ; son of Mable J Robinson and Aubrey E Robinson; married Doris A Washington; children: Paula Elaine Robinson Collins, Sheryl Louise, Jacqueline C Washington. **Educ:** Cornell Univ, BA 1943, LLB 1947. **Career:** Practiced with various law firms in WA, 1948-65; Amer Council Human Rights, gen counsel 1953-55, dir 1955; Juvenile Court DC, assoc judge 1965-66; US Dist Court, judge 1966-82, chief judge, 1982-92, senior judge, 1992-. **Orgs:** Bd dir 1954-63, vice pres 1958-61 Family and Child Services, Washington, DC; bd dir Family Services Assn of America 1958-68; bd trustees United Planning Organization, Washington, DC, 1963-66; exec comm, bd dir 1964-66, Citizens for Better Public Educ, Washington, DC; exec comm Interreligious Comm on Race Relations 1966-67; bd dir Eugene & Agnes E Meyer Foundation 1969-85; Cornell Law School Adv Council 1974-80; mem Comm on the Admin of the Criminal Law 1977-83; adj prof WA Coll of Law, Amer Univ 1975-84; bd mem Fed Judicial Center 1978-82; bd trustees Cornell Univ, 1982-; Judicial Conf of the US 1982-92; mem Amer Bar Assn. **Honors/Awds:** Distinguished Alumnus Award, Cornell Law School, 1986; Honorary Doctor of Laws Degree, Drew University, 1987; Charles Hamilton Houston Medallion, Washington Bar Association, 1989; Judicial Honoree Award, Bar Association of the District of Columbia, 1990; H Carl Moultrie Award for Judicial Excellence presented by the Trial Lawyers Assn of Metropolitan Washington, DC, 1992; The DC Bar Assn Certificate of Appreciation in recognition of unselfish service to the courts, the Community and the Bar, 1992; The Federal Bar Assn Lifetime Achievement Award, 1992; Wiley A. Branton, Sr Award, Washington Lawyers' Committee for Civil Rights and Urban Affairs, 1995. **Military Serv:** US Army, First Sergeant, 1943-46. **Business Addr:** Senior Judge, US District Court of DC, US Ct House, Washington, DC 20001.

ROBINSON, BARRY LANE
Government official. **Personal:** Born Jun 5, 1943, White Plains, NY; divorced; children: 2. **Educ:** State Univ of Buffalo, BA 1980. **Career:** Johnson & Johnson, salesman 1974-75; Attica Correction Ctr, corrections officer 1975-79; Masten Park Secure Ctr, child care worker 1979-; Erie Co, co legislator 1982-. **Orgs:** Mem NAACP 1985; mem Ellicott Dist Concerned Taxpayers 1985; mem Operation PUSH. **Honors/Awds:** Mr Black America 1981; Dale Carnegie Awd Public Speaking/ Univ; training course NY State Police. **Military Serv:** AUS sp/5 trans 1966-80; Honorable Discharge. **Business Addr:** County Legislator, Erie Co Dist 3, 25 Delaware Ave, Buffalo, NY 14202.

ROBINSON, BENJAMIN ELLISON, III
Banking officer. **Personal:** Born Nov 11, 1963, Philadelphia, PA; son of Mildred Jolly Robinson and Benjamin Robinson Jr. **Educ:** Bates College, Lewiston, ME, BA, 1986; Trinity College, Hartford, Ct, MA, 1991. **Career:** Connecticut National Bank, Hartford, CT, correspondent banking officer, 1986-91; Mellon Bank, Pittsburgh, PA, west coast cash management officer, 1991-. **Orgs:** Vice-chairman, American Red Cross, 1988-; board of directors, Urban League of Greater Hartford, 1988-; president, North Hartford Federal Credit Union, 1988-90. **Honors/Awds:** Thousand Points of Light, President Bush, 1990; Star Player Award, National Red Cross, 1990; Future Leader, Ebony Magazine, 1990. **Business Addr:** Cash Management Officer, Mellon Bank, Global Cash Management Dept, 3 Mellon Center, Pittsburgh, PA 15206.

ROBINSON, BEVERLY JEAN
Publishing company executive. **Personal:** Born Dec 15, 1957, Bath, NY; daughter of Alice Jackson Robinson and George Wesley Robinson; married Christopher K Chaplin, Aug 30, 1981; children: Christopher, Khalif. **Educ:** Dowling Coll, Oakdale, NY, BA (magna cum laude), 1979; New School for Social Research, New York, NY, Masters, 1988. **Career:** Random House, New York, NY, advertising asst, 1979-82; Ballantine Publishing Group, New York, NY, publicity coordinator, 1982-87, publicity mgr, 1987-90, asst publicity dir, 1990-93, associate, director of press relations, 1993-, One World Books dept, dir of publicity, currently. **Orgs:** Mem, Women in Communications, 1983-85. **Honors/Awds:** Member of Publicity Dept that received Excellence in Publicity Award, Literary Market Place, 1991. **Special Achievements:** Member of the team that founded One World, the first multicultural imprint at a major publishing house, 1992. **Home Addr:** 135 Clinton St, #4V, Hempstead, NY 11550.

ROBINSON, BILL, JR. (WILLIAM HENRY)
Professional baseball player (retired). **Personal:** Born Jun 26, 1943, McKeesport, PA; married Mary Alice Moore; children: William III, Kelly Ann. **Career:** Atlanta Braves, outfielder 1965-66; New York Yankees, outfielder 1967-69; Philadelphia Phillies, outfielder 1972-74; Pittsburgh Pirates, outfielder 1975-82; Philadelphia Phillies, outfielder 1982-83; New York Mets, batting coach, 1st base coach.

ROBINSON, CARL CORNELL
Attorney. **Personal:** Born Sep 21, 1946, Washington, DC; son of Florence A Robinson and Louis W Robinson. **Educ:** Univ of Michigan, BS Aero Eng 1969; Golden Gate Univ, MBA 1974; UCLA, JD 1977. **Career:** O'Melveny & Myers, attorney 1977-84; Robinson & Pearman, partner 1984-. **Orgs:** Dir San Fernando Valley Neighborhood Legal Serv 1981-91, chair, 1982-86; dir UCLA Public Interest Law Foundation 1982-89, chair, 1982-84; vice pres Natl Black MBA Assn Los Angeles 1985; mem Legal Serv Trust Fund Commn CA 1985, Judicial Evaluation Comm Los Angeles County Bar Assn 1986, 1988, 1990, 1994, 1998; dir Natl Assn of Securities Profls 1986-94, dir, John M Langston Bar Assn 1987-94; dir, Western Center on Law and Poverty, Inc, 1988-94; dir, UCLA Law Alumni Association, 1977, 1997. **Military Serv:** USAF capt 1969-74. **Home Addr:** 3924 S Sycamore Ave, Los Angeles, CA 90008. **Business Addr:** Partner, Robinson & Pearman, 1055 W 7th St, Ste 2800, Los Angeles, CA 90017, (213)627-9060.

ROBINSON, CARL DAYTON
Pediatrician. **Personal:** Born Jun 14, 1942, Tallulah, LA; son of Emily Parker Robinson and Bernie Dayton Robinson; married Sandra Lawson, Aug 14, 1965; children: Michael, Carla. **Educ:** Howard Univ, BS 1964, MD 1968; Tulane Univ Sch of Public Health, MPH 1977. **Career:** Letterman Army Med Ctr, chf prenatal/infant serv 1971-73; Flint Goodridge Hospital, dir sickle cell pgm 1973-78; Natl Sickle Cell Adv Comm, mem 1976-78; Reg Med Pgm, LA, mem 1976-78; LA Commsn on Prenatal Care, mem 1977-81; Genetic Disease Ctr, med dir 1978-81; Tulane Univ Med Sch, cln asst prof pediatrics 1973-; Robinson Med Grp, pres 1978-; Childrens Hospital of New Orleans, pres medical staff 1986-88; Developmental Center of America, New Orleans, LA, president, 1990-; Key Management, Birmingham, AL, vice president/medical director, 1990-. **Orgs:** Consultant to sec Dept of Health & Human Resources LA 1984; vice pres Southeast LA Med Qlty Review Found 1979-81; pres APTECH Inc 1978-; pres LA Health Corp 1984-; life mem Alpha Phi Alpha; mem Amer Public Health Assn; president, Orleans Parish School Board, 1990. **Honors/Awds:** Fellow Amer Acad of Pediatrics; fellow Intl Coll of Pediatrics; elected to Orleans Parish School Bd 1989. **Military Serv:** AUS major 1971-73. **Business Addr:** President/CEO, Robinson Medical Group, 2600 Ursuline Ave, New Orleans, LA 70119.

ROBINSON, CAROL EVONNE
Newspaper reporter. **Personal:** Born Sep 15, 1959, Sacramento, CA; daughter of Claudia Cleatus Buford Robinson and Herbert Allen Robinson. **Educ:** Univ of California, Davis, CA, BA, 1983; Cosumnes River College, Sacramento, CA, 1984-86; Summer program for Minority Journalists, Berkeley, CA, 1988. **Career:** Meracor Mortgage, Sacramento, CA, assistant loan closer, 1986-87; California Personnel Service, Sacramento, CA, word processor, 1988; Bellingham Herald, Bellingham, WA, education writer, 1988-89; Daily Republic, Fairfield, CA, education writer, 1989-. **Orgs:** Member, National Assn of Black Journalists, 1989-; member, Sacramento Black Journalists Assn, 1990-; member, Society of Professional Journalists, 1989-. **Honors/Awds:** First Place, Government Reporting, Society of Professional Journalists, Northwest Chapter, 1989. **Business Addr:** Staff Writer, Editorial, The Daily Republic, 1250 Texas St, Fairfield, CA 94533.

ROBINSON, CAROL W.
Librarian. **Personal:** Born Dec 4, 1953, New Rochelle, NY; daughter of Dorothy Clark Word and Richard Word; married Curtis Robinson (died 1982); children: Ujima, Zakiyyah, Saliym. **Educ:** WEB Dubois Seminar at Atlanta University, Atlanta, GA, 1973; Northeastern University, Boston, MA, BA, 1976; Pratt Institute, Brooklyn, NY, 1981-82; Queens College, Flushing NY, MLS, 1984. **Career:** Library of Congress, Washington, DC, library intern, 1973; MIT Historical Collections, Cambridge, MA, museum intern, 1974-76; Coopers & Lybrand, Washington, DC, library asst, 1976-78; Washington, DC Public Schools, Washington, DC, teacher, 1978-80; Mount Vernon Public Library, Mount Vernon, NY, librarian, beginning 1981, asst dir, acting dir, 1997. **Orgs:** Member, Westchester Library Association, 1981-; member, New York Black Librarians Caucus, 1984-; member, Black Caucus of American Library Association, 1990-; member American Library Association, 1982-; vice president Sons and Daughters of African Unity, Inc; New York Library Assn, 1994-; chair, African American Librarians of Westchester, 1994-. **Honors/Awds:** Phi Alpha Theta, Zeta-Tau Chapter, 1975-; Beta Phi Mu, Beta Alpha Chapter, 1985-. **Business Addr:** Asst Director, Mount Vernon Public Library, 28 S First Ave, Mount Vernon, NY 10550, (914)668-1840.

ROBINSON, CARRIE C.
Educator, librarian (retired). **Personal:** Born Apr 21, 1906, St Madison County, MS; daughter of Cordelia Julia Harris Coleman (deceased) and James S Coleman (deceased); married Thomas L Robinson, Jun 12, 1935 (died 1989). **Educ:** Tougaloo College, Tougaloo, MS, AB, 1931; Hampton Univ, Hampton, VA, BLS, 1932; Columbia Univ, New York, NY, 1940-41; Univ of Illinois, Urbana, IL, MLS, 1949, advance studies, 1953-55. **Career:** West Kentucky Industrial College, Paducah, KY, head librarian, 1932-34; Avery Institute, Charleston, SC, head librarian, 1934-35; Tillotson College, Austin, TX, head librarian, 1935-37; Dorchester Academy, McIntosh, GA, head librarian, 1938-40; Grambling College, Grambling, LA, head librarian, 1942-43; Louisiana Library Comm, Scotlandville, LA, branch library supervisor, 1943-45; Alcorn College, Lorman, MS, head librarian, 1945-46; Alabama State University/State Dept of Education, Montgomery, AL, assistant professor, 1946-62; Purdue Univ, Lafayette, IN, associate professor, summer, 1963, 1964; Alabama State Dept of Education, Montgomery, AL, school libraries consultant, 1946-72; Auburn University, Auburn, AL, associate professor, 1972-75. **Orgs:** American Library Assn, 1946-; American Assn of School Librarians, 1946-76; Alabama Assn of School Librarians, 1947-75; Alabama Library Assn, 1949-75; ALA Committee of Accreditation of Library Schools, 4 years; member, Standards Committee, American Assn of School Libraries, 4 years; life member, National Education Association; co-founder, School of Library Media, Alabama A&M University, 1969; trustee, Freedom to Read Foundation, 1969-74; First Congregational Christian Church of Montgomery, AL, 1946-, mem of the trustee board, 1989-, chair of mission and outreach committee, teacher of church school. **Honors/Awds:** Alabama LAMP Workshops, Meritorious Service Award, 1979; Southern Poverty Law Center, Outstanding Service to Cause of Human Rights and Equal Justice, Certificate, 1990; Freedom to Read Foundation Award for, School Library Administration, Library Educator, Intellectual Freedom Advocate, Service and Commitment, 1991; Alabama Assn of School Librarians' Award; Distinguished Service, 1947-70; Personalities of the South Award, 1976-77; Alpha Kappa Alpha Sorority Award for Courageous Pursuit and Accomplishments in Civil Rights, 1971; Black Caucus of ALA Award, 1974; Alumnae of the Year Award; Tougaloo College, 1970; Distinguished Service Award, Alabama Library Assn, 1980. **Special Achievements:** Alabama LAMP Workshops, Meritorious Service Award, 1979; Southern Poverty Law Center, Outstanding Service to Cause of Human Rights and Equal Justice, 1990; Freedom to Read Foundation, School Library Administration, Library Educator, Intellectual Freedom Advocate, Service and Committment, 1991. **Home Addr:** 155 Pinetree Dr, Montgomery, AL 36117.

ROBINSON, CATHERINE
Educator. **Personal:** Born Sep 11, 1904, Petersburg, VA; widowed; children: Lynne, McDonald II, Valarie. **Educ:** RI Coll, atnd, Univ of RI. **Career:** So Prov Proj Univ of RI Coop Exten Serv, asst home econ ldr 1963-75; Family & Bus Relo Serv, field interviewer 1959-63; TV Series in Home Econ & Other Areas, hostess 2 yrs. **Orgs:** Mem bd dir Oppor Ind Ctr; mem Women's Counc of United Way; mem Civil Rights Commn RI Adv Commn of US Commn on Civil Rights; mem bd dir Black-Heritage Soc; fndr Scitamard Players 1937. **Honors/Awds:** Comm ldr award United So Providence Block Club 1971; comm serv award 1973; cit for disting serv Univ of RI Coop Exten Serv 1974; RI Heritage Hall of Fame 1975; hon PdD RI Coll; schlrshp Nat Conf of Christians & Jews Rutgers U. **Business Addr:** City Hall, Metter, GA 30439.

ROBINSON, CECELIA ANN
Educator. **Personal:** Born May 28, 1948, Dallas, TX; married Kenneth E. **Educ:** Prairie View A&M University, BA, 1969; University of Missouri, Columbia, MEd, 1970, education spec, 1971. **Career:** William Jewell College, English instructor, 1979-; Maple Woods Community College, English instructor, 1979; Pennsylvania Valley Community College, English instructor, 1976-79; Oak Park HS, English teacher, 1972-79; Prairie View A&M University, English instructor, 1972. **Orgs:** Sigma Tau Delta, English Honor Society, 1972-; National Council Teacher of English, 1972-; Missouri State Teacher of English, 1972-; Missouri State Teacher of English Association, 1979-; William Jewell Woman's Committee, 1974-80; corresponding secretary & journalist, Delta Sigma Theta, 1976-; board of directors, Mid-Continent Council of Girl Scouts, Kansas City, 1979-. **Honors/Awds:** EPDA Fellowship Univ of MO 1970-71; English Speaking Union Fellowship Univ of Oxford Eng 1976; MO Writer's Proj Grant Univ of MO 1979. **Business Addr:** Assistant Professor of English, William Jewell College, Department of English, Liberty, MO 64068.

ROBINSON, CHARLES
Actor. **Career:** Television credits include: ''Night Court,'' ''Love and War, ''Home Improvement'', ''Ink'';'' film credits include: ''Together Brothers,'' ''Sugarhill,'' ''Black Gestapo,'' ''Uncle Joe Shannon,'' ''Apocalypse Now,'' ''The River;'' plays include: ''My Sweet Charlie,'' ''Spoon River Anthology,'' ''The Night Thoreau Spent in Jail,'' ''Othello,'' ''Set It Off''. **Business Phone:** (310)277-7779.

ROBINSON, CHARLES
Educational administrator. **Personal:** Born Mar 19, 1940, Philadelphia, PA; married Bernice Ann Baker; children: Deborah Ann, Lesly Denise. **Educ:** Cheyney State Univ, BS 1966. **Career:** Philadelphia Dept of Recreation, dec leader 1962-66; Philadelphia Public Schools, teacher 1966-75, admin asst 1975-84, teacher 1984-85; NJ School Bd Assn, vice pres. **Orgs:** Scout master Troop 713 1968-74; chmn Edgewater Pk Twp Juvenile Conf Comm 1970-85; bd of educ Edgewater Pk Twp 1977-87; adv bd Burlington Co Voc Tech 1978-85; pres bd of trustees Edgewater Pk Football Assn 1981-83; vice pres Burlington Co Sch Bds Assn 1982-86; vice pres NJ Sch Bd Assn 1984-85. **Military Serv:** AUSR sgt E-5 6 yrs. **Business Addr:** Vice President, NJ Sch Bds Assn, 22nd & Chestnut St, Philadelphia, PA 19103.

ROBINSON, CHARLES E.
Psychiatric social worker. **Personal:** Born Aug 31, 1926, Indianapolis, IN; married Ann Garrett; children: Angela, George. **Educ:** IN Univ, BS 1950, MSW 1952. **Career:** Robinson & Robinson Behavioral Sci Cons, co-partner; Hallie Q Brown Settlement House St Paul, group soc worker 1952-54; Central State Hosp, psychiatric social worker 1954-64; IN Bd of School Comm, school social worker 1964-68; CMHC, dir of social work; Yale Univ Dept of Psychiatry, asst clinical prof of soc work in psychiatry, currently. **Orgs:** Bd of deacons Immanuel Baptist Church; IN Alumni Assoc; Jr C of C; Acad of Cert Soc Workers; Natl Assoc of Soc Worker; treas, bd of dir Newhallville Comm Action 1971-73; natl bd mem Family Serv Assoc 1973-; pres New Haven Family Serv Assoc of Amer 1974-78. **Honors/Awds:** Outstanding Human Serv Professional of Amer; Outstanding Comm Serv Awd, United Newhallville Org. **Military Serv:** AUS 1945-47. **Business Addr:** Assistant Clinical Professor, Yale University, Dept of Psychiatry, 34 Park St, New Haven, CT 06510.

ROBINSON, CHARLOTTE L.
Educator, consultant. **Personal:** Born Jun 13, 1924, Long Island, NY; widowed; children: Barry, Cherylyn. **Educ:** BA 1948; MA 1967; Univ of PA, dr degree 1976. **Career:** Philadelphia Pub Sch Sys, asst dir curriculum & instr multimedia instructional resources; City Univ of NY, cons; Sears Roebuck & Co Phila, cons. **Orgs:** Phi Delta Epsilon; Am Women in Radio & TV; Media Adv Com for Commonwealth of PA; Assn for Educ Communications & Tech; PA Learning Resources Assn, Philadelphia Unique Communications Project, 1974. **Business Addr:** 43 W Tulpehocken St, Philadelphia, PA 19144.

ROBINSON, CHRIS (CHRISTOPHER SEAN)
Professional basketball player. **Personal:** Born Feb 17, 1973, Columbus, GA. **Educ:** Western Kentucky. **Career:** Vancouver Grizzlies, guard, 1996-98; Sacramento Kings, 1998-. **Business Addr:** Professional Basketball Player, Sacramento Kings, One Sports Parkway, Sacramento, CA 95834, (916)928-6900.

ROBINSON, CLARENCE B.
Legislator (retired). **Personal:** Born Feb 4, 1911, Chattanooga, TN; son of Katie Robinson and Lewis Robinson; married Lillian Davis. **Educ:** TN State Univ, BS; Atlanta Univ, MEd; Univ of WI, post graduate. **Career:** Orchard Knob Baptist Church, trustee, chmn, bd of dirs; real estate broker self-employed; Alton Park Jr HS, Calvin Donaldson, principal; House of Reps TN, legislature, 1974-92. **Orgs:** Chmn emeritus, House Black Caucus; vice chmn, House Democratic Caucus; Natl Business League Bd; pres ETN Chap of TN Voters Council; life mem NEA, NAACP, NAASP, Kappa Alpha Psi; founder & co-chairman, State of TN Voters Council; Adv Bd of Human Relations; mem, Democratic Platform Adv Comm 1980. **Honors/Awds:** Certificate, Chattanooga Ambassador of Good Will 1968; Achievement Award, Natl Assn for the Study of Afro-Amer Life & History 1977; Distinguished Serv Award, TN State Univ, 1981; Meritorious Serv Appreciation Award, Chattanooga City Coll; Distinguished Serv Plaque, Chattanooga Chapter, NAACP; CB Robinson Bridge, Chattanooga, named in honor; CB Robinson Classroom, OKB Church; CB Robinson Scholarship Fund, OKB Church; Tenn Teachers School Bell, 1992; WJTT Lifetime Achievement; Retired Chairman Emeritus, 1992; TN Black Caucus of State Legislators, 1992. **Special Achievements:** Served on commissions under four US presidents; honored at Kennedy Center, Washington DC; Tennessee State University, library room dedicated to him. **Home Addr:** 1909 E 5th St, Chattanooga, TN 37404.

ROBINSON, CLARENCE G.
Internist, consultant. **Personal:** Born Sep 19, 1920, Chicago, IL; son of Mary Taylor Robinson and Dr Clarence G Robinson, Sr; married Dr Thelma M Lennard Robinson, May 28, 1946; children: David L, Michael O, Mary Robinson Cohen. **Educ:** Univ of Chicago, BS 1942; Meharry Med Coll, MD 1945. **Career:** Coney Island Hosp, chief ambulatory care serv 1967-72; City of NY, police surgeon 1970-73; New York City Police Dept, 1st black chief surgeon 1973-85, 1st full-time police surgeon, suprv chief surgeon 1980-85; Intl Assn of Chiefs of Police, chmn police physicians section 1986-89; Coney Island Hospital, Brooklyn, NY, consultant in quality assurance, 1990-93. **Orgs:** Assoc mem 1955, Fellow 1964, Amer Coll of Physicians; assoc attending physician Maimonides Med Ctr certified 1955, recertified 1974 Amer Bd of Intl Med; clinical instr med SUNY Downstate Med Ctr 1962-69; dir, med ed Coney Island Hosp 1967-70; scy 1969-70, pres med bd 1970-72, Coney Island Hosp; clinical asst, prof of med SUNY Downstate Med Ctr 1969-; vice chmn 1970-71, chmn 1971-72 Adv Council of Med Bds of Municipal Hospitals; attending physician Kings Cty Hosp Ctr 1971-; medical board member, New York City Employees Retirement System, 1988-97, chmn, 1997-; founding mem & pres-elect Amer Academy of Police Medicine 1976-80, pres 1981-85. **Honors/Awds:** Certificate of Advanced Achievement in Internal Medicine, Amer Bd of Internal Medicine, 1987; had self-teaching room dedicated in his honor, Coney Island Hospital, 1973; Special Award, Honor Legion of New York City Police Dept, 1981; Commendation, President's Council on Physical Fitness and Sports, 1983. **Military Serv:** US Air Force, capt, 1953-55. **Home Addr:** 2652 E 21 St, Brooklyn, NY 11235.

ROBINSON, CLIFFORD RALPH
Professional basketball player. **Personal:** Born Dec 16, 1966, Buffalo, NY. **Educ:** Connecticut. **Career:** Portland TrailBlazers, forward, 1989-97; Phoenix Suns, 1997-. **Honors/Awds:** NBA Sixth Man Award, 1993; NBA All-Star, 1994. **Business Addr:** Professional Basketball Player, Phoenix Suns, PO Box 515, Phoenix, AZ 85001, (602)379-7867.

ROBINSON, CRYSTAL
Professional basketball player. **Personal:** Born Jan 22, 1974. **Educ:** Oklahoma State Univ. **Career:** Colorado Xplosion, forward, 1996-. **Honors/Awds:** US Sports Festival, Most Valuable Player, 1993. **Business Addr:** Professional Basketball Player, Colorado Xplosion, 800 Grant St, Ste 410, Denver, CO 80203, (303)832-2225.

ROBINSON, CURTIS
Educator. **Personal:** Born May 12, 1934, Wilmington, NC; married Joan Elenor Williams; children: Debra D, Milton C, Cheryl A. **Educ:** Morgan State University, BS, 1960; Howard University, MS, 1968; University of Maryland, PhD, 1973. **Career:** Edinboro University of PA, professor, 1973-; Radiation Biology Lab, Smithsonian Institution, Rockville, MD, research biologist, 1962-69; Williston Sr HS, North Carolina, science/math teacher, 1961-62; Lincoln HS, North Carolina, science/math teacher, 1960-61. **Orgs:** American Society of Plant Physiologists, 1970-; National Education Association, 1973-; American Association of University Professors, 1978-; Alpha Phi Alpha, 1959-; Association of Pennsylvania State College Biologists, 1973-; NAACP, 1975. **Military Serv:** AUS spec-3 3 yrs. **Business Addr:** Biology & Health Sciences, Edinboro University of Pennsylvania, Edinboro, PA 16444-0001.

ROBINSON, CURTIS L.
Marketing project consultant engineer. **Personal:** Born Jan 21, 1958, Startex, SC; son of Dorothy Robinson and Willie Robinson; married Verneda F Robinson, Mar 30, 1991. **Educ:** South

Carolina State College, Orangeburg, SC, BS, civil engr; Rockhurst College, Kansas City, MO, MBA, financial, 1987. **Career:** Kansas City Power & Light Co, plant engineer, 1981-83, grade II engineer, 1983-85, turbine/generator engineer, 1985-90, marketing project consultant, 1990-. **Orgs:** Secretary, American Association of Blacks in Energy, 1990, Association of Demand Side Professionals, 1990, American Black MBA Association, 1987-; treasurer, Kansas City Alumni Chapter of Kappa Alpha Psi, 1988-; charter member, MBA Network of Kansas City, 1988-; citizen review committee member, United Way, 1988-90.

ROBINSON, DAMIEN
Professional football player. **Personal:** Born Dec 22, 1973. **Educ:** Univ of Iowa. **Career:** Tampa Bay Buccaneers, defensive back, 1997-. **Business Addr:** Professional Football Player, Tampa Bay Buccaneers, One Buccaneer Place, Tampa, FL 33607, (813)870-2700.

ROBINSON, DANIEL LEE
Business owner, chef. **Personal:** Born May 7, 1923, York County, SC; married Evelyn Young; children: Daniel Jr, Robert, Marilyn. **Educ:** Friendship Jr Coll, attnd. **Career:** Desales Hall Theol Sem, chef 1977; Colonial Villa Manor Care, kitchen mgr 1965-74; Fed Cab Co, taxicab owner, operator 25 yrs; Taxicab Ind Assn, rep 1972; NIH, 1953-63; PTA & Emery Sch, pres 1967; Langley Jr HS PTA, pres 1972; McKinley Sr High School PTA, vice pres 1974. **Orgs:** Mem DC Dem Central Com 1973-76; bd mem Ctr City Comm Corp 1967-; vice pres Three A Area Counc Cong of Parents & Tchrs 1973; pres adv counc Emery Comm Sch 1975; Ward 5 campaign coord Mayor Walter E Washington 1974; chmn 5th Ward Dem 1973-77; 1st vice pres Edgewood Civic Assn 1977; commr Single Mem Dist 5c-06; Adv Neighbrhd Commn DC Govt 1976; active in sch bd campaigns 1972; worked in CORE & ACT 1950'; ward coord Barbara Sizemore Campaign 1977; trstee Franklin P Nash United Meth Ch; chrpsn area of Christian Soc Concerns. **Honors/Awds:** Serv award Mattie G Taylor 1973; serv & award Ward 5 Counc William Spaulding 1976; grass roots hon DC Fdn of Civic Assns 1976; ten yr serv cert US Govt 1963. **Military Serv:** AUS staff-sgt 1943-47. **Business Addr:** 5001 Eastern Ave, Hyattsville, MD.

ROBINSON, DAPHNE MCCASKEY. See MCCASKEY, DAPHNE THEOPHILIA.

ROBINSON, DAVID MAURICE
Professional basketball player. **Personal:** Born Aug 6, 1965, Key West, FL; married Valerie; children: David Maurice Jr, Corey, Justin. **Educ:** United States Naval Academy, Annapolis, MD, 1983-87. **Career:** San Antonio Spurs, center, 1989-. **Honors/Awds:** All-NBA Third Team, 1990; NBA All-Defensive Second Team, 1990; NBA Rookie of the Year, 1990; NBA All-Rookie First Team, 1990; Schick Pivotal Player Award, 1990; NBA All-Star, 1990-98; NBA Most Valuable Player, 1995. **Special Achievements:** US Olympic Basketball Team, 1988, 1992, 1996; Selected as one of the 50 Greatest Players in NBA History, 1996. **Business Addr:** Professional Basketball Player, San Antonio Spurs, 600 E Market St, San Antonio, TX 78205, (210)554-7773.

ROBINSON, DAWN
Vocalist, songwriter. **Personal:** Born in New London, CT. **Career:** Member of the group En Vogue, 1988-97; albums include: Born to Sing, 1990; Remix to Sing, 1991; Funky Divas, 1992; EV3, 1997: singles include: ''Hold On,'' ''Lies,'' ''Free Your Mind,'' ''This Is Your Life,'' ''My Lovin' (You're Never Gonna Get It),'' ''Desire,'' ''Yesterday.''. **Honors/Awds:** Born to Sing, platinum, 1990; National Academy of Recording Arts and Sciences, Grammy nominations: rock duo or group, best short video, ''Free Your Mind''; r&b duo or group, Funky Divas. **Business Addr:** Singer, En Vogue, c/o David Lombard, Lombard Management, 4859 W Slauson Ave, Los Angeles, CA 90056, (213)962-8016.

ROBINSON, DEANNA ADELL
Convention service manager. **Personal:** Born Jul 31, 1945, Chicago, IL; married Willie. **Educ:** MI State Univ, BS 1967. **Career:** Hilton Hotels, 20 yrs serv with a wide range of positions, currently convention service mgr Palmer House Hotel. **Orgs:** Mem Natl Coalition of Black Meeting Planners 1986. **Business Addr:** Asst Dir Convention Serv, Palmer House-Hilton Hotel, 17 E Monroe St, Chicago, IL 60690.

ROBINSON, DENAUVO M.
Director of special services. **Personal:** Born Apr 10, 1949, Quincy, IL. **Educ:** Northeast MO St U, BS 1971; MA 1971; Northern IL U, EdD 1977. **Career:** Drexel U, dir of Specl Srv; Northern IL Univ CHANCE Dekalb, IL, assoc dir 1974, counselor 1972-74; Western IL U, Macomb, counselor 1971-72. **Orgs:** Mem APGA; ANWC; IGPA; IANWC; NIU; APGA; NAACP; Civil Liberties Union. **Business Addr:** Drexel University, 32nd & Chestnut Streets, Philadelphia, PA 19104.

ROBINSON, DONALD LEE
Dentist. **Personal:** Born Jul 25, 1930, Indianapolis, IN; married Juanita Cook; children: Carmaletus F, Donald L II, Kimberly P. **Educ:** AB 1955; DDS 1960; IN U. **Career:** Private Practice, dentist. **Orgs:** Mem, Am Dental Assn; Nat Dental Assn; IN Dental Assn; Indianapolis Dist Dental Soc; Indianapolis Dental Study Club; IN Branch, Natl Dental Assn; life mem, NAACP; life mem, Kappa Alpha Psi Fraternity, Mt Zion Baptist Church; bd mem, Indianapolis Alumni of Kappa Alpha Psi Frat. **Military Serv:** AUS 1952-54. **Business Addr:** 3721 N Illinois St, Indianapolis, IN 46208.

ROBINSON, EDDIE
College football coach. **Personal:** Born Feb 13, 1919, Jackson, LA; son of Lillie Stewart (deceased) and Frank Robinson (deceased); married Doris Mott Robinson, Jun 24, 1941; children: Lillian Rose Robinson Watkin, Eddie, Jr. **Educ:** Leland College, Baker, LA, English, 1937-41; Univ of Iowa, Iowa City, IA, physical education. **Career:** Grambling Univ LA, football coach 1941-, vice president, athletic relations. **Orgs:** Member, American Football Coaches Assn; member, Alpha Phi Alpha. **Honors/Awds:** Holds record of most college football victories; Horatio Alger Award, 1988; Maxwell Award, Maxwell Foundation, 1991; National Football Foundation & College Hall of Fame, Outstanding Contribution to Amateur Football Award, 1992; SWAC Hall of Fame, 1992; Maxwell Club, Francis J Reds Bagnell Award, 1991; Disney Pigskin Classic, Heritage Award, 1990; National Association for Sports and Physical Education Hall of Fame, 1990; B'nai B'rith International, Molder of Champions Award, 1988; New York Urban League, Whitney M. Young Jr Memorial Award, 1983; Bobby Dodd Award, 1993. **Business Addr:** Coach, Grambling University, PO Box 868, Grambling, LA 71245.

ROBINSON, EDDIE JOSEPH, JR.
Professional football player. **Personal:** Born Apr 13, 1970, New Orleans, LA; married Tonja. **Educ:** Alabama State University, bachelor's degree in chemistry, 1993. **Career:** Houston Oilers, linebacker, 1992-95; Jacksonville Jaguars, linebacker, 1996-. **Orgs:** Omega Psi Phi Fraternity. **Honors/Awds:** Second round draft pick, 1992. **Business Addr:** Professional Football Player, Jacksonville Jaguars, One Stadium Place, Jacksonville, FL 32202, (904)633-6000.

ROBINSON, EDITH
Business executive. **Personal:** Born Dec 31, 1924, Buffalo, NY; married James C. **Educ:** Wilberforce U, BS 1946; State Univ NY, MSW. **Career:** Erie Co Dept of Social Svcs, asst dep commr; Pub Welfare, caseworker, sr caseworker, unit supr, dist supr 1947-77; State Univ Coll SEEK Prgm, adj prof 1969-70. **Orgs:** Past pres Nat Assn of Social Workers ACSW; exec bd NY State Welfare Conf 1970-72; chmn Nat Field Adv Cncl Alexandria Am Red Cross 1977-78; vice-chmn Greater Buffalo Chap ARC 1971-; Resolutions Com ARC 1978; publicity chmn Am Lung Assn of NY 1977; Zonta Club of Buffalo 1970; YWCA 1972; Links Inc; Comm Adv Council State Univ NY at Buffalo. **Honors/Awds:** Alumna of year Wilberforce Univ 1967; outst serv award Bronze Damsels 1968; 1st disting womans serv award Buffalo Urban Ctr 1971; comm serv award Buffalo Urban League 1975. **Business Addr:** 95 Franklin St, Buffalo, NY 14202.

ROBINSON, EDSEL F.
Cleric, real estate broker. **Personal:** Born May 5, 1928, Wrightsville, GA; son of Tressie Robinson and Rev Jasper Robinson; married Pearlie Haynes; children: Edsel Jr, Desiree. **Educ:** Morris Brown Coll, 1959; Turner Theological Seminary, BD; Interdenominational Theological Center; Turner Theological Seminary of Interdenominational Theological Center Atlanta, Honorary DD candidate 1980. **Career:** EF Robinson Realty Co, pres; Augusta Athens District, AME Church, presiding elder, currently. **Orgs:** Mem NAACP, YMCA, AME Ministers' Union, SCLC, Empire Real Estate Bd, Operation Breadbasket, Natl Assn Real Estate Brokers 1974; mgmt broker Veterans Admin 1970-73; organizer Doraville Community Org 1974. **Honors/Awds:** Salesman of the Year 1971-72; Special Award for Outstanding Serv to AME Church; recipient E F Robinson Day Proclamation for Outstanding Contribution to the city & people of all races, City of Doraville GA 1976; Outstanding Georgia Citizen, 1995. **Home Addr:** 3322 Rabun Dr, SW, Atlanta, GA 30311. **Business Addr:** Broker, E F Robinson Realty Co, Inc, 195 Auburn Ave, NE, Atlanta, GA 30303.

ROBINSON, EDWARD A.
Educator. **Personal:** Born Jun 13, 1935, Gary, IN; married Lavada Hill; children: Edward Allen, Arlen Yohance. **Educ:** Howard University, BA, 1959; University of Chicago, MAT, 1970; Northwestern University, PhD, 1974. **Career:** Northeastern Illinois University, assistant professor; Lake Forest College, IL, English instructor, 1970-72; Chicago Board of Education, HS English consultant, 1970-72; Wendell Phillips & Summer HS, Chicago, instructor, 1961-64; English Department, Harlan HS, Chicago, instructor & chairman, 1960-69; Carver HS, Chicago, instructor, 1959-60; Emmy Award Winning TV Prog, ''The Giants'', ''The Common Men'', narrator, 1967; ''Like It Was the black man in America'', teacher/host, 1969; Midwest Modern Language Association convention, presented paper, 1973; NDEA Institute, University of Chicago, summer participant, 1965. **Orgs:** South Shore Valley Community Organization, 1969-74; Faulkner School Association, 1974-75; Faulkner School Father's Club, 1974-75; National Urban League, 1968-74; Operation PUSH, 1972. **Honors/Awds:** Recipient, Experienced Teacher Fellowship, University of Chicago, 1969-70; Ford Foundation Fellowship for Black Americans, 1973-74; Author of numerous publications. **Military Serv:** Served in AUS 1953-55. **Business Addr:** Ciriculum & Instruction, Northeastern Illinois University, 550 N St Louis Avenue, Chicago, IL 60625-4625.

ROBINSON, EDWARD ASHTON
Attorney. **Personal:** Born 1949, Hammond, LA. **Educ:** Grambling U; State Univ NY; Rutgers U. **Career:** Private Practice, atty 1979-; Baton Rouge LA, chf adminstr, state atty gen. **Honors/Awds:** Outsdng yng man LA Jaycees 1977. **Business Addr:** PO Box 3131, 4962 Florida Blvd, Baton Rouge, LA 70821.

ROBINSON, ELLA S.
Educator. **Personal:** Born Apr 16, 1943, Wedowee, AL; daughter of Mary Ella MacPherson Scales and Less Scales; married John William Robinson, May 9, 1980 (deceased); children: John William, Jr. **Educ:** AL State Univ, BS 1965; Univ of NE, MA 1970, PhD 1976. **Career:** Univ of IL, assistant prof 1975-77; Atlanta Univ, assistant prof 1977-79; Univ of Nebraska-Lincoln, professor of English, beginning 1979; Tuskegee University, assoc prof, currently. **Orgs:** Mem MLA 1974-87; chair afro-lite session MMLA 1985-86; life time mem NAACP 1986-; ALA; African Amer Poet for the Heritage Room, Bennet Martin Library, 1989. **Honors/Awds:** Travelled throughout Nigeria in order to do research for poetry, paintings and articles. **Special Achievements:** Painted 85 oils & acrylics; author, ''Selected Poems,'' 1995; ''To Know Heaven,'' 1996; ''Love the Season and Death,'' 1996; ''Heritage: Tuskegee Poems a Celebration,'' 1997; numerous articles. **Business Addr:** Prof of English, Tuskegee Institute, Tuskegee Institute, AL 36087.

ROBINSON, ERIC B.
Management consultant. **Personal:** Born Nov 4, 1961, Long Branch, NJ; son of Beverly Gilmore Robinson and Bruce Robinson; married Maribelle Vargas Robinson, Jul 29, 1990. **Educ:** Edinboro University, Edinboro, PA, BA, Business, 1984. **Career:** Bruce Robinson Associates, New York, NY, vice pres, partner, 1984-. **Orgs:** President, KPK, 1983; chairman, promotion, Concert Committee, 1983. **Honors/Awds:** America's Best and Brightest, Dollars & Sense Magazine, 1988.

ROBINSON, ERNEST PRESTON, SR.
Motivational consultant, sales trainer. **Personal:** Born Aug 15, 1947, Detroit, MI; son of Willie B Robinson and Andy ''Pop'' Brown; married Sheila M Boswell, Aug 9, 1980; children: Ernie Jr, Eric. **Educ:** Detroit Coll of Business, Dearborn MI, BS Mktg, 1971. **Career:** J L Hudson Co, Detroit MI, sales supvr, 1971-72; Allstate Insurance Co, Southfield MI, mktg sales mgr, natl sales trainer, 1972-88; Self-Employed, Farmington Hills MI, president, owner, 1988-. **Orgs:** Mem, Natl Assn of Life Underwriters, 1972-, Life Underwriting Training Council, 1978-, Veterans Boxing Assn, Ring 32, 1983-, Southern Christian Leadership Conf, 1987-, NAACP, 1987-, Thursday Luncheon Group, 1988-, Greater West Bloomfield Chamber of Commerce, 1988-, Michigan Coalition for Human Rights, 1988-; dir, Drama Soc of St John CME Church, 1988-. **Honors/Awds:** Author of poem, ''Detroit Fate Train on the Move,'' 1967; Master Speech Award, Dale Carnegie, 1980; Key Mgr, Allstate Insurnce Co, 1985, 1986; Natl Sales Trainer Award, Allstate Insurance Co, 1987; Speaker of the Year, Southern Christian Leadership Conf, 1988; Actor of the Year, St John CME Church, 1988; Producer/Director/Actor in the dramatization, The Resurrection of the Spirit of Dr Martin Luther King Jr, 1988-.

ROBINSON, EUGENE
Professional football player. **Personal:** Born May 28, 1963, Hartford, CT; married Gia; children: Brittany, Brandon. **Educ:** Colgate, bachelor's degree in computer science. **Career:** Seattle Seahawks, defensive back, 1985-95; Green Bay Packers, 1996-; InterMix Records, co-owner. **Honors/Awds:** Pro Bowl, 1992, 1993. **Business Addr:** Professional Football Player, Green Bay Packers, 1265 Lombardi Ave, Green Bay, WI 54304, (414)494-2351.

ROBINSON, EUGENE HAROLD
Editor. **Personal:** Born Mar 12, 1954, Orangeburg, SC; son of Harold I & Louisa S Robinson; married Avis Collins Robinson, Sep 23, 1978; children: Aaron E, Lowell E. **Educ:** Univ of MI, BA, 1974; Harvard Univ, Nieman Fellow, 1988. **Career:** San Francisco Chronicle, reporter, 1975-80; Washington Post, city hall reporter, 1980-82, asst city editor, 1982-84, city editor, 1984-87, South American correspondent, 1988-92, London correspondent, 1992-94, foreign editor, 1994-. **Orgs:** Natl Assn of Black Journalist, 1987-; Council on Foreign Relations, 1995-. **Special Achievements:** Several Journalism Awards. **Business Addr:** Foreign Editor, Washington Post, 1150 15th St, NW, Washington, DC 20071, (202)334-7400.

ROBINSON, EUNICE PRIMUS
Counselor. **Personal:** Born Oct 17, 1935, Hardeeville, SC; married DeWitt T Jr; children: Janice, De Witt III, Glenn. **Educ:** Savannah State Coll, BS Elem Educ 1953; Univ of SC, MEd 1972. **Career:** Midlands Tech Coll, couns; Benedict Coll, dean women, couns 1968-71; Rosenwald Elem Sch, tchr 1965-67; Allen U, couns, dir student activities 1959-63; SC State Coll, couns 1955-59; Hardeeville Elem Sch, tchr 1953-55. **Orgs:** Mem Zeta Phi Beta Sor; SC Pers & Guid Assn 1975; Nat Dirs Orientation Assn; fdr, adv Afro-Am Club of Midlands Tech Coll 1972-; mem Scholarship Found, Booker T Washington 1975; sec Fairwald Elem Sch PTA 1974-; treas Fairwald Middle Sch PTA; sec Altar Guild, St Luke's Epis Ch 1974-; sec Omega Psi Phi Frat Wives 1974-75; team mother Pony League, Dixie Youth League Baseball Prgm 1972-75. **Honors/Awds:** Chosen by survey Counselor Most Seen by Students, Midlands Tech Coll 1973; Mother of Yr, Zeta Phi Beta Sor 1959; Mother of Yr, Afro-Am Club, Midlands Tech Coll 1975. **Business Addr:** Midlands Tech Coll, PO Drawer Q, Columbia, SC 29250.

ROBINSON, FISHER J.
Clergyman. **Personal:** Born Aug 12, 1929, Abbeville, LA; son of Winnie Smith Robinson and Fisher Joseph Robinson. **Educ:** Divine Word College, Epworth, IA, BA, 1952; Society of the Divine Word, ordination, 1958; Catholic University, Washington, DC, MA, 1959; Rome, Italy, sabbatical, 1966-67. **Career:** St Augustine Seminary, Bay St Louis, MI, formation dir, 1959-61; Notre Dame Church, St Martinville, LA, associate pastor, 1961-63; Divine Word Seminary, Riverside, CA, instructor and formation dir, 1963-67; Verbum Dei High School, Los Angeles, CA, principal, 1967-80; St Malachy Church, Los Angeles, CA, pastor, 1980-89; Archdiocese of Los Angeles, Los Angeles, CA, vicar of African-American Catholics (first black), 1986-. **Orgs:** Member, Los Angeles Archdiocesan Council of Priests, 1976-80; consultant, Archdiocesan Board of Consultors for Los Angeles, 1979-; board member, Ecumenical Center for Black Church Studies, 1980-; chairman of Los Angeles archdiocesan team, National Black Catholic Pastoral Plan on Evangelization, 1987-; commissioner, Los Angeles County Probation Committee, 1986; St Anne's Maternity Home for Unwed Mothers, board member, 1992-; Regions XI and XII for the National Black Catholic Congress, coordinator, board member, 1992; National Black Catholic Administrators, bd, 1992-; National Black Roman Catholic Rite, committee, 1993-. **Honors/Awds:** Co-author, Pastoral for Black Catholics for the Archdiocese of Los Angeles, 1988. **Home Addr:** 6028 Victoria Ave, Los Angeles, CA 90043. **Business Addr:** Vicar, African-American Vicariate, Archdiocese of Los Angeles, 3424 Wilshire Blvd, Los Angeles, CA 90010-2241, (213)637-7435.

ROBINSON, FLOYD A.
Construction company executive, real estate developer. **Personal:** Born May 9, 1936, Prescott, AR; son of Lois Sandifer Piggie and George Robinson; married Sandra Authur Robinson, Dec 31, 1963; children: Kevin, Rhonda. **Career:** Chicago White Sox, baseball player, 1960-66; Cincinnati Red, baseball player, 1967; Oakland Athletics, baseball player, 1968; self-employed real estate developer, chief executive, currently. **Orgs:** Board member, Boy's Club; board member, SEDC, 1983-87; board member, BBA of San Diego, 1983-87; board member, East-West Optimist Club. **Honors/Awds:** Hall of Fame, Boy's Club of America, 1991; Housing Achievement, San Diego Housing Commission; Hall of Fame, San Diego Balboa Park. **Business Addr:** President & Chief Executive Officer, Robinson Development Inc, 5843 Market St, San Diego, CA 92114.

ROBINSON, FRANK
Professional baseball executive. **Personal:** Born Aug 31, 1935, Beaumont, TX; son of Ruth Shaw and Frank Robinson; married Barbara Ann Cole; children: Frank Kevin, Nichelle. **Career:** Cincinnati Reds farm system teams, 1953-56; Cincinnati Reds, player, 1956-65; Santurce Cangrejeros PR, manager, beginning 1968; Baltimore Orioles, outfielder, 1965-71, manager, 1988-91, assistant general manager beginning 1991; LA Dodgers, player, 1972; CA Angels, 1973-74; Cleveland Indians, manager, 1975-77; Rochester Red Wings, manager, 1978; San Francisco Giants, manager, 1981-84; Arizona Fall League, director of baseball operations, 1997-. **Honors/Awds:** Natl League Rookie of Yr 1956; Baseball Writers Assn 1956; Most Valuable Player 1961; Amer League Triple Crown 1966; Most Valuable, AL 1966; tied world series record for most times hit by pitcher 1961; appeared in 11 All Star games; author (with Al Silverman) ''My Life Is Baseball'' 1968; elected to Hall of Fame at Cooperstown 1982. **Special Achievements:** Became baseball's first African American manager with the Cleveland Indians, 1974; first African American manager in the National League with the San Francisco Giants. **Business Addr:** Director of Baseball Operations, Arizona Fall League, 350 Park Ave, New York, NY 10022.

ROBINSON, FRANK J.
Educator, clergyman. **Personal:** Born Nov 18, 1939, Montgomery, TX; married Reecie (deceased); children: Lady Robinson Nelson, Portia Elaine, Frank J Jr, Gusta Jovon. **Educ:** Texas Southern Univ, BS, 1964. **Career:** Bowid Dance Studio, Houston, instr of dramatics; Houston Comm Coll, instr; Urban Theatre, tech dir; Assured Blessing Ministry Ch 39, tech dir; treasurer Central Convention of TX Brotherhood; Greater St Matthews Baptist Church, clergyman; Greater Second Baptist Church, assist pastor. **Orgs:** Chmn Comm Coord TX State Conf of Br NAACP; vice pres Alpha Mu Omega; mem West End Civic Club. **Military Serv:** USMCR 1957-68. **Business Addr:** Clergyman, Greater St Matthews Baptist Church, 7701 Jutland, Houston, TX 77027.

ROBINSON, GENEVIEVE
Educator, educational administrator. **Personal:** Born Apr 20, 1940, Kansas City, MO; daughter of Helen Williams Robinson and James L. Robinson. **Educ:** Mt St Scholastica Coll, BA history 1968; New Mexico Highlands Univ, MA history 1974; Catholic Univ of Amer, history 1978-79; Boston Coll, PhD history 1986. **Career:** Lillis HS, history teacher 1969-73, 1974-75, history dept chairperson 1970-73, admin/curriculum dir 1974-75; Donnelly Comm Coll, instructor 1976-78; Boston Coll, instructor 1983; Rockhurst Coll, instr 1985-86, asst prof 1986-91, dir, honors program, 1990-, associate professor, 1991-, chair of dept of history, 1994-. **Orgs:** Mem Phi Alpha Theta, Kappa Mu Epsilon, Organization of Amer Historians, Immigration History Soc, Pi Gamma Mu; mem Ethical Review Board 1988-; Notre Dame de Sion Schools, board of directors, 1990-95; National Assn of Women in Catholic Higher Education, regional rep. **Honors/Awds:** Gasson Fellowship Boston Coll 1984-85; Natl Endowment for the Humanities Coll Teachers Summer Seminar Grant 1987, Presidential Grant, Rockhurst Coll, 1988; Natl Endowment for the Humanities Summer Inst, NEH, 1990; Lilly Workshop on the Liberal Arts, Lilly Endowment, Inc, 1990; Rockhurst College, Presidential Grant, 1988, 1992. **Business Addr:** Chair/History Dept, Assoc Prof, Rockhurst College, 1100 Rockhurst Rd, Kansas City, MO 64110-2508, (816)501-4108.

ROBINSON, GEORGE ALI
Analyst. **Personal:** Born Apr 16, 1939, Americus, GA; children: Ali, Omari, Khalid. **Educ:** Shaw Univ, AB 1965, MDiv 1975; Neotarian Coll, DD 1976; Metanoia Univ, PhD 1981. **Career:** Ed Black Bus Awareness Mag; comm rel spec US Dept Justice Col writer ''Moving On''; pastor Ridgeway Baptist Church; social worker Raleigh; prog analysisDHEW; pres A&G Enterprises Raleigh; consult MKT Pol Camp; HEW, soc sci analyst; CEO, Georgian For Two Party State. **Orgs:** Consult AMEC Press; lecturer Chris Ed in Black Religion Conv, Black Theol Mason, PUSH, ASPA; author ''Metanoia Conv, The need for the Black Church;'' The Republican Council of Georgia. **Military Serv:** AUS sgt 1957-62.

ROBINSON, GLENN A.
Professional basketball player. **Personal:** Born Jan 10, 1973, Gary, IN. **Educ:** Purdue. **Career:** Milwaukee Bucks, forward, 1994-. **Honors/Awds:** John Wooden Award, 1994; NBA All-Rookie Team, 1995. **Special Achievements:** Selected in first round, first pick of NBA draft, 1994. **Business Addr:** Professional Basketball Player, Milwaukee Bucks, 1001 N Fourth St, Bradley Center, Milwaukee, WI 53203, (414)227-0500.

ROBINSON, GLORIA
Government official. **Career:** City of Detroit, Planning, Community & Economic Development departments, dir; HUD, asst secy, 1997-. **Business Addr:** Assistant Secretary, HUD, 451 7th St SW, Rm 10226, Washington, DC 20410, (202)708-4093.

ROBINSON, HARRY, JR.
Museum administrator. **Career:** Museum of African-American Life and Culture, director, currently. **Business Addr:** Director, Museum of African-American Life & Culture, PO Box 150153, Dallas, TX 75315-0153, (214)565-9028.

ROBINSON, HARRY G., III
Educator, architect, city planner. **Personal:** Born Jan 18, 1942, Washington, DC; son of Gwendolyn Herriford Robinson and Harry G Robinson Jr; married Dianne O Davis; children: Erin K, Leigh H, Kia L. **Educ:** Howard Univ, BArch 1966, MCity Plng 1970; Harvard Univ, MUrban Design 1972. **Career:** DC Redevelopment Land Agency, arch, planner 1968-72; Univ of the DC, prof 1969-70, 1971-74; Morgan State Univ, chmn, prof 1971-79; Howard Univ, dean arch & plng, 1979-95, vice president, 1995-. **Orgs:** The Robinson Group, principal, 1976-; DC Bd of Exam & Reg of Arch, president, 1983-; Amer Inst of Arch, 1976-; Amer Inst of Cert Plnrs, 1974-; Natl Building Museum, trustee, secretary; Natl Council of Architectural Registration Bds, president; Cooper-Hewitt Museum, trustee; African-American Architect Initiative, founder, director; Arch Adventure/City Place, foundation director; African-American Architect Archive, Howard University, director; The Chauncey Group Intl, director; Natl Architectural Accrediting Board, president; US Commission of Fine Arts, vice chairman; Pennsylvania Avenue at the White House Presidential Committee, chairman. **Honors/Awds:** Lasker Fellow in City Plng Lasker Found 1969-70; Martin Luther King Jr Fellow Woodrow Wilson Found 1969-70; Urban Transp Rsch Fellow US DOT 1969-70; Faculty Gold Medal in Design Howard Univ 1965; Silver Medal, Tau Sigma Delta, 1988; American Institute of Architects, elected of College of Fellows, Whitney M Young Jr Citation. **Military Serv:** AUS 1st lt 2 yrs; Ranger Tab; Bronze Star; Purple Heart 1966-68. **Business Addr:** Vice President, Howard Univ, 2400 6th St NW, Washington, DC 20059, (202)806-2272.

ROBINSON, HENRY
Mayor. **Personal:** Born Oct 2, 1936, Port Royal, SC; married Jannie Middleton; children: Elizabeth, Tracy, Stephanie. **Career:** Town of Port Royal, council & mayor pro-tem, mayor. **Orgs:** Pres, Comm Ctr Port Royal; 2nd vice pres Dem Party Port Royal Prec. **Honors/Awds:** Outstanding Comm Svc. **Business Addr:** Mayor, Town of Port Royal, Drawer 8, Port Royal, SC 29935.

ROBINSON, HERBERT A. See Obituaries section.

ROBINSON, HOLLY
Actress. **Personal:** Born 1965, Philadelphia, PA; daughter of Dolores and Matt Robinson; married Rodney Peete, 1995. **Educ:** Sarah Lawrence College, graduated. **Career:** Actress; appeared in movie Howard the Duck; guest starred in This Is the Life; 21 Jump Street; Hanging W/Mr Cooper.

ROBINSON, HUGH GRANVILLE
Business executive. **Personal:** Born Aug 4, 1932, Washington, DC; son of Wilhelmina and James; married Matilda; children: Hugh G Jr, Mrs Susan Gardner, Mia Turner. **Educ:** US Military Acad West Point, BS 1954; MIT, MS 1959. **Career:** Tetra Group, chmn & CEO, currently; Grigsby Brandford Powell Inc, sr vice pres, 1988-. **Orgs:** Bd dir Federal Reserve Bank of Dallas; bd chairman, Museum of African-Amer Life & Culture, bd dir, LBJ Foundation; bd trustees Dallas Museum of Fine Arts, vice chairman, North Texas Public Broadcasting; bd chairman Dallas Youth Services Corps, chairman advisory Comm United Negro College Fund; bd dir Texas Utilities, The Belo Corp, Columbus Realty Trust; Guaranty Federal Savings Bank; Canonie Environmental Services Co, Inc; Univ of TX Eng Foundation, bd of dirs. **Honors/Awds:** Fellow, Soc of Amer Military Engineers; Williams College, honorary LD, 1983. **Military Serv:** US Army Corps of Engineers, major general, 1954-83; Distinguished Serv Medal; Legion of Merit (with Oak Leaf Cluster); Bronze Star (with Oak Leaf Cluster); Meritorious Serv Medal; Air Medal (with two Oak Leaf Clusters); Joint Serv Commendation Medal; Army Commendation Medal (with Oak Leaf Cluster); Vietnamese Cross of Gallantry (Gold Star); Vietnamese Serv Medal; Vietnam Campaign Medal; Amer Defense Medal. **Business Phone:** (214)828-7906.

ROBINSON, ISAIAH E.
Association executive. **Personal:** Born Feb 17, 1924, Birmingham; son of Willia A Willis Robinson and Isiah E Robinson; married Sylvia Lawson Robinson, Jul 25, 1959; children: Larry A. **Educ:** Tuskegee Inst Flying Sch, 1944. **Career:** New York City Bd of Edn, pres 1971-72; Borough Pres of Manhattan, educ cons; Delmar-Raywin Lithographers, art dir; USPO 1944-54; Commission of Human Rights , New York, NY, commissioner, 1978-84. **Orgs:** Mem Conf of Large City Bds of Educ of NY; dir Ex-Officio; bd dir NY State Sch Bd Assn; NY State Del to the Nat Sch Bds Assn; mem Fed Rel Network of Nat Sch Bds Assn; Tchrs Retirement Sys of NYC; Leg Advocacy Com Council of Great City Bd of Edn; past chmn Harlem Parents Com; past assoc dir of Harlem Freedom Sch for study of Afro-Am Hist & Culture; past trustee Pub Educ Assn; pres Harlem Commonwealth Council for Econ Devel; Progressive Ninety-Niners Investin Club; chmn bd Commonwealth Holding Corp; chmn of bd, Harlem Commonwealth Council, 1967-; vice pres, America-Israel Friendship League, 1978-; chmn of bd, Freedom Natl Bank, 1988-90. **Honors/Awds:** NY Assn of Black Educators Comm Ser Award Kappa Beta Sigma Chap 1973; Carter G Woodson Award African-Am Hist Assn; Pub Ser Award NY Br of NAACP 1958; Intl Elec Workers Union Aweard 159th St Block Assn 1966; Pub Ser Award Martin Luther King Dem Club; Public Serv, NY Chapter United Negro Coll Fund, 1977; Man of the Year, Tuskegee Airmen, Inc, NY Chapter, 1984; Partner in Educ, Malcolm-King Coll, 1986. **Military Serv:** USAAF 1943-46.

ROBINSON, JACK, JR.
Attorney. **Personal:** Born Mar 20, 1942, Chicago, IL; son of Clara L Jones Robinson and Jack Robinson Sr; married Flora G; children: Jacqueline, Craig, Christopher. **Educ:** Chicago Teachers Coll, BE 1963; Chicago Kent Coll Law, JD 1970. **Career:** Argonne Natl Lab, atty 1971-; Miller & Pomper, atty 1970-71. **Orgs:** Natl Bar Assn; Mem Natl Cook Co Bar Assn; Omega Psi Phi Fraternity. **Business Addr:** Attorney, Argonne Natl Laboratory, 9700 S Cass, Argonne, IL 60439.

ROBINSON, JACK E.
Editor, publisher. **Personal:** Born in Indianapolis, IN; son of Billie and Jack; divorced; children: Jacqueline, Errol, Sarah. **Educ:** Boston U, AA, BS, grad study. **Career:** Washington Globe, editor, publisher; Park Dale Nursing Home; Burton Nursing Home; Compact Advt; Burton Realty Trust; Amer Business Mgmt; Consolidated Liquors; Amer Beverages Corp; Robinson Construction Corp; Universal Distributing; Compact Corp; Apex Construction Co, Boston, MA, CEO. **Orgs:** Pres Commonwealth Rep Club; Boston NAACP; Sportsmen Tennis Club; State Enterprises; Nat Assn Minority Contractors; Real Estate Owners Assn; bd dirs Voluntary Action Center; ABCD; Circle Assos; pres Am Motorist Assn; mem Omega Psi Phi Frat; Phi Epsilon Kappa Frat; Bay State Golf Club; pres Oak Bluffs

Tennis Club; Alliance for a Safer Greater Boston; pres NAACP 1973-84. **Honors/Awds:** Civil Liberties Union Adv Com Man of Yr Construction Engineering News Mag; Man of Yr Boston Bldg Dept; Savenergy Award Dir US Dept Commerce. **Military Serv:** AUS. **Business Addr:** President, Bulletin Corporation, 61 Arborway, Boston, MA 02130.

ROBINSON, JACK E.
Telecommunications company executive. **Personal:** Born May 12, 1960, Boston, MA; son of Lillian Byers Granderson and Jack E Robinson. **Educ:** Brown University, BS, 1982; Harvard Law School, JD, 1985; Harvard Business School, MBA, 1986. **Career:** Texas Air Corp, director of strategic planning, 1987-88; MasterCard International, assistant to president, 1988-89; Bar Harbor Airways, airline consultant, 1989-90, president, 1990-91; Florida Air, president, 1991-94; National Telecom, president, 1994-. **Orgs:** Harvard Club of New York City, 1988-; US Colored Troops Memorial Comm, Civil War, 1992; Martha's Vineyard Racquet Club, director, 1987. **Honors/Awds:**. **Special Achievements:** Author, FreeFall: The Needless Destruction of Eastern Airlines, 1992; author, American Icarus: The Majestic Rise & Tragic Fall of Pan Am, 1994. **Business Addr:** President/CEO, National Telecom Inc, 101 Park Ave, 26th Fl, 101 Park Ave, 26th Fl, New York, NY 10178, (212)557-6500.

ROBINSON, JACQUELINE J. See Obituaries section.

ROBINSON, JAMES
Profeesional basketball player. **Personal:** Born Aug 31, 1970, Jackson, MS. **Educ:** Alabama. **Career:** Portland Trail Blazers, guard, 1993-96; Minnesota Timberwolves, 1996-97; Los Angeles Clippers, 1997-. **Business Addr:** Professional Basketball Player, Los Angeles Clippers, 3939 S Figueroa St, Los Angeles Sports Arena, Los Angeles, CA 90037, (213)748-8000.

ROBINSON, JAMES EDWARD
Business executive. **Personal:** Born Aug 31, 1943, Asheville, NC; married Shirley Byrd; children: Geno Nigel, Tajuana Yvette, Tanya, Aisha Monique. **Educ:** Taylor Sch of Broadcast Tech, AA 1969; Elkins Inst of Broadcasting, certificate 1971. **Career:** Model Cities Agency, public info asst 1971-74; City of Asheville, public info officer 1974-76; Radio Station WBMU-FM, pres/gen mgr 1975-. **Orgs:** Mem Natl Assn of Black Owned Broadcasters; mem NC Soc of Public Relations Dirs. **Honors/Awds:** Rec'd Awds for, Principles of Supervision, Supervisory Comm, Effective Mgmt NC State Univ at Raleigh, Comm Develop NC Dept of Natl & Economic Resources; Comm Broadcaster of the Year Optimist Intl; Asheville Chap NAACP Cert of Merit; Asheville Chap Sickle Cell Anemia Comm Svcs; W Carolina Univ Cert of Appreciation. **Military Serv:** AUS 82nd airborne div 9 yrs. **Business Addr:** Engineering Physics, McMaster University, Hamilton, ON, Canada L8S 4K1.

ROBINSON, JAMES L.
Architect, developer, urban planner, builder. **Personal:** Born Jul 12, 1940, Longview, TX; son of Ruby Newhouse Robinson and W L Robinson; married Dame Annabell Hilton, Sep 10, 1985; children: Kerstin G, Maria T, Jasmin Marisol, Ruby Nell, Kenneth, James L Robinson Jr. **Educ:** Southern Univ, B Arch 1964; Pratt Inst, MCP 1973. **Career:** Herbst & Rusciano AIA, architect 1964; Carson Lundin & Shaw, architect 1965; Kennerly Slomanson & Smith, architect 1966-68; Carl J Petrilli, architect 1968-69; James L Robinson PC, architect 1970-84; Robinson Architects PC, architect 1984-. **Orgs:** Mem, Independent Platform Assn; former Bd of Dirs, Boys Clubs of America; arbitrator, American Arbitration Assn, 1979. **Honors/Awds:** Martin Luther King Fellow Pratt Inst 1972-74; Natl Housing Award Design & Environ 1976; AIA Design Citation Stuyvesant Height Christian Church; Bard Award Fulton Ct Complex 1977; Knighthood, Order of St Johns, Knights of Malta; Designer the Nehemiah Plan, NYC, Casas Theresa Homes, Jasmin Houses, Stuyvesant Learning Center, Lenoxville Houses, David Chavis House, Sojourner Truth, Eliot Graham Houses; numerous residential developments. **Military Serv:** AUS Pfc 1966; Good Conduct Medal 1966. **Business Addr:** Robinson Architects, PC, 314 Scotland Rd, South Orange, NJ 07079.

ROBINSON, JAMES WAYMOND
Physician (retired). **Personal:** Born Nov 6, 1926, Wilmington, NC; son of Addie Best Robinson and Sam Robinson; married Carol Blackmar Robinson, Sep 18, 1979. **Educ:** NC Coll at Durham, BS 1950; Meharry Med Coll, MD 1960; internship 1960-61; resident 1961-65. **Career:** Joint Disease N General Hospital, asst attending physician beginning 1979; Beth Israel's Methadone Maintenance Treatment Prgm, assoc chief beginning 1975; Beth Israel's Methadone Maintenance Treatment Program Harlem Unit, unit dir 1965-75; Arthur C Logan Memorial Hospital, assoc attending physician 1965-79; Harlem Hospital, asst attending physician 1965-92. **Orgs:** Med Soc of State & Co of NY; Omega Psi Phi Frat; ASIM; NYSSIM; NYCSIM. **Special Achievements:** Author: ''Methadone Poisoning, Diagnosis & Treatment''; ''Methadone Treatment of Randomly Selected Criminal Addicts''. **Military Serv:** Military serv corporal 1945-46.

ROBINSON, JANE ALEXANDER
Clinical psychologist. **Personal:** Born Jan 17, 1931, Chicago, IL; daughter of Janie Burruss-Goodwin Alexander and Cornelius Alexander; divorced; children: David, Amorie, Richard. **Educ:** BS 1952, MS 1963, PhD 1978. **Career:** Detroit Publ Schools, elem teacher 1957-63; Southfield Bd of Ed, school psych 1964-68; Detroit Bd of Ed, school psych 1968-70; Private practice, clinical psych. **Orgs:** Mem, founder, sec 1968-70, pres, 1975-76, MI Assoc Black Psych; consult, Rape Counseling Ctr, Detroit Receiving Hosp; mem, Psi Chi Natl Hon Soc Psych, Univ of Detroit Chapt. **Honors/Awds:** Natl Assoc of Black Psych Awd for Org Leadership 1976; dissertation ''Self-Esteem, Racial Consciousness & Perception of Difference Between the Values of Black & White Amers'' 1977. **Business Addr:** Clinical Psychologist, Fisher Bldg, Ste 1125, 3011 W Grand Blvd, Detroit, MI 48202.

ROBINSON, JASON GUY
Actor, stuntman, director, poet. **Personal:** Born Aug 8, 1934; son of Mabel Walker Robinson and John Robinson; married Jean Wentz, Jan 30, 1977; children: Michelle. **Educ:** Philadelphia Coll, BA 1961. **Career:** Actor, model, artist, disc jockey, poet under professional name of Jason Guy; has appeared in movies, numerous plays, TV shows; WHAT & WXPN, disc jockey; Third World News WXPN, editor, newscaster; model in various advertisements; Japanese Karate Assn, instr Martial Arts; R & J Prod, partner; two albums ''Jason Roars'', ''Jason Reads in the Lion's den''. **Orgs:** Founder Drama III Theatre Projects Co Inc; mem Philadelphia Jazz Soc; Positive Thinking Parents Assn; East Coast Stuntmens Assn; AFTRA-SAG; founder, dir Citizens Against Drugs (CAD). **Honors/Awds:** Holder of Black Belt (Nidan). **Military Serv:** USMC sgt 1953-57. **Business Addr:** Substance Abuse Prevention Specialist, Philadelphia Anti-Drug Anti-Violence Network, 121 N Broad St, 6th Floor, Philadelphia, PA 19107.

ROBINSON, JAYNE G.
Educator. **Personal:** Born Aug 22, 1912, Freeport, TX; daughter of Rachel Rebecca Bush Glenn and Ernest Glenn; married Clarence Arthur Robinson, Jun 2, 1934. **Educ:** TX Southern Univ, 1938; KS State Univ, 1939; NY Univ Drexel Inst, additional study; Univ of IL; TX Women's Univ. **Career:** TX Southern Univ, asst prof 1939-75; Riverside Hospital, 1941-45; NYA Center Houston TX, teacher 1940-41. **Orgs:** Mem Am Dietetic Assn; Am Home Econ Assn; TX Dietetic Assn; TX Home Econ Assn; Am Pub Health Assn; TX Pub Health Assn; Assn of Sch of Allied Health Professions; life mem YWCA; life mem Zeta Phi Beta; elder, mem of serv comm, Pinecrest Presb Church; mem, Fifth Ward Housing Corp of The Metropolitan; mem, Fifth Ward Area Planning & Advisory Council, Health & Human Serv Dept; mem, trustee bd, Fifth Ward Community Devel Corp; mem, Texas Southern Univ Recruitment Council; bd mem, St Elizabeth Hospital, 1977-87. **Honors/Awds:** Texas Assn of Coll Teachers Service Award, Texas Southern Univ, 1975; Certificate of Recognition for Excellence in Humanitarian Achievement, 1982. **Home Addr:** 5202 Arapahoe, Houston, TX 77020.

ROBINSON, JEANNETTE
Educational administrator. **Personal:** Born Jul 8, Atlanta, GA; daughter of Mary Robinson and Reginald Robinson; children: Yolanda C Wade. **Educ:** Essex Co Coll Newark, AS 1975; Rutgers Univ, BS 1977; Fairleigh Dickinson Univ, MBA 1980. **Career:** Newark Educational Inst, administrator 1973-80; Dept of Planning & Economic Development Div of Employment Training, contract mgmt supvr 1980-83; Essex County College, Newark, NJ, director of personnel, director of human resources, currently. **Orgs:** Business administrator IEE 1976-; pres Management Business Advisors 1980-; arbitrator Better Business Bureau NJ 1982-; mem NJ Educ Assoc, NJ Assoc for Equality and Excellence in Educ, Assoc of Black Women in Higher Educ, Delta Sigma Phi Frat, Natl Assoc of Colleges and Universities Personnel Administrators. **Honors/Awds:** Publications ''People Just Like You: A Guide for the Employer of the Handicapped'' 1982, ''People Just Like You: A Guide for the Teacher of the Handicapped'' 1982. **Home Addr:** 18 Goldsmith Ave, Newark, NJ 07112. **Business Addr:** Director, Human Resources, Human Resources Department, Essex County College, 303 University Ave, Newark, NJ 07102.

ROBINSON, JIM C.
Educator. **Personal:** Born Feb 9, 1943, Ackerman, MS. **Educ:** CA St, BA 1966; CA St, MA 1968; Stanford U, MA 1972; Stanford U, PhD 1973. **Career:** CA St Univ Long Beach, assoc prof Black Studies; CA St, spec asst vice pres acad affrs; CA St, dean faculty & staff affairs; San Jose St Coll, teacher. **Orgs:** Mem, Nat Alliance of Black Sch Educators; Am Assn of Univ & Prof; dir of Reg Programs in W for Am Assn for Higher Edn; chmn Assn of Black Faculty &Staff of So CA; mem Mayor's Task Force Fiscal Mgmt & Cntrl, Compton. **Business Addr:** Calif State University, 1250 Bellflower Blvd, Long Beach, CA 90840.

ROBINSON, JOHN E.
Insurance company administrator. **Personal:** Born Jul 12, 1942, Hollywood, AL; son of Anna Naomi Ellison Edwards and John Karie Robinson; divorced; children: Dana L. **Educ:** Clark Coll, BA 1979; Atlanta Univ, MBA 1979. **Career:** Soc for Savings Bank, asst branch mgr 1964-69; Wesleyan Univ, asst personnel dir 1969-73; WSC Corp, admin vice pres 1973-77; Aetna Life & Casualty, administrator; Aetna Inc, mktg consultant, currently. **Orgs:** Past pres Beta Sigma Lambda Chapter Alpha Phi Alpha 1981-; mem Sigma Pi Phi 1983-; mem Univ Club of Hartford 1983-95; producer/host 30 min talk show WVIT Channel 30 1983-; bd mem Greater Hartford Business Develop Ctr 1984-; bd mem Trinity Coll Comm Child Center 1986-94; bd mem, Univ Club Scholarship Fund; Youth Program Service Committee, YMCA, chairman, 1992-95; Alpha Phi Alpha, life mem; chairperson Craftery Art Gallery, 1994-. **Honors/Awds:** Outstanding Business Student Clark Coll 1979; Leadership of Greater Hartford Chamber of Commerce 1982; founded a network group F-200 1983; The Pinnacle Men Awd, 1994. **Home Addr:** 485 High Street, Unit E, New Britain, CT 06053. **Business Addr:** Mktg Consultant, Aetna Inc, 151 Farmington Ave, MCC1, Hartford, CT 06156.

ROBINSON, JOHN F.
Business executive. **Personal:** Born May 3, 1944, Brooklyn, NY; children: Timothy. **Educ:** AAS; BBA; New York City Community Coll; Baruch Coll Office Serv. **Career:** F Chusid & Co, office serv dupr 1966-68; Cancer Care Inc, dupr 1968-76; NY Educ & Training Consortium Inc, pres, exec dir; Natl Minority Business Inc, pres & CEO, currently. **Orgs:** Mem Amer Mgmt Assn; mem Soc for Advancement of Mgmt; chmn Alliance of Minority Business Organizations Inc; bd of Harlem YMCA; Service for the Underserved, president board of directors, 1989-92. **Honors/Awds:** Published several mgmt articles in the monthly and quarterly journals of the Amer Mgmt Assn; minority business advocate Small Business Admin 1986 & Minority Business Development Agency 1986; pres Minority Business Exec Prog; admin assoc Tuck Business School; mem, Small Business Admin Advisory Council. **Business Addr:** President and CEO, Natl Minority Business Council Inc, 235 E 42nd St, New York, NY 10017.

ROBINSON, JOHN G.
Business executive. **Personal:** Born Feb 22, 1942, Birmingham, AL; son of Addie B Robinson and Johnny G Robinson Sr; married Yvonne R Young, Feb 29, 1980; children: Brittany Ann. **Educ:** Miles College, BA, 1963; University of Minnesota, attended, 1968. **Career:** Control Data Corp., compensation consultant, 1971-75; Magnetic Peripherals Inc, staffing, employee relations and training manager, 1975-79, remote site personnel manager, 1979-80, division personnel manager, 1980-82; Control Data Corp., human resources manager, 1982-86; ETA Systems Inc, human resources manager, 1986-89; John Robinson & Associates, president, 1989-; County of Anoka, diversity coordinator, 1993-. **Orgs:** National Association of Public Sector Equal Opportunity Officers, 1996-; Minnesota Association of Human Righs Workers, 1993-; Twin City Personnel Association, 1986-89; Board of directors, Law Enforcement Opportunities, 1995-; Alpha Phi Alpha Fraternity, life member 1961-; Minnesota Vikings Public Relation Game Staff, 1968-93; United Way of Minneapolis, Fund Disturbution committee, 1992-. **Honors/Awds:** Miles College, Sports Hall of Fame, Inducted 1980; Alpha Phi Alpha Fraternity, Distinguished Chapter Service Award, 1982. **Military Serv:** US Army Security Agency, 1965-67. **Business Addr:** President, John Robinson & Associates, 14620 Carriage Ln, Burnsville, MN 55306.

ROBINSON, JOHN L.
Television broadcaster (retired). **Personal:** Born Dec 15, 1930, Atlantic City, NJ; son of Beatrice Johnson Robinson and John L Robinson; married Louise J Lambert (deceased) (died 1995); children: Tracy R Crew, Jefrey L Robinson; married Anita B. Johnson. **Educ:** Lincoln Univ, 1948-49; Xavier Univ, 1949-50; TV Workshop of NY, 1955. **Career:** Crosley Broadcasting Corp, film librarian 1955-62; WTEV-TV, film dir 1962-65, prod mgr 1965-68, prg mgr 1968-79. **Orgs:** Corporator New Bedford Five Cents Savings Bank 1970-; mem RI Broadcasters Assn 1970-79, treas 1975-76; mem MA Broadcasters Assn 1970-79; mem Natl Assn TV Prg Execs 1970-79; mem Human Relations Comm New Bedford, MA 1975-76; mem Govs Council on Civil Rights RI; vice pres New Bedford Branch NAACP; mem NAACP. **Honors/Awds:** NAACP, New Bedford, MA, Humanitarian Award, 1970; Marian Award, 1980. **Military Serv:** USAF stf/sgt 1951-55; Occupation Medal (Japan), Korean Service Medal; United Nations Service Medal; Natl Defense Service Medal; Good Conduct Medal. **Home Addr:** 111 Brandt Island Rd, Mattapoisett, MA 02739.

ROBINSON, JOHN M.
Metalworking company executive. **Personal:** Born May 22, 1949, Philadelphia, PA; son of Janie Hines and Marvin Robinson; married Alisa Ramsey, Mar 12, 1988; children: Faith Caryn. **Educ:** Edward Waters College, 1971; Dartmouth University, Amos Tuck, 1991. **Career:** SI Handling Systems, sales engineer, 1971-76; Black Diamond Enterprises, Ltd, chief executive officer, 1976-. **Orgs:** NAACP, life member; Society Manufacturing Engineers; Omega Psi Phi, life member; International Materials Management Society; Operations Crossroads Afric, Inc, alumni; Minority Business Education Legal Defense Fund. **Honors/Awds:** Edward Waters College, Visiting Professor, 1989; Maryland Deed, Small Business of the Year, 1989. **Business Phone:** (301)336-4466.

ROBINSON, JOHNATHAN PRATHER
Sales promotion executive. **Personal:** Born Apr 7, 1953, Cleveland, OH; son of Robbie Luster Robinson and Verdix Robinson; married Deborah Lynn Turner Robinson, Apr 12, 1980; children: Rikki Lauren, Jorie Patrice. **Educ:** Northwestern University, Evanston, IL, BS, radio-tv film, 1975. **Career:** National Talent Associates, Chicago, IL, assistant manager, 1975-77; Washington National Insurance Co, Evanston, IL, marketing asst, 1977-80; WorldBook Childcraft Intl, Chicago, IL, project supervisor, 1980-81; Kemper Financial Services, Chicago, IL, sales promotion specialist, 1981-82; ShopTalk Publications Inc, Chicago, IL, vice president, 1982-90; Burrell Consumer Promotions Inc, Chicago, IL, senior vice president/managing director, 1990-92; The Career Television Network Inc, vice pres marketing/sales, 1992-. **Orgs:** Steering committee, Promotional Marketing Assn of America, 1990-; member services comm, board of directors, Howard/Paulina Development Corp, 1989-; member, Omega Psi Phi Fraternity Inc, 1972-. **Honors/Awds:** Editor: Who's Who in American Beauty, 1990. **Home Addr:** 1440 W Birchwood, Chicago, IL 60626. **Business Addr:** Vice Pres, Marketing Sales, The Career Television Network Inc, 4343 Commerce Ct, Ste 600, Lisle, IL 60532.

ROBINSON, JONTYLE THERESA
Educator, author, curator. **Personal:** Born Jul 22, 1947, Atlanta, GA. **Educ:** Clark College, BA, Spanish, 1968; Univ of Georgia, MA, art history, 1971; Univ of Maryland, PhD, contemporary Caribbean and Latin American art history, 1983. **Career:** University of Georgia, Study Abroad Program (Europe) Fellowship, research assistant, 1970; Atlanta University, instructor, summer 1971, 1972; Philander Smith College, acting chairperson, 1971-72; University of Maryland, Eastern Shore, instructor, 1972-75; Emory University, instructor, 1978-83, assistant professor, joint appointment in African-American and African Studies Program/art history, 1983-86, director, designer, African-American and African studies/art history, Summer Study Abroad Program, Haiti, Jamaica, 1984, 1986, Haiti, The Dominican Republic, Puerto Rico, 1985; West Virginia State College, associate professor, 1986-87; Smithsonian Institution/Archives of American Art, research for a retrospective exhibition, catalogue raisonne, American painter Archibald John Motley Jr, 1986-88; Kenkeleba Gallery, research fellow, cocurator, Three Masters: Cortor, Lee-Smith, Motley, 1987-88; Winthrop College, associate professor, 1989; Spelman College, Department of Art, associate professor, 1989-. **Orgs:** Delta Sigma Theta; National Conference of Artists, national executive secretary, 1971-72; Phi Kappa Phi Natl Hon Society. **Honors/Awds:** Spelman College, Coca-Cola Fund Grant for presentation/lecture for the African Americans in Europe Conference, Paris, France, 1992, Department of Art, Amoco Faculty Award, nominee, 1992, Bush Faculty Development Grant, Research for African American Architects, City Planners, Artisans, and Designers 1619-1850, 1993; Bessie L Harper Estate, Grant for The Art of Archibald J Motley Jr, 1990-91; numerous others. **Special Achievements:** Author, works include: Archibald John Motley Jr, Chicago Historical Society, 1991; ''Archibald John Motley Jr: Painting Jazz and Blues,'' paper, College Art Association, Chicago, Feb 13-15, 1992; ''Archibald John Motley Jr: The Artist in Paris, 1929-1930,'' paper, African-Americans and Europe International Conference, Paris, Feb 5-9, 1992; review: ''Black Art-Ancestral Legacy: The African Impulse in African-American Art,'' African Arts Magazine, Jan 1991; judge: Contemporary Art Exhibition, National Black Arts Festival, Atlanta, 1988; consultant: Archibald John Motley Jr Exhibition, Your Heritage House, Detroit, 1988; curator: ''VH-4 Decades: The Art of Varnette P Honeywood,'' Spelman College, 1992; numerous other television/public lectures, tours, panels, publications. **Business Addr:** Associate Professor, Department of Art, Spelman College, 350 Spelman Ln SW, Box 265, Atlanta, GA 30314.

ROBINSON, JOSEPH, JR.
Clergyman. **Personal:** Born Jul 28, 1940, Orangeburg, SC; married Lizzie Miller; children: Jonathan, Joseph C, Jason. **Educ:** Claflin Coll, Orangeburg, SC, BA 1964; Interdenominational Theological Center, Atlanta, BD 1967, MDiv 1973. **Career:** Morris Brown Coll, chaplain 1965-66; Turner Theo Sem, tchr 1966-67; Woodbury, NJ, Campbell AME Ch 1967-68; St of NJ, soc wrkr 1967-68; St Johns AME Church, Brooklyn, minister, 1968-72; Grant AME Church Boston, minister 1972-78; Bethel AME Church Freeport NY, minister 1978-86; Bethel AME Church New Haven CT minister 1986-. **Orgs:** Phi Beta Sigma; mem bd dir Mass Cncl of Chs; mem Family Serv Div Prof Couns Staff Boston; pres bd dir Brightmoor Terr Inc Boston; mem Minstl All Grtr Bstn; v chmn trustee bd New England Annual Conf AME Ch; delegate Gen Conf AME Ch Atlanta 1976; pres NAACP Freeport/Roosevelt Branch 1978-79; commnr Human Relations Cncl of Freeport; trustee NY Annual Conf; mem bd of examiners NY Annual Conf; coord of 1st dist Episcopal Headquarters; bd of dirs Liberty Park Housing; chmn of bd, Paul Quinn Federal Credit Union; trustee, New York Annual Conf, AME Church, 1976-; mem, Self Help, First Episcopal District, 1989; NF Housing Authority, hearing officer; Christians and Jews in America, board of directors. **Honors/Awds:** Phi Beta Sigma Schl Awd 1964; Jackson Fisher Awd 1964; Intrdenmntl Theol Ctr Schlrshp Awd 1966-67; Turner Memorial Awd 1967; Mortgage Reduction Citation; 19 years ahead of time Leadership Awd Macedonia AME Church 1986. **Special Achievements:** Morehouse Coll, Martin Luther King Coll of Ministers, Religious Emphasis Week, speaker. **Business Addr:** Pastor, Bethel AME Church, 255 Goffee St, New Haven, CT 06511.

ROBINSON, JOSEPH WILLIAM, SR.
Architect. **Personal:** Born in Georgetown, SC; married Willie Louise Taylor; children: Joseph William Jr, Jeffrey Leonardo, Janice Burns. **Educ:** Hampton University, BS, 1949. **Career:** JW Robinson and Associates, president, currently. **Orgs:** American Institute of Architects, Atlanta Chapter, past director; National Organization of Minority Architects, past director; National Council of Architectural Registration of Boards; Atlanta Business League Leadership; Georgia World Congress Center, board of governors, past secretary; Butler Street YMCA, 1982-90; West End Merchants Commercial Development Association; Phi Beta Sigma Fraternity, Inc. **Honors/Awds:** ICBO, Southeastern Region, Catalyst Award, 1975; National Hampton Alumni, Lambda Sigma Chapter Leadership Atlanta, 1974; Atlanta Business League, Outstanding Leadership in the Field of Architecture, 1984; Big Bethel AME Church, Lay Fellowship Service Award, 1987; Elevated to Fellowship, American Institute of Architects, FAIA, 1995. **Business Addr:** President, J W Robinson & Associates, 1020 Ralph David Abernathy Blvd, Atlanta, GA 30310, (404)753-4129.

ROBINSON, KENNETH
County official. **Personal:** Born Dec 10, 1947, Chicago, IL; son of Seayray Govan Robinson and Henry Lee Robinson; married Etta D Clement, Jun 7, 1987. **Educ:** IL State Univ, BA Bus Admin 1975. **Career:** Amer Hosp Supply Corp, tax accountant; Abbott Labs, staff tax admin; IL Dept of Revenue, revenue auditor; Lake Co Comm Action, economic develop coord, administrative director, currently. **Orgs:** Pres, Five Points Economic Development Corp, 1981-; Bd mem Lake Co Urban League 1981-; bd mem N Chicago Plan Comm 1982-; sch bd mem Dist #64 No Chicago 1984-; bd mem, Lake City Private Industry Council, 1994. **Military Serv:** AUS sp/4 2 yrs. **Home Addr:** PO Box 1181, North Chicago, IL 60064-8181.

ROBINSON, KENNETH EUGENE
Educator. **Personal:** Born Mar 9, 1947, Hannibal, MO; married Cecilia. **Educ:** William Jewell Coll, BS; Northwest MO State U, Ms Ed; Univ of MO Kansas City, Ed Spec 1980. **Career:** Liberty Sr HS, psychology/sociology instr 1972-80; Moberly Pub Schs, social studies instr 1969-71; Liberty Pub Schs, asst football & head track coach1972-80; Clay Co Juv Justice Center, detention officer 1977-78; Franklin Life Ins, ins agent 1979-80. **Orgs:** Mem Parks & Recreation Bd Liberty MO 1977-80; pres Liberty Tchrs Assn 1979-80; Minority Studies Task Force William Jewell Coll 1979-80; pres elect Libert CTA 1978-79; campaign chmn United Way Liberty Pub Schs 1979; mem Pub Relations Com MSTA 1980. **Business Addr:** Agent, State Farm Insurance, 7211 NW 83rd St, Kansas City, MO 64152.

ROBINSON, KITTY (WILLIE MAE KIDD)
Educator (retired). **Personal:** Born Jan 7, 1921, West Point, MS; widowed. **Educ:** TN St U, BS 1942; DePaul U, M Supvis & Admin 1960; NW U, PhD 1974. **Career:** Chicago St U, asst dean; Chicago St U, early child educ 1967-76; Chicago Pub Sch, pr tchr 1956-66. **Orgs:** Chrmn Assn for Child Educ 1974; pan mem Coop Urban Tchr Educ Wrkshp; mem Amer Assoc of Univ Prof; Natl Educ Assoc Intl; Assn for Child Educ Intl; IL Assn for Supvis & Curr Devel; Nat Coun of Tching Engl Res Assn; bd mem Assn of Mammequins; mem Nat Reading Conf; mem Chicago Urban League; S Shore Comm Serv; Women Mobil for Change; PUSH; Assn of Mannequins; Trophy Schol Fund Bd Jeffery-Yates Neigh; base oper Shore Patrol; past pres 79th St Block Club; mem Widows Club. **Honors/Awds:** Cit sch comm Phi Delta Kappa Educ Honors Soc; recip Indep Wrkshp Fellowship Univ of Chicago 1967; award IL Assn for Supvis & Curric Devel 1974; publ dissert ''A Descrip Eval of the Disting Coop Tchr Prgm at Chicago & St U''; poetry Ebony Jr Magz Johnson Publ Co; pub coll text ''Putting It All Together'' Univ Press of Am 1977.

ROBINSON, LARRY
Professional basketball player. **Personal:** Born Jan 11, 1968, Bossier City, LA. **Career:** Washington Bullets, 1990-91; Golden State, 1991; Boston Celtics, 1991; Rapid City Thrillers, 1991-92; Washington Bullets, 1993; Houston Rockets, 1993-. **Business Addr:** Professional Basketball Player, Houston Rockets, PO Box 272349, Houston, TX 77277.

ROBINSON, LAUREN DANIELLE
Journalist. **Personal:** Born Nov 30, 1964, Glen Ridge, NJ; daughter of G. Nina Scott Robinson and Lawrence D. Robinson. **Educ:** Princeton University, Princeton, NJ, BA, English/creative writing, 1985; Columbia University, New York, NY, MS, journalism, 1986. **Career:** Gateway Cable, Newark, NJ, educational access coordinator/video manager, 1986-87; Newark Star Ledger, Newark, NJ, reporter, metro desk, 1988-89; Dallas Times Herald, Dallas, TX, reporter, city hall, 1989-. **Orgs:** Member, National Association of Black Journalists, 1988-; member, Dallas Fort Worth Association of Black Communicators, 1991-; member and executive committee member, Association of Black Princeton Alumni, 1985-. **Honors/Awds:** Easter Seal Journalism Award, Newark Star Ledger, 1989; Publishers Award, 1990, Employee of the Month, 1990, Coverage Beyond the Call of Duty, 1990, Dallas Times Herald; New York Times Scholarship, Dow Jones Scholarship, Geraldine Livingston Thompson Memorial Scholarship, Class of 1915 Memorial and Frank L. Wright Scholarship, Newel Rodney Fiske Memorial Scholarship, Charles T. Hanna 1910 Scholarship.

ROBINSON, LAWRENCE B.
Educator. **Personal:** Born Sep 14, 1919, Tappahannock, VA; married Laura G Carter; children: Lyn, Gwen, Lawrence Jr. **Educ:** VA Union U, BS 1939; Harvard U, MA 1941; Harvard U, PhD 1946; VA Union U, ScD 1968. **Career:** Univ of CA LA, prof engineering 1962-; asso prof 1960-62; part time lecturer 1957-60; Technische & Hochschule Aachen Germany, visiting prof 1966-67; BrooklynColl, asst prof physics 1954-56; Howard U, asso Prof 1948-51, asst prof 1946-47; Univ of Chicago, instr 1947-48; Ramo-Woolridge Corp & Space Tech LabInc, mem tech staff 1956-60; Naval Research Lab Washington DC, research physicist 1953-54; N Am Aviation Downey CA, research engr 1951-53; US NavalResearch Lab, 1954; Lockheed Aircraft Corp, consult 1955; Aerospace Corp, 1960-66. **Orgs:** Charter mem LA Co Art Museum 1963-; mem SW Museum Highland Park 1963-; Buffalo Bill Hist Cntr Cody WY 1963-; Whitney Gallery of Western Art Cody WY 1963-; Westerners LA Corral 1969-; memshp NY Academy of Sci 1965. **Honors/Awds:** Hon DSc VA Union Univ 1968. **Military Serv:** AAC WWII. **Business Addr:** Sch of Engineering & Applied Sci, U of CA, Los Angeles, CA 90024.

ROBINSON, LAWRENCE D.
Physician, educator. **Personal:** Born Sep 20, 1942, Baltimore, MD; married; children: one. **Educ:** Univ Pittsburgh, BS 1964; Howard U, MD 1968. **Career:** Allergys & Immunology, asst prof pediatrics, dir; Martin L King Jr Hosp; Charles R Drew Postgrad Med Sch UCLA Immunology Fellowship 1973-; US Army Ped Dir Sicle Cell Dis Prog 1971-73; Johns Hopkins Hosp, intern 1968-69; res 1969-70; Sinai Hosp Baltimore, chief res 1970-71. **Orgs:** Nat Med Assn; Scien Adv Com of Nat Assn for Sickle Cell Dis; Bd Cert by Am Bd of Ped; Bd of Allery & Immunology 1975; mem Am Thoracic Soc; mem Am Acad of Ped; mem bd Am Lung Assn LA; Immunization Action Com 1978-80; co-chmn Nat Immunization Prog LA. **Honors/Awds:** Has written & present many pub at meet of Am Ped Soc Atlantic City, Am Ped Soc Wash; contributing editor Essence Mag; presented papers to Am Acad of Allergy.

ROBINSON, LEARTHON STEVEN, SR.
Attorney. **Personal:** Born May 8, 1925, Pittsburgh, PA; son of Mamie Miller Robinson and Learthon Steven Robinson; married Beulah Beatrice Brown, Aug 26, 1950; children: Deborah L Flemister, Learthon S Jr, Iris R Rodgers, Michael J, Denise E Baba. **Educ:** Univ of Pittsburgh, BA 1948; Univ of WI, Grad Study 1950; Cleveland-Marshall Sch of Law/Cleveland State U, JD 1952. **Career:** Ohio Cvl Rgts Commsn, jdcl hrng ofcr 1964-65; Warren, OH Law Dept, city prsctr 1967-71, 1st dpty law dir 1971-; Montford Point Marines Assn, Inc national office, general counsel, 1990-. **Orgs:** Pres PA-OH Blk Lwyrs Assn Inc 1981-; pres Shenango Vly Svcs, Inc 1985; comm mem Pblc Rels Spkrs Bureau Trumbull Co Bar Assn 1985; mem OH Bar, Amer Bar, DC Bar, Natl Bar Assocs; bd of trustees Goodwill Industries Warren/Youngstown Area 1986-89; member, Omega Psi Phi Fraternity, 1947; life mem, NAACP, 1973; life mem, National Bar Association, 1980; life mem, Montford Point Marine Association, Inc, 1993. **Honors/Awds:** Congressional Citation and Proclamation for Exemplary Professional Serv City of Warren OH 1971-87; State of OH Citation and Proclamation for Exemplary Professional Serv City of Warren OH 1971-87; City Council of Warren Citation and Proclamation for Exemplary Professional Serv City Council of Warren OH 1971-87; Man of Yr Urban League Warren/Trumbull Chptr 1976; Cmnty Serv Trumbull Co NAACP 1982; Outstanding Leadership 17th Congressional Dist Caucus 1984; Montford Point Assn, Inc, National Semper Fidelis Award for Outstanding Service to the Assn, 1994; National Bar Association, Hall of Fame, 1995; Iwo Jima Medal, 1995. **Military Serv:** USMC gnry sgt 1942-46; Honorably Discharged; 4 mjr cmpgns, Awrd 4 battle stars 1942-46; Pres Unit Citation, WWII Vctry Medal, 2 Purple Hrts, Navy Commendation for Bravery in Combat, Asiatic-Pacific Medal in Combat, Japanese Occupation Medal, Marine Corps Service Medal. **Home Addr:** 4119 Chevelle Dr SE, Warren, OH 44484. **Business Addr:** Attorney, Robinson Professional Bldg, 179 W Market St, Warren, OH 44481.

ROBINSON, LEONARD HARRISON, JR.
Executive. **Personal:** Born Apr 21, 1943, Winston-Salem, NC; son of Winnie Cornelia Thomas Robinson and Leonard H Robinson; married Cassandra Maria; children: Kimberly Michelle, Rani Craft. **Educ:** OH State University, BA 1964; SUNY Binghamton, grad work 1966-67; American University, MA, PhD candidate 1982-89. **Career:** Peace Corps, India/Washington DC 1964-71; ATAC, economic/mgmt analyst 1971; Inner City Comm Prog, EPA, dir 1971-72; FPIA, Africa region dir 1972-78; US Congress, task force dir 1977-78; Office of Pop AID, chief, Africa div 1978-79; HARC Battelle, dir, intl devel study 1979-83; Dept of State for African Affairs,deputy asst sec of

state 1983-85; African Development Foundation, president, 1984-90; US Dept of State, deputy asst secretary, 1990-93; The Washington Strategic Group, Inc, vice chairman, cheif operating officer, 1993-. **Orgs:** Kappa Alpha Psi 1963-; Washington Ballet 1982-85, vice pres of board, 1986-89; Men's Republican Club Montgomery County 1982-85; bd of dir, Coalition for Equitable Representation in Government, Montgomery Co 1985-89; Sigma Pi Phi 1984-; bd of dir, JACC 1985-86; board member, Academy Review Bd, State of MD, Sen Chas McMathias, 1986-88; board of visitors, Shaw University, 1986; dir, Sevin Development Group, 1986; board member, Montgomery County Board of Social Services, 1986-; Council on Foreign Relations. **Honors/Awds:** Le Droit d'Honneur, OH State University 1963; Outstanding Black American Contribution, Sears Roebuck & Co 1971; Doctor of Law Degree, Shaw University 1983; many publ & papers including: "Assessment & Analysis," Tanzania Battelle Memorial Inst 1981, "Non-Academic Careers for Minority Scientists," Natl Inst of Health 1982, "Battelle PDP Draft India Country Strategy," w/James E Kocher, Office of Population Agency for Intl Devel, Battelle Mem Inst 1982; Commandeur de l'Ordre National du Niger (highest honor given by the Republic of Niger) 1988; special achievement award, Africare, 1990; City of Greensboro, NC, awarded key to city, 1991; LLD, Huston-Tillot-Son College, 1991. **Business Addr:** Vice-Chairman, Chief Operating Officer, Washington Strategic Group, Inc, 805 15th St NW, Washington, DC 20005.

ROBINSON, LUTHER D.
Physician, educator. **Personal:** Born Dec 22, 1922, Tappahannock, VA; son of Fannie E Robinson and William H Robinson; married Betty Boyd; children: Jan, Barry, Vance. **Educ:** VA State Coll, BS 1943; Meharry Med Coll, MD 1946. **Career:** St Elizabeths Hosp Washington, supt 1975-; St Elizabeths Hosp, staff 1955-; Mercy Hosp Phila, intern 1946-47; Lakin State Hosp Lakin WV, staff 1947-49; Freedmen's Hosp Washington, psychiatric residency 1953-54; St Elizabeths Hosp, 1954-55; Howard Univ Coll Med, clin instr 1956-68; vis lectr 1974-; Gallaudet Coll, lectr 1968-; Georgetown Univ Sch Med, fac mem 1974-; Geo Washington U, clin assoc prof 1969-. **Orgs:** Mem Medico Chirurgical Soc; Med Soc DC; Washington Psychiatric Soc; AMA; natl chmn Commn Med & Audiology 7th World Cong; World Fedn Deaf Originated Mental Health Prog Deaf St Elizabeths Hosp 1963; co-founder AA Prog St Elizabeths Hosp. **Honors/Awds:** Hon DSc Gallaudet Coll 1971; Edw Miner Gallaudet Award 1974. **Military Serv:** AUS capt 1949-52.

ROBINSON, MARCUS
Professional football player. **Personal:** Born Feb 27, 1975. **Educ:** South Carolina, attended. **Career:** Chicago Bears, wide receiver, 1997-. **Business Addr:** Professional Football Player, Chicago Bears, 1000 Football Dr, Halas Hall at Conway Park, Lake Forest, IL 60045-4829, (847)295-6600.

ROBINSON, MARTHA DOLORES
Educational administrator, editor. **Personal:** Born Aug 19, 1956, Halls, TN. **Educ:** TN State Univ, BS, 1978, MBA, 1991; Memphis State Univ, MA; Vanderbilt Univ, doctoral scholarship, currently. **Career:** TN State Univ, production asst 1976-78; Lau-Fay-Ton, teacher 1978; Lauderdale Cty Enterprise, reporter 1978-79; Lane Coll, dir of publ relations and alumni affairs; Univ of Tennessee at Martin, executive asst to chancellor, beginning 1989; Meharry Medical College, publications editor, assoc dir of college eelations, director of college relations, currently. **Orgs:** Public Relations Soc of Amer 1985, TN Coll Public Relations Assoc, Council for the Advancement & Support of Educ, NAACP, Tau Beta Sigma Natl Hon Band Sor, TSU Natl Alumni Assoc, Alpha Kappa Alpha Sor Inc; Board of Directorss: United Way of West TN, The Jackson Arts Council, Jackson City Beautiful Commission. **Honors/Awds:** Honor Student TN State Univ 1975-78; Plaque Disting Serv Lane Coll Pre Alumni 1980; Cert of Awd Alpha Kappa Alpha Sor 1980-82; Outstanding Serv Lane Coll Student Gov Assoc 1982; Guest of the White House by Pres Reagan 1983. **Business Addr:** Director of College Relations, Meharry Medical College, 1005 DB Todd Blvd, Nashville, TN 37208.

ROBINSON, MATT
Writer, producer. **Personal:** Born Jan 1, 1937, Philadelphia, PA; son of Mamie Camilla Henson Robinson and Matthew Thomas Robinson; married Dolores James Robinson (divorced 1981); children: Matthew Thomas IV, Holly Elizabeth. **Educ:** Penn State University, BA, 1958. **Career:** WCAU-TV, writer/producer, 1963-68; Children's Television Workshop, producer/performer, "Sesame Street," 1968-72; Paramount Pictures, writer/producer, Save the Children (film), 1972-73; United Artists, writer/producer, Amazing Grace (film), 1973-74; self-employed free-lance writer/producer, 1974-82; "The Cosby Show," writer/producer, 1987-91. **Orgs:** Writers' Guild of America; Dramatists' Guide; American Federation of Television and Radio Artists; American Society of Composers, Authors and Publishers. **Honors/Awds:** NAACP, Image Award, for writing of "The Cosby Show," 1988; Humanitas Award, for writing of "The Cosby Show," 1985; Black Film Festival, Jamaica, award for producing film Save the Children, 1973; Emmy, for producing "Sesame Street," 1970; Penn State Distinguished Alumni Award, 1994. **Special Achievements:** Movies and plays written include: "The Possession of Joel Delaney," "Keyboard," "The Confessions of Stepin Fetchit," books include: "The Gordon of Sesame Street Storybook.". **Business Addr:** 9171 Wilshire Blvd, Ste 541, Beverly Hills, CA 90210.

ROBINSON, MAUDE ELOISE
Nursing educator. **Personal:** Born Jan 18, 1927, New York, NY. **Educ:** St John's Episcopal School of Nursing, RN 1955; Jersey City State Teachers Coll, BA, BS 1970; Hunter Coll CUNY, MS, MPH 1974; Walden Univ, PhD 1976; Hunter Coll, CUNY, BSN 1982, postgraduate, gerentology 1985; PhD Walden University, 1993. **Career:** Hospital in Brooklyn, supvr operating room 1960-65; St John's Episcopal School of Nursing, instructor, 1965-70; Hospital for Joint Diseases, instructor, 1970-74; Church of Christ Bible Inst NYC, health educator 1968-80; Nursing/Health/Safety ARC, intl instructor 1968-present; BRAVO/youth groups/church groups/BC/BS March of Dimes & Nat Council of Negro Women, lecturer/prof comm health educ 1970-; consultant various natl comm health agencies, 1970-; Nursing Resources Journal Nursing Admin, consultant 1978-80; St Joseph's Coll, prof 1978-, preceptor-counselor; Hunter Coll, coordinator seek health science & nursing 1974-94; Coll of New Rochelle, prof, consultant, 1988-96. **Orgs:** Business and Professional Women, ENY branch, 1990-93; Nurses Sorority Chi Eta Phi Inc, 1984; Natl Black Professional & Business Women, ENY Chap. **Honors/Awds:** Faculty of the Year Award, St Johns School of Nursing Brooklyn 1965-67; pub health/nursing articles NY Amsterdam News 1972; co-author, health career textbook Bd of Educ NY 1975; "Women in Am" 1977-; Impact Remediation Nursing Aspirants Nat Black Nurses Assn Newsletter 1977; Laurel Wreath Doctoral Assn NY Educators 1977; health/nursing articles Everybody's Journal 1979; appeared on "News Center 5 Live at Five" Channel 4 WNBC-TV 1980; Top Ladies of Distinction Award 1983; Business & Professional Women, ENY branch, Sojourner of Truth Awd, 1990; Outstanding Faculty Year, St Joseph's College, 1996; Fac of Year, Hosp for Joint Diseases, School of Nsg, 1971-72; Faculty of the Year, Hunter Coll, 1988-90; Faculty of the Year, St. Joseph's Coll, 1994-95. **Special Achievements:** Author, Significant Racial Factors Related to Enrollments in Math/Science Courses, 1992; Author: Impact Remediation Nursing Aspirants in Schools of Nursing, 1976. **Business Addr:** Preceptor Community Health, Human Services, St Joseph's College, 265 Clinton Ave, Brooklyn, NY 11205.

ROBINSON, MAURICE C.
Attorney. **Personal:** Born Mar 4, 1932, St Andrew, Jamaica; son of Mildred Anastasia Magnus Robinson (deceased) and Herbert Ulysses Robinson (deceased); married Hazel Thelma Chang Robinson, Nov 24, 1990; children: Mark Wayne, Janet Marie, Wade Patrick. **Educ:** Univ Coll of West Indies, BA 1951-54. **Career:** Manton & Hart, assoc, 1959-64 partner 1964-77; Myers, Fletcher & Gordon, 1977-. **Orgs:** Dir Victoria Mutual Bldg Soc, Stresscon Jamaica Ltd, Eric Fong-Yee Engrg Co Ltd, chmn Public Utility Comm 1972-76; legal officer Air Jamaica Ltd 1970-80; sec Air Jamaica Ltd 1968-69; dir Travel Planners Ltd; Dyoll/Wataru Coffee Company Limited; dir Security Advisory & Management Services Ltd; dir Victoria Mutual Investments Ltd; mem Inst of Trade Mark Agents; director, Victoria Mutual Property Services Ltd; director, Victoria Mutual Insurance Company Ltd; Restaurant Associates Ltd, Burger King Franchisee, director; International Trademark Association, associate mem; Alpha Financial Services Ltd, dir; Secadman Holdings Ltd, dir. **Honors/Awds:** Full Univ Colours for Field Hockey 1953. **Business Addr:** Attorney, Myers, Fletcher & Gordon, 21 East St, Kingston, Jamaica, (809)922-5860.

ROBINSON, MELVIN P.
Entrepreneur. **Personal:** Born Feb 12, 1935, Atlantic City, NJ; son of Marcella Derry Robinson and Warren Robinson; children: Tiffany, Michael Ribando. **Educ:** Villinova Univ, Villinova PA, 1952-54. **Career:** Self-Employed, 1965-. **Orgs:** Mem, Amer Inst of Organbuilders, 1990-. **Business Addr:** Melvin P Robinson Pipe Organs, 12 Irving Pl, Mount Vernon, NY 10550.

ROBINSON, MICHAEL DAVID
Consultant. **Personal:** Born May 17, 1953, Phoenix, AZ; son of Edith Leonia Cole Robinson and Peter James Robinson Sr; married Debra Jean Rogers Robinson, Aug 28, 1976 (divorced 1980); children: Dante Alonzo, Marcus Ian. **Educ:** Westchester College, White Plains, NY, AS, 1985. **Career:** New York Telephone Co/Nynex, New York, NY, senior systems analyst, 1974-89; Trecom Business System, Edison, NJ, consultant, 1989-90; Robinson-Cole & Associates, Atlanta, GA, president, 1990-. **Orgs:** Advisory board member, Urban Women's Shelter, 1988-89; president, New York City Chapter, Black Data Processing Associates, 1987-89; board member, National Black Data Processing Associates, 1987-; member, Black Achievers in Industry Alumni Association, 1989-; charter member, New York Area Minority Management Association, 1986-89; member, Data Processing Management Association, 1990-; board member, Volunteer Resource Center Metro, Atlanta United Way, 1990-; board of directors, Bedford Pine Family Resource Center; board of directors, Aid to Imprisoned Mothers. **Honors/Awds:** Black Achievers in Industry Award, Harlem YMCA, 1989; Black Achievers in Industry Award, Nynex Corp, 1989. **Military Serv:** US Navy, Petty Officer, 3rd Class, 1971-77, Honorman Award 1975. **Business Addr:** Consultant, Robinson-Cole & Associates, 205 C Winding River Dr, Atlanta, GA 30350.

ROBINSON, MILTON BERNIDINE
Clergyman, editor. **Personal:** Born Jun 29, 1913, Forest City, NC; married Lois Mosley; children: Evelyn Mercer, Essie McDaniel, Connie Foust, Milton Bernidine, Arthur, Charles, Annie Evans, Bettie McKesson, Priscilla Hodge, Phylias, Kenneth. **Educ:** Johnson Comm Coll, AB 1963; A&T State Univ Greensboro NC, MS 1967. **Career:** Former school bus driver, farmer, pullman porter, builder, brick mason, editor; AME Zion Church, ordained to ministry 1949; Rutherford Cty Carver HS, teacher 1965-69; Star of Zion, editor 1969-80; St John AME Zion Church, pastor 1965-76; Isothermal Community Coll, Hindale, NC, teacher, 1984-86 (retired). **Orgs:** Del Gen Conf AME Zion Church 1960, 1964, 1968, 1972, 1976, 1980, 1984; conn mem bd christian ed home-ch div 1968-; del World Meth Conf 1971; mem gov bd Natl Council Church Christ in USA 1972-; chmn Rutherford Cty Human Relations Council; 2nd vchmn Rutherford Cty Dem Exec Comm 1970-74; trustee Winston-Salem State UnivClinton Jr Coll Rock Hill SC; mem NAACP, Mason; presiding elder York-Chester Dist SC Conf African Meth Episcopal Zion Church 1981-87; trustee Isothermal Comm Coll Spindale 1983-91; chmn trustees, Doggett Grove AME Zion Church, Forest City, NC. **Honors/Awds:** Honorary DD, Livingston Coll, 1973; Lincoln Univ Award for helping famine-struck people in Africa in the 1970's.

ROBINSON, MILTON J.
State official. **Personal:** Born Aug 16, 1935, Asbury Park, NJ; married Sadie Pinkston; children: Valerie, Patricia. **Educ:** Univ of MI, BS 1958; Columbia Univ, MA 1962; Univ of MI, MSW 1966, PhD 1980. **Career:** Battle Creek Urban League, exec dir 1966-69; Flint Urban League, exec dir 1969-70; Dept of Civil Rights State of MI, exec dir 1970-72; State of MI, parole board member 1972-; Wayne State Univ Sch of Social Work, adjunct prof 1975-, GMI Engineering & Mgmt Inst, admissions & corporate relations consultant 1985-; State of Michigan, exec sec parole and review bd, currently. **Orgs:** Mem Kappa Alpha Psi Frat; bd mem United Neighborhood Cntrs of Am 1972-; pres Cath Youth Orgn 1978-; mem Lions Intl 1979-; bd mem Detroit Metro Youth Program 1985-. **Honors/Awds:** Comm Serv Award City of Battle Creek 1969; Outstanding Professional Serv Award Flint Urban League 1978; Outstanding Contrib to Continuing Judicial Educ MI Judicial Inst 1979; Meritorious Serv Awd Catholic Youth Org 1984; Certificate of Achievement Natl Cncl of Juvenile & Family Court Judges 1986. **Military Serv:** AUS Sp 4 1958-60. **Business Addr:** Executive Secretary, Parol & Review Board, State of Michigan, 1200 6th St, Detroit, MI 48226.

ROBINSON, MURIEL F. COX
Physician. **Personal:** Born Nov 6, 1927, Columbus, OH; daughter of Veola Isbell Cox and Henry W. Cox; divorced. **Educ:** Attended, Ohio State Univ 1945-48; Meharry Medical Coll, MD 1952. **Career:** Homer G Phillips Hospital affiliated w/Washington Univ Sch of Medicine, psychiatry resident 1953-56; St Louis Municipal Child Guidance Clinic, staff psychiatrist 1956-57; Napa State Hosp, staff psychiatrist 1958; Richmond Mental Health Center, staff psychiatrist 1959-75; East Oakland Mental Health Center, staff psychiatrist 1976-79; Private Psychiatric Practice, psychiatrist 1960-79; CA Youth Authority, staff 1979-92; Locum Tenens Group, 1992-94. **Orgs:** Former mem advisory bd Contra Costa Mental Health Advisory Bd; former mem bd of dirs North Richmond Neighborhood House; mem American Psychiatric Assn 1957-; member Black Psychiatrists of America; mem NAACP Sacramento 1987-; life member, American Psychiatric Assn, 1991-; member, American Medical Assn, 1957-; member, American Assn for Advancement of Science, 1989-; member, National Medical Assn, 1960-. **Home Addr:** PO Box 292148, Sacramento, CA 95829-2148.

ROBINSON, MYRON FREDERICK
Organization executive. **Personal:** Born Dec 15, 1943, Youngstown, OH; son of Virginia L Robinson-Robinson and Romeo Robinson; married Brenda King Robinson, Dec 15, 1987; children: Myron Rodney, Myra Michele. **Educ:** Ohio State University, Youngstown, OH, BA; University of Pittsburgh, Pittsburgh, PA; University of Wisconsin; National Urban League Executive Development Training. **Career:** Urban League of New Haven Connecticut; Urban League of Madison Wisconsin; Greenville Urban League, Inc, Greenville, CS, president/CEO, 1972-. **Orgs:** Board of directors, American Federal Bank; member, board of directors, YMCA; member, Greenville South Carolina, Rotary Club; member, The Governor's Task Force in Reducing Health Cost; member, board of directors, Christ Episcopal Church. **Business Addr:** President/CEO, Greenville Urban League Inc, 15 Regency Hill Drive, Greenville, SC 29607.

ROBINSON, NATHANIEL. **See Obituaries section.**

ROBINSON, NINA
Newspaper public relations coordinator. **Personal:** Born Jul 17, 1943, Stamford, CT; daughter of Olga Larianova Scott (deceased) and Henry Scott (deceased); married Lawrence Donniva Robinson, Jul 28, 1962 (divorced); children: Lawrence Damian, Lauren Danielle. **Educ:** New York University, New York, NY, 1961-62. **Career:** The New York Urban League, New York, NY, administrator, Brownstone Prep, 1968-72; The Newark Board of Education, Newark, NJ, staff trainer, researcher, 1972-74; The Chad School, Newark, NJ, administrator, 1974-82; The New York Times Co, New York, NY, public relations coor, 1983-. **Orgs:** Board member, The Newark Board of Education, 1982-83; New York Association of Black Journalists (NYABJ), 1992-93, Executive Board, fund raising chairwoman, 1992-; Newark Citizen Education Committee; A Better Chance, 1980-83. **Honors/Awds:** Miss Manhattan, 1961. **Special Achievements:** Contributing writer, New York Times, New Jersey Edition. **Business Addr:** Coordinator Public Relations/Media, Corporate Communications & The New York Times Co., 229 W 43rd St, Rm 1042 W, New York, NY 10036, (212)556-1982.

ROBINSON, NOAH, SR. See Obituaries section.

ROBINSON, NOAH R.
Construction executive. **Career:** Precision Contractors, Inc, Chicago IL, chief executive officer, currently.

ROBINSON, NORMAN T., JR.
Educator, clergyman, business executive. **Personal:** Born Aug 31, 1918, Bennettsville, SC; married Mayme Adams; children: Norman III, Mansel, Lyndon. **Educ:** SC State Coll, BSA 1939, MS 1964; Columbia Univ, post grad study. **Career:** Chesterfield-Marlboro EOC OEO, exec dir; Society Hill SC, teacher; Smith Elem School, principal; Shawton HS, teacher of vets; Dale SC, teacher; Petersburg Elem School Pageland SC, principal; Stuckey HS Johnsonville SC, teacher; St James Baptist Church Bonnettsville, pastor; Mt Tabur Bapt Church Clio SC, pastor; Marlboro Branch of SCLG, vice pres; Fine Print News, publisher; Marlboro Co Dist 4, councilman. **Orgs:** Vice pres Cherow Alumni Chap Kappa Alpha Psi Frat; mem NAACP, Marlboro Betterment League; mem SC Comm Action Agy; moderator Marlboro Union; sec exec bd Borea Assn; vice pres BTU Conv; chmn bd dir BTU Rest Home. **Honors/Awds:** Comm Leader of Amer 1969; Certificate of Awd Leadership Inst for Comm Devel. **Military Serv:** AUS 1943-46. **Business Addr:** Councilman, District 4 Marlboro Co, 514 Cherad St, Bennettsville, SC 29512.

ROBINSON, PATRICIA JERVIS
Acct executive. **Personal:** Born Apr 18, 1951, Miami, FL; children: Lennard, Patrice. **Educ:** Miami-Dade Community Coll, AA, 1981; Barry Univ, BS, 1983. **Career:** Dade Cty Circuit Court, court calendar clerk, 1974-77; Dade County Dept of Human Resources, admin officer, 1977-83, newsletter asst editor, 1983-87, administrator, 1987-89; Thomas & Doyle Real Estate, Inc, assoc realtor, 1979-85; ERA Empress Realty Inc, assoc realtor, 1985-86; Coldwell Bankers, referral agent, 1986-87. **Orgs:** Mem, Natl Forum of Black Public Admin, Iota Phi Lambda Sor, NAACP; trustee, bd chair, Valley Grove MB Church; Natl Assoc of Life Underwriters; Barry Univ, Alumni Assn; Florida Real Estate Council; Natl Assn of Female Exec. **Honors/Awds:** Employee of the Year Dept of Human Resources Office of Admin, 1985; Honored for Outstanding Business Achievement, 1989; Natl Quality Award; Natl Sales Achievement Award; Million Dollar Round Table Qualifier. **Business Addr:** Administrator, Dade County Dept of Human Resources, 8390 NW 53rd St, #301, Miami, FL 33166.

ROBINSON, PETER LEE, JR.
Fine artist, graphics designer, consultant. **Personal:** Born Jan 16, 1922, Washington, DC; married Romaine Frances Scott. **Educ:** Howard Univ, AB 1949. **Career:** USN, supr illustrator 1957-62; Natl Aeronautics & Space Admin, dir, visual info officer 1962-77; Self employed, fine artist, graphics designer, consultant. **Orgs:** Dir, founder HEM Rsch Inc Past Inc; pres, treas DC Art Assn; past vice pres Soc of Fed Artists & Designers, Fed Design Council; exhibits at the Corcoran Gallery of Art, Atlanta Univ Gallery, Smithsonian Inst, The Artists Mart, Howard Univ Gallery, Barnett Aden Gallery, Collectors Corner, The Potters House Gallery, The Smith-Mason Gallery, The Anacostia Nghbrd Mus, Univ of PA, Martin Luther King Jr Gallery, The Art Barn; US State Dept ''Arts for the EmbassiesProg''; speaker Rice Univ 1969, 16th Intl Tech Comm Conf 1969, Morgan State Coll 1969, 19th Intl Tech Comm Conf 1970, NAIA 1971, 19th Intl Tech Comm Conf 1972, 1st Indust Graphics Intl Conf 1974, 4th Tech Writing Inst 1974, Natl Conf of Artists 1980. **Honors/Awds:** Award of Excellence in Visiting Comm Soc of Fed Artists & Designers 1961; Meritorious Civilian Serv Award 1960; Apollo Achievement Award 1969; NASA Exceptional Serv Medal 1973; NASA Outstanding Performance Award 1975; NASA Spaceship Earth Award 1975. **Military Serv:** USAAC 1943-46. **Business Addr:** Fine Artist, Graphics Designer, 1900 Tulip St NW, Washington, DC 20012.

ROBINSON, PREZELL RUSSELL
Educational administrator. **Personal:** Born Aug 25, 1923, Batesburg, SC; married LuLu Harris; children: JesSanne. **Educ:** St Augustine's Coll Raleigh NC, AB 1946; Bishop Coll, LLD 1951; Cornell Univ NY, MA 1951, EdD 1956. **Career:** Voorhees School & Jr Coll Denmark SC, instructor of French/math/science, 1948-54; Univ of Nairobi Kenya, visiting prof, 1973; Univ of Dar es Salaam Tanzania, vstg prof, 1973; Haile Selassie I Univ Addis Ababa Ethiopia, vstg prof, 1973; Univ of Guyana, vstg prof, 1974; Cornell Univ Ithaca NY, fellow, 1954-56; St Augustine's Coll, prof of sociology 1956-, dean 1956-64, exec dean 1964-66, acting pres 1966-67, pres 1967-95, president emeritus, 1995-; Alternate Representative to the General Assemlby of the United Nations, 1996. **Orgs:** Mem Phi Kappa Phi, Delta Mu Delta, Alpha Kappa Mu, Phi Delta Kappa, Amer Social Soc, NC Social Soc, Amer Acad of Political Sci, So Social Soc, Amer Assn for Advancement of Sci, Study of Negro Life & History, Amer Acad of Pol & Soc Sci; mem bd of dir Wachovia Bank & Trust Co; state bd of ed NC; exec comm NC Assn of Coll & Univ; bd of dir Natl Assn for Equal Oppty in Higher Ed; bd dir Tech Asst Consortium to Improve Coll Svc; pres United Negro Coll Fund, 1978-80; bd of dir Occoneechee Cty BSA; pres Natl Assoc for Equal Oppty in Higher Educ, 1981-84; bd dir C of C; pres Cooperating Raleigh Colls, 1981, 1986-88; mem exec comm Assn of Episcopal Coll, Omega Psi Phi; 47th General Assembly, UN, public member ambassador, 1992; Alternative Representative of US to UN, 1992; vice chmn, NC State Board of Education. **Honors/Awds:** Recipient Fulbright Fellow to India 1965; Tar Heel of the Week Raleigh News & Observer 1971; Recognition for Services Rendered Awd 2nd highest Awd from Liberia 1971; Outstanding Service Award, Alpha Phi Alpha, 1977; Citizen of the Year Award, Omega Psi Phi, 1979; Silver Anniversary Award, N Carolina Community Coll System, 1989; author of more than 21 articles in professional journals. **Military Serv:** US Army. **Business Addr:** President Emeritus, St Augustine's College, 1315 Oakwood Ave, Raleigh, NC 27610-2298.

ROBINSON, R. DAVID
Professional football player (retired), business executive. **Personal:** Born May 3, 1941, Mount Holly, NJ; son of Mary E Gaines Robinson and Leslie H Robinson; married Elaine Burns Robinson, Mar 22, 1963; children: Richard, David, Robert. **Educ:** Penn State Univ, BS, 1963. **Career:** Linebacker: Green Bay Packers, 1963-72; Washington Redskins, 1973-74; Schlitz Brewing Co, Youngstown OH, district sales manager; Mars Dist Co, executive vice pres, 1984-. **Orgs:** Mem NFL Players Assn; NFL Player rep 1967-70; vice pres Players Assn 1968-70; YMCA; Big Bros; board of directors, Pro Football Hall of Fame, 1990-. **Honors/Awds:** Liberty Bowl 1960; Gator Bowl (1st Black) 1961; 62 MVP; All Amer 1962; Hula Bowl 1962; All Star Game 1963; All Pro 1965-69; MVP Pro Bowl 1968; 1st Black Linebacker NFL. **Business Addr:** Executive Vice President, Mars Dist Co, 425-27 Victoria Rd, Austintown, OH 44515.

ROBINSON, RANDALL S.
Association executive. **Personal:** Born in Richmond, VA; married; children: Anikie, Jabari, Khalea. **Educ:** Virginia Union Univ, Grad 1967; Harvard Law School, JD, 1970. **Career:** US Rep Diggs, administrative asst; TransAfrica, executive dir. **Honors/Awds:** Ford Fellowship; Received Ebony's MLK Public Service Award. **Special Achievements:** Author, Defending the Spirit.

ROBINSON, RANDALL S.
Educator. **Personal:** Born Nov 26, 1939, Philadelphia, PA; married Janice Whitley; children: Randall, Ginger. **Educ:** OH St U, BS 1961; Univ of PA, MS 1965; Temple U, EdD 1972. **Career:** Philadelphia Bd of Educ, teacher 1961-65; Glassboro St Coll NJ, assoc prof, dept of elem & early childhood educ, currently; Egg Harbor School System NJ, consultant Summer School Improvement Project 1967; Educational Materials Co, project coord, research & devel 1668-69; Templ Univ, adjunct prof 1968-69; Temple Univ, consult & Group Leader annual summer workshop in lang arts; Tioga Community Youth Council, educ consultant for disruptive youth 1971. **Orgs:** Mem Curriculum Revision Com; Glassboro St Coll early childhood educ & curriclum devel com; dept Tenure & Recontracting Com Urban Educ Curriculum Devel Com; faculty adv Black Cultural Leg; cnslr & Adv Upward Bound Students; cnslr & adv Martin Luther King Scholars Faculty; mem Glassboro St Fdrtn of Coll Tchrs; mem Nat Council for the Social Studies; mem Washington Township Bd Educ 1973-76; mem Negotiations Com, Washington Township of Edn; mem Curriculum Com; Washington Township Bd of Edn; chmn Policy Com Washington Twnship Bd of Edn; mem Balanced Group of Washington Township. **Honors/Awds:** Plaque, Tioga Community Youth Council 1973. **Business Addr:** Associate Professor, Elem & Early Childhood Educ, Glassboro State College, Glassboro, NJ 08028.

ROBINSON, RENAULT A.
Government official. **Personal:** Born Sep 8, 1942, Chicago, IL; married Annette Richardson; children: Renault Jr, Brian, Kivu, Kobie. **Educ:** Roosevelt Univ, BS 1970, MS Urban Studies 1971; Northwestern Univ, Urban Fellow 1972-73. **Career:** Chicago Police Dept, police officer & vice detective 1965-83; Chicago Housing Authority, chmn bd of dirs, 1979-87, chmn bd of commrs 1983-87; ASI Personnel Service, Inc, sr management associate, 1989-. **Orgs:** Chmn bd dir Afro-American Police League 1983-; exec dir Afro-American Police League 1968-83; mem NAACP; Chicago Urban League; Natl Forum for Black Public Admin. **Honors/Awds:** Author ''The Man Who Beat Clout City'' 1977; Renault A Robinson Award Natl Black Police Assn 1979; Youth Award John D Rockefeller III Found 1979. **Business Addr:** Sr Management Associate, 2 Illnois Ctr, 233 N Michigan Ave, Ste 2306, Chicago, IL 60601.

ROBINSON, ROBERT G.
Medical researcher, educator. **Personal:** Born Aug 11, 1943, New York, NY; son of Dorothy May Wilson Robinson and Garl Robinson. **Educ:** City College of New York, BA, 1967; Adelphi University, MSW, 1969; University of California, Berkeley, MPH, 1977, DrPH, 1983. **Career:** Adelphi University, chairperson, assistant professor, 1969-76; REACH, Inc, psychotherapist, 1973-75; University of California, Berkeley, various consulting/teaching positions, 1977-84; American Cancer Society, principal investigator, 1983-85; National Cancer Institute, cancer control science associate, 1985-88; Fox Chase Cancer Center, associate member, 1988-90, director of community planning and development, 1990-92; Centers for Disease Control, assoc director for program development, 1993-; Emory Univ, School of Public Health, adjunct prof, 1997-. **Orgs:** American Public Health Association; National Medical Association; American Association for Advancement of Science; Stop Teenage Addiction to Tobacco, board of directors, 1990-; Tobacco Control: An International Journal, editorial adv board, 1992-; Journal of Health Care for the Poor & Underserved, national editorial board, 1990-; Uptown Coalition for Tobacco Control & Public Health, board of directors, 1989-93; National Black Leadership Initiative on Cancer of Philadelphia, chairperson, 1988-93. **Honors/Awds:** American Medical Women's Association, Community Health Award, 1990; National Association of Health Service Executives, Community Service Award, 1990; Commonwealth of Pennsylvania, Pennsylvania Heritage Award, 1992; Uptown Coalition for Tobacco Control & Public Health, Outstanding Leadership, 1992; National Black Leadership Initiative on Cancer, Outstanding Leadership Award, 1992. **Special Achievements:** ''Pathways to Freedom,'' video, 1990; ''Cancer Awareness Among African-Americans,'' 1991; ''Pathways to Freedom,'' guide 1992; ''Smoking and African-Americans,'' publication of Henry J Kaiser Foundation, 1992; ''Report of the Tobacco Policy Group,'' Tobacco Control: An International Journal, 1992; CDC ASTDR Honor Awd, Svc to the Public, 1995; NCCDPHP, Outstanding Performance in International Health, 1996. **Business Addr:** Associate Director for Program Development, Centers for Disease Control and Prevention, Office of Smoking and Health, 4770 Buford Hwy NE, K50, Atlanta, GA 30341, (404)488-5709.

ROBINSON, ROBERT LOVE, JR.
Accountant. **Personal:** Born Apr 21, 1961, Madera, CA; son of Evelyn Barnes Robinson and Robert L Robinson, Sr. **Educ:** The Univ of Pacific, BS 1982. **Career:** Price Waterhouse, auditor 1982-85; Sun Diamond Growers of CA, internal auditor 1985-86; The Grupe Co, Stockton, CA, sr accountant 1986-89, manager, accounting operations, 1989-92; staff consultant, Delta Systems Associates, 1993-. **Orgs:** Mem CA State Soc of CPA's 1985-; advisor, 1985-, president, 1989, Sacramento Valley Chapter Natl Assn of Black Accountants 1985-; mem UOP Alumni Assn 1986-. **Honors/Awds:** Award of Excellence, The Grupe Company, 1990. **Business Addr:** Staff Consultant, Delta Systems Associate, 2295 Gateway Oaks Dr, #165, Sacramento, CA 95833.

ROBINSON, ROBIN
Journalist. **Personal:** Born Aug 4, 1957, Chicago, IL; divorced. **Educ:** Journalism, BA, 1981. **Career:** KGTV, McGraw Hill, 1978-81; KMGH-TV, McGraw Hill, reporter, 1981-83; WBBM-TV, CBS, anchor, 1983-86; WFLD-TV, Fox, anchor, 1986-. **Orgs:** Chicago Assn of Black Journalists, 1985-; Child Abuse Prevention Services, spokeswoman, 1995; South Central comm Services, bd mem, 1993-. **Honors/Awds:** Natl Academy of TV Arts & Sciences, Chicago Chapter, Emmy Awards on Art Achievement, (5), 1985-87, 1993 (2); San Diego Chapter, Emmy Awards on Art Achievement, 1980. **Business Addr:** Anchor, Fox-News/WFLD - TV, 205 N Michigan Ave, Chicago, IL 60601.

ROBINSON, RONNIE W.
Apparel company executive. **Personal:** Born Dec 26, 1942, Louisville, KY; son of Donetta L Smith Robinson and Lawrence Robinson; married Veronices Gray, Jul 14, 1973; children: Kelli, Ronnie, Jr. **Educ:** Kentucky State Univ, Frankfort KY, BS, 1964. **Career:** ICI Americas Inc, Charlestown IN, mgr ballistics lab, 1965-71, mgr EEO, 1971-73, mgr employment, 1973-77; Johnson & Johnson, Chicago IL, mgr personel admin, 1977-82; Hart Schaffner & Marx, Chicago IL, dir human resources administration 1982-88, vice pres of human resources 1988-. **Orgs:** Bd mem, Society of Human Resources Professionals, 1982-83; bd mem, Cosmopolitan Chamber of Commerce, 1983-; mem, Chicago Urban Affairs Council, 1983-; chairman, Human Resources Committee, IL State Chamber of

Commerce, 1986-87; mem personnel comm, Chicago Youth Centers, 1986-; bd mem, Duncan YMCA, 1987-. **Business Addr:** Vice President of Human Resources, Hart Schaffner & Marx, 101 N Wacker Drive, Chicago, IL 60606.

ROBINSON, ROSALYN KAREN
Attorney. **Personal:** Born Dec 5, 1946, Norristown, PA. **Educ:** Dickinson Coll Carlisle, PA, AB 1968; Boston Coll Law Sch Newton, MA, JD 1973. **Career:** Chemical Bank NY, NY, mgmt trainee/ofcr's asst 1968-70; Hon Doris M Harris, Crt of Common Pleas, law clrk 1973-74; Philadelphia Dist Atty's Ofc, asst dist atty 1974-79; PA Dept of Aging, chf cnsl 1979-83c of Gen Cnsl, dpty gen cnsl 1983-. **Orgs:** Treas Brstrs Assn 1973-; mem Philadelphia Bar Assn 1973-; mem PA Bar Assn 1982-; mem Am Bar Assn 1979-83; cls chmn Dickinson Coll Annl Giving 1984; vice pres Dickinson Coll Alumni Cncl 1974-80; mem PA Coalition of 10 Black Women 1984-, Harrisburg Chap of Links Inc 1984-, Dickinson Coll Bd of Trustees 1985-; Alpha Kappa Alpha Sorority Inc, Rho Theta Omega Chapter 1990-. **Honors/Awds:** One of 79 to watch in 1979 Philadelphia Mag January 1979. **Business Addr:** Deputy General Counsel, Office of General Counsel, 17th Flr Harristown II, 333 Market St, Harrisburg, PA 17108.

ROBINSON, RUMEAL JAMES
Professional basketball player. **Personal:** Born Nov 13, 1966, Mandeville, Jamaica. **Educ:** Univ of Michigan, Ann Arbor, MI, 1986-90. **Career:** Atlanta Hawks, guard, 1990-92, New Jersey Nets, 1992-93; Charlotte Hornets, 1994; CBA: Rapid City Thrillers, 1994-95; Shreveport Crawdads, 1995; Connecticut Pride, 1995; NBA: Portland TrailBlazers, 1996; Los Angeles Lakers, 1996; Portland TrailBlazers, 1997; Detroit Pistons, 1997. **Special Achievements:** NBA Draft, First round pick, #10, 1990. **Business Phone:** (248)377-0100.

ROBINSON, S. BENTON
Business executive (retired). **Personal:** Born Jun 5, 1928, Parsons, KS; married Dymple O McIntyre; children: Benton, Karen, Arthur. **Educ:** WV St Coll, BS 1950; Univ of Chgo, MBA 1970. **Career:** Supreme Life Ins Co, dist mgr 1950-54, field auditor 1954-55, mgr field accounting 1955-62, vice pres controller 1962-70, first vice pres 1970-73 sr vice pres 1973, exec vp/sec 1980; BRASS Foundation Inc, controller 1984-91. **Orgs:** Asso Life Ofc Mgmt Assn; vice pres United Charities of Chgo, bd dir; Exec Prog Club Univ of Chgo, bd dir; mem Univ of IL Citizens Com; Alpha Phi Alpha Frat; 1971-72 co-chmn United Negro Coll Fund. **Military Serv:** USN 1946-48. **Home Addr:** 1641 E 92 St, Chicago, IL 60617.

ROBINSON, S. YOLANDA
Educational administrator. **Personal:** Born Oct 1, 1946, Columbus, OH; daughter of Lucy M and Rudolph V; children: Chad Heath. **Educ:** University of Massachusetts, Amherst, medicine, 1981. **Career:** Midwest Institute for Equal Education, administrative assistant, 1971; Institute for Black Community Research and Development, research coordinator, 1980-81; THe Ohio State University, administrative secretary, 1980-81, program coordinator, currently. **Orgs:** African-American Triumphs Consortium, president, 1992-; National Council for Black Studies, conference chair, 1978-; OSU Affirmative Action Committee, 1985; Ohio Black Political Assembly, vice pres, 1978-81; Cardinal 9 to 5, president, founder, 1985-86; Call VAC, board member, 1990. **Honors/Awds:** Natl Council for Black Studies President's Award, 1988; Coalition of 100 Black Women, Mwanawake, 1992. **Special Achievements:** Blue Chip Profile, 1992; International Business and Professional Women, 1990; editor: "Research Profiles," OSU Dept of Black Studies, 1982. **Business Addr:** Program Coordinator, The Ohio State Univ, 905 Mt Vernon Ave, Columbus, OH 43203, (614)292-4459.

ROBINSON, SAMUEL
Educational administrator. **Personal:** Born Dec 18, 1935, Memphis, TN; son of Sarah Robinson and Omar R Robinson Sr (deceased); married Hugh Ella Walker; children: Debra, Charlotte. **Educ:** TN State Univ, BS 1956, MS 1958; IN Univ, EdD 1974. **Career:** Lincoln Inst, dean of ed 1964-66; Lincoln School, principal 1967-70; Shawnee High School, principal 1970-73; Lincoln Found, exec dir 1974-; pres, currently. **Orgs:** Matl exec dir Phi Beta Sigma Ed Found 1980-; mem Sigma Phi Phi 1983-; bd mem Presbyterian Health Ed & Welfare Assoc 1982-, Black Achievers Assoc 1980-, Assoc of Black Found Exec 1974-, Louisville Presbyterian; chmn KY Humanities Council 1984-; Kentucky Center for the Arts, 1988-; Kentucky State Board of Education, 1991; bd of trustees, Bellarimme Coll, 1990; Outstanding Community Service, National Conference of Christians and Jews, 1993; KY Bd of Education; KY Civiliam Aide to the Sec of the Army. **Honors/Awds:** Recipient Outstanding Young Man Awd Louisville C of C 1963; Outstanding Young Educator Awd Shelbyville Jr C of C 1966; Disting Serv Awd Zeta Phi Beta 1974; Outstanding Citizen Awd Louisville Defender 1975; Comm Serv Awd Alpha Kappa Alpha 1976; Social Action Awd Phi Beta Sigma; Outstanding Black Achiever Awd Louisville 1980; Disting Citizen Awd Alpha Kappa Alpha 1980; Man of the Year Sigma Pi Phi 1986; Achiever of the Year Black Achievers Assn 1987; Berea College Community Service Award 1986. **Military Serv:** AUS sp4 1958-60. **Business Addr:** Pres, Lincoln Foundation, Inc, 233 W Broadway, Louisville, KY 40202.

ROBINSON, SANDRA HAWKINS
Attorney. **Personal:** Born Jul 17, 1951, Lynchburg, VA; daughter of Mary Alice Hawkins-Baker and William Sterlon Hawkins; divorced; children: Mary Alysia. **Educ:** Oberlin College, BA, 1973; Howard University Graduate School, attended, 1973-75; Catholic University School of Law, JD, 1982. **Career:** Robinson & Robinson, partner, attorney, 1985-87; Federal Election Commission, senior attorney, 1987-90; Jack H Olender & Associates PC, attorney, 1990-. **Orgs:** National Association of Black Women Attorneys, program coordinator, 1985-; National Bar Association; American Bar Association; Trial Lawyers Association of Metropolitan Washington, DC, board member, president-elect; Maryland Trial Lawyers Association; Washington Bar Association. **Business Addr:** Associate Attorney, Jack H Olender & Associates, PC, 1634 I Street NW, 11th Flr, Washington, DC 20006, (202)879-7777.

ROBINSON, SANDRA LAWSON
Physician, medical administrator. **Personal:** Born Mar 22, 1944, New Orleans, LA; daughter of Elvera Martin and Alvin J Lawson; married Carl Dayton Robinson (divorced); children: Michael David, Carla Marie. **Educ:** Howard Univ Clg Liberal Arts Washington, DC, BS 1965; Howard Univ Clg Medicine Washington, DC, MD 1969; Hlth Care Admn Tulane Univ Sch Pblc Hlth & Tropical Medicine New Orleans, LA, MPH 1977; Pediatric Intrnshp Childrns Hosp Natl Med Ctr Dist Columbia, 1969-70; Pediatric Resdnc Chldrns Hosp Natl Med Ctr Dist Columbia, 1970-71; Pediatric Residency Flwshp Ambulatory Care Univ CA San Francisco San Francisco Gen Hosp, 1971-72. **Career:** Neighborhood Health Clinics New Orleans, med dir 1973-77; Ambulatory Care/Outpatient Serv Charity Hosp, dir 1977-81; Minority Afrs LA State Med Ctr, coordinator 1979; Ambulatory Care Serv Childrens Hosp, dir 1981-84; LA State Univ & Tulane Univ Sch of Medicine, clncl asst prof of peds; Tulane Univ Sch Pblc Hlth & Tropical Med, adjunct asst prof; Dept of Hlth & Human Resources, sec/commissioner, 1984-88; Robinson Medical Group, vice president, 1988-92; Children's Med Care, president, 1992-. **Orgs:** Med cnsltnt to Lrng Disabilities Teams Pilot Proj Mission Area Sch Unified Sch Dist San Francisco 1971-72; team pedtrcn Family Clncs San Francisco Gen Hosp; mem Med Advsry & Sickle Cell Anemia Rsrch Found San Francisco; med cnsltnt of Sch & Behavoir Unit Mt Zion Hosp San Francisco, CA; Prvt Practice of Peds San Francisco 1972-73; Proposal Dev Comprehensive Hlth Serv New Orleans Parish Prison Inmates 1974; Common Hlth Problem Manual Neighborhood Hlth Clncs 1974; Coordination Preventive Medicine Pgm Natl Med Assc Convention 1974; mem Ross Roundtable Upper Respiratory Disease 1974; Project Analysis Paper New Orleans Neighborhood Hlth Clncs 1975; bd mem Kingsley House 1976-79; bd mem Family Serv Soc 1976-79; cnsltnt Westington Corp Headstart Pgm 1976-80; bd memNew Orleans Area Bayou River h Systms Agcy 1977-82; mem Plan Dev Com Hlth Systms Agcy 1978-82; mem Com Use of Human Subjects Tulane Univ 1974-; bd mem Urban League of Greater New Orleans 1967-82; bd mem Isidore Newman Sch 1978-88; board of administrators, Tulane University, 1989. **Honors/Awds:** Howard Univ Alumni Region V Awrd; Black Orgnztn for Ldrshp Dev Outstndg Comm Serv Awrd; Woman of the Year, National Association of Black Social Workers, 1987; The Scroll of Merit, National Medical Assn Award, 1988. **Business Addr:** President, Children's Medical Care, 2602 Ursulines Ave, New Orleans, LA 70119.

ROBINSON, SHARON PORTER
Government official. **Educ:** University of Kentucky (Lexington), doctorate, education. **Career:** Classroom teacher; National Education Association, program director; Office of Educational Research and Improvement, assistant secretary of education, currently. **Special Achievements:** First African American to fill the research and planning post within the Department of Education. **Business Addr:** Asst Secretary of Education, Office of Educational Research & Improvement, US Dept of Education, 555 New Jersey Ave, NW, Rm 602, Washington, DC 20208, (202)219-1385.

ROBINSON, SHERMAN
Business executive, consultant. **Personal:** Born Sep 16, 1932, Piqua, OH; son of Anna Lou Robison and Sherman Robinson; married Beverly J Clark; children: Tod, Tina, Tracy. **Educ:** Central St Coll, 1952-53; OH U, 1953-56, 58-59. **Career:** Sherman Robinson Inc, pres 1970-; Saylor, Rhoads Equip Co, designer, draftsman 1969-70; JG Richards & associates, draftsman, designer, vice pres 1961; Western Fixture Co, equip dealer 1959. **Orgs:** Consult Food Facilities Soc; asso mem AIA Rippledale Optimist Club; past pres Keystone Optimist Club 1972-73. **Honors/Awds:** Instns VF Awd 1975. **Military Serv:** AUS sp3 1956-58. **Business Addr:** 708 Bungalow Ct, Indianapolis, IN 46220.

ROBINSON, SMOKEY (WILLIAM JR.)
Musician, business executive. **Personal:** Born Feb 19, 1940, Detroit, MI; son of William Robinson Sr; married Claudette Rogers, Nov 7, 1959 (divorced 1985); children: Berry William, Tamla Claudette; children: Trey. **Educ:** Attended Jr Coll. **Career:** Detroit Nightclub, performer; Smokey Robinson & The Miracles, recording artist 1957-72; solo recording artist, 1972-; Big Time, exec producer 1977; Motown Record Corp, vice pres; has made numerous television appearances, including his own special in 1971; appeared in Broadway in "An Evening With Smokey Robinson," 1985. **Honors/Awds:** Author, Smokey: Inside My Life, 1989; albums with The Miracles: Hi, We're the Miracles, 1961, Shop Around, 1962, Doin' Mickey's Monkey, 1963, The Fabulous Miracles, 1964, Going to a Go Go, 1964, Away We Go, 1965, Make It Happen, 1968, Special Occasion, 1969, Time Out, 1970, Four in Blue, 1970, Smokey and the Miracles, 1971, The Miracles, 1977; solo albums: Renaissance, 1973, Smokey, 1973, Pure Smokey, 1974, A Quiet Storm, 1974, City of Angels, 1974, Love Machine, 1975, Smokey's Family Robinson, 1975, Power of the Music, 1977, Deep in My Soul, 1977, Love Breeze, 1978, Warm Thoughts, 1980, Being with You, 1981, Yes It's You, 1981, Touch the Sky, 1983, Essar, 1984; Rock and Roll Hall of Fame, 1986; Songwriters Hall of Fame, 1986; Grammy Award for "Just to See Her," 1987. **Business Addr:** Vice President, Motown Record Corp, 5750 Wilshire Blvd, Ste 300, Los Angeles, CA 90036-3697.

ROBINSON, STEVE
Basketball coach. **Career:** University of Tulsa, head basketball coach; Florida State Univ, head basketball coach, 1997-. **Special Achievements:** First African American coach at Florida State Univ; only African American coach in the Atlantic Coast Conference. **Business Addr:** Head Basketball Coach, Florida State University, Attn Steven Robinson, PO Box 2195, Tallahassee, FL 32316, (904)644-2525.

ROBINSON, THELMA MANIECE
Educator. **Personal:** Born May 1, 1938, Tuscaloosa, AL; married. **Educ:** AL St U, BS 1960; Univ of AL Tuscaloosa, MA 1970, currently working toward EdS. **Career:** TVA, personnel clk, examining officer; Florence Bd of Edn, presently guidance counselor. **Orgs:** Mem Am Personnel & Guidance Assn; Am Sch Counselor Assn; AL PGA & AL SCA; st sec for AL PGA; mem NEA; AEA; Florence Educ Assn; pres Delta Sigma Theta Sor; AL Assn of Univ Women; Florence League of Women Voters; mem Lauderdale Co Chpt, ARC, treas; vice pres Muscle Shoals Assn for Mental Hlth. **Honors/Awds:** Chosen Outstanding Secondary Educator 1974. **Business Addr:** Senior Guidance Counselor, Coffee High School, North Cherry St, Florence, AL 35630.

ROBINSON, THOMAS DONALD
Hospital executive. **Educ:** Marshall Univ, BBA 1964; Georgia State Univ, MHA 1977. **Career:** Welch Emergency Hosp, administrator 1977-80; Parkway Regional Medical Ctr, asst administrator 1980-84; Newport News General Hosp, administrator 1984-85; Tyrone Hosp, chief exec officer 1985-92; Pennsylvania State University, Continuing Education Faculty, 1988-; Quoram Health Resources, Robinson Group, Pittsburgh Office, group, vp, currently. **Orgs:** Fellow Amer Coll of Health Execs 1981-; bd Tyrone Salvation Army 1986-, past pres Tyrone Rotary Club 1986-; past pres Tyrone Area Chamber of Commerce 1987-; bd Blair County United Way 1987-; public affairs comm Hospital Assoc of Western PA 1987-; Mellon Bank, regional advisory board; Blair County Human Services Board; advisory board, McDowell College of Business; advisory board, Marshall University. **Honors/Awds:** Fellow, American College of Healthcare Executives. **Business Addr:** Group VP, Quoram Health Resources, 101 N Meadows Drive, Bldg 200, Ste 230, Wexford, PA 15090, (412)934-2882.

ROBINSON, VERNEDA
Executive recruiter. **Personal:** Born Dec 17, 1960, Memphis, TN; daughter of Rev CL & Wilma Bachus; married Curtis Robinson, Mar 30, 1991; children: Bria, Bryan. **Educ:** Washburn Univ, BBA, 1985; Webster, Univ, MA, 1992, MBA, 1995. **Career:** Western Resources, Inc, vp of customer svc, 1990-94; Missouri Gas Energy, vp of customer svc & accounting, 1994; V Robinson & Company, Inc, president/CEO, 1995-. **Orgs:** Jr Achievement Middle America, bd mem; Gem Theater, bd mem; Kansas City Public TV, bd mem; Negro Leagues Baseball Museum, bd mem; National Association of Women Business Owners, mem; Kansas City friends of Alvin Riley, mem; Greater Kansas city Chamber of Commerce, mem; Minority Supplier Coun, mem. **Honors/Awds:** Minority Enterprize Development, New Business of the Year, 1997. **Special Achievements:** Featured by Fox 4 News, Women On the Move Segment, 1997. **Business Addr:** President/CEO, V Robinson & Co., Inc, 1044 Main St, Ste 600, Kansas City, MO 64105, (816)421-4944.

ROBINSON, VERNON EDWARD
Government official. **Personal:** Born Jul 21, 1959, Florence, SC; son of Edward G & Madaline H Robinson; married Barbara J Robinson, Jan 25, 1992. **Educ:** Claflin Coll, BA, 1982; SC State Univ, MA, 1984; Interdenominational Theological Ctr, Morehouse School of Religion, pursuing MDiv, 1994. **Career:** SC Vocational Rehabilitation Dept, evaluator, 1984-87; SC Dept of Mental Health, counselor, 1987; Babcock Ctr Inc, unit supervisor, 1987-90; Friendship Ctr, Inc, group leader, 1987-90; Babcock Ctr Inc, prog mgr, 1989-90; Fulton County Board of Education, teaching assist, 1993-94; US Dept of Justice, Federal Bureau of Prisions, federal officer, 1994-. **Orgs:** Prince Hall Lodge of Free & Accepted Masons, 1991; Pi Gamma Mu International Social Science Honor Society, 1979; Assn of Study of Afro-Amer Life & History, 1978.

ROBINSON, WALKER LEE
Educator. **Personal:** Born Oct 13, 1941, Baltimore, MD; son of Wilma L Walker and Edward F Robinson; married Mae Meads Robinson, Apr 9, 1966; children: Kimberly Yvette, Walker Lee Jr. **Educ:** Morgan State College, BS, 1962; Univ of Maryland Medical School, 1970; Univ of London, Fellowship, 1975. **Career:** Univ of Maryland Medical School, Baltimore, MD, assistant professor, 1976-90; Univ of Maryland Medical School, Baltimore, MD, associate professor, division of neurosurgery, 1990-97; Seton Hall School of Graduate Medical Education, Pediatric Neurosurgeons, head. **Orgs:** President, Clarence S Green, Maryland Neuro Surgical Soc, 1984-87; president, Baltimore Urban Services Foundation, 1986-87; president, Black Faculty & Staff Assn Univ of Maryland, 1989-90; member, board of directors, Variety Club of Baltimore, 1988; member, board of directors, Urban Cardiology Research Center, 1986-91; Intl Soc for Pediatric Neurosurgery; fellow, American Coll of Surgeons; fellow, American Academy of Pediatrics; American Society for Pediatric Neurosurgery Univ of Maryland Medical Systems, Cancer Committee, 1989-94. **Honors/Awds:** Paul Harris Fellow, The Rotary International, 1989; Honoree, AFRAM Expo-City of Baltimore, 1988, 1997; Fellow, Stroke Council, American Heart Association; American Coll of Surgeons, fellow; American Academy of Pediatrics, fellow; African American heritage Society, Living Legend Honoree, 1995; Fund for Educational Excellence, Distinguished Alumnus Award, 1991; Consultant NIH, NCI, CDC. **Business Addr:** Professor, Head of Ped Neurosurgery, Seton Hall School of Medical Education, 65 James St, Edison, NJ 08818.

ROBINSON, WALTER G.
Educator. **Personal:** Born Oct 16, 1928, Chgo; married Jean Dorsett; children: Walter III, Waddell Craig, Keith Jones. **Educ:** Lincoln U, BS 1955; Univ of MO Social Work, MSW 1965; So IL U, PhD 1976. **Career:** Rehabilitation Institute Southern IL Univ, asst prof, asst to dir, former dir Black Amer Studies, asst to pres, asst to chancellor, asst to vice pres for Area & Internatl Serv Coordinator Univ Serv to Carbondale & Environs 1968-73; Neighborhood Youth Corp St Clair, Madison Co, dir; Social Work Serv, Child Welfare Serv, MO Div of Welfare, St Louis, supvr 1962-68. **Orgs:** Mem bd dirs Nat Council on Aging; bd dirs So IL Instrctl TV Assn; elected Jackson Bd of Comm; Certified IL Social Worker; cert rehab couns & mem NASW; AAVP; Nat Rehab Assn; Nat Assn Black Social Workers; Nat Assn Non-white Rehab Workers; Assn Black Psychologist; African Assn Black Studies; African Heritage Studies Assn; Buc Merit Acad; IL Council Educ Svc; Nat Caucus on Black Aging; IL St Adv & Council Title I Higher Act 1965; memNAACP; Omega Psi Phi Frat; Phi Delta Kappa Frat. **Honors/Awds:** Recip Merit Comm Serv Awd E St Louis 1968; Merit Awd for Youth Prog E St Louis 1967; listed Comm Ldrs & Noteworth Ams 1973-74. **Military Serv:** AUSR capt 1968. **Business Addr:** Rehabilitation Inst, So IL Univ, Carbondale, IL 62901.

ROBINSON, WILL
Sports administrator. **Educ:** West Virginia State College; University of Michigan, master's degree. **Career:** Cass Technical High School, teacher; Miller High School, teacher; Pershing High School, teacher; Ilinois State University, educator, starting 1970; Detroit Pistons, administrative assistant to general manager, currently. **Special Achievements:** First African American head coach in top college basketball. **Business Addr:** Administrative Assistant to General Manager, Detroit Pistons, The Palace, 2 Championship Dr, Auburn Hills, MI 48326, (313)377-0100.

ROBINSON, WILLIAM
Federal official. **Personal:** Born Jun 30, 1920, Harrisburg, PA; son of Saddie Robinson and Earnest Robinson; married Beatrice S; children: Paula, Evelyn, Nancy. **Educ:** Lincoln Univ, BA; Pennsylvania State Extension Courses, accounting; Air Force & Army, management courses. **Career:** US Civil Service Air Force & Army, supply & logistics management; real estate sales. **Orgs:** Former mem Harrisburg City Council; former mem Vestry St Stephens; Cathedral Dioces of Central PA; mem Bd of Realtors PA & Natl Assn of Realtors; mem Harristown Bd of Directors; Comm on Ministry Episcopal Dioces of Central PA; life mem NAACP and Omega Psi Phi; lay deputy 1985/1988 Gen Natl Convention of Episcopal Church; bd mem PA Council of Churches, trustee, Lincoln Univ, PA.

ROBINSON, WILLIAM ANDREW
Physician. **Personal:** Born Jan 31, 1943, Philadelphia, PA; son of Lillian Robinson and Colonial Robinson; married Jacqueline E Knight; children: William Jr, David. **Educ:** Hampton Inst, BA 1964; Meharry Medical Coll, MD 1971; Johns Hopkins School of Hygiene & Public Health, MPH 1973. **Career:** George W Hubbard Hosp Nashville, emergency room physician 1972; Food and Drug Admin, reviewing medical officer 1973-75; Health Resources & Services Admin, medical officer 1975-80, deputy bureau dir 1980-87, chief medical officer 1987-89; Public Health Service, Office of Minority Health, dir 1989-91; Health Resources and Service Admin, acting administrator, 1993-94, chief medical officer, 1994-; Center for Quality, HRSA, dir, 1997-. **Orgs:** Mem Amer Public Health Assn, Sr Executives Assn, Federal Physicians Assn; Amer Acad of Family Physicians, National Medical Assn, American Medical Assn. **Honors/Awds:** Temporary health consultant US House of Representatives; Diplomate Natl Bd of Medical Examiners; Special Recognition Awd Public Health Serv 1980; Sr Exec Service US Govt 1984; Distinguished Alumnus in Medicine, Meharry Medical College, 1991; HRSA Administrator's Awd for Excellence 1987; Meritorious Executive, Sr Exec Service; Delta Omega Honorary Public Health Society, 1993; Hildrus Poindexter Memorial Award, 1994. **Military Serv:** AUS Medical Service Corps capt 1964-67; Natl Defense Medal, Army Commendation Medal 1967. **Home Addr:** 16608 Frontenac Terrace, Rockville, MD 20855. **Business Addr:** Director/Chief Medical Officer, Center for Quality, Health Resource & Services Administration, 5600 Fishers Ln, Rm 14-39, Rockville, MD 20857.

ROBINSON, WILLIAM EARL
City government official, consultant. **Personal:** Born Nov 18, 1940, Morton, MS; son of Gladys Robinson and P B Robinson; divorced; children: Jacqueline, William E II. **Educ:** MS Valley State Univ, Soc Sci & Pol Sci 1958-62. **Career:** North Las Vegas Chamber of Commerce, hon dir 1972-82; City of North Las Vegas, councilman 1983-; School Success Monitor Clark County School Dist. **Orgs:** Gaming policy comm State of NV 1973-81; life mem US Jaycees, NV Jaycees, North Las Vegas Jaycees; hon dir North Las Vegas Chamber of Commerce 10 yrs; second vice pres NV League of Cities; first vice pres NV League of Cities; pres, NV League of Cities, 1987-88; chairman of the board, NV League of Cities, 1988-89; chairman, North Las Vegas Housing Authority 1988-; State Gaming Policy Committee; board of directors, North Las Vegas Democratic Club; chairman, Crime Prevention Task Force; Clark County Health District; Environmental Quality Policy Review Board; steering committee, National League of Cities, CED; Job Training Board; chmn, Clark County Health Dist; NLV Library Dist. **Honors/Awds:** Jaycee of the Year North Las Vegas Jaycees 1972, 1974, 1975; Appointed to the State Gaming Policy Comm by Gov of NV 1973; JCI Senate 28596 1976; One of the Hundred Most Influential Blacks in NV 1984-87; Public Official of the Year, Nevada League of Cities, 1989. **Home Addr:** 2815 Bassler St, North Las Vegas, NV 89030.

ROBINSON, WILLIAM HENRY
Educator. **Personal:** Born Oct 24, 1922, Newport, RI; son of Julia W. S. Robinson; married Doris Carol Johnson, Jun 8, 1948. **Educ:** New York Univ, BA, 1951; Boston Univ, MA, 1957; Harvard Univ, PhD, 1964. **Career:** Prairie View Agr & Mech Coll, Prairie View TX, English instructor, 1951-53; NC Agr & Tech State Univ, Greensboro, mem of English faculty, 1956-61, 1964-66; Boston Univ, MA, assoc prof of English & humanities, 1966-68; Howard Univ, Washington DC, prof of English, 1968-70; Rhode Is Coll, Providence, prof of English and dir black studies, 1970-85; vis prof of Amer & English lit, Brown Univ, 1987—. **Orgs:** Bd mem, RI Commn on the Humanities; Bd mem, RI Black Heritage Soc; Intl Lecture Platform Assn; mem, NSLCAH; Nat Com on Black Studies; NAACP; Urban League; Coll Language Arts Assn; Assn for Study of Negro Life & Culture. **Honors/Awds:** Editor of Early Black American Poets, W.C. Brown, 1969, Early Black American Prose, W.C. Brown, 1970, Nommo: An Anthol of Modern Black African & Black American Lit, Macmillan, 1972, Critical Essays on Phillis Wheatley, G.K. Hall, 1982; author of Phillis Wheatly in the Black American Beginnings, Broadside, 1975, Phillis Wheatley: A Bio-Bibliography, G.K. Hall, 1981, Phillis Wheatley and Her Writings, Garland, 1984; also autho of num TV, stage, radio scripts; contr to journals. **Military Serv:** US Army, 1942-45. **Business Addr:** English Dept, Rhode Island College, 600 Mt Pleasant Ave, Providence, RI 02908.

ROBINSON, WILLIAM JAMES (BILLY)
Clergyman. **Personal:** Born Feb 24, 1933, New Rochelle, NY; son of Millie Royster Robinson (deceased) and Thomas Robinson (deceased); divorced; children: Daryl Anderson. **Educ:** Trinity College & Seminary, Sprinfield, IL, DDiv, 1972. **Career:** Bronx Dist, superintendent; Milinary Shop, owner; The Garden of Prayer Ch of God in Christ, bishop, currently. **Orgs:** Pres Bronx Shepherds Restoration Corp 1989; bd of dirs, Tremont Day Care Center; mem United Black Church Appeal; mem bd Intl Home & Foreign Mission; professional gospel singer for 30 years; 8 religious music albums; active in police & comm relations in 48th precinct; composer, author "Come and Stroll down Blessing Boulevard"; latest record-composer "Ooh Whee"; pres, 4th Saturday Conference, 1st Eccl Jurisdiction COGIC Eastern NY. **Honors/Awds:** Largest Pentecostal Church in the Bronx; Awd for Best Choir of 1984 Gospel Acad Awds by ballots; award Bronx Shepherds Restoration Corp 1986; proclamation from Borough president 1988; Pillar of Fire Coll & Pent Seminary of York Eng, Honorary Degrees: DCnL, 1970, DD, 1972, DHL, 1979; Proclamation, Councilman, 9th District, Bronx, 1989. **Home Addr:** 1281 E 223rd St, Bronx, NY 10466-5860.

ROBINSON, WILLIAM PETERS, JR.
State official. **Personal:** Born Oct 14, 1942, Washington, DC; son of William P Robinson Sr and Agnes R Watson Butler; married Sylvia F Thompson, 1966; children: William P III, Trevor J, Justin M, Danica A. **Educ:** Morehouse College, BA, 1964; Harvard University, LLB, 1967. **Career:** Commonwealth's Attorney's Office, assistant, 1968-70; assistant attorney general, 1970-72; Mason & Robinson Ltd, partner, 1972-78; Robinson, Eichler, Zaleski & Mason, partner, 1978-; State of Virginia, District 90, state representative, 1981-. **Orgs:** Virginia State Legislative Black Caucus; Friends of the Norfolk Juvenile & Domestic Relations Court; Norfolk City Democratic Committee & Conference of Southern Legislators; Industrial Development Authority of Norfolk; Tidewater Area Business & Contractors Association; Twin City Bar Association; Norfolk-Portsmouth Bar Association; Old Dominion Bar Association; Virginia State Bar Association; Virginia Trial Lawyers Association; Association of Trial Lawyers of America; Southeastern Virginia Advisory Council for the Arts; Virginia Association of Black Elected Officials. **Special Achievements:** Author: "Handling Narcotic Cases," Law Enforcement Training Manual, 1979. **Business Addr:** State Representative, Virginia House of Representatives, 256 W Freemason St, Norfolk, VA 23510, (804)786-8826.

ROBINSON, WILLIE C.
Business executive. **Personal:** Born Dec 13, 1934, Dunn, NC; son of Willa Moore Robinson and John L Robinson; married Ojetta Dowdy; children: William, Kevin, Lewis. **Educ:** Agr & Tech Coll, BS; Univ of Bridgeport, MA; Tchrs Coll Columbia NY, EdD, LHD. **Career:** Yale Univ, dir mid-career prog in city school admin 1971-74, acting dir of teaching prep prog 1974-75; Yale Child Study Prog, research assoc 1975-76, special asst to pres 1976-77; FL Meml Coll Miami, pres; William C Robinson and Asociates, pres, currently. **Orgs:** Bd of govs & exec comm Gr Miami C of C 1979-80; vice chairman Gr Miami C of C 1983-84; vice pres exec bd Miami Dade Co Water & Sewer Auth 1979-80; bd of dirs Dade Co United Way 1979-80; past pres bd dir Urban League of Greater New Haven; dir & mem exec bd United Negro Coll Fund; dir Eastern Airlines Inc, Southeast Bank Holding Co, Southeast Bank NA, Sharon Steel Corp, assoc mem Orange Bowl Comm; past pres Alpha Phi Alpha Frat Inc Eta Alpha Lambda Chapt; dir NVF Co. **Honors/Awds:** Outstanding Young Men of Amer Natl Jr C of C 1967; consult Tchrs Coll Columbia Univ Tchrs Corps; Outstanding Leadership Awd Dade Co NAACP; OutstandingCom Serv Awd Greater Miami Chap Alpha Phi Omega; Silver Medallion for serv to brotherhood Natl Conf of Christians and Jews 1985; Dr Willie C Robinson Day April 17 1982 City of Hialeah.

ROBINSON-FORD, DENISE RENEE
Organization executive. **Personal:** Born Apr 24, 1953, Detroit, MI; daughter of Josephine Wilson Holloway and Beryl Holloway; married Rufus Ford, May 23, 1987; children: Raymond, Toya, Tamara Robinson. **Educ:** Wayne State University, Detroit, MI, 1990; Word of Faith Christian Center, Detroit, MI, Ministry, 1990. **Career:** Hudson's Dept Store, Southfield, MI, area sales mgr, 1972-75; RuDee's Floral Expressions, Detroit, MI, florist, 1986-; Saving Our Kids, Detroit, MI, exec dir, 1986-. **Orgs:** Girl Scout leader, Girl Scouts of America, 1990; exec dir, Saving Our Kids, 1986-; parent volunteer, Truman High, 1991; member, Beaubien Parent Club, Beaubien Jr High, 1990. **Honors/Awds:** Community Service Award, Michigan Coalition Safety Belt Use, 1988, Burger King, Keys Group, 1988, Hometown Hero, WJBK-TV2, 1990, Michigan Governor Blanchard, 1989, 1990, Detroit City Council, 1987.

ROBINSON-JACOBS, KAREN DENISE
Journalist. **Personal:** Born Aug 21, 1956, Chicago, IL; daughter of Dymple Orita McIntyre Robinson and S Benton Robinson; married Ralph M. Jacobs. **Educ:** Univ of Illinois, Champaign, IL, BS, journalism, 1979; Univ of Wisconsin, Milwaukee, Milwaukee, WI, 1983-85. **Career:** The Champaign News-Gazette, Champaign, IL, reporter, 1977-80; Milwaukee Journal, Milwaukee, WI, assistant metro editor, assistant state editor, north suburban editor, reporter, 1980-89; Los Angeles Times, Los Angeles, CA, assistant metro editor, 1989-91, Times New Media Unit, associate editor, 1991-. **Orgs:** Bd of directors, Black Journalists Assn of Southern California, 1991-; vice president, Wisconsin Black Media Assn, 1982-89; bd of directors, Hansberry Sands Theatre Co, 1986-89; member, Delta Sigma Theta Sorority, 1976-; Volunteer, United Negro College Fund, 1988-; chair, Minority Editors Caucus: Los Angeles Times, 1990-. **Honors/Awds:** Black Achiever Award, YMCA, 1986. **Business Addr:** Associate Editor, Times New Media Unit, Los Angeles Times, Times Mirror Square, Los Angeles, CA 90053, (213)237-4751.

ROBINSON-WALKER, MARY P.
Library services administrator. **Personal:** Born in Pittsburgh, PA; daughter of Eula Robinson and William Robinson; divorced. **Educ:** Iron City College; Rose Demars Legal Sec School; French Institute; Henry George School of Social Sciences; Hunter College. **Career:** Amer Comm on Africa, sec 1960-64; Artist Civil Rights Asst Fund, special projects dir 1965-66; Savings Bank Assoc of NY, sec 1967-68; Metro Applied Rsch Ctr, sec 1968-70; Black Economic Rsch Ctr, admin asst 1970-76; Pearl Bailey Review, Phillip-Fort Dancers, former professional dancer, dance instr; Ctrs for Reading and Writing of the New York Public Library. **Orgs:** Emcee Comm on Discrimination in Housing; performed by New York City Youth House, New School for Soc Rsch, US Naval Hosp, West-

ern PA Psych Hosp; mem of bd of dir Harlem Philharmonic Soc 1969-; admin asst 21st Century Found; co-chmn American Red Cross, Harlem Div 1974-; mem Central Baptist Church, 1993-.

ROBY, REGINALD HENRY
Professional football player. **Personal:** Born Jul 30, 1961, Waterloo, IA; married Melissa; children: Brittany, Bry, Julian. **Educ:** Univ of Iowa, attended. **Career:** Miami Dolphins, punter, 1983-92; Washington Redskins, 1993-94; Tampa Bay Buccaneers, 1995; Houston Oilers, 1996; Tennessee Oilers, 1997-. **Orgs:** Charity Work for Special Olympics, United Way, Make-a-Wish Foundation, Shriners Hospital, and National Drug Awareness Program. **Honors/Awds:** Played in Pro Bowl, 1984, 1989, 1994; NFL Players Assn, NFL Kicker of the Year, 1984. **Business Addr:** Professional Football Player, Tennessee Oilers, c/o Baptist Sports Park, 7640 H 70-5, Nashville, TN 37221.

ROCHA, JOSEPH RAMON, JR.
Educator. **Personal:** Born Dec 4, 1925, Boston, MA; son of Odie L. and Joseph R.; married Enid Josephine Terrelonge; children: Ramona J Wilbun, Roxana L, Jeffrey R. **Educ:** Northeastern Univ, BS 1948; New York Univ, MBA 1954; Howard Univ, JD 1960; Univ of IA, PhD 1966. **Career:** Morgan State Univ, asst to pres & asst prof 1963-65; Ball State Univ, assoc prof of econ 1965-73; Univ of Rhode Island, special asst to pres 1973-76; Chicago State Univ, prof of econ & chmn 1976-77; Univ of Lowell, prof of mgmt. **Orgs:** Labor arbitrator AAA & FMCS Natl Panels 1969-; training consultant City of Lowell, MA 1977-81; bd of dir Wilbun Entrepreneurs Inc Memphis 1984; mem Kappa Alpha Psi Frat 1947; pres Community Action Agency Delaware Co, IN 1969-71; mem IRRA; bd of dirs Elder Serv of the Merrimack Valley Inc Lawrence MA 1986-. **Honors/Awds:** Delivered papers at various professional meetings; published articles on mgmt, labor relations & training. **Military Serv:** AUS corporal 1950-52. **Business Addr:** Professor of Management, Univ of Lowell, One Univ Ave, Lowell, MA 01854.

ROCHESTER, GEOF
Travel industry executive. **Personal:** Born Sep 20, 1959, St Michael, Barbados; son of Elma I Rochester and Edric G Rochester. **Educ:** Georgetown University, BSBA, 1981; University of Pennsylvania Wharton School, MBA, 1985. **Career:** Procter & Gamble, sales, Folgers Coffee, 1981-83, product manager, Bain de Soleil, Oil of Olay, Clearasil, 1985-89; Marriott Hotels, director business transient marketing, 1989-91; Radisson Hotels, sr vice pres marketing, 1991-. **Orgs:** Georgetown University Alumni, board of governors, advisory council, 1990-92; Hoya Hoop Club, board of directors, 1990-92. **Business Addr:** Sr VP of Marketing, Radisson Hotels International, 12755 State Hwy 55, Minneapolis, MN 55459, (612)449-3460.

ROCHON, LELA
Actress. **Personal:** Born in Torrance, CA. **Educ:** California State University, BA, communications. **Career:** Fred Amsel & Associates Inc, modeling: Spudette for Bud Lite TV commercial; dancer: music videos for Lionel Richie, Luther Vandross, and Levert; television: appeared on "The Cosby Show," "Amen," "Facts of Life," "21 Jumpstreet," and "A Bunny's Tale"; films include: Harlem Nights; Boomerang; Waiting to Exhale; Mr and Mrs Loving; The Chamber; Gang Related; Knock Off. **Business Addr:** Actress, c/o Gersh, 10100 Santa Monica Blvd, 25th Fl, Beverly Hills, CA 90210, (310)274-6611.

ROCK, CHRIS
Actor, comedian. **Personal:** Born 1968, Bedford-Stuyvesant, Brooklyn, NY; son of Rose Rock and Julius Rock (deceased); married Malaak Compton, 1996. **Career:** Stand-up comedian, actor, experience includes: Beverly Hills Cop II; I'm Gonna git You Sucka, 1988; Comedy's Dirtiest Dozen, 1989; New Jack City, 1991; Saturday Night Live, series regular, 1990-; Boomerang, 1992; CB4, 1993; Born Suspect, comedy album; 1996 Billboard Music Awards, host; HBO, "The Chris Rock Show.". **Honors/Awds:** CableAce, Award, Best Entertainment Host, Best Variety Special/Series, The Chris Rock Show, 1998. **Business Addr:** Actor/Comedian, c/o HBO, 1100 Avenue of the Americas, New York, NY 10036, (212)512-1000.

ROCKETT, DAMON EMERSON
Elected official & business executive. **Personal:** Born Nov 13, 1938, Chicago, IL; married Darlene Sykes; children: Deborah, Sean Damon. **Educ:** Drake Univ, BS/BA 1960. **Career:** Allstate Ins Co, claims super 1964-69; City of Harvey, comm public health & safety; IL Bell Telephone Co, bus office mgr 1969-80, phone ctr mgr 1980-81, staff-assessment ctr 1981-82, comm relations mgr; South Suburban College, academic skills advisor, currently. **Orgs:** Pres Harvey Rotary Club 1971-80; mem S Suburban Human Relations Comm 1973; bd mem & policy comm chmn Thornton Comm Coll 1975-79; bd mem CEDA 1980; YMCA Task Force 1984; mem Rotary Club of Park Forest 1984-; mem S Suburban Assn of Commerce & Industry 1984-; mem S Suburban Mayors & Mgrs Assn 1984-; bd mem Red Cross 1985; chmn African Relief Campaign 1985; mem NAACP. **Honors/Awds:** Ten Outstanding Young People Harvey Jaycees 1975; Outstanding Citizen UHURU Black Student Org Thornton Comm Coll 1979; Outstanding Citizen S Suburban Chamber of Commerce & Industry 1979. **Home Addr:** 731 Sunset Dr, Glenwood, IL 60425. **Business Addr:** Academic Skills Advisor, South Suburban College, 15800 S State St, South Holland, IL 60473.

RODDY, HOWARD W.
Health administrator. **Personal:** Born Feb 28, 1950, Nashville, TN; son of Marie Bright Roddy and Howard Walden Roddy; married Donna Norwood Roddy; children: Howard Carthie, John Travis. **Educ:** Austin Peay State Univ, BS 1971; East TN State Univ, MS Environ Health Admin 1974. **Career:** Chattanooga-Hamilton Co Health Dept, environmentalist & dir of vector control project 1971-76; Alton Park/Dodson Ave Comm Health Ctrs, asst admin for planning/evaluation 1976-81; Chattanooga Hamilton Co Health Dept, administrator 1981-. **Orgs:** Mem Amer Public Health Assn 1977-; mem TN Public Health Assn 1981-; board member Chattanooga-Hamilton County Air Pollution Control Bureau 1983-96; treas Leadership Chattanooga Alumni Assoc 1985-89; bd mem exec comm Chattanooga Area Urban League 1986-93; board member United Way of Greater Chattanooga 1987-92, 1995-97; president, Friends of the Festival, Inc, 1991-92; president, Tennessee Public Health Assn, 1991-92; board member, Chattanooga Venture, 1991-96; Bd, East TN Area Health Education Center, 1991-97, president, 1993-95; First vice president, Southern Health Assn, 1995; 100 Black Men of America, Inc-Chattanooga Chapter, 1992-; president, Development Corp of Orchard Knob, 1995-; board member, Volunteer Community School, 1993-96; Chancellor's roundtable Univ TN at Chattanooga, 1991-94; bd mem, Univ of Chattanooga Foundation, 1997-; bd mem, Community Foundation of Greater Chattanooga. **Honors/Awds:** Omega Man of the Year Kappa Iota Chapter of Omega Psi Phi Frat Inc 1981; Omega Citizen of the Year 1992; Honorary Staff Mem State of TN 28th Dist Adv Comm 1982. **Business Addr:** Administrator, Chattanooga-Hamilton Co Hlth, 921 E Third St, Chattanooga, TN 37403, (423)209-8000.

RODEZ, ANDREW LAMARR
Chief of police. **Personal:** Born Oct 9, 1931, Chicago, IL; married Patricia Lander; children: Angelina, Andy, Rita. **Educ:** VA Union Univ, AB; NE IL State Univ, MA; MI State Univ, PhD; FBI Natl Acad NW Traffic Inst, Diploma. **Career:** Off-The-Street-Boys Club, group worker 1956-57; Cook County Welfare Dept, case worker 1957-58; Evanston Police Dept, police officer 1958; Chicago Bd of Educ, teacher 1958-64; Benton Harbor, chief of police 1973-79; Benton Harbor Area School Dist, asst principal 1979-82; Maywood Police Dept, chief of police 1982-. **Orgs:** Charter mem Natl Org Black Law Enforcement Reg IV, vice pres NOBLE 1984; adj prof Triton Coll; mem Kappa Alpha Psi, NW Univ Traffic Inst Alumni, ChessmenSocial/Civic Org, FBI Natl Acad Alumni Assoc, Phi Delta Kappa Ed, IL Assoc Chiefs of Police, West Suburban Chiefs of Police, VFW, NAACP; pres Task ForceYouth Motivation 1970. **Honors/Awds:** Outstanding Citizen Awd NAACP 1970; Model Cities Awd 1974; Outstanding Alumni Awd Kappa Alpha Psi 1968; Bicent Awd Lake MI Coll 1976; All CIAA Football &Track 1951-52; Negro Coll All-Amer 1952. **Business Addr:** Chief of Police, Maywood Police Dept, 125 S 6th Ave, Maywood, IL 60153.

RODGERS, ANTHONY RECARIDO, SR.
Law enforcement officer. **Personal:** Born Apr 2, 1951, Jacksonville, FL; son of Clara Lee Maddox Washington and Clarence Rodgers; divorced; children: Anthony Jr, Martisha, Edward, Eric. **Educ:** Florida Jr Coll, Jacksonville, FL, 1971-72; Northeast Florida Criminal Justice Educ & Training Center, 1973. **Career:** Duval County Sheriffs Office, Jacksonville FL, School Attendance Officer, Abandoned Property Officer, Certified Radar Operator, Field Training Officer, Deputy Sheriff 1973-, Honor Guard 1973-, School Resource Officer, 1990-; PAL Officer, 1996-. **Orgs:** Mem, Jacksonville Urban League, 1973; president, Jacksonville Brotherhood of Police Officers, Inc, 1978; President Bliss Sertoma Club, 1979; treasurer, Viking Athletic Booster Club of Raines High School, 1980; mem, Jacksonville Job Corps Community Relations Council, 1983; pres, Jacksonville Branch NAACP, 1995-96; mem, Moncrief Improvement Assn, 1984; vp, Southern Region of Natl Black Police Assn, 1996; JUST US Comm on Community Problems, 1986; mem, FL Community Coll at Jacksonville Advisory Bd on New Direction, 1987; Jacksonville Brotherhood of Police Officers, Inc, president, 1981-91; 100 Black Men of Jacksonville, charter member, 1992; Northeast Florida Community Action Agency, Inc, board of directors, 1992; pres, Edward Waters Coll, Tiger Athletic Booster Club, 1994. **Honors/Awds:** Community Service Awd, Operation Respect, 1981; Outstanding Sec Northwest Jacksonville Sertoma Club, 1984; Community Service Awd, Northeast FL Community Action Agency, 1984; Achievement Awd, Natl Black Police Assn Southern Region, 1985; Charlie Sea Police Officer of the Year, Jacksonville Brotherhood of Police Officers, 1988; Community Svc Role Model, El Bethel El Divine Holiness Church, 1989; Sallye Mathis Community Svc, Jacksonville Branch, NAACP, 1989; Principal's Alumni Awd, William M Raines Senior High School, 1990; Coalition for Respect, First Civil Rights Awd, 1992; National Black Police Association, Inc, Southern Region Achievement Awd, 1991; Jacksonville Branch NAACP, Rutledge Pearson, Civil Rights Awd, 1996. **Home Addr:** 5720 Oprey St, Jacksonville, FL 32208.

RODGERS, AUGUSTUS
Educator. **Personal:** Born Jan 27, 1945, Columbia, SC; son of Susanne Gaymond Rodgers and William Augustus Rodgers; married Claudia Taylor Rodgers; children: Christopher Augustus, Mark Adejolah, Shaundra Ave Rodgers. **Educ:** Benedict Coll, Columbia, SC, BA, 1965; New York Univ, New York, NY, MSW, 1969; Univ of South Carolina, Columbia, SC, PhD, 1977; Luthern Theological Southern Seminary, Columbia, SC, MDir, 1988. **Career:** SC Dept of Mental Health, psychiatric worker, 1965-71; Univ of SC, Columbia, SC, prof, 1971-. **Orgs:** Dir, Natl Black Family Summit, 1986-; vice basileus, Omega Psi Phi Fraternity, Omicron Phi Chapter; mem, Phi Delta Kappa; mem, Natl Assn of Social Work; mem, Natl Assn of Black Social Workers. **Honors/Awds:** Order of the Palmetto. **Home Addr:** 112 Charring Dr, Columbia, SC 29203.

RODGERS, BARBARA LORRAINE (BARBARA RODGERS DENNIS)
Broadcast journalist. **Personal:** Born Sep 27, 1946, Knoxville, TN; daughter of Anna Connor Rodgers and Jackson Rodgers; married James Dennis, Sep 2, 1972. **Educ:** Knoxville College, Knoxville, TN, BS, business education, 1968; SUNY at Buffalo, Buffalo, NY, 1976; University of Chicago, Chicago, IL, 1985-86. **Career:** Eastman Kodak Co, Rochester, NY, public affairs researcher, computer programmer, 1968-71; Educational Opportunity Center, Rochester, NY, department head/instructor, 1971-76; WOKR-TV, Rochester, NY, anchor/reporter/show host, 1972-79; KPIX-TV, San Francisco, CA, anchor/reporter, 1979-. **Orgs:** Co-founder, past president, board member, treasurer, Bay Area Black Journalists Assn, 1981-; board member, World Affairs Council of North CA, 1990-; board member, Regional Cancer Foundation, 1989-; board member, Western Center for Drug Free Schools and Communities, 1987-90; quarterly chair, The Commonwealth Club of California, 1990; member, Alpha Kappa Alpha Sorority, 1966-. **Honors/Awds:** Emmy, North California Chapter/Nat'l Academy of Televison Arts & Sciences, 1980-88; William Benton Fellowship in Broadcast Journalism, University of Chicago, 1985-86; Eugene Block Journalism Award, 1990; Miss Knoxville College, 1968. **Business Addr:** Anchor/Reporter, KPIX-TV (Ch 5), 855 Battery St, San Francisco, CA 94111.

RODGERS, CAROLYN MARIE
Author, lecturer, teacher. **Personal:** Born Dec 14, 1943, Chicago, IL; daughter of Bazella Colding and Clarence. **Educ:** Univ of Illinois, Navy Pier, 1960-61; Roosevelt Univ, Chicago, IL, BA, 1981; Univ of Chicago, MA, 1984. **Career:** Columbia Coll, Chicago, IL, Afro-Amer lit instructor, 1969-70; Malcolm X Coll, Chicago, IL, writer-in-residence, 1971-72; Indiana Univ, Bloomington, IN, visiting prof of Afro Amer lit, 1973; Roosevelt Univ, Chicago, IL, writer-in-residence, 1983; Chicago State Univ, Chicago, IL, lecturer, 1985; Eden Press, Chicago, IL, editor/publisher, currently; Columbia College, English & poetry workshop instructor, currently. **Honors/Awds:** Soc of Midland Authors, Poet Laureate, 1970; Natl Endowment for the Arts, 1970; PEN, 1987; author: Paper Soul, Third World Press, 1969, Songs of a Blackbird, TWP, 1970, How I Got Ovah, Doubleday/Anchor, 1975, The Heart as Evergreen, Doubleday, 1978, Echoes, From a Circle Called Earth, Eden Press, 1988, A Little Lower Than The Angels, Eden Press, 1988, Morning Glory, Eden Press, 1989, Eden & Other Poems, Eden Press, 1987; We're Only Human, Eden Press, Poems, 1994 (reprinted 1996); A Train Called Judah, Eden Press, 1996; The Girl with Blue Hair, Eden Press, 1996. **Home Addr:** 12750 S Sangamon, Chicago, IL 60643. **Business Addr:** Editor-Publisher, Eden Press, PO Box 804271, Chicago, IL 60680.

RODGERS, CHARLES
Clergyman. **Personal:** Born Jul 28, 1941, Memphis, TN; married Gloria Dickerson; children: Adrian, Victor, Allison, Carlos. **Educ:** Attennded LeMoyne Owen Coll. **Career:** Memphis Press-Scimitar, staff writer 1969; Covington Church of God in Christ, pastor, 1969-; Memphis Publ Co, recruiting & job counseling 1973; Central TN Jurisdiction of Church of God in Christ, second asst to Bishop 1982-; Raleigh Church, pastor, 1985-; Fifth Jurisdiction of TN Church of God in Christ, adm asst to the Bishop, 1989. **Orgs:** Bd dir Memphis Teen Challenge; mem Intl Bd of Trustees of Church of God in Christ 1972-84; mem Shelby United Neighbors 1973-74; dir of News Serv for Church of God in Christ Intl Convention 1981-. **Honors/Awds:** Man of Yr Congressman H Ford 1976; cert Outstanding & Meritorious Serv mayor W Herenton 1976. **Business Addr:** Pastor, 3607 Frayser-Raleigh Blvd, Memphis, TN 38128.

RODGERS, DERRICK
Professional football player. **Personal:** Born Oct 14, 1971; married Sherron, Aug 19, 1992; children: Elasia. **Educ:** Arizona State. **Career:** Miami Dolphins, linebacker, 1997-. **Business Addr:** Professional Football Player, Miami Dolphins, 2269 NW 199th St, Miami, FL 33056, (305)620-5000.

RODGERS, EDWARD
Judge (retired). **Personal:** Born Aug 12, 1927, Pittsburgh, PA; married Gwendolyn; children: 3. **Educ:** Howard U, BA 1949; FL A&M U, LLB 1963. **Career:** Palm Beach Co Sch Sys, tchr; asst co Solicitor; Cities of W Palm Beach & Riviera Beach FL,

prosecutor ad litem; City of W Palm Beach, judge ad litem; Private Atty; Palm Beach Co Bd, circuit ct judge, until 1995. **Orgs:** Bd dir Cancer & Soc; mem Masons; mem Visiting Nurses Assn; mem Mental Hlth Assn; mem PB Community Foundations, Urban League; mem Palm Beach Co Bar Assn; mem Nat Bar Assn. **Honors/Awds:** Natl Jefferson Award. **Military Serv:** USN pharmacist mate 3/c 1944-46.

RODGERS, HORACE J.
Mortgage banker. **Personal:** Born Dec 10, 1925, Detroit; married Yvonne Payne; children: Kimberly, Pamela. **Educ:** Univ of MI, BA 1948; Univ of MI Sch of Law, JD 1951. **Career:** Rodgers & Morgenstein, Attys, partner present; asst US Atty; Fed Housing Adminstrn, reg atty; Standard Mortgage Corp & Bert L Smokler & Co, vp; Premier Mortgage Corp, founder & chmn bd. **Orgs:** Mem adv bd Govt Nat Mortgage Assn; mem Com of Visitors, Univ of MI Law Sch; past adv bd mem Fed Nat Mortgage Assn; Nat Corp for Housing Partnerships; chmn Nat Urban Affairs Com MBA; dir Nat Bank of Southfield; life mem NAACP; Alpha Phi Alpha; mem Sigma Pi Phi; chm Class Officers & Ldrs Council, Univ of MI Alumni Assn; dir Univ of MI Alumni Assn; trustee & v Chancellor Episcopal Diocese of MI. **Military Serv:** AUS 1944-46. **Business Addr:** 26011 Evergreen, Ste 315, Southfield, MI 48076.

RODGERS, JOHNATHAN A.
Television executive. **Personal:** Born Jan 18, 1946, San Antonio, TX; son of Barbara Rodgers and M A Rodgers; married Royal Kennedy; children: David, Jamie. **Educ:** Univ of CA-Berkeley, BA 1967; Stanford Univ, MA 1972. **Career:** Newsweek Magazine, assoc editor 1968-73; KCBS-TV, news dir 1978-82, station manager 1982-83; CBS News, exec producer 1983-86; WBBM-TV gen mgr 1986-90; CBS Television Stations Div, pres; Discovery Networks, pres, currently. **Orgs:** Alpha Phi Alpha, mem. **Military Serv:** US Army, sergeant, 1969-71. **Business Addr:** President, Discovery Networks, US, 7700 Wisconsin Ave, Bethesda, MD 20814.

RODGERS, JOSEPH JAMES, JR.
Educational administrator. **Personal:** Born Nov 22, 1939, Hopewell, VA; son of Mary Rodgers and Joseph J Rodgers Sr. **Educ:** Morehouse Coll, BA 1962; Univ de Grenoble France, Cert d'etudes 1960; Univ of WI, MA 1965; Univ of So CA, PhD 1969. **Career:** Los Angeles City Coll, lecturer 1966-67; Univ of So CA, instr 1968-69; Occidental Coll, asst prof 1968-73; VA State Coll, prof & chmn 1970-71; Intl Curriculum Devel Program Phelps-Stokes Fund, reg coord 1975-; Carib-Amer School to Dominican Republic, 1975; Lincoln Univ, chmn, prof 1973-; Center for Critical Care Languages, dir, 1990-; American Univ of Uzes, France, pres, 1990-. **Orgs:** Pr tutor Stanley Kramer's son 1966-67; mem African Ethnic Herit Sem 1974, 1975. **Honors/Awds:** Merrill Travel Study Group to Europe 1959-60; W Wilson Fellowship to Harvard 1962-63; NDEA & Oakley Fellow Univ of So CA 1965-69; numerous articles in Maghreb Digest 1966-67; Distinguished Teaching 1974; "African Leadership Ideology" (w/Ukandi Damachi) Praeger 1976; "Sacrificing Qual Lang Learn for Pol Exped" 1977; Lindback Awd Pi Delta Phi Frat Honor Soc; Alpha Mu Gamma Natl Foreign Language Honor Soc; Honored Nominee, CASE Professor of the Year 1989; Distinguished Faculty Award for Scholarship Lincoln Univ, 1989. **Business Addr:** Dept of Languages/Linguistics, Lincoln University, PA 19352.

RODGERS, NAPOLEON
Banker. **Career:** Comerica Bank, Detroit, MI, first vice president, currently.

RODGERS, NILE
Musician, producer. **Career:** Chic, group member, 1970s; Ear Candy Records, co-president; Let's Dance, album by David Bowie, producer, 1983; Nile Rodgers Productions Inc, pres, currently. **Business Addr:** President, Nile Rodgers Productions Inc, 310 W 52nd St, New York, NY 10019, (212)420-8700.

RODGERS, PAMELA E.
Automobile dealer. **Personal:** Born May 8, 1958, Detroit, MI; daughter of Horace J Rodgers & Yvonne S Rodgers. **Educ:** University of Michigan, BA, Econ, 1980; Duke University, MBA, 1983. **Career:** Ford Motor Co, Car Product Dev, financial analyst, 1984-86, dealer candidate, 1988-90; Heritage Ford of Flint, Inc, pres, 1990-92; Harrell Chev, general mgr, 1992-93; Ford Motor Co, All American Ford, dealer candidate, 1992; Flat Rock Chevrolet-Oldsmobile, Inc, pres, 1993-96; Rodgers Chevrolet, Inc, pres, 1996-. **Orgs:** National Association of Minority Automobile Dealers, scy; General Motors Minority Dealer Association, bd; Family Svc of Wayne Cty, bd; Flat Rock Rotary Club, pres; Big Brothers-Big Sisters; Detroit Metro Chevrolet Dealer Association; Links; National Women Auto Association; Girlfriends. **Honors/Awds:** State of Michigan, Special Tribute, 1992, Kizzy Award, 1997. **Special Achievements:** Museum of Automotive History, Display, 1996; General Motors, Featured in Diversity Advertising, 1997. **Business Phone:** (313)676-9600.

RODGERS, ROD AUDRIAN
Performing arts. **Personal:** Born Dec 4, 1937, Cleveland, OH; son of LaJune Rodgers and Ernest Rodgers; divorced; children: Jason Delius, Kalan Windsor, Kaldar Audrian, Jamal Kenmar. **Educ:** Detroit Society of Arts & Crafts; scholarships at several major professional dance studios in New York City. **Career:** Choreographer, free-lance community arts consultant, master tchr, lecturer; Rod Rodgers Dance Co, fndr, artistic dir, principal choreographer; staged & directed "The Black Cowboys" comm by the Afro-Amer Singing Theatre; choreographed "The Prodigal Sister"; choreograph & act in ABC-TV spec "Like It Is"; choreographed & dir CBS-TV spec "Journey Into Blackness" & "Martin Luther King" for the Voices Inc Co; Rod Rodgers Dance Co has had ext natl tours & served as cult emmissaries for US, touring Africa, Portugal, & Syria for US Intl Comm Agency; orig dance theatre works incl Percussion Suite, Tangents, Rhythm Ritual, Ictus, Langston Lives, Box 71, Echoes of Ellington, the Legacy, Against Great Odds, In Hi-Rise Shadows, El Encounter. **Orgs:** Rod Rodgers Dance Co celebrated 20th anniversary in 1987-88 via natl & intl tour featuring poets & peacemakers series of thematic tributes to Langston Hughes, Duke Ellington, Harriet Tubman & other landmark figures from Black History. **Honors/Awds:** Recipient of an AUDELCO Award; recipient of a John Hay Whitney Fellowship; commissions from numerous state and federal agencies including the NY State Council on the Arts, the Natl Endowment for the Arts, and the Rockefeller Foundation. **Business Addr:** Artistic Dir/Prin Choreog, The Rod Rodgers Dance Company, 62 East 4th St, New York, NY 10003, (212)674-9066.

RODGERS, SHIRLEY MARIE
Payroll supervisor. **Personal:** Born Dec 29, 1948, Saginaw, MI. **Educ:** MI State Univ, 1966-70, BA 1984. **Career:** Blue Cross of MI, serv rep 1970-71; MI State Univ, tutor for athletic dept 1970-71; Lansing School Dist, comm relations liaison 1972, tutor 1972; MI State Univ, prog coord Teach-a-Brother 1972-73; Meridian 4 Theaters, cashier 1973; MI State Univ, prog coord Natl Jr Tennis League 1973; Lansing School Dist, clerk Personnel Dept 1975-76, payroll clerk IV 1976-81, lead sec V to dir of adult & continuing educ 1981-82, administrative sec to the deputy supt, 1982-94, payroll supervisor, 1995-. **Orgs:** Zeta Phi Beta Sor Inc MI State Univ 1970; mem Lansing Assn of Educ Sectys 1976-82 (held various positions); mem MI Democratic Party 1980-; mem Ingham Co Democratic Party 1980-; mem, held various positions, MSU Black Alumni Inc 1980-; mem Ingham Co Sch Officers Assn 1981-; mem MSU Alumni Assn 1984; mem Gr Lansing MSU Black Alumni Chap 1983-; State Adv Council for Voc Educ 1983-84; mem NAACP 1985; Lansing Comm Coll, bd of trustees, 1981-93; mem State Council for Vocational Educ 1985. **Honors/Awds:** Citizen of the Year in Educ Phi Beta Sigma Frat Inc 1985; MSU Black Alumni Distinguished Alumni, 1989; Governors Award, Outstanding Local Elected Official, 1989; Certificate of Recognition, American Citizens for Justice, Detroit Chapter. **Business Addr:** Payroll Department, Lansing Public School District, 519 W Kalamazoo St, Lansing, MI 48933.

RODGERS, VINCENT G.
Educator. **Personal:** Born Feb 17, 1958, St Louis, MO; son of Frances Rodgers and Bennie Rodgers; married Padmini Srinivasan, Dec 23, 1989. **Educ:** University of Dayton, BS, 1980; Syracuse University, MS, 1982, PhD, 1985. **Career:** University of Iowa, physics and astronomy professor, currently. **Business Addr:** Professor, University of Iowa, Department of Physics & Astronomy, Iowa City, IA 52242, (319)335-1219.

RODGERS, WILLIAM M., JR.
Engineer. **Personal:** Born Dec 22, 1941, Friars Point, MS; son of Leanna Felix (deceased) and William M Rodgers, Sr; married Venora Ann Faulkerson; children: William III, Melita Elizabeth, Steven Eric. **Educ:** Tennessee State Univ, BS 1963; Dartmouth Coll, MS 1970. **Career:** Natl Institutes of Health, Maryland, mathematician, 1963-64; Electronic Data Processing Div, Honeywell Inc, Virginia, systems analyst, 1964-66; Data Analysis Center of Itek Corp, Virginia, senior scientific programmer, 1966-67; Bell Telephone Labs, New Jersey, technical staff mem, 1968; Exxon Refinery TX, systems analyst 1970-75; Lockheed Elect Co Inc TX, staff engr 1975-77; Xerox Corp, mgr computer graphics requirements & appl 1977-82, proj mgr CAD/CAM acquisition 1982-83, mgr CAD/CAM acquistion & integration 1983-87, CAD/CAM strategy and planning, 1987-88, principal engr 1988-. **Orgs:** Mem Assn of Computing Machinery; Soc for Professional Engrs; Dartmouth Soc of Engrs; mem Dartmouth Alumni Orgn; Dartmouth Soc of Engrs Student Exec Comm 1969-70. **Honors/Awds:** Univ Scholar Awd; Univ Counselor Tennessee State Univ 1961-62; Sears Roebuck Scholarship 1959;conducted presentation on large scale CAD/CAM Acquisitions, NCGA, 1989; conducted presentation on CAD/CAM system acquisition and related topics, Univ of Wisconson 1985, Rochester Inst of Tech 1987. **Business Addr:** Principal Engineer, Advanced Systems Tools for Prduct Devel, Xerox Corp, 800 Phillips Rd, Mail Code 147-59C, Pittsford, NY 14534.

RODMAN, DENNIS KEITH
Professional basketball player. **Personal:** Born May 13, 1961, Trenton, NJ; divorced; children: Alexis. **Educ:** Cooke County Junior College, 1982-83; Southeastern Oklahoma State University, 1983-86. **Career:** Detroit Pistons, forward, 1986-93; San Antonio Spurs, 1993-95; Chicago Bulls, 1995-; Rodman Excavating Company, owner; Illusions, owner. **Honors/Awds:** NBA Defensive Player of the Year, 1990, 1991; NBA All-Defensive Team, 1989-93, 1996; NBA All-Star, 1990, 1992. **Special Achievements:** Author, Bad As I Wanna Be; coauthor with Michael Silver, Walk on the Wild Side, 1997; film, Double Team with Jean Claude Van Damme; holds the NBA record for most seasons leading the league in rebounds per game (6); TV: "Bad As I Wanna Be," ABC, special appearance, 1998. **Business Addr:** Professional Basketball Player, Chicago Bulls, 1901 W Madison St, Chicago, IL 60612, (312)455-4000.

RODMAN, JOHN
Computer company executive. **Career:** Federal Information Exchange Inc, president, currently. **Business Addr:** President, Federal Information Exchange Inc, 555 Quince Orchard Rd, Ste 200, Gaithersburg, MD 20878, (301)975-0103.

RODMAN, MICHAEL WORTHINGTON
Banker. **Personal:** Born Sep 29, 1941, Indianapolis, IN; son of Faye R Dabner and Hubert E Dabner; married Kaaren, Oct 23, 1965; children: Michael H, Heather L. **Educ:** Indiana University, BS, education, MBA, 1990. **Career:** Midwest National Bank, assistant cashier, 1972-74; INB National Bank, branch manager and AVP, 1974-81, AVP, CRA officer, 1981-86, vice pres, senior compliance officer, 1986-; NBD Neighborhood Revitalization Corp., president, 1986-. **Orgs:** Indianapolis School Board, secretary, 1994, president, 1996; Ardyth Burkhart Series; Indiana Housing Policy Study Commission, 1989-; Indianapolis Urban League, education committee chairman, 1992-; 100 Black Men, 1991-; Frontiers, 1991-; Volunteer Action Center. **Honors/Awds:** ABA, Presidential Citation, 1986; United Way, Outstanding Service Award, 1984; CLD, Outstanding Achievement in Business, 1983; INB National Bank's, HOURS Award for Community Service, 1979. **Business Addr:** President, NBD Neighborhood Revitalization Corp., 1 Indiana Square, Ste M560, Indianapolis, IN 46266, (317)266-6906.

RODNEY, KARL BASIL
Publisher. **Personal:** Born Nov 29, 1940, Kingston, Jamaica; married Faye A; children: Michele, Denine, Karlisa. **Educ:** Hunter Coll CUNY, BA 1966, MA 1970. **Career:** Equitable Life Assurance Soc of US, analyst/project mgr/div mgr 1967-82; New York Carib News, publisher. **Orgs:** Chmn Caribbean Education & Cultural Inst 1976-; dir Martin Luther King Jr Living the Dream Inc NY 1985-. **Honors/Awds:** Community Serv Award 1980; WA Domingo Award 1980; Excellence in Ethic Journalism Harlem Week 1985; Black Journalist Award, Pepsi-Cola NY 1986. **Business Addr:** Publisher, New York Carib News, 28 West 39th St, New York, NY 10018.

RODNEY, MARTIN HURTUS
Dentist (retired). **Personal:** Born Mar 4, 1909; son of Blanche McKenzie Rodney and Charles Rodney; married Olga Eskimo Hart. **Educ:** Howard Univ Wash DC, Pre-Dental 1934; Meharry Med Coll, DDS Honors 1938. **Career:** Retired Dentist. **Orgs:** Mem, Natl Dental Assns; mem Baltimore City Dental Assn; past pres MD Dental Assn; mem Fellow Acad of General Dentistry; mem Chi Delta Mu Fraternity; mem Omega Psi Phi Fraternity; mem, OKU Natl Hon Soc; life mem NAACP; mem Douglass Memorial Church, Baltimore City; bd mem and past pres AARP; Queen Anne's Commission on Aging, 1994; Meharry National Alumni Assn Award, 1993. **Honors/Awds:** Louise Charlotte Ball Awd Ball Fdn 1938; Guggenheim Dental Scholarship Guggenheim Found 1938-39; Dentist of Yr Awd MD Acad of Gen Dentistry 1973; various articles pub Dental Digest; Gov's Citation State of MD 1975; Recognition Awd MD Dental Soc 1975; President's Award for Service to Mankind, Meharry Medical College, 1938-87. **Special Achievements:** Author "Success," (autobiography), Commonwealth Publications, Alberta, Canada.

RODRIGUEZ, DORIS L.
Association executive. **Personal:** Born Mar 8, 1927, New York City; married Jules S; children: Anna, Julio, Louis. **Educ:** Queens Coll. **Career:** Orginals of Jamaica Inc Urban Ctr, exec dir; Private Nurse, 1948-51; Manhattan Gen Hosp, obstet nurse 1951-58; Litman Dept Store NY, comparison shopper,interpretor 1946-48; Bilingual Adv Dists 27 & 28. **Orgs:** Mem bd dir Youth Consultation Serv 1972-; Concerned Parents Day Care Ctr 1969; Queensboro Council for Soc Welfare 1971; exec bd mem PTA Manlius Mil Acad; 103rd Precinct Comm Council 1969; mem Musical Art Group 1950; asso St Marys Sch for Girls & Convent 1950; adv council for Reimbursable Funds, Dist 27& 28 Citywide; queens Child Guidance Commn; mem founding com Ida B Wills Sch; mem Christ Ch Sag Harbor NY.

RODRIGUEZ, RUBEN
Recording company executive. **Career:** Pendulum Records, president, CEO, currently. **Business Addr:** President & Chief Executive Officer, Pendulum Records, 1290 6th Ave, 9th fl, New York, NY 10019, (212)397-2260.

ROE, JAMES EDWARD, II
Professional football player. **Personal:** Born Sep 23, 1973, Richmond, VA. **Educ:** Norfolk State, attended. **Career:** Baltimore Ravens, wide receiver, 1996-. **Business Addr:** Professional Football Player, Baltimore Ravens, 11001 Owings Mills Blvd, Owings Mills, MD 21117, (410)654-6200.

ROEBUCK, GERARD FRANCIS
Entrepreneur. **Personal:** Born Sep 26, 1953, New York, NY; son of Gladys Johnson Roebuck and Waldamar Roebuck; married Sharon Jeffrey Roebuck, Nov 4, 1985; children: Jared, Jashaun. **Educ:** City College of New York, New York, NY, BA, 1978; Pratt Institute, Brooklyn, NY, MLS, 1980. **Career:** New York Public Library, New York, NY, supervising librarian, 1980-89; Black Expo USA, New York, NY, founder and chairman, 1987-; New York City Board of Education, New York, NY, media director, 1989-90. **Orgs:** National Association of Market Developers, 1989-; NAACP; board of directors, OLMEC Toy Corporation; member, Atlanta Chamber of Commerce; Black Librarians Caucus. **Honors/Awds:** Class Leader, Xavier Summer Program Higher Achievement Program; Promoter of the Year, New York City Promoters Organization, 1981; concert and rap group promoter.

ROEBUCK, JAMES RANDOLPH, JR.
State representative. **Personal:** Born Feb 12, 1945, Philadephia, PA; son of Cynthia Compton Roebuck and James Randolph Sr. **Educ:** VA Union U, BA (cum laude), 1966; Univ of VA, MA 1969, PhD 1977. **Career:** Drexel Univ, lect history 1970-77, asst prof history 1977-84; City of Philadelphia, leg asst Office of the Mayor 1984-85; Commonwealth of PA, rep in the gen assembly 1985-. **Orgs:** Phila Council Boy Scouts of America; Child Crisis Treatment Ctr; NAACP; Phila Intl House; Univ of VA Alumni Assn; Mt Olivet Tabernacle Baptist Church, bd of deacons; PA Higher Education Assistance Agency; Phila Community College. **Honors/Awds:** United Negro Coll Alumni Recognition Awd 1978; Chapel of the Four Chaplians Legion of Honor Awd 1980; Boy Scouts of Amer, Conestoga Dist Awd of Merit 1983, Silver Beaver Awd 1986; VA Union Univ Alumni Achievement Awd in Public Serv 1986; Natl Assoc for Equal Oppty in Higher Educ Citation 1987; Fellowships: Foreign Affairs Scholars Program, Washington, DC, Southern Fellowships Fund, Atlanta, GA, Mutual Educ Exchange Grant, US Office of Educ & Fulbright Prog, Washington, DC, Natl Endowment for the Humanities Grant, German Federal Republic Grant. **Business Addr:** State Representative, Commonwealth of Pennsylvania, 211 South Office Bldg, Harrisburg, PA 17120.

ROEBUCK-HAYDEN, MARCIA
Publishing company executive. **Career:** ScottForesman Publishing, Research and Cirriculum, editorial director, English as a Second Language, Adult Basic Education, editorial vice president, currently. **Business Addr:** Editorial VP, English as a Second Language, Basic Adult Education, ScottForesman Publsihers, 1900 E Lake Ave, Glenview, IL 60025, (708)729-3000.

ROGERS, ALFRED R.
Public utilities executive. **Personal:** Born Apr 7, 1931, Hartford, CT; son of Oretta Rogers and John Rogers; married Alice. **Educ:** Univ of CT, BA 1953, JD 1963; Amer Inst of Real Estate Appraisal; Rensselar Polytechnic Inst of CT; Univ of MI, Public Utilities Exec Program 1982; Edison Electric Inst, Public Utilities Exec Program. **Career:** Bureau of Rights of Ways CT Dept of Transp, chief public utilities sect 1957-64; Hartford Elec Light Co Legal & Real Estate Dept, sr land agent 1964-69; Hartford Electric Light Co, mgr 1970-85; Northeast Utilities Central Region, vice pres 1985-. **Orgs:** Pres & sec Bd of Educ Hartford 1965-73; trustee YMCA 1990-; state treasurer CT Assn of Bds of Educ 1966-69; Gov Advisory Council on Vocational Educ 1967-71; Gov Clean Air Task Force 1967-69; exec bd Long River Council BSA 1973-; advisory bd Salvation Army 1973-; corporator Newington Childrens Hospital 1975-; dir Hartford Hospital 1982-; trustee Boys Club of Hartford; dir Mechanics Savings Bank Hartford; St Joseph College, West Hartford, trustee. **Honors/Awds:** Commendation Medal AUS. **Military Serv:** AUS 2nd lt 1953-56.

ROGERS, BERNARD ROUSSEAU
Physician. **Personal:** Born Jan 17, 1944, Winston-Salem, NC; married Linda Hargreaves, May 21, 1986. **Educ:** NC Central Univ, BS 1966; Meharry Medical Coll, MD 1971; University of Minnesota, residency, radiation oncology, 1973-76. **Career:** Youngstown Hosp, intern and resident in pathology 1971-72; Private Practice, physician; Oncology Services, director, brachytherapy, 1991-. **Orgs:** Amer Medical Assn 1976-; Amer Coll of Radiology 1977-; American Endocurietherapy Society 1985-; American Society of Therapeutic Radiologists & Oncologists 1976-. **Home Addr:** 50 Dana Ave, Auburn, ME 04210. **Business Addr:** Director, Brachytherapy Service, Oncology Services Inc, 110 Regent Ct, State College, PA 16801.

ROGERS, CARLOS DEON
Professional basketball player. **Personal:** Born Feb 6, 1971, Detroit, MI. **Educ:** Arkansas-Little Rock; Tennessee State. **Career:** Golden State Warriors, forward-center, 1994-95; Toronto Raptors, 1995-98; Portland TrailBlazers, 1998-. **Special Achievements:** NBA Draft, First round pick, #11, 1994. **Business Addr:** Professional Basketball Player, Portland TrailBlazers, 1 Center Ct, Portland, OR 97227, (503)234-9291.

ROGERS, CHARLES D.
Educator, artist. **Personal:** Born Jan 5, 1935, Cherokee County, OK; son of Alberta Lay and Henry Rogers; divorced; children: Warren Donald Rogers. **Educ:** CA State Coll, BA 1963; OH State U, MA 1971; Univ of North Carolina, Greensboro, NC, MFA, 1977. **Career:** Johnson C Smith Univ Charlotte NC, dept of communications, assoc prof, 1972-, art program director, currently; Bennett Coll Greensboro NC, produced Harlem Renaissance 1972; Vanguard Studios Van Nuys CA, commercial designer 1970; Watts Summer Festival Watts CA, co-dir 1967-69; Artcraft Studios Los Angeles, commercial designer 1964-69. **Orgs:** Mem Black Arts Council Los Angeles CA; works displayed in numerous one-man group shows; member, National Conference of Artists, 1986-; member, Charlotte Guild of Artists, 1980-. **Honors/Awds:** Author of Prints by Am Negro Artists & Black Artists On Art; Teaching Fellow, African/American Institute, 1974; Scholar in Residence, New York Univ, 1993.

ROGERS, CHARLES LEONARD
Aerospace engineer. **Personal:** Born Jul 27, 1951, Decatur, AL; son of Felix M E & Estelle Holmes Rogers; married Ramona, Oct 22, 1988. **Educ:** Northern Illinois University, BS, 1976; West Coast University, MS, 1986. **Career:** Commonwealth Edison, technical staff engineer, 1976-80; Lockheed Martin Astronautics, chief launch operations, 1988-97; Athens/MSLS Launch Operations, pres/mgr, 1997-. **Orgs:** National Management Association. **Honors/Awds:** Martin Marietta, Jefferson Cup, 1992; Black Engineer Magazine, Certificate of Recognition, 1992; Dollars & Sense Magazine, Americas Best & Brightest, 1993. **Military Serv:** US Army. **Home Addr:** 161 Galaxy Way, Lompoc, CA 93436.

ROGERS, DAVID WILLIAM
Broadcast journalist. **Personal:** Born Feb 2, 1959, Cleveland, OH; son of Thelma Elizabeth Grahma and David Louis Rogers. **Educ:** Temple Univ, Philadelphia, PA, journalism, 1983. **Career:** WCAU-TV, Philadelphia, PA, news producer, 1979-85; WBBJ-TV, Jackson, TN, news anchor, 1985-86; WTVR-TV, Richmond, VA, 1986-87; WJBK-TV, Detroit, MI, weather anchor, 1987-. **Orgs:** Mem, YMCA, 1979; NAACP, 1989; mem, Natl Assn of Black Journalists, 1985; project coord, United Negro Coll Fund, 1986; mem, Westland Cultural Soc, 1987; mem, Muscular Dystrophy Assn, 1987. **Honors/Awds:** Various articles published in the Philadelphia Inquirer, 1979-81; Award of Outstanding Achievement, United Negro Coll Fund, 1986; Barrier Awareness Award, Amer Assn of Handicapped Persons, 1987; Award of Appreciation, Amer Cancer Soc, 1988. **Business Addr:** Weather Anchor, WJBK-TV News, PO Box 2000, Southfield, MI 48037.

ROGERS, DECATUR BRAXTON
Educational administrator. **Career:** Tennessee State University, College of Engineering and Technology, Nashville, TN, dean, currently. **Orgs:** ASEE; ASME; NAMEPA; NSPE; NAACP; Phi Delta Kappa; Pi Tau Sigma, Mechanical Engineering Honor Society; Tau Beta Pi, National Engineering Honor Society; Phi Kappa Phi. **Business Addr:** Tennessee State University, College of Engineering & Technology, 3500 John Merritt Blvd, Nashville, TN 37209-1561.

ROGERS, DESIREE GLAPION
Utility company executive. **Personal:** Born Jun 16, 1959, New Orleans, LA; daughter of Joyce Glapion and Roy Glapion; married John W Rogers Jr, May 18, 1988; children: Victoria. **Educ:** Wellesley College, political science, 1981; Harvard University, MBA, 1985. **Career:** AT&T, custom service marketing manager; Levy Organizations Lobby Shop Division, director of development; Museum Operations Consulting Associates, president; Illinois State Lottery, directory; Peoples Energy Corporation , vp of communications, currently. **Orgs:** WTTW Channel 11, board of directors; Chicago Children's Museum, board of directors of dir; Museum of Contemporary Art; board of directors, Smithsonian; board of direectors, Museum of Science & Industry; board of Trustees, Harvard Business School Club of Chicago. **Honors/Awds:** League of Black Women, Black Rose Award; Harvard Graduate School of Business Administration, COGME Fellowship. **Business Addr:** Vice President, Peoples Energy Corporation, 130 E Randolph Dr, Chicago, IL 60601, (312)240-4000.

ROGERS, DIANNA
Educator. **Personal:** Born in Baltimore, MD; children: Marcus. **Educ:** Univ of MD Eastern Shore, BA 1969; Coppin State Coll, MEd 1972; Johns Hopkins Univ, MS 1984. **Career:** Baltimore City Public Schools, teacher 1969-77, guidance counselor 1978-. **Orgs:** Mem Delta Sigma Theta Sor, NAACP, Black Mental Health Alliance, Inter-Alumni Council of Black Colls & Univs; consultant MD State Dept of Educ; governor'sappointee Baltimore City Foster Care Review Bd 1984-. **Honors/Awds:** Congressional Fellow US House of Representatives 1983. **Home Addr:** 3700 Glen Ave, Baltimore, MD 21215. **Business Addr:** Guidance Counselor, Baltimore City Public Schools, 501 Althol Ave, Baltimore, MD 21229.

ROGERS, DONNA WHITAKER
Journalist. **Personal:** Born Sep 11, 1960, Columbia, SC; daughter of Ernestine Peay Whitaker and Charles James Whitaker Sr; married Ronald Lancaster Rogers, Jul 28, 1984. **Educ:** University of North Carolina-Chapel Hill, Chapel Hill, NC, BA, 1982. **Career:** The Courier-Journal, Louisville, KY, copy editor, 1982-84; The State, Columbia, SC, reporter, copy/layout editor, 1984-87; Austin American-Statesman, Austin, TX, copy/layout editor, 1987-88; The Tuscaloosa News, Tuscaloosa, AL, copy/layout editor, 1988-89; Fort Worth Star-Telegram, Fort Worth, TX, Features copy desk chief, 1989-. **Orgs:** Assistant leader 1987-88, troop resource person 1984-85, Girl Scouts; member, National Assn of Black Journalists, 1982-; member, Orangeburg Chapter, American Business Women Assn, 1985; announcement clerk, Sunday school teacher, Mount Carmel Missionary Baptist Church, 1990; teacher's asst, Adopt-a-School Program, 1987-88. **Honors/Awds:** Adjunct Professor, University of South Carolina Journalism School, 1987; copy editing intern, Dow Jones Newspaper Fund, 1981; Quincy Sharpe Mills Scholarship, 1981, North Carolina Fellow, 1979, Valkyrie, Order of the Grail-Valkyries honorary group, 1982, University of North Carolina-Charlotte; Honorable Mention, Poets of Tarrant County, 1990.

ROGERS, EARLINE S.
State senator. **Personal:** Born Dec 20, 1934, Gary, IN; daughter of Robbie Hicks Smith and Earl Smith; married Louis C Rogers Jr, Dec 24, 1956; children: Keith C Rogers, Dara Dawn. **Educ:** Indiana University-Northwest; Indiana University, Bloomington IN, BS, 1957, MS, 1971. **Career:** Gary Common Council, member, 1980-83; State of Indiana, General Assembly, state representative, 1983-86, state senator, 1990-. **Orgs:** Mem, League of Women Voters; mem, NAACP; mem, National Council of Negro Women; mem, Indiana Women's Political Caucus. **Home Addr:** 3636 W 15th Ave, Gary, IN 46404.

ROGERS, ELIJAH BABY
Business executive. **Personal:** Born Nov 2, 1939, Orlando, FL; married Jean Doctor. **Educ:** SC State Coll, BA 1962; Univ of SC, 1965; Howard Univ, MSW 1967, MA 1972. **Career:** SC Dept of Corrections, suprv soc work serv 1967-69; WA Bur Natl Urban League, asst dir 1968-70; Natl Urban League, sr field rep 1969; Bowie MD, asst mgr, chief of staff 1970-71; Richmond VA, asst city mgr 1972-74; Berkeley CA, asst city mgr, mgr 1974-76; City of Berkeley, city manager, 1976-79; District of Columbia, Washington, DC, city administrator, 1979-83; Grant Thornton, asst managing partner 1983-88; Delon Hampton & Associates, president, chief operating officer, currently. **Orgs:** Mem Natl Assn of Soc Workers, Acad of Cert Soc Workers, Incl City Mgmt Assoc, Young Professional Task Force 1971-72, Special Task Force on Minorities 1973-74; chairperson Minority Exec Placement Bd 1975-; mem Comm on Mgmt Labor Rel 1976; adv comm Econ Devel Natl Inst of Advanced Studies 1977; transp steering comm Natl League of Cities 1977; bd of dirs Met Wash Council of Govts 1980; bd of dir Gr Richmond Transit Co 1973-74; mem adv comm School of Soc Work 1972-73; adj prof Urban Studies 1973-74; fellow Intl City Mmgt; vice chairman, Washington Metropolitan Airports Authority, 1986-88; The Foundation for the National Capital Region, board of trustees, 1993; chairman, Wm B Fitzgerald Scholarship Fund, 1994-; Chairman, Mayor's Blue Ribbon Panel on Health Care Reform, 1994; mem, Mayor-Elect Marion Barry's Financial Transition Team, 1994. **Honors/Awds:** Outstanding Serv Awd Gavel Club #29 1969; "ICMA/COG Minority Internship Prog Dept of Urban Studies Howard Univ Reflect" ICMA Newsletter 1971; "A Career in Municipal Govt for Blacks-Why Not?" Publ Mgmt 1972; "The Minority Exec-Which Way ICMA" Publ Mgmt 1975; SC State Coll, Distinguished Alumnus Award, 1979; Howard Univ, School of Soc Work, Community Services Award; Natl Assn for Equal Opportunity in Higher Education Award, 1984; Natl Forum for Black Public Administrators, "Hall of Fame" Award, 1994. **Business Addr:** President/Chief Operating Officer, Delon Hampton & Associates, 800 K St NW, Suite 720, North Lobby, Washington, DC 20001.

ROGERS, FREDDIE CLYDE
City official. **Personal:** Born Feb 15, 1922, Sumter County, AL; son of Corean Densmore Jackson and Eddie Jackson; married Pearlie McCarthy Rogers, Jun 30, 1951; children: Jocelyn, Belinda, Eric, Karen, Brian, Emily. **Educ:** Fairfield Industrial, AL, business, 1950; Faith Bible Coll, Birmingham, AL, MA, 1988. **Career:** Pyramid Sporting Goods Inc, co-owner, currently; Ad hoc Comm NAACP, business mgr; US Steel Fairfield, AL, laborer, 1950-80; Flame Club, Birmingham, AL, owner, 1950-60; Rogers Dry Cleaning, Docena, AL, owner, 1954-80. **Orgs:** Mayor Roosevelt City Vice Pres Roosevelt Voters League; vice pres security investments & past pres Roosevelt Branch NAACP; mem Jefferson Co Mayors Assn; mem Nat League of Cities; mem Black Mayors Assn; mem Civic League; Roosevelt Civic League; Roosevelt Chamber of Commerce; chmn, AD Hoc Comm, 1950-80; pres, NAACP, 1950-85. **Honors/Awds:** Sr Citizen Inc Outstanding Citizen Award Alpha Phi Alpha Fraterity, 1968; ALBeauticians Citation; Dynamic Leader Builder, 1978; Natl Conference of Black Mayors Recognition of Vision, 1981. **Military Serv:** US Navy, S 2/C, 1947-49. **Business Addr:** 4543 Bess Super Hwy, Bessemer, AL 35020.

ROGERS, GEORGE
Educator. **Personal:** Born Sep 23, 1935, McKeesport, PA; married Emalyn Martin; children: Cheryl Jeanne Mincey, Rhea Avonne, Emalyn Cherea. **Educ:** Langston Univ, BS Educ 1961; Central State Univ, MS Educ 1968; Univ of KS, EdD 1971. **Career:** AL A&M Univ, asst prof 1968-71; Wichita State Univ, assoc prof 1971-83; Langston Univ, vice pres academic 1983-86, prof special asst to the president 1986-. **Orgs:** Mem Phi Delta Kappa 1969; mem Alpha Phi Alpha Frat 1970; pres George Rogers & Assocs 1972-; mem Sigma Pi Phi Frat 1986. **Honors/Awds:** Ford Foundation Fellow 1969-70; Honor Graduate Univ of KS 1971; Disting Young Black Amer Incentive Assoc Tallahasse, FL 1972. **Military Serv:** AUS SP-3 3 yrs. **Home Addr:** 10201 C N Finely Rd, Oklahoma City, OK 73120. **Business Addr:** Prof Special Asst to Pres, Langston University, Langston, OK 73050.

ROGERS, GEORGE, III
Educational administrator. **Personal:** Born Jan 8, 1947, Chicago, IL; son of Gertrude Ellington Rogers (deceased) and George Rogers, II; married Rita F Guhr; children: Tara M, Bret Z. **Educ:** Wilson City Coll, AA 1967; Bethel Coll, BS 1969; Wichita State Univ, MEd 1969-72; Univ of AR, PhD Candidate 1979-. **Career:** Bethel College, track coach 1969, dir of athletics, asst to coach, assoc prof of phys ed. **Orgs:** Mem Newton Jaycee's 1970; bd of dir FARM House (Alcohol & Drug Rehabilitation) 1975; mem adv bd First Step Industries; president, USD #373 School Board, 1987-88, 1994-95; pres, Harvey County Rural Water District #3, 1987-88; National Association for Student Personnel Administrators; Meadowlark Homestead, Inc, board of directors, 1996; Mirror, Inc, board of directors, 1996. **Honors/Awds:** Coach of Yr NAIA Area 3 Track Coach 1975; grad asst Track Coach Univ of AR 1979; Athletic Administrator of the Year, Kansas, NAIA, 1989-90. **Home Addr:** 3219 Royer West Drive, Newton, KS 67114. **Business Addr:** Dean of Students, Bethel Coll, Hwy, K 15 & 27th St, North Newton, KS 67117.

ROGERS, GWENDOLYN H.
Executive director. **Career:** Equal Business Opportunity Commission, executive dir; Columbus (OH) City Council, legislative analyst. **Special Achievements:** First African American female executive director of the EBOC, Columbus. **Business Addr:** Legislative Analyst, Columbus City Council, 90 W Broad St, Columbus, OH 43215, (614)645-7380.

ROGERS, JOHN W.
Judge. **Personal:** Born Sep 3, 1918, Knoxville, TN; son of Mary Turner Rogers and John W. Rogers Sr.; divorced; children: John Jr. **Educ:** Chicago Tchr Coll, BEd 1941; Univ of Chicago, LLD 1948. **Career:** Circuit Ct of Cook Co, judge 1977-. **Orgs:** Former member, bd trustees, Met Sanitary Dist of Greater Chicago; former treasurer & gen counsel, Sivart Mortgage Co Chicago; admitted to IL Bar 1948; admitted to practice US Supreme Ct; former member, bd dir Chicago Council on Human Relations; former board member, Ada S McKinley; Chicago Bar Assn; Cook County Bar Assn; Judicial Council; National Council of Juvenile and Family Court Judges; Ill Council of Juvenile and Family Court Judge's Assn. **Honors/Awds:** Congressional Black Caucus Award, Recognition of Courageous Leadership and Discipline in the Air and on the Ground during World War II, 1991. **Military Serv:** USSA, original 99th Squadron, fighter pilot, capt, WW II; Air Medal. **Business Addr:** Judge, Circuit Court of Cook County Juvenile Division, 1100 S Hamilton, Chicago, IL 60612.

ROGERS, JOHN W., JR.
Management company executive. **Personal:** son Of Jewel Lafontant (deceased) and John W Sr; married Desiree Glapion Rogers. **Educ:** Princeton University, BS, economics, 1980. **Career:** William Blair & Co, broker; Ariel Capital Management, founder, president, currently. **Orgs:** Chicago Urban League, board of directors; Family Focus; Chicago Symphony Orchestra, board of directors; Lake Forest College, board of directors; American National Bank, board of directors; Aon Corp., board of directors; Burrell Communications Group, board of directors; Chicago Park District. **Honors/Awds:** Honorary Degree, Columbia College, 1996-; Time Magazine, "40 Leaders of the Future," 1994. **Business Addr:** President, Ariel Capital Management, Inc, 307 N Michigan, Ste 500, Chicago, IL 60601, (312)726-0140.

ROGERS, JUDITH W.
Federal judge. **Career:** US Court of Appeals, judge, currently. **Business Addr:** Circuit Court Judge, US Court of Appeals-DC Circuit, 333 Constitution Ave NW, Rm 5800, Washington, DC 20001-2866, (202)482-5728.

ROGERS, LAWRENCE F.
Association executive. **Personal:** Born Mar 18, 1937, Nashville; divorced; children: Robin. **Educ:** Fisk U, BA 1967. **Career:** Environ Planning & Mgmt Prof, lic gen contr, cons; World Book Ency, salesman; Fish U, dir alumni fund 1969-70; Metro Action Commn, field rep 1969-70; JW Thompson Adv Agcy NYC, acct exec 1967-68. **Orgs:** Mem Middle TN Bus Assn; NAACP; life mem Kappa Alpha Psi 1st black appointed Davidson Co Election Commn 1971-73 reg 10000 in one day to vote; IL NG 1960-66.

ROGERS, NORMAN
Physician, educator. **Personal:** Born Oct 14, 1931, Cairo, GA; son of Willie Mae Lester Hall and Norman Rogers; married Juanita L Slack; children: Saundra, Norman III, Robert. **Educ:** A&M U, BS 1957; Howard U, MS 1959; Howard Univ Coll of Med, MD 1963. **Career:** Howard Univ, clinical asso prof 1985; private practice of surgery & teaching 1969-; Tumor Clinic Howard Univ Dept of Surgery Freedmen's Hosp, clinical cancer fellow 1968-69; Howard Univ Freedmen's Hosp, surg resd 1964-68; Howard Univ Coll of Med, instr surgery 1968; Howard Univ Coll of Med, asst prof surgery 1971-; VA Hosp, vis prof 1973. **Orgs:** Nat Med Assn 1968; AMA 1968; Medico-Chirurgical Soc of DC 1968; DC Med Soc 1968; Diplomate Am Bd of Surgery 1969; fellow Am Coll of Surgeons 1971; The Assn of Acad Surgery 1972; fellow Intl Coll of Surgeons 1974; Soc of Sigmz Xi 1959; Beta Kappa Chi 1959; Soc of Surgical Gastro Endosopist, 1988-; Prince George's Health Professionals, 1975-. **Honors/Awds:** Recpt Charles R Drew Nat Med Assn Fundamental Forum Award 1967; Congressional Citation for Breast Cancer Proj 1974; Good Conduct Medal; United Natl Medal; Korean Serv Medal; Nat Def Serv Medal. **Military Serv:** USAF s/sgt 1951-55; USPHS lt comdr 1965-66. **Business Addr:** Physician, 601 Eastern Ave NE, Ste 101, Capitol Heights, MD 20743.

ROGERS, ORMER, JR.
Federal official. **Personal:** Born Jul 23, 1945, Mount Vernon, TX; son of Susie Rogers and Ormer Rogers Sr; married Helen Pettis, Sep 27, 1983. **Educ:** Dallas Baptist University, BCA, 1977; Abilene Christian University, MS, 1978; Massachusetts Institute of Technology, attended, 1990. **Career:** United States Postal Service, director, customer service, 1983-86, operations program analyst, 1986-87, field director, marketing, 1987-88, director, city operations, 1988-91, field director, operations support, 1991, district manager, postmaster, 1991-92, area manager, Great Lakes, 1992-. **Orgs:** Rotary of Chicago, 1992-93; Federal Executive Board, 1991-93; University of Illinois, Chicago, Department of Medicine, development council, 1992-93; Combined Federal Campaign, chairman, 1993; LifeSource, bone marrow donor committee, 1992-93; United Way, Crusade of Mercy, minority outreach committee, 1992-93. **Honors/Awds:** United States Postal Service, Regional Postmaster General Award for Excellence, 1989, 1991, 1992; Abilene Christian University, Service Achievement Award, 1978. **Military Serv:** US Army, ssg, 1965-68; Bronze Star, Army Commendation Medal, Combat Infantry Badge, Senior Parachutist Wings, Good Conduct, Vietnam Campaign Medal, Vietnam Service Ribbon, Unit Citation. **Business Addr:** Area Manager, Great Lakes Area, US Postal Service, 433 W Van Buren, Rm 1134, Chicago, IL 60699-0100.

ROGERS, OSCAR ALLAN, JR.
Educational administrator, minister. **Personal:** Born Sep 10, 1928, Natchez, MS; son of Maria Rogers and Oscar Rogers; married Ethel Lee Lewis; children: Christopher, Christian, Christoff. **Educ:** Tougaloo Coll, AB (Summa Cum Laude) 1950; Harvard Divinity Sch, STB 1953; Harvard Univ, MAT 1954; Univ of AR, EdD 1960; Univ of Washington, Postdoctoral study 1968-69. **Career:** Natchez Jr Coll, dean/registrar 1954-56; AR Baptist Coll, pres 1956-59; Jackson State Univ, dean of students/prof of social science 1960-69, dean of the grad school 1969-84; Claflin Coll, pres; Oklahoma City University, DHL, 1992; Claflin College, president, 1984-94. **Orgs:** Pastor Bolton-Edward United Methodist Church 1961-84; dir Orangeburg Chamber of Commerce 1987-90. **Honors/Awds:** "My Mother Cooked My Way Through Harvard With These Creole Recipes," 1972; "Mississippi, The View From Tougaloo," 1979. **Military Serv:** USN stm 3/c 1946-47. **Business Addr:** President, Claflin College, 400 College Ave, Orangeburg, SC 29115.

ROGERS, PEGGY J.
Educator. **Personal:** Born Aug 19, 1951, Starkville, MS; daughter of Irene Jones Rogers and David Rogers. **Educ:** Rust Coll, Holly Spring, MS, BS, 1969-73; MS State Univ, State Coll, MS, MA, 1975; MS State Univ, State Coll, MS, Spec, 1988. **Career:** Clay County Schools, West Point, MS, counselor, 1984-84; Oktibbeh County Schools, Starkville, MS, supt of educ, 1987; E Jasper Schools, Heidelberg, MS, curriculum coord, 1988; Oktibbeha County Schools, Starkville, MS, counselor, teacher; Lowndes County Schools, Columbus, MS, asst supt, 1990-. **Honors/Awds:** NAACP; MS Assn for Educator; Phi Delta Kappa; Delta Sigma Theta; MS/Natl Assn of School Administrators; Teacher of the Year, Clay County Teacher Assn, vice chmn of the Democratic Party Oktibbeha County; approved, MTAI, MPAI, MPPI for the MS State Dept of Educ; consultant for Educ Equity Technical Assistance. **Business Addr:** Asst Superintendent, Lowndes County School District, 201 Airline Rd, Columbus, MS 39702.

ROGERS, RODNEY RAY, JR.
Professional basketball player. **Personal:** Born Jun 20, 1971, Durham, NC; married Tisa; children: Roddreka. **Educ:** Wake Forest University. **Career:** Denver Nuggets, forward, 1993-95; Los Angeles Clippers, 1995-. **Special Achievements:** NBA Draft, first round, ninth pick, 1993. **Business Addr:** Professional Basketball Player, Los Angeles Clippers, 3939 S Figueroa St, Los Angeles Sports Arena, Los Angeles, CA 90037, (213)748-8000.

ROGERS, ROY, JR.
Professional basketball player. **Personal:** Born Aug 19, 1973, Linden, AL. **Educ:** Alabama. **Career:** Vancouver Grizzlies, forward, 1996-97; Boston Celtics, 1997-98; Toronto Raptors, 1998-. **Business Addr:** Professional Basketball Player, Toronto Raptors, 150 York St, Ste 110, Toronto, ON, Canada M5H 3S5, (416)214-2255.

ROGERS, SAMMY LEE
Professional football player. **Personal:** Born May 30, 1970, Pontiac, MI; married Leslie; children: Sam Jr, Aaron, Areil. **Educ:** University of Colorado. **Career:** Buffalo Bills, linebacker, 1994-. **Business Addr:** Professional Football Player, Buffalo Bills, One Bills Dr, Orchard Park, NY 14127, (716)648-1800.

ROGERS, TIMMIE
Comedian, dancer, singer, composer. **Personal:** Born in Detroit, MI; son of Lillian Ancrum Rogers and Henry Rogers; married Barbara; children: Joy, Gaye. **Career:** CBS-TV Network, Sugar Hill Times 1948; dancer, singer, composer, musician, comedian, actor; Crazy Music Publishing, 1954-. **Orgs:** Member, ASCAP, 1954-; Friars Club. **Honors/Awds:** Launched first all black show; made TV appearances Sammy Davis, Jr, Melba Moore, Jackie Gleason, Ed Sullivan, Merv Griffin, Johnny Carson; appeared in Las Vegas, Canada, Australia, Germany, Japan, England, Vietnam, NY & Miami; composer, Nat King Cole, Tommy Dorsey, Sarah Vaughan; movie appearances: Sparkle, 1976; The Five Heartbeats, 1991; referred to as Dean of Black Comedians; has inspired such black entertainers as Nipsey Russell, Dick Gregory, Redd Foxx, Slappy White, Bobby Short, Harry Belafonte, and George Benson; Black Comedy Award, AHAA; Theatrical Award, Lafayette Players West; Award for contributions in the entertainment field, City of Los Angeles, LA Mayor Tom Bradley, LA City Council. **Special Achievements:** Composed "If You Can't Smile and Say Yes, Please Don't Cry and Say No," for Nat King Cole, 1944; "Everybody Wants To go To Heaven But Nobody Wants To Die," for Tommy Dorsey, 1948; Made TV appeareances on Sanford and Son, City of Angels. **Home Addr:** 1911 Garth Ave, Los Angeles, CA 90034.

ROGERS, VICTOR ALVIN
Cleric, educator. **Personal:** Born Oct 2, 1944, St Peter, Barbados; son of Violet Simmons and Grafton Simmons; married Gloria Bock, Feb 4, 1984; children: Nicholas, Paul, Matthew. **Educ:** University of the West Indies, LTH, 1971; Laurentian University, BA, 1973; Jackson State University, MA, 1977; Mississippi State University, PhD, 1987. **Career:** Diocese of Barbados, St Paul's Church, curate, 1969-70, St Philip's Parish Church, curate, 1970-71; Diocese of Long Island, St Philip's Episcopal Church, 1973-74; Diocese of Mississippi, St Mark's, rector, 1974-83; St Luke's Episcopal Church, rector, 1983-; Southern Connecticut State University, assistant professor, 1992-. **Orgs:** Society for the Increase of the Ministry, board member, 1992; Habitat for Humanity, board member, 1988; Downtown Cooperative Ministry, board member, 1986. **Honors/Awds:** Aldermanic Citation, Outstanding Community Service. **Special Achievements:** Co-author, with VV Prakassa Rao, Sex, Socio-Economic Status, and Secular Achievement Among High School Students, The Researcher, Vol 9 winter, p 25-36. **Business Addr:** Assistant Professor, Southern Connecticut State University, 501 Crescent St, New Haven, CT 06511.

ROGERS-GRUNDY, ETHEL W.
Insurance company executive. **Personal:** Born Dec 3, 1938, Macclesfield, NC; daughter of Martha Pitt Wooten and Russell Wooten; married Sherman Grundy; children: Duane A Rogers, Angela S. **Educ:** St Augustines Coll, BA 1960; Temple Univ, MEd 1970; Catholic Univ of Amer, additional study; Univ of MD. **Career:** Franklin Life Ins Co, district mgr, currently; DC Bd of Educ, coordinator office; Fed City Coll Washington, adj prof 1975; Woodson St HS, chmn, bus dept 1972-74; Johnston Co Sch Smithfield NC, asst dir of headstart 1966-67; St Augustines Coll NC, asst dean of students 1965-66. **Orgs:** Mem Eastern Bus Tchr Assn; Nat Bus Educ Assn; DC Bus Educ Assn; charter pres Prince Georges Co Alumnae Chap Delta Sigma Theta Inc; pres MD Council of Deltas; sec St Augustines Coll Nat Alumni Assn; mem bd of dir Lung Assn of So MN Inc; mem Alpha Zeta Chap Delta Phi Epsilon; Prince Georges Co MD NAACP; Womens Polit Caucas of Prince Georges Co MD; Pan Hellenic Council of Prince Georges Co MD; elected to Membership in Delta Phi Epsilon 1969. **Honors/Awds:** Female Business Leader of the Year, Maryland Chamber of Commerce, 1976; Female Business Leader of the Year, Franklin Life Insurance Co, 1981, 1983. **Home Addr:** 11111 Lochton St, Upper Marlboro, MD 20772.

ROGERS-LOMAX, ALICE FAYE
Physician, educator. **Personal:** Born Jan 20, 1950, Darlington, SC; daughter of Alice McCall Rogers and James Rogers; married Michael W Lomax, May 5, 1979; children: Lauren, Whitney. **Educ:** Holy Family Coll, BA 1972; Philadelphia Coll of Osteopathic Med, DO 1976; HPCOM, Pediatric Residency 1977-79. **Career:** Philadelphia Coll of Osteopathic Medicine, asst prof pediatrics 1979-80; NY Coll of Osteopathic Medicine,

visiting lecturer 1980; Philadelphia Coll of Osteopathic Medicine, chmn div ambulatory pediatrics 1981-; School of Nursing of the Univ of PA; adjunct clinical preceptor 1981-; Osteopathic Medical Center of Philadelphia, chmn div of ambulatory pediatrics 1981-89; Lomax Medical Associates, Philadelphia PA, private pediatric practice 1989. **Orgs:** Mem Amer Osteopathic Assn 1976-, Amer Coll of Osteopathic Ped 1977-, PA Osteopathic Med Soc 1979-, Student Admissions Comm 1982-, Philadelphia Pediatrics Soc 1983-, Ambulatory Pediatrics Assn 1983-, Student Admissions Comm, Osteopathic Medical Center 1982-86, Medical Soc of Eastern Pennsylvania 1987-. **Honors/Awds:** Mem Beta Beta Beta Natl Biology Honor Soc 1972; Legion of Honor Mem Chapel of the Four Chaplains Philadelphia 1983. **Business Addr:** Lomax Medical Associates, 300 N 52nd St, Philadelphia, PA 19139.

ROGERS NELSON, PRINCE. See THE ARTIST.

ROGERS-REECE, SHIRLEY
Educational Administrator, company executive. **Personal:** Born in Carson, CA. **Career:** McDonald's Corporation, 1981, restaurant manager, area supervisor, 1982-83, operations consultant, 1983-85, Hamburger University, professor, 1986-87, training mgr, 1987-88, operations manager, 1988-90, field service mgr, 1990-91, dean, 1991-94, Indonesia, dir of operations, 1995-97, gen manager, 1997-. **Honors/Awds:** McDonald's President's Award; Revlon Kizzy Award, Outstanding Women of America. **Business Addr:** Director of Operations, McDonald's Indonesia, Plaza Bapindo 11, 3rd Fl, JL Jend Sudirman Kav 54-55, 12190 Jakarta, Indonesia.

ROHADFOX, RONALD OTTO
Construction company executive. **Personal:** Born Mar 12, 1935, Syracuse, NY; son of Rita Rohadfox and Otto Rohadfox; children: Renwick, Roderick, Reginald, Rebekah. **Educ:** IN Inst of Tech, BSCE 1961; Woodbury Univ, MBA 1980; Century Univ, PhD 1984. **Career:** Analytic Construction Co, pres; Construction Control Serv Corp, pres, currently. **Orgs:** Kappa Alpha Psi 1960, Amer Soc of Civil Engrs 1969, fellow, 1996; Amer Public Works Assn 1977, Soc for Mktg Professional Serv 1982; Natl Assn of Minority Contractors 1985. **Honors/Awds:** One of the Top 100 Black Successful Businessmen Black Enterprise Mag 1974; mem Republican Inner Circle 1985; NC Transportation Bd, Appointment, 1991-92. **Business Addr:** President, Construction Control Serv Corp, 115 W Main St, Durham, NC 27701, (919)682-5741.

ROHR, LEONARD CARL
Business executive (retired). **Personal:** Born Sep 29, 1921, Kimball, WV; son of Irma Rohr and David Rohr; widowed; children: Ronald, Carol. **Educ:** Univ Denver, BS, ME 1950. **Career:** Leonard C Rohr Assocs Consulting Mech Engr, owner 1962-87; Koebig & Koebig Inc, chf mech engr 1957-62; Co Los Angeles, commr mech bd. **Orgs:** Mem Am Soc Mech Engr; Am Soc Heating Refrigeration & Air Conditioning Engr. Consulting Engineers. **Honors/Awds:** Silver Star. **Military Serv:** AUS 1st lt 1942-46.

ROLAND, BENAUTRICE, JR.
Staff supervisor. **Personal:** Born Dec 11, 1945, Detroit, MI; married Brenda Thornton; children: Michele S, Michael L. **Educ:** Univ of Detroit (cum laude), BS Finance 1972; Wharton Grad Sch Univ of PA, MBA Finance 1974. **Career:** MI Bell Tele Co, staff supr 1979-; Ford Motor Co, financial analyst 1975-79; Morgan Guaranty Trust of NY, euro-currency trader 1974-75. **Orgs:** Bd of dirs Univ of PA Alumni Club of MI; co-chmn Secondary Sch Com Univ of PA Alumni Club of MI. **Military Serv:** USAF sgt 1964-67.

ROLAND, JANNON
Professional basketball player. **Personal:** Born Feb 3, 1975. **Educ:** Purdue Univ. **Career:** New England Blizzard, guard, 1997-. **Honors/Awds:** Big Ten Female Athlete of the Year, 1997. **Business Addr:** Professional Basketball Player, New England Blizzard, 179 Allyn St, Ste 403, Hartford, CT 06103, (860)522-4667.

ROLAND, JOHNNY E.
Businessman, professional football coach. **Personal:** Born May 21, 1943, Corpus Christi, TX; son of Willie Mae Roland and Vernon L Roland; children: Johnny Jr, James E, Cynnamon Aisha. **Educ:** Univ of MO, BS Bus Admin, Personnel Mgmt 1966. **Career:** St Louis Football Cardinals, player 1966-72; NY Giants, player 1973; Green Bay Packers, asst coach spec assignments 1974; Univ of Notre Dame Wide Receivers, asst coach 1975; Philadelphia Eagles Runnings Backs, asst coach 1976-78; Chicago Bears Running Backs, asst coach 1983-; Bronco Broadcasting Co Inc KIRL-AM Radio, pres and owner 1979-. **Orgs:** Mem Kappa Alpha Psi, Natl Football League Players Assn, Natl Football League Alumni St Louis Chap, Univ of MO Alumni Assn; bd mem United Way 1980-83; bd mem St Louis Children's Hospital Devel Fund 1980-83; St Louis Advertising Club 1979; Kiwanis Club 1970-73. **Honors/Awds:** 1st black capt Univ of MO Football team 1965; mem TX Football Hall of Fame; Running Back All State TX 1960; Parade HS All Amer Team 1960; All Big Eight 1962, 1964-65; Walter Camp, Sporting News, AP, UPI, Kodak Coll All Amer 1965; NFL Pro Bowl 1966, 1967; NFL Rookie of the Year 1966; St Louis Cardinals Rookie of the Year 1966; St Louis Cardinals MVP 1967.

ROLARK, M. WILHELMINA
Attorney. **Personal:** Born Sep 27, Portsmouth; married Calvin W. **Educ:** Howard U, AB 1936, MA 1938; Terrell Law Sch, LLB 1944. **Career:** Pvt practice 1947-; Elected to DC City Counc Dem Ward 8, mem 4 yr; Nat Assn Black Wmn Attorneys Inc, pres 1973-; Nat Bar Assn, asst sec; DC Human Rights Commn, commr. **Orgs:** Bd mem Legal Aid Aoc; gen counsel United Black Fund; mem Wash & DC Bar Assn Vice Pres DC Bi-Centennial Assembly; bd mem Wash Organization Wmn; Early Childhood Devel Cntr; DC Bd of Labor Rels. **Honors/Awds:** Distinguished Serv Award Phyllis Wheatley 1966; Citation United Black Fund; Grassroots Award.

ROLLE, ALBERT EUSTACE
Surgeon. **Personal:** Born Aug 3, 1935, Miami, FL; son of Bessie Rolle and Jerod Rolle; married Josephine James; children: Allyson, Jonathan. **Educ:** FL A&M Univ, AB 1954; Univ of Pittsburgh, BS 1960; Univ of Pittsburgh Sch of Med, MD 1965. **Career:** Georgetown Univ Med Ctr, clin asst prof of surgery 1972-; DC Board Police/Fire Surgeons, surgeon 1973-78; Capital Area Permanent Med Group, general surgeon 1985. **Orgs:** Fellow Amer Coll of Surgeons 1973-; mem DC Med Soc 1970-; mem Washington Acad Surgery 1975-; past master Fellowship Lodge 26, F & AM, PHA 1973-; mem Kappa Alpha Psi Frat 1952-. **Honors/Awds:** Outstanding Performance Award Metro Police Dept Bd of Police Surgeons 1977; Physicians Recognition Award Amer Med Assn 1972. **Military Serv:** USAFR lt col Med Corps. **Business Addr:** Surgeon, Kaiser Permanente Medical Group, 1011 N Capitol St NE, Washington, DC 20002.

ROLLE, ESTHER
Actress. **Personal:** Born Nov 8, Pompano Beach, FL; daughter of Jonathan Rolle. **Educ:** Attended, Spellman Coll, Hunter Coll, New School for Social Rsch. **Career:** "The Blacks", off-broadway debut 1962; "God is a (Guess What?)", London stage debut 1969; Shogala Obola Dance Co, dancer; numerous stage appearances; toured Australia/New Zealand with Black Nativity/US w/Purlie; Bethune, 1991; numerous films; "Maude", 1972-74; "Good Times", 1974-77, 1978-79; performed in several stage productions including, Nevis Mountain Dew, Dame Lorraine, The River Niger, Member of the Wedding, A Raisin in the Sun, Blues for Mr Charlie, Amen Corner, Don't Play Us Cheap; TV guest star: Flamingo Road, Up and Coming, Darkroom, The New Odd Couple, Love Boat, Fantasy Island; performed one woman show "Ain't I A Women"; feature films include, "Petaluma Pride", "A Fools Dance", "Grand Baby", "Driving Miss Daisy". **Orgs:** Grand marshal Cherry Blossom Festival Washington 1975; hon chmn President's Comm on Employment of Handicapped. **Honors/Awds:** Woman of the Yr 3rd World Sisterhood 1976; first Black woman to serve as Grand Marshal of the Annual Cherry Blossom Festival in Washington DC; Emmy Award 1979; Image Award, NAACP, 1979; Leadership Award, NAACP, 1990; Black Filmmakers Hall of Fame, 1992.

ROLLE, JANET
Entertainment company executive. **Personal:** Born Dec 25, 1961, Mount Vernon, NY; daughter of William Sr & Barbara Rolle; married Mark Keye, Apr 14, 1995. **Educ:** State Univ of NY at Purchase, BFA, 1984; Columbia Univ Graduate School of Business, MBA, 1991. **Career:** HBO, special assistant to the chairman, 1991-92; mgr, multiplex marketing, 1992-93; dir of marketing, 1993-. **Orgs:** New York Coalition of 100 Black Women, 1992-; Black Filmmaker Foundation, 1990-; New York Women in Film & Television, 1991-; Harlem YMCA Mentoring Program, 1993-. **Honors/Awds:** Harlem YMCA, Black Achievers in Industry, 1993. **Business Addr:** Director of Marketing, HBO Home Video, 1100 Avenue of the Americas, Ste G9-10, New York, NY 10036, (212)512-7645.

ROLLINS, AVON WILLIAM, SR.
City official. **Personal:** Born Sep 16, 1941, Knoxville, TN; son of Josephine Rollins Lee and Ralph Kershaw; married Sheryl Clark, Sep 28, 1974; children: Avon Jr, Avondria F. **Educ:** Knoxville Coll; Univ of TN. **Career:** Student Nonviolent Coord Comm, natl exec; Southern Christian Leadership Conf, spec asst; TN Valley Authority, mgr; Clark Rollins & Associates, pres, currently. **Orgs:** One of co-founders, former natl exec, SNCC Raleigh NC 1960; asst to the late Rev Dr Martin Luther King Jr; mem, bd of dir, Mgmt Comm Knoxville Intl Enrgy Exposition 1982; chmn, Magnolia Fed Savings & Loan Assn; adv, former chmn & founder ,TVA Employees Minority Investment Forum, mem Chancellors Assn, The Univ of TN; mem, Pres Round Table Knoxville Coll; chmn emeritus, former chmn of bd, founder, Greater Knoxville Minority Business Bureau Inc; former chmn, pres, Knoxville Comm Coop, former mem, Natl Rural Cable TV Task Force; co-founder, Greater Knoxville Urban League; co-founder, former mem of bd of dir, Knoxville Oppty Indust Ctr Inc. **Honors/Awds:** TN 94th Gen Assembly, Untiring Service to Humanity, US Dept of Commerce, Nashville Bus Devt Ctr, Bus Advocate of the Year, 1987, 1993; song entitled "Avon Rollins" recorded by MAtt Jones depicting Rollins' involvement in civil rts movement; Natl Assn of Human Rights Workers, dedication of 47th Annual Conf to Rollins, 1994; Natl Civil Rights Museum, named annual Heritage Award after Rollins; Natl Assn of Black Legislatures, Nation Builder Award, 1994; Natl Bus League Award; Booker T Washington Foundation, Leadership & Achievement Award; numerous other awards; Top Ladies of Distinction, Inc, Outstanding Lard, 1995. **Special Achievements:** Publications include: "Minority Economic Development/Problems & Opportunity"; "The Tennessee Black Economy", 1972-; numerous other articles on the civil rights struggle and minority economic development. **Business Addr:** Pres & CEO, Rollins & Associates Inc, 2765 Sunset Ave, Knoxville, TN 37914.

ROLLINS, ETHEL EUGENIA
Social worker (retired). **Personal:** Born Feb 16, 1932, Paris, TX; daughter of Julia Grant and Elisha Grant; married Edward C Rollins; children: Vyla LeJeune, Rojeune Bali. **Educ:** Jarvis Christian Coll, BA 1954; Univ of Pittsburgh, MSW 1958. **Career:** Dayton Children Psych Hosp & Child Guidance Clinic, psych soc worker 1958-62; Family & Childrens Serv Assoc Dayton, psych soc worker 1964-65; Denver Cty Publ School Psych Svc, school social worker 1965-68; Denver Univ, assoc prof soc work 1975-; Ft Logan Mental Health Ctr Denver, psych soc worker 1972-95. **Orgs:** Mem CO Christian Home Bd, CO Christian Home for Children Denver 1970-75; human svcs, adv bd Metro State Coll Denver 1979-84, chairperson 1984-; week of compassion comm Christian Ch Disciples of Christ Indianapolis 1975-80; adv bd Mother to Mother Ministry 1978-80; bd & comm mem Habitat for Humanity 1979-80; leg & social concerns CO Council of Church 1980-82; sec CO Council of Churches 1981-82; chmn Outreach Christian Church Disciples of Christ CO, WY Reg Outreach on Reg Needs 1982-83; activist Peace/Justice Movement/Nuclear Freeze Movement 1982-84; Information and Services, Christian Church (Disciples of Christ) General Assembly, volunteer/lay ministry/vice chairperson, 1997. **Honors/Awds:** Hon Awd for Leadership State Fair of TX 4-H Club 1949; Jarvis Christian College, "Student Contributing Most to the Religious Life of Campus" Award, 1952; author "Changing Trends in Adoption" Natl Conf Social Welfare 1971; Colorado Christian Home, Outstanding Leadership Award, 1971-75; Rojeune, Edward & Ethel appeared as family on KCNC NBC Affil Denver CO 1983 discussing film "The Day After"; Human Services Department/Human Serv Education Organization, Outstanding Member/Chair, 1988. **Home Addr:** 2439 S Dahlia Ln, Denver, CO 80222.

ROLLINS, LEE OWEN
Business executive. **Personal:** Born Dec 22, 1938, Kansas City, KS; married Rosalie D; children: Lori, Linda, Larry, Lonny, Lyle. **Educ:** Univ of NE, psychology 1956-63. **Career:** San Diego Gas & Elec, mgr employment 1979-, employment rep 1968-78, license negotiator 1966-68; Flintkote Co Los Angeles CA, marketing rep 1963-66. **Orgs:** Bd mem Western Coll Placement Assn 1975-80; chmn Affirmative Action Com WCPA 1975-78; vice pres campus relations Soc for Advancement of Mgmt 1979-; vice pres transportation SD Jr C of C 1970-74; dir Southeast Rotary 1974-79; dir Amigos del Ser 1979-80; Outstanding Kappa Man ETA Chap Univ of NE 1960. **Honors/Awds:** Community Serv Award Nat Alliance of Businessmen 1968; Outstanding Serv Award Urban League 1979. **Business Addr:** 101 Ash St, San Diego, CA 92101.

ROLLINS, RICHARD ALBERT
Educator. **Personal:** Born Nov 30, 1927, Philadelphia, PA; married Audrey J King. **Educ:** Lincoln Univ, AB 1952; Union Theological Seminary, MDiv 1955; Boston Univ School of Theology, STM 1960; Claremont School of Theology, RelD 1969. **Career:** Bishop Coll, chmn div of rel 1958-67, assoc dean/admin 1969-70, dean of the college 1970-77, vice pres for pme/prof of religion 1977-83, exec asst to pres dean of chapel 1983-. **Orgs:** Mem Goals for Dallas, Natl Urban League, NAACP, Natl Campus Ministry Assoc, Acad of Religion, TX Alcohol/Narcotics Assoc; bd of dirs Dallas YMCA; chmn-Moorland Branch YMCA 1969-85. **Honors/Awds:** Danforth Foundation Teacher Awd 1960-62; Ford Foundation Fellowship Awd 1967; Dallas Citizenship Awd Radio Station KNOK 1970. **Military Serv:** AUS corpl 2 yrs. **Home Addr:** 630 Woodacre Dr, Dallas, TX 75241. **Business Addr:** Exec Asst to the President, Bishop Coll, 3837 Simpson Stuart Rd, Dallas, TX 75241.

ROLLINS, SONNY. See ROLLINS, WALTER THEODORE.

ROLLINS, TREE (WAYNE MONTE)
Professional basketball player. **Personal:** Born Jun 16, 1955, Winter Haven, FL; children: Nicolas, Undria, Katreesa. **Educ:** Clemson Univ, Clemson, SC, 1973-77. **Career:** Center: Atlanta Hawks, 1977-88, Cleveland Cavaliers, 1988-90, Detroit Pistons, 1990-91, Houston Rockets, 1991-93; Orlando Magic, 1993-. **Honors/Awds:** NBA All-Defensive First Team, 1984; NBA All-Defensive Second Team, 1983; led NBA in blocked shots, 1983. **Special Achievements:** Orlando Magic, player/asst coach, 2nd season; NBA Player, 18th season; 3rd oldest active player behind Robert Parrish & Moses Malone, 1994-95; Atlanta Hawks Career Record, most games played 814; blocked

shots 2,283; defensive rebounds 4,092. **Business Addr:** Professional Basketball Player, Orlando Magic, 1 Magic Pl, Orlando, FL 32801.

ROLLINS, WALTER THEODORE (SONNY ROLLINS)
Composer, musician. **Personal:** Born Sep 7, 1930, New York City, NY; son of Valborg and Walter; married Lucille. **Career:** Recording career started in 1949, involved in modern jazz movement; travelling & rec band; has recorded with: Bud Powell, Dizzy Gillespie, Max Roach, Clifford Brown and Thelonious Monk; discography contains 71 recordings, 1997. **Honors/Awds:** Numerous trade mag awds abroad & in US; Guggenheim Fellow 1972; Hall of Fame Downbeat Mag; Honorary Doctorate of Music Bard College, 1992. **Special Achievements:** His Freedom Suite, 1957, anticipated the jazz protest movement of later years. **Business Addr:** PO Box 175, Route 9G, Germantown, NY 12526.

ROMANS, ANN
Association executive, educator. **Personal:** Born Apr 3, 1929, Wetumpka, AL; daughter of Tumpa Riley Varner (deceased) and John Varner; married Lawrence Jones, Mar 9, 1960 (divorced); children: Anthony L Jones. **Educ:** Knoxville College, Knoxville, TN, BA, education, 1952; University of Tennesse, Knoxville, TN sp education; Case-Western Reserve University, Cleveland, OH, 1965; John Carroll University, Cleveland, OH, computer education, 1985, master's degree, 1996. **Career:** Cleveland School Bd, Cleveland, OH, teacher/sub teacher, 1952; Comedian, Cleveland, OH, 1979; Help Educate for Service, Cleveland, OH, director, 1979-; Cleveland Black Writers, Cleveland, OH, president, 1986-. **Orgs:** Alpha Kappa Alpha Sorority, 1951-; Political Black Caucus, 1973-; 21st District Caucus, 1973-; St Mark's Presbyterian Church, 1948-. **Honors/Awds:** 21st District Caucus Community Award; Ohio Director of Miss Galaxy Black Pageant, 1968; Comedy Award, Cleveland Comedy Club, 1989. **Home Addr:** 3685 Winchell Rd, Cleveland, OH 44122.

ROMES, CHARLES MICHAEL
Professional football player (retired). **Personal:** Born Dec 16, 1954, Verdun, France; married Redalia; children: Twila Redalia. **Educ:** Lake City Junior College; North Carolina Central Univ. **Career:** Cornerback: Buffalo Bills, 1977-86; San Diego Chargers, 1987; Seattle Seahawks, 1988.

ROMNEY, EDGAR O.
Labor union official. **Personal:** Born Feb 9, 1943, New York, NY; son of Ida Johnstone Romney and Edward Romney; married Gladys Talbot Romney, Oct 20, 1972; children: Juliette, Monique, Nicola, Edgar Jr. **Educ:** Hunter College, Queens, NY, 1972-75; Empire State Labor College, New York, NY, 1979-82. **Career:** Local 99, ILGWU, New York, NY, organizer/business agent, 1966-75; Local 23-25, ILGWU, New York, NY, dir of organization, 1976-78, asst manager, 1978-83, manager/secretary, 1983-; ILGWU, New York, NY, executive vice president, 1989-; UNITE!, exec vp, 1995-. **Orgs:** 2nd vice president, New York City Labor Council AFL-CIO, 1992-; board of directors, Garment Industry Development Corp, 1987-; board of directors, New York State Dept of Labor Garment Advisory Council, 1988-; board of directors, Bayard Rustin Fund, 1989-; national secretary, A Philip Randolph Institute, 1987-; board of directors, New York Urban League, 1987-; board of directors, American Labor ORT Federation, 1986-; co-chair, New York Labor Committee Against Apartheid, 1989-94; co-chairman, NY Committee for African Labor Solidarity, 1994-; membership, Congressional Black Caucus, Braintrust on Labor Issues, 1991-. **Honors/Awds:** Achievement Award, NAACP, New York Branch, 1987; Outstanding Leadership in Labor & Community Service, Borough of Manhattan Community College, 1989; Outstanding Service & Commitment/Hispanic Labor Committee, 1989; Distinguished Service Award AFL-CIO, 1990; Nelson Mandela Award, Coalition of Black Trade Unionists, 1984, 1989 Recognition Award, Chinatown, YMCA, 1988; NAACP Man of the Year Award NAACP, 1987; Recognition Award, Negro Labor Committee, 1984; Roberto Clemente Appreciation Award/Hispanic Labor Committee, 1987; Leadership Award, American ORT Federation, 1989. **Business Addr:** Exec VP, UNITE!, Manager Secretary, Local 23-25, 275 7th Ave, 10th Fl, New York, NY 10001.

RONEY, RAYMOND G.
Educator, publisher. **Personal:** Born Jul 26, 1941, Philadelphia, PA; son of Rosezell Harris Roney and Wallace Roney; married Ruth A Westgaph; children: Andre. **Educ:** Central State Univ, BA Pol Sci 1963; Pratt Inst, MS Library Science 1965; Catholic Univ, Post Grad, 1980-85. **Career:** Howard Univ Library, supr ref dept 1965-66; Natl League of Cities/US Conf Mayors, dir library serv 1966-70; Washington Tech Inst, dir library services 1970-78; Wash Tech Inst, chmn med tech dept 1971-78; Univ of the District of Columbia, deputy dir learning resources, 1978-83; El Camino Coll, assoc dean learning resources 1984, dean instructional serv 1988-; publisher Library Mosaics Magazine 1989-. **Orgs:** Pres Cncl on Lib/Media Tech 1983; bd mem COLT 1978; mem ALA, ACRL, AECT, COLT 1970; mem Phi Delta Kappa 1980; pres Shepherd Park Citizens Assn (DC) 1972-74; exec bd Paul Comm School 1974-83; United Way Advisory Board 1988-; dir California Library Employees Assn 1988; library advisory board, Afro-American Museum of CA 1989-; long range planning committee member, 1988-91, membership committee, 1989-91, California Library Assn; program planning committee member, CARL, 1989-91; Learning Resources Association of California Community Colleges, bd mem 1994-. **Honors/Awds:** Outstanding Achievement Bright Hope Baptist Church 1963; Grass Roots Award DC Fed Civic & Citizens Assn 1975; Outstanding Achievement Shepherd Park Citizens Assn 1975; Book Intro to AV for Tech Assts 1981; Book Classification Index for Urban Collections 1969; Book Job Descriptions for Library Support Personnel, 1986; Audiovisual Technology Primer, Libraries Unlimited 1988; Directory of Institutions Offering Training Programs for Library/Media Technicians, 1992; INTELECOM, Administrative Excellence Award, 1993; California Assn of Post Secondary Educ and Disabilities, Administrator of the Year Award, 1997. **Business Addr:** Dean, Instructional Services, El Camino Coll, 16007 Crenshaw Blvd, Torrance, CA 90506.

ROOKS, CHARLES SHELBY
Theologian (retired). **Personal:** Born Oct 19, 1924, Beaufort, NC; son of Maggie Hawkins Rooks and Shelby A Rooks; married Adrienne Martinez; children: Laurence Gaylord, Carol Ann. **Educ:** VA State Coll, AB 1949; Union Theol Sem, MDiv 1953; Coll of Wooster, DD 1968; Interdenominational Theol Ctr, DD 1979; VA Union Univ, DD 1980. **Career:** Shanks Vill Protestant Church Orangeburg, pastor 1951-53; Lincoln Meml Temple United Church of Christ Washington, pastor 1953-60; Fund for Theol Educ Princeton, assoc dir 1960-67, exec dir 1967-74; Chicago Theol Sem, pres 1974-84; United Church Bd for Homeland Ministries, exec vice pres, 1984-92. **Orgs:** Pres Commun Recruitment & Training Inc; bd of dir Office of Comm United Church of Christ; Pres, Soc for the Study of Black Religion, 1970-74, 1980-84. **Honors/Awds:** Distinguished Service Medal, Association of Theological Schools in the US and Canada, 1992; Numerous honorary degrees. **Special Achievements:** Author of Rainbows and Reality, Atlanta, The ITC Press 1984; The Hopeful Spirit, New York, Pilgrim Press 1987; Revolution in Zion; Reshaping African American Ministry, 1960-74, New York, Pilgrim Press, 1990. **Military Serv:** US Army, SSgt, 1943-46. **Home Addr:** 83 Riverbend Dr, New Brunswick, NJ 08902.

ROOKS, SEAN LESTER
Professional basketball player. **Personal:** Born Sep 9, 1969, New York, NY. **Educ:** Arizona, 1992. **Career:** Dallas Mavericks, center, 1992-94; Minnesota Timberwolves, 1994-96; Atlanta Hawks, 1996; Los Angeles Lakers, 1996-. **Business Addr:** Professional Basketball Player, Los Angeles Lakers, PO Box 10, Inglewood, CA 90306, (213)419-3100.

ROPER, BOBBY L.
Educational administrator. **Personal:** Born in Chicago, IL; son of Irvia Carter Roper and William Roper; children: Reginald. **Educ:** Chicago Teachers College, BED, 1959; Chicago State University, MS, 1966. **Career:** Chicago Public School master teacher 1962-64, adjustment teacher 1965-68, asst principal 1968-71; Lawndale Comm Academy, principal, currently. **Orgs:** Board of dirs Lawndale Homemakers 1970-75; board of directors Chicago Youth Center 1975-; board of directors Marcy Newberry Center 1982-83. **Military Serv:** US Army, corporal, 1954-56. **Business Addr:** Principal, Lawndale Community Acad, 3500 W Douglas Blvd, Chicago, IL 60623.

ROPER, DEIDRE (SPINDERELLA)
Rapper, business owner. **Career:** Mem, rap group Salt-N-Pepa, currently; owner, She Things Salon and Day Spa, currently.

ROPER, GRACE TROTT
Librarian (retired). **Personal:** Born Sep 8, 1925, New York, NY; daughter of Erma Trott and Edwin Trott; married Ivan Roper; children: James, Eric, Johanna, Robert. **Educ:** City Coll of NY; Newark St Coll. **Career:** NY Public Library, asst to children lib 1950-54; Belmar Public Library, library dir 1962-93. **Orgs:** Chmn Monmouth Council of Girl Scouts 1974-76; mem & sec The Vestry 1975; Belmar Bd of Educ 1976-; bd dir Monmouth Coun of Girl Scouts 1976; rec sec Monmouth Cty Lib Assn 1976-77; vice pres Monmouth Cty Lib Assn 1977-; Belmar Wom Club; Jersey Ctrl Bus Prof Wom Club; St Agnes Guild St Augustine's Epis Ch; Art on Belmar in Am Ency; pres of Belmar Bd of Educ 1983-85; Belmar Bd of Education, 1985-. **Honors/Awds:** Wrote and published book on Belmar history, copyright 1978. **Home Addr:** 406 9th Ave, Belmar, NJ 07719.

ROPER, RICHARD WALTER
Executive. **Personal:** Born Sep 20, 1945, Deland, FL; son of Dorothe Roper and Henry Roper; married Marlene Peacock; children: Jelani, Akil. **Educ:** Rutgers Univ, BA 1968; Princeton Univ, MPA 1971. **Career:** NJ Department of Higher Education, Trenton, NJ, asst to the vice chancellor, 1968-69; Dept of Transportation and Planning Greater London Council, London, England, research asst, 1971; Mayor's Education Task Force, Office of Newark Studies, Newark, NJ, staff coordinator, 1971-72; NJ Dept of Institutions and Agencies Div of Youth and Family Services, Trenton, NJ, 1972-73; Greater Newark Urban Coaltion, NJ Education Reform Project, Newark, NJ, director, 1973-74; Mayor Kenneth A Gibson, Newark, NJ, legislative aide, 1974-76; Office of Newark Studies, Newark, NJ, director, 1976-78; US Dept of Commerce, Office of the Secretary, Washington, DC, director, 1979-80; Woodrow Wilson School of Public and Intl Affairs, Program for NJ Affairs, PrincetonUniversity, Princeton, NJ, director, 1980-88, asdean for graduate career services and governmental relations, 1988-1992; Port Authority of NY & NJ, director, Office of Economic and Policy Analysis, 1992-. **Orgs:** Bd trustees, Newark Public Radio; mem Governor's Taskforce on Child Abuse and Neglect, 1984-; NJ Child Life Protection Comm; bd dirs, NJ Public Policy Research Institute; bd trustees, exec committee member, Boys' & Girls' Clubs of Newark, NJ; board director, Associate of Black Princeton Alumni; bd of dirs, Greater Jamaica Development Corp, NY; bd of dirs, Assn of Black Princeton Alumni; bd of overseers, Rutgers University Foundation; advisory committee, Center for Government Services, Rutgers University; advisory bd, New Jersey Natl Center for Public Productivity. **Honors/Awds:** Distinguished Princeton Alumni, 1992; NJ NAACP Service Award, 1990; NJ Legal Services Recognition Award, 1989. **Special Achievements:** ''Building One New Jersey,'' New Jersey Reporter, February 1990; ''New Jersey's Crunch: Better to Take the Hit Now,'' Commentary, Asbury Park Press, April 1990; ''Florio's Fiscal Plan Makes Sense,'' coauthor, Trenton Times, October 1990; ''The 1991 Legislative Election in New Jersey: An Analysis,'' Black Issues Convention Quarterly, December 1991; ''An Analysis of Changes in Population, Education and Income for African-Americans in New Jersey: 1980-90 (Northern Counties)'', New Jersey African-Americans and the 1980 Census, New Jersey Public Policy Research Institute, Inc, February, 1994. **Home Addr:** 12 Rutgers St, Maplewood, NJ 07040. **Business Addr:** Director, Office of Economic and Policy Analysis, Port Authority of NY & NJ, One World Trade Center #545, New York, NY 10048.

ROSCOE, WILMA J.
Association executive. **Personal:** Born Aug 24, 1938, Kershaw, SC; daughter of Estelle Harris and Chalmers Harris; married Alfred D Roscoe Jr, Jul 6, 1963; children: Alfred D Roscoe III, Jenae V, Jeneen B. **Educ:** Livingstone College, Salisbury, NC, BS, 1960. **Career:** Howard University, Washington, DC, admissions assistant, 1963-69; Fayetteville State University, Fayetteville, NC, director of tutorial program, 1969-74; National Association for Equal Opportunity in Higher Education, Washington, DC, 1975-. **Orgs:** Member, American Personnel and Guidance Association; member, National Coalition of Black Meeting Planners; member, Delta Sigma Theta. **Honors/Awds:** Distinguished service award, National Association for Equal Opportunity in Higher Education, 1986; DHL, Livingstone College, Salisbury, NC, 1989; National Business League Award. **Home Addr:** 6001 Joyce Drive, Camp Springs, MD 20748. **Business Addr:** Vice President, National Association for Equal Opportunity in Higher Educati, 400 12th Street, NE, Lovejoy Building, Washington, DC 20002.

ROSE, ALVIN W.
Educator. **Personal:** Born Feb 14, 1916, New Haven, MO; married Helen Cureton. **Educ:** Lincoln U, BA 1938; Univ of IA, MA 1942; Univ of Chicago, PhD 1948; Sorbonne Paris, postdoctoral study 1952. **Career:** Fisk Univ, prof of Sociology 1946-47; NC Coll, prof 1948-56; Wayne State Univ, prof 1956-72; Dept of Sociology Wayne State Univ, chmn 1968-72; Univ of Miami, prof 1972-; visiting prof & lectr at numerous coll & univ. **Orgs:** Mem Am Social Assn; Soc for Study of Social Problems; Am Assn of Univ Prof; Intl Soc for Scientific Study of Race Relations; So Social Soc; AmAcad of Political & Social Sci; Phi Delta Kappa Social Sci Soc; Alpha Kappa Delta Social Soc; Nat Assn of Intergroup Relations Officials; FL Social Soc; African Studies Assn; NAACP; mem bd of Govs Museum of Sci; bd dir United Nations Assn; chmn Intergroup Relations Sect Soc for Study of Social Problems; mem Univ of Miami Com on Salaries Rank & Promotion; mem Univ of Miami Grad Com on Degrees & Acad Prog; Univ of Miami Faculty Com for Afro-Am Studies; mem exec com Univ Cntr for Urban Studies; Author of Numerous Publications. **Business Addr:** Ashe Adminstrn Bldg, U of Miami, Coral Gables, FL 33124.

ROSE, ARTHUR
Artist, educator. **Personal:** Born May 26, 1921, Charleston; married Elizabeth; children: 4. **Educ:** Claflin Coll, BA 1950; NYU, MA 1952; IN Univ, post graduate, 1966-68. **Career:** Claflin Coll Orangeburg SC, head of art dept 1952-; Holmes Elem School, teacher, 1950-51. **Orgs:** Mem, Natl Conf Artists; SC Assn School Art; Smithsonian Assn; AAUP. **Honors/Awds:** Best in Show Award JO Endris & Sons Jewelers 1967; Second Award Nat Conf Artists 1970. **Military Serv:** USNR ship serviceman 3rd class 1942-45.

ROSE, BESSIE L.
Electrical engineer. **Personal:** Born Mar 2, 1958, Lafayette, LA; daughter of Iritha Stevens Rose and Andrew Rose. **Educ:** Southern Univ, Baton Rouge, LA, BSEE, 1980. **Career:** Naval Air Rework Facilities, Pensacula, FL, co-op student, 1976-78; Xerox, Rochester NY, summer intern, 1979; Commonwealth Edison, Chicago, IL, electrical engr, 1980-. **Orgs:** Mem, Alpha Kappa Alpha, 1977-; mem, Natl Black MBA Assn, 1990-;

mem, League of Black Women, 1990-. **Honors/Awds:** Section Engr (responsible for defining, developing and implementing an entirely new dept on quality control). **Business Addr:** Section Engineer, Distribution Engineering Services, Commonwealth Edison Co, 1319 South First Ave, Maywood, IL 60153.

ROSE, JALEN
Professional basketball player. **Personal:** Born Jan 30, 1973, Detroit, MI. **Educ:** Univ of Michigan. **Career:** Denver Nuggets, guard, 1994-96; Indiana Pacers, 1996-. **Honors/Awds:** NBA All-Rookie Second Team, 1995. **Special Achievements:** Member of the Fab Five, Univ of Michigan Basketball Team, 1991-94; NBA Draft, First round pick, #13, 1994. **Business Addr:** Professional Basketball Player, Indiana Pacers, 300 E Market St, Indianapolis, IN 46204, (317)263-2100.

ROSE, MALIK JABARI
Professional basketball player. **Personal:** Born Nov 23, 1974, Philadelphia, PA. **Educ:** Drexel. **Career:** Charlotte Hornets, forward, 1996-97; San Antonio Spurs, 1997-. **Business Addr:** Professional Basketball Player, San Antonio Spurs, 600 E Market St, San Antonio, TX 78205, (210)554-7773.

ROSE, RACHELLE SYLVIA
Clinical social worker. **Personal:** Born Aug 19, 1946, Chicago, IL. **Educ:** District of Columbia Teachers Coll, BS Educ 1974; Howard Univ Grad Sch of Social Work, MSW 1976. **Career:** Kaiser Permanente Hospital, licensed clinical social worker. **Orgs:** Past mem Kappa Delta Pi Natl Teachers Honor Soc,Howard Univ; mem Natl Assoc of Social Workers; Calif Soc of Clinical Social Workers; Alpha Kappa Alpha Sorority, Mu Lambda Omega Chapt, Culver City, CA. **Business Addr:** Clinical Social Worker, Kaiser Permanente Hospital, 1505 Sunset Blvd, Los Angeles, CA 90027.

ROSE, RAYMOND EDWARD
Engineer. **Personal:** Born Jul 17, 1926, Canton, OH; married Jessica Mack (divorced); children: Sharon, Critchett, Dan, Tim. **Educ:** Univ of Kansas, BA, 1951; Univ of Minnesota, MSAE, 1956, PhD, 1966. **Career:** Rosemount Aero Labs, Univ of Minnesota, jr engr to scientist aerodyn, 1951-62, res fel, 1962-66; Honeywell, Inc, Minneapolis, MN, sr prin res scientist, 1966-72, sr prin res scientist prog mgr, 1972-74, proj staff engr scientist, 1974-76; Aerodyn & Active Controls, prog mgr aircraft energy efficiency, 1976-79, prog mgr of gen aviation, subsonic aircraft technol, 1979-84; NASA Headquarters, Washington, DC, gen aviation & commuter aerodynamics & coordinator, manager, 1984-. **Orgs:** American Helicopter Soc, American Inst of Aeronautics & Astronautics; Tau Beta Pi; Sigma Gamma Tau; Sigma Tau. **Honors/Awds:** Space Ship Earth Award, NASA, 1980. **Special Achievements:** 22 Publications, 1953-73; 12 Presentations at Tech Conf, Symposiums, Universities, etc, 1971-75; Control Apparatus-Shock Swallowing Air Data Sensor for Aircraft, patent, 1971; numerous contributions to the research & development of aviation. **Military Serv:** USAAF, 1945-46.

ROSE, SHELVIE
Educator, city official. **Personal:** Born Jan 5, 1936, Covington, TN; married Odessa White; children: Delores, Shelvie Jr, Saundra, Kelda La Trece, Kenny. **Educ:** TN State U, BS; Memphis State Univ Univ of TN, Grad Study. **Career:** Tipton Co Bd of Educ, health & driver educ instr; Aquatics, pro boy scout instr 1959-63; Tipton Co Pub Sch System, instr 1959-; Tipton Co, alderman, District 1, commr, currently. **Orgs:** Alderman Committee; Finance and Administration; General Welfare-Public Relations; Tipton Co Pub Works; bd of control; Tipton Co Voters Council; Tennessee Voters Council, board member. **Business Addr:** Instructor, Brighton High School, Brighton, TN 38011.

ROSEMAN, JENNIFER EILEEN
Public information director. **Personal:** Born Sep 6, 1952, Spokane, WA; daughter of Jerrelene Hill Williamson and Sam Williamson; married Larry Roseman Sr, May 13, 1983; children: Larry Jr, Maya. **Educ:** New York University, New York, NY, BA, journalism, 1974; Gonzaga University, Spokane, WA, MA, organizational leadership, 1989. **Career:** New York Daily News, New York, NY, intern, 1973-74; The San Diego Union, San Diego, CA, reporter, 1974-78; The Spokesman-Review, Spokane, WA, editor/editorial writer, 1978-92; Community Colleges of Spokane, director of communications & development, 1992-. **Orgs:** Junior League of Spokane; chair, Instructional Equity Committee; Spokane School District 81; cultural awareness trainer, City of Spokane, 1990; Links, Inc. **Business Addr:** Director, Communications & Development, Community Colleges of Spokane, N 2000 Greene St, Spokane, WA 99207.

ROSEMOND, JOHN H.
Physician. **Personal:** Born Oct 17, 1917, Jacksonville, FL; married Rosalie Edge; children: John Jr, Janith, Ronald. **Educ:** FL A&M Univ, BS 1941; Howard Univ, MD 1951; DC General Hosp, intern 1951-52. **Career:** AUS Fort Belvoir VA, civilian phy one yr; Ohio Univ Coll Med, instr; physician private practice; Columbus OH Mem Soc Tchr Family Med 1985. **Orgs:** Mem med staff Grant St Anthony Mt Carmel Childrens & Univ Hosp; Flying Phy Assn; Fellow Am Acad Family Phy; pres bd trustees Columbus Tech Inst; chmn Freedom Fund; OH N AACP; Basileus Omega Psi Phi Frat 1970; mem bd dir Beneficial Acceptance Corp; exec bd Central OH Council; Boy Scouts Am 1968; chmn Columbus UN Festival; city councilman 1969-; chmn Service & Airport Com; mem Columbus Airport Commn & Council Rep Columbus Bd Health; elder Bethany Presb Ch; bd trustees Nat Med Assn; diplomate Am Bd of Family Practice; pres pro-team Columbus City Council; mem Min Affairs Com Am Acad of Family Physicians; Columbus Acad of Medicine; Ohio State Medical Assn; Central Ohio Acad of Family Physicians; Amer Acad of Family Physicians; Natl Medical Assn. **Honors/Awds:** Frontiers Man Yr Columbus Chap Frontiers Intl 1969; Omega Man Yr 1970; Gen Practitioner Yr Nat Med Assn 1970; Layman Yr United Presb Ch 1973; Family Phy Yr OH Acad Family Phy 1974. **Military Serv:** USAAF navigator-bombardier WWII 1st lt discharged 1946.

ROSEMOND, LEMUEL MENEFIELD
Physician. **Personal:** Born Jan 23, 1920, Pickens, SC; married Gloria Gardner; children: Reginald, Wanda, Lisa. **Educ:** Benedict Coll Columbia SC, BS 1941; Meharry Med Coll Nashville TN, MD 1950. **Career:** Physician private practice 1985; Cherokee, chief of staff. **Orgs:** Mem Hosp 1969-71; Cherokee Med Soc; Am Med Assn 1955-80; Nat Med Assn 1955-80; Am Acad of Family Physicians 1970-80; sec/treas Cherokee Co Med Soc 1973-76; pres Palmetto Med Dental Pharmaceutical Assn SC 1977; adv bd Salvation Army 1970-76; C of C 1974-78; adv bd Bank of Gaffney 1975-78. **Honors/Awds:** Omega Man of the Year Omega Psi Phi Frat 1974; Twenty Five Year Award Meharry Med Coll 1975; Twenty Five Year Serv Award Palmetto Med Dental & Pharm Assn 1979. **Military Serv:** AUS 1st lt 1941-46. **Business Addr:** 313 W Meadow St, Gaffney, SC 29340.

ROSEMOND, MANNING WYLLARD, JR.
Dentist. **Personal:** Born May 20, 1918, Toccoa, GA; married Edrose Smith; children: Manning III. **Educ:** Claflin Univ, AB 1940; Atlanta Univ, MS 1949; OH State Univ, DDS 1956. **Career:** Private practice, dentist, currently. **Orgs:** Mem Pres Adv Bd; pres 1973-74, chmn bd, pres elect 1972-73, vice pres 1971, 1972, exec bd 1967-71 NDA; pres Forest City Dental Study Club 1973-74; founder Buckeye State Dental Assn 1974; dir Jane Adams Dental Clinic 1977-; pres CRC Enterprises; pres Romac Cty; mem Omega Psi Phi, NAACP, Frontiers Intl; holder, pvt pilots license; mem Aircraft Owners & Pilots Assn; mem Amer Dental Assn, OH Dental Assn; pres Max's Aerial Photographic Svcs. **Military Serv:** AUS 1st lt 1942-46,50-52; Bronze Star. **Business Addr:** 1296 Hayden Ave, Cleveland, OH 44112.

ROSENTHAL, ROBERT E.
Business executive. **Personal:** Born Apr 9, 1945, Phillips, MS; son of Inez Rosenthal and J R Rosenthal; children: Robert E Jr. **Educ:** Univ of FL, 1967; Jackson State Univ, BS 1971; Jackson State Univ, Grad Work 1973. **Career:** Whitten Jr High Jackson, teacher 1972; PO Jackson, EEO couns 1974; PO Dist Jackson, EEO spec 1976; PO Edwards MS, postmaster 1978; Mid-South Records Inc Jackson, vp, co-owner 1978; mgmt & mktg consult for artists & record co's; Who's Who in Black Music, editor 1986; Who's Who in Music, editor 1987; Programming Ratio, editor 1987; Rosenthal & Maultsby-Music Research Intl, natl public relations mgr for The Young Black Programmer Coalition & The Black Music Assn; Philadelphia International Records, natl public relations manager; Philadelphia Intl Records, natl public relations mgr; Corps of Engineers, equal emp oppty ofcr, currently. **Orgs:** Mem MS Teachers Assoc, Natl Bus League, Natl Assoc of Postmasters, NAACP, NAREB Realist, Urban League, Jackson State Univ Alumni, Natl Counsel on Affirm Action; mem Minority Bus Brain Trust for the Congressional Black Caucus 1982-83, 1984, 1986, 1987-; Rock Music Assoc; Young Black Programmers Coalition. **Honors/Awds:** Best All Around Student Awd, Rosa Scott HS Madison MS 1963; Music Scholarship Jackson State Univ 1964; Good Conduct Medal. **Military Serv:** USAF 1968. **Business Addr:** Equal Empl Oppty Officer, Corporations of Engineers, Lower Mississippi Valley Div, PO Box 80, Vicksburg, MS 39180.

ROSS, ANTHONY ROGER
Educational administrator. **Personal:** Born Jan 28, 1953, Jamaica, NY; son of Esther Ross and Abram Ross; children: Jamal, Shama. **Educ:** St Lawrence Univ, BA Sociology 1975, MEd Counseling 1978; Northern AZ Univ, EdD 1984. **Career:** Utica Coll of Syracuse Univ, counselor higher educ opportunity prog 1975-76; St Lawrence Univ, dir higher educ opportunity prog 1976-81; St Lawrence Univ, asst basketball coach 1977-80; Northern AZ Univ, asst/assoc dean 1983-84, dean of students 1985-, adjunct professor, 1986-, asst vice president of student services, 1989-. **Orgs:** Amer Coll Personnel Assn 1978-, Amer Assn for Counseling & Devel 1978-; pres Higher Educ Opportunity Prog Professional Org 1976-81; board of directors, 1992-94, Natl Assn of Student Personnel Admin 1980-; NAACP 1982-; Coach, Youth League Basketball & Soccer 1982-, Big Brothers of Flagstaff 1983-, Buffalo Soldiers of Flagstaff 1984-; bd of dirs, Coconino Community Guidance Ctr 1986; Commissioner on Flagstaff Cty Parks and Recreational Commission, 1986-92; president, Arizona Assn of Student Personnel Administrators, 1990-91; member, Blacks for Progress in Higher Education, 1985-; pres, Higher Education Opportunity Program 1979-80. **Honors/Awds:** Athlete of the Year, St Lawrence Univ, 1975; Hall of Fame, St Lawrence Univ, 1986; Distinguished Service Award, Arizona Alliance of Black School Educations, 1992; Distinguished Alumni Award, Northern Arizona University, 1989; America's Best & Brightest Young Business and Professional Men, Dollars & Sense Magazine, 1992. **Business Addr:** Assistant Vice President for Student Services, Northern Arizona University, PO Box 6015, Flagstaff, AZ 86011-6015.

ROSS, CATHERINE LAVERNE
Educator. **Personal:** Born Nov 1, 1948, Cleveland, OH; married Dr Thomas Daniel. **Educ:** Kent St U, BA History/Sociology 1971; Cornell U, M of Regnl Plnning 1973; Cornell U, PhD City & Reg Plnning 1979. **Career:** GA Inst of Tech, asst prof 1976; Atlanta U, asst prof 1977-79; Cornell U, rsrch asst offc of transport 1975-76; Daton Dalton Little Newport Shaker Hgts, OH, transp planner 1973-74; Reg Planning Commn Cleveland, grad Asst 1972; GA Tech Engineering Experiment Sta, consult 1979; Comm Serv Admin Atlanta, consult resrchr 1979. **Orgs:** Mem N At Assn for the Advncmnt of Sci 1978; mem Black Women Academicians 1979; policy analyst, Am Planning Assn Wash DC 1979. **Honors/Awds:** Ford found flwshp Am Soc of Plng Ofcls 1971-73; outstndg women Essence Mag 1974; sci & tech del Six Pan-African Congress Tanzania 1974; Rockefeller found flwshp Cornell Univ 1975. **Business Addr:** Georgia Inst of Technology, College of Architecture, Graduate City Planning Program, Atlanta, GA 30332.

ROSS, CLARENCE S.
Company financial services administrator. **Personal:** Born May 29, 1955, Philadelphia, PA; married Carolyn; children: Three. **Educ:** Dickinson College, BA, economics; Harvard Business School, MBA, general management. **Career:** Coopers & Lybrand, account manager, 1976-78; Corning Glass Works, senior financial analyst of Latin America/Asia, 1980-81, financial supervisor, 1981-82, business controller-consumer products division, 1982-83; PepsiCo Inc, manager of business planning international division, 1980-91, manager of operations analysis-international division, 1984-87; Pepsi Cola Company of Northern California, area chief financial officer, 1987-90; Quaker Oats Company, director of customer financial services, 1990-92, vice president of customer financial services, 1992-. **Business Addr:** VP, Customer Financial Services, Quaker Oats, PO Box 049001, Chicago, IL 60604, (312)222-7111.

ROSS, DIANA
Singer. **Personal:** Born Mar 26, 1944, Detroit, MI; daughter of Ernestine Ross and Fred Ross; married Robert Ellis Silberstein, 1971 (divorced 1976); children: Rhonda Suzanne, Tracee Joy, Chudney; children: Ross Arne. **Career:** Singer, actress; The Primettes; The Supremes; Diana Ross and The Supremes, lead singer, 1960-68; solo performer, 1970-; Diana Ross Enterprises Inc, pres; Anaid Film Productions; RTC Management Corp; Chondee Inc; Rosstown; Rossville Music Publishing Companies; films include: Lady Sings the Blues, 1972; Mahogany, 1975; The Wiz, 1978; TV Specials include: An Evening with Diana Ross, 1977; Diana, 1981. **Honors/Awds:** Grammy Award for Best Female Vocalist, 1970; Billboard, Cash Box, and Record World Awards for Best Female Vocalist, 1970; Female Entertainer of the Year, NAACP, 1970; Academy Award nomination, Best Actress, Lady Sings the Blues, 1972; Cue Award, 1972; Tony Award, 1977; Inductee, Rock 'n' Roll Hall of Fame, 1988; hits include: "Where Did Our Love Go,"; "Baby Love,"; "Come See About Me,"; "Stop! In the Name of Love"; "Back in My Arms Again"; "I Hear A Symphony"; "Reflections"; "Love Child"; "Someday We'll Be Together"; numerous hit singles and albums as a solo performer including Diana Ross, Everything is Everything, Ross, Why Do Fools Fall in Love, Silk, Take Me Higher. **Business Addr:** Singer, Actress, RTC Management, PO Box 1683, New York, NY 10185.

ROSS, EDWARD
Cardiologist. **Personal:** Born Oct 10, 1937, Fairfield, AL; son of Carrie Griggs Ross and Horace Ross; married Catherine I Webster; children: Edward, Ronald, Cheryl, Anthony. **Educ:** Clark Coll Atlanta, GA, BS 1959; IN Univ Schl of Med, MD 1963. **Career:** Edward Ross, MD, Inc, pres (CEO) 1970-; Medical Cardiovascular Data, Inc, pres (CEO) 1982; Private practice, cardiologist; Methodist Hospital of Indiana, director of cardiovascular patient care programs, chief of cardiovascular medicine and surgery, 1989-95. **Orgs:** Cntrl IN Comprehensive Health Plng Cncl; Comprehensive Health Plng Cncl Marion Cnty 1972-73; Marion Cnty Medcl Soc; IN State Mdcl Assoc; Royal Soc for the Promotion of Health (London); Amer Soc of Internal Med; Aesculapean Mdcl Soc; NMA pres Hoosier State Mdcl Assoc 1980-86; Natl Mdcl Assoc; Amer Coll of Cardiology; Amer Coll of Angiology; clncl asst prfsr IN Univ Schl of Med 1970-75; sec Div Natl Mdcl Assoc 1972-73; pres elec Mdcl-Dental Serv Inc 1971-78; brd dir Cntrl IN TB & Resp Diseases Assoc 1971-74; apt Natl Cntr for Health Serv Rsch & Dvlpmnt 1970; med dir Martindale Health Center, 1968-71;

member, Indiana State Medical Assn; member, Council on Scientific Assembly; board of directors, Assn of Black Cardiologists, 1990-92. **Honors/Awds:** Fellowship Woodrow Wilson 1959, IN Heart Assoc 1961-62; Dept of Cardiology, Research Fellow in Cardiology Dept of Med 1968-70; chief fellow int med IN Univ 1969-70; Certificate of Merit Scientific Achievements in Biology 1959; natl Fdn Health Schlrshp 1955; Fellow Royal Soc for the Promotion of Health, 1974; Fellow, Amer Coll of Angiology; Fellow, Amer Coll of Cardiology; Fellow, International College of Angiology, 1971-. **Military Serv:** USAAF, captain, Certificate of Appreciation SAC 1966-68. **Business Addr:** Chairman Cardiovascular Medicine and Surgery, Methodist Hospital of Indiana, 3737 N Meridian, #400, Indianapolis, IN 46208.

ROSS, EMMA JEAN
Educator. **Personal:** Born Sep 6, 1945, Independence, LA; daughter of Lillie Leola Brown Ross and Isaac E Ross Sr. **Educ:** Southern University, BS, 1970; Southeastern Louisiana University, MA, 1974, admin, supervision, 1979. **Career:** Washington Parish School, librarian, 1970-84, guidance counselor, 1984-; Licensed Professional Counselor, 1990-; Varnado High School, principal, 1993-. **Orgs:** Theta Theta Zeta, 1974-; Louisiana School Counselor's Association, 1989-; Louisiana Counseling Association, 1989-; Louisiana Association of Multi-Cultural Development, 1989-. **Home Addr:** PO Box 202, Varnado, LA 70467, (504)986-2491. **Business Addr:** Guidance Counselor, Varnado High School, 25543 Washington St, Guidance Dept, Angie, LA 70426, (504)732-2025.

ROSS, FRANK KENNETH
Certified public accountant. **Personal:** Born Jul 9, 1943; son of Ruby Ross and Reginald Ross; married Cecelia M Mann; children: Michelle, Michael. **Educ:** Long Island Univ, BS 1966, MBA 1968. **Career:** Peat, Marwick, Mitchell & Co CPA, partner 1966-73; Ross, Stewart & Benjamin, PC, CPA, pres/owner 1973-76; KPMG Peat Marwick, partner 1976-96; Washington DC Office and Midatlantic Area, managing partner, 1996-. **Orgs:** 1st natl pres/founder Natl Assn of Black Accountants 1969-70; mem Amer Inst of CPA's 1969-; tresurer Ellington Fund 1982-; mem Bd of Councillors, Coll of Business & Public Mgmt, Univ of the District of Columbia 1983-; treas Washington Urban League 1986-; pres, bd mem Iona Senior Services; vice pres, treasurer Corcoran Museum & School of Art, 1994-; visiting prof Howard Univ 1982-; KPMG, board of directors, 1993-96, management committee, 1996-. **Honors/Awds:** Black Achievers in Industry YMCA of Greater NY 1980; Outstanding Achievement Award Washington DC Chapter NABA 1984; Distinguished Serv Awd NABA 1985; Accountant of the Year, Beta Alpha Psi, 1994. **Business Addr:** Partner, KPMG Peat Marwick, 2001 M St, Washington, DC 20036.

ROSS, JOANNE A.
Association executive. **Personal:** Born Jun 24, 1929, East Falmouth, MA; children: Margo Ross, Nathan G, Armond. **Career:** Univ Yr for Action Univ MS Boston Harbor Campus, dir 1985; Boston Univ Sch of Urban Studies & Planning, visiting lectr 1974-75; Tufts Experimental Coll Sociology Dept, faculty 1966-69; Commonwealth Serv Corps Boston, dir regional; Orgn for Social & Tech Innovations, consult 1968-71; Mustang Industrial Cleaners Inc, pres 1974-. **Orgs:** Mem Review Com Nation Cntr for Health Svcs; incorporating mem Elma Lewis Sch of Fine Arts MS; chrprsn Statewide Council Ofc for Children 1974-; interimchrprsn TCHUBA Cape Verdean Am Releif Orgn 1975; vol Lobbyist Welfare Rights & Civil Libs. **Honors/Awds:** Recip NASW Comm Serv 1965; Columbia Point Civic Assn Comm Serv 1963, 1965, 1966; Lambda Kappa Contrib of Pub Serv 1968.

ROSS, KEVIN ARNOLD
Attorney. **Personal:** Born Apr 22, 1955; married Gornata Lynn Cole; children: Kelly Alexis, April Whitney. **Educ:** Dartmouth Coll, BA 1973-77; Emory Law School, JD 1977-80. **Career:** Kilpatrick & Cody, summer legal clinic 1979; Long & Aldridge, assoc attny beginning 1980; Hunton & Williams, 1992-, managing partner, 1994-. **Orgs:** Staff lawyer Volunteer Lawyer for the Arts 1981-84; sec, vp, pres elect, pres Gate City Bar Assoc 1982-85; vice pres Amer Diabetes Assoc 1982-84; mem StateLicensing Bd of Used Car Dealers 1984-89. **Honors/Awds:** Leader Under 30 Ebony Mag 1985. **Business Addr:** Managing Partner, Hunton & Williams, Nations Bank Plaza, 600 Peachtree St, Ste 4100, Atlanta, GA 30308.

ROSS, LEE ELBERT
Educator. **Personal:** Born Mar 16, 1958, Shorter, AL; son of Geneva Trimble & Silas Bates Ross Sr; married Leslie Ann, Aug 31, 1985; children: Christopher Daniel, Alexander Nelson. **Educ:** Niagara University, BA, 1981; Rutgers University, The Graduate School of Criminal Jus, MA, 1983, PhD, 1991. **Career:** NY State Sentencing Guidelines Commission, 1984; US Treasury Department, customs officer, 1984-91; University of Wisconsin-Milwaukee, associate professor of criminal justice, 1991-. **Orgs:** Academy of Criminal Justice Sciences, 1991-; American Society of Criminology, 1984-; National Organization of Black Law Enforcement Executives, 1991-; American Civil Liberties Union, board member, 1992-; Journal of Crime & Justice, editor/board member, 1996-98; Journal of Criminal Justice Education, editorial board member, 1996-98. **Honors/Awds:** Wisconsin Teaching Fellow, 1996; Patricia Harris Fellowship, 1981-84; Michael J Harasmik Fellowship, 1982-83. **Special Achievements:** "African American Criminologists: 1970-1996," 1997; "School Environment, Self-Esteem & Delinquency," Journal of Crim Justice, 1995; "Religion, Self-Esteem & Deliquancy," Journal of Crime & Justice, 1996; "Religion & Deviance: Exploring the Impact..," Sociological Spectrum, 1992; "Black, Self-Esteem & Delinquency:..," Justice Quarterly, 1992; Expert witness in areas of Crime Causation Theory. **Business Addr:** Associate Prof, Criminal Justice, University of Wisconsin-Milwaukee, School of Social Welfare, PO Box 786, Milwaukee, WI 53201.

ROSS, MARTHA ERWIN
Entrepreneur. **Personal:** Born Jun 4, 1944, Tyler, TX; daughter of Miner Mae Jackson Erwin and Carvie Earnest Erwin Sr; married Lamont W Ross, Oct 27, 1961; children: Stetron Proncell, Trelitha Rochelle Ross Bryant. **Educ:** Business degree in secretarial science, 1967; Bellevue University, management degree (with honors), 1994. **Career:** AT&T, secretary, 1964-66, public relations, 1966-80, network sales support information rep, 1980-85, United Way of Midlands Western/Central, region marketing manager, loaned executive, 1986-88, customer service training technician, 1988-91; OSHA safety inspector, 1991-94, materials auditor, 1994-; Quality Nutrition & Painting Contractors, president, 1985-. **Orgs:** Chamber of Commerce, 1985-; Urban League of Nebraska, 1970-; Urban League Guild, 1970-; Youth Motivation Task Force, marketing manager, 1991; United Way of the Midlands, ambassador, 1978-86; Nebraska for Public Television, auctioneer, 1985, ambassador, 1985-86; YMCA Youth Camp Campaign, 1985-86; Church of Christ, numerous auxiliaries. **Honors/Awds:** KETV Channel 7, Top 10 in Jefferson Award, 1988; United Way, Loaned Executive Honor, Commercial Division, 1988; NPTV, top ambassador, 1987, 1988; Chamber of Commerce, Top Honors, Annual Campaign, 1988-89; Urban League of Nebraska, Top Honors, Membership Drive, 1987-89; Omaha Opportunities Industrialization Center, Honors, 1992, 1993. **Home Addr:** 5741 Tucker St, RR 46, Omaha, NE 68152.

ROSS, MARY OLIVIA
Association executive. **Personal:** Born in Georgia; daughter of Beatrice Taylor Brookins (deceased) and Solomon Brookins (deceased); married Rev Solomon D Ross, May 28, 1930 (deceased); children: Abigail E, Judson B (deceased), William T (deceased), Angelene D, Olivia D McKinney. **Educ:** Spelman Coll, graduate; Wayne State Univ, Univ of MI, grad studies. **Career:** Walker Institute, teacher, 1928-30; Detroit Board of Education, teacher, 1934-44; Natl Baptist Convention USA Inc, pres the women's convention aux. **Orgs:** Bd of trustees Amer Baptist Theol Seminary; bd of mgrs Church Women United; Women's Planning Comm Japan Intl Christian Univ Foundation; exec comm North Amer Baptist Women's Union; bd of trustees Morehouse School of Religion Atlanta; dir minister's wives div Natl Bapt Congress of Christian Educ; Natl Sor of Phi Delta Kappa; life heritage mem NAACP; golden life mem Delta Sigma Theta Sor Inc; Top Ladies of Distinction Inc; guest lecturer/seminar leader First Asian Baptist Congress Hyderabad India; delegate 6th Assembly of the World Cncl of Churches Vancouver BC Canada; central comm World Cncl of Churches. **Honors/Awds:** Hon DD Interdenominational Theol Ctr Atlanta 1982; Founder's Day Speaker Spelman Coll 1983; author "The Minister's Wife" and "New Women for a New World for Christ"; co-author "The Natl Missionary Study Guide"; editor "The Mission"; also has written several brochures and contributed to numerous religious journals and magazines; apptd by Gov of MI to Dr Martin Luther King Jr Holiday Commn 1985; Living Legacy Awd 1986; Honorary Doctorate of Literature, Natchez College, Natchez, MS; Honorary Doctorate of Humane Letters, Bishop College, Dallas, TX; Honorary Doctorate of Humane Letters, Arkansas Baptist College of Little Rock, AR; author, From Crumbs to Gravy, Harlo Press, 1990; Spelman College, doctor of humane lettes, founders day award. **Special Achievements:** Author, Looking Back but Moving ON, 1992; author, The Life & Leadership of Dr S Willie Layten, First President of the Woman's Convention, 1991; author, From Crumbs to Gravy, "From the crumbs of commitment to Jesus Christ, to the gravy of God's grace and boundless love"; appointed life mem, bd of trustees, Spelman College. **Home Addr:** 584 Arden Park Blvd, Detroit, MI 48202.

ROSS, N. RODNEY
Graphic designer, photographer. **Personal:** Born Jun 28, 1957, Indianapolis, IN; son of Virginia Cottee Ross and Norman Ross. **Educ:** Indiana University, Herron School of Art, BFA, 1982. **Career:** Noble Industries, Indianapolis, IN, art dir, 1984-87; Poster Display Co, Beach Grove, IN, graphic artist, 1987-91; Ross Concepts, Art Dept, Indianapolis, IN, pres, 1982-90; Career Com, Advertising Design, prof, 1990-92; Turner, Potts & Ross, Indianapolis, IN, vice pres, currently. **Orgs:** Youth leader/counselor, Community Outreach Ctr, 1985-; mem, Central IN Bicycling Assn, 1988-; African Based Cultures Study Group of Indianapolis, 1989-; Indy Rennaissance, African-American Artists Network, 1990-. **Honors/Awds:** Addy Award, 1992. **Business Addr:** Vice President, Turner, Potts & Ross, 9675 E 300 S, Zionsville, IN 46077-8825.

ROSS, PHYLLIS HARRISON
Educator, psychiatrist. **Personal:** Born Aug 14, 1936, Detroit, MI; married Edgar. **Educ:** Albion Coll Albion MI, BA 1956; Wayne State Univ Detroit 1959, MD; Kings Co Hosp Brooklyn, internship 1959-60. **Career:** NY Med Coll, prof of Psychiatry 1972-; Metropolitan Hosp Comm Mental Health Cntr, dir 1972-; physician pediatrics adult & child psychiatry 1959-; Jacoby Hosp Albert Einstein Coll of Med, residency-adult & child psychiatry 1962-66; NY Hosp/Cornell Med Coll, residency-pediatrics 1960-62. **Orgs:** Bd of dir Empire State Coll of State Univ of NY 1972-79; bd of dir Bank St Coll 1972-79; bd of dir Children's TV Workshop 1976-; pres Black Psychiatrists of Am 1976-78; mem Med Review Bd NYS Commn of Corrections 1976-; mem Minority Adv Comm to Sec of HEW & Adminstr ADAMHA 1978-; author "Getting It Together A Psychology Textbook" plus Tchng Guide 1972; author "The Black Child A Parents Guide" 1973. **Honors/Awds:** Achievement Award Greater NY Links 1973; Distinguished Alumnus Award Albion Coll 1976; Leadership in Med Award Susan Smith McKinney Steward Med Society 1978; Award of Merit Pub Health Assn of New York City 1980. **Business Addr:** Met Hosp CMHC, 1900 Second Ave, New York, NY 10029.

ROSS, RALPH M.
Educator, clergyman. **Personal:** Born Dec 23, 1936, Miami, FL; son of Effie Mae Ross and Leroy Ross; married Gertrude; children: Sharlene, Lydia, Ralph, Ray, Simona, Randall. **Educ:** AB 1961; BD 1965; MDiv 1970; DMin, 1988. **Career:** Beth Salem United Presb Ch Columbus, GA, minister 1965-66; Eastern Airlines Atlanta, ramp agt 1965-66; Mt Zion Baptist Church Miami, asso minister 1966-68; Urban League Miami, field rep 1967-68; Knoxville Coll, campus minister 1968-70; UT Knoxville, lecturer/religious dept 1969-; Knoxville Coll, dean of students; NC A&T State U, dir religious activities 1978-86, asst dean student devel 1986-90; Mount Zion Baptist Church, Miami, FL, pastor/teacher, 1990-. **Orgs:** Mem bd dir Ministries to Blacks in Higher Edn Knoxville; Knoxville Interdenominational Christian Ministeral Alliance; life mem Alpha Phi Alpha; NAACP; Baptist Ministers Council & Faith In The City; ROA. **Honors/Awds:** YMCA Best Blocker Award Knoxville Coll 1959; Rockefeller Fellowship Award 1964; Theta Phi Hon Soc 1965. **Special Achievements:** Named first African-American captain in the US Naval Reserve Chaplains Corps. **Military Serv:** USNR Chaplains Corps capt. **Home Addr:** 501 NE 96th St, Miami, FL 33138. **Business Addr:** Pastor/Teacher, Mt Zion Baptist Church, 301 NE 9th St, Miami, FL 33136.

ROSS, WILLIAM ALEXANDER JACKSON
Physician. **Personal:** Born Nov 26, 1937, Detroit, MI; son of Julia Ross and Turner W Ross; married Etna; children: William Jr, Peter, Benjamin, Roxanne. **Educ:** Univ MI, Wayne State Univ, 1956-60; Meharry Med Coll, MD 1964. **Career:** Private practice, orthopedic surgeon; Childrens' Hosp, teacher; USN, intern 1964-65; USN, resident 1969-73; USN Hosp, physician 1969-73; W Oak Health Ctr, ortho cons; Herrick Hospital, chief of orthopedics; Arlington Medical Group, orthopedic surgeon. **Orgs:** Mem Arlington Med Group, Natl Med Assoc, AMA, Alpha Phi Alpha, NAACP; mem, Sigma Pi Phi. **Honors/Awds:** First black submarine officer, US Navy, 1966; qualified submarine med officer, 1966. **Military Serv:** USN commander 1964-74. **Business Addr:** Orthopedic Surgeon, Arlington Medical Group, 5709 Market St, Oakland, CA 94608.

ROSS, WINSTON A.
Social service director. **Personal:** Born Dec 2, 1941; son of Ruby Swanston Ross and Reginald Ross; married Rosalind Golden. **Educ:** NY City Commnty Coll, AAS 1961; NYU, BS 1963; Columbia Univ Sch of Social Work, MS 1971; Adelphi Univ Sch of Social Work, Doctoral Candid. **Career:** New York City Dept of Social Svcs/Preventive Svcs/Bureau of Child Welfare, caseworker, supr 1966-73; St Dominic's Home, Blauvelt NY, exec supr 1973-74; Graham Home & Sch, Hastings NY, social work supr 1975-76; The Wiltwyck Sch, Yorktown NY, unit dir 1976-78; Westchester Commnty Opportunity Prg, Inc, exec dir, currently. **Orgs:** Chmn Westchester Div, NYS Chap NASW 1979-80, & secy 1981-83; chmn Minority Affairs Com, NYS NASW 1979-84; co-chmn 5th Annual Whitney M Young Conf on Racism & Del of Human Svcs, NASW 1978-83; chairperson Nat Nominations & Leadership Com, NASW 1984-; pres Yonkers, NY Branch NAACP 1971-78; dir Westchester Regnl NYS Conf NAACP 1977-; chmn trustee bd Metropolitan AME Zion Ch 1969-; chmn Career Guidance Advisory Council, Educ Oppor Cntr of Westchester 1979-85; mem Statewide Advisory Council, NYS Div of Human Rights 1984-; mem New York State Bd of Social Work 1987-. **Honors/Awds:** Freedom Fighter Award Yonkers NAACP 1978; Eugene T Reed Medalist, NYS Conf NAACP 1983; Social Worker of The Yr West Div NASW 1982; Citizen of The Yr Omega Psi Phi Frat, Beta Alpha Alpha Chap 1983; delegate Nat Delegate Assemblys NASW, Portland 1977, Philadelphia 1981, Washington DC, 1993. **Military Serv:** AUS sp 4th class 1963-66; National Social Worker of the Year, 1989, National 1st vp, NASW, 1989-91, 1st vp, NACAA, 1992-94. **Home Addr:** Rt 2 Box 327, Yorktown Heights, NY 10598. **Business Addr:** Executive Director, Westchester Comm Opportunity Program, 2269 Saw Mill River Rd, Elmsford, NY 10523.

ROSS-AUDLEY, CHERYL JVONNE
Personnel administrator. **Personal:** Born Sep 25, 1950, Chicago, IL; daughter of Victoria Ross Smith and John Smith; divorced; children: Claude H Audley III. **Educ:** Northern Illinois Univ, Dekalb, IL, BA, 1973, MSE, 1975. **Career:** City of Seattle, Seattle, WA, personnel analyst II, 1981-84; Seattle Public Schools, Seattle, WA, personnel admin, 1984-91; Puyallup Public Schools, Puyallup, WA, exec dir, human resources, 1991-. **Orgs:** President, Benefit Guild Assn, 1989-91; Delta Sigma Theta, 1987; chair, King County Sickle Cell Assn Bd, 1984-. **Honors/Awds:** Outstanding Woman of the Year, Women's Educ Network, 1989; Merit & Special Recognition Award, Black Educators of Greater Puget Sound, 1991; Special Recognition, Washington Assn of School Personnel Administrators, 1991; Top 10 Women in Busines, 1994.

ROSSER, JAMES M.
Educational administrator. **Personal:** Born Apr 16, 1939, East St Louis, IL; son of Mary Bass Rosser and William Rosser; married Carmen Rosita Colby; children: Terrence. **Educ:** Southern IL Univ, Carbondale, BA 1962, MA 1963, PhD 1969. **Career:** Holden Hospital, diagnostic bacteriologist 1961-63; Health Educ & Coordinator of Black Amer Studies, instructor 1962-63; Eli Lily & Co, research Bacteriologist 1963-66; Southern IL Univ, mem graduate faculty 1966-70; Univ KS, ten assoc prof & assoc vice chancellor 1971-74; Dept of Higher Educ, acting vice chancellor 1974-79; Dept of Higher Ed, acting chancellor 1977; California State Univ, Los Angeles, president, 1979-. **Orgs:** Board of governors, American Red Cross, 1986-; board of directors, FEDCO Inc, 1987-; vice chair, Disaster and Community Services Committee, 1990-; advisory board member, Blue Cross of California, 1989-; board of directors, Hispanic Urban Center, Los Angeles, CA, 1979-; board of directors, Los Angeles Urban League, 1982-95; board of directors, Southern California Edison, 1985-; board of directors, Los Angeles Philharmonic Assn, 1986-; bd of dirs, American Council for the Arts, 1991-; advisory council member, Natl Science Foundation Directorate for Education and Human Resources, 1989-96; board of directors, Natl Health Foundation, 1990-; bd of dirs, California Chamber of Commerce, 1993-; bd of dirs, Sanwa Bank of California, 1993-; bd of trustees, The Woodrow Wilson Natl Fellowship Foundation, 1993-; vice chair, American Assn of State Colleges and Universities-Steering Committee for the Council of Urban and Metropolitan Colleges and Universities, 1993-. **Honors/Awds:** Certificate of Merit, City of Los Angeles Human Relations Commission, 1982; Alumni Achievement Award, Southern Illinois Univ, 1982; Leadership Award, Department of Higher Education/EOP Fund, State of New Jersey, 1989; Medal of Excellence, Golden State Minority Foundation, 1990; "Teacher Education: The Linchpin in a Changing Social Order," Southern Illinois Univ, 1986; "Strategic Planning and Management Methodology for Responsible Change," Journal of Library Administration, 1990; Honorable Mention, Outstanding Support of Teacher Education, American Assn of Colleges for Teacher Education, 1992; Watts Foundation Comm Trust, Ed Award, 1995. **Business Addr:** President, California State University, 5151 State University Dr, Los Angeles, CA 90032.

ROSSER, PEARL LOCKHART
Physician. **Personal:** Born Dec 27, 1935, Miami, FL; married Dr Samuel B Rosser; children: Charles. **Educ:** Howard Univ, BS 1956, MD 1960. **Career:** Freedman's Hosp, intern 1960-61, pediatric resd 1961-63; Howard Univ Coll of Med, prof of pediatrics, 1964-85; consultant in Development Pediatics, currently. **Orgs:** Fellow Amer Acad of Pediatrics; Amer Pediatric Soc; Soc for Rsch in Child Develop; Assn for Children with Learning Disabilities; Natl Council on Black Child Development. **Honors/Awds:** Co-editor "The Genetic Metabolic & Devel Aspects of Mental Retardation," 1972; author of numerous other articles and chapters in professional textbooks. **Home Addr:** 2222 Westview Dr, Silver Spring, MD 20910.

ROSSER, SAMUEL BLANTON
Physician, educator. **Personal:** Born Jul 13, 1934, Tallapoosa, GA; married Pearl; children: Charles. **Educ:** Clark Coll, BS 1954; Wayne State Univ, MS 1956; Howard Univ Coll Med, MD 1960. **Career:** Freedmen's Hospital, resident general surgeon 1961-66; Children's Hospital Natl Medical Center, resident 1970-72; Howard Univ Coll Med Pediatric Surgery, assoc prof 1972-. **Orgs:** Pres 1976-77, mem Assoc of Former Interns & Residents of Howard Univ Hosp; fellow Amer Coll Surgeons;, mem Amer Acad Pediatrics, Amer Pediatric Surg Assoc. **Military Serv:** US Army, national guard, major. **Business Addr:** Associate Professor of Surgery, Howard University College of Medicine, 2041 Georgia Ave NW, Washington, DC 20060.

ROSS-LEE, BARBARA
Educational administrator. **Personal:** married Edmond Beverly; children: five. **Educ:** Michigan State Univ, Coll of Osteopathic Medicine, DO. **Career:** Michigan State Univ, assoc dean, until 1993; Ohio Univ Coll of Osteopathic Medicine, dean, 1993-. **Orgs:** Ohio Osteopathic Assn, 1993-; Amer Osteopathic Assn, 1974-; Amer College of Osteopathic General Practitioners, 1982-; Ingham County Osteopathic Society, 1984-; Natl Assn of Medical Minority Educators, 1985-; Osteopathic General Practitioners of Michigan, 1985-; Amer Assn of Family Practitioners, 1986-; Michigan Assn of Family Practitioners, 1986-; Natl Academies of Practice, 1986-; Academy of Osteopathy Directors of Medical Education, 1988-91; Amer Medical Assn, 1989-; President, Natl Osteopathic Medical Assn, 1992-. **Honors/Awds:** Distinguished Alumni Award, Wayne State Univ, 1994; Women's Health Award, Blackboard African-American Bestsellers, Inc, 1994; Magnificent 7 Award presented by Business and Professional Women/USA, 1994; Faculty Member, Phi Kappa Phi Honor Society, 1994. **Special Achievements:** First African American woman to head an American medical school. **Military Serv:** US Naval Reserve, captain. **Business Addr:** Dean, Ohio University, College of Osteopathic Medicine, 204 Grosvenor Hall, Athens, OH 45701, (614)593-2178.

ROTAN, CONSTANCE S.
Educator (retired), attorney. **Personal:** Born Apr 19, 1935, Baton Rouge, LA; married James Rotan Jr; children: Kevin, Michael. **Educ:** Southern Univ,BA (Cum Laude) 1956; Howard Univ Grad School, 36 hrs toward MA 1968; Howard Univ School of Law, JD (Hon Grad) 1967. **Career:** US Dept of Justice, gen trial atty 1968-70; United Planning Org, asst gen counsel 1970-72; Howard Univ School of Law, asst dean, asst prof 1972-75; Howard Univ, exec asst to the vice pres for admin 1975-87, vice pres for administration 1975-87, university secretary, board of trustees secretary, 1987-92, vice pres for administration, 1989-92. **Orgs:** Mem Natl Bar Assoc 1970-, Kappa Beta Pi Intl Legal Sor 1965-, Alpha Kappa Alpha 1977-, Assoc of Amer Law Schools, Natl Assoc of Coll & Univ Attnys, US Dist Ct for DC, US Ct of Appeals for DC; dean Howard Univ Chap Kappa Beta Pi Intl Legal Sor 1963-64; co-chmn Comm on Age of Majority of DC; mem DC Bar, Phi Sigma Alpha; founding mem, officer Waring/Mitchell Law Soc; mem Public Mem Assoc of Foreign Svc. **Honors/Awds:** Public Mem of USIA Selection Bd 1986. **Home Addr:** 9216 Creekbed Ct, Columbia, MD 21045.

ROULHAC, EDGAR EDWIN
Educational administrator. **Personal:** Born Sep 28, 1946, Chicago, IL; son of Portia Goodloe Roulhac and Edgar Elijah Roulhac; married Patricia Gayle Johnson. **Educ:** Southern IL Univ Carbondale, BS 1969, MS 1970, PhD 1974; Johns Hopkins Univ School of Public Health, MPH 1975, postdoctoral studies 1974-75; Harvard Univ, Inst for Educ Mgmt, 1987. **Career:** Southern IL Univ School of Medicine, prof of health care planning 1972-74; Towson State Univ, prof of health science 1975-78; Johns Hopkins School of Public Health, dean of students 1978-86; asst provost 1986-93; John Hopkins Univ, provost's office, vice provost and interim vice president, 1993-. **Orgs:** Kappa Alpha Psi Fraternity 1965-; MD Soc for Medical Research, vice pres 1981-84; Sigma Pi Phi Fraternity 1986-, AAHE, APHA, BCHW, SOPHE; advisory board, Drew-Meharry-Morehouse Medical School Cancer Prevention Consortium, 1987-; trustee, Provident Hospital of Baltimore, 1978-82; governing board, Central Maryland Health Systems Agency, 1976-80. **Honors/Awds:** Hon Educ Phi Delta Kappa 1972-; Hon Educ Kappa Delta Pi 1972-; postdoctoral fellow Johns Hopkins Univ School of Public Health 1974-75; Hon Public Health Delta Omega 1982-; Sigma Pi Phi 1986-; Academic Public Health Recognition Award, Assn of Schools of Public Health, 1985; Meritorious Service Award, Johns Hopkins Minority Medical Faculty Assn, 1986; Meritorious Service Award, Johns Hopkins Alumni Assn Executive Committee, 1983. **Business Addr:** Vice Provost, Johns Hopkins University, 3400 N Charles Street, Baltimore, MD 21218.

ROULHAC, JOSEPH D.
Judge (retired). **Personal:** Born Aug 18, 1916, Selma, AL; son of Minerva Roulhac and Robert D Roulhac; married Frances; children: Delores. **Educ:** Stillman Coll, cert 1936; Lincoln Univ, AB 1938; Univ of PA, MA 1940, JD 1948. **Career:** Lincoln Univ, instr 1938-39; Ft Valley St Coll, instr 1940-41; Summit Cty OH, asst county pros 1957-63; Akron Municipal Ct, judge (retired). **Orgs:** Mem OH, Natl, Amer Bar Asoc; mem Amer Judic Soc, OH Mun Judges Assoc; trustee Baldwin Wallace Coll & Stillman Coll; mem NAACP, VFW, Amer Leg, Phi Beta Sigma Dist Serv Chapt, Phi Beta Sigma. **Military Serv:** M sgt 1942-46. **Home Addr:** 381 Sun Valley Dr, Akron, OH 44333.

ROULHAC, NELLIE GORDON
Educator. **Personal:** Born Jun 5, 1924, Washington, DC; daughter of Agnes Pauline Lee Gordon and Levi Preston Morton Gordon; married Dr Christopher M Roulhac Jr, Aug 1, 1944; children: Christopher M III, Dr Yvonne Agnes Roulhac Horton. **Educ:** Cheyney State Univ, BA; Teachers Coll, Columbia Univ, MA; University of Pennsylvania and Temple Univ Post Grad, Cert Special Educ; Univ of Sarasota, EdD 1978. **Career:** Westmoreland County, VA, principal sch 1945; Albany State Coll, Albany GA, instructor engl 1949; Memphis Public Sch, classroom tchr 1954; Sch Dist of Phila, supvr special educ 1971-83. **Orgs:** National Foundation for Infantile Paralysis, 1954; Chair Personnel Comm Delta Sigma Theta Sor, Inc; commr Mayor's Commn for Women 1984-91; pres Bd of Trustees Pennhurst State School and Hospital, Spring City, PA, bd of trustees Pennhurst, 1970-80; pres Natl Jack & Jill of Amer 1954-58; pres Jack & Jill of Am Found 1975-78; bd of trustees The Free Library of Philadelphia 1985-96; founder Thirty Clusters; mem The Links Inc Philadelphia Chapter; former chair Eastern Area Links Inc; chair Services to Youth Comm; organizer Friends of Combs Coll of Music 1978; bd of trustees, Combs Coll of Music 1979-83; natl sec Delta Sigma Theta Sorority Inc 1954-58; board of directors, charter member, Friends of Moore College of Art; United Cerebral Palsy Assn of Philadelphia and Vicinity, 1974-80; member, Inauguration and Investiture Committee for the city of Philadelphia, 1988; steering committee member, American Foundation for Negro Affairs, 1987; member National Association of Parliamentarians, 1993. **Honors/Awds:** First Prize, Best Student Teaching, Cheyney State University; Meritorious Service Volunteer Instructor,; American Red Cross First Aid Classes; In Appreciation for Service with the National FND for Infantile Paralysis, Recognition of Outstanding Contribution Field of Special Educ/Mainline Comm Philadelphia Grand Opera Co; Continued Distinguished Serv to Jack & Jill of Amer Found 1972, 1974; Outstanding Serv Field Special Educ Div Philadelphia PA 1982; Century Club Awds, 1966-69, in Recognition Serv to Youth YMCA Memphis, TN, Philadelphia PA; author, "Seventeen Days of Jimmie" 1981; Fund Raisers From A-Z 1984; Sadie T M Alexander Award, Philadelphia Alumnae Chapter, Delta Sigma Theta Sorority Inc, 1988; In Recognition of Your Contribution to Pennhurst's History of Service, Pennhurst State School & Hospital 1987; Outstanding Service Award, Jack & Jill of Amer, 1988; Citation, City of Phila City Council, 1994; author History of Jack and Jill of America Inc 1990: "Work, Play, and Commitment: The First Fifty Years Jack and Jill of America, Inc;" author, "Jumping Over the Moon," biography; Alice Coachman, Olympic Champion, 1948, 1993; Honorary Chair, Greater Philadelphia March of Dimes, 1990; Humanitarian Service Awd, Liberian Children Rehabilitation Network, 1995. **Home Addr:** 7137 Lincoln Dr, Philadelphia, PA 19119.

ROULHAC, ROY L.
Judge. **Personal:** Born Mar 27, 1943, Marianna, FL; son of Ge-Hazel Gibson Rolack (deceased) and J Y Rolack (deceased); children: Sheryl LaSonya McGriff. **Educ:** Wayne State University, BS, business mgmt, 1970; University of Detroit School of Law, JD, 1975. **Career:** Wayne County Prosecutor's Office, asst prosecutor, 1976; Michigan Dept of State, admin law judge, 1977-79; Michigan Dept of Labor, admin law jude, 1979-. **Orgs:** Pres, Michigan Assn of Admin Law Judges, 1982-84; bd of dir, Natl Alliance Against Racist & Political Repression, 1985-94; treasurer, Amer Assn of Jurist, 1987-89; Omega Psi Phi, 1987-; pres, Assn of Black Judges of Michigan, 1988-89; pres, Admin Law Section, State Bar of Michigan, 1989-90; bd of dir,secretary, Music Hall Center of Detroit, 1988-; President, Fred Hart Williams Gen Soc 1992-; editor, FHWGS Newsletter, 1994-; founder, Roulhac Family Assn, 1990; The Roulhac Quarterly, editor/publisher, 1990-; founder, THe Gilmore Academy, Jackson County Training School Alumni Association, 1996; editor/publisher, Gilmore Academy, CTS Newsletter, 1996-. **Honors/Awds:** Admin Law Judge of the Year, Michigan Assn of Admin Law Judes, 1986; Certificate of Appreciation, Office of Governor, 1989; Senate Concurrent Resolution #277, Michigan Legislature, 1989; Testimonial Resolution, Detroit City Council, 1989; Testimonial Resolution, County of Wayne & Office of County Executive, 1989. **Military Serv:** US Army Reserves, Livonia, MI; Washington DC Natl Guard; 1st lieutenant, 1964-70. **Business Addr:** Administrative Law Judge, Michigan Department of Consumer & Industry Svcs, Michigan Employment Relations Commission, 1200 6th St, 14th Fl, Detroit, MI 48226.

ROUNDFIELD, DANNY THOMAS (ROUNDS)
Professional basketball player. **Personal:** Born May 26, 1953, Detroit, MI; married Bernadine Owens; children: Corey, Christopher. **Educ:** Central MI U, BS Bus 1975. **Career:** Indiana Pacers, 1976-78, Atlanta Hawks, 1979-84, Detroit Pistons, 1985, Washington Bullets, 1986-87. **Honors/Awds:** 1st Team All-Pro 1980, 1st Team All-Defense 1980, 30th Team All-Star 1980 all in the NBA.

ROUNDTREE, DOVEY
Lawyer, clergy. **Educ:** Spelman College; Howard University School of Law. **Career:** Lawyer, criminal, civil; African Methodist Episcopal Church, ordained minister. **Military Serv:** US Army, commissioned officer, teacher, 1942-45. **Business Addr:** Criminal/Civil Lawyer, 1822 11th St, NW, Washington, DC 20001-5007, (202)234-1722.

ROUNDTREE, EUGENE V. N.
Business executive. **Personal:** Born Dec 19, 1927, Roxbury, MA; married Jacqueline Marie; children: Gene Jr, Nicholas, Nancy, Christopher, Phillip, Stephen, Anne Marie, Mary. **Educ:** Bates Coll ME, BS 1951. **Career:** Black Corporate Pres of New Eng, dir; All-Stainless Inc, pres 1951-. **Orgs:** Dir New Eng Iron & Hardware Assn; past natl dir MA Jaycees; mem S Shore Cit Club; dir Nat Minority Prchsg Cncl; mem Hingham Rotary Club; past pres S Shore C of C; bd mem Mayor's Adv Cncl; dir Rockland Credit Union, Scoot, MA Mental Health Assoc. **Business Addr:** President, All-Stainless, Inc, 75 Research Rd, Hingham, MA 02043.

ROUNDTREE, NICHOLAS JOHN
Marketing manager. **Personal:** Born May 4, 1956, Quincy, MA; son of Camilla Lea Roundtree and Eugene V Roundtree. **Educ:** Northeastern Univ, BS 1979, Bus Admin, Marketing Rsch 5 yrs. **Career:** Gillette, mfg planning 1975; Merriman Corp/Litton Ind, inside sales expediting 1976; Boston Globe, merchandising/promo 1977; Gen Elec, sales rep 1977; IBM, sales rep 1978-79; All-Stainless Inc, natl sales mgr beginning 1979, vice pres, currently. **Orgs:** Mem So Shore Chamber of Commerce 1979-. **Business Addr:** Vice President, All-Stainless, Inc, 75 Research Road, Hingham, MA 02043.

ROUNDTREE, RICHARD
Actor. **Personal:** Born Jul 9, 1942, New Rochelle, NY; son of Katheryn Roundtree and John Roundtree; married Karen Roundtree; children: Kelly, Nicole, Morgan Elizabeth. **Educ:** Southern Illinois Univ, attended. **Career:** Barney's, suit salesman; model; Stage appearances: Negro Ensemble Co, Kongi's Harvest, Man, Better Man, Mau-Mau Room, The Great White Hope, Shaft in Africa ; recorded several songs, including St Brother: Films: What Do You Say To A Naked Lady? 1970, Shaft 1971, Shaft's Big Score 1972, Parachute to Paradies, Embassy 1972, Charley One-Eye, Earthquake 1974, Man Friday 1975, Diamonds 1975, Escape to Athena 1979, An Eye for an Eye 1981, The Winged Serpent 1982, The Big Score 1983, City Heat 1984, Killpoint 1984, Portrait of a Hitman 1984; Television app earances: The Merv Griffin Show, Search for Tomorrow, The New Yorkers, Inside B edford-Stuyvesant, The Dean Martin Show, Shaft 1973-74, Outlaws 1987; The Man From Shaft, recorded album; Sitcom, 413 Hope Street, 1997-. **Business Addr:** Actor, Agency Performing Arts Inc, 9200 W Sunset Blvd, #900, Los Angeles, CA 90069.

ROUNDTREE, SAUDIA
Professional basketball player. **Personal:** Born Oct 4, 1974. **Educ:** Univ of Georgia, attended. **Career:** Atlanta Glory, guard, 1996-. **Honors/Awds:** National Junior College Player of the Year, 1994; SEC Female Athlete of the Year, 1996; Naismith Award, 1996. **Business Addr:** Professional Basketball Player, Atlanta Glory, 2100 Powers Ferry Rd, Ste 400, Atlanta, GA 30339, (770)541-9017.

ROUNSAVILLE, LUCIOUS BROWN, JR.
Senior specialist transportation. **Personal:** Born Apr 14, 1954, Atlanta, GA. **Educ:** GA State Univ, BBA 1977; Atlanta Univ, MBA 1983. **Career:** Colonial Pipeline Co, various positions clerk, analyst, staff analyst, sr staff analyst 1977-86, sr specialist property tax 1987-. **Orgs:** Mem Alpha Phi Alpha Frat 1976-, Natl Black MBA Assoc 1979-; treas Colonial Pipeline Co Employees Club 1981-83; mem The Atlanta Exchange Foundation 1983-, LA Assoc of Tax Representatives 1983-; mem The Atlanta Tax Club 1984-; treas Natl Black MBA Assoc Atlanta Chap 1984-85, exec comm 1987-; 2nd vice pres bdof dirs Yard Wide Federal Credit Union 1987-; pres Atlanta Univ Sch of Business Admin Alumni Assoc Atlanta Chap 1987-88; mem Cosmopolitan AME Church. **Honors/Awds:** Mortar Board Outstanding Leadership Awd GA State Univ 1977; 5 Year Serv Awd 1982, 10 Year Serv Awd 1987 Colonial Pipeline Co; Outstanding Young Men of Amer US Jaycees 1984. **Business Addr:** Sr Specialist Property Tax, Colonial Pipeline Co, 3390 Peachtree Rd NE, Atlanta, GA 30326.

ROUNTREE, ELLA JACKSON
Educator. **Personal:** Born Feb 27, 1936, Griffin, GA; widowed. **Educ:** Ft Valley State Coll, BS 1957; Western CT State Coll, MS 1973. **Career:** Grassy Plain School, teacher 1963-; Moore Elem School, 1960-63; AL St Elem School, 1957-60. **Orgs:** Mem Bethel Educ Assn; Danbury City Cncl 1973-77; CT Educ Assn; Nat Educ Assn; Phi Lambda Theta; Nat Hon & Professional Assn in Edn; mem NAACP; AlphaKappa Alpha Sor; Black Dem; Waterbury Chap LINKS; Mt Pleasant AMEZ Ch; cnclpers Danbury City Cncl 6th Ward 1973-. **Honors/Awds:** Outstand Elem Tchr of Am 1974. **Business Addr:** 241 Greenwood Ave, Danbury, CT 06810.

ROUNTREE, LOUISE M.
Librarian (retired). **Personal:** Born Aug 16, 1921, Barnwell, SC; daughter of Mary M Patterson Rountree and Clarence C Rountree. **Educ:** Morris Coll, AB 1941; Atlanta Univ, BLS 1950; Syracuse U, MLS 1956; Columbia Univ 1961; W Africa, ethnic heritage seminar 1974. **Career:** Estill HS Estill, SC, librarian; Allendale Co HS SC, librarian 1948-51; Livingstone Coll, asst librarian 1951-, acting head 1969-70, head librarian 1970-87, assoc prof 1978-87; Historian, 1985-89, 1993-97. **Orgs:** Mem Southeastern Library Assn; NC Lib Assn; sec 1972; cood ICDP 1976-; mem Mayor's Historic Commn 1975-77 & 1978-80; mem/bd mem Amer Assn of Univ Women 1971, topic chmn 1973, historian 1971-73; Rowan Historical Properties Commn 1972; Rowan Bicentennial Commn 1974-76; special events com RCCM 1974; Dial Help Back Up 1972-; chairperson Centennial Program Commn 1978 & 1980; chmn JC Price Marker Com 1978; rededication comm Dodge Hall 1981-82; chairperson for Inauguration of the 7th pres of Livingstone Coll 1984; mem NC Afro-Amer Genealogical Soc 1985-; mem Arts in Public Places Panel 1986-88; comm researcher, Arts in Public Places, 1986-88; Historian, Woman's Baptist Home and FMC on NC, 1985-89, 1993-; historian, Church Women United, Salisbury, 1987-92. **Honors/Awds:** Recip Jennie Smallwood Price Award 1970; Dedication Coll Yearbook 1971; Plaque for 25 yrs of serv Friends of Livingstone Coll Library 1977; Scholarship in Honor of Louise M Rountree for Significant Serv AAUW Salisbury Chapter 1977; Certificate of Appreciation Rowan Public Library 1977; Certificate of Appreciation Athletic Dept 1979; Centennial Recognition Plaque for 25 plus yrs 1979; DAR Comm Serv Award 1983; Minority Woman of the Yr Award Zeta Phi Beta Sor 1985; Athletic Dept Serv Award for Preservation of Records 1985; apptd State Baptist Historian 1985; research editor State Baptist History (women) 1985; Livingstone Coll Alumni Meritorious Serv Award 1986; An Appreciation Award, Livingstone College 1989; Livingstone Coll Centennial Celebration Plaque, 100 yrs of Black Coll Football for Preservation, 1992; First Calvary Baptist Church, Black History Service Plaque, 1993; NAACP Distinguished Citizenship Award, 1994; Woman's Baptist Home & FMC of NC, Service Plaque, 1995; Livingstone Coll, DHL, Hon, 1996. **Special Achievements:** Research and Publications: 8 Bibliographies; 2 Indicies; 6 Brief Histories; 8 Handbooks; 4 Brochures. **Home Addr:** PO Box 2472, Salisbury, NC 28144.

ROUSE, GENE GORDON, SR.
Federal official (retired). **Personal:** Born Apr 23, 1923, Mt Vernon, OH; son of Louise Carrington Rouse and Horace K Rouse; married Estelle Lewis Rouse, Jun 4, 1949; children: Gene G Jr, Eric V. **Educ:** Central State Univ OH, BS 1951; Chicago State Univ, 1960-61. **Career:** US Post Office, clerk 1952-60; Chicago bd of Ed, teacher 1960-65; Dept of Human Resources (Comm on Youth Welfare), neighborhood Worker 1966-68; Dept of Human Resources, unit dir 1968-80. **Orgs:** Chmn Englewood Inter Agncy Cnsl 1975-; selecting brd NROTC 1971-73; mem NACD 1969-; mem Kappa Alpha Psi 1974-75; pres Mendel Booster Club 1974-75; blood donor Englewood Hosp 1979-89. **Honors/Awds:** Hnry mem Puerto Rican Congress 1972; Great Guy Award-Radio Sta WGRT 1971; Midwest All-Conference football 1950; Athletic Acmplshmnt Award Austin Town Hall 1971; Certificate of Appreciation Englewood Hosp 1974; Outstanding Serv from 17th Ward Young Dem Org 1974; Certificate of Appreciation Natl Found for Cancer Rsch 1983; services rendered Dept Ag Univ of IL Circle Campus 1983; Appreciation Award, Englewood Inter City Council, 1990; Negro All American, 1950; Central State College, Football Hall of Fame, 1990. **Military Serv:** AUS sgt 1943-45; Good Conduct Medal, ETO Ribbon.

ROUSE, JACQUELINE ANNE
Educator. **Personal:** Born Feb 1, 1950, Roseland, VA; daughter of Fannie Thompson Rouse. **Educ:** Howard University, Washington, DC, 1968-72; Atlanta University, Atlanta, GA, MA, 1972-73; Emory University, Atlanta, GA, PhD, 1983. **Career:** Pal, Beach Jr College, Lake Worth, Florida, senior instructor, 1973-80; Georgia Institute of Teachers, Atlanta, GA, guest lecturer, 1983; Morehouse College, Atlanta, GA, associate professor, 1983-; American University/Smithsonian Institute, Landmarks professor of history, beginning 1989; Georgia State Univ, prof of history, currently. **Orgs:** Assistant editor, Journal of Negro History, 1983-89; advisor/reference, Harriet Tubman Historial & Cultural Museum, Macon, GA, 1985; panelist, American Association University of Women, 1985-; principal scholar/member, Steering Committee, National Conference of Women in Civil Rights Movement, 1988; panelist, Jacob Javits Fellowship, Department of Education, 1989; national vice director, Assistant of Black Women Historians, 1989-; first vice president, Association of Social & Behavorial Scientists, 1989-; consultant/advisor, Atlanta Historical Society, 1989; historian consultant, Apex Collection of Life & Heritage, 1989. **Honors/Awds:** FIPSE, Curriculum on Black Women's History, Spellman College, 1983-84; NEH Summer Grant for College Teachers, 1984; UNCF Strengthening the Humanities Grant, 1985. **Business Addr:** Professor of History, Georgia State University, Dept. of History, Atlanta, GA 30303.

ROUSE, TERRIE
Museum director. **Personal:** Born Dec 2, 1952, Youngstown, OH; daughter of Florence Rouse and Eurad Rouse. **Educ:** Trinity Coll, BA 1974; Cornell Univ, Master Professional Studies 1977; Columbia Univ School of Intl Affairs, Cert 1979; Columbia Univ, MA 1979. **Career:** School of Intl Affairs, rsch asst 1977; Special Serv Project Hunter Coll, coord 1978-79; Adam Clayton Powell Jr State Office Bldg, mgr, curator 1979-81; Studio Museum in Harlem, sr curator; New York Transit Museum, dir; California Afro-American Museum, dir, currently. **Orgs:** Bellevue Hosp Art Bd; Literary Society; mem African Amer Museum Assn, Amer Museum Assn; member, American Assn of Museums; member, Jack & Jill, Inc, Metropolitan Chapter. **Honors/Awds:** Honor Civil Rights Awd Trinity Coll 1974; Graduate Fellow Columbia Univ 1977, 1978; Graduate Fellow Cornell Univ 1974, 1976; Unit Citation, New York Transit Authority.

ROUSSELL, NORMAN
Educator. **Personal:** marrled Dorothy McCullum; children: Michael K. **Educ:** Dillard Univ, BA 1960; Fisk Univ, MA 1965; Wayne State Univ, EdD 1974. **Career:** Orleans Parish School Systems, chmn science dept 1960-66; Dillard Univ, assoc dean of students 1969-75; Loyola Univ, dir title III 1976-79, exec asst to the pres 1979-86, vice pres for administration beginning, 1986; Dillard Univ, assoc vp, currently. **Orgs:** Mem bd of trustees NO Museum of Art 1973-86; mem Amer Assoc of Higher Educ 1977-86. **Honors/Awds:** Charles S Mott Fellowship 1972; Danna Faculty Improvement Grant Dillard Univ 1973; Academic Scholarship Wayne State Univ 1973. **Military Serv:** USAF staff sgt 4 yrs; Korean Serv Medal, Good Conduct Medal. **Home Addr:** 7441 Bullard Ave, New Orleans, LA 70128. **Business Addr:** Associate Vice Pres, Dillard University, 2601 Gentilly Blvd, New Orleans, LA 70122.

ROUTTE-GOMEZ, ENEID G.
Journalist. **Personal:** Born May 16, 1944, Long Island, NY; daughter of Maud Gomez Routte and Jesse Wayman Routte. **Educ:** University of Missouri School of Journalism, multicultural management program, 1984; University of Puerto Rico. **Career:** San Juan Star, San Juan, PR, editor/special writer, 1964-94. **Orgs:** President, Caribbean Women's Network, 1984-; director, Displaced Homemakers Council Region II, 1990-; director/ex-president, Overseas Press Clubs of Puerto Rico, 1975-; member, National Association of Black Journalists, 1984; member, Puerto Rico Endowment for the Humanities, 1990. **Honors/Awds:** Numerous civic and press awards. **Business Addr:** PO Box 58, Old San Juan Station, Old San Juan, Puerto Rico 00902.

ROUX, VINCENT J.
Physician. **Personal:** Born Apr 27, 1937, New Orleans, LA; son of Beatrice Grammer Roux and John Roux; married Lois Milton; children: Bridgette, Vincent Jr, Denise. **Educ:** Xavier Univ, BS 1961; Howard Univ Coll of Med, MD 1965; Natl Bd of Med Bd of Examiners, Diploma 1966; Amer Bd Surgery, Cert 1971; Amer Coll of Surgeons, Fellow 1975. **Career:** Howard Univ Hosp, med dir 1972-; Howard Univ Coll of Med, assoc dean/clinical affairs 1972-75; Dept of Comm Health Practices, clinical instr 1972; Dept of Surg, asst prof 1971-; chief resident 1969-70; resident gen surgeon 1966-70; Freedmen's Hosp, intern 1966; Montreal Neurol Inst, extern 1964. **Orgs:** AMA; Natl Med Assn; Amer Coll of Surgeons; Med Chirurgical Soc of DC; chmn/bd dir DC Chap United Way 1974-76; mem/bd dir Natl Cap Med Found 1975-; mem DC C of C 1976-. **Honors/Awds:** Publ, ''The Stimulation of Adenosine 3', 5' Monophosphal Prodn by Antidiuretic Factors'', ''The CV Catheter, An Invasive Therapeutic Adj'' 1977; Daniel Hale Williams Award 1966; Physician's Recog Award AMA 1969; Charles R Drew Meml Award 1965; 1st Annual Clarence Sumner Green Award 1965. **Military Serv:** AUS specialist 3rd cl E-4 1955-58. **Business Addr:** Medical Dir, Howard University Hospital, 2041 Georgia Ave, Washington, DC 20059.

ROWAN, ALBERT T.
Educator, clergyman. **Personal:** Born May 15, 1927, Kansas City, MO; son of Florence Marion Diggs (deceased) and Albert Thomas Rowan (deceased); married Carrie Mae McBride Rowan, Feb 15, 1948; children: Richard, Brenda Moore, Stephen, Allana Wheeler, Allan. **Educ:** MI State U, 1946; Western Baptist Bible Coll, BRE, BTh 1955-59; Ashland Theological Sem, MDiv 1976; Trinity Theol Sem, DMin 1987. **Career:** First Baptist, Quincy IL, pastor 1955-60; Zion Baptist, Springfield IL, pastor 1960-61; Salem Baptist, Champaign IL, pastor 1961-64; Bethany Baptist, Cleveland OH, pastor 1964-; Trinity Theological Seminary, adjunct professor, 1990-95, course assessor, 1995-. **Orgs:** 1st vice pres Baptist Minister's Conf of Cleveland; pres Northern OH Dist Congress 1955-60; past pres Cleveland Baptist Assn 1983-; mem exec bd OH General Baptist State Convention; mem Cleveland Library Bd of Trustees 1976-78; first vice moderator, Northern Ohio Baptist District Assn, 1987-; City Planning Commission of Cleveland, Ohio, chairman, mem, 1976-. **Honors/Awds:** Proclamation ''Rev Albert T Rowan Day'' Mayor Carl B Stokes 1970; Certificate of Appreciation Champaign County Urban League 1963; elected to Lincoln High School Hall of Fame 1981; Hon Dr of Div Am Bible Inst 1969; Hon Dr of Div VA Seminary & Coll 1975; Outstanding Pastor of the Year, Baptist Ministers Conference of Cleveland, 1983; Hall of Fame, Lincoln High School, Kansas City, MO, 1981. **Military Serv:** AUS Specialized Training Corps cadet student 1944-45. **Home Addr:** 3716 Langton Rd, Cleveland, OH 44121. **Business Addr:** Pastor, Bethany Baptist Church, 1201-1225 E 105th St, Cleveland, OH 44108.

ROWAN, CARL THOMAS
Journalist. **Personal:** Born Aug 11, 1925, Ravenscroft, TN; son of Johnnie Bradford Rowan and Thomas David Rowan; married Vivien Louise Murphy, Aug 2, 1950; children: Barbara, Carl Thomas Jeffrey. **Educ:** Tennessee State Univ, 1942-43; Washburn Univ, 1943-44; Oberlin Coll, AB 1947; Univ of Minnesota, MA 1948. **Career:** Minneapolis Tribune, Minneapolis MN, copywriter 1948-50, staff writer, 1950-61; US Dept of State, Washington DC, deputy asst sec for public affairs 1961-63; US ambassador to Finland, based in Helsinki, 1963-64; US Information Agency, dir 1964-65; Chicago Sun-Times (formerly Chicago Daily News), Chicago IL, columnist for Field Newspaper Syndicate (formerly Publishers Hall Syndicate), 1965-; natl affairs commentator on ''The Rowan Report,'' heard nationally on radio five days a week; Post-Newsweek Broadcasting Co, Washington DC, political commentator for radio and television stations; ''Agronsky & Co,'' nationally syndicated public af-

fairs television show, regular panelist; ''Meet the Press,'' frequent panelist; lecturer. **Orgs:** Dir, DC Natl Bank; mem Comm of 100 Legal Def Fund; NAACP 1964-; chmn adv comm Natl Comm Against Discrimination in Housing 1967; mem Sigma Delta Chi. **Honors/Awds:** Author, ''South of Freedom'' 1953, ''The Pitiful & The Proud'' 1956, ''Go South to Sorrow'' 1957, ''Wait Till Next Year'' 1960, ''Between Us Blacks'' 1974, ''Breaking Barriers'' (memoir) 1990; Sidney Hillman Found Award 1952; Amer Teamwork Award, Natl Urban League 1955; Distinguished Achievement Award, Regents of Univ of Minnesota 1961; Golden Ruler Award, Philadelphia Fellowship Commn 1961; Communications Award in Human Relations, Anti-Defamation League of B'Nai B'Rith 1964; Distinguished Serv Award, Capital Press Club 1964; Natl Brotherhood Award, Natl Conf of Christians & Jews 1964; Elijah P Lovejoy Award 1968; a Detroit, MI, public school named in his honor, 1993; National Press Foundation, Distinguished Contribution to Journalism, honoree, 1998; numerous honorary degrees. **Special Achievements:** Breaking Barriers, 1991. **Military Serv:** US Navy, World War II. **Business Addr:** 1101 7 St NW, Washington, DC 20036.

ROWAN, MICHAEL TERRANCE
Hospital administrator. **Personal:** Born in Indianapolis, IN; son of Charles & Odessa. **Educ:** Miami Univ, BA, 1980; Univ of MI, masters, health services admin, 1982. **Career:** District of Columbia Gen Hosp, admin extern, 1981; Hosp of the Univ of Pennsylvania, admin resident, 1982-83, dir, Transport Svs Dept, 1982-83; St Vincent's Hosp, outpatient admin, Dept of Psychiatry, 1983-84; St Vincent Med Ctr, asst vp, 1985-87; Memorial Med Ctr, vp, admin, 1987-92; Sarasota Memorial Hosp, exec vp, COO, 1993-. **Orgs:** Amer Coll Healthcare Executives, 1981-; United Way of Coastal GA, health div chairman, 1991; Amer Heart Assn, Southwest FL, bd mem, 1994-; Savannah Area Chamber of Commerce, Southside, bd mem, 1989-92; Sarasota Family Counseling Ctr, bd mem, 1994-; JH Floyd Sunshine Manor Nursing Home, bd mem, 1994-. **Honors/Awds:** National Assn of Public Hospitals, Fellow, 1989. **Special Achievements:** Washington Univ School of Medicine, adjunct instructor. **Business Addr:** Executive Vice Pres, Sarasota Memorial Hospital, 1700 S Tamiami Trail, Sarasota, FL 34239.

ROWE, ALBERT P.
Minister. **Personal:** Born Sep 22, 1934, Columbia, SC; married Dorothy Collins. **Educ:** Morgan St Coll, BA 1958; Crozer Theol Sem, 162; Princeton Theol Sem, 1969. **Career:** Central Bapt Ch, pastor 1962-68; Adult Basic Educ Prog, chief recruiter; Wilmington Brd Ed, 1966-68; Calvary Bapts Ch, pastor 1968-; Calvary Bapt Ch Day Care Ctr, advisor/cons; Voc Exploration Ctr & Progressive Reading & Rec Prog, 1972-. **Orgs:** Pres PUADA; bd of trustees Barnert Meml Hosp; commnr Paterson Bd of Edn; chmn Fund Renewal; bd dir/chrmn Civic Organ; vice pres Wilmington NAACP 1966-68. **Honors/Awds:** Paterson NAACP Comm Serv Award 1974; Nominated Young Man of the Yr Wilmington JC'S 1967; Disting Serv Award Calvary Bapt Ch 1973. **Military Serv:** AUS 1st lt 1958-59. **Business Addr:** 575 E 18th, Paterson, NJ 07504.

ROWE, AUDREY
Educator. **Personal:** Born Nov 4, 1946, New York, NY; divorced. **Educ:** Fed City Coll, BA 1971; George Washington Univ, Public Administration; John F Kennedy School of Govt, Harvard Univ, Fellow at Institute of Politics. **Career:** DHS, commr social servs present; CPB dir Womens Activities; Natl Yough Alternative Proj, cons; Child Defense Fnd, education specialist/child advocate; Natl Welfare Rights Org, spec asst to ex dir 1972; Proj New Hope, ed dir 1972-72; SASA House Sum Prog, consult 1969; Pupil Inctv Prog NAACP, asst dir 1967-68; Natl Womens Pol Caucus, Natl vice chairperson 1973-75; natl Chairperson 1975-77; Natl Commn on Observance of Intl Womens Year, commr; Womans Adv Com to Sec Lbr 1973; Rockefeller Foundation, Equal Opportunity Division, consultant, 1988-91; Dept of Social Services of Connecticut, commissioner; Natl Urban League, Inc, executive vice pres, currently. **Orgs:** Mvmt for Econ Jstc pres of bd 1974; mem 1965; sec of bd; mem Nat Cncl Negro Womn 1967; chrprsn Juvenile Justice Adv Grp of DC (apptmnt of mayor); fndr DC Wmns Pol Caucus 1972; bd mem rep Womens Task Force; bd mem Womens Campaign Fund; DC Comm Mgmtn; Natl Commission on Family Foster Care, chair; Joint Center for Political and Economic Studies, bd member; American Public Welfare Assn, bd member; Child Welfare League of America, bd member. **Honors/Awds:** Org Awd DC Black Econ Union Comm; nom Sojourner Truth Awd 1974. **Business Addr:** 120 Wall St, 7th Fl, New York, NY 10005.

ROWE, CHRISTA F.
Educator, religious sister. **Personal:** Born Jun 10, 1959, Clearwater, FL; daughter of Theresia Roberson Rowe and Peter John Rowe Sr. **Educ:** Intl Religious Studies, Dublin, Ireland, 1979-80; San Diego Community Coll, San Diego, CA, 1982; Hillsborough Community Coll, Tampa, FL, AA, 1986; St Leo Coll, St Leo, FL, BSW (magna cum laude), 1988; Boston College, 1992-. **Career:** Holy Family Catholic Church, San Diego, CA, sec, 1980-82; St Lawrence Catholic Church, Tampa, FL, pastoral minister, 1983-87; Diocese of St Petersburg, Office for Black Catholic Ministries, St Petersburg, FL, assoc dir, 1988-90; Diocese of St Petersburg, St Petersburg, FL, columnist, 1988-90; Diocese of St Petersburg, Tampa, FL, productions coordinator, innervision radio program, 1988-90; Our Lady Queen of Peace Church, New Port Richey, FL, dir of religious education, 1990-96; Sisters of St Clare, New Port Richey, FL, formation director, 1996-. **Orgs:** Mem, Fools for Jesus Mime & Pantomine Clown Troup, 1976-79; vocations promoter, Sisters of St Clare, 1986-91; mem, Natl Assn of Social Workers, 1987-89; mem, Campaign for Human Devt, 1988-91; mem, Natl Assn Black Catholic Administrators, 1988-89; Liturgical Commission of the Diocese of St Petersburg, 1991-94; Vocations Team, 1992-96, and Regional Team, 1992-95, Sisters of St Clare. **Honors/Awds:** Outstanding Scholar in Religious Studies, St Leo Coll, 1987; Outstanding Academic Performance Award, St Leo Coll, 1987; Natl Dean's List, 1987-88. **Home Addr:** 10544 Brian Ln, New Port Richey, FL 34654. **Business Addr:** Formation Director, St Clare's Convent, 10544 Brian Ln, New Port Richey, FL 34654.

ROWE, JASPER C.
Attorney. **Personal:** Born Aug 27, 1945, Kilgore, TX; married Susan Adams. **Educ:** Univ of TX, BA Physics 1968; Univ of TX, BA Math 1968; Univ of TX Sch of Law, JD 1971. **Career:** Texas Instrument Electronics Inc, elec engr & physicist 1965-68; US Army Corps of Engrs, constrn unit comdr 1970-74; AUS Judge Advocates Gen Corps, atty 1974-; US Dept of HHS Dallas, atty. **Orgs:** Bd dirs NBA 1968; vice pres HEW Employees Assn 1973; mem pres Dallas Ft Worth Black Lawyers Assn 1977; pres Black United Dallas Govt Employees Assn 1977-79; secty-treas bd of dirs Dallas Legal Serv Inc 1978; exec comm mem bd of dirs Dallas Legal Serv Inc 1978; membership chmn Dallas FedBar Assn; chmn Admin Law Sect NBA 1978; mem ABA, TX Bar Assn, Dallas Black C of C; mem Natl Urban League, NAACP, Fed Bus Assn; mem Reserve Officers Assn; mem 1st Baptist Church of Hamilton Park, Alpha Phi Alpha, Alpha Kappa Mu. **Military Serv:** AUS corps of engrs 1st lt 1972. **Business Addr:** Attorney, US Dept of HHS, HHS Office of Reg Atty, Ste 1300 1200 Main St, Dallas, TX 75202.

ROWE, JIMMY L.
Association executive. **Personal:** Born Dec 6, 1932, Haskell, OK; married; children: Dianna, Leonardo, James, Kimberly, Michael. **Educ:** SC St Coll, BA Industrial Educ 1956. **Career:** Sons Watts Own Recog Proj, dir 1971-74; Trans Oppor Prog Pico Rivera, CA, acting dir 1971-72, asst dir 1968-71, training coord 1967-68. **Orgs:** Tulsa Personnel Assn; Nat Assn Pretrial Release Assn; Comm Rel Commn Employment Com; dir coalition Los Angeles Model Ctys; mem Tulsa Urban League; asst pastor/minister christian ed St Luke Bapt Ch; youth minister Doublerock BC Compton, CA; Truevine BC Hawthorne, CA; NAACP; Black Econ Union Los Angeles; Mexican Am Political Assn. **Honors/Awds:** Received Resolution Los Angeles City Cncl Outstand Leadership. **Military Serv:** AUS Signal Corp 1956-58.

ROWE, MARILYN JOHNSON
Government consultant. **Personal:** Born Nov 9, 1954, Batesburg, SC; married Thaddeus E Rowe Jr; children: Brandolyn, Alesia. **Educ:** Univ South Carolina, BA Educ 1977. **Career:** SC Human Affairs Commission, sr equal employment oppty consultant; Olive Branch Baptist Church, dir of music. **Orgs:** Member Amer Assoc Affirmation Action 1979-; member Nat'l Assoc Hmn Rgts Wrkr 1979-; Tau Beta Sigma USC 1976; member State Employees Assn; volunteer, Guardian Ad Litem, Richland County Family Court; volunteer, Rape Crisis Network, Richland, Lexington, Fairfield Counties; volunteer, Metro Comm Relations Council 1989-90. **Honors/Awds:** SC Human Affairs Commission, Employee of the Year, 1990. **Business Addr:** Senior Consultant, South Carolina Hmn Affrs Comm, PO Box 4490, Columbia, SC 29240.

ROWE, NANSI IRENE
Business executive. **Personal:** Born May 6, 1940, Detroit, MI; children: Leslie Anika-ayoka. **Educ:** Detroit Inst of Tech, BBA, 1965; Wayne State U, JD, 1973; Candidate for MDIV-Garette Evangelical Theological Seminary. **Career:** City of Detroit Corp, corp counsel, dep corp counsel 1974-78; Detroit Econ Growth Corp, vp, gen counsel, sec to bd of dir 1979-82; EO Constructors Inc, pres, chairperson of the bd 1980-; Nansi Rowe & Assoc PC, pres, chief counsel, partner 1982-. **Orgs:** Secy, treas Wayne Cnty Com Coll Found; secy, genl cnsl Detroit Eco Growth Corp; bd mem Southeastern MI Transit Auth; former bd mem Homes for Black Chldrn; bd mem United Community Serv 1978-81; State Bar of MI; Amer Arbitration Assoc; NAACP; Inner-City Bus Improvement Forum, Southeastern MI Bus Devel Ctr; mem Amer Bar Assoc, Detroit Bar Assoc; life mem Natl Bar Assoc; Wolverine Bar Assoc; Southeastern Michigan Transit Authority, former board mem; Brent General Hospital, former board mem. **Honors/Awds:** Woman of the Yr United Cncl of Churches 1981; Bus Woman of the Yr Nat Assn of Professional Women 1976. **Business Addr:** Nansi Rowe & Assoc, 1420 Washington Boulevard, Detroit, MI 48226, (313)963-6110.

ROWE, RICHARD L.
Executive. **Personal:** Born Sep 21, 1926, New York, NY; married Mercedes L Walker; children: Delena Pugh, Patricia Anderson, Richard Jr. **Educ:** City Coll, B Industrial Mgmt; City Univ, MBA. **Career:** Port Authority of NY & NJ, asst mgr operating personnel personnel dept 1968-70, mgr equal opportunity prog personnel 1970-72, mgr operating personnel 1972-76, mgr employee relations 1976-78, asst dir aviation dept 1978-83, general mgr JFK Intl Airport 1983-. **Business Addr:** General Manager, John F Kennedy International, Port Authority of NY & NJ, Building 141, Jamaica, NY 11430.

ROWE, WILLIAM LEON
Publishing executive. **Personal:** Born Dec 31, 1915, St Matthews, SC; son of Josephine Rowe and John Rowe; married Isadora Viola Smith. **Educ:** Southern U, SC, PhD. **Career:** New York City Police Dept, deputy police commr 1951; WW II, sr war corr; Interstate Tattler/Harlem News/Pittsburgh Courier, theatre editor; MGM & 20th Century Fox, press agent/pr Cons; Mayor of New Rochelle, cons; Entre Marketing City of New Rochelle, American Black Male Magazine, International Photo News Service; founder/exec ed, International Historical Publishing Co, founder/pres, host/exec producer Conversation Rowe, Radio Show. **Orgs:** Capital Press Club Press Organ; Publicity Club of NY PR Organ; EDGES Organ of Corporate Exec; Nat Assn of Black Police Officers; exec bd mem/chrmn pr com Ed Newsletter New Rochelle NAACP; pres Afro-Amer Guild of Performing Artists; bd of dirs Natl Dropout Prevention Fund; adv bd Natl Inst Against Prejudice and Violence; founding mem 100 Black Men Inc. **Honors/Awds:** Half Century Award Natl Newspaper Pub Assn 1985; Appreciation Award Sickle Cell Disease Found of Greater NY 1985; Northside Center for Child Devel; 1986 Ken Knight Awd given in Recognition for total involvement in Black Radio and Black Music at the Family Affair; New Rochelle NAACP Business Award, Life member, NAACP.

ROWELL, VICTORIA LYNN
Actress. **Personal:** Born in Portland, ME; children: Maya, Jasper Armstrong Marsalis. **Career:** Distinguished Gentleman, Disney, w/Eddie Murphy, 1992; Full Eclipse, w/Mario Van Peeples, 1993; Secret Sins of the Father, w/Lloyd & Beau Bridges, 1993; Dr. Hugo, Independent, w/Vondi Curtis Hall, 1994; Dumb and Dumber, New Line Cinema, w/Jim Carrey, 1994; CBS-TV, The Young and The Restless, plays Drucilla Winters, 1990-; Viacom Prod, Diagnosis Murder, plays Amanda Bently, 1993-. **Orgs:** The Rowell Foster Children's Postive Plan, founder, 1990-; The St Lucian Board of Tourism, ambassador, 1995; The Child Welfare League of America, spokesperson, 1992-. **Honors/Awds:** NAACP, Best Actress in a Daytime Drama, 1993, 1994, 1995, 1998; Soap Opera Awards Scene Stealer, 1994. **Special Achievements:** Full Scholarship Recipient of the American Ballet Theatre School of NYC; American Ballet Theater II, NYC; Guest Teacher, resident of the Elma Lewis School of Fine Arts/Mass; Guest resident teacher of the Roxbury Ctr of the Performing Arts, Roxbury, MA. **Business Addr:** Actress, The Young & the Restless, c/o CBS-TV, 7800 Beverly Blvd, 3rd Fl, Los Angeles, CA 90036, (213)852-2532.

ROWLAND, JAMES H. **See Obituaries section.**

ROXBOROUGH, MILDRED
Association executive. **Personal:** Born 1927, Brownsville, TN; married John W II. **Educ:** Howard Univ; New York Univ, AB 1947; Columbia Univ, MA 1953; Univ of Paris; Univ of Mexico. **Career:** Natl NAACP, asst dir 1975-, exec asst, admin asst to exec dir 1963, natl staff field sec 1954, 1st woman admin asst, exec asst & asst dir. **Orgs:** Life mem, NAACP, 1958-. **Business Addr:** Deputy Dir Corp Dev, NAACP, 260 5th Avenue, 6th Floor, New York, NY 10001.

ROY, AMERICUS MELVIN
Church administrator. **Personal:** Born Apr 12, 1929, Baltimore, MD; son of Evelyn Frisby and Melvin Roy; married Doris Johnson, Apr 3, 1955. **Educ:** Credits in sociology & polit sci. **Career:** Archdiocese of Baltimore, cath clergyman/permanent deacon; US PO Baltimore, distrib clerk 1968-72; Dept of Educ Baltimore, stationary engr 1960-68; counsels pre-trial releases & ex-offenders; St Ambrose Cath Ch, assoc pastor; St Pius V Church, pastoral director, currently. **Orgs:** Mem Black Cath Clergy Caucus; pres St Vincent DePaul Soc; co-chmn Baltimore Alliance Against Racist & Polit Repression; pres NW Emergency Needs Assn; pres St John's Cncl on Criminal Justice; mem Coalition to End Med Experimentation of Prisoners; member/secretary, St Pius V Housing Committee Inc, 1985-; member, Interdenominational Ministerial Alliance; member/vice pres, Council of Clergy Advisory Div of Public Safety/Correctional Services, 1989-. **Honors/Awds:** 1st Black Permanent Deacon in US ordained June, 1971; Medal of the Holy Cross, Ecclesia Et Pontifice, 1990. **Military Serv:** AUS 1948-50. **Business Addr:** Pastoral Director, St Pius V Roman Catholic Church, Archdiocese of Baltimore, 521 N Schroeder St, Baltimore, MD 21223.

ROY, JAN S.
Corporate executive. **Personal:** Born Jan 19, 1954, Chicago, IL; daughter of Bedford McCowan; married Anthony E Roy, Jun 11, 1980; children: Harrison, Erica. **Educ:** Harold Washington College, AS, hospitality management, 1991; Roosevelt

University, BS, hospitality management, 1997. **Career:** Ramada Hotel, convention sales mgr, 1987-89; Sheraton International Hotel, convention sales mgr, 1989-91; American Medical Association, sr representative, 1991-94; McCormick Place Convention Ctr, mgr sales promo, 1994-96; Chicago Convention Bureau, dir of sales, 1996-. **Orgs:** Meeting Professionals International, bd mem, 1997-; Harold Washington College, advisory bd mem, 1996-; NEWH Network of Executive Women in Hospitality, bd, 1995-96. **Honors/Awds:** Franklin Honor Society, 1997. **Business Addr:** Director, Corporate Sales, Chicago Convention & Tourism Bureau, 2301 S Lake Shore Dr, at McCormick Pl, Chicago, IL 60616.

ROY, JASPER K.
Behavior management specialist. **Personal:** son Of J W Roy; married Barbara Miller; children: 13. **Educ:** Denver Ctr for Grad Studies, MBA 1978; Loyola Univ of Chicago, MPS 1986. **Career:** Roys Food Prod Inc Mfg Canned Meats, vice pres 1945-62; Arch of Chicago, ordained perm deacon 1974; Cook County Dept of Corrections, volunteer Catholic chaplain 1974-. **Orgs:** Deacon, Catholic Church; American General Life & Accident Insurance Co, LUTCF, insurance counselor. **Honors/Awds:** Received 3 President's Trophies. **Home Addr:** 125 S Waller, Chicago, IL 60644, (773)287-4321. **Business Phone:** (708)383-4735.

ROY, JOHN WILLIE
Automobile dealership executive. **Career:** Southland Chrysler-Plymouth, president, currently. **Special Achievements:** Co. is ranked #85 on Black Enterprise magazine's list of top 100 auto dealers, 1992. **Business Addr:** President, Southland Chrysler-Plymouth, 3674 Elvis Presley Blvd, Memphis, TN 38116, (901)398-1500.

ROYAL, ANDRE TIERRE
Professional football player. **Personal:** Born Dec 1, 1972, Northport, AL; children: Tierra. **Educ:** Univ of Alabama. **Career:** Carolina Panthers, linebacker, 1995-. **Business Addr:** Professional Football Player, Carolina Panthers, 800 Mint St, Ericsson Stadium, Charlotte, NC 28202, (704)358-7000.

ROYAL, DONALD
Professional basketball player. **Personal:** Born May 2, 1966, New Orleans, LA. **Educ:** Notre Dame. **Career:** NBA career: Minnesota Timberwolves, 1989-90; San Antonio Spurs, 1991-92; Orlando Magic, 1992-96; Charlotte Hornets, 1996-; CBA career: Pensacola Tornados, 1987-88; Cedar Rapids Silver Bullets, 1988-89; Tri-City Chinook, 1991-92. **Business Addr:** Professional Basketball Player, Charlotte Hornets, One Hive Dr, Charlotte, NC 28217, (704)357-0252.

ROYE, MONICA R. HARGROVE
Lawyer. **Personal:** Born Feb 7, 1955, Atlanta, GA; daughter of Bettye Forston Hargrove and Ernest Crawford Hargrove; divorced; children: Stephen Paul Roye. **Educ:** Dartmouth College, Hanover, NH, BA, 1976; University of Michigan Law School, Ann Arbor, MI, JD, 1979. **Career:** Kutak Rock & Huie, Atlanta, GA, paralegal, 1976; IBM Legal Dept, Armonk, NY, summer law clerk, 1978; US Department of Justice, Antitrust Division, Washington, DC, trial attorney, 1979-83; USAir, Inc, Arlington, VA, from attorney to asst gen counsel, 1983-. **Orgs:** Henry and Mayme Sink Scholarship Fund, chairperson, 1986-91; Bicentennial Revival Committee, chairperson, 1996; Celestial Echoes, mem, 1986-91, associate pastor, 1993-96; Lomax AME Zion Church; USAM Corporation, secretary, 1988-96; member, judicial counsel, AME Zion church. **Honors/Awds:** Outstanding Performance Award, US Dept of Justice, 1980. **Home Addr:** 1330 Kingston Ave, Alexandria, VA 22302, (703)370-1418. **Business Phone:** (703)418-5230.

ROYE, ORPHEUS
Professional football player. **Personal:** Born Jan 21, 1974, Miami, FL. **Educ:** Florida State Univ, attended. **Career:** Pittsburgh Steelers, defensive end, 1996-. **Business Addr:** Professional Football Player, Pittsburgh Steelers, Three Rivers Stadium, 300 Stadium Circle, Pittsburgh, PA 15212, (412)323-1200.

ROYSTER, DON M., SR.
Business executive. **Personal:** Born Mar 12, 1944, Baltimore, MD; married Vertie M Bagby; children: Don M Jr, Denise C. **Educ:** Morgan State Univ, 1962-63; Agr & Tech Univ of NC, 1963-64; Natl Coll, BA, 1970; Amer Coll, CLU, 1976; Life Office Mgmt Assoc, FLMI, 1977. **Career:** Washington National Insurance Co, 1967-85, assistant vice pres, administrator, 1985-89, assistant vice pres, marketing service officer, 1989-92, vice pres of operations; Atlanta Life Insurance Co, president, COO, 1992-93, pres/CEO, 1993-. **Orgs:** Martin Luther King, Jr, Center for Nonviolent Social Change, director, bd of advisors, 1992-; Chicago Chap Chartered Life Underwriters, 1976-92; Chicago Chap FLMI, 1977-92; Chicago Assn of Health Underwriters 1979-92; Mental Health Assn of Evanston, vice pres, director, 1981-83; Evanston Human Relations Commission, chairman, commissioner, 1981-84; Sweet Auburn Area Improvement Association of Atlanta, secretary, board of directors, 1992-; Atlanta Business League, board of directors, 1993-; Central Atlanta Progress, board of directors, 1993-; Clark Atlanta Univ, dir, board of visitors, 1993-; Emory University, board of visitors, 1994-; Georgia Institute of Technology, director, Ivan Allen College Executive Advisory bd, 1994-; Life Insurers Conference, board of directors, 1994-; Martin Luther King Jr Center for Nonviolent Social Change, dir, bd of advisors, 1992-. **Honors/Awds:** Young Men's Christian Association of Chicago, Black & Hispanic Achievement Award, 1980. **Business Addr:** Exec Vice Pres for Distribution, Life of Georgia, 5780 Powers Ferry Rd NW, Atlanta, GA 30327.

ROYSTER, PHILIP M.
Educator. **Personal:** marrIed Phyliss M Royster; children: Rebecca Suzanne, Francesca Therese, Barbara Kaye Hammond, Tara Lynn Hammond. **Educ:** University of Illinois, 1960-62; DePaul University, BA, 1965, MA, 1967; Roosevelt University, Black Cultures Seminar, 1969; Loyola University, PhD, American and British Literature, 1974. **Career:** Dept of African/Afro-Amer Studies, SUNY Albany, asst prof, 1975-78; English Dept, Fisk Univ, asst prof, 1974-75, instructor, 1970-74; Syracuse University, Department of Afro-American Studies, associate professor, 1978-1981; Kansas State University, Department of English, associate professor, 1981-85, professor, 1985-88, American Ethnic Studies Program, coordinator, 1984-88; Bowling Green State University, Department of Ethnic Studies, professor, 1987-92, assistant chair, 1990-91; University of Illinois at Chicago, Department of English, professor, 1991-, Department of African-American Studies, professor, 1991-, African-American Cultural Center, director, 1991-. **Orgs:** Society for New Music, board member, 1979-81; The African-American Drum Ensemble, 1987-; Honor Society of Phi Kappa Phi, 1992-; Illinois Committee of Black Concerns in Higher Education, 1992-; University of Illinois at Chicago Black Alumni Association, 1992-; Association of Black Cultural Centers, 1991-, National Steering Committee, 1991-, Constitution Bylaws Subcommittee, 1991-; Popular Culture Association, 1976-; Modern Language Association; College Language Association; National Council of Black Studies; National Association of the Church of God Summit Meeting Task Force; Emerald Avenue Church of God, Historical Committee, chairperson. **Honors/Awds:** Bowling Green State University, Faculty Research Committee Basic Grant Award, 1988, Black Student Union and Board of Black Cultural Activities, Certificate of Appreciation, 1988; the Seaton Third Poetry Award, 1983; Kansas State University, Faculty Research Grant, 1981, 1982; Mellon Foundation, Mellon Project, 1980; Syracuse University, Senate Research Committee Grant, 1979; Fisk University, Study Grant, 1971, 1974; Loyola University, Assistantship, 1967-68, Fellowship, 1968-69; DePaul University, Arthur J Schmitt Scholarship, 1967. **Special Achievements:** Author, ''The Rapper as Shaman for a Band of Dancers of the Spirit: U Can't Touch This,'' The Emergency of Black and the Emergence of Rap Special Issue of Black Sacred Music: A Journal of Theomusicology, pages 60-67, 1991, ''The Sky is Gray: An Analysis of the Story,'' American Short Stories on Film: A Series of Casebooks, Langenscheidt-Longman, ''The Curse of Capitalism in the Caribbean: Purpose and Theme in Lindsay Barrett's Song for Mumu,'' Perspectives in Black Popular Culture, The Popular Press, pages 22-35, 1990; Literary & Cultural Criticism: ''In Search of Our Fathers' Arms: Alice Walker's Persona of the Alienated Darling,'' Black American Literature Forum, 20.4, 347-70, 1986; ''The Spirit Will Not Descend Without Song: Cultural Values of Afro-American Gospel Tradition,'' Folk Roots: An Exploration of the Folk Arts & Cultural Traqditions of Kansas, Ed Jennie A Chinn, Manhattan: Univ for Man, 19-24, 1982; ''Contemporary Oral Folk Expression,'' Black Books Bulletin, 6.3, 24-30, 1979; ''A Priest and a Witch Against the Spiders and the Snakes: Scapegoating in Toni Morrison's Sula,'' Umoja 2.2, 149-68, 1979; ''The Bluest Eye: The Novels of Toni Morrision,'' First World, 1.4, 34-44, 1977; Suggestions for Instructors to Accompany Clayers' and Spencer's Context for Composition, Co-authored with Stanley A Clayes, New York: Appleton-Century-Crofts, 1969; Books of Poetry: Songs and Dances, Detroit, Lotus Press, 1981; The Back Door, Chicago, Third World Press, 1971; Photography: A Milestone Sampler: Fifteenth Ann Anthology, Detroit, Lotus Press, ''Samuel Allen,'' 10, ''Jill Witherspoon Boyer,'' 22, ''Beverley Rose Enright,'' 40, ''Naomi F Faust,'' 44, ''Ray Fleming,'' 50, ''Agnes Nasmith Johnston,'' 56, ''Delores Kendrick,'' 68, ''Pinkie Gordon Lane,'' 74, ''Naomi Long Madgett,'' 80, ''Haki R Madhubuti,'' 86, ''Herbert Woodward Martin,'' 92, ''May Miller,'' 104, ''Mwatabu Okantah,'' 110, ''Paulette Childress White,'' 122, 1988; Master Drummer & Percussionist: ''Earth Blossom,'' The John Betsch Society, Strata-East Recording Co, #SES-19748, 1975; Received a four and a half star review in Downbeat, 24-26, May 1975; ''A White Sport Coat and a Pink Crustacean,'' Jimmy Buffet, Dunhill ABC, DSX 50150, 1973; ''Hanging Around the Observatory,'' John Hiatt, Epic KE 32688, 1973; ''We Make Spirit (Dancing in the Moonlight),'' John Hiatt, Epic, 5-10990, ZSS 157218, 1973; ''Backwoods Woman,'' Dianne Davidson, Janus, JLS 3043, 1972; ''The Knack,'' The Interpreters, Cadet LP 762, 1965. **Business Addr:** Director, African-American Cultural Center, University of Illinois at Chicago, Rm 208 Addams Hall, 830 S Halsted Street, Chicago, IL 60607-7030, (312)413-2705.

ROYSTER, VIVIAN HALL
University library administrator. **Personal:** Born Feb 21, 1951, Monticello, FL; daughter of Emma L Hall and Henry Hall (deceased); married Charles E Royster (divorced); children: Renee Gwendolyn-Juanita. **Educ:** Florida A&M Univ, Tallahassee, FL, BS (magna cum laude), 1973; Atlanta Univ, Atlanta, GA, MSLS (summa cum laude), 1974; Florida State Univ, Tallahassee, FL, PhD candidate, 1990. **Career:** Florida State Univ, Tallahassee, FL, associate univ librarian, 1974-80; Univ Maryland, East Shore Princess Anne, MD, admin librarian, 1980-83; Florida A&M Univ, Tallahassee, FL, associate director, Title III program, 1982-84, associate professor/foreign languages, 1984-86; Florida A&M Univ Libraries, Tallahassee, FL, univ librarian/head acquisitions dept, 1986-. **Orgs:** Secretary, board of directors, Assn of College & Research Libraries, Florida Chapter, 1989-; library advisory board, Bond Community Branch Library-Leon County Public Library System, 1989-; member, American Library Assn Black Caucus, 1978-; steering committee member, E A Copeland Scholarship Drive, Florida A&M Univ Foundation, 1989-; member, American Library Assn, 1976-; financial secretary, Florida A&M Univ Friends of the Black Archives, 1988-. **Honors/Awds:** Grant Award, Of Black America, Natl Endowment for the Humanities Maryland, 1980-82; Education Fellowship, Atlanta Univ GSLIS, 1973-74; State of Florida Bd of Regents Doctoral Fellowship Award, 1984; Selected as Host, Florida Governor's Conference on the White House Conference on Library & Information Services, 1990; Beta Phi Mu Graduate Honor Soc, library science; Alpha Beta Beta Alpha Undergraduate Library Science Honor Society, FAMU, 1972; Undergraduate Advisor Awards, Alpha Kappa Alpha Sorority, Inc, 1974-1980; Florida A&M University, Professional Developmental Grant-in-Aid, 1988, 1993, 1994. **Business Addr:** University Librarian & Head, Acquistions Department, The Florida A&M University Libraries, 1500 S Martin Luther King Blvd, Tallahassee, FL 32307, (904)599-3314.

ROZIER, CLIFFORD GLEN, II
Professional basketball player. **Personal:** Born Oct 31, 1972, Bradenton, FL. **Educ:** North Carolina; Louisville. **Career:** Golden State Warriors, forward-center, 1994-96; Toronto Raptors, 1996-97; Minnesota Timberwolves, 1997-. **Special Achievements:** NBA Draft, First round pick, #16, 1994. **Business Addr:** Professional Basketball Player, Minnesota Timberwolves, 600 First Ave N, Minneapolis, MN 55403, (612)337-3865.

ROZIER, GILBERT DONALD
Business executive, organization executive. **Personal:** Born Oct 19, 1940, West Palm Beach, FL; married Juanella Miller; children: Ricardo, Rellisa. **Educ:** Benedict Coll, AB 1963; Southern Connecticut State Coll, masters, Urban Studies, 1973. **Career:** Kentucky Fried Chicken Restaurants, franchise owner, currently; Urban League of S Weston, exec dir; Urban League of Union CO, pres 1974; Urban League of S Weston Fairfield, asso dir 1970-74; Stamford Neighborhood Youth Corp, dir 1967-74; W Main St Comm Ctr, prog dir 1966-67; W Side YMCA NYC, youth worker 1963-66. **Orgs:** Sec CT State Fed of Demo Clubs 1974; pres AFLO Am Dem Club 1979; life mem, Kappa Alpha Psi; bd of trustees, Benedict Coll; trustee, Stamford Bethel AME; board member, Stanford Planning. **Honors/Awds:** Outstand Young Man of the Yr; outstand Young Men of Am 1973; Outstand Citizen Union Co NJ Human Resources 1979; Outstand Citizen St John Lodge #14 Stamford, CT 1980. **Business Addr:** 285 West Main St, Stamford, CT 06902.

RUCKER, ALSTON LOUIS
Banker. **Personal:** Born Aug 29, 1949, Greenwood, SC; son of Annie Rucker and Thomas L Rucker (deceased); married Shirley Gordon, Jul 12, 1975; children: Montrice Ginelle, Aaron Louis. **Educ:** South Carolina State College, BA, business administration, 1971. **Career:** LaSalle Bank FSB, savings representative, 1973-81, retirement account specialist, 1981-84, human resources mgr, 1984-85, assistant secretary, 1985-86, branch mgr, 1986-87, branch officer, 1987-91, assistant vice pres, 1992-. **Orgs:** Lillydale Progressive Missionary Baptist Church, 1985-; South Carolina State College, Chicago Chapter, 1975-; Dolton School District #149, PTA, 1990-; Chicago Association of Commerce and Industry, Youth Motivation Program, program speaker, 1981-; Teen Living Programs Inc, bd mem, 1993-; Thornton High School, District #205, PTA, 1992; The Harvey 100 Club, Inc, bd mem/treas, 1995-. **Honors/Awds:** Chicago South Side YMCA, Black and Hispanic Achievers, 1991; Dollars and Sense Magazine; America's Best and Brightest Young Business & Professional Men, 1992; LaSalle Bank, FSB, Branch Administration Certificate of Achievement, Certified Manager Program, 1994. **Business Addr:** Assistant Vice Pres, LaSalle Bank, NA, 1701 River Oaks Dr, Calumet City, IL 60409, (708)730-8518.

RUCKER, NANNIE GEORGE
Educator. **Personal:** Born Apr 21, 1914, Murfreesboro, TN; married James I. **Educ:** TN State U, BS Elem Educ 1950, MS Educ Psych 1958; Fisk U; George Peabody Coll; Middle TN State U; Tuskegee Inst. **Career:** Middle TN State Univ Campus School, lab teacher. **Orgs:** Mem Middle TN Tchrs Assn; Sigma Gamma Rho; Rutherford Co Tchrs Assn; Am Assn of Univ

Women; pres/sec Tchrs Assn; Pub Serv Comm Panel; sec State Fed of Dem Women 1975; mem State Dem Exec (2nd term); Steering Com of Intl Women's Yr 1975; League of Women Voters; Women's Round Table; 1st v chrprsn Dem Party for Middle TN 1976; mem TN State Bd of Edn/State Bd for Voc Educ 1979; mem admin & policy com State Bd of Edn/State Bd for Voc Educ 1979; bd dir Wee Care Day Care Child Devel Ctr 1980; mem 1st Bapt Ch; mem Delta Kappa Gamma; Alpha Kappa Mu; del Intl Reading Assn 1965; Dem Nat Conv(served as sec of TN Delegation 1972); NEA. **Honors/Awds:** ''Nannie G Rucker Day'' Doylestown PA; Elected Del-at-Large Nat Dem Conv 1980. **Business Addr:** 2419 Bennington Dr, Murfreesboro, TN 37130.

RUCKER, ROBERT D., JR.
Judge. **Personal:** Born in Canton, GA. **Educ:** Indiana University; Valparaiso University School of Law, JD. **Career:** Lake County, IN, deputy prosecutor, 1979-85; City of Gary, IN, deputy city attorney, 1987-88; private practice, 1985-90; Indiana Court of Appeals, judge, 1990-. **Orgs:** National Bar Association; Marion County Bar Association; Indiana State Bar Association. **Honors/Awds:** First black appointed to Indiana Court of Appeals. **Business Addr:** Judge, Indiana Court of Appeals, 1270 South Merchants Plaza, Indianapolis, IN 46204.

RUCKS, ALFRED J.
Engineer (retired). **Personal:** Born Oct 20, 1935, Bellwood, TN; son of Horty Rucks and Alfred Rucks. **Educ:** TN A&I State Univ, BSEE, 1958. **Career:** Defense Atomic Support Agency, 1958-62; White Sands Missile Range, electronics engr, 1962-85, EEO counselor 1973-85, chief safety engrg branch 1985-93. **Orgs:** Mem IEEE 1959-; assoc mem NSPE; trustee N Mesquite St Church of Christ 1962-; chmn Minority Housing Bd City of Las Cruces NM 1968-80; pres NM State NAACP 1970-86; chmn Reg VI NAACP 1974, 1979, 1984; natl bd of dir NAACP 1981-87; pres, Dona Ana County NAACP, 1990-; State of NM Martin Luther King Commission, 1985-86; Las Cruces Community Development Bd, 1990-; NM Private Industry Council, 1994-. **Honors/Awds:** Commanders Awd White Sands Missile Range 1975, 1982, 1993; NM NAACP Award, 1972, 1979, 1986, 1992; Natl Mert Acad Award, 1973; Region VI award, 1990; City of Las Cruces, NM Award, 1980; NM Governor, 1975, 1985, 1993; Omega Psi Phi, NMSU chapter, Citizen of the Year Award, 1992; Hispanic Leadership and Development Program Award, 1993; NMSU African-American Citizen of the YEar, 1993; Tennessee NAACP, 1994.

RUDD, AMANDA S.
Library consultant. **Personal:** Born Apr 9, 1923, Greenville, SC; daughter of Delarion Moore Sullivan and Wesley Sullivan; divorced; children: Lt Cmdr Grover Randle USN, Mrs Loretta Randle O'Brien. **Educ:** FL A&M Univ, BS Ed; Western Reserve Univ, MLS. **Career:** SC, AK, FL, OH, school librarian, elem teacher; Cleveland Public Schools, asst suprv of libr 1965-70; Field Enterprises Educ Corp, consultant educ serv dept 1970-75; The Chicago Publ Library, asst chief librarian comm rel & special prog of serv 1975, dep commissioner 1975-81, commissioner 1981-85; library consultant, currently. **Orgs:** Mem Amer Library Assn Planning Comm 1985, ALA Intl Relations Comm, ALA Legislative Comm Amer Library Trustee Assoc 1983-85, ALA Conf Comm, Metro Library Sect, Public Library Assoc 1984; chairperson Local Arrangements Comm Gen Conf, Intl Fed of Library Assoc & Inst 1985; mem, adv bd Grad School of Library & Info Sci Rosary Coll; mem Citizens Adv Bd of Channel 20 WYCC-TV Chicago, IL Literacy Council; ad hoc comm Plan for Implementation of Multitype Library Syst, IL Library Assn; mem visiting comm, Bd of Overseers for the School of Library Sci, Case Western Reserve Univ; mem Chicago Educ & Cultural Cable TV Consortium; mem bd of dir, Chicago Metro History Fair; mem Truman Coll Adv Bd Chicago; mem adv comm, The Stages of Shakespeare; mem adv comm, IL StateLibrary; mem Read IL Comm, IL Statibrary; mem adv comm, Future of IL Publ Library; mem bd of dir, Human Serv Prov ider Tech Serv Inst; mem Women's Comm, 1982 Worlds Fair Chicago; chair Intl Relations Comm, ALA; treas North Shore Chap of Links Inc. **Honors/Awds:** Marshall Bynum Humanitarian Awd for Civic & Social Achievement by Dress Horsemen Inc; Bethune Tubman Truth Awd for Community Serv & Professional Accomplishment by Black Women, Hall of Fame Found; Vivian C Harsh Awd, Afro-Amer Genealogical & Historical Soc of Chicago; ''Profile in Accomplishments'' A Salute to Black Amer on Black Entertainment TV Cable Network; Tribute for Outstanding Contrib in the Field of Library Serv, South Suburban Chicago Chap, Links Inc; Beta Phi Mu, Natl Library Sci Hon Soc; Alpha Gamma Pi Sor for Civic & Soc Achievement; numerous speaking engagements incl, ''The Perfection of the Process of Living'' Case Western Reserve Univ, ''Challenges & Pleasures of Library Serv in the 1980's'' Chicago Library Club,''The Chicago Publ Library, Reaches Out to its Youth, Public Libra& School Cooperate in Chicago'' Intl Assn of Metro City Libraries; ''Traditional & Nontraditional Career Options in the Public Library'' Univ of IL Champaign.

RUDD, CHARLOTTE JOHNSON
Educator. **Personal:** Born Jul 4, 1948, Columbus, OH; daughter of Helen Johnson and James W Johnson; divorced; children: Toyia Lynn. **Educ:** Ohio State University, BS, 1970, MS, 1985. **Career:** Columbus Public Schools, junior high English teacher, 1970-73, Drop Out Prevention Project: Move Ahead, coordinator, 1973-79, middle school reading/language arts teacher, 1980-83, Human Relations, staff development specialist, 1983-85, middle school assistant principal, 1985-91, Effective Schools Process, district administrator, 1991-. **Orgs:** National Alliance of Black School Educators, 1989-93; Franklin Alternative Middle School, department/team leader, 1979-83; National Education Association, board of directors, 1981-83, professional development committee, 1979-83; Ohio Education Association, executive committee, 1978-83, Minority Caucus, treasurer, 1974-76; Ohio House of Representatives, chair, campaign fundraising, 1983-90; Ohio State University, Commission on Interprofessional Education and Practice, child abuse and neglect advisory board; House of Representative Miller's, Community Clothes Drive, 1992-93. **Honors/Awds:** Ohio State University, Mortor Board, 1970, Phi Delta Kappa, 1979. **Special Achievements:** Co-Founder: Doris L Allen Minority Caucus-OEA, 1974; PRIDE Inc, group to develop student self-esteem and leadership, 1974; designer: Staff Development Model for School Improvement, 1984; Effective Schools Process, start-up model for middle and high schools, 1992-93. **Business Addr:** Administrator, Effective Schools, Columbus Public Schools, Columbus Education Center, 270 E State St, Columbus, OH 43215, (614)365-5738.

RUDD, DWAYNE
Professional football player. **Educ:** Alabama. **Career:** Minnesota Vikings, 1997-. **Special Achievements:** NFL Draft, First round pick, #20, 1997. **Business Addr:** Professional Football Player, Minnesota Vikings, 9520 Viking Dr, Eden Prairie, MN 55344, (612)828-6500.

RUDD, JAMES M.
Logistics manager. **Personal:** Born Dec 19, 1916, Granite Springs, VA; son of Grace Twyman (deceased) and James Melvin Rudd (deceased); married Rebecca Ryan; children: Dorothy Rudd Moore, Jacqueline May, Rosalind, James, Simone, Carolyn. **Educ:** DE State College/ Univ of DE, Certificates Council Effectiveness Training 1981/82; Natl Acad and Institute of Corrections Univ of CO, Certificate 1986. **Career:** US Civil Service, served in various supervisory capacities with the US Army electronics command, logistics administration and management field 1941-73 (retired); Bd of Educ Millside School Dist, pres 1947-50; Dept of Corrections State of DE, mem council on corrections 1982-. **Orgs:** Mem Citizen Adv Council Colonial School Dist 1982-; chairperson Citizen Adv Council William Penn HS; mem State Adv council for Adult and Community Educ; mem bd of dirs Delaware Assn for Adult and Community Educ; mem Benevolent Order of Elks Philadelphia, Kiwanis Club of New Castle Hundred, Assn of the United States Army; pres bd of dirs New Castle Comm Progressive Club; mem Governor's Task Force on Correction Security 1986-. **Honors/Awds:** Outstanding Performance US Army Matl Readiness Cmd Washington DC; Commendation US Aviation Systems Command St Louis, MO. **Home Addr:** 15 Holcomb Ln, New Castle, DE 19720.

RUDD, WILLIE LESSLIE
Business executive. **Personal:** Born Sep 22, 1944, Sardis, MS; married Barbara A; children: Jacqueline Yvette, Lynda Yvonne, Anita Michelle, Leslie Ann. **Educ:** Booker T Washington HS, 1963. **Career:** NBFI Furniture Co, upholster 1964-72; United Furniture Workers AFL-CIO, intl rep 1972-76; United Furniture Wokers Intl Union AFL-CIO, intl vice pres 1976-;United Furniture Workers Local 282 AFL-CIO, pres 1976-. **Orgs:** Mem A Phillip Randolph Org 1970-, Union Valley MB Church 23 yrs; mem NAACP 1964, Union Valley Bapt Church 1964; 1st vchmn A Phillip Randolph Inst Memphis Chap 1978-; bd of dir Girls Clubs of Amer Memphis 1978. **Honors/Awds:** Outstanding Youn Man of Amer Natl C of C 1980; Hon Sgt-at-Arms John Ford State Senator 1976; Key to Shelby Cty Commiss 1977. **Business Addr:** President, United Furniture Workers of Am, 1254 Lamar Ave, Memphis, TN 38104.

RUDD-MOORE, DOROTHY
Composer. **Personal:** Born Jun 4, 1940, New Castle, DE; married Kermit Moore. **Educ:** Howard Univ Sch of Music, B Music (Magna Cum Laude) 1963; American Conservatory Fontainebleau France, diploma 1963. **Career:** Harlem School of the Arts, teacher piano & music theory 1965-66; NY University, teacher music history appreciation 1969; Bronx Comm Coll, teacher music history appreciation 1971; Private Instructor, voice theory piano; composer, singer-performer. **Orgs:** Founder Society of Black Composers 1968; bd mem 1986, mem Amer Composers Alliance 1972-; mem Broadcast Music Inc 1972-; composer mem of recording panel Natl Endowment for the Arts 1986, 1988; served on New York State Council on the Arts, 1988-90. **Honors/Awds:** Lucy Moten Fellowship Howard Univ; grant from NY State Council on the Arts 1985, Amer Music Ctr 1985; compositions include ''From the Dark Tower'' for voice orchestra, ''Frederick Douglass'' full length opera, ''Dirge and Deliverance'' for cello and piano, ''Three Pieces'' for violin and piano, Piano Trio No 1, ''Dream and Variations'' for piano, ''Weary Blues'' for voice, cello and piano, ''Modes'' for string quartet. **Home Addr:** 33 Riverside Dr, New York, NY 10023. **Business Phone:** (212)787-1869.

RUFF, JAMIE CARLESS
Journalist. **Personal:** Born May 16, 1962, Greensboro, NC; son of Janie Catherine Ruff. **Educ:** North Carolina A&T State Univ, Greensboro, NC, history, 1984. **Career:** Richmond Times-Dispatch, reporter, currently. **Honors/Awds:** Second Place North Carolina Press, Association Award for Spot News Reporting, 1988. **Business Addr:** Reporter, Richmond Times-Dispatch, 30 Franklin St, PO Box 342, Petersburg, VA 23804.

RUFFIN, BENJAMIN S.
Company executive. **Personal:** Born Dec 11, 1941, Durham County, NC. **Educ:** North Carolina Central University, BA. **Career:** North Carolina Mutual Insurance Co, senior vice president, special asst to the president; RJR Nabisco Co, Public Affairs Programming, director, currently; RJ Reynolds Tobacco Co, vp of corp affairs, currently. **Orgs:** Vice president, UDI; consult, John Avery Boys Club; comm org, Opera Breakthrough; dir, United Organization for Community Improvement; Congress of Racial Equality; Natl Assn for Community Development; Durham Committee of Negro Affairs; secretary, Durham Homes Inc; Low-Income & Housing Development Inc; NAACP; Natl Welfare Rights Movement; Natl Business League, chairman of board; Durham Business & Professional Chain; secretary, Durham Legal Aid Society; People's Ath Concern Committee; treasurer, REMCA Housing Inc; Coordinating Council for Senior Citizens. **Business Addr:** VP, Corporate Affairs, RJ Reynolds Tobacco Co, 401 N Main St, Winston-Salem, NC 27102.

RUFFIN, JANICE E.
Psychologist, psychiatric nurse. **Personal:** Born Dec 6, 1942, Cleveland, OH. **Educ:** Ohio State Univ, School of Nursing, BS 1964; Rutgers The State Univ Coll of Nursing, MS Psychiatric Nursing 1967; CUNY Grad Ctr, MPhil 1984, PhD Clinical Psychology 1985. **Career:** CT Mental Health Ctr New Haven, dir of nursing 1974-77; Yale Univ Sch of Nursing, asst prof grad prog in psychiatric nursing, assoc prof 1975-77; City Coll CUNY, lecturer dept of psychology 1978-80; Bronx Psychiatric Ctr, psychologist Highbridge out-patient clinic 1980-85; Baruch Coll Office of Counseling & Psychological Svcs, psychologist 1985-, dir 1986-94, director, Student Health Services, 1990-. **Orgs:** Mem bd dir NY Black Nurses' Assn 1971-74; chmn 1969-71 mem 1971-72 Com on Nursing in a Soc in Crisis; Affir Action Task Force 1972-76; mem editorial bd Perspectives in Psychiatric Care 1973-83; historian Natl Black Nurses Assoc 1972-82; bd dir Nat Black Nurses' Assn 1972-74; chmn 1971-72 & vice pres 1972-73; Operation Success in Nursing Educ; mem Inst for Comm Organ & Personal Effectivesness bd dir 1974-77; mem Nurse Training Review Com NIMH 1974-78; mem AK Rice Inst 1979-; mem Sigma Theta Tau 1968-; certification and licensure as psychologistNY State Educ Dept 1986. **Honors/Awds:** Certificate and Gold Medal OH State Univ Sch of Nursing 1970; Certificate of Excellence in Psychiatric Nursing Amer Nurses' Assoc 1975; Certificate in Psychiatric Mental Health Nursing by Amer Nurses Assoc 1975; Awd Natl Assoc Negro Business & Professional Women's Clubs Inc 1977; Dedicated Professional Service Awd Natl Assoc of Negro Business and Professional Womens Clubs Inc 1977; excellence in psychology, City Coll, CUNY, 1987. **Business Addr:** Dir, Student Health Services, Baruch College, CUNY, 17 Lexington Avenue, P O Box F-1702, New York, NY 10010.

RUFFIN, JOHN
Educator. **Personal:** Born Jun 29, 1943, New Orleans, LA; married Angela Beverly; children: John Wesley, Meeka, Beverly. **Educ:** Dillard Univ, BS 1965; Atlanta Univ, MS 1967; KS State Univ, PhD 1971; Harvard Univ, Post Doctoral 1975-77. **Career:** Southern Univ Baton Rouge, biol instructor 1967-68; Atlanta Univ, asst prof 1971-74; AL A&M Univ, assoc prof 1974-75; NC Central Univ, prof biol, 1978-86, chmn biol, dean coll of arts & sciences 1986-. **Orgs:** Consult Natl Inst of Health Governor 1978-; consult Bd of Sci & Tech 1983-; consult ADAMHA, Natl Inst Mental Health 1984. **Honors/Awds:** Beta Beta Beta Natl Hon Soc 1965-; Natl Sci Found Fellowship 1969; Natl Inst Health Fellowship 1974; Cabot Rsch Fellow Harvard Univ 1975. **Business Addr:** Dean, Coll of Arts & Sciences, North Carolina Central Univ, 1801 Fayetteville St, Durham, NC 27707.

RUFFIN, JOHN H., JR.
Judge. **Personal:** Born Dec 23, 1934, Waynesboro, GA. **Educ:** Morehouse College, BA, 1957; Howard Univ, LLB, 1960. **Career:** Ruffin & Watkins, Augusta, GA, partner, 1961-63; Ruffin & Brown, Augusta, GA, partner; Augusta Judicial Circuit, superior court judge, 1986-94; Court of Appeals of Georgia, judge, currently. **Orgs:** Member, National Bar Assn; member, Augusta Bar Assn; member, National Lawyers Guild; member, Georgia Assn Criminal Defense Lawyers. **Business Addr:** Judge, Court of Appeals of Georgia, 40 Capitol Square, State Judicial Building, 4th floor, Atlanta, GA 30334.

RUFFIN, JOHN WALTER, JR.
Business executive. **Personal:** Born Jun 15, 1941, Moncure, NC; son of Theima Harris Ruffin and John Ruffin Sr; married Dorothy L Walton; children: Jonathan, Jehan. **Educ:** Morgan State Univ, AB 1963; Cornell Univ, MS 1970. **Career:** Pantry

Pride Inc, vice pres 1980-85; Paradies Airport Shops, partner/consultant; JD Ruffin Assoc, Inc, pres chief exec officer; Sunao Broadcasting Co Inc, pres & gen mgr 1986-92; Business Equipment Co, pres, CEO, 1988-91; JD Ruffin Associates Inc, CEO, currently. **Orgs:** Chmn of the bd Urban League Broward 1984-87; adv bd Barnett Bank 1985-87; chmn Broward Employ & Training 1986; chmn, Coral Springs Economic Development Foundation, 1995-97; president, Sigma Pi Phi Fraternity, Alpha Rho Boule, 1997; 33rd Degree Mason, 1996. **Honors/Awds:** Special Recognition by US Congress 1985; Sen Lawton Chiles Commendation Outstanding Citizen City of Fort Lauderdale 1986; Great Achievement NAACP Broward 1986; State Top Ten Awds Natl Business League. **Business Addr:** President & Chief Executive Officer, J D Ruffin Associates Inc, PO Box 8589, Coral Springs, FL 33075.

RUFFIN, PAULETTE FRANCINE
Military officer, educator, educational administrator. **Personal:** Born Dec 13, 1956, Alexandria, VA; daughter of Paul Ruffin and Rosetta Payton Ruffin; divorced; children: M Joshua, D Christopher. **Educ:** Lehigh, Bethlehem, PA, BS mktg, 1978; UNC, Chapel Hill, NC, MA soc psyc, 1987. **Career:** US Army, Ordinance School, APG, MD, student, basic course, 1978, Student Officer Co, APG, MD, executive officer, 1978-79, US Military Academy, West Point, NY, admissions officer, 1979-80, 9th INF Div, Ft Lewis, WA, Co CDR, asst scy to the general staff, 1980-85, US Military Academy, West Point NY, assoc prof, 1987-90, 41st Area Spt Group, Panama, Log Ops, material off, exec off, 1990-93, Army Material Command HQ, special asst to commanding general, speechwriter, 1994-96, Georgetown Univ, dir of Army ROTC, 1996-. **Military Serv:** US Army, ltc, 1978-; Legion of Merit, 1996; Meritorious Service Medal, 1990, 1993; Army Commendation Medal, 1979, 1985; Army Achievement Medal, 1983, 1984, 1993. **Home Addr:** 8126 Clifforest Dr, Springfield, VA 22153. **Business Addr:** Director, GU Army ROTC, Georgetown University, 3520 Prospect St, Ste 305, Washington, DC 20057, (202)687-7023.

RUFFIN, RICHARD D.
Physician (retired). **Personal:** Born Jul 7, 1924, Cairo, IL; son of Alpha Mae Curtis Ruffin (deceased) and Edward David Ruffin (deceased); married Yvonne White; children: Richard David Jr, Patti Yvonne, Kenneth George. **Educ:** Northern IL Univ Dekalb IL, 1940-41; IL State Univ Bloomington Normal, 1941-43; Univ of IL, 1946-47; Coll of Mortuary Sci, St Louis, B of Mortuary Sci 1948; Meharry Med Coll Nashville TN, MD 1953. **Career:** Homer G Phillips Hosp St Louis, MO, internship 1953-54, residencies surgery 1954-55, residencies urology 1955-58; private practice, urologist 1959-92. **Orgs:** Chmn Section of Urology, St Anthony Hospital 1975-78; urological consultant State of OH, Dept of Rehabilitation & Correction 1975-78; secy/treas Central OH Urological Soc 1964-65, pres 1967-68; vice chief Med & Dental Staff, St Anthony Hosp 1973-76; Columbus Acad of Med 1958-; OH State Med Assn 1958-; Am Med Assn 1958-; Central OH Urological Soc 1959-; N Central Sect; Am Urological Assn 1961-; Columbus Assn for Physicians/Dentists 1971-. **Honors/Awds:** Citation Citizenship City of Columbus, OH Div of Police 1971; Outstanding Am Bicentennial Ed 1975; President's Award; Meharry Med Coll Nashville 1978; The Blue Book of Franklin County 1980-82; Children's Hosp Award 1984; Grant Hospital Award, 25 Years Service, 1984; St Anthony Hospital Awrd, 25 Years Service, 1984. **Military Serv:** AUS 1943-45. **Home Addr:** 3236 E Livingston Ave, Columbus, OH 43227.

RUFFIN, RONALD R.
Government official. **Personal:** Born Jul 23, 1947, Saginaw, MI; son of William & Catherine Ruffin; married Verlie M Ruffin, Oct 31, 1970; children: Tulani M, Omari A. **Educ:** MI State Univ, BS, 1970; Atlanta Univ, MA, 1990. **Career:** Lakeside Labs, pharmaceutical rep, 1970-73; Ayerst Labs, pharmaceutical rep, 1973-77; CYSP (Ceta), exec admin, 1977-78; City of Detroit, mgr, Neighborhood City Halls, 1978-81, exec admin, Municipal Parking Dept, 1981-94; Wayne County Comm Coll, part-time instructor, 1990-; City of Detroit, dir, Municipal Parking Dept, 1994-. **Orgs:** Institutional & Municipal Parking Congress, 1994-; Municipal Parking Assn, 1983-; NAACP, 1965-; Museum of African American History, 1995; Kappa Alpha Psi Fraternity, 1967-; Prince Hall F & A Masons, 1993-; Detroit Zoological Society, 1993-; Motown Athletic Club, 1982-. **Special Achievements:** Developed a Practitioner's Manual: Total Fitness for Law Enforcement Officers, 1989; First appointed African-American Parking Dir, City of Detroit, 1994. **Business Addr:** Dir, City of Detroit, Municipal Parking Dept, 200 Civic Center Dr, Detroit, MI 48226, (313)877-8030.

RUFFINS, REYNOLDS
Illustrator, designer. **Personal:** Born Aug 5, 1930, New York, NY. **Career:** Cooper Union, 1951; Dept Visual Communications Coll Visual & Performing Arts Syracuse Univ, visiting adjunct prof 1973-; School Visual Arts, instructor, 1967-70. **Orgs:** Designer illustrator 7 Books for Children; Annual Riddle Calender; Charles Scribners's Sons; Family Cir Mag. **Honors/Awds:** Best illus awrd NY Times Book Rev 1973; Bologna (Italy) Children's Book Fair 1976; Am Inst Graphic Arts Art Dir Clb; CA mag awrd; soc illus awrd;profl achvmt awrd Cooper Union 1972; 200 Yrs Am Illus NY Hist Soc. **Business Addr:** Dept of Fine Arts, Parsons School of Design, 66 Fifth Ave, New York, NY 10011.

RUFFNER, RAY P.
Insurance executive. **Personal:** Born Aug 11, 1946, Washington, DC; married Patricia Smith; children: Damien Earl. **Educ:** Washington Lee HS, Grad 1964; Acct Correspondence Course, 1966-67. **Career:** Larry Buick Ar/VA, body & fender mech 1969-71; United Co Life Ins Co, ins sales 1971, ins sale & mgmt 1971-77; Ruffner & Assoc, ins sales & mgmt, sole proprietor 1977-. **Orgs:** Investor Real Estate 1973-. **Honors/Awds:** Renovating homes for low income, 5 town homes currently in progress 1985; Public Service to High School & Coll 1984. **Military Serv:** USMC E-5 4 yrs; NCO Awd 1966. **Home Addr:** 10605 Shadow Ln, Fairfax Station, VA 22039. **Business Addr:** President, Ruffner & Assocs, PO Box 290, Lorton, VA 22079.

RUMPH, ANNIE ALRIDGE
Elected official. **Personal:** Born Oct 5, 1917, Ellaville, GA; widowed. **Educ:** Fort Valley State Coll, BS 1950; Albany State Coll, 1951; Tuskegee Inst, 1953-54. **Career:** St Peter AME Church, lay organization sec 1977-84, steward bd vice pres 1981-83; Operation Cure, co-chmn 1983-84; Peach County Chap of GA Coalition of Black Women, pres 1984-85; Peach County Bd of Com, county commissioner. **Orgs:** Mem State & County Retired Teachers Assoc 1977-85; Steward Board, president, 1991-92; Teens on Action, advisor, 1985-92; Peach Co Comm Partnership Coalition, coordinator, 1990-92; Peach County Comm Organization, pres, 1985-; St Peter AME Church, pres/sr steward bd mem. **Honors/Awds:** Certificate of Appreciation Citizenship Educ Com 1981; Distinguished Serv Fort Valley State Coll 1982; Community Serv Awd Delta Pi Sigma Chapter Sigma Gamma Rho Sor 1982-83; Outstanding Achievement End Zoners Club 1984.

RUNDLES, JAMES ISAIAH
Government official. **Personal:** Born Jul 9, 1920, Jackson, MS; married Mattie Singleton. **Educ:** Tougaloo So Christian Inst, bA 1940; Univ of HI Honolulu, 1944-45; Johnson Sch of Bus, Bus Ed 1948-49. **Career:** City of Jackson, MS, exec asst to mayor 1977-; Gov of MS (First Black), exec asst 1972-76; Pittsburg Courier/Chicago & Defender, civil rights rprtr 1960-71. **Orgs:** Fndr Rundles & Assc Pub Relations Consult 1960-71; natl pub affairs dir Montford Point Marines Assc 1960-66; news dir Radio WOKJ/JaCKSON, MS 1954-60; assc edtr The Jackson Advocate/Newspaper 1946-50; bd dir MS Bar Legal Assc 1973-76; adv comm relations Div US Justice Dept 1972-76; bd dir Am Red Cross 1973-; bd dir Boys Clubs of Am 1977-. **Honors/Awds:** Black journalism awrd Nat Proj Media Assc 1975; Humanitarian Endeavors MS Independent Beauticians Assc 1975; outst & dedicated serv Gov Cncl for Minority Afrs 1975; efforts achvmt in the humanities Nine Iron Golf Assc SE 1979. **Military Serv:** USMC sgt maj 1942-45; Prsidential Unit Citation (Iwo Jima) 1945. **Business Addr:** PO Box 3953, Jackson, MS 39207-3953.

RUNNELS, BERNICE
Educational administrator. **Personal:** Born Aug 29, 1925, Memphis, TN; daughter of Susie Bradd and Ben Bradd; married Ike (deceased); children: Patricia Teague, Isaac Jr, Reginald, Maurice. **Career:** Pembroke District 259, president 9 years, board mem 1963-84. **Orgs:** Mem Three Rivers Division of the Ill Board Assn 1975-83. **Honors/Awds:** State Board Education. **Home Addr:** PO Box 149, Hopkins Park, IL 60944.

RUSH, BOBBY
Congressman. **Personal:** Born Nov 23, 1946. **Educ:** Roosevelt Univ, BA, 1974; University of Illinois, MA, 1994. **Career:** Insurance salesman; Chicago City Council, 1983-92; US House of Representatives, representative, 1992-. **Business Addr:** Congressman, US House of Representatives, 131 Cannon HOB, Washington, DC 20515, (202)225-4372.

RUSH, EDDIE F.
Professional sports official. **Career:** NBA, referee, currently. **Home Addr:** PO Box 490838, Atlanta, GA 30349.

RUSH, SONYA C.
Brand manager. **Personal:** Born Aug 23, 1959, Columbia, LA; daughter of Shirley Cross Rush and Walter C Rush. **Educ:** GA Inst of Tech, BChE 1981; Univ of MI, MBA 1983. **Career:** Philip Morris USA, operations analyst, 1983-88, superintendent-manufacturing, 1988-90, MBA associate, 1990-92, senior planning analyst, 1992, assistant brand manager, 1992-93, associate brand manager, 1993-94, brand manager, 1994-. **Orgs:** Chmn economic develop Alpha Kappa Alpha Sor 1985-; allocations mem United Way; advisor Junior Achievement; recruiter Univ of MI Grad Sch of Business; mem Natl Coalition of 100 Black Women; mem Alpha Kappa Alpha Sor Inc; mem The Friends of Art; Leadership Metro Richmond. **Honors/Awds:** President's Award, Philip Morris USA, 1989; Visting Professor, Black Execut ive Exchange Program. **Home Addr:** 424 W End Ave, Apt 6-B, New York, NY 10024-5777.

RUSHEN, PATRICE
Recording artist, film composer. **Personal:** Born Sep 30, Los Angeles, CA; daughter of Ruth L Rushen and Allen Roy Rushen; married Marc St. Louis, Jan 4, 1986. **Educ:** University of Southern California, Los Angeles, CA, music education/piano performance, 1972-76. **Career:** Recording artist, composer; recorded nine albums, which produced the hit singles ''Haven't You Heard,'' ''Never Gonna Give You Up,'' ''Don't Blame Me,'' ''Remind Me,'' ''Feels So Real,'' ''Forget Me Nots''; musical director, conductor, and arranger for ''The Midnight Hour,'' CBS-TV; musical director and arranger for John Lithgow's Kid-Size Concert Video; composed score for the films Without You I'm Nothing, Hollywood Shuffle; composed score for the TV movie ''The Women of Brewster Place'' and for the TV series of the same name; musical director for NAACP Image Awards TV Special, 1989, 1990; composed score for Robert Townsend and His Partners in Crime Part I, II, III, IV, HBO; composed theme for Pacific Bell radio campaign, 1988; composed music for Kid's Talk; has toured extensively;musical director of's highest honor, The Emmy Awards, 1991, 1992, making her the first African-American and first Women to do so; musical director for ''Comic Relief V,'' 1992. **Honors/Awds:** National Academy of Recording Arts and Sciences, Best R&B Vocal Performance, ''Forget Me Nots,'' 1982, Best R&B Instrumental, ''Number One,'' 1982; ASCAP Songwriter's Award, for ''Watch Out,'' 1988. **Business Addr:** Recording Artist/Composer, c/o Shelley, Jeffrey & Associates, 433 N. Camden Drive, 6th Fl., Beverly Hills, CA 90210.

RUSHING, BYRON D.
State representative. **Personal:** Born Jul 29, 1942, New York, NY; son of Linda Turpin Rushing and William Rushing; children: Osula. **Career:** Northern Student Movement, community organizer 1964-65; Community Voter Registration Project, dir 1964-66; Commn on Church & Race MA Council of Churches, field dir 1966-67; Ctr for Inner-City Change, administrator 1969-70; Museum of Afro-American History, pres 1972-84; Commonwealth of Massachusetts, House of Representatives, state representative, 1983-; Episcopal Divinity School, adjunct faculty, 1991-. **Orgs:** Pres Roxbury Historical Soc 1968-; lay deputy General Convention of Episcopal Church 1974-, chaplain, 1994; treas St John's/St James Episcopal Church 1975-; co-chair citizens adv comm Roxbury Heritage Park 1985-. **Honors/Awds:** Author, ''I Was Born,'' Black Power Revolt, 1968; author, ''Afro-Americana,'' Museum News 1982; author, The Lost and Found Paintings of Allan Rohan Crite 1982; author, ''A Justice That Is Real,'' Plumbline, 1987; author, ''An Ideology of Struggle,'' Forward Motion, 1988; author of numerous articles on historic archaeology; Black Heritage Trail Walking Tour Brochure, Boston African Amer Natl Historic Site; Awd, Human Rights Campaign Fund, 1985; Bay State Banner 20th Anniversary Celebration, 1985; Public Official of the Year, Boston Teachers Union, 1987; Honorary Degree, Roxbury Community Coll, l989; Action for Boston Community Development Awd, 1992; Honorary Degree, Episcopal Divinity School, 1994. **Business Addr:** State Representative, House of Representatives, Commonwealth of Massachusetts, State House, Boston, MA 02133, (617)722-2220.

RUSS, TIMOTHY DARRELL
Actor. **Personal:** Born Jun 22, 1956, Washington, DC; son of Walter H & Josephine D Russ. **Educ:** Illinois State Univ, Bloomington IL, post graduate theater; St Edwards Univ, BS, theater, psych, 1978. **Career:** Paramount Pictures Inc, actor, 1994-. **Orgs:** NAACP Hollywood Branch, 1986-. **Honors/Awds:** Sony Innovator Award, 1991; NAACP, Image Award, theater, 1987. **Special Achievements:** Films: Star Trek-Generations; Dead Connection; Mr Staurday Night; Night Eyes II; Eve of Destruction; Pulse; Fire With Fire; Death Wish IV; Crossroads; Spaceballs; Bird; TV: Star Trek-Voyager; Melrose Place; Living Single; Sea Quest; Hangin' With Mr Cooper; Deep Space Nine; Murphy Brown; Star Trek-The Next Generation; Journey to the Center of The Earth; Fresh Prince of Bel Air; Dead Silence; The Jon Lovitz Special; The Highwayman; The People Next Door; Stage: Romeo & Juliet; Barrabas; Dream Girls; As You Like It; Twelfth Night; Cave Dwellers.

RUSSELL, BEVERLY A.
Librarian, supervisor. **Personal:** Born Jan 15, 1947, Riverside, CA; daughter of Hazel M Hawkins-Russell and James H Russell (deceased). **Educ:** CA State Coll, BA 1971; CA State Univ, MS 1973. **Career:** Riverside Public Library, library asst 1974; CA State Dept of Rehab, librarian 1978; Magnavox Rsch Labs, library tech 1978-84; Burbank Unified Sch Dist, bookroom librarian 1986-90; Social Vocational Services, community supervisor, 1990-94; Pleasant Valley State Prison, librarian, currently. **Orgs:** Alpha Kappa Alpha 1973-; Intl Black Writers and Artists 1983-; Black Advocates in State Service (BASS) of California, 1995-; California Association of Black Correctional Workers, ABCW. **Honors/Awds:** Co-author, On Being Black, 1990, Bearers of Blackness, poetry published February 1987 by Guild Press MN; co-author of Three Women Black, Guild Press 1987; published in Roots and Wings, An Anthology of Poems for African-American Children, published by New York City Schools 1988; Published in River Crossings, Voices of the Diaspora, Intl Black Writers and Artists, 1994. **Home Addr:** 250 Truman Street #250, Coalinga, CA 93210.

RUSSELL, BILL (WILLIAM FELTON)
Sports announcer, former professional basketball player. **Personal:** Born Feb 12, 1934, Monroe, LA; son of Katie Russell and Charles Russell; married Rose Swisher, 1956 (divorced); children: Three. **Educ:** Univ of San Francisco, graduated. **Career:** Boston Celtics, center, 1956-69, coach, 1966-69; NBC-TV, sportscaster, 1969-8, CBS, 1980-83; Seattle SuperSonics, head coach, 1973-77; The Superstars, co-host, 1978-79; Sacramento Kings, head coach, 1987-88, director of player personnel, 1988-89. **Honors/Awds:** Podoloff Cup, National Basketball Assn, 1958, 1961, 1962, 1963, 1965; Most Valuable Player, US Basketball Writers 1960-65; author: Go Up for Glory, 1966, Second Wind: The Memoirs of an Opinionated Man, 1979; Inducted into Basketball Hall of Fame, 1975; Olympic Gold Medal for basketball, International Olympic Committee, 1956; selected as Greatest Player in the History of the NBA, Professional Basketball Writers Assn of America, 1980. **Special Achievements:** Author, Go up for Glory, MacMillan, 1966; Second Wind, Random House, 1979.

RUSSELL, BRYON DEMETRISE
Professional basketball player. **Personal:** Born Dec 31, 1970, San Bernardino, CA; married Kimberli; children: Kajun. **Educ:** Long Beach State. **Career:** Utah Jazz, forward, 1993-. **Business Addr:** Professional Basketball Player, Utah Jazz, 301 W South Temple, Salt Lake City, UT 84101-1216, (801)575-7800.

RUSSELL, CAMPY (MICHAEL)
Professional basketball player (retired). **Personal:** Born Jan 12, 1952, Jackson, TN; married Robyn; children: Oyin, Mandisha Iman. **Educ:** MI 1974. **Career:** Cleveland Cavaliers, 1975-80, 1985, New York Knicks, 1981-82. **Honors/Awds:** Athlete of yr Pontiac-Waterford Times 1978-79; pro of yr Cleveland Touchdown Clb 1978-79. **Business Addr:** Professional Basketball Player, New York Knicks, 1981-82, c/o NBA Players Assn, 1775 Broadway, Ste 2401, New York, NY 10019.

RUSSELL, CHARLIE L.
Director, playwright, educator. **Personal:** Born Mar 10, 1932, Monroe, LA; children: Michael R, Katheryn K. **Educ:** Univ of San Fran, BS eng 1959; NY U, MSW 1967. **Career:** Afro-Am Theater Conta Costa Coll, dir; NY U, asst prof 1975-77; City Coll NY, asst prof 1969-74; Am Place Theatre, writer in resid 1976. **Honors/Awds:** Image Awd Best Filmscript NAACP 1975; Playwright Awd Rockefeller Found 1976; publ plays, ''Five on the BlacK Hand Side'', ''The Incident at Terminal Ecstasy Acres'', filmscript ''Five on the Black Hand Side''; publ novellas, short stories. **Military Serv:** AUS pfc 1953-55.

RUSSELL, DARRELL
Professional football player. **Educ:** Southern Cal. **Career:** Oakland Raiders, 1997-. **Special Achievements:** NFL Draft, First round picck, #2, 1997. **Business Addr:** Professional Football Player, Oakland Raiders, 7000 Coliseum Way, Oakland, CA 94621, (510)638-0500.

RUSSELL, DEREK DWAYNE
Professional football player. **Personal:** Born Jun 22, 1969, Little Rock, AR; children: Nicolis. **Educ:** Univ of Arkansas, attended. **Career:** Denver Broncos, wide receiver, 1991-94; Houston Oilers, 1995-96; Tennessee Oilers, 1997-. **Business Addr:** Professional Football Player, Tennessee Oilers, c/o Baptist Sports Park, 7640 H 70-5, Nashville, TN 37221.

RUSSELL, DIAN BISHOP
Media coordinator. **Personal:** Born Sep 24, 1952, Rich Square, NC; daughter of Genora Tann Bishop and Paul A Bishop Jr (deceased); married Larry Russell, Sep 21, 1971; children: Tammy, Paula, Letitia. **Educ:** Fayetteville State University, Fayetteville, NC, BS, 1976; North Carolina Central University, Durham, NC, MLS, 1980, North Carolina educational administration certification, 1985; Durham City School, Durham, NC, North Carolina mentor certification, 1988. **Career:** T S Cooper Elementary, Sunbury, NC, librarian, 1974-77; Durham County Schools, NC Testing Consortium, Durham, NC, testing clerk, 1978; Durham County Library, Project LIFT, Durham, NC, special asst to the dir, educational brokering, 1979; Durham City Schools, Durham, NC, lead teacher, summer computer programs, 1986-89, media coordinator, 1980-, site coordinator for summer enrichment, 1990-. **Orgs:** Association rep 1985-, past treasurer 1987, past secretary 1988, Durham City Educators; special registration commissioner, Durham County Board of Elections, 1988-; treasurer, Eta Beta Zeta Chapter, Zeta Phi Beta Sorority, 1990-; past vice pres, Eta Phi Beta Chapter, Zeta Phi Beta, 1985; directress, Union Baptist Youth Choir, 1985-. **Honors/Awds:** Durham City Schools Superintendent's Creative Teaching Award, 1985; Scholarship, North Carolina Central University, 1985; Gold Star Awards, Final Four Teacher of Year, 1987, Women in Achievement, 1989, Durham City Schools.

RUSSELL, DOROTHY DELORES
Publishing company executive. **Personal:** Born Sep 11, 1950, Hayti, MO; daughter of Carrie Vianna Lewis Russell and Jimmie Russell, Sr. **Educ:** Southeast MO State Univ, attended; Three Rivers Comm Coll, attended; Lincoln Univ, attended. **Career:** Univ of AR CES, clerk steno I 1973-76; Dept of Natural Resources, clerk steno II 1976-78; MO Exec Office, sec receptionist 1978-79; MO Patrol State Water, admin sec 1979-80; Community Review Newspaper, editor/writer/photographer, 1983-84; Pemiscot Publishing Co, copysetter, circulation/classified manager, 1989-. **Orgs:** Former asst 4-H Leader; former bd mem/vice pres Community Review Paper expired 1983-84; editor/writer/photographer Community Review Newspaper 1983-84; missionary Church of Jesus Christ Congregation; organized Southeast Missouri Black Writers Club, 1989. **Honors/Awds:** Certificate of Appreciation, Univ of Missouri Extension Program, Pemiscot County, 1983; Certificate of Appreciation, Hayti Junior High School, 1985; Certificate of Appreciation, Education and Public Service, Central Star Chapter #114, Order of Eastern Star, 1988; Certificate of Appreciation, St James Word of Faith, 1988; established first minority newspaper with paid ads in southeast MO; established first minority chamber of commerce in Southeast MO & Northeast AR area; organized 4-H Club in Hayti/Hayti Heights; promoted minority interest in the print media in three city area; writer of ''Jussilo Salvo'' a satirical column.

RUSSELL, ERMEA J.
Attorney, educator. **Personal:** Born Sep 2, 1953, Toxey, AL; daughter of Abbie L Winston Jackson and Willie Eddie Jackson (deceased); children: Remarque, Ayla. **Educ:** Meridian Jr College, 1971; Livingston University, bachelor's, 1974, master's, 1987; Mississippi College Law School, JD, 1985. **Career:** Livingston University, admissions counselor, 1975-77; Neely College, registrar/office manager, 1978-79; Life Insurance Co of Georgia, agent, 1979-80; Meridian Housing Authority, counselor, 1980-82; Mississippi Secretary of State, staff attorney, 1985-86; Mississippi State Senate, staff attorney, 1986-90; Mississippi Institutions of Higher Learning, Minority Affairs and Affirmative Action, director, 1990-92; Legal Counsel, lieutenant governor of Mississippi, 1992-93; State of Mississippi, secretary of the senate, 1993-. **Orgs:** Black Women in Higher Education, 1990-; American Association for Affirmative Action, 1990-; Alpha Kappa Alpha Sorority, secretary, 1988-89; Order of Eastern Star, 1972-; Daughter of Elk, 1978-; Pearl City Leadership 2000, 1987-; Phi Alpha Delta Law Fraternity, treasurer, 1983-84; Mississippi State Bar Association, 1986-, Minority Involvement Committee, chair, 1991; American Bar Association; 100 Black Women; Miss Bd of Bar Commissioners. **Honors/Awds:** Alpha Kappa Alpha Sorority, Outstanding Service, 1977. **Military Serv:** United States of America Reserve, Major, 1974-; Army Commendation Medal, Army Achievement Medal, Army Service Ribbon, NCO Development Ribbon, National Defense Service Medal, Southwest Asia Medal.

RUSSELL, ERNEST
Administrator. **Personal:** Born Feb 16, 1933, Massillon, OH; son of Alzater (Carter) Russell and Ernest Russell; married Signe Hippert; children: Robert, Koren. **Educ:** Attended Western Reserve Univ Cleveland 1951-53; Univ of KS Lawrence, BA 1958; attended Harvard Univ summer 1978. **Career:** KS State Employment Serv, employment interviewer 1959-60; Topeka KS Commn on Civil Rights, educ dir 1960-62; Des Moines Commn on Human Rights, exec dir 1962-65; Charlotte NC Bur of Employment Training & Placement, dir 1965-66; DC VISTA/OEO, vocational training officer 1966-67; CA VISTA Office of Econ Oppor, sr prog analyst 1967-69; NY VISTA Office of Econ Oppor, regional admin 1969-70; DC VISTA Office of Econ Oppor, natl dept dir 1970-71; Office of Econ Oppor, assoc dir for admin 1971-73; Natl Inst of Educ DHEW, assoc dir/admin & mgmt 1973-76; Natl Labor Relations Bd Washington, dir of admin 1976-. **Orgs:** Guest lectr numerous progs sponsored by coll & univ labor/mgmt groups; mem Amer Soc for Pub Admin; supr group training for individuals & groups CSC CA; labor mgmt & super training tchr CSC Washington; tchr managing mgmt time DHEW/USDA Washington; mem NAACP 1950; mem Natl Urban League 1950; mem Operation PUSH 1977; mem Gov's Commn on Human Rights IO; mem Amer Educ Inst Valpraiso IN; mem Inst on Human Relations Fisk Univ. **Honors/Awds:** Human Rights Awd KS & IO 1960 & 1964; Awd Natl Assn of Equal Housing Oppor 1962; Awd for Work with Juveniles Natl Assn of Colored Women's Clubs 1963; Awd NAACP 1964; Meritorious Serv Awd Settlement House Des Moines 1965; Outstanding Performance Awd 1970; Outstanding & Sustained Superior Performance Awd OEO 1971; Quality Increase Awd OEO 1972; Highest Awd for Exceptional Serv OEO 1973; Boss of the Yr Awd L'Enfant Chap Amer Bus Women's Assn Wash DC 1973; Sustained Superior Performance Awd NLRB 1977; Quality Within-Grade Awd NLRB 1977; Recommendation for the Career Serv Awd Natl Civil Serv League NLRB 1978; EEO Outstanding Contribution Awd NLRB 1978; Special Achievement Awd NLRB 1978; Recommendation for Roger W Jones Awd for Exec Serv NLRB 1979; Sr Exec Serv CashBonus Awd 1980, 1984, 1985987; Special Act Award for Exceptional Contributions by the Chmn, NLRB, 1987; Presidential Rank Award: Meritorious Exec, NLRB, 1988. **Military Serv:** US Army, private first class, 1953-55. **Business Addr:** Dir of Admin, Natl Labor Relations Bd, 1717 Pennsylvania Ave NW, Room 400, Washington, DC 20570.

RUSSELL, GEORGE A.
Composer, music theoretician, teacher, band leader. **Personal:** Born Jun 23, 1923, Cincinnati; son of Bessie Sledge Russell and Joseph Russell; married Alice Norbury Russell, Aug 4, 1981; children: Jock Russell Millgardth. **Educ:** Wilberforce University, OH, 1940-43. **Career:** New England Conservatory of Music, Boston, MA, professor in jazz studies, 1969-; George Russell Living Time Orchestra, conductor, 1977-; lecturer at Harvard Univ, Tufts Univ, New Music Gallery in Vienna, Sibelius Academy in Helsinki; School Jazz Lenox MA, 1959-60; Swedish Labor Org, 1965; Fesitval of the Arts Finland, 1966-67; Lund University Sweden, Vaskilde & Summerschule, 1971; appointed to panel of National Endowment for the Arts Washington DC, 1975; mem, International Society of Contemporary Musicians; Norwegian Society of New Music; American Federation of Musicians Local 802; adv council MA state Council on the Arts; adv bd Third Street Music School Settlement; and others. **Honors/Awds:** Author of ''George Russell's Lydian Chromatic Concept of Tonal Organization'' 1953; Natl Endowment for the Arts Award 1969; Guggenheim fellowship 1972, 1973; natl music award 1976; composition fellowship Natl Endowment for the Arts 1976, 1979, 1980, 1981; George Russell Day proclaimed by Gov of MA, 1983; two Grammy nominations, 1985; Jazz Master Award, Afro-American Museum Philadelphia PA, 1985; John D & Catherine MacArthur Foundation Fellowship, 1989; Natl Endowment for the Arts Jazz Master Award, 1990; Natl Endowment for the Arts Composition Fellowship, 1990; British Music Award, 1989; New England Foundation Jazz Master Award, 1996; numerous recordings, US & abroad; performances in Europe, Japan and in the US with the George Russell Living Time Orchestra. **Business Addr:** Professor, Jazz Studies, New England Conservatory of Music, 290 Huntington Ave, Boston, MA 02115.

RUSSELL, GEORGE ALTON, JR.
Bank executive. **Personal:** Born in Boston, MA; married Faye Sampson; children: Martin Bakari. **Educ:** Clark Univ, BA 1972; NY Univ, MBA 1974. **Career:** Urban Bus Assistance Corp, pres 1972-74; State St Bank & Trust Co, vice pres 1979-84; City of Boston, collector-treas; Freedom Natl Bank of NY, chief executive, currently. **Orgs:** Dir Dimock Comm Hlth Ctr 1983-; bd mem Boston Indus Develop Finance Auth 1984-; treas-custodian State Boston Retirement System 1984-; comm Boston Arson Comm 1984-; custodian Boston Public Sch Teachers Retirement Fund 1984-; mem Business Assoc Club 1984-; mem Govt Finance Officers Assn 1984-; mem MA Collector-Treas Assn 1984-; trustee Boston Concert Opera; mem of corp Boston Science Museum; dir Organization for a New Equality 1985-; trustee United Methodist Church 1985-. **Honors/Awds:** Prof Achievement Awd Boston Urban Bankers Forum 1984; Ten Outstanding Young Leaders Awd Boston Jaycees 1985; Professional Achievement Awd Boston Urban Banker's Forum 1985; Industrial/Service 100, Freedom Natl Bank of NY, Black Enterprise, 1990.

RUSSELL, HARVEY CLARENCE. **See Obituaries section.**

RUSSELL, HERMAN JEROME
Company executive. **Personal:** Born Dec 23, 1930, Atlanta, GA; married Otelia; children: Donata, Michael, Jerome. **Educ:** Tuskegee Inst, attended. **Career:** City Beverage Co Inc Atlanta GA, pres, chmn bd; Atlanta Enquirer Newspaper Inc, chmn bd dir; Enterprise Investments Inc, chmn bd; Concessions IntlInc, pres, chmn bd; GA Southeastern Land Co Inc, pres chmn bd; Paradise Apts Mng Co Inc, pres; H J Russell Plastering Co & Constr Co, pres, owner, chmn bd; H J Russell & Co's Atlanta, pres, owner, until 1997, chairman of the board, currently. **Orgs:** Chmn of bd DDR Intl Inc Atlanta GA; bd of dir World Congress Ctr Auth Atlanta GA; chmn bd dir Cit Trust Co Bank; mem bd dir YMCA; mem bd of trustees Morris Brown Coll Atlanta GA; life mem NAACP; mem natl adv bd GA Inst of Tech; mem African Meth Episcopal Church; mem bd of trustees AfricanEpiscopal Church; chmn bd Russell/Rowe Commun Inc; bd dir Prime Cable Inc; mem bd dir 1st Atlanta Corp; past pres Atlanta C of C; mem bd dir GA C of C, Central Atl Prog, Tuskegee Inst. **Honors/Awds:** Natl Assoc of Market Developers Awd 1968; Meritorious Bus Achievement Awd Atlanta Comm Relations Comm 1969; Equal Oppty Day Atlanta Urban League 1972; African Meth Episcopal Outstanding Bus of the Year 1973; Winter Conf Awd Affiliate Contractor of Amer Inc 1973; Disting Serv Awd Empire Real Estate Bd 1973; Black Enterpise Mag Annual Achievement Awd 1978; Jr Achievement Awd (Bus & Youth) 1979; Natl Alumni Awd Tuskegee Inst. **Business Addr:** Chairman of the Board, H J Russell & Co, 504 Fair St NW, Atlanta, GA 30313.

RUSSELL, JAMES A., JR.
Educator (retired). **Personal:** Born Dec 25, 1917, Lawrenceville, VA; son of Nellie P. Russell and Dr. J. Alvin Russell; married Lottye J Washington; children: Charlotte R Coley, James A III. **Educ:** Oberlin Coll, BA 1940; Bradley Univ, MS 1950; Univ of MD, EdD 1967; St Paul's Coll LLD 1984. **Career:** Norfolk Naval Shipyard, electrician 1941-42; US Naval Training School, instructor 1942-45; St Paul's College, asst prof 1945-50; Hampton Univ, prof & div dir 1950-71; St Paul's Coll, pres 1971-81; VA Comm Coll Sys, dir of instr prog 1981-

82; WV State Coll, prof & div chmn 1982-86, Interim President 1986-87; West Virginia Community College, interim president, 1988-89. **Orgs:** Pres Peninsula Council on Human Relations 1962-65; mem Richmond Metro Authority 1981-82; sen warden & vestryman St James Episcopal Church 1982-; member/board of directors, West Virginia Public Radio, 1988-; jury commissioner, Kanawha County, 1990-. **Honors/Awds:** Space scientist McDonnell Douglas Astronautics 1968; NAFEO Study Group Republic of China Taiwan 1979; Hon Degree LLD St Paul's College 1984; Distinguished Alumnus Award Bradley Univ 1984. **Home Addr:** 811 Grandview Dr, Dunbar, WV 25064.

RUSSELL, JEROME
Construction company executive. **Personal:** Born 1962?. **Career:** HJ Russell & Company, president/chief operating officer, 1994-. **Special Achievements:** President of Atlanta's largest minority-owned firm. **Business Addr:** President/COO, HJ Russell & Co, 504 Fair St SW, Atlanta, GA 30313, (404)330-1000.

RUSSELL, JOHN PETERSON, JR.
Educational administrator. **Personal:** Born Aug 26, 1947, Cora, WV; son of Mary Louise Thompson Russell and Johnnie P Russell Sr; married Gail P Davis, May 31, 1968; children: Kim, Janelle. **Educ:** Bluefield State Coll, BS 1970; WV Coll of Grad Studies, MA 1975; VPI & SU, CAGS 1978. **Career:** Nathaniel Macon Jr HS, secondary teacher 1970-71; Omar Jr & Logan HS, secondary teacher 1971-74; Southern WV Comm Coll, counselor 1974-76, dean of students 1979-81, asst to dean of students, director of financial aid, 1986-87; Walters St Community College, Morristown, TN, coordinator of training, 1987-. **Orgs:** Chmn, bd of dir New Employment for Women Inc 1981-; mem appt Amer Friends Serv Comm Relation Comm 1982-; mem elected Amer Friends Serv Exec Comm 1983-; polemarch, Knoxville Chapter, 1989-, field deputy, Eastern Region, 1990-, Kappa Alpha Psi Fraternity; chairman, community relations committee, American Friends Serv, 1985-86; Kappa Alpha Psi, Polemarch South Central Province, senior vice, 1994, Polemarch, South Central Province, 1994. **Honors/Awds:** Community Service Award, Mechanicsville Community Development Corporation, 1991; Bronze Man of the Year, Iota Phi Lambda Business and Professional Sorority. **Home Addr:** 1608 Blackwood Dr, Knoxville, TN 37923.

RUSSELL, JOSEPH D.
Educator. **Personal:** Born Aug 11, 1914, Richmond, KY; married Josie Marie Ruffin; children: Joseph III, Cirus, Candace. **Educ:** Wilberforce Univ, BS 1937; OH State Univ, MA 1939; Univ of WI, Univ of IL, IL State Univ, attended. **Career:** Mounds Douglass HS, teacher basketball & track coach 1939-42; Attucks HS, teacher athletic coach 1943-57; Eisenhower HS Decatur IL, teacher basketball-tennis coach 1957-69; Bradley Univ, past asst prof 1960-80. **Orgs:** Mem bd YMCA 1963-65; bd mem Garden Angel Home for Dependant Boys & Girls 1975-76; multimedia instr ARC 1977-80. **Honors/Awds:** Partic black coaches & principal giving black school the ability to partic in state tournaments 1945; 1st black coach of a predominantly white school in IL 1957-69; Coach of the Year Southern IL 1969; Hall of Fame Coach IL Hall of Fame 1976. **Business Addr:** Bradley University, Peoria, IL 61614.

RUSSELL, JOSEPH J.
Educator. **Personal:** Born Apr 11, 1934. **Educ:** VA State Clg, BS 1960; IN U, MS 1968, EdD 1970. **Career:** Global Team America, Inc, 1995-; OSU, vice provost, 1989-94; IN Univ, chmn 1972-, dir 1970-72; Richmond Public School, visiting teacher 1964-67; Richmond Social Serv Bur, social worker 1960-64. **Orgs:** Chpn Dept of Afro-Am Studies; exec dir Natl Cncl for Black Studies; adv com Urban Affairs 1973-; adv com Univ Div 1974-; standing com Blo Omington Campus 1974-; faculty hearing ofcr 1974-; chmn Afro-Am Conf Grp IHETS 1974-; mem Stdnt Life Study Commn 1977; mem IN State Adv Bd 1974-. **Honors/Awds:** Comm serv awrd 2nd Bapt Ch 1976; outst educator awrd Phi Beta Sigma 1976; serv appreciation plaque NM Black Studies Consortium 1977; natl Dev & ldrshp awrd Natl Cncl for Black Studies 1977; 100 Most Influential Friends for 1977; Black Jour 1977; Num Presentation & Papers; OSU African American Student Affairs Council of Honor, 1995. **Military Serv:** USAF airman 1954-58.

RUSSELL, KAY A.
Sales manager. **Personal:** Born Jul 12, 1954, Charleston, SC; daughter of Mary Forrest Russell and John Henry Russell. **Educ:** Trident Technical Coll, Charleston, SC, 1974; Univ Dist of Columbia, Washington, DC, BA marketing, 1979. **Career:** Marriott, Washington, DC, sales mgr, 1980-82; Omni Shoreman, Washington, DC, sales mgr. 1982-83; Westin Hotel Detroit, Detroit, MI, natl sales mgr, 1983-88; Minneapolis Convention & Visitors Assn, Minneapolis, MN, natl account mgr, 1988-94; Grand Hyatt, sales manager, 1994-. **Orgs:** Mem, Exec Women Intl, 1983-85; mem, Coalition Black Meeting Planners, 1984-; mem, NAACP, 1985-; Natl Urban League. **Honors/Awds:** Golden Egg Award, Natl Assn of Media Women, 1987; Sales Manager of the Year, The Westin Hotel Detroit, 1988; Imperial Potentate Achievement Award, AEOANMS, 1988.

RUSSELL, KEITH BRADLEY
Ornithologist. **Personal:** Born Aug 13, 1956, Augusta, GA; son of Barbara Elaine Jefferson Russell and John Raphael Russell. **Educ:** Cornell Univ, Ithaca NY, BS, 1977; Clemson Univ, Clemson SC, MS, 1981. **Career:** Academy of Natural Sciences, Philadelphia PA, collection mgr, 1982-92, ornithologist, 1992-. **Orgs:** Mem, Delaware Valley Ornithological Club, 1973-. **Honors/Awds:** Coordinator, Philadelphia Mid-Winter Bird Census, 1987-. **Business Addr:** Ornithologist, Department of Ornithology, Birds of North America, Academy of Natural Sciences of Philadelphia, 1900 Benjamin Franklin Pkwy, Philadelphia, PA 19103-1195, (215)299-3783.

RUSSELL, LEON W.
County official. **Personal:** Born Nov 3, 1949, Pulaski, VA. **Educ:** East TN State Univ, BS 1972; East TN State Univ Sch of Grad Studies, attended 1972-74. **Career:** TN State House of Reps, legislative intern and asst 1973; East TN State Univ Dept of Political Science, grad teaching asst 1972-73; TN Municipal League, mgmt intern and rsch asst 1974; KY Commission on Human Rights, field rep 1975-77; Pinellas County Govt Office of Human Rights, affirmative action/EEO officer 1977-85, human rights/EEO officer, 1985-. **Orgs:** Charter mem Beta Zeta Alumni Chap Alpha Kappa Lambda Frat; mem natl bd dirs Natl Assoc of Human Rights Workers; mem Intl City Mgmt Assoc; bd dirs OIC of the Suncoast; Clearwater Branch NAACP; pres, FL State NAACP Conf of Branches; mem East TN State Univ Alumni Assoc; allocations comm bd dirs United Way of Pinellas Co; bd dirs FL Assoc of Comm Relations Professionals; board of directors, Florida Assn of Equal Opportunity Professionals, Inc; member, American Society for Public Administration; national board of directors, NAACP, 1990-98. **Honors/Awds:** Pi Gamma Mu Natl Social Science Honor Soc. **Business Addr:** Human Rights/EEO Officer, Pinellas County Government, 400 S Ft Harrison, Rm 300, Clearwater, FL 34616.

RUSSELL, LEONARD ALONZO
Dentist. **Personal:** Born Dec 27, 1949, Paris, KY. **Educ:** Easter KY, BS Indust 1971; Central State, BS Biology 1978; Case Western Reserve Univ, DDS 1982. **Career:** Private Practice, dentist. **Orgs:** Natl parliamentarian Student Natl Dental Assoc 1981-82; mem Acad of General Dentistry 1981-; mem Ohio Dental Assoc 1982-; pres Forest City Dental Soc 1986-87. **Honors/Awds:** Leonard A Russell Awd Kappa Alpha Psi Frat 1971; Kenneth W Clement Awd Cleveland City Council 1981; Outstanding Young Man of Amer US Jaycees 1984. **Business Addr:** 2204 South Taylor Rd, Cleveland Heights, OH 44118.

RUSSELL, MAURICE V. See Obituaries section.

RUSSELL, MILICENT DE'ANCE
Educational administrator. **Personal:** Born Jul 10, 1950, Chicago, IL; daughter of Mildred Iles Lavizzo and Robert Richard Lavizzo; married Clifford M Russell, Aug 29, 1970; children: Clifford, Corey, Kimberly. **Educ:** Chicago State University, BS, education, 1972; Roosevelt University, MA, administration, sup, 1984; Nova University, EdD, early middle/childhood, 1989. **Career:** Chicago Board of Education, teacher, 1972-90, acting assistant principal, 1985-86; Kennedy King College, lecturer, 1988-89; Chicago Board of Education, assistant principal, 1990-96, principal, 1996-. **Orgs:** Parent Volunteer Program, coordinator, 1988-89; Local School Council, secretary, 1989-; Woodlawn Organization, consultant, 1992; Roosevelt University, alumni, 1984-; Nova University, alumni, 1989-; NAEYC, 1986-89; CAEYC, 1992; Association for Sup & Curriculum Development, 1992. **Honors/Awds:** Project Choice, $1,000 grant, 1986, 1989; Joyce Foundation, $5,000 grant, 1990; ISBE Urban Partnership Grants-$9,600 & $7,000, 1994; Project Canal, $1.5 Million, 1997. **Special Achievements:** "Increased Home and School Involvement of Parents of Primary Grade Students, 1989, Imporved Math Skills of Second Grade Students," 1988, Resources in Education. **Home Addr:** 8936 S Leavitt St, Chicago, IL 60620. **Business Phone:** (312)535-5300.

RUSSELL, NIPSEY
Comedian, actor. **Personal:** Born Oct 13, 1924, Atlanta, GA. **Educ:** Univ of Cincinnati, BA, 1946. **Career:** Stand-up comedian; Television appearances: Car 54, Where Are You?, 1961-62; The Les Crane Show, 1965; Barefoot in the Park, 1970-71; The Dean Martin Show, 1972-73; The Dean Martin Comedy World, 1974; Masquerade Party, 1974-75; Rhyme and Reason, 1975; Nipsey Russell's Juvenile Jury, 1986-; films: The Wiz, 1978; Nemo, 1984, Wildcats, 1985, Posse, 1993; numerous appearances on talk shows and game shows. **Orgs:** Member, Screen Actors Guild; member, American Federation of Television and Radio Artists. **Honors/Awds:** First Black emcee on a national television program; first Black to be featured on a television game show. **Military Serv:** US Army, Capt. **Business Addr:** c/o Joseph Rapp Enterprises, 1650 Broadway, Suite 705, New York, NY 10019.

RUSSELL, SANDRA ANITA (SANDRA ANITA)
Writer, vocalist. **Personal:** Born Jan 16, 1946, New York, NY; daughter of Gazetta and James Oliver. **Educ:** Syracuse University, AB, music, 1968; New York University, graduate studies, 1968-69; Hunter College, graduate studies, 1970-71. **Career:** New York Board of Education, teacher, 1968-76; self-employed, jazz vocalist, 1977-81; San Francisco Clothing Co, manager, 1981-84; self-employed, writer, jazz vocalist, 1984-. **Honors/Awds:** CP Memorial Fund, CP Memorial Award, 1990; Society of Authors, Author's Foundation Award, 1991; Northern Arts Award, 1993. **Special Achievements:** Essay: "Minor Chords/Major Changes," in Glancing Fires, ed Lesley Saunders, Women's Press, London, 1987; author, Render Me My Song: African-American Women Writers, Pandora Press/St Martins, NY, 1990; theatrical performance, "Render Me My Song! One-Woman Show in Words and Song," 1990; contributing editor, The Virago Book of Love Poetry, London/NY, 1990; Sister, short story in Daughters of Africa, ed, Busby, London, Cape Pantheon, NY, 1992. **Business Addr:** Writer, c/o St Martin's Press Inc, 175 Fifth Ave, New York, NY 10010-7848, (212)674-5151.

RUSSELL, WESLEY L.
Electronics company executive. **Personal:** Born Nov 6, 1938, Camp Hill, AL; son of Cordie Mae Mennifield Russell and Pearlie L Russell; married Geraldine K; children: Derek, Dante, Deirdre, Derwin. **Educ:** Tuskegee Inst, BS 1963; San Diego State Univ, attended. **Career:** General Dynamics Electronics, assoc engr 1963, electrical engr 1964, sr electrical engr 1968, hw mgr, tactical system, section head 1984-, program mgr, 1990-. **Orgs:** National Management Assn. **Honors/Awds:** Letter of Commendation in support of initial operational evaluation of P5604 Secure Telecommun Terminals Tinker AFB OK 1974; numerous extraordinary achievement awards. **Business Addr:** Program Mgr, GDE Systems Inc, PO Box 509008, MZ 6164-P, San Diego, CA 92150-9008.

RUTH, JAMES
Judge. **Career:** Jacksonville, FL, prosecuting attorney, 1984-91; Duval County, judge, 1991-. **Business Addr:** Judge, Duval County Courthouse, 330 East Bay Street, Room 324, Jacksonville, FL 32202, (904)630-2568.

RUTHERFORD, HAROLD PHILLIP, III
Educational administrator. **Personal:** Born Sep 3, 1951, New York, NY; son of Ethel Leona Hollinger Rutherford and Steve Rutherford; married Vancenia Dowdell; children: Paitra. **Educ:** John Carroll Univ, AB 1974; Kent State Univ, MA 1977. **Career:** Kent State Univ, asst to the dean 1976-80; City of East Cleveland, vice-city mgr 1980-83; RDR Mgmt Consultants, exec dir 1982-85; Fort Valley State Coll, dir of develop 1985-. **Orgs:** Consultant East Cleveland Sch Bd 1980-83; consultant City of Maywood, IL 1982-85; mem Sigma Pi Phi Frat 1983; mem Portage County NAACP 1984; bd mem Reccord & Associates 1984-86. **Honors/Awds:** Woodrow Wilson Natl Fellowship 1985-86; Management Develop Program, Harvard Univ 1986; Management Awd Certificate, The Wharton School 1986; Regents Fellow, University of the State of New York, 1988-89. **Home Addr:** 18 Turf Lane, Albany, NY 12211-1528.

RUTLAND, WILLIAM G.
Deputy director. **Personal:** Born Jun 28, 1918, Cherokee, AL; married Eva E Neal; children: Elsie, Billy, Patty Jo, Ginger. **Educ:** Morehouse Clg, BS; Wayne State U; Grad; MI Clg; Bergamo Ctr. **Career:** Sacramento Air Logis Ctr McClellan AFB, deputy chief dir of plans & pgms; USAF, dir of materiel mgmt operations elect sys & div. **Orgs:** Pres Sacramento Unified Sch Dist Bd of Ed 1970, 77; mem Rotary Intrntl Sacramento Symphony; Mental Hlth Assc; Am Red Cross. **Business Addr:** Mc Clellan AFB, Sacramento, CA.

RUTLEDGE, ESSIE MANUEL
Educator, sociologist. **Personal:** Born in Midway, AL; daughter of Ollie M Jordan Jones and Algie L Manuel Sr (deceased); married Albert C Rutledge; children: Jeffrey A. **Educ:** FL A&M Univ, BA 1958; Univ of WI Madison, MA 1965; Univ of MI, PhD 1974. **Career:** 16th Street Jr HS, St Petersburg, social studies teacher 1958-61; Gibbs & St Petersburg Jr Coll, instr 1961-67; Macomb County Comm Coll, asst prof of sociology 1968-71; Univ of MI Flint, asst prof of sociology 1974-76; Western IL Univ, assoc prof & chairperson of Afro-Amer Studies 1976-84, prof 1984, prof of sociology 1985-. **Orgs:** Mem, Amer Sociological Assn, 1967-; mem, membership chmn, 1970-84, president, 1985-86, executive officer, 1996-99, Assn of Black Sociologists; mem, Com on Status of Women of the Amer Sociological Assn, 1978-80; mem, IL Council of Black Studies, 1979-; adv bd, McDonough Co Health Dept, 1979-81; mem, Ch Women United, 1980; mem, Pi Gamma Mu Natl Social Sci Honor Soc, Florida A&M Univ, 1965; Equal Opportunity & Fair Housing Commission of City of Macomb Illinois, 1986-, chair, 1994-; publications committee, Sociologists for Women in Society, 1993-96; Southern Sociological Society, 1992, honors committee, 1995-98; executive board, University Professionals of Illinois, local 4100, 1990-97. **Honors/Awds:** Faculty Excellence Award, Western Illinois Univ, 1991; award for service to enhance position of women through scholarship, teaching, and committee participation, Western Organization for Women, Western Illinois University, 1990; Postdoctoral Fellow of Gerontological Society of America, Program in Applied Gerontlogy 1989; Inducted into the College of Arts and Sciences Gallery of Distinction at Florida A&M Univ 1987;

Summer grants Natl Sci Found 1965-67; Rackham Fellowship Univ of MI 1971-74; Awd for Serv to Enhance Position of Women Western Orgn for Women Western IL Univ 1979; pub articles on Black Women, Role Knowledge, Black Husbands & Wives, Separatism, Black Families, racism, socialization, and suicide in the following books, documents, and journals: The Black Woman, ERIC Documents, Reflector, Genetic Psychology Monograph, Journal of Negro History, Marriage and Family Therapy, Contemporary Sociology, Journal of Comparative Family Studies, Minority Voices, Ethnic Issues in Adolescent Mental Health, 1970-; Blue Key Fraternity, Honorary Faculty, WIU, 1993; Inducted into Gamma Lambda Chapter, Honorary Order of Omega, 1990.

RUTLEDGE, GEORGE
Automobile dealer. **Career:** Rutledge Chevrolet-Oldsmobile-Cadillac-Geo Inc, chief executive officer, currently. **Special Achievements:** Company is listed #11 on Black Enterprise's list of top 100 auto dealers, 1994. **Business Addr:** CEO, Rutledge Chevrolet Olds-Cadillac-GEO Inc., 107 E Jackson, Sullivan, IL 61951, (217)728-4338.

RUTLEDGE, JENNIFER M.
Management consultant. **Personal:** Born Sep 12, 1951, White Plains, NY; daughter of Elizabeth Rutledge and James Rutledge. **Educ:** MI State Univ, BS industrial psych 1973; Pace Univ Lubin School of Business, MBA 1980. **Career:** Allstate Ins, personnel 1973-76; NAACP Legal Defense & Educ fund, dir of personnel 1976-79; Natl Council of Negro Women, natl coord work exp prog 1979-80; Girls Clubs of Amer Inc, director northeast serv ctr 1983-86; Delphi Consulting Group Inc, partner 1984-. **Orgs:** Bd mem Westchester Community Foundation, 1996-; bd mem Westchester Urban League 1976, Afro-Amer Cultural Assn 1976; bd mem, vice pres Afro-Amer Civic Assn 1978; Natl Assn MBA's; guest lecturer Business & Professional Women's Clubs; mem Meeting Planners Intl; bd mem Lubin Grad School of Bus Alumni Assn, Pace Univ; bd mem Support Network Inc 1988-; bd member, Greenwich Girls Club 1989-; Member Delta Sigma Theta; board member, Yonkers Private Industry Council Affiliated with National Center for Non-Profit Boards Member-Research Board of Advisors-ABI. **Honors/Awds:** Business Woman of the Year, Afro-Amer Civic Assoc 1987; contributing writer Human Resources Development Review 1988-; Professional of the Year, Westchester Chapter of Negro Business & Professional Women's Club Inc, 1993. **Business Addr:** Partner, Delphi Consulting Group, Inc, 399 Knollwood Rd, Ste 108, White Plains, NY 10603, (914)684-2400.

RUTLEDGE, PHILIP J.
Educational administrator (retired). **Personal:** Born Oct 15, 1925, Dawson, GA; son of Bessie Perry and John Rutledge; married Violet Eklund; children: Phyllis, Janet, Edward, Patricia. **Educ:** Roosevelt University, BA 1952; University of Michigan, MPH 1958; additional graduate study: Wayne State University; Univ of Michigan, Rackham Graduate School; Indiana University, LLD 1980. **Career:** Detroit Dept of Health, sr health inspector 1955-60, dir, Bureau of Health Education, Detroit and Wayne Co, 1960-64; Mayor Comm for Human Resources Development, dir 1964-67; US Dept of Labor, exec dir, Presidents Committee on Manpower, dep Manpower Admin 1967-69; Stanley H Ruttenberg & Assoc, sr assoc 1969; Comm for Human Resource Programs, asst to mayor 1969-70, dir, Dept of Human Resources 1970-71; DC Government, SRS Dept of HEW, dep admin 1971-73; Howard University, School of Business & Public Administration, professor/chairman 1973-80; Natl League of Cities, US Conference of Mayors, dir, Office of Policy Analysis, 1973-77; Natl Inst of Public Management, pres, 1977-82; Indiana University Northwest, dir, professor, Division of Public & Environmental Affairs and Political Science, dir, Great Lakes Center for Public Affairs, int programs coordinator 1982-89; Indiana University Center for Global Stus, special asst to pres 1989-96, professor emeritus, 1996-. **Orgs:** Chmn United Black Fund Lake County Crime & Criminal Justice Task Force; Lak e Country Comm Development Comm; Lake County Private Industrial Council; Rotary y Club; pres, Gary Redevelopment Commission; Lake County Job Training Corp; Gov's Task Force on Welfare & Poor Relief; NAACP; chmn, SSI Study Group 1975-; chmn, Com on Evaluation of Employment & Training Programs; Natl Research Council; Natl Academy of Science; pres, Greater Washington Research Center; adjunct prof public admin, Fairleigh Dickinson University; gov bd, Center for Public Affaris & Admin, Nova University; advisory bd, Salvation Army; World Future Society; AAAS; American Political Science Assn; American Sociology Assn; Natl Council on Employment Policy, Harvard University, Bd of Overseers Visiting Comm to JFK School of Government, Intl City Management Assn; Natl Planning Assn; American Public Welfare Assn; bd trustees, DC Inst of Mental Hygiene; bd dir, Natl Center for Public Serv Internships; fellow Amer Public Health Assoc; mem bd of dir ARC DC Chapter; advisory comm Evaluation of Urban Transportation Alternative Natl Research; chmn, Urban League of Northwest IN; pres World Affairs Council NW IN; pres, IN Council on World Affairs; bd dir Mid-west Univ Consortium for Intl Activities; vice chair, Lake Co Private Industry Council; Indianapolis Comm on Foreign Relations; chmn, Indiana Job Training Coordinating Council, director, Washington leadership program, IN, 1989-94. **Honors/Awds:** Fellow Institute of Politics Harvard Univ; pres Amer Soc Public Admin; Fellow, Natl Acad Public Admin; international lecturer US State Dept; numerous Citizen of the Year awards. **Home Phone:** (317)254-9463. **Business Addr:** Prof Emeritus, Public & Env Affairs and Political Science, School of Public & Environmental Affairs, Indiana Univ, Bloomington, IN 47405, (812)855-7980.

RUTLEDGE, WILLIAM LYMAN
Surgeon. **Personal:** Born Jun 27, 1952, Little Rock, AR; children: Rodney B, Estelle A, Jessica M. **Educ:** TX Southern Univ, BA (Cum Laude) 1975; Meharry Medical Coll, MD (w/ Honors) 1979. **Career:** Arkansas Surgical Assocs, pres 1984-. **Orgs:** Mem Alpha Omega Alpha Honor Medical Soc 1978-, Natl Medical Assoc 1979-; dist commnr Boy Scouts of Amer 1986; sec Scott Hamilton Drive Medical Clinic Inc 1986; Urban League of Arkansas, executive board; University of Arkansas Medical Science Campus, minority advisor board. **Business Addr:** President, Arkansas Surgical Assocs, 5800 West 10th Ste 305, Little Rock, AR 72204.

RYAN, AGNES C.
Attorney. **Personal:** Born Sep 17, 1928, Houston, TX; widowed; children: 3. **Educ:** Howard U, BA 1947; Fordham U, Juris Doc 1950. **Career:** Legal Aid Bureau, vlntr lawyer 1951-52; Private Prac, lawyer 1952-53; Legal Aid Bureau, staff lawyer 1955-, supervisory lawyer. **Orgs:** Mem Chicago Bar Assn 1968-, bd of mgrs 1976-78; mem Am Bar Assn 1971-; bd mem Bartelme Homes 1977-. **Honors/Awds:** Educ Award Elks 1971; consult to author of "Consumers in Trouble". **Business Addr:** Supervisory Lawyer, Legal Aid Bureau, 14 E Jackson Blvd, Chicago, IL 60604.

RYAN, MARSHA ANN
Business executive. **Personal:** Born Mar 12, 1947, New Orleans, LA; married Cecil James; children: Michelle, Marisa. **Educ:** Fisk U, BA 1968; TN State U, Tchr Cert 1970. **Career:** OR Adult & Fam Serv Dir Multnomah Reg Off, pgm exec bd/supr pre-admsn screening/resource unit 1980-; OR Dept of Hmn Resources Dir Ofc, pgm anls 1979-80; OR Motor Vechicles Div, pgm dev 1978-79; OR Dept of Transp, afrmtv action & ofcr 1977-78, career dev anlyst 1975; Singer, area sls mgr 1974; Xerox Ed Products Div, area sls rep 1973; Gen Elec Co, data processing instr 1971; Neely's Bend Jr H, tchr 1970-71; OR Department of Transportation, Community Service Employment Program, manager, 1984-. **Orgs:** Am Assn of Affirmative Action; Gov Tri-Co Affirmative Action Assn; Affirmative Action Ofcrs Assn dev for state gov publ "OR dept of Transp's Oral Interviewers Manual The ODOT Employee Orientation Pgm"; Washington County Dpt of Aging Services, advsy council; Washington County Retired Senior Volunteer Program, advsy cmte; Portland Community Clg Professional Skills Program, advsy board. **Business Addr:** Manager, Employment Program Office, ODOT Community Service, 4900 SW Griffin Dr, Ste 100, Beaverton, OR 97005.

RYAN-WHITE, JEWELL
Association executive, producer. **Personal:** Born May 24, 1943, Columbus, MS; daughter of Martha Ryan and Larry A Ryan Sr; divorced; children: Donald Willard Rodgers. **Educ:** Alcorn A&M Coll; Joliet Jr Coll; Olive Harvey Coll; IL State Univ; Rueben Cannon Master Series, screenwriting. **Career:** IL Bell Tel Co, opr investigator dial serv clerk 1967-76; Comm Wkrs of Amer Loca 5011, pres 1972-86; American Cablesystems Midwest, comm TV 1986-87, public relations/promotions coord 1987; California School Employees Assn, CBS program analyst; American Film Inst, admin campus oprs, 1990-; Marla Gibbs Crossroads Arts Academy, administrator, 1991-; independent producer, currently. **Orgs:** Black Trade Unionists; Urban League; Oper PUSH; Vol Parent Guardian Angel Home; St John Vianney Cath Church; SCLC; Cath Educ Assn; Smithsonian Assoc; personnel & public policy cmtes Natl Campaign Human Dev 1985-87; Joliet Jr Coll Minority/Intercultural Affairs, bd of dirs, 1985-87; Women in Cable 1986-87; commnr 1986, chairman of the board 1987 Housing Authority of Joliet; Natl Assn of Housing & Redevelop Officials 1986-87;bd of dirs Sr Serv Ctr 1987; bd of dirs Sr Companion Prog 1987; chmn EOC Comm, Natl Federation of Local Cable Programmers 1988-90; vp of bd of dir, arbitrator, Natl Bd of Arbitrators 1989; NAACP, Beverly Hill/Hollywood Chap 1989-90; Los Angeles Urban League 1989-92; master plan cmte, City of Los Angeles Cultural Arts; Los Angeles Black Educ Commission, 1989-93. **Honors/Awds:** Schlrshp in Clothing 1961; Awd Salesclerking RE Hunt HS 1961; Awd Newly Elected Officers Training Sch CWA 1973; Cert of Merit IL Bell Tele Co 1974; Awd of Appreciation CWA 1976; United Way of Will Co 1977; City of Hope COPE 1977; Pace Setter Awd City of Hope 1979; Crusade Awd Amer Cancer Soc 1980; Citizen of the Month City of Joliet 1982; Certificate of Achievement Pro-Skills 1986, Achievement Awd 1986, American Ambassador Awd 1986 American Cablesystems; Awd of Appreciation Campaign Human Develop Joliet Catholic Diocese 1986; Awd of Appreciation Natl Campaign Human Dev Washington DC 1987; Awd for Cable Excellence, Cable Television Administration and Marketing Society 1987; 3 awds for overall contribution to field of adult educ/illiteracy, Jolliet JuniorCollege 1987; Public Speaking Awdmerican Cable Systems 1987; named to Natl Bd of Consumer Arbitrators 1989; NFLCP, Cultural Diversity Award. **Business Addr:** 1171 Reynolds Ct, Morrow, GA 30260.

RYDER, GEORGIA ATKINS
Educational administrator (retired). **Personal:** Born Jan 30, 1924, Newport News, VA; daughter of Mary Lou Carter Atkins (deceased) and Benjamin F Atkins, Sr (deceased); married Noah Francis, Aug 16, 1947 (deceased); children: O Diana Jackson, Malcolm E, Aleta R Mellon. **Educ:** Hampton Inst, BS Music (Summa Cum Laude) 1944; Univ of MI, MusM 1946; NY Univ, PhD Music 1970. **Career:** Alexandria VA Public Schools, music resource teacher 1945-48; Norfolk State Univ, music prof 1948-79, dept head of music 1969-79; NY Univ, lecturer 1968-69; Norfolk State Univ, dean school of arts & letters 1979-86. **Orgs:** Mem Alpha Kappa Mu 1943-; past pres Intercollegiate Music Assoc 1975-78; commissioner Norfolk Commission on the Arts & Humanities 1978-92; council mem Coll Music Soc 1980-82; panelist Natl Endowment for the Arts 1980-83; exec commn mem Natl Consortium of Arts & Letters for HBCU's, 1983-; dir of finance Southeastern VA Arts Assoc 1983-; panelist VA Commn for the Arts 1984-87; trustee Bank St Memorial Baptist Church 1983-90; judge Governor's Awards for the Arts in VA 1985; bd mem Center for Black Music Research, Columbia Coll, Chicago l984-; board member/trustee, Virginia Symphony, 1970-; board member, MENC Black Music Caucus, 1986-90; scholarship chair, Tidewater Area Musicians, 1989-; board member, Virginians for the Arts, 1996-; trustee, Virginia Wesleyan College, 1992-; member, Delta Sigma Theta Sorority, Inc. **Honors/Awds:** Grant Southern Fellowships Fund 1967-69; Founders Day Awd for Distinguished Scholarship NY Univ 1970; Citation Distinguished Serv Norfolk Comm for Improvement of Educ 1974; Citation Leadership in Teacher Educ Norfolk State Coll 1969; Distinguished Service in the Performing Arts, City of Nortolk, VA, l986; Service to Community, State, Nation, Southeastern VA Arts Assn, l986; Martin Luther King: Living the Dream/Community Service Award, Links, Inc, 1988; Distinguished Contribution Award, National Assn of Negro Musicians, 1989; Sisterhood Citation for Humanitarian Service, National Conference of Christians and Jews, 1990; Outstanding Contribution Award, Cultural Alliance of Greater Hampton Roads, 1992; Laureate of Virginia, field of music, 1992; Distinguished Alumni Award, Hampton Univ, 1993; Achievement Award, Norfolk State University, 1994; Pioneer Award, Maude Armstrong Foundation, 1995. **Special Achievements:** Published articles in professional publications, 1973-82; contributor, Black Music and the Harlem Renaissance, S A Floyd, 1990; contributor, New Perspectives on Music, J Wright with S A Floyd, 1992. **Home Addr:** 5551 Brookville Rd, Norfolk, VA 23502.

RYDER, MAHLER B.
Educational administrator, visual artist. **Personal:** Born Jul 7, 1937, Columbus, OH; son of Virginia Ryder and Mahler Ryder; divorced; children: Ulli Kira. **Educ:** Coll of Art and Design, Columbus, OH, 1956-58; Artillery School Ft Sill OK, 1960; OH State Univ, 1963; Provincetown Workshop, 1964; Art Students League NY 1965-66; School of Visual Arts NY 1967-68; RI School of Design, 1978. **Career:** Project Turn-On NY Board of Ed, part-time faculty/asst admin 1969; SOMSEC Art Program New York City Board of Ed 1969; New School for Soc Research, part-time faculty 1969; Providence School Dept 1969-72; RI School of Design, instructor 1969-70, asst prof 1970-81, assoc prof 1981-88, prof 1988-; Providence Pub Lib, dir Special Children's Art Program 1972-73. **Orgs:** Mem comm to establish the Studio Museum in Harlem 1967; mem Comm Talented & Gifted Children RI Dept of Educ 1977; exec comm Natl Conference of Christians and Jews 1977; council mem 1978-82, juror 1989, RI State Council on the Arts; bd mem RI Volunteer Lawyers for the Arts 1978-80; chmn RI Governors Arts Awards Comm 1981; New England Foundation for the Arts 1981-83, 1990-; juror Newport Art Assn 1983; juror Arts Fellowship Boston MA 1988; juror, Manchester Art Assn 1988; project dir, Jazz, devoted to jazz music featuring established artists & musicians, 1989. **Honors/Awds:** Lectures including, Univ of Saarbruecken, Germany 1962; Wheeler School, Providence, RI 1982; Natl Center of Afro-Amer Artists 1983; Smithsonian NEH Grant Afro-Amer Art Symposium 1985; nom Loeb Fellowship for museum concept for jazz Harvard Univ 1984; solo artist Pugilist Series as part of the kick off for 1988 World Trade Ctr New York City 1984; artwork selected for office of Sen Robt Kennedy; Artists Against Apartheid UN Sponsored Exhibit 1984; org exhibit, Artists in Uniform Germany US Diplomatic Serv & Germany Gov 1962, J F Kennedy Performing Arts Ctr; has exhibited: USA, Canada, Germany, & Italy; has copyright on the Jazz Museum's Natl Jazz Medal design. **Military Serv:** US Army, Airborne Artillery PFC 1960-63; Good Conduct, Expert Rifle, Machine Gun, European Service Ribbon. **Business Addr:** Professor, Illustration, Rhode Island School of Design, 2 College St, Providence, RI 02903.

S

SAAR, BETYE I.
Artist, designer, educator. **Personal:** Born Jul 30, 1926, Los Angeles, CA; daughter of Beatrice Brown and Jefferson Brown; divorced; children: Lesley, Alison, Tracye. **Educ:** UCLA, BA 1949; American Film Institute, attended 1972. **Career:** Artist; numerous exhibits; Whitney Museum Modern Art, solo exhibit 1975; Studio Museum in Harlen, solo exhibit 1980; Monique

Knowlton Gallery NY, solo exhibit 1981; Jan Baum Gallery LA, solo exhibit 1981; Quay Gallery San Francisco, 1982; WAM & Carnberra School of Art Australia, solo exhibit 1984; Georgia State Univ Gallery, 1984; Museum of Contemporary Art LA, solo exhibitions in context 1984; MIT Center Gallery 1987; exhibitions Tai Chung Taiwan, Kuala Lumpur Malaysia, Manila Philippines, 1988; solo exhibitions: Connections: Site Installations, 1989, Sanctified Visions, 1990, Sentimental Souvenirs, 1991, Signs of the Times, 1992, Betye Saar: The Secret Heart, 1993, Limbo, 1994, Personal Icons, 1996, Tangled Roots, 1996; group exhibitions: Secrets, Dialogues, Revelations: The Art of Betye & Alison Saar, 1990-91, 500 Years: With the Breath of Our Ancestors, 1992, In Out of the Cold, 1993, Generation of Mentors, 1994, The US Delegation Fifth Biennial of Havana, 1994, The Art of Betye Saar and John Otterbridge, 1994, 1995. **Honors/Awds:** Award, Natl Endowment of Arts 1974, 1984; Spirit Catcher-The Art of Betye Saar, film featured on Women in the Art Series, WNET-TV, New York City; J Paul Getty Fund for the Visual Arts Fellowship, 22nd Annual Artist Award, 1990; Brandywine Workshop, James Van Der Zee Award, 1992; Fresno Art Museum, Distinguished Artist Award, 1993; honorary doctorates: CA College of Arts and Crafts, 1991, Otis/Parson, 1992, San Francisco Art Institute, 1992, MA College of Art, 1992, CA Institute of the Arts, 1995.

SABREE, CLARICE SALAAM
Program administrator, musician. **Personal:** Born Oct 25, 1949, Camden, NJ; daughter of Clara Ingram and Roy McClendon; divorced; children: Zahir, Anwar, Ameen, Hassan. **Educ:** Rutgers Univ Camden, BA 1978. **Career:** Lawnside Bd of Educ, teacher 1978-80; Camden Bd of Educ, elem teacher 1980-82; DMC Energy Inc, office mgr 1983-87; Maximum Persuasion, vocalist/songwriter/musician, 1984-89, solo jazz vocalist, 1989-; CAPEDA, energy analyst 1987-88; Energy Conservation, supervisor of monitors, 1988-; NJ Dept of Community Affairs, Division of Housing and Community resources, Office of Low-Income Energy Conservation, administrator, currently, program supervisor, 1993-. **Orgs:** Researcher/collector/lecturer Intl Black Dolls 1979-; board member, South African Freedom Comm; Retail Sales- Camden Culture Corner, Wearing Apparel, jewelry. **Honors/Awds:** Outstanding Volunteer Headstart Camden 1978; Cultural Awareness Council for the Preservation of African-Amer Culture 1985-87; Dark Images Award, for contributions to Black Doll Collecting, 1992; Homelessness Prevention Award, 1993. **Home Addr:** 1476 Mt Ephraim Ave, Camden, NJ 08104, (609)541-6221. **Business Addr:** Administrator, New Jersey Department of Community Affairs, Division of Housing and Community Resources Office of Low-Income Energy Conservation, 101 S Broad St, CN 806, Trenton, NJ 08625.

SADLER, KENNETH MARVIN
Dentist. **Personal:** Born Oct 12, 1949, Gastonia, NC; son of Mildred Jackson Sadler and Edward Dewitt Sadler Sr (deceased); married Brenda Arlene Latham MD; children: Jackson Lewis Ezekiel, Raleigh DeWitt Samuel. **Educ:** Lincoln Univ, BA 1971; Howard Univ Coll of Dentistry, DDS 1975; Golden Gate Univ, MPA 1978. **Career:** Howard Univ Coll of Dentistry, instructor/coordinator 1972-76; US Army Dental Corps, captain/dentist 1975-78; Winston-Salem Dental Care Plan, dir of quality assurance and referral serv 1978-. **Orgs:** Omega Psi Phi, life mem 1969; Natl Dental Assn, 1975-; Amer Dental Assn, 1975-; Academy of General Dentistry, 1976-; Lincoln Univ, chmn, bd of trustees 1983-; Old North State Dental Soc, chmn peer review committee 1986; bd of dir Old Hickory Council Boy Scouts of Amer 1988-; Lewisville Town Council, mayor pro tempore, 1991-; American Association of Dental Schools, consultant 1991; BSA, Old Hickory Council, vice president 1990; Forsyth Technical Cmnty Clg, bd of trustees; Winton-Salem Forsyth County Appearance Cmsn; Winston-Salem Forsyth County Industrial Financing Pollution Control Authority. **Honors/Awds:** Omicron Kappa Epsilon, mem 1975-; Intl Coll of Dentistry Award 1975; The Amer Assn of Endodontics Award 1975; US Army, dental diploma-general practice 1976; Academy of Gen Dentistry, fellow 1982; Recognition Cetificate, Chicago Dental Soc, 1989; Plaque-Appreciation, Fifth Dist Dental Soc, 1989; Lecture/Table Clinic, Chicago Mid-winter Meeting, 1989; Table Clinic, Thomas P Hinman Dental Meeting, 1989, 1996; United Way Forsyth County, chairman budget review panel, 1991; Forsyth County Dental Hygiene Soc, lecturer, 1991; NAFEO, Distinguished Alumni of the Year, 1986; Citizenship Award, 1996, NCDS; Mastership Academy of General Dentistry; Silver Beaver Award, OHC BSA; Fellow, American College of Dentists, 1995. **Special Achievements:** Presentations include: DC Dental Society; Howard Univ, Post-graduate Seminar; Pellican State Dental Society; Natl Dental Society; Forsyth County Dental Assistant Society; Lincoln Univ, Chemistry Department; American Academy of Dental Group Practice; Palmetto State Dental Medical Pharmaceutical Assn; author: "Resin Bonded Retainers," Journal of Natl Dental Assn, 1984. **Military Serv:** US Army, ltc; Commendation Medal; Army Achievement Medal. **Business Addr:** Director of Quality Assurance, Winston-Salem Dental Care, 201 Charlois Blvd, Winston-Salem, NC 27103.

SADLER, WILBERT L., JR.
Educator. **Personal:** Born Nov 17, Atlanta, GA; son of Willie Mae Sanford Sadler and Wilbert Sadler Sr; married Carolyn Johnson; children: Anthony Lee, Wilbert Bryant, Crystal Yolanda. **Educ:** Paine Coll, BS 1970; Morgan State Univ, MS 1972; Boston Univ, EdD 1981; Univ of Pennsylvania, Post Doctorate study 1981; Columbia Univ, post doctorate study, 1988. **Career:** Morgan State Coll, instructor 1970-74; Boston Univ, grad asst 1974-76; Livingstone Coll, asst prof 1976-82; Winston-Salem State Univ, assoc prof 1982-1992, professor, 1992-. **Orgs:** Mem Pinehurst Comm Club 1976-; mem Salisbury Rown Symphony Guild; mem Optimist Club; mem Assn of Coll & Univ Profs; NAACP; life mem, Alpha Upsilon Alpha (Read Honor Society), NC College Read; Coll Reading Assn, Intl Reading Assn, Alpha Kappa Mu Hon Soc; mem Beta Mu Lambda, Alpha Phi Alpha Frat Inc. **Honors/Awds:** Natl Endowment for Humanities Fellowship; Published 2 books, 5 articles; member, Alpha Upsilon Alpha, National Reading Honor Society, 1989-90; member, Phi Delta Kappa, National Education Honor Society, 1989-90. **Military Serv:** US Army, sp/4 2 yrs. **Business Addr:** Professor, Winston-Salem State University, Education Department, Martin Luther King Jr, Dr, Winston-Salem, NC 27101.

SAFFOLD, OSCAR E.
Physician. **Personal:** Born Feb 20, 1941, Cleveland, OH. **Educ:** Fisk U, BA 1963; Meharry Med Coll, MD 1967. **Career:** Grg W Hbbd Hosp, intern 1967-68; Tafts Univ Sch Med, asst resd derm 1968-72; Boston City Hosp, chf resd derm 1972-73; Case Wstrn Res Med Sch, asst derm dept med 1974-, clncl instr 1973-. **Orgs:** Sec Derm Sect Nat Med Assn 1975-; dir Medic-Scrn Inc 1975-; staff St Vncnt Chrty Hosp; Shkr Med Hosp; Univ Hosp Cleve 1973-; mem MA St Bd; OH St Bd; Am Bd Derm 1974; mem Am Acad Derm; Am Soc for Derm Srgry Inc; AMA; Cleve Acad of Med; Cleve Derm Assn; Nat Med Assn; OH St Med Assn. **Honors/Awds:** Publ Gundala Schmbrg Lever MD, Histlgy & Ultrstrctr of Herpes & Gstns, Fred S Hirsh MD, Oscar E Saffold MD, Mycbctrm Kansasii Infctn With Derm Mnfstns; Arch Derm 1973, 1976. **Business Addr:** Central Med Arts Bldg, 2475 E 22nd St, Cleveland, OH 44115.

SAFFOLD, SHIRLEY STRICKLAND
Judge. **Personal:** married Oscar E Saffold; children: Sydney. **Educ:** Central State Univ, bachelor's degree; Cleveland-Marshall College of Law, JD. **Career:** Cuyahoga County Court of Common Pleas, judge, currently. **Orgs:** National Bar Association; National Association of Women Judges; American Judges Association, pres. **Honors/Awds:** Dew Ward Club, Judge of the Year. **Special Achievements:** First African American woman to serve in an executive position in the American Judges Assn. **Business Addr:** Judge, Cuyahoga County Court of Common Pleas, 1200 Ontario St, Court Rm 18A, Cleveland, OH 44114, (216)443-7000.

SAGERS, RUDOLPH, JR.
Marketing representative. **Personal:** Born Feb 14, 1955, Chicago, IL; married Carol Hillsman; children: Ryan Christopher. **Educ:** Univ of IL, BS 1978; Univ of Cincinnati, MS 1980. **Career:** Veterans Administration, mgmt analyst trainee 1979-80, mgmt analyst 1980-81, health systems specialist 1981-84; Intl Business Machines, marketing rep 1984-. **Orgs:** Mem Amer Coll of Hospital Administrators 1982, MI Health Council 1982, Amer Health Planning Assoc 1983, Soc for Hospital Planning 1983, Black Data ProflAssoc 1986-. **Honors/Awds:** Outstanding Young Man of Amer Awd 1983; Veterans Admin Achievement of Service Awd 1983; Veterans Admin Superior Performance Awd 1983; Veterans Admin Special Contribution Awd 1984; Medical Ctr Director's Commendation of Excellence Awd; Intl Business Machines Branch Mgr Awd 1985,86; Intl Business Machines Natl 100% Sales Club Awd 1985,86. **Home Addr:** 2737 Tarpon Ct, Homewood, IL 60430. **Business Addr:** Marketing Representative, Intl Business Machines, One IBM Plaza, Chicago, IL 60611.

SAILOR, ELROY
Legislative special assistant. **Personal:** Born Oct 26, 1969, Detroit, MI; son of Clarence & Rev DeAnna Sailor. **Educ:** Morehouse College, BA, political science, 1990; Michigan State University, certificate, public policy, 1994; Wayne State University, master's, urban planning, 1996-98. **Career:** Governor John Engler, assistant to governor, 1991-93, re-election campaign, deputy politicl director, 1993-94; US Senator Spencer Abraham, special assistant, 1995-. **Orgs:** US Senate Black Legislative Staff Caucus, executive board member, 1995-96; "Youngbloods" National Empowerment TV, co-host, 1995-96; The Sailor Co. Vending Machines, president/owner, 1996-; Fellowship Chapel, 1990-; COTS - Homeless Shelter, volunteer, 1991-92. **Honors/Awds:** Detroit News, Detroit's Five Future Leaders, 1995; MPLP Michigan St University, Fellowship, Public Policy Program, 1994. **Special Achievements:** Entered Morehouse College at age 16, 1986. **Home Addr:** 431 W Grixdale, Detroit, MI 48203.

SAINTE-JOHNN, DON
Communications. **Personal:** Born Jul 9, 1949, Monroeville, AL; son of Nell B Henderson and Walter Johnson; married Brenda L Hodge; children: W Marcus, J'Michael Kristopher. **Educ:** LA City Coll, 1968; Cal-State Long Beach, 1969; San Francisco State University. **Career:** XEGM Radio San Diego, prog dir 1968-69; KWK St Louis, prog dir 1969-71; KYUM Yuma AZ, sports dir 1969; Aradcom Prod of St Louis, pres 1970-71; WJPC Radio Chgo, am air personality 1971-74; KFRC RKO Broadcasting Inc, air personality; KSFM-FM Sacramento, air talent. **Orgs:** Mem Natl Assoc Radio-TV Ammoun; lic CA Real Estate; mem bd E Bay Zoological Soc; mem Bay Area March of Dimes Superwalk, Natl Acad TV Arts & Sci, Amer Fed TV & Radio Art, Alpha Epsilon Rho, SC Broadcaster Assoc,; mem bd of dir Paul J Hall Boys Club; spearheaded on air int WJPC Chicago to support black boxers; athletic dir St Davids School; bd mem Diocesan Boys Athletic Council of Oakland; former basketball coach Richmond Police Activities League, El Sobrante Boys Club, St Davids Schools. **Honors/Awds:** Billboard Air Personalities of the Year 1973,74; Prod Special on Sickle Cell Anemia Channel 26 Chicago 1971; Hon as Concerned Spon for Chicago Pin-Killers Bowl Club 1974; Most Outstanding Radio Student at LA City Coll 1967; Hon for Cont in Law Enf St Louis MO 1971; Air Personality of the Year Billboard Mag 1974,75; air Personality on Pop Radio Awd Black Radio Exclusive Mag 1980. **Business Addr:** KFRC-AM, 500 Washington St, San Francisco, CA 94111.

ST. ETIENNE, GREGORY MICHAEL
Bank executive. **Personal:** Born Dec 24, 1957, New Orleans, LA; son of Geraldine and Emanuel. **Educ:** Loyola University, BBA, 1979, MBA, 1981; Graduate School of Banking of the South, certificate of completion, 1988. **Career:** Laporte, Sehrt, Romig & Hand, CPA's, senior auditor, 1981-85; Liberty Bank and Trust Co, exec vp, 1985-. **Orgs:** Kingsley House, past president, 1986-; National Bankers Association, secretary, 1991-; New Orleans Urban Bankers Association, president, 1992; 100 Black Men, New Orleans Chapter, 1992; St Thomas, Irish Channel Consortium, treasurer, 1990-; Institute of Mental Hygiene, secretary, 1994-; Louisiana State Museum Foundation, director, 1996-.

SAINT JAMES, SYNTHIA
Artist, illustrator, author. **Personal:** Born Feb 11, 1949, Los Angeles, CA. **Educ:** Attended Los Angeles Valley Coll, Dutchess Community Coll. **Career:** Artist. First commissioned paintings, 1969; Inner City Cultural Center, first one-woman show, 1977; Musee des Duncans, Paris, group exhibition; House of Seagram commission for Black History Month, 1989; designed cover art for Terry McMillan's Waiting to Exhale, international edition, 1992, among others; has own signature clothing line and signature line of clocks; illustrator of 6 children's books, including two which she authored; has also written two books of poetry and prose. **Honors/Awds:** Prix de Paris, 1980; Gentlemen Concerned (an AIDS foundation) Service Award, 1995; UNICEF Greeting Card Artist Award, 1995. **Special Achievements:** Designed first Kwanzaa stamp commissioned by the US Postal Service, 1997.

SAINT-JEAN, OLIVIER. See ABDUL-WAHAD, TARIQ.

ST. JOHN, KRISTOFF
Actor. **Career:** "Young and the Restless," actor, currently. **Business Addr:** Actor, Young & The Restless, c/o CBS/TV, 51 W 52nd St, ATTN: Stone Manners, New York, NY 10019, (212)654-7575.

ST. JOHN, PRIMUS
Educator. **Personal:** Born Jul 21, 1939, New York, NY; son of Pearle E Hall and Marcus L St John Hall; married Barbara Jean Doty; children: Joy Pearle, May Ginger. **Educ:** University of Maryland; Lewis and Clark College. **Career:** Mary Holmes Junior College, West Point, MS, teacher; University of Utah, teacher; Portland State University, Portland, OR, associate professor of English, professor of English, currently; Portland Arts Commission, member, 1979-81; educational consultant; Primus St. John, professor of English. **Orgs:** Copper Canyon Press, board of directors. **Honors/Awds:** National Endowment for the Arts, Fellow, 1970, 1974, 1982; Oregon Book Award, 1991. **Special Achievements:** Author, Skins on the Earth, 1976; author, Love Is Not a Consolation; It Is a Light, 1982; co-editor, Zero Makes Me Hungry, anthology, text, 1976; Dreamer, collection of poems, 1990; coedited, Skins on the Earth, 1978; coedited, From Here We Speak, Oregon State University, 1993. **Home Addr:** PO Box 93, West Linn, OR 97068-0093. **Business Addr:** Professor of English, Portland State University, Portland, OR 97207.

SAINT-LOUIS, RUDOLPH ANTHONY
Attorney. **Personal:** Born Dec 28, 1951, Port-au-Prince, Haiti; son of Georgette Saint-Louis and Libner Saint-Louis; divorced; children: Shaundri, Melissa. **Educ:** Saint Joseph's College, BA, 1973; University of Wisconsin's Law School, Madison, JD, 1976. **Career:** Wisconsin Department of Ind, Unemployment Division, hearing examiner,1976-77; ICC, attorney, advisor, 1977-81; U S Attorney Office special, assistant U S attorney, 1980-81; ICC, SBA, staff attorney, 1981-83; ICC, OPA, acting director, three times, 1983, staff attorney, 1983-. **Orgs:** ICC, chairman, Employee Board of Education, 1988-; LFRA, presi-

dent, 1993-95; In-Com-Co Club, president, 1991-; ICC Toastmasters, president, 1988, 1990; Federal Bar Association, agency representative, 1980. **Honors/Awds:** ICC, EEO Award, 1991, Community Service Award, 1990, 1991. **Special Achievements:** Interviewee on teleconference on racism, 1991; video on Basilica in Africa-Ivory Coast, assistant producer, 1990; Black Catholic Televangelization Network, vp, 1983-; Search For Black Christian Heritage, asst producer on video, 1995. **Home Addr:** 6500 Killarney St, Clinton, MD 20735, (301)856-7174. **Business Phone:** (202)565-1590.

ST. MARY, JOSEPH JEROME
Union official. **Personal:** Born Oct 27, 1941, Lake Charles, LA; married Elaine Guillovy; children: Jennifer Ann, Lisa Rene, Joseph J. **Educ:** Sowela Tech Inst, business 1968; Loyola Univ, labor course 1984. **Career:** Plasterers & Cement Mason #487, recording sec 1962-69, fin sec & bus mgr 1970-; Calcasieu Parish Police Jury, vice-pres 1979, 1980, 1993, pres 1981-82. **Orgs:** Exec bd Southwest Central Trades Council 1974-; vice-pres Southwest LA Bldg Trades Council 1974-; fin sec A Phillip Randolph Inst 1974-; vice pres LA AFL-CIO 1975-. **Honors/Awds:** Calcasieu Parish Police Jury, Outstanding Leadership, 1979-86; Calcasieu Private Industry Council JobMatch, Outstanding Contribution, 1987-89; Faithful, Devoted, Unfailing Support for the City Wide Easter Egg Hunt, The Coalition for Community Progress, 1989; 10 Years of Dedicated and Untiring Services, Calcasieu Parish RSVP, 1990; Dedicated and Outstanding Services, Cal Parish Police Jury, 1992; Recognition of Services as Secretary-Treasurer, Black Caucus, 1976-82; State of Louisiana Police Jury Association, 1988-92. **Home Addr:** 414 N Simmons St, Lake Charles, LA 70601. **Business Addr:** Police Juror, Calcasieu Prsh, Lake Charles, LA 70601.

ST. OMER, VINCENT V. E.
Educator, consultant. **Personal:** Born Nov 18, 1934, St Lucia, St. Lucia; married Margaret Muir; children: Ingrid, Denise, Jeffrey, Raymond. **Educ:** Ontario Vet College, DVM, 1962; University Manitoba, MSc, 1965; Ontario Vet College, University Guelph, PhD, 1969. **Career:** Hamilton & Dist Cattle Breeders Association, field veterinarian, 1962-63; Ontario Vet College, University Guelph, lecturer, 1965-67; University of Kansas, Bureau of Child Research, research associate, 1968-71, adj professor, 1970-73; Kansas State University, Bureau of Child Research, adj research associate, 1972-74; University of Medicine, School of Medicine, assistant professor, 1974, associate professor, 1974; University of Missouri, College of Veterinary Medicine, Department of Veterinary Biomedical Sciences, associate professor, 1974-83, professor, 1984-, director of graduate studies, 1976-79, director, Minority High School Student Research Apprentice Program, 1986-89; University of West Indies, School of Veterinary Medicine, special leave from University of Missouri, professor, director, 1989-91; Tuskegee Univ, School of Veterinary Medicine, prof & assoc dean of academic affairs, 1991-. **Orgs:** Sigma Xi; American Society of Veterinary Physiologists & Pharmacologists; Society of Neuroscience; Missouri Veterinarian Medical Association; Conference of Research Workers in Animal Disease, New York Academy of Sciences; Research Interests, Neuropharmacology & Neurotoxicology; Behavioral Teratology Society; Caribbean Academy of Sciences. **Honors/Awds:** American Academy of Veterinary Pharmacology and Therapeutics, Fellow. **Business Addr:** Assoc Dean of Academic Affairs, School of Veterinary Medicine, Tuskegee Univ, Tuskegee Institute, AL 36088.

SALAAM, ABDUL (LEO MCCALLUM)
Dentist. **Personal:** Born Aug 18, 1929, Newark, NJ; son of Katie Allen McCallum and Roosevelt McCallum; married Khadijah, May 14, 1954; children: Sharonda Khan, Valerie Best, Robert, Darwin, Abdul II. **Educ:** Wash Sq Coll, NYU, BS 1952; Columbia Univ Sch of Oral/Dental Surgery, DDS 1956; Acad of Genl Dentistry, FAGD 1973. **Career:** NYU Wrestling Team, capt 1950; Jarvie Hon Soc, Columbia U, mem 1954; Lincoln Dental Soc Bulletin, editor 1972; Guaranty Bank, Chicago IL, bd of dir 1976; First Africa Capital Investment Corp, Chicago, IL, treasurer, 1988-. **Orgs:** Post grad instructor Inst for Grad Dentists 1966-72; pres Commonwealth Dental Soc of NJ 1964; pres Specialty Promo Co Inc Import Export 1959-; organ pres Nation of Islam 1976; pres bd of dir New Earth Child Care Community Network 1984-88; teachers certificate in general semantics from Inst of General Semantics Englewood NJ 1986; pres-elect Kenwood Hyde Park Br of Chicago Dental Soc 1987-88; bd of dir Masjid Al' Fatir 1987-; treasurer Muhammad Ali Investment Corp 1988-90; guest lecturer Inst for General Semantics 1988-; newspaper columnist Amer Muslim Journal; mem bd of dirs Amer Muslim Journal, 1982-84; rep Chicago Dental Soc in Dialogue in Dentistry an agency for helping employers to understand dental ins programs 1987-89; mem, American Equilibration Society, 1963-; Pierre Fauchard Soc; mem, American Dental Assn, 1956-; Chicago Dental Society, bd of dirs, 1993-96; Construction Systems Inc, chairman. **Honors/Awds:** Man of the Yr Commonwealth Dental Soc of NJ 1966; fellow The Acad of Genl Dentistry IL 1973; 1st Dentist of the Year Award, Lincoln Dentl Society, Chicago, IL, 1989; Dr Abdul Salaam Day, Mayor's Office, City of Newark, NJ, 1989. **Special Achievements:** Contributor of Archival Film & Consultant to "Malcolm X, An American Experience," TV Documentary. **Military Serv:** US Army, Medical Corp pvt 1st class 1947-48. **Business Addr:** Dentist, 1335 E 87th St, Chicago, IL 60619, (312)721-7000.

SALAAM, RASHAAN
Professional football player. **Personal:** Born Oct 8, 1974, San Diego, CA. **Educ:** University of Colorado. **Career:** Chicago Bears, running back, 1995-. **Special Achievements:** Selected in the 1st round/21st overall pick in the 1995 NFL Draft. **Business Addr:** Professional Football Player, Chicago Bears, 1000 Football Dr, Halas Hall at Conway Park, Lake Forest, IL 60045-4829, (847)295-6600.

SALES, RICHARD OWEN
Business executive. **Personal:** Born Aug 12, 1948, New York, NY; married Dorethye Ann; children: Doricha, Brandy. **Educ:** Rochester Inst of Tech, BS, Printing Mgmt 1970; Northeastern Univ, Boston MA, MBA 1985-89. **Career:** MIT Press, Cambridge MA, prod mgr 1970-72; Williams Graphic Serv Wakefield MA, prod mgr 1972-74; Houghton Mifflin Co, Boston MA, vice pres, dir production 1974-. **Orgs:** Secy bd mem Soc of Printers 1983-; past pres Bookbuilders of Boston 1982-83; mem of partnership, Boston Fellows 1988-. **Honors/Awds:** Black Achievers Award Greater Boston Black Achievers 1979.

SALLEY, JOHN THOMAS (SPIDER)
Professional basketball player. **Personal:** Born May 16, 1964, Brooklyn, NY; son of Mazie Carter Salley and Quillie Salley; married Natasha; children: Giovanna. **Educ:** Georgia Institute of Technology, BA, 1988. **Career:** Power forward, Detroit Pistons, 1986-92, Miami Heat, 1992-95; Toronto Raptors, 1995-96; Chicago Bulls, 1996-; Funkee's Enterprises, president, currently; Bad Boys, film appearance, 1995. **Orgs:** Be The Best You Can Be program; Metro Youth Foundation; Cancer Assn; Omega Phi Psi; NBA Stay in School, Hepatitis B Campaign. **Honors/Awds:** Unsung Hero Award; I Have a Dream Award. **Business Addr:** Professional Basketball Player, Chicago Bulls, 1901 W. Madison, Chicago, IL 60612-2459, (312)943-5800.

SALMON, JASLIN URIAH
Educator. **Personal:** Born Jan 4, 1942, Darliston, Jamaica; son of Jane Sylent Salmon and Leaford Salmon; married Dr Anita Hawkins Salmon; children: Janet Felice, Jennifer Renee. **Educ:** Olivet Nazarene Univ, BA 1969; Ball State U, MA 1970; Univ of IL Chicago, PhD 1977. **Career:** Ball State U, teaching asst 1969-70; George Williams Coll, asst prof of sociology 1970-76; Triton Coll, prof of sociology 1976-77; Human Resource Devel Govt of Jamaica, dir 1977-79; Triton Coll, prof of soc 1979-, dir center for parenting 1985-88. **Orgs:** Social worker Dept of Mental Health IL 1968-69; dir HOP 1973-75; dir & mem Chicago Forum 1971-72; chmn Academic Senate George Williams Coll 1974; consult Parenting/Women & Minorities at the work place; pres, NAACP Oak Park IL Branch 1989-94. **Honors/Awds:** Teacher of the Year George Williams Coll 1973; author, "Black Executives in White Business" 1979; "Teaching and Learning in a Multicultural and Multiracial Environment," editor. **Home Addr:** 713 S Humphrey, Oak Park, IL 60304. **Business Addr:** Prof Soc, Triton Coll, 2000 5th Ave, River Grove, IL 60171.

SALMON CAMPBELL, JOAN MITCHELL
Clergywoman. **Personal:** Born Mar 31, 1938, St Louis, MO; daughter of Corleda Brady Mitchell and David Andrew Mitchell; married James Campbell Jr, Jan 17, 1977; children: Rebecca, David, Jeanne Salmon Stowe, Peter, Paul. **Educ:** Univ of Rochester Eastman School of Music, Rochester NY, BM, 1959; Inter-Met Theological Center, Washington DC, Master of Divinity, 1977. **Career:** Piano and voice teacher, concert singer, Rochester NY, 1959-66; asst pastor, St Mark Presbyterian Church, Rockville MD, 1974-77; interim pastor, Arlington Presbyterian Church, Arlington VA, 1976-78; co-pastor, Linwood United Church, Kansas City MO, 1978-80; pastor, St Paul Presbyterian Church, Kansas City MO, 1978-82. **Orgs:** Chairman of bd, Sickle Cell Anemia, Kansas City MO Chapter, 1980-82; basileus, Delta Nu Omega Chapter, Alpha Kappa Alpha Sorority, 1963; pres, Ujoma Consultant Network, Kansas City MO, 1980-82; pres, chairman of bd, Shalom Ministries Inc, Exton PA, 1982-89. **Honors/Awds:** Black Folks Legacy to America, History of Black Religious Music, 1966; Doctor of Divinity, Central American Univ, 1981; Vice Moderator of Presbyterian Church, Reunion Assembly, 1983; Moderator of 201st GA Presbyterian Church, 1987.

SALMOND, JASPER
Professional service consultant. **Personal:** Born Jul 5, 1930, Camden, SC; son of Dora James Salmond and James Salmond (deceased); married Thelma Brooks, May 25, 1954; children: Jeryl Stanley, Jenita Salmond Jumper Belton. **Educ:** Benedict College, BA (magna cum laude), education, 1954; Columbia University, Teachers College, MA, education administration, 1960; Atlanta University, certificate, School Systems Administration, 1963; University of SC, extension course. **Career:** Richland Co School District One, school teacher, principal, 1954-72; Wilbur Smith Associates Inc, principal associate, United Nations contact, proj development, community involvement planning, senior marketing coordinator, 1972-. **Orgs:** Alpha Phi Alpha Fraternity, Alpha Psi Lambda Chapter, past president, past chairman youth leadership, chairman scholarships; American Red Cross, past chapter chairman, Convention Plenary Presenter, chairman, national nominations; Columbia Kiwanis Club, executive committee mem, chairman, Terrific Kids Program, 1975-95; SC School Boards Association, 1990-, secretary, 1995-96, vice pres, 1996-97, board of directors, 1992-98; Midlands Technical Coll, board of comm, 1975-91; Association of Community College Trustees, Afro-American Coalition Committee, regional representative, 1990-91; Benedict College National Alumni, past pres, parliamentarian, 1960-; Richland Co School District One, board of commissioners, 1990-, chairman, 1993-94; NEA, National Principal Association; past vp, SC Elem School Principals, 1971-72; NAACP, life mem; Parliamentarian, chairman finance and facilities comm, 1995-97; Republic Natl Bank, bd of dirs, 1992-94; Greater Columbia Chamber of Commerce, exec comm, 1996-98; Carolina First Bank, bd of dirs, technology comm, 1994-; B/R Health Systems, bd of dirs, 1996-98. **Honors/Awds:** Alpha Psi Lambda Chapter, Man of the Year, 1976, 1992; Alphas of Columbia, Achievement Award, Education, 1992; Midlands Technical College, Meritorious Service, African-American Association, 1989, Outstanding Service as Commissioner, 1991; Benedict College, Dedicated Service Board of Trustees, 1980, Outstanding Alumnus; Columbia Chamber of Commerce, Service Award, Community Relations Council Chairman, 1971, advisor, 1975-; Level III School Boardmanship Inst Training Award, 1992; Lula J Gambrell Award, Top Distinguished Alumnus, 1995; numerous others. **Special Achievements:** Guardian Ad Litem, board of directors, 1993-, chairman, 1996-97; Toastmasters International, regional officer, completing distinguished toastmasters requirements, 1993-; Midlands Technical College, commission secretary, 1989-90. **Military Serv:** US Army, military police, cpl, 1954-56; Good Conduct Metal. **Home Addr:** 4035 Coronado Dr, Columbia, SC 29203, (803)765-2795.

SALONE, MARCUS
Judge. **Personal:** Born Apr 28, 1949, Chicago, IL; son of Anna Rae and Herbert Spencer; married Valee Glover, Oct 29, 1976; children: Lisa Michelle, Andrea Valee. **Educ:** University of Illinois, Chicago Circle Campus, BA, 1974; John Marshall Law School, JD, 1981. **Career:** Cook County State's Attorney's Office, assistant, 1981-83; Salone, Salone, Simmons, Murray & Associates, 1983-91; Circuit Court of Cook County, associate judge, 1991-. **Orgs:** Kappa Alpha Psi Fraternity, life member, 1970-; Cook County Bar Association, board of directors, 1988-; Ancona Montessori School, board of directors, 1988-90; John Howard Association, board of directors, 1994-. **Honors/Awds:** Cook County Bar Association, Meitorious Service Award, 1988, Judiciary Service Award, 1991; Alpha Kappa Alpha Sorority, Monarch Award, 1992. **Military Serv:** US Army, Spc4, 1969-71; Vietnam campaign award; service award. **Home Addr:** 6830 S Bennett, Chicago, IL 60649.

SALT. **See JAMES, CHERYL.**

SALTER, KWAME S.
Food company executive. **Personal:** Born Jan 31, 1946, Delhi, LA; son of Reva Daniels Salter and Samuel Leon Salter (deceased); married Phyllis V Harris, Jan 31, 1987; children: Kevin-Jamal, Keri-JaMelda, Matthew-Harrison. **Educ:** WI State Univ Whitewater, EdB (magna cum Laude) 1968; Univ of WI Madison, MA Ed Admin 1970. **Career:** Milwaukee Pub Sch Bd of Edn, teacher 1968-69; WI State Univ Whitewater, acad counselor 1968-70; Univ of WI Madison, project asst 1969-70; UW Madison Afro-Amer Cultural Ctr, exec dir 1970-73; Dane Co Parent Council Inc, exec dir 1976-86; Bd of Educ Madison Met Sch Dist, president 1982-86; Oscar Mayer Foods Corp, director of employment and public relations, currently. **Orgs:** Pres Exec Council for Cultural Interaction & Awareness Inc 1973; vice pres NAACP Madison Chap 1974-75; mem Madison Downtown Optimist Serv Club 1977; pres Common Touch Inc 1977-; mem Admin Mgmt Soc 1978-; vice pres Madison Met Sch Dist Bd of Educ 1980; mem Phi Delta Kappa 1980-; chrmn WI State Advisory Comm to US Civil Rights Commission 1985-87; chairman, Student Readiness Committee, Governor's Commission in the 21st Century. **Honors/Awds:** Fellow in Educ Ford Found (UW Madison) 1970; Outstanding Leader/Educator WI Omega Psi Phi-Kappa Phi Chap Milwaukee 1979; State Leaders for the 80's WI, The Milwaukee Journ Newspaper 1980; Outstanding Recent Alumni UW-Whitewater 1986. **Business Addr:** Director of Employment and Public Relations, Oscar Mayer Foods Corporation, 910 Mayer Ave, Madison, WI 53704.

SALTER, ROGER FRANKLIN
Business executive. **Personal:** Born Jul 15, 1940, Chicago, IL; married Jacqueline M Floyd; children: Dawn, Roger J, Marc CPres, Sanmar Fin. **Educ:** Chicago Tchrs Coll, BE 1962; DePaul U. **Career:** Sanmar Fin Plng Corp, pres; Blkbrn Agency Mut Benft Life, asst gen agt 1970-74; Mut Benfit Life, agt 1965-70; Ins Sales, asst mgr 1964; Chicago MetAsrnc Co, 2nd ldng agt 1962-63. **Orgs:** Dir sec 2nd vice pres 1st vice pres S Side Br Chicago Assn of Life Undrwrtrs; exec dir Fin for S Shore Comm; pres Ekrsll Nghrs Comm Grp; bd dir Mile Sqr Hlth Ctr; mem NAACP; Chicago Urban League; Nat Bus League; Chicago Area Cncl Boy Scts of Am; Omega Psi Phi Frat; life mem Mlln Dllr Rnd Tbl 1972-; 4th Blk in US. **Honors/Awds:** 10 Outst Bus Awd Jycs 1972; Nat Qulty Awrd Ins Sales 1971; Man of Yr 1965-67. **Business Addr:** 9730 S Western, Evergreen Park, IL 60642.

SAM, SHERI
Professional basketball player. **Personal:** Born May 5, 1974. **Educ:** Vanderbilt Univ. **Career:** San Jose Lasers, guard, 1996-. **Business Addr:** Professional Basketball Player, San Jose Lasers, 1530 Parkmoor Ave, Ste A, San Jose, CA 95128, (408)271-1500.

SAMARA, NOAH AZMI
Satellite company executive. **Personal:** Born Aug 8, 1956, Addis Abeba, Ethiopia; son of Yeshiemebet Zerfou-Samara and Ibrahim Azmi Samara; married Martha Debebe, May 6, 1989; children: Leila N. **Educ:** East Stroudsburg Univ, East Stroudsburg, PA, BA, 1975-78; UCLA, Los Angeles, CA, MA, history; Georgetown Univ, Washington, DC, Law, 1985, MS, School of Foreign Service, 1985. **Career:** Law Offices of Rothslatt & Millstein, Washington, DC, law clerk, 1981-84; Geostar Corp, Washington, DC, staff attorney, 1984-86, dir intl affairs, 1986-88; Robbins & Laramie, Washington, DC, of counsel, 1988-89; Venable, Baetjer & Howard, Washington, DC, of counsel, 1989-90; World Space Inc, Washington, DC, CEO, pres, 1990-. **Home Addr:** 8903 Ellsworth Ct, Silver Spring, MD 20910. **Business Addr:** CEO & President, World Space Inc, 11 Dupont Circle NW, Washington, DC 20036.

SAMKANGE, TOMMIE MARIE
Educational psychologist. **Personal:** Born Aug 1, 1932, Jackson, MS; daughter of Marie Hughes Anderson and Harry Anderson; widowed 1988; children: Stanlake, Jr, Harry M. **Educ:** Tougaloo Coll, BS 1953; Indiana Univ, MS 1955, PhD 1958. **Career:** Tougaloo Coll, assoc prof 1955-56; Tuskegee Inst, assoc prof 1964-67; Tennessee State Univ, prof 1967-71; Afro-Amer Studies Dept Harvard Univ, lecturer head tutor 1971-74; Stnlk Smkng, prof; Salem State Coll, asst dir minority affairs; Tufts Univ, asst prof 1979; Northeastern Univ, lecturer 1979; Ministry of Education and Culture, Zimbabwe, chief education officer, psychology, special education and early childhood education, 1981-94. **Orgs:** Amer Psychological Assn; League Women Vtrs; Health Professions Council of Zimbabwe (Psychologist); Zimbabwe Psychological Assn; Ranche House College of Citizenship, chairman. **Honors/Awds:** Mellon Found Grant 1977; Fellow Amer Assn Advncmnt Science; Consortium of Doctors, Women of Color in the Struggle, 1993.

SAMPLE, HERBERT ALLAN
Newspaper reporter. **Personal:** Born Mar 19, 1961, Los Angeles, CA; son of Ramona Adams Sample and Herbert Warner Sample. **Educ:** Pepperdine University, Malibu, CA, 1978-81; California State University, Sacramento, CA, BA, government, journalism, 1983. **Career:** Los Angeles Times, reporter, 1983-85; Sacramento Bee, reporter, capitol bureau, 1986-91, 1992-; Dallas Times Herald, chief of capitol bureau, 1991; McClatchy Newspapers, Washington Bureau, reporter, 1993-. **Orgs:** Black Journalists Association of Southern California, vp, 1985; Sacramento Black Journalists Assn, president, founder, 1988-; National Association of Black Journalists, 1986-; Washington Association of Black Journalists, 1993-. **Business Addr:** Reporter, Washington Bureau, McClatchy Newspapers, National Press Bldg, Ste 624, Washington, DC 20045, (202)383-0007.

SAMPLE, JOE
Musician, activist. **Personal:** Born in Houston, TX; children: Nicklas. **Educ:** Texas Southern University, piano. **Career:** The Crusaders, co-founder; pianist, 30 years; solo artist, 1978-. **Special Achievements:** Has recorded with Miles Davis, Joni Mitchell, Minnie Riperton, Michael Franks, Marcus Miller; Albums: Old Places, Old Faces, 1996; Sample This, 1997. **Business Addr:** Composer/Musican, Patrick Rains & ASC, 29171 Grayfox St, Malibu, CA 90265.

SAMPLE, WILLIAM AMOS
Professional athlete, broadcaster, writer. **Personal:** Born Apr 2, 1955, Roanoke, VA; son of Nora Sample and William T Sample; married Debra Evans; children: Nikki, Ian, Travis. **Educ:** James Madison U, BS Psychology 1978. **Career:** Texas Rangers, outfielder 1978-84; New York Yankees, 1985; Atlanta Braves, 1986; ESPN, broadcaster, 1991-93; Baseball Weekly, USA Today, writer; Atlanta Braves, television and radio broadcaster, 1988-89; ESPN and Universal 9 WWOR-TV, broadcaster, 1990; ESPN, studio analyst, color analyst, 1991; broadcasted select games for CBS Radio Saturday "Game of the Week", 1992; Seattle Mariners, television broadcaster, 1992; California Angels, radio analyst, play by play broadcaster, 1993-94; The Pennant Chase-Baseball Inside Out, Phoenix Comm, 1996. **Orgs:** Member, Major League Baseball Player's Association's Licensing Committee, 1986-87; consultant, Major League Baseball-Umpire Review Board, 1995-. **Honors/Awds:** Man of the Year, Texas Rangers Women's Club, 1984; Topps All-Rookie Team, 1979; 5th in American League Stolen Bases, 1983; outfielder on Topps Major League All-Rookie Team; Inducted into the Inaugural Roanoke-Salem Baseball Hall of Fame, 1992. **Special Achievements:** Articles published in The National Sports Daily, 1990; Articles published in the New York Times, "Views of Sport," 1987; Article published in Sports Illustrated, "The Point After," 1987; Voice used for voice-over in industrial films. Movie consultant, "Joe Torre: Curveballs Along the Way," Showtime Network Inc., 1997.

SAMPLES, BENJAMIN NORRIS
Judge. **Personal:** Born Aug 5, 1935, Baton Rouge, LA; married Tobortha M; children: Benjamin N II. **Educ:** Bishop College, BA Pol Sci 1965; St Mary's Univ School of Law, JD 1970. **Career:** Bexar Co Legal Aid, staff atty 1970-71, private practice 1971-78; San Antonio Civil Service Commission, chmn 1975-78; Bexar Co Juvenile Dept, judicial referee 1976-78; City of San Antonio, municipal court judge 1978-81; Bexar Co TX, judge 1981-. **Orgs:** Bars admitted to, State Bar of TX 1970, US Dist Court Western Dist of TX 1972, US Court of Appeals 5th Cir 1971, US Supreme Court 1973; mem San Antonio, American Bar Assns; mem San Antonio Trial Lawyers Assn; mem Judicial Section State Bar of TX. **Honors/Awds:** Delta Theta Phi Fraternity 1969; bd of dirs Bexar Co Easter Seals 1972; chmn trustee bd St James AME Church 1972; bd of dirs St Mary's Univ AlumniAssn 1983.

SAMPLES, JARED LANIER
City government official. **Personal:** Born Jan 22, 1965, Atlanta, GA; son of Dorothy Burns Samples and Cadmus Allen Samples. **Educ:** Georgia State University, Atlanta, GA, BS, 1989. **Career:** Atlanta Housing Authority, Atlanta, GA, weatherization specialist, 1982; Northwest Perry Recreation Center, Atlanta, GA, youth counselor, 1985; Georgia State University, Atlanta, GA, handicapped service counselor, 1988; Metropolitan Atlanta, Rapid Transit Authority, Atlanta, GA, internship, 1989. **Orgs:** Councilmember, Atlanta City Council; board member, Board of Commissioners-Atlanta, Housing Authority; board member, Economic Opportunity Atlanta, Board of Directors; board member, Atlanta Police Citizen Review Board; vice president, Perry Homes Tenant Association. **Honors/Awds:** Martin Luther King Tribute Speaker Award, J C Harris Elementary School; 50 Most Young Promising Black American, Ebony Magazine; Lt Colonel, Aide De Camp, Former Governor Joe Frank Harris; Proclamation for Outstanding Community Service, State of Georgia. **Business Addr:** Councilmember, Atlanta City Council, 55 Trinity Ave, SW, Atlanta, GA 30335.

SAMPSON, ALBERT RICHARD
Cleric. **Personal:** Born Nov 27, 1938, Boston, MA; son of Mildred Howell and Paul Sampson; divorced. **Educ:** Shaw Univ, BA 1961; Governor's State Univ, MA 1973; McCormick Theological Seminary, DIV 1977. **Career:** Newark NJ Poor People's Campaign, project director; Zion Baptist Church Everett MA, pastor; Fernwood United Methodist Church, pastor. **Orgs:** Community org consultant for poverty programs in Syracuse NY, Wilmington DE, Indianapolis IN, Boston MA; pres Council of Black Churches; spokesman Ministers Action Comm for Jobs 1985-92; intl vice pres for training of Allied Workers Intl Union; vice chmn Mayor Harold Washington's First Source Task Force; vice pres Roseland Clergy Assoc; traveled extensively in Europe to study industrialized Housing Systems as SCLC Natl Housing Director; pres, Natl Black Farmers Harvest and Business Corp 1989-; Biblical Scholar, Original African Heritage Bible; chmn, Million Man March MAPCO, Metro Area, planning corp in Chicago; national field secy, National African-American Leadership Summit; board member, Univ of Illinois Coll of Urban Business; chaplain, World Conference of Mayors; speaker, Million Man March, Oct 16th, 1995. **Honors/Awds:** Featured in Jet Magazine, Minority Builders Magazine, Chicago Sun-Times, Chicago Tribune; Christian Award 1981; Westside People for Progress Award 1983, South Shore Chamber of Commerce Award 1983; Martin Luther King Jr Award Intl Black Writer's Assn 1983; organized Dr Martin Luther King's low income cooperative housing program entitled 221d3, the only one of its kind in the nation; traveled fact finding mission to Angola, South Africa, Israel, Lebanon, Kenya, Tanzania, Zaire, Caribbean, Bermuda; publications: From Africa to the Americas: One God for One People, 1979, The Market Place from 1990-2000, Professional Agricultural Workers Conference, 1990; Only Christian Minister Traveled 18 African Countries, Friendship Tour with the Honorable Minister Louis Farrakhan. **Home Addr:** 10056 S Parnell, Chicago, IL 60628.

SAMPSON, CALVIN COOLIDGE
Educator. **Personal:** Born Feb 1, 1928, Cambridge, MD; son of Hattie Mae Stanley Sampson (deceased) and Robert Henry Sampson (deceased); married Corrine Delores Pannell; children: Cathleen Dale, Judith Gail. **Educ:** Hampton Inst U, BS Chem 1947; Meharry Med Coll, MD 1951. **Career:** Episcopal Hosp Philadelphia PA, asst dir of lab 1956-58; Freedmen's Hosp Howard U, dir of lab 1958-75; Howard Univ Coll of Med, asst prof of Path beginning 1958, prof of pathology, emeritus prof of pathology. **Orgs:** Vp bd of trustees Hosp for Sick Children Washington DC 1979-1985. **Honors/Awds:** Editor Journal of The Nat Med Assn Washington DC 1978-; 105 scientific articles published in med journals. **Military Serv:** US Army col 1953-76. **Home Addr:** 1614 Varnum Pl NE, Washington, DC 20017. **Business Addr:** Professor Emeritus of Pathology, Howard Univ, 520 West St NW, Washington, DC 20059.

SAMPSON, CHARLES
Rodeo performer. **Personal:** chilDren: Laurence Charles, Daniel. **Educ:** Attended Central Arizona Coll. **Career:** Joined Professional Rodeo Cowboys Assoc circuit, 1977; became World Champion bull rider, 1982; performed in 1983 Presidential Command Performance Rodeo; was hired by Timex to promote the durability of their watches; signed endorsement contract with Wrangler jeans; appeared 10 times in National Finals Rodeo. **Special Achievements:** Championships: Sierra Circuit, 1984, Turquoise Circuit, 1985-86, Copenhagen/Skoal, 1992, Calgary Stampede, Pendleton (OR) Round-Up, Grand National Rodeo, California Rodeo, Del Rio bull-riding buckle, Rodeo Superstars; named to Professional Rodeo Hall of Fame, 1996.

SAMPSON, DOROTHY VERMELLE
Attorney. **Personal:** Born Aug 4, 1919, Sumter, SC; daughter of Bessie Moore Sampson and William B Sampson. **Educ:** Hampton Inst, BS 1941; Atlanta Univ, MSW 1952; North Carolina Central Univ, LlB 1963, JD 1969. **Career:** Private Practice, atty 1964; Veteran's Admim, psychologist, social worker 1956. **Orgs:** Mem US Supreme Court 1967; 4th Circuit Court of Appeals 1966; Head Start Org 1965; IPAC 1949-53; ind sec Baltimore Urban League 1947; Natl Aux Epis Women 1941-42; bd of dir YWCA; candidate South Carolina Senate 1968; bd of dir South Carolina Farm Migrants Commn 1967-70; subscrib life mem NAACP. **Honors/Awds:** Award United Found 1968-69; Leadership Award, Marry Coll; Leadership Award, Youth Council 1977; Leadership Award, Mount Pisjah AME 1966; Martin Luther King Jr Civil Rights Award, Martin Luther King Jr Birthday Comm 1987. **Business Addr:** 204 W Oakland Ave, Sumter, SC 29150.

SAMPSON, HENRY THOMAS
Engineer. **Personal:** Born Apr 22, 1934, Jackson, MS; divorced; children: Henry III, Martin. **Educ:** Purdue Univ, BS 1956; MSc Univ of IL 1965; UCLA, MSc 1961; Univ of IL, PhD 1967. **Career:** US Naval Weapons Ctr, rsch chem engr 1956-61; rsch consult several documentary films; Pioneer Black Filmmakers, lecturer; Aerospace Corp, proj engr spaceflight S81-1 1967-. **Orgs:** Mem AAAS, Amer Nuclear Soc, Omega Psi Phi; fac adv comm Nuclear Eng 1976-. **Honors/Awds:** Author "Blacks in Black & White-A Source Book on Black Films 1910-50"; US Naval Ed Fellowship 1962; AEC Fellowship 1962-67; several patents engrg devices 1957-65; Scarecrow Press 1977; author "Blacks in Blackface, A Source Book on Early Black Musical Shows" Scarecrow Press 1980, "The Ghost Walks, A Chronological History of Blacks in Show Business 1863-1910" Scarecrow Press 1987, "Blacks in Black and White" Scarecrow Press, 1995. **Business Addr:** Director, Planning STP, Aerospace Corp, 125/1270 PO Box 92957, Los Angeles, CA 90009.

SAMPSON, KELVIN
Basketball coach. **Career:** Washington State Univ, basketball coach, currently. **Honors/Awds:** Named US Olympic Festival, Basketball Coach, 1993; Associated Press Coach of the Year, 1995. **Business Addr:** Basketball Coach, Washington State University, Pullman, WA 99164.

SAMPSON, MARVA W.
Human resources executive. **Personal:** Born Sep 4, 1936, Hamilton, OH; daughter of Willie Ray Sudbury (deceased) and Isiah Wells (deceased); married Norman C Sampson, Sep 29, 1956; children: Raymond, Anthony. **Educ:** Miami Univ; Univ of Dayton, MPA, 1976. **Career:** Hamilton OH City School System, priv sec 1954-58, ofc mgr 1958-59; Citizens Council on Human Relations, coor sec 1966-70; City of Middletown, dept of comm dev relocations officer 1964-66, dir dept of human resources 1971-. **Orgs:** Bd dir YMCA 1971; OH Mncpl Leag 1978; bd of trust ASPA 1978; pres Pi Alpha Alpha 1979; pres Ctr for Frnsc Psychiatry 1979-80; choir dir, pianist 2nd Bapt Church; exec bd mem Arts in Middletown; bd of trustees Central Ohio River Valley Assn; exec comm mem Butler County Children Services Bd; pres Middletown Area Safety Council; sec/coord Middletown Job Opportunity Inc; exec comm mem Middletown Area United Way; Natl Assn for Social Workers; Ohio Public Health Assn; Human Services Council; Friends of the Sorg; Ohio Parks and Recreation Assn; Natl Parks & Recreation Assn; American Society of Public Administration; Human Resources Committee; International Personnel Management Assn; State of OH, Alcohol and Drug Addiction Services Bd, executive mbr. **Honors/Awds:** Certs of Merit Serv C of C 1968; Lady of the Week Woman of the Year WPFB Radio Sta 1970; Red Triangle Award YMCA 1971-76; Outstanding Citizens Awd Knights Social Club 1972; Community Center Selective Award; Ohio Parks and Recreation Assn, Leisure Professional Certification, 1992-95; NAACP, NAACP & Southside Comm Image Awd, 1994; Volunteer of the Yr, Middletown United Way, 1996; JC Penney, Golden Rule Awd, 1997; Butler County, Woman of the Yr, 1997. **Business Addr:** Dir Dept of Human Resources, City of Middletown, One City Centre Plaza, Middletown, OH 45042.

SAMPSON, RALPH
College basketball coach. **Personal:** Born Jul 7, 1960, Harrisonburg, VA; married Aleize Rena Dial. **Educ:** Univ of VA, BA Speech Comm 1983. **Career:** Univ of VA, center basketball player; Houston Rockets, 1984-88, Golden State Warriors, 1988-89, Sacramento Kings, 1990-92; James Madison Univ, asst coach, 1992-. **Honors/Awds:** 3 times NCAA Player of the Year; 4 times All Amer; Rookie of the Year; MVP 1985 All Star game; mem 36th & 37th NBA All Star Teams. **Business Addr:** Asst Basketball Coach, James Madison University, Harrisonburg, VA 22807.

SAMPSON, ROBERT R.
Pharmacist. **Personal:** Born Oct 17, 1924, Clinton, NC; son of Annie Curry Sampson and Frank J Sampson; married Myrtle B; children: Frank R Sampson. **Educ:** Fayetteville State Univ, Fayetteville NC 1942-43; Howard Univ, Washington DC BS Pharmacy 1946-50. **Career:** Sampson's Pharmacy, owner. **Orgs:** Pres NC Old N St Pharm Soc; mem-at-large NPhA; Incorp Chtr Stockholder Gtwy Bank; mem Amer Pharm Assn; Natl Assn of Retail Druggists; mem Greensboro Med Soc; Greensboro Soc of Pharm; Omega Psi Phi Frat; Natl Pharm Assn; UMLA; Greensboro C of C. **Military Serv:** AUS combat infantry. **Home Addr:** 4608 Splitrail Ct, Greensboro, NC 27406.

SAMPSON, RONALD ALVIN
Advertising executive. **Personal:** Born Nov 13, 1933, Charlottesville, VA; son of Lucile Mills Martin and Percy Sampson; married Norvelle Johnson Smapson, Aug 8, 1959; children: David, Cheryl. **Educ:** DePaul U, BS commerce 1956. **Career:** Ebony Mag, adv sales rep 1958-63; Foote Cone & Belding Advert, merchandising supr 1963-66; Tatham Laird Kudner Advert, partner/mgmnt supr 1966-78; Burrell Advert, exec vice pres 1978-81, senior vice president, 1990-; D'Arcy MacManus Masius Advert, sr vp, 1981-89. **Orgs:** Advisor Am Assn of Advert Agencies 1972-; deacon, Chicago United, 1990-; vice president/board of director, Community Renewal Soc, 1973-. **Honors/Awds:** Vp bd of dir Community Renewal Soc 1973-; mem Chicago Forum 1978-. **Military Serv:** AUS sp 4 1956-58. **Home Addr:** 6715 S Oglesby, Chicago, IL 60649. **Business Addr:** Senior Vice President, Dir Development, Burrell Advertising Inc, 20 N Michigan Ave, Chicago, IL 60602.

SAMPSON, THOMAS GATEWOOD
Attorney. **Personal:** Born Oct 4, 1946, Durham, NC; son of Daniel & Claretta (deceased) Sampson; married Jacquelyn Sampson, MD, Jun 5, 1968; children: Thomas G II, Alia J. **Educ:** Morehouse College, BA, 1968; University of NC, School of Law, JD, 1971. **Career:** Thomas, Kennedy, Sampson & Patterson, managing partner, 1971-. **Orgs:** NC & Georgia Bar Assn; Natl Bar Assn, regional dir, 1974-75, mem, currently; Atlanta Council of Younger Lawyers, vp, 1974-75; Gate City Bar Assn, pres, 1977; Atlanta Legal Aid Society, 2nd vp, 1979; Georgia Supreme Court Commission on Racial & Ethnic Bias; Atlanta Bar Assn, bd of dirs, 1992-93; State Bar of Georgia, bd of governors, 1994-. **Honors/Awds:** American Bd of Trial Advocates, inducted, 1993; Bleckley Inn of the American Inns of Court, Master; Logan Inn of the American Inns of Court, Master; Omega Psi Phi, Psi Chap, Man of the Year, 1991. **Business Addr:** Sr Partner, Thomas, Kennedy, Sampson & Patterson, 55 Marietta St NW, Ste 1600, Atlanta, GA 30303, (404)699-4503.

SAMUEL, FREDERICK E.
Government official. **Personal:** Born Jan 22, 1924. **Educ:** McGill U, BS 1949; NY U, MA 1949; Fordham U, LLB 1953. **Career:** NY City, city ofcl; Atty, pvt prac. **Orgs:** Mem NY City Counc 1974; chmn bd Haryou Act Dist Ldr Dem Party 1971; chmn NY Co Dem Com 1973; NY Bar 1954; mem Harlem Lawyers Assn 1966-68. **Business Addr:** 2315 7th Ave, New York, NY 10030.

SAMUEL, JASPER H.
Printing company executive. **Personal:** Born Dec 13, 1944, Brooklyn, NY; son of Ruby Samuel and Frederick Samuel. **Career:** Jasper Samuel Printing Co, president, currently. **Orgs:** NAACP. **Military Serv:** US Air Force, lt, 1966. **Business Addr:** President, Jasper Samuel Printing Co, 406 W 31st St, Ste 12W, New York, NY 10001, (212)239-9544.

SAMUEL, LOIS S.
Educator (retired). **Personal:** Born May 26, 1925, Boston, MA; widowed; children: David, Judith. **Educ:** Simmons Coll, BS; Columbia Univ Sch, SSW, soc wrk. **Career:** Leake & Watts Childrens Home, social worker 1947-49; Youth Consultant Serv, social worker 1949-51; New York City Bd Educ Bureau, child guidance 1955-73, suprv 1973-79; District 29 Drug Abuse Prevention & Educ Program, dir, 1971-79; Queens High School Unit, clinical supervisor, 1979-85. **Orgs:** Academy of Certified Social Workers; Nat Assn Soc Wrkrs; Nat Assn Blk Soc Wrkrs; NAACP, br pres 1972-76; Com Adv Cncl; Hempstead Sch Bd; bd mem, Wndhm Chldrns Svc; trustee, Congreg Ch S Hempstead; Delta Sigma Theta Sor; past pres, Nassau Alm Chpt. **Honors/Awds:** Simmons Honor Soc Num Publs in Field. **Home Addr:** 243 Carolina Ave, Hempstead, NY 11550.

SAMUELS, ANNETTE JACQUELINE
Public affairs consultant. **Personal:** Born Jul 27, 1935, New York, NY; daughter of Mattie Annette Lindsay Duke and Fred Douglas Duke Jr; divorced; children: Linda, Shelly, Angelique (deceased), Micheal, Douglas, Melvin. **Educ:** New York U; New Sch for Soc Rsrch; Sch of Visual Arts; Amer U; Harvard University, JFK School of Government, Cambridge, MA, sr exec fellow, 1987, MPA, 1989. **Career:** Essence Mag, fashion editor 1969-70; Family Circle Mag, asst fashion editor 1970-71; Tuesday Publ, sr editor 1972-73; Continental Group, coor envir affairs 1973-74; Community News Svc, exec ed 1974-76; freelance jrnlst 1976-77; Women's Div NYS Exec Chamber, assoc dir pub info 1977-79; The White House, asst presidential press sec 1979-81; City of Washington, Mayor's Office, press secretary to the mayor, 1981-87; public affairs/relations consultant, 1990-92; DC Commission for Women, executive director, 1992-94. **Orgs:** Women of Washington; Women in Comm Inc; Coalition of 100 Black Women; Capital Press Club. **Honors/Awds:** Comm Serv Awd, Natl Assn of Media Women 1976.

SAMUELS, CHARLOTTE
Educator. **Personal:** Born May 27, 1948, Philadelphia, PA. **Educ:** Central State Univ, BS Educ 1969; Temple Univ, MEd 1973. **Career:** School District of Philadelphia, mathematics chairperson, currently. **Orgs:** Mem Assoc for Supervision & Curriculum Development, Natl Council of Teachers of Math, Assoc of Teachers of Math of Philadelphia and Vicinity, Black Women's Educ Alliance, Assoc of Professional & Exec Women, Joint Center for Political Studies, COBBE; mem NAACP, Big Sisters of America, Campaign Comm for State Rep Dwight Evans; volunteer Victim of Crime Program; mem Natl Forum for Black Public Administrators Philadelphia Chapt. **Military Serv:** AUS Reserves Sp5 3 yrs; Civil Affairs Awd for Disting Svcs. **Home Addr:** 9 Plum Ct, Lafayette Hill, PA 19444-2503.

SAMUELS, EVERETT PAUL
Company executive. **Personal:** Born Aug 27, 1958, Tulsa, OK; son of Gwendolyn Verone Busby Samuels and Chester R Samuels; married Patricia Ann Harris Samuels, Sep 4, 1982; children: Everett Paul II, Paige Noelle. **Educ:** Central State Univ, BS 1980. **Career:** Westin Hotel, Tulsa, OK, hotel management, 1980-82; Xerox Corp, sr marketing rep 1983-84, marketing exec 1984-85, account exec 1985-86; Progressive Mgmt Assocs, exec vice pres 1985-; EPS Management Services, Tulsa, OK, pres/owner, 1989-; Dean Witter, vp, 1991-. **Orgs:** Mem, tutor Tulsa Public Schools 1982-; bd dirs 1984-, pres 1987-89 Tulsa Economic Dev Corp; asst treasurer Bd of Trustees 1985-, assistance sec Deacon Bd 1986-, Friendship Baptist Church; mem Phi Mu Alpha Fraternity, NAACP; volunteer United Negro College Fund; bd mem Sickle Cell Anemia Foundation 1987-; bd mem Gilcrease Hills Homeowners Assoc 1989-; pres, Tulsa Economic Dev Corp, 1990-; board member, North Tulsa Heritage Foundation, 1990-. **Honors/Awds:** Inter-Univ Counsel/State of OH. **Home Addr:** 1814 N Xenophon Ave, Tulsa, OK 74127. **Business Addr:** President, EPS Management Services, PO Box 27671, Tulsa, OK 74149-0671.

SAMUELS, JAMES E.
Business executive, land developer. **Personal:** Born Jun 9, 1928, Detroit; married Eleanor M; children: 6. **Educ:** Brooklyn Coll. **Career:** VI Civil Rights Commission, exec dir 1982-; V I Trnscrbn Arwys, dir 1968-70; V I Pt Auth, asst to exec dir 1966-68; V I, asst to atty gen 1961-66; radio TV 1961-; Rltns Inc, self emplyd pub rltns advrtsng cmmnctn splst. **Orgs:** Pres Tmrnd Ntch Ltd St John; vice pres bd dirs USVI Nat Assn TV & Radio Announcers 1966-72; Cubmaster BSA 1972-74; mem Prsch Club Am; Early Fd V8 Club Am. **Honors/Awds:** Cubmaster of Yr 1973; Apprctn & Excellnce Awd Nat Assn TV & Radio Announcers 1969. **Military Serv:** AUS sgt 1950-52.

SAMUELS, LESLIE EUGENE
Government official. **Personal:** Born Nov 12, 1929, St Croix, Virgin Islands of the United States; son of Annamartha Venetia Ford (deceased) and Henry Francis Samuels; married Reather James; children: Leslie Jr, Venetia, Yvette, Philip. **Educ:** NY Univ/Carnegie Hall Music Sc, BM 1956; Blackstone Sch of Law, LLB, JD 1969-75; Columbia Pacific Univ, MBA, PhD 1981-85. **Career:** Van Dyke Studios, concert artist 1956-66; NY Dept of Housing Preservation & Develop, dir of city serv 1966-; New York State, bandmaster 1967-76, committeeman/representative, district leader, 86th AD, Bronx County, New York City, 1969-73; Massachusetts Institute of Technology, Sloan Management Review, 1986; Samuels Institute, pres/CEO, 1993; Summitt Univ of LA, prof/mentor, 1994; St Martin's Coll & Seminary, prof/mentor, 1995; College of Philosophy & Education, pres/CEO, 1997-. **Orgs:** Comm bd mem Astor Home for Children 1975-; mem Amer Mgmt Assoc 1984-; bd chmn Samuels & Co Inc 1985-; mem NY/NJ Minority Purchasing Cncl 1986, Natl Black MBA Assoc 1986-; Harvard Business Review Harvard Grad Sch of Business Admin 1987; mem Intl Traders 1988-90; task force mem Republican Presidential Task Force 1989; natl mem The Smithsonian Associates 1989-90; Natl Republican Senatorial Committee, 1994; Penthouse Dance & Drama Theatre, 1949. **Honors/Awds:** Performance Role of Dr Herdal in Henrik Ibsen's Master Builder 1950; Concert Artist Tenor Carnegie Hall 1951-; mem of cast in Langston Hughes', Simply Heavenly 1957; Marketing Thesis Columbia Pacific Univ 1984; Presidential Merit Award, Republican Presidential Task Force 1989. **Military Serv:** AUS pvt 1st class 2 yrs. **Home Addr:** 2814 Bruner Ave, Bronx, NY 10469. **Business Addr:** Dir, Dept of Housing Preservation, 100 Gold St, New York, NY 10007.

SAMUELS, MARCIA L.
Real estate broker. **Personal:** Born Dec 13, 1937, Columbus, OH; daughter of Flora Lee Agnew Samuels and Wilson Samuels; children: Kyle. **Educ:** Ohio State University, Columbus, OH, BA, communications, 1955-59. **Career:** Burns Public Relations, Cleveland, OH, media manager, 1963-70; M L Samuels & Co, Columbus, OH, president, 1981-83; McMullan Realty Inc, Beachwood, OH, managing broker, 1973-. **Orgs:** Member, Cleveland Assoc of Real Estate Brokers, Board of Directors CAREB, 1984-; member, Sickle Cell Association Board of Directors. **Honors/Awds:** Dedicated Service Award, CAREB, 1989; Realtist of the Year Award, CAREB, 1990. **Home Addr:** 3689 Gridley Rd, Shaker Heights, OH 44122. **Business Addr:** Managing Broker, McMullan Realty Inc, 17017 Miles Ave, Cleveland, OH 44128.

SAMUELS, OLIVE CONSTANCE
Educator, nurse manager. **Personal:** Born Aug 30, 1926, Montclair, NJ; daughter of Roslyn M Samuels and Cyril Samuels (deceased). **Educ:** Attended, Harlem Hosp Ctr Sch of Nursing; Seton Hall Univ So Orange NJ, BSN 1965, MA 1972; Columbia Univ, post grad courses; Montclair State Tech Coll, post grad courses. **Career:** Possaic Co Comm Coll NJ, prof 1979-; Newark Beth Israel Med, pen nurse spec 1978-79; Bell Lab Mrry Hill NJ, ind nursing 1977-78; Long Island U, asst prof 1974-79; Essx Co Comm Coll Newark, instr of nurses 1970-74; Harlem Hosp Cntr, inst of nurs stud 1959-70, head nurse 1952-58, staff nurse 1950-52. **Orgs:** Mem, AKA Omicron XI Omega NJ 1989-; Baselius Omicron Chap Chi Eta Phi Sor Inc 1978-80; mem, Tau Chi Chapter NJ Nursing Sorority Chi Eta Phi Inc 1981-; mem, ANA NY Bus Prof Women; mem, Alumni Assoc Seton Hall Univ, Harlem Hosp Ctr School of Nursing; mem, YWCA, The Sickle Cell Disease Foundation of Greater NY; pres/choir mem, Trinity Episcopal Church; member, ELW. **Business Addr:** Clinical Coordinator, St Mary's Hospital, 211 Pennington Ave, Passaic, NJ 07055.

SAMUELS, ROBERT J.
Business executive. **Personal:** Born Aug 14, 1938, Philadelphia, PA; son of Lorraine Samuels and Hubert Samuels; divorced; children: Robert Jr, Anthony, Christopher. **Educ:** Attended Amer Inst of Banking, NY Inst of Credit, NY Univ; graduate Stonier Graduate School of Banking. **Career:** Manufacturers Hanover Trust Co, NY, credit investigator, 1969-71, asst sec, 1971-73, asst vice pres, 1973-75, vice pres, 1975-; 1st Pennsylvania Bank, former loan mgr. **Orgs:** Pres Natl Assn of Urban Bankers; dir NY Urban League; chmn United Negro Coll Funds NY Corp Matching Gifts Program; visiting prof, Natl Urban League Black Exec Exchange Program; trustee, NY State Higher Educ Serv Corp, 1987; chair, HESC Audit Comm; bd member, Aaron Davis Hall; chair, NYC Bd of Educ Adopt-a-Class Corp advisory comm. **Honors/Awds:** Named Philadelphia's Outstanding Jaycee, 1968; Robert J Samuels Founder's Award established by Natl Assn of Urban Bankers, 1984; Outstanding Citizen Award, United Negro Coll Fund, 1987; Roy Wilkins Humanitarian Award, NAACP, 1988. **Military Serv:** USAF 1956-60. **Business Addr:** Vice President, Manufacturers Hanover Trust, 270 Park Avenue, New York, NY 10017.

SAMUELS, RONALD S.
Attorney. **Personal:** Born Jun 17, 1941, Chicago, IL; son of Lena and Peter; married Melva; children: 4. **Educ:** Chicago State Univ, BA 1964; John Marshall Law Sch, JD 1969. **Career:** Chicago Bd Educ, teacher 1964-69; Attorney, 1969-70; Leadership Council for Metro Open Housing, chief trial lawyer 1970-73; Cook Co States Atty Office, chief fraud div 1974-77; Ronald S Samuels and Associates, partner/attorney. **Orgs:** Natl, Cook Co, Chicago, IL State, Amer, Bar Assns; dir Legal Oppor Scholarship Prog; chmn Consumer Task Force; Chicago Urban League; Kappa Alpha Psi Alumni Chapt; CSU Alumni Assn; PUSH. **Honors/Awds:** Amer Jurisprudence Awd; William Ming Award; Richard E Westbrooks; PUSH Outstanding Public Service; Distinguished Service Award, Natl Bar Assn. **Business Addr:** Attorney, Ronald S Samuels & Associates, 111 W. Washington, Chicago, IL 60602, (312)263-6600.

SAMUELS, WILFRED D.
Educator. **Personal:** Born Feb 7, 1947, Puerto Limon, Costa Rica; son of Lena Jones Samuels and Noel L Samuels, Sr; married Barbara Fikes Samuels, Jun 1980; children: Michael Alain Fikes-Samuels, Detavio Ricardo Fikes-Samuels. **Educ:** Univ of California, Riverside, CA, BA, 1971; University of Iowa, Iowa City, IA, MA, PhD, 1971-77. **Career:** Univ of Colorado, Boulder, CO, asst prof, 1978-85; Benjamin Banneker Honors Coll, Prairie View AM, TX, assoc prof, 1985-87; Univ of Utah, Salt Lake City, UT, assoc prof, 1987-. **Orgs:** Popular Culture; MLA; Am Literature Assn. **Honors/Awds:** Ford Foundation Post Doctoral Fellow, Ford, 1984, 1985; CAAS UCLA, Postdoctoral Fellow, 1982, 1983; NEH Symposium Grants, 1980, 1984, 1989; Outstanding Teacher Award, several, 1978-84; Ramona Cannon Award for teaching Excellence in the Humanities, 1992; Student's Choice Award, 1993; The University of Utah, Distinguished Teaching Award, 1994. **Business Addr:** Professor, Department of English, University of Utah, 3407 LNCO, Salt Lake City, UT 84112, (801)581-5206.

SANCHEZ, SONIA BENITA
Author, educator. **Personal:** Born Sep 9, 1934, Birmingham, AL; divorced; children: Morani, Mungu, Anita. **Educ:** Hunter College, BA, 1955; New York University, 1957. **Career:** San Francisco State College, instructor, 1966-67; University of Pittsburgh, instructor, 1968-69; Rutgers University, assistant

professor, 1969-70; Manhattan Community College, assistant professor, 1970-72; Amherst College, associate professor, 1973-75; Temple University, poet, professor. **Orgs:** Pennsylvania Council on the Arts; contributing editor to "Black Scholar" and "Journal of African Studies"; advisory board, SISA, MADRE, and WILPF. **Honors/Awds:** PEN Writing Award, New York City, 1969; National Institute of Arts & Letters Grant, 1970; Honorary PhD, Wilberforce University, 1972; NEA Recipient, Washington, DC ,1978-79; American Book Award for "Homegirls and Handgrenades"; National Endowment for the Arts, Lucretia Mott Award, 1984; Pennsylvania Coalition of 100 Black Women, Outstanding Arts Award; National Black Caucus of State Legislators, Community Service Award; American Book Award, 1985; Honorary PhD, Trinity College, 1987; Governor's Award for Excellence in the Humanities, 1988; Women International League for Peace and Freedom, Peace and Freedom Award, 1989; Pew Fellowship in the Arts, 1992-93; Honorary PhD, Baruch College, 1993. **Special Achievements:** Author of: Homecoming, It's a New Day, We a BaddDDD People, Love Poems, I've Been a Woman: New and Selected Poems, A Sound Investment and Other Stories, Homegirls and Handgrenades, Under a Soprano Sky, Wounded in the House of a Friend; edited two anthologies: We Be Word Sorcerers: 25 Stories by Black Americans and 360 Degrees of Blackness Coming at You; author of play "Sister Sonji," Joseph Papps Public Theatre, New York; author, Does Your House Have Lions?, 1997. **Business Addr:** Professor, Temple University, Women's Studies, Philadelphia, PA 19122-2585.

SANDERLIN, JAMES B.
Judge. **Personal:** Born Jan 2, 1929, Petersburg, VA. **Educ:** Howard U, BS 1950; Boston U, 1957, JD 1962; Nat Coll of the St Jdcry, 1973. **Career:** Cir Ct St of FL, co jdg; Fed Dist Ct, jdg 1965; US Ct of Appeals 50th Cir, jdg 1966. **Orgs:** Past chmn Civil Ser Comm City of St Ptrsbrg; past pres St Ptrsbrg Cncl on Hum Rel; mem FL Adv Comm to US Comm on Cvl Rghts; past bd mem Fam & Chldrns Serv Inc; Adult Mtl Hlth Clnc; 1st pres Pnlls Co Hdstrt Inc. **Military Serv:** USAR 2nd lt 1950-53. **Business Addr:** Judge, 2nd District Court, 801 Twiggs St, Tampa, FL 33602.

SANDERS, ARCHIE, JR.
Councilman. **Personal:** Born Sep 6, 1937, Hughes, AR; married Bernice Dawkines; children: Tommy, Willie C, Bonnie, Archie III, Theresa, Diann. **Educ:** Kansas Comm Jr Coll, attended. **Career:** Adult educ adv council, 1972-73; Bonner Springs KS, councilman. **Orgs:** Mem Jaycees, Police Reserve, Fire Dept; bd dir C&D Ctr; treas NAACP. **Honors/Awds:** NAACP Achievement Awd 1971. **Home Addr:** 14011 Stillwell Rd, Bonner Springs, KS 66012-9530.

SANDERS, AUGUSTA SWANN
Health services administrator (retired). **Personal:** Born Jul 22, 1932, Alexandria, LA; daughter of Elizabeth Thompson Swann and James Swann; divorced. **Educ:** Provident Hospital School of Nursing/Morgan State Coll, nursing 1953-56. **Career:** Augustus F Hawkins Comprehensive Mental Health Ctr, mental health services coordinator, retired; First Black Nurse, Huntington Hospital, Pasadena, CA; VA Hospital, Brentwood, Los Angeles, acting evening supv; Los Angeles Amer Red Cross, venipuncture nurse; Public Health Nurse, Washington, DC; Los Angeles County Sheriff's Dept, staff nurse, mental health senior counselor. **Orgs:** Pres MD State Student Nurses 1955-56; sec Mu Chi 1975; mem Sen Diane Watson's Comm on Health Problems 1980-; mem CA State Board of Medical Quality Assurance 1981-; mem Assemblyman Mike Roos' Comm on Women's Issues 1982-; pres Wilshire Bus and Professional Women 1982-83; comm LA Unified school board 1985; pres Los Angeles Sunset Dist CA Fedn of Bus and Professional Women 1988-89, San Orco District, membership chairman, 1992-93; vice pres Calfornia Fedn of Bus and Professional Women 1995-96; mem Victor Valley African-American Chamber of Commerce 1995-; founding mem Southern CA Black Nurses Assn, 1960; founding mem Victor Valley League of Women Voters, 1960. **Honors/Awds:** Woman of the Year, Crenshaw LaTijera BPW, 1985; Woman of the Year, Wilshire BPW, 1987; Woman of the Year, Victor Valley BPW, 1994-95. **Home Addr:** 13338 Apple Blossom Ln, Apple Valley, CA 92308-5415.

SANDERS, BARBARA A.
Automotive company executive. **Personal:** Born in New Orleans, LA; daughter of Arma L Atkins Miles and Otis Miles; married Joe Sanders Jr. **Educ:** Southern Univ, BS 1969; Rutgers Univ, MS 1972; Indiana Exec Program, Certificate 1981-82; Harvard Univ PMD Program, Certificate 1985. **Career:** General Motors Corp, composites materials dept head 1979-81, composites processing manager 1981-83, CAD/CAM dir 1983-85, artificial intelligence dir 1985-87, advanced manufacturing engineering dir 1987-89, program mgr, 1989-90; Truck & Bus Baltimore Assembly Plant, Paint System, General Motors Tech Center, Advanced Engineering Staff, director, 1991-. **Orgs:** Mem Engrg Soc of Detroit 1981-86; mem Soc of Mfg Engrs 1983-86; key executive GM/Southern Univ Key Inst Program 1984-86; chairperson entrepreneurs comm Minority Tech Council of MI 1985-89; class sec Harvard Univ PMD-49 1985-87; mem Women Economic Club. **Honors/Awds:** Outstanding Alumni Southern Univ Alumni Detroit Chap 1982, 86; Disting Alumni NAFEO 1986; numerous articles/presentations in Tech Area, Lasers, CAD/CAM, AI, Composite Materials 1979-86; Honorary Doctorate, Southern Univ 1988. **Business Addr:** Director, Advanced Development, Inland Fisher Guide Divisional Engineering, 6600 E 12 Mile Rd, Warren, MI 48092-5905.

SANDERS, BARRY
Professional football player. **Personal:** Born Jul 16, 1968, Wichita, KS; children: Barry James II. **Educ:** Oklahoma State Univ, attended. **Career:** Detroit Lions, running back, 1989-. **Honors/Awds:** Sporting News NFL Rookie of the Year, 1989; NFL All-Star Team, Sporting News, 1989; Heisman Trophy winner, 1988; College Football Player of the Year, Sporting News, 1988; running back, Sporting News College All-America Team, 1988; kick returner, Sporting News College All-America Team, 1987; NFL Players Assn, NFC Most Valuable Player, 1991; Pro Bowl, 1989, 1990, 1991, 1992, 1993, 1994, 1995, 1996, 1997; NFL MVP, 1992, 1998; Associated Press, Offensive Player of the Year, 1994; NFL, Player of the Year, 1998. **Business Addr:** Professional Football Player, Detroit Lions, 1200 Featherstone Rd, Pontiac, MI 48342, (248)335-4131.

SANDERS, CHARLES LIONEL
Educator. **Personal:** Born Aug 10, 1936, Lakeland, FL; son of Eleather Sanders and Willie A Sanders; divorced. **Educ:** Howard Univ Coll of Liberal Arts, Bachelor 1959, Schl of Social Work, Masters 1961; NY Univ Grad Schl of Public Admin, Doctorate 1972. **Career:** WYCB Radio Wash DC, dir of pub affairs 1978-86; McKinley-Penn Comm Schls, prog dir 1982-84; DC Pub Schls, spec asst supr of schls 1982-84; pres Natl Capital Radio Corp 1983-; Amer Council of Educ, consult 1984-; Univ of DC, professor, College of Business and Public Management 1985-. **Orgs:** Consult, Control Data Inst Arlington VA 1984-85, Amer Council on Educ Wash DC 1984-85, Opport Advertising Inc Wash DC 1984; Amer Soc of Pub Admin Howard Univ Alumni 1984; Amer Mgmt Assc Capital Press Club 1984; Natl Black Media Coalition NY Univ Alumni Assc 1984; bd of dirs, Metropolitan Boys & Girls Club, Natl Capital Radio Corp; pres Natl Capital Broadcast 1985. **Honors/Awds:** Mental Health Ach Award Psych Inst 1982; CEBA Award 1981; Man of the Year, Annual Love Club Awd 1986; Fellow, Center for Applied & Urban Research Univ of DC 1988-89; Fellow, Amer Assn of State Coll and Univ-Japanese Studies Inst 1989. **Military Serv:** AUS Med Srv Corp cpt 1962-64.

SANDERS, CHRIS
Professional football player. **Personal:** Born May 8, 1972, Denver, CO; married Stacie; children: Chris Jr. **Educ:** Ohio State Univ, attended. **Career:** Houston Oilers, wide receiver, 1995-96; Tennessee Oilers, 1997-. **Business Addr:** Professional Football Player, Tennessee Oilers, c/o Baptist Sports Park, 7640 H 70-5, Nashville, TN 37221.

SANDERS, DEION LUWYNN
Professional football player. **Personal:** Born Aug 9, 1967, Fort Myers, FL; married; children: Diondra, Deion Luwynn Jr. **Educ:** Florida State Univ, attended. **Career:** New York Yankees, outfielder, 1989-90; Atlanta Braves, outfielder, 1991-94; Atlanta Falcons, defensive back, 1989-93; San Francisco 49ers, 1994; Cincinnati Reds, 1994-95; San Francisco Giants, 1995; Dallas Cowboys, 1995-. **Honors/Awds:** Jim Thorpe Award; Pro Bowl, 1991, 1992, 1993, 1994, 1995, 1996; NFL Defensive Player of the Year, 1994. **Business Addr:** Professional Football Player, Dallas Cowboys, 1 Cowboys Pkwy, Irving, TX 75063, (214)556-9900.

SANDERS, DORI
Author, farmer. **Personal:** Born 1935, York, SC. **Career:** Author, peach farmer in South Carolina, banquet manager. **Honors/Awds:** Author, Clover, 1990; Her Own Place, 1993; Lillian Smith Book Award, 1990. **Business Addr:** Author, Clover, c/o Algonquin Books, PO Box 2225, Chapel Hill, NC 27515.

SANDERS, FRANK VONDEL
Professional football player. **Personal:** Born Feb 17, 1973, Fort Lauderdale, FL; married Tracy. **Educ:** Auburn, attended. **Career:** Arizona Cardinals, wide receiver, 1995-. **Special Achievements:** Selected in the 2nd round/47th overall pick in the 1995 NFL Draft. **Business Addr:** Professional Football Player, Arizona Cardinals, 8701 S Hardy, Tempe, AZ 85284, (602)379-0101.

SANDERS, GEORGE L.
Physician. **Personal:** Born Jul 4, 1942, Vidalia, GA; son of Eva Mae Sanders (deceased) and Felton Sanders (deceased); married Frances; children: G Eldridge, Cleaver. **Educ:** Morehouse Coll, 1965; Univ Miami Sch Med, 1969; Jackson Meml Hosp, intern 1970, resd 1974, fellow cardiology 1976; Air War College, graduate, 1992. **Career:** Private practice, phy internal med & cardiology; US Air Force, Eglin AFB, Cardiopulmonary Laboratory, director, 1992-. **Orgs:** Life mem Phi Beta Sigma Frat; Phi Delta Epsilon; bd dir Spectrum Prog Inc 1977; associate clinical prof Univ Miami Sch Med; former vice pres Greater Miami Heart Assn; American College of Physicians; former medical dir North Shore Medical Center Cardiology 1985-90; NAACP, life mbr. **Honors/Awds:** American College of Cardiology, Fellow, 1992; American Bd of Internal Med, Diplomate; Student of Yr Phi Beta Sigma, 1966; Natl Med Assn, Student Awd, 1976; Natl Med Foundation, Fellowship, 1965-69. **Military Serv:** US Army, capt, 1970-72, US Air Force, lt colonel, 1990-; US Army, Commendation Medal, 1972; US Air Force Commendation Medal, 1992. **Business Addr:** USAF, 646 Medical Group (SGH), 2825 Boatner Rd, PSC Box 7193, Eglin A F B, FL 32542-5300.

SANDERS, GLENN CARLOS
Consultant. **Personal:** Born May 24, 1949, Bastrop, TX; son of Marjorie Sanders and Charles Sanders, Sr; married Catherine McCarty; children: Chandra, Brian. **Educ:** Texas Southern Univ, attended 1967-69; California Baptist Coll, BS 1987; CNE (certified netware engineer), 1995. **Career:** Zales Jewelers Inc, asst mgr 1973-76; TRW Information Svcs, Programmer analyst 1976-80; Riverside Co Data Processing, data base analyst 1980-83; Transamerica Life Companies, senior systems programmer, 1983-95; Sandcastle Enterprises, consultant, 1995-. **Orgs:** Mem Phi Beta Sigma 1968-, Planetary Soc 1985-; vice pres Southwestern Information Mgmt Users Group 1986-88; bd mem Parents Against Gangs 1989-92. **Honors/Awds:** Natl Student Merit Qualifying Test Commended Candidate; Who's Who in Amer High School Students 1967; Deans List Freshmen Year TX Southern Univ 1968; Top DivSales Zales Jewelers 1973; 1st Place State Extemporaneous Speaking Competition 1967; 2nd Place State Debate Competition 1967. **Military Serv:** USN machinist mate 3rd class 2 yrs. **Business Addr:** Lan Administrator, Riverside County, 4080 Lemon St, 10th Fl, Riverside, CA 92501.

SANDERS, GWENDOLYN W.
Educational administrator. **Personal:** Born Dec 17, 1937, St Louis, MO; daughter of Burnette D Harris Fletcher and Adolph Fisher; married Gordon B; children: Darrell F, Romona R Sanders Fullman, Jocelyn M. **Educ:** St Louis U, BS 1956; Harris Tchrs Coll, BA 1962; St Louis U, MEd 1967; Nova Univ, EdD; Univ of DE & Glassboro St Coll, undergrad work; graduate inst, Harvard. **Career:** DE Tech & Comm Coll, dean of development, 1989-, dean of student serv 1973-89; Univ of DE, instr 1973-75; DE Tech & Comm Coll, plng coord 1972-73; Cty Demonstration Agy, educ cons-planner 1969-72; St Peters Cathedral-Wilmington Pub Sch, tchr dir 1968-70; Oppor Indust Cntr, tchr 1969-70; Lincoln Pub Sch, tchr 1966-68; St Louis Pub Sch, master tchr 1962-68; Harris Tchrs Coll St Louis, lab asst 1959-62; pvt phy St Louis, med tech 1956-59. **Orgs:** Delta Sigma Theta; National Women's Political Caucus; United Way Critical Issues Taskforce; Headstart Adv Bd; vice pres Educ Com NAACP; consult US Dept of Justice; pres, Northeast Council Black Amer Affairs; bd mem, Natl Council Black Amer Affairs, AACJC; consultant, NJ Dept of Higher Educ, Middle States Commn Higher Educ; reader/evaluator, US Dept of Higher Educ; vice pres, Brandywine Professional Assn, AACD, 1980-; DCPA; NAFSA; AAHE; NCRD; People to People Intl; exec bd, Delaware Academy for Youth; field reader, Oklahoma Board of Regents. **Honors/Awds:** Developed bilingual bi-cultural day care center, 1970; developed and initiated ESL Prog, Delaware Tech, 1976; Outstanding Achievers Award-Education, BPA, 1989; Outstanding Community Service Award, Alliance of Ministers Businesses and Agencies, 1988; Outstanding Community Service Award, Delaware Head Start, 1988; developed freshman orientation course, human potential and career & life planning courses; developed and initiated career centers Stanton and Wilmington campuses. **Business Addr:** Dean of Development, Delaware Technical & Community Coll, 400 Stanton Christiana Rd., Newark, DE 19713.

SANDERS, HANK
State senator, attorney. **Personal:** Born Oct 28, 1942, Baldwin County, AL; son of Ola Mae Norman Sanders and Sam Sanders; married Rose M Gaines Sanders, Jan 23, 1970; children: Malika A, Kindaka J, Ainka M, Charles, Maurice. **Educ:** Talladega Coll, BA 1967; Harvard Law School, JD 1970. **Career:** Stucky Lumber Co, saw mill worker 1960-61; Honeywell, elec tech 1962-63; Chestnut Senator, Sanders Sanders & Pettway, attorney 1972-; Alabama State Senate, 1983-. **Orgs:** Harvard Black Law Students Association, past president; co-founder, former pres AL Lawyers Assn 1973; co-founder, former pres, Campaign for a New South 1982; co-founder, former pres, Alabama New South Coalition 1988-90; co-founder, former chairman, National Voting Rights Museum and Institute; co-founder & former board member, 21 Century Youth Leadership Project; co-founder & former chairman, CARE (Coalitions of Alabamians Reforming Education). **Honors/Awds:** Catherine Waldell Award, 1964; Felix Frankfuther Award, Harvard Law School, 1967; Middle East & Africa Fellowship Ford Found 1970-; Reginald Heber Smith Fellowship Legal Service Corp 1971; 2nd Annual Awd for Outstanding Service Natl Assn of Landowners 1979; Outstanding Senator, 1986; New South Leadership Award, 1989; Lawyer of the Year National Conference of Black Lawyers, 1990; The Senate Finance and Taxation Committee Education Fund, chairman, 1995-; Martin Luther King Community Svc Awd. **Business Addr:** Senator, Alabama State Senate, PO Box 1305, Selma, AL 36701, (334)875-9264.

SANDERS, HOBART C.
Physician, surgeon. **Personal:** Born Aug 19, 1929, Boley, OK; son of Thelma Curtis Sanders and Hobart M Sanders; married Maurine Lee; children: Thelma, Alice, Hobart, Jr. **Educ:** Lincoln Univ, AB 1949; Meharry Med Coll, MD 1954; Gen Hosp KC MO, Jr Internship Ob & Gyn Res. **Career:** Physician, private practice, Tulsa 1958-79. **Orgs:** Oklahoma Med Dental Pharm Assns; Natl Med Assn; Tulsa County Ob Gyn Soc; Tulsa County Med Soc; Amer Med Assn; Amer Bd Observ & Gyn; Central Assn of Ob & Gyn; YMCA; Tulsa Urban Leage; Alpha Phi Alpha; Tulsa Bd Educ 1972-; life mem NAACP; Tulsa Grnwd Bly OK C of C; fld faculty Meharry Med Coll & Univ of Oklahoma School of Med; asst state dir, Amer Assn of Retired Persons, Ok. **Honors/Awds:** American College of Obstetricians & Gynecologists, fellow. **Business Addr:** 10915 E 76th St, Tulsa, OK 74133-2621.

SANDERS, ISAAC WARREN
Educational administrator. **Personal:** Born Aug 9, 1948, Montgomery, AL; son of Bertha Lee McKenize Sanders and Hurley W Sanders Sr; married Cora Allen, May 29, 1975; children: W Machion, Christin Machael, Bryant Allen. **Educ:** Tuskegee Univ, BS 1971; Cornell Univ, MS 1973; KS State Univ, PhD 1984; Columbia Univ, New York NY, post doctoral certificate 1988. **Career:** Ft Valley State Coll, instructor/rsch assoc 1973-75; Claflin Coll, federal relations officer 1975-76; AL State Univ, dir fed relations 1976-82; Woodrow Wilson Natl Fellowship Found, vice pres 1984-86; Natl Action Council for Minorities in Engrg, dir 1986-90, vice pres 1990-91; Tuskegee Univ, Tuskegee, AL, vp emss, 1991-96; AL State Univ, exec asst to the pres, staff asst to the bd of trustees, 1996-. **Orgs:** Mem Natl Soc for Fundraising Execs 1980-; bd mem Greater Trenton NJ Mental Health 1984-; vice pres and bd mem Optimist Club Lower Bucks PA 1985-; vice pres Blanton and Assocs 1986-; pres Tuskegee Univ Philadelphia Area Alumni Assn 1986-; assoc dir Northeast Region Tuskegee Alumni Assoc 1986-; mem Kappa Alpha Psi; bd of dir NAACP Bucks Co PA 1989. **Honors/Awds:** United Negro College Fund Mind Fire Award 1982; Phi Delta Kappa KS State Univ 1983; Kellogg Natl Fellowship, Kellogg Foundation, 1990-93. **Business Addr:** Executive Assistant to the President, AL State University, PO Box 271, Montgomery, AL 36101.

SANDERS, JAMES WILLIAM
Cleric. **Personal:** Born Sep 17, 1929, Union, SC; married Ruby Lee Corry; children: Jewette LaVernae, James William Jr, Ruzlin Maria. **Educ:** Benedict Coll Columbia SC, BA 1951; A&T State Univ Greensboro NC, MEd 1961; Friendship Coll Rock Hill SC, DD 1973; Morris College, LHD, 1991. **Career:** Union SC, elementary school prin 1961-65, HS asst prin 1965-72; Union Co Educ Assn, treas 1964-69; Union SC Adult Educ Prog, co coord 1970-72; Bethel Baptist Church, minister, 1949-; Island Creek Baptist Church, pastor, 1971-; J & R Fine Jewelers, owner. **Orgs:** Pres Cherokee Co Black Ministers Alliance 1965-79; mem Planning & Zoning Comm for City of Gaffney 1980-; mem Election Comm of Cherokee Co 1980-; chmn Area Agency for the Aging for 6 county region 1979-; mem Gov's Task Force to Study Health Needs of the State of SC; bd mem Habilitation Serv for Cherokee Co Inc 1981-; vice chmn Cherokee Co Comm of the Food & Shelter Emergency Fund 1984-; moderator Co Bapt Assn 1973-; finance committeeman Natl Baptist Conv of Amer 1979-; pres NAACP of Cherokee Co Gaffney SC 1962-68; exec bd mem Appalachian Council of Govts 1972-; mem Mayor's Human Relations Comm of Gaffney SC 1972-; vice pres Cherokee Co Dem Party 1978-; trustee board member, Morris Coll, Sumter, SC, 1986-94; trustee board member, South Carolina State Univ, Orangeburg, SC, 1993-; exec board member, Financial Corporation, 1988-; vice chair, trustee bd, South Carolina State University, 1996; chairman, South Carolina Appalachian Council of Government, 1996. **Honors/Awds:** Leadership Awd Boy Scouts of Amer 1960; Human Serv Awd Comm Action Prog 1971; Citizen of the Yr Awd Phi Alpha Chap Omega Psi Phi Frat Inc 1975; State of South Carolina, Palmetto Gentleman's Award, 1980; State of South Carolina, House of Representatives Award, 1994; State of South Carolina, State Senate Award, 1994; NAACP, Cherokee County Chapter, Hall of Fame, 1996. **Business Addr:** Minister, Bethel Baptist Church, 332 W Meadow St, Gaffney, SC 29340.

SANDERS, JOSEPH STANLEY
Attorney. **Personal:** Born Aug 9, 1942, Los Angeles, CA; son of Eva Sanders and Hays Sanders; married Melba Binion, Mar 17, 1984; children: Edward Moore, Justin Hays, Alexandria Thedarin, Chelsea Winifred. **Educ:** Whittier Coll, BA 1963; Magdalen Coll Oxford Univ, BA/MA 1965; Yale Law Sch, LLB 1968. **Career:** Yale Univ Transitional Year, dir pro tem & instr 1967-68; Western Center on Law & Poverty Los Angeles, staff atty 1968-69; Lawyer's Com for Civil Rights Under Law LA, exec dir 1969-70; Wyman Bautzer Finell Rothman & Kuchel Beverly Hills, assoc 1969-71; Rosenfeld Lederer Jacobs & Sanders Beverly Hills, partner 1971-72; Sanders & Tisdale LA, partner 1972-77; Sanders & Dickerson Los Angeles, atty partner 1978-94; Barnes, McGhee & Pryce, currently. **Orgs:** Co-founder Watts Summer Festival 1966; mem Amer Bar Assn 1969-; mem bd of dirs W LA United Way 1970; mem LA World Affairs Council 1971-; trustee Ctr for Law in the Pub Interest 1973-80; mem bd of trustees Whittier Coll 1974-; bd of dir Econ Resources Corp 1974-; mem Mayor's Com on Cultural Affairs 1975-; mem bd of dir Amer Red Cross LA 1975-; bd of dir Arthritis Found So CA Chap 1976-; co-chmn CA Dem Party Rules Comm 1976-; pres LA Recreation & Parks Committee1986-93; mem LA Memorial Coliseum Comm 1980-; dir Black Arts Council; mem Langston Law Club LA Co Bar Assn; chmn United Way Task Force on Minority Youth Employment 1985-; NCAA Foundation, bd of trustees; Museum of Contemporary Art, Los Angeles, bd of trustees. **Honors/Awds:** Pub "I'll Never Escape the Ghetto" Ebony Mag 1967, "Rhodes Scholar Looks at South Africa" Ebony Mag 1970; Rhodes Scholarship; 1st Team NAIA All-Amer Football 1961; Small Coll NAIA Discus Champion 1963; Ten Outstanding Young Men of Amer Awd 1971; Fifty Disting Alumni Awd Los Angeles City Sch Bicentennial 1976. **Business Addr:** Attorney, Barnes, McGhee & Pryce, 333 S Grand Ave, Ste 2000, Los Angeles, CA 90071, (213)626-0999.

SANDERS, LARRY KYLE
Educator. **Personal:** Born Oct 16, 1970, Hammond, LA; son of Frank & Shirley Sanders. **Educ:** Southern Univ, BA, journalism, 1993, MA, mass communications, 1994. **Career:** Wiley College, instructor, 1997-. **Orgs:** American Assn of Univ Professors, 1997-; NAACP, 1997-; Intl Communication Assn, 1997-; Assn for Education in Journalism & Mass Communications, 1997-; Natl Assn of Black Journalists, 1997-; Prince Hall, Lodge #174, mason, 1993-; Southern Univ Alumni Federation, life mem. **Honors/Awds:** Southern Univ, Southern Univ Media Club Award, 1994. **Special Achievements:** Contributed to: Southern Univ Digest, articles and poems, 1988-94; Southern Univ Yearbook, poem, 1991; The Morning Advocate, article, 1991; Clark Atlanta Univ Panther, poem, 1996. **Home Addr:** 8100 Pines Rd, Apt 26-C, Shreveport, LA 71129, (318)688-7317. **Business Addr:** Instructor, Mass Communications, Wiley College, 711 Wiley Ave, Student Union Bldg, Rm 301, Marshall, TX 75670, (903)927-3363.

SANDERS, LAURA GREEN
Employment executive. **Personal:** Born Nov 14, 1942, Victoria, TX; daughter of Althea McNary Green and Cluster Green; married Willie Sanders; children: Laresee Sanders Harris. **Educ:** Victoria Junior Coll, attended 1968; TX State Management Develop Ctr, Managers Program 1986. **Career:** TX Employment Commn, area mgr, currently. **Orgs:** African Amer Chamber of Commerce of Victoria; Victoria Hispanic Chamber of Commerce; Victoria Area Chamber of Commerce; DeWitt County Chamber; Calhoun County Chamber; Victoria Financial Educ Coalition; Golden Crescent Private Industry Council; FW Gross Alumni; Victoria Prof Women's Group; Victoria County Sr Citizens, bd of dirs; Univ of Houston-Victoria Presidents Advisory Council; Women In Partnership for Progress; International Assn of Personnel in Employment Service; Texas Public Employee Assn; Mt Nebo Baptist Church. **Honors/Awds:** State of Texas, Outstanding Women in Texas Awards, 1995; Nominee for Outstanding Professional Development, Presented Certificate signed by Governor George Bush. **Business Addr:** Area Manager, TX Employment Commission, PO Box 2149, Victoria, TX 77902, (512)578-0341.

SANDERS, LINA
Educator. **Personal:** Born Apr 9, 1937, Johnston Co; children: Gary, Gretchen. **Educ:** Fyttvl St U, BS 1964; NC St U; E Crln U; UNC-G. **Career:** John Co Bd of Edn, tchr; Smthhfld Jr HS, tchr; John Tech Inst Sec, prt-tm instr. **Orgs:** Sec Lcl Nat Assn of Univ Wmen; past pres Lcl NC Assn of Ed; NC Assn of Ed; NEA; Assn of Clsrm Tchrs; chrpsn Polit Act Com for Ed; prlmntrn Dist 2 ACT; NCAE Commn on Frng Bnfts & Spl Serv; NCAE Professional Negoti Com; Civic Mdrntts Club; apptd commmnd to serv on bd of dir Atlntc & NC Rr; mem Galilee Bapt Ch; mem Mizpah Ct 79 Dau of Isis; mem NAACP; mem NCACT-NCAE Women's Ccs. **Honors/Awds:** Outstn Elem Tchr of Am 1973; Tchr of the Yr Smthfld Jr HS 1975-76; NCAE Hum Rel Nom 1977; inttd 1st Sal Sup for Tchrs John Co.

SANDERS, LOU HELEN
Library administrator. **Personal:** Born Mar 2, 1951, Bolton, MS; daughter of Irene Singleton Devine and Eddie Devine; divorced; children: Nicol. **Educ:** Jackson State University, Jackson, MS, BA, 1973, Eds, 1981; University of Michigan, Ann Arbor, MI, AMLS, 1974; University of Pittsburgh, Pittsburgh, PA, PhD, 1989. **Career:** Jackson State University, Jackson, MS, reserve/asst cir librarian, 1974-76, science technology div lib, 1976-77, instructor of library sci, 1977-87, asst professor of lib science, 1983-87, dean of libraries, 1989-. **Orgs:** American Library Association, 1974-; University of Michigan Alumni Association, 1977-, African-American life member; Jackson State University Alumni Association; Education for Bibliographic Instruction, American Library Association, 1990-92; Southeastern Library Association, 1979-; Mississippi Library Association, 1974-; ASIS, Information Analysis and Evaluation, vice chairman, 1990, chairman, 1991; Alpha Kappa Alpha, 1983-; Beta Phi Mu, 1989-; State of Mississippi Libraries Director's Council, chairman1990-; American Society of Information Science, 1988-. **Honors/Awds:** University of Pittsburgh, Provost Development Fund Scholarship, 1988; Atlanta University, FIPSE Internship, 1985-88; Phi Kappa Phi, 1976. **Special Achievements:** Author: Faculty Status of Academic Librarians in Four Year State-Supported Colleges and Universities, Univ Microfilms, International, 1989; reviewed in: "Social Responsibility in Librarianship: Essays on Equality," RQ, 1990; "Staff Training Programs for State and Local Government for Publication," Document to the People, vol, 17, 1989; "Faculty Status for Academic Librarians," Encyclopedia of Library and Information, vol 48, Marcel Dekker, 1991; "The Commitment of a Dean at a Predominately Black University," The Black Librarian in America Revisited, 1994. **Business Addr:** Dean of Libraries, Jackson State University, Henry T Sampson Library, PO Box 17745, Jackson, MS 39217-0445.

SANDERS, MICHAEL ANTHONY
Professional basketball player. **Personal:** Born May 7, 1960, Vidalia, LA; married Crystal Tate. **Educ:** UCLA, BA 1982. **Career:** San Antonio Spurs, 1982-83, Philadelphia 76ers, 1984-88, Indiana Pacers, 1990-. **Honors/Awds:** Named CBA Rookie of Yr; 1st Team All-CBA; 2nd team hnrs on the CBA All-Defensive Team; team capt 2 yrs; twice named All-PAC 10; MVP soph yr; Westrn Reg NCAA MVP. **Business Addr:** Professional Basketball Player, Indiana Pacers, 300 E Market St, Indianapolis, IN 46204-2603.

SANDERS, PATRICIA ROPER
International business consultant. **Personal:** Born Dec 23, 1945, Tulsa, OK; daughter of Rev & Mrs Harold M Anderson; married C Edward Sanders; children: Lark Nanette, Thomas Bradford. **Educ:** Lincoln Univ, BA 1966; PRSA, accreditation 1977. **Career:** US Senate Cand, dir research & policy info 1970-71; Blue Cross Hosp Serv St Louis, pub rel spec 1971-73; Western Elect Co St Louis, managing ed/comm aff spec 1973-77; Philip Morris Indsl Milwaukee, mgr communications 1977-78; Transatlantic Link, founder; The Rhopar Report/RHOPAR, pres/publisher, 1978-85; PR Associates, 1979-86; TRB Speakers Agency, public relations consultant, 1986-90; Intl Black Network Exchange, dir, 1990; International Business Consultants, director, 1990-. **Orgs:** Panel of judges Coro Found St Louis 1976; Pub Rel Soc of Amer 1977-80; bd dir Chicago Forum 1979; dir of pub rel/adv bd mem UNCF OIC Sherwood Forest St Louis 1974-77; bd of adv Lincoln Univ Jefferson City, MO 1975-77; chmn steering com Comm Pride Expo Milwaukee 1977; Tour of South Africa to establish professional networking ties 1985; bd Winnie Mandella Women's Ministries 1987; Alpha Kappa Alpha; The Links; executive director/co-founder, RMBD, 1990-92. **Honors/Awds:** Spl Citation for Documentary on Pre Con-Con OK Hist Soc 1970; Disting Serv Awards UNCF/OIC/Lincoln Univ/Milwaukee Journal/Jus Frens Milw/Coro Foundation, 1974-77; honored by Black Business and Prof Women of Los Angeles County at Fifth Annual Directory Reception; Key Speaker at the CA Governor's Conf 1985; CA Governor honored Woman of the Year 1985; Golden Phoenix Award, 1983. **Special Achievements:** Author: Public Relations for Small Business; producer, moderator/host: "A Woman's Place," WYMS; "Focus on Black Business Woman," KJLH; "Ask Me," KACD, 1977-80; "Living Positively"; Black Wallstreet, producer, 1990; African Heritage World Celebration, special events coordinator, 1995. **Business Addr:** Publisher/Lecturer, 14999 Preston Rd, Rm 212, Suite 184, Dallas, TX 75240, (214)233-3282.

SANDERS, REGINALD LAVERNE (REGGIE)
Professional baseball player. **Personal:** Born Dec 1, 1967, Florence, SC. **Educ:** Spartanburg Methodist. **Career:** Cincinnati Reds, outfielder, 1991-. **Business Addr:** Professional Baseball Player, Cincinnati Reds, 100 Riverfront Stadium, Cincinnati, OH 45202, (513)421-4510.

SANDERS, RHONDA SHEREE
Newspaper reporter, columnist. **Personal:** Born Jun 25, 1956, Montgomery, AL; daughter of Marie Williams Hamilton and Isaac Sanders. **Educ:** University of Michigan, Ann Arbor, MI, BA, 1978, MA, 1979; Wayne State University, Detroit, MI, 1990-. **Career:** Flint Journal, Flint, MI, reporter, columnist, 1980-. **Orgs:** Mid-Michigan Association of Black Journalists, 1982-92; member, National Association of Black Journalists, 1987-. **Honors/Awds:** Media Award, Natl Assn of Media Women, 1983, 1990; Wade McCree Memorial Award, Justice Award Media, 1989; Press Award, Michigan Press Association, for series on crack cocaine, 1989; author, Bronze Pillars: An Oral History of African-Americans in Flint, 1996. **Business Addr:** Reporter, Columnist, Flint Journal, 200 E First St, Flint, MI 48502.

SANDERS, RICKY WAYNE
Professional football player. **Personal:** Born Aug 30, 1962, Temple, TX; married Michelle; children: Ashlynn, Richard Wayne. **Educ:** Southwest Texas State Univ, attended. **Career:** Houston Gamblers (USFL), 1984-85; Washington Redskins, wide receiver, 1986-. **Honors/Awds:** Selected to all-Madden team, 1989; MVP, Washington Redskins, 1988; post-season play: NFC Championship Game, 1986, 1987, NFL Championship Game, 1987; MVP, Palm Bowl, 1982. **Business Addr:** Professional Football Player, Atlanta Falcons, Two Falcon Place, Suwanee, GA 30174.

SANDERS, ROBER LAFAYETTE
Engineer, scientist. **Personal:** Born Feb 14, 1952, Raleigh, NC. **Educ:** NC State Univ, BSEE 1973; Univ of AZ Phoenix, MBA 1983; MIT, MSEE, 1976. **Career:** IBM, program manager, currently. **Orgs:** Vice pres IEEE, 1973, 1986; ACME, 1973-; Amer Physicists, 1973-; basileus Omega Psi Phi Frat, 1982-90; president Scholastic Aptitude, 1983-; treas Tucson Black Forum, 1985-87; treas Tucson Democratic Party 1986-87; Black Engineers of America, president, 1989-; State NAACP, president, 1983-90; Branch NAACP, president, 1983-90; Optimist Club, vice pres, 1985-91. **Honors/Awds:** Jaycees, Outstanding Young Man, 1985, 1986; BEA, Engineer of the Yr, 1986; Omega Psi Phi, Man of the Year, 1986; Citizen of the Year; Omega Psi Phi, Assistant KF, 1994. **Home Addr:** 429 N St SW #S702, Washington, DC 20024. **Business Addr:** Program Manager, IBM Corp., 9221 Corporate Blvd, Rockville, MD 20850.

SANDERS, ROBERT B.
Educator, administrator. **Personal:** Born Dec 9, 1938, Augusta, GA; son of Lois Jones Sanders and Robert Sanders; married Gladys Nealous Sanders, Dec 23, 1961; children: Sylvia Sanders Schneider, William. **Educ:** Paine Coll Augusta GA, BS 1959; Univ of MI Ann Arbor, MI 1961, PhD 1964; Univ of WI Madison, Post Doctorate 1966. **Career:** Battelle Memorial Inst, visiting scientist 1970-71; Univ of TX Med Schl Houston, visiting assoc prof 1974-75; Natl Science Found, prog dir 1978-79; Univ of KS Lawrence, asst prof, assoc prof, full prof 1966-, assoc dean, The Graduate School 1987-96, assoc vice chancellor, Research Graduate Studies and Public Service, 1989-96, coord of minority Graduate Student Support, currently. **Orgs:** Mem bd dir United Child Devl Ctr 1968-93; consult Natl Sci Fnd 1983-94, Dept of Educ 1993-96, Natl Inst of Health 1982, Interx Research Corp 1972-80, Natl Research Councl 1973-77, mem Bd of Higher Educ United Meth Church 1976-80; mem American Soc for Biochemistry and Molecular Biology; Amer Soc for Pharmacology and Experimental Therapeutics, American Assoc of Univ Prof, and Sigma Xi. **Honors/Awds:** Postdoctoral Fellowship Natl Inst of Health 1974-75, Amer Cancer Soc 1964-66; fellowship Battelle Mem Inst 1970-71; more than 50 scientific articles; more than 50 research grants. **Military Serv:** AUSR e-4 1955-62; Honorable Dischardge. **Business Addr:** Professor Biochemistry, University of Kansas, Dept of Biochemistry, Lawrence, KS 66045-2106.

SANDERS, SALLY RUTH
Registered nurse. **Personal:** Born Jun 1, 1952, Tyler, TX; married Donald Ray Sanders; children: Carla, Candace, Christopher. **Educ:** TX Eastern Sch of Nursing, Tyler Jr Coll, diploma in nursing asst 1973-75, 1972-74; Univ of TX at Tyler, BSN 1982-84. **Career:** Relief Health Care Svcs, dir 1985-86; Triage, head nurse; Progressive Health Care, asst adminis 1986-. **Orgs:** Historian Diabetes Assoc 1984-85; asst dir Marche Incorp 1986-; mem Negro Business & Professional Women's Org; mem Rose Bud Civitan Club, Civitan. **Honors/Awds:** Woman of the Year UTHCT 1985. **Business Addr:** Nurse Clinician/Asst Adminis, Progressive Health Care, PO Box 2003, Tyler, TX 75710.

SANDERS, STEVEN LEROY
Investment advisor. **Personal:** Born Oct 26, 1959, Philadelphia, PA; son of Elouise Tooten Sanders and Willie E Sanders; married Kelly DeSouza Sanders, Jun 3, 1989; children: son. **Educ:** Howard University, Washington, DC, BBA, 1982. **Career:** Aetna Life & Casualty, Pittsburgh, PA, employee benefit representative, 1982-85; Mellon Bank, Philadelphia, PA, credit analyst, 1985-86; Hunt & Sanders Financial Advisors, Philadelphia, PA, partner/founder 1986-; MDL Capital Management, pres; Your Money Matters Program, New York, NY, Citibank Master Card & Visa lecturer, 1989-. **Orgs:** Board of Dirs, Freedom Theatre, 1990-; board of directors, Help Line, 1984-85; member, Business Education Advisory Committee, 1987-89; president, Howard University Alumni, Pittsburgh Chapter, 1984-85; Scout Master Troop 629, Boy Scouts of America, 1986-88. **Honors/Awds:** Leaders Club, The New England, 1990; Chairperson of the Month, Vectors Pittsburgh, 1985; National Speaker-Citibank Master Card & Visa Money Matters for Young Adults, 1989-. **Home Addr:** 13 Stockton Dr, Voorhees, NJ 08043. **Business Addr:** President, MDL Capital Management, 260 S Broad St, The Atlantic Bldg, Ste 1600, Philadelphia, PA 19102.

SANDERS, VICTORIA LYNN
Business executive. **Personal:** Born in Aurora, IL; divorced. **Educ:** Drake U, BS; Bradley U, MBA; Univ of Chigo. **Career:** First Womens Corp, resrch analyst; Stock Broker; Iknvestment Adv; established A Hlth Servs & Consult Orgn composed of 5 Cos Hot Line, Womens Care Ltd, Chic Womens Ctr Found Servs; has Co which supports First Womens in the investor info & finan plng for the individual; prod Money Talk TV Prgm for investor info; Great Talent Mgmt, assists promising entertainers with their careers; instr Marion Bus Coll Operation PUSH. **Orgs:** Cosmo C of C; Chicago C of C; Links; Alpha Kappa Alpha Sor; Phi Gamma Nu Bus Sor; NAACP; prog com Duncan UMCA; Black Exec Exzchange Prgm; bd of regents; mem Daniel Hale Williams U; finan edtr Chicago Post; author Victoria Letter; varius Educ Radio & TV prgms First Annual Top Rung Citation, Chicago Opptys Indusltn Ctr 1970; Achvmt Awd Cosmo C of C 1971; Black Bus Otst Serv Rendered to Profession & Comm Blackbook 1974; Black Women in Bus in NY, Black Enterprise 1974. **Honors/Awds:** We Need More of You Awd Kennedy & Co Channel 7, 1974; Women With Real Power Who Cal Help Hou, Cosmo 1975; Intl Womens Yr Awd PUSH, Spl Marketing Consult TIFCO Fiberglass Pool Renovation. **Business Addr:** 2nd Office, 185 N Wabash 1806, Chicago, IL 60611.

SANDERS, WENDELL ROWAN
Physician. **Personal:** Born Dec 12, 1933, Vicksburg, MS. **Educ:** Morehouse Coll, BS (summa cum laude) 1954; Meharry Med Coll, MD (cum laude) 1958. **Career:** Wayne St Univ Sch of Med, instr psych 1978-; Pvt Prac, 1978-; Harreld Ctr for Yng Adlts, dir 1972; Comm Mntl Hlth, agency dir 1973; Wayne Co Gen Hosp, psych 1965-68; MS St Hosp, psych 1960-62; Gen Prac, 1959-60. **Orgs:** Clncl dir SE Oakland Prgm 1971-73; psych consult various cts in Met Rgn for yng adlts; guest lctr Wayne St U; lctr Oakland Co Comm Coll; prsnl analysis 1965-70; Pres MI Soc ofr Study of Adolscnts 1973-74; pres Med staff Northville St Hosp 1975-77; mem APA; MI Soc for study of adolscnts; MI Soc of Adolscnt Psych; MI Assn of Tchrs of Emtnly Dstrbd Chldrn; NAACP; NRA; mem Detroit Educ TV Network. **Honors/Awds:** Papers ''Trtmnt Plan for Adolscnts at Wayne Co Gen Hosp''; ''A Trtmnt Plan for Black Patients''; ''Trtmnt of Black Yng Adlts''. **Business Addr:** Northville State Hosp, Northville, MI 48167.

SANDERS, WESLEY, JR.
City official. **Personal:** Born Feb 7, 1933, Los Angeles; married Benrice Jackson; children: Malinda Gale, Douglas Edward, Wesley III, Kenneth Wayne, Derlwyn Mark, Jeffery. **Educ:** Harbor Coll, 1952. **Career:** Triple Quality Meats, founder 1961; John Morrell Meat Co, salesman 1966-71; City of Compton, reserve police officer, city treas 1973-. **Orgs:** Mem Compton C of C; Negro Bus & Prof Mens Assn; BF Talbot #8 Prince Hall Masons; welfare Planning Council, mem Nat Municipal Treas Assn; CA Municipal Treas Assn; NAACP. **Honors/Awds:** Otstndng Salesman Awd, John Morrell Meat Co 1966-67-68; Otstndng Reserve Police Officer Awd 1974; Achievement Awd, Model Cities; Otstndng Awd Block Central. **Military Serv:** USAF; sgt; 1952-56. **Business Addr:** 600 N Alameda, Compton, CA.

SANDERS, WOODROW MAC
Educator. **Personal:** Born Aug 4, 1943, Luling, TX; son of Alburnice Stewart Sanders and R V Sanders; married Estella Gonzales; children: Rodrigo R, Justin W, Jennifer M. **Educ:** Univ of Alaska; Univ of ND, 1964-66; TX A&I Univ Kingsville, BA 1970; TX A&I Univ Corpus Christi, MS 1977; Uniersity of North Texas, Denton, TX, 1979-81; Bee County College, 1989-; PhD, 1992; Social Work Licenses, 1993. **Career:** Bee Co Coll, Beeville, TX, counselor/instructor 1978-81; Nueces Co Mental Health/Mental Retardation Center, dir of outpatient serv 1972-78; Gateway Wholesale Sporting Goods, asst mgr 1971-72; USN Counseling & Asst Cntgr Corpus Christi, TX, consult assn psychologist 1973-78; Univ of TX Austin, inst of Alcohol Studies 1977; S TX Housing Corp, bd pres 1978; Southwestern Bell Telephone Co, Laredo, TX, manager engineering, 1981-89; Bee County College, Beeville, TX, counselor/instructor, 1989-91; TX Dept of Health-Social Work Services, part time instructor Bee County Coll. **Orgs:** Adv bd mem Nueces House TX Youth Council 1977-78; bd mem Coastal Bend Bus & Indsl Devel Inc 1977-; life mem NAACP; mem US Rifle Marksmanship Team USAF 1962-64; vice president, board of directors Children's Heart Institute of Texs, 1985-; member, Texas Association of Telecommunication Engineers, 1981-89; Southwest Association of Student Special Services Programs, 1989-; member, Texas Association of Counseling and Development, 1989-91. **Honors/Awds:** Presidential Unit Citation USAF 1965; Republic of Vietnam Medal of Valor USAF 1966; Youth Serv Awd Corpus Christi Police Dept 1967; Awd for Ser in Drug Abuse - Prevention, Coastal Bend Council of Govts Drug Abuse Adv Com Corpus Christi 1976-77; flwshp TX Research Inst of Mental Sci Houston 1978. **Military Serv:** USAF, staff sgt, 1961-66. **Business Addr:** Texas Dept of Health-Social Work Services, 1322 Agnes St, Corpus Christi, TX 78401, (512)888-7762.

SANDERS-OJI, J. QEVIN (QEVIN Q. WEATHERSBY)
Newspaper publisher, arts administrator. **Personal:** Born May 23, 1962, Los Angeles, CA; son of Betty Lou Weathersby and James Edward Woods-Sanders; divorced. **Educ:** Los Angeles Cultural Center, Certificate, theatre craft, 1983; Los Angeles City College, AA, American cultures, 1985; Howard University, BA, film production/design, 1989. **Career:** The American Film Institute, administrative assistant, 1988-91; DC Commission of Public Health, intern, 1987-89; DC Public Schools, elementary teacher, 1991-92; The Anacostia Grapevine, publisher, editor, currently; Washington Project for the Arts, open city director, currently. **Orgs:** The Frederick Douglass Historical Society; The Anacostia Garden Club, newsletter editor; Howard University Alumni Association. **Honors/Awds:** Urban Profile Magazine, 30 Under 30, Finalist, 1992; Howard University, Community Conference Film Competition, First Place, 1988. **Special Achievements:** Curator, ''Options 1993,'' 1993; curator/coordinator, ''Face to Face,'' 1992. **Home Phone:** (202)889-8463.

SANDERSON, RANDY CHRIS
Assistant controller. **Personal:** Born Dec 23, 1954, St Louis, MO; married Toni M Harper. **Educ:** Univ of MO at St Louis, BS 1977. **Career:** May Dept Stores, staff/sr accountant mgr plans 1977-81, dir capital/pland/expense analysis 1984-87; May Company CA, dir adv acctg/financial plans 1981-84; Caldor Inc, assistant controller 1987-. **Orgs:** Chmn Natl Alumni Assoc Inroads 1985-87. **Honors/Awds:** John C Willis Awd Natl Assoc of Black Accountants 1976; CPA State of MO. **Business Addr:** Assistant Controller, Caldor Inc, 20 Glover Ave, Norwalk, CT 06850.

SANDERS-WEST, SELMA D.
Consultant. **Personal:** Born Jan 2, 1953, Farrell, PA; daughter of Martha J Wiley Sanders and Henry K Sanders; married Robert M West, Sep 13, 1986; children: Phebe Joy West. **Educ:** Pennsylvania State Univ, 1970-75; Univ of Massachusetts, Amherst MA, MRP, 1986. **Career:** Mercer County Community Action Agency, Farrell PA, program coord, 1980-81, economic devel specialist, 1981-84; Chicago Bd of Educ, Chicago IL, special asst to gen supt, 1985-86, consultant, 1986-87, press officer, speech writer, 1987-88; West & Assoc, Sharon PA, pres, 1988-. **Orgs:** Former bd of dir, Mercer County Branch, NAACP, Farrell PA, 1980-; former bd mem, newsletter editor, National Urban/Rural Fellows, 1986-88, mem, 1986-; Farrell Area School Bd, Farrell PA, 1989-01, vice president, 1993, board president, 1993-94; founding pres, Tri-County Affilate of Penna Conference on Black Basic Educ (COBBE), 1995-97; founding pres, Farrell-Wheatland, PEG/PTA, 1996-98. **Honors/Awds:** Natl Rural Fellow, Natl Urban/Rural Fellows Inc, 1985-86; contributing editor, Beautiful for Him Magazine, a Chicago-based Christian women's magazine, 1986-87; Woman of the Year, Clarion Univ, PA, Women of Color Committee, 1997. **Home Addr:** 902 Beechwood Ave, Farrell, PA 16121-1109, (412)981-8555. **Business Addr:** President, West & Associates, PO Box 865, Sharon, PA 16146, (412)981-9378.

SANDIDGE, KANITA DURICE
Telecommunication company executive. **Personal:** Born Dec 2, 1947, Cleveland, OH; daughter of Virginia Louise Caldwell Sandidge and John Robert Sandidge Jr. **Educ:** Cornell Univ, BA 1970; Case Western Reserve Univ, MBA 1979. **Career:** AT&T Network Systems, acting section chief 1970-72, section chief cost control 1972-78, dept chief data processing and accounting 1978-79, dept chief account analysis 1979-80, administration mgr 1980-83, sales forecasting and analysis mgr 1983-86, planning and devel mgr 1986-87, admin serv dir, 1987-89, div staff dir, 1990-. **Orgs:** Beta Alpha Psi Accounting Honorary, Amer Mgmt Assn, The Alliance of AT&T Black Mgrs, Natl Black MBA's, Natl Assn for Female Executives; life mem NAACP; black executives exchange prog NUL 1986-; bd of dir, East-West Corporate Corridor Assn (Illinois), 1987-90, Quad County Urban League (Illinois), 1988-90. **Honors/Awds:** Harlem YMCA Black Achiever in Industry 1981; Tribute to Women & Industry Achievement Award YWCA 1985. **Home Addr:** 10 Trade Winds Dr, Randolph, NJ 07869. **Business Addr:** Division Staff Director, Customer Support & Operations, AT&T Network Systems, 475 South St, Morristown, NJ 07960.

SANDIFER, JAWN A.
Judge. **Personal:** Born Feb 18, 1919, Greensboro, NC; married Laura; children: 1. **Educ:** C Smith Univ, AB 1938; Howard Law Sch, LlB 1941; Johnson, Hon LlD. **Career:** PRIVATE PRACTICE, 1 Child Atty; Civil Ct NYC, 10 Yr Term Judge 1964; NY Supreme Ct, term justice 1969; Criminal Br Supreme Ct, appted supr judge 1973; Criminal Branch NYC, dep admin judge 1974; Equal Employ Ofcr Unified Cy Sys State of NY; US History, Globe Press, NY, gen ed Afro-Am In; Minorities USA Globe Press, NY, co-author. **Orgs:** Mem Am Nat Bar Assns; Harlem Lawyers Asn; NY County Trial - Lawyers Assn; New York City Bar Assn; US Supreme Ct Bar Assn; mem Alpha Phi Alpha Frat; bd trustees Harlem Eye, Ear, Nose Hosp; gen counsel, NY State Conf N Aacp, past pres, NY Br; former mem Adv Com NY State Dept Edn; former bd mem, sec HARYOU ACT; mem Steward's Bd, St Marks Meth Ch ; former bd dirs, Hope Day Nursery & Windham Children's Svc; mem Resource Com, Bd Edn, NYC. **Military Serv:** USAF. **Business Addr:** Supreme Ct State NY, 100 Centre St, New York, NY.

SANDLE, FLOYD LESLIE
Educator. **Personal:** Born Jul 4, 1913, Magnolia, MS; son of Essie Hampton-Sandle and Leslie Sandle; married Marie Johnson; children: Gail Synette, Ava Leslie, Wanda Marie, Floyd Leslie Jr, Anthony Wayne. **Educ:** Dillard Univ, AB, 1937; Univ of Chicago, MA, 1947; NY Univ, postgraduate, 1951-52; LA State Univ, PhD, 1959. **Career:** Grambling State Univ, prof emeritus, 1985; Grambling Coll, instructor, prof, dept head, speech & dean, div general studies, 1951-78; Dillard Univ, prof, Speech & Drama, chair, Humanities Div, 1978-86; Louisiana State University, visiting professor of speech, 1972-73. **Orgs:** Mem, Southern Speech Assn; Natl Assn Dramatic & Speech

Arts; Am Educ Theatre Assn; mem, Theta Alpha Phi, Kappa Delta Phi, Omega Psi Phi; author ''The Negro in the American Education Theatre'', 1964; Orientation An Image of the College, 1967; contributed articles to professional journals; pres conference of LA Coll & Univs, 1977; mem, LA State Literacy Task Force, LA Council on Aging, GSU Foundation, pres, Lion's Club, Grambling, LA. **Honors/Awds:** Inducted to Hall of Fame, Grambling State Univ, 1986. **Special Achievements:** First African American to receive PhD from La State Univ. **Military Serv:** USN boatswain's mate 2/c 1943-45; instructor USAFEI Prog South Pacific 1944-45.

SANDLER, JOAN D.
Association executive. **Personal:** Born Oct 2, 1934, NYC, NY; divorced; children: Eve, Kathe. **Educ:** Attended, City Coll of NY, Univ of Mexico. **Career:** Bloomingdale Family Svc, tchr dir 1963-66; Metro Applied Rsch Ctr, researcher 1966-68; Dept Cultural Affairs, prog specialist 1968-72; Black Theatre Alliance, exec dir 1972-77; The Senghor Found, 1977-80; Metro Museum of Art, assoc museum educ in charge of comm educ. **Orgs:** Panelist & consult Natl Endowment of Arts 1971-74; consult NY State Council for Arts 1972-; adv VISIONS KCET/TV Pub Broadcasting Corp 1974; theater panel The Theater Develop Fund; bd dirs Natl Council of Women; bd dirs Children Arts Carnival; Oppor Resources; adv Gov's Task Force; lecturer Scripps Coll, BankSt Coll, Rutgers Univ, Baruch Coll, The Inst of Contemporary Arts, Hunter Coll, Princeton Univ; bd of dirs 1st Amer Congress of Theatre, NSINGHA; mem Natl Coalition of 100 Black Women, The Amer Museum's Assn, Museum's Educators Roundtable. **Honors/Awds:** American Biographies; Kellogg Fellow Smithsonian Inst; Audelco Awd 1973. **Business Addr:** Assoc Museum Educ-Comm Educ, Metropolitan Museum of Art, 1564 Broadway, New York, NY 10036.

SANDOVAL, DOLORES S.
Educator. **Personal:** Born Sep 30, 1937, Quebec. **Educ:** Institute of Chicago, art, 1956-58; University of Michigan, BSD, 1958-60; Indiana Univ, MS, 1968, PhD, 1970; Harvard University Institute for Educational Management, IEM, 1975. **Career:** University of Vermont, assoc prof of education, 1971-, Middle East studies, co-chair, 1994-, assistant to the president for human resources, 1972-77; State University College at Buffalo, assoc prof, 1970-71; Author/Illustrator of ''Be Patient Abdul,'', Margaret McElderry Books, 1996; Paintings and photography of Africa, Middle East & Latin America exhibited in Europe, Canada and USA, 1987-; Represented by program Corp. of America, 1994; consultant on Race Relations & Diversity Programming. **Orgs:** Partners of the Americas, Vermont/Honduras, president, 1997-, vice pres, 1994-96, board member, 1992-; Sister Cities, Burlington, (VT) Arad (Israel & Bethlehem), board member, 1995-96; Public Access Government TV, Channel 17 (VT), board member, 1991-95. **Honors/Awds:** Elected Democratic candidate for Congress from VT, 1990; Primary candidate, 1988; President's Fellow, Rhode Island School of Design, 1981, mem board of trustees, 1976-82; University Senate, University of VT, chair, 1981-82; Fellowship Challenges to Unity: The European Community, 1995, Maastricht, 1995; Fellow, University of New Mexico College of Fine Arts National Arts Project, Daring To Do It, 1993-94; Malone Alumni Fellow to Jordan, Israel, Palestine and Syria, summer, 1991; Malone Fellow in Arab and Islamic Studies in Tunisia, summer, 1989; Award from Black American Heritage Foundation, NYC for Contributions to Duke Ellington Concert & Speech Series, 1989-92; Fellow, National Endowment for the Humanities Summer Institute on African & African-American Culture, 1987.

SANDOZ, JOHN H.
Commissioner. **Career:** County of Los Angeles, commissioner; LA Superior Court, judge. **Business Addr:** Judge, Pasadena Superior Court, County of Los Angeles, 300 E Walnut St, Department NE-L, Pasadena, CA 91101, (213)974-5581.

SANDRIDGE, JOHN SOLOMON
Artist. **Personal:** Born May 10, Gadsden, AL; son of Edward (deceased) & Lucille Sandridge; married Frances Sandridge, Feb 7, 1975; children: Peter, Priscilla, David. **Educ:** Certified ND, 1983. **Career:** Creative Displays, supervisor; Gadsden City Bd of Ed, teacher; Luvlife Collectibles, Inc, CEO, founder, pres, currently. **Orgs:** Carver Theatre, president; Sandridge Museum of Living History. **Honors/Awds:** Governor of Alabama, Certificate of Appreciation, 1982; Black Business Assn, Certificate of Appreciation, 1983; JC Penney's, National Vendors Award, 1993; Roberta Watts Medical, Outstanding Citizen's Award, 1993; many first place ribbons throughout the country. **Special Achievements:** The First African-American to be licensed by the Coca-Cola Co to do a series of Blacks Incorporating a Black Theme; The FIrst Lithographs, Delicious & Refreshing Winning Smiles, & Delightful; The First African-American Serigraph Licenced by the Coca-Cola Co. **Business Addr:** President & CEO, LuvLife Collectibles, Inc, PO Box 1628, Gadsden, AL 35902-1628, (205)549-1534.

SANDS, DOUGLAS BRUCE
Government official, minister. **Personal:** Born Mar 1, 1934, Cooksville; son of Bess Sands and Alexander Sands; married Barbara Jean Corpening; children: Dellyne Ivy Monroe, Douglas B, Jr, Curtis O, Cecelia O. **Educ:** Morgan State Coll, BS (with High Honors/Distinguished mil student/Cadet Comdr/Student govern pres) 1956; Howard Univ School of Divinity, Masters of Divinity. **Career:** Minority & Affairs State of Maryland, exec asst to gov and dir of office 1979-; Robert Clay Inc Contracting Co, vice pres proj mgr 1977-79; High Ridge Land Devel Co, pres 1973-79; AlasKa Asso Arctic Pipeline Constrn, gen mgr 1975-77; Maryland Minority Contractors Assn Inc, founder, pres 1975-79. **Orgs:** Founder/Dir New Community Inc Community Devel Corp 1971; bd of dirs Workhorse Club Community Serv 1971; exec dir Washington DC Metro Area Southern Christian Leadership Conf 1973-79; program dir Volunteers in Tech Asst 1974-75; mem Alpha Phi Alpha Frat Inc 1953-; organ com Cantonville Community Coll & Howard Community Coll 1963-72; lay speaker & local pastor United Methodist Church 1975. **Honors/Awds:** Outstanding Commendations AUS 1957-58; Outstanding Community Serv Omega Psi Phi Frat Award 1962; Superior Public Serv Maryland State Conf of NAACP Branches 1966; Public Serv Award Washington DC Metro SCLS 1974; Outstanding Public Serv Award Maryland Minority Contractors Assn. **Military Serv:** AUS 1st lt 1956-58.

SANDS, GEORGE M.
Management consultant/trainer. **Personal:** Born Jan 15, 1942, Port Chester, NY; married Mary Alice Moxley; children: Jeffrey, Kenneth. **Educ:** Western MI Univ, BS 1964; Hunter Coll Sch of Social Work, MSW 1970. **Career:** Cage Teen Center Inc, exec dir 1972-78; Empire State Coll, lecturer 1981-; Westchester Comm Coll, adjunct prof 1973-; Sands Assocs, owner/dir 1978-; Westchester Community College, assoc prof, 1988-. **Orgs:** Educ chmn Middletown NAACP; mem Amer Soc for Personnel Admin; bd of dirs Michael Schwerner Found 1970-72; personnel chmn Middletown Bd of Educ 1976-82; consultant/trainer Stony Brook Univ 1977-; bd mem Orange Co Private Indus Council 1983-; trainer Cornell Univ School of Industrial Labor Relations. **Honors/Awds:** Teacher of the Yr Westchester Comm Coll 1982; Service Awd Middletown Bd of Educ 1982. **Business Addr:** Director, Sands Associates, PO Box 352, New Hampton, NY 10958, (914)692-6296.

SANDS, MARY ALICE
Educational administrator. **Personal:** Born Oct 20, 1941, Indianapolis, IN; daughter of Velma Goodnight Moxley and Frank O Moxley; married George M Sands; children: Jeffrey, Kenneth. **Educ:** State Univ of IA, 1959-60; Western MI Univ, BS 1964; Bank St Coll of Ed, MSEd 1982. **Career:** Bronx Municipal Hosp Ctr, asst chief OT Dept 1965-70; Harlem Hosp OT Dept, supervisor Clinical Ed 1971; Rockland Community Coll, chair OTA Prog 1973-77; Orange Cty Community Coll, chair, full professor, OTA Prog 1977-; 1986 Founder & Co-Owner Occupational Therapy Plus. **Orgs:** Mem NAACP, Alpha Kappa Alpha, Amer OT Assoc; mem AOTA Program Adv Comm 1983-86; mem bd of directors Orange Cty Cerebral Palsy Assoc 1984-87; chair, NYS Board of Occupational Therapy, 1986-89. **Honors/Awds:** Awd of Merit for Practice NYS OT Assoc 1985; contributing author Service Learning in Aging, Implications for Occupational Therapy; Contributing Author Target 2000; chair, Amer Occupational Therapy Assn Commn on Educ 1989-92; Service Award, American Occupational Therapy Assoc, 1992; Hudson-Taconic District NYSOTA, Certificate of Appreciation, 1992; Fellow of American Occupational Therapy Assn, 1994; contributing author, Willard & Spackman's Occupational Therapy, 1997. **Home Addr:** 16 Ross Lane, Middletown, NY 10940. **Business Addr:** Chairperson-OTA Program, Orange County Community Coll, 115 South St, Middletown, NY 10940.

SANDS, ROSETTA F.
Educational administrator. **Personal:** Born in Homestead, FL; daughter of Annie Pickett Harriel Ford and John H Ford; married Charles H Sands, Jun 9, 1956 (divorced); children: Michael H Sands. **Educ:** Harlem Hospital School of Nursing, New York NY, Diploma, 1954; Univ of Maryland School of Nursing, Baltimore MD, BSN, 1966, Univ of Maryland-College Park, MS, 1970; Johns Hopkins Univ, Baltimore MD, postgraduate study, 1970-77; The Union Graduate School, Cincinnati OH, PhD, 1980. **Career:** Univ of MD School of Nursing, Baltimore MD, instructor of medical/surgical, nursing, 1970-71, asst prof of registered nursing prog, 1971-83, team coordinator, 1971-74, asst dean, 1974-79; Tuskegee Univ, Tuskegee Inst AL, dean & assoc, 1983-87; The William Paterson Coll, Wayne, NJ, dean & prof, 1987-93; Student Retention In Academic Nursing, nurse consultant, 1993-. **Orgs:** Mem, 1968, trustee of Natl Sorority House, 1976-79; Chi Eta Phi Sorority for Nurses; mem, Sigma Theta Tau Intl Honor Society for Nursing, 1969; mem, Peer Review Panel, Special Project Grants, Dept of Health and Human Services, 1976-85; mem, Task Force on Teaching Culturally Diverse Students, 1977-82; mem, Phi Kappa Phi Honor Society, 1977; pres, bd of trustees, Provident Hospital, 1978-81; mem, bd of dir, Maryland Blue Cross, 1980-83; mem, Maryland Advisory Committee, US Civil Rights Committee, 1981-83; pres, Maryland Nurse Assn, 1981-82; mem, bd of dir, Amer Assn of Colleges of Nursing, 1986-88; mem, Zeta Phi Beta Sorority, Inc; bd of trustees, United Hospitals Medical Center, 1993-96. **Honors/Awds:** Author of Consumer Perception of the Expanded Role of the Nurse, Glowing Lamp, 1973; Certificate of Recognition of Leadership in Nursing, Univ of MD Nursing Faculty, 1976; Community Service and Nomination for Mary E Mahoney Award, Resolution, MD Senate, 1979; Professional Leadership in Nursing, Award, Chi Eta Phi Sorority, Gamma Chapter, 1980; Superior Leadership as President of Board of Trustees, Provident Hospital Board of Trustees, 1981; Finer Womanhood Award for Work with Youth in Health Careers, 1981; author of The 1985 Resolution and the Nursing Shortage, MD Nurse, 1981; author of Cultural Conflict in Nurse, Client Interactions, Videocassette, 1983; Excellence in Professional Achievements Award, Black Nurses Assn of Baltimore, 1983; author of Enhancing Cultural Sensitivity in Clinl Practice, 1987; author of The Predictive Potential of Social Variables for Black Students, Performance on NCELX, 1988; Author, Hospital Governance: Nurse Trustee Vis-A-Vis Nurse Executive, Nursing Management, 1990; Author, Black Nurses As Mentors: Linking The Past With Our Future, The Glowing Lamp, 1990. **Business Addr:** IMS, Consultants, 4406 Norfolk Avenue, Baltimore, MD 21216.

SANFORD, ISABEL G. (ISABEL RICHMOND)
Actress. **Personal:** Born Aug 29, 1927, New York, NY; daughter of Josephine Perry Sanford and James Edward Sanford; married William Edward Richmond (deceased); children: Pamela Richmond Ruff, William Eric Richmond, Sanford Keith. **Career:** Television appearances: Bewitched, 1968, Mod Squad, 1971, The Interns, 1971, Love American Style, 1972, The Great Man's Whiskers, 1973, Sanford and Son, 1973, Temperatures Rising, 1973, Kojak, 1974, The Love Boat, 1980, The Shape of Things, 1982, The Carol Burnett Show, All in the Family, 1971-75, The Jeffersons, 1974-85; films: Guess Who's Coming to Dinner, 1967, Young Runaways, 1968, The Comic, 1969, Pendulum, 1970, Hickory and Boggs, 1972, The New Centurians, 1972, Soul Soldier, 1972, Lady Sings the Blues, 1972, Love at First Bite, 1979. **Orgs:** Corr sec Kwanza Found 1973. **Honors/Awds:** Trouper Awd ''Y'' Drama Guild YMCA New York City 1965; Best Actress in Comedy Role, Image Awd NAACP 1975; 20 Grand Salutes ''Outstanding Actress'' 1976; Best Actress in TV Image Awd NAACP 1978; Best Actress in a Comdey Series Emmy Awd for ''The Jeffersons'' 1981.

SANFORD, MARK
Health services executive. **Personal:** Born Nov 24, 1953, St Louis, MO; son of Mr & Mrs Levi Sanford; children: Tifani Iris, Marcus L Alexander. **Educ:** Washington Univ, BA (Magna Cum Laude) 1975; St Louis Univ, MHA 1981. **Career:** St Louis Univ Med Ctr, staff assoc 1981-82; St Mary's Hospital, vice pres 1982-89; People's Health Centers, director of operations, 1989-. **Orgs:** Mem Amer Coll Healthcare Execs 1981-; bd mem Black Music Society; St Louis Chap Black MBA's 1985-; youth chairman, UNCF Telethon; African-American Chamber of Commerce, board member; 100 Black Men; past president, National Black MBA Association St Louis Chapter; National Society of Fund Raising Executives, 1992; national conference chairman, National Conference NBMBAA; Amer Heart Assn, board member; Natl Black MBA, board member; BABAA, board member. **Honors/Awds:** MBA of the Year, St Louis Chapter, Natl Black MBA Assn, 1988; EA Shepley Award. **Home Addr:** 5103 Washington, St Louis, MO 63108. **Business Addr:** 5701 Delmar, St Louis, MO 63112, (314)367-7848.

SANTIAGO, ROBERTO
Writer, journalist. **Personal:** Born Jun 30, 1963, New York, NY; son of Francisca Castro and Fundador Santiago. **Educ:** Oberlin College, BA, history/creative writing, 1985. **Career:** McGraw Hill Inc, NY, corporate writer, 1985-87; Times Mirror Inc, NY, sports writer, 1987-88; Emerge Magazine, NY, staff writer, 1989-92; The Plain Dealer, columnist, 1992-. **Orgs:** Mystery Writers of America; professional member, Natl Assn of Black Journalists; The Newspaper Guild. **Honors/Awds:** International American Press Assn, Award for Commentary, 1991; Guest Lecturer: Rutgers Univ; Princeton Univ; Vassar Clg; Oberlin Clg; CBS-TV; Columbia Univ; Trenton State Clg; Tennessee Department of Energy. **Special Achievements:** Author: Our Times 2, Bedford Books, 1991; The Contemporary Reader, Harper Collins, 1992. **Home Addr:** PO Box 6617, New York, NY 10128.

SANTOS, HENRY J.
Educator, pianist. **Personal:** Born Aug 29, 1927, Lewistown, ME; son of Beulah Benjamin Santos and Henry Santos; married Leola Waters. **Educ:** Boston Univ Sch of Fine & Appl Arts, BMus; Harvard U, Grad Stdy; Boston U, pvt study piano Alfredo Fondacaro 1952-60; Arturo Benedetti Michaelangli Lugano, Switzerland, study 1969; Boston U, condctng Allan Lanom 1972, piano Edith Stearns 1975, study theor wrk Dr H Norden 1975; Boston Univ, Boston, MA, MMus, 1980. **Career:** Bridgewater St Coll, professor of music, 1988-, asst prof music 1970-75; Perkins School for Blind, 1956-70. **Orgs:** Mem Music Ed Nat Conf; Nat Entmnt Conf Am; Assn for the Instru for the Blind; Adv Bd Fuller Art Museum; visiting member, Blue Ribbon Commission, Rhode Island Arts Council, 1991; support panel member, Rhode Island Arts Council, 1987, 1989. **Honors/Awds:** Piano recitals chamber mus progs in major cities of NE US & Europe; chosen instr perf Albert Schweitzer Fest 1950; rec cits Ach Awd Cape Verdean Benef Soc 1968; semifin 1st Louis Moreau Gottschalk Intl Compet for Pianists & Comp Dillard Univ 1970; perf of classical mus for piano by

Afro-Am Cmpsers; TV prog Say Bro 1971; prog WGBH Perf European & Afro-Am Composers for Piano 1972; lectr recital St Estrn Reg Conf Music Educ Nat Conf 1973; aptd Ethnic Herit Task Force of Commnwlth of MA by Gov Francis Sargent 1974; grant MA Council on Arts & Humanities for Trad Europe & Afro-Am music progs for elem & sec sch child Bridgewater St Coll 1974; compositions: Androscoggin Pines, 1983, Sonata for Piano, 1985, Mass in G Major, 1987, Two Dances for Piano, 1988, Healing Song,1988, Movement for Piaand Brass Quintet, 1990, Songs of Innocence, 1990. **Military Serv:** US Army, 418th Army Bad, private, 1946-47. **Business Addr:** Professor, Music Dept, Bridgewater State Coll, Bridgewater, MA 02324.

SANTOS, MATHIES JOSEPH

State official. **Personal:** Born Jan 10, 1948, Providence, RI; son of Rosemarie Lopes Santos and Matthew J. Santos; married Michelina Doretto Santos, Sep 6, 1969; children: Chiara C., Mathies-Kareem. **Educ:** Brown University, Providence, RI, BA, 1977; Rhode Island College, Providence, RI, BA, 1982. **Career:** Rhode Island College, Providence, RI, financial aid officer, 1978-80; State of Rhode Island, Department of Education, consultant, 1980-82, project director, 1983-85, Governor's Office, senior policy analyst, 1985, Department of Administration, executive assistant, 1985-90, special assistant to the commissioner of education, currently; Lippitt for Mayor, Providence, RI, campaign manager, 1982. **Orgs:** Corp. member, Delta Dental of Rhode Island; Brown University Third World Alumni Activities Committee; board member, Rhode Island College Alumni Association; member, Rhode Island Black Heritage Society; member, NAACP; member, Governor's Advisory Committee on Refugee Resettlement Management; trustee, The Wheeler School. **Military Serv:** Rhode Island Air National Guard, Capt, 1982-; Air Force Achievement Medal; sr air weapons director; military aide-de-camp to the governor, 1985-. **Business Addr:** Special Assistant to the Commissioner of Education, State of Rhode Island, 22 Hayes St, Providence, RI 02908.

SAPP, LAUREN B.

Librarian. **Personal:** Born Aug 22, Smithfield, NC; daughter of Senoria Burnette Sapp and Lee Sapp; children: Corey, Christopher, Cheston. **Educ:** North Carolina Central Univ, Durham, NC, BA, 1967; Univ of Michigan, Ann Arbor, MI, AMLS, 1971; Florida State Univ, Tallahassee, FL, AdvMS, 1979, PhD, 1984. **Career:** Voorhees College, Denmark, NC, instructor/librarian, 1971-74; Florida State Univ, Tallahassee, FL, librarian, 1974-84; North Carolina Central Univ, Durham, NC, visiting professor, 1985-96; Duke Univ, Durham, NC, librarian, 1984-96; Florida A-M University, Tallahassee, Fl, Director of Libraries, 1996-; Univ of NC at Chapel Hill, 1993-95. **Orgs:** Amer Library Assn; Black Caucus, GODORT, RASD, ACRL, BIS; Southeastern Library Association; chair, documents caucus, Florida Library Assn, 1982; chair, Documents Section North Carolina Library Association, 1988-89; secretary, State and Local Documents Task Force GODORT, 1987-88; ACRL International Relations Committee, 1994-98; mem, Beta Phi Mu Honor Society, 1980-; Lama Cultural Diversity Committee, 1997-; Lama Publications Committee of Fund Raising and Financial Development Section, 1997-. **Honors/Awds:** EEO Fellowship, Board of Regents, State of Florida, 1978-79, 1982; Title II Fellowship, University of Michigan, 1970-71; Women of Achievement Award, YWCA, Durham, NC, 1988; Star Award, Perkins University, Duke Library, 1989, 1991. **Home Addr:** PO Box 6326, Tallahassee, FL 32314. **Business Addr:** Director of Libraries, Coleman Library, Florida A & M University, Tallahassee, FL 32307.

SAPP, WARREN

Professional football player. **Personal:** Born Dec 19, 1972, Plymouth, FL. **Educ:** Miami (Fla.), attended. **Career:** Tampa Bay Buccaneers, defensive tackle, 1995-. **Honors/Awds:** Lombardi Award. **Special Achievements:** 1st round/12th overall NFL draft pick, 1995. **Business Addr:** Professional Football Player, Tampa Bay Buccaneers, 1 Buccaneer Pl, Tampa, FL 33607, (813)870-2700.

SARKODIE-MENSAH, KWASI

Librarian. **Personal:** Born Jun 13, 1955, Ejisu, Ashanti, Ghana; son of Margaret Akua Barnieh and Thomas Kwaku Mensah; married Elizabeth Oppong, Sep 21, 1980; children: Kofi, Kwame, Nana Akua. **Educ:** Universidad Complutense, diploma, 1978; University of Ghana, BA (w/honors), 1979; Clarion University, MSLS, 1983; University of Illinois, PhD, 1988. **Career:** Ahmadiyya Secondary School, teacher, 1979-80; Origbo Community High School, teacher, 1980-82; Clarion University, graduate asst, 1982-83; University of Illinois, graduate asst, 1984-86; Xavier University of Louisiana, head of public services, 1986-89; Northeastern University, library instruction coordinator, 1989-92; Boston College, chief reference librarian, 1992-95; Commonwealth of Massachusetts, court interpreter, 1992-; US Attorney General's Office, Boston, consultant, African languages; College of Advancing Studies, Boston College, faculty, 1996-; Boston College Libraries, manager of instructional services, 1995-. **Orgs:** American Library Assn, 1984-; Massachusetts Faculty Development Consortium, advsry bd mbr, 1992-; ACRL/IS Diverse Committee, chair, 1993-95; Northeastern University Committee to Improve College Teaching, 1989-92; Multicultural Network, 1992-; Boston College, Martin Luther King Committee, 1993-; ACRL/IS Committee on Education for Library Instructors, ACRL/IS Award Committee. **Honors/Awds:** University of Illinois, Fellow, 1986-87; Research Strategies, Top 20 Articles in Library Instruction, 1986; Origbo Community High School, Best Teacher, 1981, 1982; Spanish Government, Scholarship to study abroad, 1978; University of Ghana, Scholarship, 1975-79. **Special Achievements:** Author, works include: Making Term Paper Counseling More Meaningful, 1989; Writing in a Language You Don't Know, 1990; The Intl Ta: A Beat from a Foreign Drummer, 1991; Dealing with Intl Students in a Multicultural Era, 1992; Paraprofessionals in Reference Services: An Untapped Mine, 1993; editor: Library Instruction Roundtable Newsletter, 1991-92; consultant: Northeastern Univ Project on the History of Black Writing, 1990-; The International Student in the US Academic Library: Bldg Bridges to Better Bibliographic Instruction. **Home Phone:** (617)729-6759. **Business Addr:** Manager, Instructional Services, Boston College, 307 O'Neill Library, Chestnut Hill, MA 02167, (617)552-4465.

SARMIENTO, SHIRLEY JEAN

Educator, arts administrator. **Personal:** Born Nov 28, 1946, Buffalo, NY; daughter of Claudia Hall Laughlin and John C Laughlin; divorced; children: Tolley Reeves, William Jr. **Educ:** Medaille Coll, BS 1980; Canisius Coll, attended 1980-83; NY State Univ at Buffalo American studies/women's studies 1988-. **Career:** Offender Aide & Restoration, coord family support mgr 1982-83; Night People (homeless), worker 1985-86; Buffalo Bd of Educ, sub teacher; Jesse Nash Health Ctr, family life prog; Gowanda Psychiatric Ctr, WNY Peace Ctr, rep/peace educator; NY State Univ at Buffalo, lecturer 1989; St Ann's Community Ctr, director, learning club, 1990; Langston Hughes Inst, court advocate. **Orgs:** Organizer/active mem Sister-Hood Assn; mem NAACP, WNY Peace Ctr, Natl Women's Studies Assn, Educators for Social Responsibility, Christian Ministeries Prison Prog; panel mem Peace Women & Employment; member, Nat'l Women's Studies Association; board member, Jubilee Community Loan Fund, 1988-90; Burchfield/Penny Art Center, volunteer, 1992-; WNY Civil Liberties Union, committee member. **Honors/Awds:** Certificate Head Start; Certificate Offender Aid & Restoration; The Urban Arts project An African American Artist Agenda, founder, 1994. **Special Achievements:** Editor, Drumbeats: An Urban Arts Anthology, 1996. **Military Serv:** US Army Reserves, spec-4, 1977-80; 2 Appreciation Awards. **Home Addr:** 205 Marine Dr #4D, Buffalo, NY 14202.

SARREALS, E. DON

Scientist. **Personal:** Born Sep 22, 1931, Winston-Salem, NC; married Florence B Coleman; children: Cheryl Lynn, Esquire. **Educ:** City Coll of NY, BS Meteorology 1957; New York Univ, MS Meteorology 1961. **Career:** Natl Weather Serv Forecast Office, NYC, supr radar meteorologist 1961-69; WRC TV Natl Broadcasting Co, TV meteorologist 1969-75; Storm Finders Inc , pres/cons meteorologist 1969-76; Natl Weather Serv Headquarters, dissemination meteorologist 1976-80; MD Center for Public Broadcasting, TV meteorologist 1976-81; NEXRAD Project, NOAA/NWS, chief, Oper 1981-92; Federal Coordinator for Meteorology, assistant federal coordinator, NOAA/NWS, 1992-. **Orgs:** Lecturer/meterology City Coll of NY 1957-69; chmn bd dir 157th St & Riverside Dr Housing Co Inc 1966-68; mem Natl Acad of Sci Committee on Common Disasters & Media 1977-75; mem Natl Telecommunications Info Agency's Teletext Comm 1978-80; prof mem Amer Meteorological Soc 1955-; mem Natl Weather Assn 1980-; lecturer Smithsonian Inst Washington DC 1972; mem Montgomery Center School Comm on Secondary School 1976-78; bd mem D Rumaldry Homes Assn 1984-; National Science & Technology Council/Committee on Environment & Natural Resources/ Subcommittee on Natural Disaster Reduction, 1994-. **Honors/ Awds:** Ward Medal Meteorology City Coll of NY 1957; Teaching Fellowship CCNY 1957; Community Serv River Terrace Men's Club New York City 1969; Service Awards NWS 1964-65, 1980, 1984; publ NWS Forecasting Handbook #2 NWS 1978; Next Generation Weather Radar (NEXRAD) Operators Concept 1983, Product Description Document 1984, second edition 1987; ''NEXRAD Products'' 23rd Amer Meteorological Soc Con on Radar Meteorology 1986; ''NEXRAD Operational Capability'' proceedings of 1987 annual meeting of the Natl Weather Assoc; ''NEXRAD Products and Operational Capability'' proceedings of 25th Aerospace Sciences meeting Amer Inst of Aeronautics & Astronautics 1987. **Military Serv:** US Army, cpl; Natl Defense Serv Ribbon; Good Conduct Medal 1953-55. **Home Addr:** 6300 Contention Ct, Bethesda, MD 20817. **Business Addr:** Asst Federal Coordinator for NOAA, NWS, Office of the Federal Coordinator for Meteorology, 8455 Coleville Rd, Ste 1500, Silver Spring, MD 20910.

SARTIN, JOHNNY NELSON, JR.

Television photojournalist. **Personal:** Born Nov 29, 1960, Hattiesburg, MS; son of Corean Anderson Sartin and Johnny N Sartin Sr; married Natalie Renee Bell Sartin, Jun 9, 1990. **Educ:** Univ of Southern MS, Hattiesburg, MS, BS, 1982. **Career:** WLOX-TV, Biloxi, MS, TV news photojournalist, 1982-86; WKRG-TV, Mobile, AL, TV news photojournalist, 1986-88; KFOR-TV, Oklahoma City, OK, TV news photojournalist, 1988-. **Orgs:** Mem, Natl Assn of Black Journalists, 1988-; mem, Natl Press Photographers Assn, 1984-; mem, Alpha Phi Alpha Fraternity Inc, 1979-82; mem, OK City Black Media Associates, 1990-. **Honors/Awds:** Award of Excellence/ Photojournalism, Natl Assn of Black Journalists, 1989, 1990. **Business Addr:** Television Photojournalist, KFOR-TV, 444 E Britton Rd, Oklahoma City, OK 73120.

SATCHELL, ELIZABETH

Educator. **Personal:** Born in Eastville, VA; daughter of Alice Watson Satchell; children: Troi Eric. **Educ:** Drake Coll of Business, graduate 1969; Temple Univ; Charles Morris School of Advertising & Journalism; Union Co Coll; Amer Acad of Broadcasting; Kean College, BS, MPA. **Career:** CBS/WCAU-TV Channel 10, sales asst 1970-75, news prod asst 1975-77, newswriter/reporter 1977-79; WNJR Radio, dir pub rel/news editorials 1979-80, prog dir 1980-81, vp/prog dir 1981-82, vp/ station mgr 1982-; Realty World Professional Associate, Scotch Plains NJ realtor assoc 1989; Kean College, Center for Integration of Math and Science, currently. **Orgs:** dir Board of Dir Future Devel Group 1986; dir Board of Dir NYMRAD, (NY Market Radio Braodcasters Assn) 1989; Natl Assn of Broadcasters; Natl Assn of Black Owned Broadcasters; Radio Advertising Bureau; Greater Newark Chamber of Commerce; Pi Alpha Alpha Honor Society; Amer Society for Public Adm; Natl Women's Political Caucus. **Honors/Awds:** Black Achiever/ Business and Education YM-YWCA Newark & Vicinity 1982; diploma Radio Sales Univ, Radio Advertising Bureau 1988; diploma NJ Realty Institute 1989; NJ Real Estate License 1989; NJ Insurance Producers License, 1994. **Home Addr:** 948 West 8th St, Plainfield, NJ 07060.

SATCHELL, ERNEST R.

Educator. **Personal:** Born Jul 29, 1941, Exmore, VA; married Elsa Martin; children: Kwame, Keita. **Educ:** Towson State College, MEd, 1971; Maryland State College, BS; St Joseph's College, Philadelphia, advanced study. **Career:** University of Maryland, Eastern Shore, chairman, art education department, instructor of ceramics; Boeing Vertol Corporation, Philadelphia, commercial art director; Virginia Hospital, Philadelphia, art the rapist. **Orgs:** National Conference of Artists; Ant Art Education Association; Maryland State Teachers Association; NEA; Alpha Phi Alpha; board director, Somerset Co Art Association; Union Baptist Church, Committe on Higher Education. **Honors/Awds:** One-man Show, Academy of the Arts, Easton, Maryland, 1974; Exhibits: Towson State College, 1974, Pennsylvania State University, 1971. **Military Serv:** USS Forrestal 1968.

SATCHER, DAVID

Federal official. **Personal:** Born Mar 2, 1941, Anniston, AL; son of Anna Satcher and Wilmer Satcher; married Nola; children: Gretchen, David, Daraka, Daryl. **Educ:** Morehouse Coll, BS 1963; Case Western Reserve Univ, MD, PhD 1970. **Career:** Strong Meml Hosp Univ Rochester, resd 1971-72; King-Drew Med Ctr, dir 1972-75; Charles Drew Postgrad Med School, Macy faculty fellow 1972-75; King-Drew Sickle Cell Ctr, assoc dir 1973-75, asst prof, interim chmn 1974-75; UCLA School of Med, asst prof 1974-76, resd 1975-76; King-Drew Med Ctr, prof, chmn, dept of family med; Morehouse Coll School of Med, pres; Centers for Disease Control, head, 1994-97; US Surgeon General, 1998-. **Orgs:** Med dir 2nd Bapt Free Clinic; Amer Acad of Family Physicians, Amer Soc of Human Genetics; bd of dir Soc of Teachers of Fam Med, Joint Bd of Family Practice of GA, Phi Beta Kappa chap Delta 1977; mem Alpha Omega Alpha Hon Medical Soc, Amer Assn for the Advancement of Science, Amer Cancer Soc, AMA, Amer Health Assn, Natl Medical Assn; life mem NAACP; mem Urban League; bd of directors, First American Bank of Nashville; visiting committee member, Univ of Alabama School of Medicine; board of trustees, Carnegie Foundation for the Advancement of Teaching; Inst of Medicine; Natl Academy of Sciences; Alpha Omega Alpha. **Honors/Awds:** Outstanding Morehouse Alumnus Awd 1973; Awd for Med Ed for Sickle Cell Disease 1973; Macy Found Faculty Fellow Comm Med 1972-73; Dudley Seaton Meml Awd Outstanding Alumnus Case Western Res Univ 1980-; numerous publications. **Business Addr:** US Surgeon General, 200 Independence Ave SW, Washington, DC 20201, (202)443-4000.

SATCHER, ROBERT LEE, SR.

Chemist, educational administrator, educator, consultant. **Personal:** Born Sep 18, 1937, Anniston, AL; son of Anna Curry Satcher and Wilmer Satcher; married Marian Hanna; children: Serena, Robert Jr, Rodney, Robin. **Educ:** AL State Univ, BS 1959; AZ State Univ, MS 1963; OR State Univ, PhD 1971; further studies at Univ of Missouri, Oklahoma Univ, Tufts Univ, TX A&M Univ, MIT. **Career:** Booker T Washington HS, sci & math instructor 1959-62; AL State Univ, instructor, chem, phys science, 1963-65; Hampton Inst, chief planning officer, instructor to assoc prof, chem, 1965-79; Tororo Women Coll, Uganda, E Africa, prof chem, sci adv, 1973; Voorhees Coll, exec vp, acad dean, prof of chem 1979-82; Fisk Univ, interim pres 1984, acad dean/provost, professor chem, 1982-88; St Paul's Coll, acting pres/provost, 1988-89, vice president, academic affairs/provost, 1988-92, professor chem, 1988-. **Orgs:** Consult USOE/AIDP, Univ Assn, Washington, DC, 1975-78; Moton Inst Capahosic VA 1977; Comm on Colls SACS, Atlanta GA 1978-86; Operation PUSH; NAACP; SCLC; Amer Nuclear Soc; AKM National Honor Society; BKX Natl Hon Sci Soc; Natl Inst Sci; AAAS; Soc of Coll & Univ Planning; AIR; external evaluation, TN State Univ 1977-81; Norfolk State Univ 1980-83; eval Title III US Dept Ed WA 1980-83; president, Conf Academic Deans Southern States, SACS, 1990. **Honors/Awds:** Seven articles, Natl Inst of Sci, Journal of Photochem, 1968-75; fellowship grants, US Atomic Energy Comm, Ford Found, 1968-71; seven articles, Higher Educ Condensed, Assn of Inst Rsch, 1974-78; fellow, acad admin Amer Council on Educ, 1975-76; Citizen of the Year, Zeta Omicron Chap, Omega Psi Phi, 1977; Change Mag, 1978; co-author, Photochem of Thymine, 1972; author, Long Range Planning, 1978; NIH grantee, 1972-77; Ford Found fellow, 1969-71; Silver Beaver, BSA, 1988; Paper, Photochem of Thymine, International Cong Photobivl in Bochum, Germany, 1977; Omega Man of the Year, Omicron Omega Chapter, Omega Psi Phi, 1990; Outstanding Service Awards: Epsilon Gamma Chapter, Omega Psi Phi, 1992, CIC, Washington, DC, 1992; Paper, The Acting Presidency: Privileges vs Priorities, Ace Fellows Annual Meeting, Nov 1994. **Business Addr:** Prof of Chem, Dept Natl Sci & Math, St Paul's Coll, 406 Windsor Ave, Lawrenceville, VA 23868.

SATTERFIELD, PATRICIA POLSON
Judge. **Personal:** Born Jul 10, 1942, Christchurch, VA; daughter of Thea A Polson and Grady H Polson; married Preston T Satterfield, Aug 29, 1966; children: Danielle Nicole. **Educ:** Howard University, BME, 1964; Indiana University, MM, 1967; St Johns University, School of Law, JD, 1977. **Career:** Sewanhaku High School District, vocal music teacher, 1968-77; UCS Counsels Office of Court Administration, assistant deputy counsel, senior counsel, 1978-90; Unified Court System of State of New York, judge, 1991-. **Orgs:** St John's University, cultural diversity committee, School of Law, 1991-, board of directors, law alumni, 1991-; Queens Women's Network, co-chair, board of directors, 1983-90; Human Resources Center of St Albans, board of directors, 1990-; Association of Women Judges, 1991-; Metropolitan Black Lawyers Association, 1988-; Queens County Bar Association, 1989-; Jack and Jill of America Inc Queens Co, president, 1978-87. **Honors/Awds:** Alpha Kappa Alpha, Epsilon Omega Chapter, Outstanding Community Leader of the Year, 1991; Queens County Women's Bar Association, Ascension to Bench, 1991; Alva T Starforth, Outstanding Teacher of the Year, 1976. **Special Achievements:** First Black female judge elected in Queens County, New York, 1990. **Business Addr:** Civil Court of the City of New York, 120-55 Queens Blvd, Borough Hall, Jamaica, NY 11413.

SATTERWHITE, FRANK JOSEPH
Business executive. **Personal:** Born Oct 3, 1942, Akron, OH; son of Ethel Gindraw Satterwhite and Arthur Satterwhite; married; children: Frank Jr, Kuntu, Onira, Kai. **Educ:** Howard Univ, BA Educ 1965; Southern IL Univ, MS Coll Admin 1967; Stanford Univ, PhD Coll Admin 1975. **Career:** College Entrance Exam Bd, asst dir 1968-71; Oberlin Coll, assoc dean 1971-72; Ravenswood School Dist, asst to the supt 1972-76; Comm Develop Inst, pres 1978-. **Orgs:** Councilman EPA Municipal Council 1974-78; mem Narobi Secretarat 1979-85; planning comm SMC Planning Comm 1980-83; mem BAPAC 1981-85; mem Mid-Peninsula Urban Coalition 1982-85; councilman EPA City Council 1983-85. **Honors/Awds:** Comm Serv EPACCI 1983; Comm Serv EPA Chamber of Comm 1983; Champion OICW 1985; Kellogg Natl Fellowship 1986-89. **Home Addr:** 2275 Euclid Ave, East Palo Alto, CA 94303. **Business Addr:** President, Comm Develop Institute, P O Box 50099, East Palo Alto, CA 94303.

SATTERWHITE, JOHN H.
Educator. **Personal:** Born Jan 1, 1913, Newberry, SC; married Lucille C Mills; children: Joan Cecille, John Mills. **Educ:** Benedict Coll, AB; Oberlin Grad Sch Theol, BD, STM; Boston Univ Sch Theol, ThD; Johnson C Smith U, DD; Benedict Coll, DD. **Career:** Livingstone Coll, instr 1938-40; Hood Theol Sem, dean, prof 1940-57; Wesley Theol Sem, prof 1958-74; AME Zion Ch Phila-Balti Conf, clrgymn; AME Zion Qrtrly Rev, edtr. **Orgs:** Gen Sec Consult on Ch Union Adv 4th Asmbly World Coun of Chs Sweden 1968; mem Fllwshp of Profs of Missions & Ecumncs; N Am Acad Ecumncs; Inter-Relg Com on Race Rel; Oxford Theol Sem; Wrld Meth Coun; Div of Chrstn Unity; Nat Coun Chs; past pres Am Soc of Christian Ethics; dir Gastave Weigel Soc Cont Edn. **Business Addr:** 228 Alexander St, Princeton, NJ 08540.

SAULNY, CYRIL
Association executive. **Career:** NAACP, New Orleans chapt, pres, currently. **Business Addr:** President, NAACP, PO Box 8010, New Orleans, LA 70182-8010, (504)949-1441.

SAULSBERRY, CHARLES R.
Attorney. **Personal:** Born Sep 4, 1957, Goshen, AL; son of Ruby Lee Saulsberry and Asia William Saulsberry; married Dana Scott Saulsberry, Jun 28, 1986; children: Kara, Kalyn. **Educ:** Harvard University, AB, 1979; Northwestern University, School of Law, JD, 1982. **Career:** Winston & Strawn, summer associate, 1980-81, associate, partner, 1982-92; Parker, Chapin, Flattau & Klimpl, summer associate, 1981; Thompson & Mitchell, partner, 1992-. **Orgs:** Bar Association of Metropolitan St Louis, 1992-; Chicago Council of Lawyers, secretary, board of directors, 1985-86; Cabrini Green Legal Assistance Foundation, board of directors, 1985-86; Minority Legal Education Resources Inc, secretary, board of directors, 1986-87; American Bar Association, 1982-; Illinois State Bar Association, 1982-; Natl Bar Assn, 1982- Chicago Bar Association, 1982-; Cook County Bar Association, 1982-; National Association of Securities Professionals, 1982-. **Honors/Awds:** Council on Legal Opportunities Commission, Outstanding Student, 1979; Earl Warren Foundation, Earl Warren Scholar, 1979. **Special Achievements:** Bond counsel to city of Chicago on $489,735,000, O'Hare International Terminal special revenue bonds, 1990; underwriters' counsel on over $1.9 billion housing bonds for Illinois Housing Development Authority, 1984-91. **Business Addr:** Partner, Thompson & Mitchell, One Mercantile Center, St Louis, MO 63101, (314)342-1708.

SAULTER, GILBERT JOHN
Senior executive (retired), consultant. **Personal:** Born Apr 20, 1936, Seattle, WA; son of Bernice Saulter and Gerald Saulter; married Mae Frances; children: Bradford, Melonie, Daryl. **Educ:** Univ of WA, BSEE 1962; UCLA & Univ of WA, postgrad work; registered professional engr, 1969. **Career:** Boeing Co, engr aid 1958-62; Northrop, 1962-65; Itek, 1965-67; Sundstrand Data Control, 1967-71; US Dept of Labor, saf engr 1971-74, area dir 1974-76, reg admin Northeast Region, 1976-1978, reg admin, Southwest Region 1978-95; consultant. **Orgs:** Chair, YMCA Youth Comm, Indian Guide prog, 1970; vice chair, adv comm Boy Scouts of America, 1970-74; NAACP; Kappa Alphi Psi; past pres Northwest Council of Black Professional Engineers; board of directors Opportunity Industrialization Center 1985-88; board of directors Classical Guitar Soc 1986-87; board of directors Family Place 1987-90; US delegate Petroleum Conf, Lagos, Nigeria 1985; chief US delegate Intl Labor Organization Geneva, Switzerland 1986; chair Dallas/Ft Worth Combined Federal Campaign 1989-91; chair DFW Federal Executive Bd 1993-94; head of US delegation NAFTA Joint Technical Conf on Safety and Health in the Petrochemical Industry, Edmonds, Canada 1994. **Honors/Awds:** Hon Roll Univ of WA 1961, 1962; Merit Awd Northrop Corp 1963, 1965; Merit Awd ITEK Corp 1967; Publ "Act Network Compen for Adap Cont Syst," 1967; Trail Blazer Awd, SO Dallas Business and Professional Women's Club, 1983; Outstanding Sr Executive Awd 1985, 1989, 1990, 1991; Presidential Rank of Meritorious Executive, 1992. **Military Serv:** National Guard, 8 yrs, honorable discharge 1962. **Home Addr:** 525 Missionary Ridge, DeSoto, TX 75115-5233.

SAUNDERS, BARBARA ANN
Tourism/travel administrator. **Personal:** Born Jun 5, 1950, Roanoke, VA; married Byron Creighton Saunders. **Educ:** Hampton Univ Hampton, VA, BA Fine Arts 1972. **Career:** Amer Security Bank WA DC, cust serv rep 1973-75; GA Film & Videotape Office, pr specialist 1976-80; freelance writer; freelance commercial voice-over talent 1985-; GA Dept Ind, Trade and Tourism, acct asst, 1975-76, pr program coordinator, 1980-90, tour and travel development assistant director, 1990-94, tourism mktg consultant, 1994-. **Orgs:** Bd dir Women In Film-Atlanta 1977-79; pres Sigma Gamma Nu Social Club, Hampton Univ, 1971. **Business Addr:** Tourism Mktg Consultant, Tour and Travel Development, Georgia Dept Industry, Trade and Tourism, PO Box 1776, Atlanta, GA 30301.

SAUNDERS, DORIS E.
Educator, educational administrator (retired), editor, consultant. **Personal:** Born Aug 8, 1921, Chicago, IL; daughter of Thelma C Rice Evans and Alvesta Stewart Evans; divorced; children: Ann Camille, Vincent Ellsworth III. **Educ:** Roosevelt U, BA 1951; Boston U, MS Journ 1977, MA Afro-Am Studies 1977; Vanderbilt Univ, ABD, history, 1984. **Career:** Johnson Publishing Co Chicago, ed sp library, 1949-60, director, book div, 1960-66, 1972-78; Chicago Daily Defender, columnist 1966-70; The Plus Factor/Inf Inc, pres 1966-72; Chicago State Univ, dir comm relations, inst development, 1968-70; Univ of IL Chicago, staff associate, office of the chancellor 1970-72; Chicago Courier Newspaper, columnist 1970-72; Jackson State Univ, prof of journalism, 1978-96, prof mass communications, 1985-96, acting chair, 1990, chair 1991-; Ancestor Hunting, pres; Kith and Kin Geneolgical Newsletter, publisher. **Orgs:** Mem adv com Fed Reserve Bd 1968-71; mem adv com Dept of Labor Bureau of the Census 1972-80; consultant Lilly Endowment 1978-; mem Sigma Delta Chi; Natl Assn Black Journalists; ACEJME; vip & pres elect, Black College Communications Association (BCCA). **Honors/Awds:** National Black Media Coalition, Outstanding Women Communicators, 1994; Co-author with Gerri Major, Black Society, Johnson Publishing Co, 1976; in progress biography of William L Dawson (D.Ill), 1886-1970.

SAUNDERS, EDWARD HOWARD
Physician. **Personal:** Born Aug 16, 1926, Sumter City, SC. **Educ:** Morehouse Coll, BS 1949; Howard Univ Coll of Med, MD 1957. **Career:** Freedmans Hosp, chief res urol 1962-63; private practice, physician. **Orgs:** Morehouse College & Morehouse School Medicine, brd of trustees; Nat Med Assn; American Urologic Association; DC Med Soc; Med & Chirug Soc of DC; Diplomate Am Bd of Urol 1966. **Business Addr:** 715 Florida Ave, NW, Washington, DC 20001.

SAUNDERS, ELIJAH
Physician. **Personal:** Born Dec 9, 1934, Baltimore, MD; married Monzella Smith; children: Kevin, Donna, Monzella. **Educ:** Morgan State Coll, BS 1956; Univ of MD Sch of Med, MD, 1960; Univ of MD Hosp, intern 1960-61, asst res 1961-63; Univ of MD Hosp, flwshp 1963-65. **Career:** Provident Hosp, chief of cardiol 1966-84, dir 1968, chief 1969-71, acting chief 1973-75; MD Gen Hosp, asso cardiol 1965-84; Univ of MD School and Hospital, instr 1965-84, assoc professor and head, Hypertension Division, 1984-; Private Practice, 1965-. **Orgs:** Num pos Am Heart Assn: Cntrl MD Chpt, MD Affil, Natl Dallas, chmn Nat Schlarshp Fund; Unit Ch of Jesus Christ Apost; mem Med & Chirurgi Fac of MD; mem Am Med Assn; President Medical Staff, Provident Hosp 1966-74; admsns com Univ of MD 1970-75; mem Edtl Bd Spirit; trste bd 1st Un Ch of Jesus Christ Apost; chmn steer com Hyperten Contr Prgm; chmn, Adv Council of MD on Related end right factors; Hyperten Contr Prgm; mem MD Soc of Cardiol; Am Coll of Physic; Fellow Am Coll of Cardiol; Fellow Am Coll of Angiol; num other assns & com. **Honors/Awds:** Author/producer numerous film strips; num appear on TV & radio; num lect; Bronze Serv Medal; Pres Awd, 1975, Silver Disting Serv Medal, 1976, American Heart Assn; Pres Plaque Cntrl MD Heart Assn 1975; House Resol 15 Del Webs 1976; founder, Heart House; fellow Am Coll of Cardiol 1976; Disting Leadership Plaque MD High Blood Pressure Coordinating Cncl 1982; Outstanding Achievement in Health Care Awd Black Nurses Assn of Baltimore 1985; Marcus Garve Memorial Foundation Plaque, 1987; Louis B Russell Award, American Heart Assn, MD Affiliate, 1991; Honoree, Natl Kidney Foundation of MD, 1994; Keynote Speaker, Egyptian Hypertension League and Israel Hypertension Committee Program, 1994. **Military Serv:** Army NG maj 1960-66. **Business Addr:** Assoc Prof of Medicine, University of Maryland Professional Building, 419 W Redwood St, Suite 620, Baltimore, MD 21201.

SAUNDERS, ELIZABETH A.
Educator. **Personal:** Born Apr 12, 1948, Centralia, IL. **Educ:** Freed Hardeman College, AA, 1967; Memphis State University, BS, 1969; Memphis State University, MA, 1979. **Career:** Freed Hardman College, Henderson, Tennessee, academic advisor & instructor, 1978-; Haywood High School, Brownsville, Tennessee, instructor of English & reading, 1977-78; Anderson Grammar School, Brownsville, instructor of reading, 1976-77; Haywood High Jr Division, Brownsville, instruction of English & reading lab, 1970-76. **Orgs:** HEA/WTEA/TEA/NEA, 1970-78; Tennessee Association for Super & Curriculum Development, 1978-; International Reading Association, 1979-; American Pers & Guid Association, 1980; NAACP; Alpha Kappa, 1969-; committee chairman, FHC Women's Club & Student Relations Committee, Faculty Self-study Committee, 1979-; teacher, Lucyville Church of Christ. **Honors/Awds:** Freed Hardeman College, scholarship, 1966; elected representative, Tennessee Education Association, General Assembly, 1975; cert as spec in devel educ, Appalach State University, Boone, North Carolina, 1980. **Business Addr:** Education, Freed Hardeman College, Henderson, TN 38340.

SAUNDERS, JERRY
Association executive, business executive. **Personal:** Born Apr 23, 1953, Columbus, OH; son of Rosalie Saunders and Earl Saunders. **Educ:** Ohio Wesleyan University Upward Bound, completion certificate, 1967-71; Oberlin College, BA, 1975; Ohio State University, 1975-76. **Career:** Futon Corporation, draftsman, 1976-77; Las Vegas Dealers Basketball Team, player, 1977-79; Ohio Wesleyan University, associate director of Upward Bound, 1979-80; JC Penney Insurance, insurance adjuster, 1980-87; Waiters & Associates, vice pres, 1990-; Eldon W Ward YMCA, executive director, 1988-. **Orgs:** Unique Community and Neighborhood Networks, 1989-; Columbus Urban League, 1991-95; Flintridge Baptist Church, chairman of trustee board, 1979-; Columbus Public Schools, advisory board, 1991-; MVP Basketball Camps, program director, 1989-; Make the Right Choice, program coordinator, 1992-; Blue Chip Magazine Awards Gala, chairman, 1992-. **Honors/Awds:** 20 various plaques and certificates for community service. **Business Addr:** Executive Director, Eldon W Ward YMCA, 130 Woodland Ave, Columbus, OH 43203, (614)252-3166.

SAUNDERS, JOHN EDWARD, III
State labor official. **Personal:** Born Jan 17, 1945, Bryn Mawr, PA; son of Eleanor Smith Saunders and John Edward Saunders; married Vivian E Williams; children: John Edward IV, Jason Elliott, Shanna Marie. **Educ:** Central State Univ, BS Business Admin 1968; LaSalle Coll & Univ of PA, Social Serv Agency Mgmt Educ & Develop Prog certificate 1982; IBM Comm Exec Seminar, certificate 1982; Lincoln Univ, MA Human Serv Admin 1983; Duke University, Sanford Institute of Public Policy, Strategic Leadership Seminar, 1993. **Career:** Dun & Bradstreet Inc, credit analyst 1972-76; Urban League of Philadelphia, prog dir 1976-78, sr vice pres 1978-83; Urban League of Greater Hartford Inc, pres & CEO 1983-88; State of Connecticut, deputy labor commissioner 1988-97; Natl Forum for Black Public Adm, exec dir, 1997-. **Orgs:** Mem Hartford Rotary Club; mem Assn of Black Social Workers; mem CT Civil Rights Coordinating Comm; chmn Hartford Health Network Inc 1984-88; bd mem Almada Lodge Times Farm Camp Corp 1985-; chmn, Operation Fuel Inc 1986-97; bd mem, Science Museum of Con-

necticut 1988-96; trustee, Watkinson School 1988-96; bd mem, Connecticut Law Enforcement Foundation 1987-90; bd mem, Connecticut Prison Assn 1986-92; bd mem, Salvation Army, 1990-; bd mem, World Affairs Council, 1986-90; corporator, St Francis Hospital, 1986-96; trustee, Watkinson School, 1987-; trustee, Institute of Living, 1992; vice chairman, American Lendership Forum, 1992; mem, Tuscan Lodge #17, F&AM, PHA. **Honors/Awds:** ML King Jr Awd Hand in Hand Inc Philadelphia 1984; Fellow Amer Leadership Forum Hartford 1985; Doctor of Laws Honorary Briarwood College, 1983. **Military Serv:** AUS specialist 6, 3 1/2 yrs; Bronze Star; Army Commendation w/OLC; Air Medal; Vietnam Serv & Campaign Medal. **Business Addr:** Exec Dir, Natl Forum for Black Public Administrators, 777 N Capitol St, Ste 807, Washington, DC 20002.

SAUNDERS, JOHN P.
Sportscaster. **Personal:** Born Feb 2, 1955, Ontario. **Educ:** Western Michigan Univ, 1974-76; Ryerson Univ, 1976-77. **Career:** ESPN, host, basketball and hockey, 1986-; ABC Sports, host, football and baseball, currently. **Honors/Awds:** Emmy Nominee, 1994. **Business Addr:** Sportscaster, Entertainment & Sports Programming Network, 935 Middle St., ESPN Plaza, Bristol, CT 06010, (203)585-2000.

SAUNDERS, KENNETH PAUL
Navy lieutenant. **Personal:** Born May 15, 1948, Philadelphia. **Educ:** Univ of Dayton, BEE 1970; OCS USN, 1971; Armed Forces Air Intel Training Ctr Denver, 1975; Naviga Flight Training Pensacola 1975. **Career:** NYC, minor affairs off 1972-74; Small Combat Norfolk, weap off 1971-72; Gen Elec Philadel, systems & Analys 1970. **Honors/Awds:** Art public Am Contemp Artist Bicent Issue; gall Ligoa Duncan Gall New York City 1973; Bros Two Gall of New Mast TX 1975; Gall Ray Duncan Prix De Paris France 1975. **Military Serv:** USN lt. **Business Addr:** Lt Saunders AFAITC, Lowry AFB, Denver, CO 80230.

SAUNDERS, MARY ALICE
Educator. **Personal:** Born Feb 19, 1938, Waynesboro, GA; daughter of Claudia Hatcher Bell and James G Bell (deceased); widowed; children: Michael R. **Educ:** CCNY, MS 1971; New York University, New York, NY, MA, supevision & ed, 1972. **Career:** Dist 9 New York City Bd of Educ, asst dir sites & bldgs; SS New York City Bd of Educ, teacher; Educ & Employ Prog, dir; teacher computer language oper of different program machines; Reg Atty for Fed Housing Administration, admin asst. **Orgs:** Mem Protest Tchrs Assn; Fordham Univ Sch Adminstrs Assn; Black Tchrs Assn; Nat Black Caucus of Sch Bd Mem; vice pres Comm Sch Bd 6 NYC; mem Comm Plann Bd 9; Borough Pres Commn to imp the Waterfront; v chmn Area 145, Comm Corp; Hamilt Grange Bd Dirs; NAACP; chairperson, WESCAP, Inc; New York Club; prof, Black Women, 1979. **Honors/Awds:** Recpt Good Cit Awds 1967, 1969, 1972; Hamilton Grange Day Care Cntr & Bd of Edn. **Business Addr:** Instructor, SS NYC Board of Education, 620 W 150 St, New York, NY 10031.

SAUNDERS, MAUDERIE HANCOCK
Educator. **Personal:** Born Jun 13, 1929, Bartlesville, OK; children: Cheryle M Crawford, Leonard Anthony. **Educ:** Langston Univ Langston OK, BA 1947; Univ of OK Norman, MEd 1950; Univ of OK, PhD education & Psychology, 1961; Univ of Chicago, 1965. **Career:** Howard Univ, coordinator special educ prof of educ 1979-, chmn & prof of educ psychoednl studies dept 1976-79, prof dir special educ 1974-76; Howard Univ Center for the Study of Handicapped Children, asst dir 1973-74; Eastern Il Univ Charleston IL, prof 1970-73; WV State Coll Inst, prof 1966-70; Minot State Coll Minot ND, prof 1963-66; So Univ Baton Rouge, asso prof 1960-62; OK City Public Schools, visiting counselor school psychology 1950-59; Child Serv State Dept of Welfare Minot ND, psychol 1963-66; WV State Dept Mental Health, psychology consultant 1966-70; WV St Dept of Health. **Orgs:** Mem Am Psychol Assn 1961-; mem Alpha Kappa Alpha 1972; sponsor Chartered Chap Eta Gamma East IL campus 1972; spons Charter Chap #253 Counc of Except Child Howard Univ 1976. **Honors/Awds:** Listed in black OK res guide Archives of OK 1950; first black wom to rec PhD Univ of OK Norman 1961; "Teach the Educ Mental Retard Reading" Curr The Pointer 1964; outst W Virginians 1969; analys of cult diff Jour of Negro Educ 1970, and other publications. **Business Addr:** Professor of Education, Howard University, 2400 6th St, NW, Washington, DC 20059.

SAUNDERS, MEREDITH ROY
Ophthalmologist. **Personal:** Born Apr 15, 1930, Mason City, IA; son of Edna Marie Saunders and Albert J Saunders; divorced; children: Meredith Jr, Desda C, Brita B, Alaire M. **Educ:** Mason City Jr Coll, AA 1949; Univ of Iowa, BA 1952, MD 1956. **Career:** Private practice, ophthalmologist. **Orgs:** AMA; NMA; AAO. **Home Phone:** (515)274-4790. **Business Addr:** Ophthalmologist, 2101 Westown Pkwy, West Des Moines, IA 50265.

SAUNDERS, ROBERT EDWARD
Educator, historian. **Personal:** Born Jul 28, 1959, Hartford, CT; son of Styron Lucille Sanford Saunders and William Kershaw Saunders. **Educ:** Clark College, Atlanta, GA, BA, 1978-83; University of Wisconsin, Milwaukee, Milwaukee, WI, MA, 1989. **Career:** Chester-Upland School District, Chester, PA, teacher, 1986-87; Baptist Childrens Services, Thornbury, PA, youth worker, 1988-89; Community Occupational Readiness and Placement Program Inc, Philadelphia, PA, employment development council, 1989-90. **Orgs:** Member, Organization for Social Change, Clark, 1979-82; student life chair, Clark College Student Government, 1981-83; member, Organization for the Study of Negro Life & History, 1985. **Honors/Awds:** Advanced Opportunity Program Fellowship, Univ Wisconsin, Milwaukee, 1984-85.

SAUNDERS, ROBERT WILLIAM, SR.
Government official (retired). **Personal:** Born Jun 9, 1921, Tampa, FL; son of Christina Rogers Saunders and Willard Saunders; married Helen S Strickland, Jan 20, 1953; children: Robert W Jr. **Educ:** Bethune Cookman Coll, AA 1942; Univ of Detroit Coll of Law, 1952; Detroit Inst of Tech, AB 1951. **Career:** NAACP, field dir 1952-66; US Govt, chief office of civil rights CSA 1966-1976; Hillsborough Cty, dir equal opport office 1976-87, executive asst to Hillsborough County admin 1987-88; retired. **Orgs:** Gov appt Tampa Bay Reg Planning Cnsl 1984-86; mem FL Assc Prof Comm Human Rights Wrkr 1978-, Natl Assn of Human Rights Wrkr 1960-; vice pres FL State Conf NAACP Branches 1978-85, exec bd; mem Tampa Urban League 1960-, exec bd, 1989-; steward St Paul AME Church 1964-; treasurer, Hillsborough Co Democratic Exec Comm, 1986-91; Omega Psi Phi Frat; National Association of Human Rights Workers, 1995-; bd of county commissioners, Historic Commission Member Hillsborough County, 1996; mem, judicial nominating commission, 13th Judicial Circuit. **Honors/Awds:** Ruthledge H Pearson FL NAACP State Conf 1979; Whitney M Young, Jr Urban League Tampa FL 1982; Meritorious Award US Dept of Housing Urban Dev 1983; Nathan W Collier Award FL Memorial and Industrial Coll 1961; Outstanding Service Awrd Council of Handicapped Organizations; Gwendolyn Cherry Mem Freedom Fighters Awrd; Kentucky Colonel Commission 1974; "The Order of the Palmetto 1971;" President's Council, Univ of South FL; Bob's Corner, Column, Natl Assn of Intergroup/Human Rights Workers 1988-89; Whitney Young Memorial Award, 1986; University of South Florida, Outstanding Service Award; National Conference of Christian & Jews, Mayors Brotherhood/Sisterhood Award, 1992; Letter of Commendation on Retirement, Pres Ronald Reagan, 1988; Conference Program Dedication, Honor of Robert W Saunders, Sr, 48th Annual Conference, NAHRW, 1996. **Military Serv:** AAC sgt 1942-46. **Home Addr:** PO Box 4292, Tampa, FL 33677-4292.

SAUNDERS, THEODORE D. (RED)
Theatrical agent, musician. **Personal:** Born Mar 2, 1912, Memphis, TN; children: Theodore, Jr, Edmund, Deneen. **Career:** Chicago's top theatres and night clubs, entertainer 1958-; Club Delisa Chicago, band leader 1937-58; assoc with such stars as Count Basie, Duke Ellington, ed Skelton, Tommy Dorsey, Benny Goodman, Glenn Miller, numerous others; Annex Club, music 1935-36; Walk A Thon Band, Music 1928-33; theatrical agent 1955-. **Orgs:** Mem NAACP. **Honors/Awds:** Recipient Mahalia Jackson Award; Dick Gregory Award; Chicago Historical Soc Award; Record Music of Amer Award; Best Tune of the Year Award for "Hambone" (2 million rec seller) 1952; other recordings include "Stop Pretty Baby Stop," "Boot Em Up," "The Laraspa," "Advent in HiFi," "I Got Rhythm"; Ency of Jazz Award.

SAUNDERS, VINCENT E., III
Accountant. **Personal:** Born Jan 28, 1954, Chicago, IL; son of Doris Evans Saunders and Vincent E Saunders Jr; married Lynette Smith Saunders, Sep 23, 1984; children: Vincent IV, Asia Imani, Evan Paul. **Educ:** Howard University, Washington, DC, BA, 1976; Institute of Financial Educ, Chicago, IL, certificate, 1980; Univ of Illinois, Chicago, IL, 1986-89; Keller Graduate School of Management, Chicago, IL, MBA, 1997. **Career:** Citibank, FSB, assistant branch manager, 1978-86; Drexel National Bank, Retail Banking Department manager, vice president, 1986-89; Midway Airport Concessionaires, Office Admin/Information Systems, manager, 1989-97; Environmental Protection Agency, accountant, 1997-. **Orgs:** Alpha Phi Alpha Fraternity, financial secretary, 1986-88; Elliot Donnelley Chicago Youth Center, board member, 1986-89; Boy Scouts of America, asst scout master. **Honors/Awds:** Outstanding Young Men of America, US Jaycees, 1981; Up & Coming Bus & Professionals, Dollars & Sense Magazine, 1989. **Military Serv:** In Air Natl Guard, major, 1983-, Wing Human Relations Officer, 1986-93, Commander 126 Services Flight, 1993-97; exec officer, Logistics Group; Outstanding Unit 1984, 1989 & 1993; Outstanding Airman, Aberdeen Proving Award, MD, 1983; Officer Commendation Medal, 1993; Dept of Defense, Equal Opportunity Mgmt Inst Graduate, 1988. **Home Addr:** 9718 S Indiana Ave, Chicago, IL 60628.

SAUNDERS, WILLIAM JOSEPH
Association executive, educator. **Personal:** Born Oct 14, 1924, Washington, DC; son of Sara Mennah Hill Saunders and Edgar Eugene Saunders; married Gladys Mae Gray Saunders, Apr 19, 1947; children: Lois Camille, Ada Delores. **Educ:** Howard University, Washington, DC, BS, 1948, MS, 1952. **Career:** District of Columbia Public Schools, Washington, DC, assistant superintendent, 1952-81; National Alliance of Black School Educators (NABSE), Washington, DC, executive director, 1982-. **Orgs:** Vice president, Visiting Nurses Assn, 1983-89; member, Tandy Technology Advisory Committee, 1988-; Whittle Channel One Advisory Committee; president, Educators Leadership Consortium, 1990-; president, District of Columbia School Mens Club, 1982-89; Kappa Alpha Psi. **Military Serv:** US Army, First Sergeant, 1943-46. **Business Addr:** Executive Director, NABSE National Office, 2816 Georgia Ave, NW, Washington, DC 20001.

SAUNDERS-HENDERSON, MARTHA M.
Educational administrator, educator, museum administrator. **Personal:** Born Dec 18, 1924, Spartanburg, SC; daughter of Milderd Ruth Clemons Saunders and Alix Pinky Saunders; married Mark Henderson Jr; children: Sondra JoAnn Jones, Woodrene Ruth, Markette Harris, Mark III, Alexis Lillian Marion. **Educ:** Burlington Cty Coll, AA 1978, AS 1979; Southern IL Univ, BS 1982; Central MI Univ, MBA 1983; Rutgers Univ, Doctoral. **Career:** Governer Island Nursery School, dir 1963; Girls Scouts Far East Okinowa, coord 1965; NJ, PA Dept of Ed, consult 1970; Merabash Museum, dir of program teaching spec sch 1986-87, pres, vp, museum exec 1970-; Burlington County Coll, Pemberton NJ Instructor, Museum 1989; African American Preservation, Historical Sites & History on African Americans, consultant. **Orgs:** Bd of trustee Merabash Museum 1969-85; commiss Burl Co Cultural & Heritage NJ 1975-890; consult NJ Art Assoc NJ 1977-78, Burlington Cty Coll NJ 1980-84; instr Spec Serv School NJ 1983-84; instr Beverly City School NJ 1984; consultant Burlington Co Cultural & Heritage Ft Dix for Black History Prog; mem Burlington Coll Alumni Hall of Fame; mem Union Co Coll Fund Raising; mem Community Alert a service of WNET/Thirteen Comm Affairs Dept; mem African Amer Museum Assoc, Contemporary Educ in the Arts and Culture Rsch of Black Children. **Honors/Awds:** Outstanding Serv NJ Dept of Ed 1979; Recognition NJ Commiss 1980, Black Arts & History 1981; Hall of Fame Burlington Cty Coll 1984; Hon Mem Sigma Gamma Rho Sor 1986; NJ Historical Commn Awd of Recognition; Certificate for Outstanding Service to Public Natl Business and Professional Women's Club of NJ; Special Recognition Award Afro-One Dance, Drama and Drum Theatre Inc 1989; Burlington County Cultural and Heritage Commission, Appreciation for Service Award; Delta Sigma Theta, Service Award for Outstanding Contributions in Cultural Arts; Neighborhood Leadership Initiative, Comm Foundation of New Jersey. **Home Addr:** 59 Emerald Lane, Willingboro, NJ 08046. **Business Addr:** President, Merabash Museum, PO Box 752, Willingboro, NJ 08046.

SAVAGE, ARCHIE BERNARD, JR.
Educational administrator. **Personal:** Born Nov 12, 1929, Memphis, TN; son of Mattie Hester Savage and Archie Savage; married Susan; children: Carl, Karen, Barbara. **Educ:** Univ of Denver, BA 1966; Univ of MD, MEd 1971; Univ of Denver, PhD 1976. **Career:** US Counterintelligence Spec Agent, 1951-73; Coord of Inst Research Univ of Denver, 1973-76; Utah State Univ, Logan, UT, asst dir affirmative action prog 1976-79; Central Connecticut State University, New Britain, CT, director of affirmative action, 1980-86; ABS Enterprises, president, 1980-; University of Connecticut Health Center, Farmington, CT, director of diversity and affirmative action, 1981-95; New Britain Hospital for Special Care, director, 1992-. **Orgs:** Consult Higher Educ Admin 1979-; Assn of Black Cardiologists 1984-90; Kappa Alpha Psi Fraternity; New Britain Gen Hosp 1981-; chrmn NB Comm On Human Rights and Opport 1984-89; secretary CT Unit of Amer Assn for Aff Action 1984-89; chm, bd of trustee, YMCA of New Britain/Berlin, 1995-; president, Rotary Club of New Britain, 1991-92. **Honors/Awds:** Paul Harris Fellow in Rotary International; Henry C. Minton Fellow in Sigma Pi Phi Fraternity. **Military Serv:** Bronze Star, 1971, Army, Navy and Air Force Commendation Medal, 1973. **Business Addr:** President, ABS Enterprise, PO Box 877, New Britain, CT 06050, (860)224-0270.

SAVAGE, AUGUSTUS A. (GUS SAVAGE)
Former federal official. **Personal:** Born Oct 30, 1925, Detroit, MI; son of Molly Wilder Savage and Thomas Frederick Savage; married Eunice King, 1946 (deceased); children: Thomas James, Emma Mae. **Educ:** Roosevelt Univ, BA 1950; Chicago Kent Clge of Law, grad study 1953. **Career:** Westside Booster, newspaper editor & publ 1958-60; Woodlawn Booster, newspaper editor 1961-64; Bulletin, newspaper editor 1963-64; Citizen, newspaper editor & publ 1965-79; Chicago Weekend, newspaper editor & publ 1973-79; US House of Rep, Second District, IL, representative, 1981-92. **Honors/Awds:** Award of Merit Oper PUSH Chicago IL 1976; Merit Award Best Columnist Natl Newspaper Publ Assn 1979; Freshman of the Year NAACP Evanston IL 1981; Pres Award, Cook Cty Bar Assn 1981; Achiever of the Year, Chicago South Chamber of Commerce, 1981; author: Political Power, 1969, How to Increase the Power of the Negro Vote, 1959. **Military Serv:** US Army, 1943-46.

SAVAGE, DENNIS JAMES
State official. **Personal:** Born Jun 28, 1944. **Educ:** Cheney University, BA, secondary education, 1966; Temple University, post grad. **Career:** Delaware Office of Community Svcs, director, currently. **Business Addr:** Director, Delaware Office of Community Svcs, Carvel State Office Bldg, 820 N French St, 4th Fl, Wilmington, DE 19801.

SAVAGE, EDWARD W., JR.
Physician. **Personal:** Born Jul 7, 1933, Macon, GA; married Carole Avonne Porter; children: Cheryl, Racheal, Edward III. **Educ:** Talladega Coll, AB 1955; Meharry Med Coll, MD 1960; St Louis Univ, postgrad 1955; State Univ of NY, USPHS Flwsp Downstate Med Ctr 1967-69. **Career:** State Univ of NY Downstate Med Ctr, asst instr 1964-66, instr 1966-69; Univ of IL Med Ctr, asst prof 1969-73, assoc prof 1973; Charles R Drew Postgrad Med Sch, assoc prof 1973-80, prof, 1980-; Univ of CA, adjunct assoc prof 1977, prof, 1986; Charles R Drew Postgrad Med Sch, prof 1980, chief, Division of Gyncology, 1983; Private Practice, physician 1973-. **Orgs:** Numerous hospital apptmnts; mem various committees Univ of IL, Martin Luther King Hosp, Chas Drew Postgrad Med Sch; mem Task Force on the Assessment of Quality Health Care Amer Coll of Ob/Gyn 1977-80; consult ob/gyn Albert Einstein Eval Unit Dept of Health Educ & Welfare 1973-76; consult ob/gyn Drew Ambulatory Care Review Team Dept Health Educ & Welfare 1973-76; consult ob/gyn State of CA Health Care Evaluation Sect Alternative Hlth Systems Div 1975-77; consult The Albert F Mathieu Chrioepithelioma Registry S CA Cancer Ctr 1975; consult Dept of Health & Human Serv 1980; consult Ob/Gyn Natl Inst of Health 1981; certified Amer Bd of Obstetrics & Gynecology 1969; certified Special Competence in Gynecologic Oncology 1974; mem editorial bd Journal of the NatlMed Assn1981; specl reviewer Ob/ The Journal of the Amer Med Assn CHEST. **Honors/Awds:** Dean's list Meharry Med Coll 1960; USPHS Postdoctoral Fellowship Gynecologic Cancer 1967-69; Best Doctors in Amer 1st Ed; numerous publs abstracts & presentations including Savage EW Matlock DL Salem FA & Charles EH "The Effect of Endocervical Gland Involvement On the Cure Rates ofPatients with CIN Undergoing Cryosurgery" Gynecol Oncol 14, 194-198 1982; Savage E W "Cesarean Hysterectomy Abstracts of Semelweiss Waters" OB Conf Dec 30 1981;"Treatment of Cervical Intraepithelial Carcinoma" Meharry Med Coll Ob/Gyn Grand Rounds Nashville TN June 16 1983. **Military Serv:** USAF medical corps capt 1961-63. **Home Addr:** 28521 Covecrest Dr, Rancho Palos Verdes, CA 90274. **Business Addr:** Medical Director/Professor, King/ Drew Medical Center, 12021 S Wilmington Ave, Los Angeles, CA 90059.

SAVAGE, FRANK
Investment advisory executive. **Personal:** Born Jul 10, 1938, Rocky Mount, NC; son of Grace Vivian Pitt Savage (deceased) and Frank Savage (deceased); married Lolita Valderrama Savage, Feb 1, 1980; children: Eric, Brett, Mark, Antoine, Grace, Frank. **Educ:** Howard University, Washington, DC, BA, 1962; Johns Hopkins School of Advanced Intl Studies, Washington, DC, MA, 1964. **Career:** Citibank, International Division, 1964-70; Equico Capital Corp, New York, NY, president, 1970-73; TAW Int'l Leasing, New York, NY, executive vice president, 1973-75; The Equitable Life Assurance, New York, NY, vice president, 1976-85, senior vp, 1987-; Equitable Capital Management, New York, NY, executive vice president, 1985-86, vice chairman, 1986-92, chairman, 1992-. **Orgs:** Trustee, The Johns Hopkins Univ, 1977-; director, Lockheed Corporation, 1990-; director, Essence Communications, 1988-; member, Council on Foreign Relations, 1982-; director, Boys Choir of Harlem, 1985-; director, New York Philharmonic. **Honors/Awds:** Outstanding Alumnus, Howard University, 1982. **Business Addr:** Chairman, Alliance Capital Mgmt. Intl, 1345 Ave of the Americas, New York, NY 10105.

SAVAGE, GUS. See SAVAGE, AUGUSTUS A.

SAVAGE, HORACE CHRISTOPHER
Business executive, clergyman. **Personal:** Born Jul 30, 1941; children: Christopher, Nicholas, Carter. **Educ:** VA State Coll, BA 1968; Northwestern Univ Evanston Il , MA & PhD 1968-77. **Career:** George Mason Univ Fairfax VA, asso prof clinical psychology; Pvt Practice, 1973; Howard Univ Wash DC, lectrasst vice pres & dir of research & evaluation 1972; EMarie Johnson & Assoc Chicago, 1970-72; Lake Forest Coll IL, lecturer in psychology 1971-72; NW Univ, visiting lecturer in ed 1971-72; Chicago-read MentalHealth Cntr Chicago, 1971-72; spur of teaching interns 1970-71; Northwestern U, teaching asst 1969-70; Northwestern U, research asst 1968-69; Sesame St Evalutation Proj Ed Testing Serv 1969; USN Naval Shipyard 1968-70 Past, personnel mgt spec. **Orgs:** Eastern region chmn, Nat Assn of Black Psychologists; mem Am Psychological Assn; Am Assn Univ Profs; International Transactional Analysis Assn; Am Correctional Assn; Am Ed Research Assn; Nat & Counc for Blck Child Devel; Phi Delta Kappa Professional Ed Frat; Am Assn for the Advancement of Science; MD Pry Assn; DC Assn of Black Psychologists; DC Psychological Assn; Am Mgt Assn; mem bd of psychologists Examiners Wash DC. **Honors/Awds:** Has written many papers and publications in his field and conducted many workshops; Univ Scholarship; Northwestern Univ 1970; summer research fellowship Princeton 1970; Martin Luther King Jr Woodrow Wilson Fellowship 1970; WEB Dubois Award 1968; Alpha Mu Gamma Natl Foreign Language Honor Soc; Beta Kappa Chi Natl Scientific Honor Soc. **Military Serv:** USAF 3 yrs. **Business Addr:** 548 A N Cumberland St, Jackson, TN 38301.

SAVAGE, JAMES EDWARD, JR.
Psychologist. **Personal:** Born Jul 30, 1941, Norfolk, VA; son of Thelma Savage and James Savage; divorced; children: Jeffrey, Itayo, James. **Educ:** Norfolk State Univ, Norfolk, VA, BA 1968; Northwestern Univ Evanston, IL, MA 1970, PhD 1971. **Career:** Institute for Life Enrichment, dir 1979-; pres James E Savage, Jr & Assoc Ltd 1978-. **Orgs:** Mem Intl Transactional Analysis Assn 1972-; mem Amer Psychological Assn 1972-; past Eastern Reg chmn Natl Assn of Black Psychologists 1971. **Honors/Awds:** Martin Luther King Jr/Woodrow Wilson Fellowship, Woodrow Wilson Fellowship Found 1968-70; Educational Testing Serv Summer Research Fellowship Princeton, NJ 1970. **Military Serv:** USAF E-3 served 3 1/2 yrs. **Business Addr:** Director, Institute for Life Enrichment, 7852 16th St NW, Washington, DC 20012, (202)291-5008.

SAVAGE, VERNON THOMAS
Psychologist. **Personal:** Born Sep 13, 1945, Baltimore, MD; son of Mary Williams Savage and Theodore Savage; married Frances Sommerville Savage, Dec 16, 1970; children: Tonya, Nakia, Bariki, Jabari. **Educ:** Hagerstown Community College, Hagerstown, MD, AA, 1971-73; Syracuse University, Syracuse, NY, AB, 1974; University of Illinois, Urbana, IL, MA, 1976, PhD, 1981. **Career:** Children Psychiatrist Center, Eatontown, NJ, clinical intern, 1978-79; Oberlin College, Oberlin, OH, clinical psychologist, 1979-83; Swarthmore College, Swarthmore, PA, associate dean of students, 1983-87; Towson State Univ, Towson, MD, psychologist/senior counselor, 1987-. **Orgs:** Member, American Psychological Association, 1989-; member, Black Faculty, Administrators and Staff Assn, 1987-. **Honors/Awds:** Phi Theta Kappa, National Honor Fraternity for American Junior Colleges, 1972; Upper Division Scholarship, Ford Foundation, 1973; Traineeship, United State Public Health Administration, 1974. **Military Serv:** USMC, Pfc, 1962-68. **Business Addr:** Senior Counselor, Towson State University, Counseling Center, York Rd, Towson, MD 21204.

SAVAGE, WILLIAM ARTHUR
University administrator. **Personal:** Born in Chicago, IL; son of Marie and John Savage; children: William Jr, Michelle. **Educ:** University of Illinois, Urbana-Champaign, IL, BS, 1969; Illinois State University, Normal, IL, MS education, 1973, ABD. **Career:** Educational Assistant Program, Chicago, IL, instructor & counselor, 1969-70; Illinois State Univ, Normal, IL, assistant director & coordinator, academic support services, High Potential Students Prog, 1970-75, lecturer in history, 1971-73, advisor & coordinator, academic advisement center, 1975-77, affirmative action officer, 1977-80, University of Illinois, Urbana-Champaign, IL, assistant chancellor, AA director, 1980-91; University of Pittsburgh, assistant to the chancellor, AA director, currently. **Orgs:** American Assn for Affirmative Action; College and University Personnel Assn; NAACP; Pennsylvania Black Conference on Higher Education; Three Rivers Youth. **Honors/Awds:** Kappa Delta Pi, Education Honorary; Phi Delta Kappa, Education Honorary. **Home Addr:** 1403 N Negley Ave, Pittsburgh, PA 15206. **Business Addr:** Assistant to the Chancellor, Director of Affirmative Action, University of Pittsburgh, 901 William Pitt Union, Pittsburgh, PA 15260, (412)648-7860.

SAWYER, ALFRED M.
Business executive. **Personal:** Born Aug 8, 1934, Enterprise, OK; married Bertha L; children: Alfred Jr, Allen M, Alecia M. **Educ:** USAF Inst, 1959; Eastern NM Univ Jr Coll, 1965-66. **Career:** Gen Serv Dept, dir of EO; NM Human Rights Com, dpty dir 1969-; Albuquerque Black Econ Leag, exec dir 1976-79; EEO NM State Plng Ofc, spl asst to gov 1971-74; NM State Office of Econ Oppor, econ devel 1970; NM Human Rights Commn, civil rights investigator 1969. **Orgs:** Bd mem Albuquerque Black Econ Leag 1975-77; bd of dir Albuquerque C of C 1977-79; orgnzr consult NM Human Rights Citzns Com 1979-; pres Chaves Co Nghbrhd Assn 1966-67; vice pres Roswell Br NAACP 1966; pres Roswell Br NAACP 1967; mem Roswell Urban Renewal Housing Com 1967-68; sec Chaves Co Emplyng the Handicapped Com 1968-69; pres Roswell Youth Rsrc Devel 1968-69; panel of judges 17th Annual State DECA Ldrshp Conf 1971; adv com Title I Secondary Educ 1970-71; recruitment com mem Upward Bound Proj 1970-71; steering com mem Chaves Co Red Cross 1970-71; adv com mem Home Educ Livelihood 1971; bd mempres Sickle Cell Counc of NM 1971-72; modrtr Black Ldrshp Conf 1971-73; mem Minority Bus Oppor Com 1973-78; mem Black Merit Acad 1974; 1st vice pres NMConfs of BrsNAACP 1975-76; pres Albuquerque NAACP 1975-76; bd mem Gov's Black Task Force 1976; past 2 vice pres NM NAACP 1976; bd mem Albuquerque Fedn of Orgn 1977; mem Job Corps Friends Com 1977. **Honors/Awds:** Cert outstndg achvmnt black comm Black Merit Acad AL Chap 1973; col aide de camp Gov NM 1973; ctzn of the yr award NM Black Ldrshp Conf 1974; cert of achvmnt in econ devel Albuquerque Black Con Leag 1974; cert of nobility Sec of State of NM 1975; cert of apprec Black Student Union Univ of AL 1976; col aide de camp Lt Gov NM 1979; USAF longevity serv award USAF ; cert of nobility Sec of State of NM 1980. **Military Serv:** USAF a 2/c 1956-60. **Business Addr:** Dir of EO, General Services Dept, State of New Mexico, Santa Fe, NM 87503.

SAWYER, BROADUS EUGENE
Educator. **Personal:** Born May 4, 1921, Pinnacle, NC; married Iva. **Educ:** A&T State Univ, BS 1943; Univ of PA, MBA 1948; NY Univ, PHD 1955; CPA 1960; Univ of MI, post doctoral study 1960. **Career:** A&T Univ, asst prof 1948-50, assoc prof 1955-56; Prairie View A&M Univ, assoc prof 1954-55; Morgan State Univ School of Bus, prof, dean 1956-83, prof emeritus 1984-. **Orgs:** Mem Sharp St Memorial UM Church, NAACP, Urban League, MD Assoc of CPA's, AICPA. **Honors/Awds:** Pres Gamma Tau Chap Alpha Kappa Mu 1943; co-founder, treas Adv Fed Savings & Loan 1956; Founders Day Cert of Achievement NYU 1956. **Military Serv:** AUS tech 4th gr 1943-46. **Business Addr:** Professor Emeritus, Morgan State Univ, Sch of Bus, Morgan State Univ, Baltimore, MD 21239.

SAWYER, COREY
Professional football player. **Personal:** Born Oct 4, 1971, Key West, FL; children: Mercedes. **Educ:** Florida State Univ, attended. **Career:** Cincinnati Bengals, defensive back, 1994-. **Business Addr:** Professional Football Player, Cincinnati Bengals, One Bengals Dr, Cincinnati, OH 45202, (513)621-3550.

SAWYER, DEBORAH M.
Environmental consultant. **Personal:** Born May 11, 1956, Columbus, OH; daughter of Betty P Sawyer. **Educ:** Emory University, political science & biology, 1978; Eastern New Mexico University, petroleum microbiology, 1982. **Career:** URS Consultants, association & midwest operations manager, 1986-88; The Ohio EPA, env scientist II, solid, toxic & hazardous waste management div, 1986-89; Beling Consultants Inc, senior vp, board member, operations manager, 1988-90; Env S/E Inc, operations manager, toxic & hazardous waste management div, 1990-91; Env Design International Inc, president/CEO, 1991-. **Orgs:** National Association of Women Business Owners, Chicago Chap, president, 1996-97; Joseph Corp, board of directors, 1992-; Suburban Black Contractors Association, board of directors, 1993-; Evanston Business Advisory Committee, 1993-; Chemical Industry Council of Illinois, 1994-; Chicago Region Certified Hazardous Materials Managers, 1988-; Womens Business Dev Ctr, 1992-; Consulting Engineers Council of Illinois, 1996-. **Honors/Awds:** Small Business Association, Small Minority Business of the Year Region 5, 1994; Small Business Association, Small Minority Business of the Year, 1994; Bank of America, Small Business Awd, 1995; Bank of America, Woman of Achievement, 1996; NAWBO, Entreprenuer of the Year, 1996. **Special Achievements:** Crain's Small Business, p 34, March 1996; Pioneer Press, p 92, June 26, 1996; Chicago Sun-Times, p 65, December 6, 1995; Balck Entrepreneur, p 4, July/August 1996; Chicago Tribuen, section 3, p 3, November 12, 1996; Talking to the Boss, p 42, September, 1996. **Business Phone:** (708)449-0800.

SAWYER, GEORGE EDWARD
Attorney. **Personal:** Born May 7, 1919, Mobile, AL; married Maxine; children: Cynthia, Donald, Geoffrey, Michael. **Educ:** A&I State Coll, AB 1947; Univ of So CA, MA 1952, PhD 1955. **Career:** TX So U, pres 1968-; Huston-Tillotson Coll, form dean 1947-56, prof speech drama; TN A&I State Univ Bd dir & Nat Space Hall of Fame, form vp; Counc of Pres of TX Sr Coll & U, v chmn; So Assn of Coll & Sch, trust; Fed Facilities & Equip Grants Prog of TX Coll & Univ sys, adv com. **Orgs:** Bd mem Standard Savs Assn; pub articles on blk acad & stud dissent on blk coll campuses. **Business Addr:** 206 Reed Bldg, Richmond, IN 47374.

SAWYER, RODERICK TERRENCE
Attorney. **Personal:** Born Apr 12, 1963, Chicago, IL; son of Celeste C Taylor and Eugene Sawyer. **Educ:** DePaul University, BS, finance, 1985; Illinois Institute of Technoloy-Chicago, Kent College of Law, JD, 1990. **Career:** SNN Inc, dba S's Lounge, president, 1986-; Illinois Commerce Commission, administrative law judge, 1991-; Law Offices of Watkins and Sawyer, partner, 1992-. **Orgs:** CCBA-ARDC Liaison Committee, 1992-; Phi Alpha Delta Law Fraternity, 1990-; 6th Ward Democratic Organization, president, 1990-92; Chicago Bar Association, 1990-; Park Manor Neighbors Association, 1985-. **Business Addr:** Partner, Law Offices of Watkins and Sawyer, 120 W Madison, Ste 1118, Chicago, IL 60602, (312)239-3667.

SAWYER, WILLIAM GREGORY
Educational administrator. **Personal:** Born Nov 6, 1954, Columbus, OH; son of Mr & Mrs William Wesley Sawyer. **Educ:** Eastern MI Univ, Ypsilanti, MI, 1972; Mount Union Coll, Alliance, OH, BA, 1976; Eastern New Mexico Univ, Portales, NM, MA, 1978; Univ of North TX, Denton, TX, PhD, 1986. **Career:** Amarillo Coll, Amarillo, TX, communication instructor, 1978-80; Univ of North TX, Denton, TX, teaching fellow, 1980-83, hall dir, 1983-85, coordinator of interculture services, 1985-86, asst dean of students, 1986-88, assoc dean of students, 1988-90,

dean of students, 1990-; Florida Gulf Coast University, chief student affairs officers and dean of students, 1995-. **Orgs:** Pres, TX Assn of Coll & Univ Personnel Administrators, 1991-92, pres elect, 1990-91, vice pres, 1989-90, minority comm chair, 1987-89; mem, TX Assn of Black Professionals, 1988-92; Texas State Sickle Cell Foundation, board member; Minority Caucus Advisor Unit, 1985-; Progressive Black Student Organization, University of North Texas, advisor, 1985-. **Honors/Awds:** "Top Prof," Mortar Bd Honors Society, 1987-92; Outstanding Contributions to the Minority Community, TX Woman's Univ; Outstanding Service to the African Community, The Progressive Black Student Org; The Texas Award for Outstanding Vision and Leadership in Education. **Home Addr:** 1201 SW 44th St, Cape Coral, FL 33914-6389.

SAYERS, GALE E.

Marketing executive, professional football player (retired). **Personal:** Born May 30, 1943, Wichita, KS; married Ardythe Elaine Bullard; children: Gale Lynne, Scott Aaron, Timothy Gale, Gaylon, Guy, Gary. **Educ:** Attended, Kansas Univ, NY Inst Finance. **Career:** Chicago Bears, running back, 1965-72; Kansas Univ, asst to athletic dir; Southern IL Univ, athletic dir, 1981; Chicago Daily News, columnist; Computer Supplies by Sayers, vice pres, marketing; Sayers Computer Source, CEO, 1982-. **Orgs:** Co-Chmn, Legal Defense Fund, Sports Committee, NAACP; coord, Reach Out Program, Chicago; hon chmn, American Cancer Soc; commnr, Chicago Park District. **Honors/Awds:** Received numerous awds for playing; holder of numerous NFL records; named to Natl Football Hall of Fame, 1977; mem Kappa Alpha Psi. **Special Achievements:** Company is ranked #26 on Black Enterprise magazine's 1997 list of Top 100 Black businesses. **Business Addr:** President/Founder, Sayers Computer Source, 1150 Fee Hanville Dr., Mount Prospect, IL 60056-6007.

SCAFE, JUDITH ARLENE

Television executive. **Personal:** Born May 14, 1961, Detroit, MI; daughter of Mary A Scafe and Julious O Scafe. **Educ:** Michigan State University, bachelor, telecommunications, 1984; Wayne State University, Post-Baccalaureate, computer science, education, 1986, small business management coursework, 1991; Central Michigan University, pursuing MPA, 1991-. **Career:** WDTB News Radio, reporter, 1983-84; MCI Communications Corp., account executive, 1985-86; Detroit Public Schools, substitute teacher, 1987-88; The Polimage Group Inc, project coordinator, 1988-90; Wayne County Health & Community Services, program coordinator, 1988-92; Detroit City Council, special projects assistant, 1989-; WTVS Channel 56, City For Youth, project manager, 1992-. **Orgs:** Detroit City Council Youth Commission, commissioner, 1989-; Business United, Officers & Youth, board member, 1988-; Mumford Area Youth Assistance, advisor, 1990-; National Association of Black Journalists, 1992-; Detroit Urban League, 1991-92; American Red Cross, committee member, 1992-; United Community Services, planning committee, 1988-92; New Detroit Inc, committee member, 1990-92. **Honors/Awds:** Goodfellows Organization, Dress a Doll for Christmas, 4th place, 1992; New Detroit Inc, Special Recognition for Dropout Prevention, 1991-92; Phoenix Optimist Club, Special Recognition for Volunteerism, 1990; Barden Cablevision, Special Recognition for Producing, 1989. **Special Achievements:** Speaker, Creating Caring Communities Conference, Michigan State University, 1992; "50 Leaders of Tommorrow," Ebony Magazine, 1992. **Business Addr:** Project Manager, WTVS/Channel 56, 7441 2nd Ave, Broadcast Bldg, Detroit, MI 48202-2796.

SCAGGS, EDWARD W.

Management consultant. **Personal:** Born Mar 4, 1932, East St Louis, IL; children: Jonathan, Gregory, Helen, Keith, Edward Jr, Patricia Jean. **Educ:** IL St Normal Univ, BS 1956; Univ of IL, MS 1958; Kansas State Univ, PhD 1975. **Career:** Self-employed, consultant; PATCO, spec exec dir; Ten Cities DOL-HEW, exec dir; Univ of KS, asst prof; Training Corp of Amer, exec dir; Social Dynamics Inc; Poland Springs Eco Sys Corp, lang dir; St Paul Sch of Midwest Theol Sem; Western Auto Co; Milgrams Food Chains; Builder's Assoc; Impact Studies Inc; Wichita Fallas TX Govt, currently. **Orgs:** Mem KS City C of C, KS City Human Rel Menorah Med Ctr, Skill Upgrading Inc, Al Nellum Assoc, Al Andrews & Co; dir KC Sch Dist Bd; exec bd MO Sch Bds Assoc; adv bd MO Voc Educ Bd; adv bd Urban League; adv bd YMCA Careers; adv bd Niles Home for Children. **Honors/Awds:** Published numerous articles and manuals.

SCALES, ALICE MARIE

Educator. **Personal:** Born Nov 3, 1941, Darling, MS. **Educ:** Rust College, BS, 1963; Southern University, MEd, 1966; University of Maryland, EdD, 1971. **Career:** University of Pittsburgh, associate professor, associate professor of instructional studies, 1972-77; Indiana University, 1971-72; Westfield State College, instructor, 1970-71; Hadley School System, reading specialist, 1969-70; Ware School System, 1966-69; remedial reading teacher, 1966-67; John Hyson Elementary School, teacher, 1963-65. **Orgs:** Consultant, Carnegie-Mellon Action Project, Carnegie Mellon University; ESAA School; Banneker Contracted Curriculum Center; International Reading Association; American Personnel & Guidance Association; NAACP; National Association of Black Psychologists; Alpha Kappa Alpha; National Alliance of Black School Educators; American Educational Research Association; National Council of Teachers of English; AAUP; Black Women's Association, Inc. **Honors/Awds:** Publications: "Efficient Reading for Minorities Implications for Counselors", "Strategies for Humanizing the Testing of Minorities", "College Reading & Study Skills An Asses-Perscriptive Model", "A Comm Operated After Sch Rdg Prgm", "Preparing to Assist Black Children in the Rdg Act". **Business Addr:** Department of Instructional Study, Univeristy of Pittsburgh, 4c01 Forbes Quadrangle, Pittsburgh, PA 15260-0001.

SCALES, ERWIN CARLVET

Business executive. **Personal:** Born Dec 24, 1949, Eden, NC; son of Gwynzetta V Strong Scales and Irving L Scales; married Diana L Guster, Apr 2, 1983; children: Edwin David. **Educ:** Univ NE Lincoln, 1971; Harper Comm Coll, 1979; Wichita State Univ, 1977; Insurance School of Chicago, 1981-86. **Career:** Sears Roebuck & Co, various retail store controller assignments, asst mgr financial budgets and projections, corporate auditor, natl risk mgr; Winster Mgmt Svcs, pres; National Black Arts Festival, Inc, controller, currently. **Orgs:** mem Risk Mgmt & Insurance Soc, Natl Assoc of Black Accountants, Black Exec Support Team; advisor Junior Achievement; PHA; Mason; budget comm chmn Homeowners Assn; vice pres, County Affairs/Civic Assn. **Honors/Awds:** Jr Achievement Company of the Year Award; dir, Risk Mgmt & Insurance Soc. **Home Addr:** 1824 Clearlake Trace, Stone Mountain, GA 30088.

SCALES, JEROME C.

Pediatric dentist. **Personal:** Born Nov 21, 1942, Birmingham, AL; son of Annie Fancher Mason and J C Scales; married Sandra Wills Scales, Aug 17, 1973; children: Lia, Jerome III, Marc. **Educ:** Florida State University, 1962; University of Dayton, 1964; Tennessee State University, BS, 1969; Meharry Medical College, DDS, 1973; University of Alabama School of Dentistry, certificate in pediatric dentistry, 1975. **Career:** US Postal Service, letter carrier, 1965-66; Veterans Administration Hospital, dental intern, 1972; Meharry Medical College, student research assistant, 1970-73; University of Alabama School of Dentistry, clinical associate professor, 1975-; pediatric dentist, 1975-. **Orgs:** Birmingham Pediatric Dental Association, president, vice pres, secretary-treasurer, 1981-84; Alabama Dental Society, Zone I, Birmingham, vice pres, 1977, treasurer, 1978-90; Alabama Society of Pediatric Dentistry, president, 1989-90, vice pres, 1988-89, secretary-treasurer, 1986-88; Alabama Dental Society, president, 1989-91; Phi Beta Sigma Fraternity, 1976-; National Dental Association; American Dental Association; American Academy of Pediatric Dentistry; American Orthodontic Society; Alabama Dental Association; Southeastern Society of Pediatric Dentistry; Birmingham District Dental Association; Meharry Medical College Alumni Association; Tennessee State University Alumni Association; Dental Examiners of Alabama, bd, 1997-2002. **Honors/Awds:** Meharry Medical College, nominated for Martin L King Jr Award, 1973; University of Alabama School of Dentistry, best graduate student instructor, 1975; Straight Wire Technique Foundation, Certificate in Straight Wire Orthodontics, 1978, 1980; American Straight Wire Orthodontic Association, advisory board, 1983-84; Alabama Society of Pediatric Dentistry, plaque, services as president, 1990; Tabernacle Baptist Church, board of deacons, 1982. **Military Serv:** US Air Force, Airman 1st Class, 1960-64; Airman of the Month, 1964; Good Conduct Medal, 1962; Unit Citation Medal, 1962. **Business Addr:** Pediatric Dentist, 623 Eighth Ave W, Birmingham, AL 35204.

SCALES, MANDERLINE ELIZABETH

Educator. **Personal:** Born Mar 14, 1927, Winston-Salem, NC; daughter of Roxanne Pitts and Shakepeare Pitts; married Robert Albert Scales, Apr 9, 1955; children: Albert Marvin Scales. **Educ:** Spelman Coll, AB 1949; Univ Pittsburgh, MEd; Univ of Valencia, Spain; Univ of NC at Greensboro, doctorate. **Career:** Winston-Salem State U, prof Soc Sci Spanish; The Winston-Salem Forsyth Co Schs Forsyth Tech Inst, tchr; Assn of Classroom Tchrs, past Pres; Dist & State Levels of Foreign Lang Tchrs In NCTA, chmn; Forsyth PTA Enrich Proj, chmn; Forsyth Co YWCA, dir on bd; Winston-Salem Natl Council of Negro Women. **Orgs:** Past Loyal Lady Ruler Golden Circ, past Commandress Daughters of Isis; mem OES; Delta Sigma Theta Sor; The Delta Fine Arts Proj bd of dirs; trust Shiloh Bapt Ch; pres Union RJ Reynolds Flwshp to study in Spain; dir, Shilohi-an St Peter's Corp Family Center 1984-98; pres, Top Ladies of Distinction, Inc, 1986-89; natl pres, Nation Women of Achievement Inc. **Honors/Awds:** Recip Outstanding Woman in Civic & Comm Winston-Salem 1974; hon by 1972 class of Winston-Salem State U; Commandress of Yr Nat Organ of Daughters of Isis; Com on the Forsyth County Hall of Justice in Winston-Salem; Relationships of Members and Non-Members of Fraternities & Sororities, l982. **Home Addr:** 4000 Whitfield Road, NE, Winston-Salem, NC 27105. **Business Addr:** Past Assistant Vice-Chancellor for Student Affairs/Devt, Winston-Salem State University, 601 Martin Luther King Jr Dr, Winston-Salem, NC 27101.

SCALES, PATRICIA BOWLES

Construction company executive. **Personal:** Born Dec 13, 1939, Matinsville, VA; daughter of Irene Martin Bowles (deceased) and Tommy B Bowles; married Vesharn Nathaniel Scales, Sep 27, 1969. **Educ:** VA State Univ, BS 1963; Trinity Coll, MA 1975; George Washington Univ, EdD 1984. **Career:** MTI Const Co Inc, vice pres 1978-83; Liberty Constr Inc, pres/CEO, 1983-. **Orgs:** Pres Torchbearers Circle Shiloh Baptist Church 1981-89; chair, bd of dir Liberty Constr Inc 1983-; life mem Natl Council of Negro Women 1983-; alt del White House Conf on Small Bus 1986; mem MD Productivity Awd Comm 1986-89; MD Apprenticeship & Training Council 1986-87; mem Board of Directors for Africare, Inc 1989-96; member, The Woman's National Democratic Club, 1990-91; vice chair, Bowie State University Foundation Inc, 1994-; YMCA Urban Prog Ctr, Washington DC; board of visitors, Bennett College. **Honors/Awds:** Achievement Awd, Natl Council of Negro Women, 1986; Achievement Awd, One of Amer Top 100 Bus & Professional Women, Dollars & Sense Mag, 1986; Proclamation for Achievement from Prince George's County Council MD 1987. **Home Addr:** 12506 Pleasant Prospect Rd, Mitchellville, MD 20716. **Business Addr:** President & CEO, Liberty Construction, Inc, 6029 Dix St NE Ste 201, Washington, DC 20019.

SCALES, ROBERT L.

Politician. **Personal:** Born Sep 14, 1931, Wedeowee, AL; married Marcia. **Educ:** Allied Inst Tech, master machinist; Univ IL, num courses. **Career:** Maywood, vill trust 4th dist; Tool & Die Maker Am Can Co, 25 yrs; AFL-CIO, workmen's compen rep; United Steel Workers Am, grieve com 1972. **Orgs:** Mem bd dir Proviso Day Care Cntr; past bd mem Proviso-Leyden Counc Comm Action; Asso Dean Polit Educ Operation PUSH, mem Oper PUSH; mem Nat Blk Caucas Loc Elected Ofc; Polit organ in voter regis & Voter Edn; mem First Bapt Ch Melrose Pk; organ over 100 Vol Maywood Comm 1972 pres elec; demon vote splitting; initiated comm wide newsletter Black Men Pushing, oper PUSH. **Military Serv:** AUS 1952-54.

SCALES-TRENT, JUDY

Educator, attorney. **Personal:** Born Oct 1, 1940, Winston-Salem, NC; daughter of Viola Scales Trent and William J Trent Jr; children: Jason B Ellis. **Educ:** Oberlin Coll, BA 1962; Middlebury Coll, MA 1967; Northwestern Univ Sch of Law, JD 1973. **Career:** Equal Empl Opp Commn, spec asst to vice chmn 1977-79, spec asst to gen counsel 1979-80, appellate attorney 1980-84; SUNY Buffalo Law Sch, assoc prof of law 1984-90, professor of law, 1990-. **Orgs:** mem DC Bar; mem NY State Bar; US Ct of Appeals for the Fourth, Fifth, Sixth, Seventh, Ninth and Eleventh Circuits; mem Amer Bar Assn; mem bd dir Park School of Buffalo (1985-88 term); mem, bd of dirs, National Women and the Law Assn 1987-91; mem, bd of visitors, Roswell Park Memorial Cancer Institute, 1991-96; mem, bd of governors, Society of American Law Teachers, 1992-95. **Honors/Awds:** Articles published, "Comparable Worth: Is This a Theory for Black Workers" 8 Women's Rights L Rptr 51 (Winter 1984); "Sexual Harassment and Race, A Legal Analysis of Discrimination," 8 Notre Dame J Legis 30 (1981); "A Judge Shapes and Manages Institutional Reform: School Desegregation in Buffalo," 12 NYU Review of Law and Social Change 19 (1989); "Black Women and the Constitution: Finding our Place, Asserting our Rights," 24 Harvard Civil Rights-Civil Liberties Law Review 9 (1989); "Women of Color and Health: Issues of Gender, Power and Community," 43 Stanford Law Review 1357, 1991; "The Law as an Instrument of Oppression and the Culture of Resistance," in Black Women in America: An Historical Encyclopedia 701, 1993; "On Turning Fifty," in Patricia Bell-Scott, ed, Life Notes 336, 1994; Book published: Notes of a White Black Woman: Race, Color, Community, 1995. **Business Addr:** Prof of Law, SUNY Buffalo Law School, O'Brian Hall, Amherst Campus, Buffalo, NY 14260.

SCANTLEBURY-WHITE, VELMA PATRICIA

Transplant surgeon. **Personal:** Born Oct 6, 1955, Barbados, West Indies; daughter of Kathleen Scantlebury and Delacey Scantlebury; married Harvey White, Nov 4, 1989; children: Akela, Aisha. **Educ:** Long Island University, Brooklyn Campus, BS, 1977; Columbia University, College of Physicians & Surgeons, MD, 1981. **Career:** Harlem Hospital, intern and resident in general surgery, 1981-86; University of Pittsburgh, fellow, transplantation surgery, 1986-88; assistant professor, surgery, 1988-94, associate professor, 1995-. **Orgs:** American College of Surgeons, diplomat, 1982-90; American Medical Assn, 1987, 1991-; Natl Medical Assn, 1989-; P & S Minority Alumni Association, 1981-; Gateway Medical Society, 1991-; American College of Surgeons, 1994; American Society of Transplant Surgeons, 1994. **Honors/Awds:** Distinguished Daughter of PA, 1996; Carlow College "Women of Spirit" Awd, 1996; Triangle Corner Ltd, Celebration of Excellence Award, 1992; WPTT/Duquesne Light, Outstanding African-American Contribution, 1992; Outstanding Young Women of America, Annual Award, 1988; Harlem Hospital Center, Outstanding Service Award, 1988. **Special Achievements:** New Onset of Diabetes in FK 506 versus Cyclosporine treated kidney transplant recipients, 1991; Reproduction After Transplantation, 1991; Pregnancy and Liver Transplantation, 1990; Successful Reconstruction of Late Portal Vein Stenosis, 1989; Beneficial Effect of Dopamine on Function of Autotransplanted Kidney, 1984. **Business Addr:** Associate Professor, Surgery, University of Pittsburgh, Falk Clinic, 3601 5th Ave, 5 West, Pittsburgh, PA 15213-2583, (412)692-6110.

SCARBOROUGH, CHARLES S.
Educator. **Personal:** Born May 20, 1933, Goodman, MS; married Merion Anderson; children: Charles II, James II. **Educ:** Rust College, AB, 1955; Northwestern University, MS, 1958; Michigan State University, PhD, 1969. **Career:** Alcorn A&M College, instructor, 1957-59; Michigan State University, graduate teacher assistant, 1959-63, instructor, 1963-69, assistant professor, 1969-72, assistant director, 1971-73, associate professor, 1972-, director, 1973-. **Orgs:** American Men & Women of Science; Academic Affairs Administration; Sigma Xi; American Association for Advanced Science; Association General & Liberal Studies; Consumer Information Committee, Michigan State University Employee Credit Union, 1972-; chairman elect, Michigan State University Black Faculty & Administration Group. **Business Addr:** Natural Sciences, Michigan State University, 100 North Kedzie, East Lansing, MI 48824-1115.

SCAVELLA, MICHAEL DUANE
Attorney, advisor, realtor. **Personal:** Born Feb 5, 1955, Miami Beach, FL; son of Yvonne Scavella and Elbridge Scavella. **Educ:** Harvard College, BA, 1976; Harvard Law School, JD, 1979. **Career:** Self-employed, attorney, 1983-. **Orgs:** Metropolitan Black Bar Association; New York City Bar Association. **Business Addr:** Law Offices of Michael D Scavella, 89 Headquarters Plaza, 14th Fl, Morristown, NJ 07960, (973)629-6457.

SCHATZMAN, DENNIS CLYDE. See Obituaries section.

SCHENCK, FREDERICK A.
Human resources executive. **Personal:** Born May 12, 1928, Trenton, NJ; son of Alwilda McLain Schenck and Frederick A Schenck Sr; married H Quinta Chapman. **Educ:** Attended Howard Univ 1948-50; Rider Coll, BS Commerce 1958, MA 1976. **Career:** NJ Dept of Labor & Industry, personnel officer 1960-64; NJ Office of Econ Oppor, chief admin serv 1966-68; NJ Dept of Comm Affairs, chief pub employment career devel prog 1966-68, dir of admin 1967-72; NJ Dept of Inst & Agy, dir div of youth & family serv 1972-74; NJ Dept of Treas, dep dir admin Div of purchase & property 1974-77; US Dept of Commerce, reg rep sec of commerce 1977-78, dep under sec 1978-79; Resorts Intl Casino Hotel Atlantic City NJ, sr vice pres admin; Cunard Line Ltd, New York, NY, vice president, 1988-. **Orgs:** Mem adv bd Rider Coll; board of trustees, Sammy Davis Jr National Liver Institute, 1990-; member, Governors Task Force on Service to the Disabled, 1986-87; Bureau of National Affairs Inc, board of directors. **Military Serv:** US Navy, Seaman 1st Class, 1946-48. **Business Addr:** Vice Pres, Personnel, Cunard Line Ltd, 555 Fifth Ave, New York, NY 10017.

SCHEXNIDER, ALVIN J.
Educational administrator. **Personal:** Born May 26, 1945, Lake Charles, LA; son of Ruth Mayfield Schexnider and Alfred Schexnider; married Virginia Y Reeves. **Educ:** Grambling State Univ, BA 1968; Northwestern Univ, MA 1971, PhD 1973. **Career:** Owens-IL Inc, asst dir of personnel 1968; So Univ, asst prof 1973-74; Syracuse Univ, asst prof 1974-77; Fed Exec Inst, sr prof 1977-79; VA Commonwealth Univ, assoc dean, 1979-84; Univ of NC Greensboro, asst vice chancellor, 1984-87; vice provost for undergraduate studies, VA Commonwealth Univ 1987-95; Winston-Salem State University, chancellor, 1996-. **Orgs:** Mem Amer Pol Sci Assoc, Amer Soc for Publ Admin, Natl Conf of Black Polit Sci, Alpha Phi Alpha 1965-; Sigma Pi Phi, 1989-; fellow Inter- Univ Seminar on Armed Forces &Soc 1975-; consult VA Municipal League 1980; pres VA Chap Amer Soc for Public Admin 1983-84; gov commiss VA Future 1982-84; adv bd Greensboro Natl Bank 1986-87; bd of visitors VA State Univ 1986-87; member, State Board of Education, 1990-94; vice chair, Governor's Advisory Commission on the Revitalization of Virginia's Cities. **Honors/Awds:** Norman Wait Harris Fellow Northwestern Univ 1971-72; Ford Found Fellow Ford Found 1972; Fellow Woodrow Wilson Found 1973; Outstanding Young Men of Amer US Jaycees 1978; J Sargent Reynolds Awd Amer Soc for Publ Admin 1980. **Military Serv:** AUS sgt 1968-70. **Business Addr:** Chancellor, Winston-Salem State University, 601 Martin Luther King Jr Dr, Winston-Salem, NC 27101.

SCHMOKE, KURT LIDELL
Mayor. **Personal:** marrIed Patricia; children: Gregory, Katherine. **Educ:** Yale Univ, BA; Oxford Univ, attended; Harvard Univ, JD, 1976. **Career:** Piper and Marbury Baltimore, attorney, 1976-; White House Domestic Policy Staff, appointed by Pres Carter as asst dir, 1977; City of Baltimore, asst US atty, 1978-82, state's atty 1982-87, mayor, 1987-. **Orgs:** Admitted MD Bar 1976-; served on Governor's Commn on Prison Overcrowding, MD Criminal Justice Coord Council, Task Force to Reform the Insanity Defense; involved in a variety of civic and community associations. **Honors/Awds:** Rhodes Scholar; Honorary degrees from Western MD Coll, Univ of Baltimore. **Business Addr:** Mayor, City of Baltimore, 250 City Hall, 100 N Holliday St, Baltimore, MD 21202.

SCHOOLER, JAMES MORSE, JR.
Educator. **Personal:** Born Mar 22, 1936, Durham, NC; son of Frances W Williams Schooler and James Morse Schooler Sr; married Mignon I Miller Schooler, Aug 10, 1968; children: Wesley G, Vincent C. **Educ:** Wittenberg Coll, AB 1957; Univ of WI, MS 1959; Univ of WI, PhD 1964. **Career:** NC Central Univ, prof & chmn of chem, 1975-; Duke Univ, adjunct assoc prof, 1975-, asst prof of physiology, 1970-75; Tuskegee Inst, asst prof 1966-70; Dept of Physiology Harvard Med School, research fellow 1964-66. **Orgs:** Mem Am Chem Soc; An Assn for Advancement of Sci; Am Physiological Soc; mem BSA; Durham Com on Negro Affairs Educ Subcom; trst White Rock Bapt Ch; Sigma Xi; Beta Kappa Chi; Phi Lambda Upsilon; Phi Alpha Theta. **Honors/Awds:** Hillside HS Alumni Award 1970. **Business Addr:** Chairman of Chemistry Dept, North Carolina Central Univ, 1801 Fayetteville St, Durham, NC 27707.

SCHULTZ, MICHAEL A.
Stage, film, and television director. **Personal:** Born Nov 10, 1938, Milwaukee, WI; son of Katherine Frances Leslie and Leo Schultz; married Lauren Jones. **Educ:** University of Wisconsin, attended; Marquette University, BFA. **Career:** Theater direction includes: Waiting for Godot, 1966; Song of the Lusitanian Bogey, 1968; Kongi's Harvest; God Is a (Guess What?); Does a Tiger Wear a Necktie?; The Reckoning, 1969; Every Night When the Sun Goes Down, 1969; Eugene O'Neill Memorial Theatre, directed plays by new playwrights, 1969; Operation Sidewinder; Dream on Monkey Mountain, 1970, 1971; Woyzeck, 1970; The Three Sisters, 1973; Thoughts, 1973; The Poison Tree, 1973; What the Winesellers Buy, 1974; The New Theater for Now, director, 1974; film direction includes: To Be Young, Gifted & Black, 1971; Cooley High, 1974; Billie Holliday, 1974; Honeybaby, Honeybaby, 1974; Car Wash, 1976; Greased Lightning, 1977; Which Way Is Up?, 1977; Sgt Pepper's Lonely Hearts Club Band, 1978; Scavenger Hunt, 1979; Carbon Copy, 1981; Bustin' Loose, 1983; The Last Dragon, 1985; Krush Groove, 1985; Disorderlies, 1987; Livin' Large, 1991. **Honors/Awds:** Obie Award for best direction, Song of the Lusitanian Bogey, 1968; Tony nomination and Drama Desk Award, Does a Tiger Wear a Necktie, 1969; Black Filmakers Hall of Fame, Oscar Micheaux Award, 1991; Christopher Award, Ceremonies of Dark Old Men.

SCHUMACHER, BROCKMAN
Educator (retired). **Personal:** Born Aug 26, 1924, St Louis, MO; married Doris Goodman; children: Brockman Jr, Douglass William, Andrew Jason. **Educ:** State Univ of IA, BA 1949; Washington U, MAEd 1952, PhD 1969. **Career:** So IL U, coord rehab couns training prog rehab inst 1968-; Human Devel Corp, dir comprehen manpower progs 1966-68; St Louis State Hosp, dir of reha serv 1957-66; Halfway House for Psychiatric Patients, dir res & demon 1959-62; Webster Coll, asst prof soc scis 1966-67; Counc on Rehab, pres 1971-97. **Orgs:** Mem bd dir Nat Rehab Assn 1971-; IL bd of Mental Hlth Commnrs 1974-; IL Mental Hlth Plann Bd 1970-73; chmn com on Accreditation of rehab couns training progs Am Rehab Couns Assn 1972-. **Honors/Awds:** Recip St Louis Mental Hlth Assn Citation for comm serv in mental hlth 1963; awd for serv Human Develop Corp 1968; NRA Cert of apprec for serv on bd of dirs 1971-73; Am Rehab Couns Assn; Nat Assn of Non-White Rehab Wkrs; Nat Task Force for Rehab of the mentally ill Dept of Health Educ & Welfare;Ed Problems Uniue to the Rehab of Psychia Patients St Louis Hosp 1963; Intens Serv for the Disadvataged IL Div of Voc Rehab 1972. **Military Serv:** USAF 1943-46.

SCHUTZ, ANDREA LOUISE
Business executive. **Personal:** Born Feb 15, 1948, Natchez, MS; married Simuel. **Educ:** Tougaloo Coll, BA; Tuskegee Inst, 1966; Yale U, 1967; Princeton U, M 1971. **Career:** Mathematica Inc, vice pres 1978-84, personnel dir 1975-77; Princeton U, asst to dean of grad sch 1972-75; Urban Opinion Surveys Mathematica Inc, rsrch asso 1971; Adams-Jefferson Improve Corp, tutorial dir 1969; Educ Found, consult 1970; DC Redevel Land Agy, urban renewal asst 1970; NJ Municipal & Co Govt Study Com, researcher interviewer 1971; Alpha Kappa Alpha Sor Tougaloo Coll, pres 1966-67; Lenox Inc, dir of human resources 1984-88; Educational Testing Services, Human Resources, vice pres 1988-. **Orgs:** Mem Assn of Black Princeton Alumni 1979-; mem Tougaloo Coll Alumni Assn 1979-; bd mem, Princeton NJ YMCA; NAACP Legal Defense & Education Fund; bd of trustees The Hun School of Princeton; bd of trustees Granville Academy. **Honors/Awds:** Hon mention Danforth Found 1969; hon mention Woodrow Wilson Found 1969; ''Admin Issues in Establishing & Operating a Natl Cash Assistance Program'' Joint Econ Com US Congress Princeton, NJ 1972; frequent speaker at national conferences. **Business Addr:** Vice Pres, Human Resources, Educational Testing Servies, Rosedale Rd, Princeton, NJ 08541.

SCHWEICH, ANDERSON M.
Insurance executive. **Personal:** Born Jun 12, 1923, Chicago, IL; married Mary. **Educ:** Loyola Univ, BS 1951; Northwestern & Stanford Univ, attended. **Career:** Chicago Met Mutual Assur Co, office mgr, data processing mgr, asst sec in charge of systems & procedures, vp, controller, exec vice pres 1951-71, pres 1971-. **Orgs:** Bd dir Independence Bank of Chgo, Chicago Alliance of Businessmen, Joint Negro Appeal; chmn of the bd, ceo Chicago Metro Mutual Assurance Co 1978; bd of dir Jr Achievement of Chgo; mem Natl Insurance Assoc, Natl Insurance Assoc Corp, Chicago Econ Devel Corp; bd of trustee DePaul Univ Chgo, Natl Assoc of Accountants.

SCIPIO, LAURENCE HAROLD
Physician/urologist. **Personal:** Born Aug 15, 1942; married JoAnn Wilson; children: Kia Nicole, Courtney Lauren. **Educ:** Howard Univ, College of Liberal Arts BS 1970, School of Medicine MD 1974. **Career:** Vocational Rehabilitation, physician 1979-82; Birt & Howard PA, physician/urologist 1979-80; Constant Care Comm Health Ctr, urology consultant 1984-; Private Practice, physician/urologist 1980-; Northwest Community Health Care, urology consult 1983-. **Orgs:** Attending staff Liberty Medical Ctr Inc, Maryland General Hospital, Bon Secours Hosp, Mercy Hosp, North Charles General Hosp; mem MD Urology Assoc, Medical & Chirurgical Faculty of the State of MD, Baltimore City Medical Soc, Monumental City Medical Soc, all 1980-; urology consultant Northwest Comm Hlth Ctr 1983-, West Baltimore Comm Hlth Ctr 1984-, Care First 1986-. **Honors/Awds:** Asst Chief of Urology MD General Hosp 1985-86.

SCONIER-LABOO, ANDREA
Administrator, educator. **Personal:** Born Jun 13, 1962, East Orange, NJ; daughter of John and Ophelia Sconier; married Hayward G LaBoo, Oct 10, 1987; children: Maya. **Educ:** Swarthmore College BA, biology, black studies, 1984; Penn State Univ, MBA, 1992. **Career:** Ayerst Labs, data analyst, 1984-85; City of Philadelphia, Health Dept, surveillance officer, 1985-87; BEBASHI (Blacks Educating Blacks on Social Health Issues), manager, Women and AIDS, 1987-90; Chester AIDS Coalition, intervention specialist, 1992-93; Swarthmore College, HIV test counselor, 1987-; Mercy Health Plan, manager, health education, 1993-. **Orgs:** Health Educators for Diversity Assn; AIDS Information Network, board of directors; AIDS Coalition, board of chester; Assn of Black Public administrators; Assn of Black Trainers.

SCONIERS, DARYL ANTHONY
Professional baseball player (retired). **Personal:** Born Oct 3, 1958, San Bernardino, CA. **Educ:** Orange Coast College, Costa Mesa, CA, attended. **Career:** California Angels, infielder 1981-85. **Honors/Awds:** Voted Angels ''Rookie of Year'' by Anaheim-Los Angeles Chapter of BBWAA in 1983; tied club record by hitting pair of grand slam home runs in rookie season.

SCONIERS, ROSE H.
Judge. **Career:** New York State Supreme Court, justice, currently. **Orgs:** Childrens Hosp of Buffalo, board of trustees; Erie County Bar Foundation, board of directors; Judicial Commission on Minorities; State University of New York at Buffalo, emeritus mem. **Honors/Awds:** North Region Black Political Caucus, Outstanding Black Woman in Justice, 1984; National Bar Association, Buffalo Chap, Lawyer of the Year Awd, 1984; African-American Police Association, Frank F Hughes Memorial Awd, 1988, Community Svc Awd, 1992; National Association of Negro Business & Professional Women's Clubs Inc, Sojourner Truth Awd, 1993; Omega Psi Phi Fraternity Inc, Woman of the Year Civil Rights Awd, 1996; YWCA, Outstanding Achievement Awd, 1996; Buffalo Urban League, Humanitarian Award, 1997. **Business Addr:** Justice, New York State, Supreme Court Justice, 77 West Eagle Street, Buffalo, NY 14202, (716)851-3404.

SCOONOVER, BRENDA BROWN
Ambassador. **Career:** State Dept, ambassador to Togo, currently. **Business Addr:** US Ambassador, AM Embassy-Lome, Washington, DC 20520-2300.

SCOTT, ALBERT J.
State senator. **Personal:** Born Jan 1; married Diann Scott. **Career:** Georgia House of Representatives, District 2 representative; Georgia State Senate, District 2, senator, 1985-. **Orgs:** Chairman, Public Utilities Committee; member, Consumer Affairs Committee; member, Appropriations Committee; supervisor, Union Camp Corp. **Business Addr:** Georgia State Senator, State Capitol, Atlanta, GA 30334.

SCOTT, ALBERT NELSON
Elected official. **Personal:** Born Nov 27, 1916, Richmond, VA; married Annie Mae Smith; children: Maxine Gill, Albert N Jr, Luana Webster, Duane, Leona, Barbara, Charlene Jones, Eugene, Cynthia Henry. **Educ:** Fayette Co Schools WV. **Career:** Local Union 2325 Coal Mine, vice pres 1971; Mine Comm, chmn 1971-79; Beckley City Council, city councilman 1979-. **Orgs:** Mem Raleigh Co Commitment Comm for Democratic Party 1970; mem Recreation Bd 1971; mem Citizens Adv Comm 1972; mem WV Planning Assn 1979-84; mem Amer Legion Post 70 1982; mem St Comm 1982-84; head deacon Holiness Church of Jesus 1965-; mem NAACP 1985; appt mem Beckley Urban Renewal Auth 1985. **Honors/Awds:** Working With Youths Beckley City Youth 1981-82; Cert of Appreciation Quad Counties OIC Inc 1982; ground breaking Water Pollution Control Project 1984. **Military Serv:** AUS staff sgt 1941-45; Good Conduct Medal. **Home Addr:** 212 Antonio Ave, Beckley, WV 25801.

SCOTT, ALFRED J.
Clergyman. **Personal:** Born Oct 30, 1913, Gordon, AL; married May E Hollaway; children: Scylance B, Rubbeanuion. **Educ:** Theo Cntr Atlanta, GA, cert religious educ 1970. **Career:** Triumph The Ch & King of God in Christ in 38 states, Africa and Phillipines bishop; Interdenom Ministerial Alliance, pres 1972-73; Evangelical Min Alliance, pres 1962-63; Savannah Transit Auth, sec, currently. **Orgs:** Mem Dem Exec Com; Star of Firebell in the Night 1971; NAACP Adv Counc mem; founder Tricakogic Inc; licenced Master Barber Dist Bishop of diocee, SC,NC, NY; NJ Del Com MA; chmn gen bd of trust; mem exec bd NAACP chmn Legis Com.

SCOTT, ALICE H.
Librarian. **Personal:** Born in Jefferson, GA; daughter of Annie Colbert Holly and Frank D. Holly; married Alphonso Scott; children: Christopher, Alison. **Educ:** Spelman Clge Atlanta GA, AB 1957; Atlanta Univ Atlanta GA, MLS 1958; Univ of Chicago, PhD 1983. **Career:** Brooklyn Publ NY, libr I, Brooklyn Pub Libr 1958-59; Chicago Publ Libr, libr I, Woodlawn Branch 1959-61, libr Hall Branch 1961-67, libr Woodlawn Branch 1968-73, dir Woodson Regl Libr 1974-77, dir comm rel 1977-82, deputy comm 1982-1987, assistant commissioner, 1987-. **Orgs:** Former council mem Amer Libr Assc 1982-85; mem IL Library Assc. **Honors/Awds:** Beta Phi Mu Libr Hnr Soc 1958-; CIC Doctoral Flwshp Univ of Chicago 1974. **Business Addr:** Assistant Commissioner, Chicago Publ Library, 400 S State, Chicago, IL 60605.

SCOTT, ARTHUR BISHOP
Company executive. **Personal:** Born Jul 12, 1938, Denver, CO; married Frazier Marie. **Educ:** Univ of CA, MA 1970; California State Univ, BS 1969; Merritt Coll, AA 1967. **Career:** Log cont Office, postal clerk 1960-65, supv mgmt asst 1965-68; CA State Univ, dir inst 1969-79; Kass Mgmt Serv Inc Food Servs, chmn of bd, pres, janitorial & landscape maintenance control, 1977-. **Orgs:** Bd mem 24 Hr Adult Parent Child Ctr; bd mem OCCUR; bd mem Proj on Inst Racism; Prof Assn; Stud Serv Pers Assn; CA St Employ Assn; mem & found Niagara Move Dem Club; Nat Naval Ofcr Assn; Alpha Phi Alpha Frat; Educ Oppor Prgm Assn; Nat Coord Coun for Educ Oppor; NAACP; Comm Asst Coun Navy Rec; AD HOC Com on Ethnic Stud; AD HOC Com on Minor Stud Support Serv; AD HOC Com for Learn Asst Ctr; Educ Consort Com; Spec Adm Com; Task Force Com on Env Stud. **Honors/Awds:** Dean's List Merritt Coll 1967, CSCH, 1969; graduate fellowship of CA, 1969-70; Faculty advisor, Black Student Union, 1969-76. **Military Serv:** USNR ledr.

SCOTT, ARTIE A.
Insurance company executive. **Personal:** Born Mar 23, 1946, Americus, GA; daughter of Lee Decie Anthony and Cicero Anthony; divorced; children: Shujwana Smith, Gabriel Omari. **Educ:** Albany State College, 1965-68; Florida International University, BA, 1974; Insurance Institute of America, HIAA, 1980, 1990-; Life Office Mgmt Inst, 1993; Corp Management School, 1991. **Career:** ILA Welfare & Pension Fund, administrative clerk/examiner, 1970-76; The Equitable Life Assurance Society, examiner, supervisor 1976-86; Alexander & Alexander, Turner & Shepard, supervisor, assistant manager, 1986-88; Nationwide Life Insurance Co, manager, 1988-. **Orgs:** American Business Women's Association 1984-90; Action Alliance of Black Professionals, vice pres, secretary, 1987-; Nationwide's Civic Activities Representative, 1990-; United Negro College Fund Annual Walk-A-Thon, 1991-. **Honors/Awds:** Ohio House of Representatives, Community Clothes Drive, 1992; United Way Employee Campaign Drive, Chairperson, 1988; Action Alliance of Black Professinals, Homeless Shelter Drive, 1991, 1992. **Special Achievements:** Contributing writer, "How to File a Claim," The Total Manager Magazine, 1992; Song Dedication Ceremony for educational wing of Tabernacle Baptist Church, 1987; Soar Award recipient for Excellence in Customer Service, 1993-94. **Business Addr:** Manager, Nationwide Life Insurance Co., 3 Nationwide Plaza, Location 03-23-09, PO Box 2399, Columbus, OH 43216, (614)249-6279.

SCOTT, BASIL Y.
Educational administrator (retired). **Personal:** Born Jan 18, 1925; son of Iris Scott and James Scott; married Luna Lucille Edwards; children: Karen, Brian Y. **Educ:** CCNY, BA 1948; Columbia Univ, MA 1949; Siena Coll, MBA 1952; Syracuse Univ, PhD 1962. **Career:** NY State Dept of Motor Vehicles, various positions 1960-70, admin dir 1970-77, deputy commissioner 1977-78; NY State Dept of Educ, dep commiss 1978-83; Kutztown Univ, vice pres for admin & finance, until 1995. **Orgs:** Adjunct prof Siene Coll 1959-68, State Univ of NY 1968-70; mem bd of dir Blue Shield of Northeastern NY 1971-81; mem bd of governors Albany Med Ctr 1975-81; chmn bd of dir Blue Shield of Northeastern NY 1978-81; mem bd of dir Kutztown Univ Found 1983-; adjunct prof Kutztown Univ 1984-. **Honors/Awds:** Elected to Phi Beta Kappa 1948; Pres Appt Natl Hwy Safety Advisory Comm 1969-72, 1977-80; Sec of Transportation Appointed to Natl Motor Vehicle Safety Advisory Council 1975-77. **Military Serv:** AUS corpl 1943-46. **Home Addr:** 1927 Meadow Lane, Wyomissing, PA 19610. **Business Addr:** Vice Pres/Admin & Finance, Kutztown University, 302 Administration Bldg, Kutztown, PA 19530.

SCOTT, BECKY BECKWITH
Interior designer. **Personal:** Born Apr 4, 1947, Raleigh, NC; daughter of Laura Scott and Melvin Beckwith; married Donnell Scott, Aug 5, 1972; children: Darrin B. **Educ:** North Carolina Central University, Durham, NC, BA, 1969; New York School of Interior Design, New York, NY, 1980-81. **Career:** DHHS, Trenton, NJ, administrative assistant, 1969-80; At the Window, Sea Bright, NJ, co-owner/designer, 1980-. **Orgs:** Member, 1976-, past president, 1984-85, vice president, 1988-, United Black Families of Freehold Twp; member, Monmouth County Alumni chapter, Delta Sigma Theta Sorority, 1988-; member, 1991-, corresponding secretary, 1992-, Monmouth County Chapter, Jack & Jill of America Inc. **Business Addr:** Designer/Co-Owner, At the Window, 1486 Ocean Ave, Sea Bright, NJ 07760.

SCOTT, BENJAMIN
Business executive. **Personal:** Born Nov 30, 1929, Maringouin, LA; son of Sarah Scott and Harry Scott; married Doretha; children: Benjamin E Scott Jr, Daryl D. **Educ:** Pasadena City Coll, AA 1954; Pacific St Univ, BS 1959; UCLA, MS 1969. **Career:** US Naval R&D Lab, electrical engr 1959, proj engr 1974; Benjamin Scott Assoc & Co, Inc, consult engr 1974, chief cons. **Orgs:** Chmn Pasadena NAACP 1967; Chmn, Watts Comm Action Comm 1970; Chmn, Pasadena Urban Coalition 1968. **Honors/Awds:** Medal of Freedom, NAACP Pasadena Urban Coalition & Core 1966; Medal of Achievement by Pres Wm Tolbert, Jr 1972; Congratule Achievement by Pres Richard M Nixon 1972. **Special Achievements:** Involved in the peace process in South Africa 1987-93. **Military Serv:** AUS m/sgt 5 Yrs; Silver Star 1950. **Business Addr:** Consultant, Benjamin Scott Assoc & Co Inc, 2007 Wilshire Blvd, Los Angeles, CA 90057.

SCOTT, BEVERLY ANGELA
Government official. **Personal:** Born Aug 20, 1951, Cleveland, OH; daughter of Winifred M. Jones Smith and Nathaniel H. Smith; married Arthur F. Scott, Dec 31, 1986; children: Lewis K. Grisby, III. **Educ:** Fisk Univ, Nashville TN, BA, 1972; Howard Univ, Washington DC, PhD, 1977. **Career:** Tennessee State Univ, Nashville TN, asst prof, 1976; Metropolitan Transit Authority, Harris Co TX, asst gen mgr, 1978-83; Minority Contractors Assoc, Houston TX, exec dir, 1983-84; A. O. Phillips & Associates, Houston TX, consultant, 1984-85; New York City/Metropolitan Transit Authority, asst vice pres, 1985-89, vice pres, administration/personnel, 1989—. **Orgs:** American Public Transit Association. **Honors/Awds:** Ford Foundation fellow, 1972-76; Carnegie Foundation fellow, 1977-78; Outstanding Black Woman award, Black Media (Houston TX), 1984.

SCOTT, BRENDA M.
City official. **Personal:** Born 1956?; daughter of Rudy and Nancy M Scott. **Educ:** Wayne State University, bachelor's degree; University of Detroit, master's degree. **Career:** Political consultant; Congressman John Conyers, intern; Wayne State Univ Board of Governors, 1991-95; Detroit City Council, executive and administrative asst, councilwoman, 1993-. **Orgs:** Wayne State Univ Alumni Assn, executive board; Wayne State Organization of Black Alumni; Women of Wayne; Wayne State Univ Advisory Council College of Liberal Arts; Renaissance Women's Group; Detroit Entrepreneurship Institute, vice pres; Women's Economic Club; Monnier Elementary School Community Based Health Clinic Advisory Council; American Political Science Assn; NAACP, executive board; Michigan Democratic Party; Detroit Urban League Guild; Coalition of Labor Union Women; TULC; 12th Police Precinct Community Relations Committee; Bagley Community Council; Order of the Eastern Stars; Benevolent Order of the Elks; Alpha Kappa Alpha Sorority; Gamma Phi Delta Sorority; Detroit Zoological Society; National League of Cities; Women in Municipal Government. **Honors/Awds:** Brewsters Old Timers Sweetheart, 1996; Sisterhood Award, 1996; Detroit Science Center, Outstanding Women Award; City of Detroit, Mayoral Recognition Award; Wayne State University Organization of Black Alumni, Award for Dedication; Wayne County Board of Commissioners, Certificate of Appreciation; Wayne County Community College, Certificate of Appreciation; Greenlawn Block Club, Exemplary Public Service Award; IBPO Elks, World Award for Outstanding Community Achievements; Eastside Emergency Shelter, Humanitarian Award; Virginia Governor Jay Rockefeller, Goodwill Ambassador to the State of West Virginia. **Business Addr:** City Councilwoman, City of Detroit, City County Building, Rm 1340, Detroit, MI 48226, (313)224-4535.

SCOTT, BRENT
Professional basketball player. **Personal:** Born Jun 15, 1971. **Educ:** Rice. **Career:** Indiana Pacers, 1996-. **Business Addr:** Professional Basketball Player, Indiana Pacers, 300 E Market St, Indianapolis, IN 46204, (317)263-2100.

SCOTT, CARSTELLA H.
City official. **Personal:** Born Apr 6, 1928, Thomasville, AL; married Percy Scott Sr; children: Rosia B Grafton, Percy Jr, Maxine , Veronia, Geraldine, Katherine Y Parham, Christine, Roderick. **Educ:** Ruth's Poro Beauty Coll, BS; Southern Beauty Congress, MA; Southern Beauty Congress, PhD 1984. **Career:** Englewood Elementary Fairfield, pres 1957-67; Law Comm of AL, mem 1980-; AL Governor's Comm, mem 1983-; Fairfield Democratic Women, vp; AL Voter Ed, mem 1985; Fairfield City Council, councilwoman; Fairfield AL PTA, pres. **Orgs:** Mem NAACP, Zeta Phi Lambda Sor for Christian Women of Amer 1980; mem & exec bd mem AL Modern Beauticans, Chamber of Commerce Fairfield 1982. **Honors/Awds:** Nominating comm Women's Missionary Council; Mother of the Year Fairfield School Syst; pres missionary circle Shady Grove CME Church 1973-; Nine Year Svc Awd CME Church-Birmingham Conf 1984. **Home Addr:** 537 Valley Road, Fairfield, AL 35064.

SCOTT, CHAD
Professional football player. **Educ:** Virginia. **Career:** Pittsburgh Steelers, 1997-. **Special Achievements:** NFL Draft, First round pick, #24, 1997. **Business Addr:** Professional Football Player, Pittsburgh Steelers, 300 Stadium Cir, Three Rivers Stadium, Pittsburgh, PA 15212, (412)323-1200.

SCOTT, CHARLES E.
Realtor. **Personal:** Born Dec 4, 1940, Macon, GA; divorced; children (previous marriage): Erica, Derek; married Francenia D Hall (divorced). **Educ:** Morris Brown Coll, BS 1963. **Career:** Atlanta Bd of Educ, music teacher 1963-65; IBM Corp, sales rep 1968-71; Charles E Scott Real Estate, realtor/appraiser 1971-. **Orgs:** Appraisal Inst Candidate, 1977-; pres Natl Soc of Real Est Appraisers Inc Local Satellite Chap 1980; sec Children's Psychiat Ctr 1979-. **Military Serv:** AUS E-4 1966-68. **Business Addr:** Realtor/Appraiser, Charles E Scott Real Estate, 931 NE 79th St, Miami, FL 33138.

SCOTT, CHARLES E.
Photojournalist. **Personal:** Born Jul 23, 1949, Houston, TX; son of Marie Johnson Scott and Garret Scott; married Consulla Gipson Scott; children: Tracy, Tamara, Christopher. **Educ:** University of Houston, Houston, TX, 1968-71. **Career:** KUHT, Houston, TX, 1971-72; Independent Filmmaker, Houston, TX, 1971-73; KPRC-TV, Houston, TX, news camera manager, 1972-; Video Seminars Inc, Houston, TX, president, 1990-. **Orgs:** Member, NABJ, 1987-; founding member, HABS, 1987-; member, NPPA, 1972-85. **Honors/Awds:** Special Recognition, HABS, 1988; Unity Awards in Media, Lincoln University, 1984; UPI of Texas, Texas UPI Broadcaster, 1983; PAT Weavor, MDA, Muscular Dystrophy Assn, 1980; Film Grant, ACT/Public Television, 1973. **Business Addr:** Photojournalist, KPRC-TV, 8181 Southwest Fwy, Houston, TX 77074.

SCOTT, CHARLOTTE HANLEY
Educator. **Personal:** Born Mar 18, 1925, Yonkers, NY; daughter of Charlotte Hanley and Edgar Hanley; married Nathan A Scott Jr; children: Nathan A III MD, Leslie Ashamu. **Educ:** Barnard Coll, AB 1947; Amer Univ, attended 1949-53; Univ of Chicago Sch of Business, MBA 1964; Allegheny Coll, LLD 1981. **Career:** Natl Bureau of Economic Rsch NY, rsch assoc 1947-48; RW Goldsmith Assoc, rsch assoc 1948-55; Univ of Chicago Sch of Business, economist 1955-56; Federal Reserve Bank of Chicago, economist 1956-71, asst vice pres 1971-76; Univ of VA McIntire Schl of Commerce, Curry School of Educ, prof 1976-. **Orgs:** Mem bd dirs NationsBank of Virginia, NA 1989-95; mem Charlottesville Board of NationsBank 1977-93; mem 1980-82, vice chmn 1981, chmn 1982 Consumer Advisory Bd Fed Reserve 1980-82; mem Gov's Commn on VA Future 1982-84; mem VA Commn on Status of Women 1982-85; pres Women's Bd Chicago Urban League 1967-69; trustee Barnard Coll Columbia Univ 1977-81; treas VA Women's Cultural History Project 1982-85. **Honors/Awds:** Outstanding Woman Alpha Gamma Pi Chicago 1965; Alumni Medal Columbia Univ 1984; Public Service Citation Univ of Chicago 1990; honorary membership, Golden Key National Honor Society, 1990. **Business Addr:** Prof of Commerce & Education, Univ of VA, Monroe Hall, Charlottesville, VA 22903, (804)924-3040.

SCOTT, CORNEALIOUS SOCRATES, SR.
Clergyman, educator. **Personal:** Born Mar 25, 1909, Camden, AR; son of Elizzabeth Reed Scott (deceased) and Neal Scott (deceased); married Willie Mae Matthews; children: William McKinley, Wanda Joyce, Grace Louise, Cornealious Socrates, Jr, Steven Emerson. **Educ:** Western Baptist Seminary, BSEd 1952; Central Mo State Coll, MSEd 1970, Certificate for Admin, 1972; Central Baptist Theology Seminary, 1985, MARS. **Career:** St Convention MO Youth Dept, guidance & counselor 1951-56, 1981; Era Baptist Dist Assn KC, MO, 1953-58; pastor masonry Baptist; KS City, MO School Syst, teaching 1963-81; E Comm Cncl, pres Moderator New 1970-72; US Dept HEW, 1970-74; E Side Masonry Baptist Church, pastor. **Orgs:** Vice pres, KC MO Branch NAACP 1953-58; comm mem KC MO Human Relations Dept L1954-58; mem of Municipal Comm on UNICEF of KC Mo 1956-54; mem Natl Comm to Preserve SS & Medicare 1984-; mem KC MO Ministers Un; Annually Renewals bd mem of the New Era Masonry Baptist Dist Assn; Gamma Tou Theology Fraternity 1949. **Honors/Awds:** Honorary lifetime mem, Reserve Officers Training Corps, Lincoln Univ, Jefferson City, MO, 19774; 20 Club mem, cert J C Nichol Co, KS, MO, 1974; Women Comm Serv Inc, 1968. **Home Addr:** 2400 Norton Ave, Kansas City, MO 64127. **Business Addr:** Pastor, East Side Missionary Bapt Ch, 2303 Cleveland Ave, Kansas City, MO 64127.

SCOTT, CORNELIUS ADOLPHUS
Publisher. **Personal:** Born Feb 8, 1908, Edwards, MS; married Ruth Perry; children: Jocelyn Scott Walker, Portia A. **Educ:** Morehouse Coll, attended; Univ of KS, attended; Morris Brown Coll, attended. **Career:** Atlanta Daily World, publisher 1934-. **Orgs:** Bd mem NAACP Atlanta Chap over 30 yrs, Mutual Fed Savings & Loan Bank over 30 yrs, Carver Home Boys Club 1950's-; mem Republican Party 1955-; vchmn Atlanta Bi-Partisan Voters League; chmn of bd of dir Atlanta Consumers Club. **Honors/Awds:** Cited for numerous media awds & bus awds by org & agencies. **Business Addr:** Publisher, Atlanta Daily World, 145 Auburn Ave NE, Atlanta, GA 30335.

SCOTT, DARNAY
Professional football player. **Personal:** Born Jul 7, 1972, St Louis, MO. **Educ:** San Diego State, attended. **Career:** Cincinnati Bengals, wide receiver, 1994-. **Business Addr:** Professional Football Player, Cincinnati Bengals, One Bengals Dr, Cincinnati, OH 45202, (513)621-3350.

SCOTT, DEBORAH ANN
Physician. **Personal:** Born Oct 2, 1953, New York, NY; married Ralph C Martin II. **Educ:** Princeton Univ, BA 1975; Howard Univ, MD 1979. **Career:** Howard Univ Hosp, dermatology fellow 1982-83; Roger Williams General Hosp, dermatology fellow 1983-86; MIT, staff physician 1986-96; Harvard Comm Health plan, 1993-; Beth Israel Deaconess Med Ctr, 1996-. **Orgs:** NE Medical Soc 1983-87, Amer Acad of Dermatology 1986-, New England Medical Soc 1986, New England Dermatological Soc 1987. **Honors/Awds:** Alpha Omega Alpha Hon Soc 1979. **Business Addr:** Dermatologist, 110 Francis St, Ste 7H, Boston, MA 02215-5501, (617)632-9681.

SCOTT, DENNIS EUGENE
Professional basketball player. **Personal:** Born Sep 5, 1968, Hagerstown, MD. **Educ:** Georgia Institute of Technology, Atlanta, GA, 1987-90. **Career:** Orlando Magic, forward, 1990-97; Dallas Mavericks, 1997-98; Phoenix Suns, 1998-; 3-D Entertainment, Inc, pres. **Business Addr:** Professional Basketball Player, Phoenix Suns, PO Box 515, Phoenix, AZ 85001, (602)379-7867.

SCOTT, DONALD L.
City official. **Personal:** Born Feb 8, 1938, Hunnewell, MO; son of Amanda Beatrice Dant Scott and William Edward Scott; married Betty J Forte Scott, Mar 1962; children: Jeffrey Jerome, Merrill Edward. **Educ:** Troy State Univ, Montgomery, AL, masters counseling; Lincoln Univ Missouri, Jefferson City, MO, BA. **Career:** US Army, various positions, 1960-91; US Army, Ft McPherson, GA, chief of staff, 1988; City of Atlanta, chief of staff, 1991-. **Honors/Awds:** Distinguished Alumni of Year, Troy State, 1988; Distinguished Military Graduate, Lincoln, 1960. **Military Serv:** US Army, Brigadier General, 1960-91; 5 Bronze Stars, Defense Superior Medal, 2 Army Commendation Medals, Meritorious Service Medals.

SCOTT, DONNELL
Business executive, interior designer. **Personal:** Born Oct 25, 1947, Orange, NJ; son of Katherine Robinson Scott and Walter Scott; married Bessie Beckwith Scott, Aug 5, 1972; children: Darrin B. **Educ:** North Carolina Central University, Durham, NC, BA, 1970; Seton Hall University, S Orange, NJ, MA, 1973. **Career:** IBM Corp, 1976-80; At the Window, Sea Bright, NJ, president, 1980-; WS Pest Control, ceo, currently. **Orgs:** 100 Black Men of America, 1989-; United Black Families Freehold Twp, 1976-. **Business Addr:** Chief Executive Officer, W S Pest Control, PO Box 147, East Orange, NJ 07017.

SCOTT, ELSIE L.
Law enforcement mgr. **Personal:** Born in Lake Providence, LA; daughter of Alease Truly Scott and John H Scott; married Irving Joyner, 1983 (divorced). **Educ:** Southern Univ, BA, 1968; Univ of Iowa, MA, 1970; Atlanta Univ, PhD, 1980. **Career:** St Augustine's Coll, dir Criminal Justice Prog, 1977-79; North Carolina Central Univ, asst prof, 1979-80; Howard Univ, asst prof and research assoc, 1981-83; Natl Org of Black Law Enforcement Exec, prog mgr, 1983-85, exec dir, 1985-91; New York Police Dept, Deputy Commissioner of Training, 1991-. **Orgs:** Pres, Natl Conf of Black Political Scientists, 1980-81; sec, Rev John H Scott Memorial Fund, 1980-; National Organization of Black Law Enforcement Executives, executive board, 1991-93; advisory bd, Natl Inst Against Prejudice & Violence, 1987-93; panelist, Comm on the Status of Black Amers Natl Research Council, 1986-88; Amer Society of Criminology. **Honors/Awds:** Violence Against Blacks in the US, 1979-81, Howard Univ, 1983; co-author, Racial & Religious Violence, NOBLE, 1986; Achievement Award, 100 Black Women, 1988; African American Women of Distinction, Guardian Assoc, 1991; Louisiana Black History Hall of Fame, 1993; Blk Comm Crusade for Children, Working Committee, 1992-. **Business Addr:** Deputy Commissioner of Training, New York Police Dept, Police Academy, 235 E 20th St, New York, NY 10003, (212)477-9746.

SCOTT, GILBERT H.
Company executive. **Personal:** Born Sep 7, 1946, Richmond, VA; son of Vernell Green Dickerson and Charles Scott; married Brenda Patterson Scott, Apr 26, 1969; children: Gilbert H Jr, Cecily R. **Educ:** Hampton University, Hampton, VA, BS, economics, 1968. **Career:** US Army, Fort Carson, CO, 2nd Lt, 1968-69; US Army, Vietnam, 1st Lt, 1969-70; Virginia Electric & Power Co, Alexandria, VA, sales rep, 1970-71; Xerox Corporation, Rosslyn, VA, sales rep, 1971-96; The Bartech Group, president/COO, 1996-. **Orgs:** Vice chairman/executive member, President's Cabinet at the University of California Poly, San Luis Obispo. **Honors/Awds:** Community Involvement, Association of Black Military Officers, 1987. **Military Serv:** Army, 1st Lt, 1968-70; Two Bronze Stars for Valor, Vietnamese Cross of Galantry. **Home Addr:** 10731 Hunters Place, Vienna, VA 22181.

SCOTT, GLORIA DEAN RANDLE
Educational administrator. **Personal:** Born Apr 14, 1938, Houston, TX; married Dr Will Braxton Scott. **Educ:** IN Univ, AB, MA, PhD 1959, 1960, 1965, LLD 1977. **Career:** Inst for Psych Research, research assoc in Genetics 1961-63; Marian Coll, coll prof 1961-65; Knoxville Coll, prof 1965-67; NCA TSU, prof 1967-76; NCATSU, asst to pres 1967-68; TSU, 1977-78; Natl Inst of Educ, hd postsecondary research 1973-75; NCATSU, dir of Plng & Inst Research 1973-76; TX Southern Univ, prof 1976-78; Clark Coll, prof 1978-86, vice pres 1978-86; Grambling State Univ, prof 1987; Bennett Coll, pres. **Orgs:** Bd of dirs Southern Educ Foundation 1971-76; pres G Randle Serv 1975-; owner Scotts Bay Courts 1972-; consult Ford Fndtn, Southern Edctn Fndtn 1967-72, 76; sec Corp PREP 1966-82; pres Girl Scouts USA 1975-78, 1st vice pres 1972-75; bd of dir Nat Urban League 1976-82; mem & chw Defense Comm on Women in theServices 1979-81; chair of bd of dirs Natl Scholarship Fund for Negro Students 1984-85; delegation head 1985 UN Decade for Women Intl Forum Nairobi Kenyua 1985; contributing editor Good Housekeeping 1985; advisory bd, Historically Black Colleges, 1988-92; vice chair, Presidents Advisory HBCU Bd, 1976-83; vp, United Meth Ch Black Coll Fund, 1995-97, pres, 1997-99; natl bd dir, UNCF, 1990-97; head of delegation, Beijing, China, Women International Forum, 1995. **Honors/Awds:** Woman of Year, Past Standard Houston YMCA, 1977; Kizzie Image Award, Chicago, 1979; YWCA Acad of Women Achievers, Atlanta YWCA, 1986; In Exhibit, "I Dream A World, 75 Black Women Who Changed America", 1989; Hon Degrees: Wilson Coll, 1995; Vernon Coll, 1992; Indiana Univ, 1977; DHL Fairleigh Dickinson Univ, 1978; SCLC, Drum Major for Justice Award, 1994; Girl Scouts San Jacinto Coun, Texas Woman of Achievement, 1997. **Home Addr:** Rt 1 Box 53, Riviera, TX 78379, (512)297-5209. **Business Addr:** President, Bennett College, 900 E Washington St, Greensboro, NC 27420.

SCOTT, HAROLD RUSSELL, JR.
Director, performer, educator. **Personal:** Born Sep 6, 1935, Morristown, NJ; son of Janet Gordon Scott and Harold Russell Scott. **Educ:** Harvard Univ, BA 1957; studied acting with Robert Lewis, William Ball, Michael Howard; studied under the direction of Elia Kazan, Harold Clurman, Jose Quintero; studied voice & speech with Arthur Lessac, Kristin Linklater, Alice Hermes, Graham Bernard; studied dance with Anna Sokolow, Alvin Ailey. **Career:** Professional actor in commercial theatre, 1958-71; created roles in original New York productions for Jean Genet's Deathwatch, 1958, Edward Albee's The Death of Bessie Smith, 1961, Arthur Miller's After the Fall, 1964 & Incident at Vichy, 1965, Wole Soyinka's The Trials of Brother Jero & The Strong Breed, both 1967, Jack Gelber's The Cuban Thing, 1968, & Lorraine Hansberry's Les Blancs, 1970; appeared in approximately 50 other Broadway, off-Broadway, regional & stock theatre productions;Amer Coll Theater Festival Howard Univ "A Dialogue with Hal Scott" 1978; directed numerous stage productions including The Mighty Gents, Ambassador Theatre, NYC, & Kennedy Center Eisenhower Theatre, Washington DC (1978), A Raisin in the Sun 25th Anniversary Production, Roundabout Theatre, NYC, and KenneCenter Eisenhower Theatre, Washington DC (1986), Paul Robeson, Golden Theatre, NYC, 1988 & Kennedy Center, Washington DC, 1989, & Member of the Wedding, Roundabout Theatre, NYC, 1989; directed television productions including Monkey, Monkey,Bottle of Beer, How Many Monkeys Have We Here?, Theatre in America & The Past Is the Past; Design Inst Natl Arts Consortium NYC, artistic dir, 1979-81; Peterborough Players, NH, staff dir, 1981-85, assoc dir, 1985-88, acting artistic dir, 1989-90; Rutgers Univ, Mason Gross Sch of the Arts, coadjunct 1980-81, assoc prof 1981-83, assoc prof & head of directing prog 1983-87, prof & head of directing prog 1987-; Crossroads Theatre, New Brunswick NJ, assoc artist, 1988-. **Orgs:** Signet Soc-Harvard, 1956-; YMCA, 25 years; Harvard Club of New Jersey; Ensemble Studio Theatre; bd of dir, Non-Traditional Casting Project, 1987-; bd of dir, Theatre Communications Group, 1988-; Soc of Stage Directors & Choreographers, Actors Equity Assn, & Amer Fed of Television & Radio Artists. **Honors/Awds:** Special Award, Excellence as Actor, Director, & Teacher, New England Theater Conf, 1972; Exxon Award, 1974; Black Theatre Award for A Raisin in the Sun 25th Anniversary Production, 10 awards including best director, NAACP, 1988; Scott production of A Raisin in the Sun 25th Anniversary was produced for Amer Playhouse, PBS-TV, 1989; has made spoken word recordings of A Raisin in the Sun (Caedmon), After the Fall (Mercury), Incident at Vichy (Mercury), and God's Trombones (United Artists); recorded over 30 "Talking Books" for Amer Found for the Blind Inc, Library of Congress. **Home Addr:** 276 Delavan Ave East, Newark, NJ 07104. **Business Addr:** Prof/Hd of MFA Professional Directing Prog, Rutgers Univ, Mason Gross School of the Arts, Levin Theatre, Douglass Campus, New Brunswick, NJ 08901.

SCOTT, HATTIE BELL
Real estate executive. **Personal:** Born May 28, 1945, Fort Motte, SC; daughter of Cassie Keith Weeks and Jesse Weeks; married Leonard Henry Scott, Jun 17, 1966; children: Allen Leonard, Gregory Walter. **Educ:** Allen University, 1964-65. **Career:** Long & Foster, Camp Springs, MD, realtor associate, 1977-81, sales manager, 1981-88, Waldorf, MD, vice president/regional manager, 1988-. **Orgs:** Member, Women's Council, Prince Georges' County Board of Realtors, 1982-; member, Prince Georges' County Arts Council, 1990-; member, 1987-, chairman, 1989, Prince Georges' County Board of Realtors Political Action Committee; member, Prince Georges' County Fair Housing Committee, 1980-; member, Prince Georges' County Board of Realtors Distinguished Sales Club, 1978. **Honors/Awds:** Manager of the Year, 1984, Rookie of the Year, 1978, Top Residential New Homes Lister, 1978, 1979, 1980, Long and Foster Realtors; profiled, Washington Business Journal, June 5, 1989; profiled, Ebony Magazine, "Speaking of People," April, 1989; profiled, The Washingtonian Magazine, "People to Watch," January, 1987. **Business Addr:** Vice President/Regional Manager, Southern Maryland/Prince Ge, Long & Foster Realtors, 3165 Crain Hwy Ste 100, Waldorf, MD 20603.

SCOTT, HELEN MADISON MARIE PAWNE KINARD
Corporate executive. **Personal:** Born Jul 3, Washington, DC; daughter of Helen T Madison and David Madison; children: Lenise Sharon, Monique Sherine. **Educ:** Washington Univ, BMT 1963; Howard Univ, BA 1971, MA 1973; Grant College, PA, public administration. **Career:** Univ of West Indies, distinguished visiting prof 1971-72; Howard Univ, liaison for pres 1971; Dr Joyce Ladner, res asst 1972-74; Dept of Comm Plan, asst prof 1973-74; Howard Univ Sch of Social Work, adj prof 1973-74; TV, writer/co-star 1973; Howard Univ Sch of Communications, asst for admin/prof; Howard Univ, ad asst to mgr Cramton Aud; Travel Way Foundation, prof soc plan & policy; RLA Inc, vice president/director of the Zambia (HIRD) Project Lusaka, Zambia; Licensure Real Estate, Washington DC; LICSW Social Work, Washington DC; Assn of Black Psychologists, executive director, currently. **Orgs:** Coord 7th World Law Conf 1975; consult in soc planning Congress Black Caucus 1973; State of CA Child Care Conf 1973; Intl Manpwr Dev Sem 1972, 1974; com on Human Settlements 1976; State Organizer Natl Council of Negro Women 1973; mem Amer Ded of Radio & TV Artists, Amer Planning Assn, Amer Soc for Plan Ofcls, Delta Sigma Theta Sor, Natl Acad of Sci, Natl Assn of Soc Workers, Natl Assn of Coll & Univ Concern Mgmts, NAACP, Natl Council of Negro Women, Southern Christian Leadership Conf, Natl Assn of Black Educators; Natl Assn for the Educ of Young Children, Councl for Exceptional Children, Intl City Mgmt Assn, HU Alumni Assoc; bd of dirs Freedom Bowl Alumni Comm, Assoc of Black Psychologists, Caribbean Amer InterculturalOrg Inc, Caribbean Festivals Inc. **Honors/Awds:** Phi Delta Kappa; Phi Betta Kappa 1973; Southern CA Film Inst Award 1973; Emmy Award for TV Show 1973; Rockefeller Found Award 1973; Natl Inst for Mental Health Maint & Tuition 1973; full scholarship for con study 1972; Natl Inst for Mental Health Howard Univ Scholarship 1972; Natl Endowment for Arts Scholarship 1971; partial scholarship for continued study 1971; Outstanding Human Serv Howard Univ MS Proj 1971; Chi Lambda Phi; Bureau of Std Award for Outstanding HS Student in Math & Sci. **Business Addr:** Executive Director, Association of Black Psychologists, PO Box 55999, Washington, DC 20040-5999, (202)722-2446.

SCOTT, HOSIE L.
College executive. **Personal:** Born May 31, 1943, Clopton, AL; married Ruth. **Educ:** Kean Coll, BA, MA; Brookdale Community Coll; Lincroft. **Career:** Brookdale Community Coll Lincroft NJ, coor of affirm action & personnel admin 1972-; Red Bank YMCA, exec youth program dir 1970-72; NC Mutual Life InsCo Newark NJ, life underwriter counselor & debit mgr 1968-70; Jersey Central Power Co Sayreville NJ, techn 1967-68. **Orgs:** Mem NJ Coll & Univ Personnel Assn; Monmouth Ocean Co Prof Personnel Dir Assn; dir on affirm action NJ Prof; Nat Coun on Black Am Affairs; Am Assn Comm Jr Coll; past mem Life Underwriters Assn 1968-70; Assn of Professional Dir YMCA 1970-72; BAN-WY'S YMCA 1970-74; Am Soc of Notaries; mem Greater Red Bank NAACP; bd dir Union Co Urban League NJ; chmn Affirm Action Adv Com Brookdale Coll NJ; chmn Matawan Twp Drug Coun NJ; adv bd EOF Brookdale Coll; mem State Com Persnnl Resrcs Urban League; mem Dept of Higher Educ Affirm & Action Com; adv com mem for Inst of Applied Humanities Brkdl Comm Coll; mem Dr M Luther King Obsrvnc Com; exec com mem Monmouth Co NJ Bicentennial; past pres Tri-Comm Club Matawan NJ. **Honors/Awds:** Recipient Matawan Twp Tri-Community Club Distinguished Serv Award 1973; service award Greater Red Bank NAACP

1973; fitness finders award Nat YMCA 1972; outstanding leadership award New Shrewbury NJ Kiwanis 1972; outstndng cert of ldrshp & achie award Dept of Army 1967. **Business Addr:** Brookdale Community College, 765 Newman-Springs Road, Lincroft, NJ 07738.

SCOTT, HUBERT R.
Business executive. **Personal:** Born Sep 24, 1919, Athens, GA; married Betty DuMetz; children: Hubert, Wayne. **Educ:** Morehouse Coll, BS 1942; Atlanta U, MS 1947; Univ of MI, Addl Stud. **Career:** Pilgrim Health & Life Ins Co, 2nd vice pres & sec treas 1968-, actuary 1947-68. **Orgs:** Mem tech sect chmn actuary statistician Nat Ins Assn 1953-59; treas NAACP 1958-66; mem bd dir chmn Personnel Com YMCA 1956-; mem bd dir Shiloh Orphanage 1956-; Civil Serv Commn 1968-73. **Honors/Awds:** Citizen of yr YMCA 1956; citizen of yr Kappa Alpha Psi 1968. **Military Serv:** AUS s/sgt 1942-45. **Business Addr:** 1143 Gwinnett St, Augusta, GA.

SCOTT, HUGH B.
Judge. **Personal:** Born Apr 29, 1949, Buffalo, NY; son of Anne Braithwaite Scott (deceased) and Edward Nelson Scott; married Trudy Carlson Scott, Jun 9, 1973; children: Hugh B Jr, Everett N. **Educ:** Niagara University, Lewiston, NY, BA, 1967-71; State University of New York at Buffalo Law School, JD, 1971-74. **Career:** County of Erie Dept of Law, assistant county attorney, 1974-75; City of Buffalo Dept of Law, assistant corporation counsel, 1975-77; Dept of Justice, Buffalo, NY, assistant US attorney, 1977-79; New York State Dept of Law, Buffalo, NY, assistant attorney general, 1979-83; UB Law School, Amherst Campus, lecturer, 1980-; New York State Office of Court, Buffalo city court judge, 1983-. **Orgs:** Board of managers, Buffalo Museum of Science, 1989-; board of directors, UB Law Alumni Association, 1988-; former vice chairman, Urban League of Buffalo, 1980; advisory council, TransAfrica Buffalo, 1990-; member, Alpha Kappa Boule, 1983-. **Business Addr:** Judge, Buffalo City Court, 25 Delaware, Suite 600, Buffalo, NY 14202.

SCOTT, HUGH J.
Educator. **Personal:** Born Nov 14, 1933, Detroit, MI; married Florence I Edwards; children: Marvalisa, Hugh. **Educ:** Wayne State Univ, BS 1956, MEd 1960; Wayne State Univ, Educ Spec 1964; MI State Univ, EdD 1966. **Career:** Detroit Great Cities School Improvement Project, asst dir 1965; City of Detroit, teacher 1956-65, asst principal 1966-67, asst deputy supt school comm relations 1967-68; MI State Univ, instruct 1965-66; Washington, supt schools 1970-73; Howard Univ, prof 1973-75; Hunter Coll & City Univ NY, dean progs in educ 1975-. **Orgs:** Mem Phi Delta Kappa 1960-; mem NAACP 1967-70; mem Detroit Soc Black Educ Admins (bd dirs 1968-70); mem Amer Assn Sch Admins 1969-; mem Natl Alliance Black Sch Educators 1970-. **Honors/Awds:** Dist Serv Cert Phi Delta Kappa 1969; Dist Alumni Awd MI State Univ 1970; Dist Serv President's Medal, 1993. **Military Serv:** AUS pfc 1956-58. **Business Addr:** Dean, Programs in Education, Hunter Coll CUNY, 695 Park Ave, New York, NY 10021.

SCOTT, JACOB REGINALD
Beverage company executive. **Personal:** Born Jun 2, 1938, New York, NY; married Merri Hinkis-Scott; children: Elaine Beatrice, Lisa Anne Scott White. **Educ:** Lincoln Univ, BS in psychology, 1960; Inst African De Geneve, Geneva Switz, diploma African studies, 1971. **Career:** US State Dept Foreign Svc, econ/comm officer Ethiopia 1966-68; Seagram Africa, sales, mktg dir 1971-80, Dakar, Senegal; Seagram Overseas Sales NY, mktg dir Africa 1982-83, vice pres Africa 1984-91; Seagram Europe & Africa, vice pres Africa, 1992-94, vice pres of external affairs, 1995-. **Orgs:** Montclair Alumni Chapter, Kappa Alpha Psi, 1981-83; founding member/director, Seagram South Africa (Pty) Ltd, 1994-. **Business Addr:** Vice President, External Affairs, Seagram Europe & Africa, Seagram House, 5-7 Mandeville Place, London W1M 5LB, England.

SCOTT, JAMES HENRY
Business executive. **Personal:** Born Dec 22, 1942, St Louis, MO; married Cora Sabeta Dillon; children: James H. **Educ:** Villanova Univ, BEE 1965; Washington Univ, St Louis, MBA 1970. **Career:** Bank Morgan Labouchere NY, vice pres & dep 1979-; Morgan Guaranty Trust Co of New York, vice pres 1973-; The White House, White House fellow 1978-79; Gulf & Western Ind Inc, asst to vice pres fin 1972-73; Citibank, acct officer 1970-72; Guyana, South Amer, Peace Corps volunteer 1966-68. **Orgs:** Editor-in-chief, The Circuit, 1964-65; co-found & sec, AFRAM Enterprises Inc 1968-73; asst treas, Greater New York Coun Boy Scouts of Amer, 1976-; mem, New York Urban League, 1977-; mem, Acad of Polit Sci, 1977-. **Honors/Awds:** HT scholarship HT Dyett Found Rome Cable Corp 1960; Natl Rugby Football Team, Guyana, South Amer 1967; Outstanding Young Men of Amer, Jaycees 1979. **Business Addr:** Tesselschadestraat 12, Amsterdam, Netherlands.

SCOTT, JOHN SHERMAN
Educator, writer. **Personal:** Born Jul 20, 1937, Bellaire, OH; son of Beauta Scott and George Scott; married Sharon A Riley, 1982; children: Jon-Jama Scott, Jasmin Evangelene Scott. **Educ:** SC State U, BA 1961; Bowling Green U, MA 1966; PhD 1972. **Career:** Bowling Green State Univ OH, prof ethnic studies & resident-writer 1970-; director, Ethnic Cultural Arts Program. **Orgs:** Consultant Toledo Model Cities Prog 1969-72; consult Toledo Bd Edn; mem NY Dramatists League 1971-; Speech Comm Assn 1966-73; Eugene O'Neill Memorial Theatre Center 1970-; Frank Silvera Writer's Wrkshp 1973-. **Honors/Awds:** Pub articles Players Black Lines; plays performed, Off-Broadway, NYC; Ride a Black Horse, Negro Ensemble Company 1972; Karma and The Goodship Credit, Richard Allen Center 1978-79; Governor's Award for the Arts, State of Ohio, 1990; produced play (TV), CURRENTS, 1991, produced docu-drama (TV), Hats & Fans, 1991, PBS. **Military Serv:** AUS pfc 1961-64. **Business Addr:** Prof of Ethnic Studies & Resident-Writer, Bowling Green State Univ, Shatzel Hall, Bowling Green, OH 43402.

SCOTT, JOHN T.
Educator, artist. **Personal:** Born Jun 30, 1940, New Orleans, LA; married Anna Rita Smith; children: Maria Laland, Tyra Lurana, Lauren Rita, Alanda Judith, Ayo Yohance. **Educ:** Xavier University, BA, 1962; Michigan State University, MFA, 1965. **Career:** Xavier University of Louisiana, professor of art, 1965-85. **Orgs:** Galerie Simonne Stern, New Orleans, LA, 1984; Board of the Contemporary Art Center, 1994. **Honors/Awds:** Artist of the Year, New Orleans Mayors Award, 1979; Hand Hollow Fellow, Hand Hollow Foundation, G Rickey, 1983; McIntosh Gallery, 1993; MacArthur Fellow, 1992; Honorary Degree, Doctor of Human Letters (PhD) Madonna University, Detroit, Michigan. **Home Addr:** 3861 Pauger St, New Orleans, LA 70122. **Business Addr:** Professor of Art, Xavier University of Louisiana, 7325 Palmetto St, New Orleans, LA 70125-1056.

SCOTT, JOSEPH M.
Bank executive. **Personal:** Born Apr 2, 1945, Vicksburg, MS; son of Carrie Albert Scott and Pierre A Scott Sr; divorced; children: Bettina Harding, Patrick M Scott. **Educ:** Grambling State University, BS, 1967; Eastern Michigan University, MA, 1974. **Career:** National Bank of Detroit, assistant branch manager, 1967-68; First of America Bank, branch manager, 1971, numerous positions thereafter, senior vp and area sales manager, currently. **Orgs:** Detroit Medical Center northwest advisory bd, 1996; United Way Community Services; Leadership Detroit Alumni Assn; Urban Bankers Forum. **Honors/Awds:** Spirit of Detroit Award, 1995. **Military Serv:** Army, sp/5, 1968-70. **Business Addr:** Senior VP/Area Sales Manager, First of America Bank, 400 Renaissance Center, 26th Fl, Detroit, MI 48243, (313)396-4413.

SCOTT, JOSEPH WALTER
Educator. **Personal:** Born May 7, 1935, Detroit, MI; son of Bertha Colbert Scott and William Felton Scott; married; children: Victor, Valli, Velissa. **Educ:** Central MI U, BS (cum laude) 1957; IN U, MA 1959; IN U, PhD 1963. **Career:** Univ prof of American Ethnic Studies Dept, prof of Sociology Dept, chair of AES, 1985-90; Univ. of Washington, prof, American Ethnic Studies, 1985-97, prof, sociology, currently; Univ of Notre Dame, prof soc/anthro 1970-85; Univ of Toledo, prof of soc 1967-70; Univ of KY, prof of soc 1965-67. **Orgs:** Mem Amer Sociol Assn 1958-; vstg lectr num colls; mem NAACP; consult War on Poverty Prog in IN; Sunday school teacher Braden Meth Church in Toledo; bd mem Mt Zion Baptist Church Ethnic School; mem Rainbow Coalition Organizer in SB IN; elected del State Dem Convention; member 1970-, president 1996-97, Assn of Black Sociologists. **Honors/Awds:** ldrshp awd Mil Police Offcrs Basic Sch 1963; various rsrch grants various assn 1966-72; Fulbright Scholar Argentina 1967 & 69; fellow Rockefeller Fellow, Nigeria, 1972-73; fellow Am Council on Educ, Northwestern University, 1975-76; pub num books & arts on sociol topics 1966-. **Special Achievements:** The Martin Luther King, Cesar Chevez, Rosa Parks Visiting Professor at Michigan State University, 1990-91. **Military Serv:** USMPC capt 1963-65; ROTC Disting Military Student 1956-57. **Business Addr:** Professor, Univ of Washington, Box 354380, Seattle, WA 98118.

SCOTT, JUANITA SIMONS
Educator. **Personal:** Born Jun 13, 1936, Eastover, SC; daughter of Constinee Simons (deceased) and Christobel Simons; married Robert L Scott; children: Robert Vincent, Felicia C, Julian C. **Educ:** Clinton Jr Coll, AA 1956; Livingstone Coll, BS 1958; Atlanta Univ, MS 1962; Univ of SC, EdD 1979. **Career:** Benedict Coll, minority biomedical researcher; Area Health Educ Center Med Univ SC, consultant; Morris Coll, instructor, 1964-65; Benedict Coll, minority pre-med advisor, instructor biology 1963-64, instructor 1965-69, asst prof biology 1969-72, asst prof of biol dir of biol study project 1972-80, prof biology 1972-, chairperson, division of mathematics and natural sciences, assoc dean, arts and sciences, currently. **Orgs:** Past pres PTA UNCF Faculty Fellowship 1979; past mem Central Midlands Reg Planning Coun, Riverbanks Park Comm, past co-sec, co-chair,Carolina Assoc, Zeta Phi Beta, Antioch AME Church; faculty rep, Benedict Coll bd of trustees, 1975-76, 1988-90; SC Academy of Science; Project Kaleidoscope National Advisory Committee, 1992-96; SC Junior Academy of Science Advisory bd. **Honors/Awds:** NSF Awd 1960-61; Outstanding Educators Am 1971; YWCA Career Women's Recognition Awd 1980; Beta Kappa Chi Hon Soc; Distinguished Alumni, Livingstone College, 1984; Danforth Faculty Associate, 1978-84; National Council of Negro Women Career Role Model, 1981; Science Award, Columbia Youth Games, 1986 Recognized as one of ten women of achievement in Columbia, SC by the March of Dimes, 1988; Special Community Contribution Award, Training and Development Institute of the South, 1989; South Carolinian Vanguard Award, Visible Leadership and Community Service, 1990; Certificate of Recognition for Past Accomplishments and Public Services, Consortium of Doctors, Atlanta, GA, 1991; Special Recognition Award for Outstanding Service to Church and Community, Antioch AME Zion Church, 1994. **Business Addr:** Associate Dean, School of Arts and Sciences, Benedict College, 1600 Harden Street, Columbia, SC 29204.

SCOTT, JUDITH SUGG
Lawyer, business executive. **Personal:** Born Aug 30, 1945, Washington, DC; daughter of Bernice Humphrey Sugg and Irvin D. Sugg; married Robert C. Scott, Jan 2, 88 ; children: Carmen, Nichole. **Educ:** Virginia State Coll, Petersburg VA, BS; Swarthmore Coll, Swarthmore PA, post-bachelor degree; Catholic Univ School of Law, Washington DC, JD. **Career:** Virginia Housing Devel Authority, Richmond, VA, sr counsel in real estate and bond financing; office of Gov Charles Robb, sr counsel in policy and legislative devel and implementation; Systems Mgmt American Corp, corp vice pres and gen counsel in corp affairs, corp sec. **Orgs:** Mem, American Bar Assn, Virginia State Bar, Norfolk and Portsmouth Bar Assn; chmn, Governor's War on Drugs Task Force. **Honors/Awds:** Rockefeller Foundation fellow; Outstanding Woman Award from Iota Phi Lambda; named Virgina Woman of Achievement in Govt and Virginia's Outstanding Woman Atty. **Business Addr:** Corporate Vice President/General Counsel, Systems Mgmt Amer Corp, 5 Koger Ctr, Ste 219, Norfolk, VA 23502-4107.

SCOTT, JULIUS S., JR.
Educational administrator. **Personal:** Born Feb 26, 1925, Houston, TX; son of Bertha Bell Scott and Julius Sebastian Scott; married Ianthia Ann; children: Julius III, David K, Lamar K. **Educ:** Wiley College, Marshall TX, AB, 1945; Garrett Theological Seminary, Evanston IL, BD, 1949; Brown Univ, Providence RI, AM, 1964; Boston Univ, Boston MA, PhD, 1968. **Career:** Massachusetts Institute of Technology, Cambridge MA, Meth campus minister, 1960-61; Wesleyan Foundation, Houston TX, chair of united ministries, 1961-63; Southern Fellowships Fund, Atlanta GA, asst dir, 1967-69; Spelman College, Atlanta GA, special asst to pres, 1972-74; Paine College, Augusta GA, pres, 1970-82; Division of Higher Education, Board of Higher Education, Nashville TN, assoc gen secy, 1982-88; Paine College, Augusta GA, pres; Albany State College, interim pres; Wiley College, Marshall TX, pres, 1996-. **Orgs:** American Sociological Assn, American Assn Univ Professors, Black Methodists for Church Renewal, Society for Educational Reconstruction. **Honors/Awds:** Citizen of Year Award, Augusta Chapter Association of Social Workers, 1982; distinguished alumnus award, Boston Univ, 1987; Alumni Hall of Fame, Wiley College, 1988.

SCOTT, KENNETH RICHARD
Educator. **Personal:** Born Apr 17, 1934, New York, NY; son of Emma Eugenia Doby Scott and Howard Russell Scott; married Elizabeth Willette Miller Scott, Jun 30, 1956; children: Russell William, Preston Richard. **Educ:** Howard University, Washington, DC, BS, pharmacy, 1956; SUNY, Buffalo, Buffalo, NY, MS, pharmaceutical chemistry, 1960; University of Maryland, Baltimore, MD, PhD, organic chemistry, 1966. **Career:** SUNY, Buffalo, Buffalo, NY, fellow graduate assistant, 1956-60; University of Maryland, Baltimore, MD, terminal predoctoral, 1965-66; Howard University, Washington, DC, instructor, 1960-66, assistant professor, 1966-71, associate professor, 1971-76, professor/chairman, 1976-. **Orgs:** President, Howard University Pharmacy Alumni Association, 1972-74; president, Howard University Chapter, Rho Chi Pharmacy Honor Society, 1963-64; president, Howard University Chapter, Sigma Xi Scientific Society, 1975-77; member, board of directors, Epilespy Foundation of America, 1983-89; member, editorial advisory board, Transactions on Pharmaceutical Sciences, 1987-. **Honors/Awds:** Synthesis/Biologic Activity of Spiro Analogs of Valproic Acid, Epilepsy Foundation of America, 1982-83; Mechanism of Action of Valproic Acid, NIH/MBRS, 1987-; Synthesis/Biologic Activity of Imidooxy Carboxylates, Fulbright Fellowship, 1989-90. **Home Addr:** 9816 Cottrell Terrace, Silver Spring, MD 20903-1917. **Business Addr:** Professor & Chmn, Medical Chemistry, Howard University/College of Pharmacy, 2300 4th St, NW, Chauncey Cooper Hall, Room 319A, Washington, DC 20059.

SCOTT, LARRY B.
Actor, writer, business executive. **Personal:** Born Aug 17, 1961, New York, NY. **Educ:** John Bowne, diploma 1978. **Career:** Films, Extreme Prejudice, Spacecamp, Iron Eagle, Inside Adam Swit, That Was Then This Is Now, Revenge of the Nerds, Revenge of the Nerds Part II, Karate Kid, A Hero Ain't Nothing But a Sandwich, Thieves; TV, The Liberators, Children of Times Square, Grand Babies, All for One, Rag Tag Champs, Roll of Thunder Hear My Cry, The Jerk Too, One in a Million, Siege, Wilma, The Trial of Bernard Goetz, Magnum PI, The

Jeffersons, St Elsewhere, Hill St Blues, Trapper John MD, Benson, Quincy, Lou Grant, Teachers Only, Righteous Apples, Barney Miller, Super Force, 1990-; theater: Back to Back, Eden, The Wizard of Oz, The Tempest; Stainless Steele (radio series), writer; LBS Productions, owner. **Honors/Awds:** Best Supporting Actor Virgin Islands Film Festival movie ''A Hero Ain't Nothing But a Sandwich''; Outstanding Achievement in Theatre for play Eden, Ensemble Perf 1980; LA Drama Critics Awd. **Business Addr:** Actor, c/o Harris & Goldberg, 1999 Avenue of the Stars, Suite 2850, Los Angeles, CA 90067.

SCOTT, LAWRENCE WILLIAM
Physician, attorney. **Personal:** Born Mar 3, 1928, Oakland, CA; son of Harold Leon & Kathleen Frazier Scott; married Maria, Sep 7, 1997. **Educ:** University of California at Berkley, BA, 1952; University of California at Los Angeles, (UCLA), School of Medicine, MD, 1961; Southwestern University, School of Law, JD, 1981. **Career:** Womens Medical Ctr of Los Angeles, dir, 1975-83; Kaufler & Scott Law Offices, partner, currently. **Orgs:** UCLA Foundation, bd of trustees, 1981-91; UCLA Med Ctr, alumni bd of governors, 1994-95. **Special Achievements:** First African American Graduate of UCLA School of Medicine, 1961. **Military Serv:** US Army, infantry, 1st Lt, Korean War, 1952-54.

SCOTT, LEON LEROY
Certified public accountant. **Personal:** Born Aug 8, 1941, Charleston, SC; married Veryl J Wells; children: Leon L Jr, Helen E, Woodrow L, Frederick W. **Educ:** Howard Univ, BA 1968. **Career:** Ernst & Whinney CPA's, sr accountant 1967-72; Howard Univ, internal audit mgr 1972-74, asst to the comptroller 1974-75; Lincoln Univ, vice pres 1975-76; Metropolitan Comm Colls, comptroller/dir of accounting 1976-80; Norfolk State Univ, vice pres for finance and business 1980-. **Orgs:** Mem Amer Inst of Certified Public Accountants, Assoc of Coll and Univ Auditors, Dist of Columbia Inst of Certified Public Accountants, Norfolk Council Hampton Roads Chamber of Commerce, Inst of Internal Auditors, Natl Assoc of Black Accountants, Natl Assoc of Coll & Univ Business Officers, MO Assoc of Comm and Jr Colls, Financial Execs Inst, VA Exec Inst. **Military Serv:** USMC corpl 5 yrs; Good Conduct Medal; Marksman Awd.

SCOTT, LEONARD LAMAR. See Obituaries section.

SCOTT, LEONARD STEPHEN (STEVE)
Dentist. **Personal:** Born Feb 28, 1949, Indianapolis, IN; son of Bernice Katherine Covington Scott and Nathaniel Scott; married Christine Tyson; children: John, Bryant, Nathan, Leonard, Lynna, Melanie, Katherine. **Educ:** IN Univ Med Ctr, attended 1976; IN Univ Sch Dentistry, DDS 1973. **Career:** Leonbea Inc, pres; Tyscot Inc Recording Co, pres; private dental practice. **Orgs:** Mem Amer Dental Assn; mem Indianapolis Dist Dental Soc; IN State Health Facility Admin; mem IN Dental Assn; mem Omega Psi Phi Frat; mem NAACP; tst Christ Ch Apostolic; bd dir sec Christ Ch Apostolic; mem AO Dental Frat; mem Natl Acad of Recording Arts & Sciences; pres Gospel Excellence Ministries Inc; faculty mem, Aenon Bible Coll. **Honors/Awds:** Fellow Acad Gen Dentistry. **Business Addr:** Dentist, 3532 N Keystone Ave, Indianapolis, IN 46218.

SCOTT, LEVAN RALPH
Educational administrator. **Personal:** Born Jun 26, 1915, Muncie, IN; son of Fay Scott and John W Scott; married Ogretta M Clemens; children: Diana, Lavonne Floyd. **Educ:** Ball St U, BS 1958, MS 1963, EdD 1973. **Career:** Mammoth Life Ins Co, mgr 1948-53; Intl Harvester, ind rltns 1954-56; Ft Wayne Comm Schls, tchr 1958-62, elem prin 1965-76, reg dir elem ed 1977-80, asst supt 1980-87 (retired). **Orgs:** Bd of dir Parkview Hosp; Am Red Cross; bd of Dir Summet Bank; bd of dir Ft Wayne Chamber of Com; Kappa Alphi Pi; Phil Delta Kappa; Am Assn of Sch Adm; Natl Ed Assn. **Honors/Awds:** Liberty Bell Awd Allen Co Bar Assn 1970; Public Citizens Awd Natl Soc Wrkrs 1974; Allen Co United Way Dist Serv 1975; Dist Alum Awd Ball St Univ 1971; Honarary Degree Doctor of Human Letters IN Univ 1988. **Home Addr:** 3239 Mound Dr., Tallahassee, FL 32308-3636. **Business Addr:** Asst Superintendent, Fort Wayne Community Schools, 1230 S Clinton, Fort Wayne, IN 46805.

SCOTT, LINZY, JR.
Physician. **Personal:** Born Jul 4, 1934, Newark, NJ; son of Ruby Scott and Linzy Scott Sr; divorced; children: Gina Ann, Linzy III. **Educ:** Lincoln Univ, BA 1957; Fisk Univ, MA 1959; Howard Univ, MD 1963; NJ Orthopoedic Hosp, residency; Columbia Presbyterian Hosp, residency. **Career:** NJ NG, hdqtrs phys 1964-68; NJ Coll of Med, instr 1968-70; Crippled Children's Hosp, lectr phys 1968-70; Holy Family Hosp, phys 1970-75; SW Comm Hosp, chairperson disaster prog 1970-76; Hughes Spalding Pav, phys 1970-76; SW Comm Hosp, initiator pain clinic 1977; GA State Med Assn, clinical studies 1977; SW Comm Hosp, chief of ortho 1970-78; Morris Brown College, orthopaedic physician, 1970-; New Jersey Rehabilitation Commission, orthopaedic consultant, 1970-; Metropolitan Insurance Company, orthopaedic consultant, 1982-; Dept of Surgery, Morehouse Medical School, currently, family practice, currently. **Orgs:** Amer Med Assn; Atlanta Med Assn; Atlanta Ortho Soc; Eastern Ortho Soc; Natl Med Assn; diplomate Amer Bd of Orthopedic Surgeons; fellow Amer Acad of Orthopedic Surgeons; fellow Amer Acad for Cerebral Palsy; Gladden Memorial Orthopedic Soc, fndr, 1967; Southwest Comm Hosp, Pastoral Program, fndr. **Honors/Awds:** Amer Academy for Cerebral Palsy, Residency Fellowship, 1967-68; Olympic Team Physician, 1981; Gold Medalist Natl Amateur Basketball Team, physician, 1983; Benjamin E Mays Appreciation Awd 1983; Amer Med Assn Negotiation Awd; Howard Univ Alumni Soc; Amer Acad of Family Physicians 1983; Amer Bd of Orthopedic Surgery, Certification; numerous other awards and honors. **Special Achievements:** Inventor, Scott Spiral Knee Brace, 1980. **Military Serv:** NJ NG capt med corps 1964-68. **Business Addr:** President, SW Ortho Associates, 2085 Campbelton Rd SW, Atlanta, GA 30311.

SCOTT, MARVIN BAILEY
Educator. **Personal:** Born Mar 10, 1944, Henderson, NC; son of Gertrude Bailey Scott and Robert Scott; married Carol A Johnson, Oct 15, 1967 (divorced); children: Robert B, Cinda P; married Dr Dulce M Scott, Jun 10, 1995; children: Alex Costa, Marvin B, Scott Jr. **Educ:** Attended Univ of Allahabad, India, one yr; Johnson C Smith U, BA Psych 1966; Univ of Pittsburgh, MEd 1968, PhD 1970. **Career:** Boston Univ Sch of Ed, assoc prof dean 1970-79; Boston U, asst to Provost 1979-80; Univ of MA Office of Pres, ACE fellowship 1979-80; ATEX Computers, dir of human rsrs 1980-82; St of MA, asst to chancellor prof, 1983-86; St Paul's Coll, Lawrenceville, VA, pres, 1986-88; Marvin B Scott Assoc, pres, 1988-89; Lilly Endowment, education program officer, 1991-; Butler Univ, asst to the pres, prof of education and sociology, currently. **Orgs:** Vice Pres, Bd of Intl Visitors; NAACP Sch Desegration Cases 1981-84; vice pres Minuteman Cncl BSA; board of directors Black Media Coalition Wash DC.; mem, Old Dominion Area Coun of Boy Scouts of Amer; sec and exec bd mem, Central Intercoll Athletic Assn; mem, Comm Adv Bd, Brunswick Correctional Ctr, Lawrenceville; 100 Black Men of Indianapolis; court expert, Boston Desegregation Case, 1975-82; bd of dirs, Indianpolis Civie Theater; bd of dirs; Crossroad Council of the Boy Scouts of America; bd of dirs, Martin Luther King, Mult-Service Ctr. **Honors/Awds:** Kappa Alpha Psi Dist Serv Awd 1978; Am Cncl on Ed Flwshp in Acdmc Adm 1979-80; Silver Beaver Awd, Boy Scouts of America, 1984; host of radio talk show, WRKO, Boston, 1982-86; host of ''Central VA Focus'' TV program, WPLZ, Richmond, VA, 1987-88; author of books The Essential Profession, Five Essential Dimensions of Curriculum Design, and Schools on Trial; author of chapter in The Future of Big-City Schools. **Special Achievements:** Ran for Congress in the 10th congressional district in Indiana. **Home Addr:** 7567 Sycamore Grove Court, Indianapolis, IN 46260-3275, (317)259-1102. **Business Phone:** (317)283-9464.

SCOTT, MARVIN WAYNE
Educator. **Personal:** Born Jan 21, 1952, Philadelphia, PA; son of Maloy Scott and Albert Scott; married Marcia Annette Simons, Nov 23, 1973; children: Thembi L, Kori A. **Educ:** East Stroudsburg University, 1973; Ohio State University, MA, 1974; University of North Carolina, Greensboro, EdD, 1986. **Career:** Miami Dade Community College, assistant professor, 1974-78; Howard Community College, associate professor, 1979-87; University of Maryland, assistant professor, 1987-. **Orgs:** Scholarship committee, Maryland Association for Health, Physical Education, Recreation & Dance, 1980, 1984; Committee to investigate greater involvement, EDA American Alliance for Health, Physical Education, Recreation & Dance, 1981; Nom Committee, National Association for Sport & Physical Education, 1982; curriculum consultant, Hampton Institute, 1982, Maryland State Department of Education, 1982; program evaluator, University of Maryland, Batlimore, 1984. **Honors/Awds:** Published: ''Miami Dade South Basketball Motion Offense'', 1978, ''In Persuit of the Perfect Job, A Philosophical Fable'', 1979. **Business Addr:** Kinesiology, University of Maryland, College Park, MD 20742-0001.

SCOTT, MARY SHY
Association executive. **Personal:** Born Jul 19, Atlanta, GA; daughter of Robert & Flora Shy; married Alfred Scott; children: Alfredene Scott Cheely, Arthur Robert, Alfred Jr. **Educ:** Spelman Coll, AB 1950; NY Univ, MA 1969; post grad study, NY Univ and GA State Univ. **Career:** Atlanta Public Schools, music specialist, beginning 1950; Alpha Kappa Alpha Sorority Inc, South Atlantic regional director, 1st national vp, 1986-90, international president, 1990-94; Independent Educational Consultant, currently. **Orgs:** Natl arts chairlady Alpha Kappa Alpha Sor Inc, 1978-82; Music Educators Natl Conf, 1985; GA Music Educators Assn, 1985; steward Allen Temple AME Church, 1985-; Peachtree Chapter of LINKS Inc, president, 1987; SCLC, bd of dirs, 1986-88; Top Ladies of Distinction Inc; United Negro Coll Fund, bd of dirs, 1990-94; Educational Advancement Foundation, Alpha Kappa Alpha Inc, third vp, 1995-; Azalea City Chapter of LINKS, Inc, protocal chair, 1995-. **Honors/Awds:** Basilius Award, Alpha Kappa Alpha, 1978; Golden Dove Award, Kappa Omega Chapter, Alpha Kappa Alpha, 1980; Negro Heritage Bronze Woman of the Year Fine Arts Iota Phi Lambda Sor 1980; Meritorious Serv Award, Omega Psi Phi, 1987; Keys to the Cities of: Pansacola, Thomasville, Columbus, GA, Orlando, Augusta, Selma, Long Beach, and Kansas City; Mary Shy Scott Day in Kansas City, Macon, Fulton County, Charleston, SC, and Miami; Honorary Citizen of: Columbus, GA, Huntsville, Jacksonville, Little Rock, Baltimore, and State of AL; Honorary Lt, State of Alabama, 1988; Miles College, Honorary LHD, 1992; Presented by Pres NO Soola of Benin, OUIDAH 1992 Award, for a lifetime achievement, Republic of Africa, 1993; Portrait of Sweet Success, A Living Legend Award, Intergenerational Resource Ctr, Atlanta, GA, 1994; hon doctor of humane letters, Miles College, Birmingham, AL, 1992. **Special Achievements:** Co-author: ''And These Came Forth,'' drama, 1980; recording: ''Kappa Omega Chorus In Concert,'' Mark Records, 1980. **Home Addr:** 2781 Baker Ridge Dr NW, Atlanta, GA 30318. **Business Addr:** Education Consultant, 2781 Baker Ridge Dr, NW, Atlanta, GA 30318.

SCOTT, MELVINA BROOKS
Insurance agent, government official. **Personal:** Born Mar 19, 1948, Goodman, MS; daughter of Sabina Walker Brooks and Shed Brooks; widowed; children: Johnny F Jr, James T, Kateea P. **Educ:** Hawkeye Institute of Technology, grad life underwriting assntng; University of Northern Iowa, BA, social work 1976, masters program, currently; Wartsburg College, cert, mgmt by objective, community law, affirmative action, substance abuse, 1985. **Career:** Prudential Insur Co, dist agt 1977-81; Black Hawk Co Dept of Corr Svc, probation ofcr 1976-77; Minority Alcoholism Counc, 1975-76; Area Educ Agency VII, media clerk 1968-75; political consult 1978-86; Cutler for Congress, political cons; All State Ins, 1981-85; Waterloo Comm Schools, 7th grade basketball coach 1985-93; Nagle for Congress, political cons 1986; Congressman David Nagle, caseworker/staff asst, 1987-93. **Orgs:** President, United Sister of Black Hawk Co; polit action counc mem Life Underwriters Assn 1978-; vice pres of bd Logandate Coop Daycare 1977-78; youth adv, vice pres Black Hawk Co NAACP 1976-80; chair dem party Black Hawk Co 1974-78; civic com memberships C of C Com Delta Sigma Theta 1977-79; Comm Devel Com Funding Commission, 1980-86; Layman Orgn Payne AME Ch; mem Payne AME; com mem Minority Drug Counc Intl Women's Yr Com Del to Houston; co mem Third Dist Affir Action Com; ward leader Dem Party Central Com 1980-86; vchair IA Black Caucus; bd treas NHS 1983-86; Mayor Review Committee on Streets 1988-89; Mayor Review Committee on Area Economic Devel 1989; exec bd mem, YWCA, 1990-96; affirmative action chair, Iowa Democratic Party. **Honors/Awds:** Natl Sale Achvmt Awd 1978, 80; Serv Awd Boys Club of Waterloo 1977. **Home Addr:** 413 Oneida St, Waterloo, IA 50703.

SCOTT, MONA VAUGHN
Educator. **Personal:** Born in Jackson, MS; married Dr Richard; children: Monika, Sean, Malaika. **Educ:** Coll of Pacific, BA; Univ of Pacific, MA; Stanford U, PhD 1977. **Career:** Scotts Intl Research & Educ Consultant Organ, exec dir researcher; Univ of CA Dental School, teacher; Natl Med Assn, research cons; Golden State Med Assn, research cons; Black Repertory Group, research cons; WA Sch of Psychiatry & George Wash Univ, dir of research on soc servs 1966; Univ of CA Dental School on Minority Admissions Comm, consultant 1969; Gen Admissions Com Dental School of Univ of San Fran, consultant 1969; MAHLCOM (Min Allied Hlth League Concentration on Motivation), founder dir consultant 1970-75; Family Background & Family Lifestyles of Minorities in San Fran, dir of research 1971-73. **Orgs:** Mem CATESOL CA Assn of Tchrs of Eng as a Second Lang; dir SIRECO; mem BAABP Bay Area Assn of Blk Psychologists; mem NAACP; mem ORCHESIS; mem HonorSoc Nat Modern Dance. **Honors/Awds:** Tulley Knowles Schlrshp Philosophy Inst; Mary R Smith Schlrshp; outstdg Nat Meth Student Schlrshp; 2 time winner Nat Meth Schlrshp; Ambassadors AwdsComm Serv Wash, DC; Women of Yr Awd Delta Theta Nu 1964; Dept of Behavioral Tech Awd Westinghouse; pub ''The Efficacy of Tuition-Retention Progs for Minorities'' Westinghouse Div of Behavioral Tech 1967-68; ''White Racism & Black Power'' pub by Meth Pub House TN 1969; co-author ''Algerian Interview with Kathleen Cleaver'' Black Scholar Mag 1972; co-author ''Institutional Racism in Urban Sch'' pub by Stanford Univ Center for Educ Rsrch 1975; num other publ.

SCOTT, NATHAN A., JR.
Educator (retired). **Personal:** Born Apr 24, 1925, Cleveland, OH; son of Maggie Martin Scott and Nathan Alexander Scott; married Charlotte Hanley Scott, 1946; children: Nathan A, III, Leslie Ashamu. **Educ:** Univ of MI, BA 1944; Union Theol Sem, MDiv 1946; Columbia Univ, PhD 1949. **Career:** VA Union Univ, dean of the chapel 1946-47; Howard Univ, assoc prof of humanities 1948-55; Univ of Chicago, prof of theology and literature 1955-76; Univ of VA, Wm R Kenan prof emeritus of religious studies, prof emeritus of English 1976-90; Priest of the Episcopal Church. **Orgs:** Amer Philosophical Assn; Amer Acad of Religion; Modern Language Assn; Soc for Values in Higher Educ; advisory editor, Callalloo; mem of bd of consultants The Journal of Religion; mem advisory bd, Religion & Literature, Religion and Intellectual Life, The Journal of Literature and Theology. **Honors/Awds:** LittD, Ripon Coll, 1965; LHD, Wittenberg Univ, 1965; DD, Philadelphia Divinity School, 1967; STD, Gen Theological Seminary, 1968; LittD, St Mary's Coll Notre Dame, 1969; LHD, Univ of DC, 1976; LittD, Denison Univ, 1976; LittD, Brown Univ, 1981; LittD, Northwestern Univ, 1982; DD, Virginia Theological Seminary, 1985;

HumD, Univ of Michigan, 1988; LittD, Elizabethtown Coll, 1989; LittD, Wesleyan Univ, 1989; DD, Bates College, 1990; STD, University of the South, 1992; DD, Kenyon Coll, 1993; DD, Wabash Coll, 1996; fellow, Amer Acad of Arts and Sciences, 1979; author, 25 books; contributor, 42 books; Amer Acad of Religion vice pres 1984, pres-elect 1985, pres 1986. **Home Addr:** 1419 Hilltop Rd, Charlottesville, VA 22903. **Business Addr:** Prof Religious Studies & English, Univ of Virginia, Dept of Religious Studies, Charlottesville, VA 22903.

SCOTT, NELSON
Model. **Personal:** Born in Bronx, NY. **Career:** Model, ads include: Guess, Banana Republic, Benetton; runway shows include Ralph Lauren. **Business Addr:** Model, c/o Zoli Management, 3 W 18th St, New York, NY 10011-4610, (212)242-1500.

SCOTT, NIGEL L.
Attorney. **Personal:** Born Aug 23, 1940; married Monica Chasteau; children: Duane, Omar, Rion. **Educ:** Howard U, BS Chem 1970; Howard Univ Sch of Law, JD 1973. **Career:** Scott & Yallery-Arthur, atty 1980-; Atty, pvt prac 1975-79; Eastman Kodak, patent atty 1973-75. **Orgs:** Mem DC PA & US Patent Bars 1975-; exec dir Nat Patent Law Assn 1979-; adv mem Hum Rghts Commn Montgomery Co 1980; pres Trinidad & Tobago Assn of Wash DC 1977-79. **Business Addr:** 7603 Georgia Ave NW, #304, Washington, DC 20012.

SCOTT, OSBORNE E.
Educator, cleric. **Personal:** Born Feb 5, 1916, Gloucester, VA; married Jean Sampson (deceased); children: Osborne Jr, Michael D. **Educ:** Hampton Inst, BS 1938; Oberlin Grad Sch of Theol, BD 1941; Tchrs Coll Columbia U, MA 1951. **Career:** Dept of Black Studies City Coll of NY, prof 1972-; Dept of Urban & Ethnic Studies, prof & chmn 1969-71; Am Leprosy Missions, exec vice pres 1964-69; Hampton Inst, asst to pres 1941. **Orgs:** Sr assn Ldrshp Res Inc 1970-; bd dir Ch World Serv Natl Council of Chs; mem N Am Proj Comm Org; New York State Welfare Assn; sr asso ldrshp Res Inc WA; bd dir Cncl for Econ Devel & Empowerment Black People; co-chmn African Academy of Arts & Rsrch Inc; minister Trinity Bapt Ch Brooklyn NY; chmn fac sen City Coll of NY 1980. **Honors/Awds:** Outstndg alumnus Hampton Inst 1948; Bd of Trustees, Univ of Bridgeport. **Military Serv:** US Army, lt col, 1941-64. **Business Addr:** Professor Emeritus, City College of New York, 138 St & Convent Ave, New York, NY 10031.

SCOTT, OTIS, SR.
Educator, county councilman. **Personal:** Born Sep 19, 1919, Lynchburg, SC; son of Emma Green Scott and Ed Scott; married Wilhelmenia Dennis; children: Myrtle Scott Johnson, Otis Jr, Linda Scott Norwood. **Educ:** Morris Coll, BA; Columbia U, MA; Univ of SC. **Career:** Sumter County School District #2, teacher; Vet on the Job Training, instructor; Lower Lee School, teacher, basketball coach; Delaine Elementary School, teacher; Ebenezer Jr High School Sumter County Educ Assn, teacher; Mt Nebo, Jerusalem & Barnettesville Baptist Churches, pastor, 1952-70; Mt Moriah Baptist Church, pastor, 1970-; Sumter County, councilman, 1993-; Mulberry Baptist Church, pastor, currently. **Orgs:** Assn of Classroom Teachers; SC Educ Assn; bd dir NEA Boylan Haven-Mather Acad; bd dir Proj T Sq; Sumter County Econ Opportunity; Day Care Ctr; Sumter Co Democratic Party; pres Voters Precinct #1; Notary Public; master mason Prince Hall Affil; NAACP; Shriner; field worker Morris Coll; clerk Wateree Assn LD; moderator Lynches River Union; clerk Sunday Sch Conv; instructor Ann Inst Mt Moriah Assn; mem Natl Prog Conv; helped establish & build day care centers Rembert Horatio Comm; built churches Lee Co Clarendon Do; councilman, Natl Assn of Counties, 1984-; councilman, South Carolina Assn of Counties, 1984-; bd mem,Hillcrest High Sch Found, 1988-; bd mem, Minority Scholarship Comm, Sumter Sch District 17, 1989-; Order of Eastern Star, Cathall Chapter 315, worthy person; National Association of Counti South Carolina Association of Counties, member; Santee Lynches Regional Council of Government, Rural Transportation and Public Roads, board member. **Honors/Awds:** Distinguished Alumnus Award, Morris College, 1988; Special Recognition Award, Morris College, 1989; NAACP, Special Recognition Award, 1992. **Military Serv:** USAF, 1941-45.

SCOTT, OTIS L.
Educator. **Personal:** Born Dec 27, 1941, Marion, OH; son of Harriett Booker Scott and William Scott; married Willie Vern Hawkins Scott, Mar 2, 1963; children: William F, Byron O, David A. **Educ:** University of MD & Eastern Washington State College, Cheney, WA; Central State College, Wilberforce, OH; California State University, Sacramento, BA, 1971, MA, 1973; Union Graduate School, Cincinnati, OH, PhD, 1982. **Career:** California State University, Sacramento, CA, professor, 1974-. **Orgs:** Member, National Conference of Black Political Scientists, 1989-; member, National Council for Black Studies, 1979-; member, National Association of Ethnic Studies, 1985-; member, Sacramento Area Black Caucus, 1974-; National Association for Ethnic Studies, vice president, 1996-98. **Honors/Awds:** Journal article, Ethnic Studies Past and Present Explorations in Ethnic Studies Vol 11, No 2, 1988; Journal article, Coping Strategies of Women in Alice Walkers Novels Explorations in Ethnic Studies, Vol 10, No 1, 1987; Co-Project Director, Beyond the Canon, 1990-; CSUS Exceptional Merit Award, 1984. **Special Achievements:** Author, The Veil: Perspectives on Race & Ethnicity in the US, West Publishing Co, 1994; co-author, Teaching From A Multicultural Perspective, Sage, 1994; author, "Lines, Borders and Corrections," Kendall Hunt, 1997. **Military Serv:** Air Force, SSGT, 1960-68. **Business Addr:** Professor, Chair, Ethnic Studies Department, California State University, Sacramento, 6000 J St, Sacramento, CA 95819.

SCOTT, PORTIA ALEXANDRIA
Journalist. **Personal:** Born Jun 9, 1943, Atlanta, GA; daughter of Mr & Mrs C A Scott. **Educ:** Howard University, BA 1964; Atlanta University, MA 1972. **Career:** Atlanta Daily World, assistant to editor and general manager, managing editor, currently. **Orgs:** National Association of Negro Business & Professional Women; National Association of Media Women; National Federation of Business Professional Women; NAACP; Church Women United of Atlanta; Natl Council of Negro Women; Natl Federation of Republican Women; M L King Jr Natl Historic Site Advisory Cmsn, chairwoman, 1987-92; President Bush Advisory Bd for Historically Black Colleges and Universities, 1990-. **Honors/Awds:** Numerous civic & communications awards; Southern Bell Afro-American Black History Calendar, "Women of Achievement," 1990-91; Republican Nominee for 5th District Congressional Seat, GA, 1986; Atlanta Business League, Most 100 Influential African-American Women, 1995, 1996. **Business Addr:** Managing Editor, Atlanta Daily World, 145 Auburn Ave NE, Atlanta, GA 30335.

SCOTT, R. LEE
Communication executive. **Personal:** Born Oct 8, 1943, Hollywood, AL; son of Jannie Scott and Lee J Scott (deceased); married Mae Frances Kline; children: Ronald, Lynne. **Educ:** Univ of CT, BA 1966; Univ of Hartford, MBA 1977; Cornell Univ, Exec Dev Prog 1984; Northwestern University, attended, consumer strategy, 1989. **Career:** Aetna Life & Casualty Ins, sr underwriter 1966-70; So New England Telecom, district staff mgr int auditing, 1970-87, district marketing mgr, consumer products, 1987-, director legilative affairs, currently. **Orgs:** Mem Alpha Phi Alpha Frat 1968-; adjunct prof Univ of Hartford 1978-; mem Sigma Pi Phi Frat 1981-; pres Scott & Assocs 1983-; mem New Britain NAACP; bd dir Indian Hills Country Club Newington CT; adjunct professor University of New Haven. **Honors/Awds:** Certificate of Recognition Natl Alliance of Businessmen 1973; Outstanding Young Man of Amer Natl Jaycees 1978, 1980; Distinguished Minority Grad Univ of CT 1984; article "Make Your Class Room Time Count," Minority Educ Philadelphia 1980, preprinted by Northern MI Univ in career newsletter 1980; case study Personnel Assessment Ctrs in Collaboration in Organization, Alternatives to Hierarchy by William A Kraus, Human Sciences Press NY 1980; National Urban League, BEEP; Fayetteville State University, 1991; St Paul's College, 1992; Grambling State, 1993; Savannah State, 1994. **Home Addr:** 87 Little Brook Dr, Newington, CT 06111.

SCOTT, RACHEL LORAINE
Business executive. **Personal:** Born Jun 5, 1954, Bristol, TN; daughter of Elizabeth Gose Scott and Melton Scott. **Educ:** Radford Univ, BS 1976. **Career:** Bank of VA, admin asst 1976-77; Central Fidelity Bank NA, asst vice pres 1977-82; Nations Bank of Georgia, NA, vp/domestic funding mngr 1982-. **Orgs:** Advisor Jr Achievement of Richmond 1977-82; mem Natl Assoc of Bank Women 1980-, Jr Chamber of Commerce 1981, Career Ed Committee; mem Atlanta Urban Bankers Assoc, Atlanta Assoc of Women in Securities, Natl Assoc of Securities Professionals. **Business Addr:** Vice President, Nations Bank of Georgia, 600 Peachtree St, Atlanta, GA 30308.

SCOTT, RICHARD ELEY
Judge. **Personal:** Born Dec 25, 1945, Kilgore, TX. **Educ:** Prairie View A&M U, BA 1968; Univ of TX, JD 1972. **Career:** Travis Co TX, justice of the peace 1975-; Austin Comm Coll, part-time instr 1973; TX Stdte Rep Eddie B Johnson, legal asst 1973; Priv Prac, law 1972. **Orgs:** NAACP; Travis Co Jr Bar Assn 1973; State Bar TX 1972; sponsoring com Austin Urban League 1977; com chmn on adm State Bar of TX 1976; Rishon Lodge #1 1977; E Austin Youth Found Coach 1976; Nat Bar Assn 1975; Del Dem Nat Conv 1972; floor whip US Sen Humphrey 1972. **Business Addr:** 3230 E Martin Luther King, Austin, TX 78721.

SCOTT, ROBERT CORTEZ
Congressman. **Personal:** Born Apr 30, 1947, Washington, DC; son of Mae Hamlin Scott and C Waldo Scott. **Educ:** Harvard Coll, BA 1969; Boston Coll Law Sch, JD 1973. **Career:** Atty at law; Virginia General Assembly, delegate 1978-83; Virginia House of Representatives, state rep, 1983-93; US House of Representatives, congressman, 1993-. **Orgs:** Mem Newport News Old Dominion Bar Assn 1973-; pres Peninsula Bar Assn 1974-78; golden heritage life mem NAACP 1976-; pres Peninsula Legal Aid Cntr Inc 1976-81; chmn 1st Congressional Dist Dem Com 1980-85; vchmn VA Dem Black Caucus 1980; del Nat Dem Convention 1980; mem Hampton Inst Annual Fund Com; bd mem Peninsula Assn Sickle Cell Anemia & Peninsula Coun Boy Scouts of Am; mem March of Dimes, Alpha Phi Alpha, Sigma Pi Phi. **Honors/Awds:** Outstanding Leader Hampton Roads Jaycees 1976; Man of the Year Zeta Lambda Chap Alpha Phi Alpha Frat 1977; Distinguished Comm Serv Kennedy-Evers-King Meml Found 1977; Outstanding Achievement Peninsula Nat Assn Negro Business & Professional Women 1978; Brotherhood Citation Natl Conf of Christians & Jews 1985; Public Health Recognition Award, VA Public Health Assn, 1986; Outstanding Legislator Award, VA Chpt/Amer Pediatric Soc, 1986, honorary doctorate of govt science degree, Commonwealth Coll, 1987. **Military Serv:** MA Army Natl Guard 1970-73; AUSR 1973-76. **Business Addr:** Congressman, US House of Representatives, 501 Cannon House Office Bldg, Washington, DC 20515-4603.

SCOTT, ROBERT JEROME
Public television executive. **Personal:** Born Feb 2, 1946, San Francisco, CA; son of Mary Helen Harris Weeks and Robert Scott; divorced; children: Siiri Sativa, Jeremy Harrington. **Educ:** Wayne State University, 1964-71. **Career:** Studio Theatres of Detroit, supervisor, 1968-69; Detroit News, staff photographer, 1969-71; Optek Photographic, owner, photographer,1971; Detroit Free Press, staff photographer, jazz critic, 1971-79; Michigan Department of Commerce, director Michigan film office, 1979-85; WTVS/Channel 56, director of project marketing, 1985-87, vice pres for community development, 1987-91, vice pres for government relations and support, currently. **Orgs:** Concerned Citizens for the Arts in Michigan, board of directors, 1991-92, governors arts awards committee, 1989-92; Theatre Grottesco, board of directors, 1987-90; New Detroit, Inc, committee on racial and economic justice, 1986-88. **Honors/Awds:** National Academy Television Arts & Sciences, Michigan Emmy, 1987. **Special Achievements:** Governors' Arts Awards Program, producer, director, 1989-92; 1991 Montreux Jazz Festival television special, executive producer, 1991-92; Senzinina: What Have We Done to Deserve This? (Emmy), producer, 1987; Back to Detroit: The Future, executive producer, 1987; Spectrum, The Series on Arts in Michigan, producer, executive producer, 1987-90. **Business Addr:** VP for Government Relations and Support, WTVS/Channel 56, The Detroit Educational Television Foundation, 7441 Second Blvd, Detroit, MI 48227, (313)876-8385.

SCOTT, ROLAND B.
Physician (retired), educator. **Personal:** Born Apr 18, 1909, Houston, TX; married Sarah Rosetta Weaver; children: Roland B Jr, Venice S Carlenius, Estelle Irene Scott. **Educ:** Howard Univ, BS 1931, MD 1934; KS City Genl Hosp, internship 1934-35; Provident Hosp, pediatric residency 1935-36. **Career:** Howard Univ, faculty 1939-, prof pediatrics 1952-77, sabbatical leave July 1, 1950 thru June 30, 1951 (for study Pediatric Allergy Inst of Allergy Roosevelt Hosp NYC); Skin & Cancer Hosp, courses in pediatric dermatology 1956-59; Howard Univ, dir ctr for sickle cell disease, 1973-90, dist prof of ped & child health 1977-. **Orgs:** Editorial bd Jour Natl Med Assn 1978-; consult editor Med Aspects of Human Sexuality; Corporate Bd Children's Hosp Natl Med Ctr 1984; Cosmos Club Washington 1985; participated in numerous foreign ed travel & med meetings abroad including Children's Hosp Montreal, Canada, hospitals & univs in Caribbean Area, Univ of the West Indies Hosp, Children's Hosp Havana, Cuba, Lisbon, Portugal, Quito, Ecuador; chmn Sect on Pediatrics of the Natl Medical Assn 1952-65; bd trustees Hospital Serv Agency of Washington; Maternal & Child Health Comm of the Public Health Adv Council 1964-; Drug Experience Adv Comm & Consultant to Bureau of Medicine Public Health Serv HEW 1969-; Scientific Adv Comm of Natl Assn for Sickle Cell Disease Inc 1972-; rsch comm Children's Hosp Natl Medical Ctr Washington DC 1982-83. **Honors/Awds:** Percy L Julian Awd Phi Beta Kappa Sigma Xi Howard Univ 1977, 1979; Fellow Distinguished Awd Amer Coll of Allergists 1977, 1985; numerous publications; Gold Awd Outstanding Employee Support United Natl Capital Area 1978; plaque Outstanding & Dedicated Serv in Fighting Sickle Cell Disease 1980; Noteworthy Serv & Illustrious Career in Sickle Cell Education & Res; Distinguished Serv to Health Awd Natl Assn of Med Minority Educators 1982; People Who Matter; Plaque SectionCouncil on Pediatrics of the AMA 1985; Amer Acad of Pediatrics Jacobi Awd 1985; One of 17 Washingtonians of the Year named by Washingtonian magazine 1986; Hon DS Howard Univ 1987. **Business Addr:** Distinguished Professor, Pediatric and Child Health, Howard Univ, Washington, DC 20059.

SCOTT, RUBY DIANNE
Media company executive. **Personal:** Born Sep 19, 1951, New Rochelle, NY; daughter of Carmen Saunders & Clemmie Scott; married Raymond Williams, May 15, 1978. **Educ:** Boston University, BS, 1973; Northwestern University Management Training Ctr, 1985; Northwestern Univ, Advanced Executive Program, 1998. **Career:** Boston Globe, copy editor, 1972-75, assistant news editor, 1975-77; Chicago Tribune, copy editor, 1977-80, assistant news editor, 1980-81, assistant Sunday editor, 1981-83, science editor, 1983-86, editorial board member, op-ed page editor, 1990-93; Chicago Tribune Magazine, associate editor, 1986-87, managing editor, 1987-90; Chicago Tribune, editorial board mem/op-ed page editor, 1990-93; Tribune Publishing, director of editorial resources, 1993-. **Orgs:** National Association of Minority Media Executives, 1993-; National Association of Black Journalists, 1984-; Media Diversity Man-

agers, 1995-; American Society of Newspaper Editors Diversity Committee, 1994-; Newspaper Assn of America, recruitment and youth dev comm, 1997-. **Honors/Awds:** YMCA Black & Hispanic Achievers of Business & Industry, 1993; Chicago Tribune, Outstanding Professional Performance, 1983. **Special Achievements:** Sisters of Struggle, mentor, 1993-; co-chair, Tribune Diversity Steering Comm, 1995-. **Business Addr:** Director, Editorial Resources, Tribune Publishing, 435 N Michigan Ave, Chicago, IL 60611, (312)222-3561.

SCOTT, RUTH
Government official, company executive, management consultant. **Personal:** Born Aug 13, 1934, Albion, MI; daughter of Edna Holland and Robert Holland; married William G Scott; children: Greg, June, Chrystal. **Educ:** Albion Coll, BA, social work, 1956; Kent State Univ, ME, counseling 1961; Buffalo State, 6 hrs toward EdD 1968; SUNY, certificate, education administration, 1981. **Career:** Cleveland Public Schools, teacher, 1956-61; Valley Central School NY, teacher 1961-62; Arcade Central School NY, teacher 1964-66; Educ Serv BOCES Cattaraugus Co, consultant 1966-70; City School Dist Rochester, counsultant to nursing program 1971; Wilson Jr High School, reading lab coord 1974; City School Dist Rochester, adv specialist/human relations 1975-77; The Ford Found, consultant 1976-78; Community Savings Bank of Rochester, personnel compliance coordinator 1977-; Rochester Community Savings Bank, regional mgr; City of Rochester, city councilwoman-at-large, council pres 1986-; Scott Associates Inc, president, chief executive officer, 1989-; Multicultural Institute, Portland, developing multi-cultural workshops, 1993-. **Orgs:** WXXI bd of dirs, 1976-87; Friends of Rochester Public Library, 1976-87; adv council of Women's Career Center, 1977-; Phi Delta Kappa; exec secretary Rochester Area Foundation, president, 1992; WHEC TV-10, adv bd; chairperson Natl League of Cities Community & Economic Devel, 1987; NLC's Women in Municipal Govt, New Futures Initiative, board member; bd president Rochester Community Foundation, 1991-96; Monroe County Water Authority, board of directors; Leadership America Alumni Board, treasurer, 1990. **Honors/Awds:** Championship Debater Albion Coll 1952; Outstanding Alumni Award Albion Coll 1975; Outstanding Citizen-Politician-Christian Worker Black Student Caucus of local coll of Divinity; Honored by YWCA as one of their Women Builders of Communities and Dreams; honored as one of five businesswomen by prestigious Athena Award committee for significant conbributions in business & community; received Volunteer Serv Award Certificate from Martin Luther King Jr Greater Rochester Festival Commission; Leadership America Class of 1989, Chamber Civic Award; Alfred Univ Honors Causa, PhD, humane letters, 1997. **Business Addr:** President/CEO, Scott Associates, Inc, 30 Arvine Heights, Rochester, NY 14611.

SCOTT, RUTH PERRY. **See Obituaries section.**

SCOTT, SAMUEL
Engineer. **Personal:** Born Feb 2, 1946, San Francisco, CA; married Christine Mary Harrington; children: Stephany, Sybil. **Educ:** Wayne State U, 1964-68. **Career:** Off of Film & TV Serv MI Dept of Commerce, dir present; Detroit Free Press, photo/jazz critic 1972-79; Optek Potographic, dir/photo 1971-72; Detroit News, photo 1969-71; Studio Theaters of Detroit, supr 1968-69; Univ of MI Soc Rsrch Study, coor of persnl 1967-68. **Orgs:** Mem MI Press Photo Assn 1972-80; exec off MI Film & TV Coun; mem Nat Assn of Film Commissions 1980. **Honors/Awds:** 1st/2nd/3rd & hon ment MI Press Photo 1976-79; pub serv awd Wayne Co Bd of Commissioners 1979. **Business Addr:** 2021 Jefferson Davis Hwy, Crystal City, Arlington, VA 22202.

SCOTT, SHAWNELLE
Professional basketball player. **Personal:** Born Jun 16, 1972. **Educ:** St. John's Univ. **Career:** Cleveland Cavaliers, center, 1996-. **Business Addr:** Professional Basketball Player, Cleveland Cavaliers, One Center Ct, Cleveland, OH 44115-4001, (216)659-9100.

SCOTT, TIMOTHY VAN
Ophthalmologist. **Personal:** Born Jul 12, 1942, Newport News, VA; son of Janet H Scott and William H Scott; married Karen Hill Scott; children: Van, Lanita, Kevin, Amara. **Educ:** Fisk U, BA 1964; Meharry Med Coll, MD 1968; Hubbard Hosp Nashville Ophthalmology Res, rotating intrnshp 1968-69; Thomas Jefferson Univ Hosp Philadelphia 1969-72; HEED Ophthalmic Found Fellow Glaucoma Jules Stein Eye Inst UCLA 1972-73. **Career:** Private practice; Ophthalmology Martin Luther King Jr Gen Hosp, chief div 1973-82; Glaucoma Serv Jules Stein Eye Inst UCLA Los Angeles CA, consult 1973-; Glaucoma Serv Harbor Hosp Torrance CA, 1973-79; Ophthalmologist Kaiser Hosp Torrance CA, staff 1972-73; Am Bd Ophthalmology, dip 1973-; Charles R Drew Postgrad Med Sch, asst prof surgery; Ophthalmology UCLA Sch Med, assoc prof. **Orgs:** Amer Assn Ophthalmology; Natl Assn Res & Interns; Soc HEED Fellows; Omega Psi Phi Frat. **Honors/Awds:** Outstanding Young Men of Amer 1974. **Business Addr:** 323 N Prairie Ave #201, Inglewood, CA 90301.

SCOTT, TODD CARLTON
Professional football player. **Personal:** Born Jan 23, 1968, Galveston, TX. **Educ:** Southwestern Louisiana. **Career:** Minnesota Vikings, 1991-94; Tampa Bay Buccaneers, 1995, 1996; New York Jets, 1995; Kansas City Chiefs, 1997-. **Business Addr:** Professional Football Player, Kansas City Chiefs, One Arrowhead Dr, Kansas City, MO 64129, (816)924-9300.

SCOTT, VERONICA J.
Educator, physician. **Personal:** Born Feb 8, 1946, Greenville, AL; daughter of Mary Loys Greene Scott and C B Scott Jr. **Educ:** Howard University, BS, 1968; Albert Einstein College of Medicine, MD, 1973; UCLA School of Public Health, MPH, 1978. **Career:** Beth Israel Hospital, intern res med, 1973-75; UCLA preventive medicine resident, 1976-78, West Los Angeles VAMC, geriatric medicine fellowship, 1978-80; Birmingham VAMC, chief geriatrics sect, 1980-88; UAB/Medical Center for Aging, assistant director, 1980-; Meharry Consortium Geriatric Educ Ctr, dir, 1990-; Meharry Medical Coll Ctr on Aging, 1988-. **Orgs:** American Geriatric Society, 1978-; Geriatric Society of America, 1978-; American Society on Aging, 1978-; American Public Health Association, 1978-; committee member, Jeff Co Long Term Care Ombudsman Comm, 1982-84; Visiting Nurses Association, chairman, prof adv comm, 1983; VNA Medical Advisory Committee, co-chairperson, 1983-; Mayors Commission on the Status of Women, 1984-87; charter member, Association of Heads of Academic Programs in Geriatrics, 1991-; NA Research Task Force on Aging, 1992-. **Honors/Awds:** Govenor's Award, ITTG, Govenor G C Wallace, 1984; National Science Foundation Research Award, 1965-68; Geriatric Medicine Academic Award, National Institute on Aging, 1982-87; Associate Inv Award, West Los Angeles VAMC, 1980. **Business Addr:** Assoc Prof, Medicine/Dir, Ctr on Aging, Meharry Medical College, 1005 D B Todd Blvd, Nashville, TN 37208-3501.

SCOTT, WERNER FERDINAND
Marketing executive. **Personal:** Born Feb 27, 1957, Pfungstadt, Germany; son of Irene Schaffer Scott and Arthur Scott Jr. **Educ:** New Mexico State University, Las Cruces, NM, BBA, 1979. **Career:** Xerox Corporation, Albuquerque, NM, sales rep mgr, 1979-82; Xerox Corporation, Dallas, TX, district region mgr, 1982-86; Advantage Marketing Group, Inc, founder, currently. **Orgs:** Chairman 1989-90, board member 1990-91, Dallas International Sports Commission; member, NAACP, 1990-91; active supporter, UNCF, 1988-91. **Honors/Awds:** Quest for Success Award, Dallas Black Chamber, Morning News, 1991; Presidents Club Winner, Xerox, 1980-85. **Military Serv:** US Army, 1st Lieutenant, 1979-87; Distinguished Military Graduate, Airborne. **Business Addr:** President, CEO, Advantage Marketing Group, Inc, 5215 North O'Connor Rd, Ste 770, Irving, TX 75039.

SCOTT, WINDIE OLIVIA
Attorney. **Personal:** Born in Mobile, AL; daughter of Vivian Pugh Scott and Clifford A Scott. **Educ:** California Polytechnic Univ, BA, Political Science, 1970-74; Univ of CA, Juris Doctor, 1974-77. **Career:** State of California, tax counsel III, 1995-; State of California, Office of State Controller, sr staff counsel, 1987-95; Wiley Manuel Bar Assn, pres, 1984; CA Assn of Black Lawyers, bd mem, 1984-85; Centro de Legal-Sacramento, bd mem, 1984-85. **Orgs:** President, Sacramento County Bar Association, 1997; elected member, County Bar Counsel, 1989-92; chair, Mayor's City Affirmative Action Advisory Council, 1991-94; member, Executive Committee, State Bar Conference of Delegates, 1990-93; Pres, Women Lawyers of Sacramento, 1989; vice pres, California Assn of Black Lawyers, 1989; treasurer, Pan Hellenic Council, 1982-84; president, Alpha Kappa Alpha Sorority, 1992; mem, City Bar of Sacramento, 1984-85; mem, State Bar of CA, 1979-; mem, Natl Bar Assn, 1980-; mem, Black Women's Network. **Honors/Awds:** Sacramento 100 Most Influential Blacks, 1984; Past President Award, Wiley Manuel Bar Assn, 1985; Ernest L Robinson Jr Award, McGeorge Black Law Students Assn, 1985; Outstanding Women Award, Natl Council of Negro Women, 1988; Outstanding Woman of the Year, Government/Law Sacramento, YWCA, 1990; Unit Award, Wiley Manuel Bar Assn, 1990; 25 Blacks to Watch in 1989, Observer Newspapers, 1989; Mayor's Community Svc Awd, 1995. **Business Addr:** Tax Counsel III, State Board of Equalization, 450 N St, MC 82, Sacramento, CA 95814, (916)324-2656.

SCOTT-CLAYTON, PATRICIA ANN
Attorney. **Personal:** Born Oct 6, 1953, Chicago, IL; daughter of Merle & Verna Scott; divorced; children: Robynn. **Educ:** Northwestern University, BA, 1975; Georgetown University Law Center, JD, 1978, ML, 1986. **Career:** Department of Justice, Tax Div, trial attorney, 1978-85; IRS, sr attorney, 1985-89, employee plans litigation counsel, 1989-93, section chief, employee benefits & exempt organizations, 1991-93; Pension Benefit Guaranty Corp., assoc general counsel, 1993-97, deputy general counsel, 1997-. **Orgs:** Sidwell Friends School, parents rep, 1997-; Sheridan School, search comm chmn, 1996-97, bd of trustees, 1994-97, scy of parents association, 1993-94; The Essential Theatre, bd of dirs, 1993-96; DC Jrs Volleyball Club, travel coordinator, 1996-, chmn of fundraising comm, 1997-; Pension Benefit Guaranty Corp, chmn of combined federal campaign, 1995. **Honors/Awds:** Department of Justice, Attorney General's Award, 1979; IRS, Special Achievement Awards, 1990, 1992, 1993. **Special Achievements:** Author: Tax Qualification of Tax Sheltered Annuities, The Tax Lawyer, Fall 1995. **Business Addr:** Deputy General Counsel, Pension Benefit Guaranty Corp, Office of General Counsel, Ste 340, 1200 K St, NW, Washington, DC 20005, (202)326-4020.

SCOTT-HERON, GIL
Musician, poet. **Personal:** Born Apr 1, 1949, Chicago, IL; son of Bobbie Scott. **Educ:** Attended Fieldston School of Ethical Culture, Lincoln Univ, 1967; Johns Hopkins Univ, MA, 1972. **Career:** Creative Writing Fed City College, Washington DC, teacher; formed musical grp Midnight Band; film Baron Wolfgang Von Tripps (score) 1976; recordings include Small Talk at 125th & Lenox, The Revolution Will Not Be Televised, Winter in America, It's Your World, No Nukes, and Sun City; composer, writer, 1970-. **Honors/Awds:** Johns Hopkins Univ Fellowship; author of novels The Vulture, World Publishing, 1970, and The Nigger Factory, Dial, 1972; author of poetry collections, Small Talk at 125th & Lenox, World Publishing, 1970, and So Far, So Good, 1988; Album, Spirits, 1994. **Business Addr:** Author, So Far, So Good, Third World Press, 7822 S Dobson, Chicago, IL 60619.

SCOTT-JACKSON, LISA ODESSA
Director of black music marketing. **Personal:** Born Jul 17, 1960, Freeport, NY; daughter of Nancy Odessa Sims Scott and James Timothy Scott; married James Lloyd Jackson, Dec 21, 1990. **Educ:** Spelman College, Atlanta, GA, 1978-80. **Career:** Motown Record Corp, Atlanta, GA, regional sales assistant, 1984-89; BMG Distribution, New York, NY, national director black music marketing, 1990-.

SCOTT-JOHNSON, ROBERTA VIRGINIA
Elected government official, educator. **Personal:** Born in West Virginia; married Jesse; children: Robert Jerome Patterson, Rex Lenear Patterson, Carolyn Marie Patterson, Terrence Jerome. **Educ:** Bluefield Coll, BS Bus Admin attended; Univ of MI, MA Guidance & Counseling 1966; Univ of Edinborough, 1979. **Career:** Elkhorn HS WV, dir of commercial ed; Saginaw City School Dist, teacher, counselor; Econ Devel Corp Buena Vista Twp, directorship, township trustee, twp treasurer. **Honors/Awds:** Outstanding Serv Jessie Rouse School 1970-80; Outstanding Political Serv Six yrs at Twp Trustee 1978-84; Honorary Awd Buena Vista Twp 1980. **Home Addr:** 4636 S Gregory, Saginaw, MI 48601.

SCOTT-WARE, BARBARA ANN (BARBARA ANN WARE)
Activist. **Personal:** Born Feb 17, 1955, Brooklyn, NY; daughter of Marion Bertha James and Dudley Fairfax Scott; married Morris Wade, 1991; children: Michele C Ware, Morris Ware Jr; married Keith Brandon (divorced). **Career:** Lady Di Construction, Lady Di Production, gen contractor; Citizens Advocate For Employment & Housing, CEO, currently. **Orgs:** Corporate board mem, Assn of Minority Enterprises, 1986; bd mem, Alliance of Majority & Minority Contractors; NY State Assn of Minority Contractors; mem, Assn of General Contractors, 1985; Long Island Womens Equal Opportunity Council, 1989; bd chair, Long Island Affirmative Action, 1987; board mem, Long Island Prepared Recruitment Program, 1987; vice pres, NYS, Natl Organization for Women, 1985; trustee, Roosevelt Public Library, 1996. **Honors/Awds:** Womens Business Devt & Savvy Magazine, 1987; Essence Magazine, 1988; Outstanding Amongs Blacks, Community Service Award, 1984; Certificate of Appreciation, Long Island Womens Equal Opportunity Council, 1984; Certificate of Achievement, NYS Dept of Energy, 1987; Poet, ''So Where Does It All Go,'' poem published in Europe, 1987; ''Hope Is the Enemy of Love,'' 1989; founder, ''Project Alive, ''Lecturer on Business For World National TV, Washington, DC, 1980; LI Hist Foundation, LI Historic Women Award, 1997. **Business Addr:** CEO, Citizens Advocate, 316 Nassau Rd, Ste 426, Roosevelt, NY 11575.

SCRANAGE, CLARENCE, JR.
Emergency physician. **Personal:** Born Mar 16, 1955, Richmond, VA. **Educ:** VA Commonwealth Univ, BS Biology 1977; Meharry Medical Coll, MD 1982. **Career:** Howard Univ Hosp, emergency resident 1985; State of VA, medical examiner 1986-; Virginia EMS, medical dir 1986-. **Orgs:** Life mem Kappa Alpha Psi 1980-; regional dir VA Amer Coll of Emergency Physicians 1986-; chmn Southside Emergency Medical Serv 1986; mem Amer Medical Assoc, VA Medical Assoc. **Honors/Awds:** Outstanding Young Men in Amer Awd. **Business Addr:** Dir Emergency Unit, Community Memorial Hospital, 126 Buena Vista Circle, South Hill, VA 23970.

SCRIBNER, ARTHUR GERALD, JR.
Senior systems analyst, engineer. **Personal:** Born Nov 19, 1955, Baltimore, MD; son of Elizabeth Worrell Scribner and Arthur Gerald Scribner Sr; children: Lamara Chanelle, Arthur Gerald III, Milton Thomas. **Educ:** Univ of MD Baltimore, BA (Magna Cum Laude) 1981, BS (Magna Cum Laude) 1981; Johns Hopkins Univ School of Engineering, MS (Cum Laude) 1987. **Career:** Scribner Consulting Inc, pres 1985-; MD Medi-

cal Laboratories, pathology asst 1986-; Inner Harbor Sounds Inc, producer 1986-; US Dept of Defense, sr systems analyst/engr 1982-; A G Scribner & Associates, pres 1988-; The Consortium Inc, pres/CEO 1988-. **Orgs:** Tenor & soloist Univ of MD Chamber Choir 1978-81; public relations consultant Vivians Fashions of NY 1980-; asst instructor Univ of MD 1980-81; talent coordinator Baltimore Citywide Star Search 1985-86; vice pres Metropolitan Entertainment Consortium Inc 1985-. **Honors/Awds:** Superior Achievement Award Interprofessional Studies Inst Univ of MD 1982; Natl Security Agency, Black Engineer of the Year, 1993. **Home Addr:** 6820 Parsons Ave, Baltimore, MD 21207. **Business Addr:** Asst Dir of Special Projects, US Dept of Defense, 9800 Savage Rd, Fort Meade, MD 20755.

SCROGGINS, TRACY
Professional football player. **Personal:** Born Sep 11, 1969, Checotah, OK. **Educ:** Tulsa, attended. **Career:** Detroit Lions, defensive end, 1992-. **Business Addr:** Professional Football Player, Detroit Lions, 1200 Featherstone Rd, Pontiac, MI 48342, (248)335-4131.

SCRUGGS, ALLIE W.
Psychologist, educator. **Personal:** Born Feb 13, 1927, Akron, OH. **Educ:** Boston University, BS, education, 1958, EdD, 1971. **Career:** Lowell State College, assistant professor, associate professor, 1966-74; Boston University, instructor, psychology department, 1965-66; Ayer Public School, teacher/counselor, guidance director, assistant principal, 1959-64; University of Lowell, professor, 1974-79, professor/chairman, psychology department, 1979-. **Orgs:** New England regional chairman, Human Rights American Personnel & Guidance Association, 1972; acting director, AID University of Lowell, 1973-77; chairman, Task Force One Conference Minorities in Higher Education, Massachusetts Secondary Education Affairs Office, 1975; American Psychological Association, 1979; consultant, METCO, Boston; Education Testing Corporation, Princeton, 1980. **Honors/Awds:** Scholarship, Boston University, 1958; Scholarship, Jewish Anti-defamation League, 1963; Fellowship Grant, National Defense Education Act, 1964; Fellowship Grant, Ford Foundation, 1970. **Business Addr:** Professor & Chairman, Dept of Psychology, University of Lowell, One University Ave, Lowell, MA 01854.

SCRUGGS, BOOKER T., II
Educational administrator. **Personal:** Born Oct 2, 1942, Chattanooga, TN; son of Mabel Humphrey Scruggs and Booker T Scruggs; married Johnnie Lynn Haslerig, Oct 26, 1968 (divorced); children: Cameroun. **Educ:** Clark Coll, BA 1964; Atlanta Univ, MA 1966. **Career:** Howard High School, social science teacher 1966; Community Action Agency, coordinator research & reporting 1966-70; WNOO Radio, program moderator 1973-82; Univ TN Chattanooga, asst dir Upward Bound 1970-91, program dir, currently; Instructor of Sociology, Univ TN Chattanooga. **Orgs:** Mem Alpha Phi Alpha, Adult Educ Council; former mem bd Chattanooga Elec Power Bd 1975-85; life mem NAACP, Amer Lung Assoc; mem Chattanooga Gospel Orchestra; bd mem Methodist Student Center, University of Tennessee, Chattanooga; choir mem Wiley Methodist Church; president, TN Assn of Special Programs 1991-93; vice pres Brainerd High School PTA 1989-90. **Honors/Awds:** Jaycees Presidential Award Honor 1974; Alpha Phi Alpha Man of the Year 1986. **Special Achievements:** TV host/public affairs producer: "Point of View". **Business Addr:** Upward Bound Program Director, The University of Tennessee at Chattanooga, 615 McCallie Ave, 213 Race Hall, Chattanooga, TN 37403, (423)755-4691.

SCRUGGS, CLEORAH J.
Educator. **Personal:** Born Aug 20, 1948, Akron, OH; daughter of Mr & Mrs C Scruggs. **Educ:** Univ of Akron OH, BA Elem Ed 1970, MA Ed 1977, Admin Cert 1984; Professional Devel & Personnel Trng, Professional Cert 1981; Personal Dynamics Inst Inc, attended; Educational Specialist Degree Equivalent, 1989. **Career:** Workshop presenter; Akron Bd of Educ Akron OH, summer rec suprv 1970-73; Flint Bd of Educ, summer recreational supvr, 1974-79; Mott Adult HS Flint MI, GED instr 1974; Charles Harrison Mason Bible Coll, instr 1975-76; Flint Bd of Ed, instructor, 1970-. **Orgs:** Mem, United Teachers of Flint, Natl Educ Assn, Michigan Educ Assn, Urban League, NAACP, Natl Alliance of Black School Educ, Alpha Kappa Alpha Sorority Inc, Business & Professional Assn; Chair, Flint Community Schools Superintendent's Advisory Council, Human Relations Comm, United Way, United Negro Coll Fund; pres Young Women's Christian Council; former pres Usher Bd; founder, dir, actress, Christian Drama Guild; member, Michigan Federation of Teachers; member, American Federation of Teachers; member, Univ of Akron Alumni Assn; minority affairs comm, UTF, 1987-, prof negotiations bd, (PNB), 1987-, elementary caucus, 1987-, secretary, 1987-89, exec bd, 1987-89; NEA Delegate, 1987-; Precinct Delegate, 1990, 1994. **Honors/Awds:** Comm Serv Awd Floyd J McCree Theatre & other civic & religious assns; Masters Thesis, "Identification of Beginning Teachers' Problems" Univ of Akron 1970; Michigan Council for the Social Studies, Social Studies Educator of the Year, 1995; Social Studies Educator of the Year Award, 1995; Multicultural Diversity, 1990-, Worshop presenter for Prof Organizations, 1992-; Outcome Based Educ, 1993; Classroom Management, 1986-91; Essential Elements of Effective Instruction, 1988; Grant writer, recipient, & presenter of staff devlopment innovative grants, 1985-88; Multicultural Diversity Award, MEA Minority Concerns Comm, 1994; Excellence Award, MEA IPD, Commitment to Educ & Diversity, 1993; Comm Service Award, Humane Society, McCree Theater, Religious/Comm Organizations, 1975, 1988, 1990; nominee for Teacher of the Year, 1987; Social Studies Educator of the Year Award, 1995;. **Home Addr:** 1963 Laurel Oak Dr, Flint, MI 48507-6038. **Business Addr:** Instructor, Flint Board of Education, 923 E Kearsley, Flint, MI 48505.

SCRUGGS, OTEY MATTHEW
Educator. **Personal:** Born Jun 29, 1929, Vallejo, CA; son of Maude and Otey; married Barbara Fitzgerald; children: Jeffrey. **Educ:** Univ of CA Santa Barbara, BA 1951; Harvard U, MA 1952, PhD 1958. **Career:** Univ of CA Santa Barbara, instr to asso prof 1957-69; Syracuse Univ, prof of history 1969-94, emeritus, 1994-, chair, dept of history 1986-90. **Orgs:** Mem Assn for Study of Afro/Am Life & Hist; editl Bd Afro-ams in NY Life & Hist 1977-; mem Orgn of Am Historians; mem bd of dir Onondaga Historical Assn 1988-92. **Honors/Awds:** Syracuse Univ, Chancellor's Citation for Exceptional Academic Achievement. **Military Serv:** USNR 1948-57. **Business Addr:** Department of History, Syracuse University, Eggers 145, Syracuse, NY 13244.

SCRUGGS, SYLVIA ANN
Educator, social worker. **Personal:** Born Jun 18, 1951, Akron, OH; daughter of Deborah Scruggs and Cleophus Scruggs. **Educ:** Univ of Akron, BS 1976; Case Western Reserve Univ, MS, 1990. **Career:** Univ of Akron, clerk typist 1974-77; Akron Children's Medical Center, ward secretary 1977-78; Akron Urban League, educator 1978-82; Hawkins Skill Center, educator 1983; Department of Human Services, income maint III 1984-. **Orgs:** Counselors asst South High School 1969; big sister & tutor Univ of Akron 1970; precinct committee Community Third Wrd 1981; youth leader Youth Motivation Task Force 1982; membership committee NAACP 1981-82; volunteer, Project Learn, 1990; Volunteer, Battered Women's Shelter, 1991; Natl Assn of Social Workers, 1990. **Home Addr:** 1066 Orlando Ave, Akron, OH 44320.

SCRUGGS-LEFTWICH, YVONNE
Urban planner, executive, educator. **Personal:** Born Jun 24, 1933, Niagara Falls, NY; married Edward V Leftwich Jr; children: Cathryn D Perry, Rebecca S Perry-Glickstein, Tienne Leftwich Davis, Edward Leftwich III. **Educ:** North Carolina Central University, BA, 1955; Free Univ of Berlin, German Hochschulefur Politik, cert, 1956; University of Minnesota, MAPA, 1958; University of Pennsylvania, PhD. **Career:** Black Leadership Forum Inc, executive director/COO, 1996-; Joint Center for Political and Economic Studies, Urban Policy Institutes & Natl Policy Institute, dir, 1991-96; George Washington Univ, GSPM, prof, 1987-; YEL Corp. and Harlem USA Inc, COO, bd chair, 1987-90; Pryor, Govan, Counts & Co Inc, Investment Bankers, senior consulting vice pres, 1987-88; City of Philadelphia, deputy mayor, 1985-87; New York State Division of Housing and Community Renewal, commissioner, 1983-85, regional director, 1981-82; Dept of HUD, Community Planning & Development, deputy asst secretary, 1977-79; President's Urban & Regional Policy Group, executive director, 1977-78; Howard University, Dept of City & Regional Planning, professor, chairperson, 1974-77, professor, 1979-81; University of Pennsylvania, Wharton School HRG, faculty, administrator, 1970-74. **Orgs:** National Council of Negro Women; NAACP; Greater Washington Urban League; The Milton S Eisenhower Foundation, vp and trustee; Women of Distinction, president; National Political Congress of Black Women; Geneva B Scruggs Community Health Ctr, founding pres; American Institute of Planners; former vice pres, Assn of Collegiate Schools of Planning; vice pres, PA Housing Fin Corp, 1974; commr, Mobile Homes Commn; bd mbr, World Affairs Council, 1970-73; Philadelphia Council for Community Advancement, 1970-74. **Honors/Awds:** Fulbright Fellow, 1955-56; SAIS, Scholarship, Johns Hopkins Univ, 1956-57; Elks Scholarship, 1951-55; Howard Univ Grad Student Council Awd, Grad Educators, 1975; AIP, Diana Donald Award; Charter Membership, US Senior Executive Service; National Council of Negro Women, Leadership Award, 1975; Howard University, Outstanding Contribution to Graduate Education, 1975, Faculty Research Award, 1976; Dept of Housing and Urban Development, Outstanding Achievement Award, 1979; The Ford Foundation, Individual Grant Award, 1979; Howard University Institute for Urban Affairs and Research, Life and Culture of the Black Community Award, 1980. **Special Achievements:** First African American female elected officer of New York State Youth-in-Government; first Fulbright scholar from Buffalo, NY; first Fulbright scholar from North Carolina Central Univ; first African American Fulbright fellow from the State of North Carolina; first African American appointed as housing commissioner for New York State. **Business Addr:** Executive Director, Black Leadership Forum, Inc, 1090 Vermont Ave NW, Ste 1100, Washington, DC 20005, (202)789-1940.

SCRUTCHIONS, BENJAMIN
Educator. **Personal:** Born Aug 13, 1926, Montezuma, GA. **Educ:** Roosevelt U, BS; DePaul U, MS; Univ of Florence, Italy, further study; Northwestern U; Univ of Chicago. **Career:** Chicago Bd of Educ, dir Comm & Human Relations Dept; past positions as cons, supt of schools, asst prin & instr. **Orgs:** Mdm Kappa Alpha Psi; Phi Delta Kappa; mem various Professional & civic orgns. **Honors/Awds:** Recipient Dist Serv Awd; Alumni Awd, Roosevelt U; 1st Black Supt of Schs in IL. **Military Serv:** AUS. **Business Addr:** 1750 E 71 St, Chicago, IL 60649.

SCURLOCK, MICHAEL
Professional football player. **Personal:** Born Feb 26, 1972, Casa Grande, AZ; married Michaela; children: Vanessa, Michael III. **Educ:** Arizona, attended. **Career:** St Louis Rams, defensive back, 1995-. **Business Addr:** Professional Football Player, St Louis Rams, One Rams Way, St Louis, MO 63045, (314)982-7267.

SCURRY, FRED L.
Attorney. **Personal:** Born Dec 16, 1942, London, OH; divorced; children: Jeriah. **Educ:** Central St U, BS 1966; Howard Univ Law Sch, JD 1969. **Career:** Atty, pvt prac 1974-; London, city solic 1976-79; IRS, 1972-74; Clarence J Brown MC, staff 1967-69. **Orgs:** Mem Columbus OH Bar Assn; Madison Co Bar Assn; bd of dir Madison Co Metropolitan Housing; London Lions Club. **Military Serv:** AUS capt 1970-72. **Business Addr:** 100 W 2nd, London, OH 43140.

SEABROOK, BRADLEY MAURICE
Clergyman. **Personal:** Born Mar 12, 1928, Savannah, GA; son of Katie Lue Carpenter Seabrook and Bradley Seabrook; married Minnie Lucile Long Seabrook, May 14, 1951; children: Criss, Lilla, Tina, Lisa. **Educ:** Florida International University, Miami, FL, BT, industrial technology, 1979. **Career:** Aircraft Engine Mechanic, Air Force, Eglin AFB, FL, 1955-58, 1961-68; Naval Aviation Engineering Service Unit, Philadelphia, PA, 1968-83 (retired). **Orgs:** Past Grand knight, Knights of Columbus-5658, 1975-76; sir knight, 4th Degree, Deluwa Assembly, 1971; life member, NAACP, 1975; past commander, America Post 193 Pensacola, FL, 1956-58. **Honors/Awds:** Knight of the Year, Knights of Columbus Council-5658, 1974-75; Sustained Superior Performance Award, Dept of Navy, NAESU, 1983; Ordination to the Diaconate, Diocese of Pensacola-Tallahassee, 1980; George Washington Honor Medal, 1995; Freedom Foundation at Valley Forge Pensacola Chapter; Community Volunteer Award, NAACP Pensacola Branch, 1995. **Military Serv:** Navy 1946-48; Air Force, 1951-55. **Home Addr:** PO Box 702, Cantonment, FL 32533.

SEABROOK, JULIETTE THERESA
Real estate broker. **Personal:** Born Jan 27, 1954, Charleston, SC; daughter of Eva Wilson & Luther Seabrook; children: Gerren. **Educ:** Howard University, BA (Cum laude), 1975; University of Maryland Law School, JD, 1978. **Career:** US Department of Health & Human Services, staff attorney, 1979-85; The Space Company, broker-in-charge, 1986-. **Orgs:** The Community Foundation, advisory board, 1995-; First Union National Bank, advisory board, 1994-; Charleston County Human Services Comm, advisory board, 1994-; Charleston Local Citywide Development Corporation, advisory board, 1994-95; Charleston County Planning Board, 1993-. **Home Addr:** 220 3rd Ave, #5-B, Charleston, SC 29403, (803)577-6428. **Business Addr:** Real Estate Broker/Owner, The Space Co, 82 1/2 Spring St., Charleston, SC 29403, (803)577-2676.

SEABROOKS, NETTIE HARRIS
City official. **Personal:** Born Feb 22, 1934, Mount Clemens, MI; daughter of Ivan Joseph and Katherine Marshall Davis Harris; children: Victoria D, Franklyn E. **Educ:** Marygrove Coll, BS, chemistry; Univ of MI, MLS. **Career:** Detroit Public Library, Technology Dept, chemical librarian; TN State Univ, Nashville, instructor; General Motors, 31 years, Public Relations Staff Library, librarian, Corp Res Operations, mgr, Public Affairs Info Servs, dir, GM's Chev-Pont, Canada Group, dir of govt and civic affairs, GM's North Amrican Passenger Car Platforms, dir of government relations; City of Detroit, deputy mayor, chief administative officer, 1994-. **Orgs:** Bd mem, Museum of African-American History; Barat Human Servs; Detroit Institute of Arts Friends of African and African-American Art; Detroit Med Ctr; Music Hall; Karmanos Cancer Institute. **Honors/Awds:** Marygrove College, Honorary Doctor of Humane Letters, 1995. **Business Addr:** Deputy Mayor, City of Detroit, 1126 City-County Bldg, 2 Woodward Ave, Detroit, MI 48226.

SEABROOKS-EDWARDS, MARILYN S.
Government official. **Personal:** Born Mar 3, 1955, Allendale, SC; married Ronald Burke Edwards. **Educ:** University of South Carolina Saik Regional Campus, summer session 1974-75; Georgia Southern College, AB 1977; US Department of Agriculture, evening graduate studies 1984; Baruch College/City Univ of NY, MPA 1984. **Career:** City of Savannah Housing Department, special projects coordinator 1981-83; Department of Human Services, special assistant to the dir 1983-84; City of Savannah Housing Department, program coordinator 1984-85;

Department of Human Services, program analyst 1985-; Exec Office of the Mayor Office of the Sec of the District of Columbia, chief admin officer 1987-. **Orgs:** Secretary WVGS Radio Board Georgia So College 1976 & 1977; social studies teacher Jenkins County School System 1977-78; financial counselor City of Savannah Housing Department 1978-81; instructor YMCA 1983; membership YMCA 1983-85; membership Washing Urban League 1984-85; membership Natl Forum for Black Public Admin 1984-85; membership Intl City Management Assn 1984-85; sec Wash DC Chap natl Forum for Black Public Admin; bd mem Notary Public Bd for the Dist of Columbia; hearings compliance officer Exec Office of the Mayor. **Honors/Awds:** John Phillip Sousa Award 1973; Psi Alpha Theta Georgia So College 1975-77; Outstanding Young Women of America 1982 & 1983; Natl Urban Fellowship 1983-84. **Home Addr:** 2352 Glenmont Circle #201, Silver Spring, MD 20902.

SEAL
Vocalist. **Personal:** Born in London, England. **Career:** Folk-pop singer. **Special Achievements:** Songs include: Kiss from a Rose, Don't Cry, Prayer for the Dying. **Business Addr:** Vocalist, c/o Warner Brothers Records, 75 Rockefeller Plz, New York, NY 10020-1604, (212)275-4600.

SEALE, BOBBY
Political activist. **Personal:** Born Oct 22, 1936, Dallas, TX; married Artie; children: Malik Kkrumah Stagolee. **Educ:** Merritt College, attended. **Career:** Black Panther Party for Self-Defense, chairman, former minister of information, co-founder, 1966-74; Advocates Scene, founder, 1974-; lecturer, currently. **Honors/Awds:** Author: Seize the Time: The Story of the Black Panther Party and Huey P Newton, Random House, 1970, A Lonely Rage: The Autobiography of Bobby Seale, 1978; Barbeque with Bobby, 1987. **Military Serv:** USAF 3 yrs. **Business Addr:** Youth Employment Strategies, 6117 Germantown, Philadelphia, PA 19144.

SEALE, SAMUEL RICARDO
Professional football player. **Personal:** Born Oct 6, 1962, Barbados, West Indies. **Educ:** Western State College, attended. **Career:** Los Angeles Raiders, 1984-87; San Diego Chargers, cornerback, 1988-. **Business Addr:** Professional Football Player, San Diego Chargers, Jack Murphy Stadium, 9449 Friars Rd, San Diego, CA 92108.

SEALLS, ALAN RAY
Meteorologist. **Personal:** Born in New Rochelle, NY; son of Josephine Reese Sealls and Albert Sealls. **Educ:** Cornell Univ, Ithaca, NY, BS, 1985; Florida State Univ, Tallahassee, Fl, MS, 1987. **Career:** Florida State Univ, Tallahassee, FL, graduate assistant, 1985-87; WALB-TV, Albany, GA, Meteorologist, 1987-88; WTMJ Inc, Milwaukee, WI, meteorologist, 1988-. **Orgs:** Member, American Meteorological Society, 1984-; member, National Weather Association, 1987-; member, National Association of Black Journalists, 1989-; member, NAACP, 1989-. **Honors/Awds:** AMS TV Weathercaster Seal, American Meteorological Society, 1988; NWA TV Weathercaster Seal, National Weather Association, 1987; Distinguished Man of 1990; Top Ladies of Distinction, Milwaukee, 1990; Black Achiever, Metropolitan YMCA, Milwaukee, 1990-91. **Business Addr:** Meteorologist, WTMJ Inc, 720 E Capitol Dr, PO Box 693, Milwaukee, WI 53201.

SEALS, CONNIE C. (COSTELLO)
Business executive. **Personal:** Born Sep 1, 1931, Chicago, IL; daughter of Mary Lee Wade; married Jack Hollis; children: Theodore, Victor, Michelle, Philip. **Educ:** Accredited by Pub Relations Soc of Am, 1972; Daniel Hale Williams Univ, BA, Public Admin, 1976; Licensed IL Insurance Producer, 1992; certified, Primerica Personal Financial Analyst, 1997. **Career:** Bulletin Comm Newspaper, asst editor, 1962-63; Chicago Urban League, dir, Communications, 1963-73; IL Comm on Human Relations, exec dir, 1973-80; C-BREM Comm Corp, pres, currently; Primerica Financial Services, life insurance producer, currently. **Orgs:** APR Chair, National Accreditation Bd, PRSA, 1978; APR Chair, Minority Affairs Comm, Public Relations Soc of Amer, 1985; mem, Publicity Club of Chicago, 1985; APR Chair, Minority Affairs Comm PRSA, Chicago, 1984-85; Chair, IL Consultation On Ethnicity in Educ, ICEE, 1984-85; mem, exec comm, Chicago Tourism Council, 1985-89; co-chair, Coalition of Concerned Women in the War on Crime, 1974-80; founder, chair, Midwest Women's Center; founder, mem, League of Black Women; former book reviewer, Chicago Sun-Times; former bd mem, Natl Consortium for Black Prof Development; former vp/mem, Chicago Black United Fund; former bd mem, Urban Gateways; mem, Cit Comm for UIC; former guest lecturer, Journalism No IL U; former prog leader, AM Mgmt Assn Pub Relations Seminars. **Honors/Awds:** Hon LLD, 1977; DHWU Merit Award Beatrice Caffrey, Chicago 1981; Amer Pluralism Award, ICEE, 1982; Certificate of Appreciation, NAACP, 1984; Ten Year Service Award, 1979-89 University of Illinois at Chicago; Inducted, Alpha Gamma Pi Sorority, 1973; Recipient, 1st Communicator of the Year, WLS-TV, 1973; Woman of the Year, local and national, Natl Assn of Media Women. **Home Addr:** 7228 S Rhodes Ave, Chicago, IL 60619-1704. **Business Addr:** President, C-BREM Communications Corp, 7228 S Rhodes Ave, Chicago, IL 60619.

SEALS, GEORGE E.
Business executive. **Personal:** Born Oct 2, 1942, Higginsville, MO; married Cecelia McClellan. **Educ:** Univ of MO. **Career:** Trader, Chicago, bd of trade; WA Redskins, Chicago Bears, & KC Chiefs, former football player; Chicago Bd Options Exchange Bd, mem. **Orgs:** Mem Better Boys Found; Chicago PUSH; bd of regents Daniel Hale Williams Univ 1967; All Pro Team.

SEALS, GERALD
Appointed government official. **Personal:** Born Sep 22, 1953, Columbia, SC; son of Janet Kennerly Seals; married Carolyn E Seals; children: Gerald II, Jelani-Akil. **Educ:** Univ of SC, BA 1975; Univ of Denver, MA 1976; Southern IL Univ Carbondale, MS ABT 1978. **Career:** City of Carbondale IL, admin intern 1977-78; Village of Glen Ellyn IL, asst to village admin 1978-81; Village of Glendale Heights, asst village mgr 1981-82; Village of Glendale Heights, village mgr 1982-84; City of Springfield, asst city mgr 1984-86, city manager 1986-88; City of Corvallis, city manager, 1988-. **Orgs:** Vice chmn of bd Intergovt Risk Mgmt 1982-83; chmn DuPage Reg IV Sub-Region Regionalization Comm 1982-84; chmn of bd Intergovt Risk Mgmt Agency 1983-84; bd mem Springfield Civic Theatre 1985-88; bd mem Springfield OIC 1985-; bd of Clark County Transportation Coordinating Comm 1985-88; State of Oregon Structural Code Advisory Board, 1988-; Corvallis/Benton County United Way, 1989-; bd mem, Natl Forum for Black Public Administrators, 1989-. **Honors/Awds:** Acad Fellowship Univ of Denver 1975-76; Acad Fellowship Southern IL Univ 1976-78; Image Awd Fred Hampton Scholarship Fund 1983; Cert of Conformance GovtFinance Officers Assoc 1984; A Face of 1984 Article Springfield News Sun 1984. **Home Addr:** 230 NE Powderhorn Drive, Corvallis, OR 97330. **Business Addr:** City Manager, City of Corvallis, 501 SW Madison Avenue, Corvallis, OR 97339.

SEALS, MAXINE
Educational administrator. **Personal:** Born in Trinity, TX; married Frank Seals; children: Thaddeus, Cedric. **Educ:** Houston Community College, attended; Texas Southern University, attended. **Career:** Bd of directors, Gulf Coast School Board 1984-85; president, School Board, North Forest Independent School District, currently. **Orgs:** Fontaine Scenic Woods Civic Club; Texas Caucus of Black School Board Members, president, 1984-85. **Home Addr:** 5106 Nolridge, Houston, TX 77016.

SEALS, R. GRANT
Educational administrator. **Personal:** Born Aug 6, 1932, Shelbyville, KY; married Georgetta Angela Lynem; children: Rupert La Wendell, Rori LaRele, Regan Wayne, LaRita Angela. **Educ:** Florida A&M U, BS with honors 1953; Univ of KY, MS 1956; Washington State U, PhD 1960. **Career:** Internation Programs, FL A&M University, director, 1989-94; University of AR-Pine Bluff, interim director of Development, 1988-89; University of NV-Reno, emeritus professor, 1987-, professor of Biochemistry, 1982-87; Coll of Agr Univ of NV Reno, asso dean 1976-; US Dept of Agr, coord spl prog SEA/CR 1974-76; FA A&M U, dean prof sch of agr of agr-home econ 1969-74; IA State U, asst prof food tech 1966-69; IA State U, research asso food tech 1964-66; TN State U, asso prof dairy chem biochem 1959-64; Wash State U, research asst dairy mfg 1955-59; FL A&M U, instr dairying 1954-55. **Orgs:** Mem expt sta com on policy NASULGC 1971-73; mem overseas liaison com Am Counc on Educ Wash DC 1971-77; dir FAMU agr research & educ ctr Inst of Food & Agr Sci Univ of FL 1972-74; mem Alpha Kappa Mu Honor Soc FL A&M Univ 1951; memSigma Xi Wash State Univ 1958; chmn Ames Fair Housing Bd Ames IA 1967-69; pres Meth Men First Meth Ch Ames IA 1967-68; mem Alpha Phi Alpha; mem Gamma Sigma Delta Honor Soc 1979. **Honors/Awds:** Pub 28 sci papers/articles/abstracts 1958-. **Military Serv:** USAR e-6 8 yrs served;5. **Business Addr:** Professor Emeritus, University of NV, Reno, NV 89557.

SEALS, RAYMOND BERNARD
Professional football player. **Personal:** Born Jun 17, 1965, Syracuse, NY. **Career:** Tampa Bay Buccaneers, defensive end, 1989-93; Pittsburgh Steelers, 1994-95; Carolina Panthers, 1997-. **Business Addr:** Professional Football Player, Carolina Panthers, 800 Mint St, Ericsson Stadium, Charlotte, NC 28202, (704)358-7000.

SEALS, SHEA
Professional basketball player. **Personal:** Born Aug 26, 1975. **Educ:** Tulsa. **Career:** Los Angeles Lakers, guard, 1997-. **Business Addr:** Professional Basketball Player, Los Angeles Lakers, PO Box 10, Inglewood, CA 90306, (310)419-3100.

SEALY, JOAN R.
Physician. **Personal:** Born Apr 23, 1942, Philadelphia, PA; daughter of L Beverly Daniels Rice and John K Rice Jr; divorced; children: Desa, Denice. **Educ:** Univ of Chicago, BA 1964; George Washington Univ, MD 1968; Med Washing Hosp Ctr, internship 1968-69; Yale Univ Med Ctr, res psychiatric 1969-72; certified by Board of Psychiarty & Neurology. **Career:** Private practice, psychiatrist; George Washington Univ Med School, assoc clinical prof. **Orgs:** American Psychiatric Association; Washington Psychiatric Society; DC Medical Society. **Home Phone:** (202)244-2815. **Business Phone:** (202)244-6946.

SEALY, MALIK
Professional basketball player. **Personal:** Born Feb 1, 1970, Bronx, NY. **Educ:** St John's University, 1992. **Career:** Indiana Pacers, forward, 1992-94; LA Clippers, 1994-97; Detroit Pistons, 1997-; Malik Sealy XXI Inc, CEO, currently. **Business Addr:** Professional Basketball Player, Detroit Pistons, 2 Championship Dr, Auburn Hills, MI 48326, (248)377-0100.

SEAMS, FRANCINE SWANN
Professional fitness specialist, business owner. **Personal:** Born Sep 15, 1947, Ronceverte, WV; daughter of Virginia Caroline Swann and John Calvin Swann Sr; married Michael Hugh Seams, Dec 18, 1971; children: Scott Calvin, Coy Jvon. **Educ:** West Virginia State College, 1965-67; Marshall University, 1974-76. **Career:** C&P Telephone Co, service supervisor, 1970-77; Diamond State Telephone, market administrator, 1977-83; AT&T Information Systems, administrative supervisor, 1983-85; Aerobicize, co-owner, educational director, 1983-87; Fitness Specialists, director of education, 1988-92; State of Delaware, telecommunications consultant, 1986-; Christina School District, adult continuing education, fitness, 1987-; Body Seams, owner, director, 1987-. **Orgs:** Governor's Council on Lifestyles and Fitness, appointee, education committee, 1989-; Governor's Council on Drug Abuse, appointee, education committee, 1989-; American Council on Exercise, gold certified member, 1986-; IDEA, The Association for Fitness Professionals, chairman, Task Force on African-American Fitness Participation, 1990-; City of Hope National Workouts, chairman, Delaware Workouts, 1992-; United Cerebral Palsy Workouts, planner and presenter, 1992-; American Heart Association Dance for Heart, solicitor and presenter, 1989-. **Honors/Awds:** Christina School District, Board of Education, educator honor roll, 1992; Avia Outstanding Achievers, Avia Outstanding Professional Achievement Award, 1987; Randal, winner's cup, over 40 cycle racers, 1990; American Council on Exercise, gold certification, 1986. **Special Achievements:** Developed new exercise technique: board bounding, 1990; wrote, "An Instructor's Guide to Board Bounding," 1991; wrote, 40-hour Fitness Instructor Course, 1990; founded IDEA Task Force on African-American Fitness Participation, 1990; developed data and delivered, "Black, Bold, Beautiful-Make it Fit," series, 1992. **Business Addr:** Owner, Body Seams, The Fitness Specialists, 237 Crystal Court, Newark, DE 19713, (302)368-7721.

SEARCY, LEON, JR.
Professional football player. **Personal:** Born Dec 21, 1969, Washington, DC; married Joycelyn; children: Malika-Maya, Kenya Imani. **Educ:** Univ of Miami FL, bachelor's degree in sociology, 1992. **Career:** Pittsburgh Steelers, offensive tackle, 1992-95; Jacksonville Jaguars, 1996-. **Honors/Awds:** Sports Illustrated, All-Pro Team, 1995; Played in Super Bowl XXX, 1996. **Business Addr:** Professional Football Player, Jacksonville Jaguars, 1 Stadium Pl, Jacksonville, FL 32202, (904)633-6000.

SEARLES, CHARLES R.
Artist, educator. **Personal:** Born Jul 11, 1937, Philadelphia, PA; son of Catherine Hall and Charles Searles; married Kathleen Spicer, Dec 27, 1987; children: Vanessa Searles Mitchel, Gregory. **Educ:** Penn Academy of Fire Arts, 1968-72; Europe, Cresson Meml Traveling Scholarship 1971; Africa, Ware Meml Traveling Scholarship 1972; PA Acad Fine Arts, grad 1972; Univ of Penna, 1972. **Career:** ILE-IFE Center, asst orng art dept 1970; Peal Galleries PA Acad, mem exhibition com 1971; Philadelphia Coll Art, instr; Philadelphia Museum Art Studio Classes, instr; Univ of the Arts, instructor, drawing 1973-; Brooklyn Museum Art School, instr 1983-; Jersey State Coll, instructor, drawing 1990; Bloomfield Coll, instructor, painting 1990. **Honors/Awds:** Commissions: US Gen Serv Admin Interior 1976, mural "Celebration" Wm J Green Fed Bldg, "Play Time" Malory Publ Playground 1976, Newark NJ Amtrak Station Wall Sculpture "Rhythmic Forms" 1985, Dempsey Service Center, Wall Sculpture "Cultural Mix" 1989; collections: Smithsonian Inst 1976, "Festac77", collection NY St Off Bldg 1977, Philadelphia Museum of Art, Fed Railroad Admis, Ciba-Gigy Inc, Dallas Museum of Art, Montclair Art Museum, Philip Morris Inc, Howard Univ, Smithsonian Inst; exhibitions: one person show Sande Webster Gallery, Philadelphia PA 1984, 1986, group shows, Charlottenborg Museum Denmark 1986, Port of History Museum 1987, Sande Webster Gallery PA 1988, 1990, Dallas Museum of Art 1989, Milwaukee Art Museum 1990, High Museum Atlanta 1990, Richmond Museum of Fine Art, 1991ontclair Art Museum NJ, 1988; Noyes Museum NJ, 1989. **Business Addr:** 640 Broadway, New York, NY 10012.

SEARS, BERTRAM E. **See Obituaries section.**

SEARS, LEAH JEANETTE
Judge. **Personal:** Born Jun 13, 1955, Heidelberg; daughter of Onnye Jean Rountree Sears and Thomas E Sears; divorced;

children: Addison, Brennan. **Educ:** Cornell Univ, Ithaca NY, BS, 1976; Emory Univ School of Law, Atlanta GA, JD, 1980; Natl Judicial Coll, Reno NV, MJS, 1991; University of VA School of Law, LLM, 1995. **Career:** Columbus Ledger Newspaper, Columbus OH, reporter, 1976-77; Spirotte, Permutt et al, summer associate lawyer, 1979; Alston & Bird, practicing atty, 1980-85; City Court of Atlanta, GA, judge pro hac vice, 1982-85, judge, 1985-88; Superior Court of Fulton County, Atlanta GA, judge, 1989-. **Orgs:** Mem, Amer, Natl, Georgia, Atlanta, and Gate City Bar Assns; mem, Natl Assn of Women Judges; founding pres, comm mem, Georgia Assn of Black Women Attys; mem, exec comm, Greater Atlanta Club of Natl Assn of Negro Business & Professional Women; bd mem, Georgia Assn for Women Lawyers; bd mem, American Red Cross, Atlanta Chapter; mem, Natl Assn of Alcoholism and Drug Abuse Counselors; mem, Amer Business Women's Assn. **Honors/Awds:** NAACP Award (Atlanta Chapter) Award for Community Service; Distinguished Leadership Award for Outstanding Service in the Judiciary, 1988; founder of Battered Women's Project of Columbus, Georgia. **Business Addr:** Associate Justice, Georgia State Supreme Court, 244 Washington St SW, 572 State Office Annex, Atlanta, GA 30334.

SEATON, SHIRLEY SMITH
Educator, educational administrator. **Personal:** Born in Cleveland, OH; daughter of Cecil Stone Smith Wright and Kibble Clarence Smith; married Lawrence Seaton, Oct 2, 1965; children: Eric Dean. **Educ:** Howard Univ, Washington DC, BA, 1947, MA, 1948; Case Western Reserve Univ, Cleveland OH, MA, 1956; Institute Universitario di Studi Europei, Turin, Italy, cert. advanced study, 1959; Univ of Akron, Akron OH, PhD, 1981; Beijing Normal Univ, Beijing, China, 1982; postdoctorate. **Career:** Cleveland Board of Education, teacher, 1950-58, asst principal, 1959-65, principal, 1966-76; US Government, Department of Education, educational specialist, 1965; WEWS-TV, Cleveland OH, teacher, 1963-67; Cleveland State Univ, adjunct prof, 1977-85; Basics and Beyond Education Consultants, dir; John Carroll University, asst dir, multicultural affairs, 1989-. **Orgs:** National Alliance of Black School Educators, National Council for Social Studies, National Association of Secondary School Principals, Association for Supervision & Curriculum Development; pres, Metropolitan Cleveland Alliance of Black School Educators 1981-; Coalition of 100 Black Women 1991-; Phi Delta Kappa 1979-; Fulbright Association; board member, Western Reserve Historical Society; board member, Retired and Senior Volunteer Program. **Honors/Awds:** Fulbright grant to Italy, 1959, and to China, 1982; Martin Luther King Outstanding Educator Award, 1989; Outstanding Educator Awards, Cleveland City Cncl and Ohio State Legislature; Governor of Ohio, Martin Luther King Humanitarian Award, 1992. **Home Addr:** 3680 Bendemeer Rd, Cleveland Heights, OH 44118. **Business Addr:** Asst Director, Multicultural Affairs, John Carroll University, 20700 N Park Blvd, University Heights, OH 44118.

SEAVERS, CLARENCE W.
Business executive (retired). **Personal:** Born Aug 13, 1919, Sandusky, OH; married Juanita Jackson. **Educ:** Attended, Bowling Green Extension, Univ of HI. **Career:** Erie Co Health Dist, bd mem, 1968-; Erie Huron CAC, treasurer, 1969-; Erie County Bd of Elections, bd mem, 1981-retirement. **Orgs:** mem, OH Office of the Consumers Counsel, 1989; trustee, Providence Hospital, 1989; trustee, YMCA, 1989; mem, LEADS (Chamber of Commerce affiliate) 1984; chmn, Goodwill Industries, 1984; chmn, Youth Advisory Comm, 1985; mem, Downtown Merchants Inc, 1986; mem, Chamber of Commerce 1987; trustee, Stein Hospice Inc, 1992; bd mem, Second Harvest Inc, 1993; bd mem, Black Culture Awareness, 1995-. **Honors/Awds:** Outstanding & Dedicated Serv to the Community, Sandusky Branch, NAACP, 1982; Outstanding Citizen's Award, State of Ohio, 1983; Community Srv Award Progress Lodge #85, 1985; Gold Award, United Way, 1989. **Military Serv:** AUS tech 5 sgt 4 yrs, Good Conduct Medal, 1943, Asiatic Pacific Medal, 1944. **Home Addr:** 1490 Dixon Dr, Sandusky, OH 44870.

SEAY, DAWN CHRISTINE
Sales manager. **Personal:** Born Jan 23, 1964, Washington, DC; daughter of Ewart & Marjorie Russell; married Geoffrey V Seay, Oct 11, 1989; children: Alexandra, Ashton. **Educ:** Univ of Central Florida, BA, journalism, 1986. **Career:** Washington Hilton & Towers, guest svcs, 1986-87; Hospitality Parteners, sales mgr, 1987-89; Philadelphia Hilton & Towers, natl sales mgr, 1989-93; Philadelphia Convention Bureau, convention sales, 1993-. **Orgs:** Natl Coalition of Black Meetings Planners, assoc mem, 1989-; Hospitality Sales & Mktg Assn, chapter bd mem, 1990-93; Multicultural Affairs Congress, chair educ comm, 1994-. **Home Phone:** (215)763-0439. **Business Addr:** National Sales Manager, Philadelphia Convention & Visitors Bureau, 1515 Market Street, Ste 2020, Philadelphia, PA 19102, (215)636-4401.

SEAY, LORRAINE KING
Educator. **Personal:** Born Jun 20, 1926, Switchback, WV; married John T Seay (deceased); children: Yvonne D, Sean V. **Educ:** Bluefield St Clge, BS 1949; WV Univ, MS 1960. **Career:** Cheerleader coach 1950-71; Stratton Jr High, girls basketball/volleyball track coach 1960-78; gymnastic coach 1971-83, phyicial educ teacher 1950-85 (retired). **Orgs:** City Council Woman City of Beckley 1971-79; Phys Educ instr 1950-; coach cheerleader bsktbl vlybl track; recr bd City of Beckley 1979-85; life mem NEA; life mem NAACP; Amer Red Cross Bd of Raleigh Co; Raleigh Cty Assc Classroom Tchrs; Bluefield State Clge Alumni; TV Bd for Station WSWP/TV; mem Maids & Matrons Soc Study Club; ch clerk & sr usher bd mem Central Bapt Church; golden life mem Delta Sigma Theta Sor; bd dir Amer Cancer Soc Raleigh Co;mem Adv Commin, WV Hlth Agcy; summer recr dir City of Beckley; assc dir acrobatics Jerry Rose Dance Studio; WV Extention Agent bd dir; mem AAVW; mem Delta Kappa Gamma Intl Soc; mem WVEA Civil Serv Commn for Firemen; planning commission, City of Beckley. **Honors/Awds:** Silver Cup Vol Heart Fund Wrkr; Woman of the Year Raleigh Co Woman's Club; Outstanding Comm Work Mountainer State Bar Assn. **Home Addr:** 315 G St, Beckley, WV 25801.

SEAY, NORMAN R.
Educational administrator. **Personal:** Born Feb 18, 1932, St Louis, MO. **Educ:** Stowe Tchrs Coll, BA 1954; Lincoln Univ, MEduc 1966. **Career:** Dept of Health, Educ and Welfare, Equal Employment Opportunity specialist; Social Serv, proj dir 1971-73, dep gen mgr 1970-71; Concentrated Employment Prog, dir 1967-70; Dist OEO Ofcs, dir 1965-67; Work-Study Coord St Louis Bd Edn, tchr 1954-65. **Orgs:** Mem Bd of Adult Welfare Serv; MO Assn for Soc Welfare, exec Bd; Pub Improv Bond Issue Screening Comm; Yeatman-Central City Foods Inc, chmn bd dirs; Patrolman CC Smith's Children Educ Trust Fund Comm, numerous other civic affiliations; co-chair, Racial Polarization Task Force 1988-; co-chair, Education Advisory Committee, VP Fair 1989-. **Honors/Awds:** Distinguised Citizen Awd St Louis Argus Newspaper 1974; Oustanding Comm Serv Gamma Omega Chap Alpha Kappa Alpha; Outstanding & Dist St Louis Blk Police Assn; serv to all comm of Greater St Louis bd of mgmt Sheldon Memorial Ethical Soc of St Louis; Valiant Leadership Alpha Zeta Chap Iota Phi Lambda Sor Inc; Certificate of Achievement United Front of Cairo, IL; Comm Serv Radio Sta KATZ; Outstanding Aid to Law Enforcement St Louis Police Dept; Concern & Comm to Metro St Louis Youth St Louis Mayor's Council on Youth; comm serv St Louis CORE; Police Affairs St Louis NAACP; Gr Contrib for 1972 Natl Conf of Blk Policemen; Outstanding Comm Serv Northside Church of Seventh-Day Adventists; Outstanding civic work True Light Baptist Church; merit serv HDC Credit Union;Most Distinguished Alumni Awa Harris-Stowe State College 1989. **Military Serv:** AUS 1955-57.

SEBHATU, MESGUN
Educator. **Personal:** Born Jan 6, 1946, Eritrea; married Almaz Yilma; children: Emnet M Sebhatu, Temnete M Sebhatu. **Educ:** Haile Selassie I Univ, BSc Physics 1969; Clemson Univ, PhD Physics 1975. **Career:** Clemson Univ, grad TA 1970-75; NC St Univ, vis asst prof physics 1975-76; Pensacola Jr Coll, asst prof physics 1976-78; Winthrop University, asst prof physics 1978-84, associate professor of physics 1984-91, professor physics, 1992-; Michigan State University, King-Chavez-Parks, visiting professor physics, 1991-92. **Orgs:** Mbr Catholic Ch 1946-; mem Am Physical Soc; mem Am Assoc of Physics Tchrs. **Honors/Awds:** Grantee Rsrch Corp; published articles in Il Nuovo Cimento, Acta Physica Polonica, Physics Tchr Etc; rec'd physical science book for Prentice Hall, Inc. Research Grant, National Science Foundation 1990-91; Directed Physics for the Technologies Training Inst, Summer of 1994, 1996. **Business Addr:** Professor of Physics, Winthrop University, 101 Sims Building, Rock Hill, SC 29733.

SECHREST, EDWARD AMACKER
Electronics company executive. **Personal:** Born Oct 12, 1931, Washington, DC; son of Osie Grey and John Sechrest; married Margaret Ann Thomas; children: Edward Jr, Kim Ann, Lisa Marie Sechrest Ehrhardt. **Educ:** Lincoln University, 1948-50; US Naval Academy, BS 1952-56; US Naval Postgraduate School, BSEE 1962-64; Geo Washington Univ, MS 1966-67. **Career:** US Navy, officer 1956-85, US Naval Academy, instructor, 1967-70, USS Barry (DD-933), US Atlantic Fleet, commanding officer, 1971-73, Navy Recruiting Command, special assistant for minoirty affairs, 1974-77; AT&T Technologies, account executive 1985-86; Magnavox Electronics Co, mgr, Advanced Navy Programs 1986-. **Orgs:** Military organizations, annual speaking engagements 1974-85; Institute of Electrical & Electronics Engineers, mem 1979-86; Northern VA Special Olympics, chairman 1980-83; Alexandria-Fairfax Alumni, Kappa Alpha Psi, polemarch 1981-83; Natl Security Industrial Assn, consultant 1986. **Honors/Awds:** Naval War College, "Communism in Tanzania" publication 1966. **Military Serv:** US Navy, Capt, 1956-85; Bronze Star; Meritorious Service Medal; Joint Service Commendation; Navy Commendation, 1969-85. **Home Addr:** 8103 Touchstone Terrace, Mc Lean, VA 22102.

SECRET, PHILIP E.
Educator. **Personal:** Born in Omaha, NE; son of Louise Secret and Roscoe I Secret Sr; married Tijiuana R Smith; children: Sheila, Philip Jr, Marcus. **Educ:** Univ of Nebraska, BS 1969, PhD 1978. **Career:** Univ of Nebraska Omaha, prof 1972-, assoc dean coll of public affairs and comm serv. **Special Achievements:** "Sex, Race & Political Participation " Western Political Quarterly Mar 1981; "Race & Political Protest" Journal of Black Studies Mar 1982, "Impact of Region on Racial Differences in Attitudes Toward Abortion,"; "Political Efficacy, Political Trust & Electoral Participation," Western Journal of Black Studies Summer 1985; "Attitudes Toward The Court's Decision on Prayer in Public Schools" Social Science Quarterly, 1986; "The Supreme Court and Race-Conscious Seniority Systems," Howard Law Journal, 1988; "An Historical Description of Black Homicide & Suicide in the United States," Challenge: A Journal of Research in African American Men, December, 1994. **Military Serv:** USAF Honorably Discharged. **Home Addr:** 11536 Spaulding St, Omaha, NE 68164. **Business Addr:** Prof, Department of Criminal Justice, University of Nebraska Omaha, 60th Dodge St, Omaha, NE 68182.

SECUNDY, MARIAN GRAY
Educator. **Personal:** Born Oct 20, 1938, Baton Rouge, LA; married Robert; children: Susan, Joel. **Educ:** Vassar College, AB, political science, 1960; Bryn Mawr School for Social Work, MSS, 1962; Union Graduate Inst, PhD, medical humanities bioethics, 1980. **Career:** Howard University, College of Medicine, Dept of Community Health and Family Practice, Program in Medical Ethics, professor and dir, 1971-; College Allied Health, assistant professor, 1974; Reston Counsel Service, Inc, partner, 1971-; Psychiatric Institute, 1972-; Montgomery County Housing Authority, consultant, 1970-71; Northern Virginia Mental Health Institute, psychiatric caseworker, 1968-69; Gulf-Reston, Inc, consultant, 1968; Urban Systems, Inc, associate program director, 1967; American Friends Service Committee, associate director & director, 1965-67; Redev Auth Phila, relocation specialist, comm rel rep urban renewal caseworker, 1962-65; Department Social Work & Social Research, research assistant, 1961. **Orgs:** Reston Chap Links, 1976-; Vassar College, board trustees, 1971; Bassar Club, Washington, 1966; National Association Social Workers, 1962; Reston Black Focus, 1969; Soc Health & Human Values, 1974; National Council Negro Women, 1974; Social Teachers of Family Medicine, sp com educ com; Association Behavioral Science Med Educ, 1973; bd dir, Wider Oppt for Women, 1975; Fairfax Hosp Tst, 1975; Soc Friends Yrly Meeting Race Rels Com, 1962-63; American Friends Serv Com, 1962-69; Columbia Br, YWCA, 1964-65; Vassar Club Philadelphia, 1960-65; Alumnae Association Vassar College, 1968-71; Fairfax County League Women Voters, 1967-71; boardd director, Reston Virginia Comm Association, 1968-71; Natl Inst of Health, Natl Sickle Cell Advisory Council; Hillary Rodman Clinton's Health Care Task Force, Work Group on Ethical Foundations, co-chair; Washington DC Mayor's Task Force on Hospice Liensure; Medical Advisory Group of the District of Columbia; Howard Univ EThic Committee; Planned Parenthood of the District of Columbia, former mem of bd of dirs; Howard Univ, bd of trustees. **Honors/Awds:** Recipient $1,200 Grant, National Endowment For Humanities Study Medical Ethics, 1975; Publications: "Clinical Experiences for Freshman & Sophomor Medical Students", Journal National Medical Association, 1974; "Factors in Patient/Doctor Comm, A Commun Skills Elective", Journal Med & Educ, 1975;,"The Social Worker as Humanist", 1976, "Bereavement the role of the Family Physician", Journal National Med Association, 1977. **Business Addr:** Professor/Dir, Program in Medical Ethics, Howard Univ Coll of Medicine, Dept of Comm Health and Family Practice, 520 W St, NW, Washington, DC 20059.

SEE, LETHA A. (LEE)
Educator. **Personal:** Born Jan 23, 1930, Poteau, OK; daughter of Truppy Sanders Smith and Edward Sanders; married Colonel Wilburn R See; children: Terry L. **Educ:** Langston Univ, BA 1956; Univ of OK, EdM 1957; Univ of AR, MSW 1972; Univ of WI, Post Masters 1976; Bryn Mawr Coll, PhD 1982. **Career:** Univ of AR, asst prof 1972-77; Child Welfare Svcs, agency head 1977-80; Atlanta Univ, assoc prof 1982-83; Univ of GA, assoc prof 1983-. **Orgs:** US delegate to Soviet Union World Congress of Women 1987. **Honors/Awds:** Article "Migration and Refugees" Natl Assoc Human Rights 1986-87; editor Gerontological SW 1986; Title III Fellowship Univ WI-Madison 1987; author "Tensions & Tangles" 1987; author, Black Folk Healing, Sage Publisher, 1990; Cosmological Paradigm, Australian Social Welfare, 1986; Inequality in America, Garland Press 1991. **Home Addr:** 909 Otter Way, Marietta, GA 30068. **Business Addr:** Associate Professor, Univ of Georgia, 30068 Tucker Hall, University of Georgia(Athens), Athens, GA 30602, (404)457-1032.

SEGRE, GRETA EUBANK
Educator. **Personal:** Born Oct 9, 1932, Washington, DC; daughter of Myrtle Lomax Eubank and Theodore Eubank; married Paul Dunbar Segre, Aug 26, 1956 (died 1972); children: Inger Segre. **Educ:** Miner Teachers Coll, Washington, DC, BS, 1954; Trinity Coll, Washington, DC, MAT, 1972. **Career:** DC Government, Washington, DC, teacher, 1950-. **Orgs:** Mem, Phi Delta Kappa, 1986-91; mem, Whittier Theatrical Group, 1987-91. **Honors/Awds:** Teacher of the Year, Washington Afro-American, 1991; Special Recognition for Outstanding Dedication, Whittier ES, 1990. **Business Addr:** Teacher, Whittier Elementary School, Fifth and Sheridan Sts, NW, Washington, DC 20011.

SEGREE, E. RAMONE
Theater fundraiser. **Personal:** Born Aug 23, 1949, Chicago, IL; son of Blanche Hill Segree and Eustas Matthew Segree; married Carmen Montague Segree, Aug 18, 1984; children: Ashton Montague, Tara Montague. **Educ:** California State College, California, PA, BA, 1972; Pennsylvania State University, Middletown, PA, MPSSC, 1979. **Career:** Pennsylvania NAACP, Harrisburg, PA, executive director, 1980-82; USX Corp., Pittsburgh, PA, public & governmental affairs representative, 1982-83; Ketchum, Inc, Pittsburgh, PA, campaign director, 1983-84; United Way of SW Pennsylvania, Pittsburgh, PA, division & project director, 1984-86; University of Pittsburgh, Pittsburgh, PA, senior director of development, 1986-89; Pittsburgh Public Theater, Pittsburgh, PA, vice pres for development, 1989-. **Orgs:** President of the board, Hill House Association, 1991-; founder & co-chairman, Pittsburgh Black/Jewish Dialogue, 1984-; secretary, national foundation board, National Society of Fundraising Executives, 1994-; chairman, performing arts commissioning, Three Rivers Arts Festival, 1992; Minority Theater Panel, Pennsylvania Council of the Arts, 1993; bd mem, Pittsburgh Youth Symphony Orchestra, 1991; bd mem, Pittsburgh Community TV Programming Trust, 1987; chairman, Corporations & Foundations Committee, St Edmunds Academy, 50th Anniversary Capital Campaign. **Honors/Awds:** Certified Fund Raising Executive, National Society of Fund-Raising Executives, 1990; Honorary AS Degree, Community College of Allegheny County, 1992; Distinguished Alumni Award, Community College of Allegheny County, 1992; Service and Achievement Award, University of Pittsburgh African Heritage Classroom Committee, 1988; Pittsburgh Continuing Our Traditions Award, 1992; Council of Fund-Raisers Citation, 1989; Community Leadership Award, 100 Black Men of Pittsburgh, 1988; Service Award, Kappa Alpha Psi Fraternity, Harrisburg Alumni Chapter, 1980. **Military Serv:** US Army, & PA National Guard, SPC-5, 1969-75; Advanced Medical Training Honors Graduate, 1969. **Business Addr:** Vice President for Development, Pittsburgh Public Theater, Allegheny Square, Pittsburgh, PA 15212-5349, (412)323-8200.

SEIBERT-MCCAULEY, MARY F.
Educator, company executive (retired). **Personal:** Born Jun 21, 1930, Louisiana; daughter of M L Seibert (deceased) and Francais Seibert (deceased); widowed. **Educ:** TN State Univ, BS 1952, MA 1961; Northwestern Univ, 1957; Vanderbilt, 1966, 1967, 1977; George Peabody Vanderbilt, PhD 1983. **Career:** Future City Sch, teacher 1952-57; Roosevelt HS, English teacher 1957-62; Bruce HS, English teacher 1963-66; Dyersburg City High School, English teacher, 1966-69; Dyersburg Comm Coll, assoc prof 1969-, chmn of English 1974-84; prof of English 1985, chmn of humanities 1976-84; Union City Ford, Lincoln Mercury, Union City, TN, part owner, 1988-; Math Contracting Co, Dyersberg, TN, president, 1977-90; Dyersburg State College, Dyersburg, TN, Humanities Dept, chair, professor of English, 1969-94. **Orgs:** Mem Delta Sigma Theta Sor 1951-; WDSG, first African-American disc-jockey, WJRO, 1953-57; pres NAACP Dyersburg Chap 1963-64; pres Math Inc Construction Co 1977-; mem 1st Woman Dyer Co Bd of Educ 1977-; bd mem Dyer Co Mentally Retarded Assn 1980-; bd mem Dyer Co Cancer Assn 1982-; mem Tabernacle Bapt Ch; real estate holdings; mem Kiwanis Club 1988-; 1st Black Dyersburg City Bd of Educ 1988-; 1st Black director, First Citizen National Bank, 1991; mem, Dyersburg Dyer County Modernization Committee, 1990; West Tennessee Habitat; director, Tennessee State Alumni; Board for Dyersburg Dyer County Crimstoppers, 1990-; Dyersburg Dyer County Consolidation Committee, 1993-94; Aurora Civic and Social Club. **Honors/Awds:** Outstanding Teacher Awd, TN Governor's Comm on Handicapped 1966; First Black Teacher Dyersburg HS & DSCC 1966-; Certificate Outstanding Educator of Amer 1975; Stipend Natl Endowment for Humanities 1976; poems published in World of Poetry & The Eagle Eye, 1989-90. **Special Achievements:** Wrote first dissertation on and with assistance from Alex Haley: Alex Haley: A Southern Griot, 1988; First African-American Jury Commissioner, 1994. **Home Addr:** 604 Roberts Ave, Dyersburg, TN 38024.

SEIDENBERG, MARK
Bank executive. **Career:** Time Savings and Loan Association, San Francisco CA, chief executive. **Business Addr:** Time Savings and Loan Association, 100 Hegenberger Rd, Suite 110, Oakland, CA 94621-1447.

SEIGLER, DEXTER
Professional football player. **Personal:** Born Jan 11, 1972. **Educ:** Miami (Fla.). **Career:** Seattle Seahawks, defensive back, 1996-. **Business Addr:** Professional Football Player, Seattle Seahawks, 11220 NE 53rd St, Kirkland, WA 98033, (206)827-9777.

SELBY, CORA NORWOOD
Educator (retired). **Personal:** Born Jul 15, 1920, Nassau, DE; daughter of Martha L Maull Norwood and Clarence Page Norwood; married Paul M Selby, May 26, 1945 (deceased); children: Paul MN, Clarence PN, Clyde LN, Adrian Selby LeBlanc, Terence RN. **Educ:** Delaware State Coll, BS (valedictorian) 1940; Univ of DE, MEd 1959; Delaware State Coll, Dover, DE, BS, 1933-40; Univ of Delaware, Newark, DE, MEd 1948-59. **Career:** Ross Point School Dist, teacher 1941-64, reading teacher 1964-65, special educ teacher 1965-66, 2nd grade teacher 1966-69; Headstart Follow-through Prog, faculty advisor 1969-80; Laurel Sch Dist, gifted & talented teacher 1980; Migrant Educ Program, teacher (tutor) 1981-87; State Bd of Educ, Dover, Laurel teacher specialist 1941-87; Indian River School Dist, Millsboro, ABE Inst, beginning 1968; Sussex Technology, ABE-GED teacher, 1991-95. **Orgs:** LEA, DSEA, NEA Teacher Educ Org 1941-; sec DE State Coll 1980-, board of trustees; pres Laurel Sr Ctr 1987-; vice pres Peninsula Delaware Conf Council on Ministries UM Church 1985-; chaplain Alpha Delta Kappa State Chap 1986; mem Phi Delta Kappa; sec bd dirs Carvel Garden Housing; mem Laurel Historical Society; lay leader Peninsula Delaware Conference UM Church; state and natl PTA youth counselor; mem, Commn of Archives & History, Peninsula Delaware Conf Member Comm on Area Episcopacy - Peninsula Delaware Conf beginning 1988; Delaware Div of Literacy 1988-; Governor's Commission on Post-Secondary Education; AARP-DRSPA, SCRSPA 1987-. **Honors/Awds:** President's Awd for Volunteer Serv DAACE 1982; First Lady of Year Psi Chap Beta Sigma Phi 1983; Outstanding Educator in DE Natl Assoc of Univ Women 1983; Teacher of the Year Laurel School Dist 1985-86; Outstanding Alumnus DE State Coll NAFEO 1985-86; Doctor of Letters, Delaware State Coll, 1987; Alumni Queen, Delaware State Coll, 1988; Outstanding Volunteer, Governor of Delaware, 1990; Citizen of the Year, Town of Laurel, Delaware, 1990; Delegate to Delaware State Conference on Libraries & Information, Lieutenant Governor, 1991. **Home Addr:** Rt 2 Box 343, Laurel, DE 19956.

SELBY, MYRA C.
Judge. **Personal:** Born Jul 1, 1955, Saginaw, MI; daughter of Ralph and Archie Selby; married Bruce Curry, Aug 12, 1978; children: Lauren Curry, Jason Curry. **Educ:** Kalamazoo College, BA, 1977; Univ of Michigan Law School, JD, 1980. **Career:** Seyfarth, Shaw, Fairweather & Geraldson, assoc, 1980-83; Ice, Miller, Donadio, & Ryan, partner, 1983-93; State of Indiana, dir of health care policy, 1993-94; Indiana Supreme Court, assoc justice, 1995-. **Orgs:** Natl Health Lawyers Assn, board of directors; The Chicago Med School, Finch Univ of Health Science, 1993-94; Alpha Nursing Home, pres, board of dir; Flanner House, board of dir; Indianapolis Ballet Theatre, board of dir; Indianapolis Museum of Art, board of trustees; Indiana Univ/Purdue Univ at Indianapolis, board of adv; Stanley K Lacy Leadership Selection Comm; Big Sisters of Central Indiana, board development committee, 1995. **Honors/Awds:** Stanley K Lacy Leadership Series Class XIII, 1989; "A Breakthrough Woman" award, Coalition of 100 Black Women, 1990; Indianapolis Chamber of Commerce, Leadership Initiative, 1992-94. **Special Achievements:** Hospital and Physician Liability, A Legal and Risk Mgt Overview, NHLA Focus Series, 1992; Risk Mgt Handbook for Health Care Facilities, 1990 American Hospital Assn; Co-Editor of Chapter 5, Nonscored Objective Criteria in Employment; Discrimination Law, Schlei and Grossman, 2d Ed, 1983, Am Bar Assn; Terminating the Physician-Patient Relationship, Marion Co Medical Society Bulletin, March 1985; Geoffrey Segar and Myra Selby, Reform Revisited, A Review of the Indiana Med Malpractice Act 10 yrs Later, Ind Law Review, Vol 19, No 4 1986, Kemper, Selby, & Simmons. **Business Addr:** Associate Justice, Indiana Supreme Court, 200 West Washington St, 324 State House, Indianapolis, IN 46204.

SELBY, RALPH IRVING
Attorney. **Personal:** Born Feb 16, 1930, Omaha, NE; son of Georgia M Selby and Ralph L Selby; married Archie Mae; children: Ralph Earl, Myra Consetta, Karen Lynn, George Franklin. **Educ:** Univ Omaha, BA; Univ MI, LLB. **Career:** Baker & Selby, atty, currently. **Orgs:** Mem An Nat Wolverine Bay Co Bar Assn; Am Trial Lawyers Assn; bd dirs MI Trial Lawyers Assn; referee MI Civic Rights Comm; vice pres Bay City Jaycees; pres Boys Club Bay City; state chmn MI Area Council; bd mem Bay Co Comm Mental Health Serv Bd; vice pres Bay City Chap NAACP; pres United Way Bay Co; mem Bay-Midland Legal Aid Soc; Bay Co C of C; MI Chap Am Civil Liberties Union; Omicron Delta Kappa; Alpha Phi Alpha; bd mem United Way of MI; trst Delta Coll. **Business Addr:** Attorney, Baker & Selby, 508 Chemical Bank Bldg, P.O. Box 718, Bay City, MI 48707.

SELF, FRANK WESLEY
Accountant. **Personal:** Born Nov 2, 1949, Junction City, KS; son of Wilma Pollet Self and Nolan Self; married Shirley M Brown Self, Aug 28, 1969; children: Frank E, Shelley M. **Educ:** University of Colorado, Denver, CO, BS, accounting, 1976; State of Colorado, Denver, CO, CPA, certificate, 1979. **Career:** Ashby, Armstrong & Johnson, Denver, CO, manager, 1977-82; American Television & Communication Corp, Englewood, CO, director, 1982-; Time Warner Cable, dir of investment accounting, currently. **Orgs:** Member, American Inst of CPAs, 1981-; member, Colorado Society of CPAs, 1981-; member, National Association of Black Accountants, 1978-; member, Korean Tong Soo Do Karate Association, 1989-; member, National Association Minorities in Cable, 1985-. **Honors/Awds:** America's Best and Brightest, Dollars & Sense, 1989; Young Business and Professional Men. **Military Serv:** US Army, E-4, 1971-73. **Home Addr:** 17 Heritage Hill Rd, Norwalk, CT 06851. **Business Phone:** (203)328-4858.

SELLARS, HAROLD GERARD
Banker. **Personal:** Born May 27, 1953, Vass, NC; son of Bessie Mae Johnson Sellars and Frank Alfred Sellars; married Clara Scott Sellars; children: Dwight, Dwayne. **Educ:** North Carolina Central Univ, Durham, NC, BA, business admin, 1978. **Career:** United Carolina Bank, Whiteville, NC, senior vice president, begin 1977-; Branch Banking & Trust Company, vice pres, currently. **Orgs:** Board member, Bankers Educational Society Inc, 1985-; advisory board, North Carolina Small Business Administration Advisory Council, 1990-; advisory board member, North Carolina Rural Economic Development Center, 1990-; advisory board member, North Carolina, Small Business Technology and Development Centers, 1989-; Whiteville City Schools, Bd of Education, 1996-. **Honors/Awds:** Cum Laude North Carolina Central University, 1978. **Military Serv:** US Army, Spec 4, 1972-75. **Home Addr:** 6098 James B White Hwy-N, Whiteville, NC 28472. **Business Addr:** Vice President, Branch Banking & Trust Company, PO Box 632, Whiteville, NC 28472, (910)914-9703.

SELLERS, THERESA ANN
Accounting analyst. **Personal:** Born Jul 24, 1954, Eutawville, SC; daughter of Aslee Murray Sellers and George William Sellers. **Educ:** South Carolina State, BS 1976. **Career:** Standard Oil of IN, sr acct clerk 1979-81; SC State Coll, administrative asst 1982-85; Compton Unified School District, elementary teacher 1985-86; Great Amer Life Insurance Co, accounting analyst 1986-; Maxicare Health Plan, Los Angeles CA, assoc acct 1987-88; US Dept of Commerce, Compton CA, asst mgr admin 1989-. **Orgs:** Asst state coordinator Operation PUSH 1981-83; assoc matron SC Eutaw Chapter No 324 OES PHA 1982-84; vice pres SC State Rainbow Coalition 1984; mem Crenshaw-LaTijera BPW Org USA 1986-; mem NAACP, Black Women Forum, Natl Rainbow Coalition, Iota Phi Lambda Sorority, Brookins Community AME Church, Los Angeles CA, Mary M Kidd Missionary Society, Los Angeles CA. **Honors/Awds:** Humanitarian/Leadership Eutaw Chapter No 324 OES PHA 1982, Orangeburg Calhoun Allendale Bamberg Comm Action Agency 1983.

SELLERS, THOMAS J.
Educator (retired). **Personal:** Born Mar 17, 1911, Charlottesville, VA; son of Rachel Sellers and Thomas Sellers; married Eleanora E Brown; children: Thomassine E. **Educ:** VA Union U, AB 1938; NY U, MA 1958, post grad study 1959. **Career:** New York City, Board of Education, New York, NY, director public relations and ed information, 1965-80; consultant and free lance writer, currently. **Orgs:** Mem Council of Supervisors & Admins, NAACP, Protest Tchrs Assn NYC, Nat Sch Pub Rel Assn, Ed Writers Assn.

SELLERS, WALTER G.
Association executive, educational administrator (retired). **Personal:** Born Jul 25, 1925, Ann Arbor, MI; son of Leona Sellers (deceased) and Walter Sellers (deceased); married Irene; children: Victoria, Walter III, Ronald. **Educ:** Central State Univ, BS 1951. **Career:** Central State Univ, various admin positions from special asst to pres, 1951-93. **Orgs:** Xenia City Bd Educ, 1968-; past pres, Xenia Kiwanis Club, 1971-72; bd of dirs, Amer Alumni Council, 1972-73; mem, OH Sch Bds Tenure Study Comm, 1973; lt governor, Kiwanis Intl, 1974-75; bd trustees, Amer Alumni Council/Amer Coll Pub Relations Assn, 1974-; past pres, OH Assn Colleges Admissions Counselors; Council Admissions Officers State Assisted Colls Univs OH; mem, OH HS Coll Relations Comm; Midwestern Adv Panel Coll Entrance Exam Bd; mem, OH School Bds Assn Comm; OSBA Governance Comm; exec bd, Xenia YMCA; bd dirs, Xenia Sr Citizens; pres, OH Sch Bd Assn, 1981-82; governor, OH Dist Kiwanis Intl, 1984-85; comm chmn, Kiwanis Intl; trustee, Kiwanis International, vice pres, 1994-97, pres, 1997-. **Honors/Awds:** Alumnus of Year, CSU General Alumni Assn, 1972; Hon mem, SW Region OH School Bds Assn, 1973; FM Torrence Award for Outstanding Community Service, 1980; Hon LND, Central State Univ, 1988; Alumni Bldg, Central State Univ, named the "Walter G Sellers Alumni Center," 1988; had a senior citizen apartment building named in his honor. **Special Achievements:** First African-American president of Kiwanis International. **Military Serv:** USN, 1944-46. **Business Addr:** Vice President, Kiwanis Intl, 3636 Woodview Trace, Indianapolis, IN 46268.

SELLS, MAMIE EARL
Journalist, field representative. **Personal:** Born Feb 15, Moundville, AL; divorced; children: Marcia Lynn, Stephen Charles. **Educ:** Mary Manse Coll Toledo OH, BA 1956; Kellogg Found Leadership Training, cert 1979; Univ of Cincinnati, grad work on MA. **Career:** Cincinnati Herald, woman's editor 1977-; Neighborhood Reinvestment Corp of Fed Home & Loan Bank Bd, field rep 1980; City of Cincinnati Mayor, comm rel asst 1978-79; Central Comm Health Bd Cincinnati, prog coord 1977-78; Cincinnati Public Sch System, tchr 1965-75; Cincinnati Call-Post, woman's editor 1974-77; WGUC-; Univ of Cincinnati Radio Station, contrib interviewer 1976; Natl Newspaper Pub Assn to Nigeria, journalist special assignment 1979. **Orgs:** Bd of trst Cincinnati Comm Chest Council; comm chmn Comm Resources Div Chest Council; bd mem NAACP; Adv Bd Council on World Affaris; adv CincinnatiTech Coll; past

pres Cincinnati Chap Alpha Kappa Alpha Sorority; mem Top Ladies of Distinction; Friends of Ballet; Women Alliance; former trst YWCA; vpPlayhouse in Park; mem Cincinnati Found 1979-94; co-chmn opening night gala Cincinnati Symphony Orchestra 1975; c/-chmn Alvin Ailey City Center Ballet Co Benefit Cincinnati Arts Consortium 1976. **Honors/Awds:** Media awd Cincinnati Federated Colored Women's Club 1975; hon doc of tech letters Cincinnati Tech Coll 1977; feature story series of articles Cincinnati Enquirer 1977; cover story NIP Mag Cincinnati 1979. **Business Addr:** Cincinnati Herald, 354 Hearne Ave, Cincinnati, OH 45229-2818.

SENBET, LEMMA W.
Educator, researcher. **Personal:** Born in Ethiopia; son of Wolde Senbet. **Educ:** Haile Sellassie I Univ, Addis Ababa, BBA, 1970; UCLA, Los Angeles, CA, MBA, 1972; SUNY/Buffalo, Buffalo, NY, PhD, 1975. **Career:** Univ of Wisconsin-Madison, Madison, The Charles Albright chair, Professor of Finance, 1987-90; Professor & Dickson, Bascom, professor, 1983-87, asso prof, 1980-83; Northwestern Univ, Evanston, visiting associate professor, 1980-81; Univ of California, Berkeley, Berkeley, CA, visiting professor, 1984-85; Distinguished Research Visitor, LSE; Univ of Maryland, College Park, MD, The William E Mayer chair, professor, 1991-; The World Bank, consultant, 1989-; African Economic Research Consortium, consultant, 1994-; International Monetary Fund, consultant, 1996-; United Nations ECA, 1996-97. **Orgs:** President, Western Finance Assn, 1989-90; board of directors, American Finance Assn, 1991-; editorial board, Journal of Finance, 1983-94; editorial board, Journal of Financial and Quantitator Analysis, 1987-93; editorial board, Financial Management, 1979-; editorial bd, Journal of Banking and Finance, 1995-; chair, FMA Doctoral Panel, 1990. **Honors/Awds:** Chancellor's Gold Medal, Haile Sellassie I Univ, from Emperor Haile Sellassie, 1970; Teaching Excellence, Univ of Maryland, 1994; president, Western Finance Association, 1989-90; member, board of directors, American Finance Association; Ranked third among world-wide contributors to the Journal of Finance, 1975-86; Ethiopian Review, ''Achieving Excellence in a Foreign Land,'' April 1991. **Business Addr:** Professor of Finance, The William E Mayer Chair, Maryland Business School, University of Maryland, College Park, MD 20742, (301)405-2242.

SENDABA, S. M. (SHELEME)
Automobile company executive. **Personal:** Born in Ghion, Shoa, Ethiopia; son of Ketabe Gutama and Tollassa Sendaba; married Barbara A Porter, Jan 1, 1979; children: S Addis, Mekiel C, Alem. **Educ:** University of Illinois College of Business Admin, BS, finance & accounting, 1975; Walter Heller Graduate School of Business, MBA, 1977. **Career:** General Motors Corp, various assignments, 1979-83, General Motors Corp, Buick Motor Div, director financial staff, 1983-84; General Motors Corp, Flint Product Team, director, 1984-86; General Motors Corp, BOC Group, comptroller, 1986-87; General Motor Corp, Truck & Bus Group, comptroller, 1988-90; Nissan Motor Corp, Garden, CA, vice pres & CFO, 1990-. **Orgs:** Chairman, United Way Finance Committee; Member of the Board of Dirs, Natl Bankers Advisory Board; Nisan Performance Technology, Inc, Nissan Extended Service Corporation, Inc, Nissan Retirement Committee; Big Brothers & Big Sisters of America; and Athletes & Entertainers for Kids. **Business Addr:** VP, CFO, Nissan Motor Corp. USA, PO Box 191, Gardena, CA 90248-0191.

SENECA, ARLENA E.
Educator. **Personal:** Born Sep 9, 1919, Laurel, MS; daughter of Rev & Mrs Benjamin Seneca. **Educ:** Talladega Coll, BS, 1939; Atlanta Univ, MS, 1941; Univ of KS; Teachers Coll, Columbia Univ, 1946-48, 1952, 1954, 1965; Lincoln Univ, 1958; Harvard Univ, 1955; Univ of IN, 1959, 1960, 1962, 1966; Univ of CO, BSCS, 1960; Univ of AZ, 1956-67, 1958-59; Columbia Univ of the United Kingdom, PhD, 1983. **Career:** Carver High School, sponsor student council, instructor, 1945-53; Atlanta Univ, dir sci workshop 1946; Columbia Univ, panelist guest lecturer 1947; Carver High School, pres CTA 1950; Natl Science Teachers Assn, consultant, 1956; S Mt HS, head sci dept 1957; Sussex Co Chapter, Amer Cancer Soc Inc, resource person, 1957; AZ Educ Assn, panelist/demonstrator 1957; TX So Univ, guest lecturer 1958; Biol Sci Curric Study, participant, 1960-62; S Mt HS, dir adult educ program 1961-62; Sci Workshop, Sheraton Park Elementary School, dir 1965; Educ Tour, Europe 1966, Mexico 1967; Sky-Y-Camp AZ, adv 1968; Phoenix Union HS Syst, consult human relations; Dir/ConsDesert Services. **Orgs:** Treasurer, South Minister United Presbyterian Church, 1965-; co-sponsor Group Assn for Progress 1966-; dir/cons Desert Consultant Serv 1981-; LEAP Commn Phoenix 1968-76; chmn bd dir Proj Uplift 1967-; Delta Kappa Gamma Soc Intl; American Assn Univ Women, president, 1972-74, Arizona Division, president, 1969; bd dir Big Sisters Intl 1972-; bd dir Samaritan Health Serv 1973-; vice chmn Human Resources Citizens Bond Com 1974-; fellow Intl Inst of Comm Serv 1974; Governors 7 Mem Com to Select Future Prison Sites for the State of AZ 1979-80; Delta Sigma Theta. **Honors/Awds:** Whack that Quack, Amer Biology Teacher, 1961; A Spark for Johnny S Mountain HS Phoenix Rep 1966; Neurohumoral Changes w/Respect to Color Pattern in Ameiurus Nebulosus 1969; Root Pressure Science Teacher Workshop 1969; Phoenix Woman of the Yr 1954, 1958; National Science Teacher Achievement Recognition Award, 1956; Charles D Poston Award 1957; achievement certificate Natl Science Teacher 1960; Silver Tray Urban League Guild 1964; 1st Annual Citizens Award for Outstanding Serv to Comm Daughter Elks 1965; Phoenix Advertising Club Inc 1967-68; AAUW, Woman of Achievement Award, 1969; Society of Women Engineers, Outstanding Member Certificate, 1973; Delta Sigma Theta, Outstanding Community Service, 1975; Mayor of Phoenix, Certificate of Appreciation, 1975; International Institute of Community Service, London, Diploma of Honor Award, 1975; NAACP, Image Award,1, 1992; Leadership Award, AZ State Univ, 1986; Comm General Assembly, Presbyterian Church, 1987; Distinguished Citizen Citation, Phoenix Union High School District, 1990; Golden Diploma Award, Talladega College, 1990; Certificate of Appreciation, United States Postal Service, 1991; Arizona Alliance of Black School Educators, Distinguished Service Award, 1992; Listed in International Reg of Profiles, Cambridge, England; Oh Yes I Can!, Biography of Arlena E Seneca by Nelson L Haggerson, PhD, 1994, listed in Library of Congress; Governors Certificate, Outstanding Leadership Benefitting AZ, 1994; Amer Assn of Univ Women, Certificate, 1994; Delta Sigma Theta Sorority, Lifetime Achievement as an Educator, Fortitude Award; NAACP, Outstanding Achievement Award for Educ, 1994; Amer Assn of Univ Women, AZ Coll/Univ chair, 1994-95; Lifetime Science Educator of the Year Award, Society of Black Engineerings, 1996. **Business Addr:** System/Dsrt Consult Services, 3421 N 51st St, Phoenix, AZ 85018.

SENEGAL, NOLTON JOSEPH, SR.
Attorney. **Personal:** Born Mar 15, 1952, Lafayette, LA; son of Mr & Mrs Willie Floyd Senegal; married Patricia Dianne Frank-Senegal; children: Nolton Joseph Jr, Anysia Nicole, Terrence Jamal. **Educ:** BS, business, social studies, 1973; MED, admin, supervision, 1975; JD, 1984. **Career:** St Landry Parish Police Jury, 1975-77; Diocese of Lafayette, 1975-77; Lafayette Regional Vocational Tech School, 1977-81; Lafayette Parish School Bd, 1977-81; Acadiana Legal Service Corp, dir, 1985-. **Orgs:** Alpha Phi Alpha Fraternity, 1977-; Phi Delta Kappa Law Fraternity, 1982-; Student Bar Assn Law Ctr, pres, 1983-84; Minority Involvement Section of LSBA, chair, 1993-95; Acadia Parish School Bd, pres, 1990-, mem, 1993-; Natl School Bds Assn, Federal Relations Network, mem, 1996-. **Special Achievements:** First African-American to serve as pres of the Acadia Parish School Board; LA School Bds Assn, 1st vp, 1997-99. **Home Addr:** PO Box 564, 413 Section Street, Rayne, LA 70578, (318)334-5759. **Business Phone:** (318)237-4320.

SENEGAL, PHYLLIS J.
Lawyer. **Personal:** Born Apr 28, 1930, Cleveland, OH; married Charles; children: Gregg Spencer, Guy Spencer, Gary Spencer, Tamara. **Educ:** Western Reserve U; Cleveland Marshall Law Sch, LLB 1966. **Career:** Legal Aid Soc Gary, exec dir 1969-75; Gary, city atty 1968-69; asst city atty 1967-68, arbitrator 1976-; private practice, general counsel for Gary Regional Airport Authority 1988-. **Orgs:** Mem Gary Bar Assn; Am Bar Assn; James Kimbrough Law Assn; mem Urban League; League of Women Voters; Am Assn of Univ Women; Gary Commn on Status of Women; mem Lake County Bar Assn, IN State Bar Assn. **Honors/Awds:** Conn Serv Award City of Gary 1975.

SERAILE, JANETTE
Attorney. **Personal:** Born Oct 24, 1945, New York; daughter of Sarah Edwards Grey and Maurice W Grey; married William; children: Garnet Tana, Aden Wayne. **Educ:** Col Law School, grad, 1972; Lake Forest College, 1967. **Career:** Private practice, 1983-; Bedford Stuyvesant Restoration Corp, atty 1972-83; Chance & White, law asst 1970-72; Edwards Sisters Realty Assn, asst mgr 1967-70. **Orgs:** Mem NY co lawyers assn. **Business Addr:** 740 St Nicholas, New York, NY 10031.

SERGEANT, CARRA SUSAN
Association executive. **Personal:** Born Jul 16, 1953, New Orleans, LA; daughter of Susan Caralita Craven Sergeant and James Bernard Sergeant. **Educ:** Dillard University, New Orleans, LA, BA, 1976; University of Central Arkansas, Conway, AR, MS, 1978. **Career:** Indiana Council Against Rape, Indiana, PA, director, 1979-1980; Indiana Univ of Pennsylvania, Indiana, PA, residence director, 1978-80; Georgia Institute of Technology, Atlanta, GA, area coordinator, 1980-85; Metropolitan Developmental Center, New Orleans, LA, active treatment manager, 1985-89; Los Angeles State University, Eunice, LA, coordinator support service, 1989-90, coordinator Upward Bound, 1990-. **Orgs:** Secretary, 1991-, committee chair, 1990-, pres, 1995, Louisiana Assn of Student Assistance Program; regional newsletter editor, Southwest Assn of Student Assistance Programs, 1989-91; president, 1988-89, vice pres, 1987-89, New Orleans Chapter, Natl Organization for Women. **Honors/Awds:** Quoted in Article on Date Rape, Ebony Magazine, 1990; Cited for Community Service, New Orleans Mayor's Office, 1989. **Business Addr:** Project Coordinator, Upward Bound, Louisiana State University at Eunice, PO Box 1129, Eunice, LA 70535.

SERGENT, ERNEST, JR.
Physicist. **Personal:** Born Feb 9, 1943, New Orleans, LA; married Claudette Ruth Brown; children: Sandra Michelle, Ernest III, James Richard. **Educ:** So Univ New Orleans, BS Math & Physics 1970; Univ of MI Ann Arbor, MS Physics 1972. **Career:** Univ of MI Geology Dept, rsch assoc 1972-74; Gen Motors Rsch Ctr, jr physicist 1973; 3M Company, advanced physicist 1974-75, adv product control engr 1975-79, sr physicist 1979-. **Orgs:** Pres & vice pres Afro-Amer Art Soc of 3M Co 1978-80; bd dir Cottage Grove Jaycees 1978-79; commn mem Cottage Grove Human Serv Commn 1980-; chmn Cottage Grove Human Svcs/Human Rights Comm 1981-; pres, Cottage Grove Baseball/Softball Division, 1986-88; member, Society of Automotive Engineers, 1989-; board member, Community Volunteer Service, 1990-93. **Honors/Awds:** Special Physics Fellowship Univ of MI 1970-72. **Military Serv:** AUS sp-4 1961-64; Good Conduct Medal. **Home Addr:** 9119 79th St S, Cottage Grove, MN 55016. **Business Addr:** Senior Physicist, 3M Company, Bldg 251-2E-12, 3M Center, St Paul, MN 55144-1000.

SERIKI, OLUSOLA OLUYEMISI
Real estate development executive. **Personal:** Born Jul 12, 1958, Lagos, Nigeria; son of Olapeju Ajayi Seriki and Olumuyiwa Seriki; married Angela Kristen Jenkins, Dec 16, 1980; children: Joseph Olatunde, Oluyemisi Haniel, Angele Olufeyisayo. **Educ:** Government College Ibadan, Ibandan, Nigeria W.A.S.C. 1973; Howard Univ Washington DC, BArch 1979. **Career:** Tradex Corp Washington, project dir 1979-83; The Rouse Co Columbia MD, associate devel dir 1983-89, development director 1989-. **Orgs:** Vp Natl Assoc of Black Developers 1985/86; mem Intl Council of Shopping Centers 1985-87; assoc mem Urban Land Inst 1986-89; mem Natl Assoc of Corporate Real Estate Execs 1986-89; dir Metropolix Company 1987-89; consultant Extended Family Inc 1988-89; chairman Extended Family Day Committee 1988; advisor Crossroads Afrique 1988-89; Vp Special Projects, Access Africa International 1991-92; Vp Onings Mills Chamber of Commerce 1991-91. **Honors/Awds:** Housing for Nigerians with low income considerations 1982; a constraint to accelerated housing development in Nigeria 1982; Leadership Award, Extended Family 1988. **Business Addr:** Owner, Metro/Ventures/USA Inc., 9881 Broken Land Parkway, Ste 302, Columbia, MD 21046.

SERVICE, RUSSELL NEWTON
Appointed official. **Personal:** Born Sep 3, 1913, Boston, MA; married Dorothy; children: Russell N Jr, Michael B. **Educ:** Univ of Buffalo, BA 1938, MEd 1946. **Career:** YMCA of Buffalo & Erie Co NY, exec dir 1938-59; Bedford YMCA Brooklyn, exec dir 1959-64; YMCA of Greater NY, assoc exec vice pres for urban affairs 1964-74; Nassau Co CETA Prog, commissioner 1978-82; Nassau Co, deputy co exec 1974-77, 1982-. **Orgs:** Mem Nassau Co Village Officials 1974; life mem Hempstead Chamber of Comm 1981; deputy mayor Village of Hempstead 1967-; chairperson Hempstead Black & Hispanic Voters League 1975-; mem Natl Assn Black Elected Officials 1975-; mem Long Island Area Develop Agency 1980-; chairperson Nassau Co Affirmative Action Prog 1982-; life mem NAACP; vice chmn exec comm Nassau County Republican Comm. **Honors/Awds:** Achievement Awd Intl Key Women of America 1974; Selected Public Servant Hempstead Chamber of Comm 1981; Distinguished Serv Awd Hofstra Univ 1983; Serv Awd Afro-Amer Heritage Assn 1984. **Business Addr:** Deputy Co Exec of Nassau Co, Nassau Co Govt, One West St, Mineola, NY 11501.

SESSION, JOHNNY FRANK
Government official. **Personal:** Born Mar 2, 1949, Panama City, FL; son of Karetta Baker Alexander and Jake Session; married Linda Tibbs, May 11, 1969; children: Tomeka, Johnny Frank Jr, Marcus. **Educ:** Gulf Coast Jr College, Panama City FL, AA, 1970; Florida A&M Univ, Tallahassee FL, BS, 1973. **Career:** Deloit, Haskins and Sells, Ft Lauderdale FL, staff accountant, 1973-75; City of Hollywood, Hollywood FL, staff accountant, 1975-77, senior accountant, 1977-81, controller, 1981-84; City of Tallahassee, Tallahassee FL, controller, 1984-. **Orgs:** American Institute of CPA, National Govt Finance Officers Association, National Association of Black Accountants, Florida Institute of CPA; American Institute of CPA. **Honors/Awds:** Award for financial reporting, Govt Financial Officer Assn, 1985; WORD Award, Florida A&M Univ Alumni Assn, 1987; Distinguished Service Award, NABA Tallahassee Chapter, 1988. **Home Addr:** 2806 Sweetbriar Dr, Tallahassee, FL 32312.

SESSOMS, FRANK EUGENE
Physician. **Personal:** Born Oct 24, 1947, Rochester, PA; son of Catherine Sessoms and Frank L Sessoms; married Sandra Scalise, Jun 24, 1988. **Educ:** Harvard Univ, Intensive Summer Studies program 1968; TN State Univ, BS 1970; Meharry Medical Coll, MD 1974; Bradley Univ 1965-66. **Career:** Procter & Gamble, food products technical brand specialist 1969; US Dept of Agriculture, summer researcher animal hlth div 1970; Procter & Gamble Miami Valley Labs, summer researcher 1971; Meharry Medical Coll, student rscher 1971-74; St Margaret's Memorial Hospital, internship and residency in family practice 1974-77; St John's General Hosp, dir of emergency serv 1977, Diplomate of Amer Board of Family Practice 1977, 1983; medical consultant psychiatric dept; Private Practice, physician 1979-; prof, Univ of Pittsburgh Family Medicine &

Proc, 1994-. **Orgs:** Vice pres student council TN State Univ 1969-70; class pres Meharry Med Coll 1970-71; vice pres Pre-Alumni Cncl Meharry Med Coll 1973-74; mem Congressional Black Caucus Health Brain Trust 1974-; mem of bd Homewood Brushton YMCA 1979-83; chmn of bd Pittsburgh Black Action Methadone Maint Ctr 1985,86; mem Natl Medical Assn; medical dir Bidwell Drug & Alcohol Program; life mem Alpha Phi Alpha, NAACP; mem Urban League, Amer Medical Assn, PA Medical Soc, Undersea Med Soc, Natl Assn of Health Serv Executives; mem Pgh Chap 100 Black Men; mem Frontiers Intl; bd of governors TN State Univ Student Union; mem Univ Counselors TN State Univ; mem Alumni Bd of Mgmt Meharry Medical Coll; mem Chi Delta Mu Fraternity; member, Amen Corner, 1987-; member, Gateway Med Society; member, Allegheny County Med S; pres Meharry Natl Alumni Assn, 1993-95; commissioner PA, Gov Com on African American Affairs, 1992-; participant, President's Intercultural Task Force on Healthcare Reform, 1994; Guest Lecturer CCAC, 1994; Pittsburgh Public School's Restructing Task Force, 1992-93; Committee on African American Student's; member, Board of Management, Meharry Med College, 1995-. **Honors/Awds:** Fellow New York Acad of Science; patent holder High-Protein Fruit-Flavored Fat Stablized Spread 1969; Samuel Goldwyn Foundation Fellowship 1971-74; Pre-Alumni Council Awd 1974; Honorary Sgt-at-Arms of TN House of Representatives 1974; Presidential Citation Natl Assn for Equal Oppor in Higher Educ 1984; Fellow Amer Acad of Family Practice; paper published "Effects of Ethane 1,1 Dihydroxy Diphosphanate "EHDP" on the Collagen Metabolism in the Rat" 1971 (Procter & Gamble Res Lab); scientific articles "Uses of the Soybean and Their Prospects for the Future," TN State Univ Dept of Bio-Chemistry 1970. **Military Serv:** USAF Awd for Valor and Heroism 1968. **Home Addr:** 2777 Shamrock Dr, Allison Park, PA 15101-3146. **Business Addr:** 211 N Whitfield St, Pittsburgh, PA 15206.

SESSOMS, FURMIN DOUGLAS
Attorney. **Personal:** Born Jan 9, 1949, Rochester, PA; son of Catherine Williams Sessoms and Frank L Sessoms; divorced. **Educ:** University of California, AB, 1986; Georgetown University Law Center, JD, 1989. **Career:** US District Court, Northern District of California, extern law clerk, summer 1987; NAACP Legal Defense Fund, law clerk, summer 1988; Cook County Public Defender, assistant public defender, 1990-91; Pugh, Jones & Hubbard, PC, associate, 1991-. **Orgs:** American Bar Association, 1991-; Chicago Bar Association, 1990-; National Bar Association, editorial board member, 1981-; NAACP, 1990-. **Honors/Awds:** University California, Berkley, Minority Honors Scholar Program, 1985, commencement speaker, BLK graduation , 1986. **Home Phone:** (312)873-4246. **Business Addr:** Associate, Pugh, Jones & Hubbard, PC, 180 N LaSalle St, Ste, 2910, Chicago, IL 60601, (312)419-9330.

SESSOMS, GLENN D.
Company executive. **Personal:** Born Oct 20, 1953, Norfolk, VA; son of Clarence and Geraldine Sessoms; married Linda, Jul 14, 1979; children: Daryn, Justin, Adea. **Educ:** Virginia State Univ, BS, 1976. **Career:** Johnson and Johnson, various mgt positions, 1976-82; Federal Express Corporation, various mgt positions, 1983-88, managing dir, 1988-94, vp, 1994-. **Orgs:** Omega Psi Phi Fraternity, 1975; Partners in Quality, board of advisors; Charlotte Area Chamber of Commerce. **Honors/Awds:** VSU Sports Hall of Fame; Small College All-American. **Business Addr:** Vice President, Retail Marketing and Operations, Federal Express Corp, 2856 Directors Cove, Memphis, TN 38131, (901)922-5890.

SESSONS, ALLEN LEE
Educational administrator, physicist. **Personal:** Born Nov 17, 1946, New York City, NY; son of Albert Earl & Lottie Beatrice Leff; married Csilla Manette von Csiky, Apr 18, 1990; children: Manon Elizabeth, Stephanie Csilla. **Educ:** Union College, BS, 1968; University of Washington, MS, 1969; Yale University, M PhD, 1971, PhD, 1972. **Career:** Brookhaven National Laboratory, researcher, 1972-73; European Organization of Nuclear Research, (CERN), researcher, 1973-75; Harvard University, assoc prof of physics, 1974-81; US Dept of State, US Embassy Mexico, deputy chief of mission, 1991-93, minister counselor for political affairs, 1989-91; US Dept of State, various positions, 1980-89; Queens College, CUNY, president, 1995-. **Orgs:** US Dept of Energy, chair, scy's task force on fissile nuclear material disposition, 1996-, scy of energy advisory bd, 1996-; American Physical Society; American Association for the Advancement of Science, 1973-; New York Academy of Sciences; 100 Black Men, 1995-. **Honors/Awds:** Jewish National Fund, Tree of Life Award, 1996; State Department, Meritorious & Superior Honor Awards. **Special Achievements:** Alfred P Sloan Foundation, fellowship, 1977-81; Ford Foundation, travel and study grant, 1973-74; speaks German, Spanish and French; author of over 30 scientific publications in professional journals and US government policy papers.

SETLOW, VALERIE PETIT
Health administrator, scientist. **Personal:** Born Jan 24, 1950, New Orleans, LA; daughter of Alvin Joseph and Lorraine Kelly Petit; children: Daniel, Craig. **Educ:** Xavier Univ, BS, pre-med, chemistry, 1970; Johns Hopkins Univ, PhD, molecular biology, genetics, 1976. **Career:** Mt Sinai Hosp, Dept of Human Genetics, postdoctoral researcher, 1976-77; Natl Insts of Health, Lab of Molecular Virology, NIAMDD, 1977-79; NIH, NHLBI, Lab of Molecular Hematology, 1979-81; Scientific Prog Admin, asst to Diabetes Branch, 1981-82, Asst Diabetes Prog Dir, 1982-83; NIH, asst div dir, Diabetes, Endocrinology & Metabolism, 1983-86; Cystic Fibrosis Program Dir, 1984-86; Natl Conf on AIDS in Racial & Ethnic Populations, dir, 1989; Office of Asst Sec for Health, Biomedical Res (NIH), desk officer, 1986-88 ; NIH AIDS Policy Analyst, 1988-90, dir of policy analysis & coordination, 1990-91, deputy dir, 1991-92, acting dir, 1992-93; Natl AIDS Program Office, Howard Univ Sch of Med, Dept of Family & Community Med, adjunct appointment, 1994-97; Natl Acad of Sciences, dir, Div of Health Sciences Policy, 1993-97; CBR, dep dir, 1997-. **Orgs:** Amer Assn for the Advancement of Science; Amer Soc for Biochemists and Molecular Biologists; Junior League of Washington, adv bd, 1989-92; Natl Assn of People with AIDS, bd mem, 1993-96, vp of the bd, 1994-96, chmn of bd, 1996-97. **Honors/Awds:** US Surgeon General, Certificate of Appreciation, 1992, 1993; Office of the Asst Sec for Health, Special Recognition Group Awards, 1991, 1993, Exemplary Service Award, 1988, 1992; Asst Sec for Health, Award for Exceptional Achievement, 1990; National Academy of Sciences Award, 1995, 1997. **Special Achievements:** Research Publications include: co-author: "The Initiation of SV40 DNA Syntheseis in not Unique to the Replication Origin," Cell: Vol 20, pp 381-391, 1980; "The Roles of Simian Virus 40 Tumor Antigens in Transformation of Chinese Hamster Lung Cells: Studies with Double Mutants," Journal of Virology, 31: pp 597-607, 1979; "Lateral Phase Separation of Lipids in Plasma Membranes: Effect of Temperature on Mobility of Membrane Antigens," Science 184, pp 1183-1185, 1974; Research Abstracts include: co-author: "Construction of SV40 Recombinants Containing a Functional Gene for Dihydrofolate Reductase," Natl Clinical Res Meetings, 1981; "DNA, Synthesis in Normal and SV40 Transformed Cells," Intl Symposium on Papoviruses and Their Role in Cell Transformation and Oncogenesis; editor "Public Policy Reports of The IOM/NAS;" numerous other publications, interviews television interviews and reports. **Business Addr:** Deputy Director, Tulane/Xavier Center, Bioenvironmental Research, 1430 Tulane Ave, New Orleans, LA 70112, (504)585-6910.

SETTLES, CARL E.
Psychologist. **Personal:** Born Jul 23, 1948, Houston, TX; son of Lena Epps Settles and Paul Silas Settles; married Carol H; children: Carl, Jr, Corey. **Educ:** Prairie View Univ, BS 1970, MEd 1971; Univ of Texas, PhD 1976; Letterman Army Medical Center, Presidio of San Francisco, CA, postdoctoral fellowship in family therapy, 1989-91. **Career:** Waller Indep School Dist, teacher 1970-71; Austin Indep School Dist, 1971-73; Upward Bound Huston-Tillotson Coll, prog coord 1973-74; Dept Educ & Psychol, acad asst 1973-74; Center for Public Schools Ethnic Studies, group leader 1972-74; Univ TX, research assoc II 1974; 1st practicum student, advanced practicum student, teaching asst 1973-; Prairie View A&M Univ, dir, counseling center; USA Ft Lewis Wash, div psychologist; BSD Ft Sam Houston, chief psychopathology sect; USAMEDDAC Japan One Stop Counseling Center, dir. **Orgs:** Mem, Amer Psychol Assn, 1974-; chairperson, Ethnic Minority Affairs Comm, Div 19, Amer Psychol Assn, 1989-; member, Family Psychology, American Psychological Association, 1989-. **Honors/Awds:** Dr A I Thomas Award, 1969-70; T K Lawless Award, 1969-70; Outstanding Coll Athlete, 1970; Henderson Found Fund Fellow, 1974-75; Fellow, Univ of Texas, 1974-75; Grad Fellow, Natl Fellowship Fund, 1975-76; scholarship, Texas Center & Natl Conf of the A K Rice Inst, 1977; Honorable Mention, Young Leaders in Education Project, Phi Delta Kappa, Bloomington, IN, 1981. **Military Serv:** AUS Medical Serv Corp, Major, 1981-.

SETTLES, DARRYL STEPHEN
Restauranteur. **Personal:** Born Mar 30, 1961, Augusta, GA; son of Rebecca Settles and David Settles Jr. **Educ:** Carnegie-Mellon University, attended, 1978; University of Tennessee, Knoxville, attended, 1979-81; Virginia Polytechnic Institute & State University, BS, 1984. **Career:** General Electric Co., co-op student, 1979-81; Digital Equipment Corp., engineer, 1984-85, sales account manager, 1985-90; Commonwealth of Massachusetts, associate commissioner, 1991-; D'Ventures Unlimited Inc, president, 1990-. **Orgs:** Massachusetts Restaurant Association, board member, 1992-; Boston Fellows, 1991-; NCCJ/Lead Boston, 1991-; Greater Boston Convention and Tourism Bureau, 1991-; Boston Medical Center, Kids Fund, board member. **Honors/Awds:** Dollars & Sense Magazine, America's Best & Brightest Young Business and Professional Men, 1992; Roxbury Chamber of Commerce, Minority Business of the Year, 1991; SBA Minority Business of the Year, 1996; City of Boston, Entrepreneur of the Year, 1997. **Business Addr:** President, D'Ventures Unlimited Inc, 604 Columbus Ave, Boston, MA 02118, (617)536-6204.

SETTLES, ROSETTA HAYES
Educator. **Personal:** Born Nov 16, 1920, Little Rock, AR; married Dan. **Educ:** Wiley Coll, BA 1948; Harvard U, EdM 1951; Walden U, PhD 1977; Oakland U, Grad Study 1970; Summer Sch, Overseas Study 1971; Great Britain Sch, TourStudy 1973. **Career:** Oakland Univ, asso prof 1969-; Garden City Public School, rdng supr 1967-, first black teacher 1967-; Clintondale Public School, rdng spec, clinician 1965-67; Little Rock, remedial rdng elem teacher 1945-56; Harvard Boston Summer School Prog, team teacher 1965; Summer School Prog, asst dir; Detroit Public School, rdng consultant 1972; Garden City Summer School Prog, prin, dir 1974. **Orgs:** Fdr org Nat Dunbar HS Alumni Reunion of Classes; vice pres Detroit Chap Dunbar High Alumni 1980-; mem Nat Bd of Dir Dunbar HS Alumni Assn 1977-; mem IRA; NCTE; MRA; del NEA; mem NAACP. **Honors/Awds:** Originator, sponsor Lena D Hayes Schlrshp Award 1950; Harvard Univ Schlrshp 1951; Top Ten Outstndng Dunbar HS Alumni Nation 1973; Tribute Award 1977; Top Ten Outstndng Dunbar HS Alumni Nat, Little Rock AR Conv 1979; article "Reading & Rhythm" 1970. **Business Addr:** 31753 Maplewood St, Garden City, MI 48135.

SETTLES, TRUDY Y.
Government official. **Personal:** Born Jun 3, 1946, Springfield, OH; daughter of Ruth Dennis Settles and Nathaniel Settles. **Educ:** Central State Univ, Wilberforce, OH, BS, 1968. **Career:** Wilberforce Univ, Wilberforce, OH, sec to the pres; City of Dayton, Dayton, OH, 1971-75; RL Polk & Co, Washington, DC, office assoc, 1975-76; Southern CA Gas Co, Washington, DC, sec, 1976-82, govt affairs asst, 1982-94; Senate Judiciary Subcommittee on Immigration, staff asst, 1995-97; Columbia Gas Transmission, administrative asst to CEO, 1997-. **Orgs:** Sec, Washington, DC Metropolitan Chapter Amer Assn of Blacks in Energy, 1990-92; corresponding sec, Washington Energy Affiliates Desk & Derrick Clubs, 1986, bd of dir, 1986-88, chmn, rules comm, 1983-86, program comm, fin comm; Washington Energy Affiliates, Desk of Derrick Clubs, president, 1992-93.

SEVILLIAN, CLARENCE MARVIN
Educator. **Personal:** Born Apr 23, 1945, Buffalo, NY; married Madeline Carol Cochran; children: Clarence II, Nicole Ren. **Educ:** FL A&M U, BS 1966; Estrn MI U, MEd Admin 1974. **Career:** Northwestern HS, Flint, staff spec; Bryant Jr HS, instrumental Music teacher 1970-74; Saginaw Foundries, purch agent 1968-70; Hoxey Job Corp Center, Catillac, resident, counselor 1966-68. **Orgs:** Records keeper Saginaw Alumni, Kappa Alpha Psi; mem MI Ed Assn; NEA; United Tchr of Flint; MI Sch Band & Orch Assn; Music Educators Nat Conf; adv Bryant Band & Orch Parents Assn; first vice pres Unity Urban Comm Dev & Rehab Corp. **Honors/Awds:** Outs Secondary Educator of Am 1974; Outs Young Man of Am 1974. **Business Addr:** Deputy Principal, Beecher Community Schools, 1020 W Coldwater Road, Flint, MI 48505.

SEWELL, EDWARD C.
Business executive. **Personal:** Born Aug 18, 1946, Hanover, MD. **Educ:** IN U, MBA (magna cum laude); Bowling Green U, BA (magna cum laude) Omicron Delta Kappa. **Career:** Xerox Corp, fin anlyst 1970-72; Irwin Mgmt Co, asst to pres real est dvlpr 1972-75; Crocker Natl Bank, vice pres real est plng 1975-78; J P Mahoney & Co, real est Dvlpr 1978-; Prof Sports Ctr, pres sports agent 1983-. **Orgs:** V chm & fndr Judge Joseph Kennedy Fndtn Schlrshp Fndtn for Bay Area Mnrts; flwshp Consortium for Grad Study in Mgmt 1968-70. **Home Addr:** 1238 Cole St, San Francisco, CA 94117-4322.

SEWELL, ISIAH OBEDIAH
Government official. **Personal:** Born Nov 20, 1938, Lexington, SC; son of Annie Bell Sligh Sewell and Joseph Preston Sewell; married Julia Smith, Dec 24, 1962; children: Kevin, Kendra, Keith. **Educ:** SC State Coll, BSEE 1961; George Washington Univ, attended 1969-72. **Career:** US Dept of Navy, elec engr 1964-71, head utilities 1971-75; US Dept of Energy, Washington, DC, general engr 1975-84, hbcu liason 1984-; coordinator minority educ programs, 1986-. **Orgs:** Mem Federal Task Force Natl Power Grid Study 1979; mem Alpha Phi Alpha, Alpha Kappa Mu; Lawrence Berkeley Natl Lab/Mendez Educ Foundation Science Consortium 1986-; chmn Federal Agency Sci and Tech Bd 1986-; past pres Athenians Inc Washington DC; past pres Washington Chap SC State Coll Natl Alumni; mem, past sec, Trustee Bd Eard Memorial AMA, 1975-. **Honors/Awds:** Disting Military Grad 1961; Congressional Fellow nominee US Dept of Navy 1974; Civic Award-Service to Science & Technology, Carnegie Corp of NY, 1989; Outstanding Black Engineers in Govt, Black Engineer Magazine, 1989; SC State Coll Distinguished Alumni, Natl Assn for Loyal Opportunity in Higher Educ, 1991. **Military Serv:** US Army, 1st Lt, 3 years. **Home Addr:** 7000 97th Ave, Seabrook, MD 20706. **Business Addr:** Black Colls & Univs Liaison, US Department of Energy, 1000 Independence Ave SW, Washington, DC 20585.

SEWELL, LUTHER JOSEPH
Business executive. **Personal:** Born Aug 9, 1936, Chattanooga, TN; son of Minnie P Sloan and Luther Sewell; married Wilma Johnson, Jan 19, 1968; children: Luther J III, Lela J. **Educ:** Attended Tennessee A&I Univ 1954-56, Duquesne Univ 1956-58, Monterey Peninsula Coll 1960, Allegheny Community Coll, Univ of Arizona 1969; Trinity Hall Coll & Seminary, graduate 1971. **Career:** Talk Magazine, publisher 1962-; Luther J Sewell Inc, founder 1962-; Mellon Natl Bank, consult 1965-71; Business & Job Devel Corp, consultant, market analyst, community devel coor 1964-70; Allegheny County Civil Serv Commn, sec

1973-; Trans World Airlines, Pennsylvania Lottery, consultant, currently. **Orgs:** Mem Business & Job Devel Corp 1963; mem Amer Marketing Assn 1968-72; former vice pres Loendi Literary & Social Club 1969; mem review comm Community Chest Allegheny County 1971-73; bd dirs Pittsburgh Goodwill Industries 1972-; Mendelssohn Choir 1972-; former partner, vice pres A&S Securities Systems Inc 1973-74; bd dirs Pittsburgh Chapter NAACP 1973-; mem Pittsburgh Press Club, Gateway Center Club. **Honors/Awds:** Young Businessman of Year, AME Gen Conf 1965; Economic Devel Award, Urban Youth Action Inc 1972; Communications Award, Pittsburgh Club United 1972; Martin Luther King Award, Music & Arts Club of Pittsburgh 1972; Red Cross Volunteer Award 1973; Black Achievers Award, Centre Ave YMCA 1973; Publishers Award, Black Political Action Assn 1988; Business Award, Federal Executive Bd 1989. **Military Serv:** AUS sp4 1958-62. **Business Addr:** Founder, LJS Publishing Inc, 3423 Webster Ave, Pittsburgh, PA 15219.

SEWELL, RICHARD HUSTON
Deputy commissioner. **Personal:** Born Nov 1, 1946, Bowling Green, KY; son of Lottye Mae Hutson Cox and Richard Henry Sewell; married Iris Jean Jones, Dec 18, 1976; children: Rhonda Beth, Erica Jordon. **Educ:** Bowling Green State Univ, BS 1972; Univ of OK, MPH 1974. **Career:** Health Planning Assoc of Northwest OH, dir med care div 1971-76; Council for Comm Serv in Metro Chgo, sr planner 1976-77; Suburban Health Systems Agency, dir of planning 1977-80; Hay Assoc, consult 1980; Suburban Health Systems Agency, exec dir; Surburban Primary Health Care Council, Hinsdale, IL, pres 1987-90; Chicago Department of Health, Chicao, IL, administrator bureau of public health 1990-91, deputy commissioner public health and clinical services, 1991-. **Orgs:** Mem Alpha Phi Alpha 1964-; treas IL Assoc of Health Systems Agencies 1983-85; pres natl Black Health Planners Assoc 1984-86; bd of dir & exec comm Amer Health Planning Assoc 1984-87; vice chmn United Way Membership Comm 1984-; pres Men's Fellowship Trinity United Church of Christ 1984-85; board of directors United Way of Chicago 1989-; board of directors United Way Crusade of Mercy 1991-; board of deacons, deacon Trinity United Church of Christ 1979-. **Honors/Awds:** Invited to testify health subcommittee Inst of Med of the Natl Acad of Sci 1979.

SEWELL, STEVEN EDWARD
Professional football player (retired). **Personal:** Born Apr 2, 1963, San Francisco, CA. **Educ:** Univ of Oklahoma, graduate. **Career:** Denver Broncos, running back, wide receiver, 1985-93. **Orgs:** Denver Broncos, Youth Foundation. **Honors/Awds:** Post-season play, 1986, 1987, 1989: AFC Championship Game, NFL Championship Game; AFC Championship, 1992; Post Season Play, 1991. **Business Addr:** Retired Professional Football Player, Denver Broncos, 13655 Broncos Pkwy, Englewood, CO 80112-4151.

SEYMORE, STANLEY
Information systems manager. **Personal:** Born Jul 2, 1951, Bronx, NY; son of Ertha Mae Reese Seymore and Charles Bernard Clark; married Julia A. Williams, Feb 12, 1977; children: Kadeem Toure. **Educ:** Brooklyn College, Brooklyn NY, BA, 1980. **Career:** Blue Cross Blue Shield, New York NY, operational auditor, 1974-79, systems coordinator, 1979-81, programmer, 1981-84; Morgan Guaranty Trust, New York NY, programmer analyst, 1984-86; New York Times, New York NY, systems manager, 1986-. **Orgs:** Black Data Processing Associates, American Payroll Association. **Honors/Awds:** Member of Year, NY Chapter, Black Data Processing Associates, 1987. **Military Serv:** US Air Force, Sergeant, 1970-74. **Home Addr:** 60 East 17th St, #2G, Brooklyn, NY 11226.

SEYMOUR, BARBARA H.
Attorney. **Personal:** Born in Columbia, SC; daughter of Leroy Semon & Barbara Youngblood Seymour; divorced. **Educ:** SC State University, BS, 1975; Georgetown University Law Ctr, JD, 1979; Harvard University Graduate School of Business, MBA, 1985. **Career:** Texaco, tax attorney, 1979-. **Orgs:** Houston Area Urban League, dir, 1995-; Sickle Cell Assn of Texas Gulf Coast, treas, 1986-88, pres, 1988-90; IRS Commissioner's Advisory Group, 1995-97; American Bar Assn, Tax Section, 1979-; Leadership America, 1990-; Leadership Houston, 1989; Houston Chapter of Links, vp, 1996-; Alpha Kappa Omega Chap, Alpha Kappa Alpha, 1996-. **Honors/Awds:** National Eagle Leadership Institute, Eagle Award, 1995; Alpha Kappa Alpha, Foremost Fashionable, 1994; SC State University, School of Business, Distinguished Business Alumnus, 1991; Ebony Magazine, One of 50 Outstanding Young Leaders, 1983. **Special Achievements:** Author: The 1980 Crude Oil Windfall Profit Tax, Howard Law Journal, 1980. **Business Addr:** Tax Attorney, Texaco Inc, 1111 Bagby, Ste 2806, Houston, TX 77002, (713)752-6252.

SEYMOUR, CYNTHIA MARIA
Account representative. **Personal:** Born Sep 1, 1933, Houston, TX; married Oliver W Seymour; children: Michael Dwight Sweet, Wendell Raynard Sweet, Eugene LaValle Sweet Jr. **Educ:** John Adams School of Business, Business certificate 1965. **Career:** Gamma Phi Delta Sor, supreme anti-grammateus 1986-. **Orgs:** Vice pres San Francisco 49ers Toastmistress 1981-83; financial grammateus Gamma Phi Delta Sor Regional 1982-86; mem NAACP, Natl Council of Negro Women; mem Jones Memorial United Methodist Church; advisor Young Adult Fellowship; sec Joseph P Kennedy Foundation; bd of dirs Eleanor R Spikes Memorial; sec Finance Comm Jones Memorial United Meth Church 1986-. **Honors/Awds:** Outstanding Salesperson Lion's Club 1976,82; Certificate of Appreciation Gamma Phi Delta Sor 1983; Certificate of Appreciation Jones Memorial United Meth Church 1984,86; Certificate of Honor City and County of San Francisco 1985; Woman of the Year for Western Region Gamma Phi Delta Sor 1987; Certificate of Appreciation City of Detroit. **Home Addr:** 2535 Ardee Ln, South San Francisco, CA 94080.

SEYMOUR, LAURENCE DARRYL
Surgeon. **Personal:** Born Feb 1, 1935, Memphis, TN; children: Lauren Juanita, Eric Lawrence. **Educ:** TN St U, BS 1957; Howard U, MD 1961. **Career:** City of St Louis Hosp, intern 1961-62; resident 1962-66; Boston U, instr urology 1966-68; Univ TN Memphis, clin asso urology 1969-; Med Clinic Inc, vp 1971-. **Orgs:** Trustee Collins Chapel Hosp Memphis 1972; mem Am Bluff City Med Assns; mem Alpha Kappa Mu; Beta Kappa Chi; Omega Psi Phi; Mason; bd dirs Boys Club Memphis 1969-; Sigma Pi Phi Fraterniry; Memphis Unologic Society; fellow, International College of Surgeons; fellow, Amer Assn Clinical Urologists. **Military Serv:** USNR lt comdr 1966-68. **Business Addr:** 1325 Eastmoreland, Ste 435, Memphis, TN 38104.

SEYMOUR, ROBERT F.
Physician. **Personal:** Born Apr 8, 1926, Yonkers, NY; married Flora; children: Marc, Stephen, Lauren, Leslie. **Educ:** Howard Univ, BS 1948, MD 1952. **Career:** Cleveland Veteran's Admin Hosp, Case Western Reserve Univ, combined program urology specialty trng; Harlem Hospital, internship 1952-53; Private Practice, physician. **Orgs:** Mem Natl Medical Assoc, Cleveland Medical Assoc, Amer Urolog Assoc. **Military Serv:** AUS 1st lt 2 yrs. **Business Addr:** Urologic Surgeon, Cleveland Urologists Inc, 11201 Shaker Bl No 118, Cleveland, OH 44104.

SHABAZZ, BETTY. **See Obituaries section.**

SHABAZZ, KALEEM
Association executive. **Personal:** Born Jul 17, 1947, Atlantic City, NJ; son of Edna Evans Jowers and Theodus Jowers Sr; married Yolanda Dixon Shabazz, Jul 3, 1973; children: Anjail. **Educ:** Cheyney Univ, Cheyney, PN, 1965-68; Rutgers Univ, New Brunswick, NJ, BA, 1971; Rutgers Univ, Camden, NJ, courses towards masters, 1987-88. **Career:** County of Atlantic, Atlantic City, NJ, welfare care worker, 1979-81, information Atlantic, 1981-83, bus coordinator, 1983-85, dir comm devt, 1985-87; City of Atlantic City, Atlantic City, NJ, aide to city council pres, 1987-89; Natl Conf Christians and Jews, dir, currently. **Orgs:** Chmn, Minority Community Leaders Adv Bd, Rutgers Univ, 1987-; chmn, Institutional Review Bd for Institute of Human Devt, 1989-; sec, Atlantic City Art Ctr, 1988-; mem, United Negro Coll Fund, 1989-. **Honors/Awds:** Community Service Award, Business & Professional Women, 1984; Outstanding Community Service, Stockton State Coll Coalition, 1991; Meritorious Service, Youth Organiztion, 1990; Selection to ACT, Regional Leadership Training Program; Spoke at WN Special Comm on Apartheid , 1983; lead successful effort to halt erection of ''Sun City,'' South African backed casino in Atlantic City, 1983; raised over $7500 to benefit children in Atlanta, GA; frequent lecturer in local high schools and colleges Intro Group Relations, Prejudice Reduction; developed, organized and implemented Black/Jewish retreat 2 day session of over 20 African-American and Jewish Leaders to engage in dialogue, exchange and group dynamics around issues affecting both groups. **Home Addr:** 1258 Monroe Ave, Atlantic City, NJ 08401. **Business Addr:** Director, National Conference of Christians & Jews, 1125 Atlantic Ave, Ste 440, Atlantic City, NJ 08404.

SHACK, WILLIAM A.
Anthropologist. **Personal:** Born Apr 19, 1923, Chicago, IL; son of Emma McAvoy Shack and William Shack; married Dorothy Nash, Sep 1, 1961; children: Hailu. **Educ:** Sch of the Art Institute Chicago, BAE 1955; Univ of Chicago, MA 1957; London Sch of Economics, PhD 1961. **Career:** Northeastern IL State Coll, asst prof 1961-62; Haile Sellassie I Univ, asst prof 1962-65; Univ of IL, assoc prof 1966-70; Univ of CA Berkeley, prof 1970-91, dean of graduate div, 1979-85. **Orgs:** Fellow Intl African Inst 1959-; fellow Royal Anthropoligical Assn 1961-; fellow Amer Anthropological Inst 1961-; mem The Athenaeum London 1978-95; pres N Amer Comm Royal Anthropological Inst 1982; vice chmn, exec council Intl African Inst 1984-87; chairman Intl African Inst 1987-96. **Honors/Awds:** Fellow Amer Assn for the Advancement of Science 1984-; Chevalier l'ordre Nationale du Merite, Republic of France, 1987; Fellow, CA Academy of Sciences, 1987, Trustee, 1990-; vp, vice chmn, Science Council, 1992-96. **Military Serv:** USCG ETM 2/c 3 yrs; American Campaign Medal; Asiatic-Pacific Medal; WWII Victory Campaign Medal. **Home Addr:** 2597 Hilgard, Berkeley, CA 94709.

SHACK, WILLIAM EDWARD, JR.
Automobile dealership executive. **Personal:** Born Feb 4, 1943, Woodward, AL; married Lois D Webster; children: William Edward III, Vincent W. **Educ:** Clark Coll, 1961-62. **Career:** Thrifty Drug & Discount, mgr 1966-72; Ford Motor Co, mgr 1972-75; B & W Rent A Car, owner 1974-75; Miramar Lincoln-Mercury San Diego, Future Ford Banning, pres, owner 1983-; Miramar Lincoln Mercury Yucca Valley Ford Future Ford, pres owner; Shack-Woods Associates, Long Beach, CA, chief executive, currently. **Orgs:** Pres, Black Ford Lincoln Mercury Dealer Council, 1979, 1982, 1985; dir United Way 1977-83; mem Yucca Valley Lions 1977-84; dir Inland Area Urban League 1977-83; pres PUSH Intl Trade Bureau 1985; dir Jackie Robinson YMCA San Diego; commissioner San Diego City & County Intl World Trade Commission. **Honors/Awds:** Distinguished Achievement Award, Ford Motor Co 1977-84; Gold Award Urban League 1980-82; Gold Award United Way 1979-80; Founder Milligan Mem Scholarship 1980; Johnson Publishing Distinguished Businessman Award 1984. **Military Serv:** USAF E-4 1961-64. **Business Addr:** President, 2057 Kurtz St., San Diego, CA 92110.

SHACKELFORD, GEORGE FRANKLIN
Oil co. manager. **Personal:** Born Jun 3, 1939, Baltimore, MD; son of Doris Shackelford and George Shackelford; married Barbara Janice; children: Shawn, Terrence, Kymberly, Tanya, George. **Educ:** Univ MD, prog for mgmt devel; Harvard Univ. **Career:** Amoco Oil Co, director acquistions, gen manager, lubricants, business manager, light oils, capital investment mgr, mgr advertising & consumer affairs, dir mktg rsch, dir mktg strategies, manager special account, dist mgr, mgr mdsg, spl proj devel, pricing spec, fld sls mgr, term mgr, terr mgr, equip clk, mail boy 1965. **Military Serv:** AUS 1962-65. **Business Addr:** Director Acquistions, Amoco Oil Co., 200 E Randolph Dr, Chicago, IL 60601.

SHACKELFORD, LOTTIE H.
Corporate executive. **Personal:** Born Apr 30, 1941, Little Rock, AR; daughter of Bernice Linzy Holt and Curtis Holt (deceased); divorced; children: Russell, Karen, Karla. **Educ:** Broadway Sch of Real Est, Diploma 1973; Inst of Politics, Fellow 1975; Philander Smith Clg, BA (cum laude) 1979; JFK Sch of Govt Harvard Univ, Fellow 1983. **Career:** Urban League of Greater Little Rock, educ dir 1973-78; AR Regional Minority Council, exec dir 1982-92; Overseas Private Investment Corp, mem, 1994-. **Orgs:** Bd mem Natl League of Cities 1984-86; vice chm AR Democratic St Comm 1982-90; reg dir Natl Black Caucus Locally Elected Official; pres S Reg Cncl 1980-; bd of dir Urban League; bd mem Womens Pol Caucus; mem Delta Sigma Theta Sor; vice chmn Democratic National Comm 1989-92; mem Links Inc. **Honors/Awds:** Outstanding citizen Philander Smith Alum Awd 1982; outstanding community serv HOPE NLR 1977; trailblazer awd Delta Sigma Theta Sor 1977; outstanding citizen Bus & Prof Women 1984; Honorary Doctorate of Human Letters, Philander Smith College 1988; Honorary Doctorate of Humane Letters, Shorter College 1987; Esquire Magazine, one of the Distinguished Men and Women in US, 1987. **Business Addr:** Member, Overseas Private Investment Corp, 1615 M St NW, Washington, DC 20527.

SHACKELFORD, WILLIAM G., JR.
Scientist, consultant, educational administrator. **Personal:** Born Mar 30, 1950, Chicago; married Renee Nuckols; children: Dionne Deneen, Lenise Yvonne, Andre' Tarik. **Educ:** Clark Coll, BS 1971; GA Inst of Tech, MS 1974. **Career:** Babcock & Wilcox Navl Nclr Fuel Div of VA, quality control engr 1972-73; Clark Coll, assoc rschr physics dept 1973-74, coop gen sci prog phys dept; Natl Center for Atmospheric Rsch CO, vstg rschr 1975; Central Intelligence Agency, analyst 1975-77; Nuclear Assurance Corp, project mgr 1977-79; Atlanta Univ Center, dir dual degree engrg prog 1980-86; Knox Consultants, mktg mgr 1986-87; IEC Enterprises Inc, president, founder, currently. **Orgs:** Chmn Spectrum Club Com 1974; Leadershp GA Participant 1982; board of directors, Atlanta Camp Fire; reg pres, natl membership chmn Natl Assn of Minority Engrg Prog Administrators; Society Human Resource Management; American Society Training and Development. **Honors/Awds:** Beta Kappa Chi Natl Hon Soc Joint Mtng 1971; Judge DeKalb Co Dist Sci Fair 1974-75, 1978-84; Roster Listee, Blacks in Physics Scnd Awds Ceremony for Outstanding Black Physics 1975; First Prize, paper presented at Natl Sci Foundation. **Home Addr:** 5439 Golfcrest Circle, Stone Mountain, GA 30088.

SHACKLEFORD, CHARLES
Professional basketball player. **Personal:** Born Apr 22, 1966, Kinston, NC. **Educ:** North Carolina State. **Career:** NBA Record: New Jersey Nets, 1988-90; Philadelphia 76ers, 1991-93; Minnesota Timberwolves, 1994-; Italian League Record: Phonola Caserta, 1990-91. **Business Addr:** Professional Basketball Player, Minnesota Timberwolves, 600 First Ave N, Minneapolis, MN 55403, (612)337-3865.

SHADE, BARBARA J.
Educator. **Personal:** Born Oct 30, 1933, Armstrong, MO; daughter of Edna Bowman and Murray K Robinson; married Oscar DePreist; children: Christina Marie, Kenneth E, Patricia Louise. **Educ:** Pittsburg St Univ Pittsburg KS, BS 1955; Univ

of WI Milwaukee, MS 1967; Univ of WI Madison, PhD 1973. **Career:** Univ of WI, asst prof dept Afro-am Studies 1975; Dane Co Head Start, exec dir 1969-71; Milwaukee WI Pub Schs, tchr 1960-68; Consult parent Devel Regn V, 1973-75; Dept of Pub Instr WI, urban ed consult 1974-75; Univ of WI Parkside, assoc prof/chair div of educ; professor/dean, school of education. **Orgs:** Mem Delta Sigma Theta Sor 1952-; mem Am Psychol Assn; bd pres St Mary's Hosp Med Cntr 1978; vice pres priorities Dane Co United Way 1979; mem Assoc of Black Psychologists, Amer Educ Rsch Assoc. **Honors/Awds:** Post-doctorial Fellow, Nat Endwmnt for Hmnties 1973-74; Publ Jour of Psychol Jour of Social Psychol; Negro Educ Rvw; Review of Educational Rsch; Journal of Negro Educ; Journal of School Psychology. **Business Addr:** Dean of Education, University of Wisconsin Parkside, Kenosha, WI 53141.

SHADE, GEORGE H., JR.
Physician. **Personal:** Born Jan 4, 1949, Detroit, MI; son of George H Slade Sr and Julia M Bullard-Shade; married Carlotta A Johnson-Shade, Jul 24, 1976; children: Carla N, Ryan M. **Educ:** Wayne State Univ, BS, 1971, MD, 1974, Residency Training - OB/Gyn, 1975-78. **Career:** Wayne State Univ Affiliated Hospitals, chief resident of gynecology, 1977-78; Southwest Detroit Hospital, chief of gynecology, 1981-84; Detroit Receiving Hospital, vice chief of gynecology, 1982-87; Wayne State Univ School of Medicine, clinical instructor of gynecology, 1983-87, clinical asst prof, 1987-; Detroit Riverview Hospital, dir of resident education in gynecology, 1991-, chief ob/gyn dept, 1995-. **Orgs:** American Medical Assn; National Medical Assn; Michigan State Medical Society; Wayne County Medical Society; Detroit Medical Society; fellow, American College of Obstetricians and Gynecologists; fellow, American Society for Laser Medicine and Surgery; International Correspondence Society in Obstetrics and Gynecology; bd of directors, Detroit-Macomb Hospital Corp, 1996-; bd of directors, Wayne State Univ Alumni Assn, 1983-87. **Honors/Awds:** American Legion Scholarship Award; David S Diamond Award for Obstetrics and Gynecology; Chrysler Youth Award; Outstanding Senior Residence Award, Obstetrics and Gynecology; Boy Scouts of America, Eagle Scout Award; Detroit Medical Society, Service Award. **Special Achievements:** Presentations: ''Paradoxical Pelvic Masses,'' Hutzel Hospital, 1986; ''Viral Infections in Ob/Gyn,'' Detroit Riverview Hospital, 1992; ''Urinary Stress Incontinence,'' Detroit Riverview Hospital, 1992; ''Pelvic Endometriosis: Diagnostic Challenges,'' Henry Ford Hospital, 1993; ''Endoscopy in Modern Gynecology,'' The Detroit Medical Society, 1995. **Business Addr:** Chmn, Dept of Obstetrics and Gynecology, Detroit Riverview Hospital, 7733 E Jefferson, Detroit, MI 48214, (313)499-4915.

SHADE, SAM
Professional football player. **Personal:** Born Jun 14, 1973, Birmingham, AL. **Educ:** Univ of Alabama, attended. **Career:** Cincinnati Bengals, defensive back, 1995-. **Business Addr:** Professional Football Player, Cincinnati Bengals, One Bengals Dr, Cincinnati, OH 45202, (513)621-3550.

SHAH, KHALID IBN (BOB WATKINS)
Associate publisher, executive director. **Personal:** Born Jun 6, 1954, Los Angeles; son of Bartha & Mary Watkins; married Audrey Watkins, Jun 1972; children: Lawanda, Robert Khalid Jr. **Educ:** Questa College, Radiology, 1984. **Career:** Economic & Youth Opportunity Agency, prog asst II, 1970-73; Martin Luther King Hosp, radiology tech, 1985-88; Community Collabs, youth counselor, comm organizer, 1987-89; Stop the Violence Foundation, executive director, 1989-97; Rapid Publishing Inc, associate publisher, currently. **Orgs:** NAACP, mem; Muslim Business Association, vice chmn, 1992-97; Recycling Black Dollars Assn, bd mem, 1990-97; Violence Prevention Coalition, bd mem, 1995-97; Drug & Violence Prevention Agency, bd mem, 1996-97. **Honors/Awds:** California State Legislature, Assembly Resolution, 1994; Turning Point Mag, Living History Maker, 1996; County of Los Angeles, Award of Honor, 1996; City of Lynwood, Outstanding Leadership Award, 1997; Office of Criminal Justice Planning, Comm Svc Award, 1997. **Special Achievements:** Promotion of Violence, Awareness Through billboard, radio and print media campaign; created Peace Clubs in various schools and affiliate chapters of the Natl Violence Prevention Coalition. **Business Addr:** Associate Publisher, Rapid Publishing Inc, 349 W Compton Blvd, Green Fronts, Compton, CA 90220, (213)774-0018.

SHAKESPEARE, EASTON GEOFFREY
Insurance consultant. **Personal:** Born Mar 20, 1946, Kingston, Jamaica; son of Easton G Shakespeare & Leone Williams-Phillips; married Maria A, Apr 20, 1968; children: Christopher G, Collin M. **Educ:** The College of Arts, Science & Technology, 1960; Senera College, 1969; The College of Insurance, 1992; The American College, CLU, CHFC, 1993. **Career:** Island Life Insurance Co-Kingston Jamaica, rep, 1974-77; The Guardian Life Insurance Co, group rep, 1978-87; ERA Realtors, real estate assoc, 1990-91; Easton Shakespeare & Assoc, insurance broker, 1987-; FF&G Inc, Newark, NJ, vp/treasurer, 1991-93; Financial Supermarket Insurance School, partner/instructor, 1992-; Capital Employee Benefit Services, Inc, pres, 1993-97; EMCC Marketing Corp, pres, 1997-. **Orgs:** Amer Society of Chartered Life Underwriters & Chartered Financial Consultants, 1983-; New Jersey Society of CLU's & ChFC, 1985-; New York Society of CLU & CHFC, 1983-85; Monmouth County, NJ Board of Realtors, 1990-; Natl Assn Life Underwriters, 1988-. **Honors/Awds:** Health Insurance Assn of America-HIAA Group Insurance, 1982; Life Insurance Marketing & Research Assn, International Quality Award, 1975. **Business Addr:** President, EMCC Mktg Corp, PO Box 55, Lithonia, GA 30058, (770)484-8779.

SHAKIR, ADIB AKMAL
Educational administrator. **Personal:** Born Jun 15, 1953, Richmond, VA; married Dr Annette Goins; children: Ameenah N, Yusuf S. **Educ:** Morehouse Coll, BA (cum laude) 1976; Norfolk State Univ, MA 1980; Florida State Univ, PhD 1985. **Career:** Florida A&M Univ, instructor of psychology 1981-83; Bethune-Cookman College, dir counseling ctr 1983-85, asst to the pres for govtl affairs 1985-86, intvp acad afrs/dean of faculty 1986-88; Tougaloo College, president, 1988-. **Orgs:** Mem East Central FL Consortium for Higher Educ/Industry; mem Natl Council for Black Studies; mem Natl Assoc of Black Psychologists; mem North FL Chapt of the Assoc of Black Psychologists; board of directors, Mississippi Museum of Art; board of directors, United Negro College Fund; board of directors, Amistad Research Center. **Honors/Awds:** Merrill Study/Travel Scholarship Morehouse College 1973; Psychology Dept Honors Morehouse Coll 1976; McKnight Jr Faculty Develop Fellowship McKnight Foundation 1984-85; Knight Foundation, Presidential Leadership Award, 1991. **Business Addr:** President, Tougaloo College, 500 E County Line Rd, Tougaloo, MS 39174.

SHAKOOR, ADAM ADIB
Attorney. **Personal:** Born Aug 6, 1947, Detroit, MI; son of Esther Caddell and Harvey Caddell; divorced; children: Shair, Lateef, Keisha, Malik, Khalidah, Koya, Kareena, Jelani. **Educ:** Wayne State Univ, Univ of MI Labor Sch, certificate 1969; Wayne State Univ, BS 1971, MEd 1974, JD 1976; King Abdul Aziz Univ Saudi Arabia, certificate 1977. **Career:** Wayne County Comm Coll, Detroit MI, prof bus law & black studies, 1971-93; Marygrove Coll, Detroit MI, prof real estate law, 1984; 36th Dist Court, Detroit MI, chief judge, 1981-89; City of Detroit, deputy mayor, chief administrative officer, 1989-93; Reynolds, Beeby & Magnuson, partner, 1994-. **Orgs:** Consult in comm affairs New Detroit Inc 1973-74; pres Black Legal Alliance 1975-76; founding mem Natl Conf of Black Lawyers Detroit Chap 1975-; com mem New Detroit Inc 1977-81; president of bd, Boysville, Inc, 1994; club pres Optimist Club of Renaissance Detroit 1982-83; pres Assoc of Black Judges of MI1985-86; life mem Kappa Alpha Phi. **Honors/Awds:** Grnd Fellowship HUD 1971-73; Grad Fellow SE MI Council of Govt 1971-73; Wolverine Bar Assn Scholarship Natl Bar Assn 1975; Cert of Distinction Com for Student Rights 1979; Certificate of Merit for Exceptional Achievement in Govt Affairs MI State Legislature 1980; Resolution of Tribute MI State Legislature 1981; numerous others. **Business Addr:** Partner, Reynolds, Beeby & Magnuson, 615 Griswold, Ste 531, Detroit, MI 48226.

SHAKOOR, WAHEEDAH AQUEELAH (SANDRA SHORT ROBERSON)
Education administrator, elected official. **Personal:** Born Feb 11, 1950, Washington, DC; married; children: Barella Nazirah. **Educ:** Wilberforce Univ, 1968-71; Univ of Cincinnati, BS 1973; Univ of DC, MEd 1980; Trinity Coll, 1977-84. **Career:** Cincinnati Recreation Commiss, prog dir, mentally retarded 1973; Cincinnati Public Schools, teacher spec ed 1973-74; Univ of Islam, teacher, elem ed 1974-75; Charles Cty Schools, teacher spec ed 1976-79; Dist of Columbia Public Schools, teacher, dept chairperson spec ed 1979-85. **Orgs:** Mem Council for Exceptional Children 1971-84; coach Spec Olympics 1974-77; mem Marshall Hts Civic Assoc 1981-84; adv neighborhood commiss DC Govt 1981-83; mem Capitol View Civic Assoc 1981-85; consult bd of ed Sis Clara Muhammad School 1981-85; exec bd mem Marshall Hts Comm Devel Org 1981-84; ed, pr Washington Saturday Coll 1982-85; pres Bilal Entr Inc 1983-85; mem Friends of the DC Youth Orchestra 1985-. **Honors/Awds:** Dedication to Spec Olympics 1974; Serv Handicapped Parent Assoc Learning Disabled 1978; Outstanding Serv DCPS Eastern HS 1981; Serv Title I DCPS Title I Private School 1982; coord Far NE, SE Coalition for Mayoral Forum 1982; Serv to Community Marshall Hts Community Devel Org 1983; Hajij Rep Amer Muslim Mission 1984. **Home Addr:** 5340 East Capitol St, Washington, DC 20019. **Business Addr:** Chairperson Spec Ed, DCPS-Anacostia High, 2406 21st Pl NE, Washington, DC 20018.

SHAMBERGER, JEFFERY L.
Automobile dealer. **Personal:** married Regina; children: Jason, Jessica. **Educ:** Wilberforce University, BS, 1971. **Career:** Shamrock Ford-Lincoln-Mercury, owner, currently. **Business Addr:** President, Shamrock Ford-Lincoln-Mercury, 829 Tecumseh Rd, Clinton, MI 49236, (517)456-7414.

SHAMBORGUER, NAIMA
Vocalist. **Personal:** Born Apr 18, Detroit, MI; daughter of Julian Thomas & Cleopatra Davis Jones; married George L G Shamborguer, Oct 6, 1975; children: Michael Julian Griffin, David William Griffin, James Keith Griffin. **Educ:** Peralta Junior College, 1965-66; Highland Park Community College, 1969-70; Wayne State Univ, 1971-76, 1980-85. **Career:** Vernor Pre-School, head teacher, 1968-72, 1977-79; Story Book Nursery, head teacher-director, 1972-73; Grand Circus Nursery, head teacher supervisor, summer, 1974; Michigan Employment Security Commission, mail clerk, 1978-79; Greenfield Peace Lutheran School, program director, 1979-80; Action Head Start, parent involvement coordinator, 1980-85; Detroit, Montreux Jazz Festival, performer, 1980-96; Clark & Associates, psychologist assistant, 1986-93; Skyline Club, performer, 1988-89; Renaissance Club, house performer, 1989-. **Orgs:** Vernor Pre-School, head teacher, 1968-72, 1977-79; Story Book Nursery, head teacher/dir, 1972-73; Grand circus Nursery, head teacher supervisor, summer, 1974; MI Employment Security Commission, mail clerk, 1978-79; Greenfield Peace Lutheran School, program dir, 1979-80; Action Head Start, parent involvement coordinator, 1980-85; Detroit Montreux Jazz Festival, performer, 1980-93; Skyline Club, performer, 1988-89; Renaissance Club, house performer, 1989-; Jazz Alliances of Michigan, board member; Center for Musical Intelligence, board member. **Honors/Awds:** City of Detroit, Spirit of Detroit Award, 1984; Societies of the Culturally Concerned, Outstanding Service Award, 1992; BET Jazz Discovery, Best Jazz Video, 1994; Friends School Children's Festival, Artisans Award, 1995; Nat Soc of Fund Raising Exec, Special Volunteer, 1997. **Special Achievements:** Vocal Workshop, Technique and Song, 1989-; Voted number 1 female vocalist by the Southeastern Jazz Assn Musicians Poll, 1989; Michigan Heart Assn Fundraiser, Opening act for Phyllis Diller/Ruda Lee, 1988; Michigan Cancer Foundation Fundraiser, Opening act for Lainie Kazan, 1988; Featured Black History Month WEMU, Eastern Michigan University Radio, Recording ''Naima's Moods,'' 1994; Featured in Michigan Touring Arts Guide, 1986-; Studio 15, Jazz Video, 1997; has performed with Marvin Gaye, The Four Tops, Dizzy Gillespie, Wynton marsales, and others; Composed original songs: Music In the Air, Good to be Home Again, Willy Nilly. **Home Addr:** 19760 Hartwell, Detroit, MI 48235, (313)863-7168.

SHAMMGOD, GOD
Professional basketball player. **Personal:** Born Apr 29, 1976. **Educ:** Providence. **Career:** Washington Wizards, guard, 1997-. **Business Addr:** Professional Basketball Player, Washington Wizards, MCI Center, 601 F St NW, Washington, DC 20071, (202)661-5000.

SHAMWELL, JOE
Radio executive. **Personal:** Born Aug 29, 1944, District of Columbia; married Marcia L; children: Kenneth, Jehad, Ayanna, Ebay, Aisha. **Educ:** Jackson State Univ, Mass Communications. **Career:** Songwriter/Producer/Recording Artist, 1966-; East Memphis Music Inc, professional mgr 1974-76; Groovesville Music Inc, dir of operations 1977-79; Lee King Productions, dir publicity & promotion 1976-84; J Shamwell Creative Svcs, pres 1977-; Jackson State Univ, adjunct prof mass comm 1980-84; WOKJ/WJMI, acct exec 1983-85; WACR AM/FM, genl mgr 1985-. **Orgs:** Vp Golden TRiangle Advertising Federation 1987-88; chmn Comm Affairs & Hospitality Columbus/Lownoes Chamber of Commerce 1987-88; acting pres Regional Assoc of Radio Execs 1987; mem NAACP, Main St Adv Bd Columbus 1987, Natl Black Media Coalition 1987. **Honors/Awds:** Jingle of the Year Jackson Music Awds 1978-84; Songwriter of the Year Jackson Music Awds 1978,80,84; Disting Sales Awd SME 1984; Employee of the Year WOKJ/WJMI 1984; Outstanding Volunteer Serv Awd Governor of MS. **Military Serv:** AUS personnel mgmt specialist 1969-72. **Home Addr:** 2705 5th St No #147, Columbus, MS 39701. **Business Addr:** General Manager, WACR AM/FM, PO Box 1078, Columbus, MS 39703.

SHAMWELL, RONALD L.
Executive director. **Personal:** Born Nov 8, 1942, Philadelphia; married Jean; children: Nathan, Monique. **Educ:** Winston-Salem St U, BS 1969; Temple U, MSW 1973. **Career:** Philadelphia Schs, tchr 1970-71; asst Exec dir 1973; Antioch Coll, instr 1974; Wharton Cntr, exec dir 1974-. **Orgs:** Mem Assn Balck Social Wrkrs; Nat Fed Settlements; bd mem Urban Priorities; chmn bd North Central Dist Ylth an Dwelfare Coun; mem Delaware Valley Assn Dirs Vol Prog; bd mem Comm Concern #13; mem Rotary Club; consult Temple Univ Massiah Coll, Antioch Coll; chmn Yth Task Force North Central Phila; mem Philadelphia Chp Operation Breadbasket. **Honors/Awds:** Honor awd Temple U; merit awd Antioch Coll. **Business Addr:** 1708 N 22 St, Philadelphia, PA 19121.

SHANDS, FRANKLIN M., SR.
Teacher (retired), coach. **Personal:** Born Aug 11, 1920, Cincinnati; son of Dessie and Thomas; married Christine Culvert Shands, Aug 15, 1977; children: Sharon Adell, Franklin, Jr. **Educ:** Miami Univ, Oxford, OH, BFA 1946, MFA, 1984. **Career:** DePorres HS, teacher coach 1947-64; Purcell HS, teacher Coach 1964-70; Princetion HS, 1970-90; artist illustrator 1944-46; Independent Life Insurance Agent, 1968-; track coach, 1992-. **Orgs:** Pres SW OH Track Coach Assn 1968-70; fndr dir Viking Relays & Cavalier Relays; pres fndr Rembrandt Const Co and Shands Inc Builders 1947-70; contrib numerous art collections. **Honors/Awds:** Coach of yr ''A'' OH St 1961, 1963,

Nt Dist 2 1969; Miami Univ Track Hall of Fame 1970; Fred Hutchinson Meml Awd 1972; dinstgd serv awd Miami Univ 1971; Bishop Alumni Medal, Miami Univ, 1971.

SHANGE, NTOZAKE
Poet, playwright. **Personal:** Born Oct 18, 1948, Trenton, NJ. **Educ:** Barnard Coll, BA, American studies (cum laude) 1970; Univ of Southern California, MA 1973. **Career:** Former teacher at Mills College, Sonoma State Univ, Medgar Evers College, Univ of California at Berkeley; Univ of Houston, drama instructor, currently; author: For Colored Girls Who Have Considered Suicide When the Rainbow Is Enuf, 1976; Sassafrass: A Novella, 1976; Nappy Edges, 1978; Three Pieces, 1981; Cypress & Indigo, 1983; A Daughter's Geography, 1983; From Okra to Greens, 1984; Betsey Brown, 1985; Ridin' the Moon in Texas, 1988; If I Can Cook, You Know God Can, 1998. **Orgs:** Member, Poets and Writers Inc; member, New York Feminist Art Guild; member, Institute for Freedom of Press. **Honors/Awds:** Outer Critics Circle Award, 1977; Obie Award, 1977; Audelco Award, 1977; Frank Silvera Writers Workshop Award, 1978. **Business Addr:** Department of Drama, University of Houston, University Park, 4800 Calhoun Rd, Houston, TX 77004.

SHANKS, JAMES A.
Mayor. **Personal:** Born Feb 7, 1912, Tutwiler, MS; son of Dora and T.A.; married Willye B Harper. **Educ:** MS Valley State Coll, BS Ed 1958; Univ of St Louis, 1961; MS State U, 1964-65. **Career:** Town of Jonestown, mayor 1973-, alderman 1973; Coahoma Co Sch Sys, tchr 1938-77. **Orgs:** Sec & treas NAACP 1944; exec com Dem Party for the Co & Dist 1974; deacon/supt & tchr Met Bapt Ch 1942; mem MACE 1944; mem Elks Club 1946; asst to prgms Elderly Hsng Inc/Manpower Proj Clarksdale MS 1978. **Honors/Awds:** Outstdng Achvmnt in Pub Serv MS Vly State Coll Itta Bena 1977; MS Intrnl Dev Sys Gov of MS 1978. **Business Addr:** Town of Jonestown, PO Box 110, Jonestown, MS 38639.

SHANKS, WILHELMINA BYRD
Retail executive. **Personal:** Born Jul 19, 1951, Atlanta, GA; daughter of Annie Beatrice Byrd Watkins and T J Watkins Sr; divorced; children: Harold Jerome, Jr. **Educ:** Morris Brown College, Atlanta GA, BA, 1973; Georgia State Univ, Atlanta GA, 1973-74. **Career:** Rich's, Atlanta GA, sales mgr, 1973-75, buyer, 1975-78; Jordan Marsh, Fort Lauderdale FL, divisional mgr, 1978-80; Macy's South, Atlanta GA, merchandise mgr, 1980-84, store mgr, 1984-, vice pres, 1986-, vice pres/administrator, 1986-90; Foley's, Dallas, TX, vice pres/gen mgr, 1990-92; Ashford Management Group, Atlanta, Georgia, retail account executive, 1992-94; Shanks and Assoc Exec and Temporary Placement Services, president, 1994-; Atlanta Committee of Olympic Games, dir of merchandising, 1996; Reebok Intl, dir of apparel forecasting/inventory mgt, 1996-. **Orgs:** American Business Women's Association; member, board of directors, Family Life Services, 1986, ex bd Romar Academy. **Honors/Awds:** English Award, Teachers Guild, 1973; Outstanding Leadership Award, Junior Achievement, 1974; NAACP, Outstanding Business Leaders, 1989. **Business Addr:** Directory of Apparel Forecasting/Inventory Management, Reebok Intl, 100 Technology Ctr Dr, Stoughton, MA 02072.

SHANKS, WILLIAM COLEMON, JR.
Physician. **Personal:** Born May 10, 1917, Burlington, NC; married Mary Louise Loritts (deceased); children: William DeWitt MD, Elissa Stewart. **Educ:** Shaw Univ Raleigh NC, BS 1939; Meharry Med Coll Nashville TN, MD 1943. **Career:** Meml Hosp of Alamance, mem staff 1970-; Dept of Gen Pract, chief 1975-78; Alamance Co Hosp, staff mem 1955-80; Sharks Clinic, physician, currently. **Orgs:** Pres Old N State Med Soc 1957-58; 1st black mem Burlington City Bd of Educ 1964-87, chairman, 1978-80; bd mem Alamance-Caswell Reg Mntl Hlth Bd 1968-80; v chmn Burlington City Bd of Educ 1972-87; exec bd hlth & sfty chmn Boy Scouts of Am Cherokee Cncl 1972-74; life mem Alpha Phi Alpha. **Honors/Awds:** Recipient 3 bronze stars & A-P Ribbon AUSMC 1945; Silver Beaver Awrd BSA 1974; Award of Merit Alamance Co Commn on Civic Afrs 1979. **Military Serv:** AUSMC capt 1944-46. **Business Addr:** Physician, Shanks Clinic, 532 Shepard St, Burlington, NC 27215.

SHANNON, DAVID THOMAS, SR.
Educational administrator. **Personal:** Born Sep 26, 1933, Richmond, VA; married Shannon P Averett; children: Vernitia, Davine, David Jr. **Educ:** Virginia Union University, BA, 1954; Virginia Union School of Religion, BD, 1957; Oberlin Graduate School of Theology, STM, 1959; Vanderbilt University, DMin, 1974; University of Pittsburgh, PhD, 1975. **Career:** Fair Oaks Baptist Church, pastor, 1954-57; Antioch Baptist Church, student assistant, 1957-59; Oberlin Graduate School of Theology, graduate assistant, 1958-59; Virginia Union University, lecturer, 1959-69; Virginia Union University, university pastor, 1960-61; Ebenezer Baptist Church, pastor, 1960-69; Howard University, Div School, visiting lecturer, 1968; American Baptist Board of Education & Public, director, 1969-71; St Mary's Seminar, visiting professor, 1969-72; Bucknell University, professor & director, 1971-72; Pittsburgh Presbyterian Theological Seminary, dean of faculty, 1972-79; Hartford Seminary Foundation, Biblical Scholar professor of biblical studies, 1979; Virginia Union University, president, 1979-1985; Inter denominational Theo Center, vice pres for academic affairs, beginning 1985-91; Andover Newton Theological School, pres, 1991-94; Allen Unit, pres, 1994-. **Orgs:** Chairperson, Baptist Task Force of the World Baptist Alliance for Dialogue with the Secretariat of the Roman Catholic Church; Society for Biblical Lit; unit comm, National Coun Ch; comm on theological concerns, American Baptist Convention; coun comm, United Presbyterian Church, USA; board of directors, First & Merchants National Bank of Richmond; Baptist World Alliance; general board of American Baptist Church, USA; American Association Higher Education; American Academy of Religion, Richmond Rotary Club, Society for Biblical Lit, Society for Study of Black Religion; broadcast series, American Baptist Convention, 1973-74; scholarship selection committee, Phillip Morris, New York City, 1980-; board of directors, Sovran Bank, Richmond, 1980-; board directors, Urban Training, Atlanta, 1985-; NAACP; Alpha Kappa Mu; Phi Beta Sigma. **Honors/Awds:** Man of the Year, NCCJ, 1981; Numerous Publications: "Theological Methodology & The Black Experience", "The Future of Black Theology", 1977; "The Old Testament Exper of Faith", Judson Press, 1977; "Roots, Some Theological Reflections", Journal of Interdenom Sem, 1979. **Business Addr:** Pres, Allen Univ, 1530 Harden Street, Columbia, SC 29204.

SHANNON, GEORGE A.
Mayor. **Personal:** Born Sep 17, 1918, Pleasant Hill, LA; son of Elma Jones Shannon and Wilkin Shannon; married Elvera Ricks, Apr 19, 1984; children: W Ronald, Michael K. **Educ:** Southern Univ, Baton Rouge LA, BS, 1949; Bishop College, Marshall TX, MS, 1955. **Career:** Sabine Parish School Board, Many LA, principal, 1949-79; Pleasant Hill, LA, mayor, currently. **Orgs:** Carver Civic Org. **Honors/Awds:** State of Louisiana, Mason of the Year, 1993. **Military Serv:** US Army, 1st sergeant. **Home Addr:** 8653 Texas St, PO Box 127, Pleasant Hill, LA 71065. **Business Addr:** Mayor, Town of Pleasant Hill, 100 Pearl St, PO Box 125, Pleasant Hill, LA 71065.

SHANNON, JOHN WILLIAM
Federal official. **Personal:** Born Sep 13, 1933, Louisville, KY; son of Alfreda Williams Shannon and John Shannon; married Jean Miller Shannon, Apr 21, 1956; children: John W, Jr. **Educ:** Central State Univ, BS 1955; Shippenburg Coll, MS 1975, US Army War College, Carlisle, PA, 1975. **Career:** Office of Sec, Army, Washington, congressional liaison officer 1972-74; Dept Director for Manpower and Reserve Affairs Office, assistant secretary of defense for LA, 1975-78; Dept of the Army Washington, deputy dir for manpower and res affairs 1978-81; Office of the Asst Sec of Defense Legislative Affairs, special asst for manpower res affairs/logistics 1978-81, deputy under sec 1981-84, asst sec for installations/logistics 1984-89; Under Secretary of the Army, 1989-. **Orgs:** Member, Kappa Alpha Psi Fraternity. **Honors/Awds:** Distinguished Civilian Service Award, Department of the Army; Secretary of Defense Award for Outstanding Public Service; Defense Superior Service Award; Roy Wilkins Meritorious Service Award. **Military Serv:** US Army, Colonel, 1955-78; Legion of Merit, Bronze Star, Combat Infantry Badge, others.

SHANNON, MARIAN L. H.
Counselor (retired). **Personal:** Born Oct 12, 1919, Escambia Co, FL; daughter of Lacey Sinkfield Harris and James Henry Harris; married TJ. **Educ:** Hampton Inst, BS 1944; Univ Miami MEd 1964. **Career:** Dade Co Public School, school counselor chairperson Student Serv Guid & Tstng; Booker T Washington Jr HS; Curr Writer Fed Proj, "Self Concept", "Images in Black" & "Counseling the Minority Student"; Business Educ Courses Social Studies Courses, teacher, test chairman. **Orgs:** Miami Chap March of Dimes Fnd; tutor, mentor at elementary schools, 1986-88; vice president, Black Archives History & Research Foundation South Florida; 1987-91; project coordinator, The R Gibson Oratorical/Declamation Contest, 1989-; Phylacter Florida State Leadership Conference, Zeta Phi Beta Sorority, Inc, 1995-98; historian emeritus, Southeastern Region, Zeta Phi Beta Sorority Inc; participant, Intergenerational Project Dade Public Schools, 1993-97; sr adult ministry, Greater Bethel AME, 1996. **Honors/Awds:** Outstndng Cit Omega Psi Phi Frat 1967; Meritorious Serv Awrd Outstndng Zeta, Zeta Phi Beta Sor 1965, 1970; Outstndng Serv Awrd professional orgns 1971-73; Shannon Day, Miami City and Dade County; Zeta Hall of Fame, Florida, 1986; Educator Trail Blazer Award, Delta Sigma Theta Sorority, 1990; Editor AAUW Informat, Miami Branch; Ewd Waters College, Honorary Doc, 1954; Dade County, Woman of Impact Honoree; Dade County Co of Women Award, 1995.

SHANNON, ODESSA M.
County government official. **Personal:** Born Jul 4, 1928, Washington, DC; daughter of Gladys McKenzie and Raymond McKenzie; divorced; children: Mark V, Lisa S. **Educ:** Smith Coll, BA 1950. **Career:** EEOC, dep dir field serv 1979-81, dir prog planning & evaluation 1981-82, prog dir 1982-84, ex asst Off of Research; Bureau of Census, comp syst analyst; Baltimore Public School, teacher; special asst to county exec 1984-86; Montgomery County MD, dir human serv coord & planning 1986-89, dep dir family resources, 1990-94; Montgomery County Maryland Human Relations Commission, exec dir, 1994-. **Orgs:** Elected mbr bd of ed Montgomery Co, MD 1982-84; reg bd of dir Nat Conf of Christians & Jews 1980-89; Local Council; United Way; mem Alpha Kappa Alpha Sor; NAACP; chmn of bd dir Regional Inst for Children & Adolescents; bd dir MT Co Arts Council; chmn of bd Coalition for Equitable Representation in Govt 1986-; bd dir, Mont Housing Partnership; bd dir National Political Congress of Black Women, 1985-86; bd dir, National Coalition of 100 Black Women, Montgomery County, 1989-; bd dir Round House Theatre, 1990-92; bd dir Metropolitan Boys & Girls Clubs 1990-92; bd dir Christmas in April 1989-. **Honors/Awds:** Am Assoc Pub Adm Outstand Pub Serv 1984; NAACP Legal Def & Ed Fund Excptnl Achvmnts 1984; Outstand Pub Serv AKA 1984; Kappa Alpha Psi 1982; Alpha Phi Alpha 1978; Omega Psi Phi 1977; Outstanding Achievements in Human Rights, TX State NAACP, 1983; Intl Book of Honor 1986; International Professional and Business Women Hall of Fame, 1994; Woman of Distinction, Commission for Women, 1997; Leadership Montgomery, 1997. **Home Addr:** 13320 Bea Kay Dr, Silver Spring, MD 20904. **Business Phone:** (301)468-4260.

SHANNON, ROBERT F.
Educator. **Personal:** Born Jul 15, 1920, Montgomery, AL; married Eloise Wynn; children: Robert, Yolanda, Valerie, Charles. **Educ:** AL State Tchrs Coll, BS 1940; Wayne State U, MA 1955, EdS 1974. **Career:** Detroit Bd Educ In-School Neighborhood Youth Corps, proj dir; Detroit Bd Educ, admin 1968-, elem staff coord 1967-68, job upgrading & Couns 1965-67, teacher1964-65; Neighborhood Serv Org, group worker 1954-64. **Orgs:** Mem educ com Detroit Urban League 1972-73; trustee Detroit Counc for Youth Serv Inc 1971-; subcom on Juvenile Delinq State of MI 1968-71; pres bd trust Afro-Am Museum of Detroit 1974; deacon Tabernacle Bapt Ch 1961; mem bd dir Met Detroit Soc of Black Educ Adminstrs 1971. **Honors/Awds:** Outstanding serv to sch & comm Wash Sch PTA 1963; Outstndng Man of Year Tabernacle Bapt Ch 1964; Youth Serv Awrd Hannan Br YMCA 1969-71; Crisis Team Intervention in Sch-Comm Unrest Social Casework 1971. **Military Serv:** AUS pfc 1943-46. **Business Addr:** 10100 Grand River, Detroit, MI 48204.

SHANNON, SYLVESTER LORENZO
Clergyman. **Personal:** Born May 25, 1935, Pelham, GA; son of Maude Kelly Shannon and J Powell Shannon; married Doris Brooks Shannon, Dec 28, 1957; children: Glenn Leroy, Keith Lester, Theresa LaVonne. **Educ:** Florida A&M Univ, AB/BS, 1955; Duke Univ Divinity School. BDiv/MDiv, 1966, ThM, 1973; Univ of Kansas, PhD, 1974. **Career:** US Army, staff chaplain, 1966-81; Laconia Assocs, pres/CEO, 1979-99; Thyne Memorial Presbyterian Church, pastor, 1987-90; Siloam Presbyterian Church, senior pastor, 1990-. **Orgs:** President, Duke Divinity School National Alumni Council, 1992-93; convention chaplain, Alpha Phi Alpha Frat, 1979-97; candidate for general president, Alpha Phi Alpha Fraternity; chairman of the board, Living Water Ministries International, 1979-. **Honors/Awds:** Eagle Scout, 1948; House of Reps Scholarship, 1951-55; Mary Reynolds Babcock Scholarship, 1963-66; Legion of Merit, 1968. **Business Addr:** Senior Pastor, Siloam Presbyterian Church, 260 Jefferson Ave, Brooklyn, NY 11216, (718)789-7050.

SHARP, CHARLES LOUIS
Business executive. **Personal:** Born May 19, 1951, Madisonville, KY; son of Macindy and Charlie Sharp. **Educ:** General Motors Scholar, 1969-73; Millikin Univ, BS 1973; Washington Univ, MBA 1975. **Career:** RJ Reynolds Tobacco USA, brand asst 1975-77, brand mgr 1978-81, planning mgr 1982-86, group mgr 1986-90; Winston-Salem State Univ, Winston-Salem, NC, instructor, 1990; Univ of Louisville, Louisville, KY, instructor, mgt sci; UW-Madison, School of Business, instructor, currently. **Orgs:** Big Brother/Big Sister 1983-87; mem YMCA 1984-; treas Civic Devel Council 1987. **Honors/Awds:** Appreciation Cert Black Exec Exchange Prog, Amer Marketing Assn. **Home Addr:** 905 Lime Spring Way, Louisville, KY 40223. **Business Addr:** Instructor, Univ of Wisconsin-Madison, Madison, WI 53706-1323, (608)265-4830.

SHARP, J. ANTHONY
Educational administrator, aviation consultant. **Personal:** Born Dec 27, 1946, Norfolk, VA; son of Viola Brown Sharp and James A Sharp; married Khalilah Z Sharp, Jan 1975 (divorced 1986); children: Tahmir T, Aleem S. **Educ:** Norfolk State University, Norfolk, VA, undergraduate study, 1968-70; Long Island University, Brooklyn, NY, BA, political science, (cum laude), 1971; New York University, New York, NY, MA, political science, 1972; Yavapai Community College, Prescott, AZ, AA, general education, 1982; University of Miami, Coral Gables, FL, PhD, higher education. **Career:** US Air Force, aircraft mechanic, 1964-68; Embry-Riddle Aero University, flight instructor & flight supervisor, 1978-81; Hawthorne Aviation, contract & charter pilot, 1982-83; Elizabeth City State University, adjunct instructor airway science, 1986; Hampton University, assistant professor airway science, 1986-89; Florida Memorial College, Division of Airway & Computer Sciences, chairperson, 1989-94; Nova Southeastern Univ, prof of technology, 1994-96. **Orgs:** Aircraft Owners & Pilot Association, 1976-; president, National Association of Minorities in Aviation,

1976-; Tuskegee Airmen, Inc, 1987-90; University Aviation Association, 1989-; Negro Airmen International, 1990-; 100 Black Men of South Florida, 1991-; American Institute of Aeronautics and Astronautics, 1989-; Magnet Educational Choice Association Inc of Dade County, board member, 1992. **Honors/Awds:** Arizona Flight Instructor of the Year, Scottsdale, AZ, 1980. **Military Serv:** US Air Force, sgt, 1964-68; US Armed Forces Air Medal, 1968. **Business Addr:** 449 South 51st Ct, Renton, WA 98055.

SHARP, JAMES ALFRED
Company executive. **Personal:** Born May 28, 1933, New York, NY; married Tessie Marie Baltrip; children: Owen, Jacqueline A, James A III, LaTanya M. **Educ:** Univ of CA San Diego, attended; Harvard Univ, attended. **Career:** US Marine Corps, retired 1st sgt 20 yrs; US Senate, Senator Donald Riegle Jr, mgr state serv 11 yrs; City of Flint MI, mayor, 1983-87; City Mgmt Corp, vice pres of community & government affairs, 1988-. **Military Serv:** USMC 20 yrs; Served in Korea, Cuba, Vietnam; Vietnam Cross of Gallantry; 3 Navy Commendation Medals for Valor; Purple Heart. **Business Addr:** VP, Community and Government Affairs, City Management Corp, 3400 E Lafayette, Detroit, MI 48226.

SHARP, JEAN MARIE
Educational administrator. **Personal:** Born Dec 31, 1945, Gary, IN. **Educ:** Ball State U, BA 1967; IN U, MA Tchng 1969; Columbia Univ Tchrs Coll, EdM 1975, EdD 1976. **Career:** Montclair Bd of Educ, dir of pupil 1978-, asst supt for admin serv 1978; Office for Human & Devel Serv, special asst to asst sec 1977; Gen Asst Center Columbia Univ, field specialist 1976; W Side HS Gary IN, dept chmn/teacher 1969-72; Froebel HS Gary IN, teacher 1966-68. **Orgs:** Mem Am Assn of Sch Admnstrs 1980; mem Black Child Dev Inst 1980; mem Kappa Delta Pi 1980; coord 1st & 2nd Annual Black Representation Org Symposiums1973-74; tchr (vol) Uhuru Sasa Sch Brooklyn 1975; vice pres Nu Age Cntr of Harlem 1979-. **Honors/Awds:** Outstndng Yng Women of the Yr United Fedn of Women 1971; Doctoral Prgm in Educ Ldrshp Flwshp Ford Fdn 1973-76; Student Sen Awrd of Merit & Serv Columbia Univ New York City 1974; Human Resources Flwshp Rockefeller Fnd 1977. **Business Addr:** Montclair Board of Education, 22 Valley Road, Montclair, NJ 07042.

SHARP, SAUNDRA
Writer, actress, filmmaker. **Personal:** Born Dec 21, 1942, Cleveland, OH; daughter of Faythe McIntyre Sharp and Garland Clarence Sharp. **Educ:** Bowling Green State Univ, Bowling Green OH, BS, 1964; attended Los Angeles City Coll, Los Angeles CA, 1980-84, 1989. **Career:** Plays: ''Black Girl,'' ''To Be Young, Gifted, and Black,'' ''Hello, Dolly!''; TV series: ''Wonder Woman,'' ''Knots Landing,'' ''St. Elsewhere''; author: Typing in the Dark, poetry, Harlem River Press, 1991; From The Windows of My Mind, poetry volumes, 1970; In the Midst of Change, 1972; Soft Song, 1978; Black Women For Beginners, Writers and Readers Publishing, 1993; playwright: ''The Sistuhs''; Voices Inc, Los Angeles, CA, head writer, 1988-; Black Film Review, former associate editor; Black Anti-Defamation Coalition, newsletter, former editor; publisher/editor: The Black History Film List; Poets Pay Re Too, 1989; publisher: Blood Lines, Robert Earl Price, 1978; Directory of Black Film/TV Technicians and Artists, West Coast, 1980; Actress, tv appearances include: The Learning Tree, Hollow Image, Minstrel Man, One More Hurdle: The Donna Cheek Story; Produced, wrote, and directed: Picking Tribes, Life is a Saxaphone, Back Inside Herself. **Orgs:** Black American Cinema Society; founding member, Reel Black Women; Atlanta African Film Society; literacy tutor/volunteer. **Honors/Awds:** 1st place, Black American Film Society, 1984, 1989, for film production; 1st place, San Francisco Poetry Film Festival, 1985; Heritage Magazine Award for outstanding journalism, 1988; Paul Robeson Award, Newark Black Film Festival, 1989; California Arts Council, Artist Grant, 1992; Black Filmmakers Hall of Fame, Best Script Award, 1992. **Business Addr:** PO Box 75796, Sanford Sta, Los Angeles, CA 90075.

SHARPE, AUDREY HOWELL
Educator, educational administrator. **Personal:** Born Dec 14, 1938, Elizabeth City, NC; daughter of Essie Griffin Howell and Simon Howell; married Willie M, Aug 7, 1964; children: Kimberly Y. **Educ:** Hampton Inst, BS 1960; Northwestern Univ, MA 1966; Ball State Univ, EdD 1980. **Career:** State of IN Ft Wayne, speech & hearing therapist 1960-62; State of IL Dixon, hearing & speech specialist 1962-64; Ft Wayne, speech & hearing therapist 1964-65; Univ of MI Children's Psychiatric Hospital Ann Arbor, educational diagnostician language pathic asst prin 1965-68; E Wayne State Center Ft Wayne, Headstart dir 1968-69; Purdue Univ, lecturer in educ 1968-69; East Allen Co School, Title I teacher 1973-74, Title I coordinator, 1974, principal; Village Woods Jr High, asst principal 1980-81; Village Elementary School, principal 1981-84; School & Community Relations, dir, 1994-. **Orgs:** Amer Speech & Hearing Assn 1961-74; Assn for Children with Learning Disabilities 1968; bd dir Three Rivers Assn for Children with Learning Disabilities 1969-72; Delta Sigma Theta; Alpha Kappa Mu; Kappa Delta Pi; First Presbyterian Church of Ft Wayne, IN; Delta Sigma Theta Sorority; Assn for Supervision & Curriculum Devel; board of directors Erin's House; Leadership, Ft Wayne; bd dir YWCA 1984-87; Jr League of Ft Wayne; Ft Wayne Alliance of Black School Eductors. **Honors/Awds:** Delta Sigma Theta, Woman of the Year, 1973; Florene Williams Service Award, 1986; Phi Beta Sigma, Educator of the Year, 1987, Educational Service Award, 1988; Kappa Alpha Psi Fraternity, Service Award, 1984-85. **Special Achievements:** Author: ''Another View of Affective Education: The Four H's-Honesty, Humaneness, Humility, and Hope,'' Principal, Fall 1985; ''Language Training in Headstart Programs,'' ISHA, Spring 1969; ''Pass Me That Language Ticket,'' Principal, Spring 1986; ''Physical Education, A No Frills Component to the Elementary Curriculum,'' Principal, Fall 1984; guest columnist: Fort Wayne News-Sentinel; Frost Illustrated. **Home Addr:** 6727 Lakecrest Ct, Fort Wayne, IN 46815. **Business Addr:** Director, School & Community Relations, East Allen County Schools, 1000 Prospect Ave, New Haven, IN 46774.

SHARPE, CALVIN WILLIAM
Educator, arbitrator. **Personal:** Born Feb 22, 1945, Greensboro, NC; daughter of Mildred Johnson Sharpe and Ralph David Sharpe; married Janice McCoy Jones; children: Kabral, Melanie, Stephanie. **Educ:** Clark Coll, BA 1967; Oberlin Coll, Post-Baccalaureate 1968; Chicago Theological Seminary, attended 1969-71, MA, 1996; Northwestern Univ Law Sch, JD 1974. **Career:** Hon Hubert L Will US District Court, law clerk 1974-76; Cotton Watt Jones King & Bowlus Law Firm, assoc 1976-77; Natl Labor Relations Bd, trial attorney 1977-81; Univ of VA Law School, asst prof 1981-84; Case Western Reserve Univ, prof of law (tenured) 1984-; Arizona State University College of Law (Tempe), scholar-in-residence, 1990; George Washington University National Law Center, DC, visiting professor, 1991; Case Western Reserve University Law School, professor/associate dean, academic affairs, 1991-92; De Paul Univ College of Law, Distinguished Visiting Professor, 1995-96; Chicago-Kent Coll of Law, visiting scholar. **Orgs:** National Academy of Arbitrators 1991-; convener/first chair, Labor and Employment Law Section, IRRA, 1994-96; labor panel Amer Arbitration Assoc 1984-; bd of trustees Cleveland Hearing & Speech Ctr 1985-89; mem OH State Employment Relations Bd Panel of Neutrals 1985-; Phoenix Employment Relations Bd Panel of Neutrals; Los Angeles City Employee Relations Bd Panel of Neutrals; chair-evidence section Assn of Amer Law Schools 1987; Assn of Amer Law Schools Committee on Sections and Annual Meeting 1991-94; exec bd Public Sector Labor Relations Assoc 1987-89; Federal Mediation and Conciliation Serv Roster of Arbitrators 1987-; Permanent Arbitrator State of Ohio, OH Health Care Employees Assoc Dist 1199, 1987-92; AFSCME/OCSEA, 1987-92; State Council of Professional Educators OEA/NEA 1989-; Federation of Police 1988-92; Youth Services Subsidy Advisory Bd of Commissioners, Cuyahoga County Ohio 1989. **Honors/Awds:** Publications: ''Two-Step Balancing and the Admissibility of Other Crimes Evidence, A Sliding Scale of Proof,'' 59 Notre Dame Law Review 556, 1984; ''Proof of Non-Interest in Representation Disputes, A Burden Without Reason,'' 11 Univ Dayton Law Review 3, 1985; ''Fact-Finding in Ohio, Advancing the Pole of Rationality in Public Sector Collective Bargaining,'' Univ of Toledo Law Review, 1987; ''NLRB Deferral to Grievance-Arbitration, A General Theory,'' 48 Ohio St LJ No 3, 1987; Introduction, The Natl War Labor Bd and Critical Issues in the Development of Modern Grievance Arbitration, 39 Case W Res L Rev No 2, 1988; A Study of Coal Arbitration Under the National Bituminous Coal Wage Agreement-Between 1975 and 1991, vol 93, issue 3, National Coal Issue, West Virginia Law Review; ''The Art of Being A Good Advocate,'' Dispute Resolution Journal, January 1995; ''Judging in Good Faith — Seeing Justice Marshall's Legacy Through A Labor Case,'' 26 Arizona State LJ 479 (1994); ''From An Arbitrator's Point of View—The Art of Being a Good Advocate;'' Dispute Resolution Journal, 1995; Book Review: Edward J Imwinkelreid, Evidentiary Distinction: Understanding the Federal Rules of Evidence, 1993; and Arthus Best, Evidence and Explanations, 1993; 46 J Legal Ed 150, 1996. **Home Addr:** PO Box 606078, Cleveland, OH 44106. **Business Addr:** Prof of Law, Case Western Reserve Univ, 11075 East Boulevard, Cleveland, OH 44106.

SHARPE, RONALD M.
Law enforcement executive. **Personal:** Born Apr 16, 1940, Philadelphia, PA; son of Elizabeth Morgan Sharpe and Cornelius Wendell Sharpe; married Jessie L. Sowell, May 1, 1965; children: Martin, Tracey, Jennifer. **Educ:** Northwestern Univ, Evanston IL, Police Admin Trng, 1968; Elizabethtown College, Elizabethtown PA, BA, 1975; St Francis College, Loretto PA, MA, 1978; additional graduate study at Temple Univ. **Career:** Pennsylvania State Police, Hershey PA, 1962, Harrisburg PA, corporal, 1969, Washington PA, sergeant, 1976, Lancaster PA, lieutenant, 1977, Milesburg PA, captain, 1985, Harrisburg PA, major, 1986, deputy commissioner, 1987, commissioner, 1987—. **Orgs:** International Association of Chiefs of Police, National Org of Black Law Enforcement Executives, Pennsylvania Chiefs of Police Association, NAACP. **Honors/Awds:** Law Enforcement Oscar, Philadelphia Housing Police & International Union of Police Assn; achievement awards from Optimist Club, Lions Club, 5th Masonic District, and 111th Tactical Air Support Group. **Business Addr:** Commissioner, Pennsylvania State Police, 1800 Elmerton Ave, Harrisburg, PA 17110.

SHARPE, SHANNON
Professional football player. **Personal:** Born Jun 26, 1968, Glenville, GA. **Educ:** Savannah State. **Career:** Denver Broncos, tight end, 1990-. **Honors/Awds:** Pro Bowl appearances, 1992-96. **Business Addr:** Professional Football Player, Denver Broncos, 13655 Broncos Pkwy, Englewood, CO 80112, (303)649-9000.

SHARPE, V. RENEE
Technical consultant. **Personal:** Born Oct 24, 1953, Jackson, TN; daughter of Vermon Huddleston Cathey and Marvin Cathey. **Educ:** Memphis State University, Memphis, TN, BBA, 1974; MBA, 1979; State Technical Institute, Memphis, TN, AAS, 1976. **Career:** Transamerica Insurance, Los Angeles, CA, project leader, 1979-81; Federal Express Corp, Memphis, TN, technical consultant, 1981-. **Orgs:** National corr secty, Black Data Processing Associates, 1991-92; president, Memphis chapter, Black Data Processing Associates, 1989-90; student tutor, Neighborhood Christian Center, 1982-95, member, NAACP, 1989-90; member, Association of Female Executives, 1986-95; Allocations Committee, United Way of Greater Memphis. **Business Addr:** Technical Consultant, Systems & Sort Engineering Dept, Federal Express Corp, 2955 Republican Dr, Memphis, TN 38118.

SHARPER, DARREN
Professional football player. **Personal:** Born Nov 3, 1975. **Educ:** William & Mary, BA degree in sociology. **Career:** Green Bay Packers, defensive back, 1997-. **Business Addr:** Professional Football Player, Green Bay Packers, 1265 Lombardi Ave, Green Bay, WI 54304, (414)494-2351.

SHARPERSON, MICHAEL TYRONE
Professional baseball player. **Personal:** Born Oct 4, 1961, Orangeburg, SC. **Educ:** DeKalb Community College South. **Career:** Toronto Blue Jays, professional baseball player, 1987; Los Angeles Dodgers, third baseman, shortstop, 1987-. **Business Addr:** Professional Baseball Player, Los Angeles Dodgers, 1000 Elysian Park Ave, Los Angeles, CA 90012, (213)224-1530.

SHARPLESS, MATTIE
Federal government official. **Educ:** North Carolina Central Univ. **Career:** USIA Foreign Service, minister/counselor, currently. **Business Addr:** Minister/Counselor, USDA Office of Agricultural Affairs, 2, Ave Gabriel, 75008 Paris, France, 33-1-43-12-22-77.

SHARPP, NANCY CHARLENE
Social service administrator. **Personal:** Born in Pine Bluff, AR; married Tilmon Lee Sharpp; children: Tilmon Monroe. **Educ:** Wayne St Univ, BA 1961; Governors St Univ, MA 1976. **Career:** IL Dept of Corrections Juvenile Div, supervisor, admin 1966-79; IL Dept Children & Family Services, manager for support services 1979-81, case review admin 1981-; West Maywood Park Dist, pres bd of commrs. **Orgs:** Panelist Panel of American Women 1968-72; founder/past pres Chicago Area Club-Nat'l Assoc of Negro Business & Prof Womens Clubs, Inc 1977-82; founder Ascension to Manhood, Inc 1982; life mem Nat'l Assoc of Negro Business Prof Womens Clubs, Inc; appointed commr of West Maywood Park Dist 1981; elected to 2 yrunexpired term 1983; elected to 6 yr term 1985. **Honors/Awds:** Nat'l Presidents Award Nat'l Assoc of Negro Business & Prof Womens Clubs, Inc 1977; Sperry-Hutchins Comm Service Award Sperry-Hutchins Corp/NANBPW, Inc 1981; Comm Image Award Fred Hampton Mem Scholarship Fund, Inc 1983. **Business Addr:** President Bd of Commissioners, West Maywood Park District, 16th and Washington, Maywood, IL 60153.

SHARPTON, ALFRED CHARLES, JR. (AL)
Clergyman. **Personal:** Born Oct 3, 1954, Brooklyn, NY; son of Ada Richards Sharpton and Alfred C Sharpton Sr; married Kathy Jordan, Oct 31, 1985; children: Dominique, Ashley. **Career:** SCLC Operation Breadbasket, NY, youth director, 1969-71; National Youth Movement Inc, founder, president, 1971-86; Washington Temple Church of God in Christ, junior pastor; National Action Network Inc, founder, president, 1991-. **Orgs:** National Rainbow Coalition's Minister Division, national coordinator, 1993-; Bethany Baptist Church, Bklyn, associate minister, 1994-. **Honors/Awds:** Man of the Year Award, Omega Psi Phi Fraternity; City of Orange, Key to the City, 1993; New York State Cultural Society, Man of the Year, 1993; SCLC, Buffalo Chapter, Community Service Award, 1992; Goldsmith College, London, England, Fellow Award, 1991; Caribbean-American Lobby, Man of the Year, 1992. **Special Achievements:** First African-American Senate candidate in New York history, US Senate Democratic Primary, New York State, 1992; US Senate NY Democratic Primary received 27% of statewide vote, 90% of black statewide vote; Go and Tell Pharaoh: The Autobiography of Al Sharpton, 1996; NYC Mayoral candidate, 1997. **Business Addr:** President, National Action Network, 1941 Madison Ave, New York, NY 10035, (718)398-1669.

SHARPTON, DENISE
Public relations executive. **Personal:** Born Jul 18, 1958, Vero Beach, FL; daughter of Raymond Sharpton. **Educ:** Florida A&M University, 1976-78; Florida State University, BS, 1979. **Career:** KKDA Radio, news anchor, public affairs host; SHARP/PR, president, currently. **Orgs:** Multi-Ethnic Heritage Foundation, chairman. **Honors/Awds:** Iota Phi Lambda, Businesswoman of the Year, 1993. **Business Addr:** President, Sharp/PR, PO Box 710452, Dallas, TX 75371, (214)821-9000.

SHARRIEFF, OSMAN IBN
Journalist. **Personal:** Born May 9, 1935, Corinth, MS; son of Maryam Bankhead Sharrieff and Osman Sharrieff; married Gloria Howard Sharrieff, May 7, 1989; children: Sabakhan, Laela. **Educ:** Univ of Bordeux France, Journalism 1958-59; Chicago Loop Jr Coll, Polit Sci 1960-62; Univ of Chicago, Linguistics 1961; Al-Azhar Univ Egypt, Islamic Culture 1970-71. **Career:** Tri-City Journal, publisher. **Orgs:** Chmn Black Media Reps 1974; vice pres Black Media Inc 1975-87. **Honors/Awds:** Black Media Rep Serv 1974; Best Feature Article NNPA 1976; Best News Picture NNPA 1977. **Military Serv:** AUS pfc 2 yrs. **Business Addr:** Publisher, Tri-City Journal, 18 South Michigan, Chicago, IL 60603.

SHAW, ALVIA A.
Clergyman. **Personal:** Born May 7, 1915, Duarte, CA; married Ruth; children: Alvia, Jr, Wendell. **Educ:** Univ of So CA;; BA; Pacific Sch of Religion, MDiv. **Career:** St James AME Ch Cleveland, pastor 1968-; St Paul AME Ch Columbus OH, former pastor; First AME Ch, former pastor 1951-56. **Orgs:** Mem OH AME Conv; consult Nat Council of Ch; mem NAACP. **Honors/Awds:** Recipient hon DD Payne Theol Sem. **Military Serv:** AUS chaplain 1942-46. **Business Addr:** St James AME Church, 8401 Cedar Ave, Cleveland, OH 44103.

SHAW, ANN
Banking executive. **Personal:** Born Nov 21, 1921, Columbus, OH; daughter of Sarah Roberts White and Pearl Daniel White; widowed; children: Valerie, Leslie Jr, Rebecca, Dan. **Educ:** Univ of Redlands, LHD 1971; Univ So CA, MSW 1968; OH State U, MA 1944; Univ Redlands, AB 1943. **Career:** UCLA, tchr; LA Job Corps Ctr Women, exec asst 1965-66; LA City Sch, tchr 1949-51; Central St Coll, asst prof 1946-48; VA Union U, instr; Founders Savings & Loan Assoc, chmn of the bd, 1986-87. **Orgs:** Bd mem, The California Community Found, The California Medical Center Found, The Cathedral Corp of the Episcopal Church; appointed to serve on California Joint Select Task Force on the Changing Family; alumni assn; Univ So CA; OH State & Redlands U; PTA; Nat Council Negro Women; NAACP; appointed by Gov of CA 1st Black 1st Women to serve on State Commn on Judicial Performance 1976; mem YWCA World Serv Council; pres Wilfandel Club; mem Awds & Recognition Comm; sec corporate bd, United Way Inc; mem bd of visitors UCLA School of Med, Loyola Law School. **Honors/Awds:** Agency leadership awards & com Womens Div United Way; certificate merit Assn Study Negro Life & Hist 1964; Univ Redlands 1964; Woman of the Year LA Sentinel Newspaper 1964; Mother of the Year CA State Assn Colored Women Clubs 1967; Royal Blue Book; NAACP Legal Defense & Educ Fund Award Black Women of Achievement 1985; Big Sisters of Los Angeles Awd 1986; CA Senate Woman of the Year Awd for Senatorial Dist 30, 1987; United Way's Highest Honor The Gold Key Award; The Athena Award, YWCA, 1989; Community Serv Award, YWCA, 1989; The Key Council Award, California Afro-Amer Museum, 1989.

SHAW, ARDYTH M. (ARDY)
Newspaper executive. **Personal:** Born Feb 13, 1941, San Diego, CA; daughter of Louise White Love and Joseph Estes; married Solomon Shaw (divorced 1976); children: Rodney Terrence Shaw, Tiffani Aaris Shaw. **Educ:** University of California at San Diego, San Diego, CA; National University, San Diego, CA; San Diego City College, San Diego, CA. **Career:** City Attorney, San Diego, CA, confidential secretary, 1962-77; KPBS Radio, San Diego, CA, talk show hostess/producer, 1974-80; The San Diego Union, San Diego, CA, executive assistant to the editor, 1978-; KSDO Radio, San Diego, CA, talk show hostess/producer, 1981-89; The San Diego Union-Tribune, comm relations coord, 1993-. **Orgs:** Member, San Diego Press Club, 1978-; chair, YMCA Human Development Services, 1987-; member, National Organization of Black Journalists, 1982-; State of California Youth in Government, board of governors; San Diego Opera, board of directors, 1991-; Villa View Community Hospital, women's advisory board, 1991-; San Diego Lions Club, 1995-; Gaslamp Quarter Foundation, 1993-95; bd of dir, San Diego Community Foundation, 1996-. **Honors/Awds:** Civic Leadership Award, Mexican-American Foundation, 1990; Best Editorial of San Diego County (radio), National Council of Christians and Jews, 1989; Award of Achievement (journalism), Action Enterprise Development, 1980; featured in San Diego Woman Magazine (cover story), 1987; featured, "What It's Like to Work for a Newspaper," Cosmopolitan Magazine, July, 1985; Profile of Achievement, Career Focus Magazine, April, 1989; "Woman of the Year," Alvarado Parkway Institute, 1992; YMCA Golden Triangle Award, highest volunteer award, 1994; Woman of Distinction, La Jolla Soroptimists, 1994.

SHAW, BERNARD
Television news anchor. **Personal:** Born May 22, 1940, Chicago, IL; son of Camilla Murphy Shaw and Edgar Shaw; married Linda Allston, Mar 30, 1974; children: Amar Edgar, Anil Louise. **Educ:** University of Illinois at Chicago Circle, history, 1963. **Career:** WYNR/WNUS-Radio, Chicago IL, reporter, 1964-66; Westinghouse Broadcasting Co, Chicago IL, reporter, 1966-68; correspondent in Washington DC, 1968-71; Columbia Broadcasting System (CBS), Washington DC, television reporter, 1971-74, correspondent, 1974-77; American Broadcasting Co (ABC), Miami FL, correspondent and chief of Latin American bureau, 1977-79; Cable News Network (CNN), Washington DC, television news anchor, 1980-. **Orgs:** National Press Club; Sigma Delta Chi. **Honors/Awds:** Honorary doctorate, Marion College, 1985; Distinguished Service Award, Congressional Black Caucus, 1985; named to top ten outstanding business and professional honorees list, 1988; Natl Academy of Cable Programming, Golden Award for Cable Excellence, ACE, 1991; George Foster Peabody Broadcasting Award, 1990; Gold Medal, International Film and TV Festival; National Headliner Award; Overseas Press Club Award; Lowell Thomas Electronic Journalism Award, 1988; Natl Academy of Cable Programming, Golden Award for Cable Excellence, Best New Anchor, 1988, Best Newscaster, 1991, Best Newscaster, 1993; NAACP, Chairman's Award for Outstanding Journalistic Excellence, 1992; Eduard Rhein Foundation, Cultural Journalistic Award, 1991, first non-German to receive; Italian Government, President's Award, 19 Barry University, David Brinkley Award, Excellence in Communications, 1991; Society of Professional Journalists, Fellow; Congress of Racial Equality, Dr Martin Luther King Jr Award for Outstanding Achievement, 1993; University of Missouri, Honor Medal for Distinguished Service in Journalism, 1992; Natl News & Documentary Competition, Emmy Award, with CNN, 1992; Univ of Kansas, William Allen White Medallion for Distinguished Service, 1994; Natl Conference of Christians and Jews-Miami Region, Natl Headliner Award, 1994; Best Newscaster of the Year ACE for "Inside Politics '92," 1993; Congress of Racial Equality, Dr MArting Luther King Jr Award for Outstanding Achievement, 1993; Natl Assn of Black Journalists, Journalist of the Year, 1989; Univ of Chicago, Honorary Doctor of Humane Letters Degree, 1993; Northeastern Univ, honorary doctorate, 1994; Trumpet Award, 1997. **Special Achievements:** Held exclusive interview with Saddam Hussein, Operation Desert Storm, October 1990; presidential debate moderator, second debate in Los Angeles, 1988; Democratic presidential candidates' debate moderator, third debate, 1992; first correspondent/anchor to break the news of Jan 17, 1994, Los Angeles earthquake; anchored CNN's live coverage of President Bill Clinton's first Economic Summit from Tokyo, 1993. **Military Serv:** US Marine Corps, 1959-63. **Business Addr:** Principal Washington Anchor, CNN America, Inc, The CNN Building, 820 First St NE, 11th Fl, Washington, DC 20002.

SHAW, BOOKER THOMAS
Judge. **Personal:** Born Sep 14, 1951, St Louis, MO. **Educ:** Southern IL Univ at Carbondale, BA, govt, 1973; Catholic Univ of Amer, JD, 1976; MO Bar, 1976; Natl Judicial Clg, 1983; Amer Academy of Judicature, 1989. **Career:** Fed Trade Commiss, law clerk 1974; Columbus Comm Legal Svcs, law clerk 1975-76; Circuit Attny Office, asst circuit attny 1976-83; MO 22nd Circuit Court, judge 1983-. **Orgs:** Mound City Bar Assn; Metro Bar Assn; St John AME Church, trustee; Natl Bar Assn. **Honors/Awds:** Southern IL Univ, Scholarship Awd in Music, 1970-72; Spirit of St Louis Scholarship Awd, 1975; Am-Jur Book Award, 1976; Distinguished Service, Mound City Bar, 1983; Distinguished Service, Circuit Attny, St Louis, 1983; Black Law Students, Washington University, Outstanding Service, 1989; Judicial Cncl, Natl Bar Assn, Outstanding Service, 1992. **Business Addr:** Judge, Missouri 22nd Circuit Court, #10 N Tucker, Civil Courts Bldg, St Louis, MO 63101.

SHAW, BRIAN K.
Professional basketball player. **Personal:** Born Mar 22, 1966, Oakland, CA. **Educ:** St Mary's College, Moraga, CA, 1983-85; Univ of California at Santa Barbara, Santa Barbara, CA, 1986-88. **Career:** Boston Celtics, guard, 1988-89, 1990-91; played in Italy, 1989-90; Miami Heat, 1991-94; Orlando Magic, 1994-97; Golden State Warriors, 1997-98; Philadelphia 76ers, 1998-. **Honors/Awds:** NBA All-Rookie Second Team, 1989. **Business Addr:** Professional Basketball Player, Philadelphia 76ers, One Corestates Complex, Philadelphia, PA 19148, (215)339-7676.

SHAW, CARL BERNARD
Restaurateur, entrepreneur. **Personal:** Born Jan 4, 1964, Detroit, MI; son of Cyrus & Louise. **Educ:** Eastern Michigan University, Business/Information Systems, 1990. **Career:** Detroit Public Schools, adult education teacher, 1985-87; Automatic Data Processing, sr computer operator; The Stroh Brewey Co, business analyst, 1987-; Cafe Mahogany, Inc, pres, currently. **Orgs:** Alpha Phi Alpha Fraternity Inc, 1984-. **Business Addr:** President, Cafe Mahogany, 1465 Centre, Detroit, MI 48226, (313)235-2233.

SHAW, CHARLES A.
Judge. **Personal:** Born Dec 31, 1944, Jackson, TN; son of Sarah and Alvis Shaw; married Kathleen Marie Ingram; children: Bryan Ingram. **Educ:** Harris-Stowe Coll, BA, 1966; Univ of Missouri, MBA, 1971; Catholic Univ of Amer, JD, 1974. **Career:** Berlin Roisman & Kessler, law clerk, 1972; Dept of Justice, Law Enforcement Asst Admin, law clerk, 1972-73; Office of Mayor, DC, assigned to DC publ school, hearing officer, 1973-74; Natl Labor Relations Bd (enforcement litigation div DC), attorney, 1973-76; Lashly-Caruthers-Thies-Rava & Hamel (law firm), attorney, 1976-80; Dept of Justice, E Dist of Missouri, asst US attorney, 1980-87; State of Missouri, circuit judge, 1987-94; US District Judge, currently. **Orgs:** Chairperson, labor mgmt relations comm, Amer Bar Assn Young Lawyers Div, 1976-77; MO state vice chairperson, Econ of Law Section Amer Bar Assn, 1976-77; comm mem, Lawyers Fee Dispute Comm, St Louis Met Bar Assn, 1979-80; mem, Am Bar Assn, MO Bar Assn, DC Bar Assn, MO State & Corporate Comm, United Negro Coll Fund, 1978-80, NAACP, Catholic Univ Law School Alumni Assn, Harris-Stowe Coll Alumni Assn; bd mem, St Louis Black Forum, 1979-80, bd of trustees, St Louis Art Museum, 1979-80, 1992-96; Mound City Bar Assn, 1976-; Sigma Pi Phi Fraternity 1988-. **Honors/Awds:** St Louis Leadership Fellow, Danforth Found, 1978-79; Distinguished Serv Citation, United Negro Coll Fund, 1979; St Louis Public Schools Law and Education Service Award, 1984; Wellston School District Service Award, 1987-; Harris Stowe State College Distinguished Alumni Award, 1988; Catholic Univ, BLSA Distinguished Alumni Award, 1994. **Business Addr:** US District Ct, 1114 Market St, St Louis, MO 63101.

SHAW, CURTIS MITCHELL
Attorney. **Personal:** Born Apr 13, 1944, Jacksonville, TX; married Ann (divorced); children: Caja, Curtis Jr, Alexis. **Educ:** Univ of NM, BS 1967; Loyola Univ of LA, JD 1975. **Career:** Priv Prac, atty; Musical Entertainers & Motion Picture Personalities, rep; Denver Public Schools, educator; LA Unified School Dist Bd; Hollywood Chamber of Commerce; LA Co Bar Assn; Langston Law Club; Amer Bar Assn; Beverly Hills Bar Assn. **Orgs:** Dir num motion picture & prod cos. **Business Addr:** 6255 Sunset Blvd, Ste 2000, Hollywood, CA 90028.

SHAW, DENISE
Attorney. **Personal:** Born Feb 19, 1949, Los Angeles, CA. **Educ:** Bard Coll, AB 1971; Univ of PA Sch of Law, JD 1974. **Career:** US Dept of HUD Ofc of Reg Couns, atty; Texaco, law clk 1972; Yvonne Burke Asmblywmn, legis intern 1970. **Orgs:** Mem PA Bar Assn; bd dir Bishop RR Wright Meml Hlth Ctr; civ rghts com PA Bar Assn; Legal Educ Com Nat Bar Assn; Hous Com; Civ Rghts Com;adminstrv law com Fed Bar Assn. **Honors/Awds:** Prfrmnc awd Ofc of Gen Couns Dept of HUD. **Business Addr:** Brad College Alumni Office, c/o Susan Mason, Annandale on Hudson, NY 12504.

SHAW, FERDINAND
Educator. **Personal:** Born May 30, 1933, McDonough, GA; children: Mark, Gail. **Educ:** OH State U, BS Nursing 1955; Boston U, MS 1957; Union Grad Sch, PhD cand 1980. **Career:** OH State Univ Sch of Nursing, asso prof 1973; OH State U, instr/asst prof 1957-73; Cincinnati Gen Hosp, staff nurse/asst head nurse 1955-56. **Orgs:** Adv com Am Nrs Assn RN Maternity Flwshp Prog 1973-; 2nd vice pres Am Nrs Assn 1974-76; chrprsn Am Nrs Assn Com on Human Rights 1976-; consult & review panel mem Div of Nrsng Dept of HEW 1965-74; bd mem Sex Info & Educ Council of US 1971-74; consult Womens Rsrch Staff Nat Inst of Educ Dept of HEW1975. **Honors/Awds:** Recipient Mortarboard Awrd OH State Univ 1970; Centennial Awrd OH State Univ Sch of Nursing 1970; awrd for Contrib to Orgn Nat Black Nurses Assn 1974-77; Flwshp Am Acad of Nursing Am Nurses Assn 1979. **Business Addr:** 830 K St Mall, Sacramento, CA 95814.

SHAW, HENRY
Automobile dealer. **Career:** Knox Ford, Inc, CEO, currently. **Special Achievements:** Company is ranked #80 on Black Enterprise's list of top 100 Auto Dealers, 1994. **Business Addr:** CEO, Knox Ford Inc, PO Box 759, Muldraugh, KY 40155, (502)942-2363.

SHAW, LEANDER J., JR.
State supreme court justice. **Personal:** Born Sep 6, 1930, Salem, VA; son of Margaret W Shaw (deceased) and Leander J Shaw Sr (deceased); children: Sean, Jerry, Sherri, Dione, Dawn. **Educ:** WV State Coll, BA 1952; Howard Univ, JD 1957. **Career:** FL A&M Univ, asst prof 1957-60; private practice, attorney 1960-69; Duval Co, asst pub defender 1965-69, asst state atty 1969-72; private practice Jacksonville, FL, attorney 1972-74; FL Industrial Relations Comm, comm 1974-79; State of FL 1st Dist Court of Appeal, judge 1979-83; FL Supreme Ct, justice 1983-, chief justice, 1990-92, justice, currently. **Orgs:** Chmn, bd of elections Amer Bar Assn, FL Bar Assn, Natl Bar Assn, FL Gov Bar Assn; dir FL Bar Found; adv Judicial Admin Commiss, State Traffic Courts Review Comm; chmn State Courts' Restructure Commiss; mem FL Assoc of Volunteer Agencies for Caribbean Action, Most Worshipful Union Grand Lodge Free & Accepted Masons of FL PHA Inc, Alpha Phi Alpha; Tallahassee Bar Assn; Amer Judicature Society; Natl

Ctr for State Courts; Appointment by Mayor of Jacksonville, FL, Police Advisory Comm, Human Relations Council, Jacksonville Jetport Authority, Bd Chairman of Jacksonville Opportunities Industrialization Ctr, Offender Research Advisory Committee; FL Standard Jury Instructions, Civil Comm, advisor; Ethnic Bias Study Commission, advisor; Guardian Ad Litem Program, advisor; FL Sentencing Guidelines Commission, chairman; Governor Chiles' Criminal Justice Task Force, chairman; Conference of Chief Justices, second vp; FL State Univ, Coll of Law, Bd of visitors; Natl Ctr for State Courts, bd of dirs; Amer Judicature Society, bd of dirs; Judicial Fellows Program of the Supreme Court of the US. **Honors/Awds:** Dedication to Justice FL Chap Natl Bar Assn 1977; Comm Service Jacksonville Bar Assn 1978; Exemplary Achievement in Judicial Serv State of FL Natl Bar Assn 1984; Honorary Doctor of Laws Degree, WV State Coll, 1986; FL Humanist of the Year Award, St Petersburg FL, 1991; Ben Franklin Award, St Petersburg FL, 1992. **Military Serv:** US Army, Lt, 1952-54. **Business Addr:** Florida Supreme Court, Supreme Court Building, 500 South Duval Street, Tallahassee, FL 32399-1925.

SHAW, MARIO WILLIAM
Administrator. **Personal:** Born Jan 9, 1929, Montgomery, AL; son of Alma Eliz Paige Shaw and James Henry Shaw Sr. **Educ:** St Johns Univ Collegeville, MN, AB 1954, STB 1956; Univ of Ottawa Can, STL 1960, STD (Cand); George Washington Univ, DC, post graduate study 1979. **Career:** St Maurs Sem, prof of Scripture 1956-59; Univ of Ottawa, inst in Rel 1960-61; St Maurs Sem, prof of Scripture 1960-65; Cath Sem Found of Indianapolis, adm 1965-75; St Augustine Manor, adm, 1976-. **Orgs:** Comm Peoria Housing Auth 1980; mem Pres Cncl Diocese of Peoria 1984-88; Clg of Cnsltrs 1984-88; vice pres Natl Black Catholic Clergy Caucus 1972-76; exec bd mem Crossroads of Amer Council BSA 1973-75; mem Sr Citizens Found 1977-80; chm Peoria Housing & Rehab Comm 1978-80. **Honors/Awds:** Rev & the Bible "Focus on Faith" (Wkly TV Prog) Channel 6 Indianapolis 1969-71; Rsrch Stds "Buffalo, NY, A Study of Dem Change 1940-70" 1974, "Christian Anti-Jewish Polemic" 1973. **Business Addr:** Administrator, St Augustine Manor, 1301 NE Glendale, Peoria, IL 61603.

SHAW, MARTINI
Cleric. **Personal:** Born Nov 6, 1959, Detroit, MI; son of Joyce Shaw and Melton Shaw. **Educ:** Wayne State University, BS, psychology, 1983, BA, biology, 1983; McCormick Theological Seminary, MDiv, 1988; Seabury-Western Theological Seminary, certificate of Anglican Studies, 1988. **Career:** Detroit Public Schools, teacher, 1983-85; St Johns Church, assistant to the rector, 1988-90; St Thomas Church, rector, 1990-. **Orgs:** NAACP, executive board, 1988-; Alpha Kappa Alpha, 1985-; Chicago Urban League, 1986- ; Church Federation of Chicago, chair, Ecumenical Affairs, 1988-90; Illinois Commission African-American Males, 1992-; Cook County Democrats, 1990-; Chase House Child Care, board of directors, 1988-; Union of Black Episcopalians, convention chaplain, 1993; Desegragation Monitoring, Chicago Bd of Ed, commissioner, 1995-. **Business Addr:** Rector, St Thomas Episcopal Church, 3801 S Wabash Ave, Chicago, IL 60653, (773)268-1900.

SHAW, MARY LOUISE
Educator. **Personal:** Born Mar 7, 1928, Oklahoma; married Ellis. **Educ:** Marinello Comer Beauty Sch 1964. **Career:** Bakersfield City School Dist, comm contact aide; Lincoln Jr HS, instructional aide; Fremont School, aide to school counselor. **Orgs:** Mem Bakersfield City Sch Dist Title I-SB 90, adv com; Region IV Parent Dir of CA Assn of Compensatory Educ 1975; mem Coalition ESEA Title I Parents 1975; conf seminar leader CACE Leadership Inservice 1975; mem Nat Cncl of Negro Women; CA State Assn of Colored Women's Club Inc; chmn Central Dist Parliamentarian CA State Assn of Colored Women's Club Inc 1968; pres Golden W Federated Women's Club Inc; pres Parent-Tchr Assn. **Business Addr:** Educ Center, 1300 Baker St, Bakersfield, CA 93305.

SHAW, MELVIN B.
Educational administrator. **Personal:** Born Dec 23, 1940, Memphis, TN; married Gwendolyn; children: Remel, Dana, Randall, Renee. **Educ:** Lane Coll, BS 1962; Memphis State Univ, MB Ed 1968; Harvard Business School, Ed Mgmt 1970. **Career:** Shelby Cty Bd of Ed, teacher 1962-68; Lane Coll, dir of devel 1968; TX Assoc of Coll, dir of devel 1970, exec dir 1973; United Negro Coll Fund, natl dir spec promos. **Orgs:** Mem Omega Psi Phi 1959. **Business Addr:** Vice Pres for Development, Charles R. Drew University of Medicine & Science, 1621 E. 120th St., Los Angeles, CA 90059-3025.

SHAW, NANCY H.
Executive director. **Personal:** Born Sep 24, 1942. **Educ:** Jarvis Christian Coll Hawkins TX, BA 1965. **Career:** Human Rights Commn Indianapolis & Marion Co, exec dir 1971-; IN Civil Rights Commn, dep dir 1970-71; Bd Fundamental Edn, spl asst pres 1969-70, mgr adminstrv servs 1968-69, adminstrv asst dir & educ 1967-68; Manpower Training Prog, employment counselor 1966-67; VISTA Training Prog, couns 1966; Flanner House, research asst 1965-66; Indianapolis Bus Dev Fndtn, vp; Comm Action Against Poverty, vp. **Orgs:** Mem Comp Health Planning Coun; Citizens Com Full Employment; bd dirs Comm Serv Coun Gr Indpls; racism com Episcopal Diocese So IN; All Saints Epis Ch.

SHAW, SEDRICK
Professional football player. **Personal:** Born Nov 16, 1973. **Educ:** Univ of Iowa, attended. **Career:** New England Patriots, running back, 1997-. **Business Addr:** Professional Football Player, New England Patriots, 60 Washington St, Foxboro Stadium, Foxboro, MA 02035, (508)543-7911.

SHAW, SPENCER GILBERT
Librarian, educator, consultant. **Personal:** Born Aug 15, 1916, Hartford, CT; son of Martha A Taylor Shaw and Eugene D Shaw. **Educ:** Hampton Univ, BS 1940; Univ WI Sch of Librarianship, BLS 1941; Univ Chicago, Grad Library Sch, advanced studies, 1948-49. **Career:** Hartford CT, br librarian 1940-43, 1945-48; Brooklyn Public Library, prgm coord, storytelling spec 1949-59; Nassau Co NY Library System, consult pub lib svc to children 1959-70; visiting faculty member at numerous universities: Queens Coll 1958-60, Drexel Univ 1962, Syracuse Univ 1964, Kent State Univ 1965, Univ MD 1968, Univ of IL 1969, Univ HI 1969-70, Univ WA 1961, Univ AK Anchorage 1974, Univ WI Madison 1979, University of North Carolina, 1992, University of North Texas, 1990-93; Univ WA, prof 1970-86, prof emeritus, 1986-; lecturer in Australia, New Zealand, Cyprus, Japan, Hong Kong, Canada, Mexico, England, Holland, France, Switzerland. **Orgs:** Amer Library Assn 1950-; WA Lib Media Assn 1970-; Pacific Northwest Lib Assn 1978; WA Lib Assn 1970-; Natl Council of the Tchrs of English 1970-; Beta Phi Mu 1949; Intl Reading Assn, 1970-. **Honors/Awds:** Carnegie Fellowship 1940; keynote speaker, 23rd World Congress, Intl Soc for Educ through Art, 1978; author, raconteur, film narrator 1945-; Spencer G Shaw Research Storytelling Collection, Invergargill Pub Lib, NZ, 1978; Grolier Found Award, 1983; profiled, TV series: Upon Reflections 1984, Faces of America 1985; cert of apprec, Univ of WA, Grad School of Library & Info Sci, 1986; Black Librarians of Puget Sound Plaque, 1986; Pres Award, WA Lib Assn, 1986; recog certif, King County Co, Seattle, 1986; Disting Serv Award, Black Caucus, Amer Lib Assn, 1988; author of articles in Artin Cultural Diversity, Holt, Rinehart, 1980, Recreation Leadership, Prentice-Hall, 1987, The Day When the Animals Talked by William Faulkner, Follett, 1977; narrator of films: "Ashanti to Zulu: African Traditi," Weston Woods Studio, 1976, "Why the Sun and Moon Live in the Sky," ACI Films, 1977; recording: "Sounds of Childcraft," Field Enterprises, 1974; First Distinguished Alumnus Award, School of Library & Information Studies, Univ of Wisconsin-Madison, 1990; American Cultural Specialist in New Zealand, US Information Agency, 1990; University of Wisconsin, honorary DLit, 1992; Black Caucus of ALA, Leadership in Profession, 1992, Distinguished Service to Profession, 1992. **Special Achievements:** Author of articles in numerous publications including: Notable Black American Women, 1992; Musical Story Hours: Using Music with Storytelling and Puppetry, 1989; A Sea of Upturned Faces, 1989. **Military Serv:** US Army, lt, 1943-45. **Home Addr:** 5027 15th Ave NE, #103, Seattle, WA 98105.

SHAW, TALBERT OSCALL
Educator. **Personal:** Born Feb 28, 1928; married Lillieth H Brown; children: Patrick Talbert, Talieth Andrea. **Educ:** Andrews U, BA 1960, MA 1961, BD 1963; Univ of Chgo, MA 1968, PhD 1973. **Career:** Coll of Lib Arts Morgan State Univ Baltimore, dean 1981-; School of Religion Howard Univ, acting dean/asso prof of ethics 1972-81; Bowie State Coll, visiting prof 1974; Princeton Theo Sem, visiting prof 1975; Cath Univ of Amer, visiting prof 1973-74; Oakwood Coll, prof of chris ethics 1965-72, dean of students. **Orgs:** Mem exec bd Nat Com for the Prevention of Alcoholism; exec com Washington Theo Consortium; exec com Howard U; faculty mem Soc for the Study of BlackReligions; Am Acad of Religion; Am Socof Chris Ethics 1972. **Honors/Awds:** Voted distin tchr of yr Howard Univ Sch of Religion 1974. **Business Addr:** Sch of Religion, Howard Univ, Washington, DC 20059.

SHAW, TERRANCE
Professional football player. **Educ:** Stephen F Austin. **Career:** San Diego Chargers, 1995-. **Special Achievements:** 2nd round/34th overall NFL draft pick, 1995. **Business Addr:** Professional Football Player, San Diego Chargers, Jack Murphy Stadium, 9449 Friars Rd, San Diego, CA 92108, (619)280-2111.

SHAW, THEODORE MICHAEL
Lawyer, professor. **Personal:** Born Nov 24, 1954, New York, NY; son of Theodore Shaw (deceased) & Jean Audrey Churchill Shaw (deceased); married Cynthia E Muldrow; children: T Winston, Zora Jean. **Educ:** Wesleyan Univ, BA, Honors, 1976; Columbia Univ School of Law, JD, 1979. **Career:** US Dept of Justice, Civil Rights Div, trial attorney, 1979-82; NAACP Legal Defense Fund, asst counsel, 1982-87, western regional counsel, 1987-90, assoc dir-counsel, 1993-; Columbia Univ School of Law, anjunct prof, 1993-; Univ of MI School of Law, asst prof of law, 1990-. **Orgs:** Wesleyan Univ, bd of trustees, alumni elected trustee, 1986-89, charter mem, 1992-, sec of the bd, 1993-; Poverty & Race Research Action Council, bd mem, 1990-; Archbishop's Leadership Proj, bd mem, 1994-; Greater Brownsville Youth Council, bd mem, 1982-; Natl Bar Assn; Amer Bar Assn. **Honors/Awds:** US Dept of Justice, Civil Rights Div, Special Commendation, 1981; Aspen Inst Fellowship on Law & Society, 1987; Twentyfirst Century Trust Fellowship on Global Interdependence, London Eng, 1989; Salzburg Seminars Fellowship, Salzburg, Austria, Summer, 1991; Langston Bar Assn, (Los Angeles, CA) Civil Trial Lawyer of the Year, 1991. **Special Achievements:** Led Delegation of NAACP Legal Defense Fund Lawyers to South Africa to present seminars on consitutional litigation, 1994, 1995; Consulted with Spanish Senate Judiciary Comm and Judiciary on Jury Systems, Madrid, Spain, 1994. **Business Addr:** Assoc Director Counsel, NAACP Legal Defense & Educational Fund Inc, 99 Hudson St, 16th Fl, New York, NY 10013, (212)219-1900.

SHAW, WILLIE G.
Athletic director. **Personal:** Born Mar 29, 1942, Jackson, TN; married Brenda Joyce Robinson; children: Stacey Alexis, Daricus. **Educ:** Lane Coll, BS 1964; Univ of TN Knoxville, MS 1968; Middle TN State Univ, DA 1975; Memphis State Univ 1984. **Career:** New York Astronauts, professional basketball player 1964-65; Lane Coll, asst football coach 1965-71, basketball coach 1976-79; City of Jackson TN, gymnastics instr 1976-79; Lane Coll Natl Youth Sports Prog, proj activity dir 1976-80; Lane Coll, dir of athletics. **Orgs:** Chmn south reg Natl Collegiate Athletic Assoc Div III Basketball Comm 1977-; athletic dir Lane Coll 1979-; mem Natl Coll Athletic Assoc Comm on Committees 1979-81; proj admin Lane Coll Natl Youth Sports Prog 1980-; bd mem Jackson-Madison Cty Airport Auth Bd of Dir 1980-; natl chmn Natl CollAthletic Assoc Div III Basketball comm 1981-; bd chmn Jackson Housing Auth Anti-Crime Comm 1982. **Honors/Awds:** Coll div Basketball Scoring Leading Natl Assn of Intercoll Athletic Natl Coll Athletic Assn 1962,64; Basketball All Amer Natl Assn of Intercoll Athletics Assn Press United Press Intl 1963-64; State Fellow Middle TN State Univ 1972,73. **Home Addr:** 149 Commanche Trail, Jackson, TN 38305. **Business Addr:** Athletic Dir, Lane College, 545 Lane College, Jackson, TN 38301.

SHAWNEE, LAURA ANN
Human resources management. **Personal:** Born Sep 18, 1953, Merced, CA. **Educ:** Univ of Santa Clara, BA (Cum Laude) 1975. **Career:** NASA Ames Rsch Ctr, coll recruitment coord 1975-83, personnel mgr 1975-84, handicapped program mgr 1982-84, deputy chief eop office 1984-. **Orgs:** Cumming Temple Christian Meth Episcopal Church admin asst 1975-, church treas 1975-, pres missionary soc/ 1985; mem NAMEPA 1985-; mem Comm of Life & Witness 1986; mem comm on life & witness Christian Meth Episcopal Church, NAMEPA 1985, mem bd of dir and imperative comm to eliminate racism 1987; Mid Peninsula YWCA. **Honors/Awds:** Bank of Amer Achievement Awd 1971; Agency Group Achievement Awd Summer Med Student Intern Program NASA 1976; Special Achievement Awd for College Recruiting Program NASA 1980. **Business Addr:** Deputy Chief, EOP Office, NASA Ames Research Ctr, Mail Stop 241-7, Moffett Field, CA 94035.

SHEAD, KEN
Sportswear manufacturing company executive. **Career:** Drew Pearson Companies, president, currently. **Orgs:** National Minority Development Council. **Honors/Awds:** Black Enterprise Company of the Year, 1994. **Special Achievements:** Company is ranked #79 on Black Enterprise magazine's list of top 100 industrial/service companies, 1992. **Business Addr:** President, Drew Pearson Companies, 15006 Beltway, Addison, TX 75001, (214)702-8055.

SHEALEY, RICHARD W.
Bank executive. **Career:** First Independence National Bank, president, CEO, currently. **Business Addr:** President & CEO, First Independence National Bank, 44 Michigan Ave, Detroit, MI 48226, (313)256-8200.

SHEARIN, KIMBERLY MARIA
Journalist. **Personal:** Born Apr 1, 1964, Baltimore, MD; daughter of Mary James Withers and Matthew Shearin. **Educ:** St Mary's College, St Mary's City, MD, BA, english, 1986; Boston University, Boston, MA, MS, journalism, 1987. **Career:** The Associated Press, Providence, RI, staff reporter, 1985, 1987-89; New Haven Register, New Haven, CT, staff reporter, 1989-. **Orgs:** Member, National Association of Black Journalists, 1987-. **Honors/Awds:** National Dean's List, 1983, 1985; helped launch St Louis Sun newspaper, 1989. **Business Addr:** Reporter, Editorial Dept, New Haven Register, 40 Sargent Dr, New Haven, CT 06511.

SHEATS, MARVIN ANTHONY
Computer consultant. **Personal:** Born Nov 22, 1958, Detroit, MI; son of Evelyn Flacks and Marvin Sheats. **Educ:** Wayne County Community College, liberal arts degree, 1981; Computer Skills Training Center, certificate, computer operations, 1985; EDS, certificate, computer operations, 1986. **Career:** Electronic Data Systems, computer operator, 1985-87; Wayne County Public Service, computer operator, 1988-92; Mac Training & Design Inc, vice pres, owner, consultant, currently. **Orgs:** MacGroup Detroit, vice pres, 1990-. **Honors/Awds:** Computer Skills Training Center, Achievement Award, 1992. **Business Phone:** (313)557-0750.

SHEDD, KENNY
Professional football player. **Personal:** Born Feb 14, 1971. **Educ:** Northern Iowa. **Career:** Oakland Raiders, wide receiver, 1996-. **Business Addr:** Professional Football Player, Oakland Raiders, 1220 Harbor Bay Pkwy, Alameda, CA 94502, (510)615-1875.

SHEEN, ALBERT A.
Attorney. **Personal:** Born Jul 14, 1920, StCroix, VI; married Ada Mae Finch; children: Albert Jr, Nicole. **Educ:** Lincoln Univ, BA 1964; Howard Univ, JD 1968. **Career:** Virgin Islands, senator 1972-74; Antilles Petro Indus, pres gen counsel 1974-76; US Bankruptcy Judge Virgin Islands 1972-84; US Magistrate 1984-; Hodge& Sheen, attorney 1969-. **Orgs:** US Dist Ct DC 1969; US Ct of Appeals 3rd Circuit 1969; VI Bd of Educ 1970-72; Judicial Conf of 3rd Circuit 1973-74; VI Bar 1974-; Coll of VI 1975-; Peoples Broadcasting Corp; Rubin Bros Intl. **Business Addr:** Attorney, 46-47 Company St, Christiansted, St Croix, Virgin Islands of the United States 00821.

SHEFFEY, FRED C.
Aerospace company executive. **Personal:** Born Aug 27, 1928, McKeesport, PA; son of Julia B Richardson and Fred Culmore Sheffey; married Jane Hughes, Dec 27, 1952; children: Alan C, Steven C, Patricia C. **Educ:** Central State Coll, BS 1950; OH State U, MBA 1962; George Washington U, MS 1969; Command & Gen Staff Coll, 1965; Natl War Coll, 1969. **Career:** US Army Quartermaster Cntr & Ft Lee, commanding general, US Army Quartermaster Sch Ft Lee VA, comdt; served various duties as military career man; LTV Missiles & Electronics Group, dir of productivity; Lockheed Martin, director/ethics officer, currently. **Orgs:** Chmn of the bd Dallas Urban League; deputy bd chmn, Sunbelt Natl Bank 1982-86. **Honors/Awds:** Hall of Fame Central State Univ, 1989; Productivity With Quality Publication, 1988. **Military Serv:** US Army, Major General, 1973-1980; Legion of merit with 2 oak leaf clusters; bronze star medal; merit ser medal; army commend with 1 oak leaf custer; Purple Heart; army of Occup Medal; United Nations Serv Medal; Natl Defense Serv Medal with 1 Oak Leaf Cluster; Korean Serv Medal with three Battle Stars; Vietnamese serv medal; rep of Vietnam Campaign medal with 60 device; combat infantry badge; Inducted into US Army Quartermaster Hall of Fame, Fort Lee, VA, 1994.

SHEFFEY, RUTHE G.
Educator. **Personal:** Born in Essex County, VA; married Vernon R Sheffey; children: Illona Cecile Sheffey Rawlings, Renata Gabrielle Sheffey Strong. **Educ:** Morgan State Univ, BA 1947; Howard Univ, MA 1949; Univ of PA, PhD 1959. **Career:** Howard Univ, graduate asst in English, 1947-48; Claflin Coll, instructor, English, French, 1948-49; Morgan State Coll, asst prof, 1959-64, assoc prof, 1964-70; chairperson, English dept, 1970-74, prof, dept of English, 1975-. **Orgs:** Coll English Assn; Coll Language Assn; Modern Language Assn; Natl Cncl of the Teachers of English; Eighteenth Century Studies Assn; Middle Atlantic Writers Assn; vice pres, Langston Hughes Soc; founder, pres, Zora Neale Hurston Soc; editor, Zora Neale Hurston Forum; Assn for the Study of Afro-American Life & Culture; Kings Kids Mentor, Heritage United Church of Christ; Mayor's Cncl on Women's Rights; delegate, White House Conf on Women as Economic Equals; Morgan State, Howard Univ, & the Univ of PA Alumni Assns; communications comm, United Fund of MD, 1972-74; commnr & vice chair, Baltimore Co Human Relations Commn; MD state delegate, Paula Hollinger's Scholarship Award Panel; Maryland Council for the Humanities, 1990-96. **Honors/Awds:** Coll Language Assn Creative Achievement Award, 1974; United Fund Award for Community Serv, 1975; Community Serv Award, Jack & Jill of Amer, 1979; Distinguished Alumni Citation, Natl Assn for Equal Opportunity, 1980; Faculty Rsch Grants for studies in Shakespearean Production, 1983; Achievement Award for Preservation of Higher Educ Standards & Contributions to African-American History & Culture, 1984; Morgan State Univ Women Award, 1985; Citations for Outstanding Service to Scholarly and Literary Communities, 1985-93; Maryland Assn for Higher Education, Faculty Member of the Year Award, 1994; Howard Univ, Baltimore Chapter, Alumna of the Year, 1987; Towson State Univ, Distinguished Black Woman of America, 1984; numerous other citations and awards. **Special Achievements:** Author of numerous books, articles, and reviews. **Business Addr:** Professor of English, Morgan State University, Coldspring & Hillen Rds, Baltimore, MD 21239.

SHEFFIELD, GARY ANTONIAN
Professional baseball player. **Personal:** Born Nov 18, 1968, Tampa, FL. **Career:** Milwaukee Brewers, infielder, 1988-92; San Diego Padres, third baseman, 1992-93; Florida Marlins, 1993-. **Orgs:** The Gary Sheffield Found, 1995-; Sheff's Kitchen. **Special Achievements:** National League, batting champion, 1992, all-star team member, 1992; Sporting News NL Silver Slugger Team, 1992, 1996; holds Marlins all-time record for most home runs and highest batting average, 1997. **Business Addr:** Professional Baseball Player, Florida Marlins, Pro Player Stadium, NW 199th St, Miami, FL 33169, (305)356-5848.

SHEFTALL, WILLIS B., JR.
Educational administrator. **Personal:** Born Dec 12, 1943, Macon, GA. **Educ:** Morehouse Coll, BA 1964; Atlanta Univ, MA 1969; GA State Univ, PhD 1981. **Career:** AL State Univ, instructor in econ 1969-71; Atlanta Univ, rsch assoc 1978-80; Morehouse Coll, asst prof of econ 1976-81; Hampton Univ, chmn econ dept 1981-82, dean school of business. **Orgs:** Consult to various agencies/official bodies of City of Atlanta, State of GA, Commonwealth of VA, General Serv Admin 1977-82; mem Amer Econ Assoc, Natl EconAssoc, Intl Assoc of Black Bus Ed, Assoc of Social & Behavorial Sci; mem past & pres Natl Urban League, NAACP. **Honors/Awds:** Published articles in the areas of local public finance & urban economics; Merrill Foreign Study Travel Scholar 1968-69; Southern Fellowships Fund Fellow 1972-75. **Military Serv:** USN quartermaster 3rd class 1964-66. **Business Addr:** Dept of Economics, Moorhouse College, Atlanta, GA 30314.

SHELBY, KHADEJAH E.
City official. **Personal:** Born Feb 15, 1929, Dayton, OH; daughter of Eloise Evans Davis and Artman Davis; divorced; children: Elizabeth Diane Lugo. **Educ:** Baldwin-Wallace College, Berea, OH, 1947-49; North Carolina University, graduate, 1986; Wayne State University Professional Management and Development School, American Association of Zoological Parks and Aquariums, 1989-. **Career:** NYU Medical Center, executive asst, 1958-69; City of Detroit, administrator, 1975-82, Zoological Parks Dept, deputy director, 1982-. **Orgs:** American Association of Zoological Parks and Aquariums, fellow, 1982-; Friends of African Art, 1972-; Detroit Institute of Arts, Founders Society, 1972-; NAACP, life member. **Honors/Awds:** Wayne State University, Golden Key Honor Society, life member, 1989-; Baldwin-Wallace College, Outstanding Freshman, 1947. **Business Addr:** Deputy Director, Detroit Zoological Parks Dept, 8450 W Ten Mile Rd, PO Box 39, Royal Oak, MI 48068-0039.

SHELBY, REGINALD W.
Physician. **Personal:** Born Jul 6, 1920, Memphis, TN; son of Grace Irving Shelby and Charles H Shelby; married Jay; children: Cathi, Reginald Jr. **Educ:** LeMoyne-Owen Coll Memphis TN, BS 1940; Meharry Medical Coll, 1950; NY City Hosp, Post-Grad Training 1950-57; Intl Coll Surgeons, Fellow 1959; American Brd Surgery Chicago Illinois Member l967; American Brd Surgery Chicago Illinois re-Certified l980. **Career:** Ashtabula County Med Center, chief surgery 1987; private practice, 1959-. **Orgs:** Bd dir Western Reserve Health Plan, Ashtabula County Health Serv 1987; past pres Ashtabula County Med Soc; past chief of staff Ashtabula County Med Ctr;past mem Ashtabula City Bd of Health; mem Ashtabula C of C; bd dir Mary Chatman Comm Center; past asst coroner Ashtabula County; mem Comm Action County-wide Sickle-Cell Screening; fellow Pan-Amer Soc Med; mem OH State Med Assoc, Ashtabula County Med Assoc, Kappa Alpha Psi; legal defense contrib NAACP; Ashtabula County Health Dept medical dir l987-. **Military Serv:** AUS 1952-56; WWII Pacific Theatre m/sgt New Guinea, Philippines, Japan. **Business Addr:** Physician, Reginald W Shelby MD Inc, 524 West 24th St, Ashtabula, OH 44004.

SHELBY, REGINALD W.
Dentist. **Personal:** Born Mar 29, 1948, Laurel, MS; son of Hester and Milton; children: Jibril Muhammad. **Educ:** Flint Comm Coll, AA 1968; N MI Univ, BA 1970; Howard Univ, DDS 1975. **Career:** Private Practice, dentist 1976; Arthur Capper Dental Clinic, team leader 1981; self-employed. **Orgs:** Photographer; founder and pres Universal Peace 1983; videographer. **Honors/Awds:** Awd of Excellence DC Government 1983; produced video documentary of 1984 march on Washington 1984.

SHELL, ART
Professional football assistant coach. **Personal:** Born Nov 26, 1946, Charleston, SC; married Janice; children: two. **Educ:** Maryland State-Eastern Shore College, BS, industrial arts education, 1968. **Career:** Oakland Raiders (later, Los Angeles Raiders), offensive tackle, 1968-82, asst coach, 1983-89, head coach, 1989-95; Kansas City Chiefs, offensive line coach, 1995-. **Honors/Awds:** Inducted into Football Hall of Fame, 1989; played in Pro Bowl, 1972-78, 1980; first black head football coach in NFL; Associated Press, Coach of the Year, 1991. **Business Addr:** Offensive Line Coach, Kansas City Chiefs, 1 Arrowhead Dr, Kansas City, MO 64129, (816)924-9300.

SHELL, JUANITA
Psychologist, educator. **Personal:** Born Apr 21, 1940, Winston Salem, NC; daughter of Sallie Sanders Shell and Douglas Shell; married Alonza Peterson, Dec 24, 1961; children: Lisa, Jason. **Educ:** CCNY, BA 1971; Grad Ctr City Univ of NY, PhD 1977; NY Univ Postdoctoral Program Psychoanalysis & Psychotherapy, certificate, 1991. **Career:** Brooklyn Com Counsel Ctr, staff psychologist 1976-84; Brooklyn Coll, adj prof 1976-78; NYU Bellevue Med Ctr, assistant clinical professor/staff psych 1978-; Self-employed, psychoanalyst, currently. **Orgs:** Mem Amer Psych Assoc 1975-, Mayors Advisory Sub-com of Mental Retard & Dev Disabil 1978-; chairperson Health Com of Community Bd #4 1979-81; 1st vp metropolitan Chap of Jack & Jill of Amer 1984, pres, 1987-89; consult Shelter & Arms Child Serv 1984; mem NYAS 1981-; pres, Metropolitan Chapter of Jack & Jill Alumni Inc, 1990-; NY Univ-Bellevue Psychiatric Society; NYS Division for Women Committee; trustee, Schomburg Corp. **Honors/Awds:** Grantee NIMH 1971-74; fellow Black Analy Inc 1975-76; article, with J Campion Shell, "A Study of Three Brothers with Infantile Autism" Jrnl of the Amer Acad of Child Psych 1984; article with W Kass, "The Reactions of Black Children to the Atlanta Child Murders," 1988; Grantee, NIHM, 1971-75; Three Brothers with Infantile Autism, 1984; Governor's Award, Excellence in Mental Health, 1997; co-wote "Values of Post Partum Women From The Inner City: An Exploratory Study," with Judith Minton, PhD, and Ralph Steinberg, PhD, Journal of Child and Family Studies, 1997. **Business Addr:** Asst Clinical Instructor, Psychiatry, New York University, Bellevue Med Center, 1st Ave and 27th St, 21W23, New York, NY 10016, (212)562-4509.

SHELL, THEODORE A.
Dentist. **Personal:** marrIed Juanita Hamlin; children: Gail, Theodore Jr. **Educ:** Miles Mem Coll, AB; Wayne State Univ, MBA; CLU Am Coll of Life Underwriters. **Career:** Great Lakes Mutual Ins Co, debit mgr asst mgr & mgr 1934-44; Great Lakes Mutual Life Ins Co, exec vice pres 1944-59; Golden State Minority Foundation, various offices, pres; Golden State Mutual Life Ins Co, v chm of Bd 1960-. **Orgs:** Mem bd dir Family Savings & Loan Assn; mem Nat Assn Life Underwriters; Life Mgrs Assn; Town Hall; Chartered Life Underwriters; bd mem SCLC West; LA Urban League LA; NAACP; trustee bd Second Bapt Ch; bd of govs Town Hall; comm mem CA C of C Statewide Welfare Comm; So CA Research Comm; Community Skills Cntr Advisory Comm; chmn CA Job Creation Prog Bd; bd of commr Muncpl Auditorium; citz mngmt review comm LA Sch System; chmn sub-com on budget & finance LA Sch System; bd of trustees Pitzer Coll; bd of dir Joint Ctr Comm Studies; Grantsmanship Ctr; Fundraising Sch; develop Comm Town & Hall; United Way Study Comm; top vice pres agency dir Nat Ins Assn 1964-72. **Honors/Awds:** Olive Crosthwait Award Chicago Ins Assn; Spec Ser Award Nat Ins Assn 1973. **Business Addr:** 1931 15th St NW, Washington, DC 20009.

SHELL, WILLIAM H.
Medical social worker (retired). **Personal:** Born Aug 22, 1910, Cartersville, GA; married Ethel Margaret Moore. **Educ:** Morehouse Coll, AB 1933; Atlanta Univ, AM 1935, certificate in indus statistics 1943. **Career:** Natl Youth Admin, asst state dir 1935-38, state adv on Negro affairs 1938-42; Ft Valley State Coll, instr social studies & workshop consult 1940-41; US Post Office, railway post clerk 1943; YMCA Butler St Br, prog membership sec 1944; War Manpower Comm Region 7, placement specialist 1944-47; VA Hosp, exec sec bd of US civil serv examiners 1947-49, med social worker 1949-50; US Dept of Agriculture, admin officer 1950-53; Natl Found for Infantile Paralysis, asst Brooklyn & Manhattan dir 1953-54; New York City Health & Hosp Corp, med social worker 1954-75. **Orgs:** Consultant to many organizations; bd dir House of Friendship Comm Ctr NY; Cornerstone Baptist Church Day Care Ctr Inc mem bd trustees 1970-84; genl supt of church sch; mem Friendship Baptist Church, Nineteenth St Baptist Church, Mt Zion Baptist Church; mem Admin Com Natl Office March on Washington for Jobs & Freedom; mem Acad of Certified Soc Workers, NAACP, Amer Assn of Retired Persons; mem Atlanta Univ Alumni Assn, Morehouse Coll Natl Alumni Assn; charter mem Natl Assn of Social Workers. **Honors/Awds:** Awd of Merit Tuskegee Inst 1949; plaque for Disting Serv as Comm Leader Am Biog Inst; Herbert F Rawll Mem Awd; Pres Awd Ebony Mag 1959.

SHELLO, KENDEL
Professional football player. **Personal:** Born Nov 24, 1973. **Educ:** Southern University. **Career:** Indianapolis Colts, defensive tackle, 1996-. **Business Addr:** Professional Football Player, Indianapolis Colts, PO Box 535000, Indianapolis, IN 46253, (317)297-2658.

SHELTON, BRYAN
Professional tennis player. **Educ:** Georgia Tech, industrial engineering degree, 1990. **Career:** Professional tennis player, currently. **Honors/Awds:** Played at Wimbledon, 1994. **Business Addr:** Professional Tennis Player, Agent: Richard Howell, 3379 Peachtree Rd NE, Ste 230, Atlanta, GA 30326, (404)842-1556.

SHELTON, CHARLES E.
Newspaper company executive. **Personal:** Born Oct 5, 1945, New York, NY; son of Fredrine Bolden Shelton and Edward Shelton; married Sylvina Robinson, Oct 10, 1964; children: Helen, Charmaine, Mia. **Educ:** Northeastern Univ, Boston MA, 1963-65; Pace Univ, 1984; Stanford University, graduate school, 1991; Dartmouth, Tuck executive prog, 1994. **Career:** New York Times, New York NY, budget analyst, 1967-79, consumer marketing rep, 1979-81, city circulation mgr, 1981-83, metropolitan circulation mgr, 1983-87, metropolitan home delivery dir, 1987-88, single copy sales dir, 1988-89, dir of NY edition, beginning 1989, group dir , sales & operations, 1992, vp, distribution, currently. **Honors/Awds:** Black Achiever Award, Harlem YMCA branch, 1982. **Business Addr:** VP, Distribution, Circulation Department, New York Times, 229 W 43rd St, New York, NY 10036.

SHELTON, CORA R.
Counselor. **Personal:** Born Mar 5, 1925, Monroe, MI; married Jean C Mitchell; children: Deborah, Mark, Janice. **Educ:** Wayne State Univ Detroit, attended 1944-60; Wayne Co Community Coll, attended 1969; Univ of MI Extension Detroit, 1972. **Career:** Kent Barry Eaton Connecting Ry Inc, pres/gen mgr 1979-; Met Life Ins Co, sales rep 1973-79; Detroit St & Rys, transp equipment operator 1946-73. **Orgs:** Corp dir Kent Barry Eaton Connecting Ry 1979-; mem Nat Fedn of Independent Bus1979; mem Southcentral MI Transp Planning Com 1980; dist rep Div 26Streetcar & Bus Operators 1960-62; v chmn City-Wide Polit Action Group 1961-63; pres St Cecelia Ch Dad's Club 1968-70. **Honors/Awds:** Man of the year award Nat Life Underwriters 1974. **Business Addr:** Lexington Childrens Cntr, 115 E 98 St, New York, NY 10029.

SHELTON, DAIMON
Professional football player. **Personal:** Born Sep 15, 1972; married Stephanie; children: Aliya. **Educ:** Sacramento State, attended. **Career:** Jacksonville Jaguars, running back, 1997-. **Business Addr:** Professional Football Player, Jacksonville Jaguars, One Stadium Place, Jacksonville, FL 32202, (904)633-6000.

SHELTON, HAROLD TILLMAN
Physician. **Personal:** Born May 4, 1941, Lake Charles, LA; married Dolores Hayes; children: Keith, Sherry, Stephanie. **Educ:** McNeese State Univ, BS 1970; LA State Univ Med Sch, MD 1974; LA State Univ Med Cntr, internship 1975; LSU Med Cntr New Orleans, residency in general surgery, 1975-79. **Career:** Private Practice, General surgery, 1979; LA State Univ, Med Center, Clinical Instructor, 1980. **Orgs:** Regional dir, Region III Center Natl Med Assn 1973; mem, cand group Am Coll of Surgeons 1979-; diploma, Am Bd of Surgery 1980; mem, Amer Med Assn; LA State Med Soc; Calcasieu Parish Med Soc 1979; staff mem Lake Charles Memorial Hosp & St Patrick Hosp 1979. **Honors/Awds:** Pub "Evaluation of Wound Irrigation by Pulsatile Jet & Conventional Methods" Annals of Surg Feb 1978. **Business Addr:** 511 Hodges St, Lake Charles, LA 70602.

SHELTON, HARVEY WILLIAM
Administrator. **Personal:** Born Jan 18, 1936, Charlottesville, VA; married Delores Manly; children: Renee, Harvey Jr. **Educ:** VA State Coll, BS 1960; NC State U, cert pub policy 1967; NC State U, MEd Adult Educ 1969; VPI&SU, EdD Adult & Continuing Educ 1976. **Career:** Pittsylvania Co VA, extension agent 1963-69; VPI&SU, area resource devel agent 1969-70; Comm Resource Devel VPI&SU, program leader 1970-78; Comm Resource Devel & Energy MD Coop Ext Serv, asst dir 1978-86; MD Cooperative Extension Service, asst to the dir 1986-. **Orgs:** Kellogg Found, fellow 1966-67; Big Brothers Assoc, big brother 1971-73; mem Adult Educ Assn of USA 1972-80; Ford Found, fellow 1974-75; mem Phi KappaPhi Honorary Soc 1975-80; bd mem Boy Scout Council 1976-78; treas & bd mem Roanake NAACP1976-78; chmn professional improvement com Comm Devel Soc of Amer 1979-80, bd mem 1981-83; mem MD Assoc of Adult Educ 1980. **Honors/Awds:** Epsilon Sigma Phi Outstanding Achievement Award; VA Pol Inst & StU 1978; Army Commendation Medal; US Senator MacMathis awd 1983; Community Development Soc service awd 1985. **Military Serv:** AUS first lt 1961-63. **Business Addr:** Asst to the Dir, Cooperative Extension Service, University of Maryland, Symons Hall, College Park, MD 20742.

SHELTON, JEWELL VENNERRIE (ELVOID)
Consultant, organization administrator. **Personal:** Born Oct 9, 1928, St Louis, MO; married Robert Louis; children: Robbin M, Annora N, Alika P, Jan P. **Educ:** Pitzer Coll Claremont CA, BA sociology 1973. **Career:** San Bernardino City Unified Sch Dist, pres bd of edn, Office of Comm Devel City of San Bernardino, sr proj coor 1975-85; Proj Understanding, human relations specialist 1973-75; Univ of CA, staff asst/nutrition Educ 1969-71; KUCR-TV San Bernardino Vly Coll, consult comm resource 1967-79; Home Econs Educ Univ CA Riverside, consult 1969-71; Choice Living Consortium, founder, director, 1985-. **Orgs:** Bd of dirs GSA 1966-67; bd mem San Bernardino Pub Library 1972-75; pres NCNW Inland Empire 1974-75. **Honors/Awds:** Martin Luther King Scholarship San Bernardino Valley Coll 1968; S & H Found Award/Scholarship Claremont Coll 1970; Woman of Achievement Award Natl Council Negro Women 1974; Citizen of Achievement Award League of Women Voters Inland Empire 1975. **Home Addr:** 1146 E 38th St, San Bernardino, CA 92404.

SHELTON, JOHN W.
Sales executive. **Personal:** Born Dec 16, 1958, Buffalo, NY; son of Joyce Hargrave Shelton and John Shelton; married Martha Zehnder Shelton, Jun 8, 1986; children: John Bradford, Nicholaus Edwin. **Educ:** Valparaiso Univ, Valparaiso, IN, BBA. **Career:** MGM Grand Hotel, Las Vegas, NV, reservations, 1981-82; Flamingo Hilton Hotel, Las Vegas, NV, front office, 1982-83; Hyatt Regency Oakland, Oakland, CA, sales mgr, 1984-87; Hyatt Regency Atlanta, Atlanta, GA, sales mgr, 1987-88; Hyatt Regency Flint, Flint, MI, dir of sales, 1988-90; Zehnder's of Frankenmuth Inc, Frankenmuth, MI, dir of sales, currently. **Orgs:** Mem, MI Society of Assn Executives; mem, Big Brothers/Big Sisters East Bay, 1987; mem, Rotary Intl, 1989; membership chmn, Society of Govt Meeting Planners, 1987; mem, Natl Coalition of Black Meeting Planners. **Honors/Awds:** Natl Nominations/Elections Comm, Society of Govt Planners, 1988; Hyatt Hotels Career Dev, Hyatt Hotels Corp, 1988, 1989; Hyatt Regency Oakland Manager of the Quarter, Hyatt Hotels Corp, 1986. **Business Addr:** Director of Sales and Marketing, Zehnder's of Frankenmuth, 730 S Main St, Frankenmuth, MI 48734.

SHELTON, JOSEPH B.
General contractor, construction management co. director. **Personal:** Born Oct 12, 1946, Vicksburg, MS; son of Charlene Shelton and Joseph B Shelton (deceased); married Valeria D Bledsoe Shelton, Nov 10, 1973; children: Robert Waites Jr, Tamara, Joseph III, Jonathan. **Educ:** Hampton Institute, BS, building construction engineering, 1969. **Career:** Darin & Armstrong, field engineer, 1969-70, coordinator, 1970-75, project engineer, 1975-78, project manager, 1978-84; Walbridge Aldinger, project manager, 1984-91, project director, 1991-. **Orgs:** Engineering Society of Detroit, 1976-; St Gerard's Church, Administration Commission, past vice pres, 1989-92; St Gerard's School, School Board, past vice pres, 1987-90; North Huntington Block Club, past president, 1982-88. **Honors/Awds:** Young Men's Christian Association, Minority Achiever in Industry, 1980. **Home Addr:** 20310 Huntington, Detroit, MI 48219, (313)592-0134. **Business Addr:** Project Director, Walbridge Aldinger Co, 613 Abbott St, Detroit, MI 48226-2521, (313)963-8000.

SHELTON, LEE RAYMOND
Health services administrator, physician. **Personal:** Born Oct 25, 1927, Pittsburgh, PA; son of Mable Shelton and Lee Shelton; married Delores; children: Marva, Fawn, Gia, Raymond. **Educ:** Howard U, BS 1951; Howard Univ Med Sch, MD 1955; General Surgery Residency Certified 1973. **Career:** General surgeon, 1961-77; SW Hospital & Med Ctr, dir emergency svcs; Morehouse Coll of Medicine, clinical asst prof surgery; Atlanta Southside Comprehensive Health Ctr, dir health svcs; Health Services, director, vice pres; Health lst Foundation, director. **Orgs:** Bd dir Health 1st (HMO); life mem NAACP; Montford Point Marine Assn; Episcopal Church of The Incarnation; Omega Psi Phi Frat; Atlanta Med Assn; GA State Med Assn; MAG; NMA; Howard Univ Med Alumni Assn; YMCA. **Military Serv:** US Marine Corps, sgt, 1946-49; US Army Reserves MC, capt. **Business Addr:** Physician, 725 Lynhurst Dr SW, Atlanta, GA 30311.

SHELTON, MILLICENT BETH
Co. executive, director, screenwriter. **Personal:** Born Jan 29, 1966, St Louis, MO; daughter of Mildred E Shelton and Earl W Shelton. **Educ:** Princeton University, BA, English, 1988; New York University, MFA, 1993. **Career:** 40 Acres & a Mule Filmworks, wardrobe assistant, 1988; Cosby Show, wardrobe assistant, 1988-89; Idolmakers Films & Fat Productions, vice pres, director, 1989-92; Fat Film Productions, president, director, 1992-. **Honors/Awds:** Center for Population Options, Nancy Susan Reynolds Award, writer, 1992; Urban Profile Magazine, Thirty Under Thirty Award (2nd place), 1992; New York University, WTC Johnson Scholarship, 1989. **Special Achievements:** Directed videos for: Salt-N-Pepa, MC Lyte; wrote, directed, Ride, 1998. **Business Phone:** (212)219-9122.

SHELTON, O. L.
State representative. **Personal:** Born Feb 6, 1946, Greenwood, MS; son of Idell McClung Shelton and Obie Shelton; married Linda Kay; children: Eric, Shron, Jaimal, Kiana. **Educ:** Lincoln Univ, AB 1970. **Career:** Missouri State Legislature, state representative, 1983-. **Orgs:** Member, executive board, National Black Caucus; member, William Community School Board; chairman, Ville Area Neighborhood Housing Assn Inc; chair, St. Louis Democratic Central Committee. **Home Addr:** 1803A Cora Ave, St Louis, MO 63113.

SHELTON, REUBEN ANDERSON
Attorney. **Personal:** Born Dec 6, 1954, St Louis, MO; son of Elizabeth Shelton and Sedathon Shelton; married D'Anne Tombs; children: Christian, Heather. **Educ:** Univ of KS, BS journalism 1973-77; St Louis Univ School of Law, JD 1978-81; Washington University, MBA, 1991. **Career:** Legal Serv of Eastern MO, atty 1980-81; US District Court, law clerk 19781-83; Husch, Eppenberger, Donohue et al, litigation atty 1983-84; Union Electric Co, in house atty 1984-. **Orgs:** Mem Kappa Alpha Psi 1974-; chair of att comm United Negro Coll Fund 1983-; task force dir Bar Assoc of Metro St Louis 1984-; pres Mound City Bar Assoc 1985-86; dir Childhaven Autistic Childcare 1986-, YMCA 1986-. **Honors/Awds:** Academic All Amer Univ of KS Basketball Team 1975-76; Law Student of the Year St Louis Chapter of Black Amer Law 1981. **Business Addr:** Attorney, Union Electric Co., PO Box 149, Mail Code 1320, St Louis, MO 63166.

SHELTON, ROY CRESSWELL, JR.
Educational administrator, electrical engineer. **Personal:** Born Jun 30, 1941, Toledo, OH; son of Celestine B Campbell Shelton and Roy C Shelton; married Patricia Lee Little Shelton, Apr 24, 1976; children: Kevin Lamont, Kelly Marie, Roy C III, James Phillip, Katherine Celestine. **Educ:** Central State University, pre-engineering, 1959-61; University of Toledo,BSEE, 1964, MSEE, 1967; University of Detroit, doctorate of engineering, 1969-72, 1991-. **Career:** Lawrence Technological University, associate professor, electrical engineering, chair, Dept of Eng, currently; Badgett Industries Inc, project manager, currently. **Orgs:** Natl Society of Black Engineers, facutly advisor, 1983-; Tau Beta Pi, 1963-; Eta Kappa Nu, 1964-. **Honors/Awds:** Black Educator of the Year, Peace Corps, 1990. **Business Addr:** Chair, Dept of Engineering, Lawrence Technological University, 21000 W 10 Mile Rd, Southfield, MI 48075.

SHELTON, ULYSSES
State legislator. **Personal:** Born Jul 1, 1917; married Pearl; children: Charles, Frederick. **Educ:** Mastbaum Vocational School. **Career:** PA House of Rep 181 Dist, retired dem Mem 1960-80; US Congressman Bradley, former magistgrate's clk, dept of records, clk, aide; beer Distributor; Yorktown Civic Assn, club owner. **Orgs:** N Philadelphia Model City Prog. **Military Serv:** USAF. **Business Addr:** 1132 W Jefferson St, Philadelphia, PA 19122.

SHEPARD, BEVERLY RENEE
Reporter, lawyer. **Personal:** Born Nov 30, 1959, Jacksonville, NC; daughter of Ruth Pearson Shepard and Odis Shepard. **Educ:** Univ of North Carolina, Chapel Hill, NC, BA, journalism, 1982, law degree, 1985. **Career:** The Virginian-Pilot, Norfolk, VA, reporter,1985-. **Orgs:** NABJ; Hampton Roads Black Media Professionals. **Honors/Awds:** Virginia Press Association, team winning First Place In A Series for project concerning the Year of the Child, 1990; Virginia Press Women's Association, First Place, news writing, 1990; The Virginian-Pilot/Ledger-Star, Second Place, overall news coverage among staff, 1990; National Federation of Press Women, Honorable Mention, News Writing, 1990; Algernon Sydney Sullivan for all-around excellence to an undergraduate female: Order of the Valkyries for scholastic achievement; Society of Hellenas for contributions to sorority life; Holderness Moor Court, UNC Law School. One of three selected from 60 competitors to fill the 27-member team, 1983; Winner, Regional Team Competition, Black Law Students Association. **Business Addr:** Reporter, News Dept, The Virginian-Pilot, 150 W Brambleton Ave, Norfolk, VA 23501.

SHEPARD, GREGORY
Information technology company executive. **Personal:** Born Mar 7, 1961, Trenton, NJ; son of George Jr and Evelyn M Shepard. **Educ:** Rensselaer Polytechnic Institute, BS, electrical engineering, 1983; Wharton School, Univ of PA, MBA, 1985. **Career:** Shepard-Patterson, CEO, 1986-95; Britton Financial Group, Investment Banking, principal, 1995-97; US Web Page Co, CEO, 1997-. **Orgs:** Leadership Congress for the 21st Century, chairman, 1994-; Rensselaer Alumni Club of Washington, DC, pres, 1992-; Alpha Phi Alpha, 1982-; Osayande Partners, chairman, 1991-. **Honors/Awds:** Rensselaer Polytechnic Institute, Directors Award, 1994; Johnson and Johnson, Leadership Fellowship, 1983. **Special Achievements:** Private Pilot Certification, 1993. **Home Addr:** 1713 Leighton Wood Ln, Silver Spring, MD 20910. **Business Phone:** (301)588-4600.

SHEPARD, HUEY PERCY
Court official. **Personal:** Born Jun 19, 1936, Jefferson, TX; son of Mr & Mrs Shirley Shepard; married Elaine Blanks; children: Dawn V, Huey Jr. **Educ:** CA State Univ Long Beach, BA 1957; UCLA Law School, LLB 1960. **Career:** LA Cty Superior Court, juvenile court referee 1965-68, commr 1968-71; Compton Mun Court, judge 1971-75; LA Cty Superior Court, judge 1975-81; Court Arbitration Ctr, dir 1981-. **Honors/Awds:** Resolution of Commendation City Council Compton 1973; Resolution of Commendation City Council Long Beach 1974; Honor Grad of the Year Long Beach Unified School Dist 1975; Outstanding Alumnus CA State Univ Alumni Long Beach 1975. **Business Addr:** Dir, Court Arbitration Center, 18411 Crenshaw Blvd, Ste 110, Torrance, CA 90504.

SHEPARD, JOAN
Journalist. **Personal:** Born in Philadelphia, PA. **Career:** NBC, consumer reporter 1975-76; WINS Radio, consumer reporter 1969-73; Women's Wear Daily, editor, feature writer 1964-69; New York Daily News, reporter, consumer affairs editor, currently.

SHEPARD, LINDA IRENE
Consultant. **Personal:** Born Dec 13, 1945, St Louis, MO; daughter of Dorothy Alice McCune and Woodie McCune; widowed; children: Monica Shepard, Adrienne Fitts, Alton Fitts III. **Educ:** Merritt College, Oxford CA, AA, 1972; Mills College, Oakland CA, BA, 1975. **Career:** Assemblyman Bill Lockyear, San Leondio CA, district secy, 1975-76; Jimmy Carter for President, Atlanta GA, dir of campaign operations, 1976; BART, Oakland CA, affirmative action officer, 1976-85; Mayor Lionel Wilson, Oakland CA, campaign mgr, 1985-86; Superior Consultants, owner, 1985—. **Orgs:** National Council of Negro Women, NAACP. **Honors/Awds:** Special recognition, Metropolitan Transportation Commission, 1985, for Bay Area Rapid Transit District summer program; outstanding business achievement award, National Council of Negro Women, 1987.

SHEPARD, RAY A.
Educational publishing. **Personal:** Born Jun 26, 1940, Sedalia, MO; married Kathy Crisman; children: Jon, Alice, Austin, Semantha. **Educ:** Univ of NE, BS 1967; Harvard Grad School of Educ, MAT 1971. **Career:** Scholastic Inc, editor 1972-83; Houghton Mifflin Co, vp, editorial dir 1983-87; Globe Book Co, pres 1987-. **Military Serv:** AUS sp4 1954-61.

SHEPHERD, BENJAMIN A.
Educational administrator, educator. **Personal:** Born Jan 28, 1941, Woodville, MS; married Ann Marie Turner; children: Benjamin III, Amy Michelle. **Educ:** Tougaloo College, BS, 1961; Atlanta University, MS, 1963; Kansas State University, PhD, 1970. **Career:** Atlanta University, teacher, 1962-63; Tougaloo College, instructor, 1963-65; Kansas State University, teacher assistant, 1966-69; Southern Illinois University, assistant professor, 1970-73, associate professor, 1973-, assistant dean graduate school, 1973-74, assistant chairman, zoology, 1976-79, professor zoology, 1979, associate vice president, academic affairs & research, 1979, vice pres, academic affairs & research, 1988, vice pres, academic affairs & provost, 1992-96, professor of Zoology, 1997-. **Orgs:** President, local chapter, Omega Psi Phi; American Society Zoologists; American Association of Anatomists; Illinois Academy of Science; New York Academy of Science; American Association for the Advancement of Science (AAAS); Sigma Xi; Society for Study Reproduction; life member, NAACP; life member, Tougaloo Alumni Association. **Honors/Awds:** Mason Senior Achievement Award Biology, Tougaloo College, 1961; Reg Fellowship, Atlanta University, 1962; Best Graduate Teacher Assistant, Kansas State University, 1968; Omega Man of the Year, Tau Upsilon chapter, 1979; ACE Fellowship, LSU, Baton Rouge, 1978-79; Numerous Publications in Field. **Home Addr:** 4009 Old US Hwy 51 S, Makanda, IL 62958-2201.

SHEPHERD, BERISFORD
Musician. **Personal:** Born Jan 19, 1917; married Pearl E Timberlake (died 1996); children: Roscoe, Synthia, Keith. **Educ:** Studied percussion instruments pvt then majoring Music Mast-Baum Cons. **Career:** Jimmy Gorham's Orchestra Phila, drum & arr 1932-41; Benny Carter 1941-42; recorded Artie Shaw, Lena Horne; AUS Bands 1943-46; short tour Cab Calloway 1946; Buck Clayton Sextet 1947; 3 yrs Earl Bostic Philadelphia 1950-52; free lancing Bill Doggett Combo 1952-59; played & transcribed several Broadway shows Mr Kicks & Co, Am Be Seated, Jerico Mim Crow, Here's Love; Sy Oliver Orchestra; 1964 played "Here's Love" SF Drumming Show "Club Finocchio", until 1993; co-writer Honky-Tonk; Berisford of San Francisco, owner, designer, builder fine furniture; North Peninsula Wind & Percussion Ensemble, 2nd Trombone; John Cordoni, Big Band, drummer; Charles Brown Combo, West Coast Only, "sub" drummer. **Orgs:** Friendly World Sound Swoppers, pres; Friendly Fifty, hon mem. **Honors/Awds:** Men of Distinction, British Publication; lecturing on "The Mechanics of the Trombone," and playing with "The Blues Fuse," (duo). **Business Addr:** Fine Furniture by Berisford of San Francisco, 195 Elmira St, San Francisco, CA 94124, (415)468-4426.

SHEPHERD, ELMIRA
Bookkeeper. **Personal:** Born Sep 9, 1959, Birmingham, AL; daughter of Cordell Johnson Shepherd and Fred Shepherd. **Educ:** Lakeshore Clerical Training, Birmingham, AL, clerical certificate, 1980; Booker T Washington Jr College, Birmingham, AL, 1987; Southern Jr College, Birmingham, AL, BBA, 1989. **Career:** YMCA, Birmingham, AL, tutor, 1984-85; Lakeshore Hospital Work Lab, Birminham, AL, microfilm aide, 1984-85; Goodwill Industries, Birmingham, AL, book sorter, 1986-88; Division Four Inc, Birmingham, AL, bookkeeper, 1991. **Orgs:** Church school teacher, Bethel AME Church, 1983-91, steward, 1991. **Honors/Awds:** Valadictorian, Southern Jr College, 1990. **Home Addr:** 13-14th Ave, SW, Birmingham, AL 35211.

SHEPHERD, GRETA DANDRIDGE
Educational administrator. **Personal:** Born Aug 15, 1930, Washington, DC; daughter of Bertha Johnson Dandridge and Philip J Dandridge; married Gilbert A Shepherd (deceased); children: Michele M Murchison. **Educ:** Miner Teachers Coll Washington DC, BS 1951; DC Teachers Coll Washington DC, MA 1961. **Career:** DC Publ Schools, teacher 1951-66, asst principal, principal 1966-72; E Orange Public Schools, NJ, supt, 1980-82; Plainfield NJ, supt of schools 1982-84; NJ State Dept of Educ, cty supt of schools; mem Phi Delta Kappa 1987-; supt Essex County Vocational Schools NJ, retired; NC Educational Associates, vp, currently. **Orgs:** Mem Alpha Kappa Alpha Sor 1950; assoc CFK Ltd Found 1971; pres elect CADRE Found 1975-; bd of dir YWCA of the Oranges 1975-78; mem, bd of trustees East Orange Public Library 1981-83; bd of trustees Mercer Co Comm Coll 1984-; fed policy comm mem Amer Assoc of School Admin 1984-; mem, Phi Delta Kappa, 1987-. **Honors/Awds:** Fulbright/Hayes Fellow Intl Christian Univ 1965; Woman of the Year No Jersey Chap Zeta Phi Beta 1983; 5 Point Awd Educ No Jersey Chap Delta Sigma Theta Sor 1984; Awd of Recognition Congressional Black Caucus Educ Braintrust 1984; Educator of The Year, Northeast Coalition of Educational Leaders Inc 1988; New Jersey State Assembly Citation; Black New Jersey Magazine, Person of the Decade; National Assn for Equal Opportunity in Higher Education, Distinguished Alumni Award; Bd of Trustees, Univ of District of Columbia; Gubnertorial Appointee to NJ Educational Opportunity Fund. **Home Addr:** 6 Linden Ave, West Orange, NJ 07052.

SHEPHERD, LESLIE GLENARD
Professional football player. **Personal:** Born Nov 3, 1969, Washington, DC. **Educ:** Temple, attended. **Career:** Washington Redskins, wide receiver, 1994-. **Business Addr:** Professional Football Player, Washington Redskins, 13832 Redskin Dr, Herndon, VA 22071, (703)471-9100.

SHEPHERD, MALCOLM THOMAS
President. **Personal:** Born Sep 27, 1952, Chicago, IL; son of Christine Shepherd and Chester Shepherd; married Thelma Jones Shepherd, Nov 25, 1970; children: Monica, Malcolm Jr, Marlon, Maxwell, Makalen. **Educ:** Jackson State Univ, Jackson, MS, BA, 1976, MPA, 1981; Bernard M Baruch Coll, New York, NY, MPA, 1985. **Career:** State of NY Mortgage Agency, New York, NY, spec asst to pres, 1984-85; Dept of Eco Dev, Jackson, MS, fin consultant, 1985-88; Governor's Office State of MS, Jackson, MS, eco dev policy analyst, 1988-89; Madison Madison Intl, Jackson, MS, mgr, 1989-93; MTS Ltd, Inc, Jackson, MS, president, 1993-. **Orgs:** Pres, MS Chapter-Natl Business League, 1990-91; chmn, JSU-Small Business Dev Ctr, 1990-91; mem, NAACP, 1977; mem, Nation Urban Fellows, 1985-. **Honors/Awds:** Nation Urban Fellow; Annie Divine Community Service Award, Jackson State Univ, 1984; National HUD Fellow, Jackson State Univ, 1983. **Military Serv:** Marine Corps, corporal, 1970-72. **Business Addr:** President, MTS Ltd, Inc, PO Box 2542, Jackson, MS 39207-2542.

SHEPHERD, ROOSEVELT EUGENE
Educator. **Personal:** Born Oct 31, 1933, Elkridge, WV; married Vivian L. Diggs; children: Nathetha Chamelle Shepherd. **Educ:** Kentucky State College, BS, business administration, 1955; University of Louisville, certified in police science, Southern Police Institute, 1969; Michigan State University, MS, criminal justice, 1971; University of Pennsylvania, MGA, Government administration, 1979; University of Maryland, University of Cincinnati, Temple University, Shippensburg University, Pennsylvania State University, course work. **Career:** Cincinnati Division of Police, police officer (patrolman specialist sgt lt), 1956-71; Cincinnati, Ohio, security consultant, 1971-72; Pennsylvania Department of Community Affairs, Harrisburg, community service consultant, (police mgmt), 1972-76; Shippenburg University, associate professor of criminal justice/dept chairperson, 1976-. **Orgs:** Program chairman, Harrisburg-Riverside Optimist Club, 1977-79; Academy of Criminal Justice Science, 1978-; City of Harrisburg, PA, Civil Service Committee; district director, PA, Black Conference on Higher Education, 1979-80; Dauphin Co Pretrial Service Agency (DCPSA), board of directors; Omega Psi Phi, 1953-; Reserve Officers Association, ROA, 1968-; Phi Delta Kappa International, 1977-; consultant: Pennsylvania Department of Community Affairs, Maryland Transportation Authority, Pennsylvania Human Relations Commission. **Honors/Awds:** Law Enforcement Exec Development Fellowship, LEAA, US Department of Justice, 1970. **Military Serv:** AUS, spec 4, 1956-58; Good Conduct Medal; Soldier of the Month Award; AUS Reserves, chief warrant officer, 1958-83. **Business Addr:** Associate Professor Criminal Justice, Shippensburg University, Criminal Justice Department, Shippensburg, PA 17257.

SHEPHERD, VERONIKA Y.
City official. **Personal:** Born Apr 9, 1947, Cincinnati, OH; daughter of Leola Oliver Gibson (deceased) and Carl Nathenial Oliver; married David Louis Shepherd, Dec 3, 1981; children: Kevin, Willie, Bryan, Athena, Deja Dewberry. **Educ:** Ohio State University, Columbus, OH, AA, 1975. **Career:** State of Ohio, Columbus, OH, training coordinator, 1974-75, head start administrative coordinator, 1975-79, grants administrator, 1979-82, CCA/CSA/state administrator, 1982-84, geriatric adminstration specialist, 1985, personnel adminstrator, 1985-86; Village of Urbancrest, OH, mayor, currently. **Orgs:** Commissionaire, State of Ohio Women Research Policy Commission, 1991-93; president, Ohio Chapter of Black Mayors, Inc; first vice chair, National Chapter of Black Mayors Inc, Black Women Caucus, 1990-91; Unicare Development Board, Village of Urbancrest, 1990-94; first vice president, Columbus Metropolitan area Community Action Organization; Southwestern City School District Business Computer Programming Advisory Committee, Hayes Technical High School, 1990-91; member, Franklin County Headstart Policy Committee, 1991-93; member, Franklin County Right From the Start Community Forum Board, 1991-93; member, Mid-Ohio Regional Planning Board, 1991-94. **Honors/Awds:** Woman of the Year Award, The United Methodist Church, 1986; Ohio Community Section Award of Legislative and Community Leadership, 1984; Governor Award for Public Service, Governor of Ohio, 1984; Public Service Award, President Jimmy Carter, 1982; County Action Community Center Award for Volunteer Service, 1987-91; Sisterhood Award for Unselfish Service and Committment in the Bethune Tradition, Clark County Section, Natl Council of Negro Women, 1990.

SHEPPARD, STEVENSON ROYRAYSON
City official & educational administrator. **Personal:** Born Jan 10, 1945, Bunkie, LA; married Diana Lewis; children: Stephen, Steven. **Educ:** Grambling State Univ, BS 1967; Southern Univ, MEd 1974; Northwestern State Univ, MA 1976. **Career:** Rapides Parish School System, teacher 1967; Aroyelles Parish School System, teacher & coach 1968; Aroyelles Progress Action Com, athletics dir 1968; Sheppard& Jones Reading Clinic, dir; Town of Bunkie, alderman-at-large. **Orgs:** Dir, vice pres Zach & Shep's Skate-Arama Inc 1983. **Honors/Awds:** Wm Progressive Lodge #217 1975; chmn of bd Amazon Baptist Church 1982. **Home Addr:** PO Box 647, Bunkie, LA 71322. **Business Addr:** Alderman at Large, Town of Bunkie, Walnut St, Bunkie, LA 71322.

SHEPPHARD, CHARLES BERNARD
Educator. **Personal:** Born Sep 26, 1949, Port Gibson, MS; married Brenda Joyce Stone; children: Charles Kwame, Tenopra Me'Keda, Ashanta. **Educ:** Alcorn State Univ, BS 1970; Southern Univ, JD 1973; MS College, JD 1977. **Career:** Shepphard & Assoc, complete consulting svcs; Alcorn State Univ, prof of history/polit sci 1977-; MS House of Rep, 1980-; The Fayette Chronicle Newspaper, owner, publisher, currently. **Orgs:** Amer Historical Assn; Southern Growth Policy Bd; Amer Management Assn; Intl Affairs Assn; chmn NAACP-Fair Share Committee; chmn Local Political Party Activities; coordinator Political Sci Internship Program Black Political Sci Soc. **Honors/Awds:** Outstanding Young Men Award; Progressive Young Legislator of MS. **Home Addr:** PO Box 254, Lorman, MS 39096.

SHERMAN, BARBARA J. (BARBARA J. SHERMAN-SIMPSON)
Stockbroker, investments manager. **Personal:** Born Jul 20, 1944, Los Angeles, CA; daughter of Estelle Sherman and Ernest Sherman; married Mike O Simpson, 1989. **Educ:** California State University at Northridge, Northridge, CA, 1961; Mesa Community College, Mesa, AZ, 1971; Arizona State University, Tempe, AZ, business admin, 1972-74. **Career:** Merrill Lynch, Phoenix, AZ, acct exec, 1975-77; Dean Witter, Sun City, AZ, acct exec, 1977-80; Merrill Lynch, Sun City, AZ, acct exec, 1980-84; Prudential-Bache Securities, Sun City, AZ, vice pres, investments, 1984-. **Orgs:** The City of Phoenix Mayor's Commission on the Status of Women, 1979-82; chairperson, Black Republican Council-Phoenix, 1985; Arizona state chairperson, United Negro College Fund, 1987-88; Black Jewish Coalition, 1986-; Valley Big Sisters, 1983-86; Stockbroker's Society, 1975-; Arizona Board of Realtors, 1972-; American Red Cross, Central Arizona Chapter, board member, 1988-. **Honors/Awds:** Woman of the Year in a Non-traditional role, Delta Sigma Theta, Inc, Phoenix, AZ Chapter, 1983; numerous performance awards, Merrill Lynch and Prudential-Bache. **Military Serv:** US Air Force, E-5, 1963-71.

SHERMAN, EDWARD FORRESTER
Photographer. **Personal:** Born Jan 17, 1945, New York, NY; married Audrey Johnson; children: Edward F. **Educ:** Amsterdam Photographic Workship 1960; Bronx Comm Coll 1962-64; Univ S Marine Corps 1966; New Sch Soc Research Spring 1969; Brooklyn Coll 1970-73. **Career:** NCA New Journal, asso ed 1973-; Freelance Photographer 1969-; New Dimensions Assoc, dir 1968-; Comm Corp Lower W Side, art instr 1972; Photographic Prog, dir June-Sept 1970; Photo-Lab Tech 1968-69; Still Photographer USMC, 1965-67; freelance photographer 1962-65. **Orgs:** Co-chmn Collective Black Photographers 1971; chmn Benin Enterprises Inc 1975-. **Military Serv:** USMC sgt. **Business Addr:** 240 W 139 St, New York, NY 10030.

SHERMAN, RAY
Football coach. **Personal:** Born in Berkeley, CA; married Yvette; children: Ray II, Erica. **Educ:** Laney Junior Coll; Fresno State; San Jose State, education degree, 1975. **Career:** Michigan State Univ, coaching staff, 1974, 1976-77; California, coaching staff, 1975, 1985; Wake Forest Univ, coaching staff, 1978-80; Purdue, coaching staff, 1982-85; Georgia, coaching staff, 1986-87; New York Jets, offensive coordinator; Minnesota Vikings, quarterback coach, currently. **Orgs:** American Football Association. **Business Addr:** Quarterback Coach, Minnesota Vikings, 9520 Viking Dr, Eden Prairie, MN 55344, (612)828-6500.

SHERMAN, THOMAS OSCAR, JR.
Chief engineer, director. **Personal:** Born May 29, 1948, Elberton, GA; son of Edna Murray Sherman and Thomas Oscar Sherman, Sr; married Joyce Chestang, May 12, 1973; children: Alfred, Morris, Katherine. **Educ:** NC A&T State Univ, BSEE 1971; Golden Gate Univ, MBA Mgmt 1979. **Career:** USAF SAC, ATC, capt ewo instructor 1971-80; Ford Aerospace sr systems engr 1980-83, mgr computer systems 1983-84, mgr TREWS engrg 1984-88, SDDS/TREWS Program Manager 1988-90; Loral SRS, Ridgecrest, CA, director, E W programs, 1990-91, deputy engineering director, 1991-95; Lockheed Martin SRS, chief engineer, director, 1996-. **Orgs:** Mem Assoc of Old Crows 1976-; mem Natl Guard/Air Force Assoc 1980-; opers officer (capt) 129th Communications Flight CA ANG 1980-83; commander (major) 129th Information Systems Flight

CA ANG 1983-87; mem Union Baptist Church Ridgecrest CA; commander (lieutenant colonel) 129 Mission Support Squadron CA ANG 1987-94, commander, 129 support group (Colonel), 1994-; adult bible teacher, 1987, choirmember, 1986-94, Union Baptist Church; membership chairman, Kiwanis Club of Ridgecrest, CA, 1990-91; Emanual Baptist Church, adult bible teacher, mem, 1994-. **Honors/Awds:** Distinguished ROTC Graduate NC A&T State Univ 1971. **Military Serv:** USAF/ANG, colonel, 1971-; AF Commendation Medal (1 cluster); Natl Defense Ribbon; Coast Guard Outstanding Unit Ribbon (1 cluster); AF Outstanding Unit Ribbon; Longevity Service Ribbon (3 clusters); Armed Forces Reserve Medal; Air Force Training Ribbon, Governor's Outstanding Unit Ribbon, Meritorious Service Medal, 1 cluster, Senior Navigator Wings. **Business Addr:** Chief Engineer/Director, Lockheed Martin Western Development Labs, Systems Engineering Laboratory, 1260 Crossman, Sunnyvale, CA 94089.

SHERMAN-SIMPSON, BARBARA J. See SHERMAN, BARBARA J.

SHEROW, DON CARL
Cleric, educator. **Personal:** Born Apr 15, 1949, Gilmer, TX; married Hazel June Smith; children: Don Jr, Shuna, Kenan, Brecca, Wendell. **Educ:** Tuskegee Inst, BA English 1971; Covenant theological Seminary, MDiv 1976. **Career:** Tuskegee Inst, instructor 1971-72; Berachah Comm Church, pastor 1976-78; Westminster Schools, teacher 1978-81; Madison Ave Christian Reformed Church, minister, pastor, 1982-86; Christian Reformed Church NA, church planter, 1986-89; Gloucester County Public Schools, teacher, 1990-. **Orgs:** Bd mem Covenant Theological Seminary 1979-85; bd mem Dawn Treader Sch 1983-85; consultant and seminar leader "Racism & Reconciliation" 1983-85; chmn family select comm & bd mem Paterson Habitat for Humanity 1984-85. **Special Achievements:** Composer/arranger Religious music, 1963-85; consultant, revision of The Psalter Hymnal, 1983-84; "The Black Connection," The Banner, 1984.

SHERRELL, CHARLES RONALD, II
Broadcasting executive. **Personal:** Born May 10, 1936, Gary, IN; son of Beatrice Mariner Sherrell and George Wesley Sherrell, Jr.; married Trutie Thigpen, Nov 25, 1969. **Educ:** Mexico City Coll, Mexico, BA, 1958; Roosevelt Univ, Chicago IL, MA, 1963; Univ of Chicago, PhD, 1975. **Career:** Gary Public Schools, Gary IN, foreign language tchr, 1961-65; United States Steel, Gary IN, foreman, 1965-67; Globe Trotter Commns, Chicago IL, sales mgr, 1967-71; Bell & Howell Schools, Chicago IL, vice pres, 1971-74; Mariner Broadcasters Inc, Chicago IL, pres, 1974-. **Orgs:** Radio Advertising Bureau, 1974-; pres, Amer Soc of Linguists, 1978-80; chmn of memshp comm, Black Hispanics Assoc, 1979-84; mem of reading educ comm, New Fronteirs Inc, 1981-82; chmn, Natl Assn of African-Amer Anthropologists, 1983-85; chmn of cable TV comm, 901 Condo Bd Assn, 1987-89; pres 1988-90, chairman 1990-, Natl Assn of Black-Owned Broadcasters Inc. **Honors/Awds:** Distinguished Alumnus Award, Univ of Chicago Alumni Assn, 1979; Humanitarian Award, American Linguists Soc, 1980; Humanitarian Award, New Frontiers Inc, 1981. **Military Serv:** US Army, 1959-61. **Home Addr:** 901 S Plymouth Ct, Apt 106, Chicago, IL 60605.

SHERRILL, WILLIAM HENRY
Educator. **Personal:** Born Dec 6, 1932, North Carolina; married Gloria; children: William Jr, Adrienne Budd, Erick, Sharon, Karen. **Educ:** Shaw U, AB 1954; Univ PA 1959; Univ MI, MA 1960; Univ CA, PhD 1961-72; SF State Coll 1965. **Career:** Howard Univ, dean 1972-; Univ CA, dir 1968-72; Univ CA 1968-69; Univ CA, dir 1967-68; SF State Coll, lectr 1965-69; Berkeley HS, teacher counselor 1960-67; LH Foster HS, teacher 1954-59. **Orgs:** Mem Afro-Am Educators Assn; Am Assn of Collegiate Registrats & Admissions Officers; Am Council on Higher Edn; Am Personnel & Guidance Assn; CA Counseling & Guidance Assn; CA Tchrs Assn; Coll Entrance Exam Bd; Berkeley Tchrs Assn; No CA Counseling & Guidance Assn; Nat Assn of Berkeley Councelors;Nat Assn of Coll Deans Registrars Admissions Officers; Nat Assn of Coll Admissions Counselors; Nat Assn of Fgn Students Affairs; Consortium of Univ of the WA Metro Area; WA Area Admissions Assn; DC Orgn of Admissions & Financial Aid Personnel; Proj BOOST 1968; Upward Bound 1968; Monterey Co Counselors Assn 1968; Am Coll Test Adv Bd 1968-72; Educ Testing Serv 1969; Educ Oppty Prgms 1968-72; Coll Entrance Exam Bd Proj Acess 1969; Nat Merit Scholarship Selection Com 1971-72; NatAchvmt Scholarship Sction Com 1969-70; Nat Teamsters Scholarship Selection Com 1973-; W Reg Scholarship Selection Com 1972. **Honors/Awds:** Num Professional Confs Attended; Publ, Counseling in the Absence of Intergration, A Comparative Study of Selected Psychol & Soc Perception of Negro & Mexican-Am Adolescents.

SHERROD, CHARLES M.
Clergyman. **Personal:** Born Jan 2, 1937, Petersburg, VA; son of Martha Walker Sherrod Gibson and Raymond Sherrod; married Shirley M Sherrod; children: Russia, Kenyatta. **Educ:** VA Union Univ, AB 1958; VA Union Univ School of Religion, BD 1961; Union Theological Seminary, STm 1967; Univ of GA, Certificate of Comm Development. **Career:** Interdenominational, minister 1956-; SNCC, Field Sec 1961-67; SW GA Project, dir 1961-87; New Comm Inc, dir 1968-85; City of Albany, city commissioner 1977-. **Orgs:** 1st SNCC Field Organizer 1961; mem Freedom Ride Coordinating Comm 1963; US Govt OEO 1974; Fellow Inst for Policy Studies 1974; consultant Natl Council of Churches 1978; pres SW GA Project 1967-85; bd NAACP 1970-85; bd Slater King Center 1975-85; bd SW GA Planning Comm 1978-85; bd mem Fed of Southern Coop 1979-87; GA Coalition of Housing 1983-85. **Honors/Awds:** Omega Man of the Year Lambda Chapter Richmond 1958; Honors in Civil Rights Natl Lawyers Guild 1985; Delegate Natl Democratic Party Convention 1984; song writer, poet, singer. **Home Addr:** 201 Garden Hill Dr, Albany, GA 31705. **Business Addr:** Commissioner, City of Albany, PO Box 447, Albany, GA 31701.

SHERROD, EZRA CORNELL
Sales Executive. **Personal:** Born Jul 25, 1950, Wilson, NC; son of Mary Hester Worsely Sherrod and John Sherrod; married Charlotte Pye Sherrod, Aug 23, 1975; children: Derrick Cornell. **Educ:** Lear Siegler Inst, AA 1971; Univ District of Columbia, BA 1977; Project Management Seminars, 1977-80; People and Resources Mgmt Seminars, 1983-86. **Career:** Woodard and Lothrop, computer specialist 1970-72; Intl Business Serv Inc, project mgr 1972-80; Automated Datatron Inc, project mgr 1980-86; Sherrod Security Co, pres/owner 1986; Wilkins Systems Inc, facility mgr 1986-; Hecht's, comm sales/professional sales executive 1990-91; Advantage Mortgage Services, VP, 1993-. **Orgs:** Pres history club Univ DC 1974-76; mem Univ District of Columbia Alumni 1984; mem Minority Business Commn 1986; active mem Evangel Assembly Church Camp Springs MD; mem Business Network of Washington DC; mem Physical and Mental Self-Improvement Programs. **Honors/ Awds:** Top Five Mgrs of Year Automated Datatron Inc 1985; author letter of intro "Saga of Sidney Moore," 1985; top candidate for major exec position involving a major computer network w/Wilkins Systems Inc 1987; diamond club member Top Sales Level Hecht's, 1991. **Home Addr:** 808 Kirkwood Rd, Waldorf, MD 20602.

SHERVINGTON, E. WALTER
Physician. **Personal:** Born Jul 23, 1906, Antigua, WI; son of Ethel Julian M. and Ashley Shervington; married Charlotte; children: Anne, Walter, Carol. **Educ:** Howard U, BS 1931; Howard Univ Coll Med, MD 1934. **Career:** Retired physician internal med; VD Clinics Baltimore City Hlth Dept, dir 1954-76; Baltimore City Hosp, chf med clinic 1960-70; Johns Hopkins Sch Med, instr med 1964-80; instructor Emeritus, 1980-89, Epidemiology Sch Hlth & Hygiene Johns Hopkins U; Consult Med Ch Hosp, staff; Soc Security Medicare consultant. **Orgs:** Mem AMA; Baltimore Med Soc; MD Med Soc; Chi Delta Mu Med Frat; Flw Royal Soc Hlth; Am Coll Angiology; Am Geriatric Assn; Intl Coll Angiology; mem Am Pub Hlth Assn; Clinical Cncl Am Heart Assn. **Military Serv:** AUS MC capt 1950-52.

SHERWOOD, O. PETER
Attorney. **Personal:** Born Feb 9, 1945, Kingston, Jamaica; son of Gloria Howell Sherwood and Leopold Sherwood; married Ruby Birt; children: 1. **Educ:** Brooklyn Coll, BA 1968; NYU Sch of Law, JD 1971. **Career:** NY Civil Court, law sec to Hon Fritz W Alexander II 1971-74; NAACP Legal Def & Educ Fund Inc, atty 1974-84; NY Univ School of Law, adj asst prof of law 1980-87; State of NY, solicitor general, 1986-91; City of New York, corporation counsel, 1991-93; Kalkines, Arky, Zall & Bernstein, partner, 1994-. **Orgs:** Trustee NY Univ Law Ctr Found; co-chmn Compliance & Enforcement Comm NY & St Bar Assn; Taskforce on NY St Div on Human Rights 1977-80; board of directors New York City Comm Action Legal Serv 1971-75; 100 Black Men; Metro Black Bar Assn; Natl Bar Assn; secretary, Bar of the City of New York Association, 1992-97. **Business Addr:** Partner, Kalkines, Arky, Zall & Bernstein, 1675 Broadway, New York, NY 10019.

SHERWOOD, WALLACE WALTER
Attorney, educator. **Personal:** Born Oct 6, 1944, Nassau, Bahamas; son of Tereceta Sherwood and Walter Sherwood. **Educ:** St Vincent Coll, BA 1966; Harvard Univ, LLM 1971; George Washington Univ, JD 1969. **Career:** Legal Svcs, staff atty 1969-71; MA Comm Against Discrimination, commnr 1971-73; Roxbury Pub Def, dir 1971-73; OEO, gen counsel 1973-74; Lawyers Comm for Civil Rights under Law, exec div 1974-76; Private Practice, attorney 1976-; NE Univ Coll of Criminal Justice, assoc prof. **Orgs:** Mem MA Bar Assn 1969-; mem Boston Bar Assn 1969-; mem MA Council for Pub Justice. **Honors/ Awds:** Dulles Fulbright Awd Natl Law Ctr 1969; Teacher of The Year, 1987 Coll of Criminal Justice. **Business Addr:** Associate Professor, Northeastern Univ Coll of Criminal Justice, 360 Huntington Ave, Boston, MA 02115.

SHIELDS, CLARENCE L., JR.
Physician. **Personal:** Born Jul 19, 1940, Helena, AR; married Barbara Wilson; children: Brian, Christopher, Angela. **Educ:** Loyola Univ, Los Angeles, CA, 1958-62; Creighton Univ School of Med, Omaha, NE, MD. **Career:** UCLA Med Center, Los Angeles, CA, surgical intern, 1966-67; Southwestern Orthopaedic Med Group, Inglewood, CA, orthopaedic surgery, 1973-; Daniel Freeman Hospital, staff, 1973; Los Angeles Rams, associate physician 1973-; Viewpark Community Hosp, staff, 1973; Martin Luther King Hosp, staff, 1973; Charles Drew School of Med, Los Angeles, CA, clinical prof, 1973-; Rancho Los Amigos Hosp, staff, 1976; Los Angeles Dodgers, Los Angeles Lakers, Los Angeles Kings, California Angels, orthopedic consultant, currently; Univ of Southern Cal School of Medicine, clinical prof, 1976-; Kerlan-Jobe Orthopedic Clinic, Inglewood, CA, private practice, currently. **Orgs:** AMA; Amer Orthopaedic Soc of Sports Med; Amer Bd of Orthopaedic Surgery; Amer Acad of Orthopaedic Surgeons; diplomate, Natl Bd of Med Examiners; mem, bd of dirs, Western Orthopaedic Assn, 1979; LA Co Med Assn; Charles Drew Med Soc; CA Med Assn; Western Orthopaedic Assn; chm, orthopaedic review com, 1978-, orthopaedic comm and credential comm, Centinela Hosp; adv bd, 1973-, chm, fellowship comm, 1973-, Natl Athletic Health Inst; Alpha Omega Alpha; Herodicus Soc. **Military Serv:** US Air Force, CPT, general medical officer, 1967-69. **Business Addr:** Associate Physician, Los Angeles Rams, 505 N Tustin Ave, Ste 243, Santa Ana, CA 92705-3735.

SHIELDS, CYDNEY ROBIN
Company manager. **Personal:** Born Feb 24, 1957, Jamaica, NY; daughter of Sylvia and Waddel; divorced. **Educ:** Indiana University of Pennsylvania, BA, English, 1980. **Career:** Lockheed Management Information Systems, auditor, analyst, 1982-84, control manager, 1984-87, regional office manager, 1987-; Claims Administration Corp, division manager, 1989-. **Orgs:** Delta Sigma Theta, 1977-; American Business Women's Association, vice pres, 1988-; Black Women's Advisory Board, 1989-; National Commission of Working Women of Wider Opportunities for Women, 1992-; National Association for Female Executives; Black Women Who Win, founder, 1986-. **Special Achievements:** Co-author, Work, Sister, Work: Why Black Women Can't Get Ahead, 1992; Managing Your Writing, Management World, 1992; The Right Moves on Your New Job, Women in Business, 1991; Mounting a Career Climb, Career Focus Magazine, 1992. **Home Phone:** (301)590-0119. **Business Phone:** (301)517-2165.

SHIELDS, DEL PIERCE
Radio commentator. **Personal:** Born Apr 29, 1933, New York, NY; son of Daisy Hite Shields and Judge Pierce Shields; divorced; children: Leslie, Allyson, Cydney, Cynthia, Stacy. **Educ:** National Theological Seminary, BS, 1978, MA, 1982, MDiv, 1984; University of Santa Barbara, PhD, 1989. **Career:** WLIB, radio host, 1965-68; Independent Network-WLIB, WRVR, WWRL, radio host, 1968-70; Jemmin Inc (Bill Cosby's Production Co), assistant vice pres, 1970-77; Avant-Garde Broadcasting Inc, vp/gen manager, 1975-77; Zion Gospel Church, senior pastor, 1980-; Unity Broadcasting WWRL, Morning Fellowship host, 1986-91, Drivetime Dialogue commentator, 1991-. **Orgs:** National Association of Television & Radio, executive vice pres, 1971-73, executive director, 1974-78. **Honors/Awds:** Blanton Peale, Graduate Institute, 1981. **Special Achievements:** Moments in Meditation, 1991-92. **Home Addr:** 112-11 Dillon St, Jamaica, NY 11433, (718)658-2420.

SHIELDS, KAREN BETHEA (KAREN GALLOWAY SHIELDS)
Attorney. **Personal:** Born Apr 29, 1949, Raleigh, NC; daughter of Grace Parrish Bethea and Bryant W Bethea; married Linwood B Shields, Dec 31, 1984. **Educ:** E Carolina Univ, AB, 1971; Duke Univ, School of Law, JD, 1974. **Career:** Paul Keenan Rowan & Galloway, partner, 1974-77; Loflin Loflin Galloway & Acker, partner, 1977-80; 14th Judicial Dist Durham Cty, judge, 1980-1985; sole practitioner, Karen Bethea-Shields law firm, 1986-; attorney, counselor-at-law, currently. **Orgs:** American Bar Association; Natl Conference of Black Lawyers; jud council, Natl Bar Assn; American Civil Liberties Union; faculty mem, Natl Inst of Trial Advocacy; trial practice instructor, training of lawyers; Natl College for Criminal Defense Lawyers of NACDA; natl judicial college, Natl Bar Assn; Natl Assn of Women Judges; Amer Judicature Soc; Natl Judicial College Search & Seizure & Grad Evidence Spec Sessions, 1983; faculty mem, Women Trial Lawyers Advocacy Clinic, San Francisco, CA, 1984; guest lecturer, workshop panel member, Natl Academy of Trial Lawyers, Toronto, Canada, 1982; Intl Platform Association, 1988-89; Natl Council of Negro Women, 1989; vice chair, educ committee, Durham Committee on Affairs of Black People, 1989-; board of directors, Edgemont Community Center, 1990-; Hayti Development Corp., board of directors; Durham Community Shelter for HOPE, board of directors. **Honors/Awds:** Lawyer of the Year, Natl Conf of Black Lawyers, 1976; Outstanding Serv Awd, Raleigh Chap, Delta Sigma Theta, 1977; Outstanding Young Woman of the Year, 1983; NAACP, Distinguished Achievement Awd, 1981; Runner-up, NEXT Mag, 100 Most Powerful People for the 80's; NC Juvenile Court Judges, cert for 1982, 1984; Cert of Appreciation, NC State Assn of Black Social Workers, 1979; 1st Black female, 1st female Dist Court Judge in Durham Cty; 2nd Black female judge in NC; Joann Little Defense Team, 1974-75; Outstanding Service, Community Service, Excellence in Education, Sister Clara Muhammad Schools Education Fund for NC, 1989. **Business Addr:** Attorney, 123 Orange St, PO Box 6, Durham, NC 27702.

SHIELDS, LANDRUM EUGENE
Clergyman. **Personal:** Born Mar 17, 1927, Winston Salem, NC; son of Joanna Mary Berry and Samuel Jennings Shields; married Marjorie, Jun 11, 1955; children: Landrum Jr, Sharyn, Laurita, Andrea. **Educ:** Lincoln Univ, AB 1949; Oberlin Grad Sch of Theol; Howard Univ Sch of Religion, BD 1954; Christian Theol Sem, MRE 1960. **Career:** Witherspoon Presbyterian Church, clergyman; United Presb Ch 1985; Central State Hosp, dir tng; IN U, asso faculty; IN Central Coll, instr; Indpls YMCA, youth & adult sec; Howard U, chaplain; 1st Congregational Ch, pastor; Covenant Community Church, clergyman, currently. **Orgs:** Vp pres bd commrs Indianapolis Pub Schs; bd dir Comm Serv Cncl; Whitewater Presbytery of United Presb Ch; Marion Co Tax Adjustment Bd; Indianapolis Mayor's Task Force on Communications; UNICEF Indianapolis Com; Num Other Affiliations. **Honors/Awds:** Human Rels Roll of Honor Indpls; Recorder Newspaper 1968; Award of Merit So Cross #39 F & A M; Award for Outstanding Ldrshp & Dedication to Am Cancer Soc City of Indianapolis 1972-73; 50th Ann Distinguished Alumni Award Christian Theol Sem; 1976 Father of Yr Award Greyhound Corp; Chaplain for A Day US Senate 1977. **Home Phone:** (317)283-1627. **Business Addr:** Clergyman, Covenant Community Church, 3737 N Meridian St, Indianapolis, IN 46208.

SHIELDS, VAREE, JR.
Editor, publisher. **Personal:** Born Feb 19, 1935, Huntsville, TX; son of Robbie Hagan Shields and Varee Shields; married Johnnie Wright Shields, 1986; children: Ronald Victor Shields. **Educ:** TX Southern Univ, Houston, TX, BA 1956. **Career:** Houston Informer, gen assigments reporter 1959-60; Forward Times, Houston, TX, reporter, managing editor, 1960-86; The Houston Flame, editor & publisher 1986-. **Orgs:** Pres Vartrom Inc; chmn of bd J Wright & Associates Inc; mem bd Fannie Lou Hamer Memorial Found Inc, mem, Natl Newspaper Publisher Assn, 1963-86; pres, Huntsville, TX, Sam Houston High School, ex-students assn, 1982-84; mem, Metropolitan Transit Authrity Northeast Houston Transit Task Force, 1985-88; mem, Texas Publishers Assn, 1987-. **Honors/Awds:** Outstanding Media Award, Texas Black Media Coalition, 1977, Community Service, PABA Lynn Eusan Award, 1979. **Military Serv:** AUS Security Agency, specialist 5, 1956-59. **Home Addr:** 7401 Jay St, Houston, TX 77028.

SHIELDS, VINCENT O.
Director civil rights. **Personal:** Born Feb 20, 1924, Chillicothe, MO; married Edna Gilbert. **Educ:** Lincoln U, Attended 1946-48. **Career:** Chillicothe MO, us post office, fireman, laborer 1948-73; Fed Hwy Adm, equal oppor; Ofc of Civil Rights Fed Hwy Adm Reg 7, dir 1985; Mayor's Citizen Adv Com on Minority Housing Chillicothe, ch 1970; Chillicothe Housing Authority, 1st vp; MO State Conf NAACP, pres 1968-73. **Orgs:** Bd mem Hope Haven Ind 1968; pres Livingston Ct Human Dev Corp 1969-73; mem Amer Legion Post 25 Veterans of Foreign Ward; pres KC Chillicothe Br 1954-73; ch EEO Adv Com Green Hills Comm Action 1970-71. **Honors/Awds:** Award for Outstanding Serv Green Hill Human Dev Corp 1971; Outstanding Contribution to Improvement Social Justice Health & Welfare for People of MO MO Assn for Social Welfare 1973; Award Reg IV NAACP 1976; Bd Mem KS City Br NAACP; Plaque for Outstanding Dedicated & Loyal Leadership as Pres; MO State ConfNAACP & Branches 1973. **Military Serv:** US Army Inf 1943-45. **Business Addr:** Federal Highway Administration, PO Box 19715, Kansas City, MO 64141.

SHIELDS, WILL HERTHIE
Professional football player. **Personal:** Born Sep 15, 1971, Fort Riley, KS; married Senia; children: Sanayika, Shavon. **Educ:** Univ of Nebraska, degree in communications. **Career:** Kansas City Chiefs, guard, 1993-. **Orgs:** Marillac Center for Children, bd mem. **Honors/Awds:** Pro Bowl appearances, 1995, 1996. **Special Achievements:** Established the Will to Succeed Charitable Foundation to address the needs of battered and abused women and children in Kansas City. **Business Addr:** Professional Football Player, Kansas City Chiefs, One Arrowhead Dr, Kansas City, MO 64129, (816)924-9300.

SHIELDS-JONES, ESTHER L. M.
Dietary consultant. **Personal:** Born Dec 30, Beatrice, AL; daughter of Annie Gertrude Ishman Montgomery and Marshall A Montgomery Sr (deceased); widowed; children: Reginald A Shields, Darryl K Shields. **Educ:** Tuskegee University, Tuskegee Institute, AL, BS, 1963, dietetic internship, 1966-67; Texas Southern University, Houston, TX, MS, 1976; University of Minnesota, Minneapolis, MN, nutrition administration, 1989. **Career:** Veterans Administration Hospital, Tuscaloosa, AL, clinical dietician, 1976-78; Jefferson County Health Dept, Birmingham, AL, nutrition consultant, 1978-84; Elba General Hospital, Elba, AL, director of dietary services, 1984-85; University of Alabama at Birmingham, Birmingham, AL, clinical instructor, 1985-86; Hillhaven Corporation, Nashville, TN, staff dietician, 1985-87; Beverly Enterprises Inc, Atlanta, GA, dietary consultant, 1987-1991; Consultant dietician for Community Dialysis Centers, Salem Nursing Home and Rehab Center, Alabama Dialysis, Inc., 1993-96; Professional Directions, Consultant Dietician Group, 1996-; Healthcare Partners, Medical Group, nutritional educator, 1996-. **Orgs:** Member, American Dietetic Association, 1968-; member, Alabama Dietetic Association, 1967-; member, Consultant Dietitians in Health Care Facilities, 1988-; member, Top Ladies of Distinction, Birmingham Metropolitan Chapter, 1989-; member, Delta Sigma Theta Sorority, Birmingham Alumnae Chapter, 1984-. **Honors/Awds:** Outstanding Dietitian Nominee, Birmingham Dietetic Association, 1982. **Military Serv:** US Army, Lt Colonel, 1990-.

SHIFFLETT, LYNNE CAROL
Gallery administrator. **Personal:** Born in Los Angeles, CA; daughter of Carolyn Ellen Larkin Shifflett and James Hubbard Shifflett. **Educ:** Govt, Political Sci, Los Angeles State Coll, BA; Univ of WI, MA. **Career:** NBC, admin; Neighborhood Adult Participation Project, Watts Center Dir; Sch for Workers, Univ of WI, instructor; Communications Relations-Social Devel Commn, Milwaukee Co, urban planner, 1969-71; KMOX-TV (CBS), news writer, 1971-72, news producer, 1972-73; Columbia Univ Summer Program in Broadcast Journalism for Minority Groups, consultant and teacher 1973; WNBC-TV NewsCenter 4, weekend news producer, 1973-75, NBC Loan to Comm Film Workshop, training dir & teacher, 1975, WNBC-TV news field producer/writer, 1975-85; Shifflett Gallery, dir, 1985-; Sr news writer, KCOP Television News, 1989-91. **Orgs:** Fellowship Operations Crossroads Africa; delegate 8th Natl Conf US Natl Com for UNESCO 1961; Cert Comm Leadership Sch of Public Admin USC 1966; bd of dir Triad Inc 1977; bd of dir Henry St Settlement 1978; adv comm Edwin Grould Serv for Children 1985; Golden Life Mem, Delta Sigma Theta Sorority; Amer Women in Radio & TV; Natl Acad of Television Arts & Sciences; Natl Assn of Black Journalists. **Business Addr:** Director, Shifflett Gallery, PO Box 19159, Los Angeles, CA 90019.

SHINE, THEODIS
Educator. **Personal:** Born Apr 26, 1931, Baton Rouge, LA; son of Bessie Herson Shine and Theodis Wesley Shine. **Educ:** Howard University, Washington, DC, BA, 1953; University of Iowa, 1958; University of California, Santa Barbara, CA, PhD, 1973. **Career:** Dillard University, New Orleans, LA, instructor in drama and English, 1960-61; Howard University, Washington, DC, assistant professor of drama, 1961-67; Prairie View A & M University, Prairie View, TX, professor and head of department of drama, 1967-. **Orgs:** National Theatre Conference, National Conference of African American Theatres; Southwest Theatre Conference; Texas Educational Theatre Association; Texas Non-Profit Theatres, board member. **Honors/Awds:** Brooks-Hines Award for Playwriting, Howard University, author of "Plantation," contribution, "The Woman Who Was Tampered with in Youth," "Shoes", " Three Fat Batchelors"; Delta Sigma Theta Award-teacher; Beanie Award-Teaching; author of over sixty television scripts for series "Our Street.". **Home Addr:** 10717 Cox Lane, Dallas, TX 75229. **Business Addr:** P O Box 2082, Prairie View, TX 77446-0519.

SHINHOSTER, EARL
Association executive. **Personal:** Born in Savannah, GA. **Educ:** Morehouse College, degree in political science. **Career:** NAACP, Southeastern regional director, national field secretary, acting executive director, currently. **Business Addr:** Acting Executive Director, NAACP, 4805 Mount Hope Dr., Baltimore, MD 21215-3206, (410)358-8900.

SHIPE, JAMESETTA DENISE HOLMES
Journalist. **Personal:** Born May 30, 1956, Knoxville, TN; daughter of Lavonia Thompson Holmes and James Edward Holmes; married Abie Shipe, Oct 10, 1987; children: Kristen Janan. **Educ:** Univ of TN, BS Commun/Journalism 1980; Cooper Business School, AS (Cum Laude) Bus 1982; TN Institute, Electronics 1989-90. **Career:** FBI Office of Congressional & Public Affairs, writer, public relations rep 1982-83; Martin-Marietta Energy Systems Inc Computer Electronics Services, customer relations rep 1983-. **Orgs:** Mem Sigma Delta Chi Soc of Prof Journalists 1975-, Public Relations Soc of Amer 1977; public affairs/press consult Knoxville Women's Ctr 1979-80; mem Phi Beta Lambda Soc of Bus 1982; mem Smithsonian Institution 1987-; mem NAACP 1988-. **Honors/Awds:** PTA Scholarship Knoxville Chap 1974-75; Minority Scholarship Amer Newspaper Publ Assoc 1976-78; Dean's List Univ of TN 1980. **Home Addr:** 206 Northwestern Ave, Oak Ridge, TN 37830.

SHIPLEY, ANTHONY J.
Clergyman, educator. **Personal:** Born May 19, 1939, New York, NY; son of Lillian Hawkins Shipley and Oscar Shipley; married Barbara McCullough, Sep 3, 1960; children: Cornelia Jean. **Educ:** Drew University, BA 1961; Garrett Seminary, DMin 1964; Adrian College, DD 1974. **Career:** United Methodist Church, supt Detroit West Dist 1982-; Scott Church, pastor, 1987-; UMC, General Board of Global Ministry, deputy general secretary, 1992; Christ United Methodist Church, sr pastor, 1994. **Orgs:** Consultant NCJ Urban Network; adjunct prof Garrett Evangelical Theol Sem; bd of dir Adrian Coll; chmn Devel Commn for National Black United Fund; President's Assn of the Amer Mgmt Assn; delegate, Gen Conf of the United Methodist 1980; lecturer, Church Admin at N MS Pastors School; Inst for Adv Pastoral Studies; Oppor Indus Ctr; pres Natl Fellowship Conf Council; dir Detroit Council of Churches; MI State Council of Churches; MI State United Ministries in Higher Educ; Natl Bd of Higher Educ & Min; mgmt consultant Charfoos Christenson Law Firm; bd dir Methodist Theol School in OH; founder, McKenzie High School/Adrian College Bound Program; bd of directors, Barton McFarland Neighborhood Assn; Cuvy Leadership Center, certified trainer, 7 Habits of Highly Effective People. **Special Achievements:** Author: "The Care & Feeding of Cliques in the Church" Interpreter Magazine 1975; "The Self Winding Congregation" Interpreter Magazine 1975; "The Council on Ministries as a Support System" Letter Ctr for Parish Devel; "Everybody Wants to Go to Heaven But Nobody Wants to Die" Christian Century 1976; "Long Range Planning in the Local Church" MI Christian Advocate; "Something for Nothing" MI Christian Advocate; "Fable of Disconnection" MI Christian Advocate. **Home Addr:** 19505 Canterbury Rd, Detroit, MI 48221.

SHIPMON, LUTHER JUNE
Clergyman/social worker. **Personal:** Born Sep 24, 1932, Clarkton, NC; married Daisy Lindzy; children: Krishmu J. **Educ:** Shaw Univ, AB 1954, MDiv 1955, DD 1956; Friendship Coll, DD 1957. **Career:** LJ Shipmon Found Inc, pres 1972-85; Youngstown UN Day, chmn 1980; United Nations of YO Chapt, mem 1982; Northside Coalition YO, mem 1983; Regional Council on Alcoholism Inc, chmn bd dirs 1983. **Orgs:** Mem Mahoning Co Amer Cancer Soc 1980-; mem Health System Agency 1979-80; statistician Lott Cary Bapt Foreign Mission Coun USA 1965-81; chmn United Negro Coll Fund Inc 1979-82; clerk Steel Valley Assn Souther Bapt Con 1983; chmn NAACP membership drive 1975; minister Univ Park Bapt Ch 1962; minister Second Bapt Ch 1964; coord Mahoning Co Social Serv EPSDT 1981-83; minister First Calvary Bapt Ch YO 1965; minister/fndr St John's Bapt Temple YO 1982-85; Civil Rights Coord mahoning Co Welfare Dept YO 1974-80; delegate World Bapt Alliance in Stockholm Sweden 1975; coordinator 1st Nat'l Holiday Celebration for Martin Luther King Jr 1986; chiarman/bd dir Youngstown Food to Gleeners Inc 1986; pres Baptist Ministers Conference & Vicinity Youngstown OH 1986-88. **Business Addr:** Minister, 2801 Market St, Youngstown, OH 44503.

SHIPP, E. R.
Journalist. **Personal:** Born Jun 6, 1955, Conyers, GA; daughter of Minnie Ola Moore Shipp and Johnny Will Shipp Sr. **Educ:** Georgia State Univ, BA Journalism 1976; Columbia Univ, MA Journalism 1979. **Career:** The New York Times, natl correspondent, legal correspondent; asst metropolitan editor, currently. **Orgs:** Mem Chicago Assn of Black Journalists 1983-86; mem Natl Assn of Black Journalists 1983-; New York Assn of Black Journalists 1986-. **Honors/Awds:** Co-author, Outrage: The Story Behind the Tawana Brawley Hoax, Bantam, 1990; Pulitzer Prize, 1996. **Business Addr:** New York Daily News, 450 W. 33rd St., New York, NY 10001-2681.

SHIPP, HOWARD J., JR.
Educator. **Personal:** Born Oct 2, 1938, Muskogee, OK; married Jeanetta Combs; children: Jackie. **Educ:** Langston U, BS 1962; Northeastern State Coll, MS 1966; OK State U, post grad. **Career:** Univ Counseling Serv OK State Univ, counselor; Muskogee Public Schools, teacher football coach; Douglas HS Oklahoma City, teacher football coach; Northeast HS Oklahoma City, asst principal; Professional Baseball Player 1958-59; Professional Barber 1966-71. **Orgs:** Mem Oklahoma City Classroom Tchr Assn; Oklahoma City C of C; OK Educ Assn; Nat Assn of Edn; APGA NAACP; mem OCPA Bd Community Action Prog Stillwater OK; treas Mid Scope; chmn Minority Scholarship Com9; mem Institutional Scholarship Com; faculty advisor OSU Afro-Am Soc; sponsor Kappa Alpha Phi. **Honors/Awds:** Recipient Black Gold Award Alpha Phi Alpha Epsilon Epsilon Chap 1972-73; Co-coordinated Book "Techniques for the Low-Achiever in Science". **Business Addr:** Oklahoma State Univ, Univ Counseling Serv, Stillwater, OK 74074.

SHIPP, MAURINE SARAH
Realtor, appraiser. **Personal:** Born Mar 6, 1913, Holiday, MO; daughter of Sarah Harston and Edward Harston; widowed; children: Jerome Reynolds, Patricia R England. **Educ:** LaSalle Ext IL Univ, Ext Course Completed 1956; IL Bus Clg, Completed 1963. **Career:** Dept Agr St of IL, supv; Comm Dev Prog, appraiser; Springfield Pub Bldg, mbr; Shipp Real Estate Agcy, real est broker appraiser, currently. **Orgs:** State appraiser st of IL; bldg comm by the Mayor of Spfld 1984; National Conference Minority Women; NAACP; Natl Urban League. **Honors/Awds:** Hnry degree CO Christian Clg. **Business Addr:** Real Estate Broker/Appraiser, Shipp Real Estate Agency, 1017 S Spring, Springfield, IL 62704.

SHIPP, MELVIN DOUGLAS
Educator. **Personal:** Born Aug 10, 1948, Columbus, GA; married Dr Michele Pierre-Louis; children: Gael, Elizabeth. **Educ:** Indiana Univ School of Arts & Sci, BS 1970; Indiana Univ School of Optometry, OD 1972; Harvard Univ School of Public Health, MPH 1980; Univ of MI, School of Public Health, DRPH, 1996. **Career:** Naval Hosp Port Hueneme, chief optometry serv 1972-76; School of Optometry Univ of AL, dir optometric tech prog 1976-79, asst dean for clinical serv 1980-86;

Senator Donald W Reigle, Jr. (D-MI), health legislative assistant, 1989-90; Universtiy of Alabama at Birmingham School of Optometry, associate professor, 1983-. **Orgs:** Consult Med Info System via Telephone 1976-; panalist, consult Ophthalmic Devices Panels 1980-84; chmn, exec comm Ed Manpower Div Amer Optometric Assn 1983-; chmn Continuing Ed Comm Natl Optometric Assn 1983-; participant, guest Channel 10 PBS-TV Advances in Health 1983; American Public Health Association, governing councilor, 1990-; National Society to Prevent Blindness, scientific advisory committee, 1991-92. **Honors/Awds:** Commiss Spec Citation Food & Drug Admin 1983; National Optometric Association, Founder's Award, 1989. **Military Serv:** US Navy Reserve, 1971-; Natl Defense Medal, Armed Forces Reserve Medal, Meritorious Mast 61st Marine Amphibious Unit USCM 1978, Robert Wood Johnson Health Policy Fellow, 1989-90; Bell Ringer Awd REDCOMNINE, Navy Commendation Medal, 1992; Pew Health Policy Doctoral Fellow. **Business Addr:** Associate Professor, Univ of Alabama, School of Optometry, Birmingham, AL 35294.

SHIPP, PAMELA LOUISE
Licensed psychologist. **Personal:** Born Feb 18, 1947, St Louis, MO; daughter of Lovia L Falconer-Shipp and Mall B Shipp. **Educ:** Colorado Coll, BA 1969; George Washington Univ, MA 1973; Denver Univ, PhD 1985. **Career:** Irving Jr HS, dean of students 1975-77, counselor 1977-83; Southern IL Univ Counseling Ctr, therapist 1983-84; Palmer HS, counselor 1984-85; Colorado Coll, therapist 1985-; Pikes Peak Psychological Ctr, therapist 1985-. **Orgs:** Alumni Kappa Kappa Gamma Sor 1966-87; mem Amer Psychological Assoc Div 16 1985-87; consultant Ctr for Creative Leadership 1986-; pres Assoc of Black Psychologists Denver/Rocky Mtn Chap 1986-87; bd of dirs, Boys & Girls Club of Pike Peaks Region 1988-91; bd of dirs, World Affairs Council-Colorado Springs 1988-91. **Honors/Awds:** Publication "Counseling Blacks, A Group Approach," The Personnel and Guidance Journal 1983. **Home Addr:** 1510 Witches Willow Ln, Colorado Springs, CO 80906, (303)579-6878. **Business Phone:** (303)633-3891.

SHIPPY, JOHN D.
Foreign service officer. **Personal:** Born in Gaffney, SC; son of Hattie M Gibbs Shippy and John H Shippy; married Carmen L Richardson; children: Angela A, Tamar S, Stearmen R. **Educ:** USAF, certified master instructor, 1975; Culver-Stockton College, Canton, MO, BA, political science, 1978; Webster University, St Louis, MO, MA, personnel mgt, 1986; St Mary's University; Our Lady of the Lake University; AHMA, certified convention service manager, 1988; Dept of State Administrative Officers CRS. **Career:** US Air Force, MacDill AFB, cook, 1964-65; MACV, Compound, Pleiku AB, Vietnam, cook, 1965-66; High Wycombe Air Station, England, storeroom supervisor, 1967-69; 12th TFW Alert Facility, Cam Ranh Bay AB, Vietnam, supervisor, 1969-70; officer's op en mess, supervisor, 1970-71; 4th TFW Hospital, Seymour Johnson AFB, shift supervisor, 1970; Bien Hoa AB, Vietnam, shift supervisor, 1970; Lackland AFB, military training instructor, 1971-76; Royal Saudi Air Force, informational programmer, 1976-77, military training instructor, 1977-79; Offutt AFB, services operations officer, 1979-81; Air Force recruitment officer, 1981-83; Officer Recruitment Branch, chief, 1983-85; Kunsan AB, Korea, services operations officer, 1985-86; Central Texas College, Pacific Div, human relations management instructor, 1985-86; Kelly AFB, Base Services Div, chie1986-88; Royal Air Force, 20th Services Squadron, Upper Hayford, England, commander, 1988-91, special assistant, 1991-93; Army Air Force Exchange Service Headquarters, planning officer, retired USAF officer, The Dept of State, Foreign Service Officer, 1994; US American Embassy, Lima Peru, currently. **Orgs:** Vice president, Black Awareness Committee, 1990-91; Services Society, 1985-; Retired Office Association, 1985-; Air Force Association, 1978-; Veterans of Foreign Wars, 1972-; Vietnam Veterans of America; American Legion Services Society; HQ AAFES Food Inspection and Evaluation Program; board of governors, HQ AAFES Officers' Club, 1991-92. **Honors/Awds:** Best Recruiting Group in Nation, US Air Force, 1983; Best Innkeeper, US Air Force, 1986; Master Instructor, US Air Force, 1976; Master Drill Instructor, US Air Force, 1976; Instructor of the Quarter, US Air Force, 1976. **Military Serv:** US Air Force, Major, 1964-93; Meritorious Service Medal, 1986, 1988, 1992; Air Force Commendation Medal (6 Awards), Vietnam Service Medal. **Business Addr:** US Department of State, Washington, DC 20520.

SHIRLEY, CALVIN HYLTON
Physician. **Personal:** Born Jan 28, 1921, Tallahassee, FL; son of Stella Gertrude Shirley and Edwin S Shirley; married Jeanette Lindsey (deceased); children: Calvin H Jr, John W, Jasmin Denise, Cedric H, Carmen Anita. **Educ:** FL A&M Coll Tallahassee, pre-med 1942; Boston Coll of Physicians & Surgeons, MD 1947. **Career:** JC & SB Property Development Corp, owner/mgr; Private Practice, physician 1947-. **Orgs:** Pres Broward Co Med Dental & Pharm Assn of FL 1955-59; adv exec bd mem FL State Bur of Comprehensive Med 1969; state med dir 1977, present Grand Asst Med Dir IBPO Elks of the World; asst med dir FL State Sickle Cell Found 1979; active mem FL Med Assn, Natl Med Assn; past pres Kappa Alpha Psi Alumni Chapt; solo accompanist playing trumpet with St Christopher Episcopal Church Choir; 1st trumpet player with the Broward Comm Coll Symphony Orchestra. **Honors/Awds:** FL State Distinguished Serv Awd Gov of FL 1976; So Provincial Achievement Awd So Provincial of Kappa Alpha Psi Frat Inc 1977; Doctor of the Year Award, Caducean Soc of Greater Ft Lauderdale, 1985. **Military Serv:** USN hosp corpsman 1944-45; Asiatic Pacific Campaign. **Business Addr:** Physician, PO Box 9767, Fort Lauderdale, FL 33310-9767.

SHIRLEY, EDWIN SAMUEL, JR.
Surgeon/physician. **Personal:** Born Dec 13, 1922, Tallahassee, FL; son of Stella Gertrude Young Shirley and Edwin S. Shirley, Sr.; married Iris Mays, Jul 3, 1954; children: Edwin, John, Michael, Donald. **Educ:** FL A&M U, BS 1942; Howard Univ Grad Sch, MS 1948; Coll of Med Howard U, MD 1952; Howard Univ & USPH Staten Island, surgical residency 1953-57. **Career:** Dade Monroe Co Lung Assoc, rep dir 1966-; Chirs Hosp Miami, chief of staff 1968-; Dade Co Sickle Cell Council, chmn 1971-; Jackson Memorial Hosp, vicechmn bd trustees 1973-; Public Health Trust Miami, chmn exec com; Emergency Medicine Univ of Miami Family Practice Residents, instructor 1975-84; Ambulatory Walk-In Serv for Comm Health Inc, dir 1977-; Floral Park Med Ctr Miami, owner/director 1966-; instructor emergency medicine U of Miami Jackson Hospital Miami Florida, l975-; Floral Park Medical Center owner 1966-. **Orgs:** Mem Nat Med Assn; FL State Med Assn; Am Thoracic Soc; Dade Co Acad of Med; chmn Educ Task Force Model Cities; mem Chi Delta Mu Phi Beta Sigma Sigma Pi Phi Frats; mem Amer College of Medicine; Floral Park Medical Center owner l966-; appointed Medical Director Sunshine Health Center, Hollywood, FL, 1993. **Honors/Awds:** Oaths Honors Award in Pediatrics 1952; Merit Achievement Award FL A&M Univ 1968; Soc Action Award Phi Beta Sigma Frat 1970; Dean's Adv Com Univ of Miami Sch of Med; Disting Serv Awd Howard Univ 1975; Special Meritorious Awd Comm Health Inc 1983; the emergency room of Comm Hlth Inc of Miami renamed "The Edwin S Shirley, MD Ambulatory Walk-In Service" 1985; Ambulatory Walk-In Service C.H.I., Inc dir l978-; Man of the Year, Dade County Primary Care Consortium, 1992; Community Service Award, Natl Assn of Negro Business and Professional Women's Club, 1992; Dedicated Service Award, in primary care, Pompano Beach FL, 1994; Chief Executives Award, Sunshine Health Center, Pompano Beach, FL, 1994. **Military Serv:** UAS capt 1943-46. **Home Addr:** 2000 NW 56 St, Miami, FL 33142. **Business Addr:** Floral Park Medical Center, 1521 B NW 54 St, Miami, FL 33142.

SHIRLEY, JAMES M.
Banker. **Career:** Drexel National Bank, president and COO, currently. **Business Addr:** Pres, COO, Drexel Natl Bank, 3401 S. King Dr., Chicago, IL 60616, (312)225-9200.

SHIVER, JUBE, JR.
Journalist. **Personal:** Born May 30, 1953, South Boston, VA; son of Mildred Leigh Shiver and Jube Shiver Sr; married Tadasha Culbreath-Shiver, Nov 18, 1989. **Educ:** Syracuse University, Syracuse, NY, BS, 1975; Antioch School of Law, Washington, DC, JD, 1978; University of Southern California, Los Angeles, CA, MA, 1988. **Career:** Wilmington News-Journal, Wilmington, DE, staff writer, 1977-79; Washington Star, Washington, DC, staff writer, 1979-81; Washington Post, Washington, DC, staff writer, 1981-82; USA Today, Arlington, VA, staff writer, 1982-83; Los Angeles Times, Los Angeles, CA, staff writer, 1983-, Washington, DC, business correspondent, currently. **Orgs:** Washington Assn of Black Journalists; National Assn of Black Journalist. **Honors/Awds:** Washington/Baltimore Newspaper Guild Award, 1981; International Journalism, Fellowship USC, 1987; Author, Horizons East, 1974; Los Angeles Press Club Award, 1992. **Business Addr:** Washington Business Correspondent, Los Angeles Times, 1875 I St NW, Ste 1100, Washington, DC 20006.

SHIVERS, P. DERRICK
Multi-media company executive. **Personal:** Born Oct 30, 1964, Kansas City, MO; son of Alice L Perry and Isiah Shivers. **Educ:** Maplewoods Community College, 1984; Penn Valley Community College, AS, 1986; University of Missouri at Kansas City, 1988. **Career:** PDS Universal Entertainment Group Inc, president, 1989-92; Paradigm Entertainment, consultant, 1990-; PDS Communications Inc, chairman/CEO, 1992-; SS Sear International, Ltd, vp/gen mgr, 1994. **Orgs:** RIAA, 1991; UCC, 1991; National Association of Record Merchants, 1990; National Association of Ind Record Distributors, 1990; ASCAP, 1989; BMI, 1989. **Honors/Awds:** Black Business Association, Outstanding Achievement, 1990-91; Image Magazine, Kansas City, Entertainment Industry Top Ten, 1990. **Business Phone:** 800-473-7550.

SHIVERS, S. MICHAEL
City official. **Personal:** Born Mar 20, 1935, Madison, WI; son of Dimetra C Taliaferro Shivers and Stanley M Shivers; married Jacklyn Lee Gerth; children: Steven Michael, David Wallace, Julie Ann. **Educ:** Univ of WI, BS 1958. **Career:** WI Soc of Professional Soil Scientists, mem 1958-78; City of Madison, alderman 17th dist, 1971-73, 1975-. **Orgs:** Equal Opport Commiss, Bd of Public Works, City Parks Commiss, Transp Commiss, Legislative Comm; Madison Water Utility, Health Commiss, Dane Cty Parks Commiss, Common Council Org Comm; City-County Bldg Comm; mem NAACP, Urban League; City County Liaison Comm; City MATC Liaison Comm. **Honors/Awds:** Disting Serv Awd North Madison Jaycees 1977-78; sr mem Madison Common Council. **Business Addr:** Alderman District 17, City of Madison, City County Bldg, 210 Martin Luther King Blvd, Madison, WI 53709.

SHOCKLEY, ALONZO HILTON, JR.
Educator. **Personal:** Born Sep 30, 1920, Milford, DE; married Kay Marilyn Falke; children: Novella Shockley Randolph, Cheryl Shockley Durant, Alonzo Hilton III. **Educ:** DE State Coll, BS 1943; MI State Univ, MA 1947; NY Univ, advance cert ad/supv 1956, candidate doctoral degree; (NY Univ). **Career:** Brooks HS, science tchr 1948; Dept of Public Instruction, prin elem/jr high 1948-58; DE State Coll, rsch assoc 1958-60; Central St Dist #4, tchr 6th grade 1960-62; Union Free Sch Dist, prin 4-6 grades 1962-63; NY State Educ Dept, assoc adminstr 1964-65; Nassau Co Health & Welfare Cncl, educ coord 1965-66; Freeport Public Schs, dir state fed progs 1966-; Retired-Education Consultant 1985. **Orgs:** Pres 1984-85 bd dirs 1973- NY Univ Alumni; allocation comm United Way of Long Island 1977-; NY State Cncl of Superintendent Fed Legislation Comm 1976-; member, National Education Assn; member, Assn for Childhood Education International; member, Educational Research Assn of New York State; member, Nassau County Elementary Principles Assn; member, New York State Teachers Assn; member, Long Island National Conference of Christians and Jews; council pres, United Nation Assn; member, American Assn for School Administrators; member, New York State Council for School Superintendents; member, Assn for Supervision and Curriculum Development. **Honors/Awds:** Afro Amer Republican Cert Awd Long Island Cncl 1973; Meritorious Serv Awd Black Educators Comm of Freeport 1974; Serv Above Self Rotary Club of Westbury LI; Recog of Dedicated Serv Adminstrs in Compensatory Educ NY State 1972; Pres Mid-Long Island Chapter United Nations Assn-USA 1983-; Mem Bd of Dir Southern NY St Div-United Nations Assn of the USA 1978-; Bd of Dir, mem, Long Island Science Congress 1976-; Bd of Dirs-Alumni Federation of NYU Inc, & NYU Alumni Assn-Sch of York Univ Alumni Assn Health Nursing & Arts Profession 1984-85; Alumni Meritorious Service Award, 1988; Certificate of Appreciation, American Assn of School Administrators, 1982; Emeritus Membership, Long Island chapter, Phi Delta Kappa.Alocation Committee-United Way of Long Island-1976-; US Army 37th Special Service C942-45 (Retired). **Home Addr:** 49 Gaymore Road, Port Jefferson Station, NY 11776-1353.

SHOCKLEY, ANN ALLEN
Librarian, writer, educator. **Personal:** Born Jun 21, 1927, Louisville, KY; daughter of Bessie L Allen and Henry Allen; divorced; children: William L, Tamara A. **Educ:** Fisk Univ, BA 1948; Case Western Res Univ, MSLS 1959. **Career:** Del State Coll, freelance writer asst lib 1959-60, asst lib 1960-66, assoc lib 1966-69; Univ of MD East Shore, lib 1969, assoc lib pub serv, dir oral history; Fisk Univ, assoc lib for special collections & univ archivs, assoc prof lib sci 1970-. **Orgs:** Authors Guild; Soc of American Archivists; Amer Library Assn Black Caucus; Tennessee Archivists; Assn of Black Women Historians; College Language Assn. **Honors/Awds:** Research Grant Del State Coll; Short Story Award, AAWW, 1962; Faculty Research Grant, Fisk Univ, 1970; Fellow, Univ of Maryland Library Admin Devel Inst, 1974; ALA Black Caucus Award, 1975; Martin Luther King Black Author's Award, 1982; First Annual Hatshepsut Award for Lit, CVOBW, 1981; Susan Koppelman Award for Best Anthology of 1989 (for book Afro-Amer Women Writers 1746-1933), Popular and American Culture Associations; published works include Living Black American Authors 1973, Loving Her, Bobbs-Merrill Inc 1974, reprint 1997, A Handbook for Black Librarianship 1977, Say Jesus and Come to Me, Avon Books 1982, The Black and White of It, Naiad Press 1980, and Afro-American Women Writers 1746-1933: An Anthology and Critical Guide, G K Hall 1988; author, paperback, New American Library, 1989; Outlook Award, 1990; Black Caucus American Library Association Achievement Award for Extraordinary Achievement in Professional Activites, 1992; Additional awards:-Central High School (Louisville, KY) Class of 1944 1/2 Success Recognition Award Librarian/Author, 1997. **Home Addr:** 5975 Post Road, Nashville, TN 37205.

SHOCKLEY, THOMAS EDWARD
Educator. **Personal:** Born Mar 15, 1929, Rock Island, TN; married Dolores Janet Cooper; children: Thomas Jr, Beverly, Kimberly, Janet. **Educ:** Fisk University, BA, 1949; Ohio State University, MSc, 1952, PhD, 1954. **Career:** Meharry Medicall College, professor, chairman department of micribiology, 1971-; Ohio State University, research fellowship, 1952-54, graduate assistant, 1951-52, researcher & teacher, 1951. **Orgs:** Society of Sigma Xi; placement committee, American Society for Microbiology, 1975-78; board of trustees, Association of Medical Schools Microbiology, chairman, 1975-78. **Honors/Awds:** Rockefeller Foundation Fellowship, 1959-60; Scholar of American Cancer Society, 1960-61. **Business Addr:** Micrbiology, Meharry Medical College School of Medicine, 1005 Dr D B Todd Blvd, Nashville, TN 37208-3501.

SHOEMAKER, VERONICA SAPP
Cleric, city official. **Personal:** Born Jun 23, 1929, Ft Myers, FL; daughter of Lillian Sapp and Henry L Sapp; children: Mattie, Bennie, Duane E (deceased). **Educ:** Edward Waters Coll Jacksonville FL, 1950-51; Edison Comm Coll Ft Myers FL, 1971-72. **Career:** FL Health & Rehab Svcs, foster care home 1974-83; Sunland Deve Ctr, residenttraining instr; City of East Ft Meyers, city councilwoman-at-large 1982-90-; Veronica Shoemaker Florist, owner/designer 1974-. **Orgs:** Area dir Southwest FL State Conf of NAACP; volunteer prog Lee Cty RSVP Comm; mem Hispanic Amer Soc; mem bd Lee Cty Cemetary; school bd mem Lee Cty School Bd ESAA Comm; bd mem, charter mem Dunbar Merchants' Assn Inc; mem Greater Ft Myers Chamber of Comm, FL Conf on Children & Youth, Lee Cty Charter Comm, Lee Cty Hosp Study Comm, Lee County Human Relations Comm; past chmn Lee Cty Bi-Racial Comm, Lee Cty Mental Health Assn; past pres Dunbar HS & Elem PTA; past mem Lee Cty Council PTA; past pres & charter mem Dunbar Little League; past charter mem Ebony Parent Club; past mem Dunbar Easter Club; past charter mem, vice pres FL Women's Political Caucus; past charter mem Southwest Fl Women's Political Caucus; past mem Lee Cty League of Women Voters, Overall Econ Devel Comm; pres & charter memDar Improvement Assn 1979-; bd dir Natl League of Cities, Goodwill Indust, Metro Org, SW Fl League of Cities, Women in Municipal Govt; founder/director, Source of Light & Hope Development Center Inc, 1988. **Honors/Awds:** Woman of the Year Zeta Phi Beta; SROP for Comm Serv Plaque; Natl Assn for the Advancement of Colored People Awd FL; Pres Awd Dunbar Little League; Honor & Awd Edison Comm Coll Black Student Union; Easter Club; Dunbar Coalition; Lay Man in Ed Awd Phi Delta Kappa; High Honor Heart of Gold Gannett Found; FTP & NEA, Martin Luther King Jr Human & Civil Rights Award, 1992. **Home Addr:** 3054 Mango St, Fort Myers, FL 33916. **Business Addr:** Councilwoman, 3510 Martin Luther King Blvd SE, Fort Myers, FL 33916.

SHOFFNER, CLARENCE L.
Dentist. **Personal:** Born Dec 13, 1921, Greensboro, NC; son of Lelia Hairston Shoffner and Ira B Shoffner; married Carrie Carter; children: Selia L, Annah Y. **Educ:** A&T State Univ, BS 1942; PA Univ 1946-47; Howard Univ Coll of Dentistry, DDS 1951. **Career:** Howard Univ Coll of Dentistry, asst clin prof 1976-; Dr of Dental Surgery 1975-. **Orgs:** Past pres Old North State Dental Soc & Rocky Mount Acad Med Dentistry & Pharmaceutical Soc; past baselius Alpha Omicron Chap, life mbr Omega Psi Phi; Intl Platform Assn; Master Mason; pres Hillcrest Realty Subdivision Roanoke Rapids NC; Amer Endodontic Soc; Amer Dental Assn; other various dental socs; life mbr: Chi Delta Mu, Alpha Phi Omega; bd trustees Halifax Comm Coll; K of C; bd of ed Weldon City Schools; bd of trustees NC Community Coll System 1986-; Weldon City School Bd, 1986-92. **Honors/Awds:** Omega Psi Phi, Alpha Omicron Chapter, Omega Man of Yr, 1961, 50 Years Award, 1942-92; Pres's Alumni Pacesetter Awd A&T State Univ 1967; NC Dental Soc 5th Dist Scholar Awd continuing educ 1973-74; Howard Univ Coll Dentistry Alumni Awd 1974; Fellow Acad of Gen Dent 1976; Fellow Acad of Dentistry Intl; Masters of Acad of Gen Dentistry; Fellow of Amer Coll of Dentists. **Military Serv:** US Air Force, corpl, 1942-45. **Home Addr:** PO Box 266, Weldon, NC 27890.

SHOFFNER, GARNETT WALTER (GUS)
Counselor. **Personal:** Born Jul 12, 1934, Greensboro, NC; son of Hortense and Robert; married Doris Cole, Feb 1, 1958; children: Joseph, Robin, Debra. **Educ:** Bellevue College, BS, 1972; University of Nebraska, MPA, 1975; Creighton University, MS, 1988. **Career:** Employee Developmental Center, Enron Corp, director, 1979-87; Great Plains Counseling Center, counselor, 1988-90, director, 1990-. **Orgs:** Nova Therapeutic Community, board vice pres; Sarpy County Mental Health, board member; Bryant Resource Community Center, board member; Omaha Temporary Organizing, steering committee; Rotary Intl; NAACP; Urban League; Family Life Ministry, Creighton University, 1990-. **Honors/Awds:** Great American Family of Midlands, State of Nebraska, 1990. **Military Serv:** US Air Force, TSgt, 1952-72. **Business Addr:** Director, Great Plains Counseling Center, 205 N Galvin Rd, #B, Bellevue, NE 68005-4852, (402)292-7712.

SHOFFNER, JAMES PRIEST
Chemist. **Personal:** Born Jan 14, 1928, New Madrid, MO; married Cornelia Dow; children: Stuart, Karen, Andrew. **Educ:** Lincoln U, BS 1951; DePaul U, MS 1956; Univ IL, PhD 1965. **Career:** UOP Inc, rsrch chemist 1963-; CPC Internat, rsrch chm 1956-61. **Orgs:** Mem Am Chem Co; Catalysis Soc; Chicago Chem Club; IL Acad of Sci; Nat Councilor Am Chem Soc; chmn Chicago ACS 1976-77; bd mem NW Suburban SCLC; Dist 59 Sch Comm Council; Omega Psi Phi; Black Achievers Award YMCA 1975; pub Papers in Num Sci Jours Patents. **Military Serv:** AUS tech-5 1946-47. **Business Addr:** Research Chemist, 10 UOP Plaza, Des Plaines, IL 60016.

SHOOK, PATRICIA LOUISE
Dentist. **Personal:** Born Feb 25, 1919, Chicago, IL; daughter of Cerella Brown Shook and Conness S Shook. **Educ:** Fisk Univ, AB 1939; Meharry Med Clg, Cert of Dental Hygiene 1941, DDS 1951. **Career:** Bethune Cookman Clg, tchr 1941-42; WAC, Armed Services 1942-46; Self Employed, dentist (retired) 1951-86. **Orgs:** Amer Dental Assoc; Amer Assoc of Women Dentists; Western Dental Assoc; CA Dental Assoc; Alpha Kappa Alpha Sorority, Pi chap, 1936-. **Military Serv:** WAAC & WAC 1st lt 2 1/2 yrs. **Home Addr:** 4268 Mt Vernon Dr, Los Angeles, CA 90008.

SHOPSHIRE, JAMES MAYNARD
Clergyman, educator. **Personal:** Born Oct 7, 1942, Atlanta, GA; son of Esther Pickett Shopshire and James Nathaniel Shopshire; married Berlinda Kay Brown; children: James Jr, Anika Diarra, Ekerin Ayobami. **Educ:** Clark Coll, BA 1963; Interdenominational Theological Ctr Gammon Seminary, BD 1966; Northwestern Univ, PhD 1975. **Career:** Interdenominational Theol Ctr, asst prof 1975-80, chair of church & soc dept 1978-80; Wesley Theological Seminary, assoc prof 1980-83, assoc dean 1980-85, prof 1983-. **Orgs:** Minister Bethlehem United Methodist Church 1964-66, Burns United methodist Church 1966-71, Ingleside-Whitfield United Meth Church 1974-75. **Honors/Awds:** Rockefeller Doctoral Fellowship Fund for Theol Educ 1971-72; Crusade Scholarship United Methodist Church 1973-74. **Home Addr:** 6215 Sligo Mill Rd, NE, Washington, DC 20011. **Business Addr:** Prof of Sociology of Religion, Wesley Theological Seminary, 4500 Massachusetts Ave NW, Washington, DC 20016.

SHORES, ARTHUR D. See Obituaries section.

SHORT, BOBBY (ROBERT WALTRIP)
Entertainer. **Personal:** Born Sep 15, 1924, Danville, IL. **Career:** Specializes in songs of the 1920's & 1930's by composers such as Duke Ellington, Rodgers & Hart, Cole Porter, George & Ira Gershwin; appeared in Broadway productins 1956-; appeared almost nightly at New York City Cafe Carlyle 1968-; performed for a yr in Paris & London; teamed up with Mabel Mercer for concert in New York City Town Hall 1968 & rec of concert was a best seller; performed at the White House during the Nixon, Carter, Reagan, and Clinton administrations; appeared in TV movie "Roots, The Next Generation" 1979; produced DancEllington; appeared in motion pictures "Splash," "Blue Ice," "For Love or Money," and "Hannah and Her Sisters"; has appeared with The Boston Pops, The Chicago Symphony, the Orchestra of St Luke's, and the New York Pops; appeared on the television program "In the Heat of the Night"; appeared in a television cabaret special filmed at the White House. **Orgs:** Life mem NAACP; Duke Ellington Memorial Fund, founder/pres; Third Street Music School Settlement House, bd mem; Studio Museum in Harlem, trustee. **Honors/Awds:** Laureate of the Lincoln Acad State of IL; author "Black and White Baby," 1971; also several articles; Grammy nominations in 1993 and 1994; honorary Doctor of Arts degree from Bloomfield College; received You're the Top award from the Cole Porter family; New York State Governor's Arts Award, 1994; New York Landmarks Conservancy, Living Landmarks Award, 1994. **Business Addr:** c/o Christine Wyeth, 444 E 57th St, New York, NY 10022.

SHORT, KENNETH L.
Educator. **Personal:** Born Aug 21, 1943, Chicago, IL. **Educ:** Howard University, BSEE, 1966; SUNY at Stony Brook, MS, 1969, PhD, 1972. **Career:** State University of New York, Stony Brook, assistant professor, 1985. **Orgs:** Faculty, Department of Electrical Sciences, SUNY at Stony Brook, 1968; consultant: several industries in New York area specializing in design of instumentation & digital systems; research in design of microprocessor, Based Digital Systems Reg Professional Engineer, NY, 1970-; New York State Society of Professional Engineers, 1970-; Institute of Electrical & Electronic Engineers, 1964-; New York Karate Association, 1970-. **Honors/Awds:** Recipient, Schmitt Scholar Fellowship, National Engineering Consortium, Inc, 1974. **Business Addr:** Department of Electrical Engineering, SUNY at Stony Brook, Stony Brook, NY 11794-1400.

SHORTY, VERNON JAMES
Health services administrator. **Personal:** Born Dec 17, 1943, New Orleans, LA; son of Adries Shorty and Earl Shorty (deceased); divorced; children: Angelique, Chyna. **Educ:** Southern Univ in New Orleans, BA History 1972, BA Sociology 1973; Tulane Univ New Orleans, Fellowship Certificate 1974; Admin of Drug Abuse Prgms, entered Southern Univ in Baton Rouge MS, 1992. **Career:** Desire Narcotic Rehabilitation Ctr, Inc Exec Dir, 1970-; Southern Univ System, adj prof, 1973-; LA State Univ; adjunct instructor 1970-72; CADA Desire Florida outreach Admin Asst 1970-72. **Orgs:** Consultant technician Veterans Administration 1973-; co-chmn First Natl Drug Abuse Conference 1974; chmn LA Assoc of Program Directors 1974-86; mem Phi Alpha Theta Soc, principal investigator, NIDA AIDS Outreach Demonstration Research Project, 1989-92. **Honors/Awds:** Social Justice Awd Natl Black Policemen Assoc; HTLV III Study Rsch Triangle Inst 1985-86; published "A Situation of Desire" Org & Adm of Drug Treatment Prog 1974; America's Unsung Heroes 1988; Kool Achiever Awards Nominee; Part of Research Team, frequent isolation and molecular identification of human T-Cell Leukemia Virus Type-2 1988; Part of Research Team, High rate of HTLV-II infection in Seropositive IV Drug Abusers in New Orleans 1989; Nyswander-Dole Award, 1994. **Military Serv:** USN E-4 2 yrs; USN Reserves 4 yrs. **Home Addr:** 4760 Franklin Avenue, New Orleans, LA 70122. **Business Addr:** Executive Dir, Desire Narcotic Rehabilitation Ctr Inc, 4116 Old Gentilly Rd, New Orleans, LA 70126.

SHOTWELL, ADA CHRISTENA
Educator. **Personal:** Born Sep 5, 1940, Helena, AR; married Roy Edward. **Educ:** Southern University, Baton Rouge, BA, 1961; University of California, Berkeley, teaching certificate, 1962; Memphis State University, edM, 1976. **Career:** State Tech Institute at Memphis Correctional Center, division head, correctional education, 1978-; State Tech Institute, department head, developmental studies, 1976-78; State Tech Institute, teacher, 1975; Memphis City School, teacher, 1968-75; Clover Park School District, teacher, 1964-67. **Orgs:** AVA, 1976-; TVA, 1976-; ATEA, 1976-; TTEC, 1976-; WTEA, 1976-; MACBE, 1976-; National Association of Black Americans in Vocational Education, 1979-80; chapter, board of directors, Black on Black Crime Task Force, 1985; NAACP, 1985; PUSH, 1985. **Honors/Awds:** Outstanding Young Woman of America, 1976; Citizen of the Week, WLOK Radio Station, 1978; Teacher of The Year, Correctional Education Association, Region III, 1978; Tennessee Correctional Educator of Year, Tennessee Association, 1978; Professional of Quarter Quarterly Journal of Corrections. **Business Addr:** Religious Studies, State Tech Institute at Memphis, 5983 Macon Cove, Memphis, TN 38134.

SHOULDERS, RAMON HENKIA (RAY)
Supermarket executive (retired). **Personal:** Born Mar 8, 1924, Athens, AL; son of Susie Mae Garrison and Arthur J Shoulders; divorced 1978; children: Mary J, Walter E, Juanita E, Roland V, Darryl A, Ray H. **Educ:** Cleveland Bible College, BTh, 1949-53, MTh, 1953-57; Western Reserve University. **Career:** WJMO-Radio, Cleveland, OH, broadcaster, 1954-57; WLIN-Radio, broadcasting announcer, 1957; United Methodist minister; Ray Shoulders Markets, 1967-82; WMKM-Radio, Detroit, MI, broadcaster, currently. **Orgs:** Board member, Friends of Michigan State; board member, Michigan Food and Beverage Association; president, Northwest Black Businessmen's Association; life member, NAACP, 1985; president, Associated Food Dealers, 1978-80. **Honors/Awds:** Youth Day Award, 1988; Honorary Ambassador of the Air Defense Artillery, United States Army Air Defense Command; Executive Declaration, Boy Scouts of America, 1971. **Military Serv:** US Air Force, Capt., 1941-45; received Service Awards. **Home Addr:** 17206 San Juan Dr, Detroit, (313)863-9065, 48221.

SHOULTZ, RUDOLPH SAMUEL
Cleric. **Personal:** Born Jul 24, 1918; married Vera Pearson; children: Tony E, Michele V. **Educ:** Moody Bible Inst; Chicago Bapt Inst, BTh 1961; Ministerial Inst & Coll, DD 1967. **Career:** Bapt Gen State Cong Christian Edn, dir gen; Woodriver Bapt Dist Assn Bd, treas; St Paul Bapt Ch Freeport IL, asst pastor 1952; Second Bapt Ch Dixon IL, pastor 1956; Union Bapt Ch Springfield IL, pastor 1968-. **Orgs:** Mem IL Housing Devel Authority; bd mem Mayor's Adv Council (Dept of Community Devel & Prog); bd mem Adv Council Comprehensive Employment Act; elected bd mem Springfield Metro Exposition Auditorium Auth; IL Human Rights Commission, bd mem. **Business Addr:** Pastor, Union Baptist Church, 1405 E Monroe, PO Box 2193, Springfield, IL 62705.

SHOWELL, HAZEL JARMON
Educator. **Personal:** Born Apr 5, 1945, Macon, GA; children: Angela, Patrick. **Educ:** DE State College, BA, English, 1968; Univ of Bridgeport, MA, guidance, 1973. **Career:** Dept of Pub Instrn, state supr, adult educ, 1976-; Wm Henry Middle School, Dover DE, asso prin 1973-76, teacher of humanities 1968-73; Univ of DE, consultant for staff leadership, 1975; State of VA, cons/evaluator, 1978; State of DE, cons/police training, 1979. **Orgs:** Delta Sigma Theta, 1968; pres, Peninsula Sect of Natl Council of Negro Women, 1976-79; chairperson, Social Justice Com, NAPCAE, 1978; Teacher of the Year Award, Capital Sch Dist, Dover DE, 1972; Women of Vision Daring to Venture, Delta Sigma Theta Sor, Dover DE, 1974. **Honors/Awds:** Outstanding Young Women in America, 1978; White House Conference on Families, State of DE, 1979-80. **Business Addr:** Director of Adult Education, Miner Administration Unit, 601 15th St NE, Washington, DC 20002.

SHOWELL, MILTON W.
Military officer. **Personal:** Born Apr 19, 1936, Baltimore; married Alberta Graves; children: Keith, Kimberly. **Educ:** Morgan State Coll, BS 1958. **Career:** Logistic Vietnam, mgr med serv 1966-67; Korea 1971-72; US Army Europe, implemented race relations prog; Seminars Drug Abuse; Author Book; Dept Def RaceRelations Inst, grad; Patrick AFB FL 1974. **Orgs:** Mem Toastmasters Am; Intl Winner Toastmaster's Inernat; European Speech Contest 1975; All Europe Winner Toastmaster's Dist Speech Contest 1975 (1st American); mem First Apostolic Faith Ch Baltimore. **Honors/Awds:** AUS maj 1961. **Military Serv:** AUS maj 1961-.

SHROPSHIRE, HARRY W.
Financial administrator. **Personal:** Born Apr 13, 1934, Asbury Park, NJ; married Kathleen Rae Nelson. **Educ:** Moravian Coll, BS Econ & Bus Admin 1957; Advanced Training, Mgmt 1972, Foreign Affairs Exec Studies Prog 1974, Financial and Economic Analysis 1976. **Career:** Emerson Radio & Phonograph Corp NJ, accountant 1957-62; Hess Oil & Chemical Corp NJ, accountant 1962-65; US Dept of State AID, auditor 1965-70, acctng div 1970-75; foreign serv controller 1975-86; Self-employed, financial mgmt consultant 1986-. **Orgs:** Mem Assn of Govt Accountants 1966-; mem Am Mgmt Assns 1976-. **Honors/Awds:** Cert of Apprec for Coop in Equal Oppor Prog Dept of State AID 1974. **Military Serv:** USNR 1952-60. **Home Addr:** 592 Trout Lake Drive, Bellingham, WA 98226.

SHROPSHIRE, JOHN SHERWIN
University administrator. **Personal:** Born Sep 6, 1938, Pittsburgh, PA; son of Dr Willa Shields Johnson and John Shropshire (deceased); married Jamie Nagle Shropshire; children: Christopher, Alicia. **Educ:** Clarion Un of PA, BS 1961; Yale Un, Grad; Shippensburg Un, Grad; Penn St Un. **Career:** Central Dauphin East HS, tchr/coach 1961-72; Black History Nwspr Wrtr, Clarion University, assistant director of admissions, 1972-78, director of admissions, 1978-83, enrollment management and academic records, dean, 1983-; Elected Paint Township supervisor, three terms, 1983-. **Orgs:** Pennsylvania Black Conference on Higher Education Inc, president, 1994-96; Pennsylvania University Admissiona Association, president, 1997-98; Clarion County Municipal Officers Association, president, 1990-94; Clarion-Jefferson County Economic Development Association, board of directors; Clarion Rotary Club, past president; Association of Collegiate Registrars & Admissions Officers, enrollment management chairperson. **Honors/Awds:** NDEA Grant-Yale University, African Studies. **Special Achievements:** First African-American head coach, Central, PA, High School Sports. **Home Addr:** 512 Ridgewood Rd, Shippenville, PA 16254.

SHROPSHIRE, THOMAS B.
Brewing company executive. **Personal:** Born Oct 15, 1925, Little Rock, AR; son of Irene Shropshire and William Bruce Shropshire; married Jacqulyn Calloway; children: Terilyn, Tom Jr. **Educ:** Lincoln U, BS 1950; NY Univ Grad Sch of Business Admn, MBA 1951. **Career:** Philip Morris Inc, corporate vice pres 1978; Miller Brewing Co (Sub of Philip Morris Inc), sr vice pres tres 1978. **Orgs:** Vp Mkt Plng Miller Brewing Co; mem bd dir 1972; dir Fin Holding Co; chmn & managing dir Philip Morris Nigeria 1968 sales mgr tropical Africa 1963; coll supr 1953; sales rep Philip Morris Inc 1952; life mem NAACP; Alpha Phi Alpha; Am Mktg Assc; Intl Adv Assn; Natl Assc of Mkt Dev; tres Milwaukee Urban League; mem Cncl of Trustees Univ of WI Hosps; adv cncl of W Paul Stillman Sch of Business Seton Hall U; bd of trustees Howard Univ 1982-; bd of trustees Winthrop Rockefeller Foundation 1984-; bd of trustees Natl Urban League 1984-; bd of dir Key Banks Puget Sound 1988-89. **Honors/Awds:** Distnguished alumni award Lincoln Univ Jefferson City, MO; Dr of Law, Lincoln Univ 1980; Dr of Humane Letters, Huston-Tillotson Coll 1982; Dr of Humane Letters, Miles Coll 1984; Dr of Humane Letters, Philander Smith Coll 1985; Dr of Humane Letters, Talladega Coll 1987. **Military Serv:** USN 1944-46. **Home Addr:** 4968 Verdun Avenue, Los Angeles, CA 90043.

SHUFFER, GEORGE MACON, JR.
Military officer (retired), clergyman. **Personal:** Born Sep 27, 1923, Palestine, TX; son of Johnnie D'Ella Butler Shuffer and George Macon Shuffer Sr; married Maria Cecilia Rose; children: Gloria, David, George III, Marlene Kuhn, Rita Lloyd, Monica Thomas, Rosemary McQuillan, Joseph, Maria Wallace, Anita Shuffer, Peter. **Educ:** Monterey Peninsula Clg, AA 1953; Univ of MD, BS 1956; Univ of MD, MA 1959. **Career:** 2nd Inf US Army, battalion commander 1964-66; US Army & Sec of Def, Pentagon staff off 1967-70; 193rd US Army, brigade cmdr 1970-71; 3rd Inf Div, asst div cmdr 1972-74; assistant to Catholic chaplain at Beaumont Hosp, currently. **Orgs:** Deacon Roman Catholic Ch 1977-. **Special Achievements:** "Finish Them with Firepower," Military Review, 1967; "An Appropriate Response," Military Review, 1969. **Military Serv:** US Army brigadier gen 35 yrs; Dist Serv Medal; 3 Silver Stars; 3 Legions of Merit 1944-75; 3 Bronze Stars; 6 Air Medals; Purple Heart. **Business Addr:** Hospital Chaplain, Wm Beaumont, AMC, WBAMC, El Paso, TX 79920.

SHUFORD, HUMPHREY LEWIS
Educational administrator. **Personal:** Born Nov 18, 1945, Wetumpka, AL; son of Cora Shuford and Robert Shuford; divorced; children: M Shondia, Monique. **Educ:** AL A&M Univ, BS, 1969; Troy State Univ, advanced studies, 1973; Univ of So AL, advanced studies 1974; Auburn Univ, advanced studies 1975-76; AL State Univ, MS 1978. **Career:** Atmore State Tech Coll, coord of student personnel; Jefferson Davis St Jr Coll; part time Sociology Inst; Jefferson Davis Community College, dean, extended services. **Orgs:** Mem, AL Coll Personnel Assn 1980-86, AL Counselsor Assn 1980-86; Atmore State Tech Coll Educ Assn vice pres, 1982-84, pres 1984-86; vice pres, pres, Progressive Civic Club 1982-83; vice pres 1983, pres 1985, Atmore Alumni Chapter, Kappa Alpha Psi; bd mem, Atmore Chamber of Commerce; mem, AL Educ Assn, 1986, Natl Educ Assn, 1986, Amer Assn for Counseling 1986, AL Democratic Conf, Hermon Lodge No 260; vice chairman of the bd, Escambia County School Board, Atmore, AL. **Honors/Awds:** Achievement Awd Progressive Club 1979; Polemarch Awd 1981, Achievement Awd 1981 Atmore Alumni Chap Kappa Alpha Psi; Achievement Awd State Testing Program 1982; Special Service Awd Atmore Alumni Chap Kappa Alpha Psi 1982; Southern Province Achievement Awd Kappa Alpha Psi 1986; Chapter of the Yr Awd Kappa Alpha Psi Frat 1986. **Home Addr:** PO Box 902, Atmore, AL 36502. **Business Addr:** Coord of Student Personnel, Atmore State Tech College, PO Box 1119, Atmore, AL 36502.

SHUMAN, JEROME
Attorney, educator. **Personal:** Born Sep 24, 1937, St Augustine, FL; married Christine. **Educ:** Trenton Jr Coll, AA 1958; Howard Univ, BA 1960, LLB 1963; Yale Univ LLM 1964. **Career:** Howard Univ, prof of law 1964-69; Amer Univ, adj prof law; Univ TN, Rutgers Univ, visiting adj prof law; Georgetown Univ, prof law 1968-78; US Dept Agriculture, dir office equal oppor 1971-74; Howard Univ, prof law, currently. **Orgs:** Chmn bd of dirs District of Columbia Housing Finance Agency; bd of directors, W R Lazard & Co. **Business Addr:** Professor of Law, Howard University, 2900 Van Ness St NW, Washington, DC 20008.

SHUMATE, GLEN
Tourism executive. **Personal:** Born Sep 9, 1958, Sandusky, OH; son of Annie Ruth Henson Shumate and John Wesley Shumate; children: Darrin Wesley. **Educ:** Univ of Toledo, Toledo OH, BS Student Services, 1982. **Career:** Univ of Toledo, Toledo OH, activities coord, 1980-82, counselor asst, 1982-83; Burlington Northern, Holland OH, operations agent, 1983-84; Cimmaron Express, Genoa OH, operations mgr, 1984-86; Hillcrest Hospital, Mayfield OH, mgr patient support serv, 1986-88; Cleveland Ind, dir comm relations, 1988-95; Cleveland Convention & Visitors Bureau, vp of tourism, 1995-. **Orgs:** Esperanza Inc, board member, 1991-95; United Way, campaign coordinator, 1990-93; Rainbow Hospital, Sickle Cell Anemia Advisory Board, 1989-95. **Honors/Awds:** Glen Shumate Award, Black Faculty/Staff at Univ of Toledo, 1981; Leadership Award, Black Student Union, 1981; Unemployment in the 9th Congressional Dist, Congressional Record, 1982; Eastern Campus Honors List, Cuyahoga Community Coll, 1987; City of Cleveland, Hispanic Hertiage Award of Excellence, 1993; Natl Organization of Black Law Enforcement Executives, Humanitarian Award, 1994. **Business Addr:** VP, Tourism, Cleveland Convention & Visitors Bureau, 3100 Tower City, Cleveland, OH 44113.

SHUMPERT, TERRANCE DARNELL (TERRY)
Baseball player. **Personal:** Born Aug 16, 1966, Paducah, KY. **Educ:** University of Kentucky. **Career:** Infielder: Kansas City Royals, 1990-92, Omaha Royals, currently. **Business Addr:** Baseball Player, Omaha Royals, PO Box 3665, Omaha, NE 68103, (402)734-2550.

SHURNEY, DEXTER WAYNE
Physician. **Personal:** Born Jul 15, 1958, Loma Linda, CA; son of Dr Green & Mrs Juanita Shurney; married Wanda Whitten-Shurney, Oct 10, 1982; children: Simone, Cameron. **Educ:** Loma Linda University, BS, 1979; Howard University College of Medicine, MD, 1983; University of Detroit/Mercy, MBA, 1990. **Career:** Westland Medical Ctr, surgical staff physician, 1986-90; Blue Cross/Blue Shield, case management director, 1987-90, Network, HMO, medical director, 1990-92, planning sr assoc med dir, 1992-95, vp corp med dir, 1996-. **Orgs:** American Medical Assn, 1988-; Hospice of Southeast Michigan, bd, 1995-; Michigan AIDS Fund, bd, 1995-; Michigan Environmental Council, bd, 1997-; Journal of Manager Care, editorial bd, 1997-; Drug-Free Michigan Comm, steering comm, 1997-; Federation of Intl Health Funds, advisory panel, 1998-; Kids Immunization Initiative of Detroit/Southeast Michigan, co chair, 1998-. **Honors/Awds:** Detroit Medical Society, Community Service Award, 1998. **Home Addr:** 1497 W Boston Blvd, Detroit, MI 48206, (313)865-0987. **Business Addr:** Vice Pres, Medical Affairs/Corporate Med Director, Blue Cross/Blue Shield of Michigan, 600 Lafayette E, Ste 2030, Detroit, MI 48226, (313)225-9290.

SHUTTLESWORTH, FRED L.
Clergyman. **Personal:** Born Mar 18, 1922, Montgomery, AL; widowed; children: Patricia, Ruby, Fred, Jr, Carolyn. **Educ:** Selma U, AB; AL State Clg, BS 1955; Birmingham Bapt Clg, LlD 1969. **Career:** Greater New Light Bapt Ch Cincinnati, fndr pastor 1966-. **Orgs:** Bd mem 1st sec SCLC; former aide to Dr Martin Luther King, Jr; fndr AL & Christian Movement for Human Rights 1956-69. **Honors/Awds:** Recipient hon DD Cincinnati Bapt Bible Clg 1971; russwurm awrd Natl Nwspr Pub Assc 1958; fdr awrd SCLC 1977; ml king civil rights awrd ProgressiveNatl Bapt 1975; rosa parks awrd SCLC 1963; spec awrd Back Our Brothers Inc 1963; spec cit Natl Com for Rural Sch 1961; excellence awrd PUSH 1974; human rel awrd Press Clb 1962. **Business Addr:** Grtr New Light Baptist Church, 710 N Crescent, Cincinnati, OH 45229.

SIDBURY, HAROLD DAVID
Construction company executive. **Personal:** Born Sep 15, 1940, Hampstead, NC; married Vivian Ann Radd; children: Timothy, Channeta, Felicia, Colette, Harold Jr, Jarvis, Ingar. **Educ:** Attended, Cape Fear Tech 1960, Kittrell Coll 1966. **Career:** African Methodist Episcopal Church, pastor 1966-87; General Contractor, 1974-87; SCC Construction Company, president, currently. **Orgs:** Chmn Counsel Bd of Educ Pender co 1960-85; mem East Gate Masonic Lodge #143 1965-; chmn bd of trustees Grand United Order of Salem 1978-85; chmn bd of dirs, Grand United Order of Salem 1985-87. **Honors/Awds:** Appreciation Awd Neighborhood Housing Develop Wilmington Chap 1979; Designing & Building Awd Grand United Order of Salem Building 1982; Most Outstanding Minister of Year Black Caucus Robeson Co 1984. **Business Addr:** President, SCC Construction Company, 1301 Castle St, Wilmington, NC 28401-5422.

SIERRA, RUBEN ANGEL
Professional baseball player. **Personal:** Born Oct 6, 1965, Rio Piedras, Puerto Rico. **Career:** Texas Rangers, outfielder, 1986-. **Honors/Awds:** American League All-Star Team, 1989. **Business Addr:** Professional Baseball Player, Cincinnati Reds, 100 Riverfront Stadium, Cincinnati, OH 45202.

SIEVERS, ERIC SCOTT
Professional football player. **Personal:** Born Nov 9, 1957, Urbana, IL. **Educ:** Univ of Maryland, attended. **Career:** San Diego Chargers, 1981-88; Los Angeles Rams, 1988; New England Patriots, tight end, 1989-. **Honors/Awds:** Played in AFC Championship Game, post-1981 season. **Business Addr:** Professional Football Player, New England Patriots, Sullivan Stadium, Rt 1, Foxboro, MA 02035.

SIFFORD, CHARLIE
Professional golfer. **Personal:** Born Jun 2, 1922, Charlotte, NC. **Career:** Private golf instructor for singer Billy Eckstine, 1947-53; professional golfer, 1954-. **Honors/Awds:** First Black to achieve success on the PGA tour; first Black to win the PGA Senior Championship, 1975; won the Negro National title six times. **Special Achievements:** Just Let Me Play, autobiography, 1992. **Business Addr:** Golfer, c/o Professional Golf Association (PGA), BOX 109601, Palm Beach Gardens, FL 33418.

SIGLAR, RICKY ALLAN
Professional football player. **Personal:** Born Jun 14, 1966, Albuquerque, NM. **Educ:** San Jose State. **Career:** San Francisco 49ers, tackle, 1990; Kansas City Chiefs, 1993-96; New Orleans Saints, 1997-. **Business Addr:** Professional Football Player, New Orleans Saints, 5800 Airline Hwy, Metairie, LA 70003, (504)733-0255.

SIGLER, I. GARLAND
Business executive. **Personal:** Born Dec 7, 1932, Bessemer, AL; married Bertha; children: Glenn Garland, Ennis Stevenson. **Educ:** Pennsylvania State U; Temple U. **Career:** SE PA Transportation Authority, ino agent 1960-; Philadelphia HS for Girls, instr 1967-; Sigler Travel Serv & Ticket Agcy, pres; Comm Serv Ctr, exec dir1970-; Teamster Local 161 Intl Brotherhood Teamster, vice pres 1972-. **Orgs:** Chldren's pgm dir Natl Med Assc 1971; pres Transit Roundtable of Philadelphia; pres York 15 Home Assc; life mem NAACP; dir N Philadelphia Br 1972-73. **Honors/Awds:** Mason of yr Prince Hall Mason Tuscan Morning Star Lodge 48 1968; comm serv awrd NAACP 1971; serv awrd Natl Dairies Corp. **Business Addr:** 1330 W Olney Ave, Philadelphia, PA 19141.

SIGUR, WANDA ANNE ALEXANDER
Engineer. **Personal:** Born May 26, 1958, New Orleans, LA; daughter of Louella Clara Boyd Alexander and Alvin Maurice Alexander; married Michael Gerard Sigur, Feb 14, 1981; children: Michael Jr, Gregory. **Educ:** Rice Univ, Houston, TX, BS, natural science, engineering, 1979. **Career:** General Electric, Houston, TX, lab technician, 1977-79; Martin Marietta Manned Space Systems, New Orleans, LA, section chief, 1979-. **Orgs:** Treas, American Inst for Aerospace and Astronautics, 1988-90; mem, Soc for the Advancement of Materials and Process Engineering, 1983-90. **Honors/Awds:** Principal Investigator of the Year, Martin Marietta Corp, 1989; Author Award, Martin Marietta Corp, 1987; R&D Investigator Award, Martin Marietta Corp, 1986; Technology Disclosure Award, US Patent and Technology Disclosure Office, 1989; Author Award, AIAA, 1988. **Business Addr:** Section Chief, Composites Technology, Martin Marietta Manned Space Systems, PO Box 29304, M/S 3572, New Orleans, LA 70189.

SIKES, MELVIN PATTERSON
Psychologist, educator (retired). **Personal:** Born Dec 24, 1917, Charleston, MO; son of Dorthy E Sikes and Kimmie Sikes; married Zeta Lorraine Bledsoe. **Educ:** NC Clge Durham, BA (cum laude) 1938; Univ of Chicago, MA 1948, PhD 1950. **Career:** Wilberforce Univ OH, dean 1950-52; Bishop Clge Marshall TX, dean, admin 1952-55; VA Hosp Houston TX, clinical psych 1960-1969; Univ of TX at Austin, prof educ psych 1969-retirement; Zeta Assc Inc, dir, currently. **Orgs:** Life mem Amer

Psych Assc 1950-, Natl Educ Assc, TX Psych Assc; mem Intl Psych Assc, NAACP, Kappa Alpha Psi, 32 Deg Mason, Shriner. **Honors/Awds:** Meritorious Srv Award Amer Psych Assc for work in Area of Psych; book Harper and Rowe The Admin of Injustice; research grant; Living with Racism (with Joe Feagin) Beacon Press. **Military Serv:** USAF 2nd lt 1943-45; Amer Theatre Medal Sharpshooter. **Business Addr:** Dir, Zeta Assc Inc, 8703 Point West Dr, Austin, TX 78759.

SILAS, PAUL THERON
Professional basketball player (retired). **Personal:** Born Jul 12, 1943, Prescott, AZ; married Carolyn Silas; children: Paula, Stephen. **Educ:** Creighton Univ, Omaha, NE, attended. **Career:** Forward: St Louis Hawks, 1964-68, Atlanta Hawks, 1968-69, Phoenix Suns, 1969-72, Boston Celtics, 1972-76, Denver Nuggets, 1976-77, Seattle Supersonics, 1977-80; San Diego Clippers, head coach, 1980-83; New Jersey Nets, assistant coach, 1985-86; New York Knicks, assistant coach, 1989-. **Honors/Awds:** NBA All-Star Team, 1972, 1975; NBA All-Defensive Team. **Business Addr:** Coach, New York Knicks, 4 Pennsylvania Plaza, New York, NY 10001.

SILAS-BUTLER, JACQUELINE ANN
Attorney. **Personal:** Born Aug 20, 1959, Middletown, OH; daughter of Elizabeth Peterson Silas and Frank Silas; married Lawrence Berry Butler Jr, Jun 14, 1986. **Educ:** Ohio State University, BA, 1981; University of Akron School of Law, JD, 1984. **Career:** Parms, Purnell, Stubbs & Gilbert, law clerk 1982-83; Jones Day Reavis & Poque, law clerk 1983-84; Akron Metro Housing Auth, legal intern & Hearing officer 1983-84; Parms Purnell Gilbert & Stidham, assoc 1985-86; Summit Co Prosecutor's Office, asst prosecuting atty 1984-87; Robinson Smith & Silas Law Firm, attorney/partner 1986-87; Akron Metropolitan Housing Authority, Akron, OH, chief legal counsel, 1987-89; private practice, attorney, 1989-91; The Univ of Akron School of Law, assistant admissions director, 1990; Summit County Juvenile Court, court referee, 1991-. **Orgs:** Wesley Temple AME Zion Church; board member, Summit County American Red Cross, 1992-; Natl Council of Negro Women, 1992-; vice pres Black Law Students Assn 1981-84; president 1990-, Delta Sigma Theta Sor, Akron Alumnae Chapter 1984-; Akron Barristers Club 1984-; third vice pres 1985-87, president 1987-90 Akron Branch NAACP; vice chairperson young lawyers comm 1986-87, Akron Bar Assn 1986-91; Natl Bar Assn 1986-91; Natl Assn of Black Women Attys 1986-90; The Ohio State Bar Assn 1986-90; Business Network Connection 1986-88; board member, secretary East Akron Community House 1986-88; board member, Western Reserve Girl Scout Council, 1989-; board member, Akron Area Young Women's Christian Association, 1987-90; board member, Akron Summit Community Action Agency, 1991-; Junior League of Akron, 1989-. **Honors/Awds:** Member of the Year 1984, Senior Award 1984, Black Law Students Assn; Delta Service Award 1989, Community Service Award 1988, Delta Sigma Theta Inc, Akron Alumnae Chapter. **Home Addr:** 2081 Larchmont Rd, Akron, OH 44313. **Business Addr:** Court Referee, Summit County Juvenile Court, 650 Dan St, Akron, OH 44310.

SILER, BRENDA CLAIRE
Communications director. **Personal:** Born Oct 3, 1953, Washington, DC; daughter of Helen G Siler and Floyd Howard Siler. **Educ:** Spelman Coll, BA, English, 1975. **Career:** Natl Center for Voluntary Action, resource specialist, 1978-79; United Way of Metro Atlanta, comm assoc, 1979-82; Rafshoon Shivers Vargas & Tolpin, acct exec, 1982; Siler & Assocs, owner/pres, 1982-83; Amer Red Cross Metro Atlanta Chapter, asst dir, public rel, dir, chapter communication, dir external communications, 1983-89; AARP, communications representative, 1989-94; Council on Competitiveness, dir of communications, 1994-. **Orgs:** Membership chairperson, Atlanta Assn of Black Journalists, 1980, publicity chair, 1983, professional standards chair, 1984; public comm Minority Business Awareness Week 1982; Bronze Jubilee Task Force, WETV, 1982-83; chaplain, Natl Assn of Media Women, Atlanta, 1983; United Way's Volunteer Atlanta, advisory council, 1983-; 2nd vice pres, Natl Assn of Media Woman, 1984-85; team captain, High Museum Membership Committee, 1985; Atlanta Women's Network, board member, 1985-86, vice pres, 1987; National Association of Market Developers; International Association of Business Communicators, Atlanta Chapter, vice pres, international board director-at-large, 1979-, international chairwoman, 1998-99; Capital Press Club, 1995-. **Honors/Awds:** Gold Awd for Annual Report Writing United Way 1980; Outstanding Achievement in Public Relations Natl Assn of Media Women 1980; Outstanding Young Women in Amer 1981; President's Awd Natl Assn of Media Woman 1983-85; Chairman's Awd Atlanta Assn of Black Journalists 1984; honorable mention for Annual Report Writing, Amer Red Cross Communications Excellence 1987; honorable mention for Exhibits Amer Red Cross Communications Excellence 1989, Outstanding Atlanta honoree 1989, President's Award, Int'l Association of Business Communicators, 1990; Public Relations Society of America, Georgia Chapter, Award of Merit for Press Kits. **Business Addr:** Director of Communications, Council on Competitiveness, 1401 H St NW, Ste 650, Washington, DC 20005.

SILER, FREDDIE BUSH
Librarian. **Personal:** Born Sep 11, 1956, Marianna, FL; daughter of Mary Frances Speights Bush and Homer Bush Jr; married Tommy Edward Siler Jr, Jan 14, 1985. **Educ:** Chipola Junior College, Marianna, FL, AA, 1976; Florida State University, Tallahassee, FL, BA, 1978, MLS, 1983. **Career:** Graceville Elementary School, Graceville, FL, school media specialist, 1978-80; Altha Public School, Altha, FL, school media specialist, 1980-84; Clemson University, Clemson, SC, business/textile reference librarian trainee, 1984-85, business reference librarian, 1985-87; US Army, Ft Leonard Wood, MO, reference librarian, 1987-94. **Orgs:** Chair, Libraries Committee on the Handicapped, 1987; chair, Agricultural Reference Librarian Search Committee, 1985-86; coord, TIUC Pathfinder Committee, 1986-87; member, South Carolina Librarian Assn Awards Committee, 1987; member, Libraries Five Year Task Force on Services, 1986-87. **Honors/Awds:** Cash Award for Exceptional Performance Rating, 1989, Special Act Award, 1989, US Army, Ft Leonard Wood, MO.

SILER, JOYCE B.
Educator. **Personal:** Born Aug 1, 1945, Siler City, NC; daughter of Juanita Womble Siler and Ross Siler; married Lloyd G Flowers; children: Rashad Flowers. **Educ:** NC Central Univ, BS 1967; Hunter Coll, MS Ed 1976; Manhattan Coll, MBA 1983; Columbia University, Teachers College, EdD, 1991. **Career:** Barnard Coll, secretary 1967-68; NY City Housing Authority, housing asst 1968-70; Model Cities Admin, principal program spec 1970-74; Medgar Evers Coll, asst prof 1974-. **Orgs:** Vice pres programs, Delta Pi Epsilon Alpha Xi Chap 1988-91; historian, Coll Business Educators Assn BEA 1989-90; sec John W Saunders Scholarship Comm Conv Church 1985-94; mem, women's auxiliary bd, corresponding secretary 1986, ML Wilson Boys' Club of Harlem; state advisor, Phi Beta Lambda, 1989-; chairperson, NY State, Phi Beta Lambta, 1993; bd of trustees, Belle Zeller Scholarship Trust Fund, Professional Staff Congress/City Univ of NY, 1992-; editorial bd, Collegiate Press, 1990-. **Honors/Awds:** Article, "Advice for Business Women," Everybody's Magazine 1985; "Survey of Curriculum Patterns & Practices In Business/Marketing Education," BEA Journal researched with Robert Landberg & others; Article, "Computer Software Evaluation Model for Education," Management In Nigeria, 1991; co-author, several articles about income tax; Fannie Lou Hamer Award, Women's History Month, Center for Women's Development, 1990. **Home Addr:** 700 Columbus Ave 11G, New York, NY 10025. **Business Phone:** (718)270-5121.

SILLAH, MARION ROGERS
Educator. **Personal:** Born Aug 7, 1945, Cuthbert, GA; daughter of Mary Nell Rogers; divorced; children: Samba, Samouri, Amie. **Educ:** Tuskegee Institute, Tuskegee, AL, BS, 1967; Morgan State College, Baltimore, MD, attended, 1965-66; University of Michigan, Ann Arbor, MI, MBA, 1969; University of South Carolina, Columbia, PhD, 1986. **Career:** W R Grace & Co, New York, NY, executive assistant, 1969-71; IT & T, New York, NY, compensation analyst, 1971-72; Bloomingdale's, New York, NY, assistant department manager, 1972-74; Tuskegee University, Tuskegee, AL, instructor, assistant professor, 1974-78, 1985-87; New Horizons Realty, Tuskegee, AL, licensed agent, 1977-78; Tuskegee University Human Resource Development Center, consultant, 1985; independent consultant, 1985-; Morehouse College, Atlanta, GA, associate professor, 1987-. **Orgs:** American Real Estate and Urban Economics Association, 1979-; Rho Epsilon, real estate, 1980-85, American Real Estate Society, 1985-; Young Advisory Council, Society of Real Estate Appraisers, 1985; chairman, Education Committee, National Society of Real Estate Appraisers, 1988-; Urban Land Institute, 1988-; International Council of Shopping Centers, 1989-. **Honors/Awds:** First Black Female to receive MBA from University of Michigan, 1969; United Negro College Fund Fellowship, 1983; First Black Female to receive PhD in Real Estate from University of Southern California, 1986; Faculty Award in Research, Tuskegee University, 1987.

SILLS, GREGORY D.
Administrator. **Personal:** Born Mar 2, 1950, Newport, AR; married Wanda Lou Brown; children: Brian Keith, Phillip Lawrence. **Educ:** Crowley's Ridge Jr Clg Paragould AA 1969; Harding Univ Searcy, AR, BA 1971. **Career:** White River Voc Tech School, asst dir 1975-; AR State Juvenile Servs Div, youth serv cncl 1972-75; Jackson Co & Family & Children Serv, juvenile probation officer 1971-72. **Orgs:** Adv bd mem Retired Sr Citizens Vol Pgm 1977-; adv bd mem AR Educ TV Network 1979-; area plng bd mem State Div of Employment Dev 1980-; past pres vice pres Newport Jaycees 1973-75; mem Newport Urban League 1978-. **Honors/Awds:** Citizen of the yr WF Br HS 1965-66; outst jaycee of the yr Newport Jaycee Chap 1973-74. **Business Addr:** Dir of Student Services, White River Voc Tech Services, P O Box 1120, Newport, AR 72112.

SILLS, THOMAS ALBERT
Artist. **Personal:** Born Aug 20, 1914, Castalia, NC; married Jeanne Reynal; children: Michael, Kenneth. **Career:** Museum Collections, Metro Museum of Art Fordham U; Whitney Museum of Amer Art; Mus of Modern Art; Finch Clg Museum; Rose Museum Brandeis Coll; Syracuse Univ Mus; Sheldon Meml Gallery; Williams Coll Museum; Phoenix Art Museum; Norfolk Museum of Arts & Science; LA & Co Museum; Krannert Art Museum Chase Manhattan Collection; Rockefeller Univ; Hofstra Univ; Fisk Univ; San Francisco Museum of Art; Wichita State Univ; Ciba-Geigy Collection; Greenville Co Museum of Art; Johnson Pub Co; St Lawrence Univ; Tougallo Coll; Univ of NC. **Orgs:** 1st PA Bnkg & Trust Co; Brooklyn Mus; High Mus of Art; Trevor Farnet Lib; Univ Art Mus; Studio Mus in Harlem Exhibits, Betty Parsons Gallery 1955, 57, 59, 61, Paul Kantor Gallery 1962, Bodley Gallery 1964, 67, 70, 72; Fine Arts Gallery 1967; The Cushing Gallery; Artists Annual Stable Gallery 1955; New Sch for Soc Rsrch 1956; Artist Grp 1956; Whitney Mus of Am Art Annual 1959-60, 71, 72; Univ of CO; Fairleigh Dickinson Univ 1964; Dord & Fitz Gallery; Mus of Modern Art 1969; Stdnt Ctr Art Gallery 1969; Afro-Am Artists 1969; Wilson Clg 1968; Mt Holyoke Clg 1969; Univ Art Mus; Mus of Fine Arts; Minneapolis Inst of Art St Paul's Clg; Everson Mus of Art; Betty Parson Pvt Collection; Sidney Wolfson Gallery; PVI Gallery; CIRCAL The Art Gallery Mag Jay Jacobs 1970; TheFlowering of Thomas Sills News 1972; The Afro Am Artist Elsa Honig Fine 1973; Sills William & Noma Copley Found 1957; Landmark Gallery Exhibits 1980. **Special Achievements:** Collection of The Newark Museum, Newark, NJ; Collection of The Portland Museum of Art, Portland, MA. **Home Addr:** 240 W 11th St, New York, NY 10014.

SILVA, HENRY ANDREW
City government official, cleric. **Personal:** Born Aug 26, 1924, Worcester, MA; son of Lula and Joseph; married Celeste; children: Cherryle Goode Hooks, Kimberly. **Educ:** Howard Univ, BA, 1975; George Washington Univ; Amer Univ; Natl Anthology of Coll Poetry; Howard Univ School of Divinity, MDiv 1983, Doctor of Ministry 1985. **Career:** EEO Natl Labor Relations Bd, dir 1974-80; EEO Food & Drug Admin, dep dir 1971-74; EEO US Naval Oceanographic Office, coordinator 1965-71; St Marks United Methodist Church, pastor; SCLC, natl bd mem; natl vice pres, SCLC assigned North Atlantic Region; Dorcestor Community Assn, former chrmn, Baltimore Support Group Community for Non-Violence; Hadens Chapel, pastor, currently; City of Charlottesville, sr counselor, currently. **Orgs:** DC Metro Area EEO Council, pres, 1970-75; DC Chapter SCLC, pres; past pres, founder, Natl Union of Security Officers; Montgomery Improvement Assn, Montgomery Bus Boycott; founder, Tent City Rangers (used as security in march on WA Resurrection City Charleston Hospital Strike, Memphis Rally; War Against Repression Atlanta GA); March Forsyth GA Commr DC Human Rights Commission 1980; participant in most major rallys & marches throughout the country for the last 30 years; chairman, Maryland State Housing Now; Save Our Cities; Natl Board Policy Planner; Common Agenda; Organized Love CEO Race Relations Institute, Va, MD, DC, Feb 15, 1995. **Honors/Awds:** Mayor's Award Testimonial Dinner 1975; plaques SCLC, HEW, NLRB, USNAU, DC Metro EEO Council 1943-46; SCLC, CK Steele Award, 1984; Baltimore's Best Award 1989. **Special Achievements:** Organizer, march against drugs, Charlottesville, VA, March 10, 1992; Hands across The State of VA, 1993. **Military Serv:** US Army Air Force 1943-46.

SILVA, OMEGA C. LOGAN
Physician (retired). **Personal:** Born Dec 14, 1936, Washington, DC; daughter of Mary Ruth Dickerson Logan and Louis Jasper Logan; married Harold Bryant Webb, Nov 28, 1982; children: Frances Cecile Silva. **Educ:** Howard Univ, BS (Cum Laude) 1958, MD 1967. **Career:** Veterans Admin Medical Ctr, intern 1967-68, resident 1968-70, rsch assoc 1971-74, clinical investigator 1974-77, asst chief of endocrinology, Diabetic Clinic, chief 1977-96; Howard Univ, prof of oncology 1985-97; George Washington Univ, prof medicine 1990-97. **Orgs:** Consultant FDA Immunology Panel 1981-89; pres Howard Univ Medical Alumni 1983-88; VA Adv Comm on Women Veterans 1983-88; general rsch support review comm NIH 1984-89; pres Amer Medical Womens Assn Branch I, 1987-88. **Honors/Awds:** Letter of Commendation from the Pres of the United States 1984; Alpha Omega Alpha Honor Medical Society Howard University 1990. **Special Achievements:** First women president, Howard Univ Medical Alumni, 1983-88. **Home Addr:** 354 N St SW, Washington, DC 20024.

SILVER, JOSEPH HOWARD, SR.
Educator, administrator. **Personal:** Born Oct 19, 1953, Goldsboro, NC; son of Augusta King Silver and Joel Silver; married Rosalyn Smalls Silver, Aug 14, 1976; children: Crystal, Joseph H Jr. **Educ:** St Augustine's College, Raleigh, NC, BA, 1975; Atlanta University, Atlanta, GA, MA, 1977, PhD, 1980. **Career:** Kennesaw State College, Marietta, GA, professor political sci, 1977-83, dir minority affairs & prof/pol sci, 1983-85; Georgia Board of Regents, Atlanta, GA, assistant vice chancellor academic affairs, 1985-97; Savannah State University, vice president academic affairs, 1997-. **Orgs:** President, National Conference of Black Political Scientists, 1990-92; president, Kathryn R Woods Scholarship Fund, 1987-; president, St Augustine's College Alumni Association, 1988-; president board of directors, Girls Inc of Cobb County, 1990-92; national board of directors, Girls Inc; member, American Red Cross Metro Chapter, 1991-. **Honors/Awds:** Presidential Award for Distinguished Service at Kennesaw College, 1983; Excellence in Educ Award, Savannah State College National Alumni Assn,

1991; Selected Educator of the Year, Cobb County NAACP, 1984; Selected Outstanding Educator, Kennesaw Jaycees, 1985; Selected to Leadership Atlanta, 1990; Leadership Georgia, 1988; Leadership Cobb, 1986; Man of the Year, St Anthony's Church; Alpha Phi Alpha, Carter G Woodson Freedom Award, 1993; Kathryn Woods Foundation, Outstanding Educator, 1993; MLK Support Group, Living the Dream, 1994; Girls Inc, Youth Advocacy Award, 1995. **Business Addr:** Vice President for Academic Affairs, Savannah State University, PO Box 20411, Savannah, GA 31404.

SILVEY, EDWARD
Educational administrator. **Personal:** Born Oct 28, 1937, Jersey City, NJ; married Joan Drane; children: Adrienne, Marc. **Educ:** St Paul's Coll, BS Sec Ed 1959; NC State Univ. **Career:** New York City Dept of Soc Svcs, soc worker 1959-61, 1963-66; Harnett Cty Bd of Ed, supr 1966-68; NC Dept of Admin, dir of manpower 1968-69; Shaw Univ, asst to the pres 1969-75; Wake Tech Coll, dir of dev & inst rsch 1975-76, dean of students 1976-. **Orgs:** Pastor Pleasant Grove UCC 1982-; state advisor NC Student Govt Assoc; pers advisor State Pres NC Student Govt Assoc; task forces state level Minority Recruit, Career Caucus, Student Devel; chmn Christian Soc Ministries Comm, Southern Conf UCC; pres Ministers for Racial & Soc Justice, Eastern NC Assoc. **Honors/Awds:** Outstanding Educator Omega Psi Phi 1976. **Military Serv:** AUS E-4 2 years. **Business Addr:** Dean of Students, Wake Technical College, 9101 Fayetteville Rd, Raleigh, NC 27603.

SIMIEN, TRACY ANTHONY
Professional football player. **Personal:** Born May 21, 1967, Sweeny, TX. **Educ:** Texas Christian University, graduated. **Career:** Pittsburgh Steelers, 1989; New Orleans Saints, 1990; Kansas City Chiefs, 1991-. **Special Achievements:** Established the Simien for Seniors Foundation. **Business Addr:** Professional Football Player, Kansas City Chiefs, One Arrowhead Dr, Kansas City, MO 64129, (816)924-9300.

SIMKINS, GEORGE CHRISTOPHER
Dentist. **Personal:** Born Aug 23, 1924, Greensboro, NC; son of GuYrene Tyson Simkins and George C. Simkins, Sr.; married Anna; children: George III, Jeanne. **Educ:** Attended Herzel Jr Coll 1942, Talladega Coll 1944; Meharry Dental Sch, DDS 1948; Jersey City Med Ctr, intern 1949. **Career:** Dentist general practice 1954-. **Orgs:** Mem Amer Dental Assn, NC Dental Soc, Old N State Dental Soc, Greensboro Med Soc, Natl Dental Assn; Greensboro Br NAACP; pres Gate City Golf Assn; mem Greensboro Men's Club; mem NC Guardsman. **Honors/Awds:** Certificate of Merit Alpha Phi Alpha Frat 1964; Dentist of Yr Old N State Dental Soc 1964; Scroll of Hon Natl Med Assn 1964; 25 yrs Serv to Mankind Meharry Med Coll 1973. **Business Addr:** Doctor of Dental Surgery, 500 S Benbow Rd, Greensboro, NC 27401.

SIMMELKJAER, ROBERT T.
Educational administrator, attorney. **Personal:** Born in New York, NY; son of Lenora Simmelkjaer and Carl Simmelkjaer; married Gloria J Foster; children: Robert Jr, Mark Allen. **Educ:** CCNY, BS Pol Sci 1962, MA Pol Sci 1964; Columbia Univ Teachers Coll, EdD Ed Admin 1972; Columbia Univ Business School, MBA Bus Admin 1977; Fordham Univ School of Law, JD 1978. **Career:** Inst for Ed Devel, exec asst to pres 1969-71; NY City Bd of Ed, principal 1971-74; CCNY, prof ed admin 1974-79, dean of gen studies and vice provost for academic administration, 1979-86; attorney/arbitrator; Governor's Advisory Commission for Black Affairs, executive director 1986-88; New York City Transit Authority, administration law judge 1988-90; Joint Commission for Integrity in the Public Schools, deputy chief counsel 1989-90; Institute for Mediation and Conflict Resolution, president 1991-. **Orgs:** PERC, OCB 1977-; minority school fin network Urban League & NAACP 1980-83; bd of dir Inst for Mediation & Conflict Resolution 1980-84; consult Ford Found, Natl School Fin Proj, NY Task Force Equity & Excellence, Urban Coalition Local School Devel 1980-83; vice chmn Personnel Appeals Bd US Acctg Office 1981-84; speaker, consult US Info Agency 1981-84; consult NY Univ School of Bus 1982-83; board of directors, Institute for Mediation and Conflict Resolution, 1980-92; board of directors, National Academy of Arbitrators, 1988-. **Honors/Awds:** NY State Regents Scholarship 1957; US OE Ed Fellowship 1969-70; Great Cities Rsch Fellow 1971; Chap in "A Quest for Ed Oppty in a Major Urban School District, The Case of Washington DC" 1975; author, "From Partnership to Renewal, Evolution of an Urban Ed Reform," The Ed Forum, 1979; author, "State Aid to Substantially Black School Districts," Crisis and Opportunity; "Finality of Arbitration Awards, The Arbitration Forum," Fall 1989; author chapters on Representation, Collective Bargaining Impasses in Federal Civil Service Law and Procedures, BNA, 1990; "State Aid to Substantially Black School Districts," in Crisis and Opportunity Report (NY, NY); Federal Civil Service Law and Procedure, Washington, DC (BNA) 1990: two chapters on collective bargaining and arbitration. **Business Addr:** Attorney at Law and Arbitrator, 160 W 97th St, New York, NY 10025.

SIMMONS, ALBERT BUFORT, JR.
Social service administrator. **Personal:** Born Feb 1, 1943, Chicago, IL; son of Arnetta Woodhouse Simmons and Albert Simmons; divorced; children: Vera. **Educ:** Anderson Univ, Anderson IN, AB, 1968; Indiana Univ School of Law, Indianapolis IN, 1970-71. **Career:** Urban League of Madison County, Anderson IN, pres & CEO, 1967-; Indiana Health Careers, Indianapolis IN, dir of counseling, 1970-71; Action Inc, Muncie IN, exec dir, 1971-72; Equal Employment Opportunity, Washington DC, mgmt official, 1972-84; Equality Profits, Washington DC, pres & CEO, 1984-87. **Business Addr:** President & CEO, Urban League of Madison County Inc, 1210 W 10th St, PO Box 271, Anderson, IN 46015.

SIMMONS, ANNIE MARIE
Educator. **Personal:** Born Jul 25, 1949, Henderson, TX; daughter of Lonnie Marie Henderson Simmons and Roscoe Simmons Jr; children: Shirley N Lawdins. **Educ:** North TX State Univ, BA psychology 1970, MEd 1972, Post Grad Studies 1972-74; TX Southern Univ 1975, 1979. **Career:** NTSU Counseling Center, counselor 1970-72; Favor's Pre-School, asst dir 1970-72; Geary Elem School, para prof 1972-74; Galveston Coll, assistant dean, currently. **Orgs:** Psi Chi 1968-; TX Jr Coll Teacher's Assn 1974-; League of Women Voters 1976-; Electa Chapter Order Eastern Star 1979-; pres Black Ladies of Distinction 1980-81; pres Alpha Kappa Alpha Sor 1983-85; member, Phi Delta Kappa, 1990-; pres, GISD Board of Trustees, 1989-91, 1995-97; facilitator, co-founder, Save Our Children/Galveston, 1990-; Gulf Coast Apollo Links, Inc. **Honors/Awds:** Outstanding Grammateus-Beta Phi Omega Chap of Alpha Kappa Alpha 1978; Outstanding Achieve in Galveston Comm 1979; cert of appreciation Epsilon Mu Chap of Alpha Kappa Alpha Outstanding Alumni 1972-82; Galveston Fire Dept Training Acad most popular visiting instructor 1979-81; pres BLOD 1980-81; Distinguished Service Awd Galveston Jaycees 1981; Sigma Gamma Rho Outstanding Black Galvestonian 1982; cert of appreciation Noon Optimist Club of Galveston 1982; NTSU/TWU Black Alumni Assn Quality of Life 1982; Outstanding Citizen of the Year Gamma Phi Lambda Chap of Alpha Phi Alpha Frat 1982; elected to Galveston Independent School Dist Bd of Trustees 1982-85; NAACP Galveston Br Juneteenth Image Awd 1983; Outstanding Women of Amer 1983; appointed to Gov's Commn for Women 1983-85 by Gov of TX Markite; Exceptional Svc Awd, Galveston College, 1995; Commencement Speaker, Galveston College, 1994; Brazosport College, 1995. **Home Addr:** 3525 Avenue O, Galveston, TX 77550. **Business Addr:** Assistant Dean, Galveston College, Division of Humanities & Fine Arts, 4015 Avenue Q, Galveston, TX 77550, (409)763-6551.

SIMMONS, BELVA TERESHIA
Journalist. **Personal:** Born Jul 2, 1927, Jacksonville, FL. **Educ:** Spelman Coll, 1946-47; Lincoln Univ, BJ 1949-52. **Career:** St Louis Argus, feature editor; US Senate Constitutional Rts, prof staff 1955-69; Amer Natl Red Cross, public relations writer 1970-73; KMOX-TV, community relations coord 1973-78; Anne Beers Elem Sch Journalism, dir/instructor 1981-83; ANC 7B Newsletter, editor/writer 1981-; DC Comm Schs, editor Sound Off. **Orgs:** Mem League of Women Voters; mem NAACP. **Honors/Awds:** Alumni Achievement Awd Lincoln Univ Sch of Journalism 1975; Distinguished Serv Human Develop Corp 1978; Comm Serv Awd ANC & Southeast Neighbors Inc 1981. **Home Addr:** 3604 Austin St SE, Washington, DC 20020.

SIMMONS, BOB
Sports coach. **Career:** Oklahoma State Univ, football coach, 1995-. **Business Addr:** Football Coach, Oklahoma State University, Whitehurst, Ste 103, Stillwater, OK 74078, (405)744-5000.

SIMMONS, CHARLES WILLIAM
Educational administrator. **Personal:** Born Jun 17, 1938, Baltimore, MD; son of Vivian Jordan-Simmons and Floyd Mays Simmons; married Brenda Leola Hughes; children: Dominic, Natalie Bohannan, Wanda Williams, Anthony, Kojo, Rashida, Tacuma. **Educ:** Antioch Univ, Baltimore MD, AB, 1972; Union Graduate School, Cincinnati OH, PhD, 1978; Harvard Univ, Cambridge MA, 1984. **Career:** International Brotherhood of Teamsters, Baltimore MD, field rep, 1964-67; Baltimore City Health Department, Baltimore MD, dir of health, education & community org, 1967-74; Antioch Univ, Baltimore MD, co-dir, 1972-80; Sojourner-Douglass College, Baltimore MD, president, 1980-. **Orgs:** NAACP, African-American Empowerment Project. **Honors/Awds:** President's Award, Black Women's Political Leadership Caucus, 1988; Leadership Award, Historically Black Colleges & Universities, 1988; Pace Setter Award, African-American Heritage Inc, 1989. **Military Serv:** US Marine Corps, Sergeant, 1955-60. **Business Addr:** President, Sojourner-Douglass College, 500 North Caroline St, Baltimore, MD 21205.

SIMMONS, CLAYTON LLOYD
Probation officer (retired). **Personal:** Born Sep 11, 1918, New York, NY; son of Florence Albertha Forde Simmons (deceased) and William Arthur Simmons (deceased); married Angela L Petioni; children: Janet, Sandra, Angela, Rene. **Educ:** Columbia Univ, BS 1954, MS 1969. **Career:** New York City Dept of Probation, held various assignments as probation officer, supervising probation officer, project coord, eeo officer 1960-82; freelance pianist & keyboardist 1983-; Upjohn Health Care Svcs, contract social worker 1984-85; ABC Home Health of Florida Inc, social work consultant 1987-89; Best Western Hotel, pianist 1988-92. **Orgs:** Mem Natl Council on Crime & Delinquency 1962-83; mem Rockland Co NY Bd of Commissioners of Sewer Dist No 1 1974-78; mem bd dirs Columbia Univ Sch of Social Work 1977-80; mem Rockland Co NY Bd of Governors for Health Facilities 1977-79; jr warden St Paul's Episcopal Ch 1977-82; vice chmn Spring Valley NY Democratic Comm 1978-80; mem bd trustees Village of Spring Valley NY 1979-82; pres Martin Luther King Jr Multi-Purpose Ctr Inc 1980-82; chmn bd dirs Youth Activities Comm Inc 1972-82; mem Vestry of St Stephen's Episcopal Ch Silver Spring Shores FL 1984-88, 1995-; mem Commn on Church in Soc in the Central FL Episcopal Diocese 1984-88; 2nd vice commander Post 284 American Legion, Belleview, FL, 1988; pres, St Stephen's Episcopal Church Men's Club, Ocala, FL, 1987, 1988, 1991. **Honors/Awds:** Certificate of Merit Roberto Clemente Social & Cultural Club Inc 1974; plaque Carlton & Surrey Apts for serv to tenants 1977; Guardsman Award for patriotic service to Natl Guard Bureau 1977; Plaque for Outstanding Leadership and Intensified Struggle for Minorities, First Baptist Church, 1978; Distinguished Serv Awd Rockland Co 1977 1979 1982; Cert of Appreciation Office of the Dist Attorney Rockland Co 1980; plaque Club Personality for Magnificent Job as Pres of Spring Valley NAACP 1973-79; NY State Senate Achievement Awd 1981; NY State Assembly Cert of Merit 1981; plaques Outstanding Serv to Village of spring Valley NY 1982; plaque Outstanding & Dedicated Serv to NAACP & Comm NAACP 1982; plaque Haitian-Amer Cultural & Social Orgns for Serv to Comm 1982; Certificate of Appreciation 26th Congressional Dist 1982; Certificate of Awd Spring, Valley NY Youth Council of NAACP 1982; ML King Jr Multi-Purpose Ctr Inc 1982; plaque Black Political Caucus of Rockland Co NY for Years of Dedicated Serv 1984; Certificate of Participation Amer Legion Post 284 Bellview FL 1986; Certificate of Appreciation Office of the Governor State of FL 1986; Award Clock, Black Democratic Committee Men, 1982. **Military Serv:** AUS staff sgt 1942-45. **Home Addr:** 4 Palm Run - SSS, Ocala, FL 34472.

SIMMONS, CLYDE, JR.
Professional football player. **Personal:** Born Aug 4, 1964, Lanes, SC; married Sandra; children: Jaison, Corey, Janya. **Educ:** Western Carolina, bachelor's degree in industrial distribution, 1996. **Career:** Philadelphia Eagles, defensive end, 1986-93; Arizona Cardinals, 1994-95; Jacksonville Jaguars, 1996-. **Honors/Awds:** Pro Bowl, 1991, 1992. **Business Addr:** Professional Football Player, Jacksonville Jaguars, One Stadium Place, Jacksonville, FL 32202, (904)633-6000.

SIMMONS, CRAIG, SR.
Finance company executive. **Personal:** Born Sep 2, 1962, Riverside, NJ; son of Joan & William; married Dail St Claire Simmons, Jul 5, 1986; children: Rachel, Craig. **Educ:** Amherst College, BA, 1984; Doshisha University, exchange student. **Career:** First Boston Corporation, analyst, corporate finance, 1984-85; Sumitomo Bank NY, assistant treasurer, public finance, 1985-87; Lehman Brothers, AVP, international sales, 1987-90; Kankaku Securities America Inc, vice president, fixed income, 1990-96; Cantor Fitzgerald Co, vice pres; Ashland Capital Holdings, vice chairman, currently. **Orgs:** One Hundred Black Men Inc, vp, bd of directors, 1989-; St Bartholomew's Church, bd of vestry, 1994-; St Bartholomew's Community Preschool, advisory bd, 1994-; NAACP, NY advisory bd, 1994-95; Fifth Ave Tower Condominium, vp bd of directors, 1994-97; Boy Scouts of America, campership steering committee, 1987-. **Honors/Awds:** Dollars & Sense Magazine, Outstanding Business and Professional Award, 1993. **Special Achievements:** Fluent in Japanese. **Business Addr:** Vice Chairman, Ashland Capital Holdings, LLC, 380 Lexington Ave, 11th Fl, New York, NY 10168.

SIMMONS, DONALD M.
Business executive. **Personal:** Born Jul 3, 1935, Muskogee, OK; son of Willie Eva Flowers Simmons and J J Simmons Jr; married Barbara Jean Ford; children: Annamarie, Donna Rose, Barbara Elaine. **Educ:** OK State Univ, BS & Grad Study 1961. **Career:** Phillips Petroleum Co, Regional Mgr 1963-67; US Sen J Howard Edmondson, Legis Asst 1962; Harlem Commonwealth Council, exec dir 1967-70; Simmons Royalty Co, pres 1970-. **Orgs:** Life mem NAACP; life mem Alpha Phi Alpha Frat; mem Centennial Comm OK State Univ; mem Natl Petroleum Council 1981-; mem Bd of Trustees Musk Reg Med Ctr 1981-; mem Interstate Oil Compact Comm 1981-; gov's apptmt mem Prof Respon Tribunal 1982-; member, National Council of the National Museum of Natural History, 1991. **Honors/Awds:** Business Awd NAACP. **Home Addr:** 710 Girard St, Muskogee, OK 74401-3841. **Business Addr:** President, Simmons Royalty Co, 323 W Broadway, Manhattan Bldtg, Ste 404, Muskogee, OK 74401.

SIMMONS, EARL MELVIN
Physician, poet. **Personal:** Born Feb 20, 1931, Brooklyn, NY; son of Iris and Isaac; married Elena; children: Erin, Erlan, Elis-

sa, Erik. **Educ:** Brooklyn Coll, 1949-53; Howard Univ, BS Chem magna cum laude 1958; Howard Univ Med Coll, MD 1962; Meadowbrook Hosp, surg cert 1964; Mt Sinai Hosp, otolaryngol cert 1967. **Career:** Cook Cty Hosp, intern cert 1963; Mt Sinai Med School, clin instr 1966; East Orange NJ Gen Hosp, chief dept otolaryngol 1967-79; Newark Eye & Ear Infirmary & NJ Med School, att phys 1967-79; USAF Hosp, chief dept otolaryngol 1979-81; Encinitas CA, pvt practice 1981-. **Orgs:** Mem Council of Otolaryngology, Deafness Rsch Found, Med Soc of San Diego, AMA, NMA, Undersea Med Soc, Assn of Military Plastic Surgeons, YMCA, UNICEF, NAACP. **Honors/Awds:** AMA Phys Recog Awd 1978-80. **Special Achievements:** Author, 24 books of poetry, including Turn Hourglass, 1977, Eagle Spree, 1979; Spirit Flesh, Circles, 1984, Songs of Sunset, 1988, Sonnets and Such, 1989, Legacy, Calypso Songbook, Seasons Blendings, Slang Slants, Songs of Salutation, Illuminati; Gambits, 1991; Spirals, 1991; Palisades and Peaks, 1991; Compromise, 1991; Aspects, 1991; Come, Sing with Me, 1992; Footsteps, 1992; Shadows, 1992; Cycles of Surrender, 1992; Crucibel, 1992. **Military Serv:** USA pfc 1953-55; PHS surgeon 1963-79; USAF lt col 1979-81.

SIMMONS, EDWARD
Professional football player. **Personal:** Born Dec 31, 1963, Seattle, WA; children: Cheyanne, Olivia, Edward. **Educ:** Eastern Washington, attended. **Career:** Washington Redskins, tackle, 1987-. **Honors/Awds:** Ed Block Courage Award, 1996. **Business Addr:** Professional Football Player, Washington Redskins, 13832 Redskin Dr, Herndon, VA 22071, (703)471-9100.

SIMMONS, ELLAMAE
Retired physician. **Personal:** Born Mar 26, 1919, Mt Vernon, OH; daughter of Ella Cooper Simmons and G L Simmons; divorced; children: Delabian, Diana, Daphne, Debra. **Educ:** Hampton Inst, RN 1940, MA 1950; Meharry Med Coll, grad student 1955; Howard Univ, MD 1959; Ohio State Univ, B.S., l948; Ohio State Univ, M.A., l958. **Career:** Practiced nursing at various hosps, 1940-42, 1950-51; Bellevue Hosp, med social worker 1951-53; Wayne Co Hosp, intern; Univ Co Med Ctr, resident 1962-63; Natl Jewish Hosp, resident chest med & allergy 1963-65; Kaiser Found Hosp, allergist, retired. **Orgs:** Mem AMA; Admissions Com Univ of CA Sch of Med 1974-79; CA & San Francisco Med Soc; John Hale Med Soc; Amer Acad Allergy; Amer Med Womens Assn No CA Chmn; Mutual Real Estate Investment Trust; mem No CA Med Dental Pharmaceutical Assn 1974-; mem Univ of CA San Francisco Sch of Med Admissions Com 1974-79; NAACP, Urban League. **Honors/Awds:** Certificate of Recognition, CA State Senate & CA Legislature Assembly, 1990; Soroptomist International, Women of Distinction, 1995; Martin Luther King Family Health Center, Award for Didication & Commitment to Service, 1994. **Military Serv:** Army Nurse Corps, 1st Lt, 1942-46.

SIMMONS, ERIC O.
Telecommunications account executive. **Personal:** Born May 19, 1956, Little Rock, AR; son of Dr Otis D and Jean W Simmons; married Cynthia Rena Simmons, Aug 18, 1979; children: Derek Michael, Dominique Nicole, Kevin James. **Educ:** Auburn Univ, BS, business admin, 1979. **Career:** South Central Bell, toll special service mgr, 1979-82; IBM Corporation, advisory sales rep, 1982-92; General Electric, diagnostic imaging account mgr, 1992-94; AT&T, account exec, 1994-. **Orgs:** Omega Psi Phi Fraternity, Pledge Club pres, 1976; Inner City Jaycees, vp, 1981; South Central Bell, Toastmasters Group, vp, 1981; IBM, Junior Achievement advisor, 1982. **Honors/Awds:** Auburn Univ, Dean's List, 1978-79; South Central Bell, Toastmasters Speakoff Winner, 1981; IBM, Marketing Education, Class Pres, 1982, Branch/Regional Mgr Leadership Award, 1983-92; General Electric, Chairman of the Board, Excellence Award, 1993. **Special Achievements:** Auburn Univ, Basketball Letterman, 1975-77; Guest Speaker, ''Minorities in Technical Fields,'' Auburn Univ, 1981, Univ of Alabama, Dept of Electrical Engineering, 1981, Minorities In Business, Alabama State Univ, 1984, Blacks In Corporate America, WFSA TV, 1987. **Home Addr:** 156 Spaulding Trail, Atlanta, GA 30328, (404)481-0874. **Business Addr:** Account Executive, AT&T, 1057 Lenox Blvd., Ste 200, Atlanta, GA 30319, 800-862-5677.

SIMMONS, ESMERALDA
Attorney, educational administrator. **Personal:** Born Dec 16, 1950, Brooklyn, NY; daughter of Esmeralda Benjamin Daley and Frank V Daley; children: Marques Akinsheye, Ewansiha Elias. **Educ:** Hunter Coll CUNY, BA 1974; Brooklyn Law School, JD 1978. **Career:** New York City Law Dept, honors attorney, civil rights employment unit 1978-79; US Dist Ct US Dist Judge Henry Bramwell, law clerk 1979-80; US Dept of Educ Office of Civil Rights, regional civil rights atty 1980-82; NY Dept of Law Atty General's Office, asst attorney general 1982-83; NY State Div of Human Rights, first deputy commissioner 1983-85; Medgar Evers Coll Ctr for Law and Social Justice, dir 1985-. **Orgs:** Natl Conf Black Lawyers 1975-; Natl Bar Assn 1979-; pres Bedford Stuyvesant Lawyers Assn 1981-84; legal committee chair, Coalition for Community Empowerment 1983-91; bd dirs Metro Black Bar Assn 1984-91; vice chair, New York City Districting Commission, 1990-92; board member, Fund for the City of New York, 1990-. **Honors/Awds:** Partner in Educ Awd NY City Bd of Educ 1981; Appreciation Awd Central Brooklyn Mobilization 1982; Lawyer of the Year Bedford Stuyvesant Lawyers Assn Inc 1984; Imani Awd Weusi Shule Parents Council 1984; Professional of the Year Natl Assn of Negro Business and Professional Womens Clubs Inc 1986; Harriet Tubman Award, Fannie Lou Hamer Collective, 1987; Woman on the Move, Concerned Women of Brooklyn, 1988; Leadership Award, Asian Americans for Equality, 1990; Leadership in Civil Rights Award, United Negro College Fund, Brooklyn Chapter, 1990; Women for Racial and Economic Equality, Fannie Lou Hamer Award, 1991; council member Annette M Robenson, Spirited Leadership Award, 1992; Community Service Society, Ellen Luriel Award, 1992; Magnolia Tree Earth Center, Magnolia Award, 1992. **Home Addr:** 272 Hancock St, Brooklyn, NY 11216.

SIMMONS, FRANK
Automobile dealer. **Career:** Hill Top Chrysler Plymouth, pres, currently. **Special Achievements:** Company is ranked #99 on Black Enterprise magazine's 1997 list of Top 100 Black businesses. **Business Addr:** President, Hilltop Chrysler/Plymouth Inc, 940 N Beckley, Lancaster, TX 75146, (972)230-2300.

SIMMONS, GERALDINE CROSSLEY
Attorney. **Personal:** Born Feb 17, 1939, Chicago, IL; daughter of Ivey Moore Crossley and Hosea H Crossley Sr; divorced; children: Stacey Elizabeth. **Educ:** Roosevelt Univ, BA; John Marshall Law School, JD 1981. **Career:** Scott Foresman & Co, dir copyrights/permission contracts, 1965-80; IL Appellate Court, judicial law clerk 1981; US Court of Appeals 7th Circuit, staff atty 1981-83; Washington, Kenyon, associate, 1983-84; private practice, 1984-; Roosevelt Univ Paralegal Program, instructor 1985-86; Salone Simmons Assoc, attorney. **Orgs:** Cook County Bar Assn; American Bar Assn; Women's Bar Assn; Black Women Lawyers Assn; Illinois State Bar Assn, past governor; National Bar Assn, board of directors; Chicago Bar Assn, committee member; Sojourner's Political Action Committee; Alpha Gamma Phi; State Literacy Advisory Board; Greencastle of Kenwood Advisory Board; CCBA Community Law Project, panel attorney; Lawyers for the Creative Arts, panel attorney; Parkway Community House, board of directors; numerous others. **Honors/Awds:** Nathan Burkan Copyright Competition, John Marshall Law School 1979; Law Review, John Marshall Law School, 1981; Distinguished Serv Award, Cook County Bar Assn, 1985; Businesswoman of the Year, Parkway Community Center, 1986; Distinguished Service Award, John Marshall Law School, 1990. **Business Addr:** Attorney at Law, 737 E 93rd St, Chicago, IL 60619, (312)994-2600.

SIMMONS, HAROLD LEE
Police officer. **Personal:** Born Apr 21, 1947, Kansas City, KS; son of Jeanette Vivian Watson Turner and Herbert Lee Simmons; married Wendy Diane Milan Simmons (divorced 1991). **Educ:** Kansas City Community College, Kansas City, KS, AA, 1988. **Career:** Kansas City, Police Dept, Kansas City, KS, detective, 1968-. **Orgs:** Pres, Kansas City Black Police Assn, 1986-; information officer, Midwest Region Black Police Assn, 1988-; national board member, National Black Police Assn, 1989-; board member, Kansas City American Red Cross, 1990-; member, Kansas City NAACP, 1968-. **Honors/Awds:** Distinguished Leadership Award, National Association for Community Leadership, 1990; Community Service Award, Midwest Region Black Police Associates, 1990; Citizen Appreciation Award, Kansas Black Legislatures, 1990; Christian Service Award, Mount Olive Baptist State Laymen of New Mexico, 1990; Law Enforcement Award, Northeast Optimist Club of Kansas City, 1988. **Home Addr:** 2513 N 73rd Ter, Kansas City, KS 66109-2430.

SIMMONS, HOWARD L.
Educational administrator. **Personal:** Born Apr 21, 1938, Mobile, AL; son of Daisy Simmons and Eugene Simmons. **Educ:** Spring Hill Coll, BS 1960; IN Univ, MAT 1965; FL State Univ, PhD 1975. **Career:** Lake Shore High School, Florida, Spanish/English instructor 1960-61; Central High School, Alabama, Russian/Spanish instructor 1961-63; Forest Park Community Coll, Missouri, chmn foreign language dept 1964-69; Northampton County Area Community Coll, Pennsylvania, dean of instrnl serv 1969-74; Comm on Higher Educ, Middle States Assn, assoc dir 1974-88, exec dir 1988-. **Orgs:** Consultant to various US coll & univ 1969-; staff assoc Amer Assn of Community & Jr Coll 1972-73; bd of dirs Amer Assn for Higher Educ 1974-75; bd mem St Louis Teachers Credit Union 1965-69; mem Phi Delta Kappa 1972-; mem Kappa Delta Phi 1974-; sr researcher/visiting scholar Natl Ctr for Postsecondary Governance and Finance Rsch Ctr at Arizona State Univ 1986-87; consultant Assn of Dominican Univ Chancellors, Santo Domingo, 1987-; exec bd Amer Assn for Higher Educ Black Caucus 1989-92. **Honors/Awds:** NDEA Fellowship, Indiana Univ, 1963-64; ACE/AAIP Fellow, Amer Council on Educ, 1972-73; EPDA Fellowship, Florida State Univ, 1973-75; keynote speaker on future of higher educ in Puerto Rico, Angel Ramos Found 1987; published study ''Involvement and Empowerment of Minorities and Women in the Accreditation Process,'' 1986; Grad Made Good (Distinguished Alumnus), Florida State Univ, 1988; American Assn for Higher Education Caucuses, recipient of 1st Annual Diversity Award, 1992; various articles in professional journals. **Business Addr:** Exec Dir, Comm on Higher Education, Middle States Assn, 3624 Market St, Philadelphia, PA 19104.

SIMMONS, ISAAC TYRONE
Computer manager. **Personal:** Born Aug 9, 1946, Birmingham, AL; married Jamesena Hall. **Educ:** Knoxville Coll, BS Math 1968; Univ of TN, MS Math Ed 1970. **Career:** Robertsville Jr HS, teacher 1970-71; Atlanta Area Tech School, part time teacher 1978-83; City of Atlanta, syst & programming mgr. **Orgs:** Mem Data Processing Mgr Assoc 1979-85; pres City of Atlanta Toastmasters 1980-85; mem Amer Mgmt Assoc 1983-85; vice pres Ben Hill UMC Santuary Choir 1983. **Home Addr:** 3611 Heritage Valley Rd SW, Atlanta, GA 30331. **Business Addr:** Systems & Programming Mgr, City of Atlanta, 1201 City Hall, Atlanta, GA 30335.

SIMMONS, JAMES E.
Educator, columnist. **Personal:** Born Aug 24, 1927, New York, NY; married Cecilia Wyche-Simmons; children: Keith, Robert, Andreas; married Bettie Foster Simmons. **Educ:** Hampton Inst, BS 1955; Harvard Univ, MEd 1963; Univ CA Berkeley, PhD, 1975-76. **Career:** Hampton Institute, asst dean, 1960-62; Stanford Univ, asst pres 1968-74; Univ MA Amherst, staff asst 1976-80; Simmons and Assc, consult 1980-83, 1988-90; Stanford Univ, financial Adv , beginning 1983; Fitchburg State College, Academic Independent Progrsm, director, 1986-88; Stokes Mortuary Services, staff asst, 1991-96; Media Center, Parker Middle, asst instructor, 1991-; Evening Telegraph, columnist. **Orgs:** Exec dir Conntac Hartford CT 1967-68; ABC Boston MA 1963-67; deputy dir OEO Upward Bound DC 1965; Alpha Phi Alpha; Nash/Edgecombe Big Brothers/Big Sisters, board of directors; pres, Greater Rocky Mount; board of directors, Family Medical Center. **Honors/Awds:** Ford Fellow Harvard 1962-63. **Military Serv:** USN tm; Pacific Theater Victory Medal 44-49.

SIMMONS, JAMES RICHARD
Administrator. **Personal:** Born Mar 1, 1939, Chicago, IL; son of Phyllis Isbell Jones and Oscar Lee; married Judith Marion Albritton; children: James Jr, David. **Educ:** Grinnell Clg, BA 1961; Univ of Chicago Sch of Social Serv Admn, MA 1964; Brandeis Univ Heller School of Advanced Social Policy, MM 1984. **Career:** IL Youth Commn, caseworker/team moderator 1964-66; IL Children's Home & Aid Soc, caseworker & psychotherapist 1966-69; Volunteers of Amer, state & exec dir, dir of children's serv 1969-71; Chicago United Inc, vice president-admin 1984-. **Orgs:** Mem Natl Assn of Soc Workers 1964-72; mem Acad of Certified Soc Workers 1966-72; mem Natl Assn of Black Soc Workers 1973-75; vice pres Grinnell Coll Alumni Bd 1973; bd mem Planning Consortium for Children 1973-75; bd mem IL Child Care Assc of IL 1975-76; Natl Soc Welfare Sec Vol of Am 1980; Delegatefrom IL White House Conf Children 1970; Nat'l Assoc of Black MBA's 1986; pres Hellen School Alumni Brandeis Univ 1986-. **Honors/Awds:** Minority advocate - IL, US Small Business Admin 1989. **Business Addr:** Vice President, Chicago United, Inc, 116 S Michigan Ave, Chicago, IL 60603.

SIMMONS, JANICE
Health administrator. **Personal:** Born Sep 28, 1944, Decatur, AL; daughter of James & Ruth Mitchell; married Paul A Simmons Sr, May 1, 1965; children: Paul A Jr, Troy. **Educ:** Oakland Community College, AD; Madonna University, BSN, 1977, MSA, 1986. **Career:** St. Joseph Mercy Hospital, staff development instructor, home care coordinator, oncology unit manager, 1977-82; North Oakland Medical Center, dir maternal child health, 1982-84, dir mktg and pr, 1984-86, vp mktg and pr, 1986-94; City of Pontiac, deputy mayor, 1994; Wayne State University, asst dir ambulatory svcs, 1994-. **Orgs:** Oakland Community College, chairperson, bd of trustees, 1992-98; Alpha Kappa Alpha Sorority, basileus, 1992-96; Haven Domestic Violence Shelter, bd of trustees, 1990-95. **Honors/Awds:** YWCA, Woman Achiever, 1994; YMCA, Minority Achiever's Award, 1992; Oakland County Council of Black Nurses, Mary Mahoney Award, 1984; National Assn of Negro Business and Professional Women's Club, Sojourner of Truth, 1985; American Business Women's Assn, Boss of the Year, 1987. **Special Achievements:** First African American elected to countywide office in Oakland County, Michigan; National Healthcare Marketing Symposium, speaker; St. Joseph Mercy Hospital, The Patient Education Workshop, developer; North Oakland Medical Center, Guest Relations Program, developer. **Business Addr:** Clinical Services Administration - Womens Services, Detroit Medical Ctr, Hutzel Hosp Administration, 4707 St Antoine, Detroit, MI 48201.

SIMMONS, JOHN EMMETT
Educator. **Personal:** Born Feb 6, 1936, St Petersburg, FL. **Educ:** Morehouse College, BS, 1957; Syracuse Univ, MS, 1961; CO State Univ, PhD, 1971. **Career:** Western College for Women, asst prof of biology, 1965-68; Research Fnd Washington Hosp Cntr, research assoc, 1968-70; CO State Univ, asst prof of physiology, 1971-72; Trinity College, assoc prof, of biology 1972-82, prof of biology, 1982-. **Orgs:** Society for Neuroscience, Endocrine Society. **Honors/Awds:** Fulbright Scholar, Gezira University, Wad Medani, Sudan, Africa, 1982-

83. **Home Addr:** 31 Woodland St, Apt 5-P, Hartford, CT 06105. **Business Addr:** Professor of Biology, Trinity College, Department of Biology, Hartford, CT 06106, (860)297-2232.

SIMMONS, JOSEPH JACOB, III
Government official, judge. **Personal:** Born Mar 26, 1925, Muskogee, OK; son of Eva Flowers Simmons and Jacob Simmons Jr; married Bernice Elizabeth Miller; children: Joseph Jacob IV, Bernice Garza, Mary Agnes Bursick, Jacolyn Reade, Eva Frances. **Educ:** Univ of Detroit, 1942-44, 1946-77; St Louis Univ, BS 1949. **Career:** Amerada Hess Corp, vice pres gvt relations, 1970-82; Dept of the Interior, under sec 1983-84; Interstate Commerce Commn, commissioner 1984-85, vice chmn 1985-86, commissioner 1987-. **Orgs:** Professional Amer Assoc of Petroleum Geologists 1958-; commissioner Statue of Liberty Ellis Island Commn 1983-; mem Natl Acad of Sci Bd of Mineral and Energy 1984-; mem Dept of the Interior Outer Continental Shelf Adv Bd 1984-. **Honors/Awds:** Special Act of Service Awd, Outstanding Performance Awd, Disting Serv Awd all from Dept of the Interior; Public Service Awd Amer Assoc of Petroleum Geologists 1984. **Military Serv:** AUS sgt 2 yrs. **Home Addr:** 2736 Unicorn Lane NW, Washington, DC 20015. **Business Addr:** Commissioner, Interstate Commerce Commission, 12th & Constitution Ave NW, Washington, DC 20423.

SIMMONS, JOYCE HOBSON (JOYCE ANN HOBSON-SIMMONS)
Accountant. **Personal:** Born Aug 1, 1947, Port Jefferson, NY; daughter of Ada Rebecca Townes Hobson and Nathan Edward Hobson Sr; married Leroy Simmons Jr, Feb 21, 1978; children: Leroy III (stepson), Victor. **Educ:** Essex Cty Comm Coll, 1971; Indian River Comm Coll, AA 1973; Amer Inst of Banking, Basic Cert 1973; FL Atlantic Univ, BBA 1975. **Career:** Port of NY Authority, personnel dept, police recruitment, world trade ctr, bldg constr dept, toll collector 1969-71; First Natl Bank & Trust Co, auditorcommercial loan dept, supv proof & bkkp dept 1971-75; Homrich Miel & Mehlich, staff acct 1976-77; Westinghouse Comm Dev Group, staff supv 1977; JA Hobson Acct & Tax Svc, sole proprietor 1978-95; Dir Business & Citizens Partnerships, State Dept of Educ, dir, 1995-97. **Orgs:** Dir, Division of Administration, State Dept of Educ, 1997; Florida Education Foundation, 1997; dir United Way of Martin Cty, Stuart/Martin Cty Chamber of Comm 1980-82, 1992-95; pres Amer Bus Women's Assn 1981-82; chairperson Martin Cty School Bd 1982-86, 1993-94; dir Girl Scouts of Amer Palm Glade Council 1982-86; FAU Alumni Assoc 1982-88, IRCC Advisory Council Acct & Fin 1984-86, Martin Cty 4-H Found 1984-86; mem Martin Memorial Found Hosp Comm Council, Amer Accounting Assn; bd of trustees, IRCC, 1987; dir, Children's Serv Council, 1988; Martin County School Board 1990; Graduate Leadership Martin County, 1991-92; FL School Boards Assn, treasurer, 1992-93, pres-elect, 1993-94, pres, 1994-95; South FL Consortium of School Boards, pres, 1993-94; Martin County Economic Council Republican Club, Exec Comm Council of 100; Florida Commission on Community Service Foundation. **Honors/Awds:** Women of the Year Amer Business Women's Assn 1982; Outstanding Serv as Chmn Legislative Subcomm FL Sch Bd's Assoc 1986; Phi Delta Kappa, Community Service Award, 1993; FL Assn of Community Colleges, Leroy Collins Award, 1991; Martin County Women of Distinction, Palm Glades Girl Scout Council Inc, 1993; Commissioner's Award for Exemplary Teamwork, 1996, Black Achiever Award, Tallahassee Branch, NAACP. **Home Addr:** 2322 Tina Dr, Tallahassee, FL 32301.

SIMMONS, JULIUS CAESAR, SR.
Clergyman, educator. **Personal:** Born Nov 24, 1925, New Rochelle, NY; son of Priscilla Dilligard Simmons and Charles Simmons; married Alma May Alexander Simmons, Jul 3, 1954; children: Patricia Diane, Julius Caesar Jr. **Educ:** VA Union Univ, AB 1952; School of Theology VA Union, Master of Divinity, 1955; Fort Valley State Coll, Graduate Study. **Career:** Dayton Christian Center Dayton OH, work with boys 1955-57; Fort Valley State Coll, dean of men, dir of religious activities, 1957-70, dir of financial aid 1970-73, counselor, dept of developmental studies, 1973-. **Orgs:** Chmn Peach Cty Hospital Authority 1965-; Natl Dove of Peace Phi Beta Sigma Fraternity Inc, natl pres, 1951-; mem Citizen Educ Comm, optimist; pres Natl Pan Hellenic Council, 1959, 1961; chmn, authority mem, Peach County Hospital Authority, 1967-85. **Honors/Awds:** Citizenship Award Citizen Educ Comm 1980; Devoted Serv To Roesh Cty Alumni Assn FVSC 1977; Serv to FVS Coll Area Alumni Chapter 1983. **Military Serv:** USN stewart 2c 1944-46; Honorable Discharge WWII Victory Medal. **Business Addr:** Counselor, Fort Valley State College, Dept of Developmental Studies, State College Dr, Fort Valley, GA 31030.

SIMMONS, KENNETH H.
Architect, planner. **Personal:** Born Jun 28, 1933, Muskogee, OK; divorced; children: Margot Eva, Kenneth II, Annette, Jalia. **Educ:** Harvard Clg, AB 1954; Univ CA Berkley, BArch 1964. **Career:** Housing & Community Development Program, coordinator; San Francisco Econ Opportunity Cncl, 1964; Bay Group Architects & Planners, principal, 1965; Arch Renewal Com, co-director, 1966; Hunts Point Neighborhood Project for Urban Am Inc, executive director, 1967; University of California-Berkeley, Department of Architecture, associate professor, 1968-; Com Design Collaborative Arch & Plnrs, principal, 1989; Miller, Simmons & Grant Design Group, Architects & Urban Planners, partner, 1991-. **Orgs:** Amer Planning Association; Am Inst of Certified Plnrs; International Congress of Archetecture and Townplanning; Architects Designers and Planners for Social Responsibility; Bay Area Black Architects; National Organization of Minority Architects; African Studies Association; Association of Concerned African Scholars; TransAfrica; Washington Office on Africa; Bay Area Anti-Apartheid Network; Greenpeace; National Association of Arab Americans; San Francisco African-American Historical and Cultural Society; World Affairs Council of North California; Joint Center for Political and Economic Studies; Harvard Club of San Francisco. **Business Addr:** Partner, Miller, Simmons & Grant Design Group, 414 13th St, Ste 400, Oakland, CA 94612.

SIMMONS, LEONARD (BUD)
Public official. **Personal:** Born May 2, 1920, Goldsboro, NC; married Claudia; children: Patricia, Leonard Jr, Gloria, Dennis, Jeffrey, Pamela, Zeno. **Educ:** Browne Bus School NYC, 1941. **Career:** State of NJ, commissioner, civil service 1972-. **Orgs:** Former city councilman, pres of council & police commiss City of Roselle; former pres, mem Roselle Bd of Ed 13 yrs; original & only black mem NJ Lottery Commiss; former mem, pres Union Cty NJ Vocational & Comm Coll; former comm clerk NJ Leg; former vice pres NJ Vocational School Bd Assoc; org, past presRoselle Br NAACP; former congressional aide to congresswoman Florence P Dwyer 21st Dist NJ. **Honors/Awds:** 1st black policeman in Roselle NJ; 1st black in history of NJ to be named to State Civil Serv Comm. **Business Addr:** Commissioner, Civil Service, State of New Jersey, 1019 Chandler Ave, Roselle, NJ 07203.

SIMMONS, LIONEL J.
Professional basketball player. **Personal:** Born Nov 14, 1968, Philadelphia, PA. **Educ:** LaSalle Univ, Philadelphia, PA, 1986-90. **Career:** Sacramento Kings, 1990-. **Business Addr:** Professional Basketball Player, Sacramento Kings, 1 Sport Pkwy, Sacramento, CA 95834-2301.

SIMMONS, MAURICE CLYDE
Marketing executive. **Personal:** Born Feb 15, 1957, Washington, DC; son of Ada Blaylock Simmons and Clyde T Simmons; married Vicki Baker, Sep 1988; children: Marcus, Shaun. **Educ:** Dartmouth Coll, AB 1979; Univ of Pennsylvania Wharton Sch, MBA 1986. **Career:** Procter & Gamble, sales rep 1979-81, dist field rep 1981-82, unit mgr 1982-84; McNeil Consumer Products Co, asst prod dir 1986-; McNeil Consumer Products Co, Ft Washington PA, product dir 1986-, manager, customer support; Johnson & Johnson CFT, marketing mgr, currently. **Orgs:** Mem Natl Black MBA Assoc Philadelphia Chap 1984-; regional coord Black Alumni of Dartmouth 1984, 1987; pres Wharton Black MBA Assoc 1985; co-chmn prog develop Natl Black MBA 1987 Conf Comm. **Home Addr:** 5963 Woodbine Ave, Philadelphia, PA 19131-1206.

SIMMONS, PAUL A.
Judge (retired). **Personal:** Born Aug 31, 1921, Monongahela, PA; son of Lilly D Simmons and Perry C Simmons; married Gwendolyn; children: Paul Jr, Gwendolyn, Anne. **Educ:** Univ of Pittsburgh, 1946; Harvard Law Sch, 1949. **Career:** PA RR, employee 1941-46; SC Coll Law, prof of law 1949-52; NC Coll Law, prof law 1952-56; general practice 1956-58; Clyde G Tempest, 1958-70; Hormell Tempest Simmons Bigi & Melenyzer, law partner 1970-73; Common Pleas WA Co PA, judge 1973-78; US Dist Court for the W Dist of PA, judge 1978-91. **Orgs:** Mem: Amer Bar Assn, Amer Trial Lawyers Assn, Amer Judicature Soc, PA Bar Assn, WA Co Bar Assn, NC State Bar, NAACP, Ind Benevolent Protective Order Elks of World, PA Human Rel Comm, Commonwealth PA Minor Judiciary Educ Bd, Bethel AME Church, Alpha Phi Alpha; bd dir, Mon Valley United Health Serv; past grand atty, State of PA for Most Worshipful Prince Hall Grand Lodge F&AM PA. **Honors/Awds:** Two Human Rights Awds NAACP; Meritorious Comm Serv Awd the Most Worshipful Prince Hall Grand Lodge; Pennsylvania Bas Assn, Minority Bar Committee, Lifetime Achievement Award, 1992; Natl Bar Assn Hall of Fame, 1994. **Special Achievements:** First African American to run statewide in the Commonwealth of Pennsylvania for a judicial office; first African American in Pennsylvania to sit regularly as a Common Pleas Orphans' Ct Judge. **Business Addr:** Judge (retired), US Dist Ct for the W Dist PA, Room 620, US Post Office & Court House, Pittsburgh, PA 15219.

SIMMONS, RON
Professional wrestler. **Educ:** Florida State Univ. **Career:** Professional wrestler: tag-team member, Doom; individual pro wrestler, 1988-. **Honors/Awds:** Three-time All-American nose tackle, Florida State University. **Special Achievements:** First African American World Heavyweight Wrestling Champion, WCW, 1992. **Business Addr:** Professional Wrestler, World Wrestling Federation, c/o Titan Sports Inc, 1241 E Main St, Stamford, CT 06902.

SIMMONS, RUSSELL
Entertainment company executive. **Personal:** Born in Queens, NY; son of Daniel Simmons. **Educ:** City College of New York, Harlem Branch, sociology. **Career:** Rush Communications, chief executive officer, currently; (all following companies are a part of Rush Comms, and all are current companies in the Simmons family): Def Jam Records, co-founder, owner, 1985-; Rush Artist Management, owner, PHAT Fashion, developer, Russell Simmons' Def Comedy Jam, producer for HBO, 1992-; owner of six other recording companies, Rush Producers Management, owner, Rush Model Management, partner; Krush Groove, film co-producer; Tougher Than Leather, film co-producer; The Nutty Professor, coproducer, 1996. **Honors/Awds:** 10 Gold Albums; 6 Platinum Albums; 2 Multiplatinum Albums. **Special Achievements:** Rush Communications ranked #32 on BE's list of Top 100 Industrial/Service Companies, 1992. **Business Addr:** Chief Executive Officer, Rush Communications, 652 Broadway, 3rd Fl, New York, NY 10012, (212)979-2610.

SIMMONS, RUTH
Educational administrator. **Personal:** Born 1945. **Educ:** Dillard Univ; Harvard Univ, master's and doctorate degrees, Romance languages. **Career:** Princeton Univ, Black Studies, dir; Spelman Coll, provost; Princeton, vice provost, 1992-95; Smith Coll, pres, 1995-. **Orgs:** Pfizer Corp, dir; MetLife; JSTOR Institute for Advanced Study, trustee. **Honors/Awds:** Fellow, American Academy of Arts and Sciences. **Special Achievements:** First African American to lead one of the elite Seven Sister schools. **Business Addr:** President, Smith College, Elm St, Northampton, MA 01063, (413)584-2700.

SIMMONS, S. DALLAS
Educational administrator. **Personal:** Born Jan 28, 1940, Ahoskie, NC; son of Mary A Simmons; married Yvonne Martin; children: S Dallas, Jr, Kristie Lynn. **Educ:** North Carolina Central Univ, BS 1962, MS 1967; Duke Univ, PhD 1977. **Career:** North Carolina Central Univ, dir data processing 1962-64; Norfolk State Univ, dir data processing 1964-66; North Carolina Central Univ, asst prof business admin 1967-71, asst to the chancellor 1971-77, vice chancellor for univ relations 1977-81; St Paul's College, pres 1981-85, VA Union Univ, pres 1985-. **Orgs:** Mem Durham C of C 1971-81; liaison officer Moton Coll Serv Bureau 1972-; competency testing commiss NC State Bd of Educ 1977-81; exec comm 1981-, council of pres 1981-, fin comm 1984-85, bd of dir 1981-, Central Intercollegiate Athletic Assoc; bd dir VA Polytech Inst & State Univ 1982-83; bd trust NC Central Univ 1983-85; conf comm, 1983, chmn leadership awds comm 1984-85, bd of dir 1985 Natl Assoc for Equal Oppty in Higher Educ; exec comm mem bd of trust NC Central Univ 1983-85; exec com mem bd of dir UNCF; mem Amer Mgmt Assn, Kappa Alpha Psi, Brunswick C of C 1981-85; mem bd dir Pace Amer Bank 1984-; mem US Zuluand Educ Found 1985; exec bd John B McLendon Found Inc 1985; Data Processing Mgmt Assoc, Doric Lodge No 28 of Free & Accepted Masons, DurhamConsistory No 218 32 Degree, Zaffample No 176 Shriner, Kappa Alpha Psi, Tobaccoland Kiwanians, Sigma Pi Phi Frat Alpha Beta Boule', Optimist club, Amer Assoc of School Admin, Amer Assoc of Univ Admin, The Downtown Club. **Honors/Awds:** Kappa of the Month Kappa Alpha Psi Fraternity 1981; Citizen of the Year Omega Psi Phi Fraternity 1983-84; Black Amer Achievers 1983-84; Business Associate of the Year B&G Charter Chapter, ABWA 1984. **Business Addr:** President, Virginia Union University, 1500 N Lombardy St, Richmond, VA 23220.

SIMMONS, SAMUEL J.
Association executive. **Personal:** Born Apr 13, 1927, Flint, MI; son of Hattie Simmons and Samuel Simmons; married Barbara Lett; children: David Clay, Robert Allen. **Educ:** Western MI Univ, BA 1949. **Career:** US Dept of Housing and Urban Dev, asst secr 1969-72; Natl Ctr for Housing Mgmt, pres 1972-81; Fed Natl Mortgage Assn, dir 1978-; Natl Housing Conf, dir 1979-; Natl Comm Against Discrimination in Housing, treas 1980-; Natl Caucus and Ctr on Black Aged Inc, pres. **Orgs:** Life mem NAACP and Urban League. **Honors/Awds:** Honorary Doctor of Pub Srv Western MI Univ 1970. **Business Addr:** President, Natl Caucus & Ctr Blk Aged, 1424 K St NW 500, Washington, DC 20005.

SIMMONS, SHEILA ANNE
Journalist. **Personal:** Born Dec 8, 1965, Asheville, NC; daughter of Gralene Graves Simmons and Arthur Gene Simmons. **Educ:** North Carolina State University, Raleigh, NC, 1984-86; University of North Carolina at Chapel Hill, Chapel Hill, NC, BA, Journalism, 1988. **Career:** The News and Observer, Raleigh, NC, reporter, 1987-88; Philadelphia Newspaper Inc (Philadelphia Daily News), Philadelphia, PA, business writer, 1989-. **Orgs:** Member, National Association of Black Journalists, 1989-; member, Urban League Young Professionals, Philadelphia, PA, 1990-; member, 1989, vice president for print journalism, 1991, Philadelphia Association of Black Journalists. **Honors/Awds:** Second Place, Business Writing and Economic News, Keystone Press Association, 1989; member, Gamma Beta Phi Honor Society, North Carolina State University, 1984; Eleventh Place, William Randolph Hearst Award, College Journalism Contest, 1988.

SIMMONS, SHIRLEY DAVIS
Elected official. **Personal:** Born Sep 3, 1941, Vaughn, MS; married Princeston G Simmons; children: Brenda S Gooden, Vernadette S Gipson, Princeston Jr, Katrina, Makeba. **Educ:** Tougaloo Coll, certificate AA; Jackson State Univ, certificate; Mary Holmes Coll, certificate. **Career:** Natl Council of Negro Women, 1st vice pres 1978; NAACP, chmn of redress 1980-82; Women for Progress, publicity chmn 1982; Madison-Yazoo-Leake Health Clinic,chmn of personnel 1984; Madison Co Schools, bd member. **Orgs:** Coord Summer Feeding Program 1979; coord Energy Assistance 1984; mem Project Unity 1985; mem Madison Co School Bd 1984-. **Honors/Awds:** Outstanding Contribution to Youth Awd Project Unity 1983. **Home Addr:** Rte 3 Box 327, Canton, MS 39046.

SIMMONS, STEPHEN LLOYD
Restauranteur. **Personal:** Born Aug 4, 1958, Boston, MA; son of Herbert & Sylvia Simmons; married Elizabeth Simmons, May 14, 1994; children: Alexander Charles. **Educ:** City Coll of San Francisco, hotel restaurant management, 1984. **Career:** Stanford Court Hotel, roundsman, 1980-83; Campton Place Hotel, chef de cuisine, 1983-86; Casa Madrona Hotel, exec chef, 1986-88; SS Monterey Cruise Ship, exec chef, 1988-89; One Market Restaurant/Lark Creek Inn, chef, partner, 1989-94; Bubba's Diner, owner,chef, currently. **Orgs:** Full Circle Programs, bd mem, 1993-96; City Coll Advisory Bd, bd mem, 1992-. **Honors/Awds:** 100 Black Men, Top Black Chefs, 1993; James Beard House, Rising Star Chef, American Cuisine, 1989; Cornell Univ, Cross Country Dining Program, 1989. **Special Achievements:** Published Recipes include : Detroit Free Press, 1984-95, San Jose Mercury News, San Francisco Chronicle, Marin Independent Journal; presently working on cookbook. **Home Addr:** 182 Floribel Ave, San Anselmo, CA 94960. **Business Addr:** Owner, Bubba's Diner, 566 San Anselmo Ave, San Anselmo, CA 94960, (415)459-6862.

SIMMONS, SYLVIA J.
Educator. **Personal:** Born May 8, 1935, Boston, MA; daughter of Margaret M Thomas Quarles and Lorenzo C Quarles; married Herbert G Simmons Jr, Oct 26, 1957; children: Stephen, Lisa, Alison. **Educ:** Manhattanville Coll, BA 1957; Boston Coll, MED 1962, PhD, 1990. **Career:** ABCD Headstart Program, soc serv suprv 1965; Charles River Park Nursery School, Montessori teacher 1965-66; Boston Coll, reg school of mgmt 1966-70; Harvard Univ, assoc dean of admissions & financial aid, faculty arts & sci 1974-76; Radcliffe Coll, assoc dean of admissions, financial aid & womens educ, dir financial aid 1972-76; Univ of MA Central Office, assoc vice pres academic affairs 1976-81; MA Higher Educ Asst Corp, sr vice pres 1982-; American Student Assistance, exec vp, 1992-95, president, 1995-96; lecturer in education, Boston Univ. **Orgs:** Past mem Exec Council Natl Assoc of Student Financial Aid Admin; past 1st vice pres Eastern Assoc of Financial Aid Admin; mem MA Assoc of Coll Minority Admin; consult Dept of HEW Office of Educ Reg I; consultant Coll Scholarship Serv, MA Bd of Higher Educ; past mem Rockefeller Selection Comm Harvard Univ; mem Delta Sigma Theta Natl; bd mem Family Serv Assoc Boston, Wayland Fair Housing, Concerts in Black & White, past pres Newton Chapter of Jack & Jill Inc, Boston Chapter Links Inc, Boston Manhattanville Club; mem bd of trustees Manhattanville Coll; past bd trustees Rivers Country Day School; past bd mem Cambridge Mental Health Assn; past bd trustees Simons Rock Coll; North Shore CC, chmn bd of trustees; William Price Unit of American Cancer Soc, past pres; bd of dir Amer Cancer Soc MA Div 1-90; board of trustees, Boston College; past mem board, Mass Foundation for the Humanities, 1990-91; Merrimack Coll, bd of trustees; Mt Ida Coll, bd of overseers; Grimes-King Foundation, bd of dirs; Regis College, bd of trustees; Anna Stearns Foundation, board of directors; Exec Service Corps, bd of dir. **Honors/Awds:** Women in Politics; Outstanding Young Leader Boston Jr Chamber of Commerce 1971; Boston Coll Bicentennial Award 1976; Black Achiever Award 1976; President's Award, Massachusetts Educ Opportunity Program 1988; Human Rights Award, Massachusetts Teachers Assn, 1988; Educator of the Year, Boston Chapter Assn of Negro Business & Professional Women's Club, 1989; Recognition of Contributions to Higher Educ, College Club, 1988; Honorary Degree, St Joseph's College, 1994; Sojournore Daughters, 25 African-American Women Who Have Made A Difference, 1990; Bishop James Healey Award, 1997.

SIMMONS, THELMA M.
Regional compensation manager. **Personal:** Born Aug 10, 1942, Bastrop, LA; daughter of Leona Averitt Cross and Charlie Cross; married Arthur Simmons (divorced 1985); children: R Stevonne, Eric, Brenda. **Educ:** Western WA State Coll, Bellingham, WA, human resources, 1979. **Career:** Pacific Northwest Bell, Seattle, WA, supr, mgr, 1965-76, staff mgr, 1976-79, mgr, operator services, 1979-82, exec asst, 1982-84; AT&T, Seattle, WA, carrier selection mgr, 1984-85; AT&T, Oakland, CA, regional diversity mgr, 1985-88; AT&T, San Francisco, CA, regional compensation mgr, 1988-. **Orgs:** Mem, Seattle Women's Comm, 1981-83; lifetime mem, NAACP, 1965-; chairperson,human resource comm, Oakland Private Industry Council, 1987-; mem, Delta Sigma Theta, 1979-. **Honors/Awds:** Future Black Leaders of the 80's, Black Elected Officials, WA State, 1980; Certificate of Appreciation for Civic Service, Mayor of Oakland, 1990.

SIMMONS, WAYNE GENERAL
Professional football player. **Personal:** Born Dec 15, 1969, Beauford, SC. **Educ:** Clemson, BA in finance. **Career:** Green Bay Packers, linebacker, 1993-97; Kansas City Chiefs, 1997-. **Business Addr:** Professional Football Player, Kansas City Chiefs, One Arrowhead Dr, Kansas City, MO 64129, (816)924-9300.

SIMMONS, WILLIE, JR.
Bank executive. **Personal:** Born May 23, 1939, Meridian, MS; son of Gussie Simmons (deceased) and Willie Simmons (deceased); married Vernocia Neblett; children: Michael Anthony, Kevin Lawrence. **Educ:** Military Police Officer, advanced course 1970; Univ of Tampa, BS (sr honors) 1975. **Career:** AUS, police officer 1958-78; Ingalls Memorial Hosp, dir of security 1978-80; First Chicago Security Serv Inc, chmn CEO 1985-; First Natl Bank of Chicago, mgr of protection & security 1980-85, dir of corporate security 1985-. **Orgs:** Pres IL Security Chiefs Assoc 1982; speaker Project We Care 1982-; chmn Deacon Bd Truevine MB Church 1982-; mem Amer Soc for Industrial Security 1984-; chmn Bd of Christian Educ Truevine MB Church 1985-; vice chmn, Crime Stoppers Plus 1986-; mem, Intl Org of Black Security Executives. **Honors/Awds:** Outstanding Serv Awd Hospital Security 1980; Outstanding Serv Awd IL Security Chiefs Assoc 1980, 1981; Award of Excellence, 1986, First Chicago Corp; Appreciation Award, 1988, Natl Assn of Asian-Amer Professionals, 1986. **Military Serv:** AUS major 20 yrs; Bronze Star, Meritorious Svcs, Vietnam Serv 1958-78. **Business Addr:** Director/Vice President, First Natl Bank of Chicago, One First Natl Plaza, Chicago, IL 60670.

SIMMONS-EDELSTEIN, DEE
Business executive. **Personal:** Born Jul 1, 1937, New York, NY; daughter of Gertrude Dobson and Tonsley Dobson; divorced. **Educ:** City Coll of NY. **Career:** Ophelia DeVore Assn, vp; mistress of ceremonies; fashion commentator; Grace Del Marco, professional commercial model; WNJR-AM, NJ, Dee Simmons Radio Show; Nat Shoes, NYC, statistical bookkeeper; mag cover girl; lectr; New York Images & Voices, host, currently. **Orgs:** Mem Am Fedn of TV & Radio Assn; mem Nat Assn of Women in Media; 100 Coalition of Black Women; Affairs Com for Freedom Fund Drive; NAACP; Nat Drive Cerebral Palsy Telethon. **Honors/Awds:** Spl Achvmt Award 1973; Pharmaco Products Award for first model of color to do TV commercial 1962; Ms Empire State 1962; Model of the Year 1963; Ms Beaux Arts for Schaefer Brewery 1962-63; hon award United Negro Coll Fund; Comm Serv Award for anti-narcotic rehab Prgm; NY Evvy Fashion Award, 1994; Ophelia DeYore & Florence M Rice Positive Image Award, 1994; Host of New York Images And Voices; Models of the South Convention Award, 1994.

SIMMS, ALBERT L.
Clergyman. **Personal:** Born Jan 21, 1931, Claremont, WV; son of Mr & Mrs Robert T Simms; divorced; children: Div. **Educ:** Appalachian Bible Inst, grad; So Baptist Sem Ext Sch, 1973; Hilltop Baptist Ext Sem, grad 1976; North Gate Bible Coll, BA. **Career:** First Baptist Church Harlem Heights, pastor, currently. **Orgs:** Past treas New River Valley Missionary Baptist Assn; asst dir Hill Baptist Ext Seminary; historian New River Valley Bapt Assn; mem Hist Comm WV Baptist State Conv; ch Dist Assn new River Educ Com; Hill Top Baptist Ext Sem adv bd; mem WV Baptist Minister Conf; past vice pres Fayette Ct Com Action; mem Crippled Children Div Assn Huntington; active in Bible Integratged camps & 4H camps as youth counselor. **Honors/Awds:** Award of Merit Profiles of a Christian 1972. **Home Addr:** 216 Broadway Ave, Oak Hill, WV 25901.

SIMMS, CARROLL HARRIS
Artist, educator. **Personal:** Born Apr 29, 1924, Bald Knob, AR; son of Rosa Hazel Harris Sims (deceased) and Tommie Wesley Sims. **Educ:** Cranbrook Art Acad, BFA 1950, MFA 1960. **Career:** Toledo State Mental Hosp, 1948-49; Detroit Art Inst Art Sch, 1950; TX So Univ, prof art 1950-87. **Orgs:** Assoc life mem Inst African Studies Univ Ibadan Nigeria; TX So Univ Group Study Abroad Project Natl Univ of Haiti Port-au-Prince/Henriquez Padre Urena Natl Univ Santo Domingo Dominican Republic West Indies 1981 East/West, Contemporary American Art July 1984; mem 1984, 1986-, secretary 1987-91, Houston Municipal Art Comm Houston TX; Dallas Mus Fine Arts 1952, 1953; mem Amer Soc African Culture; assoc life mem Inst African Culture Univ Ibadan Nigeria; life mem Inst Intl Educ; life mem Slade Soc Univ Coll London England; mem TX Assn Coll Tchrs; adv panel TX Comm on Arts & Humanities 1972-79; Natl Humanities Fac 1975-77; volunteer, Texas Southern University Select Committee/Recruitment of Students. **Honors/Awds:** 1st Awd Toledo Mus Fine Arts 1949-50; Purchase Awd Cranbrook Mus Art 1953; Fulbright Fellow 1954-56; Scholarship Swedish Inst Stockholm Survey Contem Ceramic Pottery 1964; TX So Univ Awd; Cert of Recog for Exemplory Representing Afro-Amer Artistic & Cultural Expression Second World Black & African Festival of Arts 1977; contrib author "Black Art in Houston, The TX Southern Univ Experience" TX A&M Univ Press 1978; "Black Artists/South 1800-1978" Huntsville Museum of Art AL 1979; Carroll Sims Day, Mayor of City of Houston, 1977; exhibition "African-Amer Artists" 1978; Griot Awd Southern Conf on Afro-Amer Studies In-cHouston 1984; "He's Got the Whole World In His Hands" bronze sculpture permanent collection the new CA Afro-Amer Museum LA CA; Alpha Kappa Omega Chap Alpha Kappa Alpha Sor Inc Edtor and Outstanding Achievement in Visual Arts; Sculpture bronze permanent collection Texas Southern Univ title "A Tradition of Music" 1986; published numerous books, articles, illustrations and periodicals; numerous exhibitions and sculpture commissions; Texas Southern Univ dedicated a sculpture to Carroll Harris Sims, 1996. **Special Achievements:** Forerunners and Newcomers: Houston's Leading African-American Artists, 1989-; Our Commonwealth: Our Collections, Works from Traditionally Black Colleges and Universities.

SIMMS, DARRELL DEAN
Consultant, writer. **Personal:** Born in New Orleans, LA; son of Elleneese Brooks Simms and Melvin Simms; married Nelda Conde Simms, Aug 17, 1977; children: Darsha, Thorin. **Educ:** University of Washington, BSIE, 1982. **Career:** Westinghouse Corp., nuclear safety engineer, 1982-83; IBM, systems engineering manager, 1983-91; City of Portland, executive assistant to commissioner, 1992-93; Management Aspects Inc, president, currently. **Orgs:** Business-Education Compact, board of directors, 1991-; Black United Fund of Oregon, allocations committee, fund disbursements committee; Urban League of Portland, Business Corp. Partnerships, 1992-; Black Contractors Alliance, executive secretary, 1993. **Honors/Awds:** IBM, Management Excellence Award, 1990. **Special Achievements:** Author, Black Experience, Strategies and Tactics, 1992; co-founder, Project MISTER, Male Information to Encourage Responsibility. **Military Serv:** US Navy, hm2, 1973-77. **Business Phone:** (503)591-7498.

SIMMS, JAMES EDWARD
Educational administrator, cleric. **Personal:** Born Dec 14, 1943, Richmond, VA; married Emmajane Miller; children: Rachael, Eboni, James. **Educ:** VA Union Univ, BA 1967; Pgh Theological Seminary, MDiv 1972, Dr of Ministry 1974. **Career:** Pgh Human Relations Comm, exec dir 1972; Allegheny Co Comm Coll, student serv coord 1973; Chatham Coll, instructor 1974; Comm Release Agency, exec dir 1974; Comm Action Pgh Inc, neighborhood admin 1977; City of Pittsburgh, asst exec sec office of the mayor. **Orgs:** Chmn United Negro College Fund Telethon 1983; pastor St Paul Baptist Church; pres Amer Baptist Theological Seminary; chmn Municipal Campaign United Way; mem Natl Forum of Black Public Admin; pres Homer S Brown Alumni Assn of VA Union Univ; pres bd of dirs Hill House Comm Serv Inc; mem bd of dirs Hill House Assn; mem bd of dirs Volunteer Action Center; mem bd of dirs Action Housing; mem Bd of Garfield Jubilee Housing Inc. **Honors/Awds:** Varsity Letters Inter-Collegiate Football VA Union Univ 1965-67; Distinguished Serv Awd Conf of Minority Public Admins 1978; Political Awareness Awd Young Republican Council 1979; Civil Rights Awd Hand in Hand Inc 1980. **Business Addr:** Asst Exec Secretary, Office of The Mayor, 517 City County Bldg, Pittsburgh, PA 15219.

SIMMS, MARGARET CONSTANCE
Economist. **Personal:** Born Jul 30, 1946, St Louis, MO; daughter of Margaret E Simms and Frederick T Simms. **Educ:** Carleton Coll, Northfield, MN, BA 1967; Stanford Univ, MA 1969; Stanford Univ, PhD 1974. **Career:** Univ of CA, Santa Cruz, acting asst prof 1971-72; Atlanta Univ, asst prof School of Business 1972-76; Atlanta Univ, Econ Dept, assoc prof & dept chair 1976-81; The Urban Inst, sr rsch assoc 1979-81, dir minorities & social policy prog 1981-86; The Joint Center for Political Studies, dep dir of rsch, 1986-. **Orgs:** Edtr The Review of Black Political Econ 1983-; mem Natl Economic Assoc 1971-, pres 1978-79; bd mem Council on Economic Priorities 1979-85; bd mem Women's Equity Action League 1984-; mem Fed Advsry Panel on Financial Elem & Secondary Ed 1979-82. **Honors/Awds:** Selected Publs ed. "Black Economic Progress: An Agenda for 1990s" with Julianne M Malveaux, Slipping Through the Cracks, The Status of Black Women 1986, with Kristin A Moore & Charles L Betsey, Choice & Circumstance, Racial Differences in Adolescent Sexuality & Fertility (New Brunswick, NJ, Transaction Books, 1985) "The Economic Well-Being of Minorities during the Reagan Years," Urban Inst Paper 1984; "The Impact of Chgs in Fed Elem & Secondary Ed Policy," Urban Inst Discussion Paper 1984. **Business Addr:** VP, Research, Joint Ctr for Political & Economic Studies, 1090 Vermont Ave NW, Washington, DC 20005.

SIMMS, ROBERT H.
Company executive, consultant. **Personal:** Born Oct 2, 1927, Snowhill, AL; son of Alberta Simms and Harry Simms; married Aubrey Watkins, Nov 27, 1953; children: Leah Aliece Simms-Graham, David Michael. **Educ:** Xavier Univ, BS 1949; Tuskegee Inst; NY Univ, Advanced Study; Univ of Miami; Univ of MA. **Career:** Bob Simms Assoc Inc, pres/CEO currently; Comm Rel Bd Metro Dade Co, exec dir, 1967-83; Small Business & Development Center, exec dir 1965-66; Dade Co Bd of Educ, teacher 1953-65; Macon Co Bd of Educ, teacher 1949-50, 1952-53. **Orgs:** Founder Miami Varsity Club; mem Orange Bowl Com; mem Kappa Alpha Psi; mem Sigma Pi Phi; Creator of Inner City/Minority Experience for Defense Dept's Race Relations Inst 1972; Trustee, Univ of Miami. **Military Serv:** AUS

sgt e5 1950-52. **Business Addr:** President-CEO, Bob H Simms Assoc, Inc, 7020 Glenoogle Dr, Miami Lakes, FL 33014, (305)821-6558.

SIMMS, STUART OSWALD
Attorney. **Personal:** married Candace Otterbein; children: Marcus. **Educ:** Harvard Law School, 1975. **Career:** US Attny's Office US Courthouse, attny 1978-. **Orgs:** Pres Black Alumni Assoc 1979-81. **Business Addr:** Attorney, US Attorneys Office, US Courthouse, 101 West Lombard St, Baltimore, MD 21201.

SIMMS, WILLIAM E.
Insurance company executive. **Personal:** Born Aug 23, 1944, Indianapolis, IN; son of Rosa Lee Smith Simms (deceased) and Frank T Simms Sr (deceased); married Maxine A Newman Simms, Jul 3, 1971; children: Terry Denise Reddix-Simms, Randall L. **Educ:** Univ of Southern California, Los Angeles CA, BS Business Admin, 1971, MBA Marketing, 1976. **Career:** Transamerica Occidental Life, Los Angeles CA, mgr, 1969-77; Lincoln Natl Reinsurance Co, Fort Wayne IN, second vice pres, 1977-80; Transamerica Occidental Life, Los Angeles CA, vice pres reinsurance mktg, 1980-84, vice pres sales/admin, 1984-86, vice pres reinsurance, 1987, sr vice pres reinsurance, beginning 1988; Transamerica Life Companies, reinsurance division, president, currently. **Orgs:** California Life Insurance Companies Assn; Los Angeles Jr Chamber of Commerce; Natl Urban Leauge; bd of trustees, Los Angeles Summer Games Found; Los Angeles Open Gulf Found; advisory bd, United Negro Coll Fund. **Special Achievements:** Second African-American member of the exclusive Augusta Natl Golf Club, 1995. **Military Serv:** US Air Force, staff sergeant, 1963-67. **Business Addr:** President, Reinsurance Division, Transamerica Life Companies, NationsBank Corporate Center, 100 N Tryon St, Ste 2600, Charlotte, NC 28202-4004.

SIMON, ELAINE
Cosmetologist. **Personal:** Born Nov 30, 1944, St Johns, Antigua-Barbuda; daughter of Rosalyn Richards Jarvis and Hubert Phillips; divorced; children: Denise, Francine, Sheldean. **Educ:** Bay Coll of Baltimore, Baltimore MD, AA, 1976; Univ of Baltimore, attended, 1977-78; Natl Beauty Culturist League, Washington DC, Doctorate, 1987; Catinsville Community Coll, Certificate, 1982; Central State Univ, Columbus OH, Certificate, 1985; Coppin State Coll, Certificate, 1985. **Career:** Bay Coll of Maryland, lounge mgr, 1985-76; Johnsons Product Co, lecturer, technician, 1979-85; Touch of Paris Coiffure, owner, mgr, 1978-. **Orgs:** Natl Beauticulturist League, Baltimore MD, public relations dir, 1978-89; exec dir, Natl Black Women Consciousness Raising Assn, 1980-89; public relations dir, Master Beautician Assn, 1982-89; educ dir, Maryland State Beauty-Culture Assn, 1982-89; public relations dir, Theta Mu Sigma Natl Sorority, Zeta Chapter, 1985. **Honors/Awds:** Civil Rights Humanitarian Award, Maryland Special Inaugural Comm, 1981; Governor's Citation, Governor of Maryland, 1983; Resolution, City Council of Baltimore 1989; Booker T Washington Citation Honor, Business League of Baltimore, 1989; Economic Stress Threaten Black Salon (shop talk magazine), 1983; "Pocket News Paper," 1983; Business Award, Mayor Baltimore City, 1994; Natl Black Women Consciousness Raising Assn Inc; natl exec dir, Baltimore Response Assn; Rosa Pryor Music Scholarship Fund, admin advisor. **Home Addr:** 20 N Kossuth St, Baltimore, MD 21229.

SIMON, JEWEL WOODARD
Artist. **Personal:** Born Jul 28, 1911, Houston, TX; daughter of Rachel Williams Woodard and Chester Arthur Woodard; married Edward Lloyd Simon, Feb 19, 1939 (died 1984); children: Edward L Jr, Margaret Jewel Summerow. **Educ:** Atlanta Univ, AB (summa cum laude) 1931; Commercial Art, grad cert 1962; Atlanta Coll Art, BFA 1967. **Career:** Jack Yates High School, math dept head 1931-39; artist, many one-woman shows. **Orgs:** Charter-patron, High Museum, Theater Guild, Atlanta Coll Art; past pres Mosolit Literary Cir, life mem AKA Sor; Amer Assn Univ Women; Natl Council of Negro Women; GA Council Arts; past bd mem YWCA; Atlanta Civic Design Comm; Jack & Jill of Amer, past natl serv project chmn, Atlanta Chapter, past pres; past pres Grady Metro-Atlanta Girls Club; past pres E R Carter School PTA; Girls Clubs of Amer; life mem Church Women United; Amer Assn Univ Women; 1st Congregational Church; vice pres Assn Emory Sch of Nursing; past treas, Black Artist Atlanta; First Congregational Church, past vice chair, past deaconess bd; Special Audiences, bd of dirs, Handicapped Artist Show, judge. **Honors/Awds:** NCA Awds Mental Health Assn 1958; Atlanta Univ Alumni Awd 1966; WSB Beaver Awd 1968; Recognition Awd Simon Family Natl Conf of Christians & Jews 1971; Outstanding Leadership Awd 1975; Amer Assn Univ Women; Distinguished Serv March of Dimes; Mother of the Yr Awd; Bronze Woman Yr Fine Art; 8 purchase awds; Golden Dove Heritage Awd; First Pres Alumni Awd for Outstanding Achievement Artist Teacher Humanitarian 1984; Valiant Woman Award CWU 1987; Lifetime Deputy Governor, ABIRA; Golden Girl Award, Alpha Kappa Alpha Founders Day Celebration, 1991; Golden Poet Awards, 1985-86, 1990; World of Poetry Convention, numerous awards, 1985, 1990. **Special Achievements:** Artist, exhibitions/showings and private collections include: Amer Negro Art, Cedric Dover; Black Dimensions in Contemporary Amer Art; Women Artists in America; Amer Printmakers; Leading Contemporary Amer Artists, Les Krantz; Carver Museum; DuSable Museum; Kiah Museum; Ringling Museum, Education Department; Atlanta Univ; Clark Clg; Natl Archives; Carnegie Institute; numerous other museums, colleges, universities, and publications in the US and Canada; author: Flight, Preoccupation with Life, Death and Life Eternal, 1990; contributor: "Three Women," show, Ariel Gallery, Soho, NY, 1990-91.

SIMON, JOSEPH DONALD
Clergyman, education administrator. **Personal:** Born Jun 30, 1932, Natchitoches, LA. **Educ:** Attended Divine Word Seminary, Epworth, IA, 1955; Divine Word Seminary, Bay, St Louis, BA, 1961; Gregorian University, Rome, Italy, MA, eclec history, 1963. **Career:** Divine Word Seminary, Bay, St Louis, professor history, 1963-66; Divine Word College, Epworth, director of development, 1975-80, assistant professor history, 1966-81, academic dean/vice president, 1981-87, president, 1987-. **Orgs:** City council, Epworth, IA, 1976-85; chairman, Area Council of Government, Dubuque County, 1976; chairman, East Central Intergovernmental Association, 1977; board of trustees, Divine Word College, 1975-80; board of directors, League of Iowa Municipalities, 1979-80; executive committee, East Central Intergovernmental Association, 1980-; chairman, East Iowa Regional Housing Authority, 1982, 1983-; chairman, East Central Intergovernmental Association Business Growth, Inc, 1985-. **Business Addr:** President/ Chancellor, Divine Word College, Center Ave, Epworth, IA 52045.

SIMON, KENNETH BERNARD
Surgeon. **Personal:** Born Sep 29, 1953, San Francisco, CA. **Educ:** Univ of AZ-Tucson, BS RN 1976; Meharry Medical Coll, MD 1980; American Bd of Surgery, Specialty Certification 1986. **Career:** DC General Hosp, staff surgeon/instructor in surgery 1985-86; Univ of Alberta Hospitals, resident in cardiac surgery 1986-87; Univ of Mississippi, Jackson, MS, asst prof of surgery, 1987-90; VA Hospital, Jackson, MS, staff surgeon, 1987-90; Cleveland Clinic, Cleveland, OH, fellow in vascular surgery, 1991-; VA Hospital, chief, surgical service; Univ of Mississippi Medical Ctr, asst prof of surgery, 1992-. **Orgs:** NMA; American Coll of Surgeons; Assn of Academic Surgeons; Natl Med Assn; Assn of VA Surgeons. **Honors/Awds:** Kim Meche Scholar Univ of AZ 1974-75. **Home Addr:** 863 Rutherford Dr, Jackson, MS 39206.

SIMON, LONNIE A.
Clergyman. **Personal:** Born Mar 23, 1925, East Mulga, AL; son of Tempie Haywood Simon and William Simon; married Florence, May 14, 1949; children: Janet Write, Lonita Ross, Kenneth, Cynthia Layton. **Educ:** Central Bible Coll, 1963; Amer Baptist Theol Sem, 1975; Trinity Theological Seminary, enrolled master of theology program, Newburgh IN 1983-; Youngstown Coll, 1959. **Career:** Eastern OH Baptist Assn, moderator 1968-76; New Bethel Baptist Church, 1962-95; Jerusalem Baptist Church 1960-62; Elizabeth Baptist Church 1954-59; US Post Office Youngstown OH, letter carrier 1955-65. **Orgs:** Song leader exec bd mem Lott Carey Bapt Foreign Mission Conv; mem Youngstown Bd of Ed 1972-75; missionary Guyana South Amer 1968, 1976; instr Yo Ext Unit of the Amer Baptist Theol Seminary; past pres Intl Ministerial Alliance; past pres Youngstown Council of Churches; past pres Youngstown Urban League; past vice pres Youngstown Br NAACP; former mem Health & Welfare Council; former mem Mayor's Human Relations Commn; Downtown Kiwanis; Moderator Northern OH Baptist Assn 1993-97; Co-chairman, Inter-Racial Clergy Dialogue 1982-97; Ohio Commissioner Socially Disadvantaged Black Males 1990; Ohio advisory bd Ohio Dept of Ecomonic Development 1991-; Mayor's Bi-Centennial Committee, 1996. **Honors/Awds:** Received ten week Ford Found grant to attend Urban Training Ctr Chicago 1967; Natl Inst of Mental Health four-week grant to attend Case Western Res Univ 1969; observer All African Council of Churches, Partners in Ecumenism, 1987; Jesse Jackson delegate Natl Democratic Convention 1988; Committee Member Award; Ohio Commission Martin Luther King Holiday 1989-; Natl Leadership Award, 1991; State of Ohio-"Martin Luther King Award," 1995. **Special Achievements:** Published: An Anthology, "Songs of Simon," 1993. **Military Serv:** USN 3rd class officer's steward 1943-46. **Business Addr:** Pastor, Friendship Baptist Church, 3395 Spearman Ave, Farrell, PA 16121.

SIMON, MATT
Sports coach. **Career:** Univ of North Texas, head football coach, 1995-. **Business Addr:** Head Football Coach, University of North Texas, Athletic Department, PO Box 13917, Denton, TX 76203, (817)565-2000.

SIMON, ROSALYN MCCORD
Management consultant. **Personal:** Born Dec 2, 1946, Baltimore, MD; daughter of Jacolian McCord (deceased) and Moffett McCord; children: Monica Lynnette. **Educ:** Coppin State Coll, BS 1973; Morgan State Univ, MS 1981, University of Maryland at College Park, PhD candidate currently. **Career:** Admin on Develop Disabilities, consultant 1982-84; Amer Assoc of Univ Affiliated Progs, project dir 1984-86; Natl Information Ctr for Handicapped Children & Youth, consultant 1986-; Mass Transit Admin, management consultant, 1988-. **Orgs:** Consultant Developmental Disabilities Law Project Inc 1980-82, DC Commn on Public Health DC District Govt 1986.

SIMON, WALTER J. **See Obituaries section.**

SIMONE, NINA
Singer, composer, pianist. **Personal:** Born Feb 21, 1940, Tryon, NC; daughter of Mary Kate Waymon and John D Waymon; children: Lisa Celeste. **Educ:** Juilliard Sch of Music (Carl Freidberg), student 1954-56; Curtis Inst Music (Vladimir Sokoloff), student 1950-53; Malcolm X College, DH; Amherst College, DMusic; private study, with Clemens Sandresky, Grace Carrol. **Career:** Private music teacher 1954; Composer, Mississippi Goddam 1963; Four Women 1964 (with Langston Hughes); Backlash Blues 1966; recording for RCA Victor Records; accompanist for vocal student Arlent Smith Studio Phila; Film, actress "Someone to Watch Over Me" 1987; Composer, "Young, Gifted & Black" was named Natl Anthem of Black America by CORE, composed 500 songs, made 58 albums. **Orgs:** Mem ASCAP, AFTRA, Amer Federation Musicians, SAG. **Honors/Awds:** Albums incl, Silk & Soul, Emergency Ward, It Is Finished, Here Comes the Sun, Young Gifted & Black; Recip YMCA Life Award for Fund Raising; Named Woman of the Year Jazz at Home Club Philadelphia 1966; Hits from albums are "Porgy" from Porgy & Bess, "Life" from Rock Opera Hair, My Baby Just Cares For Me; Awarded keys to 7 major US cities. **Business Addr:** Sibongile Music & Publishers, Mail Boxes USA, 7095 Hollywood Blvd, West Hollywood, CA 90046.

SIMONS, RENEE V. H.
Consumer products company executive. **Personal:** Born May 27, 1949, New York, NY; daughter of Phyllis Harley Phipps and Charles Leroy Moore; married Eglon Simons, Nov 29, 1969; children: Kimberly, Cameron, Kourtney. **Educ:** Hunter College, New York, NY, BA, 1971; Fordham Graduate School of Education, New York, NY, MS, education, 1974; Columbia Graduate School of Business, New York, NY, MBA, 1978. **Career:** General Foods, White Plains, NY, asst brand manager, Kool-Aid, 1978-80; American Can/James River, Greenwich, CT, brand manager, Dixie/Northern, 1980-83; Seven-Up, St Louis, MO, brand manager, 1983-85; Philip Morris USA, New York, NY, exec asst to exec vice pres, 1985-86; Philip Morris USA, New York, NY, brand manager, 1986-89; Philip Morris Management Corp, New York, NY, director, special projects, 1989-91, group director in marketing, 1991; Trade Marketing, Sales Promotions and Information, director, 1991-93; Marketing, dir consumer marketing svcs, 1993-94; Marketing, dir of media, 1994-. **Orgs:** Member, PTA, 1980-; member, Links, 1990-; Delta Sigma Theta Sorority, 1968-; Covenant House, New York Board of Dirs. **Honors/Awds:** Outstanding Professional Women in Advertising Award, Dollars & Sense, 1989; Black Achievers Award, YMCA, 1981-82; Fellow, COGME, 1976-78. **Business Addr:** Director, Media, 120 Park Ave, New York, NY 10017.

SIMPKINS, CUTHBERT O.
Dentist, state government official. **Personal:** Born Jan 13, 1925, Mansfield, LA; married Elaine J. Shoemaker; children: four. **Educ:** Wiley College; Tennessee State University; Meharry Medical College, DDS, 1948. **Career:** Dentist in private practice; Louisiana House of Representatives, 1992-. **Orgs:** National Society of Dental Practitioners; National Dental Association; Academy of General Dentistry; American Analgesic Society; American Dental Association; New York State Dental Society; Queens County Dental Society; Queens Clinical Society; Alpha Phi Alpha Fraternity; charter member, Institute of Continuing Dental Education of the Eleventh District; Biracial Commission; 4th vice president, Southern Christian Leadership Conference; Sigma Pi Phi Fraternity. **Honors/Awds:** First Civil Rights Award, 1970, President's Appreciation Award, 1975, NAACP; Martin Luther King Award for Outstanding Contributions to the Civil Rights Movement, 1989; Southern University Leader of the Year Award, 1988-89; Civil Rights Award, National Dental Association, 1970; Distinguished Service Award, New Elizabeth Baptist Church, 1989; Meharry Medical College President's Award for 25 Years of Service to Mankind, 1973; Dedication to Mankind Award, Airport Park Advisory Council, 1989; Louisiana State Beauticians Award for Achievement in Civil Rights, 1989; Arthritis Humanitarian Award, recipient, 1992; Founders Day Award, York Coll, New York, 1993; Bill of Rights Award, 1994. **Military Serv:** US Air Force, Capt, 1951. **Business Addr:** Dentist, 4001 Lakeshore Drive, Shreveport, LA 71109, (318)635-2382.

SIMPKINS, DICKEY (LUBARA DIXON SIMPKINS)
Professional basketball player. **Personal:** Born Apr 6, 1972, Fort Washington, MD. **Educ:** Providence. **Career:** Chicago Bulls, forward, 1994-97, 1998-; Golden State Warriors, 1997. **Business Addr:** Professional Basketball Player, Chicago Bulls, 1901 W Madison St, Chicago, IL 60612, (312)455-4000.

SIMPKINS, J. EDWARD
Educator. **Personal:** Born Oct 18, 1932, Detroit, MI; married Alice Marie Mann; children: Edward, Ann Marie, Evelyn.

Educ: Wayne State University, BA, 1955, edM, 1961; Harvard University, CAS, 1969, edD, 1971. **Career:** College of Education, Wayne State University, dean, 1974-; Center for Black Students, Wayne State University, 1972-74; Pennsylvania Public Schools, chief negotiator, 1971-72; Faculty & Executive Director of Center for Urban Students at Harvard Graduate School of Education, assistant & dean, 1970-71; History Department, Tufts University, Lecturer, 1968-71; Detroit Federation of Teachers, executive vice president, 1965-68; High School English Journ History, teacher, 1956-65. **Orgs:** American Arb Association; Ind Rel Res Association; Phi Delta Kappa; president, Association for the Study of Afro American Life & History St of Michigan. **Honors/Awds:** Human Rights Award, 1968; Spirit of Detroit Award, 1974; Martin Luther King Award; Woodrow Wilson Foundation; Harvard University Fellowship. **Military Serv:** USNA pvt 1956-58. **Business Addr:** Education Administration, Wayne State University, 323 Education, Detroit, MI 48202.

SIMPKINS, WILLIAM JOSEPH
Military. **Personal:** Born Dec 30, 1934, Edgefield, SC. **Educ:** NC A&T State Univ, BS 1952-56; Attended, Univ of MD; Baylor Univ, MHA 1969. **Career:** 121 Evc Hosp Repub of Korea, exec officer 1969-70; Mcdonald Army Hosp Ft Eustis VA, exec officer 1970-71; HQ AUS Ofc of Surgeon Genl, asst chief personnel serv 1971-75; Eisenhower Med Ctr Ft Gordon, chief/personnel div troop comdr 1975-78; AUS Med Command Korea, exec officer 1978-79; Walter Reed Army Med Ctr, col AUS dir of personnel & comm activities 1979-83; US Army Medical Dept Personnel Support Agency Office of the Surgeon Genl, commander 1983-. **Orgs:** Mem Natl Assn of Health Serv Exec 1971-80; mem US Military Surgeons Assn; mem Amer Hosp Assn; mem Keystone Consistory #85 Free & Accepted Masons; mem NAACP; life mem Alpha Phi Alpha Frat Inc. **Honors/Awds:** Legion of Merit Office of Surgeon Gen HQ AUS; Bronze Star Medal Republic of Vietnam; Meritorious Serv Medal Ft Gordon GA; Meritorious Serv Medal Repub of Korea. **Military Serv:** AUS col 1956-. **Business Addr:** AUS Med Dept Personnel Sup Agency, Office of the Surgeon Genl, 1900 Half St SW, Washington, DC 20024.

SIMPSON, CARL WILHELM
Professional football player. **Personal:** Born Apr 18, 1970, Baxley, GA. **Educ:** Florida State, bachelor's degree in criminology. **Career:** Chicago Bears, defensive tackle, 1993-. **Business Addr:** Professional Football Player, Chicago Bears, 1000 Football Dr, Halas Hall at Conway Park, Lake Forest, IL 60045-4829, (847)295-6600.

SIMPSON, CAROLE
Journalist. **Personal:** Born Dec 7, 1940, Chicago, IL; daughter of Doretha Viola Wilbon Simpson and Lytle Ray Simpson; married James Edward Marshall, Sep 3, 1966; children: Mallika Joy. **Educ:** Univ of Illinois, 1958-60; Univ of Michigan, BA, 1962; Univ of Iowa, 1964-65. **Career:** WCFL Radio, news reporter, 1965-68; WBBM Radio, reporter, 1968-70; WMAQ-TV, news reporter, 1970-74; NBC News, news correspondent; ABC News, news correspondent, weekend anchor, currently. **Orgs:** Member, Radio-TV Correspondents Assn; member, Theta Sigma Phi. **Honors/Awds:** Media Journalism Award, AMA; Outstanding Woman in Communications, YWCA of Metro Chicago, 1974; Natl Assn of Black Journalist, Journalist of the Year, 1992. **Business Addr:** Correspondent/Weekend Anchor, ABC News, 1717 DeSales St NW, Washington, DC 20036.

SIMPSON, DARLA
Professional basketball player. **Personal:** Born Apr 11, 1969. **Educ:** Univ of Houston. **Career:** Atlanta Glory, forward, 1997-98; Colorado Xplosion, 1998-. **Business Addr:** Professional Basketball Player, Colorado Xplosion, 800 Grant St, Ste 410, Denver, CO 80203, (303)832-2225.

SIMPSON, DAZELLE DEAN
Physician. **Personal:** Born Aug 28, 1924, Miami, FL; married George Augustus Simpson Sr MD; children: George Jr, Gregory, Gary. **Educ:** Fisk Univ, BA magna cum laude 1945; Meharry Med Coll, MD highest honors 1950. **Career:** Private practice physician, currently. **Orgs:** Bd trustees Meharry Med Coll 1977-; diplomate Amer bd of Pediatrics 1957; fellow Amer Acad of Pediatrics; Alumnus of Year Meharry Coll 1974; chmn (pediatric sec) Natl Med Assn 1975-77; natl pres Meharry Alumni Assc 1976-77; life mem NAACP; mem Delta Sigma Theta Sor Head Start Consult Force on Pediatric Educ 1974-78; Task mem Amer Acad of Ped; mem bd of dirs, Miami Childrens Hospital 1988-. **Honors/Awds:** Contributing editor Current Therapy 1980. **Business Addr:** Physician, 1001 NW 54th St, Ste C, Miami, FL 33127.

SIMPSON, DIANE JEANNETTE
Social worker. **Personal:** Born Sep 20, 1952, Denver, CO; daughter of Irma Virginia Jordan Simpson and Arthur H Simpson (deceased); children: Shante Nicole. **Educ:** NE Wesleyan Univ, BS 1974; Univ of Denver Grad School of Social Work, MSW 1977. **Career:** Girl Scouts Mile Hi Council, summer asst 1971-77; Denver Public Schools, social worker asst, 1974-75, social worker, 1977-; Univ of Denver Grad School of Soc Work, field instr 1984-. **Orgs:** Mem Natl Assoc of Black Soc Workers 1980-86, Natl & CO Assn of Ed 1980-; sec of bd of trustees Warren Village Inc 1982-83; nominations & personnel comm Christ United Methodist Church 1981-84; mem Denver Chap Black Genealogy Org 1981-87; chairperson of minority adult recruitment team Girl Scouts Mile Hi Council 1982-84; mem Black Women's Network 1983-86; natl council delegate Girl Scouts 1984-87; chairperson planning comm Creative Ctr for Children 1984, adv bd 1984-86, Christ United Meth Church; mem traveler Denver Sister Cities Inc 1984; admin bd, staff, parish relations, Council of Ministries Christ United Methodist Church 1984-87; vice pres, United Methodist Women, Christ United Methodist Church, 1989-91; Education Scholarship Comm of Shorter African Methodist Episcopal Church. **Honors/Awds:** Selectee to Ghana West Africa Girl Scouts of the USA/Oper Crossroads Africa 1974; Crusade Scholar Bd of Global Ministries, United Methodist Church 1976-77; Spec Mission Recognition United Methodist Women, United Methodist Church 1982; Elizabeth Hayden Award for Outstanding Serv Girl Scouts Mile Hi Council 1983; Young Alumni Loyalty Awd NE Wesleyan Univ 1985; Woman of the Year Award Aurora Area Business & Professional Women's Org 1986; Excellence in Education Award, Black Educators United, Denver Public Schools, 1990. **Home Addr:** 6865 E Arizona Ave, #D, Denver, CO 80224.

SIMPSON, DONNIE
Radio & television host. **Personal:** Born Jan 30, 1954, Detroit, MI; son of Dorothy Simpson and Calvin Simpson; married Pamela; children: Donnie Jr, Dawn. **Educ:** Univ of Detroit, BA, communications. **Career:** WJLB Detroit, air personality 1969-77; Black Entertainment TV, host of "Video Soul," currently; WPGC Radio, morning show personality, currently, Top 30 USA, host, currently. **Orgs:** Supporter United Negro Coll Fund, Big Brothers, Easter Seals. **Honors/Awds:** Program Dir of the Year, Billboard Magazine 1982; Superstar of the Year, The National Urban Coalition 1989. **Business Addr:** Morning Show Personality, WPGC Radio, 6301 Ivy Ln, Ste 800, Greenbelt, MD 20770.

SIMPSON, FRANK B.
Educational administrator (retired). **Personal:** Born Dec 21, 1919, Jewett, TX; son of Annie Matson Simpson and Herman W Simpson; married Estelle Martin, Dec 28, 1945; children: Rosetta S Hassan, Oliver B. **Educ:** Kentucky State Univ, BS 1942; Univ of Kentucky, MS 1956; Univ of Kentucky & Univ of Louisville, postgrad. **Career:** Todd Co & Christian Co, high sch principal, 21 yrs; Hopkinsville Sch System, asst supt, 1967-69; Jefferson Co Sch System, asst supt 1969-80. **Orgs:** Mem: KEA, NEA, KASA; past pres 3rd Dist Tchrs Assn; 2nd Dist Principals Assn; KY HS Athletic Assn; mem Gov Commn for High Educ, 1967-70; mem Gov Adv Commn on Local Govt, 1969-71; life mem, NAACP, Urban League; mem Alpha Phi Alpha Frat; Mason; mem Gov Comm for Improving Educ, 1978-86; mem Sigma Pi Phi Frat Boule Louisville Chpt; bd mem USO; steward Miles Meml CME Ch; past vice pres, past pres, KSU Natl Alumni Assn; mem, past pres, KSU Foundation; past pres, State Bd of Athletic Control; past pres, East 41 Athletic Assn. **Honors/Awds:** Man of Year, Alpha Phi Alpha Gamma Epsilon Lambda 1966; Distinguished Alumni Award 1970, Distinguished Service Award 1981, Meritorious Sevice Award 1984, President Club Award 1984, KY State Univ; Lucy Hart Smith-Atwood S Wilson Award, KY Educ Assn, 1974; Distinguished Alumni Award, Natl Assn of Black Colleges, 1989; served on Kentucky Commn on Human Rights Comm on Black History, which wrote "Kentucky Black Heritage," used in Kentucky schools. **Military Serv:** US Army, staff sgt, 1942-46. **Business Addr:** 3332 Newburg Rd, Louisville, KY 40218.

SIMPSON, GREGORY LOUIS
Physician. **Personal:** Born Feb 16, 1958, Columbus, OH; married Alena M Baquet-Simpson MD; children: Gregory II, Nathaniel. **Educ:** VA Union Univ, attended 1976-79 (achieved early acceptance into 2 medical schools without BS); Meharry Medical Coll, MD 1983. **Career:** Martin Luther King Jr General Hosp, internship 1983-84, residency 1984-86, chief resident 1984-86; Los Angeles Co Court System, medical expert on call list 1984-; Los Angeles Co Dept of Hlth Svcs, medical expert panel for child abuse 1984-, medical expert witness for child abuse 1984-; Private Practice, pediatrician 1986-; Martin Luther King Jr General Hosp, fellow child abuse/child develop 1986-. **Orgs:** Mem NAACP 1976-, Amer Medical Student Assoc 1979-83, Student Natl Medical Assoc 1979-83; assoc minister Southfield Comm Missionary Bapt Church ColumbusOH 1979-; licensed baptist minister 1979-; mem Los Angeles Pediatric Soc 1983-, Amer Medical Assoc 1983-, Physician Housestaff Educ Comm ML King Genl Hosp 1984-86; mem Suspected Child Abuse and Neglect Team ML King Jr Genl Hosp 1984-; mem Patient Care Fund 1984,85; mem Joint Council of Residents and Interns 1985-; mem Los Angeles Co Medical Assoc 1987-. **Honors/Awds:** Mem Alpha Kappa Mu Natl Honor Frat 1978, Beta Kappa Chi Natl Honor Frat 1978; Student Rsch Fellowship Natl Insts of Health Washington DC 1979; Outstanding Young Man of Amer 1981; Housestaff of the Year Awd Dept of Pediatrics Charles R Drew Medical Sch Martin Luther King Jr Genl Hosp 1985,86. **Home Addr:** 2301 West 115th Place, Inglewood, CA 90303. **Business Addr:** Child Abuse Consultant, Martin Luther King Genl Hosp, 12021 So Wilmington Ave, Los Angeles, CA 90059.

SIMPSON, HARRY L.
Organization executive. **Personal:** Born Mar 21, 1950, Birmingham, AL; son of Dorothy & Calvin; married Rosalind, Apr 27, 1985; children: Daren, Ramon & Rosalind Rolack. **Educ:** Oakland Community College, associate degree, mental health, 1986; Wayne State University. **Career:** Eastwood Community Clinics, acting prog dir, 1985-89; MI Dept of Public Health, HIV/AIDS Section, public health consultant, 1989-94; Community Health Awareness Group, exec dir, 1994-. **Orgs:** Southeastern MI HIV/AIDS Council, bd member; Community Health Outreach Workers, bd member; Southeastern MI Regional Community Planning Council, advisory member; MSU Community HIV/AIDS & Mental Health, minority advisory committee, 1991-93; Midwest AIDS Prevention Project, bd secretary, 1991-94; Metro Detroit Substance Abuse AIDS Prevention, task force member; Statewide Community Prevention Planning Group, community co-chair; Community Health Outreach Workers, past president. **Honors/Awds:** Centers for Disease Control & Prevention (CDC), Price Fellow, 1996; Boston University School of Public Health, Join Together Fellow, 1997; Spirit of Detroit Award, 1997. **Military Serv:** US Army, specialist, 1968-72; Purple Heart, Army Accomodation Medal/Valor. **Business Addr:** Executive Director, Community Health Awareness Group, 3028 E Grand Blvd, Detroit, MI 48237.

SIMPSON, JAMES ARLINGTON. See SIMPSON, NORVELL J.

SIMPSON, JOHN
Educational Administrator. **Personal:** marrled Rita; children: John. **Educ:** West Chester University, BA, music education, 1970, MA, vocal pedagogy, MEd, 1975; University of Delaware, educational leadership, 1981; University of Michigan, PhD, educational policy, 1983. **Career:** Newark, DE, Philadelphia, music teacher; Washington, assistant junior high principal, 1984-86; Washington, DC, elementary principal, 1986-88; Oklahoma City, 29 public elementary schools, director, 1988-91; North Chicago Public Schools, superintendent, until 1993; Ann Arbor Board of Education, superintendent, 1993-. **Orgs:** Rotary Club; board of directors, Hands-On Museum, Washtenaw County Red Cross, University Musical Society; American Association of School Administrator; National Association of Black School Educators; Michigan Association of School Administrators. **Business Addr:** Superintendent, Ann Arbor Public Schools, 2550 S State St, Ann Arbor, MI 48104, (313)994-2230.

SIMPSON, JUANITA H.
Retired educator. **Personal:** Born Aug 27, 1925, Terre Haute, IN; daughter of Cornelia Williams Hatchett and Will Hatchett; married William Simpson, May 15, 1949; children: Barton A, Cathy L MD, Capt Dorothy E. **Educ:** Northwestern Univ, Evanston IL, BA Music Educ, 1947; Roosevelt Univ, Chicago IL, MA Music Educ, 1964, MA Arts, 1973. **Career:** Chicago Bd of Educ, Chicago IL, teacher, 1947-86, asst principal, 1980-85. **Orgs:** Bd mem, School Dist 163, Park Forest IL, 1973-75; pres, Illinois State Conference NAACP Branches, 1986-89. **Home Addr:** 403 Wilshire, Park Forest, IL 60466.

SIMPSON, MERTON DANIEL
Artist, business executive. **Personal:** Born Sep 20, 1928, Charleston, SC; married Beatrice Houston; children: Merton Daniel Jr, Kenneth Charles. **Educ:** NYU, Attended; Cooper Union Art School. **Career:** Merton D Simpson Gallery Inc, pres & owner. **Orgs:** Mem Curatorial Counc Studio Mus Harlem 1977-; Red Cross Exchange Exhibit Paris & Tokyo 1950; Intercultural Club 1951; SC Cultural Fund 1951; Gibbes Art Gallery 1956. **Honors/Awds:** Publ Young Amer Painters 1954; Amer Negro Art 1960; comtemporary Artists of SC 1970; The Afro Amer Artist 1973; numerous exhibits, permanent collections. **Military Serv:** USAF artist 1951-54. **Home Addr:** 1063 Madison Ave, New York, NY 10028.

SIMPSON, NORVELL J. (JAMES ARLINGTON SIMPSON)
Human relations administrator (retired). **Personal:** Born Mar 25, 1931, Rochester, NY; son of Martha Perlina Jentons Simpson (deceased) and Frank Douglas Simpson (deceased); married Alice Elizabeth Saxton Simpson, Jul 11, 1953; children: Gary A, Sharon R, Leslie A. **Educ:** Park Clge, BA Econ and Bus 1970; Univ of CO, MA Cand Guid and Couns 1981. **Career:** USAF, sr mstr sgt 1949-71; Pikes Peak Comm Action Prog, exec dir 1972-74; El Paso Cty CO, dir comm serv dept 1974-79; TRW/EPI, prop mgr 1980-86; Colorado Springs Public Schools Dist 11, human relations adminstrator 1986-94. **Orgs:** Dir United Way Pikes Peak Reg 1978-93; Schl Dist 11 1975-85; CO Assc of Schl Bd 1983-84; comm Colo Sprngs Human Rel 1973-79; Alpha Phi Alpha, Kadesia Shrine Temple #135. **Honors/Awds:** Citizen of the Year Alpha Phi Alpha 1979 1981 1982; Omega Psi Phi 1978; Comm Ldr of Amer 1979-81; TRW Leadership Award TRW 1979; The Norvell Simpson Community Center, The Colorado Educ Assn Lion II Award. **Military Serv:** USAF sr mstr sgt 1949-71. **Home Addr:** 4880 Topaz Dr, Colorado Springs, CO 80918.

SIMPSON, O. J. (ORENTHAL JAMES)
Former professional football player, sports commentator, actor. **Personal:** Born Jul 9, 1947, San Francisco, CA; son of Eunice Simpson and Jimmy Simpson; married Marquerite Thomas, 1967 (divorced 1979); children: Arnelle, Jason; married Nicole Brown Simpson (divorced); children: Sydney, Justin. **Educ:** San Francisco City Coll, 1965-67; Univ of Southern California, 1967-69. **Career:** Buffalo Bills, halfback, 1969-78; San Francisco 49'ers, 1978; actor: The Towering Inferno, 1974, The Klansman, 1974, Killer Force, 1975, Cassandra Crossing, 1976, Capricorn I, 1977, Firepower, 1978, Hambone & Hilly, 1983, The Naked Gun, 1989, The Naked Gun 2 1/2, 1991; appeared on various TV productions; Orenthal Productions, owner, exec producer of several TV productions; ABC-TV Sports 1969-77, sports color commentator, Monday Night Football, 1983-86, Rose Bowl color commentator, 1979, 1980; competed in and won the 1975 Superstars Competition; 1976 Summer Olympics, color commentator; NBC-TV Sports 1978-82, NFL Live, co-host, beginning 1989; 1984 Summer Olympic Sports special events; several TV commercials; appears in own exercise video. **Honors/Awds:** Coll of San Francisco, All American 1965-66; USC, All American 1967-68; world record 440 yd relay team 1967; Heisman Trophy winner 1968; UPI & AP, college athlete of the year 1968; voted coll player of the decade ABC Sports 1970; Named Amer Football League All Star Team 1970; named collegiate athlete of the decade 1972; Most yds gained in a season 2,003 1973; Most games in a season with 100 yds or more 11 1973; Most rushing attempts in a season 332, 1973; Hickok Belt recipient 1973; NFL most valuable player 1975; AFC most valuable player 1972, 1973, 1975; Most yds gained rushing in a game 273, 1976; Most yds rushing gained in a game; Pro Bowl 1972, 1974, 1975, 1976; named NFL Player of the Decade 1979; College Football Hall of Fame induction 1983; 2nd leading rusher in NFL history; Pro Football Hall of Fame induction 1985.

SIMPSON, RALPH DEREK
Professional basketball player. **Personal:** Born Aug 10, 1949, Detroit, MI; married Joyce McMullen. **Educ:** MI State, attd 1973. **Career:** Denver Rockets, 1971-76, Detroit Pistons, 1977-78, Denver Nuggets, 1978, Philadelphia 76ers, 1979, New Jersey Nets, 1979-80.

SIMPSON, SAMUEL G.
Clergyman. **Personal:** Born Dec 6, 1931; married Lola Campbell; children: Erica, Stephen, Kim. **Educ:** BRE 1967; student of MDiv. **Career:** Jamaica, civil servant treas 1955-59; Bronx Bapt Ch NY, pastor 1964-74; So Bapt Chs Bronx, pastor dir. **Orgs:** Pres East Tremont Ch Coun; vice pres Counc of Ch Bronx Div; vice pres Met NY Bapt Assc; vice pres Bapt Conv of NY; chmn Nominating Com of Council of Chs New York City Sec Comm Planning Bd No 6 Bronx; treas Twin Parks Urban Renewal Bronx; 46 pct exec bd mem Alumni of Year 1974; of Northeastern Bible Clge. **Honors/Awds:** Award Bapt Conv of MD. **Business Addr:** 331 E 187, Bronx, NY 10458.

SIMPSON, STEPHEN WHITTINGTON
Attorney. **Personal:** Born Mar 14, 1945, Philadelphia, PA; married Audrey C Murdah; children: Stephen Jr, Christopher Lindsey. **Educ:** Harvard Univ, AB 1966; Univ of PA, JD 1969. **Career:** Suns Co, Inc, chief counsel, 1978-87; Goodrs Greenfield, atty 1973-77; Dechert, Price & Rhoades, atty 1970-73; PA Superior Ct, law clerk 1969-70; Vance, Jackson, Simpson & Overton, attorney, currently. **Orgs:** Amer Bar Assc; Philadelphia Bar Assc; Barristers Club. **Business Addr:** Attorney, Vance, Jackson, Simpson, & Overton, 1429 Walnut St, 8th Floor, Philadelphia, PA 19107.

SIMPSON, VALERIE
Singer, songwriter. **Personal:** Born in New York, NY; married Nicholas; children: Nicole. **Career:** Songwriter/singer with Nick Ashford, worked for Motown Records; wrote songs for, Diana Ross, Marvin Gaye & Tammi Terrell, Ray Charles, Chaka Khan, Gladys Knight & the Pips. **Honors/Awds:** Songs incl, So, So Satisfied, Send It, Reach Out and Touch, Ain't Nothing Like the Real Thing, Your Precious Love, It's My House, Ain't No Mountain High Enough. **Business Addr:** c/o Patty Keller, 1260 Avenue of the Americas, New York, NY 10020.

SIMPSON, WILLA JEAN
Child development coordinator. **Personal:** Born May 15, 1943, Little Rock, AR; married Earl Henry Simpson; children: Desiree, Jill, Earla. **Educ:** Kennedy King Clge, AA 1969; Chicago State Univ, BS 1974; Governors State Univ, MA 1975; Fielding Inst, PhD 1981. **Career:** Golden Gate Cons, child family therapist 1981-; Malcolm X Coll Chicago IL, instr 1981-84; Dept of Army Savanna IL, educ spec 1984; BCDI Chicago affiliate, rec secr 1982-85; AUS Dept Defense Rock Island Arsenal, child devel serv coord; Fort Hood Army Base, child develop serv coord 1987-. **Orgs:** Handicap coord Dept Human Srv Chicago IL 1982-1983; spec needs mgr Ebony Mgmt Assc Chic 1980-82; deputy dir CEDA Chicago 1976-78; rec sec Black Child Dev Inst 1982-85; mem Natl Phi Delta Kappa Inc 1983; pres Golden Gate Bd of Dir 1971-81; mem Pi Lam Theda 1985-. **Honors/Awds:** Biog study of Black Educ PhD Dissertation GGDCC Pub 1981; Srv Award Harris YWCA Chic 1974, Holy Cross Child Care Ctr 1984, Gldn Gate Day Care Ctr Chic 1984; Special Act Awd Rock Island Arsenal 1985; Exceptional Performance Awd Rock Island Arsenal 1986.

SIMPSON-TAYLOR, DOROTHY MARIE
Educator. **Personal:** Born Jun 25, 1944, Pickens, MS; daughter of Mary Jane Young-Simpson and Willie Andrew Simpson; married Harold J Taylor, Nov 26, 1965; children: Harold Duane, Robert Lance. **Educ:** University of Nebraska, Omaha, BGS, urban studies, 1972, MS, guidance & counseling, 1974; University of Denver, PhD, counseling psychology, 1988. **Career:** Pikes Peak Counseling Center, mental health therapist, 1978-83; Iowa State University, psychology intern, 1984-85; VA Veterans Readjustment Centers, team leader, counselor, 1985-88; University of Northern Colorado, assistant professor, counseling psychology, 1988-90; Indiana State University, assistant professor, africana studies, 1990, assist to the pres for Ethnic Diversity, 1995. **Orgs:** Wabash Valley Critical Incident Stress Debriefing Team, steering committee, 1992-93; Indiana Association of Blacks in Higher Education, government affairs, 1991-93; Indiana State Board of Health, HIV/AIDS program review board, 1991-93; Vigo County AIDS Task Force, 1991-93; National Association of Black Psychologists; National Black Storytellers Association. **Honors/Awds:** Fullbright Hayes Scholar, 1993; NAACP Community Service Award, 1993. **Military Serv:** US Air Force, A-1C, 1963-66. **Home Addr:** 1819 S 8th St, Terre Haute, IN 47802, (812)235-0139. **Business Addr:** Professor, Indiana State University, Department of Africana Studies, Terre Haute, IN 47809, (812)237-2550.

SIMPSON-WATSON, ORA LEE
Educator. **Personal:** Born Jul 7, 1943, East Chicago, IN; children: Ronald Damon, Kendyl Joi. **Educ:** Ball State Univ, BA 1965; Purdue Univ, MA 1969, PhD 1977. **Career:** Dallas Independent School District, dir learning 1977-80, dean of instruction 1981-83; Dallas County Comm College, div chair North Lake College 1983-. **Orgs:** School bd trustee Dallas Independent School Dist; mem Natl Assn Black School Educators; mem Alpha Kappa Alpha; mem Links, Texas Assn of School Boards; consultant Republic of Suri Name 1986, Child Care, Dallas 1986. **Honors/Awds:** Hon mem Dallas Regional NABSE 1986. **Business Addr:** Div Chair Humanities/Comm, North Lake College, 5001 N Mac Arthur Blvd, Irving, TX 75038.

SIMS, ADRIENNE
Financial consultant. **Personal:** Born Apr 1, 1952, Tacoma, WA; daughter of Mary Sims and Alfred Sims. **Educ:** Univ of CA-Irvine, BA 1974; CA State Univ-Los Angeles, MS 1978; Pepperdine Univ, EdD 1987. **Career:** LA Comm Coll Dist, student/comm serv rep 1976-77; Long Beach Comm Coll Dist, student advisor coord 1978-81; Univ of Phoenix, coordinator of admissions 1981-84; Univ of Redlands, asst dean of admissions 1985-90; Rancho Santiago College, director of student transition and retention, 1990-92; Mainway Services Group, vice pres of operations, 1992-. **Orgs:** Mem Pacific Assoc of College Registrars/Admission Officers 1981-, Phi Delta Kappa 1983-, Natl Assoc of Coll Admission Counselors 1985-, mem Natl Assoc for Foreign Student Affairs 1985-, mem Third World Counselors Assoc 1985-, mem CA Coll Personnel Assoc 1985-; pres CA Counselors for Minority Success 1986; Natl Assn of Women Deans and Administrators. **Business Addr:** Vice Pres, Operations, Mainway Services Group, Ontario Airport Center, 337 N Vineyard Ave, Ste 202, Ontario, CA 91764.

SIMS, BARBARA M.
Judge. **Personal:** Born in Buffalo, NY; married William Sims; children: Frank William, Sue Cynthia. **Educ:** State Univ Clge at Buffalo, BS; State Univ of NY at Buffalo Law Sch, JD. **Career:** City Ct of Buffalo, city ct judge 1977-; City of Buffalo Parking Violations Bur, hearing ofcr 1975-77; State Univ of NY Buffalo, asst to pres 1969-74; State Univ of NY Buffalo Law Sch, lectr; Erie Co DA Office, asst district attorney, 1964-1968. **Orgs:** Mem Natl Bar Assc; Women's Polit Caucus; natl vice pres Natl Assc of Black Women Attys 1975-80; mem Erie Co Bar Assc; former pres Women Lawyers of W NY; numerous law assc; mem NAACP; mem bd dir NAACP; bd dir BC/BS of W NY; mem United Fund Natl Fnd for Birth Defects; mem Natl Assc of Negro Bus-Prof Women Buffalo Chpt. **Honors/Awds:** Recipt Comm Srv Award 1968; Fight for Freedom Award 1968; Distg Achievement Award 1968; chosen One of 100 Black Women Chicago Conv 1972; del Natl Women's Year Conf Houston 1977; Distg Srv Award Grand United Order of Oddfellows 1978. **Business Addr:** 50 Delaware Ave, Buffalo, NY 14202.

SIMS, CALVIN GENE
Journalist. **Personal:** Born Dec 17, 1963, Compton, CA; son of Calvina Odessa Borders Sims and Lonnie Gene Sims. **Educ:** Yale University, New Haven, CT, BA, 1985. **Career:** The New York Times, New York, NY, reporter, 1985-. **Orgs:** Member, Scroll and Key, 1985-; staff worker, Coalition for the Homeless, 1985-87. **Honors/Awds:** Fellow, American Association for the Advancement of Science, Mass Media, 1984; Poynter Fellowship in Journalism, 1985; New York Times Publisher's Award, 1990. **Business Addr:** Natl Correspondent, The New York Times, Los Angeles Bureau, 6500 Wilshire Blvd, Ste 1820, Los Angeles, CA 90048.

SIMS, CARL W.
Newspaper editor. **Personal:** Born Apr 29, 1941, Washington, DC; married Barbara Lindsey; children: 1 son. **Educ:** Howard Univ, 1960-62; Univ of MN, 1987-. **Career:** Peace Corps Sierra Leone, vol 1962-63; WA Post, reporter 1965-70; Boston Globe, copy editor 1970; Bay State Banner Boston, editor 1970-72; Newsweek, assoc editor 1973-74; Minneapolis Star Tribune, natl editor 1974-. **Orgs:** Mem Capital Press Club 1966-69, Harvard Club of MN; member, National Assn of Black Journalists, 1990-. **Honors/Awds:** Nieman Fellow Harvard Univ 1972-73. **Business Addr:** National Editor, Minneapolis Star Tribune, 425 Portland Ave, Minneapolis, MN 55488.

SIMS, CONSTANCE ARLETTE
Educational administrator. **Personal:** Born Nov 26, 1940, Detroit, MI; married Dr Joseph William Sims; children: Andre-Marc, Nicole Danielle. **Educ:** MI State Univ, BA 1962; Univ of MI Flint, MA 1970; Nova Univ, EdD 1983. **Career:** Flint Primary School, teacher 1962-66, title I reading spec 1966-68; MI Coord of Early Childhood Genesee Comm Coll, project dir 1968-70, coord 1970-72; Univ of MI, coord of student teaching 1971-75; Unified School Dist Oakland CA, reading resource teacher 1975-76, tech asst; Park Forest School Dist 163, title vii spec 1976-77; Dogwood Elementary School, principal 1977-82; Lakewood School, elem sch principal 1982-84; Pine Bush Schls, dir of continuing educ 1984-85; Netherwood Elem School, principal 1985-. **Orgs:** Mem IL Principal's Assoc 1977-84, Phi Delta Kappa 1983-; Urban League, NAACP, Second Baptist Church ASCD 1985-, Mid-Hudson Reading Assoc 1986-. **Business Addr:** Principal, Netherwood Elementary School, Netherwood Rd, Hyde Park, NY 12538.

SIMS, DIANE MARIE
Government contractor, entrepreneur. **Personal:** Born Feb 22, 1955, New York, NY; daughter of Sarah Sims and Oscar Sims; divorced; children: Arik A Sims-Marrow. **Educ:** Suny, BA, 1973; University of Cincinnati, MPA, 1975. **Career:** University of Cincinnati, instructor, 1975; University of District of Columbia, instructor, 1987-79; International City Management Association, assistant director, productivity projects, 1975-77; Pabon, Sims, Smith, president/chief executive officer, 1977-. **Orgs:** Compass of Hope, trustee/board member, 1991-; Hands-On Corporation, board member, 1982-; JSJ Corporation, board member, 1990-; Group Health Association, trustee, 1989; ICMA, 1975-86. **Honors/Awds:** US Department of Transportation, Women Owned Business of the Year, 1988; Meridian Hill Organization, Community Service Award, 1991. **Special Achievements:** Productivity Measurements Improvement, 1976; Water Conservation Makes Cents, 1980; Motivational Strategies to Encourage Employees to use Safety Belts, 1985. **Business Addr:** President/Chief Executive Officer, Pabon, Sims, Smith, Inc, 644 Massachusetts Ave NE, Ste 500, Washington, DC 20002, (202)331-1110.

SIMS, EDWARD HACKNEY
Physician, surgeon. **Personal:** Born Sep 5, 1944, Atlanta, GA; children: Jessica Carolyn. **Educ:** Morris Brown Coll Atlanta, BS 1965; Meharry Medical Coll, MD 1972. **Career:** King/Drew Medical Ctr, chief of general surgery, 1983-87; Private Practice, currently. **Military Serv:** USAF E-4 3 yrs.

SIMS, ESAU, JR.
Food service company executive. **Personal:** Born Apr 14, 1953, Barberton, OH; son of Eleanor Sims and Esau Sims Sr; married Sarah Harris, Dec 1972; children: Esau Jaques, Rashawn, Jeffrey. **Educ:** National College of Education, BS, 1972. **Career:** Arthur Treacher's Fish 'n Chips, district manager, 1973-75, area manager, 1975-78, assistant director, franchise operation, 1978-79; Burger King, district manager, 1979-83, area manager, 1985, vice pres operations, 1989, vice pres, franchise sales & service division, currently. **Orgs:** Swift Creek Athletic Association, vice pres, 1986-92; Spring Creek Baptist Church, chairman, trustee, 1992-93; Chesterfield County Athletic Association, vice pres, 1991. **Business Addr:** Vice Pres, Franchise Sales and Services, Burger King Corp, 9200 Arboretum Pkwy, Ste 104, Richmond, VA 23236, (804)330-0308.

SIMS, GENEVIEVE CONSTANCE
Attorney. **Personal:** Born Nov 4, 1947, Baltimore, MD; daughter of Fannie Sims and Joe Sims. **Educ:** North Carolina State Univ, BA, 1969; Univ of Southern California, MPA, 1976; North Carolina Central Univ, JD, 1986. **Career:** Law Offices of Genevieve C. Sims, lawyer, 1987-; Merit Sys Protection Bd, special asst, 1979-81; US Civil Serv Commn, special asst commr, 1977-78; Office of Mgmt & Budget Exec Office Pres, mgmt analyst, 1976-77; US Civil Serv Commn, personnel mgmt spec, 1972-76; Office of State Personnel, North Carolina State Govt, econ analyst 1969-72; North Carolina State Univ, Raleigh, NC, asst professor, 1982-93; North Carolina Central Univ, Durham, NC, visiting instr, 1982-92. **Orgs:** Former chairperson, bd of dir, Shelley School; bd of dir, North Carolina Assn Black Lawyers, 1989-92; board of directors, North Carolina Academy of Trial Lawyers, 1995-; North Carolina Bar Assn; board of directors, United Black Fund of Washington, 1976-81. **Honors/Awds:** Award, North Carolina Special Olympics, 1982. **Business Addr:** 313 S Blount St, PO Box 987, Raleigh, NC 27601, (919)834-7775.

SIMS, HAROLD RUDOLPH
Business Executive. **Personal:** Born Jul 25, 1935, Memphis, TN; son of Geraldine Rayford Sims and Benjamin Webster Sims; married Lana Joyce Taylor, Jun 25, 1962; children: Douglass D, Kimberly J. **Educ:** Southern Univ, BR, LA, BA (cum laude) 1957; Univ of Poona, Poona, India, certf 1956; Geo Washington Univ, MS 1967; Johns Hopkins Univ, Baltimore, Grad Study 1961-62. **Career:** Ofc Econ Oppor Exec Ofc Pres White House, exec sec 1967-69; National Urban League, deputy executive director, 1969-71, executive director, president, 1971-72; Johnson & Johnson, vice pres 1972-79; Sims & Assoc/Sims Intl, pres 1979-; Sound Radio WNJR, CEO, gen mgr, pres 1984-92; MLK Jr NJ Commission, Office of Governor, exec dir 1985-86; Ebony Magazine, sr account exec 1986-87; Uni-Med Consulting, chairman, executive committee, 1992-; Centennial Concepts, 1992-. **Orgs:** Pres, Sims-Sutton Indstrl Dev Group 1982-; natl advsry brd Natl Science Foundation 1977-82; exec vp Gibson-Wonder Film Co/Jos P Gibson Fdn 1983-; life member, Alpha Phi Alpha Fraternity, NAACP; commissioner NJ MLK Jr Commission 1984-86; brd dir, 1972-, sr intl advisor and UN rep, 1986-, Martin Luther King Jr Ctr 1972-96; intl brd advsr African-American Inst 1976-; advsry brd (Soc) Princeton Univ 1971-82; board of trustees, St Louis Univ, 1974-84; board of dirs, Near East Foundation, 1976-; co-founder, King-Luthuli South African Transformation Center, 1989-; PUSH, Eastern Region Operation, vice pres, 1972-74; Nat Assn of Marketing Development, NY Chapter, pres, 1974-76; Friends of the Congressional Black Caucus, chair, 1973-78; US Army Special Forces Assn, 1996-. **Honors/Awds:** Spcl citation Martin L King Jr Cntr for NVSC, Atlanta 1981; spcl citation/comm Congrsnl Black Caucus Inc (DC) 1973; spcl citation Friends of Harold R Sims, Waldorf Astoria 1972; spcl citation/Resolution Natl Urban Bd of Dir 1971; numerous articles, artistic acmplshmnts, awards, citations; Outstanding Graduate-First Century, Southern Univ, 1980; Doctor of Humane Letters, King Memorial College, 1977; cert, urban fellow, Yale Univ, New Haven, CT, 1969; Award of Merit, Natl (South) African Chamber of Commerce (NAFCOC), 1978; National Assn of Marketing Development, Forty Living Legends Award, 1996. **Military Serv:** US Army, Major, 1957-67; Bronze Star, Army Commendation Medal w/Oak Leaf Cluster, 1963, 1967, Purple Heart, 1964, Army Parachutist Badge, 1963; Joint Staff Campaign, Certs of Achvmnt 1957-67. **Home Addr:** 1274 Carlisle Rd, North Brunswick, NJ 08902.

SIMS, JOHN LEONARD
Computer company executive. **Personal:** Born Jul 1, 1934, Wilmington, DE; son of Ella Gibbs Sims and Thomas A Sims; married Shirley (Horton) Sims, Jun 14, 1962; children: John Jr, Kevin, Joe. **Educ:** Delaware State Coll, Dover DE, BS, 1962; Ohio State Univ, Columbus OH, Graduate Work; Columbia Univ, New York NY, Mgmt Training Courses. **Career:** E I Du Pont de Nemours Co Inc, mgmt positions, chemist; Champion Intl Corp, mgmt positions, govt relations; Digital Equipment Corp, Maynard MA, corp mgr EEO/AA, 1974-75, dir of manf personnel, 1975-81, corporate staff mgr, 1981-84, vice pres personnel, 1984-87, vice pres strategic resources, 1987-. **Orgs:** Mem, Natl NAACP, The Boston Private Industry Council, Northeast Human Resources Assn, Exec Leaderhsip Council; bd of trustees, The Natl Urban League; SBI Roundtable at Florida A&M; board of directors, The Boston Bank of Commerce, 1983-; bd of governors of ASTD, 1987-; chmn, Freedom House, 1987-; bd of governors, Boston Chamber of Commerce, 1992-. **Honors/Awds:** Top 25 Most Powerful Black Managers, Black Enterprise Magazine, 1988; Award for Service, Freedom House; Award for Service, Alpha; Award for Contributing, Natl Urban League, 1988; Award for Achievements, Several Colleges and Minority Organizations. **Military Serv:** US Army Corps, 1955-57. **Business Addr:** Vice President, Strategic Resources, Digital Equipment Corporation, 146 Main St, ML012-1/A51, Maynard, MA 01754.

SIMS, JOSEPH WILLIAM
Educational administrator. **Personal:** Born Feb 14, 1937, Detroit, MI; married Constance A Williams; children: Nicole, Andre. **Educ:** MI State Univ, BA 1961, MA 1962; Univ of MI, PhD 1972. **Career:** Prairie State Coll Chicago Heights IL, vice pres student serv 1976-83; Oakland & Berkeley School Dist CA, Rockefeller intern 1975-76; Flint Community School Flint MI, asst principal/deputy principal/principal 1968-75; Southwestern High School Flint MI, French teacher 1967-68; AC Spark Plug Flint MI, supvr 1965-67; Southwestern High School, French & Spanish teacher 1962-65. **Orgs:** Mem Amer Assn for Higher Educ; mem Natl Assn of Student Personnel Admin; mem Alliance of Black School Educ; mem IL Council Community Coll Admin; mem IL Coll Personnel Assn Natl Defense Educ Act Grant US Govt 1968; Mott Found Grant Charles S Mott Found Flint MI 1970-71. **Honors/Awds:** Superintendency Training Grant Rockefeller Found NY 1975-76; Distinguished Serv Award City of Detroit 1975. **Military Serv:** USAF s/sgt 1954-58.

SIMS, KEITH
Professional football player. **Personal:** Born Jun 17, 1967, Baltimore, MD; married Cammy; children: Cairo. **Educ:** Iowa State, BS in industrial technology. **Career:** Miami Dolphins, guard, 1990-97; Washington Redskins, 1998-. **Honors/Awds:** Pro Bowl, 1993, 1994, 1995. **Business Addr:** Professional Football Player, Washington Redskins, 13832 Redskin Dr, Herndon, VA 22071, (703)471-9100.

SIMS, KEITH EUGENE
Oil company executive. **Personal:** Born Jul 30, 1953, Louisville, KY; son of Alfred and Anna Sims; married Cathy, Jan 15, 1983; children: Andre Tremayne, Ariel JoAnna. **Educ:** United States Military Academy, West Point, NY, BS, 1976; Houston Baptist University, MBA, 1987. **Career:** Mobil Oil Corporation, lubrication engineer, 1985-87, area sales mgr, 1987-88, chief engineer, 1988-90, special assignment, 1990-91, division mgr, 1991-; Mobil Lubricants Canada, Ltd, dir, 1994-; Mobil Marketing Canada, Inc, pres, 1991-. **Orgs:** Alpha Phi Alpha, 1981-; Natl Petroleum Refiners Assn, 1991-; Independent Lube Manufacturers Assn, 1991-; Black Exec Exchange Program, Natl Urban League, 1994; Black Employee Success Team, 1991-; West Point Society, 1972-; Mobil Goodwill Ambassador, 1991-. **Military Serv:** US Army, Captain, 1976-82, Airborne Wings, Aviator Wings, Army Commendation Medal. **Business Addr:** Division Mgr. of Specialty Products/Pres, Mobil Marketing Canada, Mobil Oil Corp., 3225 Gallows Rd., Fairfax, VA 22031, (703)849-3796.

SIMS, LOWERY STOKES
Curator. **Personal:** Born Feb 13, 1949, Washington, DC; daughter of Bernice Banks Sims and John Jacob Sims Sr. **Educ:** Queens Coll, BA 1970; Johns Hopkins Univ, MA 1972; CUNY, New York, NY, MA, philosophy, 1990, PhD, 1995. **Career:** Metro Museum of Art, asst museum educ 1972-75; Queens Coll Dept Art, adjunct instructor 1973-76; Sch Visual Arts, instructor 1975-76, 1981-86; Metro Museum of Art, assoc curator beginning 1979-, curator, currently. **Orgs:** Mem grants comm, Metro Museum Art, 1975-77; museum aid panel, NY State Council on Arts, 1977-79; mem, Art Table, College Art Assn 1983-, Assn of Art Critics, Amer Sect Intl Art Critics Assn 1980-, Natl Conf of Artists; visual arts panel, New York State Council on Arts 1984-86; council mem, New York State Council on Arts, 1987-92; bd, College Art Association, 1994-97; bd, Tiffany Foundation, 1995-97; advisory bd, Center for Curational Studies, 1995-; chair, Forum of Curators and Conservator, Metro Museum of AA, 1996-97. **Honors/Awds:** Fellowship for Black Dr Students, Ford Found, 1970-72; Employee Travel Grant, Metro Museum Art, 1973; numerous publications; Amer Artists & Exhibition Catalogs; Hon Doctor of Humane Letters, Maryland Inst Coll of Art, 1988; Frank Jewett Mather Award, College Art Association, 1991. **Business Addr:** Curator, Metro Museum of Art, Dept of 20th Century Art, New York, NY 10028.

SIMS, LYDIA THERESA
Retired city administrator. **Personal:** Born Nov 18, 1920, Pennsgrove, NJ; daughter of Helen Hoskins Williams (deceased) and Clifton Williams (deceased); married James M Sims Sr; children: James M Jr, Ronald C, Donald C. **Educ:** NY Business Sch, attended 1941; WA State Univ, attended 1971; E WA State Coll, attended 1974-77. **Career:** YWCA/Spokesman Review Newspaper, stenographer/sec 1951-66; Eastside Neighborhood Ctr, dep dir 1968-70; Comm Action Council, manpower training specialist/personnel 1970-73; City of Spokane, affirmative action dir 1975-89. **Orgs:** Pres Spokane Br NAACP 1976-80; mem OIC Bd of Dirs 1978-80; pres NAACP Northwest Area Conf of Branches 1980-82; mem WA State Adv Com US Commn on Civil Rights 1978-84; mem League of Women Voters 1970-; mem Amer Assn of Affirmative Action 1978-89; precinct comm mem Spokane Co Central Com 1980-; mem NW Women's Law Ctr 1980-; Amer Mgmt Assn 1983-89; Amer Soc for Personnel Directors 1980-89; YWCA Spokane Bd of Dir vice pres chrp Mutual World Serv Comm 1981-88; vice chrpsn Interstate Task Force on Human Relations 1979-; mem Women in Municipal Govt 1982-88; mem Citizen Adv Comm Pinelodge Correctional Ctr 1980-86; mem Blacks in Govt; Black elected and appointed officials Treasurer Amer Assn of Affirmative Action Region X 1985-89; Life member NAACP, Life member LincolnUniv PA Women's Auxiliary, irp task force on Minority aged, Eastern WA Area Agency on Aging; member Greater Spokane Women's Commission 1986-87; Magnuson Democratic Club 1986-; Spokane Falls AARP Chpt 1989; mem Spokane Chpt United Nations 1978-; WA State Commissioner, Martin Luther King Celebration 1985-89; exec committee Spokane Branch NAACP 1982-, president Church Women United 1990-. **Honors/Awds:** First black hired Spokesman Review Newspaper 1964; first black personnel officer Spokane Comm Action Council 1972; first female pres NAACP NW Conf of Branches 1980; first female pres Spokane NAACP 1976; Human Relations Awd Fairchild AFB 1977; 1983 NAACP Awd NW Area Conf of Branches; rsch & devel dir "Brief History Black Americans in Spokane Co 1878-1978" 1979; Awd of Appreciation Kiwanis; First Black Female Adminstr City of Spokane 1979; Governing Board East Central Comm Center Award of Appreciation 1979-81; 1982 Spokane Co Black Students Awd of Appreciation; 1980 Awd of Appreciation Black Students Lewis & Clark HS; Amer Assoc for Affirmative Action Award for Dedication 1985; Outstanding Leadership Award in Government and Politics YWCA1986; Cert of Appreciation, Eastern WA Univ 1986; BCertificate of Appreciation, City Univ 1987.

SIMS, NAOMI R.
Author, business executive. **Personal:** Born Mar 30, 1949, Oxford, MS; married Michael Alistair Findlay. **Educ:** Fashion Inst Tech NY; NYU, 1967. **Career:** Fashion Model, 1967-73; Fashion & Beauty, freelance writer, many articles; Naomi Sims Collection, owner founder bd chmn chief exec. **Orgs:** Mem, bd dirs Northside Center Child Devel Harlem; NAACP; mem, Womens' Firm Inc 1977; panel mem lecturer; Sickle Cell Anemia Dr; NY St Drug Rehabilitation Program; Play Schools Assn NY. **Honors/Awds:** Model of the Year Award, 1969, 1970; Modeling Hall of Fame Intl Mnqns 1977; Intl Best Dressed List 1971-73, 1976, 1977; Women of the Country Intl Mnqns 1977; proclaimed Sept 20 Naomi Sims Day Gov Walker, IL 1973; Women of Achievement Lds Home Jour 1970; Women of Achievement Amer Cancer Soc 1972; Ebony Success Library; Top Hat Award New Pitts Courier 1974; Key to City Cleveland 1971; NY City Bd Educ Award 1970; devel new fiber for wigs 1973-. **Business Addr:** Chairman, Naomi Sims Beauty Products Ltd, 435 W 57th St, New York, NY 10019.

SIMS, PETE, JR.
Business executive. **Personal:** Born May 11, 1924, El Dorado, AR; widowed. **Educ:** Atlnt Coll of Mrtry Sci, 1950. **Career:** Sims Mrtrty Inc, pres; El Dorado Hsng Athrty, pres 1970-; NFDMA AR St Fnrl Dirs, past pres dist gov; Sims-Shaw Burial Ins Assn, sec; Sims Entrprs, pres 1973-; AR Fun Dirs & Mrtcns Assn, pres 1974. **Orgs:** Natl Funeral Directors and Morticians, Inc, bd member; Natl Funeral Directors Assn; Arkansas Officials Assn; NAACP; Operation PUSH; DeSota Area Council of Boys Scouts; Past Ex-Ruler, IBPOE OF W; Chamber of Commerce, El Dorado, Arkansas; chm of budget & finance for 25 years, First Baptist Church; Natl Ex-Ruler Council of Elks; Arkansas State Elk Assn, past state pres; Past District Governor, District VI; The Exchange Club, charter member; State Board of Burial Assn (Arkansas), past bd member; Arkansas Funeral Directors Assn; North East Louisiana Funeral Directors Assn; Booker T Washington Alumni Assn, past president. **Honors/Awds:** United Way, Outstanding Citizen Award, 1969; Boys Club of America, Public Service Award, 1979; Personality of the South Award, 1977; Guaranty Natl Insurance Co, Sales Award, 1980; Elk of the Year, 1982; Boy Scouts of America, Century Member Award, 1983; Outstanding Contribution to Elkdom, 1988; Working to promote Human and Civil Rights in Education in the El Dorado Public School, 1984; The Boys Club Movement, Outstanding Public Service, 1979; US Small Business Administration for Successful Community Outreach Activity, 1994. **Military Serv:** AUS m/Sgt WW II. **Business Addr:** Sims Mortuary, PO Box 967, El Dorado, AR 71730.

SIMS, RIPLEY SINGLETON
Educator. **Personal:** Born Jul 5, 1907, Mobile, AL; married Dorothy Revalion. **Educ:** Talladega Clge, AB 1931; Northwestern Univ, MA 1939; Univ of Chicago, postgrad 1940-42. **Career:** Teacher math 1931-32; private hs prin 1932-38; Univ of Chicago, research asst 1940-42; USAAF, math-electricity instr 1942-46; USAF Inst, educ spec 1946-54, head educ div 1954-68; assoc deputy dir for acad prog 1968-; Educational Consultant. **Orgs:** Mem Amer Assc Higher Educ; Adult Educ Assc; Amer Educ Research Assc. **Honors/Awds:** Contrb articles to prof jours; author "An Inquiry into Correspondence Educating Processes"; Univ Extension Assoc Awd for Achievement. **Military Serv:** USAAF civilian instructor 1942-46.

SIMS, RONALD CORDELL
County official. **Personal:** Born Jul 5, 1948, Spokane, WA; son of Lydia Williams Sims and James M. Sims; married Cayan Topacio; children: Douglas, Daniel, Aaron. **Educ:** Central Washington State University, Ellensburg, WA, BA, psychology, 1971. **Career:** Washington State Attorney General, Seattle, WA, investigator, 1971-72; Federal Trade Commission, Seattle, WA, senior investigator, 1972-78; City of Seattle, WA, director, 1978-81; Washington State Senate, Olympia, WA, leadership coordinator, 1981-86; King County Council, Seattle, WA, councilman, 1986-. **Orgs:** Presidential commission on trade/investment policy in Asia; Seattle Human Rights Commission, 1984-86; volunteer, Meany Middle School; lay minister, Operation Nightwatch; former president, Rainier District Youth Athletic Association; member, board of directors, Planned Parenthood; board member, Families First Children's Home Society. **Honors/Awds:** World Affairs Fellow, James Madison Foundation, 1986-87; Progressive Animal Welfare Society, Humanitarian of the Year Award, 1993. **Home Addr:** 3227 Hunter Blvd S, Seattle, WA 98144.

SIMS, THEOPHLOUS ARON, SR.
Pharmacist. **Personal:** Born Mar 17, 1939, Jefferson, TX; married Nancy Jayne Wattley; children: Theophlous Jr, Shannon D'Lynne, Stephanie Racquel. **Educ:** Texas Southern University, BS, pharmacology 1961. **Career:** Forth Worth Independent School District 4, secretary, currently; pharmacist, currently. **Orgs:** Natl Assn of Retail Druggist; life mem, Kappa Alpha Psi; Alpha Phi Alpha 1983; bd mem, Texas Enterprise Foundation 1984; advisory comm, Texas Girls Choir 1984; Natl Institute of Health (Sickle Cell) 1984-. **Honors/Awds:** Black Achievers Award 1980; Outstanding Business Award, Fannie Brooks/Heath Club 1984; TSU Shining Star, Texas Southern University 1985; Quest for Success Award 1985. **Home Addr:** 4421 King-

sdale Dr, Fort Worth, TX 76119. **Business Addr:** School Board Member, Secretary, Fort Worth Independent School District 4, 944 E Berry St, Fort Worth, TX 76110.

SIMS, WILLIAM
Attorney, judge, businessman. **Personal:** Born May 28, 1922, Hughes, AR; son of Sephronia Sims and John Sims; married Barbara Merriweather; children: Sue Cynthia, Frank William. **Educ:** Univ of Buffalo BA 1947; Univ of Buffalo, LLB 1950; Suny at Buffalo, JD 1966. **Career:** Law Office Buffalo, sole proprietor 1976-; Robinson Sims Gibson & Green, law partner 1971; Sims & Purks, law partner 1968; Buffalo Cty Ct, assoc judge 1966; Sims & Sims Law Firm, partner 1956; Law Office, sole proprietor 1951. **Orgs:** Pres Buffalo Chap NAACP 1953; ofcr dir Ellicott Lanes Inc 1959-; dir vice pres Heart Assn of Western NY 1967-73; natl atty Grand United Order of Oddfellows 1974-; dir Nghbrhd House Assn 1975-; mil judge USMC Reserve. **Honors/Awds:** Recip 3 battle stars for overseas duty ETO USMC 1942-45; merit award for comm serv P Ballantine & Sons 1966; founding mem Judicial Counc NBA 1971; regional dir NBA 1973; dir at Large NBA 1972 & 74. **Military Serv:** US Army (SGT) 1942-45, 1973-80 major USMCR, military judge. **Business Addr:** 280 Humbolt Parkway, Buffalo, NY 14214.

SIMS-DAVIS, EDITH R.
Educational administrator. **Personal:** Born Dec 24, 1932, Marion, LA; daughter of LuEllen Nelson Robinson and Rich Louis Robinson; married Samuel C Davis, Jun 15, 1984; children: Cynthia Laverne Sims, William Sims Jr. **Educ:** AM&N Coll, BS (cum laude) 1955; Tuskegee Inst, MS 1960; Univ Buffalo, post grad study 1961-62; Chicago State University, Chicago, IL, 1962-66. **Career:** Merrill HS, teacher 1955-59; Englewood HS, 1961-66, counselor 1966-68; Fenger HS, 1968-69; Calumet HS, asst prin, acting prin 1969-71; Caldwell & McDowell Schools, prin 1971-82; Corliss HS, prin 1982-. **Orgs:** Mem Chicago Bd Educ, SE Comm Org, IL Prin Assn; Chicago Prin Assn; Ella Flagg Young Chap Natl Alliance of Black Sch Edns; Natl Council of Admin Women in Educ; Crerar Presb Ch; Chicago Urban League; mem Beta Kappa Chi Sci Frat; member, Univ of AR Alumni Assn, 1969-; member, Delta Sigma Theta Sorority, 1953-; member, Chicago Principal Assn, 1971-; Samuel B Stratton Assn, 1980-; Natl Council of Negro Women. **Honors/Awds:** Univ of AR Alumni Assn at Pine Bluff "Miss Alumni" 1955; Alpha Kappa Mu Natl Honor Soc; Roseland Comm Grit Award 1986; Outstanding Chicago Principal Award Dist 33 1986; Outstanding Principal Award, Superintendent of Schools Chicago Board of Education, 1986; Distinguished Alumni Award, Univ of AR, Pine Bluff, 1987; Whitman Award, Excellence in Educational Management, Whitman Corporation, 1990; Phi Delta Kappa Award, 1992. **Home Phone:** (312)649-1425. **Business Addr:** Principal, Corliss High School, 821 E 103rd St, Chicago, IL 60628, (312)535-5125.

SIMTON, CHESTER
Librarian. **Personal:** Born Jan 28, 1937, Longstreet, LA; son of Umie Crowell Simton and James Simton; married Peggy I Nabors, Jul 4, 1978; children: Jessica, Jennifer, Annelle M, Mary Lee. **Educ:** University of California, Berkeley, CA, BS, 1976, MLS, 1977; Matanuska Susitna Community College, Palmer, AK; Norton Sound College, Nome, AK; University of Anchorage, Anchorage, AK. **Career:** Matanuska Susitna Borough School District, Palmer, AK, librarian/media, 1973-; Nome Public School District, Nome, AK, library/media specialist, 1980-83; King Cove City School District, King Cove, AK, library/media specialist. **Orgs:** Media round table, Alaska Library Assn, 1987-88; Teachers Right Committee, executive board, NEA Alaska, 1989-; Diversified Occupation Palmer High School, 1987-90; multicultural chairman, State of Alaska, 1992-93. **Home Addr:** PO Box 3429, Palmer, AK 99645.

SINBAD (DAVID ATKINS)
Comedian, actor, talk show host. **Personal:** Born 1957, Benton Harbor, MI; son of Donald Atkins; divorced; children: Paige, Royce. **Educ:** University of Denver. **Career:** Opening act for music groups such as the Pointer Sisters, Kool and the Gang; Actor: The Redd Foxx Show; The Cosby Show; A Different World; Hollywood Squares; The Sinbad Show, 1994; Showtime at the Apollo, host, beginning 1989; Films: Houseguest, w/ Phil Hartman, 1995; Cherokee Kid; Jingle All the Way w/ Arnold Schwarzenegger, 1996. VIBE, tv talk show, host, 1997-. **Honors/Awds:** Star Search, seven time winner. **Special Achievements:** Author, Sinbad's Guide to Life. **Military Serv:** US Air Force, until 1983. **Business Addr:** Actor/Founder, David and Goliath Production Company, 11330 Ventura Blvd, Studio City, CA 91604.

SINCLAIR, BENITO A.
Consulting structural engineer, building & safety commissioner. **Personal:** Born Aug 18, 1931, Colon, Panama; son of Isabel Darshville Sinclair and Arthur Donovan Sinclair; married Helen Rahn Sinclair, Sep 7, 1963; children: Marcia Yvette, Shana Elida. **Educ:** California Polytechnic State University, San Luis Obispo, CA, BS, architectural engineering, 1957. **Career:** B A Sinclair & Assoc Inc; Lon Angeles, CA, president/CEO, 1964-. **Orgs:** Los Angeles city commissioner, Building & Safety, 1984-; director, Structural Engineers Association of California, 1982-83; founding member/president, Los Angeles Council of Black Professor of Engineers; founding member/president, California Association of Minority Consulting Engineers; member, National Association of Black Consult Engrs, ASCE, ACEC, EERI. **Honors/Awds:** Excellence in Design, AM Inst of Architects, 1984; Tom Bradley Terminal, LAX, Prestressed Conc Inst, 1987; Distinguished Alumnus, California Polytechnic Univer Arch Engr, 1969; Special Honoree, Los Angeles Council of Black P E, 1987; Outstanding Contributions to Community American Soc of Civil Engineers, 1976. **Business Addr:** President/CEO, B A Sinclair & Assoc Inc, 5601 W Washington Bl, Los Angeles, CA 90068.

SINCLAIR, CLAYTON, JR.
Attorney. **Personal:** Born Jul 4, 1933, Wadesboro, NC; married Jeanette B. **Educ:** Univ ME, BA 1955; Howard Univ Law Sch, LLB 1960. **Career:** Sinclair & Dixon, sr partner 1976-; Patterson Parks & Franklin Atlanta, atty 1971-76; Goodis, Greenfield & Mann Phila, atty 1970-71; Scott Paper Co, 1969-70; NY State Banking Dept NYC, asst coun 1968-69; O'Donald & Schwartz NYC, atty 1960-68. **Orgs:** Mem Bar States NY, PA, GA; US Fed Dist Ct; So & Eastern Dist NY; US Sup Ct; Amer Bar Assn; Natl Bar Assn; Atlanta Bar Assn; GA Trial Lawyers Assn. **Business Addr:** Senior Partner, Sinclair & Dixon, 100 Peachtree St, Suite 301, Atlanta, GA 30303.

SINCLAIR, MICHAEL GLENN
Professional football player. **Personal:** Born Jan 31, 1968, Galveston, TX; married Betty, May 25, 1991; children: Michael, Michaela, Johnnie Glenn. **Educ:** Eastern New Mexico, bachelor's degree in physical education. **Career:** Seattle Seahawks, defensive end, 1991-. **Business Addr:** Professional Football Player, Seattle Seahawks, 11220 NE 53rd St, Kirkland, WA 98033, (206)827-9777.

SINDLER, MICHAEL H.
Executive director. **Personal:** Born May 15, 1943, District of Columbia; married Louise Bates. **Educ:** Georgetown Sch Foreign Srv, BS 1965; Georgetown Law Sch, JD 1968; further study. **Career:** DC Legislation & Opinions Div, asst corp counsel 1969-73; Motor Vehicles DC, asst dir 1973-74, spl asst to dir 1974-. **Orgs:** Mem numerous offices, coms & Washington Bar Assc; DC Bar Assc; Fed Bar Assc; mem DC Municipal Officers Club 1973-. **Honors/Awds:** Amer Jurisprudence Award. **Business Addr:** 301 C St NW, Washington, DC 20001.

SINGER, ENOS LEROY
Construction company executive. **Personal:** Born Jul 25, 1943, Marietta, OH; son of Virginia H Singer and Kenneth E Singer (deceased); married Patricia Ann Burke Singer; children: Misty D, Mischa D, Corey E. **Educ:** Ohio State University, 1961-63. **Career:** Selby General Hospital, office mgr, 1969-72, patient account mgr, 1972-74, patient account mgr/purchasing agent, 1974-75; Washington County Home Nursing Service, director, 1975-80; WORDS-8, Inc, vice pres, 1980-81; Singer Construction Company, Inc, president/chief executive officer, 1981-; PDK Construction, Inc, president/chief executive officer, 1987-. **Orgs:** Ohio 8A Association, 1989-; National Association of Disadvantaged Business, 1989-; Democratic County Chairmans Association of Ohio, president, 1989-; Buckeye Contractors Association, 1990-; National Association of Small Business, 1989-; Ohio Small Business Council, 1989- Marietta Community Foundation Board, 1991-; Washington Democratic Party, chairman, 1984-. **Honors/Awds:** National Jaycees-JCI Senate #19447, life member, 1975; Ohio Democratic Party, Democrat of the Year, 1991; Outstanding Young Man of Marietta, Distinguished Service Award, 1974; One of America's Outstanding Young Men, 1973-80. **Military Serv:** US Army Reserves, sp-5, 1964-70.

SINGH, RAJENDRA P.
Educator. **Personal:** Born May 6, 1934, Mnagar; married Sneh P; children: Ram C, David A. **Educ:** Agra Univ, BScI 1952; King George's Dental Coll & Hosp, BDS 1964; Guggenhiem Dental Ctr, Cert Clinical Dentistry 1966; Univ of Pittsburgh, Grad Studies in Endodontics 1975. **Career:** King George's Dental Hosp, house surgeon 1964-65; Murry & Leonie Dental Clinic, fellow of the dental staff 1965-66; Howard Univ Coll of Dentistry, instr 1969-77, asst prof 1977-. **Orgs:** Rsch assoc in oral surgery NJ Coll of Dentistry 1966-69; mem Amer Dental Assoc 1970-; Amer Assoc of Endodontists 1975-; lecturer Adv in Sci 1978-79; Black Brotherhood Week Key Jr High 1983; nom judge Montgomery County Debating Contest 1985; Washington DC Dental Society 1977; Edward C Penne Endodontic Club 1978; official delegate, Citizen Ambassador Program-People to People International (visited People's Republic of China); American College of Dentists, fellow. **Honors/Awds:** Outstanding Clinical Teacher Student's Council Coll of Dentistry 1973-74; Louise C Ball Fellowship Awd Coll of Dentists 1974-77; Outstanding Faculty Award, Student Council of Dentistry 1973, 1989. **Special Achievements:** Author: "Endodontic Considerations of Tricanaled Mand Premolar," Journal of Maryland Dental Assn, 1987; "Evaluation of Optimal Site Maxi Teeth," thesis, Library of Congress, 1977. **Home Addr:** 8822 Sleppy Hollow Ln, Potomac, MD 20854.

SINGLETARY, INEZ M.
County health administrator. **Personal:** Born in New York, NY; daughter of Adina Maloney and Edison Maloney; married Samuel P Singletary; children: Shauna K Singletary Alami, Samuel P III. **Educ:** Hunter Clge, BA, MA. **Career:** PS 99 Bronx, school teacher 1947-64; Ferris Ave Neighborhood Center, exec dir 1965-68; White Plains Comm Action Prog Inc, exec dir 1968-69; Day Care Council Westchester Inc, exec dir 1969-81; College of New Rochelle, Grad School of Education, prof; West County Dept Comm Mental Health, dir comm rel, currently. **Orgs:** Chairperson, special events, Child Care Council of Westchester Inc; co fndr past pres NY St Child Care Coord Cncl Inc; bd mem Oak Lane Child Care Ctr Inc; The Children's Place at the Plaza Albany NY; chrpsn Westchester Women's Council; Task Force on Worship; chairperson, admin bd, Pleasantville United Meth Church; chairperson, Board of Women's News. **Honors/Awds:** Outstanding Srv to Humanity Church of our Savior United Meth Church Yonkers NY 1971; Invaluable Srv to Comm Yonkers Child Care Assc Yonkers NY 1975; Woman of the Year Cty of Westchester 1979; Sojourner Truth Award Natl Assn of Negro Bus and Prof Women Inc West Cty Club 1981. **Business Addr:** Dir of Community Relations, West County Dept Comm Mental, 112 E Post Rd, White Plains, NY 10601.

SINGLETARY, REGGIE
Professional football player. **Personal:** Born Jan 17, 1964, Whiteville, NC; son of Notredane Pridgen Singletary and Dan Arron Singletary; married Janice Jeffires Singletary, May 21, 1988; children: Reginald L II. **Educ:** North Carolina State Univ, attended. **Career:** Philadelphia Eagles, guard/offensive tackle, 1986-. **Honors/Awds:** Dick Christy Award, North Carolina State, 1985; All Rookie Team Defense, NFL, 1986. **Business Addr:** Professional Football Player, Philadelphia Eagles, 1989, Broad St & Pattison Ave, Veterans Stadium, Philadelphia, PA 19143.

SINGLETON, ALSHERMOND
Professional football player. **Personal:** Born Aug 7, 1975. **Educ:** Temple Univ, bachelor's degree in sport recreation management. **Career:** Tampa Bay Buccaneers, linebacker, 1997-. **Business Addr:** Professional Football Player, Tampa Bay Buccaneers, One Buccaneer Place, Tampa, FL 33607, (813)870-2700.

SINGLETON, BENJAMIN, SR.
Deputy sheriff, business owner. **Personal:** Born Dec 17, 1943, Summerville, SC; son of Catherine Fludd and Clement Addison Singleton Sr; married Dorothy Abraham, May 2, 1964; children: Benjamin Jr. **Educ:** Vocational Training, Columbia SC, Certificate, 1977-81; Atlanta Univ Criminal Justice Institute, Miami FL, Certificate, 1985. **Career:** Dorchester County Sheriff's Dept, St George SC, lieutenant, deputy sheriff, 1971-; Knightsville Dry Cleaners, Summerville SC, owner, 1986-. **Orgs:** Life mem, Cannan United Methodist Church, United Methodist Mens Club; mem, New Eden Lodge #32, 1984-, NAACP, 1985-, The Upper Dorchester Civic Club, 1985-; vice pres, Palmetto State Law Enforcement Office Assn, 1985-87, pres, 1987-89; mem, The First Congressional Dist Black Caucus, 1986-90; bd mem, South Carolina Attorney General Advisory Bd for State Grand Jury, 1988-92, Univ of South Carolina Police Census, 1988-92. **Honors/Awds:** Sponsor, Annual Senior Citizens Dinner for the Tri-County; Co-Sponsor, Dixie League Baseball Team for the Community, 1967-; Co-Founder, The Berkeley-Dorchester Chapter of PSLEOA, 1977; Outstanding Services, Palmetto State Law Enforcement, 1982; Sponsor, Dixie League Baseball Team, 1984; Speaker to varied church youth groups on law enforcement, 1985-90; Community Service, Berkeley-Dorchester Chapter, 1989. **Home Addr:** 406 E Old Orangeburg Rd, Summerville, SC 29483. **Business Addr:** Owner, Knightsville Dry Cleaners, 1580 Central Ave, PO Box 515, Summerville, SC 29483.

SINGLETON, CHRIS
Professional football player. **Personal:** Born Feb 20, 1967, Parsippany, NJ. **Educ:** Univ of Arizona, sociology major, 1986-89. **Career:** New England Patriots, outside linebacker, 1990-. **Honors/Awds:** Two-time All-Pac 10 selection; second-team All-American, Sporting News, 1989. **Business Addr:** Professional Football Player, New England Patriots, Sullivan Stadium, Rt One, Foxboro, MA 02035.

SINGLETON, ERNIE
Record company executive. **Personal:** Born in New Orleans, LA. **Career:** Radio station, New Orleans, host; radio station, Jacksonville, host, music director, program director, morning newsman; Fantasy, Mercury Records, regional promotions manager; Casablanca Records, regional promotions manager; national promotional director; PolyGram Records, national promotional director, 1978-83; Warner Brothers Records, senior vice pres, Reprise Records promotion staff head, 1987; MCA Records, Black Music promotion national director, beginning 1983, Urban and Jazz Music promotion, vice pres, Black Music Division, president, 1990-. **Orgs:** Young Black Programmers Coalition, founding member. **Honors/Awds:** Urban Network, Impact, Black Radio Exclusive, Executive of the Year, 1990; Young Black Programmers Coalition, Award of Excellence,

1987; Bobby Poe Executive of the Year Award, 1985. **Special Achievements:** Organized local and national radiothons to raise funds for sickle-cell anemia research; worked with Quincy Jones, Prince, Madonna, and numerous others. **Business Addr:** President, Black Music Division, MCA Records, 70 Universal City Plaza, Universal City, CA 91608.

SINGLETON, HAROLD DOUGLAS
Clergyman (retired). **Personal:** Born Dec 10, 1908, Brunswick, GA; son of Annie King Singleton and Joseph Singleton; married Mary; children: Mercedes, Harold Jr, Alvin, Kenneth, Marilyn, Dwight. **Educ:** Oakwood Coll, 1928; Union Coll, attended; 7th Day Advent Sem, attended. **Career:** Pastor 1929-42; S Atlantic Conf SDA, pres 1946-54; NE Conf SDA, pres 1954-62; N Amer Black SDA Prog, dir 1962-75; retired clergyman.

SINGLETON, HARRY M.
Attorney. **Personal:** Born Apr 10, 1949, Meadville, PA; son of Rose A Fucci Singleton and G T Singleton; divorced; children: Harry Jr, Leah. **Educ:** The Johns Hopkins Univ, BA 1971; Yale Law School, JD 1974. **Career:** Houston & Gardner Law Firm, assoc 1974-75; Consult Amer Enterprise Institute 1975; Office of General Counsel/Fed Trade Commiss, attny 1975-76; Covington & Burling Law Firm, assoc 1976-77; Comm on the Dist of Columbia/US House of Reps, dep minority counsel 1977-79, minority chief counsel & staff dir 1979-81; Office of Congressional Affairs/US Dept of Commerce, dep asst sec 1981-82; US Dept of Ed, asst sec 1982-86; Harry M Singleton & Associates Inc, pres 1986-91; private practice, attorney, 1991-. **Orgs:** Pres, bd of trustees Barney Neighborhood House 1978-80; corp board of directors Childrens Hosp Natl Med Ctr 1984-88; board of directors, DC Chap, Republican Natl Lawyers Assn, 1990-91; bd of dirs, Council of 100 Black Republicans, 1991-92; DC Black Republican Council, 1991-93, chairman, 1992-93; Republican National Hispanic Assembly of the District of Columbia, 1991-93; District of Columbia Republican Committee, 1991-; Republican National Committeeman, District of Columbia, 1992-; Republican National Committee Executive Council 1993-95; Republican National Committee, Resolutions Comm 1997-; Lions Club, District 22-C, 1991-; natl chairman, Republican National African-American Council, 1993-; chairman, DC Chapter Republican National African-American Council, 1993-; Boys and Girls Clubs of Greater Washington, 1994-. **Honors/Awds:** Disting Hon Alumnus Awd Langston Univ 1984. **Business Addr:** Attorney at Law, 2300 N St, NW, Ste 600, Washington, DC 20037.

SINGLETON, HERBERT
Investment company executive. **Personal:** Born Jul 21, 1947, Jacksonville, FL; son of Henrietta Wallace Singleton and Henry Baker Sr; married Brenda Ann Oliver; children: Wanda Y, Chante L. **Educ:** Morris Brown Coll, BA 1969; St Francis Coll, MBA 1979, MSBA 1978. **Career:** Lincoln Natl Corp, programmer 1974-1978, mgr professional dev & training 1978-80, data processing devel mgr 1980-83; Lincoln Natl Investment Mgmt Co, dir invest sys 1983-84, asst vice pres 1984-. **Orgs:** Mem Assoc of MBA Exec 1980-83; chap pres Alpha Phi Alpha 1984-86. **Honors/Awds:** Computer Programmer Cert 1970; Cert Teacher CA Commun Coll Syst 1974; Outstanding Coll Alumnus Morris Brown Coll 1983. **Military Serv:** USAF, SSgt, 1970-74; Outstanding Airman of the Month 1973, 1974. **Business Addr:** Assistant Vice President, Lincoln Natl Invest Co, 1300 S Clinton St, Fort Wayne, IN 46801.

SINGLETON, ISAAC, SR.
Pastor. **Personal:** Born Mar 31, 1928, Tallulah, LA; married Pearl B; children: Gloria Hayes, Isaac Jr, Charles, Barbara Edward, Valerie Gaffin, Willie D. **Educ:** Lincoln Christian Coll, BA 1962; Bearea Sem, M Div 1983. **Career:** Lebanon Bapt Dist Assoc, moderator 1963-75; Joliet Chptr Oper PUSH, pres 1974-; Joliet Reg Chmbr of Comm, v pres 1978-80; Operation Push, natl brd 1979-. **Orgs:** Pres PUSH 1974-; adv bd Children & Family of IL 1980-, chmn 1986-; vice pres Bapt Gen Congress of Chris Ed 1980-; chrmn rgnl brd Children & Family 1983-. **Honors/Awds:** Dr of Divinity Miller Univ Plainfld, NJ 1969; Hon Citizen of New Orleans 1978. **Military Serv:** USAAF sgt 1945-47; Good Conduct. **Business Addr:** Pastor, Mt Zion Baptist Church, McKinley & Erie, Joliet, IL 60436.

SINGLETON, JAMES LEROY
Podiatrist. **Personal:** Born Jul 20, 1944, Beaufort, SC; married Maxine; children: Daphne, Andrea, Krystal. **Educ:** VA Union Univ, BS 1967; VA State College, 1969; OH College of Podiatric Med, DPM, 1973; Sidney A Sumby, resident, 1973-74. **Career:** Richmond Public School System. **Orgs:** Mem Amer Podiatry Assc; MI State Podiatry Assc; diplomate Natl Bd Podiatry Exmnr; VA Podiatry Soc; staff mem Sidney A Sumby Mem Hosp; Norfolk Comm Hosp; Med Ctr Hosp; Chesapeake Gen Hosp; mem Noble Mystic Shrine; 32nd degree Mason; OH Royal Arch Mason; Eureka Lodge 52 Most Worshipful Prince Hall; Alpha Phi Alpha Frat; bd dir Jamson Bible Inst. **Honors/Awds:** Christian Physician Award Jamson Bible Inst 1975; OH College Podiatric Award 1973; Natl Fed March of Dimes 1974; PA Podiatry Assn Surg Seminar 1972; Pres's Award 1966. **Business Addr:** PO Box 5402, Chesapeake, VA 23324.

SINGLETON, JAMES MILTON
City government official. **Personal:** Born Aug 10, 1933, Hazlehurst, MS; married Allie Mae Young; children: James Jr, Jacquelyn. **Educ:** So Univ of Baton Rouge LA, BS; Xavier Univ New Orleans, Health Plnng; Loyola Univ, attended; Univ of OK, attended. **Career:** Orleans Parish School Bd, teacher 1956-70; Natl Urban Health New Orleans, consult 1970-71; City of New Orleans Mayors Office, spec consult on health 1971-78; City of New Orleans, city councilman 1978-. **Orgs:** Pres Central City Econ Corp 1965-78, Total Comm Action Inc 1975; chmn Dryades St YMCA; chmn Heritage Aq Adv Comm, Bd of LA Health Plan, Total CommAction Inc. **Honors/Awds:** Past Pres Awd Total Comm Action Inc 1976; Past Pres Awd Dryades St YMCA 1977. **Military Serv:** AUS lt col 16 yrs. **Business Addr:** City Councilman, City of New Orleans, 1300 Perdido St, Room 2W50, New Orleans, LA 70112.

SINGLETON, JOHN
Screenwriter, filmmaker. **Personal:** Born in Los Angeles, CA; son of Sheila Ward and Danny Singleton; married Akosua Busia (divorced 1997); children: Hadar. **Educ:** University of Southern California, School of Cinema-Television, BA, 1990; Columbia Studios, internship. **Career:** Boyz N the Hood, director, screenwriter, 1991; Poetic Justice, director, screenwriter, 1993; Higher Learning, director, screenwriter, producer. **Honors/Awds:** Oscar nominee, Best Original Screenplay, Best Director, both for Boyz N the Hood, 1992. **Special Achievements:** Testified before Senate Subcommittee examining violence and children, 1992; "Remember the Time," directed music video for Michael Jackson, 1992; youngest person and first African American nominated for Best Director Academy Award, 1992; author of articles: "The Fire This Time," Premiere, p 74, July 1992; "Coolin' with Spike," Essence, p 64, November 1991. **Business Phone:** (310)288-4545.

SINGLETON, KATHRYN T.
Business executive. **Personal:** Born May 15, 1951, Orange, TX; daughter of Gertie M Singleton and Lester B Singleton Sr (deceased); married Lonnie M Cane, Apr 18, 1992. **Educ:** Incarnate Word College, BS, 1973; State University of New York, MS, 1977. **Career:** Highsmith Rainey Memorial Hospital, director, Medical Record Department, 1973-76; Henry Ford Hospital, assistant director, Medical Record Department, 1978-79; University of Wisconsin, assistant professor, 1978-80; Holy Cross Hospital, administrator, Medical Record Department, 1980-82; Tascon, Inc, president/chief executive officer, 1982-. **Orgs:** American Medical Record Association; District of Columbia Medical Record Association, executive board member; Hospital Council Medical Record Director's Division, chairperson, National Capitol Area; Maryland Director's Division; University of Wisconsin, faculty senate member; Alpha Kappa Alpha Sorority; Metropolitan Baptist Church, chair, New Member Orientation Program. **Honors/Awds:** Young Comunity Leadership Award, 1989-91. **Special Achievements:** New Technologies Affecting Medical Records, Journal of American Medical Record Association, 1987; Portable Information Technology, Journal of American Medical Record Association, 1987. **Business Addr:** President/Chief Executive Officer, Tascon, Inc, 7101 Wisconsin Ave, Ste 1125, Bethesda, MD 20814, (301)907-3844.

SINGLETON, KENNETH WAYNE
Professional baseball player (retired). **Personal:** Born Jun 10, 1947, New York, NY. **Educ:** Hofstra Univ, Hempstead, NY, attended. **Career:** New York Mets, outfielder, 1970-71; Montreal Expos, outfielder, 1972-74; Baltimore Orioles, outfielder, 1975-84; The Sports Network Canada, analyst. **Honors/Awds:** American League All-Star Team, 1977, 1979, 1981.

SINGLETON, LEROY, SR.
Funeral director. **Personal:** Born Oct 8, 1941, Hempstead, TX; son of Rosie Lee Singleton-Moore and Oscar Singleton (deceased); married Willie E. Franklin, Apr 25, 1977; children: LaRonda K, Leroy Jr, Kaye, Erica, Kareen, Garard W. **Educ:** Prairie View A&M Univ, Prairie View TX, BS, 1968; Prairie View A&M Univ, Prairie View TX, MEd, 1971; Commonwealth School of Mortician, Houston TX, diploma, nortuary science, 1982. **Career:** Dallas ISD, Dallas TX, teacher, 1968-69; Prairie View A&M Univ, Prairie View TX, associate teacher, 1971-75; Singleton Funeral Home, Hempstead TX, owner/mgr, 1982-; mayor of Hempstead TX, 1984-; Singleton Trucking, owner & manager, 1975-82. **Orgs:** Independent Funeral Directors Assn, Texas Independent Funeral Directors Assn; Kiwanis International; Lone Star Masonic Lodge #85; 1980-; American Legion Post 929; 1966-; National Conference of Black Mayors/World Conference of Mayors; charter member, Lion Tamer, Lion's Club, 1972-; Amer Personnel & Guidance Assn; Amer Coll Personnel Assn; Admin Student Personnel; Prairie View Alumni Assn; Assn for Counselor Educ & Supervision; Amer School Counselor Assn; TX Admin Student Personnel; Phi Delta Kappan; Omega Psi Phi Fraternity, Inc; TX Coalition of Black Democrats; NAACP; Appointed to the TX State Review Bd, representing Houston-Galveston Area Council in Austin, TX, by Governor Mark White, 1986-89; Appointed to the Appraisal Licensing & Certification Bd, by Governor Ann Richards, 1991-94; Reappointed to the Appraisal Licensing & Certification Bd, by Governor George Bush, 1995-. **Honors/Awds:** First Black Mayor, Lone Star Lodge #85; 1985; Plaque, Boy Scouts of America, 1985; Plaque, Vocational Guidance Service, 1986; Natl Technical Assn, Houston Chapter Comm Service Award; Outstanding Service Award, First Black Mayor of Hempstead, TX. **Military Serv:** US Navy, E-4, 1962-65; Navy Unit Citation, 1964; Expeditionary Service Medal. **Home Addr:** PO Box 344, Hempstead, TX 77445.

SINGLETON, NATE
Professional football player. **Personal:** Born Jul 5, 1968, New Orleans, LA. **Educ:** Grambling State. **Career:** San Francisco 49ers, wide receiver, 1993-96; Tennessee Oilers, 1997; Baltimore Ravens, 1997-. **Business Addr:** Professional Football Player, Baltimore Ravens, 11001 Owings Mills Blvd, Owings Mills, MD 21117, (410)654-6200.

SINGLETON, ROBERT
Association executive. **Personal:** Born Jan 8, 1936, Philadelphia, PA; married Helen Singleton; children: Robby, Damani, Malik. **Educ:** Univ of CA, BA 1960, MA 1962, PhD 1983. **Career:** Pacific Hist Review Univ CA, asst editor 1958-60; Univ of CA, rsch asst 1961-63; Inst Indus Relations Univ CA, chief rscher 1963-64; US Labor Dept,rsch economist 1964-66; Educ Assoc Inc Wash, consul; Univ of CA, rsch economist 1967-69; Afro-Amer Studies Ctr Univ CA, dir & Prof 1969-70; Univ of CA, economist 1969-71; Robert Singleton & Assoc, pres 1979-; Loyola Marymount Univ, economics prof 1980-. **Orgs:** Past pres UCLA-NAACP; past chmn Santa Monica Venice Congress Racial Equality; mem Chancellors Adv Com Discrimination, Amer Civil Liberties Union, Soc Science Rsch Council Com Afro-Amer Studies; consultant staff Senate Select Subcom, OP-EN; HEW; Urban Educ Task Force; Natl Urban League Educ Task Force; mem Natl Assn Planners; founder & chmn Journal Black Studies; founding dir UCLA Ctr Afro-Amer Studies. **Honors/Awds:** John Hay Whitney Fellowship 1963; US Dept Labor Grant support dissertation 1966; Order Golden Bruins Chancellors Secret Hon Soc 1963-; John Hay Whitney Grant problems Black Educ 1972; Assembly Rules Com CA Legislature Resolution 1974. **Business Addr:** Economics Prof, Loyola Marymont University, 80th St & Loyola Blvd, Los Angeles, CA 90045.

SINGLETON, WILLIAM MATTHEW
Clergyman, educator. **Personal:** Born Oct 12, 1924, Conway, SC; married Florence Revels; children: Margaret, Elizabeth, William Jr. **Educ:** VA Union Univ, BA 1946; Howard Univ Sch of Religion, BD 1949; Drew Univ, MRE 1951; Western Bapt Bible Clge, DD 1959. **Career:** Western Bapt Bible Clge, pres 1965-, tchr dean 1954-61; 1st Bapt Ch, pastor 1951-52; Butler Clge, dean of chapel 1947-50; 2nd Bapt Ch Miami MO, pastor 1964-69; 2nd Bapt Ch Columbia MO, interim pastor 1969-71; Ward Memorial Baptist Church Sedalia MO 1982-87. **Orgs:** Mem Inst of Religion Howard Univ; mem KS City Theol Soc; mem Natl Bapt Conv USA Inc; mem NAACP; Urban League; Omega Psi Phi Frat; KS City Bapt Ministers Union. **Honors/Awds:** Num publ 1946-71. **Business Addr:** 2119 Tracy, Kansas City, MO 64108.

SINGLEY, ELIJAH
Librarian. **Personal:** Born Jan 29, 1935, Bessemer, AL; son of Pearl Whitman Singley and Daniel Singley; married Yvonne Jean; children: Jennifer. **Educ:** Miles Coll, AB 1958; Atlanta Univ, MS in LS 1963; Sangamon State Univ, MA 1980. **Career:** VA State Coll, asst ref librarian 1960; AL State Univ, library dir 1963-71; Lincoln Land Comm Coll, asst librarian 1971-. **Orgs:** Mem Alpha Phi Alpha Frat; mem Amer Numismatic Assn; mem Natl Urban League; mem IL Sociological Assn; mem IL Library Assn; mem White House Conf on Library & Info Serv 1978-79; NAACP. **Honors/Awds:** Sports Hall of Fame Miles Coll Birmingham, AL, 1981. **Military Serv:** AUS spec 4th class 1960-63; Good Conduct Medal; Natl Defense Serv Medal. **Home Addr:** 2301 Noble Ave, Springfield, IL 62704. **Business Addr:** Assistant Librarian, Lincoln Land Comm College, Shepherd Rd, Springfield, IL 62708.

SINGLEY, YVONNE JEAN
Educational administrator. **Personal:** Born Jun 18, 1947, Gary, IN; daughter of Mary Williams and William Webb; married Elijah Singley, May 24, 1980; children: Jennifer. **Educ:** Memphis State Univ, BA, Latin, 1969; Univ of IL, Urbana, MUP, 1974, Normal, IL Campus, doctoral studies, education administration, currently. **Career:** Indiana Univ-Northwest, social researcher, 1969-72; Opportunities Indus Ctr, CETA, manpower training, education coordinator, 1974-75; Division of Vocational Rehabilitation, program evaluation unit, methods and procedures advisor, 1975-78; Illinois Department of Public Aid, Title XX Program, social service planner, 1978-79; Illinois Board of Education, academic and health affairs, assistant director, 1979-87; Illinois Community College Board, director of instructional & student development, 1987-. **Orgs:** Springfield Magical Event, volunteer, 1991; YMCA, board member, 1985-91; Illinois Committee on Black Concerns in Higher Education, cofounder; AAWCC State Executive Committee; Springfield Junior League, board member, 1987-88; Access to Housing, president, 1981-86; Springfield League of Women Voters, board member, 1979-84; Kappa Delta Pi, Intl Honor Society, 1995; Springfield Urban League, board member, 1977-80.

Honors/Awds: Illinois Association for Personalized Learning, Program Award, 1992; AAWCJC, National Leadership Development Award, 1991, 1992; Illinois Community College Faculty Association, Honorary Membership Award, 1991; University of Illinois, Graduate College, graduate fellowship. **Special Achievements:** Volunteer chair, ''The Nuts and Bolts of Fund Raising,'' WSEC public television fund raising event, 1992; consulted with the US Department of Education in reviewing proposals for the distribution of Title III Disadvantaged Student Grant and Challenge Grant funds; presentations: ''Cultural Diversity, Goals, Plans and Strategies,'' Interassociation Conference, 1992; ''Movin' Up with Intergenerational Programs: College and Community Coalitions that Work,'' League of Innovation, Leadership 2000, 1992. **Home Addr:** 2301 Noble Ave, Springfield, IL 62704. **Business Addr:** Director, Instructional & Student Development, Illinois Community College Board, 509 South 6th Street, Room 400, Springfield, IL 62701.

SINKLER, GEORGE
Educator (retired). **Personal:** Born Dec 22, 1927, Charleston, SC; son of Mary Sinkler and Moses Sinkler; married Albertha Amelia Richardson, Aug 19, 1949; children: Gregory, Kenneth, Georgette Alberta. **Educ:** Augustana Coll (RI, IL), AB 1953; Columbia Univ (Tchrs), MA 1954; Columbia Univ (Tchrs), Ed D (History) 1966. **Career:** Bluefield State Coll, instr 1954-55; Prairie View A&M Coll, instr assoc prof 1955-65; Morgan State Univ, prof history 1965-88, professor emeritus, history. **Orgs:** Visiting prof Jackson State Coll 1969; visiting prof Amherst 1969, Baltimore Comm Coll 1972, Frostburg State Univ 1969, Youngstown State Univ 1969, Univ of NE (Omaha) 1971, Catonsville Comm Coll 1971; mem Govans United Meth Church 1967-; cncl mem Govans Comm 1967-79; mem York Road Plng Comm 1967; Amer Hist Assoc; Orgn of Amer Historians. **Honors/Awds:** Phi Beta Kappa, Phi Alpha Theta, Kappa Delta Augustiana Coll 1953; Mr Friednship 1953; Augustana Grad Flwshp 1953; Post Doctoral Flw Johns Hopkins Univ 1972-73; NEH Summer Stipend for Coll Tchrs 1980; book Racial Attitudes of Amer Pres, Doubleday 1971; articles in OH Hist, Vol 77 1968; IN Magazine of Hist Vol 65 1969; newspapers Afro-Amer Baltimore 1972; Amsterdam News 1976; publications incl, ''What History Tells Us About Presidents and Race'' Afro-American Feb 19, 1972; ''Blacks and American Presidents'' New York Amsterdam News Summer 1976. John Hay Whitney Opportunity Fellow, 1958; Southern Fellowship Fund Grant 1957; Danforth Fellowships 1961, 1964. **Military Serv:** USN 1st class stewards mate 1946-49; Partcptd Navy Golden Gloves; Good Conduct Medal. **Home Addr:** 821 Beaumont Ave, Baltimore, MD 21212.

SINNETTE, CALVIN HERMAN
Physician (retired). **Personal:** Born Aug 30, 1924, New York, NY; son of Frances Sinnette and Norman J Sinnette; married Elinor Kathleen DesVerney; children: Caleen S Jennings, Darryle S Craig. **Educ:** City Coll of New York, BS 1945; Howard Univ Coll of Medicine, MD 1949. **Career:** Univ of Ibadan & Zaria Univ, prof pediatrics 1964-70; Columbia Univ, prof pediatrics 1970-75; Univ of Nairobi Kenya, prof pediatrics 1975-77; School of Medicine Morehouse Assoc, dean clin affairs 1977-79; Howard Univ, asst to vice pres health affairs 1979-88, asst vice pres health affairs, 1988-91. **Orgs:** Mem Natl Medical Assoc 1977-; bd of dirs TransAfrica 1981-89; mem Alpha Omega Alpha 1978-. **Honors/Awds:** Professor Emeritus, Pediatrics, Howard University, College of Medicine. **Military Serv:** USAF capt 1 1/2 yrs. **Home Addr:** 1016 S Wayne St, #409, Arlington, VA 22204-4435.

SINNETTE, ELINOR DESVERNEY
Librarian (retired). **Personal:** Born Oct 8, 1925, New York, NY; daughter of Elinor Adams Calloway DesVerney and James C DesVerney; married Dr Calvin H Sinnette, Nov 19, 1949; children: Caleen Sinnette Jennings, Darryle Sinnette Craig. **Educ:** Hunter Coll of the City Univ of New York, AB, 1947; Pratt Inst School of Library Serv, MLS, 1959; Columbia Univ School of Library Serv, DLS, 1977. **Career:** The New York City Public Library, New York NY, librarian, 1947-54; New York City Bd of Educ, New York NY, school librarian, 1960-65; Inst of African Studies, Univ of Ibadan, Nigeria, lecturer, Institute of Librarianship, 1965-69; Ahmadu Bello Univ, Zaria, Nigeria, lecturer, 1969-70; Moorland-Spingarn Research Center, Howard Univ, 1980-. **Orgs:** Life mem, The Oral History Assn, Oral History Middle Atlantic Region, mem, Black Caucus of the American Library Assn. **Honors/Awds:** Distinguished Service Award, 92nd Infantry Div, World War II Assn, 1986; The Forrest C Pogue Award for Significant Contributions to Oral History, OHMAR, 1991; The BCALA Professional Achievement Award, 1992; author of ''Arthur Alfonso Schomburg, Black Bibliophile and Collector, A Biography,'' The New York Public Library and Wayne State Univ Press, Detroit MI, 1989; editor ''Black Bibliophiles and Collectors; Preservers of Black History,'' Wash, DC, Howard University Press, 1990. **Home Addr:** 1016 S Wayne St, Apt 409, Arlington, VA 22204-4435.

SIRMANS, MEREDITH FRANKLIN
Educator, physician. **Personal:** Born Aug 22, 1939, New York, NY; son of Audrey Elizabeth Gray Sirmans and Booker Tariaffero Sirmans; divorced; children: M Franklin Jr, Meryl D, Traci D. **Educ:** Lincoln Univ, AB (Cum Laude) 1961; Meharry Medical Coll, MD (Cum Laude) 1965. **Career:** Presbyterian Hospital, asst attending Ob-Gyn 1972; Harlem Hospital Center, assoc attending Ob-Gyn 1975; Med Serv for Women PC, med dir 1975-; Coll of Physicians & Surgeons Columbia Univ, asst prof clinical Ob-Gyn. **Orgs:** Exec comm NAACP 1984-85; pres Manhattan Center Med Soc 1983-85; lecturer graduate program, nurse midwifery Columbia Univ 1971-74; rsch clerk Tissue Bank Natl Naval Med Center 1963; lecturer Human Sexuality Program NY, Amer Coll of Ob-Gyn, Amer Coll, Coll of Surgeons, Amer Assoc of Gyne Laparscopists, Amer Fertility soc, Amer Assoc of Sex Educs Counselors & Therapists; physician advisor NY City Health Science Review Org, 369th Veterans Assoc, Omega Psi Phi; pres Black Caucus of Harlem Health Workers; diplomate Amer Bd of Ob-Gyn, Natl Bd of Med Examiners; rschr, fellowship biochem Meharry Medical Coll 1962-63; panelists, sex therapy NY Assoc of Black Psychologists 1977; mem Rotary Club; chmn Region I Natl Medical Assn 1988-89. **Honors/Awds:** Acad Scholarship Meharry Med Coll 1962-65. **Military Serv:** USN, MC, LCDR 1966-69; Vietnam Serv Medal, Natl Defense.

SIZEMORE, BARBARA A.
Educator. **Personal:** Born Dec 17, 1927, Chicago, IL; daughter of Delila Mae Alexander and Sylvester W Laffoon; children: Kymara Chase, Furman G. **Educ:** Northwestern Univ Evanston IL, BA 1947, MA 1954; Univ of Chicago IL, PhD 1979. **Career:** Chicago Pub Schl Chicago IL, tchr, elem prin, hs prin dir of Woodlawn Exper Schl Proj 1947-72; Amer Assc of Schl Admin, assc sec 1972-73; Washington DC, supt of schls 1973-75; Univ of Pittsburgh, assc prof 1977-89, prof, 1989-92; DePaul University, School of Education, dean, currently. **Orgs:** Consult, Chicago Public Schools, 1992-; University of Alabama at Birmingham AL, 1992-; mem Delta Sigma Theta; Natl Alliance of Black Schl Educ; bd mem Journal of Negro Educ 1974-83. **Honors/Awds:** Honorary Doctor of Letters Central State Univ 1974; Honorary Doctor of Laws DE State Coll 1974; Honorary Doctor of Humane Letters Baltimore Coll of the Bible 1974; Honorary Doctor of Pedagogy, Niagara Univ, 1994; Northwestern Univ Merit Alumni Awd 1974; United Nations Assoc of Pittsburgh Human Rights Awd 1985; Racial Justice Awd, YWCA, 1995; The Ruptured Diamond: The Politics of the Decentralization of the DC Public Schools, Lanham, MD: Univ Press of America, l981. **Home Addr:** 1350 N Lake Shore Dr, Apt #1111, Chicago, IL 60610. **Business Addr:** Dean, School of Education, DePaul University, Chicago, IL 60614.

SKEENE, LINELL DE-SILVA
Physician. **Personal:** Born Nov 6, 1938, Brooklyn, NY. **Educ:** Temple U, BA 1959; Meharry Med Coll, MD 1966. **Career:** Maimonides Med Ctr, atdng surg 1973-; Metro Hosp, 1971-72; NY Med Coll, instr surg 1971-72. **Orgs:** Mem AMA; Am Med Women's Assn; NY St Med Soc; mem Nat Cncl of Negro Women; NAACP. **Honors/Awds:** Outstdng Yng Women of Am 1974. **Business Addr:** 25 Dunhill Rd, New Hyde Park, NY 11040.

SKERRETT, PHILIP VINCENT
Pathologist (retired). **Personal:** Born Aug 10, 1923, Lincoln Univ, PA; son of William D. Skerrett; married Dolores Evon Barksdale; children: Philip V II, Donna L Tabrizi, Stephanie M. **Educ:** Lincoln Univ, AB 1947; Meharry Medical Coll, MD 1951. **Career:** Mercy-Douglas Hospital, internship 1951-52; T Jefferson Med Sch, instruction in pathology 1958-66; Univ of PA Med Sch, asst prof pathology 1964-76; Medical Coll of PA, assoc prof of pathology 1976-; Veterans Admin Hospital Philadelphia, asst chief lab serv 1957-64, chief lab serv 1964-78; chief anatomic pathology 1978-l988; dir Blood Bank/Hematology Labs l988-retirement. **Orgs:** Mem Alpha Phi Alpha Frat 1946-, AMA, PMS, PCMC, NMA, MSEP 1956-; diplomate AM Bd of Pathology Coll AM Pathology 1956; mem Int Acad Pathology Philadelphia PathSoc 1957-; diplomate AM Bd of Clinical Pathology 1964; mem Med Lab Tech Adv Commn Comm Coll of Phila. **Honors/Awds:** Beta Kappa Chi Hon Scientific Soc Lincoln Univ 1943; Kappa Phi Hon Soc Meharry Medical Coll 1950; pres Philadelphia Alumni Lincoln Univ PA 1960-64; presidentMeharry Medical College Alumni Philadelphia 1982-. **Military Serv:** AUS staff sgt 3 yrs.

SKINNER, BYRON R.
University president. **Career:** Univ Maine Augusta, pres 1983-. **Business Addr:** President, University of Maine at Augusta, University Heights, Augusta, ME 04330.

SKINNER, CLEMENTINE ANNA MCCONICO
Educator (retired). **Personal:** Born Feb 9, 1916, Birmingham, AL; daughter of Alice Burnett McConico and John F A McConico; married Herbert Skinner Sr (deceased); children: Herbert Jr, Kenneth C. **Educ:** Wilson Jr Coll, AA 1959; Chicago Teachers Coll, BE 1961, ME 1963; Univ of Chicago, Loyola Univ, graduate work 1964-74; Nova Univ, EdD 1976. **Career:** Manley Vocational High School, school library clerk 1950-53; Wadsworth Elementary School, teacher/librarian 1960-68; Kenwood Acad, teacher/librarian 1968-70; South Shore High School, special asst principal in charge of curriculum 1970-82. **Orgs:** Elder former clerk of session Sixth Grace Presbyterian Church 1939-; Presby of Chicago, former moderator, 1987; United Presbyterian African Methodist Episcopal Conf Inc 1969-; former chmn Woodlawn Adv Council DHS 1970-80; bd mem YWCA of Metro Chicago, YWCA Harris Center; chmn bd of dirs Plano Child Devel Center; mem Exec Serv Corp Chicago; bd mem exec council Assoc for Study of Afro-Amer Life and History. **Honors/Awds:** CRRT Award Children's Reading Round Table 1976; Soror of the Year Natl Sorority of Phi Delta Kappa Mu Chapter 1976; honoree Alpha Gamma Pi Sorority 1976; Ralph Metcalfe Award Plano Child Devel Center 1980; Sr Citizens Hall of Fame City of Chicago 1983; Hall of Fame Wendell Phillips High School 1983; Distinguished Serv Award ASALH-Chicago Branch 1989; Connectional Humanitarian Award, MDC-African Methodist Episcopal Church 1989; Golden Apple Award, The JL of Negro History, 1996; Mary McLeod Bethune Service Award, 1996; Natl Retired Educator Award, AARP, 1997. **Military Serv:** WAC tech/cpl 2 yrs; Good Conduct Medal, American Theatre; 404th ASF Band (played trumpet/french horn). **Home Addr:** 8245 So Champlain Ave, Chicago, IL 60619.

SKINNER, ELLIOTT P.
Educator. **Personal:** Born Jun 20, 1924, Port-of-Prince, Trinidad and Tobago; son of Ettice Francis and Joseph McDonald Skinner; married Gwendolyn Mikell, May 28, 1982; children: Victor, Gale, Sagha, Toure, Luce. **Educ:** New York University, University College, New York, NY, BA, 1951; Columbia University, New York, NY, MA, 1952, PhD, 1955. **Career:** Columbia University, New York, NY, assistant prof, 1957-1959; New York University, New York, NY, assistant prof, 1959-1963; Columbia University, New York, NY, associate prof, 1963-70, Franz Boas professor of anthropology, 1970-. **Orgs:** Past Pres, Assn of Black Amer Ambassadors, 1987-92; Council on Foreign Relations, 1976-; board member, Fulbright Assn, 1988-; ACLS rep for African Studies Assn, 1990-; pres, General Anthropology Section of the American Anthropological Assn, 1996-98. **Honors/Awds:** Distinguished Fulbright Professor to Ivory Coast, 1987; Woodrow Wilson International Scholor, Smithsonian Instit, 1980; Guggenheim Fellowship, Center for Adv Study in Behavorial Sciences, 1975; Grand Commander of Upper Volta National Order, 1969; Melville J Herskorits Book Award, African Studies Assn, 1975; Distinguished Africanist Award, African Studies Assn, 1985; Lincoln Univ, (Penn), Honorary Degree, 1994. **Military Serv:** US Army, Tech 4th grade, 1943-46. **Business Addr:** Franz Boas Prof of Anthropology, Columbia University, 116th and Broadway, New York, NY 10027.

SKINNER, EUGENE W.
Educator. **Personal:** Born Jul 25, 1935, Bristow, VA; son of Doris Thomas Skinner and Harrison E Skinner Sr; married Rosamond Anderson; children: Inez India, Eugene Jr, Carl Edward, Paul Wesley. **Educ:** VA Union Univ, BS 1957; Howard Univ, MS 1967; Advance Studies at Amer Univ of MD; Univ of VA; Hampton Univ; Old Domin Univ; Madison Univ; VA Tech & ST Univ, VA ST Univ, William & Mary Coll; Nova Univ; Montgomery Coll MD, OK ST Univ. **Career:** Fairfax County School Bd, science supvr VA Union Univ, asst coach 1958; Luther Jackson HS, chmn, science dept 1959-60; Luther Jackson, asst football & asst baseball coach, 1959; Vernon HS, chmn science 1960-67; Fort Hunt HS, asst principal 1981-1985; Hayfield Secondary Sub School Principal, beginning 1987, retired. **Orgs:** Mem NAACP, Urban League, Fairfax Hosp Assoc; pres Randall Civic Assoc 1969-; founder, pres Psi Nu Chap Omega Psi 1971; pres VA Union Athletic Alumni Assoc; Manassas Elks; Focus Club; mem Dept Progressive Club Inc; Fairfax Retired Teachers Assn, 1988; Fairfax Retired Coaches & Administrators Assn, 1989. **Honors/Awds:** Outstanding Sci Teacher 1961; Omega Man of the Year Psi Nu Chap 1971; Top Ten Class Leadership School; Cert of Award in Recog of Dedication in Ed to Young People, Outstanding Serv to Prof of Teaching & Guidance in Sci & Math The Joint Bd of Sci & Engrg Ed of Greater WA Area 1975; Scroll of Honor for Outstanding Serv to the Chap & the Comm Psi Nu Chap 1981; All CIAA Center Football, 1953; 25 Year Certificate of Award, Omega Psi Phi, VA Union Univ, 1989. **Military Serv:** AUS sfc 1953-55.

SKINNER, EWART C.
Educator. **Personal:** Born Jan 2, 1949. **Educ:** Univ of Hartford, Hartford, CT, 1967-69; Tarkio Coll, Tarkio, MO, BA, 1971; American Univ in Cairo, Cairo, Egypt, MA, 1974; MI State Univ, East Lansing, MI, PhD, 1984. **Career:** Self-employed media consultant, Trinidad and Tobago, 1975-79; UNESCO, Trinidad and Tobago, West Indies, 1987; MI State Univ, East Lansing, MI, instructor, 1983-84; Purdue Univ, West Lafayette, IN, asst prof, 1984-. **Orgs:** Intl Assn for Mass Communications Research; Intl Communication Assn; Intl Peace Research Assn; Semiotics Society of America; Assn for Education in Journalism ans Mass Communication; Caribbean Studies Assn. **Honors/Awds:** Specialist in Caribbean Mass Media Systems and Intl Media; Poet. **Business Addr:** Assistant Professor, Purdue University, Department of Communication, 1366 Heavilon Hall 304, West Lafayette, IN 47907-1366.

SKINNER, ROBERT L., JR.
Airline executive. **Personal:** Born Oct 5, 1941, Chicago, IL; son of Willie Louise Jemison Skinner and Robert L Skinner Sr. **Educ:** Chicago City Coll, Chicago IL, attended, 1959-61; Univ

of Wisconsin, Madison WI, attended, 1963; Northeastern Univ, Boston MA, attended, 1978-79. **Career:** American Airlines, Chicago IL, passenger serv representative, 1965-66, passenger serv mgr, 1966-69, sales representative, 1969-77, Boston MA, supvr flight serv, 1977-80, Chicago IL, account exec, 1980-84, mgr convention and company meeting sales, 1984-88, Rochester MN, gen mgr, 1988-91, gen mgr, Indianapolis, IN, 1991-96; Atlanta GA, gen manager, 1996-. **Orgs:** Bd of dir, Rochester Convention and Visitors Bureau, 1989-91. **Military Serv:** US Air Force, Airman First Class, 1961-64. **Business Addr:** General Manager, American Airlines, Hartfield Atlanta International Airport, PO Box 45238, Atlanta, GA 30320.

SKLAREK, NORMA MERRICK (NORMA MERRICK-FAIRWEATHER)
Architect (semi-retired). **Personal:** Born Apr 15, 1928, New York, NY; daughter of Amelia Willoughby Merrick and Walter Merrick; married Cornelius Welch, Oct 12, 1985; children: Gregory Ransom, David Fairweather, Susan. **Educ:** Columbia Univ NYC, BArch 1950. **Career:** Skidmore Owings Merrill, architect 1955-60; New York City Coll, arch faculty mem, 1957-60; Gruen Assoc, dir of arch 1960-80; UCLA, arch faculty mem, 1972-78; Welton Becket Assocs, vice pres 1980-85; Own architectural firm, 1985-89; Siegel-Sklarek-Diamond, AIA Architects; The Jerde Partnership, principal, 1989-92; conducts classes and seminars for the state, NCARB arch licensing exam. **Orgs:** Commr California Bd of Arch Examiners 1970-; dir LA/AIA, vp, CC/AIA 1973-; dir USC Arch Guild 1984-87; master juror for NCARB. **Honors/Awds:** First African-American Woman Licensed as an architect in the US; First African-American female Fellow of AIA; Fellow of Amer Inst of Architects 1980; YWCA of Los Angeles, Professional Achievement Award, 1987, 1989; YWCA of Cincinnati, Keynote Speaker, Award Recipient, 1990. **Special Achievements:** Guest lecturer or keynote speaker: Howard University, Columbia University, Hampton University, Southern University, Cal Poly San Louis Obispo, University of Utah, Kansas State University, Tuskegee University, Yale.

SLADE, CHRISTOPHER CARROLL
Professional football player. **Personal:** Born Jan 30, 1971, Newport News, VA. **Educ:** Univ of Virginia, attended. **Career:** New England Patriots, linebacker, 1993-. **Honors/Awds:** 1776 Quarterback Club, Defensive MVP, 1994; Pro Bowl alternate, 1995. **Business Addr:** Professional Football Player, New England Patriots, 60 Washington St, Foxboro Stadium, Foxboro, MA 02035, (508)543-7911.

SLADE, JOHN BENJAMIN, JR.
Physician. **Personal:** Born Dec 20, 1950, Columbus, OH; son of Betty Buckner and John Benjamin Slade Sr; married Rischa Ann Williams, Mar 8, 1980; children: Danielle, Alana. **Educ:** US Air Force Academy, BS, 1972; Case Western Reserve Medical School, MD, 1978. **Career:** USAF, Beale AFB, Family Practice Clinic, chief, 1981-84; USAF David Grant Medical Center, Travis AFB, family practice staff, 1984-86; USAF, Iraklion Air Station, Crete, Greece, chief, hospital services, 1986-88; USAF School of Aerospace Medicine, fellow, hyperbaric medicine, 1988-89; USAF, David Grant Medical Center, Travis AFB, chairman, Department of Hyperbaric Medicine, 1989-96, chief of the medical staff, 1996-97; Hyperbaric Medicine, Doctors Medical Center, San Pablo, CA, assoc dir, currently. **Orgs:** American Academy of Family Practice, 1981-; Aerospace Medical Association, 1989-; Wound Healing Society, 1990-. **Military Serv:** US Air Force, colonel, 1972-97, retired; Meritorious Service Medal, 1988; Legion of Merit, 1997. **Home Addr:** 131 Blackwood Ct, Vacaville, CA 95688-1058.

SLADE, KAREN E.
Business executive. **Personal:** Born Oct 18, 1955, Cleveland, OH; daughter of Violette Gohagan and Charles Slade (deceased). **Educ:** Kent State University, BS, 1977; Pepperdine University, MBA, 1991. **Career:** Xerox Corporation, senior account executive, 1978, marketing consultant, project mgr, dealer sales mgr, regional sales mgr, 1988-89; Taxi Productions, vice pres/general mgr, 1989-. **Orgs:** Urban League, board member, 1989-; MOSTE, mentoring program w/junior high school students, 1989-; Black Media Network, 1989-; National Association of Black Owned Broadcasters, 1989-. **Honors/Awds:** Peabody Award, 1992; NAACP, Image Award, Recognition of Broadcast Achievement, 1993. **Business Addr:** VP, General Mgr, Taxi Productions, Inc, DBA KJLH Radio, 161 N La Brea Ave, Inglewood, CA 90301, (310)330-5550.

SLADE, PHOEBE J.
Educator, sociologist. **Personal:** Born Oct 17, 1935, New York; married Robert H; children: Robert, Paula. **Educ:** Columbia University, EdD, 1976, MA, 1960; Jersey City State College, BS, 1958; Bellevue Nursing School, RN, 1957; Hunter College, 1954. **Career:** Jersey City State College, chair, dept of sociology and anthropology, 1985-, professor, 1977-, associate professor, 1975-77, assistant professor, 1963-74; chairman department of health sciences, 1968-69; assistant director dorm, 1966-67; Hunter College, lecturer, 1965-71; New Jersey State Deptartment Health, consultant, 1961-63; New York City Department Health, public health nurse, 1959-61. **Orgs:** Jersey City State College Faculty Association, 1963-; Association New Jersey College Faculties, 1963-; Delta Sigma Theta, 1954-; American Public Health Association, 1962-; National Council Family Relations, 1966-; Tri-State Council Family Relations, 1968-; Royal Soc Health, London, England, 1969-; National Education Association, 1972-; Board of Ethics, Teaneck, 1976-; Jersey State College, 1975-; Archdiocean Board of Education, 1976-; vice president, Hawthorne's PTA, 1977; Afro-American Committee Political Act, 1985; Mayors Special Task Force Research, Teaneck, 1985; board, Teaneck & Together, 1973-; Mayors Task Force Ed, Jersey City, 1972-; Jersey City Board Ed, 1971-74; board, Jersey City Public Library, 1970-74; Jersey City Com Criminal Justice, 1970-75; ANSSCF; HCEA; National Geographic Society; Museum of National History; New Jersey State Board of Human Services, 1991-; NAACP, 1960-; Zonta International, 1994-. **Honors/Awds:** Pi Lamda Theta, National Scholastic Organization for Women in Education, 1967; Citation Award, Com Civil Rights Met, New York, 1963; Board of Trustee's Service Award, Jersey City Public Library, 1975; Tribute to Mother's Award, Hudson County Sickle Cell Anemia Association, 1989; Teaneck Pioneer Recognition Award, Teaneck Centennial Committee of 100, 1995. **Special Achievements:** Author: "Evaluating Today's Schools: Reelevancy of the Open Classroom," NJ E Pac, May 1978; co-author: The Complete Guide to Selected Health and Health Related Careers, 1980. **Business Addr:** Sociology, Jersey City State College, 2039 Kennedy Blvd, Jersey City, NJ 07305-1527.

SLADE, WALTER R., JR.
Physician. **Personal:** Born Nov 11, 1918, Knightsdale, NC; son of Blonnie Pair Slade and S Walter R Slade; married Ruth D Sims. **Educ:** St Augustine's Coll, BS tchrs cert 1939; Meharry Med Coll, MD 1947. **Career:** Brooklyn VA Med Ctr, staff Neurologist 1954-59, staff psychiatrist 1960-1962, staff neurologist 1963-1970, chief neurology 1970-. **Orgs:** Attending neurologist Kingsbrook Jewish Med Ctr 1966-; Kings Cty Hosp Ctr 1967-; clinical prof Downstate Med Ctr 1980-; consult Baptist Hosp of Brooklyn 1973-80; bd trustees Kingsbrook Jewish Med Ctr 1976-77; vice pres Midwood Dev Corp 1980-; Amer Coll of Angiology 1978-; chmn of the bd Midwood Devel Corp 1985. **Honors/Awds:** Doctor of the Year Award TAN Magazine 1952; Family of the Year Award Brooklyn Council of Churches 1982; Distinguished Brotherhood Award William Moss Brotherhood 1979; living treas View from the Torch 1986; editor, Geriatric Neurology, 1980; editor, Angiology (journal), 1970-; more than 30 publications 1950-88; past president medical/dental staff, Kingsbrook, JMC; vice president, American College Angiology, 1987-88. **Business Addr:** Chief Neurology Service, Brooklyn VA Med Ctr, 800 Poly Place, Brooklyn, NY 11209.

SLASH, JOSEPH A.
Business executive, CPA. **Personal:** Born Aug 25, 1943, Huntington, WV; son of Clara Rose Slash and Joseph Autumn Slash; married Meredith; children: Alexandria Dawson, Adrianne Letetia. **Educ:** Marshall Univ, BBA 1966. **Career:** Sears Roebuck & Co, comptroller asst 1966; Arthur Young & Co, audit mgr 1968-78; City of Indianapolis IN, dep mayor 1978-89; Indianapolis Power & Light Co, Indianapolis, IN, vice pres, 1989-. **Orgs:** United Way Greater Indianapolis; mem Indiana Assoc CPA's Adv Forum 1976-78, Amer Inst CPA, Indiana Assoc CPA's; bd of dir Indianapolis Chap Indiana Assoc CPA's; mem Kappa Alpha Psi, Alpha Eta Boule, Sigma Pi Phi; bd of dirs, United Way of Central Indiana, 1985-; exec comm, Commission for Downtown, 1991-; exec comm, Indiana Sports Corp, 1991-. **Honors/Awds:** Outstanding Black Alumni, Marshall Univ, 1986; Professional Achievement Award, Center for Leadership Devel, 1987; Kappa of the Month, Kappa Alpha Psi, 1978. **Home Addr:** 1140 Fox Hill Dr, Indianapolis, IN 46208. **Business Addr:** Vice President, General Services, Indianapolis Power & Light Co, PO Box 1595, Indianapolis, IN 46206.

SLATER, HELENE FORD SOUTHERN
Public relations executive. **Personal:** Born in Philadelphia, PA; daughter of Henrietta B Ford-Southern (deceased) and William B Southern (deceased); married Chester E Slater (divorced). **Educ:** New School for Social Rsch, BA, 1955, MA 1959; Howard Univ, Temple Univ, City Coll of NY, Yeshiva Univ, Fordham Univ, Bank State Coll of Ed, Postgraduate. **Career:** Various newspapers, reporter, columnist, feature writer 1940-; New York City Bd of Ed, teacher retired; Southern-Slater Enterprises Public Relations, pres, 1955-. **Orgs:** Editor, The Acorn, LKM House Org, 1960-65, 1978-81; mem of bd, 1963-65, 1977-81, NW regional dir, 1967-68, NE regional dir, 1968-70 Lambda Kappa Mu Sor Inc, Natl Epistoleus; natl publ relations dir, 1969-71, 1973-75, 1978-83, 1984; Natl Assn of Media Women Inc; chmn, Natl Const 1971-73; public relations specialist, publicity dir, 1970-85; Shirley Chisholm Comm Action Assn, 1972; pres, Howard Univ Alumni Club of New York City, 1975-79; public relations dir, UNCF/Arthur Ashe Tennis Benefit, 1978-82; mem, Amer Social Soc, Natl Assn of Univ Women, Negro Business & Professional Women's Club, 100 Black Women, Bd of New Harlem YWCA. **Honors/Awds:** Citation of Merit, Lambda Kappa Mu Sor, 1973; Founders Cup, Natl Assn of Media Women Inc, 1974; Certificate of Merit, Howard Univ Alumni Club of New York City, 1975; Distinguished Serv Key Lambda Kappa Mu Sorority, 1977; Achievement Award, Howard Univ Alumni Club of New York City, 1980; Outstanding Person in Communications, WNYE-FM Medgar Evers Coll Comm Radio 1983; Prizes for Excellence in Latin & Greek upon grad from HS; Citation-Honorary Barbadian, Barbados Bd of Tourism, 1983; Special Recognition Award for Excellence in Public Relations and Editorial Ability, Lambda Kappa Mu Sorority, 1987. **Business Addr:** President, Southern-Slater Enterprises, 1060 Amsterdam Avenue, #216, New York, NY 10025.

SLATER, JACKIE RAY
Professional football player (retired). **Personal:** Born May 27, 1954, Jackson, MS; married Annie; children: Matthew. **Educ:** Jackson State Univ, BA; Livingston Univ, MS, currently. **Career:** Los Angeles Rams, offensive tackle, 1976-89, 1993-. **Orgs:** Active in Rams' Speaker's Bureau during off season. **Honors/Awds:** All-American (Pittsburgh Courier) at Jackson State; played in College All-Star game after senior season; first recipient of Walter Payton Physical Education Award, Jackson State; All-NFC and All-NFL (second team), UPI, 1983, 1985; named All-NFC, Football News, 1985; played in Pro Bowl, 1983, 1985-89 seasons.

SLATER, PHYLLIS HILL
Company executive. **Personal:** Born Oct 16, 1945, New York, NY; daughter of Yvonne Redding Hill and Philbert D Hill; married Gordon H Slater (divorced 1976); children: Gina, Lisa, Tanya. **Educ:** Bronx Community College, Bronx, NY; Nassau Community College, Nassau County, Long Island, NY. **Career:** Hill, Jenkins, Gaudt & Assoc, Lynbrook, NY, principal administrator, 1969-85; Hill Slater Inc, Lynbrook, NY, president, 1984-. **Orgs:** Trustee, National Minority Business Council, 1987-90; director, Long Island Association, 1989-; director, WLIW Public Television, 1989-; director, SUNY Old Westbury Foundation, 1990-; assoc trustee, North Shore University Hospital, 1991-; president, Natl Assn of Women Business Owners, 1987-89. **Honors/Awds:** Excellence in Business, SUNY/Old Westbury, 1991; Leadership Woman of Record, The Women's Record, 1990; Women in Business, US Small Business Association, 1987; Business Recognition, Negro Business & Professional Women Club, 1988; Path Finder, Town of Hempstead, NY, 1990. **Business Addr:** President, Hill Slater Inc, Engineering & Architectural Support Systems, 149 Broadway, Lynbrook, NY 11563.

SLATER, REGGIE (REGINALD DWAYNE)
Professional basketball player. **Personal:** Born Aug 27, 1970, Houston, TX. **Career:** Argal Huesca (Spain), forward, 1992-93; Denver Nuggets, 1994-95; Portland Trail Blazers, 1995; Denver Nuggets, 1996; Dallas Mavericks, 1996; Chicago Rockers (CBA), 1996; Toronto Raptors, 1996-98; Portland Trail-Blazers, 1998-. **Business Addr:** Professional Basketball Player, Portland TrailBlazers, One Center Ct, Portland, OR 97227, (503)234-9291.

SLATER, RODNEY E.
Government official. **Personal:** Born Feb 23, 1955, Tutwiler, MS; married Cassandra Wilkins; children: one daughter. **Educ:** Eastern MI Univ, BS 1977; Univ of AR, JD 1980. **Career:** State Atty General's Office, asst atty 1980-82; AR Gov Bill Clinton, staff special assistant 1983-85, exec asst 1985-87; AR Hwy & Transportation, commissioner; AR State Univ, dir of govt relations, beginning 1987; US Federal Highway Administration, federal highway administrator, 1993-96; Secretary of Transportation, 1997-. **Orgs:** Campaign mgr Gov Bill Clinton's Staff 1982-86; pres W Harold Flowers Law Soc; founding mem AR Children's Hosp Comm for the Future; former bd mem GW Carver YMCA of Little Rock; mem John Gammon Scholarship Found of AR, former bd mem United Cerebral Palsy of Central AR; appointed by Fed Judge Henry Woods to serve as mem of Eastern District of AR Comm on the Bicentennial of the US Constitution; volunteer & supporter of Boy Scouts of Amer, Gyst House, March of Dimes, Sickle Cell Anemia Found, Thurgood Marshall Scholarship Fund, United Negro Coll Fund; mem Eastern Arkansas Area Council bd of dir of the Boy Scouts of Amer; mem AR Advocates for Children and Families Bd of Dir; Sec-Treasurer of the AR Bar Assn; mem Commission on AR's Future; bd mem, John Gammon Scholarship Foundation of Arkansas; numerous others. **Honors/Awds:** Elton Rynearson Grid Scholar Award, 1976; Eastern Michigan Univ Top Ten Student Award, 1977; Eastern Michigan Univ Natl Championship Forensics Team 1977; Univ Political Science Hon Soc of Phi Sigma Alpha. **Business Addr:** U.S. Department of Transportation, 400 7th St SW, Rm 10200, Washington, DC 20590.

SLATON, GWENDOLYN C.
Librarian. **Personal:** Born Jun 19, 1945, Philadelphia, PA; daughter of LaFronia Delorial Dunbar Childs and George Alexander Childs; married Harrison Allen Slaton, Sep 17, 1966; children: Kimberly Dawn, Leigh Alison. **Educ:** Pennsylvania State University, University Park, PA, BA, history, 1970; Seton Hall University, South Orange, NJ, MA, education, 1975; Rutgers University, New Brunswick, NJ, MLS, 1982. **Career:** Essex County College, Newark, NJ, librarian, 1976-81, library administrator, 1981-. **Orgs:** Board of dirs, Family Service Child Guidance Center, 1977-83; advisory board, Youth Center/South Orange-Maplewood, 1983-89; exec board, Essex-Hudson Re-

gional Library Coop, 1986-91; secretary, Maplewood Cultural Commission, 1986-91; member, Delta Sigma Theta Sorority, 1966-; member, Delta Sigma Theta Sorority, North Jersey Alumnae Chapter, 1982-, pres, 1993-95. **Home Addr:** 620 Prospect St, Maplewood, NJ 07040. **Business Addr:** Associate Dean/Learning Resources, Essex County College, 303 University Ave, Newark, NJ 07102.

SLAUGHTER, CAROLE D.
Testing expert. **Personal:** Born Jul 27, 1945, Chatanooga, TN; daughter of Rebecca Jones and Preston Jones; married Thomas F Slaughter Jr; children: Kelli, Eric. **Educ:** Douglass Coll-Rutgers Univ, AB 1972; Princeton Univ, MA 1975. **Career:** Educ Testing Services, assoc examiner 1974-79, grad record exams assoc program dir & dir develop 1979-86, coll & univ programs prog dir 1986-87, Office of Corp Secretary, dir, 1987. **Orgs:** Chairperson ETS Comm on Personnel Equity 1983-85; chairperson League of Women Voters Women's Rights Study Group; mem Highland Park NJ School Bd. **Honors/Awds:** Ford Foundation Fellowship 1972-76; Test Preparation Specialist. **Business Addr:** Dir, Office of Corp Sec, Educational Testing Service, Rosedale Rd, Princeton, NJ 08541.

SLAUGHTER, FRED L.
Educator, attorney. **Personal:** Born Mar 13, 1942, Santa Cruz, CA; married Kay Valerie Johnson; children: Hilary Spring, Fred Wallace. **Educ:** UCLA, BS 1964, MBA 1966; Columbia U, JD 1969. **Career:** Practicing atty 1970-; School of Law, UCLA, asst dean, lecturer 1971-80; real est broker 1974-; assoc campus advocate 1971-72; spec asst to chnclr 1969-71. **Orgs:** Mem LA Co, CA St Am Bar Asn; licensed to prac law before the US Supreme Ct, US Fed Cts, CA St Cts; life mem UCLA Alumni Assn. **Home Addr:** Box 3522, Santa Monica, CA 90408.

SLAUGHTER, JEWELL L.
Insurance company executive. **Personal:** Born Nov 24, 1924, Lagrange, GA; son of Samuel & Azella Slaughter; married Ann Slaughter, Oct 15, 1943; children: Aaron, Juanita Kirsey, Larry. **Educ:** Tennessee State Univ; Life Underwriters Training Council, graduate. **Career:** Willie Burton Insurance Agency, 1958-60; Mammoth Life Insurance Co, 1960-85; Wright Mutual Insurance Co, 1985-. **Orgs:** Temple Bapt Church Credit Union, auditor, pres, 1960-75; Natl Insurance Assn, Agency Division, asst sect; Longacre St Block Club, past pres; Schoolcraft Improvement Assn; Wright Mut Ins Co., board of directors; National Ins Association, sec, mktg section, 1996, bd of dirs, 1997, elected vp of mktg section, 1997. **Honors/Awds:** Winner of Class AAA Olive Trophy, Natl Insurance Assn; Life Insurance Agency Management Assn, Certificate; Universal Sales Training Agencies, Certificate; Life Insurance Mktg & Research Assn; Certificate; Wayne County Bd of Commissioners, Certificate of Appreciation; Recipient of the Thelma J Hall Award; Office of Wayne County Execs, Community Service Award; Certificate of Appreciation, City of Memphis TN, 1996; Certificate for Outstanding Svcs/Appointed Legislative Advisor, State Senate, State of TN, 1996; Silver Awd, National Ins Weeks New Business Production Leader, National Ins Association, 1996; numerous others. **Special Achievements:** NIA Examiner Issue II, p 4, July 1994. **Military Serv:** Army, corporal, 1943-46; Marksmanship Award, 1943. **Business Addr:** VP, Agency Director, Wright Mutual Insurance Co, 2995 E Grand Blvd, Detroit, MI 48202, (313)871-2112.

SLAUGHTER, JOHN BROOKS
Educational administrator. **Personal:** Born Mar 16, 1934, Topeka, KS; son of Reuben Brooks and Dora (Reeves) Slaughter; married Ida Bernice Johnson, Aug 31, 1956; children: John II, Jacqueline Michelle. **Educ:** KS State Univ, BSEE, 1956; UCLA, MS, Eng, 1961; Univ of CA-San Diego, PhD, Eng Sci 1971. **Career:** General Dynamics Convair, electronics engineer, 1956-60; Naval Elec Lab Center, 1960-75, div head 1965-71, dept head 1971-75; Applied Physics Lab Univ of WA, dir 1975-77; Natl Science Fnd, asst dir 1977-79; WA St Univ, acad vice pres and provost 1979-80; Natl Science Fnd, dir 1980-82; Univ of MD Coll Park, chancellor, 1982-88; Occidental Coll, president, 1988-. **Orgs:** Pres Zeta Sigma Lambda Chap of Alpha Phi Alpha 1956-60; board of directors San Diego Urban League 1962-66; mem San Diego Transit Corp 1968-75; mem Amer Assoc Adv ofSci 1984-; board of directors Baltimore Gas and Elec Co 1984-88; bd dir Comm Credit Co 1983-88; bd of dirs Sovran Bank 1985-88; Medical Mutual Liability Insurance Soc of MD 1986-88; Nat Collegiate Athletic Assn, chairman President's commission, 1986-88; board of directors Martin Marietta Corp 1987; LA World Affairs Council, board of directors 1990-96; Town Hall of California, bd of governors, 1990-94; board of directors Monsanto Co., 1983-; board of directors IBM, 1988-; board of directors Northern Grumman, 1993-; board of directors Avery Dennison, 1989-; board of directors Atlantic Richfield, 1989-. **Honors/Awds:** UCLA, Distinguished Alumnus of the Year Award, 1978; NSF, Distinguished Service Award, 1979; Kansas State Univ, Service in Engineering Award, 1981; Univ of California-San Diego, Distinguished Alumnus of the Year Award, 1982; Topeka High School Hall of Fame, 1983; American Society of Engineering Education Hall of Fame, 1993; Kansas Native Sons and Daughters, Kansan of the Year, 1994. **Business Addr:** President, Occidental College, 1600 Campus Rd, Los Angeles, CA 90041, (213)259-2500.

SLAUGHTER, JOHN ETTA
Educator. **Personal:** Born Nov 3, 1929, Beaumont, TX; married Murray L Slaughter; children: JoAnne Brunson, Beverly Janine. **Educ:** Howard University, BA, MA, 1946-51. **Career:** San Antonio Independent School District, teacher, 1957-69; St Philip's College, professor history, 1969-, chairman social sciences, 1978-. **Orgs:** Faculty senate president, St Philips College, 1978-80; project director grants, NEH, TCH, TCA, 1980-85; Phi Delta Kappa, Delta Kappa Gamma, Texas Junior College Teachers Association; scholarship chairman, Delta Sigma Theta; NAACP; president, San Antonio Alumnae Chapter, Delta Sigma Theta; Bexar County Historical Commission; Martin Luther King Memoiral City County Commission. **Honors/Awds:** Graduate Scholarship in History, Howard University; Master Teacher Award, University of Texas, Austin. **Business Addr:** Chairman, Social Sciences Department, St Philips College, 2111 Nevada St, San Antonio, TX 78203.

SLAUGHTER, PETER
Physician. **Personal:** Born May 15, 1928, Detroit; married Geraldine; children: Chevon, Karen, Tracy. **Educ:** Wayne U, BS 1955; Univ of MI, MD 1963. **Career:** Samaritan, medical dir; Clinical Operations, Dmic Prescad, dir. **Orgs:** Mem Detrt Ped Soc. **Honors/Awds:** Felw Am Acad of Ped 1973; Spec Acvmnt Galen's Hon Soc 1961. **Military Serv:** AUS sfc 1950-52. **Business Addr:** Midical Dir, Samaritan, 10201 E Jefferson, Detroit, MI 48226.

SLAUGHTER, VERNON L.
Attorney. **Personal:** Born in Omaha, NE. **Educ:** Univ of NE Lincoln, BA 1972. **Career:** CBS Records Washington DC, local promo mgr 1973-76; CBS Records NY, assoc dir album prmo 1976-77, dir jazz/prog mktg 1977-79; Katz, Smith & Cohen, entertainment attorney, currently. **Orgs:** Mem Country Music Assoc 1976-80; mem exec council Black Music Assoc 1980. **Honors/Awds:** Black Achievers Awd Harlem YMCA New York City 1980. **Business Addr:** Entertainment Attorney, Katz, Smith & Cohen, 3423 Piedmont Rd, Ste 200, Atlanta, GA 30305, (404)237-7700.

SLAUGHTER-DEFOE, DIANA T.
Psychologist, educator. **Personal:** Born Oct 28, 1941, Chicago, IL; daughter of Gwendolyn Malva Armstead and John Ison Slaughter; married Michael Defoe, Sep 16, 1989 (divorced). **Educ:** BA (with Honors) 1962, MA 1964, PhD 1968, The University of Chicago. **Career:** Univ of Chicago Grad School of Educ, rsch assoc 1966-67; Howard Univ School of Med, instr in psychiatry 1967-68; Yale Univ School of Med, asst prof psych 1968-70; Univ of Chicago, asst prof behavioral sci human devel, educ 1970-77; Northwestern Univ, asst prof 1977-80, assoc prof 1980-90, professor 1990-. **Orgs:** Mem African Seminar sponsored by Inst for Intl Educ in New York & Inst for African Studies Univ of Ghana 1972; elected chairperson Black Caucus of the Soc for Rsch in Child Devel 1979-81; appt Natl Adv Bd of Child Abuse & Neglect 1979-81; elected mem Governing Council Soc for Rsch in Child Devel 1981-87; mem Soc Rsch Child Devel Study Tour to the Peoples Republic of China 1984; mem Amer psych Assn, Soc for Rsch in Child Devel, Amer Educ Rsch Assn, Natl Assn Black Psych, Groves Conf on the Family, Delta Sigma Theta, Natl Assoc Educ of Young Children; American Psychological Association, bd of ethnic & minority affairs, 1986-88, bdo of scientific affairs, 1995-97; mem Committee on Child Development Research and Public Policy, National Research Council, 1987-92; bd of dir, Ancona School, Chicago IL, 1989-91; mem adv panel, Head StaBureau, ACF, 1988-. **Honors/Awds:** First Pi Lambda Distinguished Rsch Awd for Most Outstanding Thesis conducted by women in educ 1969; first Black Scholar Achievement Award, Black Caucus of the Society for Research in Child Development, 1987-; published books, Visible Now: Blacks in Private Schools (Greenwood Press) 1988, and Black Children and Poverty: A Developmental Perspective (Jossey-Bass Press) 1988; Elected Fellow, American Psychological Association, 1993; Distinguished Contribution to Researching Public Policy, American Psychological Association, 1994. **Business Addr:** Professor, Northwestern University, School of Education & Social Policy, 2115 N Campus Dr, Evanston, IL 60208.

SLEET, GREGORY M.
Attorney. **Personal:** marrled Mary G Sleet. **Career:** District of Delaware, US attorney, 1994-. **Orgs:** Delaware, Pennsylvannia, New York State Bars; American Bar Association; National Bar Association. **Honors/Awds:** NAACP Freedom Fund Distinguished Service Award, 1994. **Special Achievements:** First African American US attorney for Delaware. **Business Addr:** US Attorney, State of Delaware, Chemical Bank Plaza, 1201 Market St., Ste. 1100, Wilmington, DE 19899-2046, (302)573-6277.

SLIE, SAMUEL N.
Educator, clergyman. **Personal:** Born Jun 8, 1925, Branford, CT; son of Hannah Brown Slie and Robert Slie. **Educ:** Springfield Clge, BS 1949; Yale Div Schl, BD 1952, STM 1963; NY Theological Seminary, Dr of Ministry 1985. **Career:** Natl Student Council YMCA, southern area staff 1952-55; Student Christian Movement, United Church of Christ staff 1955-63; Yale Univ, assoc pastor and lecturer in higher educ 1965-; Southern CT State Univ, dir united ministry in higher educ 1976-86; coordinator Downtown Cooperative Ministry, New Haven 1986-94. **Orgs:** Mem United Church of Christ Task Force on World Hunger 1972-73; corp mem United Church Bd World Ministries 1973-81; past pres Natl Campus Ministers Assn 1973-74; mem Theological Comm Worlds Alliance of YMCA's 1981-86; treas CT United Nations Assn USA 1984-92; adv council Natl Ecumenical Student Christian Council 1984-86. **Honors/Awds:** Distinguished Serv Awd Alpha Phi Omega Gamma Eta, Springfield Coll, 1949; Intl Distinguished Serv Awd, Natl YMCA Boston, 1981; Elm-Ivy Awd for Contributions to Town-Govt Relations by Mayor of New Haven and Pres of Yale Univ 1985; distinguished educational service Dixwell Community House 1989; National Negro Professional & Business Women, New Haven Chapter, Man of the Year, 1991; Distinguished Alumnus Award, Yale Divinity School, 1993. **Special Achievements:** Author of articles: "The Black Church in Theology;" "Identity in the United Church of Christ," 1990; article The New National Ecumenical Journal 1981. **Military Serv:** US Army infantry staff sgt 1943-46; Mediteranean and European Theatre Medals, 2 Battle Stars, Combat Infantry Medal. **Home Addr:** 188 W Walk, West Haven, CT 06516. **Business Addr:** Associate Pastor, Church of Christ, Yale University, PO Box 200258, New Haven, CT 06520.

SLOAN, ALBERT J. H., II
Educational administrator. **Personal:** Born Aug 24, 1942, Atlanta, GA; married Emma Lillian; children: Ashaki Nicole. **Educ:** Albany State College, BA; Interdenominational Theological Center, MDiv; Miles Law School, JD; further study at various institutions. **Career:** City of Atlanta Recreational Department, center director, 1968-69; Alabama State University, Upward Bound, counselor, assistant director, 1969-71; Miles College, professor, dean of chapel, dean of students, president, currently. **Orgs:** Omega Psi Phi, Alpha Phi chapter; National Bar Association; Fairfield City Board of Education, president; Alabama Council on Human Relations, board; Montgomery Association for Retarded Children, board; NAACP; pastor of numerous denominations. **Honors/Awds:** Omega Man of the Year, 1965, Outstanding Achievement Award, 1971, Omega Psi Phi; Ford Foundation Fellow. **Business Addr:** President, Miles College, PO Box 3800, Birmingham, AL 35208, (205)923-2771.

SLOAN, DAVID E.
Attorney. **Personal:** Born Apr 23, 1923, Baltimore, MD; son of Zelia Sloan and Eugene Sloan; married Jo Rogers; children: 1. **Educ:** St Coll, AB 1944; Howard Univ, JD 1950; Temple Univ, grad cert 1970. **Career:** DC law practice 1954-65; Afro-Amer News Baltimore, sr ed 1966-71; private practice, 1971-; Baltimore Contractors, house counsel 1971-. **Orgs:** Org Urban Task Force BS Amer, Amer Bar Assn, DC Bar Assn, NAACP, Urban League, Alpha Phi Alpha, Baltimore City Bar Assn, MD Bar Assn; member, Baltimore School Board, 1976-79; chairman, Baltimore Frontiers Intl, 1981-82; hearing officer, Baltimore City Civil Service Dept, 1991-. **Military Serv:** USNR 1944-46. **Home Addr:** 5315 Norwood Ave, Baltimore, MD 21207.

SLOAN, EDITH BARKSDALE
Attorney. **Personal:** Born Nov 29, 1940, New York, NY; married E Ned Sloan; children: Douglass Ned. **Educ:** Hunter Coll, BA 1960; Cath Univ of Am, JD 1974. **Career:** Cncl on Std Travel, mgr of info office 1960-61; US Peace Corps Philippines, 1962-64; Eleanor Roosevelt Human Rel NY Urban League, intern 1964-65; US Commn on Civil Rights, pub info spce 1965-68; Natl Com on Household Emp, exec dir/cnsl 1969-75; DC Office of Consumer Protection, dir 1976-77; US ConsumerProduct Safety Commn, 1978-. **Orgs:** Mem PA Bar 1974, DC Bar 1977; mem Community Adv Com Howard Univ Cancer Rsch Ctr, Women's Div Nat Bar Assn, Inst on Women Today; adv com Natl Ctr Policy Rev; mem bd dir The Lupis Fndtn; fndr Black Am Law Stds Assoc; Catholic Univ; Delta Sigma Theta Inc; bd mem Greater Washington Rsch Ctr, Natl Consumers League, Public Voice. **Honors/Awds:** Adam Clayton Powell Award 1974; named One of 75 Outstndng Black Women in Pub Srv 1974; subject of NBC-TV Documentary "a woman is " 1974. **Business Addr:** Attorney at Law, 1200 29th St NW, Washington, DC 20007.

SLOAN, MACEO ARCHIBALD
Business executive (retired). **Personal:** Born Aug 10, 1913, Newport, AR; married Charlotte Kennedy (deceased); children: Sylvia S Black, Maceo K. **Educ:** Prairie View State Coll, BS, 1937; Wharton Sch Univ of PA, Temple Univ, CLU Seminars Univ of WI. **Career:** NC Mutual Life Ins Co, agent, asst mgr, exec asst mgr, asst agency dir, vice chmn prod, exec vp, vice chmn bd of dirs 1938-86. **Orgs:** Emeritus bd mem Salvation Army Natl Adv Cncl, Salvation Army Boy's Club Adv Bd; former mem bd govrs Univ of NC; former bd mem Natl Bus League; Fund for the Advancement of Sci & Math Educ in NC; past chmn bd Fed Reserve Bank of Richmond; Amer Soc Chartered Life Underwriters, Amer Mgmt Assn; former pres & chmn bd Natl Ins Assn; Durham Comm on the Affairs of Black People; Alpha Phi Alpha; Sigma Pi Phi. **Honors/Awds:** Cert of Achievement Prairie View State Coll 1955; Cert Quarter Million Dollar Round Table Natl Ins Assn; Honorary Dr of Laws, Livingstone Coll, 1977. **Home Addr:** 2100 Otis St, Durham, NC 27707.

SLOAN, MACEO KENNEDY
Investment manager. **Personal:** Born Oct 18, 1949, Philadelphia, PA; son of Charlotte Kennedy Sloan and Maceo Archibald Sloan; married Melva Iona Wilder; children: Maceo S, Malia K. **Educ:** Morehouse Coll, BA 1971; Georgia State Univ, MBA (w/Honors) 1973; NC Central Univ Law School, JD (w/Honors) 1979. **Career:** NC Mutual Life Insurance Co, investment analyst trainee 1973-75, investment analyst 1975-77, asst to treasurer 1977-78, asst vice pres 1978-83, treasurer 1983-85, vice pres/treasurer 1985-86; NCCU School of Law, adjunct visiting prof 1979-86; Study Seminar for Financial Analysts, workshop review leader 1980-; Moore & Van Allen Attorneys at Law, of counsel 1985-86; NCM Capital Mgmt Group Inc, president/CEO beginning 1986; Sloan Financial Group Inc, chair, pres/CEO, currently. **Orgs:** Mem Financial Analysts Federation 1974-; mem Durham Chamber of Commerce 1974-; mem, vice pres 1977-78 NC Soc of Financial Analysts 1974-; bd of visitors NCCU School of Law 1979-86; mem NC State Bar 1979-; bd of dirs Mechanics & Farmers Bank 1979-; bd of dirs Natl Insurance Assoc 1980-; bd of dirs United Way of Durham 1980-89; vice chmn/treas Urban Ministries of Durham 1983-88; mem Univ Club 1986-, The Georgetown Club 1988-; founder & chairman Natl Investment Managers Assn. **Honors/Awds:** Resolution in Appreciation The Durham City Council; Certificate of Service city of Durham; Outstanding Service as Pres Better Business Bureau 1980; Freedmon Guard Award, Durham Jaycees 1981; Outstanding Leadership Award, United Way Durham 1984; featured on "Bridgebuilders," 1998. **Business Addr:** President/CEO, Sloan Financial Group Inc, Two Mutual Plaza, 501 Willard St, Durham, NC 27701.

SLOCUMB, HEATHCLIFF
Professional baseball player. **Personal:** Born Jun 7, 1966, Brooklyn, NY; son of Mattie Louise & Karl Paul Slocumb; married Deborah, Mar 4, 1986 (deceased); children: Jessica, Heather. **Career:** Chicago Cubs, pitcher, 1991-93; Cleveland Indians, 1993; Philadelphia Phillies, 1993-96; Boston Red Sox, 1996-97; Seattle Mariners, 1997-. **Special Achievements:** Winner of 1995 All-Star Game. **Business Addr:** Professional Baseball Player, Seattle Mariners, 83 King St, 3rd Fl, PO Box 4100, Seattle, WA 98104, (206)628-3555.

SLOSS, MINERVA A.
Educator (retired). **Personal:** Born Jun 2, 1921, Waco, TX; daughter of Ruby M Jones and Earnest Grantt; married Curley L Sloss Sr; children: Curley L Jr. **Educ:** Wiley Coll, Marshall, TX, AB, 1942; Univ of Oklahoma, Norman, OK, Master Sec Educ, 1953; Central State Univ, Edmond OK, Certificate, Guidance and Counseling, 1970. **Career:** Oklahoma City Public School, attendance secretary, 1947-49, English and journalism teacher, 1949-69, sec guidance counselor, 1969-75, language arts consultant, 1975-77; Rose State Coll, English instructor, 1977-1986 (retired); Part-time English teacher, Rose State Coll, 1988-retirement. **Orgs:** Pres Okalahoma City Minority Pol Assc Women, 1984-; area I chairperson, Okalahoma Conf WMS 12th Epis Dist AME; 1st vice pres Avery Chapel AME Church WMS 1978-; workshop coord Oklahoma Delta Sigma Theta's Membership Seminar, 1984; regl dir Central Region Delta Sigma Theta Inc 1961-66; parliamentarian Blanche M Bruner Order of the Eastern Star, 1982-86; mem Natl Council of Teachers of English, Rose State Coll Faculty Assn; chairperson Tenure Comm Rose State Coll Humanities Div, 1983-84; rep Annual Scholastic Contest Humanities Div; mem North Central State Cert Team Putnam City JHS, 1983-84; mem sponsor Phi Theta Kappa Honorary Soc Rose State Coll; mem Oklahoma City Set Club Inc, Links Inc; part time english teacher, Rose State Coll, 1988; bd of dir, SunbeamHome Serv, 1987; equity comm, Ohoma City Public Schools, 1988; area I chairperson, Oklahoma, Conf, WMS,12th African Methodist Episcopal. **Honors/Awds:** Fellowship Grant Wall St Journal, 1961; articles pub in The Black Chronicle The Former Black Dispatch, Oklahoma Today, Oklahoma Educ Journal For English Teachers, Oklahoman and Times, Oklahoma Sage, Pittsburg Courier and Kansas City Coll. **Home Addr:** 12120 NE 50th Street, Spencer, OK 73084.

SMALL, ISADORE, III
Sales engineer. **Personal:** Born Apr 27, 1944, Pontiac, MI; married Earline Olivia Washington; children: Michael, Brian, Vanessa. **Educ:** Univ of MI, BS Elect Engr 1967; Wayne State Univ, Masters Bus Admin 1981. **Career:** Cutler-hammer Inc Milwaukee WI, design engr 1967-74; Detroit MI, sales engr 1974-82; Eaton Corp Southfield MI, sales mgr 1982-83; Eaton Corp Grand Rapids MI, sales engr 1984-. **Orgs:** Mem Soc of Automotive Engr 66-67; Assc of Iron and Steel Engr 1974-84; Elect Manuf Rep Assc 1979-; state youth dir Churchs of God WI 1969-74; Alpha PiOmega Frat 66-67; chrmn bd of trustees Metropolitan Church of God 1974-84; chrmn Bus Assembly; Men of Church of God, state men's cabinet, 1983-90; Division of Church Extension, chair, 1988-94; Orchard View Church of God, church council chairman, 1987-93; Kentwood Schools Legislative Committee, parent advisory, 1986-91; National Division of Church Extension, Church of God, 1994-. **Honors/Awds:** Electronic Patent US Patent Office 1972, 1974; Eaton Soc of Inventors 1980; Man of the Year, 1984. **Business Addr:** Executive Sales Engineer, Eaton Corp, 161 Ottawa NW, Grand Rapids, MI 49503.

SMALL, ISRAEL G.
Administrator. **Personal:** Born Feb 26, 1941, Rincon, GA; married Jenetha Jenkins. **Educ:** Savannah St Coll, BS 1963; GA S Coll, Grad Study; Ft Valley St Coll; Univ of GA; Comm Planning & Evaluation Inst, Washington DC. **Career:** Bur of Pub Dev, Savannah, dir, hum serv 1985; City of Savannah, model cities admin; Model Cities Prog, served in various capacities 1970. **Orgs:** Mem Kappa Alpha Psi; past mem GA Tchrs Ed Assn; Nat Ed Assn; Am Tchrs Assn; YMCA; Savannah Drug Abuse Adv Cncl; mem NAACP; mem People United toSave Humanity; completed training in Municipal & Comm Plng. **Military Serv:** AUS e-5 1966-68.

SMALL, KENNETH LESTER
Association executive. **Personal:** Born Oct 1, 1957, New York, NY; son of Catherine Johnson Small and Julius Small; married Patricia A Cooper, Nov 8, 1988; children: Catherine Louise. **Educ:** Fordham Univ at Lincoln Center, BA 1979; Long Island Univ at Brooklyn Center, MA 1981. **Career:** Long Island Univ, rsch asst 1979-80, adjunct prof, currently; Bureau of Labor Statistics US Dept of Labor, economist 1980-81; The New York Public Library, information asst 1981-84; Natl Urban League, New York, NY, program evaluator, 1984-86; Natl Urban League, Inc, asst dir, 1985-86, exec asst 1986-89, strategic planner, 1986-95, assoc dir, research and evaluation, 1994-95; Citizen Advice Bureau, dev dir, 1995-; KTL Associates, prin consultant, 1990-; Sphinx Communications Group, associate consultant, 1989-. **Orgs:** New York Urban League; Natl Economic Assoc, 1990-; Co-op Amer; Friends of the Black Scholar; Hunger Action Network of New York State, board member, 1993-95; National Coalition of Blacks for Reparations in America, mem, 1993-. **Honors/Awds:** Connolly School Graduate Assistantship, Long Island University, 1979-80; HW Wilson Scholarship, Pratt Institute, 1990. **Home Addr:** 1485 Park Ave, Apt 17C, New York, NY 10029-3525. **Business Addr:** Dev Director, Citizens Advice Bureau, 2054 Morris Ave, Bronx, NY 10453-3538, (718)365-0910.

SMALL, LILY B.
Educator. **Personal:** Born Sep 1, 1934, Trelawny, Jamaica; married Sylvester; children: Dale Andrew, Donna Marie. **Educ:** California State University, Fresno, BA, 1970, MA, 1971; University of Pacific, Stockton, California, EdD, 1976. **Career:** California State University, Fresno, California, associate professor, affirmative action coordinator, 1975-; Stockton University School District, Stockton, California, reading specialist, 1973-74; Ministry of Education, Kingston, Jamaica, teacher. **Orgs:** American Association for Affirmative Action; American Association of University Women; San Joaquin Reading Association; chapter sec, Phi Kappa Phi, 1978-80; teacher, supr, Sun School Church of God; Black Faculty & Staff Association. **Honors/Awds:** Nominated Member, Phi Kappa Phi, UOP, Stockton, California, 1976. **Business Addr:** Ethnic Studies, California State University, Fresno, 2225 E San Ramon, Fresno, CA 93740.

SMALL, STANLEY JOSEPH
Educational administrator. **Personal:** Born Jun 1, 1946, Weeks Island, LA; married Dorothy Collins; children: Keith V, Keisha L, Kory K. **Educ:** Southern Univ Baton Rouge, BS Math & Sci 1968, MS Admin & Super 1973. **Career:** New Iberia Middle Sch, teacher 1968-70, assistant principal; Anderson St Middle Sch, teacher 1970-81, principal, 1992-; Iberia Parish Council, elected parish official 1984-; Lee Street Elementary, principal, 1989-92. **Orgs:** Mem Natl Educ Assn 1969-85; pres Neighborhood Comm Serv Coalition 1978-85; mem LA Assn of Ed/Pol Action Comm 1979-85; chmn Human Serv Comm Iberia Parish Council 1984; mem NACO Human Serv Steering Comm 1984; mem Parish Bd (SMILE) Comm Action Agency 1984. **Honors/Awds:** Outstanding Teacher of the Yr Assn of Classroom Teachers 1978; developed and implemented motivation prog for students New Iberia Middle Sch 1981. **Home Addr:** 816 Francis St, New Iberia, LA 70560. **Business Addr:** Principal, Anderson St Middle Sch, 1059 Anderson St, New Iberia, LA 70560.

SMALL, SYDNEY L.
Business executive. **Personal:** Born Feb 18, 1941, Brooklyn, NY. **Educ:** Pace U, BA 1961. **Career:** Unity Broadcasting Network Inc, exec vice pres & co-found; Nat Black Network NYC, vice chairman 1973; Unity Broadcasting Network PA Inc WDAS AM/FM Phila, PA; ABC, bus mgr 1963-69; Time, Inc, 1969-71; Unity Broadcasting Network Inc, exec vp; Queens Inner Unity Cable Systems NYC, pres; NBN Broadcasting Inc, pres. **Orgs:** Mem Intl Radio & TV Soc; Nat Assn of Bdcstr; Nat Assn of Black-Owned Bdcstr; mem NAACP; NY Urban League; bd of dir World Insto of Black CommInc 1978; mem New York C of Comm Com 1979; pres World Inst of Black Commun 1986; pres Natl Assoc of Black Owned Broadcasters 1987. **Honors/Awds:** AUS 1961-63. **Military Serv:** AUS 1961-63. **Business Addr:** Chairman, NBN Broadcasting Inc, 505 8th Ave, 9th Fl, New York, NY 10018.

SMALL, TORRANCE
Professional football player. **Personal:** Born Sep 6, 1970. **Educ:** Alcorn State University. **Career:** New Orleans Saints, wide receiver; St Louis Rams, wide receiver, currently. **Business Addr:** Professional Football Player, St Louis Rams, One Rams Way, St Louis, MO 63045, (314)982-7267.

SMALL, WILLIAM
Administration. **Personal:** Born Dec 5, 1940, Elizabeth, NJ; married Carolyn; children: William, Michael. **Educ:** Howard U, AB 1962; Howard U, JD 1965. **Career:** Contract Adminstrn, dir 1975-; William Paterson Coll, dir acad serv 1971; William Patterson Coll, asso prof 1970; Newark State Coll, instr 1970; CAFEO, dep dir, acting exec dir 1969; Union Co Legal Serv Corp, chf investigator 1968-69; Domar Buckle Mfg Corp, laborer 1959; Astro Air Products Corp,laborer 1960-61; Western Elec Corp, laborer 1962; Union Co Legal Serv Corp, 1968-69; Polit Sci Soc; The Promethean Vice Pres Summer of Serv Corp, publicity & circulation mgr 1969; Title 1, asv com; Plans for Progress Task Force on Youth Motivation, part; Mayors Task Force o. **Orgs:** Bd trustees Urban League of Eastern Union Co; Concern Inc; adv various comm-based youth groups. **Honors/Awds:** Outst Achvmt Award in Fed Jurisdiction; Outst Serv Award William & Paterson Coll Student Govt Assn; Serv Award Nat Headquarters Boy Scouts of Am 1974-75; Outst Trainee Univ Co 3re BCT Bde; Outst Trainee postwide competition; Nat Def Serv Medal; Vietnamese Serv Medal; Vietnamese Campaign Medal; Good Conduct Medal; Army Commedation Medal. **Military Serv:** Military Serv #E-5 1956-67. **Business Addr:** Dean of Social Sciences, William Patterson College, 300 Pompton Rd, Wayne, NJ 07470.

SMALLEY, PAUL
Relations manager. **Personal:** Born Dec 8, 1935, Gay Head, MA; married; children: Polly, Patrick. **Career:** Comm Rel NE 1969-; Gen Dynamics 1958-69; Adv Com OIC Nat Tech V. **Orgs:** Chmn OIC Reg I; Deep River Dem Town Chmn 1980-82; v chman Reg Bd of Ed #4 1973-79; CT NAACP St Bd of Fin; mem bd of dir Urban League of Gr Hartford; min adv bd chmn WFSB-TV-3. **Military Serv:** USMC #E-4 1954-75. **Business Addr:** PO Box 270, Hartford, CT 06101.

SMALLS, CHARLEY MAE
Scientist. **Personal:** Born Oct 22, 1943, Charleston, SC; daughter of Ida Mae White Smalls (deceased) and Charles A Smalls Sr. **Educ:** Knoxville Coll, BS 1965; Univ of MD, MS 1972. **Career:** Medical Univ of S Carolina Dept of Anatomy, lab technician, 1965-68; Johns Hopkins Univ Dept of Pathology, research technician, 1968-70; Dept Zoology Univ of MD, grad asst 1970-72; Dept Anatomy Milton S Hershey Med Ctr, research asst 1973-79; US EPA, EPA asst 1980-81, environmental scientist 1981-88, HMC/EPA Environmental Monitoring Lab, environmental radiation specialist, 1988-90, environmental radiation specialist, 1990-94, division of health physics. **Orgs:** Capital Presb Church, deacon, 1986-90, elder, 1992-; Microscopy Soc of Amer; PA Alliance for Environmental Education; Susquehana Valley Health Physics Soc; Alpha Kappa Alpha Sorority. **Honors/Awds:** Bronze Medal US EPA 1980; CM Smalls & MD Goode 1977 "Ca2 Accumulating Components in Dev Skeletal Muscle" J Morph 1977; Bronze Medal, US Environmental Protection Agency, 1988. **Home Addr:** 1901 Herr St, Harrisburg, PA 17103.

SMALLS, DOROTHY M.
Educator. **Personal:** Born Jan 2, 1920, Georgetown, SC; divorced; children: Eleanor J, Carla S, Lois D. **Educ:** SC State Coll, BS 1940; SC State Coll, MS 1960; Univ of SC; Univ of Chgo. **Career:** Bd End Georgetown, english teacher; JB Beck Elem Georgetown, elem school teacher; Kensington School Georgetown, reading consultant; Wm C Reavis School Chicago, teacher; Beck Jr HS Georgetown, teacher english, reading. **Orgs:** Mem United Tchng Profession; Pee Dee Reading Council; Nat Council of Reading; past pres SC State Alumni; past sec GC Educ Assn; past pres Dis Missions; mem NAACP; Voter Registration; Home Missions.

SMALLS, JACQUELYN ELAINE
Speech-language pathologist, consultant. **Personal:** Born Nov 16, 1946, Charleston, SC; daughter of Ida Mae White Smalls (deceased) and Charles Augustus Smalls Sr; married Willard Goodnight Jr, Oct 12, 1991. **Educ:** Hampton Inst, BA 1968; Penn State Univ, MA, 1976; Howard Univ, MS 1980, PhD 1984. **Career:** Blast IU #14, coordinator 1975-76; York City Public Schools, speech pathologist 1968-78; Public School Program, consultant, program evaluator 1982; DC Public Schools, speech pathologist 1982-, Mentally Retarded Children and Adults, consultant 1987-; Functional Communication Associates, Inc, partner. **Orgs:** Consult Natl Educ Assn 1975; Philadelphia Public Schools 1982; mem Amer Speech Language and Hearing 1982-; Sargent Memorial Presbyterian Church 1983-. **Honors/Awds:** Distinguished Amer; Rec Graduate Fellowship Penn State Univ 1970, 1971, 1973; Fellowship Howard Univ 1978-83. **Special Achievements:** MD Licensure, 1995. **Business Addr:** Speech, Language, Pathology Consultant, District of Columbia Public Schools, 100 Gallatin St NE, Washington, DC 20011.

SMALLS, MARCELLA E.
Account executive. **Personal:** Born Sep 30, 1946, McClellanville, SC; children: Marcus. **Educ:** Voorhees Coll, 1963-65; Durham Coll, BA 1968. **Career:** South Santee Germantown Action Group, fin sec 1980-83; SC Charleston Chap Natl Sec Assoc, name tag comm 1982; South-Santee Comm Ctr, bd of dir 1983; Howard AME Church, asst sec 1982-; Amoco Chem

Co., accountant, currently. **Orgs:** Treas Amoco Chem Recreation Club 1983; secty/trustee Bldg Fund for Howard AME Church; financial advisor for Jr Achievement Cainhoy HS 1986-87; chairperson, March of Dimes, Amoco Chemical Co., 1989-91; March of Dimes Advisory Bd, Charleston Chapter, currently; treasurer, PTA, St James Santee Elementary School, McClellanville, SC; past chairperson, Quality Awareness Recognition SubCommittee; Amoco Cooper River Wellness Focus Committee, Amoco Bonner and Moore; COMPASS implementation team member. **Honors/Awds:** Employee of the Month, Jan 1989; Opportunity for Improvement Winner, 1991. **Home Addr:** 1940 Hill Rd, McClellanville, SC 29458.

SMALLS, MARVA
Communications company executive. **Career:** Nickelodeon/Nick at Nite, network relations, sr vp. **Business Addr:** Sr Vice Pres, Network Relations, Nickelodeon/Nick at Night, 1515 Broadway, 38th Fl, New York, NY 10036, (212)258-8000.

SMALLS, O'NEAL
Educator. **Personal:** Born Sep 7, 1941, Myrtle Beach, SC. **Educ:** Tuskegee Inst, BS 1964; Harvard Law Sch, JD 1967; Georgetown Univ, LLM 1975. **Career:** Amer Univ, assoc prof 1969-76; Systems & Applied Sci Corp, bd of dirs, 1974-85; George Washington Univ Sch of Law, prof law 1976-79; American Univ, prof of law 1979-88; Univ of SC School of Law, professor, 1988-. **Orgs:** Mem Harvard Law Sch Res Com 1966-67; asst dir Harvard Law Sch Summer Prog for Minority Students 1966; dir of admissions & chmn of Com Admissions & Scholarships Amer Univ 1970-74; mem DC, Natl, Amer Bar Assns; chmn bd dir Skyanchor Corp; exec bd DC Bapt Conv; Services Com & bd trustees Law Sch Admissions Coun Princeton 1972-76; adv com Leg Serv Plan Laborers' Dist coun of Washington DC 1973-75; bd dir Systems & Applied Sci Corp 1974-85; bd chmn, Frewood Foundation, 1987-; Freedoms Foundation, pres/chair of bd, Myrtle Beach, SC, currently. **Honors/Awds:** Articles "Class Actions Under Title VII" Amer Univ Law Review 1976; "The Path & The Promised Land" Amer Univ Law Review 1972; booklets "New Directions, An Urban Reclamation Program for the Dist of Columbia" July 1982; "Manhood Training An Introduction to Adulthood for Inner City Boys Ages 11-13" April 1985. **Military Serv:** AUS capt 1967-69. **Business Addr:** Professor of Law, University of South Carolina, Main & Green Streets, #410 Law School, Columbia, SC 29208.

SMALLWOOD, OSBORN TUCKER
Educator. **Personal:** Born Aug 12, 1911, Hillhouse, MS; married Hazel Demouy; children: Angela Cockfield, Osborn Jr, Glenn Hazelton, Carl. **Educ:** NC A&T Univ, BS 1937; Howard Univ, MA 1939; NY Univ, PhD 1948. **Career:** Samuel Huston Coll, chmn dept of English 1939-42; Office of Price Admin, History rsch specialist 1942-44; St Matthews Lutheran Church, pastor 1944-46; Howard Univ, instructor, assoc prof 1947-61; Foreign Serv Office W Germany, cultural officer consultant 1961-70; OH State Univ, dir intl program, asst vice pres, prof of comm 1970-80, prof emeritus 1980-. **Orgs:** Chmn OH Fulbright Hayes Scholarship Comm 1970-72; mem advisory comm Inst for Intl Educ, mem bd of dir Columbus Area Intl Program Tau Kappa Alpha Forensic Honor Soc, Speech Communications Assoc, NAACP, Natl Assn of Foreign Student Affairs, Torch Intl; pres Intl Educ Assn of OH Coll & Univ 1973-74, United Nations Assoc, Phi Beta Sigma. **Honors/Awds:** Citizen of the Year Woodridge Civic Assoc 1954; Fulbright Guest Prof Anatolia Coll Salonica Greece 1955-57; Merit Serv Award US Info Agency 1967; Outstanding Serv Award Intl Educ Assoc of OH Coll & Univ 1975; Merit Serv Award Inst of Intl Ed 1977. **Business Addr:** Professor Emeritus, Ohio State Univ, 154 N Oval Mall, Columbus, OH 43210.

SMALLWOOD, WILLIAM LEE
Educational administrator. **Personal:** Born Sep 2, 1945, York, PA; son of Herman L & Vera Horton Smallwood; divorced; children: Yolanda M Sherrer, Aundrea L, Liza D. **Educ:** USAF Personnel Technical School, Personnel Certificate, 1963; LaSalle Extension Univ, Accounting Certificate, 1968; Penn State Univ, Continuing Ed, 1970-71; Empire State College-State Univ of NY, Distance Learning, 1983. **Career:** US Civil Service, accounting clerk, 1967-68; LIAB Aircraft Corp, admin, 1968-69; WJ Grant Co, credit mgr, 1969-70; Caterpillar Inc, track press operator-material handler, 1970-71; Community Progress Council Inc, bus mgr, 1971-74; Pennsylvania Dept of Community Affairs, admin officer, 1974-79; York County Office of Employment & Training, exec dir, 1979-80; Crispus Attucks Assn Inc, housing financial coor, 1980-88. **Orgs:** York County Industrial Dev Corp, 1994-; South Pershing Comm Dev Corp, 1994-; William C Goodridge Bus Resource Ctr, pres, 1993-; Office of Minority Bus Dev, 1992-; York County Planning Commn, 1977-80; York City Council, 1977-80, president, 1984-; Minority Bus Assn Inc, founder-past pres, 1983-; Leadership York, bd mem, 1983-87. **Honors/Awds:** Minortiy Bus Assn Inc, Public Service Award, 1992; Natl Conference on School/College Collaboration, President's Salute, 1991; Natl Univ Continuing Education Assn, Awarded Honorable Mention, 1991; Crispus Attucks Assn Inc, Cert of Merit, 1985; City of York, PA, Resolution for Service, 1980. **Special Achievements:** York's 250th Celebration 1741-1991, African Americans of Note, 1991; African American History, York PA & Throughout the US, 1990; Operations Manual, Office or Employment & Training, 1979; Personnel Policies, Office of Employment and Training, 1979; Fiscal Management Guide, Bureau of Human Resources, PA Dept of Community Affairs, 1978. **Military Serv:** USAF, E-4, AIC, 1963-67; Air Force Longevity Service Medal 1967; Vietnam Service Medal, 1967. **Home Phone:** (717)854-0642. **Business Addr:** Area Rep, Pennsylvania State Univ, 1031 Edgecomb Ave, Continuing Education, York, PA 17403, (717)771-4067.

SMART, EDWARD BERNARD, JR.
Clergyman. **Personal:** Born Jun 23, 1949, Dothan, AL; son of Barbara Smith Smart and Edward B Smart Sr; children: Belinda. **Educ:** Fisk Univ 1967; Harrisburg Area Comm Coll, AA 1969; PA State Univ, BA 1975; Shipperburt Univ, attended; Univ of CA, PhD, 1988. **Career:** HBE Redevel, relocation office 1970-72; Warner Lambert, sales rep 1972-79; St John AME Church, pastor 1979-80; Scotland School for Vet Children, chaplain 1982-; St James AME Church, pastor 1980-86; St Stephena Comm AME Church, pastor 1986-. **Orgs:** Councilman Borough of Chambersburg 1981-85; past pres Chambersburg Black Ministry 1982; chaplain Scotland School for Vet Children 1982-, Franklin Cty Migrant Ministry 1983-85; pres Chambersburg Comm Improve Assoc 1983-; bd of dir South Central Comm Action Program 1983-; past pres Chambersburg Ministry 1984;trustee Philadelphia Annual Conf 1984,85,86; mem Mayor's Task Force on Racism 1986; trustee NY Annual Conference 1986-87; bd of examiners, NY Annual Conf, 1989-; sec, AME Ministerial Alliance NY Vicinity, 1989-; pres, sec, NY Annual Conference, 1990-. **Honors/Awds:** Fisk JS Fisk Univ 1967; Father of the Year Daughters of Fkd Co 1982; Honorary Doctorate, Univ of CA, 1989; Sanhedrin Man of the Year, Sanhedrin Ministries, 1988.

SMEDLEY, ERIC
Professional football player. **Personal:** Born Jul 23, 1973, Charleston, WV. **Educ:** Indiana. **Career:** Buffalo Bills, defensive back, 1996-. **Business Addr:** Professional Football Player, Buffalo Bills, One Bills Dr, Orchard Park, NY 14127, (716)648-1800.

SMILEY, EMMETT L.
Dentist. **Personal:** Born Jun 14, 1922, Montgomery, AL; son of Hattie Dabney Smiley (deceased) and George Washington Smiley (deceased); married Mary Jo Carter Smiley, Aug 14, 1953; children: Lynn S Hampton, Karen J, Kim A, George Wesley. **Educ:** AL State Univ, BS 1945; Prairie View Univ, Hempstead TX; Univ of Florence, Florence Italy; Meharry Med Coll, DDS 1950. **Career:** Den Practice since 1950. **Orgs:** Pres AL Dental Soc 1964-66; exec bd AL Dental Soc 1966-; pres Capitol City Med Soc 1968-70; Nat Dental Assn; Mid-century Dental Assn; Ewell Neil Dental Soc; Delta Dental Care Inc; adv bd Urban League; mem Montgomery Area C of C; Mayors Com on Comm Affairs 1964-70; Montgomery Improvement Assn; Alpha Phi Alpha Frat past pres; Cligue Social Club past pres; Cleveland Ave Branch YMCA; Century Club mem; member, Phi Boule. **Honors/Awds:** Listed in AL Dept of Archives History under "Men of Prominence"; Service Award, Alabama Dental Society, 1990. **Military Serv:** US Army, Corporal, 1942-45. **Home Addr:** 4601 Lawnwood Dr, Montgomery, AL 36108. **Business Addr:** Dentist, 1031 Oak St, Montgomery, AL 36108.

SMILEY, JAMES WALKER, SR.
Postal director (retired). **Personal:** Born May 19, 1928, Selma, AL; son of Sophia Deanna Bonner Smiley and David Smiley, Sr.; married Lillian; children: James W Jr, Gloria Jean, Jacqueline, Carolyn Smiley-Robinson. **Educ:** Evening Coll, 1964-68; Univ of Cincinnati. **Career:** US Postal Serv, line foreman 1967-68, exec secretary, 1968-69, gnrl foreman 1969-74, operations mgr 1974-78, mgr mail distrib 1978-81; US Postal Service Cincinnati, OH dir mail processing 1981-85; Village of Woodlawn, Woodlawn, OH admin 1989-92. **Orgs:** NAACP; Natl Assoc of Postal Spvsrs; councilman Woodlawn, OH 1980-81 & 1983-87; natl vice pres Natl Phoenix Assoc of Postal Mgrs 1983-1985; Board of Directors Cincinniti Hypertension Education pres 1989-95; Ideal Investment Club pres. **Honors/Awds:** Dedicated Service Cint Local NAPFE 1981; Outstanding/Dedicated Service Natl Phoenix Assoc Postal Mgrs 1983; Superior Accomplish Award US Postal Serv 1969. **Military Serv:** RA sfc 5 years; WW II Victory, Good Conduct 1946-52. **Home Addr:** 1122 Prairie Ave, Woodlawn, OH 45215.

SMILEY, TAVIS
Broadcast journalist. **Personal:** Born Sep 13, 1964, Biloxi, MS; son of Joyce M Smiley and Emory G Smiley. **Educ:** Indiana University, attended, 1982-86. **Career:** Mayor Tomilea Allison, assistant to the mayor, 1984-85; council president Pat Russell, council aide, 1987; SCLC, LA, special asst to the executive director, 1978-88; Mayor Tom Bradley, administrative aide, 1988-90; self-employed, The Smiley Report, radio/television commentator, 1990-. **Orgs:** LA's Young Black Professionals, chairman, operations committee, 1988-90; Inner City Foundation for Excellence in Education, advisory board, 1989-91; Challengers Boys and Girls Club, board of directors, 1989-; Los Angeles Black College Tour, board of directors, 1991-; Kappa Alpha Psi; Martin Luther King Jr Center for Non-violent Social Change, advisory board, 1992-93; After Class Scouting, Scouting USA, advisory board, 1991; United Way of Greater Los Angeles, steering committee, 1989-90. **Honors/Awds:** Dollars & Sense Magazine, Outstanding Business & Professional Award, 1992; Vanity Fair, Hall of Fame, 1996. **Special Achievements:** US Debate Team, "International Dialogue,", 1986; Author, Straight Talk About the Wrongs of The Right, Anchor/Doubleday. **Business Addr:** 3870 Crenshaw Blvd, Ste 391, Los Angeles, CA 90008, (213)295-3543.

SMILEY, WILLIAM L.
Physician. **Personal:** Born Nov 14, 1912, Alabama; married Adella; children: Michele, Nina. **Educ:** OH State U, BA 1933; OH State Univ Med Sch, MD 1937. **Career:** City of St Louis Div of Health & Hosp, deputy asst health commr; Homer Phillips Hosp, acting path & chief of Labs 1944-46; Homer Phillips Hosp, assoc chief dept ob-gyn 1946-47. **Orgs:** Dir Cancer Screening Prog 1953-57; co-dir Sch for Continued Educ & Med Care of Pregnant Girls 1968-; chmn bd St Louis Comprehensive Health Ctr 1969-70; FACS, FACOG. **Business Addr:** 1421 N Jefferson, St Louis, MO 63106.

SMILEY-ROBERTSON, CAROLYN
Systems analyst. **Personal:** Born Aug 26, 1954, Cincinnati, OH; daughter of Lillian Anderson Smiley and James W Smiley; married Tommie L Robertson, Nov 19, 1983; children: Kevin James, Michael John. **Educ:** Wellesley College, BA, 1976. **Career:** Western Southern Life Insurance, programmer 1976-78; AT&T, systems development specialist 1978-83; Village of Woodlawn, councilmember 1978-84; AT&T Communications, mgr, systems analyst 1984-85, mgr, information mgmt 1985-. **Orgs:** Woodlawn Bd of Zoning Appeals 1978-82; Woodlawn Planning Comm 1978-84; trustee Woodlawn Comm Improvement Corp 1981-; economic consult Village of Woodlawn 1984-. **Honors/Awds:** Ambassador, Village of Woodlawn 1980; vice mayor, Village of Woodlawn 1982; YMCA Black Achiever, Cincinnati OH 1983. **Business Addr:** Manager & Information Mgmt, AT&T Communications, 221 East Fourth St, Cincinnati, OH 45202.

SMIRNI, ALLAN DESMOND
Attorney. **Personal:** Born Aug 27, 1939, New York City, NY; son of Ruby and Donald; married Barbara Smirni; children: Amie. **Educ:** Brooklyn Coll CUNY, BA 1960; Law Sch Univ of CA Berkeley, JD 1971. **Career:** Brobeck Phleger & Harrison, asso atty 1971-74; Envirotech Corp, asst gen cnsl/asst sec 1974-81; TeleVideo Systems Inc, chief cnsl & sec 1982-86; Memorex Corp vice pres general counsel & secretary 1987-89; Siemens Pyramid Info Systems, Inc, vice pres general counsel, secretary, 1989-. **Orgs:** State of CA Job Training/Devel 1970-72; trustee Envirotech Foundation 1978-81; trustee TeleVideo Found 1983-; State Bar of CA 1972-; Am Soc of Corporate Sec 1976-; Charles Houston Bar Assn 1972-; Amer Assn of Corporate Counsel 1982-. **Military Serv:** USAF capt; AF Commendation Medal 1966. **Business Addr:** Siemens Pyramid Info Systems, Inc, Pyramid Technology Corp, 3860 N 1st St, San Jose, CA 95134-1702, (408)428-8486.

SMITH, A. WADE
Educator, sociologist. **Personal:** Born Aug 29, 1950, Newport News, VA; son of Eunice Gray Smith and A Wade Smith; married Elsie Gloria Jean Moore; children: Arthur Wade, Aaron Webster, Allen Weldon. **Educ:** Dartmouth Coll, AB 1972; Univ of Chicago, MA 1976, PhD 1977. **Career:** Univ of SC, asst prof 1977-80; Natl Opinion Rsch Ctr, rsch assoc 1977-86; Ctr for the Study of Youth Develop, vstg rsch scientist 1980; AZ State Univ, asst prof beginning 1980, prof and chairman, currently. **Orgs:** Membership chmn Assoc of Black Sociologists 1984-88; mem AZ Law Enforcement Adv Council 1986-90; assoc editor Journal of Marriage and the Family 1986-; assoc editor Amer Sociological Review 1987-90; editorial bd, Social Forces, 1990-; associate editor, Sociological Quarterly, 1991-. **Honors/Awds:** Articles "Racial Tolerance as a Function of Group Position" 1981, "Cohorts, Education, and the Evolution of Tolerance" 1985, "Sex and Race Differences in Mathematics Aptitude" 1986, "Problems & Progress in the Measurement of Black Public Opinion" 1987; "Maintaining the Pipeline of Black Teachers for the 21st Century", 1988; "Racial Insularity at the Core: Contemporary American Racial Attitudes," 1988; "Finding Subgroups for Surveys", 1989. **Business Addr:** Professor, Arizona State Univ, Dept of Sociology, Tempe, AZ 85287-2101.

SMITH, A. Z.
Association executive. **Personal:** Born Jun 16, 1938, Grand Junction, TN; married Mattie Lou Peterson; children: Burnett, Azell, Wanda, Jovernia. **Educ:** Air Conditioning Training Co, Inc, degree 1961; Rust College 1961-62. **Career:** Church Deacon Board, deacon 1969; Hardaways MB Church, choir president 1971-84, superintendent sunday school 1971-; Carrier A/C Inc Co, machine set-up and operator. **Orgs:** General staff Mississippi Governor's Colonel 1976-80; school board Benton Cty MS Bd of Education 1981-; member NAACP. **Honors/Awds:** Best all-around for religious activities, Old Salem School 1960; Golden Circle Club Collerville 1985. **Business Addr:** Carrier A/C Inc Co, 97 South Byhalia Road, Collierville, TN 38017.

SMITH, AL FREDRICK
Professional football player. **Personal:** Born Nov 26, 1964, Los Angeles, CA. **Educ:** California State Poly Univ, attended; Utah State Univ, BS, sociology, 1987. **Career:** Houston Oilers, linebacker, 1987-. **Business Addr:** Professional Football Player, Houston Oilers, 4400 Post Oak Pkwy, #2800, Houston, TX 77027-3400.

SMITH, ALBERT E.
University president. **Personal:** Born Oct 24, 1932, Sioux Falls, SD; son of Ethel Johnson Smith and Calvert Smith; married Sadie Burris, Jan 27, 1956; children: Albert Clayton, Robbin Renae, Angela E. **Educ:** North Carolina A&T State Univ, Greensboro NC, BS, 1956; George Williams Coll, Downers Grove IL, MS, 1963; Univ of Pittsburgh, Pittsburgh PA, PhD, 1984. **Career:** Knoxville Coll, Knoxville TN, dir of student center & head baseball coach, 1964-66; North Carolina A&T State Univ, Greensboro NC, dir of intercollegiate athletics & the memorial student union, 1968-71; Univ of Pittsburgh, Pittsburgh PA, exec asst dir of intercollegiate athletics & lecturer, 1971-75; Eastern Michigan Univ, Ypsilanti MI, dir of intercollegiate athletics & assoc prof of educ, 1975-76; North Carolina A&T State Univ, Greensboro NC, vice chancellor for devel & univ relations, 1976-86; South Carolina State Coll, Orangeburg SC, pres, 1986-. **Orgs:** Chmn, council of presidents, South Carolina State Colleges & Universities; mem, advisory comm, Office of Advancement for Public Black Colleges; mem, advisory bd, Governor's Agricultural & Rural Economic Devel Task Force; commr, Commn of the Future of South Carolina; bd of dir, South Carolina Heart Assn, First Natl Bank of Orangeburg, City Industrial Devel Commn, South Carolina Business Week. **Honors/Awds:** North Carolina A&T Sports Hall of Fame, North Carolina A&T State Colleges & Universities, 1988; Hall of Fame, Mid-Eastern Athletic Conf; 2nd Annual Golden Achievement Award, Afro-Amer History Club, George Washington Carver High School; Inventor, Combined Clock & Advertising Display, 1984; Inventor, Desk Ornament, 1982; "A Plan for the Development of the Afro-American Cultural and Entertainment Complex, Univ of Pittsburgh, Pittsburgh PA," 1974; "Reach for Progress," Greensboro Business, (Greensboro Chamber of Commerce Publication) Greensboro NC, 1968; Weekly Sports Column, Carolina Peacemaker, Greensboro NC, 1968. **Military Serv:** US Army, 2nd lieutenant. **Business Addr:** President, South Carolina State College, 300 College St, NE, Orangeburg, SC 29117.

SMITH, ALFRED J., JR.
Educator. **Personal:** Born Jul 9, 1948, Montclair, NJ; married Judith Moore. **Educ:** Boston U, BFA 1970; Boston U, MFA 1972. **Career:** Howard Univ, assoc art 1972-; Norfolk Correct Inst, inst art 1970-72; Boston U, asst inst 1970-72; Boston Univ Afro-Amer Center, dir cult affrs 1970-71; NatlCenter Afro-Amer Art, inst art 1969-72; prof pntr sculp & crafts. **Orgs:** Mem Nat Conf of Art. **Honors/Awds:** "Educ to Africa Assn" Afric Am Inst Tchrs Assist grant Boston Univ 1970-72; art awd Boston Univ 1967-68, 1970; comm from City of Boston in "Grtr Walls & Spaces" compet 1972; partic in num exhib; recpt Nat Endow grant for crafts 1975. **Business Addr:** Howard University, College of Fine Arts, 6th & Fairmont Streets NW, Washington, DC 20059.

SMITH, ALICE
Education administration. **Educ:** Ft Valley State Coll, BA French Lit 1968; Atlanta Univ, MA French Lit 1969; Yale Univ New Haven CT, Intensive Lang & Lit 1970; MI State Univ, French Lit 1971-72; Sorbonne, Paris, France, Modern French Lit 1972-73; Columbia Univ NY, German Lang 1973; Univ of MA, PhD French Lit 1978. **Career:** Hawkinsville HS, instr 1967; Ft Valley State Coll, instr 1969-71; Univ of MA, teaching asst 1973-77; Univ of MA, placement counselor 1979-80, dir resource ctr 1979-81, asst dir placement serv 1979-. **Orgs:** Mem Alpha Kappa Mu Natl Hon soc, Alpha Kappa Alpha, Phi Delta Kappa 1980. **Honors/Awds:** Acad Scholarship Paris France 1966; Natl Defense Scholarship Ft Valley State Coll 1964-68; The Atlanta Univ Fellowship 1968-69; Natl Fellowships Fund 1976-78.

SMITH, ALLEN JOSEPH, SR.
Educational administrator. **Personal:** Born Mar 10, 1936, Chicago, IL; divorced; children: Allen J Jr, Wendy M, Anthony R. **Educ:** Roosevelt Univ, BA 1960, MA 1966; Nova Univ, EdD 1981. **Career:** Chicago Bd of Educ, teacher 1960-67, adult educ teacher 1964-67, counselor 1967-69, guidance coord 1969-82, dir bureau of guidance 1982-. **Orgs:** Bd of dirs Parliamentarian Assoc for Multicultural Counseling and Development 1978-82, 1985-86; bd of dirs Human Resource Develop Inst 1984-. **Honors/Awds:** Disting Volunteer Awd UNCF 1984; 1984 Educator of the Year Phi Delta Kappa 1984; Special Appreciation Awd ANWC 1985; Certification of Appreciation Natl Beta Club 1985. **Business Addr:** Director, Bureau of Guidance, Chicago Public Schools, 1819 W Pershing Rd 6th Fl, Chicago, IL 60609.

SMITH, ALONZO NELSON
Educator, social service agency official. **Personal:** Born Oct 11, 1940, Washington, DC; son of Marie Wright Smint and Alonzo de Grate Smith; married Susan T Cramer; children: Anne Marie, Alexander. **Educ:** Georgetown Univ, BS Foreign Service 1962; Howard Univ, MA African Hist 1967; UCLA, PhD Afro-Amer Hist 1978. **Career:** Black Studies Center of the Claremont Colleges, lecturer 1970-75; Cal Poly State Univ, inst history 1976-77; Univ of NE, asst prof 1978-86; National Consulting Systems, writer, researcher, 1986-89; Urban League of Nebraska, vice president, 1989-. **Orgs:** Mem Omaha NAACP 1985; mem Central Comm NE State Democratic Party 1985. **Honors/Awds:** Article Afro-Americans and the Presidential Election of 1948-Western Journal of Black Studies 1984. **Military Serv:** Peace Corps W Africa 1962-64. **Home Addr:** 2048 N 54th St, Omaha, NE 68104. **Business Addr:** Vice President, Urban League of Nebraska, 3022 N 24th St, Omaha, NE 68110.

SMITH, ALPHONSO LEHMAN
Educational administrator. **Personal:** Born Feb 27, 1937, Memphis, TN; divorced; children: Angela, Anthony, Audrey. **Educ:** Fisk University, 1955-57; Ohio State University, BS, 1964. **Career:** Wright State University, director affirmative action programs, 1973-; Wright State University, assistant director of affirmative action for faculty, 1972-73; Wright State University, math instructor, 1964-68; assistant professor of computer science, 1970-. **Orgs:** American Math Society, 1961-; former chairman, Ohio Affirmative Action Officers Association, 1973-; Yellow Springs Title, IX Adv Com, 1976-77; National Science Foundation Fellow, 1956-72; Pi Mu Epsilon, 1958-; honorary member, Phi Beta Kappa, 1960-. **Business Addr:** Math, Wright State University, 3640 Col Glenn Hwy, Dayton, OH 45435-0002.

SMITH, ANDRE RAPHEL
Music conductor. **Personal:** Born in Durham, NC. **Educ:** Univ of Miami, BM, trombone; Yale Univ, MA; Curtis Institute of Music; Julliard School of Music. **Career:** St Louis Symphony Orchestra, assistant conductor, 1991-94; Philadelphia Orchestra, assistant conductor, 1994-. **Orgs:** In Unison. **Business Addr:** Assistant Conductor, Philadelphia Orchestra, 1420 Locust St., Philadelphia, PA 19102, (215)893-1900.

SMITH, ANDREW W.
Vocalist, educational administrator. **Personal:** Born Aug 24, 1941, Lexington, KY; married Yvonne Bransford; children: Auron W, Alicia Y. **Educ:** KY State Univ Frankfort, KY, BS 1964; Roosevelt Univ Chicago, MM 1970. **Career:** Opera Orch of NY 1979-; Met Opera, opera singer 1976-; Markham Roller Rink Markham IL, asst mgr/co-owner 1972-76; City of Markham, acting city mgr 1972-73, dir urban dev 1971; Chicago Bd of Ed, tchr 1964-70; Kentucky State Univ, Department of Music, assistant prof, currently. **Orgs:** Opera singer New York City Opera 1977-79/Houston Grand Opera/MI Opera/Boston Opera/Atlanta Symphony/Grand Park Summer Festival/Art Park Music Festival/Chicago Sinai Congregation Cantorial Soloist 7 Yrs; mem Kappa Alpha Phi. **Honors/Awds:** Winner Of Chicagoland Music Festival 1965; WGN Audition of the Air Met Audition; Emmy award for One of prin soloists for Best Opera Rec 1977; Tony Awrd for Principal Soloist on a recording of "Porgy & Bess"; Natl Acad of Rec Arts & Sci 1977. **Business Addr:** Professor, Kentucky State Univ, Frankfort, KY 40601.

SMITH, ANN ELIZABETH
Educational administrator. **Personal:** Born Aug 17, 1939, Poplar Bluff, MO; daughter of Hallie W Smith and Leland G Smith (deceased). **Educ:** Lincoln Univ, BA 1960; Univ of IA, MA 1962; Union Institute, PhD, 1974. **Career:** Univ of Illinois at Chicago, Chicago, IL, associate chancellor, 1988-; Endow Inc, Chicago, IL, vice pres, 1978-88, Prudential Ins Co, sales mgr 1978-; Acad Affairs, acting vp, Speech & Performing Arts NE IL Univ, assc prof 1975-77; NE IL Univ, asst to pres 1969-75; instr 1966-69; Univ of IN Black Theatre, lecturer 1971; Theatre E IL Univ, instr 1962-66; English Central HS, instr 1960. **Orgs:** Consultant Dramatic Art; consult for Women's Pgm Regnl Office of HEW & HUD 1972-73; prod coordinator, Org of Black Am Culture 1967-; bd mem League of Black Women 1976-80; Delta Sigma Theta Sorority, 1957, natl policy bd mem 1972-75; chairperson, 1974-75; Union Graduate School; Coll in the City, Commuters & Comm Houses; Improving Coll & Univ Teaching 1974; board member, Chicago Access Corporation, 1989-; board member, Gamaliel Foundation, 1990-; board member, PUSH Womens Benefit Board, 1979-90; bd of trustees, Univ of IL, 1985-88. **Honors/Awds:** NE IL Univ Intl women's yr awrd 1975; PUSH excellence awrd 1977; legionaire awrd Prudential Ins Co 1978-79; pres citation Prudential Ins Co 1979; Million Dollar Roundtable Prudential Ins Co 1980; Honorary Doctor of Humane Letters, Lincoln Univ, 1987; Top 100 Black Business & Professional Women, Dollars & Sense Magazine, 1988. **Home Addr:** 505 N Lake Shore Dr, Chicago, IL 60611. **Business Addr:** Associate Chancellor, University of Illinois at Chicago, 2503 University Hall M/C 102, 601 S Morgan, Chicago, IL 60607-7128.

SMITH, ANNA DEAVERE
Playwright. **Career:** Playwright, currently. **Honors/Awds:** John D. and Catherine T. MacArthur Foundation, "genius" award for theater work, 1996.

SMITH, ANNE STREET
Social worker. **Personal:** Born Mar 19, 1942, Spartanburg, SC; daughter of Sallie McCracken Amos and Willie L Amos; married Douglas M Smith, May 11, 1991; children: Michael D Street, Jerome Smith, Jared Smith. **Educ:** Howard Univ, BA 1964, MSW 1969; Ctr for Group Stds, completed 1 yr of 2 year program, 1974. **Career:** Dept of Human Rsrcs, social wrkr 1969-72; Howard Univ Hosp Psych & Social Serv Dept, social wrkr/instr 1972-80; Howard Univ Hosp Social Work Serv Dept asso dir 1980-86; Howard Univ Hospital Washington DC, dir of social services 1986-93; Sabbatical Leave, 1993-94; Howard Univ Hosp, social worker, 1994-. **Orgs:** Mem Gamma Sigma Sigma Natl Service Sorority 1963-; Realtor assoc Jackson Realty 1989-91; corres sec bd dir Ionia R Whipper Home, Inc 1984-85; rcrdng sec DC Hook-Up of Blck wmn 1980-84; mem Natl Asso of Social Wrkrs 1969-; mem Society of Hospital Social Work Dirs of the Amer Hospital Assn 1986-93; mem Amer Public Health Assn 1986-. **Honors/Awds:** Flwshp Grant Natl Endwmnt for Humanities 1980; Pres Meritorious Awrd DC Hook-Up of Black Women 1983; Training Stdtn Natl Inst of Mental Health 1967-69. **Business Addr:** Social Worker, Howard University Hospital, 2041 Georgia Ave NW, Washington, DC 20060.

SMITH, ANTHONY
Professional football player. **Personal:** Born Jun 28, 1967, Elizabeth City, NC. **Educ:** Communications major: Univ of Alabama, three years; Univ of Arizona, one year. **Career:** Oakland Raiders, defensive end, 1991-. **Honors/Awds:** All-PAC-10 selection, senior year; played in Aloha, Sun, Hall of Fame, and Copper Bowls. **Business Addr:** Professional Football Player, Oakland Raiders, 1220 Harbor Bay Pkwy, Alameda, CA 94502, (510)615-1875.

SMITH, ANTHONY EDWARD
Operations manager. **Personal:** Born Nov 14, 1961, Harvey, IL. **Educ:** Univ of IL at Urbana, BS Engrg 1983. **Career:** Owens-Corning Fiberglas, engrg intern 1981-82; IL Bell Telephone Co, asst mgr 1983-86, area mgr 1986-. **Orgs:** Mem Amer Youth Foundation 1978-; pres Black Student Union Univ of IL 1980-81; mem IL Soc of General Engrs 1982-83; mem Rotary Intl Harvey Club 1986-; mem Natl Black MBA Assoc. **Honors/Awds:** Larson Awd for Creative Solutions to Complex Engr Problems Univ of IL 1983; featured in US Black Engr High Tech Jobs in Midwest 1987.

SMITH, ANTOWAIN
Professional football player. **Personal:** Born Mar 14, 1972, Montgomery, AL. **Educ:** Houston. **Career:** Buffalo Bills, running back, 1997-. **Special Achievements:** NFL Draft, First round pick, #23, 1997. **Business Addr:** Professional Football Player, Buffalo Bills, 1 Bills Dr, Orchard Park, NY 14127, (716)648-1800.

SMITH, ARTHUR D.
Educational administrator (retired). **Personal:** son Of Augusta Banks Smith and Adolphus Smith; divorced. **Educ:** Kent State Univ, BS 1957, MA 1962; Yale Univ, PhD 1973. **Career:** Transitional Program Yale Univ, dir 1968-70; Baldwin-King Program Yale Child Study Center, dir 1970-73; Yale Univ, asst dean 1973-74; Northwestern Univ, assoc prof 1974-78; Northeastern Univ, dean 1978-80, assoc provost 1981-86, dir of planning beginning 1986, director of operations until 1992. **Orgs:** Educ consultant Amer Friends 1974-; chmn of bd Northcare 1976; assoc provost Northeastern Univ 1980-; program volunteer evaluator United Way Boston 1979-80. **Honors/Awds:** John Hay Fellow John Hay Whitney Found 1964; Branford Coll Fellow Yale Univ 1972.

SMITH, ARTHUR D.
Business executive, educator (retired). **Personal:** Born Feb 5, 1913, Sailes, LA; son of Rev & Mrs S Smith; married Lucille T Walton; children: Arthur D Jr, Billy C, Lonnie B, Cassandra. **Educ:** Leland Coll, AB 1939; Western Reserve Univ, MA 1949; further study Western Reserve, Univ of SC, Univ of CO, LA State Univ. **Career:** Teacher, 1939-42; Grambling Coll, assoc prof ed 1946-70; Smith Ins, owner/oper 1961-77; A D Smith Insurance Inc, principal owner/pres 1978-. **Orgs:** Mem Phi Delta Kappa Prof Frat; Natl Assn Ins Agents; mem Grambling Town Council (retired 1985 after 20 yrs svcs); mem bd dir two bus corps; 33rd Deg Mason; deacon & fin sec Mt Zion Bap Church; mayor-protem of Grambling; mem NAACP; pres Grambling Voters League; American Society of Notaries; Optimists International; Lions Club. **Honors/Awds:** Grad High Hon Leland Coll 1939; Citizen of Yr Awd of Grambling by Phi Beta Sigma Frat 1965; Citizen of Yr Awd of Grambling by Phi Beta Sigma Frat 1965; Hon 33rd Deg 1972; Silver Beaver Awd serv to Scouting 1974; inductee, Grambling State University Hall of Fame, 1990. **Military Serv:** Chief warrant off 1942-46. **Business Addr:** President, AD Smith Insurance Co, 102 W Grand Ave, PO Box 628, Grambling, LA 71245.

SMITH, ARTHUR L., JR. See ASANTE, MOLEFI KETE.

SMITH, AUBREY CARL, JR.
Laboratory official. **Personal:** Born Mar 12, 1942, Clarksdale, MS; son of Mattye Alice Johnson Smith and Aubrey Carl Smith Sr; married Marie Joyce Smith, Jun 17, 1967; children: Nicole Denise, Aubrey Brian. **Educ:** University of Illinois, Chicago, IL, 1961-63; Thornton Community College, Harvey, IL, AA, science, 1968; Illinois Institute of Technology, Chicago, IL, BA, chemistry, 1972. **Career:** A B Dick Company, Niles, IL, toner chemist, 1972; Arco Petroleum Products Co, Harvey, IL, analytical chemist, 1974, lubricants chemist, 1983, supervisor, health, safety and environmental protection, 1985; Argonne National Laboratory, Argonne, IL, supervisor, waste management operations, 1986, laboratory environmental compliance officer, 1988, manager, waste management operations, 1988, deputy building manager, environmental compliance rep, 1990-92, building mgr, environmental compliance rep, 1992-. **Orgs:** Member, American Chemical Society, 1983-; member, American Society of Lubrication Engineers, 1983-85; member, Society of Automotive Engineers, 1983-85; member, Chicago National Safety Council, 1983-85; member, American Society for Testing Materials, 1983-85. **Honors/Awds:** Elected to Dwight D Eisenhower High School Hall of Fame, Blue Island, IL; Selected by Ebony and Jet Magazines ''Speaking of People'' Sections, 1989; First black person to hold the following positions at Argonne National Laboratory: Laboratory Environmental Compliance Officer; Manager, Waste Management Operations. **Military Serv:** US Army, Specialist E-4, 1964-66; Vietnam Good Conduct Metal. **Business Addr:** Deputy Building Manager, Argonne National Laboratory, 9700 S Cass Ave, Bldg 212, Argonne, IL 60439.

SMITH, AUDREY S.
Human resources executive. **Personal:** Born Feb 24, 1940, Upper Marlboro, MD; daughter of Mary Henry Spriggs and Frank Spriggs; married Lynn H Smith (divorced 1983); children: Michael, Lisa Miller. **Educ:** Hampton University, Hampton, VA, 1957-61; Roger Williams College, Bristol, RI, BS, 1976; University College, University of Maryland, College Park, MD. **Career:** Brown University, Providence, RI, training assistant, 1971-73, director employment & employee relations, 1973-75, associated director of personnel, 1975-78, director of personnal, 1978-81; Montgomery College, Rockville, MD, director of personnel, 1981-89; Princeton University, Princeton, NJ, vice president of human resources, 1989-. **Orgs:** Committee on the Sttus of Women, member, Princeton University, 1989-; member, Multicultural Studies Project, 1990-; member, College & Universities Personnel Assn, 1975-; member, Urban League, 1963-; member, ACE/NIP, 1975-; American Council Education, National Identification Program. **Business Addr:** Vice President of Human Resources, Princeton University, Clio Hall, Princeton, NJ 08540.

SMITH, BARBARA
Restauranteur. **Career:** Former model; B Smith's restaurant, owner, 1986-; TV culinary hostess, 1997. **Honors/Awds:** Mademoiselle, first black woman on cover, 1976. **Special Achievements:** B Smith's Entertaining and Cooking for Friends, Artisan, 1995.

SMITH, BARBARA
Writer. **Personal:** Born Nov 16, 1946, Cleveland, OH. **Educ:** Mount Holyoke Coll, BA 1969; Univ of Pittsburgh, MA 1971. **Career:** Univ of MA, instructor 1976-81; Barnard Coll, instructor 1983; NY Univ, instructor 1985; Univ of MN, vstg prof 1986; vstg prof Hobart William Smith Coll, 1987; Kitchen Table Women of Color Press, director, 1981-95. **Orgs:** Mem/founder Combahee River Collective 1974-80; artist-in-residence Hambidge Ctr for the Arts & Sci 1983, Millay Colony for the Arts 1983, Yaddo 1984, Blue Mountain Ctr 1985; bd of dir NCBLG 1985-; mem NAACP. **Honors/Awds:** Outstanding Woman of Color Awd 1982; Women Educator's Curriculum Awd 1983; Books, ''Conditions, Five The Black Women's Issue,'' co-editor 1979; ''But Some of Us Are Brave, Black Women's Studies,'' co-editor 1982; ''Home Girls, A Black Feminist Anthology,'' editor 1983; ''Yours in Struggle, Three Feminist Perspectives on Anti-Semitism and Racism,'' co-author 1984; The Readers' Companion to US; Women's History, co-editor 1998; The Truth That Never Hurts: Collected Writing 1968-1998, 1998.

SMITH, BARBARA WHEAT
Educational administrator, educator. **Personal:** Born May 28, 1948, Mobile, AL; daughter of Rosetta W Wheat and Sidney W Wheat; divorced; children: Daryl E, Yuri J, Afra S, Mastaki A. **Educ:** Tuskegee University, BA, 1969; University of Wisconsin-Madison, MA, 1972, Ph D, 1982. **Career:** University of Wisconsin, School of Nursing, Equal Opportunities Program, director, 1973-75, academic advisor, 1976, College of Agricultural & Life Sciences, 1978-80; BJ Smith Co Inc Mobile, president, 1982-88; United States Census Bureau, Mobile Alabama, recruiting operations manager, 1990; Searcy Hospital, psychiatric rehabilitation counselor, 1990-91; University of Wisconsin, College of Agricultural & Life Sciences, assistant dean, 1991-. **Orgs:** National Association of Minorities in Agriculture, Natural Resources and Related Sciences, national secretary; Madison Metropolitan Links, Inc, historian; State of Alabama Mental Health Technicians, board of directors; Progressive League, Inc, board of directors; National Assault on Illiteracy, board of directors; Association of Women in Agriculture, cooperation board of advisors; National Conference of Black Mayors, Guyana, South American, trade delegation; American Ethnic Science Society, National Council on Negro Women, Alabama state president; Delta Sigma Theta Sorority. **Honors/Awds:** Governor, State of Alabama, Service Appreciation Award; Delta Sigma Theta Sorority Service Award, 1974; Vilas Fellow, 1975; Advance Opportunity Fellow, 1976-78; Pi Lamba Theta 1976; University of Wisconsin Administrative Development Program; Parents of Minority Students Advisory Council (POMSAC), Distinguished Leadership Award, 1994; Natl Society of Minorities in Agriculture Natl Resources & Related Sciences, Appreciation Awards, 1993, 1994; Dean of Students, Student Organization Service Appreciation Award, Univ of Wisconsin-Madison, 1994; Highlighted in articles appearing in the spring issue of Home Address & Wisconsin Week, Advising Role to Student Clubs, 1993. **Special Achievements:** Articles published, The Black Collegiate Magazine, 4th edition, 1992; article published, Proceedings of the North Central Teaching Symposium, University of Wisconsin-Madison, June 24-26 1991; 2 articles published, The New Times Newspaper Vol, no 7; article published, Wisconsin Agricultural and Life Sciences Alumni Associate, vol 7, no 3, Fall 1978. **Home Addr:** 103 Grand Canyon Dr, Madison, WI 53705. **Business Addr:** Assistant Dean, College of Agricultural & Life Sciences University of Wisconsin, 116 Agriculture Hall 1450 Linden Dr, Madison, WI 53706, (608)262-3003.

SMITH, BEN
Professional football player. **Personal:** Born May 14, 1967, Warner Robbins, GA; son of Bennie Joe. **Educ:** Univ of Georgia, social work, three years; Northeastern Oklahoma A & M, one year. **Career:** Philadelphia Eagles, free safety, 1990-. **Honors/Awds:** First-team All-Southeast Conference, 1988, 1989; second-team All-America, Football News, 1989; team defensive MVP honors, 1989. **Business Addr:** Professional Football Player, Philadelphia Eagles, Veterans Stadium, Broad St & Pattison Ave, Philadelphia, PA 19148.

SMITH, BENJAMIN FRANKLIN
Educator. **Personal:** Born in Martinsville, VA; son of Jessica Smith and Benjamin Smith; married Dorothy P (deceased); children: Pamela Elizabeth. **Educ:** VA Union Univ, BS 1940; Univ of IL, BS 1941, MS 1945; NY Univ, MA 1949, PhD 1951. **Career:** NC Col, prof of psychology 1947-64; Univ of IL, vis prof grad sch 1964; Towson State Univ, part-time prof 1966, 1967; Jessup State Hosp, psychologist 1969-70; Howard Univ, part-time prof 1970-72; Morgan State Univ, prof, Educ Psychology, chairman, Department of Educational Leadership, director, Doctoral Program, 1972-. **Orgs:** Amer Legion State of NC, talent scout, 1960-63, vice commander; dir Off-Duty Educ Prog for Enlisted Men AUS 1942-45; Amer Psychol Assn; MD Psychol Assn, chmn human resources com, 1977; Amer Educ Rsch Assn; Phi Delta Kappa; NAACP; elder Grace Presbyterian Church; Amer Acad of Social Sciences; pres NC Library Assn; American Sociological Assn. **Honors/Awds:** Omega Man of the Yr; elder & clerk of sessions Grace United Presby Ch; mem evaluation teams for the State Dept of Pub Instr, So Assn of Schs & Colls, Natl Council for the Accreditation of Tchr Edn; mem Prgm Com of Div 16 APA 1975-77. **Military Serv:** AUS. **Business Addr:** Professor of Psychology, Morgan State Univ, 315 Jenkins Bldg, Baltimore, MD 21239.

SMITH, BENNETT W., SR.
Clergyman. **Personal:** Born Apr 7, 1933, Florence, AL; son of Pearlene Smith; married Marilyn J Donelson, Dec 29, 1985; children: Debra T, Bennett W Jr, Lydia R Matthew T. **Educ:** TN State Univ, BS 1958; Cinn Bapt Theo Sem, DD 1967; Medaille Clge, LLD 1979; Colgate Divinity School, MDiv, 1994; Temple Bible Coll & Seminary, Cincinnati, OH, Dr, Sacred Theology, 1997. **Career:** Oper Breadbasket Cinn OH, dir 1967-70; Oper PUSH Buffalo NY, pres 1973-; Oper PUSH, Natl bd mem 1973-; VA MI Housing Co, bd chrmn 1981-; Pres Oper PUSH Buffalo, pastor St John Baptist Ch. **Orgs:** Life mem NAACP 1978-, Kappa Alpha Psi Frat 1979-; Prog Natl Bapt Conv vp, 1984-94, pres, 1994-; trustee, Sheenan Memorial Hospital, 1988-; trustee, Amer Bapt Seminary of the West, 1994. **Honors/Awds:** Medgar Evers NAACP Buffalo NY 1982; Outstanding Bl Ach 1490 Enterprise 1981; author, Handbook on Tithing, PNBC Publishing House, 1980-; Honorary DDiv from the American Bapt Seminary of the West, 1994; Evans/Young Award, Urban League, Buffalo, NY, 1996. **Military Serv:** USAF s/sgt. **Business Addr:** Senior Pastor, St John Baptist Church, 184 Goodell St, Buffalo, NY 14204.

SMITH, BERNICE LEWIS
Educational administrator. **Personal:** Born in St Louis, MO; married Thomas Peter (deceased); children: Karla Denyce. **Educ:** Stowe Tchrs Clge, AB 1948; Univ of IL, MA 1951; St Louis Univ, 1963; Univ of Chicago, 1952; SE MO State Univ, 1972; Harris-stowe State, 1976; Univ of MO, Post Grad 1980. **Career:** Riddick School, teacher 1948-51; Riddick Branch School, teacher 1950-51; Clark Elem School, principal 1956-58; Clark Branch 1 School, teacher 1958-67; Clark Branch 2 School, principal 1967-84; Arlington Elem School, principal 1984-. **Orgs:** Bd mem MO Kidney Fnd 1976-83; courtesy comm Elem Schl Admin 1978-; corr secr Sigma Gamma Rho Sor Inc 1982-84; lecturer and TV appearances Kidney Fnd 1976-; pres Wayman AME Church Schlrshp Council 1984-. **Honors/Awds:** Mother of the Year Sigma Gamma Rho 1982; Apple for the Teacher Iota Phi Lambda 1983; Outstanding Comm Srv St Louis Ambassadors 1983; 1988 Bould Hostess Sigma Gamma Rho Sor Inc.

SMITH, BETTIE M.
Educator. **Personal:** Born Apr 26, 1914, Knoxville; married David L. **Educ:** TN A&I Univ Nashville, BS; NY U, MA, EdD. **Career:** Catoosa & Whitfield Cts GA, teacher; Emory St HS Dalton, GA, teacher coach; Stephens School Calhoun, GA, prin; Harrison HS West Point, prin; NY Univ, instr; FL A&M, assc prof; School Food Serv Program GA State Dept of Educ, instr; Twin Cities Ext Am Theol Sem Nashville, instr; Stillman Coll Tuscaloosa, AL, prof. **Orgs:** Mem Natl Assc; GA Cncl Scndry Sch; prins Natl Ed & GA Assc Ed; Am Assc AL Assc For Hlth, Phy Ed & Recreation; Am Sch Food Assc; Am Sch-Hlth Assc; Schlmstrs Clb GA; GA State Bd Am Cancer Soc; GA Chap Pi Lambda Theta; Alpha Kappa Mu; Alpha Kappa Alpha; former Mem GA Textbook Selection Com; rep NY Univ at World Hlth Orgn Helsink, Finland; mem GA Com White House Conf on Ed. **Honors/Awds:** Woman of yr Dalton GA. **Business Addr:** Box 4901, Stillman Coll, Tuscaloosa, AL 35401.

SMITH, BEVERLY EVANS
Telecommunications co. executive. **Personal:** Born Apr 12, 1948, Massillon, OH; daughter of Willa Dumas Evans and Louie Edward Evans; married Stephen J Smith, Aug 28, 1970; children: Brian S, Stacy N. **Educ:** Bowling Green State Univ, Bowling Green OH, BS, 1970; Kent State Univ, Kent OH, MEd, 1973; Babson Coll, Wellesley MA, Exec Devel Consortium, 1987. **Career:** Kent State Univ, Kent OH, asst dir, Financial Aids, 1972-74, dir, Upward Bound, 1974; Georgia State Univ, Atlanta GA, asst dean, Student Life, 1976-78; Southern Bell, Atlanta GA, staff manager, 1978-83; AT&T, Atlanta GA, dist mgr, transition planning, 1990-; Delta Sigma Theta, Washington DC, exec dir, 1988-90. **Orgs:** Past officer, mem, Delta Sigma Theta Sorority Inc, 1967-; past pres, Jack & Jill Inc, North Suburban Atlanta Chapter, 1981-84; state commr, Georgia Clean & Beautiful Commn, 1984-88; chair, Adult Educ, St Catherine's Episcopal Church, 1986-88; mem, Leadership Cobb, Cobb County Georgia Selection, 1987-91, Project Mgmt Inst, 1987-89, Assn Chief Exec Council, 1988-89; bd mem, Women for a Meaningful Summit, 1989; adv bd, United Way, Cobb County, 1991. **Honors/Awds:** Outstanding Freshman & Senior Woman, Bowling Green State Univ, 1967, 1970; Mortar Bd Honor Soc, 1969; Omicrom Delta Kappa Honor Soc, 1977; Georgia Woman of the Year in Business, Cobb County Georgia, 1984; Outstanding Business Professional, Washington DC Business Professional Assn, 1988. **Business Addr:** District Manager, HR-Performance Mgnt, Rm 23W23, 1200 Peachtree St, NE, Atlanta, GA 30309.

SMITH, BOB
Businessman, artist. **Personal:** Born Apr 3, 1932, Chicago, IL; son of Lois Etta Bullock Smith and Henry D Smith; married Rosemary Booker Smith, Aug 24, 1952; children: Laura Susan, David Bernard, Stacy Donnell. **Educ:** East Los Angeles Coll, LA, CA, AA, 1952; California School of Art, Los Angeles, CA, 1948; Art Center School of Design, Los Angeles, CA, BPA, 1958. **Career:** Merville Studios, Los Angeles, CA, illustrator, 1959-60; ACP Graphic Art Studio, Los Angeles, CA, illustrator, 1960-62; freelance illustrator, Los Angeles, CA, 1962-67; Tri-Arts Studio, Los Angeles, CA, illustrator, 1967-75; freelance Illustrator, Los Angeles, CA, 1975-; Blacksmiths Cards and Prints, Altadena, CA, owner, pres, 1980-. **Orgs:** member, Los Angeles Society of Illustrators, 1958-; member, Graphic Arts Guild; advisory committee, Los Angeles Trade Technical College. **Honors/Awds:** CEBA Award of Distinction, World Institute of Black Communications, Graphics Annual International Annual of Advertising & Editorial Art, 1979-80; Best Black & White Illustration, Society of Illustrators, 1960; Exhibitor International Exhibition of Media Arts Communication Arts Magazine, 1976, 1978, 1979. **Military Serv:** US Army, Sgt, 1952-54. **Business Addr:** President, CEO, Blacksmiths Cards & Prints Inc, PO Box 623, Altadena, CA 91003, (818)794-1167.

SMITH, BOBBY ANTONIA
Government official. **Personal:** Born Feb 12, 1949, West Palm Beach, FL; daughter of Ida Mae Smith and Will Smith; divorced; children: Antonia, Erika. **Educ:** Florida A&M Univ, BS, 1970; Florida State Univ, MPA, 1972; Nova Univ, 1983-. **Career:** Broward County School District, Pompano Beach FL, instructor, 1970-73; Florida Dept of Community Affairs, Tallahassee FL, local govt spec II, 1973-75; Florida WPB, asst county administrator, 1975—. **Orgs:** NAACP; Urban League of Palm Beach County. **Honors/Awds:** Public service award, Florida A&M Univ, 1979. **Business Addr:** Asst County Administrator, Palm Beach County, Board of County Commissioners, 301 N Olive, Governmental Center Complex, 11th Fl, West Palm Beach, FL 33402.

SMITH, BRUCE BERNARD
Professional football player. **Personal:** Born Jun 18, 1963, Norfolk, VA; married Carmen; children: Alston. **Educ:** Virginia Tech, attended. **Career:** Buffalo Bills, defensive end, 1985-. **Honors/Awds:** Sporting News NFL All-Star Team, 1987, 1988; post-season play: AFC Championship Game, 1988, Pro Bowl, 1987, 1988, 1989, 1990, 1992, 1993, 1994, 1995, 1996; Outland Trophy recipient, 1985; NFLPA, AFC Defensive Player of the Year, 1985; Ed Block Courage Award, 1992; Newspaper Enterprise Assn, George Halas Trophy, 1993. **Business Addr:** Professional Football Player, Buffalo Bills, One Bills Dr, Orchard Park, NY 14127, (716)648-1800.

SMITH, BRUCE L.
Automotive company executive. **Personal:** Born Oct 15, 1962, McKeesport, PA. **Educ:** Carnegie-Mellon University, BS, 1985; Harvard University, MBA, 1989. **Career:** Delphi, General Motors maintenance super, 1985-86, manufacturing engineering, 1989, manufacturing general supervisor, 1989-90; ITT manager of manufacturing systems, 1993-94, executive assistant to CEO, 1994-95, plant manager, 1995-97; Diesel Technology Co, pres, CEO, currently. **Military Serv:** Air Force, cadet, 1980-81. **Business Addr:** President/CEO, Diesel Technology Co, PO Box 888653, Grand Rapids, MI 49588-8653, (616)554-6501.

SMITH, BUBBA
Former professional athlete, actor. **Personal:** Born 1947; divorced. **Educ:** MI State, Sociology. **Career:** Baltimore Colts, defensive lineman 1967-71; Oakland Raiders; defensive lineman 1972-74; Houston Oilers, defensive lineman 1975-77; Actor, Blue Thunder 1984, Half Nelson 1985, Police Academy, Police Academy II, Black Moon Rising, The Fun Buch; Video, Until It Hurts; Miller Beer Co, spokesman 1976-. **Orgs:** Vol Young People in LA Area. **Honors/Awds:** All American MI State 1965, 1966; All American Team Sporting News 1966; First Player selected NFL Draft 1967; AFC All Star Team Sporting News 1970, 1971; player Super Bowl 1969, 1971; player AFC Championship 1973, 1974. **Business Addr:** Spokesman, Miller Beer, 3939 West Highland Blvd, Milwaukee, WI 53201.

SMITH, C. MILES, JR.
Broadcast journalist. **Personal:** Born Apr 2, 1950, Atlanta, GA; son of Margaret N Smith and C Miles Smith; married Jul 19, 1975 (divorced); children: Calvin Miles III, Nina Patrice, Che Lena. **Educ:** Morehouse College, BS, 1979. **Career:** WGST-AM, News Radio 640, talk show host, currently. **Orgs:** Omega Psi Phi, Psi Chapter, Morehouse, 1969. **Home Addr:** 1216 New Hope Rd, Atlanta, GA 30331, (404)703-1089.

SMITH, CALVERT H.
Educational administrator. **Career:** Morris Brown College, pres; Cincinnati Public Schools, deputy superintendent, 1992-. **Business Addr:** Deputy Superintendent, Cincinnati Public Schools, 230 E Ninth St, Cincinnati, OH 45202.

SMITH, CALVIN MILES
Dentist. **Personal:** Born Dec 11, 1924, Atlanta, GA; son of Stella Smith and Harvey Smith; married Margaret Odessa Nixon; children: Calvin Miles, Stephen LaCoste, Lynne LaVada, Kim Clarice. **Educ:** Morehouse Coll, BS 1948; Howard Univ, DDS 1953. **Career:** Ballard HS Macon, teacher 1948-49; Atlanta Res Manpower Training Ctr, den consul; Dentistry, Atlanta 1953-. **Orgs:** Mem Amer Den Soc; pres GA Den Soc 1964-65; pres N GA Den Soc 1963-64; mem N Dist Den Assn; mem house del GA Den Assn; sports comm chmn Natl Den Assn; panel chmn Atlanta Comm Chest 1966-67; pres Atlanta NAACP 1963-64, treas 1962, 1965-66; Atlanta Comm Coop Act 1961-; Mayor's Comm Hot & Res Deseg 1961; mem Atlanta C of C; Gr Atlanta Hous Dev Coop; mem Exec Atlanta Model Cities Prog vice chmn 1967-75; Atlanta Youth Coun 1968; vice pres Fulton Co Dem Club 1963-71; chmn bd Sadie G Mays Mem Inst Care Nurs Home 1953-; 32nd Degree Mason. **Honors/Awds:** Citizen Yr 1964; Ach Awd from Guardsmen 1964; Pgh Civic League Awd for Ded Serv in Model Cities 1974; Dist Serv Awd Morehouse Club 1961; Unheralded Citizens Awd Atlanta Job Corps 1977; Outstanding Achievement Awd Radio Station WLTA-100 1979; Disting Alumnus Achievement Awd Morehouse Coll 1976; 25th Anniversary Awd Howard Univ Alumni Assn 1978; Appreciation Awd North GA Dental Soc 1979; Appreciation Awd Atlanta Guardsmen 1980; Atlanta Magazine as one of Atlanta's City Shapers; Harper Awd & Procalmation for Contributions NAACP; AB Cooper Awd & Past Pres Awd 1983 from N Ga Dental Soc; honorable fellow awd GA Dental Assn 1983. **Military Serv:** USMCR pto 1944-46.

SMITH, CARL WILLIAM
Administrator. **Personal:** Born Jun 8, 1931, Raleigh, NC; married Pearl Mitchell Wilson; children: Wanda, Wendi. **Educ:** St Augustine Coll, BA (Honors) 1954; NC Central Univ, MSC 1962; Univ of WI-Madison, attended 1965; The Exec Program Univ NC-Chapel Hill, Certificate1981. **Career:** CE Perry HS, asst principal/teacher 1954-55; St Augustine's Coll, administrator/instructor 1955-60; NC Central Univ, asst chmn/faculty 1961-72; Univ NC-Chapel Hill, asst to the provost 1972-. **Orgs:** Consultant PPG Industries 1969, 70, 71; mem Amer Mgmt Assoc, Amer Marketing Assoc, Amer Assoc of Higher Educ. **Honors/Awds:** Alpha Phi Alpha Frat Inc; Alpha Kappa Mu; Fellowship Natl Urban League 1968. **Military Serv:** USAF airman 1949. **Home Addr:** 1310 Oakwood Ave, Raleigh, NC 27610. **Business Addr:** Asst to the Provost, University of North Carolina, 104B South Bldg UNC-CH, Chapel Hill, NC 27514.

SMITH, CAROL BARLOW
City official. **Personal:** Born Mar 9, 1945, Atlanta, GA; married Douglas Smith; children: Eric Douglas. **Educ:** AK Business College, attended 1965; Wayland Baptist University, BA (cum laude), 1996. **Career:** Gr Anchorage Area Comm Action Agency Northwest Rep of Women's Caucus, public information specialist; BLM Anchorage, asst to chief br of field surveys; City of Anchorage, eeo officer; Municipality of Anchorage, affirm action compliance officer, currently. **Orgs:** Mem Intl Assn of Official Human Rights Agencies; bd dir AK Presswomen; Council on Drug Abuse; Council for Planned Parenthood; bd dir Citizens for Consumer Protection; YWMU; pres New Hope Bapt Ch; mem bd commrs AK State Human Rights Commn; past 2nd vice pres NAACP; AK Presswomen; Anchorage Bicentennial Commn; chmn AK State Human Rights Comm 1976; Anchorage Equal Rights assn; chairperson NAACP Freedom Fund Banquet 1972; vice chairperson AK State Human Rights Commn. **Honors/Awds:** Business Leader of the Day 1974; Outstanding Student Award, Wayland Baptist University. **Business Addr:** Affirmative Action Compliance Officer, Municipality of Anchorage, 632 W 6th Ave, Ste 720, Anchorage, AK 99501.

SMITH, CAROL J. (CAROL J. HOBSON)
Private consultant. **Personal:** Born Dec 24, 1923, Houston, TX; daughter of Julia Augusta Somerville Andrews (deceased) and Richard T Andrews, Sr (deceased); divorced; children: Julius W Hobson Jr, Jean M Hobson. **Educ:** Prairie View, BA 1944; Howard Univ, MA 1948. **Career:** US Office of Education, deputy acting asst commn for spec concern 1971-74; US Dept of Educ Office of Postsecondary Educ, liaison for minorities & women in higher educ 1974-84, prog delegate natl adv committee on black higher educ & black colls & univs 1976-82; US Dept of Educ Office of Higher Educ Progs, dir; Div of Student Serv 1984-86; Howard Univ, Washington, DC, conf coordinator, 1989-90; private practice, consultant, currently. **Orgs:** Elder Church of the Redeemer Presbyterian; mem adv consult to NAFEO Educ Braintrust, Congressional Black Caucus; vice pres B May's Research Center. **Honors/Awds:** Graduate Fellowships Howard Univ 1944-45 1947-48; Superior Serv Awd US Office of Educ 1970; Cert for Outstanding Performance US Dept of Educ Office of the Postsecondary Educ 1979; Achievement Awd Natl Alliance of Black Sch Educators 1982; Leadership Awd in Higher Educ Natl Assn for Equal Oppor in Higher Educ 1983; Honored by Natl Council of Educ Oppor Assoc 1986; Phenomenal Women Tribute, 1997. **Business Addr:** Consultant, 4801 Queens Chapel Terr NE, Washington, DC 20017.

SMITH, CAROLYN LEE
Business executive. **Personal:** Born Nov 14, 1942, Lakewood, NJ; daughter of Arline Erwin Knight and Davis Lee; married Vernon, Oct 16, 1965 (deceased); children: Sonia, Angela. **Educ:** Howard University, BA, 1965; University of Maryland, MBA, 1994. **Career:** DC Dept of Fin & Revenue 1979-82, dir govt dc, tres 1977-79; Cooper & Lybrand, audit mgr 1971-77; natl inst for comm dev, vice pres fin mgmt 1972-73; United Plng Orgn, bkpng methods specIst 1965-66; Coopers & Lybrand, audit mgr 1982-85, dir, mgmt consult 1985-86, partner 1986. **Orgs:** Mem Natl Assoc Black Accts; past pres Met Wash DC Chapt; mem Greater Wash Bd of Trade 1983-; treas Public Access Bd 1985-87; chmn DC Bd of Accountancy 1985-88; bd of gov DC Inst of CPAs 1985-87; mem DC Retirement Bd 1988-92; chairman, DC Retirement Board, 1990-92. **Honors/Awds:** DC CPA 1969; Meritorious Service Awds from DC Govt 1979,80; Outstanding Achievement Awd Natl Assoc of Minority CPA Firms 1979; Key to the City of Cleveland 1981; Proclamation from the Mayor of the District of Columbia for Outstanding Service 1982. **Business Addr:** Partner, Coopers & Lybrand, 1530 Wilson Blvd, Arlington, VA 22209.

SMITH, CARSON EUGENE
Educational administrator. **Personal:** Born Dec 23, 1943, Louisville, KY; son of Louise Bernadine Carson Smith and Fred Eugene Smith; married Gleneva McCowan, Dec 26, 1965; children: Mark, Shanna, Angela, Andrew. **Educ:** KY State Univ, BA History & Pol Sci 1965; Univ of KY, MA Pol Sci 1972, Dissertation Stage 1973. **Career:** Office for Policy & Mgmt State Govt, policy adv for higher educ 1973-74; Council on Higher Educ, coor for fin planning 1974-77; Univ of KY, asst budget dir 1977-80; Univ of MO, asst dir budget 1980-83; KY State Univ, vice pres business affairs; Univ of KY, Coll of Medicine, Lexington, KY, business mgr, 1990-. **Orgs:** Mem Central Assoc of Coll & Univ Bus Officers, Southern Assoc of Coll & Univ Bus Officers, Natl Assoc of Coll & Univ Bus Officers, Alpha Phi Alpha 1962-. **Military Serv:** USAF capt 4 yrs. **Home Addr:** 169 Bellemeade Dr, Frankfort, KY 40601. **Business Addr:** Business Manager, College of Medicine, University of Kentucky, 800 Rose St MN 140 Chandler Medical Ctr, Lexington, KY 40536-0084.

SMITH, CEDRIC DELON
Professional football player. **Personal:** Born May 27, 1968, Enterprise, AL; married Nicole; children: Chandler, Canyon. **Educ:** Florida, bachelor's degree in rehabilitative counseling. **Career:** Minnesota Vikings, running back, 1990; New Orleans Saints, 1991; Washington Redskins, 1994-95; Arizona Cardinals, 1996-. **Business Addr:** Professional Football Player, Arizona Cardinals, 8701 S Hardy, Tempe, AZ 85284, (602)379-0101.

SMITH, CHARLES
County official (retired). **Personal:** Born Oct 4, 1914, Lowndes, AL; son of Odell Pradd Smith and Nathaniel Smith; married Ella Mae Timmon Smith, Oct 26, 1936; children: Jess C, Charles E, Mary Lu Allen, Doris Collier, Lonnie, Josephos, El oise, Ferlonia Davis, Eli B, Jeremiah, Theo. **Educ:** Univ WI, Cert from Flwng Inst 1968; Penn Comm Ctr 1968; Lowndes Co Training Sch. **Career:** Shipyard Mobile, AL, erector 1942-45; Farmer 1945-65; Lowndes Co Bd Deacons Mt Calvary Bapt Ch, co commr; Lawndes Co State of AL, county commissioner, currently. **Orgs:** Chmn Lowndes & Co Christian Movement; mem adv coun of Title I Pgm in Lownde Co; bd dir Lowndes Co Hlth Serv Assc. **Honors/Awds:** Awrd Natl Urban League for Equal Opportunity 1969; Ford Fellowhship 1970-71; Citation of Merit Award Auburn Univ AL. **Home Addr:** RFD 1 Box 271, Letohatchee, AL 36047.

SMITH, CHARLES C.
Professional basketball player. **Personal:** Born Aug 22, 1975. **Educ:** New Mexico. **Career:** Miami Heat, guard, 1997-98; Los Angeles Clippers, 1998-. **Business Addr:** Professional Basketball Player, Los Angeles Clippers, 3939 S Figueroa St, Los Angeles Sports Arena, Los Angeles, CA 90037, (213)748-8000.

SMITH, CHARLES DANIEL, JR.
Professional basketball player, youth foundation founder. **Personal:** Born Jul 16, 1965, Bridgeport, CT; son of Dorthy J Childs Lee and Charles D Smith. **Educ:** Univ of Pittsburgh, Pittsburgh, PA, 1984-88. **Career:** Center/forward: Los Angeles Clippers, 1988-92, New York Knicks, 1992-96; San Antonio Spurs, 1996-; Charles Smith Educational Center, Bridgeport, CT, owner, founder, 1991-. **Orgs:** Founder, Charles D Smith Jr Foundation, 1989-. **Honors/Awds:** NBA All-Rookie First Team, 1989; member of the US Olympic team, 1988; Outstanding Serviceman, Assemblywoman Maxine Waters, 1990; Services Appreciation, 5th Central LA YMCA, 1989; Key to the City, City of Bridgeport, 1990. **Business Addr:** Professional Basketball Player, San Antonio Spurs, 600 E Market St, Ste 102, San Antonio, TX 78205.

SMITH, CHARLES EDISON
Educator. **Educ:** California Polytechnic, BS, 1965; Georgetown University, Washington, DC, JD, 1972; Duke University, LLM, 1983. **Career:** US Patent and Trademark Office, Washington, DC, Patent Examiner, 1967-69; Xerox Corp, Patent Attorney, 1972-75; Bechtel Corp, Patent Attorney, 1975-78; Golden Gate University, Assistant Professor of Law, 1977-79; Con Edison, Consultant, 1987-; North Carolina Central University School of Law, Durham, NC, Professor, currently. **Orgs:** Arbitrator, American Bar Assn, 1979-, state reporter (NC), ABA Limited Partnership Laws, 1986-; member, Delta Theta Phi Law Fraternity, 1970-; commissioner, North Carolina Statutes Commission, 1987-; attorney volunteer, AIPLA Inventor Consulting Service, 1985-; state reporter (NC), ABA Limited Liability Company Act, 1993-. **Honors/Awds:** Fellowship Grant, Duke University, 1982-83; American Jurisprudence Award, Lawyers Cooperative Publishers. **Military Serv:** US Army, Spec E-5, 1960-63; Good Conduct Medal, Expert Marksman, 1963. **Business Addr:** Professor of Law, North Carolina Central University School of Law, 1512 S Alston Ave, Durham, NC 27707.

SMITH, CHARLES F., JR.
Educator. **Personal:** Born Jan 5, 1933, Cleveland, OH; son of Julia Anna Worthy and Charles Frank Smith, Sr; married Lois Thompson; children: Carolyn Adelle, Charles Frank III. **Educ:** Bowling Green State Univ, BS 1960; Kent State Univ, EdM 1963; Harvard Univ Grad School Ed, CAS 1965; MI State Univ, EdD 1969. **Career:** Elementary School Teacher Lorain OH 1960-62; Peace Corps Field Trgn Ctr Puerto Rico, dir 1962-63; Peace Corps, spec asst 1963; Flint Publ Schools, asst dir elem ed 1965-66; MI State Univ, instr ed 1966-68; Boston Coll, assoc prof ed, prof emeritus, currently. **Orgs:** Mem adv task force MA Comm Crim Justice; adv council MA Council Bilingual Ed; adv comm MA Comm Minority Higher Ed; bd of dir School Vols Boston; adv task force, implement phase I deseg Boston Publ School; chmn Area Welfare Bd; vice pres Black Citizen of Newton; chmn Black Faculty Staff and Administrators Assoc of Boston Coll; mem Curriculum Comm Natl Cncl for the Social Studies; bd of dir MA Council of the Social Studies; bd of dir, Natl Council for the Social Studies. **Honors/Awds:** Phi Delta Kappa Teaching Fellow Harvard Univ Grad School Ed 1963-65, Danforth Assoc 1974; Traveling Fellowships Cameroons & Nigeria, Africa, 1958, 1960, Canada 1957, Germany 1954, Jamaica 1953; Visiting Scholar Univ of MI, 1988, Atlanta Univ, 1991, Yale Univ, 1995. **Military Serv:** US Army medic 1954-56. **Business Addr:** Professor Emeritus, Education, Boston College, Campion Hall, 140 Commonwealth Ave, Chestnut Hill, MA 02167.

SMITH, CHARLES HENRY, III
Professional football player. **Personal:** Born Dec 21, 1969, Athens, GA. **Educ:** Tennessee, attended. **Career:** Atlanta Falcons, defensive end, 1992-. **Business Addr:** Professional Football Player, Atlanta Falcons, Two Falcon Place, Suwanee, GA 30174, (404)945-1111.

SMITH, CHARLES JAMES, III
Educational administrator (retired), consulting company executive. **Personal:** Born Oct 7, 1926, Savannah, GA; son of Katrina Smith and Charles Smith; married Wilma Anis; children: Donna, Charles IV. **Educ:** TN State Univ, AB 1947; St Univ of IA, MA 1948; Univ of MN, Postgrad; FL A&M Univ, attended. **Career:** Savannah State Coll, dir publicity & publ , instructor of journalism, 1948-50; FL A&M Univ, dir publ rel, assoc prof, journalism, 1950-63; Royal Crown Cola Co, dir, spec mkts 1963-71; The Greyhound Corp Phoenix, asst to vice pres special mkts 1971-78; TX So Univ, dir media relations, 1978-90, dir of public affairs and marketing research; Texas Southern University, special asst to the pres, 1993; ceo, Office of Institutional Advancement, 1993; The Chuck Smith Organization, Cultural Diversity Marketing Communications Consultants, consultant, currently. **Orgs:** Art on black consumer mkt Annual Emphasis 1966-87; pres 1970-71, bd chmn 1971-75 Natl Assoc of Mktg Dev; mem Sigma Delta Chi Prol Jrnl Soc, Publ Rel Soc of Amer, Amer Mkt Assoc, Delta Phi Delta Natl Jrnl Soc; former bd mem, vice pres 1973-75, budget comm chmn 1974-76 Phoenix Scottsdale United Way; bd mem Valley Big Bros; past bd mem Phoenix Urban League & Lead Conf on Civil Rights; former mem adv comm US Census Bur for Accurate Black Count 1980. **Honors/Awds:** Newspaper Fund Fellow Mass Media Univ of MN 1971; author A Guide to Total Mkt Penetration 1968. **Business Addr:** Principal, The Chuck Smith Organization, Cultural, Diversity Marketing Communications Consultants, PO Box 45418, Phoenix, AZ 85064-5418.

SMITH, CHARLES LAMONT
Attorney, business executive. **Personal:** Born Jun 24, 1956, Omaha, NE; son of Yvette Wilson and Wilber Smith. **Educ:** Langston University, 1974-76; Clark Atlanta University, BA, 1978; Howard University, School of Law, JD, 1984. **Career:** Gorsuch, Kirgis, Campbell, Walker and Grover, 1984-85; Faegre and Benson, 1985-87; All Pro Sports and Entertainment, Inc, president, CEO, 1987-; Smith and Schaffer, PC, 1987-. **Orgs:** Black Entertainment and Sports Lawyers Association, vp; National Football League Players Association, advisory board member; Clark Atlanta University, School of Sports and Entertainment Management, advisory board; Sam Carey Bar Association, former secretary; Sam Carey Bar Assn. **Honors/Awds:** Mass Communications, Merit Award for Dedicated Service and Scholastic Excellence, 1978; Howard School of Law, American Jurisprudence Award for Scholastic Excellence in the Study of Contracts; Colorado Black Leadership Profile, Trail Blazer, 1989; first Black American agent to represent a Heisman Trophy winner; Howard University, School of Law, Alumni Entrepreneur Award, 1992. **Business Addr:** President/Chief Executive Officer, All Pro Sports and Entertainment, Inc, 1999 Broadway, Ste 3125, Denver, CO 80202, (303)292-3212.

SMITH, CHARLES LEBANON
Administrator. **Personal:** Born Apr 30, 1938, Neptune, NJ; married Muriel Lyle; children: Stacey, Romy, Kecia. **Educ:** Albright Coll Reading PA, BA psychology 1960. **Career:** US Dept of Labor, Labor Mgmt Svc, compliance officer, 1966-70, sr compliance officer, 1970-74, field liaison officer, 1974-75, dep asst reg administrator, 1975-77, asst reg administrator, 1977-78, reg administrator, 1978-89, Office of the Assistant Secretary for Administration & Management, regional administrator, 1989-. **Orgs:** So of Fed Labor Relations Professional 1972-; Indsl Relations Research Assn 1978-; Omega Psi Phi Frat Inc 1974-; former chmn NJ Black Heritage Festival 1978-79; Monmouth Men's Club. **Honors/Awds:** Secretary's Spl Commendation US Dept of Labor 1973. **Business Addr:** Regional Administrator, Office of the Assistant Secretary for Administration & Management, 201 Varicks, Rm 807, New York, NY 10014.

SMITH, CHARLES LEON
Automobile dealer. **Personal:** Born Feb 7, 1953, Charleston, WV; son of Frances Elizabeth Brown Smith and James Smith; married Emma Ruth Witten Smith, Feb 26, 1977; children: Charles, Andrew. **Educ:** West Virginia Wesleyan College, Buckhannon, WV, BS, business administration, 1972-76; West Virginia School of Banking, Charleston, WV, banking degree, 1979-83; National Automobile Dealers Association Dealer Academy, 1985-86; Ford Motor Co. Dealer Academy Program, Detroit, MI, 1986-88. **Career:** CL Smith Enterprises, Clarks Summit, PA, president/owner, 1977-; Kanawha Banking & Trust, Charleston, WV, vice president of loans, 1978-85; Ford Motor Co., Detroit, MI, dealer candidate, 1985-88. **Orgs:** Member, Kiwanis Club, 1990; vice president, Lackawanna Valley Auto Dealers Association, 1988-; member, Black Ford Lincoln Mercury Dealers Association, 1988-; member, Scranton Chamber of Commerce; board of directors, Optimist Club, 1980-85; advisory board member, West Virginia State Community College, 1982-85; treasurer, Charleston Professional and Business Club, 1978-85; member, West Virginia State Senate Small Business Advisory Board, 1982-85; board member/treasurer, Charleston Housing Board, 1979-83; selective service board member, Charleston, WV, 1982-85. **Honors/Awds:** Black Enterprise 100 Top Black Auto Dealers, Black Enterprise, 1989; Outstanding Achievement Award, Ford Motor Credit Co., 1989.

SMITH, CHARLES U.
Educator (retired). **Personal:** Born in Birmingham; married; children: Shauna. **Educ:** Tuskegee Inst, BA 1944; Fisk Univ, MA 1946; WA State Univ, PhD 1950; Univ of MI, postdoctoral study 1958. **Career:** FL A&M Univ, grad dean beginning 1974. **Orgs:** Pres So Sociol Soc; mem Amer Sociol Assn 1960-; Natl Soc Study Educ 1973-; Amer Acad Polit Soc Sci 1969-; WFSU TV adv Com 1973-; edit bd Journal Soc & Behavioral Sci 1973-; adj prof sociol FL State Univ 1966-; state committeeman 1975; mem Leon Co Dem exec comm 1969-; bd dir Leon Co CAP 1972-; bd of advisors FL Mental Health Inst; pres Conf of Deans of Black Grad Schs; mem Council of Grad Schls in US; Conf of So Grad Schs; editoral bd Negro Ed Review 1976-; editor FL A&M Rsch Bulletin 1960-; consul SC Comm on Higher Educ 1984. **Honors/Awds:** Honor Societies, Sigma XI, Alpha Kappa Delta, Pi Gamma Mu, Alpha Kappa Mu, Phi Delta Kappa, Sigma Rho Sigma, Phi Kappa Phi, Lambda Alpha Epsilon; plaque Serv Dept Sociol 1970; Coll Athletics 1966; Cert Serv State FL 1965 1972; Silver Mental Health Serv 1966; Gold Medallion 1970; FL delegate White House Conf 1960 1965 19701971; DuBois Awd Scholarship Serv 1973; FL A&M Univ Merit Achievement Awd 1973; plaque Sociol 1974; FAMU Martin Luther King Leadership Award, 1995; Southern Sociological Society Distinguished Career Award, 1997. **Special Achievements:** Author, editor, co-author: 14 books, 8 monographs, appox 80 scholarly and research journals, 10 book reviews, 12 copyrighted songs and lyrics; emeritus distinguished professor and graduate dean at FAMU.

SMITH, CHARLIE CALVIN
Educator. **Personal:** Born Jun 12, 1943, Brickeys, AR; son of Estella Smith and Charlie Smith; married Earline Williams. **Educ:** AM & N Coll Pine Bluff AR, BA history 1966; AR State Univ Jonesboro, MSE social science 1971; Univ of AR Fayetteville, PhD US history 1978. **Career:** AR State Univ, asst prof of History 1978-; AR State Univ, instructor in History 1970-78; Lee Co Public School Marianna AR, Social Studies teacher, asst football coach 1966-70; Arkansas State Univ, assoc prof of History, 1982-86, asst dean 1986-. **Orgs:** Comm mem AR Endowment for the Humanities 1975-77; gov appointee bd mem AR Student Loan Assn 1975-76; gov appointee bd mem AR Historic Preservation Program 1979-84; mem Jonesboro Rotary Club, 1987-; pres Southern Conference on Afro-Amer Studies, 1988-. **Honors/Awds:** Published ''The Oppressed Oppressors Negro Slavery among the choctaws of OK'' red river valley history review vol 2 1975; published ''the civil war letters of John G Marsh'' Upper OH Valley History Review 1979; published ''The Diluting of an Inst the social impact of WWII on the AR family'' AR history quarter (spring) 1980; published biographical sketches of AR Governors J Marion Futrell & Homer M Adkins AR Ednowment for the Humanities 1980; Presidential Fellow, Arkansas State Univ, 1982; Outstanding Black Faculty Member/Teacher, Black Student Body ASU, 1984-86, 1988; War and Wartime Changes; The Transformation of Arkansas, 1940-45, U of A Press, 1987. **Business Addr:** Assistant Dean, College of Arts & Sciences, Professor of History, Arkansas State University, PO Box 1030, State University, AR 72467.

SMITH, CHARLOTTE
Professional basketball player. **Personal:** Born Aug 23, 1973. **Educ:** Univ of North Carolina. **Career:** San Jose Lasers, forward, 1996-. **Business Addr:** Professional Basketball Player, San Jose Lasers, 1530 Parkmoor Ave, Ste A, San Jose, CA 95128, (408)271-1500.

SMITH, CHELSI
Miss Universe, 1995. **Career:** Winner of Miss Universe pageant, 1995. **Business Addr:** Miss Universe, 1995, c/o Miss Universe, 1801 Century Park East, Ste 2100, Los Angeles, CA 90067.

SMITH, CHESTER B.
Government official. **Personal:** Born Jul 1, 1954, Mound Bayou, MS. **Educ:** Tufts Univ, BA 1976; Northwestern Univ, MBA 1977, JD 1980. **Career:** Delta Capital Corp, vice-pres 1980-84; Pro-Mark Inc, financial consultant 1984-85; Private Practice, attorney 1983-86; US Dept of Commerce Minority Business Dev Agency, asst dir 1986-. **Orgs:** Vstg prof Black Exec Exchange Program 1981-83; former dir New Memphis Dev Corp 1981-84; founder Ctr for Economic Growth 1982; mem MS State Bar Assoc 1982-87; consultant Project Business 1982-85; consultant TN Valley Authority 1985-86. **Honors/Awds:** Junior Achievement 1983-85; Disting Serv Awd Natl Business League 1986; Executive Forum Dept of Commerce 1987. **Home Addr:** PO Box 2746, Arlington, VA 22202. **Business Addr:** Assistant Dir, US Dept of Commerce, 14th & Pennsylvania Ave, Room 5096, Washington, DC 20230.

SMITH, CHRIS G.
Professional basketball player. **Personal:** Born May 17, 1970, Bridgeport, CT. **Educ:** Connecticut, 1992. **Career:** Minnesota Timberwolves, guard, 1992-. **Business Addr:** Professional Basketball Player, Minnesota Timberwolves, 600 First Ave N, Minneapolis, MN 55403, (612)337-3865.

SMITH, CLARENCE O.
Publishing company executive. **Personal:** Born Mar 31, 1933, Bronx, NY; son of Millicent Fry (deceased) and Clarence Smith (deceased); married Elaine Goss Smith, Jun 22, 1963; children: Clarence, Craig. **Educ:** Baruch School of Business, 1960-61. **Career:** Prudential Insurance Co of America, NY, special rep, 1963-69; Investors Planning Corp, New York, registered rep, 1966-69; Essence Communications Inc, New York, pres, 1969-. **Orgs:** Chmn, African American Marketing & Media Assn, 1991; Dir-at-large, the Advertising Council; mem, Amer Mgmt Assn; bd of dirs, Cosmetic, Toiletry & Fragrance Assn; mem, African American Task Force of Media-Advertising Partnership for Drug-Free America. **Honors/Awds:** Communicator of the Year, Natl Assn of Market Developers, 1990; Meritorious Serv Award, UNCF, 1990; Annual Achievement Award, Black Enterprise Magazine, 1980; Principal's Award, Henry Highland Garnet School for Success, 1988-89; Black Achievement Award, The Equitable Assurance Soc of US, 1985. **Military Serv:** US Army, Spl 4th Class, 1957-59. **Business Addr:** President, Essence Communications Inc, 1500 Broadway, New York, NY 10036.

SMITH, CLEVELAND EMANUEL
Physician. **Personal:** Born Oct 5, 1924, Panama; married Beatrice; children: Nancy, Cleveland Jr, Clifford. **Educ:** Howard U, BS 1950; Howard U, MD 1955; resd 1961; cert ob gyn. **Career:** Dept Ob Gyn Howard Univ Coll Med, asst prof 1961-75; Ob Gyn Serv Columbia Hosp for Women, chf; Cleveland E Smith Flw Am Coll Ob Gyn, pres. **Orgs:** Mem Nat Med Assn; Med Chirurgical Soc DC; Dist Med Soc; Med Bd Dir Planned Parenthood. **Business Addr:** 29 Grant Cir NW, Washington, DC 20011.

SMITH, CLIFFORD V., JR.
Educational administrator. **Personal:** Born Nov 29, 1931, Washington, DC; married Nina Marie Singleton; children: Sharon, Debra, Patricia. **Educ:** Univ of Iowa, BSCE, 1954, MSE, 1960, PhD, 1966. **Career:** Pennsylvania Dept of Health, chief engineer, water supply section, 1959-61; Univ of Connecticut, asst prof, 1961-63; Johns Hopkins Univ, research & teaching asst, 1963-65; Univ of Massachusetts, asst prof, 1965-66; Tufts Univ, asst prof, 1966-68; Dorr-Oliver Inc, Stamford, CT, sanitary technology manager, 1968-70; City College of New York, asst prof, 1970-72; US Environmental Protection Agencey, administrator, 1972-74; Univ of Wisconsin at Milwaukee, chancellor/pres, currently. **Orgs:** Member, New England Health Physics Society; member, American Water Works Assn; member, Water Pollution Control Federation; member, International Assn for Water Pollution Research.

SMITH, CONRAD P.
Attorney, political consultant. **Personal:** Born Feb 15, 1932, Detroit, MI; son of Minnie J Smith and Alfred Smith; married Elsie May Smith, Nov 27, 1957; children: Judy E Smith, Conrad W Smith. **Educ:** Howard Univ, BS 1962; Howard Univ, JD 1969. **Career:** US Justice Dept, statistical analyst 1962; US Dept of Labor, manpower research analyst 1962-64; US Comm on Civil Rights, soc sci analyst 1964-66; US Comm on Civil Rights, asst gen counsel 1969-73; private practice law, 1979; political consultant, currently. **Orgs:** Chmn Ward 1 Dem Comm Wash DC; mem ACLU; NAACP; Urban League; People's Involvement Corp; Civic Assn; DC Bar Assn; Danford Fellow 1961; candidate DC City Council 1974; mem DC Bd of Educ 1976-; pres DC Bd of Educ 1978; chmn DC Parent-Child Center Wash DC 1980-85. **Honors/Awds:** Falk Fellowship, Falk Foundation, 1962. **Military Serv:** AUS. **Home Addr:** 722 Fairmont St NW, Washington, DC 20001.

SMITH, CONRAD WARREN
Cleric, physician (retired). **Personal:** Born May 10, 1919, St Thomas, VI; son of Florence Stevens Smith (deceased) and Conrad V Smith (deceased); married Marjorie Estella Weston, Jun 10, 1957; children: Conrad, Arlene Smith Lockridge, Craig, Riise Richards. **Educ:** Lincoln University, BA, 1941; Howard University, School of Medicine, MD, 1944; Harvard University, School of PH, MPH, 1952; El Semnario Episcopal del Caribe, Certificate, theology. 1975. **Career:** Knid-Hansen Hospital, chief of pediatrics, 1955-75; Government of the Virgin Islands, commissioner of health; Episcopal Diocese of the Virgin Islands, vicar of St Ursula Church, currently. **Orgs:** Virgin Islands Medical Society, mem, past president and secretary; Americal Medical Association; Pan American Medical Association; Alpha Phi Alpha Fraternity, chaplin; VI Board of Veterinary Medicine. **Honors/Awds:** St Thomas Hospital, C Warren Smith Pediatric Wing, 1984; VI Boy Scouts Annual Award Distinguished Service, 1986; The Virgin Islands Medical Society Physician of the Year Award, 1986. **Special Achievements:** Physician for the Virgin Islands Olympic Teams in the Caribbean and World Olympics; Developed public health services in the Virgin Islands; Publication: Tables of Maximum Breathing

Capacities in Female Children; Numerous publications of public health reports on the Virgin Islands and Ciguatera. **Military Serv:** US Army, 1st lt, 1943-44, certificate in Medicine, and Good Conduct Medal. **Home Phone:** (809)775-1225.

SMITH, DANIEL H., JR.
Attorney. **Personal:** Born Apr 27, 1933, Chicago, IL; married Joyce; children: David, Robin. **Educ:** Howard University, BA 1959, JD 1966. **Career:** Urban Renewal, consultant; Robin Shore Realty & Ins Agency, pres; self-employed, attorney, currently. **Orgs:** American Bar Assn; Natl Bar Assn; Chicago, IL State Bar Assns; bd dir Legal Assit Found of Chicago; panelist for American Arbitration Assn; The American Judicature Society; Natl Assn of Real Estate Brokers; Dearborn Real Estate Bd; S Shore Gardens Comm Org; Phi Alpha Delta Law Frat; bd dirs Media Inc; J Leslie Rosenblum Chicago Boys Club; South Shore YMCA; Kuumba Comm Theater; VIP Associates. **Military Serv:** US Air Force, 1st lt, 1952-56. **Home Addr:** 655 W Irving Park Rd, No 301, Chicago, IL 60613, (312)528-5422. **Business Addr:** Attorney at Law, Daniel H Smith Jr & Associates, 721 E 75th St, Chicago, IL 60619-1907, (312)483-1688.

SMITH, DARRIN ANDREW
Professional football player. **Personal:** Born Apr 15, 1970, Miami, FL. **Educ:** Miami (Fla.), bachelor's degree in business management, 1991; master's degree in business administration, 1993. **Career:** Dallas Cowboys, linebacker, 1993-96; Philadelphia Eagles, 1997-. **Business Addr:** Professional Football Player, Philadelphia Eagles, 3501 S Broad St, Philadelphia, PA 19148, (215)463-2500.

SMITH, DARRYL C.
Public radio station manager. **Personal:** Born Aug 8, 1966, Baltimore, MD; son of Dorothy C Smith and Elmer N Smith; married Pheorma N Davis, Sep 21, 1991. **Educ:** Morgan State University, 1984-86; Towson State University, BS (cum laude), 1989. **Career:** WJHU-FM, operations manager, 1988-90; WETA-FM, operations manager, 1990-91; KL UM-FM/KJLU-FM, general manager, 1991-. **Orgs:** United Way Communications Committee, 1991-; Blacks in Public Radio, 1991-; Aircraft Owner's and Pilot's Association, 1991-; United Sportsmen's Club, 1991-; Capital JazzFest Committee, 1991-. **Honors/Awds:** US Achievement Academy, All-American Scholar, 1989; Towson State University, dean's list, 1987-88; FAA, Pilot Proficiency Award, 1991. **Business Addr:** General Manger, KJLU-FM, 1004 E Dunklin St, Jefferson City, MO 65102, (314)681-5301.

SMITH, DAVID R.
Attorney. **Personal:** Born Sep 27, 1946, Loveland, OH; son of Mamie Robinson Smith and William E Smith; children: Kimberly K. **Educ:** Central State Univ, Wilberforce OH, BA, 1969; DePaul Univ Coll of Law, Chicago IL, JD, 1974. **Career:** US Dept of Energy, asst chief counsel, 1972-83; Cole & Smith, partner, 1983-85; The MAXIMA Corp, corporate senior vp, gen counsel sec, 1985-; Reed, Smith, Shaw & McClay, counsel; Alexander, Gebhardt, Aponte & Marks, partner, currently. **Orgs:** Alpha Phi Alpha Frat, 1969; Amer Bar Assn; Maryland Bar Assn; Natl Bar Assn; Illinois Bar Assn; admitted to practice: US Supreme Court; US Claims Court; Federal Trial Bars: Illinois; Maryland; Virginia; District of Columbia. **Special Achievements:** Author: "Contracting with The Federal Government: 10 Key Areas," Chicago Bar Association, 1984; Small Business and Technology Devel Contract Mgmt Magazine; Sphinx Magazine, 1983; "Exploring The Energy Frontier," Natl Bar Assn, 1982.

SMITH, DAWN C. F. (DAWN SMITH ROBERTSON)
Marketing director. **Personal:** Born Dec 23, 1960, London, England; daughter of Mavis Collier Smith and George Smith; married Elbert Robertson, Nov 3, 1990. **Educ:** Brown Univ, BA 1982; Univ of MI, MBA 1985. **Career:** Black Student's Guide to Colleges, co-mng editor, 1982; General Mills, market rsch intern 1984; Colgate Palmolive, asst brand mgr 1985-87; Kraft Inc, assoc brand mgr 1987-88; Jacobs Suchard, brand mgr 1988-90; Citicorp's Diners Club, dir mktg, 1990-. **Orgs:** Mem Natl Black MBA Assn 1983-; interviewer, National Alumni Schools Program, Brown University, 1985-. **Honors/Awds:** MBA Consortium Fellowship 1983-85; Natl Black MBA Scholarship 1984.

SMITH, DEBBIE A.
Association executive. **Personal:** Born Apr 12, 1959, Washington, DC. **Educ:** The Catholic University of America, BA, 1981; Howard University, MBA, 1985. **Career:** Xerox, mktg rep, 1985-87; Riggs National Bank, corporate lending officer, 1987-90; Signet Bank, corporate lending officer, 1990-93; US House of Representatives, staff director small business, subcommittee, 1993-94; The National Association of Investment Cos, vice pres, 1994-95; The National Association of Urban Bankers, executive director, currently. **Orgs:** Washington DC Mayor's Congressional Affairs Advisory Group, 1991-; Organization for a New Equality, advisory board member, 1996-. **Honors/Awds:** Organization For a New Equality, Pioneer Awd, 1997. **Business Addr:** Executive Director, National Association of Urban Bankers, 1801 K Street NW, Suite 200-A, Washington, DC 20006, (202)861-0000.

SMITH, DEBORAH P.
Educator, journalist. **Personal:** Born May 6, 1951, Dayton, OH; daughter of Mae Mack Pridgen and John Pridgen; children: Rahsaan, Hakim. **Educ:** Univ of California-Berkeley, Berkeley, CA, certificate, Journalism; Seton Hall Univ, South Orange, NJ, BS, English/History/Secondary Education; Montclair State Coll, Montclair, NJ, postgraduate studies. **Career:** NJ Afro-American newspaper, Newark, NJ, reporter, 1985-88, resident editor, 1988-89; NJ Perspectus News Magazine, Newark, NJ, editor-in-chief, 1989-; Newark Bd of Education, Newark, NJ, educator, 1974-; NJ Perspectus News Magazine, 1989-93; DP Smith Associates, Public Relations, Publishing Co, pres, 1994-. **Orgs:** Mem, Natl Assn of Black Journalists, 1989-; mem, Garden State Assn of Black Journalists, 1990-; mem, NAACP, 1989-; pres of bd of dir, United Academy, 1990-. **Honors/Awds:** Media Woman of the Year, YWCA/Orange, NJ, 1990; Commendation, Newark City Council, 1987. **Home Phone:** (201)733-2260.

SMITH, DEHAVEN L.
Attorney. **Personal:** Born Aug 10, 1928, Baltimore, MD; married Gertrude Jackson; children: Rubye. **Educ:** VA Union Univ, AB 1949; Univ MD School of Law, JD 1958. **Career:** Williams, Smith & Murphy, attorney. **Orgs:** Mem Am Bar Assn, Nat Bar Assn, Monumental City Bar Assn, Baltimore City Bar Assn Judicature Soc; World Peace through Law Comm; NAACP. **Military Serv:** AUS 1950-52.

SMITH, DENNIS
Professional football player. **Personal:** Born Feb 3, 1959, Santa Monica, CA; married Andree; children: Tiffany Diamond, Armani Joseph. **Educ:** Univ of Southern California, attended. **Career:** Denver Broncos, safety, 1981-. **Honors/Awds:** Played in Rose Bowl, Bluebonnet Bowl; named All-NFL Pro Football Weekly, College and Pro Football Newsweekly, 1984; All-AFC, Pro Football Weekly, UPI second team, 1985; played in Pro Bowl, 1985, 1986, 1989, 1991, 1992.

SMITH, DENNIS RAE
Engineer. **Personal:** Born Oct 23, 1961, Lewisville, AR; son of Ardenia L Smith and Lannie A Smith; married Penny Harris Smith. **Educ:** Southern Methodist Univ, BSEE 1985. **Career:** Rockwell International, test engineer. **Orgs:** Vice pres student chap Natl Soc of Black Engrs 1984-85; natl mem at large NAACP 1987; sec Hewlett-Packard Users Group l987-88; volunteer Big Brothers & Sisters l988-. **Honors/Awds:** Featured in article "The Pulse-First Jobs" The Minority Engr Magazine 1986.

SMITH, DENVER LESTER
Insurance agent. **Personal:** Born Sep 21, 1946, Detroit, MI; son of Hattie M Smith and Henry L Smith. **Career:** Denver Smith Insurance Agency, president, currently. **Business Addr:** President, Farmer Insurance Group of Companies, Denver Smith Insurance Agency, 28475 Greenfield, Ste 112, Southfield, MI 48076.

SMITH, DEREK ERVIN
Professional basketball player. **Personal:** Born Nov 1, 1961, Lagrange, GA; married Monica. **Educ:** Louisville, 1982. **Career:** Golden State Warriors, 1982-83; San Diego Clippers, 1983-84; Los Angeles Clippers, 1984-86; Sacramento Kings, 1986-89; Philadelphia 76ers, 1989-90; Boston Celtics, 1990-. **Honors/Awds:** Was a 1st Team Metro Conf All-Tournmnt selection in each of his last 3 seasons at Louisville; also selected Co-Metro Conf Player of Year in 1980-81 as jr.

SMITH, DETRON NEGIL
Professional football player. **Personal:** Born Feb 25, 1974, Dallas, TX. **Educ:** Texas A&M. **Career:** Denver Broncos, running back, 1996-. **Business Addr:** Professional Football Player, Denver Broncos, 13655 Broncos Pkwy, Englewood, CO 80112, (303)649-9000.

SMITH, DOLORES J.
Company executive. **Personal:** Born Feb 10, 1936, Lockport, IL; daughter of Mira Ellen Bills Spinks and Ernest Gill Jones (deceased); married Paul R Smith; children: Kathleen, Robert, Debra, Alan, Paul II, Dolores II. **Educ:** Roosevelt Univ, BS 1979; Ohio Univ Athens OH, MA 1983; Gestalt Inst of Cleveland, Post-Graduate Studies in Organization and Systems Devel 1989. **Career:** Smith's Office Serv, owner/mgr 1959-65; Suburban Echo Reporter, advertising mgr 1965-67; Jewel Cos Inc, area Personnel mgr 1967-79; Bausman Assocs, mgmt consultant 1979-80; WTTW Chicago, dir admin serv 1980-82; Ohio Univ, instructor/grad asst 1982-83; Columbia Coll Chicago, instructor 1983-; NBC WKQX Radio, producer/host 1983-86; DJ Smith Enterprises, pres 1983-. **Orgs:** Exec comm bd of dir Midwest Women's Ctr 1977-; mem NAACP, Soc for Human Resources Mgt, Soc for Training and Devel; trustee Wieboldt Found 1982-; bd of dirs Women and Foundations Corp Philanthropy 1984-; exec comm bd of dir Lambda Alpha Omega Chap Alpha Kappa Alpha Sor 1986-. **Honors/Awds:** Appointed to Governor's Adv Council on Employment and Training 1977-82; Corporation for Public Broadcasting Scholar at Ohio Univ 1982-83; lecturer, moderator and panelist appearing before profl, univ and TV audiences on selected topics. **Home Addr:** PO Box 1083, Maywood, IL 60153. **Business Addr:** President, DJ Smith Enterprises, PO Box 1083, Maywood, IL 60153, (708)343-4499.

SMITH, DONALD HUGH
Educator (retired). **Personal:** Born Mar 20, 1932, Chicago, IL; son of Madolene and William H; divorced. **Educ:** Univ of IL, AB 1953; DePaul, MA 1959; Univ of WI, PhD 1964. **Career:** Baruch Coll, prof, chairman, dept of educ; Chicago Pub Sch, tchr 1956-63; Cntr for Inner City Studies Northeastern IL U, asst prof asso prof dir 1964-68; Univ Comm Educ Prgms Univ of Pitts, prof dir 1968-69; Nat Urban Coalition Washington DC, exec asso 1969-70; Educ Devel Baruch Coll Cty of NY, prof dir 1970-97, associate provost, retired. **Orgs:** Exec dir Chancellor's Task Force on SEEK Cty Univ of NY 1974-; Nat Adv Counc Voc Educ 1968-70; adv Doctoral Prgm in Educ Adminstrn Atlanta Univ 1975; chairman of Black Faculty of Cty Univ of NY, 1989-92; mem InterAm Congress of Psychology 1972-; advisor Martin Luther King Jr Ctr for Social Change; mem Nat Study Commn of Tchr Educ 1972-75; chmn task force NY State Dropout Problem; bd of dir NY Serv to Older People; consult to numerous schools & univs; pres Natl Alliance of Black School Educators 1983-85; advisory board, African Heritage Studies Assn. **Honors/Awds:** Recip Chicago Bd of Educ Flwshp 1962; Univ of WI Flwshp 1963; del White House Conf on the Disadvantaged 1966; Disting Leadership Awd Natl Alliance of Black School Educators 1986; Awd for Distinguished Serv NY State Black & Puerto Rican Legislation, 1986. **Military Serv:** US Army, 1954-55. **Home Addr:** 250 W 103rd St, Apt 4A, New York, NY 10025.

SMITH, DONALD M.
Business manager. **Personal:** Born Jul 12, 1931, Elgin, IL; married Jeanette M Smith; children: Tracy, Tiffany. **Educ:** Purdue Univ, BA 1956, MA 1961. **Career:** Hills McCanna, shop supt 1960-69; Hemmenns Auditorium, gen mgr 1969-80; Rockford Metro Centre, oper mgr 1980-. **Orgs:** Mem Intl Assoc of Aud Mgr 1964, Amer Legion 1969-, Prince Hall Masons 1980-. **Honors/Awds:** Founder of the Performing Arts for Young People 1969-80; Founder of the Elgin Area Arts Council 1969-80. **Military Serv:** US Army, USAF sgt 5 yrs; Bronze Star, Korean Service Medal, Far East Campaign Medal 1949. **Business Addr:** Operations Manager, Rockford Metro Centre, 300 Elm St, Rockford, IL 61101.

SMITH, DOROTHY LOUISE WHITE
Educator. **Personal:** Born Sep 28, 1939, Memphis, TN; daughter of Ellie Mae Turner White (deceased) and Theodore Everett White (deceased); married Carl Smith, Nov 26, 1958; children: Carlton Edward Smith, Sharian Smith Lott. **Educ:** Philander Smith Coll, Natl Methodist Scholar 1957-59; Cuyahoga Comm Coll 1963-64; Case-Western Reserve Univ, BA, English, 1966; California State Univ, MA, English 1969; Univ of Southern California, EdD, intercultural education, 1992. **Career:** Glenville High School, instructor of English 1966-67; Millikan High School, instructor of English 1969-70; Long Beach City Coll, instructor of English 1970-73; San Diego City Coll, instructor of English and African-American literature, 1973-; San Diego Unified Sch Dist, mem bd of Educ 1981-88; San Diego State Univ School of Teacher Educ, 1989-91; education consultant, 1988-. **Orgs:** Alpha Kappa Alpha Sorority 1958-; Women Inc 1974-; adv comm mem Allensworth State Historic Park 1977-86; mem Assn of CA Urban School Dist 1982-87; mem CSBA Curriculum & Rsch Task Force 1983-85; mem Delegate Assembly CA School Bds Assn 1981-88; mem Delegate Assembly, Natl School Bds Assn 1983-85; mem Steering Comm Council of Urban Bds of Educ 1985-88; adv comm San Diego State Univ Teacher Educ 1986-89; mem CA Middle Grades Task Force, 1986-87; pres bd of dirs, San Diego School of Success, 1989-; vice pres, San Diego Mathematics Collaborative, 1989-91; San Diego Dialogue, 1990-; Center City Development Committee, Martin Luther King Promenade, 1991-. **Honors/Awds:** Distinguished School Bd Award 1984; Distinguished Public Serv Award Alpha Kappa Alpha 1985; Woman of Achievement Award 1985; Woman of the Year Award 1984; Achievement in Politics Award 1982; Salute to Black Women Achievement Award 1984; County of San Diego Proclamation of Community Service 1984, 1988; (3) City of San Diego, Special Commendations; Urban League Award for Outstanding Leadership as President of Board of Education; Women in Government Tribute to Women, 1985; Phi Delta Kappa Community Service Award, 1988; Samaritan of the Year Award, 1988; Intl Reading Association, Literacy Award, 1989; Magnet Schools Leadership Award, 1989; Phi Delta Kappa Honor Society, 1990-; Phi Kappa Phi Honor Society, 1969; San Diego State University, School of Teacher Education, Outstanding Faculty Award, 1990, School of Success, Founder's Award, 1995. **Home Addr:** 2650 Blackton Dr, San Diego, CA 92105. **Business Addr:** Professor of English and African-American Literature, San Diego City College, 1313 Twelfth Ave, San Diego, CA 92103.

SMITH, DOROTHY O.
Mayor. **Personal:** Born May 28, 1943, Lawrence County, AL; daughter of Cornelia Swoope Owens and James Samuel Owens

Sr (deceased); divorced; children: Derra S Warren, Leo Smith Jr, Kathleen R Smith. **Educ:** John C Calhoun, Decatur AL, Business, 1969. **Career:** South Central Bell, Decatur AL, network, 1971; City of Hillsboro, Hillsboro AL, mayor, 1989. **Orgs:** Sec, Black Mayors Conf, 1988; mem, Natl Black Women Mayors Caucus, 1988; Martin Luther King Jr Profiles in Courage, ADC, Lawrence County Chapter, 1988. **Honors/Awds:** Award for Church Sec, 1987; Award from The Lawrence County Extension Serv, 1989; Award from The Lawrence County Chamber of Commerce 1989; numerous community serv awards for speaking.

SMITH, DOUG
Professional basketball player. **Personal:** Born Sep 17, 1969, Detroit, MI. **Educ:** Missouri. **Career:** Dallas Mavericks, forward, 1991-. **Business Addr:** Professional Basketball Player, Dallas Mavericks, ReUnion Arena, 777 Sports St, Dallas, TX 75207, (214)988-0117.

SMITH, DOUGLAS M.
Journalist. **Personal:** Born Apr 18, 1942, Hampton, VA; son of Virginia Jones Smith and Samuel R Smith; married Shirley Thomas-Smith (divorced 1984); children: Jerome, Jared; married Anne Street-Smith, May 11, 1991. **Educ:** Hampton University, Hampton, VA, BA, math, 1964. **Career:** Newsday, Garden City, NY, reporter/editor, 1970-77; New York Post, New York, NY, reporter/editor, 1977-78; Newark Board of Education, Newark, NJ, public relations specialists, 1978-79; Howard University Hospital, Washington, DC, editor/writer, 1980-85; USA Today, Arlington, VA, reporter, 1986-; Hampton University, Department of Mass Media Arts, journalist-in-residence, 1993-94. **Orgs:** US Tennis Writers Association, 1990-; member, American Tennis Association, 1979-86; member, United States Tennis Association, 1979-88; member, National Association of Black Journalists, 1990-; USTWA, president, 1990-92, vice president, 1994-95. **Honors/Awds:** Great American Tennis Writing Award, Tennis Week, 1990; Media Person of the Year, Women's International Tennis Assn, 1989; Lifetime Achievement Award, United States Tennis Association, 1988; Appreciation Award, American Tennis Association, 1985. **Military Serv:** US Army, Captain, 1964-70; Bronze Star w/"V" Device, Army Commendation Medal, Purple Heart, Vietnam Service and Campaign Medals. **Business Addr:** General Assignment Reporter/Tennis Writer, USA Today, 1000 Wilson Blvd, Arlington, VA 22209.

SMITH, EARL BRADFORD
Social worker. **Personal:** Born Sep 28, 1953, St Louis, MO; married Treva Talon Smith. **Educ:** Thiel Coll, BA Psych, Sociol 1977; Marywood Coll, MSW 1979; Univ of Pittsburgh, PhD Candidate Ed. **Career:** Vet Admin Hospital, social work assoc 1976-78; Susquehanna Human Serv, human resources spec 1979-; Lackawanna Cty Child & Youth Serv, social worker II 1979-82; Pittsburgh Bd of Educ, school social worker 1982-. **Orgs:** Mem Natl Assoc of Social Workers 1979-; lector St Peters Cathedral Soc 1977-82; lector St Benedicts & St Marys Lectureship Soc 1982-. **Honors/Awds:** Outstanding Male Model NE PA Model's Assoc 1979; Dance Awds Acquired from various Modern Dance-Jazz Performances; All Amer In Football & Track Pres Athletic Conf 1974-77. **Military Serv:** USMC corpl 2 yrs; Expert Rifleman 1972-74. **Home Addr:** 1616 Meadville, Pittsburgh, PA 15214.

SMITH, EDDIE D., SR.
Clergyman. **Personal:** Born Jun 8, 1946, Macon, GA; son of Mattie Mae Smith and Rev Jack Smith Jr (deceased); married Verlene Fields; children: Charlitha S Austin, Edwanna L, Eddie Jr, Corey, Alvy. **Educ:** Ft Valley State Coll, BS 1968, MS 1971; Universal Bible College, Alamo, TN, D Div. **Career:** Bibb Co Sch, tchr 1968-82; City of Macon, councilman 1975-78; Bibb Co, bd of educ 1985-; Macedonia Missionary Baptist Church, pastor 1972-. **Honors/Awds:** Minister of the Day GA State Legislature 1981; 3 Yr Serv Award for City Cncl City of Macon 1979; Medgar Malcolm Martin's Award SCLC 1979; Dr E D Smith Day Proclamation City of Macon 1977; dir Disting Am 1981; Natl Alumni Cert of Achievement Ft Valley State Coll 1978; Cert of Appreciation Bibb Co Voter's League 1977; Citizens Award Macon Courier 1977. **Business Addr:** Pastor, Macedonia Missionary Baptist Church, 928 Anthony Rd, Macon, GA 31204.

SMITH, EDDIE GLENN, JR.
Educator, health care administrator, dentist. **Personal:** Born Nov 13, 1926, Palatka, FL; married Callie Glasby; children: Katressia M, Katherine J. **Educ:** BS 1952; DDS 1959; FACD 1972. **Career:** Private Practice, dentist 1960-80; Howard Univ Coll of Dentistry, asst prof 1969-80; Comm Group Health Found Washington, exec dir Health Center 1970-77; Coll Med, staff 1974; dentist. **Orgs:** Pres Howard Univ Dental Alumni Assn 1967-69; pres Robt T Freeman Dent Soc 1968-71; spl consult Sec HEW 1968-72; chmn DC Med Care Adv Com 1974-80; mem Nat Dental Assn (pres 1972); NAACP; Urban League; YMCA; Intl Platform Assn; ARC; Am Dental Assn; DC Dental Soc; Natl Assn Neighborhood Health Cntrs; Am Pub Health Assn; consult Howard Univ Cntr Sickle Cell Anemia; bd adv Urban Health Mag; adv com TB & Respiratory Diseases Assn; consult Robert Wood Johnson Found; consult Am Fund Dental Health; Omega Psi Phi; President's bd regents Nat Lib Med Nominee. **Honors/Awds:** Dentist of the Year Award 1969; Speaker's Award 1970; Keys to City Miami Beach 1971, New Orleans 1972; President's Award 1972; Civil Rights Award 1972; aide-de-camp Gov Dunn, TN 1972; Keys to City of Detroit 1973; Listing "100 Most Influential Black Americans" Ebony 1973; President's Award Nat Dental Assn 1973; Freedom Award NAACP 1974; Dentist of the Year Natl Dental Assoc 1986; President Gerald Ford's nominee, NAH Library, Board of Regents. **Military Serv:** USAAF 1945-47. **Business Addr:** 740 Sixth St NW, Washington, DC 20001.

SMITH, EDGAR E.
Educator (retired), consultant. **Personal:** Born Aug 6, 1934, Hollandale, MS; son of Augusta McCoy Smith and Sam Smith; married Inez O; children: Edwin D, Anthony R, Stephen S, Gregory S. **Educ:** Tougaloo Clg Tougaloo, MS, BS 1955; Purdue Univ Lafayette, IN, MS 1957; Purdue Univ Biochemistry, PhD 1960. **Career:** Dept of Biochemistry Purdue Univ Lafayette, IN, rsrch asst 1955-58; Dept Biochemistry Purdue Univ Lafayette, IN, tchg asst 1958-59; Harvard Med Sch Boston, MA, rsrch flw surg biochemistry 1959-61; Beth Israel Hosp Boston, MA, assc surg rsrch 1959-68; Harvard Med Sch Boston, MA, rsrch assc surg biochemistry 1961-68; Boston Univ Sch Med Boston, MA, asst prof surg chem 1968-70; Natl Cancer Inst, rsrch career dev awrdee 1969-74; Boston Univ Sch Medicine Boston, MA, assc prof surg chem 1970-73; Univ of MA Med Center Provost/Assoc Prof 1974-83; Univ of MA, system vice pres 1983-91; Nellie Mae, vice pres, 1991-93; Tougaloo College, acting president, 1995; consultant, 1993-97. **Orgs:** Trustee Alcohol Bev Med Rsrch Found 1982-94; governing bd Rob Wood Johnson Hlth Policy Flwshp Pgm 1978-85; Am Soc Biological Chemists; consultant Natl Inst Hlth; trustee Morehouse Sch Medicine 1976-89; trustee Tougaloo Clg 1968-90; trustee Metco Schlrshp Fund 1969-86; board of directors Planned Parenthood MA 1984-90; Am Association for Higher Ed; Natl Forum Systm Chief Acad Ofcr; NASULGC Cncl on Acad Afrs; American Society of Biological Chemist; Am Chem Soc Div Biological Chem; Am Assc Advncmnt Sci; NY Acad Sci; Am Assc Cancer Rsrch; Flw Am Inst Chem; mem Boston Cancer Rsrch Assc; Sigma Xi; Phi Lambda Upsilon Natl Chem Hon Soc; Am Pol Sci Assc; NAMME Natl Association of Minority Med Educators; chrmn Dean's Ad Hoc Com Black Grad Stdnts; administration committee School of Medicine; chairman Black Faculty Caucus; editorial board Centerscope; committee American Cancer Institute Grant; liaison Div Med Sci Biochemistry; joint com Admission to Six Yr Pgm; promotion com Six Yr Pgm. **Honors/Awds:** Res cancer dev awrd Natl Cancer Inst 1969-74; alumnus of yr Tougaloo Clg 1969; NAACP hlth awrd NAACP Boston Brnch 1977; Rbt Wood Johnson Hlth Policy Flwhsp Inst of Medicine 1977; awrd outstndg achvmnt Field Biochemisty Natl Consortium Black Profsnl Dev 1976; human relations awrd MA Tchrs Assc 1977; old master Purdue Univ 1978; distngshd alumnus Natl Assc Equal Opportnty Higher Ed; natl foud flw Purdue Univ Lafayette, IN 1958-59; Distgnshd Ldrs Hlth Care 1978; Directory Distngshd Am 1981; Honorary Doctor of Science, Morehouse School of Medicine 1989; University of Massachusetts Medical School, Professor Emeritus, 1991.

SMITH, EDITH B.
General manager. **Personal:** Born Jan 18, 1952, Norfolk, VA; daughter of Nannie Ruth Winstead Codrington and Elijah J Billups; married Joseph Smith, Aug 1970 (divorced 1988); children: Kelley N. **Educ:** Norfolk State University, Norfolk, VA, BA, 1970-74. **Career:** The Virginian-Pilot, Norfolk, VA, reporter, 1972-80; WHUR Radio, Washington, DC, promotions director, 1981-84; Mondale-Ferraro Campaign, Washington, DC, advance press person, 1984; WDCU-FM Radio, Washington, DC, general manager, 1985-. **Orgs:** Member, Capitol Press Club, 1994-95. **Honors/Awds:** Natl Black Media Coalition, for achievements in broadcasting, 1994. **Business Addr:** General Manager, WDCU-FM Radio, 4200 Connecticut Ave, NW, Bldg 38, Room A-03, Washington, DC 20008, (202)274-5090.

SMITH, EDWARD CHARLES
City official. **Personal:** Born Jan 21, 1949, Pueblo, CO; son of Marguerite Kiterell and Robert L Smith; married Gwendolyn F Creighton; children: Damon, Marcus. **Educ:** KS State Univ, BS 1971. **Career:** City of Kansas City, manpower program (CETA) 1974; manpower serv coord 1975; asst dir mgmt coord City Planning Dept 1975; comm devel coord 1976; dir comm devel div 1977-83, neighborhood preservation director, 1983-87, housing director, 1987-. **Orgs:** Mid Am Reg Cncl 1975; bd of dir United Way of Wyandotte Co 1975-77; United Comm Serv Inc 1975-77; mem KS League of Municipalities 1976-77; Nat Assnfor Comm Devel 1977; Nat Assn of Housing & Redevel Ofcl 1977; Nat Comm Devel Assn 1977; Legislative Comm mem Natl Comm Devel Assn 1978-80; Natl Urban Affairs Council 1978-80; mem bd of governors United Way 1980; sec Minority Municipal Employees Organiz 1980; pres of Region VIII Nat Comm Develop Assn 1982; first vice pres of Nat Comm Develop Assn 1982; past pres Natl Assn for Comm Development 1983-84; dir Neighborhood Preserv Dept City of Kansas City, Kansas 1983. **Business Addr:** City of Kansas City, 701 N 7th Municipal Ofc Bldg, Kansas City, KS 66101.

SMITH, EDWARD NATHANIEL, JR.
Physician, educator. **Personal:** Born Jul 28, 1955, Elizabeth City, NC; son of Georgia Long Smith and Edward Nathaniel Smith Sr; married Mona LaMothe, Nov 26, 1983; children: Edward N III, Arianne LaMothe. **Educ:** Morehouse Coll, BS 1976; Howard Univ Coll of Medicine, MD 1980. **Career:** US Public Health Svcs, medical officer 1980-82; Emory Univ Sch of Medicine, clinical assoc 1982-84; Howard Univ Hospital, radiology resident 1984-87, asst prof of radiology 1988-. **Orgs:** Mem Omega Psi Phi Frat 1974-; mem Amer Cancer Soc 1980-; bd of dirs Omega Diversified Investment Corp 1982-; mem Piney Branch Sligo Civic Organization 1984-; mem Natl Medical Assoc Radiology Sect 1985-, Radiological Soc of North America 1985-; mem American Roentgen Ray Society 1988-; American College of Radiology 1989-; American Heart Association 1990-; board of directors, Homemaker Health Aide Service, Washington, DC, 1992-; Society of Cardiovascular & Interventional Radiology, 1991-. **Honors/Awds:** Phi Beta Kappa, Delta of GA 1976; mem Alpha Omega Alpha Howard Univ College of Medicine Chap 1980-. **Business Addr:** Asst Professor of Radiology, Dept of Radiology, Howard Univ Hospital, 2041 Georgia Ave NW, Washington, DC 20060.

SMITH, ELAINE MARIE
Government employee. **Personal:** Born Nov 30, 1947, Mobile, AL; children: Vernon Leon York Jr. **Educ:** AL A&M Univ, BS; Merced Coll, AA 1972. **Career:** USAF, staffing asst 1976-77, personnel staffing specl 1977-78; US Army Corps of Engrs, staffing asst 1978, affirmative action recruiter 1978-. **Orgs:** Mem Youth Motivation Task Force 1980-86; vice pres sec Blacks in Govt 1980-86; sec Carver State Tech Coll Adv Bd 1982-86; mem Southern College Placement Assoc 1982-86; mem Southeastern Federal Recruiting Council 1982-86; mem Black Execs Exchange Program 1986. **Honors/Awds:** Outstanding Young Woman of Amer 1981; Quality Salary Increase US Corps of Engrs 1984; Sustained Superior Performance Awd US Corps of Engrs 1982, 86. **Business Addr:** Affirmative Action Recruiter, US Army Corps of Engineers, Personnel Office, P O Box 2288, Mobile, AL 36628.

SMITH, ELEANOR JANE
Educational administrator. **Personal:** Born Jan 10, 1933, Circleville, OH; daughter of Eleanor J Dade Lewis and John A Lewis (deceased); married Paul M Smith Jr, Dec 27, 1972; children: Teresa Marie Banner. **Educ:** Capital Univ, BSM 1955; Ohio St Univ, 1966; The Union Graduate School/UECU, PhD 1972. **Career:** Board of Ed, Columbus, OH 2nd-6th grd tchr 1956-64; Board of Ed, Worthington OH 6 & 7th grd tchr 1964-69; Univ of Cinn, prof, Afro-Am Studies 1972-82; vice provost Faculty & Acad Affairs; Smith Coll, dean of institutional affairs, 1988-90; William Paterson College, vice president for academic affairs and provost, 1990-94; Univ of Wisconsin-parkside, chancellor, currently. **Orgs:** Assoc of Black Women Historians, natl co-founder & co-director 1978-80; mem Natl Council for Black Studies 1982-88; mem Natl Assn Women in Education, 1986-; American Assn for Higher Education; American Council on Education; American Assn of State Colleges and Universities. **Honors/Awds:** Historical Presentation, Black Heritage, History, Music & Dance written & produced 1972-; numerous publications; YWCA Career Women of Achievement 1983; Capital Univ, Alumni Achiev Awd 1986. **Home Addr:** 40 Harborview Dr, Racine, WI 53403. **Business Addr:** Chancellor, 900 Wood Rd, 2000, Univ of Wisconsin Parkside, Kenosha, WI 53141-2000, (414)595-2211.

SMITH, ELIJAH (WYRE SMITH)
Clergyman. **Personal:** Born Dec 28, 1939, Peach County, GA; son of Ola Mae John Smith and Samuel Lee Smith; married Janet Broner, Jun 7, 1987; children: Audrey Maria Diamond, Elijah Jr, Sonja A, Avice D, Richard A, Mark A, D'ete Smith, LaShaunda R Thomas, Velecia Thomas. **Educ:** Turner Theol Seminary, diploma in Theol 1975. **Career:** Blue Bird Body Co, utility man 1964-66; Robins Air Force Base GA, electronic repairman 1966-75; Eastman Circuit Eastman GA, pastor 1967-71; Allen Chapel & Mountain Creek AME Chs, pastor 1971-84; D&S Florist, owner 1974-76; St John AME Church, pastor; Eastern District of Southwest GA, Sixth Episcopal District of the African Methodist Episcopal Church, presiding elder, 1994-. **Orgs:** Mem Columbus & Phoenix City Ministerial Alliance 1984-; mem Masonic Lodge 134 Powersville GA 1965-; mem Columbus Branch NAACP 1984-; mem Public Affairs Cncl of Columbus 1984-; mem AME Church Ministers Alliance of Columbus; mem South Columbus Exchange Club 1989; member, A J McClung YMCA; member, Columbus Urban League Inc. **Honors/Awds:** Oscar Maxwell Awd, Man of the Yr Americus Boy Scouts 1978; Minister of the Yr Black Youth in Action 1979; Tomorrow's Leaders Awd, Georgia Power 1979; Outstanding Pub Serv Awd, Sumter Co Bd of Gov of C of C 1980; Outstanding Serv & Dedication Awd, Kent Hill Youth Develop Prog 1984; Disting & Devoted Serv Awd, Americus-Sumter Co NAACP 1984; Comm Serv Awd, Mayor City of Americus 1984; Serv Awd, Chief of Police Americus GA 1984; Outstanding & Dedicated Serv Awd, Americus Police Dept & Comm of Americus & Sumter Co 1984; Devoted Leadership Sevice to St John & Community, St John AME Church, 1989; The Martin Luther King Sr, Minister's Community Service Award, PUSH, 1991; Pastor of the Year, The Sons of Allen of the Southwest GA Annual Conference of the AME

Church, 1992; Pastor of the Year, Lay Organization of Southwest GA, Annual Conference of the AME Church, 1992. **Home Addr:** 248 Brookdale Dr, Americus, GA 31709-2877.

SMITH, ELMER G., JR.
Physician. **Personal:** Born May 22, 1957, Chicago, IL; son of Joyce and Elmer; married Ingrid S P, Jun 4, 1983; children: Brittany Francoise, Harrison Monfort, Samantha Dominique, Alexander Jean-Marc. **Educ:** Univ of IL-Chicago, BS 1980; Howard Univ Coll of Medicine, MD 1983. **Career:** Norwalk/Yale Hospital, resident physician 1983-86; Northwestern Med School, clinical medicine instructor 1989; Northwestern Memorial Hospital, active attending 1990; Cook County Hospital, medicine consultant 1988-93, dir of ambulatory screening, 1993-. **Orgs:** Alpha Phi Alpha Frat Inc 1980-; Amer Medical Assoc 1980-; Amer Coll of Physicians 1985-; IL State Medical Soc 1986-; Chicago Medical Soc 1986-; pres American Cancer Society, Illinois Division, Austin Unit, 1987-89; Society of General Internal Medicine 1991. **Honors/Awds:** Vice President, Public Relations, Senior Class, Howard Univ 1982-83; Psychiatry Rsch Awd, Howard Univ Coll of Medicine 1983; Diplomate Amer Bd of Internal Medicine 1986; Chicago's Caring Physicians Award, Metropolitan Chicago Health Care Council 1987; Cook County Hospital, Acute Pharyngitis, 1989, syphilis, 1990; WVAZ, Heat Syndromes 1991. **Special Achievements:** Round Table Moderator, Hypertension Management, 1993; Cook County Hospital, Hypertension, 1991. **Business Addr:** Dir of Ambulatory Screening, Cook County Hospital, 1835 W Harrison, Chicago, IL 60612, (312)633-8160.

SMITH, ELSIE MAE
Nurse (retired). **Personal:** Born Feb 27, 1927, Erin, OK; daughter of Laura Latour and Isadore Brooks; married Dr James Almer Smith Jr., Oct 15, 1949; children: Dr James, Dr Roger, Dr Margo, Melanie. **Educ:** St Mary's School of Nursing, St Louis, MO; American International College. **Career:** Bay State Medical Center, gastro enterology, staff RN, 1973-90. **Orgs:** Links, Greater Springfield Chapter Inc; docent, Museum of Fine Arts, Springfield, MA; cooperator, Springfield Museum & Library Assn; member, president, 1980-82, Springfield Chapter Girl Friends; board of directors, secretary, Springfield Girls Club Family Center; board of directors, Connecticut Valley Girl Scouts; president, Springfield Alpha Wives, 1961-63; world traveler; volunteer, Housing For Habitant; volunteer, Springfield Tech Comm Coll, Tutor for students foreign taking English; mem, African Hall Steering Comm, Science Museum, Springfield, MA; Cooperator Bay State Med Ctr; Comm of St Michaels Cathedral. **Honors/Awds:** Achievement Award, McKnight Neighborhood; Cert for Training, Springfield Library & Museum Assn, 1989; United Church of Christ, Travel Nurse to 3 Countries in West Africa, for College student & others. **Home Addr:** 96 Dartmouth St, Springfield, MA 01109.

SMITH, EMMITT J., III
Professional football player. **Personal:** Born May 15, 1969, Pensacola, FL; son of Mary and Emmitt Smith Jr. **Educ:** Univ of Florida, bachelor's degree in public recreation, 1996. **Career:** Dallas Cowboys, running back, 1990-. **Orgs:** Make a Wish Foundation; Emmitt Smith Charities, Inc, "Emmitt Smith Scholarship Program," founder; Just Say No Anti-Drug Campaign, spokesperson, 1986. **Honors/Awds:** Surpassed the 1,000-yard rushing mark earlier than any other player in college football history; Freshman of the Year, UPI, Sporting News, 1987; Pro Bowl, 1991, 1992, 1993, 1994, 1995, 1996, 1997; Miller Lite NFL Player of the Year, 1993; National Football League, Most Valuable Player Award, 1993; Super Bowl XXVIII Most Valuable Player, 1993; Four NFL Rushing Titles; holder of numerous Cowboys & NFL records; Two consecutive Jim Thorpe Football Awards. **Special Achievements:** Coauthored his autobiography entitled The Emmitt Zone, Crown Publishing, 1994; Super Bowl 27, 28 & 30; NFL Draft, first round pick; 1st Dallas Cowboy Player to lead the league in rushing. **Business Addr:** Professional Football Player, Dallas Cowboys, One Cowboys Parkway, Irving, TX 75063, (214)556-9900.

SMITH, EMMITT MOZART
Educational administrator, cleric (retired). **Personal:** Born Jun 6, 1905, Homer, LA; married Naomi L Malone. **Educ:** Philander Smith College, BA, 1934; Fisk University, MA, 1936; New Mexico State University, education specialist degree, 1947; Reed College of Religion, DDiv, 1969. **Career:** City of Carlsbad, New Mexico, high school teacher, basketball coach, 1934-35, high school principal, 1949-52, elementary school principal, asst to superintendent, 1953-57, principal, 1957-73; Rice Memorial Methodist Church, pastor, 1962-74. **Orgs:** Presiding elder emeritus, Arizona-New Mexico District, CME Church; council delegate, New Mexico Education Assn, 1956-64; Carlsbad Education Assn, vice president, 1952; NM State University, advanced degree work, coordinator, 1950-57; S Eddy Co Red Cross, secretary, 1958-63; Lion's Club, 1964-; City Park & Recreation Bd, 1964-74. **Honors/Awds:** Elementary school renamed in honor, Aug 28, 1989, Carlsbad, NM. **Business Addr:** 2601 S Carver St, Carlsbad, NM.

SMITH, ERNEST HOWARD
Physician. **Personal:** Born Nov 9, 1931, Bethlehem, PA. **Educ:** Lincoln U, AB cum laude 1953; Howard U, mD 1957; Children Hosp Philadelphia DC Gen Hosp, studied pediatrics; Childrens Hosp Philadelphia, Henry FordHosp Detroit, pediatric cardiology. **Career:** US Pub Health Cheyenne Sioux Reservation Eagle Butte SD, med officer in charge 1958-61; Henry Ford Hosp, staff pediatric cardiologist 1965-71; Detroit, priv prac pediatric cardiology 1964-68; Drew Med Sch Los Angeles CA, asst prof pediatrics, pediatric cardiologist head of community pediatrics 1972-. **Orgs:** Mem Catalytic Community Assn Detroit 1968-70; South Central Planning Coun Los Angeles 1973-; Southeast Mental Health Liason Coun 1973-; Cit for Youth Employment 1973-; organist Pilgrim Congregational Ch Eagle Butte SD; Christ United Ch of Christ Detroit; Hartford Ave Bapt Ch Detroit; First Bapt Ch Warrenton VA; St Pauls Bapt Ch Bethlehem PA; accompanist Lincoln Univ Glee Club PA. **Honors/Awds:** Recipient Quinland Prize Biology Lincoln Univ 1953; Kappa Alpha Psi Award Mu Chap 1953; Cheyenne Sioux Tribal Citation 1961; President's Award South Central Planning Coun 1974; Educ Frat Award for So CA outstanding contrib in field on scndry educ Phi Delta Kappa 1975. **Business Addr:** 12021 S Wilmington Ave, Los Angeles, CA.

SMITH, ESTELLA W.
Utility company executive. **Educ:** Univ of Bloomington, BS; Memphis State Univ, MS, PhD. **Career:** Univ of Pittsburgh, asst prof; Memphis State Univ, instructo; Heritage National Bank, CEO; Duquesne Light Company, dir of investment & bank relations, community relations manager, 1991-.

SMITH, ESTUS
Foundation executive. **Personal:** Born Oct 13, 1930, Crystal Springs, MS; son of Margaret (deceased) and David (deceased); married Dorothy Triplett; children: Donald Gregory. **Educ:** Jackson State Univ, BS 1953; IN Univ, MME 1961; Univ of IA, PhD 1970; Eastman Sch of Music, addl studies. **Career:** Dade City, McComb MS, Jackson, band dir; Jackson State Univ, dean, vice pres acad affairs, prof of music 1973-84; Kettering Found, vp/COO, currently. **Orgs:** IN Univ, Jackson State Univ, Univ of IA Alumni Assns; fellow Amer Coun Higher Educ 1969; former chmn Com for Mississippi Humanities; former bd trustees Dept of Archives & Hist State of MS; past pres, vice pres So Conf Deans of Faculty & Acad; past chmn bd dir State Mutual Fed Savings & Loan Assn; past pres Opera/S Co; mem, NAACP, Omega Psi Phi, Phi Delta Kappa, Phi Kappa Phi, Beta Beta Beta; bd of trustees, Centerville/Washington Township Education Foundation, 1990-; Sigma Pi Phi Fraternity; Alpha Lamba Delta; Phi Kappa Phi Fraternity; Kappa Psi Fraternity; bd of dirs, Dayton Education Alliance, trustee for Dayton Foundation, 1990-; trustee, St George's Episcopal Church. **Honors/Awds:** Episcopalian Outstanding Amer, 1970; Outstanding Alumni & Scholar 1970; Outstanding Educ of America; Jackson State University Sports Hall of Fame, (football, basketball) 1980; Archon of the Year, Sigma Pi Phi Fraternity 1988. **Military Serv:** US Army.

SMITH, EUGENE
Business executive. **Personal:** Born Sep 1, 1929, Miami, FL; married Josephine Scott; children: Michael, Milton Brown (foster). **Educ:** FL A&M Univ, BS 1954-58. **Career:** HUD, asst dir mgmt, north central dist dir. **Orgs:** Deacon 1972, Sunday school teacher, business mgr Glendale Baptist Church; mem NAHRO 1979-. **Military Serv:** AUS pfc 2 yrs. **Business Addr:** North Central Dist Dir, HUD, 325 NW 62 St, Miami, FL 33150.

SMITH, EUGENE
Business executive. **Personal:** Born Aug 13, 1938, Alquippa, PA; married Jacquelyn; children: Charmaine, Deborah, Carlton. **Educ:** Geneva Coll; Univ Duquesne. **Career:** Aliquippa Water Authority, ast mgr. **Orgs:** Bd mem, vice pres Alquippa Pub Sch Dist; bd mem Beaver Co Hosp Authority; mem bd of dir PA Minority Bus Devel Commn; mem US Mil Selection Com; mem Zion Hope Lodge #72; St Cyprian Consistory #4; Sahara Temple #2. **Honors/Awds:** Man Yr Award Negro Bus Professional Women Beaver Co. **Business Addr:** 160 Hopewell Ave, Aliquippa, PA 15001.

SMITH, EUGENE DUBOIS
Athletic director. **Personal:** Born Dec 18, 1955, Cleveland, OH; son of Elizabeth DuBois Smith and Theodore Smith; married Paula Griffin Smith, May 6, 1977; children: Nicole Dawn Smith, Lindsey Rose Smith, Summer Denise Smith. **Educ:** University of Norte Dame, Notre Dame, IN, Bachelor, Business Management, 1977. **Career:** University Notre Dame, IN, asst football coach, 1977-81; IBM, South Bend, IN, marketing representative, 1981-83; Eastern Michigan University, Ypsilanti, MI, asst athletic director, 1983-85, athletic director, 1985-93; Iowa State Univ, athletic dir, 1993-. **Orgs:** Executive board, National Associate Collegiate Directors of Athletics, 1990-; board member, Chamber of Commerce, Ypsilanti, MI, 1989-; member, NAACP, Ypsilanti Chapter, 1988-; board member, NCAA Track/Field Rules Committee, 1987-89. **Business Addr:** Athletic Director, Iowa State University, Ames, IA 50011, (515)294-4111.

SMITH, FERNANDO DEWITT
Professional football player. **Personal:** Born Aug 2, 1971, Flint, MI; children: Quantiash, Tyna. **Educ:** Jackson State, attended. **Career:** Minnesota Vikings, defensive end, 1994-. **Business Addr:** Professional Football Player, Minnesota Vikings, 9520 Viking Dr, Eden Prairie, MN 55344, (612)828-6500.

SMITH, FRANCES C.
Funeral director. **Personal:** Born Jun 21, Williamston, NC; daughter of Omenella Riddick Cherry and Leo Cherry (deceased); married Alfred J Smith Jr; children: Randy, Trent. **Educ:** Attended, McAllister Sch of Embalming; Amer Acad Sch of Embalming, grad studies. **Career:** Smith Funeral Home, owner/funeral director. **Orgs:** Mem NJ State Bd of Mortuary Science; mem Elizabeth Development Co; mem Garden State Funeral Dirs; past pres Urban League Guild; past matron Lincoln Chap OES; pres Union Co Unit of Natl Assn of Negro Bus & Professional Womens Clubs; past pres Womens Scholarship Club of Elizabeth; mem Elizabeth Bd of Educ; mem Soroptimist Intl of Eliz; mem Union County Association of Women Business Owners; Governor's Commission on Quality Education for State of New Jersey 1991-. **Honors/Awds:** Achievement Awd Urban League of Eastern Union Co; Professional Woman of Yr Awd N Jersey Unit of Natl Assn of Negro Bus & Professional Womens Clubs; first Black bd mem Egenolf Day Nursery in Elizabeth presently on adv bd of nursery; Honored by receiving Key to City by Mayor 1st Black woman to receive such honor; Appreciation Awd Elizabeth Br NAACP 1980; Business Woman of Yr Awd Union Co NANBPW.

SMITH, FRANK
Clergyman, educational administrator. **Personal:** Born Dec 3, 1910, Camden, AL; married Etta Pearl Martin; children: Carolyn S Taylor, Gwendolyn Geraldine, Jesse J, Larry Whittie. **Educ:** AL State Univ, BS 1955, MS 1971; Selma Univ, Hon Dr of Divinity 1977. **Career:** Elem School AL, GA, OH teacher 1941, 1967, 1968, 1977; Rock Hill Bapt Church, pastor 1945-50; Star Hope Sunday School/BTU Congress, dean 1955-65; Lower Peach Tree Troup #171, scout master 1957. **Orgs:** Principal Lower Peach Tree Jr High 1951-55; chmn Human Relation Comm 1971; chaplain 5th St Intl W's Men Club 1976; youth advisor NAACP 1976-77; pastoral Marengo, Clarke, Dallas, Wilcox Counties 1977-85; counselor & supervisor Selma Univ 1978-79; mem Wilcox Cty AL School Bd 1980. **Honors/Awds:** Teacher of the Year Green Cty Ed Assn GA 1968; Leadership Awds Boys' Scouts of Amer; Protest Articles Southern Courier Montg Advertiser; Citation OH Ed Assn Comm on Human Relations; Citation Robert A Taft Inst of Government. **Home Addr:** Rt 1 Box 178-A, Lower Peach Tree, AL 36751.

SMITH, FRANK, JR.
City official. **Career:** City of Washington, DC, city councilman, currently. **Orgs:** Civil War Foundation, chair. **Business Addr:** Councilman, DC City Council, 1350 Pennsylvania Ave NW, Washington, DC 20004, (202)724-8181.

SMITH, FRANK JUNIUS
Management consultant. **Personal:** Born Oct 21, 1937, Richmond, VA; married Shirley E Carter; children: Monica T, Frank J Jr, Leah F. **Educ:** Hampton Inst, BS 1960; Amer Univ, MBA 1967; Rensseleaer Polytechnic Inst, certificate 1972. **Career:** Melpar Inc, methods engr, 1962-64; Vitro Corp of Amer, staff specialist 1964-67; Pratt & Whitney Aircraft, staff indus engr, 1967-69; CT Gen Ins Co, supr 1969-74; Travelers Insurance Co, 2nd vice pres agency mgmt consult 1974-90, financial services, vice pres, 1990-. **Orgs:** Sr mem, Am Inst of Indus Engrs 1962-; professional mem Assn for Systems Mgmt 1975-; Professional mem Assn of Intl Mgmt Consultant 1976-; Incorporator Manchester Mem Hosp 1979; dir CT Savs & Loan Assn 1980; Manchester Memorial Hospital, trustee, currently. **Honors/Awds:** Ujima Award Ujima Inc 1977; Chap Pres Award Am Inst Indus Engrs 1978; Distinguished Alumni Award Hampton Inst 1980. **Business Addr:** Vice President, Financial Services, Travelers Insurance Co, 1 Tower Sq, Hartford, CT 06115.

SMITH, FRANKIE L.
Professional football player. **Personal:** Born Oct 8, 1968, Fort Worth, TX. **Educ:** Baylor, attended. **Career:** Miami Dolphins, defensive back, 1993-95; San Francisco 49ers, 1996-. **Business Addr:** Professional Football Player, San Francisco 49ers, 4949 Centennial Blvd, Santa Clara, CA 95054, (415)562-4949.

SMITH, FRANKLIN L.
Educational administrator. **Personal:** Born May 26, 1943, Cape Charles, VA; son of Margaret Dixon Smith and Frank Smith; married Gloria H Smith, Jul 30, 1977; children: Franklin L Jr, Frederick L, Ericka, Delvin L, Kristy. **Educ:** Virginia State University, Petersburg, VA, BS, 1967, MEd, 1972; Nova University, Ft Lauderdale, FL, EdD, 1980. **Career:** Petersburg Public Schools, Petersburg, VA, health, physical ed & drivers ed teacher, 1968-72, asst principal, 1972-74, principal, 1975-82, asst superintendent, 1982-85; Dayton Public Schools, Dayton, OH, asst superintendent, 1985, interim superintendent, 1985-86, superintendent, 1986-91; District of Columbia Public Schools, Washington, DC, superintendent, 1991-. **Orgs:** Mem-

ber, YMCA Advisory Board; Jack & Jill; life member, NAACP; Dayton Area Superntendents Assn; Buckeye Assn of School Administrators; National Alliance of Black School Administrators; Natl Assn of Elementary School Principals, American Assn of School Administrators; Natl Assn of Secondary School Principals; member, Kappa Alpha Psi Fraternity Inc; Phi Delta Kappa, Virginia State University Chapter; member, Sigma Pi Phi Fraternity. **Honors/Awds:** Kappa Alpha Psi Achievement Award, 1987; Smitty Award, Dayton's Top Communicator of the Year, Dayton-Miami Valley Chapter of the Public Relations Society of America, 1989; presented the Exemplary Leadership Award for Region IX of the State of Ohio by the Buckeye Assn of School Administrators, 1988; Ohio Superintendent of the Year, American Assn of School Administrators, 1988; Annie E Casey Grant for At-Risk Students; Communication Award, Dayton School Toastmasters Club, Toastmasters Intl, 1989; Outstanding Community Service Award, Amer Temple #107 Inc AEAONMSPHA, 1990; Certificate of Achievement for Successfully Completing the Madeline Hunter Seminar on IncreasingTeacher Effectiveness, 1984; Certificate for Virginia Right to Read Leadership Training Institute.

SMITH, FREDDIE ALPHONSO

Surgeon (retired). **Personal:** Born Sep 29, 1924, Athens, GA; son of Forstella Robinson Smith and Arnett Smith (deceased); married Mary W Smith, Oct 1976; children: Althea S England, Amaro Cedric Wilson, Sandra K Weaver. **Educ:** FL A&M Univ, BS (highest honors), 1949; Meharry Med Coll, MD (honors), 1950. **Career:** General Practice Sanford, FL 1952-57; Tuskegee Veterans Administration Hospital, Tuskegee, AL, general surgery resident, 1957-60, staff surgeon, 1960-64; general surgeon, Tampa, FL, 1964-89 (retired). **Orgs:** Diplomate Amer Bd of Surgery 1963; fellow Amer Coll of Surgeons 1966; former mem Hillsborough County Med Assn; mem FL Med Assn; mem Amer Med Assn; mem Natl Med Assn; FL Med, Dental & Pharmaceut Assn; NAACP; Tampa Urban League; Alpha Phi Alpha; past pres FL Med, Dental & Pharmaceut Assn; Bellmen-Waiters Club. **Honors/Awds:** Citizen of the Year 1967; Achievement Award Frontiers of Amer 1972. **Military Serv:** US Air Force, Private 1st Class, 1943-46. **Home Addr:** 2108 Riverside Dr, Tampa, FL 33602.

SMITH, FREDERICK D.

City official, attorney. **Personal:** Born Mar 29, 1917, Ellsworth, KS. **Educ:** University of Iowa, BA; Hastings College of Law, JD, 1954. **Career:** Public Defenders Office of San Francisco, chief of courts, chief trial attorney, currently. **Military Serv:** US Army, captain, 1942-45. **Business Addr:** Chief Trail Attorney, 850 Bryant St, San Francisco, CA 94103.

SMITH, FREDERICK ELLIS

Dentist. **Personal:** Born Oct 23, 1928, Dayton, OH; married Dolores J Miles; children: Frederick M, Katherine D. **Educ:** OH State U, BS 1950; OH State U, DDS cum laude 1958; Univ Detroit, orthodontia 1977-78. **Career:** Dentist pvt prac 1958-; Tempora Mandibular Joint Clinic Miami Valley Hosp, co-dir 1973. **Orgs:** Mem Am Dental Assn; AR Weprin Maxillo Facial Study Grp; Nat Dental Assn; Am Acad Craniomandibular Ortho; OH Commn Dental Testing; pres Western OHAcad of Dental Practice Adminstrn 1979-81; mem NAACP; Urban League; Alpha Phi Alpha Frat; mem Pierre Fauchard Acad 1977; Aca. **Honors/Awds:** Recipient Outstanding Table Clinic Dayton Dental Soc 1969; Golden Award for Teaching OH State Med Assn 1969. **Military Serv:** AUS 1951-53. **Business Addr:** 133 N Gettysburg, Dayton, OH 45417.

SMITH, FREDRICK E.

Educator. **Personal:** Born Oct 27, 1935, Mound City, IL; married Mary L; children: David E, Melissa L. **Educ:** Lincoln Univ of MO, AB 1960; Atlanta Univ Sch of Social Work, MSW 1962; St Louis U, PhD 1976. **Career:** Washington Univ St Louis, asst prof 1969-; Med Security Inst St Louis, dir of social serv 1967-69; Urban League St Louis, dist coord 1965-67; Health Welfare & Housing MN Urban League, asso dir 1963-65; Kingdom House St Louis, dir of children's prog 1962-63. **Orgs:** Consult Jeff-Vander-Lou Corp; Nat Urban Coalition; pres Natl Com on Neighborhoods; adv Nat Urban League's Coop Energy Educ Proj; Congresional Black Caucus Energy Adv Braintrust; chmn Nat Assn of Black Social Workers Energy/Envir Com; bd mem, chmn St Louis Chap NABSW Energy/ Environment Com; Council on Social Welfare Educ; MW Coord Project 80 Coalition for black Coll, 1980. **Honors/ Awds:** Conduct med; pres citation; parachutist badge; Strivers Community Leadership Award Narcotics Serv Council 1970; St Louis Met Found Fellow Award Danforth Found St Louis 1970-74; Community Leaders & Noteworthy Americans Award 1976-77; "Task Force on Energy Final Report" Nat Assn of Black Social Workers 1980; "Energy/Environment & the Black Community" Proud Mag 1980; Fellowship Award Nat Inst for the Study of Race in the Mil 1980; hon mem 9th & 10th Cavalries "The Buffalow Soldiers". **Military Serv:** AUS 1953-56. **Business Addr:** Washington Univ Campus, Box 1196, St Louis, MO 63130.

SMITH, FRONSE WAYNE, SR.

Chemical company manager. **Personal:** Born Aug 11, 1946, Chicago, IL; son of Floy Smith and Elmer Smith; married Germaine Pellebon-Smith, Jan 20, 1972; children: Alonda Fleming, Lehia Franklin, Fronse Jr, Gamal-Azmi, Julius. **Educ:** University of Illinois at Chicago, BS, chemistry, 1970; Grand Valley State University, MBA, international new ventures, 1980. **Career:** Glidden Co, quality control technician, 1965-67; DeSoto Inc, research chemist, 1968-75; W-L Co, Parke Davis Div, Paints, analytical chemist, 1977-81; Warner Lambert Co, Pharmaceuticals, senior buyer, 1981-83, purchasing manager, 1983-88, Sterile Products, purchasing agent, 1988-92; May Day Chemical Co Inc, general manager, chemical distribution, 1992-96; president, BPS International Ltd, Consultants for Africa Chemical Procurement and Business Match-making, currently. **Orgs:** Prince Hall, FAM, Tyrian Widows & Sons Lodge 34, master mason, 1987; Hope Reformed Church, deacon and elder, 1977-96; Bethel AME Church, steward, 1982-83; Holland Coalition, People of Color, co-founder, 1989; National Association of Purchasing Managers, national associate member; University of Illinois at Chicago, Black Alumni Association; University of Illinois Alumni Association, life member. **Honors/Awds:** State of Michigan, Department of Corrections, Certified Volunteer, 1979-82. **Special Achievements:** Contributor, "Dew Freeze Vacuum, Wet Adhesion Test," Journal of Coatings Technology, 1973; amateur painter and exhibitor in Holland, MI, 1981; Eagle scout, 1961. **Home Addr:** 601 Douglas Ave, Holland, MI 49424, (616)396-4854. **Business Addr:** BPS International Ltd, 977 Butternut Dr, Ste 125, Holland, MI 49424, (616)396-1082.

SMITH, G. ELAINE

Organization executive. **Career:** American Baptist Churches USA, pres, 1996-97; US government, attorney. **Orgs:** TN Bar Assoc; PA Bar Assoc; New Jersy Bar Assoc; Alpha Kappa Alpha Sorority. **Honors/Awds:** Honorary Doctorate, Ottawa University. **Special Achievements:** First African American female president of the American Baptist Churches USA. **Business Addr:** President, American Baptist Churches USA, N Gulph Rd & 1st Ave, King of Prussia, PA 19406, (610)768-2000.

SMITH, GEORGE BUNDY

Judge. **Personal:** Born Apr 7, 1937, New Orleans, LA; married Alene Jackson; children: George Jr, Beth. **Educ:** Inst d'Etudes Politiques Paris, CEP Inst 1958; Yale Univ, BA 1959; Yale Law School, LLB 1962; NYU, MA 1967, PhD 1974. **Career:** New York City Civil Court, judge 1975-79; Supreme Court State of NY, justice 1980-87; Supreme Court Appellate Div State of NY, first dept assoc justice 1987-92; New York State Court of Appeals, 1992-. **Orgs:** Past Admin of Model Cities NYC; admitted to NY State Bar Assn 1963; admitted to Washington DC bar 1980; Metropolitan Black Bar Assn. **Business Addr:** New York State Court of Appeals, 20 Eagle Street, Albany, NY 12207.

SMITH, GEORGE S.

Government administrator. **Personal:** Born Jan 6, 1940, Terry, MS; children: George Jr, Tosha, Eric, Carol. **Educ:** Utica Jr Coll, AA; Jackson State Univ. **Career:** State Bldg Comm, suprv 1979; Governor of MS, sr staff 1966; State Medicaid Comm, comm mem 1966; Hinds Cty Dist Five, suprv 1979,83, pres 1984-. **Orgs:** Mem TC Almore Lodge #242, Jackson Chap of Natl Business League, Jackson Urban League, Natl Assoc for the Advancement of Colored People; mem bd of dir Smith-Robertson Comm, Metropolitan Young Men Christian Assoc, Goodwill Indust, Central MS Planning & Devel Dist Advisory Council on Aging, Centre South Industrial Devel Group, Jackson Chamber of Commerce. **Honors/Awds:** Appointed 1st black to the State Bldg Comm; 1st black to be sr staff mem to Gov of MS, 1st black to be appointed as commiss mem of State Med Commiss; One of two blacks to be elected suprv of Hinds Cty Dist Five 1979, re-elected suprv 1983; 1st black to serve as pres of Hinds Cty Bd of Suprvs 1984. **Business Addr:** President, Hinds Cty Bd of Suprvs, PO Box 686, Jackson, MS 39205.

SMITH, GEORGE V.

Businessman. **Personal:** Born Mar 19, 1926, Livingston, TX; married Evie Lee Flournoy; children: Charles, George Jr, Jacquelyn Eastland. **Career:** Smith Pipe Supply Inc, pres/owner 1974-; Seaboard Pipe Testers, vp/gen mgr 1970-74; Atlans Bradford Co (pipe co), field supr 1952-70. **Orgs:** Bd of dir Houston Regnl Minority Purchasing Coun 1976-78; bd of dirs Am Business Coun 1978; bd of trustees St Elizabeth Hosp 1978-; bd of dirs TX Occupational Safety Bd 1979; bd of dirs Houston Br Fed Res Bank of Dallas 1980. **Honors/Awds:** Named in Top 100 Black Businessmen Black Enterprise 1977-78; Outst Achvmnt by a Vendor Co Houston Regnl Minority Purchasing Coun 1978; Excel in Achvmnt Awd TX So Univ 1979; Bus Achvmnt Awd Houston Citizens C of C 1980; Top Hat Awd Pittsburgh Courier 1980; Distng Achvmnt Awd Nat Assn of Black Acctnts Inc 1980. **Military Serv:** USAF t5 1945-47. **Business Addr:** 12615 E Freeway, Ste 410, Houston, TX 77015.

SMITH, GEORGE WALKER

Clergyman. **Personal:** Born Apr 28, 1929, Hayneville, AL; married Elizabeth; children: Anthony, Carolyn, Joyce. **Educ:** Knoxville Coll, BS 1951; Pittsburgh Theol Sem, MDiv. **Career:** Golden Hill United Presby Ch, minister; Nat Sch Bd Assn, 1st vp. **Orgs:** Appt to serve on CA Ad Hoc Comm; sec treas Nat Sch Bd Assn; apptd CA Savs & Loan Leag; past pres Council of Great City Schs; mem San Diego Bd Edn; one of fndrs dir vice pres Pacific Coast Bank; served in various capacities on various org; Kappa Alpha Psi; Soclia Club; chrtr mem San Diego Chap Alpha Pi Boule; Sigma Pi Phi. **Honors/Awds:** Received various honors & awards. **Business Addr:** 2130 Market St, San Diego, CA 92102.

SMITH, GERALD WAYNE

Television broadcasting director - tv host. **Personal:** Born Jul 26, 1950, Detroit, MI; son of Antoinette T. Howard Smith and Jacob M. Smith; divorced; children: Adanna Nekesa Smith. **Educ:** Highland Park Community College, Highland Park, MI, 1968-69; University of Detroit, Detroit, MI, BA (magna cum laude), 1974, graduate studies, 1974-75; American Society for Industrial Security, Detroit Chapter, Certificate, 1983; The Real Estate Institute, School of Continuing Education, New York University, New York, NY, Certificate, 1984; Crittenton Real Estate Institute, Chicago, IL, Certificate, 1984; National Society of Fund Raising Executives, Detroit, MI, Certificate, 1990; Wayne State University, Detroit, MI, 1991-. **Career:** New Detroit, Inc, Detroit, MI, administrative services asst, 1968-69; City of Detroit Model Neighborhood Agency, Detroit, MI, community organizer, 1969-71; Wayne County Community College, Detroit, MI, instructor, 1972-80; Wayne County Circuit Court, Probation Dept, Detroit, MI, social service worker, 1974-75; Wholesale Distribution Center Citizens District Council, Detroit, MI, administrator, 1976-80; Detroit Economic Growth Corporation, development associate, 1980-85; Wayne State Univ, Dept of Africana Studies, assistant professor, 1980-; WTVS-TV/Channel 56, Detroit, MI, Detroit Public TV, director community development, 1985-; TV/Radio Host, "Back to Back," Detroit Public TV/WQBH AM 1400, 1992-. **Orgs:** Board of Directors, Big Brothers/Big Sisters, 1997; scy, bd of dirs, Central Educ Network, Chicago, IL, 1996-97; chmn, Detroit Cable Communications Comm, 1994-; chairman, Friends of African Art, 1988-90; trustee, Detroit Institute of Arts, 1988-90; member, Move Detroit Forward, 1980-; member, Arab-American Community Center. **Honors/Awds:** Spirit of Detroit Award, 1978; Afro-American Benefactor's Award, 1980; Crime Prevention Citation, 1982; Mayor's Award of Merit, 1982; Wayne County School District Merit Awards, 1984, 1985; Michigan Legislative Resolution, 1986; Michigan Senate Tribute, 1986; Certificate of Appreciation, Literacy Volunteers of America, 1986; Certificate of Appreciation, Greater Detroit Community Outreach Center, 1986; Carter G. Woodson Award, Educator of the Year, Creative Educational Concepts, 1987; Certificate of National Recognition, 7 Mile-Livernois Project, US Dept of Housing and Urban Development, 1986; Arab Community Center for Economic and Social Services Award, 1990; Haitian American Award, 1990; Black Educator of the Year, US Peace Corps, 1990; author, Arab-American Directory, 1990. **Business Addr:** Director, Community Development/ Program Production, Detroit Public TV/WTVS-TV Channel 56, 7441 Second Blvd, Detroit, MI 48202-3489.

SMITH, GERALDINE T.

Social worker, educator (retired). **Personal:** Born Sep 14, 1918, Cave Spring, GA; daughter of Cora L Johnson Turner and Dallas C Turner; divorced; children: Karen T Smith Watts (deceased). **Educ:** Hunter Coll, BA 1943; Columbia Univ, MA 1947; Smith Coll Sch for Social Work, MSS 1952. **Career:** Bureau Child Welfare, social worker 1952-57; Pgh Public Schs, sch social worker 1957-58; Western Psychiatric Inst, sr psychiat social worker 1958-68; Univ of Pgh, asst prof 1965-87; Neighborhood Psychiat Unit & Counseling Serv 1966-68; Western Psychiatric Inst Univ of Pgh, dir social work 1968-75; Pgh Model City Agency, consult, 1968-69;asst dir of educ CMH/ MRC 1975-78; Dixmont State Hosp Social Serv, consult 1973-74; Pgh Model Cities Agency, consul, 1968-69; WPIC Hill Satellite Ctr Western Psych Inst Univ of Pgh, dir 1979-87. **Orgs:** Sec adv bd New Opportunities for the Aging (NOFA) 1984, adv bd mem 1981-; mem Natl Assn of Social Workers; Acad Certified Social Workers; Council on Social Work Educ; Natl Conf Social Welfare; Soc for Hosp Social Work Dirs; United Mental Health of Allegheny County; bd mem, Bethesda Ctr, Inc, 1988-94. **Home Addr:** 1710 Swissvale Ave, Pittsburgh, PA 15221.

SMITH, GLORIA DAWN

Hospital administrator. **Personal:** Born Oct 2, 1947, Jones, LA; daughter of Hazel and Alvin Hayes; divorced; children: Lawonda and Orlando. **Educ:** University of San Francisco, BS, 1982; Golden Gate University, MBA, 1989-90. **Career:** Real Estate Consultant, 1984-87; Stanford University, human resources mgr, 1968-85; Children's Hospital at Stanford, dir of personnel, 1985-88; Woodland Memorial Hospital, vp human resources, 1988-91; Children's Hospital, Oakland Ca, dir of personnel, 1991-93; Univ Health Center at Tyler, vp human resources, 1993-. **Orgs:** Bureau of Natl Affirs Forum, 1995-97; Parkinsonian, Tyler, TX, 1994-; Child Care Commission City of Woodland, Ca, 1990-91; YMCA, Board of Dir, Woodland, Ca, 1989-91; Neighborhood Housing, Menlo Park, Ca, president,

1980-82; NAACP, 1995; Democratic Central Committee, 1990-91; Professional Woman Assn, 1995. **Special Achievements:** Compenation Strategies, "Splitting the Difference," 1990; American Society Human Resource Assn (ASHRA), Conference Presentation. **Business Addr:** Asst Dir. of Human Resources, University of Texas Health Center at Tyler, PO Box 2003, Tyler, TX 75710.

SMITH, GLORIA R.
Nurse, educator. **Personal:** Born Sep 29, 1934, Chicago, IL; married Leroy. **Educ:** Wayne U, BS 1955; Mich U, MPH 1959; Univ CA, cert 1971; Univ of OK, MA 1977; Union for Experimenting Coll & U, phD 1979. **Career:** Detroit Visiting Nurse's Assn, public health nurse 1955-56; sr public health nurse 1957-58; asst dist office supr 1959-63; Tuskegee Inst, asst prof 1963-66; Albany State Coll, 1966-68; Okla State Health Dept, dist nurse supr 1968-70; medicare nurse consultant 1970-71; Univ Okla, coor asst prof 1971-73; interim dean asso prof 1971-73; dean & prof 1975-83; MI Dept Public Health, dir 1983-. **Orgs:** Mem & officer Am Assn of Coll of Nursing; comm & Am Academy of Nursing; mem past officer Nat Black Nurses Assn; mem steering Com & first bd of dirMidwest Alliance in Nursing 1977-80; Nat Student Nurses Assn; bd of dir Nat League for Nursing; OK State Nurses Assn; officer Am Nurses Assn; Okla Pub Health Assn; Wayne State Alumni & Nursing Alumni Assns; Sigma Gamma Rho Sor Sigma Theta Tau; Inter Greek Council; Interagency Com Health Serv Task Orce;bd dirs YMCA 1972-; steering com Human Relations Council Greater Okla City; bd dirS St Peter Claver Community Credit Union 1961-63; Mayor's Com to Study In-migrants Detroit 1963. **Honors/Awds:** Outstanding Serv Awd Franklin Settlement Detroit 1963; Outstanding Sigma of the Year 1963; Cert OK State Nurses' Assn Black Nurses' Caucus 1973; Key to the City Miami Beach 1974; 1st Speaker Katherine Faville Disting Lecturer Series Wayne State Univ 1975; Leaders in Educ 1975; Cert of Recognition NBNA 1976; Cert & Plaque Sigma Gamma Rho 1977; Hall of Fame Sigma Gamma Rho Sor 1974; Community Serv Awd for Leadership; Soul Bazaar Coord Clara Luper 1980; Plaque of Appreciation presented by Pres Banowsky Univ of OK 1983; Plaque of Appreciation presented by Assn ofBlack Personnel 1983; Hon Mem Chi Eta Phi Sor 1984; Hon Recognition Awd OK Nurses' Assn 1984; Disting Alumni Awd Wayne State Univ 1984; Disting Scholar Amer Nurses Found 1986. **Business Addr:** Dir, Michigan Dept of Public Health, 3500 N Logan, PO Box 30035, Lansing, MI 48909.

SMITH, GORDON ALLEN
Educational administrator. **Personal:** Born May 8, 1933, Detroit, MI; married Patricia Evon Ware; children: Dorel, Gordon, Brian, Stephanie. **Educ:** Wayne State U, BS 1966; No IL U, MS 1969; No IL U, EdD 1977. **Career:** IL Office of Educ, affirmative action officer 1975-; No IL Univ, asst to pres 1973-75; No IL Univ, counselor 1970-73; Detroit & Public School, teacher 1965-68; Detroit, public aid worker 1968; Inland Steel Recruitment Com; Natl Assn Affrm Act Officers; IL Affrm Action Officers Assn Commr Dekalb Human Rel, 1973-75; commr IL Commn on Human Rel, 1974. **Military Serv:** AUS 1954-56. **Business Addr:** 100 N 1st St, Springfield, IL 62777.

SMITH, GRANVILLE L.
Insurance company executive. **Career:** Benevolent Life Insurance Co Inc, cheif executive officer, currently. **Business Addr:** CEO, Benevolent Life Insurance Company Inc, 1624 Milam, Shreveport, LA 71103.

SMITH, GRANVILLE N. See Obituaries section.

SMITH, GREGORY ALLEN
Obstetrician/gynecologist. **Personal:** Born Sep 12, 1952, Detroit, MI; married Jennifer; children: Amber, Camille. **Educ:** MI State Univ, BS 1974; Howard Univ, MD 1978. **Career:** Wayne State Univ, resident ob/gyn 1978-82; AMI Doctors Medical Ctr, chief ob/gyn 1987-88; Associated Women's Care of Tulsa, pres. **Orgs:** Mem Natl & Amer Medical Assocs, OK State Medical Soc, Tulsa Co Medical Soc; adv bd Sickle Cell Anemia Rsch Foundation of OK. **Honors/Awds:** Diplomate Amer Bd of Obstetrics-Gynecology. **Business Addr:** President, Associated Women's Care of Tulsa, 730 Peachtree St NE #920, Atlanta, GA 30308-1212.

SMITH, GREGORY KEVIN PRILLERMAN
Sports administrator. **Personal:** Born May 8, 1964, Los Angeles, CA; son of L LaDonna Prillerman and Ernie Smith. **Educ:** Tennessee State University, BS, 1987; Temple University, MEd, 1989, EdD, 1991. **Career:** Temple University, graduate assistant, 1987-91; West Virginia State College, director of intercollegiate athletics, 1991-. **Orgs:** National Association of Collegiate Directors of Athletics, 1988-; National Football League Players Association, 1988-91; National Basketball Players Association, 1988-91; Association of Representatives of Professional Athletics, 1988-91; Sports Lawyers Association, 1988-91; American Bar Association Forum on the Entertainment & Sports Industries, 1988-91; Tennessee Association of Health, Physical Education, Recreation and Dance, 1986-87; American Alliance of Health, Physical Education, Recreation and Dance, 1985-87. **Honors/Awds:** NCAA, Ethnic Minority Post Graduate Scholarship, 1988, 1989; TAHPERD, Outstanding Undergraduate HPERD, Major of the Year, 1986-87; Scholastic Achievement Academy, Academic All-American, 1985, 1986; National Dean's List, 1985. **Special Achievements:** Congressional Black Caucus Mid-Year Sports Forum, panelist, 1989; An Investigation of State Legislation Enacted to Regulate and Monitor the Practices of Athlete's Agents within the United States, Master's Thesis, 1989; A Survey of Qualifications of Competent Contract Advisers as Perceived by Members of the Association of Representatives of Professional Athletes, doctoral dissertation, 1991. **Business Phone:** (304)766-3165.

SMITH, GREGORY ROBESON, SR.
Organization executive. **Personal:** Born Sep 22, 1947, Philadelphia, PA; son of Bennie Ryan and Louis Smith; married Brenda Lee Galloway Smith, Jun 28, 1969; children: Gregory Robeson Jr, Avery Vaughn, Whitney DeAnna. **Educ:** Livingstone College, BA, 1969; University of Wisconsin, MBA, 1972; Union Theological Seminary, MDiv, 1985; Columbia University Teacher's College, courses towards EdD, 1986-91. **Career:** Lever Brothers Co., product manager, 1975-77; Revlon Inc, marketing manager, Marketing Manager Group I Classic Revlon, 1977-80, Polished Ambers, 1977-79, Classic Revlon, 1979-80; Joseph E Seagram & Sons Inc, national product manager, 1980-82; National Council of Churches, Church World Service, director, international disaster relief, 1983-88; Mt Hope AME Zion Church, pastor, 1986-; Antonovich Inc, director of marketing, 1988-91; African Development Foundation, president/chief executive officer, 1991-. **Orgs:** NAACP, White Plains/ Greenburgh, NY Chapter, vice pres; African-American Men of Westchester; Omega Psi Phi Fraternity Inc, Beta Alpha Alpha Chapter; National Black Republican Council; New York State Conference of Black Republicans, former state vice pres, regional vice pres, executive board member; Bush for President, national steering committee, 1988; Council of 100. **Honors/ Awds:** No 17, Holy Royal Arch Masons, King David Consistory, No 3 ASSR 33 Degree Mason; 14th Session of the World Methodist Council, Delegate; Mother AME Zion Church, Former Trustee; White House Fellow, National Finalist, 1976. **Special Achievements:** Author, thesis: "Ghetto as a Marketing Segment," MBA, Univ of Wisconsin, 1972; "Towards a more Perfect Union between the AME, AME Zion, and CME Denominations," MDiv, Union Theological Seminary, 1985; General Officer, AME Zion Church, youngest person in history, elected in 1976. **Business Addr:** President, African Development Foundation, 1400 Eye St NW, 10th fl, Washington, DC 20005, (202)673-3916.

SMITH, GUY LINCOLN, IV
Company executive. **Personal:** Born Mar 16, 1949, New Orleans, LA; son of Laura Louise Orr Smith and Guy Lincoln Smith III; married Marjorie Whaley Russell, Jun 19, 1971; children: Abigail, Guy, Laura. **Educ:** Bowling Green State Univ, 1967-68; Univ of Tennessee, 1968-70; American Univ, 19711 US Dept of Agriculture Graduate School, 1971. **Career:** Knoxville Journal, reporter, 1967-68, asst city editor, 1968-70; Appalachian Regional Commission, Washington, DC, asst director of information, 1970, director of information, 1970-72; City of Knoxville, press secretary, 1972-76; Miller Brewing Company, Milwaukee, WI, manager of corporate affairs, 1976-79; Seven-Up Co, St Louis, MO, vice president of corporate affairs; Phillip Morris Companies Inc, vice president of corporate affairs, currently. **Orgs:** Board of directors, Laumeir International; board of directors, Jackie Robinson Foundation; board of directors, Opera Theatre of St Louis. **Honors/Awds:** Excellence in News Writing Award, William Randolph Hearst Foundation, 1970; Award for Communications Excellence to Black Audiences, Black Communications Institute, 1982. **Business Addr:** Vice President, Corporate Affairs, Philip Morris Companies, Inc, 120 Park Ave, New York, NY 10017-5592.

SMITH, H. RUSSELL
Attorney, entrepreneur. **Personal:** Born Oct 8, 1957, Detroit, MI; son of Mildred A Smith and Oliver H Smith. **Educ:** University of Michigan, BBA, 1979; Northwestern University, MBA, MM, 1983, JD, 1983. **Career:** Dykema, Gossett, et al, attorney, 1983-85; Burroughs Corp./Unisys, attorney, 1985-87; Growth Funding Ltd, attorney, consultant, 1987-88; H Russell Smith Esq, attorney, 1988-89; Lewis, White & Clay PC, senior attorney, 1989-92; Blacks Factor Inc, president, 1992-. **Orgs:** Wolverine Bar Association; Detroit Bar Association; Michigan Bar Association. **Business Addr:** President, Blacks Factor Inc, 22757 Woodward, No 240, Ferndale, MI 48220, (810)542-2707.

SMITH, HALE
Composer, editor, educator. **Personal:** Born Jun 29, 1925, Cleveland, OH; son of Jimmie Anne Clay Smith and Hale Smith; married Juanita R Hancock; children: Hale Michael, Marcel Hancock, Robin Alison, Eric Dale. **Educ:** Cleveland Inst of Mus, BM 1950; Cleveland Inst of Mus, MM 1952. **Career:** Composer of music; Univ of CT, prof emeritus of music; freelance composer-arranger 1945-; Edward B Marks Mus Corp, ed-consult 1962-63; Frank Mus Corp, 1963-65; Sam Fox Music Publ, 1967-71; CF Peters Corp, 1962-; CW Post Coll, adj assoc prof of mus 1969-70. **Orgs:** Freelance consult to Performers, Composers, Diverse Music Publishing Firms; consult Copyright Infringement; lectr numerous coll throughout the US; former mem Bd of Gov of the Am Comp All; Composers Recording Inc, bd of dirs; former pres Freeport Arts Counc; former mem Freeport Bd of Ethics; New York State Council For The Arts, board member, 1993-. **Honors/Awds:** BMI Student Composers Awd 1952; Cleveland Arts Prize 1973; Distinguished Scholar Xavier Univ of New Orleans LA; Amer Academy Institute of Arts and Letters Award 1988; Honorary Doctorate of Music, Cleveland Institute of Music 1988; numerous commns maj perf & publ. **Military Serv:** Military Serv private 1943-45. **Home Addr:** 225 Pine St, Freeport, NY 11520.

SMITH, HAROLD GREGORY
Cleric. **Personal:** Born Dec 7, Chicago, IL; son of Mable Lee Cline Smith Jenkins and Harold Smith. **Educ:** Bradley University, BS, 1974; Nashotah House Theological Seminary, MDiv, 1980. **Career:** American National Red Cross, program development, 1974-76; Executive Office of the President of USA, staff writer, 1976-77; Church of the Holy Cross, rector, 1980-85; St Simon Episcopal Church, rector, 1985-88; Church of St Luke & St Simon Cyrene, rector, 1988-90; St Timothy Episcopal Church, rector, 1990-93; Church of the Holy Redeemer, rector, 1993-. **Orgs:** Oregon-Leopold Day Care Center, board member, 1988-90; Rochester Society for the Prevention of Cruelty to Children, board member, 1985-88; Judicial Process Commission; Bishop Sheen Ecumenical Housing Foundation, board member; Episcopal Church Home, board member; American Cancer Society, Rochester Chapter, board member; American Heart Association, Rochester Chapter, board member; Project Open Hand, volunteer; The Place Ministry, chair; Chaplain to the Colorado State House of Representatives; Economic Advisory Bd, City of Denver; Commissioner. **Home Phone:** (404)816-2916. **Business Addr:** Church of the Holy Redeemer, 2552 Williams Street, Denver, CO 80205, (303)831-8963.

SMITH, HAROLD TELIAFERRO, JR. (H. T)
Attorney. **Personal:** Born Apr 10, 1947, Miami, FL; son of Harold & Mary Smith; divorced; children: Katrell, Talia. **Educ:** Florida A&M University, BS, math, 1968; University of Miami, JD, 1973. **Career:** Dade County Public Defenders, attorney; Dade County Attorneys Office, Long and Smith PA, H T Smith PA, president, currently. **Orgs:** National Bar Association, president, 1994-; Miami Partners for Progress, co-chair, 1993-; Inroads/Miami, secretary, 1993-; Community Partnership for the Homeless, board, 1993-94; Kappa Alpha Psi Fraternity, 1983-; Miami Dade Branch, NAACP, executive committee, 1990-; Boyscott Miami Campaign, co-spokesperson, 1990-93; Coalition fo a Free South Africa, chair, 1985-90. **Honors/Awds:** Best Lawyers in America, 1995-96; National Conference of Black Lawyers, Service Award, 1991; Miami Herald, Charles Whited Spirit of Excellence Award, 1993. **Special Achievements:** Wrote numerous articles for publication and gave hundreds of speeches and seminars. **Military Serv:** US Army, 1st lt, 1968-70; Bronze Star (valor), Vietnam Service. **Business Addr:** President, H T Smith, P A, 1017 NW 9th Court, Miami, FL 33136, (305)324-1845.

SMITH, HEMAN BERNARD
Attorney, educator. **Personal:** Born Aug 20, 1929, Alexandria, LA; son of Rosa Smith and Heyman Smith; married Ina Jean Washington, Dec 26, 1952; children: Heman III, Lanie C, Paula Barnes. **Educ:** Univ of Maryland (Far East Div), attended, 1958-60; Univ of Pacific, McGeorge School of Law, JD, 1971. **Career:** Smith, Hanna, de Bruin & Yee, Sacto CA, partner, sr attorney, 1971-78; Smith & Yee, Sacto CA, partner, 1978-84; Smith & Assoc, Sacto CA, sr attorney, 1984-; Univ of Northern California, L P School of Law, Sacto CA, exec dean, 1988-. **Orgs:** Bd mem, Amer Red Cross, Sacto CA, 1980-87; mem, Minority Steering Comm California Youth Authority, 1985-87, Sacto Urban League, currently, Sacto NAACP, currently; pres, Zeta Beta Lambda, 1987-88, Wiley Man Bar Assn, 1988-. **Military Serv:** US Air Force, 1948-69. **Home Addr:** 6370 Havenside Dr, Sacramento, CA 95831. **Business Addr:** Attorney, Smith & Associates, 2710 X St, Ste 1, Sacramento, CA 95818, (916)452-5891.

SMITH, HENRY R., JR. See Obituaries section.

SMITH, HENRY THOMAS
Physician. **Personal:** Born Mar 31, 1937, Portsmouth, VA; son of Mr & Mrs Julius Smith; married Diane; children: Robert, Alicia. **Educ:** Howard Univ, BS 1957; Univ of Rochester, MD 1961. **Career:** MN Gen Hosp, intern 1961-62; Hennepin Co Gen Hosp, resd 1964-67; Hennepin Co Med Ctr, asst dir chronic dialysis unit 1967-69; Pilot City Hlth Ctr, physician 1969; Modern Med Jour, assoc editor 1970-72; Geriatrics Jour, abstract editor 1970-72; Nephrology Modern Med Jour, consult 1975-77; Park Nicollet Medical Ctr, 1971-94; Univ of MN Sch Med, clinical prof of med; Hennepin Faculty Assoc, 1994-. **Orgs:** Sister Kenny Inst 1972-75; MN Heart Assn 1974-76; president Natl Kidney Foundation of Upper Midwest 1982-84; mem Minneapolis Soc of Internal Med; mem Natl Med Assn; Am Soc Nephrology Fellow; Am Coll Physicians; American Heart Assn, Minnesota Affiliate, bd of dirs; Natl Kidney Foundation of the Upper Midwest, med advisory bd; Hennepin Faculty Associates, chief of internal med; Hennepin County Med Ctr, exec comm; Univ of Minnesota Health System, bd of governors;

Minnesota Medical Association, bd of trustees. **Honors/Awds:** Cert Internal Med 1969, Nephrology 1974; Phi Beta Kappa; Commanding General Awd for Medical Service, 1964; Awd of Excellence, Communities of Color, 1997; Best Doctors in America: Central Region, 1996-97. **Military Serv:** AUS Capt 1962-64; Kenner Army Hosp, 1964. **Business Addr:** Physician, HFA Internal Medicine, 825 South 8th Street, Ste 206, Minneapolis, MN 55404, (612)347-7534.

SMITH, HERALD LEONYDUS
Clergyman, printer. **Personal:** Born Apr 20, 1909, Smithfield, OH; married Dorothy Irene Mcclinton; children: Herald, Verl, Rosalie, David. **Educ:** Wilberforce, bachelors of theology, 1945; Monrovia W Africa, DDiv, 1955; Wilberforce Dept of Christian Edn, honors 1959. **Career:** AME Church, clergyman; Cleveland Clinic, chapel organist 1978-80; Smith Typing-mimeograph & Multigraph, owner 1963-; Quinn Chapel AME Cleveland, church builder & pastor 1963-; St Mathews Lorain OH, pastor 1967; "The Herald", editor, 1959-80; Boyd Funeral Home & House of Wills & Others, eulogist/sermon builder 1957-80; Rotary Club Ironton OH, speaker 1952; St John AME Cleveland, asst pastor 1962-66; St James AME Cleveland Branch of Payne Theol Seminar of Wilberforce OH, theol tchr 1965. **Orgs:** Pres AME Ministers Fellowship Cleeland 1971-80; vice pres NAACP Cincinnati Br; adult educ tchr Smithfield OH; master mason; mem Alpha Phi Alph Frat Wilberforce U. **Honors/Awds:** Cert Kiwinis Club of Cleveland 1963; invited to attend inaugural Pres Jimmy Carter; communication from King of Saudi Arabia in response to Article & invitation to visti Saudi Arabia 1979; cert of Honor St Paul AME Ch Cincinnati; plaque The Clevelanders Musical Group; letter of congratulations upon building church Gov Rhodes; respones to articel "Extending the Pulpit" Gov Wallace. **Business Addr:** Episcopal Headquarters Univ Ci, 2767 Halleck Dr, Columbus, OH.

SMITH, HERMAN BRUNELL, JR.
Educational administrator (retired). **Personal:** Born Feb 12, 1927, Mansfield, OH; married Annie Mae Lavender, Dec 26, 1951; children: Gregory B., Terri Lynne. **Educ:** Knoxville College, Knoxville, TN, BA, 1948; University of Wisconsin, Madison, WI, MS, 1955, PhD, 1960. **Career:** Southern Education Foundation, Atlanta, GA, consultant, 1966-68; National Assn of Land Grant Colleges, Washington, DC, director, 1968-74; University of Arkansas, Pine Bluff, AR, president, 1974-81; Atlanta University, Atlanta, GA, vice president, 1981-82; Kettering Foundation, Dayton, OH, consultant, 1982-88; University of Georgia, Athens, GA, consultant to the president, 1985-88; Jackson State University Jackson, MS, interm president, 1991-92. **Orgs:** Vice president, West End Rotary Club; president, Knoxville College National Alumni Assn, 1988-91. **Honors/Awds:** Distinguished Alumnus, University of Wisconsin Alumni Assn, 1988; Outstanding Service Award, City of Knoxville, TN, 1986; Outstanding Service Award, Sigma Pi Phi, 1986; Outstanding Service Award, Phi Delta Kappa, Atlanta University, 1989; Doctor of Laws Degree, Stillman College, Tuscaloosa, Alabama, 1991; School of Education Alumni Achievement Award, University of Wisconsin, Madison, 1992. **Military Serv:** US Army, 1st lt, 1951-53. **Home Addr:** 3380 Benjamin E Mays Dr SW, Atlanta, GA 30311.

SMITH, HERMAN TALLIFERRIO
Attorney. **Personal:** Born Oct 6, 1915, Fulton, AR; married Celestine Reed; children: Herman T; Reginald (dec). **Educ:** Prairie View Univ, BA 1937; Southwestern Univ, JD 1954. **Career:** 55th Assembly Dist State of CA, LA, rep nominee 1958; US Congress 23rd Congr Dist State of CA, LA, rep nominee 1962; Smith & Glasco, LA, atty. **Orgs:** Mem LA Cnty Judicial Procedure Comm 1962-; coop atty Legal Def Fund NAACP 1960-; chmn Watts Br NAACP Legal Redress Comm 1965-69; chmn LA Br NAACP Legal Redress Comm; pres LA Chap Prairie View Alumni Assn; mem bd of Trustees Bel Vue Comm United Presb Ch 1958-61 & 1975; Orgn & Ext Chmn BSA 1956-61; mem CA State Bar Assn; Natl Black Lawyers Assn. **Honors/Awds:** Co-author "CA Politics & Policies"; pub serv awards LA Cty, City of LA, LA Cty Council, State Leg Rules Comm.

SMITH, HOWLETT P.
Musician. **Personal:** Born Feb 29, 1933, Phoenix, AZ; son of Josephine Cox Smith (deceased) and Howard Lowell Smith (deceased); married Judith Celestin; children: Juliette, Rachel, Mark, April, Sandra, Peter. **Educ:** Univ Ariz, BM 1955. **Career:** Composer, pianist, singer, arranger, vocal coach, numerous public appearances. **Orgs:** Lectr & demonstrations concerning use of jazz in church; life mem Psi Mu Alpha Univ Ariz Alumni Asn; Kappa Kappa Psi Mr Newmanite 1955. **Honors/Awds:** Musical dir, "Me & Bessie," Mark Taper forum vol title i program la city unified dist.

SMITH, IRVIN MARTIN
Professional football player. **Personal:** Born Oct 13, 1971, Trenton, NJ. **Educ:** Univ of Notre Dame, bachelor's degree in marketing. **Career:** New Orleans Saints, tight end, 1993-. **Business Addr:** Professional Football Player, New Orleans Saints, 5800 Airline Hwy, Metairie, LA 70003, (504)733-0255.

SMITH, ISABELLE R.
Educator. **Personal:** Born Jun 8, 1924, Woodstown, NJ; married Daniel; children: Brenda, Roger, Debra, Karen, Randall, Douglas. **Educ:** Wayne State Univ, BS 1946; Univ of KS Med Ctr, 1947; Western MI Univ, MS, 1965. **Career:** Univ KS, sub dietitian 1947; Rochester Gen Hosp, floor dietitian 1947-48; Receiving Hosp, diabetic dietitian 1948-50; Battle Creek HS, instr 1964-68; W MI Univ, instr 1968-70; asst prof 1970-74; dept chmn 1974-. **Orgs:** Mem Am Assn Univ Women 1959-63, 1974-; MI Home Economics Assn 1965-; Am Home Economics Assn 1950-; mem Urban League & Urban League Guild, 1950-; NL Am Assn Univ Profs 1969-72; State Scholarship Com, 1971-74; MI Home Economics Scholarship Com 1972-74; Goodwill Industry Auxillary, 1973; vice pres Urban League Guild, 1973; dept rep Affirmative Action 1974-. **Honors/Awds:** Plaque Urban League 1973. **Business Addr:** Administrator, Dietitian, Western Michigan University, Dept of Home Economices, Kalamazoo, MI 49008.

SMITH, J. ALFRED, SR.
Cleric. **Personal:** Born May 19, 1931, Kansas City, MO; son of Amy Smith; married Joanna Goodwin; children: J Alfred Jr, Craig, Anthony, Amy Jones, Shari Rigmaiden, Ronald Craig. **Educ:** Western Baptist Coll, BS, Elementary Educ, 1952; Missouri School of Religion, Univ of MO, Columbia, BD, 1959; Pacific School of Religion, Berkeley, CA, 1962; Inter-Baptist Theological Center, TX, Church & Community, ThM, 1966; Amer Baptist Seminary of the West, 1970, ThM 1972; Golden Gate Baptist Theological Seminary, DM 1975. **Career:** Licensed minister, 1948-; ordained minister, 1951-; American Baptist Seminary of the West, acting dean, 1975-87, professor, 1975-; Graduate Theological Seminary, professor; Fuller Theological Seminary, visiting professor; Allen Temple Baptist Church, senior pastor, 1970-;. **Orgs:** Howard University School of Divinity, advisory board; United Theological Seminary, advisory board; University of California-Berkeley, community advisory board; American Baptist Churches USA, past representative; Bay Area Black United Fund, founding chairperson; Baptist Pastors/Ministers Conf of Oakland and the Easy Bay, president, 1986-; Progressive Natl Baptist Convention, president, 1986-88; board of directors: Metropolitan YMCA; Natl Cncl of Churches; Congress of Natl Black Churches; Bread for the World; Natl Conf of Black Seminarians; Howard Thurman Educ Trust; Bishop Coll Renaissance campaign. **Honors/Awds:** Over 100 local and national awards, including: Morehouse College, Martin Luther King International Chapel; Natl Council of Negro Women; Prince Hall, Free and Accepted Masons, elevated to 33rd Degree; AFRICARE; Alpha Phi Alpha; Man of the Year Award Golden West Mag LA 1976; Award for Outstanding Accomplishments at Grass Roots Level New Oakland Com 1976; Man of the Year Award Sun-Reporter/Metro Reporter 1976; Recognition for Distinguished Serv, Boy Scouts of Amer 1986; Bishop Coll Renaissance Campaign; Earl Lectures, Pacific School of Religion, 1989; Hay Lecturer, Drake Univ, 1989; Addressed United Nations on South African Apartheid, 1989; Lecturer, Hampton Univ, 1979; Honorary Doctorate of Humane Letters, ABSW, 1990; Outstanding Citizen of the Year, Oakland Tribune; Three awards named in honor. **Special Achievements:** Co-author, works include: Giving to a Giving God: Basic Bible Sermons; The Study Bible, Holman Bible Publishing; Preaching As a Social Act; Guidelines for Effective Urban Ministry; listed in Ebony Magazine as one of the fifteen greatest African American preachers in America. **Business Addr:** Senior Pastor, Allen Temple Baptist Church, 8500 A St, Oakland, CA 94621.

SMITH, J. CLAY, JR.
Government Official, attorney, educator. **Personal:** Born Apr 15, 1942, Omaha, NE; son of Emily V Williams Smith and John Clay Smith, Sr; married Patti Jones; children: Stager Clay, Michael Laurel, Michelle Lori, Eugene Douglas. **Educ:** Creighton Univ Omaha, NE, AB 1964; Howard Law Sch Washington, DC, JD 1967; George Washington Law Sch Washington, DC, LLM, 1970, SJD 1977. **Career:** US Army Judge Advocates Gen Corp, capt lyr 1967-71; Arent Fox Kintner Plotkin & Kahn Washington, DC, assc 1971-74; Fed Commctn Cmsn, deputy chf cable TV bureau 1974-76; Fed Communications Commission, assc gen cnsl 1976-77; Equal Emplymnt Opprtnty Cmsn, us cmsnr apptd by Jimmy Carter 1977-82, actng chrmn apptd by Ronald W Reagan 1981-82; Howard Univ Sch of Law, prof of law 1982-86, dean & professor of law, 1986-88. **Orgs:** NE Bar Assoc 1967; mem Howard Law Sch Alumni Assc 1967-; Dist of Columbia Bar 1968; pres bd dir Washington Bar Assc 1970; US Supreme Court 1973; advsr pres Natl Bar Assc 1973-; mem NAACP 1975-; mem Urban League 1975-; natl pres mem Fed Bar Assc 1979; utlty spec Pblc Serv Cmsn 1982-; editorial board ABA Compleat Lawyer 1984; Advisory Committee, DC Bar Exam; bd mem Natl Lawyers Club; planning committee for Task Force on Black Males, AM Psyh Assn 1986-90; mem Am Law Inst 1986-88; chair Natl Bar Assn Comm on History of Blk Lawyers; legal counsel for the Elderly Policy Bd 1986-88. **Honors/Awds:** First African American elected as natl pres, Fed Bar Assn 1980-81; founder juris art movement Washington Bar Assn 1978; Am Bar Assn 1982-; order of the coif hon George Washington Law Sch 1978; Ollie May Cooper Award, 1986; The C Francis Stradford Award 1986; Outstanding Alumni Achievement Awards from Howard University, 1981, Creighton University, 1989, George Washington University, 1990. **Special Achievements:** Publications, Fed Bar Assn Natl Pres Messages, Fed Bar News, CIVICS LEAP, Law Reason & Creativity, Mgng Multi-ethnic Multi-racial Workforce Criminal, Chronic Alcoholism — Lack of Mens Rea — A Dfns Pblc Intoxication 13 Howard Law Journal, An Investment in a New Century, Wash Afro Am; The Black Bar Assn & Civil Rights; A Black Lawyer's Response to the Fairmont Papers; Memoriam: Clarence Clyde Ferguson, Jr, Harvard Law Rev; Forgotten Hero: Charles H Houston, Harvard Law Rev; Justice & Jurisprudence & The Black Lawyer, Notre Dame Law Rev; Emancipation: The Making of The Black Lawyer, 1844-1944; National Book Award of the Natl Conference of Black Political Scientist, 1995; Rebels in Law: The Voices in History of Black Women Lawyers, 1998; Served on the transition team of President Clinton & Vice Pres Gore, 1992. **Business Addr:** Professor of Law, Howard Univ Sch of Law, 2900 Van Ness St NW, Washington, DC 20008.

SMITH, J. HARRY
Educator. **Personal:** Born Aug 22, 1922, Newport News, VA; married Marilyn Horton; children: Danielle, Stephanie, Judith. **Educ:** Seton Hall U, LLD, MA, BA. **Career:** Essex Co Coll, pres, vp, chf exec officer 1969-. **Orgs:** Mem Commission on Higher Educ of Middle States; Assn of Coll & U; pres Assn of Comm Coll; pres NJ Assn of Coll & Univ 1976; bd tsts Seton Hall U; dir Yorkwood Savings & Loan Assn; mem Cncl for Ocptnl Edn; Am Assn of Comm & Jr Coll; chmn Govtl Affairs Commn; NJ State Schlrsp Commn Bd of Tsts; Grtr Newark Hosp Fund; mem 4th Degree KC; past mem Nat Adv Cncl on Adult Edn; mem Commission for the Prison Complex in the State of NJ; past chmn Newark-Essex Chap of Congress of Racial Equality; Nat Ass of Negro Bus & Professional Women's Club 1975; trustee Cancer Inst of NJ; mem trustee bd Blue Cross of NJ; rep Amer Assn of Comm and Jr Colls and Amer Council on Education before Subcomm on Educ of the Senate Commn on Labor and Public Welfare. **Honors/Awds:** President's Medal for Distgshd Serv Seton Hall U; Man of Yr Award So Ward Boy's Clubs of Newark NJ 1975; Leadership Award B'nai B'rith Career & Cnslg Serv; Educator of Yr Award NJ GOP Heritage Found Inc; apptd to Pres Nixon's Adv Cncl on Adult Educ; Brotherhood Awd Natl Conference of Christians and Jews; Service Awd Citizens for All People; Educator of the Yr New Jersey GOP Heritage Foundation, Inc; Achievement Awd Frontiers Intl; Man of the Yr Awd North Jersey Unit Natl Assn of Negro Business and Professional Women's Clubs; numerous articles published in professional journals. **Military Serv:** USAF capt. **Business Addr:** President, Darren Services, 4 Sloan St, South Orange, NJ 07079.

SMITH, JAMES, JR.
Personnel director. **Personal:** Born Nov 10, 1932, Beckley, WV; married V Anne Smith; children: Byron A. **Educ:** Spokane Falls Comm Coll, AAS 1978; Fort Wright Coll, BS Mgmt 1981. **Career:** USAF, security police 1953-70, training admin 1970-75; City of Spokane, personnel tech 1978-81, asst personnel dir 1981-83, personnel dir 1983-. **Orgs:** Pres WA Council of Public Admin 1987-; chmn of the bd Natl Mgmt Assn 1983-87; mem Natl Forum for Black Public Admin 1983-; mem Alpha Phi Alpha Frat 1983-; pres Pine State Athletic Club 1984-87; bd dir NFBP 1985; mem bd dir Assn of Negotiators & Contr Administrators. **Honors/Awds:** Superior Serv Awd City of Spokane 1985. **Military Serv:** USAF msgt 1953-75; Commendation Medal; Good Conduct Medal. **Business Addr:** Personnel Dir, City of Spokane, W 808 Spokane Falls Blvd, Spokane, WA 99201.

SMITH, JAMES A.
Association executive. **Personal:** Born Oct 5, 1927, Ruther Glen, VA; married Katherene Stucky; children: Sherley, Willette. **Educ:** Empire State Coll, BA 1975. **Career:** Human Resources Devel Inst AFL-CIO, area rep. **Orgs:** Mem New York City Taxi Drivers Union 1963-66; financial sec Black Trade Unionist Leadership Committee, NYC Central Labor Council AFL-CIO 1966-; area rep New York City Central Labor Council Job Placement Prog 1968-73; sec New York City Taxi Drivers Joint Industry Bd; elected mem Comm Sch Bd Dist 3 Manhattan; Industry Educ Coord Com NY; Chancellors Com promote equal opportunity prevent sex discrimination employment; New York City Bd Edn; mem of NAACP 125th St Manhattan Branch, Chairman of Selective Services Board 125th St NYC. **Military Serv:** AUS 24th inf regt 1946-48; recalled Sept 1950-52. **Home Addr:** 65 W 96 St, Apt 22C, New York, NY 10025.

SMITH, JAMES ALMER, JR.
Physician, educator. **Personal:** Born May 30, 1923, Montclair, NJ; son of Carrie Elizabeth Moten Smith and James A Smith; married Elsie Brooks Smith, Oct 15, 1949; children: James A III, Roger M, Margo A, Melanie K. **Educ:** Howard Univ, BS 1947, MD 1948. **Career:** Homer G Phillips Hosp, intern 1948-49, resd psychiat 1949-51; Washington Univ, child psychiat 1952-53; Mental Hygiene Clinic Group Co, 1953-55; Hartley Salmon Child Guidance Clinic, staff psychiat 1955-60; Childrens's Serv of CT, 1956-60; Juv Ct Hartford, consult 1956-61; Bay State Med Ctr, asst vis psychiat 1960; Childrens Study Home, consultant 1960-; Kolburne Sch New Marlborough medical dir 1968-; Springfield Child Guidance Clinic, assoc psychi-

atrist 1960-83; Tufts Sch Med, asst clinical prof 1977-. **Orgs:** Mem Human Rel Commn Springfield 1961-62; mem Am Psychiat Assn; fellow Am Ortho Psychiat Assn; Am Assn of Psychoanalytic Physicians Inc; Amer Society of Psychoanalytic Physicians Fellow 1987-; Bd Negro Catholic Scholarship Fund 1980-. **Honors/Awds:** AM Acad Human Serv Award 1974-75; Community Leaders and Noteworthy Americans Awd 1978; Int'l Directory of Distinguished Psychotherapists 1981/82; Dr Anthony L Brown Award WW Johnson Center 1987. **Military Serv:** AUSR MC Capt 1953-55. **Home Addr:** 96 Dartmouth St, Springfield, MA 01109.

SMITH, JAMES ALMER, III
Psychiatrist. **Personal:** Born May 24, 1950, St Louis, MO; married Sandra Wright; children: Anthony, Jason, Brian. **Educ:** Howard Univ, BS 1972, MD 1976. **Career:** Harlem Hosp Ctr, intern 1976-77; Walter Reed Army Medical Ctr, resident 1977-80; US Army Ft Bragg, in-patient chief psych 1980-81, out-patient chief psych 1981-82; Central Prison Dept of Corrections, staff psych 1982-85, clinical dir 1985-87; NC Dept of Corrections, clinical dir of mental health. **Orgs:** Out-patient psych Wake Co Alcoholism Treatment Ctr 1983-87; mem bd dirs Drug Action of Wake Co 1986-87; president, LA Scruggs Medical Society, 1989-91; criminal adjuctant professor, Dulce Medical Center, 1989-91. **Military Serv:** AUS major 9 yrs; US Army Commendation Medal 1986; gov Council on Alcoholism 1991; LtC, 1977-91. **Business Addr:** Clinical Dir of Mental Hlth, NC Dept of Corrections, 1300 Western Blvd, Raleigh, NC 27606.

SMITH, JAMES CHARLES
Computer services company executive. **Personal:** Born Jul 27, 1936, Winnfield, LA; son of Mrs Annie Lee Rush; divorced; children: Rodney D, Michael D, Wanda T, Donna M Murphy. **Educ:** Southern Univ, & A & M Coll, BA, 1960; Saint Mary's Univ, MBA, 1971; GE Management Devt Institute, 1983-85. **Career:** US Army, Military Award Branch, chief, 1977-79; US Army Computer Systems Cmd, dir, personnel & admin, 1979-81; General Electric Co, sr systems engineer, 1981-83, mgr, 1983-86; Systems Engineering & Mgmt Assocs, Inc, founder, pres, CEO, 1986-. **Orgs:** Omega Psi Phi Fraternity, KRS, Basielus, 1985-87; INROADS-Greater Washington Inc, bd of dirs, 1991-92; George Washington Univ, adv bd, 1992-93; VA Governor's Comm of Defense Conversion, commissioner, 1992; VA Governor's Task Force on Workforce 2000, 1992-93; NASA Minority Business Resource Advisory Council, 1993-94; VA Venture Fund Foundation, bd of dirs, 1993-94; District of Columbia Math/Sci/Tech Inst, bd of dirs, 1993. **Honors/Awds:** Omega Psi Phi Fraternity, Chapter Man of the Year, 1984, Chapter & District Citizen of the Year, 1988, 1990; Merrill Lynch Inc, Mag, Ernst & Young & Washington Business Journal, Entrepreneur of the Year, 1991; N VA Minority Bus Assn, Mentor of the Year, 1989; Fairfax County Chamber of Commerce, New Bus of the Year, 1990; Black Enterprise Mag, Top 100 Black Owned Companies in US, 1994; Inc Mag, Inc 500 Fastest Growing Companies, 1993; Washington Tech Mag, Fast 50 Fastest Growing Companies, 1992-93; Government Computer News, Top 10 Fastest Growing Government Contractors, 1989, 1992; Federal Integrator, Top 25 Companies, 1994; Washington Tech Mag, Jump Start Recognition, 1990, 1991; Defense Comm Agency, Small Bus of the Year, 1989; Teledyne Brown Engineering, Outstanding Vendor Award, 1989. **Special Achievements:** Responsible for convincing Pres Jimmy Carter to award the Pres Unit Citation to the 761st Tank Battallion, 1978; First African-American to be appointed by Gov L Douglas Wilder to the three member Bd of Vistors, Gunston Hall, home of Geoorge Mason, author of the US Constitution, 1990; Testified before Congress on efforts to be made to involve more minorities in math, sci & tech, 1991, 1992; Profiled on the CBS local affiliate's TV show "Success Stories", 1991, 1992. **Military Serv:** US Army, lieutenant colonel, 1960-81; Legion of Merit, 1981; Bronze Star, 1968; 2 Meritorious Service Medals, 1973, 1974; Joint Service Commendation Medal, 1976; 2 Army Commendation Medals, 1965, 1967; Natl Defense Service Medal, 1968; Vietnamese Gallantry Cross, 1968; Vietnamese Service Medal, 1968; 4 Armed Forces Expeditionary Medals, 1965-73; The Expert Infantry Man Badge, 1962; Sr Parachutist Badge, 1966. **Business Addr:** President & CEO, Systems Engineering & Mgmt Assocs Inc, 2000 N Beauregard St, Ste 600, Alexandria, VA 22311-1712, (703)845-1200.

SMITH, JAMES DAVID
Artist, educator. **Personal:** Born Jun 23, 1930, Monroe, LA; son of Sarah Smith and Ernest Leondrus Smith; married Ruth Johnson. **Educ:** So U, BA 1952; Univ CA, 1954-55; Univ So CA, MFA 1956; Chouinard Art Inst, 1962; CO Coll, 1963; Univ OR, PhD 1969. **Career:** Santa Barbara County Schools, consultant, 1970, 1974, 1975; Univ of CA, Dept of Studio Art, prof, 1969-, Dept of Black Studies, chmn, 1969-73; Univ OR, vis asst prof 1967-69; Santa Barbara HS, instr 1966-67; So Univ, asst prof 1958-66; Prairie View Coll, instr 1956-58; So Univ, vis prof 1954-55. **Orgs:** Nat Art Educ Assn 1963-; past pres CA Art Educ Assn 1977-79; mem Kappa Alpha Psi; Phi Delta Kappa; NAACP; bd dir Self Care Found of Santa Barbara 1974-; bd dir Children's Creative Proj Santa Barbara 1975-84; pres CA Art Educ Assn 1975-77; co-orgnr Spl Art Exhibition for Hon Edmond Brown Jr, Governor of the State of California, 1975. **Honors/Awds:** Selected John Hay Whitney Fellow in the Humanities 1963; exhibited in Dallas Mus of Art; Santa Barbara Mus of Art 1973; Award of Merit, CA Art Educ, 1983; Eugene J Grisby Jr Art Award, Natl Art Educ Assn, 1981; CA Art Educ of the Year, Natl Art Educ Assn, 1986; numerous shows in galleries throughout US; University Distinguished Professor in the Arts & Humanities, 1992-93. **Military Serv:** US Army, capt, overseas service: Korea. **Business Addr:** Professor, Dept of Studio Art, Univ of California, Santa Barbara, CA 93106.

SMITH, JAMES ODELL (BONECRUSHER)
Professional boxer. **Personal:** Born Apr 3, 1953, Magnolia, NC; married Reba Sloan; children: Raymond, Jamie. **Educ:** Kenansville NC, AA Business 1973; Shaw Univ Raleigh NC, BA Business 1975. **Career:** NC Dept of Corrections, officer/counselor 1979-82; professional boxer. **Honors/Awds:** Heavyweight Champion of the World WBA 1986. **Special Achievements:** The James "Bonecrusher" Smith Educational Foundation, founder, chairman of the board, 1992-. **Military Serv:** US Army, sgt, 3 yrs; Commendation Medal 1975-78. **Home Addr:** Route 2 Box 273, Lillington, NC 27546.

SMITH, JAMES OSCAR (JIMMY)
Musician. **Personal:** Born Dec 8, 1928, Norristown, PA; married Edna Joy Goins; children: Jimmy, Jr, Jia. **Educ:** Hamilton Sch of Mus; Ornstein Sch of Music, 1946-49. **Career:** Edmy Music Pub Co, owner, dir 1962; jazz organist who heads his own jazz group The Jimmy Smith Trio; began mus career 1952; playing piano with Don Gardner & His Sonotones; began performing as a single act during intermissions at the Harlem club in Atlanta City 1954; composer num organ pieces; compiler organ books. **Honors/Awds:** Qrecipient 1st place in Downbeat Mag Jazz Poll catagory for Organ 1964; has won recognition in the poll every yr since; won Playboy Jazz Poll 1969; has been listed in that poll every yr since; Grammy Award for album The Cat 1964; other albums includ Got My Mojo Working 1966; In A Plain Brown Wrapper 1971. **Business Addr:** Musician, c/o Elektra Records, 75 Rockefeller Plaza, New York, NY 10019.

SMITH, JAMES RUSSELL
Elected official. **Personal:** Born May 2, 1931, Tupelo, MS; married Madie Ola; children: Rickey Young, Robert Young, Anita Young, Bonita Tate, Valeria Wedley, Richard. **Educ:** Jackson State Jr College, AB 1979. **Career:** Communication CGN (USAF), supervisor 1951-72; Air Refueling Tech (USAF), supervisor 1951-72; Golden Circle Life Ins Co, salesman 1972-85. **Orgs:** President Humboldt Chapter NAACP 1975-80; board member Humboldt City Schools 1982-85. **Military Serv:** USAF tsgt 1951-72; Air Medal 2 oak leaf clusters 1967; USAF oak leaf cluster 1968; retired 1972. **Home Addr:** 301 S 3rd Ave, Humboldt, TN 38343. **Business Addr:** Sales Rep, Golden Circle Life Insurance, 39 S Jackson St, Brownsville, TN 38012.

SMITH, JANE E.
Organization executive. **Career:** Carter Center's Atlanta Project; National Council of Negro Women, president, 1998-.

SMITH, JANET K.
County official. **Career:** New Castle County Police Dept, police officer, lieutenant, captain, 1973-. **Special Achievements:** First African American female to become captain in New Castle County. **Business Addr:** Captain, New Castle County Police Department, Louis Redding Bldg, 800 French St, 8th Fl, Wilmington, DE 19801, (302)571-7564.

SMITH, JANET MARIA
Publisher. **Personal:** Born Dec 12, Bluefield, WV; daughter of Edith P Patterson and John H Patterson; divorced; children: Tiffany A, Taashan A. **Educ:** Franklin University, 1984-87. **Career:** J M Smith Communications, president; The Blue Chip Profile, Inc, publisher/CEO, currently. **Orgs:** National Association of Market Developers; Columbus Association of Black Journalists, co-chair, regional conf, 1992; Columbus Urban League; NAACP, Columbus. **Special Achievements:** Founder, Blue Chip Awards, honoring African-Americans, 1992; publisher, Blue Chip Profile, resource guide for African-Americans, annual, 1991. **Business Addr:** Publisher/CEO, The Blue Chip Profile, Inc, 4313 Donlyn Ct, Columbus, OH 43232, (614)861-0772.

SMITH, JANICE EVON
Public relations. **Personal:** Born Feb 21, 1952, Warsaw, NC. **Educ:** NC A&T State Univ, BS 1974; The OH State Univ, MA 1975. **Career:** Greensboro Daily News-Record, reporting intern 1974; The Charlotte News, daily newspaper reporter 1975-79, reporter/editor 1980; Natl Urban League Washington Opers, comm assoc 1981-83; DC Office of Human Rights, special asst to the director. **Orgs:** Dist III Chair NC Press Women's Assoc 1977; publicity chair/bd dirs Charlotte Mecklenburg Afro-Amer Cultural Ctr 1978-80; forum coord Washington Assoc of Black Journalists 1982; mem Capital Press Club 1982-85; mem Washington Urban League 1982-; mem NAACP 1983-84; comm chair Natl Capital Chap Public Relations Soc of Amer 1986-87. **Honors/Awds:** Freelance articles published Essence magazine 1977-78; George Edmund Haynes Fellow Natl Urban League 1980; Outstanding Young Women of Amer 1982; Service Cert of Recognition Natl Capital Chap Public Relations Soc of Amer 1986. **Business Addr:** Special Asst to Dir, DC Office of Human Rights, 2000 14th St NW, Third Floor, Washington, DC 20009.

SMITH, JENNIFER C.
Insurance company executive. **Personal:** Born Nov 3, 1952, Boston, MA; daughter of Margaree Smith and Herman Smith; married Clement Roy. **Educ:** Union College, Schenectady, NY, BA, 1974; Fairfield University, Fairfield, CT, MA. **Career:** City of Hartford, director of personnel, assistant city manager; Travelers Insurance Company, Boston, MA, claim representative; Aetna Life and Casualty, assistant vice president, 1987, director of field operations, 1987, vice president/head of Personnel Committee, currently. **Orgs:** Board of directors, The Boys Club of Hartford; board of directors, The Martin Luther King, Jr Scholarship Foundation; board of directors, The Hartford Stage Company; trustee, Hartford College for Women; trustee, St Joseph's College. **Business Addr:** Vice President, Aetna Life & Casulty, 151 Farmington Ave, Hartford, CT 06156.

SMITH, JERALDINE WILLIAMS
Attorney, business executive. **Personal:** Born Jan 14, 1946, Tampa, FL; married Dr Walter L Smith; children: Salesia Vanette, Walter Lee II. **Educ:** Univ of FL, BS Journalism 1967; Atlanta Univ, MBA 1970; FL State Law School, JD 1981. **Career:** Freedom Savings, bank mgr 1973-75; Digital Equip Corp, admin mgr 1975-77; FL Dept of Ins, lawyer 1983-; Capital Outlook Weekly Newspaper, publ 1983-. **Orgs:** Mem Amer Bar Assoc, FL Bar Assoc, Natl Newspaper Publ Assoc, FL Press Assoc. **Honors/Awds:** William Randolph Hearst Natl Newspaper Awards Winner 1967; Businesswoman of the Year Iota Phi Lambda 1971. **Home Addr:** 2122 E Randolph Circle, Tallahassee, FL 32312. **Business Addr:** Publisher-Attorney, Capitol Outlook Newspaper, PO Box 11335, Tallahassee, FL 32302.

SMITH, JERMAINE
Professional football player. **Personal:** Born Feb 3, 1972. **Educ:** University of Georgia, attended. **Career:** Green Bay Packers, defensive tackle, 1997-. **Business Addr:** Professional Football Player, Green Bay Packers, 1265 Lombardi Ave, Green Bay, WI 54304, (414)494-2351.

SMITH, JESSE OWENS
Educator. **Personal:** Born Dec 5, 1942, Comer, AL; son of Lena Mae Corbitt Smith and Victor C Smith; married Rhoda Lee Crowe, Aug 22, 1987; children: Rhonda, Karla, Seaton. **Educ:** California State University, Los Angeles, CA, BA, 1971; University of Chicago, Chicago, IL, MA, 1973, PhD, 1976. **Career:** University of Wisconsin, Oshkosh, WI, professor, 1974-76; San Diego State University, San Diego, CA, professor, 1977-84, California State University, Fullerton, CA, professor, 1984-. **Orgs:** California Black Faculty and Staff Association, 1978-; National Conference of Black Political Scientists, 1972-; National Council of Black Studies, 1976-; American Political Science Association, 1976-; National Association for the Advancement of Black Studies. **Military Serv:** US Army, E-4, 1962-64. **Business Addr:** Professor of Political Science, California State University, 800 State College Dr, Fullerton, CA 92631.

SMITH, JESSIE CARNEY
Educator, librarian. **Personal:** Born in Greensboro, NC; daughter of Vesona Bigelow Graves and James Ampler Carney; divorced; children: Frederick Douglas Smith Jr. **Educ:** North Carolina A&T Univ, BS, home economics, 1950; Cornell Univ, 1950; Michigan State Univ, MA, child development, 1956; George Peabody College for Teachers, MA, library science 1957; Univ of Illinois, PhD, library science, 1964. **Career:** Nashville City Schools, teacher, 1957; Tennessee State Univ, head cataloger/instructor, 1957-60, coord of lib serv, asst prof, 1963-65; Univ of IL, teaching asst, 1961-63; Fisk Univ, univ librarian, prof, 1965-, univ lib, prof, fed rel officer, dir, fed progs, 1975-77; Dept of Lib Sci, Vanderbilt Univ, lecturer, 1969-, visiting prof, 1980-84 (part-time); Alabama A&M Univ, assoc prof, consultant, 1971-73; Univ of TN School of Lib Science, visiting lecturer, 1973-74; Workshop Intern Program for Librarians in Predominately Negro Coll, Atlanta Univ, assoc dir, 1969, 1970; Inst on Selection Organization & Use of Materials by & About Negro, Fisk Univ, dir, 1970; Developing Collections of Black Literature, dir, 1971; African-American Materials Project,coordinator, 1971-74; Internship in Blackudies Librarianship, dir, 1972-73; Mini-institutes in Ethnic Studies Librarianship, dir, 1974; Internship in Ethnic Studies Librarianship, dir, 1974-75; Research Program in Ethnic Studies Librarianship, dir, 1975; Library Study, TN Higher Educ Commission, dir, 1975-76; Inst on Ethnic Genealogy for Librarians, dir, 1979; Race Relations Collection Project, dir, 1980-81; Images in Black Artifacts, dir, 1980-81; Learning Library Program, dir, 1980-84; I've Been to the Mountain Top: A Civil Rights Legacy, dir, 1984-86; The Chicago Renaissance Project, dir, 1988-89; Fisk Univ, librarian, currently. **Orgs:** Amer Library Assn; TN Lib Assn; SE Library Assn; Assn of Coll & Res Lib ALA; Lib Admin Div ALA; Lib Educ Div ALA; Amer Assn of Univ Profs; Episcopacy Comm, United Methodist Church, 1984-88;

Metro Historical Commission, Nashville, 1984-88; Natl Committee on the Bicentennial Scholars Program, United Methodist Church, 1985-87; bd of dirs, Children's Intl Educ Ctr, 1986-; bd of dirs, Historic Nashville, 1986-89; advisory council, Black College Library Improvement Project, Southern Educ Foundation, 1985-; TN Advisory Council on Libraries, 1990-; chair, bd of dirs, Cooperative Coll Library Center, 1990-. **Honors/Awds:** Fellowship, Council on Library Resources, 1969; Martin Luther King Jr Black Author's Award, 1982; Academic or Research Librarian of the Year Award, Assn of Coll and Research Libraries, Amer Library Assn, 1985; Distinguished Scholars Award, United Negro Coll Fund, 1986; Distinguished Alumni Award, Dept of Library Science, Peabody Coll of Vanderbilt Univ, 1987; writings including: A Handbook for the Study of Black Bibliography, 1971, Ethnic Genealogy: A Research Guide, 1983, Images of Blacks in Amer Culture: A Reference Guide to Info Sources, 1988; Distinguished Alumni Award, Graduate School of Library & Info Science, Univ of Illinois, 1990; Natl Urban League Fellow, 1974, 1976; Certificate of Commendation, State of Tennessee, 94th General Assembly, House & Senate Concurring, 1985;publicons: co-compiler, Statistical Record of Black America, 1990, editor, Notable Black American Women, 1991. **Business Addr:** Librarian, Office of the Librarian, Fisk University, 17th Ave North, Nashville, TN 37203.

SMITH, JIMMY LEE, JR.
Professional football player. **Personal:** Born Feb 9, 1969; married Sandra; children: Jimmy Lee III. **Educ:** Jackson State University, bachelor's degree in business management, 1992. **Career:** Dallas Cowboys, wide receiver, 1992-94; Jacksonville Jaguars, 1995-. **Honors/Awds:** Mackey Award, 1996. **Business Addr:** Professional Football Player, Jacksonville Jaguars, One Stadium Place, Jacksonville, FL 32202, (904)633-6000.

SMITH, JOANNE HAMLIN
Educational Administrator. **Personal:** Born Oct 19, 1954, Pittsburgh, PA; daughter of Helen Rogers Hamlin and Robert E Hamlin; married James E Jr, May 17, 1986. **Educ:** Edinboro Univ of Pennsylvania, Edinboro, PA, BS, 1972-76; Wichita State Univ, Wichita, KS, MEd, 1977-79; Kansas State University, Manhattan, KS, PhD, 1983-86. **Career:** McPherson College, director of housing, assistant in student services, 1976-86; Arizona State Univ, assistant director of residence life, 1986-91; Southwest Texas State Univ, director of residence life, 1992-. **Orgs:** Treasurer, president-elect, president, Arizona College Personnel Assn, 1986-91; Association of College & University Housing Officers, 1986-; American College Personnel Association, 1986-; Phi Delta Kappa, 1976-; Natl Bd of Certified Counselors, certified counselor, 1980-. **Honors/Awds:** Women Helping Women Honoree, Soroptomist International, 1979; NASPA Region IV West Award for Outstanding Contributions, 1978. **Home Addr:** 13438 Forum Rd, Universal City, TX 78148-2801, (210)945-9089. **Business Addr:** Director, Residence Life, Southwest Texas State University, San Marcos, TX 78666, (512)245-2931.

SMITH, JOCK MICHAEL
Attorney. **Personal:** Born Jun 10, 1948, Manhattan-NYC, NY; married Yvette Smiley Johnson; children: Janay M. **Educ:** Tuskegee Inst, BS History 1970; Univ of Notre Dame Law School, JD 1973. **Career:** US Customs Court, clerk 1970; Police Youth Involvement Prog, instructor 1972; Natl Urban League, legal asst 1972-73; NAACP Civil Rights Project, general counsel 1973; attorney private practice; Camp Hill, AL, city judge, 1987-89; Macon County Bar Assn, pres, 1989-91; SCORING FOR LIFE!, Motivational Speaking Co, pres & founder; Macon County Commission, Tuskegee, AL, atty; self-employed atty, currently. **Orgs:** Vice pres Student Govt Assn 1969-70; chmn Notre Dame Law Sch Chap Black Amer Law Students Assn 1972-73; pres AL Lawyers Assn 1983-84; mem Alpha Phi Alpha Frat 1968-; mem AL Trial Lawyers Assn 1983-; mem Natl Bar Assn 1983-; bd of dirs, Montgomery County Trial Lawyers Assn; mem exec committee ATLA; mem ethics committee Alabama State Bar 1996-97. **Honors/Awds:** Awded Honor Roll Cert of 3 consecutive yrs 1967-70; Tuskegee Inst Dept of History Citation for Achieving Highest Average in Major 38 1968-70; Luther H Foster Awd for Outstanding Performance 1969-70; Alpha Phi Alpha Awd for academic achievement 1969-70; co-author Summer Youth Education Legal Rights Career Guidance Citizen Awareness 1972; awded 3 yr scholarship for continuing academic achievement; 3 yr academic scholarship to Notre Dame Law Sch on the basis of undergrad achievements; in 1st yr participated in the Moot Court Prog. **Business Addr:** Attorney Jock M Smith, PO Box 830419, Tuskegee, AL 36083.

SMITH, JOE ELLIOTT
Physician. **Personal:** Born Jan 28, 1938, Little Rock, AR; son of Blanche Smith and William H Smith; married Mary; children: Sharol, Gary, John. **Educ:** Philander Smith Coll, BS, 1959; Univ AR Med School, MD 1963. **Career:** VA Hospital, Univ AR Med School, 1973-; VAH, Tuskegee, AL, chief asst ophtholmology, 1969-71; private practice, physician. **Orgs:** Diplomate Amer Bd Ophthalomology 1971. **Military Serv:** USAF captain, 1964-66.

SMITH, JOE LEE
Educational administrator. **Personal:** Born May 29, 1936, Cocoa, FL; married Altamese Edmonson; children: Chyrell, Trina, Sharon, Twila. **Educ:** FL A&M Univ, BS 1959, MEd 1963; Univ of FL, Rank 1-A Ed S 1973, Doctorate Ed Admin & Supv Higher Ed 1974. **Career:** Brevard Cty Public Schools, instr 1959-63; Ft Lauderdale Broward Cty Public Schools, instr 1963-67; Miami Dade Comm Coll, instr 1967-69; Cocoa HS, asst principal 1969-70; Brevard Comm Coll, dir of student activities 1970-72; Univ of FL, rsch asst to assoc dir of inst rsch council 1972-73; Brevard Comm Coll, dir of placement 1974-75, dir of coop ed placement & follow-up 1975-77, dean of student serv 1977-. **Orgs:** Mem Phi Delta Kappa 1963, Omega Psi Phi Frat 1969; vice chmn Rockledge City Council 1972-; mem FL Assoc of Comm Coll 1974; sunday school teacher Zion Orthodox Primitive Baptist Church. **Honors/Awds:** Citizen of the Year Alpha Phi Alpha Frat 1972; recreation ctr named Joe Lee Smith Recreation Ctr 1973; Outstanding Ed of Amer 1975; Article "27 Steps to Better Discipline" 1974. **Home Addr:** 918 Levitt Pkwy, Rockledge, FL 32955. **Business Addr:** Dean of Student Services, Brevard Comm College, 1111 North US 1, Titusville, FL 32796.

SMITH, JOHN ARTHUR
Physician, educator. **Personal:** Born Aug 25, 1937, Cincinnati, OH; son of A Malvena Campbell Smith and John Douglas Smith; divorced; children: Ann, Janis, Gwen, Jill. **Educ:** Miami Univ, AB 1958; Univ of Cincinnati, MD 1964. **Career:** SUNY Downstate, physician 1971-72; Indiana Univ Sch of Medicine, professor 1972-; Harvard Univ, visiting prof 1978; Univ of West Indies, visiting prof 1992. **Orgs:** Kappa Alpha Psi, 1957; Mem/delegate NMA 1969-; bd Indianapolis Boys Club 1979-85; Alpha Eta Boule 1979-; mem chmn Soc for Pediatric Radiology 1983. **Honors/Awds:** 1-2-3 Contact PBS Feature 1985; contributor 3 books; numerous articles in professional journals; Alpha Omega Alpha, 1964. **Military Serv:** USAF capt 2 yrs; USAFE consultant radiologist 1968-70. **Business Addr:** Professor, Indiana Univ School of Medicine, 702 Barnhill Dr, Indianapolis, IN 46223.

SMITH, JOHN B.
Publisher. **Career:** Atlanta Inquirer, publisher, CEO, currently. **Business Addr:** Publisher/CEO, The Atlanta Inquirer, 947 Martin Luther King Jr Dr NW, Atlanta, GA 30314, (404)523-6086.

SMITH, JOHN L., JR.
Educational administrator, educator. **Personal:** Born Sep 14, 1938, Bastrop, LA; son of Julia S Smith and John L Smith Sr; married Juel Shannon, Aug 4, 1972; children: Kenneth, Babette, Angela, Gina, Lisa, Michael, Eva. **Educ:** Lincoln University, BME, 1959; University of Indiana, MME, 1961, performance certificate, 1961; University of Missouri at Kansas City, DMA; Harvard University, post-doctoral study, 1992. **Career:** Black Liberated Arts Center, Inc, founder, first president, 1969; Langston University, Fine Arts Series, director, 1969-72, Dept of Music, chairman, 1969-72; University of South Florida, Department of Music, acting assistant chair, 1973-74, assistant dean, coordinator of advising, 1977-86, acting dean, 1986-88, College of Fine Arts, dean, 1988-. **Orgs:** International Council of Fine Arts Deans, board of directors, 1992-94, Community Cultural Diversity & Inclusion in the Arts, chair, 1989-92; National Association of State Universities & Land Grant Colleges, Commission on the Arts, 1989-92; Florida Cultural Action & Education Alliances, board of trustees, 1990-; The Florida Orchestra, board of directors, 1989-; Hillsborough County Arts Council, board of directors, 1986-; African-American Arts Council, board of directors, 1988-90; The Mayor's Task Force on the Arts, 1991-92. **Honors/Awds:** Ringling School of Art & Design, commencement speaker, 1991; Start Together on Progress, Inc, Education Award, 1989; Pi Kappa Lambda National Music Honor Society, honorary membership, 1992; Tampa, Hillsborough County Human Rights Council, Human Rights Award, 1990; University of Missouri, Alumni Achievement Award, 1989. **Special Achievements:** National Endowment for the Arts, Grant for USF Jazz Artists' Residence Program, 1981-89; University of South Florida, Equal Opportunity Award, 1985; Summary of USF's Black Composers' Project in the Black Perspective in Music, 1983; Doctoral Diss Abstract, Missouri Journal of Research in Music Education, 1979; Florida Orchestra Brass Quintet, 1978-. **Military Serv:** US Navy, petty officer, 2nd class, 1962-66. **Business Addr:** Dean/Professor, University of South Florida, 4202 Fowler Ave, College of Fine Arts, FAH 110, Tampa, FL 33620-7350, (813)974-2301.

SMITH, JOHN RAYE (JOHN RAYE)
Motivational speaker. **Personal:** Born Jan 30, 1941, Gibson, LA; son of Vera Phillips Smith and Paul Smith; married Rosie King Smith, Aug 25, 1962; children: Michelle, Dexter Renaud. **Educ:** Southern University, BS, 1964; Columbia University, journalism, 1967; Washington Center Journalism Center, 1968. **Career:** Albany Springfield High School, Albany, LA, instructor, gen sciences, chemistry, biology, 1963-64; US Dept of Agriculture, Alexandria, LA, McMinniville, OR, soil conversationist, 1964-66; Valley Migrant League, vocational counselor, Dayton, OR, 1966-67; Moses Lakes Job Corps Center, Moses Lakes, WA, 1967-68; KREM-TV, Spokane, WA, King TV-Seattle, WA, WNBC-TV, New York, NY, WTTG-TV, Washington, DC, television reporter/anchor-producer, 1968-79; US Census Bureau, Washington, DC, 1979-83; Majestic Eagles, Inc, pres, CEO, founder, 1983-; John Raye & Associates, pres, CEO, founder, 1983-. **Orgs:** Dir of funds to secure Majestic Eagles headquartes bldg. **Honors/Awds:** Author, Born to Win: Success and Prosperity Now!, 1990; author, Think Your Way to Success and Prosperity, audio cassette tape, 1986; exec producer, BusinessLine - The Televison Program, 1988; exec producer, Making Money in the 90's: How to Get Your Share, 1991; producer, Portrait of a Queen: The Legacy of Ethel L Payne, 1987. **Business Addr:** President, John Raye & Associates, 2031 Rhode Island Ave NE, Washington, DC 20018.

SMITH, JOHN THOMAS
Educational administrator (retired). **Personal:** Born Jun 14, 1919, Lexington, KY; married Josephine Estelle Fleming; children: Thomas H, Ethelda, Nathaniel. **Educ:** KY State Coll, AB eng & soc 1940; Univ of KY, MA admin 1958; Univ of KY, EdD adminstrn 1961. **Career:** Univ KY, vice pres minority affairs 1975-retirement; Jefferson Comm Coll Univ KY, asso dir, dir 1968-75; Ashland Comm Coll Univ KY, asso prof psy & educ 1965-68; Lexington Public School, prin 1961-65; Lexington Public School, asst prin 1954-58; Lexington Public School, instr of Eng 1946-54. **Orgs:** Mem Phi Delta Kappa 1954-; mem Alpha Kappa Delta 1956-; mem Omicron Delta Kappa 1976-. **Honors/Awds:** Recipient Marksman Award AC; Order of State Performance YMCA 1964; Kiwanis Award 1965. **Military Serv:** AC corpl 3 yrs. **Business Addr:** University of Kentucky, Rm 207 Administration Bldg, Lexington, KY 40505.

SMITH, JOSCELYN E.
Judge. **Personal:** Born Feb 9, 1918, New York, NY; son of Ethel Jackson Henderson and Joscelyn E Smith; married Marion A Pinckney; children: Barbara C, Diane M, Joscelyn E. **Educ:** Howard Univ Wash DC, 1940-41; Long Island Univ Brooklyn, 1946-48; Brooklyn Law Sch, LLB 1948-50. **Career:** Atty pvt prac 1951-76; NY State Assembly, counsel to maj leader 1965-69; NY State Senate, legislative asst 1963-65; Borough of Queens NYC, borough sec 1958-60; City of New York, asst corp counsel 1956-58; Allied Real Estate Bd Queens Co, organizer, sponsor 1955-63; Civil Court, City of New York, judge, 1978-87; Supreme Ct State of NY, Supreme Ct Justice 1987-. **Orgs:** Co-fndr Macon B Allen Black Bar Assn 1970-; pres Queens Co Yth Athl Centre 1955-63; pres Queens Child Guidance Centre 1970-76; pres Mens Club Queen Co 1972-76. **Honors/Awds:** Plaque Inst Better Living 1976; plaque Women of Distinction 1976; plaque Natl Assn of Negro Business & Professional Women 1977; plaque Macon B Allen Black Bar Assn 1978. **Military Serv:** US Army, lt col, 1941-46; US Army, reserves, 35 yrs.

SMITH, JOSEPH EDWARD
Educator (retired). **Personal:** Born Jan 22, 1925, Terre Haute, IN; son of Etolia Holt Smith and Lemuel L Smith; married Betty J Wright; children: Joseph Jr, Floyd P, Andrea I. **Educ:** IN State Univ, BS 1950, MS 1955; MO Univ. **Career:** Benedict Clge, art dept chr 1951-61; Lincoln Univ, instr 1961-65; Lemoyne Clge, assoc prof 1965-69; Southern IL Univ, assc prof 1969-. **Orgs:** Mem Masonic Ldg; Omega Psi Phi Frat deacon trustee Mt Joy Bapt Ch of Edwardsville; mem Natl Conf of Artist; Am Assn of Univ Prof; Danforth Assn Prog; organizer Black Artist of Memphis Annual Exhibit 1965. **Honors/Awds:** Consult SC State Audio Visual Wrkshp 1951-61; artist demonstrater Childrens Hour TV Prog Memphis State Univ 1968-69; creator and dir Comm Art for Ghetto Children of Memphis 1969; researcher 3D Sculptured Painting Complexities Approved Proj 1978-84; consult Art Wrkshps East St Louis 1982-84. **Military Serv:** AUS sgt; Game Theater Ribbon; Bronze Stars; Victory Medal WWII; Am Theater Ribbon; Asiatic-Pacific Theater Ribbon; Good Conduct Medal 1943-46. **Home Addr:** 1916 Vassar Dr, Edwardsville, IL 62025.

SMITH, JOSEPH EDWARD
Chemist. **Personal:** Born Sep 13, 1938, Jacksonville, FL; married Mildred; children: Daryl, Ivan, Jomila. **Educ:** Allen U, BS 1960; Howard Univ Coll Dentistry, DDS 1970. **Career:** Dentist self; Jacksonville Hlth Ctr, 1974-76; Boston Univ Grad Sch Dentistry, asst prof 1970-74; Roxbury Hlth Ctr, chemist 1966-67. **Orgs:** US Bur of Mines 1964-66; sec, treas Denticare Prepaid Dental Plan of FL 1976-77; dir Denticare Prepaid Dental Plan 1976-77; Small Busmens Serv Assn 1976-77; mem Nat Dental Assn; Am Dental Assn; FL Dental Assn; VI Dental Assn; mem New Bethel AME Ch; stewart, pres Kenneth White Gospel Chorus; 3rd Sunday supt Sunday Sch; dir Northside Boys Club; bd mem Yth Congress Sickle Cell Anemia Prgm; life mem NAACP; mem Jacksonville Opt Ind Ctr 1976-77; Ribault Jr HS 1975. **Military Serv:** AUS E-5 1961-63. **Business Addr:** 1190 W Edgewood Ave, No B, Jacksonville, FL 32208.

SMITH, JOSEPH F.
Government official. **Personal:** Born Aug 22, 1945, Jacksonville, FL; son of Hazel Hall Smith and Joe Smith; married Mary Townsend Smith, Oct 15, 1974; children: Joseph Cordell, Karina Sharon. **Educ:** T Valley State Coll, BA 1967; Howard U, JD 1970; Fort Valley State College, Fort Valley, GA, BA, 1967; Howard University, School of Law, Washington, DC, JD,

1970. **Career:** WRC/NBC, Consumer Guidelines, moderator 1971-74; Consumer Liason Div Office of Consumer Affairs Dept of HUD, formerly dir; Nat Consumer Inf Ctr, producer, exec dir; WRC/NBC, It's Your World, exec producer, moderator; Am & Howard Us, prof; numerous consumer manuals, economic & political articles, editor, lct pub; Dept of Housing & Urban Developement, Washington, DC, director integovernmentl affairs, 1980-85, director of economic analysis & evaluation, 1985-89, deputy director, office of policy, 1989-. **Orgs:** Mem consult Office Consumer Affairs 1969-; mem Cong Staff; Black Caucus; Fed Trade Commn 1968-; Housing & Urban Dev; Soical Rehab Serv; OEO 1970-; Consumer Adv Com Fed Enery Office 1972-74; Cost of Living Council Assn 1974; Nat Assn Attorney Generals; Assn Home Appliances Mfgs 1974; Nat Legal Aid & Defender's Assn 1972; Nat Inst Educ in Law & Poverty 1970; Office of Gov 1973-; Atty Gen Offices of MA DC WI 1970-74; NY NV Consumer Offices 1973-74; Ohio C of C 1973; Am Bar Assn 1971; mem Alpha Phi Alpha; NAACP; Consumer Fedearation Am; Nat Conf Black Lawyers; Howard Univ Law Sch Alumni Assn; treasurer, Reid Temple AME, 1987-; secretary, Class 23 Federal Executive Institute, 1984-86. **Honors/Awds:** Certificate of Merit, Department of Housing and Urban Development, 1989; Outstanding Executive, Department of Housing and Urban Development, 1988; Federal Executive Institute Award, Department of Housing and Urban Development, 1995. **Business Addr:** Dept of HUD, 451 7th St, SW, Washington, DC 20410.

SMITH, JOSHUA ISAAC
Business executive. **Personal:** Born Apr 8, 1941, Garrard Co, KY; married Jacqueline Jones; children: Joshua I II. **Educ:** Central State Univ, BS Biology/Chemistry 1963; Univ of Akron Sch of Law, grad studies 1967-68; Univ of Delaware, association management 1975; Central MI Univ, grad studies business mgmt 1977. **Career:** Plenum Publishing Corp, mgr databook div 1969-70; Amer Soc for Information Science, exec dir 1970-76; Herner & Co, vice pres 1976-78; The MAXIMA Corp, pres & CEO 1978-. **Orgs:** Chmn 1984 United Way Fundraising Campaign; chmn of the bd Natl Business League of Montgomery Co; mem bd of dirs Intl Assn of Students in Business Mgmt & Economics; mem Minority Business Enterprise Legal Defense & Educ Fund; mem Natl Urban Coalition; dir TN Tech Foundation; mem Citizens Adv Comm for Career & Vocational Educ; mem Corporate Round Table; mem adv bd Grad Sch of Library & Info Science Univ of TN; mem adv bd NC Central Univ Sch of Library Scis; mem Amer Assn for the Advancement of Scis; mem Amer Library Assn; mem Amer Soc for Info Sci; mem Black Presidents Roundtable Washington; mem Engineering Index Inc; mem Info Industry Assn Long Range Planning Comm; mem Natl Business League of Montgomery Co. **Honors/Awds:** Minority Businessperson of the Yr Small Business Admin; Distinguished Corporate Awd US Dept of Commerce Minority Business Develop Agency; Special Recognition Awd for Valuable Commitment US Dept of Commerce Minority Business Develop Agency; numerous publications including "Library and Information Service for Special Groups" 1974; "The ERIC Clearinghouse on Library & Information Sciences (ERIC/CLIS)" The Bowker Annual Library & Book Trade Information 1973.

SMITH, JOSHUA L.
Educational administrator, educator. **Personal:** Born Dec 11, 1934, Boston, MA; son of Lorina A Henry Smith and Joshua Smith. **Educ:** Boston Univ, BA 1955; Harvard Graduate School of Educ, MAT 1959, EdD 1967. **Career:** Pittsburgh PA, admin asst to supt of schools, acting vice principal 1966-68; Ford Foundation, program officer, asst program officer, project specialist 1968-74; City Coll City Univ of New York, prof of educ 1974-76, dean school of educ 1976-77; Borough of Manhattan Community Coll, acting pres 1977-78, pres 1978-85; State of California Community Colls, chancellor 1985-87; Brookdale Community Coll, pres, 1987-90; Baruch Coll, CUNY, Department of Education, professor, 1990-, interim chair, 1992-. **Orgs:** Bd trustees Public Educ Assn 1974-; bd trustees Museums Collaborative Inc 1974-; bd trustees Natl Humanities Faculty 1974-; chmn NAACP Task Force on Quality Educ 1977-; AACJC Commn on Govt Affairs 1978-; repr CUNY to Big City Comunity Colls Pres & Chancellors AACJC 1978-; New York Co Local Devel Corp Inc 1980; bd dir AACJC 1980; vice chair Joint Comm on Fed Relations AACJC/ACCT 1982, chair 1983; AACJC, bd dir vice chair, 1983-84, bd dir chair 1984-85; bd of overseers Univ of the State of New York Regents Coll Degrees & Examination 1985-; golden heritage membership NAACP; bd of deacons Riverside Church, NY, 1977-82, bd of trustees, 1988-. **Honors/Awds:** Phi Delta Kappa Award of Achievement for Outstanding Serv to the Field of Educ AL A&M Univ 1972; Distinguished Serv Award Bilingual Vol of Amer 1973; Distinguished Serv Award Harlem Preparatory School 1973-75; Award of Appreciation Support of the Devel of the S Leadership Devel Program So Region Council 1974. **Military Serv:** US Air Force, capt, 1955-58. **Home Addr:** 315 W 70th St, New York, NY 10023. **Business Addr:** Professor, Department of Education, Baruch College, CUNY, 17 Lexington Ave, Box 505, New York, NY 10010.

SMITH, JUANITA JANE
Librarian (retired). **Personal:** Born Jun 11, 1923, Muncie, IN. **Educ:** Ball State Univ, BS Educ 1945, post grad work 1946-48; Univ of MI, AMLS 1951, grad work 1958. **Career:** Indianapolis Pub Schools, teacher 1945-46; Ball State Univ, sec to dean/sec to dir of grad studies 1946-49, catalog & ref libr 1949-75, special collections librarian 1975-83; Steinbeck Quarterly & Steinbeck Monograph Series, asst editor 1978-82, assoc editor 1983; retired librarian 1983. **Orgs:** Mem Am Lib Assn; mem IN Lib Assn; mem Soc of Am Archivists; mem Soc of IN Archivists; mem Am Assn of Univ Profs; mem Delta Kappa Gamma Soc; mem Am Assn of Univ Women; mem League of Women Voters; mem YWCA. **Honors/Awds:** Contributed articles Steinbeck Quarterly & Steinbeck Monograph Series 1978-80.

SMITH, JUANITA SMITH
City government official. **Personal:** Born Jun 28, 1927, St Petersburg, FL; daughter of Annabelle Momoan Smith and Ruffin Smith Sr; married Thomas H, Apr 13, 1956; children: Carol Tracey. **Educ:** Gibbs Jr Coll, elem educ; Tuskegee Inst, industrial arts 1947; Florida Intl Univ, BS political science 1974, extensive studies in counseling, social work, law, and criminal justice, masters, public administration, 1991. **Career:** AL Lewis Elem School, teacher; Homestead Jr HS, teacher; Dade Co Bd of Pub Instruction, teacher 1967-; Florida City, vice mayor elected 2nd term 1984. **Orgs:** Dade Co Crime Comm Court Aide; Amer Red Cross; United Heart Fund; Dade Co Cancer Soc; March of Dimes; Dade Co Comm Action Ctr; Dade Co Dept of Public Health; Hillsborough Co Juvenile Home; vice pres Dade Co Voters League; vice pres A L Lewis PTA; adv bd Protestant Christian Comm Serv Agency; adv bd FL City Parks & Rec; chairperson Public Relation Bd A L Lewis Elem School; Comm Block Club; Natl Council of Negro Women; Crime Stoppers; Children's Library Club; youth leader, welfare worker Seventh Day Adventist Church; bd member, Greater Miami Urban League, 1984-; bd member, Community Health of South Dade County, Inc, 1985-; bd mem, Dade County League of Cities, 1987-, treasurer, 1992; NAACP, 1986-. **Honors/Awds:** Woman of the Year, Links Inc 1985; Awd of Appreciation, Naval Security Group Activity 1985; Certificate and Award of Service, Dade County Community Action Ser 1985; Woman of the Year, Zeta Phi Beta 1985; Woman of the Year, Bethel Seventh Day Adventist Church. **Home Addr:** 706 NW 3rd Street, Florida City, FL 33034.

SMITH, JUDITH MOORE
Educator. **Personal:** Born Aug 3, 1948, Tallahassee, FL. **Educ:** Hampton Inst, BS summa cum laude 1970; Boston U, MA 1971. **Career:** Univ of DC, asst prof of communicative & performing arts 1978-; Univ of DC Van Ness Campus Faculty Senate, chairperson 1977-78; Cambridge High & Latin School, instr eng, comm 1971-72; WAMU-FM Radio, prod, writer, series host 1977-78; Natl Public Radio-Radio Netherlands UDC, independent prod 1978-; Univ of DC FM Radio Proj, communications cons; bd mem's newsletter 1978-80; lead dancer African Heritage Dancers & Drummers 1973-. **Orgs:** Bd of dir Friendship House 1975-; mem Nat Coun of Negro Women 1977. **Honors/Awds:** Fellowship Woodrow Wilson Doctoral 1970; fellowship Ford Found Doctoral 1970; faculty serv award Univ of DC student body 1972-74; pr intrnsp Cong Black Caucus 1977; Outstanding Young Women of Am 1978; prod radio reports Nat Pub Radio 1979-. **Business Addr:** 4200 Connecticut Ave, NW, Washington, DC 20008.

SMITH, JUDY SERIALE
Government official. **Personal:** Born Mar 10, 1953, Lafayette, LA; daughter of Vernice Bellard and Joseph Seriale; married Sylvester Lee Smith Jr, Dec 10, 1974; children: Sylvester Lee III, Joseph Seriale. **Educ:** Grambling State University, Grambling, LA, BA, social worker, 1974. **Career:** South Central Ark Community Action, Camden, AR, community service coordinator, 1980-84; PAC (People Are Concerned, Inc), Camden, AR, executive director, 1984-; state legislator, Arkansas, currently. **Orgs:** Regional coordinator, Arkansans For Drug Free Youth, 1990-; board member, Arkansas Child Abuse Prevention, 1989-; board member, Women's Crisis Center for Camden, 1988-; member, SAU Technical Branch Advisory Board, 1988-; board member, Ouachita County Emergency Food & Shelter Board, 1986-; member, Sigma Beta Omega Chapter Alpha Kappa Alpha Sorority, Inc. **Honors/Awds:** Top Ten Legislative Hall of Fame, 1993; Ark Democrat Gazette; Ark Business Weekly, Woman of Distinction, Top 100 Women in Arkansas; Flemming Fellow, Leadership Institute, 1995; ACYPL, Delegate to Japan, 1992. **Business Addr:** Executive Director, PAC (People Are Concerned, Inc), PO Box 213, Camden, AR 71701.

SMITH, KAREN LYNETTE
Education liaison. **Personal:** Born Sep 6, 1962, Baton Rouge, LA; daughter of Dorothy Turner Williams and James C Scott; married Marcus D Smith, May 30, 1987. **Educ:** Dillard University, New Orleans, LA, BS, public health, 1985; Texas Southern University, Houston, TX, MA, science, 1989. **Career:** Harris County Health Dept, Houston, TX, family planning health ed, 1984-89; LifeGift Organ Donation Center, Houston, TX, education liaison, 1989-. **Orgs:** Member, Delta Sigma Theta Sorority Inc, 1988-; chairperson of fundraising, TX Public Health Association, 1988-89; steering committee, Region II Family Planning, 1988-89; education chairperson, Information and Education Association of TX, 1987-89; camp retreat chairperson, Sickle Cell Foundation of Greater Houston, 1985-87; secretary, Texas Area Concerned with School Age Parents, 1988-89. **Honors/Awds:** Houston Presidential Scholarship, Texas Women's University, 1987; Community Service Recognition, Delta Sigma Theta Sorority, 1989; Woman on the Move, Houston Woman Magazine, 1989; Outstanding Pioneer, National Council of Negro Women, 1990.

SMITH, KATRINA MARITA
Chiropractor. **Personal:** Born Oct 1, 1958, Kosciusko, MS. **Educ:** Palmer Junior College, attended; East Carolina University, attended; University of Northern Iowa, attended; Palmer College of Chiropractic, DC 1984. **Career:** Private practice, chiropractor, currently; Forth Worth Independent School District, school bd member, sec, currently. **Orgs:** Sigma Phi Chi 1984; Intl Chiropractic Assn 1984; American Chiropractic Assn 1984; sec, Black Chiropractic Assn 1984. **Military Serv:** US Marine Corps, corporal, 4 years; Meritorious Mast, Good Conduct Medal. **Business Addr:** Chiropractic Physician, 514 W Fortification, Jackson, MS 39203.

SMITH, KEITH DRYDEN, JR.
Educational administrator. **Personal:** Born Jun 8, 1951, New York, NY; son of Marion B Sutherland Smith and Keith Dryden Smith Sr; married Heather R. Duke; children: Mitchell Duke. **Educ:** State Univ of NY, BA 1973; Syracuse Univ, MS 1978. **Career:** Red Creek Central Schools, science teacher 1974-75; Utica Coll of Syracuse Univ, HEOP counselor 1975-77, HEOP coord of academic and supportive serv 1977-79, HEOP dir 1979-81; State Univ of NY Plattsburgh, lecturer in Afro-Amer studies 1984-86, EOP dir 1981-92; SUNY Cortland, lecturer, African-American Studies, EOP dir, 1992-. **Orgs:** Amer Assn of Univ Prof 1975-81, United Univ Professors 1981-; affirmative action comm sec SUNY Plattsburgh 1983-85; inst planning comm SUNY Office of Special Programs 1985-87; human rights chair College Student Personnel Assn of NY Inc 1986-87; certified mediator, Unified Court System of NY, Community Dispute Resolution Program, 1987-; secretary, SUNY Council of Educational Opportunity Program Directors, 1988-90; senator, SUNY Plattsburgh Faculty Senate, 1990-92; SUNY Plattsburgh Presidents Advisory Committee on Affirmative Action, chairman, 1990-92; SUNY Cortland, affirmative action committee, 1992-, curriculum review committee, 1992-95, work group on multicultural fair treatment; SUNY Cortland Affirmative Action Committee, chair, 1993-95, Student Support Committee, 1992-93, 1994-95, Presidential Search Committee, 1995, treasurer, Council of Educational Opportunity Program Directors, 1994-95; Affirmative Action committee chair, SUNY Cortland, 1993-; mem bd of dirs SUNY Cortland Child Center. **Honors/Awds:** Dir of EOP Program with largest percentage of senior level students; conducted statewide survey of Minority Student Personnel Profiles 1985-; co-author, 1st comprehensive training activity for SUNY EOP Dirs, 1988; dir of EOP program with among highest graduation rates and retention rates in the state. **Special Achievements:** Co-author/collaborator: Report of Work Group on Multicultural Fair Treatment, Toward A More Equitable, Inclusive and Diverse Academic Community, SUNY Cortland, 1992. **Home Addr:** 420 Hayts Rd, #1, Ithaca, NY 14850. **Business Addr:** Director Education Oppor Program, SUNY Cortland, D-116 Cornish, PO Box 2000, Cortland, NY 13045.

SMITH, KENNETH BRYANT
Educational administrator, clergyman. **Personal:** Born Feb 19, 1931, Montclair, NJ; married Gladys Moran; children: Kenneth Bryant Jr, Kourtney Beth, Kristen Bernard. **Educ:** VA Union Univ, BA, 1953; Bethany Theological Seminary, BD, 1960; Elmhurst College, D, 1971. **Career:** Park Manor Congregational Church, Chicago, assoc minister, 1957-61; Trinity United Church of Christ, Chicago, minister, 1961-66; Urban Affairs Chicago Comm Renewal Soc, minister, 1966-68; Church of Good Shepherd Congregational, sr minister, 1968-; Chicago Theological Seminary, Univ of Chicago, pres, 1984-. **Orgs:** Nat exec council, 1967-73, chm, 1971-73, United Church of Christ; bd dirs, Urban League, Chicago; bd of trustees, Elmhurst College; Omega Psi Phi; appointed, Chicago Board of Educ, 1979. **Honors/Awds:** Author, "The Fellowship of Prayer" Lenten Season, 1976; grant, study & travel, Far East, Davella Fnd, 1952; officiated at funeral of Chicago, IL mayor Harold Washington, 1987. **Business Addr:** President, Chicago Theological Seminary, 5751 S Woodlawn, Chicago, IL 60637.

SMITH, KEVIN L.
Security guard company executive. **Career:** SC Security Inc, Charlottesville, VA, chief executive. **Business Addr:** SC Security Inc, 125 Riverbend, Charlottesville, VA 22901.

SMITH, KEVIN REY
Professional football player. **Personal:** Born Apr 7, 1970, Orange, TX. **Educ:** Texas A&M, attended. **Career:** Dallas Cowboys, defensive back, 1992-. **Business Addr:** Professional Football Player, Dallas Cowboys, One Cowboys Pkwy, Irving, TX 75063, (214)556-9900.

SMITH, LAFAYETTE KENNETH
Public administrator. **Personal:** Born Dec 17, 1947, Memphis, TN; son of Elizabeth Berniece Hodge-Smith and Joseph Smith. **Educ:** Howard Univ, Washington DC, BS, 1971; Bernard M Baruch Coll (CUNY), New York City NY, MPA, 1984. **Career:** Opportunities Industrialization Center, Washington DC, job placement specialist, 1972-75, job placement supvr, 1975-76, program supvr, 1976-78, branch mgr, 1978-81, program coord, 1981-82; Chicago Public Schools, Chicago IL, special asst to gen supt, 1982-83; Washington DC Govt, Dept of Human Serv, Washington DC, asst chief, Contracts Division, 1984-87, Youth Serv Admin, contract admin, 1987-91; DC Dept of Human Services, Washington DC, sr contracts specialist, 1993-96; Youth Services Administration, contract admin, 1996-. **Orgs:** NAACP, 1970-, Howard Univ Alumni Assn, 1971-, Big Brothers, Washington DC, 1975-82, Prince Georges County, Private Indus Council, 1979-81, State of Maryland Occupational Information, 1980-81; tutor, Washington DC Public Schools, 1980-82; scout master, Boy Scouts of Amer, 1981-81; American Society of Public Admin, 1982-, Chicago Urban League, 1982-83, Baruch Coll Alumni Assn, 1984-, Natl Forum of Black Public Admin, 1985-; bd mem, Natl Urban Fellows Alumni Assn, 1986-, Concerned Black Men Inc, 1986-95. **Honors/Awds:** Natl Urban Fellow, Natl Urban Fellows Inc, 1982; Natl OIC of Amer, 10 year Serv Award, OIC, 1982; Outstanding Young Men of Amer, US Jaycee, 1983; Enterprise Zones (Thesis), 1983; Concerned Black Men, Washington, DC Chap Appreciation Award, 1995. **Home Addr:** 2400 16th St NW #423, Washington, DC 20009, (202)232-4464. **Business Addr:** Contracts Administrator, DC Dept of Human Services, Youth Services Administration, 8300 Riverton Court, Laurel, MD 20707.

SMITH, LAMAR
Professional football player. **Personal:** Born Nov 29, 1970, Fort Wayne, IN. **Educ:** Northeastern Oklahoma A&M Junior College, Univ of Houston. **Career:** Seattle Seahawks, running back, 1994-. **Business Addr:** Professional Football Player, Seattle Seahawks, 11220 NE 53rd St, Kirkland, WA 98033, (206)827-9777.

SMITH, LASALLE, SR.
Law enforcement officer. **Personal:** Born Oct 13, 1947, Lithonia, GA; son of Ollie Tuggle Smith and Link Smith; married Evelyn Peek Smith, Dec 25, 1966; children: LaSalle Jr, Evita, Erika. **Educ:** Modern School of Music, Washington, DC, 1965-66; LaSalle Extention Univ, Chicago, IL, 1966-68; Dekalb Community, Clarkston, GA, 1974-77; Brenau College, Gainesville, GA, 1982-85; numerous other courses relating to law enforcement. **Career:** Federal Bureau of Investigation, Washington, DC, finger print sect, 1965-66; Atlanta Police Department, patroll squad, 1968, detective, 1971, police sergeant, 1973-74, police lieutenant, 1974-80; Office of the Mayor, Atlanta, executive protection commander, 1980-84; Office of the Commissioner of Public Safety, Internal Affairs Unit, commander, 1984-86; Office of the Chief of Police, commander of numerous task forces, 1986-90, Chaplaincy Corp, director, 1991-. **Orgs:** National Organization of Black Law Enforcement Executives, 1984-; National Forum for Black Public Administrators; National Black Police Association; Fulton County Task Force on Drugs and Crime; Wings of Hope Anti-Drug/Anti-Gang Task Force. **Special Achievements:** Guest lecturer and instructor for a number of agencies and organizations throughout the United States. **Business Addr:** Director, Chaplaincy Corp, Atlanta Police Department, 165 Decatur St, SE, Atlanta, GA 30303.

SMITH, LAWRENCE JOHN, JR.
Advisory services company executive. **Personal:** Born Dec 20, 1947, New York, NY; son of Jeanne Henderson Smith and Lawrence John Smith; married Ernestine Randall-Smith, Nov 27, 1985; children: Karyn Jennifer, Lawrence John III. **Educ:** University of Notre Dame, Notre Dame, IN, BBA, 1969; Harvard Business School, Boston, MA, MBA, 1971. **Career:** Honeywell Info Systems, Waltham, MA, senior financial analyst, 1972-74; Digital Equip Corp, Maynard, MA, product line controller, 1974-79; Pizza Hut Inc, Wichita, KS, US Controller, 1979-81; Wang Laboratories Inc, Lowell, MA, CEO of software subs, 1982-89; Transnational Mgmt Association, Grafton, MA, president & managing director, 1989-90; Mass Ind Fin Agency, Boston, MA, chief financial officer, 1990-94; The TM Group, pres, 1994-. **Orgs:** Trustee, Dimock Community Health Center, 1990-; trustee, Boston Opera Theatre, 1990-; member, MENSA, 1982-; member, Harvard Business School Assn of Boston, 1988-; MetroWest Medical Ctr, dir, 1994-; North American Consultants, Inc, dir, 1994-; Harvard Club of Boston, 1990-. **Honors/Awds:** Boston MBDC, Minority Business Advocate of the Year, 1993. **Business Addr:** President, The TM Group, PO Box 563, Grafton, MA 01519-0563, (508)839-1072.

SMITH, LEE ARTHUR
Professional baseball player. **Personal:** Born Dec 4, 1957, Jamestown, LA; married Diane. **Educ:** Northwestern State Univ, Natchitoches, LA, attended. **Career:** Pitcher: Chicago Cubs, 1980-87, Boston Red Sox, 1988-90, St Louis Cardinals; Baltimore Orioles, currently. **Honors/Awds:** National League All-Star Team, 1983, 1987. **Business Addr:** Professional Baseball Player, Baltimore Orioles, Oriole Park at Camden Yards, 333 W Camden St, Baltimore, MD 21201.

SMITH, LEO GRANT
Educator. **Personal:** Born Jun 21, 1940, Atlanta, GA; married Mildred Louise Hoke; children: Wendy, Kimberly. **Educ:** BA 1962, MA 1971; EdS 1982. **Career:** Hamilton HS, teacher 1962-68; Chamblee HS, asst principal 1968-72; Gordon HS DeKalb Cty Bd of Ed, principal. **Orgs:** Vp GA Assoc of Secondary Principals 1973-74; mem DeKalb Assoc of Secondary School Principals, Gordon High PTA, Venetian Hills Elem PTA; vice pres DeKalb Admin Assoc 1975-. **Honors/Awds:** ASCA administrator of the year. **Business Addr:** Principal, Gordon High School, 2190 Wallingford Drive, Decatur, GA 30032.

SMITH, LEONARD PHILLIP
Professional football player. **Personal:** Born Sep 2, 1960, New Orleans, LA. **Educ:** McNeese State Univ, attended. **Career:** St Louis Cardinals, 1983-87; Phoenix Cardinals, 1988; Buffalo Bills, safety, 1988-. **Honors/Awds:** Played in AFC Championship Game, post-1988 season. **Business Addr:** Professional Football Player, Buffalo Bills, One Bills Dr, Orchard Park, NY 14127-2296.

SMITH, LEROI MATTHEW-PIERRE, III
Social service administrator. **Personal:** Born Jan 11, 1946, Chicago, IL; son of Norma and LeRoi Jr; children: Le Roi IV. **Educ:** ID State Univ, BA 1969; WA State Univ, PhD 1977. **Career:** ID State Univ, lecturer 1969-70; WA State Univ, lecturer 1970-71; Evergreen State Coll, prof 1971-1981; Port of Seattle, director, Diversity Programs. **Orgs:** Bd dir Thurston Mason Co Mental Health 1974-81; Tacoma-Pierce Co OIC 1979-1981; consult Seattle Pub Schls 1976-85; Amer Soc for Personnel Admin 1981-; Natl Assn of Black Psychologists 1974-80; Amer Psychological Assn. **Honors/Awds:** Flwshp Lilly Fnd 1981; Danforth Fnd 1978; Natl Sci Fnd 1976; US Dept of Educ 1969. **Home Addr:** 761 S 45th St, Tacoma, WA 98408.

SMITH, LEROY VICTOR
Intramural athletic director. **Personal:** Born Aug 4, 1933, Lexington, KY; son of Mary B Smith and Henry C Smith; married Mary Levi Smith, Mar 18, 1957; children: Darryl Victor, Angela Maria, Danee LaVon. **Educ:** Jackson State Coll, BS 1958; Univ KY, MS 1963; California Western University, PhD, 1977. **Career:** Lexington Recreation Dept, supr summers 1956-63; MS Valley State Coll, 1958-59; Randolph HS, head football coach 1959-63; Meigs HS Nashville, 1963-64; Tuskegee Inst, head football coach 1964-70; KY State U, 1970-82; intramural athletic dir, currently; Comm Educ Prog Tuskegee, consult 1966. **Orgs:** Mem Am Football Coaches Assn; author of articles; mem Kappa Alpha Psi; Alpha Kappa Mu.

SMITH, LILA
Scientist. **Personal:** Born in Memphis, TN. **Educ:** Lemoyne Coll, BS Math (high honor) 1957; Howard Univ, MS Physics 1959. **Career:** FL A&M Univ, asst prof of physics 1959-62; LeMoyne Coll, asst prof of Math 1962-63; US Atomic Energy Comm, scientific analyst 1963-76; Tech Info Ctr US Dept of Energy, chief conservation & solar branch 1976-83, chief nuclear engrg & physics Branch OSTI/USDOE. **Orgs:** Pres and charter mem Blacks in Govt Oak Ridge Chap 1984; 1st vice pres Region IV Blacks in Govt Inc 1984-; vice pres Xi Iota Omega Chap Alpha Kappa Alpha Sor 1985; mem Amer Solar Energy Soc Inc; mem Natl Forum of Black Public Admins; mem Altrusa Inc Oak Ridge Chpt; mem NAACP; mem Fed Employed Women Inc; mem Negro Bus & Professional Women's Clubs; mem TN Council on Human Relations; Oak Valley Baptist Church; Toastmasters Intl. **Honors/Awds:** Sigma Pi Sigma Physics Soc; Equal Empl Opportunity (EEO); adv bd US Atomic Energy Comm Oak Ridge 1968-77; Personnel Security Bd US Dept of Energy 1974-81; Achievement Award for Outstanding Accomplishments in Sci & Civic Affairs Jack & Jill of Amer 1976; Spec Achievement Award for EEO US Energy Rsch & Develop Admin 1978; publications incl Geothermal Resources Bibliography 1975, 1976; Solar Energy Update Abstract Journal 1975. **Home Addr:** 4256 Woodcrest Dr, Memphis, TN 38111-8140. **Business Addr:** Chf Nuc Engrg & Physics Branch, US Dept of Energy Sci & Tech, PO Box 62, Oak Ridge, TN 37831.

SMITH, LONNIE
Professional baseball player. **Personal:** Born Dec 22, 1955, Chicago, IL; married Pearl; children: Yaritza LaVonne, Eric Tramaine. **Career:** Philadelphia Phillies, 1978-81; St Louis Cardinals, 1982-85; Kansas City Royals, 1985-87; Atlanta Braves, 1988-93; Pittsburgh Pirates, 1993-94; Baltimore Orioles, 1994-. **Honors/Awds:** Rookie of the Year, The Sporting News and Baseball Digest, 1980; St Louis Man of the Year, Baseball Writers Assn of America, 1982; National League All-Star Team, 1982. **Business Addr:** Professional Baseball Player, Baltimore Orioles, 333 W Camden St, Baltimore, MD 21201.

SMITH, LORETTA GARY
Banking executive. **Personal:** Born Mar 27, 1949, Detroit, MI; daughter of Luther (deceased) & Doris Gary; married Rev William J Smith, Apr 17, 1983; children: Stacey Espie, Stephanie, Ashley. **Educ:** University of Detroit-Mercy, Business Administration, 1983. **Career:** JL Hudson, clerk, 1966-67; Comerica Inc, asst vp, public affairs, 1968-. **Orgs:** Detroit & Pontiac Neighborhood Housing Svcs, Inc, bd of dirs; Habitat for Humanity, Metro-Detroit, bd of dirs; Univ of Detroit Mercy, Leadership Dev Institute, advisory bd mem; Cornerstone Schools, partner, tutor; GNL Community Dev Corp; Greater New Light Baptist Church; United Negro College Fund, advisory bd mem. **Honors/Awds:** YMCA Metropolitan Detroit, Minority Achiever, 1993; Detroit Neighborhood Housing Svcs, Award of Recognition; Black Caucus Foundation of Michigan, Pioneer Supporter Award, 1993; Minority Technology Council of Michigan, Inc, Certificate of Appreciation, 1994; City of Detroit, Spirit of Detroit Award. **Business Addr:** Assistant Vice Pres, Comerica Inc, 500 Woodward Ave, PO Box 75000, MC 3352, Detroit, MI 48275-3352, (313)222-6987.

SMITH, LOUIS
Executive, government employee. **Personal:** Born Nov 7, 1939, Ft Lauderdale, FL; married Bessie. **Educ:** Morgan State, BS 1962; NYU, MA1970. **Career:** NY Dept of Mental Hygiene Kingsboro Psychiat Center, exec dir 1974-; Morrisania Hosp, asso dir 1973-74; Sydenham Hosp, asso dir 1971-73; NY Univ MedCenter, asst adminstr, 1968-71; Goldwater Meml Hosp, asst adminstr 1970-71; NYU Bellevue Hosp Center, liaison adminstr 1965-70; NYU Bellevue Hosp Center, asst liason adminstr 1968. **Orgs:** Mem Nat Assn of Health Exec; 100 Black Men of NYC; New York City Comprehensive Health Com; Assn of Mental Health Adminstr Asso; adj prof Long Island U; doctoral cand NYU Sch of Pub Adminstration; examiner NY State Dept of Civil Serv Nat In-Door Mile Relay Team 1959-61. **Business Addr:** 681 Clarkson Ave, Brooklyn, NY 11203.

SMITH, LUTHER EDWARD, JR.
Educator, cleric. **Personal:** Born May 29, 1947, St Louis, MO; son of Clementine Smith and Luther Smith; married Beth Mclaury; children: Luther Aaron, Nathan. **Educ:** WA Univ, AB 1965-69; Eden Theological Sem, MDiv 1969-72; St Louis Univ, PhD 1973-79. **Career:** E St Louis Welfare Rgts Org, coord 1970-72; Educ for Blk Urban Mnstrs, exec coord 1972-79; Lane Tabernacle CME Church, asst pstr 1972-79; Black Church Ldrs Prog St Louis Univ, prog coord 1975-79; Candler Sch of Theology Emory Univ, prof of Church and Comm. **Orgs:** Bd chmn Northside Team Ministries 1973-79; 1st vice pres MO Assoc Soc Welfare St Louis Div 1973-79; prog coord Metropolitan Ministerial Alliance of St Louis 1975-79, Urban Churches in Community Dev Prog 1978-79; bd mem Urban Training Org of Atlanta 1980-; bd mem Inst for World Evangelism 1982-, Eden Theological Sem; Families First 1992. **Honors/Awds:** Distg srv awards St Louis and Mid St Louis Cty Jaycees 1975; member of Honor Society International Society of Theta Phi 1987; member, Omicron Delta Kappa 1991; Inducted into the Martin Luther King, Jr Collegium of Scholars, Morehouse College. **Special Achievements:** Co-author, actor: ''What's Black,'' televised KFTC, 1970, ''Earth Day,'' televised PBS, 1970; author: ''Howard Thurman, the Mystic as Prophet,'' 1992; author, Intimacy & Mission: Intentional Community as Crucible for Radical Discipleship. **Business Addr:** Prof of Church & Community, Candler Schl of Theology, Bishops Hall Emory Univ, Atlanta, GA 30322.

SMITH, MARIE EVANS
Child psychologist. **Personal:** Born Oct 21, 1928, Philadelphia, PA; daughter of Mamie Pace Evans and Frederick Evans; married Charles N Smith; children: Dianne S Partee, Dionne S Jones, Deborah S Smith. **Educ:** Temple Univ, BS 1972; Antioch Univ, MEd 1974; Kensington Univ, PhD 1985. **Career:** Greentree School, teacher 1960-65; The Inst of Human Potential, asst dir 1965-70; Parkway Day School, perceptual motor spec 1970-74; Hahnemann Medical Coll & John F Kennedy Mental Health Center, instructor and supervisor 1974-; John F Kennedy Mental Health/Mental Retardation Center, PA clinical psychologist 1974-, site director 1988-. **Orgs:** Pres Wellesley Civic Assoc 1965-; mem Temple Univ Alumni Assoc 1973-87, Antioch Univ Alumni Assoc 1974-87; mental health consultant Sch Dist of Philadelphia 1974-; mem Council for Intl Visitors Museum Civic Center 1983-87; mem Counseling Assoc of Greater Philadelphia 1985-, Natl Geographical Soc 1985-; mem at large NAACP 1985-; mem Afro-Amer Historical Cultural Museum 1985-87; bd mem Amer Black Women's Heritage Soc 1986-87; mem Zeta Phi Beta 1986-; consultant & child psychologist Minority Mental Health Advocacy Task Force; founding-mem Amer Legion Aux Henry Hopkins Post 881; member, Urban League of Philadelphia, 1990-; member, National Political Congress of Black Women, 1989-; member, Philadelphia Museum of Art, 1990; golden life member, Zeta Phi Beta Sorority, 1990. **Honors/Awds:** Legions of Honor Membership Chapel of Four Chaplains Awd 1965; Serv to Children Awd parkway Day School 1974; Certificate of Service Awd Hahnemann Medical Coll 1980; Certification of African Cultures Amer Forum for Intl Study 1981; Certificate of Merit Sch Dist of Philadelphia 1983; Recognition of Achievement Providence Baptist Church 1985; John F Kennedy Community Serv Awd Philadelphia PA 1985,86; Certificate of Achievement Behavioral Therapy Temple Univ; Womens History Month NJ Black Women's Educational Alliance 1989; Recognition of Service, John F Kennedy Mental Health/Mental Retardation Center 1988; Fellowship, Intl Biographical Assn 1989; Fellow and Diplomate, American Board of Medical Psychotherapist, 1990; Top Ladies of Distinction, 1995. **Home Addr:** 518 Wellesley Rd, Philadel-

phia, PA 19119. **Business Addr:** Mental Health Administrator, John F Kennedy Mental Health-Poplar Clinic, 321 W Girard Ave, Philadelphia, PA 19122.

SMITH, MARIETTA CULBREATH
Education administrator. **Personal:** Born Jul 11, 1933, Saulda, SC; married Sylvester Odellas Smith; children: Melvin, Darrion, Lorraine, Wardell, Sylvester Jr, Patricia Ann, Tryone. **Educ:** New York Univ, Cert 1970; Washington Tech, Cert 1971; American Univ, Cert; Pre School Day Care Div, Cert 1971. **Career:** Change Inc, board of dir, vice chmn 1970-; Neighborhood Planning, counsellor, treasure 1984-; Ward One Council on Educ, chmn Ways & Means 1980-; Advisory Neighborhood Comm, vice chmn/educational aide 1984-85. **Orgs:** Asst treas Ward I Council of Educ; sec Ward I Democrats 1985-88; bd of dirs Teachers Ctr DC Public Schools; working on computer lab Terrell Jr HS; vice chair ANC 1986-88. **Honors/Awds:** Presidential Awd 1970; Life time mem PTA Congress 1974; Appreciation Awd DC Congress 1960- & City Council 1974-88. **Home Addr:** 1351 Meridian Pl NW, Washington, DC 20010. **Business Addr:** Educational Aide, Advisory Neighborhood Comm, 104 Spring Rd NW, Washington, DC 20010.

SMITH, MARQUETTE
Professional football player. **Personal:** Born Jul 14, 1972; married Dontonya; children: Whitney. **Educ:** Central Florida. **Career:** Carolina Panthers, running back, 1996-. **Business Addr:** Professional Football Player, Carolina Panthers, 800 Mint St, Ericsson Stadium, Charlotte, NC 28202, (704)358-7000.

SMITH, MARVIN PRESTON
Police officer (retired), association administrator. **Personal:** Born May 5, 1944, Grand Rapids, MI; son of Maxine Smith and Isaiah Smith; divorced; children: Micheal, Debbie, Tracey, Preston, Marika, D'Andre. **Educ:** Jackson Community College, certification, Michigan law enforcement, 1975. **Career:** Grand Rapids Police Department, police officer, 1975-92; Grand Rapids Board of Education, building safety representative, 1992-; Project ReHab Com Alternative Program, resident counselor, 1992. **Orgs:** Officers of the Shield, president, 1988- Wealthy Street Center, director, 1990-; National Black Police Officer Association, delegate, 1989-.

SMITH, MARY ALICE. See ALICE, MARY.

SMITH, MARY CARTER
Folklorist. **Personal:** Born Feb 10, 1919, Birmingham, AL; daughter of Eartha Nowden Coleman (deceased); married Ulysses J Carter, 1946 (divorced 1950); children: Ricardo Rogers Carter (deceased); married Elias Raymond Smith, Jul 1960 (died 1962); married Eugene Thomas Grove Jr. **Educ:** Coppin State College, Baltimore, MD, BS, 1942; New York University, graduate study; Johns Hopkins University, graduate study; Rutgers University, graduate study; Queens College, graduate study; Catholic University, graduate study; University of Maryland, graduate study; Temple Buell University, graduate study. **Career:** City of Baltimore, MD, teacher/librarian, 1938-; folklorist. **Orgs:** Huber Memorial Church of Christ; NAACP; National Association of Negro Business and Professional Women's Clubs, Baltimore Club; Alpha Zeta Chapter, Zeta Phi Beta Sorority; founding member, Arena Players; founding member, board member, vice president, Big Sisters, International (now Big Brothers-Big Sisters of America), 1953-; co-founder, Big Sisters, Little Sisters (now Big Brothers-Big Sisters of Central Maryland), 1964; co-founder, Association of Black Storytellers; founder, The Griotsi Circle. **Honors/Awds:** Author: Opinionated, 1966, Vibes, 1974, Town Child, 1976, Heart to Heart, 1980; producer of audiocassette, MCS Presents; producer of videocassettes, Tell Me a Story, 1985, Cindy Ellie, 1989, A Funeral, Open the Door, Richard; has made numerous professional appearances as a storyteller and folklorist; Keeper of the Flame Award, Maryland Writers' Council, 1983; Zora Neale Hurston Folklore Award, Association of Black Storytellers, 1985; One of Twenty Women of Distinction, African-American Women's Political Caucus, 1983; Beautiful Black Woman Award, Towson State University, 1985; Great Blacks, Wax Museum of Baltimore, MD, 1989; others. **Business Addr:** Aframa Agency, PO Box 11484, Baltimore, MD 21239.

SMITH, MARY LEVI
Educational administrator. **Personal:** Born Jan 30, 1936, Hazlehurst, MS; daughter of Byneter Markham Levi and Rev William Levi; married LeRoy; children: Darryl, Angela Williams, Danee. **Educ:** Jackson State University, BS, 1957; University of Kentucky, MA, 1964, EdD, 1980. **Career:** Mississippi, Alabama, Tennessee elementary grade schools, teacher, 1957-64; Tuskegee Institute, assistant director of reading clinic, 1964-70; Kentucky State University, associate professor of education, 1970-, chairperson, department of education, 1981-83, dean, College of Applied Science, 1983-88, vice president for Academic Affairs, 1988-89, interim president, 1989-90, special assistant to president, professor of education, 1990-91, president, 1991-. **Orgs:** Commission on Colleges for the Southern Assn of Colleges & Schools, commissioner, 1992-97; Natl Assn for State Universities & Land Grant Colleges, bd of dirs; Natl Assn for Equal Opportunity in Higher Ed; Amer Assn for Colleges of Teacher Education; United Way of Frankfort; Frankfort/Franklin County Comm Education, Governmental Services Ctr for the Commonwealth of Kentucky; Amer Council on Education Comm on Women in Higher Education; Natl Bd of Examiners, Natl Council for the Accreditation of Teacher Education; Delta Sigma Theta Sorority, Inc. **Honors/Awds:** Kentucky State University, outstanding faculty of the year, 1986; Outstanding Alumnus Award, Jackson State University, 1988; Torchbearers and Trailbearers Award in Education, 1989; Young Women's Christian Association of Lexington, Women of Achievement Award, 1990; NAACP, Frankfort Chapter, Woman of the Year Award, 1990; Delta Sigma Theta, Frankfort Alumnae Chapter, Citizens Award, 1990; Louisville Defender, Prof Achievement Award; Frankfort Bus & Prof Women, Woman of Achievement Award, 1994; University of Kentucky Hall of Distinguished Alumni, 1995. **Business Addr:** President, Kentucky State University, Hume Hall, Frankfort, KY 40601.

SMITH, MARZELL
Educator. **Personal:** Born Aug 14, 1936, Conehatta, MS; married Albertine. **Educ:** Piney Woods Jr Coll; 1952-56; Jackson State Coll, BS 1958; TN A&I State U, MEd 1964; Univ Miami, 1969; Univ Miami, EdD 1973. **Career:** FL Sch Desegregation Univ Miami, staff consult 1970-; Univ Miami, flw 1969-70; GN Smith Elem Sch, asst prin 1966-69; Jim Hill Jr Sr HS, tchr 1964-66; Allen Carver Jr Sr HS, 1958-64; Douglas Elem, coord 1971-72; Monreo Co Sch System; Alachua Co, 1972; Collier Co; Dept Found FL Atlantic U, 1975. **Orgs:** Mem Am Educ Rsrch Assn; Nat Assn Sch Adminstr; BSA; Nat Assn Secondary Sch Prin; College Hill Bapt Ch; Jackson Bd Certified Officials; Phi Delta Kappa; SW Officials Assn; Kappa Alpha Psi Frat; Urban League; MTA-JTA-CTA; Miami Chap Nat Alliance of Black Sch Edr; mem FL Assn Dist Sch Supt;So Asn Black Adminstrv Personnel; Univ Miami Black Faculty Adminstr; bd dir Miami Black Arts Gallery & Workshop; mem Dept Adminstr Curriculum & Instr; NEA; Nat Alliance of Black Sch Edr; Poverty Law Ctr; NAACP; unpubl papers "An OD Analysis of Aw Soc Serv Orgn"; "Discipline Problems in a Pub Jr HS blueprints for action"; "the polit action strategies of dr martin luther king jr implications & applications"; "the role of Hallucinogenic Plants in Early Am Colonial & European Witchcraft";"Discipline Problemn Three Pub FL Sr HS implications & applications"; "Conflict Intervention Strategies in a Pub Sch System in FL; Applications". **Military Serv:** AUS pvt. **Business Addr:** PO Box 8065, Coral Gables, FL 33124.

SMITH, MAXINE ATKINS
Association executive. **Personal:** Born in Memphis, TN; daughter of Georgia Rounds Atkins and Joseph Atkins (deceased); married Dr Vasco A Smith Jr; children: Vasco III. **Educ:** Spelman Clg Atlanta, GA, AB; Middlebury Clg Middlebury, VT, MA. **Career:** Prairie View A&M Univ Prairie View, TX, instr frnch 1950-52; FL A&M Univ Tallahassee, FL, instr French 1952-53; LeMoyne Clg Memphis, TN, asst prof French & English 1955-56; Memphis Branch NAACP, exec sec 1962-. **Orgs:** Mem Delta Theta Sorority Inc Memphis Alumnae Chptr; mem Natl Smart Set Inc Memphis Chptr; mem Links Inc Memphis Chptr; mem bd of dir Democratic Voters Cncl; temporary chrmn Memphis Alliance Comm Organization; mem exec bd Memphis Com Comm Relations; bd dir Memphis Branch NAACP 1957; mem chrmn Memphis Branch NAACP 1958-61; coordinated & partcipated Freedmon Movement 1960-61; dir NAACP Annual Registration Campaigns; bd dir Voter Ed Proj Inc 1971; advsry bd Tri-State Defender 1983; hon chrprsn LeMoyne-Owen Clg 1983; bd dir Lorraine Civil Rights Museum 1984; bd trustee Ldrshp Memphis 1985; chaired NAACP's Natl Spingarn Award Com 1985; president, Memphis Board of Education, 1991; executive committee, Mayor's Task Force on Education, 1990-; Tennessee Board of Regents; NAACP, ntl bd of dirs, exec secretary emeritus. **Honors/Awds:** Woman of yr Trinity CME Chrch; achvmnt awrd Omega Psi Phi Frat; one of ten outstndg young am Pagaent Mag; woman of yr Civil Rights YWCA; annual merit awrd Memphis Brnch NAACP 1960; humanitarian of yr Alpha Pi Chi Sorority Alpha Beta Chptr 1964; woman of action awrd Alpha Kappa Alpha Sorority 1969; outstndg citizen of yr Omega Psi Phi Frat 1969; one of 5 citizens Natl NAACP Outstndg NAACP Ldrshp 1970; outstndg citizen awrd Frontier Intrl Inc 1970; distngshd citizen awrd for contributions & ldrshp Mallory Knights 1960; outstndg ldrshp in field civil rights Longview Seventh-Day Adventist Chrch; cited civil rights actvty Ward Chapel AME Church 1971; Achievement Award in Public Service, OIC, 1973; Achievement Award, Middlebury College Alumni Association, 1985.plaque for outstanding comm sereta Epsilon Omega Chptr Alpha Kappa Alpha Sorority 1972; black history week plaque of recognition Beulah Bapt Chruch 1972; Kappa Alpha Psi Plaque for Meritorious Serv to Comm Area Human Rights. **Home Addr:** 1208 E Parkway S, Memphis, TN 38114. **Business Addr:** Executive Secretary, Memphis Branch NAACP, 588 Vance Ave, Memphis, TN 38126.

SMITH, MELISSA ANN
Director of minority affairs. **Personal:** Born Jul 30, 1962, Kansas City, KS; daughter of Francella E Hayes. **Educ:** Univ of Kansas-Lawrence, BS Journalism 1984; Univ of MO - KC, working on MS in Higher Educ Administration. **Career:** RFC Intermediaries - Los Angeles, claims clerk 1984; St Mary College 2 Plus Two Prog, administrative asst 1985; Donnelly Coll, dir of publicity 1985-88; Longview College, dir of minority affairs 1989-. **Orgs:** America's Heart Co-Op, public relations consultant 1986; KCK Area Chamber of Comm, leadership 2000 participant 1986-1987; Freelance Writer and Layout Designer1986-. **Honors/Awds:** Fundraising committee mem KCK Women's Chamber of Comm 1986; mem KCK NAACP 1985-86; mem organist Pleasant Valley Bapt Church.

SMITH, MICHAEL
Professional sports official. **Career:** NBA, referee, currently. **Business Addr:** NBA Official, National Basketball Association, 645 5th Ave, 15th Fl, New York, NY 10022-5986.

SMITH, MICHAEL JOHN
Professional basketball player. **Personal:** Born Mar 28, 1972, Washington, DC. **Educ:** Providence. **Career:** Sacramento Kings, forward, 1994-98; Vancouver Grizzlies, 1998-. **Business Addr:** Professional Basketball Player, Vancouver Grizzlies, 788 Beatty St, Ste 311, Vancouver, BC, Canada V6B 2M1, (604)688-5867.

SMITH, MILDRED B.
Educator. **Personal:** Born Feb 3, 1935, South Carolina; divorced. **Educ:** SC State Coll, BS; MI State U, MA; MI State U, PhD. **Career:** Curriculum Coordinator, elementary teacher; elementary dir; u vis lectr; conselor; Flint Bd Educ, elementary dir. **Orgs:** Mem bd dir First Independence Nat Bank of Detroit; mem bd of Regents for Eastern MI U. **Honors/Awds:** Author "Home & Sch Focus on Reading" 1971; co-author "Reading Systems & Open Highways" 1971-74.

SMITH, MILLARD, JR.
US naval officer. **Personal:** Born Jul 9, 1948, Lufkin, TX; son of Gussie Mae Williams Smith and Millard Smith Sr (deceased); married Helen Jean Woodson Smith, Feb 14, 1969; children: Demethra Rochelle, Millard III. **Educ:** National Univ, San Diego CA, BA, 1980. **Career:** US Navy, Great Lakes, IL, commanding officer, currently. **Orgs:** Pres, San Diego Chapter, Natl Naval Officers Assn, 1987-88; grand chapter pres, Zeta Sigma Lambda Chapter, Alpha Phi Alpha, 1988-89; board of directors, National Naval Officers Assn, 1990-; board of directors, North Chicago School District, 1990-; board of directors, North Chicago Rotary Club, 1990-. **Military Serv:** US Navy, lieutenant/03E, 1970-; Navy Commendation, Navy Achievement 2 Awards.

SMITH, MONICA LAVONNE
Journalist, editor. **Personal:** Born Jan 26, 1966, New Haven, CT; daughter of Erma J Smith and Hulee Evans. **Educ:** Virginia State University, BA, 1988. **Career:** Comtex Scientific Corp, copy editor, 1989-90, senior editor, 1990-. **Orgs:** Natl Assn of Black Journalists, 1990-; National Assn of Negro Business & Professional Womens Clubs Inc, 1990-; NAACP, Greater New Haven Branch, election supervisory committee; Hill Neighborhood Tutoring Program, 1991-.

SMITH, MORRIS LESLIE
Researcher. **Personal:** Born May 29, 1933, Camden, NJ; son of Tamar H Smith and William E Smith; married Alice Marie Gray; children: Morris G, Wesley E, Stephen J. **Educ:** MI State Univ, BS 1959; Temple Univ, MBA Program 1978. **Career:** Magna Bond Inc, rsch chemist 1959-61; EL Conwell Inc, analytical chemist 1961; Scott Paper Co Philadelphia, rsch chemist 1961-65, sr rsch project chemist 1965-74, sect leader 1974-78, sr rsch leader beginning 1978, technology manager; The ML Smith Group, Inc., pres, currently. **Orgs:** Study prog Mt Zion United Methodist Church 1972-; mem board of directors United Methodist Homes of NJ 1980-93; mem bd dir St Peter's School Philadelphia 1970-88; mem board of directors Agape Day Care Center Marcus Hook 1982-92; pres Echelon Branch Camden Co YMCA 1983-86; exec at large Intl Soc of African Scientists 1984-; mem board of directors Camden Co YMCA; chairman, TV Mins Comm Southern New Jersey Annual Conf of United Methodist Church; treas parade marshal Lawnside 4th of July Comm Inc; president, United Methodist Homes of New Jersey Foundation; appointment to the Advisory Business Council of the R B Pamplin School of Business, Virginia Polytechnic Institute, and State University, Blacksburg, VA, to serve a 3-year term; Intensive Supervision Program (ISP), NJ Admin Office of the Courts, screening board member, 1983-; New Jersey Committee on Minority Concerns, 1996; Southern NJ Annual Conference of the United Methodist Church, Board of Pensions, vice chairperson. **Honors/Awds:** US Patent #3,389,108 1968; use of fragrance in paper Talk publ Amer Soc of Perfumers 1973; Lay Panelist Administrative Court of NJ 1984; mem NJ School Bds Assn 1975-76; Commendation Ltr Martin Luther King Mem Library DC 1984; Two US Patents, #s 4,882,221, 11-21-89 & 4,883,475, 11-28-89, chemically treated paper products-towel/tissue, US Patent Office, 1989; article, The Sweet Smell of Success, Black Enterprise Magazine, 1990; Blacks in Science Calendar, African Scientific Institute, Oakland, CA, 1991. **Military Serv:** AUS specialist 1955-57; Honorable Discharge. **Business Addr:** President, The ML Smith Group, Inc, 301 Tillman Ave, Lawnside, NJ 08045.

SMITH, NATHANIEL, JR.
Manufacturing executive. **Career:** Ver-Val Enterprises, Fort Walton Beach, FL, chief executive. **Business Addr:** Ver-Val Enterprises, 91 Heill, PO Drawer 4550, Fort Walton Beach, FL 32549.

SMITH, NEIL
Professional football player. **Personal:** Born Apr 10, 1966, New Orleans, LA; married Sheri; children: Joshua, Nesha. **Educ:** Univ of Nebraska, attended. **Career:** Kansas City Chiefs, defensive end, 1988-96; Denver Broncos, defensive end, 1997-. **Orgs:** Yes I Can Foundation, national spokesman. **Honors/Awds:** Defensive lineman, Sporting News College All-America Team, 1987; Pro Bowl appearances, 1991-95; South KC Chamber of Commerce, Super Kansas Citian Award; Lab School of Washington, Outstanding Learning Disabled Achievers Award; Ed Block Courage Award, 1994; US Junior Chamber of Commerce, 10 Outstanding Americans Award, 1996; Super Bowl, Denver Broncos, champions, 1998. **Business Addr:** Professional Football Player, Denver Broncos, 13655 Broncos Pkwy, Englewood, CO 80112, (303)649-9000.

SMITH, NELLIE J.
Educator. **Personal:** Born May 15, 1932, Meridian, MS; daughter of Nettie B Johnson (deceased) and Booker T Johnson (deceased); married Levi; children: Bobby, Paula, Perry, Joseph. **Educ:** Rust Coll Holly Spring MS, BS 1954; KS State Teachers Coll, Emporia, KS, MS, 1956; Univ of ND, PhD 1973. **Career:** Rust College, secretary to president, 1954-55; Intl Brothers Teamsters, 1st black clerical worker, 1960-62; Rust Coll, bus instr 1962-63; Harris High School, bus instr 1963-64; MS Valley State Coll, asst prof 1964-70; Rust Coll, chairperson div bus, prof bus ed 1970-. **Orgs:** National Council of Negro Women; Mem So Bus Ed Assn, UMC 1942-, A Cappella Choir Rust Coll 1950-55; voice recital MS Valley State Coll 1969; choral union Univ of ND 1971-73, Natl Bus Ed Assn, Delta Pi Epsilon, Pi Omega Pi, Phi Beta Lambda; Marshall County Election Commissioner, 1993-97; Mississippi Arts Commissioner, 1994-98; Appointed by Governor to Private Industry Council, and Commission on Temporary Assistance for Needy Families, 1997-2001. **Honors/Awds:** Publ poem "Life Its Mystery & Struggles" set to music 1969; publ 6 articles, 4 shorthand tests 1973, "How to Use Fortran Arithmetic Operators" 1973, typewriting speed test 1973; author: Doctoral Dissertation, "A Comparative Analysis of National Employment Patterns as Perceived by Minority and Non-minority Bachelor Degree, Bus Education, Graduates of 1972," 1973. **Business Addr:** Professor of Business, Rust College, 150 Rust Ave, Holly Springs, MS 38635.

SMITH, NORMAN RAYMOND
Publisher. **Personal:** Born Nov 17, 1944, New Orleans, LA; married Patricia A. Smith; children: Corey Norman, Christopher Jude. **Educ:** Southern Univ at New Orleans, BA History, 1994; Commonwealth Coll of Science, Mortuary Science 1966; Southern Univ at New Orleans, BS, 1994. **Career:** Treme Improvement Political Soc, pres/chmn of bd 1970-; Upper Pontalba Bldg Commn, mem 1980-88; Treme Cultural Enrichment Progs, secty; LA Black Culture Commn, exec bd mem 1984-88; Forget-Me-Knots Inc, pres/chmn of bd. **Orgs:** Mem New Orleans Embalmers Assoc 1966-; mem Armstrong Park Adv Comm 1983-88; grand knight Knights of Peter Claver-Thomy Lafon Council #240 1986-89; treas Greater New Orleans Black Tourism Ctr 1986; exec dir Treme Community Education Program, 1996-. **Honors/Awds:** Fellow Loyola Univ Inst of Politics 1979; publisher of "Etches of Ebony Louisiana," annual Black LA history caldenar, 1983-, incl current issue 1995. **Military Serv:** AUS sgt 1967-69; Good Conduct Medal, Vietnam Campaign Medal. **Home Addr:** 4653 Tulip St, New Orleans, LA 70126. **Business Addr:** President, Forget-Me-Knots Inc, PO Box 7332, New Orleans, LA 70186, (504)241-7179.

SMITH, OBRIE
Foundation pres. **Educ:** Lincoln Univ, BS, MA. **Career:** Pres, NC A&T University Foundation Board, Inc, currently. **Orgs:** Former vice pres, bd mem, Waukesha County NAACP; bd mem, United Way; National Hispanic Univ; Milwaukee Enterprise Ctr; Charlotte Meckleburg Ministries. **Military Serv:** US Army, 1965-67.

SMITH, ORLANDO. See SMITH, TUBBY.

SMITH, OSCAR A., JR.
Supermarket chain executive. **Career:** Community Foods Inc, CEO, currently. **Honors/Awds:** Co. is ranked #18 on Black Enterprise magazine's list of top 100 industrial/service companies, 1992. **Business Addr:** Chief Executive Officer, Community Foods Inc, 2936 Remington Ave, Baltimore, MD 21211, (301)235-9800.

SMITH, OSCAR SAMUEL, JR.
Business executive. **Personal:** Born Aug 5, 1929, Raleigh, NC; son of Sarah Smith and Oscar Smith Sr; married Gloria K; children: Robin Swinson, Oscar S III. **Educ:** St Augustine's Coll Raleigh, BA 1955; Univ of MD, MA 1968; Univ of NC, Inst of Gov't 1978. **Career:** US Info Agency DC, info specIsts 1956-65; Urban Renewal Auth MD, asso dir 1965-68; Shaw U, dir u rel 1968-72; Capitol Broadcast Co, cap news anchor/reporter 1972-77; NC Dept of Ins, dir pub affairs 1977-85; Creative Communications, pres/chrmn of the bd. **Orgs:** Pub rel consult United Communities Against Poverty 1968; pub rel consult Wk Co Sr Citizens Office 1977; minority affairs advisor Am Coll Pub Rel Assn 1972; NC State Univ Publ Rel Adv Bd 1977; mem NC Black Political Cacus; mem Wake Co Black Political Action Comm; mem St Paul's AME Ch; vice chair, board of directors, Helping Hand Mission, 1990-; Alpha Phi Alpha Fraternity, 1967-; Raleigh, Wake Citizen Assn, Legislative Review, 1978-; North Carolina/South Carolina Public Relations Society 1985-. **Honors/Awds:** Excell in Publications Am Coll Pub Rel Soc; Journalism Hall of Fame NC; Disting Serv Award St Augustine's Coll; Disting Serv Award Prince George's Co MD; Genious Gold Cup, Advertising/Marketing. **Military Serv:** AUS splst 2nd class, 1955-57; Served in Armed Forces Radio Network 7th Inf Div Hdqtrs.

SMITH, OSWALD GARRISON
Physician (retired). **Personal:** Born Sep 4, 1915, Vicksburg, MS; son of Mr & Mrs Perry Smith; married Millie (deceased). **Educ:** Meharry Med Coll, MD 1940. **Career:** Queens Hosp Ctr, asso atdng anesthesiologist; State Univ NY, asso clinical prof, Misericordia Hosp, acting dir anesth dept 1962; Bronx VA Hosp, resd anesth 1959-61; physician gen prac 1946-59. **Orgs:** Alpha Phi Alpha Frat; NAACP; Am Soc Anesthes; AMA; Nat Med Assn Chmn PM Smith Meml Schlrsp Com Diplomat Am Bd Anesthes 1964. **Honors/Awds:** Flw Am Coll Anesthes 1962; 1st black mem MS State Med Soc 1956. **Military Serv:** AUS MC 1st lt 1942-46.

SMITH, OTIS
Professional football player. **Personal:** Born Oct 22, 1965, New Orleans, LA; married Sandy. **Educ:** Missouri. **Career:** Philadelphia Eagles, defensive back, 1991-94; New England Patriots, 1995-96; New York Jets, 1997-. **Business Addr:** Professional Football Player, New York Jets, 1000 Fulton Ave, Hempstead, NY 11550, (516)560-8100.

SMITH, OTIS BENTON, JR.
Clergyman. **Personal:** Born Nov 5, 1939, Lexington, KY; son of Hattie Bibbs Smith and Otis B Smith Sr (deceased); married Bertha Odessa Stevenson; children: Otis III, Patrick Tyrone, Kenise Lynette. **Educ:** Central State Univ, BS 1960; So Baptist Theol Sem, MDiv 1969, Certificate of Merit 1984; Univ of North AL, Certificate of Continuing Educ 1985. **Career:** Natl Jewish Hosp Pediatric Sect, recreation supr & coun 1964-65; E Moline State Hosp, recreation supr 1965-66; WV Hosp Dayton, recreation spl 1966; Fifth St Baptist Ch Louisville, asst to pastor 1966-69; First Bapt Church, pastor 1969-. **Orgs:** Instr Sch of Religion N AL Bapt Acad-Courtland AL 1970-73; conv mem bd trustees Selma Univ 1973-; lecturer & Sect N AL Bapt Ministers Conf 1976-79; vice moderator Muscle Shoals Bapt Dist Assn of AL 1983-85; pres Muscle Shoals Bapt SS and BTU Congress 1981-90; lecturer AL Bapt State Conv Ministers Seminar 1980-; exec mem bd dir Muscle Shoals Area Mental Health 1971-; vice chmn bd dir Muscle Shoals Area Mental Health Cen 1983-85; exec mem bd dir Colbert Lauderdale Comm Action Agency 1973-79; 1st Black mem bd dirs Shoals Hosp 1980-82; mem NAACP, Kappa Alpha Psi, AL Bapt State Conv, NBC Inc; chmn bd of dirs Muscle Shoals Area Mental Health Ctr 1985-87; advisory council Shoals Community College 1987-; asst sec, Natl Baptist Convention USA INC, 1988-94; general secretary, Alabama State Missionary Baptist Convention, 1995-. **Honors/Awds:** Minister of the Yr NAACP Muscle Shoals AL 1976; Minister of the Yr Alpha Pi Chap Omega Psi Phi 1979; Spl Cert of Recog Tri County Branch of NAACP 1979; Citizen of the Yr Alpha Pi Chap Omega Psi Phi 1983; Honorary Doctorate of Divinity Degree, Selma University, 1991; Top Hatters Club Inc, Minister of the Year, 1987. **Military Serv:** AUS 1st lt 1960-64; Commendation Medal. **Home Addr:** 506 E 7th St, PO BOX 544, Tuscumbia, AL 35674. **Business Addr:** Pastor, First Baptist Church, 611 S High St, Tuscumbia, AL 35674.

SMITH, OTIS FITZGERALD
Professional basketball player. **Personal:** Born Jan 30, 1964, Jacksonville, FL. **Educ:** Jacksonville Univ, Jacksonville, FL, 1982-86. **Career:** Denver Nuggets, 1986-87; Golden State Warriors, 1988-89; Orlando Magic, 1989-. **Business Addr:** Professional Basketball Player, Orlando Magic, One Magic Place, Orlando, FL 32801.

SMITH, OTRIE (O. B. HICKERSON)
Psychiatrist. **Personal:** Born Mar 17, 1936, Coffeyville, KS; married Robert A Sr; children: Claude, Donna, Robert Jr. **Educ:** Howard U, BS 1958; Howard Univ Coll of Med, MD 1962; Kings Co Hosp, intnsp 1962-63; Menatl Hlth Inst, res 1963-66. **Career:** Jackson-hinds Comprehensive Hlth Ctr, dir mental 1970-; Am & Psychiat Assn, obsvr consult 1974-75; Univ Med Ctr, instr 1969-; Tougaloo Coll, 1969-72; VACtr, staff mem 1969-70; Area B Comm Hlth Ctr, chf 1967-69; Menninger Found, staff mem 1966-67. **Orgs:** Mem Minority Mental Hlth Ctr of the NIMH; Nat Med Assn; AMA; Am Psychiat Assn; Com of Black Psychiat; MS Med Assn; MS State Dept of Mental Hlth; Delta Sigma Theta Sor Consult Tougaloo Coll; friends of childredn of MS Head Start Proj; bd mem Hinds Co Proj Head Start; fld instr Jackson State U;Tougaloo Coll. **Business Addr:** 1134 Winter St, Jackson, MS 39203.

SMITH, OZZIE (OSBORNE EARL)
Professional baseball player (retired). **Personal:** Born Dec 26, 1954, Mobile, AL; married Denise Jackson; children: Osborne Earl Jr, Justin Cameron. **Educ:** California Polytechnic State Univ, San Luis Obispo, CA, attended. **Career:** San Diego Padres, shortstop, 1978-81; St Louis Cardinals, shortstop, 1982-96. **Orgs:** Worker for charity causes including Red Cross, Multiple Sclerosis, March of Dimes and Annie Malone Childrens Home; pres Cncl on Drug Abuse; natl spokesman for CPR. **Honors/Awds:** 13 Golden Glove Awds, 1980-92; voted to United Press Intl & Sporting News NL Post Season All Star Team in 1982; St Louis Baseball Man of Yr 1982; Father of the Year, National Father's Day Comm; National League All-Star Team, 1982, 1984-87; Smith's No. 1 jersey retired. **Business Addr:** Retired Professional Baseball Player, St Louis Cardinals, Busch Memorial Stadium, 250 Stadium Plaza, St Louis, MO 63102.

SMITH, PATRICIA G.
Senior executive. **Personal:** Born Nov 10, 1947, Tuskegee, AL; daughter of Wilhelmina R Griffin Jones and Douglas Jones Sr; married J Clay Smith Jr, Jun 25, 1983; children: Stager C, Michelle L, Michael L, Eugene Grace. **Educ:** Wesleyan Coll, acad exchange prog 1964; Univ of MI, acad exchange prog 1965; Tuskegee Inst, BA English 1968 (upper 10th of class); Auburn Univ, compl grad courses masters prog English 1969-71; Harvard Univ Grad Sch of Bus Admin, Broadcast Mgmt Dev Course 1976; George Washington Univ, Telecomm Policy Course 1984; Federal Executive Institute, 1997. **Career:** Tuskegee Inst, instr dept of English 1969-71; Curber Assoc, program mgr 1971-73; Natl Assn of Broadcasters, dir of placement 1973-74, dir of community affairs 1974-77; Group W Westinghouse Broadcasting Co WJZ Television, associate producer 1977, producer 1977-78; Sheridan Broadcasting Network, dir of affiliate relations and programming 1978-80; FCC, Office of Public Affairs, chief consumer assist & small business div 1980-92, associate managing director for public information and reference services, deputy director for policy, 1992-94; US Department of Transportation, Office of Commercial Space Transportation, associate managing director, 1994-95; FAA Office of Assoc Admin for Commercial Space Transportation, acting assoc admin, 1995-. **Orgs:** Trustee Natl Urban League 1976-81; vice chairperson Natl Conf of Black Lawyers Task Force on Communications 1975-; mem Communications Comm Cancer Coord Council 1977-84; mem Braintrust Subcommittee on Children's Prog Congress Black Caucus 1976-; mem Lambda Iota Tau Intl Hon Soc; mem Adv Bd Black Arts Celebration 1978-83; mem Journalism & Communications Adv Council Auburn Univ 1976-78; mem Amer Women in Radio and TV 1973-77; interim chairperson Intl Broadcasting Comm Natl Assn of Television and Radio Artists 1974; mem Natl Adv Comm Women in Communications Inc; mem Cert Prog in Communications Mgmt and Tech 1974-76; bd dirs The Broadcasters Club; mem AL State Soc 1984-; mem Washington Urban League 1983-; mem NAACP 1983-; mem DC Donor Project Natl Kidney Found of Natl Capital Area 1984-; board of advisors, Salvation Army, 1992-. **Honors/Awds:** Distinguished Alumnus Award, Tuskegee Univ, 1996; Sustained Superior Performance Awd 1981-91; commnr 1986-87, chair 1987-91, District of Columbia Commn on Human Rights; National Performance Review Award, 1994. **Home Addr:** 4010 16th St, NW, Washington, DC 20011. **Business Addr:** Acting Associate Administrator, Commercial Space Transportation, FAA, US Department of Transportation, 7th & Independence Ave SW, Rm 331, Washington, DC 20591.

SMITH, PAUL
Clergyman. **Personal:** Born Sep 20, 1935, South Bend, IN; married Frances Irene Pitts; children: Kathleen, Heather, Krista. **Educ:** Talladega Clge, AB 1957; Hartford Sem, MDiv 1960; Eden Theological Sem, DMin 1977. **Career:** WA Univ, assc vice chancellor 1974-78; Morehouse Coll, vice pres 1978-79; Columbia Theological Sem, adjunct prof 1979-; Candler School of Theology, adjunct prof 1979-; Hillside Presb Church, pastor. **Orgs:** Trustee Presby Schl of Christian Educ 1981-; consult Howard Thurman Educ Trust 1982; bd mem Child Srv Family Cnslng 1983-; Metro Fair Housing Srv Inc 1981-; Ldrshp Atlanta 1981; mem Council Atlanta Presb; former mem State Adv Comm US Civil Rights Comm 1977-1983. **Honors/Awds:** NEH Recepient 1982; publ Unity, Diversity, Inclusiveness 1985; book J Knox Press Theology in a Computerized World 1985-86. **Business Addr:** Pastor, Hillside Presb Church, 1879 Columbia Dr, Decatur, GA 30032.

SMITH, PAUL BERNARD
Priest. **Personal:** Born Sep 29, 1931, Baltimore, MD. **Educ:** Loyola Coll, BS 1956; Univ of Scranton, MA 1969. **Career:** Ordained priest 1962; Catholic Univ of Amer; Notre Dame Seminary; Malcolm X Coll, Chicago IL, English instr; Holy Angels School, Chicago, principal 1970-; Menard Central High School Alexandria, 1968-70; Holy Ghost Church & School & Marksville, asst curate & teacher 1962-67; Dept of Health &

Welfare, 1955-56. **Honors/Awds:** Tolton Award from Archdiocese of Chicago. **Business Addr:** 545 E Oakwood Blvd, Chicago, IL 60653.

SMITH, PAUL M., JR.
Educator (retired). **Personal:** Born Aug 10, 1920, Raleigh, NC; married Eleanor Jane Lewis, Dec 7, 1972. **Educ:** St Augustine's Coll, BA 1941; NC Central Univ, BLS 1947; Univ IL, MLS 1949; Indiana Univ, EdD 1957. **Career:** Shepard High School, teacher, 1941-42; Shaw University, assistant librarian, 1947-48; Dillard University, head librarian/instructor, 1950-53; Claflin College, head librarian, 1954-55; A & T State University, chief librarian, 1957-58; Albany State Coll, prof 1958-59; SC State Coll, prof 1959-60; NC Central Univ, prof 1960-69; Columbia Univ, adj prof 1969-70; Univ of Cincinnati, prof Afro-Amer Studies/prof psychology, professor emeritus. **Orgs:** Mem Assn of Black Psychologists 1980-85. **Honors/Awds:** Licensed Psychologist OH 1973-; publns in many nationally known journals. **Military Serv:** USMC Pfc 1943-46. **Business Addr:** Professor Emeritus, University of Cincinnati, Cincinnati, OH 45221.

SMITH, PEARLENA W.
Educator (retired). **Personal:** Born Apr 13, 1916, Greenwood, SC; daughter of Margie Frances Owens and David Williams; married Dr William N Smith, Jul 4, 1957 (deceased). **Educ:** SC State Coll Orangeburg, BS & MS 1950-54; NYU, attended 1962-63. **Career:** Hudson Valley Community Coll, retired prof 1979-; Hudson Valley Community Coll, prof liberal arts 1970-78; Colonie Pub Sch NY, reading supr 1968-70; Teaneck Pub Sch NJ, reading supr 1964-68; Jersey City State Coll, asst prof 1962-64; NC Coll Durham, asst prof of educ 1959-62; Voorhees Jr Coll Denmark SC, asst prof of reading & dng 1957-59; FL Normal Coll St Augustine, dean of women & asst prof 1956-57; Columbia Pub Sch Sys SC, elementary tchr 1950-56. **Orgs:** Chmn Jr Red Cross Carver Elem Sch SCH SC 1950-56; mem of Pres Adv Com Hudson Valley Community Coll NY 1972-78. **Honors/Awds:** Publ article on reading Jersey City State Coll 1963.

SMITH, PERRY ANDERSON, III
Clergyman. **Personal:** Born May 16, 1934, Mound Bayou, MS; son of Elease Wilson Smith and Perry Smith. **Educ:** Howard Univ, AB 1955, MDiv 1958. **Career:** Comm Action of PG County MD, exec dir 1965-69; Natl Civil Srv League, assc dir 1969-72; Univ of MD, chaplain 1975-82; First Bapt Church Inc, pastor 1958-. **Orgs:** Treas Prog Natl Baptist Conv 1974-76, auditor 1978-80; bd dir NAACP Prince George's Co MD; Min to Blacks in Higher Educ, board of directors; vice pres Natl Conf of Black Churchmen; advisory board member, Family Service of Prince George's County; member, Ministries to Blacks in Higher Education; member, Concerned Clergy of Prince George's County. **Honors/Awds:** Hester V King Humanitarian Award, 1985; Outstanding Community Service, Prince George's County, Maryland NAACP; Outstanding Community Service, Progressive Baptist Laymen of Washington DC; Outstanding Community Service, Frontiers International; Outstanding Community Service, Metropolitan Washington Health and Welfare Council; Outstanding Service, University of Maryland NAACP; Outstanding Service, DC Women Ministers Assn; Outstanding Service, Community Action of Prince George's County Maryland; Achievement Award, Combined Communities in Action, Prince George's County Maryland; Metropolitan Service Award, Iota Upsilon Lambda Chapter, Alpha Phi Alpha Fraternity, Inc; Martin Luther King, Jr Award, Black Student Union, University of Maryland at College Park, 1976. **Home Addr:** 7956 Quill Point Drive, Bowie, MD 20720. **Business Addr:** Pastor, First Bapt Church Inc, 4009 Wallace Rd, Brentwood, MD 20722.

SMITH, PHILIP GENE
Human rights specialist, educator. **Personal:** Born Mar 3, 1928, Chicago, IL; son of Ruth Smith McGowan and S David Smith; married Elaine J Kehrer; children: Philip G Jr, Kelyn M. **Educ:** KY State Coll, BA 1949; Chicago Teachers Coll, BE 1953; Antioch School of Law, MA 1982. **Career:** Danville IL Human Relations Comm, dir 1976-77; Detroit Human Rights Dept, commn administrative coord 1977-86; Voters Organized to Educate, dir 1986-; Highland Park Community Coll, Highland Park MI, instructor political science 1987-96; Dekalb Coll, Clarkston, GA, 1997-. **Orgs:** Political editor Dollars & Sense Magazine 1976-; precinct delegate MI Democratic Convention 1980-88; mem Kappa Alpha Psi, MI Assoc Human Rights Workers; pres Ethnic Educ Rsch Corp; chairman, Michigan Progressive Democratic Organization, 1988-96; Georgia Progressive Democratic Organization, 1996-. **Honors/Awds:** Fred Hampton Scholarship Fund Image Awd 1986; 1st annual Frederick Douglass Award, Hope and Magnolia United Methodist Churches, Southfield MI, 1988; published article "One Step Forward/Two Steps Backwards-An Analysis of Progressive Politics", Independent Press, Detroit MI 1989; Tilden Tech High School, Inducted into the Hall of Fame, 1994. **Special Achievements:** "The Life and Times of Thurgood Marshall," Dollars & Sense, 1992. **Military Serv:** AUS pvt E-II 1 yr. **Home Addr:** 955 Hargett Court, Stone Mountain, GA 30083-2401.

SMITH, PHILLIP M.
Educator (retired). **Personal:** Born Jan 24, 1937, Vulcan, WV; son of Bernice Whaley Smith and Robert Smith; married Gloria J; children: Phillip Jr, Jeffrey M. **Educ:** WV State Coll, BS 1958; City Univ of NY, MA 1969; Educ Adminstrn, diploma edna; Hofstra U, permanent certification 1970; Univ of Massachusetts, EdD, 1987. **Career:** Dept Welfare, Childrens counselor 1958-59; Dept Parks, recreation leader 1959-60; Dept Hosp, recreation & dir 1960-; Wilkyck School for Boys, childcare specialist, supervisor 1962-66; Neighborhood Youth Corps, curriculum specialist 1965-66; Roosevelt Junior and Senior High School, science teacher 1966-69, director of adult education, 1969-70, director of reading program, 1969-70, asst prin, 1969-79, director of Multi-level Alternative Program, 1973-74, principal, 1979-88; Roosevelt School District, district director of supporting services, 1988-92; St John's Univ, Queens, NY, adjunct prof, 1992-. **Orgs:** Member, NAACP, Kappa Alpha Psi, National Assn of Black School Educators, National Assn of Secondary School Principals, School Administrators Assn of New York State, Roosevelt Administrators Assn; vice president, executive board, Long Island Assn of Supervision and Curriculum Development, 1988-; vice president, executive board, PLUS Group Homes Inc, 1980-; member, advisory board, House of Good Council, 1987-; executive comm, Nassau/Suffolk School Bd Assn, 1995-; trustee, Uniondale School Bd, 1991-. **Honors/Awds:** Cover photo for feature article "Black tennis" Tennis Mag Dec 1974; 15 yrs serv awd Health & Hosp corp.

SMITH, QUENTIN P.
Educator. **Personal:** Born Jul 30, 1918, Huntsville, TX; son of Ione and Paige; divorced. **Educ:** Chicago U, MA 1947; IN U, MS 1956. **Career:** Gary Comm Sch Corp, exec dir of sec ed; W Side HS Gary, educator; guid cnsl, educator 1957-. **Orgs:** Past pres Urb Leag of IN 1967; comm of Pks Gary 1964; pres Gary Hum Rel Comm 1966; pres Gary City Cncl 1969; vice pres Am Fed of Tchrs 1957; Lk Co Bd Pub Wlfr 1973; IN Cncl of Ed 1974; Gary Redev Comm 1970-72; lctr in urb studies IN Univ NW 1974; St Josephs Calumet Coll 1973; bd trust Calumet Coll 1968-; adv bd Bk of IN 1970-. **Honors/Awds:** Recip Gary Jaycees Good Govt Awd 1971; NEA Tchr in Politics 1970. **Military Serv:** USAF 1st lt 1942-45. **Business Addr:** Exec Dir Secondary Education, Gary Community School Corp, 620 E 10th Place, Gary, IN 46402.

SMITH, QUENTIN PAIGE, JR.
Business executive. **Personal:** Born Jun 18, 1951, Gary, IN; son of Juanita Smith and Questin P. Smith, Sr. **Educ:** Purdue Univ, BS 1972; Pepperdine Univ, MBA 1976. **Career:** Hughes Aircraft Co, consult mgr 1975-77; MCA Universal, consult mgr 1977-79; Great Western Savings, data processing mgr 1979-80; Gottfried Consultants Inc, dir 1980-83; The Denver Group Inc, CEO and pres 1983-; Data Line Service Company, director and co-owner. **Orgs:** Bd mem LA Urban League 1982-; bd mem US Genl Serv Admin 1983-86; dir Armstrong Data Serv Inc 1984-; Center fro Educational Achievement, dir 1986. **Honors/Awds:** Cert of Accomplishment Dunn & Bradstreet Financial Analysis 1974; Cert of Appreciation Youth Motivation Task Force 1980; Outstanding Young Man of America US Jaycees 1980.

SMITH, QUENTIN T.
Educator, health services administrator. **Personal:** Born May 1, 1937, Seaford, DE; son of Elizabeth Holland Smith and Carlton Smith; married Marjorie McCoy Smith, Jun 19, 1967; children: Candace, Jason, Michael. **Educ:** Fisk Univ, AB 1958-61; Howard Univ, MD 1963-67. **Career:** WMHC Fulton Cty, dir 1974-75; Mental Health Grady Hosp, dir outpatient child and adolescent 1977-82; Ridgeview Inst, dir child and adolescent serivces, supervisor of psychiatry residents & child fellows; Emory Univ, assoc prof; Morehouse Medical School, prof of clinical psychiatry, dir of 3rd & 4th yr psychiatric clerkships. **Orgs:** Amer Psychiatric Assn, fellow, 1971-; Amer Acad Child Psychiatry, 1974-; public affairs committee, GA Psychiatric Assn, 1986-95; Ridgeview Institute, peer review subcommittee, nominating cmte; Emory Univ, Department of Child Psychiatry, Speakers Bureau; Morehouse School of Medicine, student acad affairs & promotions committee, residency training committee mbr, mbr of student appeals cmte, library committee mbr; Children's Trust Fund Committee State of GA; clincial advisory committee, Ridgeview Institute; 100 Black Men of Atlanta Inc, community involvement committee; membership committee; Amer Orthopsychiatric Assn; Directors of Medical Student Education in Psychiatry; Academy of Psychiatrists in Alcohol and Addictions; Natl Medical Assn; GA Psychiatric Physicians Assn; GA Cncl on Child & Adolescent Psychiatry; Black Psychiatrists of America; Guate Education in the Biomedical Sciences Cncl, associate; Atlanta Chapter of Black Psychiatrists of Amer, pres; Black Psychiatrists of Amer, regional rep. **Honors/Awds:** Phi Beta Kappa Fisk Univ Nashville TN 1961, Beta Kappa Chi 1961; Woodrow Wilson Fellowship Univ of Chicago IL 1961-62; Natl Med Fellowship Howard Univ Washington DC 1963-67; Man of the Year Awd Fisk Univ 1961. **Business Addr:** Dir Child & Adolescent Services, Ridgeview Institute, 3995 S Cobb Dr, Smyrna, GA 30080.

SMITH, RACHEL NORCOM
Association executive. **Personal:** Born Dec 10, 1925, Portsmouth, VA; daughter of Madeline Loretta Smith and James Gordon Norcom Sr; married Arthur David Smith Jr, Jun 3, 1945 (divorced 1956); children: Barry Gordon, Henry Lanier. **Educ:** Hampton Institute, Hampton, VA, BS, 1944; University of Pennsylvania, Philadelphia, PA, 1956; Virginia Polytechnic & State Univ, Blacksburg, VA, 1974. **Career:** Journal & Guide Newspapers, Norfolk, VA, typist, 1943; Hampton Instituete, Hampton, VA, clerk typist, 1943-44; Portsmouth Public Schools, Portsmouth, VA, teacher/coordinator, 1951-75; Judege James A Overton, Portsmouth, VA, legal secretary, 1981-91. **Orgs:** National president, Girl Friends Inc, 1990-92; national secretary, Girl Friends Inc, 1979-81; national secretary, The Moles, 1988-92; member, board of directors, Auxiliary, Portsmouth General Hospital, 1990-; member, board of directors, Miller Home and Day Nursery, 1985-. **Honors/Awds:** Teacher Appreciation Award, Delicados, 1988. **Home Addr:** 2228 Lansing Ave, Portsmouth, VA 23704.

SMITH, RALPH O'HARA
Marketing executive. **Personal:** Born Oct 24, 1952, Houston, TX; son of Dorothy Smith and James Smith; married Adrienne Tucker Smith, Aug 6, 1977; children: Patrick, Christopher. **Educ:** University of Southern California, BS, marketing, 1975; Loyola University, Los Angeles, CA, MBA (cum laude), 1979. **Career:** Xerox, marketing manager; Pepsico, marketing director; Time Warner, marketing director; World of Curls Products, Inc, vice pres, marketing, 1988-.

SMITH, REGINALD D.
Educator. **Personal:** Born Feb 21, 1918, Baltimore; married Euzelle Patterson; children: Andrea, Pamela, Patrice, Regi. **Educ:** Hampton Inst, BS 1940; A&T Coll Greensboro NC State Univ Raleigh, grad work. **Career:** Hampton Inst, staff 1940-42; Chapel Hill City Schools, teacher asst prin 1942-. **Orgs:** Mem NCAE; NEA; NASSP; NC League & Municipalities; Triangle J Council Govts 1970-74; Civitan Chapel Hill; Chapel Hill Planning Bd 1959-65; bdalderman 1965-74. **Honors/Awds:** NC Hamptonian of Yr 1969; Chapel Hill Father of Yr 1970; masonic distinguished serv award 1971; mayor pro-tem Chapel Hill 1969-74; Martin Luther King Community Service Award, 1988; Chapel Hill Cariboro, Sertomian of Yr Award, 1993; Mental Health Association, Outstanding Service Award, 1983; American Cancer Society, Outstanding Service Award, 1991; Chapel Hill Jaycees, Outstanding Senior Citizen, 1991-92. **Military Serv:** CAC sgt 1944-46.

SMITH, REGINALD KEITH
Educational administrator. **Personal:** Born Mar 3, 1960, Kenansville, NC; son of Willie Lucille Miller Smith and Rayford Smith; married Lisa L Nelson-Smith, Apr 14, 1990. **Educ:** North Carolina Central University, Durham, NC, BA, 1982; University of Delaware, Newark, DE, MPA, 1984. **Career:** Department of Health and Human Services, Rockville, MD, public health analyst, 1981; State of North Carolina Govenor's Office, Durham, minority affairs assistant, 1982; University of Delaware, Newark, dorm residence director and nutrition monitor, 1982; North Carolina Central University, Durham, adjunct assistant professor, special assistant, internship coordinator, 1984-87; Durham County Government, NC, assistant to the county manager, 1987-88; North Carolina University, Durham, business operations manager, 1988-. **Orgs:** Salvation Army Boys Club Board of Directors, appointed member, 1988-; Youth Services Advisory Committee, appointed member, 1985-; Durham Scouting Roundup, zone chairman, 1984, 1986; Academic Help Center, contributing founder, 1986-89; NCCU Alumni Association, parliamentarian and public relations chair, 1984-88. **Honors/Awds:** Youth for Energy Independence and Histadrut, Israel US Youth Delegate, 1983; US Department of Education, Public Service Fellow, 1982-84; Duke UNC Women Studies, Rockefeller Fellow, 1985-86; NCCU Public Administration Program, Second-Mile Award, 1981-82. **Home Addr:** 3200 Victor Ave, Durham, NC 27707.

SMITH, RENETTA
Judge. **Career:** US Immigration and Naturalization Service, trial attorney, judge, currently. **Orgs:** Louisiana State Bar Association; National Bar Association; Illinois Judicial Council; Alpha Kappa Alpha Sorority, Inc. **Special Achievements:** Currently only female & first African-American in Chicago to hold the position of US Immigration Judge. **Business Addr:** US Immigration Judge, Executive Office for Immigration Review, 546 S Clark, Ste 646, Chicago, IL 60605, (312)353-7313.

SMITH, RICHARD ALFRED
Primary care specialist. **Personal:** Born Oct 13, 1932, Norwalk, CT; son of Mabel Smith and Julius Smith; married Lorna Carrier; children: Dirk Devi, Rik Balakrishna, Erik Dibnarine, Blake Andrew, Quintin Everett. **Educ:** Howard Univ, BSc 1953, MD 1957; Columbia Univ, MPH 1960. **Career:** US Public Health Service, medical dir 24 yrs; Peace Corps Nigeria 1961-63; Washington DC, deputy medical dir 1963-65; Dept of Health & Human Serv Office of Intl Health, chief office of planning 1965-67; MEDEX Prog Univ of Washington, prof & dir 1968-72; The MEDEX Group, School of Medicine, Univ of Hawaii, dir 1972-, primary care and health specialist, currently. **Orgs:**

Fellow Amer Coll of Preventive Medicine 1961-; mem Amer Public Health Assn 1963-; mem Inst of Medicine of the Natl Acad of Science 1972-; consultant World Health Orgn 1972-. **Honors/Awds:** William A Jump Awd Dept of Health, Educ & Welfare; Gerard B Lambert Awd Lambert Foundation 1971; Rockefeller Public Service Awd Princeton Univ 1981; Outstanding Service Award, Region IX, Department of Health & Human Services for Leadership in Developing the Physician Assistant and Nurse Practitioners Movement in the USA, 1992. **Business Addr:** 666 Prospect St, Ste 610, Honolulu, HI 96813.

SMITH, ROBERT
Physician. **Personal:** Born Dec 20, 1937, Terry, MS; married Otrie Hickerson Smith; children: 4. **Educ:** Tougaloo Coll, BA; Howard Univ, MD; Cook County Hosp Chicago, rotating internship; Postgrad Courses, Univ of TN, Harvard Univ, Univ of MS. **Career:** Tufts Univ Coll of Medicine, instructor dept of preventive med 1967-69; Meharry Coll, preceptor dept of comm & family med, area dir; Univ of MS, Sch of Family Med, part-time asst prof; Univ of IA, Coll of Med & Continuing Educ, preceptor; staff: Hinds General Hospital, chief of staff, 1989-90, MS Baptist Hosp, St Dominic-Jackson Mem Hosp; MS Family Health Ctr, dir; Univ of MS, asst clinical prof, 1975-; Brown Univ, School of Medicine, guest lecturer, preceptor, asst prof, 1989-; Central MS Health Services Inc, medical dir, 1979-. **Orgs:** Charter bd Jackson Urban League; founder MS Com for Human Rights; Amer Cancer Soc MS Div; MS Med & Surgical Assn; Amer Med Assn; Natl Med Assn; MS Med Assn; charter diplomate Amer Bd of Family Practice; exec comm & delegate, MS State Med Assn, Central Medical Soc, AMA; bd of dirs, membership chmn Arts Alliance of Jackson/Hinds County; former commnr MS Health Care Commn apptd in 1984 by Atty General Ed Pittman; phys adv comm on Child Health with MS State Dept of Health Jackson MS 1987; chmn, Natl Adv Bd, Margaret Alexander Natl Research Ctr for the Study of 20th Century African Americans, JacksonState Univ, 1989-; community adv bd, Bank of MS, 1990-; bd of dirs, MINACT Inc, 1991-92. **Honors/Awds:** 1st Solomon Carter Fuller Awd Black Psychiatrists of Amer; Physician Recognition Awd Amer Med Assn 1971; charter fellow Amer Acad of Family Physicians 1972; Physician of the Yr 1974 MS Med & Surgical Assn; Honorary LHD Tougaloo Coll 1974; Disting Serv Awd MS Med & Surg Assoc 1977; Man of the Year Natl Cncl of Church of Christ Holiness 1981; Outstanding Serv rendered to the Comm Awd Natl Cncl of Negro Women 1981; Outstanding Serv Awd for Medicine Jackson Links Inc 1983; Expressions of Excellence Awd MS Cultural Arts Coalition 1984; Medgar Evers Awd MS NAACP Chap Freedom Awds Banquet 1984; Disting Serv Awd for OutstandingContributions in Serv and Delivery of Health Care Natl Assoc of Med Minority Educators Southern Region 1985; Health Serv Awd Jackson Concerned Officers for Progress 1986ppreciation Awd Natl Caucus of Black Aged 1987; Role Model of the Year in the field of Medicine Citizens HS Student Develop Fund Inc 1987; Natl Citizen of the Year, Omega Psi Phi, 1990; Distinguished Community Service Award, MS State Medical Assn, 1990. **Business Addr:** Director, Mississippi Family Health Center Ltd, 1134 Winter St, Jackson, MS 39204.

SMITH, ROBERT, JR.
Clergyman. **Personal:** Born Oct 5, 1951, Pensacola, FL; son of Ollie Mae Hale Smith and Robert Smith Sr; married Cynthia Perkins Smith, Dec 23, 1972; children: Sherique Smith, Conderidge Smith, Terique Smith. **Educ:** Lawson State Junior Coll, Birmingham, AL; Jefferson State Junior Coll, Birmingham, AL; Miles Coll, Birmingham, AL; New Orleans Baptist Theological Seminary, New Orleans, LA, Master of Divinity. **Career:** Eastern Star Baptist Church, Birmingham, AL, pastor; Mt Tabor Baptist Church, Brent, AL, pastor; First Baptist Church, Mason City, Birmingham, AL, pastor; Bethel Baptist Church, Pratt City, Birmingham, AL, pastor; recording artist; New Bethel Baptist Church, Detroit, MI, pastor, currently. **Orgs:** Chmn, Mayor Young's 1989 Re-election Comm; bd mem, Greater Opportunities Industrialization Ctr; mem, continuing steering comm, Natl Bank of Detroit; mem, Detroit Economic Club; mem, SCLC, program coordinator, Detroit Chapter; SCLC bd mem, 2nd vp of Detroit Chapter NAACP. **Honors/Awds:** Councilman David Eberhard Outstanding Community Award, 1989; Outstanding Achievement Award in the Gospel Ministry, 1982; Sermon Album of the Year, WENN Radio and Clergy That Care, 1982; Singing Preacher of the Year, WENN Radio and Clergy That Care, 1982; SCLC Minister of the Year Award, 1992. **Business Addr:** Pastor, New Bethel Baptist Church, 8430 Linwood, Detroit, MI 48206.

SMITH, ROBERT CHARLES
Educator. **Personal:** Born Feb 12, 1947, Benton, LA; son of Blanch Tharpe Smith and Martin Smith; married Scottie Gibson Smith, Aug 31, 1972; children: Blanch, Jessica Scottus-Charles. **Educ:** Los Angeles City College, Los Angeles, CA, AA, 1967; University of California, Berkeley, BA, 1970; University of California, Los Angeles, CA, MA, 1972; Howard University, Washington, DC, PhD, 1976. **Career:** Columbia University, New York, NY, research associate, 1976-80; SUNY College at Purchase, assistant professor, 1975-80; Howard University, Washington, DC, associate professor, 1980-89; Prairie View A&M, Prairie View, TX, professor, 1989-90; San Francisco, State University, San Francisco, CA, professor, 1990-. **Orgs:** Amer Poli Sci Assn, 1976-; Acad of Poli Sci, 1976-; Natl Conf Black Pol Sci; Natl Congress of Black Faculty, 1988-; CA Black Faculty, 1990-. **Honors/Awds:** Ford Foundation Fellow, Ford, 1973-76; RCA-NBC Scholar, RCA/NBC, 1972-73. **Business Addr:** Professor, San Francisco State University, Political Science Dept, 1600 Holloway Ave, San Francisco, CA 94132.

SMITH, ROBERT EDWARD
Flight officer. **Personal:** Born Mar 7, 1943, Louisville; married Constance Evans; children: Dana M, Robert E, Jr. **Educ:** Univ Louisville, BA 1966. **Career:** Eastern Airlines, dir & chief pilot 1972-; Phillip Morris, supvr 1966-72. **Military Serv:** USAF capt 1966-71. **Business Addr:** Atlanta Harsfield Intl Air, Atlanta, GA.

SMITH, ROBERT H.
University chancellor. **Career:** Southern University at Shreveport, Shreveport, LA, chancellor, currently. **Business Addr:** Chancellor, Southern University at Shreveport, 3050 Martin Luther King Jr. Dr., Shreveport, LA 71107.

SMITH, ROBERT JOHNSON
Clergyman, educator. **Personal:** Born Sep 26, 1920, Chicago, IL; married Jennie Mae; children: Estelle, Everett, Renee, Robert II. **Educ:** Morehouse Coll, AB 1937; Theol Sch, BD, STM, DMin; Bryn Mawr Coll, MSW; Morehouse Coll & VA Coll, honorary DD. **Career:** Salem Baptist Church, minister 1956-; Philadelphia School Dist, counselor 1960-; Hill St Church & 1954-56; High St Church, minister 1946-54; VA Hosp, chaplain 1945-54; AUS, chaplain 1941-45. **Orgs:** Chmn bd of trustees Berean Inst; bd mem Abington Meml Hosp VA Coll; mem Rotary Internat; Omega Psi Phi; Acad of Certified Soc Workers. **Military Serv:** AUS maj 1941-46. **Business Addr:** Salem Baptist Church, 610 Summit Ave, Jenkintown, PA 19046.

SMITH, ROBERT L. T., SR.
Clergyman, writer, poet. **Personal:** Born Dec 19, 1902, Hinds County, MS; son of Tresa Shuler Smith and James Smith; married Annie Louise Mason Smith (deceased); children: Ann Willis, Mary Peters, Roberta Atkins, Robert L T, Edward, Tresa Teague, Gloria Craven, Lawrence, Royce, Jerelyn. **Educ:** Jackson College; Alcorn College. **Career:** Oak Grove Baptist Church, pastor. **Orgs:** Civil rights leader; mem United Negro Coll Fund, MS Free Press Assn, NAACP, The Urban League Bd of Dirs Mississippi Action for Progress (administers head start programs); started Head Start Programs in MS & elsewhere in US; started Job Corps Program in MS. **Honors/Awds:** Man of the Year, Kappa Alpha Psi, Omega Psi Phi, Phi Beta Sigma; listed in Newsweek's 100 Most Influential Blacks in the US; chmn Civil Rights Movement State of MS; First Black to run for US Congress in MS since reconstruction thereby encouraging blacks to vote and political participation; Resolution Commending Outstanding Civic Leadership from MS State Legislature March 1985; Award of Distinction, Univ of MS, 1987; Omicron Delta Kappa, 1987; Struggle for Freedom for All, 1989; Honorary Doctorate of Humane Letters, Tougaloo College, 1980. **Business Addr:** Pastor, Oak Grove Baptist Church, 1253 Valley St, Ste 6, Jackson, MS 39203.

SMITH, ROBERT LAWRENCE, SR.
Educator, coach. **Personal:** Born Jul 11, 1923, Portsmouth, VA; son of Lula J Boone Smith and Frank L Smith; married Wilhelmenia Dawson; children: Robert L Jr (deceased). **Educ:** West Virginia State College, BS, mathematics, 1947; Columbia University, MA, health and physical education, 1955. **Career:** Bruton Heights High School, Williamsburg, VA, teacher/coach, 1948-50; I C Norcom, Portsmouth, VA, teacher/coach, 1950-69; Norfolk State University, physical education instructor, 1969-88. **Orgs:** President, HRBO; president, Hampton Roads Chapter, West Virginia State College Alumni; member, Zeta Iota Chapter, Omega Psi Phi Fraternity. **Honors/Awds:** Coach of the Year, Eastern District Basketball; Coach of the Year, Eastern District; Outstanding Tournament Coach, 1971; I C Norcom, Hall of Fame, 1986; West Virginia State College, Hall of Fame, 1987. **Home Addr:** 207 Wynn St, Portsmouth, VA 23701.

SMITH, ROBERT LONDON
Educator, political scientist. **Personal:** Born Oct 13, 1919, Alexandria, LA; son of Lillie Roberts Smith and Daniel C Smith; married Jewel Busch; children: Jewel Smith Feist, Robert London Jr, Karl Busch. **Educ:** Yale Univ, diploma 1944; Air Univ, diploma 1952; Coll of St Joseph, BA 1954; Univ of OK, MA 1955; The Amer Univ Wash DC, PhD 1964. **Career:** Hdqrs Office Aerospace Rsch Wash, asst dep chief of staff material 1960-62; Office of Sci Rsch Wash, asst exec dir 1963-65; Natl Acad of Sci, dir AFOSR post doctoral rsch prog 1964; Univ AK, assoc prof & dept head 1965-67; Univ AK, dean coll of bus econ & govt 1968-70, prof & head dept of polit sci 1970-80; Governor's Cabinet State of AK, commr dept of health & social serv 1983-84; Univ of AK, prof of polit sci emeritus 1984. **Orgs:** Mem Natl Acad of Polit Sci 1957; mem Natl Inst for Social & Behavioral Sci 1961; fellow and scientist AAAS 1964; mem Natl Inst for US in World Affairs 1964; mem Amer Polit Sci Assn 1965-80; educ commr AK C of C 1967; mem Men of Achievement Cambridge England 1974; mem Rsch & Advance Study Council Univ of AK 1968-70; mem Acad Council Univ of AK 1968-70; committeeman-at-large Natl Council Boy Scouts of Amer 1970-72; mem AK Govt Employment Commn; pres Fairbanks USO Council; bd dirs Artic First Fed Svgs & Loan Assn; corporator Mt McKinely Mutual Savs Bank; Governor's Cabinet, Rotary, Fairbanks Chap, 1981-84. **Honors/Awds:** Natl Polit Sci Honor Frat Pi Sigma Alpha 1962; Silver Beaver Awd Boy Scouts of Amer 1970; Outstanding Educ Awd NAACP 1970; Outstanding Prof Univ of AK 1974-75; Outstanding Educator of Amer 1975; Natl Social Science Honor, Pi Gamma Mu, 1962; American Assoc for the Advancement of Science, Fellow. **Military Serv:** USAF Lt Col 25 yrs; Commendation Medal Meritorious Serv 1956. **Business Addr:** Smithalaska, 100 Goldizen Avenue, Fairbanks, AK 99709-3436.

SMITH, ROBERT P., JR.
Educator (retired). **Personal:** Born Oct 12, 1923, New Orleans, LA; son of Leola Mitchell Smith (deceased) and Robert Smith Sr; married Arlette Marie Carlton, Nov 27, 1954; children: Arlette Therese Smith. **Educ:** Howard Univ, BA 1948; Univ of Chicago, MA 1950; DEU Univ of Bordeaux, France l953; Univ of PA, PhD 1969. **Career:** Talladega Coll, instructor French Spanish German 1953-54; Fisk Univ, asst prof French & Spanish 1954-58; Rutgers Univ, instructor, asst prof, assoc prof, chmn of French Dept 1965-73; assoc dean for academic affairs 1973-79; full prof 1984-89; emeritus l987-. **Orgs:** Mem Alpha Phi Alpha, Amer Assn of Univ Profs, Amer Assn of Teachers of French, Mod Lang Assn, African Lit Assoc; published articles in French Review, College Lang Assn Journal, Langston Hughes Review, Le Petit Courier, Celacef Bulletin, World Literature Today, Celfan Review; treasurer, College Language Assn, 1986-. **Honors/Awds:** Fulbright Fellowship to France DEU CEF Universite de Bordeaux France 1952-53; John Hay Whitney Found Fellowship 1958-59; NEH Summer Grant l981. **Military Serv:** USAF sgt 1943-45.

SMITH, ROBERT SCOTT
Professional football player. **Personal:** Born Mar 4, 1972, Euclid, OH. **Educ:** Ohio State. **Career:** Minnesota Vikings, running back, 1993-. **Business Addr:** Professional Football Player, Minnesota Vikings, 9520 Viking Dr, Eden Prairie, MN 55344, (612)828-6500.

SMITH, ROBERT W.
Auto dealer executive. **Career:** Bob Smith Chevrolet, Inc, Louisville, KY, chief executive. **Business Addr:** Bob Smith Chevrolet, Inc, 10500 Westport Road, Louisville, KY 40222.

SMITH, ROBERT W., JR.
Mathematician (retired). **Personal:** Born Apr 2, 1918, Philadelphia, PA; son of Henrietta Smith and Robert W Smith, Sr; married Helen C Harris; children: Robert III, Joyce Y, Derrick W. **Educ:** Temple Univ, AB 1941; Univ PA, MA 1948; Univ of Pittsburgh, post graduate work. **Career:** ADP Systems Br Pittsburgh Energy Tech Ctr, chief spec design & super; Authorization Systems Inc, regional dir 1981-; Carnegie Mellon Univ Pittsburgh PA Senior Lecturer Math 1954-71; Robert W Smith Enterprises, pres, 1981-95. **Orgs:** Mem Amer Assn Computing Machinery, Amer Assn for Advancement of Sci, Amer Soc of Pub Admin; mem & former vestryman Holy Cross Epis Ch Pittsburgh; past pres Homewood-Brushton YMCA; past mem exec bd & bd mgmt Pittsburgh Metro YMCA; past vice pres Pittsburgh Chap Amer Soc of Pub Admin; mem Kappa Alpha Psi; Minority Business Opportunity Committee, 1982-. **Honors/Awds:** Black Achievers Awd Pittsburgh YMCA 1973; Distinguished Serv Awd Pittsburgh YMCA 1972; Kappa Alpha Psi Pittsburgh Man of Yr 1966; Outstanding Achievement in Sci Pittsburgh Courier Newspaper 1962; Serv Awd from Pittsburgh Bd Public Educ 1965; YMCA Service to Youth Award, 1991. **Military Serv:** AUS 1941-46.

SMITH, ROBIN
Organization executive. **Educ:** Harvard Business School. **Career:** Investment banker; Goldman, Sachs & Co, corporate financial associate; One to One Partnership, vice pres of local mobilization, currently. **Orgs:** Dreyfus Corp, board of directors. **Special Achievements:** First African American, female, and youngest member to serve on the Dreyfus Corp board of directors.

SMITH, ROD
Professional football player. **Personal:** Born May 15, 1970, Texarkana, AR. **Educ:** Missouri Southern State College, degrees in economics and finance, general business, and marketing and management. **Career:** Denver Broncos, wide receiver, 1995-. **Honors/Awds:** Missouri Southern State College, Outstanding Graduate, 1994. **Business Addr:** Professional Football Player, Denver Broncos, 13655 Broncos Pkwy, Englewood, CO 80112, (303)649-9000.

SMITH, RODNEY
Olympic athlete. **Educ:** Bachelors' degree, criminal justice, 1988. **Career:** US Olympic Team, Wrestling Team, athlete, 1992. **Honors/Awds:** Olympic Games, individual wrestling competition, 68 kg Greco-Roman event, Bronze Medal, 1992;

US Olympic Wresting Team, Athlete, 1992, 1996. **Military Serv:** US Army. **Business Addr:** Olympic Athlete, Wrestling, US Olympic Committee, 1 Olympic Plz, Colorado Springs, CO 80909, (719)632-5551.

SMITH, RODNEY MARC

Professional football player. **Personal:** Born Mar 12, 1970, St. Paul, MN. **Educ:** Notre Dame, BA in economics. **Career:** New England Patriots, defensive back, 1992-94; Carolina Panthers, 1995-. **Business Addr:** Professional Football Player, Carolina Panthers, 800 Mint St, Ericsson Stadium, Charlotte, NC 28202, (704)358-7000.

SMITH, ROGER LEROY

Electrical engineer. **Personal:** Born May 15, 1946, New York, NY; divorced; children: Kim M, Lisa R, Shawnee L. **Educ:** Criminal Justice Nassau Comm Coll, AA 1975. **Career:** Federal Aviation Adminstrn/Flight Inspec, electronic technician 1976-; FAA, air traffic controller 1974-76; US customs, sec/patrol off skymarshal ; US Customs Bur, 1971-74. **Honors/Awds:** Comm pilot only black airborne tcchnician FAA Flight Inspec Div; mem 1st All Black Flight Insp Crew; vietnam serv medal USN. **Military Serv:** USN 2nd class petty ofcr 1966-69. **Business Addr:** Fed Aviation Adminstrn, FIFO NAFEC Bldg 301 Rm 407, Atlantic City, NJ 08405.

SMITH, ROLAND BLAIR, JR.

Educational administrator. **Personal:** Born Mar 21, 1946, Washington, DC; son of Annie Louise Smith (deceased) and Roland B Smith Sr; married Valerie V Peyton; children: Rovelle Louise, Roland Blair III. **Educ:** Bowie St Coll, BA Soc Anthro 1969; Univ of Notre Dame, attended 1969-70; IN Univ Sch of Pub & Environ Affairs, MPA 1976; Univ Notre Dame, Sociology 1978-80; Harvard Univ, EdD 1988. **Career:** Bowie St Coll, faculty asst sociology-anthro dept 1968-69; US Senate, intern/rsch asst 1970; PSC South Bend IN, dir of youth employment 1970-71; MAPC South Bend IN, manpower systems coord 1971-73; Univ of Notre Dame Proj Upward Bound, asst dir 1973-76 dir 1976-80; Center for Educ Oppor, dir 1980-83, 1986-92; Harvard Grad Sch of Educ, academic counselor 1984-86; Univ of Norte Dame, South Bend, IN, exec asst to the pres, assoc prof in sociology, 1988-96, freshman writing instructor, 1989-92; Rice Univ, Houston, TX, assoc provost, lecturer on education, 1996-. **Orgs:** Field reader DHEW US Office of Educ (Reg 5) 1977; bd dirs Mid-Am Assn for Educ Oppor Prog Personnel 1979-81; pres IN Assn for Educ Oppor Prog Personnel 1979-80; editorial bd Harvard Educ Review 1984-; exec bd Youth Serv Bur of St Joseph Co IN 1972-77; pres South Bend Branch NAACP 1975-76; IN Adv Com US Civil Rights Commn 1979-83; first vice pres Private Industry Council of St Joseph County 1990-92; exec committee Community Education Round Table 1988-91; chair, program committee, Minority Business Development Council 1990-92; chair, National Assn of Presidential Assist in Higher Educ, 1994-95; bd of dirs, Harvard Alumni Assn, 1995-; American Association of Higher Educ, Black Caucus, vice chair, 1995-97, chair, 1997-. **Honors/Awds:** MD State Senatorial School Awd 1968; mem Lambda Alpha Natl Anthropology Honor Soc 1969; Disting Serv Awd United Negro Fund 1974; Outstanding Achievement Awd Kappa Alpha Psi South Bend Alumni Chap 1976; Pres Citation Bowie State Coll 1977; Distinguished Alumni Award Indiana University South Bend School of Public and Env Aff, 1983; Phi Delta Kappa Harvard Chapter 1986. **Business Addr:** Associate Provost, Rice University, MS-3, 6100 Main St, Houston, TX 77005-1892.

SMITH, ROULETTE WILLIAM

Educator. **Personal:** Born Jan 19, 1942, New York, NY; children: Nicole Michelle, Todd Roulette. **Educ:** Morehouse, BS 1961; Stanford, MS 1964; MS 1965; PhD 1973; Univ CA San Francisco 1976-80. **Career:** Stanford U, research asst 1966-70; asst prof 1970-75; Univ CA Santa Barbara; BERD Univ CA, specialist assoc dir 1970-74; Inst for Postgrad Interdisciplinary Studies, dir 1984-; San Jose State Univ, asst dir, testing and evaluation, 1997-. **Orgs:** Pres Humanized Tech & Inc 1973-; editor Instructional Sci 1971-83; asso editor Health Policy & Educ 1979-83; sales mgr Stanford European Auto 1970-74; Consult Rand Corp 1970-74; Value Engineering Co 1973. **Business Addr:** Director, Institute for Postgrad Interdisc Studies, PO Box 60846, Palo Alto, CA 94306-0846, (415)493-0200.

SMITH, RUFUS HERMAN

Government official. **Personal:** Born Jun 23, 1950, Loudon, TN; married Patricia Ann Howse; children: Rufus H Jr, Courtney Danielle. **Educ:** Tennessee State Univ, BS 1972; Univ of Tennessee Knoxville, MS 1978. **Career:** TN Valley Authority, equal opportunity staff 1978-83; US Dept of Energy, equal opportunity manager 1983-. **Orgs:** Manager affirmative action program for Federal employees and direct minority educational assistance programs, including those specifically related to historically black colleges and universities. **Honors/Awds:** Alpha Phi Alpha. **Home Addr:** 304 Long Bow Rd, Knoxville, TN 37922. **Business Addr:** Program Manager, Equal Opportunity, PO Box E, Oak Ridge, TN 37831.

SMITH, SAM

City government official. **Personal:** Born Jul 21, 1922, Gibsland, LA; son of Mr & Mrs Stephen Kelly Smith; married Marion King Smith, Jan 29, 1947; children: Amelia, Carl, Anthony, Donald, Ronald, Stephen III. **Educ:** Seattle Univ, Seattle WA, BSS, 1951; Univ of Washington, Seattle WA, BA, 1952. **Career:** State of Washington, Olympia WA, state rep, 1958-67; City of Seattle, Seattle Wa, city councilman, 1967-. **Orgs:** Past mem, Board of Mgrs, Amer Baptist Churches USA; life mem, NAACP; mem, Seattle Urban League. **Honors/Awds:** Legislator of the Year Award, WA State House of Reps, 1967; Seattle Urban League Annual Award, 1968; Distinguished Alumnus Award, Seattle Univ, 1976; selected most outstanding public official, Municipal of Seattle and King County, 1985; Nat'l Conf of Christians and Jews recognition award, 1986; Booker T. Washington Award, Natl Business League, 1987; 1990 Links Distinguished Citizen, 33 Degree Mason. **Military Serv:** US Army, warrant officer jr grade, 1942-46; received Distinguished Service Award, Asiatic Pacific Medal.

SMITH, SHERMAN

Manufacturing manager, elected official. **Personal:** Born Apr 26, 1957, Earle, AR; married Odessa Pitchford; children: Margual, Sherman Jr. **Educ:** Draughon Bus Coll, Assoc in Bus Mgmt 1977. **Career:** Earle Jr HS, sub-teacher 1977-78; Halstead Indus Prod, storeroom supervisor 1981-. **Orgs:** Alderman City of Earle 1983-; minister of the gospel Earle Church of God in Christ 1983-; youth dept pres Earle Church of God in Christ; pres Student Govt 1976-77. **Honors/Awds:** Certified income tax preparer certificate from HR Block 1978. **Home Addr:** 215 Alabama St, Earle, AR 72331.

SMITH, SHIRLEY LAVERNE

Federal official, manager. **Personal:** Born Apr 2, 1951, Midlothian, VA; daughter of Thelma Draper Smith and Walter Smith. **Educ:** Virginia Commonwealth Univ, BS 1973. **Career:** Internal Revenue Service, clerk/tax examiner 1974-79, tax rep/tax specialist 1979-81, EEO specialist 1981-84, EEO officer 1984-88, recruitment coordinator 1988-92, personnel management specialist 1992-94; IRS Workers Compensation Center, manager, 1994-. **Orgs:** Northeast Region Undergrad Chap Coor Sigma Gamma Rho 1986-88; intl bd of dirs Sigma Gamma Rho Sor 1986-92; mem Federally Employed Women, Intl Training in Communication Clubs, Urgan League Guild, YWCA, NAACP, Richmond Jazz Soc, Assn for Improvement of Minorities-IRS, National Council of Negro Women; northeast regional dir, 1988-92, international secretary, 1992-94, grand antigrammateus, Sigma Gamma Rho Sorority, 1992-. **Honors/Awds:** IRS Communication Awd 1981; IRS Performance Awd 1984; Natl Achievement Awd Sigma Gamma Rho Sor 1984; Certificate of Appreciation Richmond Urban league 1982, 1984, Northeast Region Sigma Gamma Rho Sor 1984; Richmond Youth Serv Recognition Awd 1985; IRS Performance Award, numerous times, 1987-. **Home Addr:** P O Box 935, Midlothian, VA 23113.

SMITH, STANLEY G.

Attorney. **Personal:** Born Jul 21, 1940, Brooklyn, NY; married Ruth Grey; children: Craig, Carl. **Educ:** Seton Hall U, JD 1970; Rutgers U, BA Actg. **Career:** Urb Dev Res Inc, pres; Newark Hsng Dev & Rehab Corp, pres, chief exec ofcr 1980-; City Newark NJ, asst corp cncl 1972; Fed Prog Newark Hsng Dev Corp, att; Fidelity Union & Trust Co, fed asst, code enfor, fin analyst 1968-70; RCA, 1964-68; Seton Hall Univ Sch of Law, prof 1972-; Lofton Lester & Smith, att law prtnr 1985. **Orgs:** Mem Nat Bar Assn; concerned legal asso mem, bd dirs Nghbrhd Hlth Serv Corp 1972; bd dirs Voice Nwspr 1971-72; vice pres Phi Sigma Delta 1960; member, New Jersey State Bar Assn, 1990-91. **Honors/Awds:** On dean's list Rutgers Univ 1961-62; adjunct prof Seton Hall Univ 1972-; St Schlrshp (4 yrs) Rutgers Univ 1957; Hon Soc Seton Hall Law Sch 1967; Hon Schlrshp NJ Bell Elks Club. **Business Addr:** Attorney, Smith & Forbes, 1032 South Ave, Plainfield, NJ 07062.

SMITH, STARITA ANN

Journalist. **Personal:** Born Apr 23, 1949, Cincinnati, OH; daughter of Velma Anita Carter Smith (deceased) and Charles Thomas Smith (deceased); divorced; children: Emory K Rollins, Evan M Williams. **Educ:** Harvard Univ, Cambridge, MA, 1969-70; Knoxville Coll, Knoxville, TN, BA, 1970; Univ of TN-Graduate School Coll of Communication, Knoxville, TN, 1977-79. **Career:** CT Gen Ins Co, Bloomfield, CT, communications asst, 1974-77; Gary Post-Tribune, Gary, IN, reporter, 1979-82; Columbus Dispatch, Columbus, OH, reporter, 1983-85; bureau chief, 1985-88; Austin American-Statesman, Austin, TX, suburban ed, ed reporter, 1988-97. **Orgs:** Mem, Natl Assn of Black Journalists, 1985-; mem, American Mensa Ltd, 1991-93; former 1st vp, Central OH Chapter Society of Professional Journalists, Sigma Delta Chi, 1988; mem, OH Newspaper Women's Assn, 1983-88; Society of Prof Journalists, 1988-; Crohn's & Colitis Foundation of America, 1994-. **Honors/Awds:** Fellow, Knight Ctr for Specialized Journalism, Univ of MD, 1990, 1993; 3rd Place Award for Commentary Central OH Chapter, Sigma Delta Chi, 1988; Honorable Mention, Columbus OH Newspaper Women's Assn, 1987; Shared Award from Natl Council of Christians and Jews, 1980; Shared honorable mention for a team effort from the Associated Press Managing Editors of Texas, 1993. **Business Addr:** Reporter, Editorial, Austin American-Statesman, PO Box 670, Austin, TX 78767.

SMITH, STEVEN DELANO

Professional basketball player. **Personal:** Born Mar 31, 1969, Highland Park, MI. **Educ:** Michigan State. **Career:** Miami Heat, guard, 1991-94; Atlanta Hawks, 1994-. **Honors/Awds:** NBA All-Rookie First Team, 1992; Miami Heat, Most Valuable Player, 1993; NBA All-Star, 1998. **Special Achievements:** NBA Draft, First round pick, #5, 1991. **Business Addr:** Professional Basketball Player, Atlanta Hawks, One CNN Center, Ste 405, Atlanta, GA 30335, (404)827-3800.

SMITH, STEVIN

Professional basketball player. **Personal:** Born Jan 23, 1972. **Educ:** Arizona State. **Career:** Dallas Mavericks, 1996-. **Business Addr:** Professional Basketball Player, Dallas Mavericks, Reunion Arena, 777 Sports St, Dallas, TX 75207, (214)988-0117.

SMITH, SUNDRA SHEALEY

Health services administrator. **Personal:** Born Feb 9, 1948, Birmingham, AL; daughter of Eddie Griggs Harrell and John Shealey (deceased); married Marcellus L Smith Jr, Sep 9, 1978; children: Sonja Q, Stephanie M. **Educ:** Tuskegee Inst, Tuskegee AL, BS, 1970; Southern Illinois Univ, Carbondale IL, MS, 1973; Univ of Alabama at Birmingham, Birmingham AL, MPH, 1984. **Career:** Progressive Enterprises, Birmingham AL, owner, 1976-80; Alabama Christian Coll, Birmingham AL, instructor, 1981-83; Lawson State Jr Coll, Birmingham AL, instructor, 1983-86; Univ of Alabama at Birmingham, Birmingham AL, medical researcher, School Public Health, 1982-84, coord, Geriatric Medicine, 1984-86; Birmingham Reg Plan Comm, Birmingham AL, manager, Medicaid Waivers, 1987-90; AIDS Task Force of Alabama, Inc, exec dir, currently. **Orgs:** Mem, Natl Assn of Negro Business & Professional Women's Clubs Inc, 1974-, governor, SE Dist; mem, Omicron Omega Chapter, Alpha Kappa Alpha Sorority; sec, Birmingham Rose Soc; arbitrator, Birmingham Better Business Bureau, 1981-; mem, Amer Public Health Assn, 1982-, Alabama Public Health Assn, 1986-, Alabama Gerontological Soc, 1986-, Brown & Williamson, Kool Achiever Awards Screening Comm, 1986-89, Birmingham News Advisory Bd, 1986-88, Birmingham League of Women Voters, 1988-. **Honors/Awds:** Club Serv Award, Metro Birmingham Club, Natl Assn of Negro Business & Professional Women, 1986; Paper Presentation, Southern Gerontological Assn Mtg, 1986; Service Award, St Mark's Episcopal Church, 1987; District Service Award, Natl Assn of Negro Business & Professional Women, 1989; Appreciation Award, Better Business Bureau, 1989. **Home Addr:** 1569 Fairway View Dr, Birmingham, AL 35244.

SMITH, SUSAN L.

Educator, hospital administrator. **Personal:** Born Nov 15, 1959, Norfolk, VA; daughter of Rebecca J Smith and William L Smith. **Educ:** Grambling State University, 1992; Old Dominion University, 1989; Army Institute for Professional Development, US Army Training Support Center, 1988-91; Hampton University, Advanced Adult Nursing/Education, BS, 1987; Hampton Institute, AS, 1984; Norfolk State University, 1982. **Career:** 18th Field Hospital, USAR, Norfolk Virginia, coordinator of code blue team, 1985-92, assistant weight control officer, 1985-92, security clearance officer, 1986-92, head nurse ICU, 1986-92, CV Mosby Co, item writer, 1989-92; Nursing Educational Services, director, 1990-. **Orgs:** Virginia Community Colleges Association, 1990; Tidewater Heart Association, 1988; Association of Black Nursing Faculty in Higher Education, 1987; Sigma Theta Tau Society, vice pres, 1987; American Medical Detachment Regiment, 1987; National Association of Female Executives; numerous others. **Honors/Awds:** Honorary Army Recruiter Commander, US Army Recruiting, 1991; Promotion as a Reserved Commissioned Officer of the US Army, 1988; Achievement Award US 1st Army, 1987; Delta Iota Chapter, Sigma Theta Tau Honorary Nursing Society. **Special Achievements:** Guest Lectures: "Nursing Diagnosis and Process Evaluation: Implication for Nurse Managers," 1989. **Business Phone:** (804)484-2121.

SMITH, SYMUEL HAROLD

Business executive. **Personal:** Born Jun 1, 1922, Port Tampa City, FL; divorced; children: Cynthia D, Celeste D, Carmen D. **Educ:** Washington Univ St Louis, M of Hosp Admin 1965; Washington Univ St Louis, BS Bus Finance 1961; St Louis Univ St Louis, AA Pub Admin 1943. **Career:** ARSMARK Group Ltd, CEO, 1986-; Milwaukee Co Insts & Depts WI, dir beginning 1978; Detroit Gen Hosp, dir of hosps/Chf exec ofcr 1978; Wayne Co Gen Hosp MI, exec dir 1974-78; Morisania City Hosp Bronx, exec dir 1968-74; Edgecombe Rehab Cntr NY State Narcotic Addic Control Comm NYC, dir 1967-68; NY State Depart of Health NYC, hosp admin consul 1966-67; Bronx Muni Hosp Cntr Bronx, assist admin 1965-66; Flintgoodridge Hosp New Orleans, adminis resi & adminis assis 1964-65; Homer G Phillips Hosp St Louis, asst adminis 1952-63; City St Louis Depart Health 1950-52; Group Limited, Sales & Consultation, president, currently; ARSMARK Group Ltd, CEO & founder, 1989-. **Orgs:** Mem Am Hosp Assn; Fellow Am Pub Health Assn; mem Am Coll of Hosp Adminis; mem Nat Assn of Health Serv Execs; past first vP Hosp Exec Club of NYC; mem exec com Grtr Detroit Area Hosp Counc; mem MI State Arbitrtn Com; chmn Client Intervention Servs Syst

Subcom; hospadm consult City of St Louis MO; mem Naacp; mem Gov Coun Pub Gen Hosp Sec AHA mem Task Force on Nat Assess of Clinical Edu of Allied Health Manpwr Health Res Adminis DHEW Wash DC; mem Adminis Prac Comm Greater NY Hosp Assn; Cita Chi Eta Phi Sor Inc Omicron Chptr Oct 1970. **Honors/Awds:** Cita Morrisania City Hosp Employees Coun Feb 1971; cita Morrisania City Hosp Comm Licensed Prac Nurses of NY Inc Feb 1971; cita Employees of Morrisania City Hosp Oct 1971; Man of Yr South Bronx NAACP Nov 1971. **Military Serv:** US Army SSGT 1943-46. **Home Addr:** 3460 N Dousman, Milwaukee, WI 53212, (414)962-1381.

SMITH, THELMA J.
Savings & loan executive. **Career:** Illinois Service Federal Savings and Loan Association of Chicago, Chicago, IL, pres, chief executive, 1984-. **Orgs:** Chicago Theological Seminary; Community Renewal Society; North Carolina Mutual Univ of IL, business advisory council; The Chicago Network; The Links, Inc, Chicago Chapter; IL Service Federal Savings & Loan Assn; Chicago Sunday Evening Club, bd of trustees; Chicago Area IL Natl Guard and Comm Ctr of Influence, equal opportunity advisory council; Chicago Academy of Scis, bd of trustees; Chicago United, principal; Union League Club; The Congregational Church of Park Manor. **Honors/Awds:** Recipient NAACP Freedom Fund Dinner Award; Recipient, Black Book's Natl Business & Professional Award; Recipient, Dollars & Sense Magazine, Top 100 Black Business & Professional Women's Award; Recipient, Black Rose Award, 1989; Recipient, Top Ladies of Distinction, 1993; Ora Higgins Youth Fdn, Fdn Leadership Awd, 1993; Lovejoy Awd, 1995. **Business Addr:** Illinois Service/Federal Savings and Loan Association of Chi, 4619 S Dr Martin Luther King Jr Dr, Chicago, IL 60653.

SMITH, THIELEN
Collegiate football coach. **Personal:** Born Jan 23, 1954, New Orleans, LA; son of Helen Smith and McNorris Smith; married Cecilia Bonnett, Jun 11, 1982; children: Frank James, Toyah, Terrance, Temetria, Shaun. **Educ:** Louisiana State University, BS, education, 1977. **Career:** Warren Easton Senior High School, assistant football coach, 1977-78; Southwestern University, assistant football coach, 1979-84; Tulane University, assistant football coach, 1985-90; Louisiana State University, assistant football coach, 1991-. **Business Addr:** Asst Football Coach, Louisiana State University, Athletic Department, N Stadium Dr, Baton Rouge, LA 70803, (504)388-1151.

SMITH, THOMAS LEE, JR.
Professional football player. **Personal:** Born Dec 5, 1970, Gates, NC. **Educ:** University of North Carolina. **Career:** Buffalo Bills, defensive back, 1993-. **Business Addr:** Professional Football Player, Buffalo Bills, One Bills Dr, Orchard Park, NY 14127, (716)648-1800.

SMITH, TOMMIE
Athlete. **Personal:** Born Jun 12, 1944, Clarksville, TX. **Educ:** MS Phys Ed & Soc. **Career:** Olympic Team, sprinter 1968; Santa Monica; Coll, fac mem; Calohtex Inc LA, owner 1980. **Honors/Awds:** Holds world 200-m straightway & 220-yd straightway; AAU Champ 220-yd & 200-m 1967-68; Won NCAA San Jose State 220 yd 1967; Top ranked 200-m, 220-ys Man inthe World Track & Field News 1967-68; World Olympic Record Mexico City 1968; Held more world records simultaneously (13) than any other athlete in track & field Hist San Jose State Univ; Still holds World Track & Field Records in 3 individual events; Currently working on book to preceed movie of his life to be viewed on CBS 1980-81.

SMITH, TOMMIE M.
Business executive (retired). **Personal:** Born Jun 19, 1919, Pulaski, TN; married Eugene W Smith; children: Joe W London. **Educ:** Univ Louisville , 12 Hrs "Sucessful Mgmt of Indpendent Bus". **Career:** Tommie's Health Salon Inc, pres, retired in 1989. **Orgs:** Mem Am Massage & Therapy Assc Inc 1965-; mem Urban League Louisville 1982-; chrmn Voter Registration NAACP 1963-64; precinct capt 141-A 1974-84; first black chrmn 33rd Legislative Dist Dem 1984-; chrmn Political Action Com NAACP 1972-76; life mem NAACP; mem River City Bus & Profsnl Clb 1977-; first black mem Better Bus Bureau 1965; Commissioned KY Colonel 1974; mem Older Women's League 1982; pres KY Chap Massage Therapy Assocs 1983-87. **Honors/Awds:** Cert of Merits & Apprections Louisville Urban League Comm Vol Serv 1961, Ketuckiana Recruiting Serv 1971, Jefferson Cty Bd of Ed 1974, Gornr Cmsn to State Hlth Plng Cncl; Woman of Achvmnt River City Bus & Profsnl Women's Clb 1979; Achvr Awd Achievers AKA 1980; 1986 Black Women for Political Action Awd; 1986 Jefferson County Democrat Awd; first black owners of health salon in Louisville, Ky. **Home Addr:** 7104 Nachand Ln, Louisville, KY 40218.

SMITH, TONI COLETTE
Government official. **Personal:** Born Oct 31, 1952, Columbus, OH. **Educ:** Ohio State University, BA, 1974, management courses; University of Dayton, MS, 1993. **Career:** Ohio State Human Services, consultant, 1974-75; Columbus State Community College, instructor, 1990-91; Franklin County Human Services, caseworker, 1976-79, supervisor, 1979-86, administrator, 1986-91, assistant deputy director, deputy dir; Human Svcs, dep dir, 1996-. **Orgs:** American Association of University Women, corresponding secretary, 1988-; Berwick Civic Association, vice pres, 1989-91, president, 1991-; Syntaxis Residental Care for Youth, pres, executive board, 1990-92, 1996-98; United Way, admissions executive board, 1990-. **Honors/Awds:** Franklin County Human Services, Supervisor of the Year, 1983. **Home Addr:** 6740 Temperance Point St, Westerville, OH 43082. **Business Addr:** Deputy Director, Franklin County Human Services, 80 E Fulton St, Columbus, OH 43215, (614)462-3337.

SMITH, TONY (CHARLES ANTON)
Professional basketball player. **Personal:** Born Jun 14, 1968, Wauwatosa, WI. **Educ:** Marquette Univ, Milwaukee, WI, 1986-90. **Career:** Los Angeles Lakers, 1990-95; Miami Heat, 1995-96; Charlotte Hornets, 1996-. **Business Addr:** Professional Basketball Player, Charlotte Hornets, One Hive Dr, Charlotte, NC 28217, (704)357-0252.

SMITH, TOUKIE A. (DORIS)
Actress. **Personal:** Born in Philadelphia, PA. **Career:** Model, catering company owner; actress, currently. **Orgs:** President, Smith Family Foundation, founded in memory of brother renowned fashion designer Willi Smith who died from AIDS. **Honors/Awds:** Television: reoccurring role, "Miami Vice," NBC-TV; starring role, "227," NBC-TV, character artist, Eva Rawley; Movie: Me and Him, with Griffith Dunn; Talkin' Dirty After Dark with Martin Lawrence; co-host: "Joan Lunden Show". **Special Achievements:** Noted philanthorpist, art collector, political activist and renowned collector of African-American memorabilia.

SMITH, TUBBY (ORLANDO SMITH)
College basketball coach. **Personal:** chilDren: Orlando Jr. **Career:** University of Tulsa, men's basketball coach; University of Georgia, men's basketball coach, 1995-97; University of Kentucky, basketball coach, 1997-. **Special Achievements:** First African American head coach at the University of Georgia-Athens; guided the University of Tulsa's Golden Hurricane to the Sweet 16 in the NCAA men's basketball tournament; First African American coach at the Univ of Kentucky. **Business Addr:** Head Coach, Men's Basketball, Univ of Kentucky, Memorial Coliseum, Lexington, KY 40506.

SMITH, VASCO A.
Commissioner. **Personal:** Born Aug 24, 1920, Harvard, AR; son of Florence E Smith and Rev Vasco A Smith; married Georgia Maxine Atkins; children: Vasco A III. **Educ:** LeMoyne Coll, BS 1941; Meharry Med Coll, DDS 1945; TN Bapt Sch of Religion, LHD 1978; TX Coll, ScD 1983; Doctor of Science LeMoyne-Owen College, DSc, 1992. **Career:** Private practice, dentist 1946-; Memphis Branch NAACP, bd mem 1955-; Tri-State Bank of Memphis, bd mem 1970-; Shelby Co Govt, commr 1972-. **Honors/Awds:** Civil Rights Award Natl Dental Assn 1980; Merit Award Tennessee A&I Univ 1979; Merit Award West Tennessee 1980; Public Serv Award Memphis Urban League 1975; Citizen of Year Omega Psi Phi Frat 1968; Pres Award Meharry Med Coll 1970; Leadership Award IBPOE of W (Elks) 1969; Achievement Award OIC 1973; Merit Award NAACP 1961; Citation Congressional Record 1975; Citation Mallory Knights 1969. **Military Serv:** USAF cpt 1953-55. **Home Addr:** 1208 E Parkway S, Memphis, TN 38114. **Business Addr:** Commissioner, Shelby Co Govt, 1952 Lamar Ave, Memphis, TN 38114.

SMITH, VERNEL HAP
City official. **Personal:** Born Nov 12, 1924, Waycross, GA; divorced; children: Randy, Kevin. **Educ:** OH State Univ, BS; OH State Univ, MA. **Career:** US & Overseas Social Welfare, admin, lecturer, teacher, trainer; City of Oakland CA, mgr recreation serv 1966-74, dir office of parks & recreation 1974-. **Honors/Awds:** Outstanding & Dedicated Service Awd Natl Recreation & Park Assoc Ethnic Minority Soc 1984.

SMITH, VERNICE CARLTON
Professional football player. **Personal:** Born Oct 24, 1965, Orlando, FL; married Era; children: Alexandria, Vernice Jr, Mitchell. **Educ:** Florida A&M, attended. **Career:** Phoenix Cardinals, center, 1990-92; Chicago Bears, 1993; Washington Redskins, 1993-95; St Louis Rams, 1997-. **Business Addr:** Professional Football Player, St Louis Rams, One Rams Way, St Louis, MO 63045, (314)982-7267.

SMITH, VERNON G.
State representative. **Personal:** Born Apr 11, 1944, Gary, IN; son of Julia E Smith and Albert J Smith (deceased). **Educ:** IN U, BS 1966, MS 1969, Ed D 1978, post-doctoral work, 1986-90. **Career:** Gary Urban League's Operation Jobs, asst dir 1966; OEO's Operation Sparkle, asst dir 1967; John Will Anderson Boys Clb, stf asst 1967-68; Gary, IN Public Sch Systm, tchr 1966-71, resource tchr 1971-72; Ivanhoe Sch Gary, IN, asst prncpl 1972-78; Nobel Sch Gary, IN, prncpl 1978-85; Williams School Gary IN, principal 1985-; 4th district councilman, City of Gary, IN, 1972-90; state representative, 1990-; Indiana University Northwest, assistant professor, currently. **Orgs:** Pres tres Gary Downtown Merchants Assn; mem Gary Brnch NAACP; life mem IN Univ Alumni Assn; life mem Omega Psi Phi Frat; founder pres IU Gents Inc; founder pres IU Dons Inc; founder spnsr Focus Hope; founder spnsr Young Citizens League; founder spnsr Youth Ensuring Solidarity; mem Phi Delta Kappa Frat; pres Gary Comm Mental Hlth Bd; mem past pres Elem Prncpl Assn; mem Med Ctr Gary; vice pres NW IN Urban League; mem deacon, trustee, and teacher Pilgrim Bapt Chrch; mem Gary's Ed Talent Srch Bd; mem Little League World Series Bd; mem Gary Young Demo; pres, Gary Common Coun, 1976, 1983-84, vice pres, 1985, pres, 1986; chm, Gary, IN, City-wide Festivals Comm, Inc. **Honors/Awds:** GOIC Dr Leon H Sullivan Awrd 1982; Gary Community Mentl Health Ctr, Appreciation Award 1981, 10th Yr Service Award 1985; Mahalia Jackson Special Achvmnt Awrd 1980; Omega Psi Phi, Alpha Chi Chap Citizen of Yr Awrd 1980; Young Democrat's outstanding serv awrd 1979; Gary Downtown Merchants Businessman of Yr awrd 1979; Club FAB Outstndg Achvmnt citation 1978; Ebony mag most eligible bachelor 1977; Gary Jaycees, Good Govt Award 1977, Youth Award 1983;Omega Man Yr 1974; Omega Psi Phi 10th dist citizen of yr 1972, 1989; Outstanding Citizen of NW IN & Outstanding Educ Award, Info Newspaper, 1984; Blaine Marz Tap Award, Post Tribune, 1984; Focus Hope Dedication in Action Award, 1987; Gary Educator for Christ Administrator Leadership Award, 1988. **Home Addr:** PO M622, Gary, IN 46401.

SMITH, VIDA J.
Convention meeting planner. **Personal:** Born in Lynchburg, VA; daughter of Mary & Leo Jones. **Educ:** Central State Univ, 1976; Univ of the District of Columbia. **Career:** Natl Black Media Coalition, dir, black radio projects/meeting planner; Delta Sigma Theta, meeting planner, currently. **Orgs:** NCBMP; GWSAE; AMHIP, past vp; Coalition of Black Meeting Planners, bd mem. **Honors/Awds:** Meeting Planner of the Year, Coalition of Black Meeting Planners, 1996. **Business Addr:** Convention Meeting Planner, Delta Sigma Theta Sorority, 1707 New Hampshire Ave., NW, Washington, DC 20009.

SMITH, VINCENT D.
Painter. **Personal:** Born Dec 12, 1929, New York, NY; son of Louise Smith and Beresford Smith; married Cynthia Linton, Jul 12, 1972. **Educ:** Brooklyn Museum, 1954-56. **Career:** Painter one-man shows & exhibits; Whitney Mus Art Resources Ctr, instr 1967. **Orgs:** Illustrator "Folklore Stories from Africa" 1974; mem Natl Conf of Artists, African-Amer Museum Assoc, Audubon Artist, Natl Soc of Painters in Casein & Acrylics. **Honors/Awds:** Scholarship Showhegan School of Painting & Sculpture 1955; Brooklyn Museum Art School 1955-56; Fellowship John Hay Whitney Found 1959-60; Artist-in-Residence Smithsonian Conf Ctr 1967; Natl Inst of Arts & Letters Grant 1968; Childe Hassam Purchase Prize Amer Acad of Arts & Letters 1973,74; Thomas B Clarke Prize Natl Acad of Design 1974; Commd for 4 murals for New York City Bd of Ed 1975, "Impressions-Our World" Portfolio of Black Artists 1975; Participant 2nd World Black & African Festival of Arts & Culture, Lagos, Nigeria 1977; Artist-in-Residence Cite Des Arts Intl Paris France 1978; Mural Crotoma Ctr Human Resources Admin Bronx NYC; Collections Mus of Mod Art NYC, Newark Mus NJ, Brooklyn Mus NYC, Columbus Gallery of Fine Art OH; Commn Mural Oberia DDempsey Multi-Service Center for Cral Harlem NYC 1989. **Military Serv:** AUS pvt 1948-49. **Business Addr:** Artist, c/o Vicent D Smith, G W Einstein Co Inc, 591 Broadway, New York, NY 10012.

SMITH, VINSON ROBERT
Professional football player. **Personal:** Born Jul 3, 1965, Statesville, NC. **Educ:** East Carolina, bachelor's degree in communications, 1989. **Career:** Atlanta Falcons, linebacker, 1988; Dallas Cowboys, 1990-92, 1997-; Chicago Bears, 1993-96. **Business Addr:** Professional Football Player, Dallas Cowboys, One Cowboys Pkwy, Irving, TX 75063, (214)556-9900.

SMITH, VIRGIL CLARK, JR.
State senator. **Personal:** Born Jul 4, 1947, Detroit, MI; married Elizabeth Little-Smith; children: Virgil Kai, Adam Justin, Anthony Langdon. **Educ:** MI State Univ, BA Pol Sci 1969; Wayne State Law, JD 1972. **Career:** Justice Wade McCree US Appeals Ct, student clerk; Wayne Co Legal Svcs, legal advisor 1972-73; Model Cities Drug Clinic; Corporations Council City of Detroit; Michigan House of Representatives, state representative; Michigan State Senate, senator, Dem floor leader, currently. **Orgs:** Former finance, Family Law, Criminal Law & Corrections, and Reapportionment Cmtes; Law Revision Cmsn; Legislative Black Caucus; appropriations, subcommittes on Capital Outlay, Regulatory & Transportation; Families Mental Health & Human Svcs, judiciary, legislative council. **Honors/Awds:** Legislator of Year, Police Officers Association of Michigan & Michigan Judges Association, 1996. **Business Addr:** State Senator, Michigan State Senate, PO Box 30036, Lansing, MI 48909-7536, (517)373-7748.

SMITH, VIRGINIA M.
Educator (retired). **Personal:** Born May 9, 1929, El Dorado, AR; daughter of Annie Burks and Henry Burks; widowed; children: Marcia Green Hamilton, Gregory Green, Dana Paul

Green. **Educ:** Am&N College, BA, 1950; University of Illinois, MEd, 1955; University of Arkansas, 1963; Henderson State University, 1968, 1972; Arkansas State University, 1979; program management training, Title III, 1983, 1985. **Career:** Arkansas Public Schools, teacher, 1950-60; Southern University, assistant professor, 1963-65; El Dorado, counselor, 1965-70; Henderson State University, personnel dean, 1971-81, director of special services for disadvantaged students, 1982-86; Arkansas Baptist College, teacher of English, 1986-90. **Orgs:** Delta Sigma Theta; NAACP; Arkadelphia Women's Development Council; Ione Bynum Child Care Center, bd of dirs, 1992-; UAPB Alumni Assn, life mbr. **Honors/Awds:** Arkansas Baptist Clg, Teacher of the Year, 1989-90. **Home Addr:** 110 S Austin, PO Box 274, Arkadelphia, AR 71923.

SMITH, VOYDEE, JR.
Banker. **Personal:** Born Feb 14, 1949, Barton, FL; son of Fannie Colson and Voydee Smith; married Saundra Johnson, Jan 23, 1981; children: Daryl, Allen, Eric, Jason, Steven. **Educ:** North Carolina AT&T State University, BS, 1973. **Career:** US Dept of Treasury, asst bank examiner, Office of the Comptroller of the Currency, national bank examiner, 1973-85; Industrial Bank of Washington, senior vp, loan administration, 1985-95; Consolidated Bank & Trust Co, sr vp & loan administrator, 1995-. **Orgs:** Industrial Bank, management committee, 1986, loan officers committee, chmn, 1985, loan and discount committee, 1985; National Bankers Assn, 1989; Washington Area Bankers Assn, 1987. **Business Addr:** Sr. VP & Loan Administrator, Consolidated Bank & Trust Co, 320 North First St, Richmond, VA 23240, (804)771-5200.

SMITH, WALLACE CHARLES
Cleric, educator. **Personal:** Born Nov 6, 1948, Philadelphia, PA; married G Elaine Williams; children: Christen Ann. **Educ:** Villanova U, BA 1970; Eastern Bapt Sem, MDiv 1974; Eastern Bapt Sem, DMin 1979. **Career:** Eastern Bapt Sem, dir alumni affairs & asst dir field educ 1979-; Calvary Bapt Church, pastor; Prog Natl Bapt, home mission bd, 1979; Shiloh Baptist Church, pastor, 1991-. **Orgs:** Exec bd Chester Br NAACP 1974-; pres Chester Clergy Assn 1977-79; pres Chester Community Improvement Project 1979-. **Business Addr:** Pastor, Shiloh Baptist Church, 1500 9th St, NW, Washington, DC 20001.

SMITH, WALTER L.
Business executive, educator. **Personal:** Born May 14, 1935, Tampa, FL; married Jeraldine Williams; children: John, Andre, Salesia, Walter II. **Educ:** FL A&M Univ, BA Biology & Chem 1963, MEd Admin & Supv 1966; FL State Univ PhD Higher Ed Admin 1974. **Career:** Natl Educ Assn, assoc regional dir for NEA 1969-70; FL Educ Assn, admin asst 1970, asst exec sec 1970-73; Hillsborough Comm Coll, collegium dir 1973, dean employee relations 1973-74, provost 1974; Roxbury Comm Coll, pres 1974-77; FL A&M Univ, prof, president 1977-85; Education Development in South Africa, international team leader; Smith & Smith of Tallahassee Inc, president, currently; Univ of FL, visiting professor, currently. **Orgs:** Chairperson FL Supreme Ct Judicial Nominating Comm 1980-83; FL Supreme Ct Article V Comm 1983; chmn State Bd of Educ US Dept of Interior 1984; bd of dirs Natl Assoc for Equal Opportunity HE 1982-; bd dir Amer Assn of State Colleges and Univs; Urban League, chairman of the board. **Honors/Awds:** Red-X Awd Cape Kennedy IBM Corp 1966; Scholarly Distinction Awd Univs Urban League 1974; Meritorious Serv Awd Amer Assoc State Colleges & Univs 1984; Jackson Memorial Awd Assoc of Classroom Teachers 1984; Fulbright Senior Scholar 1985; Congressional recognition for international leadership. **Military Serv:** AUS sp-5 3 yrs; Commendation Medal; Natl Defense Medal; Good Conduct Medal 1953-56. **Business Addr:** Visiting Professor, Dept, Ed Leadership, University of Florida, 258 Norman Hall, Gainesville, FL 32611.

SMITH, WALTER T.
Dentist. **Personal:** Born May 25, 1927, Huntsville, AL; married Maureen; children: Shawn, Walter. **Educ:** Howard U, BS 1956; Meharry, DDS 1961. **Career:** Gary Ind, dentist private practice 1965-; Meharry Dental School, instr. **Orgs:** Mem Omega Psi Phi; ADA; Lincoln Dental Soc Chgo; NW Ind & IDA Dental Socs; NDA; Acad of Gen Dentistry; mem exec & adv Com NW Ind Sickle Cell Found; mem Gary Police Civil Serv Comm; mem United Fund. **Military Serv:** USN 1945-47; AUS 1953-55. **Business Addr:** 1706 Broadway, Gary, IN 46407.

SMITH, WARREN
Banker. **Personal:** Born Mar 12, 1949, New Britain, CT; son of Carrie Bell Morgan Smith and John Hardy Smith; married Pauline Angela Cain Smith, Jul 8, 1978; children: Marcus Alexander, Michael Warren. **Educ:** University of New Haven, BS, accounting, economics, 1972; Atlanta University, MA, economics, ABD, 1973; Babson College, MBA, finance, 1979. **Career:** Connecticut Bank & Trust, CT, credit analyst, commercial loan; New England Merchant, Boston, MA, loan officer, commercial; State Street Bank, Boston, MA, vice pres, commercial; Boston Bank of Commerce, Boston, MA, president, COO, currently. **Orgs:** Chair of ecomonics committee, Boston Urban Bankers Forum; committee finance group, Twelfth Baptist Santuary; chair, Boston Cultural Education; long range planning committee, The Cultural Ed Collaborative; sub committee comm development, American Bankers Association, 1990. **Honors/Awds:** South Shore Chamber of Commerce, Small Business Award, 1982; Boston Urban Bankers Forum, President Award, 1980; First Prize, Outstanding Citizens Award, 1989. **Business Addr:** President & COO, Boston Bank of Commerce, 133 Federal Street, Boston, MA 02110.

SMITH, WAYMAN F., III
Company executive. **Personal:** Born Jun 18, 1940, St Louis, MO; children: Kymberly Ann. **Educ:** Attended, Washington Univ 1957-59; Monmouth Coll, BS 1962; Howard Univ, JD 1965. **Career:** Missouri Commn on Human Rights, dir of concilliation 1966-68; Law Firm Wilson Smith Smith & McCullin, partner 1969; St Louis City Council, three-term alderman; City of St Louis, municipal court judge 1973-75; Anheuser-Busch Companies Inc, vice pres of corporate affairs 1980-. **Orgs:** Mem bd alderman City of St Louis 1975-; mem bd of dirs Anheuser-Busch Companies Inc 1981-; coord Lou Rawls Parade of Stars fund-raising telethon which benefits The United Negro College Fund; mem bd of admissions US District Court for the Eastern District of MO; mem ABA, Natl Bar Assoc, Mound City Bar Assoc; Bar Assn of Metro St Louis; Howard Univ, bd of trustees. **Honors/Awds:** Distinguished Alumni Howard Univ 1983;, Monmouth Coll 1983. **Business Addr:** VP, Corporate Affairs, Anheuser-Busch, One Busch Place, St Louis, MO 63118.

SMITH, WAYNE FRANKLIN
Organization executive. **Personal:** Born Feb 17, 1951, Providence, RI; married Debra Petrarca Smith; children: Marah Elizabeth Ann. **Educ:** BA, 1977. **Career:** Vietnam Veteran Readjustment Counseling Ctr, counselor; Vietnam Veterans of America, dir of membership, 1987-91; Vietnam Veterans Memorial Fund, dir of development, 1991-; The Black Patriots Foundation, president, 1996-. **Orgs:** National Veterans Legal Service Project, bd of dirs; Friends of the Vietnam Veterans Memorial, bd of dirs. **Military Serv:** US Army Medical Corp, spec 4, 1968-71; Combat Medic Badge; Army Commendation Medal, Vietnamese Cross of Gallantry, Vietnam Campaign. **Business Addr:** President, Black Patriots Foundation, Inc, 1612 K St NW, Ste 1104, Washington, DC 20006.

SMITH, WILL (FRESH PRINCE)
Actor, vocalist. **Personal:** Born 1968, Wynnefield, PA; son of Caroline and Willard; married Sheree Zampino (divorced); children: Will C. III; married Jada Pinkett, Dec 31, 1997; children: one. **Career:** Member of the duo DJ Jazzy Jeff & the Fresh Prince, beginning 1986; albums include: Rock the House, 1987, 1989; He's the DJ, I'm the Rapper, 1988; And in This Corner..,1989; Homebase, 1991; solo rapper: Big Willie Style, 1997; singles include: "Parents's Just Don't Understand"; "Girls Ain't Nothing but Trouble"; "I Think I Could Beat Mike Tyson"; television credits: "Fresh Prince of Bel Air," star, 1990-96; movie credits include: Where the Day Takes You, 1992; Made in America, 1993; Six Degrees of Separation, 1994; Bad Boys, 1995; Independence Day, 1996, Men in Black, 1997. **Honors/Awds:** Massachusetts Institute of Technology, full scholarship; He's the DJ, I'm the Rapper, double platinum; National Academy of Recording Arts and Sciences, Grammy, rap category (first year), "Parent's Just Don't Understand," 1989; NAACP, Image Award, Rap Artist, 1998; Grammy, Award for Best Rap Solo Performance, 1998. **Special Achievements:** Appeared, with DJ Jazzy Jeff, in a "Club Connect" tv episode that dealt with conflict resolution, 1991.

SMITH, WILLIAM FRED (FRED)
Human resources director (retired). **Personal:** Born Mar 22, 1938, Savannah, GA. **Educ:** Savannah State Coll; California State Univ. **Career:** GTE, dir, human resources, 1991-94; Contel Federal Systems, dir, human resources, 1986-91; Bunker Ramo Corp, mgr personnel, 1980; Litton Date Systems, mgr affirmative 1978-80; EEO Computer Sci Corp, corp mgr 1976-78; Litton Guidance & Control Sys, mgr, affirmative action 1972-76. **Orgs:** Valley Pref Empl Committee; mem Kappa Alpha Psi Frat; mem PMAA; mem LA Basin EEO; NAACP; Employment Mgmt Assn; Society for Human Resources Mgmt; Westllake Village Chamber of Commerce, bd of dirs; Natl Employee Services & Recreation Assn; Human Relation Commission; West Covina City, 1970-74; personnel mgmt assn, Aztian, 1974-93; aerospace industry, EEO Comm, 1970-93; member, JTPC/Private Industry Council, Ventura County, CA, 1987-94; member, Society for Human Resources Mgmt, 1980-94; member, Employment Management Assn, 1984-; mem, dir, California Chapter Family Motor Coach Assn, 1980-; community police advisory board, Los Angeles Police Department, 1994-. **Honors/Awds:** Comm Serv Award 1971; LA County Human Relations Commn Community Serv Award 1972; Natl Media Women Communication Award 1973; mem LA Dist Atty Comm Adv Council 1972; selective sys bd mem adv appointed by President 1971; appointed to CA Gov Comm for Employment of the Handicapped 1978; San Fernando Concerned Black Womens Award 1979; invited to White House by Pres Carter 1980; received award from Soc of Black Engineers CA State Univ Northridge 1980. **Home Addr:** 10611 Ledeen Dr, Lake View Terrace, CA 91342.

SMITH, WILLIAM FRENCH, II
Engineer. **Personal:** Born Nov 30, 1941, Bay City, TX; son of Willie Mae Perry Smith and William Smith, Sr; married Sylvia Knight Smith, Feb 4, 1977; children: William III, Maurice. **Educ:** Tuskegee Univ, BS 1959-64; Washington Univ St Louis MO, Graduate Study 1968-70; Front Range College, hazardous materials technology, 1989-. **Career:** Boeing Co, Huntsville, AL, equipment engineer, 1964-67; McDonnell Douglas Corp, St Louis, MO, plant design engineer, 1967-69; St Louis County Government, project engineer, 1969-72; E I DuPont de Nemours & Co, Inc, division engineer, Wilmington, DE and Victoria, TX, 1972-74; Westinghouse Corp, Millburn, NJ, engineering manager, 1974-76; Denver Public Schools, building safety engineer, 1976-, project administrator, 1977-, energy conservationist, 1978-; Tuskegee Univ, Denver, CO, manager of hazardous materials, 1985-88, environmental safety engineer, 1988-; Safety Engineer/Mgr Environmental Safety 1992-; Wm French Smith Consulting, CEO, currently. **Orgs:** Bd dir Denver Opportunity Industrial Center 1979-80, Natl Comm on Future of Regis Coll; mem Mayor's Citizens Adv Comm on Energy 1980-; mem Amer Soc Safety Engineers, CO Assn School Energy Coords, Amer Assn Blacks in Energy, treas Denver Public Schools Black Admin & Supvs Assn; mem CO Environ Health Assn, Natl Asbestos Council, CO Hazardous Waste Mgmt Soc, CO Hazardous Materials Assn, Natl Assn Minority Contractors, Rocky Mountain Hazardous Matls Assn, Tuskegee Univ Alumni Assn; vice president, Rocky Mountain Poison and Drug Center, 1990-; treasurer, Hazardous Materials Association; Colorado Emergency Planning Commission; Colorado Alliance for Environmental Education; Natl Black Environmental Assn; Denver Emergency Planning Commission; Senior Citizens Advisory Board. **Honors/Awds:** Nominated Black Engineer of the Year, Career Comm Group, Inc, 1990, 1991, 1992; Registered Environmental Assessor; Certified Environmental Inspector; Juanita Gray Community Service Award; President's Award on Energy Conservation. **Military Serv:** USNR 1978-80. **Home Phone:** (303)233-3335. **Business Addr:** Safety Engineer/Energy Czar, Denver Public Schools, 900 Grant St, Denver, CO 80203-1009, (303)575-4135.

SMITH, WILLIAM GENE
Bank executive. **Personal:** Born Jan 23, 1955, Windsor, NC; son of Mattie S Smith and James L Smith; married Leenora Baker, Apr 18, 1981; children: Byron Eugene, Antoine A. **Educ:** North Carolina Central University, BA, 1977; UNC, School of Banking, mid management, 1985. **Career:** First Union, branch manager, 1977-81, assistant consumer bank manager, 1984-85, Durham, consumer bank manager, 1985-88, Raleigh, consumer bank manager, 1988-90, regional consumer bank executive, 1990-92, Durham city area executive, senior vp, 1992-. **Orgs:** NCCU Foundation, board member, treasurer, 1990-; InRoads, board member two terms, 1986-92; Wake Opportunities, past treasurer, board member, currently; North Carolina Central Univ Board of Trustees, vice chairman. **Honors/Awds:** Dollars & Sense Magazine, honored as one of America's Best and Brighest Executives, 1992.

SMITH, WILLIAM HOWARD
Engineer. **Personal:** Born Dec 17, 1912, Talladega, AL; married Eva; children: Julius, Burton, Marianne, Kenneth, Harold, Patricia. **Educ:** MI State Univ, BS 1937. **Career:** Hwy design engr retired. **Orgs:** Past office, current mem NAACP; past pres Model Cities Adv Bd; chmn Tri Cty Plnng Comm; adv comm, vice pres BASE; mem Black Assoc in State Employment, CDCH. **Honors/Awds:** 39 Yr Cert & Roadside Park Name St Hwy & Transp comm; hon life mem Hwy Mens Club; AASHO 25 Yr Awd Pine & Cert.

SMITH, WILLIAM JAMES
Attorney. **Personal:** Born Mar 5, 1946, Fresno, CA; married Alice; children: Danielle, Nicole. **Educ:** UCLA, BA 1968; UCLA Sch of Law, 1972. **Career:** Trust Admin Union Bank, UCLA football; Nat Labor Relations Bd, atty; Brundage Reich & Pappy Labor Spec, atty. **Orgs:** Mem Nat Conf Black Lawyers; bd dirs Black Law Journ; mem LA Bar Assn; mem CA Bar Assn; mem Langston Law Club; Pro Bono Cases Labor Law. **Business Addr:** 13130 L St Ste E, Fresno, CA.

SMITH, WILLIAM MILTON
Clergyman. **Personal:** Born Dec 18, 1918, Stockton, AL; married Ida M Anderson; children: Eula C Goole. **Educ:** Tuskegee Inst Livingstone Coll, SMU, Perkins School of Religion, BS; AL State Univ, BS Ed. **Career:** 2nd Episcopal Dist AME Zion Church, presiding bishop; African Methodist Epis Zion Church Mobile AL, sr bishop. **Orgs:** Bd dir Gulf Fed Loan Assoc, YMCA, Mobile Co United Fund, Mobile United, Mobile Cty Red Cross, Mobile Gen Hosp, Mobile Found for Med Care, Mobile Cty Men Health, Amer Jun Miss Pagent Inc, Legal Aid Soc, Mobile Cty Palsy Inc; natl com life mem NAACP; chmn Church Ext Bd AME Zion Church; trustee Liingstone Coll, Lomax-Hannon Coll, AL State Univ 1980-; mem Cty & State Exec Com Rep Party. **Honors/Awds:** Ebony Magazine Awd 1980; various group awds. **Business Addr:** Senior Bishop, African Meth Epis Zion Church, 3753 Springhill Ave, Mobile, AL 36608.

SMITH, WILLIAM PERNELL, JR.
Educator (retired). **Personal:** Born Oct 2, 1919, Birmingham, AL; son of E Marzetta Johnson Smith and William P Smith Sr; married Dorothy Horton; children: Barbara J, William Pernell, III, Eric B. **Educ:** Tuskegee Inst, BS 1939; Rutgers U, MEd 1947; EdD 1959. **Career:** Tuskegee Inst, instr 1947-51; asso prof Educ 1960-69; VA and Constrn Cos Newark NJ, clerk 1951-52; AL State Coll Montgomery, asst prof 1952-55; asso prof educ 1956-60; Rutgers University, visiting prof, 1957-58; Office of Econ Oppor, consult in guidance and psychology, 1964-75; Stanford Research Inst, regl rep, 1968-75; AL State Univ, prof educ, chmn, dir, teacher educ & psychology 1969-71, area coordinator, guidance & psychology 1971-75, prof educ, 1975-84 (retired). **Orgs:** Mem AL Educ Assn; Am Personnel Guidance Assn; Nat Vocational Guidance Assn; Student Personnel Assn for Tchrs in Edn; Assn for Measurement & Evaluation in Guidance; NEA; VP Com for Greater Tuskegee 1969-70; pres 1970-71; mem Phi Delta Kappa; Kappa Delta Pi. **Military Serv:** AUS 1942-46.

SMITH, WILLIAM XAVIER
Banker. **Personal:** Born Dec 9, 1934, Livingston, AL; son of Daisy Jones Smith and Elijah Smith; married Cynthia Wright Smith, Jun 1, 1990; children: Molina, Xavier Gerard, Dianna, April. **Educ:** Bryant Coll, BS 1960; AIB basic & standard certificates, certificates 1970-74; Univ of WI School for Bank Admin, diploma 1975. **Career:** Liggett Drug Co, jr accountant 1960-62; Wonstop Auto Service, accountant 1962-63; US Treas Dept, intl revenue agent 1963-67; GAC Corp, tax rsch supvr, 1967-70; Unity Bank & Trust, asst treasurer 1970-72; Peoples Bank of Virgin Islands, vice pres cashier 1972-77; American State Bank, vice pres operations 1977-82, pres & dir 1982-; Gateway National Bank, St Louis, MO, pres/dir 1990-. **Orgs:** Dir/treas Boy Scouts of Amer Virgin Islands 1974-77; pres Greenwood Chamber of Commerce 1984-; dir Tulsa Comm Action Agency 1985-; director, Monsanto YMCA, St Louis, MO, 1991-. **Military Serv:** USAF airman 1st class 1954-57. **Business Addr:** President/CEO, Gateway National Bank, 3412 North Union Blvd, St Louis, MO 63115.

SMITH, WILSON WASHINGTON, III
Senior designer. **Personal:** Born Oct 2, 1957, Portland, OR; son of Mr & Mrs Wilson W Smith, Jr. **Educ:** Univ of Oregon, BArch, 1980. **Career:** Skidmore, Owings & Merrill, architect, 1981-82; self-employed, map designer, freelance architect, 1982; Portland General Elec, CAD, 1982-83; Planning Bureau, urban planner, 1983; NIKE, Inc, interior designer, 1983-86, product designer, footwear, 1986-90, sr product designer, 1990-. **Orgs:** Portland Foursquare Church, music minister, worship coord, 1987-; Worship Servants, Portland, coord, 1989-. **Honors/Awds:** Dollars & Sense Magazine, Outstanding Business & Professional Award, 1993. **Special Achievements:** Television, Breakfast Club, FX Network, "NIKE Design," Dec 1994; Television, "How'd They Do That," Presentation on NIKE Design, May 1994; Television, 20/20, Presentation on NIKE Design, Aug 1988; Music Director Summit, 1991; (6000 Youth, 3 day, 1988); National Four Square Youth Convention, 1988. **Home Phone:** (503)690-2188. **Business Addr:** Sr Footwear Designer, NIKE, Inc, 1 Bowerman Dr, MJ4, Beaverton, OR 97005, (503)671-3342.

SMITH, WYRE. See SMITH, ELIJAH.

SMITH, ZACHARY
Chef. **Personal:** Born Jul 1, 1951, Detroit, MI; son of Leola Smith and Jame Z Smith; married Donna J Alex, Jan 14, 1988; children: Chelsea, Christina. **Career:** Battery Point, chef; Hyatt Regency, San Francisco, sous chef; Benbow Inn, executive chef; Lansdowne, executive chef; Restaurant OneTwentyThree, executive chef, currently. **Orgs:** Chef Association. **Special Achievements:** Cooking demonstration for Baccat School; 4-star rating, Restaurant OneTwentyThree, in Restaurants of Detroit, 6th edition, by Molly Abraham. **Business Addr:** Executive Chef, Restaurant OneTwentyThree, 123 Kercheval, Grosse Pointe Farms, MI 48230.

SMITH-CROXTON, TERRI
Business executive. **Career:** JD & Associates, Arlington, TX, president, CEO, currently. **Orgs:** Links; League of Women Voters; WIB. **Honors/Awds:** Quest for Success, 1989; Leader of the Year, 1994; Trail Blazer, 1995. **Business Addr:** President/CEO, JD & Associates, 700 Highlander, Suite 110, Arlington, TX 76015, (817)467-7714.

SMITH-EPPS, E. PAULETTE
Librarian. **Personal:** Born Mar 6, 1947, Atlanta, GA; daughter of Viola Williams Smith and William Chauncey Smith Sr; married William Given Epps Sr, May 5, 1979. **Educ:** Spelman Coll, Atlanta, GA, BA, 1968; Atlanta Univ, Atlanta, GA, MSLS, 1971. **Career:** Atlanta Univ, Atlanta, GA, circulation librarian, 1972-73; Atlanta-Fulton Public Library, Atlanta, GA, reference librarian, 1973-76, branch mgr, 1976-82, asst branch services admin, 1982-86, branch services admin, 1986-91, central library admin, 1991-92, project manager, 1992, outreach services administrator, 1992-95, learning assistance business officer, 1995-96, public services administrator, 1996-97, assistant director of public svcs, 1997-. **Orgs:** Mem, Amer Library Assn, 1974-; mem, Black Caucus of Amer Library Assn, 1976-; mem, Metro-Atlanta Library Assn, 1971; mem, Spelman Coll Alumnae Assn, 1968-. **Home Addr:** 5160 Bruce Place SW, Atlanta, GA 30331. **Business Addr:** Public Services Administrator, Atlanta-Fulton Public Library, 1 Margaret Mitchell Square, Atlanta, GA 30303, (404)730-1790.

SMITHERMAN, CAROLE
Judge, educator. **Personal:** daugHter of Thelma Catlin and Jerry Catlin (deceased); married Rodger Smitherman; children: Rodger II, Tonya Renee, Mary Elaine. **Educ:** Spelman College, BA, political science; Miles Law School, JD, 1979. **Career:** Miles Law School, professor, 1982-; State of Alabama, circuit court judge, 1991; private practice, attorney, currently. **Honors/Awds:** Recipient of numerous honors and awards for public service. **Special Achievements:** First African-American woman deputy district attorney, State of Alabama, 1982; first appointed woman judge, City of Birmingham, 1986; first appointed African-American woman circuit court judge, 1991. **Business Phone:** (205)322-0012.

SMITHERMAN, GENEVA
Educator. **Personal:** Born in Brownsville, TN; daughter of Harry Napoleon; married Jeff R Donaldson; children: Robert Anthony. **Educ:** Wayne State University, BA, 1960, MA, 1962; University of Michigan, PhD, 1969. **Career:** Detroit Public Schools, teacher, 1960-66; Eastern Michigan University & Wayne State University, instructor, 1965-71; Wayne State University, assistant professor; Afro-American studies, Harvard University, lecturer, 1971-73; University of Michigan, adjunct professor, 1973; Wayne State University, professor, 1973-. **Orgs:** National Council Teachers of English, 1979-82; Executive Committee Conference College Composition, 1971-73; chairman, Black Literature Section, Midwest Language Association, 1972; Modern Language Association Committee, Minorities, 1976-77; Oral History Committee, Afro Museum, 1967-68; judge, Scholastic Writing Awards Contest, 1975; advisory board, Ethnic Awareness Project, 1977-78; founding member, African-American Heritage Association, 1976. **Honors/Awds:** Dean's List of Honor Students, Wayne State University; University of Michigan, Pre-Doctoral Fellowship; Award for Scholarly Leadership in Language Arts Instruction, 1980. **Business Addr:** English, Michigan State University, 201 Morrill Hall, East Lansing, MI 48824-1036.

SMITHERMAN, RODGER M.
Attorney, government official. **Personal:** Born Mar 2, 1953, Montgomery, AL; son of Ralph & Mary Smitherman; married Carole Smitherman, Nov 29, 1980; children: Rodger II, Tonya, Mary, Crystal. **Educ:** Univ of Montevallo, BBA, 1976; Miles Law School, JD, 1986. **Career:** Southern Junior Coll, Dean of Students; State of Alabama, state senator, 1994-. **Orgs:** Westimister Presbyterian Church, elder; Western Area YMCA, bd of dirs; West End High School, youth & government coach; Camp Birmingham, advisory bd; Vulcan Kiwanis; Birmingham Tip Off Club; Amateau Athletic Union, volunteer basketball coach; Police Athletic Team. **Honors/Awds:** City of Birmingham, Vulcan Award; Police Athletic Teams, Distinguished Service Award; District 18, Service Award; Westminister Presbyterian Church, Service Award. **Home Addr:** 928 Center Way, SW, Birmingham, AL 35211. **Business Addr:** Managing Attorney, Smitherman & Associates, 2029 2nd Ave, N, Birmingham, AL 35203, (205)322-0012.

SMITHERS, ORAL LESTER, JR.
Engineer. **Personal:** Born Jul 12, 1940, Columbus, OH; son of Mildred H Smithers and O Lester Smithers Sr; married Priscilla; children: Sheila, Lisa. **Educ:** Ohio State Univ, BCE 1963; Sacramento State Coll, MEngr Mech; Central Michigan Univ, MA 1982; Massachusetts Inst of Technology, Cambridge MA, MS 1985. **Career:** Aerojet Gen Corp, design engineer, 1963-68; US Air Force, aerospace engineer, 1968-85; Dept of Air Force, Wright Patterson Air Force Base, F-16 director of engineering, 1985-89, director of flight systems engineering, 1989-92; Wright Laboratory, deputy director, 1992-97, director of engineering, 1997-. **Orgs:** Ohio Society of Professional Engineers, American Association of Aeronautics and Astronautics; Clark/Champaign County Society of Professional Engineers; bd of dirs, Armed Forces Communications and Electronics Assn; past member, Clark State College Board of Trustees; Clark County/Springfield Planning Committee; past mem steward bd St Andrews AME Church; New North St AME Church; Omega Psi Phi Fraternity. **Honors/Awds:** Meritorious Civ Serv Award, Air Force Sys Command; Civil Engineering Hon, Chi Epsilon; Sloan Fellow, MIT, 1984-85; 4th District Man of the Year, Omega Psi Phi Fraternity, 1984; Senior Engineer of the Year, USAF Aeronautical Systems, 1989, Senior Executive Service Association; Exceptional Civilian Service Award, 1993; Air Force EEO Management Award, 1995. **Home Addr:** 15 Bobwhite Drive, Enon, OH 45323.

SMITHERS, PRISCILLA JANE
Association executive. **Personal:** Born Jan 2, 1942, Parkersburg, WV; daughter of Mildred Burke Spriggs and Robert D Spriggs; married O Lester Smithers Jr; children: Sheila, Lisa. **Educ:** Mtn State Coll, exec sec 1959-60; Am River Coll, part-time 1968; Clark Tech Coll, part-time 1971-73. **Career:** Cont Cablevsn of Springfield, comm serv dir, prod, hostess of wkly TV show 1973-78; City of Springfield, city clrk 1978-87; United Way, Springfield, campaign assoc, 1987-91, Alcohol, Drug, and Mental Hlth Board, executive director, 1991-96; Clark County Family Council, exec dir, 1995-96; United Way, Springfield, dir of Resource Development. **Orgs:** Past chmn Civil Serv Comm City of Springfield 1973-78; bd dir United Way 1976-87; OH Municipal Clerks Assn 1978-87; vice pres, Wittenberg Univ/Chamber of Commerce Leadership Academy Alumni, 1988-90; central cmte chairperson, Clark County Republican Party, 1994-; Key Corp, Bank Comm Advisory Comm, 1995-; Enon Historical Society, 1995-; City of Springfield, mediation bd, 1994-; Alcohol Drug Mental Health Board, bd of dirs, 1986-91; Springfield Rotary Club, 1993-. **Honors/Awds:** Prtcpnt Chmbr Comm "Leadership Academy" 1982; Citizen of the Year, pltcl ctgry, Black Women Leadership Caucus, 1979; Citizen of the Year Frntr Intl, 1978; Black History Award, St John Miss Church, 1990; Community Leadership Award, Springfield Comm Leadership Alumni Assn, 1990; Omega Phi Psi, Natl Citizen of the Year, 1994; ADMH, Employee of the Year, 1994. **Home Addr:** 15 Bobwhite Dr, Enon, OH 45323. **Business Addr:** Director of Development, United Way, 616 N Limestone, Springfield, OH 45503, (513)324-5551.

SMITHEY, ROBERT ARTHUR
Educator (retired). **Personal:** Born Dec 18, 1925, Norfolk, VA; son of Lovie Jordan Smithey and Phillip J Smithey. **Educ:** De Pauw Univ Greencastle IN, AB 1950; Univ of WI Madison, AM 1953; Univ of WI, PhD 1968. **Career:** Talladega Coll Talladega AL, chmn lower div 1960-64; Univ of MO Kansas City, asst prof English 1968-70; Univ of Houston, assoc prof English 1970-72; Norfolk State Univ VA, prof English & communications 1972-95. **Orgs:** Exec comm Conf on Coll Composition & Comm 1964-67; dir Natl Council of Teachers of English 1968-70; reader Coll Bd of Exams 1970-72; lay reader St James Episcopal Church Houston 1970-72; editorial bd Four C's 1972-76; lay reader, chalicer, Grace Episcopal Church Norfolk 1972-; pres, Natl Youth Conf; NAACP, 1944-45. **Honors/Awds:** IBM Fellow Univ of WI 1964-68; Vilas Fellow Univ of WI 1965-68; Univ Fellow Univ of WI 1966-68; Ford Fellow Univ of WI 1967-68. **Special Achievements:** Co-editor "Variations on Humankind," an anthology of world literature, Kendall How Publishers, 1995, revised 1996. **Military Serv:** AUS cpl; USAF a1/c 5 yrs.

SMITH FREEMAN, PATRICIA M.
Educator, librarian. **Personal:** Born Aug 11, 1937, Brooklyn, NY; daughter of Naomi McKeever Smith and Philip Smith; married Arnold C Freeman, Nov 28, 1981; children: Naomi Brown, Mabel Mcleod, Derek Brown, Latrice Kendall, Arnold II. **Educ:** College of New Rochelle, New Rochelle, NY, BA, liberal arts, 1979; Pratt Institute, Brooklyn, NY, MS, library & information science, 1980; College of New Rochelle, New Rochelle, NY, MA, gerontology, 1988. **Career:** Brooklyn Public Library, Brooklyn, NY, supervisor clerk/librarian, 1969-81; New York Techincal College, Brooklyn, NY, adjunct faculty, 1988-89; College of New Rochelle, New Rochelle, NY, branch librarian, 1981-, adjunct faculty, 1982-. **Orgs:** Pilgrim Church of Brooklyn, NY, 1959-; president, New York Black Librarians Caucus Inc, tenure, 1984-86; executive board member, American Library Association Black Caucus, 1985-87; member, ALA, NYLA, NYBLC, Black Women of Higher Education; Alumni Association College of New Rochelle & Pratt Institute. **Honors/Awds:** Linden Plaza Political Action Comm, 1979; Brooklyn Public Library, Ten Years of Service Award, 1979; Teacher of the Year, 1990; Computerized Career Planning, Service to the College, 1991. **Business Addr:** Associate Professor, Librarian, College of New Rochelle, 1368 Fulton St, Brooklyn, NY 11216.

SMITH-GASTON, LINDA ANN
Consumer affairs executive. **Personal:** Born Jan 17, 1949, Kingstree, SC; daughter of Frances Latimer Montgomery and George Smith; married Anthony R. Gaston (divorced); children: Taylor Aderemi Humphries, Leigh Jamila Gaston. **Educ:** University of California at Los Angeles, Los Angeles, CA, BA, 1970; California State University, Los Angeles, CA, MA, 1984. **Career:** KTTV-TV, Los Angeles, CA, host, 1978-80; Drew Postgraduate Medical School, Los Angeles, CA, program specialist, 1979-80; Consumer Credit Counselors, Los Angeles, CA, counselor, 1981-82; ARCO, Los Angeles, CA, consumer affairs specialist, 1982-84; Southern California Gas Company, Los Angeles, CA, senior consumer affairs specialist, 1984-. **Orgs:** Chairperson, KCET Community Advisory Board, 1988-90; president, Society of Consumer Affairs Professionals in Business, 1989; board member, Los Angeles County Commission on Local Governmental Services, 1990-; board member, National Coalition for Consumer Education, 1991-; state coordinator, California Agenda for Consumer Education, 1990-. **Honors/Awds:** Achievement Award, YWCA of Los Angeles, 1987. **Business Addr:** Senior Consumer Affairs Administrator, Southern California Gas Company, 810 S Flower St, ML 301V, Los Angeles, CA 90017.

SMITH-GRAY, CASSANDRA ELAINE
City administrator. **Personal:** Born Mar 7, 1947, Detroit, MI; married Charles A Gray; children: David Charles. **Educ:** Wayne State Univ, BS 1971. **Career:** Detroit Public Schools, ed 1970-74; City of Detroit Youth Dept, dir 1974-76; City of Detroit Bd of Assessors, assessor 1976-82; City of Detroit Neighborhood Svc, exec dir 1982-. **Orgs:** Mem Natl Assoc Negro Business & Prof Women 1974-; campaign mgr Mayor Young's Re-election 1981; bd mem Mayor's Anti-Crime Project 1982; trustee Ctr for Humanist Studies 1983-; bd mem Wayne Cty Child Care Council 1983-; state central mem alternate MI Democratic Party 1982-; life mem NAACP; det campaign mgr Mondale-Ferrarro Campaign 1984. **Honors/Awds:** Dir Youngest Dept Head in City's History 1974; assessor First Black Woman Assessor-Natl 1976; assessor 1st Black Woman Assessor Cert in MI 1979. **Business Addr:** Executive Dir, Neighborhood Services, 5031 Grandy, Detroit, MI 48211.

SMITH-HENDRICKS, CONSTANCE KASANDRA. See HENDRICKS, CONSTANCE SMITH.

SMITH NELSON, DOROTHY J.
Educator. **Personal:** Born Jun 24, 1948, Greenville, MS. **Educ:** Tufts University, BA, 1970, MEd, 1971; Southern Illinois University at Carbondale, PhD, 1981. **Career:** Southern Illinois University at Carbondale Office of Student Development, coordinator of student development, 1979-81; Mississippi Valley State University, assistant vice pres for academic affairs & director academic skills parlor, 1971-. **Orgs:** Board, NAACP, 1982-84; Post Doctoral Academy of Higher Education, 1979-; financial sec, Les Modernette Social Club, 1981-; International Reading Assoc, 1985; Southern Illinois University Alumni Assoc; Concerned Educators of Black Students; Southeast Regional Reading Conference; Alpha Kappa Alpha; Progressive Art and Civic Club, Mississippi Reading Assoc, Natl Assoc of Develop Educators, Mississippi Assoc of Develop Educators. **Honors/Awds:** Clark Doctoral Scholar Award for Research, Southern Illinois University, 1981; NAACP, Education Award, 1981; Education Achievement Award, Progressive Art & Civic Club, 1982; Outstanding Young Women of America, 1979-. **Business Addr:** Director, Student Counseling, Mississippi Valley State University, 14000 Highway 82 W #7232, Itta Bena, MS 38941-1400.

SMITH-SURLES, CAROL DIANN
Educational administrator. **Personal:** Born Oct 7, 1946, Pensacola, FL; children: Lisa Ronique, Philip. **Educ:** Fisk Univ, BA 1968; Chapman Coll, MA 1971; The Univ of MI, PhD 1978. **Career:** Santa Barbara County, social worker 1968-69; Allan Hancock Coll, instructor 1971-72; The Univ of MI, personnel rep 1971-77; Univ of Central FL, dir of eeo1978-84, exec asst to the pres 1982-84, assoc vice pres 1984-. **Orgs:** Mem NAACP, Urban League; mem bd trustees WMFETV and FM radio 1984-; bd mem Orlando Human Relations Bd 1984-; pres Orlando Leadership Council Orlando Chamber of Commerce 1985. **Honors/Awds:** Phi Lambda Theta Honor Soc 1977-; Outstanding Scholars Awd Delta Tau Kappa Intl Social Sci Hon Soc 1983. **Business Addr:** Assoc Vice President, Univ of Central Florida, ADM-330, Orlando, FL 32816.

SMITH-TAYLOR, DONNA LYN
Cleric. **Personal:** Born Jan 1, 1949, Detroit, MI; daughter of Georgia O Smith and Roger Brook Smith. **Career:** Carl Byoir & Associates Inc, supervisor, accounts payable, account administrator, 1978-85; Memorial Baptist Church, assistant to pastor, administrative assistant, 1985-88; Kenilworth Baptist Church, pastor, 1988-90; Empire Baptist State Convention, Empire Chronicle Newspaper, assistant editor, currently; New Progressive Missionary Baptist Church, pastor, currently. **Orgs:** Central Hudson Baptist Association, recording secretary, 1989-; Empire Baptist State Convention, assistant financial secretary, 1989-; Black Ministerial Alliance, 1991-. **Honors/Awds:** Detroit Renaissance Foundation, Certificate of Appreciation, IFF, 1981, 1982; Harlem Hospital, Certificate of Appreciation, Pastoral Care, 1987; St Clara COGIC, Certificate of Appreciation, 1991; The Thomas Whitfield Co., Certificate of Recognition, 1978. **Special Achievements:** First female elected to parent body office of Central Hudson Baptist Association, 1991; first female to pastor an African-American Baptist Church in Kingston, NY; first African-American to pastor Kenilworth Baptist Church, 1988; original member of The Thomas Whitfield Co., gospel recording/ministering choir based in Detroit, MI. **Business Addr:** Pastor, New Progressive Missionary Baptist Chruch, 10-12 Hone St, Kingston, NY 12401-6302, (914)339-0773.

SMITH-WHITAKER, AUDREY N.
Educational administrator. **Personal:** Born Mar 6, 1953, Chicago, IL; daughter of Anita Smith and Erron Smith; married Horace Edward Whitaker Jr. **Educ:** Wellesley Coll, BA 1974; Univ of ME Orono, MEd 1978. **Career:** Zayre Corp, personnel admin exec recruiter 1974-76; Univ of ME Orono, intern teacher corps 1976-78; Wellesley Coll, admission counselor 1978-79, asst dir admission 1979-80, sr asst dir admission 1980-81, assoc dir of admission 1981-85; Natl Assn of Independent Schls, dir admission and financial aid serv 1985-87; Radcliffe College-Radcliffe Seminars, Cambridge MA, recruiter/academic advisor 1987-88; Sun Financial Group, Wellesley Hills MA, registered representative 1987-88; Massachusetts A Better Chance, The College Board-Northeast Regional Office, education consultant 1987-88. **Orgs:** Mem Natl Assoc Coll Admission Counselors 1978-, New England Assoc of Black Admission Counselors Inc 1978-, Assoc of Black Admission & Financial Aid Officers of the Ivy League & Sister Schools Inc 1976-, New England Assoc Coll Admission Counselors 1979-; Black achiever Black Achievers Inc Boston MA 1981-; founding mem Wellesley Black Alumnae Network 1981-; mem School Volunteers of Boston 1982-; eval team mem New England Assoc of Schools & Coll Secondary Schools 1983-; consult Tri-Lateral Council 1984; adv council The Educ Resources Inst 1985-; mem Urban League of Eastern MA 1986-; bd mem Girl Scouts Patriots Trail Council 1986-; adv council Educ Records Bureau; mem, Links Inc 1989-. **Honors/Awds:** Black Achiever Black Achiever Assoc Inc Boston 1981; Outstanding Admin Black Grad Wellesley Coll 1982; rsch coordinator A Comparison of the Career Patterns of Black Grads of Two Selective Coll & Their Parents Morgan State Univ 1984.

SMOOT, ALBERTHA PEARL
Elected official. **Personal:** Born Oct 10, 1914, Society Hill, SC; daughter of Sally Antrum and Robert Antrum; married Clarence Smoot (deceased); children: Bruce Goldson, Jean Silva (deceased). **Career:** Macedonia Baptist Church, organist 1930-; Lily of the Valley IBPOE of W, financial sec 1965-; Second Ward, alderman. **Orgs:** Charter mem NAACP 1940-; Ansonia Republican Town Comm 1947-; Ansonia Recreation Comm 1983-85; first female appointed to Bd of Public Works 1985-; Water Pollution Control Board, 1990-92. **Honors/Awds:** Serv rendered Macedonia Baptist Church 1965; serv rendered Lily of Valley IBPOE of W 1979; 50 yr member Macedonia Baptist Church 1984; Beth Israel Synagogue Center for over 40 years of Service as being in charge of their Kitchen Affairs, 1993. **Home Addr:** 20 Hunters Lane, Ansonia, CT 06401.

SMOOT, CAROLYN ELIZABETH
Corporate consultant, educational administrator. **Personal:** Born Sep 24, 1945, Logan, WV; daughter of Mr & Mrs Edward Hickman; married Douglas B Smoot, Jan 27, 1967; children: Caroline Trucia. **Educ:** WV State Coll Inst, BS, 1967; WV Coll of Graduate Study Inst, MPA, 1975. **Career:** Mgmt & Training Corp, dir of Education & Training, 1984-; mgmt consultant/researcher, 1983-84; WV State Coll, staff assoc, Office of Development, 1982-83; mgmt consultant, researcher, 1981-82; Nemderoloc/Medlock Co Inc, corporate consultant, 1979-80; WV Dept of Employment Security, commr, 1977-78; WV State Coll Inst, part-time instructor, 1975-77; Thiokol Corp, mgr placement & records dept, 1976-77; Teledyne Economic Devel Co, dept head placement serv, 1972-76; sr instructor, 1968-72; Packard Bell Electric Corp, residential advisor, 1967-68. **Orgs:** Guest lecturer, various civic, social & comm org on topics relating to the Changing Role of Women Placement; several TV appearances; mem, Delta Sigma Theta Sorority, Phi Delta Kappa Sor; mem, Natl Womens Political Caucus & WV Women Political Caucus, asst, Durbar WV Chapter of Blue Birds Inc; homeroom mother, Dunbar Elementary School; bd dir, Multi-cap; NAACP; Amer Vocational Assn, 1984-; West Virginia Adult Educ Assn, 1984-; West Virginia Vocational Educ Assn, 1984-; West Virginia Human Resources Assn, 1984-87; Private Industry Council of Kanawha County, bd of dir, 1984-; Charleston Business & Professional Club, pres & first vice pres, 1983-86; Shawnee Community Center, bd of dir, 1984-87; political action chairman, Busines & Professional Club, 1987-; board of directors, Kanawha Countyeriff Dept, 1990-. **Honors/Awds:** Appointed West Virginia Ambassador of Good Will, 1981; Participant in the first White House Conf on Balanced Natl Growth & Economic Devel, 1978; Featured in Ebony Magazine, "The Problems of Women Bosses", 1977; Participant in the White House Conf on Science & Technology, 1985. **Home Addr:** Box 222, Institute, WV 25112. **Business Addr:** Teacher, Kanawha County School, Charleston, WV 25321.

SMOTHERS, RONALD
Restaurant executive. **Career:** Fastaurants, Inc, Los Angeles, CA, chief executive. **Business Addr:** Fastaurants, Inc, 3700 Coliseum St, Los Angeles, CA 90016.

SMOTHERS, RONALD ERIC
Reporter. **Personal:** Born Sep 3, 1946, Washington, DC; married Brenda. **Educ:** Hobart Coll, BA 1967. **Career:** Comm News Serv, editor 1969-72; Newsday, rptr 1968-69; WA Post, 1967-68. **Business Addr:** The New York Times, 229 Peachtree, NE, Suite 1103, Atlanta, GA 30303.

SMOTHERSON, MELVIN
Minister. **Personal:** Born Nov 6, 1936, Hattiesburg, MS; son of Estella S Rogers and Melvin Smotherson; married Geraldine Jackson, Jun 23, 1957; children: Charles, Bwayne, Pamela, Darren. **Educ:** Brooks Bible Coll, Cert 1965; MO Bapt Coll, BA 1974; Central Baptist Theological Seminary, DD, 1975; Webster Coll, MA 1980. **Career:** 1st Bapt Church of Creve Coeur, pastor 1963-71; Bapt State Sunday School & BTU Cong, historian 1974-75; Ministers Union of Greater St Louis, 1st & 2nd vice pres 1977-79; Washington Tabernacle Bapt Church, pastor 1971-80; Cornerstone Institutional Bapt Church, pastor 1980-. **Orgs:** Attended various conf & conv assoc with Bapt Church 1963-67; grand jr warden/grand chaplain, dep grand master Most Worshipful Prince Hall Grand Lodge; hon mem MI Grand Lodge F&AM; exec comm NAACP; deputy imperial chaplain Ancient Egyptian Arabic Order, Nobles of the Mystic Shrine of North & South Amer and its Jurisdiction 1985-; Most Worshipful Grand Master-MWPHGL of MO 1988-90. **Honors/Awds:** Various awds & certs NAACP & sororities 1965-74; Minister of the Year Awd Bapt Church 1973; Cert of Merit NAACP 1974; Doctor of Divinity Central Baptist Theological Seminary 1975; Citizen of the Year Awd George Washington Carver Assoc 1979; Citizen of the Year Awd Grand Chap OES; Knight Grand Commander of Humanity Republic of Liberia 1989; Chief of Bbandi Tribe Lofa District Monrovia Liberia; speaker in Trinidad West Indies, Seoul Korea, Rome Italy 1987-88.

SMYRE, CALVIN
State representative. **Personal:** Born May 17. **Career:** Georgia House of Representatives, District 92 representative, currently. **Orgs:** Delegate, Democratic National Party Conference, 1978; delegate, Democratic National Convention, 1980. **Business Addr:** Executive VP, Corp Affairs, Synovus Financial Corp, 901 Front Ave, Ste 301, Columbus, GA 31901.

SMYTHE, VICTOR N.
Librarian. **Personal:** son Of Agnes L. Scott Smythe (deceased) and Constantine Smythe (deceased). **Educ:** New York Univ, BA, psychology, 1964; Columbia Univ School of Journalism, 1983-84, School of Library Service, MS, 1984; Modern Archives Institute, National Archives, Washington, DC, certificate, 1989. **Career:** International Circulating Exhibitions, Museum of Modern Art, New York, NY, special assistant; Daniel Yankelovich, Inc, field supervisor; Post Exchange Services, US Fort Clayton, internal auditor; South Bronx Project, community liaison; Brooklyn College, Dept of Educational Services, chief administrative officer; New York Public Library, librarian; Schomburg Center for Research in Black Culture, heritage project, archivist, librarian, beginning 1989; Art & Artifacts Division, Schomburg Cty, curator, currently. **Orgs:** American Libraries Assn; Archives Roundtable of Metropolitan New York; Mid-Atlantic Regional Archives Conference; member, Oriental Orthodox/Roman Catholic Dialogue; director, Caribbean/American Media Studies, Inc; director, Coalition for Caribbean Interests; board member, Statue of Liberty-Ellis Island Project; executive director, 1990-, chairman of executive committee, 1982-, Ethiopian Orthodox Church; Western Hemisphere Abyssinian Cultural Center, director, 1993-; African Zion, the Sacred Art of Ethiopia, education consultant. **Honors/Awds:** Curator, Do You Know Where You Are? Maps and You, Schomburg Center, 1988-89; curator, Indians of the Americas, Brooklyn College, 1976, The Haitian Experience, 1974; curator, Native American Crafts, New York Public Library, 1978; editor of the Panama Chronicle, 1987-; author of numerous articles. **Business Addr:** Manuscript Librarian, Project Archivist, Schomburg Center for Research in Black Culture, 515 Malcolm X Blvd, New York, NY 10037-1801.

SMYTHE-HAITH, MABEL MURPHY
Editor, africanist, diplomat (retired). **Personal:** Born Apr 3, 1918, Montgomery, AL; daughter of Josephine Dibble Murphy and Harry Saunders Murphy; married Hugh H Smythe, Jul 29, 1939 (died 1977); children: Karen Pamela. **Educ:** Spelman College, 1933-36; Mt Holyoke College, BA, 1937; Northwestern University, MA, economics, 1940; University of Wisconsin, PhD, economics, law, 1942; New York University, post doctoral studies, 1948. **Career:** NAACP Legal Defense & Educ Fund, deputy dir, non-legal rsch for school segregation cases, 1953; Baruch School, adj prof of economics, 1959-60; Queens Coll, adjunct prof 1962; New Lincoln School, senior core teacher, 1954-59, coord/principal of high school, 1959-69; Encyclopedia Britannica Ed Corp, consult 1969-73; US Commn on Civil Rights, scholar-in-residence 1973-74; Phelps-Stokes Fund NY, dir rsch & publ 1970-77, vice pres 1972-77; United Republic of Cameroon, US ambassador 1977-80; Republic of Equatorial Guinea, US ambassador 1979-80; US Dept of State, dep asst sec for African Affairs 1980-81; Northwestern Univ, Melville J Kerskovits Prof of African studies 1981-83, assoc dir African studies 1983-85, prof emerita 1985-. **Orgs:** Council on Foreign Rel, Caucus of Black Econ; Amer Econ Assn; The Smithsonian Inst; Museum of the Amer Indian; Cosmopolitan Club; Refugee Policy Group; Council of Amer Ambassadors; Assn of Black Amer Ambassadors; trustee Spelman Coll 1980-; Life trustee, 1991-; US del Intl Conf to Asst Refugees in Africa Geneva 1981; Refugee Policy Group 1983-90; US del So African Devel Coord Conf Maputo Mozambique 1980; bd dir Ralph Bunche Inst on the United Nations CUNY 1986-; trustee, 1971-76, vice chair, 1975-76, trustee fellow, Mt Holyoke College, 1988-; trustee, Hampshire College, 1971-78, vice chair, 1976-77; trustee, Connecticut College, 1964-65, 1968-77; Spelman College Trustee, 1980-89, life trustee, 1991-. **Honors/Awds:** Julius Rosenwald Fellow; Harriett Remington Laird Fellow; Nat Fellow; Disting Serv Awd, NY Chap of Links, 1965; Gran Dama D'Inore; Top Hat Awd Pittsburgh Courier 1979; Grand Officer Order of Valor United Republic of Cameroon 1980; Mary McLeod Bethune Women of Achievement Awd 1981; Ella T Grasso Awd Mt Holyoke Coll 1982; Decade of Serv Awd Phelps-Stokes Fund 1982; guest scholar Woodrow Wilson Intl Center for Scholars 1982; Alumna of the Year Awd Northwestern Univ

1983; Natl Coalition of 100 Black Women Awd 1984; Assoc of Black Amer Ambassadors' Study Mission to Japan 1985; African Seminar NAFEO 1985; US Info Agency Outstanding Serv Award, 1986; Makers of History Award, Associated Black Charities, 1990;Achievement Award, American Bicentennial Presidential Inaugural Afro-American Committee, 1989; books: editor, The Black American Reference Book, Prentice-Hall, 1976; co-author with Hugh H Smythe: The New Nigerian Elite, Stanford University Press, 1960, 1971; with Alan B Howes; Intensive English Conversation (2 vols & teachers' manual), Kairyudo Press, Tokyo, 1953, 1954; honorary degrees; LHD, Mt Holyoke College, 1977; Univ of Mass, 1979; LLD Spelman College, 1980; Univ of Wisconsin, LLD, 1991; Author with Edgar S Bley, Curriculum for Understanding, Valley Stream, NY School District, 1965. **Special Achievements:** Chaired a delegation of observers (under the sponsorship of the African American Institute) to the February, 1993 election of a new president in Madagascar. **Business Addr:** 700 New Hampshire Ave, Ste 317, Washington, DC 20037-2406.

SNAGGS, CARMEN
Medford business executive. **Personal:** Born Mar 28, New York, NY; married Bert. **Educ:** City Coll, BBA 1944. **Career:** Carmen Medford, pub acct, priv prac 1944-. **Orgs:** Mem Met Soc of Acct; Empire State Assn of Acct Fin of Acct Fin sec treas N Bronx Section Nat Council of Negro Women Inc 1968-72; pres N Bronx Section Nat Council of Negro Women Inc 1972-; project dir Women in Comm Serv 1970-; oranizer & temporary chmn Black Concerned Citizens Com; fin sec bd dir Williamsbridge Sr Citizens Cntr 1972-; mem Sch Comm Adv Council Olinville Jr HS 1972-; Williamsbridge Br NAACP 1962-; Neighborhood Block Assn.

SNEAD, DAVID LOWELL
School superintendent. **Personal:** Born Oct 15, 1943, Detroit, MI; son of Edythe and Herman Snead (both deceased); married Sharon McPhail, May 27, 1995; children: Deborah, David II, Brandon. **Educ:** Tuskegee Univ, BS, 1968; Univ of Michigan, MA, 1970, PhD, 1984. **Career:** Detroit Public Schools, secondary school ed central office supv, 1985, asst principal, 1985-87, principal, 1987-93, interim asst superintendent, 1993, exec deputy interim gen superintendent, 1993, general superintendent, 1993-. **Orgs:** Amer Assn of School Admins; Detroit Police Athletic League, advisor; Health Alliance Plan, board member, 1990-92; New Detroit, Inc, board of trustees, 1994; Metro Detroit Alliance of Black School Educators, 1994; Council of Great City Schools, exec comm, 1994, board of trustees, 1994; Junior League of Detroit, commun advisory board, 1994. **Honors/Awds:** Southern Christian Leadership Conference, Septima Clark Natl Ed Award, 1995; Alpha Phi Alpha, Man of the Year Award of Merit, 1994; Michigan Assn of School Admins, Michigan Superintendent of the Year, 1994; Michigan Council of Deliberation Scholar Found, Outstanding Leadership and Service Award, 1994; Business United With Officers Youth (BOUY), Ed Award Recipient, 1994. **Special Achievements:** Education Career Directory, Teaching in Urban Schools, Gale Research Copyright Inc, 1994; Recommended Public School Finance Reforms, Detroit Free Press, March 1988; From Coach to Admin, It's All The Same, Secondary Education Today, Vol 29, No 3, Spring 1988 Edition; Dissertation, The Effects of Increased Grade Point Standards for Student Athletes, Univ of Mich Press, December 1984. **Military Serv:** US Army, personnel admin specialist, 1961-64. **Home Addr:** 18644 Shields, Detroit, MI 48234.

SNEAD, JOHN D.
Community official (retired). **Personal:** Born Nov 2, 1917, Paducah, KY; son of Mable Snead and John P Snead; widowed; children: Ronald, Jon Jr, Marva. **Educ:** AB, LUTC-IIAMA 1941; Purdue U, Marketing; KY State Univ, graduate 1941. **Career:** Gen Mtrs Lab, prof musician; UAW; committeeman; Great Lakes Mut Life Inst, insurance salesman, asst dist mgr, dist mgr, western MI mgr; Kent Co Dept of Soc Serv, caseworker, caseworker supervisor, supervisor of neighborhood ctrs & comm rel, supervisor of comm social svcs, retirement. **Orgs:** Com mem Neighborhood Health Servs; Mental Health Servs; United Comm Servs Plng Com; mem Frankln-hall Adv Cncl; bd mem Hd Strt Par Advisory Com; Model Cities HEW Com; trustee Kent Co Migrnt Affrs Cncl; mem Kent Co Jail Rehab Advisory Com; exec bd mem Grand Rapids Bus Opport; vice pres Comm Action Prog Gov Bd; mem Urban Lgue Meth Comm House; bd dir, Amer Red Cross. **Honors/Awds:** Kentucky Colonel; NAACP Man of the Year Grand Rapids; Service Awd Grand Rapids Multifamily Svc; Achievement Awd Black Business & Professional Women's Club Inc; Service Awd Michigan Senate; Kent County Youth Companion Award, Service to abused & neglected children; Giant of the Community Award; Life Enricher Award. **Military Serv:** AUS capt. **Home Addr:** 3120 Plaza Dr NE Apt #B-30, Grand Rapids, MI 49505.

SNEAD, WILLIE T., SR.
Cleric. **Career:** Greater Temple of God Missionary Baptist Church, pastor, currently. **Orgs:** National Missionary Baptist Convention of America, pres, currently. **Business Addr:** Pastor, Greater Temple of God Missionary Baptist Church, PO Box 512096, Los Angeles, CA 90051-0096, (213)582-7344.

SNEED, GREGORY J.
Company executive. **Career:** 40 Acres and a Mule Filmworks, Inc, pres/COO, 1996-; Twentieth Century Fox International, finance and administration, vp. **Business Addr:** President/COO, 40 Acres and A Mule Filmworks, 124 Dekalb Ave, Brooklyn, NY 11217, (718)624-3703.

SNEED, PAULA A.
Food and beverage company executive. **Personal:** Born Nov 10, 1947, Everett, MA; daughter of F Mary Turner Sneed and Thomas E Sneed; married Lawrence P Bass, Sep 2, 1978; children: Courtney J Bass. **Educ:** Simmons College, BA, 1969; Harvard University, MBA, 1977. **Career:** Outreach Program for Problem Drinkers, educ supvr, female coord, 1969-71; Ecumenical Center, dir of plans, Program Devel and Evaluation, 1971-72; Boston Sickle Cell Center, program coord, 1972-75; General Foods Corp, assistant product manager, 1977, vp, consumer affairs, 1986-90, svp, pres, Foodservice division, 1990-91; exec vice pres/gen manager, Desserts Division, 1991-95; Kraft Foods North America, sr vice pres, marketing services, 1995-. **Orgs:** Amer Assn of Univ Women, 1980-; Coalition of 100 Black Women, 1982-; Natl Assn of Negro Business and Professional Women, 1983-; bd of dir, Hercules Inc; mem, Exec Leadership Council; bd of dirs, Westchester/Fairfield Inroads; bd of trustees, National 4-H Council; bd of govs, Children's Miracle Network; advisory council to dean, Howard University Business School. **Honors/Awds:** Black Achiever, Harlem YMCA, 1982; MBA of the Year Award, Harvard Business School Black Alumni Organization, 1987; Benevolent Heart Award, Graham-Windham, 1987; Doctor of Business Administration Honoris Causa, Johnson and Wales University 1991; Top 100 Black Women in Corp Am, Ebony Mag, 1990, 1991; 21 Most Influential Af-Am Women in Corp Am, Black Enterprise Mag, 1991, 1997, 40 most influential Afr-Ams in Corp Am, 1993; ''Breakthrough 50'' Exec Female Mag, 1992 America's 50 Most Powerful Woman Managers, 1994; 25 Most Influential Mothers Working, Mother's Mag, 1998; Corp Achievers, Dollars and Sense Mag, 1990, ''Very Important Prestigious Woman,'' 1993; inducted into Academy of Women Achievers, New York YWCA, 1990. **Home Addr:** 158 Phelps Rd, Ridgewood, NJ 07450.

SNELL, JIMMY GREGORY. See Obituaries section.

SNELL, JOAN YVONNE ERVIN
Engineering administrator. **Personal:** Born Apr 5, 1932, Waxahachie, TX; married Clarence L Sr; children: Tyrone, Clarence Jr. **Educ:** Draughons Bus Coll, 1950; Prairie View A&M Coll, BA. **Career:** IBM Corp, field engineering adminstrn splst; Lubbock City Hall. **Orgs:** Bd of dir YWCA 1956-66; exec sec NAACP 1973-75; mem, sec New Hope Bapt Ch 1952; sec NAACP; mem Gov's Com on Higher Edn; dir New Hope Bapt Ch Yth Dept; sec W TX Bapt Dist Assn; sec Women of BM & E Conv of TX; mem Mayor's Com & C of C. **Honors/Awds:** First blk sec Lubbock City Hall 1954; first blk sec elem sch prin 1952; first blk IBM'eR hired to corp 1962; first blk elect offcl city of Lubbock 1970, 1972; 1st blk woman nomin Woman of the Yr 1969; Outstdng IBM Means Serv Aw 1968; spec hon guest to pres of corp; noble cit, gifts, & aw 1970. **Business Addr:** 1602 10th, PO Box 1890, Lubbock, TX 79408.

SNIPES, WESLEY
Actor. **Personal:** Born Jul 31, 1962, Orlando, FL; married 1985 (divorced 1990); children: Jelani. **Educ:** SUNY at Purchase, degree in theatre/dramatic art, 1985. **Career:** Actor, theatre appearances include: Execution of Justice, The Boys of Winter, and Death and the King's Horseman; film/television appearances include: Wild Cats, 1985; Streets of Gold; Michael Jackson's ''Bad'' video; Major League; HBO's Vietnam War Story; Mo' Better Blues; King of New York; Jungle Fever, 1991; New Jack City, 1990; White Men Can't Jump, 1992; Waterdance, 1992; Passenger 57, 1992; The Rising Sun, 1993; Demolition Man, 1993; Drop Zone, 1994; To Wong Foo, Thanks for Everything, Julia Newmar; Waiting To Exhale; Murder At 1600, 1997; One Night Stand, 1997; US Marshals; Down In The Delta; Blade, prod, actor; The Big Hit, co-prod; Amen Ra Films, founder. **Honors/Awds:** ACE Award, Best Actor, performance in HBO special, Vietnam War Story; won Victor Borge Scholarship to attend SUNY at Purchase; Venice Film Festival, Best Actor.

SNOOP DOGGY DOGG (CALVIN BROADUS)
Rap artist. **Personal:** Born 1972, Long Beach, CA; married Chante Taylor, Jun 14, 1997; children: Corde, Cordell. **Career:** 213, member with Nate Dogg and Warren G; vocalist on Dr Dre's album, The Chronic, 1993; solo music career, albums include: Doggy Style, debut album, 1993; Murder Was the Case, 1994. **Orgs:** Deion Sanders Primetime Shootout, 1994. **Honors/Awds:** Billboard Music Charts, #1 Album, December 1993; MTV Music Awards, presenter, 1993; Soul Train Music Award, 1995.

SNOW, ERIC
Professional basketball player. **Personal:** Born Apr 24, 1973, Canton, OH. **Educ:** Michigan State. **Career:** Seattle Supersonics, guard, 1995-98; Philadelphia 76ers, 1998-. **Business Addr:** Professional Basketball Player, Philadelphia 76ers, One Corestates Complex, Philadelphia, PA 19148, (215)339-7676.

SNOW, PERCY LEE
Professional football player. **Personal:** Born Nov 5, 1967, Canton, OH. **Educ:** Michigan State Univ, criminal justice major, 1986-89. **Career:** Kansas City Chiefs, linebacker, 1990-. **Honors/Awds:** 1989: first team All-America and All-Big Ten, Lombardi Award, Butkus Award, Big Ten Defensive Player of the Year; 1988: Sporting News first team All-America, first team All-Big Ten; 1987: first team All-Big Ten. **Business Addr:** Professional Football Player, Kansas City Chiefs, One Arrowhead Dr, Kansas City, MO 64129-1651.

SNOWDEN, FRANK WALTER
Scientist. **Personal:** Born Nov 5, 1939, New Orleans, LA; divorced. **Educ:** Xavier Univ New Orleans, BS 1960; Howard Univ Wash DC, 1960-63; Univ of New Orleans, PhD 1975. **Career:** Chemical Engineering & Material Science Dept, Inst of Tech, Univ or Minnesota, prof; Sr technical serv engr 3m; Univ of New Orleans, research & teaching 1970-73; US Dept of Agriculture So Reg Research Lab, chemist 1960-73; Howard U, teaching fellow 1960-63; US Dept of Agriculture So Reg Research Lab, student trainee 1957-60. **Orgs:** Mem Am Chemical Soc 1960-; mem Am Pub Transit Assn 1977-93; Commr Mr Met Transit Commn Twin Cities 1977-93; mem Alpha Phi Alpha Frat Inc; Several Patents/Research Publ & Presentations. **Business Addr:** Professor, Chemical Engineering & Materials Science Department, University of Minnesota, 421 Washington Ave, SE, Minneapolis, MN 55455.

SNOWDEN, GAIL
Banking executive. **Personal:** Born Jul 5, 1945, New York, NY; daughter of Muriel Sutherland Snowden and Otto Snowden; divorced; children: Leigh Trimmier. **Educ:** Radcliffe Coll, BA 1967; Simmons Coll Grad School of Mgt, MBA, 1978. **Career:** First Natl Bank of Boston, br officer 1971-76, br credit officer 1977-79, loan officer 1980, asst vice pres 1981-83, vice pres, 1984-86, division exec, 1986-88, senior credit officer, 1989-90; director, Boston First Banking/Bank of Boston, 1990-92; First Community Bank of Boston, president, 1992-. **Orgs:** Mem Natl Assoc of Bank Women 1971-; treas Radcliffe Club of Boston 1976; asst dir Boston Urban Bankers Forum 1979-80; conf steering comm Simmons Grad Prog in Man Alumnae Assoc 1979-80; steering comm of family Govt Comm on Children & Family 1980; vice pres Natl Assoc of Urban Bankers 1984-85. **Honors/Awds:** Banker of the Year, National Assn of Urban Bankers, 1989; Outstanding Alumna, Simmons Grad School of Management, 1989; Big Sister, Women of Achievement, 1992; Small Business Administration, Minority Business Advocate of the Year, 1992; Dollars & Sense Magazine Professional Women's Award, 1992. **Business Addr:** President, First Community Bank of Boston, 100 Federal St, 1-15-06, Boston, MA 02110.

SNOWDEN, GILDA
Artist, educator. **Personal:** Born Jul 29, 1954, Detroit, MI; daughter of Clara Perry Snowden and John Thomas Snowden; married William Guy Boswell II, May 29, 1987; children: Katherine Snowden Boswell. **Educ:** Wayne State Univ, Detroit, MI, BFA, MA, MFA. **Career:** Wayne State Univ, Detroit, MI, instructor, 1979-85; Ctr for Creative Studies, Detroit, MI, assoc prof, currently. **Orgs:** Mem, exhibition comm, Detroit Focus Gallery, 1984-; mem, Natl Conference of Artists; dir, Willis Gallery, 1983-84; dir, Detroit Repertory Theatre Gallery, 1987-. **Honors/Awds:** Fellowship, NEA/Arts Midwest, 1990; Grant, MI Council of The Arts, 1982, 1985, 1988, 1990. **Special Achievements:** Contributing Editors, Detroit Focus Quarterly, New Art Examiner, Natl Conf of Artists Newsletter, Ground Up Magazine; Callaloo Literary Journal, John Hopkins Press; Gumbo Ya Ya, Anthology of Women Artists, Midmarch Arts Press; Art News, Dec 1988. **Business Addr:** Associate Professor, Fine Arts, Center for Creative Studies, College of Art & Design, 201 E Kirby, Detroit, MI 48202.

SNOWDEN, PHILLIP RAY
Engineer. **Personal:** Born Dec 9, 1951, Shreveport, LA; son of Nevada Swift Snowden and Harold Phillip Snowden; married Mary Ann Robinson Snowden, Jul 6, 1974; children: Tamara Sheniki, Tariot-Phillip Ramona. **Educ:** Louisiana Tech University, Ruston, LA, BSEE, 1974; Xavier University, Cincinnati, OH, MBA, 1976. **Career:** General Electric Co, Stamford, CT, corporate management trainee-engineer, 1974-78; General Motors Corp, Detroit, MI, engineer, 1978-83; Kent State University, Warren, OH, technology/energy instructor, 1981-82; Entergy Corp, New Orleans, LA, engineer-nuclear safety, 1983-. **Orgs:** President, Louisiana Chapter of American Association of Blacks in Energy, 1991-; chairman, Computer Society Institute of Electronic Engineers, New Orleans Section, 1990-; president elect, National Association of Accountants, New Orleans Chapter, 1991; president elect, Your Metropolitan Business and Civic Club, 1991. **Honors/Awds:** Peak Performer Award, Louisiana Power and Light, Waterford 3, 1989; Black Achievers Award, Dryades YMCA, 1989; Salutatorian, Hopewell High School, 1969. **Home Addr:** PO Box 1559, Gretna, LA 70053.

SNOWDEN, RAYMOND C.
Insurance company executive. **Personal:** Born Aug 5, 1937, McNary, AZ; son of Loretta Hockett Banks and Clarence Snowden; married Bettye (divorced); children: Joni, Brian,

Eric. **Educ:** AA Psychology, 1962. **Career:** Safeway Stores Inc LA, store mgr 1965-67; Continental Assurance Co, assoc mgr 1969; Transamerica Occidental Life, beginning 1971; Ray Snowden Insurance Agency, owner, currently. **Orgs:** Pres Kiwanis Club SW LA 1976-77; mem Inglewood CA C of C; mem Salvation Army Youth Adv Council 1978; mem Life Underwriters Assn; dir Inglewood C of C 1978-80; pres Crenshaw-Imperial Sect of Inglewood C of C 1978-80; mem citizen adv com Centenila Hosp 1980-86; pres Inglewood C of C 1982-84; pres Imperial-Crenshaw Kiwanis Club 1982-83; lt governor, Kiwanis Intl, 1991-92; New Testament Church, Los Angeles CA, trustee board chairman, 1978. **Honors/Awds:** New Agency of Yr Awd Transamerica Occidental Life of CA 1972; first black general agent for Transamerica Occidental Life of CA 1971; featured in issue Sports Illus in Occidental Life's adver June 11, 1974; Kiwanis Intl Awd for Comm Serv 1974; Commendation Inglewood City Council for Comm Serv 1984. **Business Addr:** Owner, Ray Snowden Insurance Agency, 6245 Bristol Parkway #161, Culver City, CA 90230, (310)417-8372.

SNOWDEN, SYLVIA FRANCES
Artist, educator. **Personal:** Born Apr 21, 1944, Raleigh, NC; daughter of Dr and Mrs George Snowden; divorced; children: Shell Snowden, John Malik. **Educ:** Howard Univ, BA, MFA; Le Grande Chaumier, Paris, certificate; Skowhegan School of Painting and Sculpture, certificate. **Career:** Lecturer/instructor of painting, design, survey of art history at Coppin St Coll, Cornell Univ, Howard Univ, Morgan St Univ, Delaware St Coll, Community Coll of Baltimore and Univ of the District of Columbia; served as curator, juror and panelist for numerous art events. **Orgs:** Jelleff Boys and Girls Club, Arts with Elders Program, dir, 1982; Washington Women's Arts Ctr, dir, mgr, 1983. **Honors/Awds:** DC Commission on the Arts and Humanities Grants, 1978, 1979, 1989; Lois Jones Pierre-Noel Award, Water Color; Skowhegan School, First Pl Award, Oil Painting; Association of Black Arts/East, First Pl Award, Painting; Fondo del Sol Gallery, Lois M Jones Award, Recognition. **Special Achievements:** Art Shows presented in: Chile, the Netherlands, The Bahamas, Italy, Tokyo, Boston, Chicago, Los Angeles, New York City, Baltimore and Washington DC; served as visiting artist & artist-in-residence: Cornell Univ, Howard Univ, Univ of CO & the Corcoran Gallery of Art. **Home Addr:** 465 M St, NW, Washington, DC 20001, (202)347-5576.

SNYDER, GEORGE W.
Journalist, writer. **Personal:** Born Dec 6, 1944, New Orleans, LA. **Educ:** MI St U, BA 1966. **Career:** The Canadian Press, Toronto, feature editor 1967-68; Yukon Terr British Columbia, licensed prospector 1968-70; San Francisco Chronicle, reporter; KPIX TV, KGO TV, writer, producer, reporter 1970-. **Orgs:** Mem San Francisco & Black Media Assn; mem, Sonoma County Fish & Wildlife Advisory Board 1986-; vice pres, Urban Creeks Council Sonoma Chapter 1988-. **Honors/Awds:** Author, "Peyote Moon" 1973; Comm Art Workshop. **Home Addr:** P O Box 464, Occidental, CA 95465. **Business Addr:** Writer, San Francisco Chronicle, N Bay Bureau, 50 Old Courthouse Square #604, Santa Rosa, CA 95404.

SNYDER, VANESSA W.
Editor, writer. **Personal:** Born Oct 19, 1964, Washington, DC; daughter of Alvin & Dorothy Williams; married Deron K Snydar, Sep 29, 1990; children: Sierra Ngozi. **Educ:** University of Maryland, BS, 1996. **Career:** Gospel Today, contributing writer, 1996-.

SOARIES, DEFOREST BLAKE, JR.
Pastor, author, speaker. **Personal:** Born Aug 20, 1951; son of DeForest B Sr & Mary M Soaries; married Donna Soaries; children: Malcolm, Martin. **Educ:** Fordham Univ, BA; Princeton Theological Seminary, MDiv; United Theological Seminary, DMin. **Career:** Kean College Union NJ, visiting professor; Shiloh Baptist Church, assoc pastor, 1987-90; First Baptist Church-Lincoln Gardens, pastor, 1991-. **Orgs:** First Baptist Community Dev Corp, chairman of bd; New Era Bank, bd of dirs. **Honors/Awds:** NJ Superior Court, Judicial Volunteers Program, 1993; Kappa Alpha Psi Fraternity Inc, Youth At Risk-Pathway Award, 1994; Elizabeth City State Univ, MLK Award, 1994. **Special Achievements:** My Family is Driving Me Crazy, 1991; Seven Bridges to the Promise Land, 1995. **Business Phone:** (908)828-2009.

SOARIES, RAYNES L., JR.
Administrator. **Personal:** Born Jan 11, 1924, Chattanooga, TN. **Educ:** Sch of Commerce NY U, BS 1972; Grad Sch of Pub Admin NYU, post grad 1973-74. **Career:** EEO Gen Motors Acceptance Corp, staff asst 1973-; Gen Motors Corp, analyst-stock 1963-73. **Orgs:** Mem Brooklyn Rotary Club 1974-; 1st vP Brooklyn Br NAACP 1974-; bd mem Brooklyn Br Urban League 1979-; bd mem Bedford Mental Health Clinic 1976-77; exec com mem The Edges Group Inc 1976-; treas Com Planning Bd #9 1978. **Honors/Awds:** Recipient of 5 Battle Stars European Theatre 1944-45; Pub Serv Award Econ Devel Counc of New York City 1974; Black Achievers Award in Ind Harlem Br of YMCA 1974; Roy Wilkins Award Harlem NAACP New York City 1976. **Military Serv:** AUS maj. **Business Addr:** 767 5th Ave, New York, NY 10023.

SOBERS, WAYNETT A., JR.
Corporate executive. **Personal:** Born Feb 15, 1937, Bronx, NY; son of Athlene Ghyll Sobers and Waynett Sobers; married Yvonne C Barrett, Aug 23, 1969; children: Loren, Julian, Stephanie. **Educ:** CCNY, BS 1959; Sobelsohn Sch of Ins, 1965; Baruch Coll, MBA 1972; Gen Motors Dealer Devel Acad 1987-88. **Career:** Meteorologist 1959-69; WA Sobers Assoc Inc, pres 1965-69; Johnson Publ Co, advertising rep 1969-71; Black Enterprise Mag, Mktg Svc, mgr 1971-73; Advertising & Mktg, vice pres 1973; EGG Dallas Broadcasting Inc, vice pres 1977; BCI Marketing Inc, president; Earl G Graves Ltd, exec vp 1980-87; Sobers Chevorlet Inc, president, general manager, 1988-90; WayVon, business consultant, owner, pres, 1990-; Bedford Stuyvesant Restoration Corp, exec vp, 1995-97. **Orgs:** Equitable Variable Life Ins Co, former director; Amer Management Association; Amer Marketing Assn; City College NY Alumni Association; CCNY Black Alumni Association; Bernard M Baruch College Alumni Assn; Chappaqua Ridge Assn, president, 1977; Chappaqua Rotary Club, secretary, 1992-95, vice pres, 1995-. **Honors/Awds:** Salesman of the Year-Ebony 1971; Exemplary Serv Award St Luke's Epis Ch 1976; Broadcaster of the Year Natl Assn of Black-Owned Broadcasters 1984. **Military Serv:** US Navy Reserves, lt, 1959-66. **Business Addr:** President, WayVon, Inc, 32 Brook Lane, Chappaqua, NY 10514-3540.

SOCKWELL, OLIVER R., JR.
Chief executive officer. **Personal:** Born Jul 27, 1943, Washington, DC; son of Janet Sockwell and Oliver Sockwell; married Harriet E; children: Kristine, Brian, Jason. **Educ:** Howard Univ, BS Physics 1965; Columbia Univ, MBA Finance 1972. **Career:** Bell System, commun engr 1965-67; IBM, mktg rep 1967-70; Smith Barney & Co, investment banker 1972-74; Sallie Mae Student Loan Mktg Assoc, vice pres mktg 1974-83, sr vice pres operation 1983-84, exec vice pres finance 1984-87; Connie Lee (Coll Construction Loan Insurance Assn), pres and CEO 1987-. **Orgs:** Dir, Connie Lee Insurance Co; dir, Association of FinancialGuaranty Insurors; board member, Columbia University School of Business; board member, National Ctrr for Learning Disabilities; board member, Ford's Theatre. **Business Addr:** President, CEO, Connie Lee, 1299 Pennsylvania Ave, NW, Washington, DC 20004.

SODEN, RICHARD ALLAN
Attorney. **Personal:** Born Feb 16, 1945, Brooklyn, NY; son of Clara Elaine Seal Soden and Hamilton David Soden; married Marcia LaMonte Mitchell, Jun 7, 1969; children: Matthew Hamilton, Mark Mitchell. **Educ:** Hamilton Coll, AB 1967; Boston Univ Sch of Law, JD 1970. **Career:** Hon Geo Clifton Edwards Jr US Court of Appeals for the 6th Circuit, law clerk 1970-71; Boston Coll Sch of Law, faculty 1973-74; Goodwin Procter & Hoar LLP, assoc 1971-79, partner 1979-. **Orgs:** Amer Natl MA & Boston Bar Assns, pres, 1994-95; Boston Bar Association, president, 1980-81; MA Black Lawyers Assn; chairman, emeritus, trustee Judge Baker Guidance Ctr 1974-; chairman, Boston Municipal Rsch Bureau 1996-; pres United South End Settlements 1977-79; adv cncl Suffolk Univ Sch of Mgmt 1980-; faculty MA Continuing Legal Educ 1980-; pres Mass Black Lawyers Assn 1980-81; Adv Task Force on Securities Regulation Sec of State of the Commonwealth of MA 1982-; director, Greater Boston Cncl Boy Scouts of Amer 1983-; adv comm on Legal Educ Supreme Judicial Ct of MA 1984-; Mass Minority Business Devel Commn; bd of visitors Boston Univ Goldman School of Graduate Dentistry; trustee, Boston University, 1995-; co-chairman, 1991-93, Lawyers Committee for Civil Rights Under Law. **Honors/Awds:** American Bar Foundation, Fellow; Boy Scouts of America, Silver Beaver Awd and Community Youth Svc Award, Heritage District; Theodore L Storer Awd; Boston University School of Law, Silver Shingle Awd; Massachusetts Bar Association, Community Service Awd; UNICEF-Boston Local Hero Awd; Camille Cosby World of Children Medallion. **Business Addr:** Attorney, Goodwin Procter & Hoar, LLP, Exchange Pl, Boston, MA 02109, (617)570-1533.

SOGAH, DOTSEVI Y.
Educator. **Personal:** Born Apr 19, 1945, Tegbi, Ghana; son of Fiawosinu Kwawudzo Sogah and Ahiati K Sogah; married Monica Adzo Selormey; children: Senanu, Dodzie, Esinam. **Educ:** Univ of Ghana, Legon Accra Ghana, BSc (First Class) 1970, BSc (Honors) 1971; UCLA Los Angeles CA, MS 1974, PhD 1975. **Career:** UC Santa Barbara, postdoctoral 1975-77; UCLA, rsch assoc 1977-80, vstg prof 1978-80; DuPont Co, rsch chemist 1981-83, group leader 1983-84, rsch suprv 1984-90, research manager, 1990-91; Cornell University, Ithaca, NY, professor, 1991-. **Orgs:** Bd of dir, 1982-84, president, 1987-90, Intl Soc of African Sci; chmn comm ACS Delaware Wilmington DE 1984-85; chmn proj comm ISAS 1985-; NY Acad of Sci, Sigma Xi Rsch Soc; Amer Chem Soc; Amer Assn for Advancement of Sci; visit prof Columbia Univ Spring 1984; visiting committee member, Lehigh University Chemistry Dept, 1989-. **Honors/Awds:** Distinguished Service Award, State of Delaware, 1991; Distinguished CUMIRP Lecturer, University of Massachusetts, 1989; Cornell University, Bayer-Mobay Award and Lecturship, 1988; Macromolecular Reports, Distinguished Editorial Board, 1989-; Macromolecules Engineering Colloquia-ACS Short Course, Distinguished Lecturer, 1986-90. **Business Addr:** Professor, Dept of Chemistry, Cornell University, Baker Laboratory, Ithaca, NY 14853-1301.

SOLIUNAS, FRANCINE STEWART
Attorney. **Personal:** Born Feb 14, 1948, Chicago, IL; daughter of Juanita Jeanette Harris Stewart (deceased) and Wilborn Stewart; married Jonas Soliunas, Nov 17, 1973; children: Lukas, Mikah. **Educ:** DePaul Univ, Chicago IL, BS Math, 1970; DePaul Univ Coll of Law, Chicago IL, JD, 1973. **Career:** State Appellate Defender, Chicago IL, staff attorney, 1974-76; Equal Employment Opportunity Commn, Chicago IL, supervising attorney, 1976-80; Illinois Bell Telephone Co, Chicago IL, sr attorney, 1980-88, sr dir labor relations, 1988-90, senior attory labor, 1990-. **Orgs:** Mem, Cook County Bar Assn, 1972-, Iowa State Bar Assn, 1974-86, Sickle Cell Anemia Volunteer Enterprise, 1980-, Natl Bar Assn, 1982-; trustee, St Thomas Theological Seminary, 1985-88; vice pres, Sickle Cell Anemia Volunteer Enterprise, 1985-87; dir, DePaul Univ President's Club, 1986-; mem, Chicago Bar Assn Judicial Evaluation Comm, 1987-; bd of dir, DePaul Univ Coll of Arts & Sciences Advisory Council, 1987-; dir, South Central Community Services, 1988-. **Honors/Awds:** Outstanding Corporate Achiever, YMCA-Chicago Tribune, 1987; Chicago's Up & Coming, Dollars and Sense, 1988; Distinguished Alumni, DePaul Univ, 1988; Black Rose Award, League of Black Women, 1988; 100 Most Influential Black Women in Corporate America, Ebony Magazine, 1990.

SOLOMON, BARBARA J.
Educator. **Personal:** Born Sep 10, 1934, Houston, TX; daughter of Malinda Edmond Bryant Stinson and Willie Bryant; married Donald; children: Hugo, Edmund, Jeffrey, Marcia. **Educ:** Howard U, BS 1954; Sch of Social Welfare Univ of CA, MSW 1956; Univ of So CA, DSW 1966. **Career:** USC, prof 1966-; Univ of CA Los Angeles Sch of Social Welfare, field instr 1962-63; Univ of TX Sch of Social Work, field instr 1958-60; VA Hospitals Houston & Los Angeles, clinical social worker 1957-63; Alameda Co Medical Institution, clinical social worker 1956-57; vice provost for Graduate and Professional Studies and Dean of the Graduate School 1987-; professor School of Social Work, 1994; vice provost, Faculty & Minority Affairs, 1994-. **Orgs:** Mem, Natl Assn of Social Workers; Council on Social Work Education; Council of Graduate Schools; Amer Assn of Higher Educ; mem, bd of dir Greater LA Partnership for the Homeless; Sickle Cell Foundation; CA Pediatric Center; United Way of LA; mem, Alpha Kappa Alpha; Links Inc. **Honors/Awds:** Author, "Black Empowerment Social Work in Oppressed Comms," NY Columbia Univ Press, 1976. **Home Addr:** 5987 Wrightcrest Drive, Culver City, CA 90232. **Business Addr:** Univ of Southern California, Administration Building, Room 202, Los Angeles, CA 90089-4015.

SOLOMON, DAVID
Government official. **Personal:** Born May 19, 1944, Wilmington, NC; son of Helen Spaulding Solomon and Vester Solomon; divorced. **Educ:** North Carolina A&T State University, Greensboro, NC, BS, 1966; St Louis University, St Louis, MO, MBA, 1976. **Career:** McDonnell Douglas, St Louis, MO, supervisor, 1970-72; Monsanto, St Louis, MO, supervisor, 1972-85; self-employed, Mt Laurel, NJ, president, 1985-88; North Carolina Dept of Economics and Community Development, Raleigh, NC, dir, MBDA, 1988-91; NC Department of Transportation, director civil rights, 1991-93; US Dept of Housing & Urban Dev, Washington DC, EO specialist, 1994-96; US Department of Transportation/FTA, regional civil rights officer, currently. **Military Serv:** US Air Force, captain, 1966-70. **Business Addr:** Regional Civil Rights Officer, US Dept of Transportation/FTA, 55 Broadway, Ste 920, Cambridge, MA 02142, (617)494-3038.

SOLOMON, DENZIL KENNETH
Health services president. **Personal:** Born May 5, 1952, Tucson, AZ; married Kathryn Jo; children: Christopher D, Alyxzander R. **Educ:** AZ State Univ, attended 1971-75. **Career:** Non Invasive Diagnostic Lab Inc, chief technologist 1977-78; Good Samaritan Hosp, chief tech/cardiac ultrasound lab 1978-79; Cardiovascular Dynamics Inc, vice pres 1978-79; Advanced Diagnostic Tech, pres cardiovascular rsch & develop 1978-; Skylab Aviation Svcs, pres 1984-86; Hemodynamics, owner 1981-; Solomon Tech Corp, pres 1985-. **Orgs:** Designed and built prototype of all-electronic digital dashboard for automobiles 1975-79; art work currently displayed Reading Ctr AZ State Univ 1975-86; program bd mem Amer Heart Assoc 1986; mem Natl Soc for Cardiopulmonary Tech, Amer Inst of Ultrasound in Medicine, Amer Soc of Echocardiography, Amer Soc of Ultrasound Tech Specialists, AZ Soc for Cardiopulmonary Tech, Soc of Non-Invasive Vascular Tech, Natl Geographic Soc, Scottsdale Ctr for the Arts, Amer Registry for Diagnostic Medical Sonographers; registered diagnostic medical sonographer, cardiovascular tech, emergency medical tech. **Honors/Awds:** Hemodynamics awarded Service Co of the Year US Dept of Commerce 1985; cert of copyright registration Abacus Ultrasound Computer Program 1985, Abacus Ultrasound Computer Program Rev I 1985, Abacus Ultrasound Computer Users Guide 1985; illustrated textbook "Tactics and Techniques"; Solomon Tech Corp awarded ServiceCompany of the Year Dept of Commerce 1986; keynote speaker at AZ Council of Black Engineers and Scientists 1986, Minority Business Enterprise Development Program Conf 1986; 6 papers submitted for publication; 4 newspaper articles published.

SOLOMON, DONALD L.
Business executive. **Personal:** Born Feb 13, 1932, Birmingham, AL; married Clarice; children: Donald Jr, Walter Lynn, Gerald. **Educ:** Miles Coll, BA; Life Ins Mgmt Course for Staff Mgrs, grad; LUTC, cert; OH State U, Savannah State Coll, US Armed Forces Inst, Univ of CA. **Career:** Booker T Washington Ins Co, VP, 1960-. **Orgs:** Mem Indus Devel Bd Dirs Birmingham; mem Omega Psi Phi Frat; mem Triune Lodge #430 FAM Mngr of Yr 3 yrs Nat Ins Assn. **Honors/Awds:** Blount Award Nat Ins Assn 1972-73; Merit Award Booker T Washington Ins Co. **Military Serv:** Served military ssgt discharged 1958. **Business Addr:** PO Box 697, Birmingham, AL 35201.

SOLOMON, FREDDIE
Professional football player. **Personal:** Born Aug 15, 1972, Gainesville, FL. **Educ:** South Carolina State, attended. **Career:** Philadelphia Eagles, wide receiver, 1995-. **Business Addr:** Professional Football Player, Philadelphia Eagles, 3501 S Broad St, Philadelphia, PA 19148, (215)463-2500.

SOLOMON, JAMES DANIEL
Physician (retired). **Personal:** Born Jun 3, 1913, Georgia; son of Amanda Gardner Solomon (deceased) and Stephen Solomon (deceased); married Effie O'Neal; children: Elaine E Comegys. **Educ:** Cntrl YMCA Coll, Chgo, BS 1941; DePaul U, Chgo, MS 1943; Meharry Med Coll Nashvl, MD 1953; Univ of IL Chgo, PhD 1953. **Career:** Univ of IL, rsrch asst 1939-42; St Elizabeth Hosp (HEW), chf Cl Path 1954-58, dir labs 1958-83; private pract, physician. **Orgs:** Pres St Elizabeth Hosp Med Soc 1977; mem Am Med Assn, Natl Med Assn 1985; mem New York Acad Sci 1985. **Honors/Awds:** Soc of Sigma Xi 1946; Fellow Nutrition Foundation Univ of IL 1947-49; Superior Serv Awd Dept HEW, Wash, DC 1960; Outstanding Per Awd Dept of HEW, Washington, DC 1961. **Military Serv:** USAF 1st lt 4 yrs. **Home Addr:** 1919 Ruxton Ave, Baltimore, MD 21216.

SOLOMON, JIMMIE LEE
Major league baseball executive. **Personal:** chilDren: 1 daughter. **Educ:** Dartmouth College, history degree with honors; Harvard Law School, graduated 1981. **Career:** Baker & Hostetler, attorney, 1981-, partner, starting 1990; Office of the Commissioner, Minor League Operations, dir, 1991-; co-owner of travel agency and restaurant in Washington D.C. **Business Addr:** Director, Minor League Operations, c/o Office of the Commissioner, 350 Park Ave, 17th Fl, New York, NY 10022-6022, (212)339-7800.

SOLOMON, WILBERT F.
Government official. **Personal:** Born Dec 17, 1942, Littleton, NC; married Litisia R Smith; children: Roderic, Natalie, Jerold. **Educ:** Clark Coll, BA 1965. **Career:** Regional dir, UD Department of Labor, Office of Admin Support, 1997-; Deputy admini, Office of Regional Management, Dept of Labor, 1993-97; senior vice pres, Aurora Assn, Inc. 1983-87; director, Older Worker Programs US Dept of Labor 1987-; Job Corps US Dept of Labor, dep dir 1978-, ofc of youth prgms 1978; US Dept of Labor Chicago, dep regnl dir 1974-78; Job Corps US Dept of Labor Atlanta, GA, proj mgr 1968-74; Job Corps City of Atlanta, dir 1968; Econ Opportunity ATL Inc, apprentice couns 1965-67. **Orgs:** Mem Omega Psi Phi Frat 1963; Sunday sch supt Ch of Our Lord Jesus Christ 1974-80; pres International Congress, Church of our Lord Jesus Christ 1981-. **Honors/Awds:** Recip Performance Awards, US Dept of Labor 1972, 1977, 1979. **Business Addr:** US Dept of Labor, 200 Constitution Avenue NW, N-5306, Washington, DC 20010.

SOMERSET, LEO L., JR.
Mortgage executive. **Personal:** Born Aug 27, 1945, Memphis, TN. **Educ:** Memphis State Univ, BBA 1968; Indiana Univ, MBA 1973. **Career:** Citicorp Real Estate Inc & Citibank NA, vice pres 1973-83; Colwell Financial Corp, vice pres 1983-. **Honors/Awds:** Noyes Fellow Consortium for Grad Study in Mgmt Indiana Univ 1971. **Military Serv:** USAF 1st lt 3 yrs; Honorable Discharge. **Business Addr:** Vice President, Colwell Financial Corp, 3223 West 6th St, Los Angeles, CA 90020.

SOMERVILLE, ADDISON WIMBS
Educator, psychologist. **Personal:** Born Aug 6, 1927, Greensboro, AL; son of Ellen Wimbs Somerville and Ernest Somerville; married Carolyn Coffey; children: Laurene, Ernest, Christopher. **Educ:** Howard Univ, BS Psych 1948, MS Psych 1950; IL Inst Tech, PhD Psych 1963. **Career:** Crownsvl State Hosp MD, cl psych intrn 1950; Tech Vly Frg Army Hosp PA, chf cl psych 1950-52; W Charlotte H Sch NC, gdnc dir 1953-54; Elgin State Hosp Elgin, IL, stf psychlgst 1954; IIT Inst for Psych Ser, cl & cnslng psych 1954-58; Dept of Pupil Aprsl Wash, DC, sch psych 1958-59; Francis W Parker Sch Chgo, chf sch psych 1959-64; Govt of Virgin Isls St Thomas, asst dir of plng for mntl hlth 1964-65; CA State Univ, Sacto, prof emeritus psych 1965-96; California State Univ, Sacramento, project director, NIMH, 1971-79; California School of Professional Psychology, Fresno, adjunct professor, 1985-90; private practice, Somerville & Somerville Associates 1975-; consultant, Dept of Public Safety, Calif State Univ, Sacramento, 1982-94; academic liaison, Sacramento Valley Chpt, Calif Assn of Marriage & Family Therapists, 1986-92; Assn of Black Psychologists (ABPsi); African-American Mental Health Providers, Greater Sacramento Area; CSUS, chemical dependency studies certificate academic coordinator, 1990-94. **Orgs:** Alpha Phi Alpha Fraternity Inc, 1945-; American Psychological Assn, Divisions 2, 12, 17, 29, 45, 50; Western Psychological Assn, life fellow; California State Psychological Association, membership committee, continuing education committee program and arrangements committee, 1988-94, chair, committee on multi-ethnic diversity, 1989-91; MCE Review Comm, 1995. **Honors/Awds:** Excptnl Merit Serv Awrd CA State Univ 1984; diplomate Am Bd of Professional Psych, Inc 1971; Apprvd Flw in Sex Educ in Intl Cncl of Sex Educ & Parenthd(FIC), Am Univ 1981; Cert Sex Thrpst & Sex Educ, Am Asso of Sex Edctrs, Cnslrs & Thrpst 1977-; over 20 articles pblshd in professional jrnls; Fellow and Diplomate American Brd of Medical Psychotherapists l988; Diplomate American Board of Sexology l989; Exceptional Merit Service Award for Outstanding Teaching and Service to the Community, California State Univ l988; Outstanding Teaching Award, 1992-93; Clinical Supervisor, American Board of Sexology, 1990; Life Fellow, Society for Personality Assessment, 1990; Nominated for APA Education and Training Board Award for Distinguished Contribution to Education and Training in Psychology, 1988; Phi Beta Delta, Omicron Chapter, CSUS, The Honor Society for Intl Scholars. **Special Achievements:** Certified addiction specialist, American Academy of Health Care Providers in the Addictive Disorders, 1992-; Bd certified dipomate, fellow prescribing psychologists' register, Inc, 1967-; Licensed Marriage, Family & Child Therapists, 1971; Licensed Psychologists, 1971; Licensed Educational Psychologist. **Military Serv:** US Army sgt 1950-52. **Home Addr:** 61 Grand Rio Cir, Sacramento, CA 95826-1718.

SOMERVILLE, PATRICIA DAWN
Human resources manager. **Personal:** Born Nov 24, 1956, Leonardtown, MD; daughter of Agnes Elizabeth Stevens Somerville (deceased) and James Mitchell Norris Somerville (deceased). **Educ:** University of Maryland, Princess Anne, MD, 1976-78; Howard University, Washington, DC, BS, Physical Therapy, 1978-80; Troy State University, Troy, AL, MS Management, 1982-83. **Career:** St Francis Hospital, Columbus, GA, cardiac physical therapist, 1980-81; US Army Infantry Center, Fort Benning, GA, administrator, 1981-84; Headquarters, Communications-Electronics Command, Fort Monmouth, NJ, personnel manager, 1994-. **Orgs:** Alpha Kappa Alpha Sorority. **Honors/Awds:** Most Studious Student, University of Maryland, 1976. **Business Addr:** Personnel Mgmt Specialist, Personnel & Training Directorate, Communications-Electronics Command (AMSEL-PT-PL-3), Fort Monmouth, NJ 07703.

SOMMERVILLE, JOSEPH C.
Educator. **Personal:** Born Dec 28, 1926, Birmingham, AL; married Mattie Cunningham; children: Joseph Jr, Barry C. **Educ:** Morehouse College, BS, 1949; Univ of Michigan, MS, 1956, EdS, 1966, PhD, 1969. **Career:** Ohio AARP, president, 1996-; College of Education, prof emeritus, 1992; Department of Educational Leadership, department chairman, prof of Adm & Supr; Univ of Toledo, prof of educ, dir of adminstrative internships, 1970-75; Wayne Co Intermediate School Dist, The Assist Center, staff development specialist, 1968-70; Woodson School, Inkster, MI, prin, 1965-68, teacher, 1949-65. **Orgs:** State Pres Ohio AARP; OH Assn of Elem Sch Principals; Assn for Sch Curriculum Development; Phi Kappa Phi; Am Educ Research Assn; exec bd, Natl Urban Educ Assn; pres, bd trustees, Toledo-Lucas Co Library; Westmoreland Assn; Phi Delta Kappa; Model Comm Sch Com; scholarship com chmn, Omega Psi Phi. **Honors/Awds:** Citation of Outstanding Serv to Wayne Co; speaker many natl & local professional confs; author several articles in natl & state journals & books. **Military Serv:** AUS, s/sgt, 1945-46. **Home Addr:** 1919 Richmond Rd, Toledo, OH 43607.

SOREY, HILMON S., JR.
Healthcare executive. **Personal:** Born Jan 14, 1935, Bascom, FL; son of Bricy Wilson Sorey and Hilmon S Sorey Sr; married Martha; children: Carla-Maria, Hilmon III; children: Megan, Mollie. **Educ:** Florida A&M University, BS, 1957; University of Chicago, MBA, 1969. **Career:** Florida A&M University Hospital, administrator, 1965-67; Cleveland Metro General Hospital, associate director, 1969-71; Michael Reese Health Plan, founder, executive director, 1971-75; Kellogg School, HHSM Program, Northwestern University, professor, program director, 1976-87; Hilmon S Sorey Assoc, president, 1987-90; Hawthorn Mellody, Inc, president/chief executive officer, 1990-93; Northwestern Memorial Hospital, vice president of community relations and vice pres of support services, 1993-97. **Orgs:** United Charities, board of directors; Panel of Bankruptcy Trustees, Northern District of Illinois; New Medical Foundation, president; Michael Reese Health Plan Inc, past vice pres, board of trustees; American College of Healthcare Executives; American Hospital Association; Group Health Association of America Inc. **Military Serv:** US Army, 1st Lt, 1958-60. **Home Addr:** 723 20th Street, Wilmette, IL 60091. **Business Addr:** President, Management Recruiters of Evanston, Inc, 1007 Church Street, Suite 302, Evanston, IL 60201.

SOSA, SAMUEL
Professional baseball player. **Personal:** Born Nov 10, 1968, San Pedro de Macoris, Dominican Republic. **Career:** Chicago White Sox, outfielder, 1990-92; Chicago Cubs, 1992-. **Business Addr:** Professional Baseball Player, Chicago Cubs, 1060 W Addison St, Chicago, IL 60613.

SOUTH, LESLIE ELAINE (LESLIE ELAINE JACKSON)
Judge. **Personal:** Born Jan 4, 1949, Chicago, IL; daughter of Mildred Nash South and Wesley South; married Arthur Jackson, Jul 5, 1981; children: Wesley Jackson, Christopher Jackson. **Educ:** Loyola University of Chicago, BA, 1975; Northwestern University, JD, 1978. **Career:** Cook County State's Attorney, 1978-82; Chicago Transit Authority, 1984-88; Circuit Court of Cook County, judge, currently. **Orgs:** Illinois Judicial Council, board of directors, 1988-, African-American History Month Committee, chairman, 1988-; Illinois Judges Association, 1988-; South Suburban Bar Association, 1989-; Womens Bar Association, 1992-; Illinois State Bar Association, 1992-. **Honors/Awds:** Black Prosecutors' Association, Distinguished Sfs, 1991; Illinois Judicial Council, Judicial Sfs, 1992. **Business Addr:** Judge, Apellate Court, 160 N LaSalle St, Ste N-1607, Chicago, IL 60601, (312)793-5450.

SOUTH, WESLEY W.
Radio executive. **Personal:** Born Mar 23, 1914, Muskogee, OK; son of Mayme Waterford South (deceased) and Elijah Wesley South (deceased); married Mildres Lynell Nash, May 18, 1946; children: Leslie Elaine South. **Educ:** Northwestern U, BS/BA. **Career:** Radio Sta WVON, 1961-; Chicago Courier, ed 1964-68; NOW Mag, pub, ed 1961-62; Chicago Am, columnist 1957-61; Ebony Mag, asso ed 1951-57; Chicago Defender, 1950-51. **Orgs:** Bd mem NAACP 1964-68; Chicago Urban League 1967-71; co-fdr People United to Save Humanity, PUSH, 1971-76; bd mem, v chmn PUSH; bd mem Afro-Am Patrolmen's League 1975-. **Military Serv:** AUS corpl 1943-45.

SOUTHALL, GENEVA H.
Educator. **Personal:** Born Dec 5, 1925, New Orleans, LA; divorced. **Educ:** Dillard University, BA, 1945; National Guild Pianist, Artist Diploma, 1954; American Conservatory of Music, MusM, 1956; University of Iowa, PhD, 1966. **Career:** University of Minnesota, professor Afro-American Music Culture in New World, 1970-; Grambling College, professor, 1966-70; South Carolina State College, associate professor, 1962-64; Knoxville College, assistant music professor, 1959-61; United States Information Service, chamber pianist, 1955. **Orgs:** American Student Faculty Assembly, University of Minnesota; Womens Student Assembly, University of Minnesota; Field Research Activ, Haiti & Jamaica; graduate faculty, Music Department, University of Minnesota; African Studies Council, University of Minnesota; music editor, Howard University Press; board directors, Urban League; NAACP; board of directors, Urban Coalition of Minneapolis; life member, board directors, Association for the Study of Afro-American Life & History; Metropolitan Cultural Arts Center; admissions board, Park Avenue Unit Methodist Church; board directors, National Women Helping Offenders; Society for Ethnomusicology; American Musicol Society; Crusade Scholar, Methodist Church, 1961-62; Pi Kappa Lamda, National Honors Music Society. **Honors/Awds:** Published in "Reflections in Afro-American Music", "Black Perspectives in Music". **Business Addr:** Afro-American Studies, University of Minnesota, 808 Social Science, Minneapolis, MN 55455.

SOUTHERLAND, ELLEASE
Professor, writer. **Personal:** Born Jun 18, 1943, Brooklyn, NY; daughter of Ellease Dozier Southerland and Monroe Penrose Southerland. **Educ:** Queens College of the City University of New York, BA, 1965; Columbia University, MFA, 1974. **Career:** Department of Social Services, New York City, caseworker, 1966-72; Columbia University, New York City, instructor in English, 1973-76; Borough of Manhattan Community College of the City Univ of New York, adjunct asst prof of black literature, 1973-; Pace University, New York City, poet in residence in African literature, 1975-; writer. **Honors/Awds:** John Golden Award for Fiction, Queens College of the City University of New York, 1964; Gwendolyn Brooks Poetry Award, Black World, 1972; author of novella White Shadows, 1964, author of poetry collection The Magic Sun Spins, Paul Breman, 1975, author of autobiographical novel Let the Lion Eat Straw, Scribner, 1979; contributor of stories, essays, and poems to anthologies and periodicals. **Business Addr:** Professor, Department of English, Pace University, 1 Pace Plaza, New York, NY 10038.

SOUTHERN, CHARLES O.
Housing authority executive. **Personal:** Born Feb 24, 1920, Cincinnati, OH; married Ingerborg Moltke; children: Cheryle D, Charles O Jr. **Educ:** Univ of Cincinnati, BS, 1948, Cert of Real Est 1959. **Career:** Wright Aeronautcl Corp Cincinnati, OH, mtrls hndlr 1941-42; Self-emplyd, elec eng 1948-56; Gen Elec Co Cincinnati, OH, aero eng 1956-82; Cincinnati Metro Hsng Auth, vice chmn bd of dir. **Honors/Awds:** Cert of Achvmnt Outstndng Comm Serv from Gen Electrc Co 1970. **Military Serv:** US Army Air Corp, Capt, 1942-46. **Home Addr:** 6865 Cooper Rd, Cincinnati, OH 45242.

SOUTHERN, EILEEN JACKSON
Educator, professor emerita. **Personal:** Born Feb 19, 1920, Minneapolis, MN; daughter of Lilla Gibson Rose Jackson and Walter Wade Jackson; married Joseph Southern; children: April Southern Reilly, Edward Joseph Southern. **Educ:** Univ of Chicago, BA 1940, MA 1941; New York Univ, PhD 1961. **Career:** Prairie View State Coll, lecturer, 1941-42; Southern Univ, asst prof 1943-45, 1949-51; Alcorn Coll, asst prof 1945-46; Claflin Univ, asst prof 1947-49; City Univ of New York, asst to full prof 1960-75; Harvard Univ, full prof 1975-87, prof emeritus. **Orgs:** Concert pianist Touring in USA, Haiti 1942-54; co-founder/editor, The Black Perspective in Music scholarly journal 1973-; mem, Assn for Study of Afro-Amer Life & History; mem, Alpha Kappa Alpha; bd, New York City YWCA, 1950; leader, Girl Scouts of Amer, 1950-1960; American Musicological Society; Sonneck Society for American Music, International Musicological Society. **Honors/Awds:** Alumni Achievement Award, Univ of Chicago 1971; Readings in Black American Music WW Norton 1971, revised 1983; Achievement Award, Natl Assn Negro Musicians 1971; Citation Voice of Amer, 1971; Deems Taylor Awrd ASCAP 1973; Bd of Dir, Amer Musicological Soc, 1974-76; Honorary MA, Harvard Univ 1976; Honorary Phi Beta Kappa Radcliffe/Harvard Chapter 1982; The Buxheim Organ Book (Brooklyn, NY) 1963; The Music of Black Amer (New York) 1971, 2nd Ed 1983, 3rd ed, 1997; Anonymous Pieces in the Ms El Escorial IVa24 Basel, Switzerland 1981; author, Biographical Dictionary of Afro-Amer & African Musicians (Westport) 1982; author of articles in The New Grove Dictionary of Music and Musicians (Macmillan) 1980 and The New Grove Dictionary of American Music (Macmillan), 1986; Honorary DA Columbia College, Chicago,1; bd of dirs Sonneck Soc of Ame Music 1986-88; co-editor, African-American Traditions: An Annotated Bibliography, Westport: Greenwood Press, 1990; Peabody Medal, Johns Hopkins Univ, 1991; African-American Musical Theater, Nineteenth Century, 1994. **Business Addr:** PO Drawer I, Cambria Heights, NY 11411.

SOUTHERN, HERBERT B.
Architect. **Personal:** Born May 21, 1926, Washington, DC; son of Mildred R Southern and Albert Southern; married Mary Ann. **Educ:** Howard U, BS Arch 1950; Catholic U, additional graduate architecture study. **Career:** Arch, private practice 1954-; Newark, NJ, draftsman 1951-53; Southern Associates, architect, currently. **Orgs:** Mem Am Inst of Arch; NJ Soc of Arch; bd dir Harmonia Savings Bank; mem NAACP, Urban League & other orgns; chairman, Piscataway, NJ Planning Board. **Honors/Awds:** Cit for archit design of Rahway Pub Library 1967. **Military Serv:** AUS sgt 1943-46. **Business Addr:** Architect, Southern Assocs Architects, 571 E Hazelwood Ave, Rahway, NJ 07065.

SOUTHERN, JOSEPH
Educator emeritus. **Personal:** Born Nov 21, 1919, Indianapolis, IN; son of Mary Southern and John Southern; married Eileen; children: April Southern Reilly, Edward Joseph. **Educ:** Lincoln Univ, BS 1941; Univ of Chgo, MBA 1945. **Career:** Prairie View State Coll, asst rgstr 1941-42; Southern Univ, asst prof 1944-45; Alcorn Coll, bsns mgr 1945-46; Claflin Univ, bsns mgr 194 6-49; KY State Coll, prof 1950-53; Cmnty Fin Corp, NY, mgr/vice pres 1953-57; New York Pub Sch, tchr 1957-71; City Univ NY (LaGuardia Coll), prof 1971-85. **Orgs:** Co-fndr & pres Fndtn for Rsrch in Afro-Am Creative Arts, Inc 1971-; co-fndr & mgn edtr The Black Perspective in Music 1973-; Asso for Stdy of Afro-Am Life & Hist; Kappa Alpha Psi; life mem NAACP; scout ldr Boy Scouts of Am. **Honors/Awds:** Awrd Boy Scouts of Am 1960. **Business Addr:** PO Drawer I, Cambria Heights, NY 11411.

SOWELL, JERALD
Professional football player. **Personal:** Born Jan 21, 1974. **Educ:** Tulane. **Career:** New York Jets, running back, 1997-. **Business Addr:** Professional Football Player, New York Jets, 1000 Fulton Ave, Hempstead, NY 11550, (516)560-8100.

SOWELL, MYZELL
Attorney. **Personal:** Born Nov 16, 1924, Detroit, MI; married Robin Hamilton. **Educ:** Wayne State Univ, BBA 1953; Detroit Coll, LlB 1952. **Career:** Gen law practice, specialist in criminal law 1953-67; Legal Aid and Defender Assn of Detroit, Defender Office, chief defender 1968-. **Orgs:** Mem Detroit Bar Assn; mem State Bar of Michigan; mem Wolverine Bar Assn; mem Natl Bar Assn; mem Amer Bar Assn; mem Natl Lawyers Guild; pres Michigan Assn of Criminal Defense Attys; mem Natl Legal Aid and Defender Assn; referee Civil Rights Comm; mem bd dir Homes for Black Children; life mem NAACP; mem bd dir Urban Alliance; mem Mayor's Comm on Civil Disturbance; mem Booker T Washington Businessmen's Assn; mem by-laws comm, Detroit-Wayne County Criminal Justice System Coord Co; mem Judiciary and Correc Comm, New Detroit Inc; mem Michigan Comm on Law Enforcement and Criminal Justice Task Force on Adjudication; mem adv comm Min Program, Comm of Visitors of Law School, Wayne State Univ Law School; mem bd dirs Wayne State Fund, Wayne State Univ; memWayne County Jail Adv Comm; lecturer ICLE;cturer Prosecuting Attys Assn of Michigan; lecturer Natl Def Coll; lecturer Northwestern Univ Law School, Criminal Law; lecturer Yale Univ Law School; lecturer Natl Dist Atty's Coll; mem Bd Regents, Natl Coll of Criminal Defense Lawyers and Public Defenders. **Military Serv:** AUS sgt 1943-45. **Business Addr:** 462 Gratiot, Detroit, MI 48226.

SOWELL, THOMAS
Educator. **Personal:** Born Jun 30, 1930, Gastonia, NC; married Alma Jean Parr; children: two. **Educ:** Harvard Univ, Cambridge MA, AB, 1958; Columbia Univ, New York NY, AM, 1959; Univ of Chicago, IL, PhD, 1968. **Career:** US Dept Labor, economist 1961-62; Rutgers U, instr 1962-63; Howard U, lectr 1963-64; Am Tel & Telegraph Co, econ analyst 1964-65; Cornell Univ, asst prof, 1965-69; Brandeis U, assoc prof, 1969-70; UCLA, assoc prof, 1970-74, prof of econ, 1974-80; Urban Inst, Washington DC, project dir, 1972-74. **Orgs:** Consultant, Urban Coalition, Rockefeller Found, Urban Inst. **Honors/Awds:** Author numerous works in field, incl Civil Rights: Rhetoric of Reality?, Morrow, 1985, Education: Assumptions versus History, Hoover Inst, 1986, Compassion versus Guilt, and Other Essays, Morrow, 1987, A Conflict of Visions: Ideological Origins of Political Struggles, Morrow, 1987; contr to numerous periodicals. **Military Serv:** US Marine Corps, 1951-53. **Business Addr:** Hoover Institution, Stanford, CA 94305.

SPAIN, HIRAM, JR.
Attorney, director. **Personal:** Born Aug 22, 1936, Conway, SC; married Doris; children: Hiram, Nicole. **Educ:** SC State Coll, BS 1961; Howard U, JD 1971. **Career:** Columbia Urban League, exec dir 1974-; Office of Gov of SC, proj dir 1972-74; legal intern, Greenville 1971-72; tchr 1961-68. **Orgs:** Nat Assn of Black Soc Workers; Delta Theta Phi Lavy Frat; Delta Psi Omega; consult HEW 1977; NABSW Bus Conf 1975; NAACP; Kappa Alpha Psi; Masons; Columbia Black Lawyers Assn; Notary Pub, SC; Delta Psi Omega; Health Policy Council, Gov John West 1974; Nat Council of Urban League. **Honors/Awds:** Outst Employee Award, NCIC 1971; Outst Bus Student Award, UBEA 1961; Outst Soldier, Bussac, France 1956. **Military Serv:** AUS 1954-57. **Business Addr:** Exec Asst for Self Sufficiency, State Dept of Soc Services, 1520 Confederate Ave, Columbia, SC 29230.

SPAN, DERRICK L.
Association executive. **Career:** Broome County Urban League League, pres/CEO, currently. **Business Addr:** President, Broome County Urban League Inc, 43-45 Carroll St, Binghamton, NY 13901.

SPANN, NOAH ATTERSON, JR.
Plant manager. **Personal:** Born Oct 13, 1938, E Chicago, IN; married Claudette; children: Dwayne, Darren, Tyrone. **Educ:** IN State Univ. **Career:** Mayor's Office E Chgo, admin asst 1975; Bd of Commiss of Lake Cty IN, cty commiss; East Chicago Water Filtration Plant, supervisor, currently. **Orgs:** Mem E Chicago Young Dem 1956-74, E Chicago Jaycees 1963-73, Frat Order of Masons Twin City Lodge 47 1974-; pres NW IN Reg Planning Comm, IL-IN Bi-State Comm, Tri-City Compr Mental Health, NW IN Sick Cell Found, NAACP; trustee Antioch Bapt Church; pres Five Cty Drainage Bd. **Honors/Awds:** Outstanding Member Serv to Lake Cty Young Dem Ray J Madden Serv Awd; Minority Bus Ste Com for Outstanding Mem; Zion Christian Expo 1976; Awd E Chicago NAACP 1975-76. **Military Serv:** USAR 1958. **Business Addr:** Supervisor, Water Filtration Plant, 3330 Aldis Street, East Chicago, IN 46312.

SPANN, PAUL RONALD
Cleric. **Personal:** Born Nov 7, 1943, Ann Arbor, MI; son of Ruth Ann Green Spann and Paul Leon Spann; married Jacqueline Graves, Jan 4, 1976; children: Shannon Lyn MacVean-Brown, Seth David. **Educ:** Kalamazoo College, BA, 1965; University of Rochester, 1965-66; Episcopal Divinity School, MDiv, 1970. **Career:** St Timothy's Church, assistant, 1970-71; Church of the Messiah, rector, 1971-. **Orgs:** Islandview Village Development Corporation, past president, founder, vice pres, currently; Christian Community Development Association, national secretary, 1989-93; Diocese of Michigan, standing committee, 1988-92; Union of Black Episcopalians, 1976-. **Honors/Awds:** Woodrow Wilson Foundation, fellowship, 1965-66; St Cyprian's Episcopal Church, Malcolm Dade Lectureship, 1989; Economic Justice Commission of the Diocese of Michigan, 1993. **Special Achievements:** Sojourners Liturgy Magazine, "Wholeness & Community," July 1991, "Oblivion & the Ghetto," November 1987. **Business Addr:** Rector, Church of the Messiah, 231 E Grand Blvd, Detroit, MI 48207, (313)567-1158.

SPANN, THERESA TIEUEL
Educator. **Personal:** Born Apr 21, 1918, Boley, OK; married Samuel Wayne Spann. **Educ:** TX Coll, 1933-36; Langston Univ, BS 1941; OK State Univ, MS 1964. **Career:** Boley Public School, spec educ teacher 1974, grade sch principal 1984; Midway Dry Good Co, mgr & owner 1979-85; council member-at-large; Oklahoma City District, Christian education director, 1990; Oklahoma City District Update, editor, 1992-. **Orgs:** Supt of Sunday School Amos Temple CME Church 1970-84; mem Zeta Phi Beta Sor; sec, music dir Ladies Indust Club 1980-85; dir Christian Ed in the OK City Dist of the Okea-Muskogee Conf of the Christian Methodist Episcopal Church; pianist & organist, sec Amos Temple CME Church 1963-85; chmn ed comm NAACP 1985-86; deputy clerk Boley School Board, 1988. **Honors/Awds:** Woman of the Year McAlester Dist of the CME Church 1968; Amos Temple Woman of the Year 1981; Inducted in Natl Christian Eds Council of Christian Methodist Episcopal Church 1983; del Gen Conf of Christian Methodist Episcopal Church 1982; Recognized for serv to ed Lampton Univ Dr Holloway pres 1983. **Home Addr:** PO Box 266, Boley, OK 74829.

SPARKS, PHILLIPPI DWAINE
Professional football player. **Personal:** Born Apr 15, 1969, Phoenix, AZ; married Jodi; children: P.J., Jordin. **Educ:** Arizona State, attended. **Career:** New York Giants, defensive back, 1992-. **Business Addr:** Professional Football Player, New York Giants, Giants Stadium, East Rutherford, NJ 07073, (201)935-8111.

SPARROW, RORY DARNELL
Professional basketball player. **Personal:** Born 1958, Paterson, VA. **Educ:** Villanova Coll, BS Engrg. **Career:** Scranton CBA; New Jersey Nets, 1981, Atlanta Hawks, 1982-83, New York Knicks, 1983-88, Chicago Bulls, 1988, Miami Heat, 1989-90, Sacramento Kings, 1990-. **Orgs:** Founder Rory D Sparrow Found. **Honors/Awds:** Scored career high 30 points with Atlanta vs Chicago in 1982; all Big-5 First Team; US Basketball Writer's All-Dist Team; Eastern Atl Assoc All-Tour Team.

SPAULDING, AARON LOWERY
Investment banker. **Personal:** Born Mar 16, 1943, Durham, NC. **Educ:** Attended NC Central Univ Durham 1960-64; attended Wharton Grad Sch of Finance & Commerce Univ of PA Philadelphia 1966-68. **Career:** Re-Con Serv Inc, dir & co-founder 1968; JFK Center for the Performing Arts, comptroller 1972-74; Boyden Bd of Dirs Servs, exec dir 1974; B&C Assoc Washington, dir bus devel & consult 1974; Exec Office of the Pres The White House, assoc dir pres personnel office 1974-77; Salomon Brothers Inc, vice pres 1977-. **Orgs:** Pres Wharton MBA Assn; rsch asst Dept of Industry & the Placement Office (RE-CON Proj) Univ of PA. **Honors/Awds:** Outstanding Acad Achievement Awd NC Central Univ 1964. **Military Serv:** USN supply corps officer & mil social aide 1969-72. **Business Addr:** 1800 Redwood, NW, Washington, DC 20012.

SPAULDING, DANIEL W.
Real estate broker. **Personal:** Born Oct 24, 1909, Whitesboro, NJ; son of Hattie and Henry; married Hazel B; children: Donna Jefferson. **Educ:** Lincoln U, AB 1932; MD Univ, grad studies; Mortgage Loan Correspondent Taught Real Estate; North Mutual Life Insur Co, Durham NC. **Career:** Spaulding Realty Co Inc, owner; Morgan State Coll, tchr 3 yrs. **Orgs:** Pres Nat Assn of Real Estate Brokers Inc 1973-75; Maryland Real Estate Commission, 1972-75; former exec vice pres Advance Fed Savs & Loan Assn of Baltimore; former chmn Mortgage Loan Dept, Adv Fed Savs & Loan Assn of Baltimore; bd dir Real Estate Brokers of Baltimore Inc; mortgage loan ofcr NC Mutual Life Ins Co; past bd dir Council for Bus Opportunity; negotiator for Baltimore Comm & Housing Devel Vacant House Prgm; chmn Pub Affairs Com, Nat Assn of Real Estate Brokers Inc; mem Legislative Narello Com of NAREB; past pres Bus League of Baltimore City; chmn trustee bd Grace Presb Ch; chmn bldg com Grace Presb Ch; chmn Housing Com of Baltimore Br, life member NAACP; former bd dir Cit & Planning Housing Adminstr of Baltimore; past treas Urban League of Baltimore City; mem Omega Psi Frat; 33 degree Ancient & Acception-Scottish Rite Mason; Prince Hall Affiliation. **Honors/Awds:** Co-author of "History of My Native Home.".

SPAULDING, JEAN GAILLARD
Educational administrator. **Personal:** Born Feb 23, 1947, Birmingham, AL; divorced; children: Chandler, Courtney. **Educ:** Barnard College, AB, 1968; Duke Univ School of Medicine, MD, 1972. **Career:** Duke Univ Medical Ctr, Dept of Psychiatry, adjunct faculty, 1990-, vice chancellor for health affairs, 1998-; private psychiatry practice, 1977-; WNCU Public Radio, co-host of weekly radio show, 1997-; WTVD Newschannel 11, consultant, 1997-. **Orgs:** Alpha Omega Alpha Honor Society; American Psychiatric Assn; American Medical Assn; National Medical Assn; American Assn of Psychiatric Services for Children; American College of Forensic Examiners; NC Neuro-Psychiatric Assn; NC Council of Child Psychiatry; Durham-Orange County Medical Society; North Carolina Medical Society; Old North State Medical Assn; Josiah Charles Trent Memorial Foundation, bd of dirs, 1990-, vice pres, 1995-; Research Triangle Foundation, bd of trustees, 1993-; Wachovia Bank of North Carolina, bd of dirs, 1995-. **Honors/Awds:** American Medical Assn, Physician's Recognition Award. **Special Achievements:** First African American woman to attend Duke's School of Medicine; "Delayed Psychiatric Casualties from the Vietnam Conflict," Mental Health and Behavioral Science, Vol. XVIII, No. 3, August 1976; "Anniversary Reactions," Psychosomatics, Vol. XVII, No. 4, 1976, pp 210-12; "Grief: Normal or Abnormal?" North Carolina Medical Journal, Vol. 39, No. 1, January 1978, pp. 31-34. **Business Addr:** Vice Chancellor for Health Affairs, Duke Univ Medical Center & Health System, M101 Davidson Bld, Box 3071, Durham, NC 27710, (919)681-6591.

SPAULDING, LYNETTE VICTORIA
Attorney. **Personal:** Born Dec 21, 1954, Bronx, NY; daughter of Gertie Mae Spaulding and Aaron M Spaulding. **Educ:** SUNY at Stony Brook, BA 1976; Syracuse University College of Law, JD 1979. **Career:** Syracuse University Law School, secretary 1976-79; Bristol Lab, law clerk 1977-79; Legal Aid Society of Westchester Co, attorney, 1979-, sr attorney/deputy bureau chief, 1987-. **Orgs:** Chairperson, bd of trustees, Divine Light USDA Church 1985-; treasurer, NAACP at Stony Brook, 1975-76; committee chairperson, Black American Law Students Association , 1976-79; justice, Judicial Board, Syracuse University College, 1976-79; board of directors, Natl Assn of Black Women Attorneys, 1978-82; Black Lawyers of Westchester Co 1997, College of Law, Moot Court Board, 1979; New York State Bar. **Honors/Awds:** Special Recognition, BALSA & Womens Law Caucus Law Day 1977; Frederick Douglass Moot Court, BALSA Natl 1979; Reginald Heber Smith Comm, lawyer fellowship program 1979; subject of article, Defender's Digest. **Business Addr:** Attorney, Legal Aid Society of Westchester, 1 N Broadway, 9th fl, White Plains, NY 10601.

SPAULDING, ROMEO ORLANDO
Firefighter. **Personal:** Born Aug 27, 1940, Whiteville, NC; son of Sarah George Spaulding and Ralph Spaulding; married Annette Richardson Spaulding, Jan 23, 1962; children: Valerie G, Bernardine E, Alva G, Karen R, Kevin R. **Educ:** Howard University, Washington, DC, math, 1958-62; Univ of the Dist of Columbia, Washington, DC, fire service, 1969-70; University of Maryland, College Park, MD, Natl Staff & Command School, 1981. **Career:** Kenwood Golf & Country Club, Bethesda, MD, food service, 1958-59; Columbia Hospital for Women, Washington, DC, procurement, 1959-65; District of Columbia Fire Dept, Washington, DC, dir, comm relations/lt, 1965-92; International Association of Black Professional Fire Fighters, president, currently. **Orgs:** President, Intl Assn of Black Prof Fire Fighters, 1988-; executive board member, National Black Leadership Roundtable, 1981-90; president, Progressive Fire Fighter Assn, 1981-85; treasurer, PG County PTA, 1976-80; Superintendent, Sunday Sch Bethel Bible Church, 1976-. **Honors/Awds:** Firefighter of the Year, Firehouse Magazine, 1989; Natl School Volunteer of the Year, 1989; Christian Man of the Year, Bethel Bible Church, 1989; Congressional Commendation, US Congress, 1985; Community Service Award, District of Columbia Government, 1986, 1987.

SPAULDING, WILLIAM RIDLEY
Elected city official. **Personal:** Born in Clarkton, NC; married Dolores Hinton; children: Angelyn Flowers, Michelle, Deirdre. **Educ:** Howard Univ, BS Mech Engrg 1947. **Career:** DC Public Schools, instructor 1947-52; Howard Univ, instructor 1950-60; Nat Security Agency, engr 1952-74; Univ District of Columbia, instructor 1980; City Council councilman. **Orgs:** Chair Ft Lincoln Found; bd mem Kidney Found; bd mem Amer Heart Assn; chair Talent Search Inc. **Honors/Awds:** Producer Metro Talent Search 1978-85. **Home Addr:** 1905 Randolph St NE, Washington, DC 20018. **Business Addr:** Councilman, City Council, 14th & E Sts NW, Washington, DC 20004.

SPEAKS, RUBEN L.
Bishop. **Career:** African Methodist Episcopal Zion church, sr bishop. **Business Addr:** Sr Bishop, African Methodist Episcopal Zion Church, 401 E 2nd St, Charlotte, NC 28202, (704)332-3851.

SPEAR, E. EUGENE
Attorney. **Personal:** Born Apr 18, 1938, Cinn; married Delois Jean (divorced); children: Lisa Dawn, Selena Marie; married Minnie M. **Educ:** Univ of CT, BA Econ 1960; Univ of CT Sch of Law, grad 1963. **Career:** Superior Ct, CT Judicial Dept, pub defender, 1973-82; Merchant Melville Spear & Seymour, Bridgeport & Stamford, attorney, 1963-73; Juvenile Ct, Bridgeport, ct advocate 1968-70; Superior Court, judge, 1982-93; Appellate Court, judge, 1993-. **Orgs:** Past mem bd dir Bridgeport Legal Ser Inc; mem bd dir Bridgeport C of C; Org CT Savings & Loan Assn; mem Bridgeport Bar Assn; Bd of Fire Commrs, Bridgeport; chmn Bapt Hous Site Agy; pres Hall Neighborhood House; Bridgeport Bd of Edn. **Honors/Awds:** Man of Yr , Jr C of C 1968; Outs Young Man of CT, CT Jaycees 1968; Outs Young Man of New England, New England Jaycees 1968; CT Trial Lawyers, Judge of the Year Award, 1991. **Business Addr:** Superior Ct, 1061 Main St, Bridgeport, CT 06604.

SPEARMAN, LARNA KAYE
Engineer. **Personal:** Born May 7, 1945, Kokomo, IN; married Sarah Jewell Busch; children: Angela, Derek. **Educ:** Purdue U, BS 1967; IN Univ Law Sch, 1969-71. **Career:** Eli Lilly & Co, personnel 1977-; Mayor, coord 1976-77; Eli Lilly & Co, supr 1971-76; Detroit Deisel-Allison, engr 1967-71. **Orgs:** Guest lectr, mem Nat Crime Prevention Inst; Sch of Police Adminstrn, Univ of Lousiville; v-chmn Human Rights Commn of Indianapolis & Marion Co 1973-; sec Indianapolis Settlements Inc 1974-; bd mem Indianapolis Chap NAACP 1969-; Indianapolis Black Rep Cncl 1975-; Indianapolis Police Merit Bd 1970-74; Minority Contractors Adv Cncl 1970-71. **Honors/Awds:** Distshd Serv Award, Indianapolis Jaycees 1977; Outstdg Young Hoosier Award, IN Jaycees 1977; Citz Award, Police League Of IN 1977. **Business Addr:** 307 E Mc Carty St, Indianapolis, IN 46204.

SPEARMAN, LEONARD HALL O'CONNELL, SR.
Federal official. **Personal:** Born Jul 8, 1929, Tallahassee, FL; married Valeria Benbow; children: Lynn S McKenzie, Leonard Jr, Charles M. **Educ:** FL A&M Univ, BS, 1947; Univ of MI, MA, 1950, PhD, 1960, post doctoral study, 1965. **Career:** Lincoln HS, tchr biol scis 1949-50; FL A&M Univ, assoc prof of psych 1950-60; Lower Coll, prof psych, dean 1965-70; Southern Univ, prof of psych, dean 1960-70; Queens Coll of NY, visit prof of psych 1965; Rutgers Univ, Martin Luther King Scholar 1969; US Office of Educ Wash, DC, dir div of student spec serv 1970-72; Univ of DC, visit lectr 1971-80; US Office of Edn, dir div of student assist 1972-75, assoc commr for student asst 1975-78, assoc dep commr higher/cont educ 1978-80; US Dept of Education, assoc dep asst sec higher/cont educ 1980; TX Southern Univ, president, 1980-86; US Dept of State, US ambassador, Republic of Rwanda, 1988-90, Kingdom of Lesotho, 1990-. **Orgs:** Natl Adv Bd on Intl Educ Programs, 1982-85, chmn, 1985; Governor's Adv Comm on Equal Educ Oppty State of TX; Governor's Adv Comm on Women and Minorities State of TX; bd dirs Houston C of C 1985; Clean Houston Commn; founding mem bd Houston Lyceum; bd govs Houston Forum Club 1985; bd dirs Houston Chptr Natl Kidney Found 1985; bd mem Sam Houston Area Cncl Boy Scouts of Amer; bd dirs Houston Chptr Amer Red Cross; Houston Job Training Partnership Cncl; Neighborhood Adv Comm Freedmen's Town Assn Inc. **Honors/Awds:** LLD Shaw Univ NC 1970; LLD Oakland Univ MI 1973; LLD Southern Vermont 1978; DHL Edward Waters Coll FL 1975; Lincoln Univ, LLD, 1988; Meritorious Achievement Award FL A&M Univ 1972; Superior Serv Award Highest Honor in the US Office of Education 1975; Distinguished Serv Award Highest Honor in the Dept of Health, Educ & Welfare 1978. **Special Achievements:** Author: "The Key, Knowing Language," The Houston Chronicle, Nov 16, 1980; "Quality Control Will Benefit Minorities, Too," The Houston Chronicle, Jun 26, 1983; "On De-endangering: An Endangered Academic Species, Ruminations on the Status of an American Black College," Meeting of the American Cncl on Education, San Francisco, Oct 9, 1980; "Federal Roles and Responsibilities Relative to the Higher Education of Blacks since 1967," Journal of Negro Education, vol 50, num 3, Summer 1981. **Home Addr:** 631 G St SW, Washington, DC 20024. **Business Addr:** US Ambassador, Kingdom of Lesotho, Public Affairs, Department of State, CA-PA, Rm 507, Washington, DC 20520.

SPEARS, HENRY ALBERT, SR.
Insurance agent, registered representative. **Personal:** Born Jun 4, 1928, Montgomery, AL; son of Jettie Bennett (deceased) and Dan Spears (deceased); married Kathleen Stanford, Aug 18, 1947; children: Vicki Regina Truitt, Henry A Jr, Kathy Evangeline Cobbs. **Educ:** AL State Coll Lab School, Graduate (Valedictorian) 1946; AL State Univ, BS Sec Ed 1950 (third honors), MEd 1955; Springfield Coll, Grad Study 1959; NY Life Career Course & NASD Registerd Rep Courses 1973-74. **Career:** St Jude's Educ Inst Montgomery AL, teacher auto mechanics 1949-50; G W Carver High School, sci & math teacher 1950-55; Carver Adult School, instr 1954-55; Montgomery YMCA, exec sec 1955-63, 1968-69; AL State Coll, dir coll relations 1963-68; AL State Univ, vice pres for development 1969-72; NY Life Ins Co, field underwriter, 1972-, RHU designation 1979-, NYLIFE Securities, Inc, registered rep, 1986-. **Orgs:** Montgomery Athletic Boosters Club 1973-; Montgomery & National Association of Life Underwriters 1973-96; adv bd Central AL Home Health Serv Inc 1974-89; board of directors, adv bd, AL State Univ Foundation, Inc 1974-94, chairman of the board, 1992-94, exec dir, 1994-; board member Montgomery Co Bd of Educ 1976-, chairman of the board, 1988-92, vice chairman of the board, 1996-; Red Cross Three Gallon Plus Donor Club 1991-; trustee, Lomax-Hannon Jr Coll 1978-93; board of directors, adv bd, Goodwill Industries, 1983-; honorary life board member Montgomery Metropolitan YMCA; board member, Cleveland Ave Branch YMCA; past pres Dist IV and former board member, and completed Master Level School Bd Academy, 1992; AL Assn of School Bds; life mem Omega Psi Phi Fraternity, Inc; board member Omega Life Memshp Foundation, 1986-92; dist rep of 7th Dist, Omega Psi Phi Fraternity, Inc, 1989-92, Supreme Council, Omega Psi Phi Fraternity, Inc, 1989-92; former basileus, KRS and KF of Sigma Phi Chapter of Omega Psi Phi Fraternity; mem Alpha Kappa Mu, Beta Kappa Chi, Phi Delta Kappa; former steward and past trustee Mt Zion AME Zion Church Inc; life mem, National Education Association; Elks So Pride Lodge #431, W Montg Masonic Lodge #921; 33 degree Mason mem PH Consistory No 19; Montgomery Chapter NAACP; Democratic Party/Club; AL Democratic Conference; steering comm, Council of Urban Bds of Ed, Natl Sch Bds Assn, 1988-96; Committee of "100" Mgt Area Chamber of Commerce, 1990-92. **Honors/Awds:** Distinguished Serv & Prestige to the Univ, AL State Univ 1972; Outstanding Serv to Montgomery Area United Appeal 1973; Outstanding Alumni Awardees AL State Univ Centennial 1974; Omega Man of the Year Awd, Omega 7th Dist, 1992; Outstanding Leadership in the Montgomery Urban League 1979-81; qualified each year as a "Star Club Member" through a notable sales record with NY Life 1973-81; Health Ins Leader 5 yrs, RHU 1979; Citizen of the Year Awd Sigma Phi Chap 1982; 30 Yrs of Serv Plaque YMCA 1982; Natl Sales Achievement Awd 10 yrs; Natl Quality Awd 6 yrs; Health Ins Quality Award 5 yrs; Leading Producers Roundtable Health Ins 3 yrs; Reg Prof Disability Income & Health Ins Underwriter, RHU. **Home Addr:** 2069 Wabash St, Montgomery, AL 36108-4152. **Business Addr:** Agent/Registered Representative, New York Life Insurance Co, 4001 Carmichael Rd, Ste #150, Montgomery, AL 36106.

SPEARS, MARCUS
Professional football player. **Personal:** Born Sep 28, 1971. **Educ:** Northwestern State-Louisiana. **Career:** Chicago Bears, linebacker, 1995-96; Kansas City Chiefs, 1997-. **Business Addr:** Professional Football Player, Kansas City Chiefs, One Arrowhead Dr, Kansas City, MO 64129, (816)924-9300.

SPEARS, SANDRA CALVETTE
Marketing executive. **Personal:** Born Aug 9, 1964, Pontiac, MI; daughter of Sandra Wilkerson Lockett and Calvin Spears. **Educ:** Eastern Michigan University, Ypsilanti, MI, BS, 1986. **Career:** Total Health Care Inc, Detroit, MI, marketing rep, 1987-89, marketing development coordinator, 1989, new provider & marketing development coordinator, 1989-90, account executive, 1990, asst public marketin g manager, 1994-. **Orgs:** Natl Assn of Health Service Executives, 1987; Southeastern Michigan Health Executive Forum, 1987; NAACP, 1986; Booker T Washington Business Assn, 1986; EMU Alumni Assn, 1986. **Honors/Awds:** Top Sales Achiever, Total Health Care, 1987-90. **Home Addr:** 25151 Greenbrooke Dr, Southfield, MI 48034.

SPEARS, STEPHANIE
Travel consultant. **Personal:** Born Dec 9, 1949, San Francisco, CA; daughter of Richard McGee & Thadyne Black McGee; married John Spears, Jul 22, 1972; children: Mikele Adriana, Julian Richard. **Educ:** University of California, Berkeley, BA, 1972. **Career:** Scenery Unltd Tours, travel consultant, 1968-82; Empire Tours, retail office mgr, 1982-83; Blue World Travel, travel consultant, 1983-88; Adventure Express/Rascals in Paradise, operations mgr, 1988-98; Blue World Travel, dir of product development, 1998-. **Orgs:** International Federation of Women's Travel Organization, pacific governor, 1997-99; San Francisco Women In Travel, pres, 1995-97; Travel Agent Advisory Bd, Govt of the Bahamas, 1996-; African-American Historical/Cultural Society, bd mem, 1997-. **Special Achievements:** Portion of essay published in Travel Guide for African-American Women, 1997. **Home Addr:** 3450 Wyman St, Oakland, CA 94619. **Business Addr:** Director, Blue World Travel Corp., 50 First St, No 411, San Francisco, CA 94105, (415)882-9444.

SPEARS-JONES, PATRICIA KAY (PATRICIA JONES)
Poet/arts administrator. **Personal:** Born Feb 11, 1951, Forrest City, AR; daughter of Lillie B Dodd Spears Jones and Lee Spears. **Educ:** Rhodes Coll, BA Communications 1973; Vermont Coll, MFA candidate 1992. **Career:** Poet/Writer, 1974-; Samuel French Inc, mgr amateur leasing 1974-77; Coordinating Council of Literary Magazines, grants progs dir 1977-81; Freelance journalist: Essence, The Village Voice, Poetry Project Newsletter, 1978-; Heresies Collective Inc, managing coord 1982-83; Poetry Project at St Mark's Church, prog coord 1984-86; MA Council on the Arts & Humanities, program specialist 1987-; Film News Now Edn, program dir, 1990-91; New Museum of Contemporary Art, devt associate, 1991-94, director of planning devt, 1994-96; Authors Read Aloud, proj director, consultant, 1996-. **Orgs:** Vice pres Natl Assoc of Third World Writers 1979-82; consultant CCLM 1981; dir Mabou Mines 1984-86; mem Poetry Soc of Amer 1984-, NY Assoc of Black Journalists 1985-86; bd of dirs, Poetry Project, 1991. **Honors/Awds:** Panelist CCLM, OH Arts Council, MA Artists Foundation 1976-85; Fellow in Poetry CAPS 1983-84, New York Foundation for the Arts 1986; publication, "Mythologizing Always," Telephone Books CT 1981; travel/research grant, Goethe Institute 1988; mem advisory bd Artgarden, Amsterdam the Netherlands; juror, Judith's Room Emerging & Outstanding Women Poets Series, 1991; Fellow in Poetry National Endowment for the Arts, 1993; Panelist, Lifetime Program, New York State Council on the Arts, 1993-94; Author, The Weather That Kills, Coffee House Press, Minneapolis MN, 1995; Grant recipent Foundation for Contemporary Performance Arts Inc, 1996. **Business Addr:** Consultant, Project Director, Authors Read Aloud, New York City School Volunteer Program, Inc, 352 Park Ave, S, New York, NY 10010.

SPEEDE-FRANKLIN, WANDA A.
Educational administrator. **Personal:** Born Aug 1, 1956, Bronx, NY; married Melvin L Franklin; children: Ihsan K. **Educ:** Princeton Univ, BA 1978, certificate of prof in African-Amer Studies 1978; Northwestern Univ, MA 1980. **Career:** Princeton Univ, rsch asst computer ctr 1974-78, asst to dir third world ctr 1974-78; Chicago Metro History Fair, assoc dir for programs & operations 1980-82; Natl Assn of Independent Schools, minority affairs & info serv 1982-87; asst dir for admin, public affairs, Mass Bay Transportation Authority, 1987-88; dir, Newton Metco Program, 1988-. **Orgs:** Mem Natl Assn of Black School Educators; mem Amer Assn for Affirmative Action; mem Natl Assn of Negro Women; bd mem Metro Council for Equal Opportunity (METCO) 1985-; trustee Project Match Minority Student Talent Search Agency 1984-. **Honors/Awds:** Graduate Fellowship Northwestern Univ 1978-79; contributing author of

Visible Now: Blacks in Private Schools, Greenwood Press, 1988. **Business Addr:** Director, Newton Metco Program, Newton Public Schools, 100 Walnut Street, Room 112, Newtonville, MA 02160.

SPEIGHT, EVA B.
Educator. **Personal:** Born Dec 9, 1930, Snow Hill, NC; daughter of Easter B Bess and Eddie L Bess; married James Thomas Speight Jr, Aug 25, 1962; children: Sharon, Thomara, James T, III. **Educ:** Howard Univ; DC Teacher Coll; Univ of NC; NC A&T State Univ, BS 1957; Trinity Coll. **Career:** Jr HS, Washington DC Bd of Educ, teacher of English 1962-; Jones County Bd of Educ, Trenton NC, teacher 1957-62. **Orgs:** Mem Washington Teacher Union; sec, principal advisory council Sousa Jr HS; advisor Natl Jr Honor Soc; charter mem Kinston Alumnae Chapter Delta Sigma Theta Sorority; Les Torchettes Social Club, NC 1957-62; pres Washington Alumnae Chapter Delta Sigma Theta Sorority Inc 1974-76; past pres Alpha Phi Alpha Wives of Washington DC 1969-71; mem choir Ebenezer Baptist Church, NC; Natl Council of Negro Women; PTA; NC A&T State Univ Alumni Assn; Penn Branch Civic Assn; NAACP; Urban League; sec Capitol Hill Montessori School Bd. **Honors/Awds:** Pres Award, Alpha Wives of Washington, DC 1975; delegate to regional conf Delta Sigma Theta 1972 & natl convention 1975; Reclamation Award, Delta Sigma Theta, 4 yrs; Awardee Agnes G Meyer Found (one of five finalists); Citation/Plaque-Superintendent, Outstanding Teacher/Service Award. **Business Addr:** Teacher of English, District of Columbia Public Schools, 415 12th St, NW, Washington, DC 20004.

SPEIGHT, VELMA R.
Educational administrator (retired). **Personal:** Born Nov 18, 1932, Snow Hill, NC; daughter of Mable Edwards Speight and John Thomas Speight; divorced; children: T Chineta Kennedy Bowen. **Educ:** A&T State Univ NC, BS 1953; Amer Univ; Morgan St Coll, NSF Fellow 1956; Univ of Maryland, NSF Fellow 1957, MEd Guidance 1965, PhD Counseling Personnel Serv 1976; Virginia State Coll, NDEA Fellow 1963. **Career:** Kennard High Sch, teacher 1954-60; Kennard High Sch, Queen Anne's Co High Sch, counselor 1960-68, coordinator guidance dept 1966-68; NDEA Inst for Disadvantaged Youth, Univ of Maryland, Eastern Shore Br, staff consultant summer 1967; Family Life & Sex Educ, Caroline, Kent, Queen Anne's & Talbot Cos, curriculum res specialist 1969; Univ of Maryland, Johns Hopkins Univ, visiting prof, assoc prof; Equal Opportunity Recruitment Prog, Univ of Maryland, dir 1972; Maryland State Dept of Educ, asst supr compensatory urban & supplementary programs 1969-72, specialist guidance 1972-76, administrator 1976, asst state supt 1982-86; Univ of Maryland, Eastern Shore, Princess Anne MD, chair, dept of counseling educ, 1986-87; East Carolina Univ,Greenville NC, chair, dept of counseling & adult educ, bening 1987; Dept of Educ, Univ of MD Eastern Shore, chair, 1989-93; NC A & T State Univ, dir of alumni affairs, until 1997. **Orgs:** Life mem, MD State Tchr Assn; Natl Educ Assn; first black pres, Queen Anne's County Tchr Assn & Educ Assn; MD Assn for Counselor Educ & Supv; MD Sch Counselors Assn; Amer Personnel & Guidance Assn; MD Assn of Curriculum Devel, Amer Assn of School Bus Officials; Delmarva Alumni Assn, A&T State Univ; Study Group Mothers Prevent Dropouts; tchr, Summer Courses for Black Students; organizer, chmn, Youth Group to Study Problems of Integration; Queen Anne's, Kent & Talbot Cos Comm Action Agency Bd; MD & Natl Congress Parents & Tchrs; NAACP; organizer, chmn, Parent Educ Group Communication Rather Than Confrontation; chmn, Christian Social Relations Comm, Weslyan Serv Guild; Assn for Sup & Curriculum Devel, Amer Assn for Counseling & Devel, Assn for Counselor Educ & Sup, Natl Career Devel Assn, School Counselors Assn, Amer Rehabilitation Counseling Assn; Assn for Meas & Evaluation in Counseling & Devel, Assn for Multicultural Counseling & Devel, MD Assn for Counseling & Devel, MD Career Devel Assn, MD Assn for Multicultural Counseling & Devel; organizer, Black Churches for Educational Excellence, 1987-; bd of trustees, NC A&T State Univ. **Honors/Awds:** Woman of the Year, Negro Business & Professional Women's Orgn; A&T State Univ Alumni Achievement Awd 1974; Phi Delta Kappa; A&T State Univ Alumni Excellence Awd 1982; Natl Assn for Equal Opportunity in Higher Educ Presidential Citation to Distinguished Alumni 1985; Minority Achievement Award, Maryland State Teachers Assn, 1988; appointed by governor of Maryland to chair a comm to study sentencing alternatives for women convicted of crime, 1987; author of Improving the Status of the Culturally Different and Disadvantaged Minority Students in Gifted Programs, 1988-89; West Africa, Fulbright Scholar, 1991; UMES, Teacher of the Year, 1992; Appointed by the Gov Professional Standards Board, 1993; NC A&T State Univ, Administrator of the Year, 1997. **Home Addr:** 11 Carissa Court, Greensboro, NC 27407.

SPEIGHTS, JOHN D.
Dentist. **Personal:** Born Mar 5, 1926, Dickson, TN; son of Margaret and Foster; married Marian C Washington. **Educ:** Meharry Dental Coll, Cert in Dental Tech 1948; Wilson Jr Coll, AA 1953; Chicago Tchrs Coll, B Educ 1957; Howard Univ Dental Coll, DDS 1963. **Career:** Dentist, pvt prac 1963-; Chicago Pub Schs, tchr 1957-59; Dr William J Walker, Sr, dental technician 1949-59. **Orgs:** Mem Lincoln Dental Soc; Nat Dental Assn; Am Dental Assn; Chicago Dental Soc; IL State Dental Soc; Howard Univ Dental Alumni Assn. **Honors/Awds:** DH Turpin Award, outstanding perf in Prostodontia, Meharry Med Coll & Howard Dental Sch 1963. **Military Serv:** US Navy S 1st class 1944-46. **Business Addr:** 536 E 87th St, Chicago, IL 60619.

SPEIGHTS, NATHANIEL H.
Attorney. **Personal:** Born Nov 24, 1949, Bellaire, OH; son of Ollie Speights and Nathaniel H Speights; married Grace E Speights; children: Ashley, Nathaniel IV. **Educ:** Coll of Wooster, Ohio, BA, 1972; Univ of Miami, Florida, JD, 1975. **Career:** Speights & Mitchell, partner, attorney, currently. **Orgs:** Pres, Washington Bar Assn, currently. **Business Addr:** Partner, Speights & Mitchell, 1511 K St NW, Ste 811, Washington, DC 20006.

SPEIGINER, GERTHA
Educational administrator. **Personal:** Born Apr 28, 1917, St Louis; married Louis Sol; children: Delores, Doris, Deborah, Darlene, Delanya, Desiree, Delicya, Dauphne Delauna. **Educ:** Mt San Antonio Coll. **Career:** Studio Girl Cosmetic, rep; CA Polytechnic U, lecturer 1972-73; Mt San Antonio Coll Comm Cntr, dir 1970-74. **Orgs:** Pres Pomona Valley Branch NAACP; vice pres So Area Conf NAACP 1974-76; fdr, pres Pomona Parents Council 1965-68; past pres Parents for Understandin 1967-71; charter mem, treas, Pomona Day School; bd mem YWCA; Outreach Program YMCA; mem Pasadena Legal Aid Bd; Pomona Legal Aid; Nat Assn of Colores Women. **Honors/Awds:** Plaque for outs Black comm ser 1971; cert of merit for continuous service to comm; plaque for dedicated ser to comm Pomona Valley Br. **Business Addr:** 2243 Larchmont Ave, Pomona, CA 91767.

SPELLER, CHARLES K.
Orthopedic surgeon. **Personal:** Born Feb 25, 1933, Windsor, NC; married Virginia. **Educ:** NC Cent U, 1954; Meharry Med Coll, 1966. **Career:** Monmouth Med Cent Long Branch NJ; IL Masonic Hosp; Columbia Univ NY, internship. **Orgs:** Mem Harris Co Med Soc; Houston Med Forum; Nat Med Assn; Nat Trauma Soc Sovereign Grand Insp Gen of 33rd & last deg Ancient & Accept Scottish Riteof Freemasonry Adg Gen Corp 1954-56. **Business Addr:** 5445 Almeda, Ste 302, Houston, TX 77004.

SPELLMAN, ALONZO ROBERT
Professional football player. **Personal:** Born Sep 27, 1971, Mount Holly, NJ; married Lizzie. **Educ:** Ohio State, attended. **Career:** Chicago Bears, defensive end, 1992-. **Business Addr:** Professional Football Player, Chicago Bears, 1000 Football Dr, Halas Hall at Conway Park, Lake Forest, IL 60045-4829, (847)295-6600.

SPELLMAN, OLIVER B., JR.
City official. **Personal:** Born Sep 11, 1953, New York, NY; son of Iris Lawson Spellman Astwood and Oliver B Spellman; married Diane Reyes (divorced 1984); children: Qiana Marie, Robert Ellington. **Educ:** St Michael's Coll, Winooski VT, BA American Studies, 1975; Howard Univ School of Law, Washington DC, JD, 1978. **Career:** Ohio State Attorney General's Office, Columbus OH, law asst, 1978-79; Alabama State Univ, Montgomery AL, asst prof, criminal justice, 1979-82; New York City Criminal Justice Agency, New York NY, Bronx dir, 1982-84; New York City Dept of Parks, Brooklyn NY, enforcement dir, 1984-85, dir, Special Projects, 1985-87, park mgr, 1987-88, chief of Urban Park Serv, 1988-90, commissioner of Queens Parks Commission, 1990-. **Orgs:** Alpha Phi Alpha, 1982-. **Honors/Awds:** President's Award, Ebony Society, 1990.

SPENCE, DONALD DALE
Dentist. **Personal:** Born Dec 6, 1926, Philadelphia, PA; married Theresa Seltzer; children: Kenneth, Donna, Rosalynn, Melanie. **Educ:** Morris College Atlanta, attended 1950; Howard Univ Sch of Dentistry, DDS 1960. **Career:** Private Practice Pensacola, dentist. **Orgs:** Mem Staff Baptist, Univ, Sacred Heart Hosps; mem Gulf Coast, Natl, Santa Rosa-Escambia, Northwest FL, FL & AM Dental Assns; bd dirs So Fed Svgs & Loan; bd dirs Pensacola C of C; NAACP; Kappa Alpha Psi; Elks; Pensacola Jr Coll Found Bd; St Cyprians Epis Ch; pres NW FL Adv Counc Minority Affairs; Natl Guardsmen Inc FL Chapt; utility & zoning long-range planning com Pensacola City Coun 1974-; exec com Reg Planning W FL. **Honors/Awds:** Apptd by Gov Reubin Asken to Escambia Co Sch Bd highest ranking Black ofcl in NW FL 1975.

SPENCE, JOSEPH SAMUEL, SR.
Educator, attorney. **Personal:** Born Dec 20, 1950; son of Olive Maud Bambridge and Kenneth John Spence; married Sheila M Parrish-Spence; children: Joseph Jr, Joselyn Maria, Jonathan Clarence. **Educ:** Pikes Peak Coll, AA; Univ of MD, BSc; Webster Univ, MA Washburn Univ Law School, Topeka, KS, JD. **Career:** Century 21 Real Estate, realtor assoc 1978-80; United States Army, capt 1980-86; Riley County District Attorney's Office, 1987; City of Topeka Attorney's Office, 1988-89; Kansas State Senate, 1988-89; Milwaukee Area Technical College, 1991-; Spence Law Offices, Milwaukee, 1992-. **Orgs:** Alpha Phi Alpha; Rep-at-large Frederick Douglass Ctr Manhattan KS 1986-87, WSBA Washburn Law Sch 1986-87; Kiwanis Intl 1986-87; marshal Phi Alpha Delta Law Frat 1986-87; founder & charter pres NAACP Manhattan KS 1986; founder & legal advisor, Lex Explorer, Washburn Law School, 1988; assoc minister St. Mark AME Church; chairperson Legal Redress Comm NAACP KS 1987-89; mem Manhattan Kansas Chamber of Commerce, Manhattan KS Amer Red Cross; Commissioner-at-large, Amer Bar Assn, 1987-89; Christian Lawyers Assn, 1987-; Christian Legal Soc, 1987-; Americans United for Seperation of Church & State, 1987-; American Bar Assn, 1989-; Natl Bar Assn, 1992-; American Trial Lawyer Assn, 1993-; Wisconsin Academy of Trial Lawyers. **Honors/Awds:** Disting Military Student 1979, Disting Military Grad 1980 Howard Univ ROTC; Earl Warren Scholar NAACP Legal Defense Fund 1986-89; various awds for public speaking; Daughters of Amer Revolution Awd; Disting Grad Air Assault School; Disting Grad Logistics Automated Mgmt Sch; Expert Shooting Qualification; Jurcyk-Royle Oral Advocacy Competition; Certificate of Commendation, Amer Bar Assn, 1989; Certificate of Merit, Washburn Law Clinic, 1988; founder & chapter pres, Lambda Alpha Epsilon Criminal Justice Fraternity, 1985. **Military Serv:** AUS company cmdr capt 8 yrs; USAR, mjr, 1986-; Expert Infantry Badge, Airborne Air Assault Overseas Serv Ribbon, Army Achievement, NCO Develop, Army Svcs, Good Conduct; Natl Defense Ribbon; Command and General Staff Coll grad; Multi-Natl Force and Observer Ribbon. **Business Addr:** PO Box 26342, Milwaukee, WI 53226.

SPENCER, ANTHONY LAWRENCE
Government administrator. **Personal:** Born Aug 10, 1946, New York, NY; son of Gladys Harrington; married Jeanette Butler; children: Anthony. **Educ:** City Coll of NY, 1970-75; Cmd & Gen Stf Coll, 1980-84. **Career:** Inst for Mediation & Conflict Resolution, special asst to pres 1970-74; State Charter Revision Comm for NYC, asst to dir of community rels 1973-74; J P Stevens & Co, tech sales rep, 1975-79; New York Dept of State, special asst to sec of state 1979-85, deputy dir for gov black affairs adv comm beginning 1985; State of New York Banking Department, project director, currently. **Orgs:** New York Urban League, board of directors; board member of Div/ML Wilson Boys Club of Harlem 1982-; 1st vice pres Community Bd 9 New York, NY 1983-84; pres student body City Coll of New York 1972-73; vice pres Christmas Tree in Harlem 1981; mem Men Who Cook. **Honors/Awds:** Distinguished Serv Citation United Negro Coll Fund 1981; 125 Anniv Medal City Coll of New York 1972. **Military Serv:** UASF; AUS mjr 21 yrs; NDSM/AFOUA/SOGB/AFGCM/ARCOM/ARCAM; New York Army National Guard, Lt Col, 1990.

SPENCER, BRENDA L.
Industrial engineer. **Personal:** Born Jul 7, 1951, Youngstown, OH; daughter of Flonerra Henry and Walter Henry; children: Ebony Ayana. **Educ:** Kent State, BS Ind Engineering 1978; Malone College BA business 1986. **Career:** General Motors, accountant 1973-76; BL Unlimited Engrg & Consult Corp, owner; Republic Steel, indus engr; ITT Technical Institute, director of placement 1987-. **Orgs:** Natl youth leader Natl Assn of Negro Business and Prof Women 1978-80; natl dir Youth and Young Adults 1980-82; natl vice president Prof Women and Young Adults 1982-85; treasurer Kappa Nu Zeta 1983-85; treasurer Zeta Phi Beta 1983-85; membership chairman Amer Inst of Engineers 1983-84; National Coalition of Black Meeting Planners; Religious Meeting Planners Convention. **Honors/Awds:** Voluntary Leader Natl March of Dimes 1980; Leadership Natl March of Dimes 1982; Good Housekeeping 100 Young Women of Promise 1985. **Home Addr:** PO Box 5814, Youngstown, OH 44504.

SPENCER, DONALD ANDREW
Broker. **Personal:** Born Mar 5, 1915, Cincinnati, OH; married Marian; children: Donald, Edward. **Educ:** Univ of Cincinnati, AB 1936; Univ of Cincinnati, BE 1937; Univ of Cincinnati, ME 1940. **Career:** Real Estate broker 1945-83; Cincinnati Public School, teacher 1936-54. **Orgs:** Pres bd trustees OH Univ 1974-83; pres Housing Bd of Appeals 1970-95; Natl Assoc Real Estate Brokers; mem PAC Com 1967-75; orgnzr First Midwinter Conf; Estab Beta Eta Chptr of Kappa Alpha Psi Frat on Univ of Cincinnati Campus 1949; mem Admin & Fin Comm W OH & Lexington Conf of Meth Ch 1946-57; trustee OH Council of Churches; orgnzr, 1st pres Comm on Relig & Race 1960-65. **Honors/Awds:** Publ 1st Nat Song Book for Kappa Alpha Psi Frat 1951; pres Award Cincinnati Br NAACP 1975; Cincinnati Park Bd Award, 1992; Service to Cincinnati, Tri-Centennial Time Capsule, 1988; Charles P Taft Civic Gumption Award, 1997.

SPENCER, FELTON LAFRANCE
Professional basketball player. **Personal:** Born Jan 5, 1968, Louisville, KY. **Educ:** Louisville. **Career:** Minnesota Timberwolves, center, 1990-93; Utah Jazz, 1993-96; Golden State Warriors, 1996-. **Business Addr:** Professional Football Player, Golden State Warriors, 1001 Broadway, Oakland, CA 94607, (510)986-2200.

SPENCER, GREGORY RANDALL
Energy company executive. **Personal:** Born Dec 31, 1948, Washington, PA; son of William H & Anna Mae Spencer; married Janet O Spencer, Sep 8, 1973; children: Tammy Michelle, Michael Randall. **Educ:** University of Pittsburgh, BA, 1980; St Francis College, MA, 1984. **Career:** US Steel, gen mgr of human resources, 1971-93; AMSCO International, Inc, vp of human resources, 1993-94; Equitable Resources, Inc, senior vp and chief administrative officer, 1994-. **Orgs:** Wesley Institute, scy of the bd, 1990-; Inroads/Pgh, chmn of the bd, development comm, 1991-; Goodwill Industries of Pittsburgh, chmn of the bd, 1994-; Arthritis Foundation, W PA, financial dev, vice chair, 1994-; Urban League of Pittsburgh, bd of dirs, 1997-; Leadership Pittsburgh, bd of dirs, 1997. **Honors/Awds:** Renaissance Publications, Black Trailblazer Award, 1997; Eastern Stars, Black Achiever Award, 1980; US Jaycees, Outstanding Young Man of America, 1980; Ebony Magazine, 50 Future Leaders of America, 1978. **Military Serv:** US Air Force, sgt, 1968-71. **Home Addr:** 1020 Devonshire Rd, Pittsburgh, PA 15217. **Business Addr:** Senior VP/Chief Administrative Officer, Equitable Resources Inc, 420 Blvd of the Allies, Pittsburgh, PA 15219-1301, (412)553-5754.

SPENCER, JAMES ARTHUR, JR.
Professional football player. **Personal:** Born Mar 29, 1969, Manning, SC. **Educ:** Univ of Florida, attended. **Career:** New Orleans Saints, defensive back, 1992-95; Cincinnati Bengals, 1996-. **Business Addr:** Professional Football Player, Cincinnati Bengals, One Bengals Dr, Cincinnati, OH 45202, (513)621-3550.

SPENCER, JAMES R.
Judge. **Personal:** married Margaret. **Career:** Federal judge, currently. **Orgs:** Omega Psi Phi; Sigma Pi Phi; Phi Beta Kappa; Alpha Kappa Mu. **Business Addr:** Federal District Judge, 1000 E Main St, #307, Richmond, VA 23219-3525, (804)643-6081.

SPENCER, JOAN MOORE
Librarian. **Personal:** Born Feb 17, 1932, Henderson, NC; married Francis Herman; children: Francine Dejuanna, Christopher Columbus. **Educ:** NC Central U, BSC 1950-54; NC Central U, MLS 1960; NC State U, 9 hrs on PhD 1978-79. **Career:** Wake Co Pub Libraries, young adult coordinator 1977-; Wake Co Pub Libraries, asst dir 1974-77; Wake Co Pub Libraries, head reference dept 1968-73; JR Faison High Sch Wadesboro NC, sch librarian 1954-64. **Orgs:** Chmn const bylaws NC Adult Educ Assn 1975-77; pub library dir NC Library Assn Pub Sect 1977-79; com mem Am Library Assn YASD Media & Usage 1979-80; dir RAYC St Paul AME Ch 1970-; bd mem Wake Co Mental Health Assn 1977-79; mem Raleigh Chap of Natl Epicureans 1979-, Boyer Assembly of the Golden Circle 1979-; ivy leaf reporter Alpha Theta Omega Chap Alpha Kappa Alpha Inc 1980; compiler of ofcl index NC Library Assn 1976-; WNCC Branch UPD dir AME Church 1984. **Honors/Awds:** Mother of the Year Alpha Phi Alpha Frat Raleigh NC 1977; Pres Pin for Outstanding PTA Serv Aycock Sch PTA 1978; Woman of the Yr Zeta Phi Beta Sorority 1979. **Business Addr:** Local History Librarian, Wake County Public Libraries, 1930 Clark Ave, Raleigh, NC 27603.

SPENCER, LARRY LEE
Organization administrator. **Personal:** Born Oct 1948, Columbus, OH; son of Elizabeth Spencer and Hezekiah Spencer; children: Tangelia Spencer Palmer, Mark, Sharese. **Educ:** Franklin University, BS, 1983. **Career:** Franklin County Department of Human Services, contract negotiator, 1976-88; Ohio Department of Mental Health, management analyst, 1988; United Way of Franklin County, senior manager, currently. **Orgs:** Leadership Worthington, board member, 1991-; National Black Programming Consortium, outreach committee, 1991-; Department of Health, Minority AIDS Committee, 1992-; Westside/Eastside Child Day Care, board member, 1988-90; Mental Health State Afro Centric Conference Planning Committee, past; Worthington Community Multicultural Committee, past; Worthington Community Relations Commission, 1994-. **Honors/Awds:** Players Theatre, most valuable volunteer, 1991; WBNS-TV, Channel 10, Time to Care Community Award, 1992; Project Diversity participants, special acknowledgement, 1992-94; United Way of America, Second Century Initiative Award, 1991; Walter English Award, 1990. **Special Achievements:** Researched and presented: ''An Account of Underground Railroad Activity,'' which focused on Columbus and Worthington area, to community groups; information has been incorporated into a black history course in the Worthington Schools. **Military Serv:** US Army, sgt, 1968-70. **Business Addr:** Senior Manager, United Way of Franklin County, 360 S Third St, Columbus, OH 43215, (614)227-2740.

SPENCER, MARGARET BEALE
Psychologist, educator. **Personal:** Born Sep 5, 1944, Philadelphia, PA; married Charles L Spencer; children: Tirzah Renee, Natasha Ann, Charles Asramon. **Educ:** Temple University College of Pharmacy, BS, 1967; University of Kansas, MA, psychology, 1970; University of Chicago, PhD, 1976. **Career:** University of Kansas Medical Center, registered pharmacist, 1967-69; University of Chicago, research project director, 1974-77; Morehouse School of Medicine, clinical associate professor, 1982-89; Emory University, faculty, 1977-93; Univ of PA, bd of overseers professor of educ, 1993-. **Orgs:** Consultant/committee, Foundation for Child Development, 1981-85; consultant, Fulton County, Georgia Health Department, 1983-89; board executive committee, Fulton County Black Family Project, 1983-88; board, South DeKalb County, YMCA, 1984-86; W T Grant Foundation, 1986-93; National Black Child Development Institute, 1986-92; Center for Successful Child Development, 1986-88; committee chairman, Society for Research in Child Development, 1987-89; trustee & bd mem, White-Williams Foundation, 1994-; editorial review bd mem, Journal of Applied Developmental Psychology, 1992-; editorial review bd mem, Cambridge Univ Press, Development & psychopathology, 1994-; bd of scientific affairs, The Amer Psychological Assn, 1991-94; editorial advisory bd, Children, Youth & Change: Sociocultural Perspectives, 1994-; advisory bd, Center for the Study of Context, Generations, & Mental Health, 1994-; advisory bd, Center for Youth Development & Policy Research Board Member, Academy for Educ Development, 1993. **Honors/Awds:** Spencer, Ford, Commonwealth and WT Grant Foundations, Grant Reseach Support, 1984-87; Award for Service, DeKalb County, GA, YMCA, 1985; Outstanding Service Award, Delta Sigma Theta Sorority, Decatur Alumnae Chapter, 1986; Fellow Status, American Psychological Assn. **Special Achievements:** Author: Beginnings: The Affective and Social Development of Black Children, LEA Publishing, 1985; Ethnicity and Diversity: Minorities No More, LEA, in press; Over 75 published articles and chapters. **Home Addr:** 737 Cornelia Place, Philadelphia, PA 19118. **Business Addr:** Professor, Univ of Pennsylvania, Graduate School of Education, Psychology in Education Division, 3700 Walnut Street, Philadelphia, PA 19104-6216.

SPENCER, MARIAN ALEXANDER
Activist. **Personal:** Born Jun 28, 1920, Gallipolis, OH; married Donald A Spencer; children: Donald, Edward. **Educ:** Univ of Cincinnati, graduate. **Career:** Cincinnati City Council, former councilmember. **Orgs:** Cincinnati City Council: chairperson, Human Resources Comm, Urban Develop Planning Zoning & Housing Comm, vice chairperson, Law Committee, City Planning Comm; life mem, NAACP; life member, Alpha Kappa Alpha Sor; past pres, Cincinnati Chap of Links Inc; past pres, Woman's City Club, NAACP; Greater Cincinnati Occupational Health Center Board; WGUC Radio Station, advisory board; Planned Parenthood, public relations committee, personnel committee; Mt Zion United Methodist Church; Housing Opportunities Made Equal Board, vice pres; Cincinnati Public Schools, Discipline Task Force, chair, subcommittee; Center for Voting and Democracy, bd member, 1994-96. **Honors/Awds:** Brotherhood Awd Natl Conf of Christians & Jews; Woman of the Yr Awd Cincinnati Enquirer; Black Excellence Awd PUSH; Ethelrie Harper Awd Cincinnati Human Relations Comm; Disting Alumna Awd Alumna Assn of the Univ of Cincinnati; recognized by the Cincinnati Post as one of the 12 Most Influential Women in the City of Cincinnati; Career Woman of Achievement Awd YWCA 1984; recently inducted into the OH Women's Hall of Fame; ACLU, State of Ohio Award; A Phillip Randolph Institute of Greater Cincinnati, Community Activist Award, 1992; Greater Cincinnati Foundation, Jacob E Davis Volunteer Award, 1993; Urban League, Glorifying the Lions Club, 1994; Center for Voting and Democracy, award recipient, 1995. **Special Achievements:** First African-American woman elected to the Cincinnati City Council; only woman ever to serves as president, Cincinnati Branch, NAACP; honored by Black Careeer Women, Linda Bates Parker, dir. **Home Addr:** 940 Lexington Ave, Cincinnati, OH 45229.

SPENCER, MICHAEL GREGG
Engineer, professor. **Personal:** Born Mar 9, 1952, Detroit, MI; son of Laura Lee Spencer and Thomas Spencer; divorced; children: Thomas Lewis. **Educ:** Cornell Univ, Ithaca NY, BS, 1974, MEE, 1975, PhD, 1981. **Career:** General Electric, Syracuse NY, co-op engineer, 1972, 1973; Bell Laboratories, Whippany NJ, mem of technical staff, 1974-77; Howard Univ, Washington DC, asst prof, 1981-85, assoc prof, 1985-, Department of Electrical Engineering, Materials Science Research Center of Excellence, director, 1987-; SIMNET Laboratory, co-director, 1987-. **Orgs:** Mem, officer, National Soc of Black Engineers, 1977-; mem, Natl Science Found proposal review comm, 1984-, advisory council for Electrical Engineering and computer systems, 1988, advisory comm for materials research, 1989-; mem, Amer Vacuum Soc, 1985-; officer, Electron Device Soc of Inst of Electrical and Electronics Engineers, 1987-. **Honors/Awds:** Presidential Young Investigator Award, Natl Science Found, 1985; Allen Berman Research Publication Award, Naval Research Laboratory, 1986; Outstanding Faculty Award, White House Initiative on Historically Black Colls and Univs, 1988; Distinguished Visiting Scientist, JPL, 1991-92; Certificate of Recognition, NASA, 1992. **Home Addr:** 5133 8th St NE, Washington, DC 20011. **Business Addr:** Dept of Electrical Engineering, Material Science Research Center of Excellence, Howard Univ, 2300 6th St NW - Downing Hall, Washington, DC 20059.

SPENCER, ROZELLE JEFFERY
Business executive. **Personal:** Born Jul 3, 1936, Memphis, TN; son of Octavia McCormack Spencer and William Arthur Spencer; married Winifred L Jones, Jul 5, 1968; children: Jeffrey C, Derrick C. **Educ:** DePaul University, 1956-59; Northeastern Illinois University, BA, 1990, MA, candidate, 1990-91. **Career:** Santa Fe Railroad, trans rep, 1956-64; Trans World Airlines, employment supervisor, 1964-70; Aaro Medicar Transport, president, 1976-85; Hyde Park Self Storage, Inc, president, 1990-; Aaron Brothers Moving System, Inc, president/chief executive officer, 1969-. **Orgs:** Chicago Council on Foreign Relations; Association of African Historians; Task Force for Black Political Empowerment; Southside Community Art Center; National Association of Guardsmen.

SPENCER, SHANITA RENE
Attorney, community services administrator. **Personal:** Born Mar 22, 1960, Nu Ulm, Germany; daughter of Roberta Lee Gates Spencer and Charlie Richman Spencer; children: Brodrick Charles. **Educ:** Creighton University, Omaha, NE, BSBA, 1982; Cornell University, Ithaca, NY, JD, 1985. **Career:** Kutak Rock & Campbell, Omaha, NE, attorney, 1985-87; Consumer Services Organization Inc, Omaha, NE, staff attorney, 1988-89; University of Nebraska at Omaha, Omaha, NE, project coordinator, 1989-90; Resident Services, director, 1991-. **Orgs:** Northwest Oklahoma Black Lawyers Association, 1985-; Foster Care Review Board, 1990-; advisory board member, Black Homes for Black Children, 1990-; Alpha Kappa Alpha Sorority, 1981-. **Honors/Awds:** 50 Leaders of the Future, Ebony Magazine, 1990; task force appointee, Black Child Campaign, Children's Defense Fund, 1990; Leadership Oklahoma; vice pres, North Tulsa Heritage Foundation; executive bd, Girl Scouts; executive bd, Bookband.

SPENCER, SHARON A.
Physician. **Personal:** Born in Birmingham, AL; daughter of Annie M Rice Spencer and Otis Spencer Sr. **Educ:** Birmingham Southern College, Birmingham, AL, BS, 1979; University of Alabama School of Medicine, Birmingham, AL, MD, 1983. **Career:** University of Alabama, Birmingham, Birmingham, AL, asst professor, 1989-. **Honors/Awds:** Phi Beta Kappa, 1979. **Business Addr:** Assistant Professor, Radiation Oncology Dept, University of Alabama at Birmingham, 619 19th St S, Birmingham, AL 35233.

SPENCER, TRACIE
Vocalist. **Personal:** Born in Waterloo, IA. **Career:** Albums include: Tracie Spencer, 1988; Make the Difference, 1990; Love High, 1998. **Special Achievements:** Has appeared on ''The Arsenio Hall Show,'' ''Star Search''; has toured with New Kids on the Block, Kid N' Play. **Business Addr:** Singer, c/o Capitol Records Inc, 1750 N Vine St, Hollywood, CA 90028, (213)462-6252.

SPICER, CARMELITA
Business executive. **Personal:** Born Mar 14, 1946, Jacksonville, NC. **Educ:** NC Central Univ, BS 1968; Rutgers Univ, MEd 1975. **Career:** Celanese Fibers Marketing Co, coordinator, retail information; Johnson & Johnson Co., Personal Products Division, assistant director, consumer information, Baby Products Division, marketing consultant; Central City Marketing Inc, vice pres, marketing director; Spicer & Associates, Advertising/Sales Promotion, president; A/S Productions, Advertising/Sales Promotion, vice pres, co-owner; Louisville Gas & Electric Co., Customer Communications and Advertising Department, manager, currently. **Orgs:** Alpha Kappa Alpha, 1963; National Association of Media Women Inc, Chicago Chapter, president, 1981-83; Portland Neighborhood House, board member; Advertising Club of Louisville; American Gas Association, consumer information committee. **Business Addr:** Manager, Customer Communications and Advertising, Louisville Gas & Electric Co., 220 W Main, 5th fl, Louisville, KY 40202.

SPICER, KENNETH, SR.
Government official. **Personal:** Born Aug 21, 1949, Jacksonville, FL; son of Reba Spicer McKinney; married Patricia A Baker, May 25, 1972; children: Kenneth, Sherry, Michelle. **Educ:** Bethune-Cookman Coll, Daytona Beach FL, BS, business admin, 1971; Univ of Massachusetts, Boston MA, MS, public affairs, 1990; Northeastern University, PhD studies, law policy and society, 1991-93; Harvard University, JFK School of Government, Senior Executive Program, 1994. **Career:** South Florida Employment Training Consortium, Miami FL, dir public serv employment, 1980, dir of operations, 1980-81; Dade County JMH/Community Mental Health Center, Miami FL, dir of operations & finance, 1981; Dade County Haitian-Amer Community Health Center, Miami FL, exec dir, 1982-85; Office of City Manager, Tallahassee FL, dir of Minority Business Enterprise, 1985-86; EOCD, Office of Secretary, Boston MA, asst to the cabinet secretary for Affirmative Action, 1986-91, Bureau of Neighborhood Services and Economic Opportunity, Division of Neighborhood Svcs, director, 1991-. **Orgs:** Alpha Phi Alpha Frat Inc, 1971-; founding member, Boston Chapter, Natl Forum for Black Public Admin Inc. **Honors/Awds:** Appreciation Award, Boston Chapter, Natl Forum for Black Public Admin, 1989; Appreciation Award, State of Massachusetts, 1989; Governor's Quality Control Committee, 1993; Urban Edge Community Service Award, 1994. **Business Addr:** Director, Bureau of Neighborhood Svcs & Economic Opportunity, Division, Neighborhood Svcs, Massachusetts Department of Housing & Community Development, 100 Cambridge St, Rm 1804, Boston, MA 02202, (617)727-7004.

SPICER, OSKER, JR.
Journalist. **Personal:** Born Apr 12, 1949, Memphis, TN; son of Rosa Hall Spicer Sias; married Marion Wilson Spicer, Jul 31, 1970; children: Aki L. **Educ:** Lincoln University, Jefferson City, MO, journalism major, 1967-69; Morehouse College, Atlanta, GA, BA, 1972; Columbia University, New York City, NY, summer program for minority journalists, 1973; Atlanta University, Atlanta, GA, graduate studies Afro-American studies, 1984. **Career:** Atlanta Daily World, Atlanta, GA, reporter, night city editor, 1970-72, 1976-77; Pittsburgh Courier, Pittsburgh, PA, city editor, 1974-75; Clark College, Atlanta, GA, journalism instructor, 1978-81, 1984; WCLK Radio, Atlanta, GA, producer-announcer, news director, 1976-81; Charlotte News-Observer, Charlotte, NC, reporter, 1982-84; The Democrat, Tallahassee, FL, reporter/columnist, 1984-87; The Oregonian, Portland, OR, copy editor/columnist, 1987-. **Orgs:** Board member, charter member, Portland Assn of Black Journalists, 1990-; NABJ, Region X, dir, currently; board member, local chapter, Society of Professional Journalists, 1980-; member, International Organization of Journalists, 1990-; member, Institute for Journalism Education, 1973-; member, Morehouse Alumni Assn, 1972-; member, Asian-American Journalists Assn, 1988-; IRE; bd mem, West Coast Regional Directors, Natl Assn of Black Journalists, 1995-97; natl bd mem, chap pres, 9th & 10th Cav Assn The Buffalo Soldiers. **Honors/Awds:** Producer of the Year, WCLK Radio, 1979; Journalistic Excellence, Tallahassee Chamber, 1986-87. **Military Serv:** USMC Reserves, 2nd Lt, 1969-71. **Business Addr:** Copy Editor-Columnist, The Oregonian, 1320 SW Boradway, Portland, OR 97201.

SPIGHT, BENITA L.
Manager of corporate redesign implementation. **Personal:** Born Apr 21, 1963, Detroit, MI; daughter of Margaret Louise Lindsey McCray and James Easterling Jr; married Brian Wesley Spight, Apr 15, 1989; children: Richard Allen II. **Educ:** Univ of Michigan, BA, 1985, School of Business Administration, management seminar, certificate of completion, 1990; University of Denver, The Publishing Institute, certificate of completion, 1991. **Career:** Consolidated Data Tech, Dearborn, MI, clerical supvr, 1986-88; Gale Research, Inc, Detroit, MI, sr credit/acct svc rep, 1988-90, data entry supvr, 1990-93, mgr, 1993-95; Corporate Team & Work Redesign, trainer, 1993-; International Thomson Publishing, leadership trainer/customer svc exec trainee, 1995-. **Orgs:** Data Entry Mgmt Assn, 1990-93; NAACP, University of Michigan Branch, 1982-83; Detroit Zoological Society, 1992-95; Assn for Work Process Improvement, 1993-95. **Honors/Awds:** Scholarship recipient, Publishing Institute, University of Denver, Gale Research, 1991; IBM internship, Atlanta, GA, 1984. **Business Addr:** Manager, Corporate Redesign, Gale Research Inc, 645 Griswold, 835 Penobscot Bldg, Detroit, MI 48226-4094, (313)961-2242.

SPIGNER, CLARENCE
Educator, researcher. **Personal:** Born Mar 19, 1946, Orangeburg, SC; son of Carrie McDonald Spigner and Willie Spigner. **Educ:** Santa Monica College, Santa Monica, CA, AA, social studies, 1974-76; University of California, Berkeley, CA, AB, sociology, 1977-79, MPH, health, 1980-82, DrPH, health, 1983-87. **Career:** American Heart Assn, Marin, CA, evaluator, 1981-82; National Health Service, London, England, researcher/planner, 1982-83; University of California, Berkeley, CA, fitness superv, 1983-86, teaching asst/post-doc/lecturer, 1984-88; University of Oregon, Eugene, OR, assistant professor, assoc prof, currently. **Orgs:** Board mem, Womanspace, 1989-91; steering committee member, Clergy and Laity Concerned, 1990-; University of Oregon, Substance Abuse Advisory Board, 1990-92, Affirmative Action Task Force, 1990-, Council for Minority Education, chair, 1990-91. **Honors/Awds:** Phi Beta Kappa, Phi Beta Kappa Honor Society, 1979-; Chancellor's Post-Doctoral Fellow, Univ of California-Berkeley, 1987; Henrik Blum Distinguished Service Award, Univ of California-Berkeley, 1987; Outstanding Faculty Award, Office of Multicultural Affairs, Univ of Oregon, 1990; Friars Senior Honor Society, University of Oregon, 1990. **Military Serv:** US Air Force, Sergeant, 1964-68. **Business Addr:** Associate Professor, University of Washington, Department of Health Services, H681 Health Sciences Center, Seattle, WA 98195.

SPIGNER, DONALD WAYNE
Physician. **Personal:** Born Feb 14, 1940, Tyler, TX; son of Jessie Lee McCauley Spigner and Kermit Spigner; married Kathleen Hughes; children: Nicole Adeyinka, Danielle Khadeja. **Educ:** Univ of CA Riverside, BS 1962; Univ of CA San Francisco, MD 1966; Los Angeles Cty Govt Hosp, Internship 1967; board certified, Academy of Family Practice. **Career:** US Peace Corps, physician 1967-69, med dir of Africa Div 1969-70; Pilot City Health Ctr, proj dir 1970-73; Univ of MN School of Med, assoc prof 1973-75; Univ of MN School of Publ Health, lecturer 1973-75; Hamilton Health Ctr; med dir 1975-87; Comm Med Assoc, pres; Univ of PA Hershey Med Cntr, assoc prof 1975-; City of Harrisburg, city health ofcr 1977-80; Keystone Peer Review, part-time reviewer 1986-; Blue Shield of PA, medical dir. **Orgs:** PA Med Soc Liability Ins Co, bd mem; Consult Afric Care 1975-85; partner 3540 N Progress Assoc 1980-; mem Boys Club 1982-; partner Keystone Assoc 1984-; pres Dauphin Cty Med Soc 1984-; mem Dauphin Cty MH/MR Bd 1984-86; mem St Paul Baptist Church, mem, Advisory Bd of PA State Univ, Harrisburg Campus. **Honors/Awds:** Selected to represent Univ of CA Riverside on Project India 1961; mem PA State Bd of Podiatry; video tape on African/Amer Folk medicine, 1977. **Military Serv:** US Public Health Serv Surgeon 1967-69; USPMS. **Business Addr:** President, Community Medical Assoc, 3601 N Progress, Harrisburg, PA 17110.

SPIGNER, MARCUS E.
Postal executive. **Career:** United States Postal Service, postmaster, currently. **Special Achievements:** First African American postmaster in the state of Idaho. **Military Serv:** Idaho National Guard. **Business Addr:** Postmaster, United States Postal Service, 222 W State St, Eagle, ID 83616.

SPIKES, DELORES R.
Educational administrator. **Career:** Southern University System, president, until 1996; Univ of Maryland, Eastern Shore, president, 1996-. **Business Addr:** President, University of Maryland, Eastern Shore, JT Williams Hall, Rm 2107, Princess Anne, MD 21853-1299.

SPIKES, IRVING
Professional football player. **Personal:** Born Dec 21, 1970, Ocean Springs, MS; married Stacey, Sep 11, 1994; children: Ices, Irving Jr. **Educ:** Northeast Louisiana. **Career:** Miami Dolphins, running back, 1994-. **Business Addr:** Professional Football Player, Miami Dolphins, 2269 NW 199th St, Miami, FL 33056, (305)620-5000.

SPINKS, MICHAEL
Professional boxer. **Personal:** Born 1956; married Sandy (deceased); children: Michelle. **Career:** Professional Boxer, 1976-. **Honors/Awds:** Gold Medalist 1976 Olympics; World Boxing Assoc Light-Heavyweight Champion 1981; World Boxing Cncl Light Heavyweight Champion 1983-85; Intl Boxing Federation Heavyweight Champion 1985.

SPIVA, ULYSSES VAN
Educator. **Personal:** Born May 6, 1931, New Market, TN; son of Mary Ruth Spiva and Samuel Spiva; married Olivia A; children: Vanessa, Valerie, Bruce. **Educ:** Stanford U, PhD 1971; Case Western Reserve U, MA 1964; TN State U, BS 1954. **Career:** Old Dominion Univ, prof and dean emeritus; FL Intl Univ, dir spnsrd research; School Health School Serv, exec asst pres, interim dean; School Educ FL & Internat, asst dean; Natl Follow Through Program, US Office Educ, spec asst dir; Stanford Univ Graduate School Educ, asst dean; Cleveland, OH Public School, evening school prin & math dept chmn; Union Graduate School, adj prof; Nova Southeastern Univ, Ft Lauderdale, FL, senior national lecturer, 1990-. **Orgs:** Mem NABSE, Stanford Alumni Assn, VA Beach School Bd; bd dir Southeastern Tidewater Oppty Proj, Appalachia Educ Lab, Norfolk Kiwanis Inc; bd of trustees VA Beach Arts Center; chairman Council of Urban Boards of Education 1990-92; dir Virgini Beach Foundation 1990-; dir National School Boards Assn 1990-92. **Honors/Awds:** Alpha Phi Alpha Frat, Ldrshp & Eagle Awd in Pedagogy, John F Kennedy HS 1969; Phi Delta Kappa Hon soc; publ 3 books & numerous papers. **Business Addr:** Professor and Dean Emeritus, Old Dominion University, 5215 Hampton Blvd, Norfolk, VA 23508.

SPIVEY, DONALD
Educator. **Personal:** Born Jul 18, 1948, Chicago, IL; married Diane Marie; children: 2. **Educ:** Univ of IL, BA, history, 1971, MA, history, 1972; Univ of CA, PhD, history, 1976. **Career:** Univ of IL, dept of elem educ rsch asst 1971-72; Univ of CA, dept of history teaching asst 1972-74; Sacramento CA, music instructor 1972-74; Univ of CA Davis, lecturer in history 1975-76; Wright State Univ, asst prof of history 1976-79; Univ of MI, vstg asst prof of history 1978-79; Univ of CT, assoc prof of history 1979-85, prof of history 1985-90, director of Institute for African-American Studies, 1990-. **Orgs:** Mem President's Comm on Human Relations at Univ of CT 1984-85; mem Assoc for the Study of Afro-Amer Life and History, Organization of Amer Historians, Amer Historical Assoc, Popular Culture Assoc, Southwest Social Science Assoc, Natl Council for Black Studies, Southern Historical Assoc, North Amer Soc for the History of Sport. **Honors/Awds:** Publ Schooling for the New Slavery, Black Indust Educ 1868-1915, Greenwood Press 1978; Bolinga Dist Teacher-Scholar Awd Black Faculty Wright State Univ 1978; Amer Council of Learned Societies Res Grant 1980; Res Found Grant Univ of CT, 1983-84; publ The Politics of Miseducation, Booker Washington Inst of Liberia, 1928-84 Univ of KY Press 1984, Sport in Amer, Greenwood Press 1985. **Business Addr:** Director, Institute for African-American Studies, University of Connecticut, Storrs, CT 06268.

SPIVEY, WILLIAM REE
Business executive, management consultant. **Personal:** Born Nov 8, 1946, Brunswick, GA; son of Maggie Spivey and Danny Walters; married Sandra Miles, Feb 14, 1992; children: Tanya, Abagondol. **Educ:** Duquesne University, BS, physics, 1968; Indiana University of Pennsylvania, MS, physics, 1969; Walden University, PhD, management, 1990. **Career:** Indiana University, physics lab instructor, 1968-69; Bryn Mawr College, physics lab instructor, 1969-70; General Electric Co, marketing manager, 1970-78; Honeywell, Inc, vice pres and general manager, 1978-91; Tektronix Inc, vice pres, computer graphics group, 1991-. **Orgs:** Computer & Business Equipment Association, board member, 1988-; St Vincent Hospital, Advisory Board, 1991-; Executive Leadership Council, 1987-; Alpha Phi Alpha Fraternity, 1966-; Water & Sewer Department of Freeport, commissioner, 1983-85; Family Life Center, board member, 1983-85; NAACP of Freeport, consultant, 1984-86. **Honors/Awds:** Physics Honor Society, Honors in Physics, 1967. **Special Achievements:** Corporate America in Black and White, Carlton Press, 1992; Succeeding in Corporate America, Vantage Press, 1991. **Business Phone:** (503)685-3689.

SPOONER, RICHARD C.
Attorney. **Personal:** Born Jul 3, 1945, New York, NY. **Educ:** NY U, BA 1970; Fordham Univ Sch of Law, JD 1975. **Career:** Comm Devel Agency, dir of prog plan 1970-71; Human Resources Admin NYC, spl asst to gen counsel 1972-75; Carroll & Reid, assoc 1975-77; Chemical Bank, vice pres & sr counsel. **Orgs:** Mem Am Bar Assn 1977-; mem Urban Bankers Coalition 1978-, bd of dir 1980-84, gen counsel 1981-85, intl vice pres 1983; mem Nat Bar Assn 1979-; mem MetroBlack Bar Assoc 1985-, vice pres finance 1985. **Business Addr:** Vice President & Counsel, Chemical Bank, 380 Madison Ave, New York, NY 10016.

SPOTTSVILLE, CLIFFORD M.
Judge (retired), attorney. **Personal:** Born Oct 11, 1911, Independence, KS; son of Ethel Rogers Spottsville and Clarence Aaron Spottsville; married Geraldine A Rice; children: Keslie Rochelle, Shelly Rochelle. **Educ:** Univ KS, attended; Howard Univ School of Law, JD 1946; Natl Coll State Judiciary, further study. **Career:** US Coast & Geodetic Survey Commerce Dept, employee 1942-48; private practice, atty 1948-53; Jackson Cty MO, asst prosecuting atty 1953-61; Western Dist MO, asst US atty 1961-67; Jackson Cty MO, 1st asst prosecuting atty 1967-70; Municipal Court KC, judge 1970-77; private practice, atty 1977-. **Orgs:** Mem Kansas City MO, Amer, Jackson Cty Bar Assocs; mem Amer Judicature Soc; pres Municipal & Magistrate Judges Assoc MO 1974-75; bd dirs Boys Club, United Way; bd trustees Univ MO, Ottawa Univ Ottawa KS. **Home Addr:** 11715 Pennsylvania Ave., Kansas City, MO 64114-5591.

SPRADLEY, FRANK SANFORD
Educator. **Personal:** Born Oct 7, 1946, New Rochelle, NY; son of Mary Williams Baker and Frank Spradley; married Patricia Jones Spradley, Aug 23, 1972; children: Ayinde, Omolara, Ife, Naima. **Educ:** Southern Illinois Univ, Carbondale, IL, BS, accounting, marketing, 1970; Brooklyn College, New York, NY, MA, education, 1975, administration, supervision advance cert, 1981; Fordham University, New York, NY, Doctoral Candidate. **Career:** Shaw University, North Carolina, instructor curriculum writer, 1972; Board of Education, PS 137K, Brooklyn, NY, teacher, 1970-81; Board of Education, Brooklyn, NY, instructor new teacher workshops, human relation courses; College of New Rochelle, New York, NY, adjunct prof, 1989-; Board of Education, PS 137K, Brooklyn, NY, principal, 1981-. **Orgs:** Member, National Alliance of Black School Educators, political chairman, treasurer, Coalition of Concerned Black Educators, member, Council of Supervisor and Administrators. **Honors/Awds:** Outstanding Teacher Award, 1975; Outstanding Administrator Award, 1987; Rachel Jean Mitchelle Leadership Award, 1987; Excellence in Education Award, 1988. **Home Addr:** 117-15 224th St, Jamaica, NY 11411. **Business Addr:** Principal, Bd of Education, PS 137K, 121 Saratoga Ave, Brooklyn, NY 11233.

SPRADLEY, MARK MERRITT
Consultant. **Educ:** Howard Univ, BS 1983; Med Univ SC, MHSA 1986. **Career:** US Dept of State, consultant, 1979-84; Voice of Amer, consultant, 1983-84; Pres Private Sector Surveyon Cost Control, consultant, 1983-84; Mayor's Comm on Food Nutrition & Health Wash, comm, 1983-84; African Marketplace 1984 World's Fair, consultant, 1984. **Orgs:** Discussant Amer Enterprise Inst Religious & Econ Seminars 1984; chmn Charleston Co Young Republicans 1985-. **Honors/Awds:** Several newspaper & magazine articles on health & political topics.

SPRADLING, MARY ELIZABETH MACE
Librarian. **Personal:** Born Dec 31, Winchester, KY; widowed. **Educ:** KY State Coll, AB 1933; Atlanta Univ, BLS 1958; Rutgers Univ, certificate 1971. **Career:** Public Schs KY SC, tchr 1933-37; Shelbyville Sch, tchr lib 1944-47; Public Library, librn 1948-57; Kalamazoo Pub Lib, young adult dept 1957-76; Gale Rsch Co, bibliographer compiler. **Orgs:** Mem Family Serv Org Comm Cncl, Louisville Area Girl Scouts Bd, Kalamazoo Cncl on Human Relations, Kalamazoo YWCA Pub Affrs Comm, Kalamazoo Co Comm Serv Cncl, Kalamazoo Youth Comm, Kalamazoo Cncl Churches, Kalamazoo Co Library Bd, Mayor's Adv Comm on Problems of Law Enforcement, Kalamazoo Co Bi-Centennial Comms, King Meml Fund Bd Secty; Kalamazoo Branch NAACP; bd trustees Nazareth Coll; mem Delta Kappa Gamma Soc Epsilon Chapt; mem Kalamazoo Alumnae Chap Delta Sigma Theta Sor; asst supt Friendship Home; chmn Librarian's Sect KY Negro Educ Assn; KY mem

chmn Assn of Young People's Librarians; mem MI Library Assn Recruiting Comm; mem YASD Comm "Recent Adult Books for Young People"; mem Book Bait Comm ALA; guest lectr Dept of Librarianship Western MI Univ; mem bd dirs Young Adult Serv ALA; memer Lib Assn Cncl; contributor PREVIEWS Magazine; keynote spkr IN Library Assn YART, Student Library Workshop Western MI Univ. **Honors/Awds:** Listed in Notable Black Women Nancy Ellin 1984; Citations Midwest Region, Delta Sigma Theta Sor Inc, Kalamazoo Alumnae Delta Sigma Theta Sor, Adero Sisterhood Awd, Black Educators Kalamazoo; Kalamazoo NAACP Freedom Fund Humanitarian Awd 1984; "There Is No Such Book" Top of the News June 1965; Afro Amer Quiz 1976, In Black & White, Afro-Amers in Print, 2nd & 3rd ed supplement, 1985; "Black Librarians in KY" 1980. **Business Addr:** Bibliographer/Compiler, Gale Research Company, PO Box 628, Kalamazoo, MI 49005-0628.

SPRAGGINS, STEWART
Executive administrator. **Personal:** Born May 17, 1936, Pheba, MS; married Jean Caldwell; children: Renee Ericka, Stewart II. **Educ:** Mary Holmes Coll, AA 1958; Knoxville Coll, BA 1962; Fairfield Univ, MA 1972. **Career:** YMCA of Greater Bridgeport, exec mem & phys ed 1962-70; YMCA of Greater OK City, metro outreach exec 1970-72; YMCA of the Oranges, exec dir 1972-74; YMCA of Greater NY, exec dir 1974-77; JP Stevens & Co Inc, dir comm affairs 1977-. **Orgs:** Chmn Council of Concerned Black Execs; exec comm The Edges Group Inc; treas Natl Urban Affairs Council Inc; mem Corporate Coordinators Volunteers Council Inc; bd member Mary Holmes Coll 1983; bd mem NY March of Dimes 1983; bd member Accent Magazine 1984; bd mem Inst of NJ 1984. **Honors/Awds:** Outstanding Blk Amer NAACP & City of Bridgeport 1968; past state pres Elks of N America & Can 1969; Board Member of the Yr OK City Comm Action Prog 1970; Dr of Humane Letters Miles Coll 1983. **Military Serv:** AUS pvt 1 yr. **Home Addr:** 18 Maplewood Ave, Maplewood, NJ 07040.

SPRATLEN, THADDEUS H.
Educator, consultant. **Personal:** Born May 28, 1930, Union City, TN; son of Lela C Dobbins (deceased) and John B Spratlen (deceased); married Lois Price, Sep 28, 1952; children: Pamela, Patricia, Paula, Thadd Price, Townsend Price. **Educ:** OH State U, BS 1956; OH State U, MA 1957; OH State U, PhD 1962. **Career:** Howard Univ School of Business Administration, visiting research professor of marketing, 1986-87; Univ of WA, acting dir Afro-Amer Studies, 1980-81; Univ of WA, assoc dir Black Studies Program, 1979-80; Univ of WA, prof marketing 1975-; Univ of WA, assoc prof 1972-75; UCLA, 1969-72; W WA State Coll, 1961-69; author pubns; conference speaker; UCLA, consultant, adjunct assoc prof, 1972-75; Univ CA Berkeley, lecturer, 1965; Ethnic Studies Prog W WA State Coll, acting dir 1969; Black Economists Devel Proj, dir 1970-74. **Orgs:** Mem Natl Econ Assn; mem Caucus Black Economists; mem Amer Marketing Assn; mem WA State Adv Comm Minority Business 1974-76; mem Beta Gamma Sigma; mem US Census Adv Comm of Amer Marketing Assn 1975-81; United Negro Coll Fund Lecturer 1971, 1974. **Honors/Awds:** John Hay Whitney Fellowship 1958-59; Frederick Douglass Scholar Award, Natl Council for Black Studies, Pacific Northwest Region, 1986. **Military Serv:** AUSA 1st lt 1952-54; enlisted KT Corp, 1948-51. **Business Addr:** Univ of Washington, School of Business Administration, DJ-10, Seattle, WA 98195.

SPRATT, LEWIS G.
State representative. **Personal:** marrIed Annie Spratt; children: Patricia Collins, Lewis Jr, Ollie, Ronald, Angela, Rodrick, Anita Smith. **Educ:** Tuskegee Institute, attended. **Career:** Alabama House of Representatives, District 59 representative, 1985-. **Orgs:** Life member, Nat Mgmt Assn. **Business Addr:** State Representative, District 59, 3809 4th St, W, Birmingham, AL 35207.

SPRAUVE, GILBERT A.
Educator. **Personal:** Born Jun 9, 1937, St Thomas, VI; son of Eunice Sprauve and Gehardt Sprauve (deceased); married Alvara Eulalia Ritter (divorced); children: Masserae, Margaret, Janine, Singanu. **Educ:** Brooklyn Coll, BA 1960; Univ of So CA, MA 1965; Princeton U, PhD 1974. **Career:** Coll of the VI, assoc prof modern langs 1967-; LA City Schs CA, French, Spanish tchr 1963-67; Albert Acad Sierra Leone, French, Spanish tchr 1961-63; Lyce Donka Guinea, Span, Engl tchr 1960-61; Third Constitutional Conv of VI, del 1977; 14th Leg of Virgin Islands, senator at-large, vp; candidate for it gov on the runner-up Bryan/Sprauve ticket in 1986 general elections; Univ of Virgin Islands, prof of modern langs; Smithsonian Institution, Festival of American Folklife, Virgin Islands Section, general advisor & research, 1990; Smithsonian Institution, Office of Folklife Programs, senior visiting scholar, 1991 . **Orgs:** Mem VI Bd of Educ 1978-; adv bd mem Caribbean Fishery Mgmt Council 1979-; Rockefeller Foun Fellowship Grad Black Studies 1971-74. **Honors/Awds:** Pub "The Queue" The Literary Review 1974; del Pres Conf on Libraries 1979; principal role Derek Walcott's "Marie La Veau" a world premiere workshop at Coll VI 1979; authorship of numerous articles and monographs on Virgin Islands language and cultural history. **Business Addr:** Professor, Univ of the Virgin Islands, St Thomas, Virgin Islands of the United States 00801.

SPREWELL, LATRELL
Professional basketball player. **Personal:** Born Sep 8, 1970, Milwaukee, WI. **Educ:** Three Rivers Community College; Alabama. **Career:** Golden State Warriors, guard, 1992-. **Business Addr:** Pro Basketball Player, Golden State Warriors, 7000 Coliseum Way, Oakland, CA 94621-1918, (510)638-6300.

SPRIGGS, G. MAX. See Obituaries section.

SPRIGGS, MARCUS
Professional football player. **Personal:** Born May 17, 1974. **Educ:** University of Houston. **Career:** Buffalo Bills, tackle, 1997-. **Business Addr:** Professional Football Player, Buffalo Bills, One Bills Dr, Orchard Park, NY 14127, (716)648-1800.

SPRIGGS, RAY V. See Obituaries section.

SPRIGGS, WILLIAM
Economist. **Career:** Joint Economic Committee, senior economist, currently. **Business Addr:** Senior Economist, Joint Economic Committee, 1090 Vermont Ave., NW, Ste. 1100, Washington, DC 20005.

SPRINGER, ASHTON, JR.
Theatrical general manager, producer. **Personal:** Born Nov 1, 1930, New York, NY; son of Julia and Ashton; married Myra L Burns; children: Mark, Chesley. **Educ:** OH State U, BS 1954. **Career:** Theatre Mgmt Asso Inc, pres, currently, gen mgr; Bubbling Brown Sugar, Broadway musical, co-producer; No Place To Be Somebody, co-producer; Little Theatre Group, New York, NY, managing dir, Helen Hayes Theatre, 1979-85. **Orgs:** Pres Motor Car Asso 1966-70; mem League of NY Theatres & Prdcrs; mem Assn of Theatrical Press Agents & Mgrs. **Honors/Awds:** One World Award No Place To Be Somebody NAACP 1971; Philadelphia Playgoers Award Special Achievement in Theatre 1977; Pulitzer Prize No Place To Be Somebody 1970; nomination, Tony Awards, best play, A Lesson From Aloes, 1980-81; nomination, Tony Award, best musical, Bubbling Brown Sugar, 1975-76; Drama Critics Award, best play, A Lesson From Aloes, 1980-81; Life Achievement Award, Natl Black Arts Festival, Atlanta, GA, 1988; produced on Broadway the following shows: Whoppee, Eubie, A Lesson From Aloes, Cold Storage, All Night Strut, Going Up. **Business Addr:** President, Theatre Mgmt Associates, 1600 Broadway, Ste 514D, New York, NY 10019.

SPRINGER, ERIC WINSTON
Attorney. **Personal:** Born May 17, 1929, New York, NY; son of Maida S and Owen W; married Cecile Marie Kennedy; children: Brian, Christina. **Educ:** Rutgers Univ, AB, 1950; NY Univ School of Law, LLB, 1953. **Career:** Justice NY State Supreme Court, law clerk, 1955-56; Univ of Pittsburgh, rsch assoc, 1956-58; asst prof of law, 1958-64, assoc prof of law, 1965-68, dir of compliance EEOC, 1967; Aspen Systems Corp Pittsburgh, vice pres, dir, publisher, 1968-71; Horty, Springer & Mattern PC Pittsburgh, partner, 1971-82, principal, 1982-. **Orgs:** Dir Presbyterian Univ Hosp 1967-; mem NY Bar (inactive) 1953, PA Bar 1975-; dir Duquesne Light Co 1977-; mem ABA, NBA, Allegheny Cty Bar Assoc; life mem NAACP; Allegheny County Bar Association, board of governors, immediate past president; Neurological Disorders and Stroke Council; national advisor; Montefiore University Hospital, Pittsburgh, Pennsylvania, trustee; Univ of Pittsburgh Med Center, trustee. **Honors/Awds:** National Bar Assn, Hall of Fame, 1993; Honorary Fellow Amer Coll of Healthcare Execs 1978; author "Group Practice and the Law" 1969; editor "Nursing and the Law" 1970; "Automated Medical Records and the Law" 1971; contributing editor of monthly newsletter "Action-Kit for Hospital Law" 1973. **Military Serv:** AUS 1953-55. **Business Addr:** Executive Vice President, Horty, Springer & Mattern PC, 4614 Fifth Ave, Pittsburgh, PA 15213.

SPRINGER, GEORGE CHELSTON
Labor union administrator, educator. **Personal:** Born Nov 9, 1932, La Boca, Canal Zone, Panama; son of Edna Ethel Westerman-Springer and Bertley Nimrod Springer; married Gerri Brown Springer, Oct 11, 1980; children: Rosina Francesca Springer Audette, Linda Inez Springer-Broderick, George C Jr. **Educ:** Canal Zone Jr Coll, La Boca, Canal Zone, AA, 1952; Teachers Coll of Connecticut, New Britain CT, BS, 1954, Central Connecticut State Univ, New Britain CT, attended, 1955-75. **Career:** Fafnir Bearing Co, New Britain CT, hardener, 1955-57, 1959; US Army, occupational therapy tech, 1957-59; Consolidated School Dist, New Britain CT, teacher, 1959-79; Connecticut Fedn of Teachers, Berlin CT, pres, 1979-. **Orgs:** Mem, SDE Educ Equity Comm, 1979-; vice pres, Connecticut State AFL-CIO, 1979-; pres, New Britain Chapter NAACP, 1982-86; secretary, treasurer, Legislative Electional Action Program, 1982-; vice pres, United Labor Agency, 1983-; mem, advisory council, CSU Center for Educ Excellence, 1986-; mem, Connecticut Coalition for Literacy, 1986-; bd of trustees, Connecticut Law School Found, 1987-; bd of dir, Connecticut Civil Liberties Union, 1987-; bd of overseers, Regional Lab for Educ Improvement in the Northeast & Islands, 1988-; vice pres, Amer Fedn of Teachers, 1988-; fellow, Amer Leadership Forum, 1988-; co-chair, Sixth Dist Fed Priorities Project, 1988-. **Honors/Awds:** Man of the Year, St James Baptist Church, 1984; John P Shaw Award (Outstanding Serv to Community), New Britain NAACP, 1984; Meritorious Serv Award, UNCF, 1987; Educators of Distinction Award, Connecticut Coalition of 100 Black Women, 1988; Carl Huroit Award (Grassroot Politics, Progressive Issues, Coalition Building), LEAP, 1989; Harriet Tubman Award (Achievement in Pursuit of Social Justice), Connecticut NOW, 1989. **Military Serv:** US Army, Sp-4, 1957-59. **Home Addr:** 45 Glen Carlyn Rd, New Britain, CT 06053. **Business Addr:** President, Connecticut State Federation of Teachers, AFT, AFL-CIO, 1781 Wilbur Cross Pkwy, Berlin, CT 06037.

SPRINGER, LLOYD LIVINGSTONE
Clergyman. **Personal:** Born Apr 28, 1930; son of Olive Springer and Oscar (deceased); married Ottorita L Philips, May 2, 1970; children: L Addison. **Educ:** Codrington College, GOE Diploma, 1960; New York Theological Seminary, STM, 1975; New York University, MA, 1982. **Career:** St Martin Episcopal Church, asst, 1971-73; Episcopal Mission Society House of the Holy Comforter, chaplain, 1980-86; St Edmund Episcopal Church, rector, 1973-; Bronx Lebanon Hosp, pt-time chaplain. **Orgs:** North West Bronx Clergy & Comm Organization; Mt Hope Housing Corp, president, 1987-96; Pension Committee, diocese; Ecumenical Commission, diocese. **Honors/Awds:** Bronx Borough President's Award; St Edmund Episcopal, Vestry Appreciation Award; Mt Hope Organization and Community Appreciation Award for Dynamic Leadership. **Business Addr:** Reverend, St. Edmund Episcopal Church, 1905 Morris Ave, Bronx, NY 10453.

SPRINGS, LENNY F.
Business executive. **Personal:** Born Apr 25, 1947, Edgefield, SC. **Educ:** Voorhees Coll, BS 1968. **Career:** Greenville Urban League, proj dir 1976-79, deputy dir 1979-82, exec dir 1982-83; Southern Bank, comm relations officer 1983-. **Orgs:** Vice pres Greenville Branch NAACP 1976-84; chmn Legal Redress Comm SC Conf NAACP 1978-; vice chmn SC Human Affairs Comm 1983-. **Honors/Awds:** Outstanding Young Men of Amer 1973 & 1979; NAACP Legal Awd for SC 1980; Greenville Branch NAACP Awd 1984. **Military Serv:** AUS sgt E-5 2 yrs; 2 Bronze Stars; Air Medal. **Business Addr:** Vice Pres, First Union Natl Bank of Charlotte, 301 S College St, Charlotte, NC 28288.

SPRINGS, SHAWN
Professional football player. **Personal:** Born Mar 11, 1975. **Educ:** Ohio State. **Career:** Seattle Seahawks, 1997-. **Special Achievements:** NFL Draft, First round pick, #3, 1997. **Business Addr:** Professional Football Player, Seattle Seahawks, 11220 NE 53rd St, Kirkland, WA 98033, (206)827-9777.

SPRINKLE-HAMLIN, SYLVIA YVONNE
Deputy library director. **Personal:** Born Apr 25, 1945, Winston-Salem, NC; daughter of Thelma Norwood Holtzclaw and Arthur William Henry Sprinkle, Jr; married Larry Leon Hamlin, Aug 29, 1981. **Educ:** Winston-Salem State Univ, Winston-Salem, NC, BS, education, 1963-67; Atlanta University, Atlanta, GA, MA, lib science, educational administration, 1968; Cheyney State University, Cheyney, PA, institute of advance study, 1972-76; University of North Carolina-Chapel Hill, Chapel Hill, NC, certification county admin, 1986-87. **Career:** Philadelphia Public Schools, Philadelphia, PA, information specialist, 1973-77; Fashion Two Twenty Cosmetics, Winston-Salem, NC, studio owner, 1977-81; Winston-Salem State Univ, Winston-Salem, NC, assistant librarian, 1978-79; Forsyth County Public Library, Winston-Salem, NC, head, children's outreach, 1979-80, assistant director-extensions, 1980-84, deputy library director, 1984-. **Orgs:** President, Black Caucus of the American Library Association, 1996-; national planning chair, National Conference African American Librarians, 1990-92; president, Youth Opportunity Homes Inc, 1990-93; board member, National Black Theatre Festival, 1989; secretary, North Carolina Black Repertory Company, 1989-; director at large, membership committee, North Carolina Library Association, 1989-91; vice president, National Women of Achievement, 1989-91; board member, Council on The Status of Women; board member, Winston-Salem State University Diggs Gallery; BCALA, North Carolina pres. **Honors/Awds:** Annette Lewis Phinazee Award, North Carolina Central University, 1986. **Business Addr:** Deputy Library Director, Forsyth County Public Library, 660 W Fifth St, Winston-Salem, NC 27101.

SPROUT, FRANCIS ALLEN
Artist, educator. **Personal:** Born Mar 5, 1940, Tucson, AZ. **Educ:** Univ of AZ Tuscon, BFA 1967; Univ of CA San Diego, MFA 1972, MA (in progress). **Career:** Univ of Denver, CO, asst prof Art 1972-75; Univ of CO, Boulder, instr African & African Amer Vsl Traditions 1976-82; Metro State Coll Denver, CO, asso prof Art 1976-. **Orgs:** Mem African Studies Asso 1984; mem Chicano Hmnts & Art Cncl Denver 1982-; mem Alliance for Contmpry Art Denver Art Museum 1980; grant review pnl CO Cncl on the Arts & Humnts 1984-85. **Honors/Awds:** Flwshp Inst on Africa, Hamline Univ 1978; CO Rep 74th Wstn Annual Denver Art Museum 1972; Flwshp Grad Stdy Ford Fndtn 1971-72. **Military Serv:** USNG 1st lt 6 yrs. **Business Addr:** Professor of Art, Metropolitan State Coll, Art Dept Box 59, 1006 11th St, Denver, CO 80204.

SPRUCE, KENNETH L.
Educator. **Personal:** Born Mar 6, 1956, Toledo, OH; son of Helen E Jordan Spruce and George Spruce Jr (deceased); divorced; children: Sierra Monique. **Educ:** University of Cincinnati, Cincinnati, OH, BA, 1980; American University, Washington, DC, 1980-81; University of Toledo, Toledo, OH, MPA, 1982; Clark Atlanta University, Atlanta, GA, PhD candidate, 1991-. **Career:** University of Toledo, Toledo, OH, graduate teaching assistant, 1981-82; Toledo Journal Newspaper, Toledo, OH, columnist writer-reporter, 1982-85; State of Ohio, Bureau of Employment Services, Toledo, OH, personnel counselor, 1983-91; Morris Brown College, Political Science Program, Atlanta, GA, adjunct instructor, 1993; Clark Atlanta University, Political Science Dept, graduate teaching assist, 1993-94; Floyd College, Rome, GA, assist prof of political science, 1993-97, assoc prof, 1998-. **Orgs:** National Conference of Black Political Scientists, mem, 1990-95; Amer Assn of University Professors, 1994-95; Amer Political Science Assn, 1992-95; Georgia Political Science Assn, 1994-95. **Honors/Awds:** US Dept of Housing & Urban Dev, 701 Work-Study Scholarship, 1980-81; Grad Teaching Assist, Univ of Toledo, 1981-82; Merit Award, Best Editorial Nominee, Natl Newspaper Publisher's Assn, 1986; Community Service Award, Nominee, Black Student Union, Univ of Toledo, 1987; Recipient, Ford Foundations Fellowship, 1992-93; Selected Collegiate Scholastic All-American, 1993. **Home Addr:** 505 Amberlake Ln, Acworth, GA 30101. **Business Phone:** (770)975-4105.

SPRUILL, ALBERT WESTLEY
Educational administrator. **Personal:** Born Aug 5, 1926, Columbia, NC; married Pearl Floydelia Farrish; children: Albert Westley Jr, Ogden Bertrand, Ronald Conrad. **Educ:** NC A&T State Univ, BS 1949; IA State Univ Ames, MS 1951; Cornell Univ, EdD 1958. **Career:** NC Agr Ext Svc, cty agent 1949-50; MS Voc Coll, act dir div of agr 1951-52; Tuskegee Inst, teacher trainer agr ed 1952-53; NC A&T State Univ, instr prof 1955-93, dean grad studies 1970-93, retired. **Orgs:** Mem NAACP 1960-; deacon Providence Baptist Church 1970-; vice pres & pres Southern Conf of Grad Schools 1974-76; sec/treas Southern Assn Land Grant Coll & State Univ 1976-; bd of dir Council of Grad Schools in US 1985-88. **Honors/Awds:** Gate City Alumni Awd NC A&T State Univ 1949; Gen Ed Bd Fellow Gen Educ Bd 1953-54; Elected to Phi Delta Kappa Theta Chap Cornell 1954; Alumni Merit Awd IA State Univ Ames 1982. **Military Serv:** AUS pfc 1946-47. **Home Addr:** 1303 Marboro Drive, Greensboro, NC 27406. **Business Addr:** Dean, Graduate School, NC Agr & Tech State Univ, 120 Gibbs Hall, Greensboro, NC 27411.

SPRUILL, JAMES ARTHUR
Educator. **Personal:** Born Sep 28, 1937, Baltimore, MD; married Lynda; children: Robert, Joshua. **Educ:** Goddard Coll, AB 1968; Boston Univ, MFA 1975. **Career:** Boston Univ School for Arts, tenured assoc prof, 1975-; Emerson Coll, asst prof, 1970-74; Goddard Coll, visiting prof 1971-72; Boston State Coll, visiting prof 1972-75; Theatre Co of Boston, acted, production, dir, taught 1967-75. **Orgs:** Pres, New African Co Inc 1968-; co-founder New African Co Inc 1968-; mem bd trustees Metro Cultural All; mem New England Theatre Conf; sr mem Actors Equity Assn; AFTRA; SAG; past mem Theatre Advis Panel MA Coun on Arts & Human, Martin Luther King Fellow Boston Univ 1968; prod "The Blacks" Loeb Drama Center Harvard U 1969; reg cit New English Theatre Conf 1970; devel & taught course in Black Drama History Boston Coll, Emerson Coll, Boston State Coll; directed first play by an African American, published in US (1858) by W W Brown World premiere Emersol Coll 1972; directed "The Escape or a Leap for Freedom" at BU 1977; fdr mem Nat Conf on African Amer Theatre; past chair, Boston Univ Faculty Council; founding mem, Natl Conf on African American Theatre. **Honors/Awds:** Roxbury Action Program, Insight Award 1975; Vernon Blackman Drama Award, 1990; Elliot Norton Award, 1991; cited for direction of the Colored museum by George C Wolfe, Boston, 1994. **Business Addr:** Assoc Prof, Boston Univ, 855 Commonwealth Ave, Boston, MA 02115.

SPRUILL, ROBERT I.
Business executive. **Personal:** Born Jul 10, 1947, New Bern, NC. **Educ:** NC Cen U, BS 1970. **Career:** WAFRM FM Comm Radio Workshop Inc, pres & founder. **Orgs:** Mem Nat Assn of Educ Broadcasters; NC Assn Broadcasters. **Honors/Awds:** First black owned & controlled educ radio station in Am; Featured in Ebony Magazine, 1973.

SPURLOCK, DOROTHY A.
Consultant. **Personal:** Born Mar 18, 1956, Kalamazoo, MI; daughter of Della A Watson Spurlock and Jimmie Spurlock Sr. **Educ:** Western Michigan University, Kalamazoo, MI, BS, 1979, MA, 1983. **Career:** Western Michigan University, Kalamazoo, MI, manager, employment services, senior compensation analyst/coordinator, legislative affairs, 1979-84; The Popcorn Station, Kalamazoo, MI, owner/manager, 1984-88; Urban League of Greater Muskegon, Muskegon, MI, executive director, 1988-89; Nu-Way Consulting Inc, Kalamazoo, MI, vice president of operations, 1989-. **Orgs:** Council member, City of Kalamazoo, 1983-87. **Honors/Awds:** Woman of the Year, NOW, 1983.

SPURLOCK, JAMES B., JR.
Public relations executive. **Personal:** Born Jan 20, 1936, Roanoke, VA; married Nancy H; children: James B III, Deborah G, Kenneth L. **Educ:** A&t State Univ, BS (cum laude) 1959; Personnel Adm Personnel Mgmt, diploma 1960, 1962; Mgmt Training Course, grad 1968; Univ of MI, grad Advanced Mgmt Prog 1970. **Career:** AT&T Microelectronics, public relations manager, currently. **Orgs:** Mem VA State C of C; lectr Univ MI; A&T State Univ Career Convocation & Interview Clinic; mem Rotary Club Intl Salem VA; panelist for Natl Assn of Market Devel & WRFT-TV; Indus Mgmt Clubs of VA; VA Western Comm Coll; past chmn bd dir Roanoke Chap Oppty Indus Ctr Inc; bd of deacons First African Baptist Church; past mem bd trustees Sweet Union Baptist Ch; past mem Roanoke Jaycees; past mem bd dir Roanoke Valley Council of Comm Svcs; past mem bd dir Roanoke Valley Unit Amer Cancer Soc; past mem bd of Roanoke Valley Vol Bur; past mem Roanoke Selective Serv Bd; past mem Gainsboro Elec Mfg Co; past loan exec Roanoke Valley United Fund Campaign; past mem Roanoke City Sch Bd; past member, bd of visitors, James Madison University; Richmond Metro Chamber of Commerce; vice-chairman, bd of trustees, St Paul's College; RichmonNCP; Richmond Urban League; chairman of the board, RAPME; director, C W Anderson Male Chorus; Norfolk State University Foundation Board; City of Richmond, Private Industry Council. **Honors/Awds:** Publ articles "Obsolescence or Change"; "Recruiting the Qualified Minority Grad"; treas Sigma Rho Sigma Natl Honor Soc; Outstanding Citizen's Awd 1973; Outstanding Serv on the Bd of Dir VA Coll Placement Assn 1972; Outstanding Comm Ldr Burrell Meml Hosp 1974; Father of the Yr Inter-Faith Comm Choir 1971; Key to City of Roanoke 1975; Cert of Merit City Council of Roanoke for Serv on Roanoke Sch Bd 1974; Cert of Recog Natl Alliance of Busmn for Serv on Youth Motivation Task Force 1973-74; Cert of Appreciation State Dir of Selective Serv for Serv on Roanoke Selective Serv Bd; Awd of Apprec So Coll Placement Assn for Serv on Bd Dir; state chmn United Nations Day 1977; selected as one of VA Comm Ldrs. **Military Serv:** AUS capt 1960-68. **Business Addr:** 4500 S Laburnum Ave, Richmond, VA 23231.

SPURLOCK, JEANNE
Physician, educator. **Personal:** Born in Sandusky, OH. **Educ:** Howard Univ Sch of Medicine, MD 1947; Chicago Inst for Psychoanalysis, completed post-grad study. **Career:** Meharry Med Coll, ch dept psych; Michael Reese Hosp Chicago, chief of child psychiatry clinic; tchr at numerous med schs across the country; Amer Psychiatric Assn; deputy med dir 1974-. **Orgs:** Mem Natl Med Assn, Amer Acad of Child Psychiatry; mem bd dirs Urban League. **Honors/Awds:** 1st Black to receive Edward Strecker Awd Inst of PA Hosp for Outstanding Ability as a Clinician Educator & Comm Leader. **Business Addr:** Deputy Medical Dir, Amer Psychiatric Assn, 1400 K St, NW, Washington, DC 20005.

SPURLOCK, LANGLEY AUGUSTINE
Association executive. **Personal:** Born Nov 9, 1939, Charleston, WV; son of Eunice P Spurlock and Langley A Spurlock. **Educ:** WV State Coll, BS (magna cum laude), 1959; Wayne State Univ, PhD 1963. **Career:** Brown Univ, assoc prof of chemistry 1969-73; Amer Council on Educ, asst to pres 1973-76; US Dept of HEW, HEW fellow 1976-77; Natl Science Found, sr staff assoc 1977-82; Chemical Mnf Assn, dir CHEMSTAR Division, 1982-94, vice president, 1994-. **Orgs:** Mem Amer Chem Soc; Amer Society of Assn Executives; Amer Assoc for the Advancement of Science; Phi Lambda Upsilon Hon Chem Soc; Soc of Sigma Xi; Beta Kappa Chi Hon Sci Soc; Alpha Kappa Mu Hon Schol Soc; Delta Phi Alpha Hon German Soc; Kappa Alpha Psi. **Honors/Awds:** Certified Assn Executive 1989-; Alfred P Sloan Fellow 1973-75; NIH Postdoctoral Fellow Harvard Univ 1966; NIH predoctoral fellow Wayne State Univ 1961-63; author 34 publications & 3 patents.

SPURLOCK, LAVERNE B.
Educator, counseling administrator (retired). **Personal:** Born Feb 23, 1930, Richmond, VA; daughter of Mabel M Matney Beard and Joseph C Beard; married Charles T, Jun 10, 1956; children: Carla S Harrell. **Educ:** VA State Coll, BS 1950; Columbia U, MA 1954; Univ of VA, advanced study 1974; VPI & SU Blacksburg, VA, EdD, 1984. **Career:** Richmond Public Schools, Guidance Dept, coordinator 1970-91; Maggie L Walker HS, teacher 1951; John Marshall HS, guid dept head 1970-86; Richmond Public Schools, supervisor of guidance, 1986-91. **Orgs:** Mem co-chmn VA Assn for Non-White Concerns; past pres VA Sch Counselor Assn; past dir for educ & vice pres for educ Richmond Personnel & Guidance Assn; VPGA; vol listener Youth Emergency Svcs; bd mem Richmond Area Psychiatric Clinic; past mem Bd of Christian Educ Ebenezer Bapt Ch; Personnel Com Ebenezer Bapt Ch; trustee, Ebenezer Bapt Ch; past pres Richmond Chap Delta Sigma Theta; past first vice pres Richmond Chap National Coalition of 100 Black Women; secretary Henrico Area Mental Health Service Board, Human Rights Comm; past project director, SECME; president, Virginia Heroes, Inc; Pi Lambda Theta; associate director, AVID; The Moles; C-WIF. **Honors/Awds:** Boss of the Year, American Business Women's Assn, 1989; Delta Sigma Theta, Richmond Alum Chap, Education Award. **Home Addr:** 1611 Forest Glen Rd, Richmond, VA 23228.

SPURLOCK, OLIVER M.
Judge. **Personal:** Born Feb 28, 1945, Chicago, IL; son of Anna P Spurlock and Thomas L Spurlock; divorced; children: Stacey, Brandon, Marc. **Educ:** Univ of Illinois, BA, 1969; Northwestern Univ Law School, JD, 1972. **Career:** Cook County State's Attorney, assistant, 1972-75; private practice, attorney, 1975-88; Cook County Circuit Court, associate judge, beginning, 1988, Criminal Court, judge, currently. **Business Addr:** Judge, Cook County Daley Ctr, Rm 1303, Chicago, IL 60602, (312)603-7959.

SPURLOCK, RACQUEL
Professional basketball player. **Personal:** Born May 25, 1973. **Educ:** Louisiana Tech, attended. **Career:** Houston Comets, center, 1997-. **Special Achievements:** Won a gold medal with the United States Jones Cup team, 1994. **Business Addr:** Professional Basketball Player, Houston Comets, Two Greenway Plaza, Ste 400, Houston, TX 77046, (713)627-9622.

SPURLOCK-EVANS, KARLA JEANNE
Educational administrator. **Personal:** Born Jun 30, 1949, Willimantic, CT; daughter of Odessa Fuller Spurlock and Kelly M Spurlock; married Booker Evans, Jul 1, 1978; children: Mariama Ifetayo, Booker Theodore Jr. **Educ:** Barnard Coll, AB (magna cum laude) 1971; Emory Univ, MA 1972. **Career:** State Univ of NY at Albany, asst prof 1975-77; Haverford Coll, dir of minority affairs 1977-80; Lake Forest Coll, asst dean of students 1981-85; Northwestern Univ, assoc dean of students/dir Afro-Amer student affairs 1985-. **Orgs:** Bd mem Assoc for the Advancement of Creative Musicians 1981-83; mem IL College Personnel Assoc, IL Comm on Black Concerns in Higher Educ, Natl Assoc of Women Deans, Administrators and Counselors; The Chicago Reporter, editorial bd; Natl Assn of Student Personnel Administrators. **Honors/Awds:** Phi Beta Kappa; Grad Fellowship John Hay Whitney Foundation 1971-72; Grad Fellowship Danforth Foundation 1971-75. **Business Addr:** Assoc Dean/Dir of African-American Student Affairs, Northwestern University, 1914 Sheridan Rd, Evanston, IL 60201.

SQUIRE, CAROLE RENEE HUTCHINS
Attorney. **Personal:** Born Jul 21, 1953, Springfield, OH; daughter of Reva Hutchins and Robert Hutchins; married Percy Squire, Mar 18, 1978; children: Reva Marie, Deidra Renee. **Educ:** Ohio State University, BA, 1974; Ohio State University College of Law, JD, 1977. **Career:** Office of the Ohio Attorney General, assistant attorney general; private law practice, juvenile law, American University, Temple University, overseas, professorial lecturer; Office of the General Counsel of the Navy, attorney advisor, contracts; Youth Alternative Project, asst dir; The Ohio Legal Rights Service, staff attorney; Franklin County Domestic Relations Court, juvenile unit, asst prosecutor, juvenile unit referee, 1991-94. **Orgs:** Seal of Ohio Girl Scout Council, Brownie troop leader, 1991-93; Columbus Bar Association; Women Lawyers of Franklin County; Columbus Bar Foundation Fellow, 1992; Youth Advocate Services, board member, 1989-92; Community Mediation Services, bd member, 1988-92; National Association of Female Executives, 1993; Shiloh Baptist Church, Sunday Church School Youth Department Superintendent and teacher; National Conference of Black Lawyers.

STAATS, FLORENCE JOAN
Educational administrator. **Personal:** Born Nov 18, 1940, Newark, NJ; daughter of Florence Wheatley Staats and Jay M Staats. **Educ:** Parsons Sch of Design cert 1961; New York Univ, BS 1968; Pratt Inst, MFA 1970; Columbia Univ Tchrs Coll, EdD 1978. **Career:** Newark Pub Lbry, exhibit artst 1965-68; Essex Co Coll, fine arts instr 1972-78, asst prof coord of Art pgm 1978-81; Dutchess Comm Coll, asst dean 1982-84, asst to pres 1984-; Bloomfield Coll, associate dean 1985-86; Rockland Cmmty Coll, associate dean 1986-88; Acting Dir NY African American Institute SUNY 1988-89; Ulster County Community College, dir, COPE, currently. **Orgs:** Cnsltnt artst Pgm for Spcl Arts Fstvl 1981-81; cnsltnt Creative Arts Proj Dev 1982-83; bd dir Clearwater, Inc 1983-; rep ACE/NIP Instnl Am Cncl Education Mid Hudson Chptr 1983-; exec bd dir Ulster Co Cncl for Arts 1983-85; creative dir/pres The Arts Connection 1984-; pres Arts & Communication Network Inc 1985-; Bd of Dir Creative Research in African Amer Life 1986-; Executive Board/Chairperson Ulster County NAACP Education Committee; Rosendale Environmental Commission; bd of directors, vice pres, Ulster Arts Alliance. **Honors/Awds:** NEH Grant Black Exprnc in Am 1977; OE Grant (Fulbright) G7 Cmnty Coll Smnr Poland 1974; CBS/EEC Awrd for Mrktng Pln 1984; Ldrshp 80's Proj Am Assn of Wmn in Cmnty Coll 1985; Summer Research Grant NY African American Institute 1987; Grant Award, New York State Council on the Arts, 1989; Ulster County Multi Service, Martin Luther King Jr Award for Community Service, 1995. **Business Addr:** Dir, Public Assistance Comprehensive Employment Program, Ulster County Community College, Stone Ridge, NY 12484.

STACIA, KEVIN MAURICE
Senior human resources representative. **Personal:** Born Nov 1, 1958, Baton Rouge, LA. **Educ:** Southern Univ, BS (Magna Cum Laude) 1980; Atlanta Univ, Sch of Business, MBA 1982. **Career:** Fidelity Natl Bank Baton Rouge, bank teller 1977-80;

General Dynamics Corp San Diego, intern 1979; Scientific-Atlanta Inc, human resource rep 1982-86; Hewlett-Packard Co, sr human resources rep 1987-. **Orgs:** Adv bd mem Atlanta Urban League 1985-; assoc deacon and chmn of brotherhood Ebenezer Bapt Ch 1985-; trustee Atlanta Exchange Inc 1986-; co-chair programs comm metro Atlanta High Tech Personnel Assoc 1986-; pres Atlanta Chap Natl Black MBA Assoc 1987-; mem outreach prog comm Alpha Phi Alpha Frat Inc 1987-. **Honors/Awds:** Outstanding Serv Awd Natl Black MBA Assoc 1985; Professional in Human Resources Accreditation Amer Soc for Personnel Admin 1986; MBA of the Year Atlanta Chap Natl Black MBA Assoc 1986.

STACKHOUSE, JERRY DARNELL
Professional basketball player. **Personal:** Born Nov 5, 1974, Kinston, NC. **Educ:** North Carolina. **Career:** Philadelphia 76ers, forward-guard, 1995-97; Detroit Pistons, 1997-. **Honors/Awds:** NBA All-Rookie Team, 1996. **Special Achievements:** NBA, First Round Draft Pick, #3 Pick, 1995. **Business Addr:** Professional Basketball Player, Detroit Pistons, Palace of Auburn Hills, Two Championship Drive, Auburn Hills, MI 48326, (248)377-0100.

STAFFORD, DERRICK
Professional sports official. **Career:** NBA, referee, currently. **Business Addr:** NBA Official, National Basketball Association, 645 5th Ave, 15th Fl, New York, NY 10022-5986.

STAFFORD, DON
Law enforcement official (retired). **Personal:** Born Dec 14, 1934, Rusk, TX; son of L V Mitchell Stafford and Chilton Stafford; married Geraldine Doughty Stafford, Apr 5, 1985. **Educ:** Butler College, Tyler, TX, BS, 1956. **Career:** Dallas Police Department, Dallas, TX, asst chief of police, 1982-88; Dallas Police Department, Dallas, TX, exec asst chief, 1988-91. **Orgs:** Black Chamber of Commerce, Urban League, International Police Association, Blacks in Law Enforcement. **Honors/Awds:** Certificate of Civic Achievement, Dallas Police Department, 1977; Recipient of over 175 commendations from citizens and citizen groups; Formal recognition from groups including: AMVETS, Dallas Mayor, Texas Peace Officers' Association, Interdenominational Ministers Alliance; Promoted to detective in 1965 and later was reclassified to supervisory rank of Sergeant; First black to hold ranks to Lieutenant, Captain, Director, Deputy Chief, Assistant Chief, & Executive Assistant Chief; Governor's Office State of Texan, Outstanding Texan Award. **Special Achievements:** Promoted to the Rank of Sergeant, 1966; First African Amer to ever hold a Supervisor Rank in the History of the Dallas Police Dept. **Military Serv:** Air Force, A/2C, 1956-60; Received plaque for Outstanding Officer of the Month, Air Police. **Home Addr:** 2913 So Houston School R, Lancaster, TX 75146. **Business Phone:** (972)228-0280.

STAFFORD, EARL W.
Information services executive. **Career:** Universal Systems & Technology Inc (Unitech), CEO, currently. **Special Achievements:** Company is ranked #96 on Black Enterprise magazine's 1997 list of Top 100 Black businesses. **Business Phone:** (703)385-0349.

STAFFORD, TRISHA
Professional basketball player. **Personal:** Born Nov 11, 1970. **Educ:** Univ of California, Berkeley. **Career:** San Jose Lasers, forward, 1997-98; Long Beach Stingrays, 1998-. **Business Addr:** Professional Basketball Player, Long Beach Stingrays, One World Trade Center, Ste 202, Long Beach, CA 90831-0202, (562)951-7297.

STAGGERS, FRANK EUGENE
Physician. **Personal:** Born Aug 23, 1926, Charleston, SC; widowed; children: Frank Jr, Barbara, Michael. **Educ:** VA State Coll, BS 1949; Meharry Med Coll, MD 1953. **Career:** Physician urology 1963-; USN Hosp, asst chf urology 1961-63; USN, resd 1957-60; USN Hosp, intern 1953-54. **Orgs:** Mem AMA; CMA; ACCMA; NMA; Western Sect AUA; Med Staff & Survey Com CA Med Assn; sr staff surveyor 1971-; mem CA Blue Shield Policy Com 1972-; Geriatrics Com 1970-; pres Golden State Med Soc; St Luke's Soc; Nursing Educ Adv Com Merrie & Laney Coll 1971-; Sigma Pi Phi Frat; Kappa Alpha Psi; Beta Kappa Chi Nat Hon Sci Coc; co-chmn Golden State Med Assn CA Med Assn Liasion Com Recpt Carcinoma of the Prostate Gland in CA 1977; Carcinoma of the Prostate UC Med Ctr 1973. **Honors/Awds:** Publ "Treatment of the Underscended Testis With Especial Reference to Pathological Anatomy" Jour Urology 1960. **Military Serv:** AUS comdr 1945-45; AUSNR 1947-53; USN 1953-63; USNR 1963-73. **Business Addr:** 5900 Shattuck Ave, Ste 203, Oakland, CA 94609.

STAHNKE, WILLIAM E.
Bank executive. **Career:** First Texas Bank, Dallas, chief exec. **Business Addr:** First Texas Bank, 2650 Royal Ln, Dallas, TX 75229.

STALEY, DAWN
Professional basketball player. **Personal:** Born May 4, 1970, Philadelphia, PA. **Educ:** Univ of Virginia, graduate. **Career:** Philadelphia Rage, guard, 1996-. **Honors/Awds:** USA Basketball Female Athlete of the Year, 1994; Honda-Broderick Award, 1991. **Business Addr:** Professional Basketball Player, Philadelphia Rage, 123 Chestnut St, Fourth Flr, Philadelphia, PA 19106, (215)629-1976.

STALEY, DUCE
Professional football player. **Personal:** Born Feb 27, 1975. **Educ:** Univ of South Carolina, attended. **Career:** Philadelphia Eagles, running back, 1997-. **Business Addr:** Professional Football Player, Philadelphia Eagles, 3501 S Broad St, Philadelphia, PA 19148, (215)463-2500.

STALEY, KENNETH BERNARD
Construction company executive. **Personal:** Born Dec 31, 1948, Philadelphia, PA; son of Bernice Staley and Kinzy Staley; married Shelia Keeys, Apr 26, 1975; children: Tabbatha, Christina, Harrison. **Educ:** Villanova University, BSCE, 1971; Miller Theological Seminary, MDiv, 1975, DD, 1978; American Association of Marriage and Family Therapist, clinical, 1983. **Career:** Jos A McCollum Inc, engineer-in-training, 1966-69; RV Rulon Co., field engineer, 1969; United Engineers & Constructors Inc, field engineer, 1971-72; Kinzy Staley & Sons Inc, vice pres, 1972-90, president, chief executive officer, 1992-. **Orgs:** Mendenhall Ministries, board member, 1981-; Christian Research & Development, board member, 1980-; Greater Germantown Development Corp, board member, 1988-89; Philadelphia Leadership Foundation, steering committee, 1985-; Kinzy Staley & Sons Inc, board member, 1972-; Fellowship of Christian Athletes, PA state board, 1992; Billy Graham Crusade Philadelphia, steering committee, 1992. **Honors/Awds:** US Jaycees, Outstanding Young Man in America, 1980, 1981, 1983; National Society of Professional Engineers, 1988. **Business Addr:** President, Chief Executive Officer, Kinzy Staley and Sons, Inc., 5017 Wakefield St, Philadelphia, PA 19144.

STALEY, VALERIA HOWARD
Librarian (retired). **Personal:** Born May 5, 1925, Georgetown, SC; married Frank Marcellus Staley Jr; children: Frank Howard, Elisa Claire. **Educ:** Talladega Coll, BA 1945; Univ of Chicago, BLS 1946. **Career:** FL A&M Univ, ref librarian 1946-49; Howard HS, school librarian 1949-57; SC State Coll, reference and information specialist 1958-85 (retired). **Orgs:** Chmn Orangeburg Co Library Comm 1969-; bd dirs Orangeburg Co Arts Festival; mem Amer Library Assn; mem Southeastern Lib Assn; life mem SC Library Assn; mem Amer Assn of Univ Profs; mem Phi Delta Kappa Frat; mem Black Caucus Amer Library Assn; Churchwomen United; Links Inc, past pres, southern area officer; mem past pres Delta Sigma Theta sor; mem Jeddah Ct Daughters of Isis; life mem Eastern Stars; Life mem VFW Auxiliary Post 8166; past pres Jack & Jill of Amer; past pres, state vice pres NAACP; mem Wm Chapel AME CH; Life mem NAACP; bd dirs SC State Museum Foundation. **Honors/Awds:** Distinguished Service Awd, SC State Library.

STALKS, LARRIE W.
Public official. **Personal:** Born Sep 28, 1925, Newark, NJ; married Frederick Stalks. **Educ:** Rutgers U; NY U. **Career:** Essex Co, register of deeds Jan 1975-; Central Planning Bd City of Newark, former sec; Dept of Health & Welfare City of Newark, dir 1966-70; Central Planning Bd City of Newark, exec sec; Congressman Hugh J Addonizio, home dist sec. **Orgs:** Bd trustees Central Ward Girls Club; Edmund L Houston Found Rutgers Univ; Essex Co Youth House; pres Metro Urban Social Serv Inc; vice pres OMEGA InvestmentCorp (MESBIC Prog); counsellor Municipal Careerwomen of Newark; founder, sec Newark Comm Housing Corp; sec Peoples Devel Corp; former pres Esqui-Vogues of Northern NJ; past vice pres Shanley Ave Civic Assn; past life mem chrn NAACP (Newark Br); past state bd dir NAACP State Conf; past public affairs chrnNegro Bus & Prof Womens Club; past Ed Citizenship; chmn Newark Chapter Council of Negro Women; Nat Planning Assn; Am Soc of Planning Officials; various organizations; vice-chmn, past vice-chrn Newark Central Ward; co-chmn Newark Essex Co Meyner for Governor Club; Essex Co Rep Young DemConv; Newark Liaison All Co Campaigns; founder, onizer, advisor Central Ward Young Dem; Congressional Liaison Kennedy Air-Lift (Pres campaign); exec dir Hugh J Addonizio Civic Assn; Minorities Affairs; chrn Dem Party Co State. **Honors/Awds:** Recipient Comm Serv Award Afro Am Newspaper 1952; Achievement Award Iota Phi Lamba 1956; Achievement Award Frontiers of Am 1957; Newark Br NAACP Serv Award 1960; Stephen P Teamer Civic Assn Serv Award 1962; Negro Business & Professional Women Achievement Award 1963; Metro Civic Assn Serv Awd 1965; ILA Local 1233 Serv Award 1965; Ballantine Award 1965; Laura Grant Award 1965; Deomart Enterprises Woman of the Yr 1965; Newark Br NAACP 1966; Central Planning Bd Appreciation Award 1967; Iota Phi Chapter Sorority Outstanding Women 1968; South Ward Little League Serv Award 1968; Am Negro Assembly Inc Achievement Award 1968; Municipal Careerwomen of Newark Achievement Award 1968; Abraham Yecies Award 1972; After Hours Magazine Serv Award 1974; first blackdept head & cabinet mem in 300 yrs of Nrk's municipal govt. **Business Addr:** Office of the Register Hall of, Newark, NJ 07102.

STALLING, RONALD EUGENE
Federal law enforcement officer. **Personal:** Born Mar 11, 1946, Daytona Beach, FL; son of Helen Katherine Bolden Stalling and Lloyd George Stalling; married Paulette Marian Robinson Stalling, Jul 23, 1973; children: Kali, Dana. **Educ:** Southeastern University, Washington, DC, 1968-70; American University, Washington, DC, 1971-74. **Career:** US Dept of State, Washington, DC, admin asst, 1964-66, 1968-70; US Secret Service, Washington, DC, federal law enforcement officer, 1970-. **Orgs:** Member, National Black Police Association, 1989-; secretary, Alliance of Black Federal Officers Inc, 1989-. **Honors/Awds:** Sustained Superior Performance Award. **Military Serv:** US Army, E-4, 1966-68; service awards of Vietnam service; Master parachutists (Clic) jmp mstr/instr. **Business Addr:** Secretary, Local Chapter, Alliance of Black Federal Officers, PO Box 2243, Washington, DC 20013-2243.

STALLINGS, GEORGE AUGUSTUS, JR.
Clergyman. **Personal:** Born Mar 17, 1948, New Bern, NC. **Educ:** St Pius X Seminary, BA, philosophy, 1970; Univ of St Thomas Aquinas, STB, 1973; Univ of St Thomas Aquinas, MA, pastoral theology, 1974; Pontifical Univ of St Thomas Aquinas, STL, 1975. **Career:** Our Lady Queen of Peace, Washington, DC, associate pastor, 1974-76; St Teresa of Avila, Washington, DC, pastor, 1976-89; Imani Temple African-American Catholic Congregation, founder/bishop, 1989-. **Honors/Awds:** Award for Meritorious Service, Mayor of Washington.

STALLINGS, GREGORY RALPH
Educator. **Personal:** Born Dec 28, 1957, Richmond, VA; son of Mr & Mrs Steward B Stallings, Sr; married Mitzi Keyes (divorced); children: Brittny Jean. **Educ:** The College of William & Mary, BA 1980. **Career:** Boys Club of Richmond, unit dir 1980-81; Richmond Public Schools, teacher 1981-86, coord intervention progs 1986-88, instructional leader 1988-91, teacher specialist, 1991-95. **Orgs:** College advisor, Theta Rho Chap, Alpha Phi Alpha, VA Commonwealth Univ; dir of educational affairs, Xi Delta Lambda, Alpha Phi Alpha 1985-87; treas, pres male usher bd, chairman of trustee bd, First Union Baptist Church; basketball coach Recreation Dept; pres Xi Delta Lambda Alpha Phi Alpha 1988-90; area dir VACAPAF; instructor for VA Center for Educational Leadership. **Honors/Awds:** First Black "Golden Boy" Boy's Club of Richmond 1972; Outstanding Teaching Awd JL Francis Elementary School 1983-86; Xi Delta Lamba, Alpha Man of the Year, 1992; Teacher of the Year, Patrick Henry Elementary School, 1997-98; finalist for Teacher of the Year, Richmond Public Schools, 1997-98; finalist REB Award, 1997. **Home Addr:** 5110 Boscobel Ave, Richmond, VA 23225.

STALLINGS, HENRY, II
State senator. **Personal:** Born Dec 30, 1950. **Educ:** Western Michigan Univ, BA; Detroit College of Law, JD. **Career:** Art gallery and picture framing shop owner; Michigan State Senate, District 3, senator, 1995-.

STALLINGS, JAMES RAIFORD
Administrator. **Personal:** Born Oct 9, 1936, Augusta, GA; married Geneva Butler; children: Sylvia B, James R. **Educ:** Allen Univ, BS 1955-59; So IL Univ, MS 1966-68. **Career:** Richmond Co Bd of Educ, math teacher 1959-71; C&S Natl Bank, loan officer & asst branch mgr 1971-75; Augusta Coll, dir of financial aid 1975-. **Orgs:** Mem Alpha Phi Alpha; mem Natl Bankers Assn 1971-75; mem Bank PAC 1973; mem GASFAA 1975-; mem SASFAA 1975-; mem NASFAA 1975-. **Honors/Awds:** Most Outstanding Teacher Glenn Hills HS Augusta 1970; Star Teacher Glenn Hills HS Augusta 1970; first black banking officer in SC C&S Bank 1973. **Business Addr:** Dir, Augusta Coll, 2500 Walton Way, Augusta, GA 30910.

STALLINGS, RAMONDO ANTONIO
Professional football player. **Personal:** Born Nov 21, 1971, Winston-Salem, NC. **Educ:** San Diego State, attended. **Career:** Cincinnati Bengals, defensive end, 1994-. **Business Addr:** Professional Football Player, Cincinnati Bengals, One Bengals Dr, Cincinnati, OH 45202, (513)621-3550.

STALLS, M.
Educator, human services specialist. **Personal:** Born Oct 22, 1947, Metropolis, IL; daughter of Freda Mae Houston Stalls and Robert A Stalls; married; children: Robert C Goodwin. **Educ:** Southern IL Univ, BA 1970, MS 1976, PhD 1991. **Career:** IL Dept of Children & Family Svcs, child welfare worker 1970-75; IL Farmers Union, manpower coordinator 1976-78; SIU-C School of Tech Careers, researcher/service coord 1978-80; SIU-C Ctr for Basic Skills, coord of supple inst, developmental skills specialist/instructor, visiting assistant professor, Black American studies, developmental skills training specialist, currently. **Orgs:** Founder/coord Black Women's Coalition 1983; mentor SIU-C Project Magic 1984-; consultant Jack Co Public Housing Initiatives Training Prog 1985; steering committee member IL Committee on Black Concerns in Higher Educ 1985-; consultant SIU-C Women's Studies Film Project 1986-; American Assn of Counseling and Devel; National Council of Black Studies; executive director Star Human Serv Devel Corp Inc, 1987-; Founder/convener Assembly of African,

African-American Women, 1989, Kappa Delta Pi, 1987. **Honors/Awds:** Service Awd Eurma C Hayes Comp Child Care Services/PAC 1977; Fellow IL Comm on Black Concerns in Higher Educ 1984; Cert of Appreciation SIU-C HEADSTART Carbondale, IL 1986; Iota Phi Theta Quintessence Award 1984; SIU-C-BAC Academic Excellence Award 1987, Paul Robeson Award; Faculty Staff Award 1988; 5 Poems published in Literati 1989; coord Southern Region ICBCHE Regional Fall Seminar 1988; George S. Counts Doctoral Award 1990; ICBCHE, Dedicated Service Award, 1990; Alton Metropolitan Human Development Recognition Award, 1991; Humanitarian Award, SIUC Black Affairs Council, 1996; Nominee, Outstanding Professor, Graduate & Professional Education, Southern Illinois University at Carbondale, 1994; Academic Excellence Award, Black Affairs Council, Southern Illinois University at Carbondale, 1991; Vice Chair for the Southern Region, Illinois Comm on Black Concerns in Higher Education, 1997. **Business Addr:** Developmental Skills Training Specialist, Center for Basic Skills, Woody Hall, C-9, Southern Illinois University at Carbondale, Carbondale, IL 62901.

STALLWORTH, ALMA G.
Government official (retired). **Personal:** Born Nov 15, 1932, Little Rock, AR; married Thomas Jr.; children: Thomas III, Keith. **Educ:** Highland Park Jr Coll, 1948-49; Wayne State U, 1950-51; Merrill Palmer Inst, 1965. **Career:** Parent Involvement Program Headstart Archdiocesan Detroit, coor 1964-68; dir vol serv 1968-69; St John's Day Care Ctr, dir 1969-70; Oak Grove Day Care Ctr; ran for state Senator 7th Dist 1974; Historical Dept City of Detroit, dep dir 1978; State of MI, rep 1970-74, 1982-96, chair Public Utilities Committee for 14 years. **Orgs:** Mem Oak Grove AME Ch; mem Demo Party; Nat Order Women Legislators; Mayor's Citizens Task Force; Nat Orgn Women Detroit Sect; State Training Sch Adv Council; Nat Inst Women's Wrongs; Wayne County Juvenile Justice Commn; exec comm United Negro College Fund, Natl Conf of State Legislature; honorary mem Alpha Kappa Alpha Sorority; mem of bd of directors, Woman in gov't; Heat and Warmth Fund, Wayne Cty Task Force on Infant Mortality; founder, pres emeritus, Black Child Development Institute; founder, administrator, Black Caucus Foundation of MI. **Honors/Awds:** Legislator of the Year MI Assn of Children's Alliance; Community Serv Awd Lula Belle Stewart Centr; Dedicated Serv & Support Awd United Negro Coll Fund 1985; Outstanding Personal & Professional Commitment Awd Planned Parenthood 1985; Blue Cross Blue Shield Health & People PAC Awd 1986; Cert of Achievement for Maternal & Child Health Progs Gov Blanchard & Dept of Health; Spirit of Detroit Awd Gentlemen of Wall St; Distinguished Serv Awd MI Public Health Assn; Susan B Anthony Awd Detroit Chap of Natl Org of Women; Walter A Bergman Human Rights Award, Federation of Teachers; Women's Honors in Public Service, Nurses Assn; Distinguished Service Award, United Negro College Fund; Phenomenal Women Award, Natl Assn of Negro Business and Prof Women; Leader in Women's Health, Natl Women's Lobby 1995; Dedicated Service Award, Detroit East; Distinguished Service to Detroit Comm, Detroit Public Schools; Appreciation Award, Wayne County Child Coordinating Council; Legislator of the Year, Arthritis Foundation; Volunteer Service Award, United Negro College Fund; ''You Make All the Difference for Our World'' Award, Ameritech. **Business Addr:** State Representative, State of Michigan, PO Box 30014, Lansing, MI 48909.

STALLWORTH, ANN P.
City government official. **Personal:** Born May 15, 1932, DeKalb, TX; widowed; children: Charles, Patricia Banks, Lilye Chaffin, Rachel Carr, Allen O Jr, Eric Darrel. **Educ:** Langston Univ, Bus Admin; Delta Coll, unit in computer sci; Stockton Junior College, graduate, 1949. **Career:** Pacific Telephone, telephone operator, supervisor, asst operating mgr, 1963-68, personnel, employment, recruiting, and counseling, working with task force to develop affirmative action plan, 1968-72, customer services, education and training, 1972-83, marketing administrator, sales, 1982-83; AT&T Information Systems, technical consultant, marketing, 1983-85; tradeSOURCES, CEO, 1986-. **Orgs:** Co-founder, first vp, pres, chair of bylaws, nominating committee, California Coalition of Black School Board, 1974-90; education committee, NAACP, 1970-94; credential committee, Dameron Hospital Board of Membership, 1970-; pres, 1986-90, vp, 1984-86, treasurer scholarship fund, 1978-86, mem, 1974-, Stockton Chapter Links; board of dir, usher board, Christ Temple Church, 1975-. **Honors/Awds:** Hon Life Mem James Monroe PTA 1964; Commendation on Vocational Ed Dr Wilson Riles Supt of Public Instr State of CA 1974; Black Woman in Ed Stockton Comm 1974; Nominee Soroptimist Woman of the Year Awd 1978; NAACP, Women of Achievement Award, 1992; Girl Scout Role Model, 1994. **Business Addr:** CEO, tradeSources, 130 Sutter St, Ste 200, San Francisco, CA 94104.

STALLWORTH, EDDIE, JR.
Federal employee (retired). **Personal:** Born May 11, 1934, Columbia, LA; son of Eddie and Carrie Stallworth; married Luddine Stallworth, Dec 21, 1974; children: Carrie A, Anthony E, Audrey D, Patricia S, Agnis Y, Angela Y, Frances. **Educ:** Mary Etta Barber Coll, graduate; Leland Seminary School, Leland Coll, attended; Univ of Maryland, attended; Washington Tech Inst, AS, Police Sci, attended; Intl Detective School, attended. **Career:** Federal Bureau of Prinsons, District of Columbia, Dept of Corrections, 28 years. **Orgs:** The Legal Redress Committee, Prince William County Chap, NAACP, chair; Jennie Dean Museum Commission, Inc, pres; Triangle Masonic Lodge, No 293; Shriners and Consistory Lodge of Alexandria VA, bd mem; Natl Assn of Retired People; American Assn of Retired People, bd of dir; Prince William Historic Society, charter mem; Prince William County Government, community coord and liaison; Little Union Baptist Church in Dumfries, VA; numerous others. **Honors/Awds:** Received a ten year Service Awd, United States Marine Corps; Received the Community Service Awd, Dale City Christian Church; Emmit Service Awd, WUSA-TV. **Special Achievements:** First Black police officer of Quantico, VA; Owned and operated first black taxicab company in the city of Manassas, VA. **Home Addr:** 17517 Mine Rd, Dumfries, VA 22026.

STALLWORTH, JOHN LEE
Professional football player (retired). **Personal:** Born Jul 15, 1952, Tuscaloosa, AL; married Florastein Caudle; children: Johnny Lee Jr, Natasha. **Educ:** Alabama A&M Univ, BS, business, 1974, MBA. **Career:** Pittsburgh Steelers, wide receiver, 1974-86; American Amicable Insurance, salesman, beginning 1975; Alabama A&M Univ, part-time football coach. **Orgs:** Involved with MS, Amer Lung Assn, Sheriff's Boy's Ranch. **Honors/Awds:** SIAC All Confer Team, 1972-73; Senior Bowl Squad, 1974; All AL Football Squad, 1973; Pittsburgh Courier All American, 1974; Honor Ment AP Little All American, 1974; Football Digest All Rookie Team, 1974; AFC All-Star, Sporting News, 1979; holds all-time NFL record for most postseason touchdown receptions (12) and most 100-yard games (5); holds Super Bowl record for career average per catch (244); Alabama's ''Professional Athlete of the Year,'' 1979; Dapper Dan ''Man of the Year,'' 1984; played in Pro Bowl, 1979, 1982, 1984. **Business Addr:** Pittsburgh Steelers, Three Rivers Stadium, 300 Stadium Circle, Pittsburgh, PA 15212.

STALLWORTH, OSCAR B.
Engineering manager. **Personal:** Born Dec 5, 1944, Mobile; married Elsie Thigpen; children: Oscar, Jr, Brett. **Educ:** BS mech ngring 1966. **Career:** Castings & Brake Components Motor Wheel Corp subsidary of Goodyear tire & Rubber Co, manager 1971-; prod engr passenger car brakes & wheels, motor wheel 1968-71; jr proj engr motor wheel 1967-68. **Orgs:** Mem Soc of Automotive Engrs 1967; Am Soc for Metals 1967; Am Foundryman's Soc 1967; mem, bd dirs Boys Club of Lansing 1971-; chmn Voter Regis A Phillip Randolph Inst 1972-; v chmn, Ingham Co Dem Party 1970-72; advisor, solicitor Jr Achievement 1968; Alpha Phi Alpha Frat 1964; mgr Field Operations Political Campaigns 1970-; pres Coland Inc. **Honors/Awds:** Nominee Lansing Outstanding Person of Yr Lansing Jaycees. **Business Addr:** 1600 N Larch St, Lansing, MI 48906.

STAMPER, HENRY J.
Financial executive. **Career:** First Federal Savings & Loan Assn of Scotlandville, Baton Rouge, LA, chief executive. **Business Addr:** First Federal Savings & Loan Assn of Scotlandville, 7990 Scenic Hwy, Baton Rouge, LA 70807.

STAMPLEY, GILBERT ELVIN
Attorney. **Personal:** Born May 24, 1943, Baton Rouge, LA; married Ester J Francis. **Educ:** Grambling State U, BA 1965; JD Tulane Univ Sch of Law, JD 1972. **Career:** Harris Stampley Mckee Bernard & Broussard, atty; Smith & Stampley, att 1972-75 EEO Commn, case analyst 1970-72; Men's Affaird Jarvis Christian Coll, dep dir 1965-67; Am Bar Assn; Martinet Soc; LA State Bar Assn; Nat Bar Assn; Nat Conf of Black Lawyers Exec Com NAACP; Palm-air Civil Improvement Assn; Orleans Parish Prog Voters League, vp; Young Dem of Am; Urban League; LA Assn for Sickle Cell Anemia Found. **Orgs:** Mem City Plng Commn of New Orleans 1976-81; mem LA State Dem Ctrl Com Dist 62; Earl Warren Fellow 1971-72. **Military Serv:** AUS E-5 1968-70. **Business Addr:** 1440 Canal St, Ste 1714, New Orleans, LA 70112.

STAMPS, DELORES BOLDEN
Educational administrator. **Personal:** Born Mar 16, 1947, Monticello, MS; daughter of Balene Sutton Bolden and Peter James Bolden; married James L Campbell (divorced 1982); children: Keceya Campbell, Jason Campbell; married Alvin Stamps, Jun 22, 1985; children: Tiffany Stamps, Katrina Stamps. **Educ:** Tougaloo College, BA, 1968; University of Southern Mississippi, MS, 1972; Harvard University, Certificate, 1974; University of Southern Mississippi, PhD, 1985. **Career:** Jackson State University, assistant professor, education, 1985-88, director, academic skills center, 1976-88; Tougaloo College, director of institutional research, 1988-89, vice president, institutional advancement, 1987-. **Orgs:** Mississippi Museum of Art, board of trustees, 1989-; UNCF, chairperson, special events committee, 1985-; League of Women Voters, unit leader, 1975-. **Honors/Awds:** Outstanding Women Leader in Jackson, Mississippi, Jackson Advocate newspaper, 1990; participant, Leadership Jackson, Jackson Chamber of Commerce, 1988; Benjamin E Mays Scholar, Indiana University, 1986. **Special Achievements:** ''Coping Abilities as a Predictor of Student Retention, Black Student Retention in Higher Education'', 1988; ''Self Concept of Ability, Self-Esteem, Locus of Control and Perception of the Opportunity Structure as Predictors of Coping Ability Among Selected Black College Students'', Benjamin E Mays Academy Monograph Series, 1987; co-author, ''From Whence They Come: An Assessment of Black Coll Experience at Historically Black Institutions''. **Business Addr:** Vice President, Institutional Advancement, Tougaloo College, 500 W County Line Rd, Tougaloo, MS 39174, (601)977-7841.

STAMPS, HERMAN FRANKLIN
Broadcasting company executive. **Personal:** Born Jan 20, 1924, Washington, DC; son of Alice Bowman Stamps and Herman Stamps; married Ann Grigsby Stamps, Apr 4, 1987; children: Eric, Alisa, Anthony. **Educ:** Howard Univ, BS 1945, DDS 1948; Univ MI, MSc 1953. **Career:** Genl Practice, dentistry 1948-52; Diplomate American Board Endodontics l953-; Coll of Dentistry, dir clinics 1967-70, prof 1969-, coord facilities systems & planning 1970-86; Howard Univ, retired 1986. **Orgs:** Bd dirs Wash Urban League 1958-64; mem Robert T Freeman Dental Soc (pres 1959-61); bd dirs COIN 1962-65; manpower bd Labor Dept 1964-67; chmn supervisory com Armstrong Neighborhood Fed Credit Union 1964-66; mem Natl, Amer Dental Assns, DC Dental Soc, Amer Soc History Dentistry (charter); mem Amer Assn Endodontics; author ''Modern Prescription Writing'' 1954; bd dirs American Diabetes Assn l985-; Natl Comm, American Diabetic Assn Minority Perspectives l989-. **Honors/Awds:** National Honor Society of Dentistry, Omicron Kappa Upsilon, 1948. **Military Serv:** Army, Cpl, 1942-45. **Home Addr:** 57 W Church St, PO Box 169, Selbyville, DE 19975, (302)436-5508. **Business Phone:** (302)436-9725.

STAMPS, JOE, JR.
Educational administrator. **Personal:** Born Dec 3, 1939, Houston, TX; married Eloise Grant; children: Jo-Ellen, Bernadette, Joe III. **Educ:** Texas Southern Univ, 1959-62; Labor Studies, Linden-Hall Dawson, PA; 1979 & 1982. **Career:** Pct 371 Harris Co, election judge 1978-; United Steelworkers Local 7682, president 1979-82; Board of Education, legislation rep 1981-. **Orgs:** Member A-Philip Randolf Institution 1963-; NABSE; Local 7682, VP, 1993-97; NSBA Little Union Baptist Church, deacon, youth Sunday school teacher; pres of North Forest ISD Board of Trustees; life member, Texas PTA. **Honors/Awds:** Texas Congress of Parents Teacher Assn, life member; Outstanding School Board Member, Region IV of Texas. **Business Addr:** School Board Member, North Forest I S D, PO Box 2378, Houston, TX 77078.

STAMPS, LEON PREIST
City official & auditor. **Personal:** Born Dec 29, 1953, Bronx, NY; married Barbara Logan. **Educ:** Boston Coll, BS Acct 1975; Northeastern Univ, MBA Bus Policy 1976. **Career:** Arthur Anderson & Co, accountant 1977-79; Xerox Corp, equip control mgr 1979-81, ne reg control mgr 1981-84; City of Boston, city auditor/controller. **Orgs:** Bd of dir Boston Coll Alumni Assoc 1975-; accountant internship Continental Group Inc 1976; consult to dir of public serv Blue Cross & Blue Shield 1976; acctg prof Roxbury Comm Coll 1979; mem at large Natl Assoc of Black Accountants 1984-; mem Boston Black Media Coalition 1985. **Honors/Awds:** Recip The Young Alumni Achievers Award Boston Coll 1985. **Business Addr:** Auditor/Controller, City of Boston, City Hall Room M-4, Boston, MA 02201.

STAMPS, LYNMAN A., SR.
Clergyman. **Personal:** Born May 31, 1940, Utica, MS; son of Emma Ross Stamps and Milton Stamps; married Margarett C Donaldson; children: Lynman A Stamps Jr. **Educ:** Lane Coll Jackson, TN, BA 1968; Webster Univ, MAT 1972; US Dept Justice, Cert Jail Operations; Natl Inst of Correct Admin Studies; Western Interstate Comm for Higher Edn. **Career:** IL St Sch for Boys, cottage parent 1960-62; Chicago Parent Soc Adj Sch Boys, fam instr 1962-63; AUS, MP 1963-65; Trinity Temple CME Ch, 1964-66; Martin Tabernacle CME Ch, pastor 1966-69; Parkers Chapel CME Ch, pastor 1969-70; Clark Jr HS E St Louis, IL, civic tchr 1968-71; Pilgrim Temple CME Ch, pastor 1970-74; Radio Sta WESL E St Louis, mgr part owner 1972-78; E St Louis, civil serv commr 1971-74; St Louis Correc Inst, supt 1972-76; Coleman Temple CME Ch, pastor 1974-83; Parrish Temple AME Church, pastor, 1983-84; First Christian Methodist Church, St Louis, MO, pastor/founder 1983-; Normandy Jr HS Normandy, MO, tchr 1981-84; Marion Comm, pastor/managing partner; St Louis Bd of Educ, Military Specialist 1988-89; Pruitt Military Academy, St Louis, MO, military specialist, 1988-. **Orgs:** Life mem NAACP; mem The Amer Correct Assn; exec bd mem E St Louis Madison St Clair Co Urban League 1972-73; exec bd mem E St Louis Model City Agency 1972-73; vice pres Downtown Merchant Columbus, MS 1985. **Honors/Awds:** Cert of Honor Utica Inst Jr Coll 1956; Man of the Yr Award Afro-Amer Club Columbus, MS 1985; Found/Pres Trenton Civic League Trenton, TN; Cert of Award for Outstanding Achievements to Jobs Workshop Ex Offender Prog of Human Dev Corp Prog Metro St Louis 1976; Cert of Apprec Gateway Jaycees and US Jaycees 1976; Award Plaque Offenders Chap of AA 1974. **Military Serv:** AUS Spec 4th Class served 2 yrs; Good Conduct Medal 1963-65. **Home Addr:** 12031 Mereview Dr, St Louis, MO 63146.

STAMPS, SPURGEON MARTIN DAVID, JR.
Educational administrator, educator. **Personal:** Born Jul 16, 1937, Nashville, TN; son of Nina Bessie Dobbins Stamps and Spurgeon Martin David Stamps Sr; married Miriam Cunningham Burney Stamps, Dec 28, 1961; children: Monique Yvonne, Spurgeon Martin David III. **Educ:** Tennessee State University, BS, sociology, 1960; Washington State University, MA, sociology, 1965, PhD, sociology, 1974. **Career:** Cameron High School, teacher, counselor, 1960-62; Washington State University, teaching assistant, 1962-67; Norfolk State University, assistant professor to professor of sociology, 1967-77; Syracuse University, associate professor to professor of Afro-American studies and sociology, 1977-82; University of South Florida, aasoc dean and professor of sociology, 1982-95, interim dean, College of Arts and Sciences, 1995-96, dean, College of Arts and Sciences, 1996-. **Orgs:** Pi Gamma Mu, 1983-; Alpha Kappa Delta, 1965-; Kappa Delta Pi, 1957-; Southern Sociological Association, 1982-; Florida Center for Children and Youth, executive committee, 1990-; Literacy Volunteers of America, Florida, vice pres, 1990-; Tampa-Hillsborough County Human Rights Council, 1988-; Golden Key Honor Society, 1990-. **Honors/Awds:** Tennessee State University, graduated with distinction, 1960; Syracuse University, Distinguished Service Award, Office of Minority Affairs, 1982; Phi Gamma Mu, Roll of Distinction, faculty advisor, 1985. **Special Achievements:** Manpower Utilization in Tidewater, Hampton Roads, Virginia, 1969; established and served as editor, Review of Afro-American Issues & Culture, 1978-82; Participation of High School Adolescents in Volunteer Activities, 1979; Black Elderly Presbyterians in New York City, 1982; Comparative Study of Blacks, Whites and Hispanics in the Tampa Metropolitan Area, 1990; co-author, If You Can Walk, You Can Dance. If You Can Talk, You Can Sing, 1995. **Home Addr:** 6102 Soaring Ave, Temple Terrace, FL 33617. **Business Addr:** Dean and Professor of Sociology, College of Arts and Sciences, University of South Florida, 4202 E Fowler Ave, CPR 107, Tampa, FL 33620, (813)974-0853.

STANBACK, THURMAN W.
Educator. **Personal:** Born Mar 20, 1920, Washington, DC; son of Mozelle and James Stanback. **Educ:** VA Union U, BA 1941; Columbia U, MA 1947; Cornell U, PhD 1953-. **Career:** FL Atlantic U, retired prof of theatre 1986; Bethune-Cookman Coll 1953-73 & 1953-70, artist-in-residence, 1991; Storer Coll, 1947-49; Glassboro State College, guest director, 1990. **Orgs:** Mem Am Theatre Assn 1953-75; Speech Assn of Am 1953-75; Alpha Phi Alpha 1955-75; Nat Assn of & Dramatic & Speech Arts 1953-70. **Honors/Awds:** Teacher of Yr Bethune Cookman Coll 1969; Distinguished Alumni in the Arts, Virginia Union University 1986; Distinguished Alumnus, National Assn for Equal Opportunity in Higher Education 1989. **Military Serv:** AUS ssgt 1943-46.

STANCELL, ARNOLD FRANCIS
Educator, oil co. executive. **Personal:** Born Nov 16, 1936, New York, NY; son of Francis & Maria Lucas Stancell; married Constance Newton Stancell, Apr 21, 1973; children: Christine. **Educ:** City College of New York, BSChE (magna cum laude), 1958; Massachusetts Institute of Technology, Doctor of Science, ScD, 1962. **Career:** Mobil Oil Corp., Edison NJ, scientist & research manager, 1962-72, NY, planning mgr, 1972-76, vice pres chemicals div, 1976-80, manager corp. planning, 1980-82, England, regional executive of marketing and refining, 1982-84, NY, planning vice pres, 1985-87, Virginia, vice pres of US & international oil & gas business, 1988-93; Georgia Tech, Georgia, professor of chem engineering, 1994-. **Orgs:** American Institute of Chem Engineering, 1962-; Sigma Xi, 1965-; Advisory Committee to MIT, 1976-; Advisory Committee to City College, 1990-. **Honors/Awds:** Selected for Natl Academy of Engineering, 1997; Chemical Engineering Practice Award, AICHE, 1997; Career Achievement, City College of NY, 1993; Black Engineer of the Year, 1992; Outstanding Teacher Award, Georgia, Tech, 1997. **Special Achievements:** Invited Speaker, Marshall Lecture, University of Wisconsin (Madison), 1991; Invited Visiting Professor, MIT, 1970-71. **Business Phone:** (404)894-0316.

STANCELL, DOLORES WILSON PEGRAM
Attorney. **Personal:** Born Oct 26, 1936, New York, NY; married Vernon H; children: Timothy, Vernon. **Educ:** Rutgers U, BA 1970; Rutgers Sch of Law, JD 1974; MI State U, Annual Regulatory Studies Prog 1976. **Career:** NJ Dept of Pub Adv Div of Rate Counsel, asst dep pub adv; Hon David D Furman Superior Ct Chan Div NJ, law sec 1974-75; Rutgers Univ Rutgers Jour of Comptrs & the Law, admin 1973; Jersey Shore Med Ctr, nurse 1972; Middlesex Cty Legal Svcs, legal intern 1970; Rutgers Urban Studies Ctr, rsch asst 1968; Head Start MCEOC, nurse 1967; Head Start, nurse 1966; Beth Israel Hosp, staff nurse 1958-62; Fordham Hosp, staff nurse 1957-58. **Orgs:** Am Bar Assn Sect on Legal Educ & Admissions to the Bar 1977-78; Forum Comm on Hlth Law 1977-78; Gen Practice 1976-77; Natl Bar Assn 1st vp, Women's Div 1977-78; vice pres Civil Trial Advocacy Sect 1977-78; Legislation & Uniform & State Laws Comm 1977-78; nom com Women's Div 1976-77; Fed Bar Assn; Garden State Bar Assn; NJ State Bar Assn; Hlth Leg & Hlth Plng Serv Com 1976-78; Monmouth Bar Assn; Crmnl Pract Com 1976-78; treas Assn Black Women Lawyers NJ 1977-78; Rutgers Law Sch Alumni Assn; Rutgers Univ Alumni Assn; panelist MRC-TV NY Program, Medical Costs, The Breath of Life 1977; Am Nurses Assn; NJ State Nurses Assn; vol Ocean-Monmouth Legal Serv 1972; vol urban agt Rutgers Urban Studies Cen 1967-68; Pub Policy Forum on Civil Disorders & Forum on the Futureof NJ Rutgers Univ 1968; co Rutgers-Douglass Coll Elem Sch Tutorial Prog 1967-68; trustee Unitarian Soc 1970-72; Acad Adv Com 1977-78; bd Parents Assn Rutgers Prep Sch 1970-71; New Brunswick YWCA; Urban League; NAACP. **Honors/Awds:** Human Rels Awrd Fordham Hosp 1957; articles Wilson, Computerization of Welfare Recipients, Implications for the Individual & The Right to Privacy 4 Rutgers Journal of Computers and The Law 163 (1974); Minoritiy Workers 1 Womens Rights Law Reporter 71 (1972-73). **Business Addr:** 10 Commerce Ct, Newark, NJ 07102.

STANDARD, RAYMOND LINWOOD
Physician. **Personal:** Born May 20, 1925, Hartford, CT; son of Ruth Lee King and V Linwood; married Donna Ann Boddy; children: Kia Michalle, Gina Lynette, Darry Linwood. **Educ:** Howard Univ Coll of Liberal Arts, BS 1948; Howard Univ Coll of Medicine, MD 1952; Johns Hopkins Univ Sch of Hygiene & Public Health, MPH 1967. **Career:** Intl Med Provident Hosp, clinical dir 1956-60; NW Central Clinic, chief clinical serv 1960-66; Bureau of Chronic Disease Control, chief adult health & geriatrics 1967-68, chief bureau of chronic disease control 1968-69; DC Govt, dir pub health 1969-80; E of the River Health Assn, med dir 1980-81; clinical assoc prof Howard/Georgetown/GW Med Schs 1969-; Howard Univ Coll of Medicine, assoc prof. **Orgs:** Exec dir DC Office of Bicentennial Programs 1976; chmn med sub-com Pres Carter's Inaugural Com 1977; founder/past pres Standard Investment Co Inc; founder/past pres Century Limited Inc; bd of dirs United Natl Bank; published 45 health care admin articles local & Natl med journals 1969-. **Honors/Awds:** Fellowship World Health Organ Norway & Sweden Health Systems 1976. **Military Serv:** AUS pfc 1943-46; Bronze Star; Combat Medic Badge. **Business Addr:** Dir Grad Educ Public Health, Howard University, 520 W St NW, Washington, DC 20059.

STANDIFER, BEN H.
Educator. **Personal:** Born Aug 24, 1934, Itasca, TX; son of Emma Jean Standifer and Nathaniel C Standifer; married Esther; children: Sonceria, Fawn, Ben, Jr, Corey. **Educ:** Prairie View A&M Coll, BS 1959; TX Christian U, MA 1972; TX Christian U, certification supv 1973; N TX State U, certification adminstrn 1975; Carleton Coll, study 1965; Prairie View A&M Coll, 1966; N TX State U, 1967; Univ of TX 1968; IL Inst of Tech, 1969; Cornell U, 1970; TX Wesleyan Coll 1974. **Career:** Ft Worth Public School, math teacher 1959-73; FWISD, math instructional improvement specialist 1973-74; Ft Worth Public School, math improvement specialist 1974-; Dunbar Sr High School Fort Worth Indep School Dist, principal 1975-; Our Lady of Victory Priv School Bd, pres next 3 yrs. **Orgs:** Mem Ft Worth Classroom Tchr Assn; mem TX Classroom Tchr Assn; mem Nat Educ Assn; mem TX Industrial Educ Assn; mem Phi Delta Kappa Frat; mem FtWorth Area Council of Tchr of Math; mem Task Force Team Lay Acad United Meth Ch; d mem Ft Worth-tarrant Co Community Devel Fund Inc; steering com mem Conf for Advancement of Math Teaching; organized Parent Student Study Group Como High Community 1960; drew up Trigonometry Transparencies used in Ft OrthPub Sch System 1965. **Honors/Awds:** Published book "A Practical Guide to Good Study Habits" 1969; created progarm at Western Hills HS in Audio Tutorial Instruction 1970; organized tutorial program to help students in Wester Hills Eidglea Como Arlington Heights Communities 1971; published book of Audio Tutorial Instruction 1972; vice pres PTA 1973; presHom E& Sch Assn; pilot program for emotionally disturbed children 1974; publication Success in Math 1974; publication Improvement of & Curricular/Instructional System 1974; sunday sch tchr & church lay leader Morningside Meth Ch; tchr & com mem task force team of Lay Acad of TX Wesleyan Coll; recip of numerous awards including outstanding tchr & tchr of yr awards & healdiner in educ award Ft Worth Press Club; apptd adminstrvtrainee Ft Worth Pub Sch; layacademy recognition Ued Meth Ch W TX Conf S/Sgt. **Military Serv:** USAF 1954-58. **Business Addr:** Fort Worth Pub Sch, 3210 W Lancaster, Fort Worth, TX 76104.

STANDIFER, LONNIE NATHANIEL
Entomologist (retired). **Personal:** Born Oct 28, 1926, Itasa, TX; son of Emma Jean Johnson Standifer and Nathaniel Caroline Standifer; divorced. **Educ:** Prairie View A&M Coll, BS, 1949; KS State Coll, MS, botany, plant pathology, 1951; Cornell Univ, PhD, med entolmolgy, veterinary parisitology, 1954. **Career:** Campus Pest Control, suprv; Tuskegee Inst AL, instr biol sci, 1951-53; Cornell Univ, rsch asst, 1953-54; So Univ Baton Rouge, asst prof biol sci ,1954-56; US Dept of Agr Tucson AZ, rsch entomologist, 1956-70, suprv rsch entomolgist HoneyBee Research Center, lab dir, 1970-87. **Orgs:** Consult Dept Agr Biochem Univ of AZ, 1963; mem Entomol Soc Amer, USDA, SEA, AR; tech adv Rsch Prog on Nutrition on Honey Bees; natl consult USA-AZ, Intl Bee Rsch Assoc, AZ Acad Sci; mem Sigma Xi, Beta Kappa Chi. **Honors/Awds:** Outstanding Alumni Awd Prairie View A&M Coll, 1967; Honoring Dr Lonnie N Standifer for Excellence in Biological and Life Science, National Consortium for Black Professional Development, 1978. **Military Serv:** USAF WWII. **Home Addr:** 1212 Glasgow Rd, Fort Worth, TX 76134-1626.

STANFORD, JOHN H.
Educational administrator. **Personal:** married Patricia Corley; children: Steven, Scott. **Educ:** Penn St Univ, BS political sci, 1961; Central MI Univ, master's in personnel mgt and admin; Army, Infantry School, Army Aviation School, Transportation School, US Army Command and Gen Staff College, Industrial College of Armed Forces. **Career:** US Army, military assistant, 1977-79, exec assistant to Special Assistant to Sec of Defense, 1981, special assistant and exec sec to Sec of Defense; Fulton County, GA, manager; Seattle Public Schools, superintendent, currently. **Military Serv:** US Army, military assistant to Undersec, 1977-79, exec assistant to Special Assistant to Sec of Defense, 1981, special assistant and exec sec to Sec of Defense, 1981-84. **Business Addr:** Superintendent, Seattle Public Schools, 815 4th Ave, N, Seattle, WA 98109, (206)298-7000.

STANFORD, JOHN HENRY
Military officer. **Personal:** Born Sep 14, 1938, Darby, PA; son of Beatrice Burnette Stanford and Edward C Stanford; married Patricia Corley Stanford; children: Steven, Scott. **Educ:** Pennsylvania State University, BA, political science, 1961; US Army Infantry School, 1961; US Army Aviation School, 1965; US Army Transportation School; Comand General Staff College, 1972; Central Michigan University, MA, personnel mgt/admin, 1975; Industrial College of the Air Force, 1980. **Career:** US Army, Washington, DC, executive assistant to secretary of def; US Army, Oakland, CA, commander, military traffic mgmt cmd, WA; US Army, St Louis, MO, aviation systems command dep commanding gen; US Army Falls Church, VA, commander, military traffic mgmt command; US Army, Scott AFB, IL, USTRANSCOM, dir of plans & resources, USTRANSCOM deputy commander in chief. **Orgs:** National Defense Trans Association, 1987-89; board member, USO, St Louis Council, 1989-; president, Industrial College Association, 1987-89; president, Federal Executive Board of San Francisco, 1984-86; president, Army Aviation Assn America, St Louis, 1986-87. **Military Serv:** US Army, Major General, 1961-91; Defense Distinguished Service Medal, Distinguished Service Medal Army, Defense Superior Service Medal, Legion of Merit, with Oak Leaf Cluster, Distinguished Flying Cross, Bronze Star Medal with V device, with 2 Oak Leaf Clusters, Meritorious Service Medal, with Oak Leaf Cluster, 13 Air Medals, Army Commendation Medal with 3 Oak Leaf Cluster, Joint Meritorious Unit Award, Expert Infantryman Badge, and the General Staff Identification Badge. **Business Addr:** Deputy Commander, US Transportation Command, Department of Defense, Scott Air Force Base, IL 62225-7001.

STANISLAUS, GREGORY K.
Science teacher, youth minister. **Personal:** Born Jun 9, 1957, New York, NY; son of Eula James Stanislaus and Gregory Talbert Stanislaus; married Ruth Y Dyer Stanislaus, Aug 20, 1988; children: Gregory St Jacques, Asia Malone, Kyla Paris. **Educ:** Univ of Southern CA, Los Angeles, CA, BS, Biology, 1981; Western State Univ School of Law, Fullerton, CA, JD, 1985; New York Theological Seminary, New York, NY, Master of Divinity, 1987-. **Career:** McCutchen, Verleger and Shea, Los Angeles, CA, legal researcher, 1981-86; Bd of Education, Brooklyn, NY, science teacher, 1986-; Bethel Baptist Church, Brooklyn, NY, youth minister, 1988-. **Orgs:** Mem, Kings County Advisory Bd, 1990-91; mem, NAACP (Brooklyn), 1989-91; superintendent, Bethel Baptist Church Sunday School, 1990-; fndr, Stanislaus Theatrical Group, 1985; staff, Brooklyn Ctr for Urban Environment, 1987-; founder of Youth United to Change the World Intl. **Honors/Awds:** Part of Cover Story as Science Teacher for 90's, Black Enterprise, 1991; Honorary Award for Bldg Youth Ministry Bethel Baptist Church, 1991; Commendation for Feed Homeless Food Drive to Feed 5,000, City Harvest, 1990. **Business Addr:** Science Teacher, William Alexander Junior High School, 350 Fifth Ave, Brooklyn, NY 11215.

STANLEY, CAROL JONES
Administrative secretary. **Personal:** Born Mar 16, 1947, Durham, NC; daughter of Willie Lyons Jones and Doctor Young Jones; married Donald Andrew Stanley, Jul 21, 1990. **Educ:** NC Central Univ, Durham, NC, BSC, 1969; NC Central Univ School of Law, Durham, NC, 1973-74; NC Central Univ, Durham, NC, MS, 1975; Univ of NC, Greensboro, NC, 1987-90. **Career:** NC Central Univ, Durham, NC, research asst, 1980-81; Fayetteville State Univ, Fayetteville, NC, adjunct instructor, 1985-87; NC Central Univ School of Business, Durham, NC, adjunct instructor, 1989; NC Central Univ School of Law, Durham, NC, admin sec, 1991-94, assistant director of recruitment, 1994-. **Orgs:** Mem, NC Business Ed Assoc, 1990-91; chairperson, Publicity Comm NCBEA, 1990; tutor vietnamese, Immaculate Conception Church, 1990; registered reader, Delta Sigma Theta Sorority; Association for Supervision and Curriculum Development; National Business Education Association; Carolina Student Information System. **Honors/Awds:** Delta Sigma Theta Scholarship, 1988-89; Law Office Mgmt. **Home Addr:** 1611 Duke University Rd, Apt 8F, Durham, NC 27701.

STANLEY, COLUMBUS LANDON, SR.
Electrical engineer, city official. **Personal:** Born Sep 10, 1922, Fayetteville, NC; married Dorothy Bradford; children: Joyce Stanley Johnson, Columbus Jr, Charles, Kirk, Brian. **Educ:** NCA&T State Univ, attended 1945-46; SC State Univ, BSEE, 1958; SUNY, New Paltz, NY, grad courses, 1960-61. **Career:** IBM, staff engr 1955-; City of Poughkeepsie NY, asst mayor 1974-81, alderman 1967-93, vice mayor, 1993-. **Orgs:** Life mem Kappa Alpha Psi 1958-; mem All-SIAC Football & Basketball team; mem All-CIAA Football & Basketball team; founder Poughkeepsie Area Golfers League; mem NY Conf of Mayors 1967-; mem Natl League of Cities 1967-; treas founder Hudson Valley OIC Inc 1967-77; founder bd mem Mid-Hudson Valley HABITAT/Humanity 1983-; mem Natl Black Caucus/Local Elected Officials. **Honors/Awds:** Comm Serv Awd Key Women's Club Inc 1974; Comm Serv Awd Martin Luther King Commemorative Comm 1970; Alumni Achievement Awd NE Province Kappa Alpha Psi Frat Inc 1977; Comm Serv Awd Poughkeepsie Alumni Kappa Alpha Psi Frat Inc 1976. **Home Addr:** 168 N Clinton St, Poughkeepsie, NY 12601.

STANLEY, CRAIG A.
State official. **Personal:** Born Nov 20, 1955. **Educ:** Univ of Hartford, BA in political science. **Career:** YMWCA of Newark and Vicinity, director of corporate programs, currently; 28th Assembly District, assemblyman, 1996-. **Business Addr:** Assemblyman, 28th Assembly District, State of New Jersey, 1200 Clinton Ave, Ste 140, Irvington, NJ 07111, (973)399-1000.

STANLEY, ELLIS M., SR.
Government official. **Personal:** Born Jun 13, 1951, Shallotte, NC; son of Mae Belle Bryant Stanley and Lewis A Stanley; married Iris M White Stanley, May 31, 1975; children: Ellis M Jr, Christopher J. **Educ:** Univ of North Carolina, Chapel Hill NC, BA, 1973. **Career:** Brunswick County Govt, Bolivia NC, dir emergency mgmt, 1975-82; Durham-Durham County Govt, Durham NC, dir emergency mgmt, 1982-87; Atlanta-Fulton County Govt, Atlanta GA, dir emergency mgmt, 1987-97; City of Los Angeles, asst CAO, emergency prepardness div, 1997-. **Orgs:** President, Natl Forum for Black Public Admin, Atlanta Chapter; pres Natl Coordinating Council on Emergency Mgmt, 1985, state representative, 1988-; mem, Fulton Red Cross Advisory Comm, 1987-, Red Cross Emergency Community Serv Comm, 1987-, Hazardous Material Advisory Council, 1988-, Leadership Atlanta, class of 1990; president, Natl Defense Transportation Assn, Atlanta Chapter; NCCEM Certification Commissioners; board on national disasters, National Weather Svc; Modernization Transition Committee. **Honors/Awds:** Presidential Citation, US Civil Defense Assn, 1983; testified several times before the US Congress on Emergency Mgmt, 1985-86; lead Delegation to China to study Emergency Mgmt, 1988; presented at 1st Security Seminar in Caribbean, 1988; Board of Visitors of Emergency Managment Institute; Adjunct Instructor National Emergency Training Center; Certified Emergency Manager, commission member. **Business Addr:** Assistant City Administration Officer, Preparedness Division, 200 N Main St, Ste 1500, Los Angeles, CA 90012.

STANLEY, EUGENE
Education administrator. **Personal:** Born Nov 3, 1916, Rome, GA; married Dorothy P (deceased); children: Robert E, Dr William D. **Educ:** Wilberforce Univ, BS 1939; OH State Univ, MA 1946, continued study 1947-48. **Career:** NC A&T Univ, asst prof of educ, asst dean of men 1946-47; Savannah State Coll GA, asst prof, dir of student teaching 1948-49, dean of coll 1949-50; Morgan State Coll, asst prof of educ 1950-57, dir of student teaching, acting head of educ 1958-60, asst dean, dir of lower div 1960-67; State Bd for Higher Educ, dir div of inst approval & eval 1967-80, retired. **Orgs:** Consult higher ed Benedict Coll 1962, Johnson C Smith Univ 1963, Southern Reg Ed Bd 1966; author report for Middle States Accreditation Team for Morgan State Univ 1968; mem Urban League, NAACP, Assoc for Higher Ed, AARP, Phi Delta Kappa, Alpha Phi Alpha, Zeta Sigma Tau. **Honors/Awds:** Prominent Public Speaker in the Mid-West 1940's & 1950's; Articles publ in Bulletin of Negro History, Philos of Ed Society, Jrnl of Ed Sociology, School &Society; Authored studies for State of MD on need for School of Veterinary Med & Optometry; Cited as a living maker of Negro History 1950's. **Home Addr:** 2506 Overland Ave, Baltimore, MD 21214.

STANLEY, HILBERT DENNIS
Association executive, consultant. **Personal:** Born Feb 24, 1931, Cambridge, MD; children: Denise R, Guy Derek. **Educ:** Morgan State Univ, BS 1952, MS 1970; Wayne State Univ, EdD 1978. **Career:** Edmondson HS, principal 1973-75; Rockefeller Found, fellow 1975-76; Lake Clifton HS, prin 1979-81; Office of Mayor Baltimore, educ liaison officer 1981-84; Southwestern HS, principal, 1984-90 (retired); National Black Catholic Congress Inc, executive director, currently. **Orgs:** Vice basileus Pi Omega Chap Omega Psi Phi Frat 1978; pres Baltimore Chap Natl Alliance Black Sch Educators 1978-80; board of directors, National Alliance of Black School Educators Foundation, 1988-96; mem Board of Dirs Arena Players 1980-92; mem Bd of Dirs Afro Amer Newspaper 1981-83; chmn Selective Serv Local Bd 1982-85. **Honors/Awds:** Rockefeller Grant 1975; Man of the Yr Omega Psi Phi Frat 1980; Distinguished Alumni, National Association for Equal Opportunity in Higher Education, 1991. **Home Addr:** 413 George St, Baltimore, MD 21201. **Business Phone:** (410)547-5330.

STANLEY, KATHRYN VELMA
Attorney. **Personal:** Born Feb 9, 1967, Detroit, MI; daughter of A Knighton and Beatrice Perry. **Educ:** Spellman College, BA, 1989; Univ of Virginia School of Law, JD, 1992. **Career:** Children's Defense Fund, student intern, 1988-89; Alabama Capitol Representation Resource Center, staff atty, 1992-. **Orgs:** Sigma Alpha Iota Music Fraternity, vp, 1988-89; Black Law Students Assn, UVA Chapter, pres, 1991-92; Youth Entrepreneurship System, board sec, 1995-. **Honors/Awds:** Black Law Student Assn, Member of the Year, 1992. **Special Achievements:** Essence Magazine, Back Talk, December 1994; Virginia Lawyer (Alumni Magazine), Winter 1995. **Business Addr:** Staff Attorney, Alabama Capital Representation Resource Center, 114 N. Hull St., Montgomery, AL 36105, (334)269-1803.

STANLEY, LANETT
State government official. **Career:** Georgia State Representative, District 33, currently. **Special Achievements:** Only African American woman on the state Revenue Structure Commission; youngest person elected to state General Assembly. **Business Addr:** State Representative, District 33, Georgia House of Representatives, State Capitol, Rm 413, Atlanta, GA 30334, (404)656-5024.

STANLEY, WOODROW
Mayor. **Personal:** Born Jun 12, 1950, Schlater, MS; married Reta Venessa James; children: Heather Venessa, Jasmine Woodrina. **Educ:** Mott Comm Coll, 1969-71; Univ of MI, BA Polit Sci 1971-73; Univ of MI, Flint, MI, candidate for Master of Public Admin. **Career:** Whitney M Young St Acad, counselor 1974-77; Greater Flint OIC, asst services coord 1977-79, case mgt coord 1979-83, job club coord 1983-91; Flint City Council, councilman 1983-91; Mayor, Flint MI, 1991-. **Orgs:** Flint Human Relations Comm 1973-76; YMCA, board member, 1976-77; bd mem McCree Theatre & Fine Arts Centre 1975-90; Valley Area Agency on Aging, board member, chairman, 1982-91; Economic Develop Corp, board member, 1983-, chair, 1991; adv bd mem Univ of MI Flint African-Afro Amer Studies Prog 1983-; steering comm Coalition of Greater Flint African Relief Fund 1984-85; Ombudsman Adv Bd; bd mem Foss Ave Christian Sch; alternate trustee Flint Retirement Bd; MML, pres, 1990; MI Municipal League, Legislative and Urban Affairs Comm, board of directors, 1988-91; committe mem Natl League of Cities Human Devel Steering Comm 1989-90; National League of Cities, board of directors, 1992-, advisory council, 1994-; Natl Black Caucus of Local Elected Officials, 1987-; Michigan Association of Mayors, board of directors, 1992-94, pres, 1995; convener, Tri-County Council of Mayors 1992, NAACP. **Honors/Awds:** Listed US Jaycees Outstanding Young Men of America publication 1975; Cert of Achievement Leadership Flint 1975-76; Vol Service Awd Urban League of Flint 1981; Awd of Recognition Mott Adult HS 1982; Distinguished Comm Service Awd Foss Ave Baptist Church 1983; Comm Serv Awd Eureka Lodge F&AM 1986; Donald Riegle Community Service Award, Flint Jewish Federation 1993; Minority Women's Network Partners in Community, Mayor of the Year, 1994; Black Caucus Foundation of Michigan, Service Award, 1994; Sales and Mktg Executives of Flint, Booster of the Year, 1995; Dozier CME Church, African-American Man of Achievement, 1996; Forum Magazine, Pioneer Award, 1996. **Business Addr:** Mayor, City of Flint, 1101 S Saginaw, Flint, MI 48502, (810)766-7346.

STANMORE, ROGER DALE
Physician. **Personal:** Born Jan 20, 1957, Alanta, TX. **Educ:** Southwestern Union Coll, BS 1979; Meharry Medical Coll, MD 1984. **Career:** DC General Hosp, resident physician surgery 1984-85; Methodist Hosp/SUNY, resident physician 1985-86; Department of Justice, chief of medical staff; Jacksonville Medical Center, Jacksonville, AL, emergency room medical director, 1989-91. **Orgs:** Mem Amer & Natl Medical Assocs 1980-87; mem The Technology Transfer Soc 1982-87. **Honors/Awds:** Amer Coll of Surgeons Scholarship 1983; representative Joint Commn of Medical Education 1983. **Home Addr:** PO Box 18513, Huntsville, AL 35804-8513.

STANSBURY, CLAYTON CRESVELL
Educator. **Personal:** Born Mar 20, 1932, Havre de Grace, MD; married Catherine Laverne Posey. **Educ:** Morgan State Univ, BS 1955; Howard U, MS 1962; Univ of MD, PhD 1972. **Career:** Student Services, vice-pres 1978-; Morgan State Univ, Baltimore, MD, acting dean of student affairs, prof psychology, lower div, dir 1975-77, dir of the freshmen program, 1975, vice pres of student affairs, 1977-80, dir honors program, 1980-. **Orgs:** Chmn Psychology Dept 1973-75; asst dean Freshman Prgm 1970-73; psychol Couns Morgan State Univ 1967-70; instr Psychology Howard Univ 1965-67; tch asst Psychology Univ MD 1963-65; instr Psychology Howard Univ 1962-63; mem Am Psychol Assn MD Psychol Assn; Psi Chi Nat Honor Soc; mem Alpha Phi Alpha Frat; Urban League; life mem NAACP; mem bd dir YMCA; mem Little League Baseball; football promotions; Boy Scouts of Am; United Meth Men; Proj Upward Bound; Morgan ROTC; hon mem PKT; Univ chief marshal; cert YMCA. **Honors/Awds:** Author Portrait of a Colored Man; A Black Moses of Hartford Co MD 1977; 50 Years of Humanitarian Thoughts. **Military Serv:** AUS 1955-57. **Business Addr:** Dir, Honors Program, Morgan State Univ, Cold Spring Ln & Hillen Rd, Baltimore, MD 21239.

STANSBURY, MARKHUM L.
Educational administrator. **Personal:** Born Apr 5, 1942, Memphis, TN; son of Eliza Markhum Stansbury (deceased) and Willie Stansbury (deceased); married Lucy Barber Stansbury, Jun 4, 1966; children: Markhum Jr, Marlon B. **Educ:** Lincoln Univ, Jefferson City, MO, 1960; Lane College, Jackson, TN, BA, 1963; Memphis State Univ, Memphis, TN, 1965. **Career:** WDIA Radio, Memphis, TN, announcer, 1960-; Lane College, Jackson, TN, public relations director, 1966-69; Holiday Inns, Inc, Memphis, TN, public relations manager, 1969-83; Union Central Life Insurance Co, Memphis, TN, agent, 1983-84; American United Insurance Co, Memphis, TN, agent, 1984-87; State of Tennessee, Nashville, TN, special assistant to the Governor, 1987-90; Memphis State University, Memphis, TN, assistant to the president, 1990-. **Orgs:** Board vice chair, Emergency 911 Board; board vice chair, trustee, St Andrew AME Church; board member, YMCA; board member, Goals of Memphis; advisory board member, South Central Bell. **Honors/Awds:** Special Recognition Award, Rotary Club, 1988; Outstanding Service to Youth in Schools, Tennessee Child Care Facilities, 1989; Award of Merit, Mayor, 1989; Delegate to General Conference, AME Church, 1988. **Home Addr:** 1564 Westlawn Dr, Memphis, TN 38114. **Business Addr:** Assistant to the President, Office of the President, Memphis State University, Administration Bldg #337, Memphis, TN 38152.

STANSBURY, VERNON CARVER, JR.
Corporate president. **Personal:** Born Jul 13, 1939, Lexington, MS; divorced; children: Nicole Elaine, Vernon III. **Educ:** Roosevelt Univ, BS 1962; Kent Coll of Law, attended 1964; Harvard Bus Sch, MBA 1973. **Career:** IBM, sr systems engr 1962-67; Exxon Intl, head fleet analysis 1967-71; Cummins Engine Co, gen mgr serv tools 1973-78; Dept of Commerce, dir export dev 1978-81; Scientific and Commercial Systems Corp pres 1981-. **Orgs:** Chmn AASU-Harvard Bus Sch 1972; chmn ERB-Sr Exec Serv 1979; pres DC Chap Harvard Black Alumni 1980; chmn William R Laws Found 1974; chmn ColumbusUnited Negro Coll Fund 1977. **Honors/Awds:** Goldman Sachs Awd Harvard Bus Sch 1974; charter mem Sr Exec Serv of the US 1979; Outstanding Contrib White House Conf on Small Bus 1980. **Military Serv:** USAR warrant officer 1962-70. **Business Addr:** President, Scientific & Commercial Systms, 7600-B Leesburg Pike, Ste 400, Falls Church, VA 22041.

STANTON, JANICE D.
Career/placement counselor. **Personal:** Born Jun 26, 1928, Beaumont, TX; daughter of Myrtle Trimble Splane and Joseph Dewey Splane; married Rufus H Stanton Jr, Mar 7, 1944; children: Rufus H III, Deborah Stanton Burke, Robert T. **Educ:** Wiley Coll, 1942-44. **Career:** Galveston Coll, bd of regents, 1983-. **Orgs:** Pres bd of trustees Gulf Coast Regional Mental Health-Mental Retardation Ctr 1980-82; bd of councilors St Mary's Hosp 1980-86; adv bd Galveston Historical Found 1984; vice pres United Way of Galveston 1985-87; mem Grievance Committee, District 5B, State Bar of Texas 1988-90; board of directors, Lone Star Historical Drama Assn, 1989-92; President, Texas Assn of Community College Bd Mbrs & Administrators, 1990; Advisory Board, Children's Hospital, Univ of Texas Medical Branch (UTMB) Galveston, 1992-. **Honors/Awds:** Image Awd Galveston Branch NAACP 1983; Comm Achievement Awd Zeta Phi Beta Sor 1983; Outstanding Citizen of the Year, Gamma Pi Lambda Chapter, Alpha Phi Alpha, 1990. **Home Addr:** 3615 Avenue O, Galveston, TX 77550.

STANTON, ROBERT G.
Government official. **Educ:** Attended Huston-Tillotson Coll. **Career:** Grand Teton National Park, park ranger; National Parks-East, Washington, D.C., Virgin Islands National Park, superintendent; Park Service, Atlanta, deputy regional dir; National Park Service, dir. **Special Achievements:** First African American to head National Park Service. **Business Addr:** Director, National Park Service, 1849 C St, NW, Washington, DC 20240, (202)208-4621.

STANYARD, HERMINE P.
Teacher (retired). **Personal:** Born May 7, 1928, Charleston, SC; daughter of Mabel Comfort Washington (deceased) and Samuel Payne (deceased); married George Dewey Stanyard Sr; children: Geormine Deweya, George Dewey Jr. **Educ:** SC State Coll, BA 1949; New York Univ, MA 1952; Columbia Univ, Univ of SC, Adv Guid 1956,74,77; The Citadel Coll of Chas, Professional Certificate 1967, 1979-80. **Career:** Barnes Elem School Georgetown, teacher 1949-50; Wilson HS, english teacher 1952-56; Laing HS, english teacher 1956-59, guidance counselor 1959-67, english & reading teacher/reading coord 1967-85. **Orgs:** Mem campaigner Greater Chas YWCA 1966-86; pres Charleston Co Council Intl Reading Assoc 1977-79; chmn of nominating comm SC State Reading Assoc 1979-81; chmn Disting Teacher Membership 1981-85; volunteer teacher Morris St Bapt Church Tutorial Prog 1982,83,86; volunteer Laubach Reading Teacher; chairman SAT program 1976-82,

chairman elementary and middle school tutoring 1986-, Delta Sigma Theta Sorority, Inc; International Society of Poets, life mem, 1994-; chairman & co-chairman, Sundown Poetry Series of Piccolo Spoleto, 1995, 1996; co-chairman, Poetry and Storytelling Series of Moja Arts Festival, 1991-96. **Honors/Awds:** Certificates of Appreciation & Mother of the Year Morris St Bapt Church 1979, 1984, 1985; Certificate of Appreciation Greater Chas YWCA 1983; Delta of the Year Delta Sigma Theta Sor Inc 1983; Scroll of Honor Omega Psi Phi Frat 1984; Citation, Distinguished Woman of the 90's, Sigma Gamma Rho Sorority Inc, Delta Iota Sigma Chapter, 1992; Special Recognition, Literary Achievement, The Phyllis Wheatley Literary Social Club, 1992; Service Award, East Cooper Meals on Wheels, 1993; Community Service Award, Arabian Court #128, Daughters of Isis, 1994; Woman of the Year, Morris St Baptist Church, 1994; Certificate of Appreciation for Service, Minnie Hughes Elementary School, 1993, 1996; Certificate of Appreciation for Service, Wilmot Fraser Elementary School, 1996; Certificate of Appreciation for Service, Pan Hellenic Golden Voices of Greeks, 1994; Certificate of Appreciation for Service, Poetry Society of South Carolina, 1994-95; Certificate for Meritorious Service, Avery Institute of African-American History and Culture, 1995; Certificate of Appreciation, Delta Sigma Theta Sorority, Inc, 1994-96. **Special Achievements:** Publication: Book of Poetry, Lingering Thoughts, 1992; Verses for You and Me, 1995. **Home Addr:** 17 Charlotte St, Apt A, Charleston, SC 29403.

STAPLES, GRACIE BONDS
Journalist. **Personal:** Born Oct 27, 1957, McComb, MS; daughter of Freddie Felder Bonds (deceased) and Sula Bonds (deceased); married Jimmy Staples, Dec 21, 1985; children: Jamila Felder, Asha Dianne. **Educ:** Southwest Mississippi Jr College, Summit, MS, AA, 1977; University of Southern Mississippi, Hattiesburg, MS, BA, 1979. **Career:** Enterprise-Journal, McComb, MS, 1979-80; Delta Democrat-Times, Greenville, MS, 1980-82; The Raleigh Times, Raleigh, NC, reporter, 1983-84; The Sacramento Bee, Sacramento, CA, reporter, 1984-90; Fort Worth Star-Telegram, Fort Worth, TX, reporter, 1990. **Orgs:** Member, National Association of Black Journalists, 1980-. **Honors/Awds:** Maggie Award, Planned Parenthood of Sacramento Valley, 1986; California Education Writers Association Award, 1988; Dallas/Ft Worth Association of Black Communicators, Griot, 1992; American Bar Assn, Certificate of Merit, 1993; Black Image Award, Kappa Alpha Psi Fratenity, 1995; YMCA Minority Achiever, 1997; NAACP, Frederick Douglas Award for Journalism, 1997. **Business Addr:** Reporter, Features Dept, Fort Worth Star-Telegram, 400 W 7th St, Fort Worth, TX 76102.

STAPLES, ROBERT E.
Educator. **Personal:** Born Jun 28, 1942, Roanoke, VA; son of Anna Staples and John Staples; divorced. **Educ:** LA Valley Coll, AA 1960; CA State Univ Northridge, AB 1963; San Jose State Univ, MA 1965; Univ of MN, PhD 1970. **Career:** St Paul Urban League, dir of rsch 1966-67; CA State Univ, Hayward, asst prof Sociology 1968-70; Fisk Univ, asst prof Sociology 1970-71; Howard Univ, assoc prof Sociology 1971-73; Univ of CA, prof of Sociology. **Orgs:** Bd dir, Black World Found, 1980-; editor, Western Journal of Black Studies, 1978-. **Honors/Awds:** Distinguished Achievement, Howard Univ 1979; Simon Bolivar Lecture Univ del Zulia, Maracaibo, Venezeula 1979; Distinguished Achievement, Natl Council on Family Relations, 1982; Visiting Fellow Inst of Family Studies, Australia 1982; Marie Peters Award, Natl Council on Family Relations 1986. **Business Addr:** Professor of Sociology, Univ of CA, Box 0612, San Francisco, CA 94143.

STAPLETON, MARYLYN A.
Government official. **Personal:** Born Sep 25, 1936, St Thomas, Virgin Islands of the United States; daughter of Aletha C Callender John and Lambert George; married Frank Stapleton (divorced 1983); children: Linda Elaine. **Educ:** Washington Business Institute, New York, NY, AS, 1959; Hunter College, New York, NY. **Career:** Caribair Airline, St Thomas, VI, reservation agent, 1954-56; Macy's Dept Store, New York, NY, salesclerk, 1956-57; Gift Shop, New York, NY, salesclerk, 1957-63; Eastern Airlines Inc, New York, NY, supervisor, 1967-86; Caribbean Travel Agency, St Thomas, VI, travel agent, 1986-87; Government of the Virgin Islands, St Thomas, VI, deputy commissioner, 1987-91, asst commissioner, 1991-95; Small Business Ombudsman, SBTAP coordinator, 1995-. **Orgs:** State-chair, Democratic Party, 1986-; president, Lioness Club, 1987-88; treasurer, Lioness Club, 1985-86; public relations officer, Nevis Benevolent Society, 1966-85; membership chair, Lioness Club of STT, 1988-89; pageant chair, Lioness Club of STT, 1986-87. **Honors/Awds:** Melvin Jones Fellow, Lioness Club, 1989. **Home Addr:** P.O. Box 3739, St Thomas, Virgin Islands of the United States 00803.

STARGELL, TONY
Professional football player. **Personal:** Born Aug 7, 1966, LaGrange, GA. **Educ:** Tennessee State, bachelor's degree in health and physical education, 1990. **Career:** New York Jets, defensive back, 1990-91; Indianapolis Colts, 1992-93; Tampa Bay Buccaneers, 1994-95; Kansas City Chiefs, 1996; Chicago Bears, 1997-. **Business Addr:** Professional Football Player, Chicago Bears, 1000 Football Dr, Halas Hall at Conway Park, Lake Forest, IL 60045-4829, (847)295-6600.

STARGELL, WILLIE (WILVER DORNEL)
Sports administrator. **Personal:** Born Mar 6, 1941, Earlsboro, OK; married Margaret Weller; children: Wendy, Precious, Dawn, Wilver Jr, Kelli. **Educ:** Santa Rosa Junior College. **Career:** Pittsburgh Pirates, outfielder/infielder, 1962-82; Atlanta Braves, coach, special asst to player personnel director, currently. **Orgs:** Natl Adv Cncl on Sickle Cell Anemia; lectures at colls and univs in off-season; narrations to accompany symphony concerts around the country performing both at Carnegie Hall and the Kennedy Ctr. **Honors/Awds:** National League All-Star Team, 1964-66, 1971-73, 1978; Sporting News and UPI Comeback Player of the Year 1978; Sportsman of the Year, Sports Illustrated 1979; Major League Player of the Year Sporting News 1979; elected to National Baseball Hall of Fame, 1988. **Business Addr:** Special Asst to Player Personnel Director, Atlanta Braves, 521 Capitol Ave SW, Atlanta, GA 30312-2803.

STARKE, CATHERINE JUANITA
Educator (retired). **Personal:** Born Apr 5, 1913, Charlotte, NC; daughter of Sadie Spencer Gladden and Joseph Thomas Gladden; married William Campbell (deceased). **Educ:** Hunter Coll, BA 1936; Tchrs Coll, MA 1937, EdD 1963. **Career:** St Paul's Coll, 1938-46; Morgan State Univ, 1947-56; Jersey City State Coll, prof emeritus. **Orgs:** Modern Language Assn; Pi Lambda Theta. **Special Achievements:** Author, Symbolism of the Negro Coll, 1956; Black Portraiture in Am Fiction, Stock Characters Archetypes & Individuals, 1971. **Home Addr:** PO Box 650135, Fresh Meadows, NY 11365-0135.

STARKEY, FRANK DAVID
Personnel administrator. **Personal:** Born Aug 6, 1944, Indianapolis, IN; married Gunilla Emilia Ekstedt; children: Michael, Julia. **Educ:** Wabash Coll IN, AB 1966; Brown Univ, PhD Chem 1973. **Career:** IL Wesleyan Univ, prof 1971-80; General Elec Co, mgr equal oppor prog corp rsch & develop 1980-82, mgr human resource program 1982-. **Orgs:** Pres Wabash Council on Racial Equality 1965; chmn various comm Brown Univ Afro Amer Soc 1967-71; mem state council Amer Assn of Univ Prof 1972; memgrant rev panel NSF 1980; mem GE Found Minority Engrg Comm 1980-; comm mem to select the outstanding high school trainer of chemistry for the year Amer Chem Soc 1983-85; mem selection comm Outstanding State Biology Teacher Awd for Natl Assoc of Biology Teachers 1986. **Honors/Awds:** Alfred P Sloan Scholarship Wabash Coll 1962-66; NSF Traineeship Brown Univ 1966-70; Tchr of the Yr IL Wesleyan Univ 1978; Outstanding Young Man of Amer 1979; GE Honoree for Black Achiever In Industry Harlem YMCA 1986. **Business Addr:** Manager Human Resource Program, General Elec Co, PO Box 8, Schenectady, NY 12301.

STARKS, DORIS NEARROR
Educational administrator, nurse. **Personal:** Born Jul 30, 1937, Conecuh County, AL; daughter of Virgie G Jenkins and Cleveland H Jenkins; married Wilbert L Starks Sr, Dec 25, 1961; children: Wilbert L Jr, Garrick E. **Educ:** Tuskegee University, BSN, 1958; The Catholic University of America, MSN, 1965; Union Graduate School, PhD, 1978; Johns Hopkins University, post MS credits; University of Maryland, post MS credits. **Career:** Community College of Baltimore, 1968-90, Department of Nursing, professor Med Surgical Nursing, 1968-80, assistant chairperson, 1980-84, chairperson, 1984-86, Department of Health Science, chairperson, 1986-89, director of nursing and director of LPN to RN program, full professor, 1989-90; Coppin State College, Division of Nursing, assistant dean, 1990-91, dean, 1991-. **Orgs:** National Coalition of 100 Black Womn, 1991; Alpha Kappa Alpha, 1980-; Sigma Theta Tau International Honor Society of Nurses, 1977-; National Association of Black Nursing Faculty, 1990-; Continental Society, Inc, Columbia, Maryland Chapter, vice pres, 1992-; Chi Eta Phi, 1956-; Tuskegee University Alumni Association, 1958-; Club Dejour, 1992-; Epicureans, 1991-. **Honors/Awds:** American Academy of Nursing, Fellow, 1997; Tuskegee University School of Nursing, Hall of Fame Inductee, 1992; Baltimore Chapter of Black Nurses' Association, Outstanding Contribution to Nursing, 1984; Balitmore Tuskegee Alumni Club, Outstanding Assistance to Minorities in Health Careers, 1983; Community College of Baltimore Nursing Alumni, Contributions to Nursing Education, 1983; Maryland Foundation For Nursing, ''Leadership in Nursing,'' 1994. **Special Achievements:** Publications: ''Patchwork Reflection from a Nursing Instructor'', Today's O.R. Nurse, May 1984; ''How to Prevent Cold Weather Illnesses'', Black Family Magazine, Dec 1982; ''Mama Annie's Peanut Candy'', Black Family Magazine, Winter 1981; Tuskegee: A Precious Memory, ABNF Journal, p 6, March-April, 1995; ''Nursing Centers: A Resource for Underserved Communities'', Journal of the Association of Black Nursing Faculty, 1996; ''Coppin State College Nursing Center: A Community Partnership'', Journal of the Association of Black Nursing Faculty, 1996; Holistic Retention: A Practical Approach, Success Stories: Retention of African American Nursing Students, Tucker Publications, 1997. **Military Serv:** Army Nurse Corps, 1st lt, 1959-62. **Home Addr:** 9068 Bellwart Way, Columbia, MD 21045, (410)997-8036. **Business Addr:** Dean, Division of Nursing, Coppin State College, 2500 W North Ave, Baltimore, MD 21216, (410)383-5546.

STARKS, JOHN LEVELL
Professional basketball player. **Personal:** Born Aug 10, 1965, Tulsa, OK; married Jacqueline; children: John Jr, Chelsea. **Career:** Golden State Warriors, guard, 1998-89; New York Knicks, 1990-. **Honors/Awds:** NBA All-Defensive Second Team, 1993; NBA All-Star, 1994; NBA Sixth Man Award, 1996. **Business Addr:** Professional Basketball Player, New York Knicks, 2 Pennsylvania Ave, New York, NY 10121, (212)465-5867.

STARKS, RICK
Government executive. **Personal:** Born Apr 16, 1948, Scottsville, KY; son of Ruby Starks and L C Starks; married Saundra Harlin Starks, Nov 28, 1968; children: Derrick D, Shannon M. **Educ:** Western KY Univ, BS 1971, MPS 1975; Univ of OK, Economic Development Institute 1986-88. **Career:** Barren River Area Devel Dist, recreation planner/proj specialist 1972-80; Bowling Green Parks & Rec Center, dir 1971-72; Mammoth Cave Nat Park, park tech 1971; TN Valley Authority, Bowling Green, KY, economic development representative 1989-. **Orgs:** Taylor Chapel AME Church, steward brd, 1996-97; Big Brothers/Big Sister, vice pres, 1978-79; Bowling Green Human Rights Commission, past mbr, 1978; Kappa Alpha Psi Frat, vice polemarch, 1978-, keeper of records, 1989; Bowling Green NAACP, chmn action committee, 1979-, special projects advisor, 1988; Bradd Economic Devel Committee, chmn, 1988; Ky Industrial Devel Cncl, 1989; UPPRE Inc, bd of dirs, 1989-91; Bradd Private Industry Cncl, 1989-. **Honors/Awds:** Big Brother of the Year Award, Big Brothers Agency, 1979; Civitan Service Award, Bowling Green Noon Civitan, 1979; AWARE, Meritorious Service Award, 1980; developed NAACP Youth Improvement Grant, 1987. **Business Addr:** Regional Manager, Tennessee Valley Authority, 1945 Scottsville Rd, Thoroughbred Sq, Ste 201A, Bowling Green, KY 42104.

STARKS, ROBERT TERRY
Educator. **Personal:** Born Jan 24, 1944, Grenada, MS; son of Lula Ella Starks; married Judith Ann Minor; children: Kenya Mariama, Robert Willis. **Educ:** Loyola University, BS, 1968, MA, 1971. **Career:** Booz-Allen and Hamilton Inc, management & consultant, 1968-69; Chicago Urban League, research specialist, 1969-70; Northern Illinois University, director black studies, 1970-72, associate professor, 1972-; N'Digo newspaper, Chicago, columnist and political editor, 1992-; The Urban Affairs Review, editorial bd, 1992-95. **Orgs:** Council,National Conference of Black Political Scientists, 1979-81; DuSable Museum of Afro-American History, 1980-; vice pres, PUSH, International Trade Bureau, 1981-82; issues consultant, Rev Jesse L Jackson National Rainbow Coalition and Operation, PUSH, 1981-; issues consultant, Mayor Harold Washington and the City of Chicago, 1982-87; founder, chairman, Task Force for Black Political Empowerment, 1982-; founder, chairman, Free South Africa Movement of Chicago, 1985-; fellow, Leadership Greater Chicago, 1986-87; board member, Third World Conference Foundation, 1986-87; board member, Illinois Chapter, American Civil Liberties Union, 1987-88; vice chairman, 1987, chair, 1988-, Illinois Black United Fund; DAAD, Interdisciplinary German Studies, seminar, Phillips University, 1987; board of directors, South Side Community Art Center, Chicago, 1982-; African American Family Commission of Illinois, bd of dirs, 1995-. **Honors/Awds:** University of Michigan, Vstg Scholar at the Horace H Rackham School of Graduate Studies, 1976; Kellogg Foundation, Research Fellow, Northeastern Illinois University, 1978-80; National Endowment for the Humanities College Teachers Summer Seminar, 1982; Goethe Institute, Berlin, Germany, Language Fellow, 1986; National Community Service Award, The National Conference of Black Political Scientists, 1987. **Home Addr:** 1556 East Park Shore East Ct, Chicago, IL 60637. **Business Addr:** Urban Education, Northeastern Illinois University, 700 E Oakwood Blvd, Chicago, IL 60653.

STARLING, JOHN CRAWFORD. See Obituaries section.

STARR-WHITE, DEBI. See LIVINGSTON-WHITE, DEBORAH J. H.

STATEN, EVERETT R.
Company executive. **Personal:** Born Jun 17, 1951, Philadelphia, PA; son of Harris L & Juanita A; children: Kharee Harris Staten. **Educ:** Temple Univ, BA, 1980. **Career:** Bell of Pennsylvania, sales consultant, 1968-76; Metro Atlanta Black Pages, assoc publisher, 1981-85; Black Enterprise Magazine, sr account exec, 1986-88; Emerge Magazine, co-founder/adv dir, 1988-91; Black Expo USA, vp, 1991-96; Inner City Events, pres, 1991-; The Staten Group, Inc, CEO, 1991-; African American Heritage Collection, founder/CEO, 1996. **Orgs:** Natl Assn of Market Dev, 1980-; Natl Coalition of Black Meeting Planners, 1994-; African-American Chamber of Congress of Philadelphia, 1994-; Philadelphia Multicultural Affairs Congress, 1994-; National Association of Consumer Shows, 1996; International Association for Exposition Management, 1995. **Honors/Awds:** Martin Luther King Center for Non-Violent Social Change, Outstanding Service Award, 1986; Coors Brewing Co, Community Service Award, 1986. **Business Addr:** CEO, The Staten Group, Inc, 6228 N 8th St, Philadelphia, PA 19126, (215)224-2300.

STATEN, MARK EUGENE
Banker. **Personal:** Born Jan 22, 1963, Stuttgart, Germany; son of Walter (deceased) & Janette Staten; married Barbara Sandy Staten, Jul 1, 1994; children: Marylynn Staten. **Educ:** Langston Univ, 1986. **Career:** American Sate bank, branch mgr, 1981-. **Orgs:** Kappa Alpha Psi; Pyramid Lodge #69-Worshipful Master Mosonic Lodge; NAACP. **Home Addr:** 1330 North Boston Ave, Tulsa, OK 74106, (918)587-4604.

STATES, ROBERT ARTHUR
Tax executive. **Personal:** Born Mar 19, 1932, Boston, MA; son of Rosita A States and Earl H States; married Eva D Smith States, Feb 21, 1955; children: Lauren States Creary, Lisa, Robert Jr. **Educ:** Boston University, BS, 1953; Bentley College, certificate, 1957; Western New England College, JD, 1968; New York University Graduate Law School, attended, 1969-71. **Career:** US Veterans Administration, accountant, 1961-62; US Internal Revenue Service, IRS agent, 1962-69; Aetna Life & Casualty, Tax Audits, director, 1969-91; Triple Check Income Tax & Business Services, president, currently. **Orgs:** American Bar Association, 1977-; National Society of Enrolled Agents, 1991-; Conneticut Society of Enrolled Agents, 1991-; National Association of Tax Practitioners, 1992-; Town of East Hampton, Economic Development Commission, 1992-, Water & Sewer Authority, 1967-87. **Military Serv:** US Army, cpl, 1953-55. **Home Addr:** 35 Staeth Rd, PO Box 238, East Hampton, CT 06424, (203)267-9408. **Business Addr:** President/Owner, Triple Check Income Tax & Business Services, 7 Dickenson Rd, Marlborough, CT 06447, (203)295-0729.

STATHAM, CARL
Business executive. **Personal:** Born Dec 9, 1950, Macon, GA; son of Marie Statham and Carl Statham; married Gloria Marie Long; children: Stephanie, Christopher. **Educ:** Tuskegee Inst, BS 1973. **Career:** General Motors, business consultant 1973-77; Ford Motor Co, acct rep 1977-80, mgr acct reps 1980-83; Ford Motor Co, Southside Ford, acct general mgr 1983-84, pres 1984-. **Honors/Awds:** Top 100 Black Businesses, Black Enterprise, 1984-88; Top 300 Dealers Parts & Serv Volume, Ford Motor Co, 1984-88; Distinguished Serv Award, Ford Motor Co, 1984-87; Top 10 Nationally Ford Co Truck S/S, 1987; Co Ford Hwy Truck Dealer Council, 1989. **Business Addr:** President, Southside Ford Truck Sales, 810-850 W 39th St, Chicago, IL 60609.

STATON, DONNA HILL
Deputy attorney general. **Personal:** Born Dec 5, 1957, Chester, PA; daughter of Donald B & Ethel B Hill; married Kerry D Staton, 1984; children: Brooke, Lindsay. **Educ:** Princeton Univ, AB, English, 1979; George Washington Univ, School of Law, JD, 1982. **Career:** The Hon Joseph C Howard, US District Court for the District of Maryland, judicial law clerk, 1982-83; Piper & Marbury, assoc, 1983-93, partner, beginning 1993; Howard Cty, circuit court judge; MD deputy attorney general, currently. **Orgs:** Advisory Committee to the US Dist Ct, Dist of MD, 1991-95; The Attorney Grievance Comm of MD, commissioner & sec, 1991-95; Alliance of black Women Attorneys, pres, 1987-88; Maryland State bar Assn, bd of governors, 1988-90; Coll of Notre Dame of Maryland, bus advisory bd, 1993; Peoples Pro Bono Action Ctr, bd of dirs, 1990-92; Alpha Kappa Alpha Sorority, Inc, 1983-; Howard County Sexual Assault Ctr, bd of dirs, 1982-86. **Honors/Awds:** Maryland bar Foundation, Fellow; Alliance of Black Women Attorneys, Honoree, 1994; AFRAM Expo Salute to Black Women, Honoree, 1992; Emmanuel Christian Comm Church, 100 Outstanding Black Women of Baltimore. **Special Achievements:** First African American circuit court judge in Howard Cty, MD; first African American woman deputy attorney general in MD.

STEANS, EDITH ELIZABETH
Government official. **Personal:** Born Sep 4, 1929, Anderson, IN; daughter of Mary L Adams Downing (deceased) and Ernest J Downing (deceased); divorced; children: Bruce, Judith, Carol, Stacy. **Educ:** Anderson Coll, BA 1976; Ball State Univ, MAS 1978. **Career:** Madison Co Dept of Public Welfare, caseworker 1969-72; Madison Co Superior Court II, chief juvenile probation officer 1973-79; State of Indiana, affirmative action dir 1979-82; City of Anderson, affirmative action/human relations dir 1982-89; Univ of Nebraska Med Center, affirmative action/EEO dir, currently. **Orgs:** Mem Urban League 1955-, NAACP 1955-, bd dirs Comm Justice Ctr 1970-88; YWCA 1973-; mem Alpha Kappa Alpha Sor 1978-; instructor Anderson Coll 1978-88; commissioner Mayor's Economical Develop 1982-86; bd dir St John's Hospital Chemical Dependency 1982-88; bd dirs Enterprize Zone Assn 1984-87; St Benedict The Moor (Church). **Honors/Awds:** Outstanding Citizen NAACP 1983. **Home Addr:** 1619 W 15th St, Anderson, IN 46016-3205. **Business Addr:** Affirmative Action/EEO Director, University of Nebraska Medical Center, 400 S 42nd St, Administration 1003, Omaha, NE 68198-5020.

STEARNS MILLER, CAMILLE LOUISE
Attorney. **Personal:** Born Apr 25, 1956, Guthrie, OK; daughter of Lila Hobson Stearns and Hollis D. Stearns; married Daryl Lee Miller, Nov 7, 1987; children: Kristen Danielle. **Educ:** Howard University, Washington, DC, BA (magna cum laude), 1978; Case Western Reserve School of Law, Cleveland, OH, JD, 1981. **Career:** Ohio Attorney General's Office, Columbus, OH, assistant attorney general, 1981-82; Ohio Department of Natural Resources, Division of Oil and Gas, general counsel, 1982-85; Lewis, Clay & Munday, Detroit, MI, associate attorney, 1985-90, partner, 1991-. **Orgs:** Board member, secretary-treasurer, 1986-90, president elect, 1990-91, president, 1991-92, Wolverine Bar Association; member, Alpha Kappa Alpha Sorority, 1981-; National Conference of Black Lawyers, Columbus Chapter, 1981-85; Detroit Public Schools Role Model, 1985-91; National Coalition 100 Black Women, 1985-; National Bar Association, assistant secretary, 1991-, board member, 1995-; American Bar Association, 1981-; Detroit Bar Association, 1985-; Detroit Renaissance Links, 1990-; Detroit Chapter Jack & Jill of America, 1996-. **Honors/Awds:** Certificate of Appreciation, Detroit Public Schools, 1986-88; Outstanding Contributions to Legal Community, Black Law Students Association, Columbus, OH, 1984; Outstanding Service to the Black Law Students Association, Case Western Reserve School of Law, 1981; President's Award for Outstanding Service, National Bar Association, 1991-92; Resolution for Outstanding Service to the Community, US Congress House of Representatives, 1992; Resolution for Outstanding Service to the Legal Community and Community-at-large, Michigan State Legislature Senate, 1992; Resolution for Outstanding Service to the Community, Mayor of Detroit Coleman A Young, 1992; Resolution for Outstanding Service to the Legal Community, Wayne County Executive Ed McNamara; Resolution for Outstanding Service to the Community, Detroit Board of Education. **Business Addr:** Partner, Lewis, Clay & Munday, 1300 First National Bldg, 660 Woodward Ave, Detroit, MI 48203, (313)961-2550.

STEBBINS, DANA BREWINGTON
Government official. **Personal:** Born Nov 2, 1946, Baltimore, MD. **Educ:** Howard Univ Washington DC, BA 1963-67; Howard U, MSW 1967-70; Howard U, JD 1972-75. **Career:** Small Bus Adminstrn, spl asst to the asso adminstr for minority small us 1980-; Nat Bar Assn, dir commercial law proj 1978-80; Commodity Futures Trading Commn, atty/adv/spl asst 1977-78; Superior Ct for DC, judicial clk 1975-77. **Orgs:** Mem Am Bar Assn; mem Nat Assn of Black Women Attys; mem Nat Bar Assn; mem Nat Assn of Black Social Workers; mem Delta Theta Phi Legal Frat ; mem Nat Assn of Social Workers; mem Nat Conf of Black Lawyers. **Business Addr:** Small Business Adminstration, 1441 L St NW Room 317, Washington, DC 20416.

STEED, JOEL EDWARD
Professional football player. **Personal:** Born Feb 17, 1969, Frankfurt, Germany; married D'Angela; children: Traicee Eileen. **Educ:** Univ of Colorado, bachelor's degree in sociology, 1992. **Career:** Pittsburgh Steelers, nose tackle, 1992-. **Honors/Awds:** Pro Bowl alternate, 1996. **Business Addr:** Professional Football Player, Pittsburgh Steelers, Three Rivers Stadium, 300 Stadium Circle, Pittsburgh, PA 15212, (412)323-1200.

STEED, TYRONE
Hospital executive. **Personal:** Born Aug 18, 1948, Norfolk, VA; married Irene; children: Kenyatta Uniquegu. **Educ:** Newark School of Fine & Indust Art, Interior Design Diploma 1971-72; Fashion Inst of Tech AAS Interior Design 1973-75; Thomas Edison Coll, BA 1976-80;Kean Coll of NJ, MA Org Devel 1981-86. **Career:** New Horizons Inc, dist mgr, asst vice pres 1976-77; Girl Scouts of Amer, council field rep 1977-79; St Charles Kids School, teacher 1979-80; Newark Office onAging, sr commun relations spec 1980-; VA Med Ctr, chief voluntary svc, dir public relations. **Orgs:** Mem Amer Hosp Assoc 1981-, NJ Hosp Assoc 1981-, Amer Hosp Assoc Soc of PR Dir 1982-, Seton Hall Univ Gerontology Advisory Comm 1982-; NJ Assn Dir Volunteer Serv 1983. **Honors/Awds:** 20 min film on girl Scouts Girl Scout Council of Greater Essex Cty 1977-79; 50 page thesis innovation & change in org Kean Coll of NJ 1981-85. **Military Serv:** AUS sp4 3 yrs; Expert 45 Pistol 1965-68.

STEELE, BOBBIE L.
County official. **Personal:** Born Oct 18, 1937, Boyle, MS; daughter of Mary Rodges; married Robert P Steele, Apr 10, 1956; children: Valerie, Joyce, Robert, Byron, Donna, Elisha. **Career:** Chicago Bd of Educ, sch teacher, 1966-86; Cook County Bd of Commissioners, commissioner, 1986-. **Orgs:** League of Women Voters; Cook County Democratic Women; Operation Brotherhood, bd mem; Natl Assn of Black County Officials, reg dir; Co-sponsored the Purchasing Ordinance, 1988. **Business Addr:** Commissioner, Cook County Bd of Commissioners, 118 North Clark, Ste 567, Chicago, IL 60602, (312)443-3019.

STEELE, CLAUDE MASON
Educator. **Personal:** Born Jan 1, 1946, Chicago, IL; married Dorothy Munson; children: Jory, Claire, Claude, Benjamin. **Educ:** Hiram College, BA, 1967; Ohio State University, MA, 1969, PhD, 1971. **Career:** University of Utah, assistant professor, 1971-73; University of Washington, assistant professor, 1977, associate professor, 1977-85, professor, 1985-. **Orgs:** Board, Black Student Psychology Association, 1968-71; American Psychology Association, 1968-; psycho-social grant review panel, National Institute of Alcohol Abuse and Alcoholism, 1984-; associate editor, "Personality and Social Psychology Bulletin", 1984-; 20 articles published in professional journals. **Honors/Awds:** Dissertation Year Fellowship, Ohio State University, 1969-71. **Business Addr:** Psychology, Stanford University, Building 420, Stanford, CA 94305.

STEELE, CLEOPHAS R., JR.
Judge. **Personal:** Born Jul 13, 1945, Dallas, TX; married Barbara; children: Sheri, Sharron, Cheronda. **Educ:** Univ of Oklahoma, BA & BS 1967; Southern Methodist Univ, JD 1970. **Career:** City of Dallas, assoc judge 1974-76; Dallas County, justice of the peace. **Orgs:** Trustee/deacon Goodstreet Baptist Church; member Omega Psi Phi Fraternity 1965-; board member Dallas Alliance 1978-84. **Home Addr:** 1531 Cove Drive, Dallas, TX 75216. **Business Addr:** Justice Of The Peace, Dallas Co Pct 8 Pl 2, 414 South R L Thorton, Dallas, TX 75203.

STEELE, DAVID CHRISTOPHER
Sports journalist. **Personal:** Born Nov 10, 1964, Washington, DC; son of Vivian Magdalene Vaughan Steele (deceased). **Educ:** University of Maryland, College Park, MD, BS, journalism, 1985. **Career:** Evening Independent, St Petersburg, FL, sportswriter, 1986; St Petersburg Times, St Petersburg, FL, sportswriter, 1986-88; New York Post, New York, NY, sportswriter, 1988-89; The National Sports Daily, New York, NY/Washington, DC, sportswriter, 1989-91. **Orgs:** National Assn of Black Journalists, 1987-; Sigma Delta Chi/Society of Professional Journalists, 1986-87; Omicron Delta Kappa Honorary Society, 1985-. **Honors/Awds:** Author, Blacks in Sports: Unequal Opportunities, series in St Petersburg Times 1987; First Place, Florida Sportswriters Assn, investigative reporting, 1987; Honorable Mention, AP Sports Editors, enterprise reporting, 1987; Finalist, Atlantic chapter, Sigma Delta Chi, Contest, 1987.

STEELE, JOYCE YVONNE
Hair technician. **Personal:** Born Dec 8, 1930, St Johns, Antigua-Barbuda; daughter of Agatha Isaac and William Isaac; married Richard Biddy (divorced 1965); children: Richard Biddy, Mark Biddy. **Educ:** Hopes Beauty School, London, England, diploma, 1961; Loriel Beauty School, Paris, France, diploma, 1968; Lee College School of Cosmetology, Baytown, TX, diploma, 1982. **Career:** Dame Yvonne Beauty School, Leister, England, owner, 1958-74; American Caribbean Beauty Prod, Baytown, TX, owner, 1982-; Ultra Elegance Salon, Baytown, TX, owner, 1982-. **Business Addr:** President, American Caribbean Beauty Products, 823 South Pruett, Baytown, TX 77520, (713)422-5100.

STEELE, MICHAEL W.
Marketing executive. **Personal:** married. **Career:** Stroh Brewery Companies, Detroit, MI, sales rep, 1976-77, market dev rep, 1978, marketing mgr, 1979, product mgr, 1981; Brown & Williamson Corp, Louisville, KY, mgr special markets, 1981-84; Coca-Cola USA, Schaumburg, IL, market dev meg, 1984-86, Coca-Cola USA, Atlanta, GA, dir of African-American consumer markets, 1986-. **Business Addr:** Director, African-American Consumer Markets, Coca-Cola USA, 1 Coca-Cola Plaza, Atlanta, GA 30313-2419.

STEELE, PERCY H., JR.
Social service administrator (retired). **Personal:** Born Feb 4, 1920, Hopkinton, MA; children: Loretta Steele Chatmon. **Educ:** NC Central Univ, AB 1944; Atlanta Univ Sch of Social Work, MSW 1946. **Career:** Washington Urban League, comm org sec 1945-46; Morris County NJ Urban League, prog dir 1946-47, exec dir 1948-53; College of St Elizabeth, sociology instructor 1951-53; San Diego Urban League, exec dir 1953-63; Bay Area Urban League, pres 1964-90. **Orgs:** Secy & treasurer, bd of dirs, St Marys Medical Ctr; secy bd of dirs, Summit Medical Ctr; Natl Assn of Social Workers; Sigma Iota Chapter of Omega Psi Phi Fraternity; bd of dirs Bay Area Black United Fund, Bay Area Assoc of Black Social Workers, African-American Agenda Council SF, Sigma Pi Phi. **Honors/Awds:** First African-American to be apptd to exec dir of local housing authority in the US; Social Worker of the Year Natl Assoc of Social Workers 1976; Robert C Kirkwood Awd San Francisco Foundation 1985; Whitney M Young Jr, Medallion, 1990. **Home Addr:** 565 Bellevue Ave, #1901, Oakland, CA 94610.

STEELE, RUBY L.
Educator, nurse. **Personal:** Born Oct 13, Marion, AL; daughter of Mamie Whitehead & Alexander Williams (both deceased); married George W Steele, Mar 11, 1957; children: Jocelyn, Sonya, George, Christopher. **Educ:** American River College, Sacramento, CA, AA, 1970; Metropolitan State College, Denver, CO, BS, 1974; Southern Illinois University, Edwardsville, IL, MS, 1979; St Louis University, St Louis, MO, PhD, 1988. **Career:** Belleville Memorial Hospital, Belleville, IL, nurse, 1975-78; Belleville Area College, Belleville, IL, instructor, part-time, 1977-78; Southern Illinois Univ at Edwardsville, IL, instructor, asst prof, 1979-87; Webster Univ, St Louis, MO, asst prof, 1987-90; Southeast Missouri State Univ, Cape Girardeau, MO, assoc prof, 1990-94; Fort Valley State Coll, pro & dir of nursing prog, 1994. **Orgs:** Sigma Theta Tau, Nursing Honor Society, 1980-; member, House of Delegates, ANA, 1971-; steering committee, INA, 1975-; board of directors, Assn of

Black Nursing Faculty, 1987-; St Louis Univ Alumni, bd of dirs; YWCA; Belleville News Democrat, advisory bd. **Honors/Awds:** NIMH Traineeship for Graduate Study, 1977; Colorado Nurses Assoc Grant of BS Study, 1973; American Cancer Society Grant, Oncology for Nurse Educators, 1981; Sacramento Medical Society Scholarship, 1969-71; Faculty Fellowship, Purdue University, summer 1990. **Home Addr:** 537 Windrift Dr, Belleville, IL 62221, (618)277-5978.

STEELE, SHELBY
Educator. **Personal:** Born 1946. **Educ:** Univ of Utah, doctorate in history, 1974. **Career:** San Jose State University, professor of English, currently. **Honors/Awds:** Host, PBS special, Seven Days in Bensonhurst; author, The Content of Our Character: A New Vision of Race in America, 1990; Natl Book Critics Circle Award, 1990. **Business Addr:** Professor, English Dept, San Jose State University, 1 Washington Sq, San Jose, CA 95192-0001.

STEELE, WARREN BELL
Personnel administrator. **Personal:** Born Apr 14, 1923, Milledgeville, GA; married Victoria Kitchen; children: Holly Burns, Woody, William, Audrey Brown, Warren, Theresa Page, Frank. **Educ:** Paine Coll, BA 1947; The Am U, MA 1965. **Career:** Columbus Consolidated Govt Columbus GA, personnel officer 1983-; Signature Mfg Co Nashville TN, minority owner 1981-83; Cummins Charleston Urban League Columbus GA, exec on loan 1979-81; Cummins Charleston Inc Charleston SC, personnel div mgr 1975-79; Frigiking Dallas, vice pres personnel 1973-75; Cummins Engine Co Columbus IN, dir personnel & adminstr 1970-73; Cummins Engine Co Columbus IN, personnel adminstr 1969-70. **Orgs:** Mem Am Soc of Personnel Adminstrs 1976-; mem Tri-Co Personnel Assn 1976-; chmn Dorchester Co (SC) Sch Adv Bd 1977-; bd mem King's Grant Home Owners Assn 1977-78; trustee Voorhees Coll Denmark SC; friend to Educ Dorchester Cnty Tchrs Assn; friend to Educ Dorchester Cnty Tchrs Assn 1979; mem bd Columbus GA C of C. **Honors/Awds:** Bronza star; defense commen; Vietnam Def. **Military Serv:** AUS lt col 23 yrs.

STEGER, C. DONALD
City official. **Personal:** Born Aug 27, 1936, Huntsville, AL; son of Lula Cliff Steger and Fred Steger; married Elizabeth Sutton, Jun 1, 1966; children: Lisa Monique. **Educ:** Bethune Cookman Coll, BA 1964; Gammon Theol Seminary, BD 1968; Univ South Florida, PhD 1972. **Career:** WOBS Radio Jacksonville, announcer 1960-64; Tampa Inner City Programs, dir 1968-71; McCabe Black Comm Develop, dir 1972-75; Pinellas County FL Schools, administrator 1975-77; City of St Petersburg FL, deputy city mgr 1977-79; City of Charlotte, asst city mgr 1979-. **Orgs:** Consultant US Civil Serv Commn 1969-78, General Electric Co 1972-74, Honeywell 1975-77; mem bd of dirs, Rotary Club of Charlotte 1975-; pres bd Bethlehem Ctr Charlotte 1985-86; chmn Campaign for Charlotte Meckenburg United Way 1986; dir, Foundation for the Carolinas, 1986-. **Honors/Awds:** Doctoral Dissertation USF 1972; chmn, 1986 United Way Campaign, 1986. **Military Serv:** USAR corpl 1956-62. **Home Addr:** 6517 Hunter Pine, Charlotte, NC 28226-2892. **Business Addr:** Assistant City Manager, City of Charlotte, 600 East 4th St, Charlotte, NC 28202.

STEIB, JAMES T.
Clergyman. **Personal:** Born May 17, 1940, Vacherie, LA. **Educ:** Ordained 1957. **Career:** Titular Bishop of Britonia; St Louis, auxiliary bishop 1983-. **Business Addr:** Archdiocese of St Louis, 4445 Lindell Blvd, St Louis, MO 63108.

STENNIS-WILLIAMS, SHIRLEY
Educational administrator. **Educ:** Loyola & Chicago Teachers College; Jackson State Univ, Valedictorian BS 1958; Peabody Coll of Vanderbilt Univ, MA 1964, EdD 1972; Harvard Management Development Program, 1990. **Career:** Jackson State Lab School, teacher 1958-59; Chicago Public Schools, teacher 1959-64; Peabody Coll of Vanderbilt Univ, teaching assistant 1964-66; Univ of WI Oshkosh, asst prof 1966-72, coord of field experience 1975-83, assoc prof 1972-83, professor 1982-85, asst vice chancellor, 1985-91; senior system academic planner, dean of education, 1992-. **Orgs:** State delegate Founding Conv Natl Women's Studies Conf 1980; board of directors Wisc Council of Teachers of Engl 1981-83; district dir Wisc Council of Teachers of Engl 1981-83; founding president Wisc State Human Relations Assn 1982-83; board of directors Midwest Human Relations Assn 1982-83; American Association for Higher Education, Black Caucus secretary, treasurer, member of executive board, 1985-1992. **Honors/Awds:** Natl Defense Education Act Doctoral Fellowship 1963-66; Dissertation - "Student Teaching in the Chicago Public Schools 1856-1964" 1972. **Special Achievements:** First African-American asst prof, assoc prof and coordinator of field experience at the Univ of Wisconsin, Oshkosh.

STENT, MADELON DELANY
Educator. **Personal:** Born Sep 22, 1933, Washington, DC; children: Michelle, Nicole, Evan. **Educ:** Sarah Lawrence Coll, BA; Wellesley Coll, MA; Columbia U, EdD 1965. **Career:** CUNY, City College, professor of education, 1963-, Division of Interdept Studies, director, 1981-94; Teachers College; Columbia Univ; Queens College; Mills College; Random House-Knopf Mag, journalist, author. **Orgs:** Educ con planner for Voices Inc 1966-; Natl Assn Black Sch Educators 1971-; Amer Educ Research Assn 1973-; natl chpsn Higher Ed Comm Nat Alliance of Black Sch Educators; consult to numerous orgns & univs; HARYOU-ACT; US Off of Edn; Univ of P Rico; Univ of CA; etc. **Honors/Awds:** Comm Serv Soc Awd 1964; vis prof Fordham Univ Sch of Educ 1969-71; Ford Found Research Grantee 1973; Ford Found Grantee 1974; Rockefeller Scholar in Re Bellagio Italy 1975; Kappa Delta Pi Honor Educ Soc; Student Amb Awd in Spanish to Spain, 1952. **Special Achievements:** Author: Cultural Pluralism in American Higher Education, 1973; Minority Enrollment & Rep in Inst of Higher Educ, Praeger Press, Special Studies Intl, 1974; Minorities in US Institutions of Higher Education, Praeger Press, Special Studies Intl, 1976; Black Colleges: International Perspectives, 1984. **Home Addr:** 5700 Arlington Ave, #5B, Riverdale, NY 10471.

STENT, MICHELLE DORENE
Attorney. **Personal:** Born Feb 4, 1955, New York, NY; daughter of Madelon Delany Stent and Theodore R Stent. **Educ:** Univ of Puerto Rico, Certificate of Merit 1974; Univ of London, Certificate of Distinction 1975; Tufts Univ, BA 1976; Howard Univ School of Law, JD 1980. **Career:** Senator Edward W Brooke, intern 1976; Office of Civil Rights, public info consultant 1979; Congressional Black Caucus, graduate student intern 1979; Congressman Charles Rangel, legislative intern 1980; Comm on Educ and Labor US House of Reps, legislative counsel 1980-85; United Negro Coll Fund, dir govt affairs, assoc general counsel, Washington Office, vice pres 1989-. **Orgs:** Bd dirs Caribbean Action Lobby; consultant Natl Urban League; select comm Congressional Black Caucus Intern Program; mem Delta Theta Phi Law Fraternity, Natl Bar Assn; assn mem Congressional Black Assocs, NAACP, Natl Urban League, Natl Assn of Black Women Attorneys, Coalition of 100 Black Women; bd of dir, Natl Coalition Black Voter Participation 1985-; bd of dir, Capitol City Ballet, 1988-. **Honors/Awds:** Articles published Black Issues in Higher Education, Point of View; honorary doctorate, Texas Coll, Tyler, TX, 1987; Title IX Award, Natl Assn for Equal Opportunity in Higher Educ, 1987; Newspaper Articles, NY Voice, Mississippi Memo Digest, Tyler Courier Times, editor/writer, Government Affairs Reports UNCF, 1985-. **Business Addr:** Vice President, Government Affairs, United Negro College Fund Inc, 1025 Vermont Ave, #810 NE, Washington, DC 20005.

STENT, NICOLE M.
Governement, attorney, health services administrator. **Personal:** Born Jul 22, 1960, New York, NY; daughter of Dr. Madelon Delany Stent and Dr. Theodore R. Stent; married Mark A. Graham, 1993; children: Imani Simone Stent Graham. **Educ:** Dartmouth College, Hanover, NH, BA, 1982; Howard University School of Law, Washington, DC, 1985. **Career:** US House of Representatives, Congressional Black Caucus, fellow, 1983; Leftwich, Moore & Douglass, Washington, DC, legal intern, 1985; New York Supreme Court, law assistant, 1986; NYC Financial Services Corp, senior project mgr, 1987-88; City of New York, Mayor's Office of Minority Affairs, deputy director, 1988-90, Mayor's Office of African American & Caribbean Affairs, acting director, 1990; NYC Offtrack Betting Corp, assistant general counsel, 1991; NYC Health and Hospitals Corp, Affirmative Action/EEO, assistant director, 1992-97, executive assistant, corporate planning, 1998-. **Orgs:** Dartmouth Lawyers Assn, 1985-; New Jersey County Bar Assn, 1987-; New York State Bar Assn, 1990-; New York Urban League, 1990-. **Honors/Awds:** Certificate of Appreciation for support of community events, Clara Muhammed School, 1990. **Business Addr:** Executive Assistant, Corporate Planning, NYC Health & Hospitals Corp, 125 Worth St, Rm 401, New York, NY 10013.

STENT, THEODORE R.
Radiologist, nuclear medicine physician. **Personal:** Born Jan 7, 1924, Charleston, SC; son of Amelia Bores Stent and Theodore Stent; married Madelon Delany (divorced); children: Michelle, Nicole, Evan. **Educ:** Talladega Coll, AB 1944; Meharry Medical Coll, MD 1948; Sydenham Hospital, internship 1948-49, radiology residency, 1948-51. **Career:** AUS Hospital, chief radiology 1951-53; Bellevue Hospital, resident 1955; Amer Bd of Radiology, diplomat 1955; Workman Compensation NY, special radiology 1955; Bellevue Hospital, asst 1955-56; Private Practice NYC, radiology 1955-71; Bronx Hospital, adj attending roent 1956-64; Hospital for Joint Dist, adj radiologist 1955-57; Sydenham Hospital, radiologist 1955-60, phy chrg tumor clinic 1956-60; NY Medical Coll, asst prof radiology 1960-67; Columbia Univ, assoc prof radiology 1966-; Intramer Life Insurance Co, medical dir, vice pres 1966-71; Harlem Hospital, dir School for Nuclear Medical Technology 1971; clinical coord Antioch Coll, Harlem Hospital Center 1972; Nursing Home on Hill, pres medical bd 1973-; Columbia-Harlem Hosp, dir, radiology, 1964-71, dir, nuclear medicine, 1971-. **Orgs:** Mem Medical Advisory Council Natl Urban League 1970-; mem Natl Medical Assn, NY Roent Soc, Amer Coll Radiology, Radiological Soc NY Medical Coll, Amer Inst Ultrasound Medicine, Amer Coll Nuclear Medicine, Soc of Nuclear Medicine; mem HANA, Voices Inc, Symphony New World Tiffany Entertainment Corp, Phoenix Comm Group Inc, NY Prof Center bd of dirs on all above; mem Urban League Greater NY; bd dirs Greater Harlem Nursing Home Corp; mem NAACP, YMCA, Mayor's Org Task Force, 100 Black Men NYC; mem Sigma Pi Phi Frat, Omega Psi Phi, Guardsmen Inc; numerous publications; mem, Reveille Club, currently; bd of dir, Schubert Chorol Soc, 1989-; bd of dir, Honear Ebony Ensemble, LTD, 1986-; mem, Alpha Omega Alpha Honorary Medical Soc, Meharry Coll, 1991.

STEPHEN, JOYCE
Law enforcement official. **Career:** New York City Police Department, captain, deputy inspector, currently. **Special Achievements:** First African American female to attain rank of captain and deputy inspector with the New York City Police Department. **Business Addr:** Deputy Inspector, New York Police Dept HQ, 1 Police Plaza, New York, NY 10038, (212)374-5000.

STEPHENS, BOOKER T.
Judge. **Personal:** Born Nov 3, 1944, Bluefield, WV; married Gloria M Davis; children: Ciara Midori, Booker Taliaferro. **Educ:** WV State Coll, BA 1966; Howard Univ, JD 1972. **Career:** Asst prosecuting atty 1977-78; WV House of Delegates 1979-82; circuit court judge. **Military Serv:** AUS sp5 2 yrs. **Business Addr:** Circuit Court Judge, PO Box 310, Welch, WV 24801.

STEPHENS, BRENDA WILSON
Librarian. **Personal:** Born Oct 22, 1952, Durham, NC; daughter of Lucy Umstead Wilson and Leroy Wilson; married Gregory Stephens, Mar 6, 1977; children: Seth, Sara. **Educ:** Vincennes University, Vincennes, IN, 1970-71; Winston-Salem State University, Winston-Salem, NC, BS, 1974; North Carolina Central University, Durham, NC, MLS, 1981. **Career:** Orange County Public Library, Hillsboro, NC, library asst, 1976-81, asst county librarian, 1981-90, county librarian, 1990-91, regional library director, 1991-. **Orgs:** Kiwanis, 1990-, president, currently; board member, United Way of Greater Orange County, 1991-94; president, PTO-Cameron Park School, 1988-89; president, Al Stanback Middle School, currently; chair, adult services, NCLA, Public Library Section, 1987-93; North Carolina Library Assn, Public Library Section, 1983-85. **Honors/Awds:** Homecoming Queen, Vincennes University, 1970-71; NC Library Association Roundtable, Roadbuilders' Award, 1997. **Military Serv:** US Army, Sgt, 1974-76. **Home Addr:** 5807 Craig Rd, Durham, NC 27712. **Business Addr:** Regional Library Director, Orange County Public Library, 300 W Tryon St, Hillsborough, NC 27278.

STEPHENS, BROOKE MARILYN
Financial advisor, writer. **Personal:** Born Jan 1, 1944, Atlanta, GA; daughter of Charles W Stephens, Jr & Grace Anne Brooks Stephens. **Educ:** Fisk Univ, BA, 1963; Western Michigan Univ, MLS, 1967; Adelphi Univ, CFP, 1986. **Career:** Stephens & Associates, portfolio manager, currently. **Special Achievements:** Author of "Talking Dollars & Making Sense," McGraw-Hill Books, 1996; "Men We Cherish.". **Business Addr:** Portfolio Manager, Stephens & Associates, 43 Vanderbilt Ave, Brooklyn, NY 11205, (718)875-2575.

STEPHENS, CHARLES RICHARD
Educational administrator. **Personal:** Born Mar 1, 1938, McIntosh County, GA; son of L B Francis Stephens and James A Stephens Sr; married E Delores Betts Stephens, Nov 12, 1960; children: Chandra Rae, Charlita Rochelle. **Educ:** Morehouse Coll, BA 1960; Atlanta Univ, 1964-65; Springfield Coll, 1967-68; New Orleans Univ, 1977-78. **Career:** Butler St YMCA, public relations sec, asst gen exec, 1961-70; United Negro Coll Fund, city & natl campaign dir, 1970-76; Dillard Univ, New Orleans LA, vice pres for development, 1977-79; Clark College, Atlanta GA, vice pres for development, 1979-89; Clark Atlanta Univ, Atlanta GA, special asst to president, 1989-90; Morehouse College, Atlanta GA, dir of corp & foundation relations, 1991-92; Director of Development and Communications, Center on Philanthropy, Indiana University, Indianapolis, 1992-. **Orgs:** Mem, Alpha Phi Alpha Frat, 1958-; mem, Natl Soc of Fund Raisers, 1960-; pres, Natl Alumni Council, UNCF, 1982-86, 1990-; bd mem, United Negro Coll Fund, 1982-86; sec of natl bd, chair 1991, 1992, Natl Soc of Fund Raising Executives; former chair, People Television Inc, 1991. **Honors/Awds:** Outstanding Ind UNCF Perform Award, 1971; National Society of Fund Raising Executives, Indiana Chap, Fund Raising Executive of the Year, 1996. **Military Serv:** AUS, S/4, 1962-64; Commendation, Dept of the Army, 1964. **Business Addr:** Director of Development and Communications, Center on Philanthropy, Indiana University, Indianapolis, IN 46202-3162, (317)274-4200.

STEPHENS, CYNTHIA DIANE
Judge. **Personal:** Born Aug 27, 1951, Detroit, MI; daughter of Diane Shand Stephens and Nathaniel Otis Stephens; married Thomas Oliver Martin; children: Imani Diane Stephens. **Educ:** Univ of MI, BA 1971; Atlanta Univ, postgraduate 1971-72; Emory Law School, JD 1976. **Career:** Natl Conf of Black Lawyers, so regional dir 1976-77; Natl League of Cities, coord 1977-78; Pan-African Orthodox Christian Church, genl counsel 1978-82; Michigan Senate, assoc general counsel 1979-82; Wayne County Charter Commn, vice-chmn 1980-81; Law Of-

fices of Cynthia D Stephens, attorney 1981-82; 36th District Ct, judge 1982-85; Wayne County Community Coll, faculty, 1985-; Univ of Detroit Law School, faculty, 1988-; Wayne County Circuit Court, judge, 1985-; Detroit Coll of Law, faculty, 1990-95. **Orgs:** Mem Wolverine Bar Assoc 1979; bd mem Wayne Co Neighborhood Legal Serv 1980; mem New Detroit Inc 1981-; bd mem Assoc of Black Judges of MI 1982-89, MI Dist Judges Assoc 1982-85, Greater Detroit Health Care Cncl 1983-85; guest lecturer Southern Univ Women and Leadership Symposium Baton Rouge LA 1983, Western MI Univ Dept of Women Studies Kalamazoo 1983; Univ of MI Symposium series for the Ctr for African and Afro-Amer Studies 1984; mem adv bd African Diaspora Project of the Delta Inst 1984-88; mem City Wide Sch Comm Organization-at-Large 1984-86, Delta Manor LDHA 1984-, YMCA Downtown Detroit 1984; mem Amer Bar Assoc Comm on Judicial Evaluation 1984-85, Delta Sigma Theta Detroit Alumni 1984-85; mem adv bd MI Bar Journal 1985-; Amer Corporate Counsel Pro-Bono Adv Comm 1982-88; bd of commissioners, State Bar of MI 1986-94; mem Natl Conference of Black Lawyers, 1997-; Natl Assoc of Women Judges; MI Judges Assoc. **Honors/Awds:** Outstanding Woman Awd Woodward Ave Presbyterian Ch 1982; Disting Serv Awd Region 5 Detroit Public Schools 1983; Wolverine Bar Member of the Yr 1984; Little Rock Baptist Ch Golden Heritage Awd for Judicial Excellence 1984; Outstanding Woman in Law Hartford Memorial Bapt Ch 1985; publication "Judicial Selection and Diversity," MI Bar Journal Vol 64 No 6 1985; Disting Alumni Awd Cass Tech HS 1987; Susan B Anthony, Natl Organization of Women, 1988; Anita Hill Award, Detroit Human Rights Commission, 1991. **Business Addr:** Judge, 3rd Circuit Court, 1719 City-County Bldg, Detroit, MI 48226.

STEPHENS, DOREEN Y.
Marketing senior brand manager. **Personal:** Born Sep 10, 1963, Jamaica, West Indies; daughter of Lolita Stephens. **Educ:** University of Pennsylvania, BSE, chemical engineering, 1985; Columbia Business School, MBA, marketing, 1990. **Career:** General Foods, Battle Creek, MI, assistant engineer, 1985-86, Cranbury, NJ, associate engineer, 1986-88, White Plains, NY, assistant product manager, 1990-91, associate product manager, 1991-93, product mgr, 1993-95, sr brand manager, 1995-. **Orgs:** National Black MBA Association, 1990-, co-chairperson program committee, 1991; Black Scholars Mentor Program, mentor, 1991-; Columbia Business School, alumni admissions ambassador, 1992. **Honors/Awds:** Columbia Business School, Dean's List, spring 1990. **Special Achievements:** United States patent 317372, 1992. **Home Addr:** 14-2 Granada Cresent, White Plains, NY 10603.

STEPHENS, E. DELORES B.
Educator. **Personal:** Born Nov 30, 1938, Danville, VA; daughter of Henrietta H Betts and G A Betts Sr; married Charles R Stephens, Nov 12, 1960; children: Chandra R, Charlita R. **Educ:** Exeter University, Great Britain-Testamur, 1960; Spelman College, BA, 1961; Atlanta University, MA, 1962; Emory University, PhD, 1976. **Career:** Atlanta School of Business, instructor, 1962-63; Norfolk State University, instructor, 1963; Morehouse College, professor, 1964-77, 1979-, Freshman English Program, dir, 1984-94; Dillard University, associate professor/director, government rel, 1977-79; US Army, FORSCOM, education specialist, 1980-83; St Leo College, adjunct, 1987-95; Spelman College, visiting professor, 1991-94; Indiana - Purdue Univ, Indianapolis, visiting prof, 1994-95; Morehouse College, department of English, chair, 1995-. **Orgs:** National Council of Teachers of English, 1984-; National Honors Council, 1988-, teaching & learning committee, 1990-93; College Language Association, 1975-; South Atlantic Modern Language Assoc, 1994-; The Links Inc, Magnolia Chapter, 1991-; Morehouse Board of Trustees, 1990-93; Assn for the Study of Afro-American Life & History, 1994-; Sigma Tau Delta, International English Honor Society, 1976-; Upsilon Nu Chapter sponsor, 1985-; Georgia Association of Women in Education, 1995-. **Honors/Awds:** Alpha Psi Alpha, Alpha Rho, Educator of the Year, 1976; City of New Orleans, Mayoral Award, 1979; Morehouse Prospective Students Seminar, Service Award, 1989; University of Georgia Student Affairs, Parents Association, Service Award, 1989; Gold Key Society, Honorary Membership, 1991; Phi Beta Kappa Society, 1994. **Special Achievements:** Masters thesis, University of Kentucky Microfilm Series, 1964; contributor, Notable Black American Women, 1991; presenter: National Honors Council, Annual National Conference, 1990, So Regional Conference, 1991, Soapstone symposium, DeKalb College, 1989; Presenter, Coll Language Assn, 1994, 1995, 1997; numerous book reviews; Journal of Negro History, asst editor, 1993-97, assoc editor, 1997-. **Home Addr:** 2853 Wright Dr SW, Atlanta, GA 30311. **Business Addr:** Professor, Morehouse College, 830 Westview Dr SW, Brawley Hall, Rm 120, Atlanta, GA 30314, (404)681-2800.

STEPHENS, ELSIE MARIE
Library administrator. **Personal:** Born Mar 9, 1948, Java, VA; daughter of Lucy Womack Stephens and Edward Monroe Stephens. **Educ:** Virginia State University, Petersburg, VA, BS, 1970; Drexel University, Philadelphia, PA, MS, 1982; University of Pittsburgh, Pittsburgh, PA, PhD, 1987. **Career:** Wilmington School District, Wilmington, DE, librarian, 1970-84; University of Pittsburgh, Pittsburgh, PA, res asst, 1984-87; CLSI, Inc, Newtonville, MA, mgr, 1988-90; Travelers Insurance Co, Hartford, CT, dir, 1990-. **Orgs:** Member, American Library Assn, 1985-; member, Black Caucus American Library Assn, 1985-; American Society for Information Science, 1989-; Special Libraries Assn, 1990-; Delta Sigma Theta Sorority, Inc, 1989-. **Business Addr:** Director, The Information Exchange, Travelers Insurance Co, One Tower Sq, Hartford, CT 06183.

STEPHENS, GEORGE BENJAMIN DAVIS
Physician. **Personal:** Born Oct 12, 1904, Norfolk, VA; married Dolores Shirley Carr. **Educ:** Hampton Inst Hampton VA, dip 1924; Howard Univ Washington DC, BS 1930; Howard U, MD 1935. **Career:** Priv Pract, physician 1935-; blank for box structure which folds into box or box with tray, inventor 1980. **Orgs:** Mem Phi Beta Sigma Frat. **Honors/Awds:** Recip 50-Mile Swim Awd Hampton Inst ARC 1965.

STEPHENS, HERBERT MALONE
Judge (retired). **Personal:** Born Jul 10, 1918, Okmulgee, OK; married Lillian; children: Sydney, Sheri. **Educ:** Morehouse Coll, BA 1938; Univ of Washington Law School, juris doctorate 1950. **Career:** King Co Seattle WA, deputy prosecuting atty 1952-56; Seattle Dist Court, judge protem 1968-73; WA State, supreme court judge pro tem, retired 1989. **Orgs:** Past mem Amer Bar Assn; Amer Judicial Soc 1961-62; mem WA State & Seattle-King Co Bar Assns; mem chmn Seattle Civil Serv Comm 1963-71; mem WA State Human Rights Com 1965-60; chmn bd dirs Neighborhood Inc. **Military Serv:** USAF 1943-46. **Business Addr:** Superior Court Judge, Washington Superior Court, King Co Courthouse, Seattle, WA 98104.

STEPHENS, HERMAN ALVIN
Physician. **Personal:** Born Nov 19, 1914, Yazoo City, MS; married Kathryn; children: Patricia, Herman, Edgar, Thelma, Benjamin, Nelda, Alva, Yvette. **Educ:** Ferris Inst, PhC 1930; Univ Detroit, PhB 1932; Meharry Med Coll, MD 1936. **Career:** Stephens Nursing Home, fndr operator 1956-; VA Hosp, acting chf psychiatry 1966-71; VA Reg Off, psychiat 1964-66; Pvt Prac, 1942-64; VA Hosp, resd 1938-42; Provident Hosp Training Sch, intern 1936-37. **Orgs:** Mem bd dir Lexington YMCA; Meth Ch; Alpha Phi Alpha Frat; Pilgrim Bapt Ch; YMCA; flw Am Geriatric Soc; Nat Med Assn; AMA; mem Mil Surgeons US. **Honors/Awds:** Two Cerr merit Commonwealth KY 1966; cit meritorious serv Pers Com 1966; physician yr State KY 1966. **Business Addr:** PO Box 11786, Lexington, KY 40578.

STEPHENS, JAMAIN
Professional football player. **Personal:** Born Jan 9, 1974, Lumberton, NC. **Educ:** North Carolina A&T, attended. **Career:** Pittsburgh Steelers, tackle, 1997-. **Business Addr:** Professional Football Player, Pittsburgh Steelers, Three Rivers Stadium, 300 Stadium Circle, Pittsburgh, PA 15212, (412)323-1200.

STEPHENS, JAMES ANTHONY. See Obituaries section.

STEPHENS, JOSEPH, JR.
Professional basketball player. **Personal:** Born Jan 28, 1973; son of Cheryl and Joseph Stephens, Sr. **Educ:** Arkansas-Little Rock, attended. **Career:** Houston Rockets, forward, 1996-. **Business Addr:** Professional Basketball Player, Houston Rockets, PO Box 272349, Houston, TX 77277, (713)627-0600.

STEPHENS, JUANITA K.
Recording company executive. **Personal:** Born Dec 14, 1953, New York, NY; daughter of Margaret and Daniel. **Educ:** Word Processing, computers, 1978; psychology, 1979. **Career:** MCA Records, vice pres, artist development & publicity, 1983-90; recording artist Bobby Brown, independent manager, 1990-92; Mercury Records, vice pres, artist development & publicity, currently. **Business Phone:** (212)333-8017.

STEPHENS, LEE B., JR.
Educator. **Personal:** Born Oct 22, 1925, Atlanta, GA; son of Margie R Stephens and Lee B Stephens; married Betty S Stephens; children: Lee B III, Gary B, David B. **Educ:** Morehouse Coll, BS 1947; Atlanta Univ, MS 1950; State Univ IA, PhD 1957. **Career:** Dillard Univ, instr biology 1950-53; NC Coll, instr biology 1953-54; So Univ, assoc prof biology 1957-59, prof biology 1959-62; CA State Univ, asst prof biology 1962-65, assoc prof biology 1965-70, prof biology 1970-; assoc dean sch natl sci, 1975-83; prof emeritus, 1983. **Orgs:** Mem Soc of Sigma Xi; Amer Soc Zoologists; Amer Microscopital Soc; Predoctoral fellowships; Natl Med Fellowship Inc; NSF grants to study at Hopkins Marine Sta of Stanford Univ; rsch & study grant Marine Biol Lab NSF; rsch grants NSF, Long Beach State Coll Found. **Honors/Awds:** Author articles publ in sci jours, J Exp Zool, Ann Ent Soc Amer, Amer Zool, Trans Am Microscopical Socl J Histochem & Cytochem.

STEPHENS, PAUL A.
Dentist. **Personal:** Born Feb 28, 1921, Muskogee, OK; son of Maudie Wynn and Lonny Stephens; divorced; children: Marsha W Wilson, Paul A Jr, Derek M. **Educ:** Howard Univ, BS 1942, DDS 1945. **Career:** Coll of Dentistry Howard Univ, instr 1945-46; self-employed dentist, Gary, IN, 1946-. **Orgs:** Pres Gary IN Bd of Health 1973-79; pres Asso Med Cntr 1978-80; pres IN State Bd of Dental Exam 1978-80; mem IN Univ, Purdue Univ Adv Bd 1974-80; pres IN Acad Gen Dentistry 1980-81; vice pres Reg 7 OH-IN-Acad Gen Dentistry 1980-81; Chi Lambda Kappa; Amer Coll Dentistry; vice pres, Academy of General Denistry, 1990-91; president, 1992-93. **Honors/Awds:** Howard Univ Dentist of Yr Intl Coll of Dentists 1979; Alpha Phi Alpha Piere Fauchard Acad; life mem NAACP, Acad of Dentist Intl; rec of ASTP. **Military Serv:** US Army, pfc, 1943-45. **Home Addr:** 1901 Taft St, Gary, IN 46404.

STEPHENS, PHYGENAU
Editor. **Personal:** Born Jun 4, 1923, Ann Arbor, MI; widowed. **Educ:** Wilberforce Univ, BA; Univ of Detroit, currently working on MA. **Career:** Kodday Prod & Control City Marketing Inc, natl publ; MI Challenger Newspaper, women's editor; The Weldon Group Ltd, pres; Detroit Courier, writer; WGPR-FM, comm 4 yrs; pub rel 7yrs; elem tchr; business coll tchr; newspapers women's editor; newspaper food editor; lecturer. **Orgs:** Mem Nat Assn of Market Devel; pub rel Booker T Wash Bus Assn; 2nd vice pres Nat Assn of Media Women Inc; Detroit Urban League Guild; United Coll Fund;League of Cath Women; African Art Com; Nat Assn of Negro Bus Prof Women; Enconta Doras Fisher YMCA; Fund Raiser; Downtown YWCA; Wolverrine Rep Assn; Detroit Round Table of Christ Jews; Am Women in Radio & TV; Interracial Cncl; Detroit Women's Advertising Club; Black Women's Pol Caucus Group; Speakers Bur of United Found; bd mem Delta Sigma Theta Home for Girls; reg dir Capital Formation for Nat Awds. **Honors/Awds:** Pres awd NAMW; Gold Key Awd; Nat Boy's Club & Girl's Club of Am; wednesday luncheon awd BTWBA; Betty Jane Everett awd NAMWA; most outstng pub rel woman NAMW.

STEPHENS, WALLACE O'LEARY
Engineering executive. **Personal:** Born Aug 5, 1942, Macon, GA; son of Hazel Smith Stephens and Clarence Stephens; married Alexis Sellers Stephens, Jul 23, 1966; children: Jill Katrina. **Educ:** Tuskegee Institute, Tuskegee, AL, BS, electronics, 1964; Arizona State University, Tempe, AZ, 1964; George Washington University, Washington, DC, 1970-72. **Career:** US Department of the Navy, Washington, DC, engineer, 1969-74; Federal Aviation Administration, Washington, DC, engineer, 1974-79; Stephens Engineering Co, Inc, Greenbelt, MD, president and CEO, 1979-. **Orgs:** President and member, board of directors, Prince George's Chamber of Commerce, 1994-95; director, Bowie State College; steering committee, director, Prince George's School Board Council of Business and Industry; Suburban MD High Technology Council, Prince George's County Chapter, board of directors; Maryland International Trade Institute. **Honors/Awds:** Washington Technology Fast 50 CEO's, Washington Technology Publication, 1987-90; Minority Business of the Year, Federal Aviation Administration, 1986; Top 100 Minority Businesses, Black Enterprise Magazine, past 6 years; Minority Business of the Year, National Business League of Southern Maryland, 1991. **Military Serv:** US Navy, Lt, 1964-69; outstanding service. **Business Addr:** Chairman, CEO, Stephens Engineering Co, Inc, 4601 Forbes Blvd, Ste 300, Lanham, MD 20706.

STEPHENS, WILLIAM HAYNES
Judge. **Personal:** Born Mar 2, 1935, New Orleans, LA; son of Myrtle Stephens and William Stephens; children: Michael (deceased), Stuart, Patrick. **Educ:** San Jose State Univ San Jose CA, BA 1956; Univ of California Hastings Coll of Law, JD 1967. **Career:** Superior Court, County of Marin CA, judge, 1988-; Municipal Court County of Marin CA, judge 1979-; law office of William H Stephens, atty at law 1972-79; Bagley/Bianchi & Sheeks, assoc atty 1969-72; Contra & Costa Co, deputy public defender 1968-69; Natl Labor Relations Bd, atty 1968; Marin Co Bar Assn, dir 1970-73; Marin Co Human Rights Commn, chmn 1977-79; Marin Co Dist, dist counsel 1977-79; Marin Co Superior Ct, arbitrator 1977-79; California Agr Labor Relations Bd, admin law officer 1978-79. **Orgs:** Amer Heart Assn, 1985-; California Judges Assn, Natl Bar Assn, Amer Bar Assn. **Business Addr:** Judge, County of Marin Hall Justice, Civic Center, San Rafael, CA 94903.

STEPHENSON, ALLAN ANTHONY
Government official. **Personal:** Born Oct 27, 1937, New York, NY; married Deloris; children: Diane, Allan Jr. **Educ:** Morgan St Coll, BA 1960; Ny City Univ John Jay Sch of Crim Just, postgrad. **Career:** US Dept of Commerce Ofc of Minor Bus Enterprise, acting dir & dep dir for operations; reg dir 1973-77, br chief 1970-73; Assist Negro Bus, exec dir 1968-69; Urban League of Westchester Co, asso exec dir 1967-68; Urban League of Westchester Co, dir econ devel & employ 1966-67; Bus Educ Train Intgerracial Coun for Bus Oppor, asso dir 1965-66. **Orgs:** Bd mem exec com NY St Coun of Urban Leagues 1967-68; sec bd of dir Assn to Assist Negro Bus 1967-70; mem bd of dir Oakland Mills Youth Conf 1975-76; adv com Comp Statewide Plan for Vocation Rehab Serv 1967-69; mem bd of dir Sr Personnel Employ Com 1967-69; Statewide Manpwr Panel on Job Train Employ 1967-69; US Dept of Commerce Incent Awards Com 1975-77; Judo & Karate Club of Baltimore;

Roots Asso Adv Com Comp Statewide Plan for VocatRehab Serv 1965. **Honors/Awds:** Outst Perf Awd US Dept of Commerce 1974-75; Presidential Cit 1975. **Military Serv:** AUS res 1964-67; NYNG 1961-64. **Business Addr:** 14th Constitution Ave NW, Rm 5053, Washington, DC 20230.

STEPHENSON, CAROLYN L.
Educational administrator. **Personal:** Born Jul 27, 1945, Brownsville, TN; daughter of Fannie Fuqua (deceased) and James Lee (deceased). **Educ:** Univ of KY, AA, JCC Sociology 1974; Univ of Louisville, BS Guid & Cnslng 1976; Univ of Louisville Coll, MEd, student personnel 1978. **Career:** Univ of Louisville, couns Ath Dept 1977; Univ of Louisville, fncl aid & intern 1977; Univ of Louisville, couns W Louisville Educ Prog 1976; MD Sch of Art & Design, consult 1977; Louisville School of Art, Louisville, KY, assoc dir/dir of fin aid, 1977-83; Univ of Louisville, Louisville, KY, coordinator of grad/prof recruit, 1983-86, coordinator of minority student services, 1986-. **Orgs:** Chrprsn Annual Conf on Black Family Univ of Louisville Pan African Study 1979-80; panel reader Talent Srch Prog Offc Educ Washington 1980; mem KY Assn of Stdnt Fncl Aid Adminstrn; KASFAA 1977-80; mem, So Assn of Student Financial Aid Adminstrn SASFAA Z1977-80; vice chair, Services & Facilities Comm of the Univ of Louisville Staff Senate, 1991; public relations chair, INCOME, Inc, 1985-91; planning comm, Natl Conference on the Black Family in America, 1983-. **Honors/Awds:** Achievement Awd New Aid Admstrn, So Assn of Student Fin Aid Adminstrn 1977-78; grad assistantship, Univ of Louisville 1977; spkr Fncl Aid Awrnes Wk Prsntatn WLOU Educ 1979. **Business Addr:** Coordinator of Minority Student Services, University of Louisville, 120 East Brandeis St, 39G, 109, Louisville, KY 40292.

STEPHENSON, CHARLES E., III
Fast-food executive. **Career:** Stepco of South Carolina Inc, Columbia, chief exec.

STEPHENSON, DAMA F.
Banker. **Personal:** Born Oct 23, 1955, Kansas City, MO; daughter of Patricia M Stephenson and Clarence R Stephenson Sr. **Educ:** Howard University, BA, 1977; George Washington University, MBA, 1981. **Career:** US Department of State, Agency for International Development, foreign affairs specialist, 1979-80; US Department of Commercwe, International Trade Administration, trade assistant, 1980; CoreStates, Philadelphia National Bank, assistant vice pres, 1981-90; Commerce Bank of Kansas City NA, vice pres, 1990-. **Orgs:** National Black MBA Association, Chapter Advisory Board, 1990-; The Kansas City 100 Most Influential Charitable Organizations, treasurer, 1991-92; Kansas City Area March of Dimes, board member, 1992-; Are You Committed Kansas City, Inc, board member, 1992-; The Central Exchange, Annual Meeting Committee chair, 1992-. **Honors/Awds:** National Black MBA Association, Chapter Member of the Year, 1989; Dollars and Sense Magazine, Outstanding Business & Professional Award, 1991; High Twelve International, Wolcott Fellowship, 1980. **Business Addr:** Vice Pres, Commerce Bank of Kansas City, NA, PO Box 419248, BB 17-1, Kansas City, MO 64141-6248, (816)234-2709.

STEPHENSON, DWIGHT EUGENE
Professional football player (retired). **Personal:** Born Nov 20, 1957, Murfreesboro, NC; married Dinah; children: Dwight Jr. **Educ:** Univ of Alabama, attended. **Career:** Miami Dolphins, center, 1980-86. **Orgs:** Involved in charity work in South FL including efforts for Baby House (Cerebral Palsy) and Boy Scouts. **Honors/Awds:** Silver Medal of Valor (highest award that can be bestowed upon a civilian), Miami-Dade Police Dept, 1984; Man of the Year, Hampton VA; named team's outstanding offensive lineman for 4 straight seasons; All-NFL Squads, AP, NEA and PFWA; All-AFC, Football News, UPI; All-Pro, Sporting News, Pro Football Weekly; NFLPA Offensive Lineman of the Year; USA Today NFL Offensive Lineman of the Year; played in Pro Bowl, 1983-86 seasons.

STEPHNEY, BILL
Music executive. **Career:** StepSun Music Entertainment, pres/CEO, 1992-. **Business Addr:** President/CEO, Step Sun Music Entertainment, 1616 22nd St, 10th Fl, New York, NY 10010, (212)353-2900.

STEPP, MARC
Association executive. **Personal:** Born Jan 31, 1923, Versailles, KY; married Elanor. **Educ:** Wolverine Trade Sch, 1949; Lewis Bus Sch, 1951; Univ of Detroit, BBA 1963. **Career:** Intl Union, vp; UAW Region 1b, asst dir; Common Pleas Ct, clerk; UAW Region 1b, intl rep; Comm Hlth Assn, asst dir; Univ of Detroit-Mercy, Urban Community Affairs, dir, currently. **Orgs:** UAW Intl; exec bd dir UAW Soc Tech Educ Prgm; Job Devel Training Prgm, dir; UAW SE MI Comm Action Prgm, chmn; Dexter Ave Bapt Ch; NAACP; Trade Union Ldrshp Counc; Coalition of Black Trade Unionists; Demcrt Black Caucus Steering Com; mem Dem Nat Com. **Honors/Awds:** Honorary PhD, Lewis Coll of Business, 1986, Saginaw State Univ, 1990, Univ of Detroit, 1990. **Military Serv:** US Army, 1943-46. **Business Addr:** Executive Director, Urban & Community Affairs, University of Detroit-Mercy, 4001 W McNichols, Detroit, MI 48221.

STEPPE, CECIL H.
Law enforcement official. **Personal:** Born Jan 31, 1933, Versailles, KY; son of Esther Stepp and Grant Stepp; married Evelyn Lee Elliott; children: Gregory, Russell, Steven, Cecily, Annette. **Educ:** San Diego City Coll, AA 1961; CA Western Univ, BA 1964; Grossmont Coll, Teaching Credential 1972. **Career:** Grossmont Coll, instr criminology dept 1969-73; San Diego Cty CA, suprv probation officer 1968-73, dir juvenile intake 1973-75, asst supt of juvenile hall 1975, responsible for finalization of due-process system for adult inst 1975-76; dir Camp West Fork 1976-77, dir adult inst 1977-80, chief probation officer, beginning 1980; San Diego County, Department of Social Svcs, director, currently. **Orgs:** Mem Black Leadership Council 1980; co-covenor Black Cty Admin 1980; vice pres Chief Probation Officers of CA 1983; bd mem Amer Probation & Parole Assn 1984; chmn State Advisory Bd Victim/Witness Prog 1984; bd mem St Youth Prog; Mayors Crime Commiss, Criminal Justice Council; Interagency Youth Adv Comm; mem Natl Forum for Black Public Admin, CA Black Correction Coalition, Amer Probation & Parole Assoc, Chief Probation & Parole Assoc, Chief Probation Officers of CA, Black Leadership Council, San Diego Cty Exec Assoc; San Diego Rotary; CA Welfare Directors Association; American Public Welfare Association; Child Welfare League of America. **Honors/Awds:** Equal Oppty San Diego Urban League 1983; Valuable Serv San Diego Cty Foster Parent Assn 1984; National Probation Executive of the Year 1989. **Military Serv:** USAF a 1/c 1952-56. **Business Addr:** Director, Social Svcs, San Diego County, Department of Social Svcs, 1255 Imperial Ave, San Diego, CA 92101.

STEPTO, ROBERT BURNS
Educator. **Personal:** Born Oct 28, 1945, Chicago, IL; son of Anna Burns Stepto and Robert C Stepto; married Michele A Leiss, Jun 21, 1967; children: Gabriel Burns Stepto, Rafael Hawkins Stepto. **Educ:** Trinity College, Hartford CT, BA (cum laude), English, 1966; Stanford University, Stanford, CA, MA, 1968, PhD, 1974. **Career:** Williams College, Williamstown, MA, assistant professor, 1971-74; Yale University, New Haven, CT, assistant professor, 1974-79, associate professor, 1979-84, professor, 1984-. **Orgs:** Chair, MLA Commn on the Literatures & Languages of America, 1977-78; Connecticut Humanities Council, 1980-82; trustee, Trinity College, 1982-92; associate editor, Callaloo, 1984-88; advisor, Yale-New Haven Teachers Institute, 1985-, Anson Phelps Stokes Institute, 1985-; board of editors, American Literature, 1987-88; advisor, Southern Connecticut Library Council, 1987; advisory editor, Callaloo, 1988-. **Honors/Awds:** Woodrow Wilson Fellowship, Woodrow Wilson Foundation, 1966-67; Morse Fellowship, Yale University, 1977-78; From Behind the Veil: A Study of Afro-Amer Narrative, 1979; Edited with M Harper, Chant of Saints: Afro-Amer Literature, Art, Scholarship, 1979; Edited with D Fisher, D Fisher, Afro-Amer Literature: The Reconstruction of Instinction, 1979; Senior Fellowship, National Endowment for the Humanities, 1981-82; Alumni Medal, Trinity College, 1986; Editor, The Selected Poems of Jay Wright, 1987; Contributor to the Columbia Literary History of the United States, 1987; Robert Frost Professor, Brad Loaf School of English, 1995; Co-Editor of The Harpet American Literature since 1992. **Business Addr:** Professor, English American Studies, African-American Studies, Yale University, PO Box 203388, New Haven, CT 06520-3388.

STEPTOE, LAMONT BROWN
Arts administrator, poet, publisher, photographer. **Personal:** Born Feb 9, 1949, Pittsburgh, PA; son of Maybelle Dawson Steptoe Boyd (deceased) and Sam Brown (deceased); children: LaMer Belle Steptoe. **Educ:** Temple University, Philadelphia, PA, BS, 1975. **Career:** WPVI-TV, assignment editor, 1975-77; Freedom Theater, dir of public relations, 1978-79; Williams, Browne and Earle, rental, 1980-83; painted Bride Art Center, 1983-92; poetry consultant, theater mgr, 1983-; Whirlwind Press, founder, publisher, 1987-; Walt Whitman Cultural Arts Center, literary coordinator, 1992-. **Orgs:** Steering committee, Union of Writers of African Descent, 1990-; advisory board, Before Columbus Foundation, 1987-; advisory board, Moonstone, Inc. **Honors/Awds:** Grant for video, Electrical Matters, Pennsylvania Council of the Arts, 1990; Poetry Award, First Annual South Street Star Poetry Award, South Street Star, 1984; Chaplin's Award, Community Enrichment, Chapel of Four, 1989; Kwanza Award, Africa Network, poetry book, American Morning/Mourning, 1990; Kwanza Award, Africa Network, 1993; Poetry book, Mad Minute; 1994, Nomination for Pushcart Prize, Best of Small Presses by Negative Capability Press for poem, "Disappearance," about the life of Richard Wright; Pennsylvania Council on the Arts Literary Fellowship, 1996-. **Special Achievements:** Author: Crimson River, American Morning/Mourning, Small Steps and Toes, Mad Minute, Uncle's South China Sea Blue Nightmare; Dusty Road; In the Kitchens of the Masters; Spookism; and The Hotness of Blood: Part 1. **Military Serv:** US Army, Sgt, 1968-70; Army Commendation, Combat Infantry Badge, Bronze Star, Vietnam Campaign and Service Ribbons. **Business Addr:** Publisher, Founder, Whirlwind Press, PO Box 109, Camden, NJ 08101-0109.

STEPTOE, SONJA
Journalist. **Personal:** Born Jun 16, 1960, Lutcher, LA; daughter of Rosa Jane Jordan Steptoe and Eldridge W Steptoe Jr. **Educ:** University of Missouri, Columbia, MO, BJ, 1982, AB, 1982; Duke University Law School, Durham, NC, JD, 1985. **Career:** Dow Jones & Co, New York, NY, staff reporter, Wall Street Journal, 1985-90; Time Inc, New York, NY, staff writer, Sports Illustrated, 1990-96, senior editor, 1996-97; National correspondent, CNNSI, 1997-. **Orgs:** Board of directors, Associated Black Charities, New York, 1989-94; member, American Bar Association, 1986-; member, Pennsylvania Bar Association, 1986-; member, National Association of Black Journalists, 1987-; board of directors, University of Missouri Arts & Science Alumni Assn, 1986-97; natl correspondent, CNNSI, 1997-. **Honors/Awds:** Harry S Truman Scholar; Truman Scholarship Foundation, 1980. **Business Addr:** National Correspondent, CNN-Sports Illustrated, Time-Warner Inc, 1271 Avenue of the Americas, Time-Life Building, Room 1840, New York, NY 10020.

STERLING, CHARLES A.
Business executive, publisher. **Personal:** Born Aug 17, 1932, Chicago, IL; son of Delilah Sterling and Lott Sterling; divorced; children: Dana Sterling Davis. **Educ:** Lake Forest Coll, BA 1954; Northwestern Univ, Business Admin Grad; Marquette Univ, Business Admin Grad; Washington Univ, Business Admin. **Career:** Arnold & Assoc Memphis, vice pres 1959-60; Sterling & Assoc, head of firm 1960-63; Helene Curtis Inc Chicago, natl sales mgr special markets, 1963-66; Tuesday Publ Inc Chicago, acct exec 1965-66; P Lorillard Co New York, asst gen sales mgr 1966-68; Summit Lab Indianapolis Inc, gen sales mgr 1970-72; New York, dir devel council 1972-74; Black Sports Mag, vice pres mktg & devel 1974-75; Tuesday Mag, assoc publ 1974-76; Araser Inc, vice pres sales 1976-78; Waters of Saratoga Springs Inc, pres & Chief exec 1978-84; Minority Business Exchange, vice pres 1984-90; Obusty Local Development Corp, exec dir, 1990-97; Training and Employment Council(TEC)/Brooklyn, dir, 1998-. **Orgs:** Pres Detroit & New York Chap Natl Assn Market Devel 1968-70; bd mem Council Concerned Black Exec 1968-70, 1972-75; exec bd Boy Scouts of Amer Saratoga Springs 1979-83; bd mem, 1980-84, mem Private Industry Council of Saratoga Springs 1979-; state dir Jr C of C; mem Alpha Phi Alpha; vice pres Saratoga NAACP 1979-83; pres Men's Group of Northside Ctr 1972-74; former pres Chicago Pan-Hellenic Council; alumni bd gov Lake Forest Coll 1974-80; pres, Business Adv Council, Bethune-Cookman Coll, 1989-; bd mem, Staten Island Children's Council, 1989-. **Honors/Awds:** Distinguished Alumni Award Lake Forest Coll 1973; 2000 Men of Achievement Award England 1969; received recognition Natl Poetry Soc; Athletic Hall of Fame Lake Forest Coll 1976; Congressional Citation from Congressmen Edolphus Towns for Lifetime Accomplishments. **Home Addr:** 625 E 95th St, Brooklyn, NY 11236.

STERLING, H. DWIGHT, SR.
Newspaper executive. **Personal:** Born Jun 7, 1944, Waco, TX; son of Susie Lucille Sterling and Lawrence Sterling Sr; divorced; children: Sherilyn L Vaughn, H Dwight Jr, Keith Morris, Dana, Shantelle. **Educ:** Merritt College, AA, 1969; California State University, BA, 1972; University of California Berkeley, MA, 1973. **Career:** County of Alameda, regional administrator, 1974-78; City of Oakland, district coordinator, 1978-86; Oakland Cancer Control Program, public health educator, 1986-89; National University, Urban & Regional Planning, assistant professor, 1990-91; Dwight Sterling Associates, management consultant, 1986-; Post Newspaper, executive assistant, 1992-. **Orgs:** Pan African Chamber of Commerce, Planning Committee, chairman, 1991-92; Alpha Phi Alpha Fraternity, Gamma Phi Lambda Chapter, 1984; Seventh Step Foundation, board of directors, 1987-90, executive director, 1991-92; Association of Black Health Educators, 1973-92; Bay Area Black Professional Health Network, 1974; Black Public Administrator Association, 1979; American Public Health Association, 1974; Bethel Missionary Baptist Church, 1962; West Coast Black Publishers Assn, 1992; Assault on Illiteracy Process, division leader, 1993. **Honors/Awds:** US Public Health Service, Scholarship, 1972; US Defense Department, Superior Accomplishment, 1968; City of Oakland Mayor Dwight Sterling Day Proclamation, 1986; Alameda County, Certificate of Appreciation, for training 450 managers on management by objectives, 1975. **Military Serv:** US Army, e-4, 1963-66; Expert Rifle, 1963, US Defense Service Medal, 1966. **Home Addr:** 5441 Ygnacio Ave, Oakland, CA 94601, (510)533-8094.

STERLING, JEFFREY EMERY
Physician. **Personal:** Born Jan 15, 1964, Chicago, IL; son of Ollie Mae Emerson Sterling and John Estes Sterling Sr. **Educ:** Northwestern Univ, Evanston, IL, BA, psychology, 1985; Harvard Univ School of Public Health, Boston, MA, MPH, 1991; Univ of IL Coll of Medicine, Peoria, IL, MD, 1991. **Career:** Boston City Hosp Corp, Boston, MA, consultant to the Comm, 1990; Cook County Hosp, Chicago, IL, resident physician-transitional/emergency medicine, 1991-. **Orgs:** Chmn, bd of dir, Student Natl Medical Assn, Inc, 1988-91; project mgr, Wellness Council of Greater Boston Applied Research Forum, 1989-90; pres, One Step Before Premedical Or, 1982-84; vice pres, Black Student Alliance, Northwestern Univ, 1983-84; cofndr, pres, Junior Auxiliary of the Hyde Park Neighborhood

Club, 1981-82. **Honors/Awds:** Jeffrey E Sterling, MD, MPH Gen Endowment Fund established by Student Natl Med Assn, 1991; Elected Chairman Emeritus, Student Natl Med Assn, 1991; President's Certificate of Appreciation, Lincoln Univ, 1990; IL Dept of Public Health Scholarship, IDPH, 1986-1991. **Business Addr:** Chairman Emeritus, Student Natl Medical Assn Inc, 1012 Tenth St, Washington, DC 20001.

STETH, RAYMOND. See Obituaries section.

STETSON, JEFFREY P.
Educator. **Personal:** Born Jun 5, 1948, New York, NY; son of Isabella Stetson and John Stetson; married Carmen Hayward. **Educ:** Framingham State Coll, BA 1973; Boston Univ, EdM 1974, ABD 1976. **Career:** MA State Coll System, dir of affirmative action & alternatives for individual develop 1974-79; Univ of Lovell, dir of affirmative action 1979; CA State Univ, dean of faculty & staff 1979-86, dir of public affairs 1986-. **Orgs:** Pres & mem bd dirs Black Alliance for Scholarship & Educ 1981-84; pres & mem bd dirs Concerned Helpers of Inner Comm Endeavors 1984-; mem NAACP, Urban League, Amer Assoc of Affirmative Action, Dramatists Guild, Los Angeles Black Playwrights, Los Angeles Actor's Theatre Playwrights Lab; Writers Guild of Amer, West. **Honors/Awds:** Whitney Young Jr Fellowship Boston Univ 1975; CHOICE Comm Serv Awd 1984; Louis B Mayer Awd for Outstanding Achievement in Playwrighting 1985; 8 NAACP Theatre Image Awards 1987; 6 NY Audelco Theatre nominations; Theodore Ward Theatre Award 1989; Production of The Meeting, Amer Playhouse, 1989; Natl Playwrights Conf 1988. **Home Addr:** 4267 Marina City Dr. Unit 1002, Marina Del Rey, CA 90292-5812. **Business Addr:** Dean Faculty & Staff Affairs, California State Univ, 400 Golden Shore, Long Beach, CA 90802.

STEVENS, ALTHEA WILLIAMS
Educator. **Personal:** Born Oct 23, 1931, Norfolk, VA. **Educ:** CA St Univ Los Angeles, BS 1969; Rutgers U, MEd 1974; Rutgers U, doctoral Can. **Career:** Western Wyoming Coll, div chrmn, assoc prof; Bergen Co Comm Coll, prof bus admin 1977-78; Montclair State Coll, instr bus educ & off sys adm 1975-78; Camden HS, instr data processing 1970-75; Los Angeles Co Probation Dept, stat coor 196-68. **Orgs:** Consult comp Sweetwater Co WY Planning Bd 1978-79; gen prb mem WY Bd of Cert Pub Accts 1980-83; Assn Computer Mgmt AVA, NBEA,WBEA. **Honors/Awds:** Omicron Tau Theta; Delta Pi Espilon. **Business Addr:** Western Wyoming College, PO Box 428, Rock Springs, WY 82901.

STEVENS, CLEVELAND
Attorney. **Personal:** Born Mar 25, 1927, Loris, SC; married Leola M Dewitt. **Educ:** SC State Coll, AB, LLB 1953. **Career:** Legal Clerk 1953; Horry County, public defender; USAF Judge Adv Corp, 1955-59; Conway, SC, priv pract 1960-66; US Dept Agr DC, ofc gen coun 1966-70; Neighborhood Legal Assis Prog Inc & Charleston, dir 1972. **Orgs:** Mem SC Supreme Ct; US Dist Ct for SC; US Ct of Appeals, 4th Cir; US Supreme Ct. **Honors/Awds:** Reginald Heber Smith Fellow 1970-72; mem Kappa Alpha Psi, Mason & Shriner; aptd by Gov of SC to Advi Coun for Consumer Protection, Aug 1972. **Business Addr:** Horry County, PO Box 1666, Conway, SC 29526.

STEVENS, GEORGE EDWARD, JR.
Educator. **Personal:** Born Mar 7, 1942, Philadelphia, PA; son of Marstella Smalls Harvey and George Edward Stevens; married Pamela Ann Giffhorn Stevens, May 30, 1977; children: Kwanza B, Charlie E. **Educ:** Delaware State Univ, Dover, DE, BBA, 1971; Washington University, St Louis, MO, MBA, 1973; Thomas A Edison College, Princeton, NJ, BA, social sciences, 1976; Kent State University, Kent, OH, DBA, 1979. **Career:** Xerox Corporation, Rochester, NY, financial analyst, 1972; Rohm & Haas Co, Philadelphia, PA, employee relations, 1973-75; Kent State University, Kent, OH, instructor, 1978-79; Arizona State Univ, Tempe, AZ, asst prof assoc prof, 1979-83; Univ of Central Florida, Orlando, FL, assoc prof, prof interim dean, 1983-90; Oakland University, Rochester, MI, professor & dean, 1991-. **Orgs:** Academy of Management; Decision Sciences Institute; Rotary Club of Kent, OH, bd mem; KeyBank Community Service Bd, bd mem; Society for the Advancement of Management, bd mem; Small Business Council of Northeast OH, dir; Ken Regional Business Alliance, trustee; AARP Academic Advisory Council, bd mem. **Honors/Awds:** College of Business Researcher of the Year, Univ Central Florida, 1986, 1989; Scroll Club (Outstanding Research), Univ Central Florida, 1988; Quill Club, Book Authors Group, Univ of Central Florida, 1991; AARP Andrus Fund Foundation Grant, 1989; NAFEO Distinguished Alumni Award, 1986; various honor societies, Alpha Kappa Mu, Beta Gamma Sigma, Phi Kappa Phi; Golden Key Honor Society; Delaware State University Alumni Hall of Fame, 1997. **Special Achievements:** Author, Cases and Exercises in Human Resource Management. **Military Serv:** Army, Specialist 4, 1964-66; Good Conduct Medal. **Business Addr:** Dean, College of Business Administration & Graduate School of Management, Kent State University, Kent, OH 44242-0001, (330)672-2772.

STEVENS, GEORGE L.
Administrative assistant. **Personal:** Born Feb 6, 1932, Junction City, LA; married Brenda Washington; children: Marc, Michelle, Eric, Gary. **Educ:** CA Comm Coll, AA, teacher credentials in ethnic studies; San Diego State Univ, BS, MA candidate. **Career:** San Diego Jr Coll & San Diego State Univ, instructor; General Dynamics, logistic analyst & engineering admin 1958-64; Lockheed Aircraft, engineering mgmt rep 1966; San Diego Urban League, dir job devel & placement 1967-68; Philco-Ford, dir of placement 1968-69; State of CA, job agent for state 1969-72; Co of San Diego, affirmative action officer 1972; Viewpoint News, dir of marketing & sales 1972-74; US Congressman Jim Bates, special asst. **Orgs:** Participant March on Montgomery w/Dr Martin Luther King 1964; Civil Rights March on San Francisco 1965; placed 512 black people on job without staff or financial assistance from agency in 1967 while working at Urban League; chmn of CORE, 1967-69; past chmn Congress of African People 1969-72; past city commr Model City Advisory bd, 1971-72; city commr San Diego Stadium Authority 1971-; pas mem bd dir NAACP; asst to pastor of Calvary Baptist Church. **Honors/Awds:** Black Fed Award 1963; Black Man of Year, 1968 Black Congress; organized Black & Mexican Amer Convention 1968; Civic Contribution Award 1973; author City Ordinance paving way for the first black to be elected to bd of educ; Religious Leader Award 1980; Freedom Award Black Achievement 1982; Fredrick Douglass Award, 1986. **Military Serv:** AUS 1953-55; Honorable Discharge.

STEVENS, JOHN THEODORE, SR.
Brewery marketing manager (retired). **Personal:** Born Feb 2, 1924, Detroit, MI; son of Helen Valaria White Stevens (deceased) and John Arthur Stevens (deceased); married Jimmie Rose Phillips, Jun 21, 1951; children: John T Jr, Sandra J. **Educ:** Wayne State Univ, Detroit MI, attended, 1947-50; Univ of Detroit, Detroit MI, attended, 1954-56. **Career:** Anheuser-Busch Inc, Detroit MI, branch salesman, 1954-63, special representative, 1963-66, regional representative, 1963-71, Los Angeles CA, dist mgr, 1971-81, Woodland Hills CA, mgr of special markets, Western Region, 1981-. **Orgs:** Life mem, NAACP; mem, Alpha Phi Alpha Frat, 1948-, Christ Good Shepherd Episcopal Church, 1971-, LA Chapter UNCF, 1973-; bd mem, Good Shepherd Manor, 1982-95; mem, chmmr, Los Angeles County Fire Dept, 1983-87; bd mem, Golden State Minority Found, 1986-; mem, Los Angeles County Fire Dept Advisory Bd, 1988-93; Prince Hall Masons, 1989-; bd of trustees, St Augustine's College. **Honors/Awds:** Honorary Doctorate of Humane Letters, Shorter Coll, Little Rock AR, 1987; Honorary Fire Chief, Compton CA Fire Dept, 1987; Enshrined in walk at Promenade of Providence in Watts, 1994. **Military Serv:** US Navy, machinist mate 3rd class, 1943-46. **Home Addr:** 3804 Lenawee Ave, Culver City, CA 90232.

STEVENS, LISA MARIA
Zoo curator, zoologist. **Personal:** Born Nov 20, 1955, Springfield, OH. **Educ:** Michigan State University, BS, 1979. **Career:** National Zoological Park, animal keeper, 1978-81, assistant curator, 1981-. **Orgs:** Potomac Valley Dressage Association, 1981-; Capital Dog Training Club, 1993-; American Zoo and Aquarium Association, 1981-87, 1996-; National Capital Day Lilly Club, 1994-96. **Business Addr:** Associate Curator, National Zoological Park/Smithsonian Institute, 3001 Connecticut Ave, NW, Washington, DC 20008, (202)673-4888.

STEVENS, MAXWELL MCDEW
Assistant dean of instruction. **Personal:** Born Dec 3, 1942, Savannah, GA. **Educ:** St Augustine Coll, BS 1964; Atlanta Univ, MBA 1970; Rutgers Univ, Ed D 1977. **Career:** Glenbrook Labs, chemist/Group Ldr 1964-68; Allied Chemical Corp, mktg Analyst 1970-72. **Orgs:** Pres Intrnl Coop Ed Assoc 1974; pres NJ Coop Ed Assoc 1974; pres Amer Mktg Assoc; advsry brd Mid-atlantic Training Cntr for Coop Ed, Temple Univ; advsry brd Somerset Cnty Day Care Cntr; advsry brd Ed Opptnty Fund Somerset Cnty Coll 1980; advsry brd Somerset Cnty Coll. **Home Addr:** 15 Llewellyn Pl, New Brunswick, NJ 08901. **Business Addr:** Assistant Dean of Instruction, Somerset County College, P O Box 3300, PO Box 3300, Somerville, NJ 08876.

STEVENS, MICHELLE
Journalist. **Personal:** Born Feb 20, 1951, Chicago, IL; divorced. **Educ:** Northwestern Univ, BS, journalism, 1973; John Marshall Law School, JD, 1982. **Career:** Chicago Sun-Times, asst at home editor, dep ed, editorial pages, 1983-94, ed, editorial pages, 1995-97. **Business Addr:** Editor, Editorial Pages, Chicago Sun-Times, 401 N Wabash Ave, Rm 415, Chicago, IL 60611, (312)321-2153.

STEVENS, PATRICIA ANN
Educational administrator. **Personal:** Born Dec 16, 1946, Rochester, NY; daughter of Alice Gray Elliott and Allee George Elliott; married Dwight Morrow Russell; children: Kimberly, Kenneth. **Educ:** Monroe Comm Coll, AS Liberal Arts 1968; State Univ of NY Brockport, BS History/Psychology 1970, MS Educ 1972, MS Higher Educ Admin 1979; Natl Bd for Certified Counselors Inc, certificate 1984; University of Buffalo, PhD candidate, 1994. **Career:** Monroe Comm Coll, counselor 1970-76, asst dir 1976-81, dir 1981-89; EOC SUNY Brockport executive dir 1989-92; Monroe County Government, cost reduction project manager, 1992-. **Orgs:** Genesee Settlement House Inc, 1982-; vice pres United Neighborhood Ctrs of Gr Rochester, 1982-; United Way, Board, 1994; Joe Joe While Growth League, treasurer, 1994. **Honors/Awds:** Outstanding Serv & Dedication Gr Rochester Area Spec Progs 1983; Outstanding Admin Standing Comm on Blacks in Higher Educ 1984; Distinguished Service Award Council of EOP Directors 1989; Leadership Award, Education Opportunity Centers Directors Council, 1994. **Business Addr:** Cost Reduction Project Manager, Monroe County Government, County Executive Office, 110 County Office Bldg, 39 W Main St, Rochester, NY 14614.

STEVENS, REATHA J.
Association executive. **Personal:** Born Jun 21, 1931, Quitman, GA; divorced; children: Elinda, Ronald, Lavon. **Educ:** Savannah State Coll, BS; Univ GA, further studies. **Career:** Family Counseling Center Savannah, community organizer social serv visitor 1966-69; Dept Family & Children Svcs, caseworker 1969-70; Dept Family & Children Svcs, casework supr 1970-72; Wesley & Community Centers Savannah, exec dir 1972-. **Orgs:** Mem Social Planning Steering Bd Unted Way Chatham Ctny 1970-; GA Assn on Young Children 1974-75; Armstrong-Savannah State Coll Social Work Adv Counc 1974-75; den mother 1964-65; bd dirs Frank Callen Boys Club 1965-72; treas 1970-71; consult Savannah Assn for the Blind 1968-69; bd dirs Savannah Assn for the Blind 1969-; vice pres 1970-73; mem Chatham Counc on Human Relations 1973-74; hon mem Barons of Goodwill Rehab Club. **Honors/Awds:** Cert recognition for Distinguished Achvmt in Humanitarianism 1974; plaque serv rendered to Blind of Savannah 1973; plaque outstanding serv to Frank Callen Boys Club 1972. **Business Addr:** Executive Dir, Wesley Community Center, Inc, 1601 Drayton St, Savannah, GA 31401.

STEVENS, ROCHELLE
Track & field athlete. **Personal:** Born Sep 8, 1966, Memphis, TN; daughter of Beatrice Holloway and John Holloway. **Educ:** Morgan State University, BS, 1988. **Career:** Olympic silver medalist, 1992; Olympic gold Medalist, 1996. **Orgs:** Rochelle Stevens Scholarship Fund; Rochelle Stevens Invitational Track Meet; Rochelle Stevens Sports Clinic; Rochelle Stevens Fan Club. **Honors/Awds:** Morgan State University, three-time Female Athlete of the Year, 1985-88, four time Most Valuable Athlete, School Record Holder at 100, 200, 400 meters; received key to city of Memphis; honorary black belt in tae kwon do, 1992; Honorary Ambassador of Maryland; Honorary Citizen of Parades; Eleven time NCAA All American; NCAA Division I 400 Meter Champion; Memphis Business Jnl Top 40 Under 40, 1997; Morgan State Univ "Varsity M" Club Hall of Fame, 1997. **Home Addr:** 7016 Apple Creek Dr, Memphis, TN 38125, (901)753-0661.

STEVENS, SHARON A.
Journalist. **Personal:** Born Jun 14, 1949, Chicago, IL. **Educ:** Northern IL Univ, BS Journalism 1971; Columbia Univ NYC, Fellowship 1972. **Career:** WBBM Radio Chicago IL, reporter/anchor 1971-75; NBC Radio NYC, reporter/anchor 1975-78; WGBH-TV Boston MA, news reporter 1978-82; KTVI-TV St Louis MO, news reporter/anchorwoman. **Orgs:** Mem Alpha Kappa Alpha Sor Inc 1968-, Amer Fed of Radio & TV Artists 1971-; Greater St Louis Assoc of Black Journalists 1985; mem, vp-broadcast, Natl Assoc of Black Journalists, currently; board of directors Girls Inc, 1990-; board of directors St Louis Journalism Review, 1989-. **Honors/Awds:** Plexiglass Awd YMCA Black Achievers Awd 1974; Recognition Cert Outstanding Young Women of Amer Inc 1977; Emmy Nomination Natl Acad of TV Arts & Sci Boston Chap 1979, 1980; Spec Recognition Boston Mag 1979; Black Excellence Awd Best Series TV 1987, Political Coverage TV 1987; "Yes I Can", outstanding journalist, St Louis Metro Sentinel Newspaper, 1990; Emmy Nomination, NATAS, 1989. **Business Addr:** Education Reporter, KSDK-TV, 1000 Market St., St Louis, MO 63101.

STEVENS, THOMAS LORENZO, JR.
Educational administration, chancellor. **Personal:** Born Apr 9, 1933, Pine Bluff, AR; married Opal D Scott. **Educ:** University of Arkansas, Pine Bluff, BS, 1954; University of Southern California, Los Angeles, MBA, 1975. **Career:** Los Angeles Trade-Tech College, president, 1976-; Los Angeles Community College District, director of budget, 1973-76, manager retirement service, 1969-73; Los Angeles Unified School District, accounting administrator, 1969, assistant retirement systems manager, 1967-69, accounting & financial management supervisor, 1961-67. **Orgs:** Board/vice president, Western Region Council on Black American Affairs, 1977-80; commission of finance, California Community & Junior College Association, 1977-80; political action committee, Association of California Community College Adminstors, 1977-80; Commerce Association, 1975-80; Association of MBA Executives, 1975-80; board of governors & directors, Goodwill Industrial, Inc, 1978-80. **Honors/Awds:** Community Service Award, Met Council for Responsive Adminstration, 1976; Citation of Appreciation for Community Service, Mayor Tom Bradley, 1976; Notable American Award, American Biographical Institute, 1976-77; Community Service Award, Assemblywomen Gwen Moore, 1979. **Military Serv:** USN storekeeper 3/c 1955-57. **Business Addr:** President/Chancellor, Los Angeles Trade Tech College, 400 W Washington Blvd, Los Angeles, CA 90015-4108.

STEVENS, TIMOTHY S.
Association executive. **Educ:** Urban & Regional Planning, M; Political Science, BA. **Career:** Pittsburgh Br NAACP, exec dir 1970-; NAACP, youth dir 1969; Juvenile Ct, probation ofcr 1968; Humble Oil Co Wash, DC, dealer sales trainee 1967-68. **Orgs:** Mem ASCAP; mem AFTRA; mem AGVA; sec-treas Stebro Enter; vice pres Arkel Pub Co & Stebro Records; bd mem Hill Hse Assn; bd mem Hill Dist YMCA; host radio shows WAMO, WWSW 14k radio; mem Allegheny Co Manpwr Advis Coun; mem Mayor's Art Comm; guest Mike Douglas Show 1972. **Honors/Awds:** Received Whitney Young Award Poor People's Dinner Pittsburgh 1974; "He's a Black Man" Award 1973; Comm Award for Entertainmnt & Comm Award for Achieve in Youth Social Work in Black Comm Pittsburgh Clubs United 1970. **Business Addr:** 6393 Stanton Ave, Pittsburgh, PA 15206.

STEVENS, WARREN SHERWOOD
Automobile company executive. **Personal:** Born Jul 8, 1941, Urbana, OH; married Audrey Doreen Stevens, May 30, 1965; children: Warren D, Shanee A. **Educ:** Ohio State Univ, BS Business Admin 1978. **Career:** USAF, admin clerk 1960-64; Juvenile Diagnostic Center, mail clerk 1964-65; Western Electric Co, cable former 1965-68 & 1971-73, tester 1968-71, Local IBEW union steward 1970-71, chief union steward 1971-73; Intl Harvester, employee interviewer 1973-74, industrial engineer 1974-80; St Regis Co, staff industrial engineer 1981-83; Urban Univ, dir of admin; City of Urbana, city councilman; Baumfolder Corp, time study & methods engineer 1984-85; Williams Hardware, salesman, clerk, cashier 1986-; Executive Fundlife Insurance Co, insurance agent 1987-89; Hoffman Wood Products, working supvr, starting 1989; Honda of America, Associate Relations, administrative staff member, 1989-. **Orgs:** Mem MTM Assn 1974; coach Urbana City Baseball Program 1978; mem Champaign Co Amer Cancer Soc Bd 1980; pres Champaign Co Amer Cancer Soc Bd 1981; mem Kiwanis Club 1982; coach Urbana City Baseball pony league 1983; coach Urbana Baseball Boosters 1983; coach Urbana City Baseball pony league 1984; adv mem Public Educ Comm Amer Cancer Soc Bd; former mem Urbana Local Outdoor Educ Bd; former sec Urbana Men's Progressive Club; Democratic mem Champaign Co Central Comm & Exec Comm; one of three Black men to organize the first Black men's service organization (The Urbana Men's Progressive Club) in Urbana, OH; editor Urbana Lions Club Newsletter. **Honors/Awds:** 1st Black Trainee & Indus Engineer Intl Harvester 1974; Co-Chmn 1981 Annual Crusade Amer Cancer Soc Champaign Co 1981; Tape Line Project Standard Labor Cost System St Regis Co 1981-83, Baumfolder 1984-85; Standard Labor Cost Savings Baumfolder 1984-85; held highest admin position of any Black ever Urban Univ. **Military Serv:** USAF A/2C 4 yrs.

STEVENSON, BRYAN
Attorney. **Personal:** Born 1960. **Career:** Alabama Capital Representation Resource Ctr, exec dir, currently. **Honors/Awds:** MacArthur Foundation, fellow, 1995. **Business Addr:** Executive director, Alabama Capital Representation Resource Center, 201 Greenville St, Montgomery, AL 36107, (334)262-9979.

STEVENSON, JEROME PRITCHARD, SR.
Educator/clergy. **Personal:** Born Mar 28, 1941, Birmingham, AL; son of Jimmie & Dorothy Stevenson; married Ida Stevenson, Jun 20, 1981; children: Melissa, Jerome Jr, Julia P. **Educ:** Highland Park College, AS, 1971; Wayne State University, BS, 1973, MS, 1986; William Tyndale College, BRE, 1993; Ashland Theological Seminary, MA, 1995, DMin, expected 1999. **Career:** Detroit Postal Service, letter carrier, 1966-73; Detroit Public Schools, science teacher, 1975-77; Ford Motor Co, management trainee, 1977-80; Detroit Public Schools, lead teacher, 1980-; Renaissance Bapt Ch, pastor, 1997-. **Orgs:** NAACP, 1964-; American Legion, 1995-; VFW, 1997; American Association of Christian Counselors, 1995; American Counseling Association, 1996; Baptist Council, 1995; Michigan Progressive Convention, 1997; American Baptist Convention, 1997. **Honors/Awds:** Junior Achievement, Distinguished Advisor Award, 1977-78; Wayne County Executive, Distinguished Service Award, 1997; NAACP, Distinguished Service, 1982; Life Choice, Vision Award, 1997. **Military Serv:** US Army, spec 4, 1959-61; Soldier of Cycle, 1959. **Home Addr:** 19952 Vaughan St, Detroit, MI 48219, (313)592-0252.

STEVENSON, LILLIAN
Nurse. **Personal:** Born Nov 27, 1922, Indianapolis, IN; daughter of Jane Brown and George Brown; divorced; children: John Austin Anthony, Phillip Kelly. **Educ:** Indiana City Hosp Sch of Nurs, 1941-44; Mdme CJ Walker Coll of Cosmotol, 1958; Debbie's School of Cosmetology. **Career:** Nurs Serv Citz Ambulatory Health Ctr Neighborhood Hlth Care Facility, chg nurs; supvs head nurs staff nurs 36 yrs; cosmotol 1 yr; salesperson 1 yr; foot care specialist, manicurist. **Orgs:** Mem Natl Black Nurse Assoc; pres Black Nurse Assoc of Indianap Inc 1974-77; 3rd blk grad any sch of nurs in Indianap 1944; instr nurs Marion Co Gen Hosp; surg supr nurse St Monica's Hosp; Ladies Aux Knights of St Peter Claver Ct; #97 Indiana Christ Leadershp Confer; bd mem Indianap Chptr Oper PUSH; mem Nat Counc of Negro Women; bd mem Sub Area Counc Hlth Syst Agen; bd mem NE Unit Am Cancer Assn; past bd mem Model Cities Fed Cred Union; bd mem Hillside Cult Center; bd, Catholic Charities; pres, Archdiocesan Black Catholics concerned. **Honors/Awds:** IN Black Assem Cert of Distinct 1975; IN Black Bicent Commn 1976; Black Lag Book 1st edit 1976; IN Confer of Women 1976 gold medal winner Natl Knights of St Peter Claver 1979; Drum Major Award, ICLC 1983; co-mem, Sisters of St Joseph-Trton IN, CSJ, 1986; Food Pantry Coordinator, 1985; bd mem, St Vincent dePaul Society, 1984; St's Peter & Paul Cathedral, Indianapolis, Ind, Pro Ecclesia Et Pontifice Award, Long Service to the Church, 1994. **Business Addr:** 1818 Sheldon St, Indianapolis, IN 46218.

STEVENSON, MORTON COLEMAN
State official. **Personal:** Born in New York, NY; married Edith M Thompson. **Educ:** NY Univ School of Commerce, BA 1951; NY Univ Grad Sch Business, MBA 1955. **Career:** Urban League of Greater New York, asst indus rels sec 1951-53; NYS Banking Dept, admin asst 1957-62; NYS Career Dev Pgm, dpty dir 1967-71 ; City of Cleveland, OH, consultant 1970; NYS Dept of Civil Svc, dist supr, currently. **Orgs:** Mem Intl Prsnl Mgnt Asso 1963-; mem NY Prsnl Mgnt Assn 1965; mem Intl Inst of Admin Sci 1974; mem 100 Blck Men 1974; mem Grand St Boys 1962; mem Oratorio Soc NY 1955; bd dir Oratorio Soc of NY 1966-69; adv comm OIC NY 1971. **Honors/Awds:** Past Pres Award Estrn Reg Intl Prsnl Mgmt Asso 1983. **Military Serv:** AUS Sgt Mjr 3 yrs. **Business Addr:** District Supervisor, NYS Dept of Civil Service, 163 West 125th St, New York, NY 10027.

STEVENSON, RUSSELL A.
Educator. **Personal:** Born Feb 17, 1923, Bronx, NY; married Dora L Anderson; children: Vanessa, Melanie. **Educ:** Columbia University, MA, 1961; New England Conservatory of Music, BM, 1948. **Career:** Suffolk County Community College, department head, 1976-; assistant professor music, 1971-; Copiague Public School, teacher/director of music, 1956-71; Bny City Department of Parks, recreation leader, 1949-56; concert pianist & accompanist, 1949-. **Orgs:** Board of directors, Symphony of New World, 1976-; charter member, New York State Adminstration of Music, 1963-; adjudicator, New York School of Music Association; charter member, treasurer, Rolling Hills PTA, 1967-70; Alpha Phi Alpha; Phi Mu Alpha; NYSSMA; SCMEA; MENC; NAJE; Rotary International. **Honors/Awds:** 1st Black Secondary School Music Teacher, Suffolk County; Company History for 238 QM WWII; Solo, Boston Pops, 1949; Solo Concert, Town Hall, 1956; Concert Tour, University of Minnesota, 1950-51. **Military Serv:** AUS s/sgt ETO 1943-45. **Business Addr:** Music, Suffolk Community College Ammerman, 533 College Road, Selden, NY 11784.

STEVENSON, UNICE TEEN
State official. **Personal:** Born Apr 7, 1950, Columbus, MS; daughter of Carrie Stevenson and Willie Stevenson. **Educ:** Univ of Akron, BS Education 1976; Lake Erie College, MBA 1985. **Career:** Alltel Corp, plant accountant 1969-72, accountant/bkpr 1972-73, admin asst 1973-76; commer asst 1976-79; Alltel Service Corp, gen acctg supr 1979-84, spec projects coord 1984-87; State of Ohio, auditor of state, assistant auditor, 1987-91, regional project manager, 1991-. **Orgs:** Mem Natl Assn of Black MBA's; mem Mt Olive Baptist Church; past pres OH Natl Baptist Convention, Inc Youth Dept; past dir of mt Olive Baptist Church Young People's Dept; past pres Progressive Dist Young Peoples Dept; mem of National Assn of Black Accountants; mem of Government Finance Officers Assn of United States and Canada. **Business Addr:** 88 East Broad Street, 5th Floor, Columbus, OH 43266-0040.

STEWARD, EMANUEL
Business executive, boxing manager. **Personal:** Born Jul 7, 1944, Vivian, WV; son of Catherine Steward and Emanuel Steward Sr; married Marie Estelle Steel, 1964; children: Sylvia Ann, Sylvette Marie. **Educ:** Henry Ford Community Coll, grad 1970; Detroit Edison's Electrician-Apprenticeship Prog, grad Master Electrician 1970. **Career:** Detroit Edison, master electrician 1966-72; Securities and Life Insurance, salesman 1972-76; Escot Boxing Enterprises Inc, pres, currently; Emanuel Steward's Place, restauranteur, currently. **Orgs:** Life mem NAACP; franchise holder Little Caesar's Pizza Chain; pres Scholarship Fund for Children; founder Emanuel Steward Athletic Scholarship. **Honors/Awds:** Manager/Trainer of the yr Boxing Writers Assn 1980; Amateur Boxing Coach of the Yr, US Amateur Boxing Coaches Assn, 1977; Natl Golden Gloves 119 lbs Champ 1963; Manager/Trainer of the Yr WBC (World Boxing Council) 1983; Life Enrichment Award-Focus Life 1984; SCLC Youth Devel Award 1983; champions under tutelage, Thomas Hearns-WBC Super Welterweight Champion of the World; Milton McCrory-WBC Welterweight Champion of the World; Jimmy Paul-Intl Boxing Federation, Lightweight Champion of the World; Duane Thomas WBC Super Welterweight Champion of the World; Tony Tucker IBF Heavyweight Champion of the World; Afro-American Sports Hall of Fame, 1992. **Business Addr:** President, Escot Boxing Enterprises Inc, 19600 W McNichols, Detroit, MI 48219.

STEWARD, KORDELL
Professional football player. **Educ:** Colorado. **Career:** Pittsburgh Steelers, 1995-. **Special Achievements:** 2nd round/60th overall NFL draft pick, 1995. **Business Addr:** Professional Football Player, Pittsburgh Steelers, Three Rivers Stadium, 300 Stadium Cir, Pittsburgh, PA 15212, (412)323-1200.

STEWARD, LOWELL C.
Real estate appraiser. **Personal:** Born Feb 25, 1919, Los Angeles; married Helen Jane Ford; children: Pamela, Lowell, Jr, Shelley. **Educ:** Santa Barbara State Coll, BA 1942; UCLA, Real Estate Certificate 1952. **Career:** Lowell Steward Assoc, real estate appraiser. **Orgs:** Sr mem Soc of Real Estate Appraisers 1970; past mem bd dir Consolidated Realty Bd; mem bd dir Univ CA Santa Barbara Alumni Assn 8 yrs; past pres Tuskegee Airmen Western Region; mem Kappa Alpha Psi; life mem NAACP; natl chmn Tuskegee Airman Schlrsp Fund. **Honors/Awds:** Recip Distinguished Flying Cross WWII. **Military Serv:** Fighter pilot 332nd fighter group WWII major.

STEWART, ALBERT C.
Educator. **Personal:** Born in Detroit, MI; son of Jeanne B Kaiser Stewart and Albert Q Stewart; married Colleen M Hyland. **Educ:** Univ of Chicago, BS 1942, MS 1949; St Louis Univ, PhD 1951. **Career:** St Louis Univ, instr chemistry 1949-51; Knoxville Coll, prof chem/physics 1953-56; John Carroll Univ Cleveland, OH, lecturer chem 1956-63; Union Carbide Corp, intl bus mgr 1973-77, dir sales 1977-79, natl sales mgr 1979-82, dir univ relations 1982-84; Western CT State Univ, assoc dean/prof mktg, currently. **Orgs:** Mem Rotary Cleveland/NY 1962-69; mem Oak Ridge, TN town cncl 1953-57; pres/chmn Urban League Cleveland/NY 1959-69; mem trustee NY Philharmonic Soc 1975-80. **Honors/Awds:** Alumni Merit Award St Louis Univ 1958; Cert of Merit Soc of Chem Professions Cleveland 1962; Alumni Citation Univ of Chicago 1966; 2 US patents 1966. **Military Serv:** USNR Lt (JG) 1944-56. **Business Addr:** Professor of Marketing, Western CT State University, Ancell School of Business, 181 White St, Danbury, CT 06810.

STEWART, ALISON
Journalist. **Personal:** Born in Glen Ridge, NJ. **Educ:** Brown University, BA, Am lit. **Career:** MTV, gofer, 1988-91, reporter, 1991-; Brown Univ radio station, deejay, program dir, 1984-88. **Special Achievements:** First African American news reporter at MTV. **Business Addr:** News Reporter, c/o CBS, Coast to Coast, 524 W 57th St, New York, NY 10019, (212)975-4321.

STEWART, BERNARD
Cable broadcasting programmer. **Personal:** Born Jul 3, 1950, Birmingham, AL; married Alice Faye Carr; children: Anthony. **Educ:** Ball State Univ, Muncie IN, BS, 1974; Southern Connecticut State Univ, New Haven CT, MS Urban Studies, 1977, MS Media Studies, 1979. **Career:** WBZ-TV, Boston MA, exec news producer; WTNH-TV, New Haven CT, producer; Independent, filmmaker, producer; ESPN Intl, Inc, dir program planning, 1987-91, vice pres programming and production, 1991-. **Honors/Awds:** Lapides Award, Center for Urban Studies; Outstanding Young Man of Amer, US Jaycees; Emmy Nominations (2), Natl TV Academy, 1978, 1979. **Military Serv:** US Air Force, sergeant, 1971-75. **Business Addr:** VP, Programming and Production, ESPN, International, ESPN Plaza, Bristol, CT 06010.

STEWART, BESS
Educator. **Personal:** Born Jun 6, Buffalo, NY; daughter of Margaret Boyd and Curtis Boyd; married Wilbert E Smith, Nov 28, 1957; children: Kimberleyh. **Educ:** Incarnate Word College, BSN, 1976; University of Texas Health Science Center San Antonio, School of Nursing, MSN, 1978; University of Texas at Austin, PhD, 1986. **Career:** Baptist Hospital School of Nursing, assistant professor, 1976-78; UTHSCSA, School of Nursing, associate professor, 1979-. **Orgs:** American Nurses Credentialing Center, board of directors, 1991-; American Cancer Society, San Antonio, board of directors, 1988-; American Nurses Council on Cultural Diversity, chairperson, 1987-89, vice chair, 1982-87. **Honors/Awds:** American Nurses District 8, Nurse of the Year, 1991; UTHSCSA, Excellence in Education Award, 1991; Presidential Award for Excellence in Teaching, 1993; W K Kellogg Leadership for Minority Women, 1982; ANA Minority Fellowship, 1984-86; ANA Clara Lockwood Award, 1982-84; Fellow of the American Academy of Nursing. **Special Achievements:** Publications: "A Staff Development Workshop," Journal of Staff Development, 1991, "Cultural Considerations," Psychiatric Nursing, 1991, "Cultural Diversity in Nursing, A Guide to Curriculum Development," 1986, "Role Strain, Anxiety & Depression in Black Matters," 1991, "Screening for Depression in African-American Elders," 1991. **Business Addr:** Associate Professor/Asst Dean for Doctoral Studies, University of Texas Health Science Center, School of Nursing, 7703 Floyd Curl Dr, San Antonio, TX 78284, (210)567-5815.

STEWART, BRITTANICA
Salon owner, cosmetologist. **Personal:** Born Sep 16, 1950, Atlanta, GA; daughter of Bessie Gordon Stewart (deceased) and James Stewart. **Educ:** Ophelia DeVore School of Beauty & Charm, 1976; International Mannequin School for Models, 1978; Robert Fiance School of Beauty, beauty salon hair stylist, 1983. **Career:** Ophelia DeVore School of Beauty & Charm,

teacher for models, 1971-76; independent fashion model, 1975-82; Black Hair Is, assistant manager & fashion coordinator, 1984-86; Brittanica & Associates, president, 1986-; Bronner Bros Beauty, producer, summer fashion show, 1989-. **Orgs:** New Yorker Club, membership board, 1990. **Honors/Awds:** Hal Jackson's Talented Teens, Award of Appreciation for Outstanding Achievement, 1987, 1988; Arms Around Harlem for the Homeless, Award of Gratitude for Assistance, 1992; Friends of Senior Citizens of Springfield Gardens & St Albans, certificate of appreciation, 1991. **Special Achievements:** Advisor to Vogue Magazine for hair fashion, 1989-; guest speaker on WBLS Radio for hair fashion, 1988-; guest advisor on hair fashion for Essence Magazine, 1989-. **Business Addr:** President, Brittanica & Associates, 864 Lexington Ave, 2nd Fl, New York, NY 10021, (212)879-7030.

STEWART, CARL E.
Judge. **Personal:** Born 1950. **Educ:** Dillard, BA, 1971; Loyola (LA), JD, 1974. **Career:** Piper & Brown, attorney, 1977-78; Office of the Attorney General, State of Louisiana, staff attorney, 1978-79; Western District of Louisiana, Department of Justice, asst US attorney, 1979-83; Louisiana State Univ, adjunct instructor 1982-85; Stewart & Dixon, partner, 1983-85; Caddo Parish, State of Louisiana, special asst district attorney, 1983-85; City of Shreveport, asst city prosecutor, 1983-85; Louisiana District Court, First Judicial District, judge, 1985-91; Louisiana Court of Appeal, Second Circuit, judge, 1991-94; circuit judge, 1994-. **Orgs:** American Bar Assn; Black Lawyers Assn of Shreveport-Bossier; Harry Booth Chapter American Inn of Court; Louisiana Bar Assn; Louisiana Conference of Court of Appeal Judges; National Bar Assn; Shreveport Bar Assn. **Military Serv:** US Army, 1974-77. **Business Addr:** Judge, US 5th Circuit Court of Appeals, US Courthouse, 300 Fannin St, Ste 2299, Shreveport, LA 71101, (318)676-3765.

STEWART, CAROLYN HOUSE
Attorney. **Personal:** Born Nov 11, 1952, Columbia, SC; daughter of Mary Green Myers; married Delano S Stewart; children: Delsha C Stewart. **Educ:** Univ of S FL, BA 1974; Univ of SC Law Center, JD 1977. **Career:** MacFarlane, Ferguson, & McMullen, attorney, 1994-; partner & shareholder of firm, 1998; Travelers Insurance Co, staff counsel, 1989-94; Butler & Burnette, attorney, 1987-89; Hillsborough County Attorney, assistant county attorney, 1985-87; State Attys Ofc Hillsborough Co, asst state atty 1980-81; Jim Walter Corp, asso litigation couns 1977-80; Univ of SC Law Cntr, 1st black legal writing inst 1976-77; Law Inc Legal Serv to the Poor, legal intern 1976; Law Students Civil Rights Resrch Counc, legal intern 1975-76. **Orgs:** Spl consult to pres Nat Bar Assn; asst to pres FL Chap Nat Bar Assn 1979; CLE-CHRPSN, FL Chap Nat Bar Assn 1980, vice president, 1983-85; vice pres, Zeta Upsilon Chapter, Alpha Kappa Alpha Sorority 1972-74; bd of dirs Tampa Orgn of Black Affairs 1980; bd of dirs Hillsborough Co Mental Hlth Assn 1980; bd of dirs Tampa Philharmonic Soc 1980; member, Greater Tampa Chapter, Jack & Jill of America, Inc, 1990-; legal advisor, Gamma Theta Omega Chapter, Alpha Kappa Alpha Sorority, 1984-96; Gamma Theta Omega Chapter Alpha Kappa Alpha Sorority, president, 1992-95; Greater Tampa Urban League, life mem; Citizens Advisory Committee to President of University South Florida; Tampa Heights Neighborhood Revitalization Alliance. **Honors/Awds:** Lectr FL Chap Nat Bar Assn 1979; Member of the Year, Florida Chapter, National Bar Assn, 1983; Leadership Excellence Award, Epicureans International, Tampa Chapter, 1992; Soror of the Year, Alpha Kappa Alpha Sorority Inc, 1995; lecturer on Trial Advocacy and Employment Law Issues; Interviewed, Ebony Mag, Oct, 1997. **Business Addr:** Attorney, MacFarlane, Ferguson, & McMullen, 111 E Madison St, Suite 2300, Tampa, FL 33602-4997.

STEWART, CHARLES J.
Fire prevention, control administrator. **Personal:** Born Nov 7, 1930, Montgomery, AL; son of Helen Stewart (deceased) and Roy Clinton; married Annette Stokes, Jun 14, 1986; children: Malcolm Rogers, Valarie, Ellie Rose Stewart Williams. **Educ:** Richard J Daley Coll, Chicago IL, AAS Fire Science, 1976; Southern Illinois Univ, Carbondale IL, BS Fire Science, 1978. **Career:** Chciago Fire Dept, Chicago IL, firefighter, 1962-67, engineer, 1967-78, lieutenant, 1978-79, captain, 1979-88, deputy chief, 1988-. **Orgs:** Past master, King David Lodge #100 F&AM, PHA, IL, 1951; mem, Operation PUSH, 1971, Chicago Urban League; consultant, Citywide Detective Agency, 1987-; life mem, NAACP, 1987; mem, Xi Lambda Chapter, Alpha Phi Alpha Inc, 1988. **Honors/Awds:** Mason of the Year, MW Prince Hall Grand Lodge, Illinois, 1965; Award of Recognition, Illinois Council of Delibration 33 degree, 1980; Certificate of Achievement, Chicago Fire Dept, 1981; Distinguished Serv Award, Operation PUSH, 1988; Afro-Amer Symbol of Excellence, Life Center Church, 1988. **Military Serv:** US Army, Tec 5, 1946-48, 1948-50, 1950-51. **Home Addr:** 1700 E 56th St, #901, Chicago, IL 60637-1970.

STEWART, DAVID KEITH
Professional baseball player (retired). **Personal:** Born Feb 19, 1957, Oakland, CA. **Educ:** Merritt College, Oakland, CA, attended; California State Univ, Hayward, CA, attended. **Career:** Pitcher: Los Angeles Dodgers, 1978, 1981-83, Texas Rangers, 1983-85, Philadelphia Phillies, 1985-86, Oakland Athletics, 1986-92; Toronto Blue Jays, 1992-94; Oakland A's, 1994-95. **Honors/Awds:** American League All-Star Team, 1989. **Business Addr:** Assistant to the General Manager, San Diego Padres, 9449 Friars Rd, San Diego, CA 92108.

STEWART, DONALD MITCHELL
Educator. **Personal:** Born Jul 8, 1938, Chicago, IL; son of Ann Stewart and Elmer Stewart; married Isabel Carter Johnston; children: Jay Ashton, Carter Mitchell. **Educ:** Grinell Coll, BA (w/Highest Honors) 1959; Yale Univ, MA 1962; The Graduate Inst of Intl Studies Geneva Switzerland, studies in intl org and economics 1960-62; Harvard University Kennedy School of Government, MPA 1969 DPA 1975. **Career:** The Ford Foundation, asst to the rep for West Africa 1962-64, program asst Middle East Africa prog 1964-66, asst rep Cairo 1966-67, asst rep North Africa 1966-68, program officer Middle East Africa prog 1968-69; The Univ of PA, exec asst to pres 1970-72, Ford Foundation Study awd to conduct rsch in Washington DC 1972-73, dir comm leadership seminar prog 1973-75, assoc dean faculty of arts and scis, dir coll of general studies, counselor to provost, asst prof, rsch assoc & dir continuing educ sch of public and urban policy 1975-76; pres Spelman College 1976-86; pres The College Board 1987-. **Orgs:** Mem Natl Acad of Public Admin; bd of dirs, bd of trustees Grinnell Coll; bd of dirs Principal Insurance Co of Iowa; mem The Council on Foreign Relations; trustee, Teachers College Columbia University; dir The New York Times Co; bd of dirs, Campbell Soup Company. **Honors/Awds:** Publication "The Not So Steady State of Governance in Higher Education," Aspen Inst for Humanistic Studies position paper; Whittier Coll, Doctor of Humane Letters, 1992; Miami Univ, Doctor of Humane Letters, 1993; Northern Kentucky Univ, Doctor of Humane Letters, 1993; Tuskegee Univ, Doctor of Laws, 1994; Fairleigh Dickinson, Doctor of Laws, 1994. **Special Achievements:** Setting Educational Standards in a Democracy, Vital Speeches of the Day 60, p 331-33, Mar 15, 1994; Partnerships Have Never Seemed So Crucial to Reform, Education Week, Special Report, Apr 13, 1994; Building A Shared Future Preference, Educational Record 75, p 24-25, Spring, 1994; Improving Higher Education Outcomes, A House of Many Doors, Trusteeship, Mar/Apr 1995; The Public Interest Considered, Liberal Education, 1995. **Business Addr:** President, The College Board, 45 Columbus Ave, New York, NY 10023.

STEWART, DOROTHY NELL
City official. **Personal:** Born Sep 2, 1949, Centerville, TX; daughter of Artince Houston-Fortson and Murry B. Fortson Jr; children: Aretha R Ferrell, Craig-Murry III. **Educ:** Attended Tarrant County Junior Coll; Amber Univ. **Career:** Fort Worth Police Dept, Fort Worth TX, public safety dispatcher, 1973-1980; City of Fort Worth Action Center, TX, administrative aide, 1980-82, administrative asst, 1982-84, coordinator, office of city mgr, 1984-. **Orgs:** Mem, Amer Soc for Public Administrators; program chpn, 1982-83, 1984-85, sec, 1983, North Texas Conf of Minority Public Administrators; vice chpn, 1985-86, co-chpn, 1986-87, Urban Mgmt Assts of North Texas; chapter public rel officer, 1986-, Natl Forum for Black Administrators, council of pres, 1991; Texas City Mgmt Assn; Natl Forum for Black Public Admin, North TX Chapter, past pres, 1991; Forum Fort Worth, member; Sickle Cell Disease Association of America/Texas Chapter, board member; Minority Leaders and Citizen's Council, board member/nominations committee chair. **Business Addr:** Action Center Coordinator, City of Fort Worth, 1000 Throckmorton St, Fort Worth, TX 76102.

STEWART, EDWARD L.
Airline executive. **Personal:** Born Sep 17, 1957, Milwaukee, WI; son of Claud & Lena Stewart; married Carolyn, Oct 22, 1983; children: Cristin, Eric. **Educ:** University of Wisconsin, BA, 1978. **Career:** Network Affiliates for Milwaukee & Oklahoma, reporter; Southwestern Bell Telephone, pr manager; American Airlines, media spokesperson/pr; Southwest Airlines, director of public relations, 1990-. **Orgs:** Public Relations Society of America; Press Club of Dallas. **Business Addr:** Director, Public Relations, Southwest Airlines, 2702 Love Field Dr, Dallas, TX 75235, (214)792-4187.

STEWART, ELIZABETH PIERCE
Educator. **Personal:** Born Apr 18, 1947, Laurel, MS; married Valentine. **Educ:** Stillman Coll, BS 1970; Univ of AL, MSW 1972; Univ of Pittsburgh, PhD School of Social Work 1986. **Career:** HEW Washington DC, mgmt analyst 1971; Crawford Co Bd of Assistance Meadville PA, housing specialist 1973; Edinboro State Coll, asst prof social work 1973, prof. **Orgs:** Past pres & treas PA Assn of Under Grad Social Work Educ 1978-80; bd mem Community Health Services 1978-82; bd mem United Fund Crawford Co 1979-80; pres Martin Luther King Scholarship Found 1980-82; pres Pennsylvania Assn of Undergraduate Social Work Educators; bd mem Erie County Mental Health Mental Retardation Adv Bd. **Honors/Awds:** Outstanding Leadership in the Social Work Prof Local Chap NASW 1978-80; JFK NATO Ctr Award Erie PA 1978. **Business Addr:** Professor of Social Work, Edinboro University of PA, 107 Hendricks Hall, Edinboro, PA 16444.

STEWART, FREDDIE MARDRELL
Photographer. **Personal:** Born Feb 25, 1943, Glidden, TX; son of Katherine Stewart and Charlie Stewart; married Geneva Jackson Stewart, Nov 16, 1963; children: Frederick D, Toni L Stewart Rouser. **Educ:** Radio Engineering Institute, 1964; MetroTechnical Institute, 1988; Creighton University, SET. **Career:** Minolta, sales representative; United States West Communications, product manager, equipment engineer, electronics tech; AT&T, production supervisor; Stewart's Family Photography Studio, president, currently. **Orgs:** Big Brothers/Big Sisters; National Hunter Lodge #9, masonics treasurer; Clair United Methodist Church, finance manager; Nebraska Educational Television; Telephone Pioneers of America; Nebraska Black Manager Association, treasurer. **Honors/Awds:** United States West Communication, Small Business Excellence Award, 1990; Nebraska Black Managers, Honorary Member Award, 1990. **Home Addr:** 4709 N 53rd St, Omaha, NE 68104. **Business Addr:** President, Stewart's Family Photography Studio, 6311 Ames Ave, Omaha, NE 68104.

STEWART, GREGORY
Educational administrator, counselor. **Personal:** Born May 28, 1958, Cincinnati, OH; son of Margaret Marie Evans Stewart and Curtis Stewart. **Educ:** Univ of Cincinnati, BSW 1981; Miami Univ (OH), MS 1982; Ohio University, PhD, 1993. **Career:** Denison Univ, asst dir of admissions 1982-84, asst to the dean 1984-85; Univ of Cincinnati, admissions officer 1985-86; OH Univer, asst dir of admissions Coll of Osteopathic Med 1986-88; Denison University, assoc dean of students 1988-89; Talbert House Drug & Family Counseling Center, therapist 1990; Northern Kentucky University, Highland Heights, KY, dir of admissions 1989-94; The University of Akron, dir of admissions, 1994-. **Orgs:** Natl Assoc of College Admissions Counselors 1982-. **Honors/Awds:** Youth Leadership Awd Cincinnati Community Chest & Council 1976; presentor Educational Showcase Hofstra Univ 1978; author of article in the Synergist Journal 1981; presentor Natl Convention Natl Assoc of College Admissions Counselors 1985, 1987, 1992; National Certified Counselor National Board of Certified Counselors, Inc 1989-; Licensed Social Worker Commonwealth of Kentucky 1990; Licensed Social Worker State of Ohio 1991-; Northern Kentucky University Black Faculty and Staff Association, Outstanding Service Award, 1992. **Business Addr:** Director of Admissions, The University of Akron, Office of Admissions, Akron, OH 44325-2001.

STEWART, HORACE W. (NICK)
Theater founder, producer. **Personal:** Born Mar 15, 1910, New York, NY; married Edna Wortherly; children: Valarie, Roger, Christopher. **Career:** Ebony Showcase Theatre & Cultural Arts Cntr Inc, founder & managing dir 1950-; Eddie Cantor Show, Beulah Show, Rudy Valee Show Armed Forces Radio Show, radio performer; Irving Berlin's Louisiana Purchase, Carmen & Jones Midsummer Nights Dream, broadway performer 1939-; Louis Armstron, Cab Calloway Duke Ellington, Jimmy Lanceford, dancer & Comedian 1936-39; NY Cotton Club, chorus boy 1934; Amos & Andy (Lightnin), Milton Berle Show, Ramar of the Jungle Mr Ed, TV actor 1950-; Carmen Jones Cabin in the Sky, Dakota, Stormy Weather, Its a Mad Mad Mad Mad World, Silver Streak, film actor. **Orgs:** Founder Ebony Showcase Theatre (1st & longest existing black founded legitimate theater in Am) 1950-; USO entertained in Aleutian Islands 1947; LA City Counc Resolution, City of LA 1966. **Honors/Awds:** LA Drama Critics Circle Award LA Drama Critics 1969; cert of Commendation State of CA Museum of Sci & Industry; Mayor's cert of appreciation City of LA; author & producer Carnival Island, Greatest Mouse That Ever Lived, Chris Columbus Brown. **Business Addr:** Ebony Showcase Theatre & Culture, 4718-4726 W Washington Blvd, Los Angeles, CA 90016.

STEWART, IMAGENE BIGHAM
Cleric. **Personal:** Born Jan 23, 1942, Dublin, GA; daughter of Rev and Mrs Bigham. **Educ:** Univ of District of Columbia, AA, 1972. **Career:** African-American Women's Clergy Assn, natl chairperson, currently. **Business Addr:** Natl Chairperson, African-American Women's Clergy Association, 214 P St, NW, Washington, DC 20001, (202)518-8488.

STEWART, JAMES A., III
Insurance executive. **Career:** Peoples Assured Family Life Insurance Company, company executive, currently. **Business Addr:** Peoples Assured Family Life Insurance Co, PO Box 23129, Jackson, MS 39225-3129.

STEWART, JAMES BENJAMIN
Educational administrator. **Personal:** Born Jul 18, 1947, Cleveland, OH; son of Clora Stewart and Reuben Stewart (deceased); married Sharon Lynn Sullivan; children: Talibah, Lorin, Jaliya. **Educ:** Rose-Hulman Institute of Technology, BS 1969; Cleveland State Univ, MA 1971; Univ of Notre Dame, PhD 1976. **Career:** Cleveland Electric Illuminating Co, assoc tech studies engr 1969-74; Dyke Coll, part-time instructor 1972-73; Univ of Notre Dame, asst prof of economics and dir of black studies program; The Pennsylvania State Univ, assoc prof of economics, dir black studies program 1984-86, assoc prof of labor studies and industrial relations, dir of black studies program

1980-90; associate prof of labor and industrial relations 1989-; The Review of Black Political Economy, editor 1987-95; Penn State Univ, professor of labor studies and industrial relations, vice provost for educational equity, 1990-. **Orgs:** Mem Natl Cncl for Black Studies 1975-; vice chair Natl Cncl for Black Studies 1981-85; mem Assn for Social Economics 1978-; mem Soc for Values in Higher Educ 1980-; mem Black History Adv Comm and Historic Preservation Bd; mem Amer Economic Assn 1983-; bd of trustees Bethune Memorial U ME Church, 1985-; advisor Comm for Justice in South Africa 1985-87; mem OIC; Amer Archival Adv Comm 1986-88; National Economic Association, mem, 1984-, pres, 1994; Phi Delta Kappa 1988-; Opportunities Academy of Mgmt Training Inc Board 1989-. **Honors/Awds:** Pennsylvania Black Book 1985; Outstanding Volunteer Award, Rockview State Correctional Institution 1987; Phi Delta Kappa 1988-; Omicron Delta Kappa 1982-; Delta Tau Kappa 1979-; Honorary Outstanding Black Delawarean by the Black Studies Prog & Student Government Assn of Delaware State Coll 1985; First Humanitarian Service Awd Forum on Black Affairs 1985; Golden Key National Honor Society, 1989-; The National Council for Black Studies, Presidential Award Recipient, 1990; Award for Outstanding Contributions to Improving Equal Opportunity, Penn State University, 1992-. **Business Addr:** Vice Provost & Professor, Labor Studies and Industrial Relations, The Pennsylvania State University, 314 Old Main, University Park, PA 16802.

STEWART, JAMES OTTIS, III
Professional football player. **Personal:** Born Dec 27, 1971, Morristown, TN. **Educ:** University of Tennessee, attended. **Career:** Jacksonville Jaguars, running back, 1995-. **Special Achievements:** Selected in the 1st round/19th overall pick in the 1995 NFL Draft. **Business Addr:** Professional Football Player, Jacksonville Jaguars, 1 Stadium Place, Jacksonville, FL 32202, (904)633-6000.

STEWART, JERMAINE. See Obituaries section.

STEWART, JEWEL HOPE
Institutional research planning manager. **Personal:** Born Oct 31, 1948, Petersburg, VA; daughter of Pearl Sally Stewart Bonner and Wilbert L Stewart (deceased); children: Zanda Milan Stewart. **Educ:** Morgan State Univ, BA 1970; Ohio State Univ, MA 1973; Indiana Univ, EdD 1980. **Career:** Benedict Coll, asst dir planning rsch eval 1973-74; Lincoln Univ, inst rsch off 1974-76; MO Coord Bd/Higher Educ, assoc dir planning & rsch 1978-81; NC A&T State Univ, dir inst rsch & planning 1982-. **Orgs:** Exec comm NC Assn of Inst Rsch 1985-87; Southern Assn of Inst Rsch, Assn of Inst Rsch. **Business Addr:** Director, I/R Planning, North Carolina A&T State Univ, 1601 East Market St, Greensboro, NC 27411.

STEWART, JOHN B., JR.
Fire chief (retired), business executive. **Personal:** Born May 16, 1930, Hartford, CT; son of Mattie Baker Stewart and John Stewart Sr; married Gladys Strong Stewart, Jan 27, 1950; children: Wendy, William, Donald, John, Jeffrey, Holly. **Educ:** University of Massachusetts, Amherst, MA, associates, 1980; University of Connecticut, Hartford, CT, BA, 1991. **Career:** City of Hartford Fire Department, Hartford, CT, fire chief, 1952-92; City of Hartford, Hartford, CT, special assistant to city manager, 1971-76, acting deputy city manager, 1971-76; Stewart Associates, principal; Hartford Court of Common Council, majority leader, currently. **Orgs:** Consultant, International Association of Fire Chiefs, 1980-; chairman, Metropolitan Section, IAFC, 1987-89; chairman, Connecticut Career Fire Chiefs, 1990-91; founding chairperson, International Association of Black Professional Firefighters, 1969-70; chairman, Chief Officers Resource Committee, 1986-. **Honors/Awds:** Governor's Task Force on Safety; Outstanding Civic Employee Award, Greater Hartford Jaycees American Society and Black Students Union Award, Barbados, Outstanding Community Service Award, Kiwanis; Connecticut Fire Marshal's Association Recognition Award; Roy Wilkins Award, NAACP; Crispus Attucks Award. **Military Serv:** Naval Reserves, Seaman, 1947-56. **Business Addr:** Majority Leader, Hartford Court of Common Council, 550 Main St, Hartford, CT 06103.

STEWART, JOHN O.
Attorney. **Personal:** Born Dec 19, 1935, Springfield, IL; son of Helen Stewart and Arthur Stewart; married. **Educ:** Univ CA, AB 1959; JD 1964. **Career:** US Atomic Energy Commn, contract adminstr 1965-66; Econ Opport Counc, gen counsel 1968-69; Housing Opport Div US Dept Housing & Urban Devel, reg dir 1969; San Francisco Legal Assist Found, dir 1970-74; Bechtel Corp, chief counsel, currently. **Orgs:** Mem Com Bar Examiners State Bar CA; Charles Hoston Law Club; bd dirs San Francisco Gen Hosp; mem Com on Disadvantaged & the Law State Bar CA; judiciary com San Francisco Bar Assn 1970-73. **Military Serv:** US Army sp/4 1959-61. **Business Addr:** Chief Counsel, Bechtel Corporation, Legal Dept, 50 Beale St, San Francisco, CA 94105.

STEWART, JOHN OTHNEIL
Educator, author. **Personal:** Born Jan 24, 1933; son of Irene Holder and Ernest Stewart; married Sandra McDonald; children: John Malcolm, Ernest Jabali, Ruth Laini. **Educ:** CA State Univ, Los Angeles, CA, BA, 1960; Stanford Univ, MA 1965; Univ of IA, MFA 1966; Univ of CA LA, PhD 1973. **Career:** Univ of IA, English instr; CA State Univ, prof of Engl; Univ of IL, prof of anthrop/writer; OH State Univ, prof English 1984-91; UC Davis, prof of African Studies, currently. **Orgs:** Mem Inst for Advanced Study Princeton 1979-80. **Honors/Awds:** Fellow, Amer Anthropology Assn; Winifred Holtby Prize for Novel Royal Soc of Lit London 1972. **Business Addr:** Prof, African American & African Studies, 2143 Hart Hall, UC Davis, Davis, CA 95616.

STEWART, JOSEPH M.
Food company executive. **Personal:** Born Dec 23, 1942, Marinqouin, LA; son of Stella M (Patterson) Stewart and Willie Stewart Sr; married Clara J (St Amant), 1967; children: Erick J, Kendra L. **Educ:** Southern Univ, Baton Rouge LA, BA Foods & Nutrition, 1965. **Career:** Howard Univ, Washington DC, dir food serv, 1969-71; Washington DC Public Schools, Washington DC, dir of food serv & state dir child nutrition, 1971-80; Kellogg Company, Battle Creek MI, dir child feeding program, 1980-81, dir corporate communications, 1981-85, vice pres public affairs, 1985-88, sr vice pres corp affairs, 1988-. **Orgs:** Mem, past bd of dir, Amer School Food Serv Assn, 1971-; mem, IFMA, Intl Gold & Silver Plate Soc, 1971-; bd of dir, Battle Creek Area Urban League, 1983-88; bd mem, Battle Creek Area United Way, 1985-; bd of dir, PRIDE Inc, 1986-88; bd of governors, Public Affairs Council of Amer, 1987-; bd mem, Natl Agriculture-Users Advisory, 1988-, State of Michigan Food & Nutrition Advisory, 1988-; bd of trustees, Battle Creek Health System, 1988-; Battle Creek Health System, chairman of the board, 1991; Grand Valley State University, board of trustees, 1991; Michigan National Bank, regional board of directors, 1990; Second Harvest National Network of Food Banks, board of trustees, 1990; Medical Education for South African Blacks, board of directors, 1990; Executive Leadership Council, 1990; Sigma Pi Phi Fraternity, 1992. **Honors/Awds:** IFMA Silver Plate Award, 1974; Battle Creek Area Urban League Central Region Award, Natl Urban League, 1988; Whitney M Young Jr Community Serv Award, 1989; auhor of the following articles: "American School Food Services Journal,"; "Congressional Record," 1973, 1975, 1976; "Jet Magazine," 1974; "School Food Service Journal," 1987. **Business Addr:** Senior Vice President-Corporate Affairs, Kellogg Company, One Kellogg Square, Battle Creek, MI 49016.

STEWART, KEBU
Professional basketball player. **Personal:** Born Dec 19, 1973. **Educ:** Cal State-Bakersfield. **Career:** Philadelphia 76ers, forward, 1997-. **Business Addr:** Professional Basketball Player, Philadelphia 76ers, 1 Corestates Complex, Philadelphia, PA 19148, (215)339-7676.

STEWART, KENNETH C.
Clergyman,missionary. **Personal:** Born Sep 28, 1939, Washington, DC. **Educ:** St Joseph's Coll, BA 1964; Capuchin Sem of St Anthony, 1968. **Career:** NOBC Washington, DC, dir ch vocations 1974-; Queen of Angels Retreat Cntr Saginaw, retreat tm mem 1973-74; St Boniface Parish, Milwaukee, pastor 1970-73; Francis Comm Sch, Milwaukee, adminstr pub relations 1969-70; St Francis, St Elizabeth, Milwaukee, parish asso 1968-69. **Orgs:** A solemnly professed friar, St Joseph Province of the Capuchin Order 1963; mem Nat Black Cath Clergy Caucus; ordained priest 1967. **Business Addr:** Prov of St Joseph-Capuchin, 1740 Mt Elliott, Detroit, MI 48207.

STEWART, KORDELL
Professional football player. **Personal:** Born Oct 16, 1972, New Orleans, LA. **Educ:** Univ of Colorado, attended. **Career:** Pittsburgh Steelers, quarterback, 1995-. **Honors/Awds:** Pittsburgh Steelers, Rookie of the Year, 1995; Pro Bowl alternate, 1996. **Business Addr:** Professional Football Player, Pittsburgh Steelers, Three Rivers Stadium, 300 Stadium Circle, Pittsburgh, PA 15212, (412)323-1200.

STEWART, LARRY
Professional basketball player. **Personal:** Born Sep 21, 1968, Philadelphia, PA. **Educ:** Coppin State. **Career:** Washington Bullets, forward, 1991-96; Seattle Supersonics, 1996-. **Honors/Awds:** NBA All-Rookie second team, 1992. **Business Addr:** Professional Basketball Player, Seattle Supersonics, 190 Queen Anne Ave N, Seattle, WA 98109, (206)281-5850.

STEWART, LORETTA A.
Administrative secretary. **Personal:** Born Jul 30, 1930, Muskogee, OK; daughter of Agnes Taylor Berry and James A Taylor; divorced; children: Arrilinda Delgoda, Darryl Delgoda, Calvin, Kevin, Shelia Jordan. **Educ:** Detroit Business Institute, attended, 1973-74; Henry Ford Community College, attended, 1975-76; Wayne State University, attended, 1979-81. **Career:** Massey Ferguson, 1965-75; Wayne State University, 1975-79; Owens Corning Fiberglass, 1979-83; Stewart's Secretarial Service, owner, 1981-82; Wendy's Franchise; Ford Elementary School, 1984-87, administrative secretary; Southfield School District, substituting admin secretary, currently. **Orgs:** Michigan Cancer Foundation, board member; United Way; United Negro College Fund; D'Accord Society; Justice, Unity, Generosity, Service. **Honors/Awds:** United Way, Michigan Cancer Foundation, Heart of Gold Award, 1991; WWJ News Radio 95, Citizen of the Week Award, 1992. **Special Achievements:** Assists in fundraising for the fight against cancer. **Home Phone:** (810)353-8876. **Business Addr:** Substituting Administrative Secretary, Southfield School District, Southfield, MI 48034.

STEWART, MAC A.
Educator. **Personal:** Born Jul 7, 1942, Forsyth, GA; son of Zillia Stewart and Alonzo Stewart; married Ernestine Clemons; children: Bruce Kifle, Justin Che. **Educ:** Morehouse Coll, BA 1963; Atlanta Univ, MA 1965; The Ohio State Univ, PhD 1973. **Career:** Jasper County Training School, teacher/counselor 1963-64; Crispus Attucks HS, teacher 1965-66; Morehouse Coll, dir of student financial aid 1966-70; The Ohio State Univ, asst dean 1973-75, assoc dean 1975-90, acting dean, 1990-91, dean 1991-. **Orgs:** Consultant KY State Univ 1978; mem bd dirs Buckeye Boys Ranch 1979-85; mem bd dirs Bethune Center for Unwed Mothers 1980-83; consultant Wilberforce Univ 1980; faculty mem Ohio Staters Inc 1982-91; consultant The Ohio Bd of Regents 1986; consultant, US Department of Education, 1990; consultant, Temple University, 1991; board of trustees, Columbus Academy, 1991-; consultant, Virginia Commonwealth University, 1992; mem Amer Personnel and Guidance Assoc, Amer Coll Personnel Assoc, Natl Assoc of Student Personnel Administrators, Mid-Western Assoc of Student Financial Aid Administrators, Alpha Kappa Delta Natl Hon Sociological Soc, Phi Delta Kappa Natl Hon Educ Frat, Phi Kappa Phi Natl Honor Soc, Amer Assoc of Higher Educ; bd mem, Human Subjects Research Committee Children's Hospital. **Honors/Awds:** Distinguished Affirmative Action Awd The Ohio State Univ 1984; Outstanding Alumni Awd Hubbard School 1986; Distinguished Service Award, Negro Educational Review, 1992; Frederick D Patterson Award, United Negro College Fund, 1992. **Home Addr:** 930 Notchbrook Dr, Delaware, OH 43015. **Business Addr:** Dean, The Ohio State University, 154 W 12th Ave, Columbus, OH 43210.

STEWART, MAE E.
City commissioner. **Personal:** Born Jun 4, 1926, Memphis, TN; married Robert; children: Jacqueline, Robert Jr, Saundra, Ernest. **Career:** East Cleveland City Commission, city commissioner, currently. **Orgs:** Co-founder, Rozelle Superior Civic Assn 1963; co-founder, East Cleveland Scholarship Fund; Huron Road Hospital Assn; vice pres, East Cleveland 2nd Ward Democrats Club; bd trustees, Ohio Municiple League; exec bd, 21st Congressional District; Natl League of Cities, Human Resources Pol Com; bd dir, East Cleveland Police Athletic League; NAACP; Urban League. **Honors/Awds:** East Cleveland Citizen of the Year, 1971; first Black president, East Cleveland School District PTA, 1962; first Black woman elected to East Cleveland City Commission. **Business Addr:** Commissioner, City Commission of East Cleveland, 14340 Euclid Ave E, Cleveland, OH 44112.

STEWART, MALCOLM M. See Obituaries section.

STEWART, MICHAEL
Professional basketball player. **Personal:** Born Apr 24, 1975. **Educ:** California. **Career:** Sacramento Kings, center, 1997-. **Business Addr:** Professional Basketball Player, Sacramento Kings, One Sports Parkway, Sacramento, CA 95834, (916)928-6900.

STEWART, PAUL WILBUR
Curator. **Personal:** Born Dec 18, 1925, Clinton, IA; son of Martha L Moore Stewart and Eugene Joseph Stewart; married Johnnie Mae Davis, 1987; children: Mark, Tracy, Linda, Earl. **Educ:** Hampton Inst; Roosevelt Coll; Moler Barber Coll, certificate, 1947. **Career:** Black Amer W Found, curator; licensed barber, IL, WI, NY, CO; Black American West Museum, founder, curator, currently. **Orgs:** Musician, Consult Co; mem, Historical Records Advisory Bd for CO; co-producer, documentary, "Blacks Here & Now" on Educ TV, Ch 6, Denver, 1972; established Afro-Amer Bicentennial Corp of CO; Appointed Governor's Commn of Highways, Bi-Ways Committee, 1989-. **Honors/Awds:** Interviewed by Denver TV & radio stations; featured in several magazines; Barney Ford Award, 1977; Black Educators United Award 1977; George Washington Honor Medal Achievement, Valley Forge, 1985; Featured in Smithsonian Magazine (front cover), 1989. **Military Serv:** USN seaman 1st class. **Business Addr:** Museum Founder, Curator, Black American West Museum, 3091 California, Denver, CO 80205.

STEWART, PEARL
Journalist, educator. **Educ:** Howard Univ, graduated; American Univ, master's in communication. **Career:** Oakland Tribune, editor, 1992-93; Howard Univ, journalist-in-residenc e, 1994-. **Orgs:** Natl Assn of Black Journalists. **Honors/Awds:** Natl Achievement Award, Natl Assn of Negro Business & Professional Women, 1993. **Special Achievements:** First African-American woman editor of a US daily newspaper. **Business Addr:** Journalist-in-Residence, Howard Univ, 525 Bryant St, NW, Washington, DC 20059, (202)806-5123.

STEWART, RAYNA COTTRELL
Professional football player. **Personal:** Born Jun 18, 1973, Oklahoma City, OK; married Sonia, Dec 29, 1995. **Educ:** Northern Arizona, bachelor's degree in advertising, 1995. **Career:** Houston Oilers, defensive back, 1996; Tennessee Oilers, 1997-. **Business Addr:** Professional Football Player, Tennessee Oilers, c/o Baptist Sports Park, 7640 H 70-5, Nashville, TN 37221.

STEWART, RONALD L.
Manager. **Personal:** Born Apr 29, 1936, Philadelphia, PA; married Ardelia; children: Maitland, Adriane. **Educ:** Cheyney St Coll, BS 1960; Univ of PA, MS 1963. **Career:** St Govt Relat Smith Kline & Fr Labs, mgr 1979-; Smith Kline Corp Person, mgr compens 1972-73, rel consul 1969-72. **Orgs:** Natl Urban Leag Black Exec Exch Prgm 1969-; mem Bd Educ Moorestown NJ Pub Sch 1969-78; mem Kappa Alpha Psi Frat; mem NAACP So Burlngtn Co NJ. **Honors/Awds:** Publ Heil & Stewart "Key Role Awaits Comm Pharms" Am Pharm Assn 1974. **Military Serv:** USMC 1959-61. **Business Addr:** 1500 Spring Garden St, Philadelphia, PA 19101.

STEWART, RONALD PATRICK
Educator. **Personal:** Born Nov 14, 1942, Birmingham. **Educ:** Drake U, BFA 1966; OH U, MEd 1968; Univ Cincinnati, MA 1970. **Career:** Nat Tchr Corps, tchr 1966-68; Hammond Sch City, 1968-69; Englewood Community Theatre, dir 1969; Univ Cincinnati, instr 1969-71; Contemporary Arts Cntr, consult dir 1974; Univ Cincinnati, asst prof 1971. **Orgs:** Bd & dir Arts Cncl OH Rvr Vlly; exec dir Arts Consortium; co-convenor Cultural Task Force Cincinnati; consult Bicentennial Prgrms Queen City Met; adv com Beamon Hough Art Fund, Links Inc Steering Com; Individual Artist, The Arts Cncl OH Rvr Vlly; mem Nat Art Educ Assn; City Core Activity Commn; OH Art Educ Assn; Phi Delta Kappa. **Honors/Awds:** Numerous honors, prizes, awds, juried & invited art exhibitions. **Business Addr:** Arts Consortium, 1515 Linn St, Cincinnati, OH 45214.

STEWART, RUTH ANN
Public policy analyst. **Personal:** Born Apr 4, 1942, Chicago, IL; daughter of Ann M Stewart and Elmer A Stewart; married David L Lewis; children: Allegra, Jason, Allison, Eric. **Educ:** Univ of Chgo, 1961-62; Wheaton Coll Norton, MA, BA 1963; Columbia Univ, MS 1965; Harvard Univ, 1974; John F Kennedy School of Govt, 1987. **Career:** Philips Acad Andover MA, librarian 1963-64; Biology Library Columbia Univ NY, head librarian 1965-68; Macmillan Co NY, prod mgr 1968-70; Schomburg Center for Rsch in Black Culture NY, asst chief 1970-80; New York Public Library, assoc dir for ext serv 1980-86; Library of Congress Washington DC, asst librarian of Congress for natl progs 1986-89; Congressional Research Service, Library of Congress, assoc director, senior specialist in arts & humanities, 1989-, senior policy analyst, 1995-. **Orgs:** Dir Natl Park Found 1978-84; trustee Wheaton Coll 1979-; mem Council Foreign Relations 1980-; mem Harvard Univ Library Visiting Comm 1976-88; visiting comm MIT Library 1986-89; Board of Visitors, School of Library and Information Science, Univ of Pittsburgh, l987-95; dir Women's Foreign Policy Group, 1992-; trustee, Lab School of Washington, 1993-95. **Honors/Awds:** Intl Council of Museums Fellow 1974; Portia Published by Doubleday 1977. **Business Addr:** Senior Policy Analyst, Congressional Research Service, Library of Congress, 101 Independence Ave, SE LM320, Washington, DC 20540.

STEWART, RYAN
Professional football player. **Personal:** Born Sep 30, 1973, Moncks Corner, SC. **Educ:** Georgia Tech. **Career:** Detroit Lions, defensive back, 1996-. **Business Addr:** Professional Football Player, Detroit Lions, 1200 Featherstone Rd, Pontiac, MI 48342, (248)335-4131.

STEWART, SHANNON HAROLD
Professional baseball player. **Personal:** Born Feb 25, 1974, Cincinnati, OH. **Career:** Toronto Blue Jays, outfielder, 1995-. **Business Addr:** Professional Baseball Player, Toronto Blue Jays, 300 Bremmer Blvd, Ste 3200, Toronto, ON, Canada M5V 3B3, (416)341-1000.

STEWART, W. DOUGLAS
City government official. **Personal:** Born Apr 8, 1938, Paterson, NJ; son of Irene Stewart; married Norma; children: Giselle. **Educ:** Fairleigh Dickinson Univ, BS 1970. **Career:** Wend Realty, pres; NJ Bank NA, asst treas; City of Paterson, dir div real estate & assessment; City of Orange Township, tax assessor, dir finance dept; Atlantic City, tax assessor. **Orgs:** Mem Rotary; Jersey Ski; Intl Assn of Assessing Officers, Northeast Region Assn of Assessing Officers; Soc of Professional Assessors. **Honors/Awds:** Distinguished Serv Award Passaic Co Planned Parenthood 1984; Past Officers Award Passaic Co Child Care Coordinator Agency 1978. **Military Serv:** AUS 2 yrs. **Business Addr:** Tax Assessor, City of Atlantic City NJ, 1301 Bacharach Blvd, Room 606, Atlantic City, NJ 08401.

STEWART, WARREN HAMPTON, SR.
Clergyman. **Personal:** Born Dec 11, 1951, Independence, KS; son of Jessie Elizabeth Jenkins and Jesse Jared Stewart; married Serena Michele Wilson, Jun 18, 1977; children: Warren Hampton Jr, Matthew Christian, Jared Chamberlain, Justin Mitchell, Aaron Frederick Taylor, Jamila Imani. **Educ:** Bishop Coll, Dallas TX, BA, 1973; Union Theological Seminary, New York NY, MDiv, 1976, MST, 1977; Amer Baptist Seminary of the West, Berkeley CA, DM, 1982; Ottawa Univ, Doctor of Divinity Degree, 1994. **Career:** Cornerstone Baptist Church, Brooklyn NY, assoc minister, 1973-78; First Institutional Baptist Church, Phoenix AZ, 1977-. **Orgs:** Life mem, NAACP; mem, evangelical bd, Natl Baptist Convention USA; mem, American Baptist Churches, USA; mem, Amer Baptist Churches of Arizona; bd mem, pres, Amer Baptist Churches of Pacific Southwest. **Honors/Awds:** Image Award, NAACP; Amer Muslim Mission award; Reverend William Hardison Memorial Award; Roy Wilkins Memorial Award, NAACP (Maricopa County chapter); humanitarian award, Central Dist Congress of Christian Education; Martin Luther King Jr Justice Award, First Intl Baptist Church, 1988; distinguished service award, United Nations Assn (Greater Phoenix chapter); author of Interpreting God's Word in Black Preaching, Judson, 1984; established Samaritan House, emer shelter for homeless. **Special Achievements:** Led statewide campaign to win Martin Luther King Jr-Civil Rights Day, Arizona, 1992; Appointed Exec Sec of the Home Mission Bd of the Natl Baptist Convention, USA Inc. **Business Addr:** Pastor, First Institutional Baptist Church, 1141 E Jefferson St, Phoenix, AZ 85034.

STEWART, WILLIAM H.
Educator, clergyman. **Personal:** Born Apr 18, 1935, Greensboro, NC; son of Mildred Hancock Stewart and Harold W Stewart; children: Candida. **Educ:** NC A&T State Univ, BS 1960; Central MI Univ, MA 1973; Blackstone School of Law, JD 1977; Western CO Univ, DBAdm 1980. **Career:** Coop League of the USA, dir demonstration prog 1966-69; General Elect Co Chicago, training dir 1969-70; City of Ann Arbor, dir model cities prog 1970-71; US Dept of Housing Urban Dev, div dir 1971-75; Exec Seminar Ctr US Civil Serv Commiss, assoc dir 1975-78; TN Valley Authority Div of Energy Use, mgr Community Conserv Proj 1978-86; Mutual Housing Corp, exec dir, 1987-90; Knoxville College, Div of Business & Social Sciences, dir, 1987-91; Mother Love Baptist Church, pastor, 1987-92; US Department of Energy, Southeastern Power Administration, Power Marketing Division, program manager, 1991-94; Macedonia Outreach Ministries, pres, 1994-96; Rochdale Institute, ceo, 1996-. **Orgs:** Alpha Phi Alpha Fraternity 1959-; pres bd of dir The Stewart-Candida Co 1978-85; dean Chattanooga Baptist Bible Coll 1981-84; pres bd of dir Chattanooga Area Minority Investment Forum 1981-87; chmn bd of dir Sun Belt Allied Industries 1985-86; chmn Seville-Benz Corp 1986-93; pres, Operation PUSH, Chattanooga, TN, 1986-88. **Honors/Awds:** Youth & Commun Serv Frederick Douglass Chapter Hamilton Co 1981; Serv Award Lane Coll Jackson TN 1981; Distinguished Citizen City of Chattanooga TN 1981; Outstanding Mem Alpha Iota Alpha 1983; Distinguished Serv Sun Belt Assn Ind 1984; Humanitarian Award, Jas B Dudley High School Alumni Assn, 1988; Distinguished Service Award, Southeastern Power Admin, 1994; Doctorate of Divinity, Laurence Univ, 1968; Doctor of Laws, Buckner Univ, 1970. **Military Serv:** US Army, sgt, 3 years. **Business Addr:** New Monumental Baptist Church, 715 E 8th Street, Chattanooga, TN 37403.

STEWART, WILLIAM O.
Educational administrator (retired). **Personal:** Born Feb 8, 1925, Chicago, IL; son of Marvella Brewer Stewart and James Stewart; married Corinne Lucas, Jun 27, 1974 (deceased). **Educ:** TN State Univ, BS 1950; DePaul Univ, ME 1967; Univ of Sarasota, EdD 1980. **Career:** Chicago Bd of Educ, asst prinicpal 1991-; TN State Univ Alumni Assn, Mid-West vice chm 1961; Chicago Tchrs Union Dist 13, Chicago Bd of Educ, legislative coord 1976-91; Univ of Sarasota, Natl Bd of Schls & Univ, stdnt rep 1979. **Orgs:** Vice Pres Hale Med Ctr 1991; Trustee Chicago Tchrs Union 1991; asst prin John Farren Elem Sch 1991; bd dir Beatrice Caffrey Yth Ctr 1985; adv Dist 13 Educ Cncl (Bd of Ed) 1991; vice pres Daniel Hale Medical Foundation; John Farren Local School Council. **Honors/Awds:** People of Purpose Grass Roots Org 1981; Certificate of Honor Past Pres TN State Alumni 1980; Fclty Awrd John Farren Elem Sch 1976; Great Guy Awrd Radio Station WJPC 1974; Apple Award Chicago Bd of Educ 1988. **Home Addr:** 219 E 45th St, Chicago, IL 60653.

STICKNEY, JANICE L.
Biomedical consultant. **Personal:** Born Jul 21, 1941, Tallahassee, FL; daughter of Nerissa Lee Stickney (deceased) and William H Stickney (deceased). **Educ:** Oberlin Coll, AB 1962; Univ of Michigan, PhD 1967. **Career:** UCSF, postdoctoral fellow 1967-68, instructor 1968-69, assistant professor 1969-72; Michigan State Univ, asst prof 1972-75, assoc prof 1975-81, prof 1981; GD Searle & Co, sr scientist 1981-83, assoc dir of office of scientific affairs 1983-87, dir dept of medical and scientific information, 1987-88; Brokenburr Stickney Assoc, pres, 1988-. **Orgs:** Consultant law firms; serve on review comm NIH and NSF; consultant FDA 1971-80; Amer Assn for the Advancement of Science; Sigma Xi; Amer Soc of Pharmacology & Exper Therapeutics; elected to nominating comm 1978, 1989, membership comm 1981-84, councillor 1984-87; adv council NIEHS 1979-83; American Heart Association; International Society of Cardiovascular Pharmacotherapy; Drug Information Association; American Medical Writers Association. **Honors/Awds:** Author of more than 25 full length publications. **Business Addr:** President, Brokenburr Stickney Associates, 1555 Sherman, Dept 142, Evanston, IL 60201.

STICKNEY, PHYLLIS YVONNE
Actress. **Educ:** UCLA. **Career:** Television credits include: "The Women of Brewster Place," 1989; "New Attitude," beginning 1990; "Clippers," 1991; "The Colored Museum," 1991; "A Different World," "The Cosby Show," "The Late Show," "Showtime at the Apollo;" film credits include: Streets of Fire, 1984; Beat Street, 1984; Frederick Douglass: An American, 1986; House Party, 1990; Jungle Fever, 1991; Talkin' Dirty After Dark, 1991; stage credits include: Death and the King's Horseman; Striver's Row; The Contract.

STICKNEY, WILLIAM HOMER, JR.
Sportswriter. **Personal:** Born Apr 2, 1945, Nashville, TN; son of Nerissa Lee Brokenburr Stickney (deceased) and William Homer Stickney Sr (deceased); divorced 1986; children: William Homer III. **Educ:** Prairie View A&M University, BS, 1968. **Career:** Baylor College of Medicine, Houston, TX, lab tech, 1968-69; US Dept of Agriculture, Houston, TX, livestock inspector, 1969; Prairie View A&M Univ, Prairie View, TX, lab technician, 1969-70; Houston Chronicle, Houston, TX, sportswriter, 1970-. **Orgs:** US Basketball Writers Assn, 1978-; US Track & Field Writers Assn, 1989-; US Boxing Writers Assn, 1988-; Texas Sportswriters Assn, 1974-; Heisman Trophy Award Selection Committee, 1992-. **Honors/Awds:** Associated Press Managing Editors Association of Texas, Honorable Mention for Spot Sports Reporting, 1994. **Home Addr:** 2916 Meadowgrass Ln, Houston, TX 77082.

STIELL, PHELICIA D'LOIS
Government official. **Personal:** Born Jul 21, 1959, Chancellor, AL; daughter of Elnor Sconyers Hornsby; divorced; children: Justin, Brooke. **Educ:** Alabama A&M University, BS, 1981; Mississippi State University, 1983; University of West Florida, MPA, 1985; Florida State Univ College of Law, currently. **Career:** Thad Green Enterprises, career counselor, 1981-82; Community Counseling Svcs, social worker, 1982-83; Air Force Systems Command, financial management specialist, 1985-91; Air Force Special Operations Command, prog management analyst, 1991-. **Orgs:** Delta Sigma Theta Svc Sorority, secretary, 1980-; National Coalition of 100 Black Women, 1994-; Democratic Black Caucus of FL, mem, 1994, convention chair, 1994-; Alpha Kappa Mu, National Honor Society, 1979; American Society of Public Administrators, 1984-86. **Honors/Awds:** Office of Personnel Management, Presidential Management Intern, 1985; Dollars & Sense Magazine, Outstanding Business & Professional Awd, 1992; Mississippi State University, Academic Fellowship, 1983; Alabama A&M university, Academic Scholarship, 1977; Inns of Court, student member. **Special Achievements:** DOD Executive Leadership Dev, 1995; Chair Democratic Black Caucus of Florida Convention, 1994.

STILL, ART BARRY
Professional football player (retired). **Personal:** Born Dec 5, 1955, Camden, NJ. **Educ:** Univ of Kentucky, BA, 1978. **Career:** Defensive end: Kansas City Chiefs, 1978-87; Buffalo Bills, 1988-89. **Honors/Awds:** Named to The Sporting News NFL All-Star Team 1980; played in Pro Bowl, 1980-82, 1984 seasons.

STILL, BRYAN ANDREI
Professional football player. **Personal:** Born Jun 3, 1974, Newport News, VA. **Educ:** Virginia Tech, communications major. **Career:** San Diego Chargers, wide receiver, 1996-. **Business Addr:** Professional Football Player, San Diego Chargers, 9449 Friars Rd, Qualcomm Stadium, San Diego, CA 92108, (619)280-2111.

STILL, VALERIE
Professional basketball player. **Personal:** Born May 14, 1961; children: Aaron Still Lock. **Educ:** Univ of Kentucky. **Career:** Columbus Quest, forward, 1996-. **Business Addr:** Professional Basketball Player, Columbus Quest, 7451 State Route 16, Dublin, OH 43016, (614)873-6555.

STINSON, ANDREA
Professional basketball player. **Personal:** Born Nov 25, 1967. **Educ:** North Carolina State, attended. **Career:** Charlotte Sting, guard, 1997-. **Honors/Awds:** All-WNBA Second Team, 1997. **Business Addr:** Professional Basketball Player, Charlotte Sting, 2709 Water Ridge Pkwy, Ste 400, Charlotte, NC 28217, (704)424-9622.

STINSON, CONSTANCE ROBINSON
Realtor. **Personal:** Born in Ontario;daughter of Eliza Smith Robinson and Theodore R Robinson; married Harold N Stinson Sr, Jun 14, 1949 (died 1984); children: Harold N Jr. **Educ:** Barber Scotia Coll, BS 1949; Tchrs Coll Columbia Univ, MA 1962.

Career: Burke Co GA Sch Sys, tchr 1940-67; Pearl H Sch Nashvl TN, tchr 1964-65; Engl Wrkshp So Univ Baton Rouge, LA, dir NDEA 1966; Elon Miller Realty, Tuscaloosa, AL, rltr 1971-. **Orgs:** Mem AL Assn of Rltrs, Natl Assn of Rltrs, Wmn's Cncl of Rltrs 1972-; Asmbly Mission Bd Presby Chrch 1982-85, mem bd of dir Presbyt Apts Northport, AL 1982-85; elder Brown Mem Presbyt Church Tuscaloosa, AL 1972-; mem, Church Vocations Ministry Unit, Presbyterian Church USA, 1985-; charter member, life member, Million Dollar Roundtable, Bd of Rltrs, Tuscaloosa, AL, 1979-. **Honors/Awds:** Salesperson of the Year, Tuscaloosa Bd of Rltrs 1979. **Home Addr:** 1313 Wakefield Dr, Tuscaloosa, AL 35405. **Business Addr:** Realtor, Elon Miller Realty, 1410 McFarland Blvd E, Tuscaloosa, AL 35405.

STINSON, DONALD R.
Artist. **Personal:** Born Jan 29, 1929, Detroit; married Clara Key. **Educ:** E LA Jr Coll, 1948-49; Wayne U, 1950-51; Compton Jr Coll, 1960-62. **Career:** Artist, currently; Owner, 3 homes for aged persons, mentally ill, mentally retarded adults, retired; Golden St Life Ins Co, field rep 1956-71; Vets Hosp Long Bch, retired prac nurse 1955-56; City of Berkeley CA, rec dir 1949-50. **Orgs:** Mem bd dir Adv Med Diag Labs LA; prgm dir bd mem Willing Worker for Mentally Retarded LA; exec bd Com for Simon Rodias Towers in Watts LA; mem Stewart Grant AME Ch LA; Out of Home Care Tech Adv Com LA; mem Hub City Optimist Club of Compton; Art W Assn Inc; Black Art Counc; mem CA Caretakers Orgn; owner Billees Liquor; mem Nat Conf of Artist. **Honors/Awds:** Master enamelist award Ma-Donna Fest; Barnsdall all City Show LA; Watts Fest Art Show; CA Black Craftsman Show; Black Artisits in Am; won sev awards & hon while selling for Golden St Life Ins. **Military Serv:** USAF A/1c 1951-54. **Business Addr:** 17365 Parsons Rd, Riverside, CA 92508.

STINSON, JOSEPH MCLESTER
Physician, educator. **Personal:** Born Jul 27, 1939, Hartwell, GA; married Elizabeth; children: Joseph Jr, Jeffrey, Julia. **Educ:** Paine College, BS, 1960; Meharry Medical College, MD, 1964; Hubbard Hospital, intern, 1964-65. **Career:** Harvard Medical School, research fellowship, physiology, 1966-68; Meharry Medical College, associate professor physiology, 1972-74; Vanderbilt University, fellowship, pulmonary diseases, 1974-76; Meharry Medical College, associate professor, director, pulmonary diseases, 1976-81, chairman department of physiology, 1981-84, associate professor, medicine, physiology, 1984-. **Orgs:** Consultant, pulmonary diseases, Virginia Hospital, 1976-; board directors, Tennessee Lung Association, 1976-; Tennessee Thoracic Society, secretary/treasurer, 1977-; American Physiology Society; Thoracic Society Sec, St Luke Geriatric Center; Tennessee Heart Association; president, Tennessee Thoracic Society, 1985-87; Nashville Society for Internal Medicine; board of directors, Paine College National Alumni Association, 1985-. **Honors/Awds:** 24 Science Publications, 1969-76; Macy Faculty Fellowship, 1974-77; Pulmonary Academy Award, NHLBI, 1977-82; Alpha Omega Alpha. **Military Serv:** USAF maj 1968-72. **Business Addr:** Associate Professor, Meharry Medical College, 1005 Dr D B Todd Blvd, Nashville, TN 37208.

STINSON, LINDA
Information specialist, librarian. **Personal:** Born Sep 1, 1965, Boston, MA; daughter of Frances Laverne Johnston Stinson and James Stinson. **Educ:** Emmanuel College, Boston, MA, BA, 1987; Simmons College, Boston, MA, MLS, 1989. **Career:** Emmanuel College, Boston, MA, library asst, 1983-86; Boston Public Library, Boston, MA, librarian, 1987-89; Rogers & Wells, New York, NY, reference librarian, 1989-90; Forbes Magazine, New York, NY, information specialist/reference librarian, 1991. **Orgs:** Member, Black Librarians Assn, 1989; member, Special Libraries Assn, 1989-. **Honors/Awds:** Author, What Is This Sadness, American Poetry Anthology, 1987. **Business Addr:** Information Specialist, Reference Librarian, Forbes Magazine, Information Center, 60 Fifth Ave, New York, NY 10011.

STITH, ANTOINETTE FREEMAN
Marketing executive. **Personal:** Born Aug 10, 1958, Atlanta, GA; daughter of Eva Mae Cobb Freman and William Anthony Freeman; children: Larkin Antonio, Skeeter. **Educ:** Newport News Shipbuilding Apprentice School, Certificate 1981; Thomas Nelson Community Coll, Hampton, VA, Industrial Mgmt Trainee Certificate 1982, AA, business mgmt, 1990. **Career:** Newport News Shipbuilding, supervisor; Capitol Bankers Life, Norfolk, VA, marketing representative, 1990-; Reliance Standard Life, Norfolk, VA, marketing representative, 1990-; Financial Security Corp of America, Maitland, FL, marketing representative, 1991-. **Orgs:** Mem Apprentice Alumni Assn 1981-; public relations officer Coalition of 100 Black Women 1985-86; licensed real estate agent 1985-; public relations officer, charter mem The Peninsula Chapter Newport News-Hampton VA. **Honors/Awds:** Real Estate Sales Assoc of the Month 5-Star Real Estate 1987. **Business Addr:** Marketing Representative, Financial Security Corp of America, #22 Koger Executive Center, Suite 101, Norfolk, VA 23502.

STITH, BRYANT LAMONICA
Professional basketball player. **Personal:** Born Dec 10, 1970, Emporia, VA; married Barbara; children: two. **Educ:** Virginia. **Career:** Denver Nuggets, guard, 1992-. **Business Addr:** Professional Basketball Player, Denver Nuggets, 1635 Clay St, Denver, CO 80204, (303)893-6700.

STITH, CHARLES RICHARD
Clergyman. **Personal:** Born Aug 26, 1949, St Louis, MO; married Deborah; children: Percy, Mary. **Educ:** Baker Univ, BA 1973; Interdenominational Theol Ctr, MDiv 1975; Harvard Univ, ThM 1977. **Career:** Harvard Divinity School, adjunct prof; Union United Methodist Church, sr pastor 1979-94; Organization for a New Equality, pres, currently. **Orgs:** Incorporator Boston Bank of Commerce 1984; bd mem WCVB-TV Editorial Bd; trustee MLK Ctr for Nonviolent Social Change; dir United Way Mass Bay until 1986. **Honors/Awds:** Racial Harmony Awd Black Educators Alliance of MA 1984; Frederick Douglass Awd YMCA 1985; Ingram Memorial Awd Boston Urban Bankers Forum 1985. Paul Revere Bowl, City of Boston, 1989; Baker University, Honorary DD, 1991. **Special Achievements:** Author, Polical Religion, Abingdon Press, 1995. **Business Addr:** President, Org for a New Equality, 364 Boylston Street, 3rd Fl, Boston, MA 02116-3805.

STITH, MELVIN THOMAS
Educational administrator, educator. **Personal:** Born Aug 11, 1946, Portsmouth, VA; married Patricia Lynch; children: Melvin Jr, Lori, William. **Educ:** Norfolk State University, BA, sociology, 1968; Syracuse University, School of Management, MBA, 1973, PhD, 1977. **Career:** Syracuse Univ, director, MBA program 1976-77; Univ of South Florida, asst dean/asst prof 1977-82, assoc dean/assoc prof 1982; Florida A&M Univ, assoc prof 1982-85; Florida State Univ, dept chair marketing 1985-91, College of Business, dean, 1991-. **Orgs:** Polemarch Syracuse Alumni Kappa Alpha Psi Frat 1976-77; polemarch Tampa Alumni Kappa Alpha Psi Frat 1981; consulting Anheuser-Busch, Inc 1982-83; bd of directors Tampa Branch Urban League 1981; consulting The Drackett Co 1984; consulting Management Horizons 1984, Amer Hosp Supply 1985; Florida Council of Educational Mgmt 1988-; social environment comm, 21st Century Council, Tallahassee; bd of dirs, Chamber of Commerce, Tallahassee; Florida Black Business Investment Bd; bd of dirs: Esmor Corporation, New York; Tallahassee State Bank, Tallahassee; JM Enterprises Youth Automotive Program, Deerfield Beach, FL; Sprint/United Telephone Florida, Altamonte Springs, FL; Palmetto Hospital Trust Services, Ltd, Columbia, SC; Synovous Financial Corp, AACSB. **Honors/Awds:** Florida Endowment Fund, Presidential Leadership Award; Florida State University, Martin Luther King Jr Distinguished Scholar Award, 1990; Division of Student Affairs, Florida State University, Being There Award, 1989; Tallahassee Branch, NAACP, Black Achiever, 1989; Kappa Alpha Psi Fraternity, Achievement Award, 1988; Beta Gamma Sigma; Sigma Rho Sigma Honorary Society; Phi Kappa Phi Honor Society. **Special Achievements:** Author, works include: "Middle Class Values in Black & White," Personal Values and Consumer Psychology, 1984; Black Versus White Leaders: A Comparative Review of the Literature, w/Charles Evans and Kathryn Bartol, 1978; The Black Consumer and Value Systems; major program appearances include: discussant, "Off-Price Retailers Spin the Wheel of Retailing," Mid-Atlantic Marketing Assn, Orlando, FL, 1984; "The Importance of Values to the Black Consumer," 16th African Heritage Conference, Tampa, FL, 1984. **Military Serv:** US Army, Military Intelligence, captain, 1968-71. **Home Addr:** 2588 Noble Drive, Tallahassee, FL 32312-2818.

STITT, E. DON (ELLIOTT DONALD)
Zone sales manager. **Personal:** Born Dec 17, 1942, Birmingham, AL; son of Niola (Johnson) Stitt and Wilner C Stitt; married E Lois (Lowe) Stitt, Oct 17, 1973; children: Nikoal C, Kelley L. **Educ:** Central Michigan Univ, Mount Pleasant MI, BA, 1981. **Career:** Chrysler Motors, several positions from job setter to zone sales manager, 1965-. **Orgs:** Mem, Chamber of Commerce, Denver CO, Urban League of Metro Denver, Operation PUSH, Chrysler Minority Dealer Assn; life mem, NAACP, 1988. **Honors/Awds:** Mentor of the Year, Natl Assn of Black Women Entrepreneurs, 1987; Award Plaque, Chrysler Black Dealer Assn, 1987. **Military Serv:** AUS, Sergeant, 1961-64.

STOCKARD, BETSY
Local government official. **Career:** Decatur City Council, currently. **Special Achievements:** First African American woman to serve on council. **Business Addr:** Councilwoman, Decatur City Council, PO Box 488, Decatur, IL 62525, (217)355-7410.

STOCKMAN, IDA J.
Educator. **Personal:** Born Sep 6, 1942, Sumner, MS; daughter of Angie Burton Jones and Samuel Jones; married George Stockman, Oct 23, 1969; children: Demress Elise, Farah Nisa. **Educ:** Jackson State Univ, Jackson, MS, BS, 1962; University of Iowa, Iowa City, IA, MA, 1965; Pennsylvania State Univ, State College, PA, PhD, 1971. **Career:** Jackson State University, Jackson, MS, instructor, 1965-66; Rehabilitation Center, Binghamton, NY, speech/language pathologist, 1966-67; Kantonsspital St Gallen, St Gallen, Switzerland, research assoc, 1972-76 summers; Howard University, Washington, DC, asst/prof assoc, 1971-79; Center for Applied Linguistic, Washington, DC, research assoc, 1980-82; Michigan State University, East Lansing, MI, assoc prof, 1982-. **Orgs:** Board of directors, National Association Black Speech, Language & Hearing, 1989-; board of directors, Michigan Association-Deaf, Speech and Hearing Services, 1989-; editorial board, Howard Journal of Communication; Howard University, Washington, DC, 1988-; editorial board, Journal of Linguistics and Education, 1988-; educational standards board, The American Speech, Language, Hearing Association, 1990-. **Honors/Awds:** Information Exchange Scholar, World Rehabilitation Fund Inc, 1985; Research Grant Award, National Science Foundation, 1985; Research Grant Award, National Institute of Education, 1980; Outstanding Woman Achiever, Michigan State University, 1986; Phi Delta Kappa Professional Honor Society, 1981. **Business Addr:** Associate Professor, Dept of Audiology and Speech Sciences, Michigan State University, 371 Communication Arts & Sciences Bldg, East Lansing, MI 48824.

STOCKS, ELEANOR LOUISE
Company executive, association executive. **Personal:** Born May 10, 1943, Taledigga, AL; daughter of Cora Locust and Walter Locust; married James A Stocks Jr; children: Kevin, Kim. **Educ:** Central State Univ, BS Educ 1965; Ohio Univ, MEd 1971; Miami Univ, Post-grad 1976-78. **Career:** Dayton Public Schools, educator 1966-69; Ohio Univ, administrator 1970-72; Sinclair Comm Coll, assoc prof 1973-84; Ee & Jj Enterprises, pres, 1987-; DBA Cora's Inc, pres, 1987-. **Orgs:** Vice pres Dayton Chap Jack & Jill of Amer 1984; bd mem Human Serv Adv Bd 1985-; pres Ohio Council of Urban League Executives 1986-; mem Natl Urban League Educ Iniative Comm 1986; mem NAACP 1986-87; pres/charter mem Black Women for Professional Development; Natl Business League, Dayton Chapter, vice pres, 1988-; Springfield Urban League, pres/CEO, 1985-. **Honors/Awds:** Publication: Education Materials, University Press Co 1978; Service Awd Twinning Program NCNW Dayton 1980; producer Around Town with the Urban League, WIZE 1985; Jennings Scholar-Outstanding Educator, 1970.

STOCKTON, BARBARA MARSHALL
Psychologist (retired). **Personal:** Born Oct 19, 1923, Rockville, MD; daughter of Grace Elizabeth Weems Stockton and Augustus Lewis Stockton. **Educ:** Howard U, BS 1951, MS 1955; Oxford Univ UK, Certs 1966; NY Med Coll & Univ of Madrid, 1969; Univ of Athens Greece, 1970; Royal Acad London, 1971; Univ of Vienna, 1973; Univ of Bologna, 1974. **Career:** DC Pub Sch Ctr III, dir 1967-81, clinical Psychlgst 1965-67; Crownsville St Hosp MD, psychlgy intrn 1957-59; AUS Dept of Defns, anlytcl stat 1955-57, suprvsy stat clk 1948-55, stat cdng clk 1943-58; US Dept of Comrce, sctn clk 1942-43. **Orgs:** Mem Am Psychol Assn; life member, DC Psychol Assn; Nat Assn of Sch Psychol; Am Assn for Mentl Def; Am Acdmy of Pol & Soc Sci; the Counc for Excptnl Chldrn Bd of Gov DC 1972-75; mem Psi Chi 1950; Women's Leag Howard Univ Assn Womn Admin in Edn; mem Women's Nat Dem Club; Archives Assn; Nat Trst for Hist Presvtn; mem Bd Dir & Nom Com Eplpsy Found of Am; mem Bd Dir Chmn Spec Proj 1971-72; chmn Nom Com DC Mntl Hlth Assn; mem Mayor's Comm on Food Nutrtn & Hlth; chmn Child Feeding Subcom; life member, The National Council of Negro Women; member, The National Trust for Historic Preservation; member, The Washington Opera Guild; member, Washington Performing Arts; member, Friends of the Kennedy Center; member, DC Retired Teachers Assn. **Honors/Awds:** Merit civ award US Dept of Defns 1947; outst achvmt award Cncl for Excptnl Chldrn, 1972. **Home Addr:** 6430 7 St NW, Washington, DC 20012.

STOCKTON, CLIFFORD, SR.
Associate manager. **Personal:** Born Sep 16, 1932, Memphis; married Lois J Hampton; children: Angela, Clifford, Jr, Brian. **Educ:** TN St U, 1954;Memphis St Univ & TN St U, Grad Work; C of C Inst; Univ of GA. **Career:** Memphis Pub Schs, tchr 1956-68; Upward Bound Proj LeMoyne-Owen Coll, tchr 1967-68 summers; NAB Training Prgm Goldsmith's Dept Store, coord 1967-69; HumanResources C of C, asso mgr 1969-71, mgr 1971-72; Bus Resrce Ctr, exec dir 1972; Eco Dev Memphis Area C of C, asso mgr. **Orgs:** Bd dirs Boys Club of Am; OIC; Memphis Vol Plcmnt Prgm. **Honors/Awds:** Received Outst Serv to Minority Bus; Booker T Wash Award 1972 NBL. **Military Serv:** AUS spec 3rd class 1954-56. **Business Addr:** PO Box 224, Memphis, TN 38101.

STODGHILL, RONALD
Educational administrator. **Personal:** Born Dec 21, 1939, White Plains, NY; son of Marian Stodghill and Joseph Stodghill; divorced; children: Kimberly Denise Minter, Ronald Stodghill III. **Educ:** Wayne State Univ, Education Doctorate 1981; Western MI Univ, Master of Art Degree Cirriculum Dvlmnpt & Coordntr 1961. **Career:** St Louis Public School, assoc supt 1976-79; St Louis Pub School, deputy supt 1979-82; St Louis Public School, interim supt of Schools 1982-83; St Louis Public Schools, deputy Supt of instr 1983-84; City Detroit-Dept of Parks/Rec, rec instr 1961; Detroit Bd of Educ, science & eng teacher 1963; Detroit Bd of Educ, biology teacher 1963-65; Western MI Univ Custer Job Corps, team leader 1965-67; US

Ind Custer Job Corp, mtnce school ad admnstr 1967-68; MI-OH Regional Educ Lab, prog assoc 1968-68. **Orgs:** Dir ed New Detroit, Inc 1973-76; assoc dir assoc Suprvsn & Curr Dvl Mpt 1970-73; coordntr of comm MI-OH Rgnl Edctnl Lab 1968-69; exec cncl mem Assoc for Suprvsn & Curr Dvlpmt (ASCD) 1979; mem brd of dir Assoc for Suprvsn & Curr dvlmpt 1977-79; chrmn ASCD 1977 conf Assoc for Suprvsn & Curr Dvlpmt 1977. **Honors/Awds:** Special Achiever 1979; St Louis Metro Sentinel Nwspr 1979; Comm Recognition Award/Coca-Cola Btlng Co 1982; Eastern Airlines/MAJIC 108FM Radio Station. **Business Addr:** Superintendent, Wellston School District, 6574 St Louis Ave, St Louis, MO 63121.

STODGHILL, WILLIAM
Labor union official. **Personal:** Born Oct 7, 1940, Mount Vernon, NY; son of Marion (Wynn) Stodghill and Joseph Stodghill. **Educ:** Wayne State Univ, Detroit MI, attended; Univ of Detroit, Detroit MI, attended. **Career:** Local 79 SEIU, Detroit MI, organizer, 1966-74; Local 50 SEIU, St Louis MO, pres, 1978-; Serv Employees Intl Union, Washington DC, vice pres, 1979-. **Orgs:** Chmn, Local 50 Benefit Serv Trust and Pension, currently, Contract Cleaners Trust and Pension, currently; trustee, South African Freedom Fund, currently; mem, Advisory Comm on Civil Rights, currently; chmn, SEIU Health Care Div, currently; exec bd, A Philip Randolph Inst, currently; bd mem, United Way of Greater St Louis, currently, St Louis Branch NAACP, currently, Jewish labor Comm, currently; secretary/treasurer, Central States Labor Council, currently. **Honors/Awds:** Proclamation, Mayor of St Louis, 1983; Isrel Solidarity Award, 1983; Martin Luther King Award, Martin Luther King Assn; Man of the Year, Minority Women, 1986; A Philip Randolph Award, A Philip Randolph Inst, 1986. **Military Serv:** US Army, sergeant, 1962-64. **Business Addr:** President & International President, Local 50, Service Employees Intl Union, AFL-CIO, CLC, 4108 Lindell Blvd, St Louis, MO 63108.

STOKES, BUNNY, JR.
Banking executive. **Career:** Citizen's Federal Savings Bank, Birmingham, AL, chief executive. **Business Addr:** Citizen's Federal Savings Bank, 300 18th N, Birmingham, AL 35203.

STOKES, CAROLYN ASHE
Educator. **Personal:** Born Nov 18, 1925, Philadelphia, PA; daughter of Louisa Burrell Ashe Shelton and Charles Malcolm Ashe; married Joseph H Stokes, Oct 29, 1947; children: Michael, Monica, Craig. **Educ:** Howard Univ, BA 1947, Univ of CA Berkeley, grad educ, 1970; John F Kennedy Univ, MA 1983, leadership 1987. **Career:** Scott Air Force Thrift Shop, bookkeeper; Joseph H Stokes DDS, dental asst and office mgr; Citizen's for Eisenhower Congressional Comm Washington DC, dir of public relations in rsch dept; Dept of Commerce Immigration and Naturalization Serv/Office of Price Admin Washington, numerous clerical and personnel positions; The Media Group, script writer; Clas Enterprises Art Consciousness & Well-Being Workshop, dir/founder; Senior Senator, CA Senior Legislature, organizational leadership consultant; CLAS Choices-Hologramatic Planning Consultant, director/founder, currently. **Orgs:** Annual mtg chair, president, Mental Health Assn of Contra Costa Co; mem-at-large; planning chair, Adv Council on Aging; bd mem Ctr for New Amers; public relations comm Family Serv of the East Bay; Health Career assistance comm Alta Bates Hosp Assn Trustee; bd Howard Thurman Educ Trust; life mem Natl Council of Negro Women; volunteer AAUW Diablo Intl Resource Ctr; consultant Council for Civic Unity of Orinda Lafayette Moraga; leadership comm United Way Opportunity West; mem West County Women's Forum, Amer Assn of Univ Women; Entrepreneurial Skills Ctr; mem, Institute of Arts & Disabilities Board. **Honors/Awds:** AAUW Distinguished Woman Awd; Howard Univ Outstanding Graduate; Delta Sigma Theta Comm Serv Awd; United Way Volunteer Awd; Amer Christian Freedom Soc Awd; Most Valuable Honored Person Awd, Office on Aging; Ctr for New Americans; First Historical Awd Black Family Assn of Contra Costa Co; 5 Golden Poet Awards, World of Poetry and Intl Society of Poets Award; Counselor Christian Sr's Extension, Admin Assts Senior Award; 2 Awards Contra Costa County Supvr commendations; Congressman George Miller Award; Congressman Ron Dellums Award; State Assemblyman Robert Campbell Award; City of Richmond Award. **Home Addr:** 90 Estates Dr, Orinda, CA 94563.

STOKES, GERALD VIRGIL
Educator, scientist, researcher. **Personal:** Born Mar 25, 1943, Chicago, IL; son of Louise Shelman Stokes and Henry Stokes; married Charlotte M Eubanks; children: Gordon K, Garrett K. **Educ:** Wilson Jr Coll, AA 1965; Southern IL Univ, BA 1967; Univ of Chicago, PhD 1973. **Career:** Univ of CO, postdoc 1973-76; Meharry Medical Coll, asst prof 1976-78; George Washington Univ, asst/assoc prof 1976-. **Orgs:** Mem Assn of Amer Med Coll 1977-87; CSMM-chmn Amer Soc for Microbiology 1984-; pres elect Wash DC Branch Amer Soc for Microbiology 1986-87; mem review comm Minority Biomedical Rsch Support 1986-90; American Society for Microbiology; bd of Scientific Counselors, Natl Center for Infections Diseases, CDC, Atlanta, GA, 1993-96. **Honors/Awds:** ACS Fellow Univ of CO 1973-75; NIH Post Doc Fellow Univ of CO 1976; Sigma Xi George Washington Univ 1978-; American Academy of Microbiology, fellow. **Business Addr:** Assoc Prof of Microbiology, George Washington Univ, 2300 Eye St NW, Washington, DC 20037, (202)994-3535.

STOKES, J. J. (JEREL JAMAL)
Professional football player. **Personal:** Born Oct 6, 1972, San Diego, CA. **Educ:** UCLA, bachelor's degree in sociology. **Career:** San Francisco 49ers, wide receiver, 1995-. **Special Achievements:** 1st round/10th overall NFL draft pick, 1995. **Business Addr:** Professional Football Player, San Francisco 49ers, 4949 Centennial Blvd, Santa Clara, CA 95054, (415)562-4949.

STOKES, JOHNNIE MAE
Educator. **Personal:** Born Oct 15, 1941, Tuscaloosa, AL; married Julius; children: Salvatore, Zachary. **Educ:** OH St U, BS Home Ec 1962; Portland St U, MS Educ 1974. **Career:** Mt Hood Comm Coll, couns instr 1975-; Good Samrtn Hosp & Med Ctr, clinical dietitian 1971-75; VA Hosp Vancouver WA, clin dietitian 1967-69; Chicago Bd of Hlth, mem & nutritionist 1966-67; VA Hosp Hines IL, clin diettn 1963-65; Bronx VA Hosp, dietetic intrnshp 1963. **Orgs:** Adv bd mem E Multnomah Co Leag of Women Voters; mem Am & OR Dietetic Assn; mem OR Assn of Sch Couns; vice pres Portland Chap of Links Inc 1979-81; mem Alpha Kappa Alpha Sor. **Honors/Awds:** Home ec hon Phi Upsilon Omericon; educ hon Phi Lambda Theta; Outst Yng Wmn of Am 1975. **Business Addr:** Mt Hood Community College, 26000 S E Stark, Gresham, OR 97030.

STOKES, JULIE ELENA
Educator. **Career:** Calif State Univ, Fullerton, lecturer, 1995-, San Bernardino, lecturer, Life Span Devt, 1994, 1995; CSU, Long Beach, lecturer, African-American Families and Child Devt, 1994; Univ of California, Riverside, lecturer, African-American Families and Child Devt, 1994, African-American Family Research Coordinator, site supvr, 1993-94, lecturer, the Study of African American Women, 1995, Partnership for Responsible Parenting Teen Preg Prog, project dir, 1996-, African American Family Research Project, res dir, 1993-95; Social Science Research Ctr, Fullerton, research associate, 1997-; Bethel Comm Outreach & Human Development, project evaluator, 1997-; 100 Black Men, Passport to the Future, project evaluator, 1997-. **Orgs:** American Psychological Assn, 1995-; American Psychological Society, 1995-; Assn of Black Psychologists, 1992-; Western Psychological Assn, 1991-; Eccelesia Christian Fellowship Church, church administrator, Exec Comm mem. **Honors/Awds:** Univ of California, Graduate Fellowship, 1991-92; California State Univ, San Bernardino, Univ Honors, 1991. **Special Achievements:** Publications: Co-author, "Cross's Stage Model Revisited: An Analysis of Theoretical Formulations and Empirical Evidence," Advances in Black Psychology, in press, 1995; co-author, "The Development of the Black Family Process Q-sort," The Handbook of Text and Measurement of Black Population, in press, 1995; co-author, "Assessing the Validity of the African Self-Consciousness Scale," Journal of Black Psychology; co-author, "The Home Environment as a Predicator of Achievement," Journal of Negro Education. **Business Addr:** Lecturer, California State Univ Fullerton, 800 N State College Blvd, Fullerton, CA 92631, (714)278-3848.

STOKES, LILLIAN GATLIN
Nurse, educator. **Personal:** Born Feb 18, 1942, Greenville, NC; married Robert; children: Everett, Robyn. **Educ:** Kate B Reynolds Sch of Nursing, diploma 1963; NC Central Univ, BS 1966; IN Univ, MSc 1969, PhD, 1997. **Career:** Norfolk Comm Hosp, staff nurse 1963-64; Silver Cross Hosp, staff nurse 1966-67; Purdue Univ, asst prof of nursing 1969-72; Natl Inst of Health, peer review spec proj grants 1977; IN Univ, assoc prof of nursing, currently. **Orgs:** Am Nurs Assn; IN St Nurs Assn; Natl Leag for Nurs; chpn Aud Nurs Com Home Care Agency of Gr Indnpls 1974-76; bd dir IN Univ Sch of Nurs Alumni Assn 1973-; Chi Eta Phi Sor; Sigma Theta Tau; Alpha Kappa Alpha Sor; Wmn's Aux Indianapolis Dist Dental Soc; mem Jack & Jill of Amer Inc, Coalition of 100 Black Women; mem, Links, Inc; mem exec cncl IN Univ Alumni Assoc; bd of dir Girls Clubs of Greater Indianapolis. **Honors/Awds:** Co-author "Adult & Child Care a Client Apprch to Nurs" CV Mosby Co 1973 1nd ed 1977; Lucille Petry Leone Awd Natl League for Nurs 1975; Special Achievement Awd Chi Eta Phi Sor 1975; chap "Delivering Health Serv in a Black Comm" publ in Cur Prac in Family Ctred Comm Nurs 1977; chap in "Growing Oldin the Black Comm" Current Prac in Gerontological Nursing 1979; Lillian G Stokes Awd given in my honor by IN Univ Sch of Nursing Alumni Assoc annually since 1980; included in Contemporary Minority Leaders in Nursing 1983; Outstanding Service Awd Jack & Jill of Amer Inc; Disting Serv Awd Girls Clubs of Greater Indianapolis Inc; co-author "Medical-Surgical Nursing, Common Problems of Adults and Children Across the Life Span," 1983, second edition, 1987; Madame C.J. Walker Award, 1996. **Business Addr:** Nurse, 1111 Middle Drive, Indianapolis, IN 46202-5107.

STOKES, LOUIS
Congressman, attorney. **Personal:** Born Feb 23, 1925, Cleveland, OH; son of Louise Stone Stokes (deceased) and Charles Stokes (deceased); married Jeanette Frances Jay, Aug 21, 1960; children: Shelley, Louis C, Angela, Lorene. **Educ:** Case Western Reserve Univ, 1946-48; Cleveland Marshall Law School, JD, 1953. **Career:** US House of Representatives, 11th Congressional District, Ohio, rep 1968-, chairman, House Appropriations Subcommittee on VA-HUD-Independent Agencies, member, Appropriations Subcommittee on the District of Columbia, Subcommittee on Labor-Health and Human Services Education; private practice, attorney. **Orgs:** Bd of trustees Martin Luther King Jr Ctr for Social Change, Forest City Hosp, Cleveland State Univ; bd dirs Karamu House; vice chmn, trustee bd St Paul AME Zion Church; fellow OH State Bar Assn; mem Cleveland Cuyahoga Cty, Amer Bar Assn, Pythagoras Lodge #9; exec comm Cuyahoga Cty Dem Party; exec comm OH State Dem Party; mem Urban League, Citizens League, John Harlan Law Club, Kappa Alpha Psi, Amer Civil Liberties Union, Plus Club, Amer Legion, African-Amer Inst Intl Adv Council; vice pres NAACP Cleveland Branch 1965-66; vice chmn Cleveland Sub-Com of US Comm on Civil Rights 1966; guest lecturer Cleveland Branch NAACP. **Honors/Awds:** Distinguished Serv Award; Certificate of Appreciation, US Comm on Civil Rights; William L Dawson Award, 1980; honorary degrees: Wilberforce Univ, Shaw Univ, Livingstone College, Ohio College of Podiatric Medicine, Oberlin College, Morehouse College, Meharry Medical College, Atlanta Univ, Howard Univ, Morehouse School of Medicine, Central State Univ, Xavier Univ. **Military Serv:** US Army, 1943-46. **Business Addr:** Congressman, US House of Representatives, Rayburn Bldg, Rm 2365, Washington, DC 20515.

STOKES, REMBERT EDWARDS
Educator, administrator. **Personal:** Born Jun 16, 1917, Dayton, OH; married Nancy; children: Linda, Deborah, Celeste. **Educ:** Wilberforce U, BS Sacred Theol ; Boston U, STB, ThD. **Career:** African Episcopalian Church Rhodesia, bishop; Wilberforce Univ, pres 1956-76; Payne Theol Sem, dean; AME Church Jamestown Cambridge Canton, previously minister. **Orgs:** Mem Assn for Higher Edn; AAAS; mem OH Mntl Hlth Assn; trustee of Cleveland Chap of Nat Conf of Christns & Jews; mem Nat Counc of Chs. **Honors/Awds:** Recip alumni award for distngshd pub serv Boston Univ 1966.

STOKES, RUEBEN MARTINE
Transportation company executive. **Personal:** Born Mar 27, 1957, Los Angeles, CA; son of Alma M Stokes and Bailey L Stokes (deceased); married Alana Maria Fullove, Mar 30, 1985; children: Rueben Martine II, Blair Elizabeth. **Educ:** Dartmouth College, BA, 1979; National University, attended, 1986-87. **Career:** Airborne Express, sales representative, 1981-82; North American Van Lines Inc, territory sales manager, 1982-85; Advanced Traffic Services Inc, marketing manager, 1985-87; Mayflower Transit Inc, district sales vice pres, 1987-91; Allied Van Lines, national sales director, 1991-94; Ryder Move Management, natl sales dir, 1994-. **Orgs:** Dartmouth College Alumni Association; Theta Delta Chi Fraternity Inc. **Honors/Awds:** National Merit Honor Society, Letter of Commendation, 1975; William J Tucker Fellowship Award, 1979; Ivy League Champion Football Team, 1978; National University, US Senator Scholarship, 1987. **Special Achievements:** Author: Super Selling Secrets for the Real World, Fairway Press, 1994. **Business Addr:** Director of Diversity and Strategic Development, Allied Van Lines, 215 West Diehl Rd, Naperville, IL 60563, (630)717-3000.

STOKES, SHEILA WOODS
Educational administrator. **Personal:** Born Aug 6, 1949, Toledo, OH; daughter of Essie James Woods and Willie Woods (deceased); married George Farrar Stokes, Nov 30, 1974 (divorced); children: Ericka Kaye. **Educ:** University of Toledo, Toledo, OH, BA education, 1971; Ohio State University, Columbus, OH, MA, public admin, 1979. **Career:** State of Arizona, Phoenix, AZ, training officer, 1980-84; Arizona State University, Tempe, AZ, assistant to vice president, management intern training officer, 1984-. **Orgs:** Founding member, Sister Friends: African American Women of Arizona State University, 1990-; past president, member, University Career Women, 1985-; campus advisor, Delta Sigma Theta, 1988-90; civilian review member, City of Phoenix Police Department Disciplinary Review and Use of Force Board, 1985-90; NAACP; Black-Jewish Coalition; board of directors, Phoenix Black Women's Task Force. **Honors/Awds:** Outstanding Employee of the Year, State of Arizona Department of Administration, 1984; Black Directors Project Honoree; Trio Achiever Award, MAEOPP, 1992. **Business Addr:** Assistant to the Vice Provost for Administrative Services, Arizona State University, Administration Building, Room 207, Tempe, AZ 85287-2303.

STOKES, STERLING J.
Auto dealer. **Career:** Bannister Lincoln-Mercury, Inc, Kansas City, MO, chief executive, 1983—.

STONE, CHUCK
Journalist, educator. **Personal:** Born Jul 21, 1924, St Louis, MO; son of Madalence Stone and Charles Stone; married Louise; children: Krishna, Allegra, Charles III. **Educ:** Wesleyan Univ, AB, 1948; Univ of Chicago, MA, 1951. **Career:** CARE, overseas rep, 1956-57; New York Age, editor, 1958-60; Am Com on Africa, assoc dir, 1960; WA Afro-Am Newspaper,

White House corres/editor, 1960-63; Columbia College, instructor, journalist, 1963-64; Chicago Daily Defender, editor-in-chief, 1963-64; Rep Adam Clayton Powell Jr, special asst, 1965-67; Rep Robert NC Nix, editorial rsch specialist; Educ Testing Serv, dir minority affairs; Philadelphia Daily News, sr editor; Univ of Delaware, English professor; Philadelphia Daily News, sr editor, columnist, currently; Newspaper Enterprise Association, syndicated columnist, 1989-; University of North Carolina, Walter Spearman professor of journalism, 1991-. **Orgs:** Chmn, Natl Conf on Black Power; fellow, founding mem, The Black Acad Arts & Letters; council mem, Natl Conf Black Political Science; founding mem, 1st pres, Natl Assn of Black Journalists. **Honors/Awds:** First prize, Best Column of Year, NNPA, 1960; Journalist of the Yr, Capital Press Club, 1961; Annual Distinguished Citizen Award, CORE, 1964; Award of Merit for Journalist, Alpha Phi Alpha 1965; Politician-in-Residence, Morgan State Coll, 1969; Honorary LHD, Pembroke State University, NC; Honorary LittD, Rider Coll, 1985; Honorary LHD, Wilberforce Univ, 1977; Undergraduate Teaching Award, UNC-CH, 1992; Outstanding Prof, Univ of Delaware Honor Soc, 1986; Honorary Federal Warden, US Bureau of Prisons, 1983; 1st Place, column, Pennsylvania Newspaper Publishers Assn; Laubach Excellence in Teaching Award, Univ of Delaware, 1989; first Spearman professor of journalism, University of North Carolina; Univ of Missouri, Missouri Honor Medal for distinguished sev in journalism, 1996. **Special Achievements:** Author, Tell It Like It Is, 1968; Black Political Power in America, 1968; King Strut, 1970. **Military Serv:** US Air Force, navigator, 1943-45. **Business Addr:** Walter Spearman Professor of Journalism, School of Journalism & Mass Communication, University of North Carolina, Chapel Hill, NC 27599-3365.

STONE, DOLORES JUNE
Union official. **Personal:** Born Jun 16, 1939, Mount Clemens, MI; daughter of Annie R Dorsey and Charles K Dorsey; married Kenneth Eugene Stone, May 23, 1955; children: Don Rico, Joyce Graham Adams, Denise D Neal, Kenneth Jr. **Educ:** Ford Motor, 240 Hrs Sewing 1966; UAW, Black Lake Labor Class 1971; MCCC, Speech 1981. **Career:** The Fawns Temple, pdr 1964; Local 400 UAW, joint council 1970, exec board 1971; V of New Haven p comm sec 1980; Ford Motor, floor inspector; mem Order of the Eastern Star Supreme Lodge Intnl ; mem bd of dir The New Haven Public Housing; mem of The New Haven HS Citzens Advisory Comm. **Orgs:** Trustee Village of New Haven 1982; sec EI Ford Motor 1983, leader 1984; prec delegate New Haven Democrate 1984; lioness sec New Haven 1984; historian Village of New Haven; bd of dir, Downriver Medical Facility 1987; vice pres, S E MCOGS City/Village Bloc, 1989. **Business Addr:** Resident Agent, New Haven Historical Society, Reg 1989, PO Box 428, New Haven, MI 48048.

STONE, DWIGHT
Professional football player. **Personal:** Born Jan 28, 1964, Florala, AL. **Educ:** Middle Tennessee State. **Career:** Pittsburgh Steelers, wide receiver, 1987-94; Carolina Panthers, 1995-. **Business Addr:** Professional Football Player, Carolina Panthers, 800 Mint St, Ericsson Stadium, Charlotte, NC 28202, (704)358-7000.

STONE, HAROLD ANTHONY
Marketing manager. **Personal:** Born Aug 9, 1949, New Bedford, MA; married Elizabeth G Bates. **Educ:** Univ of MA Amherst, BB 1969, BBA 1973; Atlanta U, MBA 1976-78. **Career:** Coca-Cola USA Cincnnti, cntrl/Mid-east area spl mrkt mgr 1976-; Maxwell House Div/Gen Foods, sales rep 1973-76. **Orgs:** Mem Nat Assn of Mrkt Devlprs; mem NAACP; mem Operation PUSH Inc. **Military Serv:** USNR 1971-77. **Business Addr:** Coca-Cola USA, 8805 Governors Hill Dr #400, Cincinnati, OH 45249-1337.

STONE, JESSE NEALAND, JR.
Educational administrator. **Personal:** Born Jun 17, 1924, Gibsland, LA; married Willia Dean Anderson; children: Michael (deceased), Shonda D. **Educ:** Southern Univ; Southern Univ Sch of Law, JD 1946-50. **Career:** LA Comm Human Rels Rgts & Respnsblts, asso dir 1966-70; Southern Univ Sch of Law, dean 1971-72; LA State Dept of Educ, asst supt of educ 1972-74; Southern Univ System, pres 1974-; 3rd Supreme Court Dist LA Supreme Court, assoc justc 1979. **Orgs:** Sec bd dir Am Cncl Educ 1985; mem bd dir Am Cncl Educ 1984; mem cncl of trustees Gulf So Rsrch Inst 1985; mem bd dir YMCA 1985 ; mem Unvrsl Grnd Lodge of LA 32nd Degree; mem Omega Psi Phi Frat. **Honors/Awds:** "Top Hat" Awrd Pittsburgh-Courier 1978; Apprctn Awrd Am Natl Red Cross 1973; Dstngshd Serv Awrd LA Educ Assn 1969; LA Ctzn of Year Awrd Omega Psi Frat 1966. **Military Serv:** AUS 1st sgt 1943-46; Asiatic Pacific Theatre Medal & Hnrbl Dschrg. **Business Addr:** President, Southern Univ System, Southern Branch Post Office, Baton Rouge, LA 70813.

STONE, JOHN S.
Obstetrician, gynecologist. **Personal:** Born Jul 16, 1930, Tampa, FL; son of Mr & Mrs Edward W Stone; married Gertrude Jane Holliday Stone; children: Faith Stone, Enid Griner, John. **Educ:** Talladega Coll, BS 1951; Meharry Medical Coll, MD 1956; Univ of TX St Joseph Hosp, 1969-72. **Career:** Houston Medical Forum, pres 1986-88; obstetrician-gynecologist. **Orgs:** Bd mem Central Life Ins Co of FL 1973-87; founder pres St Elizabeth Hosp of Houston Found 1974-78; mem United Fund Agency Operations Comm 1975; mem Amer Med Assoc, TX Medical Assoc, Harris County Med Soc; bd mem Catholic Charities, Central Life Ins Co of FL 1978-87; pres med staff Riverside General Hosp 1981-82; bd mem Catholic Charities 1983-87; Houston Medical Forum 1986-87; mem Amer Med Assoc, Lone State State Med Assoc, TX Med Assoc, Houston Med Forum, Harris County Med Soc, Houston Acad of medicine, Nu Boule. **Military Serv:** USAF capt 1957-59. **Business Addr:** Obstetrician, Gynecologist, 5511 Austin Rd, Houston, TX 77004.

STONE, KARA LYNN
Educator (retired). **Personal:** Born Nov 30, 1929, Richmond, KY; daughter of Mr & Mrs J Lynn Stone. **Educ:** BA Knoxvl Coll, BA 1949-53; Eastern Univ, MA 1960-62. **Career:** Louisville School for Blind, teacher 1954-55; Paris KY School Sys, teacher 1963-64; Talbot Co MD School Sys, teacher 1964-68; The Lincoln School for Gifted, dorm cnslr 1968-69; Eastern KY Univ, asst prof, beginning 1969. **Orgs:** Loan sec Eastern KY Credit Union 1978-; chrtr mem initiator Eastern Credit Union 1978-; bd mem Richmond League of Women Vtrs 1980-82; mem Zeta Phi Beta Sor Inc 1951; bd mem United Way of Madison Co 1978-79; pres Madison Co NAACP 1980-. **Honors/Awds:** Gov's Comm for Drug Abuse Educ Pgm EKU 1971; Centennial Awrd for Exc in Tchr EKU 1974; Gov's Comm for Ser To KY 1978. **Special Achievements:** First full-time faculty female, Eastern KY University, 1969. **Military Serv:** WAC nco 1955-58.

STONE, MARCENIA LYLE. See STONE, TONI in the Obituaries section.

STONE, REESE J., JR.
Corporate communications executive. **Personal:** Born Feb 1946, Dublin, GA; son of Mildred Andrews Stone and Reese J Stone Sr; married Jennifer S Eng, Aug 1979; children: Meris E. **Educ:** Tennessee State Univ, Nashville TN, BS, 1966; Howard Univ, Washington DC, MPA, 1973. **Career:** Howard Univ, assoc dir student affairs, 1970-72; Natl Educ Assn, communications coord, 1972-79; Metropolitan Transit Authority, dir public affairs, 1979-85; Planned Parenthood Fed of Amer, dir of communications, 1985-87; Philip Morris Companies Inc, mgr corporate communications, 1987-91; Children's Television Workshop, vp of corporate communications, 1993-; Sandstone Associates, 1991-; LLT Advertising, vp of business devt, currently. **Orgs:** Natl Press Club; Overseas Press Club; 100 Black Men; vice pres, principal, Commercial Real Estate-Sandstone Associates Inc, Newark NJ, 1981-; mentor, Columbia Univ Mentor Program, 1987-89; bd mem, Hispanic Media Ctr, 1988-; Public Affairs Council, 1988-. **Honors/Awds:** PRSA Big Apple Award, Public Relations Soc of Amer, 1989; "Hispanic 100," Hispanic Magazine, 1991; Ohio State Award (for radio broadcast "Equal Rights Under Law: Desegregation in America,") 1990. **Military Serv:** US Army, Alaskan Command, Fairbanks, 1968-70; Honorable Discharge. **Home Addr:** 8 Maplewood Ave, Maplewood, NJ 07040.

STONE, RONALD
Professional football player. **Personal:** Born Jul 20, 1971, West Roxbury, MA; married Roxane. **Educ:** Boston College, attended. **Career:** Dallas Cowboys, guard, 1993-95; New York Giants, 1996-. **Business Addr:** Professional Football Player, New York Giants, Giants Stadium, East Rutherford, NJ 07073, (201)935-8111.

STONE, TONI. See Obituaries section.

STONE, WILLIAM T.
Attorney, business executive. **Personal:** Born Jan 8, 1931, Washington, DC; son of Beulah Stone and Thomas Stone; married Sara Cumber; children: William T Jr, Jacquelyn E, Michael R, Christopher D. **Educ:** Central State Univ, BS 1953; New Eng Inst Anatomy, attended 1956; Amer Univ, JD 1961. **Career:** Law Practice, 1962-; Williamsburg City & James City Co Cts, substitute judge 1968-; Whiting's Funeral Home, owner; Stone & Associates, PC. **Orgs:** Mem Old Dominion, PA, Amer, Williamsburg & Peninsula Bar Assns; VA Trial Lawyers Assn; Natl Funeral Dirs & Morticians Assn; VA Mortician's Assn; First Baptist Ch; Omega Psi Phi. **Military Serv:** Served from 1953-55. **Business Addr:** Attorney, 7345 Pocahontas Trail, Williamsburg, VA 23185.

STOREY, CHARLES F.
Dentist. **Personal:** Born Jul 5, 1926, New York, NY; children: bd. **Educ:** City Coll NY, BS 1950; Meharry Med Coll, DDS 1954. **Career:** Springfield, dentist 1957-73; Holyoke, dentist 1973-; Springfield Pub Sch Dntst 1961-. **Orgs:** Am Dntl Assn; 1st pres co-fdr Mt Calvary Brthrhd Fed Credit Union Sprngfld 1959; pres fdr Black Bus Assn Hampden Co Inc 1970; Phi Beta Sigma Frat; exalted ruler Harmony Lodge 1940 IBPOE of W 1963; Sprngfld Salvtn Army Adv Bd 1967; NAACP Bd Dir 1967-70; pres Comm Concern 1972; St Lukes Lodge 17 AF & AM; bd dir Holyoke Counc Chldrn 1974; Martin Luther King Jr Comm Ch. **Honors/Awds:** Diplomate Nat Dental Bd 1954. **Military Serv:** Dental Corps capt 1945-46, 55-56. **Business Addr:** 225 High St, Holyoke, MA.

STOREY, ROBERT D.
Attorney. **Personal:** Born Mar 28, 1936, Tuskegee, AL; married Juanita Kendrick Cohen, May 9, 1959; children: Charles, Christopher, Rebecca. **Educ:** Harvard University, AB, 1958; Western Reserve University, JD, 1964. **Career:** East Ohio Gas Co, atty 1964-66; Legal Aid Soc of Cleveland, asst dir 1966-67; Burke Haber & Berick, partner, 1967-90; McDonald, Hopkins Burke & Haber Co, partner, 1990-92; Thompson, Hine & Flory, partner, 1993-. **Orgs:** trustee Phillips Exeter Acad 1969-83-; vice pres Assn Harvard Alumni 1974-; trustee Cleveland St Univ 1971-80; City Plng Commn Cleveland 1966-74; trustee Univ Sch 1974-; mem bd dirs GTE Stamford, CT; trustee, Great Lakes Science Ctr; trustee, University Hospitals of Cleveland, 1982-90; director May Department Stores Co., St Louis MO; director Proctor & Gamble, Cincinnati OH; trustee, The Kresge Foundation, Troy MI; trustee, The George Gund Foundation, Cleveland OH; trustee, Spelman College. **Honors/Awds:** Top 10 Young Men of the Year, Cleveland Jr Chamber of Commerce, 1967; Chief Marshal, 25th Reunion, Harvard Class of 1958; Charles Flint Kellogg Award, Association of Episcopal Colleges, 1984. **Military Serv:** USMC capt 1958-61.

STORY, CHARLES IRVIN
Business executive. **Personal:** Born Aug 10, 1954, Richmond, VA; son of Geraldine & John R Story; married Deborah Ellis; children: Lachelle. **Educ:** Fisk University, BA, psychology, management, 1976; Univ of Tennessee, MPA 1978. **Career:** Fisk Univ, personnel dir 1977-78; First American Natl Bank, vp, 1989-91; INROADS, dir 1978-81, reg dir 1981-83, exec vice pres 1983-87, pres/CEO, 1993-; Dept of Economic & Community Development, State of TN, asst commissioner, 1987-88. **Orgs:** Alumni trustee Fisk Univ 1976-79; mem Leadership Nashville 1981-82; bd mem School of Bus TN State Univ 1982-83; bd mem Rochelle Training & Rehab Ctr 1982-83; chmn strategic plnng comm Child Guidance Ctr 1984-; vice chmn 1987, mem United Way Disabled Serv Panel 1984-; allocation comm United Way of Greater St Louis 1987; bd of dirs Life Crisis Serv St Louis MO 1987; United Way of Middle Tennessee, board of directors, 1989-93; Goodwill of Middle Tennessee, board member, 1989-, vice chairman, 1992; Nashville Area Red Cross, board of directors, 1990-; Watkins Institute, board of directors, 1990-; Ctr for Non-Profit Management, secretary, board of directors, 1990-; Nashville Business Incubation Center, board of directors, 1989-; First American Natl Bank, advisory bd, 1993-; Briggs & Stratton Corp, bd of dirs, 1994-; Hanigan Consulting Group, advisory bd, 1996-; Choice Point, bd of dirs, 1997-. **Honors/Awds:** Ranked #1 in Coll Grad Class Fisk Univ 1976; Outstanding Young Man of Amer US Jaycees 1978; Alumni Apprec Awd INROADS 1983; Disting Serv Awd INROADS 1984. **Home Addr:** 5505 Saddlewood Ln, Brentwood, TN 37027. **Business Addr:** President, CEO, INROADS Inc, 10 South Broadway, Ste 700, Saint Louis, MO 63102, (314)241-7330.

STORY, OTIS L, SR.
Hospital administrator. **Personal:** Born Nov 17, 1951, Anniston, AL; son of Martha Lou Wilson Story and Tom Elbert Story; married Ava D McNair-Story, Jan 7, 1991; children: Otis L Story II, Jasmyn E, Avana Leigh. **Educ:** Cornell Univ, Ithaca, NY, BA, 1976; Univ of Chicago, Chicago, IL, MA, 1977; Univ of Alabama-Birmingham, Birmingham, AL, MAHH, 1981. **Career:** Ochsner Foundation Hospital, New Orleans, LA, admin/asst dir, 1981-85; Univ of Alabama-Birmingham Hospital, admin/asst admin, 1985-90; Univ of Medicine & Dentistry of NJ, admin/chief operating officer, currently. **Orgs:** Natl Assn Health Care Executives, 1982-; Am Coll of Health Care Executives, 1982-; bd of dir, North Jersey Blood Center; 100 Black Men of NJ; UMDNJ, School of Health Related Professions, clinical assistant professor; One to One/New Jersey, mentor program; North Jersey Blood Center, board of trustees; New Jersey Organ and Tissue Sharing Network, advisory council; Toastmasters International, UMDNJ, University Hospital Club; Overall Economic Development Commission, County of Northhampton, Easton, PA. **Business Addr:** Chief Operating Officer, UMDNJ-University Hospital, 150 Bergen St, Rm D-217, Newark, NJ 07103.

STOTTS, VALMON D.
Clergyman. **Personal:** Born Oct 24, 1925, Detroit, MI; married Ethel; children: Valmon Jr, Angela, Valarie. **Educ:** Detroit Bible Coll, 1957; Bible Sch Comm Coll, 1958; Wayne St U. **Career:** Unity Bapt Ch, pastor (over 2200 mmbrshp). **Orgs:** Cnslr Billy Graham Campaign 1954; bd dir Oppt Ind Corp; Big Bros Am; pres Sherrill Sch PTA; chaplain Detroit Gen Hosp 1969-70; 2nd vice pres Counc of Bapt Pastors; sec St Cong Evangelism; yth ldr inst ABOUTS. **Business Addr:** Unity Bapt Ch, 7500 Tireman Ave, Detroit, MI 48204.

STOUDMAIRE, DAMON
Professional basketball player. **Personal:** Born Sep 3, 1973, Portland, OR. **Educ:** Arizona. **Career:** Toronto Raptors, guard, 1995-98; Portland TrailBlazers, 1998-. **Honors/Awds:** NBA

Rookie of the Year, 1996; Schick Rookie Game, Most Valuable Player, 1996. **Special Achievements:** NBA Draft, First Round, #7 Pick, 1995. **Business Addr:** Professional Basketball Player, Portland TrailBlazers, 1 Center Court, Ste 200, Portland, OR 97227, (503)234-9291.

STOUT, JUANITA KIDD
Judge (retired). **Personal:** Born Mar 7, 1919, Wewoka, OK; daughter of Mary Chandler Kidd and Henry M Kidd; married Charles Otis Stout, Jun 23, 1942 (deceased). **Educ:** Univ IA, BA 1939; IN Univ, JD 1948; LLM 1954. **Career:** FL A&M Univ & TX So Univ, tchr 1949; Hon W H Hastie US Ct Appeals for Third Circuit, Phila, admin asst 1950-55; Appeals Pardons & Paroles Divs DA Office Phila, chief 1956-59; City of Philadelphia, asst DA, 1956-59; Commonwealth of Pennsylvania, judge and justice, beginning, 1959; PA Supreme Court, justice, retired; PA Court of Common Pleas, sr judge, currently. **Orgs:** Amer Bar Assn, 1954; Pennsylvania Bar Assn, 1954-; Philadelphia Bar Assn, 1954-. **Honors/Awds:** Jane Addams Medal Rockford Coll 1966; Inducted into OK Hall of Fame Nov 16 1981; Distinguished Daughter of Pennsylvania, 1988; Gimbel Award, 1988; honorary doctor of laws degrees: Ursinus Coll, 1965, Indiana Univ, 1966, Lebanon Valley Coll, 1969, Drexel Univ, 1972, Rockford Coll, 1974, Univ of Maryland, 1980, Roger Williams Coll, 1984, Morgan State Univ, 1985, Fisk Univ, 1989; honorary doctor of humane letters degree, Russell Sage Coll, 1966; Delaware State Coll, Dover, Delaware, 1990. **Home Addr:** Logan Square East, #1803, 2 Franklin Town Blvd, Philadelphia, PA 19103.

STOUT, LOUIS
Association executive. **Personal:** Born May 17, Cynthiana, KY; son of John Stout (deceased) and Elizabeth; married Anna M Stout, Aug 19, 1961; children: Juan RaMon. **Educ:** Regis College, BA, 1959-63; Georgetown College, Kentucky, post grad, 1973-75. **Career:** Lookout Mountain School for Boys, Golden Colorado, counselor, 1963-65; Fayette Cty Schools, Dunbar High School, teacher/coach, 1965-67, Tates Creek High School, teacher/coach, 1967-71; KHSAA, asst commissioner, 1971-90, exec asst comm, 1990-94, comm, 1994-. **Orgs:** Ecquador, Lexington, KY, sports chair, 1978-85; Lexington Urban Co Government, bd of adjustment, 1990-; AAU, James E Sullivan Award, natl chair, 1992-, natl exec comm, chair, 1992-; AAU Zone B, chair, 1992-; Area Sports Authority Comm, Lexington KY, 1997-; Kentucky Coun on AIDS Prevention, 1990-; Natl Federation of High Schools, Hall of Fame Comm, 1995-. **Honors/Awds:** 10th Region, Central, KY, Hall of Fame, 1989; KY ASA (Softball), Hall of Honor, 1993; Amateur Athletic Union, Vision Award, 1995; High School Baseball Coaches, Hall of Fame, 1997. **Business Addr:** Commissioner, Kentucky High School Athletic Association, 2280 Executive Dr, Lexington, KY 40511.

STOUTMIRE, OMAR
Professional football player. **Personal:** Born Jul 9, 1974. **Educ:** Fresno State, attended. **Career:** Dallas Cowboys, defensive back, 1997-. **Business Addr:** Professional Football Player, Dallas Cowboys, One Cowboys Pkwy, Irving, TX 75063, (214)556-9900.

STOVALL, AUDREAN
Telecommunication specialist. **Personal:** Born Sep 18, 1933, Lexa, AR; daughter of Fredonia Little John Rice and John F Rice; married Williard Stovall; children: Darryl Byrd. **Educ:** Mercy Coll of Detroit, BS 1984; Wayne State Univ, 1986. **Career:** MI Bell Telephone Co, various positions 1953-83; Electronic Data Systems, telecommunication specialist; US Sprint, account consultant; A B Stovall Consulting, ITSI; MCI Customer Service, supervisor, 1985-86; Integrated Telecommunication Services, Inc, Detroit, MI, entrpreneur, pres, owner, 1986-; AB Stovall Consulting Inc, Detroit, MI, owner, pres, 1987-. **Orgs:** Mem business corporate comm ABWA 1963-; mem business corporate comm NBMBA 1985-86; mem AFCEA, Amer Business Women's Assn, Urban League Guild, NAACP, Junior Achievement, Pioneers of Amer; mem Founders Soc Detroit Inst of Arts; mem admissions and fund comm; mem telethon comm United Negro College Fund; Univ of Detroit Mercy Alumna Planning Comm; mem, business/corporate, Oakland County Business Consortium, 1990; mem, Northwest Area Business Assn, 1988-; mem, Greater Detroit Chamber of Commerce, 1988-; mem, Natl Assn of Female Executives, 1989-; Natl Black MBA Assn; MI Minority Bus Devt Corp. **Honors/Awds:** Jr Achievement, Project Bus Volunteer Award; Urban League, Detroit Guild Service Award (Guild Gala); Northwest Area Bus Assn, Certificate of Recognition, Comm Efforts; State of MI Special Tribute Entrepreneur; US Sprint 100% Natl Acct Club. **Business Addr:** 18023 Forrer, Detroit, MI 48235, (313)836-5478.

STOVALL, MELODY S.
Executive director. **Personal:** Born Nov 7, 1952, Salem, VA; daughter of Mildred Parker Stewart (deceased) and Lewis J Stewart (deceased); married Ricardo Stovall, Jun 21, 1975; children: Ricardo C II, Raven C. **Educ:** Hampton University, Hampton, VA, BS, marketing, 1974. **Career:** Harrison Museum of African American Culture, Roanoke, VA, executive director, 1985-; Total Action Against Poverty, Roanoke, VA, job training dev specialist, 1984-85; Automobile Club of Southern California, Inglewood, CA, field rep, 1976-82. **Orgs:** The Links Inc, Roanoke Chapter, 1988-; NationsBank, Roanoke, board member, 1990-93; Community Awareness Council of Salem, 1985-; Roanoke Arts Commission, 1989-93; The Moles, Inc, Roanoke Chapter, 1994. **Honors/Awds:** Honor Roll Awards, Automobile Club of Southern California, 1979-81. **Special Achievements:** Producer of Black History Month project, WDBJ Channel 7, Roanoke VA, 1990; Girl Scouts, Woman of Distinction, 1993. **Business Addr:** Executive Director, Harrison Museum of African-American Culture, PO Box 12544, Roanoke, VA 24026-2544.

STOVALL, STANLEY V.
Anchorman, journalist. **Personal:** Born Feb 24, 1953, Rochester, NY. **Educ:** AZ State U, BS 1971-75. **Career:** KTVK-TV, anchorman, reporter, photographer 1970-75; KTAR-TV Phoenix, anchorman, reporter 1975; KSDK-TV St Louis, anchorman, reporter 1975-78, anchorman 1983-86; WBAL-TV Baltimore, anchorman 1978-83; WCAV-TV Philadelphia, news anchor, reporter. **Orgs:** Mem Greater & St Louis Assn of Black Journalist 1975-78; mem Assn of Black Media Workers Baltimore; mem NAACP Baltimore Br 1980-83, St Louis Br 1983-86. **Honors/Awds:** First Black TV Anchorman in Phoenix, KTVK TV Phoenix 1970; Mr MD Bodybuilding Champ, Baltimore, 1980; Mr South Atlantic Bodybuilding Champ Baltimore 1980; Citizens Housing and Planning Assoc "Hard Hat" Awd Baltimore 1983; Baltimore City Council proclamation for Community Serv Baltimore 1983; Greater St Louis Assoc of Black Journalist & Journalist of the Year St Louis 1986; Emmy Awd for "Best News Anchor," St Louis 1986. **Business Addr:** News Anchor/Reporter, WCAV-TV, City Ave & Monument Rd, Philadelphia, PA 19131.

STOVALL-TAPLEY, MARY KATE
Mayor, funeral home director. **Personal:** Born Dec 13, 1921, Uniontown, AL; daughter of Estella Billingsley Sanders and Tim Sanders Sr; married Turner Stovall, 1953 (deceased); children: Kathleen D Stovall Caldwell, Audrey Y Stovall Hayes. **Educ:** AL State Univ, BS 1949, MEd 1955; Atlanta Univ, MLS 1969. **Career:** Perry County Bd of Educ AL, teacher 1943-51; Russell Co Bd of Educ AL, teacher/librarian 1951-76; Stovall Funeral Home, director/owner; Town of Hurtsboro, AL, councilwomen, 1976-84, mayor, 1984-. **Orgs:** Pres East AL Mental Health Bd Dirs; treas East AL Funeral Directors Assn; chairwoman Hurtsboro Ladies Aux; mem state democratic exec committee, Democratic Party, 1991-. **Honors/Awds:** Martin Luther King, Jr American Dream Award, Alabama Democratic Conference, 1984; Leadership in Government Award, 6th Annual Black Business Seminar, 1986; National Sojourner Truth Meritorious Service Award, National Assn Negro Businesses, 1986. **Business Addr:** Director/Owner, Stovall Funeral Home, PO Box 154, Hurtsboro, AL 36860.

STRACHAN, LLOYD CALVIN, JR.
Electrical engineer. **Personal:** Born Apr 12, 1954, Greensboro, NC; son of Dorothy B Lane Strachan (deceased) and Lloyd C Strachan Sr; married Carolyn Mintz Strachan, Oct 5, 1985; children: Camille. **Educ:** North Carolina A&T State Univ, Greensboro, NC, BS, electrical engineering, 1976. **Career:** Carolina Power & Light Co, Telecom Construction Unit, engineer, senior engineer, 1977-85, superintendent, 1985-89, Telecom Support Unit, manager, 1989-92, Telecom Services Section, project analyst, 1992-. **Orgs:** Member, American Assn of Blacks in Energy, 1989-; member, IEEE; steering committee member, Black Achievers, Raleigh Chapter, 1991; registered member, Professional engineer in North Carolina. **Business Addr:** Senior Analyst, Telecommunications Planning & Svcs Section, Carolina Power and Light, 411 Fayetteville St, MS 7C3, Raleigh, NC 27602.

STRACHAN, RICHARD JAMES
Educational administrator. **Personal:** Born Jan 21, 1928, Miama, FL; married Lorraine Farrington; children: Denia, Richard II, Reginald, Regina, Lori. **Educ:** Bethune-Cookman Coll, BS 1956; IN Univ, MS 1966; Barry Univ, MS 1972; Atlanta Univ, PhD Educ 1978. **Career:** North Dade Jr-Sr HS, teacher/athletic dir 1960-66; Miami Central, dept head/band dir 1966-72; Hialeah HS/Carol City/Norland, asst prin 1972-81; COPE School North, principal 1981-. **Orgs:** Bd mem NAACP; bd mem YMCA; bd mem Inner City Sch Dance; bd mem Dade Co Admin Assoc; bd mem FL Alternative Admin Sch Educators; bd mem Offc of Black Affairs 1981-86; bd mem Omega Psi Phi; bd mem youth Adv Council. **Honors/Awds:** Rockefeller Grant 1975; Outstanding Bethune-Cookman Coll Exelloc Club 1975; Service Award Sigma Gamma Rho DLSSA-NABSE-YMCA-NCAO Atlanta Univ 1986. **Military Serv:** USAF S/Sgt 1946-49; Soldier of the Yr 1947-48. **Home Addr:** 8841 NW 14th Ave, Miami, FL 33147.

STRAHAM, CLARENCE CLIFFORD, JR.
Investment manager. **Personal:** Born Sep 22, 1956, Fort Smith, AR; son of Fern Elizabeth Roby Straham and Clarence Clifford Straham Sr; married Carlotta Coleman Straham, Oct 22, 1987; children: Clarence Clifford III. **Educ:** North Carolina A & T, Greensboro, NC, 1972-78; Lane College, Jackson, TN, 1974-75; University of Arkansas, Little Rock, AR, 1982-83. **Career:** Lasater Farms, Little Rock, AR, personal valet/steward 1983-85; United Capital Corp, Little Rock, AR, first vice pres, dir minority affairs, 1985-88; Allison, Rosenblum & Hannahs, Inc, Little Rock, AR, first vice pres, dir minority affairs, 1988-. **Orgs:** Member, Kappa Alpha Psi Faternity, 1976-. **Honors/Awds:** Rookie Salesman of Year, United Capital Corp, 1987; Salesman of Year, Allison, Rosenblum & Hannahs, 1988; Salesman of Year, Director of Year, Allison, Rosenblum & Hannahs, 1989; Salesman of Year, Director of Year, Allison, Rosenblum & Hannahs, 1990. **Military Serv:** US Army, PFC, 1978-81.

STRAHAN, MICHAEL ANTHONY
Professional football player. **Personal:** Born Nov 21, 1971, Houston, TX; children: Tanita, Michael Jr. **Educ:** Texas Southern, attended. **Career:** New York Giants, defensive end, 1993-; Michael Strahan Enterprises, owner. **Business Addr:** Professional Football Player, New York Giants, Giants Stadium, East Rutherford, NJ 07073, (201)935-8111.

STRAIGHT, CATHY A.
Journalist. **Personal:** Born Sep 20, 1963, Ocean Springs, MS; daughter of June Rose Spears Straight and Turner Joseph Straight Sr. **Educ:** University of Southern Mississippi, BS, journalism, 1984. **Career:** The Hattiesburg American, Hattiesburg, MI, reporter/copy editor, 1982-87; The Jackson Sun Jackson, TN, feature reporter/editor, 1987-89; The Brandenton Hearld, Brandenton, FL, features reporter on aging, 1989-90; The Tennessean, Nashville, TN, general assignment/features, 1990-. **Orgs:** Member, National Association of Black Journalist, 1990-; member, Tennessee Press Association, 1990-; Mississippi Press Women Association, 1985-87. **Business Addr:** Journalist, The Tennessean, 1100 Broadway St, Nashville, TN 37203.

STRAIT, GEORGE ALFRED, JR.
Journalist. **Personal:** Born Mar 24, 1945, Cambridge, MA; married Lisa Michelle McIver; children: Eric Mathew, Kevin Michael Angelo. **Educ:** Boston Univ, BA 1967; Atlanta Univ, MS Prog 1968-69. **Career:** CBS News, Washington correspondent 1976-77, gen assign corresp 1977-81, White House corresp 1979-81, med corresp 1981-. **Orgs:** 1st black sports anchor WPVI Philadelphia 1972-74; charter mem Natl Assn Black Journalists; lay reader Episcopal Church of Amer 1984-. **Honors/Awds:** Assoc of Science Writers Awd 1985; Harvard Univ Fellow 1986; Overseas Press Club Awd 1987. **Business Addr:** Correspondent, ABC - News, 1717 Desales St, Washington, DC 20036.

STRATHER, VIVIAN CARPENTER. **See CARPENTER, VIVIAN L.**

STRATTON-MORRIS, MADELINE ROBINSON MORGAN
Educator (retired), author. **Personal:** Born Aug 14, 1906, Chicago, IL; daughter of Estella Dixon Robinson and John H Robinson; married Thomas Morgan, Jun 26, 1926 (divorced 1943). **Educ:** Chicago Normal College, certificate, 1929; Northwestern Univ, BS educ, 1936, MA educ, 1941; Univ of Chicago, post grad 1941-62. **Career:** Chicago Public Schools, teacher 1933-68; Bishop Sheil School of Social Studies, 1942-43; Triton Coll, teacher 1968-70; Mayfair City Coll, 1969-72; Chicago St Univ 1972-75; Governors State Univ 1975-1981; Chicago Bd of Ed, Human Rel Dept 1968-77. **Orgs:** League of Women Voters; Alpha Kappa Alpha, Theta Omega Chap, 1977; Urban League 1940-; pres Natl Council of Negro Women, Chicago Chap 1946-48; basileus, Phi Delta Kappa Mu Chapter 1941-43; Amer Assn of Univ Women 1950-74; life mbr NAACP, bd mbr 1950-70; Chicago Chapter, Links Inc 1953-91; Alpha Gamma Pi 1964-91; pres Chicago Br of Assn for the Study of Afro-American Life & History; founder Carter G Woodson 1970-76; Church of the Good Shepherd Congregational. **Special Achievements:** Introduced study of Afro-American history in Chicago Public Schools curriculum, grades 1st-8th, entitled: Supplementary Units in Social Studies, 1941; work out a curriculum to improve race relations which was integrated into the Chicago grade school system, 1943; author: "Negroes Who Helped Build America," Ginn Social Science Enrichment Books, 1965; "Strides Forward: Afro-American Biographies," Xerox Ginn Co, Jan 1973; "Chicago Schools Include Negro Achievements: A Suggestion for Your School," Virginia Teachers Bulletin, May 1944. **Home Addr:** 5142 S Ellis Ave, Chicago, IL 60615.

STRAUGHTER, EDGAR, SR.
Educational administrator. **Personal:** Born Feb 8, 1929, Willis, TX; son of Annie Lee Straughter and K J Straughter; married Betty Harvey, Oct 22, 1954; children: Edgar, Lewis, Ernest, Johnnie, Sherman, Betty, Debra. **Educ:** TX So Univ, 2 Yrs. **Career:** Willis Indus Public School Dist, pres (1st black); Quality Control supvr, Louisiana Pacific, presently; mayor, City of Willis, TX, 1989-93; mediator, Montomery County, currently. **Orgs:** Vp Montgomery Co Voters League; mem Willis Fire Dept 1965-; drill instructor 2 yrs; mem Willis City Planning Commn; Willis Board of Education, 9 yrs. **Honors/Awds:** AUS corpl 1950-52. **Home Addr:** Philpot St, Rt 3 Box 190, Willis, TX 77378. **Business Addr:** Mayor, City of Willis, TX, Quality Control Supvr, Lousania Pacific, New Waverly TX, New Waverly, TX 77358.

STRAWBERRY, DARRYL
Professional baseball player. **Personal:** Born Mar 12, 1962, Los Angeles, CA; married Charisse; children: Jade. **Career:** New York Mets, outfielder, 1980-90; Los Angeles Dodgers, outfielder, 1991-94; San Francisco Giants, 1994-95; New York Yankees, 1995-. **Honors/Awds:** John Murphy Awd; Doubleday Award; National League Rookie of the Year, Baseball Writers Assn of America, 1983; National League Rookie Player of the Year, The Sporting News; National League All-Star Team 1984-88, 1990. **Business Addr:** Professional Baseball Player, New York Yankees, Yankee Stadium, Bronx, NY 10451, (212)293-6000.

STRAYHORN, EARL CARLTON
Surgeon. **Personal:** Born Aug 27, 1948, Bronx, NY; son of Lydia Strayhorn Blocker and Rhudolphus Clemons Strayhorn; married Louisa Sapp, Jun 1968 (divorced); children: Kharim, Jamal. **Educ:** Harvard Univ, Cambridge MA, AB, 1971; Tufts Medical School, Boston MA, MD, 1975. **Career:** Beth Israel Hospital, Boston MA, intern, 1975, resident, chief resident, 1976-81; Massachusetts Gen Hospital, fellow in vascular surgery, 1982; Virgini Vascular Associates, Norfolk VA, vascular surgeon, transplant surgeon, 1983—; Norfolk Community Hospital, Norfolk VA, chief of vascular surgery, 1983—; Norfolk Gen Hospital, Norfolk VA, vice-chairman of surgery, 1988—; host of community health radio program on WTJZ-Radio, 1988—. **Orgs:** Mem, Urban League, National Medical Assn, American Medical Assn, all 1983—. **Honors/Awds:** Natl Science Found grant, 1969-70; Ellis Memorial Award for Achievement in Surgery, Tufts Medical School, 1975; author of articles for medical journals. **Home Addr:** 4501 Mossy Cup Ct, Virginia Beach, VA 23462.

STRAYHORN, EARL E.
Judge. **Personal:** Born Apr 24, 1918, Columbus, MS; son of Minnie Lee Davis Strayhorn (deceased) and Earl E Strayhorn (deceased); married Lygia E Jackson Strayhorn, Aug 17, 1941; children: Donald R, Earlene E. **Educ:** Univ IL, AB 1941; DePaul Univ Coll Law, JD 1948. **Career:** Cook Co, asst states atty 1948-52; City of Chicago, civil serv commr, 1959-63; Met Sanitary Dist Gr Chicago, vice pres bd of trustees 1963-70; Univ of IL Dept of Crim Justice, adj prof 1977-79; Northwestern Univ Sch of Law, instr 1977; Natl Coll of Criminal Defense Attys, instructor 1980; Emory Univ Coll of Law, instructor, 1980-; Natl Judicial Coll, discussion leader 1985; Benjamin Cardozo Sch of Law, instructor 1987; instructor trial advocacy Harvard Univ Coll of Law 1988-96; Cook Co II circuit judge 1970-; Natl inst of Trial Advocacy, instr 1977-96. **Orgs:** Mem NAACP; former vice pres & bd mem Chicago Urban League; mem Kappa Alpha Psi; past pres PTA Howalton Day Sch; 6th Grace United Presbyterian Church; former mem Comm Race & Religion United Presby Church USA. **Honors/Awds:** Parliamentarian Tuskegee Airmen Inc 1985-94. **Military Serv:** AUS, 1st lt, 1941-46; IL Army Natl Guard, 1948-69, lt col, 1968-69. **Business Addr:** Presiding Judge, 1st Municipal District Circuit Court Cook County, Richard J Daley Center, Room 1303, Chicago, IL 60602, (312)443-6132.

STRAYHORN, LLOYD
Numerologist/author/columnist. **Career:** Tree of Life Bookstore, teacher of numerology 1976-83; Big Red Newspaper, weekly columnist ''Numbers and You'' 1978-; NY Amsterdam News, weekly column ''Numbersand You'' 1979-; Project ENTER, teaching numerology to former drug/alchol abusers 1979-; Arts and Culture, teaching numerology to teenagers 1980-81; BMI Syndication, weekly column dist to over 100 newspapers ''Astro/Numerology and You'' 1980-. **Orgs:** Radio show host ''Numbers and You'' on WLIB-AM in New York. **Honors/Awds:** Author of book ''Numbers and You'' 1980. **Business Addr:** Numerologist, Abby Hoffer Enterprises, 223 1/2 E 48th St, New York, NY 10017.

STREET, T. MILTON
Government official. **Personal:** Born Apr 25, 1941, Norristown, PA. **Educ:** Oakwood Coll of 7th Day Adventist, 1960-61; Temple U, 1966-67. **Career:** PA House of Reps, state rep; Street's Quality Wig Shop, organizer 1968-69; Street's Quality Food Serv, organizer-Mgr 1969-76; N Philadelphia Block & Devel Corp, founder organizer; Philadelphia Black St Vendors Assn, founder organizer. **Honors/Awds:** Recipient award Nat Assn of Black Accountants; award Philadelphia Tribune; award Man of the Year 1980; award Main Line NANBPW. **Business Addr:** Senate of Pennsylvania, Main Capitol Bldg Rm 186, Harrisburg, PA 17120.

STREET, VIVIAN SUE
Health care administrator. **Personal:** Born Jun 21, 1954, Edgefield, SC; daughter of Susie Bell Werts-Bussey and James Harry Bussey; married Ronnie Street, Sep 24, 1978 (divorced); children: Jermaine Toriano. **Educ:** SUNY Coll at Brockport, Brockport NY, BS, 1976; Coll of New Rochelle, New Rochelle NY, MS (cum laude), 1981. **Career:** Westchester Devel Center, Orangeburg NY, special educ teacher, 1971-76; Westchester Devel Serv, White Plains NY, community residence supvr, 1977-78, Tarrytown NY, placement coord, 1978-82; Letchworth Village Devel Serv, Thiells NY, team leader, placement team, 1982-86; Westchester Devel Disabilities Serv, Tarrytown NY, program devel specialist, fiscal liaison, 1986-90, treatment team leader, 1990-. **Orgs:** Vice pres, Black Caucus of PS&T Workers PEF, 1983-; convention delegate, Public Employees Fedn, 1985-; steering comm, Black Tennis & Sports Found, 1986-; treasurer, NAACP Spring Valley NY, 1988-; bd mem, Time for Tots Nursery School, 1989-. **Honors/Awds:** Humanitarium, Public Employees Fedn, 1987; Community Serv, United Negro Scholarship Fund, 1988; Community Serv, Black Tennis & Sports Foundation, 1988; First Baptist Church, Board of Trustees Appointee; PEF Black Caucus, Service Award, 1991; Public Employees Federation Division 336, Council Leader, 1992.

STREETER, DEBRA BRISTER
Accounting executive. **Personal:** Born May 23, 1956, Birmingham, AL; daughter of Ella Scott Brister and Edward Brister; married Otis Streeter Jr, Jul 29, 1984 (divorced 1990); children: Otis Brister, Sheeba L. **Educ:** University of Alabama, Birmingham, AL, certificate accounting, 1981; Booker T Washington Business College, Birmingham, AL, certificate secretarial/science, 1984. **Career:** Turning Point Productions, Birmingham, AL, administrative secretary, 1976-84; Zegarelli & Associates, Birmingham, AL, secretary, 1984-86; Beverly Health Care Center West, Fairfield, AL, secretary/bookkeeper, 1986-87; University of Alabama, Birmingham, AL, secretary, 1987-88; Turning Point Productions, Birmingham, AL, comptroller, 1988-. **Honors/Awds:** Accounting Honor Award, Booker T Washington Business College, 1975; UAB, Special Studies, Certificate, 1981. **Home Addr:** 2448 Tempest Dr, Birmingham, AL 35211. **Business Addr:** Comptroller, Turning Point Productions, 1610 Fourth Ave, N, Suite A, Birmingham, AL 35203.

STREETER, DENISE WILLIAMS
Accountant. **Personal:** Born Apr 27, 1962, Washington, DC; daughter of Patricia A Dorn Williams and Michael G Williams; married Christopher M Streeter, Oct 5, 1985; children: Mikala P, C Kamaur. **Educ:** Howard Univ, Washington, DC, BBA, 1984. **Career:** Coopers & Lybrand, Washington, DC, staff accountant, 1984-86; ICMA Retirement Corp, Washington, DC, mgr, trust accountant, 1986-89; F S Taylor & Associates, Washington, DC, mgr, 1989-92; National 4-H Council, director, accounting & financial administration, assistant treasurer, 1992-. **Orgs:** Mem, past chapter pres, Natl Assn of Black Accountants, Inc, 1983-; mem, District of Columbia Institute of CPAs, 1986-; mem, American Institute of CPAs, 1986-; mem, Beta Gamma Sigma Natl Honor Society, 1983-; mem, past chapter pres, The Intl Fraternity of Delta Sigma Pi, 1981-; assistant treasurer, Mt Pleasant Baptist Church, 1991-; Planning Committee, 1993; Eastern Region NABA Student Conference, 1993-; American Society of Association Executives, 1992-. **Honors/Awds:** Outstanding NABA Member, Natl Assn of Black Accountants, Inc, 1991; Outstanding New Member, Natl Assn of Black Accountants, Inc, 1985; ''The History of Black Accountancy: The First 100 Black CPAs,'' Natl Assn of Black Accountants, 1990. **Home Addr:** 3500 Sunflower Pl, Mitchellville, MD 20721-2462. **Business Addr:** Director, Accounting & Financial Administration, Assistant Treasurer, National 4-H Council, 7100 Connecticut Ave, Chevy Chase, MD 20815.

STREETER, ELWOOD JAMES
Dentist. **Personal:** Born Jun 14, 1930, Greenville, NC; son of Hattie Forbes Streeter and William Streeter; married Martha; children: Agnes, Nicole. **Educ:** NC Coll, BS 1952; Howard U, DDS 1956; UCLA, cert 1969. **Career:** Perez & Streeter Dental Corp, dentist 1958-; LA Co USC Med Ctr, dental attending; Hollywood Presbyterian Med Center, attending staff. **Orgs:** Mem Am Dental Assn; CA Dental Assn; So CA Stomatognathic & Rsrch Seminar; pres So CA Acad Gen Denistry 1978, past presidents advisory council, 1979-; mem YMCA; NAACP; NC Coll Alumni Assn; LA Dental Soc Dental Care, member, 1958-; mem, Angel City Dental Society, 1956-; partner, Amalgamated Devel Assoc; treas, Amada Enterprises Inc; treas, Allied Diversified Assoc; bd dir, Delta Dental of Calif, 1994-. **Honors/Awds:** Fellowship Acad General Denistry 1972; Fellowship, American College of Dentists, 1985; Fellowship, International College of Dentists, 1983; Fellowship, Pierre Fuchard Academy, 1988. **Military Serv:** USNR, Captain, 1954-88. **Business Addr:** Dentist, 3701 Stocker St, No 405, Los Angeles, CA 90008-5108.

STREET-KIDD, MAE
Legislator, public relations consultant. **Personal:** Born in Millersburg, KY; married John Meredith III. **Educ:** Lincoln Inst; Amer Univ, attended 1966-67. **Career:** Mammoth Life & Accident Ins Co, former supr policy issues/sales rep/pub rel couns 1935-64; KY House of Reps 41st Dist, mem 1968-; Continental Bank of KY, dir prog & pub rel; free-lance mktg & pub rel cons. **Orgs:** Mem Banking & Ins Cities & Rules Comm; v chmn Elections Const Amendment Comm; sec Dem Caucus; deleg 1978 Dem Natl Party Conf; former bd mem YMCA; mem Natl Ins Assoc; charter mem Iota Phi Lambda; spearheaded fund-raising drives for GSA/NAACP Legal Fund. **Honors/Awds:** Unsung Heroine Award Natl NAACP Women's Conf; Ten Top Outstanding Kentuckian Award; Honor Award Louisville Urban League; Outstanding Serv & Dedication Award Portland Area Councl; Recogn as Outstanding Producer in Ordinary Sales 3 consec years Mammoth Life & Accident Ins Co; Humanitarian Serv Award United Cerebral Palsy 1974; Dist Citz Award Black Scene Mag 1974; Cato-Watts Award 1976; Serv Award Mammoth Employ Credit Union 1977; Outst Serv & Dedication Award Portland Area Councl 1977; Kentucky Housing Corp. Award, 1992; Chestnut Street YMCA, Adult Achiever Award, 1992; Louisville Conference of Christian & Jews, Outstanding Citizens Award, 1990. **Home Addr:** 211 W Oak, #410, Louisville, KY 40203.

STREETS, FRAN A.
Association executive. **Career:** International Women's Forum, pres, 1997-. **Special Achievements:** First African American to be named president of the International Women's Forum. **Business Addr:** President, International Women's Forum, 1826 Jefferson Pl NW, Ste A, Washington, DC 20036, (202)775-8917.

STRICKLAND, ARVARH E.
Educator. **Personal:** Born Jul 6, 1930, Hattiesburg, MS; son of Clotiel Marshall Strickland and Eunice Strickland; married Willie Pearl Elmore Strickland, Jun 17, 1951; children: Duane Arvarh, Bruce Elmore. **Educ:** Tougaloo Coll, Tougaloo, MS, BA, history, English, 1951; Univ of Illinois, Urbana, IL, MA, education, 1953, PhD, history 1962. **Career:** Chicago State Coll, asst prof, 1962-65, assoc prof, 1965-68, prof, 1968-69; Univ of Missouri at Columbia, prof, 1969-95, prof emeritus, 1995-, chmn dept of history, 1980-83, interim dir black studies program, 1986, 1994-95, Office of the Vice President for Academic Affairs, sr faculty assoc, 1987-88; interim assoc vice pres for academic affairs, 1989, assoc vice pres for academic affairs, 1989-91. **Orgs:** Amer Assn of Univ Prof; Missouri Advisory Commn on Historic Preservation, 1976-80; Gen Bd of Higher Educ and Ministry, The United Methodist Church, 1976-80, mem exec comm; commr, Columbia Planning and Zoning Comm, 1977-80; Assn for the Study of Afro-Amer Life and History; Southern Historical Assn; bd of trustees, Historical Soc of Missouri; co-chmn, Mayor's Steering Comm for Commemorating the Contribution of Black Columbians, Columbia, MO, 1980; mem, Fed Judicial Merit Selection Comm for the Western Dist of Missouri, 1982; Kiwanis Club of Columbia; Missouri Historical Records Advisory Bd; commr, Peace Officers Standards and Training Commn, 1988-89. **Honors/Awds:** Kappa Delta Pi (education), 1953; Phi Alpha Theta (history), 1960; Kendric C Babcock Fellow in History, Univ of Illinois, 1961-62; Distinguished Serv Award, Illinois Historical Soc, 1967 Honor Soc of Phi Kappa Phi, Univ of Missouri, 1973; Assoc of the Danforth Found, 1973; Omicron Delta Kappa Natl Leadership Honor Soc, 1978; Martin Luther King Memorial Comm Award for Outstanding Community Serv, 1982; Faculty-Alumni Award, Alumni Assn of the Univ of Missouri, 1983; Serv Appreciation Award, Missouri Comm for the Humanities, 1984; Thomas Jefferson Award, Univ of Missouri, 1985; Office of Equal Opportunity Award for Exemplary Serv in Enhancing the Status of Minorities, Univ of Missouri, 1985; Distinguished Alumni Award (Tougaloo Coll), Natl Assn for Equal Opportunity in Higher Educ, 1986; N Endowment for the Humanities, Travel to Collections Grant, 1986; Byler Distinguished Professor Award, Univ of Missouri, Columbia, 1994; St Louis American's Educator of the Year Award, 1994; publications: History of the Chicago Urban League, Univ of Illinois Press, 1966; Building the United States, author with Jerome Reich and Edward Biller, Harcourt, Brace Jovanovich Inc, 1971; The Black American Experience, co-author with Jerome Reich, Harcourt, Brace Jovanovich Inc, 1974; Vol I, From Slavery through Reconstruction to 1877; Vol 11, From Reconstruction to the Present Since 1877; Edited with an Introduction, Lorenzo J Greene, Working With Carter G Woodson, The Father of Black History: A Diary, 1928-30, Louisiana State Univ Press, 1989; Edited with an introduction, Lorenzo J Greene, Selling Black History for Carter G Woodson: A Diary, 1930-33, Univ of Missouri Press, 1996. **Military Serv:** US Army, Sp-4, 1953-55; Honorble discharge from reserves, 1961. **Business Addr:** Professor, Department of History, 101 Read Hall, University of Missouri-Columbia, Columbia, MO 65211.

STRICKLAND, CLINTON VERNAL, JR.
Educational administrator. **Personal:** Born Dec 19, 1950, Elmira, NY; son of Grace Brooks and Clinton V. Strickland, Sr.; married Holly E Williams, Apr 21, 1973; children: Crystal V, Cicely V, Clinton III, Christopher V. Caitlyn V. **Educ:** Univ of Rochester, BA 1974, MA 1975; SUNY Brockport, Cert Study of Ed Admin 1977; SUNY Buffalo, Doctoral Program. **Career:** Rochester City School Dist, teacher 1974-79, counselor 1979, dean of students 1980-82, jr high admin 1982-84, project mgr of schl environment prog 1984-85, vice principal Nathaniel Rochester Comm Sch 1985-. **Orgs:** Volunteer Urban League of Rochester NY Inc 1979-; bd of dir Office of Black Ministries Catholic Diocese of Rochester 1982-83; chmn Eureka Lodge #36 Ed & Charitable Trust, life mem Theta Omicron Chap Omega Psi Phi Frat; trainer/facilitator NYSCCT United Teachers; mem Phi Delta Kappa; pres founder Black Ed Assoc of Rochester. **Honors/Awds:** Gen Electric Fellowship Boston Univ General Electric Co 1975; Summer Intern Industrial Mgmt Co 1981; Outstanding Volunteer Awd Urban League of Rochester 1982, 83, 84; Disting Serv Awd to Masons Eureka Lodge 36 Prince Hall Masons.

STRICKLAND, DOROTHY S.
Educator. **Personal:** Born Sep 29, 1933, Newark, NJ; daughter of Evelyn Daniels Salley and Leroy Salley, Sr; married Maurice R Strickland, Aug 27, 1955; children: Mark, M Randall, Michael. **Educ:** Kean Coll, BS; NY Univ, MA, PhD, 1951-55; New York Univ, NY, MA, 1956-58, PH.D., 1967-71. **Career:** Kean Coll, prof 1970-80; NY Univ, adj prof; Jersey City State Coll, asst prof; Learning Disability Spec E Orange, teacher, reading consultant; Teachers Coll Columbia Univ, prof of Educ 1980-; Rutgers University, prof (state prof of reading) 1990; Teachers College, prof 1980-90. **Orgs:** Teacher, East Orange, NJ, 1955-61; reading specialist, East Orange, NJ, 1961-66; Jersey City State Coll, Jersey City, NJ, 1966-70; bd of dir Natl Council Teachers English; Educ advisory bd Early Years Magazine; chmn Early Childhood Educ; mem Journal Reading Instructor, Websters New World Dictionary, commission Sprint Magazine; pres Intl Reading Assoc 1978-79; mem Natl Comm Ed Migrant Children; trustee, Research Found, Natl Council Teachers English, 1983-86. **Honors/Awds:** Woman of the Year Zeta Phi Beta 1980; Natl Rsch Award Natl Council Teachers English 1972; Founders Day Recognition NY Univ 1971; Outstanding Teacher Educ Reading, Intl Reading Assn, 1985; Award for Outstanding Contribution to Ed, Natl Assn of Univ Women, 1987; emerging literacy, Intl Reading assn, 1989; admin & supvr, reading programs, Teachers Coll Press, 1989; Elected Reading Hall of Fame, International Reading Assn, 1990; Distinguished Alumni Award, New York University, 1990; Outstanding Alumni Award, Kean College of NJ, 1990; National Council of Teachers of English Award for Research; Rewey Bell Inglis Award as Outstanding Woman in English Education. **Special Achievements:** Author, editor, or co-editor, Language Literacy and the Child, Process Reading and Writing: A Literature Based Approach, Emerging Literacy: Young Children Learn to Read and Write, The Administration and Supervision of Reading Programs, Educating Black Children: America's Challenge, Family Storybook Reading, Listen Children: An Anthology of Black Literature, Families: An Anthology of Poetry for Young Children. **Business Addr:** Professor of Reading, Rutgers University, Graduate School of Education, 10 Seminary Place, New Brunswick, NJ 08903, (908)932-7496.

STRICKLAND, ERICK
Professional basketball player. **Personal:** Born Nov 25, 1973. **Educ:** Nebraska. **Career:** Dallas Mavericks, guard, 1996-. **Business Addr:** Professional Basketball Player, Dallas Mavericks, Reunion Arena, 777 Sports St, Dallas, TX 75207, (214)748-1808.

STRICKLAND, FREDERICK WILLIAM, JR.
Physician. **Personal:** Born Aug 24, 1944, Kansas City, MO; son of Ardene Graves Strickland and Frederick William Strickland Sr; married Marina Karvounis Strickland, Jun 2, 1990. **Educ:** Southwestern Coll, BA 1966; Drake Univ, MA 1976; Coll of Osteopathic Medicine & Surgery, DO 1978. **Career:** Oklahoma City Public Schools, science teacher 1967-69; Des Moines Public Schools, science teacher 1969-74; Des Moines General Hosp, intern/resident 1978-80; UOMHS, prof family medicine 1980-; COMS, clinic dir student trainer 1980-. **Orgs:** Mem AOA 1978-; mem ACGP 1980-; mem corporate bd Des Moines General Hosp 1983-; mem Polk Co Democratic Central Comm 1984-; mem Des Moines Art Ctr 1984-; adv commn State of IA DUR Commn 1985-; mem Plan & Zoning Commn City of Des Moines 1985-; mem DMGH Foundation Des Moines Genl Hosp 1986-; mem Assn for Retarded Citizens 1986-; mem Boys & Girls Club of Des Moines Board of Dirs 1988-; mem Bernie Lorenz Recovery House Board of Dirs 1987-; member, Central City Optimist Club, 1990-; City of Des Moines, Strategic Planning Committee; Assn of Addiction Medicine. **Honors/Awds:** The Moundbuilder Awd Southwestern Coll 1978; The DUR Awd Iowa Pharmacy Assoc 1986; "Alcohol-Induced Rhabdomyolysis," Hawkeye Osteopath Journal 1986; "Osteomyelitis of the Maxillary Antrum & Ethmoid Sinus in an Adolesent Male," Osteopath Medical News 1987; author, Don't Spoil the Broth, a paper on quality assurance, American Osteopathic Hospital Assn Newsletter, 1989. **Military Serv:** AUS Medical Corps maj IA Army Natl Guard 14 yrs; Flight Surgeon, Iowa Army Commendation Awd 1983-85. **Home Addr:** 4910 Country Club Blvd, Des Moines, IA 50312. **Business Addr:** Physician, Family Practice Dept, University of Osteopathic Medicine & Health Science, 3200 Grand Ave, Tower Medical Clinic, Des Moines, IA 50312.

STRICKLAND, FREDRICK WILLIAM, JR.
Professional football player. **Personal:** Born Aug 15, 1966, Ringwood, NJ; married Shay. **Educ:** Purdue, attended. **Career:** Los Angeles Rams, linebacker, 1988-92; Minnesota Vikings, 1993; Green Bay Packers, 1994-95; Dallas Cowboys, 1996-. **Business Addr:** Professional Football Player, Dallas Cowboys, One Cowboys Pkwy, Irving, TX 75063, (214)556-9900.

STRICKLAND, HERMAN WILLIAM, JR.
Banker. **Personal:** Born Sep 10, 1959, Blytheville, AR; son of Dr and Mrs Herman W Strickland Sr; married Rhonda, Mar 21, 1987; children: Ashlee'. **Educ:** Arkansas State Univ, BS, mgt, 1980; Univ of Memphis, MBA, finance, 1991. **Career:** First Tennessee Bank, mgt training program, 1981-83, account officer, 1983-84, vp/Jr lender medical svc, 1984-87, vp/sr lender metro, 1987-93, vp and sr credit officer, 1993-. **Orgs:** Synergy Found, board member, 1992-; Junior Achievement, loaned exec, 1984-85; Rozelle Elementary Adopt-a-School, steering comm member, 1987-; Dixie Homes Boys Club, board member, 1994-; Leadership Memphis, 1997. **Honors/Awds:** Black Business Directory, "Simply the Best" Award, 1995. **Business Addr:** SVP, Sr Credit Officer, First Tennessee Bank, 165 Madison Ave, Main Office 3rd floor, Memphis, TN 38103, (901)523-4341.

STRICKLAND, JILL
Publicist. **Personal:** Born Jan 4, 1965, Atlanta, GA. **Educ:** University of Georgia, Bachelors Degree in Journalism, 1987. **Career:** WBHP-Radio, news reporter, 1989-90; Newsradio WGST, news reporter, 1992-93; The Atlanta Project, communications asst, 1993-94; WGNX-TV 46, news assignment mgr, 1994-95; City of Atlanta Mayor's Office, press secy, 1994-96; Liaison International Inc, vp media relations, 1996-. **Orgs:** Atlanta Association of Black Journalists, 1987-97; Atlanta Midtown Alliance Leadership, 1997; Red Cross National Marrow Donor, steering committee, 1990-96. **Honors/Awds:** Atlanta Association of Black Journalists, Community Affairs-Radio, 1993; AP Broadcast Association, Best Spot News, Best Investigative Reporting, Best Feature Story, 1990. **Home Addr:** 010150.

STRICKLAND, MARK
Professional basketball player. **Personal:** Born Jul 14, 1970. **Educ:** Temple Univ. **Career:** Indiana Pacers, forward, 1994-95; Miami Heat, 1996-. **Business Addr:** Professional Basketball Player, Miami Heat, 721 NW 1st Ave, Miami Arena, Miami, FL 33136, (305)577-4328.

STRICKLAND, R. JAMES
Business executive. **Personal:** Born Feb 24, 1930, Kansas City, KS; son of Mable Yvonne Roberts Strickland and Roosevelt Joseph Strickland; married Deanna Cartman; children: James, Jay, Jeffrey, Deanna, Dori. **Educ:** KS U, BS pharmacy 1954. **Career:** Strickland Drugs Inc, pres owner 1968-; Joslyn Clinic, mgr 1954-68; boxing trainer, mgr. **Orgs:** Bd chmn Chatham Bus Assn 1676-77; bd mem Chicago Retail Druggist Assn 1977; pres Alpha Phi, Alpha Upsilon Chptr 1953-54; housing chmn W Sub NAACP 1965; vice pres NAACP West Sub Chap 1966; vice pres Met Improvement Assn 1971; bd chmn Met Improvement Assn 1972-73; vice pres Chicago Conf of Brothd 1977; dir, Maywood Committee for Special Events, 1989-. **Honors/Awds:** Award Chicago Conf for Brothd 1974. **Home Addr:** 150 N Elmwood, Oak Park, IL 60302.

STRICKLAND, RODNEY
Professional basketball player. **Personal:** Born Jul 11, 1966, Bronx, NY. **Educ:** DePaul Univ, Chicago, IL, 1985-88. **Career:** New York Knicks, guard, 1988-90, San Antonio Spurs, 1990-92, Portland Trail Blazers, 1992-96; Washington Wizards, 1996-. **Honors/Awds:** NBA All-Rookie Second Team, 1989. **Special Achievements:** NBA Draft, First round pick, #18, 1988. **Business Addr:** Professional Basketball Player, Washington Wizards, MCI Center, 601 F St NW, Washington, DC 20071, (301)622-3865.

STRICKLIN, JAMES
Cameraman. **Personal:** Born Mar 27, 1934, Chicago, IL; married Marita Joyce; children: Nicholas. **Educ:** IL Inst of Tech, BS 1958; attended Art Inst of Chicago. **Career:** Univ of Chicago, lecturer film cinematography; Can Broadcasting Corp, cameraman 1964-67; NBC-News, cinematographer/cameraman 1967-. **Orgs:** IL Arts Council 1976-77; US Yacht Racing Union, 1982-; Intl Penguin Class Dinghy Assn, 1985-; Jackson Pank Yacht Club, 1985-; Columbia Yacht Club, 1993, race committee; National Academy of Television Art and Sciences. **Honors/Awds:** Emmy Outstanding Cinematographer 1971-72; Univ IL photos exhibited Smithsonian Inst 1962; co-author "With Grief Acquainted" 1963; numerous documentary films. **Business Addr:** Cameraman, NBC-News TV, NBC-Tower, 454 N Columbus Dr, Chicago, IL 60611.

STRIDER, MAURICE WILLIAM
Educator, artist. **Personal:** Born Mar 18, 1913, Lexington, KY; married Mildred Goff. **Educ:** Fisk Univ, AB; Univ of KY, MA 1960; Univ of Cinncinnati; Univ of KY; Morehead State Univ. **Career:** Morehead State Univ, asso prof of art 1966-; Louisville Defender & Pittsburgh Courier, correspondent/photographer 1935-66; Lexington KY Public School System, instr 1934-66. **Orgs:** Past pres Lexington Tchrs Assn; Lexington Educ Assn; delegate assembly Nat Educ Assn; KY Educ Assn; mem Phi Delta Kappa; Kappa Pi; Kappa Alpha Psi; mem Black History Com KY Human Rights Commn; adv bd KY Educ TV; honored past mem Fisk U; Fisk Jubilee Singers 1972. **Honors/Awds:** John Hope Purchase Art Award Atlanta Univ 1960; represented exhibit "30 Years of Black Art" Chicago DuSable Museum 1975; exhibit Carnegie Inst KY State Univ, Lexington Public Library, Morehead State Univ, IL State Univ; award Southern Educ Assn fellowship, Univ of KY; Award, Fed rsch grants for rsch Afro-Amer Art. **Business Addr:** Professor Emeritus, Morehead State University, Morehead, KY 40351.

STRINGER, C. VIVIAN
Head coach. **Personal:** Born Mar 16, 1948, Edenborn, PA; married William Stringer (deceased); children: David, Janine, Justin. **Educ:** Slippery Rock Univ, BS 1971, MEd 1972. **Career:** Cheyney State Univ, head coach basketball; professor 1972-83; Univ of Iowa, head coach basketball 1983-. **Orgs:** Founder Natl Women's Basketball Coaches Assoc 1980; instructor Natl Kodak Basketball Clinics 1983; bd mem Amateur Basketball Assoc USA 1984-85; bd mem Nike Adv Bd 1986-95. **Honors/Awds:** Head Coach Natl Sports Festival Indianapolis IN 1982; Natl Coach of the Yr NCAA 1982; Outstanding Alumni Hall of Fame Slippery Rock Univ 1985; District 5 Coach of the Yr Natl Collegiate Athletic Assoc 1985; Head Coach World Univ Games Kobe Japan 1985; Head Coach US Pan American team Cuba, 1991; Big Ten Conference Coach of the Year, 1991; Nike, advisory bd, 1986-96; Natl Coach of the Year, 1987, 1993; Head Coach, World University Qualifer Tournament-San Paulo, Brazil; Naismith Coach of the Year, 1993; Sports Illustrated, Coach of the Year, 1993; Big Ten, Coach of the Year, 1993; 3rd Winningest Coach in the USA. **Business Addr:** Women's Basketball Coach, Athletic Department, Rutgers University, New Brunswick, NJ.

STRINGER, KOREY
Professional football player. **Personal:** Born May 8, 1974, Warren, OH. **Educ:** Ohio State. **Career:** Minnesota Vikings, tackle, 1995-. **Special Achievements:** 1st round/24th overall NFL draft pick, 1995. **Business Addr:** Professional Football Player, Minnesota Vikings, 9520 Viking Dr, Eden Prairie, MN 55344, (612)828-6500.

STRINGER, MELYIN, SR.
Business executive. **Personal:** Born May 15, 1927, Princeton, LA; married Hazel Rayson; children: Melvin II, Norbert G. **Educ:** De Paul U, BSC 1952; Northwestern U, 1951-53. **Career:** IRS, agent 1951-59; private practice acct 1960-62; Dept Ins State Ill, exam surp 1961-69; Supreme Life Ins Co, asst controller 1969, controller 1970, vice pres 1973, sr vice pres 1974-77, bd of dir 1977, sr vice pres treas/controller 1977. **Orgs:** Mem NAACP; Ins Accounting & Statistical Assn; charter mem Assn Black Accountants. **Military Serv:** AUS sgt 1945-46.

STRINGER, NELSON HOWARD, JR.
Physician. **Personal:** Born Feb 7, 1948, Savannah, GA; married Denise. **Educ:** Fisk U, BA 1969; Meharry Med Coll, MD 1973. **Career:** Cook Co Hosp, resd ob-gyn 1974-77, intern 1973-74; Presb St Lukes Hosp, atdg physician; Dept Ob-gyn Rush Med Coll, instr; Emergency Room Serv S Shore Hosp, dir 1974-77. **Orgs:** Mem AMA; IL Med Soc; Chicago Med Soc; Am Assn Gyn Laparoscopists. **Honors/Awds:** Alpha Phi Alpha Frat flw; Jessie Noyes Smith 1968-73. **Business Addr:** Rush Presbyterian, St Lukes Medical Center, 1653 W Congress Pky, Chicago, IL 60612-3833.

STRINGER, THOMAS EDWARD, SR.
Circuit court judge. **Personal:** Born Jul 8, 1944, Peekskill, NY; son of Fannie and Theordore; married Lillian Jean Cooper; children: Thomas E Jr, Daryl Q, Rhonda E, Roderick E. **Educ:** New York Univ (Washington Square Coll), BA 1967; Stetson Univ Coll of Law, JD 1974. **Career:** Hillsborough County State Atty's Office, staff atty 1974-76; Rosello & Stringer PA, staff atty 1976-84; Hillsborough County Court, county judge 1984-87; Hillsborough County, circuit judge 1988-. **Orgs:** Life mem Natl Bar Assoc 1974-; mem Hillsborough County Bar Assoc 1974-; mem bd of dirs Boys & Girls Clubs of Greater Tampa Inc 1976-; mem Omega Psi Phi Frat 1980-; mem bd of dirs Bay Area Legal Serv 1984-; mem bd of overseers Stetson Univ Coll of Law 1986-; mem Bay Area Chamber of Commerce 1986-. **Honors/Awds:** Citizen of the Year Pi Iota Chap Omega Psi Phi Frat 1984; George E Edgecomb Awd Tampa Urban League 1984. **Military Serv:** US Air Force, Capt, 1967-71. **Business Addr:** Hillsborough County Circuit Judge, State of Florida, Hillsborough County Courthouse, Room 332, Tampa, FL 33602, (813)276-2099.

STRINGER, VIVIAN
College basketball coach. **Personal:** Born in Edenborn, PA; married William D. Stringer (deceased); children: David, Janine, Justin. **Educ:** Slippery Rock State College. **Career:** Cheyney State Univ, women's basketball coach; Univ of Iowa, women's basketball coach; Rutgers State University, women's basketball coach, currently. **Orgs:** Women's Basketball Coaches Assn, co-founder; Amateur Basketball Assn of US, Voting Bd; Nike Coaches Advisory Bd; Kodak, all-America Selection Comm; Women's Sports Foundation Advisory Bd. **Honors/Awds:** Named Coach of the Year by Sports Illustrated, USA Today, Naismith, Black Coaches Assn; Natl Coach of the Year, 1982, 1988, 1993; Dist V Coach of the Year, 1985, 1988, 1993; Big Ten Coach of the Year, 1991, 1993; Carol Eckman Award, 1993. **Special Achievements:** NCAA Final Four, Cheyney State, 1982, Univ of IA, 1993; World Championship Zone Qualification Tournament, coach, 1989; World University Games, coach, 1979, 1985; US Select Team, head coach, 1981; Pan American Games, coach, bronze medal, 1991; one of the youngest women's basketball coaches to reach 500 victories; one of the top five winningest active division I women's basketball coaches.

STRINGFELLOW, ERIC DEVAUGHN
Journalist. **Personal:** Born Aug 31, 1960, Meridian, MS; son of Delores Tartt Stringfellow and Clintorice Stringfellow Sr; children: Courtney DeVon Stringfellow. **Educ:** Jackson State University, Jackson, MS, mass communications, 1978-82. **Career:** The Commercial News, reporter, 1982; The Clarion Ledger, reporter, 1982-86; The Plain Dealer, reporter, 1986-91; Jackson Clarion Ledger, political editor, 1991-94; Jackson State Univ, adjunt professor, 1991-94, professor in residence, 1994-. **Orgs:** President, Jackson Association of Black Journalists, 1985-86, 1992-; parliamentarian, Cleveland Association of Black Journalists, 1987-89; president, Cleveland Association of Black Journalists, 1989-91; president, JSU Cleveland Alumni Chapter, 1989-91; member, Black Media Workers, 1990-91; 100 Black Men of Jackson; bd mem, Voice of Calvary Ministries. **Honors/Awds:** John Hancock Award for Outstanding Financial Reporting, John Hancock Co, 1985; 2nd Place Interpretive Reporting, Mississippi/Louisiana Associated Press Contest, 1986. **Home Addr:** 117 Kilkenny Blvd, Jackson, MS 39209.

STRIPLING, LUTHER
Educator. **Personal:** Born Aug 25, 1935, Tingnall, GA; son of Catherine Stripling and Luther Stripling; married Myrtice Jones, Nov 7, 1957 (deceased); children: Cedric Ravel, Lloyd Byron. **Educ:** Clark Coll, AB 1957; Atlanta Univ, attended 1960-65; Univ KY, MMus 1968; Univ CO, DMus 1971. **Career:** Hamilton HS, teacher 1957-66, chmn music dept 1960-66; GA Interscholastic Assn, chmn vocal div 1964-66; Univ KY, instructor 1966-68; Univ CO, 1970-71; Macalester Coll, coordinator vocal activities 1971; So IL Univ at Edwardsville, assoc prof of music/dir of opera workshop; Tarrant County Jr Coll NE Campus, 1984-95; professor of vocal music/dir, Bel Canto Singles, currently. **Orgs:** Pres MN chapter Natl Opera Assn Inc; general dir Macalester Coll Opera Workshop; assn general dir Assoc Coll of the Twin Cities Opera Workshop; minister of music Pilgrim Baptist Church; pres St Louis Dist Chapter of Natl Assn of Teachers of Singing 1980-82; numerous performances orchestral appearances directing papers in field; mem, bd of governors, NE Trinity Arts Council, 1989-91. **Honors/Awds:** Contributor Burkhart Charles Anthology for Musical Analysis 3rd Ed NY Holt Rinehart & Winston 1978. **Home Addr:** 901 Woodcreek Ct, Euless, TX 76039. **Business Phone:** (817)515-6570.

STRODE, VELMA MCEWEN
Former senior executive. **Personal:** Born Oct 19, 1919, Jackson, MS; daughter of Rev & Mrs B T McEwen; married James W (deceased); children: James C. **Career:** Office of Equal Employment Opportunity, US Dept of Labor, dir 1971-; Dept of Justice, Community Relations Serv, sr community relations specialist; Community Center in Utica NY, dir; The Velma McEwen Show, broadcaster. **Orgs:** Exec Urban League 1946-57; Acad of Certified Social Workers; Alumni Assn of Fed Exec Inst; Amer Women in Radio & TV; bd of trustees, St Augustine's Coll; United Way Bd of Dist of Columbia; rep Greater Metro United Way Bd; advisor Capit Tower Proj Home for Delinquent Young Women; Exec Women in Govt Org; Natl Urban League; NAACP; Social Action Commn Delta Sigma Theta Sor; Leadership Conf on Civil Rights; advisory bd, YWCA Tower. **Honors/Awds:** Recognition for outstanding performance of duties, US Dept of Labor 1973; activist award, Cleveland OH 1974; outstanding serv to humanity, St Augustine Coll 1975; the Chapel of Four Chaplains Philadelphia 1975; the Conf of Minority Public Admin Award 1976; Amer GI Forum Award 1976; Equal Employment Opportunity Commn Award Dallas 1976; EEO award, Fed Women's Prog, Texas Region, Equal Employment Opportunity Commn 1976; hon citizen, Dallas TX 1976; labor mgmt award, Natl Black Women's Political Leadership Caucus 1976.

STROGER, JOHN HERMAN, JR.
Attorney. **Personal:** Born May 19, 1929, Helena, AR; married Yonnie Rita Bachelor; children: Yonnie Lynn, Hans Eric, Todd Herman. **Educ:** Xavier U, LA, BS 1952; DePaul Univ Law Sch, Chicago, JD 1965. **Career:** HS basketball coach 1952-53. **Orgs:** Mem Cook Co Bd of Commrs; committeeman 8th Ward Regular Dem Orgn 1968; personnel dir Cook Co Jail 1955-59; mem Cook Co Bar Assn; Chicago Bar Assn; IL Bar Assn; Am Bar Assn; bd dir Chicago Woodlawn Boys Club; mem BSA; Kiwanis Club; YMCA; Xi Lambda Chpt; Alpha Phi Alpha Frat Inc. **Honors/Awds:** Recipient award of merit Chicago Inter Alumni Council of the United Negro Coll Fund; Cook Co Bar Assn Edward H Wright Award 1973; Kiwanis Club of SE Area, Chicago; Englewood Bus Promotions Award; S Chicago Organized for People's Efforts Award; Chicago Park Dist Award 1973. **Business Addr:** 109 N Dearborn St, Ste 801, Chicago, IL.

STROMAN, CHERYL PARKER
Pharmacist. **Personal:** Born Jan 12, 1956, Gaffney, SC; daughter of Ruby White Parker and John H Parker, Sr; married Joseph B Stroman, Sep 17, 1988; children: Radhiya Marjani, Joseph B Jr. **Educ:** Univ of North Carolina, Pre-pharmacy 1974; Howard Univ, BS Pharmacy 1979. **Career:** Hill Health Center, staff pharmacist 1979-80; Comm Health Care Cte Plan, pharmacy coordinator 1980-84; Eckerd Drug Gastonia, pharmacist mgr 1985-86; Kaiser Foundation Health Plan, pharmacy supervisor 1986-. **Orgs:** Mem Alpha Kappa Alpha Sorority Inc 1975-, Amer Pharmaceutical Assn 1979-, North Carolina Pharmaceutical Assoc 1985-; mem St Stephens AME Zion Church, Gastonia, NC. **Business Addr:** Pharmacy Supervisor, Kaiser Permanente, 1867 Remount Rd, Gastonia, NC 28054.

STROMAN, KENNETH
Eeo coordinator/sr exec recruiter. **Personal:** Born Jun 19, 1948, New Rochelle, NY. **Educ:** Atlantic Union College, BA History Psychology 1970. **Career:** Drug Abuse Control Commission, narcotic parole officer 1975-76; Manufacturers Hanover Trust, exec recruiter 1978-85; Merrill Lynch & Co Inc, sr exec recruiter 1985, eeo coord 1985-. **Orgs:** Steering comm mem Harlem Branch YMCA "Salute to Black Achievers in Industry" 1986-87; Jackie Robinson Foundation 1986; mem NAACP 1986, Natl Urban League1986. **Honors/Awds:** Service Awd Southern Christian Leadership Conference 1985, 86.

STRONG, AMANDA L.
Nursing administrator. **Personal:** Born Nov 22, 1935, Marvel, AR; daughter of Early Mae & Percy Watson; widowed; children: Cheryl Beard, Pamela Tender, Jerilyn S. **Educ:** St Vincents Hospital School Nursing, Diploma 1954-57; Indiana Univ, BSN 1973; ANA, Certificate 1980; Indiana Univ, MSN 1983; Family Nurse Practitioner, Certificate 1985-90, 1995-. **Career:** Indiana Univ Med Center, asst head nurse 1959-64; Visiting Nurse Assn, supr 1964-72; Dept of Corr, family nurse practitioner 1974-80; Roudebush Vets Admin Med Center Home Based Primary Care Prog, nurse practitioner 1980-, prog dir, HBPC, 1988-; "Stuck on Wellness," Independent Distributor of Nikken Wellness Products. **Orgs:** Bd mem Capitol Improvements Bd 1978-85; pres Holy Angels Parish Cncl 1979-83; comm ch & bd mem Coalition 100 Black Women 1980-; mem black & minority health task force Indiana State Bd of Health; mem standards comm Chronic Health Indiana State Bd of Health; bd mem Indiana State Bd Nurses & Nurse Practitioner Council; pres, Indiana Univ School of Nursing, 1988-91; sec, District 5 Alumni Assn Bd of Nursing, Indiana State Nurses Assn, 1987-89; facilitator, Hospital Based Home Care Support Group, 1989-; vice chairperson, Archdiocesan Pastoral Council, Indianapolis, IN, 1994-97; elected secretary, Catholic Foundation Board, Archdiocese of Indianapolis, Multi-Cultural Ministry Advisory Committee. **Honors/Awds:** Those Special People Sigma Phi Communications Award; Cert Amer Nurses Assn Adult Practitioner 1995-2000; Martin Luther King Leadership Award SCLC; Citizen of Day WTLC Radio; chosen Hospital Based Home Care Nurse for 1985; Special Contribution to Nursing Veterans Admin Nursing, 1989; Minority Nurse Role Model, Indianapolis Star, 1989; member, Sigma Theta Tau Nursing Honorary Society, 1989-; Federal Employee of the Year (nominee), Federal Government, 1991; Amvets, Distinguished Nurse Award; American Cancer Society, Volunteer Service Award, 1995; Salute from WFMY for Volunteerism. **Home Addr:** 402 E 46th St, Indianapolis, IN 46205.

STRONG, BLONDELL MCDONALD
Management consultant, real estate agent. **Personal:** Born Jan 11, 1943, Fort Pierce, FL; daughter of Bertha McDonald and Jeff McDonald (deceased); married Charles E Kimbrough; children: Stanford II, Jeff Bertram. **Educ:** Tennessee State Univ, BS 1964; Geo Peabody Coll of Vanderbilt Univ, MLS 1967; Univ of Michigan, PhD 1983; University of Michigan, Postdoctorate, 1985. **Career:** Lincoln Jr Coll, librarian & music instructor 1964-65; Indian River Jr Coll, librarian & asst cataloger 1965-67; Meharry Med Coll, library dir 1967-77; Univ of Michigan, post-doctorate fellow 1984-85; Mamlika Enterprises Inc, pres 1989-; mgmt consultant; Bond Realty Inc, management executive 1986-88; Bordeaux Realty Plus, pres & co-owner, currently. **Orgs:** NAACP, life member, Nashville Branch, 1991; Alpha Kappa Alpha Sorority. **Honors/Awds:** Kappa Delta Pi Hon Soc; Beta Phi Mu Intl Library Science Hon Soc; General Manager & Treasurer, Fisk-Meharry Credit Union, 1976-77. **Business Addr:** President, Bordeaux Realty Plus, PO Box 180008, Nashville, TN 37218, (615)227-3898.

STRONG, CRAIG STEPHEN
Judge. **Personal:** Born Sep 5, 1947, Detroit, MI. **Educ:** Howard Univ, BA 1969; Detroit Coll of Law, JD 1973. **Career:** Wayne Co Neighborhood Legal Serv, law intern & staff atty 1970-73; Terry Ahmad & Bradfield, assoc atty 1973; Elliard Crenshaw & Strong PC, partner 1974-77; Recorder's Court City of Detroit Traffic & Ordinance Div, referee 1978; City of Detroit Recorder's Court, judge 1979-. **Orgs:** Past pres Wolverine Bar Assn; regional dir Natl Bar Assn; former recorder's ct com chmn Detroit Bar Assn; vice chmn bd of dir Wayne Co Neighborhood Legal Svcs; rep assembly State Bar of MI; mem Prince Hall Masons 32nd Degree; board of directors, Michigan Cancer Foundation; president, Assn of Black Judges of Michigan; life member, NAACP; Alpha Phi Alpha Fraternity. **Honors/Awds:** Man of the Yr Awd Detroit Urban Center 1979; Howardite of the Yr Awd Howard Univ Detroit Chap 1979; Resolution State of MI 1979; Disting Serv Awd Natl Council of Negro Women 1980; Renaissance Awd 13th Dist Democratic Party 1982; Outstanding Museum Serv Awd Afro-Amer Museum of Detroit 1983; Humanitarian Awd of Excellence Mother Waddles Perpetual Mission 1983; man of the year North End youth Improvement Council 1986; award of appreciation Boy Scouts of America Renaissance District 1988; Civic & Community Contribution Award, Native Detroiter Magazine, 1989; Legal Accomplishments Recognition, Wolverine Student Bar Assn, 1990. **Military Serv:** USNR-R, Commander, military judge, 1988-93. **Business Addr:** Judge, Recorder's Court, City of Detroit, 1441 St Antoine, Detroit, MI 48226.

STRONG, DEREK LAMAR
Professional basketball player. **Personal:** Born Feb 9, 1968, Los Angeles, CA. **Educ:** Xavier Univ. **Career:** NBA career: Washington Bullets, 1992; Milwaukee Bucks, 1993-94; Boston Celtics, 1994-95; Los Angeles Lakers, 1995-96, Orlando Magic, 1996-; CBA career: Quad City Thunder, 1992-93; played in Spain, 1990-91; Miami Tropics, 1991. **Honors/Awds:** Continental Basketball Assn, Most Valuable Player, 1993, Newcomer of the Year, 1993, All-Star first team, 1993, All-Defensive team, 1993. **Business Addr:** Professional Basketball Player, Orlando Magic, One Magic Pl, Orlando, FL 32801, (407)649-3200.

STRONG, DOUGLAS DONALD
Physician. **Personal:** Born May 31, 1938, Detroit, MI; married Helen Francine; children: Mark, Douglas Jr, Jennifer Anne, Stephen. **Educ:** Univ of MI, BA 1959; Howard Univ, MD 1963. **Career:** Grace Hosp Detroit, intern 1963-64; Mt Carmel Mercy Hosp Detroit, surgery resident 1966-67; San Francisco VA Hosp Univ of CA, post-doctoral cand 1968-70; Otolaryn/physician, currently. **Orgs:** Mem Detroit Med Soc, Wayne Co Med Soc, Natl Med Soc, Acad of Ophthal & Otolaryn; mem Alpha Phi Alpha Frat, NAACP; hosp staffs Harper Hospital, SW Hospital, Mt Carmel Hosp, Childrens Hosp; chief of otolaryngology Hutzel Hosp; instr Otolaryngology Wayne State Univ. **Honors/Awds:** Testimonial Resolution from Detroit City Council; Special Tribute from Senate of the State of MI; Service Award, Detroit Medical Society, 1986; Tribute, State of Michigan House of Representatives, 1984; Spirit of Detroit Award, City of Detroit, 1984; Special Citation, Korean Government, 1965; Flag from the State of Michigan, 1991. **Military Serv:** AUS capt 1964-66. **Business Addr:** Physician, 3800 Woodward, Detroit, MI 48201.

STRONG, HELEN FRANCINE (FRAN LANIER)
Attorney. **Personal:** Born Mar 22, 1947, Detroit, MI; daughter of Lonia and Nancy Lanier; married Douglas Donald Jr; children: Douglas Jr, Jennifer Anne, Stephen. **Educ:** Univ of Detroit, AB 1969; Univ of Detroit, JD 1972. **Career:** State of MI, asst attny gen; Detroit Edison Co, staff attny 1973-80; William C Gage PC, assoc 1980-81; Lewis White & Clay PC, partner, shareholder. **Orgs:** Mem Natl Bar Assn, Fed Bar Assoc, MI Bar Assn, Detroit Bar Assn, Wolverine Bar Assn, Amer Bar Assn,; legal adv Delta Sigma Theta 1973-75; aux to Detroit Med Soc, Natl Med Soc; life mem NAACP; founder Soc Detroit Inst of Arts; mem Assoc of Trial Lawyers of Amer, MI Trial Lawyers Assn; bd dir Founders Jr Council-Detroit Inst of Arts 1979-1988; sec bd dir Founders Jr Council Detroit Inst of Arts 1982-83; adv comm Detroit Inst of Arts Centennial Comm 1983-, Your Heritage House Inc 1983-84; bd dir Your Heritage House Inc 1984-88; chmn Exhibition Treasures of Ancient Nigeria-Legacy of Two Thousand Years Detroit Inst of Arts Founders Jr Council 1980; co-chmn Exhibition Opening Black Folk Art in Amer 1930-1980 Detroit Inst of Arts 1983; bd of trustees, Eton Academy, 1984-88; mem, Continuing EdComm, State Bar of MI, 1990-; mem, Legal Educ Comm, State Bar of MI, 1990-; adv bd, Founders Jr Council Detroit Inst of Arts, 1985-. **Honors/Awds:** Cert for Outstanding Scholarship in Intramural Moot Ct Compet 1970; Univ of Detroit Jr Natl Moot Ct Team 1970-71; Univ of Detroit Sr Natl Moot Ct Team 1971-72; Moot Ct Bd of Dir 1971-72; Univ of Detroit Law School Admiss Comm 1970-71; Cert for Outstanding Serv Univ of Detroit School of Law 1972; 1st blackatty, 1st woman atty empl by Detroit Edison Co; Award in Recognition of Service to the Detroit Medical Soc, 1986; Testimonial Resolution from the City Council of the City of Detroit for service to the community and to the profession of law, 1991; Testimonial Resolution from the Wayne County Commissioners for civic and cultural involvement, 1991; Distinguished Service Award from the Wayne County Executive in recognition of meritorious service, 1991; Seal of the State of MI inrecognition meritorious service, 1991. **Business Addr:** Shareholder/Partner, Lewis, White & Clay PC, 1300 First Natl, Detroit, MI 48226.

STRONG, MACK
Professional football player. **Personal:** Born Sep 11, 1971, Fort Benning, GA. **Educ:** Univ of Georgia. **Career:** Seattle Seahawks, running back, 1994-. **Business Addr:** Professional Football Player, Seattle Seahawks, 11220 NE 53rd St, Kirkland, WA 98033, (206)827-9777.

STRONG, MARILYN TERRY
Educator (retired). **Personal:** Born Sep 10, 1929, Hartford, CT; daughter of Odessa Callie Stewart Terry (deceased) and George William Terry (deceased); married Edward M Strong (deceased). **Educ:** Univ of CT, BA 1950, MA 1965. **Career:** Hartford Bd of Educ, elem physical educ teacher 1950-60, secondary physical educ teacher 1960-84; Weaver High School, physical educ dept head 1971-77, varsity basketball & softball coach 1972-86, continuing educ teacher 1984; retired 1989.

Orgs: Mem AAHPER 1950-; vice pres 1971-72 CAHPERD 1950-85; mem CEA & NEA 1950-; Golden life mem, pres 1963-65 Hartford Alumnae Delta Sigma Theta Sor Inc 1951-; mem Order of Eastern Star Stella Chap #16 1957-; leader chairperson bd of dirs CT Valley Girl Scouts 1951-; pres 1985-87, treas 1989-92, Hartford Jazz Soc 1977-; mem CT Black Caucus 1985-; mem, Links Inc, 1986-, treasurer, 1990-92; Docent, Conn Historical Society, 1989-; member/volunteer, Wadsworth Atheneum, 1989-; Girl Friends Inc, 1994-, recording scy, 1996-98. **Honors/Awds:** Delta Sigma Theta Comm Serv Awd 1965; Outstanding Secondary Educator 1973, 1976; Maharishi Educ Awd 1977; Hartford Teacher of the Yr Hartford Bd of Educ 1981; Comm Serv Awd Brass Key Inc 1982; Comm Serv Awd Natl Assn Negro Business & Professional Women's Clubs Inc Hartford Chap 1986; Iota Phi Lambda, Beta Chapter Apple for the Teacher Award 1988; Inspiration Award, National Assn for Sports & Physical Educ, 1989; Marilyn T Strong Female Athlete Award, Weaver High School, 1990-. **Home Addr:** 42 Canterbury St, Hartford, CT 06112.

STRONG, OTIS REGINALD, III

Consumer affairs representative. **Personal:** Born Sep 26, 1954, Norfolk, VA; son of Mallie Swinson Smith and Otis Strong; married Gloria W; children: Cayce J. **Educ:** Elizabeth City State Univ, BS 1976. **Career:** Delta Air Lines Inc, customer service support agent 1976-77, sr customer service agent 1978-83, sr passenger service agent 1983-84, consumer affairs rep 1984-, systems baggage coordinator, 1988-. **Orgs:** Mem NAACP 1976-, JOHER-AAHPR 1976-; vice pres Uni-Time Inc 1984-; pres Alumni Chap ECSU 1985-, Atlanta Alumni Chap ECSU 1985-; coach/head, Fayette County Rec Assn 1987-; coach, Fayette County AAU Basketball-GA 1988-; Alpha Phi Alpha Fraternity, 1990-. **Honors/Awds:** Distinguished Alumni Awd 1986. **Business Addr:** Consumer Affairs Rep, Delta Air Lines Inc, Hartsfield Intl Airport, Atlanta, GA 30320.

STRONG, PETER E.

Dentist. **Personal:** Born Apr 1, 1930, Detroit, MI; son of Manila Geraldine Powers Strong and Erman Peter Strong; married Helen Rowe; children: Peter Christopher, Kent Alexander. **Educ:** Univ of MI, DDS 1955. **Career:** Detroit Dept of Health, sr dentist 1957-58; pvt practice of gen dentistry 1958-; Staff Grace Hosp, 1965-74; Delta Dental Plan of MI, consult 1974-75; Hutzel Hospital, Detroit, MI, member, professional staff, 1976-. **Orgs:** President Wolverine Dental Soc 1972-73; NE Component Detroit Dist Dental Soc 1974-; exec council Detroit Dist Dental Soc 1973-75; bd of trustee Detroit Med Foundation 1972-74; bd of trustee Nat Dental Assn 1965-67; MI Dental Assn 1957-; Am Dental Assn 1953-; charter mem Am Soc for Preventive Dentistry, steering com of MI Chap 1970-75; Acad of Gen Dentistry 1973-; Alumni Visitation Com Adv on Curriculum of Univ of MI Sch of Dentistry 1971-81; Med Com of Human Rights 1964-70; life mem NAACP; American Civil Liberties Union; Alpha Phi Alpha Frat 1950-; The Moors; The Recess, 1975-80; Detroit Boat Club, 1974-84; Sch Health Council of Detroit Pub Sch System 1971-75; Preventive Dental Health & Education Program Detroit Pub Sch System; clinician MI Dental Assn Conv 1972; Phi Eta Sigma Freshman Honor Frat; RW Bunting Presidential Study Club, 1982-. **Honors/Awds:** Fellow, Academy of General Dentistry, 1985. **Military Serv:** US Army cpt Dental Corp 1955-57. **Business Addr:** Dentist, 18591 W Ten Mile Rd, Southfield, MI 48075-2619.

STRONG, WALTER L.

Educational administrator. **Personal:** son Of Dorothy Strong. **Educ:** Southern IL Univ-Carbondale, BA; Univ of NE-Lincoln, MA; Univ of IL, doctoral ABD; Golden Gate Univ, PhD. **Career:** Univ of CA Mgmt Inst, faculty mem; Univ of IL-Urbana, asst vice chancellor for academic affairs, political science faculty mem; Univ of CA-Berkeley, asst vice president for personnel development; Meharry Medical Coll, vice pres for institutional advancement; Florida Intl Univ, vice pres of univ relations/develop; Wayne State Univ, sr vice pres for univ relations, 1988-92; Meharry Med Coll, exec vice pres, 1992-. **Orgs:** Cumberland Museum of Science Tech, board of membership; The Robertson Assn; United Way of Nashville; NAACP, mem; Kappa Alpha Psi; Council for the Advancement and Support of Education; American Management Assn.

STROUD, HOWARD BURNETT, SR.

Educational administrator (retired). **Personal:** Born Mar 31, 1939, Athens, GA; son of Emma Flanigan Stroud and George E Stroud; married Bettye Moore Stroud, Dec 16, 1989; children: Howard B Jr, Kesha D. **Educ:** Morehouse Coll, BA 1956; Atlanta Univ, MA 1968; Univ of GA, Agnes Scott Coll, Appalachian State Boone NC. **Career:** Union Inst, teacher 1956; Burney Harris HS, teacher 1956-65; Lyons Middle Sch, guidance counselor asst prin teacher 1963-65; Lyons Middle School Clark Co, prin 1965-78; Clark Co School Dist, coord middle & secondary schools 1978-80, admin asst to supt 1980-81, acting supt 1981-82, assoc supt 1981-92. **Orgs:** Bd dir GA Assn of Educ Ldrs; Prin Res & Info Ctr; Editorial Bd Amer Middle Sch Educ Journal; Editoral Bd GA Assn of Middle Sch Prins Jour; bd dir GA Assn of Educ Ldrs 1976-; Natl Educ Assn; pres GA Middle Sch Prins; exalted ruler Classic City Elks Lodge; lay vice pres Athens-Clarke Cancer Soc; state bd Cancer Soc; pres exec comm Cancer Soc; Phi Delta Kappa, Kappa Alpha Psi; Mason; past polemarch Elks; charter mem Athens Area Oppors Indus Ctr; OIC bd of dir 1976-; Athens Council on Wellness 1982-83; bd dir Family Counseling; chmn steering comm Union Baptist Inst Inc; member Prestigious GA Professional Practices Comm 1983-88; GA Secondary Comm Southern Assn of Colls & Schs 1983-89; Hosp Auth Clarke Co 1983-89; chmn bd deacons Mt Pleasant Baptist Ch 1980; board of directors, Athen Regionaedical Center, 1991-97; chairman, Facilities & Program ARMC, 1991; chairman, Athens Regional Health Services Inc, 1991-; board of directors, Athens Technical Institute, 1991-; advisory board, Georgia Cooperative Extension, 1990-92; Athens Regional Hospital Authority, chairman, 1992-93; Clarke County School District, Foundation for Excellence, board of directors, East Athens Revitalization Implementation Committee. **Honors/Awds:** Presidential Citation Optimist Intl for Leadership as pres Athens Breakfast Optimist Club; Cert of Apprec Athens Rec Dept 1975; Cert of Achievement Kappa Alpha Psi Frat; Heritage Awd Optimist Intl; Outstanding Educators Awd Lyons Fac 1977; This is Your Life Lyons Fac & Student Body 1977; Serv Awd Mosley Gospel Choir 1977; Dedication & Serv Plaque Lyons Fac & Student Body; Outstanding Ldrshp GA Assn of Middle Sch Prins 1978; Portrait unveiled Lyons Middle Sch 1978; Awd of Excel Pub Sch Admin Kappa Delta; chmn steering comm Union Baptist Inst Inc; chmn Prestigious GA Professional PracPi 1984-87; Serv Awd Ga Assn Educ Ldrshp 1977-78, 1978-79; Serv Awd Citizens Group of Athens 1979; Ldrshp Awd Phi Beta Sigma Frat 1982; Mkt Place Achiev Awd Milledge Bapt Ch 1982; Outstndg Ldrshp Awd ClarkeCd Educ 1981-82; Human Relations Awd GA Assn of Educs 1983; W Judicial Circiut Liberty Bell Law Day Awd 1984; Spec Recog Awd 199 Percenters 1982; Outstndg Serv Awd Athens Cntr Rec Ctr Day 1984; Outstndg Serv Awd Athens Tech Sch 1982, Delegate-at-Large AASA Conference 1991. **Military Serv:** US Army, 1951-53.

STROUD, LAWRENCE LOWELL

Manager. **Personal:** Born Apr 26, 1935, Macon, GA; married Elizabeth Ervin; children: Larren, Sherri, Calisse. **Educ:** A&T U, Greensboro, NC, BS 1957; Glassboro State Coll, MA 1973. **Career:** US Govt, supr monitor prodn; FAA mgmt software respons nations air space environment. **Orgs:** Past pres Atlantic Co Citizens on Environment; Alpha Phi Alpha Frat; pres FAA Flying Club NAFFC; commr Pleasantville Housing Auth; adj coll prof; pastchmn personnel Pleasantville Bd of Edn; mem Toastmaster Internat. **Honors/Awds:** Citation Metoriuos Serv to City of Pleasantville, Bd of Educ 1976. **Military Serv:** USAR platoon leader.

STROUD, LOUIS WINSTON

Management consultant. **Personal:** Born Nov 21, 1946, Cincinnati, OH. **Educ:** Canisius Coll, AB Hist 1968; Harvard Grad School of Bus Admin, MBA Finance 1970; Univ of San Francisco School of Law, JD 1976. **Career:** Kaiser Aluminum & Chem Corp, merger acquisition specialist 1976; Mfrs Hanover Trust, product mgr disbursements 1974-76; Mfrs Hanover Trust, corp planner 1973. **Orgs:** Mem Harvard Bus School Club 1976-80; mem Harvard Club 1980.

STROUD, MILTON

Law enforcement supervisor. **Personal:** Born in Durham, NC; son of Verly Gay Cotton Stroud and John Milton Stroud; divorced; children: Monica Shafi, Dwayne Bland. **Educ:** Queens Coll, BA 1965; Long Island Univ, MA 1967; New York Univ, PhD 1976. **Career:** New York State Division of Parole, supervisor, currently. **Orgs:** Vice chmn Area Policy Bd Brooklyn 1980-; bd chmn Old 80 Precinct Council 1981-; exec vice pres Ebony Soc 1985-; exec bd mem Professional Employees Federation 1985-; mem Natl Assn of Blacks in Criminal Justice, Natl Acad of Criminology, Amer Sociological Assn, Natl Black Police Assn; member, New York City Community Action Board, 1986-92; recording secretary, northeastern region, National Black Police, 1990-92; recording secretary, New York State Parole Officer's Assn. **Honors/Awds:** Omega Psi Phi Man of the Year 1973; Certificate of Merit Natl Assoc of Black Counselors 1985; Delta Sigma Theta Comm Serv Award 1985; Achievement AwardEbony Soc 1986; Humanitarian Award Amer Federation of Police 1986; Certificate of Merit, Federation of African-American Civil Service Organization. **Military Serv:** NG 2 yrs. **Home Addr:** 1048 Union St, Brooklyn, NY 11225.

STROZIER, YVONNE IGLEHART

State official, educator. **Personal:** Born Nov 14, Waco, TX; daughter of Dessie Mae Truitt Iglehart and Bishop T D Iglehart; married Arthur A Strozier, Oct 13, 1974; children: William Charles Wilborn, Thaddeus Iglehart Wilborn, Desi Artrice Iglehart Strozier. **Educ:** Bishop Coll, Marshall TX, BS, 1959; Prairie View A&M, Prairie View TX, MA, 1965; San Diego State, San Diego CA, attended, 1968. **Career:** Conway Public Schools, Conway AR, teacher, 1959-60; Waco Independent School Dist, Waco TX, teacher 1961-65; El Dorado County Schools, Placerville CA, teacher, 1965-66; San Diego City Schools, San Diego CA, teacher, project dir, 1966-72; California Dept of Educ, Sacramento CA, consultant, 1972-. **Orgs:** Delta Sigma Theta Sorority, 1955-, Jack & Jill Inc, 1970-; cofounder, California Alliance of Black School Educ, 1979-; exec bd, Natl Alliance of Black School Educ, 1985-; corporate bd mem, California Assn of Compensatory Educ, 1985-; admin, Strozier Youth Center, 1986-; coord, The Speaker's Educ Breakfast Club (Speaker of the House, California State Assembly), 1986-; meeting planner, Natl Alliance of Black School Educ, 1986-; mem, Coalition of Black Meeting Planners, 1987-; bd mem, C H Mason Found-Church of God in Christ, 1988-; bd of dirs, Saints Academy and College, Lexington, Missisippi. **Honors/Awds:** Coordinator, The Proficiency in Standard English Porgarm for African-Amer Students (the first and only program operated by a state educ agency), 1979; Outstanding Achievement, California Alliance of Black School Educators, 1980; Proclamation of Appreciation, Natl Assn of Black School Educ, 1980-; Outstanding Educator, California Dept of Educ, 1983; Outstanding Achievement, California Assn of Compensatory Educ, 1985, 1986; Proclamation of Appreciation, Inglewood School Dist, Inglewood CA, 1987. **Business Addr:** Consultant, California Department of Education, 721 Capitol Mall, Sacramento, CA 95814.

STRUDWICK, LINDSEY H., SR.

Certified purchasing manager. **Personal:** Born Aug 8, 1946, Durham, NC; son of Christine Alston Strudwick and London L Strudwick, Sr; married Gladys B Strudwick, Nov 9, 1968; children: Lindsey Howard Jr, Casandra Michelle. **Educ:** Durham Business Coll, Durham NC, assoc degree in science/business admin; Shaw Univ, Raleigh NC, BA; Southeastern Univ, Greenville SC, MBA. **Career:** Intl Fertility Research, Chapel Hill NC, purchasing mgr, 1974-76; Northrop Corp, Research Triangle Pk NC, manager of purchasing and facilities, 1976-78; Gen Telephone Co, Durham NC, personnel asst, 1978-79; Northern Telecom Inc, Research Triangle Pk NC, group leader in purchasing, 1979-81; Scientific-Atlanta Inc, Atlanta GA, mgr of purchasing and contracts, 1982-86; Coors Brewing Co, Golden CO, dir of purchasing and materials, 1986—. **Orgs:** Mem, NAACP, 1978—; mem, Natl Assn of Purchasing Mgmt, 1978—; mem, Amer Prioduction and Inventory Control Soc, 1980—; mem, Amer Purchasing Soc, 1985—; mem, bd of dirs, 1986—, chmn, 1986-88, Rocky Mtn Regional Minority Supplier Develpment Council; mem, bd of dirs, Natl Minority Supplier Development Council, 1987—; mem, bd of dirs, Natl Minorities Business Directories, 1988—. **Honors/Awds:** Named Man of the Year (regional), Natl Urban League, 1986; corporate citizenship award, United Indian Develpoment Assn, 1988. **Military Serv:** US Army, first lieutenant, 1966-69.

STRUDWICK, WARREN JAMES, SR.

Physician. **Personal:** Born Dec 23, 1923, Durham, NC; son of Mabel Christina Wormley Strudwick (deceased) and William Canady Strudwick (deceased); married Dr Bette Catoe Strudwick; children: Laura Strudwick-Turner, Warren J Jr, William J. **Educ:** Howard Univ, BS 1948, MD 1952. **Career:** Howard Univ, Washington DC, instructor of surgery, 1959-61, asst prof of surgery, 1961-; Greater Southeast Community Hospital, staff; Providence Hosp, vice chair, surgery dept, attending surgeon; Howard Univ Hosp, attending surgeon; Washington Hospital Center, staff; Children's Hospital, staff. **Orgs:** Med Chirurgical Soc DC, bd of governors, past mem; Zion Bapt Church; Kappa Alpha Psi; Produffers Golf Club; Amer Bd of Surgery, diplomate, 1960; Amer Society of Abdominal Surgeons; Medical Society of the District of Columbia; Howard Univ, Med Alumni Assn, pres local chap; Amer Cancer Society; Amer Med Assn; Natl Med Policial Action Comm; NAACP; Urban League; Sigma Pi Phi. **Honors/Awds:** American College of Surgeons, fellow, 1962; Medical Society of the District of Columbia, Certificate of Meritorious Service, 1997. **Special Achievements:** Published articles: ''Biopsy in Modern Medical Practice,'' with Warren J. Strudwick and Jack E. White, JNMA, 1960; ''Cancer of the Skin in Negroes,'' with Newton W. Ricketts, Calvin Sampson, Warren J. Strudwick and Jack E. White, JNMA, 1961; ''A Clinical Study of 5-Fluoroucil in a Variety of Far Advanced Human Malignancies,'' with Newton Ricketts, Warren J. Strudwick and Jack E. White, JNMA, 1962; ''Carcinoma of the Stomach in American Negroes,'' Surg., Gynec., & Obstet., 1964. **Military Serv:** USMCR 1943-46. **Business Addr:** Surgeon, 513 Kennedy St NW, Washington, DC 20011.

STUART, IVAN I.

Military. **Personal:** marrIed Dorthey M; children: Ivan, Jr, Connie, Selwyn, JoAnn, Desire. **Career:** 20 years military service retired; Floyd Co Branch NAACP, pres. **Orgs:** Mem bd of gov's New River Comm Action & Program; delegate Dem Com; VA Deacon Little River Bapt Ch Floyd; mem Masonic Lodge 146. **Honors/Awds:** Letters of commendation military svc. **Military Serv:** AUS 1943-64. **Business Addr:** Rt 1 Box 62, Copper Hill, VA 24079.

STUART, MARJORIE MANN

Educator. **Personal:** Born Nov 12, 1921, New Bern, NC; daughter of Clara Smith Mann and William Mann, MD; divorced; children: Sandra Stuart, R Sterling Stuart. **Educ:** Hampton Inst, BS 1941; NY U, MA 1944; Universidad Inter-Americana, Mexico, PhD 1971; Univ Ghana Inst, 1971; OK Coll, 1972. **Career:** Hampton Inst, instr 1941-45; asso prof, cons, choreographer, performer, dance; dir childrens dance group Houston 1963-70; YMCA, instr 1952-68; consult headstart leadership devel 1966-; Univ of TX Sch of Edn, consult

1974-; choreographer educ TV series 1954; co-devel prog multi-ethnicity finearts 1974-75; TX Southern Univ professor,1948-83, retired 1983. **Orgs:** Mm Dance Panel of The TX Commn for the Arts & Humanities 1973-74; US Com Intl Orgn for Early Childhood Educ 1973-; Dance Adv Bd; HS Performing & Visual Arts, Houston 1972-; tech adv bd Hope Devel, Houston 1974-; exec dir Terpsilor Inc; mem Augustana Luth Ch Fellow; So Fellowshops Fund 1970. **Honors/Awds:** Serv recognition awards TSU Chap TX Assn Coll Tchrs 1974, 175; hon mem Epsilon Phi Chpt; Sigma Delta Pi; Nat Spanish Soc; Houston Woman of Courage, Houston Woman of Courage Project and the Radcliffe Club 1985; TX Black Women's Hall of Fame, Museum of African-American Life and Culture Dallas 1986.

STUART, REGINALD A.
Newspaper talent recruiter; free lance writer. **Personal:** Born Nov 26, 1948, Nashville, TN; son of Maxie Allen Stuart and William Stuart; married Daryl Thomas. **Educ:** TN State U, BS 1968; Columbia U, MJour 1971. **Career:** Nashville Tennessean, reporter, 1968-69; WSIX-AM-FM-TV, 1969-70; Jay Hay Whitney Foundation, New York, NY, consultant, 1972-74; New York Times, business/finance news reporter, 1974-76, national correspondent, 1976-87; Philadelphia Daily News, 1987-90; Knight-Ridder Newspapers, Washington Bureau, asst editor, 1990-97. **Orgs:** Mem NAACP; CME; member, NABJ; member, Society of Professional Journalists. **Honors/Awds:** Carter G Woodson Nat Educ Assn Award 1969; Nat Headliners Award Best Team News Rpting 1970; Service Award NAACP 1974; Wells Key, 1992. **Home Addr:** 13102 Tamarack Rd, Silver Spring, MD 20904.

STUBBLEFIELD, DANA WILLIAM
Professional football player. **Personal:** Born Nov 14, 1970, Cleves, OH; children: Kayla. **Educ:** University of Kansas, attended. **Career:** San Francisco 49ers, defensive tackle, 1993-97; Washington Redskins, 1998-. **Honors/Awds:** NFL Defensive Rookie of the Year, 1993; Pro Bowl appearances, 1994, 1995. **Business Addr:** Professional Football Player, Washington Redskins, 13832 Redskin Dr, Herndon, VA 22071, (703)471-9100.

STUBBLEFIELD, JENNYE WASHINGTON
Educator, government official (retired). **Personal:** Born Mar 6, 1925, Jacksonville, FL; daughter of Ira Johnson Washington and Marion Washington; married Charles Stubblefield, Jun 26, 1954. **Educ:** Tuskegee Inst, BS 1946; Rutgers State Univ, MS 1966. **Career:** Wm Jason H Sch, cafe mgr & voc foods tchr 1950-56; Helene Fuld Hosp Sch, 1964-70; St Francis Hosp Sch, nutritionist 1957-64; Middlesex County NJ Head Start Prog, dir food service 1966-67; Home Economics Hamilton Twp NJ, tchr 1967-71; Dept Health Recreation & Welfare Trenton, dir 1971-74; Aid to Low Income Alcoholics Trenton, dir 1974-76; Trenton Public Schools Bd of Educ, supervisor home economics & family life educ progs 1976-92; City of Trenton, councilwoman 1976-90. **Orgs:** Mem Amer Dietetic Assoc 1964-; mem Amer Home Economic Assoc 1967-89; chmn County Democratic Comm Mercer County NJ 1984-85. **Honors/Awds:** Plaques comm serv Carver Youth & Family Cntr 1983, Bilalian African Amer Conf 1983, Fairless Steel Black Caucus 1984, Mercer Co NW Ward Dem Club 1984; LIFT, Community Social Program, Trenton Administrators & Supervisors Association, Public Schools, 1990. **Home Addr:** 21 Alden Ave, Trenton, NJ 08618.

STUBBLEFIELD, RAYMOND M.
Association executive. **Personal:** Born Aug 3, 1945, Abilene, TX; married Pat. **Educ:** NM Highland Coll, Taft Coll, San Diego State, BS & BA 1969. **Career:** United Food & Commercial Workers Union, asst dir; Comm Rel Dept Retail Clks Intl Assn, co-dir; Big Brothers, works correction officers. **Honors/Awds:** Comm serv awd, San Diego Youth Leg 1970. **Business Addr:** Assistant to Dir, UFCW, 4552 Valley View Lane, Irving, TX 75038.

STUBBS, DANIEL, II
Professional football player. **Personal:** Born Jan 3, 1965, Red Bank, NJ; children: Elexa Briana, Sydnee Daniella. **Educ:** Univ of Miami (FL), BS in criminal justice, 1988. **Career:** San Francisco 49ers, defensive end, 1988-89; Dallas Cowboys, 1990-91; Cincinnati Bengals, 1991-93; Philadelphia Eagles, 1995; Miami Dolphins, 1996-; Natural Health Trends Corp, business development representative, currently. **Honors/Awds:** Defensive lineman, Sporting News College All-America Team, 1987; post-season play, 1988: NFC Championship Game, NFL Championship Game; works with Camp Sunburst (a foundation for children with AIDS) in the off-season. **Business Addr:** Professional Football Player, Miami Dolphins, 2269 NW 199th St, Miami, FL 33056, (305)620-5000.

STUBBS, GEORGE WINSTON
Physician. **Personal:** Born Sep 13, 1942, Brooklyn, NY; son of Beryl Hinds Stubbs and Cornelius A Stubbs; married Joyce Kennedy; children: George W II, C David L. **Educ:** Hunter Coll, AB 1964; Howard Univ, MD 1968. **Career:** Wills Eye Hospital, asst srgn 1977, assoc surgn, 1993; Med Clg of PA, asst prof of srgry 1979; G Winston Stubbs MD Ltd, pres 1982; Germantown Hosp, attndng opthlmgst; Chestnut Hill Hosp Attndn, Opthalmologist Graduate Hosp Country Staff. **Orgs:** Internatl Coll of Surgeon, flw 1979; Philadelphia Coll of Physicians, flw 1980; Amer Coll of Surgeon, flw 1981; American Academy of Ophthalmology 1977; Medical Society of Pa, pres elect, 1993, pres, 1995. **Honors/Awds:** Physician Recognition Award 1981, 1983, 1987. **Military Serv:** USPHS lt cmdr. **Business Addr:** Ophthalmologist, 2305 N Broad St, Philadelphia, PA 19132.

STUBBS, HAROLD K. See Obituaries section.

STUBBS, LEVI
Singer. **Personal:** married Clineice; children: 5. **Career:** Member of singing group The Four Tops; voice of Audrey II in Little Shop of Horrors.

STULL, DONALD L.
Business executive, architect. **Personal:** Born May 16, 1937, Springfield, OH; son of Ruth Callahan Branson and Robert Stull; married Patricia Ryder Stull (divorced); children: Cydney Lynn, Robert Branson, Gia Virginia. **Educ:** OH State Univ, BArch 1961; Harvard Grad Sch of Design, MArch 1962. **Career:** George Mason Clark, architect designer 1958-62; Boston Federal Office Bldg Architects, designer 1961-62; Samuel Glaser & Partners, proj dir 1962-66; Stull Assoc Inc Architects, pres 1966-83; Stull & Lee Inc Architects & Planners, pres 1984-; Registered Architect in numerous states. **Orgs:** Harvard Grad school of Design, visiting comm, 1988-94; Suffolk School of Business Management, advisory comm, 1989-; Rice Univ School of Architecture, visiting design studio professor, 1993; Ohio State Univ, School of Architecture, advisory comm, 1980-; Boston Architectural Ctr, mem, 1972-; Museum of the Natl Ctr of Afro-American History, advisory bd mem, 1982-; Museum of Afro-Amer History, Boston, advisory bd mem, 1979-; Historic Boston, mem, 1990-; Boston Foundation for Architecture, trustee, 1992-; The Institute of Contemporary Art, bd of overseers, 1996, 1997; Boston Civic Design Comm, 1987-; GSA's Public Bldg Service Natl Register of Peer Professionals, 1994-96; Resource Panel, Natl Endowment for the Arts, 1978-; City of Cambridge, Design Advisory Group, 1980-90, 1994-. **Honors/Awds:** Ten Outstanding Young Men Boston 1970; Outstanding Young Men Amer 1970; Design Awd Jury Progressive Architr 1972; Design Awd Amer Inst Arch; Design Awd HUD Housing 1972; 100 Top Black Businesses 1973; Presidential Design Award National Endowment for the Arts 1988; College of Fellows Amr Inst of Architects; Boston Society of Architects, Award of honor, 1997. **Business Addr:** President, Stull and Lee Inc, 38 Chauncy St, Suite ll00, Boston, MA 02111, (617)426-0406.

STULL, ROBERT J.
Educator, artist. **Personal:** Born Nov 4, 1935, Springfield, OH; married Bettye Joan. **Educ:** OH State, BS 1962, MA 1963; Japanese Language Sch, NY U, 1964-65; Kyoto City Coll, Japan. **Career:** Black Studies, adj prof; OH State Univ, pres black faculty & staff caucus; Univ MI, assoc prof 1971, asst prof 1968; Kyoto City Coll of Fine Arts, lecturer 1966-67; Greenwich House Pottery, NYC, mgr 1963-65, 1967-68. **Orgs:** Chmn Ceramic Dept Univ MI 1969-70; chmn Grad Program Black Studies, OH State Univ 1972-73; co-founder Gallery 7, Detroit 1968-; dir founder Gallery 7, Columbus; vice pres DARC Asso Consultants of Pub & Pvt Bus 1972-; C State dr Nat of OH Conf Artists 1973; bd dir Paul Lawrence Dunbar Cultural Center, Columbus; Eastside YMCA; consultant Univ MI Office of Minority Affairs. **Honors/Awds:** Exhibitions; pub books. **Military Serv:** USAF sgt. **Business Addr:** Dept of Art OH State Univ, Columbus, OH.

STULL, VIRGINIA ELIZABETH
Physician. **Personal:** Born May 7, 1939, Springfield, OH. **Educ:** TX So U, BS 1960; Am U, 1960-61; Univ TX Med Br, MD 1966; Capital U, 1970-72. **Career:** Physician pvt Prac 1967-; Bur Voc Rehab, field med consult 1968-75; Columbus Bd Edn, sch phy 1968-73; ER phy 1967-71; Med Diagnostic Serv Inc, pres, owner 1975-; Dept Physical Med & Rehab, OH State Univ Med Sch, clinical prof; St Anthony Hosp. **Orgs:** Mem Am Med Women's Assn; AMA; Acad Med Columbus & Franklin Co; Alpha Kappa Alpha Sor; Sigma Xi Am Sci Soc. **Honors/Awds:** Lambda Chi Outsdng Black Woman OH 1975; Flowers for Living Award 1975; Columbus Chpt, Natl Epicureans Inc. **Business Addr:** 4656 Heaton Rd, Columbus, OH 43229.

STURDIVANT, JOHN NATHAN. See Obituaries section.

STYLES, FREDDIE L.
Artist. **Personal:** Born May 12, 1944, Madison, GA. **Educ:** Morris-Brown Coll, 1962-65; Atlanta School Art. **Career:** Artist freelance; Natl Urban League, org art Exhibition 1975; Black Artist, Carnegie Inst, lecturer 1969; Morris Brown Coll Drama Guild, costume set designer 1963-65; Expansion Arts Project Black Artists, co-dir. **Orgs:** Mem LA Watercolor Soc 1973-74; Cooperstown Art Assn 1974-75; High Mus of Art; Black Artists; Clarence White Contemporary Art Gallery. **Honors/Awds:** Exhibitions, USA Artist I & II High Museum; Atlanta Univ Ann Exhibition; Johnsons Publishing Co; CTI Printing Co.

STYLES, KATHLEEN ANN
Educational administrator. **Personal:** Born Aug 6, 1949, Baltimore, MD; daughter of Minnie V Brown Styles and Calvin P Styles. **Educ:** Coppin State Coll, BS Elem Ed 1967-71, MS Special Ed/ED 1971-72; Univ of MD 1979-83. **Career:** Community Coll of Baltimore, employment counselor 1974-76, coll counselor 1976-76, Act dir student act 1979-80, prof devel specialist 1981-, acting dir of off campus and ext centers 1986-. **Orgs:** Housing advisor US Dept Housing & Urban Devel 1972-73; instructor CETA Program 1971-72; founder Learning Intellectual Skills for Advancement 1988-94, dir of student affairs, harbor campus, 1994-; mem Natl Task Force of Career Educ 1978-80; mem of bd SSD Inc 1982-84. **Honors/Awds:** Resolution Maryland Legislative Black Caucus 1984; sponsored workshop ''Trading Places'' 1984; resolution Maryland State Legislature 1978. **Home Addr:** 5709 Gwynn Oak Ave, Baltimore, MD 21207. **Business Addr:** Assistant Dean, Community College of Baltimore, 2901 Liberty Heights Ave, Baltimore, MD 21215.

STYLES, LORENZO
Professional football player. **Personal:** Born Jan 31, 1974, Columbus, OH. **Educ:** Ohio State, attended. **Career:** Atlanta Falcons, linebacker, 1995-96; St Louis Rams, 1997-. **Business Addr:** Professional Football Player, St Louis Rams, One Rams Way, St Louis, MO 63045, (314)982-7267.

STYLES, RICHARD WAYNE
Clergyman. **Personal:** Born Jun 22, 1939, Waterbury, CT; son of Helene Marie Copeland Styles and James Lawrence Styles, Sr; married Helen Penelope Horton; children: Richard Wayne Jr, Helene Rishae. **Educ:** Shaw Univ, AB 1965; Southeastern Baptist Theological Sem, M Div 1969; Yale Divinity School. **Career:** Burlington Housing Authority, bd of dirs 1977-; Burlington Christ Acad, bd of dir 1980-83; Access, bd of dir 1980-84; Allied Church of Alamance Cnty, vice chmn bd of dir 1983-; bd of dir Hospice of Alamanee County; bd of dir Fair Housing Committee; dean United Bible Inst; mem Ministerial Fellowship Alliance of Alamanee Cnty; First Baptist Church, pastor, currently; Shaw University Cape Fezr Center, professor of Bible, currently. **Orgs:** Exec dir Alamance Cnty Headstart 1984-; exec comm N State Legal Aid 1980-; vlntr cnslr Alamance Cnty Court Sys 1979-83; dean of inst United Bible Inst 1980-; recruiter Crop Walk 1977-; chmn of religious activities Broadview Mid Schl 1984-; bd of dir Homecare Providers; bd of dir Care Ministry; board of directors: United Way, Family Abuse Services, Christian Counseling Services, board of directors, Alamance Coalition Against Drug Abuse. **Honors/Awds:** Continuing Ed Grant Yale Div Sch 1972; Good Shepherd Awd Boy Scouts of Amer 1979; volunteer counselor Awd Gov James Hunt of NC 1983; Honorary Doctorate, United Bible Inst. **Home Addr:** 612 Crestview Dr, Burlington, NC 27215. **Business Addr:** Pastor, First Baptist Church, 508 Apple St, Burlington, NC 27215.

SUBER, TORA
Professional basketball player. **Personal:** Born Nov 23, 1974. **Educ:** Virginia, attended. **Career:** Charlotte Sting, guard, 1997-. **Business Addr:** Professional Basketball Player, Charlotte Sting, 2709 Water Ridge Pkwy, Ste 400, Charlotte, NC 28217, (704)424-9622.

SUBRYAN, CARMEN
Educator. **Personal:** Born Dec 30, 1944, Linden, Guyana; daughter of Sybil Allicock Barclay and Lawrence Barclay; divorced; children: Nicole, Natasha. **Educ:** Howard University, Washingtn DC, BA, 1971, MA, 1973, PhD, 1983. **Career:** University of the District of Columbia, Washington DC, academic support, 1973-74; Howard University, Washington DC, instructor, program coordinator, 1974-. **Orgs:** National Council of Teachers of English, 1980-84, College Language Association, 1981-86, National Association of Developmental Education, 1985-87, GUYAID, 1985-. **Honors/Awds:** Phi Beta Kappa, Howard University, 1971; Magna Cum Laude, Howard University, 1971; Reprise, a book of poetry, 1984; ''Walter Dean Myers,'' Article in Dictionary of Literary Biography, 1984; ''A B Spellman,'' article in Dictionary of Literary Biography, 1985; Woman's Survival, booklet, 1989; Black-Water Women, a novel, 1997. **Home Addr:** 11400 Pitsea Dr, Beltsville, MD 20705. **Business Phone:** (202)636-7634.

SUDARKASA, MICHAEL ERIC MABOGUNJE
Attorney, consultant. **Personal:** Born Aug 5, 1964, New York, NY; son of Niara Sudarkasa and Akin Mabogunje; married Joyce Ann Johnson, Nov 22, 1990; children: Jasmine Ayana Yetunde, Jonathan Michael Toure, Maya Elizabeth Sade. **Educ:** The University of Michigan, BA (high honors), history, 1985; Howard University, visiting student, 1983; Harvard Law School, JD, 1988; University of San Diego, Institute on International and Comparative Law, Paris, France, 1990. **Career:** African Development Bank, technical assistant, private sector development unit, 1988-89; Citibank-Abidjan, banking intern, 1988-89; 21st Century Africa Inc, founder, consultant, 1989-; Steel, Hector & Davis PC, associate, attorney, 1990; 21st Century Africa Inc, president, 1990-97; Trade & Investment Promotion Svcs, dir, 1997-; Georgetown Univ, Graduate School of Business, adjunct lecturer. **Orgs:** Overseas Development Coun-

cil, Africa Roundtable; American Bar Association, chair, Africa Law Committee; Calvert New World Fund, bd mem. **Honors/Awds:** Career Communications, Urban Profile Magazine, "30 under Thirty" Entrepreneur Award, 1992; Harvard Black Law Students Association, Distinguished Young Alumni Award, first recipient, 1992. **Special Achievements:** Author, publisher, The African Business Handbook, A Comprehensive Guide to Business Resources for US/Africa Trade and Investment, 1991-97; "Toward a Global African Economic Community: A Billion People and a Trillion Dollar Market," working papers for issues forum at Congressional Black Caucus, 1991; board member, Africa News Service; board member, Society for International Development. **Business Addr:** Director, Trade & Investment Promotion Svcs, Labat-Anderson Inc, 8000 Westpark Dr, Ste 400, Mc Lean, VA 22102, (703)506-9600.

SUDARKASA, NIARA (GLORIA A. MARSHALL)
Educational administrator. **Personal:** Born Aug 14, 1938, Ft Lauderdale, FL; married John L Clark; children: Michael Eric. **Educ:** Fisk Univ, 1953-56; Oberlin Coll, AB 1957; Columbia Univ, MA 1959; Columbia Univ, PhD Anthropology 1964. **Career:** Comm for the Comparative Study of New Nations The Univ of Chicago, fellow 1963-64; NY Univ, asst prof 1964-67; Univ of MI, asst to full prof 1967-; Center for Afro-Amer & African Studies The Univ of MI, dir 1981-84; Univ of MI, assoc vice pres academic affairs, prof anthropology; Lincoln Univ, president 1987-. **Orgs:** Mem African Studies Assn 1959-69, 1982-; fellow Amer Anthrop Assn 1964-; Fellow Amer Anthrop Assn Exec Bd 1972-75; chmn State of MI Comm on Minorities Women & Handicappers in Higher Ed 1984-; mem bd of dir Ann Arbor Comm Ctr 1983-; mem Assn of Black Anthropologists; mem American Assoc for HigherEduc 1986. **Honors/Awds:** Ford Found Scholarship for Early Admiss to Coll 1953-57; Ford Found Foreign Area Training Fellowship 1960-63; John Hay Whitney Oppty Fellowship 1959-60; Carnegie Found Study of New Nation Fellowship 1963-64; Social Science Rsch Council Fellowship 1973-74; Sr Fulbright Rsch Scholarship 1982-83; Achievement Awds from Links, Alpha Kappa Alpha, Zeta Phi Beta, Elks, City of Ft Lauderdale; publications on African Women, West African Migration, Afro-Amer and African Family and Minorities Organization in higher education. **Business Addr:** University President, Lincoln University, Lincoln University, PA 19352.

SUDBURY, LESLIE G.
Chemist. **Personal:** Born May 11, 1939, Meridan, MS; son of Mamie Sudbury and James Sudbury; married Audrey Faulkens; children: Leslie D, Pamela M, David G, Gloria M. **Educ:** Xavier U, BSc Chemistry 1961; Notre Dame Grad School, Chemistry. **Career:** Whitehall Labs, pharm control chemist 1961-65; Miles Labs Inc, rsch chemist 1966-73, supervisor control chemist 1973-78, mgr div control 1978-82, mgr biological evaluation 1982-85; ICN Immuno, Operation Manager 1985-89, dir of laboratory operations, 1989-. **Orgs:** Mem Amer Chem Soc 1966-; sec & editor newsletter Amer Chem Soc St Joseph Valley Sec 1979-83; mem Amer Soc of Quality Control 1982-86; coach IYHL Soccer 1980-82; co-chmn BAC Inter Community Commn 1980-82; bd dirs NOBC & treas 1977-85; bd mem NBLCC 1976-85; mem Knights of Peter Claver 1984-85; Sec Council #251 KPC. **Honors/Awds:** Outstanding Service Amer Chem Soc St Joe Valley Sec 1981; Outstanding Service NBLCC Midwest Regional 1978; Service St Augustine Parish South Bend IN 1974, 1976. **Military Serv:** AUS spl 4th 1962-64.

SUDDERTH, WILLIAM H.
Business executive. **Personal:** Born Nov 29, 1924, Jersey City, NJ; son of Frankie Little Sudderth and William H Sudderth Sr; married Estelle McGaney; children: William III, Philip, June, Theresa. **Educ:** Pace Univ, attended 1952-55; Monroe Flegenheimer Sch of Ins, attended 1957; Dale Carnegie Inst, attended. **Career:** General Insurance, agent, broker, currently. **Orgs:** Past pres Exchange Club of White Plains 1976-77; past pres NY State Dist Exchange Clubs 1983-84; Prince Hall Grand Lodge; Shriner; Mason; Eastern Star; fire commr Fairview Fire Dist; Greenburgh Housing Auth; NAACP; NYS Fire Chiefs Assn; Natl Assn of Housing & Redevel Officials; Ins Brokers Council of NYC; Pete Mete Chap 98 Disable Amer Vets Assn; received the 33 deg in Masonery Scottish Rite. **Honors/Awds:** Asst & Dirs Awd Dale Carnegie Courses; Bugler Awd White Plains; NY State Senate Achievement Awd 1984; Westchester Co Exec Cert of Appreciation 1984; USA Awd in recognition of exemplary comm serv in the finest Amer tradition signed by Pres Ronald Reagan, 1984. **Military Serv:** US Army SF Band & Engrs, T5, 1943-45. **Home Addr:** 32 Longdale Ave, White Plains, NY 10607.

SUGGS, ROBERT CHINELO
Educator. **Personal:** Born Dec 23, 1943, Newport, RI; son of Beatrice and Lewis; married Mary Louise Morrison; children: Lawrence, Sarah, Elizabeth, James. **Educ:** Barrington Coll, BA 1967; State Univ of NY at Albany, MS 1971, EdD 1979. **Career:** Dept of Counselor Ed State Univ, asst prof 1972-80; Comm Bible Church, pastor 1974-80; Dept of Counselor Ed Millersville Univ, adjunct asst prof 1982-85; Psychophysiological Clinic Univ of MD, clinical asst prof 1983-85; Crossroads Counseling Assocs, therapist 1983-; Christian Assoc of Psych Studies, newsletter editor 1983-; Messiah Coll, assoc prof of psychology, professor of psychology, director of personnel, 1986-; Cornerstone College, vp for academic affairs. **Honors/Awds:** Doctoral fellow State Univ of NY at Albany 1971-73; outstanding teacher Messiah Coll 1981; Named to Top 500 High School Basketball Players in the US Dell Mag 1963. **Business Addr:** Vice President for Academic Affairs, Cornerstone College, Grand Rapids, MI 49505.

SUGGS, WILLIAM ALBERT
Educator, pastor. **Personal:** Born Jun 1, 1922, Capleville, TN; married Carnelia Tate. **Educ:** Tskg Inst, 1943; TN St U, 1949, MS 1955. **Career:** Rchlnd Vocational School, teacher supr 1949-53; Hamilton HS, teacher dept chmn 1955-; Friendship Bapt Church, pastor. **Orgs:** Mem Memphis W TN TN Nat Educ Assns; Nat & Cncl Soc Stds; pres Memphis & Shlby Co Almn Assn 1970; pres Suggs Entrprss; mem Hmltn PTA. **Honors/Awds:** Cert of Merit Hmltn HS 1974; num publs in field. **Military Serv:** QMC sgt 1943-45. **Business Addr:** Friendship Baptist Church, 1355 Vollintine Ave, Memphis, TN.

SULIEMAN, JAMIL
Consultant. **Career:** Dallas Mavericks, team medical consultant, currently. **Business Addr:** Team Medical Consultant, Dallas Mavericks, 777 Sports St, Reunion Arena, Dallas, TX 75207-4499.

SULLIVAN, ALLEN R.
Educational administrator. **Personal:** Born Jul 15, 1941, Cambridge, MA; son of Dorothy Sullivan and Fernando Sullivan; married Deborah M Haywood; children: Raylene, Reginald. **Educ:** NE Univ, BS 1965; Syracuse Univ, MS 1966, Ph D 1970. **Career:** New England Home for Little Wanders, assn spvr res 1962-65; Syracuse Public Schl, spcl ed tchr 1966-68; Univ of MN, dir training of tchrs 1971-75; Univ of MN, assoc prof psych ed studies 1970-75; Dallas Independent School District, asst supt instructional support services, executive director student development. **Orgs:** Advsry bd Ft Worth State Schl 1978-; bd dir CT Gen of N Amer Cigna 1984-; min advsry comm Cncl for Excptnl Chldrn 1984-; bd chmn Jr Black Acad Of Arts & Letters 1984-; bd Friends of the Art Dist 1984-86; bd of dirs Dallas County Mental Health & Mental Retardation; Omega Psi Phi Fraternity; board of directors, Dallas Challenge; board of directors, Dallas Youth Services Corps; bd of dirs, Our Brothers Keeper. **Honors/Awds:** Northeastern University, Outstanding Alumni, 1982; State Fair of Texas, 2nd Place, color photography; Psi Chi, Psychology Honorary. **Business Addr:** Executive Director Student Development, Dallas Independent Sch Dist, 3700 Ross Ave, Dallas, TX 75204.

SULLIVAN, BRENDA ANN
Public policy analyst. **Personal:** Born 1955, New York, NY. **Educ:** University of Maryland Eastern Shore, Princess Anne, MD, BA, 1977; Atlanta University, Atlanta, GA, MA, 1979, PhD, 1988. **Career:** Atlanta University Center, adjunct faculty, 1984; Emory University Cognition Lab, research specialist, 1984-87; Research Atlanta, senior research associate, 1987-90; Spelman College, adjunct faculty, 1989; Urban Study Institute, research associate, beginning 1990; Kennesan State College, Political Science Department, currently. **Orgs:** Dancers' Collective Inc, former bd mbr; Georgia Forum, bd mbr, 1990-; committee, United Way Area of Need, 1990-; county advisory committee, United Way, 1991; Metro Atlanta Cncl on Alcohol and Drugs, bd mbr.

SULLIVAN, EDWARD JAMES
Dentist. **Personal:** Born May 7, 1932, Cleveland, OH; son of Ann Lee Ervin; married Janet Grant; children: Kathi Ann, Steven, Alicia. **Educ:** Ohio State Univ, BS 1956, DDS 1969. **Career:** Univ Hospitals Ohio State, pharmacist 1957-64; Columbus Health Dept, dentist 1969-73; dentist, private practice, 1969-; Columbus State Inst, dentist 1973-79; Dept of Pedodontics OH State Univ, clinical instructor 1981-; State of Ohio, Columbus, OH, dental consultant. **Orgs:** Bd mem, South State Health Ctr 1975-77; mem bd of dirs, Hilltop Health Ctr 1977; delegate, Natl Assn of Neighborhood Health Ctrs 1977-80; mem bd, Columbus Area Comm Health Ctr 1978-81; vice president, Buckeye State Dental Assn; president, Columbus Assn of Physicians and Dentists; Columbus Dental Assn, pres, 1994-96. **Honors/Awds:** Certificate of Appreciation Hilltop Health Ctr 1977; Mayor's Voluntary Serv Awd City of Columbus 1980. **Business Addr:** 1800 S Parsons Ave, Columbus, OH 43207.

SULLIVAN, EMMET G.
Judge. **Career:** Attorney; DC Superior Court; DC Court of Appeals, federal judge, currently. **Business Addr:** Federal Judge, DC Court of Appeals, 500 Indiana Ave NW, Washington, DC 20001, (202)273-0555.

SULLIVAN, ERNEST LEE
Banker. **Personal:** Born Dec 17, 1952, Columbus, OH; son of Emma Jane Sullivan and Robert Lee Sullivan. **Educ:** Capital University, BA, 1981. **Career:** Bank One Columbus, professional recruiter, 1976-80, employment manager, 1980-82; Rockwell International, employment manager, 1982-84, manager, staffing, employee relations, 1984-88; Bank One Ohio Columbus, NA, vice pres, executive selection, 1988-; national staffing manager, 1996. **Orgs:** Employment Managers Association, 1988-; Columbus Urban League, personnel advisor, 1991-; Central State University, advisory board, 1988-; Westerville Chamber of Commerce, board member, 1992-; Columbus Board of Education, advisory board, 1991-; Jobs for Columbus Program, pres, 1992-. **Honors/Awds:** Dollars & Sense Magazine, America's Best and Brightest, 1992; Columbus Metropolitan Housing, Hall of Fame, 1991; Pinnacle Award, 1993. **Business Addr:** VP, Executive Selection, Bank One Columbus, NA, 800 Brooksedge Blvd, Columbus, OH 43271, (614)248-8816.

SULLIVAN, J. CHRISTOPHER
Actor, performer. **Personal:** Born Sep 15, 1932, Greenville, TX; son of Veola Sullivan and Jack Sullivan; married Eloise Hicks (divorced); children: Jerome. **Educ:** Prairie View A&M Univ, BA 1953; Univ of TX, MA 1958, PhD 1964. **Career:** Abilene City Schools, teacher 1955-58; Dallas Ind Schools, teacher 1961-62; Prairie View A&M Univ, dir student acts 1962-63; Univ of TX, teacher 1963-64; Screen Actors Guild, professional actor, currently. **Orgs:** Screen Actors Guild 1968-, Amer Federation of TV & Radio Artists 1970-, Acad of TV Arts & Scis 1975-; exec bd 1980-87, interpreter French 1984, Los Angeles Olympics Org Cmte; vice pres Beverly Hills/Hollywood NAACP 1984-87. **Honors/Awds:** Distinguished Alumni Prairie View A&M Phi Beta Sigma Inc 1980; Phi Beta Kappa; Merit of Achievement Drama Univ of TX 1984; Image Awd/Best Actor NAACP Beverly Hills 1986. **Military Serv:** Infantry capt 1953-57.

SULLIVAN, JACK, JR.
Clergyman. **Personal:** Born Jun 1, 1959, Cleveland, OH; son of Gloria Mae Connor McCoy and Jack Sullivan Sr; married Gloria Jean Reeves Sullivan, Jul 28, 1984. **Educ:** Ohio University, BS, communications, 1983; Lexington Theological Seminary, MDiv, 1986; United Theological Seminary, doctoral candidate, currently. **Career:** Mid-America Region, Christian Church, Disciples of Christ, associate regional minister, 1986-89; Second Christian Church, pastor, 1986-89; Homeland Ministries of the Christian Church, Disciples of Christ, US and Canada, associate, racial/ethnic and multicultural ministries, 1989-. **Orgs:** Alpha Phi Alpha Fraternity Inc, 1984-; elder, youth director, Faith United Christian Church, 1990-; NAACP, 1978-; big brother, Big Brothers of Indianapolis, 1990-; Association of Christian Church Educators, 1988-; Urban League of Greater Indianapolis; American Heart Assn, volunteer; Boy Scouts of America. **Honors/Awds:** George V Moore Award, Outstanding Field Ministry, Lexington Theological Seminary, 1986.

SULLIVAN, LEON HOWARD
Clergyman, organization head. **Personal:** Born Oct 16, 1922, Charleston, WV; married Grace Banks; children: Howard, Julie, Hope. **Educ:** West Virginia State College, BA, 1943; Union Theological Seminary, 1945; Columbia Univ, MA, 1947; Virginia Union Univ, DD. **Career:** Zion Bapt Church Phila, pastor 1950-88; pastor emeritus, 1988-. **Orgs:** Founder/chmn Zion Home for Ret 1960-; founder, dir, bd chmn, Opp Indus Cntrs of Am Inc, 1964, Zion Investment Assoc Inc, Progress Aerospace Inc; GM Corp, bd of dirs, 1971-; Mellon Bank Corp, bd of dirs; cofounder of Self-Help. **Honors/Awds:** Russwurm Awd, Natl Publisher's Assn, 1963; Amer Exemplar Medal, 1969; Philadelphia Book Award, 1966; Philadelphia Fellowship Commn Awd, 1964; Leon Howard Sullivan Chair, School of Social Welfare, Univ of Wisconsin, 1976; Franklin D Roosevelt Four Freedom Medal Award, 1987; Leon Howard Sullivan Scholarship Fund established at Bentley Coll, Massachusetts, 1988; Hon LLD Dartmouth Coll, Princeton Univ, Swarthmore Coll; Bordoin Coll, Denison Univ, Gannon Coll, Temple Univ; Hon EdD, Judson Coll. **Business Addr:** Progress Plaza Shopping Center, 1501 N Broad St, Philadelphia, PA 19122.

SULLIVAN, LOUIS WADE
Educational administrator, physician. **Personal:** Born Nov 3, 1933, Atlanta, GA; son of Lubirda Elizabeth Priester Sullivan and Walter Wade Sullivan; married Eva Williamson; children: Paul, Shanta, Halsted. **Educ:** Morehouse Coll, BS (magna cum laude) 1954; Boston Univ, MD (cum laude) 1958. **Career:** Harvard Medical School, instructor, 1963-64; New Jersey College of Medicine, asst prof, 1964-66; Boston Univ, asst prof, 1966-68, associate prof, 1968-74; Boston City Hosp, Boston MA, dir hematology, 1973-75; Boston Univ, Boston MA, prof medicine and physiology, 1974-75; US Dept of Health and Human Services, Washington DC, secretary, 1989-93; Morehouse College, professor of biology and medicine, Medical Education Program, dean, director, 1975-, School of Medicine, dean, president, 1981-89, 1993-. **Orgs:** Ad hoc panel on blood diseases Natl Heart Lung Blood Disease Bur 1973; Sickle Cell Anemia adv com NIH 1974-75; Natl Adv Rsch Cncl 1977; Amer Soc of Hematology, Amer Soc Clin Investigation; Inst Medicine; Phi Beta Kappa; Alpha Omega Alpha; co-founder, National Assn of Minority Medical Educators; founding president, Association of Minority Health Professions; Medical Education for South African Blacks, chmn, 1997-. **Honors/Awds:** Trumpet Award, 1997. **Special Achievements:** Published over 70 articles in medical journals & magazines 1957-92; author, The Ed-

ucation of Black Health Professionals, 1977; first African American appointed to cabinet position in the Bush Administration, 1989; first dean, president, Morehouse College School of Medicine, 1981. **Business Addr:** President, Morehouse College, School of Medicine, 720 Westview Dr SW, Atlanta, GA 30310.

SULLIVAN, MARTHA ADAMS (MECCA)
Social worker, mental health administrator. **Personal:** Born Jun 13, 1952, Philadelphia, PA; daughter of Lillie B Foster Adams and Leon H Adams; married James Pearly Sullivan; children: Mecca Jamilah, Malik Khalil. **Educ:** NYU Washington Square College, BA 1974; Hunter Coll Sch of Social Work, MSW 1976; DSW, 1991. **Career:** Henry St Settlement Comm Consultation Ctr, supervising social worker/family therapist 1976-83; private practice, psychotherapist 1981-; Gouverneur Diagnostic & Treatment Ctr Dept of Psychiatry, assoc dir 1983-, asst dir, psychiatry, 1985, dir, Ctr for Older Adults & Their Families, 1983, consultant, inst for family & community care, currently; Minuchin Center for the Family, New York, NY, visiting faculty; Hunter College School of Social Work, adjunct faculty. **Orgs:** Founder and mem Source, The Black Women Therapists' Collective 1978-91; consultant Center for Women in Govt 1985-; mem Natl Assn of Social Workers 1985-; chairperson Citywide Geriatrics Comm 1988-; mem Natl Caucus and Center on the Black Aged; mem, Assn of Women in Psychology, 1990-; Ctr on Aging and the Family, Ackerman Inst on the Family, 1996-; chairperson, City Wide Geriatrics Comm, 1988-. **Honors/Awds:** Co-author "Women of Color & Feminist Practice," in Not For Women Only NASW Publ 1986; author, "The Homeless Older Women in Context: Alienation, Cutoff & Reconnection," Journal of Women & Aging, summer, 1991. **Special Achievements:** Author: "May the Circle Be Unbroken," in Across Cultural book at Death, Dying and Religion; author: "Look Back and Wonder: Developing Family - Oriented Mental Health Programs for the Elderly," newsletter of the American Family Therapy Assn, winter, 1997. **Business Addr:** Associate Director, Psychiatry, Director, Ctr for Older Adults & Their Families, Gouverneur Diagnostic & Treatment Ctr, 227 Madison, Ste 329, New York, NY 10002.

SULLIVAN, ZOLA JILES
Educator (retired). **Personal:** Born Nov 5, 1921, Tallahassee, FL; daughter of Susie Baker Jiles and Willis James Jiles; married William David Sullivan, Apr 1, 1956; children: Yolanda Sullivan Shelton, William D II, Shirley, Dexter Shelton. **Educ:** FL A M Univ Tllhs, BS MS 1950; Fisk Univ Nshvl; Univ of MI Ann Arbor; University of Miami, Miami, FL, post masters work, 1961; Oxfrd Univ Engl, 1965; Univ of IL Urbn Champ, PhD 1970. **Career:** Broward Co Public School Sys Ft Lauderdale, teacher 1942-43; Palm Beach Co Elementary School, teacher 1943-50; FL A&M Univ, instructor 1950-53; Dade Co Public Sys, prin elementary teacher 1953-71; FL Intl Univ Miami FL, asst prof educ 1971-74, assoc prof educ 1974-90; Florida Memorial College, adjunct professor, 1990-91; retired. **Orgs:** Chmn Num Chldhd Educ Com; consult Num Educ Assn; spkr lectr Num Elmntry Schs; coor Num Educ Wrkshps; mem Num Educ Assns; spkr Num Ch Grps; mem Rchmnd Hghts Women's Club FL; mem Alpha Phi Alpha Frat; Iota Pi Lambda Chap Miami; mem FL Intl Task Force on Needs Assessment to Improve Educational Opportunities in Guinea; advisory board, Black Heritage Museum of Dade Count, 1989-; member, Primary Readers and Evaluators in First Editions of Eric Early Childhood; founding member, Second Baptist Church, Miami, FL, 1963; founding professor, Florida International University, 1971. **Honors/Awds:** Recip num schol & career opport cert; pub num papers on edn; NDEA Fellwshp Univ of IL 1969-70; inttr various prog & Univ class; recip num plqs & cert for outstndng work; FL Governor's Awd for Outstanding Achievement 1986; Outstanding Serv to African Educators Political Leaders and Students, recognized by FL Chapter of the Natl Council of Intl Visitors; First Black Female to receive a PhD in Miami, Fl, Univ of IL, 1970; Consultant Ministry of Education, Nassau, BS, 1971.

SULTON, JACQUELINE RHODA
Physician, pediatrician. **Personal:** Born Mar 27, 1957, Detroit, MI; daughter of Dorothy G Johnson and Nathaniel O Holloway; married Francis Arnold Sulton; children: Carmen Denease, Jonathan Francis. **Educ:** Spelman Coll, BS 1978; Meharry Medical Coll, DM 1982. **Career:** Tulane Univ Sch of Medicine, internship/residency 1982-85; Robinson-Gouri Pediatric Group New Orleans, pediatrician 1984-85; Morehouse Sch of Medicine, student preceptor; Oakhurst Comm Health Ctr, staff pediatrician 1985-88; private practice Pediatric & Adolescent Medicine, Lithonia, GA. **Orgs:** Alpha Kappa Alpha Sor, Atlanta Medical Assoc Inc. **Honors/Awds:** Atlanta Univ Ctr Biology Honor Soc 1976; Outstanding Academic Performance in Biology 1977; life mem NAACP; Certificate of Merit Student Rsch 1980; American Academy of Pediatrics, Board Certified, 1989; American Academy of Pediatrics, Fellow, 1990. **Business Addr:** Private Physician, Pediatric and Adolescent Medicine, 5900 Hillandale Dr, Ste 355, Lithonia, GA 30058.

SULTON, JOHN DENNIS
Architect. **Personal:** Born Aug 18, 1912, St George, SC; son of Daisey Hume Sulton and John Jacob Sulton Jr; married Kathleen Hunter, Apr 24, 1943; children: Linda Nwosu. **Educ:** South Carolina State University, BS, mech arts, 1934; Kansas State University, BArch, 1941. **Career:** Office of Hilyard R Robinson, 1941, 1945-62; Office of Sulton Campbell & Associates, co-founder, 1964-82; Office of Sulton Campbell Britt Owens & Associates PC, chairman of the board, 1982-. **Orgs:** Fellow, American Institute of Architects; National Organization of Minority Architects; National Technical Association. **Honors/Awds:** District of Columbia, Meritorious Public Service Commendation, 1962; Prestressed Concrete Institute Award, 1973; National Technical Assn, Certificate of Achievement, 1979; National Organization of Minority Architects, Citation of Merit, 1984; Howard Univ, Commendation for Service to the Profession, 1984; KS State Univ, Recognition of Distinguished Service in Arch & Design, 1981. **Business Addr:** Chairman of the Board, Sulton Campbell Britt Owens & Associates, PC, 6031 Kansas Ave NW, Suite 2, Washington, DC 20011, (202)882-6360.

SUMLER-EDMOND, JANICE L.
Educator, attorney. **Personal:** Born Aug 10, 1948, New York, NY; daughter of Lucille Jones Sumler (deceased) and Ernest Sumler (deceased). **Educ:** UCLA, Los Angeles CA, BA, 1970, MA, 1971; Georgetown Univ, Washington DC, PhD, 1978; UCLA School of Law, Los Angeles CA, JD, 1985. **Career:** Spelman Coll, Atlanta GA, visiting prof, 1980-81; Reginald Heber Smith Fellowship, legal aid of Los Angeles, 1985-86; Clark Atlanta Univ, Atlanta GA, assoc prof, 1986-; Mack Haygood, McLean, Attorneys, Atlanta, GA, attorney, 1989-95. **Orgs:** Natl vice dir, Assn of Black Women Historians, 1986-88, natl dir, 1988-90; mem, Georgia Assn of Black Women Attorneys, 1987-; recruiter, Georgetown Univ, 1988-. **Honors/Awds:** Lubic Memorial Law Scholarship, 1983-84; Southern Fellowship Fund Summer Research Award, 1988; "The Forten-Purvis Women and the Antislavery Crusade," Journal of Negro History, 1981; "Personhood and Citizenship: Black Women Litigants, 1867-1890," University of Massachusetts Press, 1997; Judicine Fellow, US Supreme Court, Washington, DC, 1991-92; Panel of Neutrals, American Arbitration Association. **Home Addr:** 4192 Kings Troop Rd, Stone Mountain, GA 30083.

SUMMER, CREE
Actress. **Career:** Actress on NBC's A Different World, until 1993; appearances: Out All Night, 1994; Sweet Justice, 1995; Courthouse.

SUMMER, DONNA ANDREA (LADONNA ANDREA GAINES)
Musician, singer. **Personal:** Born Dec 31, 1948, Boston, MA; daughter of Mary Gaines and Andrew Gaines; married Helmut Sommer (divorced); children: Mimi; children: Brook Lyn, Amanda Grace. **Career:** Appeared in a German production of the rock musical "Hair", 1967; appeared in Vienna Volksoper productions of "Porgy and Bess," "Showboat," "Godspell," "The Me Nobody Knows"; solo recording artist, 1975-; albums include The Wanderer, Love to Love You Baby, On the Radio, She Works Hard for the Money, Another Place and Time. **Honors/Awds:** Top New Female Vocalist 1975; Best Rhythm and Blues Female Vocalist, National Academy of Recording Arts and Sciences 1978; Best Female Rock Vocalist 1979; Favorite Female Pop Vocalist, American Music Awards 1979; Favorite Female Vocalist of Soul Music 1979; Soul Artist of the Year, Rolling Stone Magazine 1979; Best Selling Album for Female Artist 1980; Ampex Golden Reel Award for single and album "On the Radio" 1980; Best Rock Performance, Best of Las Vegas Jimmy Award 1980; Grammy Award for Best Inspirational Performance 1984; Hollywood Walk of Fame, Star, 1992. **Business Addr:** Singer, c/o Geffen, Warner Brothers Distributors, 3300 Warner Blvd, Burbank, CA 91510.

SUMMEROUR-PERRY, LISA
Spokesmodel. **Personal:** Born Sep 5, 1962, Somers Point, NJ. **Educ:** Howard Univ, attended 1980-82. **Career:** Prudential Realty Group, legal sec 1983-84; Sughrue Mion Zinn Macpeak & Seas, legal sec 1984; Lenox China/Crystal, sec 1985; Sands Hotel Casino, exec secty 1985-86. **Orgs:** USO participation toured the Mediterranean on the 1st Annual Miss USA USO/DOD Tour 1986, USO Show Fort Eustis Hampton VA 1986, USO Show Celebrating the commissioning of the USS Roosevelt 1986, USO Show 1987 Natl Salute to Hospitalized Veterans 1987. **Honors/Awds:** Natl Quill & Scroll; Southern Univ Academic Achievement Awd. **Home Addr:** 101 Kensington Ave, Trenton, NJ 08618.

SUMMERS, DAVID STEWART
Physician, educator. **Personal:** Born Feb 16, 1932, Canton, OH; son of Stuard Jordan Summers (deceased) and William Edward Summers (deceased); married Ernestine Cumber, Nov 30, 1957; children: David S II, Timothy C. **Educ:** VA State Univ, BS 1954; VA Union Univ (Electives only) 1954-55; Univ of VA Sch of medicine, MD 1959. **Career:** SUNY Upstate Med Ctr at Syracuse, intern resident & instr 1959-63; Univ Rochester Sch Med & Strong Meml Hosp Dept of Neurology, instr asst prof dir EEG labs 1967-72; McGuire VA Hosp, neurologist 1967; Univ Utah Coll Med Dept of Neurology, asst prof & electroencephalographer 1972-76; DHEW, natl cncl serv & facilities devel disabled 1974-77; State of Utah, gov's black policy cncl 1975-77; Univ of Utah, affirm action comm 1975-77; Hill AFB Hosp & SLC VA Hosp, neurology consult 1972-76; St Vincent Health Ctr, neurologist & electroencephalographer; 1976-90; Headache Center, Neurology Institute of Western Pennsylvania, neurologist, 1991-93; Neurology Dir, Warren State Hosp, currently. Warren State Hosp, currently. **Orgs:** Mem Amer Acad of neurology 1962-; member, Erie County & Pennsylvania Medical Societies, 1976-90; neurology consul Metro Hlth Ctr 1978-94; lectr neurology Gannon Univ & Gannon-Hahnemann Med Prog 1977-89; lectr neurology St Vincent Health Ctr CME Prog 1976-89; mem E Assn of Electroencephalographers 1971-; mem Amer Epilepsy Soc 1971-; mem Epilepsy Found of Amer 1972-; mem Natl Med Assn 1977-; Gateway Med Society, 1994; life mem Erie NAACP, Univ VA Alumni Assn 1976-; cncl mem Immanuel Lutheran Ch 1980-86; member, National Multiple Sclerosis Society Northwest PA Branch, 1986-90; diplomat Amer Acad of Pain Mgt, 1991-. **Honors/Awds:** Publs of Neurology topics 1964-81; Abby Aldrich Rockefeller Scholar, John D Rockefeller, 3rd 1951-54. **Military Serv:** AUS Med Corps capt 3 yrs; Natl Def Serv Medal; Cert of Achievement-Germany 1967. **Home Addr:** 1520 Pasadena Dr, Erie, PA 16505. **Business Addr:** Neurologist, Warren State Hospital, 33 Main Dr, Warren, PA 16365.

SUMMERS, EDNA WHITE
Elected official (retired). **Personal:** Born Sep 4, 1919, Evanston, IL; married William J Summers; children: Michael, Stephen, Elizabeth, Jerome. **Educ:** Roosevelt Univ; Univ of Wisconsin. **Career:** City of Evanston, alderman 1968-81; State of Ill, social service 1974-85; City of Evanston, township supervisor 1985-92. **Orgs:** Real Estate Evanston, North Shore board; trustee Ebenezer Ame Church; life mem Illinois Parent-Teachers; life mem, NAACP, Evanston; Zonta International. **Honors/Awds:** Service Awd Evanston NAACP; Woman of the Year Delta Sigma Theta and Mens Social Club. **Special Achievements:** Lecturer, early childhood development. **Home Addr:** 1941 Hartrey Ave, Evanston, IL 60201.

SUMMERS, JOSEPH W.
State representative. **Personal:** Born Mar 8, 1930, Indianapolis, IN; son of Willie Mae Johnson and Joe; married Joyce Benson, 1948; children: 2. **Educ:** Indiana University; Indiana College of Mortuary Science, Indianapolis, IN, graduate. **Career:** Precinct committeeman in Indianapolis, 1952; Summers Funeral Chapel, Indianapolis, IN, owner and operator, 1962-; Indianapolis Board of Public Safety, Indianapolis, IN, member, 1965-68; Marion County Government, IN, chief deputy coroner, 1967-78; Indiana House of Representatives, state representative, 1976-. **Orgs:** National convention chmn, NAACP, 1973; Better Business Bureau; Funeral Directors Assn; member of board, Alpha Home; member of board, Sickle Cell Center; member of board, Indianapolis-Scarborough Peace Games; member, African Methodist Episcopal Church; member, Indiana Black Legislative Caucus. **Business Addr:** 1146 Brook Ln, Indianapolis, IN 46202.

SUMMERS, RETHA
Consultant. **Personal:** Born May 4, 1953, Goldsboro, NC; daughter of Aletha Summers and Harvey Summers (deceased). **Educ:** NC A&T State Univ, BS Bus Admin 1971-75; Campbell Univ, currently pursuing MEd Counseling & Guidance. **Career:** Employment Security Commission, employment interviewer 1976-77; Carolina Telephone, telephone co rep 1977-, engineering clerk, currently. **Orgs:** Past pres Amer Bus Women's Assoc 1984; mem Amer Assoc of Counseling & Development 1987; dir Future Christian Leaders of Amer 1987-. **Honors/Awds:** Most Outstanding bus Student Awd North Lenoir High/Future Bus Leaders of Amer 1971; Banner Awd and Woman of the Year Awd Amer Bus Women's Assoc/Ram Neuse Chap Kingston NC 1984. **Home Addr:** PO Box 366, La Grange, NC 28551.

SUMMERS, RODGER
Educational administrator. **Personal:** Born Jan 10, 1945, Philadelphia, PA; son of Viola Kemerlin Summers and Bennie Summers; married Dr Pamela F; children: Megan KF, Jordon F. **Educ:** Cheyney Univ, BS Ed, English 1968; Univ of VT, MA English 1972; IN Univ, EdD Higher Ed 1980. **Career:** Univ of VT, asst dean of students 1974-79, assoc dean of students 1979-81; North Adams State Coll, vice pres student affairs 1981-84; West Chester Univ, vice pres student affairs 1984-. **Orgs:** Mem Salvation Army Bd 1981; NASPA bd of dir, mem at large Natl Assoc of Student Personnel Admin 1983; bd mem YMCA 1985. **Honors/Awds:** Co-author "Commuter Marriages" VT Journal 1981. **Business Addr:** Vice President Student Affairs, West Chester University, Sykes Union Bldg, West Chester, PA 19383.

SUMMERS, WILLIAM E., III
Broadcast executive, clergyman. **Personal:** Born Oct 17, 1918; children: William IV, Seretha, Sherryl. **Educ:** KY St Coll; Coll of Scrip; Univ of Rome. **Career:** Summrs Brdcstng Inc, pres part owner; Radio Sta WLOU, gen mgr, sprts annouc 1951, num other pos 1972; St Pauls AME Ch Louis, pastor. **Orgs:** Mem bd KY Brdcstrs Assn; bd of dir Met YMCA; mem Ovrsrs Univ of Louis.

SUMMERS, WILLIAM E., IV
City official. **Personal:** Born Mar 11, 1943, Louisville, KY; son of Sallie Sellers Summers and William E Summers III; married Paulette Sweatt Summers, Jun 30, 1966; children: Kimberly, William, Anthony. **Educ:** Central State Univ, Wilberforce OH, 1961-62; Univ of Maryland, Far East Extension, 1964-65; Univ of Louisville, Louisville KY, 1970-71; Kentucky State Univ, Frankfort KY, 1974-76. **Career:** City of Louisville, Louisville KY, admin asst to Mayor, 1968-74; State of Kentucky, Frankfort KY, civil rights compliance officer, 1974-76; City of Louisville, Louisville KY, Dept of Sanitation, dir, 1976-79; Mr Klean's Janitor & Maintenance Serv, Louisville KY, vice pres, 1979-82; Property Maintenance & Mgmt Inc, Louisville KY, pres, 1982-86; City of Louisville, Louisville KY, Internal Operations, chief of staff, 1986-, deputy mayor of operations, currently. **Orgs:** Bd of dirs, NAACP, Louisville Urban League, Big Brothers/Big Sisters, Kentuckiana Girl Scout Council; bd of overseers, Bellermine Coll; mem, Urban Affairs Assn, 1986, Soc for Public Admin, 1986, Conference of Minority Public Admin, 1987; bd of dir, Humana Hospital-Audubon, 1988, Natl Forum for Black Public Admin, 1989; mem, Council on Higher Educ & Comm on Equal Opportunities; board of directors, Jefferson Community College and Watterson College, 1990. **Honors/Awds:** Leadership Louisville, Louisville Chamber of Commerce, 1981; Leadership Kentucky, Kentucky Chamber of Commerce, 1987; People to Watch, Louisville Magazine; several training certificates. **Military Serv:** AUS, E-5, 1963-65. **Business Addr:** Deputy Mayor of Operations, Mayor's Office, City of Louisville, 601 W Jefferson St, Louisville, KY 40202.

SUMMITT, GAZELLA ANN
Educational administrator. **Personal:** Born Feb 27, 1941, Wheatland, IN; daughter of Rhoda Gazella Howard Granger and John Ferrell Granger; married Paul O Summitt, Jul 11, 1964; children: Krista, Dana. **Educ:** Vincennes Univ, AS 1964; St Mary-of-the-Woods Coll, BS 1983; Grad Work Ballstate, ISU MS, 1993 (IN State Univ). **Career:** Vincennes Univ, sec to pres 1960-63, admin asst to pres 1963-80, asst to pres for admin and affirmative action officer 1980-91, director of personnel and AAO, 1991-. **Orgs:** Bd of trustees First Church of God Vincennes 1987-93; dir & sec Vincennes Univ Foundation 1980-; state coord Amer Assoc Women in Comm & Jr Colls 1984-94; co-chairperson Women's Div Knox Co United Fund 1985-91; sec Region V Amer Assoc for Affirmative Action 1986-88; co-chair (founding mem 1984) Indiana Coalition of Blacks in Higher Educ 1986; mem Historic Review Bd City of Vincennes 1986; Steering Committee, March of Dimes Walk America 1986-92; Steering Committee, Riley Children's Hospital Campaign 1986-92; sec Amer Assn for Affirmative Action 1988-92, president 1992-94; Board of Dirs, 1988-96; Steering Com. FCA, 1991; Vincennes Housing Authority, commissioner, 1992-96, chair, 1993-95; American Association for Affirmative Action Foundation Board, chairman, 1996-; Indiana Commission for Women, commissioner, 1997-99. **Honors/Awds:** Women of the Yr ABWA 1974; (2) Stephen Bufton Memorial Grants Amer Business Women's Assoc 1982, 1983; Vincennes Univ Blue and Gold Cord Award as Outstanding Prof Alumnus 1982; Greater Vincennes Area Church Women United Valiant Woman Award 1983; Martin Luther King Support Award 1988; President's Award American Assn Affirm Action 1990; Conducting EO/AA Training for Hawaiian Gov 1989, 1990, Sagamore of the WABASH Award from Gov of In, 1994. **Business Addr:** Director of Personnel and AAO, Vincennes Univ, Admin & Affirmative Action, 1002 North First St, Vincennes, IN 47591, (812)888-5848.

SUMNER, THOMAS ROBERT
Attorney. **Personal:** Born Dec 4, 1949, Louisville, KY; married Sherry Ann Beene; children: Nyshana, Rahman, Kamilah. **Educ:** Univ of IL Chicago, BA 1971; John Marshall Law Sch, JD 1977. **Career:** Circuit Court of Cook Co, Pub Defender's Ofc, trial atty 1977-; Univ of IL Chicago, acad coun, 1971-77; Chicago Title Ins, title examiner 1977. **Orgs:** Cook Co Bar Assn, pres 1985; mem Am & Trial Lawyers Assn 1980-; mem IL State Bar Assn 1980; mem Chicago Bar Assn 1980; mem Am Bar Assn 1980; Illinois Judges Assn, 1988. **Business Addr:** Judge, Circuit Court of Cook County, 2600 S California, Chicago, IL 60608, (312)890-3160.

SUNEJA, SIDNEY KUMAR
Radiologist. **Personal:** Born Jul 13, 1954, Chandigarh, India; married Kathleen. **Educ:** Howard Univ Coll of Medicine, MD 1976. **Career:** Case Western Reserve Univ, intern 1977; Howard Univ Hospital Family Practice, resident 1977-80, diagnostic radiology 1980-83; Johns Hopkins Hospital, nuclear medicine fellow 1983-85; Charity Hospital of New Orleans, assoc dir of nuclear medicine 1985-87; LA State Univ Medical Center, asst prof of radiology 1985-87; Howard Univ Hospital, asst prof of radiology 1987-. **Orgs:** Association of University Radiologists; American Ruentgen Roy Society; Medical Society of DC; Amer Coll of Radiology; Soc of Nuclear Medicine; Radiological Soc of North Amer; Amer Medical Assn; Southern Medical Assn; American BRD of Radiology, board member, 1985; American Board of Nuclear Medicine, board member, 1986; American Board of Family Practice, board member, 1982; radiation safety comm, LA State Univ Medical Center; NOLA. **Honors/Awds:** American Medical Assn, Physicians Recognition Award; Amer Bd of Family Practice, Recertification, 1989. **Special Achievements:** Author of numerous medical/scientific publications; lecturer: ''Neuroreceptor Imaging with Positron Emission Tomography,'' ''Nuclear Cardiology,'' New Orleans Fall Radiology Conference; ''Nuclear Medicine, Magnetic Resorarce Imaging,'' Annual Review Course, Howard Univ CME. **Business Addr:** Asst Prof of Radiology, Howard Univ Hospital, 2041 Georgia Ave NW, 1-R-14, Washington, DC 20060.

SURE, AL B. (AL BROWN)
Vocalist, songwriter. **Personal:** son Of Cassandra and Al Brown. **Educ:** Manhattan Center for the Media Arts. **Career:** Albums include: In Effect Mode, 1988; Private Times..And the Whole 9!, 1990; Sexy Venus, 1992; singles include: ''Rescue Me.''. **Honors/Awds:** In Effect Mode, platinum album. **Business Addr:** Recording Artist, c/o Warner Bros, 3300 Warner Blvd, Burbank, CA 91510.

SUTTON, CHARYN DIANE
Business executive. **Personal:** Born Apr 6, Philadelphia, PA; daughter of Martha Proudford Sutton and Charles Edwin Sutton; children: Kamal Everett Hoagland. **Educ:** Lincoln Univ, AB (magna cum laude) 1970; Temple Univ, School of Communications & Theatre, 1977-79, grad fellowship. **Career:** OIC's of Amer, communications dir 1976-77; Planned Parenthood Southeastern PA, communications dir 1978-79; Campbell Soup Co, product publicist 1979; Census Bureau US Dept of Commerce, regional public relations coord 1979-80; City of Philadelphia Employment & Training, community info dir 1980-84; GRIO Mag, exec editor, 1984-; Big Brothers/Big Sisters of Amer, dir mktg & communications, 1986-88; Charyn D Sutton Assn, owner, currently. **Orgs:** Bd, Philadelphia Urban League 1984-; board member, Action AIDS, 1989-; member, National Black Leadership Initiative on Cancer of Philadelphia; columnist, Philadelphia New Observer Newspaper, 1989-. **Honors/Awds:** Lincoln Univ Alumni Awd 1970; Leadership Awd Philadelphia Urban League 1987.

SUTTON, CLYDE A., SR.
Journalist, hardware company executive. **Personal:** Born Oct 21, 1927, Atlanta, GA; married Evelyn Cook, Jun 14, 1953; children: Roswell, Cheryl, Francis, Clyde Jr, Terri Vinson. **Career:** Atlanta Newspaper, Inc, 1962-; Sutton's Cascade Heights Hardware, owner, currently. **Orgs:** American Numismatic Association, 1956-. **Military Serv:** US Coast Guard, 1st class seaman. **Business Phone:** (404)755-1314.

SUTTON, DIANNE FLOYD
Human resource developer, educator, spokesperson, writer. **Personal:** Born Dec 6, 1948, Houston, TX; daughter of Dorothy Woods Floyd Brown and Osborne English Floyd; married Ronald N Sutton Jr, Sep 15, 1984 (died 1985); children: Anthony Specer Jones, Ronald Jr. **Educ:** Harris Stowe State Coll, BA, educ, sociology, 1970; Washington Univ, MA, educ, curriculum de, 1974. **Career:** St Louis Public School System, math instructor 1970-76; US EEOC St Louis Dist Office, EEO investigator/conciliator 1976-79, trainer/course design 1979-85; Creations by Dyan, design silk flowers and floral arrangements 1979-87; Independent mgmt consultant 1982; US Dept of Agriculture, employee develop specialist 1985-87; Sutton Enterprises, president, 1987-; American Univ, adjunct prof, 1990-. **Orgs:** Mem Natl Assoc for Female Execs 1976-; mem Training Officers Conf 1980-; mem Amer Soc of Trainers and Developers 1986, 1992-; Missionary Soc Metropolitan Baptist Church Washington DC 1987-; Delta Sigma Theta Sorority; mem, World Future Society 1987-. **Honors/Awds:** Experienced Teachers Grad Fellowship Washington Univ St Louis MO 1971; Special Achievement Award for Superior Performance US EEOC 1978, 1983; exec bd mem Training Officers Conf Washington DC 1980-; Distinguished Serv Award for EEO Training Progs Trainers Officers Conf 1982; Group Award for Organizational Needs Assessment, Training Officers Conference 1986; TOC Community Award 1994. **Special Achievements:** Managing Your Starship: Multicultural Managing for the 21st Century, 1996; testified at Senate hearing on small businesses for National Association for Self-Employed, 1996. **Business Addr:** President, Sutton Enterprises, 5702 Colorado Ave NW, Washington, DC 20011, (202)723-6870.

SUTTON, GLORIA W.
Librarian. **Personal:** Born Feb 17, 1952, Kinston, NC; divorced; children: Dimitri. **Educ:** Lenoir Comm Coll, AA 1972; East Carolina Univ, BS 1974; NC Central Univ, MLS 1987. **Career:** Lenoir Comm Coll, evening librarian 1974-75; Wayne Co Public Library, cataloguer 1975-76; Sampson Tech Coll, librarian 1976-81; Wake Technical Community Coll, librarian 1981-. **Orgs:** Mem NC Comm Coll Learning Resources Assoc 1977-; volunteer coord Garner Rd YMCA 1982-85; youth minister Wake Baptist Grove Ch 1983-; mem Shaw Div SchLibrary 1985-86, Wake Baptist Grove Ch Library 1985-, Capital Area Library Assoc 1985-, Professional Develop Comm Wake Tech Coll 1986-87, Church & Synagogue Library Assoc 1986-; bd of admin YWCA of Wake Co 1986-; church library consul NC Black Churches 1986-; vice chairperson ReHI Consortium 1986-. **Honors/Awds:** Volunteer of the Year Garner Rd YMCA 1983; Gloria Sutton Scholarship Wake Tech Coll 1984-; Youth Radio Ministry WSES Radio 1984-86; Outstanding Young Women of Amer 1985; Wake Baptist Grove Church minister of Youth Services 1983. **Home Addr:** 106 Towne View Trl, Garner, NC 27529-4598. **Business Addr:** Librarian, Wake Technical College, 9101 Fayetteville Rd, Raleigh, NC 27603.

SUTTON, JAMES CARTER
Purchasing agent. **Personal:** Born Jan 6, 1945, Lynville, TN; son of Nannie Readus Sutton (deceased) and Felton Eugene Sutton; married Joyce Roach Sutton, Mar 20, 1989; children: Kyra. **Educ:** Wayne State Univ, BS Business Admin 1975; Univ of Detroit, MBA. **Career:** Eastman Kodak Co, supervising buyer 1984, admin asst to vice pres 1984-85, proj mgr business ed 1985-86, public affairs planning dir 1986-, Worldwide Corporate Sourcing, manager & director minority supplier programs, currently. **Orgs:** Past chairman of the board, Urban League of Rochester, Natl Minority Supplier Devp Council, 1990; mem Corporate Director Minority Supplier Programs Kodak; minority employee recruiter Eastman Kodak Co 1984-; bd mem, Institute for American Business, 1992; bd mem, Otetiana Council Boy Scouts of America, Inc, 1988-; sec, Chase Manhattan-Rochester Metro Advisory Board; Fredrick Douglas African-American Historical Mus Advisory Committee; Business Policy Review Council, 1988-; Sigma Phi Pi. **Honors/Awds:** Features in company newspaper for involvement in Jr Achievement; featured in company Image Promotion for Community Involvement; Citation for involvement with Big Brother Program; Served as advisor to South African Black Business Development. **Military Serv:** USAF e-5 4 1/2 yrs. **Home Addr:** 2927 Portage Trail, Rochester Hills, MI 48309. **Business Addr:** Purchasing Agent, Chrysler Corporation, 800 Chrysler Dr, Auburn Hills, MI 48326-2757, (248)576-2783.

SUTTON, MARY A.
Senior software engineer. **Personal:** Born Oct 12, 1945, LA. **Educ:** Univ of Santa Clara, MS 1973; Prairie View A&M Coll, BS 1966. **Career:** Ford Aerospace & Communications, sr software engr; TRW Systems, proj mgr 1969-76; career lecturer for hs stud; Lockheed, asso engr 1967-69; Martin-marietta, asso engr 1966-67; Sunnyvale Employees Assn TRW, pres 1973-74. **Orgs:** Past mem Sunnyvale's TRW Affirmative Action Prog 1973-74; mem Univ of Santa Clara Alumni Orgn 1973-. **Honors/Awds:** First black, first woman mgr at TRW Sunnyvale. **Business Addr:** 1145 E Arques Ave, Sunnyvale, CA 94086.

SUTTON, MOSES
Clergyman. **Personal:** Born May 3, 1920, Morganfield, KY; married Emma Lou Forbes; children: Ethel Pierce, Alvin, Berthenia Hall, Stanley, Stephanie. **Educ:** Lane Coll, attended 1940; Louisville Municipal Coll, attended 1943; Eastern NM State Coll, attended 1945; Univ of Louisville, attended 1951. **Career:** Miles Chapel, pastor 1939; Patterson Chapel, pastor 1945; Muir Chapel, pastor 1951; Louisville District, presiding elder 1970; Christian Methodist Episcopal Church, mem judicial council 1982-86; The Lampkins Chapel Christian Methodist Episcopal, pastor, 1991-. **Honors/Awds:** KY Col Gov WH Ford 1973; Ambassador Gov JM Carroll 1976; KY Col Gov JM Carroll 1978; Key to Louisville Mayor HI Sloane 1984; Citizen Awd Co Judge M McConnell 1984; Christian Serv Awd Brown Mem Church 1984; Appreciation Awd Lanite Alumni 1984.

SUTTON, NATHANIEL K.
Automobile dealership executive. **Career:** Olympia Fields Ford Sales Inc, CEO, currently. **Honors/Awds:** Co. is ranked #27 on Black Enterprise magazine's list of top 100 auto dealers, 1992. **Business Addr:** Chief Executive Officer, Olympia Fields Ford Sales, 21000 Southwestern Ave, Olympia Fields, IL 60461, (708)747-7100.

SUTTON, NORMA J.
Attorney. **Personal:** Born Jun 11, 1952, Chicago, IL; daughter of Beatrice Ross Sams and Harry Sams; children: Edward. **Educ:** Loyola Univ, BA 1974; Governor's State Univ, MA 1976; Loyola Univ Sch of Law, JD 1980. **Career:** Cemrel Inc, office mgr 1975-77; North Amer Co for Ins, legal asst 1977-80; Appellate Court, judicial clerk 1980-82; Soft Sheen Products, corporate counsel 1982-85; Digital Equipment Corp, managing attorney beginning 1985; Central Region Law Group, mgr, currently. **Orgs:** Sec 1986-87, vice chair 1987-88 Illinois State Bar Assoc YLD; mem Amer Bar Assoc, Cook County Bar Assoc; mem Digital Equipment Corp Comm Relations Council. **Honors/Awds:** Leadership and Service Loyola Univ Sch of Law Chicago 1980.

SUTTON, OLIVER CARTER, II
Attorney, entertainment executive. **Personal:** Born Jan 31, 1948, San Antonio, TX; son of James Marcell Burley Heyward Sutton and Oliver C Sutton; children: Oliver C Sutton III, Samantha Leoma Sutton. **Educ:** Texas Southern Univ, Houston TX, BA, 1970; St. Mary's Univ Law School, San Antonio TX, JD, 1976. **Career:** Bexar County, TX, criminal investigator, asst dist atty in criminal dist atty's office; State of Texas, asst atty gen; private law practice; St. Philips Community Coll, TX, political science instructor until 1982; Alamo Community Coll Dist, San Antonio TX, trustee, 1982-86; Inner City Broadcasting Corp, asst to chmn of the board, 1986-; Apollo Theatre Records & Apollo Theatre Artist Management; Station Mgr WBLS-FM, 1994-. **Orgs:** Bd mem, Westin United; Regent,

Texas Southern Univ; bd mem, Black Entertainment Sports Lawyer Assn. **Business Addr:** Station Manager WBLS-FM, Inner City Broadcasting Corp, 3 Park Ave, 40th floor, New York, NY 10016.

SUTTON, OZELL
Appointed government official. **Personal:** Born Dec 13, 1925, Gould, AR; son of Lula Belle Dowthard Sutton and Charlie Sutton; married Joanna Freeman, May 9, 1947; children: Angela Sutton-Martin, Alta Muhammad, Dietre Jo Sutton. **Educ:** Philander Smith Coll, BA 1950, Hon D 1971; Fisk Univ, Nashville TN, attended, 1961. **Career:** AR Dem, staff writer 1950-57; Little Rock Housing Authority, relocations supervisor 1957-59; Winthrop Rockefeller, public relations 1959-61; AR Council on Human Relations, exec dir 1961-66; US Dept of Justice, field rep CRS 1966-68; Gov Winthrop Rockefeller of Ark, special asst 1968-69; US Dept of Justice, state supervisor AR state dir CRS 1969-72, reg dir SE region comm 1972-. **Orgs:** Relocation supvr, Litle Rock Housing Authority 1959-61; dir Arkansas Council on Human Relations, 1961-66; exec bd Philander Smith Coll 1971; bd of trustees Friendship Baptist Church 1974-; exec bd Atlanta Branch NAACP 1976-; gen pres Alpha Phi Alpha Frat Inc 1980; exec bd Leadership Conf on Civil Rights; exec bd Black Leadership Forum; chairperson Council of Presidents of Black Greekletter Organs; pres Voter Educ Project; chair Forum Comm Metro-Atlanta Crime Commn; co-chair Atlanta Black-Jewish Coalition; pres Inter-Alumni Council; chairman, Metro Atlanta Crime Commission 1991-; chairman, Voter Education Project 1986-; mem bd, NAACP 1990-. **Honors/Awds:** Distinguished Serv Award NAACP 1978; Distinguished Serv Award Alpha Phi Alpha Frat 1979; Outstanding Performance Award US Dept of Justice 1979-80; Distinguished Alumnus Award Philander Smith Coll; more than 100 other awards from many orgs; 2 Special Achievement Awards US Dept of Justice; ''The Black Experience in America,'' dramatic protrayal of black struggle; ''Watch Your Language,'' commentary on impact of racial & ethnic slurs; US Atty Gen Award, Distinguished Service Award- Natl Center for Missing and Exploited Children, 1994. **Military Serv:** USMC corpl 1944-46. **Business Addr:** Regional Dir, US Dept of Justice, Comm Relations Serv USD, 75 Piedmont Ste 900, Atlanta, GA 30303.

SUTTON, PERCY E.
Business executive (retired). **Personal:** Born Nov 24, 1920, San Antonio, TX; married Leatrice; children: Pierre, Cheryl, Darryl. **Educ:** Prairie View Coll, Tuskegee Inst, Hampton Inst, Columbia Univ, attended; Brooklyn Law School, LLB; Morgan State Coll, LLD (Hon) 1969. **Career:** Private practice, attny; NY State Assembly, elected 1964-66; Borough of Manhattan, pres 1966-77; Inner-City Broadcasting Corp, chmn, bd of dir, owner 1977-90 (retired). **Orgs:** Martin Luther King Dems; NAACP; Amer Museum of Natural History, Mus of City of NY; natl dir Urban League, Oper PUSH. **Military Serv:** USAF capt, combat intelligence officer, intelligence officer, judge advocate; Combat Stars for Serv in Italian & Mediterranean Theaters WWII.

SUTTON, PIERRE MONTE
Business executive. **Personal:** Born Feb 1, 1947, New York, NY. **Educ:** Univ of Toledo, BA 1968; Univ of KY, attended 1972. **Career:** Inner City Broadcasting, pres 1977-; Inner City Broadcasting Corp, vice pres 1975-77; WLIB Radio, pub affairs 1972-75; NY Courier Newspaper, exec editor 1971-72; Inner City Res & Analysis Corp, vice pres 1971. **Orgs:** Bd & mem Minority Investment Fund 1979-; first vice pres Nat Assn of Black Owned Broadcasters 1979-; chmn Harlem Oy Scouts 1975-; bd mem & exec com New York City Marathon 1979-; bd trustee Alvin Ailey Dance Found 1980-; bd mem Better Bus Bur Harlem 1972-77; bd mem Hayden Planetarium 1979-. **Military Serv:** USMC E-4 3yrs.

SUTTON, SHARON EGRETTA
Educator. **Personal:** Born Feb 18, 1941, Cincinnati, OH; daughter of Egretta Johnson (deceased) and Booker Johnson. **Educ:** Univ of Hartford, B Mus 1963; Columbia Univ, March 1973; City Univ of NY, M Phil 1981, MA Psychology 1982, PhD Psychology 1982. **Career:** Musician, orchestras of ''Fiddler on the Roof,'' ''Man of La Mancha,'' the Bolshoi, Moiseiyev and Leningrad Ballet Companies 1963-68; architect, Pratt Institute, visiting asst prof 1975-81; Columbia Univ, adj asst prof 1981-82; Univ of Cincinnati, asst prof 1982-84; SE Sutton Architect, private practice 1976-; Univ of MI, assoc prof, 1984-94, prof of architecture and urban planning, 1994-97; Univ of Washington, prof of architecture; Exhibitions, The Evans-Tibbs Collection in Washington, DC, fine artist, 1985; Your Heritage House in Detroit, MI 1986, June Kelly Gallery in NYC 1987, Univ of MI Musuem of Art 1988; Art included in collections of, The Mint Museum, The Baltimore Museum of Art, Baltimore, MD, The Wadsworth Atheneum, Hartford, CT. **Orgs:** Founder/coordinator, Urban Network: An Urban Design Program for Youth; fellow, Amer Institute of Architects; Amer Psychological Assn; American Educational Research Association; president-elect, National Architecture Accrediting Board. **Honors/Awds:** Danforth Foundation, Post baccalaureat Award 1979-81; Design Rsch Recognition Awd Natl Endowment for the Arts 1983; group VII Natl Fellowship, WK Kellogg Foundation, 1986-1989; project director Natl Endowment for the Arts, ''Design of Cities'' Grant; American Planning Assn Education Award, 1991; University of Michigan Regent's Award for Distinguished Public Service; first African-American woman to be named a full professor of architecture in the US; Second African-American Woman to be advanced to fellowship in the Amer Inst of Architects; Distinguished Professor, Association of Collegiate Schools of Architecture; Life Achievement Awd, Michigan Women's Hall of Fame, 1997. **Home Addr:** 8071 Main St, Dexter, MI 48130. **Business Addr:** Prof of Architecture & Urban Planning, Univ of Michigan, 2000 Bonisteel Blvd, Ann Arbor, MI 48109-2069, (313)936-0201.

SUTTON, STERLING E.
Business executive. **Personal:** Born Sep 7, 1928, Oklahoma City, OK; children: Valera. **Educ:** Alex Hamilton Inst, ABA 1949; Chicago Bd Underwriters, certificate 1964. **Career:** Unity Mutual Life Ins, agent 1949-52, mgr 1952-56, vice pres 1956-62; Sterling Sutton Assocs, pres 1962-. **Orgs:** Bd mem Neighborhood Housing Serv of Chicago 1979; mem Midwest Chicago Brokers Assns; bd mem Lake Grove Village; chmn trustee bd St Stephen AME Church; vice pres Professional Ins Agents & Brokers Assn; delegate Genl Conf of AME Churches 1980; vice pres Chicago Conf Laymen's Organ; pres Prof Ins Agents & Brokers Assoc of IL 1981-83, bd chmn to date. **Honors/Awds:** Natl Ins Assn Serv Awd 1956; Serv Awd Chicago Urban League 1960; Serv Awd F&AM Prince Hall AFFL 1961; Mayor Daley's Youth Serv Awd 1962; Chicago Econ Dev Corp Man of the Yr 1971; Disting Serv Awd 1974. **Business Addr:** President, Sterling Sutton Assocs, 5529 S Ashland Ave, Chicago, IL 60636.

SUTTON, WALTER L.
Educator (retired). **Personal:** Born Jul 26, 1917, Woodbury, GA; son of Carrie Sutton and Raymond Sutton; married Sammie W; children: Walter L Sutton, Jr. **Educ:** BA magna cum laude 1941; MS 1954. **Career:** Wiley Coll, asst prof hictory, phys edn, socialogy, economics 1968-; coach football, basketball, baseball 1968-; TX Schs, hS tchr & coach 1945-68. **Orgs:** Mem NEA Southwestern HPER; TX State Assn HPER; TX State & Baseball Assn; TX State Tchrs Assn; Football & Basketball State Assn; Nat Economic Assn; Kappa Alpha Psi; Mason Regular Fellows Club; Railroad Union; Southwest Football Official; umpire Little League; referee Kiwanis Club All Conf & Al Dist Football & Basketball. **Honors/Awds:** Awards NAIA Dit 8 Coach Of Yr 1974-75; Man of The Year Bethesda Baptist Church 1983; volunteer Harrison County Food Bank 1985-88; Hall of Fame Bethesda Baptist Church 1989; retired Wiley College Athletic Director. **Military Serv:** AUS stt ETO 1943-45.

SUTTON, WILLIAM WALLACE
Educational administrator, zoologist. **Personal:** Born Dec 15, 1930, Monticello, MS; son of Bessie Lewis Sutton and Talmon L Sutton; married Leatrice Eva Hubbard; children: William W Jr, Averell H, Sheryl Smith, Alan D, Allison M, Gavin J. **Educ:** Dillard Univ, BA 1953; Howard Univ, MS 1959, PhD 1965; Harvard University, Institute for Ed Management, 1991. **Career:** DC Genl Hosp Washington, med Tech 1955-59; Dillard Univ, instr to prof of biology 1959-79, chair div of natl sci 1969-79; Chicago St Univ, vice pres/acad afrs & provost 1979-85, prof of biol sci 1982-85; Kansas State Univ, vice pres educ & student svcs, prof biol 1985-88; Mississippi Valley State University, pres, 1988-. **Orgs:** Mem Amer Council on Educ 1983-; past pres Natl Inst of Sci; mem Society of Sigma Xi; reg liaison off Danforth Assoc Prog Danforth Found 1975-79; consul US Dept of Educ 1977-81, 1983-84; consul Natl Res Cncl Natl Acad of Sci 1980, 1982-83; consul 16 Inst Health Sci Consortium 1974-; deacon Chicago United 1980-82; bd of trustees WYES TV New Orleans 1973-79; bd dirs Methodist Hosp New Orleans 1975-79; bd dirs Urban League of New Orleans 1970-78; bd dirs Natl Conf of Christians & Jews 1968-79; bd dirs Amer Heart Assoc LA 1977-79; bd of dirs, Greenwood-Leflore Chamber of Commerce, 1989-91; member, Greenwood, MS Rotary Club, 1988-; advisory bd, Deposit Guaranty Natl Bank of Greenwood, MS, 1990-. **Honors/Awds:** Disting Awd Dillard Univ 1982; Presidential Citation Natl Assn for Equal Oppor 1979 1980; Disting Alumni Awd Dillard Univ 1978; Silver Beaver Awd Boy Scouts of Amer 1976; Man of the Middle South Changing Middle South Mag 1973; Sigma Xi The Research Society of America, 1955; Beta Kappa Chi Scientific Honor Society, 1955; Alpha Kappa Mu Honor Society, 1990; Dillard University, LLD, 1991. **Home Addr:** 125 Washington Ave, Itta Bena, MS 38941. **Business Addr:** President, Mississippi Valley State University, US Hwy 82 West, Itta Bena, MS 38941-1400.

SUTTON, WILMA JEAN
Business executive. **Personal:** Born Nov 11, 1933, Murphysboro, IL; married Clarence E. **Educ:** Univ of IL Urbana, cert of mgmt 1969; Univ of CT Storrs, cert 1970; Univ of IN Bloomington, cert 1976; Roosevelt Univ Chicago IL, B 1978; Roosevelt U, M 1979. **Career:** Hyde Park Fed Savings & Loan Assn of Chicago, exec vice pres 1964-; Chicago Title Ins Co Chicago IL, preliminary & examiner 1951-64. **Orgs:** Bd of dirs Hyde Park Fed Savings & Oan Assn of Chicago; bd of dirs Hyde Park Nieghborhood Club; bd of dirs Loretto Adult Educ Ctr; mem Lambda Alpha Ely Chpt; mem UNICEF; mem US Savings & Loan League; mem Chicago Urban League; mem NAACP; mem IL Commn on the Status of Women; mem Museum of Sci & Industry; mem St Thaddeus Ch Appointment; mem Savings & Loan Adv Bd Gov Daniel Walker State of IL. **Honors/Awds:** Cert of recognition Nat Alliance of Businessmen; editorial reviews Ebony Mag/Jet Mag/Chicago Sun Times/Chicgo Tribune/Real Estate News. **Business Addr:** VP/Regional Supervisor, Comm Outreach Svgs of Amer, 1000 S York Rd, Elmhurst, IL 60126-5188.

SVAGER, THYRSA F.
Educational administrator. **Personal:** Born in Wilberforce, OH; daughter of E Annie Frazier and G Thurston Frazier; married Aleksandar Svager. **Educ:** Antioch College, AB, 1951; Ohio State University, MA, 1952, PhD, 1965. **Career:** Wright Patterson AFB, Ohio, statistical analyst, 1952-53; Texas Southern University, instructor, 1953-54; Central State University, assistant professor, 1954-59, associate professor, 1959-66, professor, chair, 1966-85, academic affairs vice pres, 1985-89, executive vice pres, provost, 1989-. **Orgs:** Pi Mu Epsilon; Beta Kappa Chi; Alpha Kappa Alpha Sorority Inc; Alpha Kappa Mu Honor Society; Mathematical Association of America; National Association of Mathematicians; National Council of Teachers of Mathematics; Association for Computing Machinery. **Honors/Awds:** Jack & Jill of America, Saturday Academy Service Award, 1985; Greene County Women's Hall of Fame, Education Award, 1986; Top Ladies of Distinction, Wilberforce Chapter, Education Award, 1985; Human Needs Task Force, Challenge 95 Service Award, 1992; Central State University, Service Award, 1990. **Special Achievements:** Author: ''Access and Equity,'' St Phillips Episcopal Church, 1985; ''Compact Facts - Calculus,'' Visual Education Association, 1980; speaker: ''Software Documentation Controversy,'' Ohio State University, 1984; ''Computer Literacy,'' Minority Institutions Science Improvement Program, 1982; numerous others.

SWAIN, ALICE M.
Educator. **Personal:** Born Feb 3, 1924, Oklahoma City; married Robert; children: Robert A. **Educ:** Famous Writer's Sch Westport, BS 1946, ME 1952. **Career:** Univ of Oklahoma, graduate teaching assoc 1978-80; Langston Univ, asst prof 1973-78; reading specialist 1970-73; elem tchr 1948-69; Sigma Gamma & Rho, org local chapter. **Orgs:** Pres, vice pres & sec; chmn of bd Youth Services; vice pres & sec Nat Pan-hellenic Council Inc; pres & owner of The Together Charm & Fashion Modeling Sch; owner & producer of OK'S Hal Jackson's Miss US Talented Teen Pageant. **Honors/Awds:** Soc columnist The Black Dispatch Weekly Grand Epistoleus Sigma Gamma Rho 1974-76; Nat Pub Rel Chmn Sigma Gamma Rho 1974-76; Sowest Region Sigma of Yr 1963; one of nation's ten outstanding women 1967; local sigma of yr 1970; Sigma's Hall of Fame 1974; award of merit Nat Pan Hellenic Cncl Inc 1976; 1st gradn anti basileus Sigam Gamma Rho Sor Inc 1976-78; congratulatory plaque local Omega Psi Phi 1974; cert of merit for distinguished serv in Youth & Comm. **Business Addr:** 3016 Norcrest Dr, Oklahoma City, OK 73111.

SWAIN, HAMP
Consultant. **Personal:** Born Dec 3, 1929, Macon; son of Susie McIntosh and Hamp Swain Sr (deceased); married Zenola Hardeman; children: Ronald Leo, Ouida Louise, Natalie Valencia, Jarvis Osmond. **Career:** Little Richard and The Hamptones, band leader, sax player 1949-56; WIBB, radio broadcaster, announcer, 1957-81; pioneer broadcaster, 1954-81; Huckabee Auto Co, sales consultant, 1981-. **Orgs:** Mem local NAACP; co-sponsor Wendell Mcintosh Bowl; fighter for Human Rights. **Honors/Awds:** Golden Voice Award, Jack Gibson Organization, 1980. **Business Addr:** Sales Consultant, Huckabee Auto Co, 275 5th St, Macon, GA 31201.

SWAIN, JAMES H.
Attorney. **Personal:** Born Jul 4, 1954, Philadelphia, PA; married Sharon Matthews, Sep 1985. **Educ:** Univ of Bridgeport, BA 1975; Temple Univ School of Law, JD 1978; Univ of Pennsylvania Law School, LLM 1986. **Career:** US Atty So Dist of NY, summer intern 1977; Third Circuit Ct of Appeals, clerkship intern Hon A Leon Higginbotham 1978; US Dept of Labor, trial atty office of reg solicitor, 1978-88; US Dept of Justice, Eastern PA, asst US atty, 1989-94; US Dept of Justice, Southern FL, 1994-. **Orgs:** Barristers Assn of Philadelphia, executive committee, 1979-80, 1986-89, legislation revue committee, 1978-82; mem bd of dir, Community Legal Services, 1988-94; Wynfield Residents Assn, board of directors, 1988-94, executive vp, 1992-93; mem, Federal Bar Assn Philadelphia Chapter, 1988-; Philadelphia Bar Assn, 1989-; Federal Bar Assn, 1979-; trustee, Mount Pleasant Baptist Church, Philadelphia, PA; Federal Bar Association Miami Chapter, 1996-; Inns of Court University of Miami's Chapter, 1996-; Dade County Black Lawyers Association, 1994-; National Bar Association, Florida State Chapter, 1996-. **Honors/Awds:** Scholar of the Year Award, Omega Psi Phi Frat Inc, Rho Upsilon Chap 1975-76; Distinguished Serv Award, Black Amer Law Students Assn, 1977-78; Certificate of Appreciation, Barristers Assn of Philadelphia, 1978-79, 1979-80; Omega Psi Phi Frat Inc, Mu Omega Chap; US Department of Justice, John Marshall Award, 1992. **Special Achievements:** Author: ''Protecting Individual Employers: Is it Safe to Complain About Safety?,'' University of Bridgeport Law Review, 1988; lecturer, Asset Forfeiture, US

Dept of Justice & various Bar Associations, 1991-. **Business Addr:** Asst United States Atty, US Atty's Office, 99 NE 4th Street, Miami Beach, FL 33140, (305)530-7744.

SWAIN, MICHAEL B.
Senior systems analyst. **Personal:** Born Nov 5, 1965, Springfield, OH; son of Charlene Freeman-Swain and Melvin Swain. **Educ:** Ohio University, BBA, 1987. **Career:** Data Image, computer programmer, analyst, 1987-89; SEMCO, computer programmer, analyst, trainer, 1989-90; US Air Force, computer specialist, 1990-94; Decesion Systems Technologies, Inc, senior systems analyst/customer svc mgr, 1994-. **Orgs:** Alpha Phi Alpha, president, 1991-96; Springfield Urban League & Community Center, bd chmn, 1992-94, development chair, 1990-92; NAACP, education chair, 1991-93; Ebony Fashion Fair, general chair, 1992-93; Alpha Phi Omega National Service Fraternity, president, 1986-87. **Honors/Awds:** Wright-Patterson Air Force Base, Community Service Volunteer of the Year, 1993; Ohio University, John Newton Templeton Award, Outstanding Senior Leader, 1987. **Home Addr:** 1882 Clay St, Springfield, OH 45505-4066, (937)325-8089.

SWAIN, RONALD L.
Organization executive. **Personal:** Born Oct 9, 1948, Macon, GA; son of Evelyn Denton Swain and Hampton Swain; married Chrystle A Bullock, Jun 9, 1973; children: Ronald. **Educ:** Duquesne Univ Pgh PA, BA 1970, M Ed 1972; The Shaw Divinity Schl Ral NC, M Div 1975; The Univ of NC at Chapel Hill, M Ed 1983; George Washington University, DC Ed D 1987. **Career:** Shaw Univ, dir of counsel 1975-78; Univ of NC at CH, dir grad stud ctr 1978-80; Shaw Univ, assoc dean of stdnt 1980-81, spec asst to pres 1981-84, dir of devel 1987-88, vice pres for institutional advancement and planning 1988-94; United Negro College Fund, national development director, 1995-. **Orgs:** Bd of dir The Life Enrich Cntr 1983-; cnsltnt The UNC-CH Organ Dev Group 1979-82, Human Resources Consltnt 1978-82; bd of dir The Business Innovation Advancement Technology Center, Raleigh NC 1988-90. **Honors/Awds:** Flwshp Woodrow Wilson Natl Fellow Fdn Princeton, NJ 1984-84; proj dir NC Humanities Comm 120 yrs at Shaw Proj 1984-85; UNCF Fellowship for Doctoral Study 1985-87. **Special Achievements:** Author: Case Study of the US Dept of Education Institutional Development Program, 1986; Strategic Planning for the Use of Computer Technology in HBCU's, 1987. **Home Addr:** 4123 Trotter Ridge Rd, Durham, NC 27707. **Business Addr:** National Development Director, United Negro College Fund, Inc, 8260 Willow Oaks Corporate Dr, Fairfax, VA 22031-4811.

SWAN, EDWARD MCCALLAN, JR.
Company executive. **Personal:** Born Aug 31, 1941, Detroit, MI; son of Elizabeth Swan and Edward M Swan Sr; married Claudia Weaver, Nov 26, 1977. **Educ:** Tufts Univ, BA, 1963; Univ of Pennsylvania (Wharton School), MBA, 1974; CFA, 1981. **Career:** Univ of Pennsylvania Dental School, clinic business mgr, 1973-75; Prudential Insurance Co, director, 1975-84; Franklin Management Co, senior vice pres, 1984-85; W R Lazard and Co, vice pres, 1985-88; Mitchell Hutchins Institutional Investors, Inc, managing director, 1988-96; Union Bank of Switzerland Asset Management, vice pres, 1996-97; MFS Asset Management, vice pres, dir of marketing, 1997-. **Orgs:** 100 Black Men of New York, financial secretary, 1986-; Friends of Alvin Ailey, board member, 1989-; New York City Industrial Development Agency, board member, 1989-; Association of Investment Marketing Sales Executives, 1989-; New York City Small Business Advisory Board, 1993-; National Association of Securities Professionals, program comm, 1989-; Financial Services Fellowship Program, mentor, 1991-; Museum of Modern Art Membership Committee, 1995-; Friends of Education Museum of Modern Art, 1994-. **Honors/Awds:** Chartered Financial Analyst (CFA), 1981. **Military Serv:** USAF, captain, 1963-67. **Business Addr:** Vice President, MFS Asset Management, Inc, 500 Boylston St, Boston, MA 02116-3741, (617)954-5000.

SWAN, GEORGE W., III
Educator. **Personal:** Born Apr 4, 1957, Detroit, MI; son of George W Swan Jr & Henrene W Swan; married Deborah D Harris-Swan, Aug 16, 1980; children: George IV, Trevor Justin, Blake Aaron. **Educ:** Wayne State Univ, BA, speech comm & theatre, 1979, MEd, educational sociology, 1991, EdD, candidate, 1991-. **Career:** Lewis Coll of Bus, asst vice pres for academic affairs, assoc dir, Upward Bound, 1981-82; Project Job Club, dir, 1982, dir of coll relations & title III, 1982-86; Wayne State Univ, extention ctr prog coord, 1986; Wayne County Comm Coll, dir of comm relations, 1987-91, dir of public affairs, 1991-. **Orgs:** Child Welfare League of Amer, bd mem, 1993-; Lula Belle Stewart Ctr Inc, bd mem, imm past pres, 1987-; Evergreen Children's Service, bd mem, past chair, 1989-; Southern Wayne County Chamber of Commerce, bd mem, 1993-; New Detroit Inc, youth & young adults comm, 1994-; Detroit Educ Cable Consortium, vice chair, 1993-; DCC/Monroe County Private Industry Council, bd sec, 1990-96; Natl Council for Mktg & Public Relations, 1989-; American Heart Association, South Wayne, bd mem, 1995-. **Honors/Awds:** Downriver Council for the Arts, Outstanding Service Award; Evergreen Children's Service, Lobby Plaque for Outstanding & Dedicated Service, 1992; WDTR 90.9 FM, Outstanding Comm Involvement, 1993; News Herald Newspaper, Four Who Make A Difference, 1994; Lula Belle Stewart Ctr, Outstanding Service Award, 1994. **Business Addr:** Dir, Public Affairs, Wayne County Community College, 801 W Fort St, CAB-3, Detroit, MI 48226, (313)496-2727.

SWAN, JOHN WILLIAM DAVID
Business executive, justice of the peace. **Personal:** Born Jul 3, 1935; son of Margaret E Swan and John N Swan (deceased); married Jacqueline A D Roberts, 1965; children: 3. **Educ:** WV Wesleyan Coll, BA. **Career:** Lloyd's of London, underwriter; Rego Limited, real estate salesman, 1960-62; John L Swan Limited, founder, chairman, chief executive officer, 1962-; Justice of the Peace; Premier of Bermuda, currently. **Orgs:** Trustee, Bermuda Biological Station for Research; Young Presidents' Organization, 1974-86; World Business Council, 1986; Chief Executives Organization; Hamilton Rotary Club; elected to Parliament, 1972; Senate, Jun Chamber Internat, 1992. **Honors/Awds:** Honorary Degrees: University of Tampa, FL, 1985; West Virginia Wesleyan College, 1987; Atlanyic Union College, MA, 1991; Poor Richard Club of Philadelphia, 1987; International Medal of Excellence, 1st recipient, 1987; Lab Sch of Washington, Outstanding Learning Disabled Achiever Award, 1992. **Special Achievements:** Minister: Marine and Air Services; Labour and Immigration, 1977-78; Home Affairs, 1978-82. **Business Addr:** Premier of Bermuda, Cabinet Office, 105 Front St, W, Hamilton HM 12, Bermuda.

SWAN, L. ALEX
Education administrator. **Personal:** Born Jan 17, 1938, Grand Turk, Turks and Caicos Islands; married Karla K. **Educ:** West Indies Coll, AS 1963; Leg Aspects Bus (England), assoc cert 1964; Blackstone Law Sch, LLB 1966; Oakwood Coll, BS 1967; Atlanta U, MA 1969; Univ CA at Berkeley, MS PhD 1972. **Career:** Fisk Univ, chmn Dept Sociology; Univ CA at Berkeley & Sonoma State Coll, lectr; Miami-Dade Jr Coll & Dinthill Tech HS, instr. **Orgs:** Amer Sociological Assn; Amer Soc Criminology; Black World Foundation; NAACP, chmn, Leg Redress Comm, 1973-74.

SWAN, LIONEL F.
Physician. **Personal:** Born Apr 1, 1906; children: Alfreda, Andrea, Virginia, Lionel Jr. **Educ:** BS 1932; MD 1939. **Career:** Detroit Med & Surg Center, physician & pres; Nat Med Assn Fndtn, fndr; Nat Med Assn, past pres; Det Med Soc, past pres; Detroit Med News, ed staff. **Orgs:** Mem Nat Med Assn; Detroit Med & Soc; AMA; MI State Med Soc; Wayne Co Med Soc; MI Health Council; bd MI Health Maintenance Orgn; mem, NAACP, Golden Heritage; Phi Beta Sigma; Lions Club. **Honors/Awds:** Dist serv award MI Health Council 1968; fellow Am of Fam Prac; Alumnus of Year, 1964. **Business Addr:** 3956 Mt Elliott, Detroit, MI 48207.

SWAN, MONROE
Executive director. **Personal:** Born Jun 2, 1937, Belzoni, MS; children: Rosalyn, Cheryl, Gwendolyn, Allyn. **Educ:** Milwaukee Area Tech Coll; Univ of WI, BS. **Career:** Amer Motors Corp, material expeditor 1967-68; Local 75, head steward; Concentrated Employment Program, dir 1968-72; former WI state senator; FIRE HELP, exec dir. **Orgs:** Former pres orgn of Orgns (Triple ''O''); chmn Senate Com Govtl & Vet Affairs; mem Senate Joint Com Review of Adminstrv Rules; former supt Ch God in Christ Sunday Sch NW WI; mem Frontiers Intl. **Honors/Awds:** Mreitorious Award VFW; Damn Fine Legislator Award Vet Educ Com; Cert of Merit US Jaycees. **Business Addr:** Executive Dir, FIRE HELP of Wisconsin, 5815 W Capitol Dr, Ste 404, Milwaukee, WI 53216.

SWANIGAN, JESSE CALVIN
Accountant, auditor, retired. **Personal:** Born Nov 18, 1933, Widner, AR. **Educ:** Washington Univ St Louis, BS 1966; St Louis Univ, MBA 1977. **Career:** EB Koonce Mortuary Inc, supvr trainee 1961; Johnson Publishing Co, staff representative 1962; McDonnell Douglas Aircraft Corp, sr specialist auditing, 1963-97. **Orgs:** Ordained elder United Presbyterian Church in the USA 1976; life mem NAACP 1976; consultant United Negro Coll Fund Comm 1979; mem Natl Assn of Black Accountants 1977; mem Black Presbyterians United 1980; bd mem Natl Black MBA Assn; treasurer 100 Black Men of Amer Inc; bd mem Carver House; founder, past pres, St Louis Black MBA Assn, 1988; president, National Black Presbyterian Caucus, 1993; 100 Black Men of Metropolitan St. Louis. **Honors/Awds:** Black Leader for 1980 United Presbyterian Church in the USA 1979; Honor of Appreciation, Amer Business Women's Assn 1989.

SWANN, ERIC JERROD
Professional football player. **Personal:** Born Aug 16, 1970, Pinehurst, NC; married Celeste; children: Tevin, Austin, Eric Jr. **Career:** Phoenix Cardinals, defensive tackle, 1991-93; Arizona Cardinals, 1994-. **Honors/Awds:** Pro Bowl, 1995, 1996. **Business Addr:** Professional Football Player, Arizona Cardinals, 8701 S Hardy, Tempe, AZ 85284, (602)379-0101.

SWANN, EUGENE MERWYN
Attorney. **Personal:** Born Aug 1, 1934, Philadelphia, PA; son of Doris Swann and Earl Swann; children: Liana, Michael, Elliott. **Educ:** Temple U, BS 1957; Univ of MA, MA Econ 1959; Univ of CA Berkeley, LLB 1962. **Career:** Contra Costa Co, dep dist atty 1963-67; Contra Costa Legal Svcs, dir 1967-77; Office of Citzens Complaints, dir 1983-84; SF Police Dept, 1984-85; Self Employed, lecturer/atty 1977-83; Economics-Univ of Calif, Berkeley, and Stanford Graduate Schl of Business, private practice, currently. **Honors/Awds:** Outstand Legal Serv Attorney in Nation 1974. **Home Addr:** 43 Donald Dr, Orinda, CA 94563.

SWANN, LYNN CURTIS
Television sports announcer, professional football player (retired). **Personal:** Born Mar 7, 1952, Alcoa, TN. **Educ:** University of Southern California, bachelor degree, public relations. **Career:** ABC Sports, sports announcer, currently; Pittsburgh Steelers, wide receiver, 1974-82. **Orgs:** Member, Screen Actors Guild; member, American Federation of Television and Radio Artists. **Honors/Awds:** MVP, Super Bowl X, 1975; played in Pro Bowl, 1977-79 seasons.

SWANSON, CHARLES
Lawyer. **Personal:** Born Aug 16, 1949, Camp Hill, AL; married Anne Elizabeth Fox; children: Tesfaye C, Tonya D, Tamara A, Charles Joseph. **Educ:** Univ of WI-Madison, BA 1971; Univ of WI Law School, JD 1973. **Career:** Univ of WI-Madison, teaching asst afro-amer history 1970-73; Racine Co Public Defenders Office, asst public defender 1974-75; NAACP, legal redress 1978-; Private Practice, attorney. **Orgs:** Mem Racine County, Amer Bar Assocs; mem Natl Assoc of Criminal Defense Lawyers; mem bd dirs Racine NAACP; mem Racine Optimist Club. **Honors/Awds:** Apptd Racine County Circuit Court Commissioner 1980; Outstanding Young Man of Amer 1984; Outstanding Dir Racine Jaycees. **Military Serv:** ROTC-Army. **Business Addr:** 1006 Washington Ave, Racine, WI 53403.

SWANSON, EDITH
Educator. **Personal:** Born Jul 16, 1934, Detroit, MI; married Charles; children: Kenneth, Charles, II. **Educ:** E MI U, BS 1970; E MI U, MA 1975. **Career:** MI Educ Assn, full-time vice pres 1977-; Willow Run Comm Sch, tchr; Willow Run Educ Assn, pres 1972-75. **Orgs:** Bd of dir MI Educ Assn 1974-77; chpsn MI Educ Assn Minor Group & Task Force 1975; vice pres elect MI Educ Assn 1977; chairperson Coalition Against Parochaid 1977-; NEA Del World Confedtn of Orgns of Tchg Profession Jakarta Indonesia 1978; exec com MI Educ Assn; centr reg coord NEA Women's Caucus; mem Nat Alliance Blakc Sch Edctrs/MI Alliance Black Edctrs/Coalition of Labor Union Women/NAACP; pres Ypsilanti Palm Leaf Club 1973-75; Delta Sigma Theta Sor Grad Chap; v chpsn Washtenaw Co Black Dem Caucus 1974-77. **Honors/Awds:** Trib to outst women NEA educ awd rep aay 1976; maurine wyatt feminist award MI Educ Assn 1978; 1 Of Most Inflntl Black Edctrs Ebony Mag 1980.

SWANSON, O'NEIL D.
Funeral director. **Personal:** Born Apr 6, Birmingham, AL; children: O'Neil II, Linda E, Kimberly E. **Educ:** Central State Univ, BS 1953; Cincinnati Coll of Embalming, Mortuary Science 1956. **Career:** Swanson Funeral Home Inc, president/CEO. **Orgs:** Exec bd dir & life mem NAACP; dir First Independence Natl Bank of Detroit 1970-80; dir Natl Alumni Assoc Central State Univ 1978, Natl Funeral Dirs & Morticians Assoc 1979. **Honors/Awds:** Honorary Doctoral Degree Shaw Coll Detroit 1974; Honorary Doctoral Degree Central State Univ 1974. **Military Serv:** US Army, 1st Lt. **Business Addr:** President/CEO, Swanson Funeral Home Inc, 806 E Grand Blvd, Detroit, MI 48207, (313)923-1122.

SWANSTON, CLARENCE EUGENE
Organization executive, hospital project administrator. **Personal:** Born May 15, 1947, New York, NY; son of Beryl Ina Swaby Swanston and Norman C. Swanston. **Educ:** St John's Univ, Jamaica NY, BS, 1969; Metropolitan Training Institute, Queens College, Flushing NY, cert in counseling, 1973. **Career:** Sound of New York, Inc (CBS), New York NY, vice president finance, 1981-84; City University of New York, New York NY, budget officer, 1977-82; New Jersey Higher Education Authority, Trenton NJ, asst dir of finance, 1982-86; Planned Parenthood of America, New York NY, deputy grants dir, 1986-87; National Urban League, New York NY, asst dir, 1987-88; Urban League of the Albany Area, Inc, Albany NY, president, CEO, 1988-91; New York City Health & Hospitals Corp., deputy project executive, 1992-. **Business Addr:** President, Albany Area Urban League, 95 Livingston Ave, Albany, NY 12207.

SWEAT, KEITH
Vocalist. **Personal:** Born in New York, NY. **Educ:** College graduate. **Career:** Wall Street floor supervisor; Jamilah, singer; albums include: Make It Last Forever, co-producer, 1988; I'll Give All My Love to You, 1990; Keep It Comin', 1991; LSG with Gerald Levert and Johnny Gill, 1997; New Jack City, contributor, 1991; singles include: ''I Want Her,'' ''Make You Sweat,'' ''Merry Go Round,'' (with Gerald LeVert) ''Just One

of Them Thangs,'' ''Twisted,'' 1996; The Industry, owner. **Honors/Awds:** Make It Last Forever, double-platinum album; Black Radio Exclusive, number one new male artist, 1988. **Special Achievements:** Has performed in concert with Bell Biv Devoe, Johnny Gill, Ricky Harris. **Business Addr:** Singer, c/o Elektra Records, 75 Rockefeller Plaza, New York, NY 10019.

SWEAT, SHEILA DIANE
Investment analyst. **Personal:** Born May 8, 1961, New York, NY. **Educ:** Hampton Inst, BS 1983. **Career:** Moody's Investors Svcs, credit analyst 1984-86; Irving Trust Co, investment analyst 1986-. **Orgs:** Mem Long Island Chap Hampton Alumni Assoc 1984-. **Business Addr:** Investment Analyst, Irving Trust Company, One Wall St, New York, NY 10015.

SWEATT, JAMES L., III
Surgeon. **Personal:** Born Jul 13, 1937; married Mary Lois Sweatt. **Educ:** Middlebury College, BS, Chemistry, 1958; Washington University, MD, 1962. **Career:** Surgeon, private practice, currently. **Orgs:** Dallas County Med Society, pres, 1995, alternate delegate AMA, 1997; Texas Med Association, alternate delegate to Amer Med Assn; American College of Surgeons; Society of Thoracic Surgeons; American Med Assn; C V Roman Med Society; Southwestern Med Foundation, trustee. **Military Serv:** USAF, 1963-65.

SWEENEY, JOHN ALBERT
Educator. **Personal:** Born Jun 3, 1925, Columbus, OH; married Veronica Khan; children: Dereck, Peitra. **Educ:** New York University, BA, 1949; Trinity College, London, LTCL, 1951; American Guild of Organists, AAGO, 1953; New York University, MA, 1953; State College of Music, Munich, Germany, graduate certificate, 1954; Free University, West Berlin, Germany, PhD, 1961; Johns Hopkins University, Ed, 1965; African Studies, University of Nairobi & Kenya, East Africa, graduate certificate, 1971. **Career:** Morgan State University, professor of music, instruments, theory, musicology, ethnomusicology, 1962; University of Maryland, Extension Program, USAF, Berlin, Germany, teacher music theory, 1955-60; West Germany, guest lecturer, musicology, 1954-61; New York City St Mark's, Morgan State University, 1962-; New York, Munich, Baltimore, french hornist, bands, orchestras, 1945-70; Music Education's National Conference; Society for Ethnomusicology; Morgan State University & Baltimore Area, advanced international studies. **Orgs:** Ping Council for Annual Black Music Week, Morgan State University; Advanced Council, Left Bank & Jazz Society, Baltimore; India Forum; Dedicated to Dissemination of Indian Culture; Organist, Union Baptist Church Elected to Following Honor Society; Mu Sigma, New York University, 1968; Phi Beta Kappa, New York University, 1949; Phi Delta Kappa, Johns Hopkins University, 1965. **Honors/Awds:** Fulbright Scholar, Germany, 1953-54; Published Anthem: ''134th Psalm'', 1951; Book: The Trumpets in the cntatas of J S Bach, 1961; Book Reviews; Article: ''Guyanea & the African Diaspora'', 1976. **Military Serv:** USAF sgt 1944-46. **Business Addr:** Fine Arts, Morgan State University, 1700 E Cold Spring, Baltimore, MD 21239.

SWEET, CLIFFORD C.
Attorney. **Personal:** Born Aug 3, 1936, W Palm Beach, FL. **Educ:** San Jose State, BA 1959; Lincoln U, LLB 1965. **Career:** Legal Aid Soc Alameda Co, exec atty 1971-; Sweet & Sweet San Jose, pvt pract; Legal Aid Soc, staff atty 1967-. **Orgs:** Mem Fed & Inter-Am Bar Assns; State Bar CA; past bd mem Urban League; ACLU; Barrister's Club; Dem Lawyer's Club; legal couns Oakland Black Police Officer's Assns; Oakland Firefighter's Assn; Nat Orgn Women; NAACP; COYOTE; Asian Law Caucus; Bananas Child Care; Disability Law Resources Center; Legal Assistance for Seniors; Rubicon Battered Women. **Honors/Awds:** West Berkeley Seniors, Certificate of Award for Dedicated Services, 1991; Esperanza Resident Management Council, Certificate of Award for Assistance, 1991; Legal Service Administrators of Pacific Region, Award in Support of Standards of Excellence, 1985; West Oakland Food Project, Award in Appreciation of Support Rendered, 1984; Legal Services Corp., Certificate of Award for Dedication to the Provision of Legal Services to the Less Fortunate, 1992; Certificate of Appreciation for Outstanding Litigation and Support on Behalf of Image, California. **Business Addr:** Attorney, 510 16th Street, #560, Oakland, CA 94612.

SWEET, TERRECIA W.
Educator. **Personal:** Born Apr 17, 1955, Winona, MS; daughter of Lela Wilson and Robert Wilson; divorced; children: Dennis. **Educ:** Tougaloo College, Tougaloo, MS, BA, 1973-77; Mississippi State Univ, Mississippi State, MS, MA, 1977-79; George Washington Univ, Washington, DC, EdSpec, 1984-85; Mississippi State Univ, Mississippi State, MS, EdD, 1986-88. **Career:** Alabama State Univ, Montgomery, AL, instructor, 1984-85; Mississippi State Univ, Mississippi State, MS, assistant director, 1986-88; California State Univ, Fresno, CA, professor, 1988-; Life Choices, private counselor, 1989-; Fresno City College, mentor program director, 1990-. **Orgs:** Chairperson, Visiting Scholars' Program, 1988-; advisor, Assn of Counselor Educators, 1989-; affirmative action committee member, 1988-, univ lecture series committee member, California State Univ-Fresno, 1989-. **Honors/Awds:** Most Outstanding Student, Tougaloo College, 1977; Most Outstanding Graduate Student, Mississippi State Univ, 1988; Most Outstanding Student, Counselor Education, Mississippi State Univ, 1988.

SWEETS, ELLEN ADRIENNE
Editor. **Personal:** Born Feb 1, 1941, St Louis, MO; daughter of Melba Adrienne Ficklin Sweets and Nathaniel Allen Sweets; married Eric Dunning (divorced); children: Hannah Adrienne. **Educ:** Fairleigh Dickinson, Madison, NJ; Washington University, St Louis, MO; Antioch College, Yellow Springs, OH. **Career:** The St Louis Post Dispatch, St Louis, MO, reporter, 1969-77; The St Louis Civil Rights Enforcement Agency, St Louis, MO, exec dir, 1977-81; AT&T, Short Hills, NJ, editor, 1981-89; The Dallas Morning News, Dallas, TX, features reporter, 1989-. **Orgs:** Journalism & Women's Symposium, board member. **Business Addr:** Columns Editor, Today, The Dallas Morning News, PO Box 655237, Dallas, TX 75265, (214)977-8497.

SWIFT, KAREN A.
Personnel administrator. **Personal:** Born Mar 15, 1940, Kansas City, MO; daughter of William Reece, Jr & Velma M Bass; married Leroy Swift (divorced 1985); children: Andrea R Ingram, Lisa J. Ingram; married Walter Ingram (divorced). **Educ:** University of MO-KC, BA, secondary education, Masters, counseling guidance, education spec. **Career:** KCMO School Dist, assistant prin, Central HS, 1986-87, principal, Harrision Jr HS, 1987-88, principal, Westport HS, 1980-88; Hickman Mills School Dist, KCMO, director of personnel, 1988-95; Paseo Academy of Visual Arts, vice principal; Westport High School, evening school principal, currently.

SWIFT, LINDA DENISE
Librarian. **Personal:** Born May 27, 1965, Detroit, MI; daughter of Juliet Stanfield Swift and James Swift (deceased). **Educ:** Wayne State University, Detroit, MI, BA, 1987, MSLS, 1990. **Career:** Michigan Opera Theatre, Detroit, Mi, audience dev intern, 1987; WJBK-TV Channel 2, Southfield, MI, public service intern, 1987; BAC & K Advertising, Birmingham, MI, pub relations intern, 1987; Campbell Ewald Adv, Detroit, MI, telemarketing mfg, 1988-89; Michigan Bell, Detroit, MI, research assistant, 1989-90; Comerica Inc, Detroit, MI, research librarian, beginning 1990-93; UAW Chrysler, librarian, currently. **Orgs:** Vice Pres, Association of African American Librarians, 1990-; member, Special Libraries Association, 1990-; member, American Library Association, 1989-. **Honors/Awds:** Achievement Award, Wayne State University, 1989-90. **Business Addr:** Librarian, UAW Chrysler, 2211 E Jefferson Ave, Detroit, MI 48207.

SWIGGETT, ERNEST L.
Religious administrator. **Educ:** Drew Univ, NY Univ, Grad Courses; PA State Univ, BS; Columbia Univ, MA; Emory Univ Candler School of Theology, Cert UMCBA. **Career:** Unique NY Mag, comptroller 1974-76; Harkless & Lyons Inc, principal 1976-78; Salem United Methodist Church, bus admin 1978-87; Salem Home Care Serv Inc, dir 1980-87; NY Annual Conf of the United Methodist Church, bus admin, treasurer. **Orgs:** Cons, workshops NY & Eastern PA Conf of the United Methodist Church, Black Methodist for Church Renewal Inc, Drew & NY Theological Seminaries 1980-; mem 100 Black Men Inc, United Methodist Assoc of Church Bus Admins, AUDELCO, Black Methodist for Church Renewal Inc, Natl Assoc ofChurch Bus Admin; dir, Gen Bd of Global Ministries of The US Methodist Church; Natl Chairperson, Black Methodists for Church Renewal, Inc; mem Assn of United Methodists Conf Treasurers, Inc. **Honors/Awds:** Publ Unique NY Mag, Encore, Amsterdam News, New World Outlook, The Interpreter Mag; Pioneer Awd Salem Community Serv Council Inc; Service Award, Bethany United Methodist Church 1988; Service Award Upper Madison United Methodist Church; Layman's Award Janes UM Church; Man of the Year Salem United Methodist Church; Methodist Hospital, Brooklyn, NY, trustee. **Home Addr:** 135 Eastern Pkwy, Brooklyn, NY 11238. **Business Addr:** Business Admin, Treasurer, New York Annual Conference of, The United Methodist Church, 252 Brant Ave, White Plains, NY 10605.

SWINDELL, WARREN C.
Educational administrator. **Personal:** Born Aug 22, 1934, Kansas City, MO; son of Estella Jaunita McKittrick Swindell and John Truman Swindell, Jr; married Monica Streetman, Jun 25, 1967; children: Warna Celia, Lillian Ann. **Educ:** Lincoln Univ of MO, BS Music Educ 1956; The Univ of MI Ann Arbor, MM 1964; The Univ of IA, PhD Music Educ 1970. **Career:** Central High Sch Hayti MO, band and choir dir 1956-57, dir of musical act 1959-60; Hubbard High Sch, dir of music act 1960-61; Flint MI Public Schools, inst mus specialist 1961-67; KY State Univ, chair/prof of music 1970-79, prof of music 1979-80; Indiana State Univ, chair, dir/prof ctr, Dept of Africana Studies, 1980-96, prof, currently. **Orgs:** Evaluator Natl Assoc of Schools of Music Accred 1977-78; screening panel KY Arts Commn Project 1977-79; chaired State, Div & Natl MENC meetings 1979-80; worshipful master, Prince Hall Lodge #16, 1991-92; president, Region V, National Council for Black Studies, 1989-91; secretary, Indiana Coalition of Blacks in Higher Education, 1992-93; first vp, Indiana Coalition of Blacks in Higher Educ, 1994-95; pres, Indiana Coalition, 1996-; Prince Hall Grand Lodge Jurisdiction of Indiana, chairman of masonic history & education; chairman, School of Instruction, Prince Hall Masons; Terre Haute, Indiana Branch NAACP, first vp 1995-96, pres, 1997. **Honors/Awds:** Numerous Service Awds NAACP 1978-94; NEH Summer Seminar for College Teachers Grant 1984; Faculty Rsch Grant Indiana State Univ 1985; IN State Univ Research Grant 1987-88; Amer Philosophical Society Research Grant 1988; Lilly Endowment Faculty Open Fellowship 1993-94; Caleb Mills Award for Distinguished Teaching. **Military Serv:** AUS spl 4th class 2 yrs. **Home Addr:** 14 Douglas Place, Terre Haute, IN 47803. **Business Addr:** Professor, Africana Studies, Indiana State University, Department of Africana Studies, Stalker Hall 204, Terre Haute, IN 47809.

SWINER, CONNIE, III
Physician. **Personal:** Born Sep 8, 1959, Washington, DC; son of Esther Wallace Swiner and Connie Swiner. **Educ:** College of William and Mary, BS 1980; Howard Univ Coll of Medicine, MD 1985. **Career:** Michael Reese Hospital, Chicago, IL, resident, 1987-90; Univ of IL, Coll of Medicine, Chicago, IL, asst prof, 1990-. **Orgs:** Mem Amer Medical Assn 1982-; mem Black Physicians Assoc/Cook Co Hosp 1986-; mem Alpha Phi Alpha Frat Inc, 1978-; Howard Univ Medical Alumni Assn, 1985-; mem, American Soc of Anesthesiologists, 1987-. **Honors/Awds:** Mem Alpha Omega Alpha Honor Medical Soc Howard Univ 1985.

SWINGER, HERSHEL KENDELL
Educational administrator. **Personal:** Born Apr 16, 1939, Parsons, KS; married Sandra Marie Reese; children: Robbin D, Hershel K Jr. **Educ:** CA State Univ Los Angeles, BA Psych 1966, MS Rehab Counseling 1968; Univ Southern CA, PhD Clinical Psych 1978. **Career:** LA Cty Occupational Health Svc, dir counseling 1970-74; Reg IX Ctr on Child Abuse/Neglect, dir 1975-80; Dept Counselor Ed CA State Univ, assoc prof 1979-; Reg IX Ctr on Children Youth & Families, dir 1981-84; Southern CA Child Abuse Prevention Training Ctr, dir, prof. **Orgs:** Consult Natl Ctr on Child Abuse/Neglect 1978-; mem Black Psych Assoc 1980-; dir family crisis ctr Childrens Inst Intl 1982-; vice pres South Central LA Reg Ctr 1982-; exec mem West Area Council on Alcoholism 1983-; cons, psych El Centro Comm Mental Health Ctr 1984-. **Honors/Awds:** Outstanding Service LA Cty Supervising Soc Worker 1982; Roy Wilkins Ed Awd Inglewood South Bay NAACP 1984; Outstanding Alumni CA State Univ 1984; Outstanding Comm Service Black Soc Workers of LA 1984. **Military Serv:** AUS spc 4 1963-65. **Business Addr:** Director, Professor, So CA Child Abuse Prevent Ctr, 5151 State University Dr, Los Angeles, CA 90032.

SWINGER, RASHOD
Professional football player. **Personal:** Born Nov 27, 1974. **Educ:** Rutgers, attended. **Career:** Arizona Cardinals, defensive tackle, 1997-. **Business Addr:** Professional Football Player, Arizona Cardinals, 8701 S Hardy, Tempe, AZ 85284, (602)379-0101.

SWINNEY, T. LEWIS
Physician. **Personal:** Born Jun 3, 1946, Nashville, TN. **Educ:** Benedict Coll, BS (w/Honors) 1970; Meharry Medical Coll, MD 1975. **Career:** Staten Island Hosp, internship/residency internal medicine 1975-78; United States Navy, chief of pulmonary medicine, chief of alcohol rehab unit, staff physician internal medicine 1978-81; Self-Employed, physician. **Honors/Awds:** Physician of the Year Queens-Corona 1984. **Military Serv:** USN lt commander 1978-81. **Home Addr:** 100 Washington St #5B, Hempstead, NY 11550. **Business Addr:** 33 Front St Ste 306, Hempstead, NY 11550.

SWINTON, DAVID HOLMES
Educational administrator. **Personal:** Born Mar 18, 1943, New Haven, CT; son of Pearl Swinton and Morris Swinton; married Patricia Lewis Swinton; children: Olaniyan, Ayanna, Aisha, Malika, Omari, Akilah. **Educ:** New York University, BA, 1968; Harvard University, MA, 1971, PhD, 1975. **Career:** Harvard University, teaching fellow, 1970-71; City College of New York, lecturer, 1971-72; Black Economic Research Center, assistant director, research, 1971-73; WA Harriman College of Urban and Policy Science, assoc prof and director, Undergraduate Programs, 1973-78; The Urban Institute, director, Minorities and Social Policy Program, senior res associate, 1973-78; Clark College, director, Southern Center for Studies in Public Policy Program, professor, economics, 1981-87; Jackson State University, dean, School of Business, professor, economics, 1987-94; Benedict College, pres, 1994-. **Orgs:** Black Enterprise Board of Economist, 1990-; Tennessee Valley Authority, consultant, 1991-; Natl Urban League, economic advisor, 1980-; Capital Area Private Industry Council, board of directors, 1987-; Jackson Enterprise Center, training committee, chair, 1987-; Mississippi Business Hall of Fame, selection committee, 1989-; Review of Black Political Economy, editorial advisory board, 1974-; Economic Policy Institute, research council, 1986-. **Honors/Awds:** New York University, Phi Beta Kappa, Coat of Arms Society; Harvard University, Woodrow Wilson Fellowship, honorable mention, Ford Foundation Fellow, Graduate Prize Fellowship. **Special Achievements:** Writer, ''The Economic Status of African-Americans during the Reagan-Bush Era,'' The State of Black America, 1993; ''The Economic Status of African-Americans: Limited Ownership and Persis-

tent Inequality,'' The State of Black America, 1992; ''The Economic Status of African-Americans: Permanent Poverty and Inequality,'' The State of Black America, 1991; ''Racial Inequality and Reparations,'' The Wealth of Races, 1990; ''The Economic Status of Black Americans during the 1980's: A Decade of Limited Progress,'' The Economic Status of Black America, 1990. **Business Addr:** President, Benedict College, 1600 Harden St, Columbia, SC 29204, (803)256-4751.

SWINTON, LEE VERTIS
Attorney, legislator. **Personal:** Born Aug 9, 1922, Dardanelle, AR; married Grace Thompson. **Educ:** Pittsburg State Coll, AB 1948; Univ MO Kansas City, JD 1954-. **Career:** Kansas City, acting municipal ct judge 1963-64; MO, spl asst atty gen 1965-67; Jackson County, asst county counselor 1967-72; 9th Dist Kansas City MO, state sen 1980; Private Practice, atty. **Orgs:** Mem MO Jackson County Bar Assns; past sec Univ MO at Kansas City Law Alumni; vice pres Jackson County Bar Assn; past pres Kansas City NAACP 1960-67; past bd mem Uran League; YMCA; elder W Paseo Christian Ch; bd mem Freedom Inc. **Military Serv:** AUS 1942-45. **Business Addr:** 125 State Capitol, Jefferson City, MO 65101.

SWINTON, SYLVIA P.
Educator (retired), educational consultant. **Personal:** Born Oct 5, 1909, Hartsville, SC; married Toney Vance Swinton. **Educ:** Allen Univ, AB (Cum Laude) 1931; IN Univ Bloomington, MS Ed 1942, EdD 1956. **Career:** Barber-Scolia Coll, chair dept educ 1961-62; Morris Brown Coll, dir tchr educ 1966-67; Allen Univ, dir tchr educ 1967-73; Morris Coll, dir tchr edn1974-78, spec consult to pres 1978-,fed relations ofcr 1979-80, dir media center 1980-81; Allen Univ, spec consult to pres 1982-84, interim pres 1983-84; Morris Coll, prof emeritus/consultant. **Orgs:** Pres SCATE SC Assn Tchr Educ 1970-71; pres SRATE Southeastern Assn Tchr Educ 1971-72; pres SCIRA SC Intl Reading Assn 1974; life mem NEA, NAACP,NCNW. **Honors/Awds:** Allen Univ Alumni Award Allen Univ 1985; Reading Plaque SC State Coll; Allen Univ Athletic Hall of Fame; Living Legacy Award Natl Council of Negro Women; NY City Alumni Award; United Black Fund Award; Delta Sigma Theta, Great Teacher Award, 1992; Heritage Award, 1991. **Business Addr:** Prof Emerita, PO Box 61, Columbia, SC 29202-0061.

SWITZER, LOU
Business executive. **Personal:** Born Oct 12, 1948, Orangeburg, SC; married; children: Gregory, Rhonda. **Educ:** Pratt Inst Brooklyn NY, attended 1966-73. **Career:** The Switzer Group Inc, pres 1975-; LCL Desing Asso Inc NYC, partner 1973-75; WE Htton & Co NYC, asst dir of facilities 1971-73; Office Design Asso Inc & NYC, draftsman/designer 1970-71; Sherburne Asso Inc NYC, draftsman/designer 1966-70. **Orgs:** Member, Young President's Organization, 1989-; member, Peat Marwick Middle Market Advisory Board; member, New York Building Congress; member, Real Estate Board of New York. **Honors/Awds:** Entrepreneur of the Year, Natl Assn of Accountants, 1987; Interior Design Hall of Fame Award, 1993. **Business Addr:** Chairman, Chief Executive Officer, The Switzer Group, Inc., 535 5th Ave, Fl 11, New York, NY 10017-3610.

SWITZER, VERYL A.
Educator. **Personal:** Born Aug 6, 1932, Nicodemus, KS; married Fern N Stalnaker; children: Teresa, Veryl, Jr, Calvin. **Educ:** KS State U, 1954; Depaul U, grad work 1968-69; KS State U, MS 1974. **Career:** KS State Univ, dean for minority affairs special prgs 1973-; Minority & Cultural Programs KS State Univ, dir 1969-73; Chicago Public Schools, teacher 1959-69; Canadian, profl & football player 1958-60; Green Bay Packers, football player 1954-55. **Orgs:** Mem Faculty Senate Univ Loan Com; Univ Fair Practice & Housing Com; Phi Delta Kappa; Nat Assn of Student Personel Adminsitrs; mem bd Educ USD #383 Manhattan KS;cHMN KS Univ Athletic Counc. **Honors/Awds:** Recipient Numerous awards including Kappa Alpha Psi Achievement Award; all-armed forces football team; all-am first team NFL 1953; all-am second team 1951-52; NEA & AP. **Military Serv:** USAF 1st lt 1956-58. **Business Addr:** Holtz Hall KS State Univ, Manhattan, KS 66506.

SWOOPES, SHERYL
Professional basketball player. **Personal:** Born Mar 25, 1971; married Eric Jackson; children: Jordan. **Educ:** Texas Tech. **Career:** Houston Comets, forward, 1997-. **Honors/Awds:** NCAA Final Four Most Valuable Player, 1993; National Player of the Year, 1993; US Olympic Women's Basketball Team, Gold Medal, 1996. **Special Achievements:** First woman to have a Nike basketball shoe named after her, the Air Swoopes; had her Texas Tech jersey retired, 1994. **Business Addr:** Professional Basketball Player, Houston Comets, Two Greenway Plaza, Ste 400, Houston, TX 77046, (713)627-9622.

SWYGERT, H. PATRICK
Educational administrator. **Personal:** Born Mar 17, 1943, Philadelphia, PA; son of Gustina Huzzy and Leroy Huzzy; married Sonja E; children: Haywood Patrick Jr, Michael Branson. **Educ:** Howard Univ, AB History 1965, JD (cum laude) 1968. **Career:** Temple Univ School of Law, asst prof of law 1972-77; US Civil Serv Commiss, gen counsel 1977-79; Merit Systems Protection Bd, spec counsel, beginning 1979; Temple Univ School of Law, counsel 1980, prof of law, beginning 1982, exec vice pres admin; law clerk, Ch Judge William H. Hastie, Fed Ct of Appeals 1968-69; admin asst, Cong Charles B. Rangel, 1971-72; assoc Debevoise, Plimpton, New York, NY 1969-71; SUNY, Albany, president, 1990-95; Howard Univ, president, 1995-. **Orgs:** Mem bd of dir Wynnefield Residents Assn 1973-75; exec committee Public Interest Law Ctr of Philadelphia 1973-77, 1980-; exec comm Legal Careers Proj Amer Fed for Negro Affairs 1974-77, Minority Affairs Assn of Amer Law Schools 1974-77; vice chmn Public Serv Comm Philadelphia Bar Assn 1975, 1976; consult Univ Wide Affirm Action 1980; mem nominating comm United Way of SE PA 1981; apptd by Gov Robt P Casey as state rep on Bd of the Southeastern PA Transportation Authority; bd of dir, WHYY-TV and WHYY-FM; vice chmn, Philadelphia City Charter Revision Comm; Middle States Comm on Higher Educ; chr, New York State Special Commission on Educational Structure, Policies & Practices, 1993-94; chr, Summer Games Organizing Committee, Special Olympics New York, 1995. **Honors/Awds:** Commissioners Awd for Distinguished Serv 1978; Certificate of Appreciation HUD 1981; Black Law Students Awd Temple Univ School of Law Chap 1982; Pres Citation Natl Assoc for Equal Oppty in Higher Ed 1984, Outstanding Alumnus, Howard Univ, Washington DC, 1986; Jewish National Fund Tree of Life Award, 1994. **Business Addr:** President, Howard University, 2400 Sixth St NW, Washington, DC 20059.

SYKES, ABEL B., JR.
Educational administrator. **Personal:** Born Jun 1, 1934, Kansas City, KS; married Sylvia; children: Dawn, Daphne, Leslie. **Educ:** Univ of MO Kansas City, BA 1959; Univ of MO, MA 1960; San Diego State Coll Univ of CA, grad studies 1960-68; UCLA Grad Sch of Edn, 1968-71; Univ of CA LA, EdD 1971; Harvard Bus Sch, cert 1976. **Career:** O'Farrell Jr HS, instr 1960-64; San Diego Evening Coll, instr 1962-64; Grossmont Coll, instr 1962-68; Compton Comm Coll, dean instr 1968-69, pres/supt 1969-89; Kings River College, president; Lansing Community College, Lansing, MI, president 1989-. **Orgs:** American Assn of Community Colleges, chairman of board, 1975-76; American Council of Education, various leadership roles; Assn of Governing Boards, various leadership roles; American Assn of University Professors; American Historical Assn; Chairman of numerous college accreditation teams. **Honors/Awds:** China, Fulbright Scholar, 1986; Phi Delta Kappa, Educator of the Year, 1972; Sigma Pi Phi; Phi Delta Kappa. **Business Addr:** President, Lansing Community College, PO Box 40010, Lansing, MI 48901-7210.

SYKES, RAY
Business executive. **Personal:** Born in LeCompte, LA; divorced; children: Tracey, Raymonda, Ray Anthony. **Educ:** Attended, Santa Monica City Coll. **Career:** Douglass Aircraft, machinist; Jack in the Box Restaurant Los Angeles, owner; Superior Ford Minneapolis, pres/owner; Ray Sykes Buick Kingwood TX, president/owner. **Orgs:** Civil Service Commissioner City of Houston; exec bd of dirs Boy Scouts of Amer; bd of dir UNCF; vice pres Houston Buick Dealers Assoc; mem adv bd Sch of Business Texas Southern Univ. **Honors/Awds:** Houston Area Urban League Small Business Awd. **Military Serv:** AUS 1963-66; Purple Heart; Vietnam Veteran.

SYKES, ROBERT A.
Utility company executive. **Personal:** Born Dec 25, 1947, Gary, IN; son of Mary Campbell Sykes and Jasper Sykes; divorced. **Educ:** Fisk Univ, Nashville TN, BA Philosophy, 1969. **Career:** Natural Gas Pipeline Co of Amer, Chicago IL, employment compliance admin, 1970-75; Fermi Natl Accelerator Lab, Batavia IL, mgr EEO & community relations, 1975-78; General Mills, West Chicago IL, asst personnel mgr, 1978-79; Washington Gas Light Co, Springfield VA, vice pres human resources, 1979-. **Orgs:** American Gas Assn; American Society of Personnel Admin; American Assn of Blacks in Energy; Melwood Horticultural Training Center, president; Black Human Resources Network, founder. **Honors/Awds:** Elected to Phi Beta Kappa, 1969.

SYKES, VERNON LEE
Economist, state representative. **Personal:** Born Oct 2, 1951, Forrest City, AR; son of Valley Louise Walker Sykes and Walter Sykes Jr; married Barbara Ann, Dec 25, 1975; children: Stancy, Emilia. **Educ:** OH Univ Coll of Bus Admin, BBA, 1974; Kent State Univ, MPA, mgmt, 1985; Harvard Univ, Cambridge, MA, masters, public admin, 1986; Wright State Univ, Dayton, OH, MS, 1980; Univ of Akron, PhD, urban studies, currently. **Career:** Akron Bd of Ed, sub teacher 1974-75; UNCI-Econ Devel Program, sr mgmt spec 1975-76; Summit Cty Criminal Justice Commiss, planner Rsch & Eval 1976-79; Akron City Council, chmn, vice chmn, mem 1980-83; Univ of Akron, part time instr 1980-; Clarence Allen Realty, salesman; The Harvard Group; OH House of Rep, 44th house dist, state rep, 1983-; Univ of Akron, Akron, OH, instructor, economics, 1980-. **Orgs:** Interstate Coop, Energy & Environ, Ways & Means Reference, State Govt, Pay Equity Advisory Comm, Travel & Tourism, High Speed Rail Task Force, Job Training Coord Council; chmn Audit Committee, Recycle Energy Comm, Health & Social Svcs; vice chmn Housing & Urban Devel, Downtown Redevel; mem Parks & Recreation Comm, Finance Comm, Annexation Comm, Akron Summit/Medina Private Ind Council, Summit Cty Human Serv Advisory Comm, Mayor Roy Ray's Citizen's Financial Adv Comm, Western Econ Intl, Alpha Homes; vice pres Alpha Library Comm Inc, chmn Ed & Scholarship Comm Alpha Phi Alpha; dir The Harvard Group 1987-. **Military Serv:** USMC private 2 mos. **Home Addr:** 615 Diagonal Road, Akron, OH 44320. **Business Addr:** State Representative, Ohio House of Representative, 77 S High St, Riffe Ctr Bldg, Columbus, OH 43215.

SYKES, WILLIAM RICHARD, JR. (RICK)
Company executive. **Personal:** Born Jan 22, 1948, Saginaw, MI; son of Eleanor Wesley Sykes and William Richard Sykes; married Marguerite Irene Cain Sykes, Sep 16, 1978; children: James William Sykes. **Educ:** Delta Community College, Bay County, MI, 1970-71; Central Michigan University, Mt Pleasant, MI, BS, 1973, MA, 1980. **Career:** WNEM-TV, Saginaw, MI, production cameraman, 1973-75, reporter anchor, 1975-81, news mgr, 1981-82; WDIV-TV, Detroit, MI, sr assignment editor, 1982-90; Hermanoff and Associates, Farmington Hills, MI, vice pres, 1990-; Central Michigan University, associate prof, currently. **Orgs:** Advisory board member, Horizons Upward Bound Cranbrook, 1990; advisory trustee, Ronald McDonald Children's Charities, 1990; member, NAACP. **Honors/Awds:** Minority Achiever in Industry, YMCA of Metropolitan Detroit, 1984; National UPI Award for Spot News Coverage, Michigan UPI Award for Spot News Coverage, United Press International, 1981; Accredited member of Public Relations Society of America, 1994. **Military Serv:** US Army, cpl, 1968-69; Overseas Medals for service in Vietnam, 1969. **Business Addr:** Associate Professor, Central Michigan University, Mount Pleasant, MI 48859.

SYLER, M. RENE
TV news anchorwoman. **Personal:** Born Feb 17, 1963, Belleville, IL; daughter of F. Anne McDonald Syler and William Henry Syler. **Educ:** American River College, Sacramento, CA, 1981-83; Azusa Pacific University, Azusa, CA, 1984-85; California State University, Sacramento, CA, BA, Psychology, 1987. **Career:** KTVN-TV, Reno, NV, news reporter, 1988-89; KOLO-TV, Reno, NV, news anchor, 1989-90; WVTM-TV, Birmingham, AL, news anchor, 1990-. **Orgs:** Member, NAACP, 1988-; member, Northern Nevada Black Cultural Awareness Society, 1989-; member, National Black Journalists Association, 1988-; publicity committee, jr board, YWCA, 1990-. **Business Addr:** News Anchor, News Dept, WVTM-TV, Atop Red Mountain, Birmingham, AL 35202.

SYLVAS, LIONEL B.
Educational administrator. **Personal:** Born May 10, 1940, New Orleans, LA; son of Iona and Junius. **Educ:** Southern Univ, BS 1963; Univ of Detroit, MA 1971; Nova Univ, EdD 1975. **Career:** Ford Motor Co, indust rsch analy 1967-69, ed training spec 1969-71; Miami Dade Comm Coll, assoc acad dean 1971-74; Miami Dade Comm Coll, asst to pres 1974-77; Northern VA Comm Coll, campus provost. **Orgs:** Consult Southern Assoc of Coll & Schools Eval Team 1974-; mem advisory bd Black Amer Affairs, Natl School Volunteer Prog 1974-78; pres Southern Reg Couns 1977-88; field reader for Titles III & IV Office of Educ 1979-; mem advisory bd Amer Red Cross 1982-; consult advisory group VA Power Co 1983-87; panelist on the VA Commission of the Arts; mem Constitution Bicentennial Commiss VA. **Honors/Awds:** Outstanding Educator Miami Dade Comm Coll 1975. **Military Serv:** AUS 1st lt 1963-65. **Home Addr:** 6666 Old Blaksmith Drive, Burke, VA 22015. **Business Addr:** Campus Provost, Northern Virginia Comm Coll, 15200 Neabsco Mills Rd, Woodbridge, VA 22191-4006.

SYLVESTER, MELVIN R.
Educator. **Personal:** Born Mar 25, 1939, New Orleans, LA; son of Myrtle Howard Sylvester and John Sylvester; married Frances Modica; children: Lori Alaine, Kyle Eugene. **Educ:** Dillard Univ, BA 1961; Long Island Univ, MSLS 1966, MEd 1973. **Career:** Dillard Univ, circulation lib 1961-62; CW Post Lib, head circulation dept 1962-64; Long Island Univ B Davis Schwartz Lib, head serials records 1964-; full profssor 1988. **Orgs:** Faculty & chap adv Tau Kappa Epsilon 1965-; mem ALA, NYLA, Nassau Co Lib Assn; mem, N Amer Serials Group for Libraries, 1987-; mem Greater NY Metro Area Chap ACRL 1983-; sec Coll & Univ Div Nassau Co Lib Assn 1973-75; Martin Luther King Higher Educ Oppor Prog Adv Bd 1974-78; mem Lib Faculty Personnel Comm 1974-78; mem Melvil Dui Marching & Chowder Assn 1975-; rep CW Post Ctr Faculty Council 1974-78; adv bd Friendship House Glen Core NY 1975-78; Space Utilization Com CW Post Ctr 1975-78; mem Pre-Medical Comm CW Post 1984-; chmn Space Utilization Com 1977-78; mem Comm on the Handicapped Glen Cove Sch 1978-80; bd of dir Boy's Club at Lincoln House Glen Cove NY 1978-85, Day Care Head Start Ctr Glen Cove NY 1979-89; student affairs appeal comm CW Post Ctr 1979-82; mem 100 Black Men Nassau/Sulk Inc 1983-; Affirmative Action Task Force CW Post Ctr 1980-86, chairperson, 1984-86; mem, Lions Intl, 1983-; library bd of trust Glen Cove Public Library, 1984-93; chairperson, Instruction Committee, CW Post, 1986-88; Freshman Mentor Programm, CW Post 1987-; Bd of Dir, Alliance Counseling Center, 1986-89; mem, Career Advisor's

Group, CW Post, 1986-; Bd of Trustees, Nassau Library System, 1988-92; Campaign Committee & Youth & Family Services Panel of United Way of Long Island, 1988-89; mem Legislative Committee of Long Island Resources Council Inc (for libraries), 1988-93; served on Univ Study Group V for Long Island Univ LIU Plan, 1988; mem Advisory bd, Nassau County Dept of Mental Health, 1988-92; LILRC Lobbyist for Libraries, 1990-92; GRASP-Committee CW Post, 1991-. **Honors/Awds:** Contr screenings Lib Journal & Sch Lib Journal 1971-78; printed publs, ''Negro Periodicals in the US 1826-1960'' an annotated bibliography; ''A Library Handbook to Basic Source Materials in Guidance & Counseling'' 1973; Faculty Recog Awd Alpha Phi Alpha 1979; Serv Awd Glen Cove Public Schools Comm on the Handicapped 1980; Public Serv Awd Malik Sigma Psi 1981; Twenty-Year Metal, Service and Recognition, LIU, 1984; Serv Awd African Student Convocation 1986; Student Govt Assoc Awd for Serv to Students CW Post Campus 1986; Nassau Library System Award of Merit as Trustee, 1992; Nassau County Exec Citation as retired trustee, 1992; HEOP 25th Anniversary Service recognition Award, 1994; Newsmaker: Newsday, LI and Glencove Record Pilot, as curator of history exhibits from 1985-94, CW Post Campus. **Special Achievements:** Publications at www.liunet.edu/cwis/cwp/.

SYLVESTER, ODELL HOWARD, JR.
Law enforcement offical (retired), association executive (retired). **Personal:** Born Nov 3, 1924, Dallas, TX; son of Parthenia Wakefield-Sylvester and Odell H Sylvester Sr; married Dorothy Lanning; children: Jennifer, Jon. **Educ:** Univ Of CA, BDs 1948; Univ of So CA, MPA 1974; Harvard U, post grad. **Career:** Berkeley CA, apptd Chief of Police 1977; Oakland Police Dept Bur of Investigation, comdg ofcr 1971-77, dep chief 1971, capt 1963, lt 1961, sgt 1957, patrolman 1949; retired Berkley chief of police 1981; pres Urban Mgmt Assoc 1981-90. **Orgs:** Participated in devel of Oakland Police Dept New Careers Prgm; Model Cities Intern Prgm; dir Bay Area Minor Recruit Proj; Am Soc for Pub Admin; CA Peace Ofcrs Assn; Intl Assn of Chiefs of Police; exec com Nat Orgn of Black Law Enforcement Exec; president, board of directors Oakland Boys & Girls Club; bd of Gov Goodwill Ind; Lake Merritt Breakfast Club; Lions Intl Serv Club; Men of Tomorrow; Kiwanis Intl Serv Club; Oakland Central YMCA; Family Serv Agy; Nat Conf of Christ & Jews; NAACP; Alpha Phi Alpha; Sigma Pi Phi. **Honors/Awds:** Awds for Outst Serv to Oakland Comm 1968, 1969, 1971, 1976, 1981, 1985, 1987, 1989, 1990; Oakland Black Officers Association, Lifetime Achievement Award, 1992. **Home Addr:** 6151 Ridgemont Dr, Oakland, CA 94619.

SYLVESTER, PATRICK JOSEPH
Educator. **Educ:** St Francis Xavier Univ, Canada, BA 1960; Univ of New Brunswick, Canada, MA, 1962; Univ PA, MA 1967; Bryn Mawr College, PhD 1973. **Career:** West Chester Univ, prof econ. **Business Addr:** Professor of Economics & Finance, West Chester Univ, Dept of Business & Econ, West Chester, PA 19380.

SYPHAX, BURKE
Physician. **Personal:** Born Dec 18, 1910, Washington, DC; son of Nellie Smith Burke and William Custis Syphax; married Sarah Juanita Jamerson Syphax, Jul 1, 1939; children: Michael Burke, Gregory Custis, Stephen Wyatt. **Educ:** Howard U, BS, 1932; Howard Univ Med Sch, MD 1936. **Career:** Howard Univ Coll of Med, officer, 1936-, prof surg 1970-, chf div gen surg 1951-70, chm, dept surg, 1957-70, asso prof 1950-58, asst prof surg 1944-50, instr surg 1942-44, asst in surg 1940-41. **Orgs:** Kappa Pi Frat; Alpha Omega Alpha Hon Soc; member, National Medical Assn; member, Soc Surg Alimentary Tract; Alpha Omega Alpha; Alpha Kappa Alpha; Alpha Phi Alpha. **Honors/Awds:** Outst Alumnus Awd; NY Alumni Assn; Student Cncl Awd; 1st Disting Prof Awd 1974; Rockefeller Fellow, Strong Meml Hosp, Univ of Rochester 1941-42; Honorary Doctor of Science in Medicine, Howard Univ, 1985; Certification in Surgery, American Board of Surgery, 1944; Fellowship, American College of Surgery, 1957. **Home Addr:** 1370 Hamilton St NW, Washington, DC 20011. **Business Addr:** Professor, Howard University College of Medicine and Hospital, 2041 Georgia Ave, Rm 4-B-34, Washington, DC 20060.

T

T, MR. See TERO, LAWRENCE.

TABOR, LANGSTON
Entrepreneur. **Career:** Tabor Electric, Seattle, WA, owner, currently. **Orgs:** Electrical Code Revision Committee, co-chairman. **Honors/Awds:** Northwest Entrepreneur of the Year Award, 1991. **Business Addr:** President, Tabor Electric, 1938 Fairview Ave, Seattle, WA 98102, (206)329-5337.

TABOR, LILLIE MONTAGUE
State employee. **Personal:** Born May 13, 1933, Marianna, AR; married Norman. **Educ:** Univ MI, MSW 1961; Western MI U, BA Tuskegee Inst. **Career:** Detroit, nursery sch tchr 1951-53; Bur Soc Aid Detroit, soc worker 1954-57; Oak Co Childrens Svc, child welfare worker 1957-60; MI, psyciat soc worker 1960-62; Dept Soc Svc, admin 1965-69; MI Civil Serv Lansing, dir new careers 1969-72; Soc Serv Region 9 Wayne Co Consult Serv State MI, dep dir 1963-65; Family Life Educ Merrill Palmer Inst Detroit, asso prof 1968-71; Univ MI, field instr soc 1972-74. **Orgs:** Child Welfare League Am reg elected com mem 1964-68; bd mem Neighborhood Serv Org 1969-; adv com Vista Marie Sch 1970-; NASW; NAACP; Nat Council Alcoholism Delegate 1970, White House Conf Children; Spl Review Successful Program 1970; Nat Inst New Careers Free press Frank Angelo Interesting Action People 1971. **Business Addr:** MI State Plaza, 1200 6 St, Detroit, MI 48226.

TABORN, JOHN MARVIN
University professor. **Personal:** Born Nov 7, 1935, Carrier Mills, IL; married Marjorie Campbell; children: John Gregory, Craig Marvin. **Educ:** Southern IL Univ, BS 1956; Univ of IL, MA 1958; Univ of MN, PhD 1970; Harvard Business Sch, Mgmt Certificate 1971. **Career:** Minneapolis Public Schools, psychologist 1966-70; Univ of MN, youth develop consultant 1971-73; J Taborn Assocs Inc, pres 1979-; Univ of MN, assoc prof 1973-. **Orgs:** Mem Natl Assoc of Black Psychologists 1970-; professional mem Amer Psychological Assoc 1972-; consultant State of MN 1973-82; bd of dirs Minneapolis Urban League 1974-80; consultant Honeywell Inc 1981-84; mem Sigma Pi Phi Frat 1983-; consultant Natl Assoc Black Police 1984-, State of CA Education 1986-. **Honors/Awds:** Bush Leadership Fellow 1970; Monitor of the Year Monitors Minneapolis 1980; numerous scholarly publications. **Military Serv:** USNR capt 1959-; Natl Defense, Armed Forces Reserve, Navy Expeditionary. **Business Addr:** Assoc Professor, Univ of Minnesota, 808 Social Science Bldg, 167 19th Ave So, Minneapolis, MN 55455.

TALBERT, MELVIN GEORGE
Cleric. **Personal:** Born Jun 14, 1934, Clinton, LA; son of Florence George Talbert and Nettles Talbert; married Ethelou Douglas, Jun 3, 1961; children: Evangeline Violet. **Educ:** Southern Univ, Baton Rouge LA, BA, 1959; Gammon Theological Seminary, Atlanta GA, MD, 1962. **Career:** Boyd Chapel/ United Methodist Church, Jefferson TN, pastor, 1960-61; Wesley United Methodist Church, Los Angeles CA, assoc pastor, 1961-64; Hamilton United Methodist Church, Los Angeles CA, pastor, 1964-67; Southern California-Arizona Conf, Long Beach CA, district supt, 1968-73; General Board of Discipleship, Nashville TN, gen secy, 1973-80; United Methodist Church, Seattle WA, bishop, 1980-88; United Methodist Church, San Francisco CA, bishop, 1988—. **Orgs:** NAACP, Advisory Committee of Mayor of Seattle, member of board of Seattle United Way; pres, Natl Coun of Churches; member, Exec Comm, Central Comm, Finance Comm of World Coun of Churches. **Honors/Awds:** National Achievement Award, National Assn of Black Women, 1965, Doctor of Divinity, Huston-Tillston College, 1972; LLD, Univ of Pugent Sound, 1987. **Business Addr:** Bishop, San Francisco Area, United Methodist Church, PO Box 467, 330 Ellis St, Suite 301, San Francisco, CA 94101.

TALBERT, TED
Television producer. **Career:** WDIV-TV, producer, currently. **Honors/Awds:** Emmy Award. **Special Achievements:** Producer: television program on the history of Detroit-area African-Americans in the legal profession, 1991; ''From Randolph to the Rouge: Black in the Union Movement,'' 1992. **Business Addr:** Producer, WDIV-TV, 550 W Lafayette, Detroit, MI 48226, (313)222-0444.

TALBOT, ALFRED KENNETH, JR.
Educator. **Personal:** Born Sep 1, 1916, New York, NY; son of Sylvia L S Talbot; married Hazel Grace Greene (deceased). **Educ:** Hampton Univ VA, BS 1940, MA Educ Admin 1949; New York U, 1953-57; George Peabody Coll, 1955; Univ of KS, 1965; Coll of William & Mary VA, EdD 1985. **Career:** Laboratory School Hampton Univ VA, critic teacher/supv student teachers 1946-47; Carver Elem School Loudoun Co Public School VA, principal 1947-55; Bruton Hgts, School Williamsburg Jas City Co Pub School VA, asst prin 1955-63, prin 1963-67; Williamsburg Jas City Co Public School VA, supr elem school 1968-70 ; Salisbury State Coll, prof of sociology. **Orgs:** Mem Governor's Comm Study Merit Pay for Tchrs Commonwealth of VA 1964-66; mem bd of dir Williamsburg, VA Area Day Care Ctr Williamsburg Jas City Co Gov 1966-70; chmn bd dir VA Tchrs Assn (VTA) 1964-66, pres 1962-64. **Honors/ Awds:** Plaque for Disting Serv as Chmn Bd Dir VA Tchrs Assn 1964-66, Plaque for Disting Serv as Pres 1962-64; Plaque for Disting Serv & Leadership as Pres VA Congress of Colored Parents-Tchrs 1955-59. **Business Addr:** Professor of Sociology, Salisbury State University, College & Camden Aves, Salisbury, MD 21801.

TALBOT, DAVID ARLINGTON ROBERTS, SR.
Educator. **Personal:** Born Jan 25, 1916, Georgetown, Guyana; son of Maud Huberta Roberts Talbot and Dr David Patterson Talbot; married Phyllis S Willis, Jun 19, 1946; children: David A Jr, James P, Eric M. **Educ:** Queens Coll of Guyana, Oxford & Cambridge School, certificate 1934; Morris Brown Coll, BA (w/honors) 1939; Columbia Univ, MA 1951; Univ of AR, EdD 1966. **Career:** Morris Brown Coll, instructor 1939-40; City of New York, social worker 1947-51; Shorter Coll, prof & admin 1952-57; Univ of AR Pine Bluff, assoc dir of student personnel 1957-60, dean of students/prof 1960-68; East TX State Univ, prof of counseling & guidance 1968-86, dir of counseling ctr 1974-82, special asst to pres 1982-87, prof emeritus 1987-, educational consultant, 1987-. **Orgs:** Mem Omega Psi Phi 1936-; former treas Natl Assoc of Personnel Workers 1967-70; natl vice pres Society of Ethnic & Special Studies 1973-90; mem Kiwanis 1985-; vice chair, Hunt County Family Service; mem, Texas State Board of Examiners of Marriage and Family Therapists. **Honors/Awds:** Hon DD Jackson Theol Seminary 1960; DHL Morris Brown Coll 1976; Outstanding Alumnus Morris Brown Coll 1985; Centennial Awd Professor Shorter Coll 1986; Sadie Yancy Award, National Assn of Personnel Works, 1987; Spirit of Mayo Award, ETSU, 1992. **Special Achievements:** Author, Invocations Upon Divergent Occasions. **Military Serv:** AUS 1943-45, Technical Sergeant, Bronze Star Medal 1945. **Home Addr:** 3011 Tanglewood, Commerce, TX 75428. **Business Addr:** Professor Emeritus, Counseling and Guidance, East Texas State Univ, Commerce, TX 75428.

TALBOT, GERALD EDGERTON
State official (retired). **Personal:** Born Oct 28, 1931, Bangor, ME; son of Arvella McIntyre Talbot and W Edgerton Talbot; married Anita J Cummings Talbot, Jul 24, 1954; children: Sharon Renee, Regina L Philips, Rachel A Ross, Robin M Bradley. **Educ:** Diploma lessons in printing 1970; ME State Apprenticeship Council, cert of apprenticeship for printing 1972. **Career:** Maine State Legis 1972 1974 1976; Portland Savings Bank, corporator 1975-; Guy Gannett Publ Co, state rep. **Orgs:** Mem City Mgrs Policy Adv Comm 1979; adv council State of ME Dept Manpower Affairs 1979; mem State Bd of Educ 1980; founder Black Educ & Cultural History Inc 1980; mem Natl Assn of State Bds of Educ (GAC) 1981; mem Educ Comm Task Force on Sex Equality 1982; Congressman McKernan's Task Force on Children Youth & Families 1983; mem Maine Congressional Citizens Educ Adv Comm 1983; mem State Bd of Educ 1980, v chmn 1981, chmn 1983-84; corporator ME Med Ctr 1984; mem Gr Portland Federated Labor Council, Portland Typographical Union Local 66; life mem NAACP; mem Dem City Comm; mem ME Assn Blk Prog, ME Conf on Human Serv; mem, Southern ME Area Agency on Aging, 1986; bd, trust ME Vocational Tech Inst, 1986; bd dir, Portland United Way Inc, 1986; ME Project on Southern Africa, 1985; bd mem, USSelive Service System, Maine, 1987; mem, Veterans for Peace, 1988; mem, Community Task Force on Bias Crime, 1989; mem, bd of visitors, The Edmund S Muskie Institute of Public Policy, Univ of Southern ME, 1990; AARP, national minority spokesperson, 1992; National Black Leadership Initiative on Cancer, 1992; ALANA Conference Bd; US Comm on Civil Rights, ME; Tribute to Black Women of Maine Awards Banquet, sponsor, 1992. **Honors/Awds:** First black elected to ME Legislature; Golden Pin Awd 1967, Leadership Awd 1984, Twenty Years 1964-84, NAACP Portland Br; Hall of Fame Cert Laurel MS NAACP 1970-73; Outstanding Ser Comm & State Bangor NAACP 1974; Viva Cert of Recog & Appreciation 1974; Cert of Appreciation Natl Assn of Human Rights Workers 1979; Right-On Brother of Yr Awd; Cert of Appreciation ME Chap Multiple Sclerosis; Jefferson Awd Amer Inst for Public Serv WCSH-TV 1980; Black History Maker of ME Awd 1984; ME State Bd of Ed Awd 1984; Martin Luther King Award, Maine Martin Luther King Commission 1988; 1st Place Certificate of Excellence, Maine Multicultural Festival 1987; Friendship Award, Portland West Neighborhood Planning Council 1989; Certificate of Achievement, Peoples Regional Opportunity Program, 1990; Univ of Southern Maine, DHL, 1995; Matlovich Award, 1990. **Military Serv:** US Army pfc 1953-56. **Home Addr:** 132 Glenwood Ave, Portland, ME 04103, (207)772-6098.

TALBOT, JAMES PATTERSON, SR.
Insurance company executive. **Personal:** Born Nov 21, 1950, New York; son of Phyllis S Willis Talbot and David A Talbot Sr; married Cassaundra; children: James Jr, John David, Joshua. **Educ:** East Texas State Univ, BSc 1973. **Career:** G L Rutley & Assoc Insurance, sales 1975-78; Chapman Assocs/Protective Life, sales 1978-83; J P Talbot Insurance, pres/owner 1982-; Professional Sports Management Inc, pres/CEO. **Orgs:** Mem Dallas Assn of Life Underwriters 1979-; Dallas Estate Planning Council 1981-; registered representative GR Phelps 1985-; mem Dallas/Ft Worth Minority Business Devel Council 1986-. **Honors/Awds:** Mem Million Dollar Round Table several years; National Achievement Award, numerous times, National Quality Award, numerous times, National Association of Life Underwriters. **Business Phone:** (817)430-4996.

TALBOT, THEODORE A.
Educator. **Personal:** Born Dec 22, 1923, Guyana; married Dorothy. **Educ:** Coll of Lib Arts, BA 1949; Sch of Journalism Syracuse U, MA 1951; Baylor U, TX A&M U. **Career:** Texas State Technical Institute, vice president, secretary, board of regents; Paul Quinn College, Division of Humanities, chairman; Prairie View A&M College, Dept of English, associate professor. **Orgs:** Mem bd dir Am Tech Educ Assn; Nat Council of Tchrs of English; Conf of Coll Com Comm; S-contrl Modern Language Assn; So Council for the Humanities Monern Language Assn; Coll Language Assn; mem Edwards Chapel ANE Ch;

Alpha Phi Alpha Frat; Rotary Internatl; Minority Contractors Assn of Waco Bd Dirs; Heart of TX Council of Govt; Mclennan Co Human Serv Delivery Sys Prog Hon Consul for State of TX Coop Republic of Guyana. **Business Addr:** TX State Tech Inst, Waco, TX 76705.

TALIAFERRO, ADDISON
Government official. **Personal:** Born Dec 20, 1936, Springfield, MA; married Gayle E Wanagar; children: Cheryl, Addison Jr. **Educ:** Lincoln Univ, AB 1959; Columbia univ Sch of Pub Health, MPH. **Career:** NJ State Dept of Health, chief cancer registry. **Orgs:** Mem Upper Freehold Sch Bd; mem Mercer Co Comm Action Prog; mem Upper Freehold PTA, Upper Freehold Welfare Dir; chmn Check Mate Inc; mem Monmouth Co CAP 1983-84, treas CAP prog 2 yrs; pres PTA 1970-72. **Honors/Awds:** First black elected to Bd of Educ 1974; first vice pres, pres Bd of Educ 1975-76. **Business Addr:** Chief Cancer Registry, NJ State Dept of Health, Box 1540, CN 360, Trenton, NJ 08625.

TALIAFERRO, GEORGE
Educational administrator (retired), athlete. **Personal:** Born Jan 8, 1927, Gates, TN; married Viola; children: Linda T, Renee, Donna, Terri. **Educ:** IN Univ Bloomington, BS 1951; Howard Univ Washington DC 1962. **Career:** Lafayette Square Community Center, Baltimore, dir 1957-59; Prisoners Aid Assn Shaw Residence DC, caseworker 1959-66; United Planning Org DC, dir com action progs 1966-68; Dico Corp Martin-Marietta Corp Washington DC, vice pres/general mgr 1968-70; IN Univ, special asst to pres, beginning 1972; Morgan State Coll, dean of students 1970-72; Couns Center & Drug Abuse Authority of MD, exec dir 1970; Big Ten Athletic Conf Spl Adv Comm, chmn 1974-. **Orgs:** Mem Kappa Alpha Psi 1948-; bd of dirs Baltimore Big Bros & Druid Hill YMCA 1962-68; pres & founder Monroe Co Big Bros/Big Sisters 1973-. **Honors/Awds:** Recipient All-Am All Big Ten & All State Awards Coll Football Writers & Coaches 1945-48; Football Hall of Fame; Indiana University Hall of Fame, 1992. **Military Serv:** AUS corpl 1946-47.

TALIAFERRO, NETTIE HOWARD
Physician. **Personal:** Born Jan 1, 1944, Washington, DC; children: Carole, Kermit II. **Educ:** George Washington U, BSMT 1965; Howard U, MD 1974. **Career:** Boston City Hosp Boston, MA, intern/residency in internal med 1974-77; Mt Auburn Hosp Cambridge, MA, active staff 1972-; Santa Maria Hosp Cambridge, MA, courtesy staff 1977-; Private Practice Cambridge, MA, physician/internal med 1977-. **Orgs:** Clinical instructor in med Harvard Univ Coll of Med 1977-; mem Nat Med Assn; mem New England Med Soc; life mem NAACP S Middlesex Chap; mem, American Women Medical Assn, Massachusetts Branch; Massachusetts Med Society; Massachusetts Med Society. **Honors/Awds:** Alpha Omega Alpha Med Honor Soc. **Business Addr:** Physician, 300 Mt Auburn St, Ste 311, Cambridge, MA 02238, (617)661-9744.

TALIAFERRO, VIOLA J.
Judge. **Personal:** Born Sep 13, 1928, Evington, VA; daughter of Mary Elizabeth Claiborne Jones and Richard H Jones Sr; married George Taliaferro, Nov 24, 1950; children: Linda T Harvey, Renee A Buckner, Donna T Rutherford, Terri T Pendleton. **Educ:** Virginia State College, BS, 1947; Morgan State University, attended, 1964-65; Johns Hopkins University, MLA, 1969; Indiana University, JD, 1977. **Career:** Baltimore Department of Welfare, social worker, 1957-63; Baltimore Public Schools, teacher, department head, 1965-72; attorney, self-employed, 1973-89; Monroe Circuit Court, magistrate, 1989-95, judge, 1995-. **Orgs:** Indiana State Bar Association, delegate, lawyer discipline commission, bylaws committee chairperson, 1977-; American Bar Association, delegate, 1992-; Rotary International, 1989-; Boy Scouts of America, board member, 1992-; Bloomington Parks & Recreation, commissioner, 1992-; Indiana State Bar Association House of Delegates, chairman, 1989-90; Indiana Continuing Legal Education Forum, faculty, 1992. **Honors/Awds:** Indiana Bar Foundation, Fellow, 1989; American Bar Foundation, Fellow, 1990; Kentucky Colonel, 1989. **Special Achievements:** Published, Delinquency: Detention, Waiver, Disposition, from Indiana Continuing Education Forum, May 1992. **Business Addr:** Judge, Monroe Circuit Court, 301 N College Ave, Bloomington, IN 47404, (812)349-2629.

TALL, BOOKER T.
Educator. **Personal:** Born Dec 12, 1928, Hooker Bend, TN; son of Julia MacFulton and Booker T. Tall, Sr; married Carolyn; children: Reginald, Bruce, Victor, Christopher, Michael. **Educ:** Akron Univ, BA 1952; Case Western Reserve Univ, MA 1956; Oxford Univ England, grad study 1953; Harvard Univ, Management, 1977; Case Western Reserve, Weatherhead School of Management, 1984. **Career:** Congressman Louis Stokes, admin asst 1978-80; Cuyahoga Comm Coll Afro-Amer Studies, dept chmn; Urban Studies, dir 1968-70; Cuyahoga Comm Coll, instructor 1956-68; Akron Urban League, 1947-52, founder OIC; Cleveland 1st Black Minority Business Directory, published 1971-73; 1st Black Studies Directory, published 1972; Cit Participation Handbook, published 1972; Mt Pleasant Comm Council, pres; Minor Book Publishing Co, pres; US Conference of Mayors, Washington DC, business consultant, 1984; President Minority Franchise Assn, Cleveland Ohio, 1989. **Orgs:** Bd mem Bronze Marker Program for Distinguished Black Amer; mem N Cent Accredidation Team; mem NAACP; Greater Cleveland Cit League; VP Ludlow Assn; mem Nat Advisory Bd Assn for Study Afro-Amer Life & History; VP State of OH Assn for Study of Afro-Amer Life & History; bd mem Nigerian Sister City Program; mem, President's Bush Task Force/Inner Circle, 1989; pres, Western Reserve Historical Society, 1970-89; Black Archives Auxillary. **Honors/Awds:** Man Yr Urban League 1973; Omicron Delta Men Leadership Award 1952; Adv Yr Cuyahoga Comm Coll 1973; Good Neighbor Year 1974; recipient Alpha Fraternity Comm Serv Award 1976; publr "Black Settlers in Cleveland" 1976; Achvmnt Award Fed Exec Bd Minority Business 1980; author of numerous articles on planning & urban revitalization; Life Achievement Award, Black Professional Assn, 1987; History of Black Entrepreneur, Cleveland Ohio, 1988; State of Black Cleveland 1988 Urban League, 1989. **Military Serv:** Mil sgt 1954-56.

TALLEY, CLARENCE, SR.
Educator, clergy. **Personal:** Born Jun 12, 1951, Pineville, LA; son of Susie Edmond Newman and Albert Talley; married Carolyn Westley Talley, Nov 18, 1972; children: Clarence Jr, Crystal Ann. **Educ:** Southern University, Baton Rouge, LA, 1973; Louisiana State University, Baton Rouge, LA, 1975; Houston Graduate School of Theology, Houston, TX, 1991. **Career:** Southern University, Baton Rouge, LA, instructor, 1974; Prairie View A & M Univ, Prairie View, TX, professor of art & architecture, 1975-. **Orgs:** National Conference of Artist; Texas Sculpture Association; Texas Society of Sculptors, Texas Association of School Arts. **Honors/Awds:** 2nd Place Acrylic, Southwest Arts Society, University of Texas Institute of Texas Culture, 1985; Purchase Prize, 6th Annual Black Artist Exh First Louisville Bank, Kentucky, 1984; Honorable Mention, 1984 Regional Black Artist Ex George W Carver Museum, Austin, TX, 1984; 2nd Runner Up 1983 Regional Black Artist Ex George W Carver Museum, Austin, TX, 1983; Best of Show, Professional Division, Waller County Fair, 1985. **Home Addr:** 21119 Briarmeadow, Prairie View, TX 77446. **Business Addr:** Professor, Dept of Art and Architecture, Prairie View A&M University, Box 2134, Prairie View, TX 77446.

TALLEY, CURTISS J.
Administrator. **Personal:** Born Jul 16, 1939, Holly Springs, MS; son of Jessie Mae Rucker Draper and Curtis Talley; married Corene Davidson Talley, Dec 21, 1968; children: Chrystal DaNise, Curtiss Carlos, Chemberly D. **Educ:** Kilroe Coll of Sacred Heart, Honesdale, PA, BA, 1964; Memphis State Univ, Memphis, TN, 1982; Loyola Univ, New Orleans, LA, MPS, 1988; Shelby State Community Coll, Memphis, TN, 1990. **Career:** Cadet School, Holly Springs, MS, teacher, coach, 1966-72; Prudential Ins Co, Memphis, TN, district agent, 1972-75; Thomas J Lipton Co, Inc, Memphis, TN, sales rep, 1975-77; Wohl Shoe Co, Memphis, TN, suprv, 1977-78; St Joseph Church, Holly Springs, MS, Christian social worker, 1978-81; Catholic Diocese, Memphis, TN, administrator, dir, 1981-. **Orgs:** Mem, 4th deg, Knights of St Peter Claver, 1984-; mem, Serra Club, 1987-; mem, Natl Assn of Black Cath Admin, 1990-; mem, Natl Black Catholic Clergy Caucus, 1987; mem, Midtown Mental Health Assn Advisory Bd, 1990; Aloysius Home Inc, AIDS Hospice, 1992; St Peter Home for Children, interreligious affairs professional committee, 1992; UT Medical Center, volunteer chaplain, 1992. **Honors/Awds:** Volunteer in Prison Ministry, Shelby County Correctional Ctr, 1986-89; adv bd, Baptist Hospital Volunteer Advisory Bd, 1988; Teacher/Worker, St Joseph School, 1985. **Special Achievements:** Ordained Deacon, Catholic Diocese of Memphis, 1978. **Home Addr:** 1515 Waverly, Memphis, TN 38106.

TALLEY, DARRYL VICTOR
Professional football player. **Personal:** Born Jul 10, 1960, Cleveland, OH. **Educ:** West Virginia Univ, received physical educ degree. **Career:** Buffalo Bills, linebacker, 1983-. **Honors/Awds:** Linebacker, Sporting News College All-America Team, 1982; played in AFC Championship Game, post-1988 season. **Business Addr:** Professional Football Player, Buffalo Bills, One Bills Dr, Orchard Park, NY 14127-2296.

TALLEY, JAMES EDWARD
Educator. **Personal:** Born Aug 22, 1940, Spartanburg, SC; married Barbara J Goins; children: James Carlton, Deidra Sharee. **Educ:** Livingstone Coll, BS 1963; Converse Coll, 1968; SC State, 1972. **Career:** Bryson HS, teacher, coach 1967-68; Carver HS, teacher, coach 1968-70; WSPA-TV,TV show host 1973-75; WKDY Spartanburg, radio show host 1975-78; Wofford Coll, football coach; Spartanburg HS, teacher of math, currently. **Orgs:** Mem LD Barksdale Sickle Cell Found 1975-85; chmn Bethlehem Ctr Trustees 1978-81; chmn Cammie F Clagget Scholarship 1979-85; basileus Epsilon Nu Chap of Omega 1980-82; councilman City of Spartanburg 1981-85; exec comm Spartanburg Devel Cncl. **Honors/Awds:** Man of the Year Mt Moriah Baptist Church 1979; Omega Man of the Year Epsilon Nu Chap of Omega 1980; Human Relation Awd Spartanburg Cty Ed Assoc 1983. **Military Serv:** USN radioman 2 4 yrs; Honorman, Navy Co 473 Man of the Year 1963-67; Honorable Discharge 1967. **Home Addr:** 787 N. Vernon, Spartanburg, SC 29303.

TALLEY, JOHN STEPHEN
Educator. **Personal:** Born Dec 12, 1930, Sterlington, LA; married Furman; children: Kimberly, Stephen. **Educ:** Grambling Coll, BS 1954; Columbia, MA 1958; professional dipolma 1964. **Career:** Grambling Coll Nursery School, teacher 1954-56; dir teacher 1956-63; Coll teacher 1964-66; coordinator head start staff training progs 1966; Queens Coll Early Childhood Educ Center Flushing, head teacher, supervising teacher 1963-64; State of LA Office Econ Opportunity Grambling, regl training officer 1966-67; Grambling Coll, part-time teacher; Lincoln Parish, part-time supr kindergarten progs; S Central Regional Educ Lab Little Rock, cons; SW Region Office Child Devel, intl. **Orgs:** Mem LA Educ Assn; Assn for Childhood Edn; Intl So Assn for Children Under Six; Nat Assn for Educ Young Children; Am Assn Univ Profs; Am Home Econs Assn; Day Care & Child Devel Council Am; mem Alpha Kappa Alpha. **Business Addr:** 360 W 13th St, Indianapolis, IN 46204.

TALLEY, MICHAEL FRANK, SR.
Attorney. **Personal:** Born Aug 14, 1945, Chesterfield, SC; son of Rosena A Talley and Frank Talley Sr; married Dianne Wright, May 24, 1980; children: Michanna, Michael F Jr. **Educ:** South Carolina State College, BA, 1966; Howard University, MA, 1971, JD, 1976; Columbia University, graduate studies, 1973. **Career:** Wilson High School, South Carolina, French teacher, 1966-69; Howard University, french laboratory instructor, 1969-70; South Carolina State College, French instructor, 1970-71; Tennessee State University, french instructor, 1969-70, 1971-73; Presidential Clemency Board, the White House, staff attorney, 1975; Howard University, French laboratory instructor, 1973-76; Greenville Technical College, business law instructor, 1984-90; Michael F Talley, attorney, 1977-. **Orgs:** South Carolina Bar Association, 1976-92; National Bar Association, 1985-92; South Carolina Black Lawyers Association, 1977-92; Legal Services for Western Carolina, former mem board of directors, 1978-82; Kappa Alpha Psi, 1965-92; Howard University Alumni Association, 1971-92. **Honors/Awds:** South Carolina Bar Pro Bono Program, Certificate of Apreciation, 1991; Legal Services for Western Carolina, Plaque of Appreciation, 1981; NAACP Legal Defense Fund, Earl Warren Legal Fellowship, 1973-76; South Carolina State College, Gamma Mu Honor Society, 1966. **Special Achievements:** Premise liability case of Assault torture victim, "Daniel vs Days Inn of America," 356 South Eastern Reporter, 2d, 129, (SC App 1987); employment discrimination case, "Glymph vs Spartanburg General Hospital", 783 Federal Reporter, 2d, 476 (Court of Appeals, 4th Cir 1986); numerous landmark trials; Reapportionment voting rights case, SC NAACP et al vs Riley Governor or SC et al, 533 Federal Supplement Reporter 1178, 1982. **Home Addr:** 204 Boling Rd, Greenville, SC 29611, (803)295-0011. **Business Addr:** Attorney, 206 Green Ave, Greenville, SC 29611, (803)233-6229.

TALLEY, WILLIAM B.
Educator. **Personal:** Born Sep 22, 1955, Sumter, SC; son of Charles Winslow and Louise Bultmon Talley; married Tselate Betre Talley, Jul 27, 1993; children: Massie Winslow. **Educ:** South Carolina State, BS, 1976, MS, 1978; Southern Illinois Univ, PhD, 1986 . **Career:** State of South Carolina, counselor, trainee, 1976-78, vocational rehab coun selor, 1978-80, disability examiner, 1980-82; State of Louisiana, LSU, educator, 1986-88; PSI Inc, counselor, 1988-90; Univ of Maryland, Eastern Shore, educator, dir of rehabilitation services; Coppin State College, asst prof, currently. **Orgs:** Natl Rehab Assn, 1978-; Amer Asn of Counseling & Devt, 1982-; NAACP , 1973-; Alpha Phi Alpha, vp, Delta Omicron Lambda Chapter, 1994-; Univ of MD-E astern Shore Faculty Assembly, chair, 1993-; MD Rehab Counseling Assn, chair, m em comm, 1994-; Assn of Black Psychologists, 1988-; Amer Personnel & Guidance A ssn, 1984-; Natl Assn of Certified Hypnotherapists, 1988-; MD Rehab Assn, 1990- ; numerous other past and present memberships. **Special Achievements:** Certified Rehabilitation Counselor; Nationally Certified Counselor; License d Professional Counselor; Publications: The Predictors of Case Outcome for Clie nts in a Private Rehabilitation Program in Illinois, Dissertation Abstracts Int l, 1982; The Predictors of Case Outcome for Clients in Private Rehabilitation: An Illinois Study, The Journal of Private Sector Rehabilitation, 1988.

TANDY, MARY B.
Publisher. **Personal:** Born Jan 13, Louise, MS; daughter of Florence Coleman (deceased) and Thomas McGee (deceased); married O L Tandy (deceased); children: Bernice, Betty, Mary Ann, Alice M, Leroy Bryant. **Educ:** Ivy Tech Coll, AA 1982; Indiana Univ, 1966. **Career:** Indiana Herald, owner/publisher. **Orgs:** SProgram chmn Amer Business Women Assn 1980-82; noble gov Household of Ruth 1980-82; Democratic precinct comm 25 yrs; publicity comm NAACP life mem; mem IDEA Ind Demo Editors 1975. **Business Addr:** Publisher, Indiana Herald, 2170 N Illinois St, Indianapolis, IN 46202.

TANG, DEBORAH CANADA
Broadcast company executive. **Personal:** Born Jul 18, 1947, Chicago, IL; daughter of Mildred Russell Canada and Edward Preston Canada; married Roger Tang, Aug 1979 (divorced). **Educ:** University of the District of Columbia; Chicago State University; Columbia School of Journalism, Chicago; Loop Jr

College, Chicago. **Career:** KXAS-TV, Dallas, Fort Worth, TX, producer, 1978-80; WRC-TV, Washington, DC, producer, 1980-82; WJLA-TV, Washington, DC, producer, 1982-83; WTTG-Fox TV, Washington, DC, producer, 1983-84; WETA-TV, Washington DC, senior producer, 1984-86; Black Entertainment Television, Washington, DC, news director, 1986-92, vp, news and public affairs, entertainment, children, and sports programming, vp, news, sports, and entertainment, currently. **Orgs:** National Assn of Black Journalists; Capital Press Club; RTNDA, NAACP, Urban League; Washington Association of Black Journalists. **Honors/Awds:** Emmy Award for "The KKK March on Washington," 1983; Emmy Nomination for "Stephanie Roper's Appeal," 1983; Mental Health Outstanding Achievement Award, for The Psychiatric Institute, 1983; Emmy Nomination for "A Tribute to Paul Robeson," 1984; Emmy Nomination for "Babies Having Babies," 1985; CEBA Award for BET News, 1990; NABJ Award for In Focus, 1991. **Business Addr:** VP, News, Sports, and Entertainment, Black Entertainment Television, 1900 W Place NE, Washington, DC 20018.

TANN, DANIEL J.
Attorney. **Personal:** Born Nov 23, 1960, Philadelphia, PA; son of Gladys L Tann and Fee Otis Tann; married Kimberly A Smith, Jul 1988. **Educ:** La Salle University, BS, 1982; Drake University, JD, 1985. **Career:** Spear, Wilderman, Borish, Endy, Browning & Spear, managing attorney-general practice department, 1986-89; Pepper, Gordon, Breen & Weinberg, PC, litigation attorney, 1989-. **Orgs:** Phi Beta Sigma Fraternity Inc, eastern regional dir, 1997-, eastern regional legal counsel, 1989-94; president, NU Sigma Chapter, 1988-90, eastern Pennsylvania area director, 1981-82; American Bar Association, 1985-; National Bar Association, 1985-; NAACP, 1980-; La Salle University Alumni, board of directors, 1982-; Presidents Council of Associates, 1991-. **Honors/Awds:** Drake University, Joseph Drogan Scholarship, 1982-85; Boy Scouts of America, Appreciation Award, 1992; Phi Beta Sigma Fraternity, Membership Development Award, 1990; LaSalle University, Warren E Smith Award, Outstanding African-American Alumnus, 1996. **Business Addr:** Attorney at Law, Pepper, Gordon, Breen, & Weinberg, PC, 260 S Broad St, Atlantic Bldg, Ste 1410, Philadelphia, PA 19102, (215)546-3131.

TANNER, BARRON
Professional football player. **Personal:** Born Sep 14, 1973. **Educ:** Univ of Oklahoma, attended. **Career:** Miami Dolphins, defensive tackle, 1997-. **Business Addr:** Professional Football Player, Miami Dolphins, 2269 NW 199th St, Miami, FL 33056, (305)620-5000.

TANNER, GLORIA TRAVIS
State senator. **Personal:** Born Jul 16, 1935, Atlanta, GA; daughter of Blanche Arnold Travis and Marcellus Travis; widowed; children: Terrance Ralph, Tanvis Renee, Tracey Lynne. **Educ:** Met State Coll, BA Political Science (Magna Cum Laude) 1974; Univ of CO, Master Urban Affairs 1976. **Career:** Office of Hearings & Appeals US Dept of Interior, admin asst 1967-72; Denver Weekly News, reporter, feature writer 1972-76; 888 Real Estate Office, real estate salesperson 1976; Lt Gov of CO, exec asst 1976-78; Senator Regis Groff Comm Office, exec dir 1978, public admin 1978-; State of Colorado, state senator, currently. **Orgs:** Mem & public chmn Delta Sigma Theta 1974; chairwoman Senatorial Dist 3 Dem Party 1974-80; mem Amer Soc Public Admin 1976, CO Black Women for Political Action CBWPA 1976-80; exec bd CO Comm on Women 1976-79; mem Natl Assoc Real Estate Brokers; minority caucus chairperson. **Honors/Awds:** Outstanding Woman of the Year Award Scott United Methodist Church Denver 1974; Denver Chamber Leadership Award Denver Chamber of Commerce 1975; Outstanding Woman of the Year Award Reginas Civic Club Denver 1976; Outstanding Comm Serv Award Barney Ford Comm Serv Award Denver 1977; Senator Groffs Comm Serv Award Senator Groff 1977; Democratic Caucus Chairperson, 2nd black elected to a leadership position in the Colorado General Assembly. **Special Achievements:** First Black Female to be elected to the Colorado State Senate. **Business Addr:** State Senator, State of Colorado, State Capitol, Denver, CO 80203.

TANNER, JACK E.
Judge. **Personal:** Born 1919; married Glenda M Martin; children: Maryetta J Greaves, Donnetta M Gillum, Derrick Pleasant. **Career:** Tacoma pvt practice, 1955-78; US Dist Ct, Tacoma, WA, judge 1978-. **Orgs:** Mem Natl Bar Assn. **Business Addr:** Senior US District Court Judge, Western District of Washington, 1717 Pacific Ave, Ste 3144, Tacoma, WA 98402.

TANNER, JAMES W., JR.
Educational administrator (retired). **Personal:** Born Mar 18, 1936, Spartanburg, SC; married Priscilla; children: Tonya, Angela, James III. **Educ:** SC State Coll, BSA 1958; SC State Coll, MEd 1969; Univ of SC, advanced 1974. **Career:** Johnsonville School Dist #5 Bd, teacher coordinator dept head vo educ 1973-74. **Orgs:** Bd educ Florence Co 1973-74; Govs Commn; Florence Co Educ Assn pres 1973; vP 1971, dist rep 1970; bd dir SC Educ Assn 1974-; pres Florence CoVoters League 1970-; treas Congressional Dist 6 Voters Educ Proj 1973-74; mem Masonic Blue Lodge Master 1970; Am Vocation Assn 1962; Nat Council for Therapy & Rehab through Horticulture; Nat Vacation Agr Tchr Assn 1963; SC Vocational Assn 1962; Nat Educ Assn 1964; Nat Vo Agr Tchr Assn 1962; SC Vo Agr Tchr Assn 1962; bd dir Tri-Co Health Clinic; Johnsonville-Hemingway Drug Commn; Hickory Hill Comm Recreation dir; Johnsonville Devel Bd; Boy Scout post adv; membership chmn Local NAACP; Boy Scout Master 1970-74; Southeastern Regional Educational Bd, 1978-81; Florence Cty Dept Social Service Bd, 1989-93; SC Vocational & Technical Council, 1989-93; SC State Election Comm, 1993-96; SC State Univ, trustee bd, 1996-. **Honors/Awds:** Recipient Distinguished Serv Award Agr Educ 1969; a concurrent resolution by the SC Gen Assembly offering congratulations for being elected to SCEA bd dir & for Dedicated & inspiration serv to educ 1975; Sears Roebuck Scholarship 1953 in Agr Ed; Outstanding Secondary Educ of Am 1973. **Military Serv:** Served in military 1958-62. **Business Addr:** Dean of Student Services, Williamsburg Tech College, 601 Lane Rd, Johnsonville, SC 29555.

TANTER, RAYMOND
Educator. **Personal:** Born Sep 19, 1938; married 1969. **Educ:** Roosevelt University, BA, 1961; Indiana University, MA, PhD, 1964. **Career:** Northwestern University, assistant professor, 1964-67, associate professor, 1967-72; University of Michigan, professor, 1972-; Hebrew Univ of Jerusalem, visiting prof of intl relations, spring terms, 1973-78; has also served with various government agencies including the National Security Council and the National Republican Committee. **Honors/Awds:** Author, Modeling International Conflicts, 1974; author, Rational Decision Making, 1980; author, Who's at the Helm? Lessons of Lebanon, 1990. **Business Addr:** Professor, University of Michigan, Political Science Department, 5601 Haven Hall, Ann Arbor, MI 48109.

TAPPAN, MAJOR WILLIAM
Dentist. **Personal:** Born Mar 18, 1924, Chester, PA; son of Pernie Smith Briggs; married Maria Arias Tappan, Dec 2, 1989; children: Eric Rowland Tappan, Ameedah Abdullah, Bobbi Jill Jennings. **Educ:** Howard Univ Lib Arts, 1941-44; Howard Univ Dental Sch, DDS 1944-48; Columbia U, MPH 1965-66. **Career:** Roselle, NJ, private practitioner 1948-67; Denver Dept of Hlth & Hosp, Community Dental Services, dir beginning 1967; Colorado Dental Management, chief executive officer, currently. **Orgs:** Dir Found for Urban & Neighborhood Devel Inc 1984; pres The Mage Corp 1983-; consult US Dept of Labor Job Corps 1973-; spcl consult Am Dental Assn 1976; mem Urban League of Denver; dir Denticare of CO Inc 1983-; mem CF Holmes Dental Soc Nat Dental Assn. **Honors/Awds:** Diplomate Am Bd of Dental Pub Hlth; asso prof Univ of CO Hlth Sci Ctr Dental Sch 1970-; mem Nat Ctr for Hlth Serv Research Study Sec 1976-79. **Military Serv:** AUS 1st lt 1952-54. **Business Addr:** CEO, Colorado Dental Managementt, LLC, 1717 York St, Denver, CO 80206.

TARPLEY, NATASHA ANASTASIA
Writer. **Personal:** Born Jan 6, 1971, Chicago, IL; daughter of Marlene & Herman Tarpley. **Educ:** Howard University, visiting student, 1991-92; Georgetown University Law Ctr, 1993-94; Harvard University, BA, 1993; Northwestern University, School of Law, JD, 1996-98. **Career:** Beacon Press, author, currently. **Orgs:** Black Law Students Association, 1993-. **Honors/Awds:** National Endowment for the Arts, Fellowship for Poetry, 1994-95; Massachusetts Cultural Council, Fellowship for Poetry, 1994-95; Washington, DC, Commission for the Arts, Larry Neal Awd for Poetry, 1992, 1994; Radcliffe College, Joan Gray Undermeyer Awd for Poetry, 1993; Howard University, Awd for Poetry, 1992. **Special Achievements:** Testimony: Young African-American on Self-Discovery & Black Identity, Beacon Press, 1995; Girl in the Mirror & A Present Day Migration, for Minority from Beacon, 1997; I Love My Hair! - Childrens Book, Little Brook & Co., 1998; Written articles for Essence Magazine, Cover Story on Black College Students, Oct 1993, Inventions Piece, Nov 1994; Book Reviews for the Washington Post, Los Angeles Times, The Quarterly Black Review and Chicago Tribune. **Business Addr:** Editor, Testimony, Beacon Press, 25 Beacon St, Boston, MA 02108.

TARPLEY, ROY JAMES, JR.
Professional basketball player. **Personal:** Born Nov 28, 1964, New York, NY. **Educ:** Univ of Michigan, Ann Arbor, MI, 1982-86. **Career:** Dallas Mavericks, 1986-92; Aris Salonica, Greece, 1992-. **Honors/Awds:** NBA Sixth Man Award, 1988; NBA All-Rookie Team, 1987.

TARRY, ELLEN
Author. **Personal:** Born Sep 26, 1906, Birmingham, AL; daughter of Eula Tarry and John Baber Tarry; divorced; children: Elizabeth, Tarry Patton. **Educ:** AL State; Bank St Coll, NYC; Fordham Univ Sch Com, NYC. **Career:** Journalist; Friendship House, NYC & Chicago, co-founder 1929-; Natl Catholic Comm Serv, staff mem during WWII; Support HUD, dir fld 1958-76; Com Center Public School NYC, dir 1968; Comm Relations St Charles School Fund, dir; Womens Activities NCCS-USO, dir. **Orgs:** Mem, Catholic Interracial Counseling Commr Black Ministry; Archdiocese of NY; Coalition of 100 Blk Women; Nat Assn of Media Women Inc. **Honors/Awds:** Author of Janie Bell, Garden City Pub, 1940; Hezekiah Horton, Viking, 1942; My Dog Rinty, Viking, 1946; The Runaway Elephant, Viking, 1950; The Third Door: The Autobiography of an Amer Negro Woman, McKay, 1955; Katharine Drexel: Friend of the Neglected, Farrar Straus, 1958; Martin de Porres: Saint of the New World, Vision Bks, 1963; Young Jim: The Early Years of James Weldon Johnson, Dodd, 1967; The Other Toussaint: A Modern Biog of Pierre Toussaint, a Post-Revolutionary Black, St Paul Editions, 1981.

TARTER, JAMES H., SR.
Real estate broker. **Personal:** Born Nov 17, 1904, Riceville, TN; married Elizabeth; children: Gloria, James, III, Roger, Jerome. **Educ:** Columbia U, 1949; US Treas Dept Training Sch, cert. **Career:** James H Tarter Real Estate, real estate broker 1953-; Water Supply Mt Vernon, commnr bd 1964-67; Mt Vernon, deputy comptroller first black to be appointedto ofc; candidate Co Supvr on Dem ticket 1957; Sec to Comptroller 1954-56; Sec to Police Commnr 1952-54; first black to be appointed to position. **Orgs:** Mem Columbia Soc of Real Estate Appraisers; spl agent OPA Bur of Sp Investigation Currency protection div assigned to criminal cases 1942-47; held barious admin positions with New York City Dept of Welfare; spl investigator Mayros Commn on Conditions in Harlem 1935-36; mem Dem City Com of Mt Vernon; execbd Black Caucus Dem Party; Sacred Heart Cath Ch. **Honors/Awds:** Recip OPA Award for Superior Accomplishment; commendation US Attys ofc in Chgo. **Business Addr:** 37 Adams St, Mount Vernon, NY 10550.

TARTER, JAMES H., III
Business executive. **Personal:** Born Mar 6, 1927, New York, NY; married Marion; children: Krishna, Yasmin, Karim, James, Gamal. **Educ:** NY Univ; St Johns Univ; Inst for Advanced Marketing Studies; Advertising Club of NY, Honarary DD. **Career:** Tarter & Wetzel Co Inc, pres; NAACP Spl Contrib Fund, fund raising & pub relations natl dir of devel 1967-; Home Prods Corp, prodn mgr; F&M Schaefer Co, adv supvr; Fuller Brush Co, br mgr; So Delicious Bakeries, pres, gen mgr; NAACP Nat Dept of Tours, founder; NAACP Emergency Relief Fund, dir. **Orgs:** Mem Nat Soc of Fund Raisers; NY Soc of Fund Raising Dirs; Advtsng Club of NY; Knights of Columbus. **Honors/Awds:** Recip Hon Cit of New Orleans; awarded Jeruselem Medl Govt of Israel; Cit of Cr CTM. **Military Serv:** US Merchant Marine 1944-49. **Business Addr:** 424 Madison Ave, New York, NY.

TARTER, ROBERT R., JR.
Business executive. **Personal:** Born Jul 11, 1948, Cleveland, OH; son of Edna Tarter and Robert Tarter; married June Robinson. **Educ:** Univ of PA, BS Economics 1970. **Career:** Bankers Trust Co, asst tres 1971, asst vice pres 1973, vice pres 1976, sr vice pres 1985, managing dir 1986. **Orgs:** Dir United Bank for Africa 1985; trustee African-Am Inst 1984-; dir Black Alumni Soc Univ of PA 1984-; mem YMCA of New York City Bd of Dirs; mem 100 Black Men 1979-.

TARTER, ROGER POWELL
Physician, attorney, educator. **Personal:** Born Aug 27, 1930, New York, NY; son of James H and Elizabeth Tarter; married Ana Maria Hernandez Tarter, Oct 11, 1980; children: Roger Jr, Richard, Diana-Maria, Peter, Marcia-Elizabeth, Patricia. **Educ:** Iona College, BS, 1953; Long Island University, MS, 1959; University of Bologna, Faculty of Medicine, MD, 1964; Bernadean University College of Law, JD, 1994. **Career:** Westchester County, NY, asst pathologist-med examiner, 1967-69; Montefiore Hosp & Med Ctr-MMTP, med dir, 1971-74; Coney Island Hosp, Comprehensive Drug Abuse Treatment Prog, prog dir, 1974-78; NYC Bureau of Prison Health Servs, Health Dept, med dir, 1978-81; private practice, 1981-90; Albert Einstein Med Coll, asst clinical prof, Community Health Social Med, 1972-76; Mem of the US, Special Action Office Drug Abuse Prevention, expert, 1971-73; Maimonedes Hosp, Coney Island Hosp Afil, asst clinical prof & attending pathol & med, 1974-78; Charles R Drew, Martin Luther King Jr Medical School Foundation, scientific and medical advisor, 1986-90; Mercy Coll, Dept of Psychology, Natural Science, and Criminal Justice, assoc prof, 1994-. **Orgs:** American College of Physician Executives, 1994; American College of Medical Administrators, 1994; New York State Athletic Commission, staff physician, 1984; American Academy of Microbiologist, National Registry Specialist Microbiologist, 1970; National Association of Medical Examiners, 1969; Alpha Phi Alpha Fraternity, ETA Chapter, New York City, 1951; Kiwanis Club, 1969; Knights of Columbus, 1970; New York Academy of Sciences, 1985. **Honors/Awds:** Sloan Kettering Inst, Ochs Adler Scholarship, Post Grad Studies, 1956-58; Sloan Kettering Inst, National Inst of Health Pre Doctoral Research Fellowship, 1960; Cancirco Snell Scholar, Cancer Research, Makerere Medical Univ, Uganda, Africa, 1962; Iona College, Brother Loftus Award, Outstanding Achievements in Med Arts, 1972; City of Mount Vernon, New York, Honorary Police Surgeon, 1969; Adv Bd of Trustees, Iona College, 1972-; Psi Chi, Natl Honor Soc in Psychology; Alpha Phi Sigma, Natl Honor Soc in Criminal Justice; Beta Beta Beta, Natl Honor Soc in Biology. **Special Achievements:** Publications: JAMA, Vol 207, #7, p 1347, Sudden Death Dueto (Coronary Atherosclerotic Heart Disease), 1969; JAMA, Vol 211, #8, p 1331, Metaplasia of the Bronchial

Epith, 1970; Journal of Addictions, Vol 10(1), pp 23-27, Ocular Absorption of Naloxone, 1975; fluent in Spanish and Italian. **Military Serv:** US Army Medical Service Corp, private, 1953-55; US Army Medical Corp, major, 1963-90; US Army Medical Corp Reserves, 74th Field Hospital, chief of professional services, 1983-90; National Defense Medal; Good Conduct Medal; Combat Casualty Care Course Special Achievement, Army Service Ribbon; Army Component Reserve Medal. **Home Phone:** (914)376-2210. **Business Addr:** Associate Professor, Psychology, Mercy College, 555 Broadway, Dobbs Ferry, NY 10522, (914)693-7600.

TARVER, ELKING, JR.
Federal official. **Personal:** Born Nov 28, 1953, East Liverpool, OH; son of Elsie Tarver-Byers and Elking Tarver Sr. **Educ:** Gannon Univ, BS Accounting, 1976; Univ of Maryland graduate School, currently. **Career:** US Department of State, accountant 1976-78; US Dept of Agriculture, assistant regional inspector general, 1978-93, director, quality assurance, currently; private practice certified public accountant, 1994-. **Orgs:** Mem, Assn of Black Accountants, 1979-81; Assn of Govt Accountants 1982-; Shiloh Baptist Church 1983-; certified fraud examiner, Institute of Certified Fraud Examiners, 1989; Certified Public Accountant, American Inst of Certified Public Accountants, 1994. **Home Addr:** PO Box 4554, Capitol Heights, MD 20791, (301)420-1877. **Business Addr:** Director, Quality Assurance, US Department of Agriculture, Washington, DC 20250.

TARVER, GREGORY W.
Business executive. **Personal:** Born Mar 30, 1946, Shreveport, LA; married Velma Jean Kirksey Tarver; children: Gregory Jr, Ballestine, Lauren, Rebekah. **Educ:** Grambling State U; Centenary Coll. **Career:** JS Williams Fun Home, pres; Royal Life of LA Ins Co, pres; lic fun dir; State Senator, currently. **Orgs:** Mem Shreveport Fun Dir Caddo Parish Police Juror; mem bd of dir LA Men Health Assn; mem Zion Bapt Ch; chrmn bd of Caddo Barber Coll; pres J SWilliams Inc Co; 33rd Degree Mason; Universal Grand Lodge; Shriner; mem United Dem Campaign Com; mem Shreveport Jr C of C; Shreveport C of C; NAACP; Shreveport Negro C of C; Adv Council of YWCA. **Honors/Awds:** Army Accom Medal AUS. **Military Serv:** AUS spec 5 E-5 1968-69. **Business Addr:** 1104 Pierre Ave, Shreveport, LA 71103.

TARVER, LEON R., II
Educational administrator. **Personal:** marrIed Cynthia Loeb Tarver; children: Three. **Educ:** Southern University, BA, political science; Harvard University, John F Kennedy School of Government, MA, public administration; Union Institute, PhD, public administration. **Career:** Southern University System, Baton Rouge, LA, vice-chancellor for administration, prof of public administration, prof of public policy and urban affairs, pres, currently. **Business Addr:** President, Southern University, President's Office, Baton Rouge, LA 70813.

TARVER, MARIE NERO
Municipal government administrator. **Personal:** Born Aug 29, 1925, New Orleans, LA; daughter of Daisy Lee Blackmore Nero and Charles L Nero Sr (deceased); married Rupert J Jr; children: Rupert J, III, Charles LN, Stanley J, Gregory T, Bernard J, Cornelius A. **Educ:** Southern Univ Baton Rouge, BA Educ (cum laude) 1945; Univ of WI Madison School of Journalism, MA 1947. **Career:** New Orleans Informer Newspaper, women's editor 1945-46; Southern Univ Baton Rouge, English instructor 1947-49; Galesburg High School, Galesburg, IL, English teacher 1954-56; Dutchess Comm Coll Poughkeepsie, English instructor 1961-62; Marist Coll Poughkeepsie, English instructor 1963-68; Model City Agency, asst dir for planning 1968-70, deputy dir 1970-71, exec dir 1971-77; City of Poughkeepsie, NY, dir of social devel 1977-. **Orgs:** Pres & mem Bd of Educ Poughkeepsie City School Dist 1964-70; 1st vice pres natl Model Cities Comm Devel Assn 1975-77; bd of dirs Dutchess Co NY YMCA 1970-74; chr bd of dirs United Way of Dutchess Co NY Inc 1979; chr United Way Campaign 1982; Natl Antapokritis Zeta Phi Beta Sorority Inc 1948-52; commr chmn Poughkeepsie Housing Authority; exec com Dutchess-Putnam Private Indus Council; bd of dir Youth Resources Devel Corp; Mid-Hudson Reg Economic Devel Council; Dutchess Co Arts Council; trustee bd Vassar Bros Hospital; New York State Assn of Renewal and Housing Officials Inc; bd of dirs Dutchess County Child Devel Council, Hudson River Housing Inc; Dutchess/Dominica Partners of the Americas. **Honors/Awds:** First Recipient Sepia Award for Comm Serv Alpha Phi Alpha Fraternity Inc Mid-Hudson Chapter 1976; Merit Award Black Women's Caucus Polk, NY 1979; Amer Assn of Univ Women "Woman of the Year" 1982; Alexis De Tocqueville Award, United Way of Dutchess County 1989. **Business Addr:** Dir of Social Development, City of Poughkeepsie, Municipal Bldg, Poughkeepsie, NY 12602.

TASCO, MARIAN B.
City official. **Personal:** Born in Greensboro, NC; daughter of Alice Benton and Tom Benton; married Thomas Earle Williams (deceased); children: Charles Tasco, III. **Educ:** Bennett Coll, 1956-58; Temple Univ, BS Business Educ 1965. **Career:** City of Philadelphia, city commissioner, 1983-87, city council mem

1987-. **Orgs:** Delta Sigma Theta Sor; advisory bd, Natl Political Congress of Black Women; Women's Way, Family Planning Council of Southeastern PA; trainer YWCA Leadership Inst; bd of dirs, Natl League of Cities; Bd Health Watch, NY; bd mem, Recreation Fund; apptd delegate Democratic Convention 1984, 1988, 1992; board, Philadelphia Aiport Advisory, 1988-; board, Philadelphia Cultural Fund; board, Philadelphia Drama Guild, 1990-; chairperson, Philadelphia Gas Commission. **Honors/Awds:** Government Awd Bright Hope Baptist Church 1980; Winners Awd Women's Alliance for Job Equity 1985; Martin Luther King Jr Awd Salem Bapt Church 1986; Achievement Awds United Negro Coll Fund 1986; Outstanding Serv & Committment Awd Philadelphia Affirmative Action Coalition. **Business Addr:** City Council Member, City of Philadelphia, City Hall, Rm 577, Philadelphia, PA 19107, (215)686-3454.

TASSIE, ROBERT V.
Marketing executive. **Personal:** chilDren: James, Jonathan. **Educ:** St John's Univ, graduate; New School for Social Research, attended; The Foreign Institute, Washington, DC, attended. **Career:** CBS Television Network, account executive of network sales, vice president of sports sales, vice president of communications; Denver Nuggets, vice president of marketing, currently. **Orgs:** Life member, International Society of Television Arts and Sciences; board member, Arizona Sickle Cell Committee.

TATE, ADOLPHUS, JR.
Insurance company executive. **Personal:** Born Aug 18, 1942, Turrel, AR; son of Ruth Lee Johnson Tate and Adolphus Tate Sr; married Patricia Dawson; children: Adolphus III, Cherie Levelle, Faith Elizabeth Ann. **Educ:** LA City Coll, AZ 1964. **Career:** Western & So Life Ins Co, assoc sales mgr 1968-75, dist sales mgr 1975-85; sales manager Western Southern Life, 1988-. **Orgs:** Bowen Un Meth 1969-; pres, Gardena Interest Neighbor, 1990-, vice pres 1971-73; vice pres Un Meth 1976-86; Million Dollar Club Western & So Life Ins Co; Hollypary Comm Assn; co-chairperson Bolden United Meth; 32nd-degree Prince Hall Mason; chairperson Finance Comm Bowen Church 1983-85; sec United Methodist Men 1987; chairperson Trustee Bd Bowen Un Meth Church 1989-93; Bowen United Methodist Church, chairperson, administrative council, 1994-97; Knight of the West Club, pres, 1996; elected Worshipful Master, Western Knights #56, 1998. **Honors/Awds:** Policyholders Merit Awd 1971, 1976-79; Leader in the co field in given serv for past 6 yrs. **Special Achievements:** LUTCF, 1992. **Military Serv:** US Army 1964-66 SP/4. **Business Addr:** Sales Manager, Western & So Life Ins Co, 4300 S Crenshaw Blvd, Los Angeles, CA 90008.

TATE, BRETT ANDRE
Business executive. **Personal:** Born Apr 13, 1963, Seattle, WA; son of Margaret Tate and Willis Tate. **Educ:** Howard University, 1986; George Washington University, 1988. **Career:** Primerica Financial Services, vice pres; B&G Building Maintenance Inc, president, chief executive officer, currently. **Orgs:** Metropolitan Baptist Church, usher board, 1991-92. **Honors/Awds:** Primerica Financial Services, Most Valuable Person, 1991, Top Business Organization, 1990-91. **Business Phone:** (202)466-1688.

TATE, CORNELIUS ASTOR (NEAL TATE)
Conductor. **Personal:** Born Nov 17, 1921, Yonkers, NY; son of Cornelius & Sallie Lou; married Marzetta, Jun 10, 1984 (deceased); children: Sharon, Michael, James, Regina, Eyan, Avis. **Educ:** Julliard School of Music, 1942-44; Manhattan School of Music, 1944-46; New York University, 1951-55. **Career:** Music Director, orchestrator, conductor, arranger, currently. **Honors/Awds:** Audelco, Music Direction, "Williams & Walker," 1986. **Special Achievements:** Has directed numerous musicals including: "Hair," "The Me Nobody Knows," "Williams and Walker," has orchestrated and conducted: "Guys and Dolls," "Eubie," "Bubblin' Brown Sugar;" has written musical scores for television and film; directed commercials and original musicals including: "Sambo," "Music Magic;" arranged music for numerous people including Debbie Allen, Lena Horne and Cab Calloway. **Military Serv:** US Army, sgt, 1946-49. **Home Addr:** 2587 North Terrace Ave, Milwaukee, WI 53211, (414)332-1659.

TATE, DAVID
Professional football player. **Personal:** Born Nov 22, 1964, Denver, CO. **Educ:** University of Colorado. **Career:** Chicago Bears, defensive back, 1988-92; New York Giants, 1993; Indianapolis Colts, 1994-. **Business Addr:** Professional Football Player, Indianapolis Colts, PO Box 535000, Indianapolis, IN 46253, (317)297-2658.

TATE, DAVID KIRK
Attorney. **Personal:** Born Apr 20, 1939, Detroit, MI; son of Izona Kirk Tate and Andrew G Tate; married L Arlayne Carter, Nov 19, 1961; children: DeMarcus David Holland, Lisa Arlayne Tate. **Educ:** Michigan State Univ, East Lansing MI, BS, 1962; Univ of Detroit School of Law, Detroit MI, JD, 1973. **Career:** Patmon, Young & Kirk, Detroit MI, associate, 1973-76; Detroit Edison Co, Detroit MI, staff attorney, 1976-77; R J Rey-

nolds Tobacco Co, Winston-Salem NC, asst counsel, 1977-79, assoc counsel, 1979-82, counsel corporate and commercial, 1982-86, sr counsel and asst secy, 1986—. **Orgs:** American Bar Assn, North Carolina Bar Assn, Wolverine Bar Assn. **Military Serv:** US Army Infantry, captain, 1963-68; received bronze star and air medal, 1968, combat infantrymans badge. **Home Addr:** 2736 Woodlore Trl, Winston-Salem, NC 27103-6546. **Business Addr:** Sr Counsel/Assistant Secretary, RJ Reynolds Tobacco Co., 401 N Main St, Winston-Salem, NC 27104, (910)741-7385.

TATE, DEANNA
Professional basketball player. **Personal:** Born May 13, 1966. **Educ:** Univ of Maryland. **Career:** New England Blizzard, guard, 1997-. **Business Addr:** Professional Basketball Player, New England Blizzard, 179 Allyn St, Ste 403, Hartford, CT 06103, (860)522-4667.

TATE, EARNEST L.
Law enforcement official. **Personal:** marrIed Norma Jean; children: Ricky, Terry. **Career:** City of Selma, AL, police chief, 1997-. **Special Achievements:** First African American chief of police for the city of Selma. **Business Addr:** Chief, Selma Police Department, PO Drawer L, Selma, AL 36702, (334)874-2100.

TATE, ELEANORA ELAINE
Author, journalist. **Personal:** Born Apr 16, 1948, Canton, MO; daughter of Lillie Douglas Tate (raised by grandmother, Corinne Johnson) and Clifford Tate; married Zack E Hamlett III, Aug 19, 1972; children: Gretchen Tate. **Educ:** Drake University, Des Moines, IA, BA, journalism, 1973. **Career:** Iowa Bystander, Des Moines, IA, news editor, 1966-68; Des Moines Register & Tribune, reporter, 1969-76; Jackson Sun, Jackson, TN, staff writer, 1976-77; Memphis Tri-State Defender, free-lance writer, 1977; Kreative Koncepts, Inc, Myrtle Beach, SC, writer, 1979-81; free-lance writer, 1982-92; Postive Images, Inc, Myrtle Beach, SC, president and owner, 1983-93; Tate & Associates, media consultant, 1993-. **Orgs:** Member, Iowa Arts Council Artists in Schools/Community, 1970-89; member, South Carolina Arts Commission Artists in Education, 1982-92; member, NAACP, Georgetown chapter, Georgetown, SC, 1984-89; member, Concerned Citizens Operation Reach-Out of Horry County, 1985-; member of board of governors, South Carolina Academy of Authors, 1986-90, member of board of directors, 1986-92, vice president of board of directors, 1988-90; Horry Cultural Arts Council, president, sec, VP, 1986-92; member, Pee Dee Reading Council, Myrtle Beach, SC, 1987-90; member, Arts in Basic Currriculum Steering Committee, 1988-90; National Association of Black Storytellers, Inc, board member, 1988-92, pres, 1991-92, life member, 1992; member, North Carolina Writers Network, 1993-; mem Twin Rivers Reading Council of IRA, 1993-. **Honors/Awds:** Unity Award, Lincoln University, 1974; Community Lifestyle award, Tennessee Press Association, 1977; author of Just an Overnight Guest, Dial, 1980; fellowship in children's fiction, Breadloaf Writers' Conference, 1981; Parents' Choice award, 1987, for The Secret of Gumbo Grove, F Watts, 1987; Presidential Award, National Association of Negro Business and Professional Women's Clubs, Georgetown SC chapter, 1988; author of Thank You, Dr Martin Luther King, Jr!, F Watts, 1990; Grand Strand Press Association Award, Second Place, Social Responsibilities and Minority Affairs, 1988; Coastal Advertising Federation, Addy Award, Positive Images, Inc, 1988; Grace Brooks Memorial Humanitarian Award, SC Action Council for Cross-Cultural Mental Health and Human Services, 1991; Bd of Dir Award, Horry Cultural Arts Council, 1991; Distinguished Woman of the Year, Arts, Carteret County NC Council for Women, 1993; Excellent Communicator Award, Dept of Pupil Services, Horry County SC School Dist, 1990. **Special Achievements:** Author of Don't Split the Pole: Tales of Down-home Folk Wisdom, Delacorte, 1997; A Blessing in Disguise, Delacorte, 1995; Front Porch Stories at the One-Room School, Bantam Books, 1992; Retold African Myths, Perfection Learning Corp, 1992; Thank You, Dr Martin Luther King, Jr!, Franklin Watts, 1990; The Secret of Gumbo Grove, Franklin Watts, 1987; Just an Overnight Guest, Dial Press, 1980; "Bobby Griffin," Off-Beat, Macmillan, 1974; "An Ounce of Sand," Impossible?, Houghton-Mifflin, 1972; "I'm Life," Children of Longing, Holt, Rinehart & Winston, 1970; "Hawkeye Hatty Rides Again," American Girl Magazine, 1993; "Ethel's Story," Storyworks Magazine, 1992; "Secret of Gumbo Grove," play adapted, Scholastic Action Magazine, 1993; "A Blessing In Disguise," Delacorte, 1995; "Momma's Kitchen Table," essay published in "In Praise of Our Fathers and Our Mothers," Just Us Books Publishers, Inc, 1997; Just an Overnight Guest, re-issued, Just Us Books Publishers, Inc, 1997; Recorded Books, Inc, produced audio cassette tapes of The Secret of Gumbo Grove and Thank You, Dr Martin Luther King, Jr. **Business Addr:** Tate & Associates, PO Box 3581, Morehead City, NC 28557.

TATE, EULA BOOKER
Lobbyist. **Personal:** Born Nov 17, 1948, Ypsilanti, MI; daughter of Leslie Davis Booker (deceased) and Genia Webster Booker; married Ronnie G Tate; children: Ronald L, Donald D, Jennifer C, Stephen J. **Educ:** Univ of MI, BS 1977. **Career:** Chrysler Corp UAW Local 630, 1st vice pres 1967-80; Michi-

gan State Univ, labor educator; City of Ypsilanti MI, councilmember; UAW, legislative representative, currently. **Orgs:** Elks; BPOE; Temple 1283; National Democratic Party; NAACP; CBTU; CLUW. **Honors/Awds:** Michigan State University, Employee Recognition, 1983-84; Nominated Michigan Chronicle's Churchwoman of the Year 1984; UAW Region 1-A, Distinguished Service Award, 1989; Minority Women Network, Politician of the Year, 1990; Minority Business Owners Chamber of Commerce, Community Involvement Award, 1991; City of Ypsilanti, Service Award, 1991. **Business Addr:** Legislative Representative, UAW, 1757 N Street, NW, Washington, DC 20036.

TATE, GRADY B.
Entertainer. **Personal:** Born Jan 14, 1932, Durham, NC; married Vivian Tapp. **Educ:** NC Central Univ, BA 1959; Amer Acad Dramatic Arts NY, studied. **Career:** Positions include studio musician; NBC Tonight Show, musician; performed numerous night clubs prisons TV commercials. **Honors/Awds:** Special Awd Daytop Village Festival Music New York City 1968; Record World All Star Band New Artist New York City 1968; Awd for Outstanding Achievement in Area of Entertainment Hillside HS Durham NC 1971; 1st Humanitarian Awd NC Central Univ 1970-71; Overseas Jazz Club Awd 1971; Jazz Achievement Awd Jazz at Home Club Amer 1971. **Military Serv:** USAF s/sgt 1952-55. **Business Addr:** 185 E 85 St, New York, NY 10028.

TATE, HERBERT HOLMES, JR.
County prosecutor. **Personal:** Born Feb 22, 1953, Karachi, Pakistan; son of Ethel Harris Tate and Herbert H Tate Sr (deceased). **Educ:** Wesleyan Univ, BA (cum laude) 1978; Rutgers Univ Sch of Law, JD 1978. **Career:** Essex Co Prosecutor's Office Appellate Sect, law clerk 1977-78; Hon Van Y Clinton, judicial clerk 1978-79; Carella Byrne Bain Gilfillan, assoc 1983-85; Private Practice, attorney 1985-86; Urban Enterprise Zone Authority, public member, 1985-86; Essex Co Prosecutor's Office, asst pros 1979-83, trial sect dir of juvenile trial sect 1982-83; Bloomfield Coll, adjunct prof 1985; Essex Co Prosecutor's Office, prosecutor 1986-. **Orgs:** Mem Kiwanis Intl Newark Chapt; mem NJ Bar, Federal Bar NJ Dist, Pennsylvania Bar; mem NJ State Bar Assn Criminal Law Comm, Exec Comm for Criminal Law Sect; mem Essex Co Bar Assn, Natl Bar Assn, Natl District Attorney's Assn, Natl Black Prosecutors Assn, Natl Org of Black Law Enforcement Execs, Intl Narcotic Enforcement Officers Assn; mem, State Youth Services Comm, State of New Jersey; mem, Supreme Court Task Force on Minority Concerns; mem, County Prosecutors Assn; trustee, Boys & Girls Club of Newark; trustee, Montclair Kimberley Academy. **Honors/Awds:** Commendation City of Newark Municipal Cncl; East Orange Optomist Intl Law Enforcement Awd 1987; Bronze Shields Inc Law Enforcement Awd 1987, National Black Police Officers Assn, 1990. **Business Addr:** County Prosecutor, Essex County Prosecutor's Ofc, Essex County Courts Building, 50 W Market, Newark, NJ 07102.

TATE, HORACE EDWARD
Educator, state senator. **Personal:** Born Oct 6, 1922, Elberton, GA; son of Mattie Beatrice Harper Tate and Henry Lawrence Tate; married Virginia Cecily Barnett, Dec 23, 1949; children: Calvin Lee, Veloisa Cecil Tate Marsh, Horacena Edwean Tate. **Educ:** Ft Valley State Coll, BS 1943; Atlanta U, Masters 1951; Univ of KY, Doctorate 1961. **Career:** Georgia State Senate, senator, 1975-; Ft Valley State Coll, assoc prof 1959-61; Fairmont High School, Griffin, GA, principal, 1951-57; Greensboro High School, Greensboro, GA, teacher & principal, 1945-51; Union Point High School, Union Point, GA, teacher & principal, 1943-45. **Orgs:** Life mem Nat Educ Assn; mem Mut Fed Savs & Loan-bd of Dirs; mem Atlanta Bd of Educ 1965-69; exec sec, GA Assn of Educators, 1977-82, assoc exec, 1970-77; exec sec, GA Teachers & Educ Assn, 1961-70; mem Nat Commn on Libraries and Information Sci 1978-82; vice chmn, Georgia Democratic Party, 1969-73; mem, Natl Educ Assn Bd of Dirs, 1968-77; mem, officer, Butler St Christian Methodist Episcopal Church; mem, Educ Policies Comm; mem, Carrie Steele Pitts Childrens Home, Bd of Dirs; pres, School Buildings Inc, 1990-. **Honors/Awds:** Achievement & Serv Award The Atlanta Inquirer Newspaper 1969; Distinguished Mem Award Butler CME Ch 1969; delegate World Confederation of Orgns of the Teaching Profession Kenya Africa 1973; Most Illustrious Alumnus Award Ft Valley State Coll 1979; Distinguished Service Award, Fort Valley State Coll, 1982; Legislator of the Year Award, Mental Health Assn of Georgia, 1988; Trail Blaze Award, Antioch Baptist Church, 1988; Secular Educ Award, St Mark AME Church, 1989; author, "Equality & Opportunity," 1965; author, "Some Evils of Tolerated Tokenism," 1973; Marcus E Foster Distinguished Service Award, Natl Alliance of Black Educators, 1982; Dedicated Service Award, GA Assn of Educators, 1982; Atlanta University's Education Deans Award, 1983; Whitney M Young Award, Natl Education Assn, 1983;caton & Political Achievement Award, Early County, NAACP, 1983; Distinguished Service Award, Natl Education Assn, 1978; Distinguished Service Award, Atlanta Assn of Educators, 1982. **Home Addr:** 621 Lilla Dr SW, Atlanta, GA 30310.

TATE, JAMES A.
Educational administrator. **Personal:** Born Aug 7, 1927, Canton, MS; married Barbara; children: Lisa, Jayme. **Educ:** Jackson State Coll Jackson MS, BS 1950; MI State U, MA 1970; PhD cand 1975-. **Career:** Admissions & Scholarships MI State Univ, asso dir 1971-; dir devel prgm for admissions Office of Admissions 1977; science teacher prin elem schools 1968-70; MI, elem teacher 1959-70; Detroit, elem teacher 1955-57; MS, elem teacher, asst prin 1950-55. **Orgs:** Mem exec bd Adminstrv Professional Orgn 1974-76; mem Career Planning & Placement Council; mem Black Faculty Adminstrs Assn; adv bd Ypsilanti Area Comm Servs; Phi Beta Sigma; Am Personnell Guid Assn; MI Counselors Assn; Nat Cong Parents & Tchrs; Nat & MI Educ Assns; mem MASSP; MACAC; MAAAO; MIAssn Collegiate Registrars & Admissions Officers; Orgn MI State U; YMCA; Urban League; NAACP; Amer Assn Collegiate Registrars B Admissions Officers; exec bd Admin Professional Orgn, MI Educ Assn. **Military Serv:** AUS 1944. **Business Addr:** Associate Dir, Michigan State University, Achievement Admissions Program, 250 Administration Bldg, East Lansing, MI 48824.

TATE, LARENZ
Actor. **Career:** Actor. **Special Achievements:** Movie appearances include: Menace II Society; The Inkwell; Dead Presidents; Love Jones, The Postman, Why Do Fools Fall in Love; TV appearances include: "The Royal Family"; "South Central".

TATE, LENORE ARTIE
Psychologist, consultant. **Personal:** Born Apr 8, 1952, Los Angeles, CA; daughter of Earline Hopkins Tate and Wilbur B Tate. **Educ:** Mills College, BA, 1974; Howard University, MS, 1977; California School of Professional Psychology, PhD, 1980. **Career:** Prairie View A&M University, chairperson of psychology program, 1982-84; Arizona State University, assistant professor, 1984-86; California Legislature (Senate and Assembly), principal health policy consultant, 1986-. **Orgs:** Association of Black Psychologists, 1992-; Alpha Kappa Alpha Sorority Inc, 1986-; American Society on Aging, board member, 1985-87; Minority Concerns Committee, 1984-87; Arizona's Governors Conference on Aging, 1984, co-chair, 1985; County of Sacramento Health Services Cabinet, expert emeritus, advisory board, 1992, Sacramento County, self-esteem task force, 1988-90, mental health advisory board, 1988-90, chairman, 1989-92, vice-chairman, 1989; Maricopa County NAACP, board of directors, 1985-87. **Honors/Awds:** National Institute for Mental Health, Texas Research Institute for Mental Sciences, Geriatric Psychology Post-Doctoral Fellowship, 1980-82; Sacramento County, Outstanding Community Service Award, 1991; California School of Professional Psychology-Fresno, Dean's Award, 1980. **Special Achievements:** Author, "Life Satisfaction and Death Anxiety in Aged Women," International Journal of Aging and Human Development, 1982; "Employment Opportunities for Geropsychologists," American Psychologist; "Adult Day Care: A Practical Guidebook and Manual," Activities, Adaptation and Aging, special issue, 1988; California's Mental-Health System: The History of Neglect, Senate Office of Research, 1991. **Business Addr:** Staff Director, Principal Health Policy Consultant, California State Senate, State Capitol Room 4040, Sacramento, CA 95814, (916)445-5215.

TATE, MATTHEW
Educational administrator. **Personal:** Born Sep 16, 1940, McComb, MS; married Rosemary Brymfield; children: Mathis Melone. **Educ:** Southern Univ, BS 1963; Louisiana State Univ, additional work 1964; Southern Univ, Master of Ed in Administration 1969; Southeastern Louisiana Univ, Education Specialist 1974. **Career:** W S Young Constr Co, field coordinator; Fed Summer Nutritional Prog, bookkeeper; Louisiana Assn of Educators, representative 1978-82; Washington Parish Police Juror, juror 1984; Franklinton High School, assistant principal, currently. **Orgs:** President of Washington Parish Ed Assn 1967; president Phi Delta Kappa 1974; chairperson Supervisory Committee Washington Parish Ed Fed Credit Union 1980; secretary Franklinton Area Political League; committee person local mental health assn; president Rural Franklinton Water Dist; boardmen Review Board Capitol Region Planning Comm, Louisiana; member Congressional Contact Team LAE/NEA. **Honors/Awds:** Police Juror Washington Parrish Police Jury, Franklinton, LA. **Home Addr:** PO Box 368, Franklinton, LA 70438.

TATE, MERZE
Retired educator. **Personal:** Born Feb 6, 1905, Blanchard, MI; daughter of Myrtle K. Tate and Charles Tate. **Educ:** Western MI Univ, BA 1927; Columbia Univ, MA 1932; Oxford Univ, BLitt 1935; Harvard Univ & Radcliffe Coll, PhD 1941. **Career:** Crispus Attucks HS Indianapolis, hist tchr 1927-32; Barber-Scotia Coll, dean of women & hist 1935-36; Bennett Coll, prof of hist 1936-41; Morgan State Univ, dean of women & prof polit sci 1941-42; Howard Univ & US Army, prof of hist/polit sci geopolitics 1942-77. **Orgs:** Phi Beta Kappa; Pi Gamma Mu; AAUW; Radcliffe Club of Wash, DC (vp for 6 years); Alpha Kappa Alpha; Phi Delta Kappa; Round Table Club of Wash, DC; Writers Club of Wash, DC; Amer Historical Assn; Assn for the Study of Afro-Amer Life & Hist; Amer Bridge Assn; Howard Univ Women's Club; Howard Univ Retirees; mem of Found & President's Club at Western MI Univ; The Associates at Radcliffe; President's Club at Howard Univ; mem Phi Beta Kappa Assoc of Wash DC, Harvard Club of Wash DC, Smithsonian Assoc. **Honors/Awds:** Spirit of Detroit Awd of Merit 1978; The Amer Black Artist's Pioneer Awd 1978; The Radcliffe Coll Alumnae Achiev Awd 1979; The Promethean Plaque of Honor & Life Membership (the only woman) 1980; The Disting Alumnus Awd of the Amer Assn of State Colleges & Univs 1981; Howard Univ Doctor of Humane Letters degree 1986; Num publs incl, "The Disarmament Illusion—The Movement for a Limitation of Armaments to 1970" McMillan 1942 (reprinted by Russell & Russell 1970); "Control of Atomic Energy" pamphlet in an UNESCO kit on Atomic Energy Paris 1952, The US & Armaments Harvard Univ 1947, The US & The Hawaiian Kingdom Yale Univ 1964, Hawaii, Reciprocity or Annexation, MI State, Diplomacy in the Pacific, Howard Univ Mineral Railways & Projects in Amer under contract HowardUniv Press.

TATE, SHERMAN E.
Gas company executive. **Personal:** Born Oct 5, 1945, Marvell, AR; son of Annie B Tucker Tate and Rufus Tate Jr; married Janet Davis Tate, Dec 25, 1966; children: Amber Nicole. **Educ:** Philander Smith College, Little Rock, AR, BA, 1970. **Career:** City of Little Rock, AR, consultant, 1970; Arkansas State Personnel Division, Department of Finance and Administration, Little Rock, AR, personnel analyst, 1970-73; Arkansas Legislative Council, Little Rock, AR, personnel and budget specialist, 1973-75; University of Arkansas at Little Rock, Little Rock, AR, director of personnel, 1975-77; Arkansas State Office of Personnel Management, Little Rock, AR, administrator, 1977-80; Arkansas Louisiana Gas Company, Little Rock, AR, assistant vice president of employee relations, 1980-83, vice president of community/consumer relations, 1983-90, vice pres, customer relations, currently. **Orgs:** Treasurer, American Association of Blacks in Energy; member of national energy committee, NAACP; member, national advisory council, National Alliance of Business; member, board of directors, One National Bank; past chairman, Arkansas State Police Commission; member, board of directors, Centers for Youth and Families; chairman, Greater Little Rock Chamber of Commerce, 1989; member, board of trustees, Philander Smith College. **Honors/Awds:** Distinguished alumnus of Philander Smith College, National Association for Equal Opportunity in Higher Education; Doctor of Humane Letters, Philander Smith College, Little Rock, AR, 1988. **Military Serv:** US Army, sergeant; National Guard, major; received Bronze Star. **Home Addr:** 16 Windy Court, Little Rock, AR 72207. **Business Addr:** Vice President, Customer Relations, Arkansas Louisiana Gas Company, 400 East Capitol, Little Rock, AR 72202.

TATE, SONJA
Professional basketball player. **Personal:** Born Sep 7, 1971. **Educ:** Arkansas State Univ, bachelor's degree in physical education. **Career:** Columbus Quest, guard, 1996-. **Business Addr:** Professional Basketball Player, Columbus Quest, 7451 State Route 16, Dublin, OH 43016, (614)873-6555.

TATE, SONSYREA
Author, educator, journalist. **Personal:** Born Apr 22, 1966, Washington, DC; daughter of Meauvelle & Joseph Tate; divorced. **Educ:** University of the District of Columbia, BA, 1988. **Career:** The Washington Post, editorial aide, writer, 1986-89; The Washington Times Newspaper, reporter, 1989-91; Virginia-Pilot Newspaper, reporter, 1991-93; US House of Representatives, office of Eleanor Holmes Norton, assistant; Sylvan Learning Systems, instructor, 1997-. **Orgs:** National Association of Black Journalists, 1987-94. **Honors/Awds:** Echoes of Excellence Award, Hampton Roads Black Media Coalition, National Association of Black Journalist, 1993, Spot News, 1994, Commentary and in-depth Series, 1992; Virginia Press Association, Spot News Award, 1993; City Council Resolution for Community Service Jouranlism, Washington, DC, 1991; author "Little X: Growing Up in the Nation of Islam," Best Book for Young Adults, Best Book for Teen, American Library Association, 1998.

TATE, VALENCIA FAYE
Business manager. **Personal:** Born Sep 20, 1956, Petersburg, VA; daughter of Irene E Wilson and Henry G Wilson (deceased); married Penfield W Tate III, Sep 26, 1981; children: Elleana Elizabeth Wilson. **Educ:** Antioch School of Law, JD, 1981; James Madison University, BA, 1978. **Career:** Denver Juvenile Court, clerk, 1982-84; Colorado National Bank, account administrator, corporate trust supervisor, Mastercard and Visa, 1984-86; Denver Water, Mgr of EEO and minority business, supervisor of real estate contracts, supervisor of tap sales and records, 1986-. **Orgs:** Junior League of Denver, 1987-; Delta Sigma Theta, past president, 1976-; Mile High Council, Girl Scouts of America, bd mem; Leadership Denver Alumni Association, 1992; Historic Paramount Theatre Foundation, bd mem, 1992. **Honors/Awds:** Denver Chamber of Commerce, Leadership Denver Class, 1987; National Association of Negro Business and Professionals, Leadership 2000 Class, 1990. **Home Addr:** 2875 Albion St, Denver, CO 80207, (303)320-4665. **Business Addr:** Manager, Denver Water, 1600 W 12th Ave, Denver, CO 80254, (303)628-6119.

TATEM, PATRICIA ANN
Physical chemist. **Personal:** Born Aug 21, 1946, Wilmington, NC; daughter of Martha Louise Smith Faison and Ozie T Faison Sr; divorced; children: Paul Hadley. **Educ:** Bennett Coll, BS 1967; The George Washington Univ, MS 1970, PhD 1984. **Career:** The Naval Rsch Lab, tech editor 1967-72, rsch chemist 1972-94, supervisory rsch chemist, 1994-. **Orgs:** Mem WA Chromatography Discussion Group, Amer Chem Soc, The Combustion Inst, Sigma Xi. **Honors/Awds:** Summa Cum Laude Bennett Coll 1967; Co-recipient NRL Rsch Publ Awd for Applied Rsch, NRL, 1973; Recipient of Edison Meml Grad NRL 1978-81; Co-recipient NRL Rsch Publ Awd for Applied Rsch, NRL, 1983; Black Engr Awd, Professional Achievement, Morgan State Univ/US Black Engr Mag 1987; Council for Excellence in Government Fellow, 1994-95. **Business Addr:** Research Chemist, Naval Research Laboratory, 4555 Overlook Ave SW, Code 6180, Washington, DC 20375-5000.

TATUM, CAROL EVORA
Administrator. **Personal:** Born Feb 7, 1943, Alabama; daughter of Mary Kellum and Frank Kellum; children: Charles, Maurice, Shelly, Lisa. **Educ:** BA 1976; Antioch West, San Francisco, CA, MA, 1990. **Career:** Western Addition Project Area Comm, admin asst 1972-74; Model Cities, admin asst 1972-74; Bayview Hunter's Point Foundation Ctr for Problem Drinkers, dir 1974-88; Optimum Image, owner, 1990-. **Orgs:** Sec SF Chap Natl Assoc Bus & Professional Women 1983-; vice pres CA Black Alcoholism Council 1984-86; sec San Francisco Business & Professional Women 1985-; mem, adv bd, American Heart Assn, 1988-; mem, adv bd, American Cancer Society, 1988-; co-chair, Tobacco Control Coalition, 1990-; American Public Health Assn. **Home Addr:** 201 Ordway St, San Francisco, CA 94134. **Business Addr:** Owner, Optimum Image, 201 Ordway St, San Francisco, CA 94134.

TATUM, ELINOR RUTH
Publisher. **Personal:** Born Jan 29, 1971, New York, NY; daughter of Wilbert & Susan. **Educ:** St Lawrence Univ, BA, 1993; Stockholm Univ, 1993-94; New York Univ, Graduate School of Arts & Science, MA, 1998. **Career:** New York Amsterdam News, asst to the publisher, 1994-96, assoc publisher, COO, 1996-97, publisher, editor-in-chief, 1997-. **Orgs:** Wallenberg Committee of the US, bd mem, 1994-; NY Urban League, bd mem, 1997-; Learning Tree of Western Mass, chairwoman of the bd, 1997-; US Committee for UNIFEM, bd mem, 1997-; Greater NY Chapter of the Links, Inc, 1998-. **Honors/Awds:** Greater NY Coun of the Boy Scouts of America, Good Scout Award, 1997; NY Championship Block Rodeo, Woman of the Year, 1998. **Business Addr:** Publisher/Editor-in-Chief, New York Amsterdam News, 2340 Frederick Douglass Blvd, New York, NY 10027, (212)932-7400.

TATUM, KINNON
Professional football player. **Personal:** Born Jul 19, 1975. **Educ:** Notre Dame. **Career:** Carolina Panthers, linebacker, 1997-. **Business Addr:** Professional Football Player, Carolina Panthers, 800 Mint St, Ericsson Stadium, Charlotte, NC 28202, (704)358-7000.

TATUM, MILDRED CARTHAN
Elected official. **Personal:** Born Mar 26, 1940, Grady, AR; married Charles Leon Tatum Sr; children: Carl, Sharon, Charles, Jr, Gerald, Terrance, Edwin. **Educ:** Voca Sewing Class, 1st place 1959; Sharter College NLR, Special Ed 1979. **Career:** PTA, president 1969; Federal Program, president 1980; Regional 6 Chapter 1 Program, treasurer 1981; State Dept of PAC, treasurer 1982; Pulaski Co Special School Dist, president of school board. **Orgs:** Owner 145 St Liquors 1969; owner grocery store 1981; board of dir for Metroplan 1984; natl board for AAS board 1984; Judge Wood appointee to internal board 1985; owner rental house. **Honors/Awds:** Natl Honor Soc (1st Queen in college 10% of class) 1974; Key to City of LA Chapter PAC 1976; Outstanding Leader in School Dist 1983; 1st Black President School Board 1984.

TATUM, WILBERT A.
Business executive. **Personal:** Born Jan 23, 1933, Durham, NC; married Susan Kohn. **Educ:** Yale New Haven, Dr Humane Letters, 1988; Natl Urban Fellow, 1972; Occidental Coll, MA 1972; Lincoln Univ Pennsylvania, BA. **Career:** Health Ins Plan, vice pres marketing; City of NY, commr 1974-78; Borough of Manhattan City of NY, dep pres 1973-74; Milbank Frawley Urban Renewal Area City of NY, exec dir 1968-72; Stockholm Univ, instr; Inner City Broadcasting Corp, major stockholder 1972-80; Amsterdam News Corp, major stockholder chairman, former publisher 1972-. **Orgs:** Chmn of bd Tatum Kohn Assoc 1979-80; mem bd of mgrs Sloane House YMCA 1968-80; vice pres Educ Alliance 1970-80; v chmn of bd Coll for Human Serv 1974-95; asst to commr dir of comm relations Dept of Buildings; asst dir, housing New York Urban Coalition; headed Mayor Beame's Apparel Ofc of Plng & Devel; vice pres mktg Health Ins Plan of NY. **Honors/Awds:** Citation of merit B'Nai B'rith 1976; achievement award Nat Assn of Buying Offices 1976; Man of the Year Am Jewish Congress 1977; Man of the Year Fashion Nat & Urban Fellowship; US Conf of Mayors, Black Retail Action Group 1977. **Military Serv:** USMC corpl 1951-54. **Business Addr:** New York Amsterdam News, 2340 Frederick Douglass Blvd, New York, NY 10027.

TAULBERT, CLIFTON LEMOURE
Marketing executive, author. **Personal:** Born Feb 19, 1945, Glen Allen, MS; son of Mary Morgan Taulbert; married Barbara Ann Taulbert, Dec 22, 1973; children: Marshall Danzy, Anne Kathryn. **Career:** Spike USA Inc, pres/CEO, currently; Fremont Corp, Tulsa, OK, president; Bank of Oklahoma, Tulsa, OK, marketing vice pres; University Village Inc, Tulsa, OK, administrator, beginning 1972. **Orgs:** Board member, Tulsa United Way; bd member, Thomas Gilcrease Museum; bd member, Tulsa Goodwill Industry; executive bd member, Tulsa Metropolitan Chamber of Commerce; bd member, Business Industrial Development Corp. **Honors/Awds:** Manager of the Year, Oklahoma Chapter National Mgmt Assn, 1989; National Volunteer, National Arthritis Federation, 1985; author, Once Upon a Time When We Were Colored, Council Oak Publishing Co; 1989; author, Watching Our Crops Come In, Viking, 1997. **Military Serv:** US Air Force, Sergeant, 1964-68.

TAYARI, KABILI
Legislation analyst. **Personal:** Born Jun 26, 1950, Wilson, NC. **Educ:** Jersey City State Coll, BA Media & Health Sci 1974; Seton Hall Univ, grad study 1974-76. **Career:** Hudson Co Welfare, analyst 1974-78; Vornado Inc, mgr 1974-79; Conrail Passenger Div, operations mgr 1978-80; freelance lecturer 1980-; Natl Black Independent Political Party, natl presiding officer. **Orgs:** Mem NAACP 1968; mem African Heritage Studies Assn 1970-; exec mem NJ Assn of Black Educators 1972-; mem Amer Federation of State Co & Municipal Emps1974-76; mem coalition of Black Trade Unionists 1974-75; producer & critic Intl TV Assn 1978-; mem Amer Mgmt Assn 1978-; natl presiding officer Natl Black Independent Political Party 1980-; prog coord & tutor Title 20 Afterschool Recreation and Tutorial Prog of the Eastern Co YMCA 1980-84; mem Natl Title I/Chap I Adv Council; rep Natl Black Leadership Roundtable; sec Greenville Natl Little League; pres of Jersey City City Wide Parents Cncl May 1985-; mem NJ Black Issues Convention. **Honors/Awds:** Comm Serv Awd Black Assn of Alumni Faculty Staff & Students Organ at Jersey City State Coll 1981; Comm Serv Award from Title I/Chapter I Dist Wide Parents Adv Cncl 1985. **Business Addr:** Natl Presiding Officer, Natl Black Independent Pol Party, PO Box N Lafayette Sta, Jersey City, NJ 07304.

TAYLOR, AARON MATTHEW
Professional football player. **Personal:** Born Nov 14, 1972, San Francisco, CA. **Educ:** Univ of Notre Dame, BA degree in sociology. **Career:** Green Bay Packers, guard, 1995-. **Business Addr:** Professional Football Player, Green Bay Packers, 1265 Lombardi Ave, Green Bay, WI 54304, (414)494-2351.

TAYLOR, ALBERT, JR.
System analyst. **Personal:** Born Feb 14, 1957, Fairfield, AL; son of Voncile Taylor and Albert Taylor Sr; married Christella Simpson Taylor, Aug 6, 1983. **Educ:** AL State Univ, BS 1978; Samford Univ, MBA 1987. **Career:** John F Lawhon, data processing mgr 1978-80; Birmingham Bd of Educ, system analyst 1980-92, computer services director, 1992-. **Orgs:** Mem Kappa Kappa Psi Hon Band Frat 1975-87, Alpha Phi Alpha Frat Inc 1975-87, Data Processing Mgmt Assoc 1982-87, Neighborhood Watch Assoc 1984-87, Natl Black MBA Assoc 1986-87, Boy Scouts of Amer 1987; member, Helping Others Pursue Excellence. **Home Addr:** 1005 Woodbrook Rd, Birmingham, AL 35215. **Business Addr:** Director, Computer Svcs, Birmingham Bd of Education, 2015 Park Pl, Birmingham, AL 35203.

TAYLOR, ALMINA
Musician, educator. **Personal:** Born Mar 24, 1933, Shelby, NC; daughter of Willie Mae Roberts and Goald R Roberts; married Charles H Taylor Jr, Aug 23, 1970; children: Angela T Bunch, Charles III, Barbara Spruill, Robert Owens III. **Educ:** Virginia State University, BS, vocal music ed, 1954, MS, music ed, 1971; Norfolk State College, 1964, 1967; University of Richmond, 1980; University of Virginia, 1977; Old Dominion University, 1981, 1986; Shenandoah Conservatory, 1983; Westchester University, 1985. **Career:** Person County High School, choral directress, 1954-55; Portsmouth Public Schools, elementary grades & music teacher, choral directress, 1955-62, jr high school choral directress, 1962-79; Mt Pleasant Baptist Church, organist, choir directress, 1952-62; Norcom High School, music career teacher, choir directress, 1979-91; Fellowship United Church of Christ, organist, choir directress, 1978-. **Orgs:** National Education Association; National Music Educator's Conference; Virginia Music Educators Association; Portsmouth Education Association; Alpha Kappa Alpha Sorority; Portsmouth Chapter Delicados Inc; Portsmouth Chapter Pinochle Bugs; Portsmouth Alpha Wires. **Honors/Awds:** Choral Parents of Norcom High School, VIP, 1983; Women's Fellowship of Fellowship United Church of Christ, 10 Year Service Award, 1990; Portsmouth Chapter Delicados Inc, Black Educators' Award, 1993. **Special Achievements:** Conductor: All-City Elementary Chorus, 1972, Junior High All-City Chorus, 1976; school chorus chosen for demonstration choir with Lena McLin at Norfolk State University, 1983; chorus chosen to appear on "Music in our School Month," television special. **Home Addr:** 1409 Carson Crescent West, Portsmouth, VA 23701, (804)465-1823.

TAYLOR, ANDERSON
Educator. **Personal:** Born in Autaugaville, AL; married Virginia Burgohoy. **Educ:** Tuskegee Inst AL, BS 1956; Bradley Univ Peoria IL, MS 1963; Atlanta Univ GA, 1965; GA Tech, 1968; Univ of GA, attended. **Career:** MS Voc Coll Itta Bena MS, teacher 1957-59; Douglass School, teacher 1959-65; Carver Voc HS Atlanta, teacher 1965-74; Walter F George HS, dct coord, teacher. **Orgs:** Mem Ed Lowndes Cty Christian Movement 1966, Overseas Teacher Aid Prog in Ethiopia NEA 1967, Are Ind Arts Addis Tech TTI Univ 1970; master Boy Scouts KeyWest 1962-64; deacon Bethel AME Church 1960-65; dir Anti-Pov Prog Haynesville AL; faculty rep Carver Voc School 1971-74; chmn Ind Arts Dept. **Honors/Awds:** Awd for work in Ethiopia for Spec Summer Prog Univ of GA NEA 1967; Teacher of the Year 1974-75; Self-Study Career Ed Prog Univ of GA 6 yrs Cert in Ind Arts; Ed in Ethiopia & NEA Overseas Teach Aid Prog. **Business Addr:** DCT Coordinator, Teacher, Walter F George High School, 800 Hutchens Rd SE, Atlanta, GA 30354.

TAYLOR, ANDRE JEROME
Public utility executive. **Personal:** Born Sep 10, 1946, Mobile, AL; son of Doris Collins Taylor and Willie Taylor; married Vivian Buffis Taylor, Feb 14, 1982; children: Tara, Marla, Andre, Gordon. **Educ:** Tuskegee Institute, Tuskegee, AL, 1964-67; University of Alabama, Tuscaloosa, AL, BA, 1972. **Career:** WBRC-TV, Birmingham, AL, public affairs director, 1973-75; WACD Radio, Alexander City, AL, assistant general manager, 1975; WBLX-FM, Mobile, AL, account executive, 1975-77; Alabama Ed TV Commis, Birmingham, AL, assistant director program evaluation, 1977-79; Birmingham Cable Communication, Birmingham, AL, community relations director, 1979-84; Alabama Gas Corporation, Birmingham, AL, assistant vice president of community affairs, vice pres of communications, currently. **Orgs:** Exec committee, Jefferson Co Chap University of Alabama Alumni Assn; president cabinet, University of Alabama; executive committee, Birmingham Area Boy Scouts Council; board of directors, Birmingham Chapter, American Red Cross; board of directors, National Multiple Sclerosis Society; member, Kappa Alpha Psi; member, AABE; Birmingham Association of Black Journalists; past chairman, Alabama Veterans Leadership Program; president, Alabama Chapter Public Relations Society of America. **Honors/Awds:** Outstanding Alumni Public Relations, University of Alabama School of Communications; Entrepreneur of the Year Award, Birmingham Black MBA Association. **Military Serv:** US Army, E-5, 1967-71; Purple Heart, Bronze Star. **Business Addr:** Vice Pres of Communications, Alabama Gas Corp., 2101 6th Ave, N, Energen Plz Bldg, Birmingham, AL 35203.

TAYLOR, ANNA DIGGS
Federal judge. **Personal:** Born Dec 9, 1932, Washington, DC; daughter of Hazel B Johnston and V D Johnston; married S Martin Taylor; children: Douglass Johnston Diggs, Carla Cecilia Diggs. **Educ:** Barnard Coll, BA 1954; Yale Univ, LLB 1957. **Career:** Dept Labor, atty office solicitor 1957-60; Wayne Co MI, asst prosecutor 1961-62; Eastern Dist of MI, asst US atty 1966; Zwerdling, Maurer, Diggs & Papp, partner 1970-75; City of Detroit, asst corp counsel 1975-79; Wayne State Univ Law School, adjunct prof, 1976; Eastern Dist Detroit, MI, US Dist judge 1979-. **Orgs:** Trustee, Henry Ford Health System Eastern Region; Founders Soc, DIA; Detroit Symphony, mem Fed Bar Assn, State Bar MI, Wolverine Bar Assn, Women Lawyers Assn; trustee, Community Foundation for S Eastern MI; vice pres Yale Law Alumni Assn. **Business Addr:** Chief Judge, US District Court, Eastern District, Michigan, 740 Federal Courthouse, Detroit, MI 48226.

TAYLOR, ARLENE M. J.
Systems analyst. **Personal:** Born Aug 26, 1955, Baltimore, MD; daughter of Gladys Page Jones and Mack Christopher Jones; married O Odell Taylor Jr, May 10, 1986; children: Michael O. **Educ:** Univ of MD, BS Math 1977; OH State Univ, MS Math 1979. **Career:** OH State Univ, lecturer-mathematics 1980-81; NASA, intern programmer 1975-76; Western Elec, information systems design 1979-80; AT&T, information system staff beginning 1980, technical staff, currently. **Orgs:** Treas, life mem Zeta Phi Beta Sor Inc 1974-; life mem Phi Kappa Phi Honor Soc 1976-, Alpha Kappa Mu Honor Soc 1976-; Natl Assn for Female Executives l989; treasurer Ohio Oracle User's Group l989. **Honors/Awds:** Zeta of the Year (local chap) Zeta Phi Beta Sor Inc 1976; Disting Corporate Alumni Natl Assn for Equal Oppor in Higher Educ 1983; Alumni of the Year Univ of Md Eastern Shore l989; National Urban League BEEP presentator. **Home Addr:** 5076 Chipman Dr, Columbus, OH 43232. **Business Addr:** Member Technical Staff, AT&T, 5151 Blazer Memorial Pkwy, Dublin, OH 43017, (614)764-5217.

TAYLOR, ARNOLD H.
Educator. **Personal:** Born Nov 29, 1929, Regina, VA. **Educ:** VA Union U, BA cum laude 1951; Howard U, MA 1952; The Cath Univ of Am, PhD 1963. **Career:** Howard Univ, prof History 1972-; Univ of CT at Sterrs, prof history 1970-72; NC Central Univ, prof History 1965-70; So Univ in New Orleans, prof history chmn div of soc sci 1964-65; Benedict Coll, instr to prof of history 1955-64. **Orgs:** Mem assn for the study of Afro Am Life & History; So Historical Assn; Am Historical Assn; Orgn

of Am Historians; author Am Diplomacy & the Narcotics Traffic 1900-39, A Study in InternatlHumanitarian Reform Duke Univ Press 1969, "Travail & Triumph Black Life & Culture in the South Since the Civil War" Greenwood Press 1976; author several articles in scholarly journals Fulbright Hays Sr Lectr, Am Hist at Jadavpur Univ Calcutta India 1967-68. **Honors/Awds:** Recip post doc res grants Nat Endowment on the Humanities 1968, Am Council of Learned Societies 1969, Ford Found 1969-70, Univ of CT res found 1971-72. **Military Serv:** AUS corpl 1952-54. **Business Addr:** Prof of History & Dept Chrmn, Howard University, History Department, Washington, DC 20059.

TAYLOR, ARTHUR DUANE
Educational administrator. **Personal:** Born Jul 28, 1920, Buxton, IA; married Roberta Hudson; children: Rosylin, Roberta Elaine Lively, Arthur Duane Jr. **Educ:** Coe Coll Rapids IA, AB; IN Univ Bloomington IN, AM 1953; IN U, Supervision Credit. **Career:** Shasta Coll, dean of students 1969-80; Los Angeles School, dir multi-cultural leadership training 1968-69; Los Angeles School, consult intrgrp rltns 1966-69; Job Corps, pr, dept dir Educ & Guid 1965-66; HS IN & Denver, instr dir of phys ed, basketball coach 1950-65. **Orgs:** Commr CA Apprenticeshp Council 1970-74; p bd of dir Dynamics Rsrch Redding CA; pres Kiwanis Clb Redding 1978-79; NAACP; bd chmn Martin Luther King Cntr Redding; delegate Gov Conf Libraries 1979; del White House Conf 1979. **Honors/Awds:** 1st vice pres NAACP. **Business Addr:** Shasta Coll, 1065 N Old Oregon Trail, Redding, CA 96001.

TAYLOR, BENJAMIN GARLAND
Law enforcement official. **Personal:** Born Feb 27, 1950, Detroit, MI; son of Evelyn N & Douglas A Taylor (deceased); married Madonna Darlene; children: Angelena R. **Educ:** Wayne County Community College, AS, 1976; Wayne State University, 1979. **Career:** Detroit Police Dept, eastern operations enforcement, 1975-82; criminal investions bureau, gang squad, 1982-92; headquarters bureau, clerical operations, 1992-. **Orgs:** Wayne County Community College Alumni Association. **Honors/Awds:** Detroit Police Officers Assn, Officer of the Year, 1994; Detroit Police Dept, Lifesaving Citation, 1994; Detroit City Council, Award of Recognition, 1986; Detroit Police Dept, 20 Citations and Commendations. **Military Serv:** US Marine Corps, corporal, 1968-74; Good Conduct Medal, National Defense Service Medal, FMF. **Home Addr:** 18645 Robson St, Detroit, MI 48235, (313)273-8209.

TAYLOR, BOBBY
Professional football player. **Personal:** Born Dec 28, 1973, Houston, TX. **Educ:** Notre Dame, attended. **Career:** Philadelphia Eagles, defensive back, 1995-. **Special Achievements:** 2nd round/50th overall NFL draft pick, 1995; NFL All-Rookie Team, 1995. **Business Addr:** Professional Football Player, Philadelphia Eagles, 3501 S Broad St, Philadelphia, PA 19148, (215)463-2500.

TAYLOR, CAROL ANN
Attorney. **Personal:** Born Jan 17, 1956, Toledo, OH; divorced; children: Stephanie Travis, Jeremy Travis. **Educ:** Carleton Coll, BA, 1978; Univ of Minnesota Law School, JD, 1981. **Career:** Western Life, contract analyst, 1982-85; Northwestern Natl Life, product devel analyst, 1985-87; Amerisure Life, claims/compliance mgr, 1987-88; Michigan Mutual, assoc counsel, 1988-89, counsel, 1989-93, asst vp, counsel, 1993-. **Orgs:** Amer Bar Assn, 1988-; Minnesota Bar Assn, 1985-; Michigan Bar Assn, 1988-; Magnolia Neighborhood Bd, counsel, 1990-. **Honors/Awds:** YWCA, Minority Achievers Award, 1989; Girls Scouts of America, Parent Volunteer, 1992; Detroit Tutorial Center, Volunteer Tutor, 1993. **Business Addr:** Asst Vice President, Amerisure/Michigan Mutual Insurance Co, 25200 Telegraph, Southfield, MI 48034.

TAYLOR, CAROLE LILLIAN
Educator. **Personal:** Born in Pittsburgh, PA; children: Colette, Yvette. **Educ:** BS 1971; MEd 1972; PhD 1973; sp dipl 1975. **Career:** EPIC Inc, exec fdr; Tolafr Acad Elem Sch 1978; Tolafr Academy-Epic Inc, exec dir, currently, EPIC Pitts Bd of Edn, exec 1973-77, tchr 1972-77; Akronite Mag, fashion editor 1967-68; Univ of Pitts Am Assn of Univ Profs, model instr. **Orgs:** Speaker, 1977, Intl Platform Assn; Doctorate Assn Univ of Pitts. **Honors/Awds:** Oustdng accomplishments in letters Delta Sigma Theta 1976; Rotary club I Chicago Cleve 1978; Robert L Vann award Pittsburgh Courier; Lolette Wears a Patch 1975-77; ABC 1975-77; Essence Woman of the Year 1985, Essence Magazine 1985; Those Eyes, album (jazz) 1986; Speak and Read, text (instructional manual reading program) 1987. **Business Addr:** Executive Director, Tolafr Academy-Epic Inc, 1112 N Negley Ave, Pittsburgh, PA 15206.

TAYLOR, CASSANDRA W.
National sales manager. **Personal:** Born Oct 12, 1951, Franklin, TN; daughter of Mattie Lish Hughes Williams and Frederick Douglas Williams; married Wilbert H Taylor Jr, Apr 20, 1974; children: Frederick Delano, Kori Michelle. **Educ:** Memphis State Univ, Memphis TN, BBA, 1973. **Career:** Sears Roebuck & Co, Nashville TN, credit sales rep, 1973-74; Goldsmith's Dept Store, Memphis TN, asst buyer, 1974-77; Center City Commission, Memphis TN, marketing & promotions spec, 1977-82; Board of Education, Memphis TN, marketing spec, 1982-83; Greetings, Memphis TN, owner, 1983-85; Memphis Convention & Visitors Bureau, Memphis TN, currently national sales mgr. **Orgs:** Mem, Natl Coalition of Black Meeting Planners; assoc mem bd of dir, Hotel Sales Marketing Assn Intl; mem bd of dir, Tennessee/Arkansas/Mississippi Girl Scout Council; mem, Amer Business Women's Assn, Whitehaven Chapter; chmn, Memphis in May Intl Festival; sec, Shelby State Community Coll, Parent Advisory Bd and Early Childhood Education Center. **Honors/Awds:** Blues Lover Musician's Award, Beale Street Blues Foundation, 1980; Appreciation Merit Award, Memphis in May International Festival, 1980-82; Outstanding Young Women of American Award, 1981; Mother of the Year Award, Shelby State Early Childhood Education Center, 1981-82; Salute to African-American Business Women, Dollars & Sense Magazine, 1989.

TAYLOR, CHARLES AVON
Educational administrator. **Personal:** Born in Baltimore, MD; son of Ursula Milden Watkins Taylor and Ellsworth Howard Taylor; married Scheherazade Reed Taylor, Mar 12, 1982; children: Sherri, Charles Jr, Charlana, Aaron. **Educ:** Univ of Maryland, Baltimore MD, BA, 1973; Johns Hopkins Univ, Washington DC, 1976; Loyola Univ of Chicago, Chicago IL, EdD, 1984. **Career:** Univ of Maryland, Baltimore MD, counselor, resident life dept, 1971-73; Univ of Kentucky, Minority Affairs Accreditation Team, consultant, 1975; Catonsville Community Coll, Catonsville MD, student activities specialist, 1973-76; Loyola Univ of Chicago, Chicago IL, asst dean of students, 1976-86, instructor in counseling, psychology, and higher education, 1983-88, instructor in African American studies, 1984-88; Chicago State Univ, Chicago IL, dean of student development, 1986-88; Kellogg Community Coll, Battle Creek MI, vice pres for student services, 1988—. **Orgs:** Chmn, education committee, NAACP of Battle Creek MI; exec bd mem, Michigan Assn of Community Coll Student Personnel Administrators; American Association for Higher Education, AAHE Black Caucus; Battle Creek Area Urbn League; Parent Teachers Association, River Side Elementary, Lakeview School District PTA, Battle Creek, MI; National Council on Student Development, A Council of the American Association of Community and Junior Colleges; American Association for Counseling and Development; National Association of Student Personnel Administrators; American College Personnel Association; ACU-I Region 8 Representative Committee on Minority Programs; John Hopkins Alumni Assocation; Battle Creek Community Foundation. **Honors/Awds:** Advisor of the Year, Loyola Univ of Chicago, 1980; Community Leadership Award, Neighborhood Housing Services of Chicago, 1984; Black & Hispanic Achievers of Industry Award, YMCA of Metropolitan Chicago, 1984; Outstanding Citizens Award, Chicago Junior Assn of Commerce & Industry, 1986. **Business Addr:** Vice President for Student Services, Kellogg Community College, 450 North Ave, Battle Creek, MI 49017, (616)965-3931.

TAYLOR, CHARLES E.
Company executive. **Personal:** Born Jun 5, 1944, Columbus, OH; son of Catherine Taylor and Robert Taylor; married Judy Marshall; children: Enid, Antjuan, Jerome. **Educ:** Ohio State Univ, Columbus OH, BA, 1967, MA, 1969, PhD, 1971. **Career:** South Side Settlement House, program dir, 1967-68; Ohio State Univ, Columbus OH, teaching research assoc, 1968-69; Columbus Metropolitian Area Community Action Org, dir, 1969-70; VISTA, program officer, 1969; Urban Resources, consultant, 1970; Battelle Memorial Inst, consultant, 1970; Washington Internships in Educ, intern, 1970-71; Inst for Educ Leadership, staff assoc, 1971-72; Acad for Contemp Problems, vice pres for operations, 1972-76; Wilberforce Univ, pres, 1976-84; Standard Oil Co, dir contributions & comm affairs, 1984-86; Standard Oil Co Marine Transport, general mgr, 1986-89; Brand Implementation & Control, USA, mgr, 1989, mgr, Public Affairs, 1991; Lamadie Amrop Intl, partner, 1991-93, managing partner, 1993-. **Orgs:** Exec dir Columbus Area Leadership Program; dir Ohio Educ Sem Amer Educ Research Assn; Amer Assn of School Admin; Amer Mgmt Assn; Amer Acad of Political & Social Science; author producer Color Line WVKO radio; bd of dir, chmn, program com Columbus Urban League; bd of dir Blacks Against Drugs Uhuru Drug Treatment Facility; chmn Manpower Advisory Council for Columbus, Franklin Cos; steering comm Devel Comm of Greater Columbus 1974-76; bd of dir, chmn Govt Relations Comm Berwick Civic Assn 1974; bd of dir, treasurer Columbus Area Leadership Program 1974-75; bd of dir CARE Regional Resources Bd 1974-76; exec comm Franklin County Democratic Party 1974-76; bd of dir, chmn, personnel comm Neighborhood Devel Corp 1974-76; Full Employment Action Council; fellow,advisory bd Joint Center for Politl Studies; bd of trustees Franklin Univ 1975-76; bd of dir Campus Free Coll 1970-72; faculty inst for Pract Politics ; exec staff Natl Policy Conf on Educ for Blacks 1972; part Educ Staff Seminar Japan 1972; bd of educ Shaker Heights OH 1985-89; bd of dir Ameritrust Devel Bank 1988-; bd of trustees Univ of Akron 1988-. **Honors/Awds:** Community Serv Award, Columbus Urban League; talents, style & lead award Columbus Area Lead Program; Award for Asst to Acad for Contemp Problems, Battelle Memorial Inst; Award for Inspiration to Help Humanity, Assn of Black Sec; "Black Enterprise" top 25 black mgrs; Professional of the Year, Black Professionals Assn of Cleveland.

TAYLOR, CHARLES EDWARD
Attorney-at-law. **Personal:** Born Apr 19, 1931, Cincinnati, OH; son of Lenora Braden Taylor and I B Taylor; married Fern Godette Taylor. **Educ:** Brown Univ, Providence, RI, AB, 1957; Harvard Graduate School of Business, 1957-58; Georgetown Univ, Washington, DC, JD, 1983. **Career:** IBM Corp, various locations, branch mgr, sales, etc, 1963-89; IBM Corp, Washington, DC, dir of govt programs, 1978-89; Charles E Taylor Esquire & Associates, attorney-at-law, currently. **Orgs:** Mem, Natl Bar Assn, 1983-; mem, American Bar Assn, 1983-; mem, DC Bar, 1983-; life mem, Africare, 1987-; mem, Alpha Phi Alpha, 1963-. **Military Serv:** US Army, lt, 1951-53. **Home Addr:** 9920 Hall Rd, Potomac, MD 20854. **Business Addr:** Attorney-At-Law, Charles E Taylor, Esquire & Associates, 1367 Connecticut Ave, Ste 200, Washington, DC 20036.

TAYLOR, CHARLEY R.
Professional football coach. **Personal:** Born Sep 28, 1942, Prairie View, TX; married Patricia Grant; children: Charley, Elizabeth Erin, Erica. **Educ:** Arizona State University. **Career:** Washington Redskins, professional football player, running back, receiver, halfback, split end, 1964-78, Front Office Dept, scout, 1978-81, receivers coach, 1981-. **Orgs:** No Greater Love; Special Olympics, Mentally Retarded Bowls, 1963; Virginia Governor Charles Robb, Game and Inland Fisheries Commission, appointed member, 1983. **Honors/Awds:** NFL, Rookie of the Year, 1964, pass receiving titles, 1966-67; Pro Bowl, 8 time selection; All Pro, 1967, 1974; City of Grand Prairie, Texas, named, Outstanding Citizen, 1964; Washington Redskins, Offensive Player of the Year, 1974; Pro Football Hall of Fame, inducted, 1984; Texas Hall of Fame, inducted, 1985; Washington Touchdown Club Hall of Fame, inducted, 1992. **Special Achievements:** NFL's 4th all-time leading receiver, 649 catches for 9130 yards; Washington Redskins, first round draft pick, 1964, all-time leader in touchdowns. **Business Addr:** Washington Redskins, PO Box 17247, Dulles Intl Airport, Washington, DC 20041.

TAYLOR, CHRISTOPHER LENARD
Dentist. **Personal:** Born Dec 21, 1923, Charlotte, NC; son of Viola and Russell B; children: Ballinger, Russell III. **Educ:** Johnson C Smith Univ, BS 1945; Howard Univ Dental Sch, 1950; Jersey City Med Center, internship 1950-51. **Career:** Self-employed dentist, Los Angeles, 1951-. **Orgs:** Coast Dir Johnson C Smith Univ Alumni Assn 1954-; pres Pacific Town Club 1960; pres LA Chap NAACP 1962-64; gen chmn Com on Police Brutality; Rally 2nd Bapt Ch 1961; orgn gen chmn LA Civil Rights Rally 1963; 1st chmn United Civil Rights Comm; fdr chmn LA NAACP; life mem dinner 1963-65; num other affiliations; led num marches & boycotts; licensed to pract dentistry in CA, NJ, NY, NC; chmn bd Chris T RB III Corp; chmn bd T & T Dental Corp; charities, Johnson C Smith Univ, NAACP, CORE, Howard Univ, United Way, Urban League; Johnson C Smith Alumni Assn; Omega Psi Phi Frat; Alpha Kappa Mu Frat; Pacific Town Club; Amer Dental Assn; Natl Dental Assn; life mem NAACP; Intl Dental Soc; Angel City Dental Soc; Life mem Intl Anesthesiology Soc; Westminster Neighbrhood Assn; Howard Univ Alumni Assn. **Honors/Awds:** Howard Univ Alumni Achievement Award for Civil Rights Leadership, 1966; Scroll for Civil Rights Achievement, Los Angeles City Council, 1969; Award, Church of the Advent, 1970; ANC Mothers' Award, 1972; holds patent #2,807,818. **Military Serv:** WWII, Korean War Veteran. **Business Addr:** 8918 S Vermont Ave, Los Angeles, CA 90044.

TAYLOR, CLARENCE B.
Attorney. **Personal:** Born Jan 16, 1937, Pineville, KY; son of Frankie Love Taylor and William Morris Taylor; married Bertha M Thaxton, Feb 1, 1964; children: Tonyah, Renate, Clarence, Jr. **Educ:** OH State Univ, BA 1959; OH State Univ Coll of Law, LLB JD 1962. **Career:** US Atty's Off Cleveland, first asst US attorney 1972-1978; executive asst, US Attorney, 1978-; Veterans Admin Field Attorneys, supvr 1969-72; Judge Advocate General Corps & USAR, officer 1963-69(active duty); reserve officer, 1969-; grade lieutenant colonel. **Orgs:** Mem OH State Bar Assn; Alpha Phi Alpha; pres Cleveland Lawyers Assn 1973. **Honors/Awds:** Special Achievement Award, Attorney General, US Dept of Justice, 1988. **Military Serv:** Lieutenant Colonel, JAGC, USAR.

TAYLOR, CLEDIE COLLINS
Educational administrator. **Personal:** Born Mar 8, 1926, Bolivar, AR; daughter of Osie Gaines Collins and Dallas Collins; children: Paul Dallas. **Educ:** Wayne State U, BS 1948, MA 1957; L'Universita Per Stranieri, Cert etruscology 1968; Wayne State U, SP cert humanities/art/hist 1970; Union Grad Sch, PhD art hist 1978. **Career:** Detroit Pub Sch, art tchr 1979, supr of art 1980-; Metal Processes WSU, instructor fashion design 1981; Arts Extended Gallery Inc, dir, currently; Pri Jewelry Design, practicing metal craftsperson; Children's Museum, asst dir, 1987-91. **Orgs:** 1st chmn Detroit Cncl of the Arts 1977-81; 1st chmn Minority Arts Advisory Panel MI Cncl for the Arts 1982-; mem bd of trustees Haystack Mountain Sch of Crafts 1982-; mem Detroit Scarab Club 1983-; DPS advisor/liason De-

troit Art Tchrs Assn 1983-; mem/art advisor Nat Assn of the African Diaspora 1980-; dir Art Symposium Surinam NAAD Conf 1982; mem Berea Lutheran Ch; mem Alpha Kappa Alpha Sor; dir Art Symposium Barbados; appointed Michigan Council for the Arts 1987-; Board of Michigan Arts Foundation, 1988-. **Honors/Awds:** Contribution to Black Artist Nat Conf of Artist 1984, 1994; Spirit of Detroit Award City of Detroit 1983; book publ "Journey to Odiamola" 1978; "Words in a SketchBook" 1985; curator "African Tales in Words And Wood" 1984; curator "Tribute to Ernest Hardman" Exhibit Scarab Club 1985; award, Spirit of Detroit, City of Detroit for Small Business 1988; One Hundred Black Women for Art and Literature 1989; Governor's Award for Contribution to Art Education, 1989. **Business Addr:** Arts Extended Gallery, 1553 Woodward, Ste 212, Detroit, MI 48226, (313)961-5036.

TAYLOR, CORA (KOKO)
Musician, vocalist. **Personal:** Born Sep 28, 1928, Memphis, TN; married Robert Taylor (deceased); children: Joyce Threatt. **Career:** Singer, recording artist; albums and singles include: Coast to Coast, Capitol Records; Montreux Festival: Blues Avalanche, Chess Records; Ann Arbor Blues and Jazz Festival 1972, Atlantic Records; Koko Taylor, Chess Records; Basic Soul, Chess Records; Chicago Baby, France: Black & Blue; Blues Explosion, Atlantic Records; I Got What It Takes, Alligator Records; The Earthshaker, Alligator Records; From the Heart of a Woman, Alligator Records; Queen of the Blues, Alligator Records; Live from Chicago—An Audience with the Queen, Alligator Records; Jump for Joy, Alligator Records; Wild at Heart, feature film debut, singer, 1990. **Honors/Awds:** Grammy nominations, seven of last eight recordings; Grammy Award, Best Blues Recording, 1984; WC Handy Award, ten times. **Special Achievements:** Late Night with David Letterman, guest performance, 1988; President inaugural event, performer, 1989. **Business Addr:** Vocalist, Musician, Alligator Records, PO Box 60234, Chicago, IL 60660.

TAYLOR, DAISY CURRY
Congressional aide. **Personal:** Born Jul 24, 1948, Fort Lauderdale, FL; married Dr Theodore D Taylor; children: Tamila Annay, Tiffany Patrice. **Educ:** Bethune-Cookman, Liberal Arts 1970; Nova Univ, MPA 1975; Cong Professional Devel Cert Congressional Asst 1984. **Career:** FL Mem Coll, rsch analyst 1970-71; City of Ft Lauderdale, admin aide 1971-74; City of Oakland Park, dir comm affairs 1974-84; Exquisito Serv of Ft Lauderdale Mgmt Consult Firm, chmn of the bd/pres; Congressman E Clay Shaw, congressional aide 1984-. **Orgs:** Bd of dir Area Agency on Aging 1974-, Early Childhood Devel 1978-81, Community Action Agency 1983-; mem Urban League, NAACP, Task Force on the Black Aged, Women in Business, Amer Soc of Public Admin The Forum Black in Public Admin; Urban League Guild; E Broward Med Assoc Fndn; bd mem Black Coalition of Broward; bd mem Cncl for African Amer Econ Devel. **Honors/Awds:** Community Serv Area Agency on Aging 1979; Outstanding Citizen Community Partnership 1981; Outstanding Contribution to Broward Cty Mt Herman AME Church 1985; Women in Business 1986. **Business Addr:** Congressional Aide, E Clay Shaw, 299 E Broward Blvd, Fort Lauderdale, FL 33301.

TAYLOR, DALE B.
Educator, music therapist. **Personal:** Born Jun 13, 1939, Topeka, KS; son of Cassie L Moten Taylor and Wesley E Taylor; married Marguerite Davis, Mar 14, 1981; children: Shannon Michelle Davis, Shawn Jeffery Taylor. **Educ:** Coll of Emporia, KS, 1957-59; Univ of KS, BMus Ed 1963, M of Music Educ 1971, PhD, 1984. **Career:** Milwaukee County Mntl Hlth Ctr, music therapist 1963; Mendota State Hosp, dir music therapy 1964-67; Univ of WI Eau Claire, Dept of Allied Health Professions, chair, 1994-, dir music therapy, 1969-, affirmative action advisory and review board, 1994-. **Orgs:** Co-founder WI Chap for Music Therapy 1973; visiting clinician Univ of MO at Kansas City 1975; visiting clinician Mt Senario Coll 1975; assembly of delegates and intl relations committee, Natl Association for Music Therapy Inc 1976-83, 1985-97; clinical fac Univ of KS Dept of AMEMT 1979-80; grants review panelist WI Arts Bd 1984-90; mem Eau Claire Affirmative Action Review Comm 1984-90; vice commodore 1978-80, commodore 1985-87 Lake Wissota Yacht Club, racing chmn 1981-83; pres Great Lakes Region of the NAMT 1976-78; bd of dirs Intl Assn of Music for the Handicapped Inc 1986-91; advisory comm, Univ of Wisconsin System Inst on Race & Ethnicity, 1988-90; planning comm, Univ of Wisconsin System Design for Diversity Conf, 1989; conductor, accompanist, Eau Claire Gospel Choir, 1987-; soloist, Valley Gospel Choir, 1992-; secretary-treasurer, board of directors, International Arts MedicineSN, 1990-; book & media review editor 1990-97, international advisory committee 1990-, editor 1997-, International Journal of Arts Medicine; vice pres, Valley Gospel Choir. **Honors/Awds:** Pi Kappa Lambda Music Hon Soc; Honoree Martin Luther King Mem Lib Display 1985; US Deleg Intl Symposium on Music Ed for Handicapped 1980, 1983, 1985; Spcl Ambassador to Europe People-to-People 1962; Univ of KS Players, Univ of WI Players, Univ of WI-Stout Teleproduction Ctr actor/singer/dancer Madison Theatre Guild Mad Opera Co; US delegate Intl Society for Music Education, 1992; Biology of Music Making Intl Conference 1987; author of 20 publications in professional books and journals; 50 presentations at conferences; US Delegate, International Society for Music Education, Research Seminar of the Commission on Music in Special Education, Music Therapy and Music Medicine, Australia, 1988, Estonia, USSR, 1990, Korea, 1992, 1998; US Delegate, 1st US/Japan Intl Arts Medicine Leadership Conference, 1993; Author: Biomedical Foundations of Music as Therapy. **Business Addr:** Chair, Department of Allied Health Professions, Univ of Wisconsin-Eau Claire, Eau Claire, WI 54702, (715)836-2628.

TAYLOR, DALMAS A.
Educator. **Personal:** Born Sep 9, 1933, Detroit, MI; married Faye; children: Monique, Carla, Courtney. **Educ:** Western Res U, BA 1959; Univ DE, PhD 1965; Howard U, MS 1961. **Career:** Univ of Maryland, professor & assoc dean for Research; Wayne State Univ, Coll of Liberal Arts, dean; Univ of Vermont, provost & sr vp; Univ of TX (Arlington), provost, currently. **Orgs:** Dir minority flwsp prog Am Psychol Assn 1975-77; chmn asso prof dept psychology Fed City Coll DC 1969-70; rsrch psychologist Nat Naval Med Ctr1965-69; bd tst N VA Comm Coll 1973-77; bd dir Cncl Applied Soc Rsrch 1976-; Beacon Press 1971-; cncl rep soc psychol Study Social Issues 1977-; mem planning com Nat Conf Black Concerns with Pub Media Content; bd tst Unitarian Universalist Assn; bd dir Suburban Md Fare Housing Montgomery Co; chap Am Civil Liberties Union; pres Psi Chi Hon Soc Psychology 1961-62; Psi Chi 1964-65; postdoctoral flw Nat Acad Sci. **Honors/Awds:** Distinguished Service Award, Outstanding Contributions in Public Policy Interests, Amer Psychological Assoc, 1992; DIstinguished Contributions, Education & Training in Psychology, APA, 1991-92; Amer Men of Science Biography; Postdoctoral Fellow, Natl Academy of Science, Natl Research Council, 1965-66; Pres of Psi Chi, Honorary Society, Univ of Delaware, 1964-65; Pres of Psi Chi, Honorary Society for Psychology, Howard Univ, 1961-62. **Military Serv:** AUS 1956-58. **Business Addr:** Provost, UTA, PO Box 19118, Arlington, TX 76019.

TAYLOR, DAVID RICHARD, III
Attorney. **Personal:** Born Dec 17, 1949, Toledo, OH; son of Shirley L Swan Taylor and David Richard Taylor Jr; married Mary J Carrigan Taylor, Dec 12, 1987; children: Stacee L, Courtnee D, Davon R, Renesa Y, Evan K, Antoine L. **Educ:** University of Toledo, BA, 1971, College of Law, JD, 1974. **Career:** Lucas County Juvenile Court, referee, 1976-78; Lucas County Domestic Relations Court, referee, 1978-80, chief referee, 1980-84; State of Ohio, Attorney General, special counsel, 1989-; Lucas County Mental Health Board, attorney/counsel, 1990-; McConnell & Taylor, law partner, 1984-. **Orgs:** NAACP, Toledo Branch, president, 1997-, life member; University of Toledo, Alumni Assn, life member; Kappa Alpha Psi Fraternity, life member. **Special Achievements:** Lucas County Juvenile Domestic Relations Court, first African-American appointed attorney/referee, 1976, only African-American to serve as chief referee, 1980-84. **Business Addr:** Attorney, McConnell & Taylor, 316 N Michigan St, Toledo Bldg, Ste 700, Toledo, OH 43624, (419)241-6282.

TAYLOR, DAVID VASSAR
Educational administrator, educator. **Personal:** Born Jul 13, 1945, St Paul, MN; son of Eula Vassar Murphy and Clarence Taylor; married Josephine Reed-Taylor, Mar 27, 1976; children: Tyrone Reed-Taylor, Kenneth Reed-Taylor. **Educ:** Univ of Minnesota, BA 1967; Univ of Nebraska, MA 1971, PhD 1977; Harvard Univ, IEM Program 1985. **Career:** St Olaf Coll, Northfield MN, dir Amer minority studies program 1974-76; State Univ of New York New Paltz Campus, chairperson black studies dept 1977-78; Hubert Humphrey Collection Minnesota Historical Soc, curator 1978-79; Macalester Coll, dir minority/special serv program 1979-83; The Coll of Charleston, dean of undergraduate studies 1983-86; Minnesota State Univ System Office, assoc vice chancellor for academic affairs 1986-89; Univ of Minnesota Gen Coll, Minneapolis MN, dean 1989-. **Orgs:** Bd of dirs Hallie Q Brown Comm Center St Paul 1978-79; bd of advisors Perrie Jones Library Fund St Paul 1979-80, Minnesota Quality of Life Study 1979-80; vestry St Phillip's Episcopal Church 1978-81; bd of trustees Seabury Western Theological Seminary 1985-90; chairman, board of directors, Penumbra Theatre Co; board, Friends of the Saint Paul Public Libraries; treasurer, Jean Covington Foundation. **Honors/Awds:** Research Fellow-Dissertation Fellowship Fund for Black Americans 1975-77; consultant historian "Blacks in Minnesota" film for Gen Mills 1980; author bibliography/3 articles/chapter in book. **Military Serv:** US Army, spec 5 1969-70; Bronze Star & several commendations. **Business Addr:** Dean, General College, University of Minnesota, 128 Pleasant St, SE, Minneapolis, MN 55455.

TAYLOR, DEFORREST WALKER
City official. **Personal:** Born Jan 12, 1933, Brooklyn, NY; son of Francis A. Walker Taylor and Harold B. Taylor, Sr.; married Myrna Fraser; children: DeForrest F Jr, Minnette G, Karla M. **Educ:** John Jay Coll of Criminal Justice, BS 1972, masters program; FBI Acad, 1972; Univ of Virginia; FBI National Executive Institute. **Career:** New York City Police Dept, entered dept 1956, promoted to sgt 1965, promoted to Lt 1969, captain 1972, exec ofcr 79th Precinct, commanding ofcr 28th Precinct 1975-77, deputy inspector 1977, inspector 1980, deputy chief 1982, assistant chief 1983; chief of personnel 1989; New York City Housing Authority Police Dept, chief of department, 1990-. **Orgs:** Intl Assn of Chiefs of Police; bd dir Captains Endowment Assn, NYCPD; Am Acad for Professional Law Enforcement; Nat Acad Assoc Guardians Assn NYCPD; NAACP; NOBLE. **Honors/Awds:** Golden Rule Award, St George Association, NYCPD, 1990; Lloyd Sealy Award, Noble, 1991; Alumni of the Year, John Jay College, 1991. **Military Serv:** AUS Pfc 1953-55. **Home Addr:** 20 Melody Ln, Amityville, NY 11701.

TAYLOR, DONALD FULTON, SR.
Educational administrator (retired). **Personal:** Born Jul 10, 1932, Charles Town, WV; married Phyllis Shirley Jackson; children: Donald Jr, Keith C, Pamela Jackson, Mark J, Christy A Butts. **Educ:** Shepherd College, AB 1957; Johns Hopkins University, ScD 1971; Virginia Union University, MDiv Magna Cum Laude 1982. **Career:** Darby Twp HS, head, dept of science 1958-65; Cheyney State College, coordinator, health sciences 1970-75; Norfolk State Univ, dean 1975-95. **Orgs:** Pastor Greater Mt Zion Baptist Church 1985; chairperson Eastern Virginia Health Education Consort 1985; bd of directors Society for Aid of Sickle Cell Anemia 1985; bd of directors Natl Society of Allied Health 1985; task force Medicaid, Organ Transplant 1985; bd of directors Norfolk Area Health Education Center 1985; mem Prince Hall Masons, Norfolk Rotary Club; bd dir, treas Norfolk Area Health Ed Ctr 1985; mem Amer Public Health Assoc 1985, VA Assoc of Allied Health Professional 1985, VA Public Health Assoc 1985, Tidewater Metro Ministers Assoc 1985; bd of dir Chesapeake Hosp Authority 1986-90; vice pres Norfolk Area Hlth Educ Cntr 1986-; mem advisory bd Juvenile Court Conf Comm 1986-. **Honors/Awds:** Publication Allied Health Professions Admission Test 1984; Carl Haven Young Award American Corrective Therapy Assn 1984; Chapel of the Four Chaplins Award; Outstanding Educators of America-listing. **Military Serv:** AUS pfc 3-5 yrs; Silver Star, Bronze Star, 1948-51. **Home Addr:** 431 Ivy Crescent, Chesapeake, VA 23325.

TAYLOR, EARTHA LYNN
Attorney. **Personal:** Born Oct 28, 1957, Gary, IN; daughter of Mirtha Taylor and Silas Taylor; divorced; children: Barrett Alexander Boone. **Educ:** Indiana University, BS, 1979; Valparaiso University, School of Law, JD, 1985. **Career:** Steven Rolle & Madden, law clerk, 1986-87; Law Office of Frank Hernandez, 1987-88; Law Office of Eartha Taylor, attorney, 1988-. **Orgs:** J L Turner Legal Association, 1988-; Dallas Association of Black Women Attorneys, 1987-; Dallas Bar Association, 1989-; National Bar Association, 1988-. **Honors/Awds:** Texas Legal Services, Pro-Bono Award, 1991, 1992. **Business Addr:** Owner, Attorney, Law Offices of Eartha Lynn Taylor, 400 S Zang Blvd, Nationsbank Bldg, Ste 601, Dallas, TX 75208, (214)946-0993.

TAYLOR, EDGAR R.
Marketing exec. **Personal:** Born Sep 7, 1953, Cheyenne, WY; son of Jeanette & Edgar N Taylor; married Cheryl, Jul 12, 1975; children: Carly, Scott, Allison. **Educ:** Adelphi Univ, BA, 1975; Imede Univ, Lausanne, Switzerland, exec devt, 1990. **Career:** Carnation Co, acct exec, 1978-80, district mgr, 1980-82, region mgr, 1982-84, promotion mgr, 1984-86, merchandising dir, 1986-90, category dir, 1990-91; Nestle USA, mktg dir, 1991-. **Orgs:** Los Angeles Regional Food Bank, bd of dirs, 1990-; Promotion Mktg Asson of Amer, bd of dirs, 1989-. **Honors/Awds:** Dollars & Sense Magazine, Businessman of the Year, 1994; PMAA, Reggie Award, Marketing Effectiveness, 1989. **Special Achievements:** Proficient in Spanish & Portuguese. **Business Addr:** Marketing Dir, Nestle USA, 800 N Brand Blvd, 20th Fl, Glendale, CA 91203, (818)549-6781.

TAYLOR, EDWARD WALTER
Business executive (retired), architect. **Personal:** Born Jul 17, 1926, Baltimore, MD; son of Rebecca Taylor and Elbert Taylor; married Alene Lassiter. **Educ:** Hampton Inst, 1950; Johns Hopkins Univ, Univ of Maryland 1974. **Career:** US Govt, chief drafting 1950-59; Henry L Lives Balt, archt mgr 1958-63; Westinghouse Electric, mech designer 1960-73; Edward Q Rogers Balt, archt 1964-67; Sultor Campbell Architects Balt, acht mgr 1968-73; Atti Consult Ltd, owner 1973-90; Morgan State University, architect, 1991-. **Orgs:** Mem Natl Tech Assoc, Comm Devel Adv Comm, Howard Park Civic Assoc, AIA, NW Outer Urban Coaltion, NAACP; tech adv Pan African Congress; dir Model Cities Housing Corp; chmn MD Comm Devel Comm 1973; tech consult E Baltimore Comm Corp; graphics advisor Voc Ed Baltimore Construction Specification Institute; mem Construction Specification Institute; vice chairperson Education Committee Concord Baptist Church; Concord Baptist Church, vice chair, Christian education, 1991, church school superintnedent, 1992. **Honors/Awds:** Man of the Year Awd; Samuel Cheevers Awd; Tribute Awd Natl Tech Assoc; Service Award Concord Baptist Church 1987; Man of the Year Dunbar High School Baltimore; Baptist Educational Awardee 1988. **Military Serv:** USAF 1944-46. **Business Addr:** Architect, Morgan State University, Cold Spring Ln and Hillen Rd, Baltimore, MD 21239.

TAYLOR, ELLIS CLARENCE, SR.
Staff engineer. **Personal:** Born Feb 4, 1931, New Hebron, MS; married Marva Manning Whitney, Aug 3, 1970 (divorced 1980). **Educ:** Universal TV & Electronics Systems, diploma 1953; Cleveland Inst of Electronics, diploma 1956, second diploma 1988; Univ of Kansas City, 1959-62; Central Tech Inst 1968; Univ of Missouri Kansas City, video production studies 1977-82; received FCC First Class License 1955. **Career:** KPRS Radio, part-time engineer 1957-58; Taylor's TV Serv & Sales 1957-63; AM-FM station KPRS, chief engineer 1963-66; Forte Record Company, founder, 1966-83; Freelance Music Producer & Contractor, 1967; KMBC TV, staff engineer 1968-. **Orgs:** First African-American licensing exam bd mem, KC Radio & TV, 1961-84; IBEW Exec Council, 1977-79; mem, NAACP; founding bd mem, United Minority Media Assn of Missouri, 1974-77; mem, Black Music Assn, 1980; mem, Soc of Broadcast Engineers, 1980-; life mem, Univ of Missouri Kansas City Alumni Assn; mem, Audio Engineering Soc Inc, 1986-; mem, Natl Rep Senatorial Inner Circle, 1991-96; Recording Industry of America, 1976-83. **Honors/Awds:** Commended by high level leaders for efforts to deter youth crime 1975-76; Leader Jazz & Cultural Arts Study by Black Kansas City Economic Union & The Ford Foundation concerning Kansas City Jazz, 1980; invited guest of Recording Industry Assoc of Amer White House Reception 1979; host 11th Cultural Awards presentation of the RIAA; Senatorial Medal of Freedom, 1994. **Military Serv:** US Navy, gunnery, SN 1st Class, 1948-50; received China Service Medal. **Home Addr:** PO Box 17061, Kansas City, MO 64132.

TAYLOR, ERIC CHARLES
Attorney. **Personal:** Born Jun 25, 1962, Sacramento, CA; son of Joan E Taylor and John C Taylor Jr. **Educ:** Dartmouth College, BA, 1984; University of Virginia School of Law, JD, 1988. **Career:** Pettit & Martin, attorney, associate, 1988-90; Sonnenshein, Nath and Rosenthal, attorney, associate, 1990-92; County Counsel, County of Los Angeles, deputy county counselor, currently. **Orgs:** Career Ambitions Inc, president, 1989-. **Honors/Awds:** Dartmouth College, Edwin Gould Scholar, 1984.

TAYLOR, ERNEST NORMAN, JR.
Naval aviator. **Personal:** Born Aug 19, 1953, Chester, PA; son of Elizabeth Ann Derry Taylor and Ernest Norman Taylor Sr; married Ines Emilia Pelayo; children: Randy, Kevin, Matthew. **Educ:** Miami-Dade Comm Coll, AA 1973; Dillard Univ, BA (Cum Laude) 1975. **Career:** US Navy, 1975-, naval aviator 1976-. **Orgs:** Eastern region vice pres Natl Naval Officers Assn 1985-87; mem Tuskegee Airman Inc, Negro Airman Intl, NAACP, Aircraft Owners & Pilot Assn; Organization of Black Airline Pilots. **Honors/Awds:** Dorie Miller Awd Natl Naval Officers Assn 1986. **Military Serv:** USN LCDR/04 14 yrs; Navy Commendation Medal; Navy Achievement Medal; Meritorious Unit Commendation (3); Humanitarian Medal; Korean Presidential Unit Citation.

TAYLOR, ESTELLE WORMLEY
English professor (retired). **Personal:** Born Jan 12, 1924, Washington, DC; daughter of Wilhelmina Jordan Wormley and Luther Charles Wormley; married Ivan Earle Taylor, Dec 26, 1953. **Educ:** Miner Teachers College, Washington, DC, BS, 1945; Howard University, Washington, DC, MA, 1947; Catholic University, Washington, DC, PhD, 1969. **Career:** Howard University, Washington, DC, instructor in English and Humanities, 1947-52; Langley Junior High, Washington, DC, English teacher, 1952-55; Eastern Senior High, Washington, DC, English teacher, 1955-63; District of Columbia Teachers College, Washington, DC, English instructor, professor, 1963-76; Federal City College, Washington, DC, associate provost, 1974-75; District of Columbia Teachers College, Washington, DC, acting academic dean, 1975-76; Howard University, Washington, DC, English professor, chairman of department, 1976-85, associate dean of College of Liberal Arts, 1985-86, director of Graduate Expository Writing, 1988-91. **Orgs:** Member, National Council of Teachers of English, 1955-80; member, Modern Language Association of America, 1963-; member, College Language Association, life member, 1963-; member, Shakespeare Association of America, 1965; member, 1979-, vice president, 1979-81, corresponding secretary, 1989-91, recording sect, 1991-92, Capital City Links, Inc, Washington, DC; member, 1979-83, vice chairman, 1983, University of the District of Columbia board of trustees, Washington, DC; member of executive committee, Folger Institute, 1982-91; public member, US Department of State Foreign Service Selection Board, 1983; member, Commission on Higher Education, 1984-91; public member of Senior Threshold Foreign Service Appointments and Selections Board, Agency for InternationalDevelopment, 1984; member of research board of advis, American Bibliographical Institute, Inc, 1985-; member, Women's National Democratic Club, 1987-90; member, Malone Society, 1987-90; life member, National Council of Negro Women; member, District of Columbia Urban League; life member, NAACP; asociate editor, Journal of the Afro-American and Genealogical Society, 1990-93; Delta Sigma Theta Sorority. **Honors/Awds:** Author of Survival or Surrender: The Dilemma of Higher Education, 1975; author of The Ironic Equation in Shakespeare's Othello: Appearances Equal Reality, 1977; Rockefeller/Aspen Institute fellowship, 1978-79; Outstanding Teacher in College of Liberal Arts, Howard University, 1980; author of The Masking in Othello and the Unmasking of Othello Criticism, 1984; Outstanding Contribution to Higher Education award, University of the District of Columbia, College of Human Ecology, 1988; Middle State Association Service Award, 1989; Outstanding Contributions to Historically Black Colleges Award, 1995; Howard University, Alumni Award for Distinguished Achievement in the Fields of Education and Literature, 1997. **Home Addr:** 3221 20th Street, NE, Washington, DC 20018.

TAYLOR, EUGENE DONALDSON
Physician. **Personal:** Born Oct 10, 1922, St Louis, MO; son of Eugene T Taylor; married Carol; children: William, Eugene. **Educ:** VA State Coll, BS 1947; Wilberforce Univ, 1948; Howard Univ Med Sch, MD 1954. **Career:** Washington University, St Louis, MO, associate clinical prof of Ob-Gyn, 1985; Jewish Hosp, physician; Homer G Phillips, assoc dir Ob-Gyn 1967-; St Louis Pub Sch System, tchr 1948-49. **Orgs:** Mem FACOS 1977; FACOB-GYN 1962; Amer Bd Ob-gyn 1962; mem Amer Coll Ob-gyn 1959-61; St Louis Med Soc 1959-60; MO Med Soc 1960; Amer Med Soc 1960; St Louis Gyn Soc 1962; treas 1976-77; Amer Soc Abdominal Surgeons 1961; NY Acad Sci 1971; Pan Amer Med Assn 1975; Mount City Med Soc 1959; Natl Med Assn 1959-; MO Pan Amer Med Assn 1959-; MO Ob-gyn Assn 1973-; Med Adv Com Planned Parenthood 1973-; Amer Coll Surgery 1977. **Honors/Awds:** Publ, Hazards of Labor in the Grand Miltipara, 1968; Complications of Teenage Pregnancies as Seen in the Municipal Hosp, 1970; Recession of the Near Point of Convergence in the Toxic Hypertensive Syndrome of Pregnancy, jour NMA, 1958. **Military Serv:** AUS S/Sgt 1943-46. **Business Addr:** 2715 N Union, St Louis, MO 63113.

TAYLOR, FELICIA MICHELLE
Federal official. **Personal:** Born Feb 14, 1960, Concord, NC; daughter of Shirley Alsbrooks Taylor and Milton Lee Taylor. **Educ:** Cabarrus Community College, private pilot ground school, 1982; Univ of North Carolina, Chapel Hill, BA, sociology, 1982, Charlotte, MS, criminal justice, 1984; Florida State Univ, PhD, criminology, 1987-. **Career:** Univ of NC at Charlotte, admissions counselor, 1983-84; Barber-Scotia Clg, administrative asst for financial planning and development, 1984-85; Shaw Univ at Raleigh, professor, 1985-87, CAPE Ctr at Wilmington, adjunct professor, 1992; The Florida State Univ, instructor, 1988-91, Academic Support Services, tutor, 1989-91; Florida A&M Univ, adjunct professor, 1990-91; Florida Department of Hlth and Rehabilitative Services, abuse registry counselor, 1991; Univ of NC at Wilmington, guest lecturer, 1992; Federal Bureau of Prisons, research analyst, 1992-; Shaw University, Raleigh, NC, professor of criminal justice, 1993-. **Orgs:** Sweet Carolines 1980-82; Young Democrats 1982-83, Cloud Cappers Ltd Assn 1982-; Delta Sigma Theta, Inc 1984-; CVAN, Volunteer Assn for Battered Women, 1985; intake counselor, Probation & Parole, 1983-84; counselor Mecklenburg Co Charlotte; chmn UNICEF; Hall Rep 1980-81; UNC-Ch sec of dorm 1981-82; UNC Chapel Hill co-chmn 1st UNCF Tennis Tourn in Cabarrus Co; Advisor, Society of Criminal Justice 1985-87; Cooperative Colleges Task Force, 1986; American Criminal Justice Society, 1987-; Criminology Association, 1987-; Academy Criminal Justice Sciences, 1989-90; Guardian Ad Litem, 1988-; mediator, Durham County Mediation Svcs, 1996-; mem, Supreme Court Historical Society, 1994-. **Honors/Awds:** Honor Court, UNC Chapel Hill, 1980-82; UNC Charlotte, First graduate of Masters of Science Degree in Criminal Justice/Management Program, 1984; Patricia Roberts Harris Fellowship, 1987-. **Special Achievements:** Author, works presented: Conference for Social Problems, "Gender Bias Amongst State Institutional Drug Treatment Programs," April 1990; "Effects of Pornography on Women," April 1988; Assn of Criminal Justice Professionals, "History of Women's Prisons in the State of Florida"; Southern Conference, "Role Play," 1987. **Home Addr:** PO Box 45, Landis, NC 28088.

TAYLOR, FRANK ANTHONY
Director food, beverage. **Personal:** Born Jun 4, 1965, Galveston, TX; son of Essie L Taylor; married Carolyn A Taylor, Aug 10, 1996; children: Courtney L, Airielle V, James V. **Educ:** Alvin Sr College, degree, 1986; American Hotel/Motel, 1988. **Career:** Marriott Brookhollow, food, beverage dir, 1990-92; Holiday Inn San Antonio, resident mgr, 1992-94; Seldom Blues Inc, vp, 1994-96; Sheraton Hotel Imperial, dir of food and beverage, 1996; Doubletree Hotel Corp, dir of food and beverage, currently. **Honors/Awds:** American Hotel & Motel Association, Certified Food & Beverage Executive, 1988. **Home Addr:** 1613 King James Dr, Pittsburgh, PA 15237, (412)635-0701. **Business Addr:** Director, Food & Beverage, Doubletree Hotel of Pittsburgh, 1000 Penn Ave, Pittsburgh, PA 15222, (412)560-6304.

TAYLOR, GAYLAND WAYNE
Civil engineer. **Personal:** Born Aug 12, 1958, Midland, TX; son of Ardis Faye Taylor-Padgitt and Samuel Lee Taylor. **Educ:** Prairie View A&M University, Prairie View, TX, BSCE, 1981. **Career:** EG & G Idaho Inc, Idaho Falls, ID, field inspector/material lab tech, 1977-78; Arco, Arp, TX, corrosion engr, 1979; Arizona Public Service Co, Phoenix, AZ, civil engineer, 1982-90; FAA, civil engineer, currently. **Orgs:** Natl sect, natl fundraiser, National Council of Black Engineers and Scientist, 1985-91; public relations chr & editor, AZ Council of Black Engineers & Scientists, 1982-86; business owner, Minority Business Enterprise City of Phoenix, 1988; chairman, KPNX Minority Advisory Board, 1982-86; Phoenix City Club, Business Owner Member, 1989-91; auditor, Fair Housing, 1987. **Honors/Awds:** Idealine, Arizona Public Service, 1990; Certificate of Achievement, Transmissions & Distribution Expo, 1982; Adult Development Units, University of Boy Scouting, 1982; Outstanding Leadership, Valley Christian Centers, 1983; Nominee Candidate Volunteer, The AZ Domocratic Party, 1988. **Military Serv:** NROTC, Midshipman 3rd class, 1978-80; Navy Blue Guard Drill Team. **Home Addr:** PO Box 610449, Dallas, TX 75261-0449.

TAYLOR, GILBERT LEON
Consultant, museum curator. **Personal:** Born May 5, 1937, Indianapolis, IN; son of Irene Crystal Taylor and Hugh Ross Taylor; children: seven. **Educ:** IN Central U, BS 1958; IN U, MS 1969; Univ of MA, EdD Cand. **Career:** IN Pub Sch, tchr 1959-63; Liberia Presbyterian Sch, ed tchr consult 1963-66; Knoxville Coll, administrator 1966-68; IN U, administrator 1968-70; Coll of the Holy Cross, administrator 1970-74; The Children's Museum, administrator 1976-84; Butler Univ Administration, 1984-86; Private Practice, consult 1975-; Indianapolis Public Schools, Crispus Attucks Ctr Museum, Indianapolis, IN, curator, 1991-. **Orgs:** Pres Parent Centered Educ 1984-85; Long range plan comm African-Am Museum Assn 1983-85; coord Cncl for Black Exec 1984-; long range plan comm Madame Walker Urban Life Ctr 1984-85; advisory comm Freetown Vill 1984-85; advisory comm Training Inc 1984-85; Co-host Views & Visions TY Pgm WTTV 1983-; trainer, OAR, 1991; faculty, Witherspoon Performing Arts Center, 1991-; member, I V Tech Outreach Committee, 1989; 4 H Extension, adv bd; Etheridge Knight Festival, bd mem; Vision Indianapolis, Indianapolis progress comm. **Honors/Awds:** Ford Fellow Univ of MA 1974-76; Key to the City Tuskegee City, 1979; Featured Personality United Press Intl 1983; Recog Award Bahai Faith 1983; Ed & Human Rights Ind Tchrs Assn 1983; Award for Appreciation, Concerned Males, 1989; Outstanding Leadership, Career Beginnings, 1990; Certificate of Appreciation, Veteran's Administration, 1990; African-American Multicultural Ed, Certificate of Appreciation, 1992; IPS/IEA Multicultural Festival, Certificate of Appreciation, 1992; Indiana Watch Comm Award, Certificate of Appreciation, 1992; Annual 4H Ace Academy, Certificate of Appreciation, 1993; Our Story Newsletter, Feature Story, 1994; Martin L King Day IPS School 20, Service Award, 1994; US Dept of Housing & Devt, Certificate of Appreciation, 1994; Positive Change Network, Open Window Award, 1995; OAR, Certificate of Volunteer Service, 1995; Indianapolis Indians School 26 Reunion Award, 1997; OAR, Olendar Aid and Restoration, 1998. **Business Addr:** Curator, Crispus Attucks Ctr Museum, 1140 Martin Luther King St, Indianapolis Public Schools, Indianapolis, IN 46202.

TAYLOR, HAROLD LEON
Oral and maxillofacial surgeon. **Personal:** Born Mar 7, 1946, Memphis, TN; son of Vera Broxton Taylor and Jobe L Taylor; married Madeleine Cooper-Taylor, Aug 31, 1974; children: Reagan Michelle, Sydney Kristine. **Educ:** Morehouse Coll, BS 1968; Howard U, DDS 1972; Howard U, cert oral surg 1975. **Career:** Dentist, oral maxillofcaial surgery 1975-; TN Coll Denistry, asso prof 1975; DC Gen Hosp, chf resd 1972-74; Freedmen's Hosp, 1972; Howard U, lectr coll denistry; St Joseph Hosp, atdng oral surgeon; St Francis Hosp; Methodist Hospital Systems; Baptist Memorial Hospital, surgeon, currently; Memphis Jaw Surgery Center, oral surgeon, currently. **Orgs:** Bd Dir Memphis Chap Nat Bus League; Runaway House, Inc; house del Nat Dental Assn; mem Memphis Soc Oral Surgeons; mem Fndrs Club Boys Club Memphis; Alpha Phi Alpha Frat; Chi Delta Mu Frat; pres Shelby Co Dental Soc 1979; bd of dir Mason St Home for Boys 1979; mem Am Assn of Oral & Maxillofacial Surgeons 1978; pres, board of directors, Porter-Leath Children's Center, 1987-88; pres, board of directors, Bethany Maternity House, 1989-90; member, Delta Boule, Sigma Pi Phi Fraternity; board of directors, NAACP, Memphis; board of directors, 100 Black Men, Memphis; Memphis 2000 Educational Task Force; National Society of Oral & Maxillofacial Surgeons; Girls Inc-Church Health Ctr, board of directors. **Honors/Awds:** Deans Award Howard Univ 1972; Omicron Kappa Upsilon National Honor Society; Alumni Leadership Award, 1975; Diplomate, Amer Bd of Oral & Maxillofacial Surgery, 1982; Fellow, American College of Oral & Maxillofacial Surgery, 1985; fellow, Int Society of Plastic, Facial & Reconstructive Surgery, 1991; Dean's Odontological Society, 1992; Leadership Memphis, 1985. **Home Addr:** 4803 Hornsby Dr, Memphis, TN 38116. **Business Addr:** Oral Surgeon, Memphis Jaw Surgery Center, 1211 Union Ave, Suite 800, Memphis, TN 38104.

TAYLOR, HELEN HOLLINGSHED
Government official, social worker. **Personal:** Born in Cincinnati, OH. **Educ:** Howard University; Catholic University of America, master's degree in early childhood education. **Career:** National Child Day Care Association, executive director; Head Start Bureau, associate commissioner, 1994-. **Business Addr:** Associate Commissioner, Head Start Bureau, US Department of Health and Human Services, 200 Independence Ave SW, Washington, DC 20201, (202)401-2337.

TAYLOR, HENRY F.
Automobile dealership executive. **Career:** Smokey Point Sales and Service Inc, chief executive officer, currently. **Special Achievements:** Company ranked #61 of BE's Top 100 Auto Dealers, 1990, ranked #33, 1992. **Business Addr:** Chief Executive Officer, Smokey Pont Sales & Service Inc, PO Box 3008, Arlington, WA 98223, (206)659-0886.

TAYLOR, HENRY LOUIS, JR.
Educator. **Personal:** Born Sep 13, 1943, Nashville, TN; son of Mary Ruth Cheatham Taylor and Henry Louis Taylor Sr; married Carol Dozier Taylor, Aug 28, 1987; children: Jean-Jacques, Keeanga, Chad-Cinque. **Educ:** Tennessee State University, Nashville, TN, BS, 1965; University of Tennessee, Knoxville, TN, MA, 1966; State University of New York at Buffalo, Buffalo, NY, MA, 1973, PhD, 1979. **Career:** Hampton Institute, Hampton, VA, assoc director of hearing clinic, 1968-70; State University of New York at Buffalo, Buffalo, NY, coordinator, independent study, learning ctr, 1972-74; University of Cincinnati, Cincinnati, OH, director of employee's dev education program, 1974-76; University of Cincinnati Medical School, Cincinnati, OH, 1976-79; Ohio State University, Columbus, OH, assistant professor, 1980-87; State University of New York at Buffalo, Buffalo, NY, associate professor of American studies & founder/director, Center for Applied Public Affairs Studies, 1987-. **Orgs:** Chair & chief consultant, Buffalo Common Council-Commission on Urban Initiatives, 1988; member, Urban League Advisory Board, 1991; member, Greater Buffalo Economic Development Coordinating Committee, 1990-; member, Buffalo Private Industry Council's Economic Develop Coord Committee, 1990-; member, Greater Buffalo Development Foundation's Working Group on Minority Economic, beginning 1990; SUNY at Buffalo, assoc prof, currently. **Honors/Awds:** Consultant to Smithsonian Institution, "Field To Factory: Afro-American Migration, 1915-1940," An Exhibition at the National Museum of American History, Washington, DC, 1986; Consultant to National Afro-American Museum and Cultural Center Project, From Victory to Freedom: Afro-American Life in the 1950s, Columbus, 1986; African Americans and the Rise of Buffalo's Post-Industrial City, 1940-, Buffalo Urban League, 1990. **Business Addr:** Assoc Prof, Amer Studies, State University of New York at Buffalo, 101 C Fargo Quad, Bldg #1, Ellicott Complex, Buffalo, NY 14261.

TAYLOR, HENRY MARSHALL
Business executive. **Personal:** Born Dec 24, 1932, Indianapolis, IN; married Marcella Jean Collins; children: Cynthia J, Timothy M. **Educ:** IN Central U, BS 1959. **Career:** Crispus Attucks HS Indpls, teacher/coach 1959-68; Commnty Serv Cncl Metro Inpls, planner 1968-71; Indianapolis Bus Devel Found, pres 1971-. **Orgs:** Instructor Continuing Studies IU-PUI 1974-; pres HM Taylor & Asso 1983-; bd mem Ind Inst for New Bus Ventures 1984-; mem IN Dist SBA Adv Cncl; mem Omega Psi Phi Zeta Phi 1963-; commr Metro Dev Commn 1976-82; mem/treas bd Ind Export Adv Cncl US Doc Consortium for Urban Ed 1978-; sec Consumer Credit Cnslng Svc; chmn Cncl of Black Exec; exec chmn Central IN Bus Dev Coalition. **Honors/Awds:** Bus Achievement Award Zeta Phi Chap 1984; Delta Hall of Fame 1975; Disting Award Center for Leadership Dev 1981. **Military Serv:** AUS sgt E-5. **Home Addr:** 3423 N Lesley Ave, Indianapolis, IN 46218. **Business Addr:** President, Indianapolis Bus Dev Found, One Virginia Ave, Indianapolis, IN 46204.

TAYLOR, HERBERT CHARLES
Manufacturing company executive. **Personal:** Born Feb 2, 1948, Red Jacket, WV; children: Herbert Jr, Holly. **Educ:** Detroit Coll of Business, BA 1977; Central MI Univ, MA 1981. **Career:** General Motor Corp, purchasing mgr 1966-84; Bing Steel Inc, exec vice pres 1984-85; Superb Manufacturing Inc, pres 1985-. **Orgs:** Bd of dirs Bing Steel Inc 1984-, Superb Manufacturing Inc 1984-; mem Natl Black MBA Assoc 1985-; bd mem Natl Assoc of Black Auto Suppliers 1986-. **Business Addr:** President, Superb Manufacturing Inc, 6100 15 Mile Rd, Sterling Heights, MI 48312.

TAYLOR, HOWARD F.
Educator. **Personal:** Born Jul 7, 1939, Cleveland, OH; married Patricia A Epps. **Educ:** Yale, PhD 1966; Yale, MA 1964; Hiram Coll, AB 1961. **Career:** Princeton Univ, prof 1973; Syracuse Univ, 1968-73; IL Inst of Tech, 1966-68; Natl Acad of Scis, cons. **Orgs:** NAAS; Am Sociol Assn; E Sociol Soc; Am Assn of Univ Profs; Assn of Black Sociologists. **Honors/Awds:** Various grants; publ two books num articles. **Business Addr:** Princeton University, Afro-Amer Studies Prog, Princeton, NJ 08544.

TAYLOR, HYCEL B.
Clergyman. **Personal:** Born Apr 21, 1936, Columbus, OH; married Annie Bdallis; children: Chandra, Audreanna, Hycel, III. **Educ:** Fields Bible Inst, 1960; Kent State U, BFA 1965; Oberlin Grad Sch of Theol; Vanderbilt Div Sch, MDiv 1969; Vanderbilt Div Sch, Doctorate Ministery 1970; Univ of Chicago Divinity Sch, Post Doctoral study. **Career:** Garret-Evangelical Theol Sem, assoc prof 1970-; Fisk U, appointed dean chapel; Fisk Univ, minister instr in religion 1969-70; Howard Congregational Ch,pastor 1966-69; Elizabeth Baptist Ch, pastor 1962-66; Union Baptist Ch, youth dir 1959; No Baptist Dist Assn Union Grove Baptist Ch, license preacher 1956; Martin Luther King, Jr, consultant lectr founder; The Church and the Black Experience Garrett-Eangelical Theol Seminary Evanston, founder/developer; Second Bapt Church Evanston IL, pastor. **Orgs:** Mem scholarship fund Vanderbilt Div Sch; prac artist painting sculpture Martin Luther King Fund; mem Ch & Ministry of SE Conf of Un Ch of Christ; mem Life & Work Com of Nashville Council of Chs; Nashville Urban & Ministers Cadre; Bapt Sem Devel Assn; bd trustees Nashville OIC; Nashville Council on Human Relations. **Honors/Awds:** Recip TW Graham Award in Homiletics Oberlin Coll 1966. **Military Serv:** USMC res 1953-59. **Business Addr:** Pastor, Second Baptist Church, 1717 Benson Ave, Evanston, IL 60201.

TAYLOR, IRIS
Business reporter. **Personal:** Born in Powhatan, VA; children: Tamarra, Christian. **Educ:** Rutgers University, Livingston College, BA, journalism, 1983; Columbia University, School of General Studies, 1977-80. **Career:** Essence Magazine, New York, NY, contributing writer, 1974-86; Johnson & Johnson, Chicopee Div, editor, Horizons Magazine, 1980-83; The Star-Ledger, Newark, NJ, business reporter, 1983-. **Orgs:** Member, National Association of Black Journalists, 1989-. **Honors/Awds:** Lincoln University, Journalism Award for Excellence in Investigative Reporting, 1979; Outstanding Journalism Award, White House Conference on Small Business, Minority Delegates Caucus, 1988; Small Business Media Advocate of the Year, State of NJ, US Small Business Administration, 1989; Distinguished Service Award, New Jersey Press Women, for Advancing the Image of Women in Journalism, 1989; Journalism Award, NJ Chapter, Society of Professional Journalists, 1994; The Roses Scroll Woman of Achievement Awd, NJ Association of Women Business Owners Inc, 1994; Salute to Women Leaders Awd, NJ Association of Women Business Owners, 1995. **Business Addr:** Journalist, The Star-Ledger, 1 Star Ledger Plaza, Newark, NJ 07101.

TAYLOR, JACK ALVIN, JR.
Educational administrator. **Personal:** Born Jul 15, 1949, Pittsburgh, PA; son of Jean Taylor and Jack Taylor; married Janet Victoria Bivins; children: Marcus, Matthew, Jack III. **Educ:** California Univ of Pennsylvania, BA 1971, MEd 1975; Bowling Green State Univ, PhD 1985. **Career:** California Univ of Pennsylvania, dir counseling/spec serv 1972-75; Frostburg State Coll, asst dir minority affairs 1975-78; Bowling Green State Univ, student develop & spec serv 1978-85, asst vice pres for multicultural affairs 1985-95; asst vice pres for student affairs, 1995-. **Orgs:** Consultant Minority Affairs; consultant Educ Development Programs; Natl Assn of Student Personnel Administrators; mem Kappa Alpha Psi Frat Inc, PA Intercollegiate Athletic Assoc Championship Team 1970. **Business Addr:** Assistant Vice President for Student Affairs, Bowling Green State Univ, Bowling Green, OH 43403.

TAYLOR, JAMES
Business executive. **Personal:** Born Sep 8, 1922, Maywood, IL; married Margaret Caples. **Educ:** IL Inst of Tech, Inst of Design, BS 1951. **Career:** Community Film Workshop of Chicago, exec dir 1971; Cinema Video Concepts Prod Inc, pres 1971; Ctr ofr New Sch, media specialist 1975-76; Columbia Coll, instr 1972; Studio 402, freelance photojournalist, cinematographer 1966-71; Astra Photo Serv, photo lat tech 1956-66. **Orgs:** Mem, exec bd dir Intl All of Theatre Stage Employment & Moving Picture Machine Operators Union 666; Cameraman's Chic; bd dir Chic Filmmakers; bd of adv Black Arts Celebration Pro & Con Screening Bd. **Honors/Awds:** Union photographer feature film credits, "Am Dream" 1980; "Blue Bro" 1979; "The Duke" 1978; "The Awakening Land" 1977; "Moonbeam Rider" 1977; "Black Beauty" 1977; "Blue Collar" 1977; "FIST" 1977; "Piece of the Action" 1976; "Monkey Hustle" 1975; "Cooley High" 1975; "Lord Shango" 1974; "Cutter" 1972; prod & dir credits, "Ashes of Black" 1979; Fire Safety Films; Nation of Islam Saviors Day; Beacon House; Sea Scouts; Traffic Safety Commercials. **Military Serv:** US Army Air Corps corpl 1943-45. **Business Addr:** 441 N Clark St, Chicago, IL 60610.

TAYLOR, JAMES C.
State representative. **Personal:** Born Feb 8, 1930, Crawfordsville, AR; married Ella; children: Richard, Cassaundra, Cynthia. **Educ:** Univ of IL; Monticello Coll of IL. **Career:** State rep, currently; asst supt of sanitation; 16th Ward, ward committeeman, Chicago; hwy maintenance supt; professional prize fighter; hwy instructional equip operator; sanitation engr. **Orgs:** Mem Teamster Union Local 726; Ward Supt Assn; scoutmaster Troop 429 Southtown Dist; mem St Brendan's Cath Ch; mem IL Legislative Investigating Comm; mem, exec com Personnel & Pensions of Illinois House of Reps; chmn, Cities & Villages Com Illinois House of Rep; honor mem Boy Scouts Cherokee Tribe; mem S Town YMCA. **Honors/Awds:** Recipient IL Fair Employment Practices Commn Spl Recognition Award; registered Sanitation Dept of Registration & Edn; achievement award US Dept of Labor Bur of Labor Standard. **Military Serv:** AUS, corporal, Korean Conflict. **Business Addr:** State Representative, State of Illinois, 2104 State Office Bldg, Springfield, IL 62706.

TAYLOR, JAMES ELTON
Educational administrator. **Personal:** Born Jul 6, 1947, Edenton, NC; son of Mary Taylor (deceased) and Joe Taylor (deceased); married Catherine Ward; children: Kim A, Eric C, Angela Y, Pamela Y. **Educ:** Univ of MI, Business Internship 1968; Shaw Univ, BA 1969; Atlanta Univ, attended 1968-69. **Career:** First Union Natl Bank, branch mgr 1969-73; Integon Life Ins Corp, sales rep 1973-74; Elizabeth City State Univ, fin aid admin 1974-. **Orgs:** NC Assoc of Student Fin Aid Admin consul 1976 & 1977, treas 1978-80, vice pres 1980-81; Edenton-Chowan Civic League first vice pres 1984, pres 1985-89;mem Edenton-Chowan Bd of Educ 1980-86; mem NAACP 1985-; Chowan County commissioner, 1990-, elected chairman of the board, Dec 1994. **Honors/Awds:** Governor's Bulls Eye Awd NC Democratic Party 1980; Serv Awd NC Assn of Educators 1980-81; Valuable Serv Awd NC Assn of Student Fin Aid Admin 1983 & 1984; Dedicated Serv Awd Edenton-Chowan Civil League 1984; Dedicated Service Award Education, Chowan Board of Education, 1980-86. **Home Addr:** 208 W Church St, Edenton, NC 27932. **Business Addr:** Financial Aid Administrator, Elizabeth City State Univ, 1704 Weeksville Rd, Elizabeth City, NC 27909.

TAYLOR, JANICE A.
Attorney. **Personal:** Born May 23, 1954, Brooklyn, NY. **Educ:** Coll of William and Mary, BA 1975; SUNY/Buffalo Sch of Law, JD 1978. **Career:** NY City Transit Authority, attorney 1978-81, assoc attorney 1981-86; District Council 37 AFSCME AFL-CIO, asst genl counsel 1986-87; Civil Court of the City of New York, small claims arbitrator 1987-; Macon B Allen Black Bar Assoc, pres. **Orgs:** Legal counsel Concerned Citizens of South Queens 1981-87; parliamentarian Delta Sigma Theta Inc Queens Alumnae Chap 1982; legal redress chairperson NAACP Jamaica Branch 1983-85, 1987-88, exec bd mem 1983-85, 1987-88; regional council mem Natl Bar Assoc 1983-87; deaconette Concord Bapt Church of Christ 1984-;bd mem Black Women in Transit 1985-86. **Home Addr:** 111-26 198th St, Jamaica, NY 11412.

TAYLOR, JASON
Professional football player. **Personal:** Born Sep 1, 1974. **Educ:** Akron. **Career:** Miami Dolphins, defensive end, 1997-. **Business Addr:** Professional Football Player, Miami Dolphins, 2269 NW 199th St, Miami, FL 33056, (305)620-5000.

TAYLOR, JEFFERY CHARLES
Attorney. **Personal:** Born Nov 15, 1957, Staten Island, NY; son of Pauline D Taylor and Robert D Taylor. **Educ:** Pace University, BS (cum laude), 1984; Hofstra University, School of Law, JD, 1988. **Career:** Community Legal Services Corp, intern, 1987-88; Paralegal Support Services, Inc, legal assistant, 1988-89; American Civil Liberties Union, law clerk, 1989-90; Maryland Legal Aid Bureau, Inc, staff attorney, 1990-. **Orgs:** Maryland Prison Renewal Committee, member, 1991-; Project Raise of Maryland, 1991-; Renaissance Economic Development Project of Park Heights Inc, financial director, 1993-; Project 2000 of Maryland, 1992-93. **Honors/Awds:** Mayor's Citation for Outstanding Community Service, 1993. **Military Serv:** US Air Force, a-1st class, 1976-79. **Home Addr:** 2912 W Coldspring Ln #C, Baltimore, MD 21215, (410)664-1563. **Business Addr:** Staff Attorney, Prisoner's Assistance Project, Legal Aid Bureau, Inc, 500 E Lexington St, Ste 514, Baltimore, MD 21202, (410)539-0390.

TAYLOR, JEROME
Educator. **Personal:** Born Jan 26, 1940, Waukegan, IL; son of Willie Mae Taylor and George Washington (deceased); married Tommie Nell; children: Kim, Lisa, Jacques, Zwehla. **Educ:** Univ of Denver, BA 1961; IN Univ, PhD 1965. **Career:** Mental Health Unit Topeka, dir 1968-69; Univ of Pittsburgh Clinical Psych Ctr, dir 1969-71; Univ of Pittsburgh, assoc prof of black studies and education, dir, Inst for the Black Family, currently. **Orgs:** Mem Amer Psychol Society, Assoc of Black Psych, Omicron Delta Kappa, Sigma Xi, Psi Chi; member, National Black Child Development Institute; member, National Council on Family Relations. **Honors/Awds:** Postdoctoral fellow, Menninger Found, 1965-67. **Business Addr:** Associate Professor, Black Studies and Educ, Dir, Inst for the Black Family, Univ of Pittsburgh, Pittsburgh, PA 15260.

TAYLOR, JOHN L.
Educator. **Personal:** Born May 7, 1947, Holly Springs, MS; son of Cinderella Sims Taylor and Charlie E Taylor Sr; married Naomi Ruth Thomas; children: Tony, Jonathan, Chere. **Educ:** Rust College, BS 1969. **Career:** Independence High School, teacher, currently. **Orgs:** Deacon, clerk, Baptist Church; Mason, Waterford Lodge #450; Sunday school teacher, Mt Moriah Baptist Church; elected offical, election commissioner, Marshall County District 4. **Honors/Awds:** Teacher of the Day, Radio Station 1984; Academic Career Day, Univeristy of Mississippi, 1985. **Home Addr:** Rt 4 Box 107, Byhalia, MS 38611.

TAYLOR, JOHNNY
Professional basketball player. **Personal:** Born Jun 4, 1974. **Educ:** Tennessee-Chattanooga. **Career:** Orlando Magic, forward, 1998-. **Business Addr:** Professional Basketball Player, Orlando Magic, 1 Magic Pl, Orlando, FL 32801, (407)649-3200.

TAYLOR, JOSEPH T.
Educator (retired). **Personal:** Born Feb 11, 1913, Rolling Fork, MS; son of Willie Ann Price Taylor and Joseph T Taylor; married Hertha Ward; children: Bruce T, Judith F, Joel H. **Educ:** Univ of IL, AB 1936, AM 1937; IN Univ, PhD 1952; Berea Coll KY, LLD 1969; Marian Coll, LittD 1979; IN Univ, DHL 1984. **Career:** IN Univ assoc prof 1962-66; Indianapolis Regional Campus, asst dir 1965, acting dean 1966; Fisk Univ, tcher fellow, Rosenwald fellow; Flanner House Survey Indianapolis, field worker; Carnegie-Myrdal Study The Negro in Amer, field investigator; FL A&M Coll, instr; Natl Youth Admin, area dir; FL A&M Coll, asst to pres, acting dean grad div; Albany State Coll, dir arts & sci prof; Dillard Univ, chmn div of social sci prof, acting dean; Flanner House of Indianapolis, dir prog devel; IN Univ Purdue Univ, prof of sociology beginning 1967, Dean School of Liberal Arts, 1967-78, special asst vp 1978-84. **Orgs:** Spl appointee by Fed Dist Ct Judge Dillin to devel interim plan for Court ordered desegregation of Indianapolis Pub Sch 1973; author of numerous publications; bd dir Indianapolis YMCA & YWCA; bd dir United Way of Gr Indianapolis; bd dir Urban League of Gr Indianapolis; bd trustees Berea Coll KY; bd mem Comm Serv Coun of Indianapolis; bd mem Family Serv Assn of Indianapolis; bd mem Natl Conf of Christians & Jews; bd mem New Hope Found of IN; mem Christian Theological Sem Adv Coun; mem Comprehensive Health Planning Coun of Marion Co Inc; mem Federation of Asso Clubs adv com; mem Greater Indianapolis Housing Devel Corp; mem Indianapolis Prog Com; co-chmn Citizen Adv Comm Indianapolis Bd of Sch Commrs; mem Gr Indianapolis Prog Com; commrIndianapolis Housing Auth; mem Natl Bd of Higher Educited Meth Church; mem Negro Coll Advance United Meth Ch; mem Rotary Intl, State of IN Dev Disabilities Adv Council; mem YMCA Natl Coun (Mid-Amer Region); Sigma Pi Phi, Alpha Phi Alpha Inc, Prince Hall Mason; life member, NAACP. **Honors/Awds:** Black History & Fine Arts Festival Awd E St Louis Il 1974; Man of the Yr Awd Natl Coun Christians & Jews 1974; Disting Achievement Awd Fed of Assoc Clubs 1974; Indiana Academy Fellow 1989; Paul Harris Fellow, Rotary International 1989. **Military Serv:** AUS 1942-46.

TAYLOR, JULIA W.
Bank executive. **Personal:** Born Apr 4, 1936, Durham, NC. **Educ:** NC Central Univ, 1954-55; Stonier Grad School of Banking, 1967; LaSalle Extension Univ Chicago, attended; Amer Inst of Banking, attended. **Career:** Bank of Amer, employee 1960; Broadway Fed Savings & Loan Assoc, sr clerk 1961-62; Broadway Fed Savings & Loan Assoc, escrow officer 1962, asst sec 1962-63; Mechanics & Farmers Bank, note teller 1965-66, asst cashier 1966-67, vp, mgr 1967-78, sr vp, city exec 1978-83, pres/CEO, 1983-87, chairman, president/CEO, 1987-. **Orgs:** Treas, bd mem Natl Bankers Assoc 1974-82; mem Raleigh Civic Ctr Auth 1976-80; bd mem, past 2nd vice pres Jr Achievement of Wake Cty 1976-; dir, exec comm, Mech & Farmers Bk Durham NC 1978-; mem, vchmn NC State Ed Asst Auth 1978-; bd mem, past treas Raleigh Wake Urban League 1978-; trustee St Joseph AME Church Durham 1980; mem adv bd Rutledge Coll; mem bd of dir NC Bankers Assoc, mem NC Central Univ Bd of Visitors, Greater Durham Comm found; mem bd of trustees Univ of NC Wilmington, Daisy E Scarborough Found Inc; mem bd of dir Greater Durham C of C; mem NC State Banking Commission; assoc mem State Conf Bank Supervisors; bd of dirs, Kaiser Foundation Health Plan of NC; North Carolina Bus Advisory Bd, Fuqua School of Bus, Duke Univ; NC, 4-H Development Fund Inc, bd of dirs; Africa News, bd of dirs. **Honors/Awds:** Named Tar Heel of the Week by News & Observer 1986; YMCA Women of Achievement Awd 1985; Achievement Award, Iota Phi Lambda Sorority, Rho Chapter, 1984; Distinguished Alumni Award, Hillside High School, 1985; National Minority Business Advocate of the Year Award, US Department of Commerce, 1987; Citizen Award, Independent Weekly, 1988; NC Chapter of the Natl Assn of Women Business Owners Award, 1991. **Business Addr:** President, Mechanics & Farmers Bank, 114 W Parrish St, PO Box 1932, Durham, NC 27702.

TAYLOR, JULIUS H.
Educator. **Personal:** Born Feb 15, 1914, Cape May, NJ; married Patricia Spaulding; children: Dwight, Trena. **Educ:** Lincoln Univ, AB; Univ PA, MS, PhD. **Career:** WV State Coll, dept head 1945; Morgan State Coll, assoc prof 1949, dept head & prof 1951-78; Goddard Space Flight Center, NASA, contractor, 1978-. **Orgs:** Mem Chesapeake Amer Assn Physics Tchrs; Natl Com Physics Secondary Educ; pres AAPT 1962-63; rep AAPT 1964-65; Natl Science Found; Travelers Aid Soc; Gov Science Adv Council; zone councillor Soc Physics Students Alumnus Yr Lincoln Univ 1963. **Honors/Awds:** Research award; Julius Rosenwald fellow Univ PA 1943-44. **Home Addr:** 2319 Lyndhurst Ave, Baltimore, MD 21216.

TAYLOR, KENNETH DOYLE
Engineer/scientist. **Personal:** Born Nov 5, 1949, Hartford, CT; son of Adelaide P Tweedy Jordan and Frank K Taylor; married Mattie Jane Dolphy, Aug 25, 1972; children: Jerome Daniel. **Educ:** University of CT, BS 1971, MS 1974, PhD 1981; Rensselaer Polytechnic Institute (Hartford Graduate Center) Hartford CT, MBA 1988. **Career:** Picker Corp, design engr 1973-74; St Francis Hosp & Medical Ctr, mgr rsch lab 1974-79; Natl Institutes of Health, asst to the dir 1985-86; United Technologies Rsch Ctr, sr project engr 1979-90; Pfizer Hospital Products Group, director, tech assessment, 1990-93; vice pres, Research & Development, Valleylab, 1993-. **Orgs:** Lecturer Univ of CT Dept of Elec Engrg 1977-83; chmn/treas Family Federal Credit Union 1978-80, 1983-85; adjunct lecturer Hartford Grad Ctr 1982-; sr mem IEEE 1983-; vice pres Beta Sigma Lambda, Alpha Phi Alpha Frat 1983-85; mem Sigma Pi Phi Frat 1984-; bd of dirs, Connecticut Pre-Engineering Program 1989-91; bd of dirs, Channel 3 Country Camp 1989-91. **Honors/Awds:** United Technologies Awd 1981; Univ of CT Disting Grad Awd 1982; AIAA Contribution to Society Awd 1985; President's Commn on Exec Exchange Class XVI 1985-86; Registered Professional Engineer, State of Connecticut 1977. **Home Addr:** 375 Golden Eagle Dr, Broomfield, CO 80020-1272. **Business Addr:** Vice Pres, Research & Development, Valleylab, 5920 Longbow Dr, Boulder, CO 80301, (303)581-6725.

TAYLOR, KENNETH MATTHEW
Business executive. **Personal:** Born in Jersey City, NJ. **Educ:** BS; MBA. **Career:** Witco Chem Corp NYC, sr auditor/financial analyst; Allied Chem Corp Morristown, NJ, sr auditor; Colgate-Palmolive Corp NYC, sr accountant; Philip Morris Inc NYC, sr analyst/auditor; Bache & Co Inc NYC, sr brokerage accountant. **Orgs:** Mem Am Mgmt Assn; Inst of Internal Auditors; Nat Assn of Black Accountants; Nat Assn of Accountants N Jersey Chpt; mem Omega Psi Phi Frat; chmn 2nd Dist Budget & Finance Com Newark 1972-74; mem Nat Budget & Financo Com 1973-74; keeper of finance Upsilon Phi Chap 1970-74. **Honors/Awds:** Distinguished Award as Chmn Finance Com 1974. **Military Serv:** USAF. **Business Addr:** 277 Park Ave, New York, NY 10017.

TAYLOR, KIMBERLY HAYES
Reporter. **Personal:** Born Jul 9, 1962, Louisville, KY; daughter of Loraine S Hayes and James E Hayes; married Keith L Taylor, May 28, 1983. **Educ:** Morehead State University, Morehead, KY, BA, communications, 1984. **Career:** Courier-Journal, Louisville, KY, clerk/writer, 1986-88; The Commercial-News, Danville, IL, police reporter, 1987-88; Observer-Dispatch, Utica, NY, court criminal justice reporter, 1988-; Peace On Our Minds, West Edmeston, NY, editor in chief, 1990-. **Orgs:** Executive board member, Young and Teen Peacemakers Inc, 1990-; executive board, Oneida Co Chapter NAACP, 1990-; District Committee, Boy Scouts of America, 1989-; member, Greater Utica Multiculturalism Coalition 1990-; member, National Association of Black Journalists, 1986-. **Honors/Awds:** Top Well Done Award for "Street Under Siege" series, Gannett Inc, 1991. **Home Addr:** 15 Noyes St, Utica, NY 13502. **Business Addr:** Reporter, Editorial/News Dept, Observer-Dispatch, 221 Oriskany Plaza, Utica, NY 13502.

TAYLOR, LAWRENCE JULIUS
Professional football player (retired). **Personal:** Born Feb 4, 1959, Williamsburg, VA; son of Iris Taylor and Clarence Taylor; married Linda Cooley; children: 4. **Educ:** Univ of North Carolina, attended. **Career:** New York Giants, linebacker 1981-92. **Honors/Awds:** All-American at North Carolina; Atlantic Coast Conference Player of the Year, 1980; played in East-West Shrine Game and Japan Bowl; unanimous All-NFL selection for 3 yrs; top linebacker in NFL, NFLPA for 3 yrs; 2 time defensive MVP, Associated Press; NFL Defensive Player of the Year, Seagram's Computer Awards Pgm; played in Pro Bowl, 1981-. **Business Addr:** Retired Linebacker, New York Giants, Giants Stadium, East Rutherford, NJ 07073.

TAYLOR, LEBARON
Personal: widoWed; children: son, daughter. **Career:** Sony Music Entertainment Inc, sr vp of corp affairs, currently; Sony Software Corp, vp, currently. **Orgs:** Congressional Black Caucus Foundation, chair/CEO. **Honors/Awds:** CBC Chair Award winner, twice.

TAYLOR, LINDA SUZANNA. See TAYLOR, SISTER MARIE DE PORRES.

TAYLOR, MARGARET. See BURROUGHS, MARGARET TAYLOR.

TAYLOR, SISTER MARIE DE PORRES (LINDA SUZANNA TAYLOR)
Association executive, city offical, religious sister. **Personal:** Born May 27, 1947, Los Angeles, CA; daughter of Isabel "Nick" McCoy Taylor Clarke and James "Sam" Taylor. **Educ:** Marylhurst Coll, Marylhurst OR, BA, 1970; California State Univ, San Francisco CA, MA, 1976; Pacific Lutheran Seminary, Berkeley CA, 1982; California State Univ, Hayward CA, 1986-. **Career:** Holy Names High School, Oakland CA, chair home economics dept, 1969-77; St Benedict Church, Oakland CA, assoc pastor, 1977-82; Roman Catholic Bishop, Oakland CA, dir of Black Catholics, 1982-89; National Black Sisters Conference, Oakland CA, exec dir, 1982-; Oakland Private Industry Council, Oakland CA, program coordinator, 1989-91; City of Oakland, assistant to the mayor, job training and employment, 1991-. **Orgs:** Chmn, bd of dir, Bay Area Black United Fund; pres, bd of dir, Oakland Citizens Committee for Urban Renewal (OCCUR); pres, United East Oakland Clergy; mem, bd of dir, Holy Names College, Oakland CA; vice chmn, bd of dir, Oakland Police Activity League; mem, Mayor's Committee on Homeless, Oakland CA; board member, Patrons of the Arts and Humanities, 1991-; board member, 1990-, chair, 1993-, Mary's Pence. **Honors/Awds:** Image Builders Award, College Bounders of the Bay Area, 1981; Rose Casanave Service Award, Black Catholic Vicariate, Diocese of Oakland CA, 1982; Outstanding Leadership in Bay Area Award, Links Inc, 1982; Martin Luther King Jr Award, United East Oakland Clergy, 1984; Woman of the Year, Oakland YWCA, 1988; Ella Hill Hutch Award, Black Women Organized for Political Action, 1990. **Home Addr:** 5022 Camden St., Oakland, CA 94619.

TAYLOR, MARTHA
Transportation manager. **Personal:** Born Jul 26, 1941, Shreveport, LA; daughter of Viola Harris Taylor and Henry Taylor; married Royal Odell Taylor, Feb 14, 1975; children: Valerie L Thompson, Debra L Benton. **Educ:** Merritt College, Oakland, CA, AA, 1977; University of San Francisco, San Francisco, CA, BA, 1979, MPA, 1981. **Career:** Bay Area Rapid Transit District, Oakland, CA, police officer, 1973-77, police sergeant, 1977-81, police lieutenant, 1981-83, support and analysis manager, 1983-90, department manager, station operations, 1990-92, assistant chief transportation officer, 1992-. **Orgs:** President, Black Managers and Professionals Association, 1981-; member, Conference Minority Transit Officials, 1985-; member, past member of board of directors, East Oakland Youth Development Center, East Oakland, CA, 1986-87; past second vice pres, National Forum for Black Public Administrators, Oakland chapter, Oakland, CA, 1986-88; member of executive board, Black Women Organized for Political Action, 1986-; member of Youth Mentor Program, Oakland Public Schools, Oakland, CA, 1986-; chair of committee training, Women in Transit-American Public Transit Association, 1987-; bible instructor, Bethel Missionary Baptist Church, 1987-; National Negro Council of Women. **Honors/Awds:** Certificate of Recognition, American Public Transit Association, Western Conference, 1985; Certificate for Outstanding Contributions, American Public Transit Association, 1987; author of "The Challenge of Climbing the Organizational Ladder: A Matter Of Perspective," California Law Enforcement Association Police Recorder, 1988; Meritorious Award, National Forum for Black Public Administrators, 1991. **Home Addr:** 3828 Sequoyah Road, Oakland, CA 94605. **Business Addr:** Assistant Chief Transportation Officer, Bay Area Rapid Transit Dist, 800 Madison St, Rm 214, Oakland, CA 94605.

TAYLOR, MAURICE DE SHAWN
Professional basketball player. **Personal:** Born Oct 30, 1976. **Educ:** Univ of Michigan. **Career:** Los Angeles Clippers, forward, 1997-. **Business Addr:** Professional Basketball Player, Los Angeles Clippers, 3939 S Figueroa St, Los Angeles Sports Arena, Los Angeles, CA 90037, (213)748-8000.

TAYLOR, MESHACH
Actor. **Personal:** Born in New Orleans, LA; married Bianca; children: Tamar, Yasmine, Esme. **Educ:** Attended, Florida A&M Univ. **Career:** Actor, Hair Natl Theatre Company; the Organic Theatre group; performances at the Goodman Theatre; television series: "Buffalo Bill", "Designing Women", "Dave's World," currently; movies: Welcome to Oblivion; Class Act, 1992. **Honors/Awds:** Has made guest appearances on numerous TV shows. **Business Addr:** Actor, Dave's World, c/o CBS Entertainment, 4024 Radford Ave, Studio City, CA 91604.

TAYLOR, MICHAEL
Management consultant. **Personal:** Born Oct 13, 1958, New York, NY; son of Patricia Taylor and Donald Taylor; married Sandy Jones, Sep 5, 1987. **Educ:** Stanford Univ, MBA 1984; Harvard Univ, BA 1980. **Career:** Pacific Bell, systems analyst 1980-82; Ducommon, asst mgr corp develop 1983; Booz Allen and Hamilton, assoc 1984-86; Infotech Planning Group, principal, l986-90; Amer Pop Video, corp pres, l990-91; San Francisco Consulting Group, vice pres, 1991-94; Arthur D Little Inc, North America Management Consulting, managing director, information technology, media & electronics telecommunications 1994-. **Orgs:** Natl Black MBA Assoc; charter mem UJAMAA. **Home Addr:** 128-35 Skyline Blvd, Oakland, CA 94619.

TAYLOR, MICHAEL LOEB
Educator. **Personal:** Born Jan 11, 1947, Houston, TX; children: Christopher Kirrinkai Parrish-Taylor, Jennifer Nichol Parrish-Taylor. **Educ:** UCLA, BA 1970, MA 1972, MFA 1974. **Career:** Univ of Nairobi, Kenya, lecturer, 1972-73, 1975-77; Western KY Univ, asst prof, 1977-81; Lewis & Clark Coll, assoc prof, 1981-. **Orgs:** Design consult African Heritage Ltd Nairobi, Kenya, 1972-73, 1975-77; mem/artist Blackfish Gallery Portland, OR 1984; Members Gallery 1982-83. **Honors/Awds:** Fulbright Award (declined) Turkey 1981; Commission for Washington State Arts Commission 1989. **Business Addr:** Associate Professor of Art, Lewis & Clark College, Portland, OR 97219.

TAYLOR, MILDRED D.
Author. **Personal:** Born 1943, Jackson, MS. **Educ:** Graduated from University of Toledo; received master's degree from University of Colorado School of Journalism. **Career:** Peace Corps, taught English and history in Ethiopia, became recruiter in the US; University of Colorado, organizer of black studies program and study skills coordinator; writer. **Orgs:** Member, Univ of Colorado Black Students Alumni Group. **Honors/Awds:** Author: Song of the Trees, Dial, 1975; Roll of Thunder, Hear My Cry, Dial, 1976; Let the Circle Be Unbroken, Dial, 1981; Mississippi Bridge, 1990; Award from the Council on Interracial Books for Children, 1975; New York Times Outstanding Book Award, 1975; Children's Book Showcase Award, 1976; Newbery Award, 1977; Horn Book Honor Award from Boston Globe; Coretta Scott King Award; American Library Assn, honors, 1981.

TAYLOR, MILDRED E. CROSBY
Personnel specialist. **Personal:** Born Dec 18, 1919, Centralia, IL; married David P. **Educ:** LaSalle Ext Univ, 1939-41; US Dept of Agriculture Grad Sch, certificate; Exec Inst, exec devel training; US Dept of Labor, leadership devel courses; Catholic Univ Washington DC, grad study. **Career:** Women's Bur US Dept of Labor, conv planner ret social science advisor; Surgeon General's Office Dept of Army, personnel asst; Surgeon General's Office Dept of Air Force, personnel specialist; keynote speaker panelist moderator at meetings & seminars. **Orgs:** Women's Bur liaison to black women's orngs on employment; mem Sec of Labor's Vol Day Com; bd dir Dept of Labor Recreation Assn; charter mem Toastmasters Internat; vice pres Air & Cruise Travel Adminstrs Washington DC; charter mem DC Women's Commn on Crime Prevention; charter mem bd dir Trinity AME Zion Ch Housing Corp; past pres Century Club Nat Asnn of Negor Bus & Professional Women Inc; past loyal lady ruler Order of Golden Circle; past matron Order of Eastern Star; Urban League NAACP; past commandress Mecca Ct #2 Daughters of Isis (Women's Aux to Shriners); imperial conv directness Imperial Ct Daughters of Isis; vol worker for many charitable orgns. **Honors/Awds:** Recipient outstanding serv award Prentiss Inst Hon KY Col Gov Nunn 1971; first woman to receive distinguished service award from Mecca Temple #10 Ancient Egyptian Arabic Order Nobles of Mystic Shrine (Press Release to Blak Press by Dept of Labor); honorary dr of humanities deg Ministerial Inst- Coll West Point MS 1977. **Business Addr:** 1809 Kilbourne Pl NW, Washington, DC 20010.

TAYLOR, MILES EDWARD
Engineer, pyrotechnician. **Personal:** Born Apr 25, 1964, Nyack, NY; son of Lillian Murray Taylor and Aubrey Taylor. **Educ:** C W Post College, Long Island University, Brookville, NY, BA, 1986. **Career:** Nyack High School, Nyack, NY, head cross country coach, 1987; Black Magic Video Production, Nyack, NY, owner, 1987-; Fire Works by Grucci, Brookhaven, NY, pyrotechnician, 1983-; CNN New York, New York, NY, engineer, 1987-. **Orgs:** Vice president, Nyack Fire Dept, Jackson Fire Eng Co #3, 1980; member, Tau Kappa Epsilon, 1983-.

TAYLOR, NOEL C.
Clergyman, mayor. **Personal:** Born Jul 15, 1924, Bedford City, VA; married Barbara Jean Smith; children: Sabrina T Law, Deseree Charletta. **Educ:** Bluefield State Coll, BS(with honors) 1949; VA Sem & Coll, BD 1955, DD 1959; NY Univ, MA Religious Educ 1963; Ordained to Ministry of Baptist Ch. **Career:** Bedford City Pub Sch, teacher 1949, elem sch prin 1950-52; First Baptist Ch Clifton Forge, VA, pastor 1955-58; First Baptist Ch Norfolk, VA, pastor 1958-61; High St Baptist Ch, pastor. **Orgs:** Councilman Roanoke City Council 1970-; vice-mayor Roanoke, VA 1974-75; mayor Roanoke, VA 1975-; dir Dominion Bank; bd dir Local Arc & Blue Cross & Blue Shield So Western VA; bd dir Bapt Children's Home; bd dir Blue Ridge Mountains Council Boy Scouts of Amer; mem NAACP, mem VA Bapt State Conv Roanoke Ministers Conf; Valley Bapt Assn Amer Baptist Conv Nat'l Baptist Conv; Lott Carey Bapt Foreign Missions Conv; US Conf of Mayors; Nat'l Conf of Black Mayors; Nat'l League of Cities; Alpha Phi Alpha; 33rd degree Masons Mem United Supreme Cncl; mem Kiwanis;Brd of Directors-Blue Ridge Mountains Council of Boy Scouts of Am; Wlm A Hunton YMCA Family Ctr; Advisory Brd of Central YWCA, Virginia Coal Research and Dev; Roanoke Valley Chpter Amer Red Cross; RoanokeMem Hospitals; Design 85 Steering ComFirst Vice Pres VA Municipal League; Brd of Dir Jobs for Virginia Graduates requested by Governor Robb. **Honors/Awds:** Man of the Year twice Omega Phi Psi; Cert of Merit Natl Phi Delta Kappa; Cert of Apprec Roanoke Jaycees; Brotherhood Award NCCJ; Tri-Ominis Celebrity Award; Man of the Year Masons; Comm Serv Award Delta Sigma Theta; Nat'l Cncl of Christians & Jews Brotherhood Awd 1974; Northwest Jaycees Awd for Outstanding Comm Serv 1976; Lions Club Outstanding Serv Awd 1977; Ivy Bpt Church Newport News VA leadership awd 1978; Delta Sigma Theta Man of the Year 1978; Omega Phi Psi Man of the Year 1978; Nat'l Comm Educ Awd for Contributing to Community Educ 1979; Blue Cross/Blue Shield Dedicated Serv Awd 1979; Zeta Phi Beta Citizen of Year 1979;Booster Club Awd for Outstanding Serv 1979; Awd of Appreciation March of Dimes 1980; VA Educ Assoc Dist Service Awd 1981; JacksonJr HS Apprec Awd 1981;Alpha Kappapha Citizen of Year 1984; Univ S A F American Spirit Awd 1984; Int'l Mgmt Cncl Top Manager of the Year 1984-85. **Military Serv:** AUS 1943-46. **Business Addr:** Mayor, High St Baptist Church, 215 Church Ave SE, Roanoke, VA 24011.

TAYLOR, NORMAN EUGENE
Government official. **Personal:** Born Nov 12, 1948, Newark, NJ; son of Martha Small Taylor and Edwin Alfred Taylor; married Theresa Singleton, Apr 26, 1980; children: Norman Assaf, Todd Farrell, Norman Amman, Joy Jamillah, Autier Dawn. **Educ:** Bethune-Cookman College, Daytona Beach FL, BA, 1970; Florida Atlantic Univ, Boca Raton FL, MPA, 1976; University of Miami School of Law, 1991-92. **Career:** October Center, Inc, Fort Lauderdale FL, director, 1973-80; Norman E. Taylor & Associates, Inc, Miami FL, president, 1980-83; Broward County Govt, Fort Lauderdale FL, public relations mgr, 1983-84, OEO director, 1984-96, office of economic development director, 1996-. **Orgs:** National Forum for Black Public Administrators, Council for Black Economic Development; member, Airport Minority Advisory Council, 1988-; member, Broward Senior Executives, 1987-; member, Florida Association of Minority Business Enterprise Officials, 1987-; chairman, Metro-Broward Capital Corp., 1987-; mem, Psi Phi Fraternity, 1967-; mem, American Economic Development Council, 1996-; mem, Urban Land Institute, 1996-. **Honors/Awds:** City and County awards, Fort Lauderdale chapter of NAACP, 1978, 1980; outstanding service award, October Center, Inc, 1980; Service of the Year, Urban League of Broward County, 1990. **Military Serv:** US Army, E-4, 1971-73; award for outstanding service in human relations, 1973. **Home Addr:** 1966 SW 94th Avenue, Miramar, FL 33025. **Business Addr:** Director, Office of Economic Development, Broward County Board of County Commissioners, 115 S Andrews Ave, Governmental Ctr, Rm A680, Fort Lauderdale, FL 33301.

TAYLOR, OCTAVIA G.
Educator. **Personal:** Born Dec 17, 1925, Lake Charles, LA; married George E; children: Andrea M, George E, Jr, Nancy E. **Educ:** So Univ Baton Rouge, BA 1946; Columbiau, MA 1953; USC, Grad Study 1963. **Career:** Calcasieu Parish HS, eng instr 1975-; WO Boston HS Lake Charles, eng drama instr 1953-62; Mt Vernon Jr HS LA, eng instr 1963. **Orgs:** Pres Classroom Tchrs Assn St LA 1970; mem LA Coun Tchrs Eng; New Sunlight Bapt Ch Order Eastern Star; pres Beta Kappa Zeta Chap Zeta Phi Beta 1970; imperial directress Region III; Imp Dep St LA Daus Isis; bd mem Nat Counc christns & Jews. **Honors/Awds:** Testimonial Banquet, LA Charities, 1974; Daus of Isis Aux Shriners.

TAYLOR, ORLANDO L.
Educational administrator. **Personal:** Born Aug 9, 1936, Chattanooga, TN; son of Carrie Lee Sanders Taylor and Leroy Taylor; married Loretta M, Jun 6, 1957; children: Orlando II, Ingrid Taylor-Boone. **Educ:** Hampton Institute, Hampton VA, BS, 1957; Indiana Univ, Bloomington IN, MA, 1960; Univ of Michigan, Ann Arbor MI, PhD, 1966. **Career:** Indiana Univ, Bloomington IN, asst prof, 1964-69; Center for Applied Linguistics, Washington DC, senior research fellow, 1969-75; University of District of Columbia, Washington DC, prof, 1970-73; Howard Univ, Washington DC, prof, 1973—; dean of communications, 1985—. **Honors/Awds:** Distinguished scholar award, Howard Univ, 1984; Award of Appreciation, American Speech-Language-Hearing Association, 1990. **Business Addr:** Dean, School of Communications, Howard University, Washington, DC 20059.

TAYLOR, PATRICIA E.
Attorney. **Personal:** Born Feb 17, 1942, New Haven; married Dr Howard F; children: Carla Y. **Educ:** IL Inst Tech, BS 1967; Yale Law School, JD, 1971. **Career:** Commun Prog Inc, commun wrkr 1963-65; Onondaga Lega Svc, law clk 1971-73; Princeton U, vis lctr 1974-. **Orgs:** Mem NJ Bar Assn; US Sup Ct Bar; Allan Guttmacher Institute, bd of dir, 1986-89; assoc Gen Couns Educ Testing Serv Princeton NJ; bd dir ARC 1972-73. **Honors/Awds:** Reginald Herber Smith Fellow 1971-73; Outst Yng Wmn Am 1974. **Business Addr:** Educ Testing Serv, Rosedale Rd, Princeton, NJ 08541.

TAYLOR, PATRICIA TATE
Manager. **Personal:** Born Jan 13, 1954, Cleveland, OH; daughter of Catherine Johnson Tate and John Henry Tate; married Jean Georges Balla, Dec 11, 1989. **Educ:** Case Western Reserve Univ, BA 1977; Harvard Business Sch, MBA 1985; Federal Executive Institute, 1994. **Career:** Standard Oil Co OH, acctg, mktg, human resources 1977-83; Deloitte Haskins & Sells, consultant 1984; Cresap McCormick & Paget, management consultant 1985-87; US General Accounting Office, management expert, 1987-90, assistant director, federal management Isses, 1990-91, assistant director, Office of Program Planning, 1992-93, Senior Executive Service, Candidate Development Program, 1993, director, Accounting & Information Management Division, 1994-97; Dept of Defense, director, Quality Management & Performance Measurement, 1997-. **Orgs:** Mem Black Professionals Assn 1979-83; industry adv bd Cornell Univ 1981-83; industry adv comm Natl Assn of Engr Prog Admin 1981-83; mem, American Management Assn 1985-; mem, Harvard Alumni Assn 1985-; mem, Natl Assn of Female Executives 1985-; mem, Black MBA Association 1985-; Executive Women in Government, 1993-. **Honors/Awds:** Scholarship, National Achievement 1972; Academic Fellowship Harvard Univ Council for Opportunity in Graduate Management Education 1985; Special Commendation Award 1988; Top Bonus Recipient, 1989, 1990, 1991; Comptroller General's Award, 1992. **Military Serv:** Army ROTC cadet sgt major 1973-75.

TAYLOR, PAUL DAVID
Health services administrator/educator. **Personal:** Born May 1, 1937, Lexington, TN; son of Jessie Mae Williams (deceased) and Ray Otis Taylor (deceased); divorced; children: Paul David Jr, Bentley Christopher. **Educ:** Garden City Comm Coll, AS 1957; Univ of KS, 1958. **Career:** Univ of CO Health Sci Ctr, biol lab tech, 1962-65, coordinator of organ transplant prgm, 1962-92, rsch assoc, 1965-67, sr instructor, 1969-92, professor emeritus, 1992; Presbyterian Univ Hospital of the Univ of Pittsburgh, transplant admin, 1989-98; Veterans Administation Hospital, Pittsburgh, PA, health tech, 1990-97. **Orgs:** Task Force on Minority Organ Donation of Western PA; National Kidney Foundation of Western PA, minority affairs cmte; Journal of Transplant Coordination, editorial bd; Department of Hlth & Human Services, Bureau of Hlth Resources Development, grant review cmte; American Society of Minority Hlth and Transplant Professionals, charter mbr; Knights of Pythagorus, KS, 1955; Prince Hall Masons, Denver, past mstr, 1967, Grand Lodge CO & Jurisdiction, chmn, jurisprudence, 1970-90, right worshipful grand trustee, 1987-90; North America Transplant Coordinators Orgnztn, 1975-98, founding mbr; CO Society to Prevent Blindness, bd of dirs, 1977-80. **Honors/Awds:** Citizenship Awd Prince Hall Masons CO & Jurisdiction 1982; Guest Lecturer Denver Public Schools Denver 1983-; Inaugural inductee High School Hall of Fame Garden City, KS May 1985; Citizenship Awrd Hattie Anthony Resource Center 1986; Man of Distinction, Lane Contempories of Lane College Alumni Assn, Denver Chapter, 1989; Colorado's Own African-American History Maker, Honoree, 1993; BTAC, Denver, Black Transplantation Committee, 1993. **Special Achievements:** Member of world's first human liver transplant team, Denver, CO, 1963; consultant/participant: Eurotransplant Coord Organization, Leiden Holland 1983; Canadian Transplant Coord, Calgary, Alberta 1983; 10th Annual Meeting of Japanese Transplantation & Artificial Organ Society, Sendai, Japan, 1985; Cardiovascular Transplantation Seminar, Osaka, Japan, 1985; National Thoracic Organ Transplant Nurses of Hospital Juan Canalejo, La Coruna, Spain, 1992; Minister of Health & Welfare, Tokyo, Japan, 1985; author or co-author of numerous scientific papers, 1965-; 16th Annual Meeting North Amer Transplant Coordinators Organization, African Americans in transplantation lecture, Halifax, Nova Scotia, 1990; XIVth International Congress of the Tranplantation Society, Paris, France, 1992; XVth International Congress of the Transplantation Society & International Transplant Coordinators Symposium, Kyoto, Japan, 1994; Inaugural Inductee, first national minority transplant, Hall of Fame, Pioneer Award, Motted, Howard Univ, 1996. **Home Addr:** PO Box 200026, Denver, CO 80220-0026.

TAYLOR, PAULINE J.
Curator. **Personal:** Born Oct 20, 1911, Bessemer, AL; married Julius C; children: Barbara McCrary Saunders. **Career:** Detroit St Rys, conductorette 1942-46; The Edison Inst, Henry Ford Museum, Greenfield Village, housekeeper of decorative arts retired. **Orgs:** Pres Detroit Bridge League 1957-61; 1st female natl pres Amer Bridge Assn 1969-73; mem Hamilton Intl Corp, Health Soc of Wayne Cty 1962; past pres,exec bd mem Amer Bridge Assn 1974; mem NAACP, Urban League, Petite Bowling League, YWCA, Motor City Duplicettes, St Johns Christian Meth. **Honors/Awds:** Citation for Bravery City of Detroit; Outstanding Serv Awd Amer Bridge Assn; Plaque, Trophy, Life Membership Amer Bridge Assn; Silver Bracelet for Serving with Excellence Women of Detroit 1974. **Home Addr:** 97 Arden Pk, Detroit, MI 48202.

TAYLOR, PRINCE ALBERT, JR.
Clergyman (retired). **Personal:** Born Jan 27, 1907, Hennessey, OK; son of Bertha Ann and Prince Albert Taylor Sr; married Annie Belle Thaxton; children: Isabella M, Taylor Jenkins. **Educ:** Samuel Huston Coll, AB 1931; Gammon Theological Seminary, BD 1931; Columbia & Union Theological Seminary, MA 1940; NY Univ, EdD 1948; Rust Coll, DD 1949; Gammon Theological Seminary, DD 1950; Philander Smith Coll, LLD 1956; Univ Puget Sound, LittD 1965; Dickinson Coll, DD 1967; Drew Univ, LHD 1972. **Career:** NC Conf, ordained pastor NC & NY 1931; St Mark's Church NYC, summer pastor 1940-42; Bennett Coll, instructor & assistant to pres 1940-43; Gammon Theological Seminary, dept head Christian educ & psychology 1943-48; Clark Coll, exchange teacher 1943-48; Natl Methodist Student Comm, adult counselor 1944-48; Central Jurisdiction Comm, dir corr school 1945-48; Central Christian Adv, editor 1948-56; Central Jurisdiction, bishop 1956, bishop Monrovia (Liberia) area 1956-64, NJ Area 1964-76. **Orgs:** Pres council bishops 1965-66; general bd mem Nat Council Churches 1966-69; chmn Commn Structure Methodist Overseas 1968-72; tst Drew Univ Madison, NJ; chmn com World Methodist Council 1971-76; chmn Div Chaplains & Related Ministries 1972-76; hon pres World Methodist Council comm 1976; Rotary Club; trustee many universities, colleges, hospitals, museums, seminaries. **Honors/Awds:** Recipient St

George's Award Medal for Distinguished Serv to Methodist Church 1964; Decorated Venerable Knighthood of Pioneers (Liberia); Rotarian; United Methodist Communicators Hall of Fame. **Business Addr:** Bishop, The Shores At Wesley Manor, 2201 Bay Ave, Ste 202, Ocean City, NJ 08226-2572.

TAYLOR, QUINTARD, JR.

Educator. **Personal:** Born Dec 11, 1948, Brownsville, TN; son of Grace (Brown) Taylor and Quintard Taylor; children: Quintard III, Jamila, William. **Educ:** St Augustine's Coll, BA 1969; Univ of MN, MA 1971, PhD 1977. **Career:** Univ of MN, instructor 1969-71; Gustavus Adolphus Coll, instructor 1971; WA State U, asst prof 1971-75; CA Polytechnic State U, prof of history; Univ of Lagos, Akoka Nigeria, visiting Fulbright prof 1987-88; Univ of OR, prof, 1990-96, dept head, 1997-. **Orgs:** Consult Great Plains Black Museum 1980-85; consult Afro-Am Cultural Arts Ctr 1977-78; reviewer Nat Endowment for the Humanities 1979-83; pres Martin Luther Fund 1983-85, mem 1979-; mem Endowment Comm "Journal of Negro History" 1983-; mem, California Black Faculty Staff Assn 1985-, Golden Key Natl Honor Society 1987-, Phi Beta Delta Society for International Scholars 1989-; bd of governors, Martin Luther King Vocational-Technical Coll, Owerri Nigeria 1989-, African-American Vocational Institute, Aba Nigeria 1989-. **Honors/Awds:** Carter G Woodson Award ASALH 1980; Kent Fellowship The Danforth Found 1974-77; Bush Fellowship Univ of MN 1971-77; NEH Travel & Collections Grant, National Endowment for the Humanities 1988; The Emergence of Afro-American Communities in the Pacific Northwest 1865-1910; Carter G Woodson Award for best article published in the Journal of Negro History 1978-79. **Special Achievements:** Written: In Search of the Racial Frontier: African Americans in the American West, 1528-1990; The Forgiving of A Black Community Seattles, Central District from 1870 Through the Civil Rights Era. **Business Addr:** Dept of History, Univ of Oregon, Eugene, OR 97403-1288.

TAYLOR, REGINALD REDALL, JR.

Educational administrator, city official. **Personal:** Born Jun 30, 1939, Waycross, GA; son of Ellen Butler Taylor and Reginald R Taylor Sr; married Laurine Williams Taylor, Aug 11, 1963; children: Robyn Michelle. **Educ:** FL A&M Univ, BS 1961; Fort Valley State Coll, MS 1973; Valdosta State College, Valdosta, GA, 1990. **Career:** Pierce Co Bd of Ed, Blackshear, GA: Lee St HS, social studies teacher & band dir 1961-69; Blackshear HS, social studies teacher & counselor 1969-72, Pierce Co HS, counselor/asst principal 1973-90, Ware Street Elementary School, principal 1990-; City of Blackshear, councilman 1979-. **Orgs:** Mem Composite Lodge #40 FA&M 1960; pres Pierce Co Assoc of Educators, 1964, 1967, 1968; pres Consolidated Mens Club Inc 1973; bd of dirs Pierce Co Chamber of Comm 1980-82; director, Waycross Chorale Ensemble, 1988-90. **Honors/Awds:** Teacher of the Year Pierce Co Teachers Assn of Educators 1965; Father of the Yr Gaines Chapel AME Church 1982; Citizen of the Year Pierce Co Chamber of Commerce 1981. **Business Addr:** Principal, Ware Street Elementary School, 623 Sycamore St, Blackshear, GA 31516.

TAYLOR, RICHARD L.

Government official. **Personal:** Born Jul 19, 1944, Richmond, VA; married Gloria Jean McLendon; children: Richard Marcus II. **Educ:** Livingston Coll of Rutgers Univ, BA 1971; Rutgers Univ, MA City & Regional Planning 1974. **Career:** Grant Ave Community Center, pres/ceo 1976-; City of Plainfield, NJ, mayor 1984-. **Orgs:** Past chmn Plainfield Democratic City Comm 1975-76 (1st Black appointed); pres City Council of Plainfield 1979, 1982-83; ranking mem Natl League of Cities Comm & Econ Devel Steering Comm; natl bd mem Operation PUSH; mem Union Co Private Industry Cncl; mem Natl Black Caucus of Local Elected Officials; chmn Union Co Employment Educ & Training Adv Cncl 1979-82; mem Plainfield Bd of Schl Estimate 1980, 1982-84; mem Plainfield Area NAACP; mem Plainfield Model Cities Cncl 1970; mem Comm Ch of God; mem Rutgers Assn of Planning Students; pres Black Cultural Assn of Middlesex Co Coll 1968. **Honors/Awds:** Plainfield Babe Rugh Award for Outstanding Serv 1985; Plainfield Clergy Assn Recogn Award for Outstanding Leadership 1979; Outstanding Young Man of Amer Award in Leadership and Exceptional Comm Serv 1980; Frederick Douglas Award for Civic Service Black Cultural & Historical Soc of Union 1983; Comm Church of God Award for Community Svc; Plainfield Science Center Award for Civic Svc; NJ Assn of Black Social Workers (Union Co Achievement Award); NJ Black United Fund Comm Serv Award 1984; panelist WNBC-TV "First Tuesday"; panelist WNDT-TV "Livingston College". **Military Serv:** AUS 1966-68; Sgt E-5; Bronze Star for Valor; Purple Heart; Vietnam Combat Infantryman's Badge; Vietnam Serv Medal; All-Star Basketball and Football Post TeamsFort Dix, NJ and Fort Riley, KS.

TAYLOR, ROBERT, III

Dentist, educator. **Personal:** Born Apr 12, 1946, Ashburn, GA; son of Susie Bell Hudson Taylor and Robert Taylor, Jr.; married JoAnne Davis; children: Robert IV, Quentin, Sonya, Bridget. **Educ:** Albany State Coll, BS 1966; Atlanta Univ, MS 1970; Medical Coll of GA, DMD 1975; Post Grad US Navy, Certificate 1976. **Career:** Telfair Co GA, chemistry instructor 1966-69; Henry Co GA, biology instructor 1969-70; US Navy, asst sr dental officer 1975-78; Turner Job Corps GA, head dentist 1978-82; general dentistry, self-employed; dental terminoly instructor, HCOP Grant, Albany State College, 1982-; Taylor's Dental Clinics, chief executive officer, currently. **Orgs:** Mem Amer Dental Assoc, Natl Dental Assoc, Amer Acad of General Dentists, Reserve Officers League, GA Acad of General Dentists, Phi Bet Sigma Frat Inc; chmn of bd NAACP; vice pres Congress of Black Organizations; mem Jack & Jill of Amer, Albany State Coll Foundation, Title Twenty Foundation, Prince HallMason Lodge 360, Knights of Columbus 4th Degree 3607, Post 512 Amer Legion, VFW Post 7491; AL Ranken 142; Dougherty County Board of Health, Sowega Health Care Providers, Education Project 2000. **Honors/Awds:** Certificates of Honor Medical Coll of GA, US Navy, NAACP; Outstanding Young Men of Amer 1980. **Military Serv:** US Navy, lt commander, 20 yrs. **Home Addr:** 512 S Monroe St, Albany, GA 31701. **Business Addr:** CEO, Taylor's Dental Clinics, 512 S Monroe St, Albany, GA 31701.

TAYLOR, ROBERT DEREK

Management consultant. **Personal:** Born Jul 2, 1961, Los Angeles, CA; son of Geneva Williams and Robert M Taylor; married Joy L Johnson, Jul 23, 1988. **Educ:** California State University Northridge, BS, engineering, 1982; Stanford Law School, JD, 1986; Stanford Graduate School of Business, MBA, 1986. **Career:** McKinsey & Co, principal, 1986-. **Orgs:** Rebuild LA, bd of dirs; Natl Urban League, bd of trustees; LA Urban League, bd of trustees; Stanford Law School, bd of visitors. **Business Addr:** Principal, McKinsey & Company, 400 S Hope, Ste 700, Los Angeles, CA 90071, (213)624-1414.

TAYLOR, ROBERT EARLINGTON, JR.

General contractor. **Personal:** Born Aug 20, 1937, Dayton, OH; married Beverly Jean Stark; children: Kevin, Robin Perkins. **Educ:** Attended, Sinclair Comm Coll Dayton 1972-73. **Career:** Lake Pleasure Fishing Lakes, mgr 1970-75; Black Game Co of Dayton OH, founder/pres 1971-79; Delco Moraine General Motors Div, 1976-; World Toy Co of Amer, owner/pres 1979-; Taylor-Made Const & Remodelling Co Inc, pres & genl mgr 1980-. **Orgs:** Mem Natl Assoc of Black Mfg Distributors 1972-; breeder Koja Kennels 1973-80; mem bd of dirs Midas Landscaping Co Inc 1986-, Carefree Property Mgmt Co Inc 1986-. **Honors/Awds:** Certificate Mgmt Training Church's Chicken Inc 1976; Merit Awd General Motors Inc 1983. **Business Addr:** President, Taylor-Made Construction, 4538 St James Ave, Dayton, OH 45406.

TAYLOR, RONALD LEWIS

Professor, sociologist. **Personal:** Born Feb 27, 1942, St Petersburg, FL; son of Lillian Bell Miller and David Taylor; married Bernice Chavis Taylor, Dec 24, 1966; children: Kevin, Darryl. **Educ:** Bethune-Cookman College, Daytona Beach, FL, BA, 1963; Howard University, Washington, DC, MA, 1965; Boston University, Boston, MA, PhD, 1972. **Career:** US Dept of Labor, research assoc. & prog. evaluator, 1963-64; Bethune-Cookman College, dean of men, 1964-65, dir., financial aid, 1965-67; Boston University, instructor/lecturer, 1967-72; Univ of Connecticut, assistant prof-full professor, 1972-, chair, sociology dept, 1981-86; Institute for African-American Studies, dir, 1993-. **Orgs:** Chair, DuBois-Johnson-Frazier Awards, Amer Sociological Assn, 1987-90; Amer Assn of University Professors, Executive Committee, 1988-; Editorial Board, American Journal of Orthopsychiatry, 1978-85; Editorial Board, Contemporary Sociology, 1980-84; Editorial Board, University Press of New England, 1984-; American Association of Univ Profs, UConn Chapter, pres; Journal of Research on Adolescence, editorial board, 1994-; Journal of Men's Studies, editorial board, 1992-; Journal of African-American Male Studies, editorial board, 1991-. **Honors/Awds:** Research fellowship, Ford Foundation, 1970-72; Research fellow, National Endowment for the Humanities 1978-79; Distinguished Scholastic Achievement Award, University of Massachusetts, 1991. **Special Achievements:** Co-author: The Black Male in America, Nelson-Hall, 1977; Editor, American-American Youth, Praeger, 1995; Editor, Minority Families in the US, Prentice-Hall, 1994; Co-editor, Black Adolescence, GK Hall, 1990. **Business Addr:** Professor of Sociology, University of Connecticut, 344 Mansfield Rd, 225 Manchester Hall, Storrs, CT 06268.

TAYLOR, ROY MARCELLUS

Dentist. **Personal:** Born Feb 12, 1925, Sumter, SC; son of Ada Taylor and W M Taylor; married Virginia Marlene Beverly; children: Wayne M Taylor DDS, Sheryl Taylor Bailey, RDH; Anthony M. **Educ:** Howard Univ, BS 1950; Meharry Med Coll, DDS 1954; Amer Univ of Oriental Studies, PhD 1984; Acupuncture Found of Sri Lanka, DSc 1984. **Career:** Aetna Life Ins Co, consult 1960-70; TV Dental School, asst prof of dentistry 1967-71; Temple Univ Comp Health Svcs, chf of dental serv 1967-70, centerdir 1970-72; Roy M Taylor Assoc, dentist/clinician 1954-. **Orgs:** Dir Wm H Feronce Co 1960-66; dir/treas Project IN 1966-69; memAcad of Stress and Chronic Diseases; mem Acad of Gen Dentistry; mem Acad of Endosseous Implants; mem Amer Acad for Funct Prosthodontics; mem Amer Dental Assn; mem Natl Dental Assn; mem Intl Assn for Orthodontics; mem Amer Endodontic Soc; mem Intl Coll of Oral Implantology; PA Dental Assn; mem Philadelphia Cnty Dental Soc; mem Philadelphia Soc of Periodontology; Northeast Gnathological Soc; mem Inst of Med and Dent Hypnosis; mem Amer Pub Health Assn; memNew Era Dental Soc; mem Chi Delta Mu Frat; mem Acupuncture Found. **Honors/Awds:** Omicron Kappa Upsilon Natl Hon Soc 1954; Kappa Sigma Pi Honor Soc 1954; The Legion of Honor The Chapel of Four Chaplains Philadelphia in recognition of Outstanding Comm Serv 1969; Fellowship Acad of General Dentistry 1972; mem Intl Coll of Oral Implantology 1972; President's Award for Outstanding Serv to Chi Delta Mu Frat 1973; President's Award for Scientific Contrib Natl Dent Assn 1970-71; NY Acad of Sciences 1979; President's Award Med Coll 1979; Listed "The First Five Hundred" Libr Edn; publications including, "Dental Health Problems in the Ghetto"; "The Treatment of Occlusal Disturbances, The Study Cast" Quarterly of the Natl Dent Assn Vol 28 No 4 1970; "My Story of West Nicetown - Tioga Neighborhood Family Health Center" PA Dental Journal 1971; "Atlas of Complete Dentures" Lippint 1970. **Military Serv:** USMC Pvt 1st Class 1943-45; AUS Cpt 1954-56. **Home Addr:** 2 Herford Pl, Yeadon, PA 19050.

TAYLOR, RUTH SLOAN

Educator. **Personal:** Born Jun 8, 1918, Greenville, SC; widowed. **Educ:** EdD 1962. **Career:** IN Univ Nw, asst chrmn div of ed 1969-; Summer HS Cairo, IL, engl teacher 1946-48; Roosevelt HS Gary, IN, eng 1948-66; Title I E SEA Gary, IN, sup 1966-68. **Orgs:** Coop Ed Res Lab Pgm Assc Northfield, IL 1967; asst prof IN Univ Nw 1969; assc prof IN Univ NW 1972; pres bd of trustee Gary Comm Sch; consult leec chmn Bi-Cen Comm IN Univ Nw United Way Camp City Met Chmn 1974; mem Natl Soc Act Comm Delta Sigma Theta Sor 1973; asst chmn Div of Ed IN Univ NW 1974-75; elected Natl Sec Delta Sigma Theta Sor Inc. **Honors/Awds:** Auth of "Teaching in the Desegregated Classroom"; outst cit awrd for ed IU Dons Inc 1974. **Business Addr:** Indiana Univ NW, 3400 Broadway, Gary, IN 46408.

TAYLOR, S. MARTIN

Utility company executive. **Personal:** Born in Bangor, MI; married Anna Diggs. **Educ:** Western Mich Univ, BS political science and economics, 1964; Detroit College of Law, law degree, 1967. **Career:** New Detroit Inc, pres; Michigan Dept of Labor and the MI Employment Security Commission, dir; Detroit Edison, Detroit, MI, vice president of govt relations, currently.

TAYLOR, SANDRA ELAINE

Psychologist. **Personal:** Born Aug 8, 1946, New York, NY; daughter of Berthenia Turner Taylor and Floyd L Taylor; married Alvin Green (divorced); children: Kwam Taylor Green. **Educ:** Bronx Comm Coll of the City Univ of NY, AAS 1965, AA 1969; City Coll of NY, BA 1970; City Univ of NY, PhD 1976. **Career:** Bronx Psychiatric Ctr, head nurse 1965-73; Albert Einstein Clinical Internship Prog in Psychology, intern psychologist 1973-74; City College, City University, New York, adjunct lecturer, 1974-75; Bronx Psychiatric Ctr, staff psychologist 1974-76; St Joseph's College, adjunct asst prof, 1976-77; Marymount College, adjunct asst prof, 1976-79, counseling psychologist, 1976-77; City College/Harlem Hosp Ctr Physician Asst Prog, educational coord 1977-80; Brooklyn Developmental Ctr, principal psychologist & exec Asst to the dir 1980-81; Bronx Develop Ctr, deputy dir treatment svcs, 1981-90; pres, Kwam SET Publishing Co, Inc, 1989-. **Orgs:** Member, Natl Assn Female Executives 1983-. **Honors/Awds:** Numerous honors, awards, special achievements, publications such as "The New York Urban League Presents," WBLS radio station guest speaker 1976; recipient of the First Pamela Galiber Memorial Scholarship Awd for Doctoral Dissertation Rsch in memory of NY State Senator Jos Galiber's late daughter The City Univ of NY 1976; "The Meaning of Scholarship" New York Eastern Star Annual Scholarship Awd presentation principal speaker 1976; "Ethnic Self-Hatred in Black Psychotics, A Preliminary Report" Journal of the Bronx State Hosp Vol 1 No 2 Spring 1973; "Racism and Psychiatry" Bronx Psychiatric Ctr guest lecturer for visiting medical residents 1973. **Home Addr:** 1000 Grand Concourse, Bronx, NY 10451. **Business Addr:** President, Kwam SET Publishing Co, Inc, 1000 Grand Concourse, 5-8G, Bronx, NY 10451.

TAYLOR, SCOTT MORRIS

Physician. **Personal:** Born Oct 10, 1957, Berkeley, CA; son of Dr & Mrs Robert L Taylor. **Educ:** Morehouse Coll, BS 1980; Meharry Medical School, MD 1984. **Career:** Highland Hospital, surgery resident 1984-86; Martin Luther King Hospital, orthopedic resident 1987-.

TAYLOR, SINTHY E.

Company executive. **Personal:** Born Aug 18, 1947, Dayton, OH; married Vivian Lorraine Lundy. **Educ:** Union for Experimenting Colls & Univ Cincinnati, BS 1977. **Career:** Dayton Model Cities Planning Council, youth coord 1968-70; Dayton Youth Coalition, exec dir 1970-75; Dayton Voter Registration Educ Inst, adminis 1975-80; State of OH Dept of Administrative Svcs, job recruitment specialist 1980-83; Taylor-Made Construction Co Inc, vice pres of bd of dirs 1980-; Care-Free Property Mgmt Co Inc, consultant 1986-; Midas Landscaping & Develop Co Inc, pres and ecological planner 1986-; Dayton

Democratic Progressive Club, pres; commissioned Notary Public 1980-. **Orgs:** Chmn of bd Wesley Comm Ctr 1975-76; mem Miami Consistory #26 1981-; mem Ancient Square 1981-, chaplin 1983; mem Royal Arch Masons 1982-, Boone Commandery of Knights Templar 1982-; Solomon Johnson Council #4 Royal & Select Masters 1982-; Knights of the Mystic Shrine 1982-; order of Easter Star 1983-, past worthy patron 1984; assoc pastor St Paul AME Zion Church Dayton 1983-; chmn ward & precinct Democratic Voters League 1985-86; chmn voter registration Democratic Voters League 1986-87; mem Heroines of Jericho, Heroines of the Templars Crusade. **Honors/Awds:** Letter of Commendation President of the United States 1976; Elected Worthy Patron Deborah Chap #19 Order of the Eastern Star 1984; Evangelist of the Year Awd AME Zion Church Connection 1985. **Home Addr:** 4526 Alfred Drive, Dayton, OH 45417.

TAYLOR, STERLING R.
Finance company executive. **Personal:** Born Jan 5, 1942, Philadelphia, PA; son of Ellanora K Bivens and Willie Ray Taylor; married Sonia E Madden (divorced); children: Tiarzha M, Khara D. **Career:** Army & Air Force Exchange Svc, buyer, 1964-70; The Equitable Companies Incorporated, life underwriter, registered representative, 1970-. **Orgs:** Past pres So AK Life Underwriters 1974-75; past pres, AK State Assn Life Underwriters; life mem, exec comm, NAACP Anchorage Branch; founder, past pres, AK Black Caucus; comm chmn, Alaska Black Leadership Conf; ambassador, Life Underwriters Political Action Comm; life mem, past pres, Alpha Phi Alpha, Nu Zeta Lambda Chapter; junior grand warden, Prince Hall Masons, Alaska; bd chmn, Anchorage Community Health Center; chmn, Anchorage Transportation Commission. **Honors/Awds:** Natl Sales Achievement Awards; Natl Quality Awards; Life Mem, Million Dollar Round Table, 1986; Hall of Fame, The Equitable Companies Incorporated, 1982; Natl Community Leadership Award, 1993. **Business Addr:** Registered Representative, The Equitable Companies Incorporated, 200 W 34th Ave, #376, Anchorage, AK 99503.

TAYLOR, STEVEN LLOYD
Association executive. **Personal:** Born Jun 8, 1948, New York, NY; son of Marie Taylor; married Dr Dolores Y Straker; children: Brian K Taylor. **Educ:** Queens Coll (City Univ of NY), BA 1969; Fordham Univ, MSW 1971; Columbia Univ, DSW 1984. **Career:** Comm Serv Soc of NYC, research assoc 1971-73; Fordham Univ, adjunct prof 1972-; New York City Human Resources Admin, rsch scientist 1975-76, dir of prog eval 1976-78, dir research 1978-83, deputy commr 1983-87, 1991-93; United Way of New York City, senior vice pres, 1987-91; American Red Cross, chief program officer, 1993. **Orgs:** ACSW Natl Assn of Soc Workers 1973-; NY State Cert Soc Worker 1971-; mem Natl Assn of Soc Workers 1971-. **Honors/Awds:** Black Achievers Award, Harlem YMCA 1988; Fordham School of Social Service, Alumnus of the Year, 1993. **Business Addr:** Chief Program Officer, American Red Cross, 150 Amsterdam Ave, New York, NY 10023.

TAYLOR, STUART A.
Educator. **Personal:** Born Jul 2, 1936, Providence, RI; married Ella Marie; children: Sandre, Stuart, Sabrina, Scott. **Educ:** Oakwood Clg, BS Acct Bus 1960; Univ RI, MS Grad Sch Bus 1963; IN U, PhD Indsl Mgmt & Psych 1967. **Career:** Grad Sch of Bus Harvard U, assc prof; mgmt consult to various major corp. **Orgs:** Mem Acad of Mgmt; bd adv to Natl Urban League; fdr RI Com for Advancement of Negro Ed; mem White House Fellows Pgm. **Honors/Awds:** Enabled him to research US Dept of Urban Dev & Study Abroad; 1st Black to become Licensed Pblc Acctnt in RI & to Teach Full-time at Harvard Bus Sch.

TAYLOR, SUSAN CHARLENE
Dermatologist. **Personal:** Born Oct 7, 1957, Philadelphia, PA; daughter of Ethel & Charles Taylor; married Kernel W Dawkins, Mar 5, 1983; children: Morgan Elizabeth, Madison Lauren. **Educ:** University of Pennsylvania, BA, 1979; Harvard Medical School, MD 1983. **Career:** Society Hill Dermatology, physician 1989-. **Orgs:** American Med Association; American Academy of Dermatology; Pennsylvania Med Society; Medical Society of Eastern Pennsylvania; Pennsylvania County Med Society; Philadelphia Dermatology Society; Joseph J Peters Institute, board member; University of Pennsylvania, associate trustee. **Special Achievements:** Subungual Osteochondroma j Dermatol Surg Oncol, 1992; Nodular vulvar amyloid as a presentation of systemic amyloidosis, J Am Acad Dermatol, 1991; Post-Surgical Zosteriform Herpes Simplex II in Non-Contiguous Dermatomes, J Am Acad Dermatol, 1990; and numerous others. **Business Addr:** Dermatologist, Society Hill Dermatology, 932 Pine St, Philadelphia, PA 19107.

TAYLOR, SUSAN L.
Publishing company executive. **Personal:** Born Jan 23, 1946, New York, NY; daughter of Violet Weekes Taylor and Lawrence Taylor; married William Bowles, Jan 3, 1967 (divorced 1971); children: Shana-Nequai; married Khephra Burns. **Educ:** Fordham University, BA, social science, 1991. **Career:** Negro Ensemble Company, former actress; licensed cosmetologist; Nequai Cosmetics, founder, president, 1970-72; Essense magazine, free-lance writer, beauty editor, 1970-71, fashion/beauty editor, 1971-81, editor-in-chief, 1981-; Essense Communications Inc, past tv host, past executive coordinator, sr vice president, 1983-; Executive producer of Essence Awards, producer Essence Music Festival. **Orgs:** American Society of Magazine Editors; Women in Communications; Natl Assn of Black Journalists; Black Women in Publishing. **Honors/Awds:** Natl Assn of Negro Business & Professional Women's Clubs, Business Awards, 1983; Howard Univ, Excellence in Media Award, 1982; 5th Annual Kizzy Image and Achievement Award, 1981; Women in Communications Matirx Award, 1982; Lincoln Univ, Honorary Doctorate of Human Letters, 1988; Delaware State Univ, Honorary Doctorate, 1991; Spelman Coll, Honorary Doctorate, 1994. **Special Achievements:** Author, In the Spirit: The Inspirational Writings of Susan L Taylor, 1993; Lessons in Living, Anchor Books, 1995; Confirmation, coauthor, editor, 1997. **Business Addr:** Editor-in-Chief, Essence Magazine, attn: Debra Parker, 1500 Broadway, New York, NY 10036.

TAYLOR, T. SHAWN
Journalist. **Personal:** Born Aug 23, 1966, Alton, IL; daughter of Armelia Armsterd & Robert Taylor. **Educ:** University of Missouri-Columbia, bachelor's degree, journalism, 1987. **Career:** Detroit Free Press, writer, copy editor, 1988-89; Kansas City Star, copy editor, 1989-90; Chicago Tribune, copy editor, 1990-96, reporter, 1996-. **Orgs:** Alpha Kappa Alpha Sorority Inc, 1986-; National Association of Black Journalists, 1987-; Big Brothers/Big Sisters of Metro Chicago, 1992-. **Business Addr:** Reporter, Chicago Tribune, 9220 W 159th St, Orland Park, IL 60462.

TAYLOR, THAD, JR.
Dentist, educator. **Personal:** Born May 6, 1937, Waxahachie, TX; married Emma L Choice; children: Thao IV, Tracye Lashon. **Educ:** Prairie View A&M Coll, BS 1957; Howard Univ, DDS 1963. **Career:** Tulsa Jr Coll Bd of Regents, mem 1972-, chmn 1976-77, 1981-82; OK Coll of Osteopathic Med & Surgery, assoc prof oral pathology. **Orgs:** Life mem NAACP 1968-; pres OK Med Dental & Pharmaceutical Assoc 1982-84. **Military Serv:** AUS Infantry capt 2 yrs. **Business Addr:** Assoc Professor Oral Surgery, The Oklahoma College, Osteopathic Medicine & Surgery, PO Box 6428, Tulsa, OK 74106.

TAYLOR, THEODORE D.
Educational administrator. **Personal:** Born Mar 29, 1930, Ocala, FL; married Daisy R Curry; children: Tiffany, Tamila, Cedric, Theodore N, Patricia. **Educ:** FL A&M U, BS 1950, MS 1956; Atlanta U, MS 1962; Nova U, EdD 1972. **Career:** Marion Co Sch Dist, tchr 1954; Marion Co Sch Dist Ocala FL, admin 1958; Broward Co Sch Dist, cncl 1962; Broward Co Sch Dist Ft Lauderdale, admin 1963; Broward Comm Coll, dir of special serv 1970-85, dir of admissions/coll equity officer 1985-. **Orgs:** Desegregation cncl Univ of Miami 1972; mem Local Draft Bd 151 1973; basileus Omega Psi Phi Frat Zeta Chi Chap 1976-78; pres Kiwanis Clb of Cntrl Broward1978; exalted ruler Elks Clb 1978; chmn Equal Access/Equal Opprty Com for Broward Co Govtl Empl 1978-; mem Fac Task Force of Supt Commn on Pub Ed Broward Co Schs; mem Broward Co Detention Adv Bd, Broward Bar Special Comm for Children. **Honors/Awds:** Omega man of yr 1956, 1965, 1976; ndea flw Atlanta Univ 1961; a study of attrition of a select grp of disadvantaged stdnt ERIC 1976. **Military Serv:** USMC s/sgt 1950-53. **Business Addr:** Equity Officer, Broward Community College, 225 E Las Olas Blvd, Fort Lauderdale, FL 33301.

TAYLOR, TIMOTHY MERRITT
Association executive. **Personal:** Born Aug 8, 1931, New York, NY; married Nell Cochrane; children: Timothy Jr, Stuart, Blair, Scott, Marshall. **Educ:** Yale U, BA 1953; NY U, LlB 1956. **Career:** Westchester Urban League, ofcr bd dir 1969-. **Orgs:** Mem Bd of Cnslr Fordham Univ 1969-; co-fdr Urban Ed Inc 1968; mem Harlem Lawyers Assc 1956; NY Co Lawyers Assc 1956; pres W Side Sch Comm Ctrs; exec com NY NAACP; v chmn bd trustee New Lincoln Shc; chmn New York City Confed of Local Sch Bds. **Business Addr:** 277 Broadway, New York, NY 10007.

TAYLOR, TOMMIE W.
Public relations representative (retired). **Personal:** Born Mar 4, 1929, Blytheville, AR; married Aubrey Taylor Sr; children: Aubrey Jr, Darryl E, Roderic K, Cabot O. **Educ:** Licensed cosmetologist 1948; Philander Smith Coll, BA 1955; Univ of AR at Little Rock, Graduate Study. **Career:** Johnson Publ Co, stringer 1954-65; Radio Station KOKY-AM, prog asst 1957-59; AR Baptist Coll, registrar psych instructor 1959-61; Teletype Corp, civil rel assoc 1962-75; AT&T Information Systems, public relations rep 1982-87; Rolyat Fashions, owner/manager, currently. **Orgs:** Pres Urban League of Greater Little Rock 1971-75; tammateous Sigma Gamma Rho Sor 1984-85, 2nd anti basileus 1985-86, 1st anti basileus 1986-87; dir of YoungPeoples Bapt Training Union Dept NH Zion Bapt Church. **Honors/Awds:** Outstanding Serv Awd Urban League of Greater Little Rock 1973,75; Outstanding Volunteer Serv Awd Urban League 1975; Volunteer & Comm Serv Awd Urban League Guild 1975; Appreciation Awd for Service Rendered as Bd Mem Youth Home Inc 1979; Outstanding Serv Awd AR Bapt Coll Camera Club 1979; Appreciation Awd Natl Alumni Assoc of AR Bapt Coll 1984; Disting Serv Awd Philander Smith Coll United Negro Coll Fund 1987; Active Participant Awd Natl Alumni Assoc AR Bapt Coll 1987; Honorary Drs Degree, Humane Letters, AR Bapt Coll, 1987; ABC Natl Alumni Assn, Outstanding Service Award, 1988; Philander Smith Coll, Natl Alumni Assn Award, 1991; State of AR Certificate of Merit, 1994. **Home Addr:** 806 S Mississippi Ave, Little Rock, AR 72205, (501)227-4565. **Business Phone:** (501)663-3661.

TAYLOR, TYRONE
Animal trainer. **Personal:** Born in New York City, NY; married Linda; children: Emerald, Chelsea, Tevin. **Career:** Ringling Bros and Barnum & Bailey Circus, 17 year veteran, tiger trainer, 1994-. **Special Achievements:** First African American to train and perform with tigers in the Ringling Bros and Barnum & Bailey Circus. **Business Phone:** (703)448-4000.

TAYLOR, VALERIE CHARMAYNE
Adverstising/marketing executive. **Personal:** Born Jan 19, 1962, Chattanooga, TN; daughter of Geneva Williams and Harvey E Taylor. **Educ:** Austin Peay State University, 1980-82; Michigan State University, BA, telecommunications, 1985; Institute for Educational Leadership, certificate, 1987-88. **Career:** Michigan Department of Natural Resources, community Relations Representative, 1983-85; Federal Social Security Department, claims rep/assistant special emphasis coordinator, 1985-86; Lansing Community College, community relations manager, 1986-88; State Bar of Michigan, communications manager, 1988-89; Michigan Travel Bureau, marketing manager, 1989-91; Jamestown-Yorktown Foundation, Commonwealth of Virginia, director public affairs and marketing, 1991-94; Siddall Matus and Coushter, Advertising and Public Relations, account supervisor, 1994-. **Orgs:** Delta Sigma Theta Sorority Inc, national pr chair, 1987-91; Public Relations Society of American, ad-hoc Ecos board; Assn Travel Marketing Executives, 1991-; National Association Market Developers; African-American Public Relations Society; Michigan Black Media Association, charter mem, vp, 1987-89; Lansing Martin Luther King Commission, secretary (mayoral appointment), 1989-90; Lansing Food Bank, board of directors, 1987-90; Lansing Branch NAACP, co-chair citywide radiothon, 1988; Williamsburg Hotel/Motel Association, board of directors, 1991-. **Honors/Awds:** United States Department Health and Human Services "Outstanding Service Award," 1986; Delta Sigma Theta Sorority Inc, "Service Appreciation Recognition," 1987; Lansing United Negro College Fund "Service Appreciation Certificate," 1988. **Special Achievements:** Instituted museums first-time co-op ticket program, generating mor than $200,000 in sales revenue and increasing visitation by 29% for record high levels; Implemented national media relations campaign for Virginia museums, resulting in first time feature coverage by CNN Headline News, Time Life Books, Americana Magazine, Los Angeles Time and Walt Disney Productions, 1992; implemented Michigan segmented marketing program focusing on Chicago, increased visitation by 18% first year, 1991; developed Michigan co-op travel marketing program, increased travel budget by $4.5 million - generated 190,000 additional travel inquires. **Business Addr:** Account Supervisor, Siddall, Matus & Coushter, Inc. Advertising and Public Relations, 801 East Main St, Ross Building, Richmond, VA 23219, (804)253-4138.

TAYLOR, VANESSA GAIL
Law enforcement (retired). **Personal:** Born Sep 15, 1960, Lafayette, LA; daughter of Mr & Mrs Dalton Belson Jr; married John F, Sep 15, 1979; children: Tiffany, Timothy. **Educ:** Univ of Southwestern Louisiana, AS, 1982; Acadiana Law Enforcement Training Academy, 1985; Drug Abuse Resistance Education Training, 1991; Univ of Southwestern Louisiana, BS, 1994. **Career:** Lafayette Parish Juvenile Detention Ctr, 1981-82; Lafayette Police Dept, clerk II, 1982-85, corporal, 1985-. **Orgs:** Magnolia Peace Officers Assn, 1988-; Louisiana Peace Officers Assn, 1987-; Municipal Police Officers Assn, 1987-; Police Assn of Lafayette, 1989-; Lafayette Youth Conference Comm, 1991-; Black Adoption & Foster Care Advocacy Bd, 1991-. **Honors/Awds:** National Assn of Blacks in Criminal Justice, Officer of the Year, 1993; Knights of Columbus #3202, Officer of the Year, 1992; Kiwanis Club, Officer of the Year, 1994; Crime Prevention Advisory Comm Nominee, Officer of the Year, 1993; Lafayette Police Dept, Officer of the Month, Jan, May & Dec, 1992; Trio Achievers Award, 1994. **Business Addr:** Corporal, Lafayette Police Department, PO Box 4308, Lafayette, LA 70502, (318)261-8641.

TAYLOR, VERNON ANTHONY
Army officer. **Personal:** Born Jul 31, 1946, Easton, MD; son of Evelyn S Taylor and Wayman W Taylor Sr; married Judith Woodson, Oct 27, 1973; children: Anne Marie. **Educ:** Morgan State University, BS, 1969; Delaware Law School, Widener University, JD, 1980. **Career:** US Army Delaware National Guard, lt; magistrate, State of Deleware. **Orgs:** Rotary International. **Military Serv:** US Army/Delaware National Guard, lt, March, 1970-96; Legion of Merit; Meritorious Service Medal; Army Commendation Medal. **Home Phone:** (302)762-8488.

TAYLOR, VERONICA C.
Educational administrator. **Personal:** Born May 17, 1941, Pensacola; married Raymond. **Educ:** TN State Univ, BS 1962; Trenton State Coll, MA 1970. **Career:** Booker T Wash HS,

instr 1962-67; Trenton Publ School, speech therapist, 1967-88; Trenton State Coll, coadj faculty beginning 1985; Jefferson School, faculty, currently. **Orgs:** Pres Trenton Delta Sigma Theta 1973-75; pres TABS 1974-77; vice pres Trenton Ed Assoc; mem NJ Ed Assoc Pol Action Fund 1974-75; mem, bd of dir NJ Sickle Cell Soc 1972-74; pres, vice pres Trenton Pan Hellenic Council; bd of dir, chmn NJ EOF; pres Womans Steering Comm Shiloh Bapt Church, NAACP; mem Natl Scholarship Comm Delta Sigma Theta 1983-88; Governor's Task Force on Higher Education; board of dirs Merabash Museum; NJ State Social Action, chairperson DST; natl exec bd, Delta Sigma Theta 1988-92; Membership Intake Trainer DST; Governor's Review Committee on Minorities in Higher Education; exec bd, Trenton Administrators and Supervisors Assn; New Jersey Coordinator Collegiate Advisors DST. **Honors/Awds:** Most All Around, Most Outstanding Female Grad Wash HS; Winner many essay contests; toured USO; Outstanding Comm Serv Trenton Delta Sigma Theta Inc; Outstanding Serv Awd NJ Dept Higher Ed 1982, 1985, 1987; Outstanding Service Awards, Shiloh Baptist Church, Tri State Social Action Commission DST, New Jersey Educational Opportunity Fund Leadership Award, Eastern Region DST; biography listed in Notable Americans; Pearl Certificate, Eastern Reg Conf, 1995; Outstanding Service Award-Students, Robbins School, 1996. **Business Addr:** Interim Principal, Grant Elementary ntary School, 108 N Clinton Ave, Trenton, NJ 08609.

TAYLOR, VIVIAN A.
Elected official. **Personal:** Born Oct 27, 1924, Maryland; married Lula M; children: Lavon E, Myron A. **Educ:** Stillman Coll, attended 1942-43; Fisk Univ, attended 1946-48; State Univ of NY, BA 1973; attended Coll of Fredonia. **Career:** Jamestown Parks Dept, parks commissioner 1976-85; Black Awareness Studies, dir 1984-85; TRW, bearings div; City of Jamestown, city councilman. **Orgs:** Bd of dirs Jamestown Better Living; former mem Environmental Council; original appointee Jamestown Human Rights Comm; bd of dirs Jamestown Family Svcs; former chmn bd of trustees Blackwell Chapel AME Zion Church; former Boy Scout Comm; chmn Jamestown Interacial Forum 1962-65; mem City Charter Adv Comm 1977; mem of governing bd Chautauqua Oppors Inc Anti-Poverty Agency 1977-79; bd of dirs Crystal Ballroom Sr Citizens Ctr 1981-84; mem United Auto Aerospace & Implement Workers of Amer 1985; committeeman Chautauqua Co Democratic Comm 1985; committeeman Jamestown City Democratic Comm 1985. **Honors/Awds:** Cert of Honor AME Zion Church 1978; Martin Luther King Jr Peace Awd Southern Tier Peace Ctr 1982. **Military Serv:** Engineers demolition specialist 3 yrs. **Home Addr:** 31 W 18th St, Jamestown, NY 14701. **Business Addr:** City Councilman, City of Jamestown, Municipal Bldg, Jamestown, NY 14701.

TAYLOR, VIVIAN LORRAINE
Vocational educator. **Personal:** Born Jun 28, 1948, Philadelphia, PA; married Sinthy Eugene Taylor. **Educ:** Antioch College, BA 1970; Antioch Putney Graduate School, MA 1971. **Career:** Dayton Bd of Educ, English & history teacher, 1970-72; Natl Boys Clubs of Amer, dir of youth girls prog, 1970-72; Dayton Bd of Educ, counselor, 1970-79, teacher-coordinator of occupational work adjustment prog, 1972-; Midas Landscaping Development Co, co-owner and business mgr, 1986-; MacFarlane Intermediate School, business mgr, 1986-. **Orgs:** Mem, Natl Educ Assn, Ohio Educ Assn, Dayton Educ Assn, 1970-; recording sec, Democratic Progressive Club, 1976-; mem, Miami Assembly #22 Order of Golden Circle, 1982-; 3rd vice chmn, Montgomery County Republican Party, 1982-83; financial sec, Order of Eastern Star Chap PHA, 1983-85; mem, Burning Bush Court #3 Heroines of Jericho; mem, Amer Court #65 Daughters of Isis, 1984-; mem, Truth Guild #2 Heroines of the Templars Crusade, 1984-. **Honors/Awds:** Outstanding Democrat of the Year, Democratic Progressive Club, 1977; Outstanding Young Woman of Amer, 1977; Academic Achievement Award, Dayton Bd of Educ, 1979; Kizzy Award, Kizzy Scholarship Fund, 1983; Vocational Teacher of the Year, Dayton Bd of Educ 1984. **Home Addr:** 4526 Alfred Dr, Dayton, OH 45417.

TAYLOR, WALTER SCOTT
Clergyman. **Personal:** Born Dec 12, 1916, Jackson, MS; married Odella Wykle; children: Mary Overton, Susie England, Walter S, Jr. **Educ:** Clark Clg Atlanta, AB 1943; Gammon Theol Sem, BD 1946. **Career:** Galilee Un Meth Ch Englewood, NJ, minister 1952-; Trinity Meth Ch Bronx, NY, assc minister 1945-52; Meth Chs Edwards, MS & Franklin, NC, pastor. **Orgs:** Spnsr Home State Bk Teaneck, NJ; chmn bd Christian Soc Concerns No NJ Conf UMC; mem bd Pensions No NJ Conf UMC; mayor Englewood, NJ 1972-75; mem NAACP; commr Urban Renewal 1953-61; commr Englewood Housing Auth; ldr Successful Intergrate Pub Schs; fdr past pres Gr Englewood Housing Corp 1968; mem Bergen Co Hlth & Wel Cncl; bd dir Bergen Co Philharmonic Soc; bd dir Peace Ctr Bergen Co Del; Dem Natl Conv 1973; Natl League Cities Task Force Study. **Honors/Awds:** Mayor of yr awrd 1975; outst achvmnt human re Bergen Co Urban League; Natl Black Bus & Professional Women's Assc; Natl Conf Black Women; Bergen Co CnclChs. **Business Addr:** Galilee United Methodist Churc, 325 Genesee Ave, Englewood, NJ.

TAYLOR, WELTON IVAN
Consulting microbiologist. **Personal:** Born Nov 12, 1919, Birmingham, AL; son of Cora Lee Brewer Taylor and Frederick Enslen Taylor; married Jayne Rowena Kemp; children: Karyn, Shelley. **Educ:** Univ of Illinois, AB 1941, MS 1947, PhD 1948. **Career:** Univ of Illinois, asst prof 1948-54; Swift & Co, micro 1954-59; Children's Memorial Hospital, micro-in-chief 1959-64; consultant, microbiologist 1963-; Micro-Palettes Inc, pres 1977-. **Orgs:** Founding chmn Chicago Chapter Episcopal Soc for Cultural & Racial Equality 1961; bd of Scientific Advisors 1970-82; bd dir Amer Bd Bioanalysis 1973-82; Amer Assn of Bioanalysts 1970-82; vice pres, pres Chicago Medical Mycological Soc 1967-69; Acad appointments, Assoc Dept Pathology NW Medical School 1961-67; asst prof Univ Illinois School of Medicine 1965-69; assoc prof Univ of Illinois School of Medicine 1969-86. **Honors/Awds:** James M Yard Brotherhood Award, Natl Conf Christians & Jews 1961; Special Research Fellowship, Natl Inst Health 1961-62; Diplomate Amer Bd Med Microbiology 1968; Fellow Amer Acad Microbiology 1974; Editorial Boards Applied Microbiology/Amer Soc Microbiology 1968-70; Lab Med Amer Soc Clinical Pathology 1971-77; Test of Month Amer Assn Bioanalysts 1971-82; Journal of Clinical Micro Amer Soc Microbiol 1975-84; new species of bacterium "Enterobacter taylorae" named for him 1985; Special Research Fellowship, NIAID: Pasteur Inst, Lille, France, 1961; Central Public Health Laboratory, Colindale, London, England, 1962; Intl Dissemination of Salmonellae by Import/Export Foods; written more than 50 original scientific publications, book chapters and patents; formulated media/methods Salmonella/Shiqella detection used by FDA and Western Nations since, 1975; Invented, patented, manufactured and marketed microbiological diagnostic kits, founded Micro-Palettes Inc, 1977-89; Alumni Achievement Award, University of Illinois, Urbana, 1996; Pasteur Award, Illinois, Soc Microbiology, 1996. **Special Achievements:** Expert Witness: food poisoning/infection, Hospital-acquired (nosocomial) infections, doctor-caused (iatrogenic) infections. **Military Serv:** AUS 1st lieutenant, liaison pilot, 1941-46; Illinois Natl Guard major 1948-55.

TAYLOR, WILFORD, JR.
District court judge. **Personal:** Born Jan 15, 1950, Newport News, VA; son of Zenobia Miller Taylor and Wilford Taylor Sr; married Linda Holmes Taylor, Jul 3, 1976; children: Patrice D, Derek H. **Educ:** Hampton University, Hampton, VA, BS, 1972; University of Richmond, Richmond, VA, MA, 1975; Marshall-Wythe School of Law, College of William & Mary, Williamsburg, VA, JD, 1978. **Career:** Scott, Coles, Brown, Taylor & Melvin, PC, Newport News, VA, attorney, 1979-82; City of Hampton, Hampton, VA, deputy city attorney, 1982-85; Commonwealth of Virginia, Hampton, VA, general district court judge, 1985-. **Orgs:** Member, Virginia State Bar; member, Peninsula Bar Assn; member, Old Dominion Bar Assn; member, Assn District Court Judges of VA; member, Hampton Bar Assn; member, NAACP (Hampton Chapter); advisory board member, Metropolitan YMCA; affirmative action comm member, Marshall-Wythe School of Law, College of William & Mary; member, Hampton Rotary Club; president, Langley, PTA, 1990-. **Honors/Awds:** Member of Criminal Justice Services Board, Appointed by governor Lawrence D Wilder, 1990-; Member of Commission on Jail & Prison Overcrowding in VA, Appointed by Governor Gerald Baliles; Man of the Year, Mega Psi Phi (Newport News Chapter), 1990; Man of the Year Alpha Kappa Alpha Sorority (Hampton Chapter), 1986. **Military Serv:** US Army Reserve, Lt Col, currently, Army Commendation Medal, Meritorious Service Medal. **Business Addr:** Judge, Hampton General District Court, 136 King's Way Mall, PO Box 70, Hampton, VA 23669.

TAYLOR, WILLIAM EDWARD
Jazz musician. **Personal:** Born Jul 24, 1921, Greenville, NC; married Theodora Castion; children: Duane, Kim. **Educ:** VA State, BS 1942; Univ of MA, EdD 1975. **Career:** Pianist, Composer, Recording Artist, Arranger/Conductor, Actor, Author, Teacher & Lecturer. **Orgs:** Mem Natl Cncl on the Arts; guest artist at White House; bd dir Am Soc of Composerrs & Authors & Publs; Creative Artist Pub Serv; Newport Jazz Festival; NY Jazz Reperatory Co; sec NY State Com Cultural Resources; vice pres Natl Assc of Rec Arts & Sci; fdr pres fdr Jazzmobile; consult adv mus schs Civic& Cultural Grps; mentor to Jazz Orgn; worked with Dizzy Gillespie, Roy Eldridge, Wilbur DeParis, Sid Catlett, Cozy Cole; featured pianist Slam Stewart Trio; soloist Don Redman Orch; featured soloist with groups as Charlie Parker, Dizzy Gillespie, Miles Davis, Kai Winding, Jo Jones, Lester Young, Oscar Pettiford; composer "I Wish I Knew How It Would Feel To Be Free"; selected by NY Times as One of The Great Songs of the Sixties; compositions Heard On Such Pgms As,Sesame Street, The Electric; written Spl Material for Ethel Smith, Charlie Parker & Many Other Top Entertainers; composed ragtime dance score for Anna Sokolow'sTV Spl; composed ballet music for "Your Arms Too Short To Box With God". **Honors/Awds:** Written svrl Movie Scores "A Morning For Jimmy" Northside Ctr; freelance rec artist working With, David Frost, Ella Fitzgerald, Sarah Vaughn, Bing Crosby, Sammy Davis, Jr, & Many Others; muscl dir awrd winning "David Frost Show"; actor in hit "The Time of Your Life"; spokesman in Commercials for such products as, Cold Power, Schaefer, Budweiser, Schmidt's, Ballantine Bee, Pespi Cola, Peugeot, Campbell Soup, Coca Cola, Canada Dry & Many Others; author of 12 Books on Jazz & Jazz Plaing; articles written for Cue, Downbeat, Saturday Rev, Tchr, CW Post Clg, Fellow At Yale; designer of Jazz Course For Manhattan Sch of Music;lectr 1st Intrntl Music Industry Conf, Berklee Clg of Music, Music Edctrs Natl Conf; Univ of PA, Columbia Univ & Many Others; cert of appreciation CityofNY; key to city Celand; numerou awrds from Jazz Comm; hon MusD VA State; Fairfield Univ & Clark Clg; Billy Taylor Collection of Original Manuscripts;Clg of Fine Arts Howard Univ; Billy Taylor Lect Series Howard Univ; President George Bush, Natl Medal of Art Award, 1992; Natl Black College Alumni Hall of Fame, 1991. **Business Addr:** 119 W 57th St, New York, NY 10019.

TAYLOR, WILLIAM GLENN
Business executive. **Personal:** Born Oct 17, 1942, Loma Linda, CA; son of Lucille Taylor and W G Taylor; married Gwendolyn A Mayeaux. **Educ:** Riverside City College, 1963; Univ of San Francisco, BS 1979. **Career:** First Interstate Bank, business services super 1965-72; Union Bank of CA, admin officer 1972-76; Bank of CA, opers super 1976-77; Home Savings of America, branch mgr 1977-83; Saving Administration Specialists 1983- . **Orgs:** Member Pasadena Jr Chamber of Commerce 1965-67; member Oakland Chamber of Commerce 1977-82; member San Francisco Chamber of Commerce 1982-83; member Optimist Intl 1982-83. **Business Addr:** Vice President, Home Savings of America, 6955 Sierra, Dublin, CA 94568.

TAYLOR, WILLIAM HENRY, SR.
Labor leader. **Personal:** Born Aug 28, 1931, Eathel, LA; married Thelma Watkins; children: Daryl, William Jr, Dawn, Diane. **Educ:** Univ of IL Chicago, 1954-56; Roosevelt Univ, 1965-69. **Career:** Oil, Chem & Atomic Workers Union, Corn Council, pres 1973-; Inter-Union Wet Corn Milling US & Canada Council, chairperson 1979-; OCAW Comm on Minority Affairs, chairperson 1975-79, 1983; OCAWIU Local 7-507, pres 1971-. **Orgs:** Mem advisor council Amer Arbitration Assoc 1971-75, 1982-84; pres Bowen HS PTA 1973-75; instr Roosevelt Univ Labor Ed Prog 1975-; mem advisory council Comm Fund 1975-79; pres CEDA Southwest Devel Assoc 1977-80, 1983-; dir Cook County CEDA Bd of Dir 1978-81; exec comm Labor Coalition Publ Util 1981-. **Honors/Awds:** Special Citation Crusade of Mercy 1977; Humanitarian Awd St Matthew AME Church 1974. **Military Serv:** AUS sgt E-5 2 yrs; UN Ribon, Good Conduct 1952-54. **Home Addr:** 9608 S Yates St, Chicago, IL 60617. **Business Addr:** President, OCAWIU Local 7-507, 6305 S Archer Rd, Argo, IL 60501.

TAYLOR, WILLIAM L.
Educator. **Personal:** Born Oct 4, 1931, Brooklyn, NY; married Harriett Rosen; children: Lauren R, Deborah L, David S. **Educ:** Brooklyn Coll, BA (cum laude) 1952; Yale Law Sch, LLB 1954. **Career:** NAACP Legal Def & Educ Fund, atty 1954-58; Ams for Dem Action, legis rep 1959-61; US Comm on Civil Rights, gen counsel 1963-65, staff dir 1965-68; Cath Univ Law Sch, adj prof; Natl Policy Review, dir 1970-86; Private Practice, law 1986-. **Orgs:** Mem exec comm Natl Bd of Ams for Dem Action 1971-; author "Hanging Together, Equality in an Urban Nation" 1971; bd Puerto Rican Legal Def Fund 1976-; Met Washington Planning & Housing Assn 1976-; mem Bars of NY, DC, US Supreme Ct; adjunct prof Georgetown Law School 1986-. **Honors/Awds:** Sr Fellow Yale Law Sch 1969-70; Natl Endowment for Humanities Grant 1974. **Military Serv:** AUS 1956-58. **Business Addr:** Attorney-at-Law, William L Taylor, 1730 M St NW, Ste 600, Washington, DC 20036.

TAYLOR-ARCHER, MORDEAN
Educational administrator. **Personal:** Born Jul 13, 1947, North Little Rock, AR; daughter of Louella Henry Taylor and John L Taylor; married Dwain E Archer, Sep 4, 1984. **Educ:** University of the Ozarks, Clarksville, AR, BS, 1969; University of Arkansas, Fayetteville, AR, MA, 1972; Brandeis University, Waltham, MA, PhD, 1979. **Career:** University of Arkansas, Little Rock, AR, instructor, 1970-74; Boston College, Chestnut Hill, MA, asst professor & coordinator of field work, 1975-78; Virginia Comonwealth Univ, Richomnd, VA, asst dean & asst professor, 1978-90; Kansas State University, Manhattan, KS, asst provost, multicultural affairs, 1990-96; Diversity and Dual Career Development, assoc provost, 1996-. **Orgs:** Member, Assn of Black Women in Higher Education, 1990; member, American Assn of Higher Education, 1990; member, National Assn of Black Social Workers, 1978-90; member, National Assn of Social Workers, 1987-90; member, National Assn of Student Personnel Administrators, 1988-90; League of Women Voters, 1996-; Manhattan Retory Clubs, 1993-; Amer Assn of Higher Education, 1992-; Kansas Assn of African Americans of Higher Education, founder, mem, 1992-. **Honors/Awds:** Ford Foundation Fellowship, National Research Council, 1974-77; Fellowship for Human Rights, Herr Foundation, 1978; Outstanding Faculty Award, School of Social Work, Virginia Commonwealth Univ, 1981, 1984; Outstanding Admin Award, Multicultural Student Council & Blue Key Honor Society, Kansas State Univ, 1993; Appreciation Award, Founding Kansas Assn of African-American in Higher Education, 1994; Barbara Jordan Outstanding Role Model Award, Big 12 Council on Black Student Government, 1996; Martin Luther King Drum Major Award, Kansas State Univ, 1997. **Home Addr:** 1205 Greystone Pl, Manhattan, KS 66502-7562. **Business Addr:** Asst Provost, Multicultural Affairs, Kansas State University, 122 Anderson Hall, Manhattan, KS 66506.

TAYLOR-THOMPSON, BETTY E.
Educational Administrator, educator. **Personal:** Born Feb 6, 1943, Houston, TX; daughter of Johnnie Mae Hart Brooks and John Charles Taylor; married Oliver B Thompson Jr, Oct 20, 1985; children: Amnon James Ashe II, Ida Elizabeth Thompson. **Educ:** Fisk Univ, Nashville TN, BA, 1963; Atlanta Univ, Atlanta GA, MLS, 1964; Howard Univ, Washington DC, MA, 1972, PhD, 1979. **Career:** Washington DC Public Library, technology librarian, 1969-72; Texas Southern Univ, Houston TX, instructor in English, 1974-75; Houston Independent Schools, Houston TX, English teacher/librarian, 1965-68, 1982-84; Texas Southern Univ, Houston TX, assoc prof of English, 1984-89, chair, Dept of English and Foreign Language, 1989-91, associate professor of English, 1991-, prof of English, currently. **Orgs:** Mem, College Language Assn, co-chair, Black Studies Comm; mem, National Council of Teachers of English; mem, Southern Conf of Modern Language Assn, sec of Afro-Amer Section; pres, Southern Conf of Afro-Amer Studies, 1990-92; Conference of College Teachers of English; American Literature Assn; Southern Conference of Afro-American Studies (past president); Natl College of Teachers of English; American Assn of University Women; Multi Ethnic Literature of the United States. **Honors/Awds:** National Endowment for the Humanities; University of Illinois at Urbanna, Institute for African Studies for the General Curriculum, Fellow; Director, Masterworks Seminar on the Harlem Reniassance; Phi Beta Kappa; National Endowment for the Humanities (NEH) Director; Masterwork Project on the Harlem Renaissance; Masterwork Project on African American Autobiographies; Study Grant on African and African American Women Writers; Director Focus Grant on Literature, Art and Music of the Harlem Renaissance; Participant, Literature and Modern Experience Institute, Accra Ghana; Tanzania, Study & Research, Fulbright Award, summer 1997; Univ of Dar Es Saalam, Africa, Institute for Arts in Education, Humanities Scholar, summer 1997. **Special Achievements:** Publications: Oxford Campanion to African American Literature, 1997; Essays: Grant and Proposal Writing Hand Book, 1997. **Business Addr:** Professor of English, Dept of English and Foreign Language, Texas Southern Univ, 3100 Cleburne St, Houston, TX 77004, (713)313-7616.

TEAGLE, TERRY MICHAEL
Professional basketball player. **Personal:** Born Apr 10, 1960, Broaddus, TX. **Educ:** Baylor Univ, BS Phys Ed 1982. **Career:** Houston Rockets, 1983-84, Detroit Pistons, 1985, Golden State Warriors, 1985-90, Los Angeles Lakers, 1990-. **Honors/Awds:** 3-time All-SWC first team under Coach Jim Haller; 2nd team All-Am as sr.

TEAGUE, GEORGE THEO
Professional football player. **Personal:** Born Feb 18, 1971, Lansing, MI; married Consuela; children: James II. **Educ:** Univ of Alabama. **Career:** Green Bay Packers, defensive back, 1993-95; Dallas Cowboys, 1996; Miami Dolphins, 1997-. **Business Addr:** Professional Football Player, Miami Dolphins, 2269 NW 199th St, Miami, FL 33056, (305)620-5000.

TEAGUE, GLADYS PETERS
City official, account executive. **Personal:** Born Sep 14, 1921, Muskogee, OK; married LD Teague; children: Merron, Charles. **Educ:** Draughon's Bus Coll, 1956-57; Correspondence Course for Postal Clerks, 1946. **Career:** Taft Post Office, postal clerk 1946-63; 1st Baptist Church, asst church clerk 1965-; Muskogee Cty, voter registrar 1984-; Town of Taft, city clerk 1984; Muskogee Cty Clerk, cty clerk deputy 1981-. **Orgs:** Mem Starlight Chap #11 OES 1949-; beautician Taft's Beauty Shop 1951-53; notary Muskogee Cty 1962-; mem school bd Dist I-17 Muskogee Cty 1972; hon aux mem Amer Legion Post #84 1973-; mem Muskogee Cty Fed Dem Women 1981-. **Honors/Awds:** Superior Accomplishment Post Office Dept 1959. **Business Addr:** County Clerk Deputy, Muskego County Clerk, c/o Merron Teague, 19423 Cluster Oaks Dr, Humble, TX 77346.

TEAGUE, ROBERT
Health care executive. **Personal:** Born Oct 26, 1929, Durant, MS; married Tresa Marie Smith. **Educ:** Tougaloo Clg, BA 1955; Univ IL, MSW 1961, USC 1966. **Career:** Psychiatric Pgms S Bay Mental Htlh Ctr, dir 1974-; Whitney M Young, Jr Psychiatric Hosp, dir owner prof placement serv pres exec dir 1971-74; Harbor View House, dir part owner 1966-; CA Dept Mental Hygiene, pgm consult 1965-67, sr psychiatric soc worker 1964-65; Pvt Marital Cncl Clinic, assc dir 1962-64; Sepulveda VA Hosp, sr psychiatric soc worker 1961-64; Danville VA Neuropsychiatric Hosp, psychiatric team 1960-61; IL Pub Aid Comm 1959-60; Ed Oakley Training Sch, playground dir 1958-59. **Orgs:** Chmn Soc Work Res Com VA Hosp Sepulveda 1961-64; co-fdr Pvt Marital Guidance Clnc; bd dir W Reg Conf Mental Hlth Pgm Mgmt 1974-76; mem Ad HocCom Mntl Hlth Ctrs 1974; consult Westminister Neighbrhd Assc Mental Hlth Clnc 1964-65; Greater LA Mental Hlth Assc; bd dir Natl Assc Soc Workers; LA Welfare Plng Cncl; elder Westminister Presb Ch; pres Clg Alumni 1965-67; bd dir STEP Job Training Proj; bd dir S Cen Welfare Plng Cncl 1969-;mem Natl Assc Soc Workers; CA Registered Soc Workers; Am Psy Assc; CA Welfare Conf; Acad Certified Soc Workers; Clg of Nursing Home Admn. **Honors/Awds:** LA men of tomorrow YMCA; comm serv awrd LA Sentinel 1972; author of Var articles & resolutions. **Military Serv:** USAF crypot oper 1950-54.

TEAMER, CHARLES C.
Educational administrator. **Personal:** Born May 20, 1933, Shelby, NC; married Mary Alice Dixon; children: Charles Carl, Roderic F, Cheryl R. **Educ:** Clark Coll, BA 1954; Univ of Omaha, post grad 1962-63; Tulane Univ, post grad 1965-66. **Career:** SC State Coll Orangeburg, acct 1955-56; TN State Univ Nashville, asst bus mgr 1958-62; Wiley Coll Marshall, TX, bus mgr 1962-65; Dillard Univ New Orleans, vice pres fiscal affairs 1965-. **Orgs:** Dir, New Orleans Pub Serv Co; bd dir Common Fund; vice pres, United Way New Orleans; mem, past dir, pres, Natl Assn Coll & Univ Bus Officers; vice pres, bd dir, New Orleans Area Council; treas, M & T Area Com Lafon Protestant Home; bd dir, Ochner Med Found Children's Hosp; mem, New Orleans Chamber of Commerce; mem, Alpha Phi Alpha; life mem, Natl Comptroller Methodist Clubs; mem, Masons; mem, Shriners. **Honors/Awds:** Silver Beaver Award Boy Scouts of Amer 1968; 1 of 10 Outstanding Citizens of New Orleans 1979. **Military Serv:** US Army, 1956-58. **Business Addr:** Vice President of Administration & Finance, Clark Atlanta University, James Brawley at Fair Street, Atlanta, GA 30314.

TEARNEY, RUSSELL JAMES
Educator. **Personal:** Born Aug 10, 1938, Syracuse, NY; son of Barbara; married Katherine; children: Russell, William (deceased), Michele. **Educ:** VA Union U, BS 1961; Howard U, MS 1969, PhD 1973. **Career:** Howard Univ, asst prof physiology & biophysics 1973-, dir of multi-discipline laboratory, 1981-; clerk 1961-65, US Postal office; University of the District of Columbia, Washington, DC, sr research associate, adjunct assoc professor of biology, beginning 1988-; cardiovascular sr research assoc, 1991. **Orgs:** Mem Am Heart Assc Inc; Sigma XI; AAAS; Black Sci Am; Pub Hlth Serv 1966-69; Am Physiol Soc 1977; grad asst prof Grad Sch Arts & Sci 1977; member, American College of Sports Medicine, 1987-; Amer Society of Hypertension, charter mem. **Honors/Awds:** US Public Health Fellow, National Institutes Health, 1966-68; Porter Fellow, American Physiological Society, 1969-73. **Business Addr:** 520 W St NW, Washington, DC 20059.

TEASLEY, LARKIN
Business executive. **Personal:** Born Sep 23, 1936, Cleveland, OH; married Violet M Williams; children: Lisa, Erica, Laura. **Educ:** Fisk Univ, BA Magna Cum Laude 1957; Occidental Coll LA, grad work in Actuarial Sci 1957-58; Univ of CA, LA, Grad Sch of Bus Exec Prgm 1971-72. **Career:** Golden State Mutual Life Ins Co, LA, asst actuary 1958-63; NC Mutual Life Ins Co, Durham, NC, actuary 1963-69; Golden State Mutual Life Ins Co, president 1970-, CEO, 1991-. **Orgs:** Dir Golden State Mut Life Ins Co 1971; dir Golden State Minority Found; dir Broadway Fed Sav & Loan Assn; dir California Chamber of Commerce; dir LA Cty Retirement Assn; fellow Soc of Actuaries; mem Am Acad of Actuaries; mem Nat Assn of Bus Economists; mem Alpha Phi Alpha; Phi Beta Kappa; Beta Kappa Chi Scientific Honor Soc. **Business Addr:** President/CEO, Golden State Mutual Life Ins Co, 1999 W Adams Blvd, Los Angeles, CA 90018.

TEASLEY, MARIE R.
Newspaper editor (retired). **Personal:** Born in Hannibal, MO; daughter of Rose Trott Wright (deceased) and George A Wright (deceased); married Ronald; children: Ronald Jr, Timothy, Lydia. **Educ:** Wayne State Univ; Univ of Detroit. **Career:** Writer for Black Publications, Aged 14; Fame Magazine writer; Pittsburgh Courier writer; WSU campus paper; Philip Morris Co; NW Papers; Food & Music Radio, host; Regular TV Show Guest; MI Chronicle, club & soc writer, 1966, women's editor, 1991 (semi-retired), cruise rep, 1991-98, press assignment to Brazil, 1992, Los Angeles, Chicago and Dallas, 1993-94. **Orgs:** mem, Women in Communications; advisory bd, WXYZ; advisory bd, Highland Park YWCA; Northwestern High School Alumni Assn; Detroit Chapter of Natl Assn of Media Women; Cancer Soc; numerous Civic Orgs; chmn, founder, Detroit Science Center Business Fund, 1983; pres, Madonna Women on Action; Coalition of 100 Black Women; member, Urban League Guild; member, National Assn of Travel Editors; member, Gamma Phi Delta Sorority, Delta Nu Chapter. **Honors/Awds:** Named Natl Media Woman of Year, 1974-75; Bridal Book edited NAAPA Award, 1974; Woman of Year, Catholic Archidose of Detroit, 1974; SCLC Award, Top Communicator, 1973; Employee of the Year, MI Chronicle, 1972; Detroit Chapter of Negro Business & Professioanl Women Top Serv Award, 1974; Woman of Year, Detroit Chapter Media, 1974; NNAPA Best Women's Pages San Francisco 1975; profiles in black CORE NY Publication, 1977; Top Journalism Award, Business & Professional Women, Natl Negro B&P Detroit Chapter, 1977; Turner Broadcasting, Goodwill Ambassador to Moscow, 1986; Coalition of 100 Black Women; Outstanding Journalism & Reporting, 1987; Community Service Award, WC Executive William Lucas, 1986; New York Black Fashion Museum Reporting Award; Education and Civics Awards, 1994-96. **Home Addr:** 19317 Coyle St, Detroit, MI 48235.

TEE, MASTER. See THOMAS, TERENCE.

TEEKAH, GEORGE ANTHONY
Physician. **Personal:** Born Mar 29, 1948; son of Lottie Wason Teekah and George D Teekah; married Theresa Riley. **Educ:** Howard Univ, BS (hon) 1971, MD 1975. **Career:** Greater SE Comm Hosp, med dir of icu, respiratory therapy 1980-83; Richmond Comm Hosp, med dir respiratory therapy 1984-. **Honors/Awds:** Beta Kappa Chi Scientific Honor Soc 1972. **Business Addr:** Medical Dir, 505 W Leigh St, Richmond, VA 23220.

TEELE, ARTHUR EARLE, JR.
Attorney. **Personal:** Born May 14, 1946, Washington, DC; children: Arthur Patton. **Educ:** FL A&M Univ, BA 1967; Army Ranger Sch, certificate 1970; Army Airborne School, certificate 1970; FL State Univ Coll of Law, JD 1972; Judge Advocate Gen School, certificate 1973. **Career:** US House of Reps, congressional intern 1966-67; US Army, sr aide-de-camp 1974-76; US Dept of Labor, expert consultant 1976-77; Private Practice, attorney atlaw 1976-81; US Dept of Trans, transition team leader 1980-81; Urban Mass Trans Admin, administrator 1981-83; Anderson Hibey Nauheim & Blair, partner 1983-85; Sparber Shevin Shapo & Heinbronner, of counsel 1983-90; Truxpacker Inc, chmn & CEO, 1984-; Natl Bus League, pres & CEO, 1984-89; Metro-Dade Board of County Commissioners, chairman, 1993-96. **Orgs:** Amer, Natl, FL, Dist of Columbia Bar Assns; Supreme Court of the State of FL; US Court of Appeals for the Fifth Dist; US District Court for the Northern Dist of FL; Phi Alpha Delta Law Frat; Assn of the Army; bd of dir FL Voters League; Jefferson Island Club; Pi Gamma Mu Natl Honor Soc; life mem Natl Assn for the Advancement of Colored People; life mem Kappa Alpha Psi Frat; FL State Univ Gold Key Soc; Alumni Assns of FL A&M Univ and FL State Univ; pres S FL Business League of Miami; bd of dir Coalition for Black Colleges; 1980-; vice pres & gen counsel Assn Indus of FL 1983-84; chmn of bd John G Riley Foundation 1983-; Jefferson Island Club 1983-; dir Silver Star Comm of FL 1983-; dir People's Natl Bank of Commerce 1983-; pres S FL Business League 1984-; dir Rehom Corp 1984-; dir Booker Washington Found 1984-; partner 1712 Assocs 1984-; chmn & ceo Mfg Tech Indus Inc 1984-. **Honors/Awds:** FL NAACP Gwendolyn Sawyer Cherry Awd 1981; Hon Doc of Aviation Mgmt Embry-Riddle Univ 1982; Frontiers Intl Achievement and Serv Awd 1985; FL Gold Key; FL NAACP Medgar Evers Award, 1979; Honorary Doctorate of Arts, FL Memorial College, 1995. **Military Serv:** AUS capt 1967-76; Bronze Star for Valor; Bronze Star for Svs; Purple Heart; Combat Infantry Badge; Cross of Gallantry; Meritorious Svs Awd w/Cluster. **Business Addr:** 3500 Pan American Dr, Miami, FL 33133-0708.

TEER, BARBARA ANN
Cultural leader, writer, producer. **Personal:** Born Jun 18, 1937, East St Louis, IL; daughter of Lila Benjamin Teer and Fred Lewis Teer; children: Omi, Folashade. **Educ:** Univ of IL, BA, 1957. **Career:** Natl Black Theatre, visionary, inst builder, founder & CEO, writer, dir, actress, producer, real estate developer, educator, 1968-. **Orgs:** Mem Theatre Com of Second World Black & African Festival of Arts & Culture Lagos, Nigeria 1975; mem Delta Sigma Theta Commn on Arts; mem Black Theatre Collective; member, Dramatists Guild, Inc, 1976-. **Honors/Awds:** Honorary Doctorate of Humane Letters, Southern Univ of Illinois, 1995; 3rd Annual Founder's Award, Black Agency Execs, 1992; Osceola Award, Delta Sigma Theta Sorority, 1992; Cert of Appreciation, Day of the African Child, 1993; Annual Natl Conf of Artists' Award, 1993; Harlem Comm Builder's Award, Harlem Churches for Comm Improvement, 1993; Positive Black Woman's Image Award, Sisters Helping In Education, Learning & Development, 1994; Honorary Doctorate of Letters, Univ of Rochester, 1994; Women Who Dared Award, Natl Black Women's Health Project, 1994; Winona Lee Fletcher Award, 1994; Cert of Participation FESTAC North Amer Region 1977; Cultural Arts Serv Awd Black Spectrum Theatre Co 1978; Universal Awareness Awd Toward A New AGe Inc1979; For Creative Excellence Harlem Week Blackafrica Promotions 1980; Comm Serv Awd Reality House Inc 1980; For Contribution to the Field of the Performing Arts Natl Assoc of Negro Business and Professional Women's Club Inc 1981; For Outstanding Contributions to the Performing and Visual Arts Natl Cncl for Cultureand Art 1983; Annual Positive Image of the Eighties Awd Rickey Productions Inc 1984; For Her Outstanding Contribution to Black Amer Theater The Natl Black Treasure Awd Hamilton Hill Arts Ctr 1984; Sojourner Truth Award, Harlem Women's Committee, 1987; Certificate of Appreciation Award, Marie BrooksCaribbean Dance Theatre, 1988pecial Achievement Award, Audience Development Committee, Inc, 1989; Legends in Our Time, Essence Magazine, May 1990; Barbara Ann Teer Day, City of East St Louis, IL, 1991. **Business Addr:** Founder/Chief Exec Officer, NBT, 2033 Fifth Ave, New York, NY 10035, (212)926-1049.

TEER, WARDEEN
Government official. **Personal:** Born Jul 8, 1945, Marvell, AR; daughter of Walter & Lillie M Townes; married Michael C Teer Sr, May 10, 1969; children: Michael Jr, Monte. **Educ:** Southern Illinois Univ, BA, 1970. **Career:** City of East St Louis, senior planner, 1970-74; National Urban League, regional research dir, 1974-76; City of Riverside, admin analyst, 1982-86, council relations admin, 1986-. **Orgs:** UCR Botanical Gardens, bd mem; Alpha Kappa Alpha Sorority. **Special Achievements:** Exec Management Program, Univ of CA Riverside, 1992; Earth

Day Coordinator, 1990. **Business Addr:** Council Relations Administrator, City of Riverside, 3900 Main Street, 7th Fl, Riverside, CA 92522, (909)782-5640.

TEEUWISSEN, PIETER
Attorney. **Personal:** Born Sep 26, 1966, Ann Arbor, MI; son of Charlotte E Teeuwissen and John Teeuwissen. **Educ:** Princeton University, 1986; Tougaloo College, BS, 1987; University of Minnesota, JD, 1990. **Career:** Mississippi Department of Human Services, attorney, special assignments, 1990-91; self-employed, attorney, 1991-92; Cherry, Givens, Lockett, Peters & Diaz, litigation attorney, 1992-93; Dockins, Simon and Teeuwissen, partner, 1993-. **Orgs:** Assn of Trial Lawyers of America; American Bar Association, 1990-; Natl Bar Assn; Mississippi State Bar, vice chair, minority involvement committee; Magnolia Bar Association, chair, special projects committee; Omega Psi Phi. **Honors/Awds:** Sloan Foundation, Sloan Fellowship, 1986; University of Minnesota, Royal Stone Scholarship, 1987-89. **Home Addr:** 5920 Dabney Dr, Jackson, MS 39206. **Business Addr:** PO Box 9187, Jackson, MS 39286, (601)969-2221.

TELFAIR, BRIAN KRAIG
Attorney. **Personal:** Born Aug 11, 1961, Jacksonville, FL; son of Roberta E & Kenneth L Telfair. **Educ:** Virginia State Univ, BS, 1983; Univ of Massachusetts, Amherst, MEd, 1985, College of William & Mary, Marshall-Wythe School of Law, JD, 1990. **Career:** Adult Career Devt Ctr, teacher, 1985-87; Sands Anderson Marks & Miller, legal intern, 1988-89; Commonwealth of VA, Office of the Attorney General, legal intern, 1989; The Dow Chemical Co, attorney, 1990-92; Miller, Canfield, Paddock & Stone, PLC, attorney, 1992-. **Orgs:** State Bar of MI, negligence, sports & entertainment law sections, 1990-; American Bar Assn, 1990-; Wolverine Bar Assn, 1992-; Omega Psi Phi Fraternity, 1987-. **Honors/Awds:** College of William & Mary, Marshall-Wythe School of Law, The Order of Barristers, 1990. **Business Addr:** Attorney, Miller, Canfield, Paddock, & Stone, PLC, 150 W Jefferson, Ste 2500, Detroit, MI 48226.

TEMPLE, DONALD MELVIN
Attorney. **Personal:** Born May 27, 1953, Philadelphia, PA; son of Ursula Temple and Joseph Temple; married Vonterris Hagan; children: Caira Suki Temple, Imani Korina Temple. **Educ:** Howard Univ, BA 1975; Univ of Santa Clara Law Sch, JD 1978; Georgetown Univ Law Ctr, LLM 1982. **Career:** US Dept of Housing, attorney advisor 1978-80; US House of Representatives, sr staff counsel 1980-90; Donald M Temple PC, 1991-. **Orgs:** Former chmn, District of Columbia Civilian Complaint Review Board, 1991-94; pres Student Bar Assoc Univ of Santa Clara School of Law 1977-78; mem Natl Bar Assoc 1980-97; pres Natl Conf Black Lawyers DC 1980-81; pres DC Chap Concerned Black Men Inc 1982-83; natl chmn 21st Century PAC 1983-87; mem WA Bar Assoc 1984-97; chairman Charles Hamilton Houston Legal Educ Inst 1984-97; mem Kappa Alpha Psi Frat 1985-, Prince Hall Masonic Lodge 1985-; chmn Adam Clayton Powell Soc 1987; mem Wash DC and PA Bars. **Honors/Awds:** Role Model of Year in Legal Educ Natl Black Law Student Assoc 1985; Best of Washington Hall of Fame 1986; Harriet Tubman Awd Congressional Black Assoc 1987; Outstanding Black Professional Business Exchange Network 1987; Natl Bar Assn Gertrude E Rush Award, 1990; Alumni of the Year, Geortown Law Ctr Black Student Assn, 1988; candidate for US House of Representatives, DC Delegate, 1990. **Business Addr:** Attorney at Law, Donald M Temple, PC, 1200 G St NW, Ste 370, Washington, DC 20005.

TEMPLE, EDWARD STANLEY
Educator, track coach (retired). **Personal:** Born Sep 20, 1927, Harrisburg, PA; son of Ruth N Ficklin Temple and Christopher R Temple; married Charlie B Law Temple, Jul 22, 1950; children: Lloyd Bernard, Edwina R. **Educ:** Tennessee State University, BS, 1950, MS, 1953; Pennsylvania State University, 1954. **Career:** Tennessee State University, associate professor, sociology, head coach, women's track, 1950-94. **Orgs:** Kappa Delta Pi Education Fraternity; Golden Key Honor Society; Intl Track and Field Committee; The Nashville Sports Council, exec committee; Tennessee State University Alumni Assn, life mbr; United States Olympic Committee, 1960, 1964, 1968, 1972, 1976, 1980, 1984. **Honors/Awds:** Helms Hall of Fame, Life Membership; Bob Douglas Hall of Fame, NY, 1988; Natl Track and Field Hall of Fame, 1989; Tennessee Sports Hall of Fame, 1972; Black Athletes Hall of Fame, 1977; Pennsylvania Sports Hall of Fame, 1985; Special Olympics, Outstanding Service Award, 1978; Athletics Congress/USA President's Award, 1986; Tennessee State University, Edward S Temple Track, dedicated, 1978. **Special Achievements:** Has Coached: 23 Olympic Medal Winners; 34 National Team Titles; 30 Pan-American Games Medal Winners; 8 National Track and Field Hall of Fame Inductees; 40 Olympians (39 have 1 or more college degrees). **Home Addr:** 2628 Delk Ave, Nashville, TN 37208-1919, (615)244-5711.

TEMPLE, HERBERT
Graphic artist. **Personal:** Born Jul 6, 1919, Gary, IN; married Athelstan. **Educ:** The Art Inst of Chgo, 1945-48. **Career:** "Ebony Ebony Jr" & "Black World" Mags, art dir; Supreme Beauty Prod Co, designs spl advertising & promotional material & packaging. **Honors/Awds:** Illustrated a number of books including "The Ebony Cook Book", "Negro & Firsts in Sports", "The Legend of Africana"; Chmn Art Com Which Selected & Purchased$250,000 Worth of Paintings, Sculptures & Other Art Objects by Black Artists Around World for Perm Exhbn in Johnson Pub Co Bldg; judge for Numerous Art Shows. **Business Addr:** Art Dir, Johnson Publishing Co, 820 South Michigan Ave, Chicago, IL 60605.

TEMPLE, ONEY D.
Automobile dealer. **Career:** Town & Country Lincoln-Mercury-Merkur Inc, Brunswick, OH, chief exec. **Business Addr:** Town & Country Lincoln-Mercury-Merkur, 1700 Pearl Rd, Brunswick, OH 44212.

TEMPLE, RONALD J.
Educational administrator. **Personal:** Born Sep 10, 1940, Chicago, IL; married Juanita Simpson; children: Ronald, Jr, Karyn A; Randall. **Educ:** Eureka Coll, BA; Univ Cincinnati, MA; Univ MI, advanced study; Univ of Cincinnati, PhD History/Social Science. **Career:** Lyons Twp HS & Jr Coll, instructor 1965-67, asst dean men & instr history 1967, asst dean student groups & univ prog 1971, special asst to pres 1974; Univ of Cincinnati, dean univ coll & assoc prof of gen studies; Wayne County Comm Coll, pres, beginning 1985; City Colleges of Chicago, chancellor, 1993-. **Orgs:** Appointed bd Children Protective Serv 1969; appointed by Mayor Cincinnati Human Relations Comm 1969-72; appointed b Natl Conf Christians & Jews 1970; elected Cincinnati Bd Educ 1971; appointed by gov to Natl Museum of Afro-Amer History & Culture Planning Council 1974-78; mem and 1982 pres Cincinnati Bd ofHealth 1979-82; bd trustees Cincinnati Historical Soc 1982-; consultant & moderator Progs sponsored by OH Humanities Council 1983-; consultant & evaluator of College & Univ Progs; co-chmn & co-founder "Conf of Major Univs which Offer Assoc Degree Progs on the Main Campus"; mem Amer Hist Assn, Amer Assn Univ Prof, Assn Study Negro Life & History. **Honors/Awds:** Natl Conf Chief Order of Arrow Boy Scouts Amer 1961; elected Phi Alpha theta Natl Hon Scholarship History 1965; elected Omicron Delta Kappa Hon Scholarship & Leadership 1973; mem Alpha Phi Alpha and Sigma Pi Phi Fraternities. **Business Addr:** Chancellor, City Colleges of Chicago, 226 W Jackson, Chicago, IL 60606.

TEMPLETON, GARRY LEWIS
Professional baseball player (retired). **Personal:** Born Mar 24, 1956, Lockey, TX; son of Otella Willims Templeton and Spiavia Templeton; married Glenda Glenn Templeton, Dec 17, 1977; children: Garry II, Gerome, Genae Nicole. **Career:** St Louis Cardinals, shortstop, 1976-81; San Diego Padres, infielder, 1982-91; New York Mets, 1991. **Honors/Awds:** Youngest shortstop in modern baseball history to reach the 200-hit plateau and only the 14th shortstop to ever reach the mark 1977; selected Baseball Digest and Topps Chewing Gum Rookie All Star Team 1977; 9 game stretch batted 400 12 for 30; finished 1st month of season hitting 338; matched his career high of 4 RBI; finished yr with a league leading 23 intentional walks; 1st season as Padre led Natl League shortstops in runs scored 76, RBI 64, game winning RBI 8; named to UPI & The Sporting News All-Star Teams; 1st Team selection to AP & The Sporting News All-Star Squads; 34 Stolen Bases; 148 games more than any other shortstop in Natl Legue 1984; MVP Awd 1985; mem All Star Team 1977 and 1985; first player to get 100 hits batting left handed & right handed in a season; most games playby San Diego Padre Player, 1990. **Home Addr:** PO Box 1196, Poway, CA 92074.

TENNANT, MELVIN, II
Convention sales manager. **Personal:** Born Jul 2, 1959, Bryan, TX; son of Cora Tennant and Melvin Tennant; children: Caroline, Brian, Matthew, Melanie. **Educ:** Rice Univ, BA 1982. **Career:** Houston Convention and Visitors Bureau, associate director, 1980-87; Corpus Christi Convention and Visitors Bureau, convention division director, 1987-88; Irving, TX, Convention and Visitors Bureau, associate director, 1988-90; Oakland Convention and Visitors Bureau, president and CEO, 1990-. **Orgs:** Mem Houston Area Urban League 1984-, Natl Coalition of Black Meeting Planners 1985-, Amer Soc of Assn Execs; board member, Patrons for the Humanities; board member, United Negro College Fund, East Bay Chapter; chair, International Association of Convention and Visitors Bureaus; board member, Western Association of Convention and Visitors Bureaus. **Honors/Awds:** Certificate of Appreciation Natl Tour Assn 1984. **Business Addr:** President and CEO, Oakland Convention & Visitors Bureau, 1001 Broadway, Oakland, CA 94607-4019.

TERBORG-PENN, ROSALYN M.
Educator, historian. **Personal:** Born Oct 22, 1941, Brooklyn, NY; daughter of Jeanne Van Horn Terborg and Jacques Terborg Sr; divorced; children: Jeanna C. **Educ:** Queens Coll CUNY, BA 1963; George Washington U, MA 1967; Howard U, PhD 1977. **Career:** Morgan State U, prof of history, coordinator of graduate programs in history, 1986-. **Orgs:** History editor Feminist Studies, 1984-89; commr Howard Cty MD Commn for Women 1980-82; chair, American Historical Association Comm on Women Historians, 1991-93; Research & Publications Comm, Maryland Historical Soc, 1989-; Alpha Kappa Alpha Sorority, Inc; Association of Black Women Historians, founder, 1978. **Honors/Awds:** Grad History Essay Award Rayford Logan, Howard Univ 1973; Grad Fellowship in History Howard Univ 1973-74; Post Doct Fellowship for Minorities Ford Found 1980-81; Visiting Scholar Grant Smithsonian Inst 1982; Travel to Collections Grant Nat Endowment for the Humanities 1984; Association of Black Women Historians, Letitia Woods Brown Award for Best Article Published on Black Women, 1987-88. **Special Achievements:** Author: Afro-American Woman-Struggles and Images, 1978, 1981; Women in Africa and the African Dispora, 1987. **Business Addr:** Professor of History, Morgan State Univ, History Dept, Baltimore, MD 21239.

TERO, LAWRENCE (MR. T)
Actor. **Personal:** Born 1952, Chicago, IL; children: Lesa. **Educ:** Attended Prairie View A&M. **Career:** Muhammed Ali, Leon Spinks, Donna Summer, Diana Ross, Rev Jesse Jackson, Michael Jackson, bodyguard; DC Cab, Rocky III, The A-Team, actor. **Orgs:** Donated to churches & orgs to feed the hungry & clothe the naked. **Honors/Awds:** Football Scholarship. **Military Serv:** Military policeman. **Business Addr:** Actor, c/o Gersh Agency, PO Box 5617, Beverly Hills, CA 90210.

TERRELL, CATHERINE MILLIGAN
Educator. **Personal:** Born Oct 28, 1944, St Croix, Virgin Islands of the United States; daughter of Exira Milligan and Hugh Milligan; divorced; children: Natalie, Omar, E'Alafio. **Educ:** Temple Univ, Philadelphia, PA, BS, 1973; Antioch Univ, Yellow Springs, OH, MEd, 1974; Columbia Univ, New York, NY, PhD, 1991. **Career:** School Dist Philadelphia, Philadelphia, PA, assistant principal, 1980-86; St Dunstan's Episcopal School, St Croix, VI, head, 1986-. **Orgs:** Member, Phi Delta Kappa, 1987-. **Honors/Awds:** Educational articles, 1986, 1987; Pan African National Support Group, 1989; Business & Professional Women's Club, 1990, Women of the Year, 1991. **Business Addr:** Headmaster, St. Dunstan's Episcopal School, 21 Orange Grove, Christiansted, St Croix, Virgin Islands of the United States 00820.

TERRELL, DOROTHY
Computer company executive. **Personal:** Born Jun 12, 1945, Fort Lauderdale, FL; daughter of Pearl Weeks Terrell and Charles W Terrell Sr; married Albert H Brown; children: Dorian. **Educ:** FL A&M Univ, BA 1966. **Career:** Digital Equip Corp, plant personnel mgr 1978-80, group personnel mgr 1980-84, plant mgr 1984-87, group mgr 1987-; Sun Express, president, currently. **Orgs:** Mem Delta Sigma Theta 1965-; adv comm OIC 1984-87; comm mem Boston C of C 1984-88; trustee Social Policy Rsch 1985-89; bd mem Boston YWCA 1985-89; bd mem Lera Park Comm Dev 1985-89; bd mem Boston Club 1986-89. **Honors/Awds:** Achievement Awd Snowden Assoc 1984; Film "Choosing to Lead" AMA 1986; Achievement Awd YWCA 1986; Black Achievers YMCA 1987; Hecht-Shaw Award 1987; Museum of Afro-American History Award 1988; Leadership Pioneer Award 1988; Edges Group Award, 1992: Natl Council of Negro Women, Women of Courage and Conviction Award, 1993. **Business Addr:** President, Sun Express, 2 Elizabeth Dr, Chelmsford, MA 01824.

TERRELL, FRANCIS
Educator. **Personal:** Born Nov 25, 1944, Greensboro, GA; son of Carrie Terrell and Emery Terrell; married Sandra L; children: Ivanna Samal, Amani Shama, Elon Jadhal. **Educ:** Wilmington Coll (OH), BS 1968; Univ of Pittsburgh, MS 1972; Univ of Pittsburgh, PhD 1975. **Career:** Univ of Pittsburgh, post-doctoral fellow 1975-76; TX Christian Univ, asst prof 1976-80; N TX State Univ, dir of clncl training, 1981-89, assoc prof of psychology, currently. **Orgs:** Mem Am Psychol Assn 1976-80; mem Black Psychol Assn 1976-80; mem Sigma Xi 1976-80; rgnl mental health consultant US Labor Dept 1978-. **Honors/Awds:** Pub "Self Concept of Jnvls Who Commit Black on Blacks Crimes" Corrective & Social Psychiatry 1980; pub "Effects of Race of Examiner & Type of Reinforcement on the Intelligence Test of Black Children" Psychology in the Schs 1980; fellow Amer Psychological Assn 1984; fellow Soc for Study of Personality 1984; Over 40 Jrnls Publshd; fellow, American Psychological Society. **Military Serv:** USN 2nd class petty ofcr 1978-84. **Business Addr:** Associate Professor, North Texas State Univ, Psychology Dept, Denton, TX 76203.

TERRELL, FRANCIS D'ARCY
Attorney. **Personal:** Born May 13, 1940, Caledonia, NY; married Mary Jane Hawthorne; children: Derek M, Randall D. **Educ:** Univ of Toledo, BS 1970; Columbia Law School, JD 1973. **Career:** Shearman & Sterling, assoc attorney 1973-75; Private Practice, attorney 1975-77; Jones & Terrell, partner 1977-82; Bronx Comm Coll, deputy chmn/prof 1982-. **Orgs:** Mem Amer Business Law Assocs 1984-. **Honors/Awds:** Lt col 20 yrs; Bronze Star; Air Medal; Meritorious Serv Medal; Commendation Medal; Combat Infantry Badge. **Home Addr:** 788 Riverside Dr, Apt 3AA, New York, NY 10032. **Business Addr:** Deputy Chairman, Bronx Comm College, Dept of Business, W 181st & Univ Ave, Bronx, NY 10453.

TERRELL, FREDERICK
Banker, entrepreneur. **Personal:** Born in Hamtramck, MI. **Educ:** La Verne College, BS; Occidental College, MA; Coro Foundation, post-graduate fellowship; Yale School of Management. **Career:** CS First Boston Corporation, senior banker, managing director; Provender Capitol Group LLC, co-founder, currently. **Special Achievements:** One of 25 "Hottest Blacks on Wall Street" listed in Black Enterprise, October, 1992. **Business Addr:** Partner, Provender Capital Group, 17 State St, New York, NY 10004, (212)271-8888.

TERRELL, HENRY MATTHEW
Attorney, city government official. **Personal:** Born Dec 6, 1940, Caroline County, VA. **Educ:** Howard Univ Sch Law, JD 1971; VA State Clg, BA 1963. **Career:** EGS Fin Mgmt Cons, pres 1971-; CT Hellmuth & Assc, mr 1975-; Aetna Ins Co, brokerage mgr 1973-75; Am Security & Trust Co, estate & pension admn 1971-72; Prudential Life Ins Co, mktg & sls rep 1965-71. **Orgs:** Bd of Dirs, VA State Coll Alumni Assn; past pres, Howard Univ Law School Alumni Assn; Alpha Phi Alpha; Delta Theta Phi Law Fraternity; pres, VA State Coll Alumni Assn, 1966-68; bd of trustees, VA State Coll Found, 1974; regional dir, VA State Coll Alumni Assn, 1974; business mgr, Nubian Enterprises; dir DC Chap Intl Assn Financial Planners; Natl Patent Assn. **Military Serv:** US Army capt 1963-65.

TERRELL, JOHN L.
Educational administrator (retired). **Personal:** Born May 19, 1930, Forest City, AR; son of Velma Mclemore (deceased) and Willie L; married Betty R Phillips Terrell, Aug 16, 1950; children: Debra, Lanette, John, DeAnna. **Educ:** Muskegon Business Coll, Business Admin 1956. **Career:** Howmet Corp, x-ray tech 1956-88; UAW Local 1243, sec-treasurer 1958; Howmet Employee Credit Union, pres 1962; Muskegon Heights School Bd, treasurer 1969-79, vice pres 1979-85. **Orgs:** Pres, Muskegon Intermediate School District, 1989, 1991; pres, Muskegon County School Board Assn, 1987-91; mem, VFW, currently. **Military Serv:** AUS pfc 1952-54; Combat Medic Badge. **Home Addr:** 2336 Maffett St, Muskegon Heights, MI 49444.

TERRELL, MABLE JEAN
Association executive. **Personal:** Born Aug 2, 1936, North Little Rock, AR; daughter of Mable Edwards Webb and Rudolph C Webb; married William B Terrell, Nov 4, 1955 (deceased); children: Venita Terrell-Chew, Vickie Terrell-Quinn, Camelia Terrell-Cox. **Educ:** Roosevelt Univ, Chicago IL, BA, 1970. **Career:** Honeywell, Inc, Chicago IL, senior rep, 1972-82; Walter E Hellen, Chicago IL, senior analyst, 1982-84; International Black Writers, pres and exec dir, 1984-. **Orgs:** Mem, NAACP; mem, Trans Africa; mem, Urban League; bd mem, Systems Programmers Soc; pres, Jones Alumni Assn. **Honors/Awds:** Arkansas Travelers Award, 1984; Kool Achiever Award nominee, 1989; Chicago's Black Gold, 1986. **Business Addr:** President/Executive Director, International Black Writers Conference, Inc, PO Box 1030, Chicago, IL 60690.

TERRELL, MARY ANN
Judge. **Personal:** Born Jun 3, 1944, Jacksonville, FL; daughter of Minnie Armstrong Gooden and Quincy Gooden; married James Edward Terrell; children: Angela Rani, Mariessa Rebecca, James Stephen. **Educ:** Howard Univ, BA 1966; Antioch Univ, MAT 1969; Georgetown Univ Law Ctr, JD 1980. **Career:** Peace Corps/India, volunteer 1966-68; Antioch Coll, dir of admin asst prof history 1969-73; Dix St Acad, dir/founder 1974-80; Mental Health Law Project, lawyer 1980-81; Dist of Columbia City Council, exec asst to council chmn 1981-82; DC Dept of Public Works, hearing examiner 1983-84; Antioch School of Law, adjunct prof 1987-; Office of US Attorney, asst US attorney, 1984-89; Federal, Home Loan Bank Bd, Washington,DC, sr atorney, 1989; FDIC/RTC, Washington, DC, counsel litigation, 1989-90, counsel, corporate affairs, 1990-92; counsel, Outside Counsel Management Section, RTC, 1992-95; Department of Legal Programs, RTC, sr counsel dir, 1993-95; FDIC, associate director, begin 1995; Superior Ct of DC, judge, currently. **Orgs:** Treasurer Natl Pol Congress Black Women 1985-91; mem Natl Assoc of Black Women Attorneys 1985-, Women's Div of NBA 1986-; mem Women's Bar Assoc of DC 1987, Federal Bar Assoc 1987, The Washington Bar; board of directors, Women Bar Assn, Washington, DC, 1990-92; co-chair, committee exec & judicial appts, GWAC-NBA, 1990-91; co-chair, person to person committee, THIS Meridan House International, 1990-; board of directors, Federal Bar Assn, DC Chapter, 1988-; District of Columbia Bar, 1983; Bar Assn of the District of Columbia, committee chair, 1988-89; Federal Bar, DC Chapter, bd of dirs; Washington Bar, NBA Convention Steering Committee, 1988, Law Day Dinner Committee, 1993; Natl Bar Assn, GWAC, judicial exec nomination comm, 1990-91; Natl Assn of Black Women Attorneys, Conference Steering Comm, 1990; Women's Bar Assn, bd of dirs; Washington Lawyers Against Drugs, vice chair; Black Asst US Attorney Assn; Asst US Attorney Assn; Executive Women In Government; US International Cultural & Trade Ctr, advisory comm mem; Young People Communicating Inc, vp; Temporary Panel for Employees Appeal, appointed, 1992; Mayor's Citizen Budget Advisory & Review Comm, appointed, 1992; Howard Univ Alumni Assn, Ad Hoc Executive; Comm of the Executive Bd, mem; Voting Delegate, District of Columbia Judicial Conference, 1985, 1986, 1987; DC Bar, secretary, elected, 1994. **Honors/Awds:** Outstanding Comm Serv Awd in Educ 1980; apptd Mayor's Intl Adv Council 1983-; selected DC State Adv Comm for Hands Across Amer 1986; apptd Legal Serv Bd Antioch School Law 1986-; selected vice chair Washington Lawyers Against Drugs Comm 1987; Appointed Mayor's Citizen's Budget Advisory & Review Comm, 1992-94; Appointed Mem Temporary Panel for Employees Appeal, 1991-93. **Business Addr:** Judge, Superior Ct of DC, 500 Indiana Ave, NW, JM-610, Washington, DC 20001.

TERRELL, MELVIN C.
Educational administrator, educator. **Personal:** Born Oct 5, 1949, Chicago, IL; son of Ethel Lee McNeal Terrell and Cleveland Terrell. **Educ:** Chicago State Univ, BSEd 1971; Loyola Univ of Chicago, MEd 1974; Southern Illinois Univ at Carbondale, PhD 1978; Inst for Educ Mgmt Harvard Univ, Post-Doctoral Study/Mgmt Devel Program summer 1986; Univ of Virginia Annual Summer Professional Dept Workshop Educ Mgmt Strategies, 1987; Natl Assn of Student Personnel Admin, Richard F Stevens Inst, 1989; Amer Council on Educ, Fellow, Florida State Univ, 1993-94. **Career:** Kennedy-King Coll Chicago, student devel specialist, counseling instructor 1973-75; Eastern New Mexico Univ, coordinator/counselor of black affairs & asst prof ethnic studies 1977-78; Chicago State Univ, project director/asst professor of education, 1978-79; Univ of Arkansas at Monticello, dir learning devel center 1979-80; Univ of Wisconsin-Oshkosh, dir multicultural educ center 1981-85; Univ of Toledo, dir of minority affairs & adjunct asst prof 1985-88; Northeastern Illinois Univ, full professor of counselor education, 1988-, vice president for student affairs, 1988-; Illinois State Univ, visiting prof, summer 1991. **Orgs:** Vice chmn of educ comm NAACP Toledo Branch 1985-; educ bd Natl Assoc of Student Personnel Admin Journal 1986-89 on Leadership Educ, 1986-; chair educ comm Alpha Phi Alpha 1986-88; natl chmn, Ethnic Minority Network, Natl Assn of Student Personnel Assn, 1988-90; vice chmn, Amer Assn of Higher Educ, 1989; chmn, Amer Assn of Higher Educ, Black Caucus Exec, 1991-93; life mem, Alpha Phi Alphi Fraternity, Inc; evaluation team mem, Middle States Assn of Colls & Univs; consultant evaluator, North Central Assn of Colleges & Universities, 1988-; member, National Assn of Student Personnel Administrators; natl coord, Minority Undergraduate Fellows Program, Natl Assn of Student Personnel Admini, 1994-98; chair, exec comm, Ill Comm on Blacks Concerned in Higher Ed (IC-BCHE), 1995-. **Honors/Awds:** Outstanding Admin, Univ of Toledo 1985, 1986, Administrator of the Year, 1986-88; author, "From Isolation to Mainstream, An Institutional Committment" 1987; co-author, Model Field Based Program in Multicultural Educ for Non-Urban Univs 1981, "Multicultural Educ Centers in Acad Marketplace" 1987; author, Racism: Undermining Higher Education, 1988; editor, NASPA Journal Series on Cultural Pluralism, 1988; Scott Goodnight Award for Outstanding Performance of a Dean, 1990; co-editor, From Survival to Success: Promoting Minority Student Retention, 1988; recipient of a Ford Foundation Grant on Cultural Diversity, co-principal investigator, 1992-94; Identified as an Exemplary Leader in "Effective Leadership in Student Services," written by Linda M Clement & Scott T Rickard, Jossey-Bass, 1992. **Special Achievements:** "Diversity, Disunity and Campus Community," National Association of Student Personnel Administrators Monograph, 1992; Source of funding for minority student programming and its implications; Fund raising and development for student affairs; "Developing Student Government Leadership," New Directions for Student Services Monograph, Summer, 1994. **Business Addr:** Vice President for Student Affairs, Northeastern Illinois University, 5500 N St Louis Ave, Rm B-104, Chicago, IL 60625.

TERRELL, REGINALD V.
Attorney. **Personal:** Born Mar 23, 1959, Vallejo, CA; son of Codessa M Terrell and Harold D Terrell. **Educ:** Saint Mary's College of California, BA, 1981; University of California, JD, 1984. **Career:** Burris Law Office, law clerk, lawyer, 1984-. **Orgs:** Charles Houston Bar Association, 1984-; Saint Mary's College of California, trustee, board mem, 1997-; California State Bar, 1987-; National Bar Association, 1984-; California Trial Lawyers Association, 1988-. **Special Achievements:** University of California Davis Law Review, staffer, 1984. **Business Addr:** Attorney, Burris Law Office, 1212 Broadway, 12th Fl, Ste 1200, Oakland, CA 94612, (510)839-5200.

TERRELL, RICHARD WARREN
Business manager. **Personal:** Born Nov 16, 1946, Fort Riley, KS; son of Mary Terrell and Warren Terrell; married Phyllis Eileen Hargrove; children: Wesley, Rodney. **Educ:** CA Poly SLO, BSEL 1968; San Jose State, MSEE 1974. **Career:** Prairie View A&M, adj prof 1976-77; IBM, engr, mgr lsi packaging 1968-90; Tandem Computers, storage and printer systems staff, 1990-. **Orgs:** Mem Alpha Phi Alpha, NAACP, Antioch Baptist Church; Jack & Jill of America. **Home Addr:** 4959 Massachusetts Dr, San Jose, CA 95136.

TERRELL, ROBERT E.
Government official. **Personal:** Born Oct 4, 1943, Terry, MS; son of Rosie McNeil; married Karen K; children: Kelley L Carson. **Educ:** KS Univ, BS 1966, MPA 1975. **Career:** Turner House Inc, exec dir 1971-74; City of Ft Worth, budget analyst 1974-77; Ft Worth Econ Dev Corp, exec dir 1977-79; City of Ft Worth, asst to city mgr 1979-85; assistant city mgr, 1985-92, city mgr, 1992-. **Orgs:** Past officer, Kappa Alpha Psi Frat 1962-; life mem, 1989-, mem 1977-, NAACP; Natl Bd Conf of Minority Public Admin 1979-81; mem Amer Soc of Public Admin 1979-; asst steering com Intl City Mgmt Assn 1979-81; Natl Forum for Black Public Administrators, North Texas Chapter, pres, 1987-89; ICMA Council, Task Force manager, 1993-95; Public Technology Inc, steering committee, 1992-; Texas City Management Association. **Honors/Awds:** Fellowship NASPAA 1974-75; North Texas ASPA Public Administrator of the Year, 1988; Public Technology, Inc, Technology Leadership Award, 1997. **Business Addr:** City Manager, City of Fort Worth, 1000 Throckmorton, Fort Worth, TX 76102.

TERRELL, ROBERT L.
Educator, writer. **Personal:** Born Jul 19, 1943; married. **Educ:** Morehouse Coll Atlanta, BA 1969; Univ CA Berkeley, MA 1971; Univ of CA Berkeley, PhD 1970. **Career:** Publ poems short stories books 1967-; NY Post, reporter 1967-68; So Reg Council Atlanta, rsch writer 1968-69; Newsweek Mag, stringer 1968-69; Univ of CA,teaching asst 1969-70; Golden Gate Coll, instr 1969-71; San Francisco Crhonicle, copy ed 1970; CA Jrnl Teacher Ed, asst prof 1971-76, ed 1972-73; OffRsch & Plnng, coord 1974-75; St Mary's Coll Morage CA, office experimental progs 1975-76; Stanford Univ, asst prof 1976; Univ of MO, assoc prof jrnlsm 1976-; School of Jrnlsm Univ of CA Berkeley, vstg prof 1979; Beijing Review Mag Beijing China, copy ed 1981-82; NY Univ Dept of Jrnlsm & Mass Commun, vstg prof 1985-86; Univ Nairobi School of Jrnlsm, fulbright prof 1984-85. **Orgs:** Mem Amer Assoc Colls Teacher Ed, Amer Assoc Higher Ed, Amer Ed Rsch Assoc; bd dir CA Council Teacher Ed, Soc Coll & Univ; managing ed CA Jrnl Teacher Ed 1973; ed referee CA Jrnl Teacher Ed 1974-; adv screening comm commun Council for Intl Exchange of Scholars Fulbright Prog 1980-83. **Honors/Awds:** Fellowship CA State 1969-72, Grad Minority 1969-72, Fund for Peace 1970-71, NDEA 1971-74; Deans Fellowship Univ of CA 1974-75.

TERRELL, STANLEY E.
Newspaper reporter. **Personal:** Born Feb 16, 1949, Newark, NJ; son of Wilda M Johnson and Millard E Terrell; children: Salimu Amini. **Educ:** Hampton Inst, 1966-68; Essex Co Coll, 1969-70. **Career:** The Star-Ledger, gen assignment news reporter 1968-88, editorial writer/columnist, 1988-. **Orgs:** Contrib articles to numerous magazines; lectr, worked closely with NAACP; Urban League; Cong African People; Human Rights Commn; various tenant groups, juvenile programs, prison reform groups, drug rehab projects; founding member, Black Heritage Day Parade Comm, 1979-. **Honors/Awds:** Merit Awd Newark Tenants Cncl 1974; Outst Achiev Awd Newark Hum Rights Commn 1974; Awd from Newark Title I ESEA Prog for Outst Serv to Newark Comm 1975; Star-Ledger Bonus 1971; New Jersey Black Achievers Award, 1989; Distinguished Service Award, Black Heritage Day Parade Comm, 1990. **Business Addr:** Columnist, Star-Leder, 1 Star Ledger Plaza, Newark, NJ 07102.

TERRILL, W. H. TYRONE, JR.
Business executive. **Personal:** Born Aug 30, 1953, Kansas City, MO; married Suzanne E Fuller; children: Whitney Nicole, Phillip Richard Tyrone. **Educ:** Bemidji State Univ Bemidji MN, BS 1976. **Career:** MN Dept of Human Rights, compliance dir 1976-80; Minneapolis Dept of Civil Rights, dep dir 1980-87; Terrill and Associates, president 1987-. **Orgs:** Mem MN Afirmative Action Assoc 1978-; founder, mem Inter-Govt Compliance Inst 1978-; mem Minneapolis Urban League, Minneapolis Br NAACP 1984-; former chairperson Hennepin County MECAC 1986-. **Honors/Awds:** Community Serv Minneapolis Urban League 1984. **Business Addr:** President, Terrill and Associates, 2110 Lyndale Ave, #3, Minneapolis, MN 55405, (612)870-8118.

TERRY, ADELINE HELEN
Attorney (retired). **Personal:** Born Apr 17, 1931, Wichita, KS; daughter of Narcissus O'Grady Johnson and Clifford Johnson; children: Catherine. **Educ:** CA State Coll, BA Sociology 1960; Southwestern Univ of Law, LLB 1968. **Career:** LA Co Dist Attorney, investigator 1960-62; LA Co Superior Ct, domestic rel investigator 1962-65; LA Co Probation Dept, 1965-69; LA Co Dist Atty, dep dist atty 1969-. **Orgs:** Mem Assn of Dep Dist Atty of LA; mem CA Dist Atty's Assn; Black Women's Lawyers of LA; Langston Law Club; Women Lawyers of LA; State Bar of CA. **Business Addr:** Retired Deputy District Attorney, Los Angeles Co Dist Atty, 210 W Temple St, Ste 17 1013, Los Angeles, CA 90012.

TERRY, ANGELA OWEN
Educational administrator. **Personal:** Born Feb 13, 1941, Memphis, TN; daughter of Addie Griffin Owen and William Franklin Owen, Sr; married Elbert A Terry (deceased); children: Angela Daphne, Warren Marshall. **Educ:** The Univ of Vienna, Cert 1963; Spelman College, BA 1962; Fisk Univ, MA 1964; The Univ of CT, PhD 1973; Harvard Univ Cambridge MA certificate July 1987 Management Development Program for College & University Administrators Institute for Educational Manage-

ment. **Career:** Albany State Coll, asst prof psych 1964-69; Prospect Psycholog Serv Ctr, psychological serv worker 1969-71; CT State Dept of Educ, educ consul psych serv 1973-77; Univ of CT, asst dir dept of counseling serv 1978-83, asst to the vice pres for program evaluation & rsch 1983-89, assistant vice pres, student affairs, 1989-93; NC Central Univ, Durham, NC, vice chancellor for student affairs, 1993-94; Univ of CT, assoc vice pres for student affairs, 1994-. **Orgs:** Amer Assoc for Counseling & Devel; Amer Coll Personnel Assoc; Assoc for Institutional Rsch; Delta Sigma Theta Sorority Inc, National Association of Student Personnel Administrators; Amer Assoc for Higher Educ; Coalition of 100 Black Women; editorial board, NASPA Journal, 1988-1991, 1993-96; Natl ID Program for Advancement of Women (ACE), state coord, 1992-93; NASPA Region I, advisory bd, 1996-98; Enrollment Mgmt Network, chair, 1996-. **Honors/Awds:** Scholarship Univ of Vienna 1963; Fellowship Harvard Univ 1969; Doctoral Fellowship The Univ of CT 1971-73; Pi Lambda Theta Natl Educ Honor Soc; Phi Delta Kappa; National Education Honor Soc; Service Award, African-American Cultural Center, University of CT; Recognition Award, The Women's Center, University of CT; Outstanding Educator Award, Windham-Willimantic Chapter, NAACP; NC Central Univ, Leadership Award, 1994; Honorary Member, Golden Key Natl Honor Society, 1990. **Home Addr:** 36 Patriot Rd, Windham, CT 06280. **Business Addr:** Associate VP for Student Affairs, University of Connecticut, 4 Gilbert Rd, U-109, Storrs Mansfield, CT 06268-1109, (860)486-1668.

TERRY, BOB (NIGHTHAWK)
Business executive. **Personal:** Born Jan 6, 1936, Franklin, KY; divorced; children: Donald, Mia. **Educ:** NY Sch of Announcing & Speech, 1960. **Career:** WLIB NY, air personality; "Shade of Soul" Metromedia, Wash, DC, exec prod, host 1969-72; WRMA MT, AL, prog dir 1960-62; WTMP, Tampa, FL, prog mus dir 1962-63; WAME Miami, prog & mgr, oper mgr 1963-65; WOL, DC, Announcer, prog dir 1965-71; WHUR-FM, oper, mgr, air personality 1971-75. **Orgs:** Mem bd dir NATRA 1971-73; mem bd dir AFTRA 1971-73; bd mem Mayor's Proj Awareness Com 1968-70; bd mem Mayor's Youth Coun 1968-70; mem Mayor's Civ Def Commn 1968. **Honors/Awds:** Best air personality of year, WOL-AM, 1966-70; best air personality of year, Ex-Consult Inc 1971; best comm of year, Eastman Kodak Co 1967; best comm of year,Natl Brewing Co 1966-; co-star of "Trouble Man" Universal Pictures 1972. **Military Serv:** USN 1954-58. **Business Addr:** 310 Lenox Ave, New York, NY 10027.

TERRY, CLARK
Music company executive. **Personal:** Born Dec 14, 1920, St Louis, MO; married Pauline Reddon. **Educ:** Private studies. **Career:** Pastel Music, pres; Etoile Music Prod Inc, pres; Clark Terry Big Bad Band; Itinerate Jazz, clinician & educator, currently. **Orgs:** Exec dir Int Art of Jazz. **Honors/Awds:** Honorary Doctorates from Teikyo Westmar Univ, Berklee School of Music, and the Univ of New Hampshire; received numerous awards. **Military Serv:** USN.

TERRY, FRANK W.
Federal official (retired). **Personal:** Born Jan 23, 1919, Los Angeles; son of Jessie L Terry and Woodford H Terry; married Valdoras Hancock; children: Charles Love, Susan Samples, Mike Terry. **Educ:** Los Angeles City Coll, 1948-49; Army Officers Candidate School, 1942. **Career:** Freelance photographer reporter 1946-50; Joseph V Baker Assoc, west coast rep 1950-56; Douglas Aircraft Co, 1956-60; US Dept of Labor Office of Information, 1962-78; US Veterans Admin, 1978; Los Angeles Library, commr 1978-93. **Orgs:** Chmn Los Angeles Fed Exec Bd 1975-76; bd mem CA Governor's Comm for Employment of Handicapped; bd mem Coll Fed Coun of Southern CA 1965-70; third vice pres LA Library Assn; bd mem Cultural Heritage Found; bd mem Fed of Black History & Arts; LA Urban League. **Honors/Awds:** Various publications 1946-50; recipient Certificate of Merit, LA Fed Exec Bd 1967; Meritorious Achievement Award US Dept of Labor 1970; Lula Fields Exec Award Extraordinaire 1972; Aztec Award Mexican Amer Opportunities Found 1974. **Military Serv:** AUS 1st lt 1941-46. **Home Addr:** 5350 Stillwater Dr, Los Angeles, CA 90008.

TERRY, GARLAND BENJAMIN
Dentist. **Personal:** Born Mar 27, 1927, Norfolk, VA; married Marie Walker; children: Michael Quentin. **Educ:** OH State Univ, BS 1953; Coll of Dentistry Howard Univ, DDS 1957. **Career:** AUS Dental Corps, 1957-60; Private practice, dentist 1960-. **Orgs:** Mem NJ Dental Assoc, Amer Dental Assoc, Omega Psi Phi, Capitol City Golf Club. **Military Serv:** AUS 1946-49; Dental Corps 1957-60. **Business Addr:** 701-703 Rutherford Ave, Trenton, NJ 08618.

TERRY, RICK
Professional football player. **Personal:** Born Apr 5, 1974; children: Jasmine. **Educ:** Univ of North Carolina. **Career:** New York Jets, defensive tackle, 1997-. **Business Addr:** Professional Football Player, New York Jets, 1000 Fulton Ave, Hempstead, NY 11550, (516)560-8100.

TERRY, ROY
Apparel company executive. **Personal:** Born Dec 27, 1944, Dayton, OH; son of Velma G Terry and Jesse A Terry; married Willo; children: Corey, Cotina. **Educ:** Morehouse Coll, BA, 1966. **Career:** Terry Manufacturing Co Inc, president, CEO, 1972-. **Orgs:** Am Apparel Mfrs Assn, 1969-; Minority Business Enterprise Legal Def & Education Fund, founding board member, 1980-; NAACP, life member, 1970-; Federal Reserve Bank, Birmingham Branch, chairman of the board, 1985-92; Alabama Democratic Conference, voting rights coordinator, 1980-; Operation PUSH, World Trade Council, 1986-. **Honors/Awds:** US Dept of Defense, initial Shared Production Award, 1992; Morehouse College, Bennie Award, 1993; US Dept of Commerce, Minority Manufacturer of the Year, 1989; Black Enterprise Magazine, Minority Manufacturer of the Year, 1974; Alabama Demovratic Conference, AG Gaston Award, 1980. **Special Achievements:** Author: Shared Production Concept, adopted as model, $3.5 billion Defense Agency, 1992. **Business Addr:** President, Terry Manufacturing Co, Inc, 924 South St, PO Box 648, Roanoke, AL 36274, (205)863-2171.

TERRY, SAUNDERS
Entertainer. **Personal:** Born Oct 24, 1911, Greensboro, GA; married Emma Taylor. **Career:** Professional Entertainer, harmonica plyr & singer; Buck & The Preacher, mus sound tracks 1971; Cisco Pike, 1972; Book of Numbers, 1973; Leadbelly, 1976; Finnians Rainbow, mus featured 1946; Cat on A Hot Tin Roof, 1955. **Orgs:** Num radio & TV mus shows; recording artist since 1936; num records & albums on the market; tchr Harmonica Playing; films; mem Comm Civic Assn; mem Am Fedn of Musicians Local #802; mem AFTRA. **Honors/Awds:** Certificate, Preservation & Advancement of the Harmonica 1963; autobiography published, The Harp Styles of Sonny Terry 1975.

TESSEMA, TESFAYE
Artist. **Personal:** Born May 5, 1951, Addis Ababa, Ethiopia. **Educ:** Fine Arts School, Addia Ababa, Diploma, 1970; Howard Univ, MFA 1976. **Career:** Arts DC, Washington, DC, mural program coordinator, 1978-80; Museum of African Art Washington DC, designer/graphic artist 1977-78; City of Washington, muralist/program coordinator, 1976-77; muralist; sculptor; interior decorator; designer. **Honors/Awds:** Arts competition Addis Ababa Ethiopia 1967; mural Howard Univ, Washington, DC 1975; graphics for film "The Harvest" Washington DC 1976; mural Museum of African Art, Washington DC 1978.

THACKER, FLOYD GARY
Construction company executive. **Personal:** Born Nov 26, 1955, Alton, IL; son of Yvonne Boyd Thacker and Floyd Oscar Thacker; married Mary Barnes, 1977; children: Julie Ann, Floyd Oscar II, Ashley Nicole, Suretha Yvonne. **Educ:** Southern Illinois University, civil engineering, business administration, attended. **Career:** Thacker Organization, vice pres, 1984-87; Thacker Construction & Development Inc, president, 1987-89; Thacker Organization, president, 1989-; Thacker Engineering Inc, president, chief executive officer, 1989-. **Orgs:** Society of American Military Engineers; Alpha Phi Alpha Fraternity Inc; Cement Masons Local #90. **Special Achievements:** Served on President's Board on African Affairs; worked extensively in minority business development programs. **Business Addr:** President, Chief Executive Officer, Thacker Engineering Inc, 450 Seventh Ave, Ste 308, New York, NY 10123, (212)714-1119.

THAMES, UVENA WOODRUFF
Educator. **Personal:** Born Apr 15, 1944, Detroit, MI. **Educ:** Wilberforce U, BS 1965; Wayne St U, MEd 1970; Georgia State University, post-graduate study; Michigan State University, post-graduate study. **Career:** Wayne Co Children's, mntl hlth tchr 1976-; Detroit Pub Schs, pre-vocational; eval, learning disabilities specialist, 1975; Weldon Grp-Pub Rels, admin asst 1973-74; Atlanta & Area Tech, chld dev inst 1972; Emory U, dept of soc change 1972; Clark Coll, psychlgy instr 1970-72; Detroit Pub Schs, 1968-70; Highland Pk Pub Schs,spl ed tchr 1965-68; Wayne St U, Proj Right to Read Dept HEW 1977-78; St Theresa-Visitation Sch, 1979-80; MI Inst of Child Dev, 1980-81; Lewis Coll of Busn, instr, psychometrist counselor 1981-82; Wayne State Univ, tutorial coord Project 350 1983-; City of Detroit, Career Exploration Grant, counselor, 1988; Detroit Public Schools, instructor, adult education, currently. **Orgs:** Mem Delta Sigma Theta Sor Inc 1965; Atlanta Mntl Hlth Assn 1970; exec bd Atlanta NAACP; adv Sigma Chap Delta Sigma Theta Sor; Nat Assn of Black Psychlgsts 1973; MI Assn of Learning Disabilities; MI Assn of Emotionally Disturbed Chidren; Coalition of 100 Black Women. **Honors/Awds:** Schlrshp Nat Assn of Crippled Children 1967; fellow MI Dept of Ed 1968; National Dept of Education, 1978-79.

THARPE, LARRY
Professional football player. **Personal:** Born Nov 19, 1970, Macon, GA. **Educ:** Tennessee State, attended. **Career:** Detroit Lions, tackle, 1992-94, 1997-; Arizona Cardinals, 1995; New England Patriots, 1996. **Business Addr:** Professional Football Player, Detroit Lions, 1200 Featherstone Rd, Pontiac, MI 48342, (248)335-4131.

THAXTON, JUNE E.
Electrical engineer. **Personal:** Born May 28, 1961, Baltimore, MD; daughter of Mildred Thaxton and Fred Thaxton (deceased); divorced. **Educ:** Howard Univ, BSEE 1984. **Career:** Potomac Electric Power Co, engr electric system 1985-. **Orgs:** Mem IEEE 1986, AABE, 1991-. **Honors/Awds:** Biographical article US Black Engineer Magazine 1986, Ebony Magazine 1987. **Business Addr:** Engineer-Electric System, Potomac Electric Power Co, 1900 Pennsylvania Ave NW, Washington, DC 20068.

THE ARTIST (PRINCE ROGERS NELSON)
Singer, composer, producer. **Personal:** Born Jun 7, 1958, Minneapolis, MN; son of Mattie D Shaw Nelson and John L Nelson; married Mayte Jannell Garcia, Feb 14, 1996. **Career:** Singer, songwriter, actor, producer, director, currently; Albums include: For You, 1978; Prince, 1979; Dirty Mind, 1980; Controversy, 1981; 1999, 1982; Purple Rain, 1984; Around the World in a Day, 1985; Parade, 1986; Under the Cherry Moom, 1986; Sign O' the Times, 1987; The Black Album, 1988; Lovesexy, 1988; Graffiti Bridge, 1990; Emancipation, 1996; others; Motion picture soundtracks include: Purple Rain, 1984; Under the Cherry Moon, 1986; Batman, 1989; Graffiti Bridge, 1990; films include Purple Rain, 1984; Under the Cherry Moon, 1986; Sign O' the Times, 1987; Graffiti Bridge, 1990. Has written numerous hit singles for other artists including I Feel For You and Nothing Compares 2 U. **Honors/Awds:** Academy Award Best Original Song Score for Purple Rain, 1985; three American Music Awards; three Grammy Awards; 3 gold albums; 2 platinum albums; #1 album of the year Purple Rain; Rhythm and Blues Musician of Year, down beat Readers Poll, 1984; Best Soul/Rhythm and Blues Group of Year, downbeat Readers Poll, Prince and Revolution, 1985. **Business Addr:** The Artist, c/o EMI, 304 Park Ave South, New York, NY 10010.

THELWELL, MICHAEL M. EKWUEME
Educator, author. **Personal:** chilDren: Chinua, Mikiko. **Educ:** Howard University, BA, English lit, 1964; University of Massachusetts, Amherst, MFA, 1969. **Career:** Jamaica Industrial Development Corp., public relations assistant, 1958-59; Student Nonviolent Coordinating Committee, director, Washington office, 1963-64; Mississippi Freedom Democratic Party, director, Washington office, 1964-65; University of Massachusetts/Amherst, W E B DuBois Department of Afro-American Studies, chairman, 1969-75, associate professor of literature, 1972, professor, 1980-. **Honors/Awds:** National Endowment for Arts, Writers Fellowship, 1980-81; Institute of Jamaica Centennial Medal for Literature, 1980; "American Experience," WGBH TV, PBS, senior advisor, 1989; "Eyes on the Prize II," PBS TV series, Blacksides, Inc, senior advisor, 1990; author, with Chinua Achebe, John Edgar Wideman, Andrew Salkey, et al, Black Writer's Redefine the Struggle (tribute to James Baldwin), book, Amherst Institute for Humanities, 1989; Editor in Chief, Howard University, Hilltop, 1962; Rockefeller Foundation Literacy Award, 1970; Fellowship, Society for Humanities, Cornell University, 1968; Advisor/Consultant, National Endowment for the Arts, 1970. **Special Achievements:** The Harder They Come, Novel, Pluto Press, London, 1980; Pleasures, Duties, and Conflicts, University of MA, 1987; Rage, Carroll & Gref, NY, 1992.

THEODORE, KEITH FELIX
Dentist. **Personal:** Born Dec 28, 1948, Port-of-Spain, Trinidad and Tobago; married Deborah Ann Corbett; children: Tony, Jamal. **Educ:** Howard Univ, BS 1974, DDS 1980. **Career:** Robert T Freeman Dental Soc, fin sec 1987-, chmn mem comm 1987-; Tooth-N-Nail Inc, pres 1985-. **Honors/Awds:** Story published in Washington Post Newspaper 1987;TV documentary done on bus & profession. **Home Addr:** 7249 G St, Seat Pleasant, MD 20743. **Business Addr:** President, Tooth-N-Nail Inc, 7845 Eastern Ave, Silver Spring, MD 20910.

THEODORE, YVONNE M.
Educational administrator. **Personal:** Born Mar 16, 1939, Prince Georges Co, MD; divorced. **Educ:** Mt St Agnes Coll, BA 1961; Makerere Univ Uganda E Africa, MA 1962; Johns Hopkins U, Cand M Lib Arts 1976; Fisk U, Spl Courses Race Rels 1964. **Career:** Mt St Mary's Namagunga, Uganda E Africa, grad, std, flw tchr, 1961-64; Baltimore City Comm Rels Commn, intrgrp rels spl, 1965-68; Provident Comp Nghbrhd Hlth Ctr, asst to dir, 1968-69; Johns Hopkins U, 1971-. **Orgs:** Mem Nat Cncl of Negro Womn; Coll & Univ Pers Assn; Kampala Sngrs, Interracial, Intercltrl Classical Sngng Grp Uganda E Africa; Black Professionals in Tnternational Affairs; Amer Assn of University Women; Phi Delta Kappa Fraternity; Amer Council on Alcoholism; Maryland Tech Asst Program; Programmer of In Good Taste, Manford Radio Reading Station; Amer Assn for Higher Education, Black Caucus; Internatioal Duke Ellington Society; Maryland Ass of Affirmative Action Officers; Nation's Capital Area Disabled Student Services, coordinator; Baltimore Metro Area Job Service Employer Committee. **Honors/Awds:** Recip Recog for Yth Motivation Nat Alliance of Busmn 1973-74; named Illustrious Wmn Baltimore Afro-Am Nwspr 1971; Acad Schlrshp HS, Music SchlrshpThe Cath HS of Baltimore; Acad Schlrshp Mt St Agnes Coll; Recognition ofr Employement Recruitment of American Indians. **Business Addr:** Johns Hopkins University, Garland Hall Room 205, 3400 N Charles Street, Baltimore, MD 21218.

THERMILUS, JACQUE E.
Business executive. **Career:** Urban Organization Inc, CEO, currently. **Special Achievements:** Company is ranked #85 on Black Enterprise magazine's 1997 list of Top 100 Black businesses. **Business Phone:** (305)870-0684.

THEUS, LUCIUS
Health care company executive. **Personal:** Born Oct 11, 1922, Near Bells, TN; married Gladys Marie. **Educ:** Univ of MD, BS 1956; Geo Wash U, MBA 1957; Harvard Bus Sch, Grad Adv Mgmt Prgm 1969; Armed Forces Staff Coll, Disting Grad 1960; Air War Coll,1966; Indust Coll of Armed Forced (off campus), honor grad 1965. **Career:** Bendix Corp, asst corp controller; USAF, major gen; AF Accounting & Finance Center & HQ USAFF, dir of Accounting and Finance, commander; Wellness Group Inc, dir, principal, currently. **Orgs:** Exec coun Harvard Bus Sch Assn; Harvard Club; vice-Pres & mem bd dir Harvard Bus Sch Club Wash DC 1972-74; bd dir mem Harvard Bus Sch Club Denver; mem Nat Assn of Acctnts; mem Nat Assn of Black Acctnst; mem Nat Black MBA Assn; Geo Wash Univ Club; Assn for Comput Mach; AF Assn; chmn Mile High United Way 1976; dir & vice-chm Explorers Denver area couns BSA; mem dir AF Assn; mem Am Legion; mem Am Radio Relay Leag; mem & bd dir ARC Mile High Chrtr; pres Am Soc of Military Compt Wash Chptr 1973-74; pres Mile High Chptr 1975; mem Assn of Govt Accts; mem Denver C of C Military Aff Com; regl chmn Explorers BSA; mem & natl vice pres Tuskegee Airmen Inc; mem USO Denver Bd of Dir. **Honors/Awds:** Decorated Disting Serv Medal with Oak Leaf Cluster; Legion of Merit Bronze Star Medal; AF Commend Medal with Oak Leaf Cluster; Denver Fed Exec Bd Dstng Fed Serv Awrd; Pitts Cour Top Hat Award; 1000 Successful Blacks. **Military Serv:** USAF 3rd black to be prom to gen ofcr rank. **Business Addr:** President, The US Associates, 4520 Stony River Dr, Birmingham, MI 48010.

THEUS, REGGIE
Professional basketball player. **Personal:** Born Oct 13, 1957, Ingelwood, CA. **Educ:** Univ of Las Vegas NV, 1979. **Career:** Chicago Bulls, 1979-84, Kansas City Kings, 1984-85, Sacramento Kings, 1986-88, Atlanta Hawks, 1989, Orlando Magic, 1990, New Jersey Nets, 1990-. **Orgs:** Involved various clubs Little City Prog, Athletes For Better Educ 1979, Natl Comm Against Child Abuse. **Honors/Awds:** MVP, UNLV 1979; Coached All-Star Team IL HS; led Bulls in scoring (238), assists (59), steals (17) 1981-82,82-83; led the club 20 times with 6 double figure outings & a season high 13 vs Portland; had 23 doubled figure scoring nights, 7 of 20 or more points & a season-high 36 vs Los Angeles; Kings were 16-14 after he joined club; UNLV All-Amer selection; led the Rebels jr year in scoring with 190 ppg & scored in double figures in all 28 games; after jr campaign was named Rebel's MVP; in 3 seasons with Rebels UNLV posted a 78-13 mark. **Business Addr:** Professional Basketball Player, New Jersey Nets, Brendan Byrne Arena, East Rutherford, NJ 07073.

THIBODEAUX, MARY SHEPHERD
Educator. **Personal:** Born Aug 11, 1945, Homer, LA; daughter of Arquilla B Shepherd and Ross Shepherd; married Alton Thibodeaux, Aug 20, 1966; children: Edward Shepherd. **Educ:** Grambling State Univ, BS, 1965; Eastern New Mexico Univ, MBEd, 1966, Univ of North Texas, PhD, 1976. **Career:** Grambling State Univ, instructor 1966-69, assistant professor, 1969-75; Univ of North Texas, assistant professor, 1976-82, associate professor, 1983-95, prof, 1995-. **Orgs:** International Academy of Business Disciplines, board of directors, 1991-94, president, 1993-94; Southwest Academy of Management, track chair, 1993-94; Denton Area Teacher's Credit Union, board of directors, 1990-97; Cross Timbers Girl Scout Council, board of directors, 1976-82. **Honors/Awds:** Distinguished Teaching Award, 1979; Honor Professor Award, 1989; Academy of Business Administration, Outstanding Interdisciplinary Paper, 1992; JH Shelton Excellence in Teaching Award, 1994; President's Council Teaching Award, Univ of North Texas, 1994. **Special Achievements:** Author: "Organizational Politics and Planned Organizational Change: A Pragmatic Approach," Group and Organizational Studies, 1990; "Self-Managed Work Teams: Innovation in Progress," Business and Economic Quarterly, vol 4, num 1, Fall/Winter 1990-91; "Evaluating Merger Performance on a Longitudinal Basis: An Empirical Investigation," Journal of Business Strategies, vol 9, num 2, Fall 1992; "Strategic Management and Organizational Effectiveness within Colleges of Business," Journal of Education for Business, Spring, 1995; "Organizational Design of Self Directed Work Teams, Industrial Management & Data Systems," Fall, 1994; "Strategic Management and Organizational Effectiveness within Colleges of Business," Journal of Education for Business, March/April 1995; "Differences in Value Systems of Anglo-American and Far Eastern Students: Effects of American Business Education," Journal of Business Ethics, 1997; "Cross-Cultural Differences in the Personal Value Systems of Managers: Implications for Differences in Management Orientation," Intl Assoc of Management Journal, 1996; "Value Profiles of Business Students in the 1990s and the 1990s, Similarities and Differences," Jnl of Education for Business, Jan/Feb, 1997. **Home Addr:** 1501 Ridgecrest, Denton, TX 76205, (817)382-5656. **Business Addr:** Associate Dean, University of North Texas, College of Business Administration, Box 13677, Denton, TX 76203, (817)565-3086.

THIBODEAUX, SYLVIA MARIE
Educator. **Personal:** Born Nov 26, 1937, Breaux Bridge, LA; widowed. **Educ:** BA 1967; MA 1973. **Career:** Tulsa, elem teacher 1960-62; Opelousa, teacher 1962-63; Tulsa, teacher 1963-65; Proj Commitment & Assn of Urban Sisters Boston 1968-69; Witness Prog Educ Component New Orleans, dir 1967-68; St Joseph Comm Sch Boston, principal 1970-74; mem Tchr Training Coll & Religious Formation Benin City Nigeria W Africa. **Orgs:** Bd mem, Campaign for Human Devel, Natl Office for Black Catholics; Natl Black Sisters Conf; DESIGN; Minority Evaluators Ginn & Co; bd trustees, Educ Devel Ctr; consul, AFRAM Assoc; mem, Planning Comm, Black Educ Conf. **Honors/Awds:** NIA Awd Spec Achievement for Innovative Educ Prog; Outstanding Contrib to Black Comm Awd Roxbury Action Prog; SCLC Most Creative Educ Prog; Outstanding Educator of Amer Awd. **Home Addr:** Bishop's House, PO Box 35, Benin City, Bendel, Nigeria.

THIERRY, JOHN FITZGERALD
Professional football player. **Personal:** Born Sep 4, 1971, Opelousas, LA. **Educ:** Alcorn State, attended. **Career:** Chicago Bears, defensive end, 1994-. **Business Addr:** Professional Football Player, Chicago Bears, 1000 Football Dr, Halas Hall at Conway Park, Lake Forest, IL 60045-4829, (847)295-6600.

THIGPEN, CALVIN HERRITAGE
Physician, attorney. **Personal:** Born Jan 7, 1924, Greenville, NC; married Vera Belle Crawford; children: Calvin Jr, Karen. **Educ:** VA State Coll, BS 1953; Univ VA, MD 1962, JD 1974. **Career:** Hopewell, VA, teacher 1953-58; Stuart Prod Co, cosmetics/chem plant mgr 1957-58; Med Coll VA, intern 1962-63; Petersburg General Hosp, staff mem 1963; private practice 1963; VA State Coll, assoc & physician 1964-71; Petersburg Gen Hosp, vice chief/general practice section 1969-70; Office Attorney General VA, intern 1972-73; Univ VA, rsrch asst legal adv 1973-74; Private Practice, attorney 1975-. **Orgs:** Mem, Sigma Pi Sigma Natl Physics Hon Soc; Beta Kappa Chi Natl Sci Hon Soc; Phi Delta Phi Legal Fraternity; Dem Com Hopewell 1965-75; bd dir Salvation Army; Hopewell Chamber of Commerce; Old Dominion Med Soc; exec com Old Dominion Med Soc 1965. **Honors/Awds:** pres, Natl Guardsmen Inc 1967-70; Library Human Resources Amer Bicentennial Rsch Inst 1973; Fellow Amer Coll Legal Med 1976; Mem Bd of Visitors VA State Univ 1978-82; VA Delegate to the White House Conf on Library & Info Serv 1979; Chief of Staff Petersburg Gen Hosp 1980; Diplomate Amer Bd of Legal Med 1982. **Military Serv:** AUS lst Lt 1944-49. **Home Addr:** 19801 Oakland Ave, Colonial Heights, VA 23834. **Business Addr:** Physician Attorney, 734 South Sycamore St, Petersburg, VA 23803.

THIGPEN, EDMUND LEONARD
Musician. **Personal:** Born Dec 28, 1930, Chicago, IL; son of Mary Berry Thigpen and Benjamin Thigpen; widowed; children: Denise Mary, Michel Edmund. **Educ:** Los Angeles City Coll, 1949; Manhattan Sch of Mus, student 1955. **Career:** Performed with Cootie Williams 1951, Dinah Washington 1954, Johnny Hodges & Bud Powell 1955-56, Billy Taylor Trio 1957-58, Oscar Peterson Trio 1959-65; Ella Fitzgerald 1968-72; freelance musician in Los Angeles, movies, jingles etc & working with Johnny Mathis, Pat Boone, Andy Williams, Peggy Lee, Oliver Nelson, Gerald Wilson; re-joined Ella Fitzgerald as permanent member of her trio until 1972; from 1973, based in Copenhagen, freelance solo/guest artist and instructor, working with Kenny Drew, Thad Jones, Ernie Wilkins, Clark Terry; leader of ensembles "ETE" & Action Reaction; Univ of IL, Champaign/Urbana, visiting prof of Jazz Studies, 1994-95. **Orgs:** Percussion Arts Soc, mem, bd of directors; National Assn of Jazz Educators, co-natl chairman, 1991-94, dr-set & pecussion; International Association of Jazz Educators, co-chair of dr-set, 1991-93. **Honors/Awds:** Author with Ray Brown, "Be Our Guest" Ed Thigpen "Talking Drums"; "Rhythm Analysis and Basic Co-ordination"; "The Sound of Brushes"; "Rhythm Brought to Life"; videos include Ed Thigpen on Jazz Drumming, The Essence of Brushes; New Star Award, Down Beat, 1959. **Military Serv:** US Army, 1952-54. **Home Addr:** Bagerstraede 3, 2nd, t h, DK-1617 Copenhagen, Denmark.

THIGPEN, LYNNE
Actress. **Personal:** Born Dec 22, Joliet, IL. **Educ:** University of Illinois, work on masters degree, acting. **Career:** Theater appearances include: The Magic Show, 1976; But Never Jam Today, 1979; Tintypes, 1980-81; And I Ain't Finished Yet, 1981; More of a Loesser, 1982; Educating Rita, 1983; Full Hookup, 1983-84; Balm in Gilead, 1984; "D," 1985; A Month of Sundays, 1987; The Best Man, 1987; Fences, 1988; Boesman and Lean, 1992; television appearances include: Love, Sidney, 1982-83; The News Is the News, 1983; Pottsville, 1980; The Equalizer, 1987; Gimme a Break; Rockabye, 1986; The Cosby Show; Dear John; The Days and Nights of Molly Dodd; L A Law; Where in the World Is Carmen Sandiego?; Fear Stalk, 1989; film appearances include: Godspell, 1973; The Warriors, 1979; Tootsie, 1982; Streets of Fire, 1984; Sweet Liberty, 1986; Hello Again, 1987; Lean on Me, 1989; Bob Roberts, 1992; An American Daughter, 1996 (won Tony Award for role). **Honors/Awds:** An American Daughter, Tony Award, 1997. **Business Addr:** Actress, c/o Michael Thomas Agency, 305 Madison Ave, Ste 4419, New York, NY 10165, (212)867-0303.

THIGPEN, YANCEY DIRK
Professional football player. **Personal:** Born Aug 15, 1969, Tarboro, NC. **Educ:** Winston-Salem State, attended. **Career:** San Diego Chargers, wide receiver, 1991; Pittsburgh Steelers, 1992-. **Honors/Awds:** Pro Bowl appearance, 1995. **Business Addr:** Professional Football Player, Pittsburgh Steelers, Three Rivers Stadium, 300 Stadium Circle, Pittsburgh, PA 15212, (412)323-1200.

THOMAS, ALVIN
Government official (retired), cleric. **Personal:** Born Apr 11, 1951, New Orleans, LA. **Educ:** So Univ A&M Coll, BA Pol Sci 1969-74; Union Bapt Theolog Sem, 1974; Univers Bible Inst. **Career:** Gov of LA, spec asst 1976; Iberville Parish Police Jury, police juror 1972-76; Bechtel Power Corp, ofc mgr 1975; LA House of Rep, page 1972; Indsl Plant Maint, supr 1972-74; US Pub Hlth Serv Hosp, clrk 1968-72; Jerusalem Bapt Ch St Gabriel, pastor 1973-74; Mt Zion Bapt Ch #1, asst pastor 1967-69; Mt Bethel Bapt Ch, sec 1964-68. **Orgs:** Iberville Parish Hsng Auth 1972; LA Police Jury Assn 1972-76; Nat Assn of Co of Elect Ofcl 1972-76; Iberville Parish Person Com 1972-76; Iberville Parish Fin Com 1972-76; Iberville Parish Gas Com 1972-76; Iberville Parish Law Enforce Com 1972-76; E Iberville Recreation Ass 1972; Iberville Parish Indsl Voters Leag 1971; ward ldr Iberville Parish 1971-73; Iberville Parish Minis Counc 1972; mem 2nd Dist Bapt Assn 1972; mem 4th Dist Bapt Assn 1972; mem LA Bapt Convent 1972; mem Nat Bapt Convent USA Inc 1972; LA Hlth Assn Com 1972-76; fndr & pres E Iberville Vol Fire Dept 1972; vice pres E Iberville Imprv Assn 1971; mem Lemoyne Comm Action Fin Com 1968-70; dir Stud Govt Assn So Univ 1970-71; mem Nat Foreign Miss Bd USA Inc 1972; youngest elect ofcl State of LA 1972;youngest Nat elect ofcl 1; chmn 1st Nat Black Polit Convent 1972; deleg Nat Dem Convent 1972; vice pres Nat Assn of Black Counties Ofcls 1975-76; rep Natl Legislat Confer of NACO 1975; rep Iberville Parish Police Jury. **Honors/Awds:** Outst Stdnt Govt Assn Wrkr So Univ 1970-71. **Business Addr:** Rt 1 Box 44 A St, St Gabriel, LA 70776.

THOMAS, ARTHUR E.
Educational administrator. **Personal:** son Of Janie R Bradley (deceased); married Dawn Thomas. **Educ:** Central State Univ, Wilberforce, OH, graduate 1962; Miami Univ, MEd; Univ of Massachusetts, EdD. **Career:** Dayton Public School System; Wright State Univ; Central State Univ, Wilberforce, OH, vice president of academic affairs, 1977-85, president, 1985-. **Business Addr:** President, Central State University, Wilberforce, OH 45384.

THOMAS, ARTHUR LAFAYETTE, III
Videographer, editor. **Personal:** Born Jan 14, 1960, Trenton, NJ; son of Hermione Smith Thomas and Arthur Lafayette Thomas; married Robin M Golden Thomas, Sep 5, 1992; children: Sydney Golden, Paige Leigh, Arthur IV. **Educ:** Rutgers University, BA, 1982; American University, attended, 1986-87. **Career:** Powell Bros Inc, technical services manager; Black Entertainment Television, videographer, currently. **Business Addr:** Black Entertainment Television, 1900 W Pl, NE, Washington, DC 20018-1230.

THOMAS, AUDRIA ACTY
Physician, allergist, immunologist, pediatrician. **Personal:** Born Jun 6, 1954, Washington, DC; divorced; children: Shaunta Lindsey, Shavon Thomas. **Educ:** Meharry Medical Coll, MD 1980; Fellowship, HUH, 1983-86. **Career:** Howard Univ Hosp, resident 1980-83; St Thomas/St John Medical Soc, chief allergy dept; Roy L Schneider Hosp, medical staff, 1986-. **Orgs:** Soloist VI Chriistian Ministries, 1959-86; mem Natl Medical Assoc 1980-86; pediatric consultant 15-24 Free Clinic for Teenagers 1980-86; consultant Virgin Island Lung Assoc 1986-. **Honors/Awds:** Howard Univ Fellowship in Allergy Immunology 1983-86; published paper "Cystic Fibrosis in Black," Layman's Journal update in allergy 1985. **Home Addr:** PO Box 595, Charlotte Amalie, St Thomas, Virgin Islands of the United States 00804. **Business Addr:** Chief Allergy Department, Roy L Schneider Hospital, # 1, 3rd St, Decastro Bldg, Charlotte Amalie, St Thomas, Virgin Islands of the United States 00801, (809)776-5507.

THOMAS, BENJAMIN
Publisher. **Personal:** Born Sep 17, 1910, Pine Bluff, AR; widowed; children: Barry, Kevin. **Educ:** Attended OH State Univ 1933. **Career:** St Louis Evening Whirl, founder/publisher/editor 1938-. **Orgs:** Mem NAACP, YMCA. **Honors/Awds:** Citations many civic groups. **Business Addr:** Publisher, St Louis Evening Whirl, P O Box 5088, Nagal Station, St Louis, MO 63147.

THOMAS, BLAIR
Professional football player. **Educ:** Penn State Univ, attended. **Career:** New York Jets, running back, 1990-. **Honors/Awds:** Leading rookie rusher (326 yards), American Football Conference, as of 2 Nov1990; second-leading career rusher (3,391 yards), Penn State Univ. **Business Addr:** Professional Football Player, New York Jets, 1000 Fulton Ave, Hempstead, NY 11550.

THOMAS, BRODERICK
Professional football player. **Personal:** Born Feb 20, 1967, Houston, TX; children: Broderick Trevon. **Educ:** Univ of Nebraska, attended. **Career:** Tampa Bay Buccaneers, linebacker, 1989-93; Detroit Lions, 1994; Minnesota Vikings, 1995; Dallas Cowboys, 1996-. **Business Addr:** Professional Football Player, Dallas Cowboys, One Cowboys Pkwy, Irving, TX 75063, (214)556-9900.

THOMAS, CALVIN LEWIS
Professional football player (retired). **Personal:** Born Jan 7, 1960, St Louis, MO; married Bernadine; children: Nikkita. **Educ:** Univ of Illinois, BA, 1984. **Career:** Fullback: Chicago Bears, 1982-87; Denver Broncos, 1988. **Orgs:** Involved in Red Cloud Athletic Fund, Jr Variety Club, Big Brothers.

THOMAS, CARL ALAN
Educator, clergyman. **Personal:** Born Mar 21, 1924, Jersey City, NJ; children: Edward, Algynan, Elaine, Stanley. **Educ:** Rutgers U, BA 1946; Union Sem, BD 1949; NY U, MA 1950; Univ of KS, DD 1970. **Career:** Community Coll of Phila, dir/dean 1968-; Lincoln Univ of PA, dean 1968; Wilberforce Univ, dean 1964-66; FL A&M Univ, prof 1960-64; Exper In Intl Living, dir 1960; AME Zion Church, pastor; Lincoln Univ Oxford, prof of Black studies; Training Inst Lincoln Univ, teacher. **Orgs:** Mem Alpha Psi Omega Frat; mem Kappa Alpha Psi Frat Swords & Shields Wilberforce OH; Sons of Wilberforce OH. **Business Addr:** Community College of Philadelp, 34 S 11th St, Philadelphia, PA.

THOMAS, CARL D.
Coordinator. **Personal:** Born May 13, 1950, Kansas City, MO; married Dana Morris. **Educ:** Univ MA Amherst, BS 1973. **Career:** Office of Minority Business City of Boston, business develop specialist 1978-81; MA Dept of Commerce & Development, business educ training dir 1980-81; US Small Business Admin, ace counselor 1983-; Contractor's Assoc of Boston Inc, small business develop coord 1983-. **Orgs:** Mem Natl Assn of Minority Contractors 1984; mem Natl Business Admin 1984; steering comm Mass Minority Business Assistance 1985; mem NAACP Boston Chapt1984; mem ACE US Small Business Admin 1983. **Honors/Awds:** Minority Advocate of Yr US Small Bus Admin 1985; Minority Advocate of Yr Commonwealth of MA 1985. **Business Addr:** Small Business Coordinator, Contractor's Assoc of Boston, 25 Center St, Roxbury, MA 02119.

THOMAS, CAROL M.
Federal government executive. **Personal:** Born Dec 23, 1930, Washington, DC; married Laura Pedro; children: Kevin, Marla, Paul. **Educ:** Yale U, BA 1953; John Hopkins U, MA 1961. **Career:** Navy Dept, management intern 1961; Navy Dept Washington, contract negotiator 1961-64; Office Econ Opportunity Wash, br 1964-65; Job Corps, project mgr 1965-67; Contracts Div Peace Corp Wash, dep dir 1967-69; Peace Corps Sierraieone, dir 1969-71; Office Civil Rights & Urban Affairs US Environmental Protection Agy, dir 1972-74; Office Civil Rights US EPA Wash, 1974-77; Fed Trade Commn, sec 1977-; Am Acad Polit & Social Scis, 1973-; Am Soc Pub Adminstrs, 1972-; Manasas Educ Found. **Orgs:** Mem exec Com Bd Dir 1972-; Alpha Phi Alpha Frat; Federal City Club Wash 1972-; Reston Golf & Country Club 1971-. **Military Serv:** USAF 1954-59.

THOMAS, CHARLES COLUMBUS
Educator. **Personal:** Born Sep 10, 1940, McAlester, OK. **Educ:** Langston Univ, BA 1962; Brooklyn Coll, MFA 1972 City Univ NY, 1977. **Career:** Coll of Staten Island City Univ NY, asst prof; Afro-Amer Inst Richmond Coll, dir 1972-73; Univ Ghana, vis prof 1972; NY Comm Coll, asst prof 1971-74; Lefferst Jr HS, chmn 1966-69; Staten & Island Repertory Ensemble, dir; Mayor's Council on Youth & Physical Fitness, 1969; NY State Council on the Arts, 1968-70; OEO Proj, dir 1968; Egbe Omo Nago Folklorio Ensemble, dir 1967-69; Afro-Amer Folkloric Troupe, artistic dir 1963-70; African Heritage Studeis Assn; Big Bros; Epsilon Chap Omega Psi Phi; Natl Acad Rec Arts & Sciences; Natl Academy TV Arts & Sciences; Screen Actors Guild; Kappa. **Honors/Awds:** Ebony Success Library, 1972; Research Award, CUNY faculty, 1972; Contributing author, We Speak as Liberators, 1971, Probes an introduction to & poetry 1973, Yarbird Reader 1977, Rinds for Revolution 1971. **Business Addr:** 130 Stuyvesant Pl, Staten Island, NY 10301.

THOMAS, CHARLES RICHARD
Educator. **Personal:** Born Jun 6, 1933, Evanston, IL; widowed; children: Charles Jr, Markham. **Educ:** Univ of WI, BS 1957; NW U, MA 1966; NW Attended, Teachers Coll Columbia U, PhD 1978; Univ 1970. **Career:** N Chicago School Dist 64, supt 1973; IL Office of Educ, asst supt 1971-73; Evanston Public School, prin 1968-71; Evanston HS, asst prin 1964-67; Evanston HS, athletic coach 1957-68. **Orgs:** Mem IL Assn of Sch Admnstr; Am Assn of Sch Adminstr; Nat Alliance of Black Sch Educr; Lake Co Assn of Sch Adminstr; IL Assn of Sch Bd Assn; Am Assn of Sch Personnel Adminstr; Assn of Sup & Curriculum Devel; pres Phi Delta Kappa, N Chicago Rotary Club; N Chicago C of C; bd of dir LakeCo Urban Leg. **Honors/Awds:** NAACP N Chicago Br Awd, Citz Participation in Sch Desegregation, IL Jour of Educ 1972; publ ''Unique Problems Confronting the Black Sch Admnstr'' , Eric Document Reprod Serv, 1972; ''The Purpose & Value of HS Athletics'', Univ of MI 1976; ''Sch Desegregation what makes it work?'' IL sch bd jour 1977. **Military Serv:** AUSR capt 1957-65. **Business Addr:** Superintendent, Board of Education, 2000 Lewis Ave N, North Chicago, IL 60064.

THOMAS, CHARLES W.
Transportation company executive. **Personal:** Born Mar 9, 1940, Boston, MA; son of Pauline Delores Walker Thomas and Charles Edward Thomas; married Ellen V Bell; children: Kevin Charles, Tracey Ann. **Educ:** Northeastern Univ, Boston AS, 1963, BS, 1967; Univ of Redlands, Redlands CA, MA, 1983. **Career:** Raytheon Co, Bedford MA, draftsman, 1961-64, engineer, 1964-67; RCA, Chelmsford MA, engineer mgr, 1967-70; Regional Transit, Sacramento CA, asst gen mgr, 1970-78, gen mgr, 1978-81; SEPTA, Philadelphia PA, chief trans officer, 1981-85, deputy assistant general manager, operations, 1985-87, assistant general manager, operations, 1987-92, assistant general manager, safety and risk management, currently. **Orgs:** Alpha Phi Alpha Fraternity Inc. **Business Phone:** (215)580-3500.

THOMAS, CHRIS ERIC
Professional football player. **Personal:** Born Jul 16, 1971, Ventura, CA. **Educ:** Cal Poly-S.L.O. **Career:** San Francisco 49ers, wide receiver, 1995; Washington Redskins, 1997-. **Business Addr:** Professional Football Player, Washington Redskins, 13832 Redskin Dr, Herndon, VA 22071, (703)471-9100.

THOMAS, CLARENCE
Supreme Court Justice. **Personal:** Born Jun 23, 1948, Pin Point, GA; son of Leola Anderson Williams and M C Thomas; married Kathy Grace Ambush, 1971 (divorced 1984); children: Jamal Adeen. **Educ:** Immaculate Conception Seminary, 1967-68; Holy Cross College, BA, 1971; Yale University Law School, JD, 1974. **Career:** Hill, Jones & Farrington, legal aid, summers, 1971-74; Attorney General John Danforth, State of Missouri, staff member, 1974-77; State of Missouri, asst attorney general, 1974-77; Monsanto Corp, legal counsel, 1977-80; Senator John Danforth, legislative asst, 1979-81; US Federal Govt, Dept of Education, asst secretary for civil rights, 1981-82; Equal Employment Opportunity Commission, chairman, 1982-89; US Court of Appeals for District of Columbia Circuit, appointed circuit judge, 1990-91; United States Supreme Court Justice, confirmed, 1991-. **Orgs:** Black Student Union, Holy Cross College, founder, 1971. **Business Addr:** Supreme Court Justice, Supreme Court of the United States, 1 1st St NE, Washington, DC 20543-0001.

THOMAS, CLAUDE RODERICK
Judge. **Personal:** Born Mar 15, 1943, Clarksdale, MS; son of Pearl E Thomas and George A Thomas; children: Claude Roderick II, Jerry Jason, Patrick James, LaTonya Lizzie, Alexandra Nicole, Andrea Lauren. **Educ:** MI State Univ, BA 1972; Thomas M Cooley Law School, JD 1976. **Career:** Lansing Police Dept, police officer 1969-75; Ingham Cty Pros Office, asst prosecutor 1976-80; Lansing Community College, Lansing, MI, adjunct prof, 1976-; Thomas M Cooley Law School, Lansing, MI, adjunct professor, 1988-; 54A Dist Court, district judge 1981-. **Orgs:** Mem State Bar Character & Fitness 1977-, Boys Club; bd dir Cooley Credit Union 1980-81; member, Phi Beta Sigma, 1983-. **Honors/Awds:** Alumni of the Year Cooley Law School 1981. **Military Serv:** USMC corpl 4 years; Good Conduct Medal 1964. **Business Addr:** Judge District Court, 54A Judicial Dist, Lansing City Hall #6, 5th Floor, Lansing, MI 48933.

THOMAS, DAVE G.
Professional football player. **Personal:** Born Aug 25, 1968; children: Zachary. **Educ:** Univ of Tennessee, attended. **Career:** Dallas Cowboys, defensive back, 1993-94; Jacksonville Jaguars, 1995-. **Business Addr:** Professional Football Player, Jacksonville Jaguars, One Stadium Place, Jacksonville, FL 32202, (904)633-6000.

THOMAS, DAVID ANTHONY
Educator. **Personal:** Born Sep 26, 1956, Missouri; son of Jewell Williams and David Thomas; married Willetta Lewis, Aug 11, 1984; children: Sommer Iman, David Jr, Nelson Dubois. **Educ:** Yale College, BA, 1978; Columbia University, MA, 1981; Yale University, M Philsophy, 1984, PhD, 1986. **Career:** The Wharton School, asst prof, 1986-90; Harvard Business School, asst pro, 1990-93, assoc prof, 1993-. **Orgs:** The Partnership, bd mem, 1997-; Shady Hill School, trustee, 1996-; WGBH Community Advisory, bd mem, 1993-96; Journal of African American Politics, Harvard University, editorial bd, 1992-. **Honors/Awds:** Academy of Management, Best Symposium Award, 1997; Wharton School, Atlantic Richfield Foundation, 1986-90; Yale University, Term Chair, Graduate Fellowship, 1981-85; Columbia University, Graduate Fellowship, 1980-81; Yale University, Victor Wilson Scholar, 1974-78. **Business Addr:** Associate Professor, Harvard Business School, Morgan Hall 340, Soldiers Field Rd, Boston, MA 02163, (617)495-6327.

THOMAS, DEBI
Professional ice skater. **Personal:** Born Mar 25, 1967, Poughkeepsie, NY; married Chris Bequette; children: Christopher Jules Bequette II. **Educ:** Stanford Univ. **Career:** World Class figure skater; performed in London for Live Aid; appeared at Celebration America on Ice in Indianapolis for 25th Anniversary of US Figure Skating Assoc Memorial Fund; special guest star Stars on Ice. **Honors/Awds:** Winner 1985 Natl Sports Festival in Baton Rouge; two gold medal victories Skate America Intl Minneapolis and at St Ivel Intl Great Britain; United States Ladies Figure Skating Champion 1986; World Champions 1986; Olympic Bronze Medalist 1988. **Special Achievements:** First African American to win the US Figure Skating and World Figure Skating Championship Senior Titles, 1986.

THOMAS, DEON
Professional basketball player. **Personal:** Born Feb 24, 1971, Chicago, IL. **Educ:** Illinois. **Career:** Dallas Mavericks, 1994-. **Business Addr:** Professional Basketball Player, Dallas Mavericks, Reunion Arena, 777 Sports St, Dallas, TX 75207, (214)988-0117.

THOMAS, DERRICK VINCENT
Professional football player. **Personal:** Born Jan 1, 1967, Miami, FL. **Educ:** Univ of Alabama, attended. **Career:** Kansas City Chiefs, linebacker, 1989-; Derrick Thomas Clothiers, owner. **Honors/Awds:** Linebacker, Sporting News College All-America Team, 1988; played in eight Pro Bowls; NFL Man of the Year Award, 1993; Byron ''Whizzer'' White Humanitarian Award, 1995. **Business Addr:** Professional Football Player, Kansas City Chiefs, One Arrowhead Dr, Kansas City, MO 64129, (816)924-9300.

THOMAS, EARL
Oil company executive. **Career:** Chicago Bears, tight end, wide receiver, starting 1971; St Louis Cardinals, tight end, wide receiver; home building companies, project manager; oil equipment company, sales trainee, 1980; Gold Line Supply, founder, 1980; Gold Line Refining Ltd, founder, president, managing general partner, 1990-. **Special Achievements:** Black Enterprises Top 100 list of Industrial/Service Companies, #28, 1992. **Business Addr:** President, Gold Line Refining Ltd, 7324 Southwest Freeway, Suite 400, Houston, TX 77074, (713)271-3550.

THOMAS, EARLE FREDERICK
Business executive. **Personal:** Born May 6, 1925, Preston, MD; married Bettie; children: Rodney, Sherri. **Educ:** Morgan State Coll U, 1942; Hampton Inst; VA Bankers Sch, life underwriters. **Career:** VA Nat Bank, mgr 1975; loan exec 1975; asst mgr 1974-75; mktg ofcr 1974; Atlantic Nat Bank, pres, chf exec ofcr, dir sec 1972-74, vice pres dir sec 1971-72, org 1968-71; John Hancock Mutual Life Ins Co, underwriter 1966-68; Am Tobacco Co, state rep 1959-68; Newport New Shipyard, machinist 1951-59. **Orgs:** Mem bd visitors Norfolk State Coll 1977-; bd mem Retail Merchants Assn 1977-78; vice pres dir Tidewater Cncl Boy Scouts; bd mem Tidewater Red Cross; dir sec Tidewater Area Minority Contractors; bd mem Sickel Cell Anemia; mem adv cncl 4h Club; mem Sales Mktg & Exec Club; pres Club; Norfolk C of C; budget com United Fund; treas Norfolk State Coll Found Martin Luther King Comm. **Honors/Awds:** Achvmt award 1975. **Business Addr:** 3300 Princess Anne Rd, Norfolk, VA 23502.

THOMAS, EDITH PEETE
Government official, nutritionist. **Personal:** Born Jul 30, 1940, Memphis, TN; daughter of Carrie Bell Peete and James Walter Peete; married Charles L Thomas, Aug 25, 1962; children: Stephanie Lynne, Charles Stephen. **Educ:** Fontbonne College, AB, dietetics, 1960; St Louis University, MS, nutrition, 1966; Columbia University, EdM, nutrition education, 1971; Indiana University, PhD, nutrition & adult education, 1977; University of Iowa, postdoctoral studies, pediatric nutrition, 1980. **Career:** Johns Hopkins Hospital, assistant director of dietetics and chief project nutritionist, 1966-68; Indiana University, lecturer in adult education, 1973-76; The University of North Carolina, Chapel Hill, Department of Nutrition, assistant professor, 1977-78; Nutrition Consultant Associates, director, 1978-80; US Department of Agriculture Extension Service, national program leader for the Expanded Food and Nutrition Education Program, 1980-86; Goerge Mason University, visiting research professor, 1986-88; US Department of Agriculture Extension Service, national program leader for organization development, 1988-. **Orgs:** American Dietetic Association, 1960-; District of Columbia Dietetic Association, program chairperson, 1980-81, member, 1980-; American Educational Research Association, 1978-; American Home Economics Association, program planning committee, 1982-88; District of Columbia Home Economics Association, president-elect, 1983-84, president 1984-85, member, 1982-88; American Evaluation Association, chairelect, Topical Interest Group, Minority Issues, 1992, member, 1989-; Alpha Kappa Alpha Sorority, 1959-. **Honors/Awds:** Columbia University, Mary Swartz Rose Scholarship, 1970; Teachers College, Columbia University, Public Health Traineeship, National Institutes of Health, 1970; Indiana University, Pi Lambda Theta, National Honor and Professional Association in Education, 1975; Army War College, national security seminar

participant certificate, 1989; US Department of Agriculture Extension Service, certificate of merit, 1992. **Special Achievements:** March of Dimes Fellow, 1984; National Training Laboratories, Organization Development Program, postdoctoral program, 1987-89. **Business Addr:** National Program Leader, US Department of Agriculture, 12th & Independence Ave SW, 3428 South Bldg, Washington, DC 20250-0900, (202)690-4550.

THOMAS, EDWARD ARTHUR
Health insurance executive. **Personal:** Born Dec 30, 1952, Georgetown, GU; son of Andrew & Eunice Thomas; married Cecelia, Jun 12, 1976; children: Erklin, Arthur, Carla, Mahala. **Educ:** York College of CUNY, BA, 1977; Polytechnic Institute of NY, MS, 1982; Univ of Toledo, College of Law, JD, 1988. **Career:** Blue Cross/Blue Shield of Greater NY, internal auditor, 1977-80; Metropolitan Life Insurance Co, sales rep, 1980-81; Insurance Services Office, actuarial assistant, 1982-85; Blue Cross/Blue Shield of Ohio, actuarial analyst, 1985-88; Pennsylvania Dept of Insurance, chief of HMO/PPO, 1988-91; Keystone Health Plan East, vp & general counsel of review div, 1991-92; Lomax Health System, vp of managed care services, 1992-94; New Century Consultants, Inc, pres & CEO, 1994-. **Orgs:** Pennsylvania Bar Assn, 1989-. **Business Addr:** President & CEO, New Century Consultants, Inc, 900 E Eighth Ave, Ste 300, King of Prussia, PA 19406, (610)768-8078.

THOMAS, EDWARD P.
Physician. **Personal:** Born Jul 26, 1920, Mississippi; married Ruby; children: Paul A, Bradford E, Leeland M, Leah Ann. **Educ:** Butler U, 1941; Meharry Med Coll, MD 1944. **Career:** Pvt Practice, physician practicing allergist, Indpls. **Orgs:** Mem AMA IN Med Assn; Nat Med Assn; Aesculapian Med Soc; mem staff Meth Hosp Winona Hosp St Vincent & Hosp Inspls; mem Medical Council MethHosp; mem Am Coll of Allergists; Am Acad of Allergy; Am Coll of Chest Physicians; Am Coll of Gastroenterology; mem Chi Delta Mu; Omega Psi Phi. **Military Serv:** USN lt cmdr med corp 1954-56. **Business Addr:** 3450 N Illinois St, Indianapolis, IN 46208.

THOMAS, EDWARD S.
Hospital administrator. **Career:** Detroit Receiving Hospital, president, currently. **Honors/Awds:** Michigan Hospital Association, Meritorious Service Key Award, 1994. **Business Addr:** Sr Vice Pres, Northwest Region, Detroit Receiving Hospital, 4201 St. Antoine, Detroit, MI 48201, (313)745-3102.

THOMAS, ERIC JASON
Professional football player. **Personal:** Born Sep 11, 1964, Tucson, AZ. **Educ:** Attended: Pasadena City College, Tulane Univ. **Career:** Cincinnati Bengals, cornerback, 1987-93; New York Jets, 1993-. **Honors/Awds:** Post-season play, 1988: AFC Championship Game, NFL Championship Game, Pro Bowl. **Business Addr:** Professional Football Player, New York Jets, 1000 Fulton Ave, Hempstead, NY 11550.

THOMAS, ERMA LEE LYONS
Elected official, educator. **Personal:** Born Jul 7, 1928, Rentiesville, OK; married Joe Elihue Thomas; children: Lee Wilbur, Dianna Kaye, Cheryl Lynn, Bonnie Sue, John Robert. **Educ:** Langston Univ OK, BS 1951; Northeastern State Coll OK, ME. **Career:** St Thomas Primitive Bapt Church, treas 1974-80; Alpha Epsilon Omega Chap Alpha Kappa Alpha Sor Inc, basileus 1974-76; Local Langston Univ Alumni, sec 1977-85; Langston's Reg Midwestern Conf, sec 1980; State Dept OK, comm mem 1984-85; Muskogee School, lang arts teacher; City of Summit, mayor, trustee. **Orgs:** Democrat; Community Activist; OK Educators Assn; and Amer Assn of Retired Persons. **Honors/Awds:** Received Key to the City from Mayor J Ford of Tuskegee, AL. **Home Addr:** 5805 Oktaha Rd, Muskogee, OK 74401.

THOMAS, EULA WILEY
Educator. **Personal:** Born Apr 30, 1948, Arkadelphia, AR; daughter of Pernella Weaver Wiley and Elmore Wiley Sr; married Herman L Thomas; children: Traci A, Tiffani A. **Educ:** Ouachita Baptist Univ, BA Speech & Drama 1970; Henderson State Univ, MASAC Soc Agency Counseling 1976; Univ of CO Training Inst, attended 1980; Marquette Univ Training Inst for Spec Prog, attended 1981; Wichita State Training Inst, attended, 1984. **Career:** AR Human Dev Ctr, recreation leader 1970, speech pathologist 1971-76; Henderson State Univ, coord of handicapped serv 1984-, counselor/instructor 1976-. **Orgs:** Clerk, sec, deaconess Greater Pleasant Hill Baptist Church; cosponsor Henderson State Univ Minority Students Org 1979-; pres Arkadelphia Women's Devel Council 1980-; bd of dir Arkadelphia Chamber of Commerce 1983; chairperson Arkadelphia Christmas Parade 1983, 1984; mem AR Counselor Assoc, AR Assoc for Student Assoc Programs, NAACP; executive board, Arkadelphia Housing Authority, 1989-; United Way Allocation Committee, 1991; Delta Sigma Theta Sorority, Inc. **Honors/Awds:** WP Sturgis Found Grant for Continuing Educ, 1966; AR Handicapped Award for Special Educ 1971; Arkansas Black Students Assn, Outstanding Advisor of the Year, 1991. **Special Achievements:** Arkansas Black Students in Teacher Education. **Home Addr:** #4 Friendship Dr, Arkadelphia, AR 71923. **Business Addr:** Coordinator of Minority Affairs, Counselor/Instructor, Counseling & Speech Communications, Henderson State Univ, PO Box 7764, Arkadelphia, AR 71999-0001.

THOMAS, EUNICE S.
Federal official, association executive. **Career:** Affiliated with US Dept of Transportation, Washington, DC; Family Support Admin, US Dept of Health and Human Services, dir of community services, 1989-. **Orgs:** Grand Basileus, Zeta Phi Beta Sorority Inc, Howard Univ, Washington DC. **Business Addr:** Grand Basileus, Zeta Phi Beta Sorority, 1734 New Hampshire Avenue, NW, Washington, DC 20009.

THOMAS, FRANCENA B.
Educator, consultant. **Personal:** Born Mar 23, 1936, Belle Glade, FL; daughter of Lovella Bingham Bruton (deceased) and Andrew Bruton; married Joseph Thomas, Nov 2, 1962; children: Nifretta, Joseph Nicholas, Nigel Edward. **Educ:** FL A&M, BS 1959; Univ Miami, MEd 1971. **Career:** Dept Program Devel, teacher special assignment 1970-71; Little Rivere Elem, inservice coord curriculum specialist 1971-73; Olinda Center, summer school coordinator 1972; WSVN Weekly TV Show, hostess of Perspectives; WNWS Radio, host of weekly 3 hr talk show; "Degrees of Blackness", prod dir & appeared (a show based on contributions of Black poets); Miami Times, columnist 1972-; FL Intl Univ, dir div of univ relations 1973-87; Pres, Achievers Success Seminars, 1988-present. **Orgs:** Mem Dade Co Comm Relations Bd, FL Reg Manpower Planning Bd, FL Equal Educ Oppor Adv Council, Inner City Educ Found; Natl Org of Women "Her Story";Delta Sigma Theta; TV appearances; reading program instructor; literary workshops women prisoners Dade Co Jail; writer essays Black Lit 1971; Dade Co Comm Relations Bd; mem NOW; cochairperson Greater United Miami 1984; vice chairperson, Greater Miami United Jri Ethnic Bd, 1981-present. **Honors/Awds:** Best Columnist Award NNPA 1976; Second Best Columnist Award NNPA 1979; 1980 Headliner Award Women in Communications; 1982 Sara Weintraub Award of Excellence; Outstanding Journalist Concerned Black Women's Communications Award; Delta Sigma Theta Sorority Gold Key Award Intercollegiate Forensic Conf; Delta Sigma Theta Distinguished Minerva Award; Apptd by Pres Carter to be mem of Fed Judicial Screening Comm for 5th Circuit; Sigma Tau Mu Award Excellence in Debate; certificates from various comm org & school; one of 13 Miami "Young Success Stories" Miami Phoenix Newspaper; lead role play "The Man Nobody Saw"; also acted in several plays; Several others. **Business Addr:** Special Projects Administrator, Metro-Dade Police Dept, 1320 NW 14th St, Suite 319A, Miami, FL 33125.

THOMAS, FRANK EDWARD
Professional baseball player. **Personal:** Born May 27, 1968, Columbus, GA; children: Sterling, Sloan. **Educ:** Auburn University. **Career:** Chicago White Sox, infielder, 1990-. **Orgs:** President, Frank Thomas Charitable Foundation. **Honors/Awds:** American League MVP, 1993, 1994. **Business Addr:** Professional Baseball Player, Chicago White Sox, 333 W 35th St, Chicago, IL 60616, (312)924-1000.

THOMAS, FRANKIE TAYLOR
Librarian (retired). **Personal:** Born Oct 3, 1922, Samantha, AL; daughter of Frankie Walker Taylor and Nathan Taylor; married Ervin V Thomas, Jan 25, 1941 (deceased). **Educ:** Stillman College, Tuscaloosa, AL, diploma, 1945; Alabama State University, Montgomery, AL, BS, 1949; University of Wisconsin, Madison, WI, MLS, 1960. **Career:** Fayette County Schools, Fayette, AL, teacher, 1946-48; Tuscaloosa County Schools, Tuscaloosa, AL, teacher, 1949-58, librarian, 1958-61; Alabama A&M University, Normal, AL, head reference librarian, 1961-67; Stillman College, Tuscaloosa, AL, asst librarian/cataloging, 1967-68; Alabama A&M University, Normal, AL, head catalog librarian, 1968-69; University of Alabama, Tuscaloosa, AL, reference librarian/head reference dept, dir of staff development, 1969-84. **Orgs:** Member, American Library Assn, 1960; member, Southeastern Library Assn, 1962-; member, Alabama Library Assn, 1961-; member, Alabama Association of School Boards, 1988-, board of directors, 1992-94; National School Boards Association, 1988-; member, Tuscaloosa County Board of Education, 1988-. **Honors/Awds:** Northport Citizen of the Year, Chamber of Commerce, 1989; "S" Award, Stillman College, National Alumni Association, 1994; Long Distance Runner Award, NAACP, 1995. **Home Addr:** 1012 Mockingbird Ln, Northport, AL 35476.

THOMAS, FRANKLIN A.
Attorney. **Personal:** Born May 27, 1934, Brooklyn, NY; son of Viola Thomas and James Thomas; children: Keith, Hillary, Kerrie, Kyle. **Educ:** Columbia Coll, BA 1956; Columbia Law School, LLB 1963. **Career:** So Dist of NY, asst us atty 1964-65; New York City Police Dept, dep police commissioner in charge of legal matters 1965-67; Bedford-Stuyvesant Restoration, pres, ceo 1967-77; Private Practice, atty 1977-79; The Ford Found, pres 1979-96; TFF Study Group, 1996-. **Orgs:** Columbia University, trustee, 1969-75; board of directors, Aluminum Co of Amer, Cummins Engine Co Inc, Citicorp/Citibank NA; Lucent Technologies, PepsiCo; mem Sec of State's Adv Comm on South Africa 1985-87. **Honors/Awds:** Hon LLD Yale Univ 1970, Fordham Univ 1972, Pratt Inst 1974, Pace Univ 1977, Columbia Univ 1979; Awd for Contribution to the Betterment of Urban Life Lyndon B Johnson Found 1974; Medal of Excellence Columbia Univ 1976; Alexander Hamilton Awd Columbia Coll 1983. **Special Achievements:** Recipient LBJ Foundation award for contribution to betterment of urban life, 1974; Columbia Univ, Medal of excellence, 1976, Alexander Hamilton Award, 1983. **Military Serv:** USAF SAC capt, navigator 1956-60. **Business Addr:** TFF Study Group, 595 Madison Ave, 33rd Fl, New York, NY 10022.

THOMAS, FRANKLIN WHITAKER
State official. **Personal:** Born Nov 20, 1925, Winston-Salem, NC; son of Winnie Cornelia Whitaker Thomas (deceased) and Rev George J Thomas Sr; married Erma Jean Sampson; children: Donald, Ronald, Franklin, Jr, Jean-Agnes, Peter. **Educ:** Talladega Coll (AL), BA 1946; Chicago Theological Seminary, 1947; George Williams Coll, MS 1950. **Career:** Butler St YMCA-Atlanta, prog dir 1950-53; Tulsa & Denver YMCA's, exec dir 1953-65; Butler St YMCA-Atlanta, gen exec 1965-69; City of Atlanta, dir of personnel 1971-74; Nat'l Brd of YMCA'S-NYC, dir of personnel serv 1969-71 & 1974-76; Metro Atlanta Rapid Transit Authority, dir of personnel 1976-77; GA State Merit System, deputy commissioner, 1977-92; Harvard Univ School of Business, guest lecturer, summer 1977; GA Inst of Technology, adjunct professor, 1978-. **Orgs:** Mem gvnrg brd Natl Cncl of Churches 1979-82; cnsultnt-trner Indstrl Mgmnt Inter 1979-; bd mem, United Church Bd for Homeland Ministries 1985-92; moderator, Central Cong'l UCC 1991-93; asst moderator, Gen Synod UCC 1989-91; mem, Alpha Phi Alpha Fraternity, 1944-; mem, Kappa Boule of Sigma Pi Phi Fraternity, 1990-. **Honors/Awds:** Dist Serv Awd Washington HS, Atlanta 1973; Outstanding Achvmnt Award Omega Y's Men's Club, Atlanta 1983. **Business Addr:** Deputy Commissioner, State Merit System of GA, 200 Piedmont Ave SE, Atlanta, GA 30334.

THOMAS, FRED
Law enforcement official. **Career:** District of Columbia Police Dept, police official, until 1985; Metropolitan Police Boys and Girls Club, head, 1985-92; District of Columbia Police Department, chief of police, 1992-. **Special Achievements:** Appointed Chief of Police by DC May Sharon Pratt Kelly, Nov 1992. **Business Addr:** Chief, Washington, DC Police Department, Municipal Center, Rm 5080, 300 Indiana Ave NW, Washington, DC 20001.

THOMAS, FRED
Professional football player. **Personal:** Born Sep 11, 1973, Grand Rapids, MI. **Educ:** Tennessee-Martin. **Career:** Seattle Seahawks, defensive back, 1996-. **Business Addr:** Professional Football Player, Seattle Seahawks, 11220 NE 53rd St, Kirkland, WA 98033, (206)827-9777.

THOMAS, GERALD EUSTIS
Military officer (retired), educator. **Personal:** Born Jun 23, 1929, Natick, MA; son of Leila L Jacobs Thomas and Walter W Thomas; married Rhoda Holmes Henderson, Oct 3, 1954; children: Kenneth A, Steven E, Lisa D Jacobs. **Educ:** Harvard Univ, BA 1951; George Washington Univ, MS 1966; Yale Univ, PhD 1973. **Career:** US Navy, commanding officer USS Impervious, 1962-63; College Training Programs Bureau of Naval Personnel, head, 1963-65; US Navy, commanding officer USS Bausell, 1966-68; Prairie View A&M Coll Naval ROTC Unit, prof of naval science & commanding officer, 1968-70; US Navy, commander Destroyer Squadron Five, 1973-75, rear admiral, 1974-81; US Dept of Defense, acting deputy asst sec of defense for intl security affairs & dir of Near East, South Asia, & Africa Region, 1976-78, Comtrapac, US Pacific Fleet, 1978-81, retired, 1981; State Dept, US ambassador to Guyana 1981-83, US ambassador to Kenya 1983-86; Yale Univ, lecturer, Davenport College, master, currently. **Orgs:** Overseer, Bd of Overseers, Harvard Univ, 1981-88; bd of trustees, Univ of San Diego, 1981-86; life mem, Org of Amer Historians. **Military Serv:** US Navy, rear admiral, 1951-81. **Home Addr:** 271 Park St, New Haven, CT 06511-4751.

THOMAS, GLORIA V.
Educator. **Personal:** Born Mar 23, Brenham, TX; divorced; children: Dino, Paul, Edwin. **Educ:** Btx Southern U, BS 1953; TX Southern U, MS 1965; TX Southern U, Adm Cert 1968; Sorbonne, France, Cert in French; Baylor Univ & Univ So MS, Cert. **Career:** Phillis Wheatley HS Houston Indep School Dist, rgstr; Phyllis Wheatley Sr HS, chem teacher 1959-72. **Orgs:** Basileus Gamma Omega Zeta Zeta Phi Beta Sor 1971-72; mem Civil Rights Commn 1973-; ofcr Houston Tchrs Assn 1971-72; United Fund Budget Panel 1973-; Human Rel Commn & Sexism Commn Huston Ind Sch Dist; mem Houston Tchrs Assn; TX Statetchrs Assn; TX Clsrm Tchrs Assn; NEA; Nat'l Sci Tchrs Assn;MacGregor Park Civic Club; E Bethel Bapt Ch; TX Atomic Energy Commn; Black Caucus NEA; mem aux Big Bros of Houston 1965-; vol Multi Schlerosis 1972; sickle cell anemia 1973-74; cancer fund 1970-74. **Honors/Awds:** Scholarship Sorbonne 1954-56; res particip grant 1961; TX AEC Univ TX; Dr IGE Outcomes Achvmnt 1974; outstanding ldrshp Award Zeta Phi Beta Sor 1971; 15 awards NSF 1961-74; Nat'l Educ Award 1968. **Business Addr:** Income Tax Consultant, 4900 Market, Houston, TX 77020.

THOMAS, HARRY LEE
Physician. **Personal:** Born Apr 5, 1919, Richmond, VA; married Betty; children: Harriet, Harry. **Educ:** Lincoln Univ, AB 1939; Howard Univ, MD 1946. **Career:** Howard Univ, intern 1946-47, surg res 1947-52, instr 1952-53; USAF Hosp, chief surg 1953-56; VA Outpatient Facility, consult 1956-60; Mercy Douglass Hosp, sr attending surgeon; Med Coll of PA, clinical prof surgery, currently. **Orgs:** Dir Cancer Detection Proj Mercy Douglass Hosp 1958-63; bd dir Amer Cancer Soc 1977. **Honors/Awds:** Medical College of PA, Distinguished Service Award; Golden Apple Teaching Award. **Military Serv:** USAF capt 1953-56. **Business Addr:** Clinical Professor, Surgery, Med Coll of PA, 5555 Wissahickon Ave, Philadelphia, PA 19144.

THOMAS, HENRY LEE, JR.
Professional football player. **Personal:** Born Jan 12, 1965, Houston, TX; married Eyvonne; children: Natasha, Sydney. **Educ:** Louisiana State. **Career:** Minnesota Vikings, defensive tackle, 1987-95; Detroit Lions, 1995-96; New England Patriots, 1997-. **Honors/Awds:** Pro Bowl, 1991, 1992. **Business Addr:** Professional Football Player, New England Patriots, 60 Washington St, Foxboro Stadium, Foxboro, MA 02035, (508)543-7911.

THOMAS, HERMAN EDWARD
Educator. **Personal:** Born Dec 12, 1941, Bryson City, NC; married Mary Knox Thomas; children: Terence, Maurice, Katrina. **Educ:** Hartford Sem Fdn, PhD 1978; Duke Univ Divinity Schl, ThM (honors) 1969; Duke Univ Divinity Schl, BD 1966; NCA&T State Univ, BS (cum laude)1963. **Career:** Berkley HS, Aberdeen, NC, HS teacher 1966-67; Student Affrs, Morris Coll, Sumter, SC, 1968-69; Religion & Phil, Springfield Col, Sprg, MA, instr 1969-74; Black Studies, Springfield Coll, Sprg, MA, coord 1971-74; Rel Stud, asst prof, assoc prof, currently; AAA Studies UNCC, asst dir 1974-86; UTOP, director, 1986-. **Orgs:** Mem Am Acdmy of Religion 1973-; chair steer commit NC Cncl of Black studies 1975-76; assoc Mnstr First Baptist Church-West 1975-; fdng mem Natl Cncl for Black Studies 1975-; chrmn brd of dir Afro-Amer Cultural Cntr 1979-84; mem Soc for the Study of Black Religion 1980-, recording sec and historian, 1994-97; brd mem Charl-Merk Arts & Science Cncl 1984-. **Honors/Awds:** Mary Reynolds Babcock Schlrshp Duke Divinity Schl 1963-66; coord-Humanist Afro-Am Hist Project in Charlotte, NC Humanities Comm 1983-83; Religion & Slavery in JWC Pennington Jrnl of ITC 1979; Author, Biographies (5) Encylopedia of Pel in the South 1984. **Special Achievements:** Author, ''A Summary and Critical Analysis of the 'Color of God: the Concept of God in Afro American Thought','' Amez Quarterly, v 102, n 1, pp 38-41, 1990; ''Revisioning the American Dream: Individualism and Community in African American Perspective,'' Star of Zion, v 14, n 21, January 21, 1993; James WC Pennington: African American Churchman and Abolitionist, Garland Publishing, 1995. **Home Addr:** 5913 Craftsbury Dr, Charlotte, NC 28215. **Business Addr:** Associate Prof, Religious Studies, UNCC, 121 Garinger Bldg, 9201 University City Blvd, Charlotte, NC 28223.

THOMAS, HOLLIS
Professional football player. **Personal:** Born Jan 10, 1974, Abilene, TX. **Educ:** Northern Illinois, attended. **Career:** Philadelphia Eagles, defensive tackle, 1996-. **Honors/Awds:** NFL All-Rookie Team, 1996. **Business Addr:** Professional Football Player, Philadelphia Eagles, 3501 S Broad St, Philadelphia, PA 19148, (215)463-2500.

THOMAS, ISAAC DANIEL, JR.
Business executive. **Personal:** Born Jan 31, 1939, Birmingham, AL; married Mary E Ellison; children: Peter Neil, Isaac Daniel III. **Educ:** Eastern MI Univ, attended; Wayne State Univ, BA 1960; LA City Coll, attended 1966; Pasadena City Coll, attended 1968. **Career:** Wayne Cty Boys Detention Home, boys group leader 1 1960; Allstate Ins Co, casualty claims suprv 1966, div personnel mgr 1969, western zone human resources mgr 1971, urban affairs dir 1976, asst vice pres employee relations. **Orgs:** Bd mem Oper Snowball Mental Health Assoc of Greater Chicago; bd of dir So Christian Leadership Council, DuSable Mus Chicago, SAFER Found Chicago; memKappa Alpha Psi. **Honors/Awds:** Motivator of Youth Awd, YMCA of Met Chicago Black & Hispanic Achievers of Indust Recognition 1978. **Military Serv:** AUS sp 4 1960-62. **Business Addr:** Assistant Vice Pres Employee Rel, Allstate Insurance Co, Allstate Plaza, Northbrook, IL 60062.

THOMAS, ISIAH LORD, III
Sports administrator, professional basketball player (retired). **Personal:** Born Apr 30, 1961, Chicago, IL; son of Mary Thomas; married Lynn Kendall, Jul 1985; children: two. **Educ:** Indiana Univ, attended. **Career:** Detroit Pistons, professional basketball player, 1981-94; Toronto Raptors, vp of basketball operations, 1994-98; NBC, NBA analyst. **Honors/Awds:** NBA All-Star Team 1982-93; Most Valuable Player 1984, 1986. **Business Addr:** Vice President, Basketball Operations, Toronto Raptors, 20 Bay St, Ste 1702, Toronto, ON, Canada M5J 2N8, (416)341-2400.

THOMAS, JACQUELINE MARIE
Journalist. **Personal:** Born Aug 31, 1952, Nashville, TN; daughter of Dorothy Phillips Thomas and John James Thomas Jr. **Educ:** Briarcliff Coll, AA 1970, BA (Cum Laude) 1972; Columbia Univ Sch of Intl Affairs, MA 1974. **Career:** Chicago Sun Times, reporter 1974-85; Courier Journal & Louisville Times, assoc editor 1985-86; Detroit Free Press, assoc editor, 1986-92; Detroit News, news editor, 1992-94, Washington bureau chief; The Baltimore sun, editorial page editor, currently. **Orgs:** Mem Natl Assoc of Black Journalists; mem American Society of Newspaper Editors; mem Natl Conf of Editorial Writers. **Honors/Awds:** Nieman Fellow Harvard Univ 1983-84. **Business Addr:** Editorial Page Editor, Baltimore Sun, 501 North Calvert St, Baltimore, MD 21278.

THOMAS, JACQUELYN SMALL
Educator, educational administrator. **Personal:** Born Oct 25, 1938, Jacksonville, FL; daughter of Lillian Louise Graham Small and James Purcell Small; married Willie Thomas, Mar 30, 1970; children: Nicole Jacquelyn. **Educ:** Hampton Univ, Hampton, VA, BS, 1959; Columbia Univ, New York, NY, MA, 1963. **Career:** Richmond Public Schools, Richmond, VA, teacher, 1959-65, guidance counselor, 1965-67, asst principal, 1967-72; J Sargeant Reynolds Community Coll, Richmond, VA, adjunct teacher, 1979-82; The Children's Ctr, Richmond, VA, dir, 1983-. **Orgs:** Coalition of 100 Black Women, 1989-91; fin sec, James River Valley, Links, Inc, 1991-93; pres, Richmond Chapter, Jack & Jill of America, 1983-85; pres, Richmond Chapter, Delta Sigma Theta Sorority, 1960-72; vice pres, Old Dominion Volunteer League, 1979-80; advisory bd mem, Mayors Comm on Young Children, 1989-91; bd mem, VA Day Care Council, VA Dept for Children, 1987-89. **Honors/Awds:** Volunteer Service Award, Old Dominion Volunteer League, 1979; Jill of the Year, Richmond Chapter, Jack & Jill of America, 1982. **Business Addr:** Director, The Children's Center of Richmond, Inc, 2715 Chamberlayne Ave, Richmond, VA 23222.

THOMAS, JAMES L.
State representative. **Personal:** Born Jun 29, 1943, White Hall, AL; son of Rebecca Gregory and James McKinley Thomas; married Evelyn Juanita Hatcher, 1971; children: Angela Rose. **Educ:** AL State Univ, BS, 1965, MEd, 1975. **Career:** Camden Academy High School, teacher, 1965-84; Wilcox County High School, teacher, 1974-82, vocational dir, 1982-89; Wilcox Central High School, principal, 1989-; State of AL, House of Representatives, state rep, 1981-. **Orgs:** Natl Black Caucus of State Legislators, NBCSL treasurer, 1990-94, vp, 1994-; National Assn of Secondary School Principals; Wilcox County Admins Assn; National Education Association; AL Education Association; Wilcox County Educ Assn; AL Dem Conf; New South Coalition. **Honors/Awds:** WCEA, Teacher of the Year, 1972; CAPA, Outstanding Leadership Award, 1986. **Business Addr:** State Representative, Dist 69, AL House of Representatives, PO Box 1089, Camden, AL 36726.

THOMAS, JAMES O., JR.
Federal official (retired). **Personal:** Born Feb 12, 1930, Screven Co, GA; married Jacqueline Seward; children: Toniae, James O III. **Educ:** Savannah State Coll, BS Chemistry 1956; George Washington Law, 1957. **Career:** US Patent Office, primary examiner 1967; US Patent Office, supvr patent exr 1975; US Patent Office, group direction, 1979, Patent Process Services, deputy assistant commissioner. **Orgs:** Pres Assoc Investors Inc 1957; pres Savannah State Coll Alumni 1973; pres Far NE-SE Cncl 1974; chrmn brd Capitol View Development, Inc 1978; vice pres HELP, Inc 1981; chrmn Savannah State Fdn 1983; pres 3847 Corp Inc 1984. **Honors/Awds:** President's Club Savannah State Coll 1973-81; Cynus Wiley Savannah State Coll 1979; NAFEO Distinguished Alumni Savannah State Coll 1981; Alumnus Of Year Savannah State Coll 1982; Gold Medal US Patent Off 1983; Medallion of Excellence Savannah State Coll 1986; EEO Supervisory Achievement Awd Patent and Trademark Office 1986. **Military Serv:** US Army, sgt, Korean Medal, Good Conduct, Defense Medal etc 1951. **Home Addr:** 4339 H St SE, Washington, DC 20019. **Business Addr:** Deputy Assistant Commissioner, Patent Process Services, US Patent Office, Commissioner of Patents, Washington, DC 20003.

THOMAS, JAMES SAMUEL
Clergyman. **Personal:** Born Apr 8, 1919, Orangeburg, SC; married Ruth Naomi Wilson; children: Claudie Williamson, Gloria Jean, Margaret Yvonne, Patricia Elaine. **Educ:** Clafin Coll Orangeburg, AB 1939; DD 1953; Gammon Theol Sem Atlanta, BD 1943; Drew U, MA 1944; Cornell U, PhD 1953; Bethune-Cookman Coll, LLD 1963; Simpson Coll, 1965; Morningside Coll, 1966; IA Wesleyan Coll Coe Coll, 1968; Cornell Coll, LHD 1965; OH Weslyan U, 1967. **Career:** Meth Ch, ordained to ministry 1942; Orangeburg Circuit, pastor 1942-43; York, SC, 1946-47; SC State Coll, chaplain 1944-46; Gammon Theol Sem, prof 1947-53; Meth Bd Edn, asso dir 1953-64; IA Area Meth Ch, bishop 1964-; Meth Bd Edn, chmn dept educ insts; Meth Commn Christian Vocations, vice-chmn; Negro Colls Danforth Found, consult 1957-60; Perkins Sch Theol So Meth U, vis prof 1958. **Orgs:** Tst Vbennett Simpson Claflin Clark Morningside Colls Gammon Theol Sem; mem Kappa Delta Pi; Phi Delta Kappa; Phi Kappa Phi.

THOMAS, JANICE MORRELL
Educator. **Personal:** Born Oct 6, 1946, Elizabeth, NJ; married Aaron D. **Educ:** Rutgers U, AB 1968, EdM 1975. **Career:** Rutgers Univ, sr admiss officer Newark Campus 1985, acting dir of admiss 1972-73, assoc dir of admiss 1971-72, asst dir of admiss 1970-71, Asst to dir of admiss 1969-70. **Orgs:** Mem Am Assn of Collegiate Registrars & Admiss Ofcrs; Middle Sts Assn of Collegiate Registrars & Admiss Ofcrs; Nat Assn of Coll Admiss Cnslrs; AmColl Prsnl Assn; Assn of Non-White Cncrns; Rutgers Univ Black Org of Fclty; mem NJ Unit of Nat Assn of Negro Bus & Pro Wmns Clubs Inc; NAACP; UrbLeag Union Co; NJ Assn of Coll Admiss Cnslrs; NJ Assn of Black & Puerto Rican Admiss Cnslrs; Am Prsnl & Guidance Assn. **Business Addr:** Rutgers State Univ of NJ, Newark Campus, 249 University Ave, Newark, NJ 07102.

THOMAS, JANIS P.
Advertising executive. **Personal:** Born Nov 23, 1954, Frankfurt; married Edmond A Tapscott III. **Educ:** Tufts Univ, BA English, BA French, 1976; Howard Univ, MA Mass Comm, 1978. **Career:** WTTG-TV, started 1978; NBC/WRC-TV Washington DC, sales rsch coord 1980-82; Black Entertainment Television, dir of adv 1982-83, vice pres advertising 1983-93; exec vp of mktg and merchandising, 93-; pres of BET Direct Inc., currently. **Business Addr:** Vice President Advertising, Black Entertainment TV, 1232 31st St NW, Washington, DC 20007.

THOMAS, JEWEL M.
Cosmetics consultant, educator. **Educ:** Miles Coll, BA 1960; Univ of AL, EdS 1976; CP Univ, EdD 1984. **Career:** Lawson State Comm Coll, grad adv, sophomore class adv 1980-; Kappa Delta Epsilon, pres 1981-84; Twentieth Century Club, pres 1982; Lawson Comm Coll, prof; City of Brighton, mayor; A&M University, part-time instructor; Independent Mary Kay Consultant, currently; Miles College, associate professor, currently. **Orgs:** Lecturer Natl Baptist Conv USA 1980; speaker AL Women's Natl Conv 1980; lecturer AL Jr Coll Assn 1980; pres AL Ed Assn 1984; 1st Lady Mayor of Brighton City of Brighton 1984; Served Alabama League of Municipalities Executive Committee, 6th district, 1990, 1992; National League of Cities Committee & Advisory Human Development; ARC, board of directors, 1991; JCCEO Board of Directors, vice-pres, 1991; Western Area Democratic Club, first black pres, 1995. **Honors/Awds:** Soror of the Year Alpha Kappa Alpha 1980; The Writing Lab Dir AL Jr Coll Jrnl 1982; Outstanding Ed UAB School of Ed 1984; KDE Pres Awd Univ Coll 1984; Award for an Advocate of the Poor, 1995, 1996; Jefferson County Commissioners, MMRD Honor. **Home Addr:** 4900 Letson St, Brighton, AL 35020.

THOMAS, JIM
Professional basketball player. **Career:** Minnesota Timberwolves, currently. **Business Addr:** Basketball Player, Omaha Racers, 6300 Shirley, Omaha, NE 68106.

THOMAS, JOAN MCHENRY BATES
Elected official, business executive. **Personal:** Born Jun 26, 1928, Atlanta, GA; daughter of Pearl Bonnett McHenry and Henry McHenry; married Lee E Thomas (deceased); children: Edwin T Bates, Judith Z Stratton. **Educ:** Dept US Ag, 1960; Temple Business School, 1963. **Career:** Catering Business, pres; Dept Human Resources, social worker retired after 31 yrs; community service worker, currently. **Orgs:** Chairperson, US Military Widow 1980; pres, Amer War Mothers 1984-87; chairperson, Adv Neighborhood Comm 1984; vice pres, treasurer, Ward 4 Democrats; North West Boundary Civic Association, 1980-; treasurer, DC Democratic Committee 1988-92; chairperson, Advisory Neighborhood Comm, 1989-90; natl carnation chmn, National American War Mothers, 1989-92; DC convention chmn, American War Mothers, 1989-. **Honors/Awds:** Cert of Apprec from President Ronald Reagan 1980; Cert of Apprec from Mayor Marion Barry 1984; Outstanding Volunteer from American Red Cross 1974; Outstanding Community Volunteer 1984; Community Award, Rock Creek Church 1988; Dedicated, Outstanding Northwest Boundary Civi Assn; delegate to Democratic National Convention, 1992; Outstanding Community Service Award, School Board, 1992. **Home Addr:** 715 Varnum St NW, Washington, DC 20011.

THOMAS, JOHN
Boxing referee (retired). **Personal:** Born Sep 21, 1922, Meridian, LA; son of Sylvia Thomas and Clifton Thomas; married Kathryn; children: Diane. **Career:** Open novice amateur champion 1938; AAU Feather Champ 1939; Pacific Coast Golden Gloves 1940; CA Lightweight Prof Champ 1943-47; CA Athletic Comm, boxing ref; Four Roses Distillers Co, sales suprv; Athletic Comm, 2nd black referee; Four Roses Co House Seagrams, public relations. **Military Serv:** AUS pvt 1945.

THOMAS, JOHN
Athlete. **Personal:** Born Mar 3, 1941, Boston, MA. **Educ:** Boston Univ, BS Phys & Psych Rehab 1963; Boston Conserv of Music, Ballet 1962-64; Boston School of Bus, Acctg 1969; Amer Red Cross, Basic Life Support Course in CPR. **Career:** Neighborhood Youth Corps, vocational counselor 1 1/2 yrs;

Hawthorne House Neighborhood Ctr, dir 2 yrs; City of Boston, probation officer Roxbury Court 7 yrs; WCVB-TV Channel 5, acct exec 5 yrs; General Motors Truck Div, acct exec 3 yrs; New England Telephone, acct exec 3 yrs; AT&T Commun, acct exec 1 yr; Boston Univ, track coach part time 15 yrs. **Orgs:** Jr usher, bd Ebanzer Baptist Church; mem Cub Scouts, Boy Scouts, Eagle Rank, Silver Palms, Explorer Scouts-Apprentice Rank; chmn Explorer; bd mem Boys Clubs of Boston, Cooper Comm Ctr; bd mem Cambridge YMCA; mem Gov Council on Phys Fitness; mem pres Council on Physical Fitness; mem US Olympic Comm Spirit Team; intl dir Athlets United for Peace. **Honors/Awds:** HS Capt Tennis Team, Capt Track Team, State Champ High Jump, State Champ Hurdles; Natl Champ High Jump; Natl & World Interscholastic Record Holder High Jump; New England Champ High Jump; New England Champ High Hurdles; All Amer Sr Yr High Jump US Natl Team High Jump; Boston Univ, 1st man to jump 7' indoors, Capt Track Team, Former School Record Holder Hurdles, Record Holder High Jump 7'3 3/4'', IC4A Champ & Record Holder Indoors & Outdoors, NCAA, NAAU Champ & Record Holder High Jump Indoors & Outdoors, Former World Record Holder Running, High Jump Broken 13 Times 7'4'', Bronze Medalist Rome Olympics, Co-Olympic Champ Tokyo Olumpics, Silver Medalist; Hall of Fame Inductee Helms Found, Boston Univ, US Track & Field. **Home Addr:** 51 Mulberry St, Brockton, MA 02402.

THOMAS, JOHN
Professional basketball player. **Personal:** Born Sep 8, 1975. **Educ:** University of Minnesota. **Career:** Boston Celtics, forward, 1997-98; Toronto Raptors, 1998-. **Business Addr:** Professional Basketball Player, Toronto Raptors, 150 York St, Ste 110, Toronto, ON, Canada M5H 3S5, (416)214-2255.

THOMAS, JOHN HENDERSON, III
Psychologist. **Personal:** Born Sep 7, 1950, Washington, DC. **Educ:** Univ of Detroit, AB 1972; Univ of Cincinnati, MA 1976, DEd 1982. **Career:** Mott Adults HS, consult 1972; Univ of Cincinnati, minority gp counseling ctr 1973; Mott Adult HS, instr psych, soc, engl 1973; Univ of Cincinnati Consult Svc, psychologist 1975; Univ of Cincinnati Walk-In-Clinic, psych; Ctr Devel Disorders, psych 1976; Ct Domestic Rel Ct Common Prac, psych 1976, cntrl clinic 1976; Inst of Psych Univ of Cincinnati, psych; Sonlight Lectures Inc, founder, pres. **Orgs:** Mem Urban League, NAACP, Black Student; grad student Psych Assoc, Kappa Alpha Psi. **Honors/Awds:** Vocational Rehab Scholarship 1968-72; Avhievement Ed Awd Urban League 1968; Scholarship Grad Studies Univ of Cincinnati 1073-76; Miss Black Amer Leadership Awd 1973. **Business Addr:** President, Sonlight Liectures Inc, PO Box 29842, Cincinnati, OH 45229.

THOMAS, JOHN WESLEY
Psychiatrist. **Personal:** Born Feb 13, 1932, Birmingham, AL; son of Leila Berry Hatcher and James Thomas; divorced; children: Courtland W, Stephen M. **Educ:** TN State Univ, BA 1953; Meharry Medical Coll, MD 1959; Rollman Inst of Psychiatry, Cincinnati, OH, Psychiatric Residency 1960-61; Western Psychiatric Inst Pgh, PA, Psychiatric Residency 1961-63. **Career:** Gen Psychiatry, Pittsburgh, PA, priv pract 1963-; various hosp & ints in Pgh Area, psychiatric cnsltnt & staff 1963-; Univ of Pittsburgh, School of Medicine, clinical instructor in psychiatry, 1963-89. **Orgs:** Bd of dir Amer Group Psychotherapy Assn 1980-83; Natl Med Assn, Amer Group Psychotherapy Assn, Amer Psychiat Assn, Soc Keystone State Med Soc, Tri-State Grp Psychotherapy Soc, Pittsburgh Psychiatric Soc, Omicron Lambda Chapter, Alpha Phi Alpha, Pi Chapter, Chi Delta Mu; American Med Assn; Psychiatric Physicians of Pennsylvania. **Honors/Awds:** George W Carver Award Natl Achvmnt Club, Inc 1980; fellow Amer Group Psychotherapy Assn 1985.

THOMAS, JOHNNY B.
Elected official. **Personal:** Born Nov 30, 1953, Glendora, MS; married Ella Rean Johnson; children: Leslie. **Educ:** MS Valley State Univ, 1977,78. **Career:** Tallahatchie Cty, constable 1976-80; Town of Glendora, alderman 1981-82, mayor 1982-. **Orgs:** Chmn Anti Crime Commiss 1976-80, Voters League 1978-81; mem Criminal Justice Planning Commiss 1980-85, NAACP. **Honors/Awds:** Mem Kirskey Foundation for Equity & Justice. **Business Addr:** Mayor, Town of Glendora, PO Box 90, Glendora, MS 38928.

THOMAS, JOSEPH EDWARD, JR.
Law enforcement official. **Personal:** Born Jun 22, 1950, Mattson, MS; son of Clara R Thomas and Joseph E Thomas Sr; married Carol Wynne Carmody, Oct 15, 1983; children: Shayla Y, Joseph III, Daniel Wesley. **Educ:** Alcorn State University, BS, mathematics, 1972; Jackson Community College, AS, law enforcement, 1984; Michigan State Police School of Management, graduated, 1985; American Management Association, graduated, 1986; Michigan Criminal Justice Institute, graduated, 1989; FBI National Academy, attended, 1989; University of Virginia, additional studies, public administration, 1989; Western Michigan University, MS, public administration, 1989; National Fire Academy, attended, 1989, 1991-92; Michigan State School of Traffic Engineering I, attended, 1990; US Secret Service Executive School, attended, 1992; Oakland Community College, additional studies, 1992; Eastern Michigan University, educational leadership, Doctoral program currently. **Career:** Goodyear Tire and Rubber, supervisor, 1972-73; Montgomery Wards, salesperson, 1973-74; City of Jackson, detective, lieutenant, 1974-88; City of Albion, director, public safety, 1988-91; City of Southfield, chief, police department, 1991-. **Orgs:** Oakland County Sheriff Association, 1991-; Police Executive Research Forum, 1991-; Oakland County Police Chiefs Association, alt district representative, 1991-; Oakland County Narcotics Enforcement Team, board of directors, 1991-; FBI National Academy Associates, 1989-; National Fire Academy Associates, executive fire officer, 1988-; National Public Safety Directors Association, 1988-; International Fire Chiefs Association, 1988-; International Police Chiefs Association, 1988-; Michigan Association of Chief of Police, board of directors, 1988-. **Honors/Awds:** Southeastern Substance Abuse Council, Distinguished Service Award, 1992, 1996; Michigan Association of Chiefs of Police, Distinguished Service Award, 1991; State of Michigan, Senate Resolution, Outstanding Service, 1991; International Police Management Association, Outstanding Professional Award, 1990; FBI National Academy, Section Representative, 1989; Jackson Citizen Pagaent, Citizen of the Year, finalist; 1988; Boy Scouts of America, Silver Beaver-Bronze Big Horn Awards, 1987. **Business Addr:** Chief of Police, Southfield Polic Department, 26000 Evergreen Rd, Southfield, MI 48076.

THOMAS, JOSEPH H.
Attorney. **Personal:** Born May 16, 1933, Baltimore, MD; son of Dr & Mrs Joseph H Thomas; married Lois A Young (deceased); children: Nina, Donna, Beth, Laura, Joseph III, Gordon. **Educ:** Brown Univ, BA 1954; Univ of MD School of Law, LLB 1964. **Career:** Securities Inc, pres 1959-65; self employed attorney 1964-; Thomas & Welcome, 1988-89; Joseph H Thomas and Associates, currently. **Orgs:** Pres, Baltimore Alumni Kappa Alpha Psi 1964-65; pres Provident Hospital Found 1981-; pres Lafayette Square Comm Center 1982-84; Thomas letter 1983-85. **Military Serv:** USMCR capt 1954-58.

THOMAS, JOSEPH W.
Attorney. **Personal:** Born Aug 2, 1940, New Orleans, LA; son of Edith Winand Thomas and Gerald H Thomas; married Sandra Green; children: Jeffery, Anthony, Aisha, Adelle, Anne, Winand Jr, Elizabeth, Alice, Shpard. **Educ:** Loyola Univ of Chicago, BS; 1967; Loyola of New Orleans, JD 1973; Tulane Univ, MBA 1984. **Career:** New Orleans Legal Asst, staff attorney 1973; LA Dept of Justice, asst atty gen 1974-80; private law practice 1980-. **Orgs:** Mem Louis-Martinet Legal Soc; bd mem New Orleans Legal Asst Corp; mem DC Bar Assn; partner in firm Thomas & Davis; mem Amer, Louisiana Bar Assns; mem NAACP; bd of dirs, Urban League of New Orleans, 1990-91. **Business Addr:** Law Offices of Joseph W Thomas, Poydras Center, 650 Poydras St, #1020, New Orleans, LA 70130.

THOMAS, JOYCE CAROL
Author, educator. **Personal:** Born May 25, 1938, Ponca City, OK; daughter of Leona Thompson Haynes and Floyd Haynes; children: Monica Pecot, Gregory, Michael, Roy. **Educ:** Stanford Univ, MA 1967; San Jose State Univ, BA (with honors) 1966. **Career:** Full-time writer, 1981-84; Purdue Univ, visting professor of English, 1984; University of Tennessee, Knoxville, Dept of English, full prof, creative writing, 1989-. **Orgs:** Dramatist Guild; Author's Guild. **Honors/Awds:** Best Book, Young Adult Serv, Amer Library Assoc, 1982; New York Times Outstanding Book of the Year, 1983; The Amer Book Award (formerly Natl Book Award), 1983; award winning novels: Marked by Fire, Avon Books, 1982, Bright Shadow, Avon Books, 1983; Outstanding Woman of the Twentieth Century, Sigma Gamma Rho, 1986; Chancellor's Award for Research and Creativity, University of Tennessee, 1990; Citation, Oklahoma Senate, 1989; A Gathering of Flowers: Best Book for Young Adults, Voice of Youth Advocates nominee, 1991; Millionith Acquisition for the University of California, Santa Cruz, Special Collections, 1991; Kentucky Blue Grass Award, 1995; National Conference of Christians and Jews, 1994; National Council of the Teachers of English, 1994; American Library Assn, 1994; YWCA, 1993; New York Public Library, 1993. **Special Achievements:** Author of fiction books in the series about Abyssinia Jackson and her people; other works include: Marked by Fire, 1982; Bright Shadow, 1983; Water Girl, 1986; The Golden Pasture, 1986; Journey, 1988; A Gathering of Flowers, 1990; ''The Gingerbread Grandma,'' in Poems for Grandmothers, 1990; When the Nightingale Sings, 1992; Brown Honey in BroomWheat Tea, 1993; Gingerbread Days, 1995. **Business Addr:** Author, c/o Mitch Douglas International Creative Management, 40 W 57th St, New York, NY 10019.

THOMAS, J.T. (JOHNNY LE'MON)
Professional football player. **Personal:** Born Dec 15, 1971, San Bernardino, CA. **Educ:** Arizona State, attended. **Career:** St Louis Rams, wide receiver, 1995-. **Business Addr:** Professional Football Player, St Louis Rams, One Rams Way, St Louis, MO 63045, (314)982-7267.

THOMAS, JUANITA WARE (JUANITA GLEE WARE)
Educator. **Personal:** Born Oct 30, 1923, Little Rock, AR; married Morris E Thomas Sr; children: Roumania T Wiggins, Morris, Jr, Veronica T Gray, Etelka, Pearl Thomas. **Educ:** Philadners Smith & Dunbar Jr Coll, AA (elem ed) 1944; DC Tchrs Coll 1970; Howard Univ, 1974; N VA Comm Coll, 1984. **Career:** George W Carver Elementary School (No LR), elementary teacher 1944; War Dept (DC), typist 1945; Hibbler & Hibbler Attys at Law, law firm secy, notary 1946; US Navy Dept, congressional typist 1948; US Navy Dept, examiner 1949-51. **Orgs:** Elem sec Nalle Elem Schl (DC) 1956-63; elem sub tchr DC Public Schls 1963-; elem tchr Patterson Sch Admidon Schl 1974, 1980-81; tchr Headstart Pre-School-UPO 1982-; sec SE Civic Assoc 1963-65; chrmn SECA Beautification Progm 1965-68; pres PTA Buchanan Elem Sch 1957-65; advsry comm Adv Neghbrhd Comm 1975-85; prlmntrn W&V Womens Clubs-Natl Assoc C W Clubs 1985. **Honors/Awds:** ''Grass Roots Honoree'' SE Civic Assocn 1965; ''Woman of the Year'' NE Federation Womens Clubs 1976; ''Advisory Neighborhoods Comm Outstanding Serv'' 1981-84; celebrating 10 yrs ''Home Rule in DC'' Since 1975; ANCS 1985. **Home Addr:** 1528 E St SE, Washington, DC 20003. **Business Addr:** Teacher, United Planning Organization, 1288 Upshur St NW, Washington, DC 20011.

THOMAS, KENDALL
Educator. **Personal:** Born Feb 22, 1957, East Chicago, IN. **Educ:** Yale College, New Haven, CT, BA, 1978; Yale Law School, New Haven, CT, JD, 1982. **Career:** Columbia University in the City of New York, New York, NY, asst/associate professor, 1984-92, prof, 1992-. **Business Addr:** Professor, Columbia University, School of Law, 435 W 116th St, New York, NY 10027.

THOMAS, KENNETH ROGER. See Obituaries section.

THOMAS, KURT VINCENT
Professional basketball player. **Personal:** Born Oct 4, 1972, Dallas, TX. **Educ:** Texas Christian. **Career:** Miami Heat, forward, 1995-96; Dallas Mavericks, 1996-. **Special Achievements:** NBA, First Round Draft Pick, #10 Pick, 1995. **Business Addr:** Professional Basketball Player, Dallas Mavericks, Reunion Arena, 777 Sports St, Dallas, TX 75207, (214)748-1808.

THOMAS, LAMAR NATHANIEL
Professional football player. **Personal:** Born Feb 12, 1970, Ocala, FL; children: Chandler. **Educ:** Miami (FL). **Career:** Tampa Bay Buccaneers, wide receiver, 1993-95; Miami Dolphins, 1996-. **Business Addr:** Professional Football Player, Miami Dolphins, 2269 NW 199th St, Miami, FL 33056, (305)620-5000.

THOMAS, LATTA R., SR.
Educator, clergyman. **Personal:** Born Oct 12, 1927, Union, SC; son of Alsie Creshaw Thomas (deceased) and Pickett R Thomas (deceased); married Bessie Lowery Thomas; children: Latta, Jr, Ronald. **Educ:** Friendship Jr College, AA, 1949; Benedict College, AB, 1951; Colgate Rochester Divinity School, BD, 1955; Andover Newton Seminary, STM, 1966, DMin, 1973. **Career:** Monumental Baptist Church, pastor, 1952-63; Mt Olive Baptist Church, pastor, 1963-65; Benedict College, chaplain, 1965-85, acting dean, Student Affairs, 1974-75, professor, Dept of Religion and Philosophy, 1965-95; Second Calvary Baptist Church, pastor, 1975-96; Morris College, professor of Religion, currently. **Orgs:** SC Academy of Religion; NAACP; SC Council on the Holocaust, 1990-96; American Assn of University Professors, 1970-95; Kappa Alpha Psi; pres, Elmira Branch, NAACP, 1957-62; faculty rep, bd of trustees, Benedict College, 1973-75; exec bd, Friendship Center, 1978-82; Richland-Lexington Council on Aging, 1980-84; Clinical Pastoral Educ Advisory Council, 1984-90; Kiwanis; SC Democratic Party; executive board, Greater Columbia Community Relations Council; Martin Luther King Jr Memorial Foundation Inc, 1984-96; Fighting Back Anti-Drug Abuse Council, 1990-96. **Honors/Awds:** Cited for civic serv by Elmira Civic Improvement Club 1960; Elmira Neighborhood House 1961; Elmira Br NAACP 1972; publication ''Biblical Faith and the Black American,'' Judson Press 1976; Author the Biblical God and Human Suffering, David C Cook, 1987. **Business Addr:** Professor of Religion, Division of Religion & Humanitus, Morris College, 100 W College St, Sumter, SC 29150.

THOMAS, LILLIE (MICKEY)
Radiology technologist. **Personal:** Born Oct 20, 1950, St Louis, MO. **Educ:** Forest Park Comm Coll, AAS 1970. **Career:** Peralta Hosp, spec procedure tech 1975-79; MO Baptist Hospital, rad tech 1970-74, spec procedure tech 1979-. **Orgs:** Mem Amer Registry Radiological Tech 1970-, Amer Soc Radiological Tech 1970-; mem Bd of Christian Educ 1982-; asst financial sec bd of trustees 1986-, youth dir New Sunny Mount Bapt Ch 1986-. **Home Addr:** 22 St Gabriel Ct, St Louis, MO 63114.

THOMAS, LINDA
Company executive. **Educ:** Kent State Univ, bachelor's degree in business admin. **Career:** Taco Bell Express, general mgr of northeast zone, currently. **Special Achievements:** First African American to be named general manager of the northeast zone. **Business Addr:** General Manager, Northeast Zone, Taco Bell Express, 11 Ves Dr, Ste 170, Marlton, NJ 08053.

THOMAS, LIZ A.
Legislative assistant. **Personal:** Born Apr 13, 1946, Portland, OR; daughter of Mildred E Squires Reynolds and Walter C Reynolds; married David A Thomas (divorced 1982); children: Ife-Airegin V E. **Educ:** Mills College, Oakland, CA, BA, sociology/anthropology, 1968; University of California at Berkeley, MSW, 1970; University of Washington, Seattle, WA, health and social behavior, 1975, quantitative methods, 1979. **Career:** Emanuel Hospital, Portland, OR, emergency medical staff, 1964-66; The Community Action Program, Portland, OR, community assistant, 1966; Health Testing Services, Berkeley, CA, medical intake, 1967; People Pledged for Community Progress, Richmond, CA, planner/evaluator, 1968-69; National Committee Against Discrimination in Housing, San Francisco, CA, research assistant/coordinator, 1969; Berkeley Unified School District, Berkeley, CA, program assistant, 1969-70; College of San Mateo, CA, academic counselor, 1970-73, instructor in writing and research skills, 1970-73; University of Washington, Seattle, WA, assistant director of career planning and placement office, 1973-85; Better Prepared, career consultant, 1984-;King County Councilman Ron Sims, Seattle, WA, legislative assistant, 1985. **Orgs:** Vice president, Seattle Chapter, LINKS, 1989-91; vice president, board of directors, International Resource Center, 1989-91; vice president, 1989-91, co-chair, 1990-91, Long Range Planning Committee, Seattle Children's Theatre; Nominating Committee, Seattle/King County Campfire Council. **Honors/Awds:** Commissioner at Large, The Goodwill Games, 1988-90; Leadership America, The Foundation for Women's Resources, 1989; Participant, The ALKI Foundation (Political Involvement Institute), 1988; Leadership Tomorrow, 1985; Finalist, Fellowship in Cable Management, The Walter Kaitz Foundation, 1985; guest speaker, lecturer, and presenter. **Business Addr:** Legislative Assistant, King County Councilman Ron Sims, 402 King County Courthouse, Seattle, WA 98104.

THOMAS, LLOYD A.
Pediatrician, educator. **Personal:** Born Nov 3, 1922, New York, NY; son of Ethel Thomas and Lionel Thomas; married Mary Elaine Haley; children: Fern Leigh, Guy Roger, Tobi Thomas Nava. **Educ:** City Coll of NY, BS 1943; Howard Univ Med Schl, MD 1946. **Career:** State Univ of NY, clinical asst 1955-; Downstate Medcl Cntr, clinical assistant professor of pediatrics 1955-; private practice, physician, currently. **Orgs:** Consltnt Head Start 1960-65; pres Ped Sec Med Soc of Mc County of Kings 1974-75; aux brd Brooklyn Urban League 1954-57; brd chrmn W Hardgnow Mental Health Clinic 1960-70; brd Bedford Stuyvesant Comm MH Ctr. **Honors/Awds:** Kappa Pi Hon Soc Howard Univ Med Schl 1945; Black Brooklynite The New Muse 1978. **Military Serv:** AUS capt med corps 2 yrs; chief of Ped Camp Stoneman, CA 1951-53. **Business Addr:** Physician, 825 Lincoln Pl, Brooklyn, NY 11216.

THOMAS, LOUPHENIA
Business executive, educator. **Personal:** Born Jan 19, 1918, Coaso Co, AL; daughter of Addie Sims and Richard Sims; widowed; children: Dr Juanita Thomas Whatley. **Educ:** Miles Coll Birmingham, AL, AB Soc Sci w/minor in Engl; Univ of AL in Birmingham, MA Voc Educ. **Career:** Beauty Salon & Restaurant, business owner 1950-76; Lawson Comm Coll, instructor 1970-80; LSCC, tech dir chairperson 1980-84 retired. **Orgs:** Mem Kappa Delta Pi; mem AL Educ Assn; mem Natl Educ Assn; mem Lawson State Educ Assn; mem AL Voc Assn; mem Bus & Prof Women Birmingham Chapt;mem Birmingham Urban League; mem NAACP; past coord Affairs of the AL Democratic Conf; pres emeritus Women Activities Comm of the Progressive Democratic Council of Jefferson Co; mem Amer Assoc of Univ Women; mem Nat'l Woman's Political Caucus. **Honors/Awds:** Outstanding Achievement in Politics Omega Psi Phi Frat 1972; Woman of the Year Natl Bus & Prof Women 1973; Women of Distinction Iota Phi Lambda Sor 1976; Distinguished Serv Awd Delta Sigma Theta Sor 1976; Ms Democrat Loyalty & Dedication to the Democratic Party Jefferson Co Democratic Women Club 1976; Outstanding Achievement in Politics Awd Jefferson Co Progressive Democratic Council of Jefferson Co; Meritorious Serv Awd Metro Democratic Women's Club 1977; Hon Mem Gov's Staff State of AL 1976; Historic Achievement Awd in Recognition of Leadership & Representation of Black Women in Amer AL Black Mayors Conf 1978;first Black elected to the Natl Democratic Comm in the history of the Party from the State of AL; first Black Woman elected to the House ofRepresentatives in the history of the te of AL Legislative Dist 39 Jefferson Co. **Home Addr:** 2736 Bush Blvd, Birmingham, AL 35208.

THOMAS, LUCIA THEODOSIA
Judge (retired). **Personal:** Born Mar 10, 1917, Cheyenne, WY. **Educ:** Xavier Univ, BA 1936; Terrell Law Sch, LLB 1940; John Marshall Law Sch, LLM 1942, MPL 1943, JD 1970. **Career:** George A Parker, assoc atty 1940-41; Richard E Westbrooks, 1941-42; Prescott, Burroughs, Taylor & Corey, 1942-43; investigator atty 1943-47; Ben H Crockett, 1948-56; Soc Sec Admin, claims exam 1956-57; Cook Co, asst state's atty 1957-61,65-69; Juv Ct, asst to judge 1969-73; Appt Ct, law clerk 1973-74; City of Chicago, asst corp council 1974-77; Circuit Ct Cook County IL, judge 1977-87. **Orgs:** Mem, ABA, CBA, CCBA, FBA, WBAI, NBA, NAWL; IBA-FIDA; Cath Lawyers Guild; Amer Judicature Soc; life mem NAACP; Natl Bar Assc; Delta Sigma Theta Sor; mem Chicago Urban League; Field Mus; Art Inst of Chgo; DuSable Mus; Beatrice Coffrey Yth Srv; King Comm Srv Ctr. **Honors/Awds:** Richard Westbrooks Awd Cook Co Bar Assoc 1969; Silver Medal of Merit Natl Order of Knights & Ladies 1971; Merit Award Chicago Alumnae Chap Delta Sigma Theta, Pres Citation Cook & City Bar Assc 1979; Extra Mile Award Delta Sigma Theta Sor 1980; Judicial Award We Can Found Inc 1980; John Marshall Alumni Awd 1982-84; Judicial Council Awd 1984; Gold Medal Knights & Ladies of Peter Claver 1984; Chicago Sr Citizens Hall of Fame; NBA Hall of Fame; Meritorious Serv Awd Knights & Ladies of Peter Claver; Meritorious Awd 4th Degree Odel Stadeker Chap KSPC Ladies Aux; Augustine Tolton Awd 1st Black Catholic Woman of the Year.

THOMAS, LUCILLE COLE
Educator. **Personal:** Born Oct 1, 1921, Dunn, NC; daughter of Minnie Lee Cole and Collie Cole; married George Browne (deceased); children: Ronald C, Beverly G Thomas. **Educ:** Columbia Univ Schl of Lib Serv, MS 1957; NY Univ, MA 1955; Bennett Coll, BA 1941. **Career:** Bibb County Bd of Educ, teacher 1947-55; Brooklyn Public Library, librarian 1955-56; NY City Public School, librarian 1956-68; NY City Bd of Educ, supvr of Library 1968-77; NY City Bd of Educ, dir elementary school library 1978-83; Weston Woods Inst, consultant 1983-86; New York City Board Of Examiners, examination specialist, 1985-90; Graduate School of Library and Info Studies Queens Coll CUNY, visiting prof 1987-90. **Orgs:** NYS Regents Advsry Cncl on Lrng Technologies 1982-89; Amer Libr Assn, exec bd, 1985-91, cncl, 1980-91, international relations committee; coordinator UNESCO/IASL Book Prog 1980-89; pres NY (state) Libr Asssn 1977-78; pres NY Libr Club 1977-78; pres NY Black Librns Caucus 1974-75; pres Columbia Univ Schl of Libr Serv Alumni Assn 1980-81; chair, 1988-93, sec, 1985-, Sch Libraries Sect of Intl Federation of Library Associations; Schomburg Corp and Schomburg Commn for the Preservation of Black Culture; Centennial Comm for Columbia Univ Sch of Library Svcs; bd of dirs, American Reading Council, 1976-89; pres, Intl Assn of School Librarianship, 1989-95; vice pres, 1992; chair, education comm, Women's City Club, 1989-92; parliamentarian, Pi Phi Omega Chapter, Alpha Kappa Alpha Sorority, 1991-94, fir vice pres; Pres, Pi Phi Omega Chapter, Alpha Kappa Alpha Sorority, 1992-94, pres, 1994-; St Johns Episcopal Church of Brooklyn, Stewardship Committee, chairman, usher, vestry member, 1986-88; New York State Education Committee, English language arts assessment committee; American Association of Schools Librarians, international relations committee; International Federation of Library Associations, representative to United Nations and UNICEF; Brooklyn Public Library, trustee, appointed by New York City mayor, 1993-, scy to bd of trustees, 1997-; dir, US Board on Books for Young People, 1995; co-coord of Cluster III in AKA Sorority, North Atlantic Region; chair, Legislative Committee of Trustees Divsion of ALA, 1994; vice pres, Region II Trustees Division of ALA, 1993-94; honorary chair, Twenty-First Century Fund, Women's City Club of NY, 1996-97; ALA Legislation Assembly, 1995-; vice chair, Natl Alumnae Leadership Committee, Bennett Coll Capital Compaign. **Honors/Awds:** Fndr Schl Libr Media Day in NY State 1974; fndr Annual City-Wide Storytelling Cont New York City Bd of Ed 1978; recp Medal of Excellence by NY State Brd of Regentss 1984; participant/cultural Exchg Prog (Guest of French Govt for 2 wks) 1982; Programs of Service Awd by Eta Omega Omega Chap Alpha Kappa Alpha Sor; Grolier Award, American Library Assn, 1988; ALA, Black Caucus, Service Award, 1992; AASL, Distinguished Service Award, 1994; ALA, Humphrey Award, 1995; Trail Blazers Award, ALA Black Caucus, 1995; Silver Award US National Commission for Library & Information Science, 1996; Awarded Honorary Doctorate by Bennett College, 1996. **Home Addr:** 1184 Union St, Brooklyn, NY 11225.

THOMAS, LYDIA WATERS
Business executive. **Personal:** Born Oct 13, 1944, Norfolk, VA; daughter of Lillie Ruth Roberts Waters and William Emerson Waters; married James Carter Thomas (divorced 1970); children: Denee Marrielle Thomas. **Educ:** Howard University, Washington, DC, BS, zoology, 1965; American University, Washington, DC, MS, microbiology, 1971; Howard University, Washington, DC, PhD, cytology, 1973. **Career:** American University, Washington, DC, graduate teaching assistant, 1969-71; Howard University, Washington, DC, graduate teaching assistant, 1971-73; Mitrelek Systems, McLean, VA, vice pres, 1973-96, president/CEO, currently. **Orgs:** Past member, Environmental Advisory Board, US Corp of Engrs; past chairman, Chemicals Regulation Sub-Group of the USEA; appointee to the Strategic Environmental Research & Devt Scientific Advisory Bd; American Association for the Advancement of Science; American Society of Toxicology; American Defense Preparedness Association; American Management Association; George Washington University Industrial Advisory Board; advisory bd, INFORM, NYC; Sigma Xi Steering Committee; National Energy Resources Organization; Society of Macro Engineering; United States Energy Association; Superintendent's Business/Industry Advisory Council for Fairfax County Public Schools; American Inst of Aeronautics and Astronautics. **Honors/Awds:** TWIN (Tribute to Women in the Intl Industry), YWCA, 1986; EBONE Image Award (public service), Coalition of 100 Black Women, Northern, VA, 1990; Deans' Award, Black Engineer of the Year Award, 1991. **Business Addr:** President/CEO, Mitrelek Systems, 7525 Colshire Dr, Mc Lean, VA 22102.

THOMAS, MABLE
State representative. **Personal:** Born Nov 8, 1957, Atlanta, GA; daughter of Madie Broughton Thomas and Bernard Thomas. **Educ:** GA State Univ, BS Public Admin 1982, working on Masters in Public Admin; Atlanta School of Real Estate, Atlanta GA, Salesperson License, 1987. **Career:** GA Dept of Natural Resources, personnel asst 1978-79; City of Atlanta Parks & Recreation, recreation super 1980-81; GA State Univ Educ Talent Srch, rsch asst 1981-82; City of Atlanta Comm Develop, worksite monitor 1983; Univ of Black Life & Culture Comm, chairperson GA State 1982-83; GA Gen Assembly, senate intern 1984; Dist 31, state representative, currently, serves on house, educ, special judiciary & indust relations standing committees, served on State of GA housing needs study comm. **Orgs:** Vice pres GA State Univ Student Govt Assn 1983, 1984; consultant GA Democratic Party 1984; adv council Salvation Army Bellwood Boys & Girls Club 1984, 1985; bd of dirs GA Legislative Black Caucus 1985; membership chair Black Women's Health Project 1985; Hon mem chair NAACP Annual Membership Drive 1985; vol worker S Christian Leadership Conf 1981-; vol Martin Luther King Ctr for Nonviolent Social Change 1981-; vol United Way of Metro Atlanta 1982-; natl bd mem Natl Political Congr of Black Women 1985; bd mem West End Medical Ctr; bd of dirs Economic Opportunities Atlanta; bd mem, Georgia Housing Coalition, 1988-89. **Honors/Awds:** GA State Univ Mortar Bd Leadership Awd 1982; Salvation Army Bellwood Girls Club Comm Serv Awd 1983; GA State Univ Women of Excellence Awd 1983; Top Jesse Jackson Delegate to the Democratic Natl Convention 1984; City of Atlanta Cultural Affairs Bronze Jubilee Awd 1984; Royal Ark Worshipful Masters Legion of Honor Awd for Social Justice 1985; Ebony Magazine 30 Leaders of the Future 1985; Outstanding Serv Award Tony Garden Civic Assn 1985; NAACP Civic Award 1985; featured in Essence magazine August 1986 as Essence Women; Natl Assn of Black Social Workers Human Serv Awd 1986; Outstanding Freshman Legislator GA Legislative Black Caucus 1986; featured in December 1986 Washington Post "New Black Women-Mold Breakers in the MainStream"; voted one of 20 Atlantans to Watch in 1987 by Atlanta Trib newspaper; featured, Essence Magazine Profile, 1988; front page coverage Fast Forward Magazine, 1989; featured, India's national newspaper, India Times, 1988; Outstanding Georgia State University Alumni, GA State Univ, 1989.

THOMAS, MARLA RENEE
Heathcare company executive. **Personal:** Born Apr 21, 1956, Weisbaden, Germany; daughter of Laura Pedro Thomas and Carol Monroe Thomas; married Keith Gregory Barnes, Jun 4, 1988; children: Lindsay Carol Barnes, Laura Janice Barnes. **Educ:** Wellesley College, BA, 1978; Harvard Business School, MBA, 1982. **Career:** Morgan Stanley, analyst, 1978-80; Drexel Burnham, first vice pres, 1982-90; American Shared Hospital Services, president, chief executive officer, 1990-. **Home Addr:** 2041 Sacramento St, San Francisco, CA 94109. **Business Phone:** (415)788-5380.

THOMAS, MARVETTE JERALDINE
Educational administrator. **Personal:** Born Jan 27, 1953, Montgomery, AL; daughter of Bernice Morgan Thomas (deceased) and Robert Marvin Thomas (deceased); married Allen H. Jackson; children: Janel Bernice Cobb. **Educ:** Austin Peay State Univ, BS 1977; Murray State Univ, MS 1980; George Peabody Coll of Vanderbilt Univ, EdD 1984. **Career:** Northwest HS, spec ed teacher, chair spec ed spec needs counselor 1979-83; Vanderbilt Univ, teaching, grad asst 1981; Women in Nontraditional Careers WINC, dir proj 1986-; LA State Univ Eunice, counselor 1984, acting dir spec serv & devel ed, dir spec serv 1985-89, dir Academic Assistance Programs 1989-; AA/EEO, 1990. **Orgs:** Mem Natl Assn of Univ Women, Amer Assn of Counseling & Devel, Natl Council of Negro Women, Amer Coll Personnel Assn, LA Assn for Devel Ed, Southwest Assn of Student Asst Prog, Socialite Soc & Civic Club; sec Opelousas Alumnae Chap Delta Sigma Theta Inc; past pres Clarksville TN Alumnae Chapt Delta Sigma Theta; bd dir Eunice C of C; mem bd of dir Bayou Girl Scout Council 1987-; mem bd of dir Moosa Memorial Hospital 1988-; pres LA Assn of Student Assistance Programs 1988-89; mem bd of dir Southwest Assn of Student Assistance Programs 1988-90; pres-elect LA Assn of Student Assistance Programs 1989-90; pres, Opelousas Alumnae Chapter, Delta Sigma Theta, 1990-; pres, Socialite Club of Eunice, 1989-. **Honors/Awds:** Inductee Phi Delta Kappa 1979; Natl Cert Counselor 1983; Chi Sigma Iota 1985; Outstanding Woman of Eunice, The Eunice News 1987; mem President's Council Natl Council of Educ Opportunity Assn 1988. **Business Addr:** Dir, Academic Assistance Programs, Louisiana State Univ, PO Box 1129, Eunice, LA 70535.

THOMAS, MARY A.
Nurse, educator (retired). **Personal:** Born Jul 22, 1933, Gary, IN. **Educ:** Homer G Phillips Hosp Sch Nursing St Louis 1956; IN Univ, BS 1968; Valparaiso Univ, MLA Sociol; Univ IL Med Ctr, attd. **Career:** Cook Hospital Chicago, head nurse Obstetric 1957-63; Chicago Osteop Hospital Chicago, head nurse Med Unit 1963-64; Visiting Nurse Assoc E Chicago IN, staff nurse 1964-68; Gary IN, school nurse 1968-71; Gary Health Dept, asst dir nurses 1972-74; Gary Health Dept, dir nurses 1974-95; Purdue Univ Calumet Hammond IN, asst prof nursing, until 1995. **Orgs:** Consult Sr Cit Prog Gary IN 1972-; cnslr Sickle Anemia Proj 1975; schrlshp chmn Midtown Reg Nurses Club 1971-; alumni IN Univ & Valparaiso Univ; bd mem Fed Credit Union St Monica Ch 1973; parish council mem 1974.

THOMAS, MARY MAXWELL
Circuit court judge. **Personal:** Born Mar 18, 1943, Waukegan, IL; daughter of Isaiah Williams Jr and Mary Etta Jordan; married James A Cooper, Nov 21, 1987; children: Stacy L Thomas-Mosley, Owen L II. **Educ:** Michigan State Univ, 1961-63; New Mexico State Univ, BA, 1966; Univ of Chicago Law School, JD, 1973; Univ of Nevada-Reno, master of judicial studies, 1996. **Career:** US Navy, computer programmer, 1967-70; Chicago Title Ins Co, atty title examiner, 1973-74; City of Evanston, Il, asst city atty, 1974-77; US Attorney's Office, asst us atty, 1977-87; Sulzer and Shapiro, Ltd, partner, 1987; Circuit Court of Cook County, judge, 1987-. **Orgs:** Illinois Judicial Council, chairperson, law related activities and scholarship; past chairperson, sec, board, 1987-; Cook County Bar Assn, former board member, 1983-; National Bar Assn, 1983; Women's Bar Assn of IL, 1987-; Natl Judicial Council, 1987-; Alpha Kappa Alpha Sorority, silver star member, 1962-; NAACP, life member, 1993-. **Honors/Awds:** Natl Council of Negro Women, Pacesetter Award, 1994; Black Women Lawyer's of Chicago, Honoree, 1991; Kentucky Colonel from Commonwealth of KY, 1994; Ebony Man Magazine, Woman of Distinction for 1992, 1992; Illinois Judicial Council, Chairperson's Award and Meritorious Svc, 1992-94; elected to Phi Kappa Phi Honor Society, 1996. **Business Addr:** Judge, Circuit of Cook Cnty Illinois, 2600 S California, Courtroom 604, Chicago, IL 60608, (773)869-3183.

THOMAS, MATTHEW MANJUSRI, JR.
Artist, educator. **Personal:** Born Jun 12, 1943, San Antonio, TX; son of Matthew & Ella Thomas; married Bee Thomas, May 9, 1990; children: Illah, Hashim. **Educ:** San Fernando Valley Coll, Van Nuys, CA, 1961-63; Honolulu Academy of Arts, Honolulu, HI, 1963-64; Chouinard School of Fine Arts, Los Angeles, CA, 1965-67. **Career:** Visual artist, self employed, 1975-. **Honors/Awds:** Helen Londeberg L Feitelson, Art Fellowship Fund, CA Arts Council Grant, (Five Time Recipient), 1982-87; Artist in Residence, Temecula CA; Artist in Residence, Pyong, TAEK Intl, Korea; Artist in Residence, Tacikawa Intl, Japan. **Special Achievements:** First African American in art collection of the Natl Museum of Contemporary Arts, Korea; First African American in the art collection of Taiwan Museum of Art; had works of art exhibited in Spain, India, New Delhi, Korea, Japan, Taiwan, USA. **Home Addr:** 1704 S Pacific Ave, No 17, San Pedro, CA 90731-4761. **Business Phone:** (310)829-3300.

THOMAS, MAURICE MCKENZIE
Librarian. **Personal:** Born May 1, 1943, St Croix, Virgin Islands of the United States; son of Florence Bovell and Maurice Thomas; married Monica Primas; children: Charles Randall, Onika Michelle. **Educ:** Long Island Univ, BA History 1973; Atlanta Univ, 1982; Ball State Univ, MLS Libr & Info Sci 1983. **Career:** Abraham & Strauss NY, sales person 1969-73; Dept of Ed of The VI, social studies teacher 1973-82, librarian/information spec; coordinator of social studies Dept of Educ of the V.I. 1987-. **Orgs:** Mem Courtyard Players Comm Theatre 1973-, Friends of Petersen Public Libr 1983-, School Libr Assoc 1983-, Amer Libr Assoc 1983-; bd mem Theatre DanceInc 1983-84; Phi Delta Kappa. **Honors/Awds:** Libr Career Fellowship US Dept of Ed & Ball State 1982-83; Territorial Scholarship VI Govt 1982-83; joint author, Virgin Islands and Caribbean Communities. **Military Serv:** AUS corpl sp4 1962-65. **Home Addr:** PO Box 7475 Sunny Isle, Christiansted, St Croix, Virgin Islands of the United States 00820. **Business Addr:** Coordinator of Social Studies, Dept of Educ of the Virgin Islands, PO Box I, Christiansted, St Croix, Virgin Islands of the United States 00820.

THOMAS, MAXINE F. See Obituaries section.

THOMAS, MAXINE SUZANNE
Educator. **Personal:** Born Jan 23, 1948, Junction City, KS; daughter of Morris Daniels; married Larry Thomas; children: Lauryn, Noel. **Educ:** Univ of WA, BA 1970, JD 1973. **Career:** Univ of OR Schl of Law, asst prof 1976-89; Univ of OR, asst dean 1976-79; WA, asst atty gen 1973-76; assoc dean and assoc prof Univ of Georgia 1989-. **Orgs:** Mem Natl Assc of Clge & Univ Attys 1974-76; standing com on environmental law Amer Bar Assc 1979-; honorary mem Phi Delta Phi 1977-; mem OR Amer Counc on Educ Com to Promote Women to Higher Educ Admin 1978-. **Honors/Awds:** Nominated OR Outst Young Women 1978, Kellogg Natl Fellow 1985-1988, Fulbright lecturer 1988. **Business Addr:** University of Georgia School of Law, Athens, GA 30602.

THOMAS, MITCHELL, JR.
Human resources executive. **Personal:** Born Oct 19, 1952, Daytona Beach, FL; son of Dorothy Thomas Gilley and Mitchell Thomas Sr; married Orlando Pierce Thomas, Mar 2, 1981; children: Mitchell Thomas III. **Educ:** Morris Brown College, Atlanta, GA, BS, hotel & restaurant management, 1974. **Career:** ARA Services, Philadelphia, PA, assistant manager food & bev, 1974-76; Walt Disney World Co, Lake Buena Vista, FL, sr prof staffing rep, 1976-95, mgr of diversity recruiting, 1995-. **Orgs:** Member, Historically & Predominantly Black College & University Hospitality Management Consortium, 1987-91; advisor board, Grambling State University, 1988-91; advisor board, Bethune Cookman College, 1989-91; Orlando Fights Back Drug Rehabilitation & Crime Prevention, 1991-; Greater Orlando Urban League; Orange County Compact, Prevention of High School Dropouts, 1991-. **Business Addr:** Mgr, Diversity Recruiting, Walt Disney World Co, 1515 Buena Vista Dr, Casting Center, Professional Staffing, Suite 220, Lake Buena Vista, FL 32830.

THOMAS, MONICA MARIA PRIMUS
Educator. **Personal:** Born May 3, 1954, San Fernando, Trinidad and Tobago; daughter of Christine Primus Constable; married Maurice McKenzie Thomas, May 7, 1977; children: Charles Randall, Onika Michell. **Educ:** University of the Virgin Islands, St Croix, 1984; St Augustine's College, Raleigh, NC, BS, magna cum laude, early childhood, 1989. **Career:** Emma Conn Gifted and Talented School, Raleigh, NC, teacher, 1988-89; Claude O Markoe Elementary School, Frederiksted, St Croix, Virgin Islands, second grade teacher, 1989-90; Elena Christian Jr High, Christiansted, St Croix, Virgin Islands, resource teacher, 1990-. **Orgs:** Member, Alpha Kappa Alpha Sorority, 1988-; member, Kappa Delta Pi Honor Society, 1988-; member, dancer, Street Theatre Inc, 1986-. **Home Addr:** PO Box 7475, Sunny Isle, Christiansted, St Croix, Virgin Islands of the United States 00823.

THOMAS, N. CHARLES
Clergyman, administrator. **Personal:** Born Jun 24, 1929, Jonesboro, AR; son of Linnie and Willie James; married Mary Elizabeth. **Educ:** MS Indsl Clge, BA 1951; Lincoln Univ Theol Sem, BD 1954; Lancaster Theol Sem, MDiv 1974. **Career:** CME Chs Waterford MS, pastor 1949-51; Roanoke VA, 1954; Wrightsville AR, 1954-57; Hot Springs AR, 1957-60; Little Rock AR, 1960-62; Memphis TN, 1966-67; CME Church, general secretary; pastor, Greenwood CME Church, 1980-81; pastor, Featherstone Temple, 1994. **Orgs:** Dir of Christian educ 1st Dist CME Ch 1958-74, admin asst to presiding bishop 1954-74; admin Ministerial Salary Supplement Prog CME Ch Gen Bd of Pensions CME Ch 1974-; sec Gen Conf CME Ch 1970-; presiding elder S Memphis Dist 1971-74; Mem Gen Bd of Christian Educ CME Ch 1958-; sec Gen Correctional Bd CME Ch 1971-; mem bd trustees Smith-Keys Housing Project Texarkana AR 1969-; bd dir Haygood-Neal Housing Project Eldorado AR 1970-; bd dir E Gate Vlge Union City TN 1970-; bd trustees Collins Chapel Hosp Memphis TN 1974-; bd dir Memphis OIC 1972-; mem CME Ministers Alliance Memphis; Interdenom Ministers Alliance Memphis; gen sec Gen Bd of Personnel Srv 1978; board member, Metropolitan Interfaith Association, 1989-; member, Shelby County Interfaith Association, 1990-; exec dir, New Day Cooperative, 1992. **Honors/Awds:** Dr of Humanities TX Clge Tyler 1980; Golden Heritage Member, NAACP. **Business Addr:** General Secretary, CME Church, 531 S Parkway East, Memphis, TN 38101.

THOMAS, NATHANIEL (NATE)
Film producer, director. **Personal:** Born May 22, 1957, Warren, OH; son of Rose Thomas and Ace Thomas (deceased). **Educ:** St Edward's Univ, BA Theatre Arts 1979; Univ of TX at Austin, grad study in film 1979-80; Univ of S CA, MFA Cinema Prod 1984. **Career:** Actor in TV commercials for Coca-Cola & New York Life Insurance, 1978; actor in stage productions of ''The Petrified Forest'' w/Greg Morris & ''Room Service'' w/ Godfrey Cambridge, 1975; producer of award-winning PBS film ''The Last of the One Night Stands,'' 1982-83; Walt Disney Productions/The Disney Channel, asst to production exec, 1984; dir/producer of ''The Zone,'' anti-alcohol public service announcement geared for black women, 1987; dir/producer of ''Under the Rainbow: Jesse Jackson '88 for President,'' 1988; dir/producer of featurette for Universal Picture's ''Ghost Dad'' starring Bill Cosby, 1989; dir/producer of various 35 mm television commercials, music videos, etc, 1987-; California State Univ, Northridge, film professor, 1989-;line producer for ''Itchin' In My Heart,'' music video for ''The Good Girls''; dir/producer, commercials for Main Place Mall, Valencia Town Center, Fox Hills Mall, Glendale Galleria, 1988-92; writer, dir, producer feature film ''East of Hope St,'' 1996; Nate Thomas and Associates, film producer, currently. **Orgs:** mem Screen Actors Guild 1979-; mem AFTRA 1979-. **Honors/Awds:** Spec Youth Citation Urban League 1975; Scholarship Morning Star Grand Chap Order of Eastern Star 1976; Student Activities Awd of Excellence St Edward's Univ Austin TX 1978-79; Dean's List St Edwards Univ 1977-79; nominee Man of Yr St Edward's Univ 1979; pres Jr Class St Edward's Univ Austin 1977-78; The Natl Dean's List 1979; Scholarship USC Ebonics Support Group 1981; USC Cinema Fellowship from Warner Brothers 1982; USC Tommy Awd for Outstanding Achiev in Cinema TV 1984; Cine Golden Eagle & Honors at San Francisco Intl Film Festival for PBS film ''The Last of the One Night Stands'' 1984; Awd Black Amer Cinema Soc for PBS film ''The Last of the One Night Stands''; Sony Innovator Award, Sony Corporation, 1991; Honorable Mention for PBS film ''The Last of the One Night Stands,'' Wellington Film Festival, New Zealand, 1984; recognition/resolution from Warren, Ohio City Council, 1992; inducted into Trumbull County Afro-American Hall of Fame, Warren Ohio, 1992; Outstanding Teaching Award, California State Univ, Northridge, 1993; Inducted Warren High Schools, Distinguished Alumni Hall of Fame, Warren, Ohio, 1994. **Business Addr:** California State University, Northridge Dept of Radio-TV-Film, 18111 Nordhoff St, Northridge, CA 91330-8317.

THOMAS, NIDA E.
Assistant deputy commissioner (retired). **Personal:** Born Jun 19, 1914, Goldsboro, NC; widowed; children: Lutrica, Rosemary. **Educ:** NY Univ Sch of Educ, BS 1942; Atlanta Univ Sch of Social Work, MSW 1944; Cntr for Human Relations Studies NY Univ, adv study. **Career:** EEO State of NJ Dept of Educ, asst deputy commr, until 1994. **Orgs:** Chief Bur of Educ Integration NY State Dept of Educ; exec dir Urban League of Bergen Co Englewood NJ; comm org secr Union Co Urban League Elizabeth NJ; mem Natl Assc of Intergroup Rel Ofcls; Delta Kappa Gamma Soc; Alpha Kappa Alpha Sor; Mem bd dir YWCA Elizabeth NJ; bd of Theol Educ; mem at large Reformed Ch in Amer; Assc of Theol Schs US & Can; bd dir Occupational Ctr Union Co; Union Co Urban League; Union Co Urban League Guild; Natl Council of Negro Women. **Honors/Awds:** Distg Srv Award Urban League Union Co 1979; recip The Arch Award Student Council of NY Univ; outst ldrshp serv in student activities; portrait includedin UN Disting Cits Gallery Garden State Plaza; Outst Cits in Bergen Co; citation Empire State Fed Women's Club Outst Contrib & Ldrshp in comm & state; cert of appreciation NE Region NY State Conf, NAACP; Earnest O Melby Award Human Rel NY Univ Sch of Educ Alumni Assc 1971; Outst Educator AwardAcad of Amer Educators 1973-74; others.

THOMAS, NINA M.
Law enforcement. **Personal:** Born Jul 29, Bridgeport, CT; daughter of Eleanor McGarah Thomas and Livingston Thomas. **Educ:** Univ of Connecticut, Storrs CT, 1975-78; Univ of New Haven, New Haven CT; Housatonic Comm Coll, Bridgeport, CT 1997; Criminal Justice Command Inst, Farmington, Conn; Tunix Com-Tech Coll, 1997; Charter Oak State Coll, 1997; Teikyo Post Univ, 1998. **Career:** Mechanics & Farmers Savings Bank, Bridgeport CT, mortgage rep, 1978-83; Bridgeport Police Dept, Bridgeport CT, police officer, 1983-. **Orgs:** Mem, National Black Police Assn; mem, Bridgeport Guardians Inc; First Baptist of Stratford, Conn; Natl Organization of Black Women's Political Congress; Natl Organization of Women in Policing; Phi Theta Kappa; Waterbury Democratic Club; volunteer, 1996 Olympics. **Home Addr:** 72 Hamden Ave, Waterbury, CT 06704. **Business Phone:** (203)576-7671.

THOMAS, OLIVIA SMITH
Advertising account executive. **Personal:** Born Sep 20, 1956, Brookhaven, MS; daughter of Eunice Trass Smith and Charlie James Smith; married Louis Anderson Thomas, Jun 7, 1980; children: Jonathan, Sara. **Educ:** Jackson State University, Jackson, MS, BS, mass communication, 1978; Ohio State University, Columbus, OH, MA, journalism, 1980. **Career:** Tougalou College, Director Journalism Program, Tougalou, MS, 1979-82; Jackson State Univ, Jackson, MS, instructor, 1982-84; SMI, Memphis, TN, sales administrator, 1985-87; The Group Ad Agency; Memphis, TN, copywriter, 1987-88; Jackson State Univ, Jackson, MS, director of student publications, 1988-90; Network, Memphis, TN, account executive, 1991-. **Orgs:** Member, Women in Communications Inc, 1989-; board member, Women of achievement, 1990-; training volumteer, Memphis Urban League, 1985-87; member, Delta Sigma Theta, 1975-.

THOMAS, ORA P. (ORA P. WILLIAMS)
Accountant, historian, executive producer. **Personal:** Born Dec 24, 1935, Montgomery, AL; daughter of Delia Webb Pugh and Henry Pugh, Sr; married Benjamin Thomas, Jun 10, 1987; children: Tanja Bernadette Williams, Chandra D W Brady. **Educ:** Alabama State Univ, Montgomery AL, BA, 1985, MS, 1986, EdS, 1987. **Career:** Alabama State Univ, Montgomery AL, clerk/typist, 1964-65, data processor, 1965-77, accountant, 1977—; executive producer of BOT Productions (Ben, Ora Thomas), 1987—. **Orgs:** Mem, Amer Assn of Black Women Entrepreneurs, founder of Montgomery chapter; mem, National Assn of 100 Black Women; member, Alpha Kappa Alpha Sorority, 1978-; member, Alpha Kappa Mu Honor Society; member, Kappa Delta Phi Honor Society. **Home Addr:** 2014 Grande Ave, Montgomery, AL 36116.

THOMAS, ORLANDO
Professional football player. **Personal:** Born Oct 21, 1972, Crowley, LA; children: Elena. **Educ:** Southwestern Louisiana, attended. **Career:** Minnesota Vikings, defensive back, 1995-. **Business Addr:** Professional Football Player, Minnesota Vikings, 9520 Viking Dr, Eden Prairie, MN 55344, (612)828-6500.

THOMAS, PAMELLA D.
Medical director, physician. **Personal:** Born May 11, 1947, Westmoreland, Jamaica; daughter of Hyacinth Muir and Wellesley Johnston; married Earl A Thomas, Apr 9, 1977; children: Ramogi O, Monifa J. **Educ:** University West Indies, Jamaica, MD, 1974; University of Wisconsin, Medical College, MPH, 1990. **Career:** Brookdale Hospital, emergency room attending, 1979-83; New York City Transit, assistant medical director, 1983-89; Lockheed Aeronautical Systems Co, medical director, 1989-; Emory University, School of Public Health, assistant adjunct professor, 1991-. **Orgs:** American College of Occupational & Environmental Medicine, 1983-; American Public Health Association, 1986-; American College of Preventive Medicine, 1989-; Cobb County Medical Society, chair, public relations, 1989-95; Aerospace Medical Association, 1989-; Medical Association of Georgia, 1990-; American Medical Association, 1990-; Cancer Society, North Cobb Unit, board of directors, 1990-; Emory University, School of Public Health, faculty advisory board, 1991-, Environment and Occupational Health Division, academic advisory council, 1992. **Honors/Awds:** American Coll, Occup & Env Medicine, Fellow; Amer Coll, Preventive Medicine, Fellow. **Business Addr:** Medical Director, Lockheed Aeronautical Systems Co., 86S Cobb Dr, Zone 0454, Marietta, GA 30063, (404)494-4134.

THOMAS, PATRICK ARNOLD
Business executive. **Personal:** Born Oct 6, 1956, Columbus, OH; son of Lucille W Thomas and Benjamin Thomas; married Shirley A Henry, Nov 25, 1979; children: Michelle, Kenneth, Nicholas. **Educ:** Kent State University, BA, business administration, 1979; Nashville Technical Institute, AS, electronic engineering; ICS certificate in electrical and electronic engineering, 1980; Karras Seminar, certificate in effective negotiating skills, 1981. **Career:** Johnson & Johnson Permacel Tape Division, region representative, 1979-80; Ownes-Illinois Forest Products Division, regional representative, 1980-82; National Search Firm, senior technical recruiter, 1983-85; Engineering & Executive Search, Inc, president/owner, 1985-. **Orgs:** Kentuckiana Minority Supplier Development Council; National Association of Personnel Consultants; First International Personnel Consultants; Institute of Electrical & Electronic Engineers; Louisville Chapter, Urban League; Louisville Chapter, NAACP; Gerald Neal State senate Campaign, asst director, speakers bureau; Louisville PTA; Little League Basketball Coach Newburg Community Center, division champion, 1989, runner-up 1990, 1991. **Business Addr:** President/Owner, Engineering and Executive Search Inc, 141 N Sherrin Ave, Ste 221, Louisville, KY 40207, (502)895-3055.

THOMAS, PHILIP MICHAEL
Actor. **Personal:** Born May 26, 1949, Columbus, OH. **Educ:** Oakwood Coll, Huntsville, AL, religion and philosophy, one year; Univ of CA at Riverside; Univ CA Berkeley. **Career:** Actor. Plays include: Hair, No Place to Be Somebody (1971); films include: Sparkle (1975), Mr Ricco (1974), Book of Numbers (lead role, 1973), Wizard of Speed and Time (1988); TV appearances include: Medical Center, Police Woman, Toma, Good Times, Society's Child, Fight for Jennie (1986), False Witness (1989), Roots: The Next Generation, Miami Vice (costar, 1984-89). **Orgs:** Member, Screen Actors Guild, Actors' Equity, American Federation of Television and Radio Artists. **Honors/Awds:** Recorded Living The Book of My Life (album), Just the Way I Planned It (single, 1985); Image Award, NAACP, 1987; promoted PMT women's clothing line, beginning 1985; Hon doctor of arts degree, 1997. **Business Addr:** Actor, PO Box 611222, North Miami Beach, FL 33261.

THOMAS, PHILIP S.
Performing arts producer/administrator. **Personal:** Born May 24, 1946, Accommac, VA; children: Terrance Seegers. **Educ:** Montclair State Coll, BA Theater 1976. **Career:** Greater Paterson Arts Council, exec dir 1977-80; NJ State Council on the Arts, arts devel coor 1980-82; Newark Symphony Hall, dir of mktg 1982-84; Newark Bd of Educ, grants analyst 1984-85; Carter G Woodson Found, artistic dir 1985-92; New Jersey Performing Arts Center, director of arts education, 1992-. **Orgs:** Bd of dirs, Carter G Woodson Found 1974-; evaluator Natl Endowment for the Arts 1981-; bd of dir NJ Black Issues Convention 1984-. **Honors/Awds:** Montclair State Coll Speech & Theater Alumni Award 1975; Fellowship Natl Endowment for the Arts 1976; Freedom Fund Award Paterson NJ NAACP 1984; Scholarship-Martin Luther King Jr Community Nonviolent Training Program 1982; Duke Ellington Award in the Arts Paterson NJ 1985. **Military Serv:** AUS Spec 4 1965-67. **Business Addr:** Director, Arts Education, New Jersey Performing Arts Center, Gateway Center, Newark, NJ 07102.

THOMAS, PRISCILLA D.
County commissioner. **Personal:** Born Oct 26, 1934, Savannah, GA; daughter of Marie Edwards Baker and Henry Robinson; married Nathaniel Thomas, Sep 5, 1954; children: Deborah. **Educ:** Savannah State College, Savannah, GA, BS, 1955; Bradley University, Peoria, IL, MS, 1960; Univ of North America, St Louis, MO, PhD, 1988. **Career:** Savannah Bd of Public Education, Savannah, GA, elem teacher, 1956-67; American Broadcasting Co, Savannah, GA, producer/hostess, TV public service programming, 1976-83, principal, 1968-86; Iota Phi Lambda Sorority Div, Savannah, GA, international president, 1987-89; County Commission-Chatham, Savannah, GA, county commissioner, 1990-, vice chair, 1997-; Thomas & Associates, Savannah, GA, CEO, president, 1988-; Summer Bonanza Partnership, president, currently; State Board of Education, 11th Congressional District-Atlanta, GA, rep; Savannah Convention & Visitors Bureau, vp, marketing, 1995. **Orgs:** International president, Iota Phi Lambda Sorority Inc, 1987-89; Public Relations Director, Savannah Urban Dropout Collaborative, 1986-90; member, steering committee, National Council of Negro Women, 1989-91; local coordinator, National Assn of Counties-Health & Human Services, 1990-; national liaison member, National Legislative Network, CBC, 1987-; commissioner, Citizens Crime Commission, 1986-; Coalition of Black Meeting Planners. **Honors/Awds:** "Mrs Black Heritage," Afro American Life and History, 1976-77; "On Air Personality Pioneer," Gospel Music Awards, 1983; Producer of the Year, Gospel Music Awards, 1983; 100 Top Black Bus & Professional Woman, Dollars and Sense Magazine, 1987; Kool Achiever Finalist, Kool Achievers, 1988; Woman Against the Odds, Political Action Council (PAC), 1988; Outstanding Woman of the Year, Savannah Business & Professional Women's, Inc, 1991; WTOC-TV, Hometown Hero, 1994; Masons International, Savannah Chapter, Outstanding Citizen of the Year, 1994; MLK Day Celebration in Savannah, Parade Marshall; Dollars and Sense Magazine, Hall of Fame, 1994; Aunt Jemima Brands of the Quaker Oats Co, National Community Leader of the Year, 1996. **Home Addr:** 1727 Chester St, Savannah, GA 31415.

THOMAS, RALPH ALBERT
Banker. **Personal:** Born Aug 5, 1954, Washington, DC; son of Lucille Wade Thomas and Joseph Samuel Thomas; married Valerie Thornton Thomas, Jun 9, 1990. **Educ:** Lehigh University, Bethlehem, PA, BS, accounting, 1976, MBA, finance, 1977. **Career:** Price Waterhouse and Co, Washington, DC, intern, 1974, 1975, 1976, audit senior, 1976-80; Potomac Electric Power Co, Washington, DC, project systems accountant, 1980-82; AT&T Information Systems, Murray Hill, NJ, manager, cost and government accounting, 1982-84, manager, corporate accounting policy and research, Murray Hill, NJ, 1984-85, manager, financial analysis, large business systems, Morristown, NJ, 1985-87; Citicorp, NA, New York, NY, vice president, region audit head, 1987-. **Orgs:** Member, executive council and board of directors, 1980-, president, 1990-, National Association of Black Accountants; member, Urban Bankers Coalition, 1988-; member, American Institute of CPA's, 1983-; member, DC Institute of CPA's, 1982-; member, Lehigh University Black Alumni Association, 1983-; chairman, by-laws committee, Northern New Jersey Chapter of the National Association of Black Accountants, 1985-. **Honors/Awds:** Professional Achievement Award, National Association of Black Accountants, Northern New Jersey Chapter, 1990; Outstanding Member Award, National Association of Black Accountants, 1988; Alumni Award, Lehigh University Black Alumni Council, 1989; holds CPA from District of Columbia; guest lecturer at several colleges and universities. **Home Addr:** 21 Ireland Brook Dr, North Brunswick, NJ 08902-4762. **Business Addr:** Vice President, Corporate Capital, Citicorp, NA, 641 Lexington Ave, 5th Fl, New York, NY 10043.

THOMAS, RALPH CHARLES, III
Attorney. **Personal:** Born Apr 10, 1949, Roanoke, VA. **Educ:** US Int'l Univ, AA; Univ of CA, BA 1975; Harvard Law School, JD 1978. **Career:** Bergson, Borkland, Margolis, & Alder, attorney assoc 1978-80; George Washington Univ Nat'l Law Center, clinical law inst 1982-83; Law Offices of Ralph C Thomas, III, chief counsel 1980-85; Nat'l Assoc of Minority Contractors, exec dir 1985-92; NASA, assoc administrator, 1992-. **Orgs:** Univ of Maryland, Eastern Shore, chancellor's advisory committee on construction mgmt, 1986-92; American Council on Construction Education, bd of trustees, 1991-92; Construction Writers Assn, 1990-; Construction Business Review, editorial advisory bd, 1990-92. **Honors/Awds:** Natl Assn of Minority Contractors, Certificate of Appreciation, 1993; Minority Business News, Outstanding Men of Minority Business Devt, 1992; DC Contractors Assn, Humanitarian Award, 1992; American Contract Compliance Assn, President's Award, 1990; Alabama Minority Contractors Assn, Plaque of Appreciation, 1990; Assn of Minority Contractors of Houston, Distinguished Service Award, 1990. **Special Achievements:** "Giant Step for NASA," MBE Magazine, 1993. **Military Serv:** USAF, staff sergeant 1967-71; Air Force Commendation Medal, Vietnam, 1970. **Business Addr:** Associate Administrator, NASA Headquarters, Mail Code K, Washington, DC 20546.

THOMAS, REGINALD MAURICE
Emergency medical technician. **Personal:** Born Jan 4, 1964, San Angelo, TX; son of Devada Roberts Thomas and Claude Leon Thomas Jr; married Lynn Regina Scott Thomas, Jun 15, 1985; children: Brittney Regina, Reginald Maurice Thomas II. **Educ:** Morehouse College, Atlanta, GA, 1982-83; Wayne State University, Detroit, MI, 1983-84. **Career:** The GAP, Southfield, MI, salesman, 1981-83; Metric Medical Lab, Southfield, MI, supervisor of the motor pool, 1983-87; City of Detroit Parks & Rec, Detroit, MI, landscaper, laborer, 1987-88, Detroit Fire Dept, Detroit, MI, emergency med tech, 1988-, fire fighter, currently. **Honors/Awds:** Lifesaver of the Year, East Detroit Medical Authority, 1990. **Home Addr:** 18375 Grayfield, Detroit, MI 48219.

THOMAS, ROBERT CHARLES
Musician, composer. **Personal:** Born Nov 14, 1932, Newark, NJ; son of Virginia Harris and Theophilus Thomas; married Nicole Hebert-Thomas, Oct 22, 1966; children: Lorna, Marc. **Educ:** Juilliard Sch Music, BS 1961. **Career:** Billy Taylor Prods, musician & composer 1975-; perfomed with, Wes Montgomery, Herbie Mann, Carmen McRae, Burt Bacharach, Billy Taylor Orch (David Frost TV Show); Ballets USA, 1961-63; Billy Taylor Trio, drummer & lecturer, 1979-; A Chorus Line, New York, NY, music coordinator, 1975-90; Rutgers University's Mason Gross School of The Arts, associate prof of jazz percussion, 1993-96. **Orgs:** Consult E Harlem Tutorial Prog 1960-74; co-produced, composed music & lyrics "Sugar Boogie" 1976; wrote theme Black Jour for WNET 1975; mem NY Jazz Repertory Co; Jazz Mobile; wrkshps & seminars Univs & Clges. **Honors/Awds:** Shakespeare Key to City Cleveland; mem of Billy Taylor Trio two command perf at White House 1973-75; Theater World Award for "A Chorus Line," 1976-; New York University Tisch School of The Arts, Best Musical Score Award for Score of "Notes in A Minor Key", Best Short Film, 1994. **Special Achievements:** Co-chair and percussion instructor at "Jazz in July" workshops, Univ. of Massachusetts at Amherst. **Military Serv:** AUS corpl 1953-55.

THOMAS, ROBERT LEWIS
Educator. **Personal:** Born Sep 25, 1944, Brewton, AL; son of Earnestine Lane Thomas (deceased) and Robert Lewis Thomas, Sr (deceased); married Wyvonnia Thompson, Jun 6, 1969; children: Michelle, Tiffani. **Educ:** Stillman Coll, BA 1967; Troy State Univ, MS 1975. **Career:** Escambia County Bd of Educ, teacher 1967-83; Brewton Police Dept, patrolman 1969-; Faulkner State Jr Coll, professor, history, 1983-. **Orgs:** Mem Alabama Assn of Historians, NAACP; lifetime mem Kappa Alpha Psi Fraternity 1969-; delegate Conf on Black Amer Affairs 1984-86; vice pres AEA Faulkner State 1986-87; pres AEA Faulkner State 1987-88; delegate AEA Convention 1987-88; mem Alabama Peace Officers Assn, Alabama High School Athletic Assn; mem, bd of trustees Zion Fountain AME Church; NAACP, 1983-. **Honors/Awds:** Achievement Award, Kappa Alpha Psi Fraternity 1972; Operation Crossroad African Alumni; Achievement Award, Brewton Police Dept, 1980; Outstanding Police Officer, 1991. **Home Addr:** 612 Liles Blvd, Brewton, AL 36426.

THOMAS, RODERICK
Organization development consultant. **Personal:** Born Jan 12, 1939, Philadelphia, PA; son of Virginia B Mosley-Thomas and Wiliam A Thomas; divorced; children: Jeffri Pierre, Roderick Jr, Shelley McGill. **Educ:** Temple University, BS, 1970; Drexel University, MBA, 1973. **Career:** DuPont Co., organization development consultant, 1973-78; Rod Thomas Associates, director, 1978-. **Orgs:** Foundation for Community Encouragement, director, board of directors. **Special Achievements:** Produced a video, Diversity: Making It Work for You, 1992. **Business Addr:** Principal, Rod Thomas Associates, 1400 East West Hwy, No 405, Silver Spring, MD 20910.

THOMAS, RODNEY DEJUANE
Professional football player. **Personal:** Born Mar 30, 1973, Groveton, TX. **Educ:** Texas A&M, attended. **Career:** Houston Oilers, running back, 1995-96; Tennessee Oilers, 1997-. **Business Addr:** Professional Football Player, Tennessee Oilers, c/o Baptist Sports Park, 7640 H 70-5, Nashville, TN 37221.

THOMAS, RODNEY LAMAR
Professional football player. **Personal:** Born Dec 21, 1965, Los Angeles, CA. **Educ:** Brigham Young Univ, attended. **Career:** Miami Dolphins, cornerback, 1988-. **Business Addr:** Professional Football Player, Miami Dolphins, 2269 NW 199th St, Miami, FL 33056-2600.

THOMAS, RODOLFO RUDY
Law enforcement official. **Personal:** Born Feb 19, 1949, Highland Park, MI; son of Porter & Consuela Thomas; married Anna, Oct 3, 1990; children: Kimberly Stewart, Malia, Lattimer, Matthew Rodriguez. **Educ:** Highland Park College, AA; Eastern Michigan University, BS, police administration; Masters, interdiciplanary technology. **Career:** Detroit Police Dept, police officer, 1974-83; sergeant, 1983-85; lieutenant, 1985-87; inspector, 1987-89; commander/narcotics division, 1989-94; deputy chief police, 1994-. **Orgs:** Optimist Club; Golden Key Honors Society; Chamber of Commerce Law Enforcement Consultant; Drug Education Advisor; Community Policing Advisor; City Heroin Task Force Member; Detroit Public School Mentor; Adjunct Professor Eastern Michigan Univ. **Military Serv:** US Air Force, ssgt, 1969-73. **Business Addr:** Deputy Chief, Detroit Police Department, 1300 Beaubien St, Rm 820, Detroit, MI 48226, (313)596-1870.

THOMAS, RON (RONALD FOWLER)
Sportswriter. **Personal:** Born Sep 13, 1949, Buffalo, NY; son of Laughton F and Ormah Dennis Thomas; married Iris T

Crossley, Aug 7, 1982; children: Kali C Thomas. **Educ:** Univ of Rochester, BA, political science, 1971; Northwestern Univ, Masters, journalism, 1973. **Career:** Rochester Times-Union, prep sports reporter, 1973-75; Chicago Daily News, college basketball, football reporter, 1975-78; San Francisco Chronicle, pro basketball reporter, 1978-82; USA Today, pro basketball editor/reporter, 1982-84; San Francisco Chronicle, sportswriter, 1984-93, news copy editor, 1994; Home Box Office, documentary researcher/feature producer, 1995; Marin Independent Journal, sportswriter 1995-. **Orgs:** National Association of Black Journalists, 1978-; Bay Area Black Journalists Association, 1980-; Pro Basketball Writers Association, 1984-94; Pro Football Writers Association, 1987-91; North American Society for Sports History, 1992-96. **Honors/Awds:** Associated Press Sports Editors, Top 10 Features and Top 10 News stories for under 50,000 circulation, 1997; Associated Press News Executives Council, California & Nevada, Second place for sportswriting, 1997; United Press Intl, California & Nevada, Best Sports Story Award, 1980; San Francisco Press Club, Best Sports Story Award, 1980; Bay Area Black Journalists Assn, Honored for Excellence, 1987; Natl Assoc of Black Journalists, Third place, Sportswriting, 1997. **Special Achievements:** Wrote chapter entitled ''Black Faces Still Rare in the Press Box'' in sports sociology textbook, ''Sport in Society: Equal Opportunity or Business as Usual?,'' edited by Richard E Lapchick, 1996; APSE, NABJ & AP Awards were for ''College of Marin Star Fought Beyond Basketball Court,'' a Marin IJ article about Don Barksdale, first black basketball Olympian, 1997; ''Best Sports Story'' awards were for San Francisco Chronicle series entitled ''The Black Coach Barrier'' about lack of pro baseball, basketball and football coaches, 1980. **Home Addr:** 9 Washington Ave, San Rafael, CA 94903, (415)492-9243.

THOMAS, RONALD F.
Educator. **Personal:** Born Jul 2, 1944, Wilmington, DE; married Marva Wyche, Dec 23, 1967; children: Ronald LeRoy, Olivia Necole. **Educ:** Delaware State Coll, BS 1967; Central MI Univ, Master 1979, postgraduate studies, 1987. **Career:** 7th grad math teacher 1977; Capital School Dist Dover DE, math instructor 1970-74, reading & math ctr oper Title VII, Title I; Telegraph Road Learning Center, computer lab supvr, mathematics and science teacher, currently; Red Clay School Dist, Wilmington DE, math/science teacher, 1988-. **Orgs:** Groove Phi Groove Soc Fellowship 1963, VA 1967-; Del State Educ Assoc 1970-; Natl Educ Assoc 1970-; Capital Educ Assoc 1970-; Church Laymens Assoc 1970-; Human Relations Conf Represent Capital School Dist 1972, 73; Problems & Relations Comm 1971-73, 32nd Degree Mason & Shriner 1972-; lab del, assembly delegate 1973, bldg rep 1972-74 State Educ Assn; negotiation team for schools 1974; chmn nom comm Del State Educ Assembly 1974; pres DE State Minority Ed Assoc 1974-76; Del Disadvantaged Found Inc 1974-; VFW 1974-, DOIC, GED, ABE Teacher 1963; advisory Coll Gospel Youth Group 1974; vice pres DeFrontier Intl Club; Omega Psi Phi. **Honors/Awds:** State Civic Duty Award 1962; Outstanding Sr Choir & Band 1962; recorded ''Love You So Bad Come Home Girl'', ''Your on Top Girl Slide On By''; 1st pl All Army Talent Show 1969; Outstanding Leaders In Elementary & Secondary Educ 1976; Citizen of the Year Award for Dover DE 1985; Thirty-Third Degree, United Supreme Council, 1988. **Military Serv:** AUS sgt E-5 1967-70; DE NG captain.

THOMAS, ROY L.
Foreman. **Personal:** Born Jul 27, 1938, Forest, MS; married Altemese Woods; children: Micheal, Sandra, Mark. **Educ:** Univ MD. **Career:** Hercules Inc, Glen Falls, prod foreman; Minority Bus Oppor, enforcement offcr. **Orgs:** Bd chmn Local Housing Corp; Warren Co NY Sewer Dist 1; chmn NY St Conf NAACP, Prisons Affrs Com; ex dir Vol Housing Survey; bd & chmn Warren Hamilton Off Econ Oppo; bd mem E Adirondack Econ Devel Auth; bd mem, Warren Co Alcoholic Bev Con Bd; RE Salesman; pres Glen Falls Br NAACP; mem Warren Co Rep Comm; NYS Ancillary Mnpwr Plnng Bd; Senate Lodge 456 F&AM of Glens Falls. **Military Serv:** USAF 4 Yrs. **Business Addr:** 11 Darwin Ave, Glens Falls, NY 12801.

THOMAS, SAMUEL (BUZZ)
Government official. **Career:** Michigan State Legislature, state rep, 1997-. **Business Addr:** State Representative, Michigan State Legislature, State Capitol, PO Box 30014, Lansing, MI 48909-7514, (517)373-1782.

THOMAS, SAMUEL
Utility company executive. **Personal:** Born Aug 21, 1943, Malvern, AR; son of Altora Burks Boles and Robert Thomas; married Lura D Shannon Thomas, Mar 6, 1965; children: Samuel II, Jason Anthony. **Educ:** Monterey Peninsula College, Monterey, CA, AA, 1974; Golden Gate University, San Francisco, CA, BA, 1977, MBA, 1984. **Career:** Pacific Gas & Electric, pump test engineer, 1977-78, marketing repres, 1978-80, local manager, 1980-83, area manager, 1983-86, employee participation administrator, 1986-90, continuing education administrator, 1990-; America Protective Services, acct mgr, currently. **Orgs:** Subscribing life member, NAACP, 1989-91; life member, National Black MBA, 1989; member, American Legion, 1982-91; member, American Assn of Blacks in Energy, 1983-91; member, Pacifica Lions Club, 1980-91; president, Healdsburg Chamber Commerce, 1985-86. **Honors/Awds:** Dedicated Service Award, Math Engineer & Science Achievement, 1990; Community Service Award, Pacific Gas & Electric, 1989; Service Award, Healdsburg Chamber of Commerce, 1985; Service Award, American Legion, Pacifica Post, 1984. **Military Serv:** Army, Spec 4, 1962-65; Good Conduct Medal, 1965. **Business Addr:** Account Manager, American Protective Services, 120 Howard Street, No. 620, San Francisco, CA 94104.

THOMAS, SAMUEL HAYNES, JR.
Attorney, real estate executive. **Personal:** Born Oct 2, 1941, Detroit, MI; son of Samuel Sr & Margaret Thomas; married Aug 1966 (divorced); children: Samuel Thomas III. **Educ:** Lafayette College, AB, 1964; Harvard Law School, LLB, 1967. **Career:** Ford Motor Co, office of general counsel, 1967-69; Jaffe, Snider, Raitt, Garratt & Heuer PC, 1970-77; Thomas & Pomeroy Inc, president, 1977-80; Burlington Construction Co., president, 1980-; Burlington Properties, president, 1980-; Phoenix Management, vice pres, 1993-. **Orgs:** Sigma Pi Phi Fraternity, 1993-95; Det Institute of Art, executive committee & vice pres, 1985-; State Bar of Michigan, 1968-; National Bar Association; Detroit Bar Association; State of Michigan Building Authority, vice chairman; Metro Realty Corp., vice chairman. **Honors/Awds:** State of Michigan, Legislative Resolution, 1993. **Special Achievements:** Detroit Institute of Art, Chair, Bal African, 1988-. **Military Serv:** US Army, 1st lt, 1969. **Business Addr:** Vice Pres, Phoenix Management, 1900 W Liberty, Ann Arbor, MI 48103, (313)747-6666.

THOMAS, SHERRI BOOKER
Geologist. **Personal:** Born in Richmond, VA; married Norman Thomas. **Educ:** VA State Univ, BS 1980; Univ of SC, MS 1982. **Career:** Amoco, sr explor tech 1978-79; Natl Assoc of Black Geologists & Geophysicists, sec 1983-84; Conoco, geologist 1980-. **Orgs:** Mem Natl Assoc of Black Geol & Geophys 1982; sec Ella Bouldin Missionary Soc #5 1983-; mem Amer Assoc of Petroleum Geol 1984, Geol Soc of Amer 1985; mem Celestrial Choir Payne Chapel AME Church. **Honors/Awds:** Article ''Quartz Sand Provinence Changes'' S Booker, R Ehrlich 1981. **Business Addr:** Senior Geologist, Conoco Inc, 600 N Dairy Ashford Rd, Ste 3064, Houston, TX 77079.

THOMAS, SHERYL ANN BENNING
Educational administrator. **Personal:** Born in Columbus, GA; daughter of Calvin & Emma Benning; married Lee M Thomas, Jun 10, 1970; children: Khalia M, Shaura A. **Educ:** Fisk Univ, BA; Texas Southern Univ, masters; Wayne State Univ, Ed Spec. **Career:** Detroit Public Schools, teacher, counselor, asst principal; Golightly Educational Ctr, principal, currently. **Orgs:** Jack & Jill of America, national president, 1996-98; The Links Inc, Detroit chapter; Delta Sigma Theta Sorority; Phi Delta Kappa. **Honors/Awds:** US Dept of Ed, National Blue Ribbon School status, 1994; State of Michigan Dept of Ed, State Blue Ribbon School status; Phi Delta Kappa Wayne State, Educator of the Year, 1994. **Business Addr:** Principal, Golightly Ed Center, 5536 St Antoine, Detroit, MI 48202, (313)494-2538.

THOMAS, SIRR DANIEL
Construction manager. **Personal:** Born Jul 21, 1933, Huntsville, AL; married Barbara Williams; children: S. **Educ:** Tuskegee Inst, plumbing & mech drawing; Knoxville Coll, math; Howard Plumbing Co, Knoxville, journeyman plumber 1960-63; Elmer A Thomas Plumbing Co, foreman, plumber 1957-60, journeyman plumber 1953-55. **Career:** Thomas & Thomas Inc, gen contrctrs, Chattanooga, owner, mgr 1963-; Howard & Howard Plumbin Co, Knoxville, journeyman plumber 1960-63; Elmer A Thomas Plumbing Co, foreman, plumber 1957-60, journeyman plumber 1953-55; City of Chattanooga, mayor, city councilman, 1990. **Orgs:** Mem Nat Bus League; mem bd dir Eastern Seabord Plumbing & Heating Assn; mem bd dir Chattanooga Chap NAACP; mem bd dir Security Fed Sav & Loan Assn; mem bd dir Peoples Bank; chmn Chattanooga C of C Minority Bus Com; trained & tutored young black men in preparation for plumbing career. **Military Serv:** US Army pfc 1955-56. **Business Addr:** 617 Shallowford Rd, Chattanooga, TN 37411.

THOMAS, SPENCER
Physician. **Personal:** Born in Gadsden, AL; married Lela; children: Spencer Jr. **Educ:** Alabama State Univ, BS 1952; Howard Univ, MD 1959. **Career:** Mercy Douglas Hospital Philadelphia, intern/house physician 1959-61; Philadelphia General Hospital, urology special training 1972-76, asst attending physician 1976-77; Holy Name of Jesus Hospital now Riverview & Baptist Memorial (now Gadsden Regional) Hospital, Gadsden, staff physician; private practice, Gadsden AL, physician. **Orgs:** Mem Indus Devel Bd Gadsden 1968-72 & 1978-80; bd dir Gadsden Progress Council; sponsor Project Headstart 1964-72 & 1980-; pres Community League for Advancement of Social Socs Gadsden 1969; founder & mem of gov bd Colley Child Care Center Gadsden; medical dir Project Head Start 1968-72; pres Gadsden Alumni Assn of Alabama State Univ 1979-; NAACP; Alpha Phi Alpha Fraternity Inc, Alabama State Medical Assn, Natl Medical Assn, AMA, SCLC, Howard Univ Medical Alumni Assn; chmn administrative bd, trustee Sweethome United Methodist Church 1979-81; church lay leader 1981-84; mem Gadsden City Bd of Educ 1980-90, vice pres 1984; mem bd trustees Alabama A&M Univ 1980-87, chmn 1982-84; pres Gadsden-Etowah AL Branch of NAACP 1982-94; pres AL State Alumni Assn Gadsden Chapter 1979-; past mem Camber of Cerce, Gadsden Al; weekly columnist Gadsden Times Daily. **Honors/Awds:** Recipient Serv Award, Gadsden Progress Council 1972. **Military Serv:** AUS 1952-54. **Business Addr:** PO Box 57, Gadsden, AL 35902.

THOMAS, STANLEY B., JR. See Obituaries section.

THOMAS, TERENCE (MASTER TEE)
Producer, audio engineer, disc jockey. **Personal:** Born Nov 15, 1966, Brooklyn, NY; son of Tijuana G Thomas. **Educ:** Audio Recording Technical Institute, 1989. **Career:** TBTA, 1985-89; Master Lab Productions Studio, president/CEO, currently; First Priority Music, East West Records, currently. **Orgs:** SAG; AFTRA. **Honors/Awds:** Five gold records and six platinum record. **Special Achievements:** Television appearances include: ''In Living Color,'' 1992, ''Soul Train,'' 1992, ''NBA All-Star Game,'' 1992, ''The Arsenio Hall Show,'' 1990, ''Showtime at the Apollo,'' 1990; ''The Phil Donahue Show''; ''The Geraldo Show''; ''MTV''; ''Yo MTV Raps''; ''The Party Machine''; appeared in the films ''Boomerang'' and ''Mo' Money,'' ''Moesha,'' ''Joan Rivers,'' ''BET,'' ''Video Soul;'' has produced and mixed tracks for 2 Pac, New Power, Prince, New Power Generation, MCLyte, Worldwide Traveller, Janet Jackson, Mint Condition, Brandy, Mavis Staples, and Big Daddy Kane. **Business Addr:** President/CEO, Master Lab Productions Studios, 134-11 111th Ave, South Ozone Park, NY 11420, (718)322-2258.

THOMAS, TERRA LEATHERBERRY
Human resources administrator, psychologist. **Personal:** Born Oct 16, 1947, Easton, MD; daughter of Betty Leatherberry Thomas and Clarence S. Thomas; married Joe Louis Washington, Feb 1, 1987. **Educ:** Morgan State University, Baltimore, MD, BS, 1969; New York University, New York, NY, MA, 1971; Adelphi University, Garden City, NY, PhD, MA, 1973-82; Kellogg-Northwestern University, Evanston, IL, MBA, 1990-91. **Career:** Bloomfield College, Bloomfield, NJ, acting dean of women, 1969-71; Brownsville Child Development Center, New York, NY, psychological consultant, 1972-74; Northwestern University Medical School, Chicago, IL, psychology intern, 1974-75; Ada S. McKinley Community Services, Chicago, IL, psychological consultant, 1975-78; Human Resources Development Institute, Chicago, IL, senior vice president, 1978-94; Northwestern University Medical School, Chicago, IL, associate faculty, 1983-94. **Orgs:** Member, Illinois AIDS Advisory Council, 1989-91; chair education committee, Illinois Certification Boards, 1987-90; chair service provider's council, AIDS Foundation of Chicago, 1986-88; education committee co-chair, NAACP, 1989-91; member, Alpha Kappa Alpha Sorority, 1967; chair, Chicago chapter, National Association of Black Psychologists, 1976. **Honors/Awds:** Recognition for Compassion, Dedication & Generosity, AIDS Foundation of Chicago, 1989; Outstanding Alumni Award, National Association for Equal Opportunity in Higher Education, 1988; Humanitarian & Leadership Award, HRDI Drug & AIDS Prevention Class, 1987; Prevention Leadership Award, Illinois Alcoholism & Drug Dependency Association, 1987; Ten Outstanding Young Citizens Award, Chicago Junior Association of Commerce & Industry, 1986. **Business Addr:** Organization Development Consultant, Human Resources Development Institute, Inc, 222 S Jefferson St, Chicago, IL 60661.

THOMAS, THURMAN LEE
Professional football player. **Personal:** Born May 16, 1966, Houston, TX; married Patti; children: Olivia, Angelica. **Educ:** Oklahoma State Univ, attended. **Career:** Buffalo Bills, running back, 1988-. **Honors/Awds:** Pro Bowl, 1989, 1990, 1991, 1992, 1993; NFL MVP, 1992. **Business Addr:** Professional Football Player, Buffalo Bills, One Bills Dr, Orchard Park, NY 14127, (716)648-1800.

THOMAS, TIM
Professional basketball player. **Personal:** Born Feb 26, 1977. **Educ:** Villanova. **Career:** Philadelphia 76ers, forward, 1997-. **Honors/Awds:** USBWA, National Freshman of the Year, 1997. **Business Addr:** Professional Basketball Player, Philadelphia 76ers, 1 Corestates Complex, Philadelphia, PA 19148, (215)339-7676.

THOMAS, W. CURTIS
State representative. **Personal:** Born Apr 11, 1948, Philadelphia, PA; son of Hattie M Thomas and Curtis Thomas; children: Salim, Kareem. **Educ:** Temple Univ, Philadelphia, PA, BS, 1975, attended, 1975-77; graduate work, Education Admin Antioch School of Law, Washington, DC, JD, 1980. **Career:** Antioch School of Law, Washington, DC, student teacher, 1978-79; US Dept of HEW, Washington, DC, law clerk, 1979-80; Commonwealth of PA, Harrisburg, PA, law clerk, 1980-82; EPNAC, Inc, Philadelphia, exec dir, 1982-87; Commonwealth of PA, Harrisburg, PA, state rep, 1988-. **Orgs:** Bd mem, Alphonso Deal Devt Corp, 1989-; bd mem, Cunningham County House, 1990-91; vice chair, PA Legislative Black Caucus, lifetime mem, Yorktown Community Org, 1991-; founder, chmn, Legis-

lative Housing Caucus, 1990-. **Honors/Awds:** Fishtown Revitalization Project, Fishtown Civic Assn, 1989-90; E Luther Cunningham Service Award, E Luther Cunningham Community Ctr, 1990; PUC Appreciation Award, Philadelphia Urban Coalition Leadership Comm, 1990; Self Help Initiative Award, Self Help Initiative Adv Comm, 1990; MOC Volunteer Service Award, Mayors Office of Community Service, 1990. **Business Addr:** State Representative, Commonwealth of Pennsylvania, 1348 W Girard Ave, Philadelphia, PA 19123.

THOMAS, WADE HAMILTON, SR.
Management consultant, certified public accountant. **Personal:** Born May 12, 1922, Jackson, MS; son of Lealer Bandy Thomas and Harrison Spurgeon Thomas; married Mary Katherine Scruggs; children: Wade Jr, Karl, Harrison, George, Kenneth, Korda, Ren'ee, Rex, Axel, Michelle. **Educ:** TN State Univ, BS (with distinction) 1949; TN State Univ, Post Grad 1950; US Civil Serv Comm, Intern 1962; IN Central Univ, MBA 1962. **Career:** Southern Training Inst, instr 1947-49; Univ Life Ins Co, sp rep 1951-52; US Post Office Dept, gn clerk 1953-62; Drake & Thomas Pub Accts, co-ownr 1954-60; GSA, PBS, BMD (US Govt), fld mgr 1963-72; W H Thomas, Sr, Pub Acct, owner 1973-80; Confidential Assoc, Realtors, management cnslt beginning 1981; management consultant, currently. **Orgs:** Mem NY Comm to Study Housing 1981-83; mem Asheville Promo Comm 1984-; treas YMI Cultural Cntr 1984-; mem US Feed Exec Assn 1967-72; basiceus Up Omc, Chapter Omega Psi Phi Frat 1970-71; mem Nat Soc Pub Acct 1973-; chairman Asheville Civil Serv Comm 1992-; chmn Asheville Bd of Adjstmnts 1988-; board of directors Asheville Bd of Realtors 1984-; comm NC Housing Comm 1983-; past master, Capital Hill #251, F&AM, PHA, 1960; potentate, Gizen Temple #162, AEAONMS, PHA, 1989-90; sergeant of arms, Asheville Optimist Club, 1990. **Honors/Awds:** Spl Accomplishment Award-US Post Off Dept 1960; Spl Accomplishment Award Gen Serv Admin 1971; Outstanding Serv Award Omega Psi Phi Frat 1971 & 1983; Golden Anniv Award TN State Univ 1962. **Military Serv:** USAFR ofcr Tuskegee Airman, 1942-47, Reg Campaigns & Good Conduct 1945. **Home Addr:** 2 Mardell Circle, Asheville, NC 28806. **Business Addr:** Management Consultant, Certified Public Accountant, 51 Downing St, PO Box 2202, Asheville, NC 28802.

THOMAS, WILBON
Farmer, station proprietor, county official. **Personal:** Born Mar 6, 1921, Midway, AL; son of Ada Brown Thomas and Wilbon Thomas; married Mary E Warren; children: 3. **Career:** NAACP, vice pres 1954-56, pres 1964-; Midway Improvement Club, pres 1956-64; Bullock Cty Schools, bus driver 27 yrs; farmer, serv sta oper 1957-; Macon County Racing Commission. **Orgs:** Deacon, mem 1st Baptist Church Bullock Co ESPO; mem Jury Comm of Bullock Cty, Bullock Cty Dist Adv Council for Title I, BTU & Sunday School Teacher; state bd mem ESPO; supt of Sunday School; Pres of First Baptist Usher Board; Organized a Sunday School Program; Bullock County Democratic Executive Committee. **Honors/Awds:** Bullock Cty PTA Awd; Serv Awd ASCAARV; AL NAACP; Youth Councils & Coll; 2 Leadership Awds AL Baptist State Conv; Cert Personal & Family Survival; Proclamation of Achievement, Gov Guy Hunt 50th Wedding Anniversary March, 1991; Proclamation of Service, 43 Years Bus Driver Bullock Co Public School Gov Hunt, 1991. **Home Addr:** Rt 1, Box 170, Midway, AL 36053.

THOMAS, WILLIAM
Educational administrator. **Personal:** Born Jan 1, 1935, Cairo, IL; son of Claudia Mae Campbell Thomas and William H Thomas; married Majoice Lewis; children: Joyce D, Sharon S, William E, Anjanette, Marcus K. **Educ:** So IL Univ, BS 1967; Purdue Univ, MS 1969, PhD 1972. **Career:** City of Gary Schools, head teacher/teacher 1967-70; Purdue Univ, administ asst 1970-72; DePauw Univ, dir Black studies/asst prof 1972-73; Purdue Univ, dir special academic servcs/asst prof 1973-75; CIC Midwest Program for Minorities in Engrg, exec dir 1975-77; Thomas Distrib, vice pres 1977-79; Cairo School Dist #1, admin asst to supt 1979-83; Carbondale Elem School Dist #95, supt 1983-87; New Orleans Public Schools, New Orleans LA, assoc superintendent, 1987-91; Greenville Public Schools, Greenville, MS, superintendent, 1991-94; Thomas Associates, president, 1994-95; Philander Smith College, dean of instruction, 1995-. **Orgs:** Educ consultant, Joliet Area Schools 1973-74, Office of Educ Region V 1974-75, IN Dept Public Instructor 1975-77; corp dir Southern Med Center 1980-84; vp/sec/treas Kiwanis Club of Cairo 1979-83; mem Carbondale Rotary Club 1984-87; Western Reg chmn Egyptian Council Boy Scouts of Amer 1983-87; treasurer Egyptian Council Boy Scouts of Amer; mem, Partnership in Education Steering Committee, 1989; educ consultant, National School Services 1988-; educ consultant, James Nighswander Associates 1987-; educ consultant, Illinois State Bd of Eduction 1986-87. **Honors/Awds:** Maintenance Man of the Month 13th Air Div (SAC) 1963; Martin Luther King Jr Fellowship Woodrow Wilson Found 1970-72; David Ross Fellow Purdue Univ 1972; President's Award Egyptian Council Boy Scouts of Amer 1985. **Military Serv:** USAF Tech Sgt served 10 yrs; Natl Defense Serv Medal; Good Conduct Medal; Missileman's Badge. **Business Addr:** Dean, Philander Smith College, 812 W 13th St, Little Rock, AR 72202.

THOMAS, WILLIAM CHRISTOPHER
Administrator, management consultant. **Personal:** Born Feb 4, 1939, Chicago, IL; married Joan Marie; children: Gene, Sean, Dawn, Theresa, Bill Jr. **Educ:** Northeastern IL Univ, BE 1962; Harvard Grad Sch of Business, PMD 1972. **Career:** Sealy Mattress Co, personnel dir 1964-66, mfg supt 1966-67; Honeywell Inc, labor relations manager 1967-69, corporate training manager 1969-73; Univ of MN, assoc vice pres for finance, personnel and physical plant opers 1973-. **Orgs:** Pres Modern Mgmt Assoc Inc Consultants 1981-; pres MN State Affirm Action Assoc 1979-80; mem AMA Natl Adv Council 1979-82; mem Board Twin Cities Personnel Assoc 1978-79. **Honors/Awds:** Bush Fellow Bush Foundation 1972. **Home Addr:** 2149 Scott Ave N, Golden Valley, MN 55422.

THOMAS, WILLIAM HARRISON, JR.
Professional football player. **Personal:** Born Aug 13, 1968, Amarillo, TX; married Susan; children: Zion Michael. **Educ:** Texas A&M, attended. **Career:** Philadelphia Eagles, linebacker, 1991-. **Honors/Awds:** Pro Bowl, 1995, 1996. **Business Addr:** Professional Football Player, Philadelphia Eagles, 3501 S Broad St, Philadelphia, PA 19148, (215)463-2500.

THOMAS, WILLIAM L.
Business executive. **Personal:** Born Apr 3, 1938, Cleveland; married Joyce; children: Menelik, Malaka. **Educ:** OH U; Univ Madrid; Ghetto U; Univ MD; OH Drug Studies Inst, 1973-74. **Career:** City of Cleveland, engr inspector 1968-69; Black Unity House Inc, fdr, exec dir. **Orgs:** Mem exec com OH Black Polit Assembly 1974; Cleveland Black Polit Assembly 1974; trustee Community Action Against Addiction 1971-75; African Liberation Support Com 1969-75; Community Coalition on Construction 1971-75. **Military Serv:** USAF a/2c 1960-65. **Business Addr:** 1167 Hayden Ave, Cleveland, OH 44110.

THOMAS-BOWLDING, HAROLD CLIFTON
Social services executive. **Personal:** Born Jul 24, 1941, Washington, DC; son of Helen and Benjiman; married Linda M; children: Harold Jr, William Staggs, Aneara, Emmatt, James Carter, Godtheson Benjamen. **Educ:** Federal City Coll, 1970; UDC, 1974-75. **Career:** Anacostia Youth Environ Org Inc, pres 1971; DC Metro Youth Org & Enterprises Inc, pres 1976; Natl Love Comm Youth & Adult Org Inc, pres 1984-; pres Council of Peers, Inc. **Orgs:** Youth counselor SE Neighborhood House 1976; adv neighborhood comm 8B02 1979-84; AL Ave Rennisance Proj Dept of Housing/Comm Development 1982-83; adv neighborhood comm 8B01 1985-87; DC Comprehensive Plan DC Office of Planning 1983-84; Mayor's Ward 8 Adv Comm 1983-84; Mayor's Budget and Resource Adv Commappointee 1985. **Honors/Awds:** Ward 8 Constituent Serv Cert Councilwoman Rolark 1982; Recognition of Leadership Frederick Douglass Dwellings Resident Council 1984; coord of Frederick Douglass' Recogn Day; Community Olympics 1985. **Military Serv:** AUS sp/4 2 yrs; championship watch & jacket 2nd div football 1967. **Home Addr:** 1738 Stanton Terr SE, Washington, DC 20020.

THOMAS-CARTER, JEAN COOPER
Retired city official, educator. **Personal:** Born Dec 16, 1924, Baltimore, MD; married Calvin Lavette Carter; children: Jacques S Maultsby. **Educ:** Hampton Inst Hampton VA, BS 1946; Howard Univ School of Soc Work, MSW 1965; Univ of AL, Cert in Mgmt 1979. **Career:** Barrett School for Girls, teacher 1947-49; Baltimore City Dept of Soc Svcs, caseworker 1949-57, casework suprv 1957-66, dist suprv 1966-71; Logical Tech Serv Residential Drug Treatment Prog, deputy dir 1971-73; Baltimore City Dept of Soc Svcs, dist supvr group day care 1973-78, prog spec for day care 1978-79, chief/prog spec for serv to families with children 1979-80, dist mgr 1980-83, asst dir of client serv oper 1983-84, bureau chief adult & family svcs. **Orgs:** Instr Comm Coll of Baltimore 1970-; exec comm Howard Univ School of Soc Work Alumni Assoc, Mayors Advisory Council on Drug Abuse; co-chairperson awds comm Conf on Women in State Svcs; past v chairperson of bd of dir Xcell Drug Treatment Center; past bd of dir Baltimore Assoc for Retarded Citizens; pasast MD Conf of Soc Concern; past budget allocations comm United Fund; dir Youth Ministry of Our Lady of Lourdes Parish, Baltimore MD 1985-; bd mem Campfire Council of the Chesapeake 1985-; volunteer panelist Administrative Review Bd for serv to families with children, Baltimore Dept of Social Services 1989-. **Honors/Awds:** Awd of Recognition Chairperson for Annual Dr United Fund 1974; Publ "Does Existing Social Policy, Service Programs, & Support Systems Help the Children of Women Involved in the Criminal Justice System"? Natl Inst of Health 1979, "The Impact of PA Pmts & Social Policy on Family Functioning" Child Welfare League of Amer Eastern Reg Conf 1980. **Home Addr:** 2317 Monticello Road, Baltimore, MD 21216.

THOMAS-RICHARDS, JOSE RODOLFO
Surgeon. **Personal:** Born Jul 28, 1944; married Lynette; children: Jose, Raoul. **Educ:** Andrews U, BA 1966; KS City Coll Osteo Med, DO 1970. **Career:** Orthopedic surgeon, self; Martin Luther King Hosp, dir emergcy med, chmn Dept Orthopedic & Hand Surgery, dir rehab med. **Orgs:** Med sec Central State Conf of Seventh Day Adventists; mem AMA 1975; !mo State Med Assn 1975; Jackson Co Med Soc 1975; KS City Med Soc 1973; SW Clinical Soc 1974; life mem NAACP 1975; nominee, bd dir Jackson Co Med Soc 1977; MO State Med Assn 1977; bd dir Martin Luther King Hosp; mem Nat Med Assn; life mem Golden Heritage NAACP; mem bd of trustees PUSH; fdr Excel-Health, a new prgm of PUSH; phys Wyandotte Co Jail & Dep Sheriff Kansas City, KS; Coll Emergency Med 1975; Surgery of the Hand 1977-78. **Honors/Awds:** Mead-Johnson Award 1971. **Business Addr:** Metro Medic Professional Bldg, Ste 100, Kansas City, MO 64130.

THOMAS-RICHARDSON, VALERIE JEAN
Allied health & social service consultant. **Personal:** Born Apr 21, 1947, Akron, OH; daughter of Mary Carson Cooper and Rev Charles Cooper Jr. **Educ:** Akron School of Pratical Nursing, LPN 1968-69; Thomas A Edison Coll, BA Soc Sci 1969-73; Univ of Pittsburgh, MSW 1974-76; Union Grad School, PhD 1976-78; Medina Hosp, Cardiopulmonary Tech Training Prog; International Apostolic Coll of Grace & Truth, doctorate of christian education, 1994. **Career:** NEOCROSS, Inc, interim executive dir 1978-79; The Gilliam Family Service Center, exec dir 1979-82; Cleveland Adult Tutorial Services, exec dir 1983-86; Georgian Allied Health Educational Services, assoc dir; International Apostolic Coll of Grace & Truth, Richmond, IN, site coordinator, 1994. **Orgs:** Zonta Club 1969; bd mem agency rep Ohio Legal Services Commissions Consumer & Housing Task Force Comm Columbus OH 1977-78; First aid & personal safety instr, cpr instr Amer Red Cross 1975-87; former med newsletter editor "Heartbeat" Amer Heart Assoc Publ 1976; natl pres appointment exec comm Fed Council on Aging Wash DC 1978-; American Assoc for University Women 1984-86; Altrusa of Greater Cleveland 1985-86; Greater Cleveland Blood Pressure Coalition, board mem 1985-87; Ohio Entrepreneur Women's Directory 1986-87; Amer Biog Inst, honorary mem research comm; International Apostolic Coll of Grace & Truth, Richmond, IN, mem, bd of trustees, 1994. **Honors/Awds:** Many local, state natl and political proclamations commemorating "Women's Equality Day" and "Cardiopulmonary & Cardiovascular Technology Week" 1985-86; secured a natl special cardiovascular tech testing site in Northeastern OH for credentialing examination admin 1986; secured an "off-campus" site for Cuyahoga Community College's medical courses within the East Cleveland, OH community; Silver Medal of Honor Amer Bio Inst; fellow Intl Bio Assn; Dr Valerie Richardson, dir Greater Cleveland Tutorial Services, program entered into US Congressional Record by Cng Louis B Stokes 1985. **Home Addr:** 16000 Terrace Rd, East Cleveland, OH 44112.

THOMAS-SAMUEL, KALIN NORMOET
Television producer/correspondent. **Personal:** Born Nov 20, 1961, Baltimore, MD; daughter of Katherine Foote Thomas and Louis N Thomas. **Educ:** Howard University, Washington, DC, BA, Broadcast Journalism, 1983. **Career:** Cable News Network, Atlanta, GA, producer, 1984-. **Orgs:** Vice chair, Atlanta Association of Black Journalists, 1991-93; member, National Association of Black Journalists, 1983-; member, Women in Communications, 1980-83 & 1990-96; member, Sigma Delta Chi, Society of Professional Journalists, 1980-83, 1990-93,; member, Alpha Kappa Alpha Sorority Inc, 1981-. **Honors/Awds:** Media Access Awards (2), National Easter Seals, 1989; Michigan Outdoor Writer's Award, Michigan Outdoor Writer's Association, 1990; Emory O Jackson Journalism Award, Alpha Kappa Alpha Sorority, Inc, 1992; Natl Easter Seals EDI Award, 1993; Atlanta Assn of Black Journalist Award, Feature Series, 1997; Maryland Office of Tourism Development Award, 1997. **Business Addr:** Cable Network News (CNN), 1 CNN Center, Atlanta, GA 30303.

THOMAS-WILLIAMS, GLORIA M.
Association executive. **Personal:** Born Jul 5, 1938, NYC, NY; married Evrard Williams; children: Michelle. **Educ:** Attended, NY Univ, Brooklyn Coll. **Career:** Gloria Thomas Modeling Sch, prop; Schaefer Brewing Co, mgr public relations; WCBS-TV, dir comm affairs. **Orgs:** Professional Commentator; Mistress of Ceremonies. **Honors/Awds:** Outstanding Achiev Awd Bottle & Cork Sales 1970; Best Fashion Commentator Cabaret Prods 1971; Comm Serv Awd Mt Calvary Methodist Ch 1976; Awds in Black-Foundation for Educ in Sickle Cell 1973; Woman of the Yr 1972; Comm Serv Awd 1973; Awd of Merit WCBS-TV 1982; Police File Commendation 1974; Cert of Commendation Natl Assn for Visually Handicapped 1979; Mothers of Freedom Reward 1984; Outstanding Performance of Comm Serv Strivers Awd The Guardians Assn 1976; Alma John Comm Serv Awd 1984; Cert of Appreciation The Natl United Licensees Beverage Assns Inc 1972; Good Sportsmanship & Outstanding Serv WCBS-TV. **Business Addr:** Dir of Community Affairs, WCBS-TV, 524 W 57th St, New York, NY 10019.

THOMPAS, GEORGE HENRY, JR.
Law enforcement offical. **Personal:** Born Jun 26, 1941, Philadelphia, PA; son of Olliebea and George; married Sharon Patton (divorced); children: George III, Orlando, Rhonda, Troy, Derek, Tanay, Jason, Brandi. **Educ:** Federal Bureau of Law Enforcement Training Sch, Certificate 1969; Philadelphia Police Acad, police officer 1971; St Lukes and Children Medical Ctr, Certificate 1973; Community Coll of Philadelphia, AA, 1978; PA State Police Certification, Special Instructor; Municipal Po-

lice Officers Educ & Training Commn, Instructors Certification. **Career:** Reading Railroad (Conrail), railroad policeman 1968-71; City of Philadelphia, police officer 1971-85; Watterson School of Business and Technology, director of security training, 1985-; Philadelphia Housing Authority, police officer 1986-. **Orgs:** Variety Club for Handicapped Children 1968-; Guardian Civic League 1971-; Fraternal Order of Police 1971-; Missing Children Inc 1986; brethren, Mount Olive Lodge No 27 F&AM, 1988. **Honors/Awds:** Public Service Safeway demonstrations for senior citizens groups and organizations 1978-. **Military Serv:** US Army, PFC, 1963-66. **Home Addr:** 7943 Bayard St, Philadelphia, PA 19150.

THOMPSON, AARON A.
City official. **Personal:** Born Jul 23, 1930, Philadelphia, PA; son of Helen M Montier Blythe and Alonzo A Thompson; divorced 1991; children: Aaron G, Brion R, Shelley L, Lillian E, Marsha L, Eugene. **Career:** Bell Telephone of PA, Philadelphia, PA, systems technician (retired) 1986; City of Camden, Camden, NJ, councilman, 1989-90, mayor, currently. **Orgs:** Chairman, City of Camden Parking Authority, 1988-89; board member, Cooper's Ferry Development Assn; life member, Telephone Pioneers; member, Camden County NAACP; president, Parkside Little League; former president, Parkside PTA. **Business Addr:** Mayor, City of Camden, 6th & Market Streets, Camden, NJ 08101.

THOMPSON, ALBERT N.
Beverage company executive. **Career:** Vending machines, owner, 1965; Abelson's, retail beverage outlet, owner; Pabst Blue Ribbon, wholesaler, 1975; Falstaff, wholesaler, 1975; Pabst Blue Ribbon Products, New York State, master wholesaler, 1984-, Pabst Brewing Co, New York State Operations, director, currently; Housing Authority Police Force, lt, 15 years; Office of the District Attorney, Investigations Division, lt; Consolidated Beverage Corp, chief executive officer, currently. **Orgs:** Toys for Tots; Marine Corps Junior Cadets Scholarship; Bernice Riley Thompson Scholarship Fund, founder, 1985; board member of following: Urban Resource Institute, Culinary Institute of America, Regional Plan Assn, New York City Partnership, New York Urban League, Harlem Dowling Society, Service Academy Review Board Commission. **Honors/Awds:** Honored by the National Chinese Women's Society. **Special Achievements:** Black Enterprise Magazine, BE 100 List of Top Industrial Companies, Number 82, 1992. **Military Serv:** US Marine Corps, master sgt, active and reserves, 30 years; recalled to active duty, Desert Storm. **Business Addr:** Chief Executive Officer, Consolidated Beverage Corp, 235 W 154th St, New York, NY 10039.

THOMPSON, ALBERT W., SR.
State official (retired), attorney. **Personal:** Born Jun 29, 1922, Ft Benning, GA; married Ozella N; children: Eloise, Charles III, Albert. **Educ:** Savannah State Coll, BS 1942; Howard Univ Sch Law, JD 1950. **Career:** Atty Columbus, GA since 1951; Georgia General Assembly, 1965-1980; Special Judiciary Com, chmn, 1975; Chattahoochee Judicial Circuit, superior court judge, 1981-1982; Georgia Board of Workers Compensation, administrative law judge, until 1991. **Orgs:** State Crime Commn; State Bar GA; Columbus Lawyers Club; NAACP; YMCA; former mem Nat Council; dir Muscogee Co Red Cross; Social-Civic 25 Club; Dem Exec Com. **Honors/Awds:** State & Co Progressive Club's Man of Yr 1966. **Military Serv:** AUS sgt 1943-46.

THOMPSON, ALMOSE ALPHONSE, II
Attorney. **Personal:** Born Feb 12, 1942, Shawnee, OK; son of Lucille Marshall Thompson and Aimose Alphonse Thompson; married Delma Jean Thompson; children: Almose A III, Jennie. **Educ:** UCLA, BS 1962, Teaching Credential 1965, EdD 1972; Cal State Univ Long Beach, MA 1970; Vanderbilt Univ Law School, JD 1988. **Career:** LA Unified school Dist, secondary teacher 1965-68; CA State Univ, dir project upward bound & asst prof 1968-70; UCLA, part time instructor 1970-71; Holman &Thompson Inc, educ consul 1970-72; Univ of CA Santa Barbara, assoc dean of students; Portland State Univ, asst prof of curriculum & instruction 1972-74; Moorhead State Univ, asst prof of secondary educ 1974-75; CA State Univ, assoc prof & dir; Martin Luther King Jr Genl Hosp & Charles R Drew Post Grad Med School, educ eval specialist 1976-78; City of LA, prog dir 1978-79; Curatron Systems Inc, vice pres & Head of educ div 1978-79; Metropolitan Weekly, staff writer 1980-84; TN State Univ, prof of educ admin; syndicated columnist, Metropolitan Weekly; The Legal Clinic, Nashville, TN, sr partner, 1989-. **Orgs:** Bd mem Walden Univ Bd of Rsch Advisors & Readers 1984-; rsch fellow selected 3 consecutive yrs Southern Educ Found 1980-83; mem ASPA, Natl Assn of Black, State of TN Pol Sci Assn; State's Media Corp; TN Prof Educational Admin Assn; Natl Assn of Social & Behavorial Scientists. **Honors/Awds:** Awd for article "Blacks in America before Columbus" Negro History Bulletin 1975; 2 Grad Fellowships UCLA 1964 1970; Awd from The Black Caucus TN Genl Assembly 1982; Awd from the Mayor of Memphis 1982; numerous publications including, "Black Studies is Down to This" Black Times 1976; "Albina & Educational Reform" Portland Observer Special Issue Feb 15 1974; "The Student's Guide to Better Grades" NDS 1983; contributor "On Being Black, An In-Group Analysis" edited by David Pilgrim, published by Wyndham Hall Press 1986; passed written examination for Tennessee Bar, Tennessee Board of Bar Examiners, 1989. **Military Serv:** USN E III 1963-65.

THOMPSON, ALVIN J.
Physician. **Personal:** Born Apr 5, 1924, Washington, DC; son of Aurelia Pinchot Speller-Thompson and Victor J Thompson Sr; married Faye; children: Michael, Donna, Kevin, Susan, Gail. **Educ:** Howard Univ Coll of Liberal Arts, attended 1940-43, BS 1981; Howard Univ Med Sch, MD 1946; St Louis City Hosp, internship 1946-47; St Louis Hosp, residency 1947-51. **Career:** Providence Hosp, gastroenterology lab founder/dir 1963-77; Univ of Washington Sch of med, clinical prof; Providence Hosp, chief of medicine 1972-74; Veterans Adminstrn Hosp Univ Hosp, Harborview Med Ctr, attending physician; Providence Hosp, Swedish Hosp Med Ctr, attending staff; Veterans Administration Seattle, physician gastroenterologist 1953-59; Private Practice, physician gastroenterology internal medicine 1957-. **Orgs:** Certified Amer Bd of Internal Medicine 1953, recertified 1974; alternate delegate 1974-80 delegate 1980-89 Amer Medical Assn; gov Amer Coll of Physicians for WA & AK 1974-78; WA State Med Assn; WA State Soc of Internal Medicine; Puget Sound Health Planning Bd; Puget Sound Health Systems Agency; King Co Medical Soc; King Co Comprehensive Health Planning Council; King Co Blue Shield; Seattle Acad of Internal Medicine; Providence Hosp; Amer Coll of Physicians; Amer Med Assn; Amer Gastroenterologic Assn; Amer Soc for Gastrointestinal Endoscopy; N Pacific Soc of Internal Medicine; Amer Soc of Internal Medicine; Inst of Medicine Natl Acad of Sciences; Natl Med Assn; president, WSSIM, med staff Providence Hospital, KCMS, WSMA, Seattle Academy of Med, State Assoc of Black Profesionals in health care, delte AMA, President, Washington State Assoc for Biomedical Research; Seattle King County Board of Health. **Honors/Awds:** Kappa Cup for Superior Scholarship Howard Univ 1941; Robt H Williams Superior Leadership Awd Seattle Acad of Internal Medicine 1979; Inst of medicine Natl Acad of Scis 1978; Council for Cooporate Responsibility Seattle Chamber of Commerce 1983; Natl Assn of Medical Minority Educators for Outstanding Contrib in Health 1983; Philanthropist of the Year 1989; Washington Give's; Seattle Links Inc, Human Rights Day Award; Master, American College of Physicians; Alpha Omega Alpha. **Special Achievements:** Publications: "Pernicious Anemia in the Negro," co-author, Journal of the Natl Med Assn, 1948; "Klebsiella Pneumoniae Meningitis," Archives of International Medicine, 1952, "Mesenteric Valvular Insufficiency," Northwest Medicine, 1962; numerous other editorials and articles. **Military Serv:** Appointed US Naval Academy 1940; Howard Univ, ROTC, 1940-43, pfc, commanding officer, ASTP, 1943-46; US Army, 1st lt, 1946-48; US Air Force, captain, 1951-53; US Air Force Reserve, major, 1953-59. **Business Addr:** Physician, 1600 E Jefferson, #620, Seattle, WA 98122.

THOMPSON, ANNE ELISE
Federal judge. **Personal:** Born Jul 8, 1934, Philadelphia, PA; daughter of Mary Elise Jackson Jenkins and Leroy Henry; married William H Thompson, Jun 19, 1965; children: William H Jr, Sharon A. **Educ:** Howard Univ, BA 1955; Temple Univ, MA 1957; Howard Univ Law Sch, JD 1964. **Career:** Office of the Solicitor US Labor Dept Chicago, staff atty 1964-65; Legal Aid Soc of Mercer Co, staff atty 1966-67; Trenton, asst dep pub defender 1967-70; Twp of Lawrence NJ, prosecutor 1970-72; City of Trenton, municipal court judge 1972-75; Mercer Co Trenton NJ, prosecutor 1975-79; District of New Jersey, federal judge, 1979-. **Orgs:** Member, American Bar Assn; member, New Jersey Bar Assn; member, Federal Bar Assn. **Honors/Awds:** Outstanding Leadership Award, New Jersey County Prosecutors Assn, 1980; Gene Carte Memorial Award, American Criminal Justice Assn, 1980; John Mercer Langston Outstanding Alumnus Award, Howard Univ Law School, 1981. **Business Addr:** Federal Judge, U S District Court, 402 E State St, Trenton, NJ 08605.

THOMPSON, ART, III
Journalist. **Personal:** Born May 29, 1955, San Francisco, CA; son of Ocie Mae Matson Thompson and Arthur Thompson Jr; children: Arthur IV, Ania Rashida. **Educ:** West Los Angeles College, Culver City, CA, AA, general studies, 1976; California State University, Chico, Chico, CA, BA, information & communication, 1978; Valley Electronics School, Van Nuys, CA, first class broadcasters license, 1980; University of Arizona, Institute for Journalism Education, Tucson, AZ, completion of editing program for minority journalists, 1982. **Career:** Wave Newspapers, Los Angeles, CA, sports editor, 1978-81; Modesto Bee, Modesto, CA, sportswriter, 1981-84; St Louis Post-Dispatch, St Louis, MO, sportswriter, 1985-88; Orange County Register, Santa Ana, CA, sportswriter, 1988-. **Orgs:** Committee member, Los Angeles Chapter, Jack Yates Sr High Alumni; member, Baseball Writers of America Association; member, National Association of Black Journalists; Pro Football Writers of America; Southern California Association of Black Journalists; US Basketball Writers Assn; Football Writers Assn of America; NABJ Sports Task Force, western regional dir. **Honors/Awds:** Writing Award in News, catagory for newspapers of over 175,000 circulation, Associated Press Sports Editors, 1990, 1992-; Excellence Award, Greater St Louis Association of Black Journalists, 1988; APSE, Writing Award, Enterprise Catagory for Newspapers over 175,000 Circulation, 1992. **Business Addr:** Staff Writer, Sports, Orange County Register, 625 N Grand Ave, Santa Ana, CA 92711.

THOMPSON, BEATRICE R.
Psychologist. **Personal:** Born May 5, 1934, Townville, SC; daughter of Canary Rice and Elliott Rice; married Harry S Thompson; children: Randy, Stephen, Darryl. **Educ:** BA English; MA English; MA Guidance 1973; EdS Educ Psychology; Univ of GA, PhD 1978. **Career:** Anderson, SC, sch psychologist 1972-; Tri-Co Tech Coll, psychology instr 1972-74; Anderson, SC, HS guid couns 1967-71, HS Eng tchr 1954-65. **Orgs:** Mem Anderson United Way Bd; City Councilwoman, Anderson SC 1976-; mem SC Nat Bank Bd; mem Crippled Children Bd; mem Family Counseling Bd; elected SC Dem Nat Com Woman 1980; mem APGA; SCPGA; SC Pupil Pers Assn; SC Assn of Sch Psychologists; NEA; Nat Council for Excep Children; Nat Assn of Black Psychologists; sec Human Relations Council; den mother; vol Cancer Soc; chmn Sch Dist Five, Counslr Orgn; SC Pers & Guid Assn; pres Zonta Intl Bus & Professional Womens Club; mem Delta Sigma Theta Sor; Phi Kappa Phi Hon Soc; Phi Delta Kappa Hon Soc; sec-treas SC AMEG; sec-treas Anderson Family Counseling Ctr; pres, SC Municipal Assn, 1987-88. **Honors/Awds:** NDEA Guid & Counseling Fellow; Gen Elec Guid Fellow. **Business Addr:** School Psychologist, Anderson School District 5, Anderson, SC 29622.

THOMPSON, BENJAMIN FRANKLIN
Public administrator. **Personal:** Born Aug 29, 1947, Philadelphia, PA; married JoAnne Snow; children: Kaif. **Educ:** Boston State Coll, 1971-74; Antioch Univ, MEd 1979; Kennedy School Govt Harvard Univ, MPA 1982. **Career:** MA Halfway Houses Inc, prog dir 1975-78; MA Dept Corrections, dir of prog 1978-80; MA Dept Social Svcs, area dir 1980-82; Dept Social Svcs, consult 1983-84; Suffolk Cty Penal Dept, commiss 1984-; City of Boston, sr policy advisor on equal/humans rights, dep mayor 1984-. **Orgs:** Mem Intl Halfway Houses Inc 1976-84, Amer Correctional Assoc 1977-84; chmn Mayors Coord Council on Drug Abuse 1984-85; candidate Boston City Council 1984. **Military Serv:** USAF sgt 4 yrs. **Business Addr:** Senior Policy Advisor, Boston City Hall, Mayors Office, City Hall, Boston, MA 02201.

THOMPSON, BENNIE
Professional football player. **Personal:** Born Feb 10, 1963, New Orleans, LA. **Educ:** Grambling State, attended. **Career:** Winnipeg Blue Bombers (CFL), 1986-88; New Orleans Saints, defensive back, 1989-91; Kansas City Chiefs, 1992-93; Cleveland Browns, 1994-95; Baltimore Ravens, 1996-. **Honors/Awds:** Pro Bowl appearances, 1991, 1995; Ed Block Courage Award, 1995; Playoff Corporation, Unsung Hero Award, 1996. **Business Addr:** Professional Football Player, Baltimore Ravens, 11001 Owings Mills Blvd, Owings Mills, MD 21117, (410)654-6200.

THOMPSON, BENNIE G.
Congressman. **Personal:** Born Jan 28, 1948, Bolton, MS; married London Johnson. **Educ:** Tougaloo College, BA, 1968; Jackson State Univ, MS, 1972. **Career:** US House of Representatives, congressman, 1993-; Hinds County, supervisor, 1980-93; Town of Bolton, mayor 1973-79; Tri-Co Comm Cntr, proj dir 1970-74; Meadville MS, tchr 1968-70. **Orgs:** Asst dir Tchr Corps 1974-; chmn of bd Farish St YMCA; Mt Beulah Devel Found; vchmn of bd The Delta & Ministry; bd dir So Reg Cncl; Am Civil Lbrts Un. **Honors/Awds:** Otstndng Yng Men of MS Awd NAACP; Otstndng Prsnlts of S 1971; Pltcn of Yr Jcksn St Coll 1973; Alumnus of Yr Awd Utica Jr Coll 1974. **Business Addr:** Congressman, US House of Representatives, 1408 Longworth House Office Bldg, Washington, DC 20515-2402.

THOMPSON, BETTE MAE
Librarian. **Personal:** Born Nov 12, 1939, Washington, DC; daughter of Dorothy Louise Hunter Thompson and Louis Merritt Thompson; married Jerry Ward O'Dell, May 3, 1963 (divorced 1980). **Educ:** Antioch College, Yellow Springs, OH, BA, 1962; University of Michigan, Ann Arbor, MI, AMLS, 1968. **Career:** Perry Nursery School, Ann Arbor, MI, teacher, 1962-67; Detroit Public Library, Detroit, MI, children's librarian, 1969; Ann Arbor District Library, Ann Arbor, MI, reference librarian, 1970-. **Orgs:** Member, American Library Assn; member, Black Caucus of the American Library Assn; member, Public Library Assn; member, Michigan Library Assn; member, Assn of African American Librarians. **Honors/Awds:** Beta Phi Mu. **Home Addr:** 648 Cloverdale, Ann Arbor, MI 48105. **Business Addr:** Librarian, Ann Arbor District Library, Information Resources Dept, 343 S 5th Ave, Ann Arbor, MI 48104.

THOMPSON, BETTY LOU
Elected official, association executive. **Personal:** Born Dec 3, 1939, Helm, MS; daughter of Lubirtha Lacy Bolden and William Sam Bolden; married Jack Thompson, 1958; children: Anthony, Tyrone, Sonja, Kwame. **Educ:** Harris Teachers Coll, BA 1962; Hubbard Bus Coll, 1963-65; Washington Univ, certificate 1972. **Career:** Daniel Boone PTO Univ City, past pres 1977-78; Women in Municipal Govt, past pres 1983-84; Assoc

for Non-Violent Social Change for Amer, pres; KATZ Radio Station, host talk show 1963-; Human Develop Corp, area coordinator 1964-90; pres MLK MO Support Group; St Louis County Govt, special asst, 1991-. **Orgs:** Mem PUSH; mem NAACP; mem Natl League of Cities; past pres Black Women of Unity 1975-79; mem Camp Fire Girls 1982; mem Natl Assoc of Media Women 1980-; Dr MLK, past president, 1988-89; BECO, co-chair & founder, 1990-91; member, U City, City Council, 1980-. **Honors/Awds:** Comm service Zeta Phi Beta Sor 1973; comm service George Washington Carver Awd 1977; Employee of the Year Human Development Corp 1978; comm service Martin Luther King Awd 1985; Best Speaker of the Year Award 1986; 1987; Two Speaking Albums, "Do Your Best But Don't Leave God Out," "Philosophy Called Anyway"; Dr MLK Award, 1987-88; Employee of the Year Award, 1989; BECO, Black Elected County Official, 1990-91. **Business Addr:** Special Assistant to Buzz Westfall, St Louis County Government Center, County Gov, Dept of County Executive, 41 S Central, 9th Floor, Clayton, MO 63105.

THOMPSON, BOBBY E.
Mayor. **Personal:** Born Aug 15, 1937, Florence, AL; son of Althea Thompson Lovelace and William Thompson; married Vera L. Pride Thompson, Sep 3, 1960; children: Cheryl L, Karen E Thompson-Sprewer. **Career:** Uptown Meat Market, Waukegan IL, owner, 1972-75; United Insurance Co, Chicago IL, agent, 1977-83; City of North Chicago, North Chicago IL, mayor, 1983—. **Orgs:** Lake County Economic Development Commission, Community Action Board; past potentate, Prince Hall Shriners; 33rd Degree Mason, Rufus Mitchell Lodge #107 Prince Hall; member, NAACP, 1976-; blue ribbon committee member, National Prince Hall Shriners, 1988. **Honors/Awds:** Distinguished Service Award, We Do Care, 1981; Top Black Elected Official, Illinois Black Elected Official, 1990; Trend-Setter Award, LeMoyne-Owen College Alumni Assn, 1989. **Home Addr:** 1915 Dugdale Rd, North Chicago, IL 60064.

THOMPSON, BRENDA SMITH
Educational administrator. **Personal:** Born Jun 17, 1948, Richmond, VA; married Hugo Harrison Thompson; children: Rodney Harrison. **Educ:** Virginia Union Univ, B 1970; Virginia Commonwealth Univ, M 1977; Virginia Polytechnic Inst & State Univ, D 1983. **Career:** Medical Coll of VA, lab specialist 1970-75; J Sargeant Reynolds Comm Coll, instructor 1977-80; State Council of Higher Educ for VA, asst coord 1984-85; Virginia Union Univ, dir enrollment mgmt 1985-. **Orgs:** Pres Natl Assoc of Univ Women Richmond Branch 1984-85; mem Richmond Professional Women's Network, VASFAA, SASFAA, NASFAA, VACRAO, SACRAO, NACDRAO; mem NAACP, Alpha Kappa Alpha Sor. **Honors/Awds:** Doctoral Fellowship State Council of Higher Educ for Virginia 1980, 81; Disting Volunteer Parent for John B Gary Elem Sch 1981,83; Disting Alumni Awd Natl Assoc for Equal Oppor in Higher Educ 1986. **Home Addr:** 4004 Poplar Grove Rd, Midlothian, VA 23113. **Business Addr:** Dir Enrollment Mgmt Serv, Virginia Union Univ, 1500 North Lombardy St, Richmond, VA 23220.

THOMPSON, CARL EUGENE
Life insurance company executive. **Personal:** Born Aug 9, 1953, Siler City, NC; son of Minnie L Thompson and Robert L Thompson; married Karen Mechelle McClain, May 3, 1981; children: Carla Michelle, Karen Nicole, Carl E Jr. **Educ:** NC Central Univ, BA Phil 1976; Univ of MA at Amherst, Masters Reg Planning 1985. **Career:** Town of Pittsboro, patrolman 1976-78; Home Security Life Ins Co, sales rep 1978-80; North State Legal Svcs, legal asst 1980-83; licensed realtor 1982-; Charlotte Liberty Mutual Ins Co, sales rep 1984-; Chatham Co, co commissioner; Monumental Life Insurance Co, sales rep 1986-; Beulah United Church of Christ, pastor, currently; Thompson Insurance and Realty, owner, currently. **Orgs:** Bd of dirs Capital Health Systems Agency 1978; bd of dirs Joint Orange Chatham Comm Action 1980; bd of dirs Council on Aging Chatham Co 1983; CEO Capital Development Inc 1982-; CEO NC Woodcutters Assn Inc 1984-; Rural Economic Develop consultant 1984-; consultant Social Security 1984-; Wesley Chapel United Church of Christ, assoc minister 1986-; Central Caroline Tech Coll, board of trustees 1986-. **Honors/Awds:** Natl Rural Fellowship Nat Rural Fellows Inc NY 1983-84. **Home Addr:** 67 Robert Thompson Rd, Bear Creek, NC 27207.

THOMPSON, CAROL BELITA (CAROL THOMPSON COLE)
Government official. **Personal:** Born Aug 5, 1951, Washington, DC. **Educ:** Smith Coll, BA 1973; NY Univ, MPA 1975. **Career:** Govt of the Dist of Columbia, spec asst housing 1979-81, act dir licenses, inv 1981-83, dir consumer & reg affairs 1983-86, mayor's chief of staff 1986-87, dep mayor econ dev 1987-91; RJR Nabisco Inc, vice pres of govt and environmental affairs, 1991-. **Orgs:** Bd mem Natl Conf of Christians & Jews 1983-; bd mem Ronald McDonald House 1985-; bd pres Asbury Dwellings Home for Seniors 1985-; co-chairperson DC Downtown Partnership 1987-. **Honors/Awds:** NASPFAA Urban Adm Fellow; Martin Luther King Jr Fellow; Outstanding Young Women in Amer 1982; Outstanding Prof Serv Awd Natl Assoc of Negro & Professional Women 1987; Outstanding Govt Serv Awd Natl Black MBA Assoc 1987. **Business Addr:** Vice Pres, Government and Environmental Affairs, RJR Nabisco Inc, 1301 Avenue of the Americas, New York, NY 10019-6054.

THOMPSON, CECIL, SR.
Cleric, author (retired). **Personal:** Born Sep 6, 1930, Washington, DC; son of Mamie Thompson and James C Thompson; married Ann P Thompson, Jun 29, 1958; children: Vicki, Vera, Valerie, Victor, Cecil Jr, Vincent, Vance. **Educ:** Washington Bible College, 1951-55. **Career:** Shining Star Community Organization, 1967-70; Sheridan Terr Tenant Council, president, 1967-69; United Planning Organization, counselor, 1967-70; Job Developer, 1970-72; Craig Memorial Community Church, pastor, 1973. **Honors/Awds:** World of Poetry, Gold Medal, 1992, Golden Poet Award, 1988, 1989. **Special Achievements:** Author, Afro-America's Quest for Freedom, Vantage Press, 1991; Fluent in Spanish & French; Licensed Tour Guide, Washington, DC. **Military Serv:** US Marine Corps, corporal, 1951-53. **Home Addr:** 321 University Blvd West #129, Silver Spring, MD 20901-1954, (301)593-1522.

THOMPSON, CHARLES H.
Business owner. **Personal:** Born May 24, 1945, Kimball, WV; son of Ardella Richardson Thompson and Herbert Thompson; married Harriet Jones Thompson, Jul 2, 1982; children: Charles Jr, Kellye, Eric, NaShawn. **Educ:** Fisk U, BS 1967; TN St U, MA 1968; LA St U, PhD 1989. **Career:** Southern Univ, swimming coach 1968-70; Dillard Univ, swimming coach 1970-74; Tuskegee Univ, assoc prof physical educ 1975; Charlie Tees Screen Printing, owner 1982-; Tuskegee Univ, head basketball coach 1975-88. **Orgs:** Aquatics dir YMCA; Am Swmng Coaches Assoc; Am Alliance Hlth Phy Ed & Rec ARC; aquatics adv New Orleans Rec Dept 1973-74; mem Natl Assoc of Basketball Coaches; pres SIAC Basketball Coaches Assoc; information dir SIAC 1981-85; Kappa Alpha Psi, 1966-. **Honors/Awds:** 1st Black Swmng Champ So AAU Coached 1973; SIAC Coach of the Year 1979; SIAC Championships 1979, 1980, 1982. **Home Addr:** 1204 Johnson St, Tuskegee Institute, AL 36088. **Business Addr:** Owner, The Great Tuskegee Trading Co, 1311 Old Montgomery Rd, Tuskegee Institute, AL 36088, (334)724-0308.

THOMPSON, CLARISSA J.
Educator. **Personal:** Born Feb 24, 1930, Sugar Land, TX; divorced; children: Chanthini, Emmitt. **Educ:** TX So U, BA 1951, MEd 1965. **Career:** Shrpstwn Jr High Hstn, emmitt asst prin 1971-; Hstn Independent School Dist, conselor 1965-71, english teacher 1955-65; Wdsn HS Nrmng, english math teacher 1952-55; Abrhm Schwrtz Firm Hstn, asst accountant 1951-52; Neighborhood Youth Corps, council 1970. **Orgs:** Mem Assn for Super & Curr Devel; TASCD; HASCD; TX Assn of Scndry Sch Prins; TX St Tchrs Assn; Hstn Prins Assn; Hstn Cncl of Edn; Phi DeltaKaapa Frat; cncl Delta Sigma Theta Sor One Am Proj 1970-72; mem Blue Bonnet Garden Club; Macgregor Civic Club; mem Strng Com Tri-U; Hrcrt Brace Invttnl Conf 1966; del TSTA Conv Dist IV 1974; mem HPA Exec Bd 1974-75; HPA Rep Consult Com for Mntn & Ops 1974-75. **Business Addr:** Sharpstown Jr High St, 8330 Triola St, Houston, TX 77036.

THOMPSON, CLEON FRANKLYN, JR.
Educational administrator. **Personal:** Born Nov 1, 1931, New York, NY; son of Maggie Eady Thompson and Cleon F Thompson Sr; married; children: Cleondra Thompson Jones. **Educ:** NC Central Univ, BS 1954, MS 1956; Duke Univ, PhD 1977. **Career:** Shaw Univ, vice pres for academic affairs 1970, sr vice pres 1971-73; Univ of NC, acting vice pres 1975-76, vice pres student serv & special programs 1976-. **Orgs:** Mem advisory council NC Comm Coll Syst 1978-81; bd dir Shakespeare Festival 1978-81; pres Leadership Winston-Salem; mem, bd of dirs Winston-Salem Business. **Honors/Awds:** Man of the Year Kappa Alpha Psi 1970; ACE Fellowship Acad Admin Amer Council on Educ 1970-71. **Military Serv:** AUS 2nd lt 1953-55; Citation AUS Med Corps. **Business Addr:** President, Winston-Salem University, 601 Martin Luther King Jr Dr, Winston-Salem, NC 27101.

THOMPSON, DANIEL JOSEPH
Attorney. **Educ:** Tskg Inst AL, 1948; Brown Univ (cum laude), BA 1970; Hrvrd Law Sch, JD 1973. **Career:** AT&T Co Wash DC, atty 1979-; S Cntrl Bell Tele Co, atty 1978-79; Lg Aldrdg Hnr Stvns & Smmr Atlnt GA, atty 1974-77; St of AL Mntgmry, asst atty gen 1973-74. **Orgs:** Vp AL Blk Lwyrs Assn 1974; mem Nat Bar Assn; Am Bar Assn 1975-80; exec com mem Gate City Bar Assn 1977; instr Abrn Univ Mntgmry 1974; bd of dir Atlnt Urban Leag 1975-77; mem Atlnt Jdcl Commn 1977. **Business Addr:** American Telephone & Telegraph, 1120 20th St NW #1000, Washington, DC 20036.

THOMPSON, DAVID O.
Sports franchise executive. **Personal:** Born Jul 13, 1954, Shelby, NC; son of Ida Thompson and Vellie Thompson Sr; married Cathy; children: Erika, Brooke. **Career:** Denver Nuggets, guard 1975-82; Seattle SuperSonics, guard 1982-85; Charlotte Hornets, youth programs coordinator, beginning 1988; Unlimited Success, motivational speaker, currently. **Orgs:** FCA; X NBA Players Assn; YMCA. **Honors/Awds:** ABA Rookie of the Year 1975-76; All Star Game ABA 1976; All Star NBA 1977-79, 1983; only player named MVP in both ABA & NBA All Star Game; Scored 10,000th point 1981; named All Atlantic Coast Conf Player of the Year 1973, 1974, 1975; named CO Athlete of the Year 1975; Eastman Awd Collegiate Basketball Player of the Year 1974-75; Inducted into NC Sports Hall of Fame 1982; Scored 73 points in one game, 1978; Colorado Sports Hall of Fame, 1996; Naismith Natl Basketball Hall of Fame, 1996; Sports Magazine Performer of the Year, Pro Basketball, 1978; Named One of Five Best College Players in History, 1995; Leading Vote Getter, All Star Game, 1977; All NBA 1st Team, 1977, 1978; Joe Mallamo Humanitarian Award, Carolina's Athlete of the Year, 1994; Carolina's Athlete of the Year, 1973, 1974; 3 time First Team, All America, NAI Smith Award, 1975; Consensus College Player of the Year, 1975. **Business Addr:** Motivational Speaker, Unlimited Success, PO Box 13291, Charlotte, NC 28270.

THOMPSON, DEBORAH MARIA
Physician. **Personal:** Born May 4, 1958, Philadelphia, PA; daughter of Hazel Logan Thompson and William C Thompson; married Omer Abadir, May 29, 1982; children: Adam Omer Abadir, Alia Marie Abadir, Amira A Abadir. **Educ:** Howard Univ, BS (Magna Cum Laude) 1980; Howard Univ Coll of Medicine, MD 1982; Univ of MD, Post Graduate 1982-85. **Career:** Dept of Family Medicine Univ of MD, chief resident 1984-85; Community Health Ctr, medical dir 1985-89; Mid-Atlantic Permanente Medical Group, Washington, DC, physician, 1989-. **Orgs:** Mem Amer Acad of Family Physicians; MD Academy of Family Physicians 1989-. **Honors/Awds:** Mem Alpha Omega Alpha Medical Honor Soc 1982-; Diplomate Amer Bd of Family Practice 1985-92, recertified 1997-04; fellow American Academy of Family Physicians. **Business Addr:** Physician, Mid-Atlantic Permanente Medical Group, 5100 Auth Way, Suitland, MD 20746.

THOMPSON, DEHAVEN LESLIE (DEE)
Reporter, journalist. **Personal:** Born Aug 22, 1939, Philadelphia, PA; married Patricia Marlene Eberhardt; children: Shannon Leslie, Tara Neile. **Educ:** Geneva Coll, BA 1968. **Career:** WIIC-TV Pittsburgh, news & sports rprtr 1975-; WTAE-TV Pittsburgh, prdcr, assgnmnt ed 1970-75; WTAE-TV & WTAE,RADIO AM Pittsburgh, 1st blk nws ed-rptr 1966-70; Beaver Falls News Trib, 1st blk asst sprts ed 1964-66, 1st blk sprts rptr 1959-64; Black Chronicle TV Show, crtr 1968. **Orgs:** Mem Pittsburgh Press Club; bd mem Pittsburgh Pastoral Inst; mem Sigma Delta Chi; mem Pittsburgh Yth Motivation Task Force; mem Bob Moose Meml Fund Com. **Honors/Awds:** Recip PA Asso Press Award for Top Sports & News Story of Yr 1973; Golden Quill Award (Pittsburgh TV Emmy), Series on Hndcpd Athls 1977; Meritous Srv Award, Penn Hills NAACP 1977. **Military Serv:** USNG 6 yrs. **Business Addr:** WPXI-TV, 11 TV Hill, Pittsburgh, PA 15214.

THOMPSON, EDWIN A.
College president. **Career:** Atlanta Metropolitan College, GA, president, currently. **Business Addr:** President, Atlanta Metropolitan College, 1630 Stewart Ave, SW, Atlanta, GA 30310.

THOMPSON, ERIC R.
Educator. **Personal:** Born Mar 23, 1941, Warren, OH. **Educ:** Hiram Coll, BA. **Career:** Hiram Coll, asst dir of admsn. **Orgs:** Reg rep Minority Ed Serv Assn. **Honors/Awds:** Outstndng Coll Athl of Am 1970-71. **Military Serv:** USMC. **Business Addr:** Ofc of Admissions, Hiram Coll, Hiram, OH 44234.

THOMPSON, EUGENE EDWARD
Physician. **Personal:** Born Sep 25, 1938, Brooklyn, NY; son of Corrie Thompson and Eugene Thompson; married Corine; children: Eugene, Carlton, Valerie. **Educ:** Brooklyn Coll, BA 1960; Howard Univ Coll Med, MD 1968. **Career:** Dept Alchohol & Drug Abuse, med dir; NY City Fire Dept, med ofc; Mt Sinai Hosp, sr clinical asst; NIH, clinical asso 1969-71; Hempstead, pvt prac, physician, currently; South Shore Dialysis, owner, director, currently. **Orgs:** Diplomate Nat Bd Med Exmrs; Am Bd Intrntl Med; mem Am Coll Physicians; Phi Beta Sigma. **Honors/Awds:** Alpha Omega Alpha Hon Med Soc 1967; Josiah Macy Faculty Flw 1974-76. **Military Serv:** USPHS lt comdr 1969-71. **Business Addr:** Owner, Medical Director, South Shore Dialysis, 160 N Franklin St, Hempstead, NY 11550.

THOMPSON, FLOYD
Dental surgeon. **Personal:** Born Aug 5, 1914, Houston, TX; married Nellie Crawford; children: 6. **Educ:** Wiley Coll, AB 1937; Howard, dds 1942; USC dntl sch, post grad 1964. **Career:** Dr of Dent Surg, self empl 1985. **Orgs:** Mem AZ S Dent Soc; Nat Dent Assn; Am Dent Assn; mem NAACP; trustee Mt Calvary Bapt Ch; mem Urban Leag. **Honors/Awds:** Man of Yr Award, Tuscon Chptr NAACP 1961; Alumni Award for Outstndng Contri to Civic & Comm Act 1971. **Military Serv:** US Military maj 1942-46. **Business Addr:** 2600 W Ironwood Hills Dr, Apt 18190, Tucson, AZ 85745-4005.

THOMPSON, SISTER FRANCESCA
Educational Administrator, nun. **Personal:** Born Apr 29, 1932, Los Angeles, CA; daughter of Evelyn Preer Thompson and Edward Thompson. **Educ:** Marian Coll, BA 1960; Xavier Univ, MEd 1963; Univ of MI, PhD 1972. **Career:** Marian Coll Indianapolis IN, chairperson theatre dept 1966-82; Fordham Univ,

asst dean/assoc prof communications 1982-. **Orgs:** Faculty Martin Luther King Fellows 1973-; Armstead-Johnson Found for Theatre Rsch NY; Martin Luther King Jr Fellow; PUSH Adv Bd. **Honors/Awds:** Sojourner Truth Awd Marian Coll; Key to the City Clarksdale MS; 1981 Brotherhood Awd Natl Conf of Christians & Jews; Jan 12 1981 declared by Mayor of Oakland CA to be Sister Francesca Thompson Day in appreciation for being "Scholar in Residence" for Oakland Public Sch System; Dr Martin Luther King Human Rights Awd Indianapolis Educ Assn; NY State English Council Awd for Tchr of Excellence in Drama; Disting Alumnus Awd Marian Coll; Outstanding Teacher of the Year Fordham Univ 1986; Pierre Toussaint Award for Outstanding Service to the Black Catholic Community; Tony Board Nominator; Koob Award; NCEA Award, Outstanding Educator; Honorary Degrees: LeMoyne College, Syracuse, NY, St Michael College, Winooski, VT, Marian College, Indianapolis, IN; Outstanding Alumnus Award, Dept of Theatre, Univ of MI, Ann Arbor, MI. **Business Addr:** Assistant Dean, Fordham Univ, Office of Dean, Ktng Hall 302, Bronx, NY 10458, (718)817-4738.

THOMPSON, FRANK
Educator. **Personal:** Born Oct 1, 1927, West Helena, AR; married Deloise D; children: Frank Jr. **Educ:** Crescent Sch of TV & Brdcstng, Grad 1952; CUNY Vo Tech Tchr Ed, grad 1968; Adams Coll, MAED 1975. **Career:** City of NY, jr HS tchr, bd of ed; TV Sales & Srv, ownr-optr; Armed Forces, elect tech; Shoe Shine Chain, ast mgr; NY Recorder, column. **Orgs:** Fdr, pres Better TV Dlrs Assoc; union del UFT; NYSUT; AFT; NEA; pres FACEJ Srv Corp; mem Black Trade Unionists Ldrshp Comm; mem Crispus Attucks Dem Club; worshipful mstr Essene Lodge AASRFM; command in chf Grand Consist of NY; patron Excel Chap 76 OES; patron, Matron & Patrons Cncl; OES. **Honors/Awds:** Coronated "Soverign Grand Insp Gen", Supreme Cncl LA AASRFM; placque, letters of commendation Var Civ Grps. **Military Serv:** GKCS cadet corp, col.

THOMPSON, FRANK L.
Business executive (retired). **Personal:** Born Mar 28, 1903, New York, NY; son of Laura Ann Johnson and Wilson Thompson; married Marcie L Taylor, Dec 25, 1930; children: Judith Hamer, Carolyn Brown. **Educ:** Cornell Univ, CE 1924; NY Univ, MBA 1929. **Career:** Design of New York City Projects Bridges-Water Supply, civil engr designer 1924-80; FL Thompson Assoc-Design of Homes, pres 1946-58; Slingerland and Booss Arch & Engr, assoc partner 1958-67; Allied Federal Savings & Loan, pres brd chrmn 1960-80; Money Management Service, pres, owner 1985-. **Orgs:** Trustee Long Island Jewish Hosp 1978-; brd of dir Greater Jamaica Chamber of Comm; brd of dir Jamaica Devel Corp 1975-85; mem Life, Am Soc Civil Engr 1948; mem NY Soc Municipal Engrs 1946; mem Nat Techl Assn, Alpha Phi Alpha Frat, Sigma Pi Phi Frat Cornell Univ Council 1976; Frank L Thompson Asthma Seminar, Amer Lung Assn of Queens, annually, 1989-. **Honors/Awds:** Council of Black Alumni, Distinguished Alumni Award, 1989; Borough President of Queens County, Frank Thompson Day, 1993; Alpha Phi Alpha Fraternity, Distinguished Alumni Award, 1996. **Home Addr:** 85-14 150th St, Jamaica, NY 11435.

THOMPSON, FRANK WILLIAM
Physician. **Personal:** Born Jan 15, 1928, Georgetown, Guyana; married Nellie; children: Errington, Melissa, Michele, Frank II. **Educ:** Morgan State Univ, BS 1955; KS City Osteopathic Med Coll, DO 1961. **Career:** Dr Frank W Thompson & Assoc, pres. **Orgs:** Mem State Med Bd NY, OH, TX; diplomate Amer Ost Bd Gen Practice; flw Amer Coll Gen Practitioners; reg med consult Region V Job Corps 1976; adv bd TX Legislative Joint Sub-com on Pub Hlth 1974-75; mem TX Osteopathic Med Assn Govt Rels Com 1974-76; exec admissions com TX Osteo Med Coll 1974-76;hlth care com Comm Cncl Grtr Dallas 1975; mem Amer Coll Gen Prac Osteo Med & Surgery; Amer Osteo Assn; TX Osteo Med Assn; Amer Heart Assn; Natl Med Assn; Amer Public Health Assn; sec treas Alpha Phi Alpha Frat; bd mem Dallas Urban League; dir 2nd vice pres BSA; chmn W View Dist Health & Safety Comm; hon life mem US Lawn Tennis Assn; Amer Contract Bridge League. **Business Addr:** President, Dr Frank W Thompson & Assocs, 2850 Singleton Blvd, Dallas, TX 75212.

THOMPSON, FRENCH F., JR.
Small business consultant. **Personal:** Born Sep 16, 1953, Indianapolis, IN; son of Dorothy L Clark Thompson and French F Thompson Sr; married Linda Jo Paulden Thompson, Aug 7, 1977; children: Emerald Michelle, French III. **Educ:** Lincoln University, Jefferson City, MO, BS, 1975; Money Concepts University, West Palm Beach, FL, financial planner degree, 1985. **Career:** Missouri State Highway & Trnasportation, Jefferson City, MO, assistant supervisor, 1977-83; Prudential Insurance Co, Landover, MD, financial planner, 1984-86; United States Business Association, Washington, DC, account executive, 1986-87; A V Consultants, Arlington, VA, regional account executive, 1987-89; Emerald Way Enterprises, College Park, MD, president/owner, 1990-. **Orgs:** Public Relations, Maryland Health Underwiters Assn, 1989-; steward & financial committee, St Paul AME Church, 1989-; member, Concerned Black Man Inc, 1988-; events coordination, DC Chamber of Commerce, 1987-; member, Omega Psi Phi Fraternity Inc, 1972-; member, Felix Lodge #3 F&AM PHA, 1982-. **Honors/Awds:** Washington DC PTA Volunteer Award, DC Public Schools, 1989; Million Dollar Sales Club Award, Prudential Insurance, 1986; Outstanding Broker Sales, Blue Cross/Blue Shield, 1988. **Military Serv:** US Army, 1st Lt, 1975-78; Outstanding Platoon Leader, 1978.

THOMPSON, GARLAND LEE
Journalist. **Personal:** Born May 2, 1943, Chester, PA; divorced; children: Consuella Alicia, Grace Lynn. **Educ:** Temple Univ, BA, journalism, 1975, JD, 1983. **Career:** Bell Telephone of PA, switchman 1963-73; Philadelphia Inquirer, copy editor 1975-78, editorial writer 1978-81, reporter 1981-84; Philadelphia Tribune, exec editor; The Sun, editorial writer, currently. **Orgs:** Joint Comm on Minority Editorialists, Broadcast Editorial Assn 1979-81; Natl Assn Black Jrnl; Natl Conf of Edit Writers, 1979-81; faculty editor Inst for Jrnl Ed-Editing Program for Minority Journalists 1980, 1981, 1985; PA Bar Assn, 1984-. **Honors/Awds:** Temple Univ, Barrister's Award for Excellence in Trial Advocacy, student award, 1982; Univ of Kansas, Freedom Forum Professional-In-Residence, 1992-93. **Special Achievements:** First African-American mbr, Inquirer Edit Bd, 1978-81; editor of nation's oldest African-American newspaper, Philadelphia Tribune; Put together largest single editorial in the Tribunes history, 100 pages, 1984; instructor of GED preparation course, Philadelphjia Community CLG, 1975-76. **Military Serv:** USN electronics tech 2nd clas (commun) 1965-68; 2nd Honorman 1966. **Home Addr:** Editorial Writer, The Sun, 501 N Calvert St, Baltimore, MD 21278.

THOMPSON, GAYLE ANN-SPENCER
Educational administrator. **Personal:** Born Aug 17, 1956, Detroit, MI; daughter of Annie R Spencer (deceased) and Edward Spencer Sr (deceased). **Educ:** Marygrove College, BA, 1979, MA, 1989. **Career:** Marygrove College, director of residence, 1978-79, coordinator of student services, 1980-91, director of talent search, 1991-94; Marygrove College, Job Placement and Developer, coordinator, 1994-. **Orgs:** Marygrove Alumni Association, president-elect, 1990-, member at large, 1989-90; Midwest Association of Student Financial Aid Administration, 1992-; Because of Christ, tutor, 1992-; Marygrove College Alumni Assn, president, 1993-. **Honors/Awds:** Marygrove College, Iota Gamma Alpha, 1975-79; Southern Womens Athletic Conference, honorable mention, 1977; Michigan Consolidated Gas Co, Panelist Award, 1992; Martin Luther King, Chavez, Rosa Parks College Day, presenter, 1992. **Business Addr:** Director, Renaissance Talent Search Project, Marygrove College, 8425 W McNichols Rd, Rm 027, Detroit, MI 48221, (313)862-8000.

THOMPSON, GERALDINE
Educator, nurse, consultant. **Personal:** Born in Dunkirk, NY; daughter of Hattie Dickey Carter and George T Carter; married John W Thompson Sr, Nov 17, 1942; children: John Jr, Brian, Dennis. **Educ:** Jamestown School of Practical Nursing, 1954; Jamestown Comm Coll, 1968. **Career:** Jamestown Gen Hosp, staff nurse 1954-75, psych nursing 1975-85; strategic planning consultant, human service agencies, Southern Chautaugua County, currently. **Orgs:** Board of directors, Ebony Task Force, 1984-; board of directors, 1972-75, 1985-, board president, 1990-92, Jamestown YWCA; board of directors, Jamestown Community Schools Council, 1988-95; board of directors, Chautauqua County School Boards Assn, 1987-90; member, National Caucus of Black School Board Members; member, vice chair Selective Service Board, 1985-; vice president, Jamestown Democratic Women's Club, 1990-92; Jamestown Board of Public Utilities, 1991-96; The Links, Inc, Jamestown Chap, 1995-. **Honors/Awds:** 1st woman pres Jamestown School Bd 1983-85; 1st black on Selective Serv Bd; Advisory Comm on Minority Issues of the NY ST Schl Bds Assoc 1987-90; Jamestown Woman of the Year, 1991; New York State's Governors Award for African American of Distinction, 1993. **Home Addr:** 95 Liberty St, Jamestown, NY 14701.

THOMPSON, GLORIA CRAWFORD
Public affairs manager lobbyist. **Personal:** Born Aug 12, 1942, Philadelphia, PA; divorced. **Educ:** Cheyney State Univ, PA, BS Ed1968; St Joseph Coll, PA, MBA candidate 1978; Temple Univ, PA, Pub Rel 1962; Univ of PA, PA, Real Estate 1973, Master, Government Administration 1990. **Career:** SmithKline Beckman Corp, adv & sales promo 1968-72, news relations assoc 1973-75; Opportunities Industrialization Center of Amer, edtr OIC Keynens 1970-72; Natl Alliance of Businessmen, dir, coll rel 1974-76; Smithkline Beckman Corp, adv & Sales promo 1968-72, news relations assoc 1973-75, public affairs assoc 1975-87, assoc mgr Penna govt 1987-; Ross Associates, Philadelphia PA, corporate relations consultant 1989-. **Orgs:** Frmr natl sec Natl Assoc of Mkt Dvlprs (NAMD); Philadelphia Chptr Pres (NAMD); mem Public Affrs Comm PA Chamber of Comm; mem State Govt Comm Philadelphia Chamber of Comm; bd of dir Art Matters, Inc; vice chmn bd of dirs Cheyney Univ Foundation, chmn 1988-; mem Mayor's Office of Comm Serv Adv Bd; mem Minority Retention TAsk Force, Hahnemann Hosp Univ. **Honors/Awds:** Pres comdtn Pres Gerald Ford 1975; dist award Dr Charles Drew Awards Comm 1980; recogntn Natl Alliance of Businessmen 1975; mktr of the Yr Nat'l Assoc of Mkt Dvlprs 1974; hnry prfsn Prairie View State Univ 1975; Outstanding Young Women in Amer 1979-80. **Home Addr:** 2114 North 50th St, Philadelphia, PA 19131.

THOMPSON, HAROLD FONG
Architect. **Personal:** Born Sep 1, 1943, Memphis, TN; married Delilah Dianne Smith; children: Alan Craig, Kimberly Jean, Roderie, Derrell. **Educ:** Howard U, B Arch 1967. **Career:** Lyles Bissett Carlisle & Wolff, Wash, fallout shltr analyst, proj arch 1964-68; Walk Jones & Francis Mah, Memphis, proj arch 1968-69; job capt 1969-72; Clair Jones & Harold Thompson, Memphis, partner 1972-77; Thompson-Miller Arch, pres 1978-; Memphis Comm Design Ctr, vice pres 1972-74. **Orgs:** Mem Nat AIA; TN Soc Archs; Constrn Spcfctns Inst; mem Vollintine-Evergreen Comm Assn; natl trustee Hist Preservation; Ldrshp Memphis, Shelby FarmsPlng Bd 1979; mem Alpha Phi Alpha. **Business Addr:** 1420 Union Ave, Memphis, TN 38104.

THOMPSON, HERMAN G.
Attorney. **Personal:** Born in Cincinnati, OH; son of Thelma Thompson and Roscoe Thompson; married Roberta Brown; children: Collette Hill, Janice Marva. **Educ:** Ludwig Coll of Music, BME 1952; Harris Teacher's Coll, BA 1957; Howard Univ Sch of Law, JD 1968. **Career:** Charlotte, NC, asst dist atty 1972; Private Practice, atty Wash, DC 1975-77; US House of Reps Post Office & Civil Serv Comm, atty 1977-80; Private Practice, atty Southern Pines, NC 1980-. **Orgs:** Atty Commerce Dept/Ofc of Minority Bus Enterprise Wash, DC 1972; pres Moore Cty Chap NAACP 1985-; chmn Minority Affairs/Moore Cty Republican Party 1985; NC State Bd of Transportation 1987-91. **Honors/Awds:** NC Black Lawyers Assn, Community Service Award, 1994; Freedom & Justice Award, 1983, Moore County, NC, NAACP. **Military Serv:** AUS Pfc. **Home Addr:** 105 Ft. Bragg Road, Southern Pines, NC 28387. **Business Addr:** Attorney, 510 Broad Street N.W., Southern Pines, NC 28387.

THOMPSON, HOBSON, JR.
Librarian (retired). **Personal:** Born Sep 26, 1931, Tuscumbia, AL; son of Marie Belue Thompson (deceased) and Hobson Thompson Sr; married Geneva S; children: Michael Stewart, Sharon M. **Educ:** AL State Univ, BS in sec ed 1953; Atlanta Univ, MS in LS 1958. **Career:** Morris Coll, head librarian/Instr math 1954-62; Elizabeth City State Univ, head librn/asst prof math 1962-74; Chicago Public Libr, branch head 1976-98. **Orgs:** Mem Amer Libry Assoc 1953-; mem Amer Topical Assoc 1982-; mem Omega Psi Phi Frat 1951-; mem Beta Kappa Chi hnry sci soc 1952-; mem Ebony Society of Philatelic Events and Reflections 1989-. **Honors/Awds:** Masters Thesis A Study Of The Communications Behavior Of The Residents Of Census Tract F-39, Atlanta GA. **Military Serv:** USN rm/te 3rd class. **Home Addr:** 400 E 33rd St, Apt 212, Chicago, IL 60616.

THOMPSON, IMOGENE A.
Educator. **Personal:** Born Aug 13, 1927, Stonewall, MS; married Rev Marcellous C; children: Gail P. **Educ:** Jackson St U, BS 1959; UW, MS 1967; MS S & MS St, Further Study. **Career:** Meridian Public School, teacher 32 Yrs. **Orgs:** Pres Bapt Ministers' Wives Alliance 1976-80; pres Assn of Meridian Educators 1979-81; mem Ed Com C of C 1979-81; mem Lay Adv Com St Dept of Ed 1977-81; mem St Bd of Mgrs Rprsntng MS Congress of Parents & Tchrs 1977-81. **Honors/Awds:** Outstndng Ldrshp Award, St Tchrs Assn 1976; Hum Rels Award, St Tchrs Assn 1976; 11th Edition Prsnlts of the S, Am Biographical Inst 1980; MS Tchr of the Yr, St Dept of Ed 1980. **Business Addr:** Meridian Public Schools, 4101 27th Avenue, Meridian, MS 39301.

THOMPSON, ISAIAH
Government official. **Personal:** Born Nov 8, 1915, Birmingham, AL; married Lodeamer; children: Arwilda Storey. **Educ:** Fenn Coll; Cleveland State Univ. **Career:** State of Ohio, representative, District 14, 1971-. **Orgs:** Founder, 13th Dist Civic League; bd chmn, 14th Dist Civic League, 1971-; permanent mem, Natl Conf of State Legislatures, 1975-; exec vice pres, Black Elected Democrats of Ohio, 1975-; chmn, Transportation & Urban Affairs Comm, 1975-; mem, Economic Devt/Small Business Comm, 1985-; co-chair, Cuyahoga Co Delegation, 1985-; chmn, Ohio Retirement Study Commn, 1987-. **Business Addr:** Representative, 14th Dist, State of Ohio, State House, Columbus, OH 43215.

THOMPSON, JAMES W.
Dentist. **Personal:** Born Jan 8, 1943, Birmingham; married Charlie Mae; children: Scott Frederick. **Educ:** BS 1970; DDS 1974. **Career:** Jackson MI Pvt Prac, dent 1975-; Detroit Maternal & Infant Care Proj, dent 1974-75; Wayne Co Comm Coll, 1971-74; Difco Labs, 1967-71; Univ of TN 1965-67; Wayne St U, tissue culture tech 1961-65. **Orgs:** Mem Jackson Dist Dental Soc; Wolverine Dental Soc; Univ of Detroit Black Dental Alumni Assn; career prog Detroit Pub Schs; Detroit Head Start Proj, Dental Svcs; mem Detroit Jaycees; Children's Hosp Christmas Party Com; Omega Psi Phi Frat; chmn Soc Act Com. **Honors/Awds:** Recip Nat Hlth Professional Schlrshp; Robt Tindal Schlrshp. **Business Addr:** 123 N West Ave, Jackson, MI 49201.

THOMPSON, JEFFREY EARL
Certified public accountant. **Personal:** Born Apr 13, 1955, Mandiville, Jamaica. **Educ:** Univ of the District of Columbia,

BBA 1980; Certified Public Accountant 1981. **Career:** Natl Rifle Assn, asst comptroller 1978-80; Mitchell/Titus & Co, sr accountant 1980-81; Leeny Redcross & Co, mgr 1981-83; Thompson, Curtis, Bazilio & Associates PC, president, 1983-. **Orgs:** American Inst of Certified Public Accountants 1978-; Alumni Assn Coll of Business & Public Admin Univ of DC 1980-; Natl Assn of Black Accountants 1980-; chair tax issues subcommittee DC Chamber of Commerce 1985-. **Honors/Awds:** Most Outstanding Accounting Graduate Univ of DC 1980; Most Outstanding Alumni Univ of DC 1986. **Home Addr:** 322 Peabody St NW, Washington, DC 20011. **Business Addr:** President, Thompson, Curtis, Bazilio & Associates, PC, 1010 Vermont Ave NW, Ste 300, Washington, DC 20005.

THOMPSON, JESSE
Automobile dealer. **Career:** Duryea Ford Inc, chief executive officer, currently. **Special Achievements:** Company is ranked #42 in Black Enterprise's listing of the top 100 auto dealers, 1994. **Business Addr:** CEO, Duryea Ford Inc., 4875 S. Lake Rd., Brockport, NY 14420, (716)637-8134.

THOMPSON, JESSE M.
Educational administrator. **Personal:** Born Nov 3, 1946, Oxford, MS; son of Irma Thompson and Jesse Thompson; children: Stacey L Thompson, Latoya S Taylor. **Educ:** CS Mott Community Coll, AA 1968; Eastern Michigan Univ, BA 1970; Univ of Michigan, MA 1975; Central Michigan Univ, MS 1980. **Career:** Detroit College of Business, management instructor 1976-; Michigan State Univ School of Criminal Justice, staff specialist 1980-85; CS Mott Community College,treasurer, board of trustees 1980-87; Intake, Assessment and Referral Center, executive director, 1973-88; City of Flint, dir of personnel & labor relations, 1988-90; Mott Community College, dir of human resources, 1990-. **Orgs:** Chairman Genessee County Criminal Justice Staff Advisory 1981-84; member Flint Assn of Black Administrators 1981-84; Paul Harris Fellow Rotary International 1983-; Governor's Substance Abuse Advisory Commission 1989-91. **Honors/Awds:** Humanitarian of the Year Flint Inner-City Lions Club 1980; Social Worker of the Year Michigan Assn of Black Social Workers 1981. **Home Addr:** 1810 Montclair Avenue, Flint, MI 48503. **Business Addr:** Director of Human Resources, Charles Stewart Mott Community College, 1401 E Court St, Flint, MI 48503.

THOMPSON, JOHN ANDREW
Clergyman. **Personal:** Born Dec 24, 1907, McCool, MS; married Maudie Louise Lee; children: John Andrew, Karl Anthony. **Educ:** Jackson Coll, Under-grad Study; Atlanta U, Grad Study; Univ of Chicago, Grad Study; Univ of Omaha, Grad Study; Howard U, Sch of Religion, Grad Study 1950;Ministerial & Ind Coll W Point MS, DD. **Career:** Choctaw Co Sch MS, prin; Charleston MS, tchr, prin; Oakland Jr HS, 1938-41; Coll Hill HS, Pontotoc MS, prin 1941-44; Holmes Co Tr Sch Durant MS, 1944-45; Lawrence Co Tr Sch Supt 1945-46; Louisville MS Ch, pastor; Pontotoc MS, pastor; Macon MS Ch, pastor; Tabernacl Bapt Ch, W Palm Bch FL, pastor 1950; Bethel Bapt, 1951-54; Douglas Co Yth Ctr, supr 1956-66; Juveniles for NE, parole ofcr 1966-72. **Orgs:** Org Corinth Meml Bapt Ch 1955; dir Western Bapt Bible Coll, Omaha Ctr; bd mem NAACP; pres New Era Bapt St Conv of NE; fndr, pres Nat Leag ofBrthrhd & Peace; mem Interdenom Ministerial Alliance; mem Bapt Ministers Conf; Bapt Pastors Interracial Union; fdr, dir Martin Luther King Jr & Cultural Arts Ctr; bd mem Nat Bapt Conv USA Inc. **Honors/Awds:** Award Outstndng Contrib to the Comm of Omaha 1969. **Business Addr:** 3938 Florence Blvd, Omaha, NE 68110.

THOMPSON, JOHN ROBERT, JR.
College basketball coach. **Personal:** Born Sep 2, 1941, Washington, DC; son of Anna Thompson and Robert Thompson; married; children: John III, Ronald, Tiffany. **Educ:** Providence Coll, BA Economics, 1964, MA Guidance and Counseling, UDC, 1971. **Career:** Boston Celtics, player, 1964-66; St Anthony's High School, Washington DC, head basketball coach, 1966-72; Georgetown Univ, Washington DC, head basketball coach, 1972-; US Olympic Basketball Team, asst basketball coach 1976, head basketball coach 1988. **Orgs:** Past pres, bd of dir, Nat'l Assoc of Basketball Coaches 1976-; trustee, Basketball Hall of Fame; mem, selection comm for several intl and natl competitions; Nike, bd of dirs, 1991-. **Honors/Awds:** Mem of NIT Championship Team, 1963; inducted into Providence College Hall of Fame, 1974; recipient of President's Award, Patrick Healy Award, Georgetown Univ, 1982; LHD Hon, St Peter's Coll, 1982; HHD, Wheeling Coll, 1982; named US Basketball Writer's Assn Coach of the Year and The Sporting News, 1983-84, Natl Assn of Basketball Coaches, 1984-85, and twice by the Big East Conference, 1979-80, 1986-87; recipient of many other awards. **Business Addr:** Head Basketball Coach, Georgetown University, 37th & O Sts NW, Washington, DC 20057.

THOMPSON, JOHNNIE
City official. **Personal:** Born Jan 10, 1930, Walterboro, SC; married Thelma; children: Anita P Fryar, Rochelle, Ronnie. **Educ:** Palmer Coll, AS Public Serv Criminal Justice major 1976; attended Rice Bus Coll Charleston, SC. **Career:** Colleton Cty Political Action, pres & founder 1969; City of Walterboro, Teledyne Inc, production supvr 1971-83; Big-O Chrysler, new car salesman; City of Walterboro, city councilman, mayor protem, 4 yrs, council member, 18 yrs. **Orgs:** 1st exalted ruler Colleton Cty Elk Lodge 1975; 32nd Degree Mason; mem NAACP, Amer Legion, AUS Retired Assoc; Mt. Olive Baptist Church; Tuskegee Airmen Inc. **Honors/Awds:** Noble of the Mystic Shrine Arabion Temple #139; Bronze Level of Professional Sales Chrysler 1984; Salesman of the Year, 3 consecutive years, Big-O Chrysler Plymouth Dodge. **Military Serv:** AUS Armor Tank Platoon Sgt; Army Commendation; CIB; Bronze Star; Korean Pres Citation; Retired after 20 yrs hon serv served 11 mo combat in Korean War. **Home Addr:** 502 Padgett Loop, Walterboro, SC 29488.

THOMPSON, JOSEPH ALLAN
Psychiatric social worker (retired), cleric. **Personal:** Born Nov 2, 1906, Atlantic City, NJ; son of Fannie E Sims Thompson and William E Thompson; married Tracy Harvey, Dec 28, 1936 (deceased). **Educ:** Natl Training School for Boy Scout Exec Mendham NJ, 1936; Washburn Univ Topeka KS, AB 1948; Univ of Chicago School of Social Serv Admin, 1948-49. **Career:** Shawnee Cty Juvenile Cty Topeka, juvenile & adult probation officer 1932-40; Menninger Found Topeka, psychiatric aide 1950-51; US Disciplinary Barracks Ft Leavenworth, clinical social worker 1951-76; Dept of the Army, psychiatric social worker 1976-retired. **Orgs:** Deacon Grace Episcopal Cathedral Topeka 1956-; mem exec bd Jayhawk Area Council BSA, Amer Cancer Assoc KS; mem Governor's Advisory Council on Mental Health for KS; Topeka Housing Authority; Topeka Halfway House. **Honors/Awds:** Silver Beaver Awd BSA 1962; Decorated for Meritorious Civilian Svc; Distinguished Alumnus, Washburn University, 1985; St George Award, Episcopal Church, 1984; 835th Point of Light for the Nation, President George Bush, 1992; Whitney Young Jr Service Award, Boy Scouts of Amer, 1994. **Military Serv:** AUS sgt 1942-45, 1976. **Business Addr:** Deacon, Grace Episcopal Cathedral, 701 SW 8th St, Topeka, KS 66603.

THOMPSON, JOSEPH EARL, SR.
Educational administrator. **Personal:** Born in Columbia, SC; son of Margaret Elizabeth Kennedy Thompson and Hale B Thompson; married Shirley Williams, Nov 27, 1969; children: Shirley Elizabeth, Joseph Earl Jr, Amber Gale. **Educ:** Union Theological Seminary, Master of Divinity; New York Univ, MA, MEd, EdD. **Career:** Johnson C Smith University, Charlotte, NC, director of fresh/soph studies, 1970-72; Southern Assn of Colleges & Schools, Atlanta, GA, associate executive director, 1972-84; Talladega College, Talladega, AL, academic dean, 1984-88, interim president, 1988-91; Atlanta University Center, Woodruff Library, executive director, 1991-. **Orgs:** Life member, NAACP; member, Kappa Delta Pi; Natl Assn of College & University Chaplains, 1960-72. **Honors/Awds:** Honorary Doctor of Humane Letters, Talladega College, 1990; Distinguished Administrator, Alabama Assn of College Administrators. **Business Addr:** Executive Director, Atlanta University Center, 111 James P Bradley Dr, Atlanta, GA 30314.

THOMPSON, JOSEPH ISAAC
Postmaster. **Personal:** Born Aug 21, 1922, Amelia County, VA; married Mabel K; children: Sina Joann. **Educ:** VA Union U, 1942. **Career:** US Post Srv, postmaster; Postal Wrkr's Union WI, pres Madison WI, alderman 5 yrs. **Orgs:** Grand lect Prince Masonic Lodge; WI Dept of Hlth & Soc Srv Oral Exam Bd; pres City of Madison Water Commn 1970-75; Mem Nat Assn Pstmstrs US. **Honors/Awds:** Sup Accomplish Award, Postal Srv 1968. **Military Serv:** WW II vet. **Business Addr:** Postmaster, US Postal Service, 300 Mill St, Beloit, WI 53511.

THOMPSON, KAREN ANN
Financial analyst. **Personal:** Born Jun 12, 1955, Fairborn, OH; daughter of Marlien Vaughn Thompson and Jack Long Thompson. **Educ:** Univ of Dayton, BS 1977; Indiana Univ, MBA 1984. **Career:** Coopers & Lybrand, auditor 1977-79; Cummins Engine Co, intl collections manager 1979-82; Chrysler Corp, finance manager, process cost and management reporting manager, currently. **Orgs:** National Alumni Association, Univ of Dayton, president, 1993-96; Chrysler Management Club, treasurer, 1995-96. **Honors/Awds:** Certified Public Accountant State of IN 1980; Fellowship Consortium for Grad Study in Mgmt 1982-84. **Home Addr:** 17576 Glenwood Blvd, Lathrup Village, MI 48076-2707.

THOMPSON, KEVIN
Professional basketball player. **Personal:** Born Feb 7, 1971, Winston-Salem, NC. **Educ:** North Carolina State. **Career:** Portland Trail Blazers, 1993-. **Business Addr:** Professional Basketball Player, Portland Trailblazers, 1 N Center Court St, Ste 200, Portland, OR 97227-2103, (503)234-9291.

THOMPSON, LANCELOT C. A.
Educator (retired). **Personal:** Born Mar 3, 1925; son of Vera Leolyn Reid Thompson (deceased) and Cyril Alfonso Thompson (deceased); married Naomi E; children: Lancelot Jr, Carol Lynn, Angela Maria. **Educ:** BS 1952; PhD 1955. **Career:** Wolmers Boys School, teacher 1955-56; Penn St Univ, research fellow 1957; University of Toledo, asst prof 1958, asst dean 1964, vice pres, prof 1966, vice pres student affairs 1985, professor emeritus, chemistry, 1988. **Orgs:** Chmn local sect Am Chemical Soc; mem NY Acad Sci; exec com Nat Std Prsnl Adminstrs 1972; editorial bd NASPA Jrnl 1972; mem Mayor's Com on Alcoholism; Toledo Dev Com; life mem NAACP; mem, Pres local grp Torch Intl 1974; Phi Kappa Phi 1963; Sigma Xi 1956; Blue Key 1964; vice chairman, Toledo Red Cross, 1990-. **Honors/Awds:** Key to Golden Door Award, Intl Inst 1973; Distngshd Bro Award, Mdwstrn Reg, Alpha Phi Alpha Frat 1973. **Home Addr:** 2507 Cheltenham, Toledo, OH 43606.

THOMPSON, LARRY D.
Attorney. **Personal:** Born Nov 15, 1945, Hannibal, MO; son of Ruth Robinson Thompson Baker and Ezra Thompson; married Brenda Taggart; children: Larry Jr, Gary. **Educ:** Culver-Stockton Coll Canton MO, BA 1967; MI State Univ, MA 1969; Univ of MI Ann Arbor, JD 1974. **Career:** Monsanto Co St Louis MO; staff atty 1974-77; King & Spalding Atlanta GA, assoc 1977-82; US Dept of Justice, US attorney (Northern District of Georgia) 1982-86; King & Spalding Atlanta GA, partner 1986-. **Orgs:** Mem Amer Bar Assoc, Gate City Bar Assn, State Bar of GA, The MO Bar, Natl Bar Assoc, GA Comm on Bicentennial of US Constitution; bd of dir Atlanta Urban League; bd of dirs, King-Tisdale Cottage Foundation, Savannah GA; bd of dirs, Georgia Republican Foundation 1989; chmn, Georgia Lawyers for Bush 1988. **Honors/Awds:** Dist Alumni Awd Culver-Stockton Coll Canton MO 1983; AT Walden Awd Gate City Bar Assn 1984. **Business Addr:** Partner, King & Spalding, 191 Peachtree St NE, Atlanta, GA 30303-1763.

THOMPSON, LASALLE, III
Professional basketball player. **Personal:** Born Jun 23, 1961, Cincinnati, OH. **Career:** Kansas City Kings, 1983-85, Sacramento Kings, 1986-89, Indiana Pacers, 1989-. **Honors/Awds:** Top Kings rebound (82) & shot blocker (147 total 21); had 38 double figure scoring games in 83-84 season; in college led NCAA Dev rebounding in 81-82 with 135 ave; set all TX rebounding records single game (21); most rebounds season (370 in 1980-81); led TX in scoring soph & jr years. **Business Addr:** Professional Basketball Player, Indiana Pacers, 300 E Market St, Indianapolis, IN 46204-2603.

THOMPSON, LAURETTA PETERSON (LAURETTA NAYLOR)
Educator. **Personal:** Born Sep 19, Chicago, IL; daughter of Ada Ferrell Peterson and Arthur W Peterson; married Gears H, Sep 22, 1973. **Educ:** Wilson Jr Coll, 1942; Chicago Tchrs Coll, BA 1949, BE 1949; NWU, MA 1953; Vanderbilt Univ of George Peabody Coll, EdD 1983. **Career:** Wendell Smith, asst prin 1973-; McCosh Primary, asst prin 1960-69; Mntl Hlth Prog, coord dir 1969-73; rdng coord, adjstmnt cnslr 1954-60. **Orgs:** Elem Adjstmnt Tchrs Assn; Chicago Assn of Asst Elem Prins; former vice pres Woodlawn Mntl Hlth Ctr; former bd chmn Plano Child Dev Ctr; Alpha Kappa Alpha; Alpha Gamma Pi; NAACP; mem Kappa Delta Pi Hon Soc Educ; Natl Assn of Univ Wmn; vice pres Berean Ch Credit Union; 2nd vice pres Wendell Smith Hm & Sch Assn; Urban League; PUSH; gen supt Berean Baptist Church Sch; pres, Beatrice Caffrey Youth Service Inc. **Honors/Awds:** Theta Omega Chap AKA; semi-finalist K Maremont Tchr of Yr; dedication awd AME Ch 1976; plywrtr, prod Credit Union Plays 1966-68, 1970, 1974, 1976; COSROW Award, Commission On the Status and Role of Women, South Shore United Methodist Church 1989.

THOMPSON, LINDA JO
Association executive. **Personal:** Born Aug 29, 1953, Oklahoma City, OK; daughter of Emma Lucille Jones Paulden and Moses E Paulden Jr (deceased); married French F Thompson Jr, Aug 6, 1977; children: Emerald Michelle, French F III. **Educ:** Lincoln Univ, Jefferson City MO, BA, 1975; Strayer College, master of science program, business administration, currently. **Career:** Mid-American Television, Jefferson City MO, office mgr, 1978-84; Zeta Phi Beta Sorority, Inc, Washington DC, exec dir, 1984-. **Orgs:** Mem, Natl Coalition of Black Meeting Planners; bd mem, Natl Pan Hellenic Council; bd mem, Black Women's Political Action Forum; Intl Soc of Meeting Planners, 1990-91; American Soc of Assn Exec, 1989-91. **Honors/Awds:** Grantsman Training Program, Grantsmanship Ctr, 1990. **Business Addr:** Executive Director, Zeta Phi Beta Sorority, Inc, 1734 New Hampshire Ave, NW, Washington, DC 20009.

THOMPSON, LITCHFIELD O'BRIEN
Educator. **Personal:** Born Apr 15, 1937; married Bernadette Pearl Francis; children: Gennet, Hailu. **Educ:** Enfield Coll of Tech; Univ of London, London, UK, BS (Hons) Sociology 1969; Univ of OR Eugene, MA Sociology 1972, PhD Sociology 1975. **Career:** WV St Coll, prof of sociology 1974-; Barbados Advocate Barbados WI, advertising layout spec 1959-61, advertising clk 1955-59. **Orgs:** Mem Am Sociological Assn; mem N Cent Sociological Assn; Assn of Black Sociologists, West VA Sociological Assn. **Honors/Awds:** Recip Radfen Medal Aden S Arabia, RAF 1966; flwshp Ford Fund 1972-73; pub ''Black Nationalism & the Garvey Movement Toward an Understanding'', Black Sociologist Vol 7 Nos 3/4 spring/sumer 1978; How Cricket in West Indian Cricket? Caribbean Review, Vol XII, No 2, Spring 1983; Franklyn Frazier: Mainstream or Black Sociologist? An Appraisal, Sociological Focus Vol 15, #3, 1982. **Military Serv:** RAF, 1961-66. **Business Addr:** WV State Coll, Institute, WV 25112.

THOMPSON, LLOYD EARL
Physician. **Personal:** Born Apr 10, 1934, Kingston, Jamaica; married Mercedee Ball; children: Damon, Arie. **Educ:** Union Coll Lincoln NE, BA 1960; Howard Univ Washington DC, MD 1964. **Career:** Christian Welfare Hosp, chief of staff 1977-79; Homer G Phillips Hosp, supt; Washington Univ Med School, clinical instr; Private practice, physician. **Orgs:** Mem diplomate 1970, Fellow 1972, Amer Bd of Otolarynology 1970; pres St Clair Med Soc 1979; pres Comm Hosp Bd of Dir 1979; mem St Louis Ear Nose & Throat Club, Roman-Barnes Soc of Ophthalmology & Otolaryngology; bd mem So IL Med Utilization Review Org. **Business Addr:** 4601 State St, Ste 375, East St Louis, IL 62205.

THOMPSON, LOWELL DENNIS
Artist. **Personal:** Born Oct 8, 1947, Chicago, IL; children: Tanya Natasha. **Educ:** Art Inst of Chicago, 1966. **Career:** Leo Burnett Co, art dir; J Walter Thompson Co, art dir, prod, creative grp head; Needham Harper & Steers Adv, art dir, prod 1972-74; Young & Rubicam Adv, art dir 1971-72; Greenwich Vlg NY, portrait art 1971; McLann Erickson Adv, art dir 1968-71; Am Assoc of Adv Agys, tchr 1974. **Honors/Awds:** Two Awards Rep In Creativity 77 Show, Sponsored by Art Dir Magazine; Represented in Commun Arts Magazine, 1976; Honorable Mention Adv Club of NY 1971; 1st Prize Lk Meadows Art Fair 1966; scholarship Chicago Assn of Commerce & Indus Fire Prevention Poster Contest, 1966; Numerous Gold Keys & Scholarships in Scholastic Magazine Annual Art Competition. **Business Addr:** Prudential Bldg, Chicago, IL 60601.

THOMPSON, M. T., JR.
Attorney, counselor. **Personal:** Born Apr 15, 1951, Saginaw, MI; son of Pecola Matsey-Thompson and M T Thompson Sr; married Ivory C Triplet; children: Felica L, Monica R. **Educ:** Oakland Univ, BA 1973; Northeastern Univ Sch of Law, JD 1977. **Career:** Michigan Bell Telephone Co, mgr 1973-74; Natl Labor Relations Bd, attorney 1977-79; Lewis White & Clay PC, attorney 1979-83; MT Thompson Jr PC, attorney 1983-. **Orgs:** Admitted to practice MI Supreme Court 1977, US Sixth Circuit Court of Appeals 1980, US Supreme Court 1984. **Honors/Awds:** Author "Institutional Employment Discrimination as a Legal Concept," 1981.

THOMPSON, MARCUS AURELIUS
Educator/musician. **Personal:** Born May 4, 1946, Bronx, NY; son of H Louise Stewart Thompson and Wilmore Thompson. **Educ:** Juilliard Sch Lincoln Ctr NYC, BM 1967, MS 1968, DMA 1970. **Career:** Juilliard School at Lincoln Center, viola faculty, 1969-70; Oakwood Coll, Alabama, asst prof of music, 1970-71; Wesleyan Univ, Middletown CT, viola faculty, 1971-73; Mt Holyoke Coll, S Hadley MA, lecturer, 1971-73; New England Conservatory, viola faculty, 1983-; Massachusetts Inst of Technology, prof of music, 1973-; viola soloist with Chicago Symphony, Natl Symphony, St Louis Symphony, Boston Pops, Cleveland Orchestra; recitalist, Carnegie Recital Hall, Kennedy Center Terrace Theatre, Orchestra Hall Minneapolis, Grace R Rodgers Auditorium NY, Hertz Hall Berkeley CA, Herbst Theater San Francisco, Teatro Nacional Dominican Republic, etc; chamber music appearances w/ Boston Chamber Music Soc, Chamber Music Soc of Lincoln Center, Concord, Vermeer, Manhattan, Muir String Quartets,Boston Mua Viva, etc; festival appearances at Aspen, Marlboro, Spoleto, Sitka, Newport, Seattle, Dubrovnik, Santa Fe, etc. **Honors/Awds:** Recip First Prize, Hudson Vly Philharmonic Young Artists Comp 1967; winner Young Concert Artist Inc Auditions NY 1967; winner String Prize, Nat Black Colloquim Compet Kennedy Ctr for Performing Arts Wash DC 1980; NEA Solo Recitalist Fellowship; joint-recipient, NEA Commissioning Program. **Business Addr:** Professor, Massachusetts Inst of Tech, 77 Massachusetts Ave, Cambridge, MA 02139.

THOMPSON, MARTTIE L.
Attorney. **Personal:** Born Jul 5, 1930, Meridian, MS; son of Rosie L Young Thompson and Samuel L Thompson; married Cornelia Gaines; children: Sandra M Ruffin. **Educ:** Univ of Toledo, BS 1954; St Johns Univ School of Law, 1955-56; Columbia Univ Graduate School of Business Inst for Not for Profit Mgmt, 1977. **Career:** NL & JZ Goldstin Esq, tax certiorari, eminent domain 1958-62; Wolf Pepper Ross Wolf & Jones Esqs, surrogates practice 1963-65; Wm C Chance Jr, trial counselor 1965-66; Ft Green Comm Corp, house counselor, assoc dir for urban devel 1966-68; MFY legal Serv Inc, exec dir 1970-71, mng atty 1968-70; Comm Act for Legal Serv Inc, general counsel 1971-77; Seton Hall Univ School of Law, adjunct prof 1979; Legal Serv Corp, regional dir 1977-84; private practice, atty 1984-. **Orgs:** Mem Panel for Indigent Defendants, Supreme Court Appeal Div, ABA, Natl Bar Assoc, Bar of Washington DC 1980; former consultant Natl Conf on Law & Poverty, NW Univ Law School, former mem, Natl Legal Aid & Defense Assoc Chicago; mem New York County Lawyers Assoc; vice chmn, New Jersey Chapter, Americans for Democratic Action; mem of the bd of dir, NY County Lawyers Assn; Amer Bar Assn (Labor Law Section) and a fellow of the Amer Bar Found; Assn of the Bar of the City of NY and Metropolitan Black Bar Assn; mem House of Delegates; NY State Bar; chair, National Employment Law Project. **Honors/Awds:** Author, Social Activism in Legal Services, NY Law Journal Press, 1974; New York County Lawyers' Association, William Nelson Cromwell Award, 1991. **Military Serv:** USAF sgt 1946-49. **Business Addr:** Attorney, 275 Madison Ave, Ste 718, New York, NY 10016.

THOMPSON, MAVIS SARAH (MAVIS BLAIZE)
Physician. **Personal:** Born Jun 22, 1927, Newark, NJ; married James Blaize; children: Clayton, Marcia Adele Callender, Sidney, Ronald, Kevin. **Educ:** Hunter Coll, NYC, BA 1947; Howard Univ Medical School, MD 1953. **Career:** Kings County Hospital, internship 1953-54; Kings County Hospital, resident internal medicine 1954-57; Brooklyn, NY, private practice 1957-76; Lyndon B Johnson Health Complex Inc, medical dir 1970-71, 1974-76; New York City Bd of Educ, school medical instructor 1962-85; Medgar Evans Coll, teacher dept nursing 1975-76; Kingsboro Medical Group, family physician 1976-. **Orgs:** Mem bd of dir Camp Minisink New York City 1973-; mem advisory comm Gerontological Serv Ad New School for Soc Research 1983-; board of directors, Episcopal Health Svcs; mem Amer Public Health Ass, Natl Medical Assn, Amer Gerontology Assn; den mother BSA; pres Black Caucus of Health Workers of the Amer Public Health Assoc 1976-77; lic lay St Georges Episcopal Church, Brooklyn. **Honors/Awds:** Community Serv Award, St Mark's United Methodist Church 1973; past pres Award Black Caucus of Health Workers 1977; Alberta T Kline Serv Award Camp Minisink 1980; lecturer on med Care & Geriatrics 1984-; Bishop's Cross, Episcopal Church, 1990. **Business Addr:** Family Physician, Kingsboro Medical Group, 1000 Church Ave, Brooklyn, NY 11218.

THOMPSON, MILT (MILTON BERNARD)
Professional baseball player. **Personal:** Born Jan 5, 1959, Washington, DC. **Educ:** Howard University, Washington, DC. **Career:** Atlanta Braves, 1984-85; Philadelphia Phillies, 1987-88; St Louis Cardinals, outfielder, 1988-92; Philadelphia Phillies, 1993-. **Business Addr:** Professional Baseball Player, Philadelphia Phillies, PO Box 7575, Philadelphia, PA 19101, (215)463-6000.

THOMPSON, MOZELLE W.
Federal government official. **Career:** US Treasury Dept, principal deputy asst secretary; Federal Trade Commission, commissioner, currently. **Special Achievements:** Second African American to serve as a commissioner for the Federal Trade Commission. **Business Addr:** Commissioner, Federal Trade Commission, Pennsylvania Ave and 6th St NW, Washington, DC 20580, (202)326-2222.

THOMPSON, MYRON H.
Judge. **Career:** Middle District of Alabama, judge, currently. **Business Addr:** Federal Judge, Middle District of Alabama, PO Box 235, Montgomery, AL 36101, (205)223-7312.

THOMPSON, OSWALD
Security administrator. **Personal:** Born Dec 5, 1926, New York, NY; son of Leoine Dollison Thompson and Oswald Thompson; married Eileen Preece Thompson, Nov 9, 1948; children: Katrina, Raymond, Kenneth, Luisa, Toby, Mary, Desean, Elizabeth. **Career:** New York Housing Police, New York, NY, detective, 1959-86; Apollo Theatre, New York, NY, chief of security, 1986-. **Orgs:** President, delegate, National Black Police Association, 1984-; president, Guardians Association, 1981; National Grand Master, 1948-59. **Military Serv:** US Navy, Msts, Lt Cdr, 1948-59. **Home Addr:** 1695 Grand Concourse, Bronx, NY 10453.

THOMPSON, PORTIA WILSON
Government official. **Personal:** Born Oct 23, 1944, Washington, DC; children: Lisa-Marie, Joseph M, Jared M. **Educ:** Howard Univ, BA 1968. **Career:** Bd of Governors of Federal Reserve Syst, rsch asst 1968-71, programmer 1971-74, economic system analyst 1974-80, asst to EEO dir 1980-81, mgr, bd EEO programs, 1982-84, EEO programs officer 1984-. **Orgs:** Consultant, Soul Journey Enterprises 1979-; life mem, NAACP 1980-; mem, Amer Assn of Affirmative Action, 1980-; sec, Natl Black History Observance Comm 1982-83; treas Natl Black Heritage Observance Comm 1983-; mem Friends Bethune Museum Archives Inc 1984-; mem, Natl Assn of Banking Affirmative Action Dirs 1985-, Friends of Dusable Museum 1985-; sec, Washington Metro Amer Assn of Affirmative Action, 1985-; mem Friends of Armistad, 1986. **Honors/Awds:** Outstanding contributions HD Woodson Sch of Business & Finance 1984-85. **Business Addr:** EEO Programs Officer, Bd of Governors, Federal Reserve System, 20th & C Sts NW, Washington, DC 20551.

THOMPSON, PRISCILLA ANGELENA
Government official. **Personal:** Born Oct 29, 1951, Bronx, NY; daughter of Elaine Almatha Bullard Ready and Fredric Oliver Thompson; married Clarance Patterson (divorced 1991); children: DeShield Bostwick Godet. **Educ:** Miami Dade Community College, Miami, FL, 1969-70, 1984-85, 1993; Florida Memorial College, Miami, FL, 1974-75; Barry University, Miami, FL, BSc, 1978, 1986-87; Florida Atlantic University, Boca Raton, FL, 1978-79; Florida International University, Miami, FL, 1980. **Career:** Sheraton British Col Hotel, Nassau, Bahamas, convention sales secretary, 1972-74; Dade County School Board, Miami, FL, business education instructor, 1978-81, 1990-92; Miami Dade Community College, Miami, FL, business education instructor, 1979-81; Civil Service Board City of Miami, Miami, FL, adm asst I, 1980-86; Fire, Rescue & Insp Serv, City of Miami, Miami, FL, adm asst II/senior staff analyst, 1986-90; Civil Service Board City of Miami, Miami, FL, executive secretary, 1990-. **Orgs:** Member, International Personnel Management Association, 1981-; member, Florida Public Personnel Association, 1981-89, 1991-; member, Dade County Chapter Florida Women in Government, 1989-95; member, Dade County Business Educators Association, 1978-81; member, National Association for Female Executives, 1989-; Delta Sigma Theta Sorority, Inc, 1994-. **Honors/Awds:** 2nd Place Scholarship Winner in Accounting, Dade County Assn Women Acct, 1969; Educational College Scholarship, Barry University, 1975-76; Outstanding Committee Member, Boy Scout Troop 41, 1986; Delta Sigma Theta, Sorority Inc, Chapter, UNCF, Comm Chair, 1995-96; Chap Comm Chair, Cooking Gents Affair, 1996, 1997. **Business Addr:** Executive Secretary, Civil Service Board, City of Miami, 444 SW 2nd Ave, Rm 724, Miami, FL 33130.

THOMPSON, REGINA
Nurse, educator. **Personal:** Born Dec 3, Beckley, WV; daughter of Gracie M Allen Thompson and Elder L Thompson. **Educ:** Bluefield State Coll WV, BS; Lincoln Sch for Nurses NY, Dipolma; Columbia U, MA, Post Grad Work. **Career:** Sea View Hosp, Staten Isl NY, clin instr & acting asst educ dir; Walter Reed Gen Hosp, Washington, staff nurse & acting head nurse; USPHS Hosp, NY, staff nurse; Wagner Coll Sch of Nursing, NY, instr & asst prof of nursing; Clemson Univ Coll of Nursing, SC, asst prof of nursing. **Orgs:** Natl Assn of Black Nurses; NAACP; Natl League for Nursing; SC League for Nursing; Amer Nurses Assn SC Nurses Assn; Charter Mem, Gamma Mu Chapter Sigma Theta Intl Honor Soc for Nurses; Served as first vice pres, SC League for Nurses; mem, bd of dir, Oconee chapter, Amer Red Cross; sec, SC Council on Human Relations; Orzanizer of Oconee County Chapter of MADD; Past mem, SC Joint Practice Commn; Chair, Publicity and Public Relations Comm, Oconee Cancer Trust. **Honors/Awds:** Awarded NY Regents Fellowship; Named Citizen of the Day by local Radio Station; Woman of Achievement, Lambda Chapter, Lambda Kappa Mu Sorority; Acting Dir, BS Degree Program, Clemson Univ Coll of Nursing; First advisor to student Nurse Assn, Clemson Univ; Nominated for the Jefferson Award; Certificate of Appreciation, Oconne County United Way Budget Review; Several articles published in the "Living Well" column, sponsored by the Coll of Nursing, Clemson Univ. **Special Achievements:** Research: E Colleaque, Hypertension, "Blood Pressure Patterns, Knowledge Level and Health Behaviors in Children and Adolescents," presented in Nairobi, Kenya and the University of South Alabama, 1989; Poetry: entries accepted for publication as follows, Great Poems of our times, National Library of Poetry, 1993, Library of Congress cataloging in publication Data ISBN 1-56167-044-8; named an outstanding poet of 1994 by the National Library of Poetry, Library of Congress catologing in publication ISBN 1-56167-048-0; Treasured Poems of America, any sparrow grass poetry, Forum Inc, Library of Congress catalog #90-64-0795 ISBN 5-9232-42-29-5. **Military Serv:** AUS Nurse Corps 1st lt 1957-60; USAF Nurse Corps Res capt. **Business Addr:** 714 Strode Tower Box 72, Clemson Univ Coll of Nursing, Clemson, SC 29631.

THOMPSON, RICHARD ELLIS
Educator (retired). **Personal:** Born May 5, 1935, Gary, IN; son of Roberta May Thompson and Elija Thompson; children: Kevin. **Educ:** Beatty Memorial Hospital, psych-aide training cert, 1955; Indiana University, AA, 1956; Roosevelt University, BA, 1963, MA, 1966; DePaul University, EdM, 1973; Illinois Administrators Academy, certificate, 1989. **Career:** Beatty Memorial Hospital, psychiatric aide, 1955-56, 1957-58; Lake County Children's Home, child care counselor, 1958-63; Harlan High School, Chicago Bd of Education, history teacher, 1963-70; Illinois Dept of Labor, employment counselor, 1966-67; City Colleges of Chicago, teacher/registrar/adm, 1966-70, 1973-79; Mayor's Summer Youth Program Chicago, training spec, 1976, 1977, 1980-91; Harlan HS, asst principal, 1970-97; Chicago Public Schools, consultant, 1997-. **Orgs:** Trustee, Chicago Asst Principal Assn 1973-; bd dir, Headstart Program, 1st Church of Love & Faith 1983-, trustee, 1982-; Phi Delta Kappa 1968-; notary public, Notaries Assn of Illinois 1979-; Natl Assn of Secondary School Principals 1973-; consultant, Curriculum Committee School of Education, Chicago State University 1984-. **Honors/Awds:** Kappa Delta Pi, DePaul Chapter 1973-; Achievement Award Roosevelt High School, Silver Anniv Class of '53, 1978; Eligible Bachelors, Ebony Mag 1975; Outstanding Educator of America 1975; Outstanding Secondary Educator of America 1975; Certificate of Appreciation Chicago Asst Principal's Assn 1978; Service Awd, Div of Educ Governors, State Univ Chicago 1982; 8 articles, The Administrator, Chicago Asst Principals Assn 1973-83; Distinguished Service Awared, Chicago Asst Principal's Assn, 1990. **Military Serv:** US Army, E-5, 1959-62; Good Conduct Award, 1961, Certificate of Achievement, 1962, Soldier of the Month, November 1960. **Home Addr:** 500 E 33rd St #1601, Chicago, IL 60616.

THOMPSON, ROBERT FARRIS
Educator. **Personal:** Born Dec 30, 1932, El Paso, TX; married Nancy Gaylord; children: Alicia, Clark. **Educ:** Yale U, BA 1955, MA 1961, PhD 1965. **Career:** African & Afro-Amer Art History Yale Univ, prof 1964-. **Honors/Awds:** Authored ''African Influence on the Art of the United States'' 1969; ''Black Gods & Kings'' 1971; ''African Art in Motion'' 1974; ''Four Moments of the Sun'' 1981; ''Flash of the Spirit'' 1983. **Business Addr:** Professor History of Art, Yale University, 63 Wall St, New Haven, CT 06510.

THOMPSON, ROSIE L.
Educator. **Personal:** Born Aug 16, 1950, Macon, MS; daughter of Lula B Little (deceased) and Willie Lee Little Sr; married Cornelius Thompson Sr; children: Cornelius Jr, Reginald Cornell. **Educ:** Jackson State Univ, BS, 1970, MS, 1976; Phillips Coll, AS; Univ of Arkansas, MEd, 1985; Jackson State Univ, PhD, 1997. **Career:** Canton Public Schools, science teacher, 1970-71; Tougaloo Coll, data operator, 1971, teacher, 1983; South Central Bell, data operator, 1972; Mississippi School for the Blind, teacher, 1972-79, orientation & mobility specialist, low vision clinician, 1985-92, assistant principal, 1992-96, secondary principal, 1996-. **Orgs:** Bd mem, Assn for Education of Blind; mem, Assn for Education and Rehabilitation of Blind and Visually Impaired; bd mem, Mississippi Assn for Education and Rehabilitation of Blind and Visually Impaired; mem, Black Women's Political Action Forum; life member, Zeta Phi Beta Sorority Inc, 1968-, past regional director, 1994-96; state coord, Mississippi Black Women's Political Action Forum, 1987-89. **Honors/Awds:** Outstanding Teacher's Award, Mississippi School for the Blind, 1988, 1990; Outstand Service Award, Black Women's Political Action Forum, 1988, 1989; Outstanding Service Award, Zeta Phi Beta Sorority Inc, 1988, 1991; Zeta of the Year, Zeta Phi Beta Sorority Inc, 1983; Outstanding Service Award, Mississippi Association for Education & Rehabilitation of Blind and Visually Impaired, 1991; Community Service Award, 100 Black Women's Coalition, 1993. **Home Addr:** 112 Needle Cove Dr, Jackson, MS 39206. **Business Phone:** (601)984-8211.

THOMPSON, RYAN ORLANDO
Professional baseball player. **Personal:** Born Nov 4, 1967, Chestertown, MD; son of Arrie Lee Carter and Earl Carter; married Melody Blackstone, Feb 8, 1992; children: Ryan O Jr, Camren D, Taylor A. **Career:** Toronto Blue Jays, professional baseball player, 1987-92; New York Mets, professinal baseball player, 1992-. **Orgs:** Maryland Professional Baseball Association; Professional Baseball Association. **Honors/Awds:** Maryland Professional Baseball Association, Maryland Star of the Future, 1993; Toronto Blue Jays, Labatts Player of the Year, 1989; Kent County HS, MVP in basketball, baseball and football, 1986-87. **Home Addr:** 6327 Piney Neck Rd, Rock Hall, MD 21661, (410)778-4614. **Business Addr:** New York Mets, Shea Stadium, Flushing, NY 11368, (718)565-4330.

THOMPSON, SANDRA ANN
Municipal court judge. **Personal:** Born in Hawkins, TX; daughter of Maye Thompson and L R Thompson. **Educ:** Univ of So CA, BA 1969; Univ of MI Law School, JD 1972. **Career:** Assembly Health Comm, State of California, legislative intern 1972-73; Assembly Judiciary Comm, State of California, analyst 1973-75; Dept of Consumer Affairs, State of California, legislative coord 1975-77; City Attorney's Office, City of Inglewood, CA, deputy city attorney 1977-81; Los Angeles County Dist Atty's Office, deputy district atty 1981-83; South Bay Judicial Dist, commnr 1983-84, judge 1984-86, presiding judge 1986-87, judge 1987-; chairman, Los Angeles County Municipal Court Judges Association, 1991-93. **Orgs:** CA Assn of Black Lawyers, CA Court Commnrs Assn, CA Judges Assn; life mem, CA Women Lawyers; Langston & Minority Bar Assns; chair, 1991-92, Municipal Court Judges Assn; Natl Assn of Women Judges; life mem, Natl Bar Assn, Phi Alpha Delta, Presiding Judges Assn; South Bay Bar Assn, South Bay Women Lawyers Assn; Torrance League of Women Voters 1985-; bd of trustees Casa Colina Foundation of the South Bay 1987-; Amer Assn of Univ Women, Torrance Branch, 1988-; bd of dirs, Southern California Youth & Family Center, 1988-94; Los Angeles Urban League, NAACP Los Angeles Chapter; Los Angeles County Municipal Court Judges Assn, chair, 1991-93. **Honors/Awds:** Torrance YWCA, Woman of the Year, 1992; Dr Martin Luther King Jr, Human Dignity Award, 1994; Remraw Commanders of the Rite, Distinguished Service Award, 1995. **Business Addr:** Municipal Court Judge, South Bay Judicial District, Los Angeles Municipal Court, 825 Maple Ave, Torrance, CA 90503.

THOMPSON, SHARON
Professional basketball player. **Personal:** Born Jan 21, 1976. **Educ:** Mississippi State Univ. **Career:** San Jose Lasers, forward, currently. **Business Addr:** Professional Basketball Player, San Jose Lasers, 1530 Parkmoor Ave, Ste A, San Jose, CA 95128, (408)271-1500.

THOMPSON, SHERWOOD
Chief recreation therapist. **Personal:** Born Aug 18, 1928, Poughkeepsie, NY; married Willie Bea McLawhorn; children: Anthony Edmund, Kathy Ellen. **Educ:** NC A&T State U, BS Phys Educ 1952; Tchrs Coll Columbia U, MA Spl Educ 1968. **Career:** Hudson River Psychiat Cnt Poughkeepsie, chief recreation thrpst 1964-; Mic-Hudson & Rehab Unit (narcotics) Beacon NY, cons/thrpst rec 1969; Mattewan St Hosp Beacon NY, consult thrpst recreation 1968; Dannemora St Hosp Dannemora NY, cons/thrpst receation 1966; Wassaic Dev Cnt Wassaic NY, sr institutional tchr 1962-64. **Orgs:** Pres NYS Mental Hygiene Rec Therapy Assn 1967-68; mem exec com Therapeutic Sect NYS Rec & Parks Assn 1974-77; chmn Mental Health Com NYS Rec & Parks Assn 1975-77; fndr/co-chmn/bd mem Hudson Valley Oppor Indsl Cnt 1968-; pres Catharine St Comm Cnt 1975-80; mem Poughkeepsie Rec Commn 1976-. **Honors/Awds:** Expert Infantryman's Badge AUS 1954-56; Sports Hall of Fame NC A&T St Univ Greensboro 1973-; dist serv awd NYS Rec & Parks Soc 1976. **Military Serv:** AUS 1st lt 1954-56. **Business Addr:** Hudson River Psychiat Cntr, Station B, Poughkeepsie, NY 12601.

THOMPSON, SIDNEY
Educational administrator. **Career:** Los Angeles Unified School District, superintendent, retired 1997; Univ CA at Los Angeles, sr fellow, grad school of edu, 1997-. **Orgs:** PDK; bd dir, Natl Ctr Educ & Economy; numerous other bds. **Honors/Awds:** Hon Dr Laws, Pepperdine University; numerous other awards/honors. **Business Addr:** UCLA, 705 Hilgard Ave, Moore hall GSEIS, Rm 1333, Los Angeles, CA 90024, (310)794-9290.

THOMPSON, SYLVIA MOORE
Educator (retired), business executive. **Personal:** Born Nov 4, 1937, Cincinnati, OH; daughter of Edna Moore and Clinton Moore; divorced; children: Yvette. **Educ:** Univ of Cincinnati, BS Educ 1960; OH State Univ, MA Educ 1973; OH State Univ, post grad work. **Career:** Midwest Inst for Equal Educ Oppors, consul 1973; Office of Minority Affairs OH State Univ, consul 1974; Columbus City Schools, prog coord 1975-77; Otterbein Coll Reading Ctr, tutor 1979-84; Columbus City Schools, Chapter I reading instructor, until 1991; Academic and Financial Assistance Services, owner, currently. **Orgs:** Consul Macedonia Bapt Ch Educational Facility; pres Youth Service Guild Inc 1983-85; pres Columbus Alumnae Chap Delta Sigma Theta Inc 1970-72; treas Bethune Serv Bd; bd of dirs The Learning Juncture; business mgr, Columbus Girlchoir, 1987-91; pres, Youth Service Guild, 1989-91. **Honors/Awds:** Outstanding Leadership Awd Delta Sigma Theta Inc 1975-76; Meritorious Serv Awd United Negro Coll Fund 1985, 1986. **Business Addr:** Owner, Academic and Financial Assistance Services, 1806 Andina Ave, Cincinnati, OH 45237.

THOMPSON, TAWANA SADIELA
Appointed government official. **Personal:** Born May 24, 1957, Tallahassee, FL. **Educ:** FL A&M Univ, BS Journalism/PR 1976. **Career:** FAMU Coll of Educ, editor The Educator 1976-78; Ocala Star Banner, staff reporter 1978-79; Capital Outlook Newspaper, editor in chief 1979; FL Occupational Info Coord Comm, clearinghouse coord 1979-80; Dade Co Partners for Youth, admin officer 1981-82; Metro Dade Co, public info officer. **Orgs:** Exec bd mem Dade Co Alumnae Delta Sigma Theta 1983-; mem Natl Forum for Black Public Admin 1984-85, 1987-88; consultant FL Inst of Education/Precollegiate Prog 1984-85; mem Urban League of Greater Miami 1984-; mem Coconut Grove Jaycees 1984-; deputy political dir Statewide Campaign 1986; exec bd mem Greater Miami Chap Natl Assoc of Media Women; consultant South Florida Business League. **Business Addr:** Public Information Officer, Metro Dade County, 111 NW First St Ste 2510, Miami, FL 33128.

THOMPSON, TAYLOR
Business executive. **Personal:** Born Nov 1, 1919, Forest, MS; married Rosie Hale; children: Taylor T, Bobby G, Betty J. **Career:** Thompson's Elec Supply Co Inc, pres. **Orgs:** Vice pres Nat Bus League Reg II 1980; chmn Nat Minority Purch Counc Min Input Com Pittsburgh Chap 1980; mem Nat Assn of Elect Dist; bd of dirs Brentwood-Whitehall C of C. **Military Serv:** US Army, 1941-45. **Business Addr:** 4048 Saw Mill Run Blvd, Rt 51, Pittsburgh, PA 15227.

THOMPSON, THEODIS
Health services executive. **Personal:** Born Aug 10, 1944, Palestine, AR; son of Grozellia M Weaver Thompson (deceased) and Percy Thompson (deceased); married Patricia Holley; children: Gwendolyn L Ware, Theodis E, II, Omari P Thompson. **Educ:** Tuskegee Inst AL, BS 1968; Univ Michigan Ann Arbor, MPA 1969, PhD 1972; Harvard Univ, Cambridge MA, PHSM 1977. **Career:** Sr chem tech John T Stanley Co, New York NY, 1964-66; disc jockey/News reporter, Florence SC, Portsmouth VA, St Louis MO; research assoc Inst Soc Research Univ of Michigan, Ann Arbor MI 1969-71; asst prof, chmn Health Serv Admin Dept Howard Univ, Washington DC 1973-77; Howard Univ School of Business & Public Admin, acting asst dean 1977-78; Univ of Southern California Los Angeles, assoc prof 1978-79; Memphis Health Center Inc, Memphis TN, dir planning mktg research 1979-85, chief admin officer 1985-, pres/chief exec officer 1987-88; Brooklyn Plaza Medical Center Inc, Brooklyn, NY, CEO, 1988-. **Orgs:** Mem APHA 1970-, Alpha Phi Alpha Fraternity Inc 1962-; pres Metro Washington Public Health Assn 1970-72, Black Caucus Health Workers 1974-75; pres MGNAA Inc; mem Community Health Assn of New York State Inc 1989, Natl Assn of Community Health Centers, 1979-; mem, bd of dir Community Assoc Devel Corp 1989; co-owner The Medicine Shoppe Franchise, Memphis TN 1985. **Honors/Awds:** Leadership Memphis 1982; Public Health Scholarship, Univ of Michigan School of Public Health 1970-72; Fellowship Natl Urban League 1968-69; Distinguished Service Award, New York State Association of Black & Puerto Rican Legislators, Inc, 1992. **Business Addr:** CEO, Brooklyn Plaza Medical Center, Inc, 650 Fulton St, Brooklyn, NY 11217.

THOMPSON, TINA
Professional basketball player. **Personal:** Born Feb 10, 1975. **Educ:** USC, bachelor's degree in sociology. **Career:** Houston Comets, forward, 1997-. **Honors/Awds:** All-WNBA First Team, 1997. **Business Addr:** Professional Basketball Player, Houston Comets, Two Greenway Plaza, Ste 400, Houston, TX 77046, (713)627-9622.

THOMPSON, WILLIAM COLERIDGE
Associate justice. **Personal:** Born Oct 26, 1924, New York, NY; son of Louise Thompson and William W. Thompson; married Barbara Thompson; children: William Jr, Gail. **Educ:** Brooklyn Coll, BA 1948; Brooklyn Law Sch, LLB 1954. **Career:** City of New York, councilman 1969-73; New York State, senator 1965-68; Supreme Court of the State of New York, admin judge, assoc judge, appellate div, currently. **Orgs:** One of founders with late Sen R Kennedy of Restoration Corp; one of orig dir of Bed-Stuy Youth in Action; past reg dir NAACP; dir Bed-Stuy Restoration Corp; mem Amer Bar Assn; Brooklyn Law School Alumni Assn; mem, Metro Black Bar Assn; chairman, Blacks & Jews in Conversation; treasurer, Judges & Lawyers Breast Cancer Alert; mem, Comm on Judicial Conduct. **Military Serv:** US Army, Sgt 1943-46; Purple Heart; Combat Infantry Badge; Three Battle Stars. **Business Addr:** Associate Judge, Supreme Court Appellate Div, 2nd Dept, 45 Monroe Pl, Brooklyn, NY 11201.

THOMPSON, WILLIAM HENRY
Dentist. **Personal:** Born Dec 16, 1933, Trenton, NJ; son of Fannie L Thomas Thompson and John H Thompson; married Anne E Jenkins Thompson, Jun 19, 1965; children: William Jr, Sharon. **Educ:** Lincoln Univ, BA 1956; Howard Univ Coll of Dentistry, 1963. **Career:** Private practice, dentist; State of New Jersey, Department of Corrections, director of dental services, currently. **Orgs:** Omega Psi Phi Fraternity; life mem NAACP; ADA; New Jersey DA; Mer County Dental Association; dir, Sun Natl Bank, Trenton, New Jersey, 1989-; trustee, St Lawrence Hospital, 1986-92; Sigma Pi Phi Fraternity Mu Boule, 1988. **Military Serv:** US Army, 1956-58. **Business Addr:** Director, Dental Services, State of New Jersey, Department of Corrections, CN 863, Trenton, NJ 08625.

THOMPSON, WILLIAM L.
Airline pilot, attorney, company executive. **Personal:** Born Jun 14, 1951, Orangeburg, SC; son of Pearl Richburg Thompson and Willie J Thompson; married Kathie Taylor Thompson, Oct 4, 1987; children: Taylor M, Sydney E. **Educ:** US Air Force Academy, CO, BS, commandant's list, 1973; California State University, Sacramento, CA, MA, deans list, 1977; McGeorge School of Law, UOP, Sacramento, CA, JD, 1980; Suffolk University Law School, Boston, MA, 1991-92, dean's list. **Career:** USAF, USAFA, CO, minority adv to superintendent, 1973-74; USAF, Sacramento, CA, instructor pilot, chief, life support, 1974-80; Delta Air Lines, Boston, MA, captain, 1980-; Regency Park Associaties, Boston, MA, managing partner, 1986-; The Summit Group Companies, Boston, MA, president, 1982-; Mass Aeronautics Commission, Boston, MA, commissioner, 1983-. **Orgs:** Chairman of the board, American Cancer Society, 1983-; board member, Security National Bank, 1984-86; board member, Bank of New England, 1986-90; board member, finance committee, Northeast Health Systems, 1983-; commissioner, Boy Scouts of America, 1982-89; bd mem, Eastern Bank and Trust Co, 1996-; trustee, Bridgton Academy, 1994-96; pres, Natl Assn of Guardsmen, Boston Chapter; natl b of dirs, American Cancer Society. **Honors/Awds:** Volunteer of the Year, 1992; Outstanding Service, 1986; American Cancer Society; Distinguish Achievement, Boy Scouts of America, 1986; Distinguished Contributions, Massachusetts Airport Managers Association, 1995; Distinguished Service, American Cancer Society, 1996; Bell South, African American History Calendar, 1998; Guardsman of the Year. **Military Serv:** USAF, Captain, 1973-80; Air Force Commendation Medal, 1980, ATC Safety Award, 1978, Vietnam Service Medal 1972, Presidential Unit Citation, Longivity Medal. **Home Addr:** 60 Lothrop St, Beverly, MA 01915, (978)927-7432. **Business Addr:** President, The Summit Group Companies, 7 Charlton St, Everett, MA 02149, (617)389-3700.

THOMPSON, WILLIAM S. (TURK)
Judge (retired). **Personal:** Born Nov 21, 1914, Mebane, NC; son of Willie Mae Hughes Thompson and Samuel Thompson; married Melvalee ''Mickey'' Mitchell, Apr 5, 1994; children: William Waller. **Educ:** Howard Univ, Washington, DC, BS, 1934; Robert H Terrell Law School, Washington, DC, LLB, 1939. **Career:** Private Practice of Law, Washington, DC, sr partner, 1944-69; DC Govt, Washington, DC, councilmember,

1966-69; DC Superior Court, Washington, DC, assoc judge, 1969-92. **Orgs:** Pres, Kiwanis Club of Georgetown, DC, 1990-91; chmn, Judicial Council of the NBA, 1989-90; sec-general, World Peace Through Law Center, 1963-67, 1972-89; pres, Washington Urban League BD, 1966-69; mem, Junior Citizen Corps Inc Adv Bd, 1976-; pres, Natl Bar Assn, 1957-59. **Honors/Awds:** Charles H Houston Medallion of Merit, Washington Bar Assn, 1983; Honorary Degrees: LLD/Howard Univ, 1975, Lincoln Univ, 1981, St Augustine's, 1983; Distinguished Service Award, Natl Bar Assn, 1977; Whitney M Young Jr Memorial Award, Washington Urban League, 1974; The Intl Law Society of Howard Univ School of Law renamed ''The William S Thompson Intl Law Society,'' 1974. **Military Serv:** Army, corporal, 1942-44, Good Conduct Medal, 1944.

THOMPSON, WILLIE EDWARD
Educational administrator. **Personal:** Born Sep 30, 1940, Turbeville, VA; married Mattie Smith; children: Eric, Jason. **Educ:** Bay City Jr Coll, AA 1961; MI Univ, BSW 1964; Univ of MI, MA 1973. **Career:** City of Saginaw, asst youth ctr dir 1964-65, adult probation officer 1965-70; Delta Community College, dean of student support services 1970-. **Orgs:** Bd of dir Capital Investment Inc; pres Saginaw Bd of Ed 1976-78; vice pres Saginaw Econ Devel Corp 1976-; board member BOLD 1978-; Ruben Daniels Education Foundation. **Honors/Awds:** Liberty Bell Awd Saginaw Cty Bar Assoc 1970; Serv Awd Amer Assoc of Univ Professional 1972; Comm Serv Awd Negro Womens Professional Group 1975; Comm Serv Awd Black Nurses Assoc 1977. **Special Achievements:** Co-founder, Growth in Afrocentric Programming for Elementary Boys; coached AAU Basketball, 1980. **Business Addr:** Associate Dean, Student Support Services, Delta Community College, University Center, MI 48710.

THOMPSON, WINSTON EDNA
Educational administrator, educator. **Personal:** Born Apr 9, 1933, Newark, NJ; daughter of Cora Edna West and Dorsey Nelson West; divorced; children: Darren Eric Thompson. **Educ:** Seton Hall Univ, BA 1965; Columbia Univ, Teachers College MS 1969; Rutgers Univ, EdD 1980. **Career:** Essex County Coll, dir of advising, counselor 1968-72; Rutgers Univ, Livingston College, assoc dean of students 1972-75; Tombrock Coll, dean of student dev 1975-76; Tombrook Coll, dean of student develop 1975-76; AT & T Bell Lab, consultant 1975-77; East Orange Board of Education, adult educator 1977-78; Salem State Coll, vice pres of student services 1978-88; Connecticut State Univ, exec officer of academic affairs and research, 1988-. **Orgs:** American Council of Education, consultant 1981-; AAA of New England, advisory bd mem 1986-88; Morgan Memorial Goodwill Industries, bd of trustee, mem 1986-88; HERS Wellesley Coll, advisory bd mem, faculty 1982; bd mem, JJS Enterprise 1979-; State Education Coordinator, Natl Coalition 100 Black Women 1988-89. **Honors/Awds:** Salem State Coll, recipient women's awrd 1981; Univ of MA at Amherst, co-designer of non-traditional doctoral prog 1983; Northeastern Univ, Greater Boston Inter University Council report, minority student retention 1985; Distinguished Educator, Natl Coalition of 100 Black Women 1988; Meritorious Service Award, United Negro College Fund, Inc 1989; Black Women/Black Men lecture and writing 1989; Black Feminism, lecture and writing 1989. **Business Addr:** Executive Officer, Academic Affairs & Research, Connecticut State University, 39 Woodland St, Hartford, CT 06105.

THOMPSON-MOORE, ANN
Senior consultant education. **Personal:** Born Oct 13, 1949, Edwards, MS; divorced; children: DeAnna. **Educ:** Jackson State Univ, BA 1972, MSEduc 1974. **Career:** Jackson-Hinds County Youth Court, counselor 1972-74; MS Gulf Coast Jr Coll, dir special services prog 1974-82; Northern IL Univ, counselor 1983-84; MS Governor's Office Federal/State Prog, special project officer IV 1984-87; The Kelwynn Group, sr consultant 1987-. **Orgs:** Mem MS State Democratic Party 1980; mem Phi Delta Kappa Frat East MS Chap 1981; fundraising chair Hinds County Democratic Exec Comm 1984; pres United Black Fund of MS 1984; bd mem Hospice Friends Inc 1985; coord United Negro College Fund 1985-86, 1986-87; peer panelist MS Arts Commn 1986; mem Farish St Bapt Church; mem Delta Sigma Theta Sor Inc. **Honors/Awds:** Outstanding Young Woman in Amer 1979; new articles The MS Press 1980, The Washington Star 1980, Black Enterprise 1981; participant A Presidential Classroom for Young Americans. **Business Addr:** Senior Consultant, The Kelwynn Group, PO Box 1526, Jackson, MS 39215-1526.

THOMS, DONALD H.
Television director. **Personal:** Born Feb 28, 1948, Baltimore, MD; son of Henrietta Austin Thoms and McKinley Thoms; married Mariana Davis Thoms, Jun 6, 1970; children: Tracie Nicole, Austin Curtis. **Educ:** Morgan State University, BA, sociology, 1971. **Career:** WBAL-TV Baltimore, MD, operations director, 1967-73; Maryland Public TV, Owings Mills, MD, stage manager, 1973-75, TV director, 1975-80, producer, 1980-85, executive producer, 1985-90, senior executive producer, 1990-91, director of regional productions, 1991-93, director prog management, 1993-96, vice pres programming, 1996-. **Honors/Awds:** Cine Golden Eagle for ''Crabs,'' Best Entertainment Program Television Director, 1988; NATPE International-Iris Award Winner for ''Crabs,'' Television Director, Best Entertainment Prog, 1988; Corporation for public television, CPB Public Television Local Program Award-Silver Award for ''Outdoors Maryland,'' Executive Producer, 1990; Bronze Award-Film and TV Festival of New York, ''Couple In Crisis,'' Producer, 1989; Emmy Awards: best information program, ''Outdoors Maryland,'' live television directions, ''Crabs,'' 1990; Emmy Award Exec Producer, 1992, 1993; Telly Award, 1993. **Business Addr:** Vice Pres, Prog Management, PBS, 1320 Braddock Pl, Alexandria, VA 22314.

THOMSON, GERALD EDMUND
Physician, educator. **Personal:** Born 1932, New York, NY; son of Lloyd Thomas and Sybil Gilbourne; married Carolyn Webber; children: Gregory, Karen. **Educ:** Howard U, MD 1959. **Career:** Harlem Hosp Center, pres 1976-78, dir med 1971-85, dir nephrology, 1970-71; assoc prof med, Columbia Coll Phys & Surg, 1970-72; Columbia Univ, prof 1972-; Presb Hospital, attending physician 1970-; prec med 1963-; clin asst prof medicine 1968-70; Coney Island Hospital, assoc chief medicine 1967-70; State Univ NY Med Brooklyn Hospital, attending physician 1966-70; asst visiting physician 1963-70; Univ NY, instr 1963-68; clinical dir dialysis unit 1965-67; NY Heart Assn, fellow nephrology 1965-65; chief resident 1962-63; resident medicine 1960-62; State Univ NY Kings Co Hospital Center, intern 1959-60, chief resident, 1962-63; Samuel Lambert prof med and chief of staff, 1980-. **Orgs:** Pres Med Bd 1976-; mem Hlth Rsrch Cncl City of NY 1972-81; hypertension adv com NY City Hlth Serv Adminstrn 1972-75; adv bd NY Kidney Found 1971-72; mem Hlth Rsrch Cncl City of NY 1975-; mem NIH 1973-74; mem adv bd Nat Assn Patients on Hemodialysis & Transplantation 1973-; mem Com on Mild Hypertension Nat Heart & Lung Inst 1976; mem/clin/trials rev com, 1980-85; bd dir NY Heart Assn 1973-81 mem clin/trials rev com, 1980-85; bd dir NY Heart Assn 1973-81; chmn com high blood press 1976-81; chmn com hypertension NY Met Regnl Med Prgm 1974-76; Diplomate Am Bd Internal Med Fellow ACP, 1985-; mem AAAS 1973-74; Am Fedn Clin Rsrch Soc Urban Physicians 1972-73; Am Soc for Artificial Organs; NY Acad Med 1974-; Alpha Omega Alpha; mem adv bd Jour Urban Hlth 1974-; mem adv com Heart and Hypertension Inst of NY State, 1984; mem NY Gov's Health Adv Coun, 1981-84; pub Health Coun, NY, 1983-95; Joint Nat Com High Blood Pressure NIH, 1983-84, 1987-88; mem rev panel hypertension detection and monitoring bd study cardiovasc risk factors in young, Nat Heart, Lung and Blood Inst., 1984-90; NY State Adv Com on Hypertension, 1977-80; com on non-pharm treatment of hypertension Inst of Med Nat Acad Scis, 1980; mem med adv bd, Nat Assn Patients on Hemodialysis and Transplantation, 1973-83; mem adv bd, Scho Biomed Edn, CUNY, 1979-83; Med News Network, 1993-95; mem panel on receiving and witholding med treatment, ACLU, 1984-88; mem, Grad Med Edn Comn, State of NY, 1984-86; mem Comm on End-State Renal Disease, 1985, 1989-90; pres WA Heights-Inwood Ambulatory Care Network Corp, 1986-91; bd dirs Primary Care Devel Corp, 1993-; mem adv bd, Jour Urban Health, 1974-80; Med News Network, 1993-94; chmn ad hoc com on access to nursing homes, Pub Health Council State of NY; pres WA Hghts-Inwood Ambulatory Care Network Corp, 1986-91; chmn Federated Coun Internal Med, 1991-92; mem Mayor's Commn Health and Hosp Corp; dir Harlem Ctr for Health Promotion and Disease Prevention; bd dirs Primary Care Devel Corp. **Honors/Awds:** Recipient Nat Med Award, Nat Kidney Found, NY, 1984; Outstanding Alumnus Award, Howard University, 1987; Dean's Outstanding Teaching Award, Coll Physicians and Surgeons, Columbia Univ, 1986. **Business Addr:** Coll Physicians & Surgeons, Columbia University, New York, NY 10032.

THORBURN, CAROLYN COLES
Educator. **Personal:** Born Dec 20, 1941, Newark, NJ. **Educ:** Douglass Coll, BA Spanish 1962; Rutgers Univ, MA Spanish 1964, PhD Spanish 1972; PhD, nutrition, 1987. **Career:** Barringer HS, Spanish teacher 1964-66; Rutgers Univ, teaching asst Spanish 1966-67; Upsala Coll, prof of Spanish/coord of black studies 1967-95; Union County College, adjunct prof of Spanish, 1992-; Seton Hall Univ and E. Orange School District, educational consultant, 1995-. **Orgs:** Mem Modern Language Assoc, Natl Council of Black Studies, Amer Assoc of Univ Profs, Amer Assoc of the Teachers of Spanish & Portuguese. **Honors/Awds:** Romance Language Honor Soc Phi Sigma Iota 1972. **Special Achievements:** Author, Mastery of Conversational Spanish, 1992; author, Complete Mastery of Spanish, 1993; author, Complete Mastery of Spanish Workbook, 1994; speaks Spanish. **Business Addr:** Prof of Spanish, Educational Research Center Language School, 75 Central Avenue, East Orange, NJ 07018, (973)677-9504.

THORNE, CECIL MICHAEL
Physician. **Personal:** Born May 13, 1929, Georgetown, Guyana; married Sandra; children: Timothy, Christine, Christopher, Jonathan, Victor. **Educ:** Queens Coll; Lincoln U, AB 1952; Mainz U, MD 1957. **Career:** Newark Pathologists Inc Licking Meml Hosp, pres 1967-; OH St Univ Patho, asst prof pathol 1964-65; W MA Hosp, demonstrator res 1962-63; Springfield Hosp, intern res 1958-62. **Orgs:** Flw Am Coll Patho; mem Am Soc Clinical Patho; clinical asso prof pathology OH St Univ 1980; pres elect OH Soc of Pathologists; past pres tst OH Assn Blood Banks; past pres Central OH Soc Patho; bd gov OH Soc Pathol; lab com OH St Med Assn; mem AMA; OSMA; Licking Co Med Soc; Am Assn Blood Banks; Acad Clinical Lab Physicians & Sci; past chmn bd dir Licking Co Chap Heart Assn; Licking Co ARG; past chmn Central OH Blood Prog Com; chmn Med Adv Com Central OH Blood Prgm; past dir Newark Area C of C; chmn Licking Co Metro Park Dist; Rotary Club. **Business Addr:** 1320 W Main, Newark, OH 43055.

THORNELL, RICHARD PAUL
Educator. **Personal:** Born Oct 19, 1936, New York, NY; married Carolyn O Atkinson; children: David Evan, Paul Nolan Diallo, Douglass Vashon. **Educ:** Fisk Univ, magna cum laude, 1956; Pomona Coll, 1955; Woodrow Wilson Sch, MPA, 1958; Yale Law Sch, JD, 1971. **Career:** Howard Univ Sch of Law, prof of Law, currently, vice pres, general counsel, 1984-88; Rosenman Colin Freund Lewis & Cohen NYC, asso litigation dept 1975-76; US Comm Relations Serv Dept of Justice, chief fed progms staff 1965-66; Africa Reg Ofc US Peace Corps, chief program staff; US Dept of State Agency for Intl Develop, econ & intl rel ofcr 1958-61. **Orgs:** Bars of NY/DC/Fed Cts/US Supreme Ct; bd of dir YMCA of Wash DC 1977-83; bd of dir Africare 1977-83; trustee Phelps Stoke Fund 1980-85; lay mem bd of dir, com Nat Bd of UMCA'S of USA; exec com & gen counsel Fisk Univ Gen Alumni Assn 1977-79; Phi Beta Kappa Delta Chap, Fisk Univ 1956-; elected Council on Foreign Relations. **Honors/Awds:** Fisk Univ Serv Awd; Fisk Univ Gen Alumni Assn 1978; Grad Fellowship Princeton U; Fellowship Grant Yale Law Sch; Intl Achievement Awd Willilam S Thompson Intl Law Soc dir com Nat Bd of UMCA'S of USA; exec com m1980. **Military Serv:** US Army, pfc, 1959-61. **Business Addr:** Howard University, 2400 Van Ness St NW, Washington, DC 20008.

THORNHILL, ADRINE VIRGINIA
Business administrator. **Personal:** Born Feb 22, 1945, Birmingham, AL; divorced; children: Herschel III, Michelle Vertess, Adrienne Mychael. **Educ:** Attended, Miles Coll 1963-65, Urbana Coll 1979. **Career:** Montgomery Co Human Svcs, administrative asst 1969-76; Dr Frederick Jackson DDS, office mgr 1976-78; Columbus Comm Action Org, administrator 1978-82;Care-Free Property Mgmt Co Inc, vice pres/genl mgr 1987-. **Orgs:** Bd of dirs Taylor-Made Construction Co Inc 1980-87; office mgr NAACP Dayton Branch 1985-87; bd of dirs Midas Landscaping Co Inc 1986,87, Care-Free Mgmt Co Inc 1986-87; 1st vice pres Democratic Progressive Club 1986-87; corresponding sec Democratic Voters League 1986-87. **Honors/Awds:** Outstanding Democrat of the Year Awd Dem Progressive Club 1976.

THORNHILL, HERBERT LOUIS
Physician. **Educ:** Univ Pittsburgh, BS 1951; Howard Univ Coll of Med Wash DC, MD 1955. **Career:** Div Rehab Med Montefiore Hosp & Med Cntr, asst attending 1963-66; Montefiore Hosp & Med Cntr, adjunct attending Div Rehab Med 1966-67; Albert Einstein Coll of Medicine, Yeshiva Univ, instructor, 1963-65, asst clinical prof of rehab medicine, 1965-67; Presbyterian Hospital, asst physician in rehab service 1968-84; Harlem Hospital Center, asst dir of rehab medicine, 1967-69, attending physician, 1969-, chief, amputee service, 1969-, assoc dir of rehab medicine, 1969-78, acting dir of rehab medicine, 1979-80, dir of rehab medicine, 1980-; Columbia Univ Coll of Physicians & Surgeons, asst clinical prof of rehab medicine, 1968-73, assoc prof of clinical rehab medicine, 1973-85, prof of clinical rehab medicine, 1985-, director, department of rehab med, currently. **Orgs:** Diplomate, Amer Bd Physical Med & Rehab 1964; mem Bronx Co Med Soc; mem Pub Comm 1970; mem Med Soc of St of NY; v chmn Sec on Phys Med & Rehab 1972; chmn Sec on Phys Med & Rehab 1973; mem NY Soc of Phys Med & Rehab Prog Chmn 1970-71, vice pres 1971-72, pres elect 1972, pres 1973; fellow Am Coll of Phys 1972; fellow, Am Acad of Phys Med & Rehab, 1965; mem Con of Rehab Med; mem NY Acad of Med; Sec on Phys Med & Rehab; mem, Natl Planning Comm, President's Comm on Employment of the Handicapped, 1987-88; mem, Natl Advisory Comm, Howard Univ Research & Training Center for Access to Rehabilitation & Economic Opportunity, 1988-; surveyor, Commn on Accreditation of Rehabilitation Facilities, 1982-89; mem, 1974-87, chmn, 1981-82, Medical Advisory Comm, Greater Harlem Nursing Home; mem, Advisory Comm on the Disab, Borough of Manhattan, 1989-92; Natl Medical Assn, 1967-. **Honors/Awds:** Author of 17 publications & 9 abstracts. **Military Serv:** USN med officer 1957-59; USNR lt commander. **Business Addr:** Dir, Dept of Rehabilitation Medicine, Columbia Univ, Harlem Hospital Center, 506 Lenox Ave, Rm 3125, New York, NY 10037-1802, (212)939-4401.

THORNS, ODAIL, JR.
Auto supply company executive. **Personal:** Born Jan 3, 1943, Pine Bluff, AK; children: Michelle, Camille, Octavia. **Educ:** BS Chem 1964; KS State Univ, grad study 1964-65; Harvard Grad Sch of Business Admin, PMD 1984. **Career:** Delco-remy Div GMC, asst supt mfg; chemist, process engr, res engr mfg foreman, labor relations supr gnrl supr mfg, plant supt, plant mgr, mfg mgr, opers mgr, divisional director of personnel, director Quality Network/Synchronous Automotive Components

Group, director Engine Drive Business Unit, Saginaw Division, currently. **Orgs:** Mem Industrial Mgmt Club; bd dir St Manpower Training Comm; bd dirs IN Forum & pres; IN St Conf of NAACP Br 1971-76; chmn Region III NAACP 1974-75; chmn bd United Way 1979; mem Natl Bd NAACP 1980-84; chmn bd Comm Hosp 1983-85; trustee Peerless Lodge F & AM; mem dir Madison Co Br NAACP; bd of dirs Anderson Leadership Acad; state advisor NAACP Women's Aux; pres emeritus IN State NAACP; chmn Martin Luther King Memorial Comm. **Honors/Awds:** Finalist Jaycees Outstanding Yhoung Man 1972; gM'S Top Ten in Community Svcs; Man of Yr Urban League of Madison Co 1972; B Harry Beckham Meml Awd NAACP 1975; Loren Henry Awd NAACP 1976; Disting Serv Awd United Way 1979; Outstanding Achievement in Business & Prof Leadership Develop Ctr 1983; Disting Honoree Urban League 1983; Disting Serv Awd Comm Hosp 1985; Professional Man of the Yr Peerless Lodge F&AM 1985; Life Membership Hall of Fame NAACP 1985; City of Anderson, Indiana, Key Award, 1991. **Business Addr:** Director, Engine Drive Business Unit, General Motors, Saginaw Division, 3900 Holland Rd, Saginaw, MI 48605.

THORNTON, ANDRE
Professional baseball player (retired). **Personal:** Born Aug 13, 1949, Tuskegee, AL; married. **Educ:** Cheyney State College, Cheyney, PA, attended; Nyack College, Nyack, NY, attended. **Career:** Chicago Cubs, infielder, 1973-76; Montreal Expos, infielder, 1976; Cleveland Indians, infielder, 1977-87. **Honors/Awds:** Danny Thompson Meml Awd, Baseball Chapel; American League All-Star Team, 1982, 1984.

THORNTON, CLIFFORD E.
Educator. **Personal:** Born Sep 6, 1936, Philadelphia; widowed. **Educ:** Juiliard, BM 1968; Manhattan Sch of Mus, MM 1971. **Career:** New York City Public School, teacher 1967; Black Arts Repertory Theatre School, 1965-66; NY School of Music 1966; Wesleyan Univ, asst prof of music 1969. **Orgs:** Founded & dir prog in Afro-am Mus; continuous activities as performer, composer & producer of concerts & recordings; mem Am Fedn of Mus jazz composersorch assn; pres third world records; pres third world mus; mem broadcast mus inc; mem kappa alpha psi. **Honors/Awds:** Recipient Nat Endowment for the Arts; Jazz Composition Fellowships 1972 & 73; NY St Council on the Arts Performance Grant. **Military Serv:** AUS 1st lt 1958-61. **Business Addr:** Music Department, Wesleyan Univ, Middletown, CT 06457.

THORNTON, CLINTON L.
Farmer, elected official. **Personal:** Born Aug 3, 1907, Bullock Co, AL; married Johnnie Woods; children: Morris, Eloise, Walter, Wilbert, Mose C. **Educ:** Tuskegee Inst, BS 1955. **Career:** Bullock Cty Schools, mem bd of ed 1970-. **Orgs:** Pres Bullock Cty Improvement Org 1960-70; bd dir SE AL Self-Help Assoc 1967-, AL Assoc School Bd 1970, AL & Natl Retired Teachers Assoc 1970; mem NAACP.

THORNTON, CORA ANN BARRINGER (LADY K)
Company executive. **Personal:** Born Jun 13, 1941, Washington, DC; daughter of Pearl G Barringer and George F Barringer; children: Johnnie R, Joseph T, Jerome F, Jenese E. **Educ:** DC Teachers College, BS, 1964; Howard University, post graduate, 1966; George Washington University, post graduate, 1970; Trinity College, MA, 1982. **Career:** Taft Junior High School, instructor, mathematics, 1964-73; St Mary's School, instructor, mathmatics, 1976-79; Eastern High School, instructor, mathematics, 1979-85; Barr-Thorn Enterprises, president, chief executive officer, 1981; University of the District of Columbia, Dept of Mathematics, associate professor, 1980-86; Trinity College, Dept of Mathematics, associate professor, 1984; Lady K Corporation, president, chief executive officer, 1989-. **Orgs:** Delta Sigma Theta, 1964-; Organization of Superintendent's Award Recipients, 1982; National Council of Teachers of Mathematics; Delta Sigma Theta Sorority. **Honors/Awds:** Superintendent's Incentive Award, 1982. **Special Achievements:** Author: Learning Mathematics, LMASL, 1981; developer: Mathematics Games LMASL, 1981; organizer: Les Beaux Visages, 1981; workshop presenter: Philadelphia Council for Math Teachers, 1983.

THORNTON, CORNELIUS (PERK)
Business executive. **Educ:** University of Iowa; University of Chicago Graduate School of Business, graduated, 1973. **Career:** Aetna Life and Casualty Insurance Co, common stock analyst; Morgan Stanley, institutional equity research area; First Boston Corporation, vice president, senior securities analyst; Goldman, Sachs & Co, vice president, senior research analyst, 1992-. **Special Achievements:** Listed as one of 25 ''Hottest Blacks on Wall Street,'' Black Enterprise, 1992; one of Wall Street's most outstanding brokerage analysts for 14 straight years, Institutional Investor, 1992. **Military Serv:** US Army, paratrooper. **Business Addr:** Vice Pres & Senior Research Analyst, Goldman, Sachs & Co, 85 Broad St, 16th Fl, New York, NY 10004, (212)902-8156.

THORNTON, DOZIER W.
Educator. **Personal:** Born in Aliquippa, PA; son of Myrtle Thornton and Dozier Thornton; married Kazuko Otaki; children: Monica Thornton, Dr Lisa Thornton, Hugh Heslep. **Educ:** Univ Pittsburgh, PhD 1966. **Career:** MI St U, prof Dept Psychology/Acting Dean, Urban Affairs Programs. **Orgs:** Mem Comm Mental Hlth & Educ Cons; psychtherapist; American Psychological Assn; Michigan Psychological Assn. **Honors/Awds:** Phi Kappa Phi. **Military Serv:** AUS 1951-53. **Business Addr:** Michigan State Univ, Psychology Dept, East Lansing, MI 48824, (517)353-9533.

THORNTON, IVAN TYRONE
Investment advisor. **Personal:** Born Aug 8, 1961, Brooklyn, NY; son of Esther Thornton and Paul A Thornton; married Thomasina Toles Thornton, Apr 18, 1987; children: Ivana. **Educ:** Howard University, Washington, DC, BBA, finance, 1983; New York University, MBA. **Career:** Midas Investment Corp, Arlington, TX, manager/financial administrator, 1983-86; Merrill Lynch Pierce Fenner & Smith, New York, NY, sr financial consultant, 1986-89; Smith, Barson, Barnes, Shearson, New York, NY, vice president/registered investment advisor, 1989-96; vp, private equity sales, Donaldson, Lufkin, & Jennette, 1996-. **Orgs:** President, Howard University Alumni Assn, 1993-95; member, Alpha Phi Alpha Fraternity, 1981-; member, American Management Assn, 1991; economic development committee, One Hundred Black Men, Inc; National Association of Securities Professionals; public policy committee, Black Executive Exchange Program, National Urban League. **Honors/Awds:** Executives Club, Merrill Lynch Pierce Fenner & Smith, 1989; Division Leader, New Business Development, Shearson Lehman Brothers, 1990; Presidents Club, Smith, Barney, Shearson, 1993-96; Presidents Club, Donaldson, Lifkin & Jennette. **Business Addr:** Vice President, Private Equity Sales, Donaldson, Lufkin & Jennette, 277 Park Ave, New York, NY 10172.

THORNTON, JACKIE C.
Business executive. **Personal:** Born Apr 26, 1960, Pine Bluff, AR; daughter of Beatrice Thornton and Laudell Thornton. **Educ:** Univ of AR Pine Bluff, BS 1981; Univ of WI Madison, MS 1983. **Career:** Phillips Petroleum, accountant 1981-82; IBM Corp, mktg sales asst 1983; NCR Corp, educ analyst 1984-1988; product marketing manager Pitney Bowes 1988-91; United American Healthcare Corp, New Product Development, 1992-94; Southwest Hospital, vice president of Business Development, 1994-96; Bell South Mobility, advertising & PR regional mgr, 1997-. **Orgs:** Corres sec 1986, vice pres 1987, chpter president 1990-91; Dayton Chap Natl Black MBA Assoc; Amer Marketing Assn. **Home Addr:** 2093B Lake Park Drive, Smyrna, GA 30080.

THORNTON, JOHN C.
Food company executive. **Personal:** Born May 22, 1940, Louisville, KY; son of Alberta Thornton and William Thornton; married Rochelle A Ray; children: Ardell N, Timothy. **Educ:** KY State Univ, BS 1963; Northeastern Univ, MA 1975; Union Grad Sch, PhD 1977. **Career:** Chicago Bd of Educ, tchr 1963-66; City of Chicago, comm organizer, rsch analyst, criminal justice dir 1966-81; Columbia College, professor, 1977-84; McDonald's Franchise, owner, currently. **Orgs:** Mem Nat'l Black McDonald's Owners' Assn 1981-. **Honors/Awds:** Athletic Hall of Fame KY State Univ 1980; ''Behavior Modification-The Road to Genocide'' pub 1977. **Home Addr:** 10110 S Paxton, Chicago, IL 60617. **Business Addr:** Owner, McDonald's Franchise, 11201 S State St, Chicago, IL 60628.

THORNTON, MAURICE
Educational administrator. **Personal:** Born Dec 31, 1930, Birmingham, AL; son of Alberta and William Thornton (both deceased); married Elizabeth McDonald, Apr 15, 1961; children: Karen, Susan, Christopher. **Educ:** Alabama State Univ, BS 1952; Cleveland State Univ, MEd 1973; Nova Univ, EdD 1981. **Career:** Cuyahoga Co Welfare Dept Cleveland, investigative caseworker supervisor title V 1958-67, coord neighborhood youth corps asst dir personnel dept 1958-67; Cuyahoga Comm Coll Cleveland, eeo officer, minority recruiter dir equal oppor 1967-82; State Univ of NY Central Admin, dir affirmative action compliance, affirmative action officer 1982-90, affirmative action programs, director, 1990-. **Orgs:** Mem Capital District Black & Puerto Rican Caucus, Amer Assoc of Affirmative Action Officers, participant Loaned Exec Program, Leadership Develop Program; consultation training fund raising Cleveland Foundation; mem past chmn Lee/Harvard Branch NAACP, Urban League; fund raiser United Negro Coll Fund; mem Omega Psi Phi Frat Inc; past pres AL State Univ Alumni Assoc; sire archon Sigma Pi Phi Frat Beta Psi Chapt; treas 369th Veterans Assoc; deacon United Presbyterian Church; vice pres, pres-elect, Nova Univ Alumni Assn, New England, New York 1989-90; secretary of bd, Camp Opportunity, Albany NY 1989-90; mem, American Mathematical Assn; mem, American Mgmt Assn; Capital District Human Rights Advisory Committee. **Honors/Awds:** Academic Scholarships recipient in undergrad and grad schools; ERIC Univ of CA; published dissertation ''An Analysis of Cuyahoga Community College's Progress at Equal Opportunity Compliance''; addressed the Ohio General Assembly in Columbus OH; addressed the Assoc of Bds of Trustees of the Community Colls of the State Univ of New York (64 campuses, 30 are community colls). **Military Serv:** AUS corpl medical corpsman 2 yrs; Good Conduct Medal, Letters of Commendation. **Home Addr:** 7 Keith Rd, Delmar, NY 12054. **Business Addr:** Affirmative Action Programs Director, SUNY Central Administration, State University Plaza, Albany, NY 12246.

THORNTON, OSIE M.
Association executive. **Personal:** Born Oct 6, 1939, Tuscaloosa, AL. **Educ:** Wayne St U, BA 1961, MA 1963. **Career:** Wayne Co Bur Soc Welfare; soc worker; CA Dept Rehab Nat Rehab Assoc, voc rehab counselor; mem Am Personnel & Guidance Assoc; mem United High Blood Pressure Found; Nat Non-white Counseling Assoc & Crenshaw Center Optimist Club; Big Bro Greater Los Angeles; licensed Child Family Marriage Counselor. **Orgs:** Man of Yr Awd 1974, Optimist Club; citation for Comm Achvmnt LA Co Supv James Hayes. **Business Addr:** 10925 S Central Ave, Los Angeles, CA 90059.

THORNTON, TRACEY
Government official. **Career:** The White House, special assistant to the president for legislative affairs, currently. **Business Addr:** Special Asst to the Pres, Legislative Affairs, The White House, 107 East Wing, 1600 Pennsylvania Ave, NW, Washington, DC 20500, (202)456-6493.

THORNTON, WAYNE T.
Banker. **Personal:** Born Aug 13, 1958, Harrisburg, PA. **Educ:** Morgan State Univ, BS (Cum Laude) 1981. **Career:** Comptroller of the Currency, natl bank examiner 1979-85; Industrial Bank of Washington, asst vice president 1985-87. **Orgs:** Realtor-assoc ERA Nyman Realty 1985-; bd of dirs Univ Legal Services 1986-. **Honors/Awds:** Academic Merit Awd. **Business Addr:** CEO, The Corvus Group, Inc, 1730 K St NW, Ste 304, Washington, DC 20006, (202)508-1489.

THORNTON, WILLIE JAMES, JR.
Wholesaler. **Personal:** Born Jan 22, 1954, Nettleton, MS; son of Berdie Thornton and Willie Thornton; married L Kay Collins, Dec 10, 1977; children: Willie III, Timothy, Jessica, Monica. **Educ:** University of Nebraska, BS, 1976; Mississippi College, MBA, 1983. **Career:** The Travelers, supervisor of data processing, 1976-83; Xerox Corp, account mgr of marketing, 1983-86; Cleaning Solutions, Inc, president, currently. **Orgs:** Garland Chamber of Commerce, 1986-; Dallas Black Chamber of Commerce, 1992; Independent Small Business Association, 1989-; Dallas/Fort Worth Minority Business Development Council, 1986-; Houston Business Council, 1990-; Oklahoma Minority Supplier Development Council, 1990-; Arkansas Regional Minority Purchasing Council, 1990-; Amber University, charter member, 1983; Dallas/Fort Worth Minority Business Development Council, mentor, entrepreneur program, 1996. **Honors/Awds:** Xerox, Par Club, 1984, Certificate of Achievement, Basic Skill School, 1985, Certificate of Achievement, Account Representative School, 1984, Account Rep, 1985, Sales Rep of the Month, 1984; Certificate of Achievement, El Centro College, Bldg Better Banking Relationships, 1989; Certificate of Achievement, Frito Lay, Bidding Techniques, 1989, Marketing Techniques, 1989; Certificate of Achievement, Xerox, Foundation for Success, 1983; Honored for Service, Garland City Council's Economic Advisory Group, 1990-93; Garland Chamber of Commerce, Outstanding Service Award, for Small Business Council, 1993, Awarded Committee Chair of the Year, 1993, Outstanding Service as Member of the Bd of Dirs, 1993; Certificate of Completion for the course ''Effective Personal Leadership,'' Garland TX, 1993; Certificate of Completion for the course ''International Marketing,'' Garland TX, 1993; Certificate of Appreciation, Dallas-Fort Worth Minority Business Development Council, Contributions made as a member of the Vender Input Committee, 1994; Recognition of Achievement, 1996. **Business Addr:** President, Cleaning Solutions, Inc, 4109 Miller Pk Dr, Garland, TX 75042, (972)271-2600.

THORPE, EARL HOWARD
Computer company executive. **Personal:** Born Oct 15, 1936, Raleigh, NC; son of Lucille B Thorpe and Marvin W Thorpe; married Michelle N Thorpe; children: Eric E, Wendy M, Zoe F, Alexia M, Scarlett V. **Educ:** A&T State University, BS, 1958. **Career:** US Department of Labor, assistant director for departmental accounting operations, 1972-79; District of Columbia Office of Employment Security, director, office of budget and finance, 1979-80; US Department of Labor, director, office of financial management services, 1980-86; Thorpe International, Inc, chairman/chief executive officer, 1986-. **Orgs:** Alpha Phi Alpha Fraternity, 1956-. **Special Achievements:** Founder, Thorpe International, Inc. **Military Serv:** US Army, spc4, 1959-62. **Business Addr:** Chairman/Chief Executive Officer, Thorpe International, Inc, 2100 M St NW, Ste 606, Washington, DC 20037, (202)857-7835.

THORPE, HERBERT CLIFTON
Engineer. **Personal:** Born Jan 9, 1923, New York, NY; married Jessie M Shorts; children: Jessica Davis, R Clifton. **Educ:** NYU, BEE. **Career:** Rome Air Devel Ctr, elec engr. **Orgs:** Sec Rome Br NAACP; exec bd mem Mohawk Valley Frontiersmen; past pres Cosmopolitan Ctr. **Military Serv:** Military Serv 2nd lt 1943-46. **Business Addr:** Griffiss A F B, NY 13441.

THORPE, JOSEPHINE HORSLEY
Attorney. **Personal:** Born Jun 3, 1943, Elizabeth, NJ. **Educ:** Montclair St Coll, BA 1964; Seaton Hall Univ Sch of Law & Rutgers Sch of Law, jD 1969. **Career:** Newark Legal Serv Proj, staff atty 1969-70; Murphy Thorpe & Lewis NYC, law partner 1970-73; gen practice of law in Newark NJ 1973-74; Educ Law & Cntgr,atty 1974-75; Gen Attys Orgn Western Elec Co Inc NYC, atty 1975. **Orgs:** Mem Bar of NJ & NY; US Dist Ct for Dist of NJ; vice pres Educ Law Cntr Inc 1974-75; mem Garden St Bar Assn; Nat Bar Assn 100 Women for Integrity in Govt. **Honors/Awds:** Recipient Regional Heber Smith Fellowship 1969; first place in oral presentation of Appellants brief in Rutgers Moot Ct Competition 1968. **Business Addr:** 195 Broadway, New York, NY.

THORPE, OTIS HENRY
Professional basketball player. **Personal:** Born Aug 5, 1962, Boynton Beach, FL. **Educ:** Providence College, Providence, RI, 1980-84. **Career:** Kansas City Kings, forward, 1984-85; Sacramento Kings, 1985-88; Houston Rockets, 1988-95; Portland Trail Blazers, 1995; Detroit Pistons, 1995-97; Vancouver Grizzlies, 1997-98; Washington Wizards, 1998-. **Honors/Awds:** NBA All-Rookie Second Team, 1985; NBA All-Star, 1992. **Special Achievements:** NBA Draft, First round pick, #9, 1984. **Business Addr:** Professional Basketball Player, Washington Wizards, MCI Center, 601 F St NW, Washington, DC 20071, (202)661-5000.

THORPE, WESLEY LEE
Executive director. **Personal:** Born Nov 20, 1926, Durham, NC; married Louise; children: Angela A, Wesley L Jr. **Educ:** A&T Univ Greensboro NC, grad 1949. **Career:** Greaster New Haven Bus & Professional Mens Assn, exec dir; Delaney Cleaners Raleigh NC, asst mgr & tailor; Olin Matheson, scrap control mgr 1952-56; Siskorsky Aircraft, inspector 1956; Newhallville Cleaners, owner 1965. **Orgs:** Mem Widows Son Lodge #1 PH Mason NH; trustee Immanuel Bapt Ch; sec Club 30 Inc; asst sec Widows Son Lodge 1955-56; bd dir Community Progress Inc; bd Dir BBB; bd Dir JC of New Haven. **Military Serv:** USN 1945-46. **Business Addr:** 261 Newhall St, New Haven, CT.

THREATT, ROBERT
Educator. **Personal:** Born Apr 4, 1928, Columbus, GA; married Helen Kilpatrick. **Educ:** Morris Brown Coll, AB 1949; Atlanta U, MA 1958; Univ OK, edD 1963. **Career:** Morris Brown Coll, pres 1973-; Ft Valley St, chmn Dept Secondary Educ 1963-73; GA St Dept Educ, 1958-61; Marshall Jr High, GA, teacher 1953-58. **Orgs:** Mem NEA; Nat Assn Equal Opport Higher Edn; pres GA Assn Educators; bd mem Central Atlanta Progress; bd mem Citizens Trust Bank. **Honors/Awds:** Tchr of Yr 1956; Alumnus of Yr Morris Brown Coll 1971; Alumnus of Yr Atlanta Univ 1971. **Military Serv:** AUS corpl 1950-52. **Business Addr:** 643 Hunter St NW, Atlanta, GA 30314.

THREATT, SEDALE EUGENE
Professional basketball player. **Personal:** Born Sep 10, 1961, Atlanta, GA. **Educ:** West VA Tech, 1983. **Career:** Philadelphia 76er's, 1983-87, Chicago Bulls, 1987-88, Seattle SuperSonics, 1988-91; Los Angeles Lakers, 1991-96; Houston Rockets, 1996-. **Honors/Awds:** Was an NAIA first team All-Am in his jr and sr years. **Business Addr:** Professional Basketball Player, Houston Rockets, 10 Greenway Plaza, Houston, TX 77046, (713)627-0600.

THROWER, CHARLES S.
Editor, publisher. **Personal:** Born Sep 29, 1920, Philadelphia, PA; married Naomi Woo Yum; children: Charles Jr, Pamela, Teresa, Brian, Steven. **Educ:** Univ Pa; UCLA. **Career:** Peninsula Bulletin, ed pub founder 1967-75; freelance writer; newscaster; radio & TV producer; bd Bay Area Urban League. **Orgs:** Life mem NAACP; BSA; Mid-peninsula Stanford Urban Coal; bd United Nations Assn; bd W Coast Black Publ Assn; Sigma Delta Chi Journalism Frat. **Military Serv:** Army Vet. **Business Addr:** 2332 University Ave E, Palo Alto, CA 94303.

THROWER, JULIUS A.
Clergyman. **Personal:** Born Jul 31, 1917, Mobile, AL; married Omanda Harris; children: Yvonne, Julius, Randolph, Pearl, Leonard, Herbert, Saundra, Joseph, Orlando. **Educ:** So State Acad, 1959; Cedar Grove Theol Sem; Selma Univ Ext; Lutheran Theol Sem. **Career:** Mt Zion Missionary Bapt Ch; Lilly Bapt Ch; min; Fannie Bapt Ch, pastor; Bapt Training & Union Cong, inst. **Orgs:** Vol Youth Comm OH 1960-66; mem Ministeral All; vice pres Pastors Conf; Inst Dist Cong Christian Educ 1967-74; NAACP 1967-74; treas Human Right Fund for Jusitice 1973-74; vol Youth Comm OH 1966-74. **Honors/Awds:** Bronze Zero Defects Award. **Military Serv:** Air Force Logistics Comm 1967. **Business Addr:** 1535 Dewey Ave, Columbus, OH 43219.

THROWER, JULIUS B.
Administrator. **Personal:** Born Mar 26, 1938, Mobile, AL; married Louise Green; children: Julian, Jason. **Educ:** SD Bishop State Jr Coll, AA; AL State Coll Mobile Ctr, 1962; AL State U, BS 1964; Auburn U, MEd 1971. **Career:** SD Bishop State Jr Coll, dir of admin 1977-, veterans coord; SD Bishop State Jr Coll, dir veterans affairs 1973-77; SD Bishop State Jr Coll, coord special serv & devel 1971-73; SD Bishop State Jr Coll, plant supr 1966-70; Mobile Co Public School, high school instructor 1964-66. **Orgs:** Mem VCIP adv bd US Dept HEW 1975-76; past v chmn (Amvpa) Am Assn of Minority Prog Admin 1977-78; commr Nat Commns from Employment Policy 1979; former sr warden F & AM Onyx Ldg #676 1975-76; asst recorder Shriner Palestine Temple 1975-76; bd of mgmt Metro YMCA Mobile Deaborn St Br; adv bd Mobile Consortium CETA; commr (presdl appointee) Nat Commns for Employment Policy 1979; Jr Coll Leadership Conf Auburn Univ 1969. **Honors/Awds:** SGA Award student govt assn SD Biship State Jr Coll 1976; Good Conduct Medal. **Military Serv:** USMC col 4 yrs. **Business Addr:** Veterans Coordinator, SD Bishop State Jr Coll, 351 N Broad St, Mobile, AL 36603.

THURMAN, ALFONZO
Educator, educational administrator. **Personal:** Born Oct 24, 1946, Mayfield, KY; son of Georgia May Jones Thurman and Togo Thurman; married Brazilian Burnette; children: Alfonzo II. **Educ:** Univ of Wisconsin-LaCrosse, BS 1971, Univ of Wisconsin-Madison, MA 1973, PhD 1979. **Career:** Univ of Wisconsin-Whitewater, coordinator minority affairs 1971-75; Univ of Wisconsin-Oshkosh, dir academic devel program 1975-80; Northern Illinois Univ, dir special projects 1980-84, asst to the provost 1984-87, assoc dean, coll of educ, prof, ed policy studies, 1987-. **Orgs:** Pres Illinois Assn of Educ Opportunity Program 1983-84; chairman DeKalb Human Relations Comm 1983-86; Parliamentarian Mid-America Assn of Educ Opportunity Programs, 1989-90; bd of dirs, IL Assn of Colleges of Teacher Education. **Honors/Awds:** Outstanding Leadership Award ILAEOPP 1985; author: "Establishing Special Services on Campus" (chapter) IN Handbook of Minority Student Services, "Policy Making, Higher Education's Paradox" (article) in Thresholds 1986; Leadership of the Governing Board and Central Administration: Providing the Policy and Budgetary Framework for Incorporating Multicultural Elements into College and University Curriculum, co-authored with Carol Floyd, chapter, 1991; Trio Programs: A Proposal for Accrediting Programs Designed to Increase Underrepresented Groups in Higher Education, chapter, 1993. **Home Addr:** 527 Ridge Rd, De Kalb, IL 60115. **Business Addr:** Assoc Dean, Coll of Educ, Northern Illinois University, Graham Hall 321, De Kalb, IL 60115.

THURMAN, CEDRIC DOUGLAS
Banker. **Personal:** Born May 5, 1964, Chicago, IL; son of Walter & Cleola Thurman Jr; married Michelle Speller-Thurman, May 29, 1994. **Educ:** Univ of Illinois-Urbana, BS, 1987; J L Kellogg Grad School of Management, masters, management, 1996. **Career:** Harris Trust & Savings Bank, commercial banking trainee, 1987-89, international banking rep, Trade Finance, 1989-91, asst vp of community devt, 1991-93, vp of branch management, 1993-. **Orgs:** Univ of Illinois Commerce Alumni Assn, bd mem, 1994-; Jr Achievement of Chicago, area bd mem, 1995-; Urban Bankers Forum of Chicago, 1988-; National INROADS Alumni Assn, 1987-. **Honors/Awds:** National Assn of Urban Bankers, Scholarship, 1993, 1994; Urban Bankers Forum of Chicago, Outstanding Member, 1990; INROADS Chicago Alumnus of the Year, 1988, 1993; Religion Asst of the Year, 1982. **Business Addr:** VP, Harris Trust & Savings Bank, 111 W Monroe, Chicago, IL 60603, (312)461-2184.

THURMAN, MARJORIE ELLEN
Educator. **Personal:** Born in Whiteville, NC. **Educ:** Fayetteville State Univ, BS 1969; Seton Hall Univ, MA 1977; Montclair State Univ, Thistle Program & Administrative Certification, 1990-. **Career:** Essex Coll of Business, instructor 1975-85; Sawyer Business School, evening dean 1979-80; Senator Wynona Lipman, part-time clerical 1985-; SCS Business & Tech Inst, part-time instructor 1986-; Newark Bd of Educ, teacher 1969-. **Orgs:** YWCA 1972-83; Sunday school teacher St Paul's Church 1978-80; advisor Senior Class MX Shabazz 1985-87; mem Minority Business Org 1985-; Natl Business Educ Assn/NJ Business Educ Assn; Newark Teacher's Union; Alpha Kappa Alpha Sorority. **Honors/Awds:** Outstanding Teaching Plaque Essex Coll of Business 1983; Teacher of the Month-SCS Business & Technical Inst, 1987-88; created a successful program in Newark, NJ in 1981 called the "Newark Business Skills Olympics". **Business Addr:** Business Teacher, Malcolm X Shabazz HS, Newark, NJ 07108.

THURMAN, SUE BAILEY. See Obituaries section.

THURMOND, NATE (NATE THE GREAT)
Sports administrator, professional basketball player (retired). **Personal:** Born Jul 25, 1941, Akron, OH. **Educ:** Bowling Green State Univ, BS, 1963. **Career:** San Francisco Warriors, 1963-71, Golden State Warriors, 1971-74, Chicago Bulls, 1974-75, Cleveland Cavaliers, 1976-77; The Beginning Restaurant, San Francisco, owner; Golden State Warriors, dir community relations, 1980-. **Orgs:** Bd mem SCARE; promo appearances, youth clinics, speaking engagements throughout No CA. **Honors/Awds:** Leagues 4th all-time leading rebounder with 14,464 career bds; honored for outstanding play with Golden State 1978; mem Basketball Hall of Fame. **Business Addr:** Dir of Community Relations, Golden State Warriors, Oakland Coliseum Arena, Nimitz Freeway, Oakland, CA 94621-1996.

THURSTON, CHARLES SPARKS
Dermatologist. **Personal:** Born Mar 13, 1934, King & Queen, VA; married Marie; children: Renee, Cynthia, Patti, Carmen. **Educ:** VA St Coll, BS 1953; Meharry Med Coll, MD 1958; Wm Beaumont Army Hosp, intern 1959; Univ MI Med Ctr, res 1965-66. **Career:** Self Empl, drmtlgst; Wilford Hall USAF Hosp, training dir, chf 1974-76; USAF Sur Gen, consult 1968-70, 1974-76; Weisbaden USAF Hosp, chf gen therapy srv 1972-74, chf dermat1970-74; Andrew AFB, 1966-68; Howard U, asst clinical prof 1968-70; G Wash U, 1968-70; Georgetown U, 1968-70; Univ TX, 1974-; Santa Rosa Hosp, chf dermat 1978. **Orgs:** Pres CA Whittier Med Soc 1977-78; vice pres Lone Star St Med Soc 1977; pres Assn Mltry Drmtlgy 1975; natl chmn dermat sect Nat Med Assn 1977-79; flw Am Acad Drmtlgy 1967-; mem AMA 1968-; Mat Med Assn 1968-; San Antonio Dermat Soc 1975-; Am Coll Phy 1975-; pres local chap Alpha Omego Alpha 1957-58. **Honors/Awds:** R Braun Awd Most Outst Sr & Med Std Surg 1958; cert Achvmt Surg Gen 1970; V Marchbanks Awd Outst Air Force Phys 1974; Meritorious Srv Mdl USAF. **Military Serv:** USAF chf, aviation med 1959-63, col 1956-76. **Business Addr:** 343 W Houston St, Ste 909, San Antonio, TX 78205.

THURSTON, PAUL E.
Educator. **Personal:** Born Jul 13, 1938, Williamsport, PA; son of Helen Louise Thurston. **Educ:** Lafayette Coll, BS 1960; Cornell U, PhD 1964. **Career:** TX So U, asst prof 1966-73; TX So Univ asso prof 1973-; Texas Southern Univ Houston, TX prof, 1982-. **Orgs:** Mem Am Chem Soc; Am Assn of Univ Prof. **Honors/Awds:** Recip Danforth Fellow & Woodrow Wilson Fellow; Phi Beta Kappa; Experimental Organic Chemistry, American Press 1987; General Chemistry: A Lab Manual, Vol 1 & 2, 1989. **Military Serv:** AUS capt 1960-64. **Business Addr:** Professor, Texas Southern Univ, Dept of Chemistry, 3100 Cleburne St, Houston, TX 77004.

THURSTON, WILLIAM A.
Minister, architect, human rights activist. **Personal:** Born Jun 6, 1944, Chicago; married Silvia M Petty; children: William A, Peter O, Omyia N, Pauline A. **Educ:** Univ of IL, bA 1967; Moody Bible Inst, 1979; Candler Sch of Theol, 1980; Graham Found Scholar, 1966. **Career:** Operation PUSH, natl dir; Seymour S Goldstein Asso Chicago, arch 1965-67; Dubin Dubin Black & Moutoussamy Chicago, arch 1967-69; Envrn Seven Ltd Chicago, pntr dir of planning 1969-74. **Orgs:** Asso minister Fellowship Missionary Bapt Ch; bd mem Comprehensive Research & Devel Chicago Arch Assis Cntr; mem Nat Assn of Housing Owners & Mgr. **Business Addr:** 930 E 50 St, Chicago, IL 60615.

TIBBS, EDWARD A.
County official, business executive. **Personal:** Born Apr 12, 1940, Pittsburgh, PA; son of Mayme Yager Tibbs and Otis H. Tibbs; married Sheila Christian Tibbs, May 10, 1988. **Educ:** Allegheny Community College, associates 1976; Wilson College, certificate of instruction 1980; Univ Pittsburgh, evening studies; Wilson Coll, 1982-1989. **Career:** East Liberty-Garfield CAP, board member 1968-74; Allegheny County, democratic committeeman 1970-81, paymaster 1980-81; IBPOE of W Elks, asst to grand exalted ruler 1982-; Allegheny County, district magistrate, 1982-; Lincoln, Larimer, Lemington, Belmar, Citizens Revitalization Development Corp, executive director, currently. **Orgs:** Exec bd mem Local 2596 CWA 1973-80; chairman Allegheny County Black Political Assembly 1976-77; exalted ruler Greater Pgh Elks 1979-82; Committee on Ethics Communication Workers of Amer 1973-76; NAACP life mem Sixth Mount Zion Baptist Church; pgh Job Corps vp, community relations council, 1992-. **Honors/Awds:** Community Service Award Community Action Pgh 1975; Mr Elk IBPOE of W Pgh 1979; Meritorious Serv Awd PA Chaplains Dept IBPOE of W 1981; Disting Achievement Awd Steel City Council #8 IBPOE of W 1981; Leadership with Excellence Awd Faith Tabernacle Church 1986; Westinghouse High School, Hall of Fame, 1996. **Military Serv:** US Army, specialist 4th class, 3 yrs; Missileman of the Month 1960. **Home Addr:** 7243 Somerset Street, Pittsburgh, PA 15235. **Business Addr:** District Magistrate, Allegheny County, 1013 Lincoln Ave, Pittsburgh, PA 15206.

TIDWELL, BILLY JOE
Association executive. **Personal:** Born Jul 13, 1942, Tyler, TX; son of Verdalia Choice Tidwell and Edgar Tidwell; married Jean LaFaye Tidwell, Aug 13, 1969; children: Djenaba Kai, Moriba Ayo. **Educ:** Univ of CA, Berkeley, CA, BA, 1964, MSW, 1966; Univ of WI, Madison, WI, PhD, 1977. **Career:** IN Univ, Gary, IN, sr researcher, 1972-75; Mathematica Policy Research, Inc, Princeton, NJ, sr researcher, 1975-84; Natl Urban League, Inc, Washington, DC, dir of research, 1984-. **Orgs:** Mem, Natl Assn of Social Workers, 1975-; founding mem, Natl Assn of Black Social Workers, 1968-; assoc mem, Comm on the Skills of the American Workforce, 1990-; mem, Alpha Phi Alpha Fraternity, 1965-. **Honors/Awds:** Fellowship, Ford Foundation, 1970-71; Distinguished Community Service,

City of Los Angeles, 1967; Author of ''Stalling Out: The Relative Progress of African Americans,'' Natl Urban League, 1989; Author of ''The Price: A Study of the Losts of Racism in America,'' Natl Urban League, 1990. **Business Addr:** Director of Research, National Urban League, 1111 14th St NW, Suite 600, Washington, DC 20005.

TIDWELL, ISAIAH
Banking executive. **Personal:** Born Feb 13, 1945, Charlotte, NC; son of Anna D Tidwell and William Tidwell; married Hellena O Huntley; children: William DeVane, Damion Lamar. **Educ:** NC Central Univ, BS 1967; Wake Forest Univ, MBA 1980. **Career:** Celanese Fibers Co Charlotte, accountant 1967-70; Celanese Fibers Co Rock Hill, cost acct 1970-71, supvr cost analysis 1971-72; Wachovia Bank & Trust Co, regional vice president, currently. **Orgs:** Pres, jr & sr class NC Central Univ 1965-67; mem comm of fin, pres Charlotte Chapter, 1974-76, life mem, NC Central Univ Alumni Assoc 1967-76; various offices held Omega Psi Phi 1969-76; mem Charlotte Chamber of Commerce 1973-76; chmn of the bd Charlotte Business Devel Org 1974-76; bd mem Charlotte Business Resource Center 1975-76; mem bd of Deacons, bd of trustees, financial secretary First Baptist Church-E Winston; past pres PTA Moore Alt School; Omega Psi Phi Fraternity Inc Basileus, life mem; mem Statement Studies Comm Robert Morris Assoc; Mem Region IV Charlotte Advisory Council US Small Business Admin; mem bd of directors, chmn Business II Div 1982 Campaign United Way of Forsyth County; pres-bd of dir Winston-Salem Neighborhood Housing Serv; mem, exec bd, chmn communications comm; mem, bd of dir, Finance Comm YMCA-Metro Board, mem, City/County utility Commission of Winston-Salem & Forsyth County; 1984, mem, W/S Chamber of Commerce, W/S Rotary; mem, Bachelor Benedict's Club; mem Sigma Pi Phi Fraternity; founder, member, Piedmont Club, 1985-. **Honors/Awds:** 1st minority chmn Celriver Plant United Fund Campaign 1972; Man of the Year, Winston-Salem Chronicle, 1988; Omega Man of the Year, Psi Phi Chapter, Omega Psi Phi Fraternity, 1983; Distinguished Service Award, Bachelor Benedict's Club, 1990. **Business Addr:** Regional Vice President, Wachovia Bank & Trust Co, S Tryon St, Charlotte, NC 28202.

TIDWELL, JOHN EDGAR
Educator. **Personal:** Born Dec 13, 1945, Independence, KS; son of Verlean Tidwell and Harry Tidwell, Sr. (deceased); children: Levert, Trudy, Tuere. **Educ:** Washburn University, BA, English, 1969; Creighton University, MA, English, 1971; University of Minnesota, PhD, 1981; Yale University, visiting fellow, 1985-86. **Career:** Atchison Neighborhood Center, Atchison, KS, director, 1969-70; Maur Hill Catholic College Preparatory School, Atchison, KS, instructor, 1969-70; Creighton University, instructor, 1970-71; University of Nebraska at Omaha, instructor, 1971-73, acting chairman of Black Studies Department, 1972-73; St Olaf College, director of American Minority Studies, 1973-74, instructor, 1973-75; University of Minnesota, teaching associate II, 1975-78; Carleton College, visiting instructor, Fall 1977, Spring 1979; University of Kentucky, assistant professor, 1981-87; Miami University, assistant professor, 1987-93, assoc prof, 1993-. **Orgs:** Modern Language Association; Midwest Modern Language Association. **Honors/Awds:** American Lutheran Church Future Faculty Fellowship, 1975-77; Putnam Dana McMillan Fellowship, University of Minnesota, 1979; National Fellowships Fund Award, 1978-81; NEH Fellowship for Independent Study and Research, 1985-86; several other fellowships and grants. **Business Addr:** Associate Professor, Department of English, Miami University, Oxford, OH 45056.

TIEUEL, ROBERT C. D.
Business executive, cleric (retired). **Personal:** Born Jun 26, 1914, Boley, OK; married Mary E Porter. **Educ:** Lane Coll Jackson TN, AB & BD; TN St Coll; Langston U; TX Coll; Harvard Divinity School, spec study 1934-36. **Career:** Christ Call Mission Fund & News Serv, dir; Friendship Chapel CME Ch Pecos TX, pub rel consult journ churchman pastor; The Midland Reporter & Telegram andClovis Daily News Trib, staff col; NW TX Conf of CME Ch, circuit rider evang pastor; TX Coll Tyler, recruitment off. **Orgs:** Mem Hobbs NM C of C; Boley OK C of C; bd of Christ Edn; NW TX Conf CME Ch; Nat Retired Thcr Assn; chmn exec com Progressive Cit Leag Incof NM; mem Liano Estacado Hist Assn; sec treas United Clearing Syst Inc; mem Com of 100 to Make Boley OK a Nat Pk; ed Who's Who in the CME Ch 1962; religious editor of Southwest Digest Lubbock TX 1987; dir, public relations Christian Index. **Honors/Awds:** First Black cand for NM stae rep 1958; cited by Pres Eisenhower for efforts in build christ interracial goodwill & rel as ed of The Christ Call; dir Mary P Tieuel's Scholarship fund for deserving minorities 1987-88. **Business Addr:** Minister, Christian Meth Epis Church, 531 S Parkway East, Memphis, TN.

TILDON, CHARLES G., JR.
Government employee. **Personal:** Born Sep 10, 1926, Baltimore, MD; married Louise Smith. **Educ:** Morehouse Col; Morgan State Coll; Johns Hopkins U, BS 1954. **Career:** Dept Human Resources, asst sec community prog & admin 1980; Provident Hosp Inc, asso dir, coor, Neighborhood Hlth Cntr 1968-71; Biodynamics, consult off econ oppor 1968-70; Balt Pub Sch, tchr head science dept 1955-64; Balt City PO, postal clk 1951-55; Morgan St Coll, cnslr 1960-61. **Orgs:** Mem Adv Club Balt; mem Am Col Hosp Admin; mem Nat Assn Hlth Serv Executives (Charter mem & past vp) mem at Large, past chmn Archdiocesan Urban Comm; adv bd Advance Fed Savings & Loan, 1966; Am Cancer Soc; bd mem, mem exec comm, Citizens Planning & Housing Assn. **Honors/Awds:** Achievement Awd Archdiocesan Council Cath men; Citizens Salute to Charles G Tildon, Jr 1969; Spec Serv Awd, Urban Comm, Archdiocese Balt 1972; Med Staff Awd, Provident Hosp 1967. **Business Addr:** 1123 N Eutaw St, 605 Jackson Towers, Baltimore, MD 21201.

TILGHMAN, CYPRIAN O.
Union official. **Personal:** Born May 19, 1913, Washington, DC; married Cecilia Cooke; children: 13. **Career:** Former UCF Bd; HWC delegate; vice pres MD State/DC AFL-CIO; Hotel & Restaurant Local #25, advisor/consultant. **Orgs:** Former mem MDTA; mem Skills Bank; Urban League; Old Dem Central Com; pres JEB. **Business Addr:** Advisor/Consultant, Hotel & Rest Local #25, 1003 K St NW, Washington, DC 20001.

TILLERY, DWIGHT
City government official. **Career:** City of Cincinnati, councilmember, currently. **Business Addr:** Councilmember, City of Cincinnati, City Hall, Rm 351, 801 Plum St, Cincinnati, OH 45202, (513)352-5314.

TILLEY, FRANK N.
Physician. **Personal:** Born Jul 17, 1933, New York, NY; married Frances A Payne. **Educ:** Columbia Clge, BA 1955; State Univ of NY Sch of Medicine Downstate Med Ctr, MD 1959; Columbia Univ Sch of Pub Health & Admin Medicine, MPH 1964. **Career:** Dept of Family Prac State Univ of NY Downstate Med Ctr, clinical asst 1974-; Dept of Ambulatory Care Jewish Hosp & Med Ctr of Brooklyn Greenpoint Affil, chief 1973-; United Mutual Life Ins Co, med dir 1972-; United Mutual Life Ins Co, bd dir 1974-; Dept of Environmental Medicine & Comm Health State Univ of NY Downstate Med Ctr, lectr 1972-74; Jewish Hosp & Med Ctr of Brooklyn Greenpoint Affil, coord of Ambulatory Care 1971-73, asst dir EmerDept 1971, emer srv atndng physician 1965-7, 69-71. **Orgs:** Fellow Amer Clge of Preventive Medicine; Amer Clge of Emer Physicians; mem Med Soc of State of NY; Med Soc of Co of Kings; Provident Clinical Soc;Amer Geriatrics Soc; Amer Pub Health Assc; New York City Pub Health Assc; Amer Soc of Tropical Medicine & Hygiene; New York City Soc of Topical Medicine; mem 100 Black Men. **Honors/Awds:** Recipt Commendation Medal 1969; Certificate of Achievemnt AUS 1969. **Military Serv:** AUS major 1967-69.

TILLIS, FREDERICK C.
Composer, poet, performer, educator. **Personal:** Born Jan 5, 1930, Galveston, TX; son of Bernice Gardner and General Gardner; married E Louise; children: Patricia, Pamela. **Educ:** Wiley College, BA 1949; Univ of Iowa, MA, 1952, PhD, 1963. **Career:** Wiley College, instructor/director of instrumental music, 1949-51, assistant professor/chairman of the dept of music, 1956-61, associate professor/chairman of the dept of music, 1963-64; Grambling College, professor of music/head of theory dept, 1964-67; Kentucky State University, professor/head of the music dept, 1967-69; University of Massachusetts, associate professor of music, 1970-73, professor of music theory and composition/director of Afro American music & jazz program, 1973-, director of UMass jazz workshop, 1974-80, director of fine arts center, 1978-, associate chancellor for affirmative action and equal opportunity, 1990-. **Orgs:** Music or DA board of dir, 1995; Chancellor's Executive Advisory Council, 1994-; ALANA Honor Society Board, 1994-; Faculty Senate Council on the Status of Minorities, 1984-; Academy of American Poets; American Composers Alliance; American Federation of Musicians; Broadcast Music Industry; Center for Black Music Research; International Association of Jazz Educators; Music Educators National Conference; TransAfrica Forum; American Music Center; Massachusetts Music Educators Association; United Negro College Fund. **Honors/Awds:** Recip United Negro Coll Fund Fellowship 1961-63; recip Rockefeller Fund Grant for Devl Compstn 1978; recip Nat Endowment for the Arts, Composers Grant 1979; Chancellor of the University of Massachusetts, Distinguished Lecturer, 1980; MA Cultural Council, Commonwealth Award in organizational leadership, 1997. **Special Achievements:** Composer of more than 120 compositions spanning both the European classical & jazz traditions; Albums: ''Freedom,'' 1973; ''Fantasy on a Theme by Julian Adderley,'' 1975; ''The Music of Frederick Tillis, Vol I,'' 1979; ''Quintet for Brass,'' 1980; ''Kcor Variations,'' 1980; ''Elegy,'' 1983; ''Swing Low, Deep River,'' 1984; ''Contrasts and Diversions: The Tillis-Holmes Jazz Duo,'' 1987; ''Voices of Color,'' 1989; ''Crucificion,'' 1990; ''Paintings in Sound,'' 1990; ''The Second Time Around: The Tillis-Holmes Jazz Duo,'' 1991; ''Among Friends-The Billy Taylor Trio and Fred Tillis,'' 1992; author: In the Spirit and the Flesh, 1989; Images of Mind and Heart, 1991; In Celebration, 1993; Of Moons, Moods, Myths, and the Muse, 1994; ''Free as a Feather,'' Jazz Educators Journal, Dec 1994; Harlem Echoes, 1995. **Military Serv:** US Air Force, 1952-56. **Business Addr:** Director, Fine Arts Center, University of Massachusetts, 129 Herter Hall, Amherst, MA 01003-3910, (413)545-3517.

TILLMAN, CEDRIC
Professional football player. **Educ:** Alcorn State University. **Career:** Denver Broncos, wide receiver, 1992-. **Business Addr:** Professional Football Player, Jacksonville Jaguars, One Stadium Pl, Jacksonville, FL 32202, (904)633-6000.

TILLMAN, CHRISTINE L.
Elected official, social service. **Personal:** Born Dec 14, 1952, Richmond, VA. **Educ:** Radford Coll, BA 1975; VA Commonwealth Univ, 1976; J Seargeant Reynolds Comm Coll, 1981,84. **Career:** Richmond Oppty Indust Ctr, youth counselor 1975. **Orgs:** Basileus 1972-75, mem 1973-74 Alpha Kappa Alpha; mem bd of dir Dawn Progressive Assoc Inc 1978-; mem Caroline Co Rec Adv Comm 1984-, Caroline Co Ext Serv Adv Council, VA Politech Inst & State Univ 1984-, Caroline Co Bd of suprvs 1984-; v chmn Caroline Co Bd of Suprvs 1985, Caroline Co Local Welfare Bd 1985, NAACP Caroline Chapt; bd mem Tri-County Medical Corp 1985-; chmn Caroline Co Bd of Supervisors 1987. **Honors/Awds:** 1st Black Female Mem Caroline Co Bd of Suprvs 1984-; Honoree Negro Achievers Awd Caroline Co Chap NAACP 1984. **Home Addr:** 30372 Sadie Lane, Doswell, VA 23047.

TILLMAN, GEORGE, JR.
Film director. **Personal:** Born in Milwaukee, WI; married Marcia Wright. **Educ:** Columbia College, attended. **Career:** Director/writer; Films: Scenes for the Soul, 1995; Soul Food, 1997. **Honors/Awds:** Midwestern Student Academy Award. **Business Addr:** Director, c/o William Morris Agency, 151 El Camino Dr, Beverly Hills, CA 90212, (310)274-7451.

TILLMAN, JOSEPH NATHANIEL
Executive. **Personal:** Born Aug 1, 1926, Augusta, GA; son of Canarie Tillman and Leroy Tillman; married Areerat; children: Alice Tillman Thornton, Robert Bertram. **Educ:** Paine Coll, BA (Magna Cum Laude) 1948; Northrop Univ, MS 1975, MBA 1976; Nova Univ, DBA 1989. **Career:** Rockwell Intl, dir 1958-84; Tillman Enterprises, president 1985-. **Orgs:** Guest lecturer UCLA 1980-85; pres NAACP San Gabriel Chap 1984; pres Soc of Logistics Engrs Orange Co Chap 1985; chmn organizational behavior Acad of Mgmt 1985; consultant Natl Univ 1986. **Honors/Awds:** Presidential Citation Natl Assn for Equal Oppor in Higher Educ 1986; numerous publications including ''Computer Algorithm for Optimizing Testability'' 1976, ''Testability Optimizing at all Levels of Maintenance'' 1984; ''An Evaluation of Middle Managers Coping Strategies in Aerospace Industries as a Predictor of their Success'' 1986; ''Job Stressors and Coping Strategies of Aerospace Managers: Their Influence on Healthy Life Styles and Job Performance'' l989. **Military Serv:** USAF capt 9 yrs, navigator bombardier 1948-57. **Home Addr:** 1032 Sugarloaf Blvd, Big Bear City, CA 92314. **Business Addr:** President, Tillman Enterprises, 1550 S Rimpau Ave, #45, Corona, CA 91719-3206, (909)371-8179.

TILLMAN, LILLIAN G.
School principal. **Personal:** Born Jan 27, 1934, Jamaica, NY; married; children: Kay Lynn, James Edward. **Educ:** State Univ of New York, MS 1973-75; Roosevelt Univ, BA 1955; Russell Sage Coll, 1972-73; Hunter Coll, 1951-52, 1961; Queens Coll, 1960-61; Northwestern Univ, 1956; New York Univ, 1954. **Career:** St Acad of Albany NY, principal 1979; Arbor Hill School, Albany NY, resource teacher 1966-; Scudder Ave School, resource teacher 1962-66; Carousel Nursery School, teacher 1960-61; Albany, teacher 1956-57; Arbor Hill School, Albany NY, teacher 1956; Albany, teacher 1955-56. **Orgs:** Pres, Albany Interracial Council 1978-80; mem, City Club of Albany; mem, Phi Delta Kappa Frat; pres, vice pres, chairperson, Special Proj Comm, Albany Alumnae Chap, Delta Sigma Theta Sor Inc; first pres, Urban League Guild of Albany Area 1973-76; vice pres, chairperson, Personnel Comm, Albany Interracial Council; bd dir, Albany Co Div for Youth; chairperson, Twin Proj, Albany Dist PTA; hon life mem, PTA 1972; consultant, Natl PTA; bd dir, Albany Urban League; mem, Albany Public School Teachers Assn; NY State United Teachers; NEA; Urban League Guild; NAACP; participant in Inst for Study of Educ Problems Occasioned by Desegration State Univ NY 1967-68; Natl Staff Devel Ctr, Sem Open Classroom Denver 1971; Continuous Progress Learning Inst Albany 1972; Intl Conf &Symposium on Trans-CulturAdaptation Port-au-Prince Haiti 1973; consultant Conf of Concern for Absenteeism in Schools Chicago 1974-75; co-hostess TV prog ''Talking With the Tillmans'' 1973-76. **Honors/Awds:** Teacher Fellowship, NY State PTA 1975. **Business Addr:** Arbor Hill Elem School, Lark Drive, Albany, NY 12210.

TILLMAN, MARY A. T.
Physician. **Personal:** Born Sep 4, 1935, Bristow, OK; daughter of Ruthie English Tuggle (deceased) and Thomas Tuggle (deceased); married Daniel Thomas Tillman, Apr 20, 1957; children: Dana Tillman Chee, Daniel T Jr. **Educ:** Howard University, Washington, DC, BS, 1956, MD, 1960. **Career:** Self-employed, physician pediatrician, 1963-; City of St Louis Dept of Health and Hospitals, physician-supervisor, 1963-85. **Orgs:** National grammateus, Zeta Phi Beta Sorority, 1965-70; president, Mound City Medical Forum, 1980-82; committee on adoptions, American Academy of Pediatrics, 1970-76; president, Homer G Phillips Internes Alumni Assn, 1980-82; presi-

dent, board of directors, Annie Malone Children's Home, 1991-94; member, National Medical Association; American Medical Assn. **Honors/Awds:** Woman of Achievement in Medicine, St Louis Globe Democrat, 1982; Outstanding Alumni Award, Howard University School of Medicine, 1985; YWCA, Leader Award, YWCA, 1987; Feature article, Making Mama's Dream Come True, Good Housekeeping Magazine, 1986; Outstanding National Service Award, Zeta Phi Beta Sorority, 1986; Laymen's Awd, Cote Brilliante Presbyterian Church, 1988; Distinguished Svc Awd, Pediatric Section of National Medical Association, 1991; Barnes Hosp, 25 Years of Excellence Awd, 1994. **Home Addr:** 26 Washington Terrace, St Louis, MO 63112-1914, (314)361-1914. **Business Addr:** Pediatrician, 330 Northland Office Building, West Florissant at Lucas & Hunt, St Louis, MO 63136-1412, (314)385-5522.

TILLMAN, PAULA SELLARS
Government Official, law enforcement official, attorney. **Personal:** Born Jun 21, 1949, Chicago, IL; daughter of Sylvia L Cookman Sellers (deceased) and Herschel L Sellars (deceased); married James Tillman Sr; children: Lisa, James II. **Educ:** Loyola Univ Chicago, BA (magna cum laude) 1974; DePaul Coll of Law, JD 1979. **Career:** Chicago Police Dept, youth officer 1974-79, financial crimes investigation 1979-81, legal officer II 1981-89, sergeant, 1988-; liaison mayor's commn on women 1984-, EEO officer, 1984-; Office of the Public Defender of Cook County, labor relations counsel, currently. **Orgs:** President, co-founder, Women's Research Center, 1997-; Mem Cook County Bar Assoc 1979-; commissioner IL Attorney Registration & Disciplinary Comm 1981-; chairperson personnel comm Chicago Coalition Against Abused Women 1984-85; sec Bd of Dirs Providence St Mel High School 1984-85; fellow Leadership Greater Chicago 1985-86; board of directors Campfire Inc 1986-97; legislative chairperson, Natl Hook-Up of Black Women Chicago Chap 1986-90; vice pres, legislative affairs, Sojourner's United Political Action Comm, 1990-, president; co-chairman, Illinois Women's Committee to Elect Carol Moseley Brown; Campfire Metropolitan Chicago, pres/board of dirs, 1994. **Honors/Awds:** Natl Merit Scholar 1967. **Business Addr:** Labor Relations Counsel, Office of the Public Defender of Cook County, 200 W Adams, #900, Chicago, IL 60606.

TILLMAN, TALMADGE CALVIN, JR.
Accountant, educator, certified public accountant. **Personal:** Born Nov 26, 1925, Brunswick, GA; son of Lavonn Tillman and Talmadge Tillman; married Leola Bennings; children: Timothy, Philip. **Educ:** IN Univ, BS 1948; Syracuse Univ, MBA 1949; Univ of So CA, DBA 1967; CA, CPA 1965; Univ of MA, postdoctoral study 1972; Univ of CO, postdoctoral study 1974. **Career:** CA State Univ Long Beach, prof of acct 1968-; Price Waterhouse, faculty & flwshp 1969; E Los Angeles Clge, assc prof of acct 1962-68; Sidney Spiegel CPA, auditor-acct; Joseph S Herbert & Co, acct; Gilbert Drummont CPA Dept, acct; TX So Univ, chmn of acct 1950-51. **Orgs:** Treas Syracuse Univ Alumni Assc of LA 1953; pres IN Univ Alumni Assc of LA 1978-79; basileus Omega Psi Phi, Lambda Omicron Chpt, 1978-80; president of the Big Ten Club of Southern Cal, 1990-91; Syracuse University Alumni Association of Southern California, 1992. **Honors/Awds:** Van De Camp Award Best Article Written for Natl Assn of Acct LA Chap 1968; Natl Achievement Award in Acct Educ Natl Assn of Black Acct 1977; Citizen of Year 12th Dist Omega Psi Phi Frat; IN Alumni Assn Named Number One Chap in US during Presidency 1980; Omega Man of the Year, 1979. **Special Achievements:** First and only African-American to be president of the Big Ten Club of Southern California; first African-American to receive a Doctorate in accounting from the University of Southern California; first African-American to receive an MBA from Syracuse University; seventh African-American certified public accountant to receive a Doctorate in accounting in America. **Military Serv:** USN storekeeper 2nd Class 1944-46. **Business Addr:** Professor of Accounting, California State Univ at Long Beach, 1250 Bellflower Blvd, Long Beach, CA 90840.

TILLMON, JOEY
Law enforcement official. **Career:** Las Vegas Police Dept, chief of police, currently. **Special Achievements:** First African American chief of police in Nevada's history. **Business Addr:** Chief of Police, North Las Vegas Police Department, 1301 E Lake Mead Blvd, North Las Vegas, NV 89030, (702)649-9111.

TIMBERLAKE, CONSTANCE HECTOR
Educator. **Personal:** Born in New Brunswick;married Charles Timberlake; children: Christian, Curtis. **Educ:** Syracuse Univ, Doctorate in Educ Admin, 1979; MS; BA (cum laude); NYS, cert. **Career:** Syracuse Univ, assoc prof Col Human Develop; Syracuse Sch Dist, chief counselor & admin ABE prog; Neighborhood Ctr, exec dir; Syracuse Pub Sch Dist, commiss of educ; Adolescent Pregnancy Prevention Program, project dir, 1987-. **Orgs:** NY Sch Brds Assc; mem Prog Com; Central NY Sch Bd Inst mem planning com; AERA; AAUP; Syracuse Prof Women; HEW Task Force Social Justice Natl Literacy Volunteers Amer; Human Rights Comm of Syracuse & Onondaga Co; vice pres Syracuse NAACP; v chrprsn Coalition Quality Educ; v chrprsn Onondaga Urban League Guild; Natl Org Women; Adv Bd Onondaga Comm Clge; Neighborhood Health Ctr adv council; Metr Ch Bd Human Srv Com; Fair-Employ Review Bd Onondaga Co; PEACE Head Start Self-Evaluation & Performance Stand Improvement Plan; exec mem Black Political Caucus; numerous vol srvs; trust Pi Lambda Theta Inc; pres elect NYS Council Family Relations Council; mem SUNY at Oswego Adv Council Oswego NY; pres, New York State Council on Family Relations, 1988-89; honoraryadvisory bd mem, For Kids Sake, 1987; mem & program dir, Syracuse Boys Club of Syracuse; vice chair, Syracuse Univ Black & Latino Faculty Org, 1986-89. **Honors/Awds:** Citations, Meritorious Srvs 1972, March Wash 1963, Ldrshp Agway 1974; Jefferson Award, WTVH-TV/Amer Inst for Public Service, 1989; author of 30 journal articles & reviews, 1974-; more than 20 media presentations & documentaries, 1980-. **Business Addr:** Chair Child Family Comm Study, Syracuse University, 201 Slocum Hall CFCS Dept, Syracuse, NY 13244-5300.

TIMBERLAKE, JOHN PAUL
Business executive. **Personal:** Born Nov 12, 1950, Fackler, AL. **Educ:** NE State Jr Clge, AS engr 1969-72; AL A&M Univ, BS computer sci 1972-75. **Career:** Jackson Co NAACP, pres 1977-; Dept Ind Relation, programmer/Analyst 1977-; TN Valley Auth, engr asst 1976-77; Chattanooga Bd of Educ, sub tchr 1975-77. **Orgs:** Mem Jackson Co NAACP 1977-; mem Jackson Co Chamber of Comm 1980; mem & del Jackson Co Voter's League 1972-; mem & del AL Dem Conf 1975- sr wardenRed Rose Lodge No 352 1978-. **Honors/Awds:** Received Outst Achievement Award Jackson Co NAACP 1979; Harvester Award for Membership Jackson Co NAACP 1979.

TIMES, BETTY J.
Human resources consultant. **Personal:** Born Jan 16, 1939, Grambling, LA; daughter of Alice May Coleman and George Coleman, Sr (deceased); married John H Times; children: Anthony, John H III, Brian K, Ida L, David L. **Educ:** Hansell's Bus Coll, Certificate 1964; Coll of Marin, AS 1978; Univ of San Francisco, BS 1979. **Career:** Marin Co Library, head tech svcs, secty, typist 1964-77; Co of Marin, dir citizens serv office 1978-92; human resources consultant, currently; Marin City Project, proj admin. **Orgs:** Mem Natl Women's Political Caucas Assn of Affirmative Action Officers 1983-85; 1st vice pres Natl Women's Political Caucus; chair, Marin Co Democratic Cent Comm, 1990-92; chmn NWPC/Marin; California State Demo. Com; pres, Northern California Employment Round Table, 1990-91. **Honors/Awds:** Woman of the Year Awd Marin City Concerned Citizens 1981; Woman of the Yr Award Marin City Community Dev Corp 1982; Marin Women's Hall of Fame, Marin Commission on the Status of Women, 1991. **Home Addr:** 718 Drake Ave, Sausalito, CA 94965, (415)332-4951. **Business Addr:** Human Resources Consultant, 718 Drake Ave, Sausalito, CA 94965, (415)339-2820.

TIMM, MARION ELEANOR (MARION METIVIER)
Educational administrator. **Personal:** Born Mar 24, 1945, Meriden, CT; daughter of Mr & Mrs Frederick J Timm; children: Timm Metivier, Angelique Metivier. **Educ:** Eastern Conn State Univ, BA, 1977; Univ of New Mexico, MA, 1988. **Career:** State of Conn, publicist, 1968-74; Univ of Conn, asst dir, 1974-78; Univ of New Mexico, assoc dir, 1978-84; SUNY Stony Brook, special asst, 1984-89; Univ of Vermont, exec officer, 1989-93; Univ of CA, Irvine, asst exec vice chancellor, 1993-. **Orgs:** Natl Assn of Women in Education, ethnic wm caucus membership comm, 1976-; Best Buddies, faculty advisor, 1993-. **Special Achievements:** Author: Should Anyone Listen?, Curbstone Press, 1976; You Gonna Be the Death of Me, Yet, WTIC, 1969. **Military Serv:** US Navy, Reserve, cmdr, 1980-88; Meritorious Unit Commendation, Gold Wreath. **Business Addr:** Assistant Executive Vice Chancellor, University of California-Irvine, 524 Administration Bldg, Irvine, CA 92697-1125, (714)824-5594.

TIMMONS, BONITA TERRY
Health physicist. **Personal:** Born May 6, 1963, Norfolk, VA; daughter of Laura Mae Hines Johnson and Earl Nathanial Johnson; married Disoungh Lee Timmons, Sep 1, 1990. **Educ:** Purdue University, West Lafayette, IN, BS, 1986. **Career:** National Institutes of Health, Bethesda, MD, health physicist, 1987-89; Thomas Jefferson University, Philadelphia, PA, health physicist, 1990-. **Orgs:** Member, Health Physics Society, 1986-; member, ACURI (Appalachian Compact Users of Radioactive Isotopes), 1989-. **Honors/Awds:** Scholarship, Lions Club, 1981-82; Scholarship, Disabled American Veterans, 1981-82. **Business Addr:** Assistant Health Physicist, Radiation Safety, Thomas Jefferson University, 130 S Ninth St, 401 Edison Bldg, Philadelphia, PA 19107, (215)955-7813.

TIMMONS, OZZIE (OSBORNE LLEWELLYN)
Professional baseball player. **Personal:** Born Sep 18, 1970, Tampa, FL. **Educ:** University of Tampa. **Career:** Chicago Cubs, outfielder, 1995-96; Cincinnati Reds, 1997-. **Business Addr:** Professional Baseball Player, Cincinnati Reds, 100 Riverfront Stadium, Cincinnati, OH 45202, (513)421-4510.

TIMMONS-TONEY, DEBORAH DENISE
Cleric. **Personal:** Born Jan 8, 1961, Huntsville, AL; daughter of Lela D Timmons and Emmett Timmons; married Vincent Doyle Toney. **Educ:** J F Drake Technical College, certificate, 1981; Alabama A&M University, BS, 1987; Gammons Theological Seminary, MDiv, 1990. **Career:** Redstone Arsenal, Facilities Engineering, procurement clerk, 1980-85, Program Budget Analyst Branch, budget assistant, 1985-87; Gammon Theological Seminary, administrative assistant, 1987-89; United Way, intern, 1990-91; Emory University Hospital, clinical chaplain, 1990-91; Mt Mariah United Methodist Church, pastor, 1991-92; St Peter United Methodist Church, pastor, 1991-92; St Luke United Methodist Church, pastor, 1992-94; Asbury United Methodist Church, assoc pastor, 1994-96; Douglasville United Methodist Church, pastor, 1996-. **Orgs:** United Methodist Church, Bd of Higher Education, secretary, Seminole Service Center Board of Directors, chairperson, nominations and personnel committee, 1992; Gammon Theological Seminary, Bd of Trustees, student representative, 1988; Association for Clinical Pastoral Education Inc, 1990; Chaplain Association, 1988; National Council for Negro Women Inc; National Federation for the Blind, affiliate member; Greater Huntsville Ministerial Fellowship, correspondence secretary; Alpha Kappa Alpha Sorority Inc, Kappa Phi Omega Chapter, 1993. **Honors/Awds:** General Bd of Global Ministries, Crusade Scholar, 1988; Ford Foundation Fellow, Black Women in Church and Society, 1989; United Methodist Church Southeastern Jurisdiction, Ministrial Scholarship, 1988; Redstone Arsenal Engineering and Resources Management, Outstanding Employee Award, 1988, Program Analyst Branch, Outstanding Employee Award, 1986. **Special Achievements:** First African-American women ordained in the North Alabama Conference, UMC, 1992; first African-American women to pastor in major denomination in Northwest Alabama; first female pastor, St Peter United Methodist Church, 1992, St Luke United Methodist Church, 1992; first African-American women to be on radio program, ''United Methodist Men's Hour,'' 1992. **Home Addr:** 1500 32nd St, W, Birmingham, AL 35218-3317, (205)788-6775.

TIMPSON, MICHAEL DWAIN
Professional football player. **Personal:** Born Jun 6, 1967, Baxley, GA; married Edwena; children: Gabrielle Nicole. **Educ:** Penn State, bachelor's degree in telecommunications. **Career:** New England Patriots, wide receiver, 1989-94; Chicago Bears, 1995-96; Philadelphia Eagles, 1997-. **Business Addr:** Professional Football Player, Philadelphia Eagles, 3501 S Broad St, Philadelphia, PA 19148, (215)463-2500.

TINGLE, LAWRENCE MAY
Educational administrator. **Personal:** Born Jul 26, 1947, Canton, MS; daughter of Mamie Lee Smith and Peter L Smith; married Robert Earl Tingle; children: Aubrey F, Shella A, Robert L. **Educ:** Alcorn State Univ, BS 1968; MS State Univ, Chisanbop Instructor 1979, MEd 1981; Jackson State Univ, KS State Univ, Law Enforcement Ed; Mississippi State University Meridian, MS, MEd (AA) l987. **Career:** Newton Co Improvement Club, sec 1976-79; Newton Public Schools, classroom teacher 1972-82; NAACP, sec 1976-81; East Central Jr Coll, directress 1982-; Jackson Public Schools, health education coordinator, currently. **Orgs:** Mem Delta Sigma Theta; sec Newton Cty Heroines of Jericho; VBS instr Jerusalem MB Church 1982; deaconess Jerusalem MB Church 1973-; eval chair MS Assoc of Trio Prog for Colls 1982-; leader 4-H Club 1982-; sec l985, vice pres, MS Assoc of Ed Oppty Progs 1985; vice pres Jerusalem MB Church Home Mission Soc 1984-; associate matron Order of Eastern Star; mem Calanthe; Friends of Children MS, Inc, Jackson, MS Programs Advisor/Task Force; middle schools representative Mississippi Biology Association. **Honors/Awds:** Sec Newton Cty NAACP 1975-79; Class Room Teacher MS Outstanding Educator 1976; lecturer & writer State of MS Dept of Mathematics 1980; sec Newton Democratic Exec Comm 1981-; Peer Tutor Speaker MAEOPP/AEOPP 1984; MS Assoc of Ed Oppty Prog Personnel Serv Awd 1985; Southeastern Assoc of Ed Oppty Prog Personnel Cert of Apprec 1985; 1st African-American Female SS Directress East Central Jr Coll Decatur MS; Lifetime mem Delta Sigma Theta; mem Newton Political League. **Business Addr:** Health Education Coordinator, Kellogg Grant, Jackson Public Schools, 101 Near St, Enochs Complex, Jackson, MS 39203.

TINSLEY, DWANE L.
Insurance executive, attorney at law. **Personal:** Born Aug 12, 1953, Fayetteville, WV; son of Elizabeth Tinsley. **Educ:** Howard University School of Social Work, BA, sociology, 1975, MA, social work, 1978; WV University College of Law, Doctor of Jurisprudence, 1981; Harvard Law School, National Institute for Trial Advocacy's, Teaching Advocacy Skills, 1995. **Career:** Private, partnership, assoc law practices and instr, 1979-91; US Attorney's Office, asst US atty, 1987-91; WV Univ Coll of Law, Trial Advocacy Program, instr, 1991-95; WV Ethics Comm, hearing examiner, 1993-; WV Bd of Medicine, post-hearing advisor, 1993-; Nationwide Insurance Co, Trial Div, trial atty, 1992-95, special prosecuting atty, 1995-96, admin trial atty, 1995-96, managing trail atty, 1996-97, special investigations unit officer, 1997-. **Orgs:** American Bar Assn; Fayette County Bar Assn; International Assn of Special Investigation Unit; Mountain State Bar Assn; National Bar Assn;; WV State Bar Assn; Amer Corp Counsel Assn; Amer Bd of Trial Advocates; WV Prosecuting Attorneys Assn, former mem. **Honors/Awds:** US Dept of Justice, Special Achievement Award, 1990; Black Law Students Assn, Outstanding Black Attorney, 1987;

Brown W Bayne Fellowship, 1978-80; Georgetown Univ Fellowship Stipend, 1976-78; WV Honor Scholarship, 1971-75. **Special Achievements:** Criminal prosecutor, state and federal courts; Administrative Hearing Examiner; Insurance Defense Litigator; Instructor on Trial Advocacy and Civil Litigation. **Home Addr:** 1330 Penderson Ct, New Albany, OH 43054, (614)249-7591. **Business Addr:** Special Investigations Unit Officer, Nationwide Insurcance Enterprise, 1 Nationwide Plz, 1-24-10, Columbus, OH 43215, (614)249-7591.

TINSLEY, FRED LELAND, JR.
Attorney. **Personal:** Born Aug 30, 1944, Detroit, MI; married Ollie Brock. **Educ:** So U, BA 1969; So U, JD 1972. **Career:** Champman Tinsley & Reese, prtnr present; Lone Star Gas Co, regulatory atty 1975-77; US Secur & Exchange Commn, trial atty 1973-75; LA Constl Conv, resrch asst 1973; Reginald Heber Smith Fellow Legal Serv 1972. **Orgs:** Bd of dir Mental Hlth Assn of Dallas 1976-78; mem adv coun TX Employ Commn 1977-79; bd of dir Dallas Legal Serv Found Inc 1979-; mem exec com Dallas Co Dem Party 1980-; bd of dir Jr Black Acad of Arts & Letters Inc 1980-; asso judge Dallas Muncpl Cts 1978-. **Military Serv:** USMC corpl 1963-67. **Business Addr:** Chapman Tinsley & Reese, One Brookriver Pl Ste 370, Dallas, TX 75247.

TINSLEY, LEE OWEN
Professional baseball player. **Personal:** Born Mar 4, 1969, Shelbyville, KY. **Career:** Seattle Mariners, outfielder, 1993, 1997; Boston Red Sox, 1994-95, 1996; Philadelphia Phillies, 1996; Montreal Expos, 1998-. **Business Addr:** Professional Baseball Player, Montreal Expos, PO Box 500, Station M, Montreal, PQ, Canada H1V 3P2, (514)253-3434.

TINSLEY-WILLIAMS, ALBERTA
City official. **Personal:** Born Aug 14, 1954; daughter of Mary Louise Tinsley and Willie Tinsley; divorced; children: Carla Louise Williams. **Educ:** Eastern Michigan Univ, Ypsilanti MI, BS, 1976; Wayne State Univ, Detroit MI. **Career:** Detroit Police Dept, Detroit MI, rape counselor, 1976-78; United Auto Workers, Detroit MI, group worker, 1978-80; Comprehensive Youth Training & Community Involvement Program, Detroit MI, job development counselor, 1980-85; New Center Mental Health, Detroit MI, stress management instructor, 1985-87; Wayne County Commission, Detroit MI, county commissioner, beginning 1987; Job Connection, project specialist; Detroit City Council, councilwoman, 1993-. **Orgs:** Natl Organization of Black County Officials; Natl Assn of Counties; Women of NACO; NAACP. **Honors/Awds:** Outstanding Service Award, Govt Admin Assn, 1988; Shirley Chisholm Award, Natl Political Cong of Black Women, 1988; Spirit of Detroit Award, City of Detroit City Council, 1988; Public Citizen of the Year, 1992. **Business Addr:** Councilwoman, Detroit City Council, 1340 City-County Bldg, Detroit, MI 48226.

TIPPETT, ANDRE BERNARD
Sports administrator. **Personal:** Born Dec 27, 1959, Birmingham, AL; children: Janea Lynn. **Educ:** Ellsworth Community College; Univ of Iowa, BA, 1983. **Career:** New England Patriots, linebacker, 1982-93, dir of player resources, 1994-. **Honors/Awds:** Played in Rose Bowl; 1st team All-American, AP, UPI, NEA, Football Writers and Football News, 1981; NFL Defensive Player of the Week, Pro Football Weekly and ESPN 9/18/83; voted Best Linebacker/Defensive Back in AFC, 1984; Patriots' MVP, 1776 QB Club, 1984; AFC's Defensive Player of Week, Sports Illustrated and League Office, 11/3/85; All-NFL team; The Sporting News All-Pro team; "101" AFC Defensive Player of the Year Award; Defensive Player of the Year Award, New York Daily News; Big Brothers/Big Sisters-Tums Neutralizer of the Year Award; played in Pro Bowl, 1984-88 seasons; NFL Alumni Assn, Linbacker of the Year, 1987; NFL Player's Assn, Linbacker of the Year, 1985-87; Assoc Press Pro Football Writer's Assn, All NFL First Team; Sporting News, All Pro Second Team, 1987; UPI, All AFC, 1987; College & Pro Football Weekly, All Pro Second Team, AP Newspaper Enterprise Assn, 1986; Pro Football Weekly and UPI, All AFC, 1986. **Business Addr:** Director of Player Resources, New England Patriots, Rt 1, Sullivan Stadium, Foxboro, MA 02035, (508)543-7911.

TIPTON, DALE LEO
Physician. **Personal:** Born Jul 8, 1930, Parsons, KS; son of Ruby Tipton and Dale Tipton; children: Jill, Jan. **Educ:** Univ of CA Berkeley, AB Physiology 1952; Univ of CA San Francisco, MS Pharmacology 1959; Univ of CA Sch of Medicine, MD 1959. **Career:** Kaiser Found Hosp, intern 1959-60; Univ of CA San Francisco, resident genl surgery 1960-62; Cancer Rsch Inst Univ of CA, natl inst health fellow 1962-63; Univ of CA San Francisco, resident otolaryngology 1963-66; Univ of CA Sch of Medicine Dept of Otolaryngology, clinical prof 1976-; Private Practice, physician. **Orgs:** Delg to CA Med Assoc from San Francisco Medical Soc 1968-69; bd dirs San Francisco Med Soc 1972-75; med advisor CA Blue Shield 1977-; chmn Dept Ear Nose & Throat San Francisco Genl Hosp 1970-76; chmn Dept Ear Nose & Throat Franklin Hosp San Fran 1968-; bd dirs San Francisco Peer Review Oganization 1983-86; chief of medical staff Franklin Hosp San Francisco 1982-84. **Honors/Awds:** Diplomat Amer Bd Otolaryngology 1966; fellow Amer Coll of Surgeons 1970; Amer Acad Otolaryngology Head & Neck Surgery 1967-; publs "Changes in Golgi Apparatus of Islets of Langerhans in the Rat following Glucose & Insulin Admins" Endocrinology 1959; "Effects of Chlorpromazine on Blood Level of Alcohol in Rabbits" Amer Journal of Physiology 1961; "Duration of Bronchial Squamous Metaplasia Produced by Dogs by Cigarette Smoke Condensate" Journal of the Natl Cancer Inst 1964; "The Experimental Effects of Cigarette Smoke Condensate on Laryngeal Mucosa" published in proceedings of Int Congress of Otolaryngology 1965; "Osteochondroma of the tongue" Arch Path 1970; "Physiologic Assessment of Black People" Journal of Black Health 1975. **Military Serv:** USMC 1st lt 1953-55; USAR lt col 1984-. **Home Addr:** 458 Briarwood Drive, South San Francisco, CA 94080. **Business Addr:** Clinical Professor, University of CA Sch of Med, 45 Castro St, San Francisco, CA 94114.

TIPTON, DANELL
Sports figure. **Career:** International Professional Rodeo Association, rodeo rider, currently. **Special Achievements:** Bullriding champion, 1995. **Business Addr:** International Professional Rodeo Association, 2304 Exchange Ave, PO Box 83377, Oklahoma City, OK 73148, (405)235-6540.

TIPTON, ELIZABETH HOWSE
Educator, administrator. **Personal:** Born Oct 17, 1925, Chattanooga, TN; married B Cortex; children: Cassandra Wilson, Bensonetta Lane, Eunice Taylor, Libbee. **Educ:** Fisk Univ, BA 1945; Univ of Bridgeport, MS 1970; George Washington Univ, EdS 1974, EdD 1975. **Career:** Booker T Washington HS, teacher 1945-50; MDTA Ed Prog, dir 1965-70; Bowie State Coll, dean of students 1970-75; Bowie State Coll, vice pres student affairs 1975-. **Orgs:** Mem NAACP, NAFEO, AAHE, AAUP, AKA. **Honors/Awds:** Outstanding Admin; Noteable Amer 1976-77. **Business Addr:** Vice President Student Affairs, Bowie State College, Jericho Park Rd, Bowie, MD 20715.

TIPTON-MARTIN, TONI
Food editor. **Personal:** Born Mar 6, 1959, Los Angeles, CA; daughter of Beverly Dunbar Hamilton and Charles Hamilton; married Bruce Martin, 1992; children: Brandon, Jade, Christian. **Educ:** Univ of Southern CA, Los Angeles, CA, BA, 1981. **Career:** Waves Newspaper, Los Angeles, CA, food editor, 1980-91; Los Angeles Times, Los Angeles, CA, staff writer, 1983-91; Cleveland Plain Dealer, Cleveland, OH, food editor, 1991-. **Orgs:** Natl Food Editors & Writers Assn, 1991; Black Journalists Assn, 1980-91. **Honors/Awds:** Media Award, American Heart Assn, 1988; Nutrition Writing Award, Carnation Co, 1988; Media Excellence Award, American Heart Assn, 1989. **Business Addr:** Food Editor, The Plain Dealer, 1801 Superior Ave, Cleveland, OH 44114.

TISDALE, CELES
Educator. **Personal:** Born Jul 31, 1941, Salters, SC; son of Rachel and Norman; married; children: Yvette, Colette, Eric. **Educ:** State Univ Coll/Buffalo, BS 1963, MS 1969, PhD 1991. **Career:** PS 31 Buffalo, English teacher 1963-68; Woodlawn Jr High, English dept chmn 1968-69; WBEN TV, writer/producer 1969; WBFO-FM Radio, writer/announcer 1969-70; State Univ Coll Buffalo, English instructor 1969-72; WKBW TV, talk show host 1979-83; WKBW Radio, talk show host 1984-86; Erie Community Coll/City, prof of English. **Orgs:** Assoc dir Buffalo Urban league 1966-92; bd of dirs Artpark 1981-84; dir Adolescent Vocational Exploration 1985-88; Young Audiences, Inc, 1975-; Career Educator for Buffalo Urban League 1987-91. **Honors/Awds:** NY State Univ Chancellors Award for Teaching Excellence 1975; Man of Year, Business & Professional Women 1977; Media Award Sickle Cell Assn 1978. **Business Addr:** Professor of English, Erie Community College/City, 121 Ellicott St, Buffalo, NY 14203.

TISDALE, HENRY NEHEMIAH
Educational administrator. **Personal:** Born Jan 13, 1944, Kingstree, SC; son of Mr & Mrs Walter Tisdale; married Alice Rose Carson; children: Danica, Brandon. **Educ:** Claflin Coll, BS 1965; Temple Univ, EdM 1967; Dartmouth Coll, MA 1975, PhD 1978. **Career:** Philadelphia School Dist, math instructor, 1965-69; Univ of Delaware, special asst to the pres 1985-86; Delaware State Univ, instructor/summer engineering inst 1969-85, prof of math 1969-85, asst dir of inst rsch 1979-85, asst academic dean for admin & planning 1987-94, vp academic affairs; Claflin Coll, pres, 1994-. **Orgs:** Bd mem Holy Cross School System 1985-; mem State of DE Task Force on High Technology 1986-87. **Honors/Awds:** Southern Fellowship Fund Award 1976-78; Omega Psi Phi Man of the Year 1981, Dartmouth Fellow, 1972. **Home Addr:** 674 College St NE, Orangeburg, SC 29115-4476. **Business Addr:** President, Claflin College, 700 College Avenue, NE, Orangeburg, SC 29115-4476.

TISDALE, WAYMON LAWRENCE
Professional basketball player. **Personal:** Born Jun 9, 1964, Tulsa, OK. **Educ:** Univ of Oklahoma, Norman, OK, 1982-85. **Career:** Indiana Pacers, 1985-89; Sacramento Kings, 1989-94; Phoenix Suns, 1994-. **Special Achievements:** Olympics, US basketball, gold, 1984. **Business Addr:** Professional Basketball Player, Phoenix Suns, PO Box 1369, Phoenix, AZ 85001, (602)266-5753.

TITUS, LEROY ROBERT
Association executive. **Personal:** Born Dec 11, 1938, Pittsburgh, PA; married Anna Mary Adams; children: Shelley Meredyth, Sherre Mishel, Shelbi Melany. **Educ:** Lincoln Univ, AB 1960. **Career:** Natl Institutes of Health, microbiologist 1964-65; YMCA of Pittsburgh, program dir 1965-69; YMCA of Fort Wayne/Allen Co, exec dir 1969-72; YMCA of Metro Los Angeles, exec dir 1972-; Primerica Financial Services, reg mgr, currently. **Orgs:** Dist vice pres Assoc of Professional Directors; pres Natl Black & Non White YMCA's; pres YMCA's Serving Disadvantaged Communities; pres PANDA Productions; mem Alpha Phi Alpha Frat; delegate Natl Council of YMCA's of the USA; master trainer YMCA of the USA 1981-. **Honors/Awds:** APD Human Serv Awd Assoc of Prof Direct 1982; Outstanding Serv Awd CITIES Inc 1984; Dr Martin Luther King Human Dignity Awd LA Metro YMCA 1985; NAACP VPI Awd Los Angeles Chap 1987. **Military Serv:** AUS E-5. **Home Addr:** 13282 Briarwood St, Cerritos, CA 90703. **Business Phone:** (310)860-5866.

TITUS, MYER L.
College president. **Career:** State Board of Community Colleges and Occupational Education, Denver, CO, associate vice pres, instructional services; Philander Smith College, Little Rock, AR, president, currently. **Orgs:** Alpha Phi Alpha; Urban League, Commission on Arkansas' Future. **Honors/Awds:** University OF Missouri, Honorary LLD, 1991. **Business Addr:** President, Philander Smith College, 812 West 13, Little Rock, AR 72202.

TITUS, ROBERT P.
Accountant. **Educ:** Brooklyn College. **Career:** Nemiroff, Cosmas, Titus & Colchamiro, partner; Mitchell/Titus & Co, partner, 1973-. **Orgs:** District of Columbia Chamber of Commerce, president. **Special Achievements:** Co-founder of the largest minority-owned, certified public accounting firm in the United States. **Business Addr:** Partner, Mitchell, Titus, & Co, 1 Battery Park Plaza, 27th Fl, New York, NY 10004, (212)709-4500.

TITUS-DILLON, PAULINE Y.
Physician. **Personal:** Born Jan 1, 1938; married Owen Christopher; children: Denyse, Paul. **Educ:** Howard U, BS 1960; Howard Univ Coll of Med, MD 1964. **Career:** Howard Univ Coll of Med, prof 1981-, assoc dean acad affairs 1980-; Howard Univ Med Serv DC Gen Hosp, chief 1977-; Howard U, asso prof med 1977-; Howard U, asst prof med 1971-77; Georgetown Univ Hosp Wash DC, fellow endocrinology 1968-69; Howard Univ Hosp, post grad trainee internal medicine 1964-68; VA Hosp Outpatient Clinic Columbia SC, internist 1969-71. **Orgs:** Mem DC Med Soc; fellow Am Coll of Physicians; mem Program Dirs in Internal Med; mem Am Med Women's Assn Present; sec-treas Alpha Omega Alpha Honor Med Soc Gamma Chap Present; mem Natl Med Assoc, NY Acad of Sci, Amer med Assoc. **Honors/Awds:** Daniel Hale Williams Award Howard Univ 1965 & 68; diplomate Am Bd of Intnl Med Philadelphia 1972; fellowship NIH Bethesda 1975-77; Inspirational Leadership Award Student Counc Howard Univ Coll of Med 1979; Superior Performance Award, Howard Univ, Dept of Medicine, 1979; Excellence Award, Health Care Caribbean & American Intercultural Organization, 1996; Citation for Excellence, State of Maryland, Delivery of Health Care, 1966.

TOBIAS, RANDOLF A.
Educator. **Personal:** Born Jan 16, 1940, Bronx; married; children: Meredith, Maurice, Tonya. **Educ:** EdD 1976; MA 1968; BA 1961. **Career:** Queens Coll, CUNY, assoc dean of special programs, 1980-87; Graduate Dept of Educational and Community Programs, chair, 1988-94, assoc prof of School of Admini, 1994-; Black Studs Cert Prog Long Island Univ Brooklyn, dir 1972-74; Martin Luther King Jr Scholar Prog Long Island Univ, 1969-; Bedford Stuyvesant Talent Search, proj dir 1968-69; Mills Coll Educ, instr 1964-71; New York City Public Schools, teacher 1963-68; Teacher Educ Long Island Univ, asst prof. **Orgs:** Mem bd dir Willoughby House Settlement Brooklyn; bd dir Carlton Gardens Children's Cntr Flushing; VA Union Univ Alumni Assn Alpha Phi Alpha Frat; Am Assn Univ Prof; African Heritage Studs Assn. **Honors/Awds:** National Fraternity of Student Musicians-Performance Awards, 1956, 1957; Mellon Fellow, 1983.

TOBIN, PATRICIA L.
Business executive. **Personal:** Born Feb 28, 1943, White Plains, NY; divorced; children: Lauren. **Educ:** Levitan Bus Sch, attended 1962; Charles Morris Price Sch of Advertising & Journalism, attended 1974-77; Regional Purchasing Council LA, cert of training 1978; attended, CBS Mgmt Educ Seminar 1979. **Career:** Free lance model, 1967; Sun Oil Co, marketing rep, 1974; KNXT-TV, CBS-LA, administrative asst to manager of press information, 1979; UCLA, guest instructor, public relatins, 1983-84; Communicon Cable TV, talk show hostess, 1984; PT Enterprises, founder/pres; Tobin & Associates, Public Relations, consultant, president, chief executive officer, currently. **Orgs:** Philadelphia Club of Advertising Women 1976; Philadelphia Public Rel Assn 1977; Natl Assn of Media Women 1977; Natl Assn of Market Developers 1977; admin consult Screen Actors Guild of Amer Film Inst 1977; natl pub rels dir Spcl Markets for Sala & Associates Ltd 1977; Black Women's

Forum LA 1980; steering com BEA-West (Black Employees Assn of CBS, West Coast) 1979; dir pub rel People United to Save Humanity; African-American Film & Television Assn; American Women in Radio & Television; Black Women's Network; CA Afro-American Museum, director's advsy cncl; Ethnic Tourism Marketing Cmte; Urban Coalition Comm Task Force 1974; Sickle Cell Disease Research Foundation; Black Filmmaker Foundation. **Honors/Awds:** Black Entrepreneur Exchange/PG&E, Outstanding African-American Women in Business, 1992; Public Relations Advertising Marketing Excellence, Distinguished Public Relations Professional, 1992; Black Women in Sisterhood For Action, Distinguished Black Women, 1991; Communications Excellence To Black Audiences, Certificate of Appreciation for Services as Judge, 1991; NAACP Legal Defense & Education Fund, Black Women of Achievement Medal, 1991; California State Senate, Certificate of Recognition for Business Enterprises, 1990; NAACP Image Awards, nomination, assoc producer of "One More Hurdle"; Lt Governor, CA, Commendation for Public Service, 1987. **Special Achievements:** Host of weekly forum: "The Speakeasy for Media," 1979; press information officer: Summer Olympic Games, ABC-TV, 1984; publicity coordinator: Black Journalists Assn of So CA; Jesse Jackson for President Campaign, 1984; co-fdr of Black Public Relations Society, 1983. **Business Addr:** President, Tobin & Associates, 10911 Bluffside Dr, #20, Studio City, CA 91604.

TOBY, WILLIAM, JR.
Government official. **Personal:** Born Aug 12, 1934, Augusta, GA; son of Louise Toby and William Toby; married Diane Anderson; children: Michael, Kenneth. **Educ:** WV State Clg, BA 1961; Adelphi U, MSW 1963; Harvard Univ John F Kennedy Sch of Govt, MPA 1986. **Career:** New York City Ofc Mayor, intr-gvntl rltns ofcr 1969-71; Hlth Ed Wlfrs Soc Rhbltn Serv, regnl cmsnr 1971-77; Hlth Care Fin Admn, regnl admn 1977-. **Orgs:** Bd mem, Adelphi Univ; Natl Conf of Social Welfare; New York Univ Grad School of Public Admin, bd of overseers; US Dept of Health & Human Services, acting administrator. **Honors/Awds:** John W Davis Meritorious Awrd WV State Clg 1984; apprctn awrd Intl Hlth Ec Mgmt Inst 1984; excptnl achvmnt Sec Hlth Human Serv 1982; gubernatorial Citation Gov of NY 1982. **Military Serv:** USAF corpl 1951-55. **Business Addr:** Regional Administrator, Hlth Care Fin Admn, 26 Federal Plaza Rm 3811, New York, NY 10278.

TODD, BEVERLY
Actress, producer, director. **Personal:** Born in Chicago, IL; children: Malik Smith. **Career:** Warner Bros, Los Angeles, CA, star: "Moving," 1988, "Clara's Heart," 1989, "Lean on Me," 1989; Paramount Pictures: "Sliver"; Syndicate-It Pro, Los Angeles, CA, co-producer: "A Laugh, A Tear," 1990-91; television guest star: "Equal Justice," ABC-TV, 1991, "Falcon Crest," "Magnum P.I.," "The Redd Foxx Show," "Wise Guy," "A Different World," "Hill St Blues," "Roots"; HBO, Los Angeles, CA, co-producer: "The Don Jackson Story," 1991; director: "I Need a Man," Embassey Theatre, LA. **Orgs:** Pres, Kwanza Foundation, 1991; Delta Sigma Theta. **Honors/Awds:** Ben, Friends of Black Osar Nominees, 1990; Woman of the Year, State of CA Legislature, 1990; 4 Time NAACP Image Award Nominee, 1978, 1984, 1988, 1989; Founder of the Malik Smith Scholarship, 1989.

TODD, CHARLES O.
Educator (retired). **Personal:** Born Nov 12, 1915, Lawrence, KS; son of Mr and Mrs Hazel Todd Jr; married Geraldine Mann; children: Chrystal Todd Johnson, Karen Todd Lang. **Educ:** Emporia State Univ, BS 1940; Kansas Univ, MS 1948; Univ of So CA, MFA 1957; Univ of AZ, attended. **Career:** Douglas School, Mayview, MO, teacher, 1940; Western Univ High School, Quindaro, KS, teacher, 1941-42; Douglas Elem School, Manhattan, KS, principal 1943; Dunbar Jr High School, Tucson, AZ, teacher, 1947-51; Manfield Jr High School, teacher, 1951-67; Tucson Sr High School, teacher, 1967-82, retired. **Orgs:** Mem KS Teachers & Admin, 1943, Phi Delta Kappa, 1946, NEA, AEA, TEA, 1947-82; Alpha Phi Alpha 1950; treas Tucson Fine Arts Assn, 1950; pres NAACP Tucson Credit Union, 1964; mem Tucson Civic Chorus, 1966-67; pres, bd of dir of Tucson Civic Chorus, 1965; Tucson Big Brothers, mentor, 1966-67; treas Tucson Br NAACP, 1968-74; Mentor, APEX (Academic Preparation for Excellence), 1987-89; mem, Foster Care Review Board, 1988-96; pres, Eta Psi Lambda Chapter, Alpha Phi Alpha, 1989-. **Honors/Awds:** Service Awd Tucson Br NAACP 1975; Certificate of Recognition as a Connecting Link, Tucson Chapter, 1994. **Military Serv:** US Air Corps, Sgt, 1944-46; Air Campaign Medal. **Home Addr:** 848 E Grant Rd, Tucson, AZ 85719.

TODD, CYNTHIA JEAN
Newspaper reporter. **Personal:** Born Jan 12, 1951, Peoria, IL; children: Wendy. **Educ:** Northern Illinois Univ DeKalb, BA 1972. **Career:** Peoria Journal Star, reporter 1969-73; WMBD-AM-FM TV Peoria, reporter/anchor 1974-77; KSDK-TV St Louis, reporter/anchor 1977-79; Harris Stowe State Coll, dir publ; St Louis Post-Dispatch St Louis, reporter 1983-. **Orgs:** Mem Greater St Louis Black Journalist Assoc 1977-, AFTRA 1977, IL Newsbroadcasters Assoc 1975-77; mem adv comm Univ City HS, Univ City MO 1978; mem Alpha Kappa Alpha Sor; bd dirs New City School St Louis 1980. **Honors/Awds:** Broadcast History Awd McLean Cty IL Hist Soc 1976; Listed in Names & Faces Natl Publ 1978; Achiever in Industry Awd St Louis Metro Sentinel Newspaper 1978; NAACP Media Roole Model Award, 1989; Missouri Assn Social Welfare Media Award, 1992. **Business Addr:** Reporter, St Louis Post-Dispatch, 900 N Tucker Blvd, St Louis, MO 63101.

TODD, MELVIN R.
Administrator. **Personal:** Born Apr 24, 1933, Oklahoma City, OK; married Menzola Anderson; children: Sharon, Myra, David. **Educ:** Langston U, BA History 1954; Univ of OK, MEd Secondary 1960; Univ of OK, EdD Soc Admin/Gen Adminstrn 1973. **Career:** OK State Regents for Higher Educ, vice chancellor for academic admin 1980-; OK State Regents for Higher Educ, special asst to chancellor & stud & officer 1975-80; OK City Public School, dir of cirriculum 1973-75; Consultative Center for Equal Educ Opport Univ of OK, field consultant 1971-73; NE H School OK City, prin 1969-71; NE H School OK City, asst prin 1967-69. **Orgs:** Mem bd of dir E&C Trades Ltd 1980; mem OK Educ Assn present; corp mem Am Coll Testing Prog Corp present; mem Phi Delta Kappa present; mem Urban League present; mem NAACP present. **Honors/Awds:** Good conduct AUS 1954-56; outstndg edctr's awd OK Educ Assn 1975; distngd alumnus awd Langston Univ 1976; presidential cit Nat Assn for Equal Educ Opport in Highter Educ 1980. **Military Serv:** AUS spec 3rd 1954-56. **Business Addr:** Oklahoma State Regents for Hig, 500 Educ Bldg State Capitol Com, Oklahoma City, OK 73105.

TODD, ORLANDO
Accountant. **Personal:** Born Jan 21, 1958, Camden, AR; son of Annie Watson Todd and Oree Todd; married Glenda Faye; children: Anterryo, LaQuanta, Tiffaney. **Educ:** Southern AR Univ, BBA 1980. **Career:** Price Waterhouse, staff accountant 1980-83; AR Power & Light Co, accountant 1983-1987; AR Power & Light Co, senior accountant 1988-91, accounting supervisor 1992-. **Orgs:** Mem Central AR Chap of CPA's 1982-, AR Soc of CPA's 1982-, Amer Inst of CPA's 1982-; mem, NAACP, 1990; mem, Urban League of Little Rock, 1990. **Honors/Awds:** Certified Public Accountant 1982.

TODD, THOMAS N.
Attorney. **Personal:** Born Sep 24, 1938, Demopolis, AL; son of Alberta Todd and Cleveland Todd; married Janis Roberts; children: Traci Neuborne, Tamarla Nicole. **Educ:** Baton Rouge, BA 1959, JD 1963. **Career:** US Dept of Labor, office solicitor 1963-64; US Atty Chicago, officer 1967-70; Comm on Inquiry into Black Panthers & Law Enforcement NY, consult 1970-72; Chicago Capt So CLC, pres 1971; Oper PUSH, exec vice pres 1971-73; Midwest Task Force for Comm Report "Search & Destroy," dir; Northwestern Univ School of Law Chgo, asst prof of law, asst dir ctr for urban affairs; private practice, attorney. **Orgs:** Mem Supreme Court of LA 1963, US Court of Mil Appeals 1965, Supreme Court of IL 1967, US Court of Appeals 7th Circuit 1968, US Dist Court, No Dist of IL, US Supreme Court 1971, Chicago Comm of United Negro Coll Fund; bd of dir Legal Oppty Scholarship Prog; adv bd of IL Black Legislative Clearinghouse Chgo; adv bd of Afro-Amer Patrolmans League Chgo. **Honors/Awds:** Ammer Jurisprudence Awd; Law Week Awd; JS Clark Mem Awd; Criminal Law Awd So Univ School of Law; 1 of 10 Outstanding Young Men in Chicago Jaycees 1970; Leadership Council for Met Open Comm 1970; Cert of Achievement Kappa Alpha Phi Northwestern Univ 1971; Cert of Achievement Afro-Amer Policemens League 1971; Lawndale Peoples Planning & Action Comm 1971; SCLC Oper Breadbaskets Activist Awd 1971; IN Dem Org 1971; Achievement Awd Mens Fed So Univ 1972; Student Govt Awd So Univ 1972; Powr Inc Harambee Awd 1972; Listed One Thousand Success Stories 1973; Biog publ in Chicago Negro Almanac 1973; Outstanding Achievement Awd The Natl Consumer Info Ctr 1974; Black Excellence Awd for Comm Action PUSH Espo 1974; Natl Ed Awd Phi Beta Sigma 1975; Meritorious Serv Award Natl Assn of Black Political Sc976; Apprec Awd June tenth Comm 1976; Apprec Awd Natl Consumer Info Ctr host Tom Todd Show WLS Radio Chgo; "Voice of Ebony" Radio Commercial Ebony Mag; Honorary Doctorate of Laws, Grambling State Univ 1987; Honorary Doctorate of Laws, Syracuse Univ, 1990; Honorary Doctorate, Wilberforce Univ, 1993. **Military Serv:** AUS; capt, judge advocate ofc 1964-67. **Business Addr:** Attorney, 1 N La Salle, Chicago, IL 60602.

TODD, WILLIAM S.
Airline pilot. **Personal:** Born Mar 10, 1940, Portsmouth, VA; son of Martha E Muckle and William S Todd (deceased); divorced; children: David M, Kelly Yvette, William S IV. **Educ:** VA Union Univ, BS 1962. **Career:** USAF Commander C-135 Aircraft, lt col; USAF Acad, liaison officer, dep commander; Western Airlines, airline pilot Boeing 727 1969-87, Boeing 737 capt 1987-93; Delta 727 Airlines, 1993-96; Los Angeles, CA, Boeing 767, captain, 1996-; City of Bradbury, Bradbury, CA, chairman planning commission, 1990-; Delta Airlines, check pilot, instructor pilot, 1991-. **Orgs:** Mem Airline Pilots Assn, Alpha Phi Alpha Fraternity, US Jaycees; advtsng ed, mgr US Jaycees Publ, Accident Investigator, Engrg & Air Safety Comm Airline Pilots Assn; chmn Com to Select a City Slogan City of Cerritos CA; campaign mgr City Council Candidate 1974; mem Youth Motivation Task Force 1969-; mem Westside Fair Housing Council 1969-; owner Spectral Illuminations. **Honors/Awds:** Scholarship VA State Coll 1958; Jaycee Sound Citation Award 1974; Awards, Youth Motivation Task Force 1970, 1972. **Military Serv:** USAF captain 1963-68; USAF Reserve (retired); Air Medal w/5 Clusters, Small Arms Expert Marksman, Vietnam Expeditionary Medal 1965, USAF Meritorious Service Medal 1984, US Air Force Achievement Medal 1985, Second Meritorious Service Medal, 1991-. **Business Addr:** Airline Pilot, Delta Airlines, Hartsfield Atlanta Airport, Atlanta, GA 30320.

TODMAN, JUREEN FRANCIS
Educational administrator. **Personal:** Born Jun 30, 1935, St Thomas, Virgin Islands of the United States; daughter of Sarah Steimbergen Joshua; divorced; children: Jens, Maurice, Monigue. **Educ:** Philander Smith Coll, BA, BS 1959; NY Univ, graduate courses; Coll of Virgin Islands, graduate courses. **Career:** St Thomas Fedn of Teachers, teacher sec 1976-78, 1st vice pres 1979-80, pres 1981, teacher, sec bd of election, 1st vice pres, 1982-; Government Employees' Retirement System of the Virgin Islands, chairperson, bd of trustees, 1990-92. **Orgs:** Mem Alpha Kappa Alpha; pres Women Aux Little League 1972; treasurer Central Labor Council 1978-80; sec Bd of Election 1982-; bd of dir chairperson fund raising St Thomas East Lioness Methodist Church Choir 1974-75 & 1984-85; sec AAA Baseball League; bd dir United Way; trustee, Govt Employee's Retirement System of the Virgin Islands; pres, St Thomas East Lioness Club, 1990-91; chm, Joint Bd of Election St Thomas, St John, St Croix, 1986-88. **Honors/Awds:** Athletic Scholarship VI Educ Dept 1954; Athletic Award Softball, Volleyball, Track; Poetry published in local daily news; Teachers Fedn, Hugo Dennis Award, 1983; East Lioness Club District 60B, Outstanding Service, 1989, 100% President Award, Attendance, Participation, and Production. **Home Addr:** Box 11898, St Thomas, Virgin Islands of the United States 00802. **Business Addr:** Chairperson, Board of Trustees, Government Employees' Retirement System, 48B-50C Kronprindsens Gade, St Thomas, Virgin Islands of the United States 00802.

TODMAN, TERENCE A.
International consultant, career ambassador (retired). **Personal:** Born Mar 13, 1926, St Thomas, Virgin Islands of the United States; son of Rachel Callwood and Alphonse Todman; married Doris Weston; children: Terence A Jr, Patricia Rhymer Todman, Kathryn Browne, Michael. **Educ:** Poly Inst Puerto Rico, BA 1951; Syracuse Univ, MPA 1953; Amer Univ, post grad 1953-54. **Career:** Dept of State, intl rel ofcr 1952-54, foreign affairs ofcr 1955; UN Intern Program, US nom 1955; UN Trusteeship Cncl Petit Com & Com Rural Econ Dev, US rep 1956-57; UN Gen Assembly, adv US del 1956-57; Amer Embassy New Delhi, India, polit ofcr 1957-59; Amer Embassy Tunis, polit ofcr 1961-64; Lome, Togo, DCM & charge d'affaires 1965-68; Bur of African Affairs Dept State, country dir for Kenya, Tanzania, Uganda & Seychelles 1968; US Ambassador to Chad 1969-72; US Ambassador to Guinea 1972-75; US Ambassador to Costa Rica 1975-77; Asst Sec State for Latin American Affairs 1977-78; US Ambassador to Spain 1978-83; US Ambassador to Denmark 1983-89; US Ambassador to Argentina 1989-93. 1989-93. **Orgs:** Mem Amer Foreign Serv Assn; Academy of Public Administration; mem bd trustees Coll of the VI; Council on Foreign Relations; Assn of Black American Ambassadors; mem, Alpha Phi Alpha Fraternity. **Honors/Awds:** Sup Honor Award Dept State 1966; Medal of Honor Govt of the VI 1977; mem Hall of Fame US Army Infantry Sch Ft Benning, GA; Grand Cross of the Highest Order of Isabela la Catolica by Spanish Govt 1983; Grand Cross of Order Danebug by Govt of Denmark 1988; Disting Trustees Award Coll of the VI 1985; Presidental Distinguished Service Awd 1985; Honorary Doctor of Laws degree Syracuse Univ and honorary Doctor of Public Service degree Morgan State Univ 1986; Natl Public Serv Awd 1987; Honorary Doctor of Laws Degree Boston Univ 1987; Honorary Doctor of Laws Degree Colgate Univ 1981; Equal Employment Opportunity Award, Foreign Affairs Agencies, 1987. **Military Serv:** AUS 1st Lt 1945-49. **Business Addr:** International Consultant, 4701 Willard Ave Apt 304, Chevy Chase, MD 20815-4609.

TOKLEY, JOANNA NUTTER
Social service administrator. **Personal:** Born in Nanticoke, MD; daughter of Iolia Williams and Clifton Nutter; married E James Tokley; children: Tyrone, Charles, Michael. **Educ:** Morgan State Univ, BS 1962; Univ of S FL, further study. **Career:** Hillsborough Cty Public Schools, teacher 1962-70, human relations spec 1970-74; Tampa Urban League Inc, dep dir, econ devel, employment dir 1974-82, pres, currently. **Orgs:** Mem 1958-, pres 1966-69, 1975, Alpha Kappa Alpha; mem toastmasters Chap 1810 1980-; Regional Workforce Devel Bd; mem Governors Constituency Against Child Abuse, 1984-; Tampa Chamber of Commerce 1985; member, Leadership Tampa, 1989-; vice pres, National Coalition of 100 Black Women, 1989-; member, Committee of 100, 1990-. **Honors/Awds:** South Atlantic Region Ruby J Gainer Human Relations Awd AKA 1975; Outstanding Comm Serv The Charmettes Inc Mt Calvary of Day Adventist Church 1979,85, Eddie Mitchell Mem Comm Serv Awd City of Tampa Office of Comm Relations 1980; Dist Dramatic Speech Toastmasters of FL 1981;

Woman of the Year The Orchid Club 1983; Leadership Tampa, Greater Tampa Chamber of Commerce 1988; Martin Luther King, Jr Bust Award, Tampa Organization on Black Affairs; National Conference Medallion. **Business Addr:** President, Tampa Urban League Inc, 1405 Tampa Park Plaza, Tampa, FL 33605.

TOKUN, RALPH
Physician's assistant. **Personal:** Born Jan 25, 1952, Lagos, Nigeria; son of Marian Tokun and James Tokun; divorced. **Educ:** School of Radiological Technologist, diploma, 1977; American Registry of Radiology, radiologic technology, 1978; Webster University, BA, 1984. **Career:** Orthopedic and Sports Medicine, physician's assistant, currently. **Orgs:** American Association of Orthopedic Society; American Society of Radiological Technologists; St Joseph Hospital Employee Credit Union, supervisory committee, 1987. **Business Addr:** Physician's Assistant, Orthopedic & Sports Medicine, 439 S Kirkwood Rd, Ste 215, Kirkwood, MO 63122.

TOLBERT, EDWARD T. See Obituaries section.

TOLBERT, HERMAN ANDRE
Physician, psychiatrist. **Personal:** Born May 29, 1948, Birmingham, AL; son of Ruth Tolbert and John Tolbert. **Educ:** Stillman Coll, BS 1969; Univ CA San Diego, MD 1973. **Career:** OH State Univ, res 1973-77, child flw 1977-78, asst prof 1978-89; assoc prof 1989-; Insight Matters, editor, 1994-. **Orgs:** Mntry flw Am Psychtr Assn 1977; edtr Spectrm Nwsltr APA/NIMH Flws 1981-83; mem Amer Psychtrc Assn 1978-, Amer Acad Child Pschtry 1979-, Assn Acad Psychty 1980-; secretary, Psychiatric Society of Central Ohio 1985-88; president-elect, Psychiatric Society of Central Ohio 1989-90, president, 1990-91; dir, Division of Child & Adolescent Psychiatry, Dept of Psychiatry, Ohio State Univ. **Honors/Awds:** Fellowship Amer Psychtrc Assn 1977; dipl Amer Bd Psychtry Neurology 1980-82; bk chptrs Behavioral Prblm Childhood & Adolescence; fellow, Amer Academy of Child & Adolescent Psych 1982; fellow, Amer Psychiatric Association 1989. **Business Addr:** Assoc Prof, Ohio State Univ, 1670 Upham Drive, Columbus, OH 43210, (614)293-8234.

TOLBERT, JACQUELYN C.
Educational administrator. **Personal:** Born Dec 20, 1947, Kilgore, TX; married Melvin Eugene Tolbert (divorced); children: Alexis N. **Educ:** Kilgore Coll, AA (scholastic hnrs) 1968; Stephen F Austin St Univ, BA (Deans List) 1970, MA 1975, Mid-management administrators certificate 1980; East TX State Univ, Commerce, TX, currently. **Career:** Longview Independent Sch Dist, teacher 1970-71; Kilgore Independent Sch Dist, teacher 1971-79, public info coord 1979-. **Orgs:** Mem bd of dirs Longview Fine Arts Assn; mem Public Relations Comm Jr Achievement of East TX; mem Delta Sigma Theta Sor Longview Alumnae Chap 1973-79; vice pres TX Sch PR Assn 1983-85; mem Natl Sch PR Assn Impact Comm 1984-85; mem Natl Sch PR Assn Journal Council 1984-85; mem TX Sch Admin Assn 1984-, Professional Journalists Inc 1985; Kilgore Kiwanis; bd of dirs, Gregg County American Heart Assn; bd of dirs, Junior Achievement of East TX. **Honors/Awds:** Rookie of the Yr 1981, Bright Idea Awd 1982, 1983 TX Sch Public Relations Assn; "How to Build a Sch Comm Prog" TX Educ Agency/TX Sch PR Assn 1984; Outstanding Woman Sigma Gamma Rho 1985; Best of Contest, TX School PR Assn, 1989; Professional Achievement, TX School PR Assn, 1991. **Home Addr:** 2309 Pam St, Longview, TX 75602. **Business Addr:** Public Information Coord, Kilgore Public Schools, 711 N Longview St, Kilgore, TX 75662.

TOLBERT, JOHN W., JR.
Caterer (retired), city official. **Personal:** Born Jul 12, 1905, Charles Town, WV; son of Sarah Dabney Tolbert and John Wesley Tolbert; married Virginia Gaskins (deceased); children: Thelma V Roberts (deceased), Carolyn L Ashton, Carol M Smith, John III (deceased). **Career:** Maderia School, asst mgr & chef 13 yrs; Town of Leesburg, former council mem at large, vice mayor, currently. **Orgs:** Co-chmn March of Dimes 1940's; pres Londoun Cty Heart Assoc 1960's; mem of vestry St James E Church 1970's; mem NAACP, vice pres, 1991-92; Masonic Lodge; dir chaplain Red Cross; mem Kiwanis club; chmn Sr Citizens Volunteer Program, Community Div Incentive Prog; Leesburg Airport Commn; pres Keep Loudoun Co Beautiful; bd dir Preservation Soc Loudoun Co; mem Natl Trust for Historic Preservation; mem Natl Geographic Soc; mem Smithsonian Assoc; vice pres Leesburg Kiwanis Club 14 yrs; bd of dirs, Gen George C Marshall Home Preservation; chmn, Environmental Advisory Comm, 1990-94; President of NAACP, 1992-95; founder, London Branch of NAACP, Banquet 1996; St James Church, Faithful Witness Window Panel. **Honors/Awds:** Man of the Year Loudoun Co Chamber of Commerce 1981; Citizen of the Year, London-Times Mirror Newspaper, 1990; Tolbert Bldg, Town of Leesburg, 1990; Black History Month, Honoree, 1995; Tolbert Bridge Dedicated on Dulles Greenway; Marie Medely Award. **Home Addr:** 125-D Club House Dr, Leesburg, VA 22075.

TOLBERT, ODIE HENDERSON, JR.
Educator, archivist, catalog librarian. **Personal:** Born Aug 21, 1939, Memphis, TN; son of Odie H. Tolbert, Sr. (deceased) and Rozina Tolbert (deceased); married Maganolia Smith; children: Alisa, Carla, Odie III. **Educ:** Owen Jr Coll, AA 1959; LeMoyne-Owen Coll, BA 1962; Northern IL Univ, MA 1969; Fisk Univ, Adv Cert Black Studies Librarianship 1973. **Career:** Univ of Memphis, catalog librarian, asst prof, 1969-. **Orgs:** Mem Univ of Memphis Library Assoc 1970-, TN Library Assoc 1973-, Amer Library Assoc & Black Caucus 1973-; archivist Church of God in Christ 1986-; mem Disabled American Veterans (life mem) 1965-; assoc mem Center for Black Music Research 1988-; director of library service Pentecostal Temple COGIC (The Mother Church of the Denomination) 1984-. **Honors/Awds:** Music Scholarship Owen Jr Coll 1957-59; Internship Black Studies Librarianship Fisk Univ US Dept of Educ 1973; A Bibliography of the Dr Martin Luther King, Jr Collection in the Mississippi Valley Collection, Memphis State University Feb 1983; The Church Library in the Whole Truth newspaper, official paper of the Church of God in Christ (COGIC) April 1988; Article: "Gospel Music in the Cogic Tradition, Rejoice Magazine, 1989; Poster Presentation: "Research on African American Gospel Music, ALA Annual Meeting, 1990; Ten year supplement to a Bibliography of the Dr Martin Luther King Jr Collection in the Mississippi Valley Collection, Memphis State University, Summer 1993; Religious Workers Guild Inc, COGIC, Special Achievement Award, November 1993; Doctor of Humanities, Trinity Hall College and Seminary, April 1994. **Military Serv:** AUS sp4 1963-65. **Home Addr:** 5457 Heritage Ave, Memphis, TN 38115-2929. **Business Addr:** Catalog Librarian, Asst Prof, University of Memphis, University of Memphis Library, Memphis, TN 38152.

TOLBERT, TONY LEWIS
Professional football player. **Personal:** Born Dec 29, 1967, Tuskegee, AL; married Tasha; children: Anthony Lewis. **Educ:** Univ of Texas-El Paso, bachelor's degree in criminal justice, 1991. **Career:** Dallas Cowboys, defensive end, 1989-. **Honors/Awds:** All-Western Athletic Conference, 1988; Pro Bowl, 1996. **Business Addr:** Professional Football Player, Dallas Cowboys, One Cowboys Pkwy, Irving, TX 75063, (214)556-9900.

TOLENTINO, SHIRLEY A.
Judge. **Personal:** Born Feb 2, 1943, Jersey City, NJ; daughter of Mattie Theresa Kelly Tart and Jack Hayes; married Dr. Ernesto A. Tolentino; children: Ana Ramona, Candida. **Educ:** Coll of St Elizabeth, AB, 1965; Seton Hall Univ, Sch of Law, JD, 1971; New York Univ, Graduate School of Law, LLM, 1981. **Career:** Judge, Superior Court of New Jersey, 1984-; Jersey City Mus Ct, judge 1976-84; VA Newark, adjudicator 1971; Upward Bound Coll of St Elizabeth, asst proj dir 1966-68, 1969-71; Henry Hudson Reg Sch, Highland NJ, teacher, Latin & English, 1965-67; S HS Youngstown OH, tchr Latin & English, 1968-69; State of NJ Divof Law, dep atty gen 1976. **Orgs:** Hudson Cty Bar Assn; Garden State Bar Assn; Mem Alumnae Bd of Coll of St Elizabeth; NJ Alumnae Chap Delta Sigma Theta; Jersey City NAACP; Hudson Cty Urban League; Natl Assn of Women Judges, pres; bd of Regents St Peters College. **Honors/Awds:** Rec Scholar to Coll of St Elizabeth; 1st full time female Mun Ct Judge in NJ; 1st black female judge in Jersey City & Hudson City; grad in top 20 rec hon in Philosophy; Honorary Doctorate of Humane Letters, College of St Elizabeth 1980; 1st black female judge in Superior Court of NJ. **Business Addr:** Judge, Superior Court of NJ Admin Bldg, 595 Newark Ave, Jersey City, NJ 07304.

TOLER, BURL ABRON
Educator. **Personal:** Born May 9, 1928, Memphis, TN; married Melvia Woolfolk; children: Valerie D, Burl Jr, Susan A, Gregory L, Martin L, Jennifer L. **Educ:** Univ San Fran, BS 1952; Univ San Fran, MA 1966. **Career:** SF Comm Coll Dist, dir personnel 1972-; Natl Football League, official 1965-; SF, prin 1965; SF Unified School Dist, asst prin counselor teacher 1955-74. **Orgs:** Mem AFT; CTA; CASSA; SFASA; ERA; ACCCA; commr San Francisco Police Dept 1978-; Kappa Alpha Psi; Life mem NAACP; African Am Hist Soc; Grand Jury 1961; Juvenile Just Com; bd dir Booker T Washington Comm Cen; adv bd YMCA; bd dir Mt Zion Hosp 1976; bd of gov Univ of SF; bd of regents St Ignatius Coll Prep Sch; bd dir SF Entertainment Cen Corp 1976; Boys Cen 1977. **Honors/Awds:** CA Senate Res Sen Eugene Mcateer; All Coast Football 1949-51; All Am Jr Coll 1948; All Am Hon Ment 1951; Coll All Star Game 1952; drafted Cleveland Browns 1952; Univ of SF Hall of Fame; Africa Am Hist Soc Hall of Fame 1977; Isaac Hayes achiev in sports awd Vanguard Club 1972. **Business Addr:** Director Personnel, San Francisco Community College Dist, 33 Gough St, San Francisco, CA 94103.

TOLER, PENNY (VIRGINIA)
Professional basketball player. **Personal:** Born Mar 24, 1966. **Educ:** Long Beach State, attended. **Career:** Montecchio (Italy), guard, 1989-91; Pescara (Italy), 1991-94; Sporting Flash (Greece), 1994-96; Ramat HaSharon (Israel), 1996-97; Los Angeles Sparks, 1997-. **Business Addr:** Professional Basketball Player, Los Angeles Sparks, 3900 W Manchester Blvd, Inglewood, CA 90306, 800-978-9622.

TOLES, EDWARD BERNARD
Judge (retired). **Personal:** Born Sep 17, 1909, Columbus, GA; son of Virginia (Luke) Toles and Alexander Toles; married Evelyn Echols (deceased); children: Edward Bernard. **Educ:** Univ Illinois, AB 1932, post-graduate 1932-34; Loyola Univ, JD 1936. **Career:** Private Practice Atty Chicago, 1936-39; US Housing Authority, asst atty 1939-40; Chicago Defender, asst gen counsel/war correspondent 1943-45; US Bankruptcy Court Chicago, judge 1969-86. **Orgs:** Mem Amer Bar Assn; Natl Bar Assn; mem exec council Chicago Chapter Fed Bar Assn; former mem bd mgr Chicago Bar Assn 1969-70; former pres Cook County Bar Assn 1961-62; Amer Judicature Soc; Bar Assn of 7th Fed Circuit; World Peace Through Law Center; Natl Conf of Bankruptcy Judges; Alpha Phi Alpha; former trustee Church of Good Shipherd, United Church of Christ. **Honors/Awds:** Author Albert B George First Black Chicago Judge 1924-30; Natl Bar Assn CF Stradford Award; Awarded by US War Dept; Natl Bar Assn Judicial Council Newsletter 1982; Gertrude E Rush Award Natl Bar Assn 1982; Chicago Bar Assn Hononrary 50 Year Mem Award 1986; Illinois State Bar Assn Sr Counsellor 50 Year Award 1986; Judicial Council Natl Bar Assn 50 Year Award 1986; Special Award Past Presiding Judge and Legal Historial Judicial Council 1986; Natl Bar Assn 1986-89; Illinois Judicical Council Award, 1988.

TOLES, JAMES LAFAYETTE, JR.
Educator. **Personal:** Born May 9, 1933, Monrovia, Liberia; married Barbara R Gallashaw; children: Patricia Ann, Cynthia Annette, James Lafayette III, Celia A, Jartu G. **Educ:** Clark Coll, BS 1958; N TX State U, MBA 1962; Univ ND, PhD 1970. **Career:** Miles Coll Birmingham, asst prof 1958-59; Wiley Coll Marshall, asst prof 1960-62; Ft Valley State Coll, prof & accntg chmn div bus & econs 1962-75; Albany St Coll, prof of bus adminstr 1975-77; S Carolina State Coll, dean 1977; VA State Univ, dean School of Bus 1983-. **Orgs:** Consult in acad adminstrn Untd Bd for Coll Devel; mem Am Accntg Assn; Am Mgmt Assn; Nat Bus Tchr Educ Assn; Am Vocat Edn; Am Assn Collegiate Schs Bus; mem Com on Real Estate Law & Policy Devel GA Bd Regents; mem regl exec com BSA 1973-; mem Phi Omega Pi; Delta Pi Epsilon; Phi Beta Lambda Phi Delta Kappa; Alpha Phi Alpha; mem vestry bd Episcopalian Ch; Mason; contrib to professional publs. **Honors/Awds:** Liberian Govt Scholar 1954-58; Ford Found & Fellow 1964; Republic Steel Fellow 1964; So Fellow Fund Grantee 1969-70; Outstanding Serv Awd GA Bus & Off Educ Assn 1973.

TOLIVER, GEORGE
Professional sports official. **Career:** NBA, referee, currently. **Business Addr:** NBA Official, National Basketball Association, 645 5th Ave, 15th Fl, New York, NY 10022-5986.

TOLIVER, HAROLD EUGENE, JR.
Insurance company executive. **Personal:** Born Feb 11, 1944, Denver, CO; son of Audrey E Grey Anderson and Harold E Toliver Sr; married Georgia A Hanna Toliver, Jul 4, 1981; children: Dale L. **Educ:** West Los Angeles, Junior College, Culver City, CA, associate of arts degree, 1975; University of Southern California, Los Angeles, CA, BA, 1978; University of West Los Angeles, School of Law, Culver City, CA, 1980-81. **Career:** SSM Productions, Los Angeles, CA, marketing consultant, 1977-78; Block Drug Corporation, Jersey City, NJ, sales representative, 1978-83; Golden State Mutual Life, Los Angeles, CA, director, marketing & public relations, 1983-. **Orgs:** President, WLAJC, Alpha Gamma Sigma Honor Society, 1973-75; president, WLAJC Chess Club, 1974-75; president, Crenshaw Neighborhood Housing Assn, 1988-89; member board of directors, Ebony Showcase Theatre, 1990-; member, Community Redevelopment Agency, 1989-. **Honors/Awds:** Sales of the Sales Cycle, Blcok Drug Corp, 1981; Agent of the Month, Golden State Mutual, 1984; Leaders Roundtable, Golden State Mutual, 1984; Mentioned/Quoted in Black Enterprise Magazine, 1988. **Business Addr:** Director, Marketing & Public Relations, Marketing & Public Relations Dept, Golden State Mututal Life Insurance Co, 1999 West Adams Blvd, Los Angeles, CA 90018.

TOLIVER, PAUL ALLEN
Transportation executive. **Personal:** Born Sep 14, 1946, Baltimore, MD; son of Paul Arthur and Ruth Allen Toliver; married Jane D Toliver, Feb 15, 1969; children: Jill Arlene, Paul Russell. **Educ:** University of Cincinnati, BBA, 1968, MBA, 1973. **Career:** ATE Management & Service Comp, senior vice president, 1973-84; San Francisco Municipal Railway, deputy general manager, 1984-88; Seattle Metro, director of transit, 1988-96; King County Dept of Transportation, dir, 1996-. **Orgs:** National Urban League, board of directors, exec comm, 1994-97; Urban League of Metro Seattle, chair of board of directors, 1992-97; American Public Transit Association, vice president for management & finance, 1992-94; Conference of Minority Transportation Officials, national president, 1986-88; African American Agenda (Seattle), charter member, 1993-; Transportation Research Board, 1988-; National Forum of Black Public Administrators, 1990-; Seattle Art Museum's African-American & Carib Art Coun, 1993-; Intelligent Transportation Society of America comm chair, 1996-97. **Honors/Awds:** American Public Transit Association, Best (major city) Transit System, 1992; Conference of Minority Trans Officials, Sibling Leadership

Award, 1988; King County, Dr Martin Luther King Jr Humanitarian Award, 1995. **Special Achievements:** Co-author of paper/presentation on IVHS Tech, 2nd Ann IVHS Conf, 1992; The Walls have Come Down, Passenger Transport, 1992; Management Basics, Passenger Transport, 1991; The Manager and the Computer, Passenger Transport, 1990; Technology and the Transit Manager, Presentation at APTA Annl, 1994; Technology Holds the key to Better Customer Svc, Passenger Transport, 1996; Why Its in the First Place, Passenger Transport, 1997. **Military Serv:** US Army, spec-5, 1969-71; Leadership (basic training), Good Conduct, 1971. **Home Addr:** 2320 West Viewmont Way West, Seattle, WA 98199, (206)284-8385. **Business Addr:** Director, Department of King County Transportation, 821 Second Avenue, Mail Stop 94, Seattle, WA 98104, (206)684-1441.

TOLIVER, VIRGINIA F. DOWSING
Library administrator. **Personal:** Born Nov 1, 1948, Tupelo, MS; daughter of Jessie Spearman Dowsing and Frank D Dowsing Sr; divorced; children: Wilmetta J Toliver. **Educ:** Jackson State University, Jackson, MS, BA, 1969; University of Illinois, Urbana, IL, MSLS, 1973. **Career:** Alcorn State University, Lorman, MS, serials librarian, 1973-77, acting library dir, 1974-77; University of Southern Mississippi, Hattiesburg, MS, coord, information retrieval, 1977-81; Washington University, St Louis, MO, dir, admin and planning, 1982-. **Orgs:** Member, American Library Assn, 1982-87, 1989-; member, ALA Black Caucus, 1988-; board of directors, Rock Hill Public Library, 1988-; secretary, board of dirctors, Food Outreach, Inc, 1990-. **Honors/Awds:** Academic Library Mgmt Intern Council on Library Resources, 1981-82; Institute on Information Retrieval, Lawrence Livermore Laboratory, 1977. **Business Addr:** Director of Administration and Planning, Washington University, Olin Library, 1 Brookings Dr, Campus Box 1061, St Louis, MO 63130-4899, (314)935-5400.

TOLLETT, CHARLES ALBERT, SR.
Physician. **Personal:** Born in Muskogee, OK; son of Hattie Mae Scruggs Tollett and Dr Harrel E Tollett Sr; married Katherine; children: Lynn, Charles Jr, Frank, Jeffery. **Educ:** Howard Univ, BS 1950; Temple Univ Med School, MD 1952; Temple, intern 1953-56; Temple, surg resd 1956-57; jr instr surg 1956-57; sr surg resd 1957; Temple U, DSc (surgery) 1957; Am Bd Surgery, cert 1958. **Career:** Private practice, general surgeon, currently; St Anthony Hosp, chief of surgery, 1991-93. **Orgs:** Mem Phi Beta Kappa Med, AOA; Babcock Surg Soc; Howard Univ Alumni; Kappa Alpha Psi; Sigma Pi Phi; Philadelphia Co Med Soc; AMA; OK State Med Dental & Pharm Assn; OK Co & State Med Soc; OK Surg Assn; Am Coll Surgeons; mem bd dir Eastside Branch YMCA; Cntrl Chap OK Howard Alumni Assn; board of directors Oklahoma American Insurance Co; pres OK Hlth Sci Ctr Faculty House 1974; mem Areawide Hlth Plng Orgn; assoc clinical prof surg Univ OK Hlth Sci Ctr; mem Natl Med Assoc, Pan Pacific Surgical Assoc; pres bd City County Health Dept, 1984-89; Governor's Commission on Oklahoma Health Care, 1992-93; Allen Chapel AME Church, trustee board; NAACP, life member. **Honors/Awds:** Volunteer of the Year Awd in Recognition of Outstanding Serv to the Eastside Br YMCA 1984; Fellowhip, Amer Coll Surgeons, 1960. **Special Achievements:** Contributing author, A Century of Black Surgeons: The USA Experience. **Military Serv:** AUS m/sgt 1943-46. **Business Addr:** President/General Surgeon, Northeast Surgery Clinic, Inc, 700 NE 37th, Oklahoma City, OK 73105.

TOLLIVER, CHARLES
Trumpetist, composer, arranger, record producer, educator. **Personal:** Born Mar 6, 1942, Jacksonville, FL; son of Ruth Lavatt Tolliver and Samuel Tolliver; divorced; children: Charles Edward. **Educ:** Howard University, College of Pharmacy, 1960-63. **Career:** Strata-East Records, co-founder, president, chief executive officer, 1970-; New School of Jazz and Contemporary Music, adjunct professor, jazz orchestra, director, 1992-. **Orgs:** Broadcast Music Inc, 1964-; American Federation of Musicians, 1964-. **Honors/Awds:** Downbeat Magazine, #1 Trumpetist, 1968; New England Conservatory of Music, 1975. **Special Achievements:** Composer, conductor, arranger of orchestral suite performed at Carnegie Hall, 1975. **Business Addr:** President & Chief Executive Officer, Strata-East Records, Box 36, Grand Central Station, New York, NY 10163.

TOLLIVER, JOEL
Pastor, administrator, educator. **Personal:** Born Feb 26, 1946, Philadelphia, PA; married Sharon; children: Joel Jr, Paul. **Educ:** Lincoln Univ, BA 1969; Yale Univ, MPH 1971; Colgate Bexler Crozer Theol Sem, MDiv 1985; SUNY at Buffalo, educ admin, PhD 1995. **Career:** Univ of Rochester, health educator 1971; Empire State Coll, asst prof 1973; Radio Sta WAXI, talk show host 1973-77; City of Rochester, asst to city mgr 1974-82; Monroe Comm Coll, chaplain & administrator; Brockport State Coll, chaplain, admin and inst 1987; Devry Institute of Technology, dean. **Orgs:** Consult Brockport State Coll 1974; consult Genessee Comm Coll 1974; bd mem United Ch Ministry Inc 1979; bd mem Bridge Vol Inc 1979; mem Urban League 1979; mem Alpha Phi Alpha Frat Inc; mem Alpha Phi Omega Nat Serv Frat; mem Phi Delta Kappa Educational Society, 1989; mem Benevolent Order of Elks; mem Nat'l Sickle Cell Org; mem Martin Luther King Health Center. **Honors/Awds:** Young Man of Am Comm Serv US Jaycees 1977; Comm Serv to Black Ch & Comm United Ch Ministry Inc 1978 & 79; Comm Serv NAACP Elmira State Prison 1980; Church & Comm Serv Award United Ch Ministry, Inc 1983; ed excel awd Black Student Union Monroe Comm Coll 1984; outstanding adult & student awd Rochester Area Coll 1985; leadership dev inst awd SUNY at Brockport 1986; Organization of Students of African Descent Awd for Service to Afro-American Students 1985-89; Nat'l Assoc of Negro Women Awd for Comm Service 1986; United Ch Ministry Awd for Service to Black Family & Community 1986; Community Mediator, Hudson Valley Mohawk Association, 1986; Certificate of Achievement, Martin Luther King Center for Social Change, 1989-90; Conflict/Management Medicator, Center for Dispute Settlement, 1990; New York State Assembly Award for Community Service, 1995. **Home Addr:** 1130 S. Michigan Avenue, Apt. 2304, Chicago, IL 60605.

TOLLIVER, LENNIE-MARIE P.
Educator. **Personal:** Born Dec 1, 1928, Cleveland, OH; daughter of Marie Pickens and George W Pickens Sr; married Alonzo H Tolliver. **Educ:** Hampton U, BS 1950; Univ Chicago, AM 1952, Post Masters Cert 1961; Union Grad Sch, PhD 1979. **Career:** State NJ Mental Hygeine Clncs, psych soc wrkr 1952-55; Duke Univ Med Ctr, PSW inst actng 1956-58; Atlanta U, spvr field work instructor 1957-58; Johnston Training Rsrch Cntr NJ, soc work, spvr actg dir soc wrk 1959; Univ Chicago, fld instr 1961-64; Univ OK, prof 1964-; US Dept Hlth Human Svcs, US cmnsr aging 1981-84; Univ of Oklahoma, professor of social work, 1985-94. **Orgs:** Acrdtn rvwr Cncl Soc Wrk Ed 1972-81; mem dir prof Stndrds Natl Assc Soc Wrkr 1967-70; east pres OK Hlth Wlfr Assc 1971-72; mem Fed Cncl Aging 1974-78; frmr vice pres OK City Urban League; past pres OK City Links Inc; past natl sec Delta Sigma Theta Inc; mem advsry cncl Allied Corp Achvmnt Awrd Aging 1984; chair Commn on the Family and Primary Assocs, Natl Assoc of Social Workers Inc 1985-; chairperson, Commission on Family and Primary Association, Natl Association of Social Workers Inc, 1985-87; chairperson, OK Energy and Aging Consortium, 1986-94; mem, Governor's Commission on the Status of Women, appointed by Governor Henry Bellman, 1988; advisory comm, OK Rehabilitation Institute, Univ of OK Health Svcs Center, 1989-91; editorial bd, Journal of Multi-Cultured Social Work, New York, Harworth Press, 1989-; charter mem, OK Chap, Natl Caucus and Center on the Black Aged, 1991. **Honors/Awds:** 20 yr alumni awrd Hampton Univ 1970; Awrd Elvirita Lewis Fndtn 1982; Ellen B Winston Awrd Natl Cncl Aging 1984; equal Opprtny awrd US Dept Hlth & Human Serv 1984; OK County Chap, Natl Assn of Social Workers, 1986; Women in Communications, By Lines Awd, 1992; Betsy D Smith Awd, OK Department of Human Services, 1993. **Home Addr:** 32 N Misty Morn Ln, Ewing, NJ 08638.

TOLLIVER, NED, JR.
Educator, elected official. **Personal:** Born May 2, 1943, Woodville, MS; son of Charlotte Bonney Tolliver and Ned Tolliver, Sr; married Dorothy Bickham Tolliver, Aug 23, 1969; children: Tony L, Daphne A. **Educ:** Mississippi Valley State Univ, BS 1967; Western Michigan Univ, Certificate 1969; Jackson State Univ, Certificate 1973; Delta State Univ, MA 1983. **Career:** Negro Civic Club, corresponding secretary 1973; East Side High School, team leader, Social Studies Dept 1973-94; Summer Youth Program, coordinator 1973-94; Cleveland Area Civic Club, vice pres 1978-; Selective Service Bd, member Bolivar Cty 1982-; Cleveland Bd of Alderman, vp, 1991, West Tallahatchie High School, principal, 1994-. **Orgs:** Mem Cleveland Assn of Educ 1967-, Mississippi Assn of Educators 1967-, Natl Educ Assn 1967-; sponsor Citizenship Club, East Side High 1968-; mem Democratic Party of Mississippi 1977-; notary public Bolivar County MS 1977-; mem Trustee Bd United Baptist Church 1980-, NAACP Cleveland Chapter 1982-; pres Cleveland Area Civic Club 1986. **Honors/Awds:** Start Teacher, 1987-90; Star teacher, 1992-93. **Home Addr:** PO Box 814, Cleveland, MS 38732. **Business Addr:** Principal, Drew High School, Drew, MS 38737.

TOLLIVER, RICHARD LAMAR
Episcopal priest, educator. **Personal:** Born Jun 26, 1945, Springfield, OH; married Ann Cecile Jackson (divorced 1987). **Educ:** Miami Univ, Oxford, OH, BA, religion, 1967; Boston Univ, Boston, MA, MA, Afro-American Studies, 1971; Episcopal Divinity School, Cambridge, MA, Master of Divinity, 1971; Howard Univ, Washington, DC, PhD, political science, 1982; Boston Univ, Boston, MA, political science, 1986. **Career:** St Cyprian's Church, Boston, MA, rector, 1972-77; St Timothy's Church, Washington, DC, rector, 1977-84; US Peace Corps, Kenya, assoc country dir, 1984-86; US Peace Corps, Mauritania, country dir, 1986-88; Howard Univ, Washington, DC, prof, 1988-89; St Edmund's Episcopal Church, Chicago, IL, rector, 1989-. **Orgs:** Natl Conference of Black Political Scientists, 1982-; Beta Boule, Sigma Pi Phi Fraternity, 1991-; Omega Psi Phi Fraternity, 1968-; pres, St Edmund's Redevt Corp, 1989-; natl bd of dir, Union of Black Episcopalians; vice pres, board of directors, St Edmund's Academy; board of directors of trustees, Bennett College. **Honors/Awds:** Fellowship for Doctoral Studies, Natl Science Foundation, 1979-82; Distinguished Service Award, St Augustine's Coll, 1983; Regional Finalist, White House Fellowship, 1983; Distinguished Achievement Medal, Miami University, 1996. **Home Addr:** 5400 S Hyde Park Blvd, Unit 8D, Chicago, IL 60615.

TOLLIVER, STANLEY EUGENE, SR.
Attorney. **Personal:** Born Oct 29, 1925, Cleveland, OH; married Dorothy; children: Stephanie, Sherrie, Stanley Jr, Nathan. **Educ:** Baldwin-Wallace, Pre-Law 1948; Cleveland Marshall Law School, LLB 1951, JD, LLD 1969. **Career:** Cleveland Assoc of Realty Brokers, legal counsel 1954; Congress on Racial Equality, legal counsel 1960-66; Rev Dr Martin L King Southern Leaders Christian Conf, legal advisor 1965-68; CORE, atty 1966; prvt practice, atty. **Orgs:** Pres Natl Conf of Black Lawyers Cleveland Chap 1975; class rep Baldwin Wallace Coll 1980-82; reg dir Natl Conf of Black Lawyers 1980; natl co-chmn Natl Conf of Black Lawyers 1981; elected bd mem Cleveland School Bd 1981-; exec comm Dem Party Cuyahoga Cty 1981-; mem Cleveland Assoc of Black Ed 1981-, Natl Black School Bd 1984-; only elect publ official from OH to be elect as a delegate to the Natl Dem Conv for Rev Jesse Jackson for Pres of the US; mem bd managers Cleveland YMCA; marathon runner; elected pres Cleveland Bd of Educ 1987. **Honors/Awds:** Hon Mention & Trophy Freedom Fighters 1964; Hall of Fame East Tech HS 1978; Frank D Reeves Awd Natl Conf of Black Lawyers 1981; Bus Awd WJMO Radio Cleveland 1983; Outstanding Alumnus Baldwin Wallace Coll 1978; baritone soloist. **Military Serv:** AUS pfc army counter intelligence 1951-53; Passed OH Bar in the Army 1953. **Business Addr:** Attorney, 1464 E 105th St, Ste 404, Cleveland, OH 44106.

TOLLIVER, THOMAS C., JR.
City official. **Personal:** Born Oct 16, 1950, Woodville, MS; son of Sarah Tolliver and Tom C Tolliver; married; children: Tommie C. **Educ:** Jackson State Univ, BS 1972, MS 1979; Univ of Southern MS, MS 1978. **Career:** Wilkinson Cty High School, teacher 1972-79; Wilkinson Cty, chancery clerk 1979-. **Orgs:** Asst state dir Alpha Phi Alpha Frat 1970-75; bd of dir MS Chancery Clerk's Assn 1979-85; bd of dir, chmn Chatwell Club Inc 1982-88; bd of dir Friends of Armisted 1984-; worshipful master F&AM Prince Hall Masons 1985; 32nd degree mason, 33rd degree mason, Shriner. **Honors/Awds:** Man of the Year Alpha Phi Alpha Frat 1972-73. **Home Addr:** PO Box 1376, Woodville, MS 39669. **Business Addr:** Clerk Chancery Court, Wilkinson Co, PO Box 516, Woodville, MS 39669.

TOMLIN, JOSEPHINE D.
Banker. **Personal:** Born Jul 5, 1952, Pittsburgh, PA; daughter of Hattie Holmes Tomlin and Charles C Tomlin; married Mark Washington, Feb 22, 1990. **Educ:** Allegheny Coll, BA 1974; Univ of Pgh, MEd 1975. **Career:** Univ of Pgh, prog counselor 1975-76; LaRoche Coll, upward bound dir 1976-81; Mellon Bank, Pittsburgh, PA, corporate demand despoit mgr 1983-84, support serv sect mgr 1984-85, retail systems mgr, 1985-88, loan services mgr, 1988-90, project consultant, vice pres, 1990-. **Orgs:** Bd dir Women's Ctr of Pgh 1978-80; business & finance acad consultant Urban League 1985-86; career oppor comm advisor Allegheny Coll 1987; Perry Traditional Acad Partnership Tutor Mellon Bank/Bd of Educ 1987; steering comm, Women's Forum, 1990-. **Honors/Awds:** Premier Achievement Awd Mellon Bank 1985; Outstanding Trio Student MAEOPP 1986.

TOMLINSON, MEL ALEXANDER
Dancer. **Personal:** Born Jan 3, 1954, Raleigh, NC; son of Marjoriline Henry Tomlinson and Tommy Willie Amos Tomlinson. **Educ:** North Carolina School of the Arts, Winston-Salem NC, BFA, 1974. **Career:** Heritage Dance Theatre, Winston-Salem, dancer, 1972-74; Dance Theatre of Harlem, dancer, 1974-77, 1978-81; Alvin Ailey Dance Theatre, NY, dancer, 1977-78; New York City Ballet, dancer, 1981-87; North Carolina Dance Theatre, dir of educational services, 1988-89, dancer, 1988-; Boston Ballet, principal dancer, 1991-92, City Dance Outreach Program, master teacher, 1991-. **Orgs:** Intl Platform Assn; AFTRA; AFMA; SEG; Equity; AGMA. **Honors/Awds:** New York Times, North Carolina Prize, 1983; Elliot Award, 1993. **Special Achievements:** Choreographer: "No Right on Red," 1987; "Carnival of the Animals," 1988; "Karenda," 1990; "Sonata 5," 1991; "Alas!" 1992; "In the Beginning," 1993; "Pedipieds," 1993; filmed documentary, "With A Clear Voice," NBC-TV, 1993; " Feathers, Furs, Fins and Friends (Carnival of the Animals)," 1998; "Melody," 1990; "Eli! Eli!," 1997; author, poetry "My Life at the White House" (co-authored by William Wolfe). **Home Addr:** 6201 Whitewater Dr, Charlotte, NC 28214-2838.

TOMLINSON, RANDOLPH R.
Editor, publisher (retired). **Personal:** Born Aug 28, 1920, Rebpulic of Panama; son of Myrtle C Tomlinson-Allen; married Algean; children: Randolph Jr, William, Marta, Edward, Levette. **Educ:** Inst Nacional de Panama, 1940; Univ of Panama, 1950; NW Univ, Postgraduate Work 1958. **Career:** La Nacion Panama City, editorial page editor; The Star & Herald Panama City, reporter; The Panama Review, assoc editor; North Shore Examiner Newspaper, editor, publisher, until 1995. **Honors/Awds:** Outstanding Business Award; Outstanding Citizen Award for Public Serv Gamma Omicron Chapter Detla Sigma Theta Sorority; Candidate for Mayor of Evanston nominated by acclamation of all black citizens of Evanston; served in a civilian capacity during WWII in the Canal Zone.

TOMLINSON, ROBERT
Educator, artist. **Personal:** Born Jun 26, 1938, Brooklyn, NY; son of Julia Espeut Tomlinson and Sydney Tomlinson. **Educ:** Pratt Inst, Brooklyn, BFA 1961; Columbia Univ Teachers Coll NY, 1963; CUNY Graduate Center NY, PhD 1977. **Career:** Emory Univ Atlanta, assoc prof 1978-; Hunter Coll NY, adj asst prof 1972-78; HS of Art & Design NY, French instr 1968-72; Ministere de l'Education Nationale Paris, Eng instr 1963-68; This Week Mag, asst art dir 1961-63. **Orgs:** Mem Am Soc for Eighteenth Cent Stud mem Mod Lang Assoc; chmn Emory Univ Commn on the Status of Minorities 1980-81, 1984-85. **Honors/Awds:** Number 1 man exhibit of Painting Paris, London, NY, Washington 1968, 1971, 1979, 1984; rep in private coll; Advanced Study Fellow Ford Found, 1972-76; fellow, CUNY 1975-77; Amer Council of Learned Societies Grant 1979. **Business Addr:** Associate Professor, Emory University, Modern Languages Dept, Atlanta, GA 30322.

TOMS-ROBINSON, DOLORES C.
Educator. **Personal:** Born Dec 26, 1926, Washington, DC; married George L Robinson; children: Gigi W, Greg. **Educ:** Howard Univ, BS cum laude 1947, MS 1948; Univ of MI, PhD 1957; Univ of IL Inst for Study of Mental Retardation, post doctoral study 1956-57. **Career:** Univ of UT, rsch child psychology, 1957-58; Jarvis Christian Coll, dir of psychol testing 1960-62; Jackson State Coll, dir fresh studies 1962-64; TX So Univ, prof of psychology 1964-70; Central MI Univ, chmn 1974-76, prof 1970-. **Orgs:** Mem Council for Exceptional Children; NEA; Phi Delta Kappa. **Business Addr:** Professor, Counseling & Special Education, Central Michigan Univ, Rowe Hall 208, Mount Pleasant, MI 48859.

TONEY, ANTHONY
Professional football player. **Personal:** Born Sep 23, 1962, Salinas, CA. **Educ:** Attended: Hartnell Community College, Texas A & M Univ. **Career:** Philadelphia Eagles, fullback, 1986-. **Business Addr:** Professional Football Player, Philadelphia Eagles, Veterans Stadium, Broad St & Pattison Ave, Philadelphia, PA 19148.

TONG, DALTON ARLINGTON
Financial administrator. **Personal:** Born Apr 19, 1950, Guyana; married Linda V Smith; children: Sophia, Nicole. **Educ:** Univ of Baltimore, BS Accntg 1973; Univ of Baltimore, MBA Corp Mgmt 1975; Harvard U, Cert in Fincl Mgmt & Strategy in Hlth 1976; State of MD cpa 1978. **Career:** S Baltimore Gen Hosp, fin contrl present, contrl 1976, asst contrl 1975, reimbursement spec 1974, gen accnt 1973; MD Farm Bur of Rec & Tax Servs, accntg intern 1970. **Orgs:** Evening fac Dundalk Commun Coll 1975; evening fac Howard Commun Coll present; mem Minority Recruitment & Equal Opport MD Ass of CPAs advanced; mem Hosp Finan Mgmt Assn present; mem Am Mgmt Assn present; advisory St Frances Charles Hall Sch 1979. **Honors/Awds:** Beta Alpha Natl Hon Soc; Magna (cum laude) Univ of Baltimore 1973.

TONGUE, REGINALD CLINTON
Professional football player. **Personal:** Born Apr 11, 1973, Baltimore, MD. **Educ:** Oregon State. **Career:** Kansas City Chiefs, defensive back, 1996-. **Honors/Awds:** Mack Lee Hill Award, 1996. **Business Addr:** Professional Football Player, Kansas City Chiefs, One Arrowhead Dr, Kansas City, MO 64129, (816)924-9300.

TOOMBS, CHARLES PHILLIP
University professor. **Personal:** Born Dec 2, 1952, Indianapolis, IN; son of Stella Irene Evans Toombs and Martin Richard Toombs; married Irene Williams (divorced 1987); children: Iisha Marie. **Educ:** Purdue University, West Lafayette, IN, BA, 1976, MA, 1978, MS, 1981, PhD, 1986. **Career:** Purdue University, West Lafayette, Ind, graduate assistant, 1976-81, graduate instuctor, 1982-85; Indiana University Northwest, Gary, IN, visiting instructor, 1985-86; California State University, Bakersfield, CA, assistant professor, 1986-88; University of Georgia, Athens, GA, assistant professor, 1988-. **Orgs:** Member, Modern Language Association, 1985-; member, Research Association of Minority Professors, 1986-; member, Southern Conference on Afro-American Studies, 1988-; member, National Council for Black Studies, currently. **Honors/Awds:** Lilly Fellowship, University of Georgia, 1989-90; "Joyce Carol Thomas," Dictionary of Literary Biography, 1984; "Master Timothy," Indiana Experience, Indiana UP, 1978; "Seven Haiku," High/Coo, 1977; Howard G McCall Award, Purdue U Black Cultural Center, 1978; First Place in Fiction and Poetry, Paul Robeson Literary Awards, 1976.

TOOMER, AMANI
Professional football player. **Personal:** Born Sep 8, 1974, Berkeley, CA; son of Donald Sr. **Educ:** Univ of Michigan, attended. **Career:** New York Giants, wide receiver, 1996-. **Business Addr:** Professional Football Player, New York Giants, Giants Stadium, East Rutherford, NJ 07073, (201)935-8111.

TOOMER, CLARENCE
Library director. **Personal:** Born Jun 12, 1952, Asbury Park, NJ; son of Hazel Markham Toomer and Willie Toomer. **Educ:** Livingstone College, Salisbury, NC, BA, 1974; North Carolina State University, Durham, NC, MLS, 1975; North Carolina State University, Raleigh, NC, EdD. **Career:** North Carolina A&T State Univ, Greensboro, NC, librarian, 1975-77; Johnson C Smith Univ, Charlotte, NC, assistant librarian, 1977-80; Shaw University, Raleigh, NC, library director, 1980-88; Greensboro College, Greensboro, NC, library director, 1988-. **Orgs:** North Carolina Library Assn, 1977-; American Library Assn, 1984-; Guildford Library Club, 1988-; Assn of College & Research Libraries, 1988-. **Business Addr:** Director of Library Services, Greensboro College, 815 W Market St, Greensboro, NC 27401.

TOOMER, VANN ALMA ROSALEE
Educator. **Personal:** Born Oct 16, Franklin, VA; married J W; children: Dr Jethro W Jr. **Educ:** Benedict Coll Columbia SC, BS; Hampton Inst Hampton VA, MA; Temple Univ PA, earned 30 hrs. **Career:** Broward Co Ft Lauderdale FL, ret school prin 11 yrs; Orange Co, oral dir one yr; SC, prin school 2 yrs; Orange Co, one yr; total yrs teacher & prin of schools 28 yrs. **Orgs:** Dept elem sch prin nationally; mem FL Educ Assn; Orange Co Tchrs Assn; Nat Educ Assn; Intl Reading Assn; pres Nat Counc Negro Women 1972-74; exec bd Christian serv ctr Orlando; exec bd mem Comprehensive Hlth Prog City Orlando; Ch Women Untd Orlando; orgnzd First Pres Bapt Ministers wives Alliance Broward Co; mem bd dir Girl Scout Counc Inc; Cradle Kindergarten & Nursery Broward Co. **Honors/Awds:** Past achiev & outstndg serv to comm & state.

TOON, AL LEE, JR.
Professional football player (retired). **Personal:** Born Apr 30, 1963, Newport News, VA; married Jane. **Educ:** Univ of Wisconsin, BS, family resources. **Career:** New York Jets, wide receiver 1985-92; Investor in residential/commercial real estate, owner/mgr; Burger King Franchise, Southern WI; director/organizer, Capital Bank Corp, Madison, WI, vice pres. **Honors/Awds:** Named 1st team All Big 10; voted Badgers MVP 2 yrs in a row; MVP performance in Hula Bowl; NFL All-Rookie by Football Digest; played in Pro Bowl, 1986-88 seasons; MVP, New York Jets, 1986-88. **Business Addr:** Southern Wisconsin Foods, Inc, 710 W High Pt Rd, Madison, WI 53717.

TOOTE, GLORIA E. A.
Attorney. **Personal:** Born Nov 8, 1931, New York, NY; daughter of Lillie Toote and Frederick A Toote. **Educ:** Howard Univ School Law, JD 1954; Columbia Univ Graduate School Law, LLM, 1956. **Career:** Natl Affairs Section Time Magazine, former mem; NYC, Prac law 1954-71; Toote Town Publs Inc, pres; Action Agency Off Volunteer Action Liaison, asst director 1971-73; Dept Housing & Urban Devel, asst sec 1973-75; author & lecturer; NYC, presently engaged in practice of law; Trea Estates & Enter Inc, pres, currently. **Orgs:** Bd mem, Arbitrator Assn, Consumer Alert, Council of Economic Affairs for the Republic/Natl Black United Fund; cited by the following organizations, Natl Business League, Alpha Kappa Alpha Sorority, US Chamber of Commerce, Natl Newspaper Publication Assn; member, Hoover Institution on War, Revolution and Peace; Fannie Mae, bd of dirs, 1992-. **Honors/Awds:** Newsmakers Awd, Nat Assn of Black Women Atty, NY Fed of Civil Serv Org, Navajo Tribe, Nat Assn of Real Estate Brokers, Nat Citizens Participation Counc, Nat Bar Assn; YMCA World Serv Awd, Women's Nat Rep Club, New York City Housing Auth, Res Adv Counc MA-CT-NY-NJ, Pol Ldrshp Awd, NNPA.

TOPPIN, EDGAR ALLAN
Educator. **Personal:** Born Jan 22, 1928, New York, NY; married Antionette Lomax; children: Edgar Jr, Avis, Louise. **Educ:** Howard Univ, AB cum laude 1949, MA 1950; Northwestern Univ, PhD 1955. **Career:** AL State Coll, instr 1954-55; Fayetteville State Coll, chmn Soc Sci Div 1955-59; Univ Akron, asst assc prof 1959-64; VA State Coll, full prof 1964-; NC Coll, vis prof 1959, 1963; Western Res Univ, 1962; Univ Cincinnati, 1964; San Francisco State Coll, 1969; IN Univ, 1971. **Orgs:** Natl Pres Assc study Afro-Amer life & history 1973-76; editorial bd Journal Negro History 1962-67; exec bd Orgn Amer Historians 1971-74; mem Natl Hist Pub Commn 1972- 1st black mem; adv bd Natl Parks Historic Sites Bldgs & Monuments 1st black mem; bd dir So Flwshps Fund 1966-; World Book Encyclopedia Socl Sci Adv Com 1968-; vice pres bd Akron Urban League 1961-64; bd dir Fayetteville United Fund 1957-59. **Honors/Awds:** Author books, Pioneer Patriots 1954; Mark Well Made 1967; Unfinished March 1967; Blacks in Amer 1969; Biog History of Black in Amer 1971; Black Amer in US 1973; 30 lesson educ TV Course Amer from Africa; grad flwshps from Howard Univ 1949-50; Hearts Fnd 1950-51, 1952-53; John Hay Whitney Fnd opport Flwship History 1964; research grants from Amer Assn State Local History 1964; Old Dominion Fnd 1968; Ford Fnd 1970; Comtemporary Authors. **Business Addr:** VA State Coll, Petersburg, VA 23803.

TORAIN, TONY WILLIAM
Clergyman, educational administrator. **Personal:** Born Jun 27, 1954, Mebane, NC; son of Myrtle Juanita Woody Torain and William Torain; married Celestine Best, May 25, 1985; children: Tony William II (Nnamdi), James Best (Jay). **Educ:** Univ of NC at Chapel Hill, BA 1975; Gordon-Conwell Theological Seminary, MATS 1979; Boston Univ, MA 1980; Univ of MD at Baltimore, MSW/JD 1984-85. **Career:** Boston State Coll, campus minister 1978-80; Twelfth Baptist Church, assoc minister 1978-80; Joint Orange-Chatham Comm Action, dir elderly serv 1980-81; Office of the Atty Gen MD, clerk 1982-83; Baltimore Assoc of Retarded Citizens, counselor 1983-85; Highway Church of Christ, assoc minister 1982-85; Highway Training Inst, dean 1984-85; Ch Mason Memorial (COGIC) associate minister 1985-88; US Dept of Health & Human Svcs, employee counseling serv asst 1984-85, program/legal analyst 1985-87; The Good Shepherd Church (COGIC), Baltimore Maryland pastor/founder 1985-89; Univ of Maryland School of Social Work, bd mem, 1986-. **Orgs:** Member, Black/Jewish Forum of Baltimore; director, African-American Cultural Center, Towson State Univ. **Honors/Awds:** North Carolina Governor's School 1971; Scholarship First Federal Scholar 1973; Scholarship Turrentine Scholar 1975; Awd Martin L King Jr Awd for Ministry 1979; second person to complete Univ of Maryland's joint law/social work program, 1985. **Business Addr:** Assistant to Vice President for Student Services, Towson State University, 8000 York Road, Towson, MD 21204.

TORAN, KAY DEAN
Government official, educator. **Personal:** Born Nov 21, 1943, Birmingham, AL; married John Toran; children: Traci, John Dean. **Educ:** Univ of Portland, BA 1964; Portland State Univ, MSW 1970. **Career:** Portland State Univ, asst prof counseling 1970-71; Portland State Univ Grad School of Soc Work, asst prof soc work; Adult & Family Serv Publ Welfare,asst mgr field oper 1976-79; Office of the Govt, dir affirm action 1979-. **Orgs:** Mem Delta Sigma Theta Soc Serv Sor 1964-; dir Girl Scouts Summer Camp 1968; prog consult Girl Scouts 1969-70; bd of dir Campfire Girls Inc 1975-77; bd of dirs Met Fam Serv 1976-82; bd of dirs Portland State Univ Found 1980-; bd of dir The Catlin Gable School 1980-84. **Honors/Awds:** Rsch grant Curriculum Devel Western Interstate Comm for Higher Ed 1973; Publ "Curriculum Devel" 1974; Leader of the 80's Awd NW Conf of Black Publ Officials 1979; Outstanding Young Woman of Amer 1980; Woman of Excellence Delta Sigma Theta 1982. **Business Addr:** Dir, Office of the Government, Affirmative Action, State Capitol Bldg, Salem, OR 97310.

TORIAN, EDWARD TORRENCE
Optical company executive. **Personal:** Born Dec 20, 1933, New Rochelle, NY; son of Julia Torian and Edward Torian (deceased); married Pearl Cromartie; children: Curtis, Darlene. **Educ:** Westchester Business Inst, Certificate in Accounting 1956; Iona Coll, BBA 1968, MBA Finance (50% complete). **Career:** Perkin-Elmer Corp, sr contract accountant 1966-90; Hal-Tor Enterprises Co, partner & treasurer 1970-; Danbury Common Council, legislative leader 1983, councilman-at-large 1979-87; Hughes Danbury Optical Systems, sr admin, 1990-. **Orgs:** Mem Natl Assn of Accountants 1967-; mem Iona Coll Alumni Assn 1968-; mem NAACP 1980-; treasurer Black Democratic Assn of Danbury 1981-; sec Men's Council 1981-84, treasurer 1990-, New Hope Baptist Church; bd of trustees, board of directors, United Way of Northern Fairfield County, CT. **Military Serv:** USN petty officer 3rd class 1951-54; Natl Defense Award. **Home Addr:** 18 Indian Head Road, Danbury, CT 06811-2919.

TORRENCE, GWEN
Olympic athlete. **Personal:** Born in Decatur, GA; children: one. **Career:** US Olympic Team, track and field, currently. **Honors/Awds:** Olympic Games, Barcelona, Spain, Gold Medals (2), track & field, 1992. **Business Addr:** Gold Medalist, 1992 Games, c/o US Olympic Training Center, 1750 E Boulder St, Colorado Springs, CO 80909, (719)632-5551.

TOTTEN, BERNICE E.
Supervisor, elected official. **Personal:** Born Sep 1, 1921, Mississippi; children: Othell, Adell, Bertrial, Mack C, Mildred Mitchell, Napolian Jr, Robert, Landon, Martha Jamison. **Educ:** MS Ind Coll Holly Spring MS, Teacher License 1951; Tuskegee Inst AL, Early Childhood Ed 1968; Rust Coll, 1968-74. **Career:** Public School, teacher 1950-51; Head Start, teacher 1964-75; Marshall Cty MS, cty suprv 1974-88. **Orgs:** Mem NAACP 1965-85. **Honors/Awds:** Shield MS Ind Coll Holly Spring MS 1975; Awd Inst Comm Serv 1979-80; Shield Mid South Comm Org Tenn 1980; Cert MS Head Start Assoc. **Business Addr:** Supervisor, Marshall Cty Dist 4, Rt 3 PO Box 98, Holly Springs, MS 38635.

TOTTEN, HERMAN LAVON
Educator. **Personal:** Born Apr 10, 1938, Van Alstyne, TX; son of Dulvi Sims Totten and Derrall Scott Totten. **Educ:** Wiley Coll Marshall TX, BA 1961; Univ of OK, MLS 1964, PhD 1966. **Career:** Wiley Coll, librarian & dean 1966-71; Univ of KY, assoc dean 1971-74; Univ of OR, dean & prof 1974-77; N TX State Univ, prof 1977-. **Honors/Awds:** SEF Fellow Southern Educ Found 1964-66; ACE Academic Internship Amer Council on Educ 1970-71; CLR Fellow Council on Library Resources 1977-78. **Business Addr:** Prof Sch Library & Info, North TX State Univ, PO Box 13796, Denton, TX 76203.

TOTTRESS, RICHARD EDWARD
Cleric (retired). **Personal:** Born Nov 25, 1917, Newby Creek, OK; son of Louisa Headspoth Totress (deceased) and Rev M Totress (deceased); married Margarreau Fluorine Norton; children: 1 son (dec). **Educ:** Pacific Union Coll, BA 1943; Oakwood Coll, BA 1969; Langston Univ; Home Study Inst; Ministerial Internship Evangelism, TX 1943-47; Univ of Beverly Hills, MA and PhD 1981. **Career:** Texaco Conf/Texas SDA, minister 1943-; SW Region Conf, pastor/evangelist 1947-52; So Atlanta Conf SDA, dist pastor/youth assoc 1952-63; Oakwood Acad & Coll, dean 1963-66, coll pastor/chaplain 1965-69 and 1972-73; Oakwood Coll Ch, co-pastor 1973-79; Your Bible Speaks radio show, producer/speaker 1953-; Westend SDA Church, assoc paster, 1993-. **Orgs:** Civilian chaplain 1944; dir Bibb County March of Dimes 1961; Fellow Intl Biog Assn 1970's & 1980's; coord Metro-Atlanta Area SDA Pastors 1982-84; dir Crusade for Voters Bibb County,GA 1959-60; mem Book of Honor Amer Biogr Inst 1979; broadcast programs WEUP Radio 1971-73. **Honors/Awds:** Special Plaques Oakwood Coll Faculty & Student Ch Bld 1977; Special Plaques South Central SDA 1978; Plaque Notable Amer in the Bicentennial Era 1976; Certificate Outstanding Secondary Educator of Amer 1975; Poet and Author. **Military Serv:** ASR Chaplain 1943-44. **Business Addr:** Your Bible Speaks Inc, PO Box 310745, Atlanta, GA 30331.

TOUCHSTONE, JOHN E.
Appointed official. **Personal:** Born Jul 27, 1939, New Kensington, PA; married Mary. **Educ:** VA Union Univ, BA 1965; Howard Univ, MPA 1973. **Career:** Montgomery Co MD, admin asst 1971-72; Washington Metro COG, asst dir 1972-83; DC Dept of Public Works, dir 1983-. **Orgs:** Mem Eastland Garden Civic Assn 1977; mem DC Delphi Panel 1980; co-chair Washington Waterfront Action Grp 1981; mem 1973-85, exec bd, Intl City Mgmt Assn 1973-85; mem Coalition of Black Public Admins 1982-85; mem Intl Assn of Police; bd of dir, Natl Forum for Black Public Admin. **Honors/Awds:** Scholarship Howard Univ 1970; Fellowship Intl City Mgmt Assn 1973. **Business Addr:** Dir Public Works, District of Columbia, 2000 14th St NW 6th Fl, Washington, DC 20009.

TOURE, KWAME. **See CARMICHAEL, STOKELY.**

TOUSSAINT, ROSE-MARIE
Medical administrator. **Personal:** Born Jun 15, 1956, Port-au-Prince, Haiti. **Educ:** Loyola Univ, BS 1979; Howard Univ, MD 1983. **Career:** NIH, rsch assoc; Howard Univ Hosp, general surgery residency, board certified in General Surgery; Howard Univ Transplant Center, assistant professor of surgery, associate director, 1971-77; Horus Corp, medical director, 1995-. **Orgs:** Mem Delta Sigma Theta Sor 1978; vice pres All African Physicians of North Amer 1984; Liver Medical Advisory Committee, chairperson; Wash Regional Transplant Consortium, 1993; American Society of Transplant Surgeons; Transplant Society; Cheasepeake Transplant Society, vice president; Transplantation at the TE Starzl Transplantation Institute, fellow and funding member, 1988; American College of Surgeon, fellow. **Honors/Awds:** Best Surgical Resident DC General Hosp 1985-86; Drew-Walker Surgical Resident Award; Ferebee Award in Medicine and Pioneers in Transplantation Award. **Special Achievements:** Author, Never Question the Miracle-A Surgeons' Story, 1998. **Business Addr:** PO Box 334, Burtonsville, MD 20866, (410)724-3732.

TOVAR, STEVEN ERIC
Professional football player. **Personal:** Born Apr 25, 1970, Elyria, OH. **Educ:** Ohio State Univ, attended. **Career:** Cincinnati Bengals, linebacker, 1993-. **Business Addr:** Professional Football Player, Cincinnati Bengals, One Bengals Dr, Cincinnati, OH 45202, (513)621-3550.

TOWNES, CLARENCE LEE, JR.
Business executive. **Personal:** Born Jan 21, 1928, Richmond, VA; son of Alice S Townes and Clarence L Townes Sr; married Grace Elizabeth; children: Clarence III, Michael S, Lisa F, June E. **Educ:** VA Union Univ, BS Commerce 1951. **Career:** VA Mutual Benefit Life Ins Co, dir of training 1948-66; Republican Natl Comm, asst to chmn/dir minority affairs 1966-70; Joint Ctr/Pol Studies, dir govtl affairs 1970-74; Metropolitan Coach Corp, pres & CEO 1974-1986; Richmond Renaissance Inc, deputy dir, beginning 1982, executive director, currently. **Orgs:** Alternate delegate Republican Natl Convention 1964; comm Rich Redev & Housing Auth 1964-66; chmn Electoral Bd Richmond VA 1979-84; bd of dirs VA Mutual Benefit Life Ins Co 1985-88; mem Phi Beta Sigma Frat 1945-; pres/COO Jefferson Townhouse Corp 1964-; bd of dirs Consolidated Bank & Trust Co 1970-; bd of dirs Amer Bus Assn 1976-1982; pres Arts Council of Richmond 1986-88, Richmond Public School Bd, chairman, 1992-. **Honors/Awds:** Citizenship Awd Astoria Benefical Club Richmond 1968; Man of the Year Iota Sigma Chap Phi Beta Sigma 1969; Good Government Award Richmond First Club 1987; Brotherhood Citation Award, Richmond Chapter, Natl Conf of Christians and Jews, 1987. **Military Serv:** AUS 2nd lt 3 yrs. **Home Addr:** 3103 Hawthorne Ave, Richmond, VA 23222. **Business Addr:** Executive Director, Richmond Renaissance Inc, 600 E Broad St #960, Richmond, VA 23219.

TOWNES, SANDRA L
Judge. **Career:** City Court, Syracuse, NY, judge, currently. **Business Addr:** Judge, City Court, 511 S State St, Syracuse, NY 13202.

TOWNS, EDOLPHUS
Government official. **Personal:** Born Jul 21, 1934, Chadbourn, NC; son of Vergie Towns and Dolphus Towns; married Gwendolyn Forbes; children: Darryl, Deidra. **Educ:** NC A&T State Univ Greensboro, BS 1956; Adelphi Univ Garden City NY, MSW 1973. **Career:** Medgar Evers Coll, Brooklyn, New York City Public School, teacher, dep hosp admin 1965-71; Borough of Brooklyn, dep pres 1976-82; US House of Representatives, member, 1983-. **Orgs:** Mem adv council Boy Scouts Amer, Salvation Army, Phi Beta Sigma, Kiwanis; NAACP; American Red Cross; Guardsmen; Boule; chairman, Congressional Black Caucus , 1991-. **Honors/Awds:** Honorary degrees: DSC, North Carolina A&T University, 1985, LLD, Shaw University, 1984, LLD, Aldelphi University, 1988, LLD, Virginia Seminary at Lynchburg, 1982. **Military Serv:** AUS 1956-58. **Business Addr:** US Congressman, US House of Represenatives, 2232 Rayburn HOB, Washington, DC 20515.

TOWNS, EVA ROSE
Child psychiatrist. **Personal:** Born Feb 3, 1927, Ellwood City, PA; divorced; children: Ronald, James, Shaaron, Jennifer. **Educ:** Univ of Pittsburgh, BS 1948; Howard Univ Coll of Med, MD 1953; Freedmen Hosp Washington DC, adult psych training; Johns Hopkins Hosp Balt MD, childpsych training. **Career:** North Community Mental Health Center Washington DC, medical officer; Private practice, child adolescent adult psychiatry. **Orgs:** Mem Amer Psychiatric Assoc, Natl Med Assoc, Med Chirurgical Soc of DC. **Honors/Awds:** Prog Fellow Amer Psych Assn 1973; Fellow Amer Acad of Child Psychiatry. **Home Addr:** 7739 16th St NW, Washington, DC 20012.

TOWNS, MAXINE YVONNE
Clergyman, educator. **Personal:** Born Jan 12, 1941, Chester, PA. **Educ:** Camden Co Comm Coll Blackwood NJ, AA 1975; Notre Dame Coll Manchester NH, BA 1978. **Career:** Notre Dame Coll Manchester NH, dean of students 1978-; Camden Co Jail NJ, chaplain 1972-77; Boston MA, rec dir 1970-72; Diocese of Fresno CA, religion educ tchr 1963-70; Wade Day Care Cntr Chester PA, day care asst 1960-61. **Orgs:** Sec of bd So NJ Prison Serv Comm 1973-75; sec Nat Balck Sisters' Conf 1975-77; treas NBSC 1980-; enterd Franciscan Sisters of the Atonement 1961; planning com Annuan NBSC Meeting 1977-79; planning com NH Person & Guidance Assn 1980; chprsn NH Diocesan Vocation Commn 1980-; pres NH Coll Person Assn 1980-81. **Business Addr:** Notre Dame College, 2321 Elm St, Manchester, NH 03104.

TOWNS, MYRON B., II
Physician. **Personal:** Born Dec 18, 1943, Greensboro, NC; son of Miriam Gould Towns and Myron B Towns Sr. **Educ:** Fisk Univ, BA, foreign languages, 1970; Meharry Medical Coll, MD 1978. **Career:** The Tennesseean, copy editor, 1967-70; Waverly-Belmont Clinic Lab, co-organizer/founder 1972-74; Univ of GA Athens, electron microscopist div of genetics 1974-75; George W Hubbard Hospital Meharry Medical Coll, pathology resident 1978-83; Vanderbilt University, clinical pharmacology fellow, 1982; Hebbronville Clinical Lab, dir co-owner pathologist 1984-86; The Community Clinic, physician, 1985-86; Doctor's Clinic, associate 1986-87; Towns Clinic, primary and indigent physician, 1987-93; Clark and Associates Management Consultants, medical dir. **Orgs:** Coll of Amer Pathologists; Amer Soc Clinical Path & local med socs 1980-; American College of Forensic Examiners; consultant in automation; Sanford and Associates; IMAGE; trustee, Wildlife Rehabilitation Center, 1987-92; sec, ICS School Board, Blytheville, 1990-92; certified emergency foster parent; NAACP, life mem. **Honors/Awds:** Carter Woodson Award in journalism, 1969; honors in biochemistry and research, Meharry Medical College 1972-83;. **Business Addr:** PO Box 90159, Pittsburgh, PA 15224-0559.

TOWNS, ROSE MARY
Librarian. **Personal:** Born Jan 7, 1934, Houston, TX; married George Elbert. **Educ:** San Francisco State Coll, BA Soc Sci 1955; Univ of CA Berkeley, MLS 1956. **Career:** City Coll of San Francisco, librarian/instructor, 1987-; Laney Coll Library, 1983-87; Bay Area Library and Info System, project coord, 1982-83; N Bay Cooperataive Libr Syst, syst prgm coor 1979-82; Ref Referral Proj N Bay Coop Lib Sys, coord 1975-79; Richmond Pub Lib Richmond CA, city libr 1969-70; Richmond Pub Lib Richmond CA, asst city libr 1966-69; Oakland Pub Lib Oakland CA, sup libr 1962-66; Oakland Pub Lib Oakland CA, sr libr 1960-62; Oakland Pub Lib Oakland CA, jr libr 1956-60. **Orgs:** Mem Am Lib Assn; mem Am Lib Assn Black Caucus; mem CA Lib Assn; mem Intellectual Freedom Com CA Lib Assn 1966-69, 1980-; chpsn Intellectual Freedom Com CA Lib Assn 1967-68; Long Range Planning Com CA Lib Assn; sec CA Soc of Libr CA Lib Assn 1979; mem CA Libr Black Caucus N; sec CA Libr Black Caucus N 1972-73; mem Black Women Orgn for Polit Action. **Honors/Awds:** Delegate CA Gov Conf on Lib & Infromation Serv 1979. **Business Addr:** Librarian/Instructor, City College of San Francisco, 50 Phelan Ave, San Francisco, CA 94112.

TOWNS, SANNA NIMTZ
Educator. **Personal:** Born Oct 12, 1943, Hawthorne, NV; daughter of Margeurite Malarcher Nimtz and August H Nimtz Sr; divorced; children: Joseph IV, Jawad. **Educ:** Southern Univ, BA 1964; Teachers Coll Columbia Univ, MA 1967; Univ of Southern MS, PhD 1985. **Career:** Amer Language Prog Columbia Univ, English lang instructor 1969-71; Office of Urban Affairs SUNY at Buffalo, prog coord 1973-75; Kuwait Univ, instructor & admin 1975-79; English Dept Univ of New Orleans, lang coord & instructor 1980-82, 1985-86; Delgado Comm Coll, asst prof, asst chair, 1986-87, chair, communication division, 1987-92, associate professor of English, 1992-. **Orgs:** Mem Natl Council of Teachers of English 1980-, LA Assoc of Developmental Educ 1981-, Phi Delta Kappa 1984-, South Central Modern Language Assoc 1986-; speaker New Orleans Museum of Art Speakers Bureau 1987; member, Delta Sigma Theta Sorority, 1962-; member, Conference on College Composition & Communications, 1980-. **Honors/Awds:** State of LA Bd of Regents Graduate Fellowship 1982-85; article "Integrating Reading & Writing Instruction" in ERIC 1984; Black Achiever in Education, Dyrades YMCA, New Orleans, 1988-89; Fulbright-Hays Seminars Aboard Participant, American University in Cairo, 1988; Fulbright Scholar Award, Comenius Univ, Bratislava, Slovakia, Jan-June 1994. **Business Addr:** Associate Professor of English, Communication Division, Delgado Community College, 615 City Park Ave, New Orleans, LA 70119, (504)483-4093.

TOWNSEL, RONALD
State corrections offical (retired). **Personal:** Born Nov 25, 1934, Chicago; children: 3. **Educ:** George Williams Coll, BS 1957; Governores State U, MA 1975. **Career:** IL Dept of Corrections, st supt of adult parole beginning 1970; IL Youth Commn, area parole supr juvenile parole agt 1960-70; Chicago Fed of Settlements, youthgang worker 1958-60; Chicago Bd of Edn, tchr 1957-58. **Orgs:** Mem ACA Compact of St Governors; NICO; IPPCA. **Military Serv:** AUS 1952-54. **Business Addr:** 100 W Randolph, Chicago, IL 60601.

TOWNSELL, JACKIE MAE
City official. **Personal:** Born Apr 7, 1936, Dallas, TX; daughter of Ola Wade Howard and Jack Howard; married Jimmie Townsell, Dec 22, 1952; children: Aaron H. **Career:** City of Irving, Irving, TX, councilwoman, 1977-; Townsell Groc & Mkt, owner, mgr, currently. **Orgs:** Served Dallas Cty Grand Jury 1971; adv comm mem Legis Dist Rep 1973; nominated 1st black appt to City Park Bd 1973; appt to serve Dallas Cty Mental Health Mental Retard Bd of Trustees; Dallas Cty Grand Jury Comm 1974; delegate City Council 1st black to seek publ office 1974; testified Environ Affairs Comm for creation of a state park 1975; elected Irving City Council 1977-; bd mem Helping Hand School for Retarded Children W Irving Improvement Assoc & Day Care Ctr; Irving Planning & Adv Comm; Irving Aid Inc; Dem for Responsible Govt; Dallas Cty Child Welfare; Liaison to Dallas Cty Foster Parent; nominated 1st black appt to City Housing Code Bd; appt Screening Sub-Comm charged with responsibility to fill a vacancy in Criminal Dist Ct #1; dep voter registrar;pres Young Womens Mission, Par Leaders Org. **Honors/Awds:** Worked with City Fathers to obtain park site & construct swimming pool; Worked with City Fathers to bring water lines through the comm; Suggested to City Officials the need to installment contract payments so people of Irving would have option of paying cash or installment to tie onto city water & sewer lines; This is Your Life Pen & Plaque 1965; Cit Awd Outstanding Young Women of the Year; Cert of Apprec Irving Parks & Rec Dept 1971; Serv & Outstanding Contrib to Citizens of Irving 1972; Accomplishment Awd Serv Rendered to Dallas Cty 1974; Cert of Apprec Merit Serv Outstanding Contrib Cty of Dallas 1974. **Business Addr:** Manager, Townsell Grocery & Market, 3941 Carver St, Irving, TX 75061.

TOWNSEND, ANDRE
Professional football player. **Personal:** Born Oct 8, 1962, Chicago, IL. **Educ:** Univ of Mississippi, attended. **Career:** Denver Broncos, defensive end, nose tackle, 1984-. **Orgs:** Kappa Alpha Psi Fraternity Incorporated. **Honors/Awds:** Post-season play, 1986, 1987, 1989: AFC Championship Game, NFL Championship Game.

TOWNSEND, LEONARD
Judge. **Career:** State of Michigan, Recorder's Court, judge, currently. **Business Addr:** Recorder's Court Judge, Frank Murphy Hall of Justice Bldg, 1441 St Antoine, Courtroom 702, Detroit, MI 48226, (313)224-2437.

TOWNSEND, MAMIE LEE HARRINGTON
Business executive. **Personal:** Born Nov 20, 1920, Warwick, GA; married Calvin Louis Townsend; children: Roselyn Rochelle Greene Cole, Ervin Louis. **Educ:** Purdue Univ, 1966; IN Univ 1966-68. **Career:** Finance Ctr AUS, branch mgr 1951-66; Faith United Christian Church, diaconate & bd 1981-; Auntie Mame's Child Devel Centers, founder/pres, 1969. **Orgs:** Pres IN Licensed Child Care Assn 1975; vice chmn IN Citizens Adv Comm 1977 & 79; central reg rep IN Assn for the Educ of Young Children 1978-79; bd of dirs Metro Bd of Zoning & Appeals 1979-82; Golden Heritage NAACP 1979-; steering comm Christian Churches of IN 1981-84; vol training Amer Cancer

Soc 1982-85; steering comm mem United Negro Coll Fund Drive 1984; appty by Gov Bowen charter mem Title XX Bd, vice chmn 1975-79; mem Metropolitan Bd of License Review 1982-. **Honors/Awds:** Proclamation of Mamie Townsend Day Mayor Wm Hudnut IN 1977-79; Indiana Jefferson Award Indianapolis Star Nwsp 1978; Woman of the Year Zeta Phi Beta Sor 1979; Distinguished Serv Indianapolis Chamber of Comm; Madame CJ Walker Center for Leadership Devel 1982; Outstanding Businesswoman Iota Phi Lambda Sor 1983; Sojourner Truth Award by Natl Assn of Negro Business & Professional Women's Clubs Inc 1985 for Meritorious Svcs; Human Rights Award for Outstanding Leadership in Educ; Hon Mem Zeta Phi Beta 1986. **Business Addr:** President, Auntie Mame's Child Dev Ctrs, 3120 N Emerson Avenue, Indianapolis, IN 46218.

TOWNSEND, MURRAY LUKE, JR.
Government official (retired). **Personal:** Born Jul 6, 1919, Indianapolis, IN; son of Novella Foster and Murray L Townsend Sr (deceased); married Evelyn; children: Cheryl, Murray III, Frederick. **Educ:** Morehouse Coll, BA 1942; Boston U, LLB 1949. **Career:** PO, 1950-56; IRS, criminal investigator 1956-64; Boston and NY, dep equal employment policy ofcr 1963-66; Small Business Admin, sr compliance officer 1967-81 (retired); Consultant. **Orgs:** Mem Omega Psi Phi Frat 1939; deacon Union Bapt Ch 1955-62; mem Prince Hall Mason 1963-, mem Middleboro Lakeville Mental Health Comm Couns 1966; mem bd of deacons, Central Baptist Church 1973-; mem NAACP; 366th Infantry Vet Assn; adv com bd of dir New Eng Village for Human Rights 1979; mem Afro Am Vet US 1980. **Honors/Awds:** Citz Schrsp Found Middleboro 1968-70; Cits Schlrsp Found MA 1970-72; Paul Revere Bowl Citz Schlrsp Found Am 1976. **Military Serv:** Infantry 1942-46, 1951-54; capt 1951-54; Bronze Star w/2 Oak Leaf Clusters and V device, Silver Star Med 1951, Infantryman's Badge w/Star; Purple Heart, 1951. **Home Addr:** 95 Thomas St, Middleboro, MA 02346, (508)947-1584.

TOWNSEND, P. A.
Attorney (retired). **Personal:** Born Nov 29, 1914, Poplar Bluff, MO; son of Ava Porter Townsend and Sol Townsend; married Evelyn M; children: Prentice, Edward. **Educ:** Univ of KS, AB 1934, LLB 1937. **Career:** Gen practice of law 1937-65; State of KS, spec asst to attny gen 1937-41; State Tax Comm, asst attny 1947-52; State Corp Comm, asst attny 1947-52; Missionary Bapt State Conv of KS, gen counsel 1948-62; Interstate Assoc of Church of God, gen counsel 1948-69; Prince Hall Grand Lodge of KS F&AM, grand attny 1956-77, past grand master 1979-81; KS Conf, AME Church, attny; State of KS, pardon attny 1965-67; State Corp Comm, asst gen counsel 1967-70; Dept of Housing & Urban Devel, attny, reg counsel 1970-82; Municipal Court of Topeka, judge pro-tem 1983-90. **Orgs:** Del at large Rep Natl Conv 1960; del Gen Conf 1960, 1964, 1968, 1972, 1976, 1980, 1984, 1988; commiss Topeka Housing Auth 1963-70; exec bd Salvation Army 1965; adv comm Red Cross 1966; mem Gen Conf Comm 1964; pres Judicial Council 1968-92; vchmn Rep State Comm two terms; vchmn Shawnee Cty Central Comm; 33 Degree Mason. **Honors/Awds:** Shriner; Alpha Phi Alpha; Washburn Univ Centennial Fund Dr; Stormont-Vail Hosp Bond Dr; past comdr Jordan-Patterson Post #319, Amer Legion; former mem Legal Redress Comm, NAACP; bd of stewards, former mem, bd trustees Douglass Hosp; pres, judicial council, St John AME Church; Kansas Bar Association, certificate for 50 years meritorious service as an attorney, 1987. **Military Serv:** Capt WWII.

TOWNSEND, ROBERT
Writer, producer, director, actor. **Personal:** Born Feb 6, 1957, Chicago, IL; married Cheri Jones, Sep 1990; children: Sierra, Skylar. **Educ:** Illinois State Univ; William Paterson Coll NJ; Hunter Coll NY. **Career:** Actor, Cooley High, Ratboy, Streets of Fire, A Soldier's Story, American Flyers, The Mighty Quinn; actor/director/producer, Hollywood Shuffle; starring in "Uptown Comedy Express," HBO; writer/actor/director/producer, "Robert Townsend & His Partners in Crime," HBO, 1987-88; writer/director/actor, The Five Heartbeats, The Meteor Man; TV: Parenthood, Warner Bros, 1995-; director, "Raw," "B.A.P.S.". **Business Addr:** Owner, The Townsend Entertainment Corporation, 8033 Sunset Blvd, #890, Los Angeles, CA 90046.

TOWNSEND, RON
Broadcast company executive. **Personal:** Born Sep 23, 1941, Jacksonville, FL; married Dorothy; children: Michelle Townsend-Smith, Ronnie Jr, Gina. **Educ:** Baruch College, NY, received business degree. **Career:** CBS-TV, beginning 1960, dir of business affairs and programming 1964-69; Children's TV Workshop, dir of field services, beginning 1969; WTOP-TV (currently WUSA-TV), station manager, 1974-82, general manager, three years; Gannett Television Group, president, 1989-. **Honors/Awds:** First black member of the Augusta National Golf Club. **Business Addr:** President, Gannett Television, 1000 Wilson Blvd, Arlington, VA 22209.

TOWNSEND, WARDELL C., JR.
Government official. **Personal:** Born Oct 16, 1952, Baltimore, MD; son of Wardell Clinton Sr (deceased) and Toyoko Yonamine Townsend; married Diane Martin, May 7, 1979; children: Sarah Sachiko, Claire Keiko, Jordan Hideto, Aaron Masao. **Educ:** Western Carolina Univ, BS, psychology, social welfare, 1975; West VA Univ, MSW, 1979. **Career:** Cherokee Minority Business Devt Ctr, business devt mgr, 1982-83; Henderson County, dir, Community Devt Dept, 1980-82; Human Resource Devt Foundation, planning & devt mgr, 1979-80; Assn for Sickle Cell Disease, health educator/outreach coordinator, 1976-77; Boys Club of Asheville, group counselor, 1975-76; US Rep, Mike Espy, legislative dir, assoc staff to the Budget Committee, admin asst/chief of staff; US Rep, Doug Applegate, project dir, 1985; US Rep, Jamie Clarke, proj dir, 1983; Clinton Presidential Transition Team, 1992-93; US Dept of Agriculture, asst sec for admin, 1993-. **Orgs:** Administrative Assts Assn, bd of dirs, 1991-92, vp, 1992; Council of African-American Admin Assts; Natl Assn of Social Workers, 1974-; Academy of Certified Social Workers, 1982-; Diocesan Investment Committee, Episcopal Diocese of Washington, 1991-; Ascension Church; numerous past memberships; Japanese American Citizens League, 1993-; House Administrative Assistants Alumni Assn, 1993-; Asian American Government Executive Network, 1996-; President's Council for Management Improvement, 1993-; North Carolina Democratic Club of Washington, 1993-. **Honors/Awds:** US House of Representatives, Administrative Assistants Assn, Membership Recruitment Award, 1991; Asian Pacific American Network in Agriculture, Special Recognition, 1993; Western Carolina University Alumni Assn and Pi Gamma Mu International Honor Society, Special Recognition, 1994; Vice President Al Gore, Hammer Award, 1994; Forum on Blacks in Agriculture, Special Recognition, 1995; National Federation of Federal Employees, Honorary Member, 1995; US Department of Agriculture, African American Males Alumni Award, 1996; Executive Potential Program, Special Recognition, 1996; Defense Information Systems Agency, Special Recognition, 1996. **Business Addr:** Asst Sec for Administration, US Dept of Agriculture, 14th & Independence Ave SW, Rm 240W, Washington, DC 20250, (202)720-3291.

TOWNSEND, WILLIAM HENRY
Elected official, optometrist. **Personal:** Born Jul 30, 1914, West Point, MS; son of Annie Harris Townsend and John Henry Townsend; married Billye Gene McNeely, May 25, 1952; children: Yolanda Gene, Terezenha Ann, LaJuan Ursula. **Educ:** Tuskegee Inst, BS 1941; Howard Univ, 1946; Northern Illinois Coll of Optometry, OD, 1950. **Career:** Optometrist, Little Rock, 1950-; Arkansas House of Representatives, Dist 63 Pulaski Co state rep, 1973-. **Orgs:** 15 orgns including: life member NAACP; mem Urban League; treas Prof Serv Inc; mem Alpha Phi Alpha; mem the Masonic; 1st vice pres AR Democratic Black Caucus; mem AR Comprehensive Health Bd; mem Uptown Toastmaster Club; former mem bd of dirs 1st Natl Bank & 1st Commercial Bank Little Rock; Natl Christian & Jews, exec bd; Mount Zion Baptist Church, trustee, deacon bd; House of Representativs, educ, legislative audit committees; Arkansas Enterprise for the Blind; Aging and Legislative Affairs Committee, House of Representatives, chair. **Honors/Awds:** First licensed black optometrist in Arkansas, 1950; Citizen of the Yr Awd Omega Psi Phi 1964; Imperial Club's Awd Outstanding Serv in Politics 1975; Serv Awd for Outstanding Serv, Morris Booker Coll, 1975; Cert of Distinguished Service as mem of the State Adv Comm for Special Needs Prog 1975; AR Council of Human Relation Life Serv Awd; Optometrist of the Year Awd 1981; The Jerome S Levey Awd 1981; Martin Luther King Jr Commemorative Award, 1986; Distinguished Legislative Achievement, Alpha Phi Alpha, 1989; General C C Andrew Freedom Award, 1991; Whitney M Young Jr Service Award, 1993; Alpha Kappa Alpha Sorority, Beta Pi Omega Chapter Award, 1993; Outstanding Service to the Arkansas Beautician Assn Award, 1993, Friend of Education Award, 1993; The Natl Conference of Christians & Jews, Humanitarian Award, 1994; The Arkansas Natl Guard, Black Heritage Award, 1995; Senator David Pryor Award, 1997. **Special Achievements:** Bronze Bust of State Representative Townsend, placed on the 4th floor of the State Capitol, 1994. **Military Serv:** US Army Eng Unit, platoon sergeant, 1942-46. **Business Addr:** State Representative, Pulaski County, District 65, 1304 Wright Ave, Little Rock, AR 72206.

TRADER, HARRIET PEAT
Social work, educator. **Personal:** Born Jul 6, 1922, Baltimore, MD; married Herbert W Trader. **Educ:** Morgan State Coll, AB 1944; Columbia Univ, MS 1946; Univ of PA, DSW 1962. **Career:** Bronx Hosp NY, med social worker 1952-53; Crownsville State Hosp MD, psychiatrist caseworker suprv 1953-62; Howard Univ School of Social Work, assoc prof 1963-65; Morgan State Coll, assoc prof 1965-68; Univ of MD School of Social Work, assoc prof 1968-84; Johns Hopkins Univ, assoc prof 1968-; Morgan State Univ; vice pres acad affairs 1980-85; Baltimore Urban League, consultant 1986-. **Orgs:** Past pres Social Work Vocational Bur 1973-; chairperson Natl Cabinet on Professional Standards; mem Natl Assoc of Soc Workers, Natl Assoc of Black Soc Workers, Urban League, NAACP, YWCA; bd mem, Commission on Community Relations, Family & Children's Service, Enoch Pratt Library. **Honors/Awds:** Comm Contrib Awd Delta Sigma Theta 1969; Listed in Outstanding Ed in Amer 1971; Alumna of Year Awd Morgan State Coll 1972; 1st woman to be appt to bd trustees Enoch Pratt Library 1972; Honored as Living Maker of Negro History Delta Phi Lambda 1973.

TRAINER, JAMES E.
Automobile dealer. **Personal:** Born in Birmingham, AL; married Mattie; children: Eric, Marcus, Jameta. **Career:** Trainer Oldsmobile-Cadillac-Pontiac-GMC Truck Inc, CEO, currently. **Special Achievements:** Company is ranked #1 on Black Enterprise's list of Top 100 Auto Dealers, 1994; Trainer was first African American salesman to work for Edwards Chevrolet in Birmingham, AL, the oldest Chevrolet dealership in the US, 1971; company led all US black-owned auto dealerships with sales of $254.6 million, 1992. **Business Addr:** CEO, Trainer Olds-Cad-Pont-GMC Truck Inc, PO Box 6119, Warner Robins, GA 31095, (912)929-0222.

TRAMIEL, KENNETH RAY, SR.
Counselor. **Personal:** Born May 31, 1946, Shreveport, LA; married Sandra Mackel; children: Kenneth Jr, Kendra, Kai. **Educ:** Univ of CA, Berkeley, BA (summa cum laude) 1973; CA State Univ, MS (Summa Cum Laude) 1976. **Career:** East Oakland Youth Devel, head counselor 1979-80; Federal Govt Vietnam Outreach program, asst team leader/counselor 1980-82; Oakland Unified School Dist, head counselor, college & scholarship counselor 1982-, afrocentric curriculum and counseling techniques, post traumatic stress disorder, currently; consultant, currently. **Orgs:** Pres bd of dirs Berkeley Youth Alternative 1981-82; pres 1984-85, mem Oakland Personnel & Guidance Assoc 1982-; mem CA Assoc for the Gifted 1984; consultant CA Assoc for the Gifted State Conf 1984-85; vice pres Oakland Public Sch Affirmative Action Comm 1985-86; board member Berkeley Juneteenth Association, Inc; board member Racial & Ethnic Ministry Committee, The Presbyterian Church USA, Synod Northern California. **Military Serv:** AUS personnel sp5 2 yrs; Outstanding Section Leader 1969. **Home Addr:** 2923 Jo Ann Dr, Richmond, CA 94806.

TRAMMELL, WILLIAM RIVERS
Insurance company executive. **Personal:** Born Oct 19, 1926, Anniston, AL; son of Mattie Rivers Trammell and Edward A Trammell Sr; married Bertha Hicks. **Educ:** Clark Coll Atlanta, AB 1948; Columbia Univ NY, MA 1961. **Career:** Calhoun County Schools, jr high principal 1948-65; Anniston Public Schools, elem principal 1965-75, interim sch supt 1978-79, asst supt and dir of finance 1975-85 (retired); Protective Industrial Insurance Company of Alabama, dir 1989-. **Orgs:** Dir of pilot state kindergarten prog Anniston City Schools 1973-77; sec Anniston Airport Commn 1980-86; mem Alabama Governor's Comm on Handicapped Employment 1985-; treas Calhoun Co Economic Develop Cncl 1986-; bd of dirs Alabama Easter Seal Soc 1986-. **Honors/Awds:** Outstanding Serv Awd in Educ Alpha Kappa Alpha Sor 1984; Archon of the Year Sigma Pi Phi Frat Beta Kappa Boule 1986; Gold Awd Alabama Easter Seal Soc 1986. **Home Addr:** 2517 McKleroy Ave, Anniston, AL 36201.

TRAMMER, MONTE IRVIN
Newspaper publisher. **Personal:** Born Nov 11, 1951, Birmingham, AL; son of Edwenia Wilson Trammer (deceased) and Jimmie Trammer; married Hilda Hudson Trammer, May 20, 1972. **Educ:** Indiana University, Indianapolis, IN, 1969-75. **Career:** Indianapolis Star, Indianapolis, IN, reporter, 1970-76; Baltimore Sun, Baltimore, MD, reporter, 1977-80; Detroit Free Press, Detroit, MI, business writer, 1980-81, assistant city editor, 1981-82; USA Today, Washington, DC, deputy managing editor, 1982-86; Poughkeepsie Journal, Poughkeepsie, NY, assistant to publisher, 1986; The Saratogian, Saratoga Springs, NY, publisher, 1986-. **Orgs:** Chmn, United Way of North East New York, 1996-; NY Newpaper Publishers Fdtn, treasurer; NY Newspaper Publishers Assn, bd mbr; member, Saratoga Springs NAACP; Saratoga Spring, Rotary, Empire State Coll Foundation, board member; trustee, College of St Rose, 1997. **Honors/Awds:** Paul Harris Fellow (Rotary). **Business Addr:** President & Publisher, The Saratogian, Inc, 20 Lake Avenue, Saratoga Springs, NY 12866.

TRAPP, DONALD W.
Financial administrator. **Personal:** Born Sep 28, 1946, Hampton, VA; son of Ida Holt Trapp and Chester A. Trapp; married Shirley Ann Stokes; children: Rashaad, Brandon, Yvonne. **Educ:** Virgina State U, BS Bus Admin 1968; IN U, MBA Finance 1973. **Career:** Cummins Engine Co Inc, dir pricing 1978-82; Cummins Engine Co, asst treas 1977-78; Cummins Engine Co, finan spec 1976-77; Irwin Mngmt Co Inc, mgr treas reporting 1973-76; Cummins Engine Co Inc, dir components strategy 1982-83, dir intl logistics 1983-84; Remote Equip Corp, pres 1985; vice pres and treasurer UNC Ventures, Inc. Boston, MA, 1988-90; Cummins Engine Co, Inc, director strategic planning, 1991-92, director business development, 1992-94, director, electronics business strategy, 1994-96, exec director, electronics, 1996-97. **Orgs:** Mem C of C 1975; mem Kappa Alpha Psi Frat Inc 1967-; bd of dir William R Laws Found 1975-84; bd of dir Columbus United Way of Am 1976-79; bd of directors Accent Hair Salons 1988-90; bd of directors Xinix Corp 1989-90; National Black MBA Association, 1991-; board of directors, Columbus Enterprise Development Corp 1994-97; board of directors, Bartholomew County Big Brothers/Big Sisters 1995-; board of directors, Indiana Univ Business School Alumni Assn 1996-; board of directors, United Way of Bartholomew County 1996-. **Honors/Awds:** Achmnt awd Wall St Jour

1968; distng serv cit United Negro Fund 1977. **Military Serv:** AUS first lt 1968-70; commendation med, 1968. **Home Addr:** 3241 Beechnut Ct, Columbus, IN 47203.

TRAPP, ELLEN SIMPSON
Educational administrator. **Personal:** Born Dec 29, 1920, Chester, SC; daughter of Bessie Simpson and Furman Simpson; married Vanis W Trapp; children: Karlus, Vanis, Ellan. **Educ:** Benedict Coll Columbia, SC, BA 1943; NYU, pre-med. **Career:** Original Displays, owner/operator 1945-49; New York City Bd of Health, bacteriologist; School Bd, elected mem 1973-, chairperson 1983-. **Orgs:** Treas New York City School Bd Assn 1980-; bd mgr Soc Gifted Children 1976-; active mem LWV, served as Educ Task Force chairperson; active mem League for Better Govt; mem State Educ Adv Com 1975; Staten Island Better Govt Cncl 1961; Mayor's Comm on Inter-Group Relations 1976; Mothers March on Birth Defects/March of Dimes 1975; Staten Island Area Policy Bd 1983; Staten Isl Human Rights Comm 1984; Sixth Term, Re-elected to Community School Board, 1993. **Honors/Awds:** Rara Avis Mariners Harbor PS 44 1975; Woman of Achievement Staten Island 1979; Mills Skinner Award SI Urban League 1979; Except Childrens Club 1985; Martin Luther King Awd SI NY Richmond Occupational Training Center 1987; Maurice Wollin Educ of the Year Awd 1987; 1st Black person elected to public office on Staten Island elected to 5th term May 2, 1989; Impact on Education of Youth, Lambda Kappa Mu, 1990. **Business Addr:** Chairperson, Community School Board, 211 Daniel Low Terrace, Staten Island, NY 10301.

TRAPP, JAMES
Professional football player. **Personal:** Born Dec 28, 1969, Greenville, SC; married. **Educ:** Clemson. **Career:** Oakland Raiders, defensive back, 1993-. **Business Addr:** Professional Football Player, Oakland Raiders, 1220 Harbor Bay Pkwy, Alameda, CA 94502, (510)615-1875.

TRAPPIER, ARTHUR SHIVES
Nuclear engineer. **Personal:** Born Mar 22, 1937, Brooklyn, NY; children: Arthur S Jr, Jason M. **Educ:** Lincoln U, BA physics 1960; Polytech Inst of Brooklyn, MS bioengr 1970; IN No U, DSc med engr 1973. **Career:** Dept Physic & Nuclear Med Mt Sinai Ch fo Med City Univ of NY, research phys 198-0; Jewish Hosp Med Center of Brooklyn, radiol phys 1970-78; Downstate Med Center Kings Hwy Hosp, radio phys 1965-70; NYU Environ Med, research asst 1962-65; AUS Rockett Guided Missle Agency Red Stone Arsenal DC, physical sci 1961-62. **Orgs:** Prof of phsy Prat Inst 1978; consult phys Vet Adminstrn Med Center 1977-80; treas Grtr NY Hlth Physcis Soc 1978-79. **Honors/Awds:** Pub ''Rectum Bladder Dosimetry in the RX of Uterine Cancer'' Radiology 1969; ''Calibration of a Whole Body Counter for Clinical Investigation in a Psychiat Hosp'' Physics in Med & Biology 1971; pub ''Postmortem Exam of an X-Ray Tube'' Journ of the Natl Med Assn 1978. **Military Serv:** AUS sp-4 1960-62. **Business Addr:** 5th Ave & 100th St, New York, NY 10029.

TRAUGHBER, CHARLES M.
Government employee. **Personal:** Born Feb 13, 1943. **Educ:** TN State Univ, BS 1968, Grad School, 1970-71. **Career:** TN State Penitentiary, counselor I 1969, sr institutional counselor 1971; Adult Counseling Serv for Adult Inst State of TN, dir 1972; TN Bd of Paroles, mem 1972-. **Orgs:** Mem Amer Correctional Assoc, Natl Assoc for Advancement of Col People; enrolled MA Prog Criminal Justice TN State Univ; mem TN Correctional Assoc, Amer Paroling Assoc. **Business Addr:** Tennessee Bd of Paroles, 3rd Floor, State Office Bldg, Nashville, TN 37237.

TRAVIS, ALEXANDER B.
Business executive. **Personal:** Born Oct 19, 1930, Dallas; married Jo Ann Jones; children: Judy (erwin), Anthony, Paula. **Educ:** Compton Jr Coll; SW Business Coll. **Career:** Bell Telephone Co, various jobs in co's plant dept comm mgr spec assign 1949-. **Orgs:** Bd mem of Park So YMCA; NAACP Area Chpter; Natl Alliance Businessmen & Venture Adv Inc; mem Dallas Urban League; mem Alliance of Business, Plans for Progress, US Dept of Labor & Career Guid Inst; Dallas Negro Chamber of Commerce; Moorland Branch YMCA; Natl All Market Devel; SCLC; Black Part Program; Maria Morgan Branch YWCA; sponsor Boy Scouts & Explorer Scout Troops of Amer; Betheleham Comm Center; Community Relations Comm; B & PW; Tele Poin Amer; Dallas All for Min Enterp; Amer Assn Min Consult Dallas Branch; New Bethel Baptist Church. **Honors/Awds:** First black mgr of SW Bell Co; Presidential Citation for work with veterans & ex-offenders; Special Commendation Dallas Area former-Pres Jimmy Carter; 1st Black pres of Intl Lions Club.

TRAVIS, BENJAMIN
Attorney. **Personal:** Born in Brooklyn; married; children: 3. **Educ:** Coll of Pugent Sound, 1951; San Francisco State Coll, 1954; Univ of CA Hastings Coll of Law, JD 1960. **Career:** Alameda Superior Court, judge; atty pvt prac 1961-66; Western Addition Law Ofc, opened first neighborhodd legal serv ofc in San Francisco as chief counsel 1966-72; Community Educ Proj & Neighborhood Lega Newspaper, founded 1968-; San Francisco State Coll, lecturing prof 1971. **Orgs:** Mem, bd dir Berkeley Neighborhood Legal Serv; mem, bd dir San Francisco Local Devel Corp; mem, bd dir Bay Area Social Planning Coun; past vp, bd dir San Francisco Neighborhood Legal Asst Found; mem, bd dir Bayview Hunter's Point Community Health Cntr; mem, bd dir Tassili Sch; mem, bd dirNat Legal Aid & Defender's Assn; consult evaluator & technical asst Volt Inc Civil Defenders Com; mem, bd dir Nat Bar Assn; sec Charles Houston Law Club 1971; mem Task Force Com on Criminal Justice; mem, bd dir United Bay Area Crusade 1972; mem Judicare Experiment Prog 1973; pres Charles Houston Law Club 1973-. **Military Serv:** USAF 1950-54. **Business Addr:** Judge, Alameda Superior Court, 1225 Fallon St, Oakland, CA 94612.

TRAVIS, DEMPSEY J.
Realtor. **Personal:** Born Feb 25, 1920, Chicago, IL; son of Mittie Strickland Travis and Louis Travis; married Moselynne. **Educ:** Wilson Jr Coll, AA 1948; Roosevelt Univ, BA 1949; Northwestern Univ School Mortgage Banking, Certificate 1969; Olive Harvey Coll, Honorary Doctorate Economics 1975; Daniel Hale Williams Univ, Honorary Doctorate Business Admin 1976. **Career:** Sivart Mortgage Corp, pres 1945-78; United Mortgage Bankers of Amer, founder & pres 1960-73; Dempsey J Travis Securities & Investment Co, pres 1960-76; Urban Research Press, pres 1969-; Travis Realty Co, founder & pres 1949-. **Orgs:** Mem trustee Northwestern Meml Hosp 1975-; dir Uni Banc Trust 1976-87; trustee Chicago Historical Soc 1985-; pres Soc of Midland Authors 1988-90; Book Review Critic, Chicago Sun-Times, 1991; Chicago Board, Roosevelt University; Auditorium Theater, Black Music Center, Columbia College, advisory bd; NAACP. **Honors/Awds:** The Soc of Midland Authors Award, 1982; The Art Deco Award, 1985; The Gustavus Myers Center for the Study of Human Rights, 1st America Award, 1996; Author of Don't Stop Me Now, An Autobiography of Black Chicago, 1981; An Autobiography of Black Jazz, 1983; An Autobiography of Black Politics, 1987; Real Estate is the Gold in Your Future, 1988; Harold: The People's Mayor, 1989, Racism: American Style, A Corporate Gift, 1991; Daniel Hale Williams Univ, Honorary Doctorate Business Admin, 1976; Kennedy-King College Chicago, Honorary Doctorate of Humane Letters, 1982. **Special Achievements:** Author: I Refuse to Learn to Fail, book, 1992; Views from the Back of the Bus, During WW II and Beyond, 1995; The Duke Ellington Primer, 1996; The Louis Armstrong Odyssey: From Jane Alley to America's Jazz Ambassador, 1997; Racism: Like a Merry Go 'Round, 'Round 'N 'Round It Goes, 1998. **Military Serv:** US Army Techn Sgt served 4 years. **Business Addr:** President, Travis Realty Company, 840 E 87th St, Chicago, IL 60619.

TRAVIS, GERALDINE
Legislator. **Personal:** Born Sep 3, 1931, Albany, GA; daughter of Dorothy Marshall Washington and Joseph T Washington; married William Alexander Sr; children: William, Michael, Ann, Gerald, Gwendolyn. **Educ:** Xavier Univ, 1947-49. **Career:** Dem Natl Conv Miami, delegate 1972; Dem Mini-Conv KS, delegate 1974; Dem Natl Conv NY, delegate 1976; State of MT, legislator 1975-77. **Orgs:** Co-chmn Dem Party Minorities Comm 1972-74; mem Natl Steering Comm 1973-74; mem State Coord Comm of Intl Womens Year 1977; official observer Natl Womens Conf 1977; bd of dir YWCA Great Falls 1979; co-chmn Dem Women's Club; mem St Peter & Paul Cath Church, Natl Womens Polit Caucus, Natl Order of Women Legislators, YWCA, Natl Council of Negro Women, NAACP, natl Urban League, Amer Civil Liberties Union, Sierra Club, MT Womens Pol Caucus; MT Crime Control Bd, Human Resources Comm, Criminal Justice Info Comm; precinct comm Woman of Precinct #42 Cascade Cty; mem MT Adv Comm to US Comm on Civil Rights; chmn Cascade Cty Detoxification Adv Bd, Amer Indian Action Council; chmn sub-comm Admin of Justice; mem, Arizona Precinct Comm Women, Democratic District #17; mem, St Augustines Parish, Phoenix, Arizona.

TRAVIS, JACK
Architect, interior designer. **Personal:** Born Mar 2, 1952, Newellton, LA; son of Mary L Brown Travis and Sam L Travis. **Educ:** Arizona State University, BArch, 1977; University of Illinois at Champaign/Urbana, MArch, 1978. **Career:** Whisler-Patri, designer, architect, 1978; Pacific Gas & Electric, draughtsman, architect, 1978-79; Eyes Group Design, designer, draughtsman, architect, 1979-80; Skidmore Owings & Merrill, designer, interior architect, 1980-82; Switzer Group Inc, designer, interior architect, 1982-84; Sydney Philip Gilbert Assoc, designer, interior architect, 1984; NBC Broadcasting Co, designer, interior architect, 1985; Fashion Institute of Technology, adjunct professor; Jack Travis Architect, principal, owner, 1985-. **Orgs:** American Institute of Architects, National AIA Task Force on Civil Rights and Cultural Diversity, 1992. **Honors/Awds:** Entrepreneurship Award; Howard University, Leadership in Architecture Citation, 1992; Passive Systems Division, American Section of the International Solar Energy Society, Residential Merit Award, 1982. **Special Achievements:** Architectural consultant to Wesley Snipes in ''Jungle Fever,'' 1991; author, African American Architects: In Current Practice, Princeton Architectural Press, 1991. **Business Addr:** Principal, JTA, Jack Travis Architect, 103 E 125th St, Ste 1102, New York, NY 10035, (212)987-8300.

TRAVIS, MYRON
Law enforcement officer. **Personal:** Born Nov 16, 1963, Detroit, MI; son of Louise Barnhill Travis and Joshua Travis Sr; married Mary Reed Travis, Nov 14, 1988; children: Renell LeRon, Shae Lekarroll. **Educ:** Madonna Univ, Livonia, MI. **Career:** City of Detroit, Detroit, MI, police officer, 1985-. **Orgs:** Member, Detroit Police Officers Association, 1985-; member, Fraternal Order of Police Officers, 1985-. **Honors/Awds:** Graduate of Detroit Metropolitan Police Academy, 1986; Officer of the Month, Detroit Police Department, 1988; Officer of the Year, Detroit Police Department, 1988; Decorated Lifesaving Medal, Detroit Police Department, 1988; Decorated Commendation Ribbon, Detroit Police Department, 1990. **Military Serv:** US Marines, E-4, 1981-84; Good Conduct Medal. **Home Addr:** 15872 Monte Vista, Detroit, MI 48238.

TRAYLOR, ELEANOR W.
Educator. **Educ:** Spelman College, BA; Atlanta University, MA; Catholic University, PhD. **Career:** Department of Agriculture, Graduate School, English Department, chairperson, 1966-67; Howard University, College of Fine Arts, adjunct professor, drama, 1968-75; Hobart & William Smith Colleges, The Melvin Hill Professorship Chair, 1979; Cornell University, visiting professor, literature, 1979-80; Tougaloo College, visiting humanist, 1982; Montgomery College, professor, English, 1965-90; Howard University, professor, English, Humanities Department, chair, 1990-93, chair, Dept of English, 1993-. **Orgs:** The Larry Neal Cultural Series, designer, project director, 1984; Educators for the Advancement of American Literature in Public Schools, founder, 1984; College Language Association; Modern Language Association; Afro-American Museum Association, evaluator; The Smithsonian Institution, Program in Black American Culture, script writer; National Council of Teachers of English; National Endowment for the Humanities, panelist. **Honors/Awds:** Midwest African-American Theatre Alliance, The Hazel Joan Bryant Recognition Award, 1987; Peoples Congregational Church, The Black History Achievement Award for contributions to the advancement & preservation of African-American Literature, 1989; Catholic University, The Alumni Achievement Award, Literary criticism, 1989; The Marcus Garvey Memorial Foundation, The Larry Neal-Georgia Douglas Johnson Award, literature and community service, 1989. **Special Achievements:** Author, College Reading Skills, Random House, 1966; The Dream Awake: A Multi-Media Production, 1968; The Humanities and Afro-American Literature Tradition, 1988; Broad Sympathy: The Howard University Oral Tradition Reader, Simon and Schuster, 1996. **Business Addr:** Professor, Howard University, Department of English, Locke Hall, Rm 248, 2400 6th St NW, Washington, DC 20059.

TRAYLOR, HORACE JEROME
Educator, foundation administrator. **Personal:** Born Mar 15, 1931, LaGrange, GA; married Theola Dennis; children: Sheryl Lynn, Linda Gail, Yohanna Faye, Chequeta Renee, Tonya Yvonne. **Educ:** Zion Coll, AB 1953; Gammon Theolo Sem, BD 1958; Univ of TN Chattanooga, MEd 1965; Univ Miami, PhD 1978. **Career:** Chattanooga City Coll, pres 1964-69; Univ of TN, spec asst chancellor 1969-71; Miami-Dade Comm Coll, dean, Open Col 1971-74, pres develop 1974-79, vice pres, institutional advancement, 1980-. **Orgs:** Treas Leadership Inst Comm Develop Wash DC 1969-73; mem fndng bd dir United Bank of Chattanooga 1971-; adv bd United Bank of Chattanooga 1971; treas Counc on Black Am Affairs-Am Assn Com & Jr Coll 1974-; adv com Inst for the Study of Educ Policy Howard Univ 1967-; Miami-Dade Community College Foundation Inc, president, 1985-. **Honors/Awds:** Smith-Taylor Award for Excellence in Journalism 1958; Outstanding Young Man of Yr Award Natl Jaycees 1965; Ambassador Good Will Human Relations Counc Chattanooga 1969. **Business Addr:** Vice Pres, Institutional Advancement, Miami-Dade Comm College, Dist Adm, 300 NE 2nd Ave, Miami, FL 33132.

TRAYLOR, KEITH
Professional football player. **Personal:** Born Sep 3, 1969, Little Rock, AR; married Krista; children: Brandon. **Educ:** Central Oklahoma. **Career:** Denver Broncos, defensive tackle, 1991-92, 1997-; Green Bay Packers, 1993; Kansas City Chiefs, 1995-96. **Business Addr:** Professional Football Player, Denver Broncos, 13655 Broncos Pkwy, Englewood, CO 80112, (303)649-9000.

TREADWELL, DAVID MERRILL
Journalist. **Personal:** Born Feb 21, 1940, Dayton, OH; son of Euretta Merrill Moore Boyce (deceased) and Timothy D Treadwell Sr (deceased); divorced. **Educ:** Ohio State Univ, BA English 1964, MA Journalism 1974. **Career:** US Bureau of Land Mgmt, public relations specialist 1969-70; Ohio State Univ, asst dir intl programs 1970-73; Associated Press, reporter 1974-80; Los Angeles Times, Washington correspondent 1980-85, Atlanta bureau chief, New York Bureau correspondent 1989-93; Kean University, assistant professor of English and journalism, 1994-. **Orgs:** Mem Kappa Alpha Psi; Natl Assn of Black Journalists; Assn for Education in Journalism and Mass Communications; Natl Council of Teachers of English; New Jersey College English Assn. **Honors/Awds:** Sloan Found Fellowship in Economics Journalism Princeton Univ 1979-80. **Military Serv:**

USN lt 1964-69. **Business Addr:** Asst Professor of English and Journalism, Kean University, 305E Willis Hall, 1000 Morris Avenue, Union, NJ 07083, (908)629-7172.

TREADWELL, FAY RENE LAVERN
Music manager. **Personal:** Born May 9, 1935, Okolona, AR; daughter of Rev & Mrs James Johnson; widowed; children: Tina. **Educ:** AR Baptist Coll, AA; LA St Coll. **Career:** Drifters Inc, pres singing group that performs all over the world. **Orgs:** Life mem, NAACP; mem Personal Mgrs United Kingdom. **Business Addr:** Manager, 130 Engle St, Englewood, NJ 07631.

TREES, CANDICE D.
Government official. **Personal:** Born Jul 18, 1953, Springfield, IL; daughter of Peggie D Neal Senor and Clarence L Senor; married John F Trees; children: Peggi, Jessi, Johanna. **Educ:** Sangamon State Univ, BA 1981. **Career:** Town & Country Bank, teller 1976-77; State of IL Office of Gov, exec correspondent 1977-79; City of Springfield, city clerk 1979-86; Circuit Court of Sangamon County, clerk 1986-. **Orgs:** Mem United Way of Sangamon County 1980-, Jr League of Springfield 1984-; program vice pres Springfield Area Arts Council 1984-; treas Municipal Clerks of IL 1984-86; vice pres Lincolnfest Inc 1984-; mem Springfield Area Labor Mgmt Comm 1984-; admin vice pres Springfield Area Arts Council 1985-; mem Jr League of Springfield 1985-; chmn of the bd HAT Construction 1986-; bd of dirs Kennerer Village Children's Home 1986; sec advisory bd Salvation Army 1987-; mem Greater Springfield Chamber of Commerce 1987-88; mem. IL Assn of Court Clerks 1986; bd mem, Mental Health Centers of Central Illinois, 1987; mem, Natl Assn of Court Managers, 1988; mem, Assn of Records Managers and Administration (ARMA) 1989. **Honors/Awds:** Registered Municipal Clerk 1981; Plaque for Outstanding Serv Springfield Urban League 1985; Certified Municipal Clerk 1986; Certificate of Appreciation US Air Force 1986; State Cochring 50th Anniversary, March of Dimes, Central Illinois Chapter 1988; Plaque for Service as President, Lincolnfest 1988. **Business Addr:** Clerk of the Circuit Court, Sangamon County, County Bldg Room 412, Springfield, IL 62701.

TREMITIERE, CHANTEL
Professional basketball player. **Personal:** Born Oct 20, 1969. **Educ:** Auburn, BA in public relations, 1991. **Career:** Auburn Univ, asst coach, 1991-92; Texas Univ, asst coach, 1992-93; Univ of Massachusetts, asst coach, 1993-96; Sacramento Monarchs, guard, 1997-. **Business Addr:** Professional Basketball Player, Sacramento Monarchs, One Sports Parkway, Sacramento, CA 95834, (916)928-3650.

TRENT, GARY DAJAUN
Professional basketball player. **Personal:** Born Sep 22, 1974, Columbus, OH. **Educ:** Ohio University. **Career:** Portland TrailBlazers, forward, 1995-98; Toronto Raptors, 1998-. **Special Achievements:** NBA, First Round Draft Pick, # 11 Pick, 1995. **Business Addr:** Professional Basketball Player, Toronto Raptors, 150 York St, Ste 110, Toronto, ON, Canada M5H 3S5, (416)214-2255.

TRENT, JAMES E.
Educational consultant (retired). **Personal:** Born Jan 14, 1936, Uniontown, PA; married Rosalie Mahaley; children: Jamie, Kelly, Jill. **Educ:** Wayne State Univ, BS Bus Ad 1957; Univ Detroit, MBA 1965. **Career:** Chrysler Realty, vice pres comm opers 1970-79; City of Detroit Mayor's Office, exec asst productivity 1979-80; Chrysler Learning, vice pres govt training 1980-86; Chrysler Motors, educ consultant 1986-. **Orgs:** Polemarch Kappa Alpha Psi Detroit Alumni 1977-83; dir/secty Metro Detroit Youth Foundation 1978-95; pres Detroit Assn of Black Organ 1985-; pres Detroit Black Inter-Greek Council 1985-88; dir Univ of Detroit Black Alumni 1986-90. **Honors/Awds:** Roy Wilkins Awd Detroit Assn Black Organ 1985. **Military Serv:** AUS sgt e-5 1959-60. **Home Addr:** 5366 Briarcliff Knoll, West Bloomfield, MI 48322.

TRENT, JAY LESTER
Telephone co. manager (retired). **Personal:** Born Jan 27, 1940, Uniontown, PA; children: Vincent S, Michael J, Shane J. **Educ:** Electronic Computer Prgmng Inst, attnded 1966; Wayne St U, BS 1977; Univ of MI, public utilities exec progrm 1980; MI St Univ, MBA 1985. **Career:** MI Bell Telephone Co, analyst comp progmmng 1966-68, syst analyst comp progmmng 1968-70, sr syst analyst syst design 1970-74, staff supr person assessment 1974-76, dist data syst mgr 1976-90. **Orgs:** Mem fund raiser Univ of Detroit Titan Club 1976-78; bud consult Jr Achvmnt 1978-; Governor's Exec Corps 1985-86; MSU advanced mngmnt program; MBT minority advisory panel; NAACP; Detroit Friends of Morehouse College. **Honors/Awds:** Michigan Technological University, Martin Luther King Jr/Rosa Parks Visiting Lecturer's Fellowship, 1986. **Military Serv:** AUS specialist 5th 1962-65. **Home Addr:** 20400 Manor, Detroit, MI 48221.

TRENT, JOHN SPENCER
Electron microscopist. **Personal:** Born Feb 16, 1950, Pittsburgh, PA; son of Addie Rebecca Beaton Trent and John Peyton Trent; married Jacquelynn A Williams Trent, Mar 23, 1974; children: Joshua John, Mikah James, Bethany Spencer. **Educ:** Pennsylvania State University, University Park, PA, BS, polymer sci, 1974; Case Western Reserve University, Cleveland, OH, MSE, macromolecular science, 1979; Rutgers, The State Univ of New Jersey, Piscataway, NJ, MPhil, mechanics & material science, 1982, PhD, mechanics & material science, 1983. **Career:** Dow Chemical Co, Midland, MI, research chemist, 1974-76, consultant, 1976-79; Bell Laboratories, Murray Hill, NJ, consultant, summer, visiting professor, 1984; Pennsylvania State University, University Park, PA, assistant professor, 1983-86; Rohm & Haas Co, Spring House, PA, summer, 1985; General Electric Plastics, Mount Vernon, IN, lead polymer scientist, microscopist, 1986-. **Orgs:** Member, Electron Microscopy Society of America, 1986-; member, American Chemical Society, 1977-87; member, American Physical Society, 1977-87; member, Sigma Xi, The Scientific Research Society, 1982-. **Honors/Awds:** Discovered Ruthenium Telraoxide as a staining agent for polymers in the transmission electron microscope, which lead to revitalization of polymer microscopy, Rutgers Univ, 1980; Nominated Technologist of the Year, GE Plastics, 1989 Technologist of the Month Award, Nov 1988; Received Minority Research Initiation MRI Award, Pennsylvania State University, NSF, 1983-86.

TRENT, MARCIA M. (MARCIA M. MILLER)
Librarian. **Personal:** Born Sep 3, 1948, East Chicago, IL; daughter of Birdie J Glass Martin and Alvin G Martin; married Arlis E Trent Jr, Oct 31, 1987; children: Arlis Trent III, Ajana J Miller, Calvin L Miller. **Educ:** Calumet College, Whiting, IN, BS, 1972; Indiana University, Bloomington, IN, MLS, 1973; University of Ghana, summer institute; Alabama State University, Montgomery, AL, 1982. **Career:** East Chicago Public Library, East Chicago, IN, children librarian, 1971-72; Alabama State University, Montgomery, AL, librarian/instructor, 1973-84; Hammond Public Library, Hammond, IN, asst dir, 1984-89; Indiana University/NW, Gary, IN, adjunct faculty, 1985; NW Indiana Area Library Authority, Indiana, consultant, 1985; Kansas Public Library, Kansas City, MO, loan service coord, 1989-. **Orgs:** Board member, Altrusa Club of Kansas, 1990-; board member, Theatre for Young America, 1990; member, American Library Assn, 1983-; member, ALA/Black Caucus, 1983. **Honors/Awds:** US Office of Education Fellowship Study Award, 1973. **Business Addr:** Loan Services Coordinator, Kansas City Public Library, 311 E 12th St, Kansas City, MO 64106.

TRENT, RICHARD DARRELL
Educational administrator. **Personal:** Born Nov 23, 1925, Detroit, MI; married Cynthia Ganger; children: Giselle, Stephen, Bradley. **Educ:** MI St Univ E Lansing, AB Psychology 1950; Tchrs Coll Columbia Univ NY, MA Devel Psychology 1951; Tchrs Coll Columbia Univ NY, EdD Social Psycholoigy 1953;K. **Career:** Medgar Evers Coll of City Univ of NY, pres 1970-; Brooklyn Coll of City Univ of NY, assoc prof dept of educ 1965-69; Natl Inst of Health & Med Research Ghana Academy of Sci Accra Ghana, research off 1965-69; Puerto Rico Inst of Psychiatry Bayamon Puerto Rico, dir of research 1957-61; NY State Training School for Boys Warwick NY, staff psychologist 1954-57; City Coll of City Univ of NY, lect in educ psychology 1952-54; Youth House NY, boys supr 1950-52. **Orgs:** Bd of dir NY Urban Leag 1969-71; appointed educ chmn Brooklyn Bicentennial Commn 1974; bd of dir Brooklyn Rotary Club 1975; mem Nat Assn for Equal Opportunity in Higher Educ Wash DC 1976; mem exec com Coll Pub Agency Counc of US Civil Serv Commn 1977; mem Research Found Exec Com City Univ of NY 1978; bd of dir Counc for Higher Educ Inst of NY 1978; mem Com on Research & Liaison of Am Assn fo St Coll & Univ 1979; appointed master Fed Ct for Educ Issues So Dist US Fed Ct 1969; mgr ed ''Afro-Am Studies'' 1969-74; asso Danforth Found Asso Prog 1969-70; external examiner in psychology Univ of Lagos Lagos Nigeria 1973, 74, 80. **Honors/Awds:** Mem blue key scholastic hon soc MI St Univ 1949; man of yr Brooklyn Club of Nat Assn of Bus & Professional Women's Club 1972; educ awd Intl Inc Brooklyn NY 1973; cit for outstnd educ & civic contrbns Pres of Borough of Brooklyn 1973; awd for outsnd conrbrns Nat Conf of Christ & Jews 1974; The Reciprocal Impacl of the Brown Decision of Higher Edn; The Plignt of the Urban Coll & Minority Students; A Study of Pictorial Proj among Ghanians; A Study of Self-Concepts of Ghanian Children; The Sibling Rel in Group Psychotherapy for Puerto Rican Schizophrenics; Three Basic Themes in Mexican & Puerto Rican Family Values; The Expressed Values fo Inst Delinqueng Boys; The color of the Investigator as a Variable in Exptl Research with Negro Subject;num others pubs. **Military Serv:** AUS 1st lt 1944-47. **Business Addr:** University of NY, 1150 Carroll St, Brooklyn, NY 11225.

TRESCOTT, JACQUELINE ELAINE
Journalist. **Personal:** Born Jan 2, 1947, Jersey City, NJ; married Edward M Darden; children: Douglass. **Educ:** St Bonaventure Univ, BS 1968. **Career:** The Washington Star, reporter 1970-75; The Washington Post, reporter 1975-. **Orgs:** Mem Natl Assoc of Black Journalists; faculty Summer Program for Minority Journalists 1978-. **Business Addr:** Reporter, Washington Post, 1150 15th St NW, Washington, DC 20071.

TRESVANT, JOHN BERNARD (TRES)
Construction company executive. **Personal:** Born Nov 6, 1938, Washington, DC; son of Esther Staley Tresvant and Hammie Tresvant; married Ginny Ann Billington; children: Raquel, Sean Christopher, Kendra Ann. **Educ:** Seattle U, BA 1965. **Career:** Tresvant Construction Company, owner, 1983-; Gen Tel & Electronics, sr communications 1977-83; Shoreline Comm Coll, basketball coach 1977-78; Nat Basketball Assn, professional basketball player 1965-74. **Orgs:** Basketball coach Kirkland Boys & Girls Club 1978-80; basketball coach PAC Asian Basketball Leag Women 1980. **Honors/Awds:** Names most valuable player basketball jr & sr Seattle Univ 1963-64; outstnd athlete pro basketball Epicureans Inc 1971; oustnd youth promotion Tri-State Assn of Elks 1971. **Military Serv:** USAF airman 1st class 1958-60.

TRESVANT, RALPH
Vocalist. **Career:** Member of the musical group ''New Edition''; solo artist, currently. **Special Achievements:** Albums: ''Ralph Tresvant,'' 1990; ''It's Goin' Down''; appeared on soundtrack for the movie ''Mo' Money''. **Business Addr:** Vocalist, It's Goin Down, c/o MCA Records, 70 Universal City Plaza, Universal City, CA 91608, (818)777-4000.

TRIBBETT, CHARLES A., III
Company executive. **Personal:** Born Oct 25, 1955, Louisiana; married Lisa; children: Jason, Charles, Jillian. **Educ:** Marquette Univ, BA, 1976; Univ of VA, JD, 1980. **Career:** Russell Reynolds Assocs Inc, managing dir, currently. **Honors/Awds:** Phi Beta Kappa, 1976.

TRIBBLE, HUERTA CASSIUS
Government official. **Personal:** Born Sep 15, 1939, Terre Haute, IN; children: Huerta Lee, Steven Harold, Kevin Eugene. **Educ:** IN State U, AB 1961. **Career:** PR Mallory, pr ma eng 1966-69; Indpl Urban League Inc, proj dir asst dist 1969-81; US Small Bus Admn, dir 1983-. **Orgs:** Mem IN Mnrty Splr Dev Cncl 1983-85; trst Martin Cntr Clg 1984-85; crdntr IN Mnrty Bus Oprtnty Cncl 1983-85. **Home Addr:** 3710 N Meridian St #606, #606, Indianapolis, IN 46208.

TRIBBLE, ISRAEL, JR.
Educational administrator. **Personal:** Born Sep 4, 1940, Philadelphia, PA; son of Fannie Louise Thomas and Israel Tribble; divorced; children: Ahsha, Aiyisha. **Educ:** Montclair State Univ, Upper Montclair, NJ, BA, 1958-62; California State University, Hayward, CA, MS, 1970-72; Stanford University, Stanford, CA, MA, 1972-76; Stanford University, Stanford, CA, EdD, 1972-76. **Career:** Bethune-Cookman College, Daytona Beach, FL, provost, 1977-78; Edward Waters College, Jacksonville, FL, vice pres & dean of academic affairs, 1978-80; US Department of Education, Washington, DC, special asst of secretary, 1980-81; Department of Defense, Washington, DC, director of voluntary education, 1981-82; Board of Regents, SUS of FL, Tallahassee, FL, assoc vice chancellor, 1982-84; The Florida Education Fund, Tampa, FL, president & CEO, 1984-. **Orgs:** Sigma Pi Phi Fraternity; Education Advisory Committee, National Urban League; Greater Tampa Chamber of Commercc, chmn; bd of trustees, Univ of Tampa; Board of Directors, NCNB Bank of Florida; Tampa Bay Male Club. **Honors/Awds:** Honorary Doctorate, Montclair State Univ, 1992; Rockefeller Internship for Leadership Development, 1973-74; Carnegie Internship with Carnegie Council on Policy Studies in Higher Education, 1974-75; Marcus A Foster Award for Outstanding Service to the Institute, 1977; US Department of Education Cash Award, 1981. **Military Serv:** Army, Captain, 1964-67, Army Commendation Medal for Meritorious Service. **Business Addr:** President & CEO, Florida Education Fund, 201 E Kennedy Blvd, Ste 1525, Tampa, FL 33602.

TRIBBLE, KEITH
Sports administrator. **Career:** Univ of Nevada, Las Vegas, assoc athletic dir, currently. **Orgs:** Orange Bowl, Miami, executive dir, 1993-; Blockbuster Bowl, managing dir. **Special Achievements:** First African-American exec dir of a major bowl game (Orange Bowl), 1993. **Business Phone:** (702)895-3011.

TRICE, JESSIE COLLINS
Health services administrator. **Personal:** Born Dec 26, 1929, Baxley, GA; daughter of Hattie Eunice Peterkin Collins and Herbert Collins; married James Harold Trice (deceased); children: Bradford, Valencia Batiste. **Educ:** Grady Memorial Hosp, RN diploma 1950; Univ of MI, Certificate 1960, M Public Health Admin 1975; Univ of Miami, B Public Health Nursing 1965. **Career:** Dade Co Dept Public Health, public health nurse 1961-67; Dade Co Dept Public Health Children/Youth Project, asst county nursing dir 1967-70; Dade Co Dept Public Health, public health nurse supervisor II 1970-74, chief nursing serv 1975-80; Vstg Nurses Assoc Inc, exec dir 1975-78; Family Health Ctr Inc, chief exec officer 1980-. **Orgs:** Mem NAACP 1972-; chairperson FL Public Health Assoc 1978-79; pres FL Council Primary Care Ctrs 1984-85; pres Southeast Hlth Care Consortium 1985-86; chairperson FL State Bd of Nursing 1985-; bd of dirs Urban League of Greater Miami 1985-; mem Forum Minority Professional Assoc; mem/founder Black

Nurses Assoc; secretary, 1988-89, vice president, 1988-, Florida Association of Community Health Centers, Inc; chairperson, 1987-89, board of directors, 1990-, chairperson, National Association of Community Health Center, 1990-; chairperson, Metro Miami Health and Human Services Committee, 1988-; member, American Public Health Association, 1989-. **Honors/Awds:** Florida Nurse of the Year, Florida Nurses Association, 1984; Proclamation, Jessie Trice Day, Metro-Dade County Commission, 1984; John Gilbert Award, National Association of Community Health Centers, 1989; Citizen of Year for Outstanding Service, Omega Psi Phi Fraternity, 1989; Dedication of Jessie Trice Blvd, Metro-Dade County Commission, 1994. **Home Addr:** 18730 NW 8th Ave, Miami, FL 33169.

TRICE, JUNIPER YATES
Educator, clergyman. **Personal:** Born Aug 10, 1921, Verona, MS; married Detris Delois Scales; children: Juniper Olyen, Harriman Robert. **Educ:** AB 1942; BTh 1950; DD 1958; MEd 1961; spl degree in adminstrn 1972. **Career:** Hall's Chapel New Albany MS, pastor City Rd Corinth MS; Naylor Chapel Pontotoc MS; Aberdeen Dist, presided; Jennings Temple Greenwood MS, Pastor; The Greenwood Dist, presided; Booneville Sch, prin; Carter HS Tishomingo MS; E HS Fulton MS; W Bolivar HS Rosedale MS; Rosedale MS Sch, asst supt; City of Rosedale, mayor. **Orgs:** Mem Selective Serv Bd Bolivar Co; mem City Coun; mem bd dir S Delta Plng & Devel Dist Inc; mem exec bd Delta Area Coun BSA; mem bd trst MS Indsl Coll; presiding elder Christ Meth Epis Ch; mem Hwy Com Delta Coun; mem MS Tchr Assn; Nat Educ Assn; 32 degree Mason; sec MS Educ FinCommin; mem So Regl Educ Bd; mem MS Adult Educ Assn; exec dir Bolivar Cncl on Aging; bd of dir First Ntl Bank of Rosedale; bd of trustees BolivarCty HOsp; mem MS Employment Security Cncl. **Honors/Awds:** Listed in Outstnd Person of The S 1971; Leader of Am Sec Educ 1972; BSA awd for outstnd serv 1970; silv beaver awd Ousts Serv Yht of the Delta 1977. **Home Addr:** PO Box 819, Rosedale, MS 38769.

TRICE, TRENA
Professional basketball player. **Personal:** Born Aug 4, 1965; children: Kiana. **Educ:** North Carolina State, bachelor's degree in speech communications. **Career:** New York Liberty, forward-center, 1997-. **Business Addr:** Professional Basketball Player, New York Liberty, Two Penn Plaza, New York, NY 10121, (212)564-9622.

TRICE, WILLIAM B.
Dentist. **Personal:** Born Jan 28, 1924, Newton, GA; married Mildred Moore; children: Sheila T Bell, Angela M. **Educ:** Univ Pittsburgh, BS 1951; DMD 1953. **Career:** Private practice, dentist; Hamot Hospital, staff; Erie Univ Pittsburgh School of Dentistry, coord continuing educ; Univ of Pittsburgh School of Dental Med, lectr. **Orgs:** Mem Amer & Natl Dental Assns; Pierre Fauchard Acad; Federation Dentaire Internationale; Intl Assn for Dental Research; Amer Assn for Dental Research; Acad Gen Dentistry; Amer Acad Dental Electrosurgery; Alpha Phi Alpha; Rotary; pres Am Heart Assn; Knights Columbus; trustee Stoneleigh-Burnham School Fellow Amer Coll Dentists; Intl Dental Assn. **Military Serv:** USN 1946. **Business Addr:** 275 Professional Blvd, Erie, PA 16501.

TRICHE, ARTHUR, JR.
Public relations executive. **Personal:** Born Aug 16, 1961, Mound Bayou, MS; son of Beatrice Anderson Triche and Arthur Triche Sr; married Velma Slack Triche, Aug 16, 1986; children: Brandon Arthur. **Career:** Tulane University, New Orleans, LA, asst sports information director, 1983-86; Louisiana State University, Baton Rouge, La, asst sports information director, 1986-88; Detroit Lions, Pontiac, MI, assistant director of public relations, 1988-89; Atlanta Hawks, Atlanta, GA, dir of public relations, 1989-. **Orgs:** Member, NBA Public Relations Directors Assn, 1989-. **Business Addr:** Director of Public Relations, Atlanta Hawks Basketball, 1 CNN Center, Suite 405, Atlanta, GA 30303.

TRIM, JOHN H.
Educator. **Personal:** Born Apr 19, 1931, Ft Worth, TX; married Earnestine Trim. **Educ:** Bishop Col, BA Social Sci; Prairie View A&M U, cert vocational indust ed. **Career:** US Air Force, 1953-57; Neiman Marcus, 1957-64; Franklin D Roosevelt HS Dallas TX, cvae coord instr mstr lvl 1964-. **Orgs:** Mem Prof Tchr Org; vice pres Assn Adv Artists & Writers; Human Interest Colum Post Tribune News 1970-; columinst Porters/Quall Ecumenical News 1975; mem deacon trst Morning Star Bapt Ch; Org orginal Dalworth Ldrshp Coun Grand Prairie TX; dir comm youth mural comm cntr. **Honors/Awds:** Wrote book of poetry on life; fine arts shows; Airman of Mo 1954; cit of Mo KNOX 1954; Serv Awd 1969; Youth Awd 1973. **Military Serv:** USAF 1953-57.

TRIMIAR, J. SINCLAIR
Dentist, educator. **Personal:** Born Dec 17, 1933, Lynchburg, VA; married Anna H; children: Stefanie, Jay. **Educ:** Howard U, BS 1960; Howard U, DDS 1964; NY U, post grad oral surgery cerpt 1968. **Career:** Harlem Hosp Cntr, oral surgery intern 1964-65; Harlem Hosp Cntr, anethesia res 1965-67; Harlem Hosp Cntr, oral surgery res 1968-69; Harlem Hosp Cntr Respiratory Therapy Serv, chief 1969; Ambulatory Anethesia Harlem Hosp Cntr, chf 1970; Infections Com Harlem Hosp Cntr, cochmn 1971-74; Harlem Hosp Sch of Respiratory Therapy, dir 1974; Harlem Hosp Cntr Dept of Oral Surgery, asst vis att; Columbia Univ Coll of Physicians & Surgeons, asst prof of clinical anesthesiology. **Orgs:** Past pres Harlem Dental Soc of Grtr NY; past pres Harlem Hosp Soc of Oral Surgeons; mem Am Dental Assn; Nat Dental Assn; First Dist Dental Soc; NY St Soc of Oral Surgeons; Am Assn for Respiratory Therapy; Am Soc of Oral Surgeons; Am Soc of Dental Anesthesiology; 1st vice pres Black Caucus of Harlem Hlth Workers; One Hundred Black Men Inc; mem Omega Psi Phi Frat. **Military Serv:** USAF 1952-56. **Business Addr:** Asst Clinical Professor, Harlem Hospital Center, 506 Lenox Ave, New York, NY 10037.

TRIPP, LUCIUS CHARLES
Physician. **Personal:** Born Nov 10, 1942, Memphis, TN; son of Dorothy Watson and Luke Tripp; married Delores Whitus, Jul 23, 1963; children: Felicia. **Educ:** Univ of Detroit, Detroit, MI, BS, 1964; Wayne State Univ Medical School, Detroit, MI, MD, 1968, neurosurgery, 1974; Univ of Michigan, Ann Arbor, MI, MPH, 1983; American Society of Addiction Medicine, Inc, New York, NY, 1988. **Career:** General Motors, Detroit, MI, associate medical director, 1974; General Motors, Livonia, MI, medical director, 1974-76; General Motors Proving Grounds, Milford, MI, division medical director, 1976-79; GMAD, Warren, MI, division medical director, 1979-84; Buick-Olds-Cadillac, Warren, MI, group medical director, 1984-; General Motors, Warren, MI, regional medical director, 1988-. **Orgs:** Executive board member, Boy Scouts of America, 1984-; vice president, internal affairs, Detroit Historical Society, 1990; president, Detroit Occupational Physician Assn, 1990; state delegate, Michigan Occupational Medicine Assn, 1988-; public health committee chairman, Wayne County Medical Society, 1990-. **Honors/Awds:** Nathanial B. Rubinstein Humanitarian Award, Wayne State Univ Medical School, 1968; Award for Excellence in Community Service, General Motors, 1986; National Quality District Award, 1989, District Award of Merit, 1990, Boy Scouts of America; Boy Scouts, Silver Beaver Award, 1995; Honor Citation, Michigan Division, American Cancer Society, 1989-90. **Military Serv:** US Army, Major, 1968-81; reserves, currently. **Business Addr:** Medical Dir, General Motors Corp, 31 E Judson Street, Pontiac, MI 48342.

TRIPP, LUKE SAMUEL
Educator. **Personal:** Born Feb 6, 1941, Atoka, TN; son of Dorothy Tripp and Luke Tripp, Sr; married Hedy Bruyns; children: Ruth Sherman, Azania, Comrade. **Educ:** Wayne State Univ, BS 1966; Univ of MI, MA 1974, PhD 1980. **Career:** Community Skills Ctr, math/sci teacher 1972-73; Univ of MI, grad rsch dir 1977-80; Univ of IL, asst prof 1981-82; Southern IL Univ, asst prof 1982-89; St Cloud State Univ, asst professor, 1989-92, professor, 1992-. **Orgs:** Co-founder League of Revolutionary Black Workers 1969; dir political educ Natl Black Independent Political Party 1980-81; Natl Council for Black Studies 1983; IL Council for Black Studies 1983; Soc of Ethnic and Special Studies 1983; coord Southern IL Anti-Apartheid Alliance 1985-89; St Cloud State Univ, Minority Concerns Cmte, 1989-; founder, Human Rights Coalition, 1990-. **Honors/Awds:** Faculty Service Awd Black Affairs Council 1983; African Students Assn, Outstanding Contribution, 1985, Certificate for Distinguished Service, 1988, 1989; Outstanding Faculty Awd Black Affairs Council 1985; Outstanding Leadership Carbondale Black Coalition 1986; plaque, ''In Appreciation for Continuing the Struggle for Excellence,'' African-American Student Assn 1989; plaque, Upliftment of the Human Spirit, The Muslim Community of Southern Illinois, 1989; St Cloud State Univ, recipient of two certificates, 1992, Faculty/Staff Relations Committee, Distinguished Teacher Award, 1990, Human Relations Dept, Mary B Craik Award for Equality and Justice, 1990, Office of Academic Affairs, Outstanding Faculty Award, 1991; VCC, African-American Cmte, Comnty Serv Award, 1989; Kappa Delta Pi, Gamma Pi, plaque, Outstanding Work asHn Rights Activist, 1992. **Special Achievements:** Author: ''The Political Views of Black Students During the Reagan Era,'' The Black Scholar, vol 22, num 3, p 45-52, Summer 1992; ''Race Consciousness Among African-American Students, 1980's,'' The Western Journal of Black Studies, vol 15, num 3, p 150-168, Fall 1991; Black Student Activists: Transition to Middle Class Professionals, Univ Press of America, 1987. **Business Addr:** Associate Professor, Interdisciplinary Studies, St Cloud State University, 720 S 4th Ave, 355 Stewart Hall, St Cloud, MN 56301-4498.

TROTMAN, RICHARD EDWARD
Educator. **Personal:** Born Jun 22, 1942, East Orange, NJ; married Cordell Jones; children: Richard Jr, Raheem. **Educ:** Shaw Univ, BA 1960-64; Kean Coll, MA 1970-71; Rutgers Univ, 1975-78. **Career:** NJ Dept of Educ, supervisor 1973-76; Kean Coll of NJ, assoc dir EOF 1976-79; Bergen Cmmty Coll, dir EOF 1979-82; Somerset Cnty Coll, dir, Spec Educ Services 1982-. **Orgs:** Passaic Cnty Manpwr Prog, Mayors Planning Council - Paterson, NJ 1971-73; mem NJ Assn of Black Educators 1984-86; mem, Advisory Board, Central New Jersey Colleges, LD programs, 1989; Reach Program Advisory Board, New Jersey Social Service, 1989. **Honors/Awds:** Mem NAACP 1985-86, Natl Urban League 1985-86, NJ Educational Opportunity Funding Directors 1976-86; workshops relating to multi-cultural aspects of learning styles 1988-89. **Business Addr:** Dir Special Ed Services, Somerset County College, PO Box 3300, Somerville, NJ 08876.

TROTTER, ANDREW LEON
Government official. **Personal:** Born Sep 7, 1949, San Antonio, TX. **Educ:** New Mexico State Univ, BA 1972. **Career:** Human Services Dept, caseworker 1972-79, supervisor 1979-. **Orgs:** Sec Mt Olive Bapt State Con Laymen Aux 1974-; Christian educ dir BSBC 1983-; treas New Hope Bapt Dist Laymen's Assoc 1985-; treas Human Services Consortium; mem Amer Public Welfare Assoc; musician, BSBC Mt Olive Baptist State Congress; mem, El Paso Chap Gospel Music Workshop of Amer; mem NAACP; treasurer Association of Professional Supervisors NM; coordinator Mt Olive State Music Workshop; National Baptist Convention USA Inc, Laymens Department; board member, Adult Basic Education; Dona Ana Branch Comm Coll, 1985-95; bd mem, RSVP Dona Ana Cty; mem, Mesilla Valley Civitan; superintendent, church school BSBC, 1990-; vice-pres, New Hope District Congress of Christian Ed, 1997. **Honors/Awds:** Certificate of Achievement State of New Mexico 1982; Advanced Certificate Natl Congress of Christ Educ NBC USA Inc 1983; honored by: Dona Ana Branch Comm Coll, 1985; Social work dept, NMSU, 1996; State of NM, 1997; Career Tracks, 1996, 1997. **Home Addr:** 1440 North Paxton, Las Cruces, NM 88001. **Business Addr:** Eligibility Worker Supv II, Human Services Department, PO Box 1959, Las Cruces, NM 88004.

TROTTER, DECATUR WAYNE
State senator. **Personal:** Born Jan 8, 1932, Washington, DC; son of Bernice Trotter and Decatur Trotter; married LaGreta Trotter; children: Denise Glynn, Kathi Rieves. **Educ:** VA State Univ, BS 1956. **Career:** Town of Glenarden, mayor 1970-74; MD House of Delegates, delegate 1975-79; Prince George's Co Orphan's Court, judge 1982-83; MD State Senate, senator 1983-. **Orgs:** Kappa Alpha Psi Frat; former residential prog director, Bureau of Rehabilitation. **Honors/Awds:** Outstand Comm Serv Awd Combined Comm in Action 1981; Legislator of the Year Prince George's Chap of the MD Municipal League 1983; Distinguished Serv Awd MD Municipal League 1983; Outstanding Govt Achievement Kappa Alpha Psi Frat 1984; Distinguished Alumnus National Association for Equal Opportunity in Higher Education (NAFEO) 1989. **Business Addr:** Senator Dist 24, Maryland Senate, 313 James Senate Office Bldg, Annapolis, MD 21401.

TROTTER, DONNE
State senator. **Career:** Illinois State Senate, senator, leader of the Black Caucus, currently. **Business Addr:** State Senator/Black Caucus Leader, Illinois Senate, PO Box 3422, Springfield, IL 62708, (217)782-3201.

TROTTER, LLOYD G.
Electric company executive. **Educ:** Cleveland State University, BBA, 1972. **Career:** GE Electrical Distribution and Control, vice president/general manager, president/chief executive officer, 1992-. **Orgs:** Connecticut Pre-Engineering Program, governing board. **Honors/Awds:** Harlem YMCA, Black Achievers in Industry Award. **Business Addr:** Pres/CEO, GE Elec Dist Control, General Electric Co., 41 Woodford Ave, Plainville, CT 06062, (860)747-7508.

TROTTMAN, CHARLES HENRY
Educator, historian, scientist. **Personal:** Born Jul 29, 1934, Pine Bluff, AR; married Evelyn Marie Royal; children: Rodney, Jeniffer, Phyliss, Calliette, Charlette. **Educ:** AR AM&N Coll, BS 1957; Syracuse U, MS 1961; Univ of WI, PhD 1972; Tuskegee Inst, 1959-61; Univ of NC, 1969. **Career:** Jackson St Univ, assoc prof chem 1972-; Coleman HS, instr 1957-59; So Univ, asst prof chem 1961-67; AR AM & N Coll, asso prof chem 1967-69; Univ of WI, research asst 1969-72. **Orgs:** Consult Argonne Nat Lab 1974-76; dir Nat Sci Found 1977-78; mem Sigma Xi; Am Chem Soc; MS Acad of Sci; Hist of Sci Soc; MS Assn of Edutrs; AmAssn for Adv of Sci; NAACP; AAUP; Omega Psi Phi Frat; Nat Orgn for Prof Adv of Black Chem & Chem Eng; mem Nat Inst of Sci. **Honors/Awds:** Acad yr fllwshp Nat Sci Found 1960-61; Ford Found Fellow 1969-70; Sthrn Fllwshp Grant 1970-72; Nat Urban Leag Fellow 1974; Outst Edutrs of Am 1974; mem Fac Sen Jackson St Univ 1974-76; Outst Chem & Chem Eng 1976. **Military Serv:** AUS 1953-55. **Business Addr:** Dept of Chem, Jackson State Univ, Jackson, MS.

TROUP, ELLIOTT VANBRUGH
Ophthalmologist. **Personal:** Born Feb 28, 1938, Brunswick, GA; married Linda; children: Elliott Jr, Traci, Patrick. **Educ:** Fisk U, BA 1959; Meharry Med Coll, MD 1963; Univ MN, resd ophthal 1969. **Career:** Ophthalmlgst, pvt prac. **Orgs:** Mem Acad Ophthal & Otolaryn; pres St Paul Ophthal Soc 1977-78; mem Nat Med Assn; AMA; med & couns Med Prod Div 3m Co; mem Alpha Phi AlphaFrat. **Honors/Awds:** Cert Am Bd Ophthal 1971. **Military Serv:** USAF capt 1964-66. **Business Addr:** 2233 Hamline Ave N, St Paul, MN 55113.

TROUPE, CHARLES QUINCY
State representative. **Personal:** Born May 12, 1936, St Louis, MO. **Educ:** Washington Technical School; Denver University. **Career:** Democratic First Ward St Louis, committeeman; Amalgamated Transit Union, vice pres; Missouri House of Representatives, state representative, 1978-; electrical contractor, currently. **Honors/Awds:** Missouri State Employes Award for Exceptional Serv, 1980; Optimists' Comm Serv Award, 1980; Comm Serv Award, Natl Alliance of Postal and Fed Employees, 1981; Comm Serv Award, St Louis Ethical Police Assn, 1981; Child Care Award, Early Child Care Develop Corp, 1981; Comm Serv Award, Sigma Gamma Rho Inc, 1981; Humanitarian Award, Wellston Sch Dist, 1982; Outstanding and Dedicated Serv Award, Wellston Sch Dist, 1983; Outstanding Ded & Leadershp Black Leadership Assn, 1983; Outstanding Serv to the Comm, Firefighters Inst of Racial Equality, 1984; Comm Serv Award, Assn Black Collegians, 1984; Merit Award Ded Comm Serv, United Black Comm Fund, 1984; Recognition of Housing Rehab First Ward Northside Pres Com Awards, 1985; Comm Involvement Award Natl Black Child Devel Inst St Louis Affiliate19 Outstanding Leadership in the Interest of Missouri's Youth, Primary Care Cncl of Metro St Louis, 1986; Missouri Perinatal Assn Awd, 1986; Special Serv Award for Efforts in Reducing Teenage Pregnancy, Missouri Family Planning Assn, 1986. **Business Addr:** State Representative, Missouri House of Representatives, State Capitol Room 113, Jefferson City, MO 65101.

TROUPE, MARILYN KAY
Educator. **Personal:** Born Sep 30, 1945, Tulsa, OK; daughter of Lucille Andrew Troupe (deceased) and Ernest Robinson Troupe (deceased). **Educ:** Langston Univ, BA 1967; Oklahoma State Univ, MA 1976, EdD, occupational and adult education, 1993. **Career:** Oklahoma State Univ, history instructor 1981-82; CETA City of Tulsa, summer youth counselor 1980-; Tulsa Public Schools, teacher 1969-81, cosmetology instructor 1982-87; Oklahoma State Department of Vocational and Technical Education, curriculum specialist, 1987-94; Lane College, Teacher Education Program, coord, 1995-97; Kentucky Dept of Education, Teacher Education and Certification, dir, 1997-. **Orgs:** Catholic Daughters of Amer Tulsa Court; mem, Alpha Phi Alpha; mem Links Inc, Iota Lambda Sigma, Phi Delta Kappa, Theta Nu Sigma, Phi Alpha Theta, Langston Alumni, NAACP, Natl State Local Business and Professional Women's Club, Natl State Local Beauty Culturists League Inc, Amer and OK Vocational Assn, Voc & Industrial Clubs of Amer; mem, board of directors, Stillwater Chamber of Commerce 1988-94; Natl Assn of Minority Political Women 1988-89; charter mem, State and Natl Assn for the Advancement of Black American Vocational Educators; board member, Community Relations City of Stillwater, 1991-94; board member, Park and Recreation City of Stillwater, 1991-94; board member, Life Center for the Elderly, 1991-94; American Vocational Association, minority action committee; Alpha Kappa Alpha, Oklahoma State University, Theta Beta Chapter, graduate advis; Lane College Division of Liberal Studies & Education, chair, 1995-97, Womens Advisory Council, chair; Frankfort Soup Kitchen volunteer; Oklahoma Task Force, Goals for Tomorrow, Advisory Committee; American Association of University Women (AAUW). **Honors/Awds:** Woman of the Year North Tulsa Chap Business & Professional Women 1979, Zeta Phi Beta Sor 1985; policy leadership program for the Oklahoma State Dept of Votech 1988-89; Leadership Stillwater, City of Stillwater Chamber of Commerce, 1990; Soror of the Year, AKA Sorority Inc, Local Chapter, 1992-93. **Home Addr:** 1004 Excell Ct, Frankfort, KY 40601.

TROUPE, QUINCY THOMAS, JR.
Poet, educator. **Personal:** Born Jul 23, 1943, New York, NY; son of Dorothy Marshall Smith Troupe and Quincy Troupe, Sr; married Margaret Porter; children: Antoinette, Tymme, Quincy, Porter. **Educ:** Grambling College (now Grambling State University), BA, 1963; Los Angeles City College, AA, 1967. **Career:** Watts Writers Movement, Los Angeles CA, creative writing teacher, 1966-68; Shrewd Magazine, Los Angeles, associate editor, beginning 1968; University of California, Los Angeles, instructor in creative writing and black literature, 1968; Ohio University, Athens, instructor in creative writing and third world literature, 1969-72; Richmond College, Staten Island NY, instructor in third world literature, beginning 1972; Columbia University, New York NY, member of faculty of Graduate Writing Program, 1985—; poet. **Orgs:** Poetry Society of America. **Honors/Awds:** International Institute of Education grant for travel in Africa, 1972; National Endowment for the Arts award in poetry, 1978; grant from New York State Council of the Arts, 1979; American Book Award from Association of American Publishers, 1980, for Snake-back Solos: Selected Poems, 1969-1977, Reed Books, 1978; New York Foundation for the Arts fellowship in poetry, 1987. **Home Addr:** 1925 Seventh Ave, Apt 7L, New York, NY 10026. **Business Addr:** Department of Performing and Creative Arts, City University of New York, 130 Stuyvesant Place, Staten Island, NY 10301.

TROUPE-FRYE, BETTY JEAN
Elected official, nurse. **Personal:** Born Mar 8, 1935, St Louis, MO; daughter of Ruth Townsend Troupe and Phillip Jeffery Troupe; divorced; children: Armont, Mona Long Roberts, Evette Boykins. **Educ:** State Comm Coll, 1974; Tariko Coll, BS management 1988; Webter Univ, MA HRD 1988-91. **Career:** Wellston School Board, pres 1981-84; Wellston City Council, councilperson 1982-84; Wellston 1st Ward, pres; Nurse. **Orgs:** Nurse Olsten Health Svcs; mem chmn ANSCA 1982-; mem Campaign For Human Dignity 1984; mem St Louis Chapter 46 OES Prince Hall Affiliate; ACORN. **Honors/Awds:** Appreciation Noble 1982; Appreciation Women in Municipal Govt 1983; Appreciation St Louis Head Start 1983; Appreciation Enforcers Amateur Athletic Assn. **Home Addr:** 1538 Ogden Ave, St Louis, MO 63133.

TROUT, NELSON W.
Cleric, educator. **Personal:** Born Sep 29, 1920, Columbus, OH; married Jennie Foster; children: Cassandra Ellis, Paula Crosby, Philip. **Educ:** Capital U, AB 1948; Evang Theol Sem, 1952; Wartburg Coll, DD 1970. **Career:** Minority Minstry Stud Trinity Luth Sem, dir 1970-; Am Luth Ch, dir of urban evang 1968-70; Am Luth Ch, asso yth dir 1962-67; Eau Claire WI, pastor 1967-68; Los Angeles, pastor 1955-62; Montgomery, AL, pastor 1952-55. **Orgs:** Exec dir Luth Soc Serv Dayton OH 1970-75; pres Twin Cities Human Relat Assn 1962-67; vice pres Luth Human Relat Assn of Am 1969-70; pres Luth Human Relat 1971-72. **Honors/Awds:** Citatn for outst work Commn on Evang ALC 1970; citatn for outst work Bd for World Missin & Inter-Ch Cooprtn ALC 1976; recip Purple Heart AUS. **Military Serv:** AUS capt 21 yrs. **Business Addr:** 2199 E Main St, Columbus, OH 43209.

TROUTMAN, PORTER LEE, JR.
Educator. **Personal:** Born Apr 4, 1943, Newellton, LA; married Bobbie Jean Martin; children: Gregory, Portia. **Educ:** Univ NV, Ed Spec Degree; N AZ 19, MA; S Univ Baton Rouge LA, BS; No AZ U, EdD 1977. **Career:** Rec Center, dir 1965-66; SELD Program Title I, curr spec 1968; Clark Co School Dist, teacher 1966-71; Clark Co Teacher Assn, staff rep 1970-71; Dis Office of Professional Studies Univ of NV Las Vegas, prof 1974; Teacher Corps Univ NV, lecturer, assoc dir 1971-74; Teacher Corps Univ NV, asst prof, dir 1974-75. **Orgs:** Mem CCSD Task Force; Acting Pring; mem Clark Co Tchr Assn; Clark Co Sch Dist Adv Facilities Com; chrm Jo Mackey Elem Sch Adv Brd; Clark Co Tchr Assn; mem Human Relations Com; Alternate Sen Jo Mackey Elem Sch; mem NV State Ed Resolution Com; Adv Student Nat Ed Assn UNLV; delegate Nat Ed Assn Detroit delegate First Nat Cong Black Prof Higher Ed Univ TX; mem Nat Educ Assn; Knights Columbus; mem American Assn Sch Adm; American Assn Col Tchr Ed selected by AACTE Com on Perf Based Edn; one of twelve natl to receive training in C/PBE 1974; mem Kappa Delta Pi; Phi Delta Kappa Hon Soc in Edn. **Military Serv:** ROTC Southern U. **Business Addr:** Office of Professional Studies, Univ of Nevada at Las Vegas, 4505 S Maryland Parkway, Las Vegas, NV 89154.

TROWELL-HARRIS, IRENE
Military official. **Career:** Air Natl Guard, brigadier general, currently; Dept of Veteran's Affairs, Patient Care Inspection and Evaluation Div, dir, currently. **Orgs:** Aerospace Med Assn; ANA; APHA; NYSNA; Sigma Theta Tau; AMSUS. **Honors/Awds:** Distinguished Alumni Columbia Univ; Honorary Doctor of Humane Letters, Medical University of SC. **Special Achievements:** First African American woman in the 357-year history of the National Guard to achieve the rank of brigadier general; First female, minority and nurse in the 349th year history of the National Guard to command a medical clinic. **Business Addr:** Brigadier General, Air National Guard, HQ USAF/SGX, 110 Luke Ave, Ste 400, Bolling AFB, Washington, DC 20332-7050, (202)767-5054.

TRUEBLOOD, VERA J.
Product design engineer. **Personal:** Born Dec 10, 1962, Minneapolis, MN; daughter of Maurine Alexander Trueblood and Wiley Trueblood Jr. **Educ:** University of Minnesota, Minneapolis, MN, BS, mechanical engineer, 1985; University of Michigan, Ann Arbor, MI, currently. **Career:** Donaldson Mfg Co, Minneapolis, MN, product test eng, 1983-85; Chrysler Corporation, Highland Pk, MI, product quality engineer, 1985-. **Orgs:** Board member, scholarship committee, National Alumni, member Inroads/Metropolitan Detroit, Inroads, 1989-; member, board of directors, Youth Development Committee, Detroit Urban League, 1987-; member, community action committee, scholarship committee, Black MBA Association, 1989-; member, Explorer Scout Development Community Development, STRIVE, 1985-; member, Industry Ambassadors, Engineering Society of Detroit, 1986-; member, annual dinner chair, Single Minded Inc. **Honors/Awds:** Chairmans Award, Chrysler Corporation, 1989; Directors Award, Chrysler Corporation, 1988; Outstanding Young Woman of Year, 1987; Ebony Magazine, "10 Young Achievers," Johnson Publishing, August 1989. **Business Addr:** Design Engineer, Interior Trim Engineering, Chrysler Motors, PO Box 214468, Auburn Hills, MI 48326.

TRUEHEART, WILLIAM E.
Educational administrator. **Personal:** Born Jul 10, 1942, New York, NY; son of Louise Elnora Harris Trueheart and Junious Elton Trueheart; married Carol Ann Word, Jun 26, 1988. **Educ:** Univ of CT, Storrs, CT, BA, 1966; Harvard Univ-Kennedy School of Govt, Cambridge, MA, MPA, 1973; Harvard Univ-Graduate School of Education, Cambridge, MA, EdD, 1979. **Career:** Univ of CT, Storrs, CT, asst to the pres, 1969-70; Univ of CT-Coll of Liberal Arts & Sciences, Storrs, CT, asst to the dean and dir of the academic advisory ctr, 1970-72; Harvard Univ-John F Kennedy School of Govt, Cambridge, MA, asst dean & dir of the master in public admn program, 1979-83; Harvard Univ-office of Governing Boards, Cambridge, MA, assoc sec to the univ, 1983-86; Bryant Coll, Smithfield, RI, exec vice pres, 1986-89, pres, 1989-96; Harvard Univ, Graduate School of Education, visiting scholar, 1996-97. **Orgs:** Bd of dir, Public Education Fund Network, Washington, DC, 1990-; bd of dir, Providence Chamber of Commerce, 1990-; bd of dir, Nellie Mae, Inc, 1988-; bd of dir, Fleet Natl Bank, 1990-; bd of dir, Narragansett Electric, 1990-; American Institute of Certified Public Accountants; treasurer, Lifespan Inc; Narragansett Electric Company; New England Education Loan Marketing Corp; chmn, Rhode Island Independent Higher Education Assn; Rhode Island Public Expenditure Council; Woods Hole Oceanographic Institution. **Honors/Awds:** Littauer Fellow, Harvard Univ, 1973; Travelli Fellow, Charles I Travelli Foundation, 1973-79; Ford Foundation Fellow, Ford Foundation, 1974-79; ACE Fellow, American Council of Education, 1968-69; Black Alumni Assn Award of Excellence, Univ of CT, 1989; honorary doctorate, Bryant College, 1996, Johnson and Wales University, 1996. **Special Achievements:** First African American to head a four year, private college in New England; co-author, Production Function Analysis in Higher Education: General Methodology and Applications to Four Year Black Colleges, Government Printing Office, 1977; author, "The Underside of Federal Involvement with Higher Education," The Federal Purse and the Rule of Law, Univ of Notre Dame, 1983. **Business Addr:** Visiting Scholar, Harvard University, Graduate School of Education, One Waterhouse St, Ste 1, Cambridge, MA 02138-3619.

TRUITT, KEVIN
Government official. **Personal:** Born Jan 2, 1953, Chicago, IL; son of Ethel & Alfred Henry; married Karen, May 8, 1993; children: Marissa. **Educ:** Loyola Univ, BBA, 1975; DePaul Univ, MBA, 1977. **Career:** Arthur Young & Co, staff auditor, 1977-79; Baxter-Travenol, sr financial analyst, 1979-80; First Chicago, commercial banking officer, 1980-86; Harris Bank & Trust, asst vp, 1988-89; Bank Hapoalim, asst vp, 1987-88 & 1989-90; City of Chicago Dept of Revenue, deputy dir, revenue, 1991-. **Honors/Awds:** Dollar & Sense Magazine, Outstanding Bus & Professional Award, 1993; Pullman Education Foundation, Pullman Scholar, 1975. **Special Achievements:** The Money Yard Stick, Letter to the Editor, Financial World Magazine, 1990. **Business Addr:** Deputy Dir-Revenue Receivables, City of Chicago, 333 S State Street, DePaul Ctr, Rm LL-30, Chicago, IL 60604, (312)747-3780.

TRUITT, OLANDA
Professional football player. **Personal:** Born Jan 4, 1971, Bessemer, AL; married. **Educ:** Mississippi State. **Career:** Minnesota Vikings, wide receiver, 1993; Washington Redskins, 1994-95; Oakland Raiders, 1996-. **Business Addr:** Professional Football Player, Oakland Raiders, 1220 Harbor Bay Pkwy, Alameda, CA 94502, (510)615-1875.

TRUITTE, JAMES F.
Educator (retired). **Personal:** Born in Chicago. **Educ:** Horton Dance Theatre, 1948. **Career:** Teacher at numerous institutions, including: Lester Horton Dance Theatre, Clark Center for the Performing Arts, American Dance Center (Alley School), New Dance Group, Dance Theatre of Harlem, Yale University, New York University, Boston College, Brooklyn College, Natl Assn for Regional Ballet, Jacob's Pillow, Texas Christian University, and Balett Akademien in Goleborg, Sweden; Lester Horton Dance Theatre, former principal dancer; Alvin Alley American Dance Theatre, former principal dancer; Dayton Contemporary Dance Co, master teacher, artist-in-residence, 1976-; Philadanco Summer Program, 1979-; University of Cincinnati, CCM, associate professor of dance, 1970-87, professor, 1988-93, professor emeritus, 1993-. **Orgs:** Natl Foundation for Advancement in the Arts, Dance Adjudication Panel, 1984-88, Choreographic Fellowship Panel, 1991. **Honors/Awds:** John Hay Whitney Fellow, 1959-60; Corbett Award, finalist, 1979, 1987; Thelma Hill Dance Award, 10 Black Men in Dance, 1980; Ohio Arts Council, Individual Artist Perfoming, award recipient, 1981; Los Angeles Mayor Tom Bradley, personal commendation, 1985; Links Inc, Cincinnati Chapter, Bicentennial Award for Achievement in Dance, 1988; Ohio Dance Award for Sustained Achievement, 1992; University of Cincinnati, Award of Excellence for Teaching, 1992; CCM Tribunal, Ernest N. Glover Outstanding Teacher Award, 1993; CCM Alumni Association Faculty Recognition Award, 1993; Seventh General Conference of Blacks in Dance, Outstanding Achievement Award, 1994. **Special Achievements:** Arthur Todd in the New York Times acknowledged him as "the foremost exponent and teacher of the Lester Horton Technique".

TRUMBO, GEORGE WILLIAM
Judge. **Personal:** Born Sep 24, 1926, Newark, OH; son of Beatrice Trumbo and George Frank Trumbo; married Sara J Harper; children: Constance, James, Kimberlee, Karen, Adam. **Educ:** OH State Univ, BS; Case Western Reserve Law School, LLB. **Career:** Court of Common Pleas, referee 1977-82; Cleve-

land Municipal Court, judge 1982-. **Orgs:** Mem Mt Olive Baptist Church; past Sunday school teacher; past dir Jr Church of Mt Olive Baptist Church; mem Natl Bar Assn, Greater Cleveland Bar Assoc, OH Bar Assn, Cuyahoga Cty Bar Assn, Elks Lodge IBPOE of W, Kappa Alpha Psi, NAACP; bd of dir Judicial Council of the Natl Bar Assn; pres Shaker Square Kiwanis Club; pres trustee bd Cleveland Public Library 1984; chmn Task Force on the House of Corrections; past pres Northern OH Municpal Judges Assn; member, El Hasa Temple No 28; The United Supreme Council Ancient & Accepted Scottish Rite of Freemasonry. **Honors/Awds:** Cuyahoga Cty Criminal Court Bar Assn Awd 1973; Superior Judicial Service 1982, 1984, 1985. **Military Serv:** USN 1944-46.

TRUVILLION, WENDY
College track coach. **Educ:** Louisiana State University, 1987; Georgia State, master's degree in sports administration, currently. **Career:** Detroit Cheetah Track Club, co-founder; Georgia Tech University, assistant track coach, 1988-93, head track coach, 1993-. **Special Achievements:** 1985 NCAA champion who led off LSU's winning 1600-meter relay team; coached one national champion, eight all-Americans and nine ACC champions. **Business Addr:** Head Track Coach, Georgia Tech University, POB 1505, Lawrenceville, GA 30246-1505, (404)962-7580.

TUBBS, WINFRED O'NEAL
Professional football player. **Personal:** Born Sep 24, 1970, Hollywood, FL. **Educ:** Univ of Texas, bachelor's degree in psychology. **Career:** New Orleans Saints, linebacker, 1994-. **Business Addr:** Professional Football Player, New Orleans Saints, 5800 Airline Hwy, Metairie, LA 70003, (504)733-0255.

TUCKER, ANTHONY
Physician. **Personal:** Born Aug 14, 1957, New York, NY; son of Georgia O Tucker and James W Tucker. **Educ:** Harvard Univ Cambridge MA, AB 1980; Howard Univ Washington DC, MD 1985. **Career:** District of Columbia Hospital, physician 1985-86; Flushing Hospital & Medical Center, surgical resident 1986-89. **Orgs:** Mem US Chess Federation 1976-87; alumni interviewer Harvard Alumni Assn 1980-81; mem Student Natl Medical Assn 1980-85, Amer Medical Assn 1984-87, Harvard Club of NY 1980-82, Harvard Club of Washington DC 1983-85, Med Soc of the State of NY 1987-88, Queens County Med Soc 1987-88. **Honors/Awds:** Polaroid Scholarship 1980; Natl Medical Fellowship 1980-81.

TUCKER, BILLY J.
Physician. **Personal:** Born Feb 3, 1934, Magnolia, AR; married Cecelia; children: Karen, Kelly, Kimberly. **Educ:** MI St U, 1953; Wayne St U, 1958; Univ MI Med Sch, 1962. **Career:** Norfolk Chesapeake, phys adminstr 1965-; Norfolk Drug Abuse Rehab Prgm, dir 1970-72. **Orgs:** Fdr & 1st pres Tidewater Area Bus Leag 1967-; fdr Atlantic Nat Bank 1968; fdr 1st pres Grtr Norfolk Devel Com 1967; mem Norfolk Med Soc; Old Dominian Med Soc; Nat Med Soc; Chesapeake Med Soc; Am Acad Fam Prac; Tidewater Acad Fam Prac; Cong Black Caucus Braintrust on Hlth; Tdwtr Area Bus& Contrctrs Assn; Norfolk Com for Imprvmnt Edn; Tdwtr Reg Polit Assn. **Honors/Awds:** Serv award Tdwtr Area Bus Leag 1969; outst citz award Norfolk Chap Drifters Inc 1976; outst citz Chesapeake Chap Delicados Inc 1977; for vision & support Tdwtr Area Bus & Cont Assn 1977. **Military Serv:** USAF 1953-57. **Business Addr:** 490 Liberty St, Chesapeake, VA 23324.

TUCKER, C. DELORES
Newspaper executive. **Personal:** Born Oct 4, 1927, Philadelphia, PA; daughter of Rev & Mrs Whitfield Nottage; married William. **Educ:** Temple U; PA St U; Univ of PA; N Philadelphia Sch of Realty. **Career:** Secretary of State Pennsylvania 1971-77; Federation of Democratic Women, president, beginning 1977; Democratic Natl Comm Black Caucus, chmn, beginning 1984; Philadelphia Tribune, vice pres 1989-. **Orgs:** Mem Pennsylvania Board of Proprty; mem Pennsylvania Commn on Interst Coop; mem Gov Affirm Act Counc; mem Commnwlth Bd of Med Coll of PA; mem Bd of Martin Luther King Ctr for Soc Chng; mem Links Inc; mem-at-large Dem Natl Committee; vice pres Natl Assn of Sec of St; Natl Assn of Real Estate Brokers; Natl Assn of Mkt Devel; bd mem Natl Rainbow Coalition; mem Natl Org of Women; natl vice pres, NAACP Board of Trustees 1989; convening founder & vice chmn, National Political Congress of Black Women. **Honors/Awds:** Named best qual to be Ambass to UN by Nat Women's Pol Caucus & Redbook Mag; recog one of the 100 most influential black Am Ebony Mag 1972-77; nom wmn of yr Ladies Home Jour 1975-76; nom wmn of yr Natl Assn of TV & Radio Artists 1972; commun serv award Quaker City Chap B'nai Birth 1974; Emma V Kelly achvmt award Natl Elks 1971; mkt serv & achvmnt award Natl Assn Real Estate Devel 1971; OIC Achvmnt Award; NAACP Freedom Fund Award 1961, Thurgood Marshall Award, 1982; Martin Luther King Award Philadelphia Trade Unions Coun; The White Noose, Home and Housing Journal; ABC's of Charitable Giving. **Business Addr:** Chairperson, Dem Natl Comm Black Caucus, 6700 Lincoln Dr, Philadelphia, PA 19119.

TUCKER, CHRIS
Comedian/actor. **Career:** TV: Def Comedy Jam; films: House Party III, Friday, Dead Presidents. The Fifth Element, Money Talks. **Business Addr:** Comedian, United Talent Agency, 9560 Wilshire Blvd, Ste 500, Beverly Hills, CA 90212, (310)273-6700.

TUCKER, CLARENCE T.
Chemical plant manager. **Personal:** Born Feb 22, 1940, Elba, AL; son of Josephine Tucker and Samuel T Tucker; married Delores B Tucker, Nov 28, 1963; children: Reginald, Ryan. **Educ:** Alabama A&M Univ, Huntsville AL, BS; Atlanta Univ, Atlanta GA, MS. **Career:** Chattanooga Public Schools, Chattanooga TN, teacher & dept chair, 1962-65, 1966-68; Clark Coll, Atlanta GA, laboratory instructor, 1968-69; Polaroid Corp, Waltam MA, process eng to production mgr, 1969—. **Orgs:** Exec bd chmn, NOBCCUE. **Honors/Awds:** Outstanding Teacher Award, Chatanooga Science Fair Group, 1966; Outstanding Service Award, Atlanta Univ, 1984; Meritorious Service Award, NOBCCUE, 1985. **Home Addr:** 8 Longmeadow Rd, Westboro, MA 01581.

TUCKER, CYNTHIA ANNE
Journalist. **Personal:** Born Mar 13, 1955, Monroeville, AL; daughter of Mary Louise Marshall Tucker and John Abney Tucker; divorced. **Educ:** Auburn University, BA, 1976. **Career:** The Atlanta Journal, reporter, 1976-80; The Philadelphia Inquirer, reporter, 1980-82; The Atlanta Journal, editorial writer, columnist, 1983-86; The Atlanta Constitution, associate editorial page editor, 1986-91, editorial page editor, 1992-. **Orgs:** American Society of Newspaper Editors; American Red Cross, Atlanta Chapter, board of directors; Families First, board of directors. **Honors/Awds:** Harvard University, Nieman Fellow, 1988-89. **Business Addr:** Editorial Page Editor, The Atlanta Constitution, 75 Marietta St, Atlanta, GA 30303, (404)526-5084.

TUCKER, DONALD
Government official. **Personal:** Born Mar 18, 1938, Newark, NJ; married Cleopatra Gipson; children: Donna Marie, Kiburi. **Educ:** Goddard Coll VT, BA 1973. **Career:** Congress Racial Equality, fld orgnzr 1961-63; Operation Ironbound UCC, dir 1965-70; City of Newark, councilman-at-large 1974-; NJ State Assembly, 1998-. **Orgs:** Vice pres, Natl Black Leadership Roundtable 1981-; chmn, NJ Black Issues Convention 1984-; mem Natl Black Leadership Forum 1981-. **Military Serv:** USAF airman first class 1955-59. **Home Addr:** 84 Hansbury Ave, Newark, NJ 07112. **Business Addr:** Councilman at Large, City of Newark, City Hall Rm 304, 920 Broad St, Newark, NJ 07102.

TUCKER, DOROTHY M.
Educator, psychologist. **Personal:** Born Aug 22, 1942, Spartanburg, SC; daughter of Cleo Christine Fant Tucker and James Anderson Tucker. **Educ:** CA Sch of Professional Psychol, PhD 1976; OH State Univ, PhD 1972; Bowling Green U, BS; Univ Toledo, MEd. **Career:** Brentwood Public Schools & Ford Foundation, demonstration teacher & curriculum writer, 1963-65; Dept of Defense, Spangdahlem, Germany, educator, 1965-67; Wright Institute of Los Angeles, director of clinical teaching; California State Univ, Los Angeles, asst prof, 1968-69; Ohio State Univ, research associate, 1969-71; Bureau of Drug Abuse, Columbus, OH, consult psychologist, 1971; Florida International University, assistant associate prof, 1971-74; Charles Drew Medical School, associate prof, 1977-78; fld dir, Cranston For Senate Com, 1980; Office of the Speaker, California Assembly, Willie Brown Jr, special asst, 1981-84; Crenshaw Consortium, Los Angeles, CA, pres, 1984-; Saybrook Institute, San Francisco, CA, faculty, 1989-; Los Angeles Police Department, California Commission on Post, consulting organizational psychologist. **Orgs:** Western Psychol Assn; Am Psychol Assn; Assn Black Psychologists; So CA Assn Black Psychologists; Assn of Soc & Behvrl Scientists; governor, California State Bar Board of Governors, 1990-; pres, Los Angeles Building & Safety Commission, 1990-; past chair, California Board of Psychology; treasurer, Association of Black Psychologist, Southern California; vice pres, Board of Governors, State Bar of California; president, Convenor Alliance of African-American in Psychology; vice pres, Foundation of the State Bar of California; judicial council, Access of Fairness, California; past chair, Public Interest Division, California Psychological Association; executive committee, California Psychological Association; American Psychological Association, Urban Initiatives Task Force. **Honors/Awds:** First chair, Faculty Senate, FIU, 1972-74; First Chair, Florida State University Faculty Senate, 1972-74; Pi Lambda Theta Educ Hon; Natl Women's Polit Caucus; mem, Nat Orgn of Women 1975; charter mem, Black's Women's Forum, 1977; chmn exec com Forum 1979; commnr, CA Jud Nominees Evaluation Commn 1979; president, United Negro College Fund So CA Adv Bd 1980; cmmnr Inglewood Housing Commn 1980; nominee Sojourner Truth Awd 1974; Outstanding Woman, California Legislature, 1985; Women In Public Service Award, Westside Women's Clinic, 1987; California Psychological Association, Helen Mehr Public Interest Award, 1994; Silver Psy Award, 1995. **Business Addr:** President, Crenshaw Consortium, PO Box 62309, Los Angeles, CA 90062.

TUCKER, EDMUND ANDREW, SR.
Hotel manager. **Personal:** Born Dec 31, 1952, Paget, Bermuda; son of Violet and Shirley (father); divorced; children: Andresa Lynette, Edmund Andrew Jr. **Educ:** Bermuda Hotel and Catering Coll, Hotel Admin, 1970; America Hotel & Motel Assn, Hotel Admin, certified admin, 1991; Hotel Catering Institutional Mgt Assn, hotel admin, 1994. **Career:** Colonial House of Pancakes, personnel mgr, 1980-81; Sheraton Tara Hotel, Nashua, night mgr, 1981-84; ColorTech Printing, account exec, 1984-86; Sheraton Mansfield, asst general mgr, 1986-88; Nantucket Inn, general mgr, 1988-89; Hilton at Dedham Place, gen mgr, 1989-. **Orgs:** Mass Lodging Assn, board member/education chairman, 1995; SKAL Club of Boston, board member, 1995. **Honors/Awds:** American Hotel and Motel Assn, Certified Hotel Admin, 1991. **Business Addr:** Gen Mgr, Hilton at Dedham Place, 95 Dedham Pl., Dedham, MA 02026, (617)329-7900.

TUCKER, ERIC M.
County financial manager. **Personal:** Born Dec 22, 1950, Kansas City, MO; son of Shirley A East. **Educ:** Harvard Univ, BA Govt 1978; Northwestern Univ Kellogg Grad Sch of Mgmt, MM Fin 1980; DePaul Univ Grad Sch of Business, M Science Taxation 1990. **Career:** First Chicago, investment officer 1980-85; City of Washington DC, treasury expert 1986-87; The Univ of MD, mgr treasury operations, 1987-89; Prince George's County, finance dir, 1989-. **Orgs:** Pres Professional Financial Mgmt 1981-; bd mem Travellers Aid Soc 1984-86; mem NAACP, Natl Assoc of Black MBA's, Natl Aquarium Soc, Natl Forum of Black Public Administrators; Maryland Public Finance Officer's Assn; board member, Maryland Local Government Investment Trust; member, Gov't Finance Officers Assn; National Black MBA Association, DC Chapter, president, currently. **Honors/Awds:** Johnson & Johnson Leadership Awd; Harvard Club of Kansas City Scholarship.

TUCKER, GERALDINE COLEMAN (GERI)
Journalist. **Personal:** Born Mar 23, 1952, Cincinnati, OH; daughter of Marian Annamae Taylor Coleman and Robert A Coleman (deceased); married Michael Anthony Tucker, Aug 31, 1980; children: Christopher Coleman Tucker. **Educ:** Kenyon College, Gambier, OH, AB, 1970-74; Wayne State University, Detroit, MI, 1979; George Mason University, Fairfax, VA, 1985-86. **Career:** Beacon Journal, Akron, OH, reporter, 1975-79; Detroit Free Press, Detroit, MI, copy editor, 1979-82; USA Today, Arlington, VA, front page editor, special sections editor, 1982-87; Gannett News Service, Arlington, VA, managing editor/Midwest, 1987-. **Orgs:** Member, Washington Assn. of Black Journalists, 1982-; member, National Assn.of Black Journalists, 1976-. **Honors/Awds:** Fellowship, American Newspaper Publishers Assn., 1987; Fellow, Gannett Management Seminar, 1989; Fellow, US Dept. of Education/African Studies, 1981. **Home Addr:** 5906 Veranda Dr, Springfield, VA 22152. **Business Addr:** Managing editor/Midwest, Gannett News Service, Gannett Co Inc, 1000 Wilson Blvd, Arlington, VA 22229.

TUCKER, GERALDINE JENKINS
Attorney-at-law. **Personal:** Born May 3, 1948, Newark, NJ; daughter of Helen Jenkins and Richard Jenkins Sr; married; children: Carmen Alicia. **Educ:** Fisk Univ, BA 1970; Howard Univ, MS 1972; Univ of TX, JD 1986. **Career:** Howard Univ Wash DC, asst dir of admissions 1970-73; CA Sch of Professional Psych, dean for student affairs 1973-75; Hughes Aircraft Co LA, sr personnel rep 1975-77; ARA Food Servs LA, training mgr 15 states 1977-78; TX Rehab Commn Austin, civil rights specialist 1978-80; NuScope Cons, president 1980-85; Lower CO River Authority, dir human resources 1986-91. **Orgs:** Mem bd of trustees Fisk Univ Nashville 1970-74; columnist Village Newspaper Austin 1970-; western bd of adv United Negro Coll Fund 1975-77; bd of dir Austin Women's Center 1979-; mem Austin Area Urban League; mem Austin NAACP; mem Austin C of C; mem, Austin Children's Museum; pres, Howard Univ Alumni Assn 1989; member/bd of directors, Austin Area Urban League, 1990; Jack and Jill, 1989; founder, Black Manager's Network, 1990. **Honors/Awds:** Ford Fellowship for Graduate Study Ford Found 1970; Alumni Leadership Award Fisk Univ 1970. **Business Addr:** Attorney-at-Law, 7701 N Lamar, Ste 305, Austin, TX 78752, (512)458-6510.

TUCKER, HERBERT E., JR.
Justice (retired). **Personal:** Born Aug 30, 1915, Boston, MA; son of S Ella Fitzgerald Tucker and Herbert E. Tucker, Sr; married Mary Hill; children: Gwendolyn, Gretchen. **Educ:** Boston Latin Sch, Grad; Northeastern Sch of Law. **Career:** US Treas Dept IRS, dep clctr rvn agt 1943-52; Pvt Prac, 1952-; Cardozo & Tucker, former partner; Chf Finan Div Cmmnwlth MA, asst atty gen 1959-68; MA Dept Pub Utilties, commr 1969-72, chmn 1972-73; Muncpl Ct Dorchester Dist, spl justice 1973-74, prsdng jstc 1974-; Boston Coll, Boston U, Northeastern U, Wellesley Coll, Harvard U, lctr; Union Warren Savs Bank, corprtr 1969; presiding justice Edjartown District Court 1979-85; retired, 1985. **Orgs:** Grand basileus Omega Psi Phi Frat 1955-58; bd tst 1969-, exec comm, Simmons Coll 1969-; dir Nat Coun Northeastern U; TV Stn WGBH; Howard Benevolent Assn; mem num ofcs coms, num professional civ frat orgns. **Honors/Awds:** Omega man of yr awd Nat 1958, Cleveland Chap 1966; alumnus of yr Northeastern Univ Sch of Law 1971. **Home Addr:** 66 Gorham Ave, Oak Bluffs, MA 02557.

TUCKER, JAMES F.
Business education. **Personal:** Born Nov 2, 1924, Brooklyn, NY; married Caroline Hamblin; children: Kenneth, Lauren. **Educ:** Howard U, AB 1947, MA1948; Univ of PA, PhD 1957. **Career:** Fed Res Bank of Richmond, vice pres 1974-; VA Polytechnic Inst & State U, prof econ dept 1970-74; VA St Coll, pres 1968-70; US Dept of Labor, dir ofoper 1965-68; NC Cntrl U, chmn dept of econs 1962-65; WV St Coll, chmn dept of bus 1956-62. **Orgs:** Pres bd of dir VA Counc for Econ Edn; mem VA St Adv Counc on Vocat Edn; mem liason bd Nat Consumer Econs Proj; mem bd of vis VA Polytechnic Inst & St U; mem bd of trustees Howard U; mem adv bd of dir Richmond Mem Hosp. **Honors/Awds:** Auth Essentials of Econ Prentice-Hall Inc 1975; Current Econ Issues & Prblms Rand McNally 1976; Anathomy of High-Earning Minor Banks, Am Bankers Assn 1978; outst serv award VA Counc on Econ Educ 1978; various articles publ. **Military Serv:** AUS pvt 1942-45. **Business Addr:** 701 E Byrd St, Richmond, VA 23227.

TUCKER, KAREN
Legal editor. **Personal:** Born Jul 18, 1952, Washington, DC; daughter of Marie Roberson Tucker and Willie Tucker Jr. **Educ:** Trinity Coll Hartford, BA, 1974; Univ of Hartford, Grad Study Certificate, Business Admin 1979, Org Beh 1979; Antioch School of Law, Paralegal Certificate, 1983, MA, 1984. **Career:** CT General (CIGNA), supervisor of admin 1974-80; AT&T Long Lines, NJ opers supv 1980-81, NY cost support/admin mgr 1981-82; Pepper, Hamilton & Scheetz, legal editor 1984-89; Steptoe & Johnson, legal editor, 1989-. **Orgs:** 1974 Class agent Trinity Coll, 1980-85; panelist "Beyond the Degree" Trinity Coll 1980; speaker/facilitator Latham & Watkins, 1996-97; speaker/facilitator Dow, Lohnes & Albertson Seminar, 1985-; mem Trinity Club of Washington, Hobart Place Comm Block Club; second vp and board mem, National Capital Area Paralegal Association, 1991-93; affiliate mem, Natl Federation of Prarlegal Assn, Inc, 1990-; facilitator, Citechecking & Legal Research Seminar, Univ of Maryland, Alumni Paralegal Assn, 1993; bd of advisors, Paralegal Program, Marymount Univ, Arlington, VA, 1993; faculty mem, Legal Research & Writing for Paralegals, Practising Law Inst, Natl Broadcast Simulcast, 1994; founding bd mem, vp, Public Relations; executive committee, Natl Black Amer, Paralegal Assn, (NBAPA), 1994-96; editor emeritus, The NBAPA Review, 1994-. **Honors/Awds:** Class of 1916 Trophy, Trinity Coll, 1984; Steptoe & Johnson Public Service Award, 1993; Publications: Jurisoft News, 1992. **Special Achievements:** Publications: "Report on the Proposed Rules of Procedure and Evidence of the International Tribunal to Adjudicate War Crimes Committed in Former Yugoslavia;" chief editor, "Special Task Force of the ABA Section of International Law of Practice," 1995; "A Positive Life Step," Woman Engineer, spring 1992; Research & Writing, Practising Law Institute & Laurie Beth Zimet, Chapter 9; Basic Research & Writing for Legal Assistants; A Satellite Program, 1994; articles: "Organizing Basics," Washington Living, 1985; "Be Your Own Best Legal Editor," The Docket, 1986; "Getting the Word Out," The Docket, 1988. **Business Addr:** Legal Editor, Steptoe & Johnson, 1330 Connecticut Ave, Washington, DC 20036.

TUCKER, LEOTA MARIE
Business executive. **Personal:** Born Aug 1, 1944, New Haven, CT; daughter of Viola Kittrell Goodman and Curtis Saulsbury (deceased); married Robert Clifton, Jul 27, 1975; children: Ronald. **Educ:** So CT St Coll, BA 1968; Univ of New Haven, MA 1975; Union Grad Sch, PhD Psych 1977. **Career:** Tucker Associates, New Haven, CT, senior associate, 1989-; Karonee Inc Ctr for Appld Behav Sci, pres 1980-89; City of New Haven, dir of welfare 1978-80; Yale & Univ CT Mntl Hlth Ctr, dir preventn & commun educ proj 1975-78, mntl hlth adminstr 1973-75; Dixwell Crisis Prevntn Svc, proj dir 1973. **Orgs:** Bd dir United Way of Gr New Haven 1978-; bd dir ARC New Haven Chap 1979-; bd dir St Raphaels Hosp 1980; Theta Epsilon Omega Chapter, AKA; New Haven Chapter of Girl Friends Inc. **Honors/Awds:** Commun serv award Chi Omicron Chap Omega Psi Phi Frat 1978; Outst Yng Wmn Award 1978; commun serv award Mt Zion SDA Ch 1978; professional award New HavenChap of the Black Bus Professional Club 1979; Co-Winner, McGregor Award for Excellence in Applied Behavioral Science, 1979.

TUCKER, M. BELINDA
Educator, social psychologist. **Personal:** Born May 19, 1949, Washington, PA; daughter of Margaret Louise Jones Tucker Chandler and Robert Benjamin Tucker (deceased); married Russell L Stockard; children: Desmond Mosi Tucker Stockard, Daren Blake Tucker Stockard. **Educ:** Univ of Chicago, AB 1967-71; Univ of MI, MA, PhD 1971-75. **Career:** Univ of MI Inst for Social Rsch, study dir, 1975-78; UCLA, psych & biobehavioral sci dept, asst rsch psych, 1983-, psych dept, asst rsch psych, 1987, asst dir, Afro-Amer Studies, 1978-89, acting dir, Afro-Amer Studies, 1989-, associate prof of psychiatry, 1991-. **Orgs:** Mem Drug Abuse Clinical Behavioral & Psych Rsch Review Comm Natl Inst on Drug Abuse 1978-81; ed bd Amer Jrnl of Drugs & Alcohol Abuse 1980-; consult editor Psych of Women Quarterly 1986-. **Honors/Awds:** Research Scientists Devel Award. **Special Achievements:** Author: "Social Support & Coping, Appl for the Study of Female Drug Abuse" Jrnl of Social Issues 1982; "Coping & Drug Use Behavior Among Heroin Addicted Men & Women" Coping & Substance Use by W Shiffman & TA Wills 1985; "The Black Male Shortage in LA" Sociology & Social Rsch 1987; "Demographic Correlates of Relationship Status among Black Americas," Journal of Marriage ad the Family, 1989; co-author: with C Mitchell-Kernan, "Sex ratio imbalance among Afro-Americans: Conceptual and methodological issues," in Advances in Black Psychology, R L Jones, ed, vol 1, 1991; with C Mitchell-Kernan, "New trends in Black American interracial marriage: The social structure context," Journal of Marriage and the Family, 52, 209-218, 1990; with L M Chatter, R J Taylor, and E Lewis, "Developments in Research on Black Famil: A Decade Review," Journal of Marriage and the Family, 52, 993-1014, 1991; co-author: "Marriage and Romantic Involvement among aged African-Americans," Journal of Gerontology: Social Sciences, 1993; "Sex Ratio Imbalance among African-Americans: Conceptual and Methodological Issues," Advances in Black Psychology, vol 1, 1993; "Adolescence and AIDS in the Caribbean," Handbook on AIDS Prevention in the Caribbean, 1992; "Gender, Marital, Familial and Friendship Roles of Older Black Americans," Aging in Black America, 1992; Co-editor, The Decline in Marriage among African Americans: Causes, Consequences, and Policy Implications, Russell Sage Foundation, 1995; Co-Author, Interracial Dating and Marriage in Southern California, Journal of Social and Personal Relationships, 1995; Co-Author, The Meaning of Sexual Partnerships: Re-examining the Jamaican Family System, Bulletin of Eastern Caribbean Affairs, 19(4), 17-30, 1994. **Business Addr:** Professor, Psychiatry & Behavioral Sciences, UCLA, SBG Box 62, 760 Westwood Plaza, Los Angeles, CA 90024-1759.

TUCKER, MARCUS O., JR.
Judge, attorney. **Personal:** Born Nov 12, 1934, Santa Monica, CA; married Indira Hale; children: Angelique. **Educ:** Univ Southern CA, BA 1956; Howard Univ Sch Law, JD 1960. **Career:** Santa Monica, prv prctc law 1962-63, 1967-74, deputy city atty 1963-65; US Atty Ofc, asst us atty 1965-67; Cnty Los Angeles, spr ct cmsnr 1974-76; Long Beach Mncpl Ct, judge 1976-85; Los Angeles Superior Court, judge, 1985-, supervising judge, 1991, 1992, presiding judge, Juvenile Courts, 1993-94. **Orgs:** Pres John Langston Bar Assn 1972-73, Legal Aid Found LA 1977-78, Legal Aid Soc Santa Monica 1972-73; bd dir Boy Scouts Am Long Beach 1978-93, Long Beach C Of C 1979-82; pres Comm Rhbltn Inds Found. **Honors/Awds:** Judge of the Year Juvenile Dept of LA Superior Court 1986; Bernard Jefferson Jurist of the Year, John Langston Bar Assn, 1990; Constitutional Rights Foundation, Law-Related Education Award, 1992; Judge of the Year, Long Beach Bar Assn, 1993; Jurist of the Year, Juvenile Ct Bar Assn, 1997; First Annual Adoptions Conference, Judge of the Year, 1997. **Military Serv:** US Army, 1960-66. **Business Addr:** Judge, Los Angeles Superior Court-Juvenile Dept, 415 West Ocean Blvd, Long Beach, CA 90802.

TUCKER, MICHAEL ANTHONY
Professional baseball player. **Personal:** Born Jun 25, 1971, South Boston, VA. **Educ:** Longwood College. **Career:** Kansas City Royals, outfielder, 1995-96; Atlanta Braves, 1997-. **Business Addr:** Professional Baseball Player, Atlanta Braves, 521 Capitol Ave SW, Atlanta, GA 30312, (404)522-7630.

TUCKER, MICHAEL KEVIN
Attorney at law. **Personal:** Born Sep 16, 1957, Albany, NY; son of Norma G Foulkes Tucker and Carroll B Tucker; married Judith C Henry, May 15, 1989. **Educ:** Cornell University, Ithaca, NY, BS, 1979; Boston University School of Law, Boston, MA, JD, 1983. **Career:** IBM, Kingston, NY, recruiting specialist, 1979-80; Csaplar & Bok, Boston, MA, associate, 1983-88; Bingham, Dana & Gould, Boston, MA, associate, 1988-90; Ballard, Spahr, Andrews & Ingersoll, Philadelphia, PA, senior associate, 1990-. **Orgs:** Member, Alpha Phi Alpha Fraternity, 1976-; member, Philadelphia Bar Association, 1990-; member, American Bar Association, 1983-. **Business Addr:** Attorney, Bullard, Spahr, Andrews & Ingersoll, 1735 Market Street, 51st Floor, Philadelphia, PA 19103.

TUCKER, NORMA JEAN
Educator. **Personal:** Born Jan 28, 1932, Muskogee, OK; divorced. **Educ:** Langston Univ OK, BS 1953; Univ of OK, MEd 1966; Univ of CA Berkeley; CA St U; Hayward. **Career:** Douglass High Sch, teacher, 1953-56; Oakland Tech High Sch, teacher, 1962-68; Merritt College, instructor, 1968-72; N Peralta College, coord of instr, 1972, acting dean of instr, 1972, dean of instr, 1973, dean of college, 1974-75; Merritt College, Oakland CA, dean of instr, beginning 1975, pres, 1982-88; College of Alameda, Alameda CA, instructor in secretarial science and business, currently. **Orgs:** Sr vice pres bd of dirs United Way of the Bay Area; life mem Alpha Kappa Alpha Sor; past pres Alpha Nu Omega Chap Alpha Kappa Alpha Sor Inc; mem E Bay Area Club of Bus & Professional Wmn; The American Red Cross, Bay Area Chapter, vice pres, board of dirs, 1994-95; chairman, Alameda County board of dirs, American Red Cross, Bay Area, 1992-94; mem Kappa Delta Pi; mem Counc on Black Am Affairs; former mem Christian Edn Bd Park Blvd Presb Ch; chmn bd of dirs, American Red Cross, Bay Area Chap, 1996-98; western area vice dir, The Links, Inc. **Honors/Awds:** Reg Award Alpha Kappa Alpha Sor; Ida L Jackson Award Alpha Kappa Alpha Sor; Nat Nom Com Alpha Kappa Alpha Sor; selected as Outst Wmn of the E Bay, Allen Temple Bapt Ch; hon as an Outst Wmn in an Unusual Prof St Paul AME Ch; featured in February 1986 Ebony magazine Black Women College Presidents; 1986 Charter Day speaker for alma mater Langston Univ Langston, OK; several other hon & achvmnts. **Business Addr:** Instructor, Secretarial Science and Business, College of Alameda, 555 Atlantic Ave, Alameda, CA 94501.

TUCKER, O. RUTH. See Obituaries section.

TUCKER, PAUL, JR.
Engineering consultant. **Personal:** Born Jun 15, 1943, Detroit, MI; son of Frances Kinney Tucker Williams and Paul Tucker Sr; married Evelyn Virginia Reid; children: Kendrah, Kendall. **Educ:** Detroit Inst of Technology, BSCE 1971; Eastern Michigan Univ, MBA 1975. **Career:** Ayres Lewis Norris & May Inc, consulting engr 1970-76; Giffels & Assoc Inc, sr engr 1976-78; Bechtel Power Corp, civil/site sr engr 1978-79; Camp Dresser & McKee, sr engr/mgr 1979-81; English Tucker & Assoc Inc, vice pres/chief engr 1981-84; Tucker Young Jackson Tull Inc, pres/CEO 1984-. **Orgs:** Dir, Detroit Chap MI Soc of Professional Engrs 1986-89; Natl Soc of Professional Engrs; MI Water Environment Federation; Amer Soc of Civil Engrs; dir, Consulting Engrs Cncl of MI, 1990-94; dir, Soc of Amer Military Engrs, 1986-89. **Honors/Awds:** Order of the Engineer Ann Arbor MSPE 1970; Private Practice Division of Michigan Society of Professional Engineers, Outstanding Engineer Award, 1993. **Military Serv:** AUS 1st lt 3 yrs. **Business Addr:** President, Tucker Young Jackson Tull Inc, 565 E Larned St, Suite 300, Detroit, MI 48226.

TUCKER, ROBERT L.
Attorney. **Personal:** Born Feb 14, 1929, Chattanoga; married Shirley Cross; children: Terri E, Arnold. **Educ:** TN St U, BS 1951; NW Univ Sch of Law, JD 1955. **Career:** Tucker Watson Butler & Todd Attys Couns at Law Chgo, prtnr 1973-; NW Univ Sch of Law, mem of fclty; McCarty Watson & Tucker, prtnr 1971-73; Gen Couns, Metro Casualty Co Chgo, vice pres 1971-72; Equal Opport Chgo, asst reg asminstr 1968-71; Atty, pvt prac 1965-68; Metro Inter-Ins Exch, gen couns 1963-65; McCoy Ming & Leighton Chgo, mem of firm 1963-65. **Orgs:** Spl couns St of IL Commn on Human Rel 1974-; gen couns & trustee MERIT Real Est Invest Trust 1972-; gen couns & mem bd People United to Save Hum 1971-; mem Am Bar Assn; Chicago Bar Assn; Cook Co Bar Assn; Com on Cand Chicago Bar Assn; spl com on Civil Disorders; Phi Alpha Delta; Alpha Phi Alpha; Am Judicature Soc; PUSH; Chicago Urban Leag; NAACP; Bd Dir IL Div Am Civil Liberties Union; Roger Baldwin Found; Nat Assn of Comm Leg Couns. **Honors/Awds:** Citatn by Cook Co Bar Assn 1969; Richard E Westbrook Meml Award & Plaque Outst Contb to Legal Prfsn 1968; cited in 1000 Successful Blacks 1973; National Bar Association, Hall of Fame inductee, 1997. **Business Addr:** 111 W Washington St, Ste 1100, Chicago, IL 60602.

TUCKER, SAMUEL JOSEPH
Psychologist, neuropsychologist. **Personal:** Born Nov 5, 1930, Birmingham, AL; son of Lucille McGhee Tucker and Daniel Tucker; married Arlene Kelly, Jul 12, 1958; children: Samuel Jr, Sabrina, Sharon, Sterling. **Educ:** Morehouse Coll Atlanta, BA 1952; Columbia Univ NYC, MA 1956; Atlanta Univ, PhD 1969, Harvard Univ, Post Doctoral 1973. **Career:** Morehouse Coll, dean of students 1963-71; Univ of FL Gainesville, asst prof 1971-73; Edward Waters Coll Jacksonville, pres 1973-76; AL State Univ Montgomery, dean & prof 1976-78; Langston Univ OK, pres 1978; Atlanta Human Devel Center, psychologist & pres 1978-. **Orgs:** Consult Stanford Research Inst Menlo Park CA 1965-70; consult Princeton Univ 1965-70; consult Univ of MI Ann Arbor 1965-70; chap pres Alpha Phi Alpha Frat Inc 1971-73; mem Jacksonville Area Planning Bd 1973-76; bd of govs Jacksonville Area C of C 1973-76; member American Psychological Assn 1958-; member Natl Academy of Neuropsychologists 1988-. **Honors/Awds:** Travel Grant Ford Found 1967; Research Grant Danforth Found 1968; Research Grant Univ of FL 1972; pub "Action Counseling" Journal of Non-White Concerns, 1973; 40 articles on mental health issues published. **Military Serv:** AUS Spec Serv 1952-54. **Business Addr:** Clinical Psychologist and Neuropsychologist, 490 Peachtree Street N.E., Suite 358-B, Atlanta, GA 30308.

TUCKER, SHEILAH L. WHEELER
Public relations manager, account executive. **Personal:** Born Nov 18, 1951, Phoenix, AZ; daughter of Miriam Ashley Wheeler (deceased) and John William Wheeler, Sr (deceased); married Larry L Tucker (divorced 1983); children: Kristin Layne. **Educ:** University of Washington, Seattle, WA, BS, 1972. **Career:** Continental Airlines, Houston, TX, flight attendant, 1972-83; Crosson-Dannis Inc, Dallas, TX, legal assistant, 1984-87; Pro-Line Corp, Dallas, Tx, public relations director, 1987-89; S/T & Associates, Dallas, TX, PR entrepreneur, 1989-90; Advantage Marketng Group, Irving, TX, public relations manager/account exec, 1990-. **Orgs:** Member, Delta Sigma Theta Sorority, 1970-; member, Links Inc, 1989-90; member, Child Care Dallas, 1991-; member, St Philip's Community Development Committee, 1988-. **Business Addr:** Corporate Marketing, Advantage Marketing Group, 5215 N O'Connor Blvd, Suite 770, Irving, TX 75039.

TUCKER, SHERYL HILLIARD
Magazine editor, journalist. **Personal:** Born Jul 13, 1956, Passaic, NJ; daughter of Audrey & Arthur Hilliard; married Roger C Tucker III, Sep 15, 1985; children: Ara, Alexis. **Educ:** Cornell Univ, BA, 1978; Columbia Univ, Grad School of Journalism, MS, 1982. **Career:** CBS Special Interest Publications, editor, 1978-81; Tucker Hilliard Mktg Communications, exec vp, 1987-90; Black Enterprise Magazine, editor-in-chief, 1982-95; Your Company Magazine, editor, 1995-. **Orgs:** American Society of Magazine Editors, bd mem, 1993-95; National Assn of Black Journalist, 1992-, chair, Business Writers Task Force, 1994; March of Dimes National Communications Council, 1985-; Public Service Electric & Gas Co, 1990-92; President's Council of Carnell Women, 1991-; Carnell Mag, bd of dirs, 1992-; St James Preparatory School, bd mem, 1992-. **Honors/Awds:** Glamore Magazine, Top 10 Outstanding Young Working Women, 1986; YWCA Academy of Women Achievers, 1985; Unity Awards, Journalism; Magazine Week Editorial Excellence Award, 1992. **Business Addr:** Editor, Your Company Magazine, 1271 Avenue of Americas, Time-Life Bldg, New York, NY 10020, (212)522-5045.

TUCKER, WALTER RAYFORD, III
Former congressman. **Personal:** Born May 28, 1958, Compton, CA; son of Martha Tucker and Walter R Tucker; married Robin Smith Tucker. **Educ:** Princeton Univ, 1974-76; Univ of Southern California, BS, political science, 1978; Georgetown Univ Law Center, JD, 1981. **Career:** City of Compton, mayor; US House of Representatives, congressman, until 1996. **Orgs:** NAACP, life mbr; Kiwanis Club of Compton; LA County Bar Assn; South Central Bar Assn; Langston Bar Assn. **Business Addr:** Former congressman, US House of Representatives, 419 Cannon House Office Bldg, Washington, DC 20515, (202)225-7924.

TUCKER, WILBUR CAREY
Physician. **Personal:** Born Apr 3, 1943, Philadelphia, PA; son of Rose Tucker and Wilbur Tucker; married Faye; children: Maria, Caren. **Educ:** Temple U, AB 1965, MD 1972; Howard U, MS 1968. **Career:** Presbyterian Hospital, Dept of OB/GYN, Philadelphia, PA, acting chairman, 1990-91; Temple U, clncl instr 1975-80; University of Pennsylvania, Philadelphia, PA, clinical assoc prof, 1975-; Temple Univ Hosp, resd ob-gyn 1972-75; Ofc Naval Res, physio 1968; NASA, biochem 1965-68. **Orgs:** Mem Phi Rho Sigma Med Frat; Omega Psi Phi Fraternity, 1966; Sigma Pi Phio Fraternity, 1991-. **Honors/Awds:** Flw Am Coll Ob-Gyn; diplomate Am Bd Ob-Gyn. **Home Addr:** 24 Hazelhurst Dr, Voorhees, NJ 08043. **Business Addr:** Physician, 51 N 39th St, #200, Philadelphia, PA 19104, (215)387-8776.

TUCKER-ALLEN, SALLIE
Educational administrator. **Personal:** Born Jan 21, 1936, Union, SC; daughter of Elmira Phyllis Johnson Tucker and Reuben Tucker; married Charles Claybourne Allen, Jun 6, 1959; children: Charles II, John IV, Sallie Monique. **Educ:** Hampton University, BS, 1954-59; Hunter College, New York, NY, MS, 1967-68; Northwestern Univ, Evanston, IL, PhD, 1983-86. **Career:** Valparaiso Univ, Valparaiso, IN, assistant professor, 1969-72; Lewis Univ, Romeoville, IL, assistant professor, 1976-80; Univ of Illinois, Chicago, IL, lecturer, 1982-86; Bradley Univ, Peoria, IL, associate professor, 1986-88; Univ of Wisconsin, Green Bay, WI, chair, associate professor, 1989-91; Delaware State College, Department of Nursing, chair, professor, 1992-93; president, consultant, Tucker Publications Inc, 1988-; F&A Consultants, 1995-. **Orgs:** Founder, Assn of Black Nursing Faculty, Inc, 1987, treasurer, 1993-97; board member, Assn of Black Women in Higher Education, 1987-92; member, Amer Nurses' Assn, 1959-; member, National League for Nursing, 1990-. **Honors/Awds:** Sigma Theta Tau Nursing Honor Society, 1982; Role Model for Youth of Peoria, IL, 1986; Outstanding Woman Leader in Science & Medicine, YWCA, 1989; Hall of Fame, Hampton Univ School of Nursing, 1989; Hall of Fame, Hunter College, 1990; American Academy of Nursing, 1991. **Home Addr:** 5823 Queens Cove, Lisle, IL 60532, (630)969-3809. **Business Phone:** (630)969-3809.

TUCKETT, LEROY E.
Architect. **Personal:** Born May 21, 1932, New York City; son of Helen and Issac; divorced; children: Amy, Lori, Lee, Lise. **Educ:** Columbia Coll, 1950-52; Pratt Inst, BArch, 1960. **Career:** LaPierre Litchfield & Partners, 1961-64; Charles Luckman & Associates, project architect, 1964-67; Petroff & Jones Architects, associate partner, 1967-69; self-employed, LE Tuckett Architect PC, 1969-; State University of NY, architectural design instructor, 1983-86; L E CADDD Corp, president, 1986-. **Orgs:** Am Inst of Architects, corporate mbr, 1965-; National Organization of Minority Architects, charter mbr, 1972-; NY Coalition of Black Architects, vice pres, 1973-; Am Arbitration Assn, panelist, 1978-; CUNY, Bd of Higher Educ, A/E review committee, 1973-78; NAACP, Mentor Program, ACTSO, architecture judge, 1992. **Military Serv:** US Army, cpl, 1952-54. **Business Addr:** L.E. Tuckett Architect, P.C., 315 E Chapel Hill Street, Durham, NC 27704, (919)956-8387.

TUCKSON, REED V.
Educational administrator. **Career:** Charles R Drew University of Medicine and Science, president, currently. **Business Addr:** President, Charles R. Drew Univ of Med & Science, 1730 E. 118th St., Los Angeles, CA 90059, (213)563-4800.

TUDY JACKSON, JANICE
Attorney. **Personal:** Born Sep 30, 1945, New York, NY; daughter of Mildred Reid Tudy-Johnston and James Augustus Tudy, III; children: Pamela E. **Educ:** City Coll of New York, BA 1977; Univ of MI Labor/Industrial Relations, Certification 1983; Inst of Applied Mgmt & Law, Certification 1985; Cornell Univ/Baruch Coll NY, NY MS-ILR 1989; Columbia University Law School, JD 1992. **Career:** St Luke's Hosp Sch of Nursing, asst registrar 1970-74; Continental Grain Co, research asst 1975-77, personnel admin 1977-79, EEO officer 1979-80, mgr coll relations 1980-82, regional personnel mgr 1982-84, corp labor relations mgr 1984-86, asst vice pres human resources 1986-88, vice pres labor relations 1988-89; Morgan, Lewis & Bockius, attorney, 1992-. **Orgs:** Speaker/lecturer Cornell Univ, Purdue Univ, Atlanta Univ, Yale Univ, Howard Univ, Univ of IL 1979-; adv bd mem Atlanta Univ Grad Sch of Business 1979-82; panelist Women Business Owners of NY 1982,83; dir Tutorial Prog Manhattan Ctr for Science & Math 1985-; exec bd mem The EDGES Group Inc 1986-; life mem Delta Sigma Theta Inc 1986; aux mem NY City Commn on the Status of Women 1987-; board of trustees, Manhattan Country School, 1990-. **Honors/Awds:** Natl Selection for Weinberg Natl Labor Mgmt Certificate; Graphic Art/Design Continental Grain Co Annual Employee Statement 1976-81; article "ET to Denny - Bossism or Crucifixion," The Esplanade News 1983; editorial "Miscarriage of Justice," NY Amsterdam News 1985; International Human Rights Fellowship, Kenya, Columbia Law School, 1990; National YWCA Academy of Woman Achievers, National YWCA, 1989; Barbara Aronstein Black Scholarship, Columbia Law School, 1990; Harlan Fiske Stone Scholar; Charles Evans Hughes Fellow; Jane Marks Murphy Prize, Columbia Law School, 1992; Outstanding Woman Law Graduate, National Assn of Women Lawyers, 1992. **Business Addr:** Attorney-at-Law, Morgan, Lewis & Bockius, 101 Park Ave, New York, NY 10178.

TUFFIN, PAUL JONATHAN
Magistrate (retired). **Personal:** Born Sep 9, 1927, Charleston, WV; son of Nellie Carter Tuffin and Gerald D Tuffin; married Virginia L Hamilton; children: Paula A, J Brian. **Educ:** Bluefield State Coll, BS (Cum Laude) 1951; Cleveland-Marshall Law School, LLB 1956, JD 1968. **Career:** US Post Office, clerk 1952-55; Cleveland Bd of Educ, sub teacher 1952-54; IRS, revenue officer 1955-59; US Veterans Admin, adjudicator-section ch 1959-84; Cleveland Municipal Court, referee 1984-95, magistrate, 1990-95. **Orgs:** Asst supt of Sunday sch & atty for trustee bd St John AME Ch 1957-; natl parliamentarian Bluefield State Coll Natl Alumni Bd 1986-87; mem Pi Omega Pi; mem NAACP, Kappa Alpha Psi. **Honors/Awds:** Meritorious & Conspicuous Serv Military Order of the Purple Heart 1984; Citation of Appreciation The Amer Legion 1984; Outstanding Serv Awd Disabled Amer Veterans 1984; Disting Serv Awd VFW-Cleveland 1984. **Military Serv:** AUS corpl 1 1/2 yrs.

TUFON, CHRIS
Public utility executive. **Personal:** Born Sep 18, 1959; son of Scolastica Ngong and Elias Tufon; married Bernadette Ahlijah Tufon, Jun 6, 1990. **Educ:** Brigham Young University, Provo, UT, BS, 1984, MS, 1986; California State University, Fresno, CA, MS, 1988. **Career:** California State University, Fresno, CA, lecturer, 1988-89; Pacific Gas and Electric Co, Hayward, CA, marketing associate, 1989-. **Honors/Awds:** Student of the Year, Brigham Young University, 1985.

TUGGLE, DORIE C.
Human resources administrator. **Personal:** Born Mar 31, 1944, Detroit, MI; daughter of Pearl (deceased) and Frank (deceased). **Educ:** Detroit Institute of Commerce, AS, 1963; University of Michigan, attended, 1965; Penn State University, attended, 1978; UCLA, attended, 1980. **Career:** IBM Corp., marketing manager, 1977-79, equal opportunity program manager, 1979-80, regional personnel manager, 1980-82, management development manager, 1982-85, employee relations manager, 1985-87, division program manager, 1987-88; Lockheed, equal opportunity manager, 1989-. **Orgs:** Atlanta Industry Liaison Group, vice pres, board member, 1989-; South Eastern Consortium for Minorities in Engineering, board vice chair, secretary, 1989-; Alanta Merit Employment Association, chairperson, 1990-; Cobb County Urban League, advisory board, 1991-; Girls Inc, committee of 100, 1992-; NAACP, life member; Tuskegee Airmen, Alanta chapter, committee chairperson, 1992-; President's Council, Kennesaw State College, 1992-. **Honors/Awds:** City of Atlanta, Hearts for Youth Award, 1991; Dollars & Sense Magazine, African-American Woman Achievement Award, 1992; US Dept of Labor, Affirmative Action Achievements, 1990; Cobb County Girls Inc, Gift of Time Volunteer, 1992; Pee Dee Newspaper Group, Minority Recruiter Newspaper Positive Image Award, 1992. **Special Achievements:** Guest columnist, Michigan Chronicle, Detroit News, 1980, 1982; visiting lecturer, human resources management, labor relations, general management, 1980-; elected, Union Baptist Church Board of Trustees, 1986; consultant, trainer, human resources; speaker, motivational techniques. **Business Addr:** Manager, Equal Employment Opportunity, Lockheed Aeronautical Systems Co., 86 S Cobb Dr, Dept 90-43, Marietta, GA 30063-0330.

TUGGLE, JESSIE LLOYD
Professional football player. **Personal:** Born Feb 14, 1965, Spalding County, GA; married Dujuan; children: Justin, Jessica Dujuan. **Educ:** Valdosta State College, attended. **Career:** Atlanta Falcons, linebacker, 1987-. **Honors/Awds:** Pro Bowl, 1992, 1994, 1995; Atlanta Falcons, Man of the Year, 1993. **Business Addr:** Professional Football Player, Atlanta Falcons, Two Falcon Place, Suwanee, GA 30174, (404)945-1111.

TUGGLE, REGINALD
Cleric, publishing executive. **Personal:** Born Apr 9, 1947, Denver, CO; son of Mertis Jean Marie Hawkins and Otis Tuggle; married Marie R Peoples (deceased); children: Karleena Regina-Marie, Regine Perry. **Educ:** Central Phillippine Univ, 1968; Bishop College, BA Philosophy/Psych 1969; Univ of Ghana, Certificate Economics 1971; Union Theological Seminary, MDiv 1972; Yale Univ, Master Corporate Ethics 1975; Commonwealth Univ, Hon DD 1985. **Career:** Urban League of Long Island NY, exec dir 1975-79; Town of Hempstead Presiding Super, exec asst 1979-81; Memorial Presbyterian Church, pastor 1973-; Newsday Newspaper, community relations dir; Nassau Community College, college community relations dir, currently. **Orgs:** Chairperson Nassau County Health Systems Agency 1979; chairperson Nassau County Dept of Social Services 1980-81; vice pres Roosevelt Youth Bd 1983-; pres, Memorial Economic Development Corp; moderator, Long Island NY Presbytery. **Honors/Awds:** Community Serv Award, Nassau County Press Club 1975; Reginald Tuggle Day Award, Suffolk Co 1979; Outstanding Prof Serv, Roosevelt Inter-Agency Council 1979; Community Serv Award, 100 Black Men of Nassau/Suffolk 1982; recepient of Nassau County Martin Luther King Jr Humanitarian Award, 1987; invited on fact finding visit to USSR by Soviet govt, 1988; NATO, Keynote Speaker, 1996.

TUKUFU, DARRYL S.
Association executive. **Personal:** Born Jul 27, 1949, Cleveland, OH; married Myra C Tukufu; children: Ricky, Khari Ture. **Educ:** Youngstown State University, AB, 1976; University of Akron, MA, 1977, PhD, 1984. **Career:** Youngstown Urban League, deputy director, 1971-75; Youngstown Hometown Plan, acting director/EEO officer, 1975-76; University of Akron, graduate research assistant, 1976-77; City of Akron, EEO officer/labor standards enforcement officer, 1977-79; Akron-Summit Community Action Agency, mgr, 1979-80; Fair Housing Contact Service, executive director, 1980-82; University of Akron, graduate teaching assistant, 1982-84; Kent State University, visiting assistant professor, 1984-85; Volunteer & Employment Project, project director, 1985; Northeastern University, assistant professor, 1985-86; Memphis State University, assistant professor, 1986-90; LeMoyne-Owen College, assistant professor, 1990; Urban League of Portland, president/chief executive officer, 1990-93; Public Svcs Inst, exec dir; Corain County Comm Coll, Public Svcs Div, div dir, 1993-96. **Orgs:** Port of Portland, commissioner, 1991-93; Leaders Roundtable, executive committee member, 1991-93; Oregon Chapter, American Leadership Forum, fellow, 1991-; NIKE, Inc, Minority Affairs Review Board, 1991-93; Emanuel Medical Center Foundation Board, 1991-93; North/Northeast Economic Development Alliance Board, 1991-93. **Honors/Awds:** LeMoyne-Owen College, Outstanding Contributions to the African-American Community, 1990; Education Association, Appreciation, 1991; Governor Roberts Oregon Transition Team, Appreciation, 1991; Beaverton High School, Martin Luther King Day, Thank You, 1991; Youngstown, Ohio, Martin Luther King Day, Appreciation Award, 1992. **Special Achievements:** "Doctors of Love," Bev Johnson Show/WDIA, 1988-90; "Jesse Jackson & The Rainbow Coalition: Working Class Movement or Reform Politics?," Humanity & Society, May 1990; "Tukufu's Rap," copyrighted motivational rap for students, 1992; A Guide Toward the Successful Development of African-American Males, 1997. **Business Addr:** Executive Director/President, Greater Cleveland Roundtable, 1111 Chester Avenue, Ste 530, Park Plaza Bldg, Cleveland, OH 44114, (216)579-9980.

TULLER, JOHN
Cable company executive. **Personal:** Born Dec 6, 1961, New York, NY; son of Carrie Carter Tuller and Joseph Tuller; married Mary Mercer Tuller, Mar 7, 1987; children: Terence, Julien. **Educ:** New York School of Business, New York, NY, certificate, 1981; Bronx Community College, Bronx, NY, AAS, 1985; City College, New York, NY, 1988. **Career:** Bronx Community College, Bronx, NY, recruitment officer, 1983-85; Malcolm-King College, New York, NY, director of student life, 1986-87, director of financial aid, 1988-90; Paragon Cable-Manhattan, New York, NY, manager of community and government affairs, 1990-. **Orgs:** Board of directors, East Manhattan Chamber of Commerce, 1990; member, Corporate Volunteers, 1990; member, ROCK Foundation, 1990; alternate board member, Harlem YMCA, 1990; alternate member, Cable Telecommunications Association of New York, 1990. **Honors/**

Awds: Distinguish Award, Bronx borough president; The Sidney Silverman Award, Bronx Community College. **Business Addr:** Manager of Community and Government Affairs, Paragon Cable Manhattan, 5120 Broadway, New York, NY 10034.

TUNIE, TAMARA
Actress. **Personal:** Born Mar 14, 1959, McKeesport, PA; daughter of Evelyn Hawkins Tunie and James W Tunie; divorced. **Educ:** Carnegie-Mellon University, BFA. **Career:** Television: "As the World Turns," "Tribeca," "Spenser For Hire"; films: "Rising Sun," "Wall Street," "Bloodhound of Broadway;" Broadway: "Lena Horne," "Oh Kay," "Sweet Lorraine". **Business Addr:** Actress, As the World Turns, CBS-TV Inc, 524 W 57th St, Ste 5330, New York, NY 10019, (212)975-5781.

TUNLEY, NAOMI LOUISE
Nurse (retired). **Personal:** Born Jan 10, 1936, Henryetta, OK; daughter of Ludia B Franklin (deceased) and Alexander Tunley. **Educ:** Dillard U, BS Nurs Ed 1958; Univ of MO, KC, MA Sociology 1974; Univ Iowa 1966-67. **Career:** VA Hosp, staff nurse in service Ed; Okla City VA Hosp, assoc chf nurs serv 1958-65; Iowa Luth Hosp, Des Moines, med & Surg instr 1965-66; Mercy Hosp Iowa City, IA, emerg rm chrg nurs 1966; VA Hosp, KC, assoc chf nurs serv, chrg Nurs, psychiatric unit, staff nurs, ins instr 1967-77, head nurs; patient care surgical coord 1977; VA Medical Center, Kansas City, MO, nurse manager, 1977-94. **Orgs:** Natl Honor Soc of Nurs; Amer Red Cross; Amer Sociological Assn; Big Sisters Org Am; Iowa Nurs Assn Instr Home Nurs; Amer Red Cross; March Dimes; Muscular Dystrophy Assn; Mo Tchr Religious Ed, Faith Mission Ch; trustee, National Council on Alcoholism and Drug Abuse, 1985-. **Honors/Awds:** KC, Mo Natl Honor Soc 1953-54; State Honor Soc, 1953-54; 4 yr Scholarship, EK Gaylor Philanthropist; First Black to hold position as Assoc Chief of Nurs Serv, Okla City First Black to hold position as Medi-surgi Instr, Des Moines. **Home Addr:** 3120 Poplar, Kansas City, MO 64128.

TUNSIL, NECOLE
Professional basketball player. **Personal:** Born Aug 22, 1970. **Educ:** Univ of Iowa. **Career:** Long Beach Stingrays, forward, 1997-. **Business Addr:** Professional Basketball Player, Long Beach Stingrays, One World Trade Center, Ste 202, Long Beach, CA 90831-0202, (562)951-7297.

TUNSTALL, JUNE REBECCA
Physician. **Personal:** Born Jun 20, 1947, Baltimore, MD. **Educ:** Bennett Coll, BS 1969; Meharry Coll, MD 1974. **Career:** Surry Co Fam Hlth Grp Inc VA, staff phys, med dir 1979-80; John Randolph Hosp Hopewell VA, staff phys 1979-; Med Coll of VA Dept Fam Prac Richmond, instr 1979-80; Surry Co HURA Proj, staff phys 1978; Univ of MA, fam phys & educ coord of fam prac dept 1977, resd 1975-77; Worchester City Hosp, intern 1974-75. **Orgs:** Chprn bd dir Surry Co Fam Hlth Grp Inc 1979-80; vice pres Surry Co Unit Am Heart Assn 1979-80; pres Surry Co Unit Am Heart Assn 1980-81; mem VA Acad Fam Phys; mem Med Soc Southside VA; bd dir So Chirstian Ldrshp Conf; mem Am Acad of Fam Phys; MA Acad of Fam Phys; New Eng Med Soc Bd; dir Fam plng serv of Gr Worcester; bd dir United Way of Cntrl MA. **Business Addr:** Physician, PO Box 354, Surry, VA 23883.

TUNSTALL, LUCILLE HAWKINS
Educator. **Personal:** Born in Thurber, TX; children: Ruth Tunstall Grant, Leslie Tunstall Dawkins. **Educ:** Univ of CO Boulder, BS Med Tech 1943; Wayne State Univ, MS Biology 1959, PhD Biology 1963; Atlanta Law Sch, JD 1984. **Career:** Bishop Coll, chairperson dept of biology 1967-71; Natl Council of Churches, asst dir academic admin 1971-72; GA State Univ, clin prof physical therapy dept 1978-; Atlanta Univ, adj prof biology dept 1972-82; Clark Coll, prof of biology/chairperson allied health professions dept. **Orgs:** Consul United Bd for College Develop 1972-76; consul Moton Found 1971-78; consul Marc Prog Natl Inst of Genl Medical Sciences 1975-78; trustee Nulti-area Rape crisis Ctr Atlanta 1975-78; bd dirs Natl Soc of Health Professions 1983-; adv bd Atlanta Health Educ Consortium 1984-; pres GA Soc of AlliedHealth Professions 1978; chair biology sect GA Acad of Sciences 1976; regional vice pres Beta Kappa Chi Natl Honor Soc 1974-; treas Delta Theta Phi 1982-84; mem Sigma Xi 1958-. **Home Addr:** 620 Peachtree St NE Apt 1202, Atlanta, GA 30308.

TUPPER, LEON
Automotive executive. **Career:** Gilreath Manufacturing Inc, chief executive, currently. **Special Achievements:** Company is ranked #76 on Black Enterprise magazine's Top 100 Black businesses. **Business Addr:** President, Chief Executive Officer & Owner, Gilreath Manufacturing Inc, PO Box 408, Howell, MI 48844, (517)546-5250.

TURK, ALFRED J., II
Physician (retired). **Personal:** Born Jan 26, 1930, Atlanta, GA; married Charlotte Willis; children: Althea L MD, Alfred J Turk III Esq. **Educ:** Clark Coll, BS 1951; Howard Univ, MD 1964. **Career:** Booker T Washington High School, teacher 1951-58; Private Practice, Newnan GA, physician 1964-69; Private Practice, Atlanta GA, family practice physician 1965-90. **Orgs:** Life mem Alpha Phi Alpha Frat 1950-; trustee Beulah Baptist Church; mem Natl, GA State and Atlanta Medical Assocs; mem/supporter Clark Coll Alumni Assoc Inc, Howard Univ Alumni Assoc. **Honors/Awds:** Silver Circle Awd Clark Coll; Loyalty Club Awd Clark Coll 1981,82,83; Southwest Comm Hosp Atlanta Awd 18 yrs serv 1984; Outstanding Serv Eta Lambda Chap Alpha Phi Alpha Frat Inc 1984. **Home Addr:** 3111 Eleanor Terr NW, Atlanta, GA 30318.

TURMAN, GLYNN
Actor. **Personal:** marrIed Aretha Franklin (divorced); children: Glynn Turman Jr (deceased); children: Delena Joy. **Career:** Actor. **Honors/Awds:** Films include: Thomasine and Bushrod; Together Brothers; Cooley High; Minstreal Man; JD's Revenge; Penitentiary II; Secrets of a Married Man; Buffalo Soldiers.

TURMAN, KEVIN
Clergyman. **Career:** Second Baptist Church of Detroit, pastor, currently. **Orgs:** Michigan Progressive Baptist Convention, pres. **Business Addr:** Pastor, Second Baptist Church, 441-461 Monroe St, Detroit, MI 48226, (313)961-0920.

TURMAN, ROBERT L., SR.
Educational administrator, military officer (retired). **Personal:** Born Sep 29, 1926, Gadsden, AL; son of Lillian Long Turman and Arthur Turman; married Maggie Dossie Turman, Jun 29, 1950 (deceased); children: Daphne, Gregory, Robert II, Arthur, Oliver. **Educ:** Tuskegee Inst, BS Ed 1949; NC A&T State Univ, MS Ed Admin 1962; Univ of Northern CO, MA, psychology, 1975; Univ of CO, Post-Grad 1977. **Career:** US Army, lt col 1949-72; Carmel Jr HS, teacher 1972-74; John Adams Elementary School, asst principal 1974-75; Helen Hunt Elem School, principal 1975-77; Mark Twain Elem School, principal 1977-82; Will Rogers Elem School, principal 1982-84. **Orgs:** Mem Omega Psi Phi Frat 1948, Assoc of US Army 1955-, Phi Delta Kappa Ed Frat 1974-, Natl Assn Elem Principals 1975-, Amer Assn of School Admin 1975-, Natl Assn of School Bd 1979-, CO Black Caucus 1979-; pres Bd of Ed Harrison School Dist #2 1979-89; mem NAACP 1981-. **Honors/Awds:** Educator of the Year CO Springs Chap of Omega Psi Phi Frat 1981; Outstanding School Board Member, CO Association of School Boards 1984. **Military Serv:** US Army, lt col, 1949-72; Legion of Merit; Bronze Star Medal, 1971; Purple Heart, 1951; Joint Service Commendation Medal, 1969; Army Commendation Medal, 1962. **Home Addr:** 123 Penn Drive, Gadsden, AL 35903-3149.

TURNBULL, CHARLES WESLEY
Educator. **Personal:** Born Feb 5, 1935, Charlotte Amalie, St Thomas, Virgin Islands of the United States; son of Ruth Ann Eliza Skelton Turnbull and John Wesley Turnbull. **Educ:** Hampton University, Hampton, VA, BS, 1958, MA, 1959; University of Minnesota, Minneapolis, MN, PhD,1976. **Career:** Virgin Island Department of Education, St Thomas, VI, social studies teacher, 1959-61, assistant principal, 1961-65, principal, 1965-67, assistant commissioner of education, 1967-79; commissioner of education, 1979-87; University of the Virgin Islands, St Thomas, VI, professor of history, 1988-. **Orgs:** Member, Alpha Phi Alpha Fraternity Inc, 1958-; member, Association of Caribbean Historians; member, Organization of American Historians; member, Council of Chief State School Officers, 1979-87; member, Board of Trustees, University of the Virgin Islands, 1979-87; member, Virgin Islands Board of Elections, 1974-76; member, Virgin Islands Humanities Council, 1989-; member, Virgin Islands Board of Education, 1988-; president, Virgin Islands Historical Society, 1976-; member, American Historical Association. **Honors/Awds:** Ford Foundation Scholar, Ford Foundation, 1954-59; President Senior Class of 1958, Hampton University, 1957-58; Delegate to Four Constitutional Conventions of the US Virgin Islands, 1964-65; 1972-73; 1977-78; 1980-81; Citation for Excellence, Leadership and Service in the Field of Education, Iota Phi Lambda Sorority, 1989; Citation for Contributions to Virgin Islands History & Culture, Cultural Education Division Virgin Island Department of Education, 1987; Citation for Excellence in Teaching, Charlotte Amalie High School Class of 1964, 1989; Citation for Excellence in the Service of Humanity, Alpha Phi Alpha Fraternity Inc, Theta Epsilon Lambda Chapter, 1992. **Home Addr:** PO Box 2265, Charlotte Amalie, St Thomas, Virgin Islands of the United States 00803.

TURNBULL, HORACE HOLLINS
Administrator. **Personal:** Born Mar 26, 1949, Greenville, MS; married Eunice Carter; children: LaChandrea, Tamari, Courtney. **Educ:** Tougaloo Coll, BS 1971; Columbia U, MA 1975; Long Island Univ, MBA 1978. **Career:** Abbott House Childrens Home, cons; Childrens Village, grp home parent; Leake & Watts Childrens Agency, soc worker 1971-72; Planned Parenthood of NYC, dir, coord 1974-76; St Peters Sch, coord; St Mary's in-the-Field, res dir; Lakeside School, exec dir 1983-86; The Equitable Financial Svcs, registered rep1986-. **Orgs:** Mem 100 Black Men; vice pres Harlem Boys Choir Bd of Dir; Interest Hlth & Human Serv Adminstn. **Honors/Awds:** Acad & Athl Schlrshp 1967; hon mention Danforth Flwshp. **Business Addr:** Registered Representative, Equitable Financial Serv, 2 Corporate Park Dr, White Plains, NY 10604.

TURNBULL, RENALDO ANTONIO
Professional football player. **Personal:** Born Jan 5, 1966, St Thomas, Virgin Islands of the United States; son of Ellina Turnbull and George Turnbull; married Thea Lynn Winick-Turnbull, Mar 16, 1990; children: Royce Alexander. **Educ:** West Virginia Univ, Morgantown, WV, BA communications, 1990. **Career:** New Orleans Saints, linebacker, 1990-96; Carolina Panthers, 1997-. **Honors/Awds:** Pro Bowl, 1993. **Business Addr:** Professional Football Player, Carolina Panthers, 800 Mint St, Ericsson Stadium, Charlotte, NC 28202, (704)358-7000.

TURNBULL, WALTER J.
Educator. **Personal:** Born Jul 19, 1944, Greenville, MS. **Educ:** Tougaloo College, BA, music education, 1966; Manhattan School of Music, MA, 1968, DMA, 1984. **Career:** Educator, artist, singer, conductor, currently. **Honors/Awds:** New York UNV, NDEA title IV Fellowship, 1971; William F Sullivan Foundation, winner, 1971; Eleanor Roosevelt Community Service Award; President's Volunteer Service Award; Distinguished Black Mississippian Award, 1991; National Medal of Arts; numerous other awards; Hofstra University, Honorary Doctorate; Queens College, Honorary Doctorate of Humane Letter, 1989; Tougaloo College, Honorary Doctor of Music, 1989; numerous other honorary doctorates. **Special Achievements:** Queens College, Honorary Doctorate of Humane Letter, 1989; Tougaloo College, Honorary Doctor of Music, 1989; numerous other honorary doctorates. **Home Addr:** 484 W 43rd St #36B, New York, NY 10036. **Business Addr:** President, Director, Founder, The Boys Choir of Harlem Inc, 2005 Madison Avenue, New York, NY 10035, (212)289-1815.

TURNER, ALLEN H.
Engineer. **Personal:** Born Oct 19, 1923, Detroit; married Beverly K; children: Linda K. **Educ:** BS Elec Engr 1950. **Career:** Ford Motor Co, retired supr elec sys dept 1972-82, supr rsrch & devel ICPD Div 1965-72, rsrch engr sci lab 1952-65; Tuskegee Inst, rsrch asst 1950-52. **Orgs:** Mem Electron Microscope Soc of Am; Am Vacuum Soc; Soc of Am Engr Bd Dir Fam Svc. **Military Serv:** USAF 2nd lt WW II. **Business Addr:** Supervisor Elect Syst Dept, Ford Motor Co, Scientific Lab Ford Motor Co, Dearborn, MI.

TURNER, BAILEY W.
Consultant. **Personal:** Born Dec 18, 1932, Sadlersville, TN; married Ruby McClure; children: Carolyn, Gayle. **Educ:** TN State U, BS 1956; PA State U, MEd 1957; Union Grad Sch, PhD 1977. **Career:** Lincoln Heights Pub Schs, tchr 1960-61; Cincinnati Pub Schs, 1961-65; Comm Action Commn Cincinnati area, field rep comm organizer 1965-67; Metropolitan Life, sales rep 1967-72; Midland Nat Life, general agent; Univ Cincinnati, adj asst prof; RST Pub Relations & Consult firm, sr asso; Community Orgn, gen cons; Black-White Employee Relations, cons, mgmt tng. **Orgs:** Pres OH Black Political Assembly 1974-; chmn Coalition Concerned Black Citizens 1971-; United Black Community Orgns 1969-70; pres Avondale Commn Council 1967-69. **Honors/Awds:** PUSH Black Excellence Award 1972; SCLC Cincinnati chap Distingshd Commn Serv Award 1969; Alumnus of Yr TN State Univ 1965; Outstandng New Jaycee CincinnatiJaycees 1965. **Military Serv:** USAF 1949-53.

TURNER, BENNIE
Broadcasting company executive. **Career:** T&W Communications, WACR-AM/FM, pres, currently. **Orgs:** National Association of Black Owned Broadcasters Inc, president. **Business Addr:** President, WACR-AM/FM, T&W Communications, 1910 14th Ave N, Columbus, MS 39701, (601)328-1050.

TURNER, BILL
Automobile dealer. **Career:** Cumberland Chrysler-Plymouth Inc, chief executive officer, currently. **Special Achievements:** Company is ranked #70 on Black Enterprise's list of top 100 auto dealers, 1994. **Business Addr:** CEO, Cumberland Chry-Plymouth Inc., 5421 Raeford Rd., Fayetteville, NC 28304, (910)425-4200.

TURNER, CASTELLANO BLANCHET
Educator. **Personal:** Born Jun 14, 1938, Chicago, IL; son of Loretta Ganier Turner and James Julius Turner; married Barbara Formaniak, Apr 29, 1961; children: Adam Justin, Shomari Megan. **Educ:** DePaul Univ, BA 1962, MA 1963; Univ of Chicago, PhD 1966. **Career:** Woodlawn-Hyde Park-Kenwood Proj, prog dir 1967-68; School of Social Serv Admin Univ of Chicago, sr rsch assoc; Collegiate Ed of Black Students Univ of MA, dir counseling & tutoring prog 1969-70; Univ of MA, Amherst, prof of psych, Boston, professor & director of clinical psychology program, 1989-. **Orgs:** Mem Amer Psych Assoc, Assoc of Black Psych. **Home Addr:** 95 Wood End Rd, Newton Highlands, MA 02161-1402.

TURNER, DIANE YOUNG
Educational administrator. **Personal:** Born Jan 2, 1950, New Orleans, LA; daughter of Mary Montana Young and William Young; married John Turner, Dec 26, 1976; children: Kyra De-

nita, Jayna Ymon, John Kenneth. **Educ:** Grambling College, Grambling, LA, BA, 1972; State University of New York, Albany, NY, MA, 1974. **Career:** Renselaer Polytechnic Institute, Troy, NY, asst dir, admissions; Roxbury Community College, Roxbury, MA, dir, financial aid; Yale University, New Haven, CT, asst dir, financial aid, senior human resource specialist, director, library human resources, currently. **Orgs:** President, New Haven Chapter of Jack and Jill, 1989-94; president, Hamden PTA Council, 1989-91; member, Alpha Kappa Alpha Sorority, 1970-; pres, Hamden High School PTSA, 1993-; board member, Greater New Haven Community Action Agency, 1988-; board member, Greater New Haven Arts Council, 1990-; member, Junior League of Greater New Haven, 1985-89; board member, YWCA of Greater New Haven, 1990-, first vp. **Honors/Awds:** Participated in Leadership Greater New Haven, Institution and Volunteer Action Agency, 1989-; Elm Ivy Award, 1994; Hamden Notables Award, 1995; Jack & Jill, Distinguished Mother Award, 1993. **Special Achievements:** Special Olympics World Games, dir of volunteers at Yale Univ. **Home Addr:** 55 Chatterton Woods, Hamden, CT 06518.

TURNER, DORIS (DORIS TURNER KEYS)
Association executive. **Personal:** Born Jun 30, 1930, Pensacola, FL; married Willie D Keys. **Career:** Dist 1199 Nat Union of Hosp & Health Care Employees, exec vice pres 1961-. **Orgs:** Sec Nat Union of Hosp & Health Care Employees; union trustee Hosp League/Dist 1199 Training & Upgrading; union trustee Nat Benefit & Pension Fund for Hosp & Health Care Employees; mem Exec Com of Nat Benefit & Pension Funds; bd mem Am for Dem Action; bd mem Martin L King Cntr for Social Change; mem State of NY Comn on Health Educ & Illness Prevention; mem Coalition of Labor Union-Women; appntd mem NY State Hosp Review & Planning Cncl 1978-81. **Honors/Awds:** Dist srvcs award New York City Central Labor Counc AFL-CIO 1969; award of merit The Black Trade Unionist Ldrshp Com of NY Central Labor Counc 1974; Hispanic Labor Com Award 1978; Eugene V Debs/Norman Thomas Award 1978. **Business Addr:** President, 310 W 43rd St, New York, NY 10036.

TURNER, DORIS J.
Educator. **Personal:** Born in St Louis, MO; daughter of Adeline Herndon Turner and Julius Adams Turner. **Educ:** Stowe Coll St Louis, BA 1953; Universidade da Bahia Salvador Bahia Brazil, 1963; St Louis U, PhD 1967. **Career:** Kent State Univ, asso prof & coordinator, Latin American Studies, currently. **Orgs:** Field reader US Ofc of Educ (HEW) 1976-77, 79; elected mem & past chmn Nat Ofc Steering & Com of Consortium of Latin Am Studies Prog 1973-76. **Honors/Awds:** Fulbright Fellowship Brazil 1962-64; Research Grant to Brazil, Kent State Univ 1976; Danforth Assn 1976; NEH Summer Fellwshp Brown Univ 1979; Postdoctoral Fellowship, Ford Foundation, 1987-88; Outstanding Teaching Award, College of Arts & Sciences, Kent State Univ, 1986. **Business Addr:** Associate Professor, Romance Languages & Literatures, Kent State University, 101 Satterfield Hall, Kent, OH 44242.

TURNER, EDDIE WILLIAM
Crime prevention officer. **Personal:** Born Apr 21, 1931, Toledo, OH; married Jacquelyn H; children: Edward, Kimberly. **Educ:** Findlay Coll, 1954-56; Univ of Toledo, BS 1977. **Career:** Toledo Police Dept, crime prevntn offcr 1978-, comm relatns offcr 1968-78, detective 1962-68, patrol offcr 1959-62. **Orgs:** Mem Adv Bd Vol of Am; mem Adv Council E Toledo Helping Hand; mem Adv Bd E Mental Health Cntr; chaplin Omega Frat Xi Tau Chpt; mem City of Toledo Baseball & Softball Commn; pres Med-City Football Adv Bd. **Honors/Awds:** 100 Membership Club NAACP Toledo Chap 1976; Shoplftg Study age 11 thru 14 toledo police dept 1978-79; crime prevntn offcr of yr asso for crime Prevntn 1979. **Military Serv:** AUS corpl 1952-54. **Business Addr:** Toledo Police Department, 525 N Erie St, Toledo, OH 43604.

TURNER, EDWARD L.
Councilman. **Educ:** Univ GA, BA. **Career:** Com Preserving NE Athens, vice pres 1973; A Philip Randolph Inst, commun sec 1972-73; Clark Co Dem Club, 2nd vice pres 1972; Athens Central Labor Council, 2nd vice pres 1971; Voter Registration, chmn 1973-74. **Orgs:** Mem C of C; Jaycees; Optimist Brkfst Club; Black Professional Club; Black Bus League; mem Civic League; Generatn Gay Civic & Soc Orgn; Community Serv Club. **Honors/Awds:** Man Yr NAACP 1973. **Business Addr:** 393 3 St, Athens, GA 30601.

TURNER, ELMYRA G.
Educator. **Personal:** Born Nov 27, 1928, Longview, TX; married James M Turner; children: 3. **Educ:** BS 1952; MEd 1959; MEd 1969; TX Ksouthern U, Admin Cert 1973. **Career:** Texas Southern Univ, sec 1952; Crawford Elementary School, 1953; Elmore HS, sec/teacher 1954; Langston Elementary School, teacher 1959; Lockett Jr High, 1964; Lincoln Jr-Sr High, 1968; Sam Houston Sr High, counselor 1970; Deady Jr High, asst prin 1970; all Houston TX. **Orgs:** Mem Nat Council Negro Women 1973; NAACP 1973-74; Houston Principals Assn 1970-; Houston Council of Educ 1972; supt com on Community Relatns for Area V 1972-74; Evaluatn Panel of Intervwrs-Area V PTA Deady Jr HS; Lockhart Elem TX State Tchrs Assn vp; Top Ladiel of Distinctn Inc past pres; Beta Pi Chap Iota Phi Lambda Sor Inc past pres; organizer Houston Chap Nat Tots & Teens Inc; mem Houston League of Bus & prof Women; Home Improv & Protec Assn; chmn Youth Com; mem Delta Sigma Theta Sor Inc; mem AAUW; Univ Christian Ch publicatns "a study of Techniques for Improving Staff Morale" 1959, "The Etiology and Effect of Dialect Upon Behavior" 1969. **Honors/Awds:** President's Award 1971 Iota Phi Lambda Sor Inc; Outstndg Woman Yr 1974-75 Iota Phi Lambda Sor Inc, Beta Pi Chap Houston TX; recv 1977 Human Rel EducAward for outst achvmt in human rel Houston Ind Sch Dist in coop with Anti-Defamation Leag of B'nai B'rith Houston Met Ministries & Nat Conf of Christians-Jews; Notable Ams 1976-77. **Business Addr:** 2500 Broadway, Houston, TX 77012.

TURNER, ERIC
Professional football player. **Personal:** Born Sep 20, 1968, Ventura, CA; married. **Educ:** UCLA. **Career:** Oakland Raiders, defensive back, currently. **Business Addr:** Professional Football Player, Oakland Raiders, 1220 Harbor Bay Pkwy, Alameda, CA 94502, (510)615-1875.

TURNER, ERVIN (PETER TURNER)
Business executive. **Personal:** Born Mar 20, 1948, Monroe, LA; married Kathleen Lindsey; children: Christopher Earl, Roanita. **Educ:** Northeast LA Univ, Associate 1972; Boys' Clubs of Amer, certification 1974. **Career:** Ouachita Parish Police Jury, police juror 1979-; EPT Enterprise AAA LTD, pres/owner 1982-; Tri-District Boys' Club, exec dir 1971-. **Orgs:** Mem NAACP; mem Northeast LA Sickle Cell Anemia; mem NLU Booster Club Business Action Assoc; mem Amer Entrepreneurs Assn; mem zoological Soc of LA Purchase Gardens and Zoo; bd mem Northeast LA Indus Dev Bd; bd mem Northeast LA Indus Bd; bd mem LA Minority Bus Develop Auth Bd; BCA Professional; coord Volunteer for Job Corps; sec Luminous Civic Club; bd mem Youth House of Quachita; bd mem Business Action Assn; bd mem Better Business Bureau; exec sec LA Area Council-BCA 1974; 2nd vice pres North Delta Regional Planning 1979-. **Honors/Awds:** Man of the Year St Philip Baptist Church 1975; Man of the Year NAACP 1978; Monroe's Outstanding Young Man Monroe Jaycees 1982. **Home Addr:** 102 Roosevelt Circle, Monroe, LA 71202.

TURNER, EUGENE
Clergyman. **Personal:** Born Apr 17, 1934, Macon, GA; married Sylvia Baskerville; children: Peter Eugene, Paul Eugene, Lennie Elis. **Educ:** Knoxville Coll, BA; Pittsburgh Theological Sem, MDV; Harvard U, post grad work. **Career:** Pittsburgh, asst pastor; Patterson NJ, pastor; Philadelphia, organzng pastor; Presbeytery of Phila, assist for leadrshp devel, coord of Met Mission; Synod of the Golden Gate San Franc, asso exec; United Presby Ch Syracuse NY, exec of Synod of the Northeast. **Orgs:** Bd mem No CA Coun of Ch; bd mem Nat Planned Parenthd 1964-66; bd mem Coun of Black Clergy; bd mem Black Presby United; mem steering com Nat Black Conf 1968; bd mem Model Cities of Phila. **Military Serv:** AUS 1957-59. **Business Addr:** 3049 E Genesee St, Syracuse, NY.

TURNER, EVELYN EVON
Educator. **Personal:** Born Sep 22, 1954, Buffalo, NY; daughter of Mary Turner and Steven Turner. **Educ:** Bowie State Coll, BS 1978; Univ of Maryland at Baltimore, MSW 1980. **Career:** Homes for Black Children, social worker 1982-84; PG Dept of Social Services, social worker 1984-85; Bowie State Coll, instructor 1985-86, program coord 1986-90, instructor, 1990-. **Orgs:** Mem College Alumni Assoc 1978-; recording sec 1980-84, vice pres 1985-86 Natl Assoc of Black Social Workers; pres Sigma Gamma Nu Social Club 1981-84; sec Coalition of Black Child Welfare Advocates 1985-; mem Delta Sigma Theta Sor 1986-; member, National Association of Social Workers. **Honors/Awds:** Certificate of Appreciation Natl Alliance of Business 1981; Certificate of Appreciation Natl Assoc of Black Social Workers 1981-85; Presidential Citation Natl Assoc on Equal Oppor in Higher Educ 1984; Certificate of Appreciation, Delta Sigma Theta, 1990. **Home Addr:** 6405 Hil-Mar Drive #301, Forestville, MD 20747. **Business Addr:** Instructor, Bowie State University, Bowie, MD 20715.

TURNER, FRANKLIN JAMES
Engineer. **Personal:** Born Aug 16, 1960, Birmingham, AL. **Educ:** Alabama A&M Univ, BS 1983. **Career:** Rockwell Intl, software engr 1984-86; Northrop, software quality engr 1986—. **Honors/Awds:** Pride Awd Engrg Outstanding Achievement Rockwell Intl 1986. **Home Addr:** 19101 Pricetown Ave, Carson, CA 90746.

TURNER, GENEVA
Educator, business owner. **Personal:** Born Jul 6, 1949, Columbus, GA; daughter of Mollie Bell Turner and George Robert Turner (deceased); married 1994; children: Gennyce Ashley Nelson Turner. **Educ:** Columbus College, AAN, 1971; Georgia Southwhwestern, BSN, 1979; University of Alabama, MSN, 1982; Texas Woman's University, PhD, 1987. **Career:** The Medical Center, staff nurse, 1971; Talmadge Memorial Hospital, staff nurse, 1971-73; RE Thomason General Hospital, charge nurse, 1973-74; Convalescent Center, charge nurse, 1974; US Army Hospital, acting head nurse, 1975-77; The Medical Center, staff nurse, 1978-79; Columbus College, associate professor of nursing, 1979-93; Turner and Associates Consulting, owner, 1989-; Family Projects Publishers, owner, 1992-. **Orgs:** American Nurses Association, 1979-; Sigma Theta Tau, 1983-; National Council of Marriage & Family Relations, 1986-; Phi Kappa Phi, 1987-; Association of Military Surgeons of the United States, 1988-; Association of Black Nursing Faculty, 1989-93; National League for Nursing in Higher Education, 1990-93; National Association of Nurses in Business, 1991-93; Publishers Marketing Assn, 1992-; Network for Professionals & Executives Inc, 1994-; Alliance for Homelessness, 1994-. **Honors/Awds:** Columbus College, Outstanding Sophomore Teacher in Nursing, 1981; Columbus College, Dr John Townsend Award for Outstanding Service to the Community in Medicine, 1983; Mayor's Office, Outstanding Service to the City of Columbus, 1990; Greater Columbus Chapter of Alzheimer's Disease, Service Award, 1991; Combined Communities of Southeast Columbus, Certificate of Appreciation, 1989. **Special Achievements:** Disseminating Intravascular Coagulation, Nursing Interventions, 1991; Preceptorship Program: A Public Relations Tool, 1991; Dealing with Polychronic or Monochronic Individuals in the Work Place, 1992; Black American Folk Medicine Health Care Beliefs: Implications for Nursing, 1992; How to Plan a Spectacular Family Reunion, 1993; Fathers Cry, Too, 1995; "Theory of Homelessness Using Gibb's Paradigm," 1992. **Military Serv:** US Army Reserves, ltc, 1979-. **Home Addr:** 4815 Velpoe Dr, Columbus, GA 31907. **Business Addr:** 3009 Hamilton Rd, PO Box 6427, Columbus, GA 31907, (706)687-4296.

TURNER, GEORGE CORDELL, II
Human resources executive. **Personal:** Born Jun 3, 1937, McGehee, AR; son of George C Sr & Mary L; married Nancy C Turner, Aug 11, 1968; children: Melissa, George III. **Educ:** Univ of Ark at Pine Bluff, history & government, 1959; Further study: U of AR, Univ of FL, Univ of IL. **Career:** Helena-West Helena Public Schools, inst, 1959-64; Conway Public Schools, inst-adm, 1964-69; Consumers Power, dir human resources, 1969-. **Orgs:** Amer Assn Blacks Energy, 1988-; Michigan Chapter AABE, treasurer, 1991-; Charter Member Jackson Service Club, held all offices, 1974-. **Honors/Awds:** Nat Assn for Equal Opp in Education, National Alumni of the Year, 1994. **Business Addr:** Corp. Director, Diversity/EEO & Safety, Consumers Power Co, 212 W Michigan Ave, General Office M-565, Jackson, MI 49201, (517)788-1303.

TURNER, GEORGE R.
Podiatrist. **Personal:** Born Jun 14, 1944, Bryn Mawr, PA; married Betty; children: Gayle, Garrett, Avis. **Educ:** Lincoln U, AB 1967; Temple U, EdM 1969; PA Coll of Podiatric Med, DPM 1976. **Career:** Lawndale Commun Hosp, podiatrist; PA Coll of Podiatric Med 1972-76; IBM, marktg rep 1969-72; Philadelphia Bd of Edn, tchr 1967-69. **Orgs:** Mem Amer Podiatry Assn; bd mem Natl Podiatry Assn; PA Podiatry Assn; Metrop Podiatry Assn; Philadelphia Co Podiatry Assn; consult Hardy's Orthopedic ApplInc; mem Omega Psi Phi Frat. **Honors/Awds:** Outst Young Man in Amer 1976; Morris prize in bio 1967; Metrop Podiatry Assn achiev award 1976. **Business Addr:** 1901-03-05 74 Ave, Philadelphia, PA 19138.

TURNER, GEORGE TIMOTHY
Auto dealer. **Career:** Plainfield Lincoln-Mercury-Merkur, Inc, Grand Rapids MI, chief executive, 1986—. **Business Addr:** Plainfield Lincoln-Mercury-Merkur, Inc, PO BOX 8705, Grand Rapids, MI 49518-8705.

TURNER, HARRY GLENN
Automotive executive. **Personal:** Born Jul 23, 1951, Chicago, IL; son of Ruby Turner and William Turner; divorced; children: John, Laura. **Educ:** Kennedy-King Junior College, AA, 1971; University of Illinois, School of Engineering, BME, 1976; Oakland University, Graduate School of Business Administration, MBA, 1979. **Career:** Chevrolet, engineer, 1979-83, engineering mgr, 1983-85, executive engineering mgr, 1985-86, chief engineer, export group, 1986, chief engineer, body systems, 1987, large car product planning, 1988-90, Corvette and Camaro product planning, sporty car segment mgr, 1990-96; General Motors, motor sports strategic planning, 1996-. **Business Addr:** Motorsports Strategic Planning, Chevrolet Motor Division, General Motors Corp, 30007 Van Dyke Ave, Rm 278-05, Warren, MI 48090-2350, (313)492-1175.

TURNER, ISIAH
Commissioner of state employment security department. **Personal:** Born May 15, 1945, St Joseph, LA; son of Leona Johnson Turner and Isiah Turner; married Carmen Cayne, Jul 10, 1982; children: Damon Isiah, Terrie Lynn. **Educ:** Evergreen State College, Olympia WA, 1986; Harvard Univ, 1987. **Career:** Seattle Opportunities Industrialization Center, Seattle WA, dir of education, 1971-79; Operation Improvement Foundation, Seattle WA, dir of industrial relations, 1980-83; Washington State Employment Security, Olympia WA, asst commissioner, 1983-85, commissioner, 1985—. **Orgs:** National Job Training Partnership, National Black Public Administrators Forum, Blacks in Government, Interstate Conference of Employment Security Agencies, Northwest Conference of Black

Public Officials, Washington State Economic Development Board. **Honors/Awds:** Administrator of the Year, National Job Service Employer Committee, 1986; Job Training Professional of the Year, National Alliance of Business, 1988; award of merit, International Association of Personnel in Employment Security, 1989.

TURNER, JEAN TAYLOR
Educator. **Personal:** Born Nov 13, 1943, Philadelphia, PA; daughter of Roberta Hargrove Taylor and Clarence William Taylor (deceased); children: Christopher Francis, Sean Michael. **Educ:** University of California at Los Angeles, BSN, 1973, MN, 1975; Medical College of Virginia, Virginia Commonwealth University, PhD, health services organization and research, 1987. **Career:** Fox Hills Community Hospitals, Los Angeles, staff development director, 1974-75; Virginia Commonwwealth University, School of Nursing, Medical College of Virginia, Department of Psychiatric Mental Health, instructor, 1979-84, assistant professor nursing administration, 1984-92; University of Virginia, associate professor of nursing, 1992-. **Orgs:** Assn for Health Services Research, 1993-; American Nurses Association, 1980-; American Public Health Association, 1987-; Association of Black Nursing Faculty in Higher Education, editorial review bd, 1989-; Sigma Theta Tau International Nursing Honor Society, 1988-. **Honors/Awds:** Virginia Commonwealth University, Provost Award, 1990, Best Mentor Award, 1992; Association of Black Nursing Faculty in Higher Education, Johnella F Banks Award for Member Excellence, 1992; Virginia Department of Mental Health, Mental Retardation and Substance Abuse Services, Certificate of Recognition, 1991; National Institute of Mental Health, pre-doctoral fellowship, 1984-87. **Special Achievements:** Publications: "Recidivism and Mental Illness: The Role of Communities," Community Mental Health Journal, 1993; "Participative Management: Determining Employee Readiness," Administration and Policy in Mental Health, 1991; "Measuring Adolescent Satisfaction with Nursing Care in an Ambulatory Setting," The ABNF Journal, 1991. **Business Phone:** (804)924-5742.

TURNER, JESSE H., JR.
Banker. **Career:** Tri-State Bank of Memphis, TN, pres/chmn, currently. **Special Achievements:** Listed at #18 of 25 top financial companies, Black Enterprise, 1992. **Business Addr:** President & Chairman, Tri-State Bank of Memphis, 180 S Main St, Memphis, TN 38103, (901)525-0384.

TURNER, JOHN B.
Educator. **Personal:** Born Feb 28, 1922, Ft Valley, GA; son of Virginia H Brown Berry and Brister William Turner; married Marian Floredia Wilson; children: Marian Elizabeth, Charles Brister. **Educ:** Morehouse Coll, BA 1946; Case Western Resrv U, MSc 1948, DSW 1959. **Career:** Butler St YMCA, prog sec 1948-50; Atlanta Univ, instr 1950-52; Welfare Federation Field Serv Cleveland, dir 1959-61; Case Western Reserve Univ, chmn community orgn sequence 1957-67; School Applied Social Scis, dean 1968-73; Ency of Soc Work, editor 1977; Univ of NC School of Social Work, dean 1981-92; Univ NC, Kenan, dean and prof emeritus, currently. **Orgs:** Consult Nat Urban League 1966-71; Intl Resrch Prog Cairo Egypt 1974; chmn Social Work Training Com Nat Inst Mental Hlth 1967-68; pres Nat Conf of Soc Welfare; mem Mayor's Com on Commun Resrcs Cleveland 1968-70; Cleveland Inst Art bd trustees 1970-74; city commnr E Cleveland 1967-69; sec, bd of trust Chapel Hill YMCA 1986; bd trust Council on Social Work Educ. **Military Serv:** USAF 1st lt, pilot, 1943-45.

TURNER, JOHN BARRIMORE
Educational administrator. **Personal:** Born Feb 4, 1942, Sardis, MS; married Clevonne LaVerne Watkins; children: Stephanie, Robin, Bridget. **Educ:** Fisk Univ, BA 1965; IN Univ Bloomington, MS Student Personnel Admin 1968, EdD 1972, Post-Doctorate Internship Admin 1973; Harvard Univ Inst for EdMgmt, 1979. **Career:** Fisk Univ, teaching asst math dept 1963-65; Westinghouse Elect Corp, mgmt trainee 1965-66; McNutt Quadrangle IN Univ, resident asst 1966-67; Foster Quadrangle IN Univ, asst head counselor 1967-68; Urban League Indianapolis, ed dir 1967; Upward Bound IN Univ, asst dean, div dir 1968-74; MIT, asst dean of grad school 1974-76, assoc dean of grad school, asst provost beginning 1977; Knoxville Coll, pres, currently. **Orgs:** Natl Assn of Grad School Deans, Amer Assoc for Higher Ed, Natl Assn of Student Personnel Admin, Phi Delta Kappa, Natl Black Alliance, Assn of Black Admin & Financial Aid Officers of the Ivy League & 7 Sister School; bd of dir Natl Consortium for Grad Degrees for Minorities in Engrg Inc; steeringcomm mem Ad Hoc Consortium on Minority Grad Ed Washington DC; pres Fisk Univ Alumni Assoc of Boston 1977-. **Honors/Awds:** Outstanding Young Man of Amer Jaycees 1978; Martin Luther King Jr Awd for Disting Serv MIT Minority Comm 1978-79. **Business Addr:** President, Knoxville College, Knoxville, TN 37914.

TURNER, JOHNNIE RODGERS
Educational administrator. **Personal:** Born Jun 23, 1940, Hughes, AR; daughter of Charlie Mae Watson Rodgers and Clayton Rodgers; married Larry Turner; children: Larry R. **Educ:** LeMoyne-Owen Coll, BS 1962; Memphis State Univ, MEd 1971. **Career:** Memphis City Schools, tchr 1965-, supr; dir, Staff Develmnt 1986-90, co-director, Professional Assessment Development and Enhancement Center (PADEC), 1991-. **Orgs:** Pres Memphis Br NAACP 1977-78; pres Memphis Alumnae Chap Delta Sigma Theta Sor 1978-80; mem Leadership Memphis 1979-; ASCD 1980-; Natl Staff Dev Council 1980-; MABSE 1981-; Phi Delta Kappa 1982-; Natl Alliance of Black School Educators 1982-; bd mem, Health, Educational and Housing Facility Board of Shelby Cty, Tennessee, 1982-; pres, Memphis Alliance of Black School Educators (MABSE) 1988-90. **Honors/Awds:** Merit Awd for Outstanding Serv Memphis Br NAACP 1975; co-editor "Why Doesn't An Igloo Melt Inside?" handbook for tchrs of the gifted 1978; Citizen of the Week Gilliam Comm Station WLOK 1978; Citizenship Awd Moolah Temple #54 Shriner 1979; Delta of the Year 1983; Golden Apple Award, Natl Alliance of Black School Educators (NABSE) 1988. **Business Addr:** Co-Director, Professional Assessment Development and Enhancement Cente, r, Memphis City Schools, 2597 Avery Ave, Memphis, TN 38112.

TURNER, JOSEPH ELLIS
Commercial airline pilot, military official. **Personal:** Born Sep 2, 1939, Charleston, WV; son of Annetta Frances Malone (deceased) and Joseph Turner (deceased); married Norma Jean Sims, Apr 25, 1959; children: Alan, Brian, Joseph Jr. **Educ:** West Virginia State College, BS, math, 1961; University of Southern California, aviation safety, 1968; Command & Gen Staff College, grad; Indust College of Armed Forces, Air War College; Senior Off Chem, CSE; Force Integration, CSE; Nato Orien, CSE; BG, Orien Conf. **Career:** First Officer, L1011 Delta Air Lines, LAX, 1970-; Major General, US Army Reserves, 1992-; vice director, Directorate, Office Information Systems for Command Control Communications & Computers; Master Army Aviator; U3a U6a 1963; CV2 1963; U8D, G, F, U21A 1968; U3A 1976; Fixed wing OH58 1975; UHIH 1975; rotary wing. **Orgs:** Airline Pilots Assn, 1970-; NAI, 1969-; ROA, 1970-; American Society of Miltary Comptrollers, 1984-; Organization of Black Airline Pilots, 1984-; Senior Army Reserve Commanders Assn, 1988; Armed Forces Communications Electronics Assn, 1988-; Signal Corp Regimential Assn, 1988-; Black Military History Institute of America Inc, 1989-; Caribon Assn, Army Otter, currently. **Honors/Awds:** WV State College, ROTC Hall of Fame, 1984; NAFEO, Distinguished Alumni Citation of the Year Award, 1989; WV State College, General Officer Hall of Fame, 1988. **Military Serv:** US Army, col, 1961-70, US Army Reserves, major general, 1970-; Legion of Merit, 2 Bronze Stars, 3 Meritorious Service Medals, 3 Army Commendation Medals, 11 Air Medals, Army Achievement Medal, Presidential Unit Citation, Army Reserve Ribbon, Vietnam Service Medal w/8 Stars, Armed Forces Reserve Medal, Army Reserve Components Achievement Medal, Republic of Vietnam Campaign Ribbon, Master Army Aviator Badge, Republic Vietnam Gallantry Cross w/Palm. **Home Addr:** 1630 Loch Lomond Trail SW, Atlanta, GA 30331. **Business Addr:** Major General, US Army Reserves, Office Information Systems, Command Control Communications & Computers (ODISC4), Pentagon, Washington, DC 20310-0107.

TURNER, KIM SMITH
Associate Director of Finance and Administration. **Personal:** Born Apr 11, 1959, New York, NY; daughter of Bernice Alford Smith and Solomon Smith; married Ray Turner, Jan 19, 1980; children: Kory, Kortnie. **Educ:** Morgan State University, Baltimore, MD, 1977-79; State Univ Educational Opportunity Center, Albany, NY, Certificate, 1980; Emory University, Atlanta, GA, 1989-. **Career:** State of New York, Rochester Psychiatric Ctr, Rochester, NY, 1981; US Government Social Security Admin, Atlanta GA, secretary, 1982-83; American Rheumatism Association, Atlanta, GA, meetings coordinator, 1983-86; Emory University Business School, Atlanta, GA, departmental oper coordinator, 1986-90, business manager, 1990-94, acting assoc, dir for Executive Programs, 1995, assoc dir fin & admin, 1995-. **Orgs:** President, Emory University Employee Council, 1987-88; Emory University President's Commission on the Status of Minorities, 1989-92; Emory University President's Commission on the Status of Women, 1988-89; co-founder, Emory's Black Education Network, 1990; NAACP, Atlanta Chapter, 1988, 1990-; Emory University EEOC Task Force, 1989. **Honors/Awds:** Promotion, People Section, Jet Magazine, 1990; Promotion Article, Chicago Tribune, 1990; Emory Profile, Emory University Campus Report, 1988; Promotion Article, Atlanta Daily World, 1990. **Business Addr:** Associate Director Finance & Administration, Emory University Goizueta Business School of, 1602 Mizell Dr, Rich Bldg, Atlanta, GA 30322-2710, (404)727-6376.

TURNER, LANA
Real estate sales. **Personal:** Born Feb 8, 1950, New York, NY; daughter of Ida Ford Turner and Lee Arthur Turner; children: Eric M Fane. **Educ:** City College of New York, New York, NY, 1972-76; Sarah Lawrence College, Bronxville, NY, 1987-89. **Career:** Men Who Cook, New York, NY, president, 1982-. **Orgs:** Advisory board member, Manhattan Borough Historian Commission, 1986-; chairperson, The Literary Society, 1982-; advisory board member, Breast Examination Center, 1982-. **Honors/Awds:** Author, Travelling Light, Pictures of Fathers, New York, Sarah Lawrence College, 1988. **Home Addr:** 270 Convent Ave, New York, NY 10031.

TURNER, LESLIE MARIE
Government official. **Personal:** Born Oct 2, 1957, Neptune, NJ; daughter of Robert Turner II and Jeanette Turner. **Educ:** New York University, BS, 1980; George Town University Law Ctr, JD, 1985. **Career:** DC Court of Appeals, judicial law clerk, 1985-86; Akin Gump Strauss Hauer & Feld, sr associate, 1986-93; US Department of the Interior, assistant secretary for territorial & international affairs, 1993-95, counselor to the secretary & director of office of intergovenmental affairs, 1995-. **Orgs:** American Bar Association, vice chair of the committee on environmental justice, 1996-; District of Columbia Bar, mem community on public understanding about the law, 1996-; DC Coalition on Environmentl Justice, mem, 1995-. **Business Addr:** Counsel to the Secretary, Director Office of Intergovernmental Affairs, US Department of the Interior, 1849 C St, NW, Mail Stop 6214, Washington, DC 20240, (202)208-5336.

TURNER, LINDA DARNELL
Minority affairs officer. **Personal:** Born Mar 29, 1947, River Rouge, MI; daughter of Alean Darnell Turner and Beatreat Turner; children: Akaia. **Educ:** Mercy College of Detroit, Detroit, MI, BA, 1981. **Career:** Independence Capital Formation, Detroit, MI, manager, 1972-79; Detroit Economic Growth, Detroit MI, manager, 1979-81; Barton Malow, Southfield, MI, director, vice pres minority affairs, currently. **Orgs:** Board member, Major Corporation Program, NAMC, 1990-93; corporate urban forum representative, Corporate Urban Forum, 1983-; board member, Oakland County Private Industry Council, Oakland County, 1989-; executive committee , General Business Purchasing, MMBDC, 1987-; board member, Greater Detroit Alliance of Business, Detroit Chamber of Commerce, 1988-, committee member, EEO Committee, AGC, Detroit Branch, 1990. **Honors/Awds:** Business Development, Governor State of Georgia, 1989; Major Corporation Achievement, NAMC, 1989; Minority Achiever, Detroit YWCA, 1987; MBE Corporation Role Model, Chrysler Corp, 1996. **Business Addr:** Vice President, Minority Affairs, Barton Malow Co, 27777 Franklin Road, Suite 800, Southfield, MI 48034.

TURNER, M. ANNETTE
Administrator. **Personal:** Born Feb 17, 1953, Belhaven, NC; daughter of Edna Mae Jones Mandley and James W Mandley; married James Roderick Turner, Feb 14, 1971. **Educ:** University of Louisville, Louisville, KY, BS sociology, 1980, BS ed psychology, 1991, MS, 1987. **Career:** St Denis School, Louisville, KY, teacher, 1975-84; Regional Youth Program, Louisville, KY, coordinator, 1984-89; Human Resource Plus, Louisville, KY, diversity consultant, 1988-; Office of African-American Catholics, Archdiocese of Louisville, KY, executive director, 1989-. **Orgs:** Founder, National African American Youth Ministry Network; chair, National Federation Catholic Youth Ministry Ethnic Concern Committee, 1986-90; executive board member, National Federal Catholic Youth Ministry, 1990-; member, National Council of Negro Women, 1990-; Grand lady, Knights of Peter Claver Ladies Aux, 1989-90; board of directors, One Church One Child, 1992-; board of trustees, National Black Catholic Congress, 1992. **Honors/Awds:** International and National Youth Ministry Award, National Federation Catholic Youth Ministry, 1990; Elizabeth Lange Award, Dutshnding Leadership, Knights of Peter Claver, 1989; Kujenga Vongoni, African American Youth Leadership, 1985; Jr Horizon Youth Ministry Program, Developed for African American, 1988, 1991. **Home Addr:** 8506 Image Way, Louisville, KY 40299.

TURNER, MARCELLUS
Librarian, educator. **Personal:** Born Aug 6, 1963, Newton, MS; son of Ellestene Pilate Turner and Lucious Turner Jr. **Educ:** Utica Junior College, Utica, MS, AA, 1983; Alcorn State Univ, Lorman, MS, 1983-84; Mississippi Univ for Women, Columbus, MS, BS, 1986; Univ of Tennessee, Knoxville, TN, MSLS, 1988. **Career:** Univ of Tennessee at Chattanooga, Chattanooga, TN, reference librarian, 1988-89; McNeese St Univ, Lake Charles, LA, public services librarian, 1989-90; East Tennessee St Univ, Johnson City, TN, library instruction librarian, 1990-. **Orgs:** Member, American Library Assn, 1987; member, Southeastern Library Assn, 1990-; member, Black Caucus of the American Library Association, 1990-. **Honors/Awds:** James E Ward Library Instruction Award, April 1992 by the Library Instruction Round Table of the Tennessee Library Association.

TURNER, MARK ANTHONY
Educational administrator. **Personal:** Born Feb 23, 1951, Lynch, KY; son of Naomi Miller Randolph Turner and William Earl Turner; divorced; children: Andrea Kamille, Brittany E Nelson-Turner. **Educ:** Univ of KY Southeast Comm Coll, AA 1972; Western KY Univ, BS 1974. **Career:** Deloitte Haskins and Sells, sr asst, 1974-78; Business Resource Center, sr consultant, 1978-79; Ohio River Co, financial analyst, 1979-80; Arthur Young & Co, sr consultant-auditor 1980; Univ Coll Univ of Cincinnati, asst dean 1982-95; Mark A Turner & Associates, senior partner, 1988-; Taxx Express, founder, 1996-. **Orgs:** Treas NABA Cincinnati Chap 1980-84; founding mem Cincinnati Chap Natl Assoc of Black Accountants 1980; treas Bond Hill Comm Council 1980-84; consultant Sickle Cell Awareness Group of Greater Cincinnati 1982-84; company treas Cincinnatians for Yates for Council 1984-86; treasurer 1990-91, bd of

trustees 1989-91, Central Community Mental Health Board; member, Univ College Minority Scholarship Board, 1988-91; pres, bd of trustees, CCUB; founding treasurer, 4 Square Foundation. **Honors/Awds:** Ford Foundation Scholarship 1973; Certificate of Appreciation Junior Achievement 1977-81; Certificate of Appreciation Cincinnati Chamber of Commerce Business Resource Ctr 1979-82; Certificate of Appreciation The Union of Experimenting Colleges 1986; Distinguished Faculty-Administration, Delta Sigma Theta, 1990; Distinguished Faculty, Univ of Cincinnati Evening College, 1990; Kentucky Colonel, 1996; Lynch Colored School of Lynch West Main Historical Association, Prestigious Alumni Award. **Home Addr:** 5411 Carrahen Ct, Cincinnati, OH 45237. **Business Addr:** Mark A Turner & Associates, CPA, 3142 Losantiville Ave, Ste 4, Cincinnati, OH 45213.

TURNER, MARVIN WENTZ
Chief financial officer. **Personal:** Born Oct 17, 1959, Philadelphia, PA; son of Frances B McAlister Turner (deceased) and Gilbert Turner, Jr (deceased). **Educ:** Howard Univ, BBA, cum laude, 1981; Temple Univ, 1984-86; The George Washington Univ, MBA, 1988; Georgetown Univ Law Center, JD candidate, 1994-. **Career:** Prudential Insurance, Fort Washington, PA, external relations advisor, 1982-86; Management Enterprise, Philadelphia, PA, business advisor, 1984-86; CNA Insurance, Washington, DC, policy analyst, 1986-88; Bell Atlantic-Network Services Inc, Arlington, VA, manager of corporate financial planning and analysis, 1988-93; Local Government Insurance Trust, chief financial officer, 1993-95; Hopkins Turner Wharton Inc, Bethesda MD, managing director, 1995-. **Orgs:** Assoc of MBA Execs; Delta Sigma Pi Professional Business Frat; Assoc of Individual Investors; Howard Univ Sch of Business and Public Admin Alumni Assoc; Business and Economic Develop Comm Natl Black MBA Assoc 1986-; treasurer, Natl Black MBA Assn DC Chapter 1988-; Telecommunications Network Exchange; board member, United Way of the National Capital Area Membership and Allocations Board; National Black MBA Association Scholarship Fund, trustee; Washington Urban League, life mem; NAACP, life mem; Community of Hope, mem, board of directors; Washington Area Telephone Federal Credit Union, alternate, supervisory committee, mem, mem services committee; Washington Society of Investment Analysts, mem; Financial Executives Institute, mem; US Small Business Administration, mem, national advisors council. **Honors/Awds:** Elizabeth B Adams Memorial Award, 1988; Scholarship Recipient, National Black MBA Assn, 1987; Scholarship Recipient, George Washington University; Materials Management Cost Improvement Award, 1989. **Home Addr:** 13300 Burleigh St, Upper Marlboro, MD 20774, (301)249-0577. **Business Addr:** 1201 Pennsylvania Ave NW, Ste 300, Washington, DC 20004.

TURNER, MELVIN DUVAL
Administrator, director. **Personal:** Born Jun 10, 1949, Detroit, MI; married Connie Jean Long; children: Melvin D. **Educ:** Hartwick Coll, BA 1971; Universidad Ibero-americana, Mexico City;; attended. **Career:** CAPTURE, Citizens Crime Prevention Inc, exec dir 1974-; San Mateo Co;; adult probation officer 1972-74; OICW Job Training Ctr, bi-lingual vocational counselor 1971-72; Sickle Cell Anemia Research & Educ Found San Francisco, chmn of bd 1976-. **Orgs:** Mem Human Resource Comm City of San Mateo 1978-; mem CA Crime Prevention Officers Assn present; tech adv group mem CA Crime Resistancew Task Force, present. **Honors/Awds:** Cert of Commendation Foster City Police Dept 1980; host weekly radio talk slhow "Crime the Courts & You" 1979-80; various publs 1977. **Business Addr:** 2121 S El Camino Real, Ste 310, San Mateo, CA 94403.

TURNER, MELVIN E.
Undersheriff, chief deputy. **Personal:** Born Nov 5, 1947, Detroit, MI; son of Martha & M E Turner; divorced; children: Naetta Williams, Tramale, Dorian. **Educ:** Madonna Coll, Associate, 1976, BS, 1977; Univ of Detroit, MA, 1979. **Career:** Wayne County, police officer, 1969, investigator, 1973, sgt, 1976, lieutenant, 1980, captain, 1987, police commander, 1988, exec deputy chief, 1990, undersheriff/chief deputy, 1991-; FBI National Academy, 1986; BNDD Academy, 1973. **Orgs:** Natl Assn of Chief of Police; FBI Natl Academy Assn, 1986-; International Narcotic Enforcement Officers Assn; Michigan Sheriffs' Assn; Wayne County Awards Committee, 1993-; Wayne County Comm Corrections (Alternate), 1993-; Wayne County Ethics Bd, 1994-; Woodward Academy, board of directors. **Honors/Awds:** Citation for Valiant Service in the Line of Duty; Award of Special Honor; US Dept of Justice Commendation; 36th District Court, Certificate of Award; Sheriff's Esteem Service Award; Distinguished Service Medal. **Business Addr:** Undersheriff/Chief Deputy, Wayne County Sheriff's Dept, 1231 St Antoine, Administration Bldg, Detroit, MI 48226, (313)224-2232.

TURNER, MIKOEL
Association executive. **Personal:** Born Aug 22, 1950, New York, NY; son of Enid Gordon and Richard Turner; divorced; children: Mekell Mia. **Educ:** Cobleskill A&T Coll, New York, AAS, 1971; Cornell Univ, Ithaca NY, BS, 1974. **Career:** Marriott Corp, dept mgr, 1975-81, gen mgr, 1981-84; Fletcher Consulting Service, partner, 1982-; Board of Ed, NJ, supervisor, 1984-88; Turner & Assoc, owner; New York Board of Educ, culinary arts coordinator, 1990; Chelsea Catering, NJ, dept mgr, 1988-; Guest Services Healthcare Company, pres, 1994-; National Association of Black Hospitality Professionals, president, currently. **Orgs:** Bd mem, Union County Psych Clinic; bd mem, Plainfield Economic Development Corp. **Honors/Awds:** Food Management Professional, certified; certified teacher. **Business Addr:** President, National Association of Black Hospitality Professionals, PO Box 8132, Columbus, GA 31908-8132.

TURNER, MOSES
Educator. **Personal:** Born Mar 28, 1938, Athens, GA; son of Roberta Turner and Audly Turner; married Joan; children: Shaul, Lisa, Chris. **Educ:** Albany State Coll, BA 1962; Central Washington State Coll, MA 1969; Washington State Univ, PhD 1974; Harvard Univ Inst for Educ Mgmt 1982. **Career:** Public school teacher and Columbia Basin Comm College, chair/dir music prog 1969-72; Washington State Univ, asst dean of students 1972-77; TX Tech Univ, dean/dir student life 1977-79; MI State Univ, vice pres student affairs 1979-. **Orgs:** Bd mem Opera Company of Mid-MI, Oakes Sports Program, Boy Scouts of Amer; mem Governor's Prayer Breakfast Commn; mem MI Black Caucus Foundation; bd mem Himan Fdn for Awarding Scholarships to deserving high school students; spokesperson Youth Motivation in MI; bd mem Lansing Symphony Bd of Dirs; mem Subcomm on Fed Student Financial Assistance, Natl Assoc of State Univs and Land-Grant Colls; bd mem Golden Key Natl Honor Soc; Lansing Assn of Black Org; Lansing Chapter of Alpha Chi Boule; Editorial Bd of Natl Assn Student Personnel Administrators, Inc; member, National Congress of Black Faculty. **Honors/Awds:** President's Awd Golden Key Natl Honor Soc 1986. **Military Serv:** AUS sgt 1962-65. **Business Addr:** Vice Pres for Student Affairs, MI State University, 153 Student Serv Bldg, East Lansing, MI 48824.

TURNER, PETER. **See TURNER, ERVIN.**

TURNER, REGINALD M., JR.
Attorney. **Personal:** Born Feb 25, 1960, Detroit, MI; son of Reginald M Turner, Sr & Anne L Turner; married Marcia Holland Turner, Jun 10, 1989; children: Nia. **Educ:** Wayne State Univ, BS, 1982; Univ of Michigan, Law School, JD, 1987. **Career:** Michigan Supreme Court, law clerk to justice Dennis Archer, 1987-89; Sachs, Waldman, O'Hare, partner, 1989-. **Orgs:** State Bar of Michigan, commissioner, 1995-; National Bar Association, bd of governors exec comm, 1995-; Wolverine Bar Association, past pres, 1987-; Detroit Metro Bar Association, 1987-; Barristers of Detroit Metro Bar Association, past pres, 1987-97; American Bar Association, 1985-. **Honors/Awds:** American Bar Foundation Fellow, 1997; White House Fellow, 1996-97; Michigan State Bar Foundation Fellow, 1995; State Bar of Michigan, Outstanding Young Lawyer, 1995. **Business Addr:** Esquire, Sachs, Waldman, O'Hare, Helveston, Bogas & McIntosh, PC, 1000 Farmer St, Detroit, MI 48226-2834, (313)496-9418.

TURNER, RICHARD M., III
Educational administrator. **Personal:** Born in Charleston, SC; married Dolores Walker Turner; children: two. **Educ:** Fisk Univ; Indiana Univ-Bloomington, master of music ed, doctor of music ed. **Career:** South Central Community Coll, pres; Lane Community Coll, pres; Nashville State Technical Institute, pres; Fisk Univ, assoc prof of music, Dept of Music, chairman, Fisk Jubilee Singers, dir; Wayne County Community Coll Northwest Campus, dean; Wayne County Community Coll, interim pres, currently. **Orgs:** American Assn of Community Colleges; Intl Education Commission of the American Council on Education; Natl Commission for Cooperative Education, bd of trustees; Natl Council on Black American Affairs, bd member; United Way; American Red Cross; Natl Conf of Christians and Jews. **Business Addr:** Interim President, Wayne County Community College, 801 W Fort St, Detroit, MI 48226, (313)496-2500.

TURNER, ROBERT, JR.
Assistant head football coach. **Personal:** Born May 6, 1949, Midway, AL; son of Julia Ann Turner and Robert Turner Sr; married Kimberly Jean Turner; children: Nacole, Krishana, Kiaana. **Educ:** Indiana State Univ, Terre Haute, IN, BS, 1972, MS, 1976. **Career:** Kokomo Haworth High School, Kokomo, IN, asst football/basketball coach, admin asst, 1972-75; Indiana State Univ, special team coordinator & asst football coach, 1975-83; Fresno State Univ, asst football coach, 1983-89; Ohio State Univ, asst football coach, 1989-90; Purdue Univ, asst head football coach & offensive coordinator, 1990-. **Orgs:** American Football Coaches Association; Black Coaches Association; National Association for Advancement Colored People; Indiana State Univ Alumni Assn; Kappa Alpha Psi Fraternity; Fellowship Christian Athletes. **Business Addr:** Asst Head Coach & Offensive Coordnator, Purdue University, Football Office, West Lafayette, IN 47907.

TURNER, ROBERT LLOYD
State representative. **Personal:** Born Sep 14, 1947, Columbus, MS; married Gloria; children: Robert, Roosevelt, Ryan. **Educ:** Univ of Wisc, Parkside, BS. **Career:** Publisher; personnel manager; restaurant owner; WI State Assembly, state representative, 1991-. **Orgs:** NAACP; Urban League; Democratic Party; Amer Legion; South Gate Lodge #6 Prince Hall; Racine City Council, alderman, 1976-; City of Racine Finance Committee, chairman; State of WI Elections Bd, chairman, 1990; Community Development Committee; Economic Development Committee, City of Racine, chairman; Assembly Committee on Highways and Transportation; Assembly Committee on Urban and Local Affairs; Assembly Committee on Financial Institutions; Assembly Committee on Labor and Employment; Assembly Committee on Ways and Means; State of WI Bldg Commission; Governor's Task Force on Federal Clean Air Act Implementation. **Military Serv:** USAF sgt 1967-71; Commendation Medal for Meritorious Service Vietnam. **Home Addr:** 36 McKinley Ave, Racine, WI 53404. **Business Addr:** State Representative, Wisconsin State Assembly, PO Box 8953, Madison, WI 53708-8953.

TURNER, ROBERT S., JR.
Wholesale company executive. **Personal:** Born Sep 8, 1935, Winston-Salem, NC; son of Mary P Turner and Robert S Turner Sr; divorced; children: Terra L. **Educ:** North Carolina A&T; Fenn College; Amos Tuck School. **Career:** State of Ohio, computer/radar mechanic, 1960-65; Lear Power Equipment, electrician, 1965-66; Weathead, instrument technician, 1966-68; Philips, electron microscope repair, 1968-70; Honeywell, sales, 1970-85; The Turner Group, president, currently. **Orgs:** Omega Psi Phi Fraternity. **Military Serv:** US Army, ssgt, 1956-60. **Business Phone:** 800-553-9191.

TURNER, SCOTT
Professional football player. **Personal:** Born Feb 26, 1972, Richardson, TX; married Robin. **Educ:** Univ of Illinois, bachelor's degree in speech communication. **Career:** Washington Redskins, defensive back, 1995-. **Business Addr:** Professional Football Player, Washington Redskins, 13832 Redskin Dr, Herndon, VA 22071, (703)471-9100.

TURNER, SHARON V.
Elections director. **Personal:** Born Jul 8, 1945, Kansas City, MO; daughter of Eunice Weaver Douglass Shellner and O E Douglass; divorced; children: Sheri Lynette Turner-Duff, Paul Eugene Jr. **Educ:** Park College, BS, Psychology, Kansas City MO, 1993; Baker University, MS, Management, Overland Park, KS, 1994. **Career:** Southwestern Bell Telephone, Kansas City MO, area manager, 1966-93; Elections Director-Kansas City, MO, 1994-. **Orgs:** Secretary, Leon Jordan Scholarship fund, 1984-95; trustee, Urban League, 1985-89; trustee, Rehabilitation Loan Corp, 1987-89; chair, scholarship comm, Southern Christian Leadership Conf, 1988-95; gen telethon chair, United Negro College Fund, 1989; vice pres, Black Achievers Society, 1989-90; vice pres, Black Chamber of Commerce, 1989-90; pres, Urban League top Notch Team, 1991-93; board of directors, Kansas City Visitors and Convention Bureau, 1991-94; gala co-chair, Kansas City Friends of Alvin Ailey, 1992; first vice pres, SCLC, 1992-95; fund development chair, Jackson County Links, Inc, 1994-. **Honors/Awds:** Boss of the Year, Galaxy II Chapter ABWA, 1983; Black Achiever in Industry, 1983; Volunteer Service Award, YMCA, 1984; Kansas City's 100 Most Influential Black Women, Kansas City Globe Newspaper, 1984; Star Panelist, UNCF, 1985; Special Recognition, Black Achiever in Industry, 1987; Outstanding Business Woman of the Year, Natl Assn of Negro Business and Professional Women, 1987; Presidents Award, Black Chamber of Commerce, 1988; Juneteenth Women of Year, Black Archives, 1989; Difference Maker, Urban League, 1989; Kansas City Globe's 100 Most Influential, 1993. **Business Addr:** Director of Elections, Kansas City Board of Election Commissioners, 1828 Walnut, Ste 300, Kansas City, MO 64108.

TURNER, SHIRLEY
Educator. **Personal:** Born Mar 22, 1936, South Bend, IN; divorced; children: Dawn, Kimberly, Steven. **Educ:** WMU, BS 1972; WMU, MA 1977. **Career:** Fisk University, dean of students, dir of career planning & placement; WMU Placement Serv, asst dir; WMU Para School Learning Center. **Orgs:** Urban Leg of So Bend St Joseph Co Dir of Edn; Kalamazoo Pub Lib pub sch bd dir Planned Parenthood Assn; bd YMCA; YWCA Com Outreach Adv; Youth Serv Sys Adv Bd; Cont Educ for Young Women Adv Bd; consult Upward Boun Univ of Notre Dame; Planned Parenthood Teen Clinics; Delta Sigma Theta Serv Sor; Dulcet Club of Kalamazoo; MI Assn of No White Concerns; Kalamazoo Personnel Assn; Midwest Cool Placement Assn. **Honors/Awds:** Laubaugh Lit Inst Teach Awd; MI Nat All of Bus Career Guid Inst Awd; WMU Awds of Excel Sch of Soc Work Field Instr; Cert of Academic Apprec; Cert of Career Exploration Excel; produced, directed video tape, demo of prof interview tech. **Business Addr:** Dir of Career Placement, Rider College, 2083 Lawrenceville, Lawrenceville, NJ 08648-3099.

TURNER, TINA (ANNA MAE BULLOCK)
Singer. **Personal:** Born Nov 25, 1941, Nutbush, TN; married Ike Turner (divorced 1976); children: Craig, Ronald Revelle. **Career:** Ike and Tina Turner Revue, 1960-76; Solo albums: Private Dancer, 1984, Break Every Rule, Tina Live in Europe, For-

eign Affair; actress, Mad Max Beyond Thunderdome, 1985; Subject of the movie, What's Love Got to do with it?, 1993. **Honors/Awds:** 5 Grammy Awds incl "Better Be Good To Me" and best rock female for album Tina Live in Europe, 1989; 2 Amer Music Awds; Triple Platinum Album "Private Dancer"; Gold Single "What's Love Got To Do With It?"; Silver Disk Awd "Let's Stay Together"; Honoree, ABAA Music Award, 1985; honored with a star on the Hollywood Walk of Fame; author, I, Tina, My Life Story, 1986; Citation, Ms Magazine, 1984; MTV Video Award. **Business Addr:** Singer, c/o Roger Davies Management, 14755 Ventura Blvd, #772, Sherman Oaks, CA 91403.

TURNER, TOM
Union official. **Career:** Michigan AFL-CIO, secretary-treasurer, currently; Natl NAACP, board member, currently; Detroit Economic Growth Corp, board member, currently. **Business Addr:** Secretary-Treasurer, Michigan AFL-CIO, 2550 W Grand Blvd, Detroit, MI 48208, (313)894-6348.

TURNER, VIVIAN LOVE
Tobacco company executive. **Personal:** Born May 25, 1947, Concord, NC; daughter of Othella Spears Love and F Haywood Love; married William H Turner, Sep 6, 1969; children: Kisha, William, Hodari. **Educ:** Livingstone College, Salisbury, NC, BS, math, 1968; University of Notre Dame, South Bend, IN, MA, education, 1971. **Career:** Fisk University, Nashville, TN, programmer/analyst, 1971-73; University of Maryland, Princess Anne, MD, lecturer, 1974-77; Digital Equipment Corp, Lanham, MD, sr education specialist, 1977-79; Lexington Community College, Lexington, KY, assoc professor, data processing tech, 1980-85; R J Reynolds Tobacco Co, Winston-Salem, NC, programmer/analyst II, 1985-90, mgr community program, 1990-. **Orgs:** Board member, Winston Lake YMCA, 1990-91; Alpha Kappa Alpha Sorority, 1966-; Kentucky Academic Computer Users Group, 1980-85; student chapter sponsor, Data Processing Management Assn, 1981-85; director of Christian education, Emmanuel Baptist Church, 1989-; Links, 1996-; Forsyth County United Way, bd, 1993-; Winston-Salem State University, foundation bd, 1994-. **Honors/Awds:** United Negro College Fund Scholarship, Livingstone College, 1964-68; Alpha Kappa Mu Honor Society, 1967; Danforth Associate, 1976-85; Volunteer of Year, Winston Lake YMCA, 1994; Winston-Salem Chronicle Woman of the Year, 1995; Seedco Distinguished Svc Awd, 1997. **Business Addr:** Manager, Community Programs, RJ Reynolds Tobacco Co, PO Box 2959, Winston-Salem, NC 27102, (336)741-0049.

TURNER, VIVIAN VANESSA
Accountant. **Personal:** Born Feb 18, 1955, Kilmarnock, VA; daughter of Vivian Alease Corbin Turner (deceased) and John F Turner (deceased). **Educ:** VA State Univ, BS Acctg Fin 1977; Univ of Hartford, MBA candidate 1990. **Career:** Texaco Inc, auditor 1977-78; The Traveler, accountant 1978-79; Aetna Life & Casualty, auditor 1979-80, sr admin corp human resources 1980-84, pension invest sales consult 1984-85, mgr accounting serv 1985-. **Orgs:** Dir Red Cross 1985-; dir YWCA 1985-; mem United Way 1985-; officer Alpha Kappa Alpha.

TURNER, W. BURGHARDT
Educator. **Personal:** Born Jul 30, 1915, Jamaica, NY; son of Frosty Duncan Turner and Frank M Turner Sr; married Joyce Moore; children: Mitchell, Sylvia, Richard. **Educ:** KY State Coll, AB, Columbia Univ, MA; Colunbia Univ & NY Univ, Post Grad. **Career:** NY City, Bay Shore, Patchogue, Long Island, teacher 15 yrs; Long Island Univ Southampton Coll, assoc prof history 1965-68; State Univ of NY Stony Brook, asst prof history 1968-79, prof emeritus 1979. **Orgs:** Mem, dir Natl Ed Assn Proj Civil Rights 1965; asst dir Inst School Integration Southampton Coll 1966; pres NAACP; chmn Suffolk Cty Human Rights Comm; vice pres United Fund; dir Legal Aid Soc Suffolk Cty; chmn Equal Oppty Employment Comm SUNY Stony Brook; chmn Curriculum Comm Continuing Ed; chmn bd dir Econ Oppty Council of Suffolk 1986-87. **Honors/Awds:** Man of the Year Mens Club Temple Beth-El 1962; Man of the Year Eastern Long Island Assn Negro Bus & Professional Women 1963; Outstanding Serv Awd Natl Conf Christian & Jews 1972; co-author with Joyce Moore Turner, Richard B Moore: Caribbean Militant in Harlem, Univ of Indiana Press, Black American Writers, St Martins Press NY. **Military Serv:** US Army 92nd Infantry Div 1942-45. **Business Addr:** Assistant Professor, History, State Univ of New York, Stony Brook, NY 11794.

TURNER, WALLACE E.
Scientist (retired). **Personal:** Born Jan 2, 1923, Nashville, TN; son of Florence Jean Johnson Turner and Wallace Turner, Sr.; married Dr Jeannette M Simms; children: Reid, Lorraine, Paul, Geoffrey. **Educ:** Knoxville Coll, BS 1944; NY Univ, MA 1947; Univ of NC Chapel Hill, MPH, Dr PH 1971. **Career:** VT Dept of Health Burlington, microbiologist 1953-68; PA Dept of Health Bur of Lab, dir of office of lab safety health & rsch 1971-80; retired 1988. **Orgs:** Mem Amer Soc for Microbiologists 1970-80; former chmn for mem Amer Publ Health Assoc 1970-80; mem NAACP 1975-85, Knoxville Coll Club 1975-80. **Honors/Awds:** Several articles on Microbiology Publ in Jrnl of Mycologiaetpathologica 1974, Annals of Internal Med 1978, Jrnl of Clinical Microbiology 1980. **Military Serv:** USAF staff sgt 1944-46. **Home Addr:** 118 Petrie Ave, Rosemont, PA 19010.

TURNER, WILLIAM H.
State government official. **Personal:** Born Aug 1, 1931, Miami, FL; divorced; children: 4. **Educ:** Bethune Cookman Coll, BS 1956; Univ of Miami, MEd 1969. **Career:** City of Miami, police officer, 1956-57; Dade County Public School, teacher, asst principal for comnty eductn, school bd mem, chair, 1957-71; Florida Memorial Clg, dir of clg placement and comnty relations; Miami-Dade Rapid Transit System, consultant; Florida State Senate, District 36, senator, currently. **Orgs:** Dade County Schl Bd 1971; vice chrmn Sch bd of Dade & Co 1972-74; bd of dir Coun of Great City Sch 1974-77; intergove liaison OTA; Edison Little Rvr, self help cmte cncl 1975-77, 1977-79, advs bd, 1971 ; FL Schl Bd Assn, 1971, legsltv cmte, 1974 ; Nat Sch Bd Assn 1971; bd mem City of Miami Comm Actn; bd mem Model Cities Prgrm Admnstr 1971; adv bd Miami Dade Comm Coll; Dade Co Assn for Retarded Chldrn; v p Black Grove; plnnng com Third Century; So Assn of Black Adminstr Persnnl 1974; dir of comm educ Charles R Drew Jr HS 1969-71; Ch of Incrntn (Episcopal); Dade Co Yng Dem; YMCA, George Washington Carver Br, mgmt bd; adv bd Yth Indstrs; Dade Co Tax Adjustment Bd 1971; Released Employment Placement Srvc, advs bd; Elks Lodge, exe cmte; Demcrtc Club of Miami Beach, 1974. **Honors/Awds:** Cert Creative Writing, Bethune Cookman Coll; Sch Bell Awd Dade Co Dade Co Classroom Tchr Assn; Educ Srv Awd Miami Dade Comm Coll; Melvin Rolle Memrl Awd Liberty News Miami; Pi Beta Sigma, Tau Zeta Cit of Yr 1971; Nathan Collier Meritorious Srv Awd FL Memrl Coll 1971; Outstndng Civic Srv Awd Bethune Cookman Coll 1973; Certf Apprctn Nat Caucus Black Sch Bd Mem, Nat Sch Bd Assn 1974; Certif Apprctn FL A&M Univ 1974; Plaque Miami Nrthwstrn Parent Adv Coun Dedicated Efforts Prvd Educ Opprtnts Yth Comm 1974; Cert Apprctn Dade Co Coun PTA 1974; Plaque for Otstnding & Meritorious Srv People Brothermen 1974; Educ of Yr Orchard Villa PTA 1974; Cert Merit Srv Big Brothers, Miami, 1974; Faith Clg, Honorary LLD, 1982. **Military Serv:** US Army, personnel administrative assistant, 1951-53. **Business Addr:** State Senator, District 36, Florida State Senate, 1175 NE 125th St, Ste 320, North Miami, FL 33161.

TURNER, WILLIAM HOBERT
Educator. **Personal:** Born Jul 20, 1946, Lynch, KY; married Vivian Love; children: Kisha, William K, Hodari. **Educ:** Univ of KY, BS 1968; Univ of Notre Dame, PhD 1974. **Career:** Howard Univ, sr rsch fellow 1977-79; Univ of KY, asst prof of sociology 1979-84; KY State Univ, dean of arts and sciences 1984-85; Berea College, distinguished visiting professor of Black and Appalachian studies, 1988; Winston Salem State Univ, chairman of social sciences beginning 1985; B&C Intl Inc, senior vp; Turner & Assoc, pres, currently. **Orgs:** Eastern KY Social/Heritage Soc, historian/archivist 1977-; USAID, consultant 1986; Comm on Religion in Appalachia, commissioner 1986-; EKSC, editor/publisher; Black Mountain Improvement Association, founder, 1988; Southern Regional Council; Appalachian African American Community Development Center; Phi Beta Sigma Fraternity; Prince Hall Masons. **Honors/Awds:** Natl Rsch Council, Ford Foundation fellow 1983; Mountain Spirit Award, 1994. **Business Addr:** President, Turner & Associates, Box 4584, Winston-Salem, NC 27115.

TURNER, WILLIE
Educator. **Personal:** Born Feb 1, 1935; married Porter; children: Vincent, Austin, Nicole, Dina. **Educ:** MD St Coll, BS 1957; OH St U, MSc 1959; PhD 1961. **Career:** MD State Coll, lab asst 1954-57; MD State Coll, rsch asst 1957; MD St Coll, grad asst 1957-59; Meharry Med Coll, instr of mcrblgy 1962-63; Meharry Med Coll, asst prof microbiology 1963-66; TN St A&I Univ, lecturer 1962; Bowie State Coll, 1969; Howard Univ, prof chmn microbiology Dept 1971; OH St Univ, NIH pre doctoral fellow 1959-61; Naval Med Rsch Inst, NIH postdoctoral fellow 1961-62; Nat Cancer Inst, NCI staff fellow 1966-69; Natl Cancer Inst, NCI sr staff fellow, 1969-70; head microbiology section 1970-71. **Orgs:** Mem, Sigma Xi; Am Soc for Microbiology; Am Assn Advancement Sci; NY Acad Sci; Amer Assn Cancer Rsch; Tissue Culture Assn; Soc Experimental Biology & Med; Amer Assn Immunologists; Am Assn Med School Chmn; Am Assn Dental School Chmn. **Honors/Awds:** Recipient numerous NIH Rsch Grants; NCI Cancer Center Core Grant 1973; NIH ICC Exchange Fellow to Paris 1971. **Business Addr:** Howard Univ, Coll of Med, 520 W St, NW, Washington, DC 20001-2337.

TURNER, WINSTON E.
Educator (retired). **Personal:** Born Aug 23, 1921, Washington, DC; son of Mary Montague Turner and Frederick Finley Turner; married Helen Smith Turner; children: Lisa, Valerie. **Educ:** Miner Teachers Coll, BS 1947; NY Univ, MA 1949; St Coll Educ Plattsburgh NY; DC Tchrs Coll; Georgetown U; Univ Bridgeport Ct. **Career:** DC Pblc Schls, tchr 1947-54; Miner Tchrs Coll, monroe lab sch 1954-57; DC Tchrs Coll, asst prof educ truesdell lab sch 1957-59; HD Cooke Elem Sch Wash DC, prin 1959-69; River Terrace Elem Sch Wash DC, prin, until 1976. **Orgs:** Life mem Natl Educ Assn; Phi Delta Kappa; pres Natl Assn Elem Sch Prins 1974-75; DC Elem Sch Prins Assn; Assn Study Negro Life History; pres vice pres treas prog ch Elem Sch Prins Assn Wash DC; ch Non Graded & Team Tchng Com Model Schs Div; exec com cncl offcrs DC Pub Schs; Examining Panels Prin Asst Prins DC Pub Schs; examining asst Day Elem Sch Prins NY City; bd dirs SE Neighbrhd Hse; board of directors Columbia Hghts Boys Clb; Queens Chapel Civic Assn; life mem NAACP; Omega Psi Phi Frat; Pigskin Clb Wash DC; Mt Horeb Bapt Ch. **Honors/Awds:** Guest lectr Howard Univ 1974; Outstndng Prin Awd DC Elem Sch Prin Assn 1974; Outstanding Ret Tr Award, Jr Citizens Corps 1978; Outstanding Public Service: Mayor Baltimore Md, Afro-American Newspaper, Central Summerfield United Meth Church, 1980; Man of the Year, New Bethel Baptist Church, 1981; publications, The Black Principal and the Bicentennial, Principal, 1976; Principals in the Pressure Cooker, Principal 1977; Expanding Our Horizons through Global Education, Principal 1980. **Military Serv:** US Army 1st sgt 1942-46. **Home Addr:** 1626 Varnum Pl NE, Washington, DC 20017.

TURNER, YVONNE WILLIAMS
Community activist (retired). **Personal:** Born Apr 5, 1927, Birmingham, AL; daughter of Leitha W Williams (deceased) and John Harvey Williams; married James L Turner Sr, Jun 9, 1945; children: Philandus C, Roderick G, Keith H, Leitha B, Stanley M. **Educ:** Booker T Washington Junior College of Business, Birmingham, AL, diploma, 1952; Rosetta Reifer's School of Modeling, New York, NY, certificate, 1954; Anna Watson's School of Millinery Designing, 1958-68; Dale Carnegie School, Birmingham, AL, certificate, 1960; 100 or more workshops all descriptions. **Career:** Booker T Washington Insurance Company, Birmingham, AL, clerk, 1946-64; Clyde Kirby Insurance Agency, Birmingham, AL, secretary, 1965-66; Department of Housing and Urban Development, Birmingham, AL, clerk trypist, 1966-77, computer technician, 1977-82, community resources specialist, 1982-86, program assistant in single family division loan management, 1986-87; (Retired); Birmingham Housing Authority, Birmingham, AL, housing counselor, 1987-90. **Orgs:** Member, Alabama Christian Movement for Human Rights and Southern Christian Leadership Conference, 1956-; fund raiser, United Negro College Fund, 1965-; former member, Birmingham Design Review Committee, Birmingham, AL, 1979-85; member, 1985-, Birmingham Arts Commission, Birmingham, AL; member, Jefferson-Blount-St Clair Mental Health/Mental Retardation Authority Board, 1989-91; member, Birmingham's Image Committee 1990-91; associate member, Alabama State University Alumni, 1990-; Band Mother, Alabama State University, 1979-; president or busines manager, Wilkerson Elem & A H Parker High Band Boosters, 1975-89; member, Red Cross Minority Involvement Committee, 1989-91; chartered mem, Magic City Chapter Links, Inc, 1993; served eight years as Alabama Election Law Commissioner; presently, Deputy Registrar. **Honors/Awds:** Certificate of recognition in field of business, Booker T Washington Junior College of Business Alumni Association, 1978; plaque for 25 years of outstanding service, National Southern Christian Leadership Conference, 1982; alumni merit award, Booker T Washington Junior College of Business, 1984; named in House of Representative Resolution 125, 1988; HR and author of column "Socially Speaking," Birmingham Times, 1988-92; Honored by Gov Guy Hunt, Arts, 1989; Iota Phi Lambda Sorority, 1981; Alpha Phi Chi Sorority, 1985; Zeta Phi Beta Sorority, Women of the Year, 1990; Civil Rights Honoree during 1991 Martin Luther King Jr Birthday Celebration, Omisson Lambda Chpt; Alpha Phi Alpha Fraternity Inc; HUD's Faithful Service to US Government Award, 1987; Ladies of Distinction, Sixth Ave Bapt Church, 1992; SCLS Women, Special Award, 1991; Channel 42, WBMG/TV Jefferson Award, Bronze Medal, Documentation on Civil Rights, 1992; United to Serve Amer Diamond Award, 1992; WENN 107-WAGG 1320 and Anheuser's Citizen of the Week, 1991; 21st Century Human Rights Movement, Appreciation for Dedicated Services to Mankind, 1991; Certificate of Appreciation, AL State Univ, Connection Day Committee, 1992; Curioso Club's Rose Award, 1992; Cert of Appreciation, Birmingham City Council, District #4; Meritorious Service Award, United Negro Coll Fund, Inc, 1993; Birmingham Comm Schools Appreciation, 1991-92; Honored for 14 years, Faithful and Dedicated Services, AL State Univ Marching Band of Montgomery AL, 1994; Community Service Award, Birmingham Baptist College, Black Catholic Ministries, Nation of Islam; Invisible Giants of the Voting Rights Movement, Honored in Selma, Commendation of the Voting Rights March and Bloody Sunday, March 4, 1995; Plaque, NAACP, Outstanding African American, 1996; Academy of Fine Arts, Inc, Citizen Arts Award, 1996. **Special Achievements:** Lectured at the Birmingham Civil Rights Institute, "Yesterdays Voices of African-American Women of the Movement," 1996; Spoke at the Historic 16th Street Baptist Church where four little girls were killed, during Dr Martin Luther King's Birthday Celebration, 1997. **Home Addr:** 504-10th Court, West, Birmingham, AL 35204.

TURNER-FORTE, DIANA
Dancer, choreographer, arts administrator, educator. **Personal:** Born Aug 24, 1951, Columbus, OH; daughter of Ethel S Turner and Everhart S Turner Sr; married Kenneth T Forte, Aug 1993. **Educ:** Capital University, BA, 1985; Antioch University, MA, 1991. **Career:** Des Moines Ballet Company, dancer, soloist, 1980-81; Ohio Arts Council, minority arts assistant, 1981-83; Balitmore School for the Arts, faculty, 1983-86; BalletMet, faculty, 1986-; Antioch University, adjunct faculty, 1990-; Greater Columbus Arts Council, artists-in-schools program director, 1991-. **Orgs:** Maryland State Arts Council, dance advisory pan-

elist, 1984-86; Franklin County Educational Council, arts advisory panel chair, 1991; Ohio Dance, advisory board, 1991; Third Ave Performing Space, community fundraising committee, 1992; WOSU Radio, board of trustees, 1992. **Business Addr:** Program Director, Artists-in-Schools, Greater Columbus Arts Council, 55 E State St, Columbus, OH 43215, (614)224-2606.

TURNER-GIVENS, ELLA MAE
Consultant, educator, liaison, pianist, organist. **Personal:** Born Jun 5, 1927, Los Angeles, CA; daughter of Ruth Dean Moore and Rev Ezekiel Moore; married Walter Givens; children: Edward Samuel Turner. **Educ:** Univ of Southern California, BMusic, 1957; State of California Dept of Educ, life diploma, special secondary teaching credential in music, 1965; UCLA Graduate School Univ of California, 1965, 1966, 1968; California Dept of Educ, life diploma, standard secondary teaching credential in English, 1968. **Career:** Los Angeles Unified School Dist, teacher 1971-; Los Angeles High School, teacher 1967-71; Girls Social Adjustment School, teacher 1966-67; Markham Jr High School Summer Opportunity Center Program, teacher 1965; Manual Arts High School, teacher summer 1962; Markham Jr High School, teacher 1958-66; Foshay Jr High School, teacher 1957-58. **Orgs:** Chmn Natl Advisory Council on Environmental Educ; HEW; advisory council HUD; Urban Studies Fellowship Program: mem Textbook Adoption Comm Los Angeles Unified Schools District; adjudicator Southern California Vocal Assn; host, chmn Southern California Vocal Assn Choral Festivals; pres Secondary Music Teacher Assn; chmn, bd dir, Do Re Me Child Devel Center; member: NEA, California Teacher Assn; Los Angeles Teacher Assn; Music Educ Natl Conf, Life; Los Angeles County Music Educ Assn; Amer Choral Dir Assn; Southern California Vocal Assn; Advisory Health Council: State Dept of Health; Child Devel Advisory Bd; General State Dept of Health, consultant: California State Dept of Health, State of California Personnel Bd, W Interstate Commn on Higher Educ, California Work Incentive Plan Program, Neighborhood Adult Participation Proj, Delinquency Prevention Center; mem, Atty Gen, Vol Advisory Council, Neumeyer Found; representative State Control Comm; appointee California Gov Comm for Employment of the Handicapped; Statewide Planning Project on Vocational Rehabilition, Advisory Comm Vocational Rehabilitation; sec Advisory Comm, Urban Affairs Inst; Dist Atty Advisory Council; Dist Atty Legis Council. **Honors/Awds:** Recipient 10th Dist PTA 4 year scholarship; Delta Sigma Theta Sor Scholarship; Order of the E Star Scholarship awarded twice; Women's Political Study Club Scholarship; first black woman in US history to chair a Natl Advisory Council. **Home Addr:** 2158 W 82nd St, Los Angeles, CA 90047.

TURNIPSEED, CARL WENDELL
Banker. **Personal:** Born Dec 21, 1947, Baltimore, MD; son of Alice Poyner Turnipseed and Willis Turnipseed; married Joyce Hill, Jun 6, 1970; children: Danielle. **Educ:** Morgan State Coll, BS 1969; NY Univ Grad Sch of Business, MBA 1974. **Career:** Fed Reserve Bank of NY, over 20 yrs of mgmt experience in various areas incl acctng, govt bonds, check proc, elect funds trnsfers, personnel, foreign relations, vp, pres, personnel function, currently. **Orgs:** Urban Bankers Coalition internal vice pres; Keeper of the Exchequer Brooklyn Long Island Alumni Kappa Alpha Psi Fraternity l988-; mem Union Baptist Church 1980-; life mem NAACP 1982-; mem Assoc of MBA Executives 1982-; mem Urban Bankers Assn 1983-; mem Black MBA Assn 1983-; mem MBA Executives; member 16th SEANZA Central Banking Program 1986; vstg prof Natl Urban League BEEP; life member, Kappa Alpha Psi Fraternity; member, Society for Human Resource Management. **Honors/Awds:** Martin Luther King Jr Alumni Assoc of NY Univ Awd for Achievements in Commerce 1978; President's Award for Excellence Federal Reserve Bank of N.Y. l987; Urban Bankers Coalition, Banker of the Year, 1992. **Military Serv:** AUS 1st lt 2 yrs. **Business Addr:** Vice President, Personnel Function, Federal Reserve Bank of NY, 33 Liberty St, New York, NY 10045.

TURNLEY, RICHARD DICK, JR.
Credit union officer. **Personal:** Born Nov 15, 1933, Plaquemine, LA; son of Dorothy Banks; married Joyce Huntsberry; children: Tamera, Sharon, Richard. **Educ:** Southern Univ, BS, 1955, JD, 1972; Univ of Wisconsin, Madison, 1978. **Career:** State of Louisiana, state representative, 1972-84; Southern Teachers and Parents Federal Credit Union, treasurer and manager, currently. **Orgs:** Free and Accepted Masons; Capitol City Golf Assn; Louis Sewell Boys Scouts; life member, Southern Univ Alumni Assn. **Honors/Awds:** Outstanding Contribution in Minority Business Development; Outstanding Service Award, Louisiana Justice of Peace and Constables Assn. **Military Serv:** US Army, 1955-61.

TURNQUEST, SANDRA CLOSE
Management services executive. **Personal:** Born Jul 19, 1954, Bainbridge, GA; daughter of Daisy Close and Frank Close; married Rhett Edwin Turnquest, Dec 14, 1987; children: Austin Royce. **Educ:** Florida Agricultural and Mechanical University, Tallahassee, FL, BS, political science, magna cum laudae 1972-75; Florida Atlantic University, Boca Raton, FL, MPA, 1975-77. **Career:** South Florida Water Management, dist admin office I-III, 1977-80, administrative officer IV, 1980-84, assistant to director, 1984-87, executive assistant, 1984-87, director, administration services, 1987, dist West Palm Beach, dir human resources, 1987-94, deputy department director HRD, Management Services. **Orgs:** President, Sickle Cell Foundation of PB County, 1991-92; financial secretary, Delta Sigma Theta Sorority, 1989-91; 2nd vice pres, Business & Professional Women's Club, 1987-; member, Executive Women of the Palm Beaches; member, Vital Programs Leadership of Palm Beach County, 1987; member, chairperson, fund-raising, Florida A&M University Alumni Assn; The Links Incorporated, West Palm Beach Chapter, 1992-. **Honors/Awds:** Up & Comers Award, 1992; Finalist in Govt Sec Pricewater, 1991; Black Awards, Woman of the Year, Palm Beach County, 1988; Tri County Business League Community Service Award, 1987; J C Penney Golden Rule Award, Community Service, 1986; Sickle Cell Foundation of Palm Beach County, Outstanding Board Member, 1985; Eta Phi Beta Sorority, Community Service Award, 1985; American Business Women's Association, Woman of the Year, 1981. **Business Addr:** Deputy Department/Hrd/Administration, Management Services, South Florida Water Management District, 3301 Gun Club Rd, West Palm Beach, FL 33416-4680.

TURPIN, MEL HARRISON
Professional basketball player. **Personal:** Born Dec 28, 1960, Lexington, KY. **Educ:** Kentucky, 1979-84. **Career:** Cleveland Cavaliers, 1985-87, Utah Jazz, 1988, Washington Bullets, 1990. **Honors/Awds:** Finished career at KY with 1509 points to rank 9th on the schools all-time scoring list. **Business Addr:** Professional Basketball Player, Washington Wizards, One Harry S Truman Dr, Capitol Centre, Landover, MD 20785-4798.

TUSAN, GAIL S.
Judge. **Personal:** Born Aug 3, 1956, Los Angeles, CA; daughter of Lois Carrington Tusan and Willie Tusan Jr; divorced; children: Ashley Lauren, Shannon Kyle. **Educ:** University of California, Los Angeles, BA, 1978; George Washington University, JD, 1981; University of Nevada/National Judicial College, 1992. **Career:** U.S. Department of Justice, intern, 1980-81; Kilpatrick & Cody, associate, 1981-84; Asbill, Porter, associate, 1984-86; Joyner & Joyner, partner, 1986-90; City Court of Atlanta, judge, 1990-92; State Court of Fulton County, judge, 1992-95; Institute of Continuing Judicial Education, faculty member; Georgia State University Law School, faculty member; Superior Court of Fulton County, judge, 1995-. **Orgs:** Georgia State Bar, 1981-; Georgia Association of Black Women Attorneys, president, 1983, executive committee; Gate City Bar Association; Atlanta Bar Association; Judicial Procedure and Administration Advisory Committee; Committee on Professionalism. **Honors/Awds:** YWCA of Greater Atlanta's Academy of Women Achievers, Inductee, 1995; Cited by Georgia Informer as one of Georgia's 50 Most Influential Black Women, 1994; Justice Robert Benham, Law Related Supporter of the Year Award, 1992; Martin Luther King Jr Center for Nonviolence and Social Change Community Service Peace and Justice Award, 1991; Ebony, Thirty Leaders of the Future, 1985. **Business Addr:** Judge, Superior Court of Fulton County, 185 Central Ave SW, Rm T8955, Atlanta, GA 30303, (404)302-8520.

TUTT, LIA S.
Financial planner. **Personal:** Born May 4, 1960, Washington, DC; daughter of Julia Smith Tutt and Dr Walter C Tutt; divorced; children: Fiana T Brown. **Educ:** Howard Univ, BS 1982; George Washington Univ, 1984. **Career:** Metropolitan Life Financial Planning Dept, registered rep and financial planner; Natl Financial, Washington, DC, certified financial planner. **Orgs:** Mem various comm serv organizations 1972-85; sec Jack & Jill of Amer Assn 1972-78; mem Natl Black MBA Assoc 1986-; lecturer on financial mgmt and wealth accumulation, retirement planning, business planning. **Honors/Awds:** Certificate and Trophy Outstanding Participation & Congeniality Howard Univ 1979, l980; Certificate Tribute to Ideal Black Womanhood Ebony Magazine 1980; certificate: Outstanding Performance on the bd of dir to Biomedical Research Engineering JTF, l988; finiancial consultant to various organizations. **Business Addr:** Certified Financial Planner/Investment Consultant, PO Box 6366, Washington, DC 20015.

TUTT, WALTER CORNELIUS
Dental surgeon. **Personal:** Born Jan 29, 1918, Birmingham, AL; son of Corinne Flood Tutt and Rev. Walter Andrew Tutt; married Julia Smith (deceased); children: Lia. **Educ:** Livingstone Coll, BS 1939; Howard Univ, Grad School 1942-43, DDS 1957; Univ of Florence 1945. **Career:** NC Publ School, teacher 1941-42; VA Publ School, teacher 1947-48; private practice, dental surgeon, over 35 years. **Orgs:** Mem Robert T Freeman Dental Soc, Natl Dental Assoc, Amer Dental Assoc; formerly utilization rev sub-comm Home Care prog DC Gen Hosp; past pres Prince Williams Cty Teacher Assn 1948; mem, past pres WA Grad Chap Chi Delta Mu Natl Med Frat; grand exec comm Grand Chap Chi Delta Mu; mem Kappa Alpha Psi; past mem adv comm WA Alumni Chap Kappa Alpha Psi; bd of dir WA Alumni Chap Kappa Alpha Psi; mem Rock Creek E Neighborhood League, Pigskin Club WA, Howard Univ Gen & Dental Alumni Assoc; treas Hellians Inc. **Honors/Awds:** Conspicuous Serv Awd Chi Delta Mu; Citation Disting Alumni of Historically Black Coll Natl Assoc for Equal Oppty in Higher Ed. **Military Serv:** AUS 1944-45; Combat Infantry Badge, Three Battle Stars, Two Campaign Ribbons, Good Conduct Medal. **Business Addr:** Dental Surgeon, 4122 16th St NW, Washington, DC 20011.

TWEED, ANDRE R.
Physician. **Personal:** Born Apr 16, 1914, New York City, NY; married Ruth; children: Phyllis, Roland, Wayne, Andrea. **Educ:** Brooklyn Coll, BA 1936; Howard U, MD 1942. **Career:** Columbia Univ Montefiore Hospital, 1949; Loma Linda Univ Med esmnr Superior Ct LA Co, asso clinical prof psychiatry 1950-74; psychiatrist in private practice, 1950-; Kedren Community Mental Health Center, chief of children in patient, chief of adult day care. **Orgs:** Mem, life fellow Amer Psychiatric Assn; Black Psychiatrist of Southern CA; Black Psychiatrists Amer Hon LlD, Forensic Psychiatry CA Coll Law, 1973; diplomate, Amer Bd of Psychiatry & Neurology, 1949; AAAS; fellow, Amer Assn for the Advancement of Psychotherapy. **Honors/Awds:** Hon JD, CA College of Law; established private museum of Ethiopian religious artifacts. **Special Achievements:** Article and picture appear in book, Songs of My People. **Military Serv:** US Army, capt 1943-46, 1950-51. **Business Addr:** 3750 W 54th St, Los Angeles, CA 90043.

TWIGG, LEWIS HAROLD
Physician. **Personal:** Born Oct 5, 1937, Muskogee, OK; son of Ann R Twigg and Lewis Twigg Sr; married Myrna; children: Lewis III, Karen. **Educ:** Morehouse Coll, BS 1958; Atlanta Univ, MS 1960; Meharry Med Coll, MD 1967. **Career:** MI State Coll, assoc clinical prof dept ob-gyn & reproductive biology of human med; Hurley Med Ctr, vice chmn dept ob-gyn 1978-81; Private Practice, physician; diplomate, Amer Bd Ob-Gyn; Fellow Coll Ob-Gyn. **Orgs:** Mem Flint Acad Surgery; mem Alpha Phi Alpha Frat; diplomate Amer Bd Ob-Gyn; Fellow Coll Ob-Gyn; Sigma Pi Phi Fraternity. **Honors/Awds:** Co-author, ''Cutaneous Streptococcal Infections in Vietnam,'' Archives of Dermatology, Sept 1971. **Military Serv:** US Army, Capt, 1968-70; Bronze Star. **Business Addr:** Physician, 4250 N Saginaw St, Flint, MI 48505.

TWIGGS, LEO FRANKLIN
Artist, educator. **Personal:** Born Feb 13, 1934, St Stephen, SC; son of Bertha L Moultrie and Frank Twiggs; married Rosa Johnson, Jun 15, 1962; children: Kenneth, Darryl, Keith. **Educ:** Claflin Coll, Orangeburg, SC, BA, 1956; Art Inst of Chicago, 1961-; New York Univ, MA, 1964; Univ of Georgia, EdD, 1970. **Career:** Lincoln High School, Sumter, SC, art teacher, 1958-64; South Carolina State Univ, art prof, exec dir of the Stanback Museum. 1964-. **Orgs:** Museum committee, State Museum, 1972-; board, vice pres, South Carolina Art Foundation, 1985-; African American Museum Assn, chair, long range planning committee, 1985-; ABC Committee, South Carolina Arts Commission, 1989; trustee, New Mount Zion Baptist Church, 1987-. **Honors/Awds:** Governor's Trophy in Arts, State of South Carolina, 1981; Distinguished Prof Award, South Carolina State Univ, 1978; Batik artist, over 60 one-man shows nationwide & Rome; Decca and Togoland; featured in Ebony, September, 1988; ''On Art and Testing in a Period of Educational Reform,'' 1986; numerous other publications. **Military Serv:** US Army Signal Corp, Sp/4, 1956-58. **Home Phone:** (803)534-9796. **Business Addr:** Executive Director, Stanback Museum & Planetarium, South Carolina State University, PO Box 7191, Orangeburg, SC 29117, (803)536-7174.

TWINE, EDGAR HUGH
Attorney. **Personal:** Born Oct 9, 1935, Chicago, IL; married Lillian; children: Deborah Jeleen, Edgar H. **Educ:** Univ of IL, BS 1956; Univ of IL Coll of Law, LlB 1958, MIT, MS 1973. **Career:** US Dept of Justice, attorney, 1958-69; US Dept of Transp, member bd of contract appeals, atty, 1969-70; Atlantic Richfield Co, sr atty, 1970, gen atty, 1971-72, assoc gen couns 1973-. **Orgs:** Admitt to pract IL Sup Ct; US Ct of Claims; US Sup Ct; CA Sup Ct; DC Ct of Appeals; US Ct of Milit Appeals; bd of dir Econ Resour Corp 1974-; mem bd of visit Univ of OR Sch of Law; Com on the envior; CA State Bar Assoc; lect Black Exec Exchan Prog; mem Amer Bar Assoc; CA State Bar Assoc; lect Black Exec Exchan Prog; mem Amer Bar Assoc; CA Bar Assoc; DC Bar; Langston Bar Assoc; Los Angel Co Bar Assoc; Natl Bar Asso; Alpha Phi Alpha Frat JohnHay Whitney Flwshp 1957-59. **Honors/Awds:** Merit Serv Awd Dept of Justice 1965; Bd of Stud Editrs Univ of IL Law Forum 1956-58; Order of the Coif Univ of IL Coll of Law 1958; Sloan Fellow MIT Sloan Sch of Mang 1972-73; Outstdng Alum Achiev Awd Univ of IL Coll of Law 1976. **Military Serv:** USAR capt 1958-67.

TYEHIMBA, CHEO TAYLOR
Writer, journalist, screenwriter, author. **Personal:** Born Nov 6, 1964, Palo Alto, CA; son of Don K & Doris H Taylor; married Raina Tyehimba, Sep 22, 1993. **Educ:** San Jose State Univ, BA, 1989. **Career:** Sellectek Advertising, PR, copywriter, 1989-90; Richmond District YMCA, youth dir, 1990-91; San Francisco Bay Guardian, features writer, 1991-93; Time Warner Inc, staff writer, 1993-. **Orgs:** Simba Inc, leader, 1992-; Omega Psi Phi Fraternity Inc, 1990-; Big Brothers of the Bay Area, 1992-. **Special Achievements:** Co-author of ''The Ghetto Solution,''

1994; Anthologized in ''Brotherman: The Odyssey of Black Men in America,'' Ballantine, 1995; Founded First African American Student Magazine at San Jose State Univ, ''Forward Magazine.''. **Business Phone:** (212)522-2528.

TYLER, B. J. (BRANDON JOEL)
Professional basketball player. **Personal:** Born Apr 30, 1971, Galveston, TX. **Educ:** DePaul Univ; Texas. **Career:** Philadelphia 76ers, 1994-. **Business Addr:** Professional Basketball Player, Philadelphia 76ers, PO Box 25040, Philadelphia, PA 19147, (215)339-7600.

TYLER, CHERYL LYNNETT
Secret Service agent. **Educ:** Spelman College, bachelor's degree in sociology; Atlanta University, master's degree in sociology. **Career:** US Secret Service, agent, special agent, currently. **Special Achievements:** Highest ranking African American female in the US Secret Service; has been personally responsible for the security of the President of the United States, past presidents and their families as well as visiting dignitaries. **Business Addr:** Agent, US Secret Services, 6 World Trade Center, Rm 623, New York, NY 10048, (212)435-5100.

TYLER, GERALD DEFOREST
Educational administrator. **Personal:** Born Feb 28, 1946, Louisa Co, VA; son of Annie Tyler and John Tyler; children: Michael Jerone, Jerome Duvall. **Educ:** Norfolk State Univ, BS (honors) 1977, MA (highest honors) 1983; Old Dominion Univ, pursuing PhD 1983. **Career:** Dalmo Sales Co, salesman 1964-66; US Marine Corps, admiral's orderly 1966-69; Tidewater Regional Transit System, bus oper 1969-77; Elizabeth City State Univ, spec asst to chancellor 1977-84; Norfolk State Univ, dir of univ relations, 1984-. **Orgs:** Mem, NAACP, 1979-; Adv ECSU Student Chap NAACP 1980-84; mem NC State Employees Assn Inc 1980-84; pres Prof Business Assn 1980-81; alternate delegate 35th Annual NCSEA Convention Comm 1980-81; mem S Humanities Conf 1980-82; chmn NC State Employees Assoc Inc 1981-82; mem Greater Bibleway Temple 120 Club 1981; 1st vice pres Pasquotank Co Branch NAACP 1981-84; mem NCSEA Inc Area 24 Exec Bd 1981-84; adv ECSU Sr Class 1981-84; 1st vice chmn Pasquotank Co Voting Precinct 3B 1981-82; mem NCSEA Inc Bd of Governors 1981-82; chmn NCSEA Inc Area 24 1981-82; bd mem Gov's FOTC Assn 1982-84; bd mem Albemarle Develop Auth 1982-84; head adv ECSU Sr Class 1982-84; mem NCSEA Inc State Organ Study Comm 1982-83; mem Pasquotank Co Voting Precinct 3B 1983-84; mem Pasquotank Co Improvement Assn 1983-84; mem New Towne Civic League 1984-86; mem Tidewater Media Prof Assn 1984-89; bd mem New Towne Civic League 1984-86; mem VA Social Sci Assn 1984-94; mem Virginia Assn of Printing, Publications & Public Relations, 1986-; bd of dirs & advisors, Pepper Bird Found, 1988; bd mem, Miss Black Virginia Pageant, 1986-88; mem bd of advisors, Miss Collegiate African American Pageant, 1989-93; mem board of directors, Tidewater Charter, American Red Cross, 1990-92; Hampton Roads Black Media Professionals, 1990-; The Council for the Advancement and Support of Education District III, board of directors and nominating committee, 1993-95. **Honors/Awds:** Safe Driving Awd for operating 32 passenger bus free of accidents while employed at TRT 1969-77; Certificate of Appreciation UNCF New York 1979; Outstanding Boxer Awd USMC; First Awd Cert as Asst Head Coach for ECSU's Lady Vikings Softball Team 1980-81; NCSEA Inc Employee of the Year Awd 1981-82; Awd for Outstanding Leadership Unselfish and Dedicated Serv rendered as Sr Class Advisor 1982-84. **Military Serv:** USMC E-6/staff sgt 6 yrs; recipient of the Presidential Unit Citation; USN Commendation; Good Conduct Medal; Natl Def Medal. **Business Addr:** Dir of University Relations, Norfolk State Univ, Wilson Hall, Suite 340, 2401 Corprew Ave, Norfolk, VA 23504, (757)683-8373.

TYLER, HUBERT
Educator. **Personal:** Born May 23, 1934, Ridgeland, SC; married Jessie Wright; children: Dr Yasmin Tyler-Hill, Mrs Kahn Tyler-Smith, Khandra Y. **Educ:** Savannah State Coll; BS 1959; Armstrong-Savannah State Grad Sch, MS 1976. **Career:** Robert Smalls Jr HS, math & science teacher 1959-. **Orgs:** Mem BCEA, SCEA, NEA 1959-; leader St John Ame Church 1965-; sr warden Shiloh Lodge #92 1976-; mem Live Oak Hosp Bd 1976-86; mem Jasper Co Bd of Educ 1976-89; vice pres Ridgeland Chap of NAACP 1984-; mem Beaufort Jasper Career Ctr 1985-89. **Honors/Awds:** Family of Year Jasper Co 1980; Serv Awd Ridgeland High Athletic Dept 1980, 1983; Serv Awd Jasper Co School Dist 1983; Serv Aws Cystic Fibrosis FoundSC Chap 1983. **Military Serv:** AUS sgt 1951-54; Combat Inf Badge; Korean Serv Medal; 2 Bronze Stars; UN Serv Medal; Good Conduct Medal; Natl Defense Serv Medal.

TYLER, JOHN LEWIS
Social work executive (retired). **Personal:** Born Jan 25, 1914, Clifton Forge, VA; married Elizabeth Moultrie; children: Ingrid Elizabeth, Johnetta Louise. **Educ:** VA State Coll, BA, 1939; Loyola Univ School of Social Work, MA, 1951; St John's Univ, NY, studied law. **Career:** VA Lakeside Hospital, social work serv, 1967-; Hines Hospital, prog supvr social work serv, 1965-67, supvr, social work serv, 1955-63; Cook County, program dir, juvenile home, 1951-54, social worker, 1949-51; Farmville, VA, school teacher, 1940; Maywood, IL, social work consultant, child home, 1960-65. **Orgs:** Natl Assn of Social Work; mem, Amer Police Center Museum, 1975; Federal Exec Bd, EEOC, 1975. **Honors/Awds:** Acad of Certified Social Workers; certified social worker, State of IL, chmn, Chiefs Social Work Serv Comm, VA Med Dist No 18, 1974; Bronze Star AUS. **Military Serv:** AUS 1943-46.

TYLER, ROBERT JAMES, SR.
Real estate executive, county official. **Personal:** Born Dec 14, 1935, Darby, PA; son of Katharine Tyler and Joseph Tyler; married Phyllis E Jones-Tyler, Aug 30, 1958; children: Mary E, Robert J Jr. **Educ:** Univ of PA, ABA in Business 1978. **Career:** Philadelphia Svg Fund Soc, mortgage loan solicitor 1967; Hope Develop Corp, mgmt 1971; First PA Bank NA, appraisal dept 1973; Tyler Realty Co, owner 1978. **Orgs:** Co-chair, Equal Oppor & Govtl Agencies, PA State Realtor, 1983-84; pres, Darby-Lansdowne Rotary, 1984-85; treas, Delaware Co Bd of Realtors, 1985; Equal Opportunity co-chair Bd of Realtors 1985; Darby Salvation Army Adv Council, 1985; Wm Penn Sch Authority, 1983-; trustee, First Baptist Church of Darby, 1960-; dir, Delaware County Red Cross, 1985-88; Delaware County Association of Realtors, co-chair, equal opportunity committee, 1993-; Pennsylvania Association of Realtors, multiple listing committee, equal opportunity committee; Delaware County Board of Assessment Appeals, until 1996; Darby Free Library, board of directors, 1980-, treasurer, 1991-93; NAACP, Darby Area Branch, 1980-, executive committee, 1989-94, chairman, housing committee, 1991-94; Affordable Housing Opportunities Inc, board of directors, 1990-; Delaware Co, Bd of Realtors, pres, 1988; PA Real Estate Broker, 1978-; PA Certify Residential Appraiser, 1992-; Darby Bobo Council, chair, 1987-88; Grants, Recreation, Municipal Servs, parking authority, Darby Boro Council, chmn, 1991-95; Darby Bus Lianson, com mem; PA Notary Public, public safety, 1978-; Darby Bus Assn, 1992-; Darby Revitalization Task Force, 1994-; Delaware Co Wm Penn School District, 1995; Task Force for Sch Safety & Violence Prevention; pres, Delaware Co Bd of Realtor, 1988; PA Real Estate Broker, 1978-; PA Certify Residential Appraiser, 1992-; Darby Boro Council, 1981-88; chmn, Grants, Recreation, Municipal Servs, Parking Authority, Dary Boro Council, 1991-95; chmn, Darby Business Liaison com mem, public safety; PA Notary Public, 1978-; Darby Business Assn, 1992-; Darby Revitalization Task Force, 1994-; Delaware Co William Penn Sch District, 1995, Task Force For School Safety and Violence Prevention. **Honors/Awds:** Civic Awd The Chapel of Four Chaplains 1970; Civic Awd Penguin Club of Darby 1972; Civic Awd First Baptist Church of Darby 1980; Community Service, The Penguins of Darby 1988. **Military Serv:** USMC corpl, 12 yrs. **Business Addr:** Realtor, Self Tyler Realty Co, 850 Main St, PO Box 121, Darby, PA 19023.

TYLER, SHIRLEY NEIZER
Educational administrator. **Personal:** Born in Philadelphia, PA; daughter of Frances Washington Neizer and Raymond F Neizer; divorced; children: Richard J Jr, Kathryn T Prigmore. **Educ:** Simmons Clg, BS; Univ of VA. **Career:** Natl Schlrshp Serv Fund for Negro Stdnt, assc cnslng, pr; Arlington Cty Pblc Sch VA, edctr; Gilchrist Co Boston VA, prsnl admn; US Natl Stdnt Assc Madison, WI, exec sec; Grace Episcopal Sch, head of school, currently. **Orgs:** Former bd dir Mid Atlantic Episcopal Sch Assn; former mem Govnr Ed Block Grant Cmt; Natl Assn Elem Sch Prncpl; VA Association Elem Sch Prncpl; Natl Assc Ed Yng Chldrn; chmn, vice chmn, Alexandria City Sch Bd 1973-82; former bd dir vchrmn Alexandria Comm Hlth Clnc; mem Alexandria Hosp Corp; former bd dir Northern VA Fmly Svc; NAACP; VA Urban League; INOVA Alexandria Hosp. **Honors/Awds:** Distngshd Serv Citizens Alexandria, VA; Outstanding Serv in Education, Northern Virginia, Urban League; Outstanding Comm Serv, NAACP, Alexandria Brch; Community Activist, Hopkins House Assn. **Home Addr:** 3703 Edison St, Alexandria, VA 22305.

TYLER, VANESSA R.
Broadcast journalist. **Personal:** Born in New York, NY; daughter of Brenda Lowery and Gerald Tyler. **Educ:** Syracuse University, SI Newhouse School of Public Communications, BS. **Career:** Docuvid, news producer, 1981-82; WTTG-TV, news assignment editor, 1982-84; WMDT-TV, reporter, 1984-85; WHEC-TV, reporter, 1985-91; WSOC-TV, reporter, 1991-. **Orgs:** Natl Assn of Black Journalists. **Business Phone:** (704)335-4772.

TYLER-SLAUGHTER, CECIL LORD
Social services consultant. **Personal:** Born Oct 15, 1958, Peoria, IL; son of Verline Tyler-Scott and Willie Albert Scott. **Educ:** Illinois State Univ, cultural anthropology & microeconomics 1974-78. **Career:** Florida Job Serv, interim super to private sector 1979; Learning Tree Prep Sch, publicity dir & after school coord program 1980-84; Central IL/Eastern IA Salvation Army Headquarters, housing relocation specialist 1984; Peoria Assn Retarded Citizens, residential counselor-consultant 1985-. **Orgs:** Club leader Peoria County 4-H 1976-83; black history research reporter Traveler Newspaper 1980-84; mem Peoria Historical Soc 1982-; mem Peoria Lake View Museum for Arts Sci 1982-; media rsch consultant NAACP 1983-84; minority prog rsch journalist GE cable radio CCI 1984-. **Honors/Awds:** 4-H Bronze Leadership Peoria Co 4-H/Peoria 1982; nominated White House Fellowship US Chamber of Commerce 1982; Special Merit Citation Save the Children Fund Mayor's Office 1983. **Business Addr:** Residential Counsel-Consultant, Peoria Assn Retarded Citizens, P O Box 5942, Peoria, IL 61602.

TYNER, CHARLES R.
Clergyman, educator. **Personal:** Born Jun 23, 1950, Murfreesboro, NC; married. **Educ:** Shaw Univ Raleigh, NC, 1972; Southeastern Bapt Sem Wake Forest, NC. **Career:** Mt Moriah Bapt Church, pastor 1969-; White Oak Bapt Church, 1972-; Tarboro City Schools, admin asst supt 1972-. **Orgs:** Mem W Roanoke Bapt Assn, exec com; Shaw Theological Alumni Assn; pres Hertford Co Min Alliance; NC Assn Educ mem NAACP; Prince Hall Grand Lodge F& A Masons of NC; vice pres New Hope Bapt Assn. **Honors/Awds:** Merit Outstdg Leadership Shaw Univ 1969, 70, 71, 72; merit Great Ldrshp in Comm Murfreesboro, NC 1973; merit Outstdg Work General Bapt Conv NC 1971, 72, 73.

TYNER, MCCOY
Jazz musician. **Personal:** Born Dec 11, 1938, Philadelphia, PA; married Aisha; children: son. **Educ:** West Philadelphia Music School; Granoff School of Music. **Career:** Benny Golson/Art Farmer Jazztet, 1959; John Coltrane Quartet, 1960-65; solo performer, 1960-; recordings include: ''Inception,'' 1962, reissue, 1988; ''The Real McCoy,'' 1967; ''Sahara,'' 1972; ''Just Feelin','' 1985; ''Soliloquy,'' 1992; numerous others. **Business Addr:** Abby Hoffer Enterprises, 223 1/2 E 48th St, New York, NY 10017.

TYNER, REGINA LISA
Publishing company executive. **Personal:** Born Jul 5, 1945, New York, NY; daughter of Edith Helen Williams (deceased) and William H Kearney (deceased); married Berson J Tyner Sr, Nov 12, 1983; children: Jane Marie Glenn, Bonita Jo Glenn. **Educ:** Univ of Puget Sound, BS Bus Admin 1969, MA Bus Admin 1971; Harvard Univ, State & Local Exec Prog, 1980. **Career:** City of Tacoma, minority empl spec civil serv coord 1971-72; City of Tacoma Tech Transfer Ctr, dir 1972-77; Office of Intergovt Affairs City of Tacoma, dir 1977; WA State Dept of Retirement Systems, dep dir 1977-79; City of Seattle, dir dept of licenses & consumer affairs, 1979-86; Continental Telephone of NW, dir public affairs, 1986-88; Amer Communications Enterprises Inc, pres, 1988-; MWBE Digest, publisher, currently. **Orgs:** Mem, Alpha Kappa Alpha Sorority Inc, 1975-; Vice chair found comm Intl City Mgmt Assoc 1975; rep City of Seattle Public Tech Inc 1982; mem Amer Soc of Prof Admins 1982; bd of dir United Way of King Cty 1980-86, Leadership Tomorrow 1983-87; instr South Seattle Comm Coll 1985; mem, Ladies Auxiliary of Veterans of Foreign Wars, Post 2289, Seattle, WA, 1985-; bd of dir, Washington Leadership Inst, 1988-, Municipal League of King County, 1988-, Medina Children Services, 1988-. **Honors/Awds:** Award of Excellence, Amer Soc Public Admin, 1986. **Business Addr:** President, American Communications Enterprises Inc, 2819 1st Ave, Suite 250, Vanderveer Bldg, Seattle, WA 98121-1113.

TYNES, RICHARD H.
Engineer. **Personal:** Born Apr 28, 1942, Washington, DC; married Charlene L Bracken. **Educ:** Lake MI Coll, AA Indsl Engr 1962; Western MI U, BS Engineering 1965; MI St U, MBA 1969; Gen Motor Dealer Devel Academy, grad 1975. **Career:** Tynes Chev Cadillac Inc, pres 1976; Whirlpool Corp 1965-73; indsl & engr 1965-68; spl assingments with inner city bus 1970; budget mgr 1971-73; Notre Dame U, Engineering Dept, instr 1969-71; Lake MI Coll, instr 1968. **Orgs:** Bd mem, pres, treas, vp, So Bend Chap Am Inst of Indsl Engrs 1966-71; bd mem Mercy Hosp Benton Harbor MI 1969-76; Berrien Co Canvassars, 1970-75; bd mem, ''Y'' uncle, YMCA 1969-71; bd of dirs Grady Hosp Delaware OH; pres Benton Harbor Alumni Chap Kappa Alpha Psi; chmn NAACP Freedom Fund Banquet 1972. **Business Addr:** 680 Sunbury Rd, Delaware, OH 43015.

TYREE, PATRICIA GREY
Business executive. **Personal:** Born Nov 8, 1942; married Winston E. **Educ:** Carlow Coll, BS 1966; Antioch Coll, MA 1973; Univ Pittsburgh, PhD 1974. **Career:** Holy Family Sch, tchr 1966-67; St Mary's Sch, 1967-68; Carlow Coll, moderator couns Project Upward Bound Mt Mercy 1968; Diocesan Office Econ & Oportunity, asso dir Compensatory Educ Prog 1968-69; Nat Black Sisters' Conf, dir 1969-72; Antioch Putnam Grad Sch Educ & Carlow Coll, design training lab 1972-73; Design Progs Inc, 1972-74; Tyree Corp, corp vice pres 1974-, bd dirs; Black Women's Comm Dev Found; Design Prog Inc; num previous offices, coms proflorgan; publs in field. **Honors/Awds:** Religion in Action Awd Delta Sigma Theta. **Business Addr:** 318 Leader Bldg, Cleveland, OH 44114.

TYREE-WALKER, IDA MAY
Operations manager. **Personal:** Born Mar 16, 1941, Philadelphia, PA; daughter of Sophie & Albert Tyree; divorced; children: Dawn Walker-Anderson, Mark Gregory Walker. **Educ:** Philadelphia College Textile & Science, BS, business administration, 1975; Bowie State University, MSA, administration

management, 1990-92. **Career:** Philadelphia National Bank, sr financial analyst; Container Corp of America, controller, sales purchasing manager; Bowie State University, assistant internal auditor; Quality Care Dialysis Inc, operations manager, currently. **Orgs:** Hosanna Ministries, chair, board of directors, 1996-98; National Association of Women Business Owners, 1995-97; National Association of Health Services Executives, 1995-97; YMCA Black Achievers, board of directors, 1996-97; BEGIN Program, mentor, 1995-97. **Honors/Awds:** NAWBO, Business Owner of the Year Nominee, 1996; Phi Delta Kappa, Outstanding Leader, 1996; Meridian Bank, Certificate of Excellence, 1995. **Military Serv:** US Navy Reserve, petty officer second class, 1979-81. **Business Addr:** President/CEO, Quality Care Dialysis, Inc, 5070 Parkside Ave, Ste 5100W, Philadelphia, PA 19131.

TYRRELL, JAMES A.
Business executive. **Personal:** Born Dec 15, 1931, NYC, NY; married Ruby Belk; children: Milton, Cheryl, Joi Nandra. **Educ:** CBS Sch of Mgmt, certificate; BS Industrial Educ. **Career:** Record producer, professional musician, 1954-69; Intl Tape Cartridge Corp, vice pres 1965-70; Epic & Columbia Custom Labels, vice pres marketing & Sales 1973-74; Epic/Portrait & all CBS Assoc Labels, vice pres marketing 1974-79; T-Electric Records Co, pres chmn bd 1979-; T-Associates, owner; JTRT Corporation, owner 1980-; Safe-Waste Systems Inc, Wanamassa, NJ, mem bd of dir, corp secy, currently; Lopat Enterprises, Wonamassa, NJ, vice pres admin, mktg, secy. **Orgs:** Pres & founder NY Chap Frat of Recording Exec 1970-; bd dir Black Music Assn; mem finance com exec com Black Music Assn; ombudsman Black Record Retailers Assist Pilot Prog through BMA; bd dirs Metro Liquid Assets Inc, Melbaba Management Co, Lopat Industries Inc; advisor/lectr Inst of New Cinema Artists; advisor Youth Activists NOW Orgn; trustee vice prs gov Natl Academy Recording Arts & Scis; mem bd advisrs Natl Assn Recording Merchandisers. **Honors/Awds:** First Black vice pres CBS with appt as vice pres sales 1973; established a scholarship & career guidance awd for New York City HS students called PACE Awd; Entertainment Indus Publ Poll recognized him among 100 Most Influential Execs of the Decade 1978; Citations for Leadership, Boro President of Manhattan, MA State Legislature, New Communicators Organs, Natl Youth Movement, Youth Activists NOW, NY Media Assocs. **Business Addr:** Corporate Secretary, Safe-Waste Systems Inc, 1750 Bloomsbury Ave, Wanamassa, NJ 07712.

TYSON, BERTRAND OLIVER
Physician. **Personal:** Born Apr 3, 1931, Baton Rouge, LA; married Maureen; children: Lisa, Celeste, Bertrand Jr, Michelle, Kevin, Melissa, Amber. **Educ:** Howard U, BS 1950; Meharry Med Coll, MD 1959. **Career:** Physician; Crown City Ob Gyn Med Grp Inc, pres; Bar-Tram Ranch. **Orgs:** Mem Alpha Phi Alpha Social Frat 1947-; del Dem Nat Conv State LA 1968; ldr Civil Rights Demon 1963; fr Flw Am Coll Ob-Gyn; flw Intl Coll Surgeons; mem Am Fertility Soc. **Military Serv:** AUS corpl 1952-54. **Business Addr:** 2657 E Washington Blvd, Pasadena, CA 91107.

TYSON, CICELY
Actress. **Personal:** Born Dec 19, 1933, New York, NY; married Miles Davis, 1981 (deceased). **Educ:** Attended New York Univ, Actors Studio. **Career:** Plays: The Blacks, Off-Broadway, Moon on a Rainbow Show, Tiger, Burning Bright, The Corn is Green; TV programs: E Side W Side 1963, Miss Jane Pittman 1974, King 1977, Roots 1977, Bluebird 1976, A Woman Called Moses 1978; Films: Twelve Angry Men 1967, Odds Against Tomorrow 1959, The Last Angry Man 1959, A Man Called Adam 1966, The Comedians 1967, The Heart Is a Lonely Hunter 1968, Sounder 1972, The Blue Bird 1976, The River Niger 1976, A Hero Ain't Nothin' But a Sandwich 1978, The Concorde-Airport 79 1979, The Marva Collins Story 1981, Benny's Place 1982, Wilma; Women of Brewster Place; Riot, 1997; Ms. Scrooge, USA Network, 1997; Socrates, 1998. **Orgs:** Co-founder & vice pres, Dance Theater of Harlem; bd dir Urban Gateways; trustee Human Family Inst, Amer Film Inst. **Honors/Awds:** NAACP Awd; Awd Natl Council Negro Women; Awd Capital Press; Vernon Rice Awd 1962; Named Best Actress for Sounder Atlanta Film Fest 1972; Nom Best Actress Sounder Acad Awds 1972; Honorary Doctor of Fine Arts, Marymount College, 1979; Emmy TV Acting Trophy for ''Jane Pittman''.

TYSON, EDWARD CHARLES
Convention center manager. **Personal:** Born Jul 31, 1957, Brooklyn, NY; son of Dr Clarence and Cleo Tyson; married Diane K Tyson, Jun 27, 1992. **Educ:** Howard Univ, BA, 1979; Central Univ, MBA, 1983. **Career:** Manufacturer's National Bank, asst branch mgr, 1979-83; Life of Virginia Insurance Company, special agent, 1983-85; COBO Convention Center, event mgr, 1985-90; Tampa Convention Center, mgr of marketing and event svcs, 1990-. **Orgs:** Omega Psi Phi Fraternity, 1977-; Natl Forum for Black Public Admin, 1992-; Natl Coalition for Black Meeting Planners, 1990-; Intl Assn of Auditorium Mgrs, 1990-; Intl Assn of Exposition Mgrs, 1990-. **Honors/Awds:** Howard Univ Alumni Assn, Howardite of the Year, 1989. **Business Addr:** Manager, Mktg & Event Services, Tampa Convention Center, 333 S. Franklin St., Tampa, FL 33602, (813)274-8422.

TYSON, JOHN C.
Educator, librarian. **Personal:** Born Aug 4, 1951, Richlands, VA; son of Catherine Rutledge Tyson and Isaac McKnight Tyson, Jr.; married Rogenia Laverne Motley, Nov 22, 1973; children: Natasha Nicole. **Educ:** Concord College, Athens WV, 1969-72; Univ of Illinois at Urbana, Urbana-Champaign IL, MLS, 1976; West Virginia Univ, Morgantown WV, MPA, 1979; Simmons College, Boston MA, DALA, 1988. **Career:** Fairview Jr High School, Bluefield WV, teacher of Spanish, 1972-73; Concord College, Athens WV, circulation supervisor, 1973-75; West Virginia Univ, Morgantown WV, reference librarian, 1976-77; Univ of Wisconsin-Parkside, Kenosha WI, public services librarian, 1977-79; Northern Illinois Univ, DeKalb IL, asst dir for planning, administration & development, 1979-86; University of Richmond, Richmond VA, university librarian, 1986-90; Virginia State Library & Archives, state librarian, 1990-. **Orgs:** Black Caucus of the American Library Association; Chief Officers of State Library Agencies, board of directors, 1992-94; Black History & Culture Museum of Virginia, board of trustees, 1990-; The Edgar Allan Poe Museum, board of directors, 1990-; Southeastern Library Network, board of directors, 1990-93; Virginia Center for the Book, board of directors, 1991-. **Honors/Awds:** Outstanding Young Man of America Award, Jaycees, 1979; Distinguished Service Award, BCALA, 1992; Award of Merit, Virginia Educ Media, 1991; HEA Title II D Doctoral Fellowship. **Home Addr:** 1524 Westin Pl., Knoxville, TN 37922-8033. **Business Addr:** State Librarian, Commonwealth of Virginia, Virginia State Library & Archives, 11th St and Capitol Square, Richmond, VA 23233.

TYSON, LORENA E.
Educator (retired). **Personal:** Born Dec 1, 1933, Montclair, NJ; daughter of Clariee Love and Alfred E. **Educ:** Coll of St Elizabeth Convent Station, BS Chemistry 1956; Catholic Univ of Amer Washington DC, MS Chemistry 1965; Seton Hall Univ, South Orange NJ, Math Certificate 1966-67; Rutgers Univ, 1972; NJ Inst of Technology 1978; Kean College, NJ, Supervisors Certificate, 1994. **Career:** Sacred Heart Acad, Hoboken NJ, teacher chemistry & math 1956-59; St Joseph High School, teacher physics, chemistry & math 1959-62; St Peter & Paul High St, Thomas VI, teacher, physics, chemistry & math 1962-71; Essex County Coll, Newark NJ, adj math 1971-78; Kean Coll of NJ, adj math 1971-83; Montclair High School, Montclair Bd of Ed, chemistry teacher 1971-97; Middlesex County College, Edison, NJ, adj teacher, 1989-93; Montclair High School, dept chair science, 1994-97. **Orgs:** Mem Natl Educ Assn 1971-; New Jersey Educ Assn 1971-; Essex County Ed Assn, secretary 1973-77, treasurer 1988-97, rep council, 1972 exec bd 1974; Montclair Educ Assn 1971-95; mem, rep council, exec bd, sec 1980-84, treasurer 1980-95, corres sec 1973-77; executive bd, 1985; ACS Teacher Affiliate 1974-; League of Women Voters Montclair 1974-90; New Jersey Science Teachers 1975-; NJEA Exceptional Child Comm 1975-90; EOF Adv Bd Coll of St Elizabeth 1976-83; Natl Council of Negro Women 1978-82; consultant, editor Educ Unlimited Magazine 1978-82; mem New Jersey Math Teachers 1979-83; mem Phi Delta Kappa 1981-; treasurer Phi Delta Kappa Montclair State Coll 1987-89; Montclair Volunteer Ambulance Unit, bd of trustees, 1990-94. **Honors/Awds:** NSF Fellowship Chem Catholic Univ of Amer 1962-64; NSF Fellowship, Seton Hall 1966-67; Human Relations Award, Essex County Educ Assn, W Orange NJ 1980; Contribution to Educ Award, Montclair Educ Assn, Montclair NJ 1980; Resolution of Commendation, Montclair Bd of Educ, Montclair NJ 1980; NJ Governor's Teachers Recognition Program 1987; Montclair Teacher of the Year, Montclair Bd of Educ 1989; Eve Marchiony Outstanding Teacher Grant, Montclair Bd of Educ 1989; Edward J Merrill Award, NJ section, Amer Chem Soc, 1990; American Chem Society, Middle Atlantic Regional Award in HS Chemistry Teaching, 1992; Essex County Education Association, Educator of the Year Award, 1993; Princeton Distinguished Educator Award, 1994; Knights of Columbus Council, 1277 Montclair NJ, Public School Teacher of the Year, 1995; Weston Awd for Excellence, 1996.

TYSON, MIKE
Professional boxer. **Personal:** Born Jun 30, 1966, Brooklyn, NY; married Robin Givens, Feb 7, 1988 (divorced 1988); children: Michael, D'Amato Kilrane; married Monica Turner, Apr 1997; children: Reina, Amir. **Career:** Alternate boxer, US Olympics, 1983; professional boxer, 1985-; opponents have included Hector Mercedes, Mitch Green, Alonso Ratliff, Trevor Berbick, James Smith, Pinklon Thomas, Tony Tucker, Larry Holmes, Michael Spinks, Razor Ruddock, James Buster Douglas, and Evander Holyfield; World Wrestling Federation, special enforcer. **Honors/Awds:** Youngest Heavyweight Champion in Boxing History; Boxer of the Year, WBC Quantas, US Boxing Writers and other organizations; featured in Guinness Book of World Records; triple crown winner; Honorary Doctor of Humane Letters, Central State Univ, 1989. **Business Addr:** Professional Boxer, c/o Jeff Wald Entertainment, 8900 Wilshire Blvd, Ste 101, Beverly Hills, CA 90211.

TYUS, WYOMIA
Athlete, public relations. **Personal:** Born Aug 29, 1945, Griffin, GA; children: Simone, Tyus. **Educ:** TN State Univ, BS 1968. **Career:** Afro-Amer Cntr UCLA, research asst 1969-70; Bret Harte Jr HS Los Angeles, phys ed tchr 1970-72; Beverly Hills HS, trach coach 1972-73; Intl Track Assn, pub rel staff 1973-76; ABC coverage of Olympic Games in Montreal, commentator 1976; Councilman David Cunningham, community liason 1978; US Dept Labor sponsored Sports and Career Dev, instructor 1979-81; Coca-Cola USA, public relations 1981-84. **Orgs:** Competed in amateur and prof track & field 1963-75; for past 15 years instructed at dozens of sports clinics in US and abroad; particip in numerous panels and lectured on role of sports in culture; TV appearances include talk shows throughout US ie The Merv Griffin Show, ABC Superstars, Challenge of the Sexes. **Honors/Awds:** Publications and film appearances, ''Inside Jogging for Women'' pub by Contemporary Books Chicago 1978; ''Olympic Let Down'' Women's Sports Mag 1976; ''Women in Sports'' filmed by the Women's Sports Found 1979; ''Women Gold Medal Winners'' filmed by Bud Greenspan; TN Sports Hall of Fame Nashville 1972; US Track and FieldHall of Fame Angola, IN 1976; Black Athletes Hall of Fame New York 1978; Natl Track and Field Hall of Fame Charleston, WV 1980; Olympic Flag Carrier in the XXIIIrd Olympic Games Los Angeles 1984; Ten times AAU Natl Champ and All-Amer Athlete in both indoors and outdoors competition; Five times world record holder in 50/60/70 and 100-yard dashes and 100 meters sprint; Represented the US in more than twenty international competitions winning most;Gold Medal winner in 200 meter dain the 1967 Pan Amer Games; Winner of three Olympic Gold Medals and one Silver Medal - The only person in the hist of the modern Olympic Games among men and women to ever win a Gold Medal in 100 meter dash in two consecutive Olympics (1964 and 1968).

TZOMES, CHANCELLOR ALFONSO (PETE)
Naval officer (retired), financial executive. **Personal:** Born Dec 30, 1944, Williamsport, PA; son of Charlotte Eudora Hill Tzomes and James C Tzomes; children: Chancellor A II. **Educ:** US Naval Academy, BS 1967. **Career:** USNavy, capt, (0-6), 1967-94; USS Houston, 1983-86; dir, Navy Equal Opportunity, 1988-90; commanding officer, Recruit Training Command, Great Lakes, 1990-92; vp, Bank One, Cleveland, NA, 1994-. **Orgs:** VP, Natl Naval Officers Assn, 1989-90, mem, 1976-94; mem, US Naval Inst, 1970-; Amer Legion, 1990-; Retired Officers Assn, 1992-; Natl Assoc of Urban Bankers, 1995-. **Honors/Awds:** Black Engineer of the Year, Career Communications Group, 1991. **Special Achievements:** First African American to command a nuclear submarine. **Military Serv:** US Navy, capt, 27 yrs; Navy Commendation Medal with 2 gold stars; Meritorious Service Medal with 3 gold stars; Legion of Merit with 2 gold stars; various unit and campaign ribbons. **Business Addr:** VP, Retail Banking Division, Bank One, Cleveland NA, 600 Superior Avenue, PO Box 93108, Cleveland, OH 44101-3308.

U

UGGAMS, LESLIE
Actress, singer. **Personal:** Born May 25, 1943, New York, NY; daughter of Juanita Uggams and Harolde Uggams; married Grahame Pratt; children: 2. **Educ:** New York Professional Children's School; Juillard School of Music, 1963. **Career:** Actress and singer. Television appearances include, debut, Beulah, 1949; Your Show of Shows, 1953; The Milton Berle Show, Name That Tune, Sing Along With Mitch, featured performer 1961-64, Roots, 1979, The Book of Lists, 1982, Backstairs at the White House, 1982, Christmas at Radio City, Fantasy; plays include, Hallelujah Baby, 1967, Her First Roman, 1968, Blues in the Night, 1982, Jerry's Girls, 1985, The Great Gershwin, 1987, Anything Goes, 1989; films include, Black Girl, Skyjacked, 1972; numerous nightclub and musical variety show appearances. **Orgs:** Screen Actors Guild; Actor's Equity; American Federation of Television and Radio Artists; founder, BRAVO Chapter, City of Hope. **Honors/Awds:** Tony Award, Best Actress, Halleulajah Baby, 1967; Critics Award, Best Supporting Actress, Roots, 1979; Emmy Nomination, Roots, 1979; Emmy Award, Fantasy; Drama Critics Award, 1968; Best Singer on TV, 1962-63; author, Leslie Uggams Beauty Book, 1962. **Business Addr:** c/o William Morris Agency, 151 El Camino, Beverly Hills, CA 90212.

UKABAM, INNOCENT O.
Company executive. **Personal:** marrIed Chidi; children: four. **Educ:** Univ of Nigeria, bachelor's degree animal science; Univ of Wisconsin, doctorate meat science. **Career:** Protein Tech Intl, area dir, currently. **Special Achievements:** First African American named area director of Central American and Caribbean divisions of Protein Tech Int. **Business Addr:** Area Director, Protein Tech Intl, Checkerboard Square, St Louis, MO 63164, (314)982-1000.

UKU, EUSTACE ORIS, SR.
Attorney, business consultant. **Personal:** Born Jun 1, 1947, Ibadan, Oyo, Nigeria; son of Mabel Uku and Augustine Uku; married Jul 1, 1976 (divorced); children: Eustace Jr, Austin. **Educ:** University of Lagos, Lagos Nigeria, LLB, 1970; Nigerian Law School, Lagos Nigeria, BL, 1971; Long Island University, Brooklyn NY, MBA, 1974; Duquesne University, Pittsburgh PA, Cert in Law, 1981. **Career:** Lawrence & Co, Lagos Nige-

ria, attorney, 1971; Garrick & Co, Benin Nigeria, attorney, 1976-79; Delstacy Mgmt Serv, Benin Nigeria, managing dir, 1976-79; Greater Pittsburgh Business Development Corp, Pittsburgh PA, financial analyst, 1980-81; Equibank, Pittsburgh PA, asst vice pres, 1981-85; Exico Inc, Pittsburgh PA, pres, 1985—. **Orgs:** Mem, Pennsylvania Bar Assn; dir, Functional Literacy Ministry. **Business Addr:** Attorney/President, Exico, Inc, Federated Investors Tower, 1001 Liberty Ave, Ste 603, Pittsburgh, PA 15222.

UMBAYEMAKE JOACHIM, LINDA
Librarian, lecturer. **Personal:** Born Feb 19, 1953, Cleveland, OH; daughter of Helen Loretta Ballard McDonald and C Morgan McDonald; children: Manu Rashad, Kumar Rashad, Bari Zaka, Mayi UmBayemake, Thurayya UmBayemake. **Educ:** Cuyahoga Community College, Cleveland, OH, AA, 1980; Kent State Univ, Kent, OH, BA, 1984; Texas Women's Univ, Denton, TX, MLS, 1989; Univ of KY, Lexington, KY, MrC, 1998. **Career:** City of Denton Planning Dept, Denton, TX, planning assistant, 1986-87; Texas Woman's University, Denton, TX, library assistant II, 1988-89; University of North Texas, Denton, TX, library asst II, 1988-89; Toledo Lucas County Public Library, Toledo, OH, librarian, 1989; Cuyahoga County Public Library, Warrensville Hts, OH, librarian, 1989-90; Santa Fe Community College, Grants, NM, librarian/instructor, 1990; Owensboro Community College, Owensboro, KY, asst librarian, 1996; Kentucky State Univ, Frankfort, KY, ILL/Reference librarian, 1992-96. **Orgs:** Member, American Library Association, 1988-; member, Black Caucus American Library Assn, 1988-; member, ASCLA, 1990; member, College & Research Libraries, 1990; member, American Geographers Association, 1984-; National Rehabilitation Association, 1997-; Kentucky Blacks in Higher Education, 1993-. **Honors/Awds:** Honorary Award of Service, Kent State Student Government, 1982-85; Honorary Award of Service, COSO, 1982-85; Certificate of Service, Margaret Fain Elementary, 1990. **Home Addr:** 102 Centennial Drive, Frankfort, KY 40601.

UMOLU, MARY HARDEN
Educator. **Personal:** Born Nov 24, 1927, Newsoms, VA. **Educ:** NY U; Brooklyn Coll, MA 1951, BA 1949. **Career:** Medgar Evers Coll City Univ NY, prof dir comm art & science; Eastern Nigera Broadcasting, orgr producer artist 1960-67. **Orgs:** Bd dir Nat Assn Educ Brdcst; chmn Minoirites in Telecomm NAEB; mem Joint com on Pub Brdcstg; mem Action for Children's TV bd mem Kings Co Hosp Ctr; bd dir Comprehensive Hlth Sys NYC; mem Zeta Phi Beta Sor; Nat Sor Phi Delta Kappa. **Honors/Awds:** Brdcst Preceptor's Awd; San Francisco State Univ Tch Excellence Awd; Media Woman Yr City Univ NY; Outsdng Tchr Awd City Univ NY. **Business Addr:** 1150 Carroll St, Brooklyn, NY 11225.

UMOLU, SHEILA ANDREA
Project manager. **Personal:** Born Sep 19, 1966, Berkeley, CA; daughter of Xaythine Rogers Williams and Julius Williams. **Educ:** Stanford University, Stanford, CA, BS, industrial engineering, 1988. **Career:** Pacific Gas & Electric Co, San Francisco, CA, engineering intern, 1985, college relations representative, 1988-89, human resources representative, 1989-90, project manager, 1990-; IBM, East Fishkill, NY, engineering intern, 1986; Procter & Gamble, Sacramento, CA, summer manager, 1987. **Orgs:** National public relations chair, National Society of Black Engineeers Alumni Extension, 1991-93; chair, San Francisco State Minority Engineering Program Industry Advisory Board, 1990-91; coordinator, NAAC/NSBE Technology, Transfer Program, 1990-; Head Advising Associate, School of Engineering, Stanford University, 1987-88; president, Society of Black Scientists & Engineers, Stanford University, 1987-88. **Honors/Awds:** Lloyd W Dinkelspiel Award for Outstanding Service for Stanford University, Stanford University, 1988; School of Engineering Distinguished Service Award, Stanford University, 1988; Lewis H Latimer Award, National Society of Black Engineers, 1988; NSBE National Community Leadership Award, National Society of Black Engineers, 1987; Leadership & Service Award, Society for Black Scientists & Engineers, Stanford, 1985, 1987, 1988. **Business Addr:** Project Manager, Human Resources Computer Systems Development, Pacific Gas & Electric Company, 201 Mission St, Rm 1841A, San Francisco, CA 94105.

UNAEZE, FELIX EME
Librarian. **Personal:** Born Apr 12, 1952, Owerri, Imo State, Nigeria; son of Mary Mgbakwo Oguike Unaeze and James Unaeze; married Victoria Nwachukwu Unaeze, Dec 22, 1984; children: Obi, Kenny, Laura. **Educ:** Lincoln University, Jefferson City, MO, BA, journalism, 1980, MA, political science, 1981, MBA, management, 1983; University of Missouri, Columbia, MO, MALS, library science, 1984. **Career:** University of Lagos, Nigeria, library asst 3, 1971-73; Natl Library of Nigeria, Lagos, library asst 1, 1973-76; Lincoln University, Jefferson City, MO, periodicals librarian/administrator, ethnic studies, 1984-87; Northern Illinois University, DeKalb, IL, asst prof/business economics librarian, 1987-88; New Mexico State University, Las Cruces, NM, asst prof/business reference librarian, 1988-90; Ferris State University, Big Rapids, MI, head reference and instructional services, 1990-. **Orgs:** Member, American Library Association, 1988-; member, Black Caucus of the American Library Association, 1986-; member, New Mexico Library Association, 1988-90; member, Association of MBA Executives, 1984-88; member, Alpha Phi Alpha Fraternity, Inc, 1985. **Business Addr:** Professor, University Library, Ferris State University, 901 S State St, Big Rapids, MI 49307.

UNDERWOOD, ARTHUR C.
Attorney. **Educ:** University of Wyoming, BS, accounting, MBA; University of Denver, JD. **Career:** Peat, Marwick, Mitchell and Co, CPA's, sr accountant, 1973-75; Newman and Co, CPA's, independent consultant, 1975; US Securities and Exchange Commission, legal intern, 1976, law clerk, 1977-78; University of Wyoming, accounting instructor, 1977; US State Department, administrative officer, 1978; business consultant, 1979-80; First Financial Securities, Inc, administrative vice pres, 1980-81; Securities Clearing of Colorado, Inc, corporate attorney, account executive, 1982-84; attorney, 1981-. **Orgs:** Colorado Society of Certified Public Accountants; American Institute of Certified Public Accountants; Colorado Bar Association; Denver Bar Association; American Bar Association; Urban League of Metropolitan Denver, board of directors; Urban League of Metropolitan Denver, treasurer; Joint Center for Political Studies. **Business Addr:** Attorney, PO Box 473738, Aurora, CO 80047-3738, (303)755-2002.

UNDERWOOD, BLAIR
Actor. **Personal:** Born 1964, Tacoma, WA; son of Marilyn Underwood and Frank Underwood; married Desiree, 1994. **Educ:** Carnegie-Mellon Univ. **Career:** Actor, films include: Krush Groove, Murder in Mississippi, Posse, Heat Wave, Just Cause, Set It Off, Gattaca, Deep Impact; guest star on various TV shows including The Cosby Show, A Different World, recurring role in One Life to Live; star of LA Law; High Incident.

UNDERWOOD, FRANKYE HARPER
Educator, labor union official. **Personal:** Born Nov 19, 1953, Coal Valley, AL; daughter of Sarah Harper and Will Harper; married Harold Underwood, Dec 17, 1957; children: Angela, Harold Jr. **Educ:** Alabama State Univ, Montgomery AL, BS, 1957; Univ of Alabama, Tuscaloosa AL, MA, 1968. **Career:** Anniston City Schools, Anniston AL, teacher, 1957-62; Walker County Board of Education, Jasper AL, teacher, 1963-67; Alabama Education Assn, Montgomery AL, vice pres, 1987-88, pres, 1988-89; Jasper City Schools, Jasper AL, teacher, 1967—. **Orgs:** Mem, NEA; mem bd of dir, Alabama Education Assn; mem, Alabama Committee for Educational Excellence; trustee, Alabama State Univ. **Honors/Awds:** Teacher of Year Award, Jasper City Board of Education, 1985. **Home Addr:** PO Box 2144, Jasper, AL 35501.

UNDERWOOD, JAMES
Cleric. **Personal:** Born Apr 24, 1938, Panther Burn, MS; son of Sarah Parson Underwood and Judge Underwood; married Evelyn Miller, May 28, 1977; children: Jeff, James L Burnett, Greg, Theodore, Timothy Burnett, Angela R Patterson, Janet, Herbert D Burnett, Judy Grant, King James Jr. **Educ:** Industrial Training Institute, attended. **Career:** General Bishop, General Conference, Western Division, Free Will Baptist Inc, Ministers Conference, president; Kentucky Annual Conference of Western Division of Free Will Baptist Inc, vice bishop, bishop; Terre Haute District Ministers Conference, secretary; St James Free Will Baptist Church, assistant pastor; Emmanual Free Will Baptist Church, pastor; New Free Will Baptist Church, pastor, general contractor, builder, currently. **Orgs:** Hiram Lodge No 10, Blue Lodge, chaplain; St James No 3 Grand Consistory, AASR, Grand Hospital; Champaign County, NAACP. **Honors/Awds:** State of Illinois, Industrial Arts, 2nd Place Award, 1960; Terre Haute District Conference Education Department, Outstanding Teacher Award; Honorary Doctor of Divinity. **Military Serv:** US Navy, seaman recruit, 1961. **Home Addr:** 1310 Ellis Dr, Urbana, IL 61801, (217)367-8215. **Business Addr:** Bishop, Pastor, New Free Will Baptist Church, 601 East Grove St, Champaign, IL 61820, (217)355-2385.

UNDERWOOD, JOSEPH M., JR.
Law enforcement official. **Personal:** Born May 19, 1947, Dowagiac, MI; son of Alma L Underwood and Joseph M Underwood Sr (deceased); married Cindy L Glynn, Jul 22, 1989; children: Shannon, Sharon. **Educ:** Lake Michigan Community College, applied science, attended, 1978; Western Michigan University, criminal justice, attended, 1982; FBI National Academy, attended, 1987. **Career:** Cass County Sheriff's Dept, deputy, detective, 1973-79, lt, 1979-82, captain, 1982-85, undersheriff, 1985-88, sheriff, 1988; Haggin-Wimberly Ford, assistant business manager, fleet manager, 1989-92; Cass County Sheriff's Dept, sheriff, 1993-. **Orgs:** Civitan; Westgate Center, board member, 1988-; House of Prayer Community Church, trustee, 1987-; Dowagiac Area Federal Credit Union, past vice pres, board member; VFW. **Honors/Awds:** Sportsman Big 10 Club, Citizen of the Year Award, 1992. **Military Serv:** US Army, sgt, 1966-68; Purple Heart, Good Conduct. **Home Addr:** PO Box 291, Cassopolis, MI 49031. **Business Addr:** Sheriff, Cass County Sheriff's Department, 321 M-62, Cassopolis, MI 49031, (616)445-8644.

UNDERWOOD, MAUDE ESTHER
Broadcasting executive. **Personal:** Born Jul 7, 1930, Cotton Valley, LA; married David C Underwood; children: Marcus, Sharon, Yvonne Holmes, James. **Educ:** Ruth Beauty Sch, diploma 1958; Springhill HS, GED 1979; Northwest LA Vo-Tech School, diploma 1982. **Career:** State of LA, LSU Ext Agent 1976; City of Cullen, alderman 1982,87; Black Comm Broadcast (KBSF), producer 1983-. **Orgs:** Organizer treas Springhill-Cullen Improvement Assn 1962; organizer treas Cullen Ladies Club; chmn Cystic Fibrosis; mem Order of Eastern Star; orator Clantha Pride of LA. **Honors/Awds:** Outstanding Serv Awd Webster Parish Comm Action 1978; Black Pride Awd-Black Pride Comm 1983; Bible Teachers Awd 13th North Calvary Dist 1981. **Home Addr:** PO Box 336, Cullen, LA 71021.

UNSELD, WES
Sports administrator. **Personal:** Born Mar 14, 1946, Louisville, KY; married Connie; children: Kimberly, Westley. **Educ:** Univ of Louisville. **Career:** Baltimore Bullets, 1968-73, Capital Bullets, 1973-74, Washington Bullets, 1974-81, vice-president, 1981-96, head coach, 1987-94; Washington Bullets and Washington Sports and Entertainment, executive vice president/general manager, 1996-. **Orgs:** Head of Capital Centre Charities; volunteer at Kernan Hosp; bd trustees Mt St Mary's College. **Honors/Awds:** All-American honors at Univ of Louisville; Rookie-of-the-Year; League's Most Valuable Player; selected to play in NBA All-Star Game (1st of 5 appearances); Most Valuable Player of the 1978 NBA Championship series that brought Washington 8 first sports titles in 36 years; Bullets all-time leader in games played, rebounds, minutes played and assists; 1st Recip of Walter Kennedy Citizenship Award. **Business Addr:** Executive Vice President/General Manager, Washington Wizards, One Harry S Truman Dr, Capitol Centre, Landover, MD 20785-4798.

UPSHAW, GENE
Union official. **Personal:** Born Aug 15, 1945, Robstown, TX; son of Cora Riley Upshaw and Eugene Upshaw Sr; married Theresa; children: Eugene Upshaw III, Justin Andrew, Daniel James. **Educ:** TX A&I Univ, BS 1968; CA State Univ, 1968; Golden Gate Univ, 1980. **Career:** NFL Players Assn, player rep/alternate 1970-76, exec comm 1976-80, pres 1980-82, exec dir 1982-. **Orgs:** Partner Gene Upshaw & Assoc (Mgmt Consult Firm Oakland) 1970-78; pres Fedn of Professional Athletes AFL-CIO 1984-; CA Governor's Cncl on Wellness & Physical Fitness; CA Bd of Governors for 104 Community Colleges; former planning commr for Alameda County; coord Voter Regis/Fundraising in Alameda County; NFL Players Inc, chair, currently. **Honors/Awds:** Byron (Whizzer) White Humanitarian Awrd NFL Players 1980; A Philip Randolph Award A Philip Randolph Inst 1982; Inducted into Hall of Fame (Football) 1987. **Military Serv:** AUS Spc 4th Class 1967-73 Ft Jackson, SC. **Business Addr:** Executive Dir, NFL Players Associaton, 2021 L St NW, 6th Floor, Washington, DC 20036.

UPSHAW, REGAN
Professional football player. **Personal:** Born Aug 12, 1975, Detroit, MI. **Educ:** Univ of California, attended. **Career:** Tampa Bay Buccaneers, defensive end, 1996-. **Business Addr:** Professional Football Player, Tampa Bay Buccaneers, 1 Buccaneer Pl, Tampa, FL 33607, (813)870-2700.

UPSHAW, SAM, JR.
Photojournalist. **Personal:** Born Jan 10, 1964, Louisville, KY; son of Mary Lou Parmer Upshaw and Samuel Upshaw Sr. **Educ:** Western Kentucky University, Bowling Green, KY, photojournalism, 1987. **Career:** The Louisville Defender, Louisville, KY, Intern, 1985; the Tennessean, Nashville, TN, Intern, 1986; Los Angeles Times, Los Angeles, CA, Intern, 1987; The Courier Journal, Louisville, KY, staff photographer, 1987-. **Orgs:** Member, National Association of Black Journalists, 1986-; member, National Press Photographers Association, 1985-; member, Kentucky News Photographers Association, 1987-; co-founder and vice president, Western Kentucky University's Association of Black Communicators. **Honors/Awds:** Team (Staff) Coverage General News, Pulitzer Prize, 1989; Best of Show first Place Feature Picture Story, Third Place Sports and Honorable Mention Pictorial Kentucky News Photographers Assoc Contest, 1989; Best of Gannett, Gannett Co Inc, 1988, 1989; Honorable Mention (Photojournalism), National Association of Black Journalists, 1990. **Business Addr:** Staff Photographer, The Courier Journal, 525 W Broadway, Louisville, KY 40204.

UPSHAW, WILLIE CLAY
Professional baseball player (retired). **Personal:** Born Apr 27, 1957, Blanco, TX; married Cindy; children: Brock Anthony, Courtney, Chad. **Career:** Toronto Blue Jays, outfielder/infielder, 1978, 1980-87; Cleveland Indians, infielder, 1988.

UPTON, E. H.
Elected government official. **Personal:** Born Jan 4, 1924, Sweetwater, TN; married Edna M Roberts. **Educ:** Dale Carnegie Course, grad. **Career:** Union Carbide Corp, matls dispatching & handling, indust engrg div retired after 26 yrs. **Orgs:** Mem Commiss of the City of Oak Ridge 1974, Oak Ridge City

Council 1975-; hon mem Constitutional Convention TN 1977; mem NBC/LEO Nominating Committee 1982;Oak Ridge Masonic Lodge 345, TML Human Resources Comm, Oak Ridge Chamber of Commerce; mem bd of dir HOPE of Oak Ridge Inc, Melton Hill Reg Indust DevelAssoc; campaign chmn Jesse Jackson Committee for Pres in Oak Ridge. **Honors/Awds:** Recipient of Union Carbide Corp Comm Serv Awd, Hon Sgt at Arms of House of Rep State of TN; Hon Mem of Staff of Senator Anna Belle Clement O'Brien, Black Caucus of the TN Gen Assembly. **Business Addr:** Councilmember, City of Oak Ridge, 134 Houston Ave, Oak Ridge, TN 37830.

URDY, CHARLES E.
Educator. **Personal:** Born Dec 27, 1933, Georgetown, TX; son of Pearl Roberta Jackson Urdy and William Braxton Urdy; married Margaret Bright, Apr 7, 1962; children: Christopher Braxton Rodgers Urdy, Steven Eugene Urdy. **Educ:** Huston-Tillotson Coll, BS Chem 1954; Univ of TX at Austin, PhD Chem 1962. **Career:** Environmental Science & Technology Development, Lower Colorado River Authority, manager, 1993-; Huston-Tillotson Coll, prof of chem 1972-93; Prairie View A&M Univ, prof of chem 1963-72; NC Central Univ, prof of Chem 1962-63; Huston-Tillotson Coll, prof of chem 1961-62; Univ of TX at Austin, post-doc Fellow 1962-63; Dow Chem Co Freeport TX, summer employee 1970; MIT Lincoln Lab Boston, Natl Urban League Fellow 1972. **Orgs:** Mem Alpha Phi Alpha Frat; Am Chem Soc; Am Crystallographic Assn; Sigma Xi; Fellow in Am Inst of Chemists; mem numerous local civic organ & com; campaign mgr first Black Wilhelmina Delco elected to TX Legis from Travis Co 1974; state sec-treas TX Assn of Coll Tchrs 1970; elected chmn First Prairie View A&M Fac Council 1969; mem Hon Soc Phi Lambda Upsion Alpha Kappa Mu; Nat Sci Found Fellow 1959; Univ of TX Fellow 1960; Procter & Gamble Fellow 1960; mem Beta Kappa Chi Hon Sci Soc; mem Cty of Austin Charter Revision Com; chmn Black Voters Action Proj Pol Com; elected council mem Austin City Council 1981-94. **Honors/Awds:** Recipient Prairie View Alumni Award for Leadership 1967; Huston Tillotson Alumni Award for Acad Achievement 1967 Alpha Phi Alpha Frat Community Serv & Leadership Award 1974; NAACP commun serv award 1975; City of Austin community serv award 1976; Doctor of Science, Houston Tillotson College, 1994; Whitney M Young Awd, Austin Area Urban League, 1994; NAACP, Arthur B DeWitty Awd for Human Rights, 1977. **Military Serv:** AUS sp-3 1954-57. **Business Addr:** Manager, Env Science & Technology Development, Lower Colorado River Authority, PO Box 220, Austin, TX 78767.

URQUHART, JAMES MCCARTHA
Business executive. **Personal:** Born Jul 31, 1953, Wakefield, VA; married Linda Diane Ricks (divorced); children: Torrey. **Educ:** Paul D Camp Coll, 1975-77; Richard Bland Coll, Bus Mgmt Cert 1979; John Tyler Coll, Acct Cert 1983. **Career:** Horton Furn Co, asst mgr 1981-83; Gen Electric, serv tech 1973-81; WakefieldFurn Co, pres, currently. **Orgs:** Mgr, coach Wakefield Eagles Men League 1979-81; councilman Wakefield Town Council 1983-86; mem NAACP 1983-85, SCLC 1983-85, Union Love Lodge 153; young adult teacher 1st Baptist Church; comm chmn Wakefield Improvement Assoc; past club master Wakefield Pack 75.

USHER (USHER RAYMOND)
Vocalist. **Personal:** son Of Johnetta Patton. **Career:** Vocalist, LaFace Records, currently. **Special Achievements:** Albums: Usher Raymond; My Way; Television guest appearances: Moesha, The Parent Hood; Teen Star Search champion, 1992. **Business Addr:** Singer, "My Way", LaFace Records, 3350 Peachtree Rd NE, Ste 1500, Atlanta, GA 30326, (404)848-8050.

USRY, JAMES LEROY
Mayor (retired). **Personal:** Born Feb 2, 1922, Macon, GA; son of Louise Usry and Leroy Usry; married Lavergin Stephens, Mar 31, 1984. **Educ:** Lincoln Univ, Lincoln University, PA, BA, 1946; Glassboro State Univ, Glassboro NJ, MA, 1971; Temple Univ, Philadelphia PA. **Career:** Harlem Globetrotters and New York Rens Basketball Team, New York, NY, basketball player, 1946-51; Atlantic City Board of Education, Atlantic City NJ, teacher, principal, asst superintendent, 1952-84; City of Atlantic City, Atlantic City NJ, mayor, 1984-90. **Orgs:** Pres, Natl Conf of Black Mayors; commissioner, Natl Council on Educational Research and Improvements; mem of bd of governors, Rutgers State Univ and Lincoln Univ; dir, New Jersey Casino Reinvestment Authority; mem of bd of dir, MidLantic National Bank South; mem exec bd, Atlantic City NAACP; mem, Congress of Community Organizations; mem bd of dir, YMCA; mem, Martin L King Jr Commission of New Jersey; mem bd of overseers, Governors School of New Jersey. **Honors/Awds:** Elected to Bob Douglas Hall of Fame, 1984; Man of Year Award, Omega Psi Phi, 1986; Community Service Award, 101 Women Plus, 1986; Richard Hatcher Distinguished Black Mayor Award, 1987; elected to Lincoln University Hall of Fame, 1988. **Military Serv:** US Army.

USSERY, TERDEMA LAMAR, II
Footwear company executive. **Personal:** Born Dec 4, 1958, Los Angeles, CA; son of Jean Hendrick Ussery and Terdema Ussery; married Debra Hubbard Ussery; children: Terdema L III, Elizabeth. **Educ:** Princeton University, Princeton, NJ, BA, dept honors, 1981; Harvard University, Cambridge, MA, MPA, honors, 1984; Univ of California, Berkeley, CA, JD, 1987. **Career:** Morrison & Foerster, Los Angeles, CA, associate, 1987-90; Continental Basketball Assn, deputy commissioner & general legal counsel, 1990-91, commissioner, beginning 1991; Univ of Denver, grad school of business, prof, 1991-; NIKE Sports Management, president, 1994-. **Orgs:** Member, Denver Games Committee, 1990; Denver Games Committee, Finance Committee; member, Los Angeles Young Black Professionals, 1984; graduate member, Ivy Club, 1981-. **Business Addr:** President, NIKE Sports Management, 1 Bowerman Dr, Beaverton, OR 97005.

UTENDAHL, JOHN O.
Investment banker. **Educ:** Long Island University; Columbia Business School. **Career:** Salomon Brothers, corporate bond trader; Merrill Lynch Inc, vice president, manager, senior bond trader; Utendahl Capital Partners, LP president, CEO, currently. **Special Achievements:** Listed as one of 25 "Hottest Blacks on Wall Street," Black Enterprise Magazine, 1992. **Business Addr:** President, CEO, Utendahl Capital Partners, 30 Broad St, 31st Fl, New York, NY 10004.

UTLEY, RICHARD HENRY
Public relations marketing consultant. **Personal:** Born Jan 2, 1949, Pittsburgh, PA; married Audrey L Ross. **Educ:** Univ of Pittsburgh, BA 1972, Law School 1972-73. **Career:** PA Legal Svcs, dir of prog devel 1980-82; City of Harrisburg Dept of Public Safety, tech asst 1982-83; Auditor Gen PA, asst dir; Utley Assoc, pres; Public Affairs Consultants Inc, vp; State of PA, The Bureau of Charitable Organizations, director, currently. **Orgs:** Pres Utley Assoc; NAACP; vice chair Harrisburg Housing Authority; sec of bd Center; bd dir. **Home Addr:** 122 Locust Street, Harrisburg, PA 17104.

UWAEZUOKE, IHEANYI
Professional football player. **Personal:** Born Jul 24, 1973, Lagos, Nigeria. **Educ:** University of California, bachelor's degree in political science. **Career:** San Francisco 49ers, wide receiver, 1996-. **Business Addr:** Professional Football Player, San Francisco 49ers, 4949 Centennial Blvd, Santa Clara, CA 95054, (415)562-4949.

UZOIGWE, GODFREY N.
Educator. **Personal:** Born Sep 25, 1938; married Patricia Maria Cahill; children: Emeka Anthony, Amaechi Charles, Chinue Jaja. **Educ:** Univ Coll Dublin, BA (Hons), 1963; Trinity Coll, Dublin, Higher Diploma in Educ 1964; Christ Ch Oxford Unv England, DPhil, History, 1967. **Career:** Makerere Univ, Kampala Uganda, lecturer in history, 1967-70; University of MI, asst prof of history, 1970-72, associate professor of history, 1972-75, prof of history, 1975-84; University of Nig Nsukka, visiting prof of history, 1976-77; University of Calabar Nigeria, prof and head, dept of history, 1981-87, dean, faculty of arts, 1984-87; Imo State University, Okigwe Nigeria, prof of history, 1987-91, dean, College of Humanities and Social Sciences, 1987-91, pioneer director, Ctr for Igbo Studies, 1988-91; Cornell University, visting senior fellow, 1989; Abia State University Uturu, dean, college of humanities and social sciences, 1991-1992, prof, of history, 1991-95, dean, college of post graduate studies, 1995-96; The Presidency, Abuja Nigeria, visiting senior research prof of history, 1993-94. **Orgs:** President General, Mbaitoli Cultural Union, Imo State Nigeria 1996-; chairman, Imo State Council for Arts and Culture, 1995; chairman, Ahiajoku Lecure Planning Committee; Imo State, Nigeria 1991-95; Imo State Library Board, Owerri Nigeria, 1984-87; group chairman, Esther Thompson Consultants, Owerri Nigeria, 1995-; consultant, Danchimach Nigeria America Lab School, 1993-; chairman of the board, Esther Thompson Publishers, 1991-; Rhodes Scholarship New Panel for Nigeria, 1991-; fellow Historical Soc of Nig, 1987-; president, Historical Soc of Nigeria, 1988-92; American Historical Association, 1970-; African Studies Association, USA, 1970-; Historical Association of Nigeria, 1967-; Smithsonian Institute, 1974-; Intra University, Seminar on Armed Forces and Society, 1974-; Royal African Soc, London, 1970-; The Oxford and Cambridge Club of Nigeria, 1985-; Oxford Union Soc, Oxford, 1964-. **Honors/Awds:** Chief Ugochinyere I of Ubomiri (1996); Hon Fellow, The Institute of Administration Management of Nigeria, 1992-; Hon Fellow, the International Multi-Disciplinary Science Institute, College of William and Mary, 1985-; Sports Certificate of Honor, University of Calabar Nigeria, 1988; Fellow, The Research Club of the University of Michigan, 1978-; Commonwealth Scholar, 1964-67; Federal Government of Nigeria, Scholar, 1960-64. **Special Achievements:** Publications: "A Short History of South Africa," Esther Thompson Publishers, 1988; "Uganda: Dilemma of Nationhood," New York, Nok Publishers, 1982; "Britain and the Conquest of Africa: The Age of Salisbury" University of Michigan Press, 1974; "Anatomy of an African Kingdom: A History of Bunyoro Kitara," New York Doubleday, 1973; "Revolution and Revolt in Bunyoro Kitara," London Longman, 1970. **Business Addr:** Professor of History, Imo State University, PMB 2000, Owerri, Imo, Nigeria.

V

VAILS, DONALD. See Obituaries section.

VALBRUN, MARJORIE
Journalist. **Personal:** Born Apr 26, 1963, Port-au-Prince, Haiti; daughter of Marie-Denise Jean-Baptiste and Austrel Valbrun. **Educ:** Long Island Univ, C W Post Center, Long Island, NY, BA, communications 1985; Columbia University, New York, NY, MS journalism, 1986. **Career:** CBS News, New York, NY, researcher, 1986-87; The Journal News, Nyack, NY, reporter intern, 1986; News/Sun-Sentinel, Fort Lauderdale, FL, reporter, 1987-90; The Miami Herald, Miami, FL, reporter, 1990-. **Orgs:** South Florida Assn of Black Journalists, 1988-; Natl Assn of Black Journalists, 1988-. **Honors/Awds:** C W Post Collegial Federation Award for Academic Achievement & Service, Long Island University, 1985; Outstanding Journalism Student, American Political Journalism Conference, Washington, DC, 1984; Harvard University, Nieman fellowship, 1996.

VALDES, LAURA
Attorney. **Personal:** daugHter of Panfila Valdes and Abelaro Valdes. **Educ:** New York University, BS, 1943; New York Law School, JD, 1960. **Career:** New York State Department of Labor, es supt, 1936-73; private practice, attorney, 1973-. **Orgs:** NAACP, Co-op City Branch, president, 1973-, Day Care Center, director, volunteer; Bronx Municipal Hospital Advisory Bd, president, 1976-80; Bronx County Bar Assn; Williamsbridge Senior Citizens Assn, president, 1974-; New York State Bar Assn; New York State Supreme Court, Appeliate Court Committee on Character & Fitness, delegate. **Honors/Awds:** New York State Division Human Rights, Human Rights Award, 1970; B'nai Brith, Woman of the Year, 1973; Butler United Methodist Church, Comm Recognition Award, 1969; numerous others. **Home Addr:** 3820 Paulding Ave, Bronx, NY 10469. **Business Addr:** Attorney, 3820 Paulding Ave, Bronx, NY 10469.

VALDES, PEDRO H.
Business executive. **Personal:** Born Jan 20, 1945, Havana, Cuba; son of Hesma and Pedro H.; married Maria A Bermudez; children: Hesma, Pedro III, Xiomara. **Educ:** City Coll of NY, BA 1969; Middlebury Coll, MA 1971; SUNY at Stony Brook, attended 1972-73; NY Univ, attended 1974-75. **Career:** SEEK Prog, tutor 1963-65; NY Philantropic League, rehabilitation counselor 1966-69; Alcur Tours Inc, tour guide & planner 1968-72; Wm H Taft HS, Spanish Language tchr 1969-72; State Univ of NY Stony Brook, teaching asst dept of hispanic languages & lit 1972-73; NY Coll of Podiatric Medicine, asst dean for student affairs 1973-75, vice pres for student affairs 1975-77, exec vice pres 1977-80; Premo Pharmaceutical Labs Inc, export sales mgr 1980-81, exclusive export sales agent, intl, 1981-82; pres, Protecom Inc, currently. **Orgs:** Mem United Federation of Teachers 1969-80; mem Amer Assn of Univ Professors 1972-80; mem Amer Assn of Colls of Podiatric Medicine 1973-80; mem Amer Public Health Assn 1973-; mem Natl League of Nursing Policies & Procedures Comm 1977-; mem Natl Health Council Inc 1980-; mem Natl Ctr's Advisory Council for Rsch in Vocational Educ 1981-84. **Honors/Awds:** Outstanding Educator of Amer Awd 1974; Tching Assistantship State Univ of NY Stony Brook 1972-73. **Business Addr:** President, Protecom Inc., 262 Griggs Ave, Teaneck, NJ 07666.

VALENTINE, DARNELL
Professional basketball player. **Personal:** Born Feb 3, 1959, Chicago, IL. **Educ:** Univ of KS, BS Pol Sci 1981. **Career:** Portland Trail Blazers, 1982-86, Los Angeles Clippers, 1986-88, Cleveland Cavaliers, 1989. **Honors/Awds:** One of the most honored players in Big Eight Conf history Univ of KS; All Conf all 4 seasons; Led the Big Eight in steals all 4 seasons & was 1st in assists in 3 of 4 years. **Business Addr:** Professional Basketball Player, Cleveland Cavaliers, Gund Arena, One Center Ct, Cleveland, OH 44115.

VALENTINE, DEBORAH MARIE
Environmental protection specialist (retired). **Personal:** Born Feb 18, 1951, Boston, MA; daughter of Virginia Alleyne Valentine and Roger Valentine. **Educ:** Howard Univ, BS 1972; Howard Univ Law Sch, JD 1972-75; certificate in catering training L'Academie de Cuisine Bethesda, MD July l988. **Career:** Minority Counsel Senate Select Subcomm Small Business, legal intern 1974-75; US Securities & Exchange Comm 1975-76; Fed Energy Admn Dept Energy, regulatory analyst 1977-80; ERA Housing Ctr Inc, group sales leader 1982-84; Assoc Legal Title Co, Inc, settlement officer 1986-87; US Dept Energy, environmental protection specialist; owner Valentine's Catering Upper Marlboro, MD Nov. l988-. **Orgs:** Rise Sister Rise; Notary public State MD 1979-86; realtor assc ERA Nyman Realty; mem Natl Assc Realtors 1981-86, MD Assoc Realtors 1981-86, Prince Georges Cty Bd Realtors 1981-86, Phi Alpha Delta Legal Frat 1973-81; vp, bd of dir Prince Place III at Northampton; chairperson of social & cultural committee Howard Univ Law Alumni Assoc l988-89; senior tutor Prince Georges Literacy Council l987-. **Honors/Awds:** Outstanding Work Performance Award Dept Energy 1980; scholarship Howard Univ

1973; scholarship Alpha Kappa Alpha 1968; chairperson Environmental Reg Compliance Working Group 1986-88; Outstanding Work Performance, Dept of Energy 1989; Superior Work Performance, Dept of Energy, 1994.

VALENTINE, HERMAN E.
Business executive. **Personal:** Born Jun 26, 1937, Norfolk, VA; son of Alice (deceased) and Frank (deceased); married Dorothy Jones; children: Herman Edward Jr, Bryce Thomas. **Educ:** Norfolk State Coll, BS 1967; Amer Univ, 1968; Coll of William & Mary, 1972. **Career:** Grad School Dept of Agriculture, exec officer, 1967-68; Systems Management American Corp, chmn and pres, 1970-; Norfolk State Coll, Norfolk, VA, business mgr, 1968-70. **Orgs:** Founder/chmn Tidewater Regional Political Assoc; mem Amer Mgmt Assoc, Armed Forces Communications and Electronics Assoc; bd of dirs Cooperating Hampton Roads Org for Minorities in Engrg; bd of dirs and exec comm Greater Norfolk Corp; adv comm VA Chapter of St Jude Children's Rsch Hosp; adv council The Virginia Stage Co; Air Traffic Control Assn (ATCA); Tidewater Regional Minority Purchasing Council (TRMPC); Soc of Logistics Engineers (SOLE); bd of dir, Operation Smile; bd of dir, PUSH Intl Trade Bureau, Inc; President's Council, Old Dominion University; advisory board Tide water Veterans Memorial Project; Hampton Roads Chamber of Commerce; Downtown Norfolk Development Corporation; lifetime member Navy League of the United States. **Honors/Awds:** Presidential Citation Natl Assoc for Equal Oppor in Higher Educ 1981; named to President's Council of the Amer Inst of Mgmt; Presidential Citation Entrepreneur of the Year Dept of Commerce Minority Business Develop Agency 1984; Delicados Inc Awd for Entrepreneurship in Blazing New Horizons 1986; Citizen of the Yr Awd for Outstanding Leadership & Serv to the Comm 1986; Regional Minority Mfg of Year Award, MBDA, 1988; one of Top 10 minority owned federal govt contractor, Govt Computer News, 1988, 1989; Certificate of Recognition, lieutenant governor, Commonwealth of VA, 1987; Outstanding Org for large financial contributions and employment of minorities, NAACP Area II, 1988; Outstanding Businessperson of Year, State of VA Award, black pres Roundtable Assn, 1987; Class III Supplier of thear Award, Natl Minority Supplier Devel Council, 1987; Ambassador of the City of Norfolk, CA, 1986; Black Diamond Award, presented by Rev Jesse Jackson, Operation PUSH, 1989; Patriotic Service Award, US Savings Bond Campaign, US Treasury Dept, 1989; Comm Service Award, Exemplary Blacks in Business, Institute for American Business, 1989; Certificate of Recognition, African American Entreprener, New York City Police Dept, 1990.

VALENTINE, J. T.
Attorney (retired). **Personal:** Born Sep 21, 1918, Suffolk, VA; son of Annie Valentine and Miles E. Valentine; married Rosetta M Cason. **Educ:** Howard U, BS 1948; Howard U, LLB 1951. **Career:** Washington Contracts Office Fed Aviation Adminstrn 1970, chief contract servcs 1970; Fed Aviatio Adminstrn, suprv contracts specialist 1970; FAA, superv procurement officer 1966-; Small Business WA FAA, officer 1971. **Orgs:** Tuskegee Airmen, East Coast Chapter, past president; Israel Baptist Church; NAACP; Natl Camping & Hiking Assn. **Military Serv:** US Army, Tuskegee Airmen, 1943-46. **Home Addr:** 3608 Carpenter St SE, Washington, DC 20020.

VALIEN, PRESTON
Retired government official. **Personal:** Born Feb 19, 1914, Beaumont, TX; married Bonita Harrison. **Educ:** Prairie View State Coll TX, BA; Univ of WI, PhM & PhD; Univ of PA, postdoctoral study. **Career:** American Embassy Nigeria, cultural attache 1960-62; Brooklyn Coll NY, assoc prof sociology & anthropology 1962-65; HEW Washington, dir prog analysis br 1965, chief grad acad progs 1965-66, dir div grad progs 1966-67, assoc commr higher educ 1967-73, dir coll & univ unit 1973-82; retired federal govt executive. **Orgs:** Fellow, Amer Sociological Assn, African Studies Assn; DC Scoiol Soc (pres, 1970-71). **Honors/Awds:** Superior Serv Award Educ 1970; Hon LLD Rio Grande Coll OH 1971; Hon D Hum Rust Coll, MS 1974. **Military Serv:** AUS S/Sgt 1943-46. **Home Addr:** 8020 W Beach Dr NW, Washington, DC 20012.

VALMON, ANDREW ORLANDO
Track and field athlete, sales representative. **Personal:** Born Jan 1, 1965, Brooklyn, NY; son of Norma Haynes and Oscar Valmon. **Educ:** Seton Hall University, BA, marketing communications, 1987. **Career:** Georgetown Univ, Mens Track & Field, asst coach. **Orgs:** Founder of the Avenue Program, program to provide role models for kids; Spokesman for USOC & the current sponsors. **Honors/Awds:** NJ Athlete of the Year, 1990, 1992; inducted into the NJ Sports Hall of Fame; Olympic Games, Gold Medal, 4x400m relay, 1988, 1992; Goodwill Games, Gold Medal, 4x400m relay, 1990, 1994; World Record Holder, 4X400m Relay; Metropolitan Athletics Congress, Athlete of the Year, 1990; TAC National Championship, Silver Medal, 1991; IAAF Mobil Grand Prix, 2nd Place, 1991; World Record and Gold Medalist at the World Championships, 4X400m relay, Best Relay Ever and New World Record, 1993; Seton Hall Univ, Track and Field, Hall of Fame, 1997. **Home Addr:** 2215 Cold Meadow Way, Silver Spring, MD 20906.

VANALLEN, MORTON CURTIS
Cleric, consultant. **Personal:** Born Mar 10, 1950, New York, NY; children: Richard. **Educ:** City Coll of NY, AA 1970; Antioch Coll, BA 1972; Harvard Grad Schl of Bus, MBA 1978. **Career:** Ordained minister 1969; Youth Services Agency City of NY, asst to commissioner 1970-71; Urban Crisis Task Force, founder & chief exec officer 1971-80; servedas dir of United Black Fund of Tri State (NY, NJ & CT) 1978-80; Willing Workers Baptist Church, pastor 1976; Public Utility Review Bd NY City Cncl, chrmn 1980; consultant, currently. **Orgs:** Judicial Delegate Bronx County, 1978; Legal Services Congress of Racial Equality, director; Veterans in Distress, board member; Domestic Council of Racial Justice, chairman of the board, 1977-; City College YMCA, board member, 1969-71; Equal Time, Inc, board member. **Honors/Awds:** Black Better Business Bureau, man of the yr awd 1984; rec'd commendation from Pres James Carter; former sec'y HUD Pat Harris; Mayors Beame & Koch citationof merit from Bronx Borough president and NY Housing Auth Police Dept all for comm work in the south Bronx and Harlem area of NYC. **Home Addr:** 53 W 130th St, New York, NY 10037.

VAN AMSON, GEORGE LOUIS
Investment banking executive. **Personal:** Born Jan 30, 1952, New York, NY; son of Willie-Mae Van Amson and Adolph Van Amson; married Wendy Alicia Tempro; children: Alexandra Case, Victoria Taylor, GA Schuyler Van Amson. **Educ:** Columbia Coll, AB 1974; Harvard Business School, MBA (honors) 1982. **Career:** Revlon Inc, financial analyst 1974-76; Citibank NA, asst controller 1976-77; Goldman Sachs & Co, senior financial analyst 1977-80, vice pres 1982-92; Morgan Stanley & Co, Inc, vp, Head of Latin America Trading, 1992-94, principal, co-head, International Trading, 1995, principal sr domestic trader, 1996-. **Orgs:** Dir, Alpha Phi Alpha Fraternity, Inc, 1971-73; dir, Urban Leadership Forum 1983-88, 21st Century PAC of NY 1984-87, Minisink Townhouse Inc 1985-88; mem economic develop comm 100 Black Men 1985-; pres HBS Black Alumni Assn 1985-87; chairman intl comm Securities Traders Assn of NY 1987-89; trustee, Columbia Unit, 1994-; trustee, Riverside Church, 1994. **Honors/Awds:** Curtis Gold Medal Columbia Coll 1974; Leadership Awd Harvard Business School 1982; Distinguished Service Award United Negro College Fund 1989; Global Leader for Tomorrow, World Economic Forum, 1992. **Home Addr:** 210 West 90th St #4B, New York, NY 10024-1241. **Business Addr:** Principal, Morgan Stanley & Co., Inc, 1585 Broadway, 5th Fl, New York, NY 10036.

VANCE, COURTNEY
Actor. **Personal:** Born 1960; married Angela Bassett, 1997. **Career:** Actor, currently. **Honors/Awds:** Clarence Derwent Award, 1987; Theatre World, Citation, 1987; Obie Award, "My Children! My Africa!," 1990; Tony Award, Best Featured Actor, nominated, 1987, Best Lead Actor, nominated, 1991. **Special Achievements:** Stage: The Comedy of Errors, 1982; A Raisin in the Sun, 1983; Fences, Yale Repertory Theatre, 1985, Goodman Theatre, Chicago, 1986, Broadway, 1987; Romeo and Juliet, 1988; My Children! My Africa!, 1989-90; Six Degrees of Separation, 1990-91; Film: Hamburger Hill, 1987; Hunt for Red October, 1990; The Adventures of Huckleberry Finn, 1993; Dangerous Minds, 1995; The Last Supper, 1995; Panther, 1995; The Preacher's Wife, 1996; TV: Thirtysomething, 1989; In the Line of Duty: Street War, 1992; Percy and Thunder, 1993; Race to Freedom: The Underground Railroad, 1994; The Affair, I and II, 1995; The Piano Lesson, 1995; The Tuskegee Airmen, 1995; Picket Fences, 1995; Law and Order, 1995; Half Lives, documentary, 1995; The Boys Next Door, 1996; Twelve Angry Men, 1997; Narrated books: Bo Knows Bo, 1991; I Had A Hammer: The Hank Aaron Story, 1991; And This Too Shall Pass, 1996.

VANCE, IRVIN E.
Educator. **Personal:** Born Apr 8, 1928, Mexico, MO; son of Dorothy Ayers Vance and Virgil Lee Vance; married Ann M Graham Vance, Dec 29, 1959; children: Barbara Ann Le Cesne, Velesha Ivy Vance, Katrina Iris Vance. **Educ:** Wayne State Univ, BS 1957; Washington Univ, MA 1959; Univ of MI, EdD Math 1967. **Career:** Northeastern HS, math instr 1957-59; Southeastern HS, math instr 1959-62; Univ of MI, teachiing fellow math dept 1962-64, instr in math 1964-66; MI State Univ, asst prof of math 1966-69, assoc prof of math 1969-71; Educ Develop Ctr, dir of sch comm outreach for project one 1973-75; NM State Univ, dir of black progs 1971-72, assoc prof of math 1971-82, prof of math 1982-89; Michigan State University prof of math 1989-. **Orgs:** Consultant to numerous schools & univs; NM State Univ, chmn mem Math Educ Comm, planning grant comm, advisory comm, promotion to assoc & tenure comm, master comm, doctoral comm, comm on evalutation of ethnic progs; external affairs comm Natl Cncl of Teachers of Math; chmn bd dirs Development of Rsch & Human Resources; mem Natl Council for Accreditation of Teacher Educ; bd of dirs NAACP; reader of advance placement exam in math Educational Testing Serv 1979-84; judge at Black History Knowledge Bowl; review panel for the Minority Institution Science Improvement Program Natl Science Found; vice pres for univs NM Council of Teachers of Math 1978-81; pres NM Council of Teachers of Math 1984-85; prog chmn Annual Conf NM Council of Tchrs of Math 1984 1985; lecturerin math Boston Univ 1975, Ley Coll 1974; dir of worksh op for Coll Teachers of Math Spelman Coll 1975; fndr dir NM State Univ Elem Teachers Math Project 1977-80; Math Inst for In-Serv Teachers at MI State Univ 1968 1971; assoc dir Grand Rapids MI Middle Sch Math Lab Project 1967-68; dir MSU Math Project for Michigan Minority Youth; dir MSU Math Project for Teachers of Minority Youth 1989-; chairperson Benjamin Banneker Assn Coordinating Committee; president, Benjamin Banneker Assocation, 1993-95; board of directors, National Council of Teachers of Mathematics, 1992-95; chair, Coordinating Committee of Alliance to Involve Minorities in Mathematics, 1992-. **Honors/Awds:** Recd grants from NSF, NMSU; numerous works & papers published & presented. **Military Serv:** AUS 1950-52. **Business Addr:** Professor, Dept of Math, Michigan State University, East Lansing, MI 48824.

VANCE, LAWRENCE N.
Communications journalist. **Personal:** Born Dec 20, 1949, Chicago, IL; children: 2. **Educ:** Roosevelt Univ, BS 1973; Chicago Kent Law School, JD 1977. **Career:** Cook County Public Defender, investigator 1973-79, atty 1977-79; Private Practice, attorney. **Orgs:** Mem Natl, Cook Cty, IL and Chicago Bar Assocs 1977-87. **Business Addr:** Attorney, 201 North Wells, Chicago, IL 60602.

VANCE, TOMMIE ROWAN
Manager (retired). **Personal:** Born Apr 13, 1929, Frederick, OK; daughter of Victoria Mims Rowan (deceased) and Alfred Rowan (deceased); divorced; children: Michael, Nathan, Noretha. **Educ:** Golden Gate Univ, 1979-81. **Career:** Gary's Grocery, cashier 1955-59; Nevada Bell Telephone Co, mgr 1960-78; Pacific Telephone Co, mgr 1978-90. **Orgs:** Dem Ctr Comm 1974-78; mem NV State Dem Affirmative Action Comm 1975-76; mem, Intl Women's Yr Conf; chrpsn Reno Comm on the Status of Women 1972-74; mem Washoe Cnty Demo Women's Club 1968-72; member 4th July Committee, Carson City, NV, 1990; Reno-Sparks Negro Business and Professional Women's Clubs, club sec, 1993-95, 1st vice pres. **Honors/Awds:** Speech winner Pipe & Wire Toastmistress 1968; winner Council Level 1968; Boss of the Yr Amer Bus Women of Sparks 1971; Commendation United Fund. **Home Addr:** 1792 Gregg St, Carson City, NV 89701.

VANCE, VERA R.
Educator. **Personal:** Born Jul 11, 1908, Waskom, TX; married; children: James R. **Educ:** BA 1939; MEd 1962; Grad Stud 1971. **Career:** Notre Dame HS, consultant 1973-; JS Clarke Jr HS, teacher & counselor 1961-72 Central Jr HS, teacher 1959-61; Mooretown Elementary Shreveport, teacher 1951-56; Dixie Elementary, prin teacher 1948-81; Beaver Pond Elementary, prin teacher 1945-47; Gainsville Elementary, prin teacher 1931-45; Galilee Elementary Gilliam LA, teacher 1929-31; Velie Elem, teacher 1924. **Orgs:** Past sec Inter Scholastic League; TX & LA SS & BTU Congress 1932-50; sec Dist I SS Inst 1932-47; basileus of Sigma Gamma Rho; sec of chap 1974; mem YWCA; YMCA; Caddo Ed; ASS; Tchrs Assn Am Personnel-Guidance; LA Guidance Assn; Breezy Hill Comm Club; treas Trinity Bapt Ch. **Honors/Awds:** Award Sigma Gamma Rho 1962; award for 20 yrs contin serv Sigma Gamma Rho 1974; award in bus Sigma Gamma Rho 1974.

VANCE, WILLIAM J., SR.
Clergyman. **Personal:** Born Jan 14, 1923, Des Arc, AR; son of Esther Butler Vance and Ignatius D Vance; married Jacqueline G, Aug 24, 1947; children: Rene J Smith, William Jr (deceased). **Educ:** Roosevelt Univ, 1946-54; Moody Bible Inst, 1961; Gov State Univ, BA 1974, MA 1975; "Parish Context Training" Pastoral Psysho-Therapy Institute 1983-84. **Career:** Chicago Post Office, 1948-69; Older Boys & Girls Conf, bible teacher, couns, summer camp 1958-74; Berean Baptist Church, pastor 1969-91; Paster Emeritus, 1991-. **Orgs:** Chmn bd of dir Douglass Tubman Christian Ctr 1976-78; bd mem 1974-, ed 1969-75, Berean News. **Honors/Awds:** Great Guy of Day WVON 1970; E Chicago Heights Comm Ctr Awd 1975; Great Amer Awd 1976. **Military Serv:** USAF 1943-46. **Business Addr:** Pastor Emeritus, Berean Baptist Church, 5147 S Dearborn, Chicago, IL 60609.

VANDERBURG, CRAIG TERRENCE
Plant manager. **Personal:** Born Nov 6, 1954, Detroit, MI; son of Maudice Franklin Vanderburg and Virgil Vanderburg; married Alfrieda Dillard Vanderburg, Aug 20, 1977; children: Aurelia Nicole, Alexis Elise, Corbin Franklin. **Educ:** MI State Univ, E Lansing, MI, BS, 1976; Keller Graduate School, Chicago, IL, MBA, 1982. **Career:** Bristol-Meyers Co, pkg pro, engr, 1976-78; G D Searle Co, plant/general manager, 1978-; The Nutrasweet Co, plant mgr, currently. **Orgs:** Mem, NAACP, 1988-; mem, Natl Assn of Black MBA's, 1989-; past chap pres, mem, Alpha Phi Alpha Fraternity, 1973-; corp rep, Drug & Pharmaceutical Packaging Com of Institute of Packaging Prof, 1983-. **Honors/Awds:** America's Best & Brightest Businessmen, Dollars & Sense Magazine, 1989; Academic Scholarship Recipient, Detroit News, 1969.

VANDERPOOL, EUSTACE ARTHUR
Educator. **Personal:** Born Dec 11, 1934, Nassau, Bahamas; married Andrea Taylor; children: Sheely, Scot-Erik. **Educ:** Howard U, BS 1964; Howard U, MS 1967; Howard U, Doctorate 1971. **Career:** Howard Univ Coll of Med, asso prof 1973-; Dept Microbiology Howard Univ Coll of Med, virologist 1973; Microbiology Assoc MD, electron microscopist- Virology 1969; Naval Med Res Inst, guest scientist 1974. **Orgs:** Mem Am Soc of Microbiology 1964; mem Tissue Culture Assn 1967; mem Nat Inst of Sci 1978. **Honors/Awds:** Res grant Am Cancer Soc Institutional Res Grant #1n-132; appt asso prof grad sch of Arts & Sci Howard Univ 1979; latest pub Proc of Soc Exp Bio Med 160389-395 1979. **Business Addr:** 520 W St NW, Washington, DC 20059.

VANDROSS, LUTHER R.
Singer, songwriter, producer. **Personal:** Born Apr 20, 1951, New York, NY; son of Mary Ida Vandross. **Educ:** Western Michigan Univ, 1970. **Career:** Wrote song ''Everybody Rejoice'' featured in Broadway show The Wiz 1972; toured with David Bowie 1974; sang on albums with Bette Midler, Carly Simon, Chaka Khan, Average White Band; first Epic Solo album ''Never Too Much'' 1981 sold more than 1,000,000 copies; second solo album ''Forever, For Always, For Love'' 1982; wrote and recorded third solo album ''Busy Body'' 1984; fourth solo album ''The Night I Fell in Love'', 1985; produced albums for Dionne Warwick How Many Times Can We Say Goodbye and Aretha Franklin Jump To It, Get It Right 1983; sang backup and arranged vocals for three tracks on Diana Ross' ''Silk''; solo albums, ''Give Me the Reason,'' 1987, ''Any Love,'' 1989, ''The Power of Love'', 1991; Never Let Me Go, 1993; Songs, 1994. **Orgs:** ASCAP, SAG, AFTRA. **Honors/Awds:** Platinum LP's ''Never Too Much'', ''Forever For Always'', ''Busy Body'', ''The Night I Fell in Love'' 1981-86; received Grammy Award nominations for best new artist and best male rhythm and blues vocalist, 1981; American Music Awards (2), 1992; Grammy Awards (2), 1992. **Business Addr:** Vocalist, c/o Epic Records, Intl Creative Mgmt, 40 W 57th St, New York, NY 10019.

VAN DYKE, ALEX
Professional football player. **Personal:** Born Jul 24, 1974, Sacramento, CA. **Educ:** Nevada-Reno. **Career:** New York Jets, wide receiver, 1996-. **Business Addr:** Professional Football Player, New York Jets, 1000 Fulton Ave, Hempstead, NY 11550, (516)560-8100.

VAN DYKE, HENRY
Author. **Personal:** Born Oct 3, 1928, Allegan, MI; son of Bessie Van Dyke and Henry Van Dyke. **Educ:** Univ MI, BA 1953, MA 1955. **Career:** Basic Books, edtr 1958-66; Kent State U, writer-in-residence 1969-. **Honors/Awds:** Guggenheim 1971; literary award Acad Arts & Letters 1973; Published, Ladies of the Rachmaninoff Eyes 1965, Blood of Strawberrs 1969, Dead Piano 1971, Lunacy and Caprice 1987. **Military Serv:** AUS corpl 1947-50. **Home Addr:** 40 Waterside Plz, New York, NY 10010. **Business Addr:** Writer-in-Residence, Kent State University, Kent, OH 44242.

VAN EXEL, NICK (NICKEY MAXWELL)
Professional basketball player. **Personal:** Born Nov 27, 1971, Kenosha, WI. **Educ:** Trinity Valley Comm College; Cincinnati. **Career:** Los Angeles Lakers, guard, 1993-. **Honors/Awds:** NBA, All-Rookie second team, 1994. **Business Addr:** Professional Basketball Player, Los Angeles Lakers, PO Box 10, Inglewood, CA 90306, (213)419-3100.

VAN HOOK, GEORGE ELLIS, JR.
Judge, attorney. **Personal:** Born Aug 27, 1948; married Margaret Ann Kendrix Van Hook; children: Demetric, Alison Blossam, George Ellis III. **Educ:** University of Arkansas, BSBA, marketing, 1970; University of Arkansas School of Law, JD, 1973. **Career:** Walker, Kaplan and Mays, legal intern, 1971; Eugene Hunt, law clerk, 1973; Hunt and Van Hook, attorney, 1973-74; Arkansas State Highway Department, staff attorney, 1974-76; general practice of law, attorney, 1976-77; private practice, attorney, 1977-79; Union County Child Support Enforcement Unit, contract attorney, 1981-90; Union County Municipal Court, magistrate, 1983-90; private practice, attorney, 1979-; Union County, municipal judge, private practice, attorney, 1991-. **Orgs:** Union County Bar Association; Salvation Army, board of advisors; Union County United Way, board of directors; Progressive Gentlemen, Inc; El Dorado Chamber of Commerce; Union County Academic Foundation, Inc; Boys and Girls Club of El Dorado; Boy Scouts Union District; South Arkansas Arts Center; UALR Scholarship Program; Winthrop Rockefeller Scholarship Program; Arkansas Cost of the Judiciary Study Commission, 1986; Arkansas Municipal Judges Council; Arkansas Municipal League; Independent Living Centers, board; Harold Flowers Law Society; Union County Community Foundation; State of Arkansas Community Punishment Advisory Board. **Business Addr:** Attorney at Law, Judge, 307 S Hill St, PO Box 490, El Dorado, AR 71730, (501)863-5119.

VAN HOOK, WARREN KENNETH
Educator. **Personal:** Born Jun 26, 1920, Elverton, WV; married Cora; children: Sharyl, Warren Jr, Fay. **Educ:** WV Coll, 1941-42, 1945-47; Howard U, BS 1951. **Career:** Howard Univ, dir minority business 1976-; Inst Minority Business Educ School Business Public Admin Howard Univ, dir 1973-; Small Business Guidance & Devel Center Howard Univ, assoc dir 1968-73; Van-Park Drugs, owner 1954-68; Div Drugs Inc, mgr pharm 1951-54; United Comm Natl Bank WA, founding dir vice pres 1964-68; Antioch School Law, adv dir 1970-73; Minority Business & Orgn, mgmt consultant 1974-; DC Commn Against Drug Abuse, commr 1976-77; United Natl Bank WA, dir 1976-. **Orgs:** Co-foundr vice pres treas memsp Neighbors Inc 1958-68; mem Alpha Phi Alpha Frat; Nat Bus League; Am Soc Training & Devel; Am Pharm Assn; Nat Pharm Assn; NAACP; Urban League. **Honors/Awds:** Outsdng serv Aw Ministerial Alliance NE WA 1964; key to cty Savannah GA 1977; pbul ''Crime & Small Bus'' Black Enter 1971; ''Combating Crime in the Small Bus Arena'' Jour Small Busm Mgmt 1971; ''Tech & Asst & the Busmn'' DC Dealer 1971; bronze star aw. **Military Serv:** AUS capt 1942-45. **Business Addr:** 2361 Sherman Ave NW, Washington, DC 20059.

VANITY (DENISE MATTHEWS)
Vocalist, actress. **Personal:** Born 1958, Ontario;married Anthony Smith, 1995. **Career:** Vanity 6, former lead singer, work includes: Nasty Girls, single; Wild Animal, Skin On Skin, both with Motown; film appearances include: The Last Dragon, 1985; Never Too Young To Die, 1986; 52 Pickup, 1986; Love You To Death; Deadly Illusion, 1987; Action Jackson, 1988; television appearances include: The Late Show, 1987; The New Mike Hammer, 1987; Miami Vice, 1987; Ebony/Jet Showcase, 1988; Memories of Murder, 1990; Evangelist, currently. **Special Achievements:** Nasty Girls, Gold Single. **Business Addr:** Actress, c/o William Morris Agency, 151 El Camino Dr, Beverly Hills, CA 90212, (310)274-7451.

VAN LIEROP, ROBERT F.
Ambassador, attorney. **Personal:** Born Mar 17, 1939, New York, NY; son of Sylvia and Edward; married Toy. **Educ:** Hofstra Univ, BA Econ 1964; NY Univ Sch of Law, LLB (JD) 1967. **Career:** Asst counsel NAACP 1967-68; assoc Fleisher, Dornbush, Mensch, Mandelstam 1968-71; Atty; Self-employed, film prod photojournalist 1971-; ''Like It Is'' WABC/TV, coprod 1977-78; Privte Practice, atty 1968-71; NY City Community Bd #9 Manhattan, chairman, 1985-87; Republic of Vanuatu, Ambassador to the United Nations 1981-94. **Orgs:** Bd mem, Lawyers Comm for Human Rights; bd mem Arthur Assn Inst for Urban Health; bd of dir Black Economic Research Center; past mem exec comm Amer Comm on Africa; founding mem Natl Conf of Black Lawyers; former bd mem Harlem Children's Theatre; past mem natl exec bd Natl Lawyers Guild; past bd mem NY Civil Liberties Union; mem, bd of directors, Manhattan Borough Development Corp 1988-90. **Honors/Awds:** George M Estabrook Distinguished Service Award, Hofstra University, 1991; Hofstra Univ Award, Alumni Achievement, 1993; Vanatu Independence Medal, Republic of Vanuatu, 1991; Grand Cross of the Order of the Infante Dom Henrique, Pres of Portugal, 1993; Doctor of Humane Letters, Donoris Causor, Hofstra Univ, 1994. **Military Serv:** USAF 1956-60. **Business Addr:** Attorney & Counselor at Law, Van Lierop, Burns & Schaap, 320 Convent Ave, New York, NY 10031-6331.

VAN LIEW, DONALD H.
Educator. **Personal:** Born Oct 4, 1929, Somerville, NJ; married Ruth E Kauffmann; children: Ingrid E, Hans P, Nil C. **Educ:** Univ of New Mexico, BFA 1956; Columbia Teachers Coll, MA 1979. **Career:** Univ of MI, asst counselor intl center 1960-64; Inst of Intl Educ NYC, program specialist 1964-65; NSSFNS, assoc 1965-66, sr assoc 1966, assoc dir 1966, dir 1967-69; Columbia Univ, asst to dean of student affairs 1969-71; Marymount Coll, dir comm leadership program 1971-, dir HEOP, asst dean 1985-. **Orgs:** Mem Planning Comm NACAC 1968; pres Croton Comm Nursery School 1968; mem NY State Educ Dept Head Task Force on Consortia 1973; chairperson Cross-cultural program com Marymount Coll 1973; mem ex-officer Com on Academic Standing & Retention Marymount Coll 1971-79; sec NY State Higher educ Opportunity Program Professional Org 1975; mem Academic Dean Search Comm Marymount Coll 1977; mem Bd of Trustees Common Marketing Marymount Coll 1978; mem Commn on Independent Coll & Univ Higher Educ Oppor Program 1979; Westchester Regional Rep NY State Higher Educ Opportunity Program Professional Org 1979; mem Taks Force on Admissions Marymount Coll 1972-74; chairperson Fact Finding Comm to the Presidential Search Com 1974; mem NY State Task Force on HEOP Guidelines 1974;mem Affirmative Action Task Forcarymount Coll 1975; chmn Calendar Comm 1985-; mem national assoc of academic affairs administrators 1988; mem committee for bridging academic and student affairs 1986; mem committee on the troubled student 1986; mem committee on racial and cultural diversity 1989. **Honors/Awds:** Ford Found Grant to participate in program for educ leadership Teacher Coll Columbia Univ 1970-71. **Military Serv:** Served 1951-53. **Home Addr:** RD #1, Box 155 Wooddale Ave, Croton On Hudson, NY 10520.

VANN, ALBERT
State official. **Personal:** Born Nov 19, 1934, Brooklyn, NY; married Mildred E; children: Scott, Shannon, Fola, Binta. **Educ:** Univ of Toledo, BBA, 1959; Yeshiva Univ, MS; Long Island Univ, MS. **Career:** New York State Assemblyman, District 56, 1975-. **Orgs:** Dir Talent Serach Prog Dept HEW; mem NY State Assem; founder, pres, African-Am Teachers Assn; bd dir Bedford-Stuyvesant Restoration Corp; pres Vannguard Civic Assn; chmn NY State Blk & Puerto Rican Legis Caucus 1977; bd mem NAACP; mem Blk Educs; Medgar Evers Coll Comm Coun; mem Alpha Phi Alpha Fraternity. **Honors/Awds:** Political Achievement Award IDEA Inc; Community Service Award Bus & Professional Negro Women Inc; Outstanding Educator Award, Bro & Sister Afro-Am Unity. **Military Serv:** USMC sgt 1952-55. **Business Addr:** State Capitol, Albany, NY 12225.

VANN, GREGORY ALVIN
Consultant. **Personal:** Born Apr 17, 1954, Washington, DC; married Joan A Simpson. **Educ:** Howard Univ, BArch 1977; Univ of FL, MConst Mgt 1978; Drexel Univ, MBA 1985. **Career:** Daniel Mann, Johnson & Mendenhall, draftsman, 1974-1976, Bryant & Bryant Architects, designer 1976-77; Whiting Turner Contracting Co, Project Engr 1977; Catalytic Inc, Sr Planning Engr 1978-81; Burns & Roe Inc, Sr Planning Engr 1981-84; The Vann Organization, Pres 1984-. **Orgs:** Mem Amer Assoc of Cost Engrs 1980-; mem Amer Inst of Architects 1986-87; mem Philadelphia Chap Natl Black MBA Assoc 1986-, Cherry Hill Minority Civic Assoc 1986-. **Business Addr:** The Vann Organization, 11 Sayer Ave, Cherry Hill, NJ 08002.

VANNAMAN, MADI T.
Human resources administrator. **Personal:** Born Mar 18, 1957, Aberdeen, MD; daughter of Nobuko Otsuki Thornton and Charles Robert Thornton; married Robbie L Vannaman, Aug 8, 1987. **Educ:** University of Kansas, BS, business, 1979, JD, 1983. **Career:** E&E Specialties, personnel director, 1983-85; State of Kansas, personnel management specialist, 1985-86, management analyst, Department of Administration, 1986-89, acting benefits administrator, Department of Administration, 1989; University of Kansas, assistant director, Human Resources, 1990-. **Business Addr:** Assistant Director, Human Resources, University of Kansas, Carruth O'Leary, Room 7, Lawrence, KS 66045, (913)864-4946.

VANOVER, TAMARICK
Professional football player. **Personal:** Born Feb 25, 1974, Tallahassee, FL. **Educ:** Florida State Univ. **Career:** Kansas City Chiefs, wide receiver, 1995-. **Honors/Awds:** Mack Lee Hill Award, 1995. **Business Addr:** Professional Football Player, Kansas City Chiefs, One Arrowhead Dr, Kansas City, MO 64129, (816)924-9300.

VAN PEEBLES, MARIO
Actor, director, writer, filmmaker. **Personal:** Born in Mexico City, Mexico; son of Maria Van Peebles and Melvin Van Peebles. **Educ:** Columbia University, BA, economics, 1980. **Career:** Movies include: Heartbreak Ridge; Sweet Sweetback's Baadassssss Song; Jaws: the Revenge; Exterminator II; Cotton Club; Rappin; Solo; Riot, 1997; director, actor: New Jack City, 1991; Posse, 1993; Gunmen, co-star, soundtrack album executive producer; appeared in Off-Broadway comedy ''A Thousand Clowns''; Broadway comedy ''Waltz of the Stork''; TV movies: ''Blue Bayou,'' ''In The Line of Duty: Street War,'' ''Sophisticated Gents,'' ''Stompin' at the Savoy,'' ''Children of the Night,'' ''Third and Oak: The Pool Hall,'' ''Triumph of the Heart: The Ricky Bell Story,'' ''Emperor Jones''; star, co-director, series: ''Sonny Spoon,'' NBC-TV; co-star series: ''Orleans,'' NBC/Disney; has directed numerous TV shows including: ''21 Jump Street,'' ''Wiseguy,'' ''Top of the Hill,'' ''Gabriel's Fire,'' After School Special, ''Malcolm Takes A Shot''; co-wrote, withfer, ''No Identity Crisis''; hosted, ''The Pat Sajek Show,'' 1990; cohosted, Black Filmmakers Hall of Fame Awards, 1991. **Orgs:** Screen Actors Guild; Actor's Equity; American Federation of Television and Radio Artists; Directors Guild of America. **Honors/Awds:** Bronze Halo Award, for performance in ''Children of the Night''; Pioneers of Excellence Award, World Institute of Black Communications; Emmy Award nomination and Directors Guild Award, for ''Malcolm Takes A Shot,'' 1990; NAACP Image Award, for Heartbreak Ridge.

VAN PEEBLES, MELVIN
Writer, actor, composer, film director. **Personal:** Born Aug 21, 1932, Chicago, IL; divorced; children: Mario, Megan, Melvin. **Educ:** Graduated from Ohio Wesleyan Univ; Univ of Amsterdam, attended. **Career:** Acted with the Dutch National Theatre; writer, director, film, The Story of a Three Day Pass, 1967, in France; directed motion pictures for Columbia Studios, including Watermelon Man, 1969; wrote, directed, and financed the film Sweet Sweetback's Baadasssss Song, 1971; wrote and produced two Broadway plays Ain't Supposed to Die A Natural Death, 1971; Don't Play Us Cheap, 1972; directed a music video of the group Whodini's song Funky Beat; composer for recordings; tv writing projects: Just an Old Sweet Song, 1976; Sophisticated Gents, 1981; American Stock Exchange, floor

trader, 1984; Mabon, Nugent & Co, consultant, 1984; actor, LA Law, 1986; Jaws: The Revenge, 1987; Posse; Boomerang; Riot, 1997. **Orgs:** mem, Directors Guild of Amer; mem, French Directors Guild. **Honors/Awds:** First Prize from Belgian Festival for Don't Play Us Cheap; author, Bold Money, A New Way to Play the Options Market, Warner Books, 1986, Bold Money: How to Get Rich in the Options Market, Warner Books, 1987, No Identity Crisis: A Father and Son's Own Story of Working Together, 1990; honorary doctorate, Hofstra Univ, 1995. **Military Serv:** US Air Force, navigator-bombardier, 3.5 yrs. **Business Addr:** Author, No Identity Crisis, 1990, c/o Simon & Schuster, 1230 Ave of the Americas, New York, NY 10020-1586.

VAN TRECE, JACKSON C.

Educator (retired). **Personal:** Born Aug 31, 1928, Edwardsville, IL; married Dolores Wilson. **Educ:** KS State Tchr Coll, BS 1952; KS State Coll Pgh, MS 1960; UMKC & KS State Tchrs Coll Emporis KS. **Career:** NE Jr HS, teacher 1952-56; NE Jr HS, counselor 1965-66; Sumner HS Kansas City KS, 1966-70; Univ of MO KC, asst vice chanchellor student affairs 1980-85. **Orgs:** Admin & dir Black Motivation Training Cntr KC 1970; life mem NEA; pres Region VII Trio Proj Dir Orgn; dir Trio Progs UMKC; Boy Scouts Am Troop Ldr 1952-58; devel Turner House KC; Kappa Alpha Psi Frat; dir Area Youth Groups; YMCA exec bd KC MO 1973. **Special Achievements:** University of Missouri's first African-American Academic Dean. **Military Serv:** AUS 1946-48. **Business Addr:** 5100 Rockhill Rd, Kansas City, MO 64110.

VANZANT, IYANLA

Author. **Personal:** divoRced. **Career:** Author, currently. **Special Achievements:** Books include: One Day My Soul Just Opened Up; In the Meantime: Finding Yourself and the Love You Want; Tapping The Power Within.

VARGUS, IONE D.

Educational administrator. **Personal:** Born Jul 19, 1930, Medford, MA; daughter of Madeline Kountze Dugger-Kelley and Edward Dugger; married William H Adams (deceased); children: Suzanne Vargus Holloman; William D. **Educ:** Tufts U, AB 1952; Univ Chicago, MA 1954; Brandeis Univ, PhD 1971. **Career:** Several Yrs Social Work Practice Family Servcs, Child Welfare Public Housing Home Mgmt Informal Educ 1954-71; Brandeis Univ Waltham, MA, asst prof 1969-71; Univ IL Urbana, asst prof 1971-74; Temple Univ, dean sch social admin, 1974-91, vice provost 1991-93, presidential fellow, 1993-95. **Orgs:** Trustee Tufts Univ 1981-91; board member Juvenile Law Center 1991-; board member Tucker House II 1990-96; board member Multicultural Institute 1990-; chair, Family Reunion Inst, 1990-. **Honors/Awds:** NAACP, Founders Award, 1991; Tufts Alumni Council, Distinguished Service Award, 1993; Kwanzaa Holiday Expo Award, 1994. **Home Addr:** 429 East Durham St, Philadelphia, PA 19119. **Business Addr:** Professor & Dean Emeritus, Temple Univ, Ritter Hall Annex, Philadelphia, PA 19122, (215)204-6244.

VARNADO, ARTHUR

Business executive. **Personal:** Born Oct 19, 1932, Buffalo, NY; married Theresa E; children: Debra, Karen, Arthur. **Educ:** Cameron Coll, 1971; Dowling Coll, BS 1973; FAA Exec Sch, 1974; Univ Louisville, MS 1975; Air War Coll, Prof Diploma 1976; Auburn U, MPA 1976. **Career:** Lazard Freres & Co, vice pres of municipal finance, 1993-; Prudential Securities, vice pres, municipal finance, until 1993; FAA, spl asst to dir 1976-; Air Traffic Control Tower, chief 1973-75; Air Traffic Control Tower JFK Tower, chief 1972-73; Newark Tower, dep chief, 1971-72; radar controller 1968-71; Newark Tower, radar controller 1963-68. **Orgs:** Kappa Alpha Psi 1977; Black Controllers Coalition 1968-72; Fed Exec Assn 1973; Louisville Urban League 1973-76; Louisville Eastern Area Counc 1974-76; NAACP 1963-68; White Oaks Civic Assn 1969-73. **Honors/Awds:** Grad dean's honor awd 1976; outst rating awd FAA 1975; disting citizens awd Louisville 1975; hon Bky Col Louisville 1974; we point with pride awd FAA1966. **Military Serv:** USAF s/sgt 1952-56. **Business Addr:** Vice President, Municipal Finance, Lazard Frere & Co, 1 Rockefeller Plaza, New York, NY 10020.

VARNER, HAROLD R.

Architect. **Educ:** Lawrence Technological Univ, BS Architecture; General Services Admin, engineering cert. **Career:** Howard Sims & Assoc, joined 1973, principal 1976; Sim-Varner and Assoc, pres/CEO, currently. **Orgs:** AIA Detroit, mem, 1968-; AIA Michigan, mem, 1968-; Michigan Bds of Architecture and Engineers, former mem; New Detroit Inc, mem; Detroit Public School Vocational/Tech Centers, task force. **Honors/Awds:** Hastings Award, 1996. **Special Achievements:** Formed MI requirements for Intern Development Program (IPP); Architect of the African American Museum, Detroit. **Business Addr:** President/CEO, Sims-Varner & Associatess, 244 Penobscot Bldg, 645 Griswold, Ste 244, Detroit, MI 48226, (313)961-9000.

VARNER, JAMES, SR.

Business executive, educator. **Personal:** Born Nov 2, 1934, Jersey City, NJ; son of Mamie Dickerson Varner and Charles Varner; married Florence Johnson; children: 4. **Educ:** Univ of ME, BS 1957; Rutgers Univ, MS 1970, M City & Regional Planning 1972. **Career:** Mt Sinai Hosp, chemist 1957-58; Public School, high school teacher 1960-66; Plainfield Comm Action, assoc dir 1966; Morris Co Human Resources Agency, exec dir 1966-82; Drew Univ, counselor & lectr part-time 1 972-82; Black Enterprise Magazine, acct exec 1982-85; Fallis Communications Inc, vice pres, 1985-86; Informatoin Mgmt Resources, Inc, vice pres, 1970-; ''Community Update,'' WMTR Radio, Morristown, NJ, host and producer, 1970-; East Orange Board of Education, East Orange, NJ, teacher, 1990-92; Univ of Maine, asst dir of admissions for minority recruitment, 1993-95; Univ of Maine, advisor, lecturer and consultant, 1995-; Gov Angus King appointed me as a commisioner on the State of Maine Human Right Commission. **Orgs:** Amer Inst of Planners; Amer Soc of Planning Officials; Natl Assn of Planners; Amer Found for Negro Affairs; Congress of African Peoples; Natl Assn for Comm Devel; Rotary Club of Morristown NJ; bd mem Plainfield NJ Area YMCA; bd mem Morris Co NAACP; named chmn emeritus of Natl Assn of Planners 1972; bd mem Natl Assn of Comm Devel; past bd mem Amer Soc of Planning Officials. **Honors/Awds:** First place in NJ Jaycees Area Speak Up Finals 1967; Community Service Award, The Morris County Urban League, Inc, 1989. **Special Achievements:** Host of radio program, Community Update. **Military Serv:** US Army, Capt. **Home Addr:** 314 S Brunswick St, Old Town, ME 04468. **Business Addr:** Phi Eta Kappa, Univ of Maine, 107 College Ave, Orono, ME 04469.

VARNER, JEWELL C.

Association director. **Personal:** Born Apr 12, 1918, Tatums, OK; daughter of Janie Lovejoy Carter and Joseph Carter; married Jimmy Lee (deceased); children: Jimmie Mae, Rose Marie. **Educ:** Langston Univ, BS; KS State Teachers Coll Emporia, MS; OK State Univ, Post Graduate Studies. **Career:** Big Five Devel Found Head Start HEW, dir; Jewell's Ceramics & Gifts, owner 1975-; Tatums OK Public Schools, teacher 28 yrs; Golden Acre Enterprizes, owner, dir. **Orgs:** Mem Eastern Star; Delta Sigma Theta; vice pres OK Assn Children Under Six; OK Educ Assn; life mem NAACP; mem NTU, NAMPU, Natl Set Inc, OK Chapter Langston Alumnus Assoc; Links Inc Oklahoma City Chapter. **Honors/Awds:** Black Voise Better Business Award 1973; best dressed woman OK State Soul Bazaar 1973; Outstanding Civic Serv Fed Club Women; Tatums Comm Action Agency Chmn War on Poverty Gov's Advisory Group; Inducted into OK Afro-Amer Hall of Fame 1984. **Home Addr:** 3405 E Maxwell Drive, Oklahoma City, OK 73121.

VARNER, NELLIE M.

Educator, real estate investment broker. **Personal:** Born Aug 27, 1935, Lake Cormorant, MS; daughter of Essie Davis & Tommie Varner (both deceased); divorced; children: Janniss LaTronia Varner. **Educ:** Wayne State Univ, BS 1958, MA 1959; Univ of MI, PhD 1968. **Career:** Detroit Public School, teacher 1959-64; University of Michigan, College of Literature Science & Arts, spl asst to dean, 1968-70, Ctr for Russian & European Studies, faculty assoc, 1968-69, asst prof political science, 1968-69; Harvard Univ, rsch fellow 1970-71, rsch assoc 1970-71; University of Michigan, Affirmative Action Progs, dir, 1972-75, Rackham School of Grad Studies, assoc dean, 1976-79; Strather & Varner Inc Real Estate Invest Brokers, vice pres 1979-91; Primco Foods Inc, pres, 1988-; N M Varner Co, pres, 1991-; Atwater Entertainment Associates, vice pres, 1994-. **Orgs:** American Council on Educ Comm on Women in Higher Educ 1976-; Natl Sci Foundation Adv Com for Minority Progs in Science Education 1977-; chair Real Estate Adv Bd State of MI 1978-79; del White House Conf on Small Business 1980-; bd of regents Univ of MI 1980-; bd dir Highland Park YMCA 1980-83; exec bd Detroit Chapter NAACP 1985-86; bd dir Amer Inst for Business 1986-; Southern Oakland County Bd of Realtors, Detroit Bd of Realtors; chair Equal Opportunity Com Natl Assn of State Univ & Land Grant Coll; Econ Action Com New Detroit Inc; MI Bd of Realtors & Natl Bd of Realtors; Equal Opportunity Task Force Amer Council on Educ, Acad Affairs Faculty Analysis Proj Adv Com Univ of MI, Senate Assem Adv Com on State Real University of MI, exec bd Wayne State Univ, Univ of MI; Institute of Gerontology; exec com Ctr for Afro-American African Studies, U of MI; HEW Title I State Adv Council to Bd of Educ State of MI; consult Natl Sci Found Panel on Awds to Minority Coll & Univ, Proj for Acad Affirm Action Training Intl Assoc of Official Human Rights Agency, Dept of HUD US Govt; trustee, New Detroit Inc, 1987-; dir, Inst of Amer Business, 1986-94; trustee, WTVS Channel 56, 1990-93. **Honors/Awds:** Florence Sweeney Scholarship 1958; Detroit Women Principals Club Scholarship 1959; teaching fellowship 1964; NDFL Fellowship 1966-68; congressional internship US Congress 1966; CIC grant for Field Study in USSR 1968; Wilton Park Fellowship for Amer participation in Wilton Park Conf Steyning Sussex England 1969; social Sci Rsch Council Rsch Training Fellowship 1970-71; rsch grant Univ of MI 1970-71; recip rsch travel grant to study Black Political Elites in Africa US & the Caribbean Carnegie Endowment for Intl Peace 1970-; Distinguished Community Leadership Award Natl Assoc of Women Business Owners 1984. **Business Addr:** Vice Pres, Atwater Entertainment Associates, 300 Riverplace, Ste 6600, Detroit, MI 48207, (313)446-6900.

VARNER, ROBERT LEE, SR.

Military officer (retired), business executive. **Personal:** Born May 3, 1932, Birmingham, AL; married Annie C; children: Venetia, Dwayne, Robert II, Sherian. **Educ:** San Diego City College, 1970; University of Northern Colorado, 1973; National University, BBA, 1976, MBA, 1978. **Career:** US Marine Corps, 1950-75; Pacific Coast Bank, vice president, business development and public relations, 1975-79; Bank of American, MBA Management Training Program, commercial loan officer, financial services officer, 1979-82; Los Angeles Small Business Investment Corporation, economic development director, 1982-83; Pacific Coast Executive Management, CEO; Maestas Precision Metals Inc., CEO, 1983-87; Law Offices of G Michael Curls, administrator, 1987-91; Community Business Center, CEO, 1991-. **Orgs:** President emeritus, California Federation of Black Leadership; executive vice president, National Association of Black Military Officers; Presidential Republican Task Force; California Black Republican Council; Los Angeles County Private Industry Council; San Diego Urban League; First AME Church; numerous others. **Honors/Awds:** San Diego County Human Relations Award, community involvement; American Tennis Association, Outstanding Service; Los Angeles County Special Commendation, outstanding service as a member of the Employment and Training Program. **Military Serv:** US Marine Corps, capt, 1950-75; Vietnamese Cross of Gallantry; Presidential Unit Citation; National Defense Service Medals; Korean Service Medals; United Nations Service Medals; Good Conduct Medal; Vietnamese Combat Medal; Vietnamese Service Medal; Korean Presidential Unit Citation. **Business Addr:** CEO, Community Business Center, 8825 S Central Ave, Los Angeles, CA 90002-1123.

VASQUEZ, JOSEPH B.

Filmmaker. **Career:** Films include: Street Story, 1988, Bronx Wars, 1989, Hangin' With the Homeboys, 1991. **Honors/Awds:** Shared Best Screenwriter award with Hal Hartley for Trust, Sundance Film Festival, 1991; special audience award, US Film Festival, Deauville, France, 1991. **Business Addr:** Filmmaker, c/o William Morris Agency, 151 El Camino Drive, Beverly Hills, CA 90212, (310)274-7451.

VAUGHAN, GERALD R.

Certified financial planner. **Personal:** Born Sep 9, 1957, Bronx, NY; son of Juanita B Smith-Vaughan and Raymond Vaughan; married Ramona D Girtman. **Educ:** NC A&T St Univ, BS (Magna Cum Laude) 1980; Atlanta Univ, MBA (Magna Cum Laude) 1983; Adelphi Univ, CFP 1985. **Career:** Liberty Mutual Insurance Co, personal risk underwriter/industry regulator/tech analyst 1976-80; Citizens & Southern GA Corp, strategic planner/invest analyst 1982-83; Entrepreneur, certified financial planner 1985-; Grumman Corp, sr financial analyst 1983-89. **Orgs:** Mem Assoc of MBA Executives 1982-, Natl Black MBA Assoc 1982-; keeper of finance Omega Psi Phi Frat Inc 1985-89. **Honors/Awds:** Fellowship Grants NC A&T St Univ/Atlanta Univ 1975-83; Outstanding Young Americans Intl Biographical Inst 1978-80. **Home Addr:** 3666 Cherry Ridge Blvd, Decatur, GA 30034.

VAUGHAN, JAMES EDWARD

Broadcast minister. **Personal:** Born Mar 7, 1943, Herdford County, NC; son of Jesse Mae Majette Vaughan and John Henry Vaughan; married Della M (deceased); children: Alvin, Patrinia, Meimii. **Educ:** NC Central Univ, BA Art/English 1969. **Career:** NY Courier Newspaper, managing editor 1969; Capital Cities Comms Inc, promotions mgr 1971-74; WYAH-TV, mgr promotion/producer 1977-81; Christian TV Ministries Inc, founder/chmn/pres 1980-; Small Bus Broadcasting Serv Co, founder/chmn/pres 1982-; WJCB TV Tidewater Christian, founder/chmn/pres 1983-. **Orgs:** Bd of dirs The STOP Org; mem Amer Mgmt Assoc, Interdenominational Ministers Forum, AEHRO Broadcast Frat; vice pres Southern Christian Leadership Conf VA; chmn media Tidewater for Jesus Assoc; chmn black broadcast ownership Natl Relig Broadcasters; board of directors, Tidewater Chapter National Conference of Christians & Jews, 1991-; advisory board, Inner-City Ministers Prayer Breakfast, 1989-; member, Portsmouth Area Ministerial Assn, 1986-. **Honors/Awds:** Ex Umbra Radio/TV Broadcasts and weekly column 1977-; Citation of Merit Natl Multiple Sclerosis Soc 1984; Certificate of Service VA State Adv Comm US Commn on Civil Rights 1985; Oliver J Allen Awd WRAP Radio Gospel Music Awds 1986; Public Service Award, Portsmouth City Council, 1987; Media Service Award, Athletes for a Better America, 1990; Excellence in Broadcast Pioneering, TCC Communications, 1986.

VAUGHN, ALVIN

Educator. **Personal:** Born Aug 30, 1939, Philadelphia, PA; son of Martha Vaughn and Roger Vaughn; married Eloise Stephens; children: Lois Jonneen. **Educ:** Temple Univ, BS 1963, MS 1964; Intl Grad School, EdD 1984. **Career:** School Dist of Philadelphia, teacher 1963-70, acting super 1970-71, dept head 1971-74, asst principal 1974-; evening school principal 1976-. **Orgs:** Bd of dirs Drew Comm Mental Health Ctr 1975-85; counselor/admin Negro Trade Union Leadership Council 1978-84; bd of sch dirs Cheltenham Township PA 1978-87; bd of dirs Philadelphia PUSH 1982-87, Cheltenham Art Ctr 1982-86. **Home Addr:** 1108 Curtis Dr, Wyncote, PA 19095, (215)886-2186. **Business Addr:** Educational Administrator, School District of Philadelphia, George Washington High School, Philadelphia, PA 19116, (215)961-2001.

VAUGHN, AUDREY SMITH
Utilities company executive. **Personal:** Born May 19, 1958, Birmingham, AL; daughter of Ophelia Lyas Smith and Porter D Smith Sr; married Rudolph Vaughn Jr, Jan 2, 1982; children: Christian, Adriene. **Educ:** University of Alabama-Birmingham, Birmingham, AL, BS, 1980; Samford University, Birmingham, AL, MBA, 1984. **Career:** Social Security Admin, Talladega, AL, claims rep, 1978-80; Alabama Power Company, Birmingham, AL, manager/employee relations, 1981-91, research & planning, manager, director of constituency relations, currently. **Orgs:** American Management Association, 1990-; National Management Association, 1986-; American Association of Blacks in Energy, 1989-; Delta Sigma Theta Sorority, 1979-; National Association of Female Executives, 1989-. **Honors/Awds:** Graduate, Chamber Leadership Development, Birmingham Chamber of Commerce, 1990; Birmingham's Top 40 Under 40, 1991. **Business Addr:** Director, Consituency Relations, Alabama Power Company, PO Box 2641, Birmingham, AL 35291-0680.

VAUGHN, CLARENCE B.
Clinical scientist. **Personal:** Born Dec 14, 1928, Philadelphia, PA; son of Aretha Johnson Vaughn and Albert Vaughn; married Sarah Campbell Vaughn, Sep 14, 1953; children: Steven, Annette, Carl, Ronald. **Educ:** Benedict Coll, BS 1947- 1951; Howard Univ, MS, 1951-1953/1955, MD 1953-1957; MD 1957; DC Gen Hosp, Intern 1957-58; Freedmans Hosp, Residency 1958-59; Wayne State Univ, PhD 1965. **Career:** Rsch Physician 1964-70; Milton A Darling mem Ctr, clin dir 1970-72; SW Oncology Study Group, principle investigator 1978-; Wayne State Univ, clinical prof 1988-; Providence Hospital, dir of oncology 1973-88; Southfield Oncology Institute Inc, dir of oncology, 1988-; Oakland Univ, clinical professor. **Orgs:** Bd of dir Amer Coll Cancer Society, Amer Assoc Univ Prof, AMA; natl chmn Aerospace & Military Sect of NMA, mem Amer Soc Clin Oncology, Natl Med Assn, Wayne Cty Med Soc, Oakland Cty med Assn, Reserve Officers Assn, US Assn Military Surgeons, USAF Assn, Detroit Cancer Club, Detroit Physiological Soc; pres Amer Cancer Soc MI Div 1986-; chmn adv comm minority involvement field serv comm Amer Cancer Soc; educ review comm Natl Cancer Inst; mem Natl Surgeon of Reserve Officers Assoc; mem Metropolitan Detroit Steering Comm for The Cancer Prevention Awareness; medical dir, Oncology, Samaritan Health Center 1986-. **Honors/Awds:** Outstanding Reserve Aerospace Med Physician Awd 1974; AFRES Command Flight Surgeon of the Year 1974; Humanitarian of the Year 1988. **Military Serv:** US Air Force, caption, 1959-61; US Air Force Reserves, colonel, 1961-87. **Business Addr:** Director, Oncology, Southfield Oncology Institute, Inc., 27211 Lahser Road, Southfield, MI 48034.

VAUGHN, DAVID, III
Professional basketball player. **Personal:** Born Mar 23, 1973, Tulsa, OK. **Educ:** Memphis. **Career:** Orlando Magic, forward, 1995-97; Golden State Warriors, 1997-98; New Jersey Nets, 1998-. **Business Addr:** Professional Basketball Player, New Jersey Nets, 405 Murray Hill Parkway, Brendan Byrne Arena, East Rutherford, NJ 07073, (201)935-8888.

VAUGHN, ED
State representative. **Personal:** Born 1924?. **Educ:** Fisk University, bachelor's degree. **Career:** Detroit Public Schools, teacher; Vaughn's Book Store, owner; Michigan House of Representatives, state representative, currently. **Business Addr:** State Representative, 4th District, Michigan House of Representatives, State Capitol, PO Box 30014, Lansing, MI 48909, (517)373-1008.

VAUGHN, EUGENIA MARCHELLE WASHINGTON
Social worker. **Personal:** Born Oct 31, 1957, Columbus, OH; daughter of Lula Augusta Edwards Washington and Eugene G. Washington; married Tannis Eugene Vaughn, Jun 9, 1984; children: Shannon Eugene, Ieasha Michelle. **Educ:** Columbus Tech Inst, associate's degree, 1977; OH Dominican Coll, BA 1983; OH State Univ, MSW 1985. **Career:** Franklin Co Children Svcs, caseworker I 1977-83, child welfare caseworker II 1984; Columbus Area Mental Health Ctr, contract worker 1985; Franklin Co Children Svcs, child welfare caseworker II, III Foster Care 1985-87, social worker III 1987-89, treatment manager, 1989-91, child welfare supervisor II, 1991-. **Orgs:** Natl Assoc of Social Workers, Natl Assoc of Black Social Workers; rec'd LSW Status Natl Assoc of Social Workers 1986; initiator Scholarship Alumni Assoc; LISW, 1990. **Honors/Awds:** Minority Fellowship 1983-84, Child Welfare Traineeship 1984-85 OSU; mem Delta Epsilon Sigma Hon Soc, Alpha Delta Mu Social Work Honor Soc. **Home Addr:** PO Box 534, Galloway, OH 43119. **Business Addr:** Child Welfare Supervisor II, Franklin Co Children Services, 1951 Gantz Rd, Grove City, OH 43123.

VAUGHN, GREGORY LAMONT
Professional baseball player. **Personal:** Born Jul 3, 1965, Sacramento, CA. **Educ:** Sacramento City College; University of Miami. **Career:** Milwaukee Brewers, outfielder, 1989-96; San Diego Padres, 1996-. **Business Addr:** Professional Baseball Player, San Diego Padres, PO Box 2000, San Diego, CA 92120, (619)283-4494.

VAUGHN, JACKIE, III
State senator. **Personal:** Born Nov 17, 1939, Birmingham, AL. **Educ:** Hillsdale Coll, BA; Oberlin Coll, MA; Oxford Univ, LittB. **Career:** Univ of Detroit, instructor, Wayne State Univ, instructor; Michigan House of Representatives, former rep; Michigan Senate, District 4, senator, assoc pres pro tempore, currently. **Orgs:** Member, Fulbright Alumni Assn; member, American Oxonian Assn; past president, Michigan Young Democrats; executive board, Detroit Branch NAACP; member, Oberlin College Alumni Assn; member, Hillsdale College Alumni Assn; member, Focus: HOPE. **Honors/Awds:** Focus and Impact Award, Cotillion Club, 1980; Outstanding Achievement Award, Booker T Washington Business Association, 1980; Outstanding Community Service Award, Charles Stewart Mott Community College, 1981; Outstanding State Senator of the Year, Detroit Urban League Guild, 1983; Most Outstanding Legislator of the Year, Washburn-Ilene Block Guild, 1983; Humanitarian Award, Michigan AFSCME Council 25, 1984; Politician of the Year Award, Rosa L Gragg Education and Civic Club; Class Ambassador, Oberlin College; Class Ambassador, Hillsdale College; Distinguished Senator and Man of Peace, D'Etre University; Legislator of the Year, Jaycees; honorary degrees from Marygrove College, Shaw College, Univ of Windsor, Highland Park Community College; Elected to Omicron Delta Kappa Honor Leadership Society; Outstanding and Model Legislator, Michigan Chronicle. **Special Achievements:** First African American president of Young Democrats of Michigan; Authored important legislation including: 18-year olds' Voting Rights Act; Dr Martin Luther King, Jr Holiday Bill; Prisoners' Bill of Rights; Free College Tuition Bill; Medical Malpractice Review Panel Bill; Workers' Compensation Bill; High School Voter Registration Bill; AIDS Education Act. **Business Addr:** State Senator, The Michigan Senate, State Capitol, P O Box 30036, Lansing, MI 48909, (517)373-7918.

VAUGHN, JACQUE
Professional basketball player. **Personal:** Born Feb 11, 1975. **Educ:** Kansas. **Career:** Utah Jazz, guard, 1997-. **Business Addr:** Professional Basketball Player, Utah Jazz, 301 W South Temple, Salt Lake City, UT 84101-1216, (801)575-7800.

VAUGHN, MARY KATHRYN
Government official. **Personal:** Born Sep 20, 1949, Kansas City, KS; daughter of Kathryn Jones Parks and Edward Parks; married Harvey L Vaughn Jr (died 1983). **Educ:** Coll of Wooster, Wooster, OH, BA, 1970; Rutgers Univ, New Brunswick, NJ, MSW, 1972; Harvard Univ Program for Sr Exec in State & Local Govt, Cambridge, MA, 1985. **Career:** Jackson County Juvenile Court, Kansas City, MO, residential svcs admin, 1973-78; Univ of Kansas, Kansas City, KS, minority affairs outreach counselor, 1978-79; City of Kansas City, Kansas City, MO, dept head, 1979-. **Orgs:** Pres, US Conference of City Human Services Officials, 1985-, pres, 1990-; program coordinator, Mayor's Christmas Tree Assn, 1980-; mem, Private Industry Council, 1990-; mem, Full Employment Council, 1986-. **Honors/Awds:** NEWS-Maker of the Year, NEWS House Shelter for Battered Women, 1990; Graduate, KC Tomorrow Leadership Program, 1990; Graduate, Centurions Leadership Program, 1980. **Business Addr:** Director, Neighborhood & Community Services Dept, City of Kansas City, 414 E 12th St, 4th Floor, Kansas City, MO 64106.

VAUGHN, MO (MAURICE SAMUEL)
Professional baseball player. **Personal:** Born Dec 15, 1967, Norwalk, CT. **Educ:** Seton Hall University. **Career:** Boston Red Sox, designated hitter, 1991-. **Honors/Awds:** Baseball Writers' Assn of America, American League Most Valuable Player, 1995. **Business Addr:** Professional Baseball Player, Boston Red Sox, Fenway Park, 24 Yawkey Way, Boston, MA 02215, (617)267-9440.

VAUGHN, NORA BELLE
Artistic director. **Personal:** Born Sep 20, 1914, Crystal Springs, MS; married Birel Vaughn (deceased); children: Wilma Jones, Dr Mona Scott, Birel Vaughn Jr. **Educ:** Jackson State Univ, BA General Educ 1934; LaSalle School of Drama, 1936-38; Univ of CA Berkeley, 1968-69; State of CA, Teaching Certificate 1972. **Career:** Oak Unified School Dist, volunteer drama specialist, 1948-63; Downs Mem Methodist Church, drama specialist 1948-78; Black Repertory Group Inc, founder/executive director, 1964-; Berk Unified School Dist, workshop instructor, 1966-69; UC Berkeley, lecturer, 1971-72. **Orgs:** Mem Phyllis Wheatley Club 1979-. **Honors/Awds:** Published "Black Theatre Finds Its Place in the Community" 1971; contrib to Youth Through Involvement with Comm Awd North Oakland Baptist Church Conf on Excellence 1973; Founder of 1st Black Theatre Conf 1974; Devoted Serv to the Community Award Beta Phi Sigma Inc 1980; Outstanding Comm Serv Award Natl Council for Black Studies 1983; The Paine Knickerbocker Award Bay Area Theatre Critics Circle 1983; Pre-Kwanaaa Award Assoc of Africans & African-Amer 1983; The Fannie Lou Hamer Award presented by the Univ of CA Black Studies Dept for Contributions to Community in Black Theatre Arts. **Business Addr:** Executive Dir, Black Repertory Group Inc, 3201 Adeline St, Berkeley, CA 94703.

VAUGHN, PERCY JOSEPH, JR.
Educational administrator. **Personal:** Born Jan 11, 1932, New Orleans, LA; married Doris C; children: Percy Darrell, Rene, Denise, Tracy. **Educ:** Morris Brown Coll, BS 1957; Atlanta U, MBA 1959; TX Tech U, DBA 1975; Harvard U, Post Grad Study 1978. **Career:** Coll of Business Admin AL State Univ, dean 1975-; TX Tech Univ, instructor 1972; Southern Univ, asst prof 1968; Jackson Brewing Co, sales & pub relations rep 1960. **Orgs:** Proj dir Small Bus Inst of the US Small Bus Adminstrn 1978; chmn of bd AL Consortium of Deans of Coll of Bus Adminstrn for the estab of ASBCD 1978; pres AL Council of Deans of the AL Assn for Higher Educ in Bus 1979; faculty coord Nat Urban Leagues' Black Exec Exchange Prog 1976; mem natl advcounc Fasculty Coord Career Awareness Prog 1976; mem Active Corp of Execs of the Nat SCORE/ACE Counc 1978. **Honors/Awds:** Co-author "Managing New Enterpises" 1976; article Free Enterprise in Focus 1978; article The Approaching Eighties New Management Challenges 1979; co-author "An Investigation of Small Bus Inven Policy" 1979. **Military Serv:** AUS 1948-52. **Business Addr:** AL State University, 915 S Jackson St, Montgomery, AL 36195.

VAUGHN, WILLIAM SAMUEL, III
Physician. **Personal:** Born Jul 11, 1955, Detroit, MI; married Lauren A. Brown, Apr 28, 1988; children: William S. Vaughn IV. **Educ:** Rensselaer Polytechnic Inst, BS 1977; Howard Univ Coll of Medicine, MD 1982. **Career:** Howard Univ Hospital, attending physician emergency room; clinic physician Kaiser Permanente Washington D.C. 2-23-87; emergency Room physician Capital Hill Hosp Washington D.C. 1988-. **Orgs:** Pres Student Natl Medical Assoc Howard Univ Chap 1980-82; assoc AMA 1982-, Amer Acad of Pediatrics 1982-, Amer College of Physicians 1982-; vice pres 1984-85, pres 1985-86 Howard Hospital House Staff Assoc. **Honors/Awds:** Resident Dir Academic Opportunity Consortium 1978-80; Resident of the Year HU College of Med Student Council 1985. **Business Addr:** Kaiser Permanente, 1011 North Capital Street N.E., Washington, DC 20002.

VAUGHN, WILLIAM SMITH
Government official. **Personal:** Born Feb 19, 1930, St Louis, MO; widowed; children: La Vonna J, Lisa M, William S Jr, Michael E. **Educ:** Univ of MO, BS 1973; Webster Univ, MA 1975; Southern IL Univ, MBA 1976. **Career:** St Louis Cty Police Dept, commander 1955-81; US Dept of Justice, marshal 1981-. **Orgs:** Mem FBI Natl Acad Assoc 1977-, Intl Assoc of Chiefs of Police 1978-, NOBLE 1978-, St Louis Crusdade Against Crime 1979-, MO Peace Officers 1979-. **Honors/Awds:** Pres St Louis NOBLE 1980. **Military Serv:** USA corpl 1951-53; Good Conduct Medal 1953. **Business Addr:** US Marshal, US Dept of Justice, 1114 Market St, St Louis, MO 63101.

VAUGHNS, FRED L.
Dentist. **Personal:** Born Apr 29, 1923, Monroe, NC; son of Mrs M L Vaughns; married Frances Branson; children: William Maurice, Lisa Gayle, Dana Gareth. **Educ:** Johnson C Smith Univ, BS 1944; Howard Univ Coll of Dentistry, DDS 1949; Am Inst of Hypnosis, Certificate 1966; Post Grad Course Efficient Endodontics for Every Day Practice 1974. **Career:** Private Practice, dentist 1949-; Longshoreman, 1945-46; Curtiss Public Co, dispatcher 1944-45; Davidson HS, teacher 1944; Assoc Trasport, freight caller 1943. **Orgs:** Pierre Fauchard Intl Dental Academy; life Amer Dental Assn; PA Dental Assn; Odontological Soc W PA; past pres Fayette Co Dental Soc; past pres W PA Soc of Dentristry for Child; Assn to Advance Ethical Hypnosis; Acad of General Dentistry; Am Endodontic Soc; charter mem Brownsville-Uniontown Branch NAACP; mem past vice pres PA State Con of Branch NAACP; past pres PA State Conf of NAACP Br 1970-73; mem Hosp Assn of PA; med staff Uniontown Hosp Assn; trustee bd Uniontown Hosp Assn; bd of trustee Nursing Com Hosp; past vice pres bd dirs Fayette Co Mental Health Assn; mem Fayette Co Planning & Zoning Comm 1976; past pres PA State Conf Branch of NAACP; assoc mem Dental practice; exec bd mem Westmoreland-Fayetteville Council Boy Scouts Amer; mem Pvt Industry Council ofWestmoreland/Fayette Coun mem bd of dir Uniontown Chamber of Commerce; Uniontown Indus Fund; Ed Council of Chamber of Commerce Advisory, bd Fayette Campus of Penn State Univ; bd of dir Fayette City Devel Council, Ambassadors Club, Chamber of Commerce Univ. **Honors/Awds:** Recip Outstanding City for 1974; Natl Register 1973; nominated outstanding prof in human serv Educ Bd Am Acad of Human Serv 1974; man of yr award Harriett Beecher Class Mt Zion Church 1964; award of merit judge in PA Jr Acad of Sci 1973; testimonial dinner Brownsville, Uniontown NAACP 1973; certificate of appreciation Affirmative Action Com 1970; most outstanding negro newspaper carrier Charlotte Observer Newspaper 1943; Dr F L Vaugns Scholarship Comm. **Business Addr:** 333 Coolspring, Uniontown, PA 15401.

VAUGHT, LOY STEPHON
Professional basketball player. **Personal:** Born Feb 27, 1967, Grand Rapids, MI; son of Ozzie Friend Jager and Loy Vaught Sr. **Educ:** University of Michigan, business management, 1990. **Career:** Los Angeles Clippers, forward/center, 1990-. **Business Addr:** Professional Basketball Player, Los Angeles Clippers, 3939 S Figueroa St, Los Angeles Sports Arena, Los Angeles, CA 90037, (213)748-8000.

VAUGHTERS-JOHNSON, CECILIE A.
Attorney. **Personal:** Born Jul 29, 1953, Montclair, NJ; daughter of Vivian S Vaughters and Alans H Vaughters; married Robert W Johnson, Oct 12, 1985; children: Langston, Ciara. **Educ:** Ohio University, BBA, 1975; Georgetown University Law Center, JD, 1978. **Career:** General Motors, Inland Division, comptroller's office intern, 1972-75; Clinton Chapman Law Office, associate, 1978-82; Chapman, Norwind & Vaughters Law Firm, 1982-86; Cecilie Vaughters-Johnson, professional consultant, 1987-. **Orgs:** National Bar Association, Greater Washington Area Chapter Women Lawyers Division, president, 1983-84; Washington Bar Association, vice president, 1983-85; National Bar Association, regional director, 1984-85; NAACP, Palo Alto Chapter, vice president, 1987-89; Red Cross, Palo Alto Chapter, board of directors, 1989-96; PTA, Montclaire School, treasurer, 1992-94; Georgetown Black Law Alumni Association, regional director, 1991-94; Los Altos Parent Preschool Association, board of directors, 1992-94; Jack and Jill of America, San Jose Chap, treasurer, 1996-98; Johnson Tri-Dom Foundation, CFO, 1990-. **Honors/Awds:** African American Student Life Univ of California Santa Cruz, Humanitarian Award, 1997; Certificates of Special Congressional Recognition, 1994; East Palo Alto City Council, Certificate of Commendation, 1994; National Bar Association, Women Lawyer's Division, President's Award, 1985; Black American Law Students Association, A J Cooper Award, 1978. **Home Addr:** 1635 Candace Way, Los Altos, CA 94024, (415)961-3312.

VEAL, HOWARD RICHARD
Business executive. **Personal:** Born Oct 24, 1942, Jackson, MS; married Elizabeth; children: Howard Jr, Jason. **Educ:** Alcorn A&M Coll, BS 1966; Utcc Jr Coll, 1964; IN U, 1969; Sngmn St U, 1975. **Career:** Spfld Urban Leag, pres/CEO 1972-; Elkhrt Urban Leag, 1971-72, act exec dir 1970-71, dir hsng comm serv 1968-70. **Orgs:** Pres IL Cncl Urban Leags 1975-; sec Urban Leag Cncl; Cntrl Reg Civic Serv; mem chmn prgm rev subcom Gov Adv Cncl Emp & Training 1974; mem Bd Hghr Educ Plng Com 1975; mem adv plan com White Hs Conf of Lbrrs 1977; mem City Spfld Citz Adv Com 1974; Omega Psi Phi Frat; co-chmn Fed Jdgt JW Ackrmns Mont Commn for Spfld Sch Dsgrgtn 1976-77; 1st bd Zion Bapt Ch. **Honors/Awds:** Recpt Outsdng Citz Awd NAACP 1970, 1975; outsdng serv Spfld Urban Leag Bd Dir 1976. **Business Addr:** 100 North 11th St, Springfield, IL 62703.

VEAL, YVONNECRIS SMITH
Physician. **Personal:** Born Dec 24, 1936, Ahoskie, NC; daughter of Zeora Ida Lewis Smith and Dempsey Porter Smith; married Henry Veal Jr; children: Michael E. **Educ:** Hampton Inst, BS, 1957; Med Coll of Virginia, MD, 1962. **Career:** Jamaica Hospital, Sickle Cell Clinic, attending physician, 1967-69, Child Development Clinic, pediatrician, 1967-69; Windham, Child Care, medical staff physician, 1967-71; Private Practice Pediatrics, 1967-71; Carter Community Health Ctr, pediatrician, 1968-79; East New York Neighborhood Family Care Ctr, dir of medical affairs, 1975-81; Carter Community Health Ctr, medical dir, 1981-84; US Postal Service, contract physician, 1984-85, Long Island Div, field div medical officer, 1985-93, New York Metro Area, senior medical dir, 1993-. **Orgs:** American Medical Assn, 1968-; Medical Society, State of NY, 1968-; Queens County Medical Society, 1968-; Natl Medical Assn, numerous positions, 1973-; Queens Pediatric Society, 1973-84; American College Occupational and Environmental Medicine, 1992-; American Heart Assn, 1992-; Professional Standards Review Org, 1977-88; Health Systems Agency of NYC, Queens Sub-Area Advisory Committee, 1981-96; Community Family Planning Council, 1981-85; Delta Sigma Theta Sorority Inc, 1955-; NAACP; YWCA; Natl Council of Negro Women, 1965-67, 1980-; Dalton School PTA, 1970-81; Merrick Y Day Care; Committee for Pre-Kindergarten Education. **Honors/Awds:** US Postal Service National Medical Directors Award, 1997; Morris Brown Coll, Ivan Allen Jr Award for Excellence in Public Relations, 1993; US Postal Service, Pride in Performance Award, 1991; Susan Smith Mckinney Steward Medical Society Recognition Award, 1991; US Postal Service, Appreciation Award, 1990; NY Chapter, Morris Brown Alumni Assn, Associate Member of the Year Award, 1990; US Postal Service, Special Achievement Award, 1989; Delta Sigma Theta, Cert of Achievement, 1989; Wives of Club 50, Special Award, 1988; Morris Brown Coll, Cert of Appreciation, 1987-88; United Negro College Fund, Distinguished Leadership Award, 1984; Saint Albans Congregational Church, Special Award for Outstanding Contribution to Southeast Queens Community, 1984; East New York NFCC Community Bd Appreciation Award, 1981; New York State Senator Carol Berman, Community Service Certificate of Merit, 1979; numerous others. **Business Addr:** Senior Medical Dir, US Postal Service, New York Metro Area, Triborough Annex, 78-02 Liberty Ave, Ozone Park, NY 11417-9451.

VEALS, CRAIG ELLIOTT
Judge. **Personal:** Born Jan 21, 1955, Los Angles, CA; son of Rhoda Maida Veals and Charles Edward Veals; married Barbara Martha O'Donovan, Jul 23, 1977; children: Aaron Elliott, Philip Seth. **Educ:** Occidental College, BS, 1977; UCLA, School of Law, JD, 1980. **Career:** California State Attorney General, deputy attorney general, 1981-83; Los Angeles District Attorney, deputy district attorney, 1983-94; Los Angeles Municipal Court, judge, 1994-97; Los Angeles Superior Court, judge, 1997-. **Orgs:** LA County Bar Association, vice chairman, Environmental Law Air Quality Sub-Section, 1992-93; Los Angeles County Bar Assn, exec comm member, Criminal Law Section, 1994-; California State Deputy District Attorneys Association, 1986-94; Association of Deputy District Attorneys, 1986-1994; Assoc of Deputy Attorneys General, 1981-83; Western Regionals Moot Court Competition, judge, 1992; Los Angeles Municipal Court, temporary judge, 1992; Phi Alpha Delta Law Fraternity, 1977-; Langston Bar Assn, 1994-; Constitutional Rights Foundation, 1989-; California Judges' Assn, mem, Criminal Law and Procedure Subcommittee, 1995-96; Municipal Court Judges' Assn, 1994-; American Judges' Assn, 1994-; Attorney Screening Committee, LA Superior Court, 1994-. **Honors/Awds:** Occidental College, scholarship, 1973-77; State of California, California State Scholarship, 1973-77; UCLA Law School, law scholarship, 1977; Los Angeles County Bar Assn and Constitutional Rights Foundation, Attorney of the Year, 1993; Commendation for Los Angeles Police Dept, 1996; Service Award, Assn of Deputy District Attorneys, 1994; Service Award, LA District Attorney's Office, Environmental Crimes Division, 1994; Constitutional Rights Foundation, Judge of the Year, 1997. **Special Achievements:** Competition judge for Constitutional Rights Foundation, Mock Trial Competition, 1989-; Constitutional Rights Foundation, mem, bd of dirs, 1997-. **Business Addr:** Judge, Los Angeles Superior Court, 111 N Hill St, Los Angeles, CA 90012, (213)974-1234.

VELJOHNSON, REGINALD
Actor. **Personal:** Born Aug 16, 1952, Queens, NY. **Educ:** Long Island Institute of Music & Arts; New York University, BA, theater; studied under Lloyd Richards. **Career:** Theater appearances include: But Never Jam Today, 1979; Inacent Black, 1981; The World of Ben Caldwell, 1982; Oh! Oh! Obesity!, 1984; Spell #7, 1987-88; film appearances include: Wolfen, 1981; The Cotton Club, 1984; Ghostbusters, 1984; Crocodile Dundee, 1986; Armed and Dangerous, 1986; Die Hard, 1988; Turner and Hooch, 1989; Die Hard 2, 1990; television appearances include: Quiet Victory: The Charlie Wedemeyer Story, 1988; The Bride in Black, 1990; Jury Duty: The Comedy, 1990; Perfect Strangers, 1988-89; Grass Roots, 1992; Family Matters, 1989-. **Orgs:** Joseph Papp's Black/Hispanic Shakespeare Company, former member; Big Brothers of America, Pass It On Program, natl spokesman. **Special Achievements:** Guest appearances include: The Joan Rivers Show, 1989; Good Morning America, 1990; The Byron Allen Show, 1991; Regis and Kathy Lee, 1991; The Arsenio Hall Show, 1991. **Home Addr:** Actor, c/o Jeralyn Bagdley, Bagdley Connor, 9229 Sunset Blvd, Ste 607, Los Angeles, CA 90069. **Business Addr:** Actor, c/o Publicist Lori DeWaal, The Garrett Co, 6922 Hollywood Blvd, Ste 407, Los Angeles, CA 90028.

VENABLE, ABRAHAM S.
Business executive. **Personal:** Born Apr 10, 1930, Washington, DC; married Anna Graham; children: Karen, Douglas, Stephen. **Educ:** Howard U, BA 1951; Grand Vlly St Coll; Howard, MA; Woodrow Wilson School of Public & Intl Affairs Princeton Univ, fellow; MIT, sr exec prog. **Career:** Gen Motors Corp, exec dir urban affrs 1971-, staff coord chmn corp intrstf minrty affrs comm; US Dept Commc, dir mnrty bus entrprs 1969-71,dir affirm actn prog 1966-68; Motor Entrprs Inc, vice pres 1975-; New Cntr Devel Prtnrshp, vice pres 1975-. **Orgs:** Mem bd dirs Nat Corp Hsng Prtnrshps Wash; chmn BPRC; commr Urban Affrs Com US C of C; v chmn bd dir Nat Bus Leag; bus adv Com Congrssl Blk Caucus; Nat Advis Cncl SBA Govt; chmn Inst for Amer Bus; vice pres Motor Enterprises Inc; vchmn Greater Detroit Foreign Trade Zone; bd of dir Detroit Br NAACP. **Honors/Awds:** Man of Yr Nat Bus Leag; author Bldng Blk Bus an Anlys & a Plan; procds from bk used to estblsh Abrhm S Vnbl Stdnt Loan Fund at Sch of Bus & Pub Admin Hwrd U. **Business Addr:** Exec Dir, Urban Affairs, General Motors Corp, 3044 W Grand Blvd, 6-252 GMB, Detroit, MI 48202.

VENABLE, ANDREW ALEXANDER, JR.
Library administrator. **Personal:** Born Nov 11, 1944, Staunton, VA; married Maxine Cockrell; children: Angela, Andrew III. **Educ:** Virginia State Univ Petersburg, BS Bus Admin, 1967; Case Western Res Univ Cleveland, MSLS 1978. **Career:** Cleveland Pub Library, head comm serv 1978-, clerk treas 1976-78, dep clerk treas 1975-76, dir finance admin serv 1972-78, asst dir personnel serv 1970-71; Standard Oil Co Marketing Dept Ohio, capital budget planning controls analyst 1968-70. **Orgs:** Pres, Pub Library Employees Credit Union, 1978-; library tech adv comm, Cuyahoga Comm Coll, 1978-; mem, Ohio Library Assn; mem, Amer Library Assn, 1978-; trustee, Urban Leage of Greater Cleveland Inc, 1979-82; trustee, Consumer Protection Assn, 1979-; mem, Cleveland City Club; trustee, Harvard Community Serv Ctr; allocations pnl United Way Serv, 1979-81; mem, Beta Phi Mu Intl Library Sci Hon Soc, 1979. **Honors/Awds:** Andrew A Venable Scholar, Virginia State Univ Almumni Assn 1973; serv appreciation award, Alpha Phi Alpha Frat Inc, Cleveland Grad Chap, 1977; Outstanding Young Men of Amer, 1978; Outstanding Greek of the Year, Greater Cleveland Pan Hellenic Council, 1979. **Business Addr:** Library Dir, Gary Public Library, 220 W Fifth Ave, Gary, IN 46402.

VENABLE, HOWARD PHILLIP (PHIL DRAWOH)
Physician (retired). **Personal:** Born Jan 27, 1913, Ontario;son of Agnes Venable and William Venable; married Katie Waters Venable (deceased). **Educ:** Wayne State Univ, BS, BM, MD 1935-39. **Career:** Ethel Waters, Don Redman, Duke Ellington Orchestras, professional musician; Homer G Phillips Hosp, dir eye dept; Amer Bd Ophthalmology, assoc examiner 1959-81, St Louis Hospital, dir 1985-89 (retired). **Orgs:** Life mem Amer Acad of Ophthalmology 1941-; Royal Vaugabonds, Inc 1941-; mem Intl Congress Ophthalmology 1944-; diplomate Am Bd Oph 1944-; life mem Amer Coll of Surgeons 1952-; mem Mound City Med Forum; St Louis Med Soc; flw Amer Acad Ophth; mem Yr Diocese of MO 1967; Adminstr Elect Serv Commn Pres Roosevelt; bd of dir ARC 1979-; life mem, Oxford Academy of Ophthalmology, 1984; mem, Metropolitan Aids Commn, St Louis, St Louis County; member, board of admissions, Washington University School of Medicine 1970-77; assoc examiner, American Board Ophthalmology 1959-81. **Honors/Awds:** Ecumenical Citation Metro Church Federation 1961-62; Distinguished Merit Award Homer G Phillips Hosp Interns Alumni Assn 1967-77; Tchr Yr St Louis Univ 1963; publ "Glaucoma in the Negro" 1944, 1952, 1958; "Pseudo-Tumor-Cerebri Benigh Intraeranial Hypertention & Otitic Hydrocephalus, Are They Synonymous?", 1971, 1973, 1974; "Empty Sella Syndrome" 1977; "Sudden Blindness From Blunt Trivial Trauma" 1979; Honored by Washington Univ Med Sch for 25 years of dedicated serv to students, faculty and community 1983; Teacher of the Year St Louis University 1957; Amer Academy of Ophthalmology, Outstanding Humanitarian Service Award, 1994.

VENABLE, MAX (WILLIAM MCKINLEY VENABLE, JR.)
Professional baseball player. **Personal:** Born Jun 6, 1957, Phoenix, AZ; married Molly; children: William Dion. **Career:** San Francisco Giants, outfielder, 1978, 1982-83; Montreal Expos, outfielder, 1984; Cincinnati Reds, outfielder, 1985-87; California Angels, outfielder, 1989-. **Business Addr:** Professional Baseball Player, California Angels, PO Box 2000, Anaheim, CA 92803-2000.

VENABLE, ROBERT CHARLES
Clergyman. **Personal:** Born Jan 26, 1950, Camden, NJ; married Cherly A Pitts; children: Tisa L, Lovell V, Marc R, Alvin, Labree, Justin, Steven. **Educ:** Shaw Univ Coll of the Bible. **Career:** New Wesley AME Zion Church, assoc pastor 1975-82; Harris Temple AME Zion, pastor 1982-. **Orgs:** Camden City Bd of Educ 1982-85; dir of educ Camden Ministerial Alliance; chairperson Affirmative Action; chairperson BSIP; chairperson Finance for the Bd of Educ; chairperson Legislature; chairperson Salary; mem Camden Ministerial Alliance; mem PA Ministerial Alliance; mem Camden Dist Ministerial Alliance of the AME Zion Church; mem NAACP; mem S Christian League Conf; mem Urban League; mem Assn of Sch Business Officials of the US and Canada; mem NJ Sch Bds Assn; mem PTA; mem Boy Scouts of America; mem Natl Black Caucus of State Legislators; mem Natl Caucus of Black Sch Bd Members; mem Joint Ctr for Political Studies; mem Natl Black Elected Officials; mem NJ Pan Methodist Comm Liaison; mem PA Pan Methodist Celebration Finance; mem Camden CoDemocratic Comm; mem Natl Parks andConservationsn Wash, DC; mem Natl Trust for Historic Preservation; mem Oriental Lodge No 1 F&AM-PHA. **Honors/Awds:** New Wesley AME Zion Church, Youth Choir Christian Service, 1982; Harris Temple AME Zion Church, Christian Service Award, 1983; Elegant Charm Modeling School, Christian Service Award, 1985; 13th Ward Whitman Park Little League, 1985-92; EL L Bonsall School, School Comm Service Award, 1985; Camden County Council on Economic Opp, Inc, Community Serivce, 1985; Harris Temple AME Zion Church, Christian Service Award, 1986; Union Amer ME Church, Bishops EL Huff Comm Service, 1990; Camden City Youth Assn, Inc, Comm Service, 1991; Prida of Camden Lodge No 83, Community Service, 1993; Camden High School Outstanding Achievements, The Castle Award, 1994. **Business Addr:** Pastor, Harris Temple AME Zion Church, 926 Florence St, Camden, NJ 08104.

VENEY, HERBERT LEE
Physician. **Personal:** Born Jun 24, 1953, Baltimore, MD; son of Burnell Veney and Vinson Veney. **Educ:** Howard Univ, Coll of Liberal Arts BS (Cum Laude) 1974, Coll of Medicine MD 1978; Johns Hopkins Sch of Hygiene & Public Health, MPH 1982. **Career:** Alexandria VA YWCA, youth counselor 1973; US Dept of Housing & Urban Develop, program asst 1974; Howard Univ Hospital, resident physician 1978-81; East Baltimore Drug Abuse Ctr, staff physician 1979-81; Warsaw Health Care Ctr, medical director, 1982-84; Warsaw Medical Ctr, owner 1981-; Tidewater Memorial Hospital, chief of staff 1986-87; Riverside/Tappahannock Hospital, staff physician 1986-. **Orgs:** Fellow Amer Acad of Family Physicians 1978; mem Natl & Amer Medical Assocs 1978-; diplomate Amer Bd of Family Practice 1981; dir Richmond Community Serv Assoc 1982-; chairperson Black Business & Professional Coalition of NN VA 1985-; dir Family Focus of Richmond Co Inc 1986-90; trustee St Paul's Coll, chairman, Student Affairs Comm, 1988-91; life mbr NAACP. **Honors/Awds:** Special Achievement Awd US Dept of Housing & Urban Develop 1974; Natl Phi Beta Kappa, Natl Beta Kappa Chi Howard Univ 1978; Citation

of Recognition St Paul's College 1990; Charter Life Membership Award Howard Univ Coll of Medicine, 1988. **Home Addr:** 202 Washington Ave, Warsaw, VA 22572. **Business Addr:** Warsaw Medical Center, 404 Main St, Warsaw, VA 22572.

VENEY, MARGUERITE C.
Insurance company executive. **Personal:** Born Mar 8, 1949, Melfa, VA; daughter of George & Maggie Chandler; married. **Educ:** Virginia State Univ, BS, 1971; Northeastern Univ, MBA, 1995. **Career:** John Hancock Mutual Life Insurance Co, Contact Mgr, currently. **Honors/Awds:** Boston YMCA, Black Achievers Award, 1990. **Business Addr:** Contract Mgr, Group Life Products, John Hancock Mutual Life Insurance Co, 200 Berkley Street, B 9, PO Box 111, John Hancock Pl, Boston, MA 02117.

VENSON, CLYDE R.
Organization executive. **Personal:** Born May 8, 1936, Alexandria, LA; son of Effie Kellum Venson and Samuel S Venson; married Annette Broussard Venson, Dec 23, 1962; children: Jane A, Lisa A. **Educ:** Southern University, Baton Rouge, LA, BS, Sociology, 1960; FBI National Academy, Washington, DC, 1971; US/Japan Bilateral Session Legal Relations, Tokyo, Japan, 1988. **Career:** Shelby County Sheriff's Dept, Memphis, TN, deputy sheriff, 1960-65; TN Dept of Corrections, Memphis, TN, parole officer, 1965-68; TN Dist Atty General, Memphis, TN, asst chief criminal investigations, 1968-85; Shelby County Sheriff's Dept, Memphis, TN, dir of traffic safety, 1985-88; Shelby County Corrections, Memphis, TN, admin of security, 1988-90; Criminal Justice and Corrections Consulting Associates, Inc, president, 1993-95; Memphis Housing Authority, dir of security; Venson's Criminal Investigations & Assocs, pres, 1991-. **Orgs:** General chairman, Memphis Cotton Makers' Jubilee, Inc, 1985-; national executive dir, National United Law Enforcement Officers Assoc, 1970-; executive director/publisher, Blacks in Law Enforcement, 1986-; exalted ruler, IBP Order of Elks of W, 1965-69; member, Alpha Phi Alpha Fraternity, 1958-. **Honors/Awds:** Man of the Year, National United Law Enforcement Officers Association, 1980. **Business Addr:** President, Venson's Criminal Investigations, 256 E McLemore Ave, Memphis, TN 38106-2833.

VERBAL, CLAUDE A.
Engineer, business executive. **Personal:** Born Nov 12, 1942, Durham, NC; son of Mary Gladys Verbal and Sidney Verbal, Sr.; married Dorothy Simmons. **Educ:** NC St Univ, BSME 1964. **Career:** Buick Motor Div GMC, engr rsch devel 1964-66, experimental lab test engr 1966-69, chassis design engr 1969-73, staff proj engr supv experimental engr 1974-75, asst supt quality control 1976-77, supt quality control 1977; Milford Proving Ground, engr supv 1973-74; BOC Powertrain GMC, supt mfg 1985-87; Serv Parts Operation GM, plant mgr 1987-. **Orgs:** Pres Flint Econ Devel Corp; 1st vice pres Flint Inner City Lion's Club; Mid-Mi Govng Bd Soc of Auto Engr 1970-; mem Soc of Mech Engr; Natl Soc of Professional Engr Registered 1971; Bsls Omcrn Rho Chap Omega Psi Phi Frat Inc 1971-; mem Leadership Flint; FAM Mstr Mason Erk Lodge 32 Degree; Flnt Urban League Hrt in City Adv Bd; bd dir Hurley med Ctr 1984-; natl bd of dir Soc of Automotive Engrs 1988, pres of bd dir Hurley Med Ctr 1989; Flint Airport Authority 1991; pres, Pontiac Visiting Nurses Assn, 1991; bd of dirs, Flint Urban League; bd campaign chair, North Oakland United Way, 1992; Society of Automotive Engineers, pres, 1996; Michigan Technological Univ, bd of control, 1997-. **Honors/Awds:** Young engr of the yr Flint Chap Professional Engr 1974; Omega Man of Yr Omicron Rho Chap Omega Psi Phi 1974; Natl Media Women Award 1977; Distinguished Alumnus of North Carolina State Univ Award, 1997; Flint chapter of Natl Society of Professional Engineers, Engineer of the Year Award, 1997. **Business Addr:** Plant Manager, Serv Parts Operation GM, 4400 Mount Hope Rd, Lansing, MI 48917.

VEREEN, BEN AUGUSTUS
Entertainer. **Personal:** Born Oct 10, 1946, Miami, FL; married Nancy Brunner; children: Benjamin, Malaika, Naja (deceased), Kabara, Karon. **Educ:** Pentacostal Theological Seminary, New York, NY, attended. **Career:** Stage appearances: The Prodigal Son, Sweet Charity, Golden Boy, Hair, Jesus Christ Superstar, Pippin, Cabaret, Grind; films: Sweet Charity, Funny Lady, L ouis Armstrong-Chicago Style, All That Jazz; television appearances: Roots, 1977, Ben Vereen-His Roots, 1978, Tenspeed & Brown Shoe, Webster. **Orgs:** Celebrity spokesperson, Big Brothers; national celebrity spokesperson, A Drug-Free America. **Honors/Awds:** Theatre World Award, Jesus Christ Superstar 1972; Tony Award; Drama Desk Award; CLIO Pippin Humanitarian Award Israel 1975; George M Cohen Award, AGVA; Best Song & Dance Star; Best Rising Star; Entertainer of the Year 1976; TV Critics Award, Roots 1977; Image Awd Roots NAACP 1977, 1978; 7 Emmy Awards for Ben Vereen-His Roots; Cultural Award Roots Israel 1978; Humanitarian Award, State of Israel, 1979; Eleanor Roosevelt Humanitarian Award, 1983. **Business Addr:** c/o Lee Solomon, William Morris Agnecy, 1350 Avenue of the Americas, New York, NY 10019.

VEREEN, DIXIE DIANE
Design editor. **Personal:** Born Nov 6, 1957, Colorado Springs, CO; daughter of Dixie Lee Dorsey Vereen and Willie C Vereen. **Educ:** Randolph Technical College, Asheboro, NC, AAS photography, 1977. **Career:** Raleigh News & Observer, photographer, 1978-80; Newsday, photographer, 1980; Philadelphia Inquirer, photographer, 1981-82; USA Today, photographer/photo editor, 1982-85; USA Weekend, dir of operations, 1986-90; Wilmington News Journal, assistant managing editor, 1990; USA Today, design editor, page one, 1991-. **Orgs:** Former Minority Affairs Committee Chairperson, National Press Photographer Assn, 1988; National Assn for Black Journalists; White House Press Photographer's Assn. **Business Addr:** Design Editor/Page One, USA Today, 1000 Wilson Blvd, 16th Floor, Arlington, VA 22209.

VEREEN, MICHAEL L.
Electrical engineer. **Personal:** Born Aug 15, 1965, Southport, NC; son of Thelma L Hankins Vereen and William B Vereen; married Erdyne L. **Educ:** North Carolina State Univ, Raleigh, NC, BS, 1988. **Career:** Carolina Power & Light, Raleigh, NC, engineer, 1985-89; Glaxo Wellcome Inc, Zebulon, NC, engineer, 1989-. **Orgs:** Kappa Alpha Psi Fraternity Inc, 1987-; member, National Society of Black Engineers, 1983-; Rotary Club of Wendell, NC, bd of dirs; Eastern Wake Senior Citizen Ctr, bd of dirs; Wake County Communities In Schools Program, steering committee; Zebulon Chamber of Commerce; Vereen School of Dance Arts, Inc., board of directors; Boys Club, board of dirs. **Honors/Awds:** Copyright (Recloser Computer Program), Carolina Power & Light Co, 1989. **Home Addr:** 712 Moss Rd, PO Box 1194, Zebulon, NC 27597, (919)269-6197. **Business Phone:** (919)269-1065.

VEREEN, NATHANIEL
Mayor. **Personal:** Born Mar 3, 1924, Forest City, FL; married Rosetta G; children: Mark, Roslyn, Nathaniel Jr, Gloria Ann, Valerie. **Educ:** Svnnh St Coll, BS 1949; Brdly U, MA 1952. **Career:** Etnvll FL, mayor 1973-, prt time mayor 1963-72, cnclman 1958; Etnvll Dvrsfd Inc, owner pres; Vrn Cnstrctn Co, owner pres. **Orgs:** Mem Orng Co Cncl Lcl Gvt; Orng Co Dem Exec Com; adv bd Vlnc Comm & Smnl Comm Colls; Tri-Co Gvt Cities; sec FL Constrn Lcns Bd; New Prvdnc Bapt Ch. **Military Serv:** AUS. **Business Addr:** PO Box 2185, Eatonville, FL 32751.

VEREEN-GORDON, MARY ALICE
Educator. **Personal:** Born Jul 9, 1950, Cerro Gordo, NC; married James Leon Gordon. **Educ:** NC A&T State Univ, BS 1972; Atlanta Univ, MA 1975; Univ of WI-Madison, PhD 1983. **Career:** Winston-Salem State Univ, english instructor 1975-76; Nakina High School, english/french teacher 1976-77; KY State Univ, english instructor 1977-80; Morris Coll, academic dean 1984-. **Orgs:** Mem Phi Delta Kappa 1981-; mem Amer Educ Rsch Assoc 1981-; mem NAACP, Alpha Kappa Mu Natl Honor Soc. **Honors/Awds:** Advanced Oppor Fellowship Adv Oppor Program 1980-82; Pre-Doctoral Scholarship for merit WI Ctr for Educ Rsch 1982-83; Tribute to Women and Industry YWCA 1983. **Business Addr:** Academic Dean, Morris College, N Main St, Sumter, SC 29150.

VERNON, ALEXANDER
Organization executive. **Personal:** married Nora. **Career:** Veterans of Foreign Wars, Dept of Texas, state commander, 1996-97; VFW Post 9191, commander; VFW District 14, commander. **Orgs:** Masonic Lodge. **Honors/Awds:** Vietnam Service Medal, Silver service, two Bronze service; Republic of Vietnam Campaign Medal; Bronze Star Medal, one Oak Leaf Cluster. **Military Serv:** US Army, Vietnam, two tours, 22 yr. veteran. **Business Addr:** State Commander, Veterans of Foreign Wars, Department of Texas, PO Box 15906, Austin, TX 78761, (817)699-5296.

VERNON, EASTON D.
Consultant, financial planner. **Personal:** Born Jan 14, 1934, Montego Bay, West Indies; son of Serina (deceased) and Walter (deceased); children: Theresa Howe, Steve, Michelle Medine, Lisa Fassari, David. **Career:** IDS Financial Services, financial planner, 1973-85, district manager, 1985-87, division vice pres, 1987-92, diversity consultant, financial planner, 1992-93; Vernon & Assocs, 1994. **Orgs:** Harlem Interfaith Counselling Service, 1st vice pres, 1977-; Westchester Community College, foundation board, 1991-. **Home Phone:** (914)674-6161.

VERNON, FRANCINE M.
Educator. **Personal:** Born Nov 14, 1939, New York, NY; married Bernard R; children: Richard, Carolyn-Michelle, Michael. **Educ:** Hwrd U, BS 1961; Hntr Coll, MS 1973; Frdhm U, Prof Dip 1976. **Career:** New York City Bd of Educ, dir adult basic educ program num pos 1968-; Hunter Coll, instructor 1973-75; Dept of HEW, claims rep 1962-67. **Orgs:** NY Assn for Cntng Comm Edn; Nat Assn for Pub Cntng Adlt Edn; Kappa Delta Pi; NY St Engl as 2nd Lang & Blngl Educ Assn; Nat Assn Tchrs of Engl to Spkrs of other Langs; pres Ossng NAACP; trst Afro-Am Cltrl Found of Wstchstr Co; past pres trst Ossng Bd of Edn; bd mem Ossng Comm Actn Prgm; bd mem Ossng Coll Cltn to Fght Unemploy Agnst Infltn. **Honors/Awds:** Achvmt awd Nat Assn for Pub Contng Adlt Educ 1975; recog awd Commrs Nat Conf on Career Educ 1976; apprec awd Ossng Jycs 1977. **Business Addr:** 347 Baltic St, Brooklyn, NY 11201.

VERNON-CHESLEY, MICHELE JOANNE
Journalist. **Personal:** Born Aug 23, 1962, New York, NY; daughter of Mae Sawyer Vernon and Hayden Arthur Vernon; married Roger Thomas Chesley, Sep 19, 1987; children: Roger Thomas Jr, Christine, Maya. **Educ:** Long Island University, Brooklyn, NY, BA, journalism, 1984. **Career:** Detroit Free Press, Detroit, MI, copy editor, 1984-86, assistant news editor, 1986-88; page designer, 1988-90; reporter, 1991-93; coord, high school journalism, 1993-94; dir, Jounalism Inst of Minorities, 1994-. **Orgs:** Representive Assembly, The News Paper Guild, 1988-; member, National Assn of Black Journalists, 1984-; member, Society of Newspaper Design, 1989-; member, Detroit East Area Residents Assn, 1990-; secretary, Detroit Chapter Natl Assn of Black Journalists, 1985-86; chairwoman human rights committee, Newspaper Guild, 1990-. **Honors/Awds:** Design Award/Merit, Society of Newspaper Design, 1990; Intern of the Year, Detroit Free Press, 1984. **Business Addr:** Director, Journalism Inst for Minorities, Wayne State Univ, 199 Manoogian, Detroit, MI 48202.

VERRETT, JOYCE M.
Educator. **Personal:** Born May 26, 1932, New Orleans, LA; married Wilbert; children: Lester McKee, Jeannine, Stanley, Rory. **Educ:** Dillard U, BA 1957; NY U, MS 1963; Tulane U, PhD 1971. **Career:** Orleans Parsih LA, hs teacher 1958-63; Dillard Univ Div of Ntrl Sci, instr prof chmn. **Orgs:** Ent Soc Am; Nat Inst Sci; Beta Beta Beta Bial & Hon Soc; Beta Kappa Chi Sci Hon Soc Cncr Assn Grtr ND 1974; LA Hrt Assn 1973-; NAACP 1960-; Reg 9 Sci Fair 1958-. **Honors/Awds:** HS Vldctn 1948; Alpha Kappa Mu Nat Hon Soc 1956; Beta Kappa Chi Nat Sci Hon Soc 1956; Grad Summa Cum Laude Dillard Univ 1957; NSF Fllwshp for Adv Study 1960-62; 1st blk wmn to recv PhD in Bio from Tulane Univ 1971; Otstndng Educ of Am 1972. **Business Addr:** Dillard Univ, 2601 Gentilly Blvd, New Orleans, LA 70122.

VERTREACE, MARTHA MODENA
Educator, poet. **Personal:** Born Nov 24, 1945, Washington, DC; daughter of Modena Kendrick Vertreace and Walter Charles Vertreace. **Educ:** District of Columbia Teachers College, BA, 1967; Roosevelt University, MA, 1971, MPh, 1972; Mundelein College, MS, 1981. **Career:** Roosevelt High School, English instructor, 1967-72; Rosary College, associate adjunct professor, 1981-82; Kennedy-King College, professor, poet-in-residence, 1976-. **Orgs:** Modern Language Association, 1982-; National Council of Teachers of English, 1982-; Society for the Study of Midwestern Literature, 1987-; Midwest Modern Language Association, 1982-; Poets and Patrons, second vice pres, 1986-; Illinois Association of Teachers of English, 1986-; Kappa Delta Pi Honor Society, 1966-; Pi Lambda Theta Honor Society, 1973-. **Honors/Awds:** Hawthornden International, Writers Retreat Fellowship, 1992; Ford Foundation Fellowship, 1972; Spoon River Quarterly, Illinois Poet, publication of poems, 1988; Illinois Arts Council, literary awards, 1988, 1989, 1990; Illinois Association for Teachers of English, Excellence in Writing, 1985; National Endowment for the Arts Fellowship, 1993; Fellowship, Writers Center, Dublin Ireland, 1993; Gwendolyn Brooks Award for the Significant Illinois Poet, 1993. **Special Achievements:** Under a Cat's-Eye Moon, collection of poems, 1991; Second House from the Corner, collection of poems, 1986; Kelly in the Mirror, children's book, 1993; Oracle Bones, collection of poems, 1994; Light Caught Bending, collection of poems, 1995; Cinnabar, collection of poems, 1995; Maafa: When Night Becomes a Lion, collection of poems, 1996. **Home Addr:** 1155 E 56th St, Chicago, IL 60637-1530, (312)363-0766. **Business Addr:** Professor, Poet-in-Residence, Kennedy-King College, 6800 S Wentworth Ave, Chicago, IL 60621, (312)962-3200.

VERTREACE, WALTER CHARLES
Attorney, personnel executive. **Personal:** Born Sep 17, 1947, Washington, DC; son of Modena K. Vertreace and Walter C. Vertreace; married Peggy A, May 14, 1977; children: Bryan, Kelly, Erin. **Educ:** Howard Univ, BA 1968, MS 1970; Temple University School of Law, JD 1982. **Career:** USAF Human Resources Lab, research psychologist 1970-72; Information Science, Inc, human resources consultant 1972-75; The Hertz Corp, mgr EEO programs 1975-76; INA Corporation, mgr EEO operations 1976-80; Amerada Hess Corp, mgr corporate EEO 1980-. **Orgs:** Member board of dir Equal Employment Adv Council; president, United Way of Central Jersey, 1990-92; Amer, Ntl, New Jersey State Bar Assns; vice chairman Manhattan Affiliate NY Urban League, Philadelphia Urban League; past president The EDGES Group, Inc; mem Omega Psi Phi; president New York State Advisory Council on Employment Law; past vice chair, board of deacons Grace Baptist Church Germantown; Tri-State Corporate Campaign UNCF, chairman; major, Civil Air Patrol. **Honors/Awds:** NIMH Fellow; Howard Univ Fellow; Beta Kappa Chi Natl Scientific Honor Soc; Psi Chi Natl Honor Society in Psychology; Civil Air Patrol Lampligter Award, 1996; United Way Distinguished Volunteer, 1993. **Military Serv:** USAF First Lieutenant; Systems Command Cert of Merit 1972. **Business Addr:** Mgr Corp EEO, Amerada Hess Corp, 1 Hess Plaza, Woodbridge, NJ 07095.

VESSUP, AARON ANTHONY
Educator. **Personal:** Born Mar 28, 1947, Los Angeles, CA. **Educ:** NE Wesleyan Univ, BS 1970; IL State Univ, MA Sci 1972; Univ of Pgh, PhD 1978; Univ of Edinburgh Scotland, media studies 1984. **Career:** IL State Univ, comm instr 1971-72; City of Bloomington, human relations coord 1972-75; Univ of Pittsburgh, teaching fellow 1975-78; Rockwell Intl, communications intern 1977-78; TX Southern Univ, asst prof of communications 1978-; Intercultural Communications, cons; Elgin Comm Coll, dir of forensics. **Orgs:** Mem Soc for Intl Educ Assn; mem TX Speech Comm Assn; mem US Tennis Assn; mem Intl Comm Assn; mem Amer Mgmt Assn; mem Speech Communication Assn; edited Interracial Comm Bloomington Press 1977; pub in textbook Urban Comm Winthrop Press 1977. **Honors/Awds:** Co-author of Conflict Mgmt Acad of Mgmt Review 1979; dir of Grant Proj TX Comm for Humanities 1979-80; author Symbolic Communication, Understanding Racial Stereotypes Brethren Press 1983. **Business Addr:** Dir of Forensics, Elgin Community College, 50 Slade Ave, Elgin, IL 60120.

VEST, DONALD SEYMOUR, SR.
Business manager. **Personal:** Born Apr 5, 1930, Ypsilanti, MI; son of Vida Carter Vest and Eugene L Vest; married Hilda Freeman Vest, Jul 12, 1953; children: Karen Vest, Donald Vest, Jr, Carl Vest. **Educ:** Michigan State Univ, East Lansing, MI, BA, Social Serv, 1952. **Career:** US Army, lieutenant, 1952-54; Detroit Mutual Insurance, Detroit, MI, agent, 1954-55; City of Detroit, MI, playleader, 1955-56; State of Michigan, Detroit, MI, interviewer, 1956-57; City of Detroit, MI, recreation instructor, 1957-60; Boy Scouts of Amer, Detroit, MI, dist exec, 1960-62; Ford Motor Co, Dearborn, MI, mgr, 1962-87, personnel mgr, 1987; Broadside Press, Detroit, MI, business mgr, currently. **Orgs:** Pres bd of trustees, 1986-87, chair collections comm, 1987-88, Museum of African-Amer History; pres bd of dir, Brazeal Dennard Chorale, 1989. **Honors/Awds:** Community Serv Award, Ford Motor Co, 1968, 1969; Special Serv Award, Detroit Bd of Educ, 1977; Sankofa Award, Museum of African-Amer History, 1988. **Military Serv:** AUS, first lieutenant, 1952-54. **Business Addr:** Business Mgr, Broadside Press, PO Box 04257, Detroit, MI 48204, (313)963-8526.

VEST, HILDA FREEMAN
Publisher, editor. **Personal:** Born Jun 5, 1933, Griffin, GA; daughter of Blanche Heard Freeman and Pharr Cyral Freeman; married Donald Vest, Jul 12, 1953; children: Karen, Donald Jr, Carl. **Educ:** Wayne State Univ, Detroit, MI, BS, education, 1958. **Career:** Detroit Bd of Educ, Detroit, MI, teacher, 1959-1988; Broadside Press, Detroit, MI, publisher, editor, 1985-. **Honors/Awds:** Southeastern Michigan Regional Scholastic Award, Detroit News, 1950; author, Lyrics I, self-published poetry, 1981; Writing Award for Poetry, Detroit Women Writers, 1982; featured in Broadside Poets' Theater, 1982; featured in Detroit Sings Series, Broadside Press, 1982; scholarship to Cranbrook Writers' Conf, 1984; author, Sorrow's End, Broadside Press, 1993. **Business Addr:** Publisher, Editor, Broadside Press, PO Box 04257, Detroit, MI 48204, (313)963-8526.

VESTER, TERRY Y.
Physician. **Personal:** Born Sep 9, 1955, Houston, TX; daughter of Willie T. Busby; married Dr Alphonza Vester; children: Jennifer, Alexandria, Geoffrey. **Educ:** Univ of San Francisco, BS 1978; Howard Coll of Medicine, MD 1982. **Career:** Montgomery Residency Program, family practice 1982-85. **Orgs:** Mem Amer Acad of Family Physicians 1982-87, Natl Medical Assoc 1986-87, Southern Medical Assoc 1986-87, Medical Assoc of the State of AL 1986-87, Chambers Co Medical Assoc 1986-87. **Business Addr:** 404-B 9th St SW, Lafayette, AL 36862.

VIA, THOMAS HENRY
Manufacturing engineer. **Personal:** Born Sep 12, 1959, Martinsville, VA; son of Margaret Dandridge Via and Henry Via. **Educ:** Solano Community College, AS, welding technician, 1980, AS, machine tool technician, 1982; Community College of the Air Force, AAS, metals technology, AAS aircraft maintenance technology, 1982; Southern Illinois University, BS, industrial engineering technology, 1982; Golden Gate University, MBA, management, 1984; University of California, Berkeley Extenstion, certificate in vocational education & engineering, 1986. **Career:** Viking Steel, Anaheim, CA, ironworker/welder, 1983; Tegal Corporation, Novato, CA, electro mechanical technician, 1984; Southern Illinois University, Carbondale, IL, instructor, manufacturing engineer, 1985; Solano Community College, Suisun, CA, part-time welding, machine tool, business instructor, 1982-; United Airlines, San Francisco, CA, jet mechanic/welder, 1985; Via Technologies, Fairfield, CA, principal/manufacturing engineer, 1985-. **Orgs:** D16 committee on robotics, C2 Thermal Spray Comm, American Welding Society, 1986-; Robotic Industries Assn R15.06, safety standards comm, 1986-; technical forum, CASA/SME, 1986-; ASM International thermal spray automation committee, 1988; A15.08 sensor interfaces committee, Automated Imaging Association, 1986-; Robotics International of the Society of Manufacturing Engineers, board of advisors, 1993-94. **Honors/Awds:** Challenges & Opportunities for Manufacturing Engineers, Society of Manufacturing Engineers, Nuts & Bolts, 1989; Editor, Curricula 2000 Workshop Proceeding, Society of Manufacturing Engineers, 1990; Society of Manufacturing Engineers, Outstanding Young Manufacturing Engineer Award, 1994. **Military Serv:** US Air Force, ssgt, 1977-81; US Air Force Reserve until 1991. **Business Addr:** Manufacturing Engineer/Principal, Via Technologies, PO Box 2868, Fairfield, CA 94533-0286, (707)425-0365.

VICKERS, ERIC ERFAN
Attorney. **Personal:** Born Feb 16, 1953, St Louis, MO; son of Claire Vickers and Robert Vickers; married Judy Gladney Vickers; children: Erica, Aaron. **Educ:** Washington University, BA, political science, 1975; Coro Foundation Fellowship Program; Occidental College, MA, 1976; University of Virginia School of Law, JD, 1981. **Career:** Vickers and Associates, attorney, currently. **Honors/Awds:** Minority Business Enterprise Legal Defense and Education Fund Inc, 1988; St. Louis Chapter of Links, Outstanding Minority Effort, 1989; Mound City Bar Association, Legal Service Award, 1989; St. Louis American Merit Award, 1989; Mokan Construction Contractors, Minority Services Award, 1989. **Business Addr:** Attorney, Vickers & Associates, 7171 Delmar Blvd, #101, St Louis, MO 63130-4334, (314)367-0120.

VICKERS, KIPP E.
Professional football player. **Personal:** Born Aug 27, 1969, Holiday, FL; married Tracy; children: Treme, Trinity, Tajay. **Educ:** Miami (Fla.). **Career:** Indianapolis Colts, guard, 1994-. **Business Addr:** Professional Football Player, Indianapolis Colts, PO Box 535000, Indianapolis, IN 46253, (317)297-2658.

VICK-WILLIAMS, MARIAN LEE
Educator (retired). **Personal:** Born in Newton Grove, NC; daughter of Reverend and Mrs Milford E Lee; children: Linda Vick Davis, Charles Alphonso Vick. **Educ:** Fayetteville State Univ, BS 1948; Univ of MI, MA 1954; Syracuse Univ, CAGS 1961; Duke Univ, EdD 1968. **Career:** NC Public Schools, elementary teacher 1948-60; Bennett Coll, dir of reading center 1961-62; Winston-Salem State Univ, asst prof of reading 1962-66; Dept of Elementary Educ, acting chairperson 1977-80, chairperson 1980-83; NC A&T State Univ, assoc prof of Reading Educ 1968-70, prof of Reading Educ 1970-77, 1984-90. **Orgs:** Life mem NAACP 1979-; Alpha Kappa Alpha, Beta Iota Omega Chapter; Kappa Delta Pi; Phi Delta Kappa; NEA-NCAE; Intl Reading Assoc; St James Presbyterian Church. **Honors/Awds:** NAFEO's 1985 Distinguished Alumni Award 1985; FSU National Alumni Association. **Special Achievements:** Author of nine published articles. **Home Addr:** 1601 S Benbow Rd, Greensboro, NC 27406.

VILTZ, EDWARD GERALD
Company executive. **Personal:** Born Mar 11, 1947, Los Angeles, CA; son of Germaine Poche Viltz Smith and Oniel Edward Viltz; married Paula Smith, Jan 31, 1977; children: Simeon, Malika, Erika. **Educ:** Harvard Graduate School of Business, 1979; Southern University of New Orleans. **Career:** IBM Corp, branch manager, 1980-82, district manager, 1982-85, manager, channel development, 1986-88, regional manager, marketing programs, 1988-89, director, minority business development program, 1989-90, loaned executive, 1990-92; Pulsar Data Systems, senior vp, chief operating officer, 1992-; Integrated Systems Analysts Inc, vp & chief development officer, 1995-96; Enterprise Integration Corp., general manager, 1996-. **Orgs:** Progressive Life Institute, board of directors, vice pres, 1988-93; Pulsar Data Sustems, board of directors, 1991-93; Just Say No International, board of directors, 1992-93; Urban League, Black Executive Exchange Program, 1975. **Honors/Awds:** IBM, Manager of the Year, 1986, Community Service Award, 1990, President's Award, 1981, Golden Circle, 1983, 100% Club, 1969-85; Urban League, Certificate of Appreciation, 1976. **Special Achievements:** Developed a national network of IBM business partners, 1990; conducted Careers Day for Howard University, 1978; visiting professor, Florida Memorial College, 1975. **Business Addr:** General Manager, Enterprise Integration Corp., 8 Normandy Sq Ct, Ste 1, Silver Spring, MD 20906.

VINCENT, DANIEL PAUL
Business executive. **Personal:** Born Jun 19, 1939, New Orleans, LA; son of Josephine Vincent and Howard Vincent; married Leatha; children: Dannette, Robin, Daryl. **Educ:** Southern University, BS Loyola Univ, MBA; Univ of No CO, MA; UECU, PhD Cand; Shrtr Coll, Hon PhD. **Career:** Total Community Action Inc, exec dir 1969-; Equity Funding Corp of Amer, reg rep 1968-70; Chrysler Corp, engr 1966-68; Mayor of New Orleans, spec adv vice chmn mayor's charter rev com 1970-. **Orgs:** Pres chmn EDU Inc 1975-; consultant lecturer LSUNO; Cppn State Coll; lectr Tln U; lectr Xavier Univ; Univ of WI; adv bd NO Area Boy Scouts; chmn LA Housing Asstance Corp; pres TCA Fed Credit Union; exec bd Natl Assn for Comm Devel; pres LA Assn of Comm Action Agencies; fdr NO Human Serv Inst; mem Natl Assn of Housing & Redevelment; vice chmn NO Manpower Adv Planning Council; bd of dir NO Chap Intrcl Council for Business Opportunity; bd dir NO Area Health Planning Council; NY Stock Exchange; Attitional Study of Orlns Prsh Sch Syst. **Honors/Awds:** Beta Gamma Sigma Hon Soc; Army Commd Medal John H Whitney & Fellowship; officials publications Patterns of Poverty in NO; manpower training needs for the City of NO; Governance of New Comm; hist of other world stock exchanges. **Military Serv:** UAS capt 1960-66.

VINCENT, EDWARD
Mayor. **Personal:** Born 1934, Steubenville, OH; married Marilyn Vincent; children: Two. **Educ:** Iowa State Univ; California State Univ, BA. **Career:** City of Inglewood, CA, mayor, currently. **Orgs:** Member, AFL-CIO. **Business Addr:** Mayor, City of Inglewood, PO Box 6500, Inglewood, CA 90301.

VINCENT, IRVING H.
Producer, director, actor, educator. **Personal:** Born Nov 28, 1934, St Louis, MO; married Delora Sherleen Sinclair; children: Dr Terrel Lynn French, Mark, Paul, Samantha. **Educ:** St Louis Univ, BS Speech 1957; Brooklyn Coll, 26 MFA credits 1974; HB Studios Lee Strasberg professional acting, attended 1961-70; Third World Cinema, attended 1976-77. **Career:** Broadway, Off-Broadway, stage mgr 1961-69, stage dir 1966-; Downstate Medical Ctr, personnel dir 1966-69; Brooklyn Coll, tchr 1969-74; freelance video artist 1977-81; ABC-TV, unit mgr. **Orgs:** Bd of dir Media for the Other Arts 1981-; pres The Seminole Group 1979-81. **Home Addr:** 155 Bank St, New York, NY 10014.

VINCENT, MARJORIE JUDITH
Journalist, Miss America 1991. **Personal:** Born Nov 21, 1964, Chicago, IL; daughter of Florence Bredy Vincent and Lucien Vincent. **Educ:** DePaul Univ, Chicago, IL, 1988; Duke Univ Law School, Durham, NC. **Career:** Brooks, Pierce, McLendon Humphries, Greensboro, NC, law intern, 1989; Mudge, Rose, Guthrie, Alexander & Ferdon, New York, NY, law intern, 1990; Miss America 1991; WGBC-TV, anchor/reporter, 1993-94; WHOI TV, anchor, currently. **Orgs:** Sec, mem, Black Law Student Assn, 1988-90; sec, Alpha Kappa Alpha Sorority, 1987-; bd mem, Miss Illinois Scholarship Pageant; bd mem, Ctr for Prevention of Abuse. **Honors/Awds:** Honorary chair, Council for Safe Families; Natl Ambassador, Children's Miracle Network; Peace Begins at Home Award, Women Against Abuse; Law Scholarship, Duke Univ Law School. **Business Addr:** Anchor, WHOI-TV, 500 N Stewart, Creve Coeur, IL 61611, (309)698-1950.

VINCENT, TROY
Professional football player. **Personal:** Born Jun 8, 1970, Trenton, NJ; son of Alma; married Tommi, Mar 19, 1994. **Educ:** Univ of Wisconsin, attended. **Career:** Miami Dolphins, defensive back, 1992-95; Philadelphia Eagles, 1996-. **Honors/Awds:** Ed Block Courage Award, 1994. **Business Addr:** Professional Football Player, Philadelphia Eagles, 3501 S Broad St, Philadelphia, PA 19148, (215)463-2500.

VINSON, ANTHONY
Professional football player. **Personal:** Born Mar 13, 1971. **Educ:** Towson State. **Career:** Baltimore Ravens, running back, 1997-. **Business Addr:** Professional Football Player, Baltimore Ravens, 11001 Owings Mills Blvd, Owings Mills, MD 21117, (410)654-6200.

VINSON, CHUCK RALLEN
Television director. **Personal:** Born Jul 14, 1956, South Bend, IN; son of Charlotte Moxley and Ray Vinson. **Educ:** Ball State, Muncie, IN, 1975; Los Angeles College, Los Angeles, CA, 1977-80. **Career:** "Benson," stage manager, 1980-84; Carsey/Werner Productions, "Cosby Show," stage manager, 1984-87; HBO Special, Sinbad, Atlanta, GA, director, 1990; Carsey/Werner Productions, "Cosby Show," director, 1986-92; "Clarissa Explains It All," producer/director, 1991-93; "Apollo Comedy Hour," producer/director, 1991-93; "Thea," director, 1993; "Fresh Prince of Bel Air," director, 1993-; "Sinbad," director, 1994; "Sister, Sister," director, 1994; "All That," director, 1995. **Home Addr:** 4229 Fair Ave, Studio City, CA 91602.

VINSON, JULIUS CEASAR
Insurance salesman. **Personal:** Born Feb 16, 1926, Macon, GA; married Sara Rogers; children: Saralyn, Walter. **Educ:** CA Plytchnc at San Luis Obsp CA; Univ of GA, Cert In Mncpl Gvt. **Career:** Professional Ins Corp, life ins; Macon GA, cty cnclmn; All Star Life Ins, slsmn mnl 1974. **Orgs:** Mem GABEO; mem NAACP; mem Pres Club Ins Slsmn; GA Mncpl Assn; tst St Paul AME Ch; mem Mddl GA Area Plng & Devel Commn. **Honors/Awds:** 32nd Dgr Mason Prc Hall Affil; awd Cncrnd Ctzn Club Civil Rghts 1976; ldng slsmn Hlth Life Ins Professional Ins Co 1975; awd Mlln Dllr Rndtbl Club 1975; 1st blk city cnclmn in Macon GA. **Business Addr:** PO Box 4402, Macon, GA 31208.

VINSON, ROSALIND ROWENA
Attorney. **Personal:** Born Sep 25, 1962, Highland Park, MI; daughter of Mary S McGhee and Roosevelt Massey. **Educ:** Michigan State University, BA, 1983; Georgetown University Law Center, JD, 1987. **Career:** Equal Employment Opportunity Commission, attorney, 1989-. **Orgs:** Black Law Alumni of Georgetown University Law Center, secretary, 1992-; H Carl

Moultrie T Endowment, vice pres, 1989-; Phi Delta Phi, vice magister, 1986-87. **Honors/Awds:** Black Law Students Association, Mary McCloud Bethune Award, 1987, First Year Pacesetter, 1986, Second Year Pacesetter, 1985. **Home Phone:** (301)567-2513. **Business Phone:** (202)663-4474.

VIOLENUS, AGNES A.

Educator. **Personal:** Born May 17, 1931, New York, NY; daughter of Antonio and Constance. **Educ:** Hunter College, BA, 1952; Columbia Univ Teachers College, MA, 1958; Bank Street Coll, professional certificate computers in education, 1984; Nova Southeastern Univ, EdD, 1990. **Career:** NY State Education Department, head teacher day care ctr, 1952-53; NYC Board of Education, teacher common branches, 1953-66; City Coll of NY, adjunct advisor, open education program, 1974-75, adjunct teacher mentor program, 1990-91; York Coll, Continuing Education Div, adjunct instructor of computers, 1985-87; New York City, Bd of Education, asst principal elementary school, 1966-91; City Coll of New York, supervisor of student teachers, 1997-. **Orgs:** Schomburg Corp, pres, 1995-; Hunter Coll Alumni Assn, sec/bd of dirs, 1995-; New York Public Library Volunteers, vice pres/trea, 1996-; NY Club National Assn Negro Business and Professional Women, co-chair scholarship comm, 1991-; NY Affilate National Black Child Development Institute, chair public policy comm, 1992-; Hunter Coll Scholarship & Welfare Fund, mem, bd of dirs, 1997-; Manhattan Psychiatic Ctr, bd of visitors, pending NYS legislature approval; NY Academy of Science, participant scientist in schools prog, 1994-. **Honors/Awds:** Phi Delta Kappa, 1981; Kappa Delta Pi, 1958; Pi Lambda Theta, 1958; Council of Supervisors and Administrators, Dedicated Service Award, 1991; Aerospace Education Association, Appreciation Award, 1985; Archdiocese of NY Catholic Charities, Ministry to Seniors Certificate of Appreciation, 1996; New York Club, NANBPWC Prof Achievement Awd, 1997. **Special Achievements:** Article: African-American Historical and Genealogical Society, Local Chap Quarterly Publication, 1996; 5 Articles, NYC Bd of Education Curriculum Guide Logo: K-12, 1986; Over 100 Reviews of Educational Films, Published in Film News magazine, Film News Omnibus and Sightlines Magazine, 1963-1992; Three articles published in city college workshop center, Notes, 1972, 1973, 1978; Judge: Emmy Awards, documentories, 1995, 1997. **Home Addr:** 626 Riverside Dr, # 24P, New York, NY 10031. **Business Phone:** (212)862-3639.

VISOR, JULIA N.

Educator. **Personal:** Born May 6, 1949, New Albany, MS; daughter of Vurry Olivia Visor and A J Visor. **Educ:** Illinois State University, Normal, IL, BS, 1971; Ohio University, Athens, OH, MA, 1975; Illinois State University, Normal, IL, DA, 1987. **Career:** Cornell University, Ithaca, NY, residential area coordinator, 1973-76; Illinois State University, Normal, IL, assistant director of residential life, 1976-79, instructor of English, 1979-80, 1981-86, director, student support svcs, 1980-81, assistant director, Univ Ctr for Learning Assistance, 1986-90, assistant prof of English, 1988-; Univ Ctr for Learning Assistance, associate director, 1990-97, coordinator, 1997-. **Orgs:** President, Mid-America Assn of Educational Opportunity Program Personnel (MAEOPP), 1991-92; Mid-America Assn of Educational Opportunity Program Personnel, 1980-; Illinois Assn for Learning Assistance Professionals, 1986-; National Council of Teachers of English, 1979-; Illinois Assn of Educational Opportunity Program Personnel (ILAEOPP), 1980-; Natl Assn for Developmental Education, 1990-; Illinois Assn of Teachers of English: Modern Language Assn, 1997-. **Honors/Awds:** MAEOPP Distinguished Service Award, MAEOPP, 1982; Outstanding Svc Award, ISU Alumni Board of Directors, 1982; President's Award, ILAEOPP, 1984; Ada Belle Clark Welsh Scholarship, ISU, 1985; Outstanding Svc Award as co-editor, MAEOPP, 1989; David A Strand Diversity Achievement Award, Illinois State University, 1995-96. **Business Addr:** Coordinator, 4070 Illinois State University, University Ctr for Learning Assistance, Normal, IL 61761-4070.

VIVIAN, CORDY TINDELL

Clergyman. **Personal:** Born Jul 30, 1924, Howard County, MO; married W Octavia Geans; children: Jo Anna, Denise, Cordy Jr, Kira, Mark, Charisse, Albert. **Educ:** Western IL Univ, BA 1948; Amer Baptist Theol Sem, BD 1958; New School for Social Rsch, Doctorate 1984; Western IL Univ, Doctorate 1987. **Career:** Natl Bapt Conv USA Inc, natl dir 1955-61; 1st Comm Church, pastor 1956-61; Cosmo Comm Church, pastor 1961-63; SCLC, natl dir 1962-67; Shaw Univ, minister 1972-73, natl dir sem without walls 1974-; Black Action Strategies & Info Center Inc (BASIC), bd chmn. **Orgs:** Chmn Natl Anti-Klan Network; mem Natl Black Leadership Roundtable; chmn Southern Organizing Comm Educ Fund; bd mem Inst of the Black World; bd mem Intl United Black Fund; co-dir Southern Reg Twentieth Anniversary March on Washington For Jobs Peace & Freedom; bd mem Southern Christian Leadership Conf, Souther Organizing Comm, Natl Council of Black Churchmen, The African Inst for the Study of Human Values; mem Racial Justice Working Group Natl Council Churches; vstg prof Wartburg Theol Sem; intl lecture & consult tours Africa, Tokyo, Isreal, Holland, Manila, Japan. **Honors/Awds:** Author Black Power & The Amer Myth, Amer Joseph, Date & Fact Book of Black Amer; editor the Baptist, Layman Mag for Baptist Men; listed in 1000 Successful Blacks, The Ebony Success Library, Odyssey, A Journey Through Black Amer, From Montgomery to Memphis, Clergy in Action Training, Unearthing Seeds of Fire, The Idea of Highlander, The Trouble I've Seen. **Business Addr:** Chairman, BASIC, 595 Parsons St, Atlanta, GA 30314.

VIVIANS, NATHANIEL ROOSEVELT

Engineer, educator. **Personal:** Born Feb 6, 1937, Mobile, AL; son of Ella Lett Sellers and Charlie Vivians; married Dorothy C Willis; children: Venita Natalie, Mark Anthony. **Educ:** Tuskegee Inst, BSEE 1961; Univ Dayton, MS Eng 1973, MS Mgmt Sci 1977. **Career:** Air Defense Command, radar officer, 1961-64; Aeronautical Systs Div, Elec Eng, 1964-71, program mgr 1971-80, tech advisor 1980-85, technical dir 1985-87, co-deputy 1987-. **Orgs:** Asst prof, Univ of Wilberforce 1980-; ltc/air force officer AF Reserve 1967-; basileus Omega Psi Phi Fraternity 1957-; trustee Holy Trinity Amer Church 1975-; chptr pres Natl Soc Professional Eng 1970-; EEO counselor Aeronautical Systs Div 1969-; pres WCPOVA 1974-80. **Honors/Awds:** Outstanding Serv NSPE Greene Xenia, OH 1975; commendation ASD/AE WPAFB, OH 1978; man yr Omega Psi Phi Fraternity 1980; outstanding performance Aeronautical System Div 1983-84, 1986-90. **Military Serv:** USAF capt; USAF Reserves col; Commendation 1967, 1974, 1980. **Home Addr:** 3479 Plantation Place, Beavercreek, OH 45434. **Business Addr:** Co Deputy for Avionics Control, USAF/AFSC/ASD/AX, ASD/AX, Wright Patterson AFB, OH 45433.

VOGEL, ROBERTA BURRAGE

Psychologist, educator. **Personal:** Born Jun 13, 1938, Georgetown, SC; daughter of Vivian Helen Bessellieu Burrage and Demosthenes Edwin Burrage, Sr; divorced; children: Duane Stephen Vogel, Shoshana Lynn Vogel. **Educ:** Temple Univ, Philadelphia, PA, BA 1960, MA 1962; Michigan State Univ, E Lansing, MI, PhD 1967; Ackerman Inst of Family Therapy, New York, NY, Post-Doctoral Certificate 1981. **Career:** Michigan State Univ, E Lansing, MI, instructor 1966-67, asst prof 1967-68; Center for Change, New York, NY, co-leader and staff mem 1970-72; N Richmond Comm Mental Health, Staten Island, NY, staff psychologist 1971-72; Staten Island Comm Coll (now College of Staten Island), NY, asst prof and counselor 1972-74, assoc prof 1974-78, director of SEEK Program 1978-; consultant and eval researcher for RH Clark Associates, 1978-83, and CUNY Office of Special Prog, 1981-88; consultant and psychologist for Steinway Family & Child Devel Center, 1984-88, and Harlem-Dowling Child & Family Services, 1989-. **Orgs:** Dir of clinical serv, Black Psych Inst of NY Assn of Black Psychologists, 1978-81; advisory board mem, NY Urban League, Staten Island Branch, 1980-; pres, NY Assn of Black Psychologists, 1982-83; mem, Staten Island Human Rights Advisory Comm, 1986-; board mem, Staten Island Mental Health Society, 1987-; mem, Staten Island Task Force on AIDS, 1988-; commissioner, NY Black Leadership Commn on AIDS, 1988. **Honors/Awds:** Research fellow, Natl Insts of Health, 1964. **Business Addr:** Assoc Prof, Director/Chair, SEEK Program, College of Staten Island, City Univ of New York, 715 Ocean Terrace, Room H-11, Staten Island, NY 10301.

VOLDASE, IVA SNEED

Aerospace engineer. **Personal:** Born Nov 9, 1934, Frankston, TX; daughter of Mr & Mrs Bynus Sneed; divorced; children: Joseph Jr, Robert. **Educ:** Prairie View A&M Univ, BA, mathematics, 1954; El Camino Coll, AA, mathematics, 1977; Univ of San Francisco, BS, 1983; CA State Univ, Dominguez Hills, computer science, 1974-88. **Career:** North American Aviation, math analyst, jr eng, 1954-59; STL, computer, math analyst, 1960-61; STL becomes TRW Inc, sr mem of technical staff, 1961-. **Orgs:** Carson Black Heritage Assn, pres, 1969-; Natl Council of Negro Women, pres, 1976-90; TRW SEA Bootstrap, pres, 1976-78; Intl COCOMO Users Group, affiliate, 1989-; United Christian Women, asst general coord, 1995-97; Harriet Tubman School for Unwed Mothers, original charter bd mem, 1970-90; Soc of Cost Est & Analysis, speaker, mem, 1989-; Intl Soc of Parametic Analysts, speaker, mem, 1990-. **Honors/Awds:** TRW DSSG Natl Women's Week, Women of Achievement Award, 1978; Volunteers of America, Community Service Award, 1983; Intl Soc of Parametic Analysts, Outstanding Parametic Technical Paper, 1997; Journal of the NTA, Top Minority Women in Science & Engineering, 1996; Council of Engineering Deans of Historically Black Colleges and Career Communications Group, Black Engineer of the Year, Community Service, 1995. **Special Achievements:** Not All COCOMOs Are Alike, Technical Paper presented at a REVIC Conf, published, 1991; Parametic Modelling at TRW, SSCAG Symposium, published, 1997; The Use of Parametic Models for Historical Data, ISPA Conf, published 1997; Software Modelling Risk Management, technical class, class book, 1996; Minority Women in the Aerospace Labor Market, Career Conf for Women, 1978; speaks fluent Spanish.

VOORHEES, JOHN HENRY

Air force chief executive. **Personal:** Born Aug 12, 1936, New Brunswick, NJ; married Jeanine Carter; children: Melanie Shemyne, John Carter. **Educ:** Rutgers Univ, BS Chemistry 1958; Univ of Southern CA, MS Mgmt 1967; Harvard Univ, Senior Exec Fellow 1981. **Career:** Oklahoma City Air Logistics Ctr, chief B-52 and missile div syst 1979-81; Sacramento Air Logistics Ctr CA, dir matl mgt 1981-82; Defense Contract Admin Serv Region LA, commander 1982-84; Headquarters European Command Germany, deputy dir logistics 1984-86; Defense Personnel Support Ctr, commander. **Orgs:** Mem Air Force Assoc 1960-, Tuskegee Airman Inc 1981-, Federal Exec Bd LA 1982-84, Federal Exec Bd Philadelphia 1986-; mem Greater Philadelphia Chamber of Commerce 1987; mem exec bd United Way of SE PA 1987; chmn Combined Federal Campaign 1988. **Honors/Awds:** Senior Executive Fellow Harvard, JFK School of Govt 1981. **Military Serv:** USAF major general 29 yrs; Defense Superior Svc, Legion of Merit, Distinguished Flying Cross, Defense Meritorious Svc, Air Medal 1958-. **Home Addr:** Quarters "L", US Naval Base, Philadelphia, PA 19112.

W

WADDELL, RUCHADINA LADESIREE

Attorney, county official. **Personal:** Born Feb 21, 1965, Wilmington, NC; daughter of Ruth Weaver Waddell and Charles R Waddell. **Educ:** University of North Carolina, Greensboro, BS, 1985; University of Wisconsin, School of Law, JD, 1989. **Career:** Department of Industry Labor and Human Relations, administrative law judge, 1990-91; Department of Health Social Services, assistant legal counsel, 1992; Grant County, corporation counsel, 1992-94; Walworth County, asst corporation counsel, 1994-. **Orgs:** Wisconsin State Bar Association; Grant County Bar Association; Dane County Bar Association; Phi Delta Phi; Delta Sigma Theta Sorority. **Honors/Awds:** University of Wisconsin, Law School, AOF fellow, 1987-89. **Home Addr:** 4607 Franklin Ave #218, Wilmington, NC 28403-0603. **Business Addr:** Asst Corporation Counsel, Walworth County, State of Wisconsin, County Courthouse, 106, Elkhorn, WI 53121, (414)741-4358.

WADDELL, THEODORE R.

Electronics engineer. **Personal:** Born Mar 3, 1934, Wilmington, NC. **Educ:** NC A & T, BS 1962; Bthn Ckmn Coll, 1954; Grg Wash U, 1970. **Career:** Fed Commu Commn, chf dmstc mcrwv rd br 1980-, rep oncmps rcrtmnt of gradtng stdnts at prdmntly blk Univ 1965-; Engineer, various other postns; Common Carrier Bur, 1962-80. **Honors/Awds:** Recip cert of aw for hgh qlty prfrmnc Fed Commu Commn 1965, 1973, 1974. **Military Serv:** AUS splst 5 1955-58. **Business Addr:** 1919 M St NW, Washington, DC 20554.

WADDLES, CHARLESZETTA LINA (MOTHER WADDLES)

Mission director. **Personal:** Born Oct 7, 1912, St Louis, MO; daughter of Ella Brown and Henry Campbell; married Payton Jr (deceased); children: Beatrice, Lathet L, Latheda, Lorraine, Andrea, Dennis, Theresa, Annette, Roosevelt, Charles (deceased). **Career:** Waddles Perpetual Mission Inc, founder (1956), national director, pastor; Emergency Service Program provides clothing, food, shelter, medicine, transportation & anything required by the needy. **Orgs:** Life mem NAACP; Mayor's Task Force Committee; City's Bicentennial Committee. **Honors/Awds:** Honorary chairman, Women's Conference of Concern; received nearly 150 awards among which are Ford Motor Co Bell Ringer, Lane Bryant Citizens Award, Sojourner Truth Award, Religious Heritage Award, State of Michigan Special Tributes, State of Michigan Legislative Body, Humanitarian Award presented by President Richard Nixon, Volunteer Leadership Award presented by Governor William Milliken, Humanitarian Award presented by Mayor Roman S Gribbs of Detroit; described by Bishop Emrich as "One Husky St Joan of Arc"; "A One Woman War On Poverty," Life Magazine; "Detroit's Resident Who Really Proves Her Concern by Doing for Her Fellow Man" Detroit editorial column; included in Black Woman Oral History Project, Schlesinger Library, Radcliffe College;included in Black Woman of Courage Traveling ibit, Smithsonian Institution; Woman of Courage Exhibit, Walter P. Reuther Library, Archive of Labor & Urban Affairs, Black History Month; A. Philip Randolph Institute Special Award; Honorary Doctor of Humanities Degree; Mission & School, Kumast, Ghana, West Africa; Humanitarian Award, Urban League, 1988; Honorary Kiwanian, The Order of the Giraffe.

WADDLES, GEORGE WESLEY, SR.

Clergyman, psychologist. **Personal:** Born Jul 19, 1948, Wichita, KS; married Karen Lavern Winn; children: George Jr, Nicholas, Nathanael, Genesis Maian. **Educ:** Bethel Coll N Nwtn KS, BA Soc Wk 1974; KS Univ Lwrnc, MSW 1976. **Career:** Vncnns Univ, pastor psch conselor 1977-; 2nd Bapt Church, pastor 1977-; Ottawa Univ, prof 1976-77; KS Univ, adm asst to dean 1976-77; Mt Olive St Cngrs of Christian Educ, dean 1977-; WVUT, TV host blkns is 1977-. **Orgs:** Staff mem Nat Bapt Cngrs of Chrstn Educ 1978-; pres Grtr Vncnns Mnstrl Alli 1978-79; bd mem Knox Co Chld Protctn Team 1978-; coor hnd-cppd Vncnns Univ Stdnt Serv 1979-. **Honors/Awds:** Grad Sch Schol Nat Inst of Mtl Hlth 1974; Otstndng Yng Men of Am US Jr C of C 1977. **Business Addr:** Vincennes University, Vincennes, IN 47591.

WADDY, WALTER JAMES
Administrator. **Personal:** Born Dec 31, 1929, Irvington, VA; married Clorie M Byrd; children: Waltia Suzanne. **Educ:** George Meany Labor Studies Center, labor courses 1973; Goucher Coll, labor courses 1975. **Career:** Amer Fedn of Labor & Cong of Industrial Organizations, Region III covering 7 states & DC, dir 1973-; AFL-CIO, Region IV covering 3 states & DC, dir 1971; AFL-CIO Region IV, field rep 1961; United Papermakers & Paperworkers AFL-CIO, field rep 1959; Local #632 United Papermakers AFL-CIO, pres 1956. **Orgs:** Exec bd mem VA St AFL-CIO 1956; coord Coord Div of MD & DC Coop Orgn 1964; sec/tras Baltimore Chap APRI Orgn Cmpgn 1968; bd mem Nat APRI 1973-80; prog dir Cedar-Morris Hill Improv Assn 1974; mem Ancient Egyptian AONMS; mem Jerusalem Tmpl No 4 AEAONMS; mem 32 degree Mason Hiram Consistory No 2; mem Landmark Lodge #40 F&AM. **Honors/Awds:** Trd unionist of the yr Met Baltimore Counc AFL-CIO 1975; govr's awd for Contrib to Labor Movement MD 1975; mayor's awd for Contrib to Labor Movement Baltimore City 1975; A Philip Randolph Awd Negro Labor Union Counc 1976. **Business Addr:** 2701 W Patapsco Ave, Baltimore, MD 21230.

WADE, ACHILLE MELVIN
Educational administrator. **Personal:** Born Nov 5, 1943, Clarksville, TN; son of Electra M Freeman Wade and Bennie Albert Wade; married Angela Nash Wade; children: Chaka L. **Educ:** OK State Univ, BA 1966, MA 1969. **Career:** Black Studies Center, Univ of CA Santa Barbara, acting dir 1969-70; Black Studies Univ of Omaha NB, dir 1970-71; Black Studies Vassar Coll, dir 1971-73; Black Studies Univ of Austin TX, lecturer 1973-86; Moorhead State Univ MN, Minority Student Affairs, coordinator 1988-89; Yale Univ, asst dean of students, dir Afro-Amer Cultural Center 1989-92; Upward Bound, Univ of Bridgeport CT, dir, 1993; Multicultural Ctr, Univ of RI, Kingston, RI, 1994-. **Orgs:** Arts commission City of Austin 1981-; bd mem Laguna Gloria Art Museum 1982-84; pres TX Assn for the Study of Afro-Amer Life and History Inc 1985-88; bd mem, CT Afro-American Historical Soc, 1990-; bd mem, New Haven Ethnic History Ctr, 1990-92. **Home Addr:** 9 Alumni Avenue, #10, Providence, RI 02906. **Business Phone:** (401)874-2851.

WADE, BERYL ELAINE
Attorney. **Personal:** Born Jul 1, 1956, Wilmington, NC; daughter of Geneva M S Wade and Clarence W R Wade. **Educ:** University of North Carolina at Chapel Hill, BA, 1977; University of Michigan, School of Law, JD, 1980. **Career:** Cumberland County District Attorney's Office, assistant district attorney, 1980-82; North Carolina Senator Tony Rand, campaign coordinator, 1982; NJ Justice Academy, legal instructor, 1982-84; City of Fayetteville, assistant city attorney/police attorney, 1984-93; State of North Carolina, deputy legislative counsel, Office of the Governor, 1993-95; counsel to Governor James B Hunt Jr, 1996-. **Orgs:** North Carolina State Bar, 1980-; North Carolina Association of Police Attorney's secretary/treasurer, 1987, president, 1988; Administration Rules Review Commission, commissioner, 1985-90, 1992-; North Carolina Association of Black Lawyers, board of governors, 1985-91, assistant secretary, 1991-; Cumberland Co Bar Association, 1980-93, Cumberland Co Board of Health, 1988-94; United Way, board of governor's, 1988, chair, Nominating Committee, 1991, chair, Project Blueprint Committee, 1991-92, NAACP, 1981-; UNC-CH, board of visitors, 1996-. **Honors/Awds:** 7th District Black Leadership Caucus, Presidential Award, 1984; College Heights Presbyterian Church, Trustee, 1990. **Home Addr:** 303 S King Charles Rd, Raleigh, NC 27610, (919)250-0083. **Business Addr:** Counsel to the Governor, State of North Carolina, Office of the Governor, 116 W Jones St, Raleigh, NC 27603, (919)733-5811.

WADE, BRENT JAMES
Writer, telecommunications co. manager. **Personal:** Born Sep 19, 1959, Baltimore, MD; son of Sylvia Wade and James Bennett Wade; married Yvette Jackson, Sep 29, 1979; children: Wesley Jackson, Claymore Dotson. **Educ:** University of Maryland, BA, English, 1981. **Career:** Westinghouse Electric Corp., marketing representative, 1981-87; LSI Logic Corp., marketing manager, 1987-89; AT&T, computer systems senior project manager, 1989-. **Special Achievements:** Author, Company Man, novel, Algonquin Books, 1992. **Business Addr:** Author, Company Man, c/o Algonquin Books of Chapel Hill, PO Box 2225, Chapel Hill, NC 27515, (919)933-2113.

WADE, BRUCE L.
Musician. **Personal:** Born Jul 17, 1951, Chicago, IL. **Career:** Baltimore Symphony Orchestra, violinist 1977-; Mil Symphony, 1972-73; Grant Park Symphony of Chicago 1971-; Civic Orchestra of Chicago, 1968-72. **Orgs:** Mem Pro Musica Rara. **Honors/Awds:** $50000 Award Louis Sudler 1971. **Business Addr:** Violinist, Baltimore Symphony, 1212 Cathedral St, Baltimore, MD 21201.

WADE, CASEY, JR.
Government official. **Personal:** Born Oct 7, 1930, Pickens, MS; son of Kate Wade and Casey Wade Sr; married Doris Taylor Wade, Nov 12, 1967; children: Robert, Diane, Joycherie. **Career:** IL Dept of Mental Health, Kankakee, IL, security officer, 1966-. **Orgs:** Mem, Black Mayors Assn, 1990-; minister, Pleasant Grove Baptist Church, 1980-; mayor, Village of Sun River Terrace, IL, 1980-; Leadership Institute for Black Mayors Certificate, 1990; mem, Kankakee County Mayor's Assn, 1988; mem, NAACP, 1982-; mem, Teacher's Union, 1987-. **Honors/Awds:** Founder/mayor, Village of Sun River Terrace (plaque), 1990; Governor's Hometown Award, State of IL plaque, 1987; Certificate of Appreciation, Boy Scouts #302, 1989, 1990; Citizens United for Better Society Plaque, 1980; House Resolution #2125, IL State house of Rep Certificate, 1990; Mayor, Kankakee County Men of Progress Plaque, 1983; Natl Alliance of Business, Natl Black Mayor Assn Certificate, 1990, 1991, 1992; Natl Alliance of Leadership Natl Black Mayor Assn Certificate, 1990, 1991, 1992; IL Clean & Beautiful Award, IL Dept of Commerce & Community Affairs Certificate, 1987.

WADE, EUGENE HENRY-PETER
Physician. **Personal:** Born Nov 20, 1954, Washington, DC; son of Dorothy Heyward Vallentine and Samuel Wade; married Portia Battle; children: Kim M, Eugene Henry-Peter II, Kara. **Educ:** Brown Univ, AB, ScB, 1978; Howard Univ, Coll of Medicine, MD, 1981; Univ of Alamaba, Postgrad training. **Career:** Private Practice, family physician. **Orgs:** Co-chairman, North Carolina Acad of Family Physicians, Minority Affair Comm; mem, Indigent Care Task Force of North Carolina Medical Soc, North Carolina Gen Assembly Indigent Health Care Study Commr. **Honors/Awds:** Diplomate, Acad of Family Physicians. **Business Addr:** 1041 Kirkpatrick Rd, Burlington, NC 27215.

WADE, JACQUELINE E.
Educator. **Personal:** Born Sep 7, 1940, Murfreesboro, TN; daughter of Ellen Wade and Aaron Wade; children: Sharon Elizabeth Rose. **Educ:** Fisk Univ, BA 1962; Univ of PA, MSW 1972, PhD 1983. **Career:** Univ of PA, dir Penn Children's Ctr 1973-80, assoc dir of student life 1980-84, faculty school of social work 1973-88, dir Afro Amer studies prog 1984-88; Bennett College, Women's Research Training and Development, director, 1988-90; Ohio State University, National Council for Black Studies, exec dir, 1990-. **Orgs:** Consultant Trenton State Coll AFAMS Dept 1984-, Philadelphia Sch Dist Desegregation Office 1985-, Benj Bannekar Honors Coll Prairie View A&M 1985-, Conrad Hilton Foundation 1985-88. **Honors/Awds:** Challenge Grant, St Peter's Coll Urban Educ, 1988-. **Home Addr:** 6140-A Polo Dr W, Columbus, OH 43229. **Business Addr:** Executive Director, Natl Council for Black Studies, Ohio State University, 208 Mount Hall, 1050 Carmack Rd, Columbus, OH 43210.

WADE, JAMES NATHANIEL
Business executive. **Personal:** Born Oct 2, 1933, Patterson, NJ; children: Valarie, JaJa, Atiba. **Educ:** Voorhees Coll, AA 1982-54; St Augustines Coll, BA 1954-56; Howard Univ, MSW 1965-67; Univ of Pittsburgh, post grad 1973-75. **Career:** Erie Community Action Committee, deputy of operations 1967-69; Erie Urban Coalition, exec dir 1969-71; Dept of Community Affairs/Commonwealth, deputy sec 1971-73, gov special asst 1973-75, sec of admin 1975-79; Wade Communications, Inc, chairman of the bd. **Orgs:** First and Second Philadelphia United Negro Coll Fund, chairman; THe Basan Development, v p; Crisis Intervention Network, exec committee, mem; Philadelphia-Dance Co, bd mem; Congreso De Latinos Unidos, Inc, bd mem; NAACP, life mem; Kappa Alpha Psi, life mem; Nat'l Black MBA Association, mem; Bay City Masonic Lodge, mem. **Honors/Awds:** NAACP, presidential award 1975, humanitarian award 1976; United Negro Coll Fund, award of distinction 1976; St Augustines Coll, achievement & meritorium award; Chapel of Four Chaplains, legion of honor award; Ame Union Church, christian businessman of the year award; Nat'l Assoc for Equal Opp in Higher Ed, pres citation distinguished alumni award; Omega Psi Psi, citizen of the year award. **Military Serv:** AUS, sp 4 1956-58; Leadership Training Award, 1957.

WADE, JOSEPH DOWNEY
Educational administrator. **Personal:** Born Jan 16, 1938, Beaumont, TX; son of Lorene and Rufus; married Judith Allen; children: Stacy, Joseph Jr. **Educ:** Oregon State Univ, BS, 1959, MEduc, 1961; Univ of Oregon, PhD, 1982. **Career:** Compton Coll, head football coach, 1969-71; Univ of Oregon, asst football coach, 1972-75, assoc dir of admissions, 1975-76, assoc dir academic adv & student serv, 1976-84, dir academic adv & student serv, 1985-. **Orgs:** Commr, chair, Oregon Commn on Black Affairs; univ senate, Faculty Advisory Council; executive council, National Student Exchange. **Business Addr:** Dir, Acad Adv & Student Serv, Univ of Oregon, 164 Oregon Hall, Eugene, OR 97403.

WADE, JOYCE K.
Banker. **Personal:** Born May 2, 1949, Chicago, IL; daughter of Martha L Davis Wade and Ernest S Wade, Sr. **Educ:** Northwestern Univ, Evanston IL, BS educ, 1970; Univ of Chicago IL, MBA, 1977. **Career:** US Dept of Housing & Urban Development, Chicago IL housing rep, 1970-78; IL Housing Devel Authority, Chicago development office rep, 1978-79; Community Bank of Lawndale, Chicago loan office rep 1979-87, office CEO 1987-, mem Bd of Dir 1988-. **Orgs:** Dir, treas, Carole Robertson Center for Learning, 1980-; mem of Bd of Control, treas & chair of Loan Comm, Neighborhood Network & Housing Services, Marshall Sq & Douglas Park, 1984-; mem, Urban Renewal Bd of City of Chicago, 1987-; mem, treas, Natl Assn of Negro Business & Professional Women, 1987-; dir, Amer Civil Liberties Union of IL, 1988-; mem, Urban Bankers Forum of Chicago, 1988-. **Honors/Awds:** Marilyn V Singleton Award, US Dept HUD, 1975; Bank Operation Outstanding Student Award, Assn of Bank Oper Mgmt, 1980; Top 100 Business & Professional Women, Dollars & Sense Magazine, 1988; Positive Self Image Award, Westside Center for Truth, 1988; Outstanding Service Award, Carole Robertson Center, 1989.

WADE, KIM MACHE
Beauty salon owner, playwright. **Personal:** Born Sep 25, 1957, Manhattan, NY; daughter of Rosa Jean Wade and Curtis L Wade (deceased); children: Rossi Jewel, Courtney Semaj. **Educ:** Attended, A&T State Univ 1972-73, UNC Greensboro 1973-74, Shaw Univ 1976-78; Sandhills Comm Coll, license cosmetology 1986. **Career:** Moore County Arts Council, playwright/producer 1984; Innervision Theater Co, producer/playwright/director 1984-; Hometown News Magazine, assoc editor 1984-;Sandhills Comm College, instructor; Mache Beauty Station, owner. **Orgs:** Mem NAACP Moore Co Chap 1975-; am clerk and newsletter reporter UPS 1981-; summer youth counselor Southern Pines Recreation Dept 1984-85; missionary Harrington Chapel Young Adult Missionary 1986-; activity coord Ebonette Cultural Club 1986-. **Honors/Awds:** Young Black Achiever Awd Black History Month Observation 1986; columnist Hometown News Magazine ''WORD'' 1986-; productions performed ''Innervisions,'' ''Go Tell it on the Mountain,'' ''Black Folk Got Dey'Selves T'Gather,'' ''Can I Get a Witness,'' 1989; Production, ''Celebrating the Word.''. **Home Addr:** 240 S Stephens St, Southern Pines, NC 28387.

WADE, LYNDON ANTHONY
Social worker. **Personal:** Born Jun 30, 1934, Atlanta, GA; married Shirley M; children: Lisa, Nora, Jennifer, Stuart. **Educ:** Morehouse Coll, AB 1956; Atlanta Univ, MSW 1958; Menninger Found Topeka KS, adv cert psy soc wk 1963. **Career:** Emory Univ, asst prof 1963-68; The Atlanta Urban League Inc, pres, ceo 1968-. **Orgs:** Mem Acad of Cert Soc Workers, Atlanta Action Forum; NationsBank Comm Reinvestment Comm; Jr League Advisory Comm; Vision 20/20 Task Force; Atlanta Committee for Public Education. **Honors/Awds:** Disting Comm Serv Atl Morehouse Alumni Club 1965; Disting Serv Fulton Cty Medical Soc 1971; Social Worker of the Year North GA Chap of NASW 1971; 10 Years Outstanding Serv Atlanta Urban Leag 1978. **Military Serv:** USA Med Serv Corp, 1st lt 1958-62. **Business Addr:** President, CEO, Atlanta Urban League, Inc, 100 Edgewood Ave, NE, Ste 600, Atlanta, GA 30303.

WADE, MILDRED MONCRIEF
Nursing home administrator (retired). **Personal:** Born Feb 5, 1926, Pittsburgh, PA; daughter of Fannie Primus Moncrief and Lawrence Moncrief; divorced; children: Judith L Johnson. **Educ:** Univ of Pittsburgh, BA 1947; Tuskegee Inst, EdM 1951. **Career:** Selma AL Public Schools, teacher 1947-50; Tuskegee Inst, instr 1951-52; YWCA, prog dir 1953-55; Youth Devel Ctr, teacher 1955-59; Home for the Aged, 1959-60; Dom Rltns Ct, counselor 1960-65; Pittsburgh Publ School, teacher 1965-67; Louise Child Care Center, Pittsburgh, PA, asst executive director, 1967-90; Lemington Home for the Aged, Pittsburgh, PA, administrative liaise, beginning 1991. **Orgs:** Natl Conf of Christians & Jews, Sickle Cell Soc of Pittsburgh; mem Urban League Guild of Pittsburgh; Natl Council of Negro Women Pittsburgh section; Delta Sigma Theta Inc Pittsburgh Alumnae chapter; life mem NAACP; mem Wesley Ctr AME Zion Church, Pittsburgh, PA; mem African Heritage Room Comm, University of Pittsburgh, Pittsburgh, PA; Martin Luther King, Jr, Outstanding Citizen's Award, Hand in Hand Inc, 1986; board member, Urban League of Pittsburgh, 1990-; board member, Lincoln, Larimer Revitalization Assn, 1989-. **Honors/Awds:** Outstanding Citizen Award, Pittsburgh City Council, 1990; Councilman's Cup for Community Service, City Council of Pittsburgh, 1990. **Home Addr:** 7166 Tilden St, Pittsburgh, PA 15206. **Business Addr:** Administrative Liaise, Lemington Home for the Aged, 1625 Lincoln Ave, Pittsburgh, PA 15206.

WADE, NORMA ADAMS
Journalist. **Educ:** Univ of Texas at Austin, BJ 1966. **Career:** Dallas Morning News TX, staff writer/columnist 1974-; Post Tribune Dallas TX, staff writer/asst to editor 1972-74; Bloom Advertising Agency Dallas, advertising copywriter production asst 1968-72; Collins Radio Co Dallas, editor/proofer of tech equipment manuals 1966-68. **Orgs:** Dallas-Ft Worth Association of Black Communicators; Natl Assn of Black Journalists. **Honors/Awds:** NAACP Juanita Craft Award, 1985; Bronze Heritage Award for preservation of African-American history, 1989. **Business Addr:** Staff Writer, Columnist, Dallas Morning News, PO Box 655237, Dallas, TX 75265.

WADE, TERRELL (HAWATHA TERRELL)
Professional baseball player. **Personal:** Born Jan 25, 1973, Guayubin, Dominican Republic. **Career:** Atlanta Braves, pitcher, 1995-97; Tampa Bay Devil Rays, 1998-. **Business Addr:** Professional Baseball Player, Tampa Bay Devil Rays, One Tropicana Dr, St Petersburg, FL 33705.

WADE, WILLIAM CARL
Nutritional products co. director. **Personal:** Born Aug 24, 1934, Rocky Mount, VA; son of Della Fox Wade and William Taft Wade; married Mary Frances Prunty, May 14, 1955; children: Pamela Renee Stockard, Marcus Sidney, Carl Tracy. **Educ:** Franklin University, BS, 1968; University of Dayton, MBA, 1972. **Career:** Ross Laboratories, financial reporting supervisor, 1966-72; Xerox Inc, account analyst, 1972-74, credit manager, 1974-76; General Motors, payroll accountant, 1976; Ross Laboratories, credit manager, 1976-77, customer service & credit director, 1977-90, fiscal services director, 1990-. **Orgs:** The Executive's Club, 1977-, president, 1991-93; Central Ohio Treasury Management Association, 1990-; American Legion, 1965-; University of Dayton Alumni Association, 1972-; Franklin University Alumni Association, 1968-. **Honors/Awds:** National Association of Credit Managers, Certified Credit Executive, 1988, Credit Manager of the Year, 1989; Boy Scouts of American, Silver Beaver, 1979. **Military Serv:** US Army, e-5, 1957-59. **Home Addr:** 5700 Echo Rd, Columbus, OH 43230, (614)476-0076. **Business Addr:** Director, Account Audits/Control, Ross Laboratories, 625 Cleveland Ave, Columbus, OH 43215, (614)624-7449.

WADE-GAYLES, GLORIA JEAN
Educator. **Personal:** Born in Memphis, TN; daughter of Bertha Reese Willett and Robert Wade; married Joseph Nathan Gayles, Aug 24, 1967; children: Jonathan Gayles, Monica Gayles. **Educ:** LeMoyne Coll, AB (Cum Laude with Distinction) 1959; Boston Univ Woodrow Wilson Fellow, AM 1962; George Washington Univ, doctoral work 1966-67; Emory Univ NEH Fellow, 1975; Emory Univ, PhD 1981. **Career:** Spelman Coll, instructor of English 1963-64; Howard Univ, instr of English 1965-67; Morehouse Coll, asst prof 1970-75; Emory Univ, graduate teaching fellow 1975-77; Talladega Coll, asst prof 1977-78; Spelman Coll, asst prof 1984-90, prof, 1992-. **Orgs:** Teacher COFO Freedom School/Valley View MS 1964; mem bd dir WETV 30 -WABE-FM 1976-77; sec Guardians for Quality Educ 1976-78; mem editorial bd of Callaloo 1977-80; exec bd Coll Language Assn 1977-80; mem NAACP, ASNLC, CORE; mem Alpha Kappa Alpha Sorority Inc; partner in Jon-Mon Consultants Inc; speech writer. **Honors/Awds:** Woodrow Wilson Fellowship 1959-62; Merrill Travel Grant to Europe The Charles Merril Found 1973; Danforth Fellow 1974; Faculty Award of the Year Morehouse Coll 1975; mem Alpha Kappa Mu Natl Honor Soc; editor CLANOTES 1975-; poems published in, Essence, Black World, The Black Scholar, First World; articles published in, Callaloo, Liberator, The Atlantic Monthly; wrote the preface to " Sturdy Black Bridges" Doubleday 1979; author of "No Crystal Stair, Visions of Race and Sec in Black Women's Fiction 1946-1976" Pilgrim Press 1984 (won 1983 manuscript award); UNCF Mellon Rsch Grant 1987-88, Liaison with Natl Humanities Faculty; Presidential Award for Scholarship, Spelman Coll, 1991; Named CASE Natl Prof of the Year, 1991; Author, Anointed to Fly, Harlem River, 1991; Dana Mentor, Spelmaoll, 1989-. **Special Achievements:** Pushed Back to Strength, Beacon Press, 1993; My Soul Is a Witness, Beacon Press, Rooted Against the Wind, Beacon Press, 1996; Father Songs: Testimonies by African-American Sons and Daughters, Beacon Press, 1997. **Business Addr:** Professor, English Dept, Spelman College, 350 Spelman Lane SW, Atlanta, GA 30314.

WADEN, FLETCHER NATHANIEL, JR.
Company executive. **Personal:** Born Jan 30, 1928, Greensboro, NC; son of Rosa P Waden and Fletcher Waden Sr; widowed; children: Betty. **Educ:** American Business Institute, 1947-48; Winston-Salem State University, 1974; North Carolina A&T State University, 1975-76; University of North Carolina, 1987. **Career:** Ritz Loan Co., owner, general manager, 1951-57; Gnato's Children Clothing Store, owner, 1960-70; Gnato's Construction Co., president, owner, 1979-; National Financial & Business Consultants Inc, president, currently. **Orgs:** DAV & VFW, life member; National Minority Suppliers Development Council Inc; NAACP; National Republican Senatorial Committee; US Senator's Club; Minority Business Enterprise Legal Defense and Education Fund Inc; US Department of Defense, Defense Manufacturers & Suppliers Association. **Military Serv:** US Army, 1948-51. **Business Phone:** (919)841-3494.

WAGNER, ANNICE
Chief justice. **Educ:** Wayne State Univ, BA, JD. **Career:** National Capital Housing Authority, general counsel; Superior Court D.C., assoc judge, 1977-90; DC Ct Appeals, assoc judge, beginning 1990; DC Supreme Ct, chief judge, currently; Harvard Univ, instructor, currently. **Special Achievements:** One of six African Americans to be appointed chief justice in the US. **Business Addr:** Chief Justice, District of Columbia Supreme Court, 500 Indiana Ave NW, Rm 600, Washington, DC 20001, (202)479-3011.

WAGNER, DAVID H.
Attorney. **Personal:** Born Jul 23, 1926, Davidson Co, NC; married Mollie Craig; children: Brenda C, Davida S. **Educ:** A&T U, BS 1948; A&T State U, MS 1957; Wake Forest U, JD 1968. **Career:** Atty, pvt practice 1969-; Wachovia Bank, closing atty & housing spec 1968-69; Lexington NC, instr principal 1958-66; Pender Co, instr principal 1954-58. **Orgs:** Gen couns Winston Mut Life Ins 1969-; pres Urban Housing Inc 1970-; pres Assoc Furniture Inc 1970-; mem NBA; NC Black Bar Assn; Forsyth Co Bar Assn; NC Bar treas Goler Met AME Zion Ch; vice pres life mem NAACP; bd mem & stockhldr Vanguard Invest Co; Forsyth Econ Devel Corp; life mem Alpha Phi Alpha; life mem NEA. **Military Serv:** AUS 1st lt 1948-53. **Business Addr:** PO Box 998, Winston-Salem, NC 27102.

WAGNER, VALLERIE DENISE
Engineer. **Personal:** Born Apr 10, 1959, San Antonio, TX; daughter of Janie Powell Wagner and Jewell Wagner. **Educ:** Southern Univ, BSME 1981; Tuskegee Inst, MSEE 1983. **Career:** Detroit Diesel Allison/GM, test engr 1979; Jet Propulsion Lab, engr I 1981-82, mem tech staff 1983-. **Orgs:** Alpha Kappa Alpha Sor Inc 1979-; Eta Kappa Nu Honorary Frat 1982-; Black Gay and Lesbian Leadership Forum, board of directors, 1991-; African-American Gay and Lesbian Cultural Alliance, board of directors, 1990-; United Lesbians of African Heritage, board of directors, 1991-92. **Honors/Awds:** GM Scholar General Motors 1979; GEM Fellowship 1981-83; First female to receive MS degree in engineering Tuskegee Inst 1983; Group Achievement Award, NASA, 1986, 1989. **Home Addr:** 2108 Fair Park Ave, #110, Los Angeles, CA 90041. **Business Addr:** Member, Technical Staff, Jet Propulsion Laboratory, 4800 Oak Grove Dr, M/S 264805, Pasadena, CA 91109.

WAGONER, J. ROBERT (TOM RIVERS)
Writer, producer, director, company executive. **Personal:** Born Mar 27, 1938, Concord, NC; son of Virginia L Wagoner and Elijah James Wagoner. **Educ:** Manhattan School of Music, 1962-63; Senior Dramatic Workshop, certificate, 1962; North Carolina A&T State University, BS, English, drama, 1968; University of North Carolina, MA, film, television, drama, 1974; University of Southern California Graduate School of Cinema, 1983-84. **Career:** North Carolina A&T State University, lecturer, photography, 1964-67; Black Journal, writer, producer, director, camera, 1968-71; Fayetteville State University, communications center designer, 1971-72; Cap Cities Comm, promotions manager, 1974-75; Transvue Films, writer, director, 1975-79; California State University, Long Beach, associate professor, 1980-83; Televersity, president, CEO, 1985-. **Orgs:** Bushido International, grand master, North Carolina A&T's Alumni Karate-do, 1967-; The Greater African-American, All-American Univ Marching Band, bd chairman, 1993-. **Honors/Awds:** WGBH Ed Foundation, WGBH Fellow, 1992; CPB/SC Educational TV, delegate, International TV Screen Conference, 1992; National Academy of Television Arts & Sciences, Emmy, one of six producers, 1969; University F & V Prod Association, White House Photographer's Association Award, 1972; University of North Carolina, Special Jefferson Broadcast Fellow, 1968. **Special Achievements:** Writer, producer, director, camera, Black Journal, 1969; City of Pasadena & The Ralph Parsons Co, special directing citation, 1978; writer, director, Avenging Godfather, 1979; film retrospective, Security Pacific National Bank, 1980; International Film Seminars, Movie Lab Fellow, 1969. **Military Serv:** US Navy, photo 2nd, 1956-60; US Navy Honorman (top photographer), Music Citation. **Business Addr:** President, CEO, Televersity, PO Box 645, Chapel Hill, NC 27514-0645, (919)968-9836.

WAHLS, MYRON HASTINGS (MIKE)
Judge. **Personal:** Born Dec 11, 1931, Chicago, IL; son of Frederica Bunton Wahls; married Shirleyan Chennault; children: Myron Jr, Julie K. **Educ:** Univ of MI, BA; Northwestern Univ Sch of Law, JD; Univ of Virginia Law School, Master of Laws in Judicial Process 1986. **Career:** Keith Conyers Anderson Brown & Wahls, atty 1964-75; Wayne Co Circuit Court, judge 1975-82; MI Court of Appeals, judge 1982-, chief judge pro tem, 1988-91; Wayne State Univ Law School, associate prof, 1989-. **Orgs:** Mem MI Judicial Inst; bd mem Fund for Equal Justice; chmn MI Court Reporting/Recording Bd of Review; guest lecturer Univ of Florence Italy, Univ of Pisa Italy & Univ of Clermont Ferrand Law Sch; adjunct prof Cooley Law Sch & Amer Inst for Paralegal Studies; bd dirs Natl Cncl on Alcoholism, MUSIC, Gamma Lambda Chap Alpha Phi Alpha Frat Inc, Ashland Theol Seminary, Save Orchestra Hall Inc, Jazz Development Workshop Inc, Kenneth Jewell Chorale, Fund for Equal Justice; Univ of MI Alumni Assn, Northwestern Univ Alumni Assn, Wayne State Univ Ctr for Black Studies, Jimmy Wilkins Cultural Found Inc, Sigma Pi Phi Frat Inc Iota Boule, Tabernacle Missionary Bapt Ch; life mem NAACP; NARCO; bd of directors Harmonie Park Playhouse; bd of directors Detroit Symphony OrchestralHall; bd of directors Dett Science Center. **Honors/Awds:** Outstanding Jurist Awd 1975; Dr Martin Luther King Awd First Annual MI Elks 1976, Disting Serv Awd Courville PTA 1977; Outstanding Serv Awd Webber Middle Sch 1981; Outstanding Jurist Awd Wall St 1981; D Augustus Straker Outstanding Jurist Awd Wolverine Bar Assn 1982; H H Humphrey Humanitarian Awd Alpha Tau Chap Alpha Phi Alpha Frat Inc 1982; Disting Serv Awd Assn of Black Judges of MI; Disting Serv Awd Wayne Co Circuit Court 1982; Outstanding Serv Achievement Awd Markley Minors Affairs Cncl Univ of MI 1983; Disting Serv Awd Epsilon Chap Alpha Phi Alpha Frat Inc 1983; Appreciation Awd MI Chap Natl Mgmt Assn 1984; Cert of Recognition Tabernacle Missionary Bapt Ch 1984; Distinguished Citizen of the Year - Rush County NAACP 1989; Outstanding CommunityService United Citizens for Detroit 198Bridge Builder Award New Calvary Baptist Church 1988; Guest Jazz Pianist with Lionel Hampton Orchestra Tour of Europe 1988; album release, "You Be The Judge," Mike Wahls Trio, 1997. **Business Addr:** Judge, Michigan Court of Appeals, 900 First Federal Bldg, Detroit, MI 48226, (313)256-9291.

WAIGUCHU, MURUKU
Educator. **Personal:** Born Nov 29, 1937, Kenya; son of Waiguchu and Mugure; divorced; children: 3. **Educ:** Central Coll, BA 1965; Queens Coll, MA 1967; Temple Univ, PhD 1971. **Career:** African Studies Ctr St John's Univ, instr 1968-69; Urban Univ, Rutgers Univ, asst prof 1969-70; Office of Minority Student Ed Univ of MD Coll Park, dir 1978-80; William Paterson Coll of NJ, assoc prof, chairperson 1973-78, full prof publ admin 1980, prof sch of mgt. **Orgs:** Mem AHSA, ASA, NCBPS, ABSW, NJABE, INCCA, ASPA. **Honors/Awds:** Recipient UN Fellow 1967-68. **Business Addr:** Professor, William Paterson College, School of Management, Wayne, NJ 07470.

WAINWRIGHT, GLORIA BESSIE
Elected official. **Personal:** Born Jul 13, 1950, Cleveland, OH; married Roy Wainwright; children: Roy Jr, Jason. **Educ:** Case Western Reserve Univ, 120 hr Cert 1971; Jane Addams School of Practical Nursing, Diploma 1975; Cuyahoga Comm Coll, 3 credits 1980. **Career:** Ward 5 Block Club, pres 1980; New Bethel AME Church, steward bd 1984-85; Bathsheba Order of Eastern Star, chaplain 1983; Oakwood Village City Council, councilmem 1984-. **Home Addr:** 7226 Wright Ave, Oakwood Village, OH 44146. **Business Addr:** Councilmember, Oakwood Village City Council, 24800 Broadway Ave, Oakwood Village, OH 44146.

WAINWRIGHT, OLIVER O'CONNELL
Business executive. **Personal:** Born May 6, 1936, Nanticoke, MD; son of Victoria Nutter Wainwright and Jesse Wainwright; married Dolores Moorman; children: Oliver Jr, Stephen C, Eric C. **Educ:** Hampton Inst, BS 1959; William Paterson Coll, MA Commun 1972; Central MI Univ, MA Indust Mgmt 1974; US Army Command & Gen Staff Coll, 1975; Nova Univ, MPA 1980, DPA 1981; Rutgers University, advanced management, resident, 1985. **Career:** AUS, various positions to lt col, 1959-79; SCM Corp, mgr corp security 1979-85; Mobil Corp, Stamford, CT, corp security mgr, 1985-87; American International Group, New York, NY, asst vice pres, dir corporate security, 1987-. **Orgs:** Mem Kappa Alpha Psi; mayoral appt Human Resources Council Piscataway 1980; trustee North Stelton AME Church 1980-81; mem Assoc of Political Risk Analysts 1982; mem cert bd Acad of Security Ed & Trainers 1983-85; mem disting lecturer series Dept of Mgmt & Criminal Justice 1985; bd of dir Acad for Security Ed & Trainers 1982-85; standing comm mem Amer Soc for Indust Security Intl; assoc mem Intl Assoc of Chiefs; bd of dir Amer Soc for Indust Sec 1985-87, Amer Soc for Indust Security 1981-; International Security Management Assn, 1985-; Alliance for Concern Citizens, Piscataway, NJ; member, Board of Education, Piscataway, NJ, 1987-90; Oversea Security Council, US Dept of State, 1988-90. **Honors/Awds:** Natl Training Award Defense Intelligence School Natl Training Officers Conf 1977; Political Risk Assessment Article Risk Planning Group 1980; Cert Protection Professional Amer Soc of Indust Sec Intl 1981; Cert Security Trainer Acad Security for Security Ed & Trainers 1981; Black Achievers in Indust Award Harlem YMCA 1982; Mgmt of the Future Article Security Mgmt Mag 1984; Certificate of Appreciation, board of directors, American Society Ind Sec, 1987; Distinguished Service Award, L I University, School of Public Administration, 1985; Certificate of Appreciation, Community Service Award, Piscataway Sportsmen, 1989; Honorary Certificate, New York City Police Dept, 1990. **Military Serv:** AUS Military Intelligence lt col 1959-79; Bronze Star w/1 OLC; Air Medal w/2 OLC; Pres Unit Citation, Natl Defense Serv Medal, Defense Meritorious Svc. **Home Addr:** 63 Coventry Circle, Piscataway, NJ 08854.

WAITE, NORMA LILLIA
Physician. **Personal:** Born Oct 14, 1950, Kingston, Jamaica; married Ainsley Blair; children: Craig, Duane, Andre Blair. **Educ:** Howard University, BS 1972; Howard University Medical School, MD 1977. **Career:** Brookdale Hospital, ob resident program 1977-81; private practice, physician, currently. **Orgs:** Fellow, American College OB/GYN 1982-; attending physician, Orlando Regional Hospital, FL Hospital; Humana Hospital Lucerne; fellow, American Board of Ob/Gyn. **Honors/Awds:** Phi Beta Kappa Society. **Business Addr:** Physician, 7479 Conroy Rd, Ste B, Orlando, FL 32811.

WAITERS, ANN GILLIS
Educator. **Personal:** Born Dec 5, 1939, Philadelphia, PA. **Educ:** Cheyney State Coll, BS; Elem Educ Temple U, EdM; Elem & Urban Educ Temple U, EdD. **Career:** William Penn School District, supt of schools; Phila School District, regional supt, high school principal; Univ School Relations Temple Univ, Philadelphia; Temple Univ Coll of Educ, adjunct prof; coordinator of International Student Exchange Program; School Dist of Philadelphia, reading teacher; Performance Appraisal of Admin & Suprs, spec cons; Temple Univ, competency based

teacher educ. **Orgs:** Title 1 Review Com Educ, Educ & Human Relat Com Assn for Field Serv in Tchr Edn; Black Educ Forum; Educ Equality Leag; Nat Counc of Adminstrv women in Edn; PA Assn for Supervsn & Curr Devel; PA Congress of Sch Adminstrs. **Honors/Awds:** Principal of the Year, Educators Roundtable; Phi Delta Kappa Serv Award Temple Univ; bicentennial award Nat Assn of Univ Women; awards of apprec Linpark Civic Assn Trevose PA; Morton Mcmichael SchPhiladelphia PA; charter mem PA Congress of Sch Adminstrs; Philadelphia Black Women's Educ Alliance. **Business Addr:** Dr Ann G Waiters, Superintendent, William Penn School District, 100 Green Ave, Lansdowne, PA 19050.

WAITERS, GAIL ELENORIA
Government administrator. **Personal:** Born May 15, 1954, Kansas City, MO; daughter of Lenora Sampson Waiters and Lloyd Winfred Waiters. **Educ:** California State Univ, Hayward, BA 1981, MPA 1989. **Career:** California State Univ, Hayward, administrative services coordinator, 1974-82; Univ of California, Berkeley, administrative analyst, 1982-85; City of Sunnyvale, CA, administrative assistant, 1985-89; City of Sunnyvale, CA, assistant to the city manager, 1989-. **Orgs:** Bd dir, Berkeley YWCA 1983-85, Leadership Sunnyvale 1985-86, Natl Forum for Black Public Administrators, Oakland-San Francisco Chapter 1986-; mem, Intl City Management Assn 1987-, Org Development Network 1987-, Intl Assn of Business Communicators 1987-89; chair, California, Colorado, Arizona, Nevada Innovation Group 1989-. **Honors/Awds:** Outstanding Chapter Service, NFBPA Oakland/San Francisco Bay Area Chapter, 1991.

WAITERS, LLOYD WINFERD, JR.
Manager. **Personal:** Born Sep 28, 1948, Houston, TX; son of Lenora Sampson Waiters and Lloyd W Waiters; married Alice Jean Barnhill Waiters, Jun 5, 1971; children: Tamela, Rodney, Anthony. **Educ:** Air University, Birmingham, AL, 1970-72; Chabot, Hayward, CA, AA, 1978; California State, Hayward, CA, 1978-84. **Career:** Pacific Gas & Electric, support services director, 1969-. **Orgs:** California Assn of Public Purchasing Officers; National Association of Purchasing Management. **Military Serv:** USAF, E-5, 1969-73. **Home Addr:** 610 Tennis Ln, Tracy, CA 95376-4433.

WAITES-HOWARD, SHIRLEY JEAN
Public relations consultant. **Personal:** Born Dec 29, 1948, Philadelphia, PA; daughter of Bessie E. Hill Waites and James Harvey Waites (deceased); married Alfred Howard Jr., Dec 31, 1989; children: Demarcus Reginald. **Educ:** Pennsylvania State Univ, BA, psychology, 1971; Bryn Mawr Graduate School of Social Work, MSS, 1977; Eastern Baptist Theological Seminary, Wynnewood, PA, currently. **Career:** Mental Health Consortium Inc, consultation and education specialist/social worker therapist; West Philadelphia Community, consultation & educ, 1971-77; Women's Network Consultants, public relations consultant, 1974-; Baptist Children's Service, clinical director, 1978-80; LaSalle Univ, coordinator and instructor, social work dept, 1980-83; Villanova Univ, instructor, 1980-85; Haverford State Hospital, psychiatric social worker, 1983-85; Lincoln Univ, instructor, 1984; Priosn Project, coordinator; WDAS-AM Talk Show, program asst, 1982-84; MaGee Rehabilitation Hospital, staff social worker, 1987-. **Orgs:** Advisor/team member, Triple Jeopardy Third World Women's Support Network; member, Natl Assoc of Black Psychologists; member, Natl Assoc of Black Social Workers; member, Natl Assoc of Social Workers. **Honors/Awds:** Achievement Award, Black Students of LaSalle Univ, 1983; Achievement Award, MaGee Rehabilitation Hospital, African American History Month, February, 1989. **Home Addr:** 1708 No 55th St, Philadelphia, PA 19131. **Business Addr:** Staff Social Worker, Social Services, MaGee Rehabilitation Hospital, Six Franklin Plaza, Philadelphia, PA 19102.

WAITH, ELDRIDGE
Law enforcement officer. **Personal:** Born Jan 13, 1918, New York, NY; son of Montelle Russell Waith and George Waith; married Elsie Torres, Apr 12, 1971; children: Mariann C Ramos, Linda M Waith-Broadlick. **Educ:** John Jay Coll of Criminal Justice City Univ of NY, BS 1966. **Career:** UBA Security Serv Inc, security cons, pres 1974-; NJ Civil Serv Commn on Police Promotns, consult; Police-Comm Relations for Nat Conf of Chris & Jews; New York City Bd of Educ, chief adminstr, Sch Safety 1972-74; Coll of Virgin Islands, instr Police Sci 1971; New York City Police Dept, served every rank up to & including asst chief inspector; Virgin Islands Government, comm of public safety, 1971-72; University of Virgin Islands, chief of security, 1979-90; Virgin Islands Government, director narcotic strike force, 1990-. **Orgs:** Life mem NAACP; mem 100 Black Men; mem Guardians Assn Found of NYCPD; member, Virgin Islands Retired Police Organization; member, Council of Retired Police, NYC; member, Noble. **Honors/Awds:** Recip 17 Departmental awards for outstanding police work; numerous comm awards.

WAITS, VA LITA FRANCINE
Attorney, judge. **Personal:** Born Jan 29, 1947, Tyler, TX; daughter of Sibbie Jones Waits (deceased) and Melvin Waits Jr. **Educ:** Howard University, BA, 1969; American University, MA, 1974; Texas Southern University, Thurgood Marshall School of Law, JD, 1980. **Career:** WRC-TV/NBC, producer, 1971-74; Southwestern Bell Telephone Co, manager, 1975; Texas Southern University, instructor, KTSU-FM, manager, 1975-76; U.S. Department of Energy, regional attorney, 1980-81; National Labor Relations Board, field attorney, 1981-82; Law Office of Va Lita Waits, principal, 1982-; City of Tyler, alternate municipal judge, 1984-94. **Orgs:** Supreme Court, State of Texas, Bar Admissions Committee, 1983-; Tyler Metropolitan Chamber of Commerce, founding president, 1989-92; Delta Sigma Theta, Sorority, Tyler Alumnae Chapter, president, 1990-92; Smith County Court Appointed Special Advocates, founding board member, 1989-; Smith County Bar Association, 1982-; Natl Bar Assn, 1984-; National Association of Black Women Lawyers, 1992-; Leadership Texas, 1987-; Texas Assn of African American Chambers of Commerce, secretary, 1993-. **Honors/Awds:** Austin Metropolitan Business Resource Center, Women of Distinction, 1992; KLTV, Black History Portrait, Leading African-American in East Texas, 1991; Top Ladies of Distinction, Top Lady of the Year, 1990; Tyler Independent School District, Distinguished Graduate, 1983; Omega Psi Phi, Public Service in the Area of Law, 1983; service awards from numerous organizations including: Tyler Jaycess, Delta Sigma Theta Sorority, Rosebud Civitan Club, Longview Metropolitan Chamber of Commerce, Texas College, State Bar of Texas Admissions Committee, Bonner Elementary School, District of Columbia Commission on the Status of Women, U.S. Department of Justice, Bureau of Prisons. **Special Achievements:** College of the State Bar of Texas, 1987-93; first African-American female attorney to hold judicial position in East Texas; associate editor, Thurgood Marshall Law Journal, 1978-90. **Home Phone:** (903)595-0866. **Business Addr:** Attorney, Law Office of Va Lita Waits, 719 W Front, Tyler, TX 75702, (903)597-5900.

WAKEFIELD, J. ALVIN
Consultant. **Personal:** Born Jul 25, 1938, New York, NY; son of Dorothy Nickerson Bradshaw and James Alvin Wakefield; divorced; children: Shawna Michelle, Adam Malik. **Educ:** Syracuse Univ, Syracuse, NY, 1956-57; NY Univ, BA Eng Lit 1957-60; Pace Univ Grad Schl of Bus, MBA 1970-72. **Career:** Mobil Oil Corporation, Boston, MA, employee relations asst, 1966-68; Celanese Corporation, New York, NY, supervisor personnel, 1968-70; Singer Company, New York, NY, recruiting manager, 1970-73; Avon Products Inc, New York, NY, vice pres of administration, 1973-81; Korn/Ferry International, New York, NY, vice pres/partner, 1981-83; Wakefield Enterprises, Rutland, VT, pres, 1983-86; Gilbert Tweed Associates, Pittsford, VT, managing director/partner, 1986-93; Wakefield Talabisco International, president, managing director, currently. **Orgs:** Chrmn Cncl of Concerned Blk Execs 1970-73; brd mem NY Urban League 1980-83; board member, New England Board of Higher Education, 1990-91; executive committee, Vermont Achievement Center, 1988-91; board member, Vermont Business Roundtable, 1988-; Governor's Council of Economic Advisors; Democratic Party, executive committee, 1993-95; Trinity College, board of directors. **Honors/Awds:** Acdmc schlrshp Syracuse Univ 1956; outstanding achvmnt awd Black Retail Action Group 1979; The Career Makers: America's Top 100 Executive Recruiters, 1991, The Career Makers North Americas Top 150 Executive Recruiters, 1992, 1995; Management Concepts & Practices, 1981-83. **Military Serv:** US Air Force, Capt, 1961-66. **Business Addr:** Managing Director, Wakefield Talabisco International, Mendon Meadows, Ste 8, Rte 4, Rutland, VT 05701, (802)747-5901.

WALBEY, THEODOSIA EMMA DRAHER
Actress, singer. **Personal:** Born Apr 13, 1950, Bangor, ME; married Daniel A Draher; children: Timothy W Wright, Stephen S Wright, Daniel A Draher, Jr. **Educ:** Univ of MD; Univ of CO; Kinman Bus Univ. **Career:** Music writer; co-wrote songs on latest Ritchie Family Album "Give Me A Break"; appeared before King & Prince of Morrocco & Princess Caroline's engagement party; 2 movies "La Borbichette" & "Can't Stop the Music"; TV performances, Dinah Shore, Merv Griffin, Rock Concert, Midnight Special, Soul Train, Amer Bandstand, Mike Douglas, Dance Fever, Soap Factory, numerous countries around the world; group called "The Ritchie Family", singer 1975-; Can't Stop Productions, singer, dancer, actress; "Woman of Many Faces.". **Honors/Awds:** Gold & Platinum Records from around the world 1976-77; Featured "Ebony Magazine" 1980; Featured "Black Stars Magazine"; Featured "Blacktress Magazine". **Business Addr:** Actress/Singer/Performer, Can't Stop Productions, 65 E 55th St, Ste 302, New York, NY 10022.

WALBURG, JUDITH ANN
Fund raiser. **Personal:** Born Feb 19, 1948, New York, NY; daughter of Florence Perry Walburg and Charles A Walburg. **Educ:** Fisk Univ, Nashville TN, BA 1969. **Career:** Olivetti Corp of Amer, NYC, customer relations rep 1970-72; United Negro College Fund, NYC, asst dir of educational services 1972-75, dir of alumni natl org 1975-. **Orgs:** Mem, New York Fisk Alumni Assn 1975-79, Natl Urban Affairs Council 1984-89, Corporate Women's Network 1986-89; bd mem, Council on the Environment 1987-89. **Honors/Awds:** Outstanding Young Woman of America, 1976 & 1978. **Home Addr:** 284 Convent Ave, New York, NY 10031. **Business Addr:** Director, Alumni Groups, National Organizations, United Negro College Fund, 160 Water St Fl 23, New York, NY 10038-4922.

WALDEN, BARBARA
Cosmetics company executive. **Personal:** Born Sep 3, 1936, Camden, NJ. **Educ:** Attended, Vogue Finishing School, Eccles Business Coll. **Career:** Film and TV actress, The Ten Commandments w/Charlton Heston, What A Way to Go w/Paul Newman, Global Affair w/Bob Hope, Satin's Seven Sinners w/Mickey Rooney, Freaky Friday w/Jodi Foster; TV appearances include Hour Magazine, The CBS Morning News, The Morning Show, Newsnight, The Tom Snyder Show, AM Los Angeles plus many more; Barbara Walden Cosmetics, president, currently, founder. **Orgs:** Bd mem ACLU 1985-, United Way 1986-; bd mem May Co So CA Women's Adv Council 1986-; mem Committee of 200, Coalition of 100 Black Women; co-sponsor Self-Image workshop seminars; lectures at colleges, univs, for women's groups, orgs, caucuses and for the Los Angeles Unified School Dist yearly Career Day; keynote speaker New York's Dept of States' Comm Economic Develop Prog Syracuse NY; guest lecturer UCLA's Women in Management, Southern CA Business Women's Caucus; board of directors, Love Is Feeding Everyone. **Honors/Awds:** Women in Business Awd; YWCA's Silver Achievement Awd; Watts Summer Pageant Awd; Special Merit Awd from LA Mayor Tom Bradley; The Baptist Business Women's Assoc Awd; The Women's Network Conf Achievement Awd; The Crenshaw La Tierra Business Women's Assoc Awd; cited, Congressional Record; indepth interview in Entrepreneur Magazine entitled "Advice from Some of the Nation's Most Powerful Businesswomen"; Woman of the Year Award, State of California Legislature; First Annual Los Angeles Women Making History Award. **Business Addr:** Founder/President, Barbara Walden Cosmetics Co, 5824 Uplander Way, Culver City, CA 90230.

WALDEN, EMERSON COLEMAN
Physician. **Personal:** Born Oct 7, 1923, Cambridge, MD; son of Lillian E and Charles E; married Celonia; children: Emerson C Jr, Thomas E, Celonia. **Educ:** Howard Univ, MD 1947. **Career:** USAF Hosp Mitchell AFB, chief of surg serv 1951-53; Provident Hosp Baltimore, chief surgery 1964-68; Luther, Johns Hopkins, Provident, S Baltimore Gen Hosps, attending surg; Baltimore City Health Dept, part time school physician; Private practice, physician. **Orgs:** Past pres Natl Med Assn, pres MD Med Assn; vice pres Monumental City Med Soc; bd regents Univ of MD; mem Baltimore City Med Soc; chmn bd trustees Natl Med Assn; dir health serv Providence Comprehensive Neighborhood Health Ctr. **Honors/Awds:** One of physicians who toured People's Rep of China 1972. **Business Addr:** 4200 Edmondson Ave, Baltimore, MD 21229.

WALDEN, NARADA MICHAEL
Entertainer, producer. **Personal:** Born Apr 23, 1952, Kalamazoo, MI; married Anukampa Lisa Coles. **Educ:** Western Michigan University, attended, 1970-72. **Career:** Warner Bros Records, rec artist, writer, record producer; songwriter Gratitude Sky 1976-; drummer various groups; pianist various rec artists albums; Perfection Light Productions, pres 1976-. **Honors/Awds:** Hon Citizen Awd Atlanta 1979; Hon Shelby Co Commr Shelby Co TN 1980; Hon Citizen New Orleans 1980; Outstanding Black Contemporary Artist Awd Bay Area Music Awds San Francisco 1982; numerous albums Atlantic Records; 1986 Grammy Awd Best R&B Song "Freeway of Love" Aretha Franklin; 1986 Producer of the Year Billboard Magazine; spokesperson for "The Peace Run" 1987 (27,000 mile intl relay run for peace); Billboard Magazine, Producer of the Year, 1992. **Business Addr:** 1925-G Francisco Blvd, San Rafael, CA 94901.

WALDEN, ROBERT EDISON
Educator, psychiatrist. **Personal:** Born Apr 5, 1920, Boston, MA; son of Mary E James Walden and Charles W Walden; married Ethel Lee Bazar, Jun 24, 1953; children: Kenneth E, Roberta E Miller, Robert E Jr, Mark E, Mary E Walden Mitchell. **Educ:** Lincoln Univ Chester Cty, PA, AB 1942; Meharry Medical Coll, MD 1945. **Career:** Lakin St Hosp Lakin, WV, supt 1962-65; Oakland County CMHS Bd, psych dir 1965-68; Medical Coll of OH, assoc prof psych 1968-88; Medical Coll of OH, prof clinical psych 1988-90; prof emeritus 1990-; private practice. **Orgs:** Med dir, Cordelia Martin Health Cntr Toledo, OH 1969-72, Comm Hlth & Educ & Screen Prog 1972-76; psych dir, Adult Psych Hosp MCOH 1977-88; med dir Taft State Hosp Taft, OK 1950-53; bd mem, Comm Plann Cncl NWO 1969-72; sec, treas, prog chmn, mem of cncl, 1972-95; OH Psychiatric Assn 1969-94; president, Ohio Psychiatric Assn Educ & Research Foundation, 1990-92; chairperson, Ethics Committee Ohio Psychiatric Assn, 1985-92; president, Northwest Ohio Psychiatric Society, 1972-73; pres, OH Psychiatric Assn, 1992-93. **Honors/Awds:** Diplomate, Amer Bd Psychiatry & Neurology 1962-; life fellow, Amer Psychiatric Assn; honoree, Dist Serv Award, OH Psychiatric Assn, 1976, 1981, 1989. **Military Serv:** AUS, USAFR, USAR, Colonel; Army Achievement; Good Conduct; Victory. **Business Addr:** Professor Emeritus, Medical College of OH, 3000 Arlington Ave, Toledo, OH 43699.

WALDON, ALTON RONALD, JR.
State senator. **Personal:** Born Dec 21, 1936, Lakeland, FL; son of Rupert Juanita Wallace and Alton R Waldon, Sr; married Barbara, Jun 3, 1961; children: Alton III, Dana, Ian. **Educ:** John Jay Coll, BS 1968; NY Law Sch, JD 1973. **Career:** New York City Housing Auth Police Dept, capt 1962-75; NY State Div of Human Rights, dep commr 1975-81; County Service Grp NYS OMRDD, counsel 1981-83; New York State Assembly, assemblyman 33rd dist. 1983-86; US House of Representatives, congressman 1986-87; NY State Investigation Commn, commissioner 1987-90; New York State Senate, senator, 10th S D, 1991-. **Orgs:** Mem United Black Men of Queens, K of C, Amer Bar Assn, NAACP, Alumni Assn NY Law Sch, Macon B Allen Bar Assoc; board of directors USO Greater NY. **Honors/Awds:** NY Law Sch, Thurgood Marshall Fellowship. **Military Serv:** US Army, specialist 4th class, 1956-59. **Home Addr:** 115-103 222nd St, Cambria Heights, NY 11411.

WALDON, LORI ANNETTE
Television news producer. **Personal:** Born Aug 4, 1961, Berkeley, CA; daughter of Bess Davis Waldon and Donald Waldon; married Ted DeAdwyler Jr, May 20, 1989. **Educ:** University of Southern California, Los Angeles, CA, BA, 1983; Northwestern University, Evanston, IL, Master's Degree, 1984. **Career:** WMBD-TV, Peoria, IL, television news reporter, 1984-85; WALA-TV, Mobile, AL, television news reporter, 1985-86; WPCQ-TV, Charlotte, NC, television news reporter, 1986-87; WSOC-FM, Charlotte, NC, morning show producer, 1988-89; KOFY-TV, San Francisco, CA, special projects producer, 1989-; KPIX-TV, San Francisco, CA, news writer, freelance, currently. **Orgs:** Member, Charlotte Association of Black Journalists, 1986-89; member, Bay Area Association of Black Journalists, 1989-; member, National Association of Black Journalists, 1988-; member, National Academy of Television Arts & Sciences, 1989-; member, Alpha Kappa Alpha Sorority, Inc, 1980-. **Honors/Awds:** Best Editing Award, producer, Radio and Television News Director Association, 1990.

WALDROUP, KERWIN
Professional football player. **Personal:** Born Aug 1, 1974, Chicago, IL. **Educ:** Central State (Ohio), attended. **Career:** Detroit Lions, defensive end, 1996-. **Business Addr:** Professional Football Player, Detroit Lions, 1200 Featherstone Rd, Pontiac, MI 48342, (248)335-4131.

WALKER, ALBERT L.
Educational administrator. **Personal:** Born Aug 10, 1945, Memphis, TN; son of Mr & Mrs Roosevelt Walker; married Mary Tipler; children: Brian K, Albert Jr, Kimberly Lynn. **Educ:** Lincoln University, BS, education, 1967; Bradley University, MA, 1970, MA, 1972, MA, 1976; Indiana University, Bloomington, EdD, 1974. **Career:** Peoria Public Schools, elementary school teacher, 1967-70, director, 1970-71, elementary school principal, 1971-76; Lincoln University, associate professor of educ, 1976-79; Missouri State Dept of Elementary & Second Education, asst commissioner of education, 1979-84; North Carolina A&T State University, School of Education, dean, 1984-90; Harris-Stowe State College, vice president, 1990-. **Orgs:** Phi Delta Kappa, 1970; Alpha Phi Alpha; Jefferson City Personnel Board, secretary. **Military Serv:** US Army, NG Capt, 1979-87.

WALKER, ALBERTINA
Gospel singer. **Personal:** Born Aug 28, 1929, Chicago, IL; daughter of Camilla Colemon Walker and Ruben Walker; married Lesley Reynolds, Aug 20, 1967 (divorced); married Reco Brooks, 1991. **Career:** Has recorded over 40 albums, gospel singer, currently; performer, MGM film, Save the Children, 1976. **Orgs:** Bd mem, Operation Push, 1971-79; bd mem, Gospel Music Workshop of America, 1975-; governing board, Recording Arts and Sciences, Chicago Chapter, 1985-; honorary member, Eta Phi Beta, 1986-; life mem, Natl Council of Negro Women; founder, World Famous Caravan Singers, 1952. **Honors/Awds:** Four Gold records; Intl Woman of the Year Award, PUSH, 1975; Black History Month Tribute, University of Mississippi, 1981; 9 Grammy Award nominations, 1981-87; Albertina Walker Scholarship, founded, Central State University, 1983; appearance, 26th Annual Grammy Awards Show, 1986; Albertina Walker Day proclaimed, Mayor Harold Washington, August 29, 1986; Lifetime Achievement Award, Black Gospel Awards, London, England, 1986. **Special Achievements:** Founded Albertina Walker Scholarship Fund, 1989; Bench bearing her name placed in Grant Park, Chicago, 1994; Street Renamed Albertina Walker and the Caravans;. **Home Addr:** 7740 S Essex Ave, Chicago, IL 60649.

WALKER, ALICE MALSENIOR
Author. **Personal:** Born Feb 9, 1944, Eatonton, GA; daughter of Minnie Tallulah Grant Walker and Willie Lee Walker; married Melvyn Rosenman Leventhal, Mar 17, 1967 (divorced 1977); children: Rebecca Grant. **Educ:** Spelman Coll, 1961-63; Sarah Lawrence Coll, BA 1965. **Career:** Voter registration worker, GA; Head Start, MS, staff mem; NYC welfare dept, staff mem; writer-in-res & teacher of blk studies, Jackson State Coll 1968-69, Tougaloo Coll 1970-71; Wellesley Coll & Univ of MS-Boston, lecturer in lit, 1972-73; Univ of CA-Berkeley, distinguished writer in Afro-Amer studies, 1982; Brandeis Univ, Fannie Hurst Prof of Lit, 1982; Wild Trees Press, Navarro CA, co-founder & publisher, 1984-; author: Once, 1968, The Third Life of George Copeland, 1970, In Love and Trouble, 1973, Langston Hughes: American Poet, 1973, Revolutionary Petunias, 1974, Meridian, 1976, I Love Myself When I am Laughing, 1979, Good Night Willi Lee I'll See You In the Morning, 1979, Can't Keep a Good Woman Down, 1981, The Color Purple, 1982, In Search of Our Mothers' Gardens, 1983, To Hell W Dying, 1988, Living by the Word, 1988, The Temple of My Familiar, 1989; Possessing the Secret of Joy, 1992, Warrior Marks, 1993; The Same River Twice: Honoring the Difficult; Anything We Love Can Be Saved, Random, 1997. **Orgs:** Consultant on blk history, Friends of the Children of Mississippi, 1967; bd of trustees, Sarah Lawrence Coll, 1971-73. **Honors/Awds:** Merrill writing fellowship, 1966; McDowell Colony fellowship, 1967 & 1977-78; Natl Endowment for the Arts grant, 1969 & 1977; Radcliffe Inst fellowship, 1971-73; PhD from Russell Sage College, 1972; Lillian Smith Awd, Southern Regional Council, 1973; Natl Book Awd nomination, 1973; Rosenthal Foundatn Awd, Amer Acad & Inst Arts & Letters, 1974; Guggenheim Awd, 1977-78; Natl Endowment for Arts fellowship, 1979; Natl Book Critics Circle Awd nomination, 1982; Amer Book Awd, 1983; Pulitzer Prize, 1983; O Henry Awd, 1986; Honorary PhD, Russell Sage Univ, 1972; Honorary DHL, Univ of Massachusetts, 1983; Sheila Award, Tubman African American Museum, 1997. **Business Addr:** Author, c/o Wendy Weil, Julian Bach, 747 Third Ave, New York, NY 10017, (212)753-2605.

WALKER, ALLENE MARSHA
Health services administrator. **Personal:** Born Mar 2, 1953, Chicago, IL; daughter of Mabel H Thompson Walker and Major Walker. **Educ:** Univ of IL-Chicago, BS 1974; Michael Reese Hosp Sch of Med Tech, MT 1973; Roosevelt Univ, MS 1983. **Career:** Damon Clinical Labs, lab supervisor 1974-85; Med Care HMO, provider rep 1985-89; Med Care HMO, Maywood, IL, dir/prov serv, 1989-91, asst vp prov adm, 1991-92; HMO Illinois, supr Health Services Programs, 1993-. **Orgs:** Operation PUSH Inc, bd member, 1972-; Jacqueline Inc, sec/treas, 1989-. **Honors/Awds:** Bd Certification Amer Soc of Clinical Pathologists 1975. **Home Addr:** 1417 W 73rd Pl, Chicago, IL 60636. **Business Phone:** (312)938-5917.

WALKER, ANGELINA
Government official. **Career:** The White House, executive assistant to the counsel for the vice president, currently. **Business Addr:** Exec Asst to the Council for the Vice Pres, The White House, 1600 Pennsylvania Ave, NW, Washington, DC 20500, (202)456-1414.

WALKER, ANN
Government official. **Career:** The White House, special assistant to the president, currently. **Business Addr:** Special Assistant to the President, The White House, 1600 Pennsylvania Ave, Washington, DC 20500, (202)456-7845.

WALKER, ANN B.
Appointed government official, manager. **Personal:** Born Nov 1, 1923, Columbus, OH; married Linwood Philip; children: Phillip, Julialyn, Amelia, Keith. **Educ:** Prairie View Coll, 1942; Northwestern Coll, post-grad 1944; Geo Wms Coll, BS 1944. **Career:** Comm Serv Adminstrn Wash DC, dir media/pub liason; WCMH-TV Outlet & Broadcasting Columbus OH, dir/producer 1976-80; WLWC-TV Avco Broadcasting ColumbusOH, dir community servs 1968-76; WVKO Radio Skyway Broadcasting Columbus, asst news dir 1963-67; OH Sentienel Columbus, womans editor 1959-63; Chicago SPark YWCA Chicago, girl reserve sec 1944. **Orgs:** Reg vice pres Women in Communications 1968-; natl bd of dir Women in Communications 1974-76; reg dir Nat Assn Black Journalists 1976-78; pres Columbus Leadership Prog 1976-79; mem Columbus Consumer Affairs Commn; mem OH Bur Employ Servs Adv Council 1971-. **Honors/Awds:** Career Woman of Yr Columbus OH 1971; Talaria Award Am Women in Radio/TV 1975; Emmy Nat Acad Radio-TV Artists 1976; Gov's Award State of OH 1976; Myrtle Wreath/Comm Serv Hadassah 1977; OH Women's Hall of Fame 1978.

WALKER, ANNIE MAE
Educator. **Personal:** Born Jan 7, 1913, Daytona Beach, FL; married William H Walker; children: Garland James. **Educ:** Bethune-Cookman Coll, BS Elem Educ 1944; Bank St Coll of Edn, MS (equiv) 1946; Edn/Soc Adelphi Univ, MA 1965; East Coast Univ, PhD Anthropology 1970; Yale U, Danforth Fellow 1971. **Career:** State Univ of NY Stony Brook, prof of educ 1946-; New York City Plainedge & Plainview Public Schools, taught in elementary schools; dir pre-school progs; Amityville NY, founded & dir ''After School Tutorial Prgm''; ''in Service courses in Black Studies for Teachers in LI school dist'', conducted; Afri-Amer & Native Amer Ind History, spec; Afri Hist & Culture & Seminole Hist, prof lecturer; conduct classes in Black Comm called ''Heightened Black Awareness'' for youths 8 to 13. **Honors/Awds:** Outstndg ldrshp award 1973; outstndg comm serv Martin L King Award 1970; Danforth Found post-Doc res Black Studies Award 1970; Human Relations Award Natl Conf Chris & Jews 1969; Nat Sojourner Truth Award for serv in comm 1964; most promising tchr Bethune Cookman Coll Award 1944. **Business Addr:** State Univ of NY, Stony Brook, NY 11794.

WALKER, ANTOINE DEVON
Professional basketball player. **Personal:** Born Aug 12, 1976, Chicago, IL; children: Crystal. **Educ:** Kentucky. **Career:** Boston Celtics, forward, 1996-. **Honors/Awds:** NBA, All Rookie Team, 1997. **Special Achievements:** NBA Draft, First round pick, #6, 1996; NCAA-Division I, Championship, 1996. **Business Addr:** Professional Basketball Player, Boston Celtics, 151 Merrimac St, 5th Fl, Boston, MA 02114, (617)523-6050.

WALKER, ARMAN KENNIS
Banker. **Personal:** Born Oct 15, 1957, Minneapolis, MN; son of Anna M Gallo and Simon W Walker; divorced. **Educ:** University of California, Berkeley, BA, economics, 1979. **Career:** Wells Fargo Bank, commercial banking officer, 1979-83; Marine Midland Bank, asst vice pres, 1983-85; Sanwa Bank California, vice pres, senior manager, 1985-92; Pine Cobble Partners, managing general partner, 1990-. **Orgs:** Watts Heath Foundation, board of directors, 1992-; LA's Young Black Professionals, co-chairperson, 1989-; LA Urban Bankers Association; Church of Christian Fellowship, bd of trustees, treasurer, 1992-. **Honors/Awds:** University of California, Berkley, honor student, 1975-79, Omicron Epislon Delta, 1979; Dollars & Sense Magazine, One of America's Best & Brightest, 1988; City Attorney, Los Angeles, Commendation, 1992. **Special Achievements:** Banking & Finance Conference, co-chair, 1992; California Money Managers Networking Forum, co-chair, 1992; African-American Women of Distinction Mixer, co-chair, 1993. **Business Addr:** Managing General Partner, Pine Cobble Partners, 1533 E Edgecomb St, Covina, CA 91724, (213)934-2723.

WALKER, BETTY STEVENS
Attorney. **Personal:** Born Feb 3, 1944, New York, NY; daughter of Anne Wood; married Paul T Walker, Jun 17, 1965; children: Camarf, Tarik, Kumi. **Educ:** Spelman Coll Atlanta, BA 1964; Harvard Law School, JD 1967. **Career:** Harvard Business School, research asst 1966; Wake Opportunities Inc Raleigh, coordinator of youth program 1968; Shaw Univ, curriculum consultant 1968, asst prof political science 1968-70; So Railway Co Washington, DC, atty 1974-77; Farmers Home Admin US Dept of Agr, asst to the admin 1977-; attorney, currently. **Orgs:** Mem DC Court of Appeals; US Dist Court for DC; US Court of Appeals for DC District; Supreme Court of the United States of America; DC Bar Assn; Washington Bar Assn; Natl Bar Assn; Spelman Coll & Harvard Law Alumni Assns; mem Bethel AME Church, Baltimore; steward, Bethel AME Church, 1989. **Honors/Awds:** John Hay Whitney (2) 1964; Aaron Norman Fellowships 1964; Harvard Law School 1964; 1st Black woman to Ames Competition 2 consecutive semesters at Harvard Law; Outstanding Leadership Award, National Assn for Equal Opportunity, 1990. **Business Addr:** 701 Pennsylvania Ave, NW, Suite 1118, Washington, DC 20004, (202)842-4664.

WALKER, BRACEY WORDELL
Professional football player. **Personal:** Born Oct 28, 1970, Spring Lake, NC. **Educ:** Univ of North Carolina. **Career:** Kansas City Chiefs, defensive back, 1994; Cincinnati Bengals, 1994-96; Miami Dolphins, 1997-. **Business Addr:** Professional Football Player, Miami Dolphins, 2269 NW 199th St, Miami, FL 33056, (305)620-5000.

WALKER, CARL, JR.
Judge. **Personal:** Born May 13, 1924, Marlin, TX; son of Christina Watson (deceased) and Carl Walker (deceased); married Janice Martin Walker, Dec 28, 1976. **Educ:** Texas State Univ, BA 1950, MA 1952, LLB 1955. **Career:** US Dept of Justice, exec asst US atty 1968; So Dist TX, asst US Atty 1961; Dent King Walker & Wickliff, atty 1956-61; US Atty 1980-81; l85th district court, judge, currently. **Orgs:** Mem Houston Lawyers Assn; Houston Bar Assn; TX Bar Assn; NBA; Fed Bar Assn; ABA; Kappa Alpha Psi; past pres Houston Bus & Professional Men's Clb 1971; past chmn bd Harris Comm Action Assn; chmn bd of mgrs YMCA S Cen Br Houston; pres chmn bd TX So Univ Ex Student's Assn 1970; mem bd dir USO, ARC. **Honors/Awds:** Recip US Selective Serv System Srvc Awd with Bronze Medl 1974; cert of Merit Kappa Alpha Psi 1962; many local serv awards. **Military Serv:** US Army Air Force, Sgt, 1943-46. **Business Addr:** Judge, 185th District Court, 301 San Jacinto, Room 424, Houston, TX 77002.

WALKER, CAROLYN
State representative. **Personal:** Born in Yuma, AZ. **Career:** Arizona House of Representatives, Phoenix AZ, state representative, 1983-86; state senator, district 23, 1986-. **Business Addr:** House of Representatives, State of Arizona, State House, Phoenix, AZ 85007.

WALKER, CHARLES
Educator, actor. **Personal:** Born Jan 21, 1945, Chicago, IL; son of Robbie Edith Hutchinson Walker and Charles Walker; married Lillian Beatrice Lusk Walker, Feb 7, 1976; children: Leah Cher Walker, Chasen Lloyd Walker. **Educ:** Career Academy School of Broadcasting, Milwaukee, WI, broadcasting degree, 1967; Wilson City College, Chicago, IL, 1967; California State Univ, Los Angeles, CA, BA, 1980, MA, 1982. **Career:**

WVOL-Radio, Nashville, TN, radio news reporter, WXYZ-TV, Detroit, MI, television news reporter, 1967-68; professional actor in Los Angeles, CA, working in television, film and commercials, 1968—; Los Angeles Unified School District, Los Angeles, CA, substitute teacher for day and evening classes, 1980—; California State University, Los Angeles, CA, instructor in speech communication, 1980-81; City of Los Angeles, Los Angeles, CA, lecturer for work experience program, 1981-83; Hollywood High School, Los Angeles, CA, teacher, 1984; Los Angeles Southwest College, Los Angeles, CA, instructor in public speaking, 1984—; California State University, Dominguez Hills, CA, instructor in fundamentals of speech, acting, and intercultural communication, 1984—. **Orgs:** NAACP; Screen Actor's Guild; American Federation of Television and Radio Artists; Mt Zion Missionary Baptist Church. **Business Addr:** California State University—Dominguez Hills, Speech/Theatre Department, 1000 East Victoria St, Carson, CA 90747.

WALKER, CHARLES A.
University chancellor. **Career:** University of Arkansas, Pine Bluff AR, chancellor, currently. **Business Addr:** Chancellor, University of Arkansas, PO Box 4008, Pine Bluff, AR 71601.

WALKER, CHARLES DOUGLAS
Attorney (retired). **Personal:** Born Jan 10, 1915, Cleveland, OH; son of Lydia Ruth Coleman Jackson (deceased) and Charles Douglas Walker (deceased); married Jun 4, 1942 (widowed). **Educ:** Ball State, AB 1936, MA 1945; IN Univ, JD 1953; Attended, George Washington Univ 1955, OH State Univ 1956. **Career:** Crispus Attucks HS, teacher dept head 1936-73; IN State Dept of Public Instruction, dir adult educ 1973-77; Marion Co Municipal Courts, public defender 1981-85; private practice, atty. **Orgs:** Adv council IN Vocational Ed 1965-83; bd dir All Souls Unitarian Church 1986-; nom comm OH Valley Unitarian Univ Assn. **Honors/Awds:** Pi Gamma Mu Natl Soc Sci Hon; Phi Delta Phi Law Hon. **Military Serv:** AUSAC, 2nd lieutenant, 38 months.

WALKER, CHARLES E.
Clergyman. **Personal:** Born Jun 28, 1935, Chicago, IL; son of Mercedes Pierre Walker and Charles Walker; married Barbara Wicks Walker, Sep 16, 1989; children: Pierre, Jason. **Educ:** DePaul Univ, BM 1957, MM 1959; Colgate Rochester Div Sch, BD 1970. **Career:** 19th St Bapt Ch, pastor, currently; Requiem for Brother Martin, composer Jazz Mass & Dr Watts; Charles Walker Chorale, dir. **Orgs:** Mem Am Assn Univ Profs; Am Symphony Orchestra League; Liberian Symph Orchest 1977; Federation Musicians; Theol Commn Nat Bapt Conv schlrshp commn; exec bd Hampton Inst Ministers Conf; chairman, Foreign Mission Bd Nat Bapt Conv, National Baptist Convention, USA; natl vice pres E Reg Operation PUSH pres Philadelphia branch chairman. **Business Addr:** Pastor, 19th Street Baptist Church, 1253 S 19th St, Philadelphia, PA 19146.

WALKER, CHARLES EALY, JR.
Educator, attorney. **Personal:** Born May 1, 1951, Anchorage, AK; son of Marguerite Lee Walker and Lt Col Charles E Walker Sr,; married Dorothy Sanders, Sep 17, 1983; children: Sydney, Courtney. **Educ:** University of California Santa Barbara, BA (magna cum laude), 1973; London School of Economics, 1977; Boston College Law School, JD, 1978. **Career:** Oxnard Union High School District, teacher, 1974-75; U.S. Department of Agriculture Office of the General Counsel, attorney, 1978-79; Boston Superior Court, law clerk, 1979-80; Suffolk University Law School Council on Legal Education Opportunity, teaching fellow, 1980-82, 1987-89; University of Massachusetts, instructor, 1980-82; Massachusetts Court of Appeals, law clerk, 1980-81; Commonwealth of Massachusetts, assistant attorney general, 1981-87; New England School of Law, assistant professor, 1987-; Executive of Elder Affairs, general counsel, currently; Massachusetts Commission Against Discrimination, chmn. **Orgs:** Massachusetts Bar Association Committee for Admissions, chair; Roxbury Defenders Committee Inc, acting president, 1982-; Boston College Law School Black Alumni Network, president co-founder, 1981-; Cambridge Economic Opportunity Commission, board of directors, 1982-86; Massachusetts Black Lawyers Association Executive Board, president, 1993-95; NAACP National Urban League, 1985-; Good Shepherd Church of God in Christ Trustee Board, chairman, 1985-; Wheelock College Family Theatre, board of directors; Massachusetts Law Review, editorial board, 1990-. **Honors/Awds:** Project Commitment Inc, Distinguished Service Award, 1988; New England School of Law, Charles Hamilton Houston Distinguished Service Award, 1990; Governor of Massachusetts, Excellence in Legal Education Citation; Boston College Law School, William Kenneally Alumnus of Year, 1995. **Special Achievements:** Author, "Liquor Control Act: Alcoholic Beverages Control Commission," 1986, "Violation of Injunctions: Criminal and Civil Contempt," MBA - Restraining Orders and Injunctions, pages 1-15; Massachusetts Bar Association speaker, "Obedience is Better than Sacrifice," 1988; "The History and Impact of Black Lawyers in Massachusetts," Massachusetts Supreme Judicial Work, Historical Law Society Law Journal. **Home Addr:** 6 Marie Ave, Sharon, MA 02067. **Business Phone:** (617)727-3990.

WALKER, CHARLES H.
Attorney. **Personal:** Born Nov 11, 1951, Columbus, OH; son of Juanita Webb Walker and Watson H Walker; married Amanda T Herndon; children: Katrina Della, Allison Lyles, Carlton Wesley. **Educ:** Tufts Univ, BA (magna cum laude), 1969-73; Emory Univ School of Law, JD, 1973-76. **Career:** Bricker & Eckler, assoc, 1976-81, partner, 1982-. **Orgs:** Planned Parenthood of Central, OH, 1984; past pres & mem, Columbus Acad Alumni Assn, 1979-83; mem, Columbus Acad Alumni Assn, 1982-83, 1993-95; chmn, Tufts Univ Alumni Admissions Program, Central, OH, 1986-; bd mem, Battelle Youth Scholars Program, 1988-; mem, City of Columbus Sports Arena Commn, 1989, Ohio State Bar Assn, Professional and Legal Ethics Comm, 1988-; Columbus Light Opera, 1990-94; Columbus Neighborhood Housing Services, 1990-94; mem & president, I-670 Corridor Sydogent Corp., 1992-; mem & vice pres, Life Care Alliance, 1992-; executive director, Thomas D Lambros Dispute Management Ctr, LLC, 1996-. **Business Addr:** Attorney, Bricker & Eckler, 100 S Third St, Columbus, OH 43215.

WALKER, CHARLES W.
State senator. **Career:** The Walker Group, founder/president; Georgia Senate, state senator, currently; BL's Restaurant & Dining, owner. **Orgs:** Georgia Association of Human Relations Commission, chairman; Sickle Cell Advisory Board; CSRA Classic Football Game, founder & sponsor; Senate Budget Conference; State Commission on Mental Health, Mental Restoration and Substance Abuse Svc Delivery; Governor's Commission on Health Care Reform; Southern Conference of Legislators; National Conference of State Legislature; Alpha Phi Alpha Fraternity Inc. **Honors/Awds:** Legislator of the Year; Public Servant of the Year. **Special Achievements:** Elected Georgia State Senate's first African-American Senate Majority Leader on November 13, 1996. **Business Addr:** State Senator, Georgia Senate, 18 Capitol Sq, Rm 325, Atlanta, GA 30334, (404)656-5040.

WALKER, CHESTER
Professional basketball player (retired). **Personal:** Born Feb 22, 1940, Benton Harbor, MI. **Educ:** Bradley Univ, Peoria, IL, attended. **Career:** Forward: Syracuse Nationals, 1962-63, Philadelphia 76ers, 1963-69, Chicago Bulls, 1969-73. **Honors/Awds:** NBA All-Star Team, 1964, 1966, 1967, 1970, 1971, 1973; NBA All-Rookie Team, 1963.

WALKER, CHRIS
Vocalist. **Career:** Former music director for Regina Belle; First Time, Pendulum Records, 1992; solo artist, currently. **Special Achievements:** Recorded duet, "Someday," with Lisa Fischer, on his debut album, 1992. **Business Phone:** (212)484-7200.

WALKER, CORA T.
Attorney. **Personal:** Born Jun 20, 1926, Charlotte, NC; daughter of Benetta Jones Walker (deceased) and William H Walker (deceased); married Lawrence R Bailey Sr, Feb 27, 1948 (divorced); children: Lawrence R Jr, Dr Bruce E. **Educ:** St John's U, BS 1945, St John's U Law School, LLB/JD 1946; St John's Law Honorary Doctorate, 1992. **Career:** Atty, Priv Pract 1947-54; Doles Sandifer & Walker, 1954-58; Doles & Walker, 1958-60; priv pract 1960-; Walker & Bailey, partner 1975-. **Orgs:** Mem numerous offcs, coms, numerous professional civic political orgns; NY State Beauty Culturists Assn 1969; Bermuda Benevolent Assn 1968; Mid-Eastern Coop Inc 1969; "21" Brands Inc 1968; bd of gov Natl Bar Assoc 1977-; delegate, NYS House of Delegate, currently; treasurer, National Bar Assn, Tres Comm Law Sec, currently. **Honors/Awds:** Award Women for Achievement Inc; citation Mayor's Vol Lawyers Adv Com 1957; Hall of Fame Alumni Award James Monroe HS 1967; comm leader Congressman Adam Clayton Powell; award Nat Beauty Culturists' League Inc 1969; award Negro Women Inc; NY Club Professnl Award 1969; achvmnt award IBPOE & W Grand Temple 1967; awards Hood Memorial AME Ch 1969; Actors' Fund 1968; Woman of Yr Delta Mu Zeta Chap Zeta Phi Beta Sor Inc 1971; Malcolm X Award 1969; Only Black Mother & Son Law Firm, Walker & Bailey; founder Harlem River & Consumers Coop Inc; Recipient of Natl Bar Assoc Gertrude Rush 1986; Recipient of Judicial Friends Jane M Bolin Awd 1986; NBA Wiley Branton Award, 1994. **Business Addr:** Partner, Walker & Bailey, 270 Lenox Ave, New York, NY 10027.

WALKER, CRAIG J.
Investment banker. **Personal:** Born Aug 16, 1962, Chicago, IL; son of Joanne Bell Walker and Phillip R Walker; married Nancy Ann Rybak, Aug 23, 1986; children: Craig J Walker II. **Educ:** Univ of IL, Chicago, BS Econ, 1986. **Career:** Shatkin Securities, Chicago Options Exchange, IL, floor runner, broker's asst, 1986; Daniels & Bell Inc, Chicago, IL, vice pres, 1986-89; WR Lazard & Co, Kansas City, MO, vice pres, 1989-. **Honors/Awds:** Featured in Black Enterprise, May 1988, and Wall Street Journal, Feb 1989.

WALKER, CYNTHIA BUSH
Educator. **Personal:** Born Dec 8, 1956, Fort Benning, GA; daughter of Rev & Mrs Otis Bush; married Robert B Walker Jr, Jul 3, 87 ; children: Christa S Walker. **Educ:** Morehead State Univ, BA 1977, MHE 1978. **Career:** KY Metroversity, counselor, 1978-80; Jefferson Comm Coll, counselor, professor, 1980-. **Orgs:** KY Association of Coll and School Admissions Counselors 1981-; Educ Opportunity Center Adv Bd 1983-; president, Kentucky Association of Blacks in Higher Education; Cultural Diversity Task Force, 1990-; National Association of Student Development. **Business Addr:** Professor of Counseling, Jefferson Community Coll/SW Campus, 1000 Community College Dr, Louisville, KY 40272.

WALKER, DARNELL ROBERT
Professional football player. **Personal:** Born Jan 17, 1970, St Louis, MO; married D'Elbie; children: Darnell Robert Jr. **Educ:** University of Oklahoma, attended. **Career:** Atlanta Falcons, defensive back, 1993-96; San Francisco 49ers, 1997-. **Business Addr:** Professional Football Player, San Francisco 49ers, 4949 Centennial Blvd, Santa Clara, CA 95054, (415)562-4949.

WALKER, DARRELL
Professional basketball coach. **Personal:** Born Mar 9, 1961, Chicago, IL. **Educ:** Univ of Arkansas. **Career:** New York Knicks, 1984-86, Denver Nuggets, 1986-87; Washington Bullets, 1988-91; Detroit Pistons, 1991-92; Chicago Bulls, 1993; NBA Players Association, field rep, 1993-95; Toronto Raptors, asst coach, 1995-96, head coach, 1996-. **Honors/Awds:** NBA's All-Rookie team. **Special Achievements:** NBA Draft, First round pick, #12, 1983. **Business Addr:** Head Coach, Toronto Raptors, 150 York St, Ste 110, Toronto, ON, Canada M5H 3S5, (416)214-2255.

WALKER, DENARD
Professional football player. **Personal:** Born Aug 9, 1973, Garland, TX. **Educ:** Louisiana State Univ, attended. **Career:** Tennessee Oilers, defensive back, 1997-. **Business Addr:** Professional Football Player, Tennessee Oilers, c/o Baptist Sports Park, 7640 H 70-5, Nashville, TN 37221.

WALKER, DERRICK NORVAL
Professional football player. **Personal:** Born Jun 23, 1967, Glenwood, IL; married Rhonda. **Educ:** Univ of Michigan, education major. **Career:** San Diego Chargers, tight end, 1990-93; Kansas City Chiefs, tight end, 1994-. **Honors/Awds:** All-American honorable mention, Sporting News; all Big-Ten Conference first team. **Business Addr:** Professional Football Player, Kansas City Chiefs, One Arrowhead Dr, Kansas City, MO 64129, (816)924-9300.

WALKER, DOROTHEA BERNICE
Health services administrator (retired). **Personal:** Born Jan 10, 1906, Wiggins, MS; daughter of Verna Traylor Davis (deceased) and Wade Davis; married Ralph Walker, Jun 29, 1946. **Educ:** Western Reserve University, Cleveland, OH, BS, 1949. **Career:** City Health Department, Cleveland, OH, supervisor, 1936-70; Prospect Nursing Home, Cleveland, OH, director, 1970-71. **Orgs:** National president, 1970-74, national executive board member, 1970-, Eta Phi Beta Sorority, Inc; financial secretary, Ohio State & Cleveland Chapter, National Council of Negro Women, 1964-; treasurer, National Association of Negro Business & Professional Women, 1974-; financial secretary and treasurer, East Wood Homeowners Assn, Inc; senior citizens coordinator, Nu Theta Chapter, Zeta Phi Beta Sorority; organizer of two golf clubs, 1984-89; Congregational Church. **Honors/Awds:** Numerous awards for service and recognition, 1970-90; "The Courage to Change," Course in Nursing, Metro General Hospital; Received Plaque from the President and a Proclamation from Congressman Stokes; Mayor of Warrensville, Dorothea Walker Day, June 18; Outstanding Service Award, National Association of Business & Professional Women; Achievement Award for Outstanding Service, Zeta Phi Beta Sorority, 1989; Professional Woman of the Week, WJMO Radio; Community Service Award, National Council of Negro Women; Outstanding Service, Achievement and Organizational Merit, Female Golfers of Cleveland, 1989. **Special Achievements:** Attended Mt Union College Conservatoire, music; played the violin in the college orchestra; listed in the archives of Nursing History at Metro-General Hospital, Cleveland; picture was inducted into The Harriet Tubman Museum, exhibited along the south wall. **Home Addr:** 19101 Mayfair Lane, Warrensville Heights, OH 44128.

WALKER, DOUGLAS F.
Editor. **Personal:** Born Dec 28, 1937, Detroit, MI; married Mattie Ruth. **Educ:** LaSalle, BA; Wayne State U. **Career:** The Transition Newspaper, editor Model Neighborhood Health Prog; Library of Cong, Braille transcriber; Sound Off Newspaper, editor; author numerous articles for various publications. **Orgs:** Mem New Bethel Bapt Ch; mem Mayor's Com for Human Resources. **Honors/Awds:** Recip Outstndg Newsp Publ of Year 1973; achievmnt award Lion's 1970; Citizen of Year Medal 1971.

WALKER, EDWIN L.
State government official. **Personal:** Born Aug 29, 1956, Richmond, VA; son of Mary Ella Christopher Walker and Thomas Job Walker; married Marcia Kay Alexander Walker, Jan 8,

1977; children: Jennifer Elaine. **Educ:** Hampton University, Hampton, VA, BA (summa cum laude), 1978; University of Missouri-Columbia School of Law, JD, 1983. **Career:** The Daily Press, Inc, Newport News, VA, district manager, 1978-80; Missouri Department of Social Services, Jefferson City, MO, aging program specialist, 1984-85, management analyst specialist, 1985-87, executive assistant to the director, 1987-88, principal assistant to the director, 1988, director, division of aging, 1988-. **Orgs:** Member, Columbia Human Rights Commission, 1986; member, Missouri Board of Nursing Home Administrators, 1988; executive advisory committee member, National Leadership Institute on Aging, 1990; advisory committee member, National Resource Center on Minority Aging Populations, 1990; national advisory committee member, HealthWays Foundation, 1990. **Business Addr:** Director, Missouri Division of Aging, PO Box 1337, Jefferson City, MO 65102.

WALKER, ERNEST L.
Electrical engineer, educator. **Personal:** Born Feb 12, 1941, Montrose, MS; son of Mae Ruth Wheaton Walker and Edwin Lampkin Walker; married Vivian Lelia Huey Walker, Aug 16, 1960. **Educ:** Ind Inst of Technology, BSEE 1967; Syracuse Univ, MSEE 1973; NC State Univ, PhD 1982. **Career:** IBM Corp, sr assoc eng 1969-72, staff engr 1973-82, adv engr, 1985-90; NC Central Univ, lecturer beginning 1985; WV State Univ, Dept of Electrical & Computer Engineering, asst prof, 1990-. **Orgs:** Sr mem IEEE; mem SIAM, OSA, AAAS; Kappa Alpha Psi Fraternity. **Honors/Awds:** 5 issued patents IBM Corp 1969-80; published papers; mem NY Acad of Sci 1984. **Military Serv:** AUS e-4, 1960-63. **Business Addr:** Assistant Professor, Department of Electrical and Computer Engineering, West Virginia university, A3 Greystone Circle, Morgantown, WV 26503.

WALKER, ERNESTEIN
Educator. **Personal:** Born May 26, 1926, McDonough, GA; married Solomon. **Educ:** Spelman Coll, AB 1949; Atlanta U, MA 1953; Univ Edinburgh, 1958; Western Res U, PhD 1964. **Career:** Morgan State U, prof hist 1965-; SC State Coll, instr prof 1956-65; Fort Valley State Coll, instr 1955-56; KY State U, 1954-55. **Orgs:** Mem Am Hist Assn; Assn Study Afro Life & Hist; So Hist Assn; medieval acad pres Baltimore Chap Nat Alumnae Assn, Spelman Coll Publ, ''Disestablishment of the Ch of Ireland'', Jour Social Sci 1960; ''Age of Metternick a study in nonmenclature'' exploration educ 1962; ''the influence of Lord Liverpool 1815-1827'' Jour Higher Educ 1967; ''The Struggle for Parliamentary Reform'' 1977; ''The Black Woman'' The Black Am Ref Book 1976. **Business Addr:** Morgan State Univ, Baltimore, MD 21239.

WALKER, ETHEL PITTS
Educator. **Personal:** Born Feb 4, 1943, Tulsa, OK; daughter of Wilhelmina Teresa Miller and Opie Donnell Pitts; married Phillip E Walker, Aug 6, 1977; children: Travis Donnell. **Educ:** Lincoln Univ MO, BS Ed 1964; Univ of CO, MA Speech & Drama 1965; Univ of MO Columbia, PhD Theatre 1975. **Career:** Southern Univ Baton Rouge LA, instr 1965-68; Lincoln Univ Jefferson City MO, asst prof 1968-77; Univ of IL Urbana, asst prof 1977-79; Laney Coll Oakland CA, instr 1979-80; African Amer Drama Co San Francisco, exec dir 1980-; Univ of CA Berkeley, asst prof 1988; Wayne State Univ, visiting asst prof 1988-89; San Jose State University, San Jose, CA, professor, theatre arts dept, 1989-. **Orgs:** Mem 1984-85, chmn 1985-Amer Theatre Assoc, Natl Assoc of Dramatic & Speech Arts, Theta Alpha Phi Dramatic Frat, Speech Commun of Amer, Zeta Phi Beta; Third Baptist Church (San Fransisco), parents alliance, public relations dir; Children's Performance Center, pres of advisory council; Black Theatre Network, past pres 1985-88; member, Association for Theatre in Higher Education, pres, California Educational Theatre Association. **Honors/Awds:** Ira Aldridge Scholarship 1963; Outstanding Ed 1974; Outstanding Instr Sr Class Lincoln Univ 1977; Best Actress Awd Lincoln Univ Stagecrafters 1963, Mother of the Year, Representative Teola Hunter of Michigan, 1989; ''The Amer Negro Theatre'' Black Amers in the Theatre; study, toured with Phelps/Stokes West African Heritage Seminar 1975; article ''The Diction in Ed Bullins'' In New Eng Winter, Encore 1977; Krigwa Players: A Theatre For, By, and About Black People in Theatre Journal 1989; director, When the Jumbie Bird Calls at Bonstelle Theatre, Detroit MI 1989; director, To Be Young, Gifted And Black, 1991; ''Incorporating African-American Theatre Into A Basic Theatre Course,'' Theatre Topic, Sept 1992; honorary lifetime membership, Black Theatre Network. **Special Achievements:** Directed ''Medea,'' SJSU, 1996; editor, New/Lost Plays by Ed Bullins. **Business Addr:** Professor, San Jose State University, One Washington Square, San Jose, CA 95192-0098.

WALKER, EUGENE HENRY
Physician (retired). **Personal:** Born Sep 29, 1925, Morristown, TN; son of Mabel Walker and Eugene Walker; married Dorothy Ransburg; children: Eugene C, Paula J, Erica J. **Educ:** UCLA, BA 1950; Howard Univ Coll of Med, MD 1954; Univ of MN, Med Fellow 1955-58. **Career:** Private practice, physician, retired, 1991; Home Health Service, medical director, currently. **Orgs:** Diplomat Amer Bd Intl Med; fellow Amer Coll Chest Physicians; assoc fellow Amer Coll Physicians; mem Natl Medical Assn, Kappa Alpha Psi Fraternity. **Military Serv:** USAF sgt 1943-46. **Business Addr:** Physician, 1815 Virginia Rd, Los Angeles, CA 90019.

WALKER, EUGENE KEVIN
Hospitality executive. **Personal:** Born Aug 12, 1951, St Louis, MO; son of Nadine Walker and Willie Walker; divorced; children: Kristen V. **Educ:** Cornell University, BS, 1975. **Career:** New York Hilton Hotel, convention service manager, 1975-76, account executive, 1976-78, superintendent of front service, 1978-79; Hilton Hotel of Phildelphia, executive assistant manager, 1979-81; Washington Hilton & Tower, executive assistant manager, 1981-85; Logan Airport Hilton, resident manager, 1985-91; Greater Boston Convention & Visitors Bureau, director of convention & customer service, 1991-. **Orgs:** Coalition of Black Meeting Planners, 1991-; Academy of Travel & Tourism, chair of internship committee, 1992-; Cornell Society of Hotelmen, 1975-; Cornell Club, 1975-; Assn of Convention Operations Managers, chairman. **Honors/Awds:** Certified Meeting Professional; Privot Industry Council, Achiever Award. **Home Addr:** 20 Summer St, Apt N307, Malden, MA 02148, (617)321-5696. **Business Addr:** Director of Convention & Customer Service, Greater Boston Convention & Visitors Bureau, 20 Copley Pl, Ste 105, Boston, MA 02116-6501, (617)867-8236.

WALKER, FELIX CARR, JR.
Advertising executive. **Personal:** Born Sep 1, 1949, Memphis, TN; son of Estelle Walker and Felix Walker. **Educ:** Memphis College of Arts, BFA, 1977. **Career:** Felix Way Advertising, president/chief executive officer, currently. **Orgs:** Onyx, president. **Military Serv:** US Navy, BT2, 1969-73; Vietnam Service Award. **Business Addr:** President/Chief Executive Officer, Felix Way Advertising, 937 Peabody Ave, Memphis, TN 38104-6227, (901)529-9987.

WALKER, FRANCES
Pianist, educator. **Personal:** Born Mar 6, 1924, Washington, DC; daughter of Dr George T Walker; married H Chester Slocum (deceased); children: George Jeffrey Slocum. **Educ:** Oberlin Conservatory, BMus 1945; Curtis Inst, 1945-46; Columbia Univ Teachers Coll, MA 1952, Professional diploma 1971. **Career:** Barber Scotia, 1948-49; Tougaloo Coll, 1949-50; Rutgers Univ, 1972-76; Univ of DE, 1968-69; Lincoln Univ, 1968-72; Oberlin Conservatory, prof of pianoforte 1976-. **Orgs:** Pres Pi Kappa Lambda Theta Chap 1983-85. **Honors/Awds:** Achievement Awd Natl Assoc of Negro Musicians 1979, 1985; Lorain Co Women of Achievement Award 1984; Natl Bus & Prof Womens Club, Appreciation Award, 1995. **Business Addr:** Professor of Pianoforte, Oberlin Coll Conserv of Music, Oberlin, OH 44074.

WALKER, FREEMAN, III
Food service industry executive. **Personal:** Born Jul 18, 1965, Roxboro, NC; son of Phyllis Umstead Walker and Freeman Walker Jr; married Kimberle Wathall, Jul 22, 1989. **Educ:** University of Georgia, BA, political science, 1987; North Carolina Central University, MPA, 1991. **Career:** Nations Bank, finance banking intern, 1984-87; International Business Machines, administrative personnel intern, 1988; Orange County Department on Aging, assistant director, 1990; Durham Regional Hospital Corp., media specialist, 1991; Family Health International, assistant data coordinator, 1992; We-Saw Inc, director of administrative services, currently. **Orgs:** Rotary Club of North High Point, 1985-; Omega Psi Phi, 1988-; Alpha Kappa Psi Professional Business Fraternity, 1983-; Durham Companions, board of directors, 1993-. **Home Addr:** 830 Bluestone Rd, Durham, NC 27713, (919)544-0988. **Business Phone:** (919)544-3300.

WALKER, G. EDWARD
Physician. **Personal:** Born Apr 22, 1942, Waynesville, NC; married Patricia; children: Gregory, Michael. **Educ:** BC Central U, BS 1964; Meharry Med Coll, MD 1968. **Career:** Physician, Self-emplyd; SW Comm Hosp; Crawford W Long Hosp; GA Bapt Hosp; Meharry Med Coll, chf res 1971-72. **Orgs:** Mem adv panel Clark Coll Sch Med Tech; Nat Med Assn; GA State Med Assn; Atlanta Med Assn; Med Assn GA; mem Atlanta City Club. **Honors/Awds:** Distgsd serv medal USAF 1974. **Military Serv:** USAF MC maj 1972-74.

WALKER, GARY LAMAR
Professional football player. **Personal:** Born Feb 28, 1973, Royston, GA; children: Gary Jr. **Educ:** Auburn Univ, attended. **Career:** Houston Oilers, defensive tackle, 1995-96; Tennessee Oilers, 1997-. **Business Addr:** Professional Football Player, Tennessee Oilers, c/o Baptist Sports Park, 7640 H 70-5, Nashville, TN 37221.

WALKER, GEORGE EDWARD
Artist. **Personal:** Born May 16, 1940, Memphis, TN; married Delores Prince; children: Genene' Delise, Darren George Edward, Devin George Edward. **Educ:** Memphis State Univ, BFA, MA. **Career:** Freelance designer & artist 1969-71; NAACP (Memphis Branch) artist, 1977-; Graphic Arts Memphis, owner/artist 1978-; Shelby State Comm Coll, artist. **Orgs:** Mem Alpha Phi Alpha 1977. **Honors/Awds:** Designer & Publ ''Our Precious Baby'' (1st complete black baby book) 1971; Pyramid Award Advertising Fedn Memphis 1972 & 1977; Editirial Distinct (design) SD Warren Co 1978. **Military Serv:** AUS 1958-61. **Business Addr:** Artist, Shelby State College, PO Box 40568, Memphis, TN 38106.

WALKER, GEORGE RAYMOND
Educator. **Personal:** Born Oct 13, 1936, Little Rock, AR. **Educ:** San Franc State U, BA 1959; Univ of So CA, MS 1967; Univ of So CA, EdD 1972. **Career:** CA State Univ Dominguez Hills, dean School of Educ 1976-; CA State Univ Pomona, prof of educ 1972-76; US Dependent Schools Spain, dir of curriculum 1967-69; US Dependent Schools Germany, teacher 1962-67; San Francisco City Schools, teacher 1959-62; Compton Coll Compton CA, instr 1970; CA Commn for Teacher Prep & Licensing, consultant 1971-72. **Orgs:** Pres CSUDH Chap Phi Delta Kappa 1977-78; mem profs of secondary educ Nat Assn of Secondary Sch Prin 1979-80; mem Alpha Phi Alpha Frat. **Honors/Awds:** Rosenwald Award 1960; Ambassador's Award German-Am Serv 1964; Am Studies Hon Award Univ of Notre Dame 1968; cert of apprec Research Utilization Bd State of CA 1977. **Business Addr:** 1000 E Victoria St, Carson, CA 90747.

WALKER, GEORGE T.
Composer, pianist, educator. **Personal:** Born Jun 22, 1922, Washington, DC; son of Rosa King Walker and Dr George T Walker; children: Gregory, Ian. **Educ:** Oberlin Coll, Mus B, 1941; Curtis Inst of Music, Artist Diploma, 1945; Univ of Rochester, DMA, 1957. **Career:** Smith Coll, prof, 1961; Univ of Colorado, prof, 1968; Univ of Delaware, prof, 1975; Peabody Inst of Johns Hopkins Univ, 1975-78; Rutgers Univ, 1969-92, professor emeritus, 1992-. **Orgs:** New York City; mem ASCAP, Amer Symphony League. **Honors/Awds:** Fulbright Fellow, 1957; John Hay Whitney Fellow, 1958; Rockefeller Fellow, 1972, 1975; Amer Acad & Inst of Arts & Letters Award, 1981; Koussevitsky Prize, 1988; Guggenheim Fellow 1969, 1988; Pulitzer Prize in Music, 1996; Lafayette Coll, Hon Dr Fine Arts, 1982; Oberlin Coll, Hon Dr Music, 1983; Montclair State Univ, Hon Dr Letters; Bloomfield Coll, Hon Dr Fine Arts; Univ of Rochester, Univ Scholar, 1996; Curtis Inst of Music, Hon Dr Music, 1997. **Home Addr:** 323 Grove St, Montclair, NJ 07042.

WALKER, GROVER PULLIAM
Entrepreneur. **Personal:** Born Jan 14, 1941, Chicago, IL; son of Vernell Crawford Walker and Rice Walker; divorced; children: Jasmine. **Educ:** Univ MO, AB (summa cum laude) 1963; UCLA, JD 1967; Harvard Bus Sch, MBA 1971. **Career:** CA State, Atty Gen, deputy atty gen 1968-69; Rand Corp, consult 1969; McKinsey & Co, internatl consult 1970; Exxon Corp, corp atty 1971-73; Johnson Prod Co, gen corp counsel 1973-75; LA State Univ, asst prof law & bus admin 1973; Chicago State Univ,asst prof law and business 1974; private law practice, financial planning 1975-87; California Non-Ambulatory Medical Services Inc, president/CEO, 1987-. **Orgs:** Mem Calif Bar Assn, 1968; Mem IL Bar Assoc 1974; mem FL Bar Assn 1976; mem City of Miami FL Zoning Bd 1977-79; mem of bd New Wash Hghts Comm Devel Corp 1976-77; Total Care Home Health Agency FL 1976-77; mem Amer, Natl, CA, IL, Cook Co & Chicago Bar Assns; Harvard Bus Sch Century Club; Harvard Club Chicago; PAD Legal Frat; bd mem Afro-Amer Family Comm Serv; elected co-chmn Afro-Amer Student Union Harvard Bus Sch 1969; exec dir Black Agenda 1982-84. **Honors/Awds:** Harvard Leadership Awd 1970; Victor Wilson Scholar, Univ Mo, 1959-63. **Business Addr:** President/CEO, California Non-Ambulatory Medical Services Inc, 2012 Rimpau Blvd, Los Angeles, CA 90016-1514.

WALKER, HERSCHEL
Professional football player. **Personal:** Born Mar 3, 1962, Wrightsville, GA; son of Christine Walker and Willis Walker; married Cindy De Angelis. **Educ:** Univ of Georgia, degree in criminal justice, 1984. **Career:** New Jersey Generals (USFL), running back, 1983-85, Dallas Cowboys, 1986-89, Minnesota Vikings, 1989-92, Philadelphia Eagles, 1992-95; NY Giants, 1995-96; Dallas Cowboys, 1996-; Diversified Builders Inc, Athens, GA, owner. **Honors/Awds:** Heisman Trophy, 1982; 3 time All American; USFL Outstanding Running Back, 1983, league leading rusher, 1983, 1985, voted MVP, 1985; Pro Bowl, 1987, 1988. **Business Addr:** Professional Football Player, Dallas Cowboys, 1 Cowboy Pkwy, Irving, TX 75063, (214)556-9900.

WALKER, HOWARD KENT
Foreign service official, educator. **Personal:** Born Dec 3, 1935, Newport News, VA; son of Jean K Walker and William R Walker, Jr; married Terry B Taylor; children: Gregory, Wendy. **Educ:** Univ of MI, AB (High Honors) 1957, MA Conley Scholar in Government, 1958; Boston Univ, PhD 1968. **Career:** George Washington Univ, assoc prof 1968-70; American Consulate Kaduna, consul 1970-73; Dept of State, desk officer 1973-75; American Embassy Amman, political counselor 1975-77; American Embassy Dares Salaam, dep chief of mission 1977-79; American Embassy Pretoria, deputy chief of mission 1979-81, charge d'affiaries, a/i; American Embassy Lome, ambassador to Togo 1982-84; Foreign Service Institute, Foreign

Affairs Fellow, 1984-85; Dept of State, dir, Office of West Africa, 1985-87; sr inspector, Office of Inspector General, Dept of State, 1987-89, American Embassy Antananarivo, Ambassador to Madagascar and to the Islamic Republic of Comoros, 1989-92; Natl Defense Univ, vice pres; NATO Defense College, Rome, deputy commandant, currently. **Honors/Awds:** African Studies Fellow Boston Univ 1958-60; Foreign Affairs Fellow Center for the Study of Foreign Affairs Foreign Serv Inst 1984-85. **Military Serv:** US Air Force, 1st lt, 2 1/2 years. **Business Addr:** Deputy Commandment, NATO Defense College, Viale Della Civilta del Lavaro, 38, 00144 Rome, Italy.

WALKER, J. WILBUR

Educational administrator (retired), clergyman, activist. **Personal:** Born Jun 23, 1912, Troy, AL; son of Annie Hobbdy and Luther Walker; married Ollie Elizabeth Bridges. **Educ:** Paine Coll Augusta GA, AB 1938; Atlanta Univ, MEd 1947. **Career:** Elementary Schools, asst principal/teacher 1939; Gower Elementary School, Oscar Elementary School, Union Elementary School, supvr principal 1939-60; Washington High of Emen School, principalship 1960-70; Gower Neighborhood Assn Inc, community volunteer/chairperson. **Orgs:** Advisor to Mayor & City Officials of Greenville SC 1939-; mem Natl Ed Assn 1939-72, Palmetto Ed Assn 1939-69, Natl Dept of Elementary School Principals 195-72, Natl Assn of Secondary School Principals 1960-; bd of dir St Anthony's Catholic Church 1967-70; mem SC Ed Assn 1970-79; bd of dir Gower Neighborhood Assoc Inc 1972-, Western Carolina Clients Council 1979-; mem City of Greenville Comm Devel Advisory Comm 1980-; bd of dir Legal Serv of Western Carolina 1981-, The Human Endeavor Inc 1981-, Greenville Comm Housing Resource Bd Inc 1982-, ACLU 1983-; life mem Natl Assn for the Advancement of Colored People; mem Alpha Phi Alpha Fraternity Inc, Gamma Gamma Lambda Chapt; life mem Young Laymen Christian Methodist Church, Natl Congress of Parents & Teachers Assn. **Honors/Awds:** Organized 1st Parent Teacher Assn for Public Schools in Greenville County 1939, State-wide Elementary School Principals Assn in SC 1950; Organized Operation New Broom Clean Sweep Program 1979, Operation New Broom Clean Sweep Camera 1979; Received Most Prestigious Comm Person Award presented by Sunbelt Human Advancement Resources Inc 1980; Nominated for the Jefferson Award by the City of Greenville to persons contributing distinguished community serv; I Care Award SC Gov Volunteer Award Hon Richard W Riley Gov; The Lou Rawls 1986 Met Award; The Human Relations Commission's R Cooper White, Mayor Award, 1988; Mayor's Achievement Award, 1989; Gower Neighborhood Assn Award, 1988; Phillis Wheatley Community Center Post Fellows Assn Scholarship; A Community Profile: JWilbur Walker Involvement Race Relations Video Presentation, 1989; Hettie Rickett Award for Outstanding Contributions to Community Development, South Carolina Community Development Assn, 1990; had a housing community named in his honor; Volunteer Administrator of the Year, Operation New Broom, 1984. **Home Addr:** 214 N Leach St, Greenville, SC 29601.

WALKER, JAMES

Business executive. **Personal:** Born Jan 24, 1926, Greenville, SC; son of Della Palmore Walker and James Booker Walker; married Matilda Roumania Peters; children: James G, Frances D. **Educ:** Univ of Illinois, AB, 1954, MS, 1955; Univ of Maryland, further study; Johns Hopkins Univ, further study. **Career:** Univ of Illinois, grad asst, 1954-55; Tuskegee Inst, Morgan State, Hampton Jr Coll, math instructor, 1955-60; District of Columbia, Government-DC Public Schools, research & statistics, 1960-77; The Chelsea School, sub teacher, teacher, 1978-83. **Orgs:** Vice chmn, ANC Comm 4A, 1985-; treasurer, Walker Pharmacy Inc, 1983-; dir, Walker Pharmacy Inc, 1983-; ANC comm, 4A-03, 1977, 1990 chmn, ANC Comm 4A, 1980; treasurer, ANC Comm 4A, 1982; sec, ANC Comm 4A, 1984. **Honors/Awds:** Fellowship James Fund-Tuskegee Inst 1955. **Military Serv:** USN & USAF; Good Conduct Medal; Asiatic Pacific Medal; Victory Medal. **Home Addr:** 1412 Whittier Place NW, Washington, DC 20012. **Business Addr:** Treasurer, Walker Pharmacy Inc, 7849 Eastern Ave, Silver Spring, MD 20910.

WALKER, JAMES ZELL, II

Editor, business executive. **Personal:** Born Mar 23, 1932, Birmingham; married Jeanette Adams; children: Jimmy Zelbulg, Debra Leartine, Ronnetta Marie, Freda Michetta, James, III. **Educ:** Jr San Francisco Coll, 1953-55. **Career:** Clarion Defender Newspaper, editor; Knockout Indstrs Inc, pres; KGAR Radio, weekend disk jockey 1968-76; KNEY Radio, talk show host 1977; Organic & Bio Degradable Cleanser, mfr. **Orgs:** Voting mem Portland Local 8 & ILWU 1980; past trustee chmn Billy Webb IBPOE of W 1962-70; spnsr Campfire Bonnie Blue Birds; pres Jefferson PTA 1974-75, 1977-78; Portland City Club 1970; C of C 69 Fed Title 1 Mem 1973; co-chmn Pub Sch Career Educ 3 Yrs; bd mem Portland Br NAACP 1967; Jefferson Cluster Study Com; adv bd Beach Sch; adv com Jefferson High Portland Pub Sch; co-fndr Miss Tan Am Pageant 1965; spnsrd OR & WA, Blk Am Contest 1970-75; adv on 4 bds Portland YMCA 1959; n br Portland YMCA; Freedom Bnk of Fin 1968; fndr Jimmy Bang Bang Yth Found 1969; mem OR Black Caucus 1972; mason Odd Fellws Pact Inc 1972; Am Cancer Soc Neighborhood Chap 1978-80; mem Nat Busns Leg 1968; Nat Black Mfg 1977; chrtr Mem Albina Lions Club 1970; Cold Card Mem Billy Webb ElksLdg; Fisk Univ Boosters Club 9; Jesuit HS Parents' Grp. **Honors/Awds:** First Black nom maj Polit Party in OR GOP 1970; electd Precinct Ldr 4 dists; 1974 Delegate OR Dem Conv; Sponsor 4 Prize Winning Floats Portland RoseFestvl Parade 1968, 69, 70, 71; Spl Portland PMSC Awd 1973; Albina Women Leg Achvmt Awd 1972; 3 Time 100% UGN Portland Area Chmn 1970-73; Golden Gloves 1953-54; Diamond Belt 1950; AAU Western Boxing Champ 1954; San Francisco Pacif NW Pro Boxing Champ 1958-63. **Military Serv:** AUS s sgt 1950-53; 3 Purple Hearts Bronze Star; 5 Battle Awds. **Business Addr:** PO Box 11095, Portland, OR 97211.

WALKER, JAY

Professional football player. **Personal:** Born Jan 24, 1972; married Monique. **Educ:** Howard University, attended. **Career:** Minnesota Vikings, quarterback, 1996-. **Business Addr:** Professional Football Player, Minnesota Vikings, 9520 Viking Dr, Eden Prairie, MN 55344, (612)828-6500.

WALKER, JERRY EUCLID

Educational administrator. **Personal:** Born Sep 15, 1932, Statesbury, WV; married Patricia A; children: Faye L, Jonathan L, Sue L. **Educ:** Univ of MD ES, BA 1958; Case-Western Res U, MSSA 1962. **Career:** Los Rios Comm Coll Dist, v chancellor-personnel 1974-; Sears Roebuck & Co, corporate emplymnt speclst 1966-74; Sears Roebuck & Co Cleveland OH, dir urban affairs; Lorain Co OH, exec dir econ devel; Family Serv Assn Mansfield OH, acting dir; OH State Reformatory Mansfield, dir soc serv 1958. **Orgs:** Bd of dirs Council on Blacks in Am Affairs 1979; mem NAACP; mem Urban League bd of dirs Cuyahoga Co Red Cross 1967; bd of dirs Half-way House for Boys 1968. **Military Serv:** USAF a-1c 1949-52. **Business Addr:** Los Rios Comm Coll, Dist 1919 Spanos, Sacramento, CA 95825.

WALKER, JIMMIE

Director. **Personal:** Born Nov 4, 1945, Mendenhall, MS; married Virginia Finley; children: Baron, Lorria, Erica. **Educ:** Prentiss Jr Coll Prentiss MS, AA 1967; LA Bapt Coll, BA 1969. **Career:** Farish St Br YMCA Jackson MS, exec dir 1977-; Valley N Family Br YMCA Jackson, exec dir 1978-; Farish St YMCA, prog dir 1974-77; Voice of Calvary Mendenhall MS, rec dir/pub rel Dir 1973-74; Campus Crusade for Christ, natl Co-coord Black campus ministry 1969-73. **Orgs:** Sec Assn Professional Dir Cluster 1974; bd mem Farish St Historic Dist Revitalizatn Assn 1980; mem Noon Optimist Club of Jackson 1980; bd mem Youth for Christ 1975-; bd mem S Cntrl Rural Health Assn 1979-; bd mem Voice of Calvary Ministeries 1980. **Honors/Awds:** Outstndg basketball plyr Sports Writers Assn So CA 1969; Sports Ambassador S Pacific 1970; inductee Los Angeles Bapt Coll Hall of Fame 1971. **Business Addr:** Farish St Br YMCA, 806 N Farish St, Jackson, MS 39202.

WALKER, JIMMIE (JAMES CARTER)

Comedian, actor. **Personal:** Born Jun 25, 1947, Bronx, NY. **Career:** Film appearances include: Let's Do It Again, 1975; Rabbit Test, 1978; The Concorde-Airport '79, 1979; Airplane!, 1980; Doin' Time, 1985; Kidnapped, 1987; My African Adventure, 1987; Water, 1985; television appearances include: Good Times, 1974-79; B A D Cats, 1980; At Ease, 1983; Bustin' Loose, 1987; Matchmaker, host, 1987; The Jerk, Too, 1984; Murder Can Hurt You!, 1977; An Evening of Comedy with Jimmie Walker and Friends, 1988; Jimmie Walker and Friends II, 1989; guest appearances on numerous talk shows and game shows, 1974-1988; record album, Dyn-o-mite, Buddah Records. **Honors/Awds:** Family Circle Magazine, Most Popular TV Performer, 1975; LA Free Clinic, honorary chairman, 1977; Time Magazine, Comedian of the Decade; various awards from civic groups in regard to role as JJ Evans.

WALKER, JIMMY L.

Automobile dealer. **Career:** Laurel Ford Lincoln-Mercury Inc, chief executive officer, currently; ULW Broadcasting, Inc, owner. **Special Achievements:** Company is ranked #83 on Black Enterprise's list of top 100 auto dealers, 1994. **Business Addr:** CEO, Laurel Ford Lincoln-Mercury Inc., PO Box 2608, Laurel, MS 39442, (601)649-4511.

WALKER, JOE

Journalist. **Personal:** Born Mar 11, 1934, Buffalo, NY; son of Emma L Parker Walker and Luther D Walker; married Isabel Castro; children: Joseph. **Educ:** Champlain Coll, 1952-53; Adelphi Coll, 1953-55. **Career:** Workers Defense League, researcher, 1978-79; New York Bur Bililian News, chief journalist, 1968-77; Third World Comm Vanguard, producer, 1973-77; WBAI Radio; Drug & Hospital Union New York City, editor of pubs, 1963-68; Muhammad Speaks, staff correspondent, 1962-63; Empire Star Weekly Buffalo, ed-in-chief, 1961-62, reporter feature writer, columnist, 1957-61; Local 144 Hotel, Hospital, Nursing Home & Allied Services Union, SEIW, AFL-CIO, editor/pub relations dir, 1979-83; Public Employers Federation, AFT & SEILI, AFL-CIO, dir of pub relations, 1985-87; Local 144 Hotel, Hospital, Nursing Home & Allied Services Union, SEIU, AFL-CIO, exec asst to pres, 1988-. **Orgs:** Pres, US Chapter Inter Org of Journalists, 1971-73; mem, IOJ Harlem Writers Guild; producer moderator Buffalo Roundtable radio WUFO Buffalo, 1961-62; past vice pres, exec bd mem, Afro-Amer Labor Council, 1964-73; pub inf dir, Tri-Partisan Masten Dist Com for Rep Govt, 1957-62; public relations dir, Civil Rights Party, 1960; mem, Harlem Anti-Colonial Comm, 1962-63; Julius Fucik Med Intl & Org of Journalist, 1976; pres, USA Chapter, Intl Org of Journalists, 1989-; chmn, bd of advisors, Natl Alliance of Third World Journalists, 1989-; bd of advisors, Black Press Institute, 1989-. **Military Serv:** AUS pfc 1955-57. **Home Addr:** 334 E 108 St, #18 F, New York, NY 10029. **Business Addr:** Exec Asst to Pres, SEIU Local 114, Hotel, Hospital, Nursing Home Union, 233 W 49th St, New York, NY 10019.

WALKER, JOHN LESLIE

Banking executive. **Personal:** Born May 4, 1933, York, SC; son of Neely Walker and Walter Walker; married Mary Alberta Carlton; children: John L Jr, Karen F Walker-Spencer. **Educ:** Wilberforce Univ OH, BS 1956; Stonier Graduate School of Banking Rutgers Univ, 1972; Harvard Exec Seminar, 1978. **Career:** Cairo, Egypt Chemical Bank, vice pres 1980-83; Paris, France Chemical Bank, vice pres 1978-80; Republic Natl Bank of New York, int'l private banking officer of Middle East and Africa 1988-91; US Dept of Commerce, dept asst sec, 1994-96; Merrill Lynch, vice pres, financial consultant, 1996-. **Orgs:** Mem Natl Bankers Assn 1973-78; finance sec United Black Men of Queens Co NY 1976-78; treasurer Urban Bankers Coalition 1977-78; mem Kappa Alpha Psi Fraternity; mem Prince Hall Masons; mem NAACP; mem Urban League; chairman, bd of trustees Wilberforce Univ; bd mem Jamaica Serv Program for Older Adults; African Development Foundation, 1991-94. **Honors/Awds:** Good Conduct Medal AUS 1958; Serv Award United Black Men of Queens Co 1978. **Military Serv:** AUS sgt 1956-58.

WALKER, KENNETH

Professional basketball player. **Personal:** Born Aug 18, 1964, Roberta, GA. **Educ:** Univ of Kentucky, Lexington, KY, 1982-86. **Career:** New York Knicks, 1986-94; Washington Bullets, 1994-. **Business Addr:** Professional Basketball Player, Washington Wizards, Capital Centre, 1 Harry S Truman Dr, Landover, MD 20785.

WALKER, KENNETH R.

Educator (retired). **Personal:** Born Dec 19, 1930, East Providence, RI; son of Lillian and Frank; married Gail Beverly Smith; children: Kenneth Jr, Michele, Leanne. **Educ:** Providence Coll, AB 1957; Rhode Island Coll, MEd, 1962; Boston Univ, EdD, 1976; Providence Coll, Hon SocD, 1983. **Career:** East Providence Rhode Island School Dept, teacher, 1957-68, asst principal, 1968-70; Rhode Island Coll, assoc prof, dir, Early Enrollment Program, beginning 1970. **Orgs:** Consult HEW Title IV; mem Guidance & Personnel Assn; Intl Assn of Approved Basketball Officials; Collegiate Basketball Officials Assn; Assn Curriculum Devel Specialist; Amer Fedn Teachers; Rhode Island State Parole Bd; consult, Rhode Island State Dept Educ; Omega Psi Phi Fraternity; mem, Governor's Task Force, 1991 Report on Education Rhode Island. **Honors/Awds:** Exemplary Citizenship Award, 1974; IBA Man of Year Award, 1967; Recip Afro-Am Award EPHS, 1971; Serv to Youth Award No Kingston Jr HS 1969; RI Big Brother of Yr Award, 1963; Educ Award NAACP, 1980; East Providence High School Hall of Fame, 1987. **Military Serv:** AUS Sgt 1951-53. **Home Addr:** 399 Brown St, East Providence, RI 02914.

WALKER, KENNETH R.

Journalist. **Personal:** Born Aug 17, 1951, Washington, DC; divorced. **Educ:** Catholic Univ of Amer. **Career:** Lion House Publishing, pres, currently; Independent television producer, correspondent; Anchor for Good Morning America, USA Today: The Television Show, Nightwatch; ABC News, political correspondent, news anchor, 1981-85; Washington Star Newspaper, foreign correspondent, natl affairs journalist/staff reporter 1968-81; WJZ-TV Baltimore MD, prog moderator/asst producer 1978-79. **Orgs:** Exec vice pres Nat Media Sys Inc 1970-74; mem bd of dir Townsend Reading Ctr Inc 1976; bd of dirs, Thurgood Marshall Memorial Scholarship Fund. **Honors/Awds:** Recipient, Washington Star Univ Scholarship, 1969; First Place, Washington-Baltimore Newspaper Guild Award, 1977; Emmy Award, Natl Academy of Television Arts and Scientists, 1981; Dupont Gold Baton Award, Columbia Univ School of Journalism, 1981; Journalist of the Year Award, Natl Assn of Black Journalists, 1985; Image Award, NAACP, 1985. **Business Addr:** 1119 Staples St NE, Washington, DC 20002.

WALKER, LANEUVILLE V.

Insurance executive. **Personal:** Born Oct 13, 1947, Prospect, VA; daughter of Sophia V Scott and Moses E Scott (deceased); married Ernest L Walker II, Dec 1, 1964; children: Ernest L III, Steven S. **Educ:** Cortez Peters Business College, 1966; University of Alabama, 1968; Virginia Commonwealth University, BS, 1975. **Career:** Southern Aid Life Insurance Co, administrative assistant, 1981-82, corporate secretary, 1982-88; Atlanta Life Insurance Co, assistant vice pres, 1988-. **Orgs:** Delver Woman's Club, member of the program committee, 1982-; Friends Club of Beulah Baptist Church, assistant secretary, 1981-; Third St Bethel AME Church, Missionary Society, 1981, trustee board member, 1990; Jackson Ward Business Association, board of directors, 1990. **Honors/Awds:** Third Street Bethel AME Church, Leadership Award, Women's Day Chairperson, 1992. **Business Addr:** Assistant Vice Pres, Atlanta Life Insurance Co, 214 E Clay St, Richmond, VA 23219, (804)648-7234.

WALKER, LARRY M.
Artist, educator, administrator. **Personal:** Born Oct 22, 1935, Franklin, GA; son of Cassandra Walker and W B Walker; married Gwendolyn Elaine Howell; children: Dana, Larry, Kara. **Educ:** BS 1958; Wayne State Univ, MA 1963. **Career:** Coll of Pacific, Univ of Pacific, prof chmn dept of art, 1964-83; Detroit Public School System, art instructor 1958-64; 30 one-man exhibitions; 60 group exhibitions; GA State Univ Dept of Art, prof, chmn 1983-85; GA State Univ School of Art & Design, prof, dir 1985-. **Orgs:** Mem 1976-77, chmn 1978-80 Stockton Arts Comm; bd dir 1976-80, chmn 1978-79 Natl Council of Art Admins; mem Natl Assoc of Schools of Art & Design 1983-, bd dir, 1990-93; Marta Arts Council 1983-; mem, bd dir, sec 1985, chmn 1986, 1987 Natl Council of Art Admins; bd dir Atlanta Arts Festival 1986-89, adv council, 1989-; advisory council Binney & Smith Co 1986-90; Dekalb Council for the Arts, 1987, pres, 1989, immed past pres, 1990. **Honors/Awds:** Recipient Pacific Family Award 1968; Distinguished Faculty Award 1975; over 80 awards from 100 juried art exhibits; The Afro-Amer Slide Coll, Black Professional in Predominately White Educ Inst, Black Arts Quarterly Summer 1978; public collections; Univ of the Pacific & Oakland Art Museum, CA State Univ Stanislaus, City of Stockton; Pioneer Museum & Haggin Gallery, Fulton Co Lib, City of Atlanta; Collections: Ohio Wesleyan College, Bank of North Carolina, Lander College (South Carolina), Studio Museum, Atlanta Life Ins Co; publications, ''Univ Art Classes for Children'' School Arts Magazine, ''Pioneer, Promote & Prosper, A View on the Visual Arts in Higher Educ''; The Visual Arts in the Ninth Decade, NCAA, 1980; article ''Site Sculpture'' Atlanta Arts Festival; ''The State of the Arts in SanJoaquinunty'' 1981, San Joaquin County Arts Council reports by L Walker & C Watanabe 1982; Award for Leadership & Appreciation of Serv to the Stockton Arts Commn, Annual Recognition Awards Program, 1981; Plaque for Serv to the Arts Community Stockton City Council, 1981; Certificate of Appreciation for Serv to the Community Involvement Program Univ of the Pacific, 1982; Founders Wall Plaque La Guardia HS of the Arts NYC: Certificate of Appreciation, Natl Council of Art Admin, 1988. **Business Addr:** Director, Professor, Georgia State University, School of Art & Design, University Plaza, Atlanta, GA 30303.

WALKER, LARRY VAUGHN
Educational administrator (retired). **Personal:** Born Aug 8, 1939, Meridian, MS; children: Derrick B, Terri L. **Educ:** Jackson State Coll, BS Sci 1960; Fisk Univ, MA Sci 1964; Roosevelt Univ, MST Chem 1974; Northern IL Univ, EdD Ed Adm 1983. **Career:** Wayne Cty Schools, teacher 1961-63; Jackson Public Schools, teacher, 1964-65; Proviso Twp HS, teacher 1965-74; Proviso Twp HS, dean, asst principal 1974-82; Oak Park & River Forest HS, associate principal, assistant superintendent, associate superintendent, 1982-1993; Retired from Oak Park and River Forest High School, June 1993. **Orgs:** Bd mem Family Serv & Mental Health Oak Park 1982-; presenter Natl Assoc of Secondary School Principals 1985; bd mem Oak Park YMCA 1985-. **Honors/Awds:** NSF Summer Inst Dillard Univ 1963; NSF Acad Year Inst Fisk Univ 1963-64. **Business Addr:** Retired Associate Superintendent for Pupil Service, Oak Park-River Forest High School, 201 N Scoville, Oak Park, IL 60302.

WALKER, LEE H.
Business executive. **Personal:** Born Oct 6, 1938, Troy, AL; married Audrey Davis. **Educ:** AL State; Fordham U, BA 1975. **Career:** Sears Roebuck & Co Chicago IL, grp dist mgr 1970-; Winston-Muss Corp NY, dir employee relation 1961-70; Am Prog of NYC, ins 1960-61. **Orgs:** Mem Sears Roebuck & Co contrib com; Am Mgmt Assn; mem bd AIM; Urban Problems Com 1968-69; mem Nat Urban League Guild NYC; Westchester Co blk rep; NAACP past vice pres Brooklyn Br; AIM bd dirs 1970, chmn 1970-72; past pres political club Rep; past mem Local Draft Bd 1969-72. **Honors/Awds:** Recip Black Achievers in Industry Award Harlem Br YMCA 1972; distin serv award New Rochelle Br NAACP 1967. **Business Addr:** Sears Tower, Chicago, IL.

WALKER, LEROY TASHREAU
Educator, coach (retired). **Personal:** Born Jun 14, 1918, Atlanta, GA; son of Mary Walker and Willie Walker; widowed; children: LeRoy, Carolyn. **Educ:** Benedict Coll, Ba 1940; Columbia Univ, MS 1941; NY Univ, PhD 1957. **Career:** Benedict Coll Columbia SC, chmn phys educ, coach basketball, football, track & field 1941-42; Bishop Coll Marshall TX, chmn phys dept, coach basketball, football, track & field 1942-43; Prairie View State Univ, 1943-45; NC Central Univ Durham, chmn phys dept, coach basketball, football, track & field 1945-73, vchancellor for univ relations 1974-83, chancellor 1983-86, chancellor emeritus, 1986-. **Orgs:** Educ spec, Cultural Exchange Prog, Dept of State, 1959, 1960, 1962; dir prog plnng, Peace Corps Africa 1966-68; coach Ethiopian, Israeli, Trinidad-Tobago, Jamaica, Kenya teams Olympic Games; adviser track & field teams throughout world; US Collegiate Sports Council 1972; chmn Coll Commrs Assn 1971-74; chmn track & field com Athletic Union 1973-75; head coach US Track & Field Team Olympic Games Montreal 1976; bd dirs US Olympic Com author Manual of Adapted Physical Educ 1960; Physical Educ for the Exceptional Student 1964, Championship Tech in Track & Field 1969; bd dirs USA China Relations Com; AAHPERD 1972, NEA, US Track Coaches Assn, Intl Assn Athletic Fedns, Sigma Delta Psi, Alpha Phi Omega, Omega Psi Phi; president, National Assn Intercollegiate Athletics;pres, Central Collegiate Aetic Assn; US Olympic Committee, treasurer, 1988-92, president, 1992-; US Olympic Team, Chief of Mission, Barcelona, 1992. **Honors/Awds:** Recipient James E Shepard Outstanding Teacher Awd Hamilton Watch Co 1964; Achievement Award Central Intercollegiate Athletic Assn 1967; Disting Alumnus Awd Benedict Coll 1968; Distinguished Serv Award, Kiwanis Intl 1971, City of Durham 1971, Durham C of C 1973; Gov's Ambassador of Goodwill Awd 1974; O Max Gardner Award 1976; Named to HC Hall of Fame 1975; SC Hall of Fame 1977; Natl Assn Sport & Phys Educ Hall of Fame 1977; Robert Giegengack Award, The Athletics Congress' Highest Award; Role Model Leader, North Carolina State University, 1990; Achievement in Life Award, Encyclopedia Britannica; Athletic Congress Hall of Fame; Helms National Hall of Fame; US Olympic Hall of Fame; Mid-Eastern Athletic Conf Hall of Fame. **Business Addr:** President, US Olympic Committee, 2525 Meridian Pkwy, Ste 230, Durham, NC 27713.

WALKER, LEWIS
Educator. **Personal:** Born Oct 22, 1936, Selma, AL; son of Thelma Watts Freeman and Joseph Walker (deceased); married Georgia Doles, Apr 18, 1964. **Educ:** BA, 1959; MA, 1961; PhD, 1964. **Career:** Wilberforce Univ, student instructor, 1958-59; Ohio Higher Educ Asst Commn, admin specialist, 1962; Ohio State Univ, lecturer, 1964; Ohio Hospital Assn, research specialist, 1964; W Michigan Univ, asst professor, 1964-67, assoc professor, 1967-71, professor, 1971-, chmn, sociology, 1989-. **Orgs:** Mem, Douglass Comm Assn, 1965-69; Senior Citizens Inc, 1967; founder & dir, Kalamazoo Resources Devel Council, 1967-68; consultant & program devel, Ford Motor Co, 1968-69, Police-Comm Relations Programs, 1968-70; ARC Bd, 1969-70; adv bd, Learning Village, 1970; Amer Soc Assn, 1974-; Michigan Soc Assn, 1974-; Miami Valley Soc Assn, 1974-; numerous in-service & human relations programs; mem, Kalamazoo Co Crime Commn, 1984-; bd, Goodwill Indus, 1986-, Differential Flow Systems Inc, 1986-; pres, Walker-Taylor Thermies Inc, 1984-, Spare Time Pursuits Inc 1986-. **Honors/Awds:** Recipient, Distinguished Serv Award Jaycees, 1967; One of Five Outstanding Young Men of Michigan Jaycees, 1967; Award for Teaching Excellence W Michigan Univ Alumni Assn, 1971; inventor, US patent on low pressure boiler heating system, 1984; invention, US patent on furnace system ,1986; three US copyrights, registrations, on three separate game boards and texts; Recipient, Distinguished Service Award, Western Michigan University, 1989. **Business Addr:** Professor, Western Michigan University, Dept of Sociology, Kalamazoo, MI 49001.

WALKER, LUCIUS
Educational administrator. **Career:** Howard University, School of Engineering, dean, currently. **Business Addr:** Howard University, School of Engineering, 1016 Downing Hall, 2300 6th St, NW, Washington, DC 20059.

WALKER, LUCIUS, JR.
Clergyman. **Personal:** Born Aug 3, 1930, Roselle, NJ; married Mary; children: Lucius, Donna, Gail, Richard, Edythe. **Educ:** Shaw Univ, AB; Andover Newton Theol Sem, MDiv; Univ of Wisconsin, MA 1963; Malcolm X College (Chicago), Hon LHD; Shaw Univ, Raleigh NC, LHD. **Career:** Interreligious Found for Comm Orgn NY, exec dir 1967-73; Natl Coun of the Churches of Christ NY, assoc gen sec 1973. **Orgs:** Mem bd trustees Shaw Univ; mem bd trustees Andover Newton Theol School; mem Black Foundation Executives.

WALKER, LULA AQUILLIA
Elected official. **Personal:** Born Mar 1, 1955, Derby, CT; children: William Zimmerman Jr, Tyron, Garrett. **Educ:** Shaw Coll Detroit, Med Asst Cert 1974; US Acad of Health & Sci, Med Spec Cert 1977. **Career:** Olson Dr Tenants Assoc, pres 1979; Housing Authority City of Ansonia, asst treas (1st tenant to be appointed to Housing Auth Bd) 1980; City of Ansonia, co-chmn printing & signs 1982, chmn claims comm 1984; Ansonia Bd of Alderman, fourth ward alderman (1st Black female to be elected to Bd of Alderman); State of CT, mental health worker II. **Orgs:** Advisory bd Valley legal Asst 1980; asst recording sec A Philip Randolph Lower Naaugatuck Valley Chap 1982; mem of bd Lower Naugatuck Valley Chap ofNAACP 1983; sgt of arms Lower Naugatuck Valley Chap of Black Democratics 1983; vice dgt ruler Lily of the Valley Temple H406 IBPOE of the World 1984-; chmn Claims Comm 1986; serve on Police Comm of bd of aldermen. **Honors/Awds:** Woman of the Month Women's Center of Ansonia 1979; 3 Awds for Dedicated Serv in the Community Friends of Lulu of Ansonia 1984; Dedicated Serv Plaque in the Comm Magicians AC 1984. **Military Serv:** Army NG sgt 11 yrs; Army Natl Guard Achievement Medal 1982. **Home Addr:** 68 Jackson St, Ansonia, CT 06401-1210.

WALKER, M. LUCIUS, JR.
Educator. **Personal:** Born Dec 16, 1936, Washington, DC; son of Inez and M Lucius; children: Mark, Monique. **Educ:** Morehouse Coll, 1952-54; Howard Univ, BSME 1957; Carnegie Inst of Tech, MSME 1958, PhD 1966. **Career:** Howard Univ, School of Eng, Asst Dean, 1965-66, Acting Chmn, dept of Mechanical Engineering, 1968-73, chmn dept of mech engrg 1968-73, assoc dean 1973-74, acting dean 1977-78, dean 1978-; ECSEL, director, 1990-. **Orgs:** Consultant, Center for Naval Analyses, 1991-93; Biomedical Cardiovascular Renal Rsch Team 1966-73, consultant Ford Motor Co 1971-; mem Engr Manpower Comm of Engrs Council Prof Devel 1972-; mem Amer Soc for Engrg Ed, Amer Soc of Mech Engrs, Tau Beta Pi; former mem bd of trustees Carnegie Mellon Univ; biotech resources review comm Natl Inst of Health 1980-84; Amer Soc of Mech Engrs; Ad Hoc Visitor for Accreditation Bd for Engrg & Tech; mem, past pres Howard Univ Chap Sigma Xi. **Honors/Awds:** NYAS; Fellowship Ford Found Carnegie Inst of Tech. **Business Addr:** Dean, Howard Univ School of Engrg, 2300 6th St NW, Washington, DC 20059.

WALKER, MANUEL LORENZO
Physician. **Personal:** Born Mar 22, 1930, Battle Creek, MI; son of Manuella Beck Walker and Dr Charles S Walker; married Joan Lucille Carter Parks; children: Linda Lee Walker McIntyre, Lorenzo Giles, Gregory Tracy Parks. **Educ:** Howard Univ Coll of LA, BS 1951; Howard Univ Coll of Med, MD 1955; Philadelphia Gen Hosp, Intern 1955-56. **Career:** Mercy-Douglass Hosp, staff mem 1958-73; private practice, 1958-; Mercy Catholic Med Cntr, staff mem 1968-; Lankenau Hosp, staff mem 1979-; St Joseph's Hosp, staff mem 1987-95; St Ignatius Nursing Home, med dir 1972-; University of Pennsylvania Health System, staff mem, 1995-. **Orgs:** Mem American Medical Association; Natl Medcl Assoc, PA Med Soc & Philadelphia Cnty Med Soc; v pres Howard Univ Med Alumni Assoc 1970-75; pres Philadelphia Acadmy of Fam Phys 1982-84; Keystone State Medcl Soc 1971-73; Med Soc of Eastern PA 1968-70; Yeadon (PA) Bd of Schl Dir 1968-71; alumni pres Class of 1955-Howard Univ Med Assoc; hnr soc Kappa Pi Medical, Alpha Omega Alpha Medical; editor, MSEPulse Newsletter of Medical Society of Eastern Pennsylvania, 1969-. **Honors/Awds:** Practitioner of year Philadelphia Cnty Med Soc 1979; alumni pres Class of 1955 Howard Univ Med Schl 1955-; legion of Honor Chapel of Four Chaplains 1978-; med honor soc Kappa Pi & Alpha Omega Alpha; Practitioner of the Year Natl Medical Assoc 1986; President's Award, North Philadelphia NAACP, 1990; Mercy-Douglass Lecturship Award, Med Society of Eastern Pennsylvania, 1989. **Military Serv:** USNR lt cmdr 1956-66. **Home Addr:** 425 Jamaica Dr, Cherry Hill, NJ 08002. **Business Addr:** Family Physician/Medical Dir, St Ignatius Nursing Home, 5740 W Girard Ave, Philadelphia, PA 19131, (215)877-1110.

WALKER, MARGARET ABIGAIL (MARGARET WALKER ALEXANDER)
Author, educator. **Personal:** Born Jul 7, 1915, Birmingham, AL; daughter of Marion Dozier Walker and Sigismund C Walker; married Firnist James Alexander, Jun 13, 1943 (deceased); children: Marion Elizabeth, Firnist James, Sigismund Walker, Margaret Elvira. **Educ:** Northwestern Univ, BA, 1935; Univ of Iowa, MA, 1940, PhD, 1965. **Career:** Livingstone College, Salisbury, NC, faculty member, 1941-42, professor of English, 1945-46; author, 1942-; West Virginia State College, Institute, WV, instructor in English, 1942-43; Jackson State College, Jackson, MS, professor of English, 1949-; Institute for the Study of the History, Life, and Culture of Black Peoples, director, 1968-; Cape Cod Writers Conference, staff member, 1967, 1969; Northwestern Univ, visiting professor, spring 1969. **Orgs:** Member, National Council of Teachers of English, Modern Language Association, Poetry Society of America, American Association of University Professors, National Education Association, Alpha Kappa Alpha. **Honors/Awds:** Poetry includes: For My People, 1942; Ballad of the Free, 1966; Prophets for a New Day, 1970; October Journey, 1973; prose includes: Jubilee, 1965; How I Wrote Jubilee, 1972; A Poetic Equation: Conversation Between Nikki Giovanni and Margaret Walker, 1983; Richard Wright: Daemonic Genius, 1987; has also contributed to several anthologies and worked as an editor; Yale Series of Younger Poets Award, For My People, 1942; named to Honor Roll of Race Relations, New York Public Library, 1942; Rosenthal Fellowship, 1944; Ford Fellowship, 1954; Houghton Mifflin Literacy Fellowship, 1966; Fulbright Fellowship, 1971; National Endowment for the Humanities, 1972; Doctor of Literature, Northwestern Univ, 1974; Doctor of Letters, Rust College, 1974;Doctor of Fine Arts, Dennison Univ, 1974; Doctor ofmane Letters, Morgan State Univ, 1976; Co-author, Spirit of the Season: Three Contemporary Tales of Loe for the Holidays, Pinnacle Books, 1994. **Home Addr:** 2205 Guynes St, Jackson, MS 39213. **Business Addr:** Department of English, Jackson State College, Jackson, MS 39217.

WALKER, MARIA LATANYA
Physician. **Personal:** Born Jul 3, 1957, Greenwood, SC; daughter of Leola Grant Walker and H W Walker Jr. **Educ:** Furman Univ, Greenville, SC, BS, 1978; Harvard Medical School, Boston, MD, MD, 1982. **Career:** Emory Univ School of Medicine, faculty, clinic physician, 1983-; private practice, 1990-. **Orgs:** Mem, Delta Sigma Theta, 1976, Medical Assn of Georgia, Pea-

body Acad Soc/Harvard Medical School, Amer Medical Assn. **Honors/Awds:** Phi Beta Kappa Beta Chapter, Furman Univ, 1978. **Business Addr:** 3115 Piedmont Rd, Ste 108, Suite 206, Atlanta, GA 30305, (404)981-0600.

WALKER, MARK LAMONT
Surgeon, educator. **Personal:** Born Jan 5, 1952, Brooklyn, NY; son of Ann Boston Walker and Philip David Walker; married Alicia Watson; children: Kweli, Akilah, Olabisi, Rashanna, Sharufa, Rahsaan. **Educ:** City Coll of New York, BS 1973; Meharry Medical Coll, MD 1977. **Career:** Howard Univ Hosp, instructor dept of surgery 1983-85; Morehouse Sch of Medicine, asst prof of surgery 1985-90; associate professor & chairman, 1990-94; Surgical Residency, prog dir, 1990-96; Surgical Health Collective, 1996-. **Orgs:** Fellow Intl Coll of Surgeons 1984; mem Assn of Academic Surgery 1984, Atlanta Medical Assn 1985, Natl Medical Assn 1986, Cert Surgical Critical Care 1987; Fellow American Coll of Surgeons 1988. **Honors/Awds:** Mem Alpha Omega Alpha Honor Medical Soc 1976-; Daniel Hale Williams Awd for Residency Howard Univ 1982; Awd of Merit Dept of Surgery Howard Univ 1985; Annual Awardee Science Skills Ctr Brooklyn, NY 1986. **Business Addr:** Director, Surgical Health Collective, 777 Cleveland Ave, Ste 305, Atlanta, GA 30315, (404)761-7482.

WALKER, MARY ALICE
Educator. **Personal:** Born Feb 5, 1941, Warrenton, GA; married James. **Educ:** Brockport State U, BS 1963; Nazareth Coll, MEd 1975. **Career:** Rochester NY OIC, bd chmn 1980-; Rochester City School Dist, reading teacher 1963-. **Orgs:** Dir of Christian educ NY Dist 1973-75; rec Rochester Tchrs Assn 1976-77; mem Rochester Reading Assn 1979-80; mem NY State Tchrs Assn; mem Urban League 1978-80; chmn trustee bd New Bethel CME Ch 1970-80; mem Dem Party Com Monroe Co 1979-80. **Business Addr:** Teacher, Rochester OIC, 287 N Union St, Rochester, NY 14605.

WALKER, MARY L.
Broadcast journalist. **Personal:** Born Nov 17, 1951, Shreveport, LA; daughter of Jennie V. Johnson Wilson and Sam Walker. **Educ:** Louisiana State University, Baton Rouge, LA, BA, 1973. **Career:** KJOY Radio, Stockton, CA, advertising representative, 1974; KTBS-TV, Shreveport, LA, general assignments reporter, 1974-76; KSAT-TV, San Antonio, TX, police beat reporter, 1976-. **Orgs:** Member, National Association of Black Journalists, 1986-; member, Society of Professional Journalists, 1988-; committee member, Martin Luther King Committee, City of San Antonio, 1988-. **Honors/Awds:** Best Television News Story: Film and Script, Sigma Delta Chi, 1980; Best Television News Documentary, Sigma Delta Chi, 1982; Best Documentary, Texas Associated Press, 1982; Best Public Affairs Documentary, Texas United Press International, 1983, Best Spot News Story (Team Report), 1986; Media Awards for Excellence in Reporting Concerns of Children, Best Television Documentary, Odyssey Inst, 1980; Civilian Service Award, Television Documentary, Department of the Army, 1984; Communications Award, Iota Phi Lambda Society, 1980; Media Award, Texas Public Health Association, 1977; Outstanding Achievement in News Media, Beta Omega Sigma, 1975; Nomination for Best Television Documentary, National Academy of Televsion Arts and Sciences, 1976. **Home Addr:** 3223 Howard #57, San Antonio, TX 78212. **Business Addr:** Police Beat Reporter, KSAT-TV, 1408 N St Mary's Street, San Antonio, TX 78205.

WALKER, MAURICE EDWARD
Educator. **Personal:** Born Oct 31, 1937, Rochester, NY; son of Ethel E Walker and Maurice B Walker; married Rosie Lee Williford, Sep 4, 1964; children: Christina, Juliana, Gwendolyn, Maurice Jr, Lawrence. **Educ:** LA Tech Univ, BA Speech 1968-70; Univ of So CA, MS Ed 1977. **Career:** USAF March AFB CA, airborne controller 1963-66; USAF Osan AB Korea, Lockbourne OH, Barksdale AFB LA, command post controller 1967-70; 49 Supp Sq Holloman AFBNM, sq sect comdr 1971-73; 610 Mass Yokota AB Japan, sq sect comdr 1973-77; 2052 Comm Keesler AFB MS, sq sect comdr 1977-79; USAF Acad CO The Colorado Springs School, athletic dir and eng teacher, instructor/dep dir IM division, 1979-83; Colorado Springs School, Colorado Springs, CO, director of athletic/English & speech teacher, 1983-89; Fenster School of Southern Ariz, Tucson, AZ, dean of students, 1989-. **Orgs:** Mem 2nd deg black belt Kodokan Judo Inst Tokyo Japan 1962-; military affiliate radio oper AUS 1968-; amateur radio oper FCC licensed 1968-; life mem Amer Radio Relay League 1970-; retired Multi-WSAF, USAFA. **Military Serv:** USAF, Capt, 1956-83; AF Commendation Medal w/1st Oak Leaf Cluster 1970, 1979. **Business Addr:** Dean of Students, Fenster School of Southern Arizona, 8500 E Ocotillo Dr, Tucson, AZ 85715.

WALKER, MAY
Law enforcement official. **Personal:** Born Dec 18, 1943, New Orleans, LA; daughter of Beatrice Ball Jackson and Thomas J Jackson; married Thomas Walker Jr (divorced 1979); children: Jemal R. **Educ:** Texas Southern University, Houston, TX, BA, 1969; University of Houston, Houston, TX, MA, 1975; Texas A & M University, Bryant, TX, MIS, 1990; University of Houston, Houston, TX, doctor of jurisprudence; United Way of Texas Gulf Coast, project blue print leadership forum, graduated, 1990. **Career:** Houston Independent School District, Houston, TX, instructor, 1970-72; Lockwood, Andrews & Newman Inc, Houston, TX, specification writer & librarian, 1964-72; Light House of the Blind, Houston, TX, administrative assist, 1972-74; Houston Police Department, Houston, TX, community liaison police officer, 1974-. **Orgs:** AKA Sorority; member, NOBLE, life member, National Council of Negro Women Inc; member, National Black Police Association; member, Coalition of 100 Black Women, member, League of Women Voters & Women in Community Services; numerous others. **Honors/Awds:** Outstanding Achievement, Afro American Police Officer League; Outstanding Recognition, Black Police Association; Outstanding Leadership Award, Over the Hill Inc, Outstanding Leadership Award, National Council of Negro Women; Appreciation of Achievement Accomplished, Houston Police Dept, Black Police Selection; Outstanding Achievement Award, United States Navy; Certificate of Recognition, Sunnyside Neighborhood Center. **Home Addr:** 3810 Belgrade, Houston, TX 77045. **Business Addr:** Houston Police Department, Community Svcs Div, 61 Riesner, Houston, TX 77002, (713)247-5676.

WALKER, MELFORD WHITFIELD, JR.
Attorney. **Personal:** Born Jun 15, 1958, Winchester, VA; son of Ruth Blackwell Walker and Melford W Walker, Sr; married Emile Vanessa Siddle Walker, Sep 2, 1990. **Educ:** Hampton Inst, BS Acct (summa cum laude) 1980; Harvard Law School, JD 1986; Harvard Graduate School of Business Admin, MBA 1987. **Career:** Arthur Andersen & Co, staff accountant 1980-81; Watson Rice & Co, consultant 1983-84; Walker Rental Co Inc, asst to the pres 1984; Long Aldridge & Norman, assoc 1987-90; Resolution Trust Corporation, staff attorney, 1991-. **Orgs:** Consultant, Volunteer Consulting Org at Harvard Business School 1983; Black Law Students Assn; Harvard Law School; Afro-Amer Student Union, Harvard Business School; mem, Amer Bar Assn; State Bar of GA; mem, Atlanta Bar Assn, 1987-; Gate City Bar Assn, 1988-; board of directors, Fulton/Atlanta Community Action Authority, Inc, 1990-. **Honors/Awds:** Chapter pres and natl student rep to the exec comm Alpha Kappa Mu Honor Soc 1979-80; Fellowship, Council on Graduate Mgmt Educ 1982; co-author of Best Brief and Oral Argument Semi-Finalist, 1982 Jessup Moot Court Competition, Harvard Law School.

WALKER, MELVIN E., JR.
Educational administrator. **Personal:** Born Oct 23, 1946, Shivers, MS; son of Rosie Walker and Melvin E Walker; married Jeraldine Wooden Walker; children: Daphne Melinda, Melvin Earl III, Melanie Latrice. **Educ:** Prentiss Jr College, AS 1967; Alcorn A&M College, BS 1969; University of Illinois, Urbana-Champaign, MS 1971, PhD, 1973. **Career:** Fort Valley State University, Fort Valley, GA, asst prof 1973-77, coordinator of rural development research 1977-78, dean/research director for the School of Agriculture, Home Economics, and Allied Programs, 1978-, acting president, 1988-90. **Orgs:** Chair, Assn of Research Directors, 1982-86; chair, Assn of 1890 Agricultural Administrators, 1984-85; treas, Assn of Research Directors, 1986-; vice-pres, Camp John Hope NFA Alumni Assn, 1986-; member of Am Agricultural Economics Assn, Camp John Hope NFA Assn, Optimist Club. **Honors/Awds:** Outstanding Service Awards from USDA Honors Program 1982, US Dept of Commerce Census Advisory Bureau 1983, and FVSC Agriculture Alumni Assn 1984; Honorary State Farmers Award from FFA, 1984; author, Custom and Rental Rates Used on Illinois Farms, University of IL, 1973; author, "Poverty and Alienation: A Case Study," Journal of Social and Behavioral Sciences, 1978; author, "Effects of the Changing Structure of Agriculture on Nonwhite Farming in the US, the South, and Gerogia," Sociological Spectrum, 1984. **Home Addr:** 102 Duncan St, Fort Valley, GA 31030. **Business Addr:** Dean/Research Director, School of Agriculture, Home Ec, & Allied Programs, Ft Valley State University, PO Box 5744, Agricultural Research Sta, Fort Valley, GA 31030-3298.

WALKER, MOSES L.
Health services administrator. **Personal:** Born Oct 21, 1940, Kalamazoo, MI; son of Erie Smith Walker and Arthur Walker Sr; married Ruthie; children: Tari, Mark, Stacy. **Educ:** Western Michigan University, BS, 1966, MBA, 1990; Wayne State University, MSW, 1968. **Career:** Douglass Comm Assn, outreach worker 1966; Kalamazoo County Comm Action Prog, team capt 1966; Comm Serv Council, adminstr asst 1966; Archdiocese Detroit, comm affairs dept 1967; Douglass Comm Assn, dir, asso dir 1968-78; Borgess Mental Health Center, executive director, 1978-83; DeLano Clinic, Inc, president, 1983-91; Borgess Behavioral Medicine Services, vice president, 1992-. **Orgs:** Kalamazoo City Comm; Northside Association; Educ Advancement Scholarship Comm, chairman, 1973; National Association Social Workers; United Negro College Fund, chairman, 1973; National Association Black Social Workers, steering committee; Michigan Hospital Association, chairperson, 1988-; First of America Bank, MI, director, 1978-; Association of Mental Health Administrators, MI chapter, president, 1987-89. **Honors/Awds:** Jaycees, MI Chapter, Outstanding Young Men of MI, 1969, Kalamazoo Chapter, Distinguished Service Award, 1969; Outstanding Serv Award Northside Assn Educ Advancement 1972; Distinguished Alumni Wayne St U School of Social Work 1981; Community Service Award Southwestern MI Chapter National Association of Social Workers 1974. **Military Serv:** US Army, pfc, 1961-64. **Home Addr:** 1725 Cobb Ave, Kalamazoo, MI 49007. **Business Addr:** Vice President, Borgess Behavioral Medicine Services, 1722 Shaffer Rd, Kalamazoo, MI 49001.

WALKER, RONALD PLEZZ
Educational administrator. **Personal:** Born Oct 16, 1953, Boley, OK; married Glenda Gay; children: Terrance Scott. **Educ:** Langston Univ, BS 1974; Central State Univ, MEd 1978; OK State Univ. **Career:** OK City Schools, sci teacher 1973-76, bio-medical prog dir 1976-77, sci/eng ctr dir 1977-80; Boley Public Schools, supt 1980-. **Orgs:** Pres Natl Young Adult Council CME Church; vice pres Langston Univ Alumni Assn; vice pres Organization of Rural OK Schools; pub relations dir Zeta Gamma Lambda Chap Alpha Phi Alpha. **Honors/Awds:** Outstanding Young Man Natl Jaycees 1980; Outstanding Serv Awd Adams Day Care Ctr 1983; Outstanding Serv Awd OK City Dist Young Adults 1983; Outstanding Young Man Natl Jaycees 1984. **Business Addr:** Superintendent, Boley Public Schools, PO Box 248 St, Boley, OK 74829.

WALKER, ROSLYN ADELE
Museum director. **Educ:** Hampton Univ; Indiana Univ. **Career:** University Museums at Illinois State University, director; National Museum of African Art, curator, senior curator, director, currently. **Orgs:** African Studies Assn; Arts Council of the African Studies Assn; College Art Assn; Amer Assn of Museums, ArtTable, Inc; African American Museums Assn. **Honors/Awds:** Hampton Univ, 20 Year Student, 1966; National Black Alumni Hall of Fame, 1997. **Business Addr:** Director, National Museum of African Art, Smithsonian Institution, 950 Independence Ave SW, Washington, DC 20560, (202)357-4600.

WALKER, RUSSELL DEWITT
Safety official. **Personal:** Born Aug 30, 1946, New York, NY; son of Elizier Amos Walker & Armstead Walker; married Mary Ann Walker, Aug 30, 1968; children: Lisa, Danielle, Lael. **Educ:** Mt San Antonio College, AA, 1967; Ventura College, 1975-77; California State University, Northridge, 1977-79; University of LaVerne, BS, 1980, MS, 1981. **Career:** LA County Department of Beaches, ocean lifeguard, 1965-72, sr ocean lifeguard, 1972-78, seasonal lieutenant lifeguard, 1979-82, lieutenant ocean lifeguard, 1982-92; LA County Fire Department, captain of lifeguards, 1992-. **Orgs:** Aquatic Foundation of Metro LA, board of directors, 1994; Pat McCormick Education Foundation, board of directors, 1996-; Sickle Cell Disease Services of Ventura County, president, 1976-96; World Lifesaving Association, international training officer, 1985-; Omega Psi Phi Fraternity, 1983-; So California Public Pool Operations Association, standards committee mem, 1989-90; Association of Chiefs, 1994-. **Honors/Awds:** Burke Aquatic Foundation, Certificate of Appreciation, 1995; Zenith Youth Homes, Certificate of Appreciation, 1996; Los Angeles County Sheriff, Letter of Commendation, 1977; Romper Room Show, Letter of Appreciation, 1979; Sickle Cell Anemia Disease Services of Ventura County, Service Award, 1979. **Special Achievements:** Author of Emergency Medical Section of Ocean Lifeguard Manual, 1973; Designed & Developed Beach Lifeguard Training Program, 1977; Created, Developed & Planned Water Awareness Training Education, Recruitment Program, 1985; Initiated Planning & Implementation of Lifeguard 911 Emergency System, 1986; Established Emergency Response Guidelines Book for Central Section Ocean Lifeguards, 1993. **Military Serv:** US Navy, petty officer second class, 1967-72; National Defense Medal, 1967; Honor Student Medical Illustration School, 1969; Vietnam Service Medal, 1970, Good Conduct Medal, 1971; Marksman 45 Cal, 1971. **Home Addr:** 694 Pacific Cove Dr, Port Hueneme, CA 93041, (805)984-1221.

WALKER, SAMAKI IJUMA
Professional basketball player. **Personal:** Born Feb 25, 1976, Columbus, OH. **Educ:** Louisville. **Career:** Dallas Mavericks, forward, 1996-. **Special Achievements:** NBA Draft, First round pick, #9, 1996. **Business Addr:** Professional Basketball Player, Dallas Mavericks, Reunion Arena, 777 Sports St, Dallas, TX 75207, (214)748-1808.

WALKER, SANDRA VENEZIA
Educator. **Personal:** Born Nov 1, 1949, Little Rock, AR; daughter of Ardelia H Thomas Walker and Otis L Walker; divorced; children: Brandon. **Educ:** Little Rock University, Little Rock, AR, 1966-68; University of Missouri, Kansas City, MO, BA, 1970; University of Missouri, Kansas City, MO, MA, 1972; Washington University, St Louis, MO, PhD, 1976. **Career:** Washington University, St Louis, MO, adjunct asst professor, 1976-77; City of Kansas City, MO, director of public service/community support program, dept of housing & community development, 1977-81; University of MO, Kansas City, MO, director of affirmative action & academic personnel, 1981-85; University of MO, Kansas city, MO, assist dean, college of arts & sciences, 1985-. **Orgs:** President, Association of Black Sociologists, 1988-; secretary/treasurer, Association of Black Sociologists, 1983-86; board member, Missouri School Boards Association, 1988-90; vice president, Kansas City, MO School

Board, 1986-90. **Honors/Awds:** Image Award for Education, Urban League, Greater Kansas City, 1990; Woman's Conscience, Panel of American Women, 1987; Education Award, Black Archives of Mid America, 1990; Achievement Recognition, Missouri Legislative Black Caucus, 1985; Service Award, Missouri School Boards Association, 1990. **Business Addr:** Assistant Dean, College of Arts & Sciences, University of Missouri, Kansas City, 4825 Troost, Rm 215, Kansas City, MO 64110.

WALKER, SHEILA SUZANNE
Anthropologist, educator. **Personal:** Born Nov 5, 1944, Jersey City, NJ; daughter of Susan Robinson Walker Snell and Dr James O Walker. **Educ:** Bryn Mawr College, BA (cum laude), political science, 1966; University of Chicago, MA, 1969, PhD, anthropology, 1976. **Career:** Elmhurst College, lecturer, 1969; Chicago Model Cities Health Project, research analyst, 1970; Chicago Urban League, research specialist, 1970; World Bank, Abidjan, Ivory Coast, free-lance translator, 1972; Harvard University Divinity School, research assistant, 1972-73; University of California at Berkeley, asst prof in educ, 1973-81, Dept of Afro-Amer Studies, assoc prof, 1981-89; City College of CUNY, visiting assoc prof, 1987; Schomburg Center for Research in Black Culture, scholar-in-residence, 1987; College of William and Mary, professor, anthropology, 1989-91; University of Texas at Austin, Center for African and African American Studies, director, Dept of Anthropology Annabel Irion Worsham Centennial Professor, 1991-. **Orgs:** Intl Executive Committee, Institut des Peuples Noirs, Ouagadougou, Burkina Faso; jury member, Tenth Festival Panafricain de Cinema de Ouagadougou, 1987; International Scientific & Technical Committee, The Slave Route Project, UNESCO. **Special Achievements:** Author, Ceremonial Spirit Possession in Africa and Afro-America, 1972; co-editor, African Christianity: Patterns of Religious Continuity, 1979; author, The Religious Revolution in the Ivory Coast: The Prophet Harris and the Harrist Church, 1983; author of numerous both scholarly and popular articles on anthrolopolgy, particularly how it relates to African culture and African Drapsporan; Organizer-International Conference on the African Diaspora and the Modern World, Feb 1996, Univ of Texas; co-sponsored by the Univ of Texas & UNESCO. **Business Addr:** Director, Center for African & African American Studies, University of Texas at Austin, Jester Center A232A, Austin, TX 78705.

WALKER, SOLOMON W., II
Insurance executive. **Career:** Pilgrim Health & Life Insurance Co, Augusta GA, chief executive. **Business Addr:** Pilgrim Health & Life Ins Co, 1143 Laney Walker Blvd, Augusta, GA 30901.

WALKER, SONIA
Community relations director. **Personal:** Born Apr 10, 1937, Columbus, OH; married Walter; children: 3. **Educ:** Wilbur Force U, undergrad 1954-56; Bennett Coll, BA 1958; Howard Univ Sch of Soc Work, MSW 1963. **Career:** WHBQ-TV RKO-GEN, dir commn rel 1975-;soc work in priv & pub agenc 1963-74; Univ of Chicago Housing Staff, 1970-74; elem tchr 1958-61. **Orgs:** Mem Memphis Assn of Black Comm; bd of dir Memphis Orch Soc Memphis Urban Leag Nat Conf of Christ & Jews Beale St Reprtory Co Memphis Art & Sci Comm; prog coord TN Womens Mtg; supt adv coun Memphis Pub Sch; mem PUSH; NAACP.

WALKER, STANLEY M.
Attorney, educator. **Personal:** Born Jul 15, 1942, Chicago, IL; son of Georgia Walker and Alfred Walker; married Elizabeth Mary Pearson; children: Darryl, Edana. **Educ:** Harvard Coll, AB 1964; Yale Univ Law School, JD, 1967. **Career:** Judge A Leon Higginbotham US Dist Ct, law clerk, 1967-69; Dechert Price & Rhoads, assoc, 1969-70; Pepper, Hamilton & Scheetz, Assoc, 1970-71; Pennsylvania St Bd of Law Exam's, examiner, 1971-74; Comm Legal Services, staff & mng atty, 1971-72; Greater Philadelphia Comm Devel Corp, exec vice pres, 1972-73; The Rouse Co, sr atty, 1973-79; Univ of Texas School of Law, assoc prof, 1979-89; Exxon Co, USA, counsel, 1989-95; Friendswood Development Company, gen counsel, 1995-. **Orgs:** mem, Amer Bar Assn & Natl Bar Assn; mem, of Bars of US Supreme Court, District of Columbia, Pennsylvania, Maryland, & Texas; mem, Austin Econ Devel Comm, 1985-89; alt mem, City of Austin Bd of Adjustment 1985-86; mem, Action for Metropolitan Govt Comm, 1988-89. **Business Addr:** General Counsel, Friendswood Development Company, 17001 Northchase Drive, Ste 140, Houston, TX 77060-2139.

WALKER, STERLING WILSON
Attorney (retired). **Personal:** Born Dec 25, 1912, Wakefield, VA; married Marion B. **Educ:** VA Union Univ, BS 1938; NC Central Univ, LLB 1958. **Career:** High School, teacher 1938-42; postal employee 1944-55; Private practice, attorney 1959-93. **Orgs:** Appt by Gov Linwood Holton to serve on Council of Criminal Justice of Commonwealth of VA 1971-76; mem Amer Bar Assoc, Natl Bar Assoc, The Amer Trial Lawyers Assoc, VA Trial Lawyers Assoc, Tidewater Trial Lawyers Assoc, Old Dominion Bar Assoc, Twin City Bar Assoc. **Honors/Awds:** Honored by Tidwater Aluminae Assoc NC Univ; Plaque for work in criminal law. **Military Serv:** AUS 1942-44.

WALKER, TANYA ROSETTA
Legal assistant, office administrator, association executive. **Personal:** Born Apr 2, 1953, Philadelphia, PA; daughter of Lucille and James; divorced; children: Al Qadir R. **Educ:** Stenotype Inst of New York , Certified 1970; Rutgers State Univ, BA 1974; Essex Coll of Business, Certified Legal/Admin Asst 1977. **Career:** Lofton & Lester Esqs, paralegal 1979-83; Former Gov Brendan T Byrne, exec asst 1983-85; Althear A Lester Esq, legal asst 1985-92; Essex Cty Prosecutors Office, executive administrator, 1992-. **Orgs:** Mem Natl & Essex Cos Legal Secretaries & Paralegals Assoc 1979-89; mem Notary Public of NJ 1982-; volunteer Big Brothers & Big Sisters of Amer 1983-88; bd mem Boy Scouts of Amer 1983-; bd of dirs & vice pres Make-A-Wish Foundation of NJ 1983-86; mem Union County C of C 1986-87; pres (1st black and 1st woman) Make-A-Wish of NJ 1986-. **Honors/Awds:** Awd of Excellence Aunt Millie's Childrens Learning Ctr 1984,85; Achievement Awd Tri-City Sr Citizens Group 1986; Black Heritage Awd for Achievement Teachers' Union 1986; Recognition Awd Shearson Lehman Bros Inc 1986. **Business Addr:** President, Make-A-Wish Foundation of NJ, 326 Morris Avenue, Elizabeth, NJ 07208.

WALKER, TRACY A.
Director of community relations. **Personal:** Born Jun 12, 1969, Detroit, MI; daughter of Delma L Boyce and Charles N Boyce. **Educ:** University of Michigan at Ann Arbor, BA, communications, English, 1991; Wayne State University, MA, communications, 1997. **Career:** University of Michigan at Ann Arbor, Housing Department, minority peer advisor, 1988-90, resident director, 1990-91, spring/summer coordinator, 1991; Detroit Pistons, administrative assistant, 1991, community relations assistant, 1992, education programs coordinator, 1992, community relations supervisor, 1992-95, assistant director of community relations, 1995-97, director of community relations, 1997-. **Orgs:** Delta Sigma Theta Sorority Inc, 1989-, Detroit Alumnae Chapter, 1993-; Blacks in Advertising, Radio, and Television; NAACP, lifetime member; University of Michigan Alumni Association; Natl Assn of Female Executives; vice pres of administration, Women in Communications of Detroit, 1996-97. **Honors/Awds:** Detroit Pistons, Community Relations Department Employee of the Year, 1991, 1992, 1994. **Business Addr:** Director of Community Relations, The Detroit Pistons, Palace of Auburn Hills, Two Championship Dr, Auburn Hills, MI 48326, (810)377-8244.

WALKER, VALAIDA SMITH
Educational administrator, educator. **Personal:** Born in Darby, PA; daughter of Rosa Lee Smith and Samuel Smith; married William E Walker (divorced 1968). **Educ:** Howard University, Washington, DC, BS, 1954; Temple University, Philadelphia, PA, MED, 1970, EdD, 1973. **Career:** Temple University, Philadelphia, PA, professor, 1974-, chairperson, 1980-83, associate dean, 1983-84, assoc vice provost, 1984-90, vice provost, 1987-90, vice pres for students affairs, 1990-. **Orgs:** Former member, President's Commission on Mental Retardation; past president, American Association on Mental Retardation; PA Advisory Board on Special Education; William Penn Adult Community School Advisory Board, 1976-; Knoll/Shaffer Bi-Partisan Commission, 1989-; exec advisor, Caribbean Association on Mental Retardation. **Honors/Awds:** Chapel of the Four Chaplains Service Award; Special Educator of the Year, Sigma Pi Epsilon Delta, 1983. **Business Addr:** Vice Pres for Student Affairs, Temple University, Broad & Montgomery Ave, Conwell Hall, 4th Fl, Philadelphia, PA 19122.

WALKER, VERNON DAVID
Computer consulting company executive. **Personal:** Born Jun 16, 1950, New Rochelle, NY; son of Veronica & Edward Walker; married Sabrina Highsmith-Walker, Jun 29, 1992; children: Aminah. **Educ:** University of Maryland, BS, 1976. **Career:** Bendix Field Engineering Corp, sr buyer, 1972-77; Satellite Business Systems, sr procurement admin, 1977-82; MCI Telecommunications Corp, sr staff member; Communications Networks Co, pres, currently. **Orgs:** One Hundred Black Men of New York, 1993-; National Black MBA Assn, 1993-. **Honors/Awds:** Natl Assn of Purchasing Managers, Certified Purchasing Manager, 1986; Novell, Certified Netware Engineer, 1995. **Home Addr:** 178 Flax Hill Rd, Unit A203, Norwalk, CT 06854, (203)855-8977. **Business Addr:** President, Communication Networks Co., 178 Flax Hill Rd, A 203, Norwalk, CT 06854, (203)831-0040.

WALKER, WALTER LORENZO
Education executive. **Personal:** Born Sep 4, 1935, Chicago; married Sonia L Louden; children: Walter Noland, Aaron Jordan, Marcus Elliot. **Educ:** Brandeis U, PhD 1969; Bryn Mawr Coll, MSS 1962; Univ of Chicago, AB 1955. **Career:** LeMoyne Owen Coll, pres 1974; Univ Chicago, vice pres 1969-74; Howard Univ, staff assoc 1963-66; Philadelphia Redevelopment Assn, comm relations rep 1962-63; Fed Resrv Bank St Louis, dir 1978-80; Cmmrcl Appl, clmnst 1979. **Orgs:** Mem Nat Assn Social Wrkrs; CORE; NACP; Urbn Leg; Am Dem Actn; Cncl Scl Wrk Edn; bd Dir 1st TN Nat Bnk 1980; mem bd Amrcn Cncr Soc; mem bd vice pres Memphis Untd Way 1976; dir Memphis Area C of Co 1977-79; mem Memphis Rotary Clb; mem bd Chicago Chld Care Soc. **Honors/Awds:** Recip Golden Gavel, Chicago Caucus 1974; Educator of Yr Gr Memphis State 1977; 100 Top Yng Edctrs Change Magazine 1978; 10 Top Citizens in Memphis, Comm Appeal 1980; Edctr of Yr Memphis, Phi Beta Sigma Tau Iota Sigma Chap 1980. **Military Serv:** USAF 1st lt 1955-60. **Business Addr:** 807 Walker Ave, Memphis, TN 38126.

WALKER, WAYNE (RONALD WAYNE)
Professional football player. **Personal:** Born Dec 27, 1966, Waco, TX. **Educ:** Texas Tech Univ, attended. **Career:** San Diego Chargers, wide receiver, 1989-. **Business Addr:** Professional Football Player, San Diego Chargers, Jack Murphy Stadium, 9449 Friars Rd, San Diego, CA 92108.

WALKER, WENDELL P.
Director. **Personal:** Born Jun 6, 1930, Painesville, OH; son of Evelyn Wieker Walker and Robert M Walker; married Doris Thomas Walker; children: Kevin, Andrea, Brian. **Educ:** John Carroll University, pre-med, 1948-49; Defiance College, BA, 1951; University of KS, hematology, 1969-71; Western Reserv University, 1955-56; Lake Erie College, teaching certificate, 1972. **Career:** Poly Clinic Hospital, 1955-60; Northeastern Ohio General Hospital, director, clinical laboratory, 1960-. **Orgs:** National Board of American Medical Technologists, 1976-81; Ohio State Society of American Medical Technologists, president, 1972-75; Lake County Health and Welfare Council, president, 1973-74; Lake County Metropolitan Housing Authority, vice chairman, 1973, chairman, 1974; American Medical Technologists, national scientific committee, 1972, nominating committee, 1973, state board member, 1971-74, 1975-78; United Way of Lake County, board member, 1974-76; Central Branch YMCA, board member, 1976-, chairman, 1975-76, vice chairman, 1973-74; Lake County YMCA, board of directors, 1970-; Free Clinic, board member, president, 1975; NEO Hopital, board member; Boy Scouts of America, Dan Beard District, cub pack chairman; Catholic Service Bureau of Lake County, board president; Lifeline to Economically Disadvantaged Consumers, board president; Lake Metro Housing, board member; Coalition Homeless Task Force; Lake County Jail Commission; Society Bank; Metropolitan Health Planning Corp. of Cleveland. **Honors/Awds:** Outstanding Citizen, Painesville, 1994; OSSAMT, Journal Award, 1973, Technologist of the Year, 1974; AMT, National President's Award, 1974, National President's Letter of Recognition, 1973; Central YMCA, Board Member of the Year, 1970; National AMT, Distinguished Achievement, 1975; Defiance College, Alumnae of the Year, 1987; Leadership of Lake County, Graduate, 1988-89. **Special Achievements:** Area Chamber of Commerce; Founder, Free Clinic; Lake County Grand Jury Foreman, 1973; Painesville City Councilman, 1986-95, Last 4 years as council pres; represented Painesville School Systems for State of Ohio Consensus for Education, KEDS Program; study for Lakeland Community College, need for education and vocation project projection for future; involved in first Project Testing for Sickle Cell Anemia (county-wide); social science instructor for Painesville Night School; publication of numerous articles; Radio Personality-WBKC Radio, Fainesville, OH. **Military Serv:** US Army, ssgt, 1952-55; AMEDS. **Home Addr:** 26 Orchard Grove, Painesville, OH 44077.

WALKER, WESLEY DARCEL
Professional football player (retired). **Personal:** Born May 26, 1955, San Bernardino, CA; married Judy; children: John, Taylor, Austin. **Educ:** Univ of California; Mercy College; Fordham College, MEd. **Career:** New York Jets, wide receiver, 1977-89. **Honors/Awds:** NFL-All Rookie Team, 1977; Jets MVP and NFL Leader in Rec Yds, 1978; played in Pro Bowl, 1978, 1982. **Home Addr:** 10 Schoolhouse Way, Dix Hills, NY 11746.

WALKER, WILBUR P.
Educator (retired). **Personal:** Born May 6, 1936, Okmulgee, OK; son of Mae Ella Hill Walker and Hugh Walker; married Tomycine Lewis, Aug 30, 1958; children: Wilbur Jr, Natalie. **Educ:** Langston Univ, BA 1958; Central State Univ, MT 1968; Univ of OK, EdD 1974. **Career:** OK City Public Schools, teacher 1967-69; Urban League of OK City, dir comm org 1969; Univ of OK, special asst to pres 1970-73; OK Univ, dir special student program 1973-75; Benedict Coll, dean acad affairs 1975-78; OK State Regents for Higher Educ, director, student information services. **Orgs:** Mem Phi Delta Kappa; mem Urban League of OK City, Black Inc; Natl Assn of Student Personnel Admin; Oklahoma Coll Personnel Assn. **Honors/Awds:** Amer Council on Educ Inst Fellow 1978.

WALKER, WILLIAM B.
Auto dealership owner. **Career:** New Castle Ford Lincoln-Mercury Inc, pres, owner, 1990-. **Special Achievements:** Company is ranked #96 on Black Enterprise magazine's 1997 list of Top 100 Black businesses. **Business Addr:** President, Owner, New Castle Ford Lincoln-Mercury Inc, 221 N Memorial Dr, New Castle, IN 47362, (317)529-3673.

WALKER, WILLIAM HAROLD
Educator (retired). **Personal:** Born Jun 6, 1915, Carbondale, IL; son of Grace Kelly and James H Walker; married Viola Alba Crim; children: William Harold Jr. **Educ:** S IL Univ Carbondale, BA Educ 1937, MS Educ 1948. **Career:** Rural School

Perks IL, principal/teacher 1937-38; Douglas Grade Sch, principal 1938-41; Corporal Army Engineer Training Battalion, clerk 1941; Officer Training School, army engineer 1942; Corporal Air Corps, cadet pilot training 1942-43; 99th Fighter Squadron, pilot 1943-45; Tuskegee Army Air Base, base operations 1945-46; K thru 8 Elementary Centralia, principal 1948-75. **Orgs:** Teacher sunday sch supt deacon Second Baptist Church 1949-; life mem Natl Educ Assn 1953-; life mem IL Principals 1954; mem & chmn of comm Rotary Intl 1963; tchr high school and coll Sunday School classes, financial sec Second Baptist Church. **Honors/Awds:** Outstanding Citizen Awd Centralia Jaycees 1976; Certificate of Merit Educ Council of 100 and Educ Dept of Southern IL Univ at Carbondale 1977. **Military Serv:** USAC capt 6 yrs. **Home Addr:** Rte 6 Box 82 Airport Rd, Centralia, IL 62801.

WALKER, WILLIAM PAUL, JR.
Business executive. **Personal:** Born Jul 25, 1940, Denmark, SC; married Mamie Odena; children: Daryl Lamar. **Educ:** Howard U, BS 1963; Howard U, MD 1967. **Career:** DC Gen Hosp, chf dept rdtn thrpy; Georgetown U, asst prof; Howard U, asst prof; Radiological Assocs, dept chmn. **Orgs:** Mem DC Med Soc; Am Coll Radiology; Med Chi DC; Mid Atlantic Soc Radctn Onclgst; mem Natl Medical Assoc, Amer Cancer Soc, Southern Medical Assoc; mem Randall Memorial United Methodist Church. **Honors/Awds:** Upjohn Awd for Rsch 1967; 1985 Alumni Awd Voorhees Coll. **Business Addr:** Department Chairman, Radiological Associates, 2024 Georgia Ave NW, Washington, DC 20001.

WALKER, WILLIAM SONNY
Federal executive. **Personal:** Born Dec 13, 1933, Pine Bluff, AR; son of Mary V Coleman Bell Walker (deceased) and James D Walker; children: Cheryl D, James D II, Lesli W Williams, William L Jr. **Educ:** Univ of AR Pine Bluff, BA 1955; AZ State Univ, certification 1962; Univ of Oklahoma, certfication 1968; Fed Exec Inst, certification 1979. **Career:** State of AR/Gov Winthrop Rockefeller, agency dir/asst to gov 1969-71; US Dept of Housing & Urban Devel, div dir 1971-72; US Office of Economic Opportunity, regional dir 1972-75; US Comm Serv Admin, regional dir 1975-81; Natl Alliance of Business, vice pres, 1981-. **Orgs:** Bd of dirs United Way of Metro Atlanta 1977-87; bd of dirs Martin Luther King Jr Center, for Nonviolent Social Change 1979-; bd of dirs Southern Christian Leadership Conf 1980-87; bd of dirs Metro Atlanta Comm Design Ctr 1981-; bd of dirs Metro Atlanta Black/Jewish Coalition 1981-87; vice chair GA Assn of Black Elected Officials/Corporate Roundtable 1982-87; bd of trustees Metro Atlanta YWCA 1982-89; pres, Resurgens Atlanta 1984-85; chmn Economic Develop Task Force of Natl Conf of Black Mayors 1983-87; vice chair bd of trustees Metro Atlanta Crime Commn 1983-; chmn Collections of Life & Heritage 1984-87; bd of dirs/chr, Public Broadcasting Assn of Atlanta 1988-90; bd of dirs Consumer Credit Counseling Assn 1984-; life mem Kappa Alpha Psi Frat, NAACP; bd of trustees chr, Bennett College, 1991-; principal Center for Excellence in Government, 1988; president, 100 Black Men of Altanta, GA, 1991-; member, Metro Atlanta Rapid Transit Authority (MARTA) Board of Directors, 1990-; chairman, Sustaining Membership Enrollment (SME) Boy Scouts of America, 1990-92; Georgia Partnership for Excellence in Education, 1991-. **Honors/Awds:** State of GA House & Senate Resolutions Outstanding Public Serv 1979; Achievement Kappa Alpha Psi Frat 1980; Comm Serv Atlanta Business League 1984; Dr of Laws, Shorter Coll, Allen Univ, Edward Waters Coll, Morris Booker Coll; Atlanta Urban League Distinguished Serv Awd 1986; Roy Wilkins Awd Georgia NAACP 1986; President's Awd Natl Conf of Black Mayors Economic Devel Task Force 1986; Leadership Award Metro-Atlanta United Way 1987; President's Award National Alliance of Business 1988.

WALKER, WILLIE F.
Organization executive. **Personal:** Born Feb 6, 1942, Vernon, AL; son of Naomi Ford Walker and Willie B. Walker; married Frizal Glasper, May 22, 1971; children: Shannon, Willie Jr., Alex, Teresa. **Educ:** Southern Illinois University, BS, 1965; University of Wisconsin, Milwaukee, WI, MS, 1971. **Career:** Venice School System, East St Louis, IL, teacher, 1965-69; Venice-Lincoln Educational Center, Venice, IL, director of placement, 1971-73; Madison/St Clair County, Alton, IL, director of manpower, 1973-76; National Urban League Regional Office, Chicago, IL, regional coordinator, 1976-77; Madison County Urban League, Alton, IL, executive director, 1977-85; Dayton Urban League, Dayton, OH, president and chief executive officer, 1985—. **Orgs:** Co-chair, Black Leadership Development, 1986—; board treasurer, Dayton Free Clinic, 1987—; co-chair, Ohio Black Family Coalition, 1987—; board member, Ohio Elected Public Officials, 1987—; board secretary, Ohio Council of Urban League, 1987—; member, Black Managers Association, 1987—; president, United Way Agency of Executives, 1989; member of steering committee, Black Agenda for the Year 2000, 1989; account chair, United Way Campaign, 1989. **Honors/Awds:** Honorary member, National Business League, 1985; Gold Award, United Way of Greater Dayton, 1985-89; community service award, Dayton Jobs Corps Center, 1987; Century Club award, YMCA, 1987; honorary recognition, Black Leadership Development, 1989. **Business Addr:** President, Dayton Urban League, United Way Bldg, Ste 240, 184 Salem Ave, Dayton, OH 45406.

WALKER, WILLIE LEROY
City official. **Personal:** Born Dec 26, 1945, Detroit, MI; son of Leila & Stanley Walker; married Edna Walker, Dec 17, 1966; children: Dwayne, Takesha. **Educ:** USAF Academy Prep School, Certificate of Completion, 1966; Wayne State Univ, BS, bus admin, 1971, MBA, management, 1974; Walsh College, MBA, accounting, 1990. **Career:** City of Detroit, project mgr, productivity div, mayor's office, 1975-78, division head, program management E&T, 1978-91, coordinator, admin services, E&T, 1991-93, deputy dir, E&T, 1993, director E&T 1994-. **Orgs:** Multi Media Partnership, advisory bd, 1995; MI Jobs Commn, advisory bd mem, 1994-, workfirst, finance comm chair, 1994-; MI Dept Ed, advisory bd mem, 1984-; Booker T Washington Bus Assn, bd mem, 1995; Ebenezer AME Credit Union, audit comm mem, 1989-90, vice chair, 1991; Det Police Athletic League, mgr/asst coach, 1978-88; MI Dept Ed, MI Family Resource Coalition, 1995; Mercy College, accounting tutor-accounting club, 1987. **Honors/Awds:** Arab American & Chaldean Council, Civic & Humanitarian Award, 1994; Wayne State Univ, Beta Gamma Honorary Society, 1971; Highland Park Optimist Club, Appreciation Award, 1987; Det Police Dept, Jr Police Cadet Appreciation, 1985 & 1994. **Special Achievements:** Pee Wee Hockey Travel Team, National Champions, 1984. **Military Serv:** USAF, sgt, 1964-68. **Business Addr:** Dir, Employment/Training Dept, City of Detroit, 707 W Milwaukee, 5th Fl, Detroit, MI 48202, (313)876-0674.

WALKER, WILLIE M.
Engineer (retired). **Personal:** Born Aug 18, 1929, Bessemer, AL; son of Annie Maimie Thompson Walker and Johnnie Walker; married Mae R Fulton; children: Patricia, Mark, Karen M Stokes. **Educ:** Marquette Univ, BEE 1958; Univ Of WI, MSEE 1965. **Career:** AC Spark Plug Div GMC, devel tech 1953-56, proj engr 1956-60, engr supvr 1960-65; AC Electronics Div GMC, sr devel eng 1965-71; Delco Electronics Corp, Oak Creek, WI, senior production engineering, 1972-94; Walker Engineering, founder, 1995. **Orgs:** Mem IEEE since 1955, NSPE WI Soc of Prof Engrs 1981; reg prof Engr State of WI 1963; mem Computer Sci Adv Bd Milwaukee Area Technl Coll since 1982; pres Potawatomi Area Cncl BSA 1982-84; mem Natl Council Boy Scouts of Amer; mem usher St Mary Catholic Church Men Falls, WI; chief camp inspector Area 1 East Central Region BSA; vice pres program Area One East Central Region BSA 1987-93; chairman Computer Science Advisory Board Milwaukee Area Tech Coll 1988-89; sr mem Institute of Industrial Engineers 1988-; sr mem CASA Society of Manufacturing Engineers 1989-; certified systems integrator, Institute of Industrial Engineers, 1990-; vice president, We Four Program Inc, 1990-93; mem, BSA, Central Region Board, 1993-. **Honors/Awds:** GM Awd for Excellence Comm Act Delco Electronics 1980; Man of the Year Rotary Club Menomonee Falls WI 1983; Black Achiever Bus/Ind YMCA Milwaukee WI 1984; Silver Antelope Awd East Central Region Boy Scouts of Amer 1987; Silver Beaver Award, Potowatomi Area Council BSA, 1973; St Geo Award, Archdiocese, Milwaukee, 1975. **Military Serv:** USAF Sgt 1949-53.

WALKER, WOODSON DUBOIS
Attorney. **Personal:** Born Apr 6, 1950, Springfield, AR; married Hope Labarriteau King; children: Yedea H, Ajamu K, Fwatula, Ajani, Chike. **Educ:** AM&N Coll; Univ of AR Bine Bluff, BA History & Phil 1971; Univ of MN Sch of Law, JD 1974. **Career:** City of Allport AR, legal consult 1980; Cinula & Walker PA, Ltl Rock, partner 1978; City of Menifee AR, city & atty 1977; Walker Kaplan & Mays PA Little Rock, asso Atty 1976-77; Cntrl MN Legl Srv Corp Minneapolis, asso atty 1974-76. **Orgs:** Mem AR MN Am & Nat Bar Assn 1974; sec Ebony Plz Corp (Rtl Clthng Store) Little Rock AR 1976; mem Little Rock Wastewtr Utlty Com 1979; mem AR St Bd of Crrctns 1980; board member Boatmen's National Bank; board member AP&L Utility Co.; board member Little Rock Chamber of Commerce; member Pulaski Bar Association; member W Harold Flowers Law Society. **Honors/Awds:** Outstndng Stdnt Ldr Zeta Phi Beta Sor Univ of AR Pine Bluff 1971; Hghr Achvmnts Awd Phi Beta Omega Frat Inc Chi Psi Rho Chap Pine Bluff AR 1971; cum laude grad, Univ of AR Pine Bluff 1971. **Business Addr:** 124 W Capitol Ave, Ste 990, Little Rock, AR 72201.

WALKER, WYATT TEE
Cleric. **Personal:** Born Aug 16, 1929, Brockton, MA; married Theresa Ann Edwards; children: Wyatt Tee, Jr, Ann Patrice, Robert Charles, Earl Maurice. **Educ:** VA Union Univ, BS (magna cum laude) 1950, MDiv (summa cum laude) 1953, LHD 1967; Colgate-Rochester Div School, PhD 1975. **Career:** Historic Gillfield Baptist Church, Petersburg VA, minister, 1953-60; Dr Martin Luther King Jr, chief of staff; SCLC, Atlanta, vice pres, bd exec dir, 1960-64; Abyssinian Baptist Church, NYC, pulpit minister, 1965-66; Governor NYC, special asst on urban affairs; Cannan Baptist Church of Christ NYC, minister, CEO, 1967-; Church Housing Development Fund Inc, president/CEO, 1975-. **Orgs:** mem, World Peace Council, 1971-; Programme to Combat Racism of the World Council of Churches, world commissioner; Consortium for Central harlem Development, chairman; Religious Action Network of the American Committee on Africa, secretary general; ACOA, president. **Honors/Awds:** Author, Black Church Looks at the Bicentennial, Somebody's Calling My Name, Soul of Black Worship, Road to Damascus, The Harvard paper, Soweto Diary, Del World Conf on Religion and Peace, Japan, China Diary, Common Thieves, The Harvard Paper, Soweto Diary, Occasional Papers of a Revolutionary; Received numerous human rights awards including the Elks Human Rights Award, 1963; Natl Alpha Awards in Civil Rights, 1965; Shriners Natl Civil Rights Award, 1974; Civil Rights Award, ADA, 1975; Honorary LHD, Virginia Union University, 1967; Honorary DD, Edward Waters College, 1985; Honorary D Litt, Gettysburg College, 1988; Top Fifteen Greatest African American Preacher In the US, Ebony Magazine, 1993; roles in "Mama, I Wanna Sing," & "Malcolm X.". **Business Addr:** Minister, CEO, Canaan Baptist Church, 132 West 116th St, New York, NY 10026.

WALKER-GIBBS, SHIRLEY ANN
Women's basketball coach. **Personal:** Born Nov 19, 1945, Bude, MS; daughter of Bruno & Curlee Gibbs; married Lonnie R Walker, Dec 24, 1968; children: Lonnie R Jr, Marino L. **Educ:** Alcorn State Univ, BS, health and physical rec, MS, athletic adm/health & physical education-recreation. **Career:** Los Angeles Sch Dist, HPER & Science, teacher, coach, 1968-69; HISD, HPER & Science, teacher, 1969-72; Alcorn State Univ, senior women's administrator, head women's basketball coach, 1977-. **Orgs:** NCAA Council Committee, 1990-95; NCAA Women's Basketball, 1982-86; NCAA Basketball Officiating, 1992-94; NCAA Special Event, 1992-94; NCAA Minority Opportunity and Interest, 1990-95; NCAA Midwest Reg Advisory, 1990-93; NCAA Black Coaches Assn; Delta Sigma Theta Sorority, 1970-. **Honors/Awds:** Southwestern Conference, Coach of the Year, 1983-86, 1990-94; Alpha Phi Alpha, Outstanding Service Award, 1994. **Special Achievements:** Winner of five back-to-back championships, 1990-94. **Business Addr:** Sen Women's Administrator/ Head Women's Basketball Coach, Alcorn State University, PO Box 510, 1000 ASU Dr, Health and Physical Recreation Davey Whitney Complex, Lorman, MS 39096, (601)877-6500.

WALKER-SHAW, PATRICIA. **See Obituaries section.**

WALKER-SMITH, ANGELIQUE KETURAH
Clergywoman. **Personal:** Born Aug 18, 1958, Cleveland, OH; daughter of Geneva Willis Walker and Roosevelt V Walker; married R Drew Smith, Aug 16, 1980. **Educ:** Kent State University, Kent, OH, BA, 1980; Yale University Divinity School, New Haven, CT, master of divinity, 1983; Princeton Theological Seminary, Princeton, NJ, doctor of ministry, 1995. **Career:** WFSB-CBS TV, Hartford, CT, production asst, 1982-83; Operation Crossroads Africa, New York, NY, development dir, leader, 1983, 1984, 1985; Central Baptist Church, Hartford, CT, Hartford, CT, assoc pastor, 1983-86; TEAM, Trenton, NJ, exec minister, dir, 1986-90; Lilly Endowment, Indianapolis, IN, consultant, 1990-; The Church Federation of Greater Indianapolis, Indianapolis, IN, project dir, begin 1991, interim executive director, 1993-94, exec dir, 1995-; WKIV-Channel 6/AB, Faces of Faith, TV host, 1992-; Keturah Productions, founder/CEO; Odyssey Big Screen, co-host, currently. **Orgs:** Ecumenical Liaison, National Baptist Convention USA, Inc, 1989-94; member, central committee, World Council of Churches, 1991-; office of international affairs, Partners in Ecumenism, National Council of Churches in USA, 1986-88; secretary, board of directors, National Assn of Ecumenical Staff, 1986-89; pres, Global Exchange Study Associates, 1990-. **Honors/Awds:** State of New Jersey Commendation Proclamation, New Jersey State Legislature, 1990; Mayoral Commendation Proclamation, City of Trenton, 1990; Valiant Christian Woman's Award, Church Women United (Natl & Regional), 1990. **Business Addr:** Executive Director, The Church Federation of Greater Indianapolis, 1100 W 42nd St, Ste 345, Indianapolis, IN 46208.

WALKER-TAYLOR, YVONNE
Educator (retired). **Personal:** Born Apr 17, New Bedford, MA; daughter of D Ormonde Walker; married Robert H Taylor (deceased). **Educ:** Wilberforce Univ, BS 1936; Boston Univ, MA 1938; Univ of KS, Educ Spec 1964. **Career:** Wilberforce Univ, asst acad dean 1967-68, vice pres academic dean 1973-83, provost 1983-84, president 1984-88, president emeritus; Central State Univ, Wilberforce, OH, distinguished presidential professor, 1990-96. **Orgs:** Bd dirs Natl Commn on Coop Educ 1977-88; sec Greene Oaks Health Ctr 1983-87; chmn Culture Planning Council Natl Mus Afro-Amer History 1983-95-; bd mem Dayton Art Inst 1984-88; bd dirs United Way Xenia OH 1985; mem Links, 1959-93; Alpha Kappa Alpha, 1964; Ohio Humanities Council, 1994-. **Honors/Awds:** Woman of the Year Met Civic Women's Assoc Dayton 1984; one of Top Ten Women Dayton Newspapers Women's Coalition 1984; Outstanding Woman of Yr Iota Phi Lambda 1985; Drum Major for Justice Awd SCLC 1986.

WALKER-THOTH, DAPHNE LAVERA
Mental health official. **Personal:** Born Sep 16, 1954, St Louis, MO; daughter of Zelma J McNeil Carson and Sidney J Carson Jr; married Mark Walker (divorced 1980); children: Aaron; children: Candace Thoth. **Educ:** Northeast Missouri State, Kirksville, MO, BA, 1977; University of Missouri, MA, 1990. **Career:** Spectrum Emergency Care, MO, communications assistant, 1982-84; Boy Scouts of America, exploring executive, 1984-85; Voluntary Interdistrict Coordinating Council, assistant to director, 1985-90; Marketing Works, director of client

services, 1989-90; A World of Difference, community coordinator, 1990-91; Progressive Youth Center, director of community partnership, 1991-; MO Dept of Mental Health, Div of Alcohol and Drug Abuse, project manager, currently. **Orgs:** Board member, Counseling & Educational Support Services Inc, 1993-. **Honors/Awds:** Series of articles on the plight of children, National Newspaper Publishers Association, 1980; series of articles on the plight of the elderly, Greater St Louis Association of Black Journalists, 1979; Community Partnership Service Award, 1994. **Business Addr:** Project Manager, Missouri Department of Mental Health Division of Alcohol & Drug Abuse, 5400 Arsenal, St Louis, MO 63139.

WALKER WILLIAMS, HOPE DENISE
Educational administrator. **Personal:** Born Dec 24, 1952, Chicago, IL; daughter of Maryann Walker and Welmon Walker; children: Albert Lee, Ebony Emani Denise. **Educ:** Harvard Univ Graduate School of Design, certificate 1981; St Ambrose Univ, BA, psychology, 1985, MBA prog. **Career:** African-American Drama Co, midwest regional coord 1982-83; Dramatic Mktg Assn, opers mgr 1983-84; Scott County Davenport IA, admin intern 1985-86; Marycrest Coll Davenport, campus counselor 1986-87, asst to the dean 1987-90; Augustana Coll, assistant to dean of student services, 1990-92, assistant dean of students, 1991-. **Orgs:** Treas Quad Cities Career Womens Network 1983; student senator MBA Senate St Ambrose Coll 1985; Natl Assn of Black MBAs 1986; bd mem HELP Legal Aid 1986; panelist United Way Allocations 1987; bd mem, NACADA, 1988-. **Honors/Awds:** Certificate of Appreciation Conf of Black Families 1979/82; Certificate of Recognition Church Women United 1983; Yellow Belt Tae Kwon Do Karate 1984; Junior Achievement, Recognition for Personal Dedication, 1989-89, Hall of Fame Inductee, 1991; ACAFAD, Award for New Professionals, 1989; NAWE, Membership comm, national treasurer, 1993-95; Award for New Professionals. **Home Addr:** 1217 Ripley St, Davenport, IA 52803, (319)322-4732. **Business Addr:** Assistant Dean of Students, Augustana College, 639 38th St, Rock Island, IL 61201, (309)794-7580.

WALL, J. C. See Obituaries section.

WALLACE, AARON
Professional football player. **Personal:** Born Apr 17, 1967. **Educ:** Texas A&M. **Career:** Oakland Raiders, linebacker, currently. **Business Addr:** Professional Football Player, Oakland Raiders, 1220 Harbor Bay Pkwy, Alameda, CA 94502, (510)615-1875.

WALLACE, ARNOLD D., SR.
Communications administrator. **Personal:** Born Feb 1, 1932, Salisbury, MD; son of Margaret Townsend Wallace and Linwood Wallace; married Theresa, Sep 27, 1950; children: Deborah, Terry, Arnold Jr, Michael, Stephen, Stephanie. **Educ:** Rutgers Univ, AS 1974, BS 1977 (summa cum laude), MBA 1977; Howard Univ, MA 1986. **Career:** WCAU-TV, engr, 1963-72; WCAU-TV, dir of comm affairs 1972-79; Rutgers Univ, co-adj prof admin studies 1978-79; Howard Univ, dir univ relations 1979-80; WHMM-TV Howard Univ, gen mgr 1980-88; New Breed Media Group, Inc, pres, beginning 1988-. **Orgs:** Pres Pennsauken NJ Bd of Ed 1975-76; mem Capitol Press Club, Natl Press Club, NAACP, Legal Defense Fund Steering Comm, Friends of the Kennedy Ctr, Oriental Lodge 1 FAM Camden NJ, Zamora Temple AEONMS Camden; mem Omega Psi Phi, Kiwanis Intl, FAA Commercial Pilot Multi-Engine-Land, Aircraft Owners & Pilots Assoc, Negro Airmen Intl, NJ State Bds of Ed fin Comm; bd of dir Dist of Columbia C of C, Intl United Black Fund, Metro YMCA; sec Central Education Network bd of dir 1983-85; Nat'l Assoc of Public TV Stations, sec 1986-88; DC Youth Orchestra, bd of dir 1986-. **Honors/Awds:** Prod Negro Airmen Intl documentary film ''Journey to Paradise-Nassau'' 1972; article ''Ebony Eagles'' Flying Mag 1972; prod, wrote & filmed Negro Airmen Intl documentary ''Journey to Paradise-Barbados'' 1973; article ''Integrated Cockpit'' Aero Mag 1974; prod half-hour CBS training film ''Careers in Broadcasting'' 1974; Kappa Alpha Psi Frat Media Awd Media Accompl Exec Prod ''Year 2000 & Beyond'' Amer Found for Negro Affairs 1976; article ''The Sharecropper'' Rutgers Univ Lit Mag 1977; prod, dir film ''Reaching Out'' Camden Cty United Way 1979; the Four Chaplains Awd 1979; exec prod Profiles In Greatness series 1983-; Awd for Film ''Prime Minister Phillip Barrow''; prod, host ''Turn to Ten'' CBS-TV Philadelphia; Nat'l Assoc of Minority Contractors public service awd 1985; DCChamber of Commerce media awd l; Private Sector Initiatives, pres of US Ronald Reagan l987; Silver Circle Natl Academy of TV Arts & Sciences l988; Broadcasting Decision Making in the Area of Children's TV (dissertation) l986; Delaney's Business Report (US Govt Audio Video Contracts Newsletters) l989.

WALLACE, ARTHUR, JR.
Educational administrator. **Personal:** Born Jun 12, 1939, Muskogee, OK; son of Edna Collins Wallace and Arthur Wallace; married Claudina Young Wallace, Oct 4, 1969; children: Dwayne, Jon, Charles. **Educ:** Langston University, Langston, OK, BS, 1960; Oklahoma State University, Stillwater, OK, MS, 1962, PhD, 1964. **Career:** General Foods Corp, White Plains, NY, Dir, Commodity Res, 1964-67; Merrill Lynch, New York, NY, vice president & senior economist, 1967-71; Group IV Ecomonics, New York, NY, senior partner, 1971-76; International Paper, Purchase, NY, vice president, & corp secretary, 1976-; San Francisco State Univ, dean, School of Business, 1994-. **Orgs:** Member national advisory board, US Department of Commerce, 1973-74; member advisory board, Columbia University Workplace Center, 1985-89; member, advisory board, Scarsdale Day Care Center, 1985-88; trustee, American Management Assn, 1982-84, 1987-90; American Economic Assn; Natl Assn Business Economists; San Franciso Convention & Vishes Bureau, director; Romberg Tibron Research Center. **Home Addr:** 1085 Greenwich No 1, San Francisco, CA 94133. **Business Addr:** Dean, School of Business, San Francisco State Univ, 1600 Holloway Ave, San Francisco, CA 94132.

WALLACE, BEN
Professional basketball player. **Personal:** Born Sep 10, 1974. **Educ:** Virginia Union. **Career:** Washington Wizards, forward, 1996-. **Business Addr:** Professional Basketball Player, Washington Wizards, MCI Center, 601 F St NW, Washington, DC 20071, (202)661-5000.

WALLACE, C. EVERETT
Attorney, appointed government official. **Personal:** Born Aug 16, 1951, Chicago, IL. **Educ:** Northwestern U, BA 1969-73; Northwestern U, JD 1973-76. **Career:** US Senate Budget Comm, sr analysis & energy couns 1980; Sen Howard Baker US Sen, legal asst 1977-80; Memphis Light Gas & Water Div Memphis, staff atty 1976-77; Clausen Miller & Gorman Caffery & Witous Law Firm, rsch assoc 1975-76; Shelby Co Black Rep Council, legal counsel & co-founder 1977; Progressive Assembly Reps, gen counsel & co-founder 1979. **Orgs:** Vice chmn & cofounder Black Rep Cong Staffer's Assn 1979; counsel sec of 1980 Republican Natl Conv; mem Natl Bar Assn; mem Amer Bar Assn; pres Alpha Mu Chap; Alpha Phi Alpha Frat Inc. **Honors/Awds:** Northwestern Univ Top Ten Debator, Illinois State Contest; Natl Achievement Scholar, Thornton Township High School, Harvey IL; Natl Merit Scholar; Illinois State Scholar; Honors Grad, Northwestern Univ School of Law; admitted to Bar of Tennessee, 1977. **Business Addr:** US Senate, Washington, DC.

WALLACE, CHARLES LESLIE
Communications company executive. **Personal:** Born Dec 26, 1945, Monmouth, IL; son of Harriet Wallace and Leslie Wallace; married Marie Elizabeth Lancaster; children: Allison, Bryan. **Educ:** Northern IL Univ, BS Accounting 1967; Univ of Chicago, MBA Finance 1973; CPA 1973. **Career:** Arthur Andersen & Co, auditor 1967-74; Jos Schultz Brewing Co, financial analyst 1974-76; Univ Foods Corp, treasurer 1976-81; Pabst Brewing Co, treasurer 1981-85; Norrell Corp, treasurer 1985-87; North Milwaukee State Bank, pres 1987-89; Ameritech Mobile Communications Inc, vice president of finance and administration, 1989-. **Orgs:** Mem Finance Execs Inst Chicago Chapter, Amer Inst of CPA's, Kappa Alpha Psi. **Honors/Awds:** Black Excellence Award, The Milwaukee Times, 1989; Outstanding Accounting Alumnus, Northern Illinois University, 1991. **Military Serv:** USMC 1st lt 1967-72.

WALLACE, CLAUDETTE J.
Educator. **Personal:** marrIed Elmo; children: Elmo Jr, Renee, Andre. **Educ:** FL A&M U, BS; NY U, MS; Univ of Hartford, 6th yr prof cert; Springfield Coll, Triniy Coll, Univ of CT, Cntrl CT St Tchr Coll, grad Studies. **Career:** Barber Scotia Coll, past dir physical educ, FL Meml & Indstrl Inst, past dir girls physical educ. **Orgs:** Pres Black Bus & Professional Women Clb; area rep NY Univ Alumni Clb; mem Life Nat Educ Assn; mem Life Nat Hlth Phy Educ & Rcrtn Assn; exec sec New Britain Chap FL A&M Univ Alumni Assn; mem Coll Club; mem Am Assn of Univ Women; mem Life NAACP; mem Grtr New Britain Comm Cncl; den mother 1960-65; st pres of educ CT Diocese of the Ch of God in Christ; bd chrprsn Black Resrch Informtn Cntr 1970; dir New Britain Tutrl Schl 1969; chrtr mem Women's Aux of Salvation Army; mem New Britain Gen Hosp Vol Aux Assn; mem New Britain HS Music Club & Parents Booster's Athltc Assn; past vice pres Little Leg Basebll & Midget & Football Clubs. **Honors/Awds:** Recip Testmnl Dinner 1972. **Business Addr:** Head Dept of Physical Educ, Slade School, 183 Steel St, New Britain, CT 06052.

WALLACE, DERRICK D.
Business executive. **Personal:** Born Nov 4, 1953, Orlando, FL; son of Theressa Williams Wallace; divorced; children: Daunte, Deja. **Educ:** FL A&M Univ, BS, accounting, 1975; Rollins College, management program, attended. **Career:** Price Waterhouse & Co CPA, staff accountant 1975-77; Tuttle/White Constructors, Inc, chief accountant 1977-79; Construct Two Construction Managers, Inc. owner/pres 1979-. **Orgs:** Bd mem Central State Assn of Min Contr; mem Greater Orlando Chamber of Commerce 1984; bd mem Greater Orlando Chamber of Commerce 1989 6 yr term; past chairman Private Industry Council of Central Florida, past 2 years; commr Mayor's Commission on the Arts; subcommittee chair Mayor's Youth Comm (business involvement); class mem Leadership Orlando 1988; mem Greater Florida Minority Purchasing Council; partner Partners in Education-Washington Shores Elementary; partner Partners in Education-Rock Lake Elementary; sponsored minority (Black) Role Model Project for Orange County Schools as the Private Industry Council Chairman, gathered over 120 Black professionals to speak to children in school about what their life experiences had been and the importance of education; board member, Orlando/Ore County Compact, 1990-91; board member, Additions, 1990-91; member, Walt Disney World Community Service Award Committee, 1991; Economic Development Commission of Mid-Florida, board of directors; National Association of Minority Contractors, past bd of dirs; founder 100 Black Men of Orlando Inc; bd mem Central Florida Jobs in Education Partnership; Goodwill Industries, bd of dirs; Central Florida Fair, past bd of dirs; Mayor's Martin Luther King Commission, past chair. **Honors/Awds:** Construction Firm of the Year, US Dept of Commerce Minority Business Devel Agency 1984; Outstanding Achievement as Minority Business Entrepreneur, Central Florida Minority Development Council, Inc., 1988; named Outstanding Young Man of America in 1986; Entrepreneur of the year GFMPL; Up and Comer Award 1989 Orlando Business Journal and Price Waterhouse; Greater Orlando Chamber of Commerce ''Top 25 Small Business'' Award, 1997; Univ of FL ''Florida 100'' Award, 1997; Downtown Orlando Partnership ''Mentorship'' Award, 1995, 1997; Drum Major Award for business, Alpha Phi Alpha Fraternity, Inc, 1993; African American Chamber of Commerce ''Construction Co of the Year'' Award, 1997. **Business Addr:** President, Construct Two Construction Managers, Inc., 4409 Old Winter Garden Rd, Orlando, FL 32811, (407)295-9812.

WALLACE, HAROLD GENE
Educational administrator. **Personal:** Born Aug 13, 1945, Gaffney, SC; son of Melinda Goudelock Wallace and Charles T Wallace Sr (deceased); married Carrie Lucinda Littlejohn, Jul 13, 1963; children: Toya Bonita, Shonda Lee, Harold Gene Jr, Charles Marion. **Educ:** Claflin College Orangeburg SC, BS (summa cum laude) 1967; Duke Univ Div School Durham NC, MDiv 1971. **Career:** Bethesda Presbyterian Church, Gaffney, SC, pastor and youth counselor, 1968; Durham Community House, Inc, counselor, 1968-69; Duke Univ, Summer Transitional Program, asst director, 1969, assoc director, 1970, co-director, 1971, director, 1972, asst to dean of undergraduate education, student advisor, 1969-72, asst provost, dean of black student affairs, interim director of community and field work for Afro-American majors, seminar instructor for Afro-American studies, 1972-73; Univ of NC, Chapel Hill, assoc dean of student affairs, director of dept of special programs, 1973-79, asst vice chancellor for student affairs, 1979-80, vice chancellor for University affairs, 1980-96, special asst for minority affairs, 1996-. **Orgs:** Group moderator So Regional Educ Bd Conf on Black Students & Univ 1971; mem Nat Commn of United Ministers in Higher Educ 1971-75; consult Minority Student Progs Univ SC Furman & Wake Forest 1971-78; sec treas Black Faculty Staff Caucus Univ NC Chapel Hill 1974-80, chair, 1987-90; bd dir Wesley Found Campus Ministry Univ NC 1976-80; Institute for the Study of Minority Issues at NC Central University, 1977-; NC Cen Univ Durham NC 1977-80; pres Alpha Kappa Mu Nat & Honor Soc Claflin Coll 1966-67; chair, Black Culture Center Advisory Board University of North Carolina, 1990-; chair, Upward Bound Advisory Board, University of North Carolina, 1980-. **Honors/Awds:** Rockefeller Fellow, Duke Univ 1967; publ ''Studies in Black'' 1969; ''Three Years of the Duke Summer Transitional Program'' 1973; Faculty awards for outstanding achievements, Black Student Movement, Univ NC Chapel Hill, 1981, Univ NC Black Alumni Association, 1982; Martin Luther King Jr Award, South Orange Black Caucus, Chapel Hill, NC, 1988; Award of Commitment to Justice and Equality, Butner NC NAACP, 1989; chairman emeritus of the Sonja Haynes Stone Black Culture Center, UNC-Chapel Hill. **Business Addr:** Special Assistant for Minority Affairs, University of North Carolina at Chapel Hill, CB #9125, 02 South Bldg, Chapel Hill, NC 27599-9125.

WALLACE, HELEN WINFREE-PEYTON
Educational administrator (retired). **Personal:** Born Dec 19, 1927, New York, NY; daughter of Agnes Winfree and Hugh Winfree; married Mr Charles (divorced); children: Walter S Peyton IV. **Educ:** VA Union University, BA 1949, 1959; Northwestern University, MA 1955; Univ of California, VA State University, VCU, University of Caltolica, Di Milano Italy, 1960-68. **Career:** Richmond Public Schools, tchr 1949-69, lang arts consultant 1969-71, diagnostic & prescriptive reading, coord 1971-75; Richmond Public Schools chptr I reading coordinator 1975. **Orgs:** Consultant, Comm Groups 1975-83; pres, Elem Teachers Assn 1967; v pres, Assn Classroom Teachers 1973; Natl Ed Assn 1950; v pres, Richmond Ed Assn 1950; Crusade for Voters 1949; Exec Brd of NAACP IRA-RARC-VSRA; historian, Continental Societies, Inc 1976-91. **Honors/Awds:** Tchr First Black to integrate Westhampton Sch 1965-69; execl serv Chapter I Reading Teacher 1982; achievements Alliance for Black Social Welfare 1983; co-sponsored Book Bowl. **Home Addr:** 8222 Whistler Rd, Richmond, VA 23227.

WALLACE, JEFFREY J.
Educational administrator. **Personal:** Born Apr 7, 1946, Mobile, AL; married Patricia A Henderson; children: Jeffrey, Jennifer, Justin, Jawaan. **Educ:** State Univ College at Fredonia, BA History 1964-68; State Univ of NY at Buffalo, MEd Counseling 1973, PhD History & Philosophy of Educ 1980. **Career:** SUNY Fredonia, admin asst for adm & records 1969-72, dir EOP 1972-

81, asst vice pres for academic affairs 1977-81; State Univ College at Buffalo, dir EOP 1981-86, asst vice pres acad affairs 1986-. **Orgs:** SUNY Chancellors' Taskforce on Minority Graduate Oppor 1983; Natl Assn of Academic Advisors 1984; bd chairperson of the Buffalo Post-Secondary Consortium of Special Progs 1985; pres Special Prog Personnel Assn 1984-; evaluator/ ed consultant PNJ Consultling. **Honors/Awds:** Polotics & Precusors The EOP/SEEK at SUCB Urban Educ vol 18 no 4 pgs 503-519 Jan 1984; Special Services for Disadvantaged Students Grant SUNY 1979; SpecialServices for Disadvantaged Students Grant SUCB 1984.

WALLACE, JOHN
Professional basketball player. **Personal:** Born Feb 9, 1974, Rochester, NY. **Educ:** Syracuse. **Career:** New York Knicks, forward, 1996-97; Toronto Raptors, 1997-. **Special Achievements:** NBA Draft, First round pick, #18, 1996. **Business Addr:** Professional Basketball Player, Toronto Raptors, 150 York St, Ste 110, Toronto, ON, Canada M5H 3S5, (416)214-2255.

WALLACE, JOHN E., JR.
Judge. **Personal:** Born Mar 13, 1942, Pitman, NJ; son of Evelyn Wallace and John Wallace; married Barbara A Coles; children: John III, Andrea Lynn, Kimberly Denise, Michele Eileen, Michael Ernest. **Educ:** University of Delaware, BA 1964; Harvard Law School, LlB 1967. **Career:** State of New Jersey, Superior Court judge, currently; Atkinson Myers Archie & Wallace, attorney, partner; Washington Township, municipal court judge, 1972-81; Trustees of Pennsylvania Central Transp, attorney, 1971-75; Montgomery McCracken Walker & Rhoads Co, associate, 1969-71. **Orgs:** Secretary, Gloucester Co Municipal Court Judges Assn, 1974-; bd of trustees,treasurer, Gloucester Co College; American Bar Assn; New Jersey Bar Assn; Barrister's Club; baseball & basketball coach, Washington Township, 1970-; Community Activities Commission, Washington Township, 1971; Kappa Alpha Psi, 1978-. **Honors/Awds:** Outstanding Service Award, New Jersey State Federation of Colored Women's Clubs, 1976. **Military Serv:** US Army, captain, 1968-69; Certificate of Achievement, 1969. **Business Addr:** Superior Court, Appellate Division, State of New Jersey, 216 Haddon Ave, 7th Fl, Westmont, NJ 08108.

WALLACE, JOSEPH FLETCHER, JR.
Dean of education. **Personal:** Born Aug 3, 1921, Ethelsville, AL; married Ethel Theresa Ward; children: Patrick, Katherine T Wallace Casey. **Educ:** West Coast Univ, BA 1953; Amer Baptist Theol Seminary, Certificate 1975, Diploma 1977; Union Univ, DTh 1982. **Career:** US Government, clerk 1949-54; General Motors Corp, sr inspector 1955-82; Thomas & Sons Building Inc, consultant 1982-; The Religious Council of Amer, dean of educ. **Orgs:** Nobles of the Mystic Shrine 32 Degree Mason 1979; mem LA Police Clergy Council 1985-, NAACP. **Honors/Awds:** Awd of Merit for Outstanding Achievement USC 1975. **Military Serv:** AUS s/sgt 6 yrs; Good Conduct Medal, Combat Infantry, Bronze Star. **Business Addr:** Dean of Education, The Religious Council of Amer, PO Box 82004, Los Angeles, CA 90082.

WALLACE, MILTON DE'NARD
Educational administrator. **Personal:** Born Jul 7, 1957, Tyler, TX; son of Thelma Jackson Wallace and John Wallace; married Gwendolyn Wallace, Apr 8, 1989. **Educ:** East TX State Univ, BS 1978, MEd 1979; Univ of North Texas, Denton, TX 1988. **Career:** Commerce ISD, teacher 1978-83, asst principal 1983-84; Union Hill ISD, principal 1984-87; Denton Independent School Dist, Denton, TX, asst principal, 1987-90, head principal, 1990-. **Orgs:** Pres RAWSCO Inc 1983; vice pres Professional Men's Serv Club 1983-84; mem TX Assn of Elementary School Principals 1983; owner M & L Educational Scholarship Service; mem Texas Assn of Black School Educators 1989-; member, Texas Assn of Secondary School Principals, 1984-95; Director of Summer Workshop, Texas Assn of Student Councils, 1989, 1990; Denton Administrators Association, 1987-95, vice president, 1991, 1993, president, 1994-95; National Association of Secondary School Principals, 1991-95. **Honors/Awds:** Principal of Year, Texas Assn of Secondary School Principals, 1990. **Home Addr:** PO Box 2843, Denton, TX 76202. **Business Addr:** Principal, Denton High School, 1007 Fulton St, Denton, TX 76201, (817)382-9611.

WALLACE, PAUL STARETT, JR.
Attorney. **Personal:** Born Jan 22, 1941, Wilmington, NC; son of Mary Ligon Wallace and Paul Wallace; married Priscilla H Harris; children: Shaunia Patrese. **Educ:** North Carolina Central Univ, BS, 1962, JD, 1966. **Career:** US Copyright Office Library of Congress, copyright examiner, 1966-71; Congressional Research Serv, Library of Congress, former senior legislative atty, head of the Congress section, amer law div, Washington, DC, 1984-86, coord of multidis programs, 1986-96; Specialist in American Public Law, American Law Division, 1996-. **Orgs:** Advisory bd, Comm Action for Human Serv Inc, 1983-; Fed Bar Assn News & Jrnl, 1980-81; sec, Cncl of Crct; vice pres, Fed Bar Assn, 1981-82; pres, Capitol Hill Chapter Fed Bar Assn, 1979-80; adv bd mem, Federal Bar News & Journal, 1980-82; natl vice pres, District of Columbia Circuit Fed Bar Assn, 1981-82; chairperson, co-chair, Federal Bar Assn, natl mem committee, 1982-83; Section on the Admin of Justice, Washington, DC, 1984-89; mem, Dist of Columbia Bar Assn, US Supreme Court; continuing educ bd, Fed Bar Assn, 1985-; vice-chairperson, Library of Congress US Savings Bond Campaign, 1985; mem, Omega Psi Phi, US Dist Ct for District of Columbia; mem, US Court of Appeals for the DC Circuit; special editor Fed Bar Assn News & Journal, 1984, 1986; mem US Dist Court for the 8th Circuit, Phiha Delta Law Fraternity Intl; mem, Natl & Amer Bar Assoc; 33 Degree Mason; chairperson continuing educ bd, Fed Bar Assn, 1987-89; bd of trustees, Peoples Congregational Church, Washington, DC, 1985-90; Peoples Congregational Church, church council, 1990-; Foundation of the Federal Bar Association, board of directors, 1991-; Foundation of the Federal Bar Association, advisor, 1991; chairman, Diaconate Board, Peoples Congregational Church, 1993-95; chairman, Church Council, Peoples Congregational Church, 1996-; treasurer, Foundation of the Federal Bar Association, 1993-. **Honors/Awds:** Mem, Pi Gamma Mu Natl Science Honor Soc; Commendation Award Outstanding Qualities of Leadership & Dedicated Serv, 1980; Distinguished Serv Award, 1984; Fed Bar Assn Longstanding and Dedicated Serv Award, 1986; Omega Psi Phi Fraternity, Alpha Omega Chapter, Scroll of Honor, 1991. **Home Addr:** 3271 Van Hazen St NW, Washington, DC 20015.

WALLACE, PEGGY MASON
Government official. **Personal:** Born Sep 5, 1948, Salisbury, MD; daughter of Hattie A Mason (deceased) and Rayfield J Mason Sr (deceased); married Joseph R Wallace, Sep 15, 1979; children: Shawn. **Educ:** Morgan State University, BS, 1970; University of Illinois, MA, 1971. **Career:** Bell Laboratories, technical staff, 1972-75; Calculon Consulting Firm, systems analyst, trainer, 1975-81; Department of Navy, management information systems, manager, 1981-96, Management Information & Support Services, head, 1996-. **Orgs:** Alpha Kappa Mu Honor Society, president, 1967-70; Mathematics Club, charter mem, president, 1970; Federal Women's Program, 1982-83; Department of Navy's Tutoring Program. 1985-. **Honors/Awds:** US Navy Strategic Systems Program, Meritious Civilian Service Award, 1990; Morgan State University, four-year scholarship, 1966; University of Illinois, one-year scholarship, 1971; numerous others. **Business Addr:** Manager of Mgmt Info Systems, US Navy, Strategic Systems Programs, 1931 Jefferson Davis Hwy, Crystal Mall 3, Rm 829, Arlington, VA 22202-3518, (703)607-1542.

WALLACE, RASHEED ABDUL
Professional basketball player. **Personal:** Born Sep 17, 1974, Philadelphia, PA; son of Jacqueline; children: Ishmiel Shaeed. **Educ:** North Carolina. **Career:** Washington Bullets, center-forward, 1995-96; Portland TrailBlazers, 1996-. **Honors/Awds:** NBA All-Rookie Second Team, 1996. **Special Achievements:** NBA, First Round Draft Pick, #4 Pick, 1995. **Business Addr:** Professional Basketball Player, Portland TrailBlazers, 1 Center Court, Ste 200, Portland, OR 97227, (503)234-9291.

WALLACE, RENEE C.
Psychologist. **Personal:** Born in New Britain, CT; daughter of Chaudette J Wallace and Elmo Wallace Sr; widowed; children: Love, Lovely. **Educ:** Central CT State Univ, BA 1974; Univ of IA, MA 1975, PhD 1977. **Career:** Univ of IA, admin asst 1974-77; Morgan State Univ, admin/asst prof 1977-79; Clayton Univ, adjunct faculty 1979-; James Madison Univ, counseling psychologist 1980-84; Wallace & Wallace Assocs, dir 1980-; SUNY Potsdam, dir of counseling 1984; Dept of Corrections, administrator 1986, principal, 1986-89; Central Connecticut State Univ, New Britain, CT, asst prof, 1989-. **Orgs:** Sec Phi Delta Kappa 1979; consultant Southern Assoc of Colls & Schools 1981, 1984; educ consultant Black Educational Res & Inf Ctr 1984; bd dirs Natl Comm of Educating Youth on Energy. **Special Achievements:** Publications ''Prospective Teachers' Responses on an Adjective Checklist to Descriptions of 3 Students in 3 Different Socioeconomic Classes,'' US Govt 1978; ''Black Administrators & Career Stress,'' proceedings of the 8th Natl Conf on Blacks in Higher Educ 1983; ''The Ingredients of an Idea: Creativity in Counseling,'' Morgan Bulletin, 1979; Freshman Guide and Workbook of Morgan State University, 1978; ''Developmental Study Skills Program for Student Athletes,'' State Department of Education Virginia, Technical Assistant Division, Richomnd Virginia, 1982; ''The Dynamic of Career Stress in Black Professional Administrations on White Campuses,'' James Madison University Review, Harrisonburg, Virginia, 1982; ''Effects of Teaching Stress Reducation Coping Techniques in the Prevention of Academic Underachievement,'' Proceedings of the 16th National Conference of Blacks in Higher Education, 1991; ''Biofeedback, Biodots and Stress: A Technique for Improving Student Academic Performance,'' Proceedings of the 16th National Conference on Black in Higher Education, 1991, ''Mental Skills Training Program for Men's Collegiate Basketball Players,'' Research at Central Connecticut State University, 1992. **Home Addr:** 2334 Gail Ave Apt 6, Albany, GA 31707-2455.

WALLACE, RICHARD WARNER
Engineer (retired). **Personal:** Born Nov 6, 1929, Gary, IN; son of Ruth Wallace and Othello Wallace; married Lillian Mozel. **Educ:** Purdue U, BS 1951; George Washington U, Am Univ Wash DC, post grad studies. **Career:** USN Naval Sea Systems Command, dsgnr dvl & tstng elec, electronic systms on ships & submarines 1951, rspnsbl mngmnt tech & lgstcs support navy's deep submergence vehicle prgrms, & nuclear pwrd submarine NR 1, 1951-85, TRW Systems Integration Group, asst proj mgr 1985-94. **Orgs:** Life Mem Nat Soc Professional Engrs; board of directors, Potomac Chapter, Maryland Society of Professor Engineers; Am Soc Navl Engrs; Naval Submarine League; Marine Tech Soc; Amateur Radio; Astrnmy; Photography; life mem Alpha Phi Alpha; chartr mem Beta Mu Boule, Sigma Pi Phi; mem The Guardsmen, Wash DC Chpt; Rgstrd Prfl Engr, Wash DC, 1958-. **Honors/Awds:** Navy Meritorious Civilian Srv Awd 1974; Navy Grp Achvmnt Awd 1972; Dept of the Navy Superior Civilian Serv Awd 1985. **Military Serv:** AUS sgnl corp 1955-57. **Home Addr:** 30 Norwood Rd, Silver Spring, MD 20905.

WALLACE, RITCHIE RAY
Concrete paving company executive. **Personal:** Born Mar 9, 1955, Hastings, NE; son of Laura E Wallace and Andrew Wallace; married Kenetta Brown, Aug 28; children: Joshua, Eboni, Ritchie II. **Educ:** Kearney State College, BA, 1979. **Career:** Wallace Consulting Inc, president, 1979-. **Orgs:** Cornhusker Bank, board of directors, 1991-94; Community Business Association of Nebraska, board president, 1989-; NAACP, life-time member, 1989-; Newman United Methodist Church, treasurer, chairperson, 1992; Association of General Contractors, vice pres, 1991-92; Newman United Methodist Church, Ethnic Local Church Committee, 1992-; NAACP, 2nd vice president, 1994-; City of Lincoln Mayor's Office, economic development consultant; Lincoln Branch NAACPP, pres, 1992-97. **Honors/Awds:** City of Lincoln, Minority Business Recognition Award, 1991; Nebraska Department of Roads, Minority Business of the Year, 1987. **Special Achievements:** Lincoln Journal, Jan 27, Feb 25, 1991; Omaha World Herald, May 5, 1990. **Business Addr:** President, Wallace Consulting Inc, PO Box 81222, Lincoln, NE 68501-1222, (402)430-6442.

WALLACE, ROBERT EUGENE, JR.
Attorney, sports executive. **Personal:** Born Mar 1, 1956, New York, NY; son of Vivian A Wallace and Robert E Wallace Sr; married Julie A Hellmer, May 27, 1989; children: Grant Robert, Eric. **Educ:** Yale University, BA, American studies, 1978; Georgetown University, Law Center, JD, 1981. **Career:** Guilfoil, Petzall & Shoemake, attorney, 1981-91; Philadelphia Eagles, assistant to president/general counsel, 1991-. **Orgs:** American Bar Association, 1981-; Missouri Bar Association, 1981-; Pennsylvania Bar Association, 1991-; Bar Association of Metro St Louis, 1981-; Mound City Bar Association, 1981-91; Sports Lawyer's Association, board of directors, 1992-; Corporate Alliance for Drug Education, board of directors, 1991-; United Negro Coll Fund, PA, bd of advisors. **Honors/Awds:** St Louis Public Schools, Certificate of Recognition, 1988. **Business Addr:** Assistant to President, General Counsel, Philadelphia Eagles LP, 3501 S Broad St, 4th Fl, Philadelphia, PA 19148-5298, (215)463-2500.

WALLACE, RONALD WILFRED
Business executive. **Personal:** Born Nov 14, 1941, Aliquippa, PA; married Kay Francis; children: Duane, Ronald Jr, DuBoise, Elaine, LaRanna. **Educ:** Aliquippa HS, graduate 1956-60. **Career:** Natl Life Ins Co, agent 1966-69; LTV Steel Co, security services 1969-; Bd of Educ; secretary; Commonwealth of Pennsylvania, auditor. **Orgs:** Church in the Round bd of ministers 1979-, bd of trustees 1982-; exec bd NAACP 1983-; rep Legislative Action Comm 1984-. **Military Serv:** AUS security agency staff sgt 3 yrs; Good Conduct, Natl Defense, Oversea Medal; Vietnam Service NCO Leadership; Japan Svs Medal; Far East Svs Medal. **Home Addr:** 833 21st St, Aliquippa, PA 15001-2735.

WALLACE, STEVE
Professional football player. **Personal:** Born Dec 27, 1964, Atlanta, GA. **Educ:** Auburn. **Career:** San Francisco 49ers, tackle, 1986-96; Kansas City Chiefs, 1997-. **Business Addr:** Professional Football Player, Kansas City Chiefs, One Arrowhead Dr, Kansas City, MO 64129, (816)924-9300.

WALLACE, WILLIAM JAMES LORD. See Obituaries section.

WALLER, EUNICE MCLEAN
Educator. **Personal:** Born Jun 29, 1921, Lillington, NC; daughter of Mary Tucker McLean and Absalom McLean; married Dr William DeHomer Waller, Aug 9, 1958; children: Deborah, Kenneth. **Educ:** Fayetteville State Univ, BS (highest honors), 1942; University of Pennsylvania, MEd, 1953; North Carolina Central Univ, psychology, 1953-54; Wayne State Univ; Univ of Vermont, math, 1963. **Career:** Harnett HS, teacher, 1942-46; Shawtown HS, teacher, 1947-55; Fayetteville Univ, teacher, 1955-56; Sarah Nance Elementary School, teacher, 1956-58; Eiton Elementary School, teacher, 1958-60; Connecticut Coll, instructor, 1965-71; Clark Lane Jr High, teacher, 1961-93. **Orgs:** NCNW, New London section, president; AAUW, Delta Kappa Gamma; trustee, Waterford Country School; Waterford Educ Assn, pres, 1965-66, treasurer, 1969-75; pres, Dr Martin

Luther King Trust Fund ,1969-84; pres bd of dirs, Child Guidance Clinic, 1976-78; NEA; dir, Connecticut Educ Assn, 1979-82; corporator, Lawrence Memorial Hospitals, 1975-92; trustee, Mitchell Coll, 1975-; trustee, Connecticut Coll, 1988-89; mayor, City of New London, 1988-89; city councilor, City of New London, 1987-89; Southern Connecticut Easter Seals Rehabilitation Center, trustee; NAACP, New London Chapter, political action chairperson; New England Association of Black Educators, former president; Shiloh Baptist Church. **Honors/Awds:** EE Smith Memorial Award, Fayetteville Univ, 1942; Natl Science Fellowship, Univ of Vermont, 1963; Connecticut Educ Assn, Human Relations Award, 1980; OIC Comm Service Award, New London, 1982; NAACP McNair Award for Political Involvement, 1984. **Home Addr:** 337 Vauxhall St, New London, CT 06320-3837. **Business Addr:** Mayor, 181 Captain's Walk, New London, CT 06320.

WALLER, JUANITA ANN
Marketing research analyst. **Personal:** Born Feb 20, 1958, Gretna, VA. **Educ:** Drexel Univ, BS Marketing 1981. **Career:** Drexel Univ, student admissions counselor 1979-80; Clover Div of Strawbridge and Clothier, customer service mgr 1981-82; Drexel Univ, asst dean of admissions 1982-86; First Pennsylvania Bank, marketing research consultant 1986-. **Orgs:** Mem Urban Bankers Assoc of Delaware Valley 1986-, Natl Black MBA Assoc 1986-; mem The Natl Assoc of Negro Business and Professional Womens Clubs Inc 1986-. **Home Addr:** 10825 E Keswick Rd, Apt #260, Philadelphia, PA 19154.

WALLER, LARRY
Entrepreneur, contractor. **Personal:** Born Jun 9, 1947, Chicago, IL; son of Hulena Hubbard and Willis Waller; married Ruby L. Waller, Dec 24, 1969; children: Kelly D. Waller. **Educ:** Malcolm X College, Chicago, IL, AA 1974; Governors State Univ, Park Forest South, IL, BS 1978, MBA 1979. **Career:** Associated with Fullerton Mechanical Contractors, Elk Grove Village, IL, 1969-76; Dyd Construction, Phoenix, IL, superintendant, 1977-79; Pyramid Industries Inc, Riverdale, IL, president, 1979-. **Orgs:** Dir, Black Contractors United 1979-; mem, Natl Assn of Independent Business 1979-, Assn of Energy Engineers 1984-, Builders Assn of Chicago 1984-; founder & dir, Black Mechanical Contractors Assn 1983-; mem, original founding comm, Ben Wilson Foundation 1985-; comm mem, Black Musicians Hall of Fame 1986-87, Little Ciy Foundation 1986-. **Honors/Awds:** Became first black company to install elevators in the US, 1987; copyright on seminar material, ''Wisdom,'' 1989. **Military Serv:** US Air Force, E-4, 1965-69, honorable discharge. **Business Addr:** President/CEO, Pyramid Industries, Inc, 135 S La Salle-Maxwell St, #38 Fl, Chicago, IL 60603-4105.

WALLER, LOUIS E.
Business executive. **Personal:** Born Sep 10, 1928, Washington, PA; married Shirley James; children: Phyllis, Lorraine, Louis. **Educ:** W PA Tech Inst, Associate 1949; Univ of Pittsburgh, 1960-65. **Career:** Plaster Products Corp, mgr of estimating 1963; McAnallen Corp, pres. **Orgs:** Pres Kiwanis Club of Washington PA 1970, United Way of Washington Cty 1975; dir 1st Fed Savings & Loan; pres Interstate Contractors Supply; vice pres PA State Contractors; pres Master Builders Assoc. **Honors/Awds:** Man of the Year Jaycees 1969; Honorary Degree Waynesburg College, Waynesburg, PA 1985. **Business Addr:** President, Louis E Waller Co, Inc, PO Box 757, Washington, PA 15301.

WALLICK, ERNEST HERRON
State government official. **Personal:** Born Jan 15, 1928, Huntingdon, TN; married Jean Ellen Allen; children: Claudia Marie Barkley, John Herron. **Educ:** TN A&I State Univ, BS 1950; Michigan State Univ, MS 1955. **Career:** Carroll Co Bd of Educ, high school voc educ instr 1950-51; MI Wayne Co Dept of Soc Svcs, public welfare worker 1955-58, special investigator 1958-64,asst supv of personnel 1964-65, supv of office mgmt 1965-66, supv of mgmt planning 1966-67; MI Dept of Civil Svcs, dir of special progs 1967-72, dirspecial and regional serv div 1972-75, dir bureau of selection 1975-82, chief deputy dir 1982-. **Orgs:** Mem Lansing Comm Coll Social Work Curriculum Adv Comm 1970-75, State Voc Rehab Adv Cncl 1973-80, Governor's MI Equal Empl Oppor Cncl 1975-82; mem Trinity AME Bd of Trustees 1978-; mem & treas Alpha Chi Boule Sigma Pi Phi Frat 1982-; mem MI Correctional Officer's Training Cncl 1982-, Governor's MI Equal Employ and Business Oppor Cncl 1983-; mem bd of trustees Alpha Phi Alpha Frat 1985-; pres Natl Inst for Employment Equity 1985-; mem Natl Urban League, NAACP. **Honors/Awds:** Mem Phi Beta Kappa Honor Soc; Outstanding Public Serv & Achievements in EEO area and redesign of MI Civil Service Selection System MI Senate Concurrent Resolution 1979; Mayor's Proclamation for Outstanding Public Serv in EEO and Personnel Admin Detroit MI 1979. **Military Serv:** AUS staff sgt 1951-53. **Home Addr:** 1400 Wellington Rd, Lansing, MI 48910. **Business Addr:** Chief Deputy Director, Michigan Dept of Civil Service, 400 S Pine St, Lansing, MI 48909.

WALLS, FREDRIC T.
Clergyman. **Personal:** Born Oct 28, 1935, Denver, CO; married Delorez Louise; children: Fredric T, II, Agu Odinga-Ivan, Malaika Annina-Emma Delorez Louisa. **Educ:** LA City Coll, AA 1957; Knoxville Coll, BA 1963; Princeton Theol Sem, MDiv 1963; Union Grad Sch, PhD 1979; Urban Training Inst, Chicago, cert Univ of TN. **Career:** Self-Development of People Presbytarian Church, USA, dir, 1980-; Houston Urban U, pastor 1969-80; Univ of Houston, chmn dept religious activities 1974-; Univ Presb Ch, minister 1968-69; Knoxville Coll, dir Upward Bound 1967-68, asso dean of students 1965-68; Bel-Vue Presb Ch, LA, supply asst pastor 1964-65; Good Shepherd-Faith, Broadway & Sound View Presb Ch, stud asst pastor 1960-63; Westminister Neighborhood Assn, orgnr 1960. **Orgs:** Bd dir, vice pres Houston Met Ministries 1971-74, pres 1975-76; bd dir Ministries to Blacks in Higher Edn; mem Presb Housing Commn 1969-74; Houston JailChaplaincy Exec Com 1973-75; SW Steering Com, United Presb HEW 1971-74; Nat Communications Com, United Ministries in Higher Educ 1972-75; Gulf Coast Presb Com 1969-; exec com TX United Campus Christian Life Com 1973-75; policy bd United Ministries in Higher Edn; bd dir Cit for Good Sch 1969; Human Relations Training of Houston Police Cadets 1970-72; Bi-Racial Com HISD 1973-75; pres sr class, JCFremont Sr HS 1953-54; pres sr class, KnoxvilleColl 1959-60; treas sr class, Princeton Theological Sem 1962-63; exec dir Fund for the Self-Devel of People United Presb Ch USA NY. **Honors/Awds:** Outstanding Young Men of Am 1966; Danforth-Underwood Fellow 1976-77. **Business Addr:** Presbytrian Church (USA) Ctr, 100 Witherspoon St, Louisville, KY 40202.

WALLS, GEORGE HILTON, JR.
Military officer (retired), educational administrator. **Personal:** Born Nov 30, 1942, Coatesville, PA; son of Elizabeth Cooper Walls Gibson; married Portia D Hall Walls, Jun 12, 1977; children: George III, Steven, Kevin. **Educ:** West Chester State Univ, West Chester, PA, BS, education, 1964; North Carolina Central Univ, Durham, NC, MA, education, 1975; Natl War Coll, Washington, DC, 1982-83. **Career:** US Marine Corps, brigadier general, 1965-93; North Carolina Central Univ, special asst to the chancellor, currently. **Orgs:** Penndelphia Chapter, Marine Corps League, 1991; Montford Point Marine Assn, 1991; Chapel of the Four Chaplains, 1986-. **Honors/Awds:** Honorary Doctor of Humane Letters, Virginia Union University, 1993; NAACP, Roy Williams Meritorious Service Award, 1993; Humanitarian Service Award, Chapel of the Four Chaplains, 1993; Inductee, Chapel of the Four Chaplains, Valley Forge, PA, 1986. **Military Serv:** US Marine Corps, brigadier general, 1965-; Defense Superior Service Medal, 1992; Legion of Merit, 1987; Navy Commendation Medal, 1967; Meritorious Service Medal, 1982; Navy Achievement Medal, 1970; Distinguished Service Medal, 1993. **Home Addr:** 100 Canberra Court, Cary, NC 27513. **Business Phone:** (919)560-3222.

WALLS, MELVIN
Educator, city official. **Personal:** Born Nov 9, 1948, St Louis, MO; married Veronica Estella Robinson; children: FarRell L, Delvin L. **Educ:** Florissant Valley Comm, AA 1973; Harris Teachers, BA 1976. **Career:** St Louis City School, wrestling coach 1977-83, tennis coach 1979-80, baseball coach 1981, football coach, pe teacher; City of Northwoods, city collector. **Orgs:** Treas Boy Scouts of Amer 1981-; coord Normandy Baseball 1981-. **Honors/Awds:** St Louis City School All Conf Player 1965-67; St Louis City School All Star Player 1965-67; Project MEE Awd 1983; NMC Human Serv Awd 1987. **Business Addr:** City Collector, City of Northwoods, 4600 Oakridge Blvd, Northwoods, MO 63121.

WALSH, EVERALD J.
Mental health administrator. **Personal:** Born May 6, 1938, New York, NY; children: Evette Michelle, Eric Michael. **Educ:** City Coll of NY, BA 1963; Adelphi U, MSW 1970, CSW 1980. **Career:** Colony S Brooklyn Houses, dir mental retardation staff training prgm 1978-; Brooklyn Devel Ctr; Manhattan Childrens Psychiatric Ctr, team ldr 1974-77; Fed of Addiction Agy, exec dir 1971-74; Little Flower Children Svc, grp Hm Supr, Soc Worker 1966-71; Catholic Youth Orgn, grp Worker 1963-66. **Orgs:** Nat Fedn of Concerned Drug Abuse Workers 1972. **Business Addr:** 888 Fountain Ave, New York, NY.

WALSTON, WOODROW WILLIAM
Assistant director. **Personal:** Born Jul 12, 1918, Edgecombe County, NC; married Hazel Howell. **Educ:** NC Central U, BS 1946; Congress of the Am Coll of Hosp Adminstrs, yrly sem 1954-. **Career:** Richmond Comm Hosp Inc, adminstr 1973-80; Provident Hosp, Baltimore, asst adminstr, asst dir, asso dir for adm, dir of adm 1969-73; Richmond Comm Hosp Inc, adminstr 1958-69; Comm Hosp Martinsville, VA, 1952-58; Kate Bitting Reynolds Meml Hosp, ofc mgr 1946-52. **Orgs:** Mem Am Coll of Hosp Adminstrs 1970-; mem VA Hosp Assn & Roanoke Area Hosp Counc 1958-69; mem VA, MD, DE, DC Hosp Assn 1969-; mem Nat Assn of Hlth Serv Exec Inc 1969-; treas, bd mem MD Chap Hosp Fin Mgmt Assn; mem Am Hosp Assn 1954-; adv mem Hosp Fin Mgmt Assn 1958-; mem Cntrl VA Hosp Counc 1973-; VA Hosp Assn 1973-; mem VA Hosp Fin Mgmt Assn 1973-; Alpha Kappa 1946; bd mem Crusade for Voters; fin sec Spring Lk Golf Club; pres NC Coll Cntrl Univ Alumni Assn; bd mem, life mem Kappa Alpha Psi Frat Inc; mem Ku Wat Temple #126 Imperial Counc, Ancient Egyptian Arabic Order Nobles of the Mystic Shrine; pres Nat Assn of Hlth Svc; exec, bd mem Eastern Province Coun; treas Spartans Soc & Civic Club Inc; bd mem YMCA; bd mem NAACP; treas, deacon All Souls Presb Ch; dist commr BSA;bd mem, exec com Bros of Am; bd mem, treas Colonial Golf Club Inc; treas Pan Hellenic Counc of Richmond; mem, treas Club 533 Inc. **Honors/Awds:** Cert of Apprec, Blue Ridge Counc BSA; Outst Svcs, Pan Hellenic Counc of Richmond 1969; Cert of Apprec, Walston Group, Baltimore 1973; Cert of Apprec, Kappa Alpha Psi Frat Inc 1974; Cert of Commend, Nat Assn of Hlth Serv Exec NY 1976; recog award, Richmond Alumni Chap Kappa Alpha Psi Frat Inc 1976; Cert of Achvmt, Chap Bro of the Yr Award, VA Chap Kappa Alpha Psi Frat Inc 1977. **Military Serv:** AUS msgt 1942-46. **Business Addr:** 1500 N 28th St, Richmond, VA 23223.

WALTER, JOHN C.
Educator. **Personal:** Born May 5, 1933. **Educ:** AR AM&N Coll, BS (Cum Laude) Mech Engrg, History; Univ of Bridgeport, MA Amer History; Univ of ME at Orono, PhD Afro-Amer & US History. **Career:** Purdue Univ, instr history 1970-72, asst prof history 1972-73; IN Univ at Kokomo, vstg asst prof black politics 1971-73; John Jay Coll of Criminal Justice CUNY, assoc prof history, chmn black studies 1973-76; Bowdoin Coll, dir, asst prof history Afro-Amer Studies Prog 1976-80; Smith Coll, assoc prof Afro-Amer Studies 1980-. **Orgs:** Dir Afro-Amer Studies Prog Bowdoin Coll 1976-80; org, 1st chmn 1976-80, exec bd mem 1978- New England Conf of the Natl Council for Black Studies; exec comm Five Coll Black Studies 1982-; bridge comm & instr Smith Coll 1980-; devel & org Bridges to Pluralism 1983-; contrib ed Jrnl of Afro-Amer inNY Life & History State Univ Coll NY 1976-, UMOJA A Scholarly Jrnl of Afro-Amer Affairs Univ of CO 1976-, Review of Afro-Amer Issues & Culture Syracuse Univ 1976-, New England Jrnl of Black Studies Hampshire Coll 1981-; mem Amer Historical Assoc, Assoc of Caribbean Historians, Assoc for the Study of African-Amer Life & History, Caribbean Studies Assoc, Coll Lang Assoc, New England Historical Assoc, Natl Assoc of Interdisciplinary Ethnic Studies, Org ofAmer Historians,So Historical Assoc; consultnison Univ 1979, Wesleyan Univ 1978; reader Natl Endowment for the Humanities, Univ Press of Amer. **Honors/Awds:** Num rsch, book reviews & publ incl, A Passion for Equality 1977, Politics & Africanity in West Indian Soc Brown Univ 1983, The Black Immigrant & PoliticalRadicalism in the Harlem Renaissance 61st Annual Conf of the Assoc for the Study of Afro-Amer Life & History 1976, Franklin D Roosevelt & the Arms Limitation 1932-41 Hofstra Univ Conf 1982, Politics & Africanity in West Indian Soc Brown Univ 1983, The Transformation of Afro-Amer Politics, The Contribs of theWest Indian Immigrant Colby Coll 1983, Women & Identity in the Caribbean Smith Coll Women's Studies Cluster Comm Sem 1983, Enterprise Zones, Conservative Ideology or Free-Floating Political Fantasy? Simon's Rock of Bard Coll Bulletin 1984. **Business Addr:** Associate Professor, Department of Afro-American Studies, University of Cincinnati, Cincinnati, OH 45221.

WALTER, MILDRED PITTS
Writer. **Personal:** Born in DeRidder, LA; daughter of Mary Ward and Paul Pitts; widowed; children: Earl Lloyd, Craig Allen. **Educ:** Southern University, Scotlandville, Louisiana, BA, 1944; California State, elementary teaching certification, 1954; Antioch College, MEd. **Career:** Los Angeles City Schools District, teacher, 1955-70; Western Interstate Community Higher Education, consultant, 1970-73; writer, 1969-. **Orgs:** Society of Children's Book Writers and Illustrators; Author's Guild. **Honors/Awds:** Irma Simonton, Black Honor Book, 1981; Public Television, Reading Rainbow, 1983, 1985; Christian Science Monitor, Best Book: Writing, 1982; Parent's Choice Award: Literature, 1983-85; ALA Social Resp Round Table, Coretta Scott King Honorable Mmention, 1984, Corretta Scott King Award, 1987. **Special Achievements:** Children's Books: Ty's One-Man-Band, 1980; My Mama Needs Me, 1983; Brother to the Wind, 1985; Justin and the Best Biscuits in the World, 1986; Mississippi Challenge, 1992; Have a Happy, Lothrop, Lee & Shepard, 1994.

WALTERS, ARTHUR M.
Social service administrator. **Personal:** Born Nov 6, 1918, Magnolia, KY; married NoraLee Bryant; children: Reginald G, Artye M, Michele B. **Educ:** CO Coll, BA; Univ of Louisville, MEd; The Engr Sch, Asso Adv Engrng. **Career:** Louisville Urban League, soc serv adminstr, exec dir; past dir Econ Devel & Employ, Educ & Youth Incentives. **Orgs:** Mem Alpha Phi Alpha Frat; bd dir Boys Haven; bd dir KY Educ TV; bd dir Louisville C of C/Bus Resource Ctr; mem Louisville & Jefferson Co Human Rltns Commn Employ Com; Louisville Labor Mgmt Com; NAACP; Retired Ofcrs Assn; Soc of Am Mil Engrs; Downtown Rotary Club; adv counc KY Min Bus Enterprise; mem Pres Com on Employ of the Handicapped. **Honors/Awds:** AFL-CIO Gr Louisville Cntrl Labor Counc Comm Serv Award 1970; cited by Bd of Edn, Louisville Pub Sch 1971; Merit Comm Serv Medallion, Louisville & Jefferson Co Human Rltns Commn 1972; listed in 1,000 Successful Blacks, Ebony Success Library 1973; Outst Kentuckian, Intl Assn of Personnel In Employ Security 1974; cit, State of KY 1975; Merit Award, AKA Sor 1975; Whitney M Young Jr Award, Lincoln Found 1976; appearance on KY Educ TV, ''Bicent Profile of Outst Kentuckians'' 1976; Disting Serv Cit, United Negro Coll Fund; Young

Gifted & Blk Hon Roll, Plymouth Settlement House; cert of achvmnt, Nat Urban League Exec Devel Prgm; hon alumnus UNCF; Good Neighbor Award, LOU; Ambassador of Goodwill, City ofLouisville; Black Students Award, Univ of Louisville; AUS decorations commend medal for meritc; bronze star for heroism; Soldiers Medal for Bravery; Am Campaign Medal; European-african-middle Eastern Campaign Medal W/4 bronze serv stars; WW II Victory Medal; Army of Occupation Medal; Nat Defense Serv Medal; Korea Serv Medal w/1 silver serv star; Armed Forces Reserve Medal. **Military Serv:** AUS lt col ret 1962.

WALTERS, CURLA SYBIL
Educator. **Personal:** Born Jun 3, 1929. **Educ:** Andrews U, BA 1961; Howard U, MS 1964; Georgetown U, PhD 1969; Karolinska Inst, Post Doc 1969-70. **Career:** Howard Univ Dept Med, med asso prof 1975-; CO U, instr asst prof 1971-74; Howard U, rsrch asso 1964-65. **Orgs:** Mem Am Assn Emmunologist 1972-. **Honors/Awds:** AAS Parker Flwsp Aw 1963; flwsp Am Assn Univ Women 1969; NIH grant Aw 1974-77; biomed rsrch support grant 1975-76; natl inst ageing grant 1977; "Infection & Immun Proc Soc Exp Bio & Med & Fedn Proc". **Business Addr:** 2041 Georgia Ave, Washington, DC 20060.

WALTERS, FRANK E.
Athletic trainer. **Personal:** Born Aug 26, 1954, Munich, Germany; son of Alma & Ulysses; married Anne Marie, Aug 14, 1976; children: Jason, Tiffany. **Educ:** Brooklyn College, BS, 1976; Indiana State University, MS, 1977; Texas A&M University, PhD, 1988. **Career:** Pharr San Juan, Alamo HS, Pharr, Texas, teacher/athletic trainer, 1977-78; MB Smiley HS, Houston, Texas, teacher/athletic trainer, 1978-81; Prairie View A&M University, head athletic trainer, 1981-83; Texas A&M University, assistant professor, 1983-90; District of Columbia Public Schools, Athletic Healthcare Svcs, coordinator, currently. **Orgs:** Journal of Natl Athletic Trainers Assn, editorial bd, 1990-96; Athletic Training Sports Healthcare Perspectives, editorial bd, 1991-96; Natl Athletic Trainers Assn, Ethnic Minority Advisory Council, chmn, 1991-94; Univ of Washington, Natl Leadership Institute, guest faculty, 1991-92, 1994-95; Research Awards Committee, Mid Atlantic, 1992-95; Educational Task Force, Natl Athletic Trainers Assn, 1995-96; Natl Fed of State HS Assn's, sports medicine advisory com, 1996-97; Education Council Executive Comm, 1997-. **Honors/Awds:** University of Texas Dental School, Continuing Education, Certificate of Merit, 1983; Brooklyn College, Department of Physical Education, Sports Medicine Alumnus Award, 1986; Indiana State University, Athletic Training Department, First Outstanding Alumnus Award, 1994; Natl Athletic Trainer's Assn, Ethnic Minority Advisory Coun, Outstanding Service Award, 1995, Education Task Force, Outstanding Svc Award, 1997. **Special Achievements:** Published "Microfilm Your Student Emergency Cards," The Physician & Sports Medicine, 1981; JC Sterling & MC Meyers, "Tennis Elbow A Brief Review of Treatment," 1988; "Quarterback Mouthguards & Speech Intelligability," The Physician & Sports Medicine, with RM Morrow, W.A. Kuebker, M Golde, 1984, 1988.

WALTERS, HUBERT EVERETT
Music educator. **Personal:** Born Apr 27, 1933, Greenville, NC; divorced; children: Sonya Yvette, Hubert Sharif, Narda Rebecca, Julian Herman. **Educ:** NC Central Univ, BA 1951-55; vA State Univ, 1959; E Carolina Univ, MM 1963-65; Boston Univ, DMA (pending) 1969-; Boston University, School of Theology, pursing MDiv. **Career:** TX Coll Tyler, TX, chrmn dept of Music 1965-66; Shaw Univ Raleigh, NC, asst prof Music 1966-69; Harvard Univ, lctr on Black Music 1970-74; Goddard Coll VT, lecturer on Black Music 1971-73; Boston State Coll, asst proj of Music 1971-82; Boston Coll, lecturer on Black Music 1982-; Univ of MA-Boston, asst prof of Music 1982-. **Orgs:** V pres NC State Music Teachers 1963; mem Music Educators Natl Conf; mem Amer Choral Dir Assoc; Omega Psi Phi Frat; deacon Emmanuel Bapt Church; minister, Worship at Peoples Baptist Church, Boston MA. **Honors/Awds:** LO Kelly Award Excell in Music NC Central Univ 1955; mem Pi Kappa Lambda; Natl Music Honor Soc; Martin Luther King, Jr flwshp Award from Woodrow Wilson Fdn 1969. **Military Serv:** AUS sp 3. **Business Addr:** Assistant Professor of Music, Univ of MA, Harbor Campus Columbia Pt, Harbor Campus, Boston, MA 02125.

WALTERS, MARC ANTON
Educator. **Personal:** Born Jul 18, 1952, New York, NY. **Educ:** City College of New York, BS, 1976; Princeton Univ, PhD, 1981; Massachusetts Inst of Tech, Postdoc. **Career:** New York Univ, assoc prof, 1985-. **Orgs:** Amer Chem Society; Amer Assn for the Advancement of Science; NAACP; Natl Organization for the Prof Advancement of Black Chemists & Chemical Engineers; New York Academy of Science. **Special Achievements:** Proficient in French. **Business Addr:** Assoc Professor, New York University, 100 Washington Sq East, New York, NY 10003, (212)998-8472.

WALTERS, MARY DAWSON
Librarian, library administrator, retired. **Personal:** Born Oct 6, 1923, Mitchell Cnty, GA; married William Lamar Gantt; children: Marjorie M Smith, Robert H McCoy. **Educ:** Savannah State Coll Savannah, GA, BS; Atlanta Univ Atlanta, GA, MSLS 1957; OH State Univ Cols, OH, Russian Courses 1963; OH Historical Soc Cols, OH, Oral History Cert 1966; Miami Univ of OH, Lib Mgmt Cert 1973. **Career:** GA Public Schls, public schl tchr 1943-52; Carver Jr HS, schl librn 1952-56; Albany State Coll, libry dir 1956-61; OH State Univ Cols, OH, G&E lbrn 1961-63, head, procsng Div 1963-71; California State University, LA, head, acqstns dept 1974-78, collection development officer 1978-84, assistant university librarian, beginning 1980, mgr of collection development prog 1984-88. **Orgs:** Cnclr at large Am Lbry Assoc 1982-86; comm status women librnshp 1984-86; mem Black Caucus of AL 1974-. **Honors/Awds:** Director's Citation of Merit OH State Univ Cols, OH 1963; They Did so Can You Greyhound Bus Corp 1973; 1,001 Successful Blacks Ebony Success Libry 1973; "Black Literature, Works by Afro-Amer Writers in the United States" a bibliography of the Black History Month Exhibit in the John F Kennedy memorial Library Cal State LA 1984; "Approval Program Timing Study, Baker & Taylor vs Blackwell North Amer" Collection Bldg 1985. **Business Addr:** Manager, Collection Devt Program, CA State Univ, LA, 5151 State University Dr, 5171 State Univ Dr, Los Angeles, CA 90032.

WALTERS, RONALD
Educator. **Personal:** Born Jul 20, 1938, Wichita, KS; married Patricia Ann. **Educ:** Fisk Univ, BA History 1963; Amer Univ, MA 1966, PhD 1971. **Career:** Georgetown & Syracuse Univ, instr; Brandeis Univ African & Afro-Amer Studies, chmn 1969-71; Howard Univ, chmn pol sci 1971-74, prof of pol sci; Univ of Maryland, prof and sr fellow, currently. **Orgs:** Past pres African Heritage Studies Assoc; mem bd Natl Black Election Study, Inst of Social Rsch, Univ of MI; mem adv bd Southern Christian Leadership Conf; founder Natl Black Independent Political Party; secty/founding mem Natl Black Leadership Roundtable; founder/past mem Bd of TransAfrica; consultant United Nations Special Comm Against Apartheid of the Security Cncl. **Honors/Awds:** Speaks & writes on US Foreign Policies toward Africa & Black Amer Politics; over 70 articles in several scholarly jrnls; three books in press; Disting CommServ Awd Howard Univ 1982; Disting Scholar/Activists Awd The Black Scholar Magazine 1984; The Ida B Wells Barnett Awd Natl Alliance of Black School Educators 1985; Rockefeller Foundation Rsch Grant 1985; The Congressional Black Associates Awd 1986. **Business Addr:** Professor, Afro-American Studies Program, University of Maryland, Lefrak Hall, Ste 2169, College Park, MD 20742.

WALTERS, WARREN W.
Dentist. **Personal:** Born Nov 20, 1932, NYC; married Joan Husbands; children: Pennye, Pamela, Warren Wayne. **Educ:** Columbia Coll, BA 1953; Columbia Univ Sch of Bus, MBA 1955; Howard Univ Sch of Dentistry, DDS 1960. **Career:** Priv Prac, dent 1962-; Rotating Intrnshp Prog Harlem Hosp, coord; Intrnshp Harlem Hosp, oral surg 1960-61; NYS Unempl Ins, auditor 1955-56. **Orgs:** Vp Midtown Dental Soc; vice pres Greater Metro Dental Soc; bd of dir First Distr Dental Soc; pres progressive Com Real Estate Corp; mem Sigma Pi Phi Boule; past pres Harlem Hosp Dental Soc 1966, 74; mem ADA; NDA; Acad Gen Dentistry; dir Prog Comml Real Estate Inc; pres Howard Univ Studnt Coll of Dent 1959-60; mem Reveille Club; Omega Psi Phi. **Business Addr:** 200 W 145 St, New York, NY 10039.

WALTON, ANTHONY SCOTT
Sports writer. **Personal:** Born Mar 8, 1965, South Bend, IN; son of Judith Elaine Tidwell Walton and Cullen Walton Jr. **Educ:** Vanderbilt University, Nashville, TN, BA, 1987. **Career:** Detroit Free Press, Detroit, MI, sports writer, 1987-. **Orgs:** Alpha Phi Alpha Fraternity Inc, 1984-; mentor, Project Male Responsibility, 1988-. **Honors/Awds:** Honorable Mention, Best Enterprise Story, Associated Press, 1991. **Home Addr:** 853 Ashland, Detroit, MI 48215.

WALTON, DEWITT T., JR.
Dentist. **Personal:** Born May 25, 1937, Macon, GA; son of Dr & Mrs DeWitt T Walton Sr; married Joan G Robinson; children: Jimmie Alisa, Gwen Noel, Gayle Nicole, Joy Alexia. **Educ:** Howard Univ, BS 1960, DDS 1961. **Career:** Private practice, dentist, currently. **Orgs:** Life membership President's Club Howard Univ; mem Amer Dental Assn; Natl Dental Assn, Acad of Gen Dentistry; Amer Soc of Dentistry for Children; GA Dental Soc; AAAS; Natl Rehab Assn; life mem Fedn Dentaire Internationale; sustaining mem BSA; life mem NAACP; life mem Omega Psi Phi Frat; mem Washington Ave Presby Ch; Prince Hall Mason Local #12; mem GA Dental Assoc, Amer Endodontic Soc, Acad of Dentistry Intl, Amer Coll of Dentists, Intl Coll of Dentists; sustaining mem The Southern Poverty Law Ctr; mem Amer Fund for Dental Health-Century Club II, Amer Analgesic Soc, Acad of Continuing Educ; The Greater Macon Chamber of Commerce, board of directors, 1995-97. **Honors/Awds:** NAACP Community Serv Awd; Five Dental Fellowships; Lambda Phi Chap Omega Man of Yr 1969; Lambda Phi Chap Omega Cit of Yr 1971; North GA Dental Soc Dentist of the Year 1979; GA Dental Soc Citizenship Awd 1979-80; GA Dental Soc Humanitarian Awd 1981-82; Boy Scouts of Amer Silver Beaver Awd 1981; Alpha Kappa Alpha Sor Comm Serv Awd 1982; United Negro Coll Fund Meritorious Serv Awd 1983; Outstanding Serv Awd The Southern Poverty Law Ctr 1984; Whitney M Young Jr Serv Awd 1985; Outstanding Alumni Awd Coll of dentistry Howard Univ 1985; Boy Scouts of Amer Diamond Jubilee Awd for Serv to Youth 1985; 1st Annual James E Carter Jr Award, GA Dental Society, 1993. **Military Serv:** AUS Dental Corps capt 1961-63. **Business Addr:** Dentist, 591 Cotton Ave, Macon, GA 31201.

WALTON, EDWARD D.
Association executive, educator. **Career:** California State University, Pomona, Department of Chemistry, professor, currently. **Orgs:** National Organization for the Professional Advancement of Black Chemists and Chemical Engineers, past president. **Honors/Awds:** Comfortable Approach to Teaching Science, director, 1994-95; National Academy of Science Working Group for National Science Education Standards, 1991-94. **Business Addr:** Professor, Department of Chemistry, California State University, 3801 W Temple Ave, Pomona, CA 91768-4032, (909)869-3661.

WALTON, ELBERT ARTHUR, JR.
Attorney & elected official (retired). **Personal:** Born Feb 21, 1942, St Louis, MO; son of Luretta B Ray Hawkins and Elbert A Walton Sr; married Juanita Alberta Head; children: Rochelle, Rhonda, Angela, Elbert III, Johnathan. **Educ:** Harris Junior College, AA 1963; Univ of Missouri St Louis, BA business, 1968; Washington Univ, MBA 1970; St Louis Univ, JD 1974. **Career:** Continental Oil Corp, financial analyst 1969; Univ of Missouri St Louis, instructor of business law & accounting 1971-78; St Louis Municipal Court, judge 1977-78; attorney at law 1974-; Missouri House of Representatives, state representative 61st district 1979-. **Orgs:** Beta Alpha Psi Hon Acct Fraternity 1971; Phi Delta Phi Intl Legal Frat 1973; natl vice pres Natl Assn of Black Accountants 1976-77; parliamentarian Mound City Bar Assn 1979; parliamentarian MO Legislative Black Caucus 1979-85; grand counselor Omega Psi Phi Frat 1980-83. **Honors/Awds:** Omega Man of the Year Omega Psi Phi Fraternity, St Louis, MO 1964; Outstanding Achievement Award, Natl Assn of Black Accountants 1976; Citizen of the Year, Omega Psi Phi Fraternity St Louis, MO 1978. **Military Serv:** USNR E-4 1959-61. **Business Addr:** State Representative, 61st Dist, Missouri House of Representatives, 8776 N Broadway, St Louis, MO 63147.

WALTON, FLAVIA BATTEAU
Association executive. **Personal:** Born Apr 18, 1947, Tucson, AZ; daughter of Elgie Batteau and Matthew Batteau; married Col William Howard Walton; children: Nissa Mike, William Howard III. **Educ:** Mills College, BA 1967; Univ of AZ, MS 1968, PhD 1977. **Career:** Troy State University at Montgomery, adjunct professor 1976-77; Bexar Cty Mental Health Mental Retardation, unit coordinator 1977-80; Our Lady of the Lake University, lecturer in social work 1981; Natl Institute of Drug Abuse, special consultant 1984-1987; White House Conf for a Drug Free Amer, consultant, 1987-88; Project Lead: High Expectations, The Links Found, Inc, project dir. **Orgs:** Chapter pres vice pres comm chairs Alpha Kappa Alpha 1965-; mem Natl Rehabilitation Assn 1967-; mem natl Rehabilitation Counselors Assn 1967-; natl dir serv to youth The Links Inc 1968-; mem Personnel & Guidance Assn 1975-; chapter pres comm chairperson Jack & Jill of Amer Inc 1977-; chmn Natl Black Advisory Comm on Drug & Alcohol Abuse Policy 1984-85. **Honors/Awds:** Pi Lambda Theta Educ Honorary Univ of AZ 1968. **Business Addr:** Project LEAD: High Expectations, The Links Found, Inc, 1200 Massachusetts Ave NW, Washington, DC 20005.

WALTON, HANES, JR.
College professor. **Personal:** Born Sep 25, 1942, Augusta, GA; son of Estelle Brown Walton and Hanes Thomas Walton; married Alice Williams Walton, Apr 10, 1974; children: Brandon, Brent. **Educ:** Morehouse College, Atlanta, GA, BA, 1963; Atlanta University, Atlanta, GA, MA, 1964; Howard University, Washington, DC, PhD, 1967. **Career:** Savannah State College, Savannah, GA, professor, 1967-. **Orgs:** Member, Natl Conference of Black Political Scientists, 1971-; member, American Political Science Assn, 1967-; Southern Political Science Assn, 1967-; member, Assn for the Study of Afro-American Life and History, 1967-. **Honors/Awds:** Phi Beta Kappa; Alpha Kappa Mu; Pi Sigma Alpha, nine books, 1969-. **Business Addr:** Professor, Dept of Pol Sci, Savannah State College, Savannah, GA 31407.

WALTON, HARRIETT J.
Educator. **Personal:** Born Sep 19, 1933, Claxton, GA; daughter of Mable Rose Myrick Junior and Ester James Junior; divorced; children: Renee Yvonne, Anthony Alex, Jennifer Denise, Cyrus Bernard. **Educ:** Clark Coll, AB (Cum Laude) 1952; Howard Univ, MS 1954; Syracuse Univ, MA 1957; GA State Univ, PhD 1979; Atlanta Univ, MS 1989. **Career:** Hampton Inst, instr of Math 1954-55, asst prof of Math 1957-58; Morehouse Coll, instr of Math, asst prof of Math, assoc prof of Math, prof of Math 1958-. **Orgs:** Clerk Providence Baptist Church 1968-84; sec/treas Natl Assn of Math 1982-; treas Phi Delta Kappa 1984-85; deacon Providence Baptist Church 1984-; mem of advisory bd Benjamin E Mays Acad, MAA, AAUP, NCTM, GCTM, Pi Mu Epsilon, Beta Kappa Chi; treas/pres Delta Sigma Theta;

mem YWCA, NAACP, ACLU; consult Atlanta Publ Schls. **Honors/Awds:** UNCF Faculty Fellow 1964-65, 1975-77; NSF Sci Faculty 1965-66; Teaching Asst, Rsch Asst Howard Univ 1952-54; Proj Dir Contr for Math Educ 1981-84; Proj Dir Math for Middle Sch Tchrs 1981-82; Bronze Woman of the Yr Iota Phi Lambda Sor 1984; Phi Beta Kappa Delta of GA Morehouse Coll 1984. **Home Addr:** 860 Venetta PL NW, Atlanta, GA 30318. **Business Addr:** Prof of Mathematics, Morehouse College, 830 Westview Dr SW, Atlanta, GA 30314.

WALTON, JAMES DONALD
Sales executive. **Personal:** Born Jan 31, 1952, Albany, NY; son of Zymora Louise Burrell Walton (deceased) and Allen Walton (deceased); married Nadine Renee Walton, Aug 23, 1991; children: Darius James, Talib Justice. **Educ:** Univ of Vermont, BS 1975. **Career:** Xerox Corp, sales rep 1976-79; Abbott Laboratories, chemistry systems specialist 1979-82, natl account mgr 1982-83, district mgr 1984-87; regional marketing mgr 1987-90, regional mgr, 1990-94; Hematology Systems, national sales manager, 1995-. **Honors/Awds:** Abbott Laboratories: Presidents Club, 1980, 1981, 1986, 1991-93, 1995-97; Senior Salesman, 1980, 1st Black District Mgr, 1983; 1st Black National Sales Manager, 1995; 100% Club 1984, 1985; 1st Black Regional Marketing Manager, 1987, 1st Black Regional Manager, 1990; Regional Marketing Manager of the Year, 1988. **Home Addr:** 1133 N Edmer, Oak Park, IL 60302. **Business Phone:** 800-323-9100.

WALTON, JAMES EDWARD
Educator. **Personal:** Born Sep 13, 1944, Bessemer, AL; married Doris Dell Harrington; children: Leonard, Tiffany. **Educ:** Andrews Univ, 1962-64; Kent State Univ, BS 1964-66; University of Akron, MA 1970-73, PhD 1973-78. **Career:** Canton McKinley HS, english teacher 1967-70; Mount Union College, assoc prof of english 1970-. **Orgs:** Dir Freedom House Project 1975; member Jaycees 1975; yearbook advisor Mount Union College 1975-83; board member Stark County Fair Housing Comm 1978-; board member Assoc for Better Community Development 1984-; member Alliance City Planning Commission 1984-. **Honors/Awds:** Poetry, essays Black Arts Society, Ohio State Univ 1971; essay English Language Arts Bulletin 1980; article Natl Council of Teachers of English 1980; essayModern Language Association 1985. **Business Addr:** Associate Professor of English, Mount Union College, 1972 Clark Ave, Alliance, OH 44601.

WALTON, JAMES MADISON
Lawyer, retired judge. **Personal:** Born Aug 17, 1926, Norfolk, VA; son of Willie Ann Smallwood and Willie J Walton; married Jean Onie Barnes; children: James Jr, Janet Marie Dukes, Joan Denise Collaso, Julian Mark. **Educ:** VA Union Univ, AB (Cum Laude) 1952; De Paul Univ Coll of Law, JD 1958; Roosevelt Univ, MA 1982. **Career:** Cook Cty Dept of Public Aid, caseworker 1953-60; Cook Cty State's Atty, asst state's atty 1961-63; Cook Cty Public Defender, asst public defender 1964-65; Circuit Court Cook Cty, magistrate 1966, assoc judge 1970, appointed judge 1979; Circuit Ct of Cook County, elected judge 1980. **Orgs:** Trustee Bethany-Garfield Comm Hosp 1966, St Stephen African Methodist Church 15 years; mem Cook Co Bar Assn; Chicago Bar Assn; Natl Bar Assn; past pres IL Cncl of Juvenile Ct Judges; mem Natl Cncl of Juvenile and Fam Ct Judges; mem The Original Forty Club of Chicago. **Military Serv:** USAAF T/5 22 months; Good Conduct, Marksman, Philippine Independence 1945-46. **Home Addr:** 405 Fernwood Farms Road, Chesapeake, VA 23320.

WALTON, LLUDLOO CHARLES
Insurance company executive. **Personal:** Born Nov 24, 1950; son of Muriel A Walton and William B Walton; married Rosemerrie, Jun 18, 1975; children: Sheree Rosemerrie, Carlene Nicole. **Educ:** Attended Mico Training Coll of the Univ of the West Indies. **Career:** Mutual of Omaha, Livingston NJ, sales agent 1979-82, sales mgr 1982-84; Mutual of Omaha, Rutherford NJ, gen mgr 1984-. **Honors/Awds:** NASD License, Federal License, 1982; Mgr of Year, Mutual of Omaha, 1982 & 1983. **Home Addr:** 30 Manchester Rd, West Orange, NJ 07052.

WALTON, MILDRED LEE
Educational administrator. **Personal:** Born Dec 8, 1926, Atlanta, GA; daughter of Pauline Dickerson Collier and James Forrest Collier; married Borah W; children: Berle Burse, Denise Mickelbury, Charna Turner. **Educ:** Spelman Coll, BA 1947; Atlanta Univ, MA 1962; Nova Univ, EdD 1976; Harvard Univ, Summer Fellow 1984. **Career:** DeKalb Co School System, teacher 1947-56; Turner HS, teacher 1956-69; Harwell Elem Sch, principal 1969-73; Atlanta Univ, asst prof 1970; Miles Elementary School, principal 1973-87; Georgia Association of Elementary School Principals, executive director, 1987-. **Orgs:** SE zone dir Natl Assoc of Elementary School Principal 1980-83; adv bd Rockefellar Fund for Art Educ 1981-85; foundation bd Amer Assoc of Univ Women 1982-85, Phi Delta Kappa 1984-85; St Paul's Vestry St Paul's Episcopal Church 1984-87; pres Natl Assoc of Elementary School Principals 1985-86; mem Delta Kappa Gamma Hon Soc 1986-; pres, Natl Alumnae Assn of Spelman College. **Honors/Awds:** Boss of the Year Natl Business Women's Assoc 1983; Bronze Woman in Educ Black Heritage Assoc 1984; Georgia Educ of Excellence State Bd of Educ 1984; Natl Distinguished Principal US Dept of Educ 1986. **Business Addr:** Executive Director, Georgia Assn of Elementary School Principals, 1176 Oakcrest Drive, Atlanta, GA 30311.

WALTON, ORTIZ MONTAIGNE (ORTIZ MONTAIGNE)
Sociologist, musician. **Personal:** Born in Chicago, IL; son of Gladys Matilda Porche and Peter Leon Walton; married Carol Dozier Walton, Jun 28, 1957; children: Omar Kwame. **Educ:** Roosevelt Univ, BS, 1967; Univ of CA, Berkeley, CA, MA 1970, PhD 1973. **Career:** Musician Hartford New Haven, Springfield, Bridgeport Symphony Orchestras, 1951-54; Buffalo Philharmonic Orchestra, 1954-57; Boston Symphony Orchestra, 1957-63; prog coord, Chicago Association Retarded Children, 1964-66; musician, Cairo (Egypt) Symphony, 1963-64; dir, Chicago Fedn Settlement, 1964-68; instructor, Dept African-American Studies University of California Berkeley, 1974-76; faculty, Wright Institute of Berkeley, grad school, 1974-75; mem bd of studies in sociology University California Santa Cruz, 1975; A Sample Survey of Alcohol & Drug Use Among Adolescents & Young Adults, funded by Natl Inst on Alcohol Abuse & Alcoholism, princpl investigator 1978-81; contrabass soloist, author & composer; The Multi-Ethnic Inst for Resch & Ed, pres 1978-; Athanor Records, pres, currently. **Orgs:** Prof sociology Univ of CA Berkeley 1969-74, Univ of CA Santa Cruz 1975, The Wright Inst of Berkeley 1974-75; double bassist The Boston Symphony Orchestra 1957-63; presented NY Debut Recital at Mekin Concert Hall NYC, 1989; recorded solo contrabass works of WA Mozart & recorded premiere of The Walton Statement by Arthur Cunningham 1986; composed Night Letter for unaccompanied contrabass dedicated to Edward Kennedy Ellington 1968; Am Sociol Association, Internat Soc Bassists, Chamber Music Am. **Honors/Awds:** Author of work on the sociology of Amer music "Music, Black White & Blue" publ by William Morrow. **Business Addr:** President, Multi-Ethnic Institute for Research & Education, PO Box 2559, Berkeley, CA 94702-0559.

WALTON, R. KEITH
Educational administrator. **Personal:** Born in Birmingham, AL; son of Cynthia Williams Walton & Reginald Walton, Jr; married Aubria D Corbitt; children: Rachel. **Educ:** Yale College, BA; Harvard Law School, JD. **Career:** US District Ct, Northern District of AL, law clerk, 1990-91; King & Spalding, assoc, 1991-93; White House Security Review, deputy dir, 1994-95; US Dept of the Treasury, chief of staff, enforcement, 1993-96; Columbia Univ, univ scy, 1996-. **Orgs:** Enterprise Foundation, NY advisory bd, 1996-; Council on Foreign Relations, NY advisory bd, 1996-; Wilberforce Univ, trustee, 1997-; Alpha Phi Alpha; Sigma Pi Phi. **Business Addr:** Secretary, Columbia University/Attn: Keith Walton, 535 W 116 St, 211 L, 211 Low Memorial Lib, New York, NY 10027.

WALTON, REGGIE BARNETT
Federal official. **Personal:** Born Feb 8, 1949, Donora, PA; married. **Educ:** WV State Coll, BA 1971; Amer Univ, JD 1974. **Career:** Defender Assn of PA, staff atty 1974-76; US Atty's Office DC, asst US atty 1976-80, exec asst 1980-81; Superior Court of DC, assoc judge 1981-89, deputy presiding judge, 1986-89; Office of National Drug Control Policy, associate director, 1989-. **Orgs:** Member, American Bar Assn; member, Washington Bar Assn; member, District of Columbia Bar Assn; member, Judicial Conference for the District of Columbia, 1980-; member, National Institute of Trial Advocacy Advocates Assn, 1985-; member, Big Brothers of America, 1987-; board of directors, National Center for Missing and Exploited Children, 1990-. **Honors/Awds:** Award for Distinguished Service to the Community and the Nation, The Bar Assn of the District of Columbia Young Lawyer's Section, 1989; Community Service Award, Alpha Phi Alpha Inc, Iota Upsilon Lambda Chapter, 1990; President's Image Award, Madison County Indiana Urban League, 1990; The Distinguished Service Award, New Jersey State Assn of Chiefs of Police, 1990; James R Waddy Meritorious Service Award, The West Virginia State College National Alumni Assn, 1990.

WALTON, TRACY MATTHEW, JR.
Radiologist. **Personal:** Born Nov 12, 1930, Columbia, SC; married Mae; children: Adrienne, Tracy III, Terri, Brien. **Educ:** Morgan State Coll, BS 1953; Howard Univ Coll Med, graduated 1961. **Career:** Freedman's Hosp, asst radiology 1965-66; Howard Univ, asst radiology 1965-66; Georgetown Univ Sch of Med, clinical instr 1968; DC General Hosp, med ofcr 1967-71, acting chf med ofcr 1971, chf med ofcr 1971-80; University of DC, med dir, med radiography prog, dept of health sciences, 1994-. **Orgs:** Rgnl radiotherapy com of Met WA Regnl Med Prog 1968-; mem Cancer Aid Plan Com DC Chap ACS 1968-81; chmn Amer Cancer Soc 1968-, pres, DC division, 1984; adv bd United Nat Bank of WA 1974-; licensure SC Bd of Med Examiners 1981; vice pres DC Div Amer Cancer Soc 1983-; Natl Medical Assn (NMA), bd of trustees, chmn, 1990-91, pres, 1994-95; natl chmn Radiology Sect Natl Med Assn 1983-; Med Soc of DC, provisional speaker house of delegates, 1992; Natl Med Assn; Amer Coll of Radiology; So Med Assn; licensure MD Bd of Med Exam; DC Bd of Med Exam. **Honors/Awds:** Pres, Medico-Chirurgical Society of DC, 1975-78. **Home Addr:** 7506 9th St NW, Washington, DC 20012-5038.

WALTRIP, ROBERT. See **SHORT, BOBBY.**

WAMBLE, CARL DEELLIS
Health care administrator. **Personal:** Born Apr 11, 1952, Kansas City, KS; son of Geraldine Phillips Wamble (deceased) and Amos Sylvester Wamble Sr (deceased); married Naomi Jean Cannon Wamble, Apr 17, 1976; children: Christopher DeEllis, Christina Rochelle. **Educ:** Philander Smith College, BS, biology, 1975; Webster University, MA, health Service management, 1983. **Career:** Branch Medical Clinic, Fallon, operating room technician, 1977-78; USS McKean, DD784, communications officer, electronic platerial officer, 1979-81; USS New Jersey, BB62, weapons, 2nd battery officer, 1981-84; Organizational Effectiveness Center, Yokosuka, OE consultant, 1984-86; Naval Hospital, Yokosuka, Japan, operations management officer, 1986-87; Naval School of Health Sciences, master training specialist, 1987-90; Branch Medical Clinic, Treasure Island, officer-in-charge, 1990-93; NATO Allied Forces Southern Europe, Naples, Italy, 1993-96; Uniform Services University Medical School, company commander, asst. commandant, 1997-. **Orgs:** National Naval Officers Association, 1982-; American Academy of Medical Administrators, 1991; Alpha Phi Alpha Fraternity, 1971-; Alpha Phi Omega Fraternity, 1971-; Surface Warfare Officers Assn, 1990-; American Military Evangelizing Nations. **Honors/Awds:** Meritorious Service Medal; Joint Defense Service Medal; Naval School of Health Sciences, Master Training Specialist, 1989; Organizational Effectiveness Center, Yokosuka, Organizational Effectiveness Consultant, 1984; Navy Commendation Medal, 1984, 1990; Navy Achievemant Medal, 1986. **Military Serv:** US Navy, Lt Commander, 1975-. **Business Addr:** Uniform Services University of Health Sciences, 4301 Jones Bridge Road, Bethesda, MD 20814.

WANSEL, DEXTER GILMAN
Composer. **Personal:** Born Aug 22, 1950, Bryn Mawr, PA; married Lorna Millicent Hall (divorced). **Career:** Philadelphia Intl Records, dir of artist & repertoire 1980; Philadelphia Intl Records, musician & recording artist 1980; Wansel Interprises, indep record producer 1973-75; Various Record Companies, musician, arranger, orchestral dir, synthesizer & programmer 1973-75. **Orgs:** Mem Wissahickan Civic Assn 1978. **Honors/Awds:** 28 Gold & Platinum Records; Grammy Award Amer Assn of Recording Artists 1978. **Military Serv:** AUS e-5 3 yrs serv. **Business Addr:** Philadelphia International Records, 309 S Broad St, Philadelphia, PA 19107.

WANTON, EVA C.
Educator. **Personal:** Born 1935, Tunderbolt, GA; married Albert E Wanton; children: Jacquelyne G Maxey, Debra P Mitchell, Michelle V Jones, Dwanna Di Shon. **Educ:** Savannah State Univ, BS 1961; Interamerican Univ, MA 1964, PhD 1970; FL State Univ, PhD 1980. **Career:** FL A&M Univ, dir summer session 1971-75, asst to dean 1975-79, dir gen educ 1977-79, dean 1982-. **Orgs:** Mem The Chamettes Inc 1971-; bd mem Jack & Jill Found 1986-. **Honors/Awds:** Dean of the Year FL A&M Univ 1986. **Home Addr:** 3736 Sulton Court, Tallahassee, FL 32312. **Business Addr:** Dean, Florida A&M Univ, Martin Luther King Blvd, Tallahassee, FL 32307.

WARD, ALBERT A.
Educator (retired). **Personal:** Born Sep 20, 1929, Detroit, MI; son of Mattie Smith (deceased) and Abe (deceased); married Doris; children: Cheryl, David, Donald, Albert Michael Ward. **Educ:** Wayne State Univ, BA, 1949; Wayne State Univ, MEd, 1962; Univ Michigan, EdD, 1971. **Career:** Elliott Elementary, Wayne-Westland Comm School, principal; Inkster Public Schools, supt, 1972-75; Jackson Public Schools, principal, 1966-71; Michigan Bell Telephone Co, act commercial mgr, 1965-66; Detroit Public Schools, teacher, 1958-63; Detroit Housing Commn, public housing aide, 1955-57, 1950-53; retired, 1988. **Orgs:** Mem, Phi Delta Kappa, Amer Assn School Admin, Michigan Assn School Admin, Natl Assn Elementary School Principals, Metro Detroit Soc Black Educ Admin, Natl Alliance Black School Educ, elementary rep Michigan State Com for N Central Coll & Schools Steward, Grace CME Church, Able Toastmaster: chmn, Westland Library Bd; mem, professional vstr, AASA Natl Acad School Exec, 1969, Horace Rackham Predoctoral Fellowship, 1969, 33rd Annual Supt Work Conf Teacher Coll, Columbia Univ, 1974; national director of scouting ministries, CME Church, 1990-; AARP employment planning volunteer, AARP, 1990-; chair, Silver Awards Committee; editor, Scouting Visions; Detroit Area Council, Boy Scouts of America, 1991-. **Honors/Awds:** Silver Beaver Award, Boy Scouts of America, 1990 "Dr Albert A Ward Day," City of Westland, Mayor & City Council, 1989. **Military Serv:** AUS, 2nd lt, 1953-55; AUSR, capt, 1955-65.

WARD, ALBERT M.
City official. **Personal:** Born Aug 5, 1929, Baltimore. **Educ:** Hampton Inst, BA 1972. **Career:** Electrl Bd Cty of Hampton, 1st black chmn; Hampton Comm Fed Credit Union, vp; Diversified Serv & Commod Limited, corp Ofcr mem bd dir; Hampton Funeral Home; Hampton Roads Devel Corp, bd mem exec vp; HEW, corr clk 1949-58; Customs Woods Inc, interior designer 1958-60; King Merritt Baltimore, registred rep; Baltimore Post Ofc, distrib clk 1961-62; Bassette Real Estate, real

estate & ins agt ofc mgr 1963-67. **Orgs:** Mem VA Electoral Bd Assn Exec Bd Hampton Br NAACP 1964-; exec bd Hampton Chap Nat Hampton Alumni Assn; steering com & co-founder Comm Progress Com; steering com Pirate Boosters; adv com Comm Devel & Housing Funds; chmn W Hampton Target Area Sub Com; former v-chmn Rep Party 1st Congressnl Dist; mem VA Crusade of Voters; Esquire Inc; Hampton Cty Com Rep Party; 1st black Electoral Bd Hampton 1971-; parliamentarian & mem exec bd GROUP; mem Peninsula Heart Fund; Peninsula Cerebral Palsy; Am Red Cross; March of Dimes; Multi Sclerosis Soc; W Hampton Civic Assn; Hampton Sch Dist Supt Equal & Inequal Comm; sub-comm chmn Stud Conduct & Respons; bd dir mem Hampton Heritage Trust Inc; organizer Doctrus Sentry Soc. **Honors/Awds:** Recip merit serv award for Voter Regis & Voter Educ NAACP; merit serv award for Labor & Indust NAACP; cert of Apprec for Valuable serv Hampton Inst 1973 & 1975; listed Comm Ldr & Noteworthy Am; trhee commendation Awards AUS; competitive all expense schlrshp to Hampton Inst 1946. **Military Serv:** AUS e-4 1951-53. **Business Addr:** PO Box 544, Hampton, VA 23669.

WARD, ANNA ELIZABETH
City official, consultant. **Personal:** Born Dec 20, 1952, Miami, FL; married Sterling Andrew Ward; children: Johnathan Travis, Rochelle Marie. **Educ:** Miami Dade Com Coll, AA 1976-78; FL Intl Univ, BS Criminal Justice 1978-80, M Public Admin 1979-80. **Career:** FL Intl Univ, 1971-80; Sangamon State Univ, circulation dept admin 1980-81; City of Dallas, asst to asst city mgr 1981-83; Dallas Cty Com Coll District, asst internal auditor 1984-85; City of Emporia, VA, asst to city mngr. **Orgs:** Pres North Central TX COMPA 1982-83; teen counselor Women in Community Serv 1983; co-chairperson program com Urban Mgmt Asst of North TX 1983; mediator Dispute Mediation of Dallas Inc 1982-85, Better Business Bureau of Dallas 1982-85; bd mem North Central TX ASPA 1983-85. **Honors/Awds:** Nominee Outstanding Young Amer 1981; program moderator Intl City Mgmt Assoc 1982; author Public Mgmt ICMA 1982-84; serv awd North TX Conf of Minority Public Admin 1983. **Military Serv:** AUS Pvt 7 mo's; Defense Awd, Cert of Achievement, 1974-75. **Home Addr:** 5737 Valley Mills Drive, Garland, TX 75043. **Business Addr:** Assistant to City Manager, City of Emporia, City Hall PO Box 511, Emporia, VA 23847.

WARD, ARNETTE S.
Educational administrator. **Personal:** Born Dec 2, 1937, Jacksonville, FL; daughter of Albertha E Scott and Isiah Scott; married John W Ward; children: Elra Douglas. **Educ:** Edward Jr Coll, AA; Florida A&M Univ, BS, 1962; Arizonia State Univ, MA, 1972. **Career:** Lincoln High School, teacher, 1963; Florida A&M Univ, asst prof, 1964; Fall Recreation Dept, dir of rec, 1964; Roosevelt School Dist, elementary school teacher, 1968; Mesa Comm Coll, counselor, 1971; dean of student sevr, 1979; Chandler-Gilbert Community College, provost, 1985-92, president, 1992-. **Orgs:** Mem, Commn on Trail Court Appt, 1985; nominating comm, Arizonia Cactus Pine Girl Scout; mem, Black Women in High Educ, 1986; mem, Amer Assoc of Comm & Jr Co, 1986; mem, Natl Council of Black Amer; mem, Affairs Council of AACJS; mem, Amer Assoc of Women in Jr Coll, 1986; pres, Delta Sigma Theta, 1986; mem, National Council of Instructional Administration, AACJC. **Honors/Awds:** Music Scholarship, Edward Water Jr Coll, 1957; honorable mention as singer, Alex Haley "Author of Roots," 1974; Outstanding Participation, Tempe School Dist, Black Culture Week, 1976; Women of the Year, Mesa Soroptomist/ Delta Sigma Theta, 1977 & 1984; Merit Award, Black Youth Recognition Conf, 1982. **Business Addr:** College President, Maricopa Comm Coll District, 2411 W 14th St, Tempe, AZ 85281.

WARD, BENJAMIN
Company executive. **Personal:** Born Aug 10, 1926, Brooklyn, NY; son of Loretta Ward and Edward Ward; married Olivia; children: Benjamin, Jacquelyn Ward-Shepherd, Gregory, Margie Lewis, Mary I Littles. **Educ:** Brooklyn Coll, BA 1960, AAS 1957; Brooklyn Law Sch, LLB 1965. **Career:** NYS Dept of Correctional Svcs, commr 1975-78; New York City Housing Authority, police chief 1979; New York City Dept of Corrections, commr 1979-83; New York Police Dept, police commr 1984-89; Brooklyn Law School, adjunct prof; Medallion Funding Corp, bd of dirs, currently. **Orgs:** Bd of dirs, Police Athletic League 1972-; Crime Control Planning Bd 1980, 1984-85; bd of trustees St Josephs Coll, 1984; bd of dirs, Natl Conference of Christians & Jews; Bd of Police Foundation. **Honors/Awds:** August Volmer Awrd Wnr Am Soc of Crmnlgy 1984. **Military Serv:** AUS stf sgt 1945-46. **Home Phone:** (212)767-6109. **Business Addr:** Bd of Dirs, Medallion Funding Corp, Attn: Marie Russo, 205 E 42nd St, New York, NY 10017.

WARD, CALVIN
Banking executive. **Personal:** Born Dec 10, 1955, Chicago, IL; son of Annie M Ward and Thomas Ward (deceased). **Educ:** Illinois State University, BS, 1977; DePaul University Graduate School of Business, MBA, 1989. **Career:** OSCO Drugs Inc, assistant general manager, 1977-83; Northern Trust Co., second vice pres, vice pres, currently. **Orgs:** National Black MBA Association, Chicago chapter, president, 1985, board member; Urban Bankers Forum of Chicago, 1986; National Association of Urban Bankers, 1986; United Negro College Fund, telethon supervisor, 1987. **Honors/Awds:** Alpha Phi Alpha Fraternity Inc, Brother of the Year, 1992, Certificate of Recognition, 1990; National Black MBA Association, Chicago chapter, Member of the Year, 1991. **Business Addr:** Vice Pres, The Northern Trust Co., 50 S LaSalle St, B-2, Chicago, IL 60675, (312)444-3608.

WARD, CALVIN EDOUARD
Music educator (retired). **Personal:** Born Apr 19, 1925, Atlanta, GA; son of Effie Elizabeth Crawford Ward and Jefferson Sigman Ward; married Adriana Wilhelmina deGraaf-Ward, Oct 11, 1962 (divorced 1976). **Educ:** Northwestern University, Evanston, IL, bachelor of music, 1949, master of music, 1950; Staats Akademie fuer Musik, Vienna, Austria; University of Vienna, Vienna, Austria, doctoris philosophiae, 1955. **Career:** Florida A&M University, Tallahassee, FL, instructor, music, university organist, 1950-51; Southern University, Baton Rouge, LA, associate prof, music, university organist, 1957-59; South Carolina State College, Orangeburg, SC, prof, chairman, Dept of Music and Fine Arts, 1959-61; Kingsborough Community College, CUNY, New York, NY, 1964-66; Tuskegee University, Tuskegee Institute, AL, associate professor, chm, Dept of Music, conductor, Tuskegee Concert Choir, 1968-72; Johns Hopkins University, Peabody Institute, Baltimore, MD, faculty, theory, African-American classical music, 1972-73, applied music, organ, 1973-77; University of Maryland, Baltimore County, MD, faculty, African-American studies, 1976-77; Coppin State College, Baltimore, MD, prof, music, 1973-83; Trenton Public Schools, Trenton, NJ, music specialist, retired; professional music educator and specialist, African-American classical music; free lance consultant, choralonductor and elementary school resource person, currently; Calvin Edouard Ward Educational Fund for Minority Students, chief administrator, currently. **Orgs:** American Choral Directors Assn; American Guild of Organists; American Humanities Forum; African-American Music Opportunities Assn; Natl Education Assn; New Jersey Education Assn; Trenton Education Assn; Phi Mu Alpha Sinfonia. **Honors/Awds:** Pi Kappa Lambda, Natl Music Fraternity for Excellence in Scholarship & Performance; Fulbright Fellowship Award, 1951; Fulbright-Hays Faculty Research Aboard Award, 1977; Fulbright Senior Visiting Lecturer Award, 1986; African-American Exchange of Scholars Award, 1978-79; Caribbean-American Exchange of Scholars Award, 1980; selected for taping, Oral History Dept's Files, Maryland Historical Soc; 1st participant in Fulbright Program of Visiting Professors to the USSR to both lecture & perform; 1st visiting professor to State Conservatory of Music, Vilnius, Lithuanian SSR, USSR; 1st American to make known the classical tradition of African-American Music in the USSR; 1st American guest lecturer at the State Conservatory of Music, Riga, Latvian SSR, USSR; 1st American organist to perform upon the world-renowned pipe organ in the Dome Cathedr Riga, Latvian SSR, USSR; NJ Governor's Teacher Recognition Program Award, 1990-91. **Special Achievements:** Visiting professorships and guest lectureships: Cuttington University College, Monrovia, Liberia, West Africa, Kenyatta University College, University of Nairobi, Kenya, East Africa, St Petersburg State Conservatoire, St Petersburg, Russia, St John's Theological College, Morpeth, New South Wales, Australia. **Military Serv:** US Infantry, Sgt, Chaplain's Asst, NCO Entertainment Specialist, 1946-48.

WARD, CAROLE GENEVA
Educator. **Personal:** Born Jan 14, 1943, Phoenix City, AL. **Educ:** CA State Univ at San Jose, BA 1965; MA 1973; Univ of CA, Grad Studies 1970; Intl Comm Coll, PhD; Univ of Ile-Ife Nigeria, 1970; Univ of Sci & Tech, 1970; Kumasi Ghana Forah Bay Coll Sierra Leone, 1970; Sorbonne, 1963. **Career:** Ethnic Studies Laney Coll, chrwmn; Goddard Coll, mentor consult teacher for masters degree stud 1973-74; Laney Coll, 1970-; CA Coll of Arts Cabrillo Coll, 1970; Andrew Hill HS, 1965-69; airline stewardess, 1966-68. **Orgs:** Mem Bay Area Black Artists 1972-; Nat Conf of Artists 1973-74. **Honors/Awds:** Recip purchase award 27th Annual SF Art Festival 1973; alpha phi alphaaward outstanding black woman for achvmnt & serv 1974; selec com chmn for Black Filmmakers Hall of Fame Paramount Theatre of the Arts; publ Images of Awareness Pan Africanist Mag 1973; Afro-Am Artists Bio-Biographical Dir Theres Dickason 1973; black artist on Art Vol 2 by Samella Lewis Ruth Waddy 1970. **Business Addr:** Laney Coll, 900 Fallon St, Oakland, CA 94607.

WARD, CHARLIE, JR.
Professional basketball player. **Personal:** Born Oct 12, 1970, Thomasville, GA; married Tonja, Aug 26, 1995. **Educ:** Tallahassee Community Coll; Florida State, bachelor's degree in therapeutic recreation. **Career:** New York Knicks, guard, 1994-. **Honors/Awds:** Heismann Trophy, 1993. **Business Addr:** Professional Basketball Player, New York Knicks, 2 Pennsylvania Plaza, New York, NY 10121, (212)465-5867.

WARD, DANIEL
Educational administrator (retired). **Personal:** Born Mar 15, 1934, Memphis, TN; son of Mr and Mrs Gus Ward; married Margie Marie Brittmon; children: Muriel Dawn, Maria Diane, Marcus Daniel. **Educ:** TN State Univ, BS Music Educ 1956; USAF Multi-Engine Pilot Training Sch, Cert 1957; USAF Radar Controller Tng, Cert 1958; USAF Air Force Instr Course, Cert 1960; TN State Univ, MS Secondary Sch Instr 1960; USAF Air Command & Staff Sch, Cert 1976; Drug & Alcohol Abuse Workshop, Cert 1975; 36 post-grad hours. **Career:** USAF, pilot and radar contr 1956-59; Douglass HS, program coord 1962-65; Hyde Park Elem Sch, asst prin 1965-67; Grant Elem Sch, principal 1967-68; Porter Jr HS, principal 1968-70; Douglass HS, tchr vocal music 1960-62; Vance Jr HS, principal 1970-81; Fairley HS, principal 1981-83; Memphis City Schools, dist IV supt beginning 1983-, asst supt, secondary dept, 1987-94. **Orgs:** Assn of Supervision and Curriculum Dev; Omega Psi Phi Frat Inc; AASA; TN State Univ Alumni Assn; Natl Guard Assns of TN; mem bd trustees Metropolitan Baptist Ch; Memphis-Shelby County Airport Authority 1967-; mem NAACP. **Honors/Awds:** Four-year scholarships to, TN State Univ, AR State Univ, Howard Univ, LeMoyne Coll, Stillman Coll; Omega man of the Year Epsilon Phi Chptr 1976 nominated 1980; Omega Citizen of the Year 1992; Awarded Meritorious Serv Medal 1981 by Pres of the US; 1st Oak Leaf Cluster 1984; Minute-man Award for Outstanding Serv to the TN Air Natl Guard; Danforth Admin Fellow 1983-84. **Military Serv:** USAF Lt Col served 28 years. **Home Addr:** 3675 Woodglade Ln, Memphis, TN 38116.

WARD, DARYL
College president, cleric. **Personal:** Born Sep 12, 1957, Cincinnati, OH; son of Lester and Maudie Ward; married Vanessa Oliver Ward, Mar 27, 1982; children: Joshua, Rachel, Bethany. **Educ:** College of Wooster, BA, 1979; Georgetown University Law Center, JD, 1985; Colgate Rochester Divinity School, MDiv, 1986. **Career:** Federal Energy Regulatory Commission, legal intern, 1982; Rochester Soc for Prevention of Cruelty to Children, legal intern, 1984-85; United Theo Seminary, director of admissions, 1986-89; United Theo Seminary, dean of African American ministries, 1986-; Omega Baptist Church, pastor, 1988-; United Theo Seminary, executive vice president, COO, 1989-93; United Theological Seminary, president, COO, 1993-. **Orgs:** Good Samaritan Hospital, board of trustees, 1989-; Tony Hall's Congressional Advisory Council, Dayton, 1991-; Ohio State Bar Association; Victoria Theatre Board, 1993-96; Hospice of Dayton, 1993-96; Urban Outreach Foundation, pres; United Theological Seminary, pres emeritus. **Honors/Awds:** Parity 2000 Award, Dayton's Ten Top African American Males, 1994; Society Bank's Community Recognition Award, 1993; Inducted into Morehouse College Martin Luther King Jr Board of Preachers, 1993; Dayton Volunteers Community Service Award, Certificate of Merit, 1991; Up & Comers Award, 1990; Rochester Area College Outstanding Adult Student, 1986; Fund for Theological Education, Benjamin E Mays Fellowship, 1984, 1985. **Special Achievements:** Keynote Speaker: Central State University, Wilberforce University, College of Wooster, Mississippi Valley State, Florida Memorial State, Bishop College, University of Dayton, Wittenberg University, Mount Union College, Wright State University, Ohio Northern University Law School; Keynote Speaker: National Afro-American History Museum, "The Church and the Civil Rights Movement"; Author of Papers: Church Renewal and Recruitment for Ministry," Networking for Globalization: Creating Intercultural Partnerships in Predominantly White Settings". **Business Addr:** Pastor, Omega Baptist Church, 1821 Emerson Avenue, Dayton, OH 45406, (937)278-1006.

WARD, DEDRIC
Professional football player. **Personal:** Born Sep 29, 1974. **Educ:** Northern Iowa, bachelors degree in psychology. **Career:** New York Jets, wide receiver, 1997-. **Business Addr:** Professional Football Player, New York Jets, 1000 Fulton Ave, Hempstead, NY 11550, (516)560-8100.

WARD, DORIS MARGARET
Government official. **Personal:** Born Jan 27, 1932, Chicago, IL. **Educ:** Univ CA, PhD; San Francisco State U, MA 1974; IN U, MS 1964; IN U, BA 1953. **Career:** City and County of San Francisco, assessor, 1995-; San Francisco Bd of Supervisors, pres; Mateo Co Office of Educ, coord; San Francisco State Univ, adj lectr, 1969-70, 1972; IN State Teacher Corps, team leader, 1967-68; Indianapolis Public School, teacher 1959-67. **Orgs:** Betty J Olive Meml Found; Commn Instr CA Comm & Jr Coll Assn; vice pres San Francisco Black Ldrsp Forum; mem Black Women Orgn Action; consult Waterloo IA Sch; Sioux City; Milwaukee; MN; Dayton Police Dept on Conflict & Violence; vice pres bd Sanfracisco Comm Coll Dist Bd Tst 1972-; tst Minority Affairs Assem Assn Comm Coll; mat exec cncl Assn Study Afro-Am Life & Hist; natl bd western reg bd Cncl Black Am Affairs Assn Am Comm & Jr Coll; mem NAACP; SF Div Nat Women's Polit Caucus; Alpha Kappa Alpha. **Honors/Awds:** NDEA grant IN State Univ 1966; lilly found grant IN State Univ 1967; NDEA Univ CA 1968; rockefeller found grant 1974; gov hon Pi Sigma Alpha; educ hon Pi Lambda Theta; spl merit award Sup Reporter 1973; living legend award Black Women Orgn Action 1975; distgsd woman award Girls' Club of Med-Peninsula & Lockheed Missilies & Space Co Inc 1975; recog comm serv Kappa Alpha Psi 1975; bicentennial award Trinity Bapt Ch 1976f recog exemplary comm ldrsp Black Student Psychol Assn 1976; publ "Indianapolis Comm Ctr Proj" 1968-69.

WARD, DOUGLAS TURNER (DOUGLAS TURNER)
Playwright, actor. **Personal:** Born May 5, 1930, Burnside, LA; son of Dorothy Short Ward and Roosevelt Ward; married Diana Hoyt Powell; children: 2. **Educ:** Wilberforce University, attended; University of Michigan, attended; Paul Mann's Actors Workshop, actor training. **Career:** Theater appearances include: Lost in the Stars, 1958; A Raisin in the Sun, 1959; The Blacks, 1961-62; One Flew Over the Cuckoo's Nest, 1963; Day of Absence, actor/writer, 1965; Kongi's Harvest, 1968; Frederick Douglass..Through His Own Words, 1972; The River Niger, actor/writer, 1972; The First Breeze of Summer, 1975; The Offering, 1977; Old Phantoms, 1979; The Reckoning, actor/writer, 1969; Perry's Mission, director, 1971; Ride a Black Horse, director, 1971; A Ballet Behind the Bridge, director, 1972; Waiting for Mongo, director, 1975; Livin' Fat, director, 1976; Home, director, 1979; A Season to Unravel, director, 1979; A Soldier's Play, director, 1981; Ceremonies in Dark Old Men, 1984; film appearance: Man and Boy, 1972; co-founder/artistic director, Negro Ensemble Company, 1967-. **Honors/Awds:** Obie Award, Happy Ending, 1966; Brandeis University, Creative Arts Award, Happy Ending, 1969; Vernon Rice Drama Desk Award, Best Play, Day of Absence, Happy Ending, 1966; Obie Award, The River Niger, 1973.

WARD, EVERETT BLAIR
Political party executive. **Personal:** Born Nov 6, 1958, Raleigh, NC; son of Dorothy Williams Ward and William H Ward; married Cassandra Lloyd Ward, Jun 12, 1982. **Educ:** Saint Augustine's College, BA, 1982. **Career:** Westinghouse Electric Corp, Raleigh, marketing asst, 1980-82; North Carolina Democratic Party, Raleigh, NC, political dir, 1983-89, exec dir, 1989-93; North Carolina Dept of Transporation, administrator for local/community affairs, currently. **Orgs:** Life mem, Alpha Phi Alpha Fraternity, Inc, Phi Lambda Chapter; Raleigh Historical Properties; committee chairman, elder, Davie St Presbyterian Church USA; North Carolina Black Leadership Caucus; Raleigh-Wake Citizens Association; advisory board, Mechanics & Farmers Bank; member, Democratic National Committee; Wake County Democratic Men. **Honors/Awds:** Martin Luther King, Jr Service Award, NC Association of Educators, 1986; Distinguished Alumni Award, National Association for Equal Opportunities in Higher Education, 1990; NAACP Humanitarian Award, Wendell-Wake Chapter, 1993. **Business Addr:** Administrator for Local/Community Affairs, North Carolina Department of Transportation, PO Box 25201, Raleigh, NC 27605.

WARD, FRANCES MARIE
Reporter. **Personal:** Born Mar 23, 1964, Goldsboro, NC; daughter of Occie Whitfield Ward and Joe Ward. **Educ:** North Carolina Agricultural & Technical State University, Greensboro, NC, BA, English, 1986. **Career:** Associated Press, Raliegh, NC, bureau news reporter/broadcast writer, 1986; Wilson Daily Times, Wilson NC, feature writer, 1988-89; Greensboro News & Record, Greensboro, NC, feature writer, 1989-. **Orgs:** Member, Triad Black Media Professionals, Greensboro, NC, 1990-; member, National Association for the Advancement of Colored People, Reidsville, NC, 1991; member, National Association of Black Journalists, 1990-; member, North Carolina Press Women's Association, 1990-; member, Saint's Delight Church, Goldsboro, NC, 1981-; member, Sigma Tau Delta, National Honor Society for English Majors, 1983-. **Honors/Awds:** 2nd place award winner for Profiles, North Carolina Press Women's Association, 1990; Most Promising Journalism Student Award, North Carolina A&T State Univ, 1985; English Department Award, North Carolina A&T State University, 1986. **Business Addr:** Feature Writer, Greensboro News & Record, PO Box 645, Eden, NC 27288.

WARD, GARY LAMELL
Professional baseball player (retired). **Personal:** Born Dec 6, 1953, Los Angeles, CA. **Career:** Minnesota Twins, outfielder, 1979-83; Texas Rangers, outfielder, 1984-86; New York Yankees, outfielder/infielder, 1987-89; Detroit Tigers, outfielder, 1989-90. **Honors/Awds:** American League Rookie of the Year, Baseball Digest, 1979-81; selected to Major League All-Rookie Team, 1981; American League All-Star Team, 1983, 1985.

WARD, HASKELL G.
Consultant. **Personal:** Born Mar 13, 1940, Griffin, GA; son of Margaret Poe Dumas and George Ward; married Kathryn Lecube Ward, Jun 14, 1980; children: Alexandra, Michelle. **Educ:** Clark Coll, BA 1963; UCLA, MA 1967. **Career:** Cmnty Dvlpmnt Agncy, commr; State Dept, Africa adv/policy plng stf; City of New York, dpty mayor 1979; Hlth & Hsptls Corp City of New York, chmn of bd 1979-; Ward Associates, consultant, currently. **Orgs:** Rep Ford Fndtn, Lagos, Nigeria; pgm ofcr Ford Fndtn, New York; bd dir Am Cncl on Germany; mem Mid-Atlantic Clb; board of directors, The New York City Partnership; board of directors, The African Medical Research Foundation; board of directors, The American Council on Germany; member, United States Information Service's Speakers Program. **Honors/Awds:** Woodrow Wilson Hnry Fellowship; John Hay Whitney Fellowship; several awards for citizenship, community service and achievement. **Business Addr:** President, Ward Associates, 444 E 57th St, New York, NY 10022.

WARD, HORACE T.
Judge. **Personal:** Born Jul 29, 1927, La Grange, GA; married Ruth LeFlore Ward, Jun 9, 1956 (died 1976); children: Theodore J. **Educ:** Morehouse College, Atlanta, GA, BA, 1949; Atlanta University, Atlanta, GA, MA, 1950; Northwestern University School of Law, Chicago, IL, JD, 1959. **Career:** Hollowell, Ward, Moore & Alexander, Atlanta, GA, attorney-at-law, 1960-68; State of Georgia, Atlanta, GA, state senator, 1965-1974; City of Atlanta, Atlanta, GA, deputy city attorney, 1968-69; Fulton County, Atlanta, GA, asst county attorney, 1970-74, civil court judge, 1974-77; State of Georgia, Atlanta, GA, superior court judge, 1977-79; US District Court, judge, 1979-. **Orgs:** Member, Alpha Phi Alpha Fraternity, Inc, 1948-; member, Phi Beta Kappa, Delta of Georgia; member, American Bar Assn; member, National Bar Assn. **Honors/Awds:** Honorary Doctor of Laws, Morehouse College. **Military Serv:** US Army, Corporal, 1953-65. **Home Addr:** 215 Piedmont Ave NE, Atlanta, GA 30303. **Business Addr:** Judge, US District Court, Northern District of GA, 2388 US Courthouse, 75 Spring St SW, Atlanta, GA 30308, (404)331-2776.

WARD, JAMES DALE
Educator. **Personal:** Born Feb 3, 1959, Nettleton, MS; son of Alice Harper Marion and J L Ward. **Educ:** Univ of MS, BA Journalism/Sociology 1980; Univ of Cincinnati, M Public Affairs 1983, PhD Political Science 1988. **Career:** Knoxville News-Sentinel, staff writer 1980; WCBI-TV Columbus, TV reporter 1981; University of Alabama, Tuscaloosa, AL, instructor, 1987-88; Minnesota State University, Winona, MN, assistant professor, 1988-90; University of New Orleans, assistant professor, 1990-. **Orgs:** Member, American Society for Public Administration, member, American Political Science Association; member, Midwest Political Science Association; member, Southern Political Science Association. **Special Achievements:** Publications: The Privatization Review; Public Administration Quarterly; Public Productivity and Management Review. **Business Addr:** Asst Prof, Dept of Political Science, University of New Orleans, Lakefront, New Orleans, LA 70148.

WARD, JERRY WASHINGTON, JR.
Educator. **Personal:** Born Jul 31, 1943, Washington, DC; son of Mary Theriot Ward and Jerry Washington Ward. **Educ:** Tougaloo College, Tougaloo, MS, BS, 1964; Illinois Institute of Technology, Chicago, IL, MS, 1966; University of Virginia, Charlottesville, VA, PhD, 1978. **Career:** SUNY at Albany, Albany, NY, teaching fellow, 1966-68; Tougaloo College, Tougaloo, MS, professor of English, 1970-; National Endowment for the Humanities, Washington, DC, program officer, 1985; Commonwealth Center, University of Virginia, Charlottesville, VA, program director/professor, 1990-91. **Orgs:** Member, Alpha Phi Alpha Fraternity, Inc, 1961-; member, Black Studies Committee, College Language Assn, 1977-91; chair, Division of Black American Literature, Modern Language Assn, 1986-87; member, Mississippi Advisory Committee, US Civil Rights Commission, 1988-; member, The Authors Guild, 1988-. **Honors/Awds:** Kent Fellowship, 1975-77; Tougaloo College, Outstanding Teaching Award, 1978-80, 1992; UNCF Distinguished Scholar Award, 1981-82; UNCF Distinguished Scholar-in-Residence, 1987-88. **Military Serv:** US Army, Spec-5, 1968-70. **Business Addr:** Professor, Dept of English, Tougaloo College, 500 W County Line Road, Tougaloo, MS 39174, (601)977-7761.

WARD, JOHN PRESTON
Educator, lawyer (retired). **Personal:** Born Aug 16, 1929, Marion, IN; son of Eddie Ward & Anna Lillion; divorced; children: Eddie Howard, Jeffrey Kenneth. **Educ:** Indiana Univ, AB, 1952; New York Univ School of Law, JD, 1955; Indiana Univ, MA, 1967. **Career:** Indiana Univ, teaching fellow, 1954-57; self-employed attorney, 1955-85; Indiana Civil Liberties Union, executive dir, 1957-61, general counsel, 1957-62; Indiana Univ, instructor, 1958-62. **Orgs:** ACLU; NAACP; American Bar Assn; Indiana State Bar Assn; Indianapolis Bar Assn; National Bar Assn; Marion County Bar Assn; National Urban League; American Assn of University Professors; American Council of the Blind; American Assn of Workers for the Blind, Indianapolis Chapter; Southern Christian Leadership Council. **Home Addr:** PO Box 88392, Indianapolis, IN 46208, (317)637-8645.

WARD, KEITH LAMONT
Attorney. **Personal:** Born Nov 12, 1955, Bridgeport, CT; son of Willie & Vera S Ward; married Jacqueline; children: Alexandra. **Educ:** Southern University, BA, 1978; Southern University Law Ctr, JD, 1982. **Career:** Keith L Ward PLC, attorney, currently. **Home Addr:** 185 Devon St, Mandeville, LA 70448.

WARD, LENWOOD E.
Petroleum company human resources executive. **Educ:** North Carolina Central Univ, Durham, NC, BS, 1963. **Career:** Arco, CA, org & co adv, 1973-74, sr employee relations adv, 1974-78, employee relations mgr, 1978-, org & co mgr, 1978-80, corp employee relations mgr, 1980-89, human resources svcs mgr, 1989-. **Business Addr:** Mgr, Human Resources Services, ARCO, 515 S Flower St, AP 4265, Los Angeles, CA 90071.

WARD, LLOYD DAVID
Manufacturing executive. **Personal:** Born Jan 22, 1949, Romulus, MI; married Estralita Ward, Jun 27, 1970; children: Lloyd II, Lance. **Educ:** Michigan State University, BS, 1970; Xavier University, MBA, 1984. **Career:** Procter & Gamble, div mfg mgr, 1985-86, adv mgr, pkgd soap & det, 1986-87, vp & gen mgr, dishcare, 1987-88; PepsiCo, Inc, vp operations, Pepsi-Cola east, 1988-91, pres, west div Frito-Lay, 1991-92, pres cent div Frito-Lay, 1992-96; Maytag Corp, exec vp & president, Maytag Appliances, 1996-. **Orgs:** Executive Leadership Council; Central & South West Corp, bd of dirs, mem. **Honors/Awds:** Dollars & Sense Magazine, America's Best & Brightest Business & Professional Men and Women, 1995; Black Enterprises, Executive of the Year, 1995; Michigan State University, Jack Breslin Life Time Achievement Award, 1996. **Special Achievements:** Black Belt, Karate. **Business Addr:** Exec VP/President Maytag Appliances, Maytag Corp., 403 W 4th St, N, Newton, IA 50208, (515)791-8210.

WARD, LORENE HOWELTON
Personnel administrator. **Personal:** Born Sep 8, 1927, Menifee, AR. **Educ:** AR Bapt Coll, BA 1964; Univ of OK, 1964; Wayne U, 1965; Harding Coll, 1966; Univ of AR, 1969. **Career:** EOA, personnel adminstr 1976-; EOA, dir asst 1974-76; EOA, coord 1972-74; Nghbrhd Multi-Purpose Ctrs, dir 1968-72; Soc Serv Wrkrs, supr 1967-68;Philander & Smith Coll, asst dean 1964-67. **Orgs:** Consult Relig Comm Outreach of Archview Bapt Ch 1977; consult Volt Tech Corp 1972; mem Panel of Am Women 1976-77; bus mgr Sunday Sch Class-Grtr Archview Bapt Ch 1977; AR Food & Mut Counc 1976-; pres Sr Choir Grtr Archview Bapt Ch 1975-76; mem Area Agency on Aging 1975-; pres Nat Assn for Comm Devel Region VI affiliate 1975-77; 1st anti-basileus Sigma Gamma Rho Sor Inc 1975-; Black Female Action Inc 1974-; Fairfield Bay Comm Club 1973-; sec Ldrshp Roundtable of AR 1973-75f AR Black Citz Orgn 1972-74. **Honors/Awds:** Cert of merit Nat Inst of Sr Citz 1975-76; Betty Bumpers Immunz Prgm for Prevention of Childhood Dis 1974; achvmt Award Pro-Plan Intl Ltd Inc 1974; outst comm serv & Human Devel Shorter Coll Alumni Assn 1973; award of achvmt SE Mgmt & Tech Inst 1972; cert of merit Volt-Tech Corp 1970; Award of Aprec Laubach Literary Assn 1968; Nat Assn for Comm Devel Serv Award 1975, 77. **Business Addr:** 2501 State, Little Rock, AR 72206.

WARD, MELVIN FITZGERALD, SR.
Clergyman. **Personal:** Born Jul 2, 1918, New Bern, NC; son of Nancy Forbes Ward and Dolphin Ward; married Lessie Pratt, Sep 12, 1940; children: Dorothy Buckner, Mary Francis Martin, Nancy Bullet, Melvin F Jr. **Educ:** Nat Bible Inst, DD 1944; Lawson Bible Inst, BTh 1945; Teamers Bible Inst, DD 1972; Union Christian Bible Inst, DD 1974; Livingston Coll, Salesbury, NC, Doctor of Divinity, 1976; Clinton Jr Coll, Rork Hill, SC, Doctor of Divinity, 1975; Union Christian Bible Inst, Master's of Divinity, 1984-. **Career:** Tobacco Wrks Intl Union, rep 1977; African Meth Epis Zion Ch, minister 1943-; TWIU, pres 1950-68; Bakery Confectionery & Tobacco Workers, Union AFL-CIO-CLC, Kensington, MD, representative, retired; AME Zion Church, Fayetteville, NC, pastor, 1940-91. **Orgs:** Bd mem AME Zion Ch; bd tst Christian Bible Ins; mem Home Mission Bd AME Zion Ch; dir Pub Rel for the Virgin Islands & South AM Conf; mem Human Rel Comm 1960-65. **Honors/Awds:** Award Pres of Local 256 TWIU 25 yrs; Appreciation Award for Dedicated Service & Unselfish Service, Hood Theological Seminary, 1989. **Military Serv:** Quarter Master, tech sgt, 1944; Rifleman, Good Conduct Medal, 1943. **Home Addr:** PO Box 2035, Durham, NC 27702.

WARD, NOLAN F.
Attorney. **Personal:** Born Jan 14, 1945, Columbus, OH; son of Ethel Shaffer Ward (deceased) and Cliffom Loudin Ward; married Hazel Williams Ward, Sep 6, 1966; children: Penelope Kaye Ward. **Educ:** Prairie View A&M U, BA MA 1968; Univ of NE, 1967; So U, 1969; Univ of TX, JD 1973. **Career:** State of TX, chmn exec dir Texas Employment Commn; Gov Dolph Briscoe, legal staff 1976-; Private Practice, 1975; Co Judge Bill Elliott, clerk 1975; St Rep Anthony Hall, admin aid 1973-74; EEOC, case analyst 1970-73; Waller ISD, instr 1967-69; Job Corps, advr 1966-67; attorney general, Austin, TX, 1983-. **Orgs:** Mem NAACP; TX Bar Assn; Omega Psi Phi; Omicron Kappa Delta; Delta Theta Phi; Thurgood Marshall Legislative Sec; District & County Attorney's Assn, Urban League. **Business Addr:** Attorney General's Office, Supreme Court Bldg, Austin, TX 78711-2518.

WARD, PERRY W.
College president. **Career:** Lawson State Community College, Birmingham AL, president, currently. **Business Addr:** President, Lawson State Community College, 3060 Wilson Rd, Birmingham, AL 35221.

WARD, RONALD R.
Attorney. **Personal:** Born Jun 12, 1947, Sacramento, CA; son of Audrey Ward and Robert L Ward; married Willetta L Ward, Aug 26, 1978; children: Sara A. **Educ:** California State University, BA, 1973; University of California, Hastings College of the Law, JD, 1976. **Career:** State of Washington, Office of the Attorney General, state assistant attorney general, 1979-82;

Levinson, Friedman Law Firm, attorney at law, partner, 1982-. **Orgs:** Washington State Trial Lawyers Association, Bd of Governors, 1989-95; Loren Miller Bar Association, 1979-. **Honors/Awds:** Special Presidents Recognition Awd, Washington State Trial Lawyers Association, 1995. **Military Serv:** US Army, 1967-69. **Business Addr:** Attorney-at-Law and Partner, Levinson, Friedman, Vhugen, Duggan & Bland, 2900 One Union Square, 600 University St, Seattle, WA 98101-4156, (206)624-8844.

WARD, RONNIE
Professional football player. **Personal:** Born Feb 11, 1974. **Educ:** Univ of Kansas. **Career:** Miami Dolphins, linebacker, 1997-. **Business Addr:** Professional Football Player, Miami Dolphins, 2269 NW 199th St, Miami, FL 33056, (305)620-5000.

WARD, SANDRA L.
Broadcast industry executive. **Personal:** Born May 23, 1963, Atlanta, GA; daughter of Betty Jean Ward and Aston Roy Ward. **Educ:** Howard University, BA, 1985; Georgia State Univ, School of Law; John Marshall Law, 1995. **Career:** EPIC Radio Network, senior account executive, currently. **Orgs:** Black Entertainment and Sports Lawyers Association; National Urban League; National Association of Media Women; Howard University Alumni Association. **Honors/Awds:** America's Top Business & Professional Women Award, 1991. **Special Achievements:** "Tribute to African-American Business and Professional Men & Women," Dollars and Sense, July 1991. **Home Addr:** 275 Dix-Lee On Dr, Fairburn, GA 30213. **Business Phone:** (404)873-3100.

WARD, VELMA LEWIS
Educator. **Personal:** Born in Columbus, OH; daughter of John F & Anna C Lewis and Otis D & Dorothy J Huguley; divorced; children: Broderick Lewis. **Educ:** University of Michigan, attended, 1949; Wayne State Univ, BS, MT, 1953; Wayne State Univ Coll of Medicine, MS, biochemistry, 1961; Wayne State Univ Inst of Gerontology, graduate cert, 1986; Wayne State Univ, PhD, 1996. **Career:** Lafayette Clinic, Detroit MI, Clinical Lab, research associate, asst director, 1956-84; Detroit Area Pre-Coll Engineering Program, asst dir, 1985-91; Philadelphia Geriatric Ctr, research prof manager, 1992-94; Wayne State Univ, visiting asst prof, 1996-. **Orgs:** New York Academy of Sciences; Assn for Women in Science, AWIS-DAC, exec bd, vp; The Gerontological Society of America; American Anthropological Assn; Assn for Anthropology & Gerontology; American Assn of Univ Women; Research Review Bd, Southfield Oncology Inst; Michigan US Navy Scholarship Information Team, NAVSIT, Detroit; US Navy Official Educators Visiting Team, Pensacola, FL. **Honors/Awds:** Northville High School, Distinguished Alumna Award, 1992; America Inst of Chemists, Fellow; Sigma Xi, Fellow; The Royal Society of Chemistry, 1996; National Technical Assn of Scientists & Engineers, NTA, Top Fifty Minority Women Scientists, 1996; National Inst of Aging, Minority Graduate Research Training Award, 1992. **Special Achievements:** Has authored several papers and has presented papers widely. **Business Addr:** Visiting Assistant Professor, Wayne State University-Department of Anthropology, 137 Manoogian Hall, Detroit, MI 48202.

WARD, WALTER L., JR.
State representative. **Personal:** Born Oct 28, 1943, Camp Forest, TN; son of Kathryn Ward and Walter Ward; divorced; children: Dionne, Walter L III. **Educ:** Univ of WI, BS 1969; Univ of WI Law Sch; Milwaukee Area Tech Coll; Marquette U, grad work. **Career:** State of Wisconsin, District 17, state rep 1972-81. **Orgs:** Couns work; chmn OIC Industrial Adv Bd; Martin Luther King Orgn Bd mem. **Business Addr:** 325 W Capitol, Madison, WI 53702.

WARD, ZANA ROGERS
Association executive. **Personal:** Born Oct 18, 1915, Miller, MS; widowed. **Educ:** TN State Univ, Cert; LeMoyne-Owen Coll, BS 1955; Brooklyn Coll of NY Univ, 1966; Memphis State Univ, MEd 1971. **Career:** Pres Memphis Chap Fed of Colored Womens Clubs, pres 1966-; Memphis Sect Natl Council of Negro Women Inc, pres 1972-. **Orgs:** Mem Zeta Phi Beta 1959-, Memphis Pan-Hellenic Council 1960-, Lambda Gamma Chap of Kappa Delta Pi 1971-; fin sec SE Reg Assoc of Colored Womens Clubs 1971-73; proj dir Memphis Unit of Women in Comm Serv Inc 1972-; mem Corp of Natl Women in Comm Serv Inc 1972-74; bd of dir Comp Youth Serv 1973-; 1stvp TN State Fed of Colored Womens Clubs 1974-; bd dir Memphis Shelby Cty Unit of Amer Cancer Soc 1974-; mem YWCA; pres Council Mt Pisgah CME Church;bd mem Chris Ed; vice pres Stewardess Bd #4; pres BR Danner Club; treas Sr Choir. **Honors/Awds:** Disting Club Womans Aws Natl Assoc of Colored Womens Clubs Inc 1963; Memphis Intl Fellowship 1968; Plaque SE Region of Assoc of Colored Womens Clubs 1971; Zeta Phi Beta Sor 1973; Memphis Sec Natl Council Negro Women 1974.

WARDEN, GEORGE W.
Insurance agent. **Personal:** Born May 18, 1944, Richmond, VA; son of Hilda Y Warden and George Warden Sr; married Sylvia Washington, Apr 9, 1966; children: Monica, Nicholas, Cecilia. **Educ:** Virginia Union University, BS, 1966. **Career:** State Farm Insurance Co, insurance agent, currently. **Orgs:** Rosa Park Scholarship Foundation, vice pres; National Association of Life Underwriters, currently; Oakland County Life Underwriters, currently; Detroit Property & Casualty Agents Association, currently. **Honors/Awds:** National Association of Life Underwriters, National Achievement Sales Award, 1992, 1993, 1994, 1995, 1996. **Business Addr:** Agent, State Farm Insurance Co, Stratford Bldg, 24361 Greenfield, Ste 201, Southfield, MI 48075, (248)569-8555.

WARDER, JOHN MORGAN
Bank executive (retired), franchise owner. **Personal:** Born Jan 7, 1927, Ellsworth, KS; son of Beulah Warder and Warner Warder; married Margie (died 1989); children: Linda, Kent, David; married Benola Foster Warder, 1992. **Educ:** Univ KS BA 1952. **Career:** Litho Supply Depot Inc, Minneapolis, MN, office manager, 1952-62, vice pres, 1962-68; Plymouth Natl Bank, pres 1969-82; First Plymouth Natl Bank, chairman of the board 1982-84; First Bank Minneapolis, vice pres urban devel 1984-86; First Bank System Inc, vice pres urban devel 1987-88 (retired); Relax The Back Store Franchise, president, owner, 1992-. **Orgs:** Trust Macalester Coll 1970-81; bd mem Minneapolis Foundation 1972-81; Helen Harrington Trust 1972-; Bush Foundation Panel Judge 1973-; treas Minneapolis UNCF Campaign 1975-; mem Alpha Phi Alpha Frat; co-chmn Alpha Phi Alpha 1978; Nat Conf Com; Minneapolis Club; Prince Hall Masons; Dunkers Club; vchmn 1980-85, bd mem 1985- Nat Med Flwsps Inc; treas Delta Dental of MN 1984; trustee Univ of MN Med Found 1985-; bd mem MN News Council; treas W Harry Davis Found 1986-;bd mem MN Bus League 1985-; mem NAACP, Minneapolis Urban League, Zion Bapt Ch Cty of Mpls; chairman, Zion Baptist Church Building Council, 1962-64. **Honors/Awds:** Disting Serv Awd 1964; Outstanding Serv Awd, Afro Am Educator's Assn 1968; Gtr Mpls C of C Awd 1973; Miss Black MN Outstanding Achievement Awd 1975; Minneapolis Urban League's Cecil E Newman Humantarian Aw 1976; Man of the Year Awd Insight Publ 1977; Outstanding Serv Awd Alpha Phi Alpha 1978; Man of the Year Awd Alpha Phi Alpha 1979; Outstanding Serv Awd MN Black Chemical Abuse 1982; MN Urban League Volunteer Serv Awd 1986; Natl Conf of Christian & Jews Brotherhood/Sisterhood Humanataria, 1991. **Military Serv:** US Army 1946-47; USAF corpl 1947-48. **Home Addr:** 1201 Yale Pl #1210, Minneapolis, MN 55403-1958.

WARDLAW, ALVIN HOLMES
Educator. **Personal:** Born Jan 3, 1925, Atlanta; married Virginia Cage; children: Alvia W Shore, Joy Elaine. **Educ:** Morehouse Coll, BS 1948; Atlanta U, MS 1950; Univ MI, Further Study 1951-54, 1959-60; Univ WI, 1965-66. **Career:** TSU, asst prof 1950-65; TX Southern Univ Coop Center of MN Math and Sci Teaching Proj, dir 1963-64; Upward Bound Proj, dir 1970-73; TSU, acting dept head 1969-72; EPDA Inst TSU, assoc dir 1970-73; TX Southern Univ, asst vice pres academic affairs. **Orgs:** Consult Adminstr Conf Houston Indep Sch Dist 1960; Nat Sic Inst So U; faculty rep Athletics TSU 1969-72; Athletic Adv Counc 1974-75; mem NAIA Dist #8 eligibility com 1971-73; pres TX Assn Stud Assist Progs 1973; Rockefeller Found Fellow 1952-54; NSF Faculty Fellow 1959-60; Carnegie Found Fellow 1965-66. **Military Serv:** AUS 1944-46. **Business Addr:** 3200 Cleburne St, Houston, TX 77004.

WARDLAW, MCKINLEY, JR.
Educator. **Personal:** Born Jul 24, 1927, Columbus, GA; son of Rosa P Robinson Wardlaw and McKinley Wardlaw; married Thelma Sears Wardlaw, Aug 3, 1951; children: Pamela Lynch, Vanessa D Morrison, Marcus K. **Educ:** Tuskegee Inst, BS Chem 1951; PA State Coll, BS Meteorology 1952; Westfield State Coll, MEd 1969; Univ of DE, MEd 1973; Temple Univ, EdD 1983. **Career:** Kent Cty Vo-Tech, Woodside, DE, dir of guidance 1970-79; Dept of Public Instruction, Dover, DE, state supvervisor, 1979-89; Delaware State University, Dover, DE, associate professor, 1989-. **Orgs:** Mem Kappa Alpha Psi Frat 1949-; professional mem AMS 1960-; mem DASA 1979-, DSBA 1982-, ROA 1982-; vice pres Capitol School Dist School Bd 1982; commercial pilot; Governor's Council on Long-Term Care, 1992-. **Honors/Awds:** Kappa Man of the Year, Dover Alumni Chapter, 1983; Certificate of Appreciation, Deleware State Board of Education, 1989; Certificate of Appreciation, Capital Board of Education, 1989; Certificate of Appreciation, Kappa Alpha Psi Fraternity, 1989. **Military Serv:** US Air Force, major, 1951-70. **Home Addr:** 617 Buckson Dr, Dover, DE 19901.

WARE, ALBERT M.
Automotive executive. **Personal:** Born Oct 13, 1952, Detroit, MI; son of Albert & Bessie Ware; married Wendy R, Jun 26, 1982; children: Christina M, Albert B. **Educ:** Wayne State Univ, BSME, 1977. **Career:** Ford Motor Company, suspension systems engineer, 1977-81; General Motors, chassis systems engineer, 1981-91, supervisor, chassis systems, 1991-92, vehicle systems integration mgr, 1993-94; GM, mgr, vehicle systems integration, 1994-95, director of full size truck plant integration engineering, 1996-98, director of plant support team engineering, 1998-. **Orgs:** DAPCEP (Detroit Area Pre College Engineering Program) board of directors, chairman, finance and development committee, 1992-; SAE, dir of Pre Engineering Education Program, Detroit Section, 1987-, general member, 1992-; bd of trustees, SAE Foundation, 1996. **Honors/Awds:** Engineering Deans of Historically Black Colleges and Universities, Black Engineer of the Year President's Award, 1994; US Black Engineer Magazine & Several Corp Sponsors, 1988-89; SAE, Special Recognition Award, 1989. **Special Achievements:** 6TH Annual Aluminum Assn, Design and Fabrication Seminar Award, for developing a new innovative forged aluminum design for use in a high volume automotive application, 1985. **Business Addr:** Director, Plant Support Team Engineering, GM Truck Group, 2000 Centerpoint Pky, Mail Code 483-516-2D1, Pontiac, MI 48341-3147.

WARE, BARBARA ANN. See SCOTT-WARE, BARBARA ANN.

WARE, CARL
Bottling company executive. **Personal:** Born Sep 30, 1943, Newman, GA; son of Lois Wimberly Ware and U B Ware; married Mary Alice Clark, Jan 1, 1966; children: Timothy Alexander. **Educ:** Clark Coll, BA 1965; Carnegie Mellon Univ, postgrad 1965-66; Univ of Pittsburgh, MPA 1968. **Career:** Atlanta Housing Authority, dir 1970-73; City of Atlanta, pres city cncl 1974-79; The Coca-Cola Co, Atlanta, GA, vice president, 1974-87, senior vice president, 1987-, deputy group pres, Northeast Africa Group, 1991-92, pres, Africa Group, 1992-. **Orgs:** Mem Policy Com of Nat League of Cities; GA Muni Assn; Comm Devel Com; bd dirs Metro Atlanta Council on Alcohol & Drugs; elected to Atlanta City Council 1973; bd of dirs US Civil Rights Commn 1983, Natl Cncl Black Agencies 1983-, United Way of Metro Atlanta 1983-; trustee Clark Coll; mem Gammon Theol Sem, GA State Univ Found, Sigma Pi Phi. **Honors/Awds:** Jessie Smith Noyes Fellowship Award 1966; numerous civic awards.

WARE, CHARLES JEROME
Attorney, association administrator. **Personal:** Born Apr 22, 1948, Anniston, AL; son of Marie Ware and John Ware; married Lucinda Frances Hubbard; children: Lucinda Marie. **Educ:** Univ of FL Gainesville, fellow in med & sci 1969 & 1971; Univ of AL School of Medicine, attended 1970-71; Talladega Coll AL, BA 1970; Howard Univ Law Sch, JD 1975; Boston Univ Sch of Bus MA, MBA fellowship 1976. **Career:** Inst for the Study of Educ Policy, legal legislative & econ asst 1974-75; Boston Coll Law Sch, atty writer & consult 1975-76; Boston Univ Martin Luther King Ctr, atty 1976; Middlesex Co MA Dist Attys Ofc, asst dist atty 1976-77; Arent Fox Kintner Plotkin & Kahn, anti-trust atty 1977; Criminal Div US Dept of Justice, trial atty/appellate atty 1977-79; US Dept of Justice, anti-trust atty 1979-82; US Immigration, judge 1980-81; US Fed Trade Comm, first asst to the dir bureau of competition 1982-83, spcl counsel to the chmn 1983-86; St Paul's College Lawrenceville VA, exec vice pres and genl counsel 1986-87; private practice of law, Ware and Assoc, PA, Columbia, MD 1988-. **Orgs:** Life Mem NAACP 1966-, SCLC 1966-; mem dir & editor Amer Bar Assn, DC Bar Assn, PA Bar Assn 1975-, MD Bar Assoc, VA Bar Assoc; founder & pres The William Monroe Trotter Polit Rsch Inst 1978-; natl legal advisor Natl Tots and Teens Inc 1986-; General Counsel, Maryland State Conf of the NAACP. **Honors/Awds:** Finalist White House Fellowship Prog 1978; Outstanding Young Columbian Columbia MD Jaycees 1979; Outstanding Young Man of Amer Amer Jaycees Montgomery AL 1980. **Home Addr:** 5032 Rushlight Path, Columbia, MD 21044. **Business Phone:** (410)720-6129.

WARE, DYAHANNE
Attorney. **Personal:** Born Jul 26, 1958, Chicago, IL; daughter of Freddie Mae and Clinton; children: Sherry Goldman. **Educ:** Univ of IL, AB 1980; The John Marshall Law School, JD 1984; Univ of Chicago, Graduate School of Business, MBA, 1990. **Career:** Encyclopaedia Britannica USA, atty FTC compliance audit staff 1984-85, staff atty 1985-86, atty general counsel/dir legal compliance staff 1986-, special foreign asst, Guadeloupe, FWI; Chicago Area Daycare Center, owner; Lexis-Nexis, corporate counsel consultant, 1994-95; Commerce Clearing House, international sr attorney, 1995-96, assoc general coun, 1998-. **Orgs:** League of Black Women, legal counsel; mem Chicago Bar Assn 1985-; America Bar Assn; Chicago Volunteer Legal Services, Natl Bd of Realtors, Urban League, Natl Conference of Black Lawyers; member, Cook County Bar Assn, 1990; member, National Black MBA Assn, 1989-90; Day Care Action Council, 1992-. **Honors/Awds:** Honoree YWCA Leadership Award 1985; Honoree YMCA Black & Hispanic Leaders of Industry 1987. **Home Addr:** 3651 N Mozart, Chicago, IL 60618.

WARE, GILBERT
Educator. **Personal:** Born Jul 21, 1933, Elkton, VA; divorced. **Educ:** Morgan State Univ, BA 1955; Princeton Univ, MD, PhD 1962. **Career:** State of MD, program exec 1967-68; Washington Tech Inst, exec asst to pres 1968-69; The Urban Inst, sr rsch staff mem 1969-70; Drexel Univ, assoc prof/prof political science 1970-. **Orgs:** Life mem NAACP; exec dir Judicial Council of the Natl Bar Assoc 1971-81; bd of dirs Historical Soc of the US District Court for Eastern PA 1986-. **Honors/Awds:** Fel-

lowships, Ford Foundation, Amer Council of Learned Societies, Amer Philosophical Soc, Metropolitan Applied Rsch Ctr; Natl Bar Assoc Presidential Awd1977; publications "From the Black Bar, Voices for Equal Justice," Putnam 1976; "William Hastie, Grace Under Pressure," Oxford Univ Press 1984. **Military Serv:** AUS 1st lt 4 yrs. **Business Addr:** Professor Political Science, Drexel University, 32nd & Chestnut Sts, Philadelphia, PA 19104.

WARE, IRENE JOHNSON
Editor. **Personal:** Born Apr 24, 1935, Blacksher, AL; married Fred E; children: Darryl, Ronald. **Educ:** Allen Inst 1953; Besteda's Sch of Cosmetology 1961. **Career:** Gospel Serv ABC/Dunhill Records, dir; WGOK Radio, announcer/gen mgr 1962-; Record World Mag NYC, gospel editor 1967-. **Orgs:** Mem NATRA; BAMA; GMWA; exec dir Nat Assn Gospel Announcers & Affiliates; gospel editor Black Radio Exclusive Magazine; vice pres bd of dir Gospel Music Assn1980; bd dir OIC Mobile Area; mem Operation PUSH Chgo. **Honors/Awds:** Named 1 of Top 10 Gospel Announcers Open Mike Mag 1965; Humanitarian Award NATRA 1971; Woman of the Yr Black Radio Conf 1977; Gospel Announcer of Yr GospelMusic Workshop of Am 1979; Black Gospel Announcer of Yr Award SESAC 1978; Outstanding Citizen of the Yr Stewart Meml CME Ch 1980; Jack Walker Award for Excellence in Broadcasting NATRA 1973; Excellence in Broadcasting by Utterbach Concert Choir Carnegie Hall 1969. **Business Addr:** PO Box 2261, Mobile, AL 36601.

WARE, JANIS L.
Newspaper publisher. **Personal:** daugHter of J Lowell Ware (deceased). **Educ:** University of Georgia, bachelor's degree in business administration. **Career:** The Atlanta Voice, publisher, 1991-; Voice News Network, president, currently. **Orgs:** Summech Community Land Trust, chairman. **Business Addr:** Publisher, The Atlanta Voice, 633 Pryor St SW, Atlanta, GA 30312, (404)524-6426.

WARE, JEWEL C.
County official. **Personal:** daugHter of Mattie Ware. **Career:** Wayne County, commissioner, currently. **Orgs:** Committee on Roads, Airports and Public Services, mem, 1995-; Committee on Audit, vice chair; Subcommittee on Senior Citizen Affairs, vice chair; Health and Human Services committee, mem; Public Safety & Judiciary committee, mem; Legislative Research committee, mem. **Business Addr:** Commissioner, Wayne County, Office of the County Commission, 450 Wayne County Bldg, 600 Randolph St, Detroit, MI 48226, (313)224-0900.

WARE, JOHN
City official. **Career:** City of Dallas, city manager, currently. **Business Addr:** City Manager, City of Dallas, 1500 Marilla St, Dallas, TX 75201-6390.

WARE, JUANITA GLEE. See THOMAS, JUANITA WARE.

WARE, OMEGO JOHN CLINTON, JR.
Consultant. **Personal:** Born Mar 13, 1928, Washington, DC; son of Bertha Shipp Ware and Omego J C Ware Sr; married Elinor Gwen Smith; children: Karl R, Keith R, Karlene R. **Educ:** Georgetown Univ, BS foreign commerce 1960; USA War College, graduate 1969. **Career:** Central Intelligence Agency, sr intelligence service-office director, mem Exec Committee, dir Center for the Study of Intelligence 1955-82; UC Lawrence Livermore Natl Lab, administrator/operations specialist 1982-93; Counter Terror Specialist; US Dept of Energy, Washington, DC, consultant-advisor, currently; Eagle Star International Inc, president, currently. **Orgs:** BSA; SCIP. **Honors/Awds:** CIA Awards, charter mem, Senior Intelligence Service; First "Trailblazer" Award, Central Intelligence Agency, 1991; 50th Anniversary Trailblazer Award, CIA, 1997. **Military Serv:** RA military intelligence 1946-55. **Home Addr:** 3244 Pope St SE, Washington, DC 20020. **Business Addr:** Eagle Star International, Inc, 3201 New Mexico Ave NW, Ste 350, Washington, DC 20016.

WARE, R. DAVID
Sports attorney. **Personal:** Born May 20, 1954, Franklin, GA; son of Lorine Kelly Ware and Roosevelt Ware Sr; married Sharon Ward Ware, Sep 2, 1978; children: Jerris, Candace, Breana. **Educ:** West Georgia College, BA, English, 1976; University of Georgia School of Law, JD, 1979. **Career:** Counsel on Legal Education Opportunities, teaching assistant, 1977; Small Business Development Center, graduate staff consultant, 1978-79; Professor Larry E Blount, research assistant; Kilpatrick & Cody, associate, 1979-82; Vaughn, Phears & Murphy, associate, 1982-83; Law Offices of R David Ware, beginning 1983; Floyd, Jones & Ware, partner, 1985-89; Thomas, Kennedy, Sampson, Edwards & Patterson, partner; Ware & Associates, currently. **Orgs:** State Bar of Georgia; Gate City Bar Association, executive committee, 1984, vice pres, 1985, president, 1987-88; Atlanta Bar Association; Natl Bar Assn; American Bar Association; Atlanta Volunteer Lawyers Foundation; Fulton County Board of Ethics, 1989-. **Honors/Awds:** University of GEO School of Law, Alumnus of the Year, 1981-82; numerous college & law school honors. **Special Achievements:** "How to Select a Sports Agent," 1983; "Why Are There So Few Black Sports Agents?" Sports, Inc, 1988; The Effects of Gender and Race on the Practice of Law, State Bar of Georgia, 1992. **Business Addr:** Ware & Associates, 2200 Century Pkwy NE, Ste 980, Atlanta, GA 30345, (404)329-0800.

WARE, WILLIAM
Insurance executive. **Personal:** marrIed Carole M Wiggins Anderson. **Educ:** New York City College, business administration; Augusta College, business administration; Goddard University, business administration and insurance, master's program, degree in progress. **Career:** William J Ware & Associates, president/CEO, currently. **Orgs:** Georgia Association of Insurance Professionals, chmn & executive director; The Atlanta Exchange Foundation, Inc, pres; NationsBank/Atlanta Urban League Loan Review Bd, committee mem; Atlanta Urban League & Agents/Insurers Partnership, committee mem; Minority Advisor for the Georgia Department of Labor, committee mem; Atlanta Urban League; Marietta/Cobb Museum of Art, bd of trustees; Marietta/Cobb County Museum of Art, chmn of nominating committee, bd of trustees; Cobb County Children's Center Inc, Another Chance Program, board of directors; The Atlanta Exchange Foundation Pro/Business Project/Role Models/Career Day Programs for Students, coordinator; NAACP; Cobb County Martin Luther King, Jr Support Group; Disabled American Veterans, life mem; numerous others. **Business Addr:** President/CEO, Success Guide, 55 Marietta St NW, Ste 2000, Atlanta, GA 30303, (404)523-0303.

WARE, WILLIAM L.
Educator. **Personal:** Born May 15, 1934, Greenwood, MS; son of Katherine Bowden and Leslie Ware (deceased); married Lottie Herger, Apr 18, 1958; children: Felicia Joyner, Trevor Ware, Melvinia Abdullah. **Educ:** Mississippi Valley State Univ, Itta Bena, MS, BS, 1957; California State Univ, Los Angeles, CA, MA, 1969; Univ of Southern California, Los Angeles, CA, PhD, 1978. **Career:** Greenwood Public School, health educ/coach, 1957-63; Bellflower Public School, physical educ/coach, 1963-72; California State Univ, Northridge, CA, asst prof, 1964-78; Mississippi State Univ, Mississippi State, MS, assoc professor, 1979-90; Mississippi Valley State University, professor, education department chairman, 1990; Mississippi Valley State Univ, asst to president, currently. **Orgs:** Dir, United Way of Oktibbeha City, 1982-85; Boy Scouts of Amer, Pushmatha Council, 1983-85; Volunteers for Youth, 1985; pres, Kiwanis Club, Starkville, 1986-87. **Honors/Awds:** Leadership Starkville Starkville Chamber of Comm 1985; Serv Awd CA Congress of Parents & Teachers Inc 1969; Kiwanian of the Year 1985; Distinguished Educ Award, IDEA, 1987; Outstanding Serv Award, Phi Delta Kappa, 1989; Pres Citation; Natl Assn for Equal Opportunity in Higher Educ, 1989; Faculty Fellow/Foundation for Mid-South, 1994. **Home Addr:** 75 Choctaw Rd, Starkville, MS 39759. **Business Addr:** Assistant to the President, Mississippi Valley State Univ, Itta Bena, MS 38941.

WAREHAM, ALTON L.
Dentist (retired). **Personal:** Born Jul 1, 1920, New York, NY; son of Esther Wareham and Samuel Wareham; married Helene; children: Roger, Lynn Howell. **Educ:** Lincoln Univ, PA, AB 1938-42; Howard Univ Coll of Dentistry, DDS 1944-48. **Career:** Medicaid Comm of NYC, chmn & mem 1968; Dntl Care Serv of 125th St, asst dir 1968-69; Headstrt Pgm of NYC, chmn & mem 1970-72; Grtr Harlem Nrsng Home, dntl cnsltnt 1977-; attending Dentist Harlem Hospital staff. **Orgs:** Cnsltnt Blue Shld Blue Crs Dntl Care Pgm of New York City 1972; life mem NAACP, PA L Urban League; mem 1st Dist Dntl Soc Atndng Stf Dntst Harlem Hosp Oral Srgry Dept; life mem ADA; American College of Dentists, fellow, 1992; New York State Department of Correctional Services, Regional Division of Dentists. **Honors/Awds:** Fellow Acad of Gen Dnststry 1982; Apprctn Awrd Dedicated Serv to Harlem Hosp & Oral Srgry Clnc 1984; Fellow, Supplement Continuing Education Academy of General Dentistry, 1984. **Military Serv:** US Army Capt 1952-54; Bronz Star; Unit Awrd; Combat Medic Badge 1953. **Home Addr:** 2235 5th Ave, New York, NY 10037.

WARFIELD, MARSHA
Actress, comedienne. **Personal:** Born Mar 5, 1955, Chicago, IL; daughter of Josephine Warfield; divorced. **Career:** Actress, 1974-; stand-up comic/comedienne in clubs throughout US and Canada, 1976-; film appearances include: The Marva Collins Story, 1981; Mask, 1985; D C Cab, 1985; Gidget Goes to Harlem; television appearances include: Night Court, 1986-; Marsha, hostess, 1990; Teddy Pendergrass in Concert, comic, 1982; Harry Anderson's Sideshow, comic, 1987; Comic Relief, 1987; Just for Laughs, 1987; On Location, comic, 1987; The Richard Pryor Show, 1977; Riptide, 1983; The Thirteenth Annual Circus of the Stars, 1988. **Honors/Awds:** San Francisco National Stand-up Comedy Competition, winner, 1979.

WARFIELD, ROBERT N.
Television news executive, financial manager. **Personal:** Born Nov 29, 1948, Guthrie, KY; married Gloria Jean. **Educ:** Eastern Kentucky University, BA, 1970; Columbia University Graduate School of Journalism, attended, 1971. **Career:** Orion Broadcasting, news reporter and photographer, 1971-72, promotion/advertising manager, 1972-73; WAVE-TV, Louisville, KY, producer, 1973-75; WTNH-TV, New Haven, CT, production manager; WDIV-TV, Detroit, MI, asst news director, 1979-82, news director, 1982-84, vice pres of news, 1984-89, station manager, 1989-91; Alpha Capital Management Inc, Detroit, MI, cofounder and partner, 1991-. **Orgs:** Cofounder, Alpha-Munder Foundation, 1991.

WARFIELD, WILLIAM C.
Educator. **Personal:** Born Jan 22, 1920, West Helena, AR; son of Bertha McCamey Warfield and Robert Warfield; divorced. **Educ:** Eastman Sch of Music, BM 1942; Univ of AR, D Laws 1972; Univ of Boston, DMusic 1981; Milliken Univ, D Music 1984. **Career:** Univ of IL, chmn voice div. **Orgs:** Pres Natl Assn of Negro Mscns 1984; bd mem Opera Ebony 1983-85; music panal Natl Assn for Advncmnt in the Arts 1981-87. **Honors/Awds:** Handel Medallion New York City 1974; Govs Awrd State of IL 1979; Grammy Award NARAS 1984. **Military Serv:** AUS sgt 4 yrs. **Business Addr:** Chairman, Voice Division, Univ of IL, 1114 W Nevada, Urbana, IL 61801.

WARFIELD-COPPOCK, NSENGA
Psychologist. **Personal:** Born Oct 28, 1949, Minneapolis, MN; daughter of Grace Warfield and Walter Warfield; married Bertram Atiba Coppock, Jan 17, 1970; children: Khary Coppock, Akua Coppock, Safiya Warfield. **Educ:** The Am Univ, BA Psych 1971, MEd Spcl Ed 1972; The Fielding Inst, PhD organizational psychology 1985. **Career:** Assn of Black Psych, natl adm 1971-81, organizational psych; assistant visiting professor, School of Social Services, The Catholic University, Wash DC. **Orgs:** Consultant The Gray Panthers 1980-; consultant AMTRAK 1982; hist bd dir Assoc of Black Psych 1982-87; mem Assn of Black Psych 1971-; mem Various Chld, Aging & Women's Orgs; Office of Substance Abuse Prevention. **Honors/Awds:** Fellow HEW Washington, DC 1972; Fellow Natl Science Fndtn 1979-82; artcl "Liberation & Struggle" in Reflctns in Blk Psych 1977; num papers, presentations & wrkshps; books:Teen Pregnacy Prevention: A Rites of Passage Resource Manual 1989; Transformation: A Rites of Passage Manual for African American Girls 1988; Afrocentric Theory and Applications, Vol 1: The Adolescent Rites of Passage, 1990; Afrocentric Theory and Applications, Vol 2, 1992; African Sisterhood: Rite of Passage, 1994. **Business Addr:** President/Organizational Psychologist, Baobab Associates Inc, 7614 16th St NW, Washington, DC 20012-1406, (202)726-0560.

WARMACK, GREGORY (IMAGINATION)
Artist. **Career:** Self-employed, artist, 1978-. **Honors/Awds:** Folk Art Society of America, Artist of the Year Awd, 1997; Children's Defense Fund Awd, 1995. **Special Achievements:** "Reclamation & Transformation: Three Self-Taught Chicago Artists," Terra Museum, 1994; exhibitions: "The Spirit of Unity," Carl Hammer Gallery, Chicago, 1998; "Recycle, Reuse, Recreate," African Tour, 1996, and others in places like Atlanta, Pittsburgh, Bristol, Racine, Boulder, Richmond, Dallas and Milwaukee; commissioned to design entranceway, The Unity Grotto, House of Blues, Orlando, Fl, 1997; 11 foot Coca-Cola bottlecap sculpture for the 1996 Olympics in Atlanta; visiting artist including Wabash Coll, Dallas Museum of Art, Boston Coll of Art.

WARMACK, KEVIN LAVON
Senior compliance examiner. **Personal:** Born Dec 20, 1956, Chicago, IL; son of Jacqueline Elliott Warmack and Kenneth Warmack; married Delma LaSane; children: Delma, Kevin II, Nadia, Marcus. **Educ:** Ripon Coll, AB 1979; Keller Grad Sch of Mgmt. **Career:** Lawyer's Word Processing Ltd, mgr 1979-81; Mayer Brown & Platt, asst supervisor 1981-83; Arnstein Gluck Lehr, legal asst 1983-85; Hisaw & Schultz, legal asst 1985-86; McSherry & Gray Ltd, legal asst, 1986-87; law resources, 1987-88; Natl Assn of Securities Dealers, sr compliance examiner, 1988-95; Rodman & Renshaw, Associate, Regulatory Accounting, 1995-96; Warmack Consulting, Ltd, pres, currently; Melvin Securities Corp, mgr, currently. **Orgs:** Natl Black MBA Assn 1989-; bd mem, Harvard School; Woodgate Fathers; Church of St John The Evangelist Episcopal Church; Natl Assn of Black Accountants; Securities Industry Assn; National Assn of Securities Professionals. **Home Addr:** 50 Cloverleaf Rd, Matteson, IL 60443, (708)720-2083. **Business Phone:** (708)720-2102.

WARMLY, LEON
Store manager (retired). **Personal:** Born Apr 28, 1941, Shreveport, LA; son of Gertrude Williams (legal guardians) and Joe Williams. **Educ:** Bill Wade Sch Modern Radio, Certificate 1966; San Diego City College, AA, 1973; San Diego State Univ, San Diego, CA, BA, radio & TV arts, 1982, CA comm college instructor credentials, 1990. **Career:** KDIG-FM Radio, San Diego CA, announcer, 1966-67; KFMB Radio, San Diego, CA, new reporter, 1973-75; Toastmaster's International, District 5, San Diego, CA, publicity director, 1974-75; Monford Point Marine Association, San Diego, CA, publicity director, 1975-79; DECA Commissary, Imperial Beach CA, store manager, 1991-96. **Orgs:** Mem Toastmasters Intl Dist 5; San Diego Club Bi-Centennial 2675 1969-74. **Honors/Awds:** KFMB Radio News Scholarship 1973. **Military Serv:** USMC, Corporal E-4, 1962-66; Armed Forces Expeditionary Medal, 1963. **Home Addr:** 4079 N Euclid Ave, Apt P, San Diego, CA 92105.

WARNER, EDWARD L.
Rector. **Personal:** Born Oct 20, 1939, Franklin Twnshp, NJ. **Educ:** Rutgers U, AB 1961; MDiv 1964. **Career:** St Augustine's Episcopal Ch, rector 1968-; St Albans, vicar 1964-67. **Orgs:** Mem Diocesan Council & Steering Com of Council; Standing Com; chmn Mayor's Commn on Hum Rights New Brunswick NJ; past pres Interdenominational Ministerial Alliance; mem bd of educ & chmn Comm Rel Com Presby. **Honors/Awds:** Interracial Award 1969; Omega Si Phi Citizenship Award 1973; Citizenship Award Kansas City C Of C 1974. **Business Addr:** St Augustine's Episcopal Ct, 2732 Benton Blvd, Kansas City, MO.

WARNER, ISAIAH H.
Clergyman. **Personal:** Born May 17, 1916, Erwinville, LA; married Elvira; children: Gloria M, Mary A, Alton Ray, Carlyn Ann. **Educ:** Leland Coll, AB 1959. **Career:** Mt Bethel Alsin LA, pastor; Christ Bapt Ch; King David Bapt Ch; Union Bapt Ch 2 yrs; Colonial Funeral Home Inc Port Allen LA, part-owner. **Orgs:** Bd mem 4th Dist Missionary Bapt; asso pres WBR Ministers Conf; mem Sheriff's Planning Commn of WBR Affiliated LA Bapt State Convention; Nat Bapt Convention Inc; Nat Bapt BTU Convention; mem West Baton Rouge Parish Bicentennial Commn; mem Stone Square Lodge #8. **Honors/Awds:** Recipient Certificate of Appreciation King David Bapt Ch Baton Rouge; Certificate of Appreciation Young Adults of Shiloh Bapt Ch Port Allen LA.

WARNER, IVAN
State supreme court justice. **Personal:** Born Feb 18, 1919, New York, NY; married Augustine Warner; children: Sylvester. **Educ:** Amer Univ, attended; CCNY, attended; NY Law School, LLB 1955. **Career:** NY State, assemblyman 1958-60; NY State Senate, senator 1961-68; chmn of education committee 1965; NY Supreme Court justice, 1969-. **Orgs:** Mem 100 Black Men Inc; mem Harlem Bronx & NY State Bar Assoc; dir Supreme Ct Justices Assoc NYC; pres Bronx Council BSA; life mem NAACP; vestryman Trinity Episcopal Church; dir NY Law School Alumni Assn; trustee Metro Museum of Art NY; trustee Union Hospital Bronx NY; NY State Judicial Commission on Minorities; Judical Conference, NY State. **Honors/Awds:** Community Serv Awd Bronx Urban League 1963; Distinguished Merit Citation Natl Conf Christians & Jews 1964; Special Achievement Awd Natl Council of Negro Women 1969; Community Achievement Awd Negro Business & Professional Womens Club 1969; Citizens Achievement Awd Joppa Lodge 1969; Leadership Awd Soc Afro-American Transit Empl 1969; Life Mem Chmn Awd NAACP 1969; Outstanding Achievement & Serv to Community Awd Alumni Association Lincoln School Nurses 1969; Ecumenical Awd Council Chs 1970; Silver Beaver Awd BSA 1974; Serv Beyond Call of Duty to God & Humanity Mt Carmel Baptist Church 1974. **Special Achievements:** Founder, Judicial Council, Natl Bar Assn. **Business Addr:** Justice, New York Supreme Court, 851 Grand Concourse, Bronx, NY 10462.

WARNER, MALCOLM-JAMAL
Actor, director. **Personal:** Born Aug 18, 1970; son of Pamela Warner. **Career:** Actor. **Honors/Awds:** Actor in film The Father Clements Story, 1987; host of Friday Night Videos; The Cosby Show; Here and Now; author of Theo and Me, Growing Up Okay, Dutton, 1988; HBO Movies, Tyson, 1995; Tuskegee Airmen, lead role, 1995.

WARREN, ANNIKA LAURIN
Episcopal priest. **Personal:** Born Dec 8, 1959, Hartford, CT; daughter of Annie McLaurin Warren and Hubbard H Warren I; married Mozallen McFadden, Jul 11, 1987; children: Shomari McFadden, Catherine Alannie McFadden. **Educ:** St Augustine's College, BA, urban affairs, 1981; Virginia Theological Seminary, MDiv, 1984. **Career:** Christ Church Cathedral, staff priest, 1984-88; Greater Hartford Chambe of Commerce, Weaver High School, drop-out prevention counselor, 1983-91; St Monica's Episcopal Church, interim rector, 1991-. **Orgs:** Alpha Kappa Alpha, 1977-; Alpha Kappa Mu Honor Society, 1981-; Coalition of 100 Black Women, 1990-; Greater Hartford Urban League, board of directors, 1989-90; Greater Hartford United Way, board of directors, 1992-; Hartford Action Plan for Infant Health, board of directors, 1992-. **Honors/Awds:** Harriett Tubman Book Award, 1983. **Special Achievements:** First African-American to be ordained to the Episcopal Priesthood in the Diocese of Connecticut, 1985. **Home Addr:** 31 Woodland St, Apt 1K, Hartford, CT 06105-4301, (203)293-1076.

WARREN, CHRISTOPHER COLLINS, JR.
Professional football player. **Personal:** Born Jan 24, 1968, Silver Spring, MD. **Educ:** Ferrum. **Career:** Seattle Seahawks, running back, 1990-. **Business Addr:** Professional Football Player, Seattle Seahawks, 11220 NE 53rd St, Kirkland, WA 98033, (206)827-9777.

WARREN, CLARENCE F.
Retail automobile dealer. **Personal:** Born Feb 15, 1941, Detroit, MI; son of Opal C Warren and Clarence R Warren; married Geraldine, Sep 5, 1964; children: Uvanuka. **Educ:** Wayne State University, BA, 1963; University of Georgia, advanced studies. **Career:** Kroger Co, corp director, labor relations, 1958-86; PS I Love Yogurt, chairman, chief executive officer, 1986-89; Network Video, president, chief executive officer, 1986-89; 32 Ford Mercury, president, chief executive officer, 1989-. **Orgs:** National Association Minority Auto Dealer, director, 1990-; NAACP; Urban League; Wayne State University Alumni. **Honors/Awds:** Cincinnati Minority Supplier Development Council, Minority Supplier of the Year, 1992; Ford Motor Co, Top Profit DD Dealer in US, 1992; Ford Motor Company, Top Profit Dealer Award, 1994; Ford Lincoln Mercury Minority Dealer Association, 1994. **Special Achievements:** Opened New Store, Sidney Ford Lincoln Mercury, in Sidney, Ohio. **Business Addr:** President/Chief Executive Officer, 32 Ford Mercury Inc, 610 W Main St, Batavia, OH 45103, (513)732-2124.

WARREN, FRED FRANKLIN
Business executive. **Personal:** Born May 22, 1922, Stokesdale, NC; son of Frank Warren; married Della; children: Larry, Brenda, Bonnie, Judy, Vanessa, Gladys. **Educ:** A&T U. **Career:** Warren Carpet Serv Inc, pres 1959-; Warren Woodcraft Co 1969-72; My Ladies Sportswear 1972. **Orgs:** Bd mem Employment Training Commn; Alamance Comm Action Prgm; Alamance Co Civic Affairs; chmn Deacon Bd Glen Raven First Bapt Ch; mem Am Cancer Soc; BSA.

WARREN, GERTRUDE FRANCOIS
Educator. **Personal:** Born Jul 4, 1929, Detroit, MI; daughter of Lela Long Campbell and John Henry Campbell; married Minor Warren, Sep 20, 1979; children: Lela Valsine Battle, Herbert W Francois Jr. **Educ:** Eastern Michigan University, Ypsilanti, MI, BS, 1949, Masters degree, Special Education, PhD. **Career:** Meisners, Detroit, MI, personnel mgr, 1950-55; Ypsilanti Board of Education, Ypsilanti, MI, teacher; Detroit Board of Education, Detroit, MI, teacher, English Dept Head. **Orgs:** Member, steering committee, REACT, 1987-; membership, NAACP, 1981-; commissioner, Mental Health, Washington County, 1970-79; membership chair, Dorcas Society, 1971-; president, Palm Leaf Club, 1955-; budget chair, New Era Study Club, 1987-; secretary, Kings Daughters, 1985; commissioner, Low Cost Housing, 1971-; commissioner, Public Housing, 1965-70; advisor, Metro Women's Civic Club, 1988-; parliamentarian, Alpha Kappa Alpha Sorority, 1970-74; president, Michigan State Asociation of Colored Women's Clubs, 1987. **Honors/Awds:** Contributions to Community, William Lucas, 1987; Teaching Teachers to Teach, Detroit Board of Education, 1967; Founded Delta Psi Omega Chapter, AKA, Inc, 1953; Founded First Scholarship for Blacks, Michigan State Association, 1988; Conducting (over the air) How to Teach Reading Readiness, Detroit Board of Education, 1950. **Home Addr:** 26842 Hopkins, Inkster, MI 48141.

WARREN, GINA ANGELIQUE
Foundation executive. **Personal:** Born Jan 23, 1954, Oakland, CA; daughter of Lily Crawford and Gerald Crawford. **Educ:** Phoenix College, Phoenix, AZ, 1972; Arizona State University, Tempe, AZ, BA, Education, 1974, MA, Education, 1984. **Career:** AT&T, Phoenix, AZ, public relations manager, 1985-87, regulatory lobbyist, 1987-89; AT&T Foundation, New York, NY, vice president, health and social action program, 1989-. **Orgs:** Board Officer, Phoenix Urban League, 1986-89; advisory committee, Miss America Foundation, 1990-; advisory committee, Natl Urban League-BEEP Program, 1989-. **Honors/Awds:** Volunteer of the Year, Phoenix Urban League, 1988; Angela Woods Leadership Award, Alliance of Black Telecommunications Employees, Inc, 1990.

WARREN, HENRY L.
Electric utility company executive. **Personal:** Born Aug 27, 1940, Pine Bluff, AR; son of Rissie Combs Warren and Henry Warren; married Jean Henderson, Aug 21, 1960; children: Jacque, Gregory, Sandra. **Educ:** Univ of Arkansas, Pine Bluff, BS bio & chem, 1968; Univ of Arkansas, Fayetteville, MS oper mgt, 1978. **Career:** Arkansas Power & Light, Pine Bluff, design asst 1968-70, methods analyst 1970-74; AR Power & Light, Little Rock, office mgr 1974-77, equal employment mgr 1977-78; AR Power & Light, Conway, district mgr 1978-80; AR Power & Light, Little Rock, dir of internal auditing 1980-85, vice pres & asst to pres 1985-86, vice pres of admin services 1986-88, vice pres of planning & control 1988-. **Orgs:** Vice pres, Natl Soc to Prevent Blindness, AR Division, 1987-89; pres, Business Volunteer Council, 1988-89; vice pres, Leadership Roundtable, 1988-91; vice pres, Community Affairs, Greater Little Rock Chamber of Commerce, 1989-90; vice chair, United Way Volunteer Services, 1989-90; bd mem, Arkansas Opera Theatre, 1989-90; mem, Edison Electric Inst Strategic Planning Comm, 1989-90. **Honors/Awds:** Career for Youth award, Chicago Public School System, 1989. **Business Addr:** Vice President, Planning & Control, Arkansas Power & Light, PO Box 551, Little Rock, AR 72203.

WARREN, HERMAN LECIL
Educator. **Personal:** Born Nov 13, 1933, Tyler, TX; son of Leola Mosley Warren and Cicero Warren; married Mary K Warren, Oct 12, 1963; children: Michael J, Christopher L, Mark H. **Educ:** Prairie View A&M, BS 1953; Michigan State Univ, MS 1962; Univ of Minnesota, PhD 1969. **Career:** Olin Chem Corp New Haven CT, research scientist 1962-67; US Dept of Agriculture Beltsville MD, plant pathologist 1969-71; USDA Purdue Univ W Lafayette IN, prof & plant pathologist 1971-88; Virginia Polytechnic Institute and State Univ, Blacksburg, VA, professor, 1989-. **Orgs:** American Phytopathological Society. **Honors/Awds:** African Scientific Institute, fellow, 1993; Commonwealth Visiting Professor of Virginia. **Military Serv:** 1st lt 1953-56. **Business Addr:** Professor, Virginia Polytechnic Institute & State University, Plant Pathology, Physiology and Weed Science Department, Blacksburg, VA 24061.

WARREN, JAMES KENNETH
Technical training manager. **Personal:** Born Jan 1, 1947, Detroit, MI; son of Ocie Chapman Warren and Amos Warren; married Diedre Peterson (divorced 1978); children: Jacqueline Carmila Plair. **Educ:** Howard University, Washington, DC, BA, 1970. **Career:** BASF Corp, Dearborn, MI, manager of planning, 1976-79, area sales manager, 1979-88, special program developer, 1988-91, technical training manager, currently. **Orgs:** Member, Automotive Training Manager Council, 1991; member, Automotive Service Industry Assn, 1974-91; member, Howard University Alumni Assn, 1970-91. **Home Addr:** 20526 Basil, Detroit, MI 48235.

WARREN, JOSEPH DAVID
Educational administrator, educator. **Personal:** Born Apr 2, 1938, New York, NY; son of Geroldine McDaniel Warren and Harold H Warren, Sr; divorced; children (previous marriage): Makeda, Setti, Kara; married Martha L Warren. **Educ:** North Carolina A&T Univ, Greensboro NC, BS 1969; Brandeis Univ, Waltham MA, MA 1973, PhD 1983. **Career:** United Planning Org, Washington DC, dir of comm organization, 1965-67; Policy Management System, New York NY, natl VISTA training coordinator, 1967-69; Brandeis Univ, Waltham MA, exec dir of Upward Bound, 1970-74; Commonwealth of Massachusetts, Boston MA, asst sec of educational affairs, 1975-79; Northeastern Univ, Boston MA, urban asst to president 1979-82, dir of community affairs 1982-90, associate professor of African-American Studies, 1990-. **Orgs:** Pres, Devel & Training Associates; chair, Industrial Sites Devel Assn, Boston Mayor's Minority Business Advisory Council, MA Human Resource Center; mem, United Way of Greater Boston, Roxbury Multi-Service Center; trustee, Emmanual Coll. **Honors/Awds:** MA Black Achievers Awards; Phi Kappa Phi Society Award; First Annual MA Affirmative Action Award; award for minority business from Gov of MA; Award for Youth Service from Mayor of Boston; created & directed univ-based academy for pre-high schools; created & directed special higher educ opportunity for public housing residents; chaired Blue Ribbon Panel on Racial Incident, Newton MA; lead devel of MA business set-aside program. **Military Serv:** US Air Force & US Naval Reserve, commander, 1956-94. **Business Addr:** Associate Professor of African-American Studies, Northeastern University, 132 Nightingale, Boston, MA 02115.

WARREN, JOSEPH W.
Educator, businessman. **Personal:** Born Jul 2, 1949, Rocky Mount, NC; son of Marjorie Johnson Warren and James W Waren Jr; married Cynthia Taylor, Jul 2, 1972; children: Camille, Joseph II, Jerrick. **Educ:** Oakwood Coll, BA (summa cum laude), 1971; Ohio State Univ, MA, 1973, PhD, 1982. **Career:** Ohio State Univ, grad asst, 1973-76; Lake Michigan Coll, adjunct professor, 1978-80; Andrews Univ, assoc professor of English, 1976-. **Orgs:** Founder, Mid-Amer Network Marketing, Inc, 1984-; Inst for Christian Educ and Youth Devel, 1985-; co-founder, Scholastic Study Lab, Andrews Univ, 1984; founder, owner, Mid-Amer Premiere Brokerage, 1986-; founder, director, The Center for Building Self-Esteem in African-American Youth, 1990-. **Honors/Awds:** United Negro Coll Fund Fellowship, 1971; PhD, Fellowship, Ohio State Univ, 1971; Research Grant, Andrews Univ, 1984, 1992. **Home Addr:** 508 N Bluff, Berrien Springs, MI 49103. **Business Addr:** Associate Professor of English, Andrews University, Berrien Springs, MI 49103.

WARREN, JOYCE WILLIAMS
Judge. **Personal:** Born Oct 25, 1949, Pine Bluff, AR; daughter of Marian Williams Johnson and Albert Lewis Williams; married James Medrick Warren, Feb 26, 1972; children: Jonathan, Jamie, Justin. **Educ:** University of Arkansas at Little Rock, AR, BA, 1971, JD, 1976; University of Nevada at Reno, NV, summer college for family court judges, 1983, advanced evidence, 1990; Howard Univ, judicial education courses, 1996-97. **Career:** Governor Bill Clinton, Little Rock, AR, admin asst, 1979-81; private law practice, Little Rock, AR, attorney-at-law, 1981-82; Central Arkansas Legal Services, Little Rock, AR, staff attorney, 1982; Pulaski County, Arkansas, Little Rock, AR, juvenile judge, 1983-87, paternity judge, 1987-89; State of Arkansas, Little Rock, AR, circuit/chancery judge, 1989-. **Orgs:** Member, Arkansas State Board of Law Examiners, 1986-93; member, American, National, Arkansas, & Pulaski County Bar Associations, 1971-; member, National Council of Juvenile & Family Court Judges, 1983-; member, Arkansas Judicial Council, 1989-; member, Sigma Gamma Rho Sorority, Inc, 1968-. **Honors/Awds:** Arkansas Professional Women of Distinction, Worthen Bank Women's Advisory Board, 1988; Resolution for Outstanding Services, Pulaski County Quorum Court, 1988; Very Special Arkansas Women, Arkansas Sesquicentennial Official Event, 1986; Gold Medal for Excellence in Law,

Sigma Gamma Rho Sorority, Inc, 1986; Top 100 Women in Arkansas, 1995, 1996, 1997. **Business Addr:** Circuit/Chancery Judge, Juvenile Div, 6th Judicial Dist Chancery Court, State of Arkansas, 3001 W Roosevelt Rd, Little Rock, AR 72204.

WARREN, LAMONT
Professional football player. **Personal:** Born Jan 4, 1973, Indianapolis, IN. **Educ:** University of Colorado. **Career:** Indianapolis Colts, running back, 1994-. **Business Addr:** Professional Football Player, Indianapolis Colts, PO Box 535000, Indianapolis, IN 46253, (317)297-2658.

WARREN, LEE ALDEN
Advertising executive. **Personal:** Born Sep 17, 1954, Crestline, OH; son of Deloras Lee Warren and Harold J Warren; married Feb 14, 1988; children: Adriana Marie. **Educ:** Ohio Univ Athens OH, BS Journalism (Cum Laude) 1976. **Career:** Central State Univ Wilberforce OH, admissions counselor 1977-78; Xerox Corp Columbus OH, marketing exec 1978-83; Amer Hospital Supply Corp OH, product specialist/territory mgr 1983-86; KSBW-TV, NBC Salinas-Monterey CA, acct exec 1986-87; KIOI-FM San Francisco, CA, account exectuve, 1988; Forest Grove Advertising, Centerville, OH, vice president, client services, 1989-. **Orgs:** Past vice pres & treas Xerox Mid Ohio Corporate Few 1978-83; mem Ohio Univ Alumni Assoc 1980-, South Bay Area Urban Bankers 1986-88, San Jose Advertising Club 1986-88, San Jose Women in Advertising 1986-88, San Jose Jazz Soc 1986-88, TV Bureau of Advertising 1986-88; mem Broad Net Inc (Black Broadcasters in Northern CA) 1987-88; on air commercial announcer/radio; bd mem, Ohio University Alumni Assn, Dayton Chapter, 1990-. **Honors/Awds:** Account Rep of Month Xerox Corp 1979,80; President's Club 1979-80, Par Club 1979-80 Xerox Corp; Columbus Branch winner Xerox Sales Presentation contest 1981. **Home Addr:** 110 Monroe Ave Apt 903, Memphis, TN 38103-2518. **Business Addr:** Vice President, Client Services, Forest Grove Advertising, 571 Congress Park Dr, Centerville, OH 45429.

WARREN, MICHAEL
Actor, producer. **Personal:** Born Mar 5, 1946, South Bend, IN; married Susie W (divorced); children: Koa, Cash. **Educ:** UCLA, BA, theatre arts. **Career:** Appeared in TV series Hill St Blues, 1981-87; appeared in motion pictures Fast Break, 1979; Norman.. Is That You?, 1976; Drive, He Said, 1971; Dreamaniac (video), 1987; The Child Saver, tv, 1989; The Kid Who Loved Christams, tv, 1990; guest appearances, numerous tv series; tv pilot Home Free, actor, producer, 1988; Buffalo Soldiers, 1997. **Honors/Awds:** All-American Basketball Player UCLA; Academic All American NCAA 1966; Emmy Award nomination (Hill Street Blues). **Business Addr:** Actor, c/o Sandy Bresler & Associates, 15760 Ventura Blvd, Suite 1730, Encino, CA 91436.

WARREN, MORRISON FULBRIGHT
Educator. **Personal:** Born Dec 6, 1923, Marlin, TX; children: Morrison, Carolyn Pitts, Dwight, Wayne, Howard, Marilyn Shumate, Kevin. **Educ:** AZ State Univ, BA 1948; AZ State Univ, MA 1951, EdD 1959. **Career:** Phoenix Elem School Dist 1, teacher 1948-53, principal 1953-68; AZ State Univ Explt Progs Coll Ed, dir 1968-84, prof emeritus of education 1984-. **Orgs:** Mem 1966-70, vice mayor 1969, Phoenix City Council; pres Fiesta Bowl 1981-; life mem NEA; dir 1st Interstate Bank of AZ NA 1981-86; bd of dir Samaritan Health Svc until 1992, AZ Publ Svc, until 1994; State Bd of Education, Arizona, 1991-94; Far West Regional Laboratory for Educ, Res and Service, 1992-95. **Honors/Awds:** Named one of four Outstanding Young Men of Phoenix Jr C of C 1958; Recipient of Natl Conference of Christians and Jews, Human Relations Award w/ Sandra O'Connor, (Western Region, Arizona). **Military Serv:** AUS 1943-46. **Business Addr:** Prof Emeritus of Education, Arizona State University, Tempe, AZ 85287.

WARREN, NAGUEYALTI
Educator, educational administrator. **Personal:** Born Oct 1, 1947, Atlanta, GA; daughter of Frances Herrin; married Rueben C Warren; children: Alkamessa, Asha, Ali. **Educ:** Fisk Univ, BA 1972; Simmons Coll, MA 1974; Boston Univ, MA 1974; Univ of Mississippi, PhD 1984. **Career:** Northeastern Univ, instructor 1977-78; Univ of Calabar, lecturer 1979; Fisk Univ, asst prof and chairperson, Dept of English 1984-88; Emory University, asst dean, assoc prof, 1988-. **Orgs:** Mem College Language Assoc, Modern Language Assoc, Natl Council of Teachers of English, Southern Conf on Afro-Amer Studies; advisory board member, W E B Du Bois Foundation. **Honors/Awds:** Awd for Contribution to Black History Month Meharry Medical Coll 1984; Golden Poet Awd World Poetry Assoc 1985; poetry published in the following The American Poetry Anthology, Mississippi Earthworks, Janus, Riders of the Rainbow, Earthshine. **Special Achievements:** Book: Lodestar and Other Night Lights, New York, Mellen, 1992. **Home Addr:** 7469 Asbury Drive, Lithonia, GA 30058. **Business Addr:** Assistant Dean, Emory College Office, Emory University, 215 White Hall, Atlanta, GA 30322.

WARREN, OTIS, JR.
Real estate executive. **Personal:** Born Aug 25, 1942, Baltimore, MD; son of Rose Warren and Otis Warren Sr; married Dr Sharon Jones-Warren, Nov 22; children: Otis Warren III. **Educ:** Community College of Baltimore, AA, business. **Career:** Otis Warren & Co, president, owner, 1970-. **Orgs:** Medical Mutual, board of directors, 1988-; Nations Bank, board of directors, 1989-; Higher Education Commission, board member, 1990-; Fannie Mae Advisory Board, 1990-91; National Association of Realtors, board of directors, 1989-91; NAACP, lifetime member; Baltimore City Chamber of Commerce, 1992-; Greater Baltimore Board of Realtors, president, 1983. **Honors/Awds:** MDDC, Business Opportunity Fair Honoree, 1991; Maryland Association Realtors, Equal Opportunity in Housing, 1991; Greater Baltimore Board of Realtors, Realtor of the Year, 1976, Realtor Fair Housing Service Award, 1990; Morgan State University, Distinguished Service Award, 1990. **Special Achievements:** Obtained largest minority contract with the govt for the devt of an office bldg in downtown Baltimore, 1990. **Business Addr:** President/Chief Executive Officer, Otis Warren & Company, 10 S Howard St, Ste 110, Baltimore, MD 21201, (410)539-1010.

WARREN, RUEBEN CLIFTON
Health services administrator. **Personal:** Born Aug 16, 1945, San Antonio, TX; son of Bobbye Owens; married Nagueyalti Warren; children: Alkamessa Dalton, Asha Warren, Ali Warren. **Educ:** San Francisco State Univ, BA 1968; Meharry Med Coll, DDS 1968-72; Harvard Sch of Dental Med, residency in dental publ health 1973-75; Harvard Sch of Public Health, MPH 1973, Dr PH 1973-75. **Career:** University of Lagos, Nigeria West Africa 1975-76; Harvard School of Dental Medicine, instructor 1976-77; University of CT Health Center, assistant professor 1977-80; State of MS, dental director 1981-83; University of MS Med Center, clin associate professor 1982-83; Meharry Med College, associate professor & dean 1983-88; Centers for Disease Control and Prevention, Atlanta GA, Associate Director for Minority Health 1988-97; assoc adm For Urban Affairs Agency for Toxic Substances and Disease Registry; clinical prof, Morehouse School of Medicine, 1989-; adj prof, Emory Univ, 1996-. **Orgs:** American Dental Assn, Meharry Alumni Assn, National Dental Assn, NAACP, American Public Hlth Assn, Amer Assoc of Public Health Dentistry; NAACP; Natl Urban League; chairperson, Caucus on Public Health and Faith Communities Apha; chairperson National Dental Assn Delegation Conference to Africa, 1982; Operation PUSH. **Honors/Awds:** Dental School Student of the Yr Meharry Med Coll 1970; 2nd Place Awd Table Clinics 1971; Omega Man of the Yr Delta Chap 1971-72; Intermediate-Undergrad Omega Man of the Yr 5th Dist 1971-72; Awd for Outstanding Achievement in 4 yrs of Dental College Intl College of Dentists 1972; Comm Serv Awd Roxbury Med Tech Inst 1973; President's Awd National Dental Assn 1978; Robert Wood Johnson Health Policy Fellowship Finalist 1979; Scholar Prog Veteran's Admin Fellowship Finalist 1980; Distinguished Alumni Award, Harvard School of Dental Medicine, 1990. **Special Achievements:** Author, 54 publications including: "Implementing School-Based Dental Services, The Mississippi Model," 1984, "Community Diagnosis: A Comprehensive Needs Assessment Approach for Minority and Underserved Communities," 1996, and "Health and Well Being; A Clearer Vision," 1996; 115 presentations including: "A National Management Model to Facilitate Health Service for Head Start Children," presented at National Head Start Association 9th Annual Training Conference, 1982, "Your Cup is Half Full: Not Half Empty," at Conf Black History Makers, 1996, "HIV/AIDS in the US," at Black History Showdown, 1995, and "Higher Ground," at NC Dept of Environment, 1995. **Business Addr:** Associate for Minority Health, Centers for Disease Control and Prevention, 1600 Clifton Road, NE, Building 1, Room 32, Atlanta, GA 30333.

WARREN, STANLEY
Educator. **Personal:** Born Dec 18, 1932, Indianapolis, IN. **Educ:** Indiana Central Coll, BS 1959; Indiana Univ, MAT 1964; Indiana Univ, EdS; Indiana Univ, EdD 1973. **Career:** DePauw Univ, dir black studies prof educ; Indianapolis Publ Sch, tchr admin; Indiana-Purdue Univ; Indiana Univ; Indiana Commn for Humanities, assoc; DePauw Univ, assoc dean. **Orgs:** Fellowship & Grant, Carnegie; Wingspread; Eli Lilly; NSF; Natl Def Educ Act; John Hay; NEH; State Ethnic Studies Advisory Council; bd mem, Indiana Historical Society. **Military Serv:** AUS. **Business Addr:** Professor, De Pauw University, Asbury Hall, Greencastle, IN 46135.

WARRICK, ALAN EVERETT
Attorney. **Personal:** Born Jun 18, 1953, Hampton, VA; son of Geri Warrick-Crisman and John H. Warrick; married; children: Alan Everett II, Whitney Blair, Everett Alan. **Educ:** Howard Univ, BA (Magna Cum Laude) 1975; IN Univ Sch of Law Indianapolis, Dr of Jurisprudence 1978. **Career:** Joint Ctr for Political Studies, rsch asst 1972-74; IN Civil Rights Comm, civil rights specialist 1975; US Senator R Vance Hartke, campaign aide 1976; Marion Co Prosecutors Office, intern 1977-78; attorney, Branton & Mendelsohn, Inc. 1978-1982; City of San Antonio, Judge, municipal court; Law Offices of Alan E Warrick, attorney, 1989-. **Orgs:** Brd of directors, State Bar of Texas, 1991-93; board of directors, San Antonio Festival Inc, 1982-, executive committee, 1992-; selection panel, Golden Rule Awd JC Penney, 1984; exec bd of govs, United Way of San Antonio, 1985-; Amer Bar Assn; Natl Bar Assn Board of Governors, 1990-; Assn of Trial Lawyers of Amer; TX Young Lawyers Assn; TX Trial Lawyers Assn; San Antonio Bar Ass; San Antonio Young Lawyers Assn; bd of dirs, San Antonio Trial Lawyers Assn, 1981-82, sec, 1979-80, vice pres, 1980-81; pres, San Antonio Black Lawyers Assn, 1990-; Ancient Free & Accepted Masons; Omega Psi Phi Fraternity, Van Courtland Social Club; chair, African-American Lawyers Section, 1993-94. **Honors/Awds:** Assoc editor Indiana Law Review 1977-78; First Place Awd Winner Amer Bar Assn Regional Moot Court Competition 1978; Scroll of Honor for Outstanding Achievment Field of Law Psi Alpha Chap Omega Psi Phi Frat 1982; Achievements Recognition Van Courtlandt Social Club 1982; Man of the Year Elks Mission Lodge #499; Citizen of the Year Psi Alpha Chap Omega Psi Phi Frat 1982; Appreciation Awd Alamo Branch YMCA 1983; Outstanding Leadership Awd Alpha Tau Omega Chap Alpha Kappa Alpha Sor 1984; Recognition Awd Smart Set Social Club 1984; Phi Beta Kappa Howard Univ; Pi Sigma Alpha Political Science Honor Soc; Iota Phi Lambda Honoree Law Enforcement 1985; Outstanding Service Award Judicial Council, Natl Bar Assn l989. **Home Addr:** 7667 Callaghan, # 604, San Antonio, TX 78229.

WARRICK, BRYAN ANTHONY
Professional basketball player (retired). **Personal:** Born Jul 22, 1959, Moses Lake, WA. **Educ:** St Josephs, 1982. **Career:** Washington Bullets, 1982-84, Los Angeles Clippers, 1985, Milwaukee Bucks, 1986, Indiana Pacers, 1986; CBA. **Honors/Awds:** Was named an Honorable Mentn All-Am by AP and The Sporting News.

WARRICK-CRISMAN, JERI EVERETT
Appointed official. **Personal:** Born May 22, Gary, IN; daughter of Marguerite Glapion Graves and John Everett; married Bruce Louis Crisman, May 5, 1975; children: Judge Alan E Warrick, Ingrid-Joy. **Educ:** Hampton Univ, AB (High Honors) 1952; Univ of Chicago, BA (Magna Cum Laude) 1956. **Career:** Froebel High, guidance counselor, 1956-64; WMAQ-TV, producer, broadcast stds supvr, 1964-72; WNBC-TV, sr editor, broadcast stds, 1972-73; Natl Broadcasting Co, dir, natl comm, 1973-81; WNJR Radio, pres, gen mgr, owner, 1981-84; State of New Jersey, asst state treas, 1984-87; Port Authority of New York and New Jersey, mgr regional communications educ and govt analysis. **Orgs:** Mem, Alpha Kappa Alpha Sorority, 1950-; mem, The Doll League, 1977-; natl pres, Amer Women in Radio & TV, 1983-84; mem, Natl Women's Coalition, Republican Natl Comm, 1984; mem, Links Inc, 1987; chair, Carter G Woodson Foundation Bd of Directors. **Honors/Awds:** Benjamin Hooks Award, NAACP, Gary IN, 1979; Kappa Tau Alpha Award, Hampton Univ Communications Dept, 1983; asst sec, Republican Natl Convention, Dallas TX, 1984.

WARWICK, DIONNE (MARIE)
Singer. **Personal:** Born Dec 12, 1940, East Orange, NJ; married Bill Elliott, 1967 (divorced 1975); children: David, Damion. **Educ:** Attended, Ed Hartt College of Music, Hartford CT. **Career:** As a teen-ager formed Gospelaires, The Drinkard Singers, 1955-60; hit singles: "Don't Make Me Over," 1962, "Walk on By," " Do You Know the Way to San Jose?" "What the World Needs Now," "Message to Michael," and "I'll Never Fall in Love Again," "I'll Never Love This Way Again," "Deja Vu," "Heartbreaker," "That's What Friends are For"; albums include: Valley of the Dolls 1968, Promises Promises 1975, Dionne 1979, Then Came You, Friends 1986; screen debut The Slaves 1969, No Night, So Long; co-host TV show Solid Gold; host TV show, A Gift of Music 1981. **Orgs:** Formed own chairty group BRAVO (Blood Revolves Around Victorious Optimism); spokeswoman Amer Sudden Infant Death Syndrome Inst; participant USA for Africa song "We Are the World" and performed at Live Aid Concert; proceeds from sale of album "Friends" to the American Foundation for AIDS Research; established Warwick Foundation to help fight AIDS. **Honors/Awds:** Grammy Awds 1969, 1970, 1980; Whitney M Young Jr Awd Los Angeles Urban League; honored with a star on Hollywood Walk of Fame 1985; Entertainer of the Year 1987.

WASH, GLENN EDWARD
General contractor construction manager. **Personal:** Born Feb 26, 1931, Grand Rapids, MI; son of Ethel Wash and George Wash; children: Glennda Marie. **Educ:** Highland Park Coll; Univ of Detroit; The Builders Exchange (CAM), Urban Land Institute. **Career:** Construction supt, AJ Etkin Construction Co Oak Park, MI 1957-61; construction supt Leonard Jarosz Const Co Oak Pk, MI 1954-57; Practical Homes Builders Oak Pk, MI, const supt 1961-65; HL Vokes Co Cleveland, OH, construction supt 1965-67; Glenn E Wash & Assoc Inc, pres 1977-. **Orgs:** Mem Assoc Gen Contracts of Am Det Chptr 1977-85; mem, Better Business Bureau 1979-85; mem Eng Soc of Detroit 1977-85; mem Bd Trustees New Detroit Inc 1980-85; sec/chmn MI Minority Business Devel Council, 1979-85; mem Minority Input Comm Wayne State Univ 1984-85; mem Com on Soc Econ Policy Am Concrete Inst 1984-85; member of governors construction safety standards commission, 1986-. **Military Serv:** USN builder 2nd Class 2 yrs; Far East Construction Btln. **Business Addr:** President, Glenn E Wash & Assoc Inc, 14541 Schaefer, Detroit, MI 48227.

WASHINGTON, ADA CATHERINE
Educator. **Personal:** Born Sep 19, 1950, Shreveport, LA; daughter of Elizabeth J & Willie J Miller Sr; married Valdemar L Washington, Aug 11, 1984; children: Valdemar L Washington II, Christopher J Washington. **Educ:** Grambling Coll, BS, music education, 1972; Eastern Michigan Univ, Med, 1982. **Career:** Flint Bd of Educ, teacher, 1973-85; Mott Comm Coll, consultant, 1995; Citizens Commerical Savings bank, dir, 1993-. **Orgs:** Cedar Street Childrens Ctr, bd mem, 1986-87; Delta Sigme Theta Sorority, life mem, 1984-; Junior League of Flint, 1986-88; Pierians, Inc, Flint Chapter, past pres, 1990-93; Amer Lawyers Auxiliary, natl law day chairperson, 1994; Michigan Lawyers Auxiliary, state law day chairperson, 1993; Genesee Bar Auxiliary, past pres, 1989-90; McLaren Regional Med Ctr Foundation, bd mem, 1995-. **Honors/Awds:** Eisenhower Comm School, Ike Award, Distinguished Service, 1980; Dozier Memorial CME Church, African American Women of Acheivement Award, 1995.

WASHINGTON, ADRIENNE TERRELL
Columnist. **Personal:** Born Mar 28, 1950, Washington, DC; daughter of Gwendolyn Johnson & Anthony Randall; married Milton Robert Washington, Mar 26, 1969; children: Misti E, Mario E. **Educ:** Hampton Univ, 1968-69; Northern VA Comm Coll, 1972-76; Howard Univ, 1980-82; Amer Univ, 1984-86. **Career:** The Alexandria Gazette, reporter, 1972-73; Folger Shakespeare Library, editorial & admin asst, 1973-75; The Washington Star, reporter, editorial asst, 1975-81; WRC TV, metro editor, futures editor, 1982-87; The Washington Times, deputy metro editor, asst metro editor, district bureau chief, 1987-91, columnist, 1991-. **Orgs:** Leadership Washington, 1993-; Women of Washington, 1994-; Monroe E Trotter Group, 1994-; Natl Assn of Black Journalists, 1979-; Washington Assn of Black Journalists, 1975-86; Capital Press Club, 1993-; Natl Society of Newspaper Columnists, 1994-; Sasha Brice Youthworks Anti-Violence Campaign, 1993-. **Honors/Awds:** The Washington Baltimore Newspaper Guild, 1979; Society of Professional Journalist, 1993,1994; Natl Society of Newspaper Columist, 1994; Amer Assn of Univ Women, 1994. **Business Addr:** Columnist, The Washington Times, 3600 New York Ave, NE, Washington, DC 20002, (202)636-3182.

WASHINGTON, ALONZO LAVERT
Comic book publisher, writer, designer/activist. **Personal:** Born Jun 1, 1967, Kansas City, KS; son of Millie C Washington; married Dana D Washington, Mar 24, 1993; children: Antonio S Davis, Akeem Alonzo, Kamaal Malik. **Educ:** Kansas City Comm Coll; Pioneer Comm Coll; KC Media Project Communications. **Career:** AD HOC Group Against Crime, gang & youth couselor/intervention specialist, 1990-92; Swope Parkway Health Center, outreach specialist & counselor, 1992-94; Omega 7 Comics Inc, pres, publisher, writer, designer, 1992-. **Orgs:** Black Natl Congress, pres, 1990-; Black United Front, honorary mem, 1990-; AD HOC Group Against Crime, mem, 1990-; Assn of African Amer Comic Book Publishers, pres, 1994-; New Democracy Movement, 1993-. **Honors/Awds:** Mayor Emanuel Cleaver II, Certification of Appreciation, 1993; Black United Front, KC Chapter, Malcolm X Leadership Award, 1991; UB & UBS Communication Systems, Publisher of the Year, 1992; United Minority Media Assn, Distinguished Comm Service Award, 1993; KC Masterminds Alliance, Golden Eagle Comm Service Award, 1994. **Special Achievements:** Outstanding Intern, KC Media Communications Systems, 1989; Creator: of the 1st African American comic book to deal with social issues, 1992. **Home Addr:** 1155 E 75th Terr, Kansas City, MO 64131, (816)444-4204. **Business Addr:** Owner/President, Omega 7 Comics Inc, PO Box 171046, Kansas City, KS 66117, (913)321-6764.

WASHINGTON, ARNA D.
Educator (retired). **Personal:** Born Oct 5, 1927, Trawick, TX; married Marcellus J (deceased); children: Derek M (deceased), Deirdra M (deceased). **Educ:** Huston Tillotson Coll Austin TX, Grad; Texas Southern Univ, Masters. **Career:** Houston Tchrs Assn, sec 1968-70; HTA, vice pres 1971-72; Sch Chmn 1970 1972; Legislative, assembly person; NEA TSTA TCTA HTA Conv & Conf, del 1966-80; Classroom Reading Instr 20 yrs; Houston Comm Coll, reading instr 2 Yrs; Houston Tchrs Assn Houston Ind Sch Dist Houston Tchrs, pres; Magnet Sch, Coord 1 yr; HISD Title 1, consult 1985; Houston Independent Sch Dist, cons; Houston Ind Sch Dist, reading lab instr 1985-89. **Orgs:** TX State Tchrns Assn; TX Classroom Tchrs Assn; Nat Educ Assn; TX Assn of Intl Reading Dist Officer United Meth Women of SW; rep TX Conf at World Devel Seminar for United Meth Ch; Outstanding Meth Woman in United Meth Women; Delta Sigma Theta Sor, Houston Branch; Church Historian and Libarian, Blueridge UMC, lay leader; NEA Minority Caucus & NCATE; Texas Conference on Arhcives and History, cmte mbr. **Honors/Awds:** Tchr of Yr Reynolds Elem Sch for 2 yrs; 1974 Nominee for Outstanding Secondary Educator; Delta Sigma Theta Spl Achievement Awards; Many Spl Recog Awards; NEA Sp Serv TCTA Plaque for Bd Mem; UMW Awd for Svc.

WASHINGTON, ARNIC J.
City official. **Personal:** Born Nov 19, 1934, Ladson, SC; married Rosalee Williams; children: Myra, Raymond. **Educ:** Nielson Computer Coll Charleston SC. **Career:** Lincolnville Sc, vice mayor 1967-. **Orgs:** Chmn St Dept; mem Health Dept; Pub Bldg Dept; mem SC Municipal Assn SC; Small Towns Assn SC; Black Mayors Assn; So E Conf Black Elected Officials; So E Regional Council Inc Nat League of Cities; Berkeley Co Chap NAACP; W Master Saxon Lodge #249 FAM Midland Park SC; mem Wesley Meth ChLadson SC Chmn Trustee Bd; pres Willing Workers; Admin Bd; Council Ministries; Adult Class Tchr; vice pres Carnation Gospel Singers. **Honors/Awds:** Certificate of Recognition SC Legislature House of Rep Outstanding Contbns in Field of Comm & Pub Affairs; For Civic & Polit Leadership & Accomplishmentsin Country Charleston; Outstanding Performance as Councilman Historic Town of Lincolnville SC. **Military Serv:** USAF airman first class 1954-57. **Business Addr:** PO Box 536, Summerville, SC 29483.

WASHINGTON, ARTHUR, JR.
Social work administrator (retired). **Personal:** Born Oct 22, 1922, St Louis, MO; son of Frankey Riley Washington (deceased) and Arthur Washington Sr (deceased); married Toni; children: Steven Elliott, Marjory Anita, Tiffany Elizabeth, Nancy Wooten. **Educ:** Univ of Louisville, BA; Kent School of Social Work Univ of Louisville, MSW. **Career:** IL Dept soc Svcs, caseworker 1954-55; Fam Serv Ctr Kalamazoo, marriage counselor 1955-65; Kalamazoo Dept of Social Services, child welfare supvr 1956; Kalamazoo City, commission 1959-67; Kalamazoo Coll Social Work, instructor 1963-65; Calhoun County Dept Social Services, deputy dir 1965-72; MI Dept of Social Services, dir admin, asst payments 1972-76; Bureau of Field Op, admin consultant, asst payments; Kalamazoo City Dept of Social Services, deputy dir; Kalamazoo County Dept of Social Services, admin asst 1979-89. **Orgs:** Pres Kalamazoo Chapter NAACP 1957-60; mem County Bd Commiss 1959-65; mem, chmn Kalamazoo Recreation Comm 1959-65; bd mem Kalamazoo Human Relations Commission 1959-60; org leader Kalamazoo Bombardiers Drum & Bugle Corp 1960-71; mem Al Zabir Tpl Shriners 1966-67, 1980-; mem advisory comm Kalamazoo Valley Jr Coll; Northside Community Association, vice pres, 1992; Douglas Community Center, board mem, 1992; Family Institute, vice pres, 1992; Mayor's Task Force, 1992; Kalamazoo Department Social Serv, board mem, 1992; Pride Place, board mem, 1992; Safe House, board mem, 1992. **Honors/Awds:** Outstanding Masonic Award, Plaque Outstanding Achievement Northside Assoc; Cert & Plaque Outstanding Citizenship NAACP; other civic awards; Irvins Gilmore Lifetime Achievement Award 1989; Community Service Award, Kalamazoo NAACP 1989. **Military Serv:** AUS corpl 1943-46; reserves 1946-48. **Home Addr:** 719 Staples Ave, Kalamazoo, MI 49007.

WASHINGTON, ARTHUR CLOVER
Educator. **Personal:** Born Aug 19, 1939, Tallulah, LA; married Almrta Hargest; children: Arthur, Angela, Anthony. **Educ:** TX Coll, BS 1961; Tuskegee Inst, MS 1963; IL Inst of Tech, PhD 1971. **Career:** Talladega Coll, instructor 1965-67; City Coll of Chicago, assoc prof 1967-71; Langston Univ, prof 1972-74; Prairie View A&M Univ, dean graduate school & prof 1974-87. **Orgs:** Extramural assoc Natl Inst of Health 1979; pres Woodedge Civic Assoc 1981; natl exec sec Natl Inst of Sci 1983-. **Honors/Awds:** American Men and Women of Science 1982; several scientific articles published 1974-87. **Business Addr:** Dean, College of Arts and Sciences, Florida A&M University, 208 Tucker Hall, Tallahassee, FL 32307.

WASHINGTON, AVA F.
Human resources manager. **Personal:** Born Aug 9, 1949, New York, NY; daughter of Ivy B Philp and Robert W Francis; married Donald L Washington Jr, Apr 5, 1980; children: Damien, Darin, Ashley. **Educ:** Univ of Wisconsin, Madison WI, BA 1971; Univ of Illinois, Champaign IL, MS 1973. **Career:** Farleigh Dickinson Univ, Rutherford NY, asst dir of affirmative action, 1975-77; Exxon Corp, New York NY, mgr of headquarters employee relations office, 1977-. **Orgs:** Mem, Alpha Kappa Alpha 1968-, NAACP 1974-, St Catherine's AME Zion Church 1984-, Corporate Women's Network 1985-, exec bd of Jack & Jill of Westchester County 1986-, Edges 1987-, Amer Society fo r Personnel Admin 1989-; volunteer, Junior Achievement of NYC, 1988.

WASHINGTON, BEN JAMES, JR.
Pharmaceutical wholesale company executive. **Personal:** Born Feb 10, 1946, Chicago, IL; son of Frances Washington and Bennie Washington; divorced; children: Stephanie, Bennie III. **Educ:** Wright College, 1976; Harold Washington College, certificate, 1988. **Career:** Aldens Catalog Inc, executive, manager, 1968-76; Penn-Corp Financial Inc, manager, 1977-81; American Pet Association Inc, president, editor, 1981-86; American Animal Association Inc, president, 1977-86; Health Tech Industries Inc, president, CEO, 1985-. **Honors/Awds:** Penn-Corp Financial, Outstanding Achievement, 1981; Minority Business Enterprise, Outstanding Entrepreneur, 1987. **Military Serv:** Navy, e-3, 1963-67. **Business Phone:** (312)554-9100.

WASHINGTON, BETTY LOIS
Business executive. **Personal:** Born Apr 16, 1948, New Orleans, LA. **Educ:** So Univ New Orleans, BA 1970; MI State U, MA 1971; Tulane Univ Sch of Law, Attending. **Career:** Mgmt Asso New Orleans, pres 1985; Ward Design Team, team chief 1985; Teach A Brother, exec dir 1979-80; Desire Area Comm Council, exec dir 1975-79; NO Urban League, program dir 1973-75; So Univ in New Orleans, counselor 1972-73; Images Corp, sec 1985; Mgmt Assoc, pres; So Univ System, bd of supr 1978-80. **Orgs:** Mem Phi Alpha Theta Hist Honor Soc 1969-; mem Zeta Phi Beta Sor 1968-; credit com So Univ Alumni Assn 1977-. **Honors/Awds:** EPDA Fellowship MI State Univ 1970; Outstanding Volunteer Award Lansing MI Juvenile Court System 1971; Outstanding Women in Am Nat Affiliation 1978. **Business Addr:** Management Assoc, 8500 Fordham Ct, New Orleans, LA 70127.

WASHINGTON, C. CLIFFORD
Association executive. **Educ:** Cheyney State Normal Sch, Grad 1921; Temple Univ, Elem Educ 1923; Cheyney State Coll, BS Educ 1960; Virginia Union Univ, Post Grad 1965. **Career:** School District of Phila, teacher elem educ, special educ, coord work training and job placement prog for retarded educables 1926-69; Model Cities Sr Wheels West, dir. **Orgs:** Mem St John's Settlement House Bd of Dirs 1934-; vice pres PA State BYPU Convention 15 yrs; 1st vice pres New England Missionary Bapt Training Union Convention 1948-; chmn Martha Washington Sch Adv Cncl 1970-; mem Cheyney State Coll Past Presidents Cncl, PA Dept of Welfare Southeastern Region Adv Comm; Pennsylvania delegate White House Conf on Aging 1971; mem Bd of the Natl Caucus on the Black Aged 1972-; chmn Philadelphia Urban Coalition Sr Citizens Task Force 1976-; one of eight non-agency persons on the newly formed Affirmative Action Task Force of the State Adv Comm on Aging for the State of Pennsylvania 1976-78; chmn Coalition of Advocates for the Rights of the Infirm Elderly 1977-. **Honors/Awds:** Outstanding Educators Awd Black Educ Forum; Elder Watson Diggs Awd Kappa Alpha Psi; Dr Charles Drew Community Serv Awd.

WASHINGTON, CARL DOUGLAS
Business executive. **Personal:** Born Aug 11, 1943, Tuscaloosa, AL; son of Estella Washington and Sam Washington; married Charlene; children: Carl, Micheal, Chimiere, Jason. **Educ:** Long Beach State Univ, BA Pol Sci, Speech 1967. **Career:** Washington Bros Distr Co, pres; Freedom Inv Corp, pres 1977; Teleport Oil Co, pres; Kong TV Inc, pres chairman. **Orgs:** Bd Brown Boys Home; mem Big Brother Prog 1966; org mem SF Private Industry Council; mem Comm Improvement League 1965; comm mem Optimist Club 1966; Kappa Alpha Psi; Hunter Point Boys Club; Soc of 100 Men; S F Police Athlectic League; bd S F Black Chamber of Commerce. **Honors/Awds:** Coll Dean's List; Athlete of Year Long Beach Poly HS; Outstanding Black Bus, SF Black Chamber, Top 100 Black Businesses in American 1982-86. **Home Addr:** 1037 Longridge Rd, Oakland, CA 94610.

WASHINGTON, CLAUDELL
Professional baseball player. **Personal:** Born Aug 31, 1954, Los Angeles, CA; married Cynthia; children: Camille, Claudell III, Crystal. **Career:** Outfielder: Oakland Athletics, 1974-76, Texas Rangers, 1977-78, Chicago White Sox, 1978-80, New York Mets, 1980, Atlanta Braves, 1981-86, New York Yankees, 1986-88, California Angels, 1989-90, New York Yankees, 1990. **Honors/Awds:** American League All-Star Team, 1975; National League All-Star Team, 1984.

WASHINGTON, CONSUELA M.
Attorney. **Personal:** Born Sep 30, 1948, Chicago, IL; daughter of Conzoella Emanuelita Brulee Washington and Hilliard L. Washington. **Educ:** Upper Iowa Univ, Fayette, IA, BA, cum laude, political science, 1970; Harvard Univ, Cambridge, MA, JD, 1973. **Career:** Kirkland & Ellis, Chicago, IL, asso, 1973-74; Allis-Chalmers Corp, Corp Law Dept, atty, 1975-76; Securities and Exchange Commission, office of chief counsel, division of corp finance, atty adviser, 1976-79, special counsel, 1979; US House of Reps, Committee on Energy and Commerce, counsel, 1979-94; Committee on Commerce, minority counsel, 1995-. **Orgs:** Mem IL Bar Assn; Harvard Law Sch Assn; Harvard Club of Washington, DC; Harvard Law School Black Alumni Org; Harvard Board of Overseers, 1987-93. **Honors/Awds:** Dean's List 1967-70; Scholastic Honor Soc, Hon Leadership Soc 1968-70; Bradley Invit Speech Tourn Award of Excellence 1969; Notable Am 1978-79; Equal Employment Opportunity Award SEC 1978; Alumni Achievement Award Upper IA Univ 1977. **Business Addr:** US House of Rep Comm on Commerce, Room 2322 Rayburn HOB, Washington, DC 20515, (202)225-3641.

WASHINGTON, CRAIG A.
Congressman, attorney. **Personal:** Born Oct 12, 1941, Longview, TX; married Dorothy M Campley; children: Craig A II, Chival A. **Educ:** Prairie View A&M Univ, BS 1966; TX So Univ, JD (cum laude). **Career:** TSU Law School, asst dean 1969-70; self-employed attorney 1970-; TX House of Rep, 1973-82; TX Senate, senator, beginning 1983; US House of Representatives, member (D-TX), 1990-. **Home Addr:** 1919 Smith St Suite 820, Houston, TX 77002.

WASHINGTON, DANTE DENEEN
Athletic official. **Personal:** Born Nov 21, 1970, Baltimore, MD; son of Yolanda Robinson and Don Washington. **Educ:** Radford University, BA, 1992. **Career:** Howard County Library, library page, 1987; John Elicker, architect apprentice, 1987-88; Joe Wyzkoski, resident manager, 1990-92; Columbia Day Soccer Camp, coach, 1988-. **Orgs:** Kappa Alpha Psi Fraternity, keeper of records & exchequer, 1990-. **Honors/Awds:** NSCAA, NCAA Division I, Soccer All-American, 1991, Academic All-American, 1992; Radford University, Alumni Minority Scholarship, 1991-92. **Special Achievements:** United States Olympic Soccer Team, 1992; United States Pan American Soccer Team, 1991; United States Olympic Festival, 1989, 1990. **Home Addr:** 5352 Racegate Run, Columbia, MD 21045.

WASHINGTON, DARRYL MCKENZIE
Technical services manager. **Personal:** Born Jan 29, 1948, New York, NY; son of Leslie Taylor Washington and McKenzie T Washington; married Barbara Gore Washington, Aug 22, 1970; children: Monika, Matthew, Morgan. **Educ:** North Carolina A&T State Univ, Greensboro, NC, BSEE, 1970, 1972-74. **Career:** RJR Archer Inc, Winston-Salem, NC, engineer, 1974-78; Miller Brewing, Eden, NC, technical services manager, 1978-. **Orgs:** Member, Society of Mechanical Engineers, 1989-; member, Institute of Electrical and Electronics Engineers, 1967-; member, National Food Processors Assn, 1989-; member, American Institute of Plant Engineers, 1989-; member, Omega Psi Phi. **Military Serv:** US Army, 1st Lt, 1970-72. **Business Addr:** Plant Engineering Manager, Engineering Dept, Miller Brewing Co, PO Box 3327, Eden, NC 27288-2099.

WASHINGTON, DAVID WARREN
Director. **Personal:** Born Jan 13, 1949, Mound Bayou, MS; married Clotee Woodruff; children: Rynetta Rochelle, Vernekia Bradley, Monique Caldwell, Rodney Brown, Vietta Leflore. **Educ:** Coahoma Jr Coll, AA, 1970; Delta State Univ, BS, 1972, addtional graduate study in guidance and counseling, 1972-74; Ford Found Leadership Devel Program, Leadership Degree, 1975. **Career:** Ford Found Leadership Devel Program, 1974-75; Bolivar County Community Action Agency, equal opportunity officer, 1977-79; serving 3rd term as vice-mayor of Town of Pace, MS; Bolivar County Headstart Personnel/Training, dir. **Orgs:** Dir, Bolivar County Summer Food Serv Program; former pres, Pace Voters League; former mem, Bolivar County Democratic exec comm, 1984-86; school bd chmn, Bolivar County School Dist I; election commr, Bolivar County Dist I, 1984-88; mem, Spangle Banner MB Church; chmn, Bolivar County Election Commr, 1988-92; chmn of by-laws comm, Bolivar County Assn of Black Officials, 1989-92. **Honors/Awds:** In Appreciation for Outstanding Serv As Equal Opportunity Officer Bolivar County Community Action Agency Bd Dir, 1980; Outstanding Serv Rendered to the Town of Pace, Mississippi Pace Community Assn, 1980; Concern and Dedication Shown The Staff of the Bolivar County Headstart Training Center, 1982; Appreciation for Faithful Serv As Guest Speaker St James Missionary Baptist Church, 1983; Most Outstanding Citizen Award Pace Community Assn, 1983; Dedicated Serv Award, The Parents of the Bolivar County Headstart Training Center, 1984. **Business Addr:** Dir of Personnel/Training, Bolivar County Headstart, PO Drawer, 1329, Cleveland, MS 38732.

WASHINGTON, DENZEL
Actor. **Personal:** Born Dec 28, 1954, Mount Vernon, NY; son of Denzel Washington; married Pauletta Pearson; children: John David, Katia, Malcolm, Olivia. **Educ:** Fordham University, BA, journalism; American Conservatory Theatre, studied acting; studied acting with Wynn Handman. **Career:** Actor; theater appearances include: Coriolanus, 1979; One Tiger to a Hill, 1980; When the Chickens Come Home to Roost, 1981; A Soldier's Play, 1981-83; Every Goodbye Ain't Gone, 1984; Checkmates, 1988; Richard III, 1990; television appearances include: Wilma, tv movie, 1977; Flesh and Blood, tv movie, 1979; St Elsewhere, series, 1982-88; Licence to Kill, 1984; The George McKenna Story, 1986; American Heroes and Legends, 1992; Anansi, audio-visual, 1992; film appearances include: Carbon Copy, 1981; A Soldier's Story, 1984; Power, 1986; Cry Freedom, 1987; For Queen and Country, 1989; Heart Condition, 1990; The Mighty Quinn, 1989; Glory, 1989; Mo' Better Blues, 1990; Ricochet, 1991; Mississippi Masala, 1992; Malcolm X, 1992; Much Ado about Nothing, 1993; Philadelphia, 1993; Crimson Tide, 1995; Virtuosity, 1995; Devil In A Blue Dress, 1995; The Preacher's Wife, 1996; Courage Under Fire, 1996; Fallen, 1997; He Got Game, 1998; "In Harm's Way," directed video for BeBe Winans, 1997. **Orgs:** The Boys & Girls Clubs of America, national spokesperson. **Honors/Awds:** Obie Award, distinguished ensemble performance, A Soldier's Play, 1982; Image Award, NAACP, best actor, Cry Freedom, 1988; best performance by a supporting actor, Glory, 1990; Golden Globe Award, best supporting actor, Glory, 1989; Academy Award, best supporting actor, Glory, 1990; Audelco Award, When the Chickens Come Home to Roost; NAACP, Best Actor Award, Mississippi Masala, Youth or Children's Series or Special Performance, 1998; NY Film Critic's Circle Award, best actor, Malcolm X; Boston Society of Film Critic's Award, best actor, Malcolm X; Dallas/Ft Worth Film Critic's Association Award, best actor, Malcolm X; Chicago Film Critic's Award, best actor, Malcolm X; American Black Achievement Awards Ebony Career Achievement Award, 1994. **Business Addr:** Actor, c/o ICM, 8942 Wilshire Blvd., Beverly Hills, CA 90211.

WASHINGTON, DEWAYNE NERON
Professional football player. **Personal:** Born Dec 27, 1972, Durham, NC; married Adama. **Educ:** North Carolina State, bachelor's degree in multiple disciplinary studies. **Career:** Minnesota Vikings, defensive back, 1994-. **Business Addr:** Professional Football Player, Minnesota Vikings, 9520 Viking Dr, Eden Prairie, MN 55344, (612)828-6500.

WASHINGTON, EARL MELVIN
Educator. **Personal:** Born Jun 22, 1939, Chicago, IL; son of Hester L Washington and Henry W Washington; married Dianne Elizabeth Taylor; children: Jason Todd, Tiffany Anne. **Educ:** Western MI Univ, BA 1963, MA 1968; Univ of MI, 1971; Western MI Univ EdD. **Career:** Cleveland Public Schools, teacher 1963-68; Kalamazoo Valley CC, instructor 1968-70; Western MI Univ, asst prof communications 1975-82, assoc prof communications, dir black faculty devel prog 1982-, asst dean 1984-, associate professor, communications; The Institute for the Study of Race and Ethnic Relations, director, consultant, workshop presenter. **Orgs:** Knappen Voight Co, consultant 1977; Kalamazoo Valley Int Schl Dist, consultant 1979; WMU, dir blk college prog 1984. **Honors/Awds:** 2nd vice pres Kalamazoo PTA; various articles publ in communication, educ and communication quartery and black issues in higher education 1980-; press/publ dir Kalamazoo Metro Branch NAACP 1984-84; vice pres 100 men of Kalamazoo 1983-85; papers presented including at Natl Assn for Equal Oppty; Phi Kappa Phi. **Special Achievements:** Several papers presented; co-author, College: The First Two Years. **Business Addr:** Asst Dean Coll of Arts/Sci, Western Michigan University, 2020 Friedmann Hall, Kalamazoo, MI 49008.

WASHINGTON, EARL S.
Electronics company executive. **Personal:** Born in Los Angeles, CA. **Educ:** California State Univ, Los Angeles, CA, BS, business. **Career:** Rockwell International, Anaheim, CA, market analyst, vice president of business development, vice president of strategic management and international, Autonetics Marine Systems Division, vice president of advertising and public relations, currently. **Honors/Awds:** First African-American vice president at Rockwell International. **Business Addr:** Sr Vice President, Corporate Communications, Rockwell International, 2201 Seal Beach Blvd 001-B04, Seal Beach, CA 90740.

WASHINGTON, EARLENE
Procurement specialist. **Personal:** Born Nov 15, 1951, Brookhaven, MS; daughter of Geraldine Gaston McLaurin and Lonnie McLaurin; married Ralph Campbell Washington, Jun 16, 1973; children: Latonya, Kimberly, Jasmine. **Educ:** Alcorn State University, Lorman, MS, BS, 1973; Jackson State University, Jackson, MS, 1973; Mississippi College, Clinton, MS, MBA, 1975. **Career:** Utica Junior College, Utica, MS, accounts payable/inventory manager, 1973-79; Mississippi Power & Light, Jackson, MS, statistician, 1979-86, contract administrator, procurement specialist, 1986-. **Honors/Awds:** President Scholar, Alcorn State University, 1971-73; National Honor Society, Alcorn State University, 1969-73; Dean's List, Alcorn State University, 1969-73. **Home Addr:** 6225 Woodstock Dr, Jackson, MS 39206. **Business Addr:** Procurement Specialist, Purchasing/Material Management, Mississippi Power & Light Company, 308 E Pearl St, Jackson, MS 39201.

WASHINGTON, EDITH MAY FAULKNER
Counselor, consultant. **Personal:** Born Jul 28, 1933, Queens, NY; daughter of Edalia Magdalene O'Neal Faulkner and Henry Ozman Faulkner; married George Clarence Washington; children: Desiree Elaine Singletary, James Henry, Edalia Magdalene Kelley. **Educ:** New York State Univ Coll, Buffalo, BS, H, Ec, Ed, 1968, MS, H, Ec, Ed, 1971; Indiana No Univ, Gas City, IN, DHR, Human Relations Psych, 1973; Elmira Coll, MS, Ed, Behavior Sci, 1981. **Career:** SEEK Disadvantaged Students, coord, 1969-71; NY State Univ Coll at Buffalo, instructor, Afro-Amer studies, 1969-71; PEACE Inc, consultant, 1971; NY State Office of Drug Abuse Serv Masten Park Community Rehabilitation Center, inst teacher, 1971-76; NY State Office of Drug Abuse Serv Manhattan Rehabilitation Center, inst teacher, 1976-77; Church of God in Christ, Central Amer West Indies, mission worker/teacher, 1980-; NY State Dept of Correction Serv, acad classification analyst, correction counselor, retired 1991; Applied Christianity, Inc, consultant, counselor, currently. **Orgs:** Past state pres, Business & Professional Women, Church of God in Christ; bd mem, Church of God in Christ Dept of Missions; mem & workshop leader, Corr Educ Assn, 1971; past prod/dir, Benefits for Missions Church of God in Chrst Inc, Missions Benefit Breakfast; exec dir, Anegada House Cultural Inst; co-founder, Afro-Amer Cultural Center Buffalo, NY, 1960; bd mem, NAACP Elmira Corning Center, 1977; bd mem, Adv Council Citizens Advisory Council to the Commr of Soc Serv, 1978, Southern Tier Regional Planning Bd, 1976; Chemung Co Planning Bd, 1976, Applied Christianity Church of God in Christ, 1980-; ordained Evangelist of the Independent Holiness Assembly Church Inc, 1986; volunteer nutritionist/coord, Applied Christianity Inc, Food Pantry; admin, Applied Christianity Church of God In Christ. **Honors/Awds:** Ford Co Town Crier Award, Ford Motor Co, Outstanding Community Serv, 1969; Outstanding Community Serv Award, ACCEP Buffalo, NY, Frontier Citizens & Agng Comm, Cultural Educ Program Center, 1970; Outstanding Acad Achievement Award Pentecostal Temple Church of God in Christ, 1971; Outstanding Community Serv, Chemung Co (exec), 1979; Humanitarian Award from Natl Assn of Blacks in Criminal Justice, 1985; Mt Nebo Ministries MLK Drum Major for Freedom Award, co-recipient w/spouse, Rev G C Washington, 1986; Sigma Gamma Rho, Hon Mem, 1988. **Business Addr:** Executive Director, Consultant, Christian Counselor, Applied Christianity, Inc, 410-414 West Gray St, Elmira, NY 14901, (607)732-1142.

WASHINGTON, EDITH STUBBLEFIELD
Construction company executive. **Career:** The Stubblefield Group, pres, currently. **Special Achievements:** First African American to be elevated to "fellow" by the Constructions Specifications Institute. **Business Addr:** President, The Stubblefield Group, 1946 N 13th St, Toledo, OH 43624, (419)535-8883.

WASHINGTON, EDWARD
Business executive. **Personal:** Born May 2, 1936, Pittsburgh, PA; married Paula G; children: Felicia D, Teresa S, Jacquelyn R, Nicolas E. **Educ:** VA State Univ Petersburg VA, BS Psych 1963; Univ of Southern CA, MBA 1973. **Career:** Coca-Cola USA, acct exec 1964-75; Uniworld Advertising, acct suprv 1975-79; Del Monto Corp, eastern div sales mgr 1979-82; Mid-Atlantic Coca-Cola Bottling, gen mgr 1982-83. **Orgs:** Mem Natl Assoc of Mktg Devel 1978-85; bd of dir Jr Achievement 1982-85, Bowie St Coll 1983-85, Boys & Girls Club 1983-85, WHMM Radio 1983-85; mem Prince George Chamber of Commerce 1983-85, Natl Business League 1985. **Honors/Awds:** Achievement Spec Olympics 1983,84; Achivement Greater Wash Korean Assoc 1984; Outstanding Citizen DC Dept of Recognition 1984; PUSH Achievement Operation PUSH 1984. **Military Serv:** USAF airman 2/c 3 1/2 yrs.

WASHINGTON, EDWARD, JR.
Foreman. **Personal:** Born Nov 25, 1931, Logan Co, KY; married Ruth Shorton; children: James, Phillip, Terry, Bobby, Francine Wynn, Cherri, Nancy. **Career:** Auburn Hosiery Mill, foreman; fireman; emer worker; ambulance svc. **Orgs:** Mem Barroh River Health System; Adairville City Council; S Hogan Cham of Comm; Mason. **Business Addr:** Gallatin, Adairville, KY 42202.

WASHINGTON, ELI H.
Administrative aide. **Personal:** Born Sep 19, 1962, Cook County, IL; son of Arthester Washington and Booker T Washington; married Jeanette Williamson, Apr 21, 1990. **Educ:** Chicago State University, Chicago, IL, BS, 1991. **Career:** Marshall Fields, Chicago, IL, sales, 1986-90; Alderman John Steele, Chicago, IL, administrative aide, 1990-. **Orgs:** President, Chesterfield Community Council, 1987-91; president's advisory board, 1991; housing task force, member, First Congressional District, 1988-90; chairman, Six Ward Economic Development Committee, 1989-90; 100 black men, member, Sbaro Elementary School, 1990-. **Honors/Awds:** Fred Hampton Image Award, 1990; Black-on-Black Love Champaign, 1989; Service Award, Chicago Police Department, 1989. **Home Addr:** 722 E 87th Place, Chicago, IL 60619.

WASHINGTON, ELMER L.
Educator. **Personal:** Born Oct 18, 1935; married Anna Ross; children: Lisa, Lee. **Educ:** TX So U, BS 1957 TX So U, MS 1958; IL Inst of Tech, PhD 1965. **Career:** Univ of Chicago, research asst 1958-61; Pratt & Whitney Div of United Aircraftd asst project engr & research assoc 1965-69; chicago state univ, dean of naturalsci & math 1972-74; Chicago State Univ, former dean of coll of arts & sci; Research & Devel Chicago State Univ Consult Health Career Opportunites Program of HEW, vice pres 1975. **Orgs:** Mem Am Chem Soc; Electrochem Soc; Am Assn for Advancement of Sci; Am Assn of Univ Prof; Am Assn of Univ Adminstr Alpha Kappa Mu Honor Soc 1956. **Honors/Awds:** Welch Found Scholarship 1957; Voted Most Likely to Suceed in Class 1957; Petroleum Research Fellowship 1961-65; Phi Lambda Upsilon Scientific Honor Soc 1964. **Business Addr:** 95 King Dr, Chicago, IL 60628.

WASHINGTON, EMERY, SR.
Clergyman. **Personal:** Born Feb 27, 1935, Palestine, AR; son of Fannie Mae Norrington and Booker Taliferro Washington; married Alice Marie Bogard, Oct 1, 1965; children: Ekila Denese, Marie Antoinette, Emery Jr. **Educ:** Philander Smith College, BA, 1957; Virginia Theological Seminary, MDiv, 1961. **Career:** St Andrew's Episcopal Church, 1961-66; Christ Church Episcopal, 1961-71; Episcopal Diocese of Arkansas, 1971-76; St Michael's Episcopal Church, 1974-76; Emmanuel Episcopal Church, 1976-83; All Saints' Episcopal Church, 1992-. **Orgs:** Alpha Phi Alpha, local president, 1954-; Union of Black Episcopalians, local president, 1975-; General Convention Deputy, deputy, 1969, 1970, 1973, 1991; St Louis Clergy Coalition, community development chair, 1985; St Louis Black Leadership Roundtable, 1991-; leadership St Louis Inc, fellow, 1988-89; Confluence St Louis Inc, Valuing our Diverciy, 1989-; Racism Commission, chair, 1985-86, 1991-. **Honors/Awds:** Alpha Kappa Alpha, Literacy Promoter, 1990, John D Buckner Award, 1990, Excellence in Religion, 1992, Diocese

of Arkansas, Clergy of the Year, 1970. **Special Achievements:** Designed two stained glass windows: Baptism and Communion, 1988-; Designed the ''Sheild of All Saints,'' 1987; Author, copyright, 1987. **Business Addr:** Reverend, All Saints' Episcopal Church, 5010 Terry Ave, St Louis, MO 63115-5140, (314)367-2314.

WASHINGTON, ERIC
Professional basketball player. **Personal:** Born Mar 23, 1974. **Educ:** Univ of Alabama. **Career:** Denver Nuggets, guard, 1997-. **Business Addr:** Professional Basketball Player, Denver Nuggets, 1635 Clay St, Denver, CO 80204, (303)893-6700.

WASHINGTON, FLOYD, JR.
Automobile company executive. **Personal:** Born Jun 6, 1943, Shreveport, LA; son of Rosie Thomas Washington and Floyd Washington Sr; married Juanita Allen, Jun 20, 1969; children: Floyd III, Rosalind. **Educ:** Grambling State University, Grambling, LA, BS, 1965; University of Chicago, Chicago, IL, MBA, 1967. **Career:** Spiegel Inc, Chicago, IL, market research analyst, 1965-67; Ford Motor Company, Dearborn, MI, financial analyst, 1967-73; Ford Motor Land Development Corporation, Dearborn, MI, finance supervisor, 1973-80; Ford Land Services Corp, Dearborn, MI, finance manager, 1980-. **Orgs:** President, Delta Sigma Chapter, Alpha Phi Alpha, 1963-65; president, Phi Beta Lambda, 1963-65; president, Grambling State University Alumni Assn, Detroit Chapter; member, Kappa Delta Pi Educational Honor Society, 1963; member, Sigma Rho Sigma Social Science Honor Society, 1962; member, Board of Directors, Museum of African American History, Detroit, MI, 1986-, chairman of Audit Committee; Joint Fraternal Development Corp., president, 1992-93; Alpha Woodward Restoration Incorporated, vice pres, 1992-93; Detroit Economic Development Corp, 1992. **Honors/Awds:** Presidential Citation, Outstanding Alumnus of the Year, Grambling State University, 1983; first African-American to join Ford Motor Co finance staff, 1967. **Business Addr:** Finance Manager, Ford Motor Land Development Corp, Parklane Towers E, Suite 1500, Dearborn, MI 48126-2402.

WASHINGTON, GLADYS J. (GLADYS J. CURRY)
Educator (retired). **Personal:** Born Mar 4, 1931, Houston, TX; daughter of Anita Joseph and Eddie Joseph. **Educ:** BA 1952; MA 1955; Univ of So CA & Tulane Univ, addl study; University of London, England, summer 1981. **Career:** So Univ Baton Rouge, Eng instr; So Univ New Orleans, assoc prof of Eng; TX So Univ, assoc prof of English. **Orgs:** Mem Coll Language Assn, S Central Modern Languages Assn, Natl Council of Teachers of English, TX Assn of Coll Teachers, Women in Action; Church Women United; sec, South Central Language Assn (Women of Color Section), 1988-89; mem, Modern Language Assn & Southern Conf on Afro-Amer Studies 1988-; pres, Churches Interested in Premature Parentage 1989; artistic director, Cyrenian Productions (Drama Group) 1985-. **Honors/Awds:** Alpha Kappa Mu Natl Honor Soc; Lambda Iota Tau Literary Honor Soc; has done extensive work with school & little theatre groups in New Orleans & Houston; pub ''Viewpoints From Black Amer'' 1970; editor ''Cultural Arts Review''; A World Made Cunningly, A Closer Look at the Petry's Short Fiction, CLA Journal 1986; Teacher of the Year, Texas Southern Univ 1988; author, A Core Curriculum Approach to College Writing, Littleton, MA, Copley Publishing Group, 1987. **Special Achievements:** Ann Petry, ''The Narrows''; James Weldon Johnson, ''Autobiography of an Ex-Coloured Man''; Lorraine Hansberry, ''A Raisin in the Sun'' in *Masterplots II: African-American Literature,* 1993; Alice Childress, *The African-American Encyclopedia, Supplement,* 1996; Ann Petry ''In Darkness and Confusion'' and ''Solo on the Drums'' in *Masterplots II, Short Story, Supplement,* 1996.

WASHINGTON, GROVER, JR.
Musician, composer, producer. **Personal:** Born Dec 12, 1943, Buffalo, NY; married Christine Washington; children: Grover III, Shana. **Educ:** Temple Univ, Wurlitzer School of Music, attended. **Career:** Four Clefs, saxophonist, 1963; 19th Army Band, 1965-67; Don Gardner's Sonotones, 1967-68; made numerous recordings with Randy Weston, Bob James, Ralph MacDonald, Eric Gale, Don Sebesky; solo artist; G W Jr Music Company, president; G-Man Productions Inc. **Honors/Awds:** Albums: Come Morning, Mr Magic, Winelight, The Best Is Yet to Come, Then and Now, Time Out of Mind; 6 Gold Albums; 1 Platinum Album; Grammy Award; numerous other awards. **Business Addr:** Musician, Motown Record Corp, 5750 Wilshire Blvd, Ste 300, Los Angeles, CA 90036-3697.

WASHINGTON, HENRY L.
Clergyman. **Personal:** Born Nov 15, 1922, Earlington, KY; married Azlea; children: Argene, Lamar, Henry, Clyone. **Educ:** Ashland Theol Sem, OT-NT 1976; Dyke Coll, Cert Realtor 1978. **Career:** Metro Ins Co, sales rep 1969-76; Alpha & Omega COGIC, pastor 1970-85; City of Mansfield OH, councilman 1983. **Orgs:** Pres Concerned Black Citizens 1976-78; mem Real Estate Mgrs Assn 1978-85; comm chmn NAACP 1982-84; councilman City of Mansfield 1983-85; mem Richland Transit Bd 1983-84, Affirmative Scholarship DSU 1984-85. **Honors/Awds:** House of Rep State of OH 1979; Mayors Awd City of Mansfield OH 1982. **Military Serv:** AUS pfc 1 1/2 yrs; Purple Heart, European Theater Ribbons 1943-44. **Home Addr:** 312 Second Ave, Mansfield, OH 44905. **Business Addr:** Pastor, Alpha & Omega COGIC, 530 Pearl St, Mansfield, OH 44905.

WASHINGTON, HERMAN A., JR.
Educator. **Personal:** Born Jul 12, 1935, Norfolk, VA; son of Naomi Hucles Washington and Herman A Washington; married Daryl E Jordan, Aug 11, 1990; children: Tunja, Gina Hussain, Lori, Keith. **Educ:** Manhattan College, BEE, 1958; New York University, MBA, 1973. **Career:** Western Electric, engineer, 1958-59; G C Dewey Corp., consultant, 1959-61; IBM, programming manager, 1961-69; The Systems Discipline Inc, vice pres, sr project manager, 1969-71; City of New York Addiction Services Agency, director of MIS, 1971-72; LaGuardia Community College, professor, 1972-. **Orgs:** United Way of Long Island, board of directors, 1990-; Catholic Charities, board of directors, 1991-; Children's House, board of directors, 1988-; 100 Black Men of Nassau/Suffolk, 1974-. **Honors/Awds:** United Way of Long Island, United Caring Award, 1991; 100 Black Men of Nassau/Suffolk, Man of the Year, 1989. **Home Addr:** 261 Durkee Ln, East Patchogue, NY 11772-5820, (516)289-5828. **Business Addr:** Professor, LaGuardia Community College, 31-10 Thomson Ave, Computer Information Systems Department, Long Island City, NY 11101, (718)349-4047.

WASHINGTON, ISAIAH
Actor. **Educ:** Howard University. **Career:** Stage, Ntozake Shange's Spell #7, August Wilson's Fences, CityKids performance group; television, Strapped (HBO), Socrates (HBO); films; Crooklyn 1994, Clockers, Girl 6; Get on the Bus, Love Jones, Bullworth, Out of Sight. **Business Addr:** Actor, ICM, 8942 Wilshire Blvd, Beverly Hills, CA 90211, (310)550-4000.

WASHINGTON, ISAIAH EDWARD
Educator (retired). **Personal:** Born Oct 19, 1908, Augusta, GA; married Dr Justine E Wilkinson. **Educ:** Paine Coll Augusta, AB 1937; Temple Univ Phila, MS 1948; Allen Univ Columbia SC, LittD 1959. **Career:** Richmond County Bd of Educ, principal 1938-75; Albany State Coll, summer school instructor 1955-64; City of Augusta, councilman 1975-88. **Orgs:** Pres GA Teachers Educ Assoc 1943-45; regional dir American Teachers Assoc 1945-52. **Honors/Awds:** Silver Beaver Awd Boy Scouts of Amer. **Home Addr:** 1228 Kent St, Augusta, GA 30901.

WASHINGTON, JACQUELIN EDWARDS
Association executive. **Personal:** Born May 20, 1931, St Augustine, FL; daughter of Grace Benson Albert and Clarence Edwards; married Kenneth B; children: Saundra, Byron, Kristin. **Educ:** Fisk U, BA 1951; Wayne State U, MSW 1965. **Career:** Detroit Dept of Pub Welfare, case worker & supr, 1957-63; Detroit Public Schools, school social worker, 1965-75; New Options Personnel, Inc, pres, 1975-80; Bendix Corp, Southfield, MI, mgr, human resources, 1980-85; Vixen Motor Co, Pontiac, MI, dir, human resources, 1985-88; Pontiac Area Urban League, Pontiac, MI, pres, CEO, 1988-. **Orgs:** Mem Nat Assn of Soc Workers 1965-; mem State of MI Employ Agency Council 1978-80; trustee Detroit Inst of Arts 1975-81; pres Detroit Club Nat Assn Negro Bus & Professional Women 1978-80; 1st vice pres Girl Scouts of Metro Detroit 1979-80; mem NOW Legal Defense & Educ Fund 1979-91; board member, Michigan Abortion Rights Action League, 1990-91; board member, St Joseph Mercy Hospital, Pontiac, MI, 1990-; member, Michigan Council of Urban League Executives, 1989-; Planned Parenthood Southeast MI, exec dir. **Honors/Awds:** Spirit of Detroit Award Detroit Common Council 1978; Female Pioneer Award Women Lawyers' Assn 1978; Feminist of the Yr Award Detroit Chap Nat Orgn for Women 1978; Sojournor Truth Award, National Assn of Negro Business & Professional Women, 1987-. **Business Addr:** President/CEO, Pontiac Area Urban League, 295 W Huron, Pontiac, MI 48341.

WASHINGTON, JACQUELINE ANN
Human resources executive. **Personal:** Born May 2, 1968, Highland Park, MI; daughter of William & Cora Johnson; married Kenneth B. Washington, Jun 5, 1993. **Educ:** Eastern Michigan University, BS, 1990; Central Michigan University, MA, 1995. **Career:** City of Ypsilanti, personnel assistant, 1990-91; The Wellness Plan, human resources representative, 1992-93; Huron Valley Ambulance, human resources coordinator, 1993-. **Orgs:** Alpha Kappa Alpha, treasurer/vice president, 1989-; Ann Arbor Area Personnel Assn, 1994-; Human Resources Assn of Greater Detroit, 1993-. **Honors/Awds:** Alpha Kappa Alpha Sorority Inc, Hardest Worker Award, 1990. **Business Addr:** Human Resources Coordinator, Huron Valley Ambulance, 2215 Hogback Rd, Ann Arbor, MI 48105, (313)971-4211.

WASHINGTON, JACQUELYN M.
Sales manager. **Personal:** Born Apr 25, 1965, Philadelphia, PA; daughter of Arlene Berry Calerdale and Edward Washington Jr. **Educ:** Univ of Massachusetts, degree in hotel/rest/travel admin, 1987. **Career:** Philadelphia Convention & Visitors Bureau, PA, sales rep, 1987-89; Adams Mark Hotel, Philadelphia PA, natl sales manager, 1989-. **Orgs:** Membership chair & body rep, local Alpha Kappa Alpha; young professional mem, Philadelphia Urban League; Natonal Association of Market Developers; Chicago Society of Association Executives; American Society of Association Executives. **Business Addr:** National Sales Manager, Adams Mark Hotel, City Ave and Monument Rd, Philadelphia, PA 19131.

WASHINGTON, JAMES A.
Newspaper publisher. **Personal:** Born Apr 26, 1950, Chicago, IL; son of Cecelia Burns Jones and Frank S. Washington; married Victoria Meek, May 9, 1980; children: Patrick James, Elena Cecele. **Educ:** Southern University, Baton Rouge, LA, BA, 1971; University of Wisconsin, Madison, WI, MA, 1973. **Career:** Tennessee State University, Nashville, TN, worked in Development Office; American Heart Association, public relations specialist; Dallas Ballet, public relations manager; Focus Communications Group, Dallas, TX, founder and president, 1980; Dallas Weekly, Dallas, TX, owner, 1985; Ad-Mast Publishing Co, Dallas, TX, chairman, currently. **Orgs:** Member of board of directors, Cotton Bowl, I Have a Dream Foundation, Science Place, Dallas Zoological Society, Family Guidance Center; member, advisory council of small business and agriculture, Federal Reserve Bank of Dallas; chairman, minority business advisory committee, Dallas Independent School District; member, Dallas Together; member of executive committee and board, Dallas Chamber of Commerce, American Heart Association, Greater Dallas Planning Council, Junior Achievement; member of admissions committee, United Way, 1983; chairman of public relations committee, National Newspaper Publishers Association. **Honors/Awds:** Danforth Fellow, University of Wisconsin—Madison; Woodrow Wilson Fellow. **Business Addr:** Ad-Mast Publishing, Dallas Weekly, 3101 Martin Luther King, Dallas, TX 75215.

WASHINGTON, JAMES EDWARD
Optometrist. **Personal:** Born Jun 19, 1927, Beaufort, NC; son of Nancy Parker Sandlin and John Cole Washington; married Ethelyn Marie Irby Pigott, Jun 2, 1984; children: Jeffrey, Shelly, John. **Educ:** Fayetteville State Univ, attended; NY Univ Washington Square Coll, attended; No IL Coll of Optometry, BS 1953; No IL Coll of Optometry, OD 1954; Rutgers Univ Grad School Newark, MPA 1983. **Career:** Nation Optometric Assn reg dir 1972-79; Essex Cty Optometric Soc, pres 1974; Natl Optometric Assoc, pres 1974-75; Diversified Vision Svcs, exec dir; Private practice, solo practitioner; private practice, optometrist. **Orgs:** Chmn, bd of dir NOA 1975-76; preceptor PA Coll of Optometry; fellow Coll of Optometrists in Vision Devel; vstg lecturer New England Coll of Optometry; mem Amer Optometric Assoc, Natl Optometri Found, New Jersey Optom Assoc, Essex Cty Optom Soc, Optom Extension Program Found, Natl Optometric Asoc, NJ Eye Care Council; health adv bd East Orange Head Start; adv bd Montclair State Coll Health Careers. **Honors/Awds:** Optometrists of the Year Essex Cty Optom Assoc 1972; Optometrist of the Year Natl Optom Assoc 1973; mem Tomb & Key Honor Optom Frat; Black Heritage Awd City of East Orange 1987; Distinguished Service Award, New Jersey Optometric Assn 1987, Dr EC Nurock Award, 1993. **Military Serv:** US Army, 1946-49. **Business Addr:** Optometrist, 104 S Munn Ave, East Orange, NJ 07018, (201)675-5392.

WASHINGTON, JAMES LEE
Mayor. **Personal:** Born Jun 14, 1948, Glendora, MS; son of Ella Wee Billingsley Johnson and Jessie James Washington; married Zenolia Hayes Washington, Dec 22, 1974; children: James Jr, Jessica Nicole. **Educ:** Coahoma Community College, Clarksdale, MS, AA, 1970; Campbellsville College, Campbellsville, KY, BS, 1972; Delta State University, Cleveland, MS, MS, 1986. **Career:** Coahoma Agricultural HS, head basketball coach; Coahoma Jr Coll, head men's basketball coach; Friars Point NC, mayor. **Orgs:** Mem Natl Conf Black Mayors, Natl Conf Coaches. **Honors/Awds:** Outstanding Serv Awd N Atlantic Conf Boys Track 1976; Class A State Championship Coahoma Agricultural HS (basketball) 1984; Coach of the Year, 1984-85; Won State Championship, Jr College, 1986-87. **Home Addr:** Box 552, Friars Point, MS 38631, (601)383-2310. **Business Addr:** Mayor, Friars Point, PO Box 185, Friars Point, MS 38631, (601)383-2233.

WASHINGTON, JAMES MELVIN
Cleric, educator. **Personal:** Born Apr 24, 1948, Knoxville, TN; son of Annie B. Washington and James W. Washington (deceased); married Patricia Anne Alexander; children: Ayanna Nicole. **Educ:** Univ of TN Knoxville, BA 1970; Harvard Divinity School, MTS 1970-72; Yale Univ, MPhil 1972-75, PhD 1975-79. **Career:** Yale Divinity School, instr 1974-76; Union Theol Sem, assoc prof 1976-86, prof, currently; Haverford Coll, vstg assoc prof 1983-84; Columbia Univ, visiting assoc prof 1984-85; Oberlin Coll, vstg assoc prof 1985-86; Union Theol Sem, prof of Modern & American Church History 1986; visiting lecturer Princeton Theological Seminary Princeton, NJ 1989-90; visiting prof Princeton Univ Princeton, NJ 1989-90. **Orgs:** Bd mem Amer Baptist Churches USA 1982-85, Natl Council of Churches 1985-87, Amer Baptist Historical Soc 1977-82; mem, exec comm Faith & Order Commissof the Natl Council of Churches 1985-87; consult Religious Affairs Dept, NAACP; Publications, A Testament of Hope, The Essential Writing of Martin Luther King,Jr (Harper & Row 1986); Frustrated Fellowship, The Black Baptist Quest for Social Power

(Mercer Univ Press 1986); assoc editor American Natl Biography 1989-. **Honors/Awds:** Fellow Woodrow Wilson Found 1970-71; Protestant Fellow Fund for Theol Ed 1971-72; Rockefeller Doctoral Fellow Fund for Theol Ed 1972-74; Teaching Fellow Harvard Univ 1971-72; book Frustrated Fellowship 1985; Christopher Award for editing A Testament of Hope, The Essential Writings of Martin Luther King, Jr 1987. **Home Addr:** 99 Claremont Ave, New York, NY 10027. **Business Addr:** Professor Church Hist, Union Theological Seminary, 3041 Broadway, New York, NY 10027.

WASHINGTON, JAMES W., JR.
Painter, sculptor, printmaker. **Personal:** Born Nov 10, Gloster, MS; son of Lizzie Howard Washington and Rev James W Washington; married Janie R Miller. **Educ:** Natl Landscape Design & Gardening Inst Los Angeles CA, attended 1947; Mark Tobey, studied painting 1947-50. **Career:** Camp Joseph T Robinson, Little Rock AR, orthopedic mechanic-in-charge, 1941-43; Puget Sound Naval Shipyard, Bremerton WA, journeyman electrician, 1943-50; Washington's Studio of Fine Arts, painter & sculptor. **Orgs:** Pres Seattle Chap Artists Equity Assn 1960-61; mem Gov's State Arts Commn 1962-; NAACP; 33rd Degree Mason; exhibition Feingarten Gallery San Francisco 1958; one-man exhibitions, Haydon Calhoun Galleries Dallas 1960; Woodside Gallery Seattle 1962-65; Foster/White Gallery Seattle 1968-76; exhibition Squibb Gallery Princeton NJ 1982; represented w/writings, lectures on tape & sculpture Natl Museum of Amer Art Washington 1984; voted life mem, Intl Poetry Hall of Fame, 1997; James W Washington Foundation, est, 1997. **Honors/Awds:** Hon Degree AFD, Theological Union Center of Black Urban Studies, 1975; 2nd prize sculpture Seattle World's Fair 1962; purchase prize sculpture San Francisco Museum Art 1956; Gov's Awd Cultural Contrib State Heritage Group Exhibition Huntsville Museum of Art 1979; elected mem of Professional Artists by the Redevelop Authority of Philadelphia PA 1975; Kings Co Arts Comm Arts Serv Awd 1984; Certificate of Recognition WA State Gov John Spellman 1984; Washington State Centennial Hall of Honor Tacoma Washington 1984; Commission, 1989; ''Prestigious Award,'' King County Arts Commission, 1989; home and studio nominated as a historical landmark, 1992; Outstanding Contribution Award, Meany Magnet Middle School, 1997; History Makers Award, Arts and Humanities, 1997; Residence Declared Seattle Landmark, 1992. **Special Achievements:** Author of ''The Arts Are Color Blind,'' ''Christianity and the Arts,'' and ''Northwest Today,'' Seattle Pl, Seattle Wa, 1965-66; Lawrence H Bloedel Collection Whitney Museum of Amer Art, NY, 1976; poem: ''Sheep in the Fold,'' Natl Library of Poetry, 1993; sculpture commissions, ''Phoenix and Esoteric Symbols of Nature'' Sheraton Hotel, Seattle, 1982, ''Life Surrounding the Astral Altar, in Matrix'' law firm of Smith Rosenblume & Assoc, Seattle, 1987; ''The Oracle of Truth,'' Mt Zion Baptist Church, Seattle, 1988; ''Fountain of Trimuph,'' Tom Bangasser, 1993-94; sculpture ''Young Queen of Ethiopa'' accepted in the Smithsonian Inst Natl Museum of Amer Art, Washington DC, 1984; retrospective exhibit, Bellevue Art Museum, Seattle, 1989; ''One Man Exhibitio,'' Lee Nordness Gallery, New York, NY, 1962; sculpture, Foster/White Gallery, Seattle, 1989. **Military Serv:** 2nd World War, exempted from service to work in the Puget Sound Naval shipyard Bremerton WA. **Home Addr:** 1816 26th Ave, Seattle, WA 98122.

WASHINGTON, JESSE
Editor. **Personal:** Born Jun 3, 1969, New York, NY; son of McCleary & Judith Washington. **Educ:** Yale Univ, BA, 1992. **Career:** The Associated Press, reporter, 1992-93, national editor, 1993-95; New York City, assistant bureau chief, 1995-96; Vibe Magazine, managing editor, 1996-. **Orgs:** Kappa Alpha Psi Fraternity Inc, 1987-. **Business Addr:** Managing Editor, Vibe Magazine, 205 Lexington Ave, New York, NY 10016.

WASHINGTON, JOHN CALVIN, III
Elected official. **Personal:** Born Dec 12, 1950, Coatesville, PA; son of Mildred and John II; children: Nathaniel, John IV, Tamara. **Educ:** Coatesville Sr HS, diploma 1968; Coll Prep. **Career:** City of So Coatesville, councilmem. **Orgs:** Elk Mt Vernon Lodge #151 1975; mem NAACP 1975; volunteer VA Med Ctr 1978; mem Chester Co Recreation Council 1981; master mason Lily of the Valley #59 1981; dir S Coatesville Recreation 1981; mem FOP 1981; mem Hypertension Ctr 1981; chmn Grievance Comm for the Handicapped of S Coatesville 1984; chmn Property Comm 1984. **Home Addr:** 34 1/2 Penn Ave, Coatesville, PA 19320. **Business Addr:** Borough Councilman, Modena Rd, Coatesville, PA 19320.

WASHINGTON, JOHN WILLIAM
Physician (retired). **Personal:** Born Oct 3, 1921, Boston, MA; son of Marion Louise Underwood and Lawrence M Washington Sr; married Glynn Nell Lott; children: John III, Byron Lott. **Educ:** Northeastern, 1939; West VA State Coll, 1943; Yale Univ, 1944; Meharry Med Coll, MD 1948. **Career:** Ob-Gyn St Elizabeth Med Ctr, past chief; St Elizabeths Hosp, staff mem; Miami Valley Hosp, staff mem, emeritus staff Unity State Bank Dayton OH, dir; Private practice, physician; Wright State School of Med, asst clinical prof ob-gyn. **Orgs:** Vol faculty Wright State Med School; mem Alpha Phi Alpha, Natl Med Assoc, AMA; life mem NAACP; Dayton Ob-Gyn Soc; diplomate Amer Bd Ob-Gyn; life fellow Amer Coll Ob-Gyn; life mem Wright State Univ Acad of Medicine. **Military Serv:** AUS corpl 1942-45; AUS MC capt 1952-54; Battle Stars & Ribbons. **Home Addr:** 849 Olympian Cir, Dayton, OH 45427.

WASHINGTON, JOHNNIE M.
Clergyman. **Personal:** Born Sep 23, 1936, Paris, TX; married Naaman C; children: Mary M Jones, Leontyne. **Educ:** So Evang Assn, LVN 1970, DD 1974; Roosevelt U, BS 1979. **Career:** Full Gospel Temple, rev 1985; Hotel Dieu Hosp, endoscopy supr 1970-; McGraw Concern Munich Germay, sec & financial 1964-68; Nat Gastroenterology Tech, certified gi techn 1973-80; NY Univ Albany, ungrad nurse 1977-80. **Orgs:** Sec El Paso Black Caucus 1977-79; pres El Paso Br NAACP 1979-; corr sec El Paso Black Caucus 1979-. **Honors/Awds:** Certificate of Appreciation Black History Week 1975; Outstanding Black Citizen White Sands Missile Range 1978; Certificate of Appreciation YMCA El Paso 1979; Outstanding Civil Rights Award NAACP 6 Region Conf 1980. **Business Addr:** 4631 Atlas, El Paso, TX 79904.

WASHINGTON, JOSEPH R., JR.
Educator. **Personal:** Born Oct 30, 1930, Iowa City; married Sophia Holland; children: Bryan Reed, David Eugene. **Educ:** Iron Cross Univ of WI, BA 1952; Andover Newton Theol Sch, BD 1957; Boston Univ, ThD 1961. **Career:** Univ of CA Riverside, prof Religious Studies chmn Black Studies 1975-; Univ of VA, prof Religious Studies chmn Afro-Amer Studies 1970-75; Beloit Coll, dean of chapel prof religion 1969-70; Albion Coll, dean of chapel assoc prof of religion 1966-69; Dickinson Coll, chaplain asst prof religion 1963-66; Dillard Univ, dean of chapel asst prof philosophy religion 1961-63. **Orgs:** Mem Amer Soc of Chris Etheics; Amer Acad of Religion. **Honors/Awds:** Books publ, Black Religion 1964; Politics of God 1967; Black & White Power Subreption 1969; Marriage in Black & White 1970; Black Sects & Cults 1972. **Military Serv:** AUS lt military police 1952-54. **Business Addr:** B-12 Cocke Hall, University of Virginia, Charlottesville, VA 22901.

WASHINGTON, JOSIE B.
Educator. **Personal:** Born Mar 13, 1943, Leona, TX; daughter of Josephine Brooks and J B Brooks; married Eugene J Washington; children: Eugenia J, Giovonna J. **Educ:** AA, BA, MS. **Career:** San Juan Sch Dist 1968; Sacramento Co Welfare Dept Bur of Investigation 1972; State Dept of Rehab 1974; Sacramento City Unified Sch Dist; Sacramento Urban League, site adminis; head counselor and chief examiner, currently. **Orgs:** Sacramento Urban League; Youth Devel Delinq Proj Bd; Neighborhood Council; advr, Youth Outreach; Vista Neuva Adv Com; N Area Citizen for Better Govt; Natl Rehab Assn; CA Sch Bd Assn; San Juan Unified Sch Dist; adv com, Bus Skills Handicapped; trustee, clerk, Grant HS Dist Bd of Educ; Sacramento Area Regional Adult & Vocational Educ; council rep, Sacramento Co Sch Bd; Sacramento Co Central Democratic Comm; Sen SI Hayakawa CA Constituency Council; Comm to elect Mayor Tom Bradley for Gov of CA; Comm to elect vice pres Mondale for Pres; Comm to elect Pres Jimmy Carter; NAACP. **Honors/Awds:** Written contributions Resource Directory of Black Bus Sacramento area; 1st Black & Woman elected to Grant Bd of Educ; invited to White House by President Jimmy Carter, 1980. **Business Addr:** Head Counselor & Chief Examiner, Sacramento Urban League, 2420 N St, Sacramento, CA 95816.

WASHINGTON, KEITH
Vocalist. **Personal:** Born in Detroit, MI. **Career:** Former backup singer; Make Time for Love, QWest Records, vocalist, songwriter, 1991; Guest appearance, Martin, 1992; General Hospital, actor; Poetic Justice, actor. **Honors/Awds:** Make Time for Love, nominated for Grammy Award, 1992; single, ''Kissing You,'' one of the theme songs on General Hospital daytime drama. **Special Achievements:** Has worked with the Jacksons, George Clinton, Miki Howard and Stevie Wonder. **Business Addr:** Vocalist, c/o GHR Entertainment, 16601 Ventura Blvd, Ste 506, Encino, CA 91436, (818)789-9822.

WASHINGTON, KENNETH S.
Education administrator. **Personal:** Born Oct 19, 1922, Chicago, IL; married Henriella Dunn; children: Lordice Hopkins, Marcella Kingi, Henry Kingi, Corine DeBlane, Kim Wilkins, Kent. **Educ:** Roosevelt Univ Chicago, BA 1948; CA State Univ Los Angeles, MA 1954; Univ of So CA, PhD 1970. **Career:** City Coll of San Francisco, pres 1985; State of CA, asst supt for pub instr 1971-75; CA State Univ & Coll, asst dean for educ oppor 1968-71; UCLA, asst to chancellor 1966-68; Centennial High Compton CA, bd couns 1960-66; Centennial High, teacher Math & Sci 1951-60. **Orgs:** Pres CA Council for Educ Oppor 1964-69; dir Baskin Found 1956-66; dir KQED Pub Broadcasting Sta 1976-80; dir San Francisco Devel Fund 1976-; electedtrustee LA Comm Coll Dist 1969-75; mem ''Black BRAIN-TRUST'' of Rep Shirley Chisholm; vice pres Ocean Ave Merchants' Assn 1975-80; bd of dir SF Mus Soc 1979-80. **Military Serv:** AUS s/sgt 1940-45. **Business Addr:** c/o office of the current chancellor, City College of San Francisco, San Francisco, CA 94112.

WASHINGTON, LEONARD, JR.
Law enforcement official. **Personal:** Born Nov 3, 1945, Pittsburgh, PA; son of Anniebelle & Leonard Washington; married Celestine (Mickie) Washington, Nov 2, 1968; children: Leonard III, Maurice, Alonzo. **Educ:** Mercyhurst Coll, Erie, PA, associates degree, 1978; California Univ of Pennsylvania, BA, 1980. **Career:** North American Rockwell, draftsman, 1968-73; PA State Police, trooper, 1973-78, corporal, 1978-80, sergeant, 1980-82, lieutenant, 1982-88, captain, 1988-98, major, 1998-. **Orgs:** NAACP, 1987-; PA Chiefs of Police Assn, 1988-; Natl Organization of Black Law Enforcement Executives, 1998-. **Honors/Awds:** PA State Police, Commissioners Commendation, 1982. **Military Serv:** Army Airborne, sergeant, 1964-67. **Business Addr:** Director, Bureau of Emergency & Special Operations, Pennsylvania State Police, 171 E Hershey Park Dr, PO Box 444, Hershey, PA 17033-0444, (717)787-4600.

WASHINGTON, LEROY
Educator. **Personal:** Born May 1, 1925, Greenville, FL; married Edith; children: 3. **Educ:** FL A&M Univ, BA 1950; Univ of Miami, MA 1972. **Career:** Charlotte Jr Coll, drama coach; Dade Public School of Miami, drama coach; Booker T Washington HS; Miami Sr HS; Miami Jackson Sr HS, drama coach & teacher; SW Miami Sr HS; sabbatical; Miami Northwestern Sr HS, teacher. **Orgs:** Past pres NC HS Drama Assc; FL State Interscholastic Speech & Drama Assc; Dade Co Speech Tchr Assc; mem UTD Prof Sect; mem Screen Actors Guild; Natl TV & Radio Broadcasters Union; Youth Emphasis Club Sponsor; NW Br YMCA; block ldr Model Cities; dir/Vice Pres CL Williams Meml Schlrshp Fnd Inc; sponsor Creative Dance & Interpretative Reading Training Classes; Comm Sch Vol Work; several TV appearances; acted various prof plays Dade Co & several other states; host & prod of weekly TV show ''Amazing Grace''; managed & dir several shows for TV; mem Congregational Ch of Open Door. **Honors/Awds:** Man of Year 1975; Zeta Phi Beta Sorority Inc; Miami Chpt; Outst Cit & Civic Ldr Charles L Williams Meml Schlrshp Fnd; TV Personality of the Month BTW Alumni Assc; coached drama grp Booker T Washington HS; invited as one of top eight drama grps throughout cty to perform at Univ of IN; 2nd place Rowe Peterson's annual drama photo contest; 2nd place Natl Thespian Soc annual printed prog contest. **Military Serv:** USAF corpl WWII; 1st lt Korena Conflict. **Business Addr:** Miami Northwestern Sr HS, 7007 NW 12 Ave, Miami, FL 33150.

WASHINGTON, LESTER RENEZ
City government official. **Personal:** Born Feb 3, 1954, Kansas City, KS; son of Mable Watson Washington and Willie Washington; married Roberta Martin (divorced 1979); children: Jennifer, Lesley, Lester Jr, Travis, Corey. **Educ:** Univ of Iowa, Iowa City, IA, BBA, 1977; Univ of Missouri, KC, Kansas City, MO, 1980-. **Career:** Lunam Corp, Kansas City, MO, manager, 1979-81; Southland Corp, Kansas City, MO, manager, 1981-85; city of Kansas City, Kansas City, MO, manager MBC/WBE program, 1985-. **Orgs:** Board of directors, East Attucks Community Housing, 1990-; member: Ad Hoc Group Against Crime, 1986-, NAACP, 1980-, Prince Hall Mason Lodge #77; board of directors, Minority Network Association, 1990-; White House Delegate on Minority Business, 1989-. **Honors/Awds:** Advocate of Year, Minority Contractors Assn, 1988; Member of Year, Alpha Phi Alpha, 1976. **Business Addr:** Manager, MBE/WBE/Contract Compliance Division, City of Kansas City, Missouri, 414 E 12th St, 4th Floor, Kansas City, MO 64106.

WASHINGTON, LINDA PHAIRE
Scientist. **Personal:** Born Aug 11, 1948, New York, NY; married Joey Washington; children: Kamau, Imani. **Educ:** Boston Univ, BS Biology 1970; Mt Sinai Med Ctr CUNY, PhD 1975; Rockefeller Univ, Post Doctoral Res Fellow 1977; Ctr for Adv Training in Cell and Molecular Biol, adv rsch training 1983. **Career:** Laguardia Coll, lecturer 1973-75; Rockefeller Univ, post doctoral rsch fellow 1975-77; City Univ, asst prof 1976-77; Howard Univ Coll of Med, asst prof 1977-79; Tuskegee Inst, Dept of Biology prof 1981-; Cell Culture Science Ctr dir 1981-, prof of immunol/cell biol, Natl Sci Rsch Div dir 1984-. **Orgs:** Consultant Intl Progs Tuskegee Inst Liberia Linkage 1982-83; mem gen rsch support review comm Natl Inst of Health DRR 1983-87; proposal reviewer Nat'l Science Foundation 1985; panel reviewer Nat'l Inst of Health DRR 1986-87. **Honors/Awds:** Murray J Steele Awd for scientific rsch NY Heart Assn 1975; nominee recognition awd for young scholars Amer Assoc of Univ Women Educ Prog 1980; outstanding faculty awd in rsch Tuskegee Inst 1981; UNCF distinguished scholars awd United Negro Coll Fund 1984-85; mem GRSRC Subcommittee Natl Inst of Health DRR 1983-87. **Business Addr:** Dir Natural Sciences Rsch, Tuskgee University, Carver Research Foundation, Tuskegee Institute, AL 36088.

WASHINGTON, LIONEL
Professional football player. **Personal:** Born Oct 21, 1960, New Orleans, LA. **Educ:** Tulane Univ, received sports administration degree. **Career:** St Louis Cardinals, 1983-86; Oakland Raiders, cornerback, 1987-94, 1997-; Denver Broncos, 1995-96. **Business Addr:** Professional Football Player, Oakland Raiders, 1220 Harbor Bay Pkwy, Alameda, CA 94502, (510)615-1875.

WASHINGTON, LUISA
Business executive. **Personal:** Born Sep 7, 1946, Detroit. **Educ:** Univ of MI Ann Arbor, BA 1972; NY Univ, post grad courses. **Career:** MEC/REP/CO Inc Intl, dir pub rel N Africa. **Orgs:** Past sec Intl Afro-Amer Museum 1972. **Honors/Awds:** Teaching Fellow Univ of MI Ann Arbor 1971. **Business Addr:** 1200 6 Ave Suites M180 190, Detroit, MI 48226.

WASHINGTON, MALIVAI
Professional tennis player. **Personal:** Born Jun 20, 1969, Glen Cove, NY; son of William Washington and Christine Washington. **Educ:** University of Michigan, 1987-89. **Career:** Professional tennis player, 1989-. **Honors/Awds:** Tennis Magazine, Rookie of the Year, 1990; won 2 NCAA titles as a freshman at University of Michigan; University of Michigan, College Tennis Player of the Year, 1989; Federal Express International tennis tournament, winner, 1992; US Men's Clay Court Championships, winner, 1992. **Special Achievements:** US Davis Cup Team, 1993-94. **Business Addr:** Professional Tennis Player, c/o ProServe, 1101 Wilson Blvd, Ste 1800, Arlington, VA 22209, (703)276-3030.

WASHINGTON, MARIAN
Collegiate basketball coach. **Career:** University of Kansas, Women's Basketball Team, head coach, currently. **Orgs:** Black Coaches Association, first vice president, 1991, presiden t, 1992. **Business Addr:** Head Women's Coach, Basketball, University of Kansas, PO Box 3302, Lawrence, KS 66044, (913)864-4938.

WASHINGTON, MARVIN ANDREW
Professional football player. **Personal:** Born Oct 22, 1965, Denver, CO. **Educ:** Idaho. **Career:** New York Jets, defensive end, 1989-96; San Francisco 49ers, 1997-. **Business Addr:** Professional Football Player, San Francisco 49ers, 4949 Centennial Blvd, Santa Clara, CA 95054, (415)562-4949.

WASHINGTON, MARY HELEN
Professor. **Personal:** Born Jan 21, 1941, Cleveland, OH; daughter of Mary Catherine Dalton Washington and David C Washington. **Educ:** Notre Dame College, BA, 1962; University of Detroit, MA, 1966, PhD, 1976. **Career:** High school teacher of English in Cleveland OH public schools, 1962-64; St. John College, Cleveland, instructor in English, 1966-68; University of Detroit, Detroit MI, assistant professor of English, 1972-75, director of Center for Black Studies, beginning 1975; currently associate professor of English, Boston Harbor College, University of Massachusetts, Boston. **Orgs:** National Council of Teachers of English, College Language Association, Michigan Black Studies Association. **Honors/Awds:** Richard Wright Award for Literary Criticism from Black World, 1974; anthologist, Memory of Kin: Stories About Family by Black Writers. **Business Addr:** Department of English, Boston Harbor College, University of Massachusetts, Boston, MA 02125.

WASHINGTON, MARY PARKS
Artist, educator. **Personal:** Born in Atlanta, GA; children: Eric, Jan. **Educ:** Spelman Coll, AB 1946; Univ of Mexico 1947; Fourah Bay Coll Sierra Leon WA; Univ of Illeffe Nigeria; Univ of Science & Tech Ghana; San Jose State Univ, painting graduate; San Jose State Univ San Jose CA, MA Fine Arts 1978. **Career:** Union School Dist, teacher; Dartmouth Jr HS, teacher, 1961-80; Howard, 1948-51. **Orgs:** Mem CA Teachers Assn; Natl Congress of Artists; Natl Art Assc; counc mem CA Art Educ Assc; council dir Tutoring Program for Minority Stud; bd mem NAACP; chmn NAACP 1958-; charter mem San Jose Chapter AKA Sorority; San Jose Chapter Jack & Jill; Human Relations chmn Union School Dist Teachers Assn, 1968-72; San Jose Art League 1960, 1977; Collector's Choice chmn fund raising for San Jose Art League; vol Amer Cancer Soc; bd mem Info Referral of Santa Clara Co 1974-75; Rosenwood Scholarship Black Mt Coll, 1947. **Honors/Awds:** Artist of Year Links Inc; publ Black Artist on Art Vol 1; A Soul A Mirror by Sarah Webster Fabia; The Spelman Story; Black Soul, Ebony Mag; num one woman shows; Johnson Publ Art Coll.

WASHINGTON, MICHAEL HARLAN
Educator. **Personal:** Born Sep 25, 1950, Cincinnati, OH; son of Willa Washington and Herbert Washington; children: Michael Jr, Milo Robeson. **Educ:** Raymond Walters Coll, AA 1971; Univ of Cincinnati, BS 1973, MEd 1974, EdD 1984. **Career:** Univ of Cincinnati, learning skills specialist 1974-79; Northern KY Univ, learning skills specialist 1979-80, dir of Afro-Amer Studies program 1986-, assoc prof of history 1980-. **Orgs:** Consultations Office of In-Service Educ No KY University 1980; United Christian Ministeries and Black Campus Ministries, University of Cincinnati 1980-81; University of Cincinnati Medical Ctr 1980; No KY Univ Div of Continuing Educ 1980-81; Inservice Tchr Training, Southwestern Business Coll 1982; Diocesan Secondary Social Studies Tchr, Thomas Moore Coll 1982; KY Assoc of Teachers of History 1981-; Black History Archives Comm 1985-; Phi Alpha Theta 1985-; Minority Students Retention Scholarship, No KY University, founder, 1986; African-American Studies Prog, No KY University, founder, 1986. **Honors/Awds:** Staff Developement grant, KY Council on Higher Educ 1979, 1980; author of poem "On Time," publ in American Poetry Anthology, 1986; author of book "Academic Success & the College Minority Student," 1986; Outstanding Professor of the Year, Northern Kentucky Univ, Professor of the Year, 1996; Raymond Walters College, Distinguished Alumni Award, Raymond Walters College, 1996. **Business Addr:** Dir Afro American Studies Prog, Northern Kentucky University, 440 Landrum, Highland Heights, KY 41076.

WASHINGTON, MICKEY LYNN
Professional football player. **Personal:** Born Jul 8, 1968, Galveston, TX. **Educ:** Texas A&M, bachelor's degree in sociology, 1990. **Career:** New England Patriots, defensive back, 1990-91; Washington Redskins, 1992; Buffalo Bills, 1993-94; Jacksonville Jaguars, 1995-96; New Orleans Saints, 1997-. **Business Addr:** Professional Football Player, New Orleans Saints, 5800 Airline Hwy, Metairie, LA 70003, (504)733-0255.

WASHINGTON, NANCY ANN
Certified public accountant. **Personal:** Born Nov 30, 1938, Kansas City, KS; daughter of Essie Mae Williams Owens and E B Owens; widowed; children: Georgetta Grigsby, Bertram Grigsby, Charles Washington III. **Educ:** KCK Comm Coll, Kansas City KS, AA 1977; St Mary Coll, BSBA 1979; Univ of Missouri, Kansas City KS, MBA 1989. **Career:** Internal Revenue Service, Kansas City MO, agent, 1979-80; Washington Accounting Service, Kansas City KS, owner, 1980-83; Kansas Corp Commn, Topeka KS, senior utility regulatory auditor, 1983-88; Bd of Public Utilities, Kansas City KS, internal auditor, 1988-. **Orgs:** Mem, League of Women Voters 1985-, AICPA 1987-, KS Certified Public Accountants Soc 1988-, Inst of Internal Auditors 1988-; treasurer, American Assn Blacks in Energy; owner, Untouchable Concepts Beauty Salon, Kansas City, KS. **Honors/Awds:** Candlelight Service Award, KCK Comm Coll, 1976. **Business Addr:** Internal Auditor, Board of Public Utilities, 700 Minnesota Ave, Kansas City, KS 66101, (913)573-9123.

WASHINGTON, OSCAR D.
Educator. **Personal:** Born Feb 18, 1912, Tulsa; married Doretha Lumbard; children: Cynthia, Alisa. **Educ:** Creighton Univ, BS 1935; Univ of MI, MS 1948; St Louis Univ, PhD 1973. **Career:** St Louis Bd of Educ, teacher; poet; writer; musician; scientist; Soli Music Publishers Ballad Record Co, pres & Organizer; songwriter; US Govt, chemist 1943; St Louis Argus, newspaper columnist 1974-. **Orgs:** Mem, Broadcast Music Inc; organizer prof tchrs orgn Bristow OK 1945; Bristow Civic Impro Org; mem, Bristow Chamber of Commerce 1946. **Honors/Awds:** Recipt Quiz Kids Best Tchr Winner 1948; Star Award Winner Natl Sci Tchr Assc; 1956. **Military Serv:** Srv as govt chemist WWII.

WASHINGTON, PATRICE CLARKE
Airline pilot. **Educ:** Embry-Riddle Aeronautical Univ Daytona Beach. **Career:** Trans Island Airways, pilot; UPS Airlines, pilot, 1988-. **Special Achievements:** First African American female to receive BS from Embry's flight program; first female to fly for Trans Island Airways and Bahamasair; first African American female pilot UPS. **Business Addr:** Captain, United Parcel Service, 1400 N Hurstbourne Pkwy, Louisville, KY 40223, (502)329-3032.

WASHINGTON, PAUL M.
Clergyman. **Personal:** Born May 26, 1921, Charleston, SC; married Christine Jackson; children: Marc, Kemah, Michael, Donyor. **Educ:** Lincoln Univ, attd 1943; Philadelphia Div Sch 1946. **Career:** Ch of the Advocate, rector 1962-; St Cyprians Ch, vicar 1954-62; Cuttington Clge Liberia W Africa, tchr 1948-54. **Orgs:** Mem Philadelphia Commn on Human Rel 1964-71; host Black Power Conv 1968; host Black Panter Conv 1970; host The Philadelphia Ordinations of 11 Women to Priesthood 1974; chmn Black Polit Conv 1969; delegate 5 Gen Conv of Epis Ch; mem exec council Epis Ch; Gov Bd Natl Council of Chs Delegate to Conference on US Intervention in Iran 1980; American Institute for International Relations, Moscow, 1990. **Honors/Awds:** Five Honorary Doctorates; Philadelphia Award. **Home Addr:** 3359 Ridge Avenue, Philadelphia, PA 19121.

WASHINGTON, ROBERT BENJAMIN, JR.
Attorney. **Personal:** Born Oct 11, 1942, Blakeley, GA; married Nola Wallette, Dec 27, 1969; children: Todd, Kyle W. **Educ:** St Peter's College, BS, econ/political sci, 1967; Howard Law School, JD, 1970; Harvard University Law School, LLM, 1972. **Career:** Harvard Law School, teaching fellow, 1970-72; US Senate Comm on the District of Columbia, attorney, 1971-72; Howard Univ Law School, assoc prof of law and director of communication skills, 1972-73; Christopher Columbus College of Law, lecturer, 1972-73; US House of Representatives Comm on the District of Columbia, attorney, 1973-75; George Washington Univ Law Center, lecturer, 1975, assoc prof of law, 1978; Danzansky, Dickey, Tydings, Quint & Gordon, senior partner, 1975-81; Georgetown Law Center, associate professor, 1978-82; Finley, Kumble, Wagner, senior partner and member of the National Management Committee, 1981-87, managing partner, Washington office, 1986-88; Finley, Kumble, Wagner, Heine, Underberg, Manley, Myerson & Casey, Washington, DC, co-managing partner, 1986-88; Laxalt, Washington, Perito, & Dubuc, managing partner, 1988-91; Washington & Christian, managing partner, 1991-; Washington Strategic Consulting Group, Inc, chairman/chief executive officer, currently. **Orgs:** District of Columbia Bar Assn; American Bar Assn; Natl Bar Assn; Washington Bar Assn; Federal Bar Assn; American Judicature Society; Supreme Court Historical Society; Phi Alpha Delta Legal Fraternity; board member, Natl Bank of Washington, 1981-89; board member, Medlantic Healthcare Group; board member, Medlantic Management Corp; board member, Healthcare Partners; board member, AVW Electronic Systems Inc; advisory board, The Home Group (AmBase); board of trustees, Corcoran Gallery of Art; board member, Natl Symphony Orchestra Assn; Metropolitan AME Church. **Honors/Awds:** Cobb Fellowship, Howard Law School, 1969; Harvard Law School, teaching fellowships, 1970-72. **Business Addr:** Managing Partner, Washington & Christian, 805 15th St, NW, Washington, DC 20005.

WASHINGTON, ROBERT E.
Administrator. **Personal:** Born Jan 7, 1936, Phoenix, AZ. **Educ:** Univ of CA, BS 1958; Pepperdine Univ, MPA 1973-74. **Career:** Corp for Pub Broadcasting, asst to pres for human resources dev; Libr of Congress Research Srv HUD, fed govt 1974-79; Wells Fargo Bank, comm relations 1964-70. **Orgs:** Mem Amer Mgmt Assc; mem Intl City Mgmt Assc; mem Reserved Ofcrs Assc. **Honors/Awds:** Service Award USAR. **Military Serv:** AUS & USAR lt col 1959-. **Business Addr:** Corporation for Public Broadca, 1111 16th St NW, Washington, DC 20036.

WASHINGTON, ROBERT ORLANDA
Educator. **Personal:** Born Feb 8, 1935, Newport News, VA; son of Fannie Bates Washington and Robert Lee Washington; married Mary Lewis Washington, Apr 7, 1955; children: Robert, Glynnis, Cheryl, Nathan, Allyson, Terrence, Candace. **Educ:** Hampton Institute, Hampton, VA, BS, 1956; Marquette University, Milwaukee, WI, MA, 1966; University of Missouri, Columbia, MO, MS, 1968; Brandeis University, Waltham, MA, PhD, 1973. **Career:** Greenleigh Assoc, New York, NY, sr research assoc, 1968-72; University of Wisconsin-Milwaukee, Milwaukee, WI, assoc dean, 1972-76; Ohio State University, Columbus, OH, dean, 1976-82; University of Illinois, Champaign-Urbana, IL, dean, 1982-86; Social Policy Research Group, Boston, MA, pres, 1986-88; University of New Orleans, vice chancellor, 1988-93, professor, currently; co-editor, Journal of Planning Education and Research. **Orgs:** Member, National Assn of Social Worker, 1976-90; commissioner, Council on Social Work Education Commission on Accreditation, 1978-81; Association of Collegiate Schools of Planning; URban Affairs Association. **Honors/Awds:** Outstanding Teacher of the Year, 1975; Phi Kappa Phi, 1992; NDEA Fellow, 1968. **Military Serv:** Artillery, 2nd Lt, 1956. **Home Addr:** 7135 Benson Ct, New Orleans, LA 70127, (504)245-8245. **Business Phone:** (504)286-7102.

WASHINGTON, ROOSEVELT, JR.
Educator. **Personal:** Born Feb 8, 1932, Swan Lake, MS; married; children: LuWanna, Ronald, Kenneth, Pamela. **Educ:** Roosevelt Univ, BA 1960, MA 1962; Marquette Univ Chicago State Univ DePaul Univ, adv study; No IL Univ, EdD. **Career:** Univ of North Texas, Denton Texas prof 1974-; Harambee Indpt Comm Sch Inc, chief admin 1973-74; Marquette Univ, asst prof 1971-74; No IL Univ 1969-71; McDade Elem Sch, asst prin 1968-69; Manley Upper Grade Ctr, tchr/Dept chmn 1961-68; Center St Sch & Fulton Jr HS, tchr/Cnslr 1960-61. **Orgs:** Mem Natl Assc of Secondary Sch Prins; Amer Educ Research Assc; Assc for Supervision & Curriculum Devel; Phi Delta Kappa; Amer Assc of Sch Admin; Natl Organ on Legal Problems in Education. **Honors/Awds:** Author numerous publ for professional journals. **Military Serv:** US Navy, HM3, 1950-54. **Home Addr:** 2125 Woodbrook, Denton, TX 76205.

WASHINGTON, ROSE WILBURN
Organization executive. **Personal:** Born Sep 4, 1940, Daphne, AL; daughter of Emma L Chancley and Emory William; married Regis G McDonald, Oct 22, 1983; children: Gerald, Carlos, Werhner Von, Tanya Monica. **Educ:** State University, Oneonta, BS, 1975; Marywood College, MS Ed, 1979; City College, New York, 1988-. **Career:** Charles Loring Brace Youth Camp, dir, 1978-80; Tryon School for Boys, dir, 1980-83; Spofford Juvenile Detention Center, NYC, executive dir, 1983-85; Department of Juvenile Justice, NYC, asst commissioner, 1985-90, commissioner, 1990-94; Dallas County Juvenile Department, dir/chief probation officer, 1994-95; Berkshire Farm Center and Services for Youth, executive dir, 1995-. **Orgs:** National Juvenile Justice Coordinating Council, presidential appointee, 1994-; American Correctional Association, bd of governors; Juvenile Detention Committee, chair; Commission on Accreditation, auditor; National Association Juvenile Correctional Agencies; New York State Detention Association; National Black Child Development Institute; Westchester County Black Women's Political Caucus. **Honors/Awds:** Dallas County Juvenile Department, First African-American Director, 1994; Spofford Juvenile Center, Devotion and Leadership, 1994; NY Association Of Black Psychologists, Nelson Rohlilahla Man-

dela, 1993; Department of Juvenile Justice, NYC, Outstanding Leadership, 1994; Carter G Woodson Academy, Leadership and Support, 1988. **Special Achievements:** Presented paper at Thistletown Regional Centre, Ontario, Canada, ''Casemanagement as a Crisis Intervention In a Secure Setting,'' 1987; presented paper at the Chapel Hill Workshop, ''Accountability: Is There Light at the End of Tunnel?'' 1989, ''Black Identity, Where We've Been Where We Are,'' 1981; featured in PBS Documentary, ''In Search of Excellence,'' 1989; Kennedy School of Government Case Study, ''Taking Charge: Rose Washington and Spofford Juvenile Detention Center,'' Harvard University, 1989.

WASHINGTON, RUDY
Association executive, college basketball coach. **Personal:** Born Jul 14, 1951, Los Angeles, CA. **Educ:** University of Redlands, graduate. **Career:** Locke High School, junior varsity basketball coach, five seasons; Verbum Dei High School, basketball coach, 1976-77; University of Southern California, asst basketball coach, 1977; Los Angeles Lakers, administrative asst, 1982-83; Compton Junior College, head basketball coach, 1983-84; Clemson University, associate head basketball coach, 1984-85; University of Iowa, coaching staff, top aide, 1986-90; Drake University, head basketball coach, 1990-. **Orgs:** Black Coaches Association, founder, past president, board of directors, currently. **Honors/Awds:** Missouri Valley Conference, Coach of the Year, 1993; National Association of Basketball Coaches, Kodak District 12 Coach of the Year for 1992-93 season. **Special Achievements:** Author of two books on rebounding; US Olympics, only one of eight asst coaches invited to participate in trials, and selection of basketball team, 1988. **Business Addr:** Executive Director, Black Coaches Association, PO Box 4040, Culver City, CA 90232, (310)342-8453.

WASHINGTON, SAMUEL, JR.
Educator. **Personal:** Born Aug 28, 1933, Jacksonville, FL; son of Alphonso and Bernice Kelly; married Bessyee G Washington, Jul 8, 1955; children: Rommell E, Renee E. **Educ:** Florida Agricultural and Mechanical University, BS, 1955, MEd, 1972; Florida State University, 1979-81. **Career:** United States Army, officer, 1955-77; Florida Agricultural and Mechanical University, dir of admissions, 1977-83, university registrar, 1983-92, assoc vp, 1992-. **Orgs:** Tallahassee Urban League, bd of dirs, 1993-; Phi Delta Kappa, 1972-; National Assn College Deans, registrar, admissions, treasurer, 1978-; American Assn College Deans, registrar, admissions officer, 1983-. **Honors/Awds:** Leadership Award, Alpha Phi Alpha Fraternity, 1983; Man of the Year, Phi Delta Kappa, 1973. **Military Serv:** United States Army, lt colonel, 1955-77; Bronze Star, Meritorious Service Medal, Commendation Medal.

WASHINGTON, SANDRA BEATRICE
Educator. **Personal:** Born Mar 1, 1946, Nashville, TN; daughter of Sadie Lewis Tucker and Henry F Tucker; divorced; children: Howard LaMont. **Educ:** Loyola Univ, BA, 1968; Univ of Nebraska, MS, 1977; Vanderbilt Univ, EdD, 1990. **Career:** Sacred Heart Grade School, teacher, 1968-71; Omaha OIC, instructor, 1972-73; Greater Omaha Comm Action, counselor/supvr, 1972-75; PCC/Head Start, pi/soc serv coord, 1976-78; Metro-Tech Comm Coll, counselor/career devel, 1978-81; Computer Inst for Youth, educ coord, 1984-85; Nashville Public Schools, counselor, 1986-94, chairperson, Guidance Dept, 1994-. **Orgs:** Career consultant Girl's Club of Omaha, 1978-81; counselor-on-call Planned Parenthood of Nashville, 1985-; editor newsletter, Chi Sigma Iota, Counseling/Academic and Professional Honor Society International, 1991; editorial board, Elementary School Guidance and Counseling, 1991-94. **Honors/Awds:** Outstanding Young Women of Amer, 1978-79; Grant recipient, Metro Nashville Education Foundation, 1987, 1990; National Board of Certified Counselors, TN, State Certified Counselor; University of Tennessee, Stokley Fellow, 1992. **Special Achievements:** International Foundation for Education and Self-Help, counselor/volunteer, Nairobi, Kenya, East Africa, 1995-96. **Business Addr:** Guidance Counselor, Cohn Adult High School, 4805 Park Avenue, Nashville, TN 37209, (615)298-8463.

WASHINGTON, SARAH M.
Educator. **Personal:** Born Aug 10, 1942, Holly Hill, SC; daughter of Sarah Harmon McCord and David Harry McCord (deceased); married Jun 4, 1967 (divorced); children: Walter Dawit Washington. **Educ:** Tuskegee Inst, Tuskegee AL, BS 1964; Univ of Illinois, Urbana IL, MS 1970, PhD 1980. **Career:** Spartanburg District, Inman SC, English teacher, 1964-65; Anderson Public Schools, Anderson SC, Eng teacher, 1965-67; Sumter Schools, Sumter SC, social studies teacher, 1967-68; AL State Univ, Montgomery AL, English instructor, 1971-74; Univ of IL, Urbana IL, teaching asst, 1974-80; SC State Coll, Orangeburg SC, English prof, 1979-. **Orgs:** Pres, Orangeburg Branch, Assn of the Study of Afro-Amer Life & History, 1980-85; pres elect, 1991, chaplain, 1982-89, Phi Delta Kappa; mem, SC State Dept Writing Advisory Bd, 1983-89; mem, Amer Assn of Univ Women; reader, Natl Teachers Examination, 1989; Natl Council of Teachers of English; Natl Black Child Development Institute. **Honors/Awds:** Sigma Tau Delta Natl Eng Honor Soc, 1981; author of literary biog of Frank Horne, 1985; field coordinator, Assessment Performance in Teaching, 1988-90; Scholar, Let's Talk About It, a national reading program. **Business Addr:** Professor, English, South Carolina State College, PO Box 2034, Orangeburg, SC 29117.

WASHINGTON, SHERRY ANN
Gallery administrator. **Personal:** Born Oct 28, 1956, Detroit, MI; daughter of Virginia Hall Washington and William Washington; married Floyd Haywood (divorced 1984); children: Khalid R Haywood. **Educ:** University of Michigan, Ann Arbor, MI, Bachelors, General Studies, 1977. **Career:** Government administrator, 1981-88; self-employed gallery owner, 1988-; Wayne County Council for the Arts, arts consultant, 1989-93. **Orgs:** Member, Delta Sigma Theta Sorority, 1974-; member, NAACP, 1984-; board member, Detroit Institute of Arts, Friends of African Art, 1988-; board member, Detroit Cultural Affairs Committee; board member, Metropolitan Growth & Development Corp. **Honors/Awds:** Alumni of the Year, American Center for International Leadership, 1987; Distinguished Woman of the Year, Coalition of 100 Black Women, 1992; MI Black Caucus, Outstanding Community Service Award, 1993; The Links, Inc, Community Service Award, 1995. **Business Addr:** President, Sherry Washington Gallery, 1274 Library St, Detroit, MI 48226, (313)961-4500.

WASHINGTON, TED
Professional football player. **Personal:** Born Apr 13, 1968, Tampa, FL; married Verlisa. **Educ:** Louisville, attended. **Career:** San Francisco 49ers, nose tackle, 1991-93; Denver Broncos, 1994; Buffalo Bills, 1995-. **Business Addr:** Professional Football Player, Buffalo Bills, One Bills Dr, Orchard Park, NY 14127, (716)648-1800.

WASHINGTON, THOMAS
Educator. **Personal:** Born Dec 8, 1937, Rock Island, IL. **Educ:** Univ of IL, BA 1961, MA 1964; Univ of MN, PhD 1982. **Career:** Champaign Centennial HS, teacher English, Spanish 1968-70; Hamline Univ MN, instructor Spanish 1970-73; Univ of MN, instructor Spanish 1974-78, 1980-81; Women's Self Defense Empowering Women, lecturer, instructor 1972-. **Orgs:** Lecturer Women's Self Defense seminars & workshops 1982-; The Nodarse Language Learning Method 1978-. **Honors/Awds:** Phi Kappa Phi Natl Hon Soc Univ of MN 1977; Fulbright Scholarship Year's Study in Guatemala 1962; YMCA Scholarship Study/Travel in USSR Hungary Poland 1961; Sigma Delta Pi Spanish Hon Soc Univ of IL 1961. **Business Addr:** Director, Lecturer, Instructor, Women's Self Defense, PO Box 580528, Minneapolis, MN 55458.

WASHINGTON, TOM
Professional sports official. **Career:** NBA, referee, currently. **Business Addr:** NBA Official, National Basketball Association, 645 5th Ave, 15th Fl, New York, NY 10022-5986.

WASHINGTON, VALDEMAR LUTHER
Attorney, circuit court judge (retired). **Personal:** Born Jun 21, 1952, Baltimore, MD; son of Vivian E Washington and G Luther Washington; married Ada C Miller, Aug 11, 1984; children: Valdemar L, II, Christopher James. **Educ:** Baltimore Polytechnic Inst, B 1970; MI State Univ, BA 1974; Univ of MI Law School, JD 1976. **Career:** Baker Law Firm Bay City, 1981-86, assoc lawyer 1977; Acct Aid Soc of Flint, dir 1978; Private Practice, attorney 1978-81, 1981; Robinson Washington Smith & Stanfield, partner 1981; Circuit Court Judge Genesee Co, judge 1986-96, chief court circuit judge, 1990-91. **Orgs:** Mem, MI State Bar Assoc; past mem, Big Sisters Bd of Dirs; past pres, Theatre Adv Bd 1982-83; mem NAACP Legal Redress Comm 1984-86; mem Amer Judges Assoc 1986-87; mem MI Trial Lawyers Assoc 1986-, Amer Trial Lawyers Assoc 1986-; mem, Flint Community Foundation, Mensa, 1980-. **Honors/Awds:** University Rhodes Scholarship nom MI State Univ 1974; The Argus Award, The Genesee County Consortium on Child Abuse and Neglect, l989. **Business Addr:** Genesee County Circuit Court, 328 S Saginaw St, Ste 9001, Flint, MI 48502, (810)232-1600.

WASHINGTON, VON HUGO, SR.
Educator, actor. **Personal:** Born Mar 9, 1943, Albion, MI; son of Alice Coleman Washington and Hugh Washington; married Frances Mosee Washington, Mar 6, 1974; children: Von Jr, Alicia Rene. **Educ:** Western Michigan Univ, Kalamazoo, MI, BS, 1974, MA, 1975; Wayne State Univ, Detroit, MI, PhD, 1979. **Career:** Univ of Michigan, Ann Arbor, MI, dir, black theatre, 1975-77; Wayne State Univ, Detroit, MI, dir, black theatre, 1979-88; Western Michigan Univ, Kalamazoo, MI, dir, multicultural & performance area, theatre, 1988-, professor, currently. **Orgs:** Black Theatre Network, 1986-96; artistic dir/co-founder; Afro-American Studio Theatre, Detroit, 1983-86; president/co-founder, Washington Prod Inc, 1992-. **Honors/Awds:** Achievement Award, Michigan Foundation for the Arts, 1984; Career Development Chair, Wayne State Univ, 1983; Carter G Woodson Education Award, Wayne State Univ, 1984; Alumni Faculty Service Award, Wayne State Univ, 1988; Best Actor, Detroit News, 1990. **Military Serv:** Air Force, TSGT, 1961-72, Commendation Medal 1965, Bronze Star, 1967, Meritorious Service Awards, 1967, 1972. **Business Addr:** Professor, Western Michigan University, PO Box 3253, Kalamazoo, MI 49003.

WASHINGTON, WALTER
University president (retired). **Personal:** Born Jul 13, 1923, Hazlehurst, MS; son of Mable Washington (deceased) and Kemp Washington (deceased); married Carolyn Carter. **Educ:** Tougaloo Coll, BA 1948; IN Univ, MS 1952; Yale Univ, Cert of Alcoholic Studies 1953; George Peabody Coll, Educ Spec 1958; Univ So MS, PhD 1969; Harvard Inst for Ed Management, certificate, 1988. **Career:** Crystal Springs, MS, tchr 1948-49; Parrish HS, asst prin/tchr 1949-52; Utica Jr Coll, dean 1952-55; Sumner Hill HS, principal 1955-57; Utica Jr Coll, pres 1957-69; Alcorn State Univ, pres 1969-94. **Orgs:** Dir Middle So Utilities 1977-94; dir Miss Power & Light 1977-94; dir Blue Cross/Blue Shield of MS 1977-95; gen pres Alpha Phi Alpha Frat 1972-76; mem pres com Natl Collegiate Athletic Assn 1984-l989; pres, 1964-65, life mem MS Teachers Assn; pres MS Assn Colleges 1983-84; pres of NAC United Negro Coll Fund 1959-60. **Honors/Awds:** State & Natl 4-H Alumnus Recogn Award Coop Ext Serv 1975 & 1977; Silver Beaver Award Boy Scouts of Amer 1975; Man-of-Year in Educ total Living for Fifty Plus 1981; Disting Alumni Award Peabody Coll 1972; Alumnus of Year Tougaloo Coll 1959; Honorary Doctor of Laws: Tougaloo College, 1972, Indiana Univ, 1983; Honorary Doctor of Laws, Purdue Univ, 1993.

WASHINGTON, WALTER E.
Attorney. **Personal:** Born Apr 15, 1918, Dawson, GA; married Bennetta Bullock (deceased); children: Dr B Jules-Rosette; married Mary Burke. **Educ:** Howard Univ, AB 1938, LLD 1948; Amer Univ, grad courses 1939-43; Hon LLD Degrees, Fisk Univ, Georgetown Univ, Catholic Univ, Boston Univ, George Washington Univ, Princeton Univ, Gonzaga Coll, Washington Coll, Indiana Coll, Boston Coll, Carnegie-Mellon Univ, Howard Univ, Trinity Coll, Colgate Univ, Univ of the Dist of Columbia, Lincoln Univ. **Career:** Natl Capital Housing Authority DC, housing mgr, 1941-45, various exec positions 1945-61, exec dir 1961-66; NY Housing Authority NYC, chmn 1966-67; District of Columbia, appointed mayor 1967-74, elected mayor, 1974-79; Burns, Jackson, Summit, et al, partner, 1979-81. **Orgs:** vice chmn Human Resources Devel Comm Natl League of Cities; mem Adv Bd US Conf of Mayors; mem Cosmos Club Fed City Wash; mem Amer Bar Assn; bd dir Big Bros Inc; former trustee John F Kennedy Ctr for the Performing Arts; mem Natl Adv Bd BSA; Ctr for Internatl Scholars. **Honors/Awds:** Honorary LLD & DHL degrees from various colls & Univs; Disting Serv Awd Howard Univ Law Alumni Assn 1974; Capital Press Club 1974; Silver Beaver Awd BSA 1973; Natl Jewish Hosp Awd for Outstanding Serv 1973; Human Relations Awd DC Br NAACP 1969; a number of other honors. **Business Addr:** Mayor, 410 T St, NW, Washington, DC 20001.

WASHINGTON, WARREN MORTON
Scientist. **Personal:** Born Aug 28, 1936, Portland, OR; son of Dorothy Morton Washington and Edwin Washington Jr; married Mary C Washington, 1995; children: Teri Lyn Ciocco, Kim Ann Washington, Tracy LaRae Washington; married Joan A Washington (died 1987). **Educ:** Oregon State University, Corvallis, OR, BS, physics, 1958, MS, meteorology, 1960; Penn State University, State College, PA, PhD, meteorology, 1964. **Career:** National Center for Atmospheric Research, Boulder, CO, research scientist, 1963-, program scientist, 1972-73, project leader, 1973-74, senior scientist, 1974-87, dir, climate and global dynamics division, 1987-95; Climate Change Research Section, head, 1995-. **Orgs:** American Meteorological Society; American Association for the Advancement of Science; American Geophysical Union; National Science Board. **Honors/Awds:** Fellow, American Meteorological Society, 1980, president, 1994; Fellow, American Association for the Advancement of Science, 1981; Fellow, The Alumni Fellow Program, Pennsylvania State University, 1989; one of 16 scientists featured in the Chicago Museum of Science and Industry ''Black Achievers in Science'' Exhibit. The exhibit is touring major science centers and museums in the United States from 1988-94; Fellow, The Alumni Fellow Program, Oregon State University, 1990; Distinguished Alumni Award, Pennsylvania State University, 1991, Oregon State University, 1996; Clinton-Gore transition team, 1992-93; Sigma Xi Distinguished Lecturer, 1998-99; Dept Energy Biologican & Envir Research Program, exceptional service award, 1997; Nat Acad of Sciences Port Coll of African Am in Science, Engin & Med, 1997. **Business Addr:** Senior Scientist, National Center for Atmospheric Research, PO Box 3000, Boulder, CO 80307.

WASHINGTON, WILLIAM
Banking executive. **Personal:** Born Jul 10, Chicago, IL; son of Susie M Washington. **Educ:** Illinois Institute of Technology, BS, sociology, business economics, 1976, MS, mgt, finance, 1978. **Career:** LaSalle Home Mortgage Corp, mortgage collections, mortgage originations, home improvement loan coordinator, secondary mortgage market coordinator, mortgage loan underwriting manager, vice pres, currently. **Orgs:** New Friendship Baptist Church of Robbins, Illinois, Christian education director, currently; The Teen Living Program of Chicago; Society of Mortgage Professionals, NFBC Homeless Svcs. **Honors/Awds:** Federal Housing Administration, Direct Endorsement Residential Underwriter; Mortgage Bankers Association of American, Accredited Residential Underwriter; YMCA, Black Achiever in Industry Award, 1976, 1985. **Military Serv:** US Army, spc-4. **Business Addr:** Vice Pres, LaSalle Home Mortgage Corp., 4242 N Harlem Ave, Norridge, IL 60634-1283, (708)456-0400.

WASHINGTON, WILLIAM MONTELL
Corporate officer. **Personal:** Born Apr 2, 1939, Columbia, MO; son of Narcissia Washington and William Washington. **Educ:** Lincoln Univ MO, BS Educ/Math 1962; Univ of MO at Kansas City, MA Educ 1970. **Career:** Sprint, dir, corporate relations, 1990-; United Telecommunications Inc, affirmative action officer, 1971; Urban League of Kansas City, assoc dir econ devel, 1967-71; KC MO Sch Dist, high school teacher & coach 1963-67. **Orgs:** Chmn of bd, Urban League Kansas City 1978; mem Omega Psi Phi 1959; bd dir, Metro YMCA 1973; adv bd United Negro Coll Fund 1976; chairman, Black Community Fund; KC Harmony, 1996; Health Midwest; INROADS Kansas City; Bruce R Watkins Cultural Heritage Center; Urban League, Kansas City; YMCA Kansas City. **Honors/Awds:** Outstanding Leadership Award, Minority Business Awareness Prog, Black Econ Union, 1977. **Business Addr:** Director, Corporate Relations, Sprint, Box 11315, Kansas City, MO 64112.

WASHINGTON-WALLS, SHIRLEY
Journalist. **Personal:** Born May 28, 1962, Benton, MS; daughter of Pearline Jefferson Washington and H D Washington; married Curtis Leland Walls, Sep 3, 1988. **Educ:** Southern IL Univ, Carbondale, IL, BS, 1984. **Career:** WSIU-TV, Carbondale, IL, anchor/reporter, 1981-84; WAND-TV Ch 7, Decatur, IL, general assignment reporter, 1984-86; WQAD-TV Ch 8, Moline, IL, reporter, 1987; WHO-TV Ch 13, Des Moines, Iowa, general assignment reporter, 1987-89; WTVF-TV Ch5, Nashville, TN, general assignment reporter, 1989-. **Orgs:** Member, National Association of Black Journalists, 1988.

WATERMAN, HOMER D.
Printing company executive. **Personal:** Born Mar 17, 1915, Nashville, TN; son of Virginia Waterman and William Waterman; married Marie Kenyon; children: Homer Elton Jr, William O. **Educ:** Wayne State Univ, 1935. **Career:** Waterman & Sons Printing, pres. **Orgs:** Pres Booker T Washington Busn Assn 1969-71, 1973-75; bd mem Southwest Detroit Hosp 1970; bd mem Detroit Urban League 1969; bd mem BTWBA; past bd mem Met Fund; past bd mem United Comm SVc past bd mem Econ Edn; past bd mem Met Detroit Cit Devel Authority; past bd mem Brewster Old Timers. **Honors/Awds:** Recipient Pres Award BTWBA 1970 & 1975; Wolverine State Rep Citation 1969; Certs of Award Detroit Housewives League Detroit Area Dad's Club; Detroit Fire Dept Fire Prev Kick-off Parade 1974; Outstanding Achievement in Business World Award Wright Mutual Ins Co 1973; Cert of Excellence Award MI Office of Minority Business Enterprise 1974. **Business Addr:** President, Waterman & Sons Printing, 17134 Wyoming Ave, Detroit, MI 48221.

WATERMAN, THELMA M.
Educator. **Personal:** Born Jun 10, 1937, Hartford, CT; daughter of Lucille Fuller Hosendove and William Hosendove; divorced; children: Steven, Kevin. **Educ:** Hartford Coll for Women, Hartford CT, AA 1969; Trinity Coll, Hartford CT, BA 1971; Yale Univ Divinity School, MDiv 1978. **Career:** Proof oper bank 1956-57; dept store salesgirl 1959-61; Headstart Prog, teacher aide 1964-67; Trinity Coll, resident counselor of grad & undergrad students; City Hartford, teacher 1971; coll admin 1971-; Office of Community Affairs, Connecticut Coll, dir; New Haven Boys and Girls Club, New Haven CT, admin, 1984-85; United Way of Southeastern Connecticut, Gales Ferry CT, assoc exec dir, 1985-. **Orgs:** Conducted leadership training sessions, community leaders devel manpower prog, workshops, seminars, conf prog evaluation; co-organizer of 1st public housing proj pre-school ctr 1963; group counselor, Parker Memorial Ctr Hartford 1967-68; counselor, Drop Outs Anonymous Hartford 1967-69; comm rep, Hartford Bd of Educ 1970; vice pres, Dwight School PTA Hartford 1970-71; pres, POWER Hartford 1970-71; bd mem, OIC 1972; United Way 1972; Connecticut Talent Asst Coop 1973-76; Southeastern Connecticut Youth Serv 1973-74; Info & Referral Agency 1974-77; vice pres, Black Seminarians 1974-75; Yale Univ Divinity School Comp Youth Serv 1972-75; Catholic Charities 1971-74; Educ Task Force Model City 1972-75; Minority Navy Wives Scholarship Comm 1972-74. **Honors/Awds:** Delta Sigma Theta Sorority Award, 1965; citationist, Lane Byrant Annual Awards Competition, 1965; Rudolph Haffner Award for Community Service, Hartford Coll for Women, 1969; Samuel S Fishzoln Award, Trinity Coll, 1971; Community Service Recognition, Norwich Branch NAACP, Norwich CT, 1980; Martin Luther King Jr Community Service Award, Club Cosmos, New London CT, 1980; Certificate, Connecticut Advisory Council on Vocational and Career Education, 1985; Martin Luther King Jr Community Service Award, Club Cosmos, New London, CT, 1980. **Business Addr:** Assoc Exec Dir, United Way of Southeathern Connecticut, PO Box 375, Gales Ferry, CT 06335.

WATERS, ANDRE
Professional football player. **Personal:** Born Mar 10, 1962, Belle Glade, FL. **Educ:** Cheyney State College, received business administration degree. **Career:** Philadelphia Eagles, safety, 1984-. **Business Addr:** Professional Football Player, Philadelphia Eagles, Veterans Stadium, Broad St & Pattison Ave, Philadelphia, PA 19148.

WATERS, BRENDA JOYCE
Journalist. **Personal:** Born Jan 29, 1950, Goldsboro, NC; daughter of Dilliah Waters and Levi Waters. **Educ:** Univ of MD, BS 1973; Amer Univ, MS 1975. **Career:** WTVR-TV-6, reporter/anchor 1975-76; WLOS-TV-13, reporter/anchor 1977-79; WPXI-TV-11, reporter 1979-85; KDKA-TV-2, weekend anchor/reporter 1985-. **Orgs:** Mem NAACP 1981-. **Honors/Awds:** Cert of Recognition Jimmy Carter Fed Disaster Assist Admin 1977; First Place Assoc Press Awd 1982 and 1984. **Home Addr:** 104 Cara Lin Dr., Pittsburgh, PA 15221. **Business Addr:** Weekend Anchor/Reporter, KDKA-TV-2, One Gateway Center, Pittsburgh, PA 15222.

WATERS, CRYSTAL
Vocalist. **Career:** Vocalist, musician, albums include: Surprise, Mercury Records, 1991. **Business Addr:** Vocalist, c/o Publicity Dept, Mercury Records, 825 Eighth Ave, 19th Fl, New York, NY 10019, (212)333-8000.

WATERS, GARY
Basketball coach. **Personal:** married Bernadette; children: Sean, Seena. **Educ:** Ferris State University. **Career:** Kent State University, men's basketball coach, 1996-; Eastern Michigan Univ, associate head coach, 1989-96; Ferris State Univ, asst coach, 1975-89. **Business Addr:** Head Basketball Coach, Kent State University, 146 Mac Center, Kent, OH 44240, (330)672-2470.

WATERS, HENRIETTA E.
Educator. **Personal:** Born Jul 4, 1927, Augusta, AR; married Robert H Waters Sr. **Educ:** Central State Clge, BS 1949; Loyola Univ, 1950; Univ of KS, MSW 1961. **Career:** Barry Coll School of Social Work, assc Prof 1972-; Univ of KS School Social Welfare, asst prof 1966-72; KS Dept Social Welfare, dist off supv/Child welfare consultant 1958-66; Chicago Welfare Div, child welfare supv 1953-58; IL Child Welfare Div, child welfare worker 1950-52; Dade Co Comm Action Agency, consultant 1975-. **Orgs:** Trustee Bd of Pub Health Trust 1978-; house of Del counc on Social Work Educ 1979-80; mem Natl Assc Soc Wrks; mem Acad Cert Soc Wkrs; mem NatlAssc Black Soc Wkrs; former vice pres Greater Miami YWCA 1976-78; vice pres Greater Miami Urban League 1979-; exec com Children's Psychiatric Ctr 1979-. **Honors/Awds:** Srv Award Barry Clge Chap Natl Assc of Black Soc Work Students 1975, 1979; Barry Clge Prof Achievement Barry Clge 1979. **Business Addr:** 11300 NE 2nd Ave, Miami, FL 33161.

WATERS, JOHN W.
Educator, clergyman, financial executive. **Personal:** Born Feb 5, 1936, Atlanta, GA; son of Mary Annie Randall Waters (deceased) and Henry Waters (deceased). **Educ:** Atlanta Univ Summer School, 1955-58; Fisk Univ, BA 1957; Univ of Geneva Switzerland, Cert 1962; GA State Univ, 1964, 1984; Boston Univ, STB 1967, PhD 1970; Univ of Detroit, 1974-75. **Career:** Army Ed Ctr Ulm W Germany, admin 1960-63; Atlanta Bd of Ed, instr 1957-60, 1963-64; Myrtle Baptist Church W Newton MA, minister 1969; Ctr for Black Studies Univ of Detroit, dir, assoc prof 1970-76; Interdenom Theol Ctr, prof 1976-86; The Gr Solid Rock Baptist Church Riverdale, minister 1981-; senior vice pres 1984-; Primerica Financial Services, College Park, GA, senior vice president, 1984-. **Orgs:** Mem bd dir Habitat for Humanity in Atlanta 1983; mem bd of trustees Interdenom Theol Ctr 1980-84; vice pres Coll Park Ministers Fellowship; chair South Atlanta Joint Urban Ministry 1984-94; Prison Ministries with Women, 1988-96; American Academy of Religion, 1969-; Society of Biblical Literature, 1969-; American Association of University Professors (AAUP), 1971-. **Honors/Awds:** The Natl Fellowship Fund Fellowship in Religion 1968-70; Fellowship The Rockefeller Doctoral Fellowship in Religion 1969-70; Disting Lecturer Inst for Christian Thought John Courtney Murray Newman Ctr MI 1975; first faculty lecturer, Interdenominational Theological Center, 1979. **Military Serv:** US Army, sp 1960-63. **Home Addr:** PO Box 310416, Atlanta, GA 30331-0416, (404)344-8104. **Business Phone:** (404)762-9990.

WATERS, KATHRYN (KATHY)
Transportation executive. **Career:** Maryland Commuter Rail System (MARC), acting mgr, manager, currently. **Special Achievements:** First African American woman in Maryland to manage a commuter rail service. **Business Addr:** Manager/CEO, MARC, 5 Amtrak Way, PO Box 8718, Baltimore, MD 21240, (410)859-7422.

WATERS, MARTIN VINCENT
Attorney. **Personal:** Born Nov 5, 1917, Maryland; married Gloria Wood; children: Rita, Marcia, Martin. **Educ:** Lincoln Univ, BA cum laude 1939; Fordham Univ, JD 1942; NY Univ, LLM 1956. **Career:** Lawyer pvt prac 1964; Amer Title Ins Co, vice pres chief cnslr 1962-64; Guaranteed Title & Mortgage Co, vice pres mgr 1959-60; Home Title Guaranty Co, coun 1953-59; Amer Arbitration Assc, arbitrator; Ministry of Housing Ghana, consult 1956; Mauritania to UN, consult to Permanant Mission. **Orgs:** Mem various prof org; mem Interracial Council for Bus Opport NY, dir 1965, pres 1969-72; trustee Arthur C Logan Mem Hosp 1975-; pres Lincoln UnivAlumni 1955-58; Law Comm NY Bd of Title Underwriters 1959-64. **Honors/Awds:** Economic Mainstream Award 1964; LU Alumni Award; Interracial Council Award; Amer Arbitration Assn Plaque; Opport for Negros in Law; Assn of Amer Law Schs; Bronze Star Medal. **Military Serv:** AUS 1942-46. **Business Addr:** 29 W 57 St, New York, NY 10019.

WATERS, MARY D.
Benefit specialist. **Personal:** Born Aug 27, 1955, Greenville, AL; daughter of Willie M & William Waters. **Educ:** Detroit Business Institute, 1975; University of Michigan, BA, liberal studies, 1988. **Career:** McDonalds, 1973-75; National Bank of Detroit, 1975-76; Blue Cross/Blue Shield, benefit specialist, currently. **Orgs:** Detroit Charter Revision Commission, vice chair, currently; Collections Practices Board, state of Michigan, currently; Kids in Need of Direction, bd member, 1990-92; Metropolitan Detroit Youth Foundation, facilitator, 1988-89; Blue Cross/ Blue Shield, management assn, currently; Blues Pac, previously chaired political involvement committee, currently; International Assn Business Communicators, currently; University of Michigan Alumni, currently. **Honors/Awds:** Blue Cross/Blue Shield, Pride in Execellence; Employee Suggestion Program. **Special Achievements:** On Detroit Column, Detroit News. **Home Phone:** (313)259-7626. **Business Addr:** Benefit Specialist, Blue Cross & Blue Shield of Michigan, 600 Lafayette E, #2125, Detroit, MI 48226.

WATERS, MAXINE
Congresswoman. **Personal:** Born in St Louis, MO; married Sidney Williams; children: Edward, Karen. **Educ:** CA State Univ, Los Angeles, BA, sociology. **Career:** Head Start, asst teacher; State of CA, assemblywoman; US House of Representatives, member, 1990-. **Orgs:** Dem Natl Comm; del, alternate Dem Conventions; Comn on the Status of Women, Natl Women's Political Caucus Adv Comm; comm Black PACS; natl bd dir Trans Africa; former chief deputy, LA City Councilman David Cunningham; Black Women's Forum, pres; House Committee on Banking, Finance, and Urban Affairs; Veterans Subcommittee on Education, Employment, Training, and Housing; Banking Subcommittee on Housing and Community Opportunities; Congressional Urban Caucus, co-chair; Clinton for Pres Campaign, natl co-chair. **Honors/Awds:** First woman to be ranked #4 on the leadership team; first African American female mem of Rules Comm; first nonlawyer on the Judiciary Comm; one of the outstanding leaders at the Intl Women's Year Conf in Houston; sponsored legislation concerning tenant protection, small bus protection, the limiting of police strip-and-search authority. **Business Addr:** Congresswoman, US House of Representatives, Longworth House Office Bldg, 1207 Longworth, Washington, DC 20515.

WATERS, NEVILLE R., III
Radio program director. **Personal:** Born Feb 22, 1957, Washington, DC. **Educ:** Springfield Coll, BS (Magna Cum Laude) 1978, MEd 1980. **Career:** WMAS Radio, announcer 1980-81; A&M Records, promotion/merchandising 1982-83; WQXQ Radio, traffic dir/music dir 1983; WOL Radio, prog dir 1985-. **Business Addr:** Program Dir, WOL Radio, 400 H St NE, Washington, DC 20002.

WATERS, PAUL EUGENE, JR.
Broadcasting executive. **Personal:** Born Sep 9, 1959, Harrisburg, PA; son of Sylvia Byers Waters and Paul E Waters Sr; married Sonja Powell Waters, May 24, 1987; children: Paul E, III, Meredith Colleen. **Educ:** Lincoln University, 1977-80; Temple University, Philadelphia, PA, BA, 1984. **Career:** New York Times Cable TV, Cherry Hill, NJ, account executive, 1984-86; WHTM TV, Harrisburg, PA, account executive, 1986-88; United Artists, Baltimore, MD, general sales manager, 1988-91; CNBC, Fort Lee, NJ, director of local advertising, 1991-. **Orgs:** Omega Psi Phi Fraternity, 1978-; NAACP, 1972-.

WATERS, SYLVIA ANN
Journalist. **Personal:** Born Sep 29, 1949, Corsicana, TX. **Educ:** East Texas State Univ, BA 1971. **Career:** Corsicana Daily Sun Newspaper, reporter 1972-. **Orgs:** Publicity chairwoman Navarro Co United Fund 1975-; mem Natl Federation of Press Women, TX Press Women 1982-; pres Jackson Ex-Students Assoc Inc 1983-; mem NAACP 1986, Natl Assoc of Black Journalists 1986-, Amer Business Women Assoc Golden Horizons Chap 1986-; chairwoman Navarro Co Coalition Black Democrats 1986-. **Honors/Awds:** James Collins Scholarship 1968; TX Press Women third place awd in photography 1987. **Home Addr:** 601 E 14th Ave, Corsicana, TX 75110. **Business Addr:** Corsicana Daily Sun Newspaper, 405 East Collin, Corsicana, TX 75110.

WATERS, WILLIAM DAVID
Government executive. **Personal:** Born Sep 14, 1924, Camden, NJ; son of Rebecca Jones Waters and William A Waters; married Viva Edwards. **Educ:** Temple Univ Philadelphia, BS Acctng 1947, MBA Acctng 1948. **Career:** IRS, Mid-Atlantic Region Philadelphia fiscal mgmt & officer 1964-67; asst Dist Dir Albany 1966-67; asst dist dir Baltimore 1970-73; dist dir Baltimore 1973-74; reg commr Mid-Atlantic Region 1974-85; NJ Casino Control Commission, commissioner 1986-. **Orgs:** Vp, dir YMCA of Camden Cnty 1980-; mem St John's United Meth Ch Columbia; mem Housing Task Force Columbia, MD. **Military Serv:** AUS 1st Lt (USAR) 1943-52. **Home Addr:** 1011 Rymill Run, Cherry Hill, NJ 08003.

WATERS, WILLIAM L.
Business executive. **Personal:** Born Sep 23, 1941, Philadelphia. **Educ:** BS 1966. **Career:** Consolidated Edison of NY, design engr 1966-68, cost engr 1968-71; proj construction engr 1971-73; William L Waters Inc, pres. **Orgs:** Mem Mech Contractors Assc of Amer; Natl Assc of Minority Contractors; Council of Construction & Prof NY; Mem 100 Black Men NY. **Honors/Awds:** Recipt Black Achievers Award 1972. **Business Addr:** 211 E 43 St, New York, NY 10017.

WATERS, WIMBLEY, JR.
Business executive. **Personal:** Born Oct 3, 1943, Leesburg, GA; married Andrea Lois Hannans; children: Nina, Princey, Tia, Dana, Elissa. **Educ:** Monroe Area Voc Tech Albany GA, attd 1963; Daytona Beach Comm Clge Daytona Beach FL, attd 1968. **Career:** Daytona Typographical Union No 892, pres 1973-; News-Jour Corp, printer 1963-; Equifax Srv, ins investigator 1974-78. **Orgs:** Pres FL GA Typographical Conf 1980-; secr/Treas Union Label Srv Trades Council Cntrl Labor Union Volusia Flagler FL 1980-. **Business Addr:** Daytona Typographical Union No, PO Box 771, Daytona Beach, FL 32115.

WATFORD-MCKINNEY, YVONNE V.
Attorney, government official. **Career:** US Dept of Justice, assistant US attorney, currently. **Orgs:** State Bar of MI; State Bar of NY; Federal Bar Assn. **Business Addr:** Asst US Attorney, US Dept of Justice, 310 New Bern Ave, Suite 800 Federal Building, Raleigh, NC 27601-1461, (919)856-4530.

WATIKER, ALBERT DAVID, JR.
Construction company executive. **Personal:** Born May 16, 1938, Zanesville, OH; son of Lora Bell Watiker and Albert David Watiker Sr; married Rachel Almeda Carnes; children: Leslie, Leisha, Lionel, Lori, Lynn, Lachelle. **Educ:** Ohio Univ, Athens OH, accounting degree, 1958; Bliss Coll, Columbus OH, senior accounting degree, 1961; attended Muskingum Tech, Zanesville OH, 1973-75; attended Ohio State, Columbus OH, 1976. **Career:** Simmons Co, Pittsburgh PA, office mgr, 1961-65; United Technologies, Zanesville OH, foreman, 1965-72; City of Zanesville OH, compliance officer, 1970-72; State of Ohio, Columbus OH, deputy dir, 1973-81; Watiker & Son Inc, Zanesville OH, pres, 1981-. **Orgs:** Mem, Greater Apostolic Church 1970-, NAACP 1979-; National Assn of Minority Contractors. **Honors/Awds:** Outstanding Co award, Small Business Assn, 1987; Top 50 Black Companies in USA, Black Enterprise, 1987; Top 100 Black Companies in USA, Black Enterprise, 1986-; Outstanding Performance, City of Columbus, 1988; award for outstanding assistance to minority subcontractors; Award of Excellence, US Small Business Assn, Washington, DC. **Home Addr:** 3290 Bowers Ln, Zanesville, OH 43701.

WATKINS, ARETHA LA ANNA
Print journalist. **Personal:** Born Aug 23, 1930, Blairsville, PA; daughter of Carrie Thompson Fox and Clifford Fox, Sr.; married Angelo Watkins Sr, Apr 14, 1967; children: Angelo Watkins, Jr. **Educ:** Wayne St U, 1950; WSU Coll of Lifelong Learning; Marygrove Coll. **Career:** Detroit Courier, staff writer 1963-64, asst to editor 1964-66; MI Chronical, staff wirter, columnist 1966; MI Chronicle Publ Co, asst managing editor 1968-l981; managing editor l98l-. **Orgs:** Sigma Delta Chi Professional Journ Soc adv bd mem, Prog Comm Assn 1968; NAACP. **Honors/Awds:** Best Editorial Awd, Nat Newspapers Publ Assn 1972; Black Communicator Awd MI SCLC 1972; Dist Comm Serv Awd Lafayette Allen Sr 1974; Community Serv Awd Aopha Theta Chap GAmma Phi Delta 1981; Corp Serv Awd African Amer Museum of Detroit 1984; Sojourner Truth Awd Bus Woman of the Year Detroit Chap Natl Assoc of Negro Bus & Professional Women's Clubs Inc 1984; MI SCLC Martin Luther King Jr Awd for Journalists Achievement 1986. **Business Addr:** Managing Editor, Michigan Chronicle, 479 Ledyard, Detroit, MI 48201.

WATKINS, CHARLES B., JR.
Educator, educational administrator. **Personal:** Born Nov 20, 1942, Petersburg, VA; son of Haseltine Thurston Clements and Charles B Watkins Sr; married Judith Leslie Griffin; children: Michael, Stephen. **Educ:** Howard Univ, BSME, 1964; Univ of New Mexico, MS, 1966, PhD, 1970. **Career:** Sandia Natl Labs, staff mem 1964-71; Howard Univ, asst prof 1971-73, dept chmn 1973-86; Natl Governor's Assoc, sr fellow 1984-85; City Coll of New York, Herbert Kayser, prof and dean sch of engrg, currently. **Orgs:** Consultant US Navy 1975-82, Natl Science Foundation 1976-78, US Army 1979, natl chair dept heads comm 1986-87, mem bd on engrg educ 1986-88, vice chair engrg & public policy dir 1987-88 Amer Soc for Engrg Educ; bd of dirs, Parsons Brinkerhoff, Inc, 1994; assoc fellow, Amer Inst of Aeronautics & Astronautics, 1993. **Honors/Awds:** Elected Tau Beta Pi 1963, elected Sigma Xi 1978; Ralph R Teeter Awd Soc of Automotive Engrs 1980; Fellow, Amer Soc of Mechanical Engrs, 1990. **Business Addr:** Dean, City College of New York, School of Engineering, Convent Ave at 140th St, New York, NY 10031.

WATKINS, CHARLES BOOKER, SR.
Educator (retired). **Personal:** Born Oct 28, 1913, Richmond, VA; son of Nannie Watkins and Freeland Watkins; married Haseltine Thurston (divorced); children: Dr Charles Jr, Richard, George. **Educ:** VA State Coll, BS 1936; Univ of Pgh, MA 1947. **Career:** VA Pub Schls, teacher 1936; Pgh Public Schls, teacher 1947; Univ of Pgh Teacher Corps, coord 1969; Pgh Bd of Educ, coord 1971, 1973-79 (retired). **Orgs:** Mem VA State Coll track & football teams 1932-35; rec dir Summer Prog Pgh PA 1947; coach City Champ Track Teams 1949-56; deputy dist rep Omega Psi Phi Frat 1951-58; dist marshal Omega Psi Phi 1955, 1963; mem Pgh Sch Nutrition Prog Comm 1964-67; founder Youth Character Club 1964; exec comm Fed of Teachers 1967; mem More Effec Schls Comm 1967-68; mem Human Relations Comm 1967; mem Proj REAL Temple Univ 1969; mem Boy Scout Comm; mem Pgh Council of Men; mem F&AM Prince Hall Masons; mem NAACP; past basileus Iota Phi Omega Psi Phi; mem ESEA Comm 1972-73; mem Natl Science Found; Omega Psi Phi National Chorale; Mt Ararat Baptist Church, All Male Chorus. **Honors/Awds:** HC Frick Scholarship PA State Univ 1963; Council of Men Awd for Outstanding Serv rendered the Comm of Pgh 1984; Omega Man of the Year Pittsburgh 1985. **Military Serv:** US Army/USMC, Siapan, 1943; invasion with 4th Marine division Presidential Unit Citation, Navy Award, 1944, first and only time awarded to Negro troops. **Home Addr:** 5600 Penn Ave, Apt Z-308, Pittsburgh, PA 15206.

WATKINS, GLORIA ELIZABETH
Business executive. **Personal:** Born Nov 28, 1950, Kankakee, IL; married Darryl Louis Watkins; children: Tia Monet, Valerie Viola. **Educ:** Loyola Univ of Chicago, BA, 1977. **Career:** The First Natl Bank of Chicago, commerical loan rep, 1972-81; Drexel Natl Bank, vice pres, 1981-, sr vice pres, exec vice pres, 1989. **Orgs:** Mem, Natl Assn of Bank Women; bd of dir, Urban Bankers Forum, Kenwood-Oakland Com Org, Cosmopolitan Chamber of Commerce, 1982-, Mercy Hosp Women's Bd, ETA, Abraham Lincoln Center, Kuumba Workshop Theatre; pres, Chicago Chapter; vice pres, Illinois State Council, Natl Assn of Bank Women, 1989-90. **Honors/Awds:** "Chicago's Up and Coming Black Business and Professional Women" Dollars & Sense Magazine, 1985; Ten Outstanding Young Citizens, Chicago Jr Assn of Commerce and Industry, 1986; "Amer Top 100 Black Business & Professional Women," Dollars & Sense Magazine, 1986.

WATKINS, HANNAH BOWMAN
Health educator. **Personal:** Born Dec 23, 1924, Chicago, IL; widowed; children: Robert A, Melinda Geddes, Melanie E. **Educ:** Fisk Univ Nashville TN, BA 1947; Univ of Chgo, attended 1948-49; Jane Addams Sch of Soc Work, grad courses 1966-69; IL Dept of Pub Hlth st cert Audiometrist 1978. **Career:** Univ of Chicago, clinical rsch assoc 1947-60; IL Dept Public Aid, med soc worker 1960-73; Clinic in Altgeld Chicago, consultant 1975-; IL Dept of PublicHealth, publ health training cons/supr 1973-, grants mgmt consultant. **Orgs:** Exec com mem Chicago Hearing Conservation Com 1975-; sec alumni commn Fisk Univ 1976-; mem Natl Assoc Univ Women 1978-; vice pres midwest region Fisk Univ Genl Alumni Assoc 1979-81; mem Hlth Systems Agency Council City of Chicago Hlth Systems Agencies 1980-; exec council mem IL Pub Hlth Assn 1980-82;mem Lincoln Congregational United Ch of Christ; bd of trustees Hull House Assoc; bd of dirs Parkway Comm House; mem Black Caucus Public Health Workers,Amer Public Health Assoc; mem comm IL Public Health Assoc. **Honors/Awds:** Special Commendation Hlth Coord Patricia Hunt Chief Family Health IDPH 1977-80; Special Commendation Walter J Leonard Pres Fisk Univ 1979; publications "Effect ACTH on Rheumatoid Arthritis" Journal Amer Chem Soc, "Lipoprotein & Phospholipoid in Animals" Journal Amer Chem Soc, "Early Identification of Pregnant Adolescents and Delivery of WIC Services," Amer Journal of Public Health 1985.

WATKINS, HAROLD D., SR.
Fire chief (retired). **Personal:** Born Feb 19, 1933, Detroit, MI; son of Clara B McClenic Watkins and Jesse Watkins; married Edna Jean Ridgeley, Dec 22, 1954; children: Harold D Jr, Kevin Duane, Keith Arnette. **Educ:** Macomb Community Coll, Mt Clemens MI, AA, 1976. **Career:** City of Detroit, fire fighter, 1955-76, sergeant, 1976-78, lieutenant, 1978-84, captain, 1984-88, battalion chief, 1988, chief of fire operations 1988-93. **Orgs:** 47-4900 Spokane Block Club, 1959-; pres, Lay Ministers, CME Church, 1965-; bd of dir, Manhood Organization, 1986-; pres, Manhood Org, 1988-. **Military Serv:** US Air Force, s/sgt, 1950-1954. **Business Addr:** Former Chief of Fire Operations, Detroit Fire Department, 250 West Larned, Third Floor, Detroit, MI 48226.

WATKINS, IRA DONNELL
Educator. **Personal:** Born Feb 12, 1941, Waco, TX; son of Ira and Donnell Watkins; children: Sinah. **Career:** Family First Art Program, art teacher; Tenderloin Self Help Center; Hospitality House Art Program, art teacher; National Institute of Art, instructor; National Institute of Art and Disabilities, interim dir, currently. **Orgs:** Pro Art, artist; AMES Art Gallery, artist; John Natsoulas Art Gallery, artist; SF Rental Gallery, artist. **Honors/Awds:** Tenderloin Times Art Contest, 1991; Art in Transit Project SF, 1995. **Home Addr:** 650 44th St, Apt 3, Oakland, CA 94621, (510)420-1413.

WATKINS, IZEAR CARL
City official. **Personal:** Born Aug 19, 1926, Denver, CO; married Rose Anna Maxine Miles; children: Sheila A Delaney, Carol A Mitchell, Pamela I Elmore, Grace D Paulson, Lynda N. **Educ:** Denver Oppor School of Business & Trades 1945-47. **Career:** US Govt, vice pres mobilization of econs resources 1968-74; DFL, state affirmative action commr 1974-77; Minneapolis City Govt, city chtr commr 1977-. **Orgs:** One of founders of Legal Rights Ctr Inc 1970; bd of dir Legal Rights Ctr 1970-; bd of dir U-Meet Sr Citizens 1972-80; bd of dir Minneapolis Assn for Retarded Children 1973-80; bd mem Natl Comm Devel; del Natl Conv Washington DC 1972; bd mem and pres bd of dirs Legal Rights Ctr Inc. **Honors/Awds:** Commendation Awd & Plaque City of Minneapolis Elected Officials 1972. **Business Addr:** City Charter Commr, Minneapolis City Govt, 301 City Hall, Minneapolis, MN 55415.

WATKINS, JAMES DARNELL
Dentist. **Personal:** Born Aug 29, 1949, Reidsville, NC; son of Sadie Lamberth Watkins and James Granderson Watkins; married Hardenia; children: Daryl Granderson, Deveda Camille. **Educ:** VA Polytechnic Inst, St Univ Blacksburg VA, BS biology 1967-71; Medical College of VA, Sch of Dentistry Richmond, DDS 1971-75. **Career:** Private Practice, dentist 1977-. **Orgs:** Am Dental Assn & Acad of Gen Dentistry 1975-; sec, Old Dominion Dental Soc 1978-; vice pres, Century Investment Club 1979-; NAACP; Grad Chap of Groove Phi Groove Soc Fellowship Inc; Beau Brummels Social & Civic Club;fellow, Acad of Gen Dentistry; pres, bd dir, Citizens Boys Club of Hampton VA; Penninsula Dental Soc, VA Dental Assn; VA Bd of Dentistry, pres, 1993-; American Dental Association's Council on Dental Education/Commission on Dental Accreditation, 1995-98; International College of Dentists. **Honors/Awds:** President's Awd, Old Dominion Dental Soc 1986; Dentist of the Year, Old Dominion Dental Society, 1987, 1990; governor appointee, State Board of Dentistry, 1989; Boys Club Board of Directors, Laymen of the Year, 1995. **Special Achievements:** Elected first Black president of the Virginia State Dental Board; US Naval Reserve Dental Unit, Little Creek Amphibious Base, appointed first Black commanding officer, promoted to rank of captain in US Navy Reserve, 1991. **Military Serv:** US Navy, dental corps, lt, 1975-77; US Navy Reserves, dental corps, cpt, 1977-. **Business Addr:** Dentist, 3921 Kecoughtan Rd, Hampton, VA 23669.

WATKINS, JERRY D.
Automobile dealer. **Personal:** Born Mar 26, 1939, Guilford County, NC; son of Rosa Gorrell Watkins and Charles L Watkins; married Elizabeth Harris Watkins, Jun 20, 1960; children: Jerry D Watkins Jr, Carl B Watkins. **Educ:** Univ of Detroit MI, degree in automotive mgmt, 1979. **Career:** Jerry Watkins Catillac-GMC Truck Inc, Winston-Salem NC, currently pres; Watkins Cadillac Oldsmobile Inc, currently pres; Tot's Haven Nursery Inc, currently vice pres. **Orgs:** Past mem, Bd of Dir, Chamber of Commerce; mem, Kiwanis Club.

WATKINS, JOHN M., JR.
Military officer. **Personal:** Born Jul 2, 1942, Evergreen, AL; son of Atlonia Lee Watkins and John M Watkins Sr; married Doris Bryant Watkins, Dec 24, 1966; children: Monica, Daphne. **Educ:** Tuskegee Univ, Tuskegee, AL, BS, 1966; New York Institute of Technology, MBA; Stanford University, study-engineering for executives, 1989. **Career:** US Army Pentagon, Washington, DC, division unit, 1984-86; US Army, Fort Huachuca, AZ, army staff commander 11th, 1986-88; Joint Staff Pentagon, Washington, DC, signal brigade military secretary joint staff, 1988-90; US Army, Fort Huachuca, AZ, commanding general information systems engineering command, 1990-92; Global Information Systems Command, deputy commanding general, 1993-. **Orgs:** International board, Military Secretary, combined communications electronics, 1988-90; natonal board, US Military Communications Electronics Secretary, 1988-90; Armed Forces Commuications Electronics Association, board of directors, 1992-. **Honors/Awds:** Distinguished Military Army Graduate, 1966; Presidential Outstanding Young American, Presidential Commission, 1976. **Military Serv:** US Army, brigadier general, 1966-; Legion of Merit, 1988, 1992; Defense Distinguished Service Medal, 1990.

WATKINS, JOSEPH PHILIP
Journalist. **Personal:** Born Aug 24, 1953, New York, NY; married Stephanie Taylor; children: Tiffany Ann, Courtney Andrea. **Educ:** Univ of PA, BA History 1975; Princeton Theological Sem, MA Christian Educ 1979. **Career:** Talladega Coll, chaplain religion instructor 1978-79; IN Purdue Univ at Ft Wayne, campus minister 1979-8l; US Sen Dan Quayle, asst state dir 1981-84; US Congress, Republican nominee for 10th dist 1984; Merchants Natl Bank, commercial accts rep 1984; Saturday Evening Post, vice pres & dir of missions 1984-. **Orgs:** Bd of dir Big Brothers of Greater Indianapolis; bd of dir Arthritis Found of Indianapolis; bd of dir Poison Control Ctr of IN; Natl Assn for the Advancement of Colored People, bd of dir Salvation Army of Indianapolis; bd of dir Penrod Soc; bd of dir Children's Bureau; adv bd Training Inc; bd of dir Humane Soc; bd of dir Jameson Camp; life member NAACP. **Honors/Awds:** Selected as one of the Outstanding Young Men of Amer 1983; selected as one of 50 Young Leaders of the Future by Ebony

Magazine 1983; winner of the IN Jaycees Speak-Up Competition 1983; winner of the US Jaycees Speak-Up Competition 1983; selected as one of the 10 Outstanding Young Hoosiers by the IN Jaycees 1984. **Business Addr:** Vice Pres & Dir of Missions, Saturday Evening Post, 1100 Waterway Blvd, Indianapolis, IN 46202.

WATKINS, JUDGE CHARLES, JR.
Educator. **Personal:** Born Jan 20, 1933, Vidalia, LA; son of Ethel Griffin & Judge Watkins, Sr; married Herma Jean, Mar 10, 1957; children: Debbie Ann Mitchell, Judge C Watkins II, Carlo A Watkins. **Educ:** Wilbur Wright Jr Coll, AA, 1959; Quincy Univ, BS, 1961; Northeastern IL Univ, MEd, 1973; Souther IL Univ, PhD, 1989. **Career:** Englewood Hosp, laboratory dir, 1961-63; St Bernard Hosp, night supv, 1962-63; Jackson Park Hosp, lab dir, 1963-65; Univ of IL, biochemistry research, teacher, 1965-68; Martin Luther King Health Ctr, dir of lab, 1968-71; Malcolm X College, faculty, 1969-. **Orgs:** Amer Society of Clinical Pathologist, 1961-; IL Federation of Teachers, vp, 1980-, exec committee, 1989-; Cook County Coll Teachers Union, vp, 1973-; Lawndale People Planning & Action Comm, bd mem, 1971-74; Lawndale Comm Conservation Council, bd mem, 1977-; Lawndale Mental Health, bd mem, appointed by mayor of Chicago, 1980-. **Honors/Awds:** Our Own Comm, Outstanding Educator, 1974; Midwest Comm Council, Distinguished Westsider Award, 1987; City Coll of Chicago, Distinguished Prof Academy, 1988; Malcolm X College, Distinguished Prof, 1988; Dollar & Sense Mag, One of the 100 Outstanding African Amer Men, 1993. **Special Achievements:** History of Malcolm X College, Master's Thesis; Academic Achievement as a Predictor of Success on a Med Lab Tech Certification Examination; Health Sciences. **Military Serv:** US Air Force, airman first class, 1951-55. **Home Addr:** 1133 S Kostner Ave, Chicago, IL 60624.

WATKINS, LENICE J.
Publisher, business executive. **Personal:** Born Dec 17, 1933, Palestine, TX; son of Ruby Watkins and Will Watkins; married Ethel L Sims; children: Geraldine, Deborah, Ricky, Sabrina, Lenice. **Educ:** Univ of Denver, BA 1960. **Career:** Ethelynn Publishing Co, owner; Town of Sunset, mayor, 1976-82; Jet Mag, copy ed 1963-73; Cleveland Call & Post, gen assignment rptr 1961-63; Afro Am Newspaper Wash DC, gen assignment rptr 1960-61; Evening Times, photo-journalist, currently. **Orgs:** Marion-West Memphis Lion Club; James Green VFW Post 9934, commander; Earleand Sunset, Arkansas; East Arkansas Regional Mental Health Center, board. **Honors/Awds:** Freelance writer fiction & nonfiction; manuscript, nonfiction, writing for The Black Press; novels: "Where from Here," "Die as Fools," Ethelynn Publishing Co, 1991. **Business Addr:** Publisher-Editor, Ethelynn Publishing Co, Rt 2, Box 397-R, Marion, AR 72364.

WATKINS, LEVI. See Obituaries section.

WATKINS, LEVI, JR.
Educator, surgeon. **Personal:** Born Jun 13, 1944, Montgomery, AL; son of Lillian Watkins and Levi Watkins. **Educ:** Tennessee State Univ, BS, 1966; Vanderbilt Univ, School of Med, MD, 1970. **Career:** Cardiac Surgeon, Johns Hopkins Hospital, 1978-; Johns Hopkins University, professor, dean, currently. **Orgs:** NYAS; Soc of Thoracic Surgeons; Soc of Black Acad Surgeons; Assn for Thoracic Surgery; Amer Coll of Chest Physicians; SE Surgical Congress; North Amer Soc of Pacing & Electrophysiology; Assn of Acad Minority Physicians; Physicians for Human Rights; Baltimore City Med Soc; Soc of Univ Surgeons; Fellowship, Amer Coll of Surgeons; Assn for Acad Surgery; Hypertension Task Force, Health Systems Agency of Maryland; Bd of Dir, Amer Heart Assn of Maryland; Diplomate, Natl Bd of Med Examiners. **Honors/Awds:** Highest Honors, Pres, Student Body, Student of the Year, Tennessee State Univ, 1965-66; Natl Vice Pres, Alpha Kappa Mu Honor Soc, 1965; Natl Med Fellowship Awardee, 1966-70; Alpha Omega Alpha; Doctor of Humane Letters, Sojourner-Douglass Coll, 1988, Meharry Med Coll, 1989. **Business Addr:** Professor, Cardiac Surgery, Dean of Postdoctoral Programs, Johns Hopkins Univ, 600 North Wolfe St, Baltimore, MD 21287-4618.

WATKINS, LOTTIE HEYWOOD
Property management company executive. **Personal:** Born in Atlanta, GA; widowed; children: Joyce Bacote, Judy Yvonne Barnett. **Career:** Alexander-Calloway Realty Co Atlanta, sec 1945-54; Mutual Fed S&L Assn, teller-clerk 1954-60; Lottie Watkins Enterprises, president 1960-. **Orgs:** Sec So Christian Leadership Conf 1967; vice chmn Fulton Co Dem Party 1968; Fulton Co Jury Commr 1972-; Gov's Comm on Voluntarism 1972; Fulton Co Bd of Registration & Elections 1973-; Citizens Exchange with Brazil 1973; participant White House Conf on Civil Rights; GA Residential Finance Auth 1974; chmn Amer Cancer Soc; chmn Comm Chest; mem exec comm bd dir NAACP; mem League of Women Voters, Atlanta Women's C of C; active mem of innumerable civic & prof organs. **Honors/Awds:** Recipient of various leadership citations including citations from Pres John F Kennedy, Pres LB Johnson, vice pres Hubert Humphrey and many others; listed in many biographical publications; GA House of Reps 34th Dist; 10 Leading Ladies of Atlanta Channel 11 Comm Serv Awd. **Business Addr:** President, Lottie Watkins Enterprises, 1065 Gordon St SW, Atlanta, GA 30310.

WATKINS, MARY FRANCES
Administrator. **Personal:** Born Sep 9, 1925, Towson, MD; divorced; children: Martin, Betty Merrill, John, Ralph, 9 foster kids. **Educ:** Morgan St U, 1955; Southampton Coll NY; St Univ of NY, 1967; St Univ of NY Stony Brook, MSW 1979. **Career:** Smith Haven Ministries, proj dir emerg food 1973-; EOC Suffolk Cty, dir emerg food & med prog 1970-73; Comm Act Agency Suffolk, youth & proj dir 1969; Econ Oppty Coun Suffolk, comm orgn spec; Urban League of Long Island, dir, currently. **Orgs:** Founder/admin, Smithtown Comm Serv School, 1964; dir, Suffolk Cty Black Youth in Action; chairperson, Suffolk Ho Servs Pers Com; bd mem, Long Island Sickle Cell Proj; vice pres, Smithtown NAACP; bd mem Natl Assn of Black Social Workers. **Honors/Awds:** Foster Mother of Yr, Foster Mother Assn NY 1967; Comm Serv Awd, Central Islip Comm Act 1968; Woman of Yr, Nat Coun of Negro Women 1970; Humanitarian Awd, Suffolk Cnty Human Rights Commn 1979; conducted Minority Women of 50 Wrksp, Minority Women Hlth Conf St Univ Stony Brook, 1979. **Business Addr:** Program Director, Urban League of Long Island, 535 Broad Hollow Rd, Melville, NY 11747.

WATKINS, MELVIN
College basketball coach. **Personal:** married Burrell Bryant; children: Keia, Marcus, Manual. **Educ:** Univ of North Carolina-Charlotte. **Career:** NBA, Buffalo Baves, begin 1977; UNCC, head basketball coach, until 1998; Texas A&M University, head basketball coach, 1998-. **Honors/Awds:** Conference USA, Ray Meyer Coach of the Year Award, 1997; Sun Belt Conference, title, 1977. **Special Achievements:** Fianl Four, UNCC, 1977; C-USA White Division title, UNCC, 1997; C-USA American Division, second place, UNCC, 1998; first person in UNCC history to be involved as player or coach in all eight post-season appearances. **Business Addr:** Head Basketball Coach, Texas A&M University, Athletic Dept, PO Box 30017, College Station, TX 77842, (409)845-4531.

WATKINS, MICHAEL THOMAS
Vascular/general surgeon. **Personal:** Born Nov 17, 1954, Washington, DC; son of Muriel Knowles Watkins and Harding Thomas Watkins; married Paula Pinkston, May 25, 1985; children: Steven Thomas, Adrienne Elise. **Educ:** New York University, New York, NY, AB, 1976; Harvard Medical School, Boston, MA, MD, 1980. **Career:** Johns Hopkins Hospital, Department of Surgery, Baltimore, MD, intern, 1980-81, assistant resident, 1981-82; Uniformed Services University of Health Sciences School of Medicine, Bethesda, MD, research fellow, 1982-84, research instructor, 1983-84; Strong Memorial Hospital, Department of Surgery, Rochester, NY, senior resident, 1984-85, chief resident, 1985-86; University of Rochester School of Medicine, instructor of surgery, 1985-86; Harvard Medical School, Boston, MA, clinical fellow in surgery, 1986-87; Massachusetts General Hospital, Boston, MA, Vascular Surgery Department, chief resident, 1986-87; Boston University School of Medicine, Department of Surgery, Boston, MA, research fellow, 1987-88, assistant professor of Surgery and pathology, 1988-; Boston City Hospital, Mallory Instie of Pathology, Boston, MA, research associate, currently; Veterans Administration Medical Center, Boston, MA, general and vascular surgical consultant, currently. **Orgs:** National Medical Association; American Heart Association, Thrombosis Council; Fellow, American College of Surgeons; certified, National Board of Medical Examiners; diplomate, American Board of Surgery. **Honors/Awds:** Resident Teaching Award, Department of Surgery, University of Rochester, Rochester General Hospital, 1986; Minority Medical Faculty Development Award for In Vitro Response of Vascular Endothelium to Hypoxia and Reoxygenation, Robert Wood Johnson Foundation, 1987-91; Grant-in-Aid for Phospholipid and Free Fatty Acids in Hypoxic Vascular Cells, American Heart Association, 1990-93; author with C.C. Haudenschild, H. Albadawi, "Synergistic Effect of Hypoxia and Stasis on Endothelial Cell Lactate Production, Journal of Cellular Biology, 1990; author with M.R. Graff, C.C. Haudenschild, F. Velasques, R.W. Hobson, "Effect of Hypoxia and Reoxgenation of Perfused Bovine Aortic Endothelial Cells, Journal of Cellular Biology, 1989; author of numerous other articles and presentations; R29 Research Award, Endothelil Cell Responses to Acute Hypoxia & Reoxygenation, NIH, 1993-97; VA Merit Review Research Award, Signal Transduction in Hypoxic Vascular Cells, 1994-97. **Military Serv:** US Army Medical Corps, Capt, 1982-89; Army Commendation Medal, 1984. **Business Addr:** Dept of Surgery; VAMC-Boston (112), 150 South Huntington Avenue, Boston, MA 02130.

WATKINS, MOSE
Director. **Personal:** Born Jul 9, 1940, Eudora, AR; married Tommie Orlett White; children: Dwayne Andre, Nikole Michelle. **Educ:** Weber State Coll, BS Soc Phys Ed 1958-70; Univ of UT Salt Lake City, MSW 1972, PhD Ed Admin 1973. **Career:** Union Pacific RR, cook 1956-60; Swifts Packing Co & ZP Smith Constr Co, gen laborer; Athletic Dept Weber State Coll Ogden UT, publ relations asst 1966-67; Calgary Stampeders Canadian Football League, defensive end & offensive tackle 1967; Natl Job Corps Ctr Dir Comm, comm mem; Grad School of Soc Work Univ of UT, clinical instr; Thiokol Corp Clearfield Job Corps Ctr Clearfield UT, ctr dir, dirof group life/supr residential living/couns 1967-. **Orgs:** Jr pres Ogden Br NAACP 1959; mem Natl Soc Workers Org; vice pres NAACP; mem Clearfield & Salt Lake City C of C, Kiwanis, New Zion Bapt Church, Masonic Temple. **Honors/Awds:** Outstanding Honors as Lineman All Army Football Team 1964; Licensed Cert Soc Worker State of UT 1973; Outstanding Young Men of Amer 1977; Meritorious Serv Awd NAACP 1977; Man of the Year Clearfield Job Corps Ctr Student Govt 1979; Outstanding Serv Awd US DOL/ETA Reg 8 Job Corps 1979; Light Heavyweight & Heavyweight Championship AAU & Golden Gloves. **Military Serv:** AUS pfc 1963-65.

WATKINS, MOZELLE ELLIS
City official. **Personal:** Born May 18, 1924, Crockett, TX; daughter of Sallie Elizabeth Fleeks Ellis (deceased) and Leroy Ellis (deceased); married Charles Philip Watkins, Mar 20, 1948 (deceased); children: Phyllis Caselia Watkins Jones, Eunice Juaquina Watkins Cothran. **Educ:** Hughes Bus Coll, diploma 1944-45; Extension Sch of Law, 1960; Famous Writers Sch Hartford, certificate 1970; Catholic Univ, certificate public speaking 1970; Georgetown Univ School of Law, 1976-77; Montgomery Coll, spanish certificate 1978. **Career:** Federal Government, statistical clerk & sec 1945-69; Anacostia Citizens & Merchants Assn, admin asst 1969-70; Montgomery Co Govt Human Relations Comm, investigator 1971-93; DC Neighborhood Advisory, commissioner, 1976-96. **Orgs:** TASSL Block Club; Upper Northeast Family Day Comm; Citizens Adv Comm to the District of Columbia Bar; 1st vice president, Chinese-Amer Lions Club, 1994-95; president, Chinese-American Lions Club, 1995-96; 19th St Baptist Church; comm DC Government ANC-5A Single Member District 14 1976-92; elected comm ANC 5A Single Member District 11 1992-96; Brookland Comm Corp 1978-89; 12th St Neighborhood Corps 1979-89; 19th St Baptist Church, deaconess 1987-; president Jarvis Mem Club 1983-, board of directors Christian Ed, 1985-89; chairperson ANC 5A, 1978, 1979, 1985; elected delegate to 1986 DC Democratic State Convention; vice chairperson, DC Advisory Neighborhood Commn 5A 1989; Ward V Unity in the Community Comm 1988; Woodridge Orange Hat Team, 1992-; board of directors, National Foundation for the Deaf, 1989-96; NAACP; Montgomery County, Maryland, Committee on Employment of People with Disabilities, 1989-93; Woodridge Civic Association; Gateway Community Association. **Honors/Awds:** Author "Two Zodiac Calendars" 1975 & 1977; author proposal entitled "Resolution for the Conservation of a Section of the Nation's Capital as a Tribute to Afro-American" published in the DC Register; certificates of appreciation from Amer Red Cross, DC Chapter Howard Univ, Moorland-Spingarn Rsch Ctr, Anacostia Citizens & Merchants Assn, Dept of Defense, Bureau of Supplies and Accounts, District of Columbia Council, mayor Marion S Barry Jr of the District of Columbia, DC Ward V Council Member William R Spaulding, the Northeast News Publishers 1986, The State of Texas 1991; Outstanding Service & Dedication, Advisory Neighborhood Commn 5A 1989; Certificate of Election 1993-95; Certificate of Recognition for Contributions to American Society 1992-93; Fifth District DC Metropolitian Police Department & Citizens Advisory Council, Certificat of Recognition for Dedication & Devotion to Improving Public Safety, 1996. **Home Addr:** 3225 Walnut Street, N E, Washington, DC 20018.

WATKINS, PRICE I.
Government official (retired). **Personal:** Born Dec 27, 1925, Abbott, MS; son of Alice Brown Watkins and Wooster Watkins; married Elliott Mae Williams (divorced 1971); children: Dorrance, Bruce, Kenneth, Andre. **Educ:** San Diego City College, San Diego, CA, AA, 1966; San Diego State University, San Diego, BA, 1970; Pepperdine University, Los Angeles, CA, MPA, 1977; California Coast University, Santa Ana, CA, PhD, 1985. **Career:** US Marine Corps, Okinawa, JP, comm chief, 1958-62; US Marine Corps, San Diego, CA, training officer, 1962-69; US Marine Corps, Vietnam telephone officer, 1967-69; US Marine Corps, CA, maint officer, 1971-76; Wells Fargo Gd Serv, Los Angeles, CA, oper manager, 1978-83; Internal Revenue Serv, Elmonte, CA, taxpayer serv repr, 1986-87. **Orgs:** Life member, 1st Marine Division Assn, 1953-; member, American Political Science Asn, 1970-; life member, The American Legion, 1974-; life member, Republic National Committee, 1977-; member, Religious Science Practitioners Assn, 1986-;. **Honors/Awds:** Valley Forge Honor Certificate, Freedoms Foundation at Valley Forge, 1972, Valley Forge Honor Certificate, Freedoms Foundation, 1975. **Military Serv:** US Marine Corps, Captain, 1944-76; Good Conduct Medal, 5 awards, 1944-62, Navy Commendation Medal, 1968. **Home Addr:** 119 S Alta Ave, Monrovia, CA 91016-2723.

WATKINS, ROBERT CHARLES
Construction. **Personal:** Born Apr 6, 1927, Detroit, MI; married Cleo. **Educ:** Corning Free Acad, 1948; NY St, 1955. **Career:** Corning Glass Works; machine bldr rsrch & devel, 28 yrs. **Orgs:** Mem Finger Lakes St Prk & Rec Commn 1975-77; chmn Town of Corning Dem Com 1975-77; commn Steuben Co Dem Com 1974-77; exec Bd Stgeuben Co Dem Com 1975-77; chmn Steuben Co Manpower Planning Cncl 1975-77; dir NY St NAACP 1966-77; So Tier Legal Serv 1973-77; dir chtr mem Tier Empl Cncl 1970-77; life mem NAACP Fndr; Crystal City Social Club 1955-77; Corning Bi-racial Club 1967-69. **Military Serv:** AUS corpl 1947-50. **Business Addr:** Rsrch & Devel DV 1, Corning, NY 14830.

WATKINS, ROLANDA ROWE
Entrepreneur. **Personal:** Born Feb 22, 1956, Detroit, MI; daughter of Doris Louie Rowe and Carlos Rowe; married James Abel Watkins, Aug 30, 1986. **Educ:** Wayne State University, Detroit, MI, Exec Secretary, Stenographer, Certificate, 1973; Detroit Business Institute, Detroit, MI, Exec Secretary, Certificate, 1976; Detroit College of Business, Dearborn, MI, Associate, Business Administration, 1981, Bachelor, Business Administration, 1988. **Career:** Provident Mutual Life Insurance, Southfield, MI, secretary, 1980; Chevrolet Central Office, Warren, MI, secretary, 1981; Midwestern Associates, Detroit, MI, secretary, 1982-; Downtown Fish & Seafood, Detroit, MI, proprietor, 1987-. **Orgs:** Founder, coordinator, Caring Kids Youth Ministry, 1983-; member, Washington Boulevard Merchants Association, 1987-. **Honors/Awds:** National Sojourner Truth Award, 1990, Outstanding Entrepreneurial Achievements, 1989, National Assn of Negro Business and Professional Women's Club, Inc; Go 4 It Award, WDIV-TV 4, 1985; Dedicated Service to Community, New Detroit, Inc, 1989; Devoted and Invaluable Service to the Youth, 14th Precinct, Detroit Police Dept, 1985; Devoted and Invaluable Service to the Youth, 2nd Precinct, Detroit Police Dept, 1987; Commendations received from President Ronald Reagan, 1987, Senator Carl Levin, 1985, 1986, Governor James Blanchard, 1986, Mayor Coleman Young, 1986-93, President Gerald Ford; WDIV and Hardee's Hometown Heros Award/Senior Citizens Assistance, 1993; Key to the City of Detroit, Mayor Coleman Young, 1993; Spirit of Detroit Award, 1989. **Special Achievements:** Serving free Thanksgiving Dinner to over 4000 homeless people for the past eight years. **Business Addr:** Proprietor/Entrepreneur, Downtown Fish and Seafood, 1246 Washington Blvd, Detroit, MI 48226.

WATKINS, SHIRLEY R.
Government official. **Personal:** Born Jan 7, 1938, Hope, AR; daughter of Mr & Mrs Robert Robinson; married George T. Watkins, Jul 13, 1963; children: Robert T, Miriam Cecelia. **Educ:** University of Arkansas-Pine Bluff, BS, 1960; University of Memphis, MEd, 1970, post graduate, 1989-91. **Career:** University of Arkansas Extension Service, assistant Negro home demonstration agent, 1960-62; Memphis City Schools, 4th grade teacher, 1962-63, home economics teacher, 1963-69, food service supervisor, 1969-75, director of nutrition services, 1975-93; US Department of Agriculture, deputy assist secretary, FCS, 1993-94, deputy undersecretary, FNCS, 1994-. **Orgs:** ASBO, TASBO, NAACP, life member subscribing golden heritage, 1970-; Phi Delta Kappa, president, vice president of programs, 1991-93; Alpha Kappa Alpha, 1958-; Society Inc, financial secretary, 1992-95; MOLES, editor, 1990-93; ASFSA, president, vice president, section chair, legislative committee, 1982-90; Les Casvale, president, vice president, treasurer, hospitality, 1982-93; IFMA International Gold & Silver Plate Society, chairman, secretary, treasurer, 1982-92. **Honors/Awds:** Honorary Doctorate of Food Service, 1988; UAPE, Outstanding Alumni Award, 1993; Tennesse ADA, Iris Award, 1993; Tennesse Governor, Outstanding Achievement Award, 1989; International Food Manufacturers Association, Silver Plate, 1988; Memphis Board of Education, Outstanding Achievement Award, 1993; Memphis City Council, Outstanding Contributions to Community, 1994. **Home Addr:** 10941 Pebble Run Drive, Silver Spring, MD 20902. **Business Addr:** Deputy Under Secretary, US Dept of Agriculture, 14th Independence Ave., SW, Administration Building Room 240-E, Washington, DC 20502, (202)720-7711.

WATKINS, SYLVESTRE C., SR.
Business executive. **Personal:** Born Oct 8, 1911, Chicago, IL; son of Ada B and Charles E; married Mabel Fleming; children: Adrienne M, Sylvestre C Jr (dec). **Educ:** Northwestern Univ School of Business, attended. **Career:** Johnson Publishing Co, circulation director, 1951-57; Near South Post, editor, publisher 1959-60; Chicago Daily Defender, natl circ dir 1960-61; US Savings Bonds Div US Treas, dir 1961-68; Metro Washington, DC, dir, 1968-76; Negro/Black Heritage Magazine, editor, publisher 1961-82; Warner Cable TV, TV host, producer The Syl Watkins Show 1978-88; publisher/editor, The Syl Watkins' Drum, 1986-. **Orgs:** Pres, bd of trustees Abraham Lincoln Ctr 1956-68; mem bd of trustees Joint Negro Appeal 1961-63. **Honors/Awds:** Distinguished Serv Century of Negro Progress Exposition 1963; Mem of 150 IL Sesquicentennial Commn 1967; Freedom Eagle Award, 2 Special Achievement Awards, Superior Performance Award, Silver Platter Award 1968-70, 1974, 1976; Appreciation Award Warner Amex Cable Commn Inc 1980; Washington District of Columbia Public Schools, "In Support of Public Education," 1986; Florida Supreme Court, Orange County Court Mediator Arbitrator, 1992-; Orange Cty, Florida, Classroom Teachers Association, Human Relations in Education Award, 1997-; Florida Teaching Profession/National Education Association, Human Relations Award, 1997-. **Business Addr:** Publisher, Syl Watkins Drum, 5720 PGA Blvd #511, Orlando, FL 32839.

WATKINS, TED
Corporation executive. **Personal:** Born Sep 3, 1923, Meridian, MS; married Bernice Stollmach; children: Ted Jr, Tamlin, Timothy, Tom, Teryl, Lyssa. **Educ:** Watts Labor Comm Action Com, Adminstr 1966-; UAW, intl rep 1966-. **Career:** Watts Labor Comm Actioon Com 1966-; UAW, intl rep 1966-. **Orgs:** Mem Mayors Bicentennial Com; Jr Achievement Exec Bd; vice pres Martin Luther King Gen Hosp Auth Commn; mem United Civil Rights Cong; Watts-willowbrook -Compton Improvement Assn; STEP; LA Citizens Adv Com; Watts Citizens Adv Com; Watts Station Com; Police Adv Council; adv com Upward Bound, Univ CA; Watts Comm Dev; LA County Delinquency & Crime Commn; Watts-willowbrook Dist Hosp Med Prog; mem Citizens Resource Com, Bd Edn; LA Urban Coalition; SE Coll Adv Com; Black Heritage Subcommittee. **Honors/Awds:** Awards, Baha'i Human Rights 1970; City LA Human Relations Commn 1971; Urban League 1971; Council Comm Clubs 1973; County LA 1972; Assn Elem Sch Administrs 1968; DA County LA 1973; Interracial Council for Bus Opportunity 1971; Benedict Canyon Assn 1969; Cath Labor Inst 1968; Am Soc Pub Adminstrs 1972; Outstanding Com Serv Awd Watts NAACP 1977; Outstanding Com Serv Awd; Help Pub Serv Found 1978; Participation in Black Econ Devel Awd, Black Blusinessmens Assn of LA 1978; Recog & Apprec for Outstanding Contbns to Com, Oscar Joel Bryant Assn 1978; Outstanding Serv Awd, Training & Research Found Head Start & Pre/Sch 1979; Awd The Senate-cA Legislature 1980; Outstanding Contbns & Devotion, City of Compton 1980; Recog of Humanitarian Concepts, Black Caucus of CA Dem Party1980; Awd, Assembly-womMaxine Waters 1980; Cert of Spl Congressional Recog 1980; Honor Awd, Service Employees Joint Counc SEIU AFL-CIO 1980; Recog of Contbns WLCAC Exec Bd & Proj Dir 1980; Grateful Apprec Awd So CA CAP Council 1980; Awd as Founder of WLCAC & dedicated efforts, Mayor Tom Bradley of LA, 1980; Dedicated Serv Awd, Consolidated Realty & Bd 1980. **Military Serv:** AUS 1942-44. **Business Addr:** 11401 S Central Ave, Los Angeles, CA.

WATKINS, WILLIAM, JR.
Business executive. **Personal:** Born Aug 12, 1932, Jersey City, NJ; son of Willie Ree Blount and William J Watkins; married Sylvia I Mulzac; children: Cheryl, Rene M, Linda M. **Educ:** Pace Univ, BBA 1954; NY Univ, MBA 1962. **Career:** Consol Edison Co NY Inc, staff asst 1957-65; Volkswagen of Amer Inc, syst mgr 1965-71; Volkswagen NE Wilmington MA, exec 1971-72; New England Elect Sys Westborough MA, exec 1972-82; Naragansett Electric Co, vice pres 1982-86, exec vp 1992-; New England Power Service Co, vice pres 1986-92. **Orgs:** RI Industrial Competitiveness Alliance, chairman, 1994-; Rhode Island Hosp Trust Natl Bank, bd of dirs, 1987-; INROADS of Central New England, 1993-; Natl Conference of Christians & Jews, 1993-; Leadership Rhode Island, 1992-; Rhode Island School of Design, bd of trustees, 1992-; Rhode Island Hosp, 1994-; Lifespan, 1997-. **Honors/Awds:** Human Relations Award Urban League of Bergen Cty 1963; Urban League of RI Community Srv Award 1986; John Hope Settlement House Award 1987; SBA Minority Advocate of the Year Award, 1994; American Economic Development Council, Developer of the Year, 1996. **Military Serv:** AUS sp4 1955-57. **Home Addr:** 509 Corey Lane, Middletown, RI 02842.

WATKINS, WYNFRED C. (WYNN)
Company manager. **Personal:** Born Apr 15, 1946, Toledo, OH; son of Marie B Marr Watkins (deceased) and Clifford G Watkins; married Brenda J Sparks Watkins, Mar 18, 1967; children: Suzan Marie, Tara Edwina. **Educ:** Bowling Green State Univ, Bowling Green, OH, 1965-66. **Career:** JC Penney Co Inc, Saginaw, MI, district manager, 1990-93, Dallas, TX, director of geographic markets, 1993-. **Orgs:** Chairman, JC Penney Northeastern Regional Affirmative Action Committee, 1990-; fundraiser chairman, American Red Chapter Southwest, Cleveland, OH, 1989, 1990; spiritual aim chairman, Kiwanis Club of Saginaw Westshields, currently; member, Zion Baptist Missionary Church, Saginaw, currently; board member, Advisory Board of Parma General Hospital, Cleveland, OH, 1989. **Honors/Awds:** Store Manager of the Year Award, JC Penney, Cleveland District, 1989; various company awards for beating sales/profit objectives.

WATKINS-CANNON, GLORIA ANN
Educational administrator, educator. **Personal:** Born Apr 4, 1952, Courtland, AL; daughter of Mary Ella Mitchell (deceased) and W D Watkins Sr; divorced; children: Clifford Cannon. **Educ:** The Ohio State University, BS, home economics, liberal studies family relations human dev, MA. **Career:** Kroger Company, assistant manager, 1975-76; Grocery Products Group, sales representative, 1976-77; Borden Inc, food service unit manager, 1977-79; Advanced Business Communication, communication consultant, 1979-80; WIC Program, project assistant/nutritionist, 1980-83, public health educator, 1982-85; The Ohio State University Young Scholars Program, regional program director, 1988-. **Orgs:** The OSU Black Alumni Association, vice pres; The Ohio State University Mentor Program; Neighborhood House Inc, board of trustees; Women Infants & Children, advisory council; Delta Sigma Theta Sorority Inc, golden life member, vice pres, 1982; National Alliance of Black School Educators; Olde Orchard Alternative School Parents Association; A Gathering of Sisters; New Salem Missionary Baptist Church, Missionary Society, women's day chairperson, women's breakfast fellowship committee. **Honors/Awds:** The OSU Mentoring Program, Professional Mentor Achievement Award, 1989-91; The OSU Young Scholars Program, Outstanding Service Award, 1990. **Business Addr:** Regional Program Director, Assistant Administrative Director, The Ohio State University, Young Scholars Program, 1050 Carmack Road, 112 Mount Hall, Columbus, OH 43210, (614)292-4884.

WATLEY, JODY
Singer. **Personal:** Born 1960; married Andre Cymone (divorced); children: Lauren, Arie. **Career:** Solo recording artist, currently. **Honors/Awds:** Six top ten singles from album Larger than Life. **Special Achievements:** Appearance at the White House, 1992; Album: Affairs of the Heart, 1992; Intimacy; Affection. **Business Addr:** Singer, c/o MCA Records, Inc, 70 Universal City Plaza, Universal City, CA 91608.

WATLEY, MARGARET ANN
Educator (retired). **Personal:** Born Oct 19, 1925, Nashville; widowed. **Educ:** TN A&I St U, BS 61947; Columbia U, MA 1965. **Career:** Jasper County GA, teacher 1950-53; HM Nailor, Cleveland, MS, 1954-57; Winchester Comm School, 1958. **Orgs:** Life mem NEA; life mem NANB & PW Inc; pres New Haven Club of Nat Assn Negro Business Prof Womens Clubs Inc 1971-72; New Haven Educ Assn 1972-76;mem CT Educ Assn, CT Del NEA Rep Assembly 1972; NE Dist Orgn Nat Assn of Negro Bus & Prof Womens Clubs Inc 1976; founded & organized The Elm City Sr Club & Elm City Youth Club 1976; founded & organized The Elm City Yng Adult Club 1977; reappointed organizer NE Dist Gov of NANBPW Inc 1979; pres Elm City Sr Club of New Haven & Vicinity 1977-79 & 79-81; Christian Tabernacle Bapt Ch; League of Women Voters, New Haven; board of directors, New Haven Scholarship Fund; director of voter services, League of Women Voters; board of directors, New Haven Colony Historical Society, 1995-98; treasurer, Edgerton Garden Ctr, Library Board for city of New Haven; treasurer, African-American Women's Agenda. **Honors/Awds:** Outstanding Elem Tchrs Am 1972; Outstdng Participation Awd NANB & PW Clubs, Inc 1976, 77; "The Innavators" 1976, 77; Silver Tray 1976; Ldrshp Devel Awd CT Educ Assn; Nat Sojourner Truth Meritorius Serv Awd, Elm City Sr Club, 1978; Crystal & Silver Bud Vase for Work with Orgn Nat Assn Conv Pittsburg 1979.

WATLINGTON, JANET BERECIA
Appointed government official. **Personal:** Born Dec 21, 1938, St Thomas, Virgin Islands of the United States; married Michael F MacLeod; children: Gregory, Kafi. **Educ:** Pace Univ NY, 1957; Geo Wash Univ Wash DC, 1977. **Career:** ACTION Wash DC, asst dir cong affairs 1979-; Hon Ron deLugo US House of Reps Wash DC, adminstrv asst 1968-78; Legislalture VI St Thomas, exec sec 1965-68. **Orgs:** Co-chmn Dem Nat Conv Rules Com 1976; appointee Dem Party Commn Presidential Nomination & Party Struc 1976; dem nominee congress VI 1978; vchprsn Dem Nat Com Eastern Region, 1972; steering com Dem Nat Com Black Caucus, 1974; exec com Dem Party Chtr Commn 1974; Congressional Black Caucus, 1974; chtr mem Sr Exec Serv Fed Govt 1979. **Business Addr:** 806 Connecticut Ave NW, Washington, DC 20525.

WATLINGTON, MARIO A.
Educational administrator, elected official (retired). **Personal:** Born Nov 9, 1917, Charlotte Amalie, VI; son of Victoria Lambertis and Joseph Watlington; married Lysia Audain; children: Roy, Audrey Wood. **Educ:** Baruch School of Bus Admin, BBA 1960; Exec Mgmt Inst, Diploma 1962; NY Univ, MA 1966. **Career:** Coll of Virgin Islands, dir of admiss, registrar & admiss officer; Govt of Virgin Islands, dep commis of ed 1962-67; Foundation Univ of Virgin Islands, mem, 1986-93; Virgin Islands Joint Bd of Educ, St Thomas, Virgin Islands, pres; Univ of Virgin Islands, mem, bd of trustees, 1989-92. **Orgs:** Pres St Thomas Music Assoc 1960's; Continuing Ed Div Coll of the VI, lecturer, 1963-84; charter mem 1967, pres 1967-, St Thomas Lions Club; chmn SCORE US Small Bus Admin 1984-94; trustee Coll of VI 1984-93; dir St Thomas Racquet Club 1985-; mem nominating comm Natl School Bd Assn 1986-87; St Thomas Raquet Club Awd for promoting tennis in VI 1986; dir Natl School Bds Assn, Washington, DC, 1989-93. **Honors/Awds:** Sesquicentennial Awd Plate NY Univ 1981; Testimonial Coll of VI 1982; Cited in Book of Outstanding VI; Project Introspection Dept of Ed St Thomas 1984-86; Honored by Department of Education by Board of Education, and Public Broadcasting Corp-TV, St Thomas, VI; University of Virgin Islands, Faculty Emeritus, 1987; International Lions Club, Melvin Jones Fellow, 1993. **Special Achievements:** Delegate to the Virgin Island Episcopal, 1994-95; Diocesan Convention, 1995-96; served as delegate to 3rd & 4th Virgin Islands Constitutional Conventions. **Military Serv:** VI home guard, WW II. **Home Addr:** PO Box 771, 18 Estate Hope, St Thomas, Virgin Islands of the United States 00804.

WATSON, AARON
Educational administrator, attorney. **Career:** Attorney; Atlanta School Board, president, 1994-. **Business Addr:** President, Atlanta School Board, 210 Pryor St. SW, Atlanta, GA 30335, (404)827-8000.

WATSON, ANNE
Financial administrator. **Personal:** Born Feb 19, 1945, Belzoni, MS; married John. **Educ:** Western MI U, BA 1970; Univ of MI,

attended 1976-78. **Career:** Univ of Detroit, financial aid dir; Wayne St Univ, financial aid counselor 1974-75; Shaw Coll Detroit, financial aid dir 1971-76; Western MI Univ, tutor counselor & asst dorm dir 1967-70; Dept of HEW, consult 1976, discussion leader 1977-; MI Financial Aid Assn, presentor/panelist 1980. **Orgs:** Mem Nat Assn for Fin Aid Adminstr 1975-80; chprsn Com for the Physically/Mentally Handicap 1978-79; bd of dir Black United Fund 1979-80. **Honors/Awds:** Certificate (Proposal Writing), Moton Consortium Dept HEW 1974-75; Certificate (Professional Devel & Operational Procedures) Moton Consortium, Dept HEW 1975. **Business Addr:** 4001 W McNichols, Detroit, MI 48221.

WATSON, BEN
Television news reporter. **Personal:** Born Jan 28, 1955, Muskegon Heights, MI; son of Lionel Matthewes Watson and Bernie Watson Sr; married Mattie Thompson Watson, Dec 30, 1980. **Educ:** Central Mich Univ, Mount Pleasant, MI, BA, 1973-78. **Career:** WZZM TV, Grand Rapids, MI, tv camera operator, 1978-79; WEYI TV, Flint, MI, tv reporter, 1979-80; WDTV TV, Grand Rapids, MI, tv reporter, 1980-83; WLMT TV, Grand Rapids, MI, tv reporter, 1983-86; Grand Rapids Press, Grand Rapids, MI, newspaper weekend reporter, 1983,84; WMC TV, Memphis TN, tv reporter, 1986-. **Orgs:** Member, NAACP 1986-; member, National Assn Black Journalists, 1987-; member, Omega Psi Phi, 1975-; member, Manna Outreach, 1990-. **Honors/Awds:** Communicator Award, Am Cancer Society, 1983; Journalism Award, Flint Urban League, 1979; Achievement Award, Interpreting Serv for Deaf, 1989; Volunteer Award, Miss Blvd Ch Church, 1990. **Business Addr:** TV Reporter, News Dept, WMC-TV, 1960 Union Ave, Memphis, TN 38104.

WATSON, BERNARD C.
Educator. **Personal:** Born Mar 4, 1928, Gary, IN; son of Fannie Mae Browne Watson and Homer Bismarck Watson; married Lois Lathan, Jul 1, 1961; children: Barbra D, Bernard C Jr. **Educ:** IN Univ, BS 1951; Univ of IL, MEd 1955; Univ of Chicago, PhD 1967; Harvard Univ, Cambridge, MA, postdoctoral in advanced administration, 1968. **Career:** Gary Public Schools Gary, IN, teacher/counselor/prin 1955-65; University of Chicago, Chicago, IL, staff associate, 1965-67; Philadelphia Sch Dist, 1967-70; Temple Univ, chmn dept urban educ 1970-75, vice pres acad admin 1976-81; William Penn Foundation, pres & chief exec officer 1982-93; HMA Foundation, chair, 1994-97; Temple Univ, presidential scholar, 1994-97. **Orgs:** Bd of dirs of Comcast Corp, First Union Bancorp North, First Union Bank, AAA Mid-Atlantic, Keystone Ins Co, Philadelphia Contributionship; Natl Advisory Council on Ed Professions Development, vice chmn, 1967-70; Harvard Univ Grad Sch Edn, assoc in ed, 1970-72, mem vis comm, 1981-87; Natl Urban Coalition, steering committee and exec committee, 1973-89; Harvard Coll Dept Afro-American Studies, mem vis comm, 1974-78; Natl Council on Educational Research, 1980-82; Pennsyvania fed judiciary nominating commn, 1981-89; Natl Urban League, sr vice chmn, bd of dirs, 1983-96; Pennsylvania Conv Ctr Authority, vice chmn, bd of dirs, 1986-; Pennsylvania Council on Arts, vice chmn, 1986-1993; William T Grant Fdn Commn on Work, Family and Citizenship, 1987-88; New Jersey State Aquarium, sec of bd, 1988-93; Avenue of Arts, Inc, chmn, 1992-97; Judicial Conduct Bd, Supreme Ct of Pennsylvania, 1993-97; Thomas Jefferson Univ, trustee, 1993-94; Natl Advisory Council for Historically Black Colleges and Universities, mem, 1994-97; Am Philos Soc; Am Acad Political and Social Sci; Phi Delta Kappa; Kappa Delta Pi. **Honors/Awds:** More than 100 major awards, including 22 honorary degrees; author, In Spite of the System: The Individual & Educ Reform, 1974; Plain Talk About Educ: Conversations with Myself, 1987; Testing: Its Origin, Use and Misuse, 1996; Colored, Negro, Black: Chasing the American Dream, 1997; 13 monographs; chapters in 28 books; 100 career folios; 35 articles in professional journals; Dr Bernard C Watson Graduate Sem Room and Awd presented for best social science dissertation in Temple Univ, Coll of Educ. **Military Serv:** USAF 1st Lt 1951-54. **Business Addr:** Temple University Center City, 1616 Walnut St, Philadelphia, PA 19103.

WATSON, BETTY COLLIER
Educator. **Personal:** Born Aug 26, 1946, Thomasville, GA; married William Watson; children: Letoynia, Maxie, Mar-yoi, Lemoya, Zaittrarrio, Shartriya, Kirk, Keith. **Educ:** Fisk Univ Nashville TN, BA History, English 1967; Cornell Univ Ithaca, MA Equivalent 1968; Howard Univ Washington DC, 1968-69; Amer Univ Washington DC, PhD Econ 1984. **Career:** Cost of Living Council, labor economist 1972-73; Morgan State Univ, instr history 1969-71; Howard Univ, lecturer 1971-73; Univ of DC, asst prof of econ 1973-80; Econ Impact Rsch & Info Staff Dept of Energy, Office of Minority, consult 1980-81; Sonoma State Univ, asst prof mgmt studies 1981-84; Howard Comm Coll, asst prof bus 1983-84; Trinity Coll, asst prof econ 1984-; College of Notre Dame Baltimore MD, assoc prof. **Orgs:** Instr history Morgan State Univ 1969-71; lecturer econ Howard Univ 1971-73; Affirm Action Comm 1975-76; The Grievance Comm 1975-76; The Faculty Senate 1979-80; Grants Comm, The Sonoma Enterprises Bd of Dir, Grad Screening Comm; faculty consult San Francisco State Univ 1981-82; econ/statistician Howard Univ 1982-84; principal investigator An Analysis of the Displacement Process in the District of Columbia; bd of dir Bldg Comm ARB 1980-; ed bd Univ Renaissance Jrnl 1982-. **Honors/Awds:** Woodrow Wilson Fellow 1967-68; Publ, "On Love & Death," 1977, "Keeping Washington Beautiful," 1978; Paper "Economic Status of Women in the US," 1983; Published, "Differential Economic Status of Black Men & Women, Perception Versus Reality," 1984, "Math Bus & Textbook Constraint," 1985.

WATSON, BOB. See WATSON, ROBERT JOSE.

WATSON, CAROLE M.
Social worker. **Personal:** Born Aug 3, 1944, New Orleans, LA; daughter of Frances Chapman and Herman Chapman; divorced; children: Dionne T. **Educ:** Western MI Univ, BS 1965; Wayne State Univ, MSW 1970. **Career:** Milwaukee Area Tech Coll, instr 1972-73; TN State Univ Dept of Social Welfare, instr, curriculum coord 1973-77; Univ of TN School of Social Work, asst prof 1977-79; WZTV Channel 17 Black Pulse, hostess 1981-85; Nashville Urban League, exec dir 1979-85; Bay Area Urban League, Oakland, CA, vice president, 1985-90; United Way, San Francisco, CA, senior vice president, 1990-. **Orgs:** Mem Delta Sigma Theta Nashville Alumnae 1963-; mem Acad of Certified Social Workers 1975-; adv coun Bd of Cert for Master Soc Workers 1980-81; dir TN Chap of Natl Assoc of Social Workers 1980; 1st vice pres natl council of execs Natl Urban League; consumer adv comm South Central Bell; bd of dirs Nashville Class of 1981 Alumni 1982-83; bd of dir TN Oppor Prog Legal Serv of Middle TN, NAACP, Bay Area Assoc of Black Social Workers 1986-. **Honors/Awds:** Appreciation Awd Alpha Delta Mu Natl Soc Worker Hon Soc Iota Chap TN State Univ 1978; Citizen of the Year Riverside Seventh-day Adventist Church; Congressional Record Awd presented by Bill Booner 5th Congresional Dist State of TN 1985; Wall of Distinction Western MI Univ 1986; employee of the Year, Bay Area Urban League, 1987; Appreciation Award, California Association of Black Social Worker, 1989.

WATSON, CLETUS CLAUDE
Educator, clergyman. **Personal:** Born Nov 3, 1938, Philadelphia, PA; son of Claudie B Bridges Watson and Ernest Samuel Watson Jr (deceased). **Educ:** St Francis College, Loretto, PA, BA, 1962; St Francis Seminary, Loretto, PA, ordained, 1966; LaSalle University, Philadelphia, PA, MA, 1974; St Charles Seminary, Philadelphia, PA, MDiv, 1976. **Career:** Bishop Egan High School, Fairless Hills, PA, chairman, teacher, 1966-76; St Francis Prep School, Spring Grove, PA, chairman, dean of students, 1977-81; University of Florida Med School, Gainesville, FL, teacher, med ethics, 1981-85; Holy Faith Catholic Church, Gainesville, FL, assoc pastor, teacher, 1981-85; San Jose Catholic Church, Jacksonville, FL, assoc pastor, teacher, 1985-88; St Joseph Academy, St Augustine, FL, teacher, chairman, 1986-89; Church of the Crucifixion, Jacksonville, FL, pastor, teacher, 1988-. **Orgs:** Advisory bd member, Presbyteral Council of the Diocese of St Augustine, 1988-95; advisory board member, Afro-American Office (Diocese), 1987-; advisory board member, Catholic Charities Office (Diocese), 1991-97; advisory board member, Ministry Formation Board, 1991-92; member, National Black Catholic Clergy Caucus, 1966-; member, Black Catholic Congress, 1987-. **Honors/Awds:** Black History Month Award, Jacksonville Naval Base, 1987; commissioned in Afro-American ministry, Jacksonville, FL, 1990; One Church/One Child Award, Jacksonville, FL, 1990; Citizens Award, Jacksonville, FL, 1991; Alumni Award in Humanities, St Francis College, 1992; International Biographical Assn Man of the Year Award, 1993; Amer Biographical Inst Man of the Year Award, 1994. **Special Achievements:** Author, The Concept of Love: An Ongoing Perspective, Brentwood Christian Press; author, The Concept of God and the Afro-American, Brentwood Christian Press; poems include "A Man Called Black"; "Fifty Plus Five". **Home Addr:** 6079 Bagley Rd, Jacksonville, FL 32209-1805.

WATSON, CLIFFORD D.
Educational administrator, editor. **Personal:** Born Jan 30, 1946, Akron, OH; married Brenda Chapman; children: Angera, Amina. **Educ:** Ashland Coll, BS 1964; Wayne St, MEd 1970, PhD 1973. **Career:** Detroit Bd of Educ, staff coordinator, present, dean of students 1979, multi-ethnic studies coordinator 1974; writer educ serv 1972; contrib editor, McGraw Hill Book Co, 1979; Malcolm X Academy, principal, 1992-. **Orgs:** Pres United Black Educ Assn 1978-; pres/commn Nat Alliance of Black Sch Educ 1979; Author Pride Educ Serv Inc 1972. **Honors/Awds:** Urban League Comm Serv Awd, Urban League, 1975; contr ed for Sci Reading Series, Magraw Hill, 1979; article "Black Gifted", MI Chronicle 1979. **Business Addr:** Principal, Malcolm X Academy, 6230 Plainview, Detroit, MI 48228.

WATSON, CLYNIECE LOIS
Physician. **Personal:** Born Jan 27, 1948, Chicago, IL; married Sloan Timothy Letman III; children: Sloan Timothy Letman IV. **Educ:** Loyola Univ Chicago, BS 1969; Meharry Med Coll, MD 1973; Univ IL, MPH 1977. **Career:** Cook Co Hosp Dept Pediatrics, resident 1973-75; Provident Hosp, assoc med dir 1977; Private Practice, pediatrician. **Orgs:** Mem Am Med Womens Assn; Am Pub Hlth Assn; Black Caucus Hlth Wrkrs; mem Am Coll Prvntv Med/AMA/IL St Med Soc/Chicago Med Soc/IL Pub Hlth Assn/Am Assn Univ Women/Nat Med Assn; bd of dir Komed Hlth Ctr; mem Phi Delta Kappa Hon Educ Frat Mem, Womens Flwsp Congregation Ch, Park Manor;bd Religions Edn, Congregational Ch, Park Manor; Meharry Alumni Assn; Univ IL Alumni Assn; Martin Luther King Jr Flwsp; mem Asso Physicians of Cook Co 1971-73; mem Alpha Kappa Alpha Sor Inc Lambda Alpha Omega Chapt. **Honors/Awds:** Merit Awd, Womens Flwsp Congregational Ch, Park Manor; Outst Yng Citzn Chicago Jaycees 1980. **Business Addr:** 1750 East 87th St, Chicago, IL 60617.

WATSON, CONSTANCE A.
Public relations consultant. **Personal:** Born Aug 17, 1951, Nashville, TN; children: Shannon. **Educ:** TN State Univ, MSSW 1978. **Career:** Dede Wallace Mental Health Ctr, psychiatric social worker 1973-82; Neuville Industries, dir ocean pacific div 1982-86; W/W & Associates Public Relations, president/founder 1985-. **Orgs:** Chairperson Natl Hook-Up of Black Women 1980-82; exec comm 1984-86, 2nd vice pres 1986-, Beverly Hills/Hollywood NAACP; bd dir Found for Educ 1984-. **Honors/Awds:** Achievement Awd Golden West Magazine 1987; Public relations consultant for major Hollywood and Los Angeles celebrities and events, ie 19th NAACP Image Awdstelevised on NBC. **Business Addr:** President, W/W & Associates, 1539 West 56th St, Los Angeles, CA 90062.

WATSON, DANIEL
Owner. **Personal:** Born Apr 11, 1938, Hallettsville, TX; married Susan Smallwood; children: Pamela, Bradley, Stanley, Jodney, Narlan. **Educ:** Univ of Wash, BS 1959, MS 1965. **Career:** Washington Natl Ins Co, agent 1966-68, mgr 1968-71, gen agent 1971-. **Orgs:** Article published Psychological Reports 1965; mem Seattle Planning of Redevel Council 1967-71; mem Natl Gen Agents & Mgrs Assn 1971-; mem Wash Natl Gen Mgts Assn 1971-; mem Chicago Assn of Life Underwriters 1979-. **Honors/Awds:** Agency Builder Awd Wash Nat 1970-75, 1977; Top 10 Agencies Wash Nat 1976-78. **Business Addr:** Agent, Washington Natl Ins Co, 2603 W 22nd St Ste 18, Oak Brook, IL 60521.

WATSON, DENNIS RAHIIM
Lecturer, author, educator. **Personal:** Born May 14, 1953, Hamilton, Bermuda; son of Eula Watson-Stewart and Arthur Daniels. **Educ:** Fordham Univ Bronx NY, 1974-76; Pace Univ, 1976-78; New York Univ, 1980-. **Career:** Theatre of Everyday Life, exec dir 1980-83; New York City Council, exec asst 1983-84; National Black Youth Leadership Council, exec dir, CEO, 1984-. **Orgs:** UNCF, 1980-86; New York Urban League, 1980-86; volunteer Bayview Correctional Facility for Women NY 1980-86; Natl Alliance Black School Educators 1984-86; Council Concerned Black Execs 1980-86; NAACP, 1984-86; Black Leadership Roundtable 1984-86. **Honors/Awds:** Sigma Gamma Rho Inc, Performing Arts Award 1984; Natl Black Leadership Roundtable Awd 1984; US Dept of Justice Drug Enforcement Admin Volunteer Awd 1984; Mayors Ethnic New Yorker Awd 1985; Presidential White House Citation 1985; Private Sector Initiative Awd 1986; Bayview Correctional Facility for Women Male Performer of the Year 1986; Americas Best & Brightest Young Business & Professional Man, 1987; OIC Appreciation Award, 1988; Leadership Appreciation Award, UCLA, 1989; The Black Women Task Force Award, 1989; National Black Graduate Student Award, Mississippi State Univ, 1990; Black Student Alliance Award, Univ of Virginia; City of New York, Human Resource Administration Special Award; Apple P, Delta Sigma Theta Youth Award; Western Mich University Student Leadership Conference Awar1991; Florida International Univ Black Family Award; Aspira, Family Christian Assn of America, Youth Award; Burlington County College, Black History Month Award. **Business Addr:** Executive Dir, CEO, Natl Black Youth Leadership Council, 250 W 54th St, Suite 800, New York, NY 10019.

WATSON, DENTON L.
Author, journalist, public relations specialist. **Personal:** Born Dec 19, 1935, Kingston, Jamaica; son of Ivy L Watson and Audley G Watson; married Rosa Balfour, Sep 1, 1963; children: Victor C, Dawn M. **Educ:** University of Hartford, BA, 1964; Columbia University, Graduate School of Journalism, MS, 1965; Catholic University of Chile, Inter American Press Association Scholarship, 1967. **Career:** Hartford Courant, reporter, 1965-67; Hostos Community College, Department of College Relations, director; Time Magazine, writer; NAACP Department of Public Relations, assistant director, director, 1971; The Baltimore Sun, editorial writer; author; SUNY College at Old Westbury, American Studies, faculty, 1992-; Clarence Mitchell Jr Papers, editor, currently. **Orgs:** The American Historical Association; National Association of Black Journalists; The Authors Guild Inc. **Honors/Awds:** Ford Foundation grant, 1981, 1986. **Special Achievements:** Author: Lion in the Lobby, Clarence Mitchell Jr's Struggle for the Passage of Civil Rights Laws. **Military Serv:** US Navy, ae-3, 1957-59. **Home Addr:** 137 W Seaman Ave, Freeport, NY 11520, (516)546-3754.

WATSON, DIANE EDITH
State senator. **Personal:** Born Nov 12, 1933, Los Angeles, CA; daughter of Dorothy Elizabeth O'Neal Watson and William Allen Louis Watson. **Educ:** Los Angeles City Coll, AA; Univ

of CA Los Angeles, BA 1956; CA State Los Angeles, MS 1967; Claremont College, PhD, educ administration 1986. **Career:** LAUSD, teacher 1956-60, asst prin & teacher 1963-68; AUS Okinawa & France, teacher 1960-63; LAUSD Child Welfare & Attendance, asst supr 1968-69; Dept of Guidance LAUSD, school psychologist 1969-70; Cal State LA Dept of Guidance, assoc prof 1969-70; UCLA Secondary Schools Allied Health Proj, dep dir 1969-71; Health Occupation LAUSD, specialist 1971-73; LAUSD, school psychologist 1973-75; Bd of Educ, mem 1975-78; California State Senate, District 28, senator, 1978-, Health and Human Services Committee, chairperson 1981-. **Orgs:** Democratic National Committee; founder, president National Organization of Black Elected Legislative Women; CA Elected Women's Assn for Educ & Rsch; Natl Adv Panel mem UCLA Ctr for Study of Evaluation; mem Med Policy Comm; author & adv com mem McGraw Hill/Gregg Div; consult CA Commn on the Status of Women; participant Career Orientation Manual; mem Natl Sch Bds Assn; mem CA Sch Bds Assn; mem CA Assn of Sch Psychologists & Psychometrists; mem LA Elem Counseling & Guidance Assn; mem United Teachers of LA; mem CA Tchrs Assn; Hon Life mem PTA; mem exec bd Council of Great Cities Schs; bd mem Stevens House; mem Friends of Golden State Minority Found; mem Natl Black Womens Polit Caucus; mem Council of Black Admins; mem CA Dem Central Com Educ Comm; mem NAACP; mem Media Women Inc; Alpha Kappa Alpha National Sorority. **Honors/Awds:** CA State Univ of LA Alumnus of the Yr Awd 1980; LA Comm Coll Alumnus of the Yr Awd 1980; Outstanding Rep Awd from the Sacramento Assn of Black Attorneys 1981; UCLA Alumnus of the Yr Awd 1982; Comm Coll Senator of the Yr Awd 1983; Legislator of the Year, State Council on Developmental Disabilities, 1987; Black Woman of Achievement Award, NAACP Legal Defense Fund, 1988; CA State Psychological Assn Humanitarian Awd; Bank of Amer Awd; Outstanding Comm Serv Awd YWCA; Mary Ch Terrell Awd; author: Health Occupations Instructional Units-Secondary Schools, 1975; Planning Guide for Health Occupations, 1975; co-author, Introduction to Health Care, 1976. **Business Addr:** Senator, State of CA, 4401 Crenshaw, Ste 300, Los Angeles, CA 90043.

WATSON, EUGENIA BASKERVILLE
Educator (retired). **Personal:** Born Oct 1, 1919, Bridgeport, CT; married J Mervyn; children: James Jr, Donald, Charles. **Educ:** A&T Coll, BS 1941; Bridgewater St Coll; MEd 1964. **Career:** War Dept, Washington, secretary 1942; Army Ordinance Dept, Detroit, sec 1942-43; stat clk, homemaker, grad student to 1963; Brockton Sch Dept, Brockton, 1963-68; Bridgewater St Coll, asst prof educ 1968; Brockton Business Coll, 1964-66; student under Univ CT, traveled W Africa 1970; student under Howard Univ Washington, DC, East Africa 1971; student under NAACP, traveled W Africa 1974. **Orgs:** Lecturer African History & Culture; mem Natl Teachers Assn, MA Teachers Assn, Urban League of Eastern MA, Brockton Mayors Adv Comm for Cable TV; life mem NAACP; 2nd vice pres local br NAACP; black history instr Summer School Inst; mem Lincoln Congregational Church, Amer Mothers Assn 1969, MA State Merit Mother 1969, Natl Black All Grad Level Educ, Educators to Africa & African Amer Inst, NY Delta Kappa Gamma Intl Hon Soc, Women Educators, Alpha Kappa Chap Alpha Upsilon St Orgn, Professional Womens Club Boston, Natl Jack & Jill Amer Inc; bd trustees Brockton Library System 1971-; bd dir Brockton Vstg Nurse Assn 1972-75; pres 1977-79, membership chmn 1987- Links Inc Middlesex County Chapt; exec bd Parliamentarian Link Chap 1980-; adv bd Brockton Art Museum 1980-;professor emeritus Bridgeer State Coll 1985; vstg lecturer Bridgewater State Coll; supv of student teachers Early Childhood and Elementary 1985-. **Honors/Awds:** Distinguished Serv Awd MA Teachers Assoc 1985; Outstanding Serv Awd Bridgewater State Coll Alumni Assoc 1985; Awd of Recognition Brockton Chap NAACP 1985.

WATSON, FRED D.
Contractor. **Personal:** Born Jul 3, 1919, Loris, SC; married Ilean; children: Martin. **Educ:** Small Engine Repair 1980. **Career:** Paint Store, owner, contractor. **Orgs:** Council mem 16 yrs; deacon of church; mason for 20 yrs. **Honors/Awds:** Cert of Achievement; Outstanding Work in Loris Community. **Military Serv:** Staff sgt 4 1/2 yrs; Good Conduct Medal. **Business Addr:** Contractor, 3824 Church St, Loris, SC 29569.

WATSON, GENEVIEVE
Educator. **Personal:** Born Apr 2, 1950, Gilbert, LA; daughter of Laura Gilbert Thomas and Joe Thomas Jr; married Alvin Watson Jr, Jun 16, 1972; children: Alvin L Watson, Gene L Watson, Thomas L Watson. **Educ:** Grambling College, Grambling, LA, BA, 1972; Drake University, Des Moines, IA, MAT, 1978. **Career:** Drake University, Des Moines, IA, special services coordinator, 1974-81; asst dir of financial aid, 1981-85; associate dir of financial aid, 1985-86; University of AZ, Tucson, AZ, asst dir of financial aid, 1986-88, acting assoc dean of students, 1989-90, assoc dir of financial aid, 1988-95; Phoenix College, Phoenix, AZ, dir of financial aid, 1995-. **Orgs:** Exec council, rep at large minority concerns chair, Western Assn of Student Fin Aid Admn, 1990-92; past president, president, pres-elect, exec council, AZ Assn of Student Fin Aid Administrators, 1990-93; vice pres, 1989-90; minority concerns committee, exec council, Mid-West Assn of Student Fin Aid Admn, 1983-86; pres, IA Assn of Student Fin Aid Admn, 1986, pres-elect, 1985-86, vice pres, 1984-85, sec, 1983-84, college scholarship service governance Comm, College Bd, 1984-86, comm mem, IA Governor's Task Force on Ed, 1985-86; Tucson United Way, Fund Distribution Steering Com, 1995; College bd, Western Regional Planning Com, 1994; bd of dir, National Association of Student Financial Aid Administrators, 1996-99; Fund Development Com, co-chair, Western Assn of Student Fin Aid Admn, 1997-98. **Honors/Awds:** Nominated for UA Award for Excellence, University of AZ, 1990; presenter: "The Tax Reform Act & Student Fin Aid," NASFAA, 1988; "Successful Strategies for Ethnic Individuals," "Critical Issues in Graduate and Professional School Financial Aid," WASFAA, 1992; first Black female president of AASFAA (1991-92) and IASFAA (1986). **Business Addr:** Director, Financial Aid, Phoenix College, 1202 W Thomas Rd, Phoenix, AZ 85013.

WATSON, GEORGETTE
State official, association executive. **Personal:** Born Dec 9, 1943, Philadelphia, PA; daughter of Louise Watson. **Educ:** Univ of Massachusetts, Boston, Legal degree, 1979, BA, 1980; Antioch Univ, M Educ, 1981. **Career:** Dorchester Comm News, writer, 1982, 1983-; Massachusetts Commn Against Discrimination, investigator; Roxbury Multi-Ser Anti-Crime, assoc mem, 1984-; FIRST Inc, assoc mem, 1985-; Parent's Discussion Support, founder, 1987-; Mother's Against Drugs, co-founder, 1987-; Drop A Dime Intelligence Data Inc, pres, co-founder, 1983-; Governor's Alliance Against, Drugs, exec dir, currently. **Orgs:** Mem, NAACP, 1987-; assoc mem, United Front Against Crime Area B, 1987-; bd mem, Boston Gr Legal Comm Liaison Program; mediator Boston Urban Court Program. Mayor's Anti-Creme Council 1989-. **Honors/Awds:** Massachusetts Assn of Afro-Amer Police Inc Award, 1984; Shamnim Soc of Massachusetts In Appreciation to Georgette Watson, 1985; Comm Serv Award Boston Branch of NAACP, 1985; Martin Luther King Award Union Methodist Church, 1985; Disting Serv Award Eastern Region of Alpha Phi Alpha Fraternity, Inc, 1986; A Woman Meeting the Challenges of Time Award Boston Chapter Girlfriends Inc, 1986; Tribute to Women Award Cambridge YWCA, 1986; Citizen of the Year Award, Kiwanis Club of Roxbury, 1986; Comm Serv Award Action for Boston Comm Devel, 1986; 100 Heroes Newsweek, 1986; 1987 Black Outstanding Women, Essence Magazine, 1987; Sojourner Truth, Natl Assn of Negro Business & Professional Women's Club, 1989; President's Citation Volunteer Program, 1989. FBI Award 1990. **Business Addr:** Executive Director, Governor's Alliance Against Drugs, 1 Ashburton Place, Room 611, Boston, MA 02108.

WATSON, HERMAN DOC
Security specialist. **Personal:** Born Nov 10, 1931, Jersey City, NJ; married Shirley Moss, Apr 30, 1955; children: Phillip, Alan, Tracey, Elliott. **Educ:** Hofstra Univ, Criminal Justice course 1974; Georgetown Univ, Criminal Justice course 1977. **Career:** US Customs Svcs, criminal investigator 1952-82; Jersey City Bd of Educ, security guard 1982-. **Orgs:** Pres Jersey City Vikings Inc 1982-; vice chief antler Passexalted Ruler Council #17 IBPOE of W; scholarship and archives comm Most Worshipful Oriental GrandLodge AF&AM Masons; co-chairperson Hudson County United Negro Coll Fund Telethon. **Honors/Awds:** Outstanding Serv Awd Sentinel Soc Inc 1978; Certificate of Appreciation Concern Comm Women Inc 1981; Comm Achievement Awd Martin Luther King Jr Assoc1987; Andrew Young Black Male Achievement Awd Tau Gamma Delta Sor Inc Lambda Omega Chap 1987. **Military Serv:** NJNG sfc 10 yrs. **Home Addr:** 232 Union St, Jersey City, NJ 07304.

WATSON, J. WARREN
Judge. **Personal:** Born Feb 20, 1923, Pittsburgh, PA; son of Eula Henderson Watson (deceased) and James Warren Watson (deceased); married Carole A Whedbee; children: James Guy, Meredith Gay Young, Wrenna Leigh, Robert Craig, Sheila Tyler, Kevin McDowell. **Educ:** Duquesne Univ, BA Political Sci, Econ 1949, LLB 1953. **Career:** Private practice, atty 1954-66; City of Pittsburgh, city solicitor 1960-66; Commonwealth of PA, judge 1966-. **Orgs:** Bd mem Judicial Inquiry & Review Bd 1981-85; chmn Media Rel Comm Bd of Judges 1984; bd mem Estate Planning Comm State Trial Judges Conf 1984; pres council Carlow Coll; bd of dir Comm Action Pittsburgh; trustee Comm Serv of PA. **Honors/Awds:** Man of the Year Disabled Amer Veterans 1969; Hon Mem Chiefs of Police; Certificate of Merit Natl Assoc of Negro Business Professional Civic & Cultural & Political Endeavor 1972. **Military Serv:** USN 3 yrs. **Business Addr:** Judge, Commonwealth of Pennsylvania, 1700 Frick Bldg, Pittsburgh, PA 15219.

WATSON, JACKIE
Police officer. **Personal:** Born Oct 29, 1968, Jackson, MS; daughter of Laura & Jerry Watson. **Educ:** Criminal Justice, BS, 1994; GWP & Counseling, MSEd, 1998. **Career:** Jackson Police Dept, police woman, 1992-. **Orgs:** NAACP; Police Union Association. **Home Addr:** 340 Arbor Dr, No 2281, Ridgeland, MS 39157, (601)957-5884.

WATSON, JAMES L.
Judge (retired). **Personal:** Born May 21, 1922, New York, NY; son of Violet M Lopez and James S Watson; married D'Jaris Hinton (deceased); children: Karen, Kris. **Educ:** New York University, BA, 1947; Brooklyn Law School, JDS, 1951. **Career:** 21st Senate District, New York State Senate, senator, 1954-63; City of New York, civil court judge, 1963-66. **Orgs:** Bd of directors, 100 Black Men; American Judges Assn; bd or managers, Harlem YMCA. **Military Serv:** AUS 92nd Inf Div Comat Inf 1942-45; Purple Heart. **Business Addr:** Senior Judge, Court of Intl Trade, 1 Federal Plaza, New York, NY 10007.

WATSON, JOANN NICHOLS
Civil rights executive. **Personal:** Born Apr 19, 1951, Detroit, MI; daughter of Rev Lestine Kent Nichols Franklin and Jefferson Nichols Sr (deceased); divorced; children: Damon Gerard, Celeste Nicole, Stephen Bernard, Maya Kristi. **Educ:** Univ of Michigan-Ann Arbor, BA, 1972; Michigan State University, 1975-76; New York University, Institute for Educational Leadership, Educational Policy Fellowship Program, 1987-88. **Career:** Community Parents Child Care Center, executive director, 1973-75; Lake Michigan College, instructor, racism & sexism, 1975-76; Coalition for Peaceful Integration, editor, social worker, 1976-77; Focus Hope, resource coordinator, 1978; YWCA of Metro Detroit, branch executive director, 1976-87; YWCA of the USA, asst executive director, 1987-90; NAACP, Detroit Branch, executive director, 1990-97; Daily Urban Announcer Talk Show Host, WGPR "Wake Up Detroit, Joann Watson Show," 1996-; Editorial columnist Michigan Citizen 50,000 subscribers, 1996-. **Orgs:** Natl Council of Negro Women 1979-; MI Women's Hall of Fame Review Panel 1982-; Racial Justice Working Group of Natl Council of Churches 1987-; Assn of Black Women in Higher Educ 1987-; Black Child Devel Inst 1987-; vice pres, Mich NAACP 1982-87; exec bd, Natl Project Equality of EEO 1988-; pres, New York Alumni of NYU Inst for Educ Leadership 1988-; Natl Interreligious Civil Rights Commission 1988-; board of directors, American Red Cross, 1992; YWCA, Detroit; Center for Democratic Renewal; American Civil Liberties Union (ACLU), bod, 1992-; New Detroit, Inc, bod, 1996-; Cranbrook Peace Foundation, honorary trustee, 1992-; "Women on Board," Coalition for Women on Corporate Boards, American Jewish Committee, founder and co-chair, 1994-; National Association of Blacks in Radio, 1995-; Ctr for the Study of Harassment of African-American, co-founder, vice chair of natl board, 1991-; Natl Lawyers Guild, advisory bd mem, 1993-; Natl Council on Alcoholism & Other Dependencies, bd mem, 1991-; United Way Community Services, bd mem and exec committee mem, 1991-; Natl Alliance Against Racist and Political Repression, natl bd mem, 1992-; Self Help Addiction Rehabilitation, bd mem, 1994-; Detroit Women's Forum, bod, 1995; Women's Conference of Concerns, mem, 1979-; Wayne State Univ, Upward Bound Alumni Assn, 1980-; Pay Equity Network, Coalition of Labor Union Women, mem, 1991-; numerous others. **Honors/Awds:** NAACP, Thalheimer Awds, Newsletter Editor, Michigan Mobilizer, 1978-88; State of Mich Governor & Legislator Proclamation, 1987; City of Detroit "Spirit of Detroit" Awd, 1987; Life Achievement Awd, Womens Equality Day, City of Detroit, 1987; Hall of Fame Award, YWCA of Detroit, 1987-88; organizer & co-sponsor, Martin Luther King 1st Annual Youth Conference, 1988; vice chair, 25th Commemorative March in Washington, 1988; Minority Women's Network, "Civil Rights Activist of the Year," 1990; Natl Anti-Klan Network, "Special Recognition" Awd, 1996; The African-American Alumni of the Univ of Michigan, Distinguished Alumnus of the Year, Leonard Sain Awd, 1996; Doctor of Humane Letters, Lewis College of Business, Honorary Doctorate, 1996; Ameritech Black Advocacy Panel, Humanitarian of the Year Award, 1996; Detroit College of Law, Humanitarian Awd, 1996; Nigerian Foundation of Michigan, Special Recognition Awd, 1996; Michigan Civil Rights Commission, Distinguished Svc Commemoration Award, 1995; East Side Slate, Outstanding Comm Svc Award, 1996; Malcolm X Academy, Ancestors Day Awd, 1996; Natl Council of Negro Women, Outstanding Comm Leader Awd, Detroit Section, 1994; Detroit Urban League, Distinguished Comm Svc Awd, 1995; US Dept of Labor, Working Women Count Leadership Awd, 1996; WXYZ-TV - Channel 7, Outstanding Women Awd, 1995; Natl Lawyers Guild, Detroit Chap, Anniversary Awd, 1994; Natl Council of Negro Women, Natl Tribute to Women Awd, 1994; Alternatives for Girls, Annual Awd, 1994; Bennett Coll, Greensboro, NC, Distinguished Achievement Awd, 1994; Senate Star of MI, Tribute Awd, 1994; City Council Resolution, Tribute Awd, 1994; Wayne County Comm, Tribute Awd, 1994; City of Detroit, Mayoral Proclamation, Tribute Awd, 1994; United Comm Svcs, Tribute Awd, 1994; Natl Political Congress of Black Women, Distinguished Svc Awd, 1994; Wayne County Clerk, Tribute Awd, 1994; Detroit City Clerk, Tribute Awd, 1994; Inner City Sub Center, Distinguished Svc Awd, 1994; Annual Malcolm X Comm Ctr, African Heritage Awd, 1993; Mich Civil Rights Commission, Distinguished Achievement Awd, 1994; Zeta Phi Beta Sorority, Inc, Woman of the Year Awd, Beta Omicron Zeta Chap, 1994; numerous others. **Home Phone:** (313)934-1557.

WATSON, JOHN CLIFTON
Journalist. **Personal:** Born Jan 22, 1954, Jersey City, NJ; son of John & Clementine Watson; married Laura St Martin, Nov 13, 1994. **Educ:** Rutgers Coll, BA, 1975; Rutgers Univ, School of Law, JD, 1980. **Career:** Jersey City State Coll, writing instructor, 1992-94; Rutgers Coll Newark, journalism instructor, 1992-; The Jersey Journal, news editor, reporter, 1975-. **Orgs:** Garden State Assn of Black Journalists, 1992-. **Honors/Awds:** North Jersey Press Assn, 1st Place Spot News Reporting Award, 1983; NJ Press Assn, 1st Place Spot News Reporting Award, 1983; Hudson County Newspaper Guild, Sports Writing Award, 1983. **Business Addr:** News Editor, The Jersey Journal Newspaper, 30 Journal Sq, 3rd Fl Newsroom, Jersey City, NJ 07306, (201)217-3560.

WATSON, JOSEPH W.
Educator. **Personal:** Born Apr 16, 1940, New York, NY; married Mary Slater; children: Ruth, Jerome, Jennifer, Elizabeth. **Educ:** City Coll of NY, BS 1961; UCLA, PhD 1966, postdoctoral 1966. **Career:** UCSD, asst prof 1970-; Third Coll UCSD, provost 1970, UCSD, assoc prof, 1966, prof, 1987. **Orgs:** Mem Am Chem Soc; Nat Orgn for Professional & Advancement of Black Chems & Chem Engrs; CA Black Coll Faculty & Staff Assn Inc; CA Student Aid Commission, 1987-, chair, 1990-92; life mem, NAACP; life mem, Urban League. **Honors/Awds:** Anniversary Medal, City Coll of NY 1973; Outst Young Man, San Diego 1975. **Business Addr:** D-009, U of California San Diego, La Jolla, CA 92093.

WATSON, JUANITA
Councilwoman. **Personal:** Born Apr 26, 1923, Birmingham, AL; married Joe. **Educ:** Miles Coll. **Career:** Brownville; councilwoman 1972. **Orgs:** Mem Civic League of Brownville; Bessemer Voter League; comm mem Dem Exec Com Jefferson Co; vice pres Les Amies; vice pres Matrons, Sunday Sch Tchr & mem of Sr Choir New Bethel Bapt Ch.

WATSON, KAREN ELIZABETH
Communications company executive. **Personal:** Born Sep 11, 1957, New York, NY; daughter of James L Watson & D'Jaris E Hinton; children: Erika Faith Allen, James Austin Allen. **Educ:** Bard Coll, BA, American studies, 1979. **Career:** Mondale - Ferraro Presidential Campaign, press advance, 1984; Select Comm on Narcotics Abuse & Control, US House of Representatives, press secretary, 1983-85; Capitol Journal, Washington DC, reporter, researcher, 1985; Public Broadcasting Service, Alexandria VA, assoc dir, news & public affairs, 1985-92; Southern Ctr for Internatl Studies, Atlanta GA, television & educ consultant, 1993-94; WGBH Educ Foundation, Boston MA, deputy proj dir, Africans in America, 1992-94; Echostar Communications Corp, govt affairs director, currently. **Orgs:** Radio & Television News Directors Assn. **Honors/Awds:** WGBH Educ Foundation, WGBH Appreciation Award, 1991-93. **Special Achievements:** Judge Robert F Kennedy Awards, Outstanding Coverage of the Disadvantaged, 1990; Judge Corporation for Public Broadcasting Local programming Awards, 1985-93.

WATSON, LEONIDAS
Educator. **Personal:** Born Sep 12, 1910, Fodice, TX; married Lelia Landry. **Educ:** Prairie View U, bS 1936, MS 1952; Univ of TX, grad study; Ok St U. **Career:** San Antonio Union Jr Coll Dist, dean Evening Div; St Philips Coll, instr 1954; Ext Serv Grime Co, TX, 1943-54; Houston Co, instr 1936-43; independent real estate broker. **Orgs:** Charter mem Eastside Optimist Club; Basileus, Psi Alpha Chap Omega Psi Phi; v chmn trustee bd, St Paul Meth Ch; Charter mem bd Dir Comm Housing Assn; Century Mem UMCA; mem Epsilon Pi Tau Internat; mem City Pub Serv Bd Contracts Gas Distbr, San Antonio 1974; Phi Delta Kappa 1974; mem Jr Coll Tchrs Assn; mem Jr Coll Adminstrs. **Honors/Awds:** Spl Citation from TX Leg for Contrib to Educ 1973; Comm Awd for Contrib to Educ 1957; Citation KUKA Radio 1974; Citizen for Day WOAI Radio 1974. **Business Addr:** 2111 Nevada St, San Antonio, TX 78203.

WATSON, MILDRED L.
Attorney. **Personal:** Born May 25, 1923, Kansas City, MO; daughter of Arnicholas North Watson (deceased) and Stewart B Watson (deceased). **Educ:** Lincoln Univ MO, BS 1942; Univ Chicago, MA 1954; Univ MO Kansas City, JD 1974. **Career:** USN Dept Washington, mathematician 1943-45; Chicago Welfare Dept & Amer Red Cross Chicago, social worker 1946-52; Bureau Family Serv Chicago, child welfare supvr 1953-57; Univ KS Med Center, chief social worker 1957-62; Univ KS, assoc prof 1963-76; North Colbert Fields Law Firm, assoc 1976-81; North Watson & Bryant Law Firm, 1981-84; Jackson Co Circuit Court, comm juvenile div 1984-. **Orgs:** MO Bar Assn; mem Jackson Co Bar Assn; mem Kansas City Bar Assn; life mem NAACP; past pres Beta Omega Chapter Alpha Kappa Alpha; mem Twin Citians Club of Greater Kansas City; mem, Natl Council of Juvenile & Family Judges, 1984-; mem, advisory council, Urban League, 1984-. **Honors/Awds:** Community Serv, Natl Assn, Business & Professional Women, 1984; key woman, Urban League Guild, 1985; Educ & Social Serv, Essence Magazine, 1985; public serv, Univ of MO, Kansas City Law Found, 1989. **Business Addr:** Commissioner, Juvenile Div, Jackson County Circuit Court, 625 E 26th St, Kansas City, MO 64108.

WATSON, MILTON H.
Business executive (retired). **Personal:** Born Mar 12, 1927, Detroit, MI; son of Fannie M Watson and Elzie L Watson; married Mary Kathryn; children: Milton P, Kathryn M. **Educ:** Univ of MI, MSW 1962; Wayne State Univ, BA 1949. **Career:** OMNI Care Health Plan, corporate secretary, bd of trustees, 1971-; Health Council Inc, exec dir; Millar Agency Equitable Life Assurance Soc, asst agency mgr; State of MI, suprv childrens div dept of soc svc; Harvard Univ JF Kennedy School of Govt, lecturer 1971; Univ of MI School of Publ Health, lecturer 1971; Cottillion Club, fin sec 1971-84. **Orgs:** Mem Amer Publ Health Assoc, Natl Assoc of Social Workers. **Military Serv:** USMC. **Business Addr:** Corporate Secretary, Omni Care Health Plan, 1155 Brewery Park Blvd, Ste 250, Detroit, MI 48207.

WATSON, PERRY
College basketball coach. **Personal:** Born May 1, 1950, Detroit, MI; married Deborah; children: Paris. **Educ:** Eastern Michigan University, bachelor's degree, 1972, master's degree, 1976. **Career:** Southwestern High School, Detroit, boy's basketball coach, counselor, 1979-90; Nike all-star camp, director; University of Michigan, assistant men's basketball coach, 1990-93; Univ of Detroit-Mercy, head basketball coach, 1993-. **Special Achievements:** Team won two state championships as coach of Detroit's Southwestern High School; Top asst at the Univ of Michigan during two seasons which team reached NCAA championship game. **Business Addr:** Head Basketball Coach, University of Detroit-Mercy, PO Box 19900, 4001 W McNichols, Detroit, MI 48219-0900, (313)993-1731.

WATSON, PERRY, III
Automobile dealer. **Personal:** Born Apr 16, 1951, Muskegon Heights, MI; son of Roberta Watson and Perry Watson Jr; married Ida Janice Reynolds Watson, Aug 4, 1979; children: Perry, Robert, Anthony, Maya. **Educ:** Western Michigan University, BBA, 1973, MBA, 1976. **Career:** Keene Corp., purchasing agent, 1974; County of Muskegon, contract specialist, 1975; Xerox Corp., account representative, 1977-83, marketing mgr, 1980-83, sales operations mgr, 1983-85, district systems mgr, 1985-90; Brookdale Dodge, president, 1993-. **Orgs:** Omega Psi Phi Fraternity; Jack & Jill of America; Executive Black Forum; Boy Scouts of America; Black Men on the Rise; Chrysler Minority Dealers Association. **Business Addr:** President, Brookdale Dodge, Inc, 6800 Brooklyn Blvd, Brooklyn Center, MN 55429, (612)560-8000.

WATSON, ROBERT C.
Educator. **Personal:** Born Mar 2, 1947, Hazelhurst, MS; married Aisya JK; children: Tarik Emilio. **Educ:** Tougaloo Coll, BS 1965; Washington Univ, MA 1973. **Career:** Anderson Bank Nichols & Levanthal MS, rsch asst 1969; Manpower Inst St Louis, consult 1974; Lever Bros Co, quality control tech; Vaughn Cultural Ctr/Urban League of Metropolitan St Louis, director. **Orgs:** Counselor YMCA Camp Becket MA 1966; mem Univ City MO Comm on Human Rel; mem Big Bros of Amer Inc; mem Amer Chem Soc 1968-69; mem of experiment in Intl Living Expidition to Ghana W Africa; Operation Crossroads Africa Kenya 1984; mem Alpha Phi Alpha Frat Inc; spec achievement researched blk Historical College. **Honors/Awds:** Author "History of Black Protest vs Official Lies" 1975. **Business Addr:** St Louis Urban League, 3701 Grandel Square, ATTN: Adrian Gainesy, St Louis, MO 63108.

WATSON, ROBERT JOSE (BOB WATSON)
Former baseball administrator. **Personal:** Born Apr 10, 1946, Los Angeles, CA; married Carol, Oct 5, 1968; children: Keith, Kelley. **Educ:** Attended, LA Harbor Coll. **Career:** NY Yankees, professional baseball player, beginning 1979; Boston Red Sox, 1979; Houston Astros, outfielder; Oakland A's, full-time batting coach; Houston Astros, general mgr, beginning 1988; NY Yankees, general manager, until 1997. **Orgs:** Board member, YMCA/Metro, Houston, 1988-; honorary board member, UNCF, Houston, 1989-. **Honors/Awds:** Nat Leag All Star 1973-75; Led FL St Leag Catchers in Double Plays (14) 1966; plyd in All Star Games 1973 & 1975; established Major Leag Record by Hitting for the Cycle in both Leags 1977 & 1979; tied Major Leag Record Fewest Times Caught Stealing 1 Season (0) 1977; Hall of Fame, Houston Astros, 1989. **Military Serv:** US Marine Corps, sgt, 1966-71. **Business Addr:** Former General Manager, NY Yankees, 161st St and River Ave, Yankee Stadium, Bronx, NY 10451.

WATSON, ROBERTA CONWELL
Educator. **Personal:** Born Sep 14, Windsor, NC; daughter of Ruth E S Conwell and Johnnie E Conwell; married Leroy Watson Jr. **Educ:** George Washington Univ, MA, reading; Bowie University, BS, elem ed. **Career:** DC School Board, Washington, DC, elem ed teacher, gifted & talented teacher; Prince Georges Community College, math teacher; District of Columbia School Board, Washington, DC, reading teacher; Norfolk, Virginia, Schools, substitute teacher, currently. **Honors/Awds:** Outstanding Teacher, District of Columbia Schools, 1977; Award of Excellence, District of Columbia Schools, 1977; Principal's Award, District Schools, 1988; Embassy Adoption Program, District of Columbia Schools, 1984; Outstanding Service Award, District of Columbia Schools, 1985, written numerous children's articles, all published.

WATSON, SOLOMON B., IV
Lawyer. **Personal:** Born Apr 14, 1944, Salem, NJ; son of Denise A Jones Watson and S Brown Watson Jr (deceased); married Brenda J Hendricks Watson, Apr 28, 1984; children: Katitti M, Kira P. **Educ:** Howard University, Washington, DC, BA in English, 1966; Harvard Law School, Cambridge, MA, JD, 1971. **Career:** Bingham, Dana & Gould, Boston, MA, associate, 1971-74; New York Times Co, New York, attorney, 1974-76, asst secretary, 1976-79, secretary, 1979-89, gen counsel, 1989, asst gen counsel, 1984, general counsel/vice pres, 1990-96, sr vp & gen counsel, 1996-. **Orgs:** New York and Massachusetts Bars; Amer Bar Assn; Association of the Bar of the City of New York, committee on corporates law departments, legal affairs committee of the Newspaper Association of America, board of volunteers of Legal Services, Inc; Legal Aid Society; advisory board of the Agent Orange Settlement Fund. **Military Serv:** US Army, 1st lt, 1966-68; 2 Bronze Stars; 2 Army Commendation Medals. **Business Addr:** Senior VP, General Counsel, The New York Times Co., 229 West 43rd Street, New York, NY 10036.

WATSON, SUSAN
Journalist. **Personal:** Born 1942. **Educ:** Univ of Michigan. **Career:** Detroit Free Press, reporter, 1965-79, asst city editor, 1979, city editor, 1980-83, columnist, currently. **Honors/Awds:** Knigt-Ridder Inc, Editorial Award of Excellence, 1993. **Business Addr:** Columnist, Detroit Free Press, 321 W. Lafayette Blvd., Detroit, MI 48226.

WATSON, THERESA LAWHORN
Business executive, attorney. **Personal:** Born Jun 15, 1945, Washington, DC. **Educ:** Howard Univ Wash DC, BA (cum laude) 1969; Geo Wash Univ Nat Law Cen DC, JD 1973; Indiana Univ Grad School of Savings and Loan, certificate, 1982. **Career:** Am Savs & Loan Leag Inc, exec vice pres 1980-88; Dechert Price & Rhoads, aso atty 1979-80; Senate Subcom on Housing & Urban Affairs, asst minority cnsl 1977-79; Office of Gen cnsl HUD, atty-adv 1973-77; Practicing Attorney, 1988-. **Orgs:** Mem DC Bar 1973; mem US Dist Ct 1974; mem US Supreme Ct 1976; treas Women's Bar Assn of DC 1979-80; mem Bd of Appeals & Review DC 1979-80; mem Women in Hosing & Fin; mem Am Nat Fed Bar Assn 1973-; treas MA Black Lwyrs Assn 1976-77; mem exec com Black Senate Lgsltv Staffers 1977-78; chairman, bd of dir, DC Housing Fin Agency 1982-85; bd of dir Women in Housing & Fin 1980; 1986-90, trustee, DC Retirement board, chairman, 1988-90. **Business Addr:** 717 D St NW, Ste 210, Washington, DC 20004.

WATSON, THOMAS S., JR.
Business advisor, author, speaker. **Personal:** Born in Cleveland, OH; son of Geraldine Wray Watson and Thomas S. Watson; married; children: Kimberly, Timothy, Andrew. **Educ:** Cleveland State University, Cleveland, OH, BBA, 1970, MBA, 1976; Case Western Reserve University, Cleveland, OH, 1973-74; Harvard Business School, Boston, MA, 1979-83. **Career:** General Motors, Inc, Cleveland, OH, accountant, 1968-69; Ernst & Whinney, Cleveland, OH, accountant, 1969-70; Touche Ross, Cleveland, OH, accountant, 1970; Watson, Rice & Co, Washington, DC, chairman, author/intl advisor, 1971-91. **Orgs:** Polytech Inc, bd of dirs; life member, Alpha Phi Alpha Fraternity; life member, NAACP; North American Free Trade Agreement, GATT, US delegations for negotiations; Voices in the Glen, storyteller; Natl Assn of Black Storytellers; American Muslim Council, bd of dirs. **Honors/Awds:** Outstanding Leader, White House Conference on Small Business, 1986; Award of Excellence, Metrolina World Trade Assn, 1990; Kentucky Colonel, 1990; Small Business Champion, Congressman Andy Ireland, 1990; Distinguished Alumnus, Cleveland State Univ, 1990; Small Business Advocate of the Year, US Small Business Administration; selected to represent the United States private sector as an official member of the negotiating team for the General Agreement on Tariffs and Trade, 1990; Texas governor Ann Richards, citation, 1992; Presidents Award, Literary Excellence, 1997. **Business Addr:** Author/Intl Advisor, Watson Rice, LLP, PO Box 34071, Washington, DC 20043, (202)371-9005.

WATSON, TONY J.
Military officer. **Personal:** Born May 18, 1949, Chicago, IL; son of John & Virginia Watson; married Sharon, Jul 21, 1984; children: Erica, Lindsay. **Educ:** Harvard Univ, Natl Security Studies, 1992; US Naval Academy, BS, 1970; Golden Gate Univ, Pursuing MBA, 1989-. **Career:** Potomac Electric Power Co, operations coord, 1981-83; USS Birmingham, SSN 695, weapons officer, 1983-84; USS Hammerhead, SSN 663, exec officer, 1984-86; USS Jacksonville, SSN 699, commanding officer, 1987-89; US Naval Academy, deputy commandant, 1989-93; Submarine Squadron 7, commander, 1992-93; Ops, Natl Military Command Ctr, deputy dir, 1993-. **Orgs:** US Naval Inst, mem, 1987-; Naval Submarine League, mem, 1993-; Natl Naval Officers Assn, mem, past chapter pres, currently. **Honors/Awds:** Navy League of US, Most Outstanding Officer, 1976; Council of Deans of Engineering of the HBCU's, Black Engineer of Year, Govt, 1988; Amer Heritage & Freedom Award, 3rd Baptist Church, 1990; NAACP, Roy Wilkins Leadership Award, 1991; State of IL, Order of Lincoln Award, 1994. **Special Achievements:** Nuclear Submarine & Submarine Squad-

ron, 13 subs, Commander, 1987, 1992; Recipient of Rear Admiral Kauffman Sword, as person most likely to become future superintendent of US Naval Academy; First African American Submarine Officer ever to become US Navy Admiral. **Military Serv:** US Navy, rear admiral, 1970-; Legion of Merit Medal, 1993; 4 Meritorious Service Medals, 1987-92; 3 Navy Commendation Medals, 1976, 1983, 1985; 1 Navy Achievement Medal, 1974. **Business Addr:** Deputy Dir for Operations, Natl Military Command Center, US Navy, The Pentagon, Rm 28902, Washington, DC 20318-3000, (202)693-8199.

WATSON, VERNALINE
Educator. **Personal:** Born Jul 5, 1942, Hobgood, NC; daughter of Rosetter Watson and Thurman Watson. **Educ:** NC College, BA 1964, MA 1968; OH St U, PhD 1972. **Career:** Thomas Shields School Hobgood NC, 8th grade teacher 1966-67; Dept of Research Planning & Program Devel NC Fund Durham NC, historical writer 1968; St Augustine's Coll Raleigh NC, instr dept of sociology 1968-69; Div Disability Research OSU, research asst dept of physical med 1970; Mershon Center OH St Univ, research assoc 1971-72; Fisk Univ, asst prof sociology 1972-76; Center for Health Care Research Meharry Medical Coll Nashville, research assoc 1976-77; Middle Tenn Health Systems Agency, Nashville, TN, senior planner, 1977-80; Tenn state University, Nashville, TN, prof of sociology, 1980-. **Orgs:** Mem Am Soc Assn; Assn of Soc & Beh Scientists; Caucus of Black Sociologists; Acad of Polit Sci; rsrch activities Structure of Hlth Care Serv for Poor; Soc Psychol Studies in Afro-Am Womanhood; African-American Middle-Class Families; mem NAACP; YMCA; Am Civil Liberties Union. **Honors/Awds:** Fulbright Flwshp 1965-66; Vo Rehab Flwshp 1969-71. **Business Addr:** Pforessor, Department of Sociology, Tennessee State University, Nashville, TN 37209.

WATSON, WILBUR H.
Educator, medical sociologist, author. **Personal:** Born Apr 14, 1938, Cleveland; married Shirley Washington; children: Stephen, Sheryl Lynn. **Educ:** Kent St U, BA 1964, MA 1966; Univ of PA, PhD 1972. **Career:** Temple Univ Phila, asst prof of Soc 1973-; Rutgers Coll, asst prof of Soc 1970-74; Cheyney St Coll, asst prof of soc 1969-70; Kent St Univ, instr 1966-68; Lincoln Univ, instr 1966-68. **Orgs:** Mem Am Soclgcl Assn; Soc for Study of Soc Problems; Assn of Black Soclgsts; Assn for Study of African Am Life & Hist; Assn of Soc & Behvrl Scientests; mem bd govs Ctr for Rsrch on Acts of Man Univ of PA 1969-70; chmn steering com Proj-Learn;Exprmntl Elem Sch 1970-71; steering com Nat Black Alliance for Grad Level Ed 1972-74; cnsltng rsrch soclgst Stephen Smith Geriatric Ctr Philadelphia 1972-; founding ed The Black Soclgst 1975-. **Honors/Awds:** Numerous flwshps & awards; author of ''Hum Aging & Dying'' (with RJ Maxwell) 1977; ''Stress & Old Age'' 1980; other Publications.

WATT, GARLAND WEDDERICK
Judge. **Personal:** Born Feb 10, 1932, Elizabeth City, NC; married Gwendolyn LaNita Canada. **Educ:** Lab Sch, Prep Ed; Elizabeth City St University; NC Ctrl U, AB 1952; (magna cum laude); Harvard University, DePaul U, JD 1961. **Career:** Circuit Ct of Cook Co, judge 1975-; gen prac, atty 1961-75; DePaul Law Rev, asso ed 1960-61. **Orgs:** Past bd mem Independence Bk of Chgo; adv bd Supreme Life Ins Co of Am; mem Union Leag Club of Chgo; Econ Club of Chgo; bd mem Am Red Cross 1973; Chicago NAACP; v chmn, chmn Leagal Redress Com 1964-70; bd mem Joint Negro Appeal; Chicago Hearing Soc 1972-74; City Club of Chicago 1971-73. **Honors/Awds:** Recpt Richard E Westbrooks Award Cook Co Bar Assn 1972; Judical Award Cook Co Bar Assn 1975; PUSH Found Award 1977. **Business Addr:** Watt & Sawyer & Associates, 53 W Jackson Blvd, Suite 1120, Chicago, IL 60604-3701.

WATT, MELVIN L.
Congressman. **Personal:** Born Aug 26, 1945. **Educ:** University of North Carolina at Chapel Hill, BS, 1967; Yale Univ, JD, 1970. **Career:** Chambers, Stein, Ferguson & Becton, attorney, 1971-72; Ferguson, Stein, Watt, Wallas & Atkins Law Firm, attorney, partner, 1972-92; NC State Senate, 1985-87; US House of Representatives, congressman, 1992-. **Orgs:** Life member, NAACP; Mt Olive Presbyterian Church. **Honors/Awds:** Honorary degrees from Johnson C Smith University and NC A&T State University. **Special Achievements:** One of the first two African-Americans elected to Congress from North Carolina in the Twentieth Century. **Business Addr:** Congressman, US House of Representatives, 1230 Longworth HOB, Washington, DC 20515, (202)225-1510.

WATTERS, LINDA A.
Banking executive. **Personal:** Born Aug 7, 1953, Dayton, OH; daughter of Arlessie Cooper Davis and Arthur Davis; married Ronald Edd Watters, May 25, 1985. **Educ:** Bowling Green State Univ, BA 1975; Univ of Dayton, MBA 1979. **Career:** General Motors Corp, staff auditor 1978-80, financial analyst 1980-82, supervisor accts receivables 1982-84, sr market analyst 1984-87; Comerica Bank, corporate banking officer, 1988-. **Orgs:** Mem Detroit Chap Natl Black MBA Assoc 5 yrs; solicitor Boy Scouts of Amer 1985; bd mem Natl Black MBA Assoc 1986-88; mem Delta Sigma Theta Sor. **Honors/Awds:** Top 100 Black Business & Professional Women Dollars & Sense magazine 1986. **Home Addr:** 1332 Balfour Rd, Grosse Pointe Park, MI 48230. **Business Addr:** Corporate Banking Officer, Comerica Bank, 211 W Fort St, Detroit, MI 48275-1195.

WATTERS, RICHARD JAMES
Professional football player. **Personal:** Born Apr 7, 1969, Harrisburg, PA. **Educ:** Notre Dame, BA degree in design. **Career:** San Francisco 49ers, running back, 1992-94; Philadelphia Eagles, 1995-. **Honors/Awds:** American Cancer Society, Humanitarian of the Year, 1994; Pro Bowl, 1992, 1993, 1994, 1995, 1996. **Business Addr:** Professional Football Player, Philadelphia Eagles, 3501 S Broad St, Philadelphia, PA 19148, (215)463-2500.

WATTLETON, ALYCE FAYE (FAYE WATTLETON)
Broadcast journalist. **Personal:** Born Jul 8, 1943, St Louis, MO; daughter of Ozie Wattleton and George Wattleton; married Franklin Gordon (divorced). **Educ:** Ohio State Univ, BS, nursing, 1964; Columbia Univ, MS, nursing, certified nurse-midwife, 1967. **Career:** Miami Valley School of Nursing, Dayton, OH, instructor, 1964-66; Dayton Public Health Nursing Assn, asst dir of nursing, 1967-70; Planned Parenthood Assn of Miami Valley, Dayton, OH, exec dir, 1970-78; Planned Parenthood Federation of America Inc, pres, 1978-92; Tribune Entertainment, television show hostess, currently. **Orgs:** Chairperson, Young Presidents Organization, Metro Chapter; bd of dirs, Ecofund '92; bd of dirs, Natl Committee on Responsible Philanthropy; advisory council, Woodrow Wilson School of Public & Intl Affairs, Princeton Univ; advisory committee, The Nature Conservancy; natl advisory bd, Inst of Professional Excellence; advisory council, Young Sisters & Brothers Magazine, BET; mem, Women's Forum; mem, Amer Public Health Assn; board of trustees, California Wellness Foundation; board of trustees, Henry J Kaiser Family Foundation. **Honors/Awds:** Spirit of Achievement Award, Albert Einstein Coll of Med, Yeshiva Univ, 1991; GALA 10 Honoree, Birmingham Southern Coll, 1991; 20th Anniversary Advocacy Award, Natl Family Planning & Reproductive Health Assn, 1991; Honorary Doctor of Humane Letters, Bard Coll, 1991; Honorary Doctor of Humanities, Oberlin Coll, 1991; Honorary Doctor of Laws, Wesleyan Univ, 1991; Commencement Address, Antioch Univ, 1991; Women of Achievement Award, Women's Projects & Production, 1991; Claude Pepper Humanities Award, Intl Platform Assn, 1990; Pioneer of Civil Rights and Human Rights Award, Natl Conf of Black Lawyers, 1990; Florina Lasker Award, NY Civil Liberties Union Foundation, 1990; Whitney M Young Jr Service Award, Boy Scouts of America, 1990; Ministry of Women Award,Unitarian Universalist Women's Feation, 1990; Honorary Doctor of Law, Northeastern Univ Law School, 1990; Honorary Doctor of Humane Letters, Long Island Univ, 1990; Honorary Doctor of Humane Letters, Univ of Pennsylvania, 1990; Citations for Outstanding Achievement from State of Ohio House Rep, 1978; Citation for Outstanding Achievement Ohio State Univ, 1979; Margaret Sanger Award, 1992; Jefferson Public Service Award, 1992; Honored by: Hofstra University, 1992, Harverford College, 1992; Columbia School of Public Health, Dean's Distinguished Service Award, 1992.

WATTLETON, FAYE. See WATTLETON, ALYCE FAYE.

WATTLEY, THOMAS JEFFERSON
Entrepreneur. **Personal:** Born Aug 28, 1953, Dallas, TX; son of Johnnie Scott Wattley and Thomas Jefferson Wattley; married Cheryl Elizabeth Brown; children: Marissa, Scott, Elizabeth, Andrew. **Educ:** Amherst Coll, BA, 1975; Yale School of Org and Mgmt, MPPM, 1980. **Career:** The LTV Corp, coporate planner, 1980-82; Grant Thornton, sr mgmt project dir, 1982-86; Stewart-Wattley Material Handling Equipment Co, pres/CEO, starting 1987; TJW Enterprises Inc, president, CEO, 1991-. **Orgs:** Chmn bd of dirs, Creative Learning Center, 1981-86; mem bd of dir, Dallas Black C of C, 1983-; mem, Dallas Assembly 1984-, Mayor's Task Force on Housing and Economic Devel in Southern Dallas, 1985; mem bd of dirs, Child Care Partnership, Inc, 1986-; mem, Chief Exec Round Table, 1988; board member, St Paul Medical Center Foundation, currently; board member, Society of International Business Fellow, currently; board of trustees, Paul Quinn College, 1991; board member, Dallas Citizens Council, 1991; member, City of Dallas Planning and Zoning Commission, 1990. **Honors/Awds:** America's Best and Brightest Young Business Professional, Dollars and Sense Magazine, 1986; Quest for Success Award, 1989. **Home Addr:** 1620 Kent St, Dallas, TX 75203. **Business Addr:** President/CEO, TJW Enterprises Inc, 2911 Turtle Creek, Ste 300, Dallas, TX 75219.

WATTS, ANDRE
Concert pianist. **Personal:** Born Jun 20, 1946, Nuremberg. **Educ:** Peabody Conservatory Baltimore, grad; attended, the Philadelphia Academy of Music. **Career:** Philadelphia Orchestra Children's Concert, debut age 9; NY Philharmonic Orchestra, debut 1963, annual appearances; Los Angeles Philharmonic, annual appearances, toured Europe as soloist for US State Dept, 1967; Philadelphia Orchestra, annual appearances; Chicago Symphony, annual appearances; Boston Symphony, annual appearances; Cleveland Orchestra, annual appearances; other major orchestras, annual appearances; London Symphony, European debut 1966; toured Europe with leading orchestras, annually; toured Japan, 1969, biennially thereafter; toured South Amer, 1972; performed at Live from Lincoln Center, 1976, 1985; appeared at a United Nations Day performance with Eugene Ormandy and the Philadelphia Orchestra; performed at BBC presentations with the London Symphony and in solo recitals; two separate PBS telecasts with Seiji Ozawa and the Boston Symphony in performances of the Liszt A Major and the Saint Saens G minor concertos; performed in a 25th anniversary concert from Lincoln Center with the New York Philharmonic and Zubin Mehta, 1987-88; performed at the 38th annual Casals Festival; recordings, The Chopin Recital, The Schubert Recital. **Orgs:** Soloist for US State Dept; toured Soviet Union with San Francisco Symphony, 1973; narrated Copland's ''A Lincoln Portrait'' at Ford's Theatre, 1975; ten years on series ''Great Performers,'' Lincoln Ctr; Order of the Zaire Congo, 1970; Classical Action: Performing Arts Against AIDS, member. **Honors/Awds:** Hon Doctor of Music, Yale Univ, 1973; Lincoln Ctr Medallion, 1974; hon Doctor of Humanities, Albright Coll, 1975; recording artist, CBS Records; Gold Medal of Merit Award, Natl Society of Arts and Letters, 1982; Peabody Conservatory of Johns Hopkins University, Distinguished Alumni Award, 1984; Avery Fisher Prize, 1988; honorary doctorates, University of Pennsylvania, Miami University of Ohio, Trinity College, The Julliard School of Music. **Special Achievements:** Performed first full-length piano recital in the history of television, 1976; performed the first full-length recital to be aired nationally in prime time, 1985. **Business Addr:** Concert Pianist, c/o IMG Artists, 420 W 45th St, New York, NY 10036.

WATTS, ANNE WIMBUSH
Educator, educational administrator. **Personal:** Born Jan 1, 1943, Grambling, LA; daughter of V E Wimbush and R P Wimbush; married William C Watts, Mar 25, 1967; children: Michael Kevin, Christopher Nolan. **Educ:** Grambling State University, BS, 1962; University of Wisconsin, MA, 1964; Atlanta University, MA, 1966; Georgia State University, PhD, 1982. **Career:** Grambling State University, instructor, 1964-65; Jackson State University, instructor, 1965-66; Atlanta University, instructor, 1966-67; Spelman College, visiting professor, 1991; Morehouse College, class dean, professor, 1967-, director, summer academy, 1991-. **Orgs:** National Cancer Institute Advisory Committee, chairperson of curriculum committee, 1988-90; National Black Political Action Forum, consultant, 1987-89; Alpha Kappa Alpha Sorority, Inc, internat consultant, 1991-; Atlanta Job Corps Center, advisory committee, 1992-; National Council of Negro Women, 1990-; 100 Women of Atlanta, internat pub editor, 1988-. **Honors/Awds:** Phi Beta Kappa Honor Society, honorary member, 1992; Grambling State University Hall of Fame, inducted member, 1991; Golden Key National Honor Society, 1992; NAFEO Distinguished Alumni Award, nominated by GSU, 1990. **Special Achievements:** The Litteratus, founder and editor, 1984-; Three Voices, 1988; M J: Modern Job, 1991, 1992. **Home Addr:** 5245 Orange Dr, Atlanta, GA 30331, (404)349-4646. **Business Addr:** Dean, Professor, Director of Summer Academy, Morehouse College, 830 Westview Dr, Academic Support Center, Atlanta, GA 30314, (404)681-2800.

WATTS, BEVERLY L.
State official. **Personal:** Born Feb 4, 1948, Nashville, TN; daughter of Evelyn L Lindsley and William E Lindsley; divorced; children: Lauren. **Educ:** Tennessee State University, BS, sociology, 1969; Southern Illinois University, MS, 1973. **Career:** Chicago Model Cities Program, activity coordinator, 1972-74; US Department of Health, Education, and Welfare, equal opportunity specialist, 1974-78; Illinois Minority Female Business, executive director, 1987-89; US Department of Agriculture, Civil Rights/EEO, regional director, 1978-87, 1989-91; RGMA Inc, senior consultant, 1991-92; Kentucky Commission on Human Rights, executive director, currently. **Orgs:** National Urban Affairs Council, national board member, 1981-93; Affirmative Action Association, board of directors, former president, 1982-92; IAOHRA, 1993; Kentuckian Minority Purchasing Council, board member, 1993; Kentucky Council on Postsecondary Education Equal Opportunity Committee, 1993; National Association of Human Rights Workers, board member; March of Dimes Bd; Intl Assn of Human Rights, agencies bd; Leadership Louisville Bd. **Honors/Awds:** RGMA, Outstanding Contributor, 1991; US Department of Agriculture, OAE Partnership Award, 1990; Recipient of Women Executives in State Government, Attended Strategic Leadership for State Executives Program, Duke University, 1996. **Special Achievements:** Graduate of Leadership Kentucky Women's Leadership Network; selected to attend as an observer the UN Fourth World Conference for Women, Beijing, China. **Business Addr:** Executive Director, Kentucky Commission on Human Rights, 332 W Broadway, Heyburn Bldg, Ste 700, Louisville, KY 40202, (502)595-4024.

WATTS, CARL AUGUSTUS
Financial planning company executive. **Personal:** Born Jun 10, 1935, Greensboro, NC; son of Roas Louise Watts and Joseph Robert Watts; divorced; children: Carla Denise. **Educ:** Howard University, BA, 1961. **Career:** IRS, agent, 1961-64; Booz, Allen, & Hamilton, consultant, 1968-70; USAID, Department of State, foreign service officer, 1964-68; Equitable Financial

Companies, agent, 1970-92, district manager, 1978-80; Watts & Privott, Associates, president, 1980-. **Orgs:** International Association for Financial Planning, 1981-92; International Association of Registered Financial Planners, 1982-92; Estate Planning Council of Suburban Maryland, 1980-92; National Business League of Montgomery County; District of Columbia Chamber of Commerce. **Honors/Awds:** Equitable Financial Companies, Order of Excalibur, 1981, Hall of Fame, 1980, Distinguished Service Award, 1992. **Special Achievements:** Neighbor's Choice Award, 1993. **Military Serv:** US Army, corporal, 1953-56. **Business Addr:** President, Watts & Privott, Associates, 8630 Fenton St, Ste 615, Silver Spring, MD 20910, (301)585-0130.

WATTS, CHARLES DEWITT
Physician, surgeon (retired). **Personal:** Born Sep 21, 1917, Atlanta, GA; son of Ida N Hawes and Lewis Gould Watts; married Constance Merrick Watts, Jan 5, 1945; children: C Eileen Welch, Deborah C Hill, Charles D Jr, Winifred Hemphill. **Educ:** Morehouse Coll, BS 1938; Howard Univ Coll of Med, MD 1943; Freedmen's Hosp Wash DC, intern & residency. **Career:** Durham County Gen Hospital, attending surgeon; Howard Univ, instr of surgery; Cancer Clinic Freedmen's Hospital; NC Mutual Life Ins Co, sr vice pres, medical dir 1960-88; Private practice, surgeon; bd of dirs NC Mutual Life Ins Co 1965-89. **Orgs:** Past dir Student Health Serv NC Central Univ; bd dir Health Systems Agency Reg IV; chmn Ed Comm Staff of Durham Cty Gen Hosp; mem NC Health Ins Adv Bd, Inst of Med, Natl Acad of Sci; clinical instr Duke Med Ctr; past pres Durham-Orange County Med Soc; founder, dir Lincoln Comm Health Ctr, mem bd Durham C of C; past chmn bd Oper Breakthrough; mem Durham Human Relations Comm; mem Council of Inst of Med; bd dir Comm Plnng Bd; bd dir Durham United Fund; bd trustees Howard Univ; mem St Josephs AME Church; bd of dirs, Howard Univ 1975-89. **Honors/Awds:** Dr of the Year Awd Old No State Med Soc; Doctor Humane Letters, St Pauls Coll, Honorary; Diplomate American bd of surgery; Fellow of Amer Coll of Surgeons. **Home Addr:** 829 Lawson St, Durham, NC 27701.

WATTS, DAMON SHANEL
Professional football player. **Personal:** Born Apr 8, 1972, Indianapolis, IN; married Veronica; children: Alisha. **Educ:** Indiana, bachelor's degree in sports communication. **Career:** Indianapolis Colts, defensive back, 1994-. **Business Addr:** Professional Football Player, Indianapolis Colts, PO Box 535000, Indianapolis, IN 46253, (317)297-2658.

WATTS, FREDERICK, JR.
Attorney. **Personal:** Born Feb 9, 1929, New York, NY; married Janice A Cordes; children: Karen Rene, Frederick John. **Educ:** Brooklyn Law Sch, JD 1956; Coll of City of NY, BSS 1951. **Career:** New York City Police Dept, 1955-76; 6th Area Det Homicide Squad Cen Harlem, supr 1973-76; Det Squad Cen Harlem, supr 1971-73; 25th Det Squad Cen Harlem, supr 1967-71; Police Commr Confidential Investigation Unit, sgt 1965-67; New York City Police Legal Dept Leagal Div, atty 1957-65; attorney; New York City Transit Authority, hearing officer, 1984-95; Manhattan District Attorney's Office, administrative asst district attorney, 1996-. **Orgs:** Mem NAACP; 100 Black Men Inc. **Honors/Awds:** Hon atty Patrolmens Benevolent Assn New York City Police Dept 1977-; five commend Meritorious Police Duty; three commend Excellent Police Duty. **Military Serv:** AUS 1951-53. **Business Addr:** Administrative Asst District Attorney, Manhattan District Attorney's Office, 1 Hogan Pl, New York, NY 10013.

WATTS, J. C., JR.
Congressman. **Personal:** Born Nov 18, 1957, Eufaula, OK; son of Helen Watts and J C Watts Sr; married Frankie Jones Watts; children: LaKesha, Jerrell, Jennifer, Julia, J C Watts III. **Educ:** University of Oklahoma, Norman, OK, BA, Journalism, 1981. **Career:** Canadian Football League, Ottawa, Canada, quarterback, Ottawa Roughriders, 1981-85, Toronto Argonauts, 1986; Watts Energy Corp, Norman, OK, president-owner, 1987-89, Sunnylane Baptist Church, Del City, OK, youth director, 1987-, Oklahoma State Corporation Commission, commissioner; US House of Reps, Oklahoma, congressman, 1994. **Orgs:** Board mem, Fellowship of Christian Athletes of Okla, 1981-. **Honors/Awds:** Most Valuable Player, Orange Bowl, 1980, 1981; Most Valuable Player, Grey Cup Game, CFL, 1981; Black Achievement Award, University of Okla, 1981. **Business Addr:** Congressman, US House of Representatives, 1210 Longworth House Office Building, Washington, DC 20515.

WATTS, JOHN E.
Executive director. **Personal:** Born Oct 19, 1936, Atlanta; married. **Educ:** AL St U, BS 1958; Intrdnmntnl Theol Ctr, MDiv 1961; Pepperdine U, MA 1972. **Career:** 3 Chs, pastor, adminstr 1959-69; prog coord, writer 1966-68; City of Vallejo, asst to city mgr for com reltns 1968-70; Intrgvrnmntl Mgmt, prog mgr,lt gov ofc 1970-73; Model Cities Agency, exec dor ofc of the mayor 1973-. **Orgs:** Mem Omega Psi Phi; NAHRO; Am Soc of Urban Planners; life mem Nat Hum Rights Dir; mem Interntl Hum Rights Org. **Honors/Awds:** 1st Black City Adminstr for City of Vallejo; named Most Outstndng Young Clergyman by AME Zion Ch. **Business Addr:** 814 Mission St, San Francisco, CA 94103.

WATTS, LUCILE
Judge (retired). **Personal:** Born in Alliance, OH; daughter of Doris Bailey and George Bailey; married James. **Educ:** Detroit Coll of Law, LLB; Detroit Coll of Law, JD 1962. **Career:** Twp of Royal Oak, former gen council; House Labor Comm, former legal council; Lucile A Watts PC, pres; City of Detroit Common Pleas Court, judge; Third Judicial Circuit Court, judge, until 1992. **Orgs:** Mem Amer Bar Assoc, MI Bar Assoc, Detroit Bar Assoc, Women Lawyers of MI, Wolverine Bar Assoc; past pres Womens Div of Natl Bar Assoc; past pres Metro Soc for Crippled Child & Adults; chmn bd of dir Focus Hope; mem YWCA, Detroit Golf Course Prop Own Assoc, Delta Sigma Theta, Cath Inter-Racial Council, Womens Econ Club; life mem NAACP; past pres Assoc of Black Judges of MI; reg dir, Natl Assn of Women Judges. **Business Addr:** Judge (Retired), Third Judicial Circuit Court, 16929 Wyoming Avenue, Detroit, MI 48221.

WATTS, PATRICIA L.
Utility company executive. **Personal:** Born Apr 26, 1949, Los Angeles, CA; daughter of Marjorie A Wilson and James C Wilson; children: Marshan L Pettaway, Mondel E Pettaway. **Educ:** University of La Verne; California State University at Dominguez. **Career:** Southern California Edison, clerk trainee, 1974-75, counter cashier, 1975-76, customer service bookkeeper, 1978-79, supervisor's coordinator, 1979-80, energy services representative, 1980-87, area manager, 1987-93; Community Renewal, proj mgr, 1993-. **Orgs:** American Blacks in Energy, vice pres, 1991-; Soroptimist Inglewood/Hawthorne, president, 1991-93; Black Women of Achievement Board of Directors, chairperson, 1993-; Inglewood YMCA, board of managers, 1991-; Inglewood Chamber of Commerce, board of directors, 1991-; National Forum of Black Public Administrators, 1991-; Black Women's Forum, 1991-93; Hawthorne Chamber of Commerce, board of directors, 1991-93; Community Build, bd of dirs. **Honors/Awds:** California State Legislature 50th Assembly District, Woman of the Year; Team Kenyon Award, 1992; Fremont HS Hall of Fame, Inductee, 1992; Black Women of Achievement Award, 1991; YWCA Leader Luncheon XIV, Honoree, 1989. **Home Addr:** 2032 W 109th St, Los Angeles, CA 90047. **Business Addr:** Project Mgr, Community Renewal, Southern California Edison, PO Box 2944, Torrance, CA 90509-2944, (310)417-3318.

WATTS, ROBERTA OGLETREE
Educational administrator. **Personal:** Born May 12, 1939, Lawrenceville, GA; daughter of Jennie Ogletree and Walter Ogletree; married Roger William Watts Sr; children: Roger Jr, Roderick Dewayne. **Educ:** Tuskegee Inst, BSN 1961; Emory Univ, MN 1969; Univ of AL, EdD 1982. **Career:** VA Hosp, staff nurse 1961-62; Etowah Cty Health Dept, staff nurse 1969; Jacksonville State Univ, asst prof 1969-; Jacksonville State Univ, dean, prof 1982-. **Orgs:** Chrpsn Etowah Quality of Life Inc 1978-85, Colley Child Care Ctr Inc 1970-, Deans of Bacc & Higher Degree Prog 1984, Human Rel Council; various positions Alpha Kappa Alpha 1975, Wisteria Club 1964; Kappa Delta Pi. **Honors/Awds:** Achievement Awd NAACP 1982; Serv Awd Alpha Kappa Alpha 1983, Amer Assoc Univ Women 1982, Etowah Quality of Life. **Business Addr:** Dean, Professor, Jacksonville State Univ, LB Wallace Coll of Nursing, Jacksonville, AL 36265.

WATTS, ROLANDA
Talk show hostess. **Personal:** Born in Winston-Salem, NC. **Educ:** Spelman College; Columbia University. **Career:** NBC weekend anchor; WABC-TV, news anchor/reporter; "Inside Edition," senior correspondent/weekend anchor; "Rolanda," hostess, 1994-. **Honors/Awds:** Emmy nominee. **Business Addr:** Talk Show Hostess, Rolanda, 411 E 75th St, New York, NY 10021, (212)650-2000.

WATTS, VICTOR LEWIS
Sales manager. **Personal:** Born Mar 28, 1955, Colorado Springs, CO; son of Jeraldine Banks Watts and Amos Watts; married Martha Eiland Watts, Apr 18, 1981; children: Audrey, Amelia. **Educ:** Jackson State Univ, Jackson, MS, BS, Economics, 1984. **Career:** Coors Central Mississippi, Jackson, MS, route sales, 1981-85; Coors Brewing Co, Chicago, IL, asst area sales mgr, 1985-87; Coors Brewing Co, Jackson, MS, area sales mgr, 1987-. **Orgs:** Vice pres, Ole River Bass Club, 1988-; member, Southeastern Assn Black Bass Anglers, 1989-; member, Miss Have-A-Heart Assn, 1990-; member, BASS, 1989-. **Business Addr:** Area Sales Mgr, Coors Brewing Co, 845 Crossover Ln, Bldg D, Suite 103, Memphis, TN 38117.

WATTS, WILSONYA RICHARDSON
Educator, mortician. **Personal:** Born in Campbellsville, KY; daughter of Henrietta Fisher Richardson and Reddie Roy Richardson; married Rudolph F Watts, Aug 13, 1957; children: Endraetta. **Educ:** KY School of Mortuary Science; Kentucky State Univ, AB; Western Kentucky Univ, MA rank I. **Career:** EB Terry Elem, math teacher; Campbellsville City Elem School, elem teacher; Taylor County Elem School, teacher; Glasgow Indep Schools, teacher grades 1-3; Watts Funeral Funeral Home, mortician, currently. **Orgs:** President, vp, sec, treasurer Kay Bledsoe BPW; chairman Local Glasgow Jr Miss Pageant; Glasgow Urban Renewal & Community Dev Agency; city council rep (4 years); chairman Red Cross; co-chair Muscular Dystrophy; captain Easter Seals; Glasgow Chamber of Commerce, Glasgow Beautification Committee, Glasgow Arts Committee; Barren County Literacy Council, sec; Alpha Kappa Alpha Sorority, Anti Basileus of the graduate chapter, Omicron Sigma Omega, 1991. **Honors/Awds:** Rotary Award Campbellsville Rotary Club; (Ch) Music Award KY BPW Organization; (Ch) Business and Profess Women's Week (KY BPW Organization); Woman of Achievement Glasgow Kiwanis; Woman of Achievement Kay Bledsoe BPW; Durham High School Alumni, Outstanding Teachers Award, 1987. **Home Addr:** 506 S Lewis St, Glasgow, KY 42141.

WAUGH, JUDITH RITCHIE
Broadcaster. **Personal:** Born Jun 5, 1939, Indianapolis, IN. **Educ:** Indiana Univ, BA 1961, MA 1969. **Career:** Indianapolis Public Schools, teacher of english and humanities 1961-73; McGraw Hill Broadcasting WRTV 6, dir of public affairs 1973-. **Orgs:** Life mem NAACP; former pres Indpls Chapter of Links 1989-1991; Cathedral Arts; Crossroads Rehabilitation Center; Dance Kaleidoscope; Walker Theatre Center. **Honors/Awds:** John Hay Fellowship Northwestern Univ 1964-65; NDEA Grant, Purdue Univ, 1966. **Business Addr:** Dir of Public Affairs-WRTV, McGraw-Hill Broadcasting Co, 1330 N Meridian St, Indianapolis, IN 46202, (317)269-1408.

WAULS, INEZ LA MAR
Commissioner. **Personal:** Born Feb 11, 1924, Williamson, WV; divorced; children: Agatha Kenner, Rita, Luther J Jr, Ronald. **Educ:** Howard Univ Wash DC, BA 1951. **Career:** Natl Commiss for Women, natl dir 1978-80; Bel Vue UN Presbyterian Church, presiding elder 1977-80, 1980-81; Howard Univ Alumni Assoc, west reg rep; LA Cty Symphony League, 1st black pres 1977-79; Allpha Kappa Alpha Sor Theta Alpha Omega Chapt, gramma 1976-; Foster Care Serv LA Cty Dept of Soc Svc, soc work consult 1955-; Compton Comm on the Stat of Women, commiss. **Orgs:** Minority womens task force CA State Comm on the Stat of Women 1984-; re-elected to far west reg rep Howard Univ 1984-86. **Honors/Awds:** Consistent Serv Howard Univ Alumni Assoc So CA 1962; Jill of the Year Jack & Jill of Amer Inc So LA 1976; Sor of the Year Alpha Kappa Alpha, Theta Alpha Omega 1979; Exemplary Citizenship & 20 yrs of Civic & Cultural Serv Mayor & City Council Compton CA 1979. **Business Addr:** Commissioner, Compton Comm/Stat of Women, 205 S Willowbrook Ave, Compton, CA 90220.

WAY, CHARLES CHRISTOPHER
Professional football player. **Personal:** Born Dec 27, 1972, Philadelphia, PA; married Tahesha; children: Fallon. **Educ:** Univ of Virginia, attended. **Career:** New York Giants, fullback, 1995-. **Business Addr:** Professional Football Player, New York Giants, Giants Stadium, East Rutherford, NJ 07073, (201)935-8111.

WAY, CURTIS J.
Publishing company executive. **Personal:** Born Jun 19, 1935, Columbia, SC. **Educ:** Benedict Coll, BA 1962; NU Univ, MPA 1970; Fordham Univ, New School of Soc Rsch, Grad Stud; Nova Univ, DPA 1977. **Career:** Philadelphia Cty Juvenile Cty, prob off; Newark Title V Proj, dir training & job devel; Newark City Neighborhood Youth Corps, dep dir, summer exec dir 1965-67; NAACP & Multi-Purpose Ctr, dir, chmn of bd; Newark Inst of Urban Prog, chief exec officer; CEO, Sickle Cell Anemia Assoc, currently; Spoon Book Publishing, CEO, currently. **Orgs:** Consult Natl Alliance of Bus; dir City of Passaic NJ; proj housing consult Neighborhood Youth Corp 1967-69; planner & prog devel Early Childhood Ed; planner & prog devel NJUP Theater for Arts Newark NJ, Sickle Cell Anemia Proj; fundraiser & alumni org Amer Inst Planners; mem Amer Soc Planning Official; mem Amer Soc Publ Admin, Amer Acad Pol & Soc Sci; past trustee Benedict Coll; past mem Reg Health Planning Council, Newark Urban Coalition, Minority Econ Devel Corp; past pres NJ Chap Benedict Alumni; life mem NAACP; founder Hillcreek Commun Ctr Philadelphia, NAACP Multi-Purpose Ctr & Cultural Ctr; panelist Amer Arbitration Assoc; mem 32 Degree Mason. **Honors/Awds:** Oustanding Serv Awd Benedict Coll 1970; Outstanding Serv Awd Dept HUD 1971; Excellent Cit Serv Awd L Miller Civic Assoc 1972; Better Comm Newark Br NAACP 1973; Outstanding Comm Serv Newark 1973,79; Outstanding Leadership Awd NAACP MPC 1974. **Military Serv:** US Army, sgt, 1953-57; Appreciation Awd US Navy 1971; Outstanding Serv Awd USN Recruiting 1972. **Business Addr:** Chief Executive Officer, Sickle Cell Anemia Assoc, 870 Langford RD, Blythewood, SC 29016.

WAY, GARY DARRYL
Attorney. **Personal:** Born Feb 25, 1958, Newark, NJ; son of Pearl Rosser Childs Way and Robert Way; married Jill Green, Nov 28, 1987. **Educ:** Rutgers Coll, New Brunswick, NJ, BA 1980; New York Univ School of Law, New York City, JD 1983. **Career:** Haight, Gardner, Poor & Havens, New York City, associate, 1983-86; National Basketball Assn, New York City, staff attorney, 1986-88; NBA Properties Inc, New York City, asst general counsel, 1988-. **Honors/Awds:** Author of "Japanese Employers and Title VII," 1983. **Military Serv:** US Army, captain, 1980-; Distinguished Military Graduate, Rutgers Army ROTC, 1980; Army Achievement Award with Oak

Leaf Cluster. **Business Addr:** Assistant General Counsel, NBA Properties Inc, 645 Fifth Ave, Olympic Tower, New York, NY 10022.

WAYANS, DAMON
Actor, comedian, screenwriter. **Personal:** Born 1961, New York, NY; son of Howell and Elvira Wayans; married Lisa; children: Damon, Michael, Cara Mia, Kyla. **Career:** In Living Color, writer, actor, 1990-92; Beverly Hills Cop, 1984; Hollywood Shuffle, 1987; Roxanne, 1987; Colors, 1988; I'm Gonna Git You Sucka, 1988; Punchline, 1988; Earth Girls Are Easy, 1989; Look Who's Talking Too (voiceover); The Last Boy Scout, 1991; Mo' Money, 1992; Blankman, 1994; stand-up comedian; 413 Hope Street, creator, producer, 1997. **Business Phone:** (310)280-8000.

WAYANS, KEENEN IVORY
Comedian, actor, talk show host. **Personal:** Born in New York, NY; son of Elvira Wayans and Howell Wayans. **Career:** Films: I'm Gonna Git You Sucka, 1989; A Low Down Dirty Shame, 1994; Most Wanted, 1997; In Living Color, executive producer/head writer/actor, until 1993; The Keenan Ivory Wayans Show, talk show host, 1997-.

WAYNE, GEORGE HOWARD, SR.
Educational administrator. **Personal:** Born Mar 10, 1938, Meridian, MS; son of Mr and Mrs Jerry Wayne; married Juanita R Robinson; children: Lisa Monet, George Howard Jr, Kimberly Ann. **Educ:** Univ of NE, MA 1967; Univ of CO, MPA 1971; Univ of Denver, MA, EdD 1979. **Career:** Asst prof hist 1972-76, intelligence ofcr 1967-71; Univ of CO, asst prof 1974; USAF Academy; Colorado Dept of Education; California State Univ, Sacramento, CA, vice pres of student affairs, currently. **Orgs:** Pres Kappa Alpha Psi Frat 1978; bd of dirs Kappa Alpha Psi Frat 1980; pres Aspen Educational Consulting; member, Phi Alpha Theta; member, NAACP; member, American Society Public Admin. **Honors/Awds:** Outstndng Kappa Alpha Psi Frat 1979; Black Migration to CO Jrnl of the W 1976; Race Relations a time for phase III Air Univ Rev 1972; Industrial Use of Disadvantaged Ams, Air Univ Rev 1974; Black Alcoholism: Myth vs Research, 1978. **Military Serv:** US Air Force; Bronze Star, Meritorious Service Medal, Commendation Medal. **Business Addr:** Vice Pres of Student Affairs, California State University, Sacramento, 6000 J St, Sacramento, CA 95819.

WAYNE, JUSTINE WASHINGTON
Educator. **Personal:** Born Mar 8, 1945, Marks, MS; daughter of Arneal Johnson Washington and Booker T Washington; married James Wardell Wayne, Dec 22, 1968 (deceased). **Educ:** Harris Teachers College, San Diego, CA, BA, education, 1968. **Career:** St Louis Board of Education, St Louis, MO, teacher, 1968-69; Vallejo Unified School District, Vallejo, CA, substitute teacher, 1969; Solano Economic Opportunity Council, Vallejo, CA, part-time teacher, 1969; Long Beach Unified School District, Long Beach, CA, substitute teacher, 1969; San Diego Unified School District, San Diego, CA, substitute teacher, 1970-71, teacher, 1971-90. **Orgs:** Member, Association of Black Educators, 1985-; member, San Diego Teachers Association, 1971-90; chairperson, San Diego Teachers Association Minority Affairs Committee, 1986-89; member, National Education Association, 1971-90; member, California Teachers Association, 1971-90; member, National Foundation for Improvement of Education; member, Pepperdine Alumni Association; member, National Council of Negro Women; member, NAACP; member, National Association of Female Executives. **Honors/Awds:** Who Award, San Diego Teachers Association, 1987; Site Teacher of the Year, representative, 1988. **Business Addr:** Educator, San Diego Unified School District, 4100 Normal St, San Diego, CA 92103.

WAYNES, KATHLEEN YANES
Social worker. **Personal:** Born Aug 12, 1920, New York, NY; daughter of May Stewart and Pedro Yanes; married William D Waynes; children: Consuelo, Regina Joseph, Victoria Clement, Christina Lashley. **Educ:** Attended, Catholic Univ, Washington, DC, 1940; Coll of St Benedict, St Joseph, MN, BS, 1942; Columbia Univ, Training for Natl Cath Comm Serv, USO Div, 1944. **Career:** Friendship House of Harlem, asst dir, 1942-44; Natl Catholic Social Serv, USO asst dir, 1944-46; New Jersey Commission for the Blind, social worker, 1966-82 (retired); War Assets Admin, inspector, 1946-. **Orgs:** Mem, Assoc of Workers for the Blind, 1970-82; various positions permanent membership, US Coast Guard Aux, 1970-; mem, Black Social Workers of New Jersey, 1980-82; mem, NAACP, Aux Amer Legion, Aux Knights of Columbus, AARF; leader, Girl Scouts of Amer; artistic dir, Negro Womens Club. **Honors/Awds:** Information officer, Flotilla 13-06 Award, US Coast Guard Aux, 1984-86; liturgical chairperson, Golden Agers OLGC Church, 1985; The Zeta Amicae of Zeta Delta Zeta Chapter, Mother of the Year Award; College of St Benedict, 50th Reunion of Class of 1942, Benedictine Award, 1992. **Home Addr:** 337 Farmdale Rd, Moorestown, NJ 08057.

WAYNEWOOD, FREEMAN LEE
Dentist. **Personal:** Born Jun 30, 1942, Anson, TX; married Beverly; children: Tertia, Dorian. **Educ:** Univ of TX, attended; Univ of WA, BAED 1970, DDS 1974. **Career:** Real Estate, salesman 1968-71; Weyhauser, 1970-71; Richardson's Assoc, constr rsch 1971-73; Private practice, dentist; FL Waynewood and Associates, PA; pres. **Orgs:** Mem Amer Dental Assoc, MN Dental Assoc, St Paul Dist Dental Soc, Amer Soc Preventive Dentistry, Amer Soc Dentistry for Children; staff mem United Hosp St Paul; bd mem Model Cities Hallie Q Brown Comm Ctr; mem Alpha Phi Alpha, Flight Unltd; bd mem Webster School; mem St Paul Opera Workshop. **Military Serv:** Navy cmdr 20 yrs; Vietnam Campaign Ribbon Natl Def 1964-68. **Home Addr:** 1390 Carling Dr #211, St Paul, MN 55108-5214. **Business Addr:** President, Waynewood and Associates PA, 588 University Ave, St Paul, MN 55103.

WEAD, RODNEY SAM
Administrator. **Personal:** Born Jun 28, 1935, Omaha, NE; son of Daisy Shanks Wead and Sampson Lester Wead; divorced; children: Denise Michelle Wead Rawles, Owen Eugene, Ann Lineve Wead Kimbrough, Melissa Cheryl Wead Rivas. **Educ:** Dana Coll, Blair NE, BS Educ 1957; Roosevelt Univ, Chicago IL, MA Urban Studies 1976; The Union Inst, Cincinnati OH, PhD Sociology 1981. **Career:** Prof, Creighton Univ, 1986-; United Methodist Community Centers Inc, Omaha NE, exec dir 1983-; Community Renewal Society, Chicago IL, assoc exec dir 1973-83. **Orgs:** Life mem Kappa Alpha Psi Fraternity Inc 1955-; mem Clair United Methodist Church, Omaha NE, 1955-; life mem NAACP 1967-; mem Natl Assn of Black Social Workers 1981-; commr Metropolitan Area Transit, Omaha NE, 1985-; mem bd of dirs North Side Villa, Omaha NE, 1986-. **Honors/Awds:** Economic Democracy in Low Income Neighborhoods, research publication 1982; Outstanding Volunteer, Urban League of Nebraska-Omaha 1987; Dr Rodney S Wead Scholarship, Dana Coll, Blair NE, 1989; The African-Amer Family in Nebraska, research publication 1989. **Business Addr:** Executive Director, United Methodist Community Centers Inc, 2001 N 35th St, Omaha, NE 68111.

WEARING, MELVIN
Law enforcement official. **Educ:** University of New Haven, degree in criminal justice and law enforcement. **Career:** New Haven Police Dept, chief of police, 1997-. **Honors/Awds:** Yale Univ Child Study Ctr, fellow, currently. **Special Achievements:** First African American in New Haven police dept to hold following positions: chief of detectives, asst chief of police, chief of police. **Business Addr:** Police Chief, New Haven Police Dept, 1 Union Ave, New Haven, CT 06519, (203)946-6316.

WEARY, DOLPHUS
Minister. **Personal:** Born Aug 7, 1946, Sandy Hook, MS; son of Lucille Granderson; married Rosie Marie Camper; children: Danita R, Reginald, Ryan D. **Educ:** Piney Woods Jr Coll, AA 1967; Los Angeles Baptist Coll, BA 1969; LA Bapt Theol Sem, M Rel Ed 1971; Univ of So MS, MEd 1978. **Career:** Voice of Calvary Ministries, dir summer leadership 1968-71; LA Baptist Coll, coach freshmen team 1969-71; Voice of Calvary Ministries, dir 1971-75; Piney Woods School, coord of Christian ed 1975-84; Mendenhall Ministries Inc, president, 1986-. **Orgs:** Bd of dir Voice of Calvary Health Ctr, So Central MS Rural Health Assoc, Koinonia Farms Americus GA, Voice of Hope Dallas TX; mem Natl Alumni Assoc Piney Woods School, Mendenhall Ministries bd, Nat'l Black Evangelical Assoc bd; Faith at Work, nat'l bd; bd of dir mem Mississippi Religious Leadership Conference (MRLC); bd of dir mem Mississippi Children's Home Society (MCHS); member, Mendenhall Chamber of Commerce; member, National Black Evangelical Assn; member, National Assn of Evangelicals; Evangelical Council for Financial Accountability; Belhaven College. **Honors/Awds:** Alumnus of the Year, Los Angeles Baptist College, 1979; Mississippi Religious Leadership Award, 1985; Humanitarian Award, Central Mississippi Legal Services, 1985; Outstanding Citizen of the Year, Civic Circle Club of Simpson County; author, I Ain't Comin' Back, 1990; While President of Mendenhall Ministries, this organization was honored by former President George Bush in receiving the 541st Daily Point of Light Award; Renowned speaker for many organizations, including teams in the National Football League. **Business Addr:** President, Mendenhall Ministries Inc, 309 Center St, PO Box 368, Mendenhall, MS 39114.

WEATHER, LEONARD, JR.
Gynecologist, laser surgeon. **Personal:** Born Jul 6, 1944, Albany, GA; married Bettye Jean Roberts; children: Marcus, Kirstin. **Educ:** Howard Univ, Coll of Pharmacy, BS 1967; Rush Medical Coll, MD 1974. **Career:** Johns Hopkins Univ, intern, resident 1978; Tulane Univ, instructor 1978-86; Xavier Univ, assoc prof 1984-; Omni Fertility Inst, dir 1985-. **Orgs:** Radio host medical talk show WBOK 1980-84; dir and vice pres Bayou Federal Svgs & Loan 1983-; dir YMCA 1984-; host radio talk show Doctor's Corner WYLD AM 940 1985-; mem Omega Psi Phi Frat 1985; pres Black Leadership Awareness Council 1985; natl pres Chi Delta Mu Medical Frat 1986. **Honors/Awds:** Book "Why We Can't Have a Baby," 1985; article "Carbon Dioxide Laser Myomectomy" Journal Natl Medical Assoc 1986; "CO2 Laser Laproscopy-Treatment of Disorders of Pelvic Pain and Infertility" 1986. **Military Serv:** USAR major 19 yrs. **Home Addr:** 6831 Lake Willow Dr, New Orleans, LA 70126. **Business Addr:** Dir, Chef Women Clinic/Omni Fert, 7820 Chef Menteur Hwy, New Orleans, LA 70126.

WEATHERS, CARL
Actor. **Personal:** Born Jan 14, 1947, New Orleans, LA. **Career:** Oakland Raiders, professional football player; stage appearance: Nevis Mountain Dew, 1981; television appearances: The Hostage Heart, 1977, The Bermuda Depths, 1978, Braker, 1985, Fortune Dane, 1986, The Defiant Ones, 1986; films: Friday Foster, 1975, Bucktown, 1975, Rocky, 1976, Close Encounters of the Third Kind, 1977, Semi-Tough, 1977, Force 10 from Navarone, 1978, Rocky II, 1979, Death Hunt, 1981, Rocky III, 1982, Rocky IV, 1985, Predator, 1987, Action Jackson, 1988; Stormy Weathers Productions, founder, actor, currently.

WEATHERS, J. LEROY
Clergyman. **Personal:** Born May 21, 1936, Georgetown Co; married. **Educ:** Allen U, AB 1964; Dickerson Theol Sem SC, BD 1965; Urban Training Ctr for Christian Mission Chicago IL, attend 1970; Univ of Miami Drug Ed, 1973; Air Force Chaplain Sch, 1974. **Career:** Young Chapel AME Ch Irmo SC, pastor 1960; Mt Olive AME Ch Myrtle Bch SC, pastor 1961-; Myrtle Bch AFB SC, civilian aux chaplain 1975. **Orgs:** Del Gen Conf AME Ch 1968; civilian adv Religious Adv Com Myrtle AFB SC 1969; pres Myrtle Bch Ministerial Assn 1973-74, sec 1975-76; Mil Chaplains Asn; SC Com on Pastoral Care in Alcohol & Drug Abuse 1975-76; mem Masonic Lodge 423; life mem NAACP; fdr, pres Myrtle Bch NAACP; chmn Mayor's Biracial Com 1964; Horry-Georgetown Ec Opport Bd 1965-; trustee Allen U; asst treas SC NAACP 1969-73; Myrtle Bch C of C 1970; v-chmn Dem Party Myrtle Bch 1970-72; chaplain Myrtle Bch Jaycees 1970-74, dir 1971-72; Horry Co Ambulance Serv Commn; Fed Prog Adv Cncl, Horry Co Dept of Ed 1971; sec Kiwanis Club of Myrtle Bch 1971; numerous others com. **Honors/Awds:** Recip Outstndng Ldrshp Award, Mt Olive AME Ch 1967; cert of Merit SC NAACP 1967; cert of Appreciation Ec Opport Comm Act 1971; US Jaycees Spkr-of-the-Month Award 1971-72; Jaycee-of-the-Month Myrtle Bch Jaycees 1972; Key Man Award Myrtle Bch Jaycees 1972; Kiwanian-of-theYr 1972; Outstndng Young Man Award Jaycees 1972; Outstndng Young Man With Distinguished Serv Award SC Jaycees 1972; ed bldg at Mt Olive AME Ch named the JL Weathers Religious Ed Bldg1973; Hm Coming Award Singleton AME Ch SC 1973; Cit of Yr Beta Tau Chap of Omega Psi Phi Frat; Distinguished Unit Pres/Unit Citation; AF Outstndng Unit Award; Army Good Conduct Medal; Nat Def Serv Medal. **Military Serv:** AUS 1953-55. **Business Addr:** Route 1, Box 138, McClellanville, SC 29458.

WEATHERS, MARGARET A.
Association executive (retired). **Personal:** Born Feb 9, 1922, Forest City, AR; daughter of Lillie Allman and Oscar Allman; married Ernest A Weathers; children: Margaret Kathryn. **Educ:** Lincoln Univ; Western Reserve Univ; MS Indus Coll; Tulane Univ, Certificate, Inner City Training Program 1971; Capital Univ, BA. **Career:** MO, teacher 1940-50; GM Chevrolet Plant Cleveland, worker 1951-55; Child Welfare Dept Cleveland, operated nursery 1955-60; Head Start Comm Act for Youth & Council of Churches, teacher 1964-66; Cleveland Div Rec, 1966-70; Weathers Unique Cleaners, co-mgr; EA Weathers Realty; Weathers Travel Agcy; Mags Kustard, co-owner; Multi-Serv Center, past pres corp bd; Lk Erie Girl Scout Council, field dir beginning 1985-, membership specialist, until 1993. **Orgs:** Past mem, Health Planning & Devel Comm, Welfare Fed; past bd mem Hough Area Devel Corp & Council; president, Church Women United of Greater Cleveland, 1996-98. **Honors/Awds:** Plaques Hough Multi-Serv Center Bd 1973; Parkwood CME Church, 1973; Certificate of Merit, Hough Comm Council 1973; plaque To One Who Served with Dedication, The Hough Multi-Serv Center Bd of Trustees; Congressional Achievement Award; City of Cleveland Congratulatory Award 1977; Denominational Representative to Church Women United for the CME Church; associate director of Scouting Ministries, Girl Scouts USA, CME Church.

WEATHERSBY, JOSEPH BREWSTER
Cleric. **Personal:** Born Nov 23, 1929, Cincinnati, OH; son of Gertrude and Albert; married Louberta, Oct 28, 1950 (divorced). **Educ:** Berkeley, Div School, STM, 1960; Salmon P Chase College, BBA. **Career:** St Mary Episcopal Church, rector, 1960-68; Saginaw Urban Ministry, ombudsman, 1969-72; St Clement Episcopal Church, rector, 1972-74; Saginaw Office, Civil Rights Department, executive, 1975-83; Department of Mental Health, civil rights executive, 1986-. **Orgs:** Alpha Phi Alpha Fraternity, 1979-. **Military Serv:** UMCR, Corp. **Home Phone:** (313)699-9094.

WEATHERSBY, QEVIN Q. **See SANDERS-OJI, J. QEVIN.**

WEATHERSPOON, CLARENCE
Professional basketball player. **Personal:** Born Sep 8, 1970, Crawford, MS; married Hazel. **Educ:** Southern Mississippi. **Career:** Philadelphia 76ers, forward, 1992-98; Golden State Warriors, 1998-. **Honors/Awds:** Inducted into the Southern Mississippi Hall of Fame. **Business Addr:** Professional Basketball Player, Golden State Warriors, 1001 Broadway, Oakland, CA 94607, (510)986-2200.

WEATHERSPOON, JIMMY LEE
Elected official. **Personal:** Born Mar 10, 1947, Ft Lauderdale, FL; married Marian Wilson; children: Joy LaWest, Kendra LaVett. **Educ:** Automation School, Cert 1968; FL Atlantic Univ. **Career:** Carver Cmmty Middle Schl PTA, mem advisory bd 1981-82, vice pres 1982-83; Delray Beach Voters League, vice pres 1982-84; IBM, Asst Systems Analyst 1980-. **Orgs:** Chrmn Commty Primitive Bapt Church Trustees 1982-; rep Dist 69 Palm Beach Cty Democratic Exec Comm 1984; mem Delray Beach Democratic Club 1984; mem TheNaciremas Club, Inc 1984. **Honors/Awds:** Vice mayor polled highest vote in 1984 Delray Beach - first black so honored. **Business Addr:** Associate Systems Analyst, IBM, PO Box 1328, Boca Raton, FL 33432.

WEATHERSPOON, KEITH EARL
Investment banker. **Personal:** Born Dec 13, 1949, New Orleans, LA; married Marie L Slade, Aug 7, 1981; children: Ashley M Weatherspoon. **Educ:** Xavier Univ, BS 1970; Northeast LA Univ, MBA 1973. **Career:** McNeal Labs, medical representative, 1973-78; EF Hutton, stock broker, 1978-82; Small Business Admin, exec asst to admin, 1982-84; Donaldson, Lufkin & Jenrette, investment banker, 1984-. **Orgs:** Dir bd, LA Small Business Equity Corp, 1981-83, Bd of City Trust of City of New Orleans, 1981-, Dashiki Project Theatre, 1985-, Dryades St YMCA, 1986-; mem, Kappa Alpha Psi, Zulu Mardi Gras Club; chmn of bd, Dashiki Project Theatre.

WEATHERSPOON, TERESA
Professional basketball player. **Personal:** Born Dec 8, 1965; daughter of Charles Sr. **Educ:** Louisiana Tech, attended. **Career:** New York Liberty, guard, 1997-. **Honors/Awds:** Louisiana State Player of the Year, 1988; US Olympic Basketball Team, Gold Medal, 1988, Bronze Medal, 1992; All-WNBA Second Team, 1997; WNBA Defensive Player of the Year, 1997. **Business Addr:** Professional Basketball Player, New York Liberty, Two Penn Plaza, New York, NY 10121, (212)564-9622.

WEAVER, FRANK CORNELL
Marketing executive. **Personal:** Born Nov 15, 1951, Tarboro, NC; son of Queen Lewis Weaver and Frank B Weaver; married Kathryn Ann Hammond, Oct 11, 1980; children: Christina. **Educ:** Howard Univ, BSEE 1972; Univ NC Chapel Hill, MBA Mktg 1976; Nova University, Fort Lauderdale, FL, PhD candidate, business. **Career:** Westinghouse, asst sales engr 1972-73; NC Central Univ, asst prof 1975; Mellon Bank, credit analyst 1976-77; RCA Astro-Space Div, mgr commun satellites 1977-88; General Dynamics Comm Launch Servs, dir, Washington office 1988-90; UNET Communitcations Inc, Fort Washington, MD, president/CEO, 1990-93; Office of Commerical Space Transportation, director appointed by President Clinton, 1993. **Orgs:** Bd dir Direct Broadcast Satellite Assoc 1990-91; vstg prof Natl Urban League of BEEP 1978-; panelist Congressional Black Caucus Comm Braintrust 1983; mem NAACP, RCA Minorities in Engrg Prog, board of directors; Washington Space Business Roundtable, Society of Satellite Professionals; National Space Club, Tau Beta Pi Engr Honor Society. **Honors/Awds:** Honorary Doctor of Science, Saint Augustine's College, Raleigh, NC; "D-Sign Graphics", "UDI Supermkt" Case Studies Minority Venture Mgt 1975; "Intro to Commun Satellites" RCA Engr 1983; "RCA's Series 4000 Commun Satellites" Satellite Comm 1984; "DBS Satellite Tech" IEEE Electro 1985; Disting Author RCA 1984, 1985; Harlem YMCA Black Achiever in Industry 1986; "Atlas Family of Launch Vehicles," 1991 McGraw Hill Yearbook of Science and Technology; Via Satellite Magazine, "Satellite 100" Top Executives, "A Communication Satellite Dedicated To Delivery of Educational Programming," 29th Space Congress Proceedings, 1992. **Business Addr:** Director, Office of Commerical Space Transportation US Dept of Transportation, 400 Seventh St SW, Washington, DC 20059, (202)366-2937.

WEAVER, GARLAND RAPHEAL, JR.
Dentist. **Personal:** Born Jun 8, 1932, Baltimore, MD; married Barbara C Gee; children: Garland III, Edward. **Educ:** Howard University, BS 1958, DDS 1966. **Career:** Self-employed, dentist, currently. **Orgs:** Past pres, MD Dental Soc; mem Kappa Alpha Psi Fraternity. **Business Addr:** 5441 Park Heights Ave, Baltimore, MD 21215.

WEAVER, GARRETT F.
Lecturer. **Personal:** Born Jun 17, 1948, Durham, NC. **Educ:** NC Cntrl, Attend; Univ of NC, PhD 1987. **Career:** Univ of NC, lectr Afro-Amer studies 1985; Univ of WI, 1973-74; St Augustine Coll, 1972-73; NC St Univ, 1972-73; Rio Grande Coll; Marshall Univ; WV Univ, 1968-72; Afro-Amer & African Studies, 1985; Jackson State Univ, asst prof of history 1975-88. **Orgs:** Mem Am Historical Assn; Assn for Study of Afro-Am & Life & History; Nat Geo Soc; pres NAACP Charleston; mem Kanawha Co Div Comm Wlfr Bd; NASALH Biecennial Com; Phi Beta Sigma Frat; Afro-Am Studies Cons; Black Geneological Rsrchr; dir Public & Applied History Prop; dir of history English Link Proj Jackson State Univ. **Business Addr:** Assistant Professor of History, Jackson State Univ, 301 Peabody, UNC Chapel Hill, Chapel Hill, NC 27514.

WEAVER, GARY W.
Real estate executive. **Personal:** Born Sep 3, 1952, Washington, DC; married BV Goodrich. **Educ:** VA Commonwealth U, BS Bus Adm 1974. **Career:** Trifam Sys Inc, pres 1977-; VA Hsg Dev Auth Richmond, proj mgr 1975-77; City of Richmond, zoning ofcr insp dept 1974-75; Assn of Fed Appraisers, appraiser 1978-; Soc of Real Est Appraisers, asso 1978-; N VA Bd of Rltrs, rltr 1978-; Merit Properties, principal broker, currently. **Orgs:** Horizon Bank of Virginia, advisory bd. **Business Addr:** 501 Church St, Vienna, VA 22180.

WEAVER, GEORGE LEON-PAUL
Consultant (retired). **Personal:** Born Jun 18, 1912, Pittsburgh, PA; son of Josephine and George; married Mary. **Educ:** Roosevelt Univ, 1940-42; Howard Univ Law School, 1942-43; Howard Univ, 1962. **Career:** World ORT Union, consultant, 1975; Intl Labor Org Geneva Switzerland, special asst to dir general, 1969-retirement. **Orgs:** Mem, CIO War & Relief Comm 1941-42; asst to sec treas CIO 1942-55; exec sec AFL-CIO 1955-58; spec asst to Sec of Labor 1961; asst sec of Labor Intl Affairs 1969; mem bd United Negro Coll Fund; chmn Atlanta Univ Ctr.

WEAVER, HERBERT C.
Civil engineer. **Personal:** Born in Pittsburgh, PA; son of Lucy Gardener and Joseph G Weaver; married Rayma Heywood; children: Carol, Jonathan. **Educ:** Univ of Pittsburgh, BS 1961. **Career:** Commonwealth of PA, bridge designer, hydraulic engr; Rust Engr Co, civil engr; Pullman Swindell Co, proj engr, civil engr; Allegheny County Dept of Engrg & Construction, project manager; Herbert C Weaver Assoc Inc, pres, founder. **Orgs:** Mem ASCE, PSPE, NSPE; appt to panel arbitrators of Amer Arbitration Assn 1970; reg professional engr; reg land surveyor; trustee Grace Presbyterian Church 1963-; vice pres Booster Club of Wilkinsburg Christian School 1971-72; mem E Hills Pitt Club 1974-; asst track coach Churchill Area Track Club 1980-85; certified official, USA-Track & Field, l980. **Military Serv:** US Army. **Home Addr:** 2104 Swissvale Ave, Pittsburgh, PA 15221.

WEAVER, JOHN ARTHUR
Physician. **Personal:** Born Nov 23, 1940, Hemingway, SC; son of Winnie Mae Williams and Arthur C Weaver; married Yvonne Jackson; children: Jennifer, Jessica. **Educ:** Virginia Union Univ, BS, 1964; Howard Univ, MS, 1968, PhD, 1970, MD, 1978. **Career:** North Carolina State Univ, assoc professor of chemistry, Greensboro, NC, 1970-74, summer, 1975; Howard Univ, intern, 1978-79, resident, 1979-81; The Johns Hopkins Institutions, fellow in nuclear medicine, 1981-83; Weaver Medical Assocs, PC, pres, 1983-; Howard Univ Hosp, asst prof of radiology, 1991. **Orgs:** AMA; NMA; RSNA; SNM; Richmond Medical Society, immediate past president. **Honors/Awds:** NSF grantee 1972; NIH grantee 1972; Piedmont grantee 1973. **Business Addr:** President, Weaver Medical Assoc PC, 505 W Leigh St, Ste 102, PO Box 26448, Richmond, VA 23261, (804)344-5055.

WEAVER, JOSEPH D.
Physician. **Personal:** Born Sep 11, 1912, Winton, NC; married Rossie P Clay; children: Jesse R, Claudia P. **Educ:** Howard Univ, BS 1934; Howard Univ Med School, MD 1938. **Career:** Roanoke Chowan Hosp, staff 1972-74; ECU Med School, asst prof med family practice; Hertford Cty NC, med examiner 1971-; ECU Med School, assistant professor of family practice. **Orgs:** Mem Beta Kappa Chi Honor Soc 1935-; vice pres 1st Dist Medical Soc 1973-; treas Eastern NC Med, Dental & Pharm Soc; mem Hertford Cty Med Soc, NC Med Soc, Amer Med Assoc, Natl Med Assoc, Amer Publ Health Assoc, Amer Geriatrics Soc, Natl Rehab Assoc, Amer Acad Fam Physicians; mem Elks, 32 Deg Mason, Airplane Owners & Pilots Assoc; chmn bd Roanoke Chowa Med Ctr; grand medical dir IBPOE of W; fellow, AAFP; secretary & chmn, Roanoke Chowa Medical Ctr. **Honors/Awds:** Amer Negro Commemorative Soc Achievement Awd Kappa Alpha Psi 1964; Scroll of Hon Omega Psi Phi 1963; Dr of the Year Awd No State Med Soc 1962-63; Cert of Merit & Sel Serv Medal from Congress of US 1945; Cert of Merit, Scottish Rite, Masons; Recipient of Paul Harris Award from Rotary. **Military Serv:** AUS 1st lt 1942-44. **Business Addr:** Medical Examiner, Hertford County NC, 111 No Maple St, Ahoskie, NC 27910.

WEAVER, REGINALD LEE
Educator, association executive. **Personal:** Born Aug 13, 1939, Danville, IL; married Betty Jo Moppin; children: Reginald Von, Rowan Anton. **Educ:** IL St U, BA 1961; Roosevelt U, MA 1973. **Career:** IL Ed Assn, vice pres 1977-81, Budget Com, 1971-81; president, 1981-87; IPACE Com IL, vice chmn 1977-81, Staff & Retirement Com, chmn 1979-81; School Dist 152, teacher 1961-. **Orgs:** Tchr Certification Bd IL Ofc of Ed 1972-83; del WCOTP Wash DC Lagos Nigeria Brasilia Brazil 1976-80; Masons, 1965-; Harvey Ed Assn, president, 1967-68, vice pres Negotiatong Team, 1970; National Education Association, international relations com, 1975-81, Executive Com, 1989; National Board for Professional Teaching Standards, 1989; Dept of Ed, Hall of Fame, ISU; Natl Educ Assn, vice pres. **Honors/Awds:** Listed Outstndng Young Men of Am 1972; Hum Rels Award IL Ed Assn 1974; numerous Spkng Engagements 1977-. **Business Addr:** National Education Association, 1201 16th St, NW, Washington, DC 20016.

WEAVER, ROBERT C. See Obituaries section.

WEAVER, WILLIAM COURTSWORTHY, II
Cleric. **Personal:** Born Jul 11, 1929, Edgefield, SC; son of Minnie Simpkins Weaver and Allen Weaver; married Virginia Nadine Dawkins, Oct 28, 1969; children: William III, James Allen. **Educ:** Voorhees Junior College, AA, 1951; Allen University, BA, 1955; Philadelphia Divinity School, Bachelor of Sacred Theology, 1960; Episcopal Divinity School, Master of Divinity, 1972. **Career:** Central High School, assistant principal, 1955-57; Saint Paul's Church, rector, 1960-68; Saint Matthias Parish, rector, 1968-72; Church of the Redeemer, rector, 1972-79; Saint Andrew's Church, rector, 1979-83; Shaw University, adjunct professor, 1980-85; Epiphany Church, rector, 1992. **Orgs:** Charleston Housing Authority, commissioner, 1992; Charleston Naval Shipyard legislative Commissioner, 1991; Hanahan Academy Board of Trustees, 1983-86; Commission on the Ministry, 1979-83; Voorhees College Board of Trustees, 1960-64; Orangeburg Housing Authority, 1960-64; Orangeburg Civil Rights Movement, 1960-64; Sumter Civil Rights Movement, 1960-64. **Honors/Awds:** Charleston County Schools, Volunteer Service Award, 1992; Cities in Schools, Cities in Schools Award, 1992; City of Charleston, Certificate of Appreciation Award, 1992; Epiphany Church, Pastor's Appreciation Award, 1992; Clark Corporate Academy, Appreciation Award, 1992. **Special Achievements:** "Celebrating Time," 1991; "The Celebrated Imposter," 1981; "Who is the Man?," 1975; "Father Divine: The Genius of the Man from Georgia," 1960; "The Winds of Change," 1960. **Military Serv:** US Army, private first class, 1951-53; Good Conduct, 1952; European Occupation, 1953. **Home Addr:** 1203 Lenevar Dr S, Charleston, SC 29407.

WEBB, ALLAN
Sports franchise executive. **Personal:** Born Jan 22, 1931, Washington, DC; son of Catherine Webb and Allen Webb; married Fran; children: Lisa, Marc. **Educ:** Attended, Univ of Bridgeport, CT, (formerly Arnold Coll), 1953. **Career:** New York Giants, starting safety, 1961-65, scout, 1966-73, offensive backfield coach, 1974-78; Cleveland Browns, dir of pro personnel, 1979-82; San Francisco 49er's, dir of pro personnel, 1983-. **Honors/Awds:** Inducted into Coll Hall of Fame, 1984; inducted into High School Hall of Fame 1986. **Military Serv:** USN 2 yrs. **Business Addr:** Dir of Pro Personnel, San Francisco 49ers, 4949 Centennial, Santa Clara, CA 95054.

WEBB, CLIFTON ALAN
Television news director. **Personal:** Born Nov 3, 1950, New London, CT; son of June Mildred Hargrove Webb and Robert Lee Webb Sr; married Jacqueline Gales Webb, Oct 14, 1988. **Educ:** Southern Conn State College, New Haven, CT, BA, 1972; University of Conn Law School, West Hartford, CT, 1972-73. **Career:** National Black Network, New York, NY, anchor, 1982-83; United Press International, Washington, DC, editor, 1983-85; NBC News, Washington, DC, correspondent, 1985-87; United Press International, Washington, DC, reporter, 1987-88, Media General Cable, Fairfax, VA, news director, 1988-. **Orgs:** Mem, Northern Virginia Press Club, 1988-; mem, Radio-Television News Directors Assn, 1989-; mem, Wolf Trap Bd of Associates, 1990-; mem, Underwater Adventure Seekers (SCUBA), 1991-. **Honors/Awds:** ACE Award Nominee, National Acad of Cable Programming, 1990, 1991.

WEBB, GEORGIA HOUSTON
Educational administrator. **Personal:** Born May 16, 1951, Moorseville, AL; daughter of Annie Thatch Harris and George Houston; married Harold Webb, Jan 6, 1984; children: Ayinde Pendleton Webb. **Educ:** University of Iowa, Iowa City, IA, BA, philosophy, 1973; University of Wisconsin, Whitewater, WI, MS, counseling, 1974. **Career:** University of Wisconsin, Eau Claire, WI, career counselor, 1974-76; Cornell University, Ithaca, NY, asst director of minority affairs, 1976-80; Mount San Antonio College, Walnut, CA, instructor, 1984-88; Scripps College, Claremont, CA, senior asst director of admissions, 1988-90; The WEBB Connection, co-founder, president, 1990-; University of California, Berkley, southern area outreach coordinator, 1990-. **Orgs:** Board member, Community Friends of International Students-Claremont College, 1989-; member, Claremont League of Women Voters, 1989-; delegate, State Central Committee, California Democratic Party, 1988-; member, Pomona Valley-Nicaragua Friendship Project, 1988-; member, California Rainbow Coalition; member, Los Angeles Democratic Party; member, Upland Business and Professional Women's Club; member, League of Conservation Voters. **Honors/Awds:** Congressional nominee, 33rd District, California, 1990; campaign coordinator for Jesse Jackson, 33rd and 35th Districts, CA, 1984, 1988; delegate, Democratic National Convention, 1988; nominee, Best Play, NAACP Image Awards, 1983. **Home Addr:** 110 E Arrow Hwy, Claremont, CA 91711.

WEBB, HAROLD, SR.
Educator, consultant. **Personal:** Born Oct 28, 1933, Evanston, IL; son of Blanche Nance Webb and Zero William Webb; married Georgia Houston Webb, Jan 6, 1984; children: Harold Webb Jr., Robyn Leanae, Ayinde Pendleton. **Educ:** University of Indiana, Bloomington, IN, 1958-60; University of California at Davis, BA, 1971, MFA, 1973. **Career:** University of Califor-

nia at Davis, CA, liberal arts-career specialist 1973-80; Casa Colina Hospital Career Development Center, Pomona, CA, career decision training instructor, 1980-81; Center for Community Development, Pomona, CA, career change specialist, 1981-83; Pomona Youth Leadership Academy, YMCA, Pomona, CA, program advisor and teacher, 1982-86; National Association for the Advancement of Colored People, Pomona, CA, office manager, 1985-88, executive secretary, 1988-89; United Food and Commercial Workers, Local 1428, employment discrimination counselor, 1988-90; Georgia Houston Webb for Congress, campaign manager, 1990-; The Webb Connection, CEO, consultant, 1990-; Willie E. White for City Council, campaign manager, 1991; Sandy Hester for US Senate, campaign manager, 1992; Tony Randlle for Congress, 28th Dist, campaign mgr, 1994; Willie White for Ponnar City Council, campaign mgr, 1995. **Orgs:** California State Democratic Central Committee, 1990; regional director, California Democratic Council, Region XII, 1989-; Los Angeles County Democratic Central Committee, 1984-86; vice president, Jerry Voorhis Claremont Democratic Club, 1984-88; chairman, 1986-88, board member, currently, Los Angeles County Community Action Board; legal redress chairman, National Association for the Advancement of Colored People, California State Conference; founder, Segundo Players, UC Davis, 1971-75; founder, director, Kuumba Theatre, 1975-80. **Honors/Awds:** Author, Employment Development Manual, 1979; author with Margaret Harrison, Performing Arts Management, 1973; editor, NAACP Newsletter, Pomona Branch, 1985-87; has served on numerous election/re-election campaigns; Outstanding Comm Leader of the Year, America Bus Women Assn, Ponena Avante Chpt, 1995. **Military Serv:** US Marine Corps, Cpl, 1952-57; two Good Conduct Medals. **Business Addr:** CEO, The Webb Connection, 110 E Arrow Hwy, Claremont, CA 91711.

WEBB, HAROLD H.
Government employee, educator (retired). **Personal:** Born Apr 30, 1925, Greensboro, NC; son of Vina Wadlington Webb and Haywood Eugene Webb Sr; married Lucille Holcomb, Jan 15, 1949; children: Kaye. **Educ:** A&T State Univ Greensboro NC, BS 1949; MS 1952. **Career:** Hillsborough, tchr 1948-54; princ 1954-62; State Sci Consult Raleigh 1962-66; Nat Def Educ Act, asst dir 1966-69; Hum Rel, asst dir 1969-70; Tit I ESEA, dir 1970-73; Comp Edn, dep asst supt 1973-77; Ofc of State Personnel NC, state personnel dir, 1977-1986; NC General Assembly, legislative agent, 1992-. **Orgs:** Mem NEA; NSTA; vchmn NC Assn Adminstr Comp Edn; Nat Comp Educ Mgmt Proj; trust Wake Tech Inst; bd dir Raleigh Little Theatre; bd dir New Bern Ave Day Care Cent; bd dir Raleigh Cncl for Aging; exec com Raleigh Ctzns Assn; past mem Orng Co Bd Pub Wlfr Outstg Adminstr Orng Co Schs 1960; del Nat Conf on Educ of Poor Chicago 1973; chmn, Wake County North Carolina Planning Bd, 1988-; mem, Univ of North Carolina Bd of Governors, 1989-. **Honors/Awds:** Honorary Degree Doctor of Humanities, North Carolina A&T State Univ, 1978; Tarheel of the Week, Raleigh News and Observer, 1980. **Military Serv:** USAC 1943-46. **Home Addr:** 1509 Tierney Circle, Raleigh, NC 27610.

WEBB, HARVEY, JR.
Dentist. **Personal:** Born Jul 31, 1929, Washington, DC; married Z Ozella; children: Tomai, Harvey III, Hoyt. **Educ:** Howard Univ, BS 1956, DDS 1960; St Elizabeth's Hosp, intern 1960; Howard Univ, MS 1962; Johns Hopkins Univ, MPH 1967. **Career:** Howard Univ, fellow, 1960-62, instructor, 1962-63; private practice, 1960-77; Grp Health Assn Amer, 1962-63; Johns Hopkins Univ, 1969-71; Constant Care Comm Hlth Ctr, executive director, 1971-87; Univ of Maryland School of Nursing, 1976-77. **Orgs:** Bd mem, MD Heart Assn, 1969-74; trustee, 1978-85, bd mem, 1979-82, Howard County Genl Hosp, 1978-85; pres, Health Resources Inc 1978-80; mem Central MD Hlth Sys Agen 1980-81; mem Alpha Phi Alpha; Amer Dental Assn; Natl Dental Assn; Robert T Freeman Dent Soc; AAAS; Intl Assn Dental Rsch; DC Dental Soc; Maimonides Dental Soc; DC Pub Hlth Assn; DC Hlth & Welfare Cncl; Amer Public Hlth Assn; Polit Action Com RT Freeman Dent Soc; Amer Assn Public Hlth Dentists; MD State Pub Hlth Assn; coord Comm Vol Dental Svc; Dental Coord Provident Hosp; mem Balt City Dental Soc; life mem NAACP; mem Howard Univ Alumni; Neighbors Inc; Brightwood Civic Assn; WA Urban League; bd dir WA, DC Home Rule Comm; Sarasota County review bd, 1994-97; bd mem, South West Hospice, 1995-97; bd mem, North Port Area Chamber of Commerce, 1995-97; Tiger Bay Club, 1994-; Asolo Theatre, Angel, 1995-; Venice Foundation grant review committee, 1995-97; bd mem North County Ed. Assis. prog, 1994-; chair, Sarasota County democratic exec, 1992-, issues, 1994-95; pres, Holistic Healthworks, Inc, 1995-97; bd mem North Port Kiwanis, 1996-97; pres, N. Port Utility Adv. Committee, 1994-; mem, Unity Church of Sarasota; bd mem N. Port Democratic Club, 1992; Friends of Selby library, 1994-; Venice Hospital Community Health Assessment Comm, 1992-95; bd mem, Hispanic American Alliance, Inc, 1996-; Florida Academy of African American Culture, 1995-. **Honors/Awds:** Outstanding Men of Decade 1979; Com Serv Award Pi Eta Chi 1979; NM Carroll Meth Home Award 1980; numerous publs & presentations. **Military Serv:** US Army, 2nd Lt 1948-52; US Army Reserves, Maj 1953-70 (retired).

WEBB, JAMES EUGENE
Business executive. **Personal:** Born Aug 3, 1956, Cleveland, OH; children: Brian James, Richard Anthony, Khalam James-Kirsten, Elijah Khakmonee. **Educ:** Attended, Cleveland Institute of Banking 1976, Cuyahoga Comm Coll 1978. **Career:** Warrensville Ctr for Mentally Retarded, caseworker 1975-78; Republic Steel, mill wright 1978-82; Culligan Water Intl, sales manager, res sales, FL & IL, 1985-89; Webb Manufacturing/Webb World Inc, president, 1982-. **Orgs:** Consultant Career Programs Cleveland Public Schools 1985; vice pres Cleveland Business League 1985-86; speaker for several groups; parent advisory comm Canterbury School. **Honors/Awds:** Business of the Year for City of Cleveland (Webb Mfg) 1984; Entrepreneur of the Year City of Cleveland 1984; Man of the Year Cleveland Senior Council 1985. **Home Addr:** 12304 Buckingham Ave, Cleveland, OH 44120-1434.

WEBB, JAMES O.
General administrator. **Personal:** Born Nov 25, 1931, Cleveland, OH; son of Bessie R and James O Sr; married Frankie L Lowe; children: Lisa S, Paula R Webb Dixon. **Educ:** Morehouse Coll, BA 1953; Univ of Michigan, MBA 1957. **Career:** Mutual of NY, actuarial asst 1957-62; Supreme Life Ins co, vice pres actuary 1962-66; Blue Cross-Blue Shield of IL, sr vice pres 1966-84; Dental Network of Amer, pres & ceo beginning 1984-94, chm, bd of dirs, beginning 1990-94; James O Webb & Assoc, pres & CEO, currently; pres. Managed Dental Care of Canada 1986-94; Security Solutions Inc, chairman, 1995-; Village of Glencoe, president, 1993-; Harris Trust & Savings Bank, director; Harris Bank Corps, Harris Bankmont; Harris Bank, Glencoe, Northbrook, director. **Orgs:** Dir South Shore Bank 1975-89; dir treasurer exec comm Amer Acad of Actuaries 1975-78; mem Planning Exec Inst, Midwest Planning Assoc; founder & convenor Business Devel Inst Blue Cross-Blue Shield 1983-88; pres Glencoe School Bd 1971-77; exec comm, vice pres No Cook Cty Private Industrial Council 1983-86; founder & chmn, dir Home Investments Fund 1968; Chicago Metro Housing & Planning Council 1980-85; gov comm Health Asst Prog 1979-83. Pres Managed Dental Care of Canada 1986-94; Security Solutions Inc, chairman, 1995-; Village of Glencoe, president, 1993-; Harris Trust & Savings Bank, director; Harris Bank Corps, Harris Bankmont; Harris Bank, Glencoe, Northbrook, director. **Honors/Awds:** Outstanding Businessmen's Awd Young Blacks in Politics 1984. **Military Serv:** AUS corpl E-4 1953-55.

WEBB, JOE
Company executive, cleric. **Personal:** Born Aug 18, 1935, San Antonio, TX; married Frances; children: Joe Jr, Linda Ray, Vincent, Daniel. **Educ:** San Antonio Coll, Associates; St Marys Univ, Pre-Law Courses; HEB Mgmt School, Cert; Guadalupe Theol Seminary, Assoc Minister. **Career:** YMCA, public relations dir 1957-69; HEB Supermarket, store dir 1969-80; Neighborhood Grocery Store, independent grocer 1980-; Webb Way Supermarket, pres/owner 1983-; City of San Antonio, city councilman, 1977-91; WBS Inc, dba/Handy Stop Convience Store, secretary, treasurer, owner 1980-; Pleasant Zion Baptist Church, pastor 1986-. **Orgs:** Mem Black Congressional Caucus 1977-; state grand sr warden Masonic Lodge 1981-; assoc minister Zion Star Baptist Church 1982-; steering comm mem Natl League of Cities 1983-85; SA TX chmn Jesse Jackson Campaign 1984; chmn board of directors AAOMMS of North and South America Imperial Grand Council NBC/LEO, treasurer, 1987-89, Reg Dir XVII; mem Alamo City Chamber of Commerce. **Honors/Awds:** Father of the Year 20th Century Club; Man of the Year Elks; Patterson Awd United Negro College Fund; Honorary Doctors, Guadalupe Theol Seminary, 1985. **Home Addr:** 2226 Burnet, San Antonio, TX 78202.

WEBB, JOSEPH G.
Police officer. **Personal:** Born Dec 3, 1950, Chicago, IL; son of Mardina G Williams and Wellington M Webb; married Marilyn L Bell, Oct 23, 1978; children: Alishea R, Ami R, Ciara M. **Educ:** Attended Univ of Colorado, Boulder CO, 1969-71; attended Metropolitan State Coll, Denver CO, 1982-86, received AAs & BA; attending Univ of Denver Coll of Law, Denver CO, 1988-. **Career:** Denver General Hospital, mental health worker, 1972-77; Denver Police Dept, sergeant, 1977-. **Orgs:** Mem, Natl Black Police Assn 1983-, Colorado Business League 1985-86, Colorado Black Roundtable 1985-; consultant, Oasis Project 1986-87, NE Denver Task Force on Drug Abuse 1988-89. **Honors/Awds:** Citizens Appreciate Police Award; SCAT Appreciation Award; Peer Support Recognition Award; Black Officer of the Year; Officer of the Month; Optimist Intl Law Enforcement Recognition; Intelligence Bureau Appreciation Award; Natl Black Police Assn Leadership Award.

WEBB, LINNETTE
Hospital administrator. **Career:** Harlem Hospital Center, executive director. **Business Addr:** Executive Director, Harlem Hospital Ctr, 506 Lenox Ave, New York, NY 10037-1802, (212)939-1340.

WEBB, LUCIOUS MOSES
Labor liaison (retired). **Personal:** Born Sep 19, 1928, Canfield, AR; son of Victoria Strickland Webb and Lucious Webb Sr; married Dewene Jeanette Hale Webb, Aug 18, 1959; children: Ronnette, Richard, Steven. **Educ:** Creighton U, Attended 1953-54; Univ of Omaha, Attended 1955-56; Commercial Bus Sch, Attended; George Washington U, Attended 1969-70. **Career:** Labor Participation American Red Cross, regional dir 1968-92. **Orgs:** Mem United Packing House Workers Local #8 Armour & Co 19 Years; chmn of COPE Met Packing House Workers 10 Years; del Intl Union Conv; mem NE State& Douglas Co Dem Central Com; mem Mayor of Omaha Citizen Com & Omaha EEOC; ex-ocl YMCA; master mason Nathaniel Hunter AM & FM Lodge #12; mem Ch of Jesus Christ of Latter Day Saints. **Military Serv:** AUS corpl 2 Years.

WEBB, MELVIN RICHARD
Educator. **Personal:** Born Feb 9, 1940, Cuthbert, GA; married Brenda Janet Burton. **Educ:** Albany State Col, BS 1992; Atlanta U, MS 1968; OH State U, PhD 1977. **Career:** Clark Coll, prof biol & science educ 1972-; Resource Center for Science & Engineering Atlanta Univ, asst dir, 1978-; Atlanta Bd of Educ, biology teacher 1967-69; Dougherty Co Bd of Educ, biology and chemistry 1963-66; Lee Co Bd of Educ, science teacher 1962-63. **Orgs:** Mem Nat Sci Tchrs Assn; mem GA Sci Tchrs Assn; mem Phi Delta Kappa; mem NAACP; mem So Christian Leadership Conf. **Honors/Awds:** Sci Dept Citation Albany State 1962; STAR Tchr, GA State C of C 1969; Acad Year Grants to Atlanta Univ and OH State U; Nat Sci Found 1966-67 1969-70. **Business Addr:** 240 Chestnut St SW, Atlanta, GA 30314.

WEBB, RICHMOND JEWEL
Professional football player. **Personal:** Born Jan 11, 1967, Dallas, TX. **Educ:** Texas A&M, BS in industrial distribution, 1993. **Career:** Miami Dolphins, tackle, 1990-. **Honors/Awds:** NFL Rookie of the Year, 1990; Pro Bowl appearances, 1990-97. **Business Addr:** Professional Football Player, Miami Dolphins, 2269 MW 199th St, Miami, FL 33056, (305)620-5000.

WEBB, SCHUYLER CLEVELAND
US military officer, psychologist. **Personal:** Born Jun 28, 1951, Springfield, MA; son of Bettye Wright Webb and Cleveland Webb; children: Kayla Monique. **Educ:** Morehouse Coll, BA (Cum Laude) 1974; Amer Inst for Foreign Study, Certificate 1975; Univ of MA, MS 1978; Natl Univ, MBA 1986; Pacific Graduate School of Psychology, PhD candidate, currently. **Career:** Univ of Massachusetts, asst trainer & alcoholism counselor 1974-77; Inst for Studying Educ Policy Howard Univ, rsch asst 1978; Lawrence Johnson & Assoc Inc, tech staff/consultant 1978-81; US Navy Medical Serv Corps, rsch psychologist & hospital corpsman 1981-; Howard Univ Center for Sickle Cell Disease, Washington, DC, editorial comm mem/consultant 1979-81; Higher Horizons Day Care Center, Crossroads, VA, consultant 1980-81. **Orgs:** Mem Assoc of Military Surgeons, Human Factors Soc, Sleep Rsch Soc, Assoc of Black Psychologists, Amer Psychological Assoc; public relations & scholarship comm Natl Naval Officer Assoc San Diego Chap 1983-; co-chair Cultural Heritage & Black History Comm San Diego USN 1984-86; advanced open water diver Professional Assoc of Diving Instructors 1986-; mem NAACP, Alpha Phi Alpha, Urban League, Morehouse Alumni Assoc, Equal Opportunity Officer, Combined Federal Campaign Officer; vice pres of membership, natl Naval officers Assn 1988-89; mem Second Harvest Food Bank 1987-; member, Association for the Study of Classical African Civilizations, 1990-. **Honors/Awds:** Certificate of Achievement in Comm and Counseling Psychology 1974; Horace Barr Fellowship 1974-77; Collegiate Comm for the Educ of Black Students Fellowship1974-75; Our Crowd Scholarship; Springfield Teachers Club Scholarship; Springfield Coll Comm Serv Awd; Academic Scholarship (4 year tuition scholarship), Morehouse College 1970-74; Psychology Department honors, Morehouse College, 1974; Natl Univ leadership Scholarship, Natl Univ, 1984; ''Jet Lag in Military Operations'', Naval Health Research Center, San Diego, CA 1986; publication ''Comparative Analysis of Decompression Sickness'', Journal of Hyperbaric Medicine, 2:55-62, 1987; Duty Under Instruction Scholarship, US Navy, 1991-94. **Military Serv:** USN lt cmmdr; Leadership Awd, Pistol Sharpshooter, Physical Fitness Awd, Commendation Letter; Rifle Expert 1988; Defense Equal Opportunity Management Institute Internship, 1991. **Business Addr:** Medical Serv Corps Officer, US Navy, Naval Biodynamics Lab, PO Box 29407, New Orleans, LA 70189.

WEBB, SPUD (ANTHONY JEROME)
Professional basketball player. **Personal:** Born Jul 13, 1963, Dallas, TX. **Educ:** Midland College, Midland, TX, 1981-83; North Carolina State Univ, Raleigh, NC, 1983-85. **Career:** Atlanta Hawks, 1985-91; Sacramento Kings, 1991-. **Business Addr:** Professional Basketball Player, Atlanta Hawks, 1 CNN Center S Tower, Suite 405, Atlanta, GA 30335-0001.

WEBB, UMEKI
Professional basketball player. **Personal:** Born Jun 26, 1975. **Educ:** North Carolina State, attended. **Career:** Phoenix Mercury, guard-forward, 1997-. **Business Addr:** Professional Basketball Player, Phoenix Mercury, 201 E Jefferson St, Phoenix, AZ 85004, (602)252-9622.

WEBB, VERONICA LYNN
Model, journalist. **Personal:** Born Feb 25, 1965, Detroit, MI; daughter of Marion Stewart Webb and Leonard Douglas Webb. **Educ:** Parson's School of Design, attended; New School for Social Research, attended. **Career:** Ford Model Management, free-lance model, currently. **Orgs:** Black Girls Coalition, steering committee head, 1989-; Planned Parenthood, sustaining member, 1992-; The 21th Century Party, 1992-. **Special Achievements:** First African-American woman in the history of the fashion industry to be awarded a multi-million dollar contract by Revlon Inc, 1992; supporting role, Spike Lee's Jungle Fever, 1991; contributing editor, Interview, Andy Warhol, 1990; columnist, Paper Magazine, New York City, 1990. **Business Addr:** Contract Model, c/o Ford Models, 344 E 59th St, New York, NY 10022.

WEBB, WELLINGTON E.
City official. **Personal:** Born Feb 17, 1941, Chicago, IL; married Wilma J; children: Keith, Tony, Allen, Stephanie. **Educ:** CO State Coll, BA 1964; Univ No CO, MA 1972. **Career:** CO State Univ Manpower Lab, dir 1969-74; State Rep 1973-77; CO Carter/Mondale Campaign, 1976; US Dept Health & Human Serv, principal reg official beginning 1977; City of Denver, auditor, until 1991, mayor, 1991-. **Orgs:** Chmn Dem Caucus CO House of Rep 1975-; chmn Health Welfare & Inst Com 1975-76; del Dem Nat Conv 1976, 1992; trustee bd Denver Childrens Hosp 1975-; bd dir Denver Operation PUSH 1975-; bd dir Denver Urban Coalition 1975; chmn United Negro Coll Fund 1973-75. **Honors/Awds:** Barney Ford Award for Political Action 1976; Leadership of Yr Award Thomas Jefferson HS 1976. **Business Addr:** Mayor, City of Denver, 1437 Bannock, Room 350, Denver, CO 80202.

WEBB, WILMA J.
Labor official. **Personal:** Born May 17, 1943, Denver, CO; daughter of Frank Wendell Gerdine (deceased) and Faye Elizabeth Wyatt Gerdine; married Wellington, 1971; children: Keith, Anthony, Stephanie, Allen. **Educ:** Univ of CO, Denver, attended; Harvard Univ, John F Kennedy School of Government. **Career:** Mobil Corp, admin assoc; Bank of Denver, admin assoc; City of Denver, legislator; CO House of Rep, state rep; US Labor Dept, Reg 8, secretary's rep, 1997-. **Orgs:** Denver Children's Home; Martin Luther King, Jr. CO Holiday Commission, chair; Mayor's Commission on Art, Culture and Film, founder, chair; CO Joint Budget Comm. **Honors/Awds:** Martin Luther King, Jr Humanitarian Award; Colorado Institute of Art, hon doctorate. **Special Achievements:** First African American to serve Region 8; first woman to serve Region 8; first minority female mem of CO Joint Budget Comm. **Business Addr:** Secretary's Representative, US Labor Dept-Region 8, 1801 California St, Ste 945, Denver, CO 80202, (303)844-1256.

WEBB, ZADIE OZELLA
Physician, consultant. **Personal:** Born Aug 22, 1932, Washington, DC; daughter of Zadie O Sizemore Thompson and John V Thompson; married Harvey Webb Jr, DDS; children: Tomai Adana, Harvey III, Hoyt Kelan. **Educ:** Howard Univ Coll of Liberal Arts, BS 1954; Howard Univ Coll of Med, MD 1958; Johns Hopkins School of Hygiene & Public Health, MPH 1974. **Career:** DC Schools, school health physician 1963-64; Dept of Public health, med officer pediatrics 1963-68; Howard Univ Coll of Med, pediatric consultant 1964-68; Children in Foster Care, dir health serv 1968-73; Head Start Program Washington DC & Cambridge MD, pediatric consult 1969-76; Washington DC Govt, chief med asst div 1973-76; Washington DC Govt Health Admin, chief maternal & child health 1976-80. **Orgs:** Mem Links, NAACP, Urban League, Capezios, Carats, Parents and Alumni Univ PA, Howard Univ Medical Alumni Assn, Montague Cobb Med Soc, Natl Medical Assn. **Honors/Awds:** Fellowships NIH, Natl Inst Mental Health 1956-59; published numerous med articles 1970-75; Physicians Recognition Award AMA 1971; Certificate of Appreciation Natl Dental Assoc, 1976. **Home Addr:** 6601 Ruff St, North Port, FL 34287.

WEBBER, CHRIS (MAYCE EDWARD CHRISTOPHER WEBBER, III)
Professional basketball player. **Personal:** Born Mar 1, 1973, Detroit, MI; son of Doris Webber and Mayce Webber. **Educ:** Univ of Michigan. **Career:** Golden State Warriors, forward, 1993-94; Washington Wizards, 1994-98; Sacramento Kings, 1998-. **Honors/Awds:** Schick NBA Rookie of the Year Award, 1994; NBA All-Star, 1997. **Special Achievements:** Led the Univ of Michigan basketball team to two championship finals; NBA, first round draft pick, #1 pick, 1993. **Business Addr:** Professional Basketball Player, Sacramento Kings, One Sports Parkway, Sacramento, CA 95834, (916)928-6900.

WEBBER, PAUL R., III
Judge. **Personal:** Born Jan 24, 1934, Gadsden, SC; son of Clemmie Webber and Paul Webber Jr; married Fay DeShields; children: Paul IV, Stephen, Nikki. **Educ:** BA, 1955; South Carolina State University, JD, 1957. **Career:** Neighborhood Legal Serv Program, District of Columbia, mng atty, 1967-69; Antitrust Div US Dept Just, trial atty, 1964-67; Golden State Mutual Life Insurance Co LA, assoc counsel, 1960-64; UCLA, asst law lib, 1959-60; Allen Univ, Columbia, SC, private practice & lecturer, 1958-59; Dolphin Branton Stafford & Webber, atty, 1969-77; Howard Univ, lectr; George Washington Univ Law School, adjunct prof, summer, 1973; District of Columbia Superior Court, judge, currently. **Orgs:** Amer, Natl, District of Columbia, California & South Carolina Bar Assns; Alpha Phi Alpha; Sigma Pi Phi; The Guardsmen; past chmn Civil Practice & Family Law Sec Natl Bar Assn. **Honors/Awds:** Trial Judge of the Year, 1985-86 by unanimous vote of the Trial Lawyers Assn of Metro Washington, DC. **Military Serv:** UAS Artillery 2nd lt 1957. **Business Addr:** Judge, DC Superior Court, 500 Indiana Ave NW, Washington, DC 20001.

WEBBER, WILLIAM STUART
Elected official. **Personal:** Born Oct 17, 1942, Hartshorne, OK; children: Natalie Jewell, Stuart Franklin, Timpi Armelia. **Educ:** Eastern OK A&M, 1960-62. **Career:** Rancher Santa Gertrudis Breeder, 1958-; electronic tech, Rockwell Intl 1964-83; county comm Pittsburg County 1983-. **Orgs:** Mason AF&M, Pittsburg County Cattleman's Assn 1967-; real estate developer; professional coon hunter, Professional Coon Hunters Assn 1981-85; inducted mem Amer Cattle Breeder's Hall of Fame; mem Church of God in Christ. **Military Serv:** OK Ntl Guard, ES, 8 years. **Home Addr:** Rt 1, Box 240, Hartshorne, OK 74547.

WEBER, DANIEL
Attorney. **Personal:** Born Sep 25, 1942, New Orlean, LA; married Shirley Ann Nash; children: Akilah F, Akil K. **Educ:** Los Angeles City Coll, history 1961-63; CA State Coll LA, BA History, Sciology 1968; UCLA School of Law, JD 1971. **Career:** Los Angeles City Attny Office, law clerk 1972-73; CA State Attny Gen, grad legal asst 1973-74; Legal Aid Soc of San Diego, attny 1975; Grossmont Coll, teacher 1974-75; Employment Devel Dept State of CA, legal counsel 1975; Private Practice of Law, self employed 1975-76; Mira Mesa Jr Coll, teacher bus law 1979-82; Soc Sec Admin Office, govt lawyer 1976-83; Private Practice of Law, self employed 1983-; Earl B Gilliam Bar Assoc, president. **Orgs:** Mem 1973-, bd of dir 1979-80, NAACP; mem 1976-80, chmn 1976-80, treas 1978-79, court comm pres 1981-82 & 1984-85 Earl B Gilliam Bar Assoc; San Diego Mncpl Ct Appt Attny List 1976; bd of gov 1977, chmn 1977-80, judicial sel pres-elect 1979-80, pres 1980-81 CA Assoc of Blk Lawyers; San Diego bd of zoning Appeals 1978-82; bd of dir State Fed & Appellate Defenders Inc 1979-80;Indigents Defense Bd 1979-80; Aequus Dist Comm BSA 1980-; bd of dir 1981-, chmn 1981-, BAPAC; bd of gov San Diego Bar Assoc, Amer Bar Assoc, Natl Bar Assoc 1981-82; Phi Alpha Delta; rep, mem bar relations comm Student Bar Assoc; rep, student rep acad senate sub-comm on equal oppty, comm of housing, Grad Student Assoc; org mem Black Law Students Assoc; chmn BLSA Defense Comm,co-chmn BLSA Recruitment Comm' org mem UCLA ck Law Jrnl; courts adm to practice before, CA State Courts, NJ State Courts, US Dist Courts in NJ, Supreme Ct of US, US Cts of Appeals-9th, 5th & DC, US Tax Court, US Customs Court. **Honors/Awds:** Cert of Appreciation 1979,80, Outstanding Pres Awd 1980-81, CA Assoc of Black Lawyers; Outstanding Pres Awd 1981-82 Earl B Gilliam Bar Assoc of San Diego Cty; Cert of Appreciation for Serv on Bd of Zoning Appeals City of San Diego; Spec Commendation 1983 City Council of San Diego; Resolution for Outstanding Service to Legal Profession CA State Assemblyman Pete Chacon 79th Assembly Dist; Cert of Appreciation for Outstanding Contribs to the Delivery of VoluntaryLegal Service in CA 1983 The State Bar of CA Bd of Governors; Outstanding Serv Awd 1985 San Diego Volunteer Prog. **Business Addr:** President, Earl B Gilliam Bar Assn, 443 West C St Ste 111, San Diego, CA 92101.

WEBER, SHIRLEY NASH
Educational administrator. **Personal:** Born Sep 20, 1948, Hope, AR; married Daniel Weber; children: Akilah Faizah, Akil Khalfani. **Educ:** Univ of CA LA, BA 1966-70, MA 1970-71, PhD 1971-75. **Career:** Episcopal City Mission Soc LA, caseworker 1969-72; CA State Coll LA, instructor 1972; San Diego State Univ, prof 1972-; San Diego City Schools, San Diego, CA, president, board of education, 1990-91. **Orgs:** Bd mem CA Black Faculty & Staff 1976-80; pres Black Caucus Speech Comm Assoc 1980-82; pres Natl Comm Assn 1983-85; regional editor Western Journal of Speech 1979-; adv bd Battered Women's Serv YWCA 1981-; Council of 21 Southwestern Christian Coll 1983-; 1st vice pres Natl Sor of Phi Delta Kappa Delta Upsilon Chapt; trustee Bd of Educ San Diego Unified School District l988-96. **Honors/Awds:** Fellow Woodrow Wilson Fellowship 1970; Black Achievement Action Enterprise Develop 1981; Women of Distinction Women Inc 1984; Natl Citation Award, Natl Sorority of Phi Delta Kappa, Inc. July l989; Citizen of the Year, Omega Psi Phi Fraternity, 1989; Carter G Woodson Education Award, NAACP, San Diego, 1989. **Business Addr:** Professor & Chairperson, San Diego State University, Afro-American Studies, San Diego, CA 92182.

WEBSTER, CECIL RAY
Military officer. **Personal:** Born Mar 29, 1954, Franklin, TX; son of Ella McAfee Webster and Riley Webster (deceased); married Marsha E Burnett, Aug 13, 1977; children: Cecil Jr. **Educ:** Prairie View A&M Univ, BS 1976; Texas A&M Univ, MS 1984. **Career:** US Army Engr School, instructor 1981-82; Grad School, 1982-84; US Military Acad, asst prof 1984-87; US Army 101st Airborne Div, Fort Campbell, KY, platoon leader, co commander, 1976-81; US Army Training & Doctrine Command, Ft Monroe, VA, staff officer, 1987-90; US Army Space and Strategic Defense Command, Huntsville, AL, Kenetic Energy Weapons, deputy dir, 1990-. **Orgs:** Mem Assoc of United States Army 1976-; sec Soc of Amer Military Engrs 1984-. **Honors/Awds:** Tau Beta Pi Natl Engineering Honor Soc, Prairie View A&M Univ, 1975. **Special Achievements:** Registered and licensed professional engineer, State of Virginia, 1989. **Military Serv:** AUS, lt col, 16 yrs; Army Commendation Medal, 1981, Airborne Badge, Air Assault Badge, 1977, Army Meritorious Service Medal, 1987, 1990, Parachutes Badge, 1975, Army Service Ribbon, 1976, Natl Defense Service Medal, 1991.

WEBSTER, CHARLES
Dentist. **Personal:** Born Dec 15, 1936, LeCompte, LA; son of Carrie Hills Webster and Charles Webster Sr. **Educ:** Southern Univ, BS 1959; Howard Univ, MS 1971, Coll of Dentistry DDS 1977. **Career:** GA Ave Kiwanis Club, business mgr 1984-85; Private Practice, dentist; Dept Human Svcs, dental officer. **Orgs:** Mem Kappa Alpha Psi 1957-; dental intern St Elizabeth Hosp Washington DC 1977-78; dental dir Montgomery Co Detention Ctr 1978; mem Amer Soc of Dentistry for Children 1978; mem Amer Dental Soc 1981, Assoc of Military Surgeons 1981, Anethesiology Training Uniform Serv Medical Sch 1982-84. **Honors/Awds:** Mem Eta Chi Sigma Hon Biological Soc, Beta Beta Beta Hon Biol Soc; Certificate Amer Cancer Soc 1977. **Military Serv:** AUS ltc, Army Natl Guard 1981-97 (retired). **Home Addr:** 6713 14th St NW, Washington, DC 20012. **Business Addr:** Dental Officer, Dept of Corrections, 7723 Alaska Ave NW, Washington, DC 20012.

WEBSTER, JOHN W., III
Computer software development manager. **Personal:** Born Oct 19, 1961, Highland Park, MI; son of Melceina L Blackwell Webster and John W Webster Jr; married Michele S Peters Webster, Feb 19. **Educ:** Mass Inst of Tech, Cambridge, MA, BSCS, 1983, MSCS, 1987. **Career:** IBM Corp, Cambridge, MA, scientific staff member, 1983-87, scientific project manager, 1987-88; IBM Corp, Research Triangle Park, NC, comm & sys mgmt designer, 1988-89, development manager, 1989-. **Honors/Awds:** Outstanding Technical Achievement, IBM, 1986; Invention Achievement Award, IBM, 1989.

WEBSTER, KAREN ELAINE
Government official. **Personal:** Born Jan 7, 1960, Atlanta, GA; daughter of Donald & Isabell Gates Webster. **Educ:** University of Virginia, BA, 1982; Georgia State University, Masters, 1991. **Career:** Grocery Manufacturers of America, state legislative aide, 1983; Fulton County Government, law clerk, judge, 1984, law clerk, solicitor general, 1984-88, director, victim/witness program, 1988-91, executive asst to county mgr, 1991-92, executive director, intergovernmental affairs, 1992-94, chief of staff to the chairman, 1994-. **Orgs:** Regional Leadership Institute, bd member; YWCA of Greater Atlanta, chair of nominating committee, president elect, 1992-93; Links, Inc, southern area secretary, 1993-; Outstanding Atlantans, vice president selection committee, 1994; Atlanta Junior League, district advisor, 1994-; Regional Leadership foundation, bd of directors, 1994; The Southern Institute, bd member, 1994-. **Honors/Awds:** Regional Leadership Institute, 1993; Leadership America, 1994. **Business Phone:** (404)730-8206.

WEBSTER, LARRY MELVIN, JR.
Professional football player. **Personal:** Born Jan 18, 1969, Elkton, MD. **Educ:** Univ of Maryland. **Career:** Miami Dolphins, defensive tackle, 1992-94; Cleveland Browns, 1995; Baltimore Ravens, 1997-. **Business Addr:** Professional Football Player, Baltimore Ravens, 11001 Owings Mills Blvd, Owings Mills, MD 21117, (410)654-6200.

WEBSTER, LENNY (LEONARD IRELL)
Professional baseball player. **Personal:** Born Feb 10, 1965, New Orleans, LA. **Educ:** Grambling State University. **Career:** Minnesota Twins, catcher, 1989-94; Montreal Expos, 1994, 1996; Philadelphia Phillies, 1995; Baltimore Orioles, 1997-. **Business Addr:** Professional Baseball Player, Baltimore Orioles, 333 W Camden St, Baltimore, MD 21201, (410)685-9800.

WEBSTER, LESLEY DOUGLASS
Attorney. **Personal:** Born Jun 9, 1949, New York City, NY; married Jules A Webster; children: Jules S Webster. **Educ:** Northeastern Univ Boston, BA 1972; Georgetown Univ Law Ctr, JD 1972-75. **Career:** Cambridge Redevel Authority MA, comm org 1970-72; Criminal Justice Clinic, Georgetown Univ Law Center, prosecution coord 1974-75; US Dept of Energy Region II NY, atty, adv 1975-77; Coll of Staten Island NY, adjunct prof 1977-78; US Dept of Energy Reg II NY, deputy regional counsel 1977-79; Northville Ind Corp, compliance counsel 1979-84; NY Dept of Commerce, deputy commiss, counsel. **Orgs:** Chairwoman of bd Assoc of Energy Profls Inc 1980-84. **Honors/Awds:** Superior Serv Awd US Dept of Energy 1976. **Business Addr:** Deputy Commissioner, Counsel, NY Dept of Commerce, 1 Commerce Plaza, Albany, NY 12245.

WEBSTER, LONNIE
City official. **Personal:** Born Sep 3, 1922, Tillar, AR; married Modest Bishop; children: Earlene, Annette. **Career:** Reed AR, mayor; Webster Affiliated Food Store; Delta Fish Company; New Bethel Missionary Bapt Ch, pastor; Farm Worker. **Orgs:** Recipient Bookers Memorial College Banquet Award 1975.

WEBSTER, MARVIN NATHANIEL
Professional basketball player. **Personal:** Born 1952; married Maderia; children: Marvin Nathaniel II. **Educ:** Morgan State. **Career:** Denver Nuggets, 1977, Seattle SuperSonics, 1978, New York Knicks, 1979-84, Milwaukee Bucks, 1987. **Orgs:** Founder Galilee Baptist Ch Baltimore. **Honors/Awds:** Set NY record for shot blocks with 131 in one season in 1982-83; led Morgan State to the NCAA's Div II title in 1975; Player of the Year for a 2nd time.

WEBSTER, NIAMBI DYANNE
Educator. **Personal:** chilDren: K Tyronne Colemon. **Educ:** Drake Univ, BA, English/drama, 1973; Mankato State Coll, MS, curriculum & instruction, 1975; University of Iowa, PhD, curriculum & instruction, 1991. **Career:** Des Moines Public Schools, instructor 1975-78; Iowa Bystander, free lance writer, associate editor, 1976-80; Univ of IA, coord minority progs 1978-83, grad asst instructor 1980-83; IA Arts Council, touring music/theatre folk artist 1978-; Coe Coll, instr dir special servs; dir, multicultural & international student affairs, Skidmore College 1989-91; Sonoma State University, assistant professor, American multicultural studies department, currently. **Orgs:** Outreach counselor YMCA Des Moines 1974-78; instr Gateway Oppor Pageant 1975-78; press & publicity chair NAACP Des Moines Chap 1976-78; founder/dir Langston Hughes Co of Players 1976-82; co-chair Polk Co Rape/Sexual Assault Bd 1977-80; artist-in-the schools IA Arts Council 1978-; 6th Judicial Dist Correctional Serv CSP & News Editor Volunteer 1984-; chairperson Mid-Amer Assoc of Ed Oppty Prog Personnel Cultural Enrichment Comm 1984-; mem Delta Sigma Theta Sor, Berkeley Alumnae; Iowa City Comm Schools Equity Comm mem 1985-87. **Honors/Awds:** Comm Service in the Fine Arts NAACP Presidential 1978; Black Leadership Awd Univ of IA 1979; Social Action Awd Phi Beta Sigma Frat 1980; Outstanding Young Woman in the Arts NAACP Natl Women Cong 1981; Women Equality & Dedication Comm on the Status of Women 1981; Trio Achievers Awd Natl Cncl of Educ Oppor Assoc 1985; Outstanding Woman of the Year Awd Linn Co Comm 1986. **Home Addr:** 10 Meridian Circle, Rohnert Park, CA 94928. **Business Addr:** Assistant Professor, American Multicultural Studies Department, Sonoma State University, 1801 E Cotati Ave, Rohnert Park, CA 94928-3613.

WEBSTER, THEODORE
Engineering executive. **Career:** Webster Engineering Co, Inc, Dorchester MA, chief executive, 1977-. **Orgs:** NAMC of Massachusetts, local chapter, president, currently. **Business Addr:** Webster Engineering Co, Inc, PO Box 275, Dorchester, MA 02121.

WEBSTER, WILLIAM H.
Attorney. **Personal:** Born Oct 26, 1946, New York City, NY; son of Verna May Bailey Webster and Eugene Burnett Webster; married Joan Leslie; children: Sydney. **Educ:** New York Univ, BA (cum laude), 1972; Univ of California, Berkeley, School of Law, JD, 1975. **Career:** Black Law Journal, UCLA & Univ of California at Berkeley, research assoc, 1973; Natl Economic Devel & Law Project, post-grad, 1974-76; Natl Economic Devel & Law Center, Berkeley, CA, atty, 1976-82; Hunter & Anderson, partner, 1983-; Webster & Anderson, managing partner, 1993-. **Orgs:** Past mem bd of dirs, Natl Training Inst for Comm Economic Devel, Artisans Cooperative Inc; past mem, Mayor's Housing Task Force Berkeley; mem, State Bar of California, US Dist Ct No Dist of California, US Tax Ct, Natl Assoc of Bond Lawyers, Natl Bar Assoc, Charles Houston Bar Assn; past mem, City of Berkeley Citizens Comm on Responsible Investments; Kappa Alpha Psi. **Honors/Awds:** Martin Luther King Fellowship; New York State Regents Incentive Awards; Howard Memorial Fund Scholarship; Alpha Phi Alpha Scholarship; pub, "Tax Savings through Intercorporate Billing," Economic Devel Law Center Report, 1980; pub, "Housing, Structuring a Housing Development," Economic Devel Law Center Report, 1978; various other publications. **Business Addr:** Attorney, Webster & Anderson Law Office, 469 Ninth St, Ste 240, Oakland, CA 94607, (510)839-3245.

WEBSTER, WINSTON ROOSEVELT
Attorney. **Personal:** Born Apr 22, 1943, Nashville, TN. **Educ:** Fisk U, AB 1965; Harvard U, LLB 1968. **Career:** Practicing Atty 1971-; TX So U, mem bd of regents 1979-; TX So U, law prof 1974-77; Cable TV Info Ctr, regional dir 1972-74; Office of Legal SvcsWA, supervisory gen atty 1970-72; Urban Inst, think tank rsrchr 1969-70; Nghbrhd Legal Serv Prgm, staff atty 1968-69. **Orgs:** US Dist Ct DC & TC; Superior Ct DC; Supreme Ct TX; DC Bar Assn; TX Bar Assn; Am Assn of Trial Lawyers; Nat Conf of Black Lawyers; bd dir Nat Paralegal Inst 1972-75; legal adv com TX Assn of Coll Tchrs 1976-77; bd gov WA Athletic Club 1974. **Honors/Awds:** Prof of Year Thurgood Marshall Sch of Law 1976-77; Outst Young Men of Am 1977; KY Col 1973; Duke of Paducah 1972; Hon Citizen New Orleans 1971; Num Articles. **Business Addr:** Attorney, 2626 S Loop W, Houston, TX 77054.

WEDDINGTON, ELAINE
Sports franchise executive. **Personal:** Born 1963, Flushing, NY. **Educ:** St Vincent College of St John's, BS, athletic administration, 1984; St John's Univ School of Law, JD, 1987. **Career:** Boston Red Sox, Boston, MA, associate counsel, 1988-90, assistant general manager, 1990-. **Business Addr:** Assistant General Manager, Boston Red Sox, 24 Yawkey Way/Fenway Park, Boston, MA 02215-3496.

WEDDINGTON, RACHEL THOMAS
Educator. **Personal:** Born Mar 9, 1917, Atlantic City, NJ; daughter of Laura Frances Thomas Weddington (deceased) and Ralph Thornton Weddington (deceased). **Educ:** Howard Univ, Washington DC, AB 1938, AM 1940; Univ of Chicago, PhD 1958. **Career:** Rosenwald Foundation, fellow 1946-48; Atlantic City NJ, bd of educ 1941-45; Howard Univ, instructor 1948-57; Merrill-Palmer Inst Detroit, research assoc 1957-61; Queens Coll NY, asst, assoc prof 1961-75; CUNY, univ dean for teacher educ 1975-79, prof 1975-85, prof emerita. **Orgs:** Mem Pi Lambda Theta Univ of Chicago 1947; mem Kappa Delta Pi Howard Univ 1954. **Home Addr:** 575 Main St, New York, NY 10044.

WEDDINGTON, WAYNE P., JR.
Otolaryngologist. **Personal:** Born Dec 24, 1936, McGehee, AR; son of Amanda Tyler Weddington and Wayne Pennoyer L Weddington; married Dolores Johnson Weddington, Dec 2, 1957. **Educ:** University of Arkansas Agricultural, Mechanical and Normal College, BS, 1958; Howard University College of Medicine, Washington, DC, MD, 1963; Andrews Air Force Base, Camp Springs, MD, intern, 1964. **Career:** Temple University Health and Science Center, Philadelphia, PA, resident; ORL Germantown Hospital and Medical Center, Department of Otolaryngology, Philadelphia, PA, chairman, 1974-; Neuman Med Center, Philadelphia, PA, staff physician; St Christopher's Hospital, staff physician; Weddington Ent Associates MC, Philadelphia, PA, owner/CEO, 1981-; Episcopal Hospital, Department of Otolaryngology, section chief, 1992-. **Orgs:** Fellow, Amer Academy of Otolaryngology; 1972-; Fellow, College of Physicians of Philadelphia, 1990-; National Medical Association; Pennsylvania Academy of Otolaryngology, 1972-. **Business Addr:** Chairman, Department of Otolaryngology, Germantown Hospital & Medical Center, One Penn Blvd, Philadelphia, PA 19144, (215)438-3898.

WEDDINGTON, WILBURN HAROLD, SR.
Physician, educator. **Personal:** Born Sep 21, 1924, Hiram, GA; son of Annie Mae Moore Weddington and Charlie Earl Weddington; married Rose Carline Howard Weddington, Mar 15, 1979; children: Wilburn H Jr, Cynthia D, Kimberly K, Marisia D, Wilburn C. **Educ:** Morehouse College, Atlanta, GA, BS, 1944; Howard University, Washington, DC, MD, 1948; University of Buffalo, Buffalo, NY, Radiology; Harvard University, Electrocardiography, 1962; American Society of Hypnosis, 1963; The University of Mexico, Mexico City, Mexico, course on Obstetrics and Pediatrics; Howard University, family medical review. **Career:** Mercy Hospital, staff physician, 1957-70; Grant Hospital, staff physician, 1957-; St Anthony Hospital, staff physician, 1958-; Ohio State University, College of Medicine, Columbus, OH, staff physician, 1970-88, clinical associate professor, 1980-85, professor of clinical family medicine, 1987-, associate dean, Medicine Administration, currently. **Orgs:** American Medical Assn, 1952-; National Medical Association, 1954-; Ohio State Medical Assn, 1958-; Columbus and Franklin County Academy of Medicine, 1958-; Ohio Academy of Family Physicians, 1968-; Central Ohio Academy of Family Physicians, 1968-; member, 1968-, fellow, 1974-, American Academy of Family Physicians; co-founder, Columbus Assn of Physicians and Dentistry, 1973-; Omega Psi Phi; Sigma Pi Phi. **Honors/Awds:** Citizen of the Year, Mu Iota Chapter, Omega Psi Phi, 1985; Regional IV Award, Natl Medical Assn, 1985; Citation for Tremendous Record of Professional Achievement, General Assembly of the Ohio Senate, 1987; Ohio House of Representatives Recognition of Dedicated Service in the Field of Medicine, 1987; Special Recognition for Dedicated Service as a Member of the Governor's Task Force on Black & MNY Health, Governor of Ohio, 1987; Recognition for Outstanding Performance & Service in Columbus Black Community, Columbus Urban League, 1987; Dedication Award for Outstanding Service to Ohio State University & the Black Community, Black World Week, 1988; Citation for Dedicated Leadership as Chairman of the Committee on Minority Health Affairs, American Academy of Family Physicians, 1988; 7th Annual Distinguished Affirmative Action Award, State University, 1989; Ohio Academy of Family Physicians, Educator of the Year Award, 1991; has served on national and state medical committees and commissions. **Special Achievements:** Co-author, "Surgery Practice and Perceived Training Needs of Selected Ohio Family Physicians," Journal of Family Practice, Sep 1986; "Review of Literature Concerning Racial Effects on Medical Treatment and Outcome," Journal of American Board of Family Practice, 1990; numerous editorials. **Business Addr:** Associate Dean, Medicine Administration, College of Medicine, Ohio State University, 370 W 9th Ave, Rm 200-G, Columbus, OH 43210.

WEDGEWORTH, ROBERT, JR.
Educational administrator. **Personal:** Born Jul 31, 1937, Ennis, TX; married Chung Kyun. **Educ:** Wabash Coll, BA; Univ of IL, MS Library Sci; Park Coll, DLitt 1975; Wabash Coll, DLitt 1980. **Career:** KC Publ Library, cataloger 1961-62; Seattle Worlds Fair Library 21, staff mem 1962; Park Coll, asst librarian 1962-63, acting head librarian 1963-64; Meramec Comm Coll Kirkwood, head librarian 1964-66; Brown Univ Library, asst chief order librarian 1966-69; Library Resources & Tech Serv ofcl ALA Jrnl, ed; Rutgers Univ, asst prof; Univ of Chicago, lecturer; Amer Library Assoc Chgo, exec dir; Columbia Univ, dean, currently. **Orgs:** NAACP Public Serv Satellite Consortium Bd; ed AL Yearbook, AL World Encyc of Library & Info Svcs; trustees Newberry Library; adv comm US Book & Library; vice pres Wabash Coll Alumni Bd; mem adv council WBEZ Chgo; mem Amer Antiquarian Soc; Intl Fed of Library Assns & Institutions, pres, 1991-. **Business Addr:** Executive Dir, Amer Library Assoc, 50 E Huron St, Chicago, IL 60611.

WEEKES, MARTIN EDWARD
Attorney. **Personal:** Born Jun 6, 1933, New York, NY; son of Nettie Mullings Weekes and Wilfred Weekes; married Diana R Bichler Weeks, Dec 20, 1984; children: Shelli, Dawn, Nicole. **Educ:** Manhattan Coll NY, BS 1954; Univ of So CA, JD 1961. **Career:** Douglas Aircraft Santa Monica CA, engr draftsman 1956-60; Charles Meram Co Los Angeles, engr 1960-62; Deputy District Atty 1962-63; Div Chief; Co Counsel 1963-. **Orgs:** First pres Frederick Douglass Child Devel Cntr 1963; mem bd dir Rose Brooks Sch of Performing Arts 1974-; mem Reserve Faculty EPA; Lectured on Enviromental Law; guest lecturer USC; Twenty Publications Library of Congress; contrib author CA Adminstr Agency Practice CEB. **Honors/Awds:** Rector's Award Episcopal Ch of the Advent 1967; Finished Second in All-Army Talent Contest 1956. **Military Serv:** AUS 1954-56. **Business Addr:** Asst County Counsel, County Counsel, LA County, 648 Hall of Administration, Suite 648, Los Angeles, CA 90012.

WEEKS, DEBORAH REDD
Lawyer. **Personal:** Born Dec 23, 1947, Brooklyn, NY; daughter of Edna Loretta Mayo Redd and Warren Ellington Redd; divorced; children: Monteil Dior, Kristienne Dior. **Educ:** University of Kentucky, Lexington, KY, JD, 1978; Fisk University, Nashville, TN, BA, 1970. **Career:** Kentucky State Government, Frankfort, KY, Director of Contract Compliance State of Kentucky, 1980-83; Urban League, Lexington, KY, director adoption, 1983-85; WLEX-TV, Lexington, KY, Talk Show Host, 1984-86; SUNY Brockport, Brockport, NY, director, AA/EEO, 1986-89; Monroe County, Rochester, NY, counsel director AA/EEO, 1989-90; Health & Hospital Corp, New York, NY, associate legal, 1991-. **Orgs:** Chairman, EEO committee, Harlem Business Alliance, 1989-; member, RACOL Center Board, 1990-; member, Links, 1988-; member, Coalition of 100 Black Women, 1984-; member, Negro Business & Professional Women, 1990-. **Honors/Awds:** Kentucky Colonel, State of Kentucky, 1986; Multiculturism, New York Assn of College Personnel Administration, summer, 1987.

WEEKS, RENEE JONES
Judge. **Personal:** Born Dec 28, 1948, Washington, DC. **Educ:** Ursuline College, BA, 1970; Rutgers Law School, JD, 1973. **Career:** State of New Jersey, deputy attorney general, 1973-75; Prudential Insurance Co of America, 1975-89; State of New Jersey, Superior Court, judge, 1989-. **Orgs:** Past pres, Women's Div, Natl Bar Assn; Am Bar Assn; past pres, Assn of Black Women Lawyers of NJ; past asst treas, Natl Assn of Black Women Attorneys; Alpha Kappa Alpha; former member, Minority Interchange; former vice pres, former chair of judicial council, Natl Bar Assn; former trustee, Essex Co Bar Assn; past sec, Garden State Bar Assn; Natl Assn of Women Judges; Natl Council of Juvenile and Family Court Judges; former mem, New Jersey Family Practice Committee and Domestic Violence Working Group; former mem, NJ Supreme Court, Minority Concerns Committee; secty, Judical Council, Nat'l Bar. **Business Addr:** Judge, Superior Court of New Jersey, Essex County Hall of Records, Rm 908, New Courts Bldg, 50 W Market St, Newark, NJ 07102.

WEEMS, LUTHER B. **See AKBAR, NA'IM.**

WEEMS, VERNON EUGENE, JR.
Attorney-at-law. **Personal:** Born Apr 27, 1948, Waterloo, IA; son of Anna Marie Hickey Weems and Eugene Weems. **Educ:** Univ of IA, BA 1970; Univ of Miami Sch of Law, JD 1974. **Career:** US Small Business Admin, atty/advisor 1977-78, 1979-81; A Nation United Inc, pres/ceo/chmn bd 1982-85; Weems Law Office, attorney 1978-; Weems Productions and Enterprises, ceo/consultant 1987-. **Orgs:** Mem Amer Bar Assoc 1977-82, IA State Bar Assoc 1977-82, St Johns Lodge Prince Hall Affil 1977-86, Federal Bar Assoc 1979-82; mem bd of dirs Black Hawk County Iowa Branch NAACP. **Honors/Awds:** Publication "Tax Amnesty Blueprint for Economic Development," 1981; Leadership Awd OIC/Iowa 1982; Service Appreciation Awd Job Service of Iowa 1985; article "Chapter 11 Tax Subsidies," 1986; Recognition of Excellence 1986. **Business Addr:** Attorney at Law, Weems Productions/Enterprises, PO Box 72, Waterloo, IA 50704-0072.

WEIL, ROBERT L.
Educator. **Personal:** Born Apr 22, 1932, Alexandria, LA; married Judith Adams; children: Pam, Martha, Sarah, Mathew. **Educ:** Wayne State U, MA 1963; John Hay Whitney Fellow 1960-61; Cntr for Asian Studies Proj for Intl Communications to Make Film in Japan, award grant 1970. **Career:** Head Sculpture Dept MI State Univ, asso prof 1985; Sculptor Painter Film Maker 1985; Detroit Bd Educ, art instr 1958-60; Robt O'Boyal Assoc on Lansing MI Waterfront Park, designer 1975-76; Play Structure in Edgwood Village E Lansing MI, design installed 1973-74. **Orgs:** Co-chprsn E Lansing Fine Arts & Cultural Heratage Com. **Honors/Awds:** Recip Albert Kahn Prize for Archit Sculpture. **Military Serv:** Served USN 1949-53. **Business Addr:** Professor, Michigan State University, Kresge Art Center, East Lansing, MI 48823.

WEINER, CHARLES R.
Judge. **Career:** United States Court House, Philadelphia, PA, federal judge, currently. **Business Addr:** Federal Judge, 6613 United States Court House, 601 Market, Philadelphia, PA 19106, (215)923-4450.

WEISS, ED, JR.
Automobile dealer. **Career:** Allegan Ford-Mercury Sales, Inc, Allegan MI, chief executive, 1984—. **Business Addr:** Allegan Masonic Temple, PO Box 316, Allegan, MI 49010-1316.

WEISS, JOYCE LACEY
Educator. **Personal:** Born Jun 8, 1941, Chicago, IL; daughter of Lois Lacey Carter; divorced. **Educ:** Bennett Coll, BA 1963; Troy State Univ, MS 1971; Univ of Michigan, EdD, 1988. **Career:** Coweta County GA, elementary class teacher, 1963-64; Montgomery AL, elementary class teacher, 1964-69; Montgomery AL, elementary school principal 1969-75; Troy State Univ, instructor/supvr student teachers 1975-, asst prof/dept chmn, elementary educ, 1988-. **Orgs:** Mem Delta Sigma Theta; mem Montgomery AL Chap NAACP; mem Links Inc; mem Natl Educ Assn 1963-; mem Zeta Gamma Chapter of Kappa Delta Pi 1973-; mem Assn of Teacher Educators 1975-; mem Troy Univ Chap of Phi Delta Kappa 1980-; Intl Reading Assn; Alabama Reading Assn; Amer Educational Research Assn; Alabama Educ Assn. **Honors/Awds:** Natl Merit Scholarship Bennett College 1959; School of Educ Fellowship Univ of MI 1984-85; Rackham Grad Fellowship 1985; MI Minority Fellowship 1985-87; School of Educ, Dean's Merit Fellowship, 1988; Rackham School of Graduate Studies, dissertation/thesis grant, Univ of Michigan, 1987; Michigan Minority Merit Fellowship, 1985-87, School of Educ Fellowship, 1985-86, Univ of Michigan. **Business Addr:** Dept Curric & Instr, Alabama State Univ, Box 271, Montgomery, AL 36101-0271.

WEISSINGER, THOMAS, SR.
Librarian. **Personal:** Born Jul 29, 1951, Silver Creek, NY; son of Hattie Bryant Weissinger and Tom Weissinger; married Maryann Hunter Weissinger, Jun 2, 1973; children: Thomas Jr, Sandra, Eric. **Educ:** State University of New York at Buffalo, Buffalo, NY, BA, 1973; University of Pittsburgh, Pittsburgh, PA, MA, 1978, MLS, 1980. **Career:** Newark Public Library, Newark, NJ, branch head, 1980-82; Rutgers University Libraries, New Brunswick, NJ, bibliographic instruction corrd, 1982-85; Cornell University Library, Ithaca, NY, head, John Henrik Clarke Africana Library, 1985-. **Orgs:** Member 1980-, chair, publications committee 1984-87, Black Caucus of the American Library Assn; member American Library Association 1980-; member 1991-, executive committee 1992-94, ASA Africana Librarians Council; editor 1993-94, AFAS Newsletter, ACRL Afro-American Studies Librarian Section; Cooperative Africana Micro-filming Project, secretary, 1993-95. **Honors/Awds:** Co-compiler, Black Labor in America: A Selected Annotated Bibliography, Westport, CT, Greenwood Press, 1986; compiler, Current Bibliography, Black American Literature Forum, 1988-; asst editor, Black Caucus of ALA Newsletter, 1984-88; Author, "African American Reference Books and the Reviewing Media," The Reference Librarian, No 45/46, 137-51; Library Consultant, African Centre for Development and Strategic Studies, Ijebu-ode, Nigeria, 1994; Library Consultant, TransAfrica Forum, Washington, DC, 1996. **Business Addr:** Head, John Henrik Clarke Africana Library, Cornell University Library, 310 Triphammer Rd, Ithaca, NY 14850, (607)255-5229.

WELBURN, EDWARD THOMAS, JR.
Automobile company designer. **Personal:** Born Dec 14, 1950, West Chester, PA; son of Evelyn Thornton Welburn and Edward Welburn Sr; married Rhonda Doby Welburn; children: Adrienne, Brian. **Educ:** Howard Univ, BFA 1972. **Career:** GM Design Staff, creative designer 1972-75, sr creative designer 1976-81, asst chief designer 1981-89, Oldsmobile studio, chief designer, beginning 1989; Chevrolet, vehicle chief designer, currently. **Orgs:** Mem Founders Soc of the Detroit Inst of Art; mem of The Cabinet 1983-. **Honors/Awds:** Contribute to the design of Oldsmobile's product line 1976-96; Alumni of the Year, Howard University Student Assn, 1989. **Business Addr:** General Motors Design Center, GM Technical Ctr, 30100 Mound Rd, Warren, MI 48090-9030.

WELBURN, RONALD GARFIELD
Writer. **Personal:** Born Apr 30, 1944, Berwyn, PA; son of Jessie W Watson and Howard Watson; married Cheryl Donahue Welburn, 1988; children: Loren Beatty, Justin Beatty, Elliott Welburn. **Educ:** Lincoln University, PA, BA, 1968; University of Arizona, MA, 1970; New York University, PhD, 1983. **Career:** Syracuse University, Syracuse NY, assistant professor of Afro-American studies, 1970-75; Rutgers University, New Brunswick NJ, formerly affiliated with Institute for Jazz Studies, assistant professor of English, 1983; Western Connecticut State University, Danbury, CT, assistant professor of English, 1987-. **Orgs:** Board member, Eagle Wing Press, 1989-. **Honors/Awds:** Silvera Award for poetry, Lincoln University, 1967 and 1968; author of Peripheries: Selected Poems, 1966-1968, Greenfield Review Press, 1972; fellow, Smithsonian Institute and Music Critics Association, 1975; author of Heartland: Selected Poems, Lotus Press, 1981; Langston Hughes Legacy Certificate, Lincoln University, 1981; author, Council Decisions: Poems, American Native Press Archives, 1991.

WELCH, ASHTON WESLEY
Educator. **Personal:** Born Jun 17, 1947; son of Ina I Welch and J W Welch; married Dr Helen M Wanken, May 29, 1976. **Educ:** Univ of Hull, UK, 1966-67; Wilberforce Univ, BA, 1968; Univ of Wisconsin, Madison, certificate, 1971, MA, 1971; Univ of Birmingham, UK, PhD, 1979. **Career:** Richmond College, UK, 1987-88; Creighton Univ, coordinator of black studies, 1975-, history chairman, 1986-93, assoc prof, 1975-. **Orgs:** African Studies Assn, 1971-; Assn for the Study of Afro-Amer Life & Culture, 1973-; Natl Council on Black Studies, Committee on Ethics, 1976-; Natl Assn of Ethnic Studies, bd of dirs 1977-; Great Plains Black Museum, bd of dirs, 1975-88; Creighton Federal Credit Union, bd of dirs, 1986-. **Honors/Awds:** Creighton Univ, Robert F Kennedy Award, 1992; Creighton Univ, College of Arts and Sciences, Dean's Award, 1993; AK-SAR-BEN, Nebraska Educator Award, 1992. **Special Achievements:** "The National Archives of the Ivory Coast," 1982; "Omaha: Positve Planning for Peaceful Integration," 1980; "The Making of an African-American Population: Omaha," 1993; "Emancipation in the United States," 1993; "Jihad," Just War: Three Views, 1991; "The Civil Rights Act of 1968," 1992; "Ethnic Definitions as Reflections of Public Policy," 1983. **Business Addr:** Professor, Creighton University, 2500 California Plaza, 341 Administration, Omaha, NE 68178, (402)280-2884.

WELCH, EDWARD L.
Attorney. **Personal:** Born Mar 10, 1928, Helena, AR; son of Leola M Welch and Arthur A Welch; married Susan L Welch; children: David, Karen, Joseph, Christopher. **Educ:** St Louis Univ, BS, Commerce, 1957; Washington Univ, St Louis, MO, JD, Order of Coif, 1960. **Career:** Stockham Roth Buder & Martin, assoc atty; Univ of Wisconsin, Milwaukee, lecturer; Allis-Chalmers Mfg Co, Milwaukee, WI, & Springfield, IL, labor law atty, 1961-67; Natl Labor Relations Bd 14th Region; staff atty, 1967-69; atty. **Orgs:** Gen counsel, Natl Alliance of Postal & Fed Employees, Washington, DC, 1971-90; senior litigation specialist 1990-; adj prof, Southern Illinois Univ, Carbondale, 1974-; school bd atty, East St Louis School Dist, 189, 1978-; mem, Amer Bar Assn, Illinois State Bar Assn, Madison City Bar Assn; life mem, NAACP. **Military Serv:** USN, radioman, 3rd class, 1946-47.

WELCH, HARVEY, JR.
Education administration. **Personal:** Born Jun 5, 1932, Centralia, IL; married Patricia Kay; children: Harvey, Gordon, Karen, Brian. **Educ:** SIU-C, BS 1955; SIU-C, MS 1958. **Career:** Southern IL Univ, dean for student life 1985; Southern IL Univ Amer Assn for Counseling & Development Assn, former dean of students; Natl Assn of Student Personal Admin; Natl Assn of Student Financial Aid Admin; Natl Assn of Women Deans. **Orgs:** Mem NAACP; Cdale Planning Commn 1976-78; IL Guid & Personel Assn; adv bd IL State Scholarship Com; Mid-west Equal Educ Oppty. **Honors/Awds:** Assn Hon Sco HS Fellowship SIU-C 1958; Distgn Mil Student 1954; Hon Mention Little All Am Basketball 1954; Met Serv Med 1975; Joint Serv Com 1973. **Military Serv:** USAF Col 1955-75. **Business Addr:** Dean of Student Life, Southern Ill University, Bldg T-40, Carbondale, IL 62901.

WELCH, JESSE ROY
Educator. **Personal:** Born May 29, 1949, Jonesville, LA; married Vickie Ragsdale (divorced); children: Symia. **Educ:** Washington State Univ, BA 1971, ED Candidate 1977. **Career:** Big Brother-Big Sister Program Benicia CA, dir, head counselor 1967-68; Pullman YMCA, program adv 1968-70; Washington State Univ, fin aid counselor 1970-71, assoc dir of admissions 1971-. **Orgs:** Participant Johnson Found Wingspread Conf on Minority Groups in Coll Student-Personnel Programs 1971; mem Amer Assoc of Coll Registrars & Admissions Officers 1971-, WA State Univ Affirmative Action Council 1972-74; comm min affairs WA Council of HS Coll Rel 1973-; consultant Spokane Nursing School Minority Affairs Comm Spokane 1973-74, WICHE Faculty Devel to Meet Minority Group Needs 1973-74; advisory bd 1974-, co-chmn 1974-76 YMCA Pullman WA. **Honors/Awds:** Numerous publications & papers.

WELCH, JOHN L.
City health care official. **Personal:** Born Apr 27, 1929, Newark, NJ; married Delorian; children: Elizabeth, Anthony, Michael. **Educ:** Steton Hall Univ, 1970-72; Rampo Coll NJ, BA 1975. **Career:** US Post Office, clerk 1962-67; Bergen Cty Dept of Health Svcs, sanitary inspector 1967-78; Roman Catholic Archdiocese Newark NJ, youth minister 1976-78; Jersey Youth Drill Team Judges, chief 1977-83; Borough of Bergenfield, health admin 1978-. **Orgs:** Scout leader 1960-82; camping chmn Essex Cty Council Boy Scouts of Amer; pres bd of ed Queen of Angels Parochial School Newark NJ; track coach Queen of Angels Parochial School Newark NJ 1958-80; mem Essex Cty Park Commiss 1974-77, Boy Scout Troop 155, Queen of Angels 1960-82, Track Official Newark YMCA 1979-83; trustee Queen of Angels Church Newark NJ; pres Queen of Angels Choir 1968-75; mem Robert Treat Council BSA; olympics coord, vice pres Newark Central Ward Athletic Assoc 1968-; vice pres Frontiers Intl Newark Club 1982-84; life mem NAACP Newark Br; mem NJ Health Officers Assoc, Bergen Cty Health Officers Assoc, NJ Assoc of Public Health Admins. **Honors/Awds:** Outstanding Achievement Awds, Silver Beaver BSA 1972; Newark Central Ward Athletic Assoc 1975; Frontiers Intl 1982,83,84. **Military Serv:** USMC 1951-53. **Business Addr:** Health Administrator, Bergenfield Health Department, 198 N Washington Avenue, Bergenfield, NJ 07621.

WELCH, OLGA MICHELE
Educational administrator, educator. **Personal:** Born Dec 30, 1948, Salisbury, NC; daughter of Dr & Mrs S E Barnes; married George E Welch; children: Taja Michele, Stephani Amber. **Educ:** Howard Univ, BA (Salutatorian), history/English/educ 1971; Univ of TN, MS deaf educ 1972, EdD educ admin & super 1977. **Career:** The Model Secondary Sch for the Deaf, instructor 1972-73, The TN Sch for the Deaf, instructor 1973-75, supervising principal 1977-78; Univ of TN Dept of Spec Educ & Rehab, assoc prof & dir 1978-, dir deaf educ prog, Rehabilitation & Deafness Unit, professor, currently. **Orgs:** Council of Exceptional Children; Alexander Graham Bell Assn; Convention of Amer Instructors of the Deaf; Natl Educ Assn; Assn for Supervision & Curriculum Develop; Project HELP tutorial prog for disadvantaged students 1983; vice pres, Knoxville Chap Natl Black Women's Hook-Up 1980-81; Girl Scout neighborhood chmn "NightHawks" Neighborhood 1977-; Interdenominational Concert Choir 1975-. **Honors/Awds:** Phi Beta Kappa; Phi Delta Kappa; Phi Kappa Phi; Phi Alpha Theta; Dept Awd "Most Creative Dissertation Topic" Univ TN; appointment to the Natl Educ Adv Bd 1983; E C Merrill Distinguished Research Award, 1990, 1992. **Home Addr:** 5402 E Sunset Rd, Knoxville, TN 37914. **Business Addr:** Dir Deaf Education Prog, Univ of TN, Claxton Addition Rm 129, Knoxville, TN 37996.

WELCH, WINFRED BRUCE
Psychologist, educator. **Personal:** Born Jun 25, 1918, Atlanta; married Rizpah Louise Jones. **Educ:** Livingtone Coll, AB 1939; IN U, EdD 1952; Sch Psychology Am Bd of Professional Psychologists, diplomate 1970; VA OH, cert licensed psychologist. **Career:** Univ of Cincinnati, prof educ psychology 1969-75; Elementary Secondary School Teacher Admin; Coll Univ Prof Admin; USOM/Iran Asia, educ specialist 1954-56; USOE Specialist, disadvantaged & handicapped; Counseling Bureau of Indian Affairs Dept of Interior, chief; Rosenwald Found Scholarship; Gen Educ Bd Fellow; OH State Univ, advanced study; Columbia Univ, psychologist privt practice; Learning Personal Adjustment; School of Educ Psychology VA Union Univ, dir prof 1975-. **Orgs:** Mem VA Pastorial Care Bd; past mem Richmond Urban League Bd; Educ Therapy Cntr Bd; Richmond Mental Health Bd. **Business Addr:** VA Union Univ, Richmond, VA 23220.

WELDON, ONAH CONWAY
Civil service commissioner, teacher (retired). **Personal:** Born Jun 22, 1926, Philadelphia, PA; daughter of Onah and Nimrod; married Thomas A (deceased); children: Thomas Anthony. **Educ:** Fisk U, BA 1949; Temple U, Grad Courses. **Career:** Philadelphia Pub Sch, tchr 1954; PA Fed Conv, del; Nat AFT Conv; State AFL-CIO Conv; PA Federation of Tchrs, vp; Public School Employees Credit Union, pres; Philadelphia Federation of Teachers, union rep 1985; retired Philadelphia School District Teacher; retired Philadelphia Federation Grievance Chair person. **Orgs:** Bd mem Afro-Amer Hist & Cultural Museum; mem Educ Comm of the Black Music Assn; coordinator PFT United Negro Coll Fund Dr; bd of dir Mid-City YWCA; bd of dir Philadelphia Citizens for Children & Youth Serv Community Planning Council; chair Philadelphia Congress of the Natl Political Congress of Black Women; bd of dirs Amer Women's Heritage Soc; dir, Mayor's Office of Consumer Services; pres, Credit Union, Grace Baptist Church of Germantown, 1984-. **Honors/Awds:** Distinguished Serv Citation United Negro Coll Fund; Hobart C Jackson Memorial Award Philadelphia Inter-Alumni Council; E Roosevelt Humanities Award State of Israel Bond; Outstanding Serv Award Black Women's Educ Alliance; C. Delores Tucker Tribute, Natl Political Congress of Black Women, 1986; Leadership Award, YMCA of Germantown, 1990.

WELDON, RAMON N.
Law enforcement official (retired). **Personal:** Born Jul 26, 1932, Keokuk, IA; son of Virginia Weldon and Clarence Weldon; married Betty Jean Watkins, Jul 24, 1955; children: Ramon N Jr. **Educ:** Keokuk Senior High School, diploma 1938-51. **Career:** Keokuk Police Department, patrolman 1962-74, detective 1974-80; captain 1980-82; chief of police 1982-87. **Orgs:** Member Lee County Juvenile Restitution Bd 1982; member Keokuk Humane Society 1982; trustee Keokuk Library Board in 2nd six year term; active member Iowa Chief's Assoc Natl Chief's Assn Intl Chief's Assn 1982-; United Way Board, chairman; Hoerner Y. Center Board; chairman Tri-State Coalition Against Family Violence, 3 yrs; Lee County Compensation Board, chairman. **Military Serv:** AUS Corporal 2 yrs; Soilder of the Month 1953. **Home Addr:** 2510 Decatur St, Keokuk, IA 52632.

WELLS, BARBARA JONES
Community relations manager. **Personal:** Born Apr 18, 1939, Waterproof, LA; daughter of Ruth Lee Johnson Jones and Willie Ray Jones; married Washington Wells, Jun 1, 1968. **Educ:** Grambling State University, Grambling, LA, BS, biology, education, 1962; Southern University, Baton Rouge, LA, MS, biology, education, 1968; University of Iowa, Iowa City, IA, further study, 1972; University of New Orleans, New Orleans, LA, 1978. **Career:** Tensas Parish School, St Joseph, LA, teacher, bio/chem, 1962-68; Rapides Parish Schools, Alexandria, LA, teacher, chemistry, 1968-70; New Orleans Public School System, teacher, bio/chem, 1970-80; Xavier University, New Orleans, LA, chemistry teacher, 1980-81, summer, 1979, 1980; New Orleans Public School, New Orleans, LA, science supervisor, 1981-86; Louisiana Power & Light Co, New Orleans PSI, LA, communications representative, 1986-91, community relations manager, 1991-. **Orgs:** President, American Association of Blacks in Energy, LA Chapter, 1988-90; financial & corres secretary, Delta Sigma Theta Sorority, New Orleans Alumnae Chapter, 1981-83, 1989; treasurer/founder, Delta Sigma Theta Foundation, New Orleans Chapter, 1988-; board of directors: Natl Council of Negro Women, YWCA of Greater New Orleans, Vol of America; advisory board: New Orleans Public Schools, Community Education, Science and Engineering Fair of Greater New Orleans, Carver Health Clinic; Louisiana Literacy Foundation, New Orleans Alumnae Chapter, vice pres, 1991, board of directors, 1992; Xavier University Youth Motivation Task Force, 1990; Let's Talk! anti-pregnancy campaign for teenage boys and girls; Metropolitan Area Guild, project director. **Honors/Awds:** Links, Cresent City Chapter, Unsung Hero Award, 1990; Outstanding Service in Science; recipient of awards from: Pres Ronald Reagan, 1986; governor of Louisiana, 1986; mayor of New Orleans, 1986, 1988; state senator, 1990. **Home Addr:** 11309 Waverly Dr, New Orleans, LA 70128. **Business Addr:** Community Relations Manager, Louisiana Power & Light Co., 317 Baronne St, N-30, New Orleans, LA 70112.

WELLS, BILLY GENE
Mayor, printing company entrepreneur. **Personal:** Born Mar 30, Bluff City, TN; son of Grace Isbella Black and Harley Boyd Wells; married Irene Elizabeth Coleman, Dec 31, 1962; children: Cynthia Anita Wells, Rebecca Jean Wells. **Career:** TN Eastman Co, Kingsport, TN, printer, 1964-; B&I Offset Printing, Bluff City, TN, owner, 1971-; City of Bluff City, TN, mayor, 1985-. **Orgs:** Board member, Senior Citizens, United Way, and Teen World, all 1985-; comm member, Martin Luther King Jr State Holiday Comm, 1986-. **Honors/Awds:** First black mayor elected in Tennessee; first mayor elected 3 times in a row in Bluff City.

WELLS, BOBBY RAY
Orthodontist, assistant professor. **Personal:** Born Jan 25, 1956, Booneville, MS; son of Virginia Copeland Wells (deceased) and James Henry Wells (deceased); married Ella Austin Wells, Mar 23, 1979; children: Elisha S, Summer A, Samantha S. **Educ:** University of North Alabama, Florence, AL, BS, 1974-78; University of Alabama, Birmingham School of Dentistry, Birmingham, AL, DMD, 1978-82; University of Alabama, Birmingham Graduate School, Birmingham, AL, MS, oral biology, 1982-86; University of Alabama, School of Dentistry, Birmingham, AL, orthodontic specialty cert, 1984-86. **Career:** University of Alabama, School of Dentistry, Birmingham, AL, clinical instr,dept of oral biology prevet den, 1982-85; Univ of Alabama, Birmingham, AL, clinical instr, dept of ortho, 1985-86, assistant professor, dept oper dent, 1986-87, graduate school faculty, 1988-, assistant professor, 1987-. **Orgs:** Member, American Association of Orthondontists, 1984-; member, Southern Soc of Orthondontists, 1986-; member, Alabama Assn of Orthodontists, 1986-; member, American Dental Assn, 1978-; member, National Dental Assn, 1976-; member, International Assn for Dental Research, 1982-; member, American Assn for Dental Research, 1982-; member, Alabama Delegate, National Dentist Assn, 1989-. **Honors/Awds:** Second Prize, postdoctoral category, Edward H Hatton Awards Competition; IADR's 63rd General Session, 1985. **Home Addr:** 830 First St, SW, Birmingham, AL 35211.

WELLS, ELMER EUGENE
Educational administrator. **Personal:** Born Oct 6, 1939, Mt Pleasant, IA; married Georgia Lee Gehringer; children: Monte, Debra, Christian, Kori. **Educ:** Univ of AK, MA 1970; Univ of NM, PhD 1974. **Career:** Intl Student Serv Univ of So CO, dir 1978-; USC Teacher Corps Cycle 9 & 11 Pueblo, educ spec 1974-78; Albuquerque Public School, teacher 1973-74; Bureau of Indian Affairs Pt Barrow AK, teacher/asst prin/prin 1966-71; Office of Econ Opportunity, teen post dir 1965-66; Mobil Oil Co Santa Fe Springs CA, explorationworker 1964-65; Low Mt Boarding School Bureau of Indian Affairs AZ 1962-64. **Orgs:** Pres/founder Albuquerque Ethnic Communities Inc 1973-74; pres/founder CO Ethnic Communities Inc 1975-80; exec bd Pueblo Chap NAACP 1979-80; "Destroyinga Racial Myth" The Social Studies Vol 69 No 5 1978; pub "The Mythical Negative Black Self Concept" R & E Research Assn 1978; TV Debate Grand Wizard KKK COSprings Involvement Program Channel 11 1979. **Honors/Awds:** Speaker Annual Freedom Fund Banquet CO Springs Chap NAACP 1980. **Business Addr:** 2200 Bonforte Blvd, Pueblo, CO 81001.

WELLS, IRA J. K., JR.
Attorney. **Personal:** Born Oct 26, 1934, New York, NY; married; children: Joseph, Anita, JoAnne. **Educ:** Lincoln U, BA 1957; Temple Law Sch, LLD. **Career:** US Ct App 3rd Circ Phila, law clk/ct crier 1964-66; US Dist Ct Estn Dist PA, law clk 1966-68; US Dept Hsg & Urban Dev Phila, atty 1968. **Orgs:** Mem/bd dir Zion Invstmt Assn Inc, Zion Non-Profit Char Trst, Opport Ind Cent Inc; OIC Intl Inc 1968-; Ejay Trav Inc 1970; mem Nat/Am PA & Philadelphia Bar Assn; treas Philadelphia Intl Prog 1974-75; mem Barristers Club of Phila; mem Lawyers Club of Phila; bd dir Mental Hlth Assn PA; treas/bd dir Mntl Hlth Assn 1977-78; leg cnsl EMAN Grp Homes Inc; E Mt Airy Neighborhood Inc. **Military Serv:** AUS sp/4 1957-59. **Business Addr:** Ste 700 Robinson Bldg, 42 S 15th St, Philadelphia, PA 19102.

WELLS, JAMES A.
Business executive. **Personal:** Born Aug 13, 1933, Atlanta, GA; married Mary E; children: James A, Jr, John F. **Educ:** BSEE 1965; MSAT 1976. **Career:** Systems Test Mgr IBM-Owego, project engr 1974-; Aerospace & Avionic Computer Sys Final Test IBM-Owego 1967-74; Process Equipment Design IBM-Endicott, engineering 1965-67. **Orgs:** Assoc mem IEEE Assn; past vice pres Jaycees; den leader WEBELOS; mem Amvets; AOPA. **Military Serv:** USAF t/sgt 1952-57. **Business Addr:** IBM-FSD 001 A310 Bodle Hill Rd, Owego, NY 13827.

WELLS, JUNIOR. See Obituaries section.

WELLS, LINDA IVY
Human resources specialist. **Personal:** Born Jun 18, 1948, McKeesport, PA; daughter of Naomi Wells and William Wells; divorced. **Educ:** Allegheny County Comm College, AA, humanities, 1968; Seton Hill College, BA , history/secondary education, 1970; Howard Univ, MA, student personnel administration, 1972. **Career:** Seton Hall Coll, asst dir special servs, 1970-71; Bowie State Coll, grad coun Opportunity Unlimited Program, 1972; Howard Univ, admin asst stud per program 1972; Catholic Univ, dir minority student affairs, 1972-75; Stanford Univ, financial aid advisor, 1978-83; Stanford Univ School of Engineering, Stanford, CA, assistant dean, 1983-88; Gem Program, Notre Dame, IN, associate director, 1988-90; Intel Corporation, Folsom, CA, diverse workforce specialist, 1990-. **Orgs:** NAMEPA mem Reg E Natl Assoc MN Eng Admin; mem Amer Personnel & Guidance Assoc; member, Amer Assoc for Higher Educ; member, CA Assoc of Student Financial Aid Adminstrs; member, Amer Indian Science and Eng Soc; member, National Assn of Minority Engineering Administrators, 1983-; board member, National Society of Black Engineers, 1989-; member, American Society of Engineering Education, 1988-. **Honors/Awds:** Ford Foundation Fellowship Grant 1971-72; Thomas Lynch Scholarship 1968-70; Negro Educ Emer Drive Scholarship 1966-70; Senior Century Scholarship 1966; NatlHonor Soc 1966; Staff Appreciation Award 1983; Recognition Award, Stanford Univ, Society of Black Scientists and Engineers, 1985; Affirmative Action Recognition Award, Stanford Univ, 1986. **Business Addr:** Diverse Workforce Specialist, Intel Corporation, 1900 Prairie City Rd, FMI-60, Folsom, CA 95630.

WELLS, LLOYD C. A.
Professional football scout. **Personal:** Born Mar 2, 1924, Houston, TX. **Educ:** Texas Southern Univ, BS 1950; Univ of Hawaii. **Career:** Informer Chain of Newspapers, former sports editor/exec dir 10 years; Texas High School All Star Games, founder/dir; World Heavy Weight Boxing Champion Muhammad Ali, asst mgr; Wells All-Pro Detail Shop, president, KC Chiefs, scouting consultant, currently. **Orgs:** Mem Natl Assn Press Photographers; Professional Photographers of Amer; former coach/owner of Houston Olympians AAU Basketball Team; 100 Percent Wrong Club Atlanta GA 1962. **Honors/Awds:** 1st full time black scout in history of professional football 1963-; Sports Editor of the Year; Professional Football Scout of the Year 1970; Pittsburgh Courier RC Cola Black Coll All Amer Awards Dinner. **Military Serv:** USMC 1943-46, 1950-53.

WELLS, PATRICK ROLAND
Cleric, educational administrator, educator (retired). **Personal:** Born Apr 1, 1931, Liberty, TX; son of Stella Wickliff Wells (deceased) and Luther T Wells, Sr (deceased). **Educ:** TX Southern Univ, BS 1957; Univ of NE-Lincoln, MS 1959, PhD 1961; Sacred Heart School of Theology, MDiv, 1993. **Career:** Fordham Univ, asst prof pharmacology 1961-63; Univ of NE, asst prof of pharmacology 1963-65, assoc prof & dept chmn 1965-70; College of Pharmacy TX Southern Univ, dean & prof 1970-90; St Francis of Assisi Catholic Church, pastor, 1993-; Diocese of Galveston Houston, ordained Roman Catholic Priest, 1993. **Orgs:** Grand regent Kappa Psi Pharmaceutical 1983-87; mem TX Pharmaceutical Assn, Amer Pharmaceutical Assn, Natl Pharmaceutical Assn, Sigma Xi Science Hon, Rho Chi Pharmacy Hon; mem St Philip Neri Parish; mem, St Philip Neri Council #222 Knights of Peter Claver; lay oblate Order of St Benedict; Assn of Minority Health Professions Schools; Amer Assn of Colleges of Pharmacy; editor, Journal of the National Pharmaceutical, Assn, 1987-90; host, Radio Show "Lifeline" KTSU-FM, 1976-90; Natl Black Catholic Clergy Caucus. **Honors/Awds:** Outstanding Educator, Texas Pharm Assn; 1990; Dean Emeritus, Texas Southern University, 1990. **Military Serv:** USAF s/sgt 1951-55. **Business Addr:** Pastor, St Francis of Assisi Catholic Church, 5102 Dabney St, Houston, TX 77026-3099, (713)672-7773.

WELLS, PAYTON R.
Business executive. **Personal:** Born Jun 24, 1933, Indianapolis, IN. **Educ:** Butler Univ Indianapolis IN, 1955-57. **Career:** Payton Wells Ford Inc, pres; GM & Ford Motor Co Automotive Sch; Payton Wells Chrysler Ply, Dodge Jeep Eagle, president; Payton Wells Chevrolet, president. **Orgs:** Bd mem Jr Achievement; mem NAACP; mem Urban League; vice pres Flanner House Inc. **Military Serv:** US Army, PFC, 1953-55. **Business Addr:** President, Payton Wells Chevrolet, 1510 N Meridian St, Indianapolis, IN 46202.

WELLS, ROBERT BENJAMIN, JR.
Executive administration. **Personal:** Born May 21, 1947, Cleveland, OH; married Phillis Sharlette McCray; children: Michelle Renne', Bryan Jamison. **Educ:** Miami Dade Comm Coll, AA 1974; FL A&M Univ, BS 1976; 1st Yr NC Central Univ, Law Student 1985. **Career:** General Telephone of the Southeast, serv cost admin 19878-80, gen acct suprv 1980-81, gen tax suprv 1981-. **Orgs:** Consult Youth Motivation Task Force 1979-82; pres Employees Club 1980-81; dept rep United Way Campaign 1982-84; chair econ devel comm NC Assoc of Black Lawyers Land Loss Prevention Proj; vice pres mem & mktg Natl Assoc of Accountants; chairperson Natl Alliance of Business Youth Motivation Task Force 1982-; presDurham Area Chap Natl Assoc of Accountants 1986-87, 1987-88; GTE Loaned Exec United Way Campaign 1986; chairperson Greater Durham United Way Loaned Exec Alumni Comm 1987. **Honors/Awds:** Disting Serv Awd Miles Coll Birmingham AL 1982; Disting Serv Plaque Edward Waters Coll Jacksonville FL 1984; Disting Serv Plaque Florida A&M Univ Tallahassee 1986. **Military Serv:** USAF sgt 4 yrs; Disting Serv Medal, Bronze Medal 1966,68. **Business Addr:** General Tax Supervisor, General Telephone of the South, 3632 Roxboro Rd, PO Box 1412, Durham, NC 27702.

WELLS, RODERICK ARTHUR
Municipal government official. **Personal:** Born Feb 10, 1952, New Orleans, LA; son of Thomas L Jr & Maggie L; married Betty Lewis Wells, Dec 18, 1976; children: Rashaad Aneisha, Roderick Lewis. **Educ:** Southern Univ BR, BS, 1975, MEd, 1981. **Career:** EBR Mosquito Abatement, asst dir, 1986-, biologist, 1984-86; City of BR, Human Services Division, program planner, 1983-84; Kaiser Aluminum, production foreman, 1982-83, environmental tech, 1980-81. **Orgs:** Naval Reserve Assn, 1982-; SU Fed of Comm Officers, 1985-; LA Pesticide Applicators, 1988-; AM Mosquito Control Assn, 1988-; Naval Memorial Assn, 1989-; BR High School Football Officials, 1990-; LA Mosquito Control Assn, bd of dirs, 1991-, pres, 1994; Recruiting Assist Council, chair, 1994-. **Honors/Awds:** Brec Football Coach, Baby Jags, Coaches Award, 1990-91; Cub Scouts Pack 47, Fathers & Sons Award, 1992; LMCA, Pres Award, 1994. **Military Serv:** US Navy, cdr, 1975-80, active reserve, 1982-; Commanding Officer, 1978-80; Surface Warfare Officer, Sharp Shooter Pistol, Natl Defense, Navy Achievement, Sea Service, Expert Rifle, Navy Commendation. **Home Addr:** 10717 Foster Rd, Baton Rouge, LA 70811, (504)775-1232. **Business Addr:** Asst Dir, East Baton Rouge Mosquito Abatement, 2829 Lt General Ben Davis Ave, Metro Airport, Baton Rouge, LA 70807, (504)356-3297.

WELLS-DAVIS, MARGIE ELAINE
Human resources manager. **Personal:** Born Apr 27, 1944, Marshalltown, IA; daughter of Ida Wells and Gladstone Wells; married Allan C; children: Allana. **Educ:** Simpson Coll, AB 1966; Syracuse Univ, MA 1968; Univ of Cincinnati, PhD 1979. **Career:** Procter & Gamble, affirmative action coordinator 1977-; Cincinnati Health Dept, dir of staff & org devel 1974-77; US Public Health Service DHEW, sociologist 1973; Central Comm Health Bd, coordinator consulting educ 1972; Syracuse Univ, acting dir 1971; Univ of Cincinnati, asst dean of students 1968-70; St Louis Syracuse NY, teacher 1966-68; Procter & Gamble,

human resources mgr, currently. **Orgs:** Mem Am Soc for Training & Devel 1977-80; mem Original Devel Network 1978-80; bd mem New Life for Girls 1977-80; treasurer bd mem Cincinnati Human Relations Commn 1978-80; bd mem Cincinnati Womens City Club 1979-80; consultant E Harlem Ext Serv Jewish Hosp 1973-76; bd mem General Protestant Orphan Home. **Honors/Awds:** Resolution for Outstanding Serv City of Cincinnati Bd of Health 1976; Hon Soc Epsilon Sigma, Gold Key Hon Soc 1966.

WELLS-MERRICK, LORRAINE ROBERTA
Educator. **Personal:** Born Jan 5, 1938, Syracuse, NY; daughter of Dorothy Copes Wells and Robert Wells; married James A Merrick Jr (divorced). **Educ:** Cheyney State University, Cheyney, PA, BS, 1959; Syracuse University, Syracuse, NY, MS, 1973, doctoral candidate, currently. **Career:** City School District, Syracuse, NY, teacher, 1959-69, principal/administrator, 1970-79, deputy superintendent, 1979-88; New York State Education Dept, Albany, NY, assistant commissioner, 1988-. **Orgs:** National Grand Basileus, Lambda Kappa Mu Sorority, 1985-90; member, Syracuse Alumnae, Delta Sigma Theta Sorority, Inc, 1973-; member, Syracuse chapter, Links, Inc, 1976-; member, NCNW, 1960-. **Honors/Awds:** Post-Standard Woman of Achievement, Syracuse Newspapers, 1980; Woman of Achievement in Education, Delta Sigma Theta, Inc, 1975; Outstanding Soror, Lambda Kappa Mu Sorority, 1974; Outstanding Educator, Grade Teacher Magazine, 1973. **Home Addr:** 404 Kimber Rd, Syracuse, NY 13224. **Business Addr:** Assistant Commissioner, General and Occupational Education, New York State Education Dept, Washington Ave, 979 EBA, Albany, NY 12234.

WELMON, VERNIS M.
Educator, educational administrator. **Personal:** Born Mar 13, 1951, Philadelphia, PA; son of Sara H Welmon and Vernis B Welmon; married Pamela Blake Welmon, Oct 10, 1987; children: Ain. **Educ:** Temple University, BA, 1980; Columbia University, MA, 1982; Pennsylvania State University, attending, currently. **Career:** US State Department, Bureau of Human Rights and Humanitarian Affairs, intern, 1980 ; Multinational Management Education, intern, 1981; Pennsylvania State University, Smeal College of Business Administration, researcher, 1981, PhD and MS programs coordinator, 1983-85; University of the West Indies, guest lecturer, 1991; Pennsylvania State University, Smeal College of Business Administration, instructor, 1983-, assistant to the dean for minority affairs, 1985-. **Orgs:** Phi Chi Theta, 1991-; Academy of Political Science; American Academy of Political and Social Science; National Council on Black Studies; Pennsylvania Conference on Higher Education; The Black Resources Center; TransAfrica; numerous other civic groups. **Honors/Awds:** Pennsylvania State University, Spicher Service Award, 1986; US State Department, Rosenthal Fellow, 1980; Temple University, Phi Beta Kappa, 1980, President's Scholar, 1979, Marcus Garvey Scholastic Award, 1978. **Special Achievements:** Author: "New Economic Challenges for Africa and the Caribbean," Ember Magazine, 1991; "Africa in Perspective: Myths and Realities," The Review of Black Political Economy, 1989; "Import - Export: The International Challenge for Black Business," National Business, Dec 1988. **Business Addr:** Assistant to the Dean for Minority Affairs, Instructor in International Business, Pennsylvania State University, Smeal College of Business Administration, 106 Business Administration Bldg, University Park, PA 16802, (814)863-0474.

WELSING, FRANCES CRESS
Psychiatrist. **Personal:** Born Mar 18, 1935, Chicago, IL. **Educ:** Antioch Coll, BS 1957; Howard Univ Sch of Med, MD 1962. **Career:** Cook Co Hosp, internsp 1962-63; St Elizabeth Hosp, res gen psychiatry 1963-66; Children's Hosp, flwshp child psychiatry 1966-68; Howard Univ Coll of Med, asst prof of pediatrics 1968-75; Hillcrest Children's Ctr, clinical dir 1975-76; Private Pract. **Orgs:** Mem Nat Med Assn; Am Med Assn; Am Psychiatric Assn. **Honors/Awds:** Author, "The Cress Theory of Color Confrontation & Racism". **Business Addr:** 7603 Georgia Ave NW, Ste 402, Washington, DC 20012.

WERTZ, ANDREW WALTER, SR.
Educational administrator (retired). **Personal:** Born Dec 18, 1928, Hamlet, NC; son of Johnnie B Hodges Cooks and Andrew J Wertz; married Bernice Spires; children: Alonzo W, Janis M, Brian L, Andy Jr, Ray J. **Educ:** Lincoln Univ PA, BA 1949; USAF Command & Staff Coll, 1965; Syracuse Univ, MS, 1980. **Career:** Penn Fruit Co Inc, 1st African American Cashier, 1949; Detective Serv Inc, Private Investigator 1950; USAF, navigator/admin 1950-70; Hamilton Coll, dir Bristol Campus Center & dir student activities 1970-88; Retired, Freelance Consultant/Admin. **Orgs:** Bd mem OIC Utica, 1972-74; bd mem ARC Utica Chapter, 1973-79; bd mem Council of Churches, Mohawk Valley Area, 1974-78; pres, Mohawk Valley Club Frontiers Intl, 1975-77; mem Natl Conf Assn of Coll Unions Intl 1976; bd mem A Better Chance Inc Clinton NY 1977-80; host dir Region 2 conf Assn of Coll Unions Intl 1978; coord of minority progs Assn of Coll Unions Intl 1979; mem bd of dirs Frontiers Intl 1982-92; NAACP; Kappa Alpha Psi; Pres, A Better Chance Inc, 1988-; Frontiers International Foundation Inc, board of directors, 1987-93, president, chief executive officer, 1992-. **Honors/Awds:** Internal Serv Awd, Frontiers Intl, 1978; Pentagon Society, Hamilton College, 1975; Outstanding Service Award, First District Frontiers, Intl, 1990. **Military Serv:** US Air Force, lt col, 1950-70 (retired); Distinguished Service Award, 1968. **Home Addr:** 5 Cheriton Dr, Whitesboro, NY 13492.

WESLEY, BARBARA ANN
Educational administrator. **Personal:** Born Jun 7, 1930, Wichita, KS; widowed; children: Ronald Frank, John Edgar. **Educ:** Univ of Puget Sound, BA 1963; Univ of Puget Sound Tacoma, MEd 1972; Univ of MA, EdD 1977. **Career:** Clover Park School Dist, elem teacher 1960-64; Tacoma Public School, classroom teacher 1964-74; Westfield St Coll, proj dir/cons 1974-75; Alternative Prog Tacoma Public School, educ specialist 1975-78; Foss HS Tacoma Public Sch, high sch admin 1978-79; Wilson HS Tacoma Public School, hs admin 1979-82; Magnet Prog, dist admin 1982-. **Orgs:** Inst for Elem Tchrs Denver Univ 1969; Adult Educ Inst Univ of WI/NY State Univ of Albany 1972-73; Natl Sci Found Western MI Univ Santa Clara Univ 1972-73; bd of trustees Tacoma Comm Coll 1977-82; mem Delta Sigma Theta; bd of dirs YWCA Tacoma 1977-78; bd of dirs Campfire Tacoma 1979-83; State Vocational Council on Voc Educ 1982-; Wash Women Employ & Educ Bd of Dirs 1982-; mem Phi Delta Kappa, Delta Kappa Gamma. **Honors/Awds:** Delta Kappa Gamma Post-doctoral AZ State Univ 1978; Harvard Univ Mgmt Inst summer 1981; Baylor Univ Leadership/Development Seminar summer 1982. **Business Addr:** District Administrator, Magnet Prog Tacoma Public Sch, Central Admin Bldg, PO Box 1357, Tacoma, WA 98401.

WESLEY, CLARENCE E.
Business executive. **Personal:** Born Sep 24, 1940, Coffeyville, KS; married Peggy L; children: Keira, Marquel. **Educ:** Pittsburgh State U, BS 1962; Wichita State U, MA 1968. **Career:** Wichita Area C of C, mgr comm devel 1970-; Upward Bound Wichita State, asst dir 1969-70; Wichita State, KS State, Sterling Coll, lectr 1968-75; Wichita Pub Sch Sys, tchr/adminstrv asst 1962-70. **Orgs:** Pres Wes/Berry Intl; pres Central Sys Devel Corp; bd dir KS Ofc of Minority Bus; mem Nat Adv Cncl Small Bus Admin; pres Wichita Urban League;chmn trustee cncl Black Heritage Park of KS; trustee/dir Wichita Cncl of Ch; CETA Manpower Bd; bd dir Vet Adv Cncl. **Honors/Awds:** Recipient Outstand Young Man of KS 1973-; KS Outstand Cit 1974; KS Pub Cit of Yr 1975; NCCJ State Brotherhood Award 1975; Wichita's Disting Serv Award 1973; Cert of Merit Nat Alliance of Businessmen & Wichita Pub Sch Sys 1972. **Business Addr:** 350 W Douglas, Wichita, KS 67202.

WESLEY, CLEMON HERBERT, JR.
Telecommunications engineering systems company executive. **Personal:** Born Feb 24, 1936, Daingerfield, TX; son of Zannie Benson Wesley (deceased) and Clemon Herbert Wesley (deceased); married Modestine Delores Truvillion Wesley, Sep 27, 1958; children: Yolanda Wesley Harper, Deborah Wesley Hall, Eric. **Educ:** Prairie View A & M University, BS, 1957; attended Army War College and Armed Forces Staff College; Shippensburg State College, MS, 1970; LaSalle University, LLB, 1972. **Career:** TEXCOM, Inc, Landover, MD, founder and president, 1981—. **Orgs:** President, National Business League of Southern Maryland; board member, Coalition of Concerned Black Christian Men, Phi Beta Sigma Education Foundation; member, National Urban League Black Executive Exchange Program, Prince George's County Chamber of Commerce, Minority Business Enterprise Legal Defense and Education Fund, Mt Zion United Methodist Church, Prairie View A & M Alumni Association, US Army War College Alumni Association. **Honors/Awds:** Business achievement award, National Business League of Southern Maryland, 1986; Service Industry Award, US Department of Commerce, 1987; National Minority Small Business Person of the Year, and Minority Small Business Firm of the Year for region III, US Small Business Administration, 1988; Small & Minority Business, Advocate of the Year, 1990. **Military Serv:** US Army, Signal Corps, 2nd lieutenant, 1957, retired as colonel, 1981; served on Department of Army Headquarters, 1975-79; received Vietnam Service Medal, Bronze Star, and Legion of Merit. **Business Addr:** President, TEXCOM, Inc, 600 Washington St, Portsmouth, VA 23704.

WESLEY, DAVID
Professional basketball player. **Personal:** Born Nov 14, 1970, San Antonio, TX. **Educ:** Temple Junior Coll; Baylor Univ. **Career:** NBA career: New Jersey Nets, 1993; Boston Celtics, 1994-; CBA career: Wichita Falls Texans, 1992-93. **Business Addr:** Professional Basketball Player, Boston Celtics, 151 Merrimac St, 5th Fl, Boston, MA 02114, (617)523-6050.

WESLEY, NATHANIEL, JR.
Health care executive. **Personal:** Born Jan 13, 1943, Jacksonville, FL; married Ruby L Williams; children: Nataniel Wesley III. **Educ:** FL A&M U, BS 1965; Univ of MI, MHA 1971. **Career:** DC Hosp Assn, asst exec dir 1979-; Meharry Med Coll, asst prof 1977-79; Sidney A Sumby Meml Hosp, exec dir 1975-76; SW Comm Hosp, dept dir 1973-75; New York City Hlth & Hosp Corp, spl asst to vice pres 1972-73; Albert Einstein Coll of Med, adminstr/cons 1971-72. **Orgs:** Sec/exec Nat Assn of Hlth Serv 1974-78; pres Detroit & Nashville Chpts NAASE 1975-79; pres NRW Asso Inc; mem BCHW of Alpha; mem Am Pub HlthAssn. **Honors/Awds:** Nominee Am Coll of Hosp Adminstrs; WK Kellogg Fellow ACEHSA Wash, DC; Serv Award BSO Univ of MI Ann Arbor 1977; Comm Serv Award Peoples Comm Serv Detroit 1978; Tchr of the Yr Meharry Med Coll 1979-. **Business Addr:** DC Hosp Assn, 1725 Eye St NW Ste 301, Washington, DC 20006.

WESLEY, RICHARD ERROL
Playwright. **Personal:** Born Jul 11, 1945, Newark, NJ; son of Gertrude Thomas Wesley and George Richard Wesley; married Valerie Deane Wilson Wesley, May 22, 1978; children: 2. **Educ:** Howard University, Washington, DC, BFA, 1967. **Career:** Wesleyan University, African Cultural Institute, Middletown, CT, adjunct professor, 1974; Manhattanville College, Purchase, NY, adjunct professor, 1974; Borough of Manhattan Community College, New York, NY, instructor in Black Theatre, 1980-81, 1982-83; Rutgers University, Newark, NJ, instructor in Black Theatre, 1989; Elegba Productions, president; Black Theatre Magazine, past editor. **Orgs:** Bd of dirs, Frank Silvera Writers Workshop, 1976-84; bd of dirs, Theatre of Universal Images, Newark, NJ; mem of selection comm, Newark NJ Black Film Festival. **Honors/Awds:** Playwright "The Black Terror," Public Theatre, New York, NY, 1971, "Goin' Thru Changes," Billie Holiday Theatre, New York, NY, 1974, "The Sirens," Manhattan Theatre Club, New York, NY, 1974, "The Last Street Play," Manhattan Theatre Club, New York, NY, 1974, "The Mighty Gents," B'way Prod, 1978-, "On the Road to Babylon," Milwaukee Rep, Milwaukee, WI, 1980, "The Dream Team," Goodspeed Opera House, 1984, "The Talented Tenth," Manhattan Theatre Club, New York, NY, 1989; Drama Desk award, 1972; Rockefeller Grant, 1973; Audelco Award, 1974, 1977; author of screenplays "Uptown Saturday Night," Warner Bros, 1974, "Let's Do It Again," Warner Bros, 1975, "Fast Forward," Columbia Pictures, 1985, "Native Son," Cinecom Pictures, 1986; author of TV screenplay "The Houseof Dies Drear," PBS, 1984. **Business Addr:** President, Elegba Productions, PO Box 43091, Upper Montclair, NJ 07043.

WESLEY, VALERIE WILSON
Editor. **Personal:** childDren: Jamal. **Educ:** Howard University, degree in philosophy, 1970; Banks Street College of Education, master's degree, early childhood education; Columbia University, master's degree, journalism. **Career:** Scholastic News, assistant editor; freelance writer; Essence Magazine, executive editor, currently. **Special Achievements:** Author of four novels including: Hidden Death Comes Stealing, 1994; No Hiding Place, 1997. **Business Addr:** Contributor, Essence Magazine, 1500 Broadway, 6th Fl., New York, NY 10036, (212)642-0600.

WESLEY III, HERMAN EUGENE
Evangelist, publisher. **Personal:** Born Oct 17, 1961, Newark, NJ; son of Anne M Wesler and Herman E Wesley Jr; married Sonja McDade, Jun 22, 1985; children: Brandon JeMarcus. **Educ:** Southwestern Christian College, AS, 1981; Oklahoma Christian Univ, BS, 1983. **Career:** Church of Christ, evangelist, 1986-; Revivalist Magazine, publisher, 1989-; Ebony News Journals of Texas, publisher, 1992-; Christian Square Companies of Texas, CEO, 1992-. **Orgs:** Denton Housing Authority, commissioner, 1989-92; NAACP, Denton Branch, executive bd, 1990-; Multicultural Advisory Commission, chairman, 1989-92; Martin Luther King Jr Center Advisory Bd, chairman of the board, 1989-92; Black Leadership Coordinating Council, chairman, 1991-. **Honors/Awds:** NAACP, Denton County Chapter, President's Award, 1990; Southwestern Christian College Alumni of the Year, 1992; City of Denton, Civic Service Award, 1992. **Business Addr:** CEO, Christian Square Companies of Texas, N.A., 1121 Dallas Dr, Ste 2, Denton, TX 76206, (817)566-1912.

WESSON, CLEO
City councilman. **Personal:** Born Aug 27, 1924, Ozan, AR; married Julia (deceased); children: Helayne. **Educ:** Gary College. **Career:** City of Gary, councilman, currently. **Orgs:** John Will Anderson Boys Club; Lake City Lodge #182; King Solomon Lodge #57; Magic City Consistory #62; Mohomet Temple #134; Rebecca Chap #39; Sallie Wyatt Stewart Guild; Urban League of Northwest Indiana Inc; life mem, NAACP; Israel CME Church; bd dir, March of Dimes. **Honors/Awds:** Recipient, Certification of Merit, Gary Branch NAACP, 1965; Service Award, 3rd Episcopal District, CME Church 1965; J Claude Allen, Presiding Bishop Seepa 1967; Distinguished Service & Outstanding Leadership, president, Common Council, City of Gary 1966. **Military Serv:** US Air Force, 1943-45.

WEST, BRUCE ALAN
Sales manager. **Personal:** Born Mar 31, 1957, Los Angeles, CA; son of Lenon West & Betty West; married Cathy, Jul 22, 1982; children: Chastin, Cheldon. **Educ:** Mississippi State University, BA, 1978. **Career:** Thrifty Drug Stores, asst mgr, 1980-85; Lindsey Products Co, sales rep, 1985-86; Brown & Williamson Tobacco Corp, section sales mgr, 1986-. **Orgs:** Phi Beta Sigma Fraternity, Theta Iota Chap, 1976-; University Human Relations Comm, 1975-76; Bd of Elections, inspector, 1996-. **Home Addr:** 11943 Honeybrook Ct, Moorpark, CA 93021, (805)523-3345. **Business Addr:** Section Sales Manager, Brown & Williamson Tobacco Co., 990 Enchanted Way, Ste 104, Simi Valley, CA 93065, (805)578-9823.

WEST, CHERYL L.
Playwright. **Career:** Author of the plays "Holiday Heart," "Puddin 'n Pete," "Jar the Floor," and "Before It Hits Home". **Honors/Awds:** Susan Smith Blackburn Prize, 1990; four Audelco Awards; Helen Hayes Charles McArthur Award for Outstanding New Play, 1992. **Business Addr:** Playwright, c/o Creative Artists Agency, 9830 Wilshire Blvd, Beverly Hills, CA 90212, (310)288-4545.

WEST, CORNEL
Educator, educational administrator. **Personal:** Born Jun 2, 1953, Tulsa, OK; divorced; children (previous marriage): Clifton. **Educ:** Harvard University, bachelor's degree (magna cum laude), Near Eastern languages and literature; Princeton Univeristy, PhD work. **Career:** Yale University Divinty School, professor, 1984; Le Monde Diplomatique, American correspondent; University of Paris, educator, one semester; Princeton University, Dept of Religion, professor, Dept of Afro-American Studies, director; Harvard University, African American studies, currently. **Honors/Awds:** Harvard University, Du Bois Fellow. **Special Achievements:** Author: Race Matters, Beacon Press, 1993; co-author with bell hooks, Breaking Bread: Insurgent Black Intellectual Life, South End Press, 1992; Prophesy Deliverance! An Afro-American Revolutionary Christianity, Westminster/John Knox Press; The American Evasion of Philosophy: A Genealogy of Pragamatism, University of Wisconsin Press. **Business Addr:** Professor, African American Studies, Harvard University, 12 Quincy St., Berker Center, Cambridge, MA 02138.

WEST, DONDA C.
Educator. **Personal:** Born Jul 12, 1949, Oklahoma City, OK; daughter of Portwood & Lucille Williams; divorced; children: Kanye Omari I. **Educ:** VA Union Univ, BA, 1971; Atlanta Univ, MA, 1973; Auburn Univ, Doctorate, 1980; Stella Marris Univ, Madras India, 1981. **Career:** Tulsa Urban League, youth theatre dir, 1970; Spelman Coll, recruitment officer, 1971-72; Morris Brown Coll, instructor to dept chair, 1973-79; Columbus Coll, instructor, 1979-80; Chicago State Univ, asst prof to dept chair, 1980-; Chicago Public Schools, educational programs consultant, currently; Chicago City Colleges, educational programs consultant, 1990-. **Orgs:** Natl Council of Teachers of English, 1980-; Linguistics Society of America, 1971-74; Assn of English Dept Administrators, 1974-; Operation Push, 1988-. **Honors/Awds:** Morris Brown Coll, Outstanding Faculty Award, 1975; St Martin Credit Union, Outstanding Educator of the Year, 1987. **Special Achievements:** Foreign Expert to the People's Republic of China at Nanjing Univ, 1987-88; Fulbright Fellow to India, 1981; "How the Works of Black Women Writers Mean," presented at conference on Black Women throughout the Diaspora in Nigeria, 1992; Consultant to Chicago Public Schools & City Colleges, curriculum development, educational reform, 1984-. **Business Addr:** Dept Chair, Chicago State University, 9501 S ML King Jr Dr, Science Bldg, Rm 320, Chicago, IL 60628, (312)995-2189.

WEST, DOROTHY
Writer. **Personal:** Born Jun 2, 1907; daughter of Rachel West and Isaac Christopher West. **Career:** Challenge (periodical), founder; The Vineyard Gazette, columnist, currently. **Honors/Awds:** Author, The Living Is Easy, 1948; The Wedding, Doubleday, 1994.

WEST, DOUG (JEFFERY DOUGLAS)
Professional basketball player. **Personal:** Born May 27, 1967, Altoona, PA; married Wuela. **Educ:** Villanova Univ, Villanova, PA, 1985-89. **Career:** Minnesota Timberwolves, guard/forward, 1989-98; Vancouver Grizzlies, 1998-. **Business Addr:** Professional Basketball Player, Vancouver Grizzlies, General Motors Place, 800 Griffiths Way, Vancouver, BC, Canada V6B 6G1, (604)899-4667.

WEST, EARL M.
Business executive. **Personal:** Born Feb 15, 1912, Arkansas City, KS; married Erma Ratliff. **Educ:** Univ of KS, BA 1939; KS State Teachers Coll Emporia, attended; Univ of MD, Grad Ed Study; Amer Savings & Loan Inst, Grad Diploma 1961; Amer Univ, attended; Union Theol Sem, attended; Univ of Denver, attended. **Career:** CCC, ed adv 1940-42; USO, dir 1942-46; UNRRA European Opers, ins broker, contractor real estate broker 1946-48; Equity Fed Savings Bank, pres. **Orgs:** Mem Denver Bd of Realtors, Denver C of C; sr warden Vestry-Episcopal Church; mem Bd of Health & Hosps for City & Cty of Denver 1965-77; chmn E Denver YMCA 1975-77, Alpha Phi Alpha, Sigma Pi Phi. **Honors/Awds:** Outstanding & Dedicated Serv Awd Alpha Chi Pi Omega; Awd for Continuing Support of Comm Effort Sigma Gamma Phi; 50 Plus Years Membership Honor YMCA.

WEST, EDWARD LEE, III
Professional football player. **Personal:** Born Aug 2, 1961, Colbert County, AL; married Kecia; children: Jennifer, Edward Lee IV, Whitley. **Educ:** Auburn, attended. **Career:** Green Bay Packers, tight end, 1984-94; Philadelphia Eagles, 1995-96; Atlanta Falcons, 1997-. **Business Addr:** Professional Football Player, Atlanta Flacons, Two Falcon Place, Suwanee, GA 30174, (404)945-1111.

WEST, GEORGE FERDINAND, JR.
Attorney. **Personal:** Born Oct 25, 1940, Adams Co, MS; son of Artimese M West and George Ferdinand West, Sr; married Billie Guy; children: George III, Heath. **Educ:** Tougaloo Coll, BA 1962; So Univ Sch of Law, JD 1966; Univ MS, JD 1968. **Career:** Natchez Adams Co Sch Bd, appt/co-atty 1967; State Adv Bd for Voc Edn, appt 1968; Natchez-Adams Co C of C, appt/dir 1974; Jeff Co Sch Sys, atty 1974; MS Sch Bd Assn, dir/atty; Radio Pgm "FACT-FINDING", modrtr; Copiah-Lincoln Jr Coll Natchez Br, bus law prof; Natchez News Leader, mg edtr;Private Practice Natchez, MS. **Orgs:** Mem MS Bar Assn 1968; rsrchr/procter MS State Univ 1973; NAACP; Natchez Bus & Civ Lgue; vice pres Gov Com Hire the Hndcp; trust/sunday sch tchr Zion Chap AME Ch; contributing editor, Bluff City Post, l978-; chmn, Natchez-Adams School Bd, l988-. **Honors/Awds:** Outstand Yng Men in Am 1967-; Comm Ldr of Am 1972; Lifetime Rosco Pound Fellow 1972; Most Distinguished Black Attorney Travelers Coalition, l988; Doctor of Humane Letters, Natchez Coll, l989; Man of the Year, Natchez, MS, NAACP, 1990; Man of the Year, Natchez Business & Civic League, 1991; Most Outstanding Attorney, NAACP, 1992; Recorded first music album entitled "Ole Time Way," 1993; Outstanding Attorney for the African Methodist Episcopal Southern District & Man of the Year, Zion Chapel AME Church, 1995. **Business Addr:** Attorney, PO Box 1202, Natchez, MS 39120.

WEST, GERALD IVAN
Psychologist. **Personal:** Born Jun 3, 1937, St Louis; son of Frank and Effie West; married Blondel B McKinnie, Aug 20, 1960; children: Gerald I West, Jr. **Educ:** Univ of Denver, BA, 1958; So IL Univ, MS 1963; Purdue Univ, PhD 1967. **Career:** San Francisco State Univ, dean of faculty affairs, professor, College of Health & Human Services, currently; Chair Dept of Counseling, SFSU; Consultant, Private Practice; director, Diagnostic & Evaluation Center Contra Costa Co Hosp, California State Univ, admin fellow, 1986-87. **Orgs:** Mem, Assn of Black Psychologists; past president, Western Assn of Counselor Educators and Supervisors; Amer Psychological Assn; Counseling Assn; Amer Association Higher Education; Sigma Pi Phi; Kappa Alpha Psi. **Honors/Awds:** Recipient of Bay Area Black Student Psychology Assn Award, 1974; Danforth Associateship 1969; elected 1st Human Rights Commr of CA Personnel & Guid Assn 1973; Certificate of Honor, City County of San Francisco, 1983; Professional Devel Award, Amer Assn of Counseling & Develop, Multicultural Counseling, 1985; Annual Mem Award, Assn of Black Psychologist, 1980; Award of Merit, San Francisco State Univ, 1985; Admin Fellow, California State Univ, 1987; H B McDaniel Award, Stanford University, 1992, Annual Award, Public Advocates, 1983; lead case of Larry P vs State of California, first successfully litigated case disproving the theory of racial genetic intellectual inferiority according to IQ tests, which led to federal law prohibiting the use of IQ tests on African American children in CA (injuion granted, 1986). **Military Serv:** US Army Med Servs Corps, lt 1966; Biochemist, 374th General Hospital. **Business Addr:** Dean of Faculty Affairs, San Francisco State Univ, 1600 Holloway, San Francisco, CA 94132, (415)338-2204.

WEST, HAROLD DADFORD
Educator. **Personal:** Born Jul 16, 1904, Flemington, NJ; married Jesse Juanita Penn; children: Edna, Harold Dadford. **Educ:** Univ of I, BA 1925; Julius Rosenwald Fund Fellow, MS 1930; Rockefeller Found Fellow, PhD 1937. **Career:** Morris Brown Coll Atlanta, prof chem/head dept sci 1925-27; Meharry Med Coll, asso prof/physical chem 1927-, asso prof biochem 1927-38, prof biochem/chmn dept 1938-52, acting chmn/div basic sci 1947; mem interim com 1950, vice chmn 1951, coll pres 1952-66, prof biochem 1966-73; trustee, presently retired. **Orgs:** Mem Am Soc Biol Chemists; Soc Exptl Bio & Med; mem Sigma Xi; Kappa Delta Pi; Sigma Pi Phi; Alpha Phi Alpha; Kappa Pi; Alpha Omega Alpha; Omicron KappaUpsilon. **Honors/Awds:** Received Hon LLD Morris Brown Coll 1955; Hon DSc Meharry Med Coll 1970.

WEST, HERBERT LEE, JR.
Educator. **Personal:** Born May 4, 1947, Warrenton, NC; son of Wilhemenia Jones West and Herbert Lee West Sr; married Mary Bentley; children: Tamekah Denise, Marcus Delaney-Bentley. **Educ:** NC Central Univ, BA 1969; Univ of MN, MA 1972, PhD 1974. **Career:** Teacher asst, Univ of Minnesota, l972; asst prof, Univ of Maryland Baltimore County, l974-l980; asst prof, Howard University, l980-l985; faculty intern, House Urban Devel, 1980; advisor, Summer Work Program-Prince Georges County, Maryland; educator/admin, Howard County Bd of Education, l985-; adjunct faculty Univ of Maryland Baltimore County, l986-. **Orgs:** Mem NAACP, Triangle Geographers, Natl Council of Black Studies, Assoc for the Study of Afro-Amer Life; Black Student Achievement Program, Howard County, Maryland. **Honors/Awds:** Ford Found Fellow 1971; NEH Fellow Atlanta Univ 1978; Outstanding Teacher Univ of MD Baltimore Cty 1978,79; Smithsonian Fellow Smithsonian Inst 1985; NEH Fellow Univ of NC 1983; Summer Fellow UMTA/Atlanta Univ 1984; Univ of Indiana guest lecturer l988; NEH Fellow Columbia Univ l989; Comga Graduate Fellowship Univ of Minnesota l969; moderator, braodway show Sarifina, Kennedy Center, 1990. **Home Addr:** 9461 Riverark Road, Columbia, MD 21045.

WEST, JOHN ANDREW
Attorney. **Personal:** Born Sep 15, 1942, Cincinnati, OH; married Miriam Evonne Kennedy; children: Melissa Evonne. **Educ:** Univ of Cincinnati, BA, BS 1966; Salmon P Chase Law Sch, JD 1971. **Career:** Pitzer West Cutcher & Gilday, atty; GE Co Large Jet Engine Div, buyer & contract admin 1968-71. **Orgs:** Mem Nat/Am & OH Bar Assn 1972-; chmn Hamilton Co Pub Defender Commn 1976. **Business Addr:** Attorney At Law, 225 West Court St, Cincinnati, OH 45202.

WEST, JOHN RAYMOND
Educational administrator. **Personal:** Born Apr 9, 1931, Birmingham, AL; son of Mignonette Mason and John H West; married Suzanne Marie Lancaster; children: Ronald, John Jr, Gerald, Reginald, Teresa, Semara, Tia, Joshua. **Educ:** CA State Univ Fullerton, BA Anthro 1969, MA Anthro 1970; Nova Univ FL, EdD Admin 1975. **Career:** So Counties Gas Co, sr scheduler 1961-69; State of CA, employment serv officer 1969-70; Santa Ana Coll, anthro, sociol, prof 1970-; Nova Univ, cluster coord 1976-90; Saddleback Coll Mission Viejo, instr 1976-; Afro Ethnic Studies CA State Univ Fullerton, lecturer; Santa Ana Coll, dean student serv 1973-86; Santiago Canyon College, Humanities and Sciences, division chair, currently. **Orgs:** Mem, 100 Black Men of Orange County; founding pres Orange Cty Chap Sickle Cell Disease Rsch Found 1972; bd of dirs, vice pres Legislative Affairs Western Region Council on Black Amer Affairs; bd of dir Assoc of CA Comm Coll Admin 1972; bd of dir CA Comm Coll Extended Oppty Prog & Serv 1977-79. **Honors/Awds:** 5 publ Clearinghouse Clearing UCLA 1974-75. **Military Serv:** USMC gunnery sgt 1950-61; presidential Unit Citation/United Nations Serv 1950. **Business Addr:** Chair, School of Social Sciences, Santiago Canyon College, 8045 E Chapman Ave, Orange, CA 92869.

WEST, JOSEPH KING
County court judge. **Personal:** Born Sep 11, 1929, Yonkers, NY; son of Nellie Brown West and Ralph West; married Shirley Arvene Gray; children: Rebecca, Joseph Jr. **Educ:** Howard Univ, BS 1952; Brooklyn Law School, JD 1961. **Career:** City of Yonkers, asst corp counsel 1964-65, city court judge 1983-84; County of Westchester, deputy dist atty 1965-82; Elected County Court Judge, 1984, re-elected 1994; State of New York, 9th Judicial Dist, supervising judge, criminal court, currently. **Orgs:** Mem Alpha Phi Alpha Frat 1948-; bd of dirs Yonkers Big Brother-Big Sisters 1982-, St Joseph's Hosp 1983-; life mem, Alpha Phi Alpha Fraternity; life mem, NAACP. **Honors/Awds:** Achievement Awd Assoc of Black Lawyers of Westchester Co 1981; Comm Serv Westchester Rockland Guardians Assoc 1984; Comm Serv Awd Yonkers Cncl of Churches 1985; Civic Awd Frederick D Patterson Alpha Phi Alpha 1987. **Military Serv:** AUS 1st lt 1952-56. **Business Addr:** Judge, New York State, 111 Grove St, White Plains, NY 10601.

WEST, MARCELLA POLITE
Educator. **Personal:** Born in Savannah; daughter of Mary Smith-Polite (deceased) and James H Polite (deceased); divorced; children: Maralyn C West-Craddock, Rodney Cecil West. **Educ:** Montclair State Coll, MA 1973; St Philip School of Nursing Med Coll of VA, 1946-48; Upsala Coll, 1969; Newark State Coll, 1970-71. **Career:** Cornelius E Gallagher 13th Congressional Dist NJ, congressional staff 1957-66; NJ Comm Action & Training Inst Trenton, NJ, training officer 1966-67; Bergen Co Comm Action Program Hackensack, NJ, training dir 1967-69; Montclair State Coll, admin to vice provost 1969-71; Urban Educ Corps Montclair State Coll, dir 1971-73; Montclair State Coll Div Student Personnel Svc, educ adv counselor 1973-; Rutger's Univ Intern Program, 1966-67; Inner City Broadcasting Corp WLIB, bd dir; WLIB/WBLS AM/FM, exec com 1972-; Human Devel Consulting Serv Inc, consultant/facilitator 1975; Montclair State Coll, coord, adv, currently. **Orgs:** Mem Am Mgmt Assn 1967-71; mem Am Soc for Training & Devel 1967-73; mem/officer Local/State/Regional & Natl Participation of NAACP 1956-67; mem Delta Sigma Theta Sorority; mem Phi Delta Kappa Educ Fraternity; Hudson Co Dem & Com Woman 1959, 1964, 1975; del Nat Dem Women 1963-64; del Pres Nat Com on Civil Rights 1962-; del Educ Conf Harvard Univ Black Congressional Caucus 1972; guest journalist Jersey Journal covering civil rights/events, including 1962 March on Washington; Natl Youth Advisory Bd 1961; NJ State Conf NAACP Branch 1963; Spanish Teacher Corps 1970; corp sec, Inner City Broadcasting Corp, bd of dir, New York, NY, 1978-90; bd of trustees, Sr Care & Activities Center, Montclair, NJ, 1989. **Honors/Awds:** Recipient NAACP Serv Award Jersey City Branch 1965; Am Mgmt Assn Sup Certificate 1966; Serv, Govt of NJ Affirmative Action Awareness Program, 1986-87; Certificate of Appreciation, State of NJ, Dept of Civil Serv: The Next Phase, 1987; Merit Award Program, Montclair State Coll, Upper Montclair, NJ, 1989; Certificate of Appreciation, Minority Student Mentor Program, Montclair State, 1991. **Business Addr:** Teacher Certification Coord/Advisor, Post B, Montclair State College, Normal Ave, School of Professional Studies, Chapin Hall, Rm 102, Upper Montclair, NJ 07043.

WEST, MARCELLUS
Mayor. **Personal:** Born Oct 16, 1913, Jackson, MS; married Fannie; children: Eddie, Doris, Fannie. **Career:** Brooklyn, IL, mayor; Restaurant Bus; Lovejoy Sch, supr/maint/truant ofcr 10

yrs; Armour Packing House. **Orgs:** Chmn Lovejoy Adv Bd; 3rd v chmn EOC. **Honors/Awds:** EOC Bd Award Willing Wrkrs Assn Comm Work; Award for Serv Rendered EOC Bd; Outstand Job & as Mayor 1975.

WEST, MARK ANDRE
Professional basketball player. **Personal:** Born Nov 5, 1960, Petersburg, VA; married Elaina; children: Marcus. **Educ:** Old Dominion, BS in finance. **Career:** Dallas Mavericks, center, 1983-84, Milwaukee Bucks, 1985, Cleveland Cavaliers, 1985-88, Phoenix Suns, 1988-94; Detroit Pistons, 1994-96; Cleveland Cavaliers, 1996-97; Indiana Pacers, 1997-. **Business Addr:** professional basketball player, Indiana Pacers, 300 E Market St, Indianapolis, IN 46204, (317)263-2100.

WEST, PHEORIS
Artist, educator. **Personal:** Born Aug 17, 1950, Albany, NY; son of Mary Wilson McDowell and James West; married Michele Barbette Hoff, May 5, 1979; children: Jahlani, Adwin, Pheannah, Adji West. **Educ:** State Univ of NY Coll at Brockport, 1968-70; PA Acad of Fine Arts, 4 yr Professional Cert 1970-74; Yale U, MFA Painting 1974-76. **Career:** OH State U, asst prof to assoc prof of art 1976-; Hillhouse HS New Haven, Ct, artist-in-residence 1976; Educ Ctr for the Arts, dir/artist-in-residence 1976. **Orgs:** mem Natl Confernce of Artists 1970; mem Artist Equity 1978-; bd mem CMACAO Cultural Arts Ctr 1979-; mem Bahia Bridge 1988-; bd mem Columbus Art League 1988-. **Honors/Awds:** James A Porter Grand Prize $1000 Nat Exhibit of Black Artists 1971; Cresson Award Travelling Flwshp to Europe PA Acad of Fine Arts 1973, J Scheidt Award Travelling Flwshp to Ghana 1974; Commn Mural 8' X 12' Lower Washington Hgts New York City Commn on Arts 1975; special recognition OH House of Representatives 1988; Individual Artists Grant OH Arts Council 1988. **Home Addr:** 756 Seymour Ave, Columbus, OH 43205.

WEST, ROYCE BARRY
Attorney. **Personal:** Born Sep 26, 1952, Annapolis, MD; son of Gloria Morris Ashford and Willis West; married Carol Richard West, Jul 25, 1987; children: Steve, Tara, Royce, Remarcus, Rolando, Roddrick, Brandon. **Educ:** University of Texas at Arlington, BA, sociology, 1975, MA, sociology, 1979; University of Houston, JD, 1979. **Career:** Harris County District Attorneys Office, Houston, TX, asst district atty, 1979-80; Dallas County District Attorneys Office, Dallas, TX, asst district atty, 1979-84; Royce West and Associates, Dallas, TX, lawyer, 1984-88; Brown, Robinson, & West, Dallas, TX, lawyer, 1988-91; Robinson & West, partner, attorney, 1991-. **Orgs:** Co-chairman, United Negro College Fund, 1990; board of directors, Texas Turnpike Authority, 1983-90; secretary of board, Dallas County Dental Health, 1989-; chairman, board of directors, 1987-90; president, JL Turner Legal Association, 1990-91; deacon, Good Street Baptist Church, 1984-. **Honors/Awds:** Distinguished Service Award, Dallas Black Chamber of Commerce, 1988. **Business Addr:** Attorney, Robinson & West PC, 400 S Zang, Ste 600, Dallas, TX 75208.

WEST, TOGO DENNIS, JR.
Cabinet official, attorney. **Personal:** Born Jun 21, 1942, Winston-Salem, NC; son of Evelyn Carter West and Togo Dennis; married Gail Estelle Berry, Jun 18, 1966; children: Tiffany Berry, Hilary Carter. **Educ:** Howard Univ, BSEE 1965, JD (cum laude) 1968. **Career:** Duquense Light & Power Co, elec engr 1965; Sughrue Rothwell Mion Zinn & McPeak, patent researcher 1966-67; US Equal Employment Opportunity Comm, legal intern 1967; Covington & Burling, law clerk 1967-68, summer assoc 1968, assoc 1973-75, 1976-77; Hon Harold R Tyler Judge US Dist Court for the Southern Dist of NY, law clerk 1968-69; Dept of Justice, associate deputy atty general 1975-76; Dept of Navy, gen counsel 1977-79; Dept of Defense, special asst to sec & deputy sec 1979-80, general counsel 1980-81; Patterson Belknap Webb & Tyler, partner, 1981-90; Northrop Corp Inc, senior vice pres, government relations, 1990-93; US Army, secretary, 1993-98; Veterans Affairs, acting scy, 1998-. **Orgs:** District of Columbia Bar 1968; New York Bar 1969; US Ct Mil Appeals 1969; US Supreme Ct 1978; managing editor Howard Law Journal 1968; Amer Bar Assn; Natl Bar Assn; dir Washington Council of Lawyers 1973-75; US Court of Claims 1981; Eagle Scout with Bronze Palm; trustee The Aerospace Corp 1983-90; Natl Council of the Friends of the Kennedy Center, 1984-91, treasurer, 1987-91; Kennedy Center Community and Friends Board, chairman, 1991-; commissioner 1982-89, chairman 1985-89, District of Columbia Law Revision Commission; trustee, Institute for Defense Analyses, 1989-90; trustee, Center for Strategic and International Studies, 1987-90; chairman, Legislative Bureau, 1987-89; Greater Washington Board of Trade, board of directors, 1987-93; board of directors, DC Law Students in Court Program 1986-92; DC Committee on Public Education, 1988-93, chairman, 1990-91; St John's Church at Lafayette Square, Vestry; Alpha Phi Omega Fraternity; Phi Alpha Delta Fraternity; Sigma Pi Phi Fraternity; Omega Psi Phi Fraternity; DC Court of Appeals Committee on Admissions, 1990-93; The Riggs National Bank, board of consultants, 1990-93; Protestant Episcopal Cathedral Foundation, 1989-; trustee, Shakespeare Theatre at the Folger, 1990-93; trustee, NC School of Arts, 1990-; financial comm mem, Episcopal Diocese of Washington, 1989-. **Honors/Awds:** Boy Scouts of America, Eagle Scout Award with Bronze Palm, 1957, Distinguished Eagle Scout Award, 1995; Howard University, Service Award, 1965; Distinguished Public Service Medal Dept of Defense 1981. **Military Serv:** US Army, served to capt judge adv gen corps, 1969-73; decorated Legion of Merit. **Business Addr:** Office of Secretary of Veterans Affairs, 810 Vermont Ave, NW, Washington, DC 20420.

WEST, VALERIE Y.
Educator. **Personal:** Born Jul 8, 1965, Newport News, VA; daughter of Lula A & Woodrow W West Sr. **Educ:** Hampton Univ, BA, 1987; VA Commonwealth Univ, MFA, 1992. **Career:** Lindsay Middle School, 8th grade English teacher, 1989-90; VA Commonwealth Univ, adjunct instructor, 1990-92; VA Union Univ, asst prof, 1992-. **Orgs:** Natl Conference on African American Theatre, 1992-; Black Theatre Network, 1992-94; VA Speech Communication Assn, 1994-. **Honors/Awds:** The Aspen Inst, Wye Fellowship, 1995. **Special Achievements:** "Vinnette Carroll: A Portrait of a Director," 1995; "A Look at the Academic Significance of Educational Theatre," 1994; MLK Gala, The Carpenter Ctr, Richmond VA, stage mgr, 1995; VA Union Univ, Ain't Misbehavin, make-up artist, 1994, Livin' Fat, dir, 1994, Joe Turner's Come & Gone, asst dir, 1993, The Amen Corner, dir, 1994, Blue Blood, dir, 1993, numerous others. **Business Addr:** Asst. Prof, Speech & Drama, Virginia Union Univ, 1500 N Lombardy St, Richmond, VA 23220, (804)257-5861.

WEST, WILLIAM LIONEL
Educational administrator, educator (retired). **Personal:** Born Nov 30, 1923, Charlotte, NC; son of Cornelia T Hairston West and Lionel Beresford West; married Edythe Kearns West, Apr 27, 1972; children: William II, Edythe P. **Educ:** Johnson C Smith University, BS 1947; State Univ IA, PhD 1955. **Career:** Howard University, prof/chmn dept pharmacology 1972-92, prof dept radiology 1971-92; Coll Med Howard University, prof dept pharm 1969-72; Dept Pharm Coll Med & Howard, asso prof/asst prof/instr 1956-69; Radiation Rsrch Dept Coll Med State Univ IA, rsrch asso 1954-56; Zoology Dept State Univ IA, rsrch asst 1949-54. **Orgs:** Mem Am Soc Pharmacology & Experimental Therapeutics; Intl Soc Biochem; Am Nuclear Soc; Am Assn Clinical Chem; Am Soc Zoologist; Soc for Experimental Biology & Med; Am Physiol Soc; Am Inst Chemist; Mem Am Assn Cancer Rsrch; flw Am Inst Chem; Intl Acad of Law & Sci; Sigma Xi Sci Soc; NY Acad Sci; flw AAAS Num Publ. **Honors/Awds:** Howard University, outstanding scholar, teacher, Health & Science, 1986. **Military Serv:** Army Air Corp, T/5, 1943-46; Asiatic Pacific Service Good Conduct Medal, 2 Bronze Service Stars, World War II Victory Medal.

WESTBROOK, BRYANT
Professional football player. **Personal:** Born Dec 19, 1974. **Educ:** Texas. **Career:** Detroit Lions, defensive back, 1997-. **Special Achievements:** NFL Draft, First round pick, #5, 1997. **Business Addr:** Professional Football Player, Detroit Lions, 1200 Featherstone Rd, Pontiac, MI 48342, (248)335-4131.

WESTBROOK, FRANKLIN SOLOMON
Automobile industry engineer. **Personal:** Born May 4, 1958, Buffalo, NY; son of Daisy M Pursley Westbrook and Solomon C Westbrook Jr; married Helen Juanita Goble, Mar 28, 1980; children: Anthony F, Reyhan M, William C, Gregory R. **Educ:** General Motors Inst, Flint, MI, BEE, 1981; Purdue Univ, West Lafayette, IN, MSIA, 1988. **Career:** CPC Tonawanda Engine GMC, co-op student, 1976-81, assoc engineer, 1981-83, plant engineer, 1983-86, sr engineer, 1986-; General Motors Corp, Tonawanda, NY, sr plant engineer, 1986-87, sr mfg engineer, 1988-. **Orgs:** Pres, 1986-87, vice pres, 1982-83, mem, Rho Lambda-Alpha Phi Alpha Fraternity, 1978-; part-time instructor, Erie Community Coll, 1983-85; mem, Urban League, Coalition for the Redevelop of Unified Community Involvement and Leadership, NAACP; exec comm, United Negro Coll Fund, Buffalo, NY, 1989-. **Honors/Awds:** Serv Award, Delta Sigma Theta Sor, Mu Phi Chapter; publication "A Proprietary Monitoring System".

WESTBROOK, JOSEPH W., III
Educator (retired). **Personal:** Born Jul 13, 1919, Shelby Co, TN; son of Clara Nelson Westbrook and Joseph W Westbrook, II; married Dorothy Greene, Jul 13, 1939; children: 4 (1 deceased). **Educ:** B 1943; M 1961; D 1970. **Career:** Dev of Plan of Decentralization, dir; Supvr Scndry Instr 8 Yrs; Sr HS, asst prin 3 Yrs; Clsrm Tchr Athletic Coach 15 Yrs; area superintendant Memphis City Schools, Memphis, TN 1971-81. **Orgs:** Mem Sigma Pi Phi Fraternity; mem Natl Ed Assc; Assc for Supvsn & Curr Dev; Phi Delta Kappa Ed Frat; Natl Sci Supvrs Assc; past pres TN Ed Assc; mem Memphis Ed Assc; Natl Sci Tchrs Assc; Am Assc of Sch Admntrs; Natl Assc of Scndry Sch Prins; Exec Com Natl Cncl on Tchrs Retirement; mem bd dirs Memphis UrbanLeague; bd dirs Dixie Homes Goodwill Boys Clb; Glenview YMCA; Frontiers Clb Intrntl; Memphis Reg Sickle Cell Cncl; past pres Alpha Phi Alpha Frat; Local Chpt; mem Exec Com of Un Way of Memphis; Exec Com of LeBonheur Hosp; bd of dir Natl Urban League 1978-82; bd of dir Natl Assn of Sickle Cell Disease 1979-83; bd of dir Natl Educ Assn 1984-90; pres Natl Educ Assn 1984-90. **Honors/Awds:** Recip acad professional devel award Natl Acad for Sch Execs; Outstanding Alumnus LeMoyne-Owen Coll 1973; Greek of Year Alpha Phi Alpha Fraternity Memphis Chapter 1973. **Home Addr:** 1711 Glenview Ave, Memphis, TN 38106.

WESTBROOK, MICHAEL
Professional football player. **Personal:** Born Jul 7, 1972, Detroit, MI. **Educ:** Colorado, attended. **Career:** Washington Redskins, wide receiver, 1995-. **Special Achievements:** 1st round/4th overall NFL draft, 1995. **Business Phone:** (703)471-9100.

WESTBROOKS, LOGAN H.
Business executive. **Personal:** Born Aug 28, 1937, Memphis, TN; married Geraldine Douthet; children: Babette. **Educ:** Lincoln Univ, 1957-61; Lemoyne Coll, 1955-57. **Career:** Source Record Co Inc, founder/pres 1977-; CA State Univ LA PAS Dept, part-time prof 1977-; Intrntl Markets CBS Records, vice pres 1977; Special Markets CBS Records Intl, dir 1971-76; Special Markets Coll Records US, dir 1970-71; R&B Mercury Rec, dir natl promotion, 1970; Mkt Capitol Records Inc, admin asst to vice pres 1969-70; R&B Capitol Rec, mid-west prom mgr 1965-67; RCA Vic Dist Corp, mgmt trn asst to market mgr. **Orgs:** Co-founder, Cont Inst of Tech 1971; mem Omega Psi Phi; PUSH Chicago; FORE NY; bd trust Merit Rl Est Invst Trust Chicago 1973; consultant, Natl Med Assn 1971; pres, Westbrooks Artist management; vp of mktg, Soul Train Productions & Record Co. **Honors/Awds:** Recognition Comm cert LA City Council 1970; Certificate of Merit LA Urban League 1970; Merit citation proj 1975; Boston 1973; special pres Mrs Martin Luther King Atlanta 1974; Distinguished Alumni, Lincoln Univ, 1983. **Special Achievements:** "The Anatomy of A Record Company.". **Military Serv:** Military 1961-63. **Business Addr:** 280 S Bev Drive, Ste 206, Beverly Hills, CA 90212.

WESTER, RICHARD CLARK
Firefighter. **Personal:** Born Sep 24, 1945, West Palm Beach, FL; son of Hazel Fisher Wester and Walter Wester; married LaDarn Hudson Wester (divorced 1986); children: Anita Michelle Wester, Angela Monique Wester. **Educ:** Florida State Fire College, Ocala, FL, on going educational courses in hazordous materials, firefighting tactics, suppression, instruction, leadership; Valencia Community College, Orlando, FL, seminars, 1988; management and related seminars. **Career:** City of Riviera Beach Fire Dept, Riviera Beach, FL, chief, 1969-. **Orgs:** Member, National Forum for Black Public Administrators, 1981-; treasurer, Fire Chiefs Association of Palm Beach County, Florida, 1990-; member, Training Officers Association of Palm Beach County, Florida. **Honors/Awds:** "Ricky" Award, JFK High School Class of '65, 1990; First Black Firefighter, Palm Beach County, FL; First Black Lieutenant of Fire, Palm Beach County, FL; First Black Captain of Fire, Palm Beach County, FL; First Black Fire Chief, Palm Beach County, FL; First Black Chief in the State of Florida of a major municipality. **Military Serv:** US Army, Specialist 4th Class, 1965-67; received Expert Rifle Honorary Discharge. **Business Addr:** Chief, City of Riviera Beach, Fire Dept, 600 W Blue Heron Blvd, Riviera Beach, FL 33404.

WESTMORELAND, SAMUEL DOUGLAS
Educator. **Personal:** Born May 29, 1944, West Chester, PA; son of Ella Dee Ingram Westmoreland and Nip T Westmoreland Sr; married Mary E Hampton; children: Lesia A, Samara E, Diana Haskins. **Educ:** Kutztown State Coll, BS 1966, MEd 1971; Lehigh Univ, MA. **Career:** Reading PA, detached worker prog 1966-67; YMCA, detached worker (gang worker); 9th Grade World Cultures, teacher 1967-71; Kutztown Univ, assoc prof of sociology 1971-. **Orgs:** Consult Black Cultural Org Kutztown State Coll 1970-71; mem Eastern Sociol Soc; Assn of Social & Behavioral Sciences; Black Conf on Higher Educ 1972-74; PA Sociological Soc; Black Conf on Basic Educ 1972-73; Lehigh Valley Black Adminstr; mem NAACP; lectr Apr 1972 "Educ & The Black Child" Downington Br NAACP;TV appearances guest spot Nov 1972; mem Natl Conf on the Black Family 1976-87; chairperson and presented paper on "The Myth of the Black Matriarchy" 1977, 1979-83; guest lectr Black Hist Week Easton PA 1977; "Objectives of Black History Week" Coatesville PA 1981-83, Pine Forge PA 1984; NAACP panel discussion Feb 1972; chrpsn PA Sociological Assn Conf 1983 & 1984; elected to the exec bd Assn of Science & Behavioral Scis 1984-87; presentation "Sports &The Black Youth" Sertoma Club, Reading, PA 1983; presentation "Black History Past, Present, Future" and "Future Prospects for Blacks" 1986; elected chairperson The Anthropology/Sociology Dept 1987-90; president-elect, 1989-90, president, Assn of Social and Behavorial Scientist, Inc; chair National Conference on the Black Family 1989-90, 1991, 1992; chairman, life membership committee, ASBS, 1990-97; Association of Black Sociologists. **Business Addr:** Associate Professor, Kutztown Univ, Kutztown, PA 19530.

WESTON, LARRY CARLTON
Attorney. **Personal:** Born Jul 6, 1948, Sumter, SC. **Educ:** SC State Clg, BA 1970; Univ of SC, JD 1975. **Career:** Gray & Weston Attys at Law, atty 1976-; BF Goodrich Footwear Co, asst persnl mgr 1970-72. **Orgs:** Dist cnsl SC Conf of Br NAACP 1978-; bd of dir, v chmn Sumter Co Pub Defender Corp 1979-; adv bd YWCA 1977-78; mem Sumter Co Commn on Higher Ed 1979-; mem Sumter Co Election Commn 1980-. **Business Addr:** 110 S Sumter St, Sumter, SC 29150.

WESTON, M. MORAN, II
Association executive. **Personal:** Born Sep 10, 1910, Tarboro, NC; son of Catharine Perry (deceased) and Moran Weston (deceased); married Miriam Yvonne Drake, Jun 27, 1946; children: Karann Christine, Gregory M. **Educ:** Columbia Univ, BA 1930; Union Theol Seminary, MDiv 1934; Columbia Univ, PhD 1954. **Career:** Carver Federal Svgs Bank, founding dir chmn of bd 1948-; St Philip's Epis Church, rector/pastor 1957-82; Comm Serv Council, pres/chair 1957-85; State Univ of NY Albany Ctr, prof social hist 1969-77, prof emeritus 1977-; Douglass Circle Develop Corp, pres 1982-; Natl Assoc for Affordable Housing, co-developer w/Glick Construction Corp of 600 condo apts, 1985, sponsor NYC Housing Partnership. **Orgs:** Trustee Legal Defense Fund NAACP 1964-; founder/pres Upper Manhattan Day Care and Child Develop Ctr 1970-85; trustee Mt Sinai Medical Sch & Hosp 1971-; trustee/former chmn St Augustine's Coll 1971-; trustee emeritus 1982-, pres Greater Harlem Nursing Home 1975-; pres Sr House Co, SPOP Housing Corp 1975-; mem Grievance Comm NY Bar Assoc 1976-80; bd of dirs NY Chap of Amer Red Cross 1978-82; pres Housing for People Corp 1980-; governor Foreign Policy Assoc 1982-90; sire archon Sigma Pi Phi Zeta Boule 1985, 1986; pres non-profit housing corp which constructed 1000 housing units in Harlem; trustee, Columbia Univ, 1969-81, trustee emeritus, 1981-; founding pres, bd mem, WUCR Inc, 1985-. **Honors/Awds:** Honorary DD, Virginia Theological Seminary, 1964; Honorary STD, Columbia University, 1968; Honorary Canon The Cathedral Church of St John the Divine New York City 1980-; St Augustine's Cross, Awd Archbishop of Canterbury 1981; Humanitarian Awd Harlem Commonwelath Council 1982; Man of the Year NY Urban League 1982; Excellence Awd Columbia Univ Grad Fac 1982; Comm Serv Awd Manufacturers Hanover Bank NY 1984; Honorary LHD, Fordham University, 1988. **Home Addr:** 228 Promenade Circle, Heathrow, FL 32746.

WESTON, MARTIN V.
Journalist. **Personal:** Born Mar 14, 1947, Philadelphia, PA; son of Cozetta Walker Weston and Rubin Weston; married Brenda Catlin Weston, May 23. **Career:** Philadelphia Bulletin, Philadelphia, PA, editorial writer, 1979-82; Channel 6-TV, Philadelphia, PA, producer vision, 1982-83; W Wilson Goode, Mayor, Philadelphia, PA, special aide, 1983; Newsday, Melville, NY, editorial writer, 1984-. **Orgs:** Member, Natl Assn of Black Journalists. **Business Addr:** Editorial Writer, Newsday, 235 Pinelawn Road, Melville, NY 11747.

WESTON, SHARON
Communications consultant. **Personal:** Born Oct 1, 1956, Chicago, IL; daughter of Lucille Weston (deceased) and Willie Weston. **Educ:** Univ of WI LaCrosse, BA 1978; Regent Univ Va Beach, MA 1984. **Career:** Arts & Humanities Cncl of Greater Baton Rouge, regional develop officer 1985; Discover Magazine, sales manager 1985; Finesse & Associates, Baton Rouge, LA, executive director, 1985-; Baton Rouge Opera, mktg and promotions asst 1986; The Nathan Group, dir of communications 1987-; WKG-TV, public affairs dir, cohost ''IMPACT'' Baton Rouge, 1987; Metropolitan District 7, City of Baton Rouge, councilwoman, 1989, state representative, 1991-. **Orgs:** Advisor Love Outreach Faith Fellowship 1985-; LA Center for Women in Government; Capital Area United Way; board of directors Real Life Educ Found, 1989; American Heart Association; comm mem Louisiana Elected Women Officials; board member, finance & executive committee, Center for Women and Government, 1991. **Honors/Awds:** Certified Human Resource Consultant Performax Systems Intl 1985; Certificate of Appreciation South Baton Rouge Kiwanis Club 1985; Certificate of Appreciation Zeta Phi Beta Sorority Workshop Consultant, 1989; Achievement Award for Accomplishments, Greens Chapel AME Church 1989; Outstanding Talent and Spiritual Leadership to the Community Award, Mayor and Governor, 1990. **Home Addr:** 3352 Osceola St, Baton Rouge, LA 70805.

WESTRAY, KENNETH MAURICE
Roman Catholic priest. **Personal:** Born Jun 15, 1952, Washington, DC; son of Jean Virginia Hughes Westray and Kenneth Maurice Westray Sr. **Educ:** US Merchant Marine Acad, Kings Point, NY, BS 1974; attended Mount St Mary's Seminary, Emmitsburg, MD, 1976-78; St Patrick's Seminary, Menlo Park, CA, MDiv 1979, ordained 1981; attended Graduate Theological Union, Berkeley, CA, 1986. **Career:** Amer Export Isbrandsten Lines, New York, NY, third mate, 1974-76; Nativity Grammar School, Washington, DC, teacher, 1979; Sacred Heart Parish, San Francisco, CA, deacon/seminarian, 1980-83; Saint Elizabeth Parish, San Francisco, associate pastor, 1983-85; Sacred Heart Parish, San Francisco, pastor, 1985-. **Orgs:** Bd mem & past pres, Archdiocese of San Francisco Black Catholic (Apostolate) Affairs, 1979-; mem & former bd mem, Natl Black Catholic Clergy Caucus, 1980-; councilor, Archdiocese of San Francisco Priests Council, 1985-88; regent, Saint Ignatius High School, 1986-89; bd mem, Natl Federation of Priests Council, 1988-; bd mem, Catholic Charities of San Francisco, 1988-92. **Honors/Awds:** Rep to Intl Federation of Priests Council, Ghana, 1988. **Military Serv:** Naval Reserves, lieutenant, 1974-91.

WETHERS, DORIS LOUISE
Physician. **Personal:** Born Dec 14, 1927, Passai, NJ; daughter of Lilian Wilkinson & William A Wethers; married Garvall H Booker, DDS, Dec 25, 1953 (deceased); children: Garvall H Booker III, Clifford Wethers Booker, David Boyd Booker. **Educ:** Queens College, NY, BS, magna cum laude, 1948; Yale University, School of Medicine, MD, 1952. **Career:** St Luke's-Roosevelt Hosp Ctr, director of pediatrics, 1973-79, attending pediatrician, 1973-, director comprehensive Sickle Cell program, 1979-; Columbia Presbyterian Med Ctr, attending pediatrician, 1987-; Columbia University College of Physicians & Surgeons, professor of clinical pediatrics, 1987-, consultant, currently. **Orgs:** American Pediatric Society; Fellow American Academy of Pediatrics; NY County & State Med Societies; Susan Smith McKinney Steward Med Society. **Honors/Awds:** NYC Health Research Training Prog, Preceptor of the Year, 1991; Southern Regional Sickle Cell Association, Recognition Awd, 1993; St Luke's-Roosevelt Hosp Ctr Community Svc Awd, 1993; Hearbeats of Jamaica Inc, Recognition Awd, 1995. **Special Achievements:** Introduction to the Sickle Cell Trait Conference, 11th National Neonatal Screening Symposium, Corpus Christi TX, 1995; Newborn Screening for Sickle Cell Disease, 2nd International African Symposium on Sickle Cell Disease, 1995; Missed Diagnosis of S Korle-bu in Prenatal Diagnosis and Newborn Screening, 16th Annual Mtg of the National Sickle Cell Disease Prog in Mobile, Alabama, 1991; numerous other publications in professional journals and contributions to medical texts. **Business Addr:** Director, Comprehensive Sickle Cell Program St Lukes-Roosevelt, Hosp Center, 1111 Amsterdam Ave, New York, NY 10025, (212)523-3103.

WHALEY, CHARLES H., IV
Telecommunications company executive. **Personal:** Born Jan 15, 1958, Elmhurst, NY; son of Edna and Charles III; married Jeanette Smith, Sep 26, 1987. **Educ:** Queensborough Community College, AAS, 1979. **Career:** General Telephone and Electronics, test engineer, 1979-81; General Dynamics Communications Co, operations engineer, 1981-83; United Technologies Communications Co, project mgr, 1983-86; Telex Computer Products, project mgr, 1986; Pertel Communications Corp, president, 1986-91; Pertel Communication N/E Inc, pres, 1990-. **Orgs:** Hartford Chamber of Commerce, minority business roundtable, 1990-91; New York City High School of Telecommunications, board of directors, 1991-; Connecticut Minority Supplier Development Council, Minority Input Committee. **Honors/Awds:** SBA Award for Excellence, 1993. **Business Addr:** President, Pertel Communications N/E, Inc, 100 Constitution Plz, Ste 924, Hartford, CT 06103.

WHALEY, JOSEPH S.
Physician. **Personal:** Born Nov 29, 1933, Yuma, AZ; son of Elizabeth Whaley and Sexter Whaley; married Doris Naomi Pettie; children: Craig T, Dawna T. **Educ:** Univ Of AZ, BA 1954; Hahnemann Med Clg, MD 1958. **Career:** USAF, physician flight surg 1959-63; Private Practice Tucson, AZ 1963-. **Orgs:** St pres AZ Chptr Am Acad of Fam Physicians 1972; del Am Med Assn 1980-; bd of dir AZ Physicians IPA 1983-; Masonic Lodge; Archon Sigma Pi Phi Boule Frat; Kappa Alpha Psi. **Honors/Awds:** Phi Beta Kappa Univ of AZ 1954; Dist Military Grad Univ of AZ 1954; High Hnr Grad Univ of AZ 1954. **Military Serv:** Air Force Capt 1959-63. **Business Addr:** Physician, 368 E Grant Rd, Tucson, AZ 85705.

WHALEY, MARY H.
Educational administrator. **Personal:** Born in Clarksville, TN; daughter of Sadie Beatrice Allen Harrison and Adolphus David Harrison; divorced; children: Brian Cedric, Kevin Allen. **Educ:** Fisk Univ, AB 1959; Univ of TN Sch of Soc Wrk, MSW 1968, doctoral student 1978-, Univ of TN, Knoxville, TN, EdD, 1990. **Career:** TN Dept of Human Svcs, caseworker 1961-63, casework super 1966-72; Knoxville Coll, vis instr 1971-73; TN Dept of Human Svcs, staff consult E TN 1972-74; Knoxville Coll, asso dean students 1974-78; Univ of TN, professional asst 1978-; Knoxville Coll, Morristown, TN, assoc academic dean, 1989-90; Knoxville Coll, Knoxville, TN, Head/Div of Business & Soc Sciences, assistant acad dean, assoc prof, 1990-. **Orgs:** Chmn various com Natl Assn of Soc Wrks 1968; chmn various com Assn of Black Soc Wrks 1972; bd of dir Phyllis Wheatley 1972-74; Comm Imprvmt Found Bd 1972-74; bd of dirs Planned Parenthood 1973-77; UTSSW com Minority Admission & Retention 1974-76; mem League of Women Voters 1976; bd of dir Helen Ross McNabb 1977; edited What Next? Child Welfare Serv for the 80's 1982; proj dir and co-author Parmanency Planning, The Black Experience 1983; contributed ''Ethnic Competent Family Centered Svcs'' Basic Family Centered Curriculum for Family Serv Workers & Parent Aides; bd of dir TN NASW Chapter 1985; Friends of Black Children St Adv committee and the local affiliate; Soc Serv Panel TN Black Legislators Caucus; adv committee Child & Family Serv; bd mem NatlResource Cntron Family Based Serv Univ Iowa; Bijou Limelighters; nominating comm Girl Scout Council; RAM House Board; chairperson panel, United Way of Greater Knoxville, 1990-; Friends of Black Children, 1985-; Community Youth Mentoring, 1989-. **Honors/Awds:** In Appreciation of Service, Helen Ross McNabb Center, 1983; Appreciation of Service to Girl Scouting, 1990; Dept of Human Services for Work with Children, 1990; Plaque of Appreciation for Support and Wisdom, Knoxville College, Class of 1993; Boys and Girls Club, Laura Cansler Branch Board, 1991-, Program Chair, 1992-93; Moderator Women's Assn 1st United Presbyterian Church, 1986-, deacon, 1987-90, elder, 1990-; Zeta Phi Beta Sorority; Charter Member Knoxville Chapter of Jack and Jill; CAC Leadership Class, 1990; Commissioner-Presbytery of East TN, 1993-. **Business Addr:** Associate Professor, Sociology, Knoxville College, 901 College St, 114 Young Memorial, Knoxville, TN 37921.

WHALEY, WAYNE EDWARD
Educator. **Personal:** Born Oct 23, 1949, Lincoln, DE; married Janice Evans; children: Sean, Dane. **Educ:** Delaware State Coll, BS 1971; Univ of Delaware, MA 1977. **Career:** Red Clay School Dist, asst principal 1978-86; Smyrna School Dist, teacher 1971-75, asst principal 1978-86, teacher 1986-. **Orgs:** Volunteer YMCA and Delaware Special Olympics 1975-; mem Delaware Exceptional Childrens Council 1985; bd pres Centennial United Methodist Church 1985; mem Natl Assoc for Equal Oppor in Higher Educ 1986; bd mem Wilmington Lions Club 1986; mem Natl Sch Curriculum Assoc 1986. **Honors/Awds:** Special Mbr Governor's Task Force on Educ 1976; Man of the Year Epsilon Chap of Omega Psi Phi 1982.

WHALUM, KENNETH TWIGG
Minister. **Personal:** Born Mar 23, 1934, Memphis, TN; son of Thelma Miller Twigg Whalum and Hudie David Whalum; children: Kenneth Twigg Jr, Kirk Wendell, Kevin Henry. **Educ:** LeMoyne Coll, attended, 1951-57; Tennessee Baptist School of Religion, DD, 1975; Mgmt Programs, Univ of Michigan, Univ of Texas-Austin, Memphis State Univ, Harvard Univ, 1975-81. **Career:** US Postal Serv, mem, dir of personnel, 1968-71, mid-south asst dist mgr, e&lr, 1971-77, south reg gen mgr employee relations div, 1977-79, dist mgr, Michigan dist, 1979-81; Olivet Baptist Church, senior pastor. **Orgs:** Vice pres-at-large, 1977-81, pres, 1981-85, Tennessee Baptist M&E Convention; vice pres, 1981-85, mem bd of dirs, 1981-, Natl Baptist Convention USA Inc; bd of dirs Morehouse School of Religion, 1981-; bd of trustees, LeMoyne-Owen Coll, 1983-; vice chmn bd of trustees, LeMoyne-Owen Coll, 1985-86; bd of dirs, Goals for Memphis, 1986-; chmn labor industry comm, NAACP, 1987-; city councilman, Dist 4, City of Memphis, 1988. **Honors/Awds:** Jerry D Williams Award, Community Serv Agency, 1977; Man of the Year Award, ACT of Memphis, 1979; CW Washburn Achievement Award, Booker T Washington High School, 1982; Man of the Year Award, Shelby Co Dist Assn, 1985; Life & Golden Heritage NAACP, 1985; Golden Gallery Distinguished Alumni Award by Lemoyne-Owen Coll, Memphis, TN, 1987. **Military Serv:** USN personnel man 2nd class 1951-55; Natl Defense Medal, Korean Serv Medal, Good Conduct Medal 1951-55. **Business Addr:** Senior Pastor, Olivet Baptist Church, 3084 Southern Ave, Memphis, TN 38111.

WHARTON, A. C., JR.
Educator, attorney. **Personal:** Born Aug 17, 1944, Lebanon, TN; married Ruby; children: A C III, Andre Courtney, Alexander Conrad. **Educ:** TSU, BA 1966; Univ MS, JD 1971. **Career:** EEOC, decision drafter 1967-68; trial attorney, 1971-73; Lawyers Com for Civil Rights Under Law, proj dir 1973; Univ MS, adj prof; Shelby Co TN, pub defender 1980; Private Practice, Wharton & Wharton. **Orgs:** Past exec dir Memphis Area Leagl Serv Inc; mem Amer Bar Assn; Natl Legal Aid & Defender Assn; Natl Bar Assn; TN Bar Assn; NAACP; pres Leadership Memphis Alumni Assn 1979; Operation PUSH; Urban League. **Honors/Awds:** US Atty Gen Honor Law Grad Prog 1971. **Business Addr:** Attorney, 161 Jefferson Ave, Ste 402, Memphis, TN 38103.

WHARTON, CLIFTON R., JR.
Organization executive. **Personal:** Born Sep 13, 1926, Boston, MA; son of Harriette Wharton and Clifton R Wharton Sr; married Dolores Duncan; children: Clifton III, Bruce. **Educ:** Harvard Univ, BA (cum laude), 1947; Johns Hopkins Univ, MA, 1948; Univ Chicago, MA, 1956, PhD, 1958. **Career:** American International Association for Economic and Social Development, head of reports and analysis department, 1948-53; University of Chicago, research associate, 1953-57; Agricultural Development Council, Inc, 1957-69; University of Malaya, visiting professor, 1958-64; American Universities Research Program, director, 1964-66, acting director of council, 1966-67, vice president, 1967-69; Michigan State University, president, 1970-78; State University of New York (System), chancellor, 1978-87; Teachers Insurance and Annuity Association and College Retirement Equities Fund, chairman/CEO, 1987-93; Dept of State, Deputy Secretary of State, 1993. **Orgs:** Director, Ford Motor Co, New York Stock Exchange, Harcourt Genl Inc, Tenneco Inc,TIAA-CREFl; Former chairman of bd, Intl Food & Agr Development Aid, Deputy of State, 1976-83. **Honors/Awds:** Numerous publs & monographs; 58 Hon Degrees; Man of Yr Boston Latin Sch 1970; Amistad Awd Amer Missionary Assn 1970; Joseph E Wilson Awd 1977; named first Black chancellor of the State Univ of New York; first Black chairman Rockefeller Foundation; first Black admitted Johns Hopkins Univ Sch Adv Intl Studies; Alumni Medal, University of Chicago, 1980; Samuel Z Westerfield Award, National Economic Association, 1985; Benjamin E Mays Award, Boston Black Achievers, YMCA, 1986; Black History Makers Award, New

York Associated Black Charities, 1987; Frederick Douglass Award, New York Urban League, 1989; first Black to head a Fortune 100 service company, TIAA-CREF, 1987. **Business Addr:** Board of Overseers, TIAA-CREF, 730 Third Avenue, New York, NY 10017.

WHARTON, DOLORES D.
Association executive. **Personal:** Born Jul 3, 1927, New York, NY; daughter of Josephine Bradford Owens and V Kenneth Duncan; married Clifton R Wharton Jr; children: Clifton III, Bruce. **Educ:** Chicago State Univ, BA. **Career:** Fund for Corporate Initiatives Inc, founder, chmn, corporate director, currently. **Orgs:** Director, Kellogg Co, Gannett Co; COMSAT Corp; Capital Bank & Trust Co; trustee, Center for Strategic & International Studies; Committee for Economic Development; Glimmerglass Opera, City Center. **Honors/Awds:** Doctors of Humane Letters: Central Michigan University, College of St Rose, Wilberforce University, State University of New York, Le Moyne College, Michigan State University, Hartwick College, Marymount College, Chicago State University; author, Contemporary Artists of Malaysia: A Biographic Survey. **Business Addr:** The Fund for Corporate Initiatives, Inc, PO Box 615, Cooperstown, NY 13326.

WHARTON, FERDINAND D., JR.
Business manager. **Personal:** Born in Henderson, NC; son of Annie Malissa Harris Wharton and Fletcher Decatur Wharton; divorced; children: F D III, Tam Eric, Clifford Alan, Marc David. **Educ:** A&T Coll of NC, BS Agr Educ 1939; Univ of CT, MS Poultry Nutrition 1948; Monsanto Intl Div Key Mgmt Trng, adv mgmt course 1966. **Career:** Vocational Agriculture, instr 1940-42; Princess Anne Coll, head poultry dept 1942-43; Triumph Explosives, asst dir race relations 1943-44; Avon Training Sch, head poultry dept 1944-46; Univ of CT, rsch asst 1946-48; Dawes Lab Inc, asst dir nutrition rsch 1948-60; USAID Ghana, adv animal nutrition 1960-64; Monsanto Co, sr project mgr 1964-67, develop mgr 1967-72; Monsanto Commercial Prods Co, mgr environmental affairs 1972-77; Continental Diversified Indus, dir public affairs plastic beverage bottle div 1977-79, dir of public affairs 1979-82; Continental Can Company, dir of public affairs, 1982-84; Continental Group Inc, dir of public affairs, 1984-85. **Orgs:** Mem Soc of the Plastics Industry Inc; mem Soc of the Sigma Xi; mem Amer Inst of Nutrition; mem Amer Assn for the Advancement of Science; charter mem UN food and agricultural org/industry adv comm, 1965-66; mem food industry adv comm, Nutrition Foundation, 1967-71; bd dirs, 1966-73, treas, 1968, pres, 1969-71, St Louis Comm on Africa, St Louis, MO; bd dirs, 1969-73, treas, 1972, St Louis Comm for Environmental Information, St Louis, MO; bd dirs, 1969-73, 1975-77, treas, 1970, vice pres, 1971, pres, 1973, Grace Hill Settlement House; mem, White House Conference on Food, Nutrition, and Hunger, 1969; bd dirs Lakeside Ctr for Boys of St Louis Co, 1971-77, 2nd vice pres, 1974-; bd dirs Mark Twain Summer Inst, 1973-77; fellowScientist Inst for Public Info, 1971-; bd dirs Univ City Home Rentalust, 1971-77; bd dirs St Louis Council on World Affairs, 1971-77; mem citizens Adv Council Hogan St Regional Youth Ctr, 1975-77; bd dirs Keep Brown Univ Beautiful, 1983-84; charter mem tau iota, Hartford Chap Omega Psi Phi Frat; consult, 1985-, dir mgmt consulting, 1990-, Natl Exec Serv Corps, 1985-; exec recruiter Intl Exec Serv Corps, 1986-; mem, bd of dirs, Action Housing Inc, 1989; member, executive comm, Ch Personnel Com, 1990-; chairman site comm, 1990-; Housing Partnership, City of Norwalk, 1991-93, vice chairman, member executive committee, 1991-93 chairman Site Selection & CHAS Committee, chairman 1994-97. **Honors/Awds:** Career Achievement Award, Urban League, St Louis, MO, 1976; Black Achievement in Industry Award, YMCA, Harlem, NY, 1980; National Urban League Visiting Professor, Black Exchange Program, 1982-84; author or co-author of 45 published technical & scientific papers and 30 reports presented at scientific meetings; US Patent #3,655,869 "Treatment of Diarrhea Employing Certain Basic Polyelectrolyte Polymers"; editor "Proceedings of the Symposium Envirronmental Impact of Nitrile Barrier Containers, Lopac: A Case Study". **Home Addr:** 19 Ledgebrook Dr, Norwalk, CT 06854.

WHARTON, MILTON S.
Judge. **Personal:** Born Sep 20, 1946, St Louis, MO. **Educ:** SIU Edwardsville, BS 1969; DePaul Univ School Of Law, JD 1974. **Career:** St Clair Co Pub Defender, atty; IL Judiciary, judge 1976. **Orgs:** V chm IL St Bar Asso Standing Comm on Juvenile Justice; v chm St Louis Bi-state Chptr Am Red Cross; bd mem YMCA of So IL; bd mem St Marys Hosp of E St Louis; bd mem Higher Ed Ctr of St Louis. **Honors/Awds:** Alumnus of the Yr SIU at Edwardsville 1977; Dist Serv Awd Belleville Jaycees 1983; Man of Yr Nat Cncl of Negro Women-E St Louis 1982; Man Of Yr So Dist IL Asso of Club Women 1982; Civic Serv Phi Beta Sigma-zeta Ph I Beta 1985. **Home Addr:** 23 Hilltop Pl, East St Louis, IL 62203.

WHARTON BOYD, LINDA F.
Educator, consultant, government official. **Personal:** Born Apr 21, 1961, Baltimore, MD; daughter of Thelma L Kirby Wharton and Rev. Frank Wharton (deceased); children: Duke Boyd. **Educ:** Univ of Pgh, BA 1972, MA 1975, PhD 1979. **Career:** Howard Univ, asst prof 1979-85; Washington DC Office of the Mayor, communications specialist 1984-86; DC Department of Administrative Services, dir of public affairs 1986-88; DC Department of Recreation, director of communications, 1988-92; The Wharton Group, pres, 1990-; Alcohol and Drug Abuse Services Administration, chief of criminal justice, 1992-95; DC Dept of Human Svcs, sr asst, dir of policy and communication, currently. **Orgs:** Delta Sigma Theta Sor 1971-; exec treas Natl Speech Comm Assn Black Caucus 1975-; honorary bd mem, Pgh Black Theatre Dance Ensemble 1978-; bd mem, Natl Arts Prog Natl Council of Negro Women 1979-; consultant, NAACP Labor & Indus Sub-com on Comm; chairperson, Joint Chapter Event, Natl Coalition of 100 Black Women Inc. **Honors/Awds:** Outstanding Black Women's Awd Communication Arts Creative Enterprises 1974; Doctoral Honor's Seminar Prog Howard Univ Speech Comm 1977; Bethune Legacy Award, Natl Council of Negro Women 1986; Natl Public Radio Documentary Award 1985. **Special Achievements:** Author: "Black Dance, It's Origin and Continuity," Minority Voices, 1977; advisor: "Stuff," children's program, NBC-TV, Washington, DC. **Business Addr:** Director of Policy and Communication, DC Dept of Health, 800 9th St SE, Washington, DC 20024.

WHATLEY, BOOKER TILLMAN
Educator. **Personal:** Born Nov 5, 1915, Anniston, AL; married Lottie Cillie. **Educ:** AL A&M U, BS 1941; Ruthgers U, PhD 1957. **Career:** Univ of AR, lecturer; Univ of MD; Univ of FL; Cornell Univ, adj prof 1972-; USDA/ARS, colbtr 1970; Tuskegee Inst, prof 1969-; Peace Corp, consult 1962-66; US/AID, adv 1960-62; So Univ, prof 1957-69; Cobb High & Vet School, prin 1958-50; US Postal Serv, carrier 1947-48; Butler Co, co ext agt 1946-47. **Orgs:** Mem Am Soc for Hortl Sci; Assc of So Agr Sci; Assc for Tropical Bio; Am Soc of Plant Psysiologist; Intrntl Plant Propagators Soc; Soc of Ec Botany; Soc of Sigma Xi Sweet Potato Collaborators Grp. **Honors/Awds:** Outst Alumni Awrd AL A&M Univ 1971; faculty achvmt awrd Tuskegee Inst 1972; omega man of the yr Iota Omega & Lambda Epsilon 1974; serv to agr awrd AL Farm Bur Fed 1974; elected Fellow of Am Soc for Hortl Sci 1974; mem Sec Earl Butts' USDA Hon Award Com 1975; outst sci awrd RD Morrison & FE Evans 1976; chmn Annual & Meeting Am Soc of Hortl Sci 1976; cit State of AL House of Reps 1977; Apr 15 Booker T Whatley Day Hometown Anniston & Calhoun Co; outst sci awrd Natl Consortium for Black Professional Dev 1977; num publs. **Military Serv:** AUS maj 1975. **Business Addr:** Tuskegee Institute, Tuskegee Institute, AL 36088.

WHATLEY, ENNIS
Professional basketball player, cleric, business executive. **Personal:** Born Aug 11, 1962, Birmingham, AL; married Ritza. **Educ:** Univ of AL, 1979-83. **Career:** Chicago Bulls, 1983-85, Cleveland Cavaliers, 1986, Washington Bullets, 1986, 1987, San Antonio Spurs, 1986, Atlanta Hawks, 1988, Los Angeles Clippers, 1989; Wichita Falls Texans (CBA), 1990; Portland Trail Blazers, 1991-92, 1996-9 7; Atlanta Hawks, 1993-95; Kids in His Care Christian Daycare, minister. **Orgs:** Christian Outreach Organization, Sapphire Ministries, president & cofounder. **Honors/Awds:** Led Bulls in assists (83) & steals (15); led club in assists 57 games including 28 of last 30 contests; CBS Sports named him among their 5 All-Stars as he won MVP honors in televised games against UCLA, Tennessee, & Georgia.

WHEAT, ALAN
Company executive. **Personal:** Born Oct 16, 1951, San Antonio, TX; son of Jean Wheat and James Wheat; married Yolanda Townsend Wheat, Aug 11, 1990; children: Alynda Wheat. **Educ:** Grinnell Coll, BA 1972. **Career:** HUD Kansas City MO, economist 1972-73; Mid-Amer Reg Council Kansas City, econ 1973-75; Cty Exec Office KC, aide 1975-76; MO House of Reps Jefferson City, rep 1977-82; Congress 5th Dist MO, congressman 1983-94; CARE Foundation, vp of public policy and govt relations, 1995-. **Orgs:** Rules Comm, Select Comm on Children Youth & Families; chmn Subcomm on Govt Operations & Metro Affairs of the Comm on Dist of Columbia; Select Committee on Hunger, US House of Reps, beginning 1990; commissioner, Martin Luther King Jr, Federal Holiday Commission, beginning 1989; pres, Congressional Black Caucus Foundation, beginning 1990. **Honors/Awds:** Third freshman Congressman in history to be appointed to the Rules Committee; Best Freshman Legislator St Louisan Mag 1977-78; 1 of 10 Best Legislators Jefferson City News Tribune 1979-80; MO Times Newspaper 1979-80. **Business Addr:** Vice Pres, Public Policy & Govt Relations, CARE Foundation, 1625 K St NW, Ste 200, Washington, DC 20006.

WHEAT, DEJUAN SHONTEZ
Professional basketball player. **Personal:** Born Oct 14, 1973. **Educ:** Louisville. **Career:** Minnesota Timberwolves, guard, 1997-. **Business Addr:** Professional Basketball Player, Minnesota Timberwolves, 600 First Ave N, Minneapolis, MN 55403, (612)337-3865.

WHEAT, JAMES WELDON, JR.
Corporate treasurer. **Personal:** Born Mar 16, 1948, Tuskegee, AL; son of Emogene Dupree Wheat and James Weldon Wheat; married Panchit Charanachit Wheat, Dec 19, 1975; children: Saranya J, Annalai B. **Educ:** Grinnell College, Grinnell, IA, BA, 1969; Cornell University, Ithaca, NY, MBA, 1971; University of Chicago, certificate, advanced management, 1982. **Career:** Bankers Trust Co, New York, NY, vice pres, 1973-84; Corning, Inc, Corning, NY, asst treasurer, 1984-. **Orgs:** Member, Society for Black Professionals, 1986-. **Military Serv:** US Air Force, 1st Lt, 1971-73. **Business Addr:** Assistant Treasurer, Corning Inc, HP-CB-03-1, Corning, NY 14831.

WHEATLEY, TYRONE
Professional football player. **Personal:** Born Jan 19, 1972, Inkster, MI. **Educ:** Michigan. **Career:** New York Giants, running back, 1995-. **Special Achievements:** 1st round/17th overall NFL draft pick, 1995. **Business Addr:** Professional Football Player, New York Giants, Giants Stadium, East Rutherford, NJ 07073, (201)935-8111.

WHEATON, FRANK KAHLIL
Sports entertainment attorney. **Personal:** Born Sep 27, 1951, Los Angeles, CA; son of James Lorenzo Wheaton & Helen Ruth Alford; married Sarah Jean Perkins, Sep 23, 1975 (divorced); children: Marissiko Miriam, Summer Gwenhelen; married Robin Louise Green, Aug 6, 1988 (divorced). **Educ:** Willamette Univ, 1969-70; CA State Univ, Northridge, BA, 1973; West Los Angeles School of Law, JD, 1986. **Career:** WHUR-FM, broadcast announcer, eng, producer, 1973-74; Natl Broadcasting Co, broadcast eng, 1975-78; Freelance Television, actor/producer, 1975-; Natl Employers Council, legal rep, 1984; Law Offices of Bickerstaff & McNair, of counsel, 1993-; Root Hog Productions, co-exec producer, 1993-; The Management Group, chairman, 1984-. **Orgs:** Black Entertainment & Sports Lawyers Assn, (BESLA), bd mem, 1993-; Big Brothers of Greater Los Angeles, bd mem, 1994-; 28th Street/Crenshaw YMCA, bd mem, 1994-; Markham Theatre Project, bd mem, 1994-; Sports Lawyers Assn; Amer Bar Assn; Natl Basketball Players Assn; Screen Actors Guild. **Honors/Awds:** City of Compton, CA, Mayoral Resolution, 1986, Mayoral Proclamation, 1992. **Special Achievements:** Creator/Exec Producer, James Worthy All-Star Basketball Clinic, 1991-; Creator/Exec Producer, Michael Jordan/UNCF Celebrity Golf Classic, 1988-89; Ruth Berle Celebrity Golf Classic, Producer, 1990-91; Producer, "World's Fastest Athlete," ABC, 1990-91. **Business Addr:** Chairman, The Management Group, Sports/Entertainment Representatives, 1900 Avenue of the Stars, Ste 790, Los Angeles, CA 90067-4308, (213)979-9000.

WHEATON, KENNY
Professional football player. **Personal:** Born Mar 8, 1975. **Educ:** Univ of Oregon, attended. **Career:** Dallas Cowboys, defensive back, 1997-. **Business Addr:** Professional Football Player, Dallas Cowboys, One Cowboys Pkwy, Irving, TX 75063, (214)556-9900.

WHEATON, THELMA KIRKPATRICK
Educator (retired). **Personal:** Born Jul 29, 1907, Hadley, IL; daughter of Ophelia Walker McWorter and Arthur McWorter; married Allen J Kirkpatrick I; children: Allen J Kirkpatrick II, Dr David A Kirkpatrick, Dr Juliet E K Walker, Marye A K Taylor. **Educ:** Fisk Univ, BA 1929; Case Western Reserve Univ, MS 1931; Univ of Chicago, Graduate courses. **Career:** Cleveland Phyllis Wheatley Assoc, social worker 1929-31; St Louis MO Family Welfare AGency, social worker 1931; Chicago YWCA, comm social worker 1931-38; Chicago Bd of Educ, educator 1947-72. **Orgs:** Anti-Basileus, Theta Omega Chapter, chairperson, Theta Omega Seniors, Alpha Kappa Alpha Sor; pres IL Housewives Assoc; faculty rep Natl Educ Assoc, IL Natl Educ Assoc; pres, Wesleyan Service Guild; chairperson, program resources, United Methodist Women of Gorham Church; historian Natl Assoc Univ Women, Chicago Branch; chairperson, exhibit comm & archives, African Amer Geneological Soc of Chicago; life mem & bd mem, S Side Community Art Center; life mem, Du Sable Musuem of African Amer History; chairperson, Annual Heritage Jubilee Book Festival; life mem, Natl Assn of Colored Women; life mem, Natl Council of Negro Women. **Honors/Awds:** Volunteer Serv Awd Comprehensive Com Serv of Metro Chicago Inc 1981; Outstanding Service Assoc for Study of Afro-Amer Life and History 1984; Teacher of the Year, Doolittle Parent Teacher Assn; Mother of the Year, Gorham United Methodist Church; Mother of the Year, Illinois Mothers of the Amer Mothers Inc; Retired Sr Volunteer Program Annual Award; Intl Travelers Assn Award; Chicago Seniors Hall of Fame; University Woman of the Year, NAUW; Mid-Reg Volunteer of the Year, AARP, 1990. **Home Addr:** 7931 St Lawrence, Chicago, IL 60619.

WHEELAN, BELLE SMITH
Educational administrator. **Personal:** Born Oct 10, 1951, Chicago, IL; daughter of Adelia Smith (deceased) and Frank Smith (deceased); divorced; children: Reginald. **Educ:** Trinity Univ, BA 1972; Louisiana State Univ, MA 1974; Univ of TX, PhD 1984. **Career:** San Antonio Coll, assoc prof of psychology 1974-84, dir of devel educ 1984-86, dir of acad support serv 1986-87; Thomas Nelson Community Coll, dean of student serv, 1987-89; Tidewater Community Coll, Portsmouth Campus, 1989-91; Central VA Community Coll, pres, 1992-. **Orgs:** Alpha Kappa Alpha Sor Inc, 1969-; Amer Assn of Women in Comm & Jr Clgs, 1983-91; pres Texas Assn of Developmental Educators, 1987; Portsmouth School Bd, 1991; Portsmouth

Chamber of Commerce, 1990-91; Industrial Development Authority of Lynchburg, 1992-; Lynchburg Chamber of Commerce Bd, 1993-97; Centra Health Bd, 1993-95; Natl Conference of Christians & Jews, 1993-95; YWCA of Lynchburg, 1993-95, pres, 1994-95; Lynchburg Rotary Club, 1992-, pres elect, 1995, pres, 1996. **Honors/Awds:** Univ of Texas, College of Education, Distinguished Graduate Award, 1992; Blue Ridge Chapter of Girl Scouts, Woman of Distinction, 1994-. **Business Addr:** President, Central Virginia Community College, 3506 Wards Rd, Lynchburg, VA 24503, (804)386-4504.

WHEELER, BETTY MCNEAL
Educator. **Personal:** Born Oct 10, 1932, St Louis, MO; daughter of Claudia Smith Ambrose and Theodore D McNeal; married Samuel (deceased); children: Gayle. **Educ:** St Louis U, BS 1953; Univ of MO St Louis, MEd 1970. **Career:** Metro St Louis Public HS, prin 1971-, work study coord 1969-71, instrl coord 1967-69, reading specialist 1966-67, elec teacher 1963-66; St Louis YWCA, young adult pgm dir 1956-61. **Orgs:** Mem Natl Assn of Scndry Sch Prins; Assn for Supvsn & Curr Dev; St Louis White Hse Conf on Ed; Urban League Ed Com; mm bd dirs Urban League 1973-; bd dirs Metro YMCA; NAACP; Alpha Kappa Alpha Sor; installed mem Delta Kappa Gamma Soc; Hon Soc for Women Educators 1975; mem Danforth Found Scndry Sch Admnstr Fwlshp Pgm; Inst for Educational Leadership Fellowship Prog. **Honors/Awds:** A Salute to Excellence Award for School Administrators, St Louis American Newspaper, 1989. **Business Addr:** Principal, Metro Academic & Classical High School, 4015 McPherson Ave, St Louis, MO 63108.

WHEELER, JULIA M.
Educational administrator. **Personal:** Born Jun 22, 1932, Birmingham, AL; daughter of John Glenn & Julia Carson Glenn; married Dura Wheeler, Oct 26, 1956; children: Eric, Brenda. **Educ:** Tuskegee Institute, BS, 1957; Wayne State Univ, MA, 1972. **Career:** Wayne County, 1957-59; Arrington Medical Center, 1959-65; Clay County Board of Education, teacher, 1965-66; Detroit Board of Education, teacher, 1966-72, counselor, 1972-77; Joy Middle School, counselor, currently. **Orgs:** Michigan Guidance Assn; Amer Assn of Family Counselors; Amer Assn of Christian Counselors; Natl Assn of School Counselors. **Honors/Awds:** Booker T Washington Business Assn, Principals' and Educators' Achievement Award, 1992; Detroit Urban League, Excellence In Education Award, 1991; Detroit Board of Education, Award of Excellence, 1981; Joy Middle School, Outstanding Teacher Award, 1977; Field Enterprises Educational Corporation, Leadership Achievement Award, 1976. **Special Achievements:** A Study of Perception In The Junior High Classroom.

WHEELER, LEONARD TYRONE
Professional football player. **Personal:** Born Jan 15, 1969, Taccoa, GA. **Educ:** Troy State. **Career:** Cincinnati Bengals, defensive back, 1992-96; Minnesota Vikings, 1997-. **Business Addr:** Professional Football Player, Minnesota Vikings, 9520 Viking Dr, Eden Prairie, MN 55344, (612)828-6500.

WHEELER, LLOYD G.
Executive. **Personal:** Born Aug 26, 1907, St Joseph, MO; married Margaret. **Educ:** Univ IL, BS 1932; John Marshall Law Sch, Studied; Northwestern U. **Career:** Supreme Life Ins Co of Am Chgo, pres & chief operating ofcr, mem of bd dirs & exec com been with co since 1923-. **Orgs:** Former vice pres Natl Ins Assc; former bd mem Chicago Chap ARC; mem Kappa Alpha Psi Frat; former mem, Juvenile Inst of Chgo. **Honors/Awds:** Named man of yr Supreme Life Colleagues. **Home Addr:** 215 E 81st St, Chicago, IL 60619.

WHEELER, MARK ANTHONY
Professional football player. **Personal:** Born Apr 1, 1970, San Marcos, TX. **Educ:** Texas A&M, attended. **Career:** Tampa Bay Buccaneers, defensive tackle, 1992-95; New England Patriots, 1996-. **Business Addr:** Professional Football Player, New England Patriots, 60 Washington St, Foxboro Stadium, Foxboro, MA 02035, (508)543-7911.

WHEELER, PRIMUS, JR.
Hospital administrator. **Personal:** Born Mar 3, 1950, Webb, MS; married Earlene Jordan; children: Primus III, Niki. **Educ:** Tougaloo Coll, BS Biology 1972; Hinds Jr Coll, AD Applied Sci 1977; Jackson State Univ, MST Educ 1982; Univ of MS. **Career:** Univ of MS Med Ctr, respiratory therapy tech 1975-77, respiratory therapist 1977-78, instructor of respiratory therapy 1978-80, instructor/clinical coord respiratory therapy 1980-81, chmn asst prof respir therapy 1981-86; Africa Health Care, region vp, 1986-96; VMC, dir of ambulatory svcs, 1997-. **Orgs:** Mem MS Soc for Respiratory Therapists 1978-; mem Amer Assn for Respir Therapy 1978-; adv UMC Med Explorers Post #306 1983-; mem Natl Soc for Allied Health 1984-; mem bd of dirs Northwest Jackson YMCA 1984-. **Honors/Awds:** Scholastic Honor Phi Kappa Phi Natl Honor Soc JSU 1982; One of 30 Outstanding Mississippians; 1985 Leadership MS Delegate 1985. **Military Serv:** USAF ei Honorable Discharge 1973. **Home Addr:** 132 Azalea Circle, Jackson, MS 39206. **Business Addr:** Director, Ambulatory Services, University of MS Medical Center, 2500 N State St, Jackson, MS 39216.

WHEELER, SHIRLEY Y.
Nurse, educator. **Personal:** Born Feb 14, 1935, Pittsburgh, PA; married Bennie Jr; children: Teresa Marie, Bryan Joseph. **Educ:** Univ of Pittsburgh, BSN 1957, MNEd 1965, Post Master's Ed 1967-68. **Career:** Magee Woman's Hospital Pittsburgh, staff nurse 1957-58; Montefiore Hospital Pittsburgh, staff nurse 1958-59; Lillian S Kaufmann School of Nursing, instr & maternity nursing 1959-60; Univ of Pittsburgh School of Nursing, instr maternity nursing 1963-67, asst prof maternity nursing 1967-72; Duquesne Univ School of Nursing, assoc prof 1972-. **Orgs:** Orgn Childbirth Ed 1967-; test writer for Maternity Nurse Certification Exam; Master's Degree Rep Nrsg Alumnae Assc; Univ of Pittsburgh; moderator for Nurses Assc of Am Clg of Obstetricians & Gynecologists Conf 1974; Clinical Specist in Maternity & Infant Care 1963-; mem Sigma Theta Tau Professional Nurses Hon Soc; admsns com Univ of Pittsburgh Sch of Nrsg; coord Univ of Pittsburgh Sch of Nrsg Dept of Maternity Nrsg; adv Black Stdnt Nurses Univ of Pittsburth; 1st vp Univ of Pittsburgh Nurses Alumni Assn 1976, pres 1977; mem Resolutions Com PA Nurses Assn; com mem Minority Recruitment Univ of Pittsburgh Sch of Nrsg; nurse Am Yth Chorus Eurpoean Tour 1977; vice chairman, African American Alumnae, Univ of Pittsburgh, 1989-90; chairman, Afrtian American Alumna, Univ of Pittsburgh, 1990-91;ber, Nurse Recruitment Coalition, 1988-91; chairman, Duquesne Univ, curriculum development, 1986-88. **Honors/Awds:** Achievement Award for Teaching Friends of Braddock, 1990. **Home Addr:** 129 Mayberry Dr, Monroeville, PA 15146.

WHEELER, SUSIE WEEMS
Educator, journalist (retired). **Personal:** Born Feb 24, 1917, Bartow County, GA; daughter of Cora Smith Weems Canty and Percy Weems; married Daniel Webster Wheeler Sr, Jun 7, 1941; children: Daniel Jr. **Educ:** Ft Valley State College, BS, 1945; Atlanta University, MEd, 1947, EdD, 1978; University of Kentucky, sixth year certificate, 1960, 1977; University of Georgia, educ specialist, 1976. **Career:** Bartow County & Cartersville, classroom teacher 1938-46; Bartow Cartersville Calhoun Systems, jeanes supvr 1947-63; Atlanta University, teacher summers of 1962-64; Bartow County School System, curriculum director 1963-79; GA Student Finance Commn, 1985-89; The Daily Tribune News, columnist, 1978-83. **Orgs:** State rep Assoc for Supvr & Curriculum 1962-64; pres GA Jeanes Assoc 1968-70; pres GA Assn Supvr & Curriculum 1970-72; vice pres, Bartow Cartersville Chamber of Commerce 1980-82; ed rep Amer Assn Univ Women 1980-82; natl nominating comm Delta Sigma Theta 1985; restoration chair, Rosenwald Schl, Noble Hill-Wheeler Mem Heritage Ctr 1985, coordinator, currently; world traveler with Friendship Force 1980-92; Helen A Whiting Society; Intl Relations Chair, Amer Assn of Univ Women, 1987-89; Natl Planning & Devel Comm, Delta Sigma Theta, 1989-92; Georgia Student Finance Commn, State of GA, 1985-89, 1989-93; chair, Intl Delta Kappa Gamma, 1978-91; Minority Historic Preservation Committee, 1989-91; Georgia Trust for Historic Heritage Education Committee, 1990-91. **Honors/Awds:** Travel Study Award to West Africa, GA Dept of Educ, 1972; Johnnye V Cox Distinguished Award, GA Assn Supvr & Cur, 1975; Writing Comm Jeanes Supvr in GA Schools 1975; Bartow County Woman of the Year Professional & Business Women, 1977; Writing Comm, The Jeanes Story, 1979; Oscar W Canty Community Service Award, 1991; Bartow American Assn of University Women for Women in History Award, nominee, 1993. **Home Addr:** 105 Fite St, Cartersville, GA 30120.

WHEELER, THADDEUS JAMES
Clergyman, police officer. **Personal:** Born May 3, 1948, Rockford, IL; son of Beatrice Terrall Wheeler and Herman Wheeler; married Michele Barton Wheeler, Aug 26, 1972; children: Dwayne William. **Educ:** North Shore Community College, Beverly, MA, AS, 1971; Salem State College, Salem MA, BS, 1974. **Career:** Lynn Hospital, Lynn, MA, cert res therapist, 1969-74; MA Dept of Welfare, Lawrence, MA, social worker, 1976-77; Union Hospital, Lynn, MA, respiratory therapist, 1974-77; Imani Temple Co GTC, Lynn Police Dept, Lynn, MA, patrolman, 1977-; Imani Temple COGJC, Malden, MA, pastor, 1979-. **Orgs:** President, Black Student Union, NSCC, 1970-71; president, North Shore Afro Police, 1979-81, 1985-; president, Community Brotherhood of Lynn, 1985-90; pastor, Imani Temple COGJC, 1979-. **Military Serv:** Army, SP-4, 1965-68; Purple Heart, Vietnam Campaign Medal, 1967. **Home Addr:** 5 Buford Rd, West Peabody, MA 01960.

WHEELER, THEODORE STANLEY
Athletic coach. **Personal:** Born Jan 30, 1931, Chattanooga, TN; divorced; children: Theodore, Mary Frances, James. **Educ:** BS, 1956. **Career:** Amer Cyanamid, sales 1959-69; Presb St Lukes Hosp, admin dir 1969-72; Univ of IA, head men's track coach, head men's cross country coach. **Honors/Awds:** All Amer Cross Country 1951; All Amer Track 1952; All Serv 800 Champ 1955; US Olympic Team 1500 M 1956; Melbourne Australia Drake Hall of Fame 1962; Track Scholarship in name. **Military Serv:** AUS 1953-55. **Business Addr:** Head Men's Track Coach, Univ of Iowa, Rm 235 Carver-Hawkeye Arena, Iowa City, IA 52242.

WHIGHAM, LARRY JEROME
Professional football player. **Personal:** Born Jun 23, 1972, Hattiesburg, MS. **Educ:** Northeast Louisiana, bachelor's degree in criminal justice. **Career:** New England Patriots, defensive back, 1994-. **Honors/Awds:** Pro Bowl alternate, 1996; Mackey Award, 1996. **Business Addr:** Professional Football Player, New England Patriots, 60 Washington St, Foxboro Stadium, Foxboro, MA 02035, (508)543-7911.

WHIPPER, LUCILLE SIMMONS
State representative (retired). **Personal:** Born Jun 6, 1928, Charleston, SC; daughter of Sarah Marie Washington Simmons Stroud (deceased) and Joseph Simmons (deceased); married Rev Benjamin J Whipper Sr; children: Benjamin J Jr, Ogretta W Hawkins, Rosmond W Black, J Seth, Stanford Edley (deceased), Cheryl D, D'Jaris Whipper-Lewis. **Educ:** Talladega Coll, AB Economics Soc 1948; Univ of Chicago, MA Pol Sci 1955; SC State Coll, counseling cert 1961. **Career:** Charleston Co Sch, tchr & counselor 1949-65; Burke HS, counselor/chmn of dept 1965-73; Charleston Co Office of Econ Oppor, admin/prog dir 1966-68; Charleston Co Sch, dir proj ESAA 1975-77; Coll of Charleston, asst to the pres/dir of human relations 1973-75, 1977-81 (retired); South Carolina House of Representatives, state representative, currently. **Orgs:** Mem, SC Adv Council on Vocational & Tech Educ 1979-; mem Charleston Constituent Bd Twenty 1980-84; mem Coll Entrance Exam Bd; past pres, Avery Inst Afro-American History & Culture, 1980-84, 1987-89; past pres, Charleston, SC Chapter Links Inc, 1984-86; past pres, Gamma Xi Omega, Chapter, AKA, 1978-80. **Honors/Awds:** Fellowship grant for grad study Univ of Chicago 1954-55; Comm Serv Awd Charleston Chap Omega Psi Phi 1968; Mental Health Comm 1969-71; Mayor's Adv Comm on Human Relations 1971; Comm on Minimal Competency SC Gen Assembly 1977-78; SC Adv Tech Educ 1979-; Morris Coll, Honorary Doctorate of Humane Letters, 1989; University of Charleston, Honorary Doctorate of Humane Letters, 1992; SC Black Hall of Fame, 1995; received The Order of The Palmetto, 1996.

WHIPPS, MARY N.
Union official. **Personal:** Born Mar 23, 1945, Bolton, MS; divorced; children: Edgar Whipps Jr. **Educ:** Utica Jr Coll, attended 1964; Campbell Jr Coll, attended 1965. **Career:** IBEW Local Union 2262, negotiating comm 1970-, financial sec 1971-78, international representative, currently; Hammond Jr HS PTA, 1st vice pres; A Philips Randolph Conf, resource person & workshop instructor. **Orgs:** Corresp sec MS A Philip Randolph Inst 1973-76; sec, treas Jackson Central Labor Union AFL-CIO COPE Dir 1974-78; labor sect chrpsn United Way Kick-Off Fund Dr; sec Indust Employee Credit Union Bd of Dirs; mem Labors' Panel on Easter Seal Telethon; vp, pres Ramsey Rec Ctr Alexandria 1980-82; natl exec bd Coalition of Labor Union Women 1984-86; steering comm Natl A Philip Randolph Inst 1984; mem IBEW Minority Caucus 1974-78. **Honors/Awds:** Among first Black females at Presto Mfg Co; delegate to many Union activities including MS AFL-CIO Convention, Jackson Central Labor Union, MS Electrical Workers Assn, Natl Conference of A Philip Randolph; crowned Miss Mississippi A Philip Randolph; 2 Outstanding Serv Awds MS A Philip Randolph Inst; Serv Awds IBEW Local 2262, IBEW Syst Council EM-6; 1st black female Intl Rep of Intl Brotherhood of Elect Workers AFL-CIO (IBEW); Labor's Ad Hoc Committee of Nat'l Council of Negro Women. **Business Addr:** International Representative, Interntl Brotherhood Elec Wkrs, 1125 15th St NW Suite 1006, Washington, DC 20005.

WHISENTON, ANDRE C.
Government official. **Personal:** Born Feb 4, 1944, Durham, NC; son of Margret Y Whisenton and Andrew C Whisenton; married Vera Norman Whisenton; children: Andre Christopher, Courtney Yvonne. **Educ:** Morehouse Coll, BPS 1965; Atlanta Univ, MLS 1966. **Career:** Naval Sea Sys Command, lib dir 1973-76; US Dept of Labor, exec devpgm 1979, lib dir 1980-82, chief, EEO/AA, 1987-. **Orgs:** Bd mem Natl Asso of Blacks Within Govt 1985; mem NAACP 1988; Alpha Phi Alpha 1988; Montgomery Co MLK Jr Commem Comm 1988-89, bd member, 1990-91. **Honors/Awds:** DOL ECO Awd 1978; Fed Womens Impact Awd 1979, bd service award, 1986; Sec of Labor Rec Awd 1982. **Business Addr:** Chief, Office of EEO/AA, US Dept of Labor, 200 Constitution Ave NW, Room N4123, Washington, DC 20210.

WHITAKER, ARTHUR L.
Clergyman, psychologist. **Personal:** Born Jul 23, 1921, Malden, MA; son of Elizabeth A Hinton Whitaker (deceased) and Robert William Whitaker (deceased); married Virginia Carter, 1948; children: Ronald, Paul, Mark, Keith. **Educ:** Gordon Coll, AB 1949; Ordained Amer Baptist Churches, USA 1951; Harvard University Divinity School, STB 1952; Andover Newton Theological School, STM 1954, DMin 1973. **Career:** Calvary Baptist Church, Haverhill, MA, student pastor, 1950-55; American Baptist Home Mission Societies, New York, NY, field representative, 1955-56; Mt Olivet Baptist Church, Rochester, NY, pastor, 1956-66; University of Rochester, Rochester, NY, assistant professor of sociology, 1958-66; Pilgrim Baptist Church, St Paul, MN, pastor, 1966-70; American Baptist Churches of Massachusetts, associate executive minister, 1970-78; Gordon

College, Wenham, MA, visiting professor of Afro-American history, 1972; American Baptist Churches of New York State, Syracuse, NY, executive minister, 1978-83; Veterans Administrations Medical Center, Syracuse, NY, Protestant chaplain, 1984-86; editor, author, 1958-; private practice, Randoloph, MA, pastoral counseling, psychologist, 1986-; Harvard University Divinity School, counselor & visiting lecturer, Baptist polity practice and history, 1991-; Interfaith Counseling, Service, Inc, Newton, MA, staff Psychologist, 1990-92. **Orgs:** Rotary Club of Rochester, NY, 1960-66, Rotary Club of St Paul, MN, 1967-70; Amer Sociological Assn; Amer Psychological Assn; Rotary Club of Boston 1970-78; trustee Gordon Coll 1973-81; corporator Suffolk-Franklin Savings Bank Boston 1974-78; diplomate Prof Counseling Intl Academy of Professional Counseling Psychotherapy Inc; trustee: Keuka Coll 1978-83, Colgate Rochester Divinity School 1978-83; bd of dirs: NY State Council of Churches 1978-83, Rotary Club of Syracuse 1978-83, Hiscock Legal Aid Soc 1983-86; Harvard Divinity School Alumni Council, 1989-93; Andover Newton Theological School Alumni/ae Council, 1994-97; The New York Academy of Sciences, 1989-91; life member, Veterans of Foreign Wars, Post 639, 1956-; American Legion, Wm E Carter Post 16, Boston, MA, 1989-; St Paul Commission on Human Rights, 1967-69; American College of Forensic Examiners; Diplomate, American Bd of Forensic Examiners; Diplomate, American Board of Forensic Medicine, 1996; Charles F Menninger Soc, 1996; Pres (1996-97), Assn of Andover Newton Alumni/ae, Andover Newton Theological School; Class Agent, 45th Reunion Class, 1952, Harvard Divinity School, 1997; Amer Bd of Psychological Specialties, diplomate, 1997. **Honors/Awds:** Cited as one of Outstanding Negro Alumni at Work, The Andover Newton Theological School 1965; Alumnus of the Year Award, Gordon College Alumni Assn, 1972; Certificate, Federal Aviation Administration, 1991; Outstanding Community Recognition Award, American Baptist Churches of Massachusetts, 1992; numerous editorial citations and other distinguished service awards. **Special Achievements:** Author: The New Morality in Contemporary History: God's Doing Man's Undoing, 1967; The Urban Church in Urban Community, 1974; contributor: Divinings: Religion at Harvard 1636-92, 1998; Whitaker Hall, Education Bldg, Mt Olivet Baptist Church, 1991; The first African-American Baptist to receive a degree in divinity, Harvard Univ, 1952 in 30 years. **Military Serv:** 9th US Cavalry Band t/sgt; ETO, N Africa, Naples-Foggia, Central Europe & Rhineland; 4 Battle Stars 1943-46. **Business Addr:** Psychologist Pastoral, 39 Emily Jeffers Rd, Randolph, MA 02368.

WHITAKER, FOREST
Actor. **Personal:** Born Jul 15, 1961, Longview, TX; son of Laura Whitaker and Forest Whitaker Jr; married Keisha Nash, 1996. **Educ:** California State Polytechnic University, attended; University of Southern California, attended. **Career:** Actor, stage and feature films; film appearances include: Fast Times at Ridgemont High; The Color of Money, 1986; Platoon, 1986; Good Morning Vietnam, 1986; Stakeout, 1987; Bird, 1988; Downtown, 1989; Johnny Handsome, 1989; A Rage in Harlem, 1991; Hitman, 1992; Article 99, 1992; Dr Giggles, 1992; television appearances include: Criminal Justice, 1991; Body Snatchers, 1997. **Honors/Awds:** Cannes Film Festival, Best Actor, Bird, 1988.

WHITAKER, LOUIS RODMAN
Professional baseball player (retired). **Personal:** Born May 12, 1957, New York, NY; married Crystal McCreary; children: Asia, Sarah. **Career:** Detroit Tigers, second baseman, 1977-95. **Honors/Awds:** American League Rookie of the Year Award, 1978; named second baseman on The Sporting News Amer League All-Star Team 1983, 1984; named second baseman on The Sporting News Amer League Silver Slugger team 1983-85; American League All-Star Team, 1983-86. **Business Addr:** Former Professional Baseball Player, Detroit Tigers, 2121 Trumbull St, Detroit, MI 48216-1343.

WHITAKER, MICAL ROZIER
Theatrical director, educator. **Personal:** Born Feb 10, 1941, Metter, GA; son of Alma Mical Whitaker and Ellis Whitaker; married Georgenia; children: Mical Anthony. **Educ:** Howard Univ, 1958-61; Amer Acad of Dramatic Arts New York City, 1961-62; Circle-in-the-Square New York City, 1966; North Carolina A&T State Univ, BFA, 1989. **Career:** East River Players, founder/artistic dir 1964-76; Union Settlement's Dept of Perf Arts, founder/dir 1972-76; Ossie Davis & Ruby Dee Story Hour, producer/dir 1977-78; Richard Allen Ctr for Culture & Art, artistic dir 1978-81; Georgia Southern University, theatre dir, asst professor, currently. **Orgs:** Co-founder/coord Lincoln Ctr St Theatre Fest 1970-81; dir Black Theatre Festival USA Lincoln Ctr 1979; dir Intl Black Theatre Festival Lincoln Ctr 1980. **Honors/Awds:** CEBA for radio station production "The Beauty of Things Black" 1978; AUDELCO Awd Dir of Musical 1979; Emmy Production and Set Design "Cellar George" Seattle Chap 1979; Paul Robeson Theatre Award North Carolina A&T State Univ 1989. **Home Addr:** 515 Washington St, Metter, GA 30439. **Business Addr:** Assistant Professor, Theatre, Georgia Southern University, Landrum Box 8091, Statesboro, GA 30460.

WHITAKER, PERNELL (SWEETPEA)
Professional boxer. **Career:** World Boxing Council, welterweight titleholder, currently. **Business Addr:** Welterweight Titleholder, World Boxing Council, 412 Colorado Ave, Aurora, IL 60506, (708)897-4765.

WHITAKER, VON FRANCES (VON BEST)
Educator, psychologist, nurse. **Personal:** Born in New Bern, NC; daughter of Lillie Best (deceased) and Cleveland W Best; married Roy Whitaker Jr; children: Roy III. **Educ:** Columbia Union College, BS; University of Maryland, Baltimore City Campus, MS; University of North Carolina at Chapel Hill, MA, PhD. **Career:** Washington Adventist Hospital, staff nurse; Prince Georges County Maryland Health Department, public health nurse; Howard University, instructor nursing; Coppin State College, instructor of nursing; University of North Carolina at Chapel Hill, visiting lecturer nursing; University of Missouri-Columbia, assistant professor; Boston College, assistant professor; University of Texas Health Science Ct at San Antonio, assistant professor; Georgia Southern Univ, associate professor; Memorial Medical Ctr Hosp, Savannah GA, research coord, currently. **Orgs:** American Society of Opthalmic Registered Nurses, chairman of research committee, 1988-; American Public Health Association, Public Health Nursing Section, chair nominations committee, 1992-93; Texas Nurses Association, Membership Committee D#8, 1992-94; Planned Parenthood of San Antonio and South Texas, Board of Directors, 1993-95; Eye Bank of San Antonio, Board of Directors, 1992-94; C A Whittier Medical Auxilary, chairperson nursing scholarship, 1993; National Institute of Health, grant review panel, 1991-94. **Honors/Awds:** Fellow of the American Academy of Nursing; Agency for Health Care Policy and Research, Certificate of Appreciation, 1992; Sigma Theta Tau Inc, National Honor Society of Nursing, 1979; Bush Institute for Child & Family Policy, Fellowship, 1979-81; The University of NC at Chapel Hill, univ fellowship, 1977-78; Southeastern Psychological Association, Committee on the Equality of Professional Opportunity Student Research Competition, Co-Winner, 1988. **Special Achievements:** Numerous presentations and workshops national and internationaly, 1984-93; Whitaker & Aldrich, a breast self exam program for adolescent special education students, 1993; Sexual Dysfunction, Nursing Diagnosis In Clinical Practice, 1992; Violence Risk, Nursing Diagnosis In Clinical Practice, 1992, Whitaker & Morris Organization, The Key for a Successful Presentation, numerous other articles, 1992. **Home Addr:** 1 Chelmsford Ln, Savannah, GA 31411-3105, (912)598-1399. **Business Addr:** Research Coord, Memorial Medical Ctr Hosp, Department of Research, Savannah, GA 31411, (912)351-3000.

WHITAKER, WILLARD H.
Former Mayor. **Personal:** Born Feb 13, 1912, St Francis, AR; son of Polly Moore Whitaker and Joe Whitaker; married Erma Pitts (deceased); children: Gwendolyn Starlard, Vhaness Chambers. **Educ:** LeMoyne College, attended, two years. **Career:** Fund Director Exchange, foreman; ASCS, asst state director; Headstart Inc, director; City of Madison, mayor, 1970-94. **Orgs:** Sel Serv Bd, St Francis County Non-Partisan Voters League; executive board, Natl Conference of Black Mayors; president, Ark Delta Self Help Housing; Selective Service; Chamber of Commerce; advisory committee, Magnet School Community; Local Planning Group. **Honors/Awds:** Outstanding Contractor Award, AMCA, Little Rock, AR, 1975; 4th Annual Man of the Year, Delta Sigma Lambda Chapter, 1976; Advisory Board member to the Superintendent of Forest City Public Schools, Forest City, AR, 1976.

WHITAKER, WILLIAM THOMAS
Broadcast journalist. **Personal:** Born Aug 26, 1951, Philadelphia, PA; son of William T (deceased) & Marie Best Whitaker; married Teresita Conley Whitaker, Feb 12, 1982; children: William Thomas Jr, Lesley Rakiah. **Educ:** Hobart Coll, BA, Amer history, 1973; Boston Univ, MA, African Amer studies, 1974; Univ of CA, Berkeley, master of journalism, 1976-78. **Career:** KQED, San Francisco, researcher/writer, 1977-78, news producer, 1979-81; WBTV, Charlotte NC, reporter, 1981-84; CBS News, correspondent, Atlanta, 1984-89, Tokyo, 1989-92, Los Angeles, 1992-. **Orgs:** Natl Assn of Black Journalists, 1985-89; Los Angeles Assn of Black Journalists, 1993-; CBS Black Employees Assn, 1993-; NAACP, 1993-. **Honors/Awds:** Academy of Television Arts & Sciences, Emmy, 1988. **Business Addr:** Correspondent, Los Angeles Bureau, CBS News, 7800 Beverly Blvd, Rm 23, Los Angeles, CA 90036, (213)852-2202.

WHITE, ALVIN, JR.
Business executive. **Personal:** Born in Houston, TX; son of Louis Renee White and Alvin White Sr (deceased); married Carolyn Joyce Smith White; children: Alvin III, Daniel Lynn, Paul Christopher. **Educ:** University of Texas at Austin, BBA, 1976, MBA, 1986. **Career:** Johnson & Johnson, manager, personnel, 1968-71; PepsiCo, Inc, director personnel administration, 1971-79; ABC, Inc, director, compensation, 1979-81; United Gas Pipeline, vp, human resources, 1981-90; Ivex, vp, human resources, 1990-91; Pizza Hut International, vp, human resources, 1991-95; Frito-Lay, 1995-; AEA Service Solutions, founder, owner. **Orgs:** Alpha Phi Alpha Fraternity, 1970-; Pilgrim Rest MBC, Dallas Texas; KSU School of Business, advisory bd, 1992. **Military Serv:** US Army, sgt, 1968-72. **Home Addr:** 3700 Watercrest Dr, Plano, TX 75093-7517, (972)378-0364. **Business Addr:** Group Vice Pres, Human Resources, Frito Lay Inc, 7701 Legacy Dr, Plano, TX 75024, (972)334-2313.

WHITE, ANTHONY CHARLES GUNN. See KAMAU, MOSI.

WHITE, ARTHUR W., JR.
Business executive. **Personal:** Born Oct 25, 1943, St Louis, MO; married Virginia A Green; children: Arthur W III. **Educ:** Lincoln Univ, BS 1965; USAF Officers Training School, (Distinguished Military Grad) 1967; USAF Management Analysis School, cert of grad 1967. **Career:** Equitable Life Assurance; Society of the US, admin trainee 1965-66, group sales rep 1971-74, div group sales mgr 1974-76, dir of sales 1976-77, vice pres 1977; United Mutal Life Insurance, pres & chief exec officer 1985. **Orgs:** Vp NAACP 1961-62; mem Alpha Phi Alpha 1962; chmn social performance comm Equitable Life Assurance Soc 1984; adv bd Bronx Lebanon Hosp 1986; NJ State Investment Advisory Council, 1989; mem adv bd The Salvation Army of Greater NY 1986. **Honors/Awds:** Outstanding Performance Awd Equitable Life Assurance Soc Grp Oper 1969; Man of the Year Awd Alpha Phi Alpha; Outstanding Achiever Econ Devel New Era Demo Club 1985; TOR Special Inspiration Awd Theatre of Renewal 1986; Notable Americans. **Military Serv:** USAF, captin 1966-71. **Home Addr:** 5 Sylvan Way, Short Hills, NJ 07078.

WHITE, ARTIS ANDRE
Dentist. **Personal:** Born Sep 13, 1926, Middletown, OH. **Educ:** Morehouse Coll, BS 1951; Howard Univ, DDS 1955; UCLA, Post Doctoral Cert 1970. **Career:** UCLA, lecturer 1969-72; Drew Postgrad Med School LA, lecturer; Maxillofacial Prosthetic Div Martin Luther King Hosp LA, dir 1972-; Univ Guadalajara Mexico, lecturer 1975-; Private practice, dentist, maxillofacial prosthetics 1972-. **Orgs:** Fellow Royal Soc of Health Engr; fellow Acad of Dentistry Intl; mem Amer Prosthdontic Soc, Amer Cleft Palate Assoc, Amer Dental Assoc, Natl Dental Assoc; fellow Acad of Dentistry for the Handicapped, Amer Assoc of Hosp Dentists. **Business Addr:** 333 E Nutwood St, Inglewood, CA 90307.

WHITE, AUGUSTUS A., III
Orthopaedic surgeon, educator. **Personal:** Born Jun 4, 1936, Memphis, TN; son of Vivian Dandridge White and Augustus A White; married Anita Ottemo; children: Alissa Alexandra, Atina Andrea, Annica Akila. **Educ:** Brown Univ, BA (Cum Laude) 1957; Stanford Univ, MD 1961; Karolinska Inst Sweden, Dr Medical Science 1969; Univ Hospital, rotating intern 1961-62; Presbytery Medical Center, asst residential surgeon 1962-63; Yale-New Haven Hospital, asst residential orthopedic surgeon 1963-65, chief resident 1965; Newington Children's Hospital, resident 1964-65; VA Hospital New Haven, CT, chief resident 1966; Natl Inst Health, orthopedic trainee 1968-69; Harvard Business School, Advanced Mgmt Program 1984. **Career:** VA Hospital West Haven, CT, consulting orthopaedic surgeon 1969-78; Hill Health Ctr, consulting orthopaedic surgeon 1969-78; Yale Univ Sch of Medicine, orthopaedic surgery, assoc prof 1972-76, prof 1976-78; CT Health Care Plan, chief of orthopaedics 1976-78; Harvard Univ Sch of Med, prof orthopaedic surgery 1978-; Massachusetts General Hospital, visiting orthopaedic surgeon 1979-; Children's Hospital Medical Ctr, sr assoc in orthopaedic surgery 1979-; Peter Bent Brigham Hospital, assoc in orthopaedic surgery 1979-80; Sidney Farber Cancer Inst, consulting div surgeon 1980-; Brigham & Woman's Hospital; Beth Israel Hospital Boston, orthopaedic surgeon in chief 1978-90; Orthopadic Surgeon in Chief, emeritus, currently; Ortho Logic Corp Phoenix, AZ, chm scientific advisory bd, 1990-91;American Shared Hospital Svcs, San Francisco, CA, bd ofrs 1990-91. **Orgs:** Brown University Comm Dept of Orthopaedic Surgeons Yale Univ School of Med 1972-73; Brown Univ Comm on Medical Educ 1973-; Medical Conf Comm Beth Israel Hospital 1978-; Faculty Council Comm Harvard Medical Sch 1978-; Area Concent Adv Musculoskeletal Harvard-MIT Div of Health Science & Technology 1981-; Sub-Comm of Prof Harvard Medical Sch 1982; Editorial Bd of SPINE, Harper & Row 1976-82; Editorial Bd Annals of Sports Medicine 1983; New England Journal of Medicine, reviewer; New Haven Chapter NAACP; Sigma Pi Phi Fraternity 1979; visitng prof at over 11 colleges & univs; visiting comm to evaluate minority Life & Educ Brown Univ 1985, 1986; pres, Cervical Spine Research Soc, 1988-89. **Honors/Awds:** Honoree Ebony Magazine Black Achievement Awards in the Professions 1980; Eastern Orthopaedic Assn Award for Spine Research 1980; Bd of Fellows Brown Univ 1981-1992; Exceptional Black Scientist Ciba-Geigy Corp Poster Series 1982; Distinguished Serv Award Northfield Mt Hermon Alumni Assn 1983; Honorary Mem Liverpool Orthopaedic Soc; Honorary Citizen of New Orleans; Dir of the Partnership 1984-; William Rogers Award Assn AlumniBrown Univ & Delta Upsilon Fraternity 1984; Delta Upsilon Frat Award for Outstanding Achievement 1986; Honorary DHL Univ of New Haven, 1987; Honorary Doctor of MedicaL Science, Brown Univ, 1997; Northfield Mount Hermon, Athletic Hall of Fame, 1990; Co-author "Clinical Biomechanics of the Cervical Spine, 2nd ed", Lippincott, 1990; Author, "Your Aching Back", Revised Edition, Simon

& Schuster, translated and published in Germany 1990; Published over 150 Clinical & Scientific Articles; Selected by Natl Medical Assn as Outstanding Orthopaedic Scholar, 1994. **Military Serv:** AUS Captain Med Corps 139th Med Detachment KB Vietnam 1966-68; Bronze Star 1967. **Business Addr:** Professor of Orthopaedic Surgery, Harvard Medical School, 330 Brookline Ave, Boston, MA 02215.

WHITE, BARBARA WILLIAMS
Education administrator. **Personal:** Born Feb 26, 1943, Macon, GA; daughter of Ernestine Austin; married Julian E White; children: Tonja, Phaedra. **Educ:** Florida A&M Univ, BS, 1964; Florida State Univ, BS, 1974, MSW, 1975, PhD, 1986. **Career:** Lake County Public Schools, teacher, 1964-65; Duval County Public Schools, teacher, 1965-73; Leon County 4-C Council, dir, 1975-77; Florida A&M Univ, asst professor, 1977-79; Florida State Univ, assoc dean, 1979-92; University of Texas, Austin, School of Social Work, dean, 1993-. **Orgs:** Mem, Acad of Certified Social Workers, 1978-; natl 1st vice pres, Natl Assn of Social Workers, 1983-85; commissioner/on accreditation, Council on Social Work Educ, 1984-87; mem, Links Inc, Tallahassee Chapter, Alpha Kappa Alpha Sor; vice pres, for Planning, United Way of Leon County, 1988-91; pres, National Assn of Social Workers, 1991-93. **Honors/Awds:** Social Worker of the Year, NASW Florida Chapter, 1982; Florida Bd of Regents Grant for Grad Study, 1982-83, 1983-84; editor of book "Color in a White Society," published by NASW, 1985; Teacher of the Year Florida State Univ, 1986; Professor of the Year, School of Social Work, Florida State Univ, 1988-89; published author in professional journals & books-general theme, Black Amer. **Business Addr:** Dean, University of Texas, Austin, School of Social Work, Austin, TX 78712.

WHITE, BARRY
Vocalist, composer. **Personal:** Born Sep 12, 1944, Galveston, TX; children: eight. **Career:** Began career with Upfronts, 1960; musician with Mustang/Bronco, 1966-67; formed Love Unlimited, 1969; singer, composer, record producer. **Honors/Awds:** Wrote "Walkin In The Rain With The One I Love", "Can't Get Enough of Your Love Babe," "You're The First, My Last, My Everything", "I Belong to You"; "Practice What You Preach"; more than 60 gold records; 15 platinum records; composed music for several motion pictures. **Special Achievements:** Album, The Icon is Love, certified platinum, 1994. **Business Addr:** Vocalist/Composer, c/o A & M Records, 825 8th Avenue, 27th Fl., New York, NY 10019.

WHITE, BEVERLY ANITA
Broadcast journalist. **Personal:** Born Aug 4, 1960, Frankfurt; daughter of Modesta Brown White and Freeman White. **Educ:** University of Texas, Austin, TX, Bachelor of Journalism, 1981. **Career:** KMOL-TV (NBC), San Antonio, TX, news intern, 1980; KCEN-TV (NBC), Waco, TX, reporter, 1981-84; KENS-TV (CBS), San Antonio, TX, reporter/anchor, 1984-85; WKRC-TV (ABC), Cincinnati, OH, reporter/anchor, 1985-89; WTVJ-TV (NBC), Miami, FL, reporter/anchor, 1989-92; KNBC-TV, NBC, reporter, 1992-. **Orgs:** National Association of Black Journalists, 1985-; Black Journalists Assn of Southern California, president, 1995-96. **Honors/Awds:** WTVJ-TV/ NBC Miami, Peabody Award, 1992. **Business Addr:** Reporter, KNBC-TV, 3000 W Alameda Ave, Burbank, CA 91523.

WHITE, BILL (WILLIAM DEKOVA)
Baseball executive (retired). **Personal:** Born Jan 28, 1934, Lakewood, FL; divorced; children: Five. **Educ:** Hiram College, 1952-53. **Career:** Infielder: New York Giants, 1956, San Francisco Giants, 1958, St Louis Cardinals, 1959-65, 1969, Philadelphia Phillies, 1966-68; WPVI-Radio, Philadelphia, PA, sportscaster, 1967-68; WPIX-TV, New York, NY, broadcaster/baseball analyst, 1970-88; National League of Professional Baseball Clubs, New York, NY, president, beginning 1989. **Honors/Awds:** Named to National League All-Star team six times; winner of seven Gold Gloves; first African-American president of the National League.

WHITE, BILLY RAY
Elected government official. **Personal:** Born Jun 29, 1936, Center, TX; married Zerlene Victor; children: Elbert Ray, William Douglas, Jeanetta Marie, Johnetta Marie, Charles Vernon, Billy Ester. **Educ:** Prairie View A&M Univ TX, attended 1955-57. **Career:** Meth Hosp Lubbock TX, clerk 1957-64; Varian Assoc CA, mechanic 1964-77; Ray Chem Corp CA, buyer 1977-. **Orgs:** Mem consult gr Menlo-Atherton Bd of Raltors; mem plan bd State CA for E Palo Alto 1971-72; chmn plan comm City of Menlo Park 1974-78; chmn HCD bd Coof San Mateo 1978-; Center for Independence of the Disabled, Inc, bd of dir. **Honors/Awds:** First Black elected to Council of City of Menlo Park; Tulip L Jones Women's Club Inc 1978; Man of Yr Belle Haven Home Assn 1980. **Business Addr:** Buyer, Ray Chemical Corp, 300 Constitution Drive, Menlo Park, CA 94025.

WHITE, BOOKER TALIAFERRO
Educator. **Personal:** Born Sep 3, 1907, Tryon, NC; married Lucynda Stewart. **Educ:** WV State Clg, BS 1929; OH State U, MS 1937, PhD 1945. **Career:** AL A&M Univ, prof of chem 1968-; A&T Coll, prof dir of research 1953-61, chmn dept of chem

1947-53; AL A&M Coll, 1945-47; Morristown Coll, prin instr 1940-41; Halifax Co Training School, instr 1938-40; Brewer Jr Coll, 1937-38; Coxe HS, prin instr 1932-36; Kittroll Coll, instr 1930-32. **Orgs:** Mem Am Chem Soc; Am Dairy Sci Assc; Am Assc for Advancement of Sci; NC Acad of Sci; Beta Kappa Chi Sci Soc; Natl Institutional of Sci Author of Articles for Professional Journals.

WHITE, BRYAN
Automobile dealer. **Career:** Mission Blvd Lincoln-Mercury Inc, pres, currently. **Special Achievements:** Company is ranked #36 on Black Enterprise magazine's 1997 list of Top 100 Black businesses. **Business Addr:** President, Mission Blvd Lincoln Mercury Inc, 24644 Mission Blvd, Hayward, CA 94544, (510)886-5052.

WHITE, CHARLES R.
Civil engineer. **Personal:** Born Nov 25, 1937, New York, NY; son of Elise White and Clarence R White; married Dolores; children: Darryl, Sherryl. **Educ:** Howard Univ, BS 1959; Univ So CA, MS 1963. **Career:** Civil engr planner registered prof engr CA 1965; State CA LA Dept of Water Resources Southern Dist, prog mgr geothermal resources 1959-, chief planning branch, until 1992, chief, southern district, currently. **Orgs:** Mem Omega Psi Phi Frat 1956; Amer Soc Civil Engrs 1957; Tau Beta Pi Town Hall of CA 1970; Toastmasters Intl 1970. **Honors/Awds:** Principal author Planned Utilization of Ground Water Basins San Gabriel Valley 1969; Meeting Water Demands Chino-Riverside Area 1971; Meeting Water Demands SanJuan Area 1972; co-author Water & Power from Geothermal Resources in CA-An Overview 1974; publ paper on Lake El Sinore Flood Disaster of March 1980 Natl AcadPress 1982; author San Bernardino-San Gorgonio Water Resources Mgmt Investigation 1986. **Business Addr:** District Chief, State of CA, Dept of Water Resources, 770 Fairmont Avenue, Ste 102, PO Box 29068, Glendale, CA 91203-1035.

WHITE, CHRISTINE LARKIN
Nurse. **Personal:** Born Mar 12, 1946, Birmingham, AL; daughter of Catherine Mills Larkin and Robert Larkin; married Roger White, Dec 24, 1969; children: Eugena, Karen. **Educ:** Tuskegee Institute, Tuskegee, AL, BSN, 1968; University of Alabama, Birmingham, AL, MSN, 1976. **Career:** University Hospital, Birmingham, AL, staff nurse, 1968-70; Manpower Training & Dev, Akron, OH, instructor, 1970; Planned Parenthood, Akron, OH, clinic nurse, 1971-73; University Hospital, Birmingham, AL, staff nurse, 1974-77, staff development, 1977-80, dir of psychiatric nursing, 1980-. **Orgs:** Member, Quality Assurance Comm of the Medical and Dental Staff, University of Alabama Hospital, 1985-88; member, Nursing Research Comm University Hospital, 1986-87; member, Epsilon Beta Chapter Chi Eta Phi, 1966; Omicron Omega Chapter, Alpha Kappa Alpha, 1979. **Home Addr:** 212 4th Ave S, Birmingham, AL 35205.

WHITE, CLARENCE DEAN
Financial administrator, artist. **Personal:** Born Nov 27, 1946, Ellaville, GA; son of Tymy Hartage White and Charlie George White. **Educ:** Univ of Paris, attended 1967-68; Morehouse Coll, BA (cum laude) 1969; Northwestern Univ, MBA 1972. **Career:** First Natl Bank of Chicago, trust officer 1969-82; Artist & Art Critic, free lance basis; Clarence White Contemporary Art, art dealer 1974-95. **Orgs:** Mem Men's Council Museum of Contemporary Art Chicago; The Film Symposium, dir, 1976-85.

WHITE, CLAUDE ESLEY
Attorney. **Personal:** Born Jan 2, 1949, Bridgeton, NJ; son of Viola White and John White (deceased); married J Denise Rice; children: Claude Jr, Stephanie, Christopher, Alicia. **Educ:** Rutgers Coll, BA 1971; Rutgers Law Sch, JD 1974. **Career:** Pitney Hardin & Kipp, assoc atty 1974-76; Grand Met USA, atty 1976-85; Quality Care Inc, vice pres and general counsel 1985-87; Staff Builders Inc, vice pres/Gen Counsel 1988-89; Burns International Security Services, division counsel, 1989-91; Paragon Enterprises International, president & CEO, currently. **Orgs:** Chmn Rutgers Coll Econ Oppor Prog Adv Com; Natl Study Register 1971; bd dir Inmate-Self Help Com Inc 1974-76; chairman, bd trustees, treas St Paul Bapt Ch; mem Amer Assn of the Bar of the City of New York; adv Sigma Delta; chairman Home Health & Staffing Serv Assoc 1987-88; mem, bd of dir Natl Assoc of Home Care 1986-89; secretary, Committee of National Security Companies, 1991-; 100 Black Men of South Metro Atlanta, 1992-; Ben Hill United Methodist Church. **Home Addr:** 3589 Rolling Green Rdg SW, Atlanta, GA 30331-2323.

WHITE, CLAYTON CECIL
Educator. **Personal:** Born Nov 4, 1942, New York, NY; married Le Tretta Jones; children: Shannon. **Educ:** Temple Univ Clg of Music, MusB 1964, MusM 1969. **Career:** Comm Coll of Phila, assoc prof music dept 1970-; School Dist of Phila, music teacher dept head 1964-69; Natl Opera Ebony, chorus master & conductor 1976-; Clayton White Singers, music & dir/founder 1978-. **Orgs:** Minister of music Canaan Bapt Ch 1980; dir Cultural & Ed Ctr Heritage House 1962-69. **Business Addr:** 34 S 11th St, Philadelphia, PA 19107.

WHITE, CLOVIS LELAND
Educator. **Personal:** Born Mar 9, 1953, Rochester, NY; son of Alberta Morris White and Edward A. White; married Denise Andre White; children: Vanessa M. White. **Educ:** Southeastern MA Univ, BA 1975; State Univ of NY/Albany, MA 1977; Indiana Univ, MA, PhD 1984. **Career:** Charles Settlement House; youth worker 1977-78; Indiana Univ, instructor 1981-84; Univ of WI, asst prof of afro-amer studies 1984-88; assoc prof of Sociology, Oberlin Coll, currently. **Orgs:** Mem Amer Sociological Assoc 1981-, Assoc of Black Sociologists 1983-, Southern Sociological Soc 1984-. **Honors/Awds:** Minority Fellow CIC Minority Fellowship Program 1978-84, Amer Sociological Assoc 1983-84; Nord Faculty Fellow Oberlin Coll 1988-90. **Business Addr:** Assoc Professor of Sociology, Oberlin College, King Hall, Rm 305, Oberlin, OH 44074.

WHITE, CONSTANCE C. R.
Journalist. **Personal:** Born in London, England; daughter of Randall & Hazel White; married Denrick Cooper; children: Nefatari Cooper, Kimathi Cooper. **Educ:** New York Univ, BA, journalism. **Career:** Freelance Writer, NY Magazine, MS Magazine, Numerous underground publications; MS Magazine, assist to editor, 1985-86; Freelance; Women's Wear Daily, assoc sportswear editor, 1988-93; Elle Magazine, exec fashion editor, 1993-95; NY Times, fashion writer/reporter, 1995-. **Orgs:** Fashion Outreach, pres/founder, 1992-; Women In Need, bd mem, 1994-; Fashion Group, 1993-95. **Special Achievements:** Interviewed the world's top designers including: Calvin Klein, Donna Karan, Ken Lagerfeld, etc; author, Style Noir: The First How-to Guide to Fashion Written With Black Women in Mind, Perigree, 1998. **Business Addr:** Fashion Writer, The New York Times, 229 West 43rd St, New York, NY 10036.

WHITE, D. RICHARD
Attorney at law. **Personal:** Born Aug 5, 1947, Richmond, VA; children: Maleeka Renee. **Educ:** NY City Comm Coll, AAS 1968; Bernard Baruch Coll, BBA 1974; Kansas Univ, JD 1983. **Career:** Reliance Ins Co, claims adj; Liberty Mutual Ins Co, claims exam 1972-83; Nationwide Inter-Co Arbitration, arbitrator 1977. **Orgs:** Mem Omega Psi Phi, Dem Club of NY; fndr Coop Adventure 1977; mem Natl Free Lance Photographers Assn 1977; Com for a Better New York. **Honors/Awds:** Bedford-Stuyvesant Civ Awd 1974; Achievement Scroll Omega Psi Phi 1974; Bernard Baruch Act Collgn Awd 1974; Recog of Achvmt Reliance Ins Co 1976.

WHITE, DAMON L.
Affirmative action director. **Personal:** Born May 19, 1934, Nyack, NY; married Sheila D; children: Damon, Ramon, Patricia, Dana, Kevin. **Educ:** Univ of Detroit, PhB 1957; Wayne State Univ, MA 1966. **Career:** Western MI Univ, dir affirmative action. **Orgs:** Mem Phi Delta Kappa; Area V Coord Amer Assoc Affirmative Action; mem Public Safety Comm City of Kalamazoo; Pres Affirmative Action Computerized ResourceSystem; mem Alpha Phi Alpha; elected three 4 yr terms to City Council Highland Park MI; mem Council for Exceptional Children. **Honors/Awds:** PTA Natl Disting Serv Awd; Howardite of the Yr Howard Univ Alumni Assoc. **Military Serv:** AUS staff sgt 2 yrs; Combat Infantry Badge; Korean Service Medal; 2 Bronze Stars. **Business Addr:** Dir Affirmative Action, Western Michigan University, 3020 Administration Bldg, Kalamazoo, MI 49008.

WHITE, DEIDRE R.
Journalist. **Personal:** Born Jun 8, 1958, Chicago, IL; daughter of Vivian White and Thomas White. **Educ:** University of Illinois, Chicago, Chicago, IL, BA, 1979. **Career:** CBS/WBBM-AM, Chicago, IL, desk assistant, 1979-83; news writer, 1983-87; afternoon producer, 1987-89; managing editor, 1980-90, assistant news director/executive editor, 1990-. **Orgs:** Member, National Assn of Black Journalists; member, Radio Television News Directors Association; member, Writers Guild of America; member, board of directors, University of Illinois Alumni Assn. **Honors/Awds:** Kizzy Award, Kizzy Foundation, 1990; 100 Women to Watch in 1991, Today's Chicago Woman, 1991. **Business Addr:** Assistant News Director, Executive Editor, WBBM-AM/CBS News, 630 North McClurg Court, Chicago, IL 60611.

WHITE, DEVON MARKES
Professional baseball player. **Personal:** Born Dec 29, 1962, Kingston, Jamaica. **Career:** California Angels, outfielder, 1985-90; Toronto Blue Jays, outfielder, 1991-95; Florida Marlins, 1996-97; Arizona Diamondbacks, 1998-. **Honors/Awds:** American League All-Star Team, 1989; Gold Gloves, 1988-89, 1991-95. **Business Addr:** Professional Baseball Player, Arizona Diamondbacks, BankOne Ballpark, 401 E Jefferson, Phoenix, AZ 85004.

WHITE, DEZRA
Physician. **Personal:** Born Dec 11, 1941, Beaumont, TX; married Geraldine; children: Dezra Jr, Nicole, Darren. **Educ:** Morehouse Coll, BS 1963; Univ of TX, MD 1968. **Career:** Houston Med Forum, asst secty; Univ of TX Med Sch, clinical assoc; Dept OB/GYN St Elizabeth Hosp, chmn 1980-84, 1984-85; Hollins & Lord Assocs, physician. **Orgs:** Mem Amer Assn of

GYN LSP, Harris Co Med Soc; mem Houston GYN & OB Soc, Natl Med Assn; pres Houston Morehouse Alumni Assn; mem Alpha Phi Alpha, Tots & Teens; fellow Amer Coll of OB & GYN; certified Amer Bd of OB & GYN. **Business Addr:** Hollins, White & Assocs, 2105 Jackson St, Houston, TX 77003-5839.

WHITE, DON LEE
Educator (retired). **Personal:** Born Oct 25, Los Angeles, CA; son of Willie Rose Benson Brown and Kenneth White. **Educ:** Los Angeles City Coll, AA 1949; CA State Coll, AB 1952; Univ of S CA, MM 1959; Stanford Univ, study toward Dr of Musical Arts 1968-69; Univ of So CA, study toward Dr of Musical Arts 1970-72; Hon D Law Monrovia Coll 1984. **Career:** Prairie View A&M Coll, organist 1955-61; Los Angeles City Coll, instructor music 1961-62; Jefferson High Adult School, instructor 1961-63; Trade Tech Coll, instructor 1962-63; CA State Coll LA, lecturer 1962-64; CA State Univ LA, assoc prof 1964, prof of music, beginning 1983-. **Orgs:** Dir Music So CA Conf AME Church; dir Music Fifth Dist AME Church (14 states); 1st vice pres, 1990-92, 2nd vice pres, 1980-84, Natl Assn of Negro Musicians western regional dir Natl Assn of Negro Musicians 1984-87. **Honors/Awds:** Resolution City of Los Angeles Tribute Tenth Dist Councilman Thomas Bradley 1967; Los Angeles Philharmonic Orchestra 1974; lecture, "The Black Experience in Art, Aestetic meaning of Black Religious Music" presented at CA State Polytechnic Univ 1983; conductor for the Third annual Choral Festival for the Ecumenical Center for Black Church Studies 1983; elected First Vice Pres of the Natl Assn of Negro Musicians Inc 1983; an Annotated Biography of Negro Composers State LA Found Grant; The Afro-Amer Hymnal 1978; Organs in Historic Black Churches; choral arrangements, Blessed Are the Meek, When Shall I (we) Meet Him?, O for a Thousand Tongues (all published by Marvel Press), Rejoice the Lord is King, How Great the Wisdom, Glorious Things of Thee, The AME Hymn, Ye Are Baptised, Introit andA; organ compositions, Christmas Fantasy, Jesus Keep Me Near The Cross, Thanksgiving Prelude, Chorale Prelude on Fairest Lord Jesus, By the Waters of Babylon, Magnificat for organ; cantata "Jesus Said from the Cross"; A Musical Masque SATB Children Choir, Adult, Dancing and educ instruments; Dance elegy for Bass solo and piano; Anthem Blesed Are the Meek. **Military Serv:** USN 1945-47.

WHITE, DONALD F.
Architect, engineer. **Personal:** Born May 28, 1908, Cicero, IL; married Sue. **Educ:** Univ of MI Coll of Archt, BS Archt 1932; Rackam Sch of Grad Stud, MS Archt 1934. **Career:** White & Griffin Detroit, 1946-58; Giffels & Vallet Detroit, design archt 1950-53; Off of Gen Serv St of NY, proj chief off 1964-68; Prairie View -ICA Liberia Cont Liberia W Africa, proj archt 1954-67; Nathan Johnson & Assocs Inc, architect/engineer, currently. **Orgs:** Am Inst of Archt 1944; pres Nat Tech Assn 1949-51; Nat Soc of Prof Eng 1951; Eng Soc of Detroit 1950; Econo Club of Detroit; BT Wash Bus Assn Detroit; Detroit Bd of Commrc 1958; bd mem Albany Inter-racial Counc 1962-66; bd mem Model Nghbrhd Devel Corp; mem AIA Urban Plng & Dsgn Com; NAACP Albany Chpt; Urban Leag Albany Chpt; 5th Ave AME Zion Ch; Omega Psi Phi Frat; bd mem BT Wash Inst Kakata Liberia W Africa 1955-57. **Honors/Awds:** 1st black reg Archt St of AL 1935, St of MI 1938; 1st black reg as Reg Archt & reg Professional Eng; est 1st Off in MI 1938 which hired black archt eng & drftsmn; 1st black design archt; 1st black to hold off in chpts of AIA. **Business Addr:** Architect/Engineer, Nathan Johnson & Assocs Inc, 2512 West Grand Blvd, Detroit, MI 48208.

WHITE, DONALD R.
Government official. **Personal:** Born Oct 14, 1949, Oakland, CA; son of Barbara A Morton White and Louis R White; married Lillian P Green White, Feb 14, 1982; children: Michael, Christina. **Educ:** California State University at Hayward, Hayward, CA, BS. **Career:** Arthur Young & Co, San Francisco, CA, auditor, 1971-75; Agams, Grant, White & Co, Oakland, CA, auditor, 1975-85; County of Alameda, Oakland, CA, treasurer, 1985-. **Orgs:** Member, National Assn of Black Accountants, 1972-. **Business Addr:** Treasurer & Tax Collecter, Alameda County, 1221 Oak St, Oakland, CA 94612, (510)272-6801.

WHITE, EARL HARVEY
Computer systems company executive. **Personal:** Born Apr 8, 1934, Muskogee, OK; son of Mahtohoya Johnson and Earl White; divorced; children: Jean-Pierre, Jacques, Bryce. **Educ:** University of San Francisco, BS, 1963; Pepperdine University, MBA, 1975; Washington International University, PhD, ABD, 1981. **Career:** IBM Corp, management trainee; Marin County Probation; San Mateo County Probation; Pacific Training & Technical Assistant, 1969-71; EH White & Co, 1971-89; Systems Support Technologies, president, 1990-. **Orgs:** US Black Chamber of Commerce, past president, 1981-85; 100 Black Men of Bay Area, board of directors, 1991-; San Francisco Black Chamber of Commerce, secretary, pres. **Military Serv:** US Navy, HM3. **Business Phone:** (415)536-1890.

WHITE, ED PEARSON. See Obituaries section.

WHITE, EDWARD CLARENCE, JR.
Investment analyst. **Personal:** Born Oct 9, 1956, Newark, NJ; son of Viola L Williams White and Edward C White, Sr. **Educ:** Princeton Univ, BA Economics 1977; New York Univ, MS Quantitative Analysis 1981. **Career:** Merrill Lynch Pierce Fenner & Smith, industry analyst 1977-79; LF Rothschild Unterberg Towbin, vice pres 1979-83; E F Hutton & Co vice pres 1983-86, first vice pres 1986-1987; Tucker Anthony (John Hancock Financial Serv), New York, N.Y. first vice pres 1988; Technology LBO Partners, LP, managing general partner, 1988-90; Lehman Brothers, first vice president, 1990-92, senior vice pres, 1992-95, technology group head, 1994-, managing dir, 1995-. **Orgs:** Mem NY Soc of Securities Analysts 1978-. **Honors/Awds:** CFA Designation, Assn for Investment Management & Research, 1984; Ranked among top analysts worldwide in Euro Money Mag Global Rsch Survey 1985; ranked as runner up in Inst Investor Mag Analyst Survey 1986; Lehman Brothers Ten Uncommon Values Award, 1993, 1995; Ranked #2 out of 633 analysts in Bloomberg Business News 1995 Survey of US Stock Recommendations; Ranked #3 in Inst Investor Mag, Analyst Survey, 1995; Ranked as Runner Up, Investor Mag, Analyst Survey, 1996; Ranked #7, Reuters Survey, 1997; Cited as Institutional Investor, Mag Home Run Hitter, 1995, 1996. **Business Addr:** Managing Director, Equity Research, Lehman Brothers, 3 World Financial Center, New York, NY 10285-1400.

WHITE, ELLA FLOWERS
Educator. **Personal:** Born Apr 26, 1941, Blakely, GA; married Joseph Earl White; children: Derek, Dineen. **Educ:** Morris Brown Coll, attended 1959-61; Kean Coll Union NJ, BA 1970; Seton Hall Univ, MEd 1977. **Career:** Newark Bd of Educ, teacher 1970-87. **Orgs:** Mem NJ Educ Assoc, Newark Teachers Assoc 1970-, 13th Ave School PTA 1971-; co-chair Black History Comm 1983-; chairperson Delta Comm Awds Brunch 1983; co-chairperson Natl Jr Honor Soc 1984-; parliamentarian Delta Sigma Theta Sor Inc 1985-87. **Honors/Awds:** Appreciation Awd, Teacher of the Month 13th Ave Sch PTA 1982. **Home Addr:** 1230 E 7th, Plainfield, NJ 07062. **Business Addr:** Basic Skills Instructor, Newark Board of Education, Thirteenth Ave School, Newark, NJ 07102.

WHITE, ERNEST G.
Business owner. **Personal:** Born Dec 12, 1946, Dayton, OH; son of George W White & Fannie C White; married Mae Charlotte Lampkins; children: Yvette M White Ransan, Letika, Charika. **Educ:** Central State Univ, BA 1968; Gen Motors Dealer Devel Acad Univ of Detroit, 1973-75. **Career:** George White Oldsmobile, vp/gen mgr 1974-80; Ernest White Ford-Lincoln-Mercury, chief exec. **Orgs:** Mem Minority Dealer Operation; mem Kiwanis Delaware, OH Chpt; Frontier Intl; Operation PUSH; C of C; bd dir Black Ford-Lincoln-Mercury; natl bd dir Black Ford-Lincoln & Mercury Dealer Assn Great Lake Region. **Honors/Awds:** Outstanding New and Used Car Minority Operation 1980; Recogn from Governor for 3rd highest volume in sales minority in state of OH 1980-85; Truck Leadership Award for Ford in zone 1982; Outstanding Business Award for Delaward Comm 1983; Dealer with Direction Award from Ford Motor Co (Dealer Dev) 1984; Black Consumer Goods of the Year 1984; Lincoln and Mercury Cent Reg Linchpin Award (Breakthrough Soc 8%) 1984; Top 100 Businessmen in Nation (Black Enterprise Mag) 1984; First and only second generation Black new car dealer in America. **Business Addr:** CEO, Selective Auto Sales & Leasing, 8655 E Main St, Columbus, OH 43213.

WHITE, EVELYN M.
Government official. **Personal:** Born in Kansas City, MO. **Educ:** Central Missouri Univ. **Career:** US Department of Agriculture, deputy director of personnel, director of personnel, currently. **Honors/Awds:** USDA, Unsung Hero Award, 1993; Secretary of Agrigculture, Distinguished Service Award. **Special Achievements:** First African-American and first female to hold the position of dir of personnel for the USDA.

WHITE, FRANK, JR.
Professional baseball player (retired). **Personal:** Born Sep 4, 1950, Greenville, MS; married Gladys; children: Frank III, Terrance, Adrianne, Courtney. **Educ:** Manatee Jr Coll, Bradenton, FL; Longview Community Coll, Lee's Summit, MO. **Career:** Kansas City Royals, infielder, 1973-90; Boston Red Sox, coach, 1994-96, rookie league manager, 1992. **Honors/Awds:** Seven Golden Glove Awards; Received a special award at the 11th Annual Kansas City Baseball Awards Dinner to recognize achievements in career with Royals, 1981; Royals Player of the Year, 1983, 1986; Casey Stengel League was renamed the "Frank White League" in 1985; selected to the All-Star team that toured in Japan, 1986; Sporting News AL Silver Slugger team, 1986; Amer League All-Star team, 1978, 1979, 1981, 1982, 1986. **Business Addr:** Professional Baseball Player, Kansas City Royals, ATTN: Public Relations Dept., One Royals Way, Kansas City, MO 64129-1695.

WHITE, FRANKIE WALTON
Attorney. **Personal:** Born Sep 8, 1945, Yazoo City, MS; daughter of Serena Brown Walton and William Howard Walton; children: Carlyle Creswell. **Educ:** Wellesley College, 1964-65; Tougaloo Coll, BA (magna cum laude) 1966; Univ of CA at Los Angeles, MA 1967; Syracuse University, Syracuse, NY, 1972-73; Univ of MS, JD 1975. **Career:** Fisk Univ, instructor of English 1967-69; Wellesley Coll, lecturer in English 1969-70; Tougaloo Coll, asst prof of English 1970-71; Syracuse Univ, asst dir of financial aid 1971-72; Central MS Legal Svcs, staff atty 1975-77; State of MS, spec asst atty general 1977; TX Southern Univ, student legal counselor 1977-79; State of MS, asst atty general 1979-. **Orgs:** Alpha Kappa Alpha Sor Inc 1964-; mem Magnolia, Mississippi Bar Assn 1975-; The Links Inc 1977-; Commission of Colleges Southern Assn of Colls & Schools 1982-; bd of trustees, Southern Assn of Colleges & Schools, 1988-91; Leadership Jackson, 1989-; chairman, Council of State Education Attorneys, 1990-91; bd of dirs, Natl Assn of State Boards of Education, 1991. **Honors/Awds:** Woodrow Wilson Fellow; Reginald Heber Smith Comm Lawyer Fellow; Women of Achievement Awd in Law & Govt Women for Progress of Mississippi Inc 1981; Distinguished Alumni Citation NAFEO 1986. **Special Achievements:** First African-American female to be appointed special asst attorney general, 1977 and assst attorney general, 1986. **Business Addr:** Asst Attorney General, State of Mississippi, P O Box 220, Jackson, MS 39205.

WHITE, FREDERIC PAUL, JR.
Educator. **Personal:** Born Feb 12, 1948, Cleveland, OH; son of Ella Johnson White and Frederic Paul White; married; children: Alfred Davis, Michael Lewis. **Educ:** Columbia Coll New York, BA, 1970; Columbia Law School New York, JD, 1973. **Career:** Squire Sanders & Dempsey, assoc attny, 1973-78; Cleveland State Univ, asst professor, 1978-81, assoc prof, 1981-86, prof, 1986-, assoc dean, 1994-. **Orgs:** Mem, bd of trustees, Cleveland Legal Aid Soc, 1981-84, Trinity Cathedral Comm Devel Fund, 1981-89; pres, Norman S Minor Bar Assn, 1984; acting judge & referee, Shaker Heights Municipal Court, 1984-90; mem, Omega Psi Phi Fraternity Inc, Zeta Omega Chapter; host, CSU City Focus radio show, 1981-85; bd of advisors, African-Amer Museum, 1986-90. **Honors/Awds:** Book, "Ohio Landlord Tenant Law," Banks-Baldwin Law Publ Co, 1984, 2nd ed, 1990, 3rd ed, 1995; 2 law review articles, "Cleveland Housing Ct," "Ohio Open Meeting Law"; Contrib Author Antieau's Local Govt Law; co-author chapts "Criminal Procedure Rules for Cleveland Housing Ct"; Frequent guest on local TV/radio landlord-tenant law subjects; contributing editor, Powell on Real Property; Thompson on Real Property. **Business Addr:** Assoc Dean & Professor of Law, Cleveland State University, 1801 Euclid Ave, Cleveland, OH 44115.

WHITE, GARLAND ANTHONY
Physician. **Personal:** Born Dec 9, 1932, Alexandria, LA. **Educ:** Fisk Univ 1950-55; Meharry Med Coll, 1955-59; intern Geo Hubbard Hosp 1959-60; resd Kaiser Hosp 1963-65. **Career:** Permanente Med Group, physician 1965-. **Orgs:** Fisk Jubilee Singers 1952-54; life mem NAACP; Golden State Med Soc; Alpha Phi Alpha. **Honors/Awds:** AMA Physicians Recog Awd 1975; Cert of Achievement 1962. **Military Serv:** AUS mc capt 1960-62. **Business Addr:** Permanente Med Group, 1515 Newell Ave, Walnut Creek, CA 94596.

WHITE, GARY LEON
Former company chief executive. **Personal:** Born Dec 17, 1932, Ontario;son of Anna Louella Talbot White and George W White; married Inge Topper; children: Karen, Janet, Gary, Christopher, Steffanie. **Educ:** Univ of MD; Wayne State Univ; Carnegie Mellen Univ, Pittsburgh Grad School of Indus Administration, 1980. **Career:** Cobo Hall, convention, 1960-64; The Jam Handy Org, assoc prod 1964-65; Tom Thomas Orgn, exec vice pres & general mgr, 1965-70; The White Assoc Inc, pres 1970-75; Ford Motor Co, mgr 1977-87; City of Detroit, dir public info, 1975-77; Jones Transfer Co, former chmn, CEO; Automotive Logistics Productivity Improvement System, pres & CEO, currently. **Orgs:** Mem, bd of dir, Metro Affairs Corp, United Way, Monroe MI, Monroe High School Scholarship Fund, Natl Minority Enterprise Legal Defense Fund, Greater Detroit Interfaith Round Table of the Natl Conf of Christians & Jews, Boysville of Michigan, Nation Assn of Black Automotive Suppliers; NAACP; mem, advisory bd, Liberty Mutual Ins Co, African Devel Found; mem, regional advisory council, Small Business Admin; mem, bd of govs, Michigan Trucking Assn; mem, Jobs & Economic Devel Task Force, Detroit Strategic Planning Project, Communications Comm, Amer Trucking Assn; vice chmn, Booker T Washington Assn 1991-. **Honors/Awds:** Testimonial resolution, Detroit City Council; State of MI (Governor) State Senate, State House Resolutions; Outstanding Serv, Corp Coordinator, NMSDC; Concurrent Resolution, Michigan Legislature, 1987; Certificate of Special Tribute, Governor, State of Michigan, 1987; Letter of Commendation, Pres Ronald Reagan, 1987; Black Enterprise Magazine Top 100, 1988. **Military Serv:** USAF NCO 1952-57. **Business Addr:** President & CEO, Automotive Logistics Productivity Improvement System, Inc, (ALPIS), 24500 Northwestern Highway, Ste 203, Southfield, MI 48075, (810)353-0242.

WHITE, GEORGE
Dentist (retired). **Personal:** Born May 19, 1934, Houston Co, GA; son of Lula Woolfolk White and Robert White Sr; married Delores Foster; children: Terrilynn, George Jr, Miriam L.

Educ: Florida A&M Univ, BA 1956; Meharry Med Coll, DDS 1963; Veterans Administration, Tuskegee, AL, internship, 1963-64. **Career:** Private practice, dentist Bell Glade, FL. **Orgs:** Mem Amer Dental Assn, Natl Dental Assn, FL Dental Assn, Atlantic Coast Dist Soc, T Leroy Jefferson Med Soc, FL Med Dental Pharm Assn; mem Bell Glade C of C; Deacon St John 1st Baptist. **Honors/Awds:** Oral Surgery Honor Student; mem Soc of Upper Tenth of Meharry Med Coll; Cert of Honor Comm Serv FL A&M Univ Alumni Chap Palm Beach. **Military Serv:** AUS 1st lt 1956-58.

WHITE, GEORGE GREGORY
Journalist. **Personal:** Born Dec 3, 1953, Detroit, MI; son of Edna White and George Bernard White; divorced. **Educ:** Michigan State University, East Lansing, MI, BA (with honors), History and Journalism, 1975, MA, African History, 1981. **Career:** Minneapolis Tribune, Minneapolis, MN, reporter, 1975-79; US News & World Report, Detroit Bureau, correspondent, 1982-84; Detroit Free Press, Detroit, MI, reporter & columnist, 1984-87; Los Angeles Times, Los Angeles, CA, reporter, 1988-. **Orgs:** Director, board member, LA Chapter National Association of Black Journalists, 1990-; constitutional affairs committee member, Natl Assn. of Black Journalists, 1990-; member, World Affairs Council, LA, currently. **Honors/Awds:** Lilly Endowment Fellowship, 1979-81; Member, Honors College, Michigan State Univ., 1971-75; Los Angeles Press Club Award for coverage of the 1992 Los Angeles riots; Pulitzer Prize, member of the Los Angeles Times riot coverage team; Associated Press Award, feature writing, 1995.

WHITE, GEORGE W.
Federal judge. **Personal:** Born 1931. **Educ:** Baldwin-Wallace College, 1948-51; Cleveland-Marshall College of Law, JD, 1955. **Career:** Attorney in private practice, Cleveland, OH, 1956-68; Court of Common Pleas, Ohio, judge 1968-80; US District Court, Northern Ohio District, judge 1980-. **Orgs:** Member, American Bar Assn, Federal Bar Assn. **Business Addr:** Federal Judge, US District Court, Ohio Northern District, US Courthouse, Cleveland, OH 44114.

WHITE, GLORIA WATERS
Human resources administrator. **Personal:** Born May 16, 1934, St Louis, MO; daughter of Thelma Brown Waters and James Thomas Waters; married Dr W Glenn, Jan 1, 1955; children: Terry Anita White. **Educ:** Harris-Stowe Teachers Coll, BA 1956; Washington Univ, MA 1963, LLM, 1980. **Career:** St Louis Pub Sch Sys, elem tchr 1956-63; St Louis Pub Sch Sys, secondary counselor 1963-67; Upward Bound Washington University, assoc dir 1967-68; Washington Univ, dir ofc spcl program projs 1968-74, asst v chancellor-personnel & affirm action 1974-80, assoc v chancellor-personnel & affirm action 1980-87; vice chancellor for Personnel and Affirmative Action Officer Washington Univ St Louis, MO 1988-91; human resources, vice chancellor, 1991-. **Orgs:** Vol comm fund drives, Arts & Educ, United Way, Heart Fund, Leukemia Dr 1969-87; bd dir Amer Assn for Affirm Action 1975-77; faculty/staff relation committee Coll & Univ Personnel Assn 1978-80; vice pres Rsch & Publ Coll & Univ Personnel Assn 1980-84; desegration & monitoring comm Eastern Dist of MO 1981; Blue Cross Corporate Assemb 1984-87; bd dir St Louis Scholarship Found booster Urban League Scholarship Fund; pres elect Coll & Univ Personnel Assoc 1985-86; bd of trustees Blue Cross & Blue Shield of MO 1985-90; pres Coll & Univ Personnel Assoc 1986-87; vice pres Delta Sigma Theta St Louis Alumnae Chapter 1989-91; Delta Sigma Theta Sorority, St Louis Alumnae, president, 1991-93; Advisory Bd Mem Teachers Insurance Annuity Assn 1988-90; Blue Cross-Blue Shield Bd of Trustees 1988-96, chairman, 1994-96; member, board directors, Human Resources Certification Institute, 1990-92; commissioner, Social Action Commission, Delta Sigma Theta, board of directors, vice chairman, Caring Program for Children, 1990-96; Delta Habitat for Humanity, chair board of directors, 1993-94; Metropolitan YWCA, board of directors, 1993; chairman board of directors, American Red Cross Bi-State, 1994-96. **Honors/Awds:** Publ Affirm Action in Small Insts ERIC Microfiche Collect Rsch in Educ 1974; Outstanding Serv Awd Amer Assn for Affirm Action 1977; ''White Bibliography of Human Resource Lit'' compiled & edited for Coll & Univ Personnel Assn 1979; Creativity Awd CUPA 1981; ''Bridge Over Troubled Waters, An Approach to Early Retirement'' The Journal of the College & Univ Personnel Assn Vol 32 1981; ''Personnel Program Appraisal Workbook'' College & Univ Personnel Assn 1982; Disting Serv Awd CUPA 1983; Donald E Dickason Coll and Univ Personnel Assn 1988; Kathryn G Hanson Publications Award, College and University Personnel Associate, 1989; Distinguished Alumna Historically Black Colleges, 1991; Profiles of Success in Human Resources Management, College and University Personnel Association, 1991; YWCA Women leadership Award, 1992; Sheer Elegance Award, Mathews Dickey Boy and Girls Club, Community Service, 1992; Dollars and Sense Award, 1992; Delta Sigma Theta, Presidential Award, 1994. **Business Addr:** Vice Chancellor, Human Resources, Washington University, One Brookings Drive, Room 126, Box 1184, St Louis, MO 63130.

WHITE, GREGORY DURR (MRS)
Educator (retired). **Personal:** Born Oct 13, 1908, Birmingham, AL; daughter of Mattie Moffett Durr and Eugene Durr; widowed; children: Eugene A, Roger A. **Educ:** Fisk Univ, BA 1930; Northwestern Univ MusB 1940, MusM 1948. **Career:** Miles Coll, teacher 1930-47; Ullman High School, teacher 1947-70; Ramsay High School, teacher 1970-72; 6th Ave Baptist Ch, piano teacher, accompanist, choir dir 1955-84; Birmingham Public Schools, retired teacher. **Orgs:** Advisory Bd, YWCA, 1976-80; Natl Assn of Negro Musicians 1976; trustee AL Symphony Orchestra, 1977-80; Adv Bd, Positive Maturity, 1977-82; AAUW, 1978, NAACP, Urban League. **Honors/Awds:** Mem Alpha Kappa Alpha 1930-; Mother of the Year UNCF 1977; Golden Sor 1980; Outstanding Artist Awd Zeta Phi Beta 1975; Alpha Pi Chi Music & Religion Awd 1977; Cited by City of Birmingham & AL Sen for serv to the people of the gr Birmingham area through contribs to the cultural life of the community 1977; Serv Awd St Mark Christian Meth Episcopal Ch 1977; Hon Mem 6th Ave Baptist Church for dedicated serv as organist & choir dir 1977; Omega Psi Phi Serv Awd 1983; inducted as a mem AL Voter Hall of FAme 1986.

WHITE, HAROLD ROGERS
Retired educator. **Personal:** Born Jun 3, 1923, Durham, NC; son of Nora B and Dr John L; married Estelle Marie Brown; children: Darryl M, Constance A, John W. **Educ:** Johnson C Smith Univ, BS 1942; Univ of Buffalo, Grad Certificate 1951 & MSS 1953; Univ of Pittsburgh, attended 1965, doctoral studies. **Career:** Travelers Aid Soc of Buffalo, caseworker 1951-57; Buffalo Urban League, dir group work dept 1953-56; USO/Travelers Aid, exec dir 1953; Buffalo Youth Bd, youth proj coord 1956-61; Hollidaysburg State Hosp, dir social serv dept 1961-64; Grad School of Social Work Univ of Pittsburgh, field asst prof 1964-69; WV Univ Sch of Social Work, assoc prof of social work 1969-89. Now Emeritus Status. **Orgs:** Past mem bd of contributing editors Child Welfare League of Amer 1980-83; pt mem bd of dirs Natl Conf on Social Welfare 1979-82; pt mem West Virginia Univ Comm on Alcohol 1983-; pt sec bd dirs West Virginia Univ Employees Credit Union 1983-89; pt chair elected 1986 Behavioral Health Adv Cncl West Virginia Dept of Health 1981-88; pt bd mem & pres Monongalia Co Assoc for Mental Health 1982-86; pt bd mem Scotts Run Settlement House 1979-83; pt mem Comm on Self-Develop Help for People 1984-89; pt bd mem West Virginia State Mental Health Assoc; faculty advisor Undergrad of Alpha Phi Alpha; pt mem West Virginia Univ Affirmative Action Comm; pt faculty advisory council West Virginia Univ Black Cultural Center; pt bd mem Fraternal Order of Police Associates; pt life mem Assoc Ed to the Sphinx; pt chartermem Acad of Certified Soc Worker Natl Assoc of Soc Workers, Council on Soc Work Educ; pt mem session, First Presbyterian Church; pt mem Minority Scholarship Comm of Synod of The Trinity, Pennsylvania, West Virginia. **Honors/Awds:** Meritorious Serv Pittsburgh Pan Hellenic Assn 1969; Outstanding Teacher WV Univ 1975-76; Humanitarian Awd Dale Carnegie Assoc Altoona PA 1963; Sabbatical Leave Grant Sun Petroleum Prods Corp 1978; comm service awards 1986, 1987, 1989 Fraternal Order of Police; last published article in Arete, Vol 13 Winter 1988 Number 2 of Journal College of Social Work, Univ of South Carolina Titled: ''Pros And Cons of Student Placements with Employers''. **Military Serv:** AUS pvt 7 1/2 months medical discharge 1945. **Business Addr:** Associate Professor Emeritus, West Virginia University, School of Social Work, Morgantown, WV 26506.

WHITE, HOWARD A.
Educator, lawyer. **Personal:** Born Oct 6, 1927, New York, NY; married Evelyn, Jun 1, 1968. **Educ:** City College (CCNY), BEE, 1949; St Johns Univ, JD, 1954; New York Univ, MPA, 1959. **Career:** Powsner, Katz & Powsner, associate, 1953-62; Federal Communications Comm, general atty, (public utilities), 1962-66; Communications Satellite Corp, general atty, 1966-68; ITT Communications, general counsel & exec vp, 1968-87; St Johns Univ School of Law, prof of law, 1988-. **Orgs:** Federal Communications Bar Assn; American Bar Assn; NY State Bar Assn. **Special Achievements:** ''Five Tuning The Federal Govt Role in Public Broadcasting,'' 46 Fed Comm LJ 491, 1994. **Military Serv:** US Army, PFC, 1946-47. **Business Phone:** (718)990-6013.

WHITE, IDA MARGARET (IDA KILPATRICK JONES)
Government official (retired). **Personal:** Born Aug 1, 1924, Atlanta, GA; married Luther Randolph (deceased); children: Victor A Jones, Russell C Jones. **Educ:** Spelman Coll Atlanta, AB (Summa Cum Laude) 1945; Atlanta Univ, MA Sociology 1946; Fed Exec Inst, attended 1973; Brookings Inst, attended 1979. **Career:** New York City Dept Welfare, case work supr 1958-61; Dept HUD NY Regional Office, dir relocation 1966-70; Dept HUD NY Area Office, dir housing mgmt 1970-74; Cleveland Dept Community Devel, dep dir 1974-77; Cleveland City Council, exec asst to pres 1977-78; Dept HUD Richmond Office, mgr; HUD Washington DC, mgr until 1989; independent consultant, housing, community development, 1990-. **Orgs:** Guest lectr Practicing Law Inst 1970; lectr NYU 1971; lectr Cleveland State Univ 1976; lectr Case Western Reserve & Kent State Univ 1977; lectr Builders Inst at VPI; mem Amer Soc Pub Adminstrn; past mem bd Eliza Bryant Home for the Aged Kathryn Tyler Neighborhood Center; Real Property Inventory; Neighborhood Housing Svcs. **Honors/Awds:** 1st Black Woman NY Area Office Dept HUD 1970-74; Award Salute to Black Clevelanders The Greater Cleveland Interchurch Cncl & Cleveland Call & Post 1979. **Business Addr:** Manager (Retired), Dept Housing Urban Dev, 451 7th St SW, Washington Field Office, Washington, DC 20410.

WHITE, JACK E.
Journalist. **Personal:** Born Jun 30, 1946; married Cassandra Clayton; children: Kristen. **Career:** Washington Post, reporter, 1966-68; Race Relations Information Center, Nashville, TN, staff writer, 1968-72; Time Magazine: staff writer, 1972-79, Nairobi Bureau, chief, 1979-82, New York, correspondent, 1982-84, Chicago Bureau, chief, 1985-88, deputy chief of correspondents, 1987-88, senior editor, national editor, 1988-92; ABC-TV World News Tonight, senior producer, 1992-93; Time Magazine, senior correspondent, 1993-. **Honors/Awds:** Harvard University, Neiman Fellow, 1976-77. **Business Addr:** Senior Correspondent, Time Magazine, 1050 Connecticut Ave, NW, Washington, DC 20036, (202)861-4066.

WHITE, JALEEL
Actor. **Educ:** UCLA, attending. **Career:** Actor, currently. **Honors/Awds:** NAACP Image Award, Best Child Actor in a TV Comedy, 1992, 1993; Sammy Davis Jr Award; Youth Achievement Award, 1993; NAACP Image Award, Best Male Actor in a TV Comedy, 1997. **Special Achievements:** TV includes: Charlie & Company; Family Matters; guest appearances on: The Jeffersons; Mr. Belvedere; Step By Step; Full House; films include: Leftover; Silence of the Heart. **Business Addr:** c/o Norman Brokaw, William Morris Agency, 151 EL Camino Dr, Beverly Hills, CA 90212.

WHITE, JAMES DAVID
Senior corporate banking analyst, business consultant. **Personal:** Born Jun 22, 1964, Grand Rapids, MI; son of Lillie Pauline White and John Leon White; married Sulari Wirasinghe, Dec 30, 1992. **Educ:** Suffolk University, 1987-88; Davenport College, AS, 1987, BBA, 1992. **Career:** Old Kent Bank and Trust Co, collections adjustor, audit control balancing clerk, floor plan clerk, 1982-87; Suffolk University, research assistant, Department of Economics, 1987-88; Nordhaus Research, Inc, marketing interviewer, 1988-89; Dayton Hudson's Department Store, sales consultant, 1988-89; Steelcase, Inc, finance assistant, 1989; Michigan National Corp, commercial credit anaylst, 1989-92; senior corporate banking analyst, 1992-. **Orgs:** Community Housing Resource Board, board of trustees; Catholic Secondary Schools, multi-cultural advisory board; Jordan College, Grand Rapids Campus, advisory board; Commercial Credit Quality Improvement Team, founding member; Urban Bankers Forum; Grand Rapids Black Professionals Assn. **Honors/Awds:** 1st Annual King/Chavez Community Leadership Award, 1993; MNB, Outstanding Volunteer, Community, 1992; Career Communications, Urban Profile, Outstanding Entrepreneur, 30 Under 30. **Special Achievements:** Editorial columnist, Michigan Ethnic Business, 1992; Economic Editorial Columnist, 1993. **Business Phone:** (616)451-7920.

WHITE, JAMES LOUIS, JR.
Telephone company executive. **Personal:** Born Jul 14, 1949, Charlottesville, VA; son of Myrtle Virginia Garland White and James Louis White; married Cynthia Phina Austin, Jun 29, 1973; children: James Louis III, Charles Marquas, Matthew David. **Educ:** St Paul's Coll, Lawrenceville VA, BS 1973; Univ of Kansas, Lawrence KS, certificate 1982; Univ of Pennsylvania, Philadelphia PA, certificate 1982; attending Florida State Univ, Tallahassee FL. **Career:** Centel Telephone, div & dist eng in Charlottesville VA, 1973-74, dist mgr & personnel mgr in Des Plaines IL, 1974-75, asst staff mgr in Chicago IL, 1975-77, asst customer service mgr at Florida state operation, 1977-79, gen customer staff mgr in Chicago, 1979-84, gen customer service mgr at Florida state operation, 1984-88; Centel Cellular, FL, regional vice pres, beginning 1988-; 360 Degree Communication, regional pres, 1995-97; 360 Degree Long Distance, pres, 1997-. **Orgs:** Mem, Chamber of Commerce & Economic Club, 1985-89; pres, Big Ben Independent Telephone Pioneer Assn, 1988; mem of bd of dir, Dick Howser Center for Cerebral Palsy & Florida Special Olympics, 1989. **Honors/Awds:** Author of article ''Centel Puts Prewiring Costs Where They Belong,'' Team magazine, August 15, 1980. **Business Addr:** President, 360 Degree Long Distance, 4000 Regency Pkwy, Ste 300, Cary, NC 27511.

WHITE, JAMES S.
Attorney. **Personal:** Born Jan 8, 1930, Beaumont, TX; married Dolores; children: James, Jr. **Educ:** JD 1966. **Career:** Atty pvt prac. **Orgs:** Past pres Charles Houston Law Club; pres Lawyers Club of Alameda Co; bd dir Alameda Co Bar Assc; chmn State Bar Subcom; bar Examiner Hearings; past chmn bd dir Men of Tomorrow & Minority Adoption Com Childrens Home Soc; past pres Commnr Oakland Civil Srv Commn 1969-73. **Military Serv:** USN 1948-51.

WHITE, JANICE G.
Educational administrator. **Personal:** Born Aug 21, 1938, Cincinnati, OH; daughter of Odessa Parker Grey and Murray C

Gray; married Amos J White Jr, Sep 1, 1962; children: Janine, Amos III, David. **Educ:** Western Reserve University, BA, 1963; Capital University Law School, JD, 1977. **Career:** Legal Aid Society of Columbus, Reginald Heber Smith Community, Law Fellow, 1977-79; Franklin County Public Defender, juvenile unit, public defender, 1979-80; Ohio State Legal Services Association, legislative counsel, 1980-84; State Employment Relations Board, labor relations specialist, 1984, administrative law judge, 1984-88; Capital University Law & Graduate Center, alumni relations & multi-cultural affairs director, 1988-. **Orgs:** American Bar Association; Ohio Bar Association; Central Community House; Links Inc; National Conference of Black Lawyers; Women Lawyers of Franklin County Inc; Columbus Commission on Community Relations; Delta Sigma Theta Sorority Inc; United Negro College Fund. **Honors/Awds:** United Church of Christ, Outstanding Woman in the Ohio Conference, 1985; Columbus Alumnae Chapter, Outstanding Delta, 1986; United Negro College Fund Inc, Meritorious Service Award, 1989. **Special Achievements:** Reginald Heber Smith, Community Law Fellow, 1977-79; assisted in the negotiations for release of hostages from Teheran, 1980. **Business Addr:** Director, Alumni Relations & Minority Affairs, Capital University Law & Graduate Center, 665 S High St, Columbus, OH 43215-5683, (614)445-8836.

WHITE, JAVIER A.
Attorney. **Personal:** Born May 2, 1945, Limon, Costa Rica; married Rene M; children: Naomi N, Javier R. **Educ:** Columbia Univ Law Sch, attd 1971; Princeton Univ 1967. **Career:** Attorney, currently. **Orgs:** Mem NY Co Lawyers Assc; NY State Bar Assc; mem Assc of Black Princeton Alumni; bd mem Washington Heights Inwood Devel Corp; Sch Com of Princeton Univ.

WHITE, JESSE C., JR.
County official. **Personal:** Born Jun 23, 1934, Alton, IL. **Educ:** Alabama State Coll, BS 1957; North Texas State Univ, graduate work 1966. **Career:** Isham Memorial YMCA, physical ed dir, 1955-74; Jenner Sch, teacher, 1959-63; Schiller Elem Sch, teacher, beginning 1963; Illinois General Assembly, state rep, 1975-77, beginning 1979; Chicago Bd of Educ, consultant, beginning 1989; Cook County, recorder of deeds, 1994-. **Orgs:** Coach Jesse White Tumbling Team, l959-; scoutmaster Boy Scouts of America 1967-; consultant Northside Service Ctr 1975-; Elem & Secondary Ed Comm Assembly 1975-; chairman Human Serv Comm, Il General Assembly 1983-; Public ic Utilities, 1985-; Personnel & Pensions Comm. **Honors/Awds:** Most Dedicated Teacher Citizen's School Committee 1969; Excellence in Education Superintendent of Public Instruction 1974; Outstanding Legislator of the Year Illinois Hospital Assn 1984; Partner in Building Better Communities Gov James R Thompson 1985; Legislator of the Year Child Care Assn Cycle, Comm Service Award, l987; Excellence in Public Service, Illinois Hospital Assn, l987. **Military Serv:** US Army, 101st Airborne, 1957-59. **Home Addr:** 300 W Hill #714, Chicago, IL 60610. **Business Addr:** County Recorder of Deeds, Cook County, 118 N Clark St, Chicago, IL 60602.

WHITE, JO JO
Professional basketball player (retired). **Personal:** Born Nov 16, 1946, St Louis, MO. **Educ:** KS 1969. **Career:** Boston Celtics, 1969-79, Golden State Warriors, 1979-80, Kansas City Kings, 1981; last year in CBA: 1988. **Honors/Awds:** Player All Star Team 1970-77; US Gold Medal Olympic Bsktbl Team 1968; 2 NBA World Champ Teams; MVP Playoffs 1976; 13th All-Time NBA Scorer (13546 pts) selected by Dallas Cowboys NFL.

WHITE, JOHN CLINTON
Journalist. **Personal:** Born May 5, 1942, Baltimore, MD; married Elaine B; children: Anthony C, David E. **Educ:** Morgan State Univ, BS 1970. **Career:** The WA Star, staff writer 1972-; The Evening Sun, reptr 1969-72; The Balt Afro-Amer, reptr 1969; WJZ-TV, news prdcr/Wrtr 1968-69. **Orgs:** Treas Assc of Blk Media Wkrs 1975-77; mng ed The Spokesman Morgan State Univ 1969-70. **Honors/Awds:** Grp W Award completion of Westinghouse Broadcasting Int prog 1968. **Military Serv:** USAF 1961-64. **Business Addr:** 225 Virginia Ave SE, Washington, DC 20061.

WHITE, JOHN H.
Photojournalist. **Educ:** Central Piedmont Community College, AAS. **Career:** Chicago Daily News; Chicago Sun-Times, photojournalist, 1978-. **Honors/Awds:** Pulitzer Prize, Feature Photography, 1982; National Press Photographers Association, Joseph A Sprague Memorial Award, 1989; Chicago Journalism Hall of Fame, Inductee, 1993; National Press Photographer's Association Award of Excellence in General News Photography, 1994; National Headliner Award, 1991; Robert F Kennedy Journalism Award, 1979; Associated Press Award, 1991; World Press Photo Competition Award, 1979; Illinois United Press International Awards, 1982; Chicago Association of Black Journalists Award, Outstanding Journalist, 1984; National Press Award, Mandela Release, 1991; Illinois Press Photographer's Association, Photographer of the Year Award, 1971, 1979, 1982. **Special Achievements:** Photo exhibits: "My People: A Portrait of African-American Culture"; "The Soul of Photojournalism"; Contributed to the book and exhibit: "Songs of My People".

WHITE, JOHN LEE
Educational administrator. **Personal:** Born Jul 23, 1962, Charleston, SC; married Carmen Montgomery. **Educ:** Washington & Lee Univ, BA 1974; Radford Univ, MS 1976; Washington & Lee School of Law, JD 1985. **Career:** Radford Univ, admissions counselor 1974-75; Charleston Cty Public Schools, counselor 1975-76; Trident Tech Coll, devel coord 1976-84; Washington & Lee Univ, dir minority affairs 1979-85; Knoxville Coll, asst to pres 1985-86; Allen Univ, dir of admissions 1987-. **Orgs:** Consult Creative Vibrations Norfolk VA 1980; appt comm computerized career ed Gov of SC 1976; consult Chas YWCA 1978; Black Students at Wash & Lee, Wash & Lee Ofc of Publ 1979; special consultant KC Alumni Counsel 1985; bd of dirs Wilkinson & Perry Philadelphia PA 1985. **Honors/Awds:** Special Appreciation Awd Knoxville Optimist Club 1985.

WHITE, JUNE JOYCE
Correctional lieutenant (retired). **Personal:** Born Feb 25, 1949, Flushing, NY; daughter of Jean Dolores DeVega Hampton and Marion Luther Hampton; married James R White, Dec 1, 1984; children: Wenty Morris III, Ellie Morris, Mario St John, adopted: Lena White, James White, Clifton White, Roxanne White, Jasmine White, Chamara White. **Educ:** Attended Queens Coll, Flushing NY, 1969-71; NYC Health & Hosp, New York NY, respiratory therapy certificate, 1973; New Mexico Corrections Academy, Santa Fe NM, certified officer, 1983; received numerous law enforcement educational conference certificates, 1985-91. **Career:** New York City Hospital Police, New York NY, police officer, 1973-74; Jamaica Hospital, Jamaica NY, respiratory therapist, 1975-76; Brunswick Hospital, Amityville NY, respiratory therapist, 1978-83; New Mexico State Corrections, Central NM Corrections Facility, Los Lunas NM, officer until 1983, lieutenant 1984-88. **Orgs:** Mem, NAACP, 1969-; mem, NM Correctional Workers Assn, 1983-88; consultant, NM Multi Investors, 1983-91; pres, Black Officers Assn of NM, 1983-91; mem, NM Special Needs Children, 1984-91; NM delegate, Natl Black Police Assn, 1985-; pres, Rio Rancho Human Rights Commission, 1988-90; chair, NAACP Educ Comm, 1988; host chair, Natl Black Police Southern Region Conference, 1988; mem, Comm in Defense of Human Rights in the Workplace, 1988-91; mem, Amer Correctional Assn. **Honors/Awds:** Editor, NM Law Enforcement Journal, 1983-91; panelist, "Women Officers, Rewards & Regrets," Natl Black Police, 1986; founder, Outstanding Service Black Officers of NM, 1986; Joseph "Tree Top" Turner Achievement Award, Natl Black Police Assn, 1987; Guardian of the Treasury, Governors Office, 1988; TV special "Blacks in Law Enforcement: Racism & Sexism," 1988; 4th culture TV special "History of Black Officers Assn NM," 1988; Award of Excellence, Black Officers Assn of NM, 1989; Award of Excellence, Black Officers Assn of New Mexico, 1990. **Home Addr:** 2379 Lema Rd, Rio Rancho, NM 87124.

WHITE, KARYN
Vocalist. **Personal:** Born 1965, Los Angeles, CA; daughter of Vivian White and Clarence White; married Terry Lewis, Mar 31, 1991; children: Tremain, Chloe, Brandon, Ashley Nicole. **Career:** Flyte Time Productions, Minneapolis, vocalist; Warner Brothers Records, vocalist. Albums include: Karyn White, 1988; Ritual of Love, 1991; Make Him Do Right, 1994. **Special Achievements:** Debut album sold 2 million copies producing three Top 10 singles and four No 1 rhythm and blues hits, 1988. **Business Addr:** Singer, Ritual of Love, c/o Warner Bros Records, 3300 Warner Blvd, Burbank, CA 91505, (818)846-9090.

WHITE, KATIE KINNARD
Educator. **Personal:** Born Feb 28, 1932, Franklin, TN; daughter of Era Smith Kinnard and Arthur Kinnard; married Joseph White, Jun 29, 1963; children: Joletta, Angela. **Educ:** Tennessee State Univ, Nashville, BS 1952, MS 1959; attended Eastern Michigan Univ, Ypsilanti, 1961; attended George Peabody Coll, Nashville TN, 1965; Walden Univ, Naples FL, PhD 1976. **Career:** Bedford County Schools, Shelbyville TN, teacher 1952-53; Shelbyville City Schools, Shelbyville TN, teacher 1953-59; Nashville City Schools, Nashville TN, teacher 1959-62; Tennessee State Univ, Nashville TN, prof of sci educ 1962-70, prof of biophysical science and coordinator of teacher educ for biology, 1970-. **Orgs:** Mem, Imperial Club 1962-, Carondelet Civic Assn 1972-, Natl Assn of Biology Teachers 1972-, Natl Council of Negro Women 1980-, NAACP 1980-; life mem, Alumni Assn of Tenn State Univ 1968-, Tenn Acad of Science 1970-; honorary advisory board mem, Amer Biographical Inst 1982-89; public educ co-chair, Assault on Illiteracy Program 1988; natl pres (Grand Basileus), Sigma Gamma Rho 1988-. **Honors/Awds:** Outstanding Service Award, Sigma Gamma Rho, 1964 & 1976; citation, Outstanding Young Women of Amer, 1965; Teacher of the Year, Tenn State Univ, 1975; listed in "Salute to Business & Professional Women," Dollars & Sense, 1989; listed among 100 Most Influential Blacks, Ebony, 1989, 1990, 1991, 1992; author of articles "The Maturation of Biology as a Science" 1965, and "The Place of Biology in Family of Human Knowledge" 1971, both in Tenn State Univ Faculty Journal; co-author of books Learning About Living Things for the Elementary School, and Learning About Our Physical World for the Elementary School, both 1966, and A Laboratory Manual for the Biophysical Sciences, 1981. **Home Addr:** 9007 Oden Ct, Brentwood, TN 37027.

WHITE, KENNETH EUGENE, SR.
Military official. **Personal:** Born Mar 9, 1953, Columbus, OH; son of Helen (deceased) & David White; divorced; children: Kenneth E II, Malcolm J. **Educ:** Ohio State Univ, BS, 1977. **Career:** Investor Real Estate Services, broker, 1977-; US Army Reserves, recruiter, 1987-; 4 Life Enterprises, owner, 1991-. **Orgs:** I Know I Can, vol, 1988-; Toastmaster, 1990-; St Mark 76A Masons; Central Ohio Young Rebublican, past pres, 1979. **Honors/Awds:** US Army, Recruiter Ring, 1993; Mentor of the Year Award, Columbus Army Recruiting Baltalion, 1997. **Military Serv:** US Army/Reserves, sgt first class; Gold Badge Recruiter Ring; Member of the Glen E Morrell order of Recruiting Excellence. **Home Addr:** 1661 Franklin Park South, Columbus, OH 43205-2104, (614)252-4845.

WHITE, KERMIT EARLE
Dentist. **Personal:** Born Jul 15, 1917, New York City, NY; married Loretta Bagwell; children: Kermit Eston. **Educ:** Shaw Univ Raleigh NC, BS 1937; Meharry Med Clge Nashville TN, DDS 1950. **Career:** Elizabeth City NC, dentist pvt prac 1952; Craven Co Bd of Educ, h s sci tchr 1940-41; Beaufort Count Bd of Educ, hs sci & math tchr 1937-40. **Orgs:** Secr/Treas Old N State Dental Soc 19757-75; secr Eastern NC Med Dental & Pharm Soc 1957-; pres Old N State Dental Soc 1976-77; mem Omega Psi Phi Frat Inc 1935; pres Elizabeth City Civic Improvement Assc 1960-67; mem Elizabeth City State Univ Bd of Trustees 1967-; chmn Corner Stone Missionary BaptCh Trustee Bd 1968-79; mem 1st black Elizabeth City Pasquotank Bd of Educ 1973-; mem past chmn Elizabeth City State Univ Bd of Trustees 1976-; chmn Elizabeth Pasquotank Bd of Educ 1976-79; life mem Omega Psi Phi Frat Inc 1978. **Honors/Awds:** Pres Unit Citation 3 Bronze Stars Pacific Campaign 1942-46; European Theater Medal 1949-52; Kappa Sigma Pi Hnry Soc Meharry Med Clge 1949; Omicron Kappa Upsilon Hnry Natl Dental Soc 1950; Meritorious Srv Award NC Joint Council on Health & Citizenship 1960; Dentist of Year Old North State Dental Soc 1970; Citizen of Year Omega Psi Phi Frat Delta Iota Chap 1973. **Military Serv:** AUS 1st sgt 1942-46; Dental Corps capt 1949-52. **Business Addr:** 504 Shepard St, Elizabeth City, NC 27909.

WHITE, LEO, JR.
Military officer. **Personal:** Born Nov 3, 1957, California; son of Winifred White and Leo White; married Jacqueline Murray, Aug 1991. **Educ:** Cumberland College, BS, 1980. **Career:** US Army, Transportation, captain, 1980-. **Orgs:** United States Olympic Committee, board of directors, 1992-96, athlete advisory council, 1992-96; Virginia Pennisula Chamber of Congress. **Honors/Awds:** Southland Corp., Olympia Award, 1983. **Special Achievements:** United States Olympic Team, Judo Athlete, 1984, 1992; Military Athlete of the Year, Timmie Award, 1983; Black Belt Hall of Fame, 1983. **Military Serv:** Meritorious Service Medals.

WHITE, LOIS JEAN
Association executive. **Personal:** marrIed George; children: three. **Educ:** Fisk Univ, bachelors, music; Indiana Univ, grad work, music. **Career:** Oak Ridge Symphony, principal flutist; private flute teacher; National PTA, pres, currently. **Orgs:** National Parent Teacher Assn (PTA), Educ Commission, Individual & Organizational Devel Commission; TN State PTA, past pres, first vp, second vp, cultural arts chair; Knoxville Council PTA, first vp, third vp, parliamentarian; TN Assn of Parliamentarians, Alpha Unit; Knoxville Museum of Art, bd mem. **Special Achievements:** First African American president of the National PTA. **Business Addr:** President, National PTA, 330 N. Wabash Ave, Chicago, IL 60611, (312)670-6782.

WHITE, LUTHER D.
Real estate company executive. **Personal:** Born Mar 9, 1937, Minden, LA; married Betty Jean Haynes; children: 8. **Career:** D&H Tire Co, D&H Auto Mart, D&H Realty, owner & pres 1965-. **Orgs:** Life mem NAACP; mem Salem Bapt Church; chmn Deacon Bd; pres KS State Laymen's Movement; KC Chap Jr Achievement. **Honors/Awds:** Recipt Outst Enterprising Businessmen Award 1972; Award Cham of Comm 1973; Seller of Year Award 1974; Black Enterprise Mag Top 100; World Christian Assc 1973. **Business Addr:** President, D & H Tire Company, 919 Troup, Kansas City, KS 66104.

WHITE, LUTHER J.
Auto dealer. **Personal:** Born Feb 10, 1936, Gary, IN; son of Viarda White and Luther White; married Archousa Bobbie; children: Keith, Kelli, Eric, Alan, Scott. **Educ:** Drake University. **Career:** Westfield Ford Inc, Westfield MA, owner & chief executive.

WHITE, MABEL MESHACH
Real estate broker. **Personal:** Born in Bastrop County, TX; daughter of Mary Meshach and Benjamin Meshach; married William E White. **Educ:** Business College, Bishop College. **Career:** William E White's Real Estate Co, real estate broker, currently. **Orgs:** Pres Good St Missionary Soc; fin scry Dallas Assn RE Brokers; treas Zeta Amicae of Kappa Zeta Chap of Zeta Phi Beta; past pres, Bus & Prof Women's Club; chmn Pub Educ of Amer Cancer Soc; bd of dir Day Care Assn of Metro

Dallas; Skyline Voc Sch fin scry LK Williams Inst Bishop Clge; life mem YWCA; Natl Council of Negro Women; Natl Assn Negro Bus & Prof Women; Woman's Aux, Natl Bapt Convention; NAACP; Integrated Citizens Grp; chairman of the board, Maryland Cancer Society; board member, United Way; Dallas Civic Garden Center, 2nd vice president. **Honors/Awds:** Woman of Year 1965; Christian Srv Award Good St Bapt Ch; Natl Sojourner Truth Award; Bishop Clge Inst Award; Amer Cancer Award; Foley's Savvy Award; Dallas Black Chamber of Commerce, Willow Award, 1988; State of Texas, Yellow Rose of Texas, 1992; National Business and Professional Clubs Inc, KOOL Achievers Award. **Business Addr:** Real Estate Broker, William E White's Real Estate Co, 2509 Martin Luther King Jr Blvd, Dallas, TX 75215.

WHITE, MAJOR C.
Cleric (retired). **Personal:** Born May 13, 1926, Muskogee, OK; son of Effie White and Joseph White; married Rue Pearl Haynes; children: Major A, Marvin E, Maurice N. **Educ:** Pacific Un Coll, BA, with honors, 1948; Univ of Pacific, MA 1966. **Career:** Pastorates in Tucson 1948-51, Richmond CA 1951-61, Stockton CA 1961-68, Los Angeles 1968-70; San Jose, ch deptl dir 1970-71; Pacific Union Conf 7th Day Adventists, sec 1971-78; Glendale CA, exec sec 1979, church admin 1971-91. **Orgs:** Contra Costa Co No CA Easter Seal Soc 1954-61. **Honors/Awds:** Graduate with Honors, Lynwood, CA, Academy, 1944, Pacific Union College, 1948. **Special Achievements:** First African-American to be elected to serve as an Administrative Officer of the Pacific Union Conference of Seventh-day Adventists, 1971-91. **Business Addr:** Church Administrator (Retired), Pacific Union Conf of Seventh, Day Adventists, 2686 Townsgate Rd, Westlake Village, CA 91361.

WHITE, MARGARETTE PAULYNE MORGAN
Journalist. **Personal:** Born Sep 11, 1934, Tattnall Co, GA; daughter of Mr and Mrs Riley Morgan; married Frank White; children: Lairalaine. **Educ:** Reids Business Coll, diploma 1952; Morris Brown Coll, BA 1957; Univ of Toledo; Univ of TN; Georgia State University, certificate. **Career:** Teacher, 1957-66; communications specialist, 1967-69; Morris Brown Coll, dir Public Relations; The Atlanta Enquirer, associate editor and columnist, 1988-. **Orgs:** Natl PR dir Business & Professional Women's Assn, 1973; PR chmn Delta Sigma Theta; Guys & Dolls Inc; Amer Business Women; Atlanta Club Business & Professional Women; founder/pres Sparklers Inc; founder, Atlanta Jr Club; pres Gay G Club; Atlanta League of Women Voters; Leadership Atlanta; National Urban League; 100 Women International; life member, Award Journal Educ Assn; national treasurer, National Assn of Media Women. **Honors/Awds:** Newspaper Fund Fellow; Wall St Journal Fellow; Leading Lady of Atlanta, Assoc Editor, The Atlanta Inquirer 1977; Delta Women Breaking New Ground Award; Appreciation Award Journalism Educ Assc; Best Youth Page Award NRPA; National Media Woman of the Year; Alumna of the Year, Morris Brown College; The President's Award, Founder's Cup, Media Women Inc; Black Women Achievers, Southern Bell 1990; Bronze Woman of the Year, 1992.

WHITE, MICHAEL JAI
Actor. **Career:** Actor, currently. **Special Achievements:** Starred in HBO movie, Tyson, movie, Spawn. **Business Addr:** Actor, Gersh Agency, Inc, 232 N Canon Dr, Beverly Hills, CA 90210, (310)274-6611.

WHITE, MICHAEL REED
Mayor. **Personal:** Born Aug 13, 1951, Cleveland, OH; married Tamera. **Educ:** Ohio State, BA Educ 1973, M Public Admin 1974. **Career:** City of Cleveland, councilman 1977-84; Burks Elec Co, sales manager 1982-85; Beehive & Doan Partnership, partner 1983-84; Burks Develop Corp, assoc 1984-85; OH Senate, senator 21st Dist OH; State of Ohio, Columbus, OH, state senator, 1984-89; City of Cleveland, Cleveland, OH, mayor, 1990-. **Orgs:** Bd mem Cleveland Scholarship Prog 1981-85; bd mem Glenville Housing Found 1978-; bd mem Glenville Devel-op Corp 1978-; mem Glenville Festival Found, United Black Fund, Greater Cleveland Dome Corp, Royal Ridge-Pierce Found, Waterfront Devel Corp, Amers for Constitution Freedom- Univ Circle Inc. **Honors/Awds:** Outstanding Young Leader Cleveland Jaycees 1979; Service Awd East Side Jaycees 1979; Natl Assn of Black Vet Cleveland Chap Outstanding Serv Awd 1985; Community Serv Awd of the East Side Jaycees.

WHITE, NAN E.
Consultant (retired). **Personal:** Born Mar 15, 1931, Jacksonville, IL; daughter of Grace L. Mitchell Cook; married Wilmer M White, Apr 29, 1950; children: Michael Anthony. **Educ:** Bradley Univ, BS, 1952; George Warren Brown School of Social Work, Washington Univ, MSW, 1955; Chicago Univ School of Continuing Educ Summer Inst, 1964. **Career:** Family and Children Services of Greater St Louis, work-study student, caseworker III, student supervisor, 1954-67; Lincoln HS, East St Louis, IL, school social worker, 1967-68; Annie Malone Children's Home, social work dir, therapist, 1968-69; satellite Group Home for Girls, dir, 1971-73, exec dir, 1970-78; independent child welfare consultant, 1979-84. **Orgs:** United Way, allocations panel, 1978-88, admissions committee, 1989-, priorities committee, 1992-; St Louis Div of Family Serv, permanency planning review teams, 1982-85; various voluntary services for American Cancer Society and St Louis Public School System including counseling pregnant teenagers, 1985-; Y Read Tutoring Prog, 1996-, admissions committee, 1989-94, priorities committee, 1992-94; St Louis Public School System, 1985-89. **Honors/Awds:** Award for Civic Service, Zeta Phi Beta Sorority, 1976; George Washington Carver Award for Service to Youth, Sigma Gamma Rho Sorority; Annie Malone Children's Home, Founder's Award, 1991. **Home Addr:** 8412 Old Bonhomme Rd, St Louis, MO 63132.

WHITE, NATHANIEL B.
Printing company executive (retired). **Personal:** Born Sep 14, 1914, Hertford, NC; son of Annie Wood White and George White; married Elizabeth Jean Briscoe White, Jun 21, 1941 (deceased); children: Nathaniel B Jr, Joseph M. **Educ:** Hampton Inst, BS 1937. **Career:** Serv Printing Co Inc, pres/general mgr 1939-83; The Carolina Tribune, prod mgr 1937-39. **Orgs:** Past pres mem Exec Com Durham Business & Professional Chain; mem Natl Bus League; mem Durham Cham of Comm; mem exec com Durham Com of Affairs of Black People; chmn trustees White Rock Baptist Church; Scoutmaster 1942-68; mem bd trustees Durham Technology Community College, 1963-95; chmn Citizen Advisory Comm Workable Prog for Comm Improvement 1969-71. **Honors/Awds:** Durham Housewives League Man of Year 1953; Silver Beaver Award BSA 1953; NC Hamptonian of Year 1956; City of Durham Recreation Award 1958; Civic Award Durham Com on Affairs of Black People 1971, 1989; Ann Serv Award Durham Branch NAACP 1978; Nathaniel B White Building at Durham Technical Community Coll, 1988. **Home Addr:** 1501 S Alston Ave, Durham, NC 27707.

WHITE, PAUL CHRISTOPHER
Public health executive. **Personal:** Born Mar 23, 1947, Oklahoma City, OK; son of Minnie Clara Butler Colbert and Edward White; married Sheila Antoinette Riggins White, Jun 9, 1966; children: Paul C II, Simone Crystal, LaShelly Minnie, Corrine Jepahl Rashad, Brandon Thomas Edward, Bryson Chester Matthew. **Educ:** Fresno City College, Fresno, CA, AA, 1968; Fresno State College, Fresno, CA, BA, 1969; California State University, Fresno, CA, MPA, 1986. **Career:** St Agnes Medical Center, Fresno, CA, asst administrator, 1975-78, dir of personnel, 1978-80; Fresno County, Fresno, CA, asst hospital administrator, 1980-83, senior staff analyst, 1983-87, mental health system dir, 1987-88, asst dir of health, 1988-93, associate hospital administrator, chief operations officer, 1993-. **Orgs:** Member, NAACP, 1966-; member, California Black Infant Health Leadership, 1990-; member, Martin Luther King Unity Committee, 1990-; member, United Black Men, 1989-; first vice chairman, chairman, Fresno County Economic Opportunity Commission, 1987-94. **Honors/Awds:** NAACP Image Award, NAACP, 1989; NAACP Certificate of Appreciation, NAACP, 1988; Certificate of Appreciation, City of Fresno, 1989; African American Museum Appreciation, African American Museum Committee, 1987; Master thesis, A Framework for Understanding Comparable Worth and Its Implication for Public Policy, California State University, Fresno, 1986. **Business Addr:** Assistant Director of Health, Fresno County Health Department, PO Box 11867, Fresno, CA 93775.

WHITE, PHILLIP, III
Educator. **Personal:** Born Jun 23, 1956, Beckley, WV; son of Mary Louise Brown White and Phillip White Jr. **Educ:** Beckley Coll, AA 1974-76; WV State Coll, BSEd 1976-78; WVCOGS, MA 1980-83; WV Univ, Morgantown, WV, 1984; Univ of District of Columbia, Washington, DC, MA, 1990. **Career:** Regional Intergovernmental Council, Charleston, WV, planning technician, 1978-79; Job Corps, coll prep inst 1979-82; Raleigh Co Public Sch, spec ed teacher 1983-86; Educational Handbook/Curriculum Guide, staff writer/proofreader 1986-; DC Public Sch, instructional specialist 1986; Self Devt Inst Think Tank, founder, exec dir, 1989-. **Orgs:** Mem Alpha Phi Omega 1977, Kappa Delta Pi 1977-80; WV-W Germany Friendship Force Exchange, ambassador 1979; WV Rehab Center Vol Serv, vol 1979-81; Lambda Iota Tau, pres 1980-81; Assoc of Supervision & Curriculum Dev, mem 1980-82; Nat'l Ed Assoc, mem 1983-86; youth committee NAACP 1985-86; mem Phi Delta Kappa, Howard Univ 1988; mem National Council of Teachers of English 1980; mem Concerned Black Men, Inc 1989; mem Kiwanis 1977; mem Black Caucus - Council of Exceptional Children 1986; mem, DC Council of School Officers, 1989-; mem, DC Alliance of Black School Educators, 1987-; mem, Natl Council of Social Studies, 1984. **Honors/Awds:** Reg Intergovernmental Council, researcher/writer 1978-79; Liberty High School, teacher of the year 1985-86; guest lecturer, Higher Education Institution 1982; Highest Honors, Univ of District of Columbia Graduate School, 1990; Leadership Award, Self Devt Inst Think Tank, 1990.

WHITE, QUITMAN, JR.
Certified quality auditor. **Personal:** Born Jun 27, 1945, Newellton, LA; son of Florida Lamay White and Quitman White; married Eula M Wiley, Aug 14, 1987; children: Alphonse White, Quitman White III, Heath Kyle Davis, Lenia Wiley, Eric J Wiley, Eric D Wiley. **Educ:** Attended various colleges. **Career:** Chief inspector, machine operator, & set-up in plastics & metal industry, 1963-72; MoMac Div, Brearley Co, Rockford IL, QC mgr & safety dir, 1972-75; Anthony Co, Streator IL, QA mgr, 1975-76; Mardon Mfg, Ladd IL, QA mgr & safety dir, 1976; Babcock & Wilcox, WF & John Barnes Co, Rockford IL, audit coordinator QC, 1976-80; UNC Inc, UNC Naval Products, Uncasville CT, div audit coordinator & QCE, 1980-. **Orgs:** Mem, Natl Tech Program Comm of Amer Soc for QC 1980-, Customer Supplier Tech Comm 1980-, Quality Audit Tech Comm 1981-; exec comm mem, Tech Program, ASQC, 1986-89; IBPOE of W, exalted ruler 1986, aide to grand loyal knight 1986-, state pres 1987, grand exalted ruler 1988; IBPOE, special asst to state pres 1986-, special asst of Grand Lodge Security 1988-, exalted ruler 1988-; pres, UNC Mgmt Club, 1988-; local officer, ASQC; parliamentarian, New London Federation of Black Democratic Clubs. **Honors/Awds:** Author of several articles for ASQC, Prentice Hall, etc, 1980-; certified quality auditor, first black certified by ASQC, 1988; first ASQC certified quality auditor in Naval Reactor Program, 1988; Volunteer of the Month award, ASQC, June 1989; cited in "Speaking of People," Ebony, 1989. **Business Addr:** Division Audit Coordinator, Quality Control Engineering, UNC Inc, UNC Naval Products, 67 Sandy Desert Rd, Uncasville, CT 06382.

WHITE, RALPH
Real estate agent, commission member. **Career:** Real estate agent; Commission on the Status of African American Males, commission member, currently. **Orgs:** Stockton NAACP, president; Stockton Youth Foundation, founder. **Special Achievements:** First African American to be elected vice-mayor of the city of Stockton, 1972. **Business Addr:** Commission Member, Commission on the Status of African-American Males, State Capitol, c/o Darnelle Cooley, PO Box 942849, Sacramento, CA 94249-0001, (916)445-7442.

WHITE, RALPH L.
Manufacturing company executive. **Personal:** Born Mar 13, 1930, Decatur, AL; son of Bertha M White and Edmond White; married Chrysanthemum Robinson White, May 6, 1955; children: Rodney M, Lorrie C, Kimberly L. **Educ:** Alabama A&M Coll, Huntsville, BS, 1951; Texas Christian Univ, Fort Worth, MS, 1965; Webster Univ, St Louis MO, MBA, 1983. **Career:** Herf Industries Inc, Little Rock AR, president-founder, 1972-75; Southwestern Bell Telephone Co, AR, worked in engineering planning, switching systems engineering, outside plant construction, district personnel mgr, regional manager of external relations; MDI Inc, president/ceo, currently. **Orgs:** Consultant, AR Business Council, 1988; trustee, Hendrix Coll, 1988-; mem, Governor's Task Force on School Dropouts 1988-89, Little Rock Chamber of Commerce Education Comm 1988-, AR Private Industry Council Bd of Dir 1988-, AR Advocates for Children and Families 1989, Legislative Planning Group for Children. **Honors/Awds:** Graduated cum laude, Alabama A&M Coll, 1951; mem, Natl Biological Honor Society, 1964; author of "Effect of Capacitor Discharge on Microorganisms," 1965. **Military Serv:** US Air Force, lt colonel, 1952-72; Air Force Inst of Tech honor grad, 1958; commander of best electronics squadron in 2nd Air Force, 1967-68; Air Force Commendation Medal, 1971; Air Force Meritorious Service Award. **Home Addr:** 913 South Hughes, Little Rock, AR 72204.

WHITE, RANDY
Professional basketball player. **Personal:** Born Nov 4, 1967, Shreveport, LA. **Educ:** Louisiana Tech Univ, Ruston, LA, 1985-89. **Career:** Dallas Mavericks, 1989-. **Business Addr:** Professional Basketball Player, Dallas Mavericks, Reunion Arena, 777 Sports St, Dallas, TX 75217-4499.

WHITE, RAYMOND RODNEY, SR.
County official. **Personal:** Born Feb 15, 1953, Newark, NJ; son of Lucille M Jackson-White Sr (deceased) and Henry W White, Sr (deceased); married Linnie B Adams; children: Raymond Rodney Jr. **Educ:** Rutgers Univ, BA 1971-75; GA Inst of Tech, Master of Planning 1975-77. **Career:** Fulton Co Planning Dept, planner II; City of Plainfield, sr planner 1977-78; Williams Russell & Johnson Inc, sr planner 1981-82; Harrington George & Dunn PC, sr planner 1982; Oglethorpe Power Corp, land use analyst 1982-83; economic devt mgr, principal planner, 1983-; Dekalb Co Planning Department, director, 1992-. **Orgs:** Amer Inst of Certified Planners, 1990; Amer Planning Assn 1979-, planning task force chmn College Park Neighborhood Voters League 1980-; DeKalb Co Chamber of Comm 1983-; bd mem Foxhead Develop Corp 1983-; volunteer Habitat for Humanity in Atlanta 1984-; pres Develop Alliance Unlimited Inc 1984-; GA Indus Developers Assn 1984-; Natl Forum for Black Public Admins 1984-; Metro Atlanta Chamber of Commerce, Corporate Mktg Task Force, South Side Develop Task Force; Local Exhiits Committee Chairman, Amer Planning Assn 1988-89; GA Planning Association, secretary, 1990, director, 1991, 1992; Decatur-Dekalb YMCA Board, 1990, 1991, 1992; UNCF Business Community, co-chair, 1989-91; Georgia Industrial Developers Association, board of directors, 1991, 1992-; Dekalb Co District Boy Scouts of America committee member, 1992; 100 Black Men of America, Inc, Dekalb Co Chap, vice chair eco, dev community; male academy member, 1991, 1992, historian, 1994-96; Governor's International Advisory Council, commissioned member, 1992-; Atlanta Regional Commission, Alumni, 1992; Soccer in the Streets, Inc, dev committee chair,

1995-96. **Honors/Awds:** Departmental Distinction Academic Excellence Rutgers Univ 1975; Thesis Option Paper "Urban Homesteading Its use as a Residential Revitalization Tool" GA Inst of Tech 1977; Cert of Awd Distinguished Comm Serv College Park Civic and Educ Club 1984; Georgia Planning Assoc Certificate of Appreciation 1986; United Negro College Fund Meritorious Serv Awd 1986; Leadership DeKalb Palque 1988, DeKalb County Chamber of Commerce, GA 1988; Youth Leadership DeKalb Program Org Plaque YLD Progrm DeKalb County GA 1989; 100 Black Men of America, Inc, DeKalb County Chap, Outstanding Service Award, 1993, 1994; President's Achievement Award, 1996; Boy Scouts Atlanta Area Council, Key Leadership Award, 1994; Ninety-Nine Cents Breakfast Club, Inc, Excellence in Service Award, 1995. **Home Addr:** 3972 Cheru Dr, Decatur, GA 30034. **Business Addr:** Planning Director, Dekalb County Government, 1300 Commerce Dr, Ste 400, Decatur, GA 30030.

WHITE, REGINALD HOWARD
Professional football player (retired), minister. **Personal:** Born Dec 19, 1961, Chattanooga, TN; son of Thelma Dodds Collier and Charles White; married Sara Copeland White, Jan 5, 1985; children: Jeremy, Jecolia Regara. **Educ:** University of Tennessee, BA in human services. **Career:** Licensed minister; Memphis Showboats (USFL), defensive end 1984-85; Philadelphia Eagles, defensive tackle 1985-92; Green Bay Packers, 1993-98. **Orgs:** Fellowship of Christian Athletes; Children's Hospital of Chattanooga TN, blood drives; Highway House; active in Young Life; Eagles Fly For Leukemia; The Ram House Ministry; co-founder with wife, Hope Palace, 1991-; president, Alpha & Omega Ministry, 1988-. **Honors/Awds:** Named Southeastern Conference Player of the Year in college; made USFL all-rookie team 1984; named first team All-USFL 1985; NFC Defensive Rookie of the Year 1985; first team NFL all-rookie, Football Digest 1985; Pro Bowl team 1987, 1988, 1989, 1990, 1991, 1992, 1993, 1994, 1995, 1996, 1997; MVP, Pro-Bowl 1987; USFL Defensive Player of Year 1985; USFL Man of the Year 1985; NFL Defensive Player of Year, 1987, 1988, 1989, 1990; Washington Touchdown Club, NFL Player of the Year, 1988; Byron "Whizzer" White Humanitarian Award; Simon Wiesenthal Center, Tolerance Award; Jackie Robinson Humanitarian Award, 1996. **Business Addr:** Retired Professional Football Player, Green Bay Packers, 1265 Lombardi Ave, Green Bay, WI 54304, (414)494-2351.

WHITE, RICHARD C.
Artist manager. **Personal:** Born Feb 22, 1941, New York City, NY. **Educ:** NYU, BS 1962; Howard Univ, JD 1967. **Career:** Boston Symphony Orch, asst to mgr; pvt consult & artist mgr. **Orgs:** Mem NAACP; ACLU; Phi Alpha Delta Legal Frat. **Honors/Awds:** Ford Found fello 1967. **Business Addr:** Symphony Hall, 301 Massachusetts Ave, Boston, MA 02115.

WHITE, RICHARD H.
Educational administrator. **Personal:** Born Jun 1, 1950, Chicago, IL; son of Luvenia White and Herman White; married Valencia Peters White, Sep 4, 1982. **Educ:** Catholic Univ, Washington, DC, BA, 1973; Howard Univ, Washington, DC, MA, 1979. **Career:** American Red Cross, Atlanta, GA, dir of development, 1980-85; Civitan International, Birmingham, AL, dir of development, 1985-88; Riverside Community College, Riverside, CA, chief development officer, 1988-90; Morris Brown College, Atlanta, GA, vice pres, development, 1990-92; Emory Univ, Robert W Woodruff Library, 1992-. **Honors/Awds:** GA Joint Bd of Family Practice, Gov/State of GA, 1984; Child Abuse Prevention Board, Gov/State of Alabama, 1986. **Business Addr:** Emory University, Robert W. Woodruff Library, Atlanta, GA 30322.

WHITE, RICHARD THOMAS
Attorney. **Personal:** Born Jan 10, 1945, Detroit, MI; son of Joyce Loraine Thomas and Raymond Wendell White; married Tanya; children: Richard T Jr, Devin A, Andrew S. **Educ:** Morehouse College, BA (with honors), 1967; Harvard University Law School, JD, 1970. **Career:** Dykema Gossett, associate, 1970; Patmon, Young & Kirk, PC, associate, 1971-72; Lewis, White & Clay, PC, founder, 1972-, pres, 1981-. **Orgs:** Michigan Transportation Commission, vice chairman, 1991-; commissioner, Foreign Claims Settlement Commission, 1995-; American Bar Association, Corporations & Health Law Sections, 1970-; National Health Lawyers Association, 1975-; Detroit-Macomb Hospital, finance committee, board member; United American Health Care Corp, compensation committee, board of directors, 1983-; American Basic Industries Inc, board of directors, 1991-; Detroit Medical Center, board of directors, audit committee, 1990-95; City of Detroit Human Rights Commission, 1964-65; numerous others. **Business Addr:** President, Founder, Lewis, White & Clay, PC, 1300 First National Bldg, Detroit, MI 48226, (313)961-2550.

WHITE, ROBERT L.
Association executive. **Personal:** Born Mar 22, 1916, Jackson, MS; married Helen Harper; children: Helen Oladipo, Roberta Battle, Robert H, Ramon, William, Elizabeth, Dorothy, Mark, Mary, Stephen, Christopher. **Educ:** Howard Univ, 3 yrs. **Career:** US Post Office, employee 1943-. **Orgs:** Natl pres Natl Alliance Postal Fed Employees 1970-; pres WA Local 1953-70; past bd dir NAACP; past mem, bd dir WA Urban League; past bd mem Christ Child Settlement House; assoc mem Dem Natl Com. **Honors/Awds:** One of the 100 Most Influential Black Amers Ebony Mag 1971-74; Civil Rights Awd DC Civic Assoc 1972; Natl Urban Coalition's Disting Natl Leadership Awd 1984; Hon DL Howard Univ 1984. **Business Addr:** US Post Office, NAPFE, 1628 11th St NW, Washington, DC 20001.

WHITE, RONDELL BERNARD
Professional baseball player. **Personal:** Born Feb 23, 1972, Milledgeville, GA. **Career:** Montreal Expos, outfielder, 1993-. **Business Addr:** Professional Baseball Player, Montreal Expos, PO Box 500, Station M, Montreal, PQ, Canada H1V 3P2, (514)253-3434.

WHITE, RONNIE L.
Judge. **Personal:** Born May 31, 1953, St Louis, MO; son of Orville Jr & Dolores White; married Sylvia D White, Aug 15, 1981; children: Ronnie L, II. **Educ:** St Louis Comm Coll at Meremac, AA, 1977; St Louis Univ, BA, 1979; Univ of Missouri-Kansas City School of Law, JD, 1983. **Career:** Office of Public Defender, City of St Louis, trial attorney, 1983-87; Office of the Special Public Defender, trial attorney, 1987-89; Private Law Practice, lawyer, 1987-93; MO General Assembly, legislator, state rep-63rd dist, 1989-93; City of St Louis, city counselor, 1993-94; State of MO, judge, 1994-. **Orgs:** Missouri Bar, 1984-; Metropolitan Bar Assn of St Louis, 1984-; Mound City Bar Assn, 1984-. **Honors/Awds:** St Louis Women's Political Caucus, President's Award, 1993; Missouri Bar, Legislator's Award, 1991-93.

WHITE, RORY WILBUR
Professional basketball player (retired). **Personal:** Born Aug 16, 1959, Tuskegee, AL; married Ruth. **Educ:** South AL, Phys Ed 1982. **Career:** Phoenix Suns, 1983-84, Milwaukee Bucks, 1984, San Diego Clippers, 1984, Los Angeles Clippers, 1985-87; CBA, 1989-90. **Honors/Awds:** While a soph at South AL was voted Sun Belt Player of Year; First Team All-Conf honors his jr & sr years.

WHITE, SANDRA LAVELLE
Educational administrator. **Personal:** Born Aug 30, 1941, Columbia, SC; daughter of Rosena E. Benson and Christopher O. White; married Dr Kenneth Olden, May 19, 1984; children: Heather Alexis. **Educ:** Hampton Inst, BA Biol 1963; Univ MI, MS Microbiology 1971, PhD Microbiology 1974. **Career:** Sloan Kettering Inst for Cancer Res, res asst 1963-69; AT&T, res asst 1969; Univ MI Dept Microb, tchng asst 1969-71; Med Sch, asst lectr microb 1970; Univ MI, guest lectr in immunology 1973; Howard Univ Coll of Med, asst prof of Microbiology 1974-76; Natl Inst of Health, staff fellow 1976-79; Howard Univ Coll of Med assoc prof microbiol & oncology, member Cancer Center, 1979-92; Duke Univ Medical Ctr, associate research prof, currently. **Orgs:** Mem Amer Soc of Microbiologists, Amer Assn for Women in Cancer Research; Delta Sigma Theta Sorority Inc; mem Amer Soc of Cell Biology; mem, American Assn Cancer Research, 1990-; Amer Assn Immunol, 1991-; bd of dirs, NC Museum of Life & Sciences; bd of director, Women in Action Prevention of Violence and Its Causes; The LINKS Inc; Jack & Jill of America Inc; The Smaty Set Inc. **Honors/Awds:** Ford Found Fellowship 1970-74; Kaiser Permanente Awd for Excellence in Teaching 1982; mem Pathology B Study Section Natl Insts of Health 1980-84; Bd of Scientific Counselors, Div Cancer Biology & Diagnosis, Natl Cancer Inst, NIH l985-89; mem Natl Board of Medical Examiners, Microbiology Test Committee l989-93; Natl Science Foundation Traineeship, 1970-71; GLYCO Design Inc, bd of dir; NC Museum Life and Science, bd of dir. **Business Addr:** Assoc Res Prof, Bone Marrow Transplant Program, Dept of Medicine, Box 3410, Duke Univ Medical Ctr, Durham, NC 27710.

WHITE, SCOTT A., SR.
Clergyman. **Personal:** Born Aug 6, 1909, Wilmington, VA; married Mary Elizabeth (deceased); children: 15. **Educ:** Lincoln Univ, Cert in Religious Studies 1952; Accelerated Christian Educ Inst, Cert in Religious Admin 1982; New Jersey Bible Inst, in current studies 1984-. **Career:** First Zion Primitive Baptist Church, pastor 1950-68; 2nd Natl Ketoctan Primitive Baptist Assoc, vice-moderator 1977-84, moderator 1984-; New Hope Primitive Baptist Church, pastor 1968-. **Orgs:** Baccaulaureate speaker Steelton-Highspire HS 1962; co-hostTV program "Maranatha" 1970-74; delegate White House Conference of Natl Religious Leaders 1980; mem Interdenominational Ministers Conf 1970-; hon mem Elks, Eastern Star & Masons 1972-; chmn of bd Ministers Alliance of the 2nd Natl Ketoctan Assoc 1984-. **Honors/Awds:** Citation by House of Reps State of PA 1980 & 1984; Commendation from the Governor of the State of PA 1983; Commendation May of City of Harrisburg PA 1983. **Home Addr:** 215 N Harrisburg St, Harrisburg, PA 17113. **Business Addr:** New Hope Baptist Church, 2nd & Elm Sts, Steelton, PA 17113.

WHITE, SHARON BROWN
Educational administrator. **Personal:** Born Sep 29, 1963, Pineville, LA; daughter of Eva M Brown; married Wilbur James White. **Educ:** Grambling State Univ, Grambling, LA, BS, 1985; Alcorn State Univ, Lorman, MS, MS, 1988. **Career:** Alcorn State Univ, Lorman, MS, secretary, 1985-88, admin asst, 1988; Fisk University, Nashville, TN, secretary 1, 1989, director of career planning and placement, 1989-. **Business Addr:** Director, Career Planning and Placement, Fisk University, Box 4, 1000 17th Ave, North Basic College Bldg, Room #202, Nashville, TN 37208-3051.

WHITE, STEVEN
Professional football player. **Personal:** Born Oct 25, 1973. **Educ:** Univ of Tennessee, bachelor's degree in psychology. **Career:** Tampa Bay Buccaneers, defensive end, 1996-. **Business Addr:** Professional Football Player, Tampa Bay Buccaneers, One Buccaneer Place, Tampa, FL 33607, (813)870-2700.

WHITE, SYLVIA KAY
Fashion consultant. **Personal:** Born Dec 5, 1955, Washington, DC; daughter of James Odessa White and George D White Sr (deceased). **Educ:** Fashion Institute of Tech, AA 1975; State Univ of NY, Degree in Fashion Buying. **Career:** Alexander Inc, buyer/mens 1975-83; Montgomery Ward Inc, buyer/boys 1983-87; Nordstroms, McClean, Virginia, sales men's merchandise, l988-. **Orgs:** Trustee 1985-, chairperson budget & finance comm First Union Baptist 1986-88. **Honors/Awds:** Outstanding Young Women of Amer 1985. **Home Addr:** 7912 Grant Dr, Lanham, MD 20706.

WHITE, TOMMIE LEE
Clinical/counseling, psychologist, professor. **Personal:** Born May 20, 1944, Dublin, GA; son of Daisy and Mack F White, Sr. **Educ:** Yankton, BA 1966; Univ SD, MA 1967; California State Univ, Northridge MA 1978; Univ Southern California, PhD 1974; Univ of Southern California, PhD 1982; Board Certified Diplomate, Prescribing Psychology, (FPPR). **Career:** Clinical/counseling psychologist, private practice; CA St Univ Northridge, prof of kinesiology and sport psychology; Horace Mann Jr H LA, tchr history and phys educ 1967-70; Univ SD, grad asst 1966-67; Univ SD, asst research dir 1967. **Orgs:** The Amer Psychological Assn; Assn Black Psychologists; CA Faculty Association; California Psychological Association; Am Federation Tchrs; Clinical/counseling Sport Psychologist, US Olympic Comm & USATF; AAASP; Phi Delta Kappa, Alpha Phi Alpha Fraternity Inc, APA-Exercise & Sport Psychology. **Honors/Awds:** Alumni of yr 1976; All-Amer Track Hon 1965; SD Athlete of Yr Awd 1965; Howard Wood Hall of Fame 1978; dean's list hon student Yankton Coll 1965-66; SD Coll Track Athlete of Decade 1960-69; Nat Amateur Athlete Rep to AAU 1975-; Track & Field News All-Amer Awd 1971; World's best record 60 meter high hurdles 74 sec Moscow 1972; pr high hurdles 13.4 Sec 1973; publs "the relationship between physical educ admin values & their attitudes toward education Innovations," 1974, "The Relationship Between Cognitive Style and Locus of Reinforcement" 1978, "Essentials of Hurdling" Athletic Journ 1980, "Hurdling-Running Between The Hurdles" Athletic Journal 1980; Publications: "Reparenting Schizophrenic Youth in a Hospital Setting", 1985; Presentations: "African-American Athletes: Distorted Visions and Shattered Dreams," "Standing Alone: The Spinal Injured," 1992; "Diversity in Sports: Are We Doing Enough?," 1993. **Business Addr:** 8912 Olympic Blvd, Beverly Hills, CA 90211.

WHITE, VAN FREEMAN. See Obituaries section.

WHITE, WENDELL F.
Business executive. **Personal:** Born Aug 20, 1939, Atlanta, GA. **Educ:** Morehouse Coll, BA 1962; Atlanta Univ, MBA 1967; UCLA, post grad study. **Career:** Williamson & Co Real Estate, 1961-65; Johnson Publishing Co; General Motors Corp, 1965; Coca-Cola Co, marketing exec 1965-70; US Dept Commerce, dir office of minority bus enterprise 1970-74; Empire Investment Enterprises Inc, exec vice pres; Empire Realty, pres. **Orgs:** 1st vice pres Empire Real Estate Bd; mem Atlanta Bus League; mem Citizens Trust Bank Adv Bd; mem Natl Assn of Market Developers; mem bd of dirs Travelers Aid Soc; mem SCLC; mem NAACP, Urban League, Butler St YMCA. **Honors/Awds:** Leadership Awd Butler St YMCA; Letter of Commendation from Pres of US; Cert of Merit NAACP. **Military Serv:** AUS 1963-65. **Business Addr:** President, Empire Realty, 569 Ashby St SW, Atlanta, GA 30310.

WHITE, WILLIAM E.
Radio station executive. **Personal:** Born Jun 28, 1934, St Louis, MO; son of Laura White and Ephriam White; married Virginia M McDade; children: Diana, William Jr, Arnold. **Educ:** Attended, Lincoln Univ. **Career:** Kansas City Monarch, Memphis Red Sox, Kansas City Athletics Org Chicago White Sox, professional baseball player; Kirby Company, franchise factory distributor; WETU of Montgomery, owner; KIRL Radio, chairman/genl mgr. **Orgs:** Mem, deacon Newstead Ave Bapt Church; business mgr O'Neal Twins and Interfaith Choir; bd mem Natl Gospel Workshop of Amer, Natl Gospel Evangelist Musicians and Choral Org; mem NAACP; apptd Manpower Planning and Training Council for St Louis County by Supervisor Gene McNary, States Comm of Citizens Adv Commn on Mal-Practice by Atty Genl John Ashcroft; mem Women Self Help Bd, Salvation Army Bd, Pace Bd, St Charles County Bd of Re-

altors, Employers Support of Natl Guard and Reserve. **Honors/Awds:** Business Man of the Year Elks Lodge. **Military Serv:** Armed Forces President's Personal Honor Guard; Honorable Discharge. **Business Addr:** Chairman/General Manager, KIRL-AM, 3713 Hwy 94 North, St Charles, MO 63301.

WHITE, WILLIAM EUGENE
Professional football player. **Personal:** Born Feb 19, 1966, Lima, OH; married Nikol. **Educ:** Ohio State, attended. **Career:** Detroit Lions, defensive back, 1988-93; Kansas City Chiefs, 1994-96; Atlanta Falcons, 1997-. **Business Addr:** Professional Football Player, Atlanta Falcons, Two Falcon Place, Suwanee, GA 30174, (404)945-1111.

WHITE, WILLIAM H.
Educator. **Personal:** Born Feb 16, 1932; married Dolores; children: Michele, Michael, Sharon. **Educ:** Morgan St Coll, BS 1961; Am Coll Law, LLB 1965. **Career:** Health Dept NYC, chemist; Kings Co Research Labs, clinical lab mgr; Physicins Assoc prog Long Island Univ, clinical lab instr & coor; United Bapt Church, asst pastor 1963-74; New Revival Community Church, pastor 1974-. **Orgs:** Mem NAACP; Concerned Citz; Black Assn; Assoc Royal Soc Pub Hlthl. **Military Serv:** Paratroopers sgt 1953-56. **Business Addr:** 4037 Laconia Ave, Bronx, NY 10466.

WHITE, WILLIAM J.
Electrical engineer (retired). **Personal:** Born Aug 6, 1926, Philadelphia, PA; son of Mary Valentine White and James Earle White; married Althea de Freitas; children: Karen, William Jr. **Educ:** A&T Clg, 1943; Syracuse U, 1950; NY City U, BS 1960; Army Command & Gen Staff Clg, 1966. **Career:** Andrea Radio & TV, tech wrtr 1955; NY Transit Auth, elec engr 1958; US Navy Appl Sci Lab, elec engr 1959; Fed Aviation Adm elec engr 1961-87, mgr Systems & Equipment Branch. **Orgs:** Pres Local 2791 Am Fed of Govt Empl 1972-80; pres/mem Hempstead Bd of Ed 1973-78; pres SE Civic Asso 1972-; chm bd Trustee United Cong Ch 1970-72; pub rel Hempstead Little League 1970-78; mem Authors Guild 1974-, Natl Writers Club 1975-, Hempstead Planning Board; Hempstead editor "The Prospective" a monthly newspaper; editor, Hempstead Little League monthly newsletter; editor "Brieflines" Cong Church of So Hempstead Monthly, 1989-. **Honors/Awds:** Man of Yr Hempstead Little League 1972; Bk, Airships for the Future Sterling Pub, 1976; Free Lance Writer, Frequent Flyer, Newsday/Natl Rifleman Christian Herald; Listed in, Community Leaders & Noteworthy Americans, Contemporary Authors vols 97-100, Men of Achievement; Martin L King Jr Memorial Award, United Black Christians, 1990; Outstanding Community Service, CRUSH, 1988; Humanitarian Award, Hempstead NAACP, 1991. **Military Serv:** AUS mjr 1945-46, 1950-53; CIB; Purple Heart 2; Bronze Star; Assorted Minor Awds; USAR major, retired. **Home Addr:** 174 Lawson St, Hempstead, NY 11550.

WHITE, WILLIAM J.
Manager. **Personal:** Born Mar 3, 1935, Bouard, PA; son of Katie White and Ira White; married Idella M Hatter; children: Sheryl, Karen, Sandra. **Educ:** Westminster Coll, BA 1957; Alex Hamilton Bus Inst, atnd; Youngstown St Ud mgmt training prog metallur courses. **Career:** Weirton Steel Corp., logistics administrator, currently; Sharon Steel Corp, manager primary rolling & plant support services 1985-, supt trans labor & material control; supt material control 1969, gen foreman degassing 1968-69, sr melter 1965-68, heat balance cal 1962-65, stock foreman 1960-62, quality control analyst 1960, pit foreman 1958-60, trainee 1957-59. **Orgs:** Mem Jr Chamber 1959; Shenango Valley United Fund 1969-72; Y's Men 1962; Shenango Valley Urban Leag 1968-75; pres Kiwanis 1979; pres Westminster Coll Alumni Assn 1974; adv bd McDowell Nat Bank; dir George Jr Rep; dir NAACP; dir Boy Scouts of Am 1974; trustee, Westminster College, New Wilmington, PA, 1991. **Honors/Awds:** Recip Little All Am Football AP 1955-56; first black foreman gen foreman supt Sharon Steel Corp hist; Indiana County Hall of Fame, 1990. **Military Serv:** AUS sgt 1957-63. **Business Addr:** 400 Three Springs Dr, Weirton, WV 26062.

WHITE, WILLIAM T., III
Business executive. **Personal:** Born Nov 12, 1947, Jacksonville, FL; married Patricia E; children: William Thomas IV. **Educ:** Bethune-Cookman Coll, 1965-66; TN State Univ, BS Pol Sci 1969; Emory Univ, MA Metropolitan Govt 1970-72. **Career:** Office of the Mayor, Model Cities Atlanta GA, rsch eval spec 1973-75; Inst for School Rsch, rsch assoc 1975-78; Grassroots Inc, exec dir 1978-80; DeKalb Cty Planning Dept, human serv facilities coord 1980-. **Orgs:** Worshipful Master Royal Ark Masonic Lodge F&AA York Rite Masons 1978; past Grand Jr Warden Smooth Ashlar Grand Masonic Lodge 1978-82; mem of bd Community Relation Comm DeKalb Cty 1979-82; CEO Kirkwood/Edgewood Eastlake Econ Devel Corp 1982; mem Natl Forum for Black Public Admin 1983; mem SE Atlanta Intown Businessmen Assn 1985; mem DeKalb-Atlanta Voter's Cncl 1982; bd mem SE Atlanta YMCA. **Honors/Awds:** Grad Fellowship Emory Univ 1970; Illus Inspector Gen Natl Supreme Council Scottish-Rite 33rd degree Mason 1978; Outstanding Young men of Amer 1979; Lt Col Aid-de-Camp Office of the Govt State of GA 1983; Special Deputy Sheriff DeKalb Cty; Worshipful Master of the Year Masons 1980-81. **Home Addr:** 3316 Toney Dr, Decatur, GA 30032. **Business Addr:** Coord, Human Serv Facil, Dekalb County Plng Dept, 30 Warren St, Atlanta, GA 30317.

WHITE, WINIFRED VIARIA
Television executive. **Personal:** Born Mar 23, 1953, Indianapolis, IN; daughter of Winifred Parker White and Walter H White; married Kenneth Neisser, May 28, 1989; children: Alexis. **Educ:** Harvard Radcliffe Coll, AB, 1974; Lesley Coll, MA, Educ. **Career:** NBC, mgr, project peacock, 1981-82, children's programs, 1982-84, dir, children's programs, 1984-85, vice pres, family programs, 1985-89, dir, motion pictures for television, 1989-. **Orgs:** Bd of dirs, Harvard-Radcliffe Club, 1983-; bd of governors, TV Acad, 1986-; bd of dirs, Planned Parenthood, 1986-; bd of dires, Women In Film, 1990-.

WHITE, WOODIE W.
Cleric. **Career:** United Methodist Church, southern and central Illinois conferences, bishop, head, 1984-92, state of Indiana, bishop, head, 1992-. **Orgs:** Council of Bishops, president, 1996-97. **Honors/Awds:** Boston University School of Theology, Distinguished Alumni Award, 1970; United Committee on Negro History, Distinguished Service Award, 1974; Honorary Degrees: University of Evansville, Adrian College, Rust College, McKendree College, Illinois Wesleyan College, MacMurray College, Paine College, University of Indianapolis. **Special Achievements:** First African-American named to lead the United Methodist Church in Indiana, 1992. **Business Addr:** Bishop, United Methodist Church in Indiana, 1100 W 42nd St, Ste 210, Indianapolis, IN 46208, (317)924-1321.

WHITE, YOLANDA SIMMONS
Educator. **Personal:** Born Apr 6, 1955, Baltimore, MD; daughter of Edna Eva Johnson Simmons and Carlton Simmons; married Edward Clarence White, Jul 15, 1978. **Educ:** Princeton University, Princeton, NJ, BA, with honors, 1977; Yale University, New Haven, CT, MA, 1978, MA, philosophy, 1980, PhD, 1982. **Career:** World Without War Council, NY, project director, 1980-81; Y S White & Co., president, 1982-84; Queensborough Community College, assistant to dean, 1985-88; St Francis College, associate dean, 1988-91; various academic positions: Audrey Cohen College, Wagner College, Hofstra Univ, currently. **Orgs:** Bd of dirs, UNA-New York, 1989-91; head of membership cmte, bd of dirs, Assn of Black Women in Higher Education, 1989. **Honors/Awds:** NYNEX Corp., $11,400 Study Grant, population of African-American corporate managers. **Home Addr:** 155 W 70th St Apt 14E, New York, NY 10023-4428.

WHITEHEAD, DAVID WILLIAM
Corporate executive. **Personal:** Born Sep 7, 1946, Cleveland, OH; son of Leila Wall Thomas and Mack Thomas; married Ruvene Proa Whitehead, Oct 19, 1968; children: Lisa, Lora. **Educ:** Cleveland State University, Cleveland, OH, BA, 1968, JD, 1973. **Career:** Cleveland Bd of Education, Cleveland, OH, teacher, 1968-73; Howard, Watson & Whitehead, Cleveland, OH, self-employed attorney, 1973-79; The Cleveland Electric Illuminating Company, Cleveland, OH, attorney, 1979-, Northern region vice pres, currently. **Orgs:** Bd of dirs, United Way Services, pres, chair Board Development Comm, United Way Services; pres emeritus, Neighborhood Ctrs Assn; Cleveland Metroparks Pres, bd of commissioners; bd of dirs, Cleveland Golf Charities; bd of trustees, Cleveland Public Radio; bd of trustees, Cleveland Scholarship Programs, Inc; advisory bd, Institute for Educational Renewel. **Honors/Awds:** Distinguished Alumnus Award, Cleveland State Univ Assn of Black Faculty and Staff, 1990; Citizens League of Greater Cleveland, Civic Service Award, 1996. **Business Addr:** Northern Region Vice Pres, The Illuminating Company, PO Box 5000, Cleveland, OH 44101.

WHITEHEAD, EDDIE L.
Communications company executive. **Personal:** Born Jul 7, 1944, Clarksdale, MS; son of Myrtle Whitehead and Jodie Whitehead; married Lynn Demarest; children: Pax, Maya, Luke. **Educ:** Univ of Louisville, Kentucky, BS, 1967; Univ of California, Berkeley, MSW, 1974, MS, 1977. **Career:** Honeywell Info Systems, account exec, 1971-73; Rubicon Programs Inc, dir, 1974-78; Colonial Realty, sales, 1978-80; Whitehead & Co, owner, broker, 1980-84; Whitco Broadcasters Inc, pres, gen mgr; Silver King Broadcasting of Hollywood Inc, vice pres, gen mgr; Channel 66 of Vallejo Inc, pres, gen mgr; Whitehead Communications Inc, pres; HSN Broadcasting of Hollywood Inc, vice pres/gen mgr, currently. **Orgs:** Dir, human relations council Lajes Azores Portugal, 1969; pres, bd of dir, J-Pax Broadcasters Inc, 1981-; pres, gen mgr, Whitco Broadcasters Inc, 1984-; mem, Natl Assn of Broadcasters, 1984-87; pres, Channel 69 of Hollywood Florida Inc; mem, Natl Assn of Black Owned Broadcasters, Broward County Civilian Review Bd. **Honors/Awds:** US Olympic Basketball Training Camp, 1970; Head of Delegation, Counseil Intl du Sports Militaire, Tehran, Iran, 1970. **Military Serv:** USAF, Capt, 1967-71. **Business Addr:** Vice President/General Manager, HSN Broadcasting of Hollywood Inc, 10306 USA Today Way, Miramar, FL 33025.

WHITEHEAD, JAMES T., JR.
Pilot, flight engineer. **Personal:** Born Dec 10, 1934, Jersey City, NJ; divorced; children: Brent, Janet, Kenneth, Joel, Marie. **Educ:** Univ of IL, BS 1957. **Career:** USAF Univ of IL, commd 2nd lt 1957-AFROTC; USAF, pilot training 1958; KC-135, copilot 1959-63; KC-135, aircraft comdr 1963-65; Vietnam combat, 1965; U-2 Reconnaissance, aircraft comdr 1966-67; TWA, flight eng 1967, first officer Boeing 707 1968, flt engineer/instr/flt engr/check airman B-747. **Orgs:** Mem Airlines Pilot Assn 1967; ALPA activities; TWA co-chmn Hazardous Materials Com 1974-; TWA Master Exec Cncl Flt Security Com 1975; pres Kiwanis Madison Township NJ 1968; Jaycees Madison Township 1973-; served as squadron commander 103rd Tactical Air Support Squardon 1977-83; appointed as Hdqtrs PA Air Natl Guard dir of operations 1983-; promoted to Colonel 1983; Kappa Alpha Psi Frat; chmn 111th Tactical Air Support Group Minority Recruit com 1972-74. **Honors/Awds:** First and only Black U-2 Pilot until recently; Outstanding Assn Mem Madison Township Jaycees 1974; Pres Old Bridge Township Bd Educ elected 3 years 1975. **Military Serv:** USAF 1957-67 Colonel. **Business Addr:** Flight Engineer, TWA Building 95, JFK Airport, Jamaica, NY.

WHITE-HUNT, DEBRA JEAN
Performing arts company executive. **Personal:** Born Jul 21, 1951, Detroit, MI; daughter of Jean & Sylvester White; married Bruce James Hunt, Oct 19, 1985; children: Alise Frances. **Educ:** MI State Univ, BA, 1972; Wayne State Univ, MEd, 1975. **Career:** Detroit Public Schools, dance, health teacher, 1973-95; Detroit-Windsor Dance Academy & Co, artristic dir, 1984-. **Orgs:** Delta Sigma Theta Sorority Inc, golden life mem, 1970-; Detroit Inst of Arts Founders Society, 1994; life mem, NAACP. **Honors/Awds:** Milken Foundation, Natl Educator Award, 1990; Michiganian of the Year, Detroit News, 1990; John F Kennedy Artist Fellow, Kennedy Ctr for the Perf Arts, 1987; Dance Teacher of the Year, MI Dance Assn, 1988; Leadership, America, 1995. **Special Achievements:** Choreographed several major works of art (dance); Performed dances throughout America, Bermuda, Australia, NY, etc; Founded a dance inst with a major dance co and 300 students; Mentored, taught, and developed hundreds of dancers. **Home Addr:** 19541 Cranbrook Dr, #118, Detroit, MI 48221, (313)861-8188. **Business Addr:** Artistic Director, Detroit-Windsor Dance Academy & Co, 1529 Broadway, 3rd & 4th Floors, Detroit, MI 48226, (313)963-0050.

WHITEHURST, CHARLES BERNARD, SR.
City official (retired). **Personal:** Born Jun 4, 1938, Portsmouth, VA; son of Bernice N Whitehurst and John E Whitehurst, Sr (deceased); married Vandelyn Smith Whitehurst; children: Miriam Simmons, Lisa Boyd, Lisa Pretlow, Charles Jr. **Educ:** Norfolk State Univ, BS (Magna Cum Laude) 1978; Univ of CO-Boulder, Grad Degree Bank Marketing 1982. **Career:** United States Marine Corps, retired major 1955-76; Central Fidelity Bank, asst vice pres & loan officer 1977-85; City of Portsmouth, treasurer 1986-93. **Orgs:** Portsmouth Sch Bd 1977-81; pres Portsmouth Chamber of Commerce 1982; chmn Portsmouth Seawall Festival 1984-85; bd of dirs Old Dominion Univ 1984-88, Maryview Hosp 1985-88; pres Downtown Portsmouth Assoc, 1987-89; pres Retired Officers Association, Portsmouth Area Chapter, 1989; Eureka Club Inc, president, 1991-93, 1996-97; NAACP, golden heritage, life member; Optimist Club; pres Virginia Games, Inc; pres, Sports Mgt & Promotions, Inc; vice pres, Port City Publishing, Inc; staff writer, Port Cities Concerns; African American Historical Society of Portsmouth, VA, founder, pres. **Honors/Awds:** Alpha Kappa Mu Honor Soc Norfolk State Univ 1978; Distinguished Alumni NAFEO Washington DC 1984; Eurekan of the Year Eureka Club Portsmouth 1984; Citizen of the Year Omega Psi Phi Frat 1985; Treasurers' Association of Virginia, Treasurer of the Year, 1992; Sigma Gamma Rho, Alpha Sigma Chapter, 1992. **Special Achievements:** First African-American citizen of Portsmouth; poet: The Other Side of a Gemina, anthology, 1986. **Military Serv:** US Marine Corps, major, 21 yrs; Good Conduct, three stars; Navy Achievements; Navy Commendation w/Combat V; Staff Serv Honor Medal; Republic of South Vietnam. **Business Addr:** President, History on Metal, PO Box 1363, Portsmouth, VA 23705, (757)393-0598.

WHITEHURST, STEVEN LAROY
Educational administrator, author. **Personal:** Born Mar 3, 1967, Chicago, IL; son of Oneda Fondren-Whitehurst; married Noreen Halbert, Jun 27, 1992. **Educ:** Thornton Community College, AA, history, 1987, AS, geography, 1988; Chicago State University, BA, history, minor political science, 1990. **Career:** South Suburban College, graduate ambassador, 1988-90; Equal Employment Opportunity Commission, investigator, 1990-91; South Suburban College, academic skills/transition advisor, 1991-94, director of student development, 1994-97. **Orgs:** American Black Book Writers Assn, 1991-; Multicultural Publishers Exchange, 1992-94; Thornton Comm College Affirm Action Advisory Committee, 1988; ILAEOPP, 1991-92; MAEOPP, 1991-92; Project Vision, head of project/task force, 1994-97; Equal Employment Opportunity Committee, 1991; Cook County Board of Elections, elections judge/registrar, 1990; Phi Alpha Theta, 1997-; Phi Theta Kappa, Psi Pi Chap, 1989-. **Honors/Awds:** AFRIQUE Communications, Malcolm X Award For Self-Actualization, 1994; Black Booksellers

Trade Assn, Black Lit Achieve Award, 1993; South Suburban College, Role Model of the Year, 1993; South Suburban College, SGA, Outstanding Service Award, 1992; New Scriblerus Society, Creative Excellence Award, 1988; Hero Award, 1995; South Suburban College, Educational Talent Search, ETS Award, 1996. **Special Achievements:** Author, Words From An Unchained Mind, 1991; Contributor, Rodney King And The LA Rebellion, 1992; Rodney King and the LA Rebellion-Your Black Book Guide Bestseller; Words From An Unchained Mind: Your Black Books Guide Future Bestseller; Moderator, City of Harvey (Illinois) Mayoral Debate, 1995; Panelist, African-American History Month Round Table Discussion: The State of Black America, sponsored by The Times Newspaper, 1995. **Home Addr:** 14164 S Calumet Ave, Dolton, IL 60419.

WHITELY, DONALD HARRISON
Admissions counselor, instructor. **Personal:** Born Mar 4, 1955, Tarrytown, NJ; son of Helen Elizabeth Cardwell Whitely and Henry Harrison Whitely; married Angela Smith-Whitely, Jan 2, 1980; children: Asha Elizabeth, Maya Nicole. **Educ:** SUNY at Albany, Albany, NY, BA, 1977; John Jay College of Criminal Justice, New York, NY, MPA, 1982. **Career:** IBM, Harrison, NY, inventory control assistant, 1980-82; Jewish Child Care Agency, Pleasantville, NY, diagnostic unit counselor, 1983-88; Malcolm-King College, Harlem, NY, asst director HEOP, 1988-, director HEOP, 1988-89; Westchester, Community College, Valhalla, NY, admissions counselor/instructor, 1989-. **Orgs:** Higher Education Opportunity Program Professional Org, 1988-89; Westchester Educational Coalition, 1989-; Admissions Advisory Committee, WCC, 1989-; faculty advisor, African Cultural Club, WCC, 1990-; Middle States Association of Collegiate Registrars and Officers of Admissions, 1989-; SUNY Multicultural Comm. **Honors/Awds:** Tarrytown Community Opportunity Center, Distinguished Community Service Award, 1992. **Special Achievements:** First African-American elected, Board of Trustees, Village of Tarrytown, 1992, Relected to 3rd term, 1996; Coord, Open Views Youth Group of the Tarrytowns; asst hd coach for Tarrytown Pop Warner Football; Village of Tarrytown Liaison, Tarrytown School Bd an Municipal Housing Authority. **Home Addr:** 16 Mechanics Ave, Tarrytown, NY 10591. **Business Addr:** Admissions Counselor, Asst Prof, Westchester Community College, State University of New York, 75 Grasslands Rd, Administration Bldg, Rm 210, Valhalla, NY 10595.

WHITEMAN, HERBERT WELLS, JR. See Obituaries section.

WHITEN, MARK ANTHONY
Professional baseball player. **Personal:** Born Nov 25, 1966, Pensacola, FL. **Educ:** Pensacola Junior College. **Career:** Outfielder: Toronto Blue Jays, 1990-91, Cleveland Indians, 1991-93, St Louis Cardinals, 1993-. **Business Addr:** Professional Baseball Player, St Louis Cardinals, Busch Memorial Stadium, 250 Stadium Plaza, St Louis, MO 63102, (314)421-4040.

WHITE-PARSON, WILLAR F.
Nurse, educator. **Personal:** Born Nov 11, 1945, Norfolk, VA; daughter of Willar M White and Joseph S White; married Wayman L Parson, Aug 5, 1985; children: Davida Josette White. **Educ:** Hampton University, BSN, 1974, MA, guidance & counseling, 1976, MSN, community mental health, psy, nursing, 1979; Old Dominion University, PhD, urban service curriculum development, 1984. **Career:** Norfolk State University, associate professor of nursing, 1974; Norfolk Psychiatric Center, nursing supervisor, 1990-92; Sentara Norfolk General Hospital, psychiatric nurse consultant, 1991-; Private Practice, nurse psychotherapist, 1991-. **Orgs:** Association of Black Nursing Faculty in Higher Education, 1990-; American Nurses Association, 1990-; Virginia Nurses Association, 1990-; National League for Nursing, 1989-; Virginia League of Nursing, 1989-; Tidewater Academy of Clinical Nurse Specialist, 1991-; American Association of University Professors, 1976-; Virginia Council Clinical Nurse Specialist, 1991-. **Honors/Awds:** Association of Black Nursing Faculty in Higher Education, Research Award, 1992; Old Dominion University, Minority Fellowship, 1984; Sigma Theta Tau Honor Society, 1979; Kappa Delta Pi Honor Society, 1976; American Academy of Nursing, fellow, 1994. **Special Achievements:** LPN to ADN, BSN: An Accelerated Curriculum Track, $550,000 grant, 1988-92; "A Comparison of Parenting Profiles of Adolescent Mothers," dissertation, 1984; "Parenting Profiles of Battered Women," 1980. **Home Addr:** 5008 Kemps Farm Pl, Virginia Beach, VA 23464, (804)495-6115. **Business Addr:** Associate Professor of Nursing, Norfolk State University, 2401 Corprew Ave, Norfolk, VA 23504, (804)683-8525.

WHITESIDE, ERNESTYNE E.
Educator. **Personal:** Born Mar 4, Pine Bluff, AR. **Educ:** Mech & Normal Coll Pine Bluff, BA agri; NY U, MA; Europe, post grad; Ouachita Univ Arkadelphia; HI; OK U; Univ AR. **Career:** Dollarway Public School Dist, english instr. **Orgs:** Mem pres Jeferson Co Reading Coun; AR Educ Assn; bd AR Educ Assn; Assn Classrooms Tchrs; Nat AR Coun Tchrs English; Nat Reading Coun; Nat Assn Univ Women; Gov's Coun Aerospace Edn; St Orgn Minority Evolvement; Nat Alumni Assn A M & N Coll; Eastern Star; Delta Sigma Theta; Am Woodman Assn. **Honors/Awds:** Cert oustnd serv yth Jack & Jill 1974; hon cit Negro Yth Ogn; outsng tchr of mo Townsend Park HS; natl TV signing doc mergin st PTA with ACPT 1970; cit of day Radio St KCAT; judge Miss Black Am So Central AR Gamma Phi Delta 1972; listed in Dict of Intl Biog Vol 12.

WHITESIDE, LARRY
Journalist. **Personal:** Born Sep 19, 1937, Chicago, IL; son of Myrtis Wells Whiteside and Alonzo Whiteside Sr; married Elaine Fain; children: Anthony. **Educ:** Wilson Jr Coll, AA 1955-57; Drake Univ, BA 1957-59; Stanford Univ, John Knight Fellow 1987-88. **Career:** Johnson Publishing Co, researcher, 1958-59; Kansas City Kansan, sports reporter, asst editor, 1959-63; Milwaukee Journal, sports reporter, 1963-73; Milwaukee Sporting News, correspondent, 1970-74; Boston Sporting News, correspondent, 1974-78; The Boston Globe, sports reporter columnist, 1973-; Monroe Trotters, columnist, 1992-. **Orgs:** Mem, Kappa Alpha Psi, 1957-; mem, US Basketball Writers, 1960-80; mem, NAACP, 1970-; chmn, Boston Baseball Writers, 1979-80; mem, NBA Basketball Writers, 1975-; bd of dir, Baseball Writers Assn of Amer, 1980; delegate, Natl Assn of Black Journalists, 1982-. **Honors/Awds:** Wisconsin Sports Writer of the Year, Milwaukee Press Club, 1973; Investigative Reporting (2nd & 4th), Assoc Press Sports Editor, 1980, 1985; John S Knight Fellow, Stanford Univ, 1987-88; Best Sports Story, National Association of Black Journalist, 1989-90, runner-up, 1992, 1995. **Home Addr:** 64 Kirkstall Rd, Newtonville, MA 02160. **Business Addr:** Sports Reporter, Columnist, The Boston Globe, 135 Morrissey Blvd, Boston, MA 02107.

WHITEST, BEVERLY JOYCE
Government official, human relations consultant. **Personal:** Born Aug 28, 1951, Tarboro, NC; daughter of Barbara Pittman; divorced; children: Malik, Jelani. **Educ:** Univ of WI LaCrosse, exchange student 1973; NC A&T State Univ, BS Political Science 1974; Atlanta Univ, MPA (Carnegie Fellow) 1976; Nova Univ, 1988-. **Career:** City of Atlanta, urban planner 1977-78; Dept of Trans Nashville, trans planner 1978-80; Rsch & Policy Assn Jackson, planning consultant 1980-82; Div of Public Health, dir planning & evaluation 1982-86; Public Health, dir office of organizational develop, 1986-. **Orgs:** Conf on Minority Public Admin 1975-84; pres Black Prof Network 1984-85; Master trainer Southwest Serv Area Girls Scouts 1984-; exec sec Atlanta Health Prof Assn 1983-85; GA Public Health Assn 1984-; consultant Assoc of Creative Change 1984-; volunteer United Way; trainer Northwest Georgia Girls Scouts; mem Delta Sigma Theta Sorority Inc; bd of dir, Counsil on Battered Women and the West End Medical Center; mem, Coalition of 100 Black Women. **Honors/Awds:** Fellowship Public Admin Dept Atlanta Univ 1975-76; Serv Award Adamsville Area Girl Scouts 1984-85. **Home Addr:** 6615 Cedar Hurst Trail, College Park, GA 30349.

WHITE-WARE, GRACE ELIZABETH
Educator (retired). **Personal:** Born Oct 5, 1921, St Louis, MO; daughter of Madree Penn White and Dr James Eathel White Sr; married Aug 17, 1947 (widowed); children: Oloye Adeyemon (James Otis Ware II). **Educ:** Harriet Beecher Stowe Teacher's Coll, BA 1943; attended Columbia Univ NY 1944-45, Scott Foresman Inst summer 1951, Wayne State Univ 1966, St John Coll John Carroll Univ 1974-75, Kent State Univ 1976, Ohio Univ 1978. **Career:** St Louis, Chicago, New York, Cleveland, teacher 1946-82; Cleveland Public Sch, teacher elem & adult educ 1954-82; Delta Sigma Theta Sor Inc member founder, Tutoring & Nutrition Proj, prog admin 1983-88. **Orgs:** Greater Cleveland Neighborhood Centers Assn; Food First Prog; Black Econ Union; Youth Understanding Teenage Prog; Cleveland Council Human Relations; Cong Racial Equality; Tots & Teens; Jr Women's Civic League; Afro-Amer Cultural/Hist Soc; Talbert Clinic & Day Care Ctr; Langston Hughes Library; Women's Allied Arts Assn; NAACP; Phyllis Wheatley Assn; Natl Council Negro Women; Natl Sor Phi Delta Kappa; Top Ladies of Distinction Inc; Smithsonian Inst; regional and natl treas Eta Phi Beta Sor Inc 1980-88; Delta Kappa Gamma Soc Intl, The Natl Museum of Women in Arts; mem Kiwanis International 1987; treasurer, National Assn of University Women, 1987-; Phi Delta Kappa Fraternal Group, Inc, 1979-. **Honors/Awds:** Outstanding Volunteer of the Year, New York 1949; Outstanding Teacher Award 1973; Certificate of Appreciation Cleveland 1973; Master Teacher Award-Martha Jennings 1973; Pan-Hellenic Outstanding Greek Award 1979, 1984; Educational Serv Award Urban League of Greater Cleveland 1986; Humanitarian Award Top Ladies of Distinction Inc 1986.

WHITFIELD, ALPHONSO
Banking executive. **Educ:** Union College (NY), MA; Carnegie-Mellon Univ, MS. **Career:** Mutual Federal Savings and Loan Association, pres/CEO, 1995-; Federal Home Loan Bank of NY, vp, until 1995. **Orgs:** Regional Lender Consortia, cofounder; National Minority Supplier Developmental council, pres; Social Investments for Prudential Insurance of America, vp; Commercial Group for Progress Investment Associates, vp. **Business Addr:** President/CEO, Mutual Federal Savings & Loan Association, 205 Auburn Ave, Atlanta, GA 30335, (404)659-0710.

WHITFIELD, LYNN
Actress. **Personal:** Born Feb 15, Baton Rouge, LA; children: Grace. **Educ:** Howard University, BA. **Career:** Actress; TV credits include: Equal Justice, Heartbeat, The Women of Brewster Place, Stompin at the Savoy; The George McKenna Story, The Johnnie Mae Gibson Story, Hill Street Blues, Cosby Mysteries; The Josephine Baker Story; films include: Dr Detroit, Silverado, Slugger's Wife; A Thin Line Between Love and Hate; Eve's Bayou; The Wedding, 1998. **Honors/Awds:** Emmy Award, The Josephine Baker Story, 1991; Howard Univ, Alumni Achievement Award, 1992; NAACP, Image Award, TV Drama Supporting Actress, 1998. **Special Achievements:** "The Josephine Baker Story," HBO Presentation, 1991.

WHITFIELD, ROBERT
Professional football player. **Personal:** Born Oct 18, 1971, Carson, CA; children: Laniece, Kodi. **Educ:** Stanford, attended. **Career:** Atlanta Falcons, tackle, 1992-; Patchwerk Recordings, owner. **Business Addr:** Professional Football Player, Atlanta Falcons, Two Falcon Place, Suwanee, GA 30174, (404)945-1111.

WHITFIELD, TIMBERLY N.
Journalist. **Personal:** Born Feb 3, 1966, Kansas City, MO; daughter of Jimmye Deffebaugh Whitfield and William H. Whitfield. **Educ:** Schiller International University, Heidelberg, Germany, exchange student, 1986; Clark College, Atlanta, GA, BA, 1987; Columbia University, New York, NY, MSJ, 1989. **Career:** United Methodist Reporter, Dallas, TX, reporter, 1986; Response Magazine, New York, NY, reporter, 1987-88; Paragon Cable, New York, NY, producer/reporter, 1989-90; Bolthead Communications, New York, NY, associate producer, 1990-. **Orgs:** Mem, National Association of Black Journalists, 1989-; mem, SOS Society of Professional Journalist, 1989-; mem, Alpha Kappa Mu Honor Society, 1987-; mem, Black Filmmakers Foundation, 1989-; mem, Film Forum, 1991-. **Honors/Awds:** John M. Patterson Prize for Broadcast Reporting, Columbia University, 1989; Outstanding Student Award (Broadcast), Clark College Communications Dept, 1986; Benjamin Franklin Award for Overseas Studies, Clark College Language Dept, 1985.

WHITFIELD, VANTILE E.
Association executive. **Personal:** Born Sep 8, 1930, Washington, DC; married Lynn C Smith; children: Elizabeth, Lance, Bellina. **Educ:** Howard U, BA 1957; Univ CA, MA 1960. **Career:** Nat Endowment for the Arts, prog dir expansion arts; Howard U, instr 1957-58; Ad Graphics of Hollywood, prod mgr, art dir 1960-61; Theatre of Being, co-fdr, gen mgr 1963-64; LA Sch Dist, instr 1965-66; Universal City Studios, set designer 1966-67; KTTV LA "From the Inside Out," creator, prod-dir 1968-69; Performing Arts Soc of LA, fdr, dir 1966-71; KNXT LA, Anatomy of Change, creator-prod 1970; DC Black Repertory Co Wash DC, guest artistic dir, 1971-. **Orgs:** Mem Directors' Guild of Am 1968-; SAG 1964-; AFTRA 1965-; Set Design & Model Makers Guild 1966-; mem Banneker City Club Wash DC 1974-. **Honors/Awds:** Recip Commendation of Merit LA Co 1967; Commendation of Merit City of LA 1968; Image Award Hollywood-Beverly Hills NAACP 1969; Nat Assn of Media Women 1970; LA Critics' Cir Award 1970. **Military Serv:** USAF a/1c 1950-51. **Business Addr:** Nat Endowment for Arts, Washington, DC 20506.

WHITFIELD, WILLIE, JR.
Computer software marketing manager. **Personal:** Born Jan 17, 1947, Fairfield, AL; son of Willie & Eloise Whitfield. **Educ:** Tennessee State Univ, BSEE, 1970; Stanford Univ, MBA, 1973; Greenforest Bible Academy, AA, 1985. **Career:** Hewlett Packard Co, sales eng/fin analyst, 1973-81; GTS Comp Systems, mktg mgr, 1981-83; Private Consultant, 1983-85; Care Comp Systems, regional mktg mgr, 1985-. **Orgs:** Natl Assn of Accounts, 1973-75; Alabama Nursing Home Assn, assoc member, 1985-; TSU Natl Alum Assn, 1990-; Stanford GSB Alum Assn, 1990-. **Business Addr:** Regional Mktg Mgr, Care Computer Systems, PO Box 43901, Atlanta, GA 30336, (404)699-0466.

WHITING, ALBERT NATHANIEL
Educational administrator (retired). **Personal:** Born Jul 3, 1917, Jersey City, NJ; son of Hilda Whiting and Hezekiah O. Whiting; married Lottie Luck; children: Brooke E Whiting. **Educ:** Amherst Coll, AB 1938; Fisk Univ, MA 1941; The Amer Univ, PhD 1948 1952. **Career:** Bennett Coll, instructor sociology 1941-43 1946-47; Atlanta Univ, asst prof sociology 1948-53; Morris Brown Coll, dean of college 1953-57; Morgan State Coll, dean of college 1957-67; NC Central Univ, pres chancellor 1967-83, chancellor emeritus. **Orgs:** MD Commn for New York World's Fair; mem commn on academic affairs Amer Council on Educ 1968-70; mem bd dirs Amer Council on Educ 1970-73 1974-75; mem bd trustees Educ Testing Serv 1968-72; mem policies & purposes comm bd dirs pres Amer Assn of State Colleges & Univs; mem Coll Entrance Examination Bd; mem bd dirs Natl League for Nursing Inc 1970-71; vice pres 1971-74,1975-78, treas 1978-84 Intl Assn of Univ Presidents; mem bd dirs NC Memorial Hospital 1974-77; mem Joint Panel on the Grad Record Examinations Bd and the Council of Graduate School in the US, former mem; bd govs exec comm of bd

Rsch Triangle Inst Rsch Triange Park NC; mem bd dirs Greater Durham Chamber of Commerce; mem US Civil Serv Commn Southern Region; mem bd dirs General Telephone Co of the Southeast; mem bd dirs Rose'sres Inc 1981-; member bd of regents, Univ of MD System, 1988-. **Honors/Awds:** Natl Urban League Fellowship Univ of Pittsburgh; Teaching & Rsch Fellow Fisk Univ; Alpha Kappa Delta Hon Sociological Fraternity; numerous books reviews & contributions to professional journals; Six Hon Degrees LLD's & LHD's. **Military Serv:** AUS 1st lt 1943-46. **Home Addr:** 11253 "B" Slalom Lane, Columbia, MD 21044.

WHITING, BARBARA E.
Attorney. **Personal:** Born Jul 28, 1936, Tabb, VA; widowed. **Educ:** Hampton Inst Hampton VA, BS 1963; Howard Univ Sch Law, JD 1963. **Career:** US Customs Srv Wash, customs law spec 1964-; Howard Univ Dept Med, med sec 1957-63; Howard U, lib 1964. **Orgs:** Mem, treas Howard Law Alumni Assn Geo Wash Nat 1968-; Bar Assn; vol, rehab juv girls Operation Sue 1974. **Honors/Awds:** 1st Black female appointed Customs Law Spec US Customs Srv. **Business Addr:** Customs Law Specialist, US Customs Service, 1301 Constitution Ave, Washington, DC 20229.

WHITING, LEROY
City official. **Personal:** Born May 17, 1938, Rodney, MS; son of Gertrude Jackson Whiting and Johnnie Whiting; married Annette Mattie Watkins, Aug 24, 1959; children: Oran. **Educ:** Alcorn A&M Coll, BS, 1959; Mich State Univ, MAT, 1965; Univ of IL, Chicago, 1975-80. **Career:** Meridian Board of Educ, MS, science teacher 1959-60; Chicago Board of Educ, IL, science teacher 1960-68; City of Chicago, IL, dir of external affairs, assistant to mayor, beginning 1968, special assistant to planning and development commissioner, currently. **Orgs:** Member, Alpha Phi Alpha 1957-, Francis Parker School Bd of Trustees 1968-75, GAP Community Org 1983-, Natl Forum of Black Pub Admins 1986-89, Dental Assisting Natl Board 1988-, Alpha Kappa Mu Honorary Society; chair, User Requirement Pub Tech Inc 1980. **Military Serv:** US Army Reserves, spec 2, 1958-61. **Home Addr:** 3344 South Calumet Ave, Chicago, IL 60616.

WHITING, THOMAS J.
Government employee. **Personal:** Born Oct 1, 1923, Haverhill, MA; son of Margret DuBose Whiting and Elmer J Whiting Sr; married Florence Brock. **Educ:** Howard Univ, BA 1947; Univ of Michigan, MBA 1948; Cleveland-Marshall Law School, LLB 1956. **Career:** Fairfax VA, consultant 1988-; A T International, Washington, DC, director fin & admin 1977-87; Nairobi, Kenya, area auditor gen, 1974-75; Intl Audit AID/Washington, dep dir, 1971-74; S Asia New Delhi, dep area auditor gen, 1970-71; AID/New Delhi, chief auditor, 1967-70; AID/Washington, auditor, 1965-67; IRS Cleveland, appellate adv, 1949-65. **Orgs:** Mem OH Bar Assn 1956; CPA OH 1957; CPA VA 1977. **Honors/Awds:** Award OH CPA Soc 1957; Sam Silbert Award 1956. **Military Serv:** AUS 1943-46. **Home Addr:** 10023 Blue Coat Dr, Fairfax, VA 22030.

WHITING, VAL
Professional basketball player. **Personal:** Born Apr 9, 1972. **Educ:** Stanford Univ. **Career:** Seattle Reign, center, 1996-. **Business Addr:** Professional Basketball Player, Seattle Reign, 400 Mercer St, Ste 408, Seattle, WA 98109, (206)285-5225.

WHITING, WILLIE
Judge. **Personal:** Born in Chicago, IL; daughter of Elise Jones Whiting Harkness and James Whiting; divorced. **Educ:** Fisk Univ, attend; Roosevelt Univ; John Marshall Law School, LLB, JD, 1950. **Career:** Cook Co, circuit judge, 1978, asso judge, circuit court, 1970-78, asst state Atty, 1961-65; asst US atty, 1965-66; Circuit Court, previous magistrate; G J Harkness Law Firm, law clerk, atty, 1950-55; Cook Co Dept of Public Welfare, caseworker, resource consultant, 1955-56; Chicago NAACP, exec sec, 1957-59; City of Chicago, asst corp counsel, 1959-61. **Orgs:** Admitted to Illinois Bar, 1951; mem, Amer Assn of Univ Women; hon mem, Delta Kappa Gamma Educ Soc; mem, Natl Bar Assn; Amer Bar Assn; admitted to prac, US Dist Court & US Supreme Court, 1964-; mem, Advisory Counsel Cook County Temp Juv Detention Center, Hm Ec Related Occup; mem, Cook Coounty Natl Women's Bar Assns; adv bd, Midwest Comm Council; Amer Vets Comm; mem bd, Chicago NAACP; past pres, Professional Women's Club; life member, Zeta Phi Beta; mem advisory counsel, Urban Health Comm, Univ of Illinois, Chicago, 1984-; Illinois Judges Assn; Illinois Judicial Council; National Bar Assn. **Honors/Awds:** Young Lawyers Section, Chicago Bar Assn, Certificate of Appreciation Award, 1985-88. **Military Serv:** US Army, pfc, 1944-46. **Business Addr:** Circuit Court of Cook County, Daley Center Room 1408, Chicago, IL 60602.

WHITLEY, WILLIAM N.
Business executive, architect. **Personal:** Born Apr 29, 1934, Rochester; married Kaysonia Forney; children: Kyle, Kym, Scott. **Educ:** Kent St U, BS 1957. **Career:** Whitley-Whitley Inc, vice pres arch; Registered in OH, IL, IN. **Orgs:** Am Inst Archs; Archs Soc OH; Cleveland Eng Soc; Soc Arch Design 1974; OH Prestressed Concert Assoc Design 1973; Womn's Allied Arts Assoc 1974. **Honors/Awds:** United Torch Progressive Arch Design Award 1972; AIA Am Soc Arch 1st Hon Design 1969. **Military Serv:** USAF capt 1958-60. **Business Addr:** 20600 Chagrin Blvd, Shaker Heights, OH.

WHITLOCK, FRED HENRY
Mathematician. **Personal:** Born Jun 17, 1936, Winston-Salem, NC; married Barbara Hill; children: Carlton Fred, Kenneth Henry, Jacquelyn Ewaugh. **Educ:** NC A&T State U, BS 1959. **Career:** NASA Goodard Space Flight Cntr Greenbelt, MD, mathematician, sci programmer 1962-. **Orgs:** Mem Math Assn; Am Assn for Computing Machinery. **Honors/Awds:** Author "Orbit Prediction Accuracy Theory" 1963; "Interplanetary Trajectory Encke Method Prog anual 1" 1967, Manual 2 1967; manual for IBM OS/360 1970; also articles in field. **Business Addr:** Code 642 Bldg 1, Goodard Space Flight Center, Greenbelt, MD 20771.

WHITLOW, BARBARA WHEELER
Business Executive. **Personal:** Born Jul 20, 1939, Sale City, GA; daughter of Luecilla Donaldson Wheeler and Benjamin Wheeler Sr; married Charles E Whitlow, Dec 27, 1964; children: Charlene Gena, Darlene Denise. **Educ:** Albany State College, 1961; Atlanta Jr College, 1981. **Career:** Federal Bureau of Investigations, research analyst, 1964-67; Defense Contract Adm, quality control specialist, 1967-85; Lows Enterprise, Inc, president/CEO, 1985-. **Orgs:** Region IV 8a Contractors Association, secretary, 1991-. **Honors/Awds:** Georgia Minority Purchasing Council, Show Stoppers Award, 1992; Atlanta Tribune, Salute to Black Business Owners, 1992; Lockheed Aeronautical Systems Co, Salute to Small Business Suppliers, 1992; US Small Business Administration, Administrator's Award for Excellence, 1996. **Special Achievements:** Founder of Lows Enterprises, Inc, Minority Female-Owned Electronic Manufacturing Firm, 1985. **Business Addr:** President/CEO, Lows Enterprises, Inc, 3966 Shirley Dr, Atlanta, GA 30336, (404)699-0582.

WHITLOW, WOODROW, JR.
Supervisory aerospace researcher. **Personal:** Born Dec 13, 1952, Inkster, MI; son of Willie Mae O'Neal Whitlow and Woodrow Whitlow; married Michele C. Wimberly, Jan 6, 1971; children: Mary Annessa, Natalie Michele. **Educ:** Massachusetts Institute of Technology, Cambridge, MA, SB, 1974, SM, 1975, PhD, 1979. **Career:** NASA Langley Research Center, Hampton, VA, research scientist, 1979-86, research scientist/group leader, 1986-88, senior research scientist, 1988-89, asst head, aeroservoelasticity branch, 1990-; NASA, Washington, DC, program mgr, astrophysics, 1990, program mgr, structures and dynamics 1989-90; adjunct prof, Old Dominion University, 1987-; lecturer, Cairo University Aeronautics Seminar Series, 1988. **Orgs:** American Institute of Aeronautics and Astronautics; coach, Phillips Athletic Association Girls Softball, 1981-84; president, Hampton University Laboratory School Advisory Board, 1982-83; member, MIT Aeronautics and Astronautics Visiting Committee, 1987-; member, MIT Educational Council, 1987-; member, Women in Aerospace, 1991-. **Honors/Awds:** First place, Student Research Competition, AAIA New England Section, 1974; James Means Memorial Prize, MIT Aeronautics and Astronautics, 1974; special achievement awards, NASA Langley Research Center, 1982, 1986, 1989; Black Engineer of the Year in Government, Career Communications Group, 1989; Outstanding Performance Award, NASA Langley, 1990. **Business Addr:** Asst Head, Aeroservoelasticity Branch, Langley Research Center, Mail Stop 243, Hampton, VA 23665-5225.

WHITMAL, NATHANIEL
Certified public accountant, business executive. **Personal:** Born Jul 28, 1937, Memphis, TN; son of Eunice Whitmal Crook and Nathaniel Whitmal; married Yolanda Frances Pleasant; children: Nathaniel A, Angela M. **Educ:** Chicago City Coll Wilson Br, AA 1957; Loyola Univ Chicago, BSC 1961, post graduate studies. **Career:** Internal Revenue Serv Chicago, agent 1962-69; Booz, Allen & Hamilton Inc, tax mgr 1969-71; Mayfair Coll (Chicago City Colleges), faculty mem 1971-72; Private Practice, CPA 1971-77; Zenith Electronics Corp, manager corp tax 1977-87; Whitmal Oil Services; CEO l987-; concurrent public accounting practice. **Orgs:** Mem Tax Executives Inst 1977-87; mem Amer Inst of CPA's 1968-; mem IL CPA Soc 1971-; mem Commr of Internal Revenue Sm Bus Adv Comm 1975-76; mem Chicago Urban League; mem NAACP; alt mem Chicago Bd of Educ Citywide Adv Comm 1977-78. **Military Serv:** IL Natl Guard/AUS Reserves Sp 4 1961-67. **Business Addr:** Chief Executive Officer, Whitmal Oil Services, Inc, 11328 S Halsted St, Chicago, IL 60628.

WHITMORE, CHARLES
Government official, state conservationist. **Personal:** Born Jan 25, 1945, Mason, TN; son of Katherine and Morris Whitmore; married Cynthia M Huff, Jul 19, 1969; children: Lashawn, Charles Marcus, Corey Demond. **Educ:** Tennessee State University BS, 1969, MS, 1970. **Career:** USDA, SCS, Maine state conservationist, Illinois state conservationist, currently. **Orgs:** Association of Illinois Soil and Water Conservation; America Society of Agronomy; Professional Society of Black SCS Employees; Prince Hall Masonic Lodge, Bangor Lodge #22; Illinois Governor, land and water task force. **Honors/Awds:** USDA Superior Service Award, 1976. **Special Achievements:** Special achievement awards, 1976, 1984, 1991; Outstanding Performance Awards, 1980, 1981, 1990; Tennessee State University, Alumnus of the Year Award, 1992. **Business Addr:** State Conservationist, USDA/Soil Conservation Service, 1902 Fox Dr, Champaign, IL 61820, (217)398-5267.

WHITMORE, DARRELL
Professional baseball player. **Personal:** Born Nov 18, 1968, Front Royal, VA. **Educ:** West Virginia. **Career:** Florida Marlins, 1993-. **Business Addr:** Professional Baseball Player, Florida Marlins, 100 NE 3rd Ave, 3rd Fl, Fort Lauderdale, FL 33301, (305)779-7070.

WHITNER, DONNA K.
Librarian. **Personal:** Born Jan 24, 1951, Champaign, IL; daughter of Gladys McMullen Whitner and Lawrence Whitner. **Educ:** Western College, Oxford, OH, BA, 1973; University of Illinois, Urbana, IL, MLS, 1977; University of Missouri-Kansas City, Kansas City, MO, MBA, 1995. **Career:** Western College, Oxford, OH, work grant student, 1969-73; Urbana School District #16, Urbana, IL, asst to dir of libraries, 1973-76; University of Illinois, Champaign, IL, graduate asst, 1976-77; Women's Employment Counseling Center, Champaign, IL, researcher, 1977-78; University of Illinois, Champaign, IL, residence halls librarian, 1978-86; Kansas City Public Library, Kansas City, MO, technical processes coordinator, 1986-. **Orgs:** Member, American Library Assn, 1980-; member, Public Library Assn, 1986-; member, Missouri Library Assn, 1986-; vice-chair, technical services council, Missouri Library Assn, 1990-91. **Honors/Awds:** Graduate, Centurions, Leadership Development Program, Greater Kansas City Chamber of Commerce; Woman of the Year, Western College, American Assn of University Women, 1972-73. **Business Addr:** Technical Processes Coordinator, Kansas City Public Library, 311 E 12th St, Kansas City, MO 64106, (816)221-2685.

WHITNEY, CHRISTOPHER ANTOINE
Professional basketball player. **Personal:** Born Oct 5, 1971, Hopkinsville, KY. **Educ:** Lincoln Trail; Clemson Univ. **Career:** San Antonio Spurs, guard, 1993-95; Rapid City Thrillers (CBA), 1995; Florida Beachdogs (CBA), 1995-96, Washington Wizards, 1996-. **Business Addr:** Professional Basketball Player, Washington Wizards, MCI Center, 601 F St NW, Washington, DC 20071, (301)622-3865.

WHITNEY, ROSALYN L.
Educational administrator. **Personal:** Born Jan 12, 1950, Detroit, MI; daughter of Esther L DeCuir Hocker and Robert L Smith; children: Gina Michelle Lee. **Educ:** Oakland University, Meadowbrook, MI, School of Music, 1966; Eastern Michigan University, Ypsilanti, MI, BA, 1971. **Career:** Probe, Inc, Detroit, MI, vp marketing, 1973-78; CBS, Inc, Records Division S Detroit, MI, account executive, 1978-82; Barden Communications, Detroit, MI, director of marketing, 1984; New Detroit, Inc, Detroit, MI director of media relations, 1984-91; Detroit Public Schools, assistant superintendent communications, 1991-. **Orgs:** Board member, Non Profit Public Relations Network, 1991-92, vice chair board, Creative Arts Collection, 1982-; board mem, Detroit Wayne County Family Services, 1992; board mem, International Visitors Council Metro Detroit, 1985-92; mem, St Dunstans Guild Cranbrook, 1989-92; mem, Detroit Press Club, 1984-; Automotive Press Association; National School Public Relations; National Association of Television Arts & Sciences; Natl Assn of Black Journalists; Detroit Producers Association; American Society of Composers, Authors & Publishers. **Honors/Awds:** Spirit of Detroit, City of Detroit, City Council, 1979; Project Self Reliance, State of Michigan, 1984; Black United Fundraising, Black United Fund, 1985; Detroit Public Schools Volunteer Service, Detroit Public Schools, 1986; CBS Detroit Branch of the Year, CBS, Inc, 1980. **Home Addr:** 333 Keelson Drive, Detroit, MI 48215. **Business Addr:** Assistant Superintendent Communications, Detroit Public Schools, 5057 Woodward Ave, Rm 218, Detroit, MI 48202.

WHITNEY, W. MONTY
Educator, executive administrator. **Personal:** Born Sep 7, 1945, Philadelphia, PA; son of Bessie M Whitney and Wilbur M Whitney; married Vance Saunders; children: Erica, Michelle. **Educ:** Lycoming Coll, BA, 1967; Howard Univ, MS, Psych, 1969; Michigan State Univ, PhD, Psych, 1974. **Career:** Southern Univ, instr, 1969-71; Univ of Cincinnati, asst professor, 1974-76; Seven Hills Neighborhood Houses Inc, assoc dir. **Orgs:** Pres, Social Tech Systems, 1978-; natl pres, Assn of Black Psych, 1984-85; mem, TransAfrica, NAACP. **Home Addr:** 1478 Willis Mills Rd #SW, Atlanta, GA 30311. **Business Addr:** Director, Cau Head Start, 350 Autumn Ln, Atlanta, GA 30310.

WHITNEY, WILLIAM B.
President/CEO. **Educ:** Benedict College, BS biology, 1962; University of SC, chemistry, 1966-68; University of California, visiting scholar, 1970; Harvard University, exec management program, JFK school of business, 1981. **Career:** The Greenville

Urban League, Inc, pres/CEO, 1991-, executive director, 1973-79; The GUL Senior Housing Corp, pres/CEO, 1991-; The GUL Community Housing Corp, pres/CEO, 1995-; Whitney Corp of Columbia, pres, 1990-; Whitney Place, CEO, 1990-; Whitney & Whitney Development Corp, pres, broker in charge, 1990-92; State Board of Techinical & Comprehensive Education, special asst for employment & community affairs, 1986-91; State of SC Division of Employment & Training, exec asst to the governor, 1979-86; The Ford Foundation Fellowship, 1970-71. **Orgs:** Cities and Schools, bd of dirs; NAACP; Greenville Area Nations Bank, bd of dirs; South Carolina Commission for Poverty and Deprivation, bd chmn; Greenville YMCA, bd of dirs; Clemson University Board of Visitors, bd of dirs; Greenville Rotary Club; Palmetto Project, bd of dirs; No Name Group. **Military Serv:** October 1962-65. **Business Phone:** (864)244-3862.

WHITT, DWIGHT REGINALD
Friar, priest. **Personal:** Born Jul 17, 1949, Baltimore, MD. **Educ:** Loyola Coll, AB 1970; Pontifical Fac of Immaculate Conception, STB 1974, STL candidate. **Career:** Order of Friars Preachers, mem Friar; Dominicans; ordained Roman Cath priest, 1976; Spalding Coll, chaplain. **Orgs:** Mem Nat Black Cath Clergy Caucus.

WHITTAKER, SHARON ELAINE
Educational administrator. **Personal:** Born Sep 6, 1952, Gary, IN; daughter of Edith Elizabeth Whittaker and Robert Earl Whittaker. **Educ:** Howard University, BA, 1974, MEd, 1976; Illinois State University, PhD, 1983. **Career:** McKinley Tech High School, teacher, 1974-75; Cromwell Academy, teacher, counselor, 1975-77; Howard University, residence hall counselor, 1976-79; Illinois State University, residence life assistant director, 1979-84; Paine College, dean of students, 1984-90; Mary Holmes College, vice pres academic affairs 1990-95; Stillman College, vice pres of student affairs, 1995-. **Orgs:** National Association of Women in Education; National Association of Personnel Workers, president elect, 1993; Phi Beta Kappa; American Association of University Women; Business and Professional Women Inc; Alpha Kappa Alpha Sorority Inc. **Honors/Awds:** Howard University, Phi Beta Kappa George N Leighton Award, 1974; Illinois State, Human Relations Award, 1983. **Special Achievements:** Featured lecturer, presentor at over 150 colleges, universities, and various organizations regionally and nationally. **Business Addr:** Vice Pres for Student Affairs, Stillman College, PO Box 1430, Tuscaloosa, AL 35403, (205)366-9850.

WHITTAKER, TERRY MCKINLEY
Educational administrator. **Personal:** Born Mar 14, 1950, Newport News, VA; son of Blanche Sutton-Whittaker and Julius Whittaker; divorced. **Educ:** Univ of Wisconsin-Madison, BA 1972; Univ of Minnesota MA 1974. **Career:** Youth Counsel Bureau Brooklyn NY, juvenile delinquent officer 1973; Univ of Minnesota, pre-major advisor 1974-76, business sch coord student affairs 1976-79; INROADS, dir 1979-83; Univ of Delaware, dir minority engrg program 1983-85, dir undergrad advisement 1985-91, director Fortune 2000, 1991-, assistant dean, student special services, 1991-. **Orgs:** Mem Kappa Alpha Psi 1969-; mem Amer Soc of Training and Develop 1980-; bd dirs Forum to Advance Minorities in Engrg 1983-; mem Brandywine Professional Assoc 1984-; Natl Academic Advising Assoc 1985-; chmn Region A Natl Assoc of Minority Engrg Program Administrators 1986-; mem DE Soc of Professional Engrs Natl Engrs Week Festivities Comm 1986; mem Natl Assoc of Academic Affairs Administrators 1986. **Honors/Awds:** Ivan Williamson Award, Univ of Wisconsin 1972; Twin City Student Assembly Outstanding Contribution Award Univ of Minnesota 1979; Comm Serv Award Kappa Alpha Psi 1982; MN Guidance Assoc Award 1983; Black Alumni Achievement Award Univ of Minnesota 1983; Educ of the Year INROADS/Philadelphia Inc 1985. **Business Addr:** Director, Fortune 2000/Assistant Dean, Student Special Services, University of Delaware, College of Business and Economics, 228 Purnell Hall, Newark, DE 19716.

WHITTED, EARL, JR.
Attorney. **Personal:** Born Mar 26, 1931, Goldsboro, NC; married Ruby Weaver; children: Lynn, Stephen, Kenneth. **Educ:** NC Central U, BA LIB JD 1955. **Career:** Pvt Prac, atty 1970-; Criminal Law Legal Consult Fed Housing Prog, atty. **Orgs:** Mem Goldsboro Bd Aldermen 1964-; NAACP; Alpha Phi Alpha. **Honors/Awds:** Recip Alpha Phi Alpha Man of the Yr awd 1970. **Military Serv:** AUS 1956-58. **Business Addr:** 105 S John St, Goldsboro, NC 27530.

WHITTEN, BENJAMIN C.
Educator. **Personal:** Born Jul 25, 1923, Wilmington, DE; married Lucretia Bibbins; children: Benjamin, Jr. **Educ:** BS indl edn; PA State Coll, MS indl arts educ 1948; PA State U, EdD indl educ 1961; Rutgers U; Univ of MD. **Career:** Baltimore City Public School, asst supr Voc Educ 1968-; Cherry Hill Jr HS Balitmore, prin 1966-68; Granville Woods Gen Voc School, prin 1964-66; Edmondson HS, asst prin 1963-64; Carver Voc Tech HS, asst prin 1958-63, industriall arts teacher 1958; VA, training specialist 1946-67. **Orgs:** Bd dir MD Voc Assn chmn Voc Educ Com Counc of Great Cities Sch; chmn Am Voc Assn Task Force on Voc Educ in Urban Area 1972-; pres Nat Assn of Large City Dir of Voc Educ 1974-; mem Gov Manpower Adv Com Nat Adv Com Nat Cntr for Voc Tech Educ OH State U; Kappa Phi Kappa; Iota Lambda Sigma; Phi Delta Kappa; Pi Omega Chap of Oemga Psi Phi. **Military Serv:** AUS m/sgt 1943-46. **Business Addr:** Dept of Educ, Annex 23 Calvert Sts, Baltimore, MD 21218.

WHITTEN, CHARLES F.
Educational administrator, educator (semi-retired). **Personal:** Born Feb 2, 1922, Wilmington, DE; son of Emma Whitten and Tobias Whitten; married Eloise Culmer Whitten; children: Lisa, Wanda. **Educ:** Univ of PA, AB 1942; Meharry Med Coll, MD 1945; Univ of PA Graduate School 1954; Buffalo Children's Hospital, resd 1955, fellow 1956; Pediatric Hematology, Children's Hospital of Michigan, fellow 1957. **Career:** Detroit Receiving Hospital, dir pediatrics, 1956-62; Wayne State Univ, instructor, professor, 1962-70, dir clinical research center, 1962-73; associate dean of curricular affairs, 1976-92, professor of pediatrics 1976-92, dir comp Sickle Cell Center 1973-92, associate dean for special programs, 1992-. **Orgs:** Mem Amer Acad Pediatrics; Amer Fed Clinical Rsch; Amer Pediatric Soc; Amer Soc Clinical Nutrition; Amer Soc Hematology Mid-west Soc for Pediatric Rsch; Soc Pediatric Rsch; bd dir Gerber Prod Co 1972-92; com nutritional info Natl Acad Science; pres Natl Assn for Sickle Cell Disease Inc, 1972-92, president emeritus, 1992-; vice pres Amer Blood Commn; chmn Task Force Personal Health Serv Workshop MI Public Health Statute Revision Project; mem vice chmn Public Health Advisory Council State MI; advisory com Blood & Blood Pressure Resources Natl Heart Lung & Blood Inst; mem Ad Hoc Com S Hemoglobinpathies Natl Acad Science Mem Alpha Omega Alpha; Sigma Xi; Physician Yr Detroit Med Soc 1964 & 75; chmn Genetics Disease Advisory Comm State Health Dept; bd of dir Natl Bank of Detroit Bancorp 1988-93. **Honors/Awds:** Distinguished Achievement Award Detroit NAACP 1972; Franklin Lecturer in Human Relations Wayne State Univ 1972; Kennedy Lecturer Georgetown Univ Medical School 1973; Detroit Science Center Hall of Fame 1987; Distinguished Serv Award Wayne State Univ School of Medicine 1987; L M Weiner Award, Wayne State Univ School Med Alumni Assn, 1991; Distinguished Warrior Award, Detroit Urban League, 1990; Distinguished Professor of Pediatrics, Wayne State Univ, 1990; Distinguished Professor Pediatrics Emeritus, 1992; President's Cabinet Medallion, University of Detroit Mercy, 1993; Distinguished Svc Awd, National Medical Association, 1997. **Military Serv:** US Army Med Corp captain 1951-53; Served in Japan & Korea. **Business Addr:** Associate Dean for Special Programs, Wayne State University, School of Medicine, 540 E Canfield, Detroit, MI 48201.

WHITTEN, ELOISE CULMER
Social services executive. **Personal:** Born Apr 23, 1929, Philadelphia, PA; married Charles F Whitten; children: Lisa A, Wanda J Whitten-Shurney. **Educ:** Temple Univ, BA Political Science 1950; Univ of PA, MA Political Science, Public Admin 1951; Wayne State Univ, Univ of MI, Post-Masters Degree. **Career:** University of Pennsylvania Institute of State and Local Government, research assistant, 1951-52; Detroit Urban League, deputy director of housing department, 1963-64, deputy director of community affairs department, 1970-71; Wayne State University, executive secretary, 1966-67; Wayne County Community College, instructor, 1980; Shaw College, instructor, 1980. **Orgs:** International Planned Parenthood Federation, member of western hemisphere region board, 1990-; Michigan Department of Mental Health, member of multicultural advisory committee, 1985-; Michigan County Social Services Association, 1963-; Wayne State University, member of advisory committee to school of social work, 1993-; Family Preservation Communications Committee, 1990-; First Independence National Bank, board of directors, 1983-; Greater Wayne County Links, 1983-; Wayne County Social Services Board, 1974-; Detroit-Wayne County Community Mental Health Board, 1973-; United Community Services, 1990-; Planned Parenthood League of Detroit, 1959-; Delta Sigma Theta, 1949-; American Public Welfare Association; National Conference on Social Welfare; Michigan Association of Black Social Workers; Detroit Association of Black Human Services Administrators. **Honors/Awds:** National Organization of Black Business and Professional Women, Detroit Chapter, Sojourner Truth Award, 1980; Detroit Historical Society, Michigan's Outstanding Black Women, 1984; Dollars and Sense Magazine, National Business and Professional Women's Award for Social Activism, 1986; Michigan Youth Conference and Youth Advocacy Award, 1993; Black Caucus Foundation of Michigan, Partners in Community Services Award, 1993. **Special Achievements:** Organized the first area-wide conference on the problems of unwed pregnancy and single parents; helped found Homes for Black Children and changed adoption agency requirements to ease adoption of black children, 1967; developed the Lula Belle Stewart Center, one of the first centers in the country established to provide services for single, African American, low-income women, 1969.

WHITTEN, JAMIE L.
Congressman. **Personal:** Born Apr 18, 1910, Cascilla, MS; son of Nettie Early Whitten and Alymer Guy Whitten; married Rebecca Thompson, Jun 20, 1940; children: James Lloyd, Beverly Rebecca. **Educ:** University of Mississippi, 1926-31. **Career:** Public school principal, 1931; Mississippi House of Representatives, state representative, 1941; US House of Representatives, congressman, 1942-. **Orgs:** Phi Alpha Delta; Lions Clubs International; Beta Theta Pi; Masons. **Honors/Awds:** Author, Report on Russia, 1956; That We May Live, 1966. **Business Addr:** Representative, US House of Representatives, 2314 Rayburn, Washington, DC 20515-2401.

WHITTEN, THOMAS P.
Community center administrator. **Personal:** Born Sep 26, 1937, Anderson, SC; son of Hattie Brown Whitten and Benjamin J Whitten; married Ruthann DeAtley Whitten, Jul 26, 1964; children: Karen, Alexander, Bryan. **Educ:** Lincoln Univ, Jefferson City, MO, BA, 1963; Case Western Reserve Univ, Cleveland, OH, 1963-64. **Career:** Inner City Protestant Parish, Cleveland, OH, group unit leader, 1962; Chicago Renewal Soc, camp dir 1963; League Park Center, Cleveland, OH, dir youth employment 1963-64, dir of special interest groups 1963-65; Intl House of RI, exec dir, 1965-67; Harriet Tubman House, Boston, MA, 1967-68; Providence Human Relations Commission, field invest 1966-67, exec dir, 1970-73; Hall Neighborhood House, Bridgeport, CT, assoc exec dir, 1973-77; John Hope Settlement House, Providence, RI, executive director, 1977-. **Orgs:** Bd of dirs Decisions Inc, New Haven, CT, Lippitt Hill Tutorial, Wiggin Village Housing, 1979-, Providence Branch NAACP, West End Community Center, 1980-; Mount Hope Neighborhood Assoc; exec dir Assoc Comm, United Neighborhood Centers of America, Washington, DC; mem adv comm Central High School, Hope High School, WPRI-TV; City of Providence Affirmative Action Comm, 1975-; State of RI, Minority Adv Commission, Minority Advisory Comm, Congresswoman Claudine Schneider; Corporation mem Citizens bank, Volunteers in Action, Deputy Registrar State of RI, First Unitarian Church of Providence, RI; co-chairman, United Neighbors Centers of America, 1990-. **Honors/Awds:** Dean's List Lincoln Univ, Jefferson City, MO, 1960-61; Joseph G LeCount Medal, Providence Branch, NAACP, 1987; Agency Executive of the Year, Opportunities Industrialization Center, 1985; Citizenship Award, City of Providence, 1984. **Military Serv:** US Army, 1st Lt, 1956-59; Good Conduct Medal, Sharp Shooter, Unit Citation, 1958. **Home Addr:** 132 Colonial Rd, Providence, RI 02906. **Business Addr:** Executive Dir, John Hope Settlement House, 7 Burgess St, Providence, RI 02903.

WHITTINGTON, BERNARD M.
Professional football player. **Personal:** Born Aug 20, 1971, St Louis, MO; married Dana, Feb 14, 1997. **Educ:** Indiana, bachelor's degree in sports management. **Career:** Indianapolis Colts, defensive tackle, 1994-. **Business Addr:** Professional Football Player, Indianapolis Colts, PO Box 535000, Indianapolis, IN 46253, (317)297-2658.

WHITTINGTON, HARRISON DEWAYNE
Association executive. **Personal:** Born Jun 9, 1931, Crisfield, MD; son of Maryland Whittington; married Louise Holden. **Educ:** Morgan State Coll, BS, 1952; Pennsylvania State Univ, MEd, 1961; Nova Univ, EdD, 1980. **Career:** CG Woodson School Crisfield, teacher, 1954-62, principal, 1962-68; Somerset Co Bd Educ, coord, 1968-70, dir fed programs, 1968-70; Maryland State Dept Educ, coord human relations, 1974-81, asst superintendent, superintendent; University of Maryland, Eastern Shore, director of field experiences, currently. **Orgs:** Mem, NEA (state delegate 1968-70); chmn, Natl Hard Crab Derby Parade, 1971-73; mem, Teacher's Assn, Somerset Co; mem, Maryland State Teacher's Assn; mem, Maryland Assn Supvr & Curric Devel; mem, Maryland Council Adms Compensatory Educ; Assn School Business Officials; Phi Delta Kappa; Amer Assn Supvr & Admin; Maryland Assn Publicly Supported Con Educ; Somerset Co Admins Assn; Omega Psi Phi; mem, Maryland Adv Council; mem, Comm Coord Child Care; Maryland County Family Relations, Mason (32 deg); bd dir, Somerset Co Head Start; past chmn, bd dir, Somerset Co Soc Servs Agcy; bd dir, ARC; McCready Memorial Hospital; mem, Somerset Co Heart Assn; mem, Rec Commn; mem, C of C; pres, Intl Assn Basketball Officials; mem, Physical Fitness Comm; Comm Org for Progress. **Honors/Awds:** Rep Comm Leader of Amer Award, 1969; Omega City of Year, 1971; Outstanding Educ in Amer, 1973-74; Outstanding Black Comm Leader, 1974, 1976; Chancellors Award UNES, 1978; Omega Man of the Year, 1978; Afro-Amer of the Year, 1982; Outstanding Citizen; Comm Achievement Award, 1985. **Military Serv:** US Infantry capt 1952-54. **Business Addr:** Director, Field Experiences, University of Maryland, Eastern Shore, Princess Anne, MD 21853.

WHITWORTH, CLAUDIA ALEXANDER
Editor, publisher. **Personal:** Born Nov 7, 1927, Fayetteville, WV; married Clifton B Whitworth Jr (deceased); children: Robyn A Hale, Stanley R Hale, Eva J Crump, B Clifton Whitworth. **Educ:** Bluefield State Coll, attended; Natl Business Coll, attended. **Career:** Roanoke Tribune, linotype operator 1945; New York City, Cleveland, Columbus, Fayetteville Newspapers, linotype oper; Roanoke Tribune, owner 1971-. **Orgs:** Bd mem WBRA-TV; mem Amer Red Cross, Roanoke Fine Arts Museum, Mill Mtn Playhouse; bd of dir Roanoke Vocational Ed Found for Roanoke Public Schools; adv bd Salvation Army;

comm Roanoke Coll Constance J Hamlar Mem Fund Comm, League of Older Amers, Meals on Wheels; mem Baha'i Faith, Spiritual Assembly, life mem NAACP, YWCA. **Honors/Awds:** Outstanding Serv in News Media, 1 of 20 Civic Leaders selected from throughout the State of VA to accompany Gov Linwood Holton to Strategic Air Comm Hdq Offutt NE Roanoke Valley Bus League & Ladies Aux VFW #1444; Selected Leaders Pictorial Review Yesterday & Today 1976; Woman of the Year Omega Zeta Chap Zeta Phi Beta 1982. **Business Addr:** Editor & Publisher, Roanoke Tribune, 2318 Melrose Ave NW, Roanoke, VA 24017.

WHITWORTH, E. LEO, JR.
Dentist. **Personal:** Born in Kingston, Jamaica; son of Violet Whitworth and Eabert Whitworth; married Jennifer Ann Brown; children: Bianca, Lennox Valencia, Isaac. **Educ:** Northeastern Univ, BA 1971; Howard Univ, DDS 1976; Northeastern University, MBA, 1994. **Career:** St Anns Bay Hosp, dental surgeon 1976-77; Comprehensive Clinic Kingston Jamaica, dental surgeon 1976-77; Private Practice, dentist 1977-; Mattapan Health Clinic, dental dir 1977-79; Harvard Univ, clinical instructor operative dentistry 1981-. **Orgs:** Mem Amer & Natl Dental Assocs 1977-, Metropolitan District Dental Soc 1977-, MA Dental Soc 1977-; pres William B Price Unit of the Amer Cancer Soc 1978-80; mem Commonwealth Study Club 1979-, Acad of General Dentistry 1979-; chairperson MA Div Amer Societies Conf "Meeting the Challenge of Cancer in Black Americans" 1980-81; mem and completed post grad course Mid-Amer Orthodontic Soc 1983; mem Intl Orthodontic Org 1986; mem bd of dirs William B Price Unit Amer Cancer Soc; mem Congressional Adv Bd; life mem NAACP; Northeastern University, corporate bd, 1994; board of directors, Mattapan Community Dev Corp, 1996. **Honors/Awds:** Martin Luther King, Community Awd, 1994. **Business Addr:** Clin Instr for Oper Dentistry, Harvard University, 542 River St, Mattapan, MA 02126.

WHYTE, GARRETT
Artist, educator. **Personal:** Born Sep 5, 1915, Mt Sterling, KY; married Horrezelle E. **Educ:** NC A&T State Univ, BS Art Ed 1939; School of the Art Inst Chicago IL, Grad Study 1950-51. **Career:** Chicago Defender, artist 1947-51; Chicago Agency, art dir 1951-56; Chicago Dunbar Voc HS, art teacher 1956-72; Chicago City Coll System, art prof 1972-80 retired. **Orgs:** Bd mem Southside Comm Art Ctr 1962-85, Natl Conf of Artists, DuSable Mus of Afri-Amer Hist. **Honors/Awds:** Creator of cartoon comic "Mr Jim Crow" Chicago Defender, one of the 1st civil rights graphic satires 1946-51; 2 pg color reprod of painting Midwest Mag Chgo Sun-Times 1965; art work reprod Chicago Sun-Times Mag "Mid-West", Glory Forever 1974; cover story Chicago Defender Mag "Accent" 1974; slides & lecture on paintings at Art Inst of Chicago "The Art of Garrett Whyte" 1975; Amer Fed of Teachers Mag Chang Ed "Children of the Ghetto" 1967; art gallery mag work reprod 1968; Black Dimension in Contemp Amer Art 1971; Black Power in the Arts 1970; art exhibit Felician Coll 1975; painting Wolfson Collection NY Life Ins 1974; winner of Grand Awd for Art Teacher IL Reg Vocational Exhibit 1970-72. **Military Serv:** AUS sgt 1942-45. **Home Addr:** 8648 Kenwood, Chicago, IL 60619.

WICKER, HENRY SINDOS
Physician. **Personal:** Born Aug 8, 1928, New Orleans, LA; married Geralyn; children: Henry Jr, Stephen. **Educ:** Xavier U, BS 1948; Howard U, MD 1953. **Career:** St Elizabeth's Hosp, chf dept of ophthalgy; Am Bd of Ophthalgy, dipl; Am Acad of Ophthalgy, fellow; Howard U, asst prof; George Washington U, asst prof. **Orgs:** Mem Medico-chirurgical Soc; mem Med Soc of DC; mem Nat Med Assn; mem Amer Med Assn; bd dir Nat Conf of Christians & Jews 1971-75; bd of regents Ascension Acad 1970-74; bd dir Mater Dei Sch 1970-74; mem Common Cause; Alpha Phi Alpha frat. **Military Serv:** USAF capt 1957-60; USAFR maj 1960-75.

WICKHAM, DEWAYNE
Journalist. **Personal:** Born Jul 22, 1946, Baltimore, MD; son of DeSylvia Chase Wickham and John T Wickham; married Wanda Nadine Persons, Jun 1987; children: Vanessa Baker, Zenita Wickham, MiKella Nicole Wickham. **Educ:** Community Coll of Baltimore, 1970-72; Univ of MD, BSJ 1974, Certificate in Afro-Amer Studies 1974; Univ of Baltimore, MPA, 1982. **Career:** Baltimore Evening Sun, MD, reporter intern 1972-73; Richmond Times-Dispatch, VA, copy editing intern 1973; US News & World Report, Washington DC, Capitol Hill corresp 1974-75; Baltimore Sun, MD, reporter 1975-78; WBAL-TV, Baltimore, MD, talk show host 1976-89; Gannett News Service, Arlington, VA, columnist 1985-; USA Today, columnist, 1988-. **Orgs:** Life mem, NAACP; mem, Advisory Bd, Multicultural Management Prog of Univ of MO Journ School 1986-92; pres, Natl Assn of Black Journalists 1987-89; mem, Alumni Assn Board of Univ of Baltimore 1989-90; Board of Visitors, Howard University School of Journalism, chairman, 1992-. **Honors/Awds:** Author: Fire at Will, published by USA Today Books; Author: Woodholme, published by Farrar, Straus & Giroux, 1995; Fire at Will, published by USA Today Books, 1989. **Special Achievements:** Judge Not, United Image Entertainment, screenwriter, 1992. **Military Serv:** US Air Force, sgt, 1964-68; Vietnam Service Medal, Good Conduct Medal. **Business Addr:** Columnist, Gannett News Service/USA Today, 1000 Wilson Blvd, 10th Floor, Arlington, VA 22209.

WICKLIFF, ALOYSIUS M., SR.
Attorney. **Personal:** Born Oct 11, 1921, Liberty, TX; married Mary E Prilliman; children: 4. **Educ:** American University, BS; Cath University of America, LLB 1949. **Career:** TX So University, asso prof, 1995-58; pvt pract, atty, currently. **Orgs:** Mem Knights of Peter Claver; Eliza Johnson Home for Aged Negros; TX So Finance Corp; TX Finance & Invest Co; Comm Chapel Funeral Home; Comm Chapel Funeral Benefit Assn; MESBIC pres Harris Co Cncl of Orgn 1975, 76; Bus & Professional Men's Club 1973. **Honors/Awds:** Comm Serv Awd 1967; campaign mgr Barbara Jordan for US Congress. **Military Serv:** AUS 372nd infantry WW II. **Business Addr:** 4720 Dowling, Houston, TX 77004.

WICKWARE, DAMON
Automobile dealer. **Career:** Bayview Ford Inc, CEO, currently. **Special Achievements:** Company is ranked #92 on Black Enterprise's list of Top 100 Auto Dealers, 1994. **Business Addr:** CEO, Bayview Ford Inc, 27180 Hwy 98, Daphne, AL 36526, (205)626-7777.

WIDEMAN, JAMILA
Professional basketball player. **Personal:** Born in Amherst, MA; daughter of John Edgar Wideman. **Educ:** Stanford Univ, 1997. **Career:** Los Angeles Sparks, basketball player, 1997-. **Special Achievements:** AP All-America, honorable mention, 1996. **Business Addr:** Professional Basketball Player, Los Angeles Sparks, 3900 W Manchester Blvd, Inglewood, CA 90306, 800-978-9622.

WIDEMAN, JOHN EDGAR
Author, educator. **Personal:** Born Jun 14, 1941, Washington, DC; married Judith Goldman; children: Daniel, Jacob, Jamila Ann. **Educ:** Univ of PA, BA 1963; Oxford Univ, BPhil 1966. **Career:** Howard Univ, instr 1965; Univ of PA, instr 1966-74, dir Afro-Amer studies program, 1971-73, assistant basketball coach, 1968-72; Univ of Wyoming, Laramie, WY, prof of English, 1975-86; Univ of Massachusetts, Amherst Campus, Amherst, MA, prof of English, 1986-. **Orgs:** State Dept Lecture Tour-Europe Near East 1976; Phi Beta Kappa Assoc Lectr 1976; novelist visiting writer/lecturer at various campuses across country; mem bd dir Amer Assn of Rhodes Scholars; state & natl selection comm Rhodes Competition; Natl Humanities Faculty; consult secondary schs across country 1968-. **Honors/Awds:** Rhodes Scholar, Oxford England, 1963-66; Thouron Fellow Oxford 1963-66; Philadelphia Big Five Basketball Hall of Fame 1974; Young Humanist Fellowship 1975-; PEN/Faulkner Award for fiction, 1984, 1991; American Book Award; elected to American Academy of Arts & Sciences, 1992. **Special Achievements:** Author: A Glance Away, 1967, Hurry Home, 1970, The Lynchers, 1973, Hiding Place, 1981, Brothers and Keepers, 1984, Reuben, 1987, Sent For You Yesterday, 1983; Fever, short stories, 1989, Philadelphia Fire, novel, The Stories of John Edgar Wideman, stories, 1992, The Homewood Books, 1992, Fatheralong: A Meditation on Fathers and Sons, Race and Society, 1994. **Business Addr:** Prof of English, Univ of Massachusetts, Amherst Campus, Bartlett Hall, Amherst, MA 01003.

WIDENER, WARREN HAMILTON
Government official. **Personal:** Born Mar 25, 1938, Oroville, CA; son of Ruby Lee Epperson Brewer and Arnold Widener; married Mary Lee Thomas; children: Warren Jr, Michael, Stephen. **Educ:** Univ of California Berkeley, AB, 1960; Boalt Hall, Univ of California, JSD, 1967. **Career:** Real Estate Safeway Stores, atty 1968-70; Berkeley, CA, cnclman 1969-71; Housing & Econ Devel Law Proj Univ of CA, atty 1970-72; Berkeley, CA, mayor, 1971-79; CA NHS Found, pres 1977-; Urban Housing Inst, pres 1979-; Alameda County Supervisor, 1989-92. **Orgs:** Bd of dir Golden West Fin Corp 1980-94; bd of dir World Svngs & Loan Assn 1980-94; pres Natl Black Caucus of Local Elected Officials 1975; bd of dir, The Col Prep School 1984; bd of dir Berkeley Repertory Theatre 1984; bd dir E Oakland Youth Dev Ctr 1984. **Honors/Awds:** Chm Mayors Del to Hungary 1978; Dist Citizen Bay Area Urban League 1975. **Military Serv:** USAF capt 4 yrs. **Home Addr:** 420 Wildwood Ave, Piedmont, CA 94611.

WIEGAND-MOSS, RICHARD CLIFTON, JR.
Cable television company executive. **Personal:** Born Jul 17, 1947, Cleveland, OH; son of Ethel Carey Moss and Richard Clifton Moss, Sr; married Sara Wiegand-Moss; children: Chandra, Jason, Nicole, Adam Elliott, Jordan Sinclair. **Educ:** Borromeo Seminary Coll, BA 1970; Cleveland State Univ, Teaching Certificate 1973; John Carroll Univ, MA currently; AMA, Understanding the Computer 1985; Wright State Univ, Fundamentals of Mktg 1985; Business Week Seminar, Writing a Winning Business Plan 1985, Pricing for Profit 1986. **Career:** Medina County Youth Svcs, exec dir 1977-79; Dept of Justice, legislative lobbyist 1979-82; Continental Cablevision, vice pres & dist mgr 1982-. **Orgs:** OH Cable TV Assoc; regional grassroot organizer Natl Cable TV Assn; bd of trustee mem OH Youth Advocacy Program Inc. **Military Serv:** AUS E-4 1970-77; Graduated 4th Highest in Class 1970.

WIGFALL, SAMUEL E.
Financial administrator. **Personal:** Born May 4, 1946, Jacksonville, NC; married Mildred Z Jones; children: Tara, Darian. **Educ:** NC A&T State Univ, BS Accounting 1969; Univ of Louisville, Cost Acctg Sys 1973; Governor's State Univ IL, MBA work 1978; NY Univ, Capital Inv Acq Sem 1982. **Career:** Brown & Williamson Tobacco Co, financial accountant 1969-73; Johnson & Johnson Corp, sr cost accountant 1973-77; Brunswick Corp, sr financial analy 1977-79; Sherwood Medical Co, Div Fin Plng & Budget Mgr 1979-83, natl dealer comm mgr 1983-. **Orgs:** Scout master Broadway Temple Scout Troop 1971-72; dir B&W Employee's Credit Union 1972; advisor Jr Achievement KY 1972; pres sr choir Broadway Temple AME Zion Church 1972, 1973; vice pres Richmond Park IL Jaycees 1975; dir Brunswick Employees Credit Union 1976. **Honors/Awds:** Varsity football scholarship NC A&T State Univ 1965-69; parts control proc manual Johnson & Johnson Corp 1972; youth motivation prog Chicago Assn of Commerce & Ind 1973-74; pub annual budget manual Brunswick Corp 1978; Speaking of People Ebony Magazine 1984. **Home Addr:** 1446 Chandellay Dr, St Louis, MO 63146. **Business Addr:** Natl Dealer Comm Manager, Sherwood Medical Co, 1831 Olive St, St Louis, MO 63103.

WIGGINS, CHARLES A.
Physician. **Personal:** Born Aug 17, 1943, Pennington Gap, VA; son of Rebecca McCarrol and Charlie Wiggins. **Educ:** Morristown Coll, AA 1963; Fisk Univ, BA 1965; Meharry Medical Coll, MD 1969. **Career:** Charles A Wiggins MD, med dir; Crestview Nursing Home, med dir; Nashville Manor, med dir; Meharry/Hubbard Hosp Skilled Nursing Facility, med dir. **Orgs:** Mem Natl Medical Assn, RF Boyd Medical Scis, Southern Medical Assn, NY Acad of Sci, Amer Geriatrics Soc, TN Long Term Physician Soc. **Military Serv:** AUS Medical Corp major 2 yrs. **Business Addr:** Medical Dir, Meharry Hubbard Hosp, 1205 8th Ave So, Nashville, TN 37204.

WIGGINS, DAPHNE CORDELIA
Clergywoman. **Personal:** Born Oct 21, 1960, Newark, NJ; daughter of Thelma G. Wiggins and Arthur Lee Wiggins, Sr. **Educ:** Eastern Coll, BA 1982; Eastern Baptist Theological Seminary, MDiv 1985. **Career:** Eastern Coll, resident asst 1981-82; Second Baptist Church Wayne PA, assoc minister 1981-84; Yeadon Presbyterian Church, pastoral asst 1983; Saints Memorial Baptist Church Bryn Mawr PA, dir of youth ministries 1984-85; Union Baptist Church Pawtucket RI, assoc minister 1985-; Brown Univ, assoc chaplain 1985-; interim pastor Union Baptist Church 1989-90. **Orgs:** Natl Assn of Campus and Univ Chaplains 1985-; univ rep Soc Organized Against Racism 1985-; bd mem Dorcas Place 1986-88; bd of advisors One Church One Child Adoption Program 1987-; vice pres Society Organized Against Racism in New England 1989-91; Ministers Alliance of RI, vice pres 1987-88, treasurer 1990-; executive board, Interfaith Call for Racial Justice, 1990-; executive board, Black United Methodists and Related Ministries in Higher Education, 1990-. **Honors/Awds:** Preaching license Calvary Baptist Church East Orange NJ 1980; ordination Second Baptist Church Wayne PA 1983; Recognition of Ordination American Baptist Churches of R.I. 1987. **Home Addr:** 212 Cottage St, Apt 1, Pawtucket, RI 02860. **Business Addr:** Associate Chaplain, Brown University, Box 1931, Providence, RI 02912.

WIGGINS, EDITH MAYFIELD
Educational administrator. **Personal:** Born Mar 18, 1942, Greensboro, NC; children: Balaam, David. **Educ:** Univ of NC Greensboro, BA 1962, MSW 1962-64. **Career:** NC Memorial Hospital, pediatric clinical social worker 1964-67; Dept of Defense Middle School, Clark Air Force Base Phillipines, guidance counselor 1970-71; Inter Ch Council for Social Serv, social worker 1971-72; YMCA, YWCA, Univ of NC, dir campus 1972-; Univ of NC, asst vice chancellor and assoc dean of student affairs 1981-. **Orgs:** Mem Natl Assn Social Workers; past mem Chapel Hill Human Relation Comm Order of the Valkyries Univ of NC 1976; Order of the Golden Fleece Univ of NC 1976; Acad of Cert Social Workers Natl Assn Social Workers 1977-; bd of educ mem Chapel Hill-Carrboro 1979-. **Business Addr:** Asst V Chanc & Associate Dean, Univ of NC, Chapel Hill, NC 27514.

WIGGINS, JOSEPH L.
Educator. **Personal:** Born Feb 13, 1944, Norfolk, VA. **Educ:** State Coll, BA 1966; Old Dominion U, MS 1970, pursuing cert of adv study educ leadership serv & rsrch; Univ of NC, further study 1967. **Career:** Shelton Park Elem School VA Beach, prin 1974-; VA Beach, admin aide to supt admin coordinator of standards of quality & prog 1972-74, asst elem school prin; Norfolk City Public Schools, teacher; Norfolk State Coll, asst instr govt. **Orgs:** Mem Sigma Rho Sigma; life mem Kappa Alpha Psi Frat Inc; life mem Nat Educ Assn; VA Assn of Sch Execs; VA Educ Assn; VA Bch Educ Assn; trustee St Thomas AME Zion Ch Norfolk. **Honors/Awds:** Recip Academic Achvmt Awd Epsilon Zeta Chap Kappa Alpha Psi 1965; Active Chap Achvmt Awd Estrn Province Counc Kappa Alpha Psi 1965; Alumni Serv to theFrat Awd Estrn Province Counc Kappa Alpha Psi 1969; ldrs of Am Elem Educ Citation 1971; Achvmt in Educ Awd Estrn Province Counc Kappa Alpha Psi 1973; Outstng Young Men of Am 1974, 75; Achvmt Awd for Frat Serv Nor-

folk Alumni Chap Kappa Alpha Psi 1974. **Business Addr:** Staff Assistant, Virginia Bch City Sch Board, 2512 George Mason Dr, Virginia Beach, VA 23456.

WIGGINS, LESLIE
Business executive. **Personal:** Born Aug 18, 1936, Enfield, NC; married Pauline Faulkner. **Educ:** Lincoln U. **Career:** Delaware Trust Co, asst vice pres 1971-, various adv pos since 1955. **Orgs:** Mem bd Children's Home; Acct Rep United Way; treas bd mem Peoples Settelment Assn; vice pres Wilmington Housing Corp; Urban Coalition of Gr Wilmington; bd mem Assn Gr Wilmington Neighborhood Ctrs; mem Union Bapt Ch. **Honors/Awds:** Recip Minority Achiever of Wilmington Awd YMCA 1974. **Business Addr:** Delaware Trust Co, 900 Market St, Wilmington, DE 19899.

WIGGINS, LILLIAN COOPER
Journalist, elected official. **Personal:** Born Jun 26, 1932, Cincinnati, OH; daughter of Fannie Girdy Cooper and Ben Cooper (deceased); married Adolphus Wiggins (died 1989); children: Karen, Michael. **Educ:** Attended Cortex Peters Business Sch, 1953; attended Howard Univ, Berlitz Sch of Language Foreign Serv Inst & Inservice Training Sch, USMC, Univ of Puerto Rico 1957. **Career:** USMC, property & supply office 1950; Washington DC, Ghana Embassy 1960-65; Ghana Govt, press & info officer; Washington Afro-Amer Newspaper, journalist past editor; Lil & Face Place, co-owner; Advisory Neighborhood Commission, commissioner, currently. **Orgs:** Past pres DC Tots & Teens; pub relations dir Natl Tots & Teens; talk show hostess ''From the Desk of Lil'' sta WHUR; former membership chmn Capitol Press Club; former mem State Dept Corres Assn; mem Women in Journalism; Media Women; appt DC Commn on Status of Women; roving chair Orgn of Black Activist Women; vice pres Cornelius Wiggins Intl Black Owned Bus; appt polit action chairperson DC Br NAACP; founder DC Survival Conf; mem Eagles, Black Entrepreneurs; bd mem United Black Fund; Sigma Delta Chi; vice chair DC Charitable Games Control Bd; charter bd mem, DC Lottery, 1981-83. **Honors/Awds:** Journalist of the Yr 1965; 1st Prize Natl Publishers Convention 1974. **Military Serv:** USMCR 1957. **Business Addr:** Commissioner, Advisory Neighborhood Commission, 4040 8th St, NW, Washington, DC 20011.

WIGGINS, MITCHELL
Professional basketball player. **Personal:** Born Sep 28, 1959, Lenoir County, NC. **Educ:** Clemson Univ; FL State Univ. **Career:** Chicago Bulls, 1983-84, Houston Rockets, 1985-87, 1990; CBA, 1988. **Orgs:** US team in 1982 World Games in Columbia. **Honors/Awds:** 2nd among NBA rookies; led Chicago in steals 25 times; second team All-Junior Coll honors at Truett-McConnell in GA.

WIGGINS, PAUL R.
Banker. **Personal:** Born May 19, 1955, Sarasota, FL; son of Adele Wiggins and Paul Wiggins; married Cassandra F Robinson, Jul 21, 1984; children: Paula R, Chelsea R. **Educ:** Florida Memorial College, BS, business administration, accounting, 1981. **Career:** SunBank of Tampa Bay, vice pres/credit department mgr, currently. **Orgs:** National Association of Urban Bankers, president, 1993-94; Tampa Bay Male Club, chairman, 1989-; Florida Memorial College Board of Trustees, finance committee, 1992-; Leadership Tampa Alumni, 1988-; Tampa Bay Urban Bankers Association, board member, 1986-; Omega Psi Phi, 1979-. **Military Serv:** US Army, E-4 specialist, 1973-76; Graduate, Non-Commissioned Officers Academy. **Business Addr:** VP/Credit Department Mgr, SunBank of Tampa Bay, PO Box 3303, Tampa, FL 33601-3303, (813)224-2616.

WIGGINS, WILLIAM H., JR.
Educator. **Personal:** Born May 30, 1934, Port Allen, LA; married Janice Louise Slaughter; children: Wesley Howard, Mary Ellyn. **Educ:** OH Wesleyan U, BA 1956; Phillips' Sch of Theol, BD 1961; Louisville Prebyn Theol Sem, MTh 1965; IN U, PhD 1974. **Career:** IN Univ, asso prof 1980-, asst prof 1974-79, grad teaching asst & lecturer 1969-73; TX Coll, dir rel life 1965-69; Freeman Chapel CME Church, pastor 1962-65; Lane Coll, prof 1961-62. **Orgs:** Fellow of the Folklore Inst IN U; founder dir Afro-Am Folk Archive IN U; so reg dir IN Chap Assn for the Study of Afro-Am Life & History; mem Smithsonian Inst African Diaspora Adv Gr Com; exec bd Hoosier Folklore Soc; ed bd The Jour of the Folklore Inst; prestr Am Folklife Fest 1975-76; field wk Smithsonian Inst 1975-76; pres Assn of African -Am Folklorists Minister Christian Meth Epis Ch; mem Am Folklore Soc; Nat Cncl for Blk Studies; Assn for the Study of Afro-Am Life & History; Assn of African & African-Am Folklorists; Hoosier Folklore Soc; Pop Cult Assn;Num Grants. **Honors/Awds:** Num grants & flwhps; num publ; doc film ''In the Rapture'' anthologized wks appear in num publ & jour. **Business Addr:** Dept of Folklore, Indiana University at Bloomington, Bloomington, IN 47401.

WIGGS, JONATHAN LOUIS
Photographer. **Personal:** Born Sep 20, 1952, New Haven, CT; son of Alma Varella and Louis Wiggs. **Educ:** SUNY at Oswego, BA, 1980; Tsukuba University, Imbaraki, Japan, 1978. **Career:** Raleigh News and Observer, staff photographer, 1983-87; St Petersburg Times, staff photographer, 1987-90; Boston Globe, staff photographer, 1990-. **Orgs:** National Press Photographers Association, 1980-; Boston Press Photographers Association, 1982. **Military Serv:** US Navy, Petty Officer, 3rd Class, 1971-74; Naval Hospital Corpsman, National Defense Medal. **Business Addr:** News Photographer, Boston Globe, 135 Morrissey Blvd, Boston, MA 02107.

WILBEKIN, HARVEY E.
Government official (retired), attorney. **Personal:** Born Jun 18, 1926, Christiansted, St Croix, Virgin Islands of the United States; son of Elizabeth Barry Wilbekin (deceased) and Jeremiah Wilbekin (deceased); married Cleota Proctor Wilbekin, Jun 28, 1953; children: Erik J, Emil K. **Educ:** Hampton University, BS, 1951; Polytechnic Institute of Brooklyn, 1952-53; University of Cincinnati, grad school, 1957-61; Salmon P Chase College of Law, JD, 1970. **Career:** US Dept of Interior, Gvt of the Virgin Islands, jr draftsman, 1949; City of New York, Dept of Public Works, junior civil engineer, 1951-54; City of Cincinnati, structural design engineer, 1954-64, Building Inspection Department, engineer and superv engineer, 1964-82, commissioner of licenses, 1982-87, director, commissioner of buildings, 1987-92; self-employed (part-time), professional engineer, 1957-64; self-employed part-time, attorney at law, 1972-92, full-time, 1992-. **Orgs:** Ohio Bldg Officials Association, president, 1982-83; Southwestern Ohio Bldg Officials Association, founding president, 1977-79; Bldg Officials and Code Administrators, Inc, board of directors, 1984-88; Council of American Building Officials, board of directors, 1984-88; Cincinnati Bar Association, bd of trustes, 1989-; Black Lawyers Association of Cincinnati, treasurer, 1976-94; CINCO Federal Credit Union, chairman, board of directors, 1978-82, treasurer, 1982-. **Honors/Awds:** Hampton University, Dean's Honor Roll, 1949; Salmon P Chase College of Law, Dean's Honor Roll, 1970; Chase College of Law, junior class secretary, senior class treasurer, 1968-70; Ohio State Board Examination for Regulation of Professional Engineer, placed first, 1956; Bldg Officials & Code Administrators, Inc. Albert H Baun Award, 1991, Honorary Mem Award, 1992; The Amer Society for Public Admin, Admin of the Year Award, 1991; Black Lawyers Assn of Cincinnati, Recognition of Years of Service Award, 1994; publications: ''How You Can Contribute to the Code Change Process,'' ''OBOA's Challenges to 1982 Proposed Changes,'' Code News, May/June 1982. **Home Addr:** 6142 Hedge Ave, Cincinnati, OH 45213. **Business Addr:** Attorney at Law, 30 E Central Pkwy, Suite 1200, American Bldg, Cincinnati, OH 45202.

WILBER, IDA BELINDA
Correctional administrator. **Personal:** Born Feb 8, 1956, Jonesborough, LA; daughter of Rosie B Johnson and Clayton Johnson. **Educ:** Northern Arizona University, BS, political science, 1978; University of Arizona, College of Law, 1978-79; Northern Arizona University, MA, ed & counseling, 1991. **Career:** Arizona Department of Corrections, New Down Center for Girls, chief of security, 1985-86, New Down Juvenile Inst, program manager, 1986-88, Desert Valley, program administrator, 1988-90; Arizona Department Juvenile Corrections, transition administrator, 1990, training manager community services, 1990-91, Catalina Juvenile Institution, superintendent, 1991-92; Arizona State Department Youth Treatment & Rehab, assistant to chief of child care, 1992-. **Orgs:** National Association Blacks in Criminal Justice, publicity chair, 1991-, president, 1989-91, conference chair, 1987, national corporate chair, 1992; United Way, impact spending committee, 1991; Arizona Black Town Hall, board of directors, research & reports; American Correctional Association; Planned Parenthood of Southern Arizona, board of directors; United Negro College Fund, audience participation chair; Zeta Phi Beta, Omicron Zeta Zeta Chapter, state publicity chairman & graduate advisor. **Honors/Awds:** Department Juvenile Corrections, Professionalism Award, 1990; Northern Arizona University, Outstanding Senior Woman, 1978, President's Award, 1978, Mortar Board, 1977-78. **Special Achievements:** Author: final Report of Arizona Black Town Hall, Profile & Challenges of Black Policy Makers in Arizona, 1992; Profile & Status of Black Males in Arizona, 1991; Black Adolescents & the Juvenile Justice System in Arizona, 1990. **Business Addr:** Assistant to Chief of Child Care, Arizona Department of Youth Treatment & Rehabilitation, 1645 W Adams, Ste 331, Phoenix, AZ 85007, (602)869-9050.

WILBER, MARGIE ROBINSON
Government official, association executive. **Personal:** Born in Florence, SC. **Educ:** SC State, AB 1942; Am U, grad stdt 1955; George Wash U, 1958; Dept of Agr Grad Sch, 1966. **Career:** Washington, state dept 1945-83, supervisory editor publ div 1962-83; Neighbd Adv Comm, elec commr 1976; Marion, SC, tchr 1942-44; The Crime Stoppers Club Inc, fdr exec dir. **Orgs:** Mem bd of dirs DC Women's Commn for Crime Prevention; mem Woman's Nat Dem Club; WA Urban League; NAACP; DC Fedn of Bus Professional Women's Club; Delta Sigma Theta Sor. **Honors/Awds:** Comm Serv Awd Boy's Club of Gr WA 1968; Comm Serv Awd Sigma Gamma Rho Sor 1971; Action Fed Employee Disting Vol 1973; Comm Serv Awd Iota Chi Lambda 1973; Comm Serv Awd United Nation's Day (Human Rights) 1973; Outst Citizen Capitol Hill Restoration Soc 1974; Wash Vol Act Awd 1977; composer DC-TRIBUTE to Nation's Capital 1971; Future Am; Safe for the Children 1972; Let's Get Together, 1980; Senate Citation, Congressional Record, 1969; US Presidential Citation, 1970; honored by President Reagan, Rose Garden, 1985; ''Margie Wilber Day,'' Mayor, DC, 1987; Dedicated Community Service, DC Metropolitan Police Department, 1988; Community Leader of the Year, Kiwanis Club, 1996; Woman of the Year, Shiloh Baptist Church, Washington, DC, 1997; Allstate Insurance Co. ''From Whence We Came'' Award. **Special Achievements:** Appeared as contestant in the national television program ''To Tell the Truth,'' ''The Real Margie Wilbur,'' 1968; testimony before the Select Committee on Crime, House of Representatives, 1970.

WILBON, JOAN MARIE
Attorney. **Personal:** Born Aug 21, 1949, Washington, DC; daughter of Louise Wilbon and Addison Wilbon. **Educ:** Adelphi Univ Garden City NY, attended; New York Univ, BA (honors) 1971; George Washington Univ Law School Washington DC, JD 1974. **Career:** Dept of Labor Office of Solicitor, law clerk 1974; Equal Employment Oppor Comm, trial atty 1974-76; Howard Univ Sch of Law, supervising atty 1976; Natl Bar Assn EEO Div, dep dir 1976-78; Dept of Justice, trial attorney 1978-82; Joan M Wilbon & Assocs, attorney 1982-. **Orgs:** Mem Amer, DC, Women's, Washington Bar Assns; mem PA Bar Assn; mem bd of dirs Intergenerational Theater Co. **Honors/Awds:** Presidential Scholar Adelphi Univ 1967; Martin Luther King Scholar NY Univ 1969-71; Fed Employee Litigation Natl Bar Law Journal 1978. **Business Phone:** (202)737-7458.

WILBORN, LETTA GRACE SMITH
Educator. **Personal:** Born May 12, 1936, Magnolia, AR; daughter of Bulah Wilson Smith and Henry Smith; married Leonard B Wilborn; children: Leonardo, Leilani. **Educ:** Univ of AR Pine Bluff, BA (Cum Laude) 1958; CA State Univ Los Angeles, MA 1969; Nova Southeastern Univ, Ft Lauderdale, FL, EdD, 1994. **Career:** Simmons High School, teacher 1958-59; Rowland Unified School District, teacher 1963-. **Orgs:** Pres Ward AME Community Music School 1975-; mem Assoc for the Study of Afro-Amer Life and History 1984-; sec Blair Hills Neighborhood Assoc 1986-; chairperson Oratorical Contest/OASC Los Angeles Branch; mem Rowland Educ Assoc, CA Teachers Assoc, Natl Educ Assoc; mem Sigma Gamma Rho Sor Inc, Summit Climbers Intl Training in Communications, NAACP; president, Lay Organization, Ward AME Church, 1989-; Ward AME Church, trustee; Southern California Conference Lay Organization, asst recording secretary. **Honors/Awds:** Service Awd Our Authors Study Club/ASALH 1986; Quality of Life Awd Sigma Sigma Chap Sigma Gamma Rho Sor 1986. **Home Addr:** 5934 Blairstone Dr, Culver City, CA 90232.

WILBURN, ISAAC EARPHETTE
Educational administrator. **Personal:** Born Sep 11, 1932, Forrest City, AR; married Birdie Mae; children: Isaac E III, Berlinda, Michael E, Benjamin D, Loretta M, Darrell. **Educ:** Dunbar Jr Coll, 1953; Philander Smith Coll, BS 1955; TN State Univ Nashville, MEd 1969. **Career:** Dist 5 Admin Assn, sec/treas 1965-70; Crowley Ridge Fed Credit Union, treas 1978-83; Forrest City Fed Housing, vice chmn 1978-95; East AR Comm Coll, treasurer, trustee bd. **Orgs:** Chmn/trustee Beth Salem MB Church 1980-95; finan sec Beth Salem MB Church 1965-95. **Honors/Awds:** Forrest City Public Housing, VP, 20 year Award; Forrest City Public Schools, 20 Year Award, 30 Year Award, 35 Year Award; Board of Trustees, 20 Year Award. **Home Addr:** 822 East Garland Ave, Forrest City, AR 72335.

WILBURN, VICTOR H.
Architect. **Personal:** Born Jan 23, 1931, Omaha, NE; son of Katherine Wilburn and Victor Wilburn; married Sally (divorced); children: Kim, Diane, Susan, Leslie, Victor, Jeff. **Educ:** Univ Chicago, 1954; Harvard Univ, MArch 1959. **Career:** Victor Wilburn Assoc Architects & Managers, owner 1962-; Urban Devel Group Inc, pres 1970-; University of Virginia and Howard University, professor. **Orgs:** Mem Am Inst Architect; Amer Inst of Planners. **Business Addr:** Owner, Victor Wilburn Architects, PC, 2 Wisconsin Circle, Chevy Chase, MD 20815.

WILCHER, SHIRLEY J.
Government official. **Personal:** Born Jul 28, 1951, Erie, PA; daughter of James S Wilcher and Jeanne (Evans) Cheatham. **Educ:** Mount Holyoke College, AB cum laude, 1973; New School for Social Research, MA, 1976; Harvard Law School, 1979. **Career:** Proskauer Rose Goetz and Mendelsohn, associate, 1979-80; National Women's Law Center, staff attorney, 1980-85; US House of Representatives Committee on Education and Labor, associate counsel, 1985-90; National Association of Independent Colleges and Universities, general counsel and director for state relations, 1990-94; Office of Federal Contract Compliance Programs, deputy assistant secretary, 1994-. **Orgs:** ABA; National Bar Association; National Conference of Black Lawyers. **Honors/Awds:** Special Projects editor, Harvard Civil Rights, Civil Liberties Law, Harvard Law School, 1979. **Special Achievements:** Certificate Pratique de Langue Francaise, Paris, 1972; Several publications for the committee on Education and labor, Co-authored, 1986-89. **Business Addr:** Deputy Assistant Secretary, Office of Federal Contract Programs, Department of Labor, 200 Constitution Ave. NW, Washington, DC 20210, (202)219-9471.

WILCOX, JANICE HORDE
Educational administrator. **Personal:** Born Nov 2, 1940, Baltimore, MD; daughter of Gertrude Baker Horde and Robert Harrison Horde; married Marvin Marlowe Wilcox, Oct 14, 1972 (divorced); children: Kia Miguel Smith. **Educ:** Coppin State College, Baltimore, MD, BS 1965; Pepperdine Univ, Los Angeles, CA, MS 1976. **Career:** St Croix Public Schools, VI, teacher, 1965-66; Washington, DC Public Schools, teacher, 1966-68; Los Angeles City Schools, teacher, 1968-73, reading coordinator, 1973-75, early childhood education coordinator, 1975-77; California Committee on Teacher Prep and Licensing, consultant, 1977-78; US Department of Education, program analyst, 1978-81, education program specialist, 1983-88, special assistant for higher education programs, 1988-95, chief of staff, higher education programs, 1995-. **Orgs:** Natl Council of Negro Women 1965-; Natl Urban League 1970-; Alpha Kappa Alpha 1974-; League of Women Voters 1978-; Natl Coalition of 100 Black Women 1988-90; Patuxent Women's Coalition, president, 1987-95, founder; Association of Black Women in Higher Education, 1988-90; American Association of University Women, 1985-89; La Coterie, 1997-. **Honors/Awds:** Outstanding Fundraiser, Wilshire Heritage Group, 1973, 1976; Woman of the Year, CA Women's Assn, 1974; Distinguished Citizen, Jefferson Coalition, 1976; Outstanding Achievement Awards, US Dept of Educ, 1984, 1985, 1986, 1989. **Home Addr:** 1001 Spring St, No 905, Silver Spring, MD 20910. **Business Addr:** Chief of Staff, Higher Education Programs, US Department of Education, 600 Independence Ave, SW, Washington, DC 20202, (202)708-8596.

WILCOX, PRESTON
Association executive. **Personal:** Born Dec 27, 1923, Youngstown, OH; married Katherine (divorced); children: Gwynne, David, Susan, Liana. **Educ:** Attended, Youngstown Coll, Morehouse Coll, CUNY, NY Univ, Columbia Univ. **Career:** Parent Implementation in Educ, co-fndr; New Approach Method, an educ model, primary cons; JERE Media Features "Big Red" & "Black Am", syndicated columnist; Medgar Evers Coll, La Guardia Com Coll, archivist/soc analyst/prof; faculty positions at: Columbia University School of Social Work, Columbia College, NYU School of Continuing Educ; VISTA & Peace Corps, teacher, community organizer; Bedford Stuyvesant D & S Corp, staff; Princeton Univ, soc rsrchrs; AFRAM Assoc Inc, exec dir, currently. **Orgs:** National Association for African American Education (defunct), founding chairman; Congress of African People (defunct), founding corporate member; National Association of Black Social Workers, founding member; Harlem Commonwealth Council, founding board member; Manhattan Country School, founding board member; College of Human Services, chairman, founding board member; J Raymond Jones Democratic Club; African Americans United for Political Power; African Americans to Honor the Cuban People, co-chair; Borough President's Task Force on Education and Decentralization; New York State Task Force on Youth Gangs, NYS Div of Youth, co-chair, 1990; Black Fashion Museum, Harlem, Advisory Committee; Shawn A Lambert Scholarship Fund, consultant; National Malcolm X Commemoration Commission, 1990, 1991; Committee to Preserve the Works and Images of Malcolm X. **Honors/Awds:** Developed a copyrighted and tested educ model: Parent Implementation in Educ; served as primary consultant to The New Approach Method Reading Program; 40 Yr Plaque, Psi Chap, Omega Psi Phi Fraternity; numerous published works, including: an evaluation of Massachusetts Experimental School System, Boston, MA; Study of Negotiations Process bewteen Community Groups and Public Institutions, Institute of Labor Relations, University of Michigan; author of many funding proposals for associations and government agencies; First International Symposium on the Thought of Muammar Khadafy, Gar Unis University, Benghazi, Libya, 1983, attendee. **Business Addr:** Co-Founder, Board Chairman, CEO, AFRAM Alternative Information/Marketing Service, 271 Dr Martin L King Jr Blvd, #310, New York, NY 10027-4424.

WILCOX, THADDEUS
Banker. **Career:** Southeast Bank, eleven years; Peoples National Bank of Commerce, president/chief executive officer, currently. **Business Addr:** President/CEO, People's National Bank of Commerce, PO Box 470067 NW Branch, Miami, FL 33147-0067, (305)696-0700.

WILDER, CORA WHITE
Educator. **Personal:** Born Jul 31, 1936, Columbia, SC; married Kenneth Wilder; children: Michelle, Maxine, Marilynn, Marlene. **Educ:** Howard Univ, grad 1956; Howard Univ School of Social Work, 1958. **Career:** Dept Pub Welfare, Washington DC, child welfare worker 1958-61; VA Clinic, Brooklyn, clinical social worker 1961-63; VA Neuro-Psychiatric Hospital, Montrose, NY, 1963-64; Rockland & Co Mental Health Clinic, Monsey, NY, psychiatric social worker 1964-67; St Agatha Home for Children, supr; Fordham Univ, field work instr 1967-69; Rockland Community Coll Human Serv Dept, asst prof & coord of field instr 1969-; Rockland Comm Coll, assoc prof social sci dept 1984-. **Orgs:** Sec Amer Fed of Teachers 1973-; dir Comp Child Welfare Sem Scandinavia; mem Delta Sigma Theta Sorority; life mem NAACP; Rockland Negro Scholarship Fund; Day Care & Child Devel Coun of Rockland Co; co-hosted radio prog 1972-75; Rockland Co Cit adv comm, affirmative action comm; mem United Way 1972-74, bd dir 1974-; mem Rockland Co Bicentennial Comm 1975; comm person Rockland Co Dem Comm; gov's appointee to bd of visitors, Letchworth Vlg Devel Ctr; co-partner Kenco Art Assoc Art Dist & Cons; consultant, Staff Devel & Programming in Day Care & Child Welfare; mem Natl Conf on Artists; bd dir Assn of Community-Based Artists of Westchester. **Honors/Awds:** Outstanding Leadership Award, Spring Valley NAACP 1972. **Business Addr:** Assoc Prof, Social Sci Dept, Rockland Community College, 145 College Rd, Suffern, NY 10901.

WILDER, KURT
Judge. **Educ:** Univ of Michigan, AB in Political Science, 1981; Univ of Michigan Law School, JD, 1984; Graduated from courses in: General Jurisdiction, 1993; Financial Statements in the Courtroom, 1993. **Career:** City of Cleveland Prosecutor's Office, litigation intern, 1983; Foster, Swift, Collins & Smith, PC, litigation atty, 1984-89; Butzel Long, PC, litigation atty, 1989-92; Washtenaw County Circuit Court, circuit judge, 1992-. **Orgs:** Michigan Judges Assn, exec bd, legislative comm; American Judges Assn; State Bar of Michigan; The Fellows of the Michigan State Bar Foundation; Wolverine Bar Assn; Vanzetti Hamilton Bar Assn; American Bar Assn; Michigan Association of Community Corrections Advisory Bds, chairman; American Red Cross, Washtenaw County Chapter, bd of dirs, strategic planning comm/co-chair, financial development comm; Natl Kidney Foundation of Michigan, bd of trustees; Washtenaw Council for the Arts, advisory bd; NAACP; Ann Arbor Citizens Quality Service Comm, 1992-93; Ann Arbor Area Chamber of Commerce, human resources council, 1990-92; State of Michigan, vice-chair, corrections commission, 1991; Black Child and Family Institute, secretary, bd of dirs, 1986-89; Ingham County Bar Assn, bd of dirs, 1989-91. **Special Achievements:** First African-American judge appointed to Washtenaw County's Circuit Court, 1992. **Business Addr:** Judge, Washtenaw County Circuit Court, PO Box 8645, Ann Arbor, MI 48107, (313)994-2554.

WILDER, LAWRENCE DOUGLAS
Governor. **Personal:** Born Jan 17, 1931, Richmond, VA; married Eunice (divorced 1978); children: Lynn, Loren, Lawrence Jr. **Educ:** VA Union Univ, BS 1951; Howard Univ Sch of Law, JD 1959. **Career:** Attorney; State of Virginia: state senator, beginning 1969; lieutenant governor; governor, 1990-. **Orgs:** American Bar Assn, American Trial Lawyers Assn, Virginia Bar Assn, A merican Judicature Society, Old Dominion Bar Assn, Richmond Trial Lawyers Assn, Richmond Chamber of Commerce, Richmond Urban League, Red Shield Boys Club, Crusade for Voters, NAACP; vice president, Virginia Human Relations Council; Mason; Shriner; Guardsman; vice chairman, United Negro College Fund; past member, National Conference of Lt Governors. **Honors/Awds:** Certificate of Merit, Virginia State College, 1974; Honorary Doctor of Laws, 1979, Distinguished Alumni Award, 1979, Virginia Union University; Man of the Year Award, Omega Psi Phi; Astoria Benefit Assn Award, Delver Women's Club; Citizenship Award, 4th African Baptist Church; Alumnus of the Year, 1970, Certificate of Merit, 1974, Howard Univ Law School, 1970; Civic Award, Omega Psi Phi Third Dist; Civitan Award, Red Shields Boys Club. **Special Achievements:** First black state senator, Virginia, 1969; First black governor in the US, 1990. **Military Serv:** US Army; Bronze Star for Heroism during Korean War, 1952. **Business Addr:** Governor, State of Virginia, Office of the Governor, State Capitol Bldg, Richmond, VA 23219.

WILDER, MARY A. H.
Educator, counselor, psychotherapist. **Personal:** Born Oct 25, 1924, Philadelphia, PA; daughter of Cornelia Johnson and William Gardner Hackett; married Charles Edward Wilder, Jul 31, 1939 (died 1961); children: Richard, Agnes. **Educ:** Lincoln School for Nursing, RN, 1935; New York University, BS, 1945, MEd, 1947, MPA, 1974; Walden University, PhD, 1984. **Career:** Seaview Hospital, nurse, 1939-40; Cumberland Hospital, nurse, 1939-41; Yorkville Vocational High School, teacher, 1947-66; James Madison High School, counselor, 1966-73; Brooklyn College, Graduate School of Guidance, adjunct professor, currently; has also held numerous positions with local and state government. **Orgs:** Charter member, past president, Jack and Jill of America, Nassau Chapter; volunteer, National Save-A-Life League; Food On Wheels Program. **Honors/Awds:** Author, Practical Nursing Examination Review Book, 1965, 1968; author, Silent Epidemic, 1985. **Business Addr:** Professor/Counselor, Outreach, Holy Redeemer Church, 87 Pine St, Freeport, NY 11520.

WILDERSON, FRANK B., JR.
Psychologist, educator. **Personal:** Born Jan 17, 1931, Lutcher, LA; son of Valentean Wilderson and Frank Wilderson; married Ida Lorraine Jules; children: Frank III, Fawn, Amy, Wayne, Jules. **Educ:** Xavier U, BA 1953; Univ of MI, MS 1957, PhD 1962. **Career:** Univ of MN, prof of psychology, 1990-, vice pres student affairs, 1975-90, asst prof to prof asst dean 1962-74; Univ of MI School of Educ, lecturer 1960-62; OutPatient Educ Pgm, dir 1961-62; Reading Clinic Univ of MI, dir 1958-61; Univ of MI Child Psychiatric Hospital School, teacher 1957-58; Orleans Parish Public Schools, teacher 1953-57. **Orgs:** Mem MN Psychol Assc; Am Psychol Assc; Cncl for Exceptional Children; Cncl for Children with Behavior Disorders; natl adv com Handicapped Children; adv com US Pub Hlth Serv; natl adv com Handicapped Childrens Early Ed; chmn HEW/BEH Panel; MN Assc for Group Psychotherapy; MN Assc for Brain-Damaged Children; Assc of Black Psychologist; publ com Cncl for Exceptional Children; dir Bush Found; trustee Breck Clg Prep Sch; mem Phi Delta Kappa; mem Black Coalition; mem num task forces & spec coms; MN Bd of Ed; chmn Univ Com on devel BA Pgm in the Area of Afro-am Studies Publ; Classroom Mgmt of Withdrawn Children 1963; A Concept of an Ideal Tchrl-Pupil Relationship in Classes for Emotionally Disturbed Chldrn 1967; An Exploratory Study of Reading Skill Deficiencies & Psychiatric Symptoms in Emotally Disturbed Children 1967. **Business Addr:** Professor of Educational Psychology, University of Minnesota, 178 Pillsbury Dr, SE, 214 Burton Hall, Minneapolis, MN 55455.

WILDERSON, THAD
Educational administrator. **Personal:** Born Nov 13, 1935, New Orleans, LA; married Beverly; children: Troy, Dina, Lori, Marc. **Educ:** Southern Univ, BS 1960, MA 1968; Tulane Univ, addl psychology courses; Univ of MN, Doctoral candidate. **Career:** Tulane Univ, interviewer/analyst 1959-69; St James Parish Sch, teacher 1960-65; Orleans Parish Sch, teacher/counselor 1965-69; Juvenile Diagnostic Ctr, counselor 1966; Upward Bound, counselor 1968; psychologist private practice 1970-; MN State Dept of Educ, consultant 1973-; Carleton Coll, counselor/consultant1971-75; Macalester Coll, assoc dean of students/dir of Minority Prog Psychologist, starting 1969, coordinator of community relations, currently. **Orgs:** Mem Amer Personnel & Guidance Assn; mem MN Personnel & Guidance Assn; mem Amer Psychological Assn; mem Midwest Psychological Assn; mem MN Psychological Assn. **Honors/Awds:** "Housing Discrimination in New Orleans" published in 1970 Tulane Univ; "Impact of Model City Educ Progs upon the Model City Area" 1973; "Techniques for Assessing Minority Students" 1974; "Guidance Under the Knife A Case Study" 1974; "Factors Assoc with Drop Outs of Negro HS Students in Orleans" 1974; OutstandingComm Serv Awd from Minneapolis Urban League. **Business Addr:** Corrdinator of Community Relations, Macalester College, 1600 Grand Ave, St Paul, MN 55105.

WILDS, CONSTANCE T.
Educator. **Personal:** Born Jul 22, 1941, Stamford, CT; married Willie E; children: William Ernst. **Educ:** Fairfield U, MA 1972; Wilberforce U, BA 1969. **Career:** Western CT State Coll, counselor comm coord 1971-73; Neighborhood Youth Corps, dir manpower CTE Inc, acting dir; CTE Inc, admn asst. **Orgs:** Mem CT Sch Cnslr Assc; APGA; Am Personnel & Guidance Assc; Assc Black Persnl Higher Ed; vice pres Minority Higher Ed; Master Plan Higher Ed; mem Urban League; Mental Hlth Assc; Afro-Am Dem Clb. **Honors/Awds:** Cert Am Forum Internatl Study. **Business Addr:** 181 White St, Danbury, CT.

WILDS, JETIE BOSTON, JR.
Federal official (retired). **Personal:** Born Jan 10, 1940, Tampa, FL; son of Minnie Lee Wilds and Jetie Wilds Sr; married Ozepher Virginia Harris; children: Jemelle, Jeria. **Educ:** Morehouse Coll, BA Math 1962; Portland State Univ, MS Adm 1972. **Career:** USDA Forest Service, job corps official 1966-69, personnel mgmt specialist 1970-75, dir civil rights 1975-86, dir mgmt planning 1986-1989, special assistant to agency chief, 1992-94; US Office of Personnel Management, Quality Executive 1989-92; USDA Forest Service, special asst to agency chief, 1992-94; USDA Office of Secretary, deputy director of civil rights enforcement, 1994-96, director of Management Services, until 1997. **Orgs:** Mem Amer Mgmt Assoc, Amer Forestry Assoc, Amer Soc of Public Admin, NAACP, Omega Psi Phi Frat; Natl Forum for Black Public Administrators. **Honors/Awds:** Disting Alumni Award Natl Assoc for Equal Oppor in Higher Educ 1986; Outstanding Employee of the Year; Jaycees Man of the Year; Amer Business Women Boss of Yr; articles published in Natl Assoc of Personnel Workers, Washington State Ed Journal. **Home Addr:** 9477 Old Deep Ct, Columbia, MD 21045.

WILES, JOSEPH ST. CLAIR
Research pharmacologist (retired). **Personal:** Born Jul 27, 1914, Brooklyn, NY; son of Lillian Yearwood and Joseph Emanuel Wiles; married Esther Louise Ogburn Wiles, Jun 30, 1945; children: Carmen Christiana Hammel, Carole Lucille Gibson. **Educ:** Brooklyn Coll, attended 1932-38; Morris Brown Coll, AB Biology 1941; Atlanta Univ Grad Sch, attended 1941-42; Columbia Univ, 1950; Univ of MD Grad Sch, attended 1960-63. **Career:** Corps of Engrs, Water Lab Fort Benning GA, bacteriologist 1942-45; Medical Rsch Lab, Edgewood Arsenal MD, biologist 1946-52; Rsch Div Chem Systems Labs APG MD, pharmacologist (toxicology) 1953-80; Natl Academy of Science Washington DC, consultant 1980-85. **Orgs:** Zeta Sigma Chap, Phi Beta Sigma, pres 1976-79, vice dir 1977-79, dir 1979-81; Brotherhood of St Andrew St James Episcopal Church. **Honors/Awds:** Wm A Fountain Status Achievement Awd, Morris Brown Coll 1970; Academic Scholarship Awd, Atlanta Univ Grad Sch 1941; US Edgewood Arsenal Patent Awd Edgewood Arsenal MD 1971; Dept of Army Spec Act Awd Edgewood Arsenal Science Conf 1967. **Military Serv:**

US Army, s/sgt, 1943-46, 1950-51; American Campaign Medal, European African Middle Eastern Campaign Medal, Asiatic Pacific Campaign Medal, Good Conduct Medal. **Home Addr:** 3004 N Ridge Rd, Apt 504, Ellicott City, MD 21043.

WILES, LEON E.
Educator. **Personal:** Born May 28, 1947, Cincinnati, OH; married Maliaka Johnson; children: Tanzania, Saleda. **Educ:** Baldwin-Wallace Coll, certificate; Harvard University, certificate; Yale U, certificate; Philander Smith Coll, BA (cum laude) 1970; Univ of Pittsburg, MEd 1972; PhD candidate USC-Columbia. **Career:** Slippery Rock St Coll, chairperson, 1974-78; PA State Univ, dir of fresham studies, 1978-82; Univ of SC, dean of students, 1982, asso chancellor for student affairs, currently. **Orgs:** Phi Delta Kappa; YMCA Black Achievers, advisory comm; South Carolina Coll, personnel assn bd; Progressive Men's Club of Spartanburg. **Honors/Awds:** Natl Assoc Student Personnel Admin; Spartanburg Repertory Theater Advisory Comm; Davis Cup, 1994-95; Omega Outstanding Educator, 1996; Progressive Men's Outstanding Achievement Awd, 1995; Piedmont Assembly Outstanding Citizen. **Business Addr:** Associate Chancellor for Student Affairs, University of SC-Spartanburg, 303 Campus Luife Center, Spartanburg, SC 29303.

WILEY, EDWARD, III
Journalist. **Personal:** Born Dec 23, 1959, Baltimore, MD; son of B Maye Robinson Wiley and Edward Wiley, Jr. **Educ:** California State University, Fresno, CA, BA, journalism, 1984. **Career:** Fresno Bee, CA, staff writer, 1982-86; Rep Tony Coelho, CA, special asst, 1986-87; Education Daily, Alexandria, VA, writer, editor, 1987-88; Black Issues in Higher Education, Fairfax, VA, asst managing editor, 1988-. **Orgs:** Mem, National Assoc of Black Journalists, 1988-; mem, Education Writers Association, 1990-; life mem, Pi Eta Chi, 1983-; mem, Sigma Delta Chi, 1982-. **Honors/Awds:** Educational Press Assoc, Distinguished Achievement Award, series, 1989, feature writing, 1989; Young, Gifted and Black Award, California State Univ, 1990; Rosa Parks Meritorious Achievement Award, 1983.

WILEY, FLETCHER HOUSTON
Attorney. **Personal:** Born Nov 29, 1942, Chicago, IL; son of Mildred Berg Wiley and Fletcher Wiley; married Benaree Drew Pratt; children: Pratt Norton, Benaree Mildred. **Educ:** USAF Acad, BS, 1965; Univ of Paris (Fulbright), 1966; Georgetown Univ, 1968; Harvard Law School, JD, 1974; JFK School of Govt, MPP, 1974. **Career:** ABT Assoc Inc, consultant, 1972-75; Fine & Ambrogne, atty, 1975-78; Budd, Wiley & Richlin, PC, atty/mng partner, 1979-89; Wiley & Richlin, PC, atty/pres, 1989-91; Fitch, Wiley, Richlin & Tourse, P C, president, 1991-. **Orgs:** Assoc comm, Massachusetts Alcoholic Beverage Control Commn, 1977-81, 83-84; consvtr, Unity Bank & Trust Co, 1982; bd mem, Boston Chamber of commerce, 1980-; bd mem, Econ Devel & Indus Corp, 1981-; bd mem, Dana-farber Cancer Inst, 1978-86; bd mem, New England Aquarium, 1982-86; chmn, Govt commr on Minority Business Devel, 1985-; natl pres, Black Entertainment & Sports Lawyers Assn, 1986-; Coolidge Bank and Trust Co, bd mem. **Honors/Awds:** Flw US Fulbright Comm (Paris), 1965-66; flw Joint Center for Political Studies, 1970-71; flw Massachusetts Intl Fellowship Program (London), 1984; Ten Otstndng Young Leaders Boston Jaycees, 1978. **Military Serv:** USAF, captain, 4 years. **Home Addr:** 29 Fort Ave, Roxbury, MA 02119. **Business Addr:** 101 Federal St, #1900, Boston, MA 02110-1800.

WILEY, FORREST PARKS
Business executive. **Personal:** Born Nov 1, 1937, Weldon, NC; married Gloria; children: Joseph, John, Linda. **Educ:** Tuskegee Isnt, BS 1966. **Career:** Harris Corp Dilitho Systems, mgr sls mgr serv mgr 1975-; Letterflex Systems WR Grace, reg mgr 1973-75, system engr 1970-73; New Ventures Inc, dir rsrch 1970-73; WR Grace, rsrch asst bio chem 1967-70. **Orgs:** Pres Tuskegee Alumni Housing Found 1977-; bd dir WA Tuskegee Housing Found; mem Natl Geog Soc; Botanical Soc Am Am Soc Plant Physiologists; Am Inst Biol Sci; Tuskegee Alumni Assc; pres Wa-tuskegee Clb; mem Interntl Platform Assc. **Business Addr:** Mechanic St, Westerly, RI 02891.

WILEY, GERALD EDWARD (JOE)
Human resources executive. **Personal:** Born Jun 20, 1948, Belleville, IL; son of Mary Wiley and George Wiley; married Marquita Trenier; children: Raymond, Johanna. **Educ:** St Louis Univ, BS, Sociology, 1970, MA, Urban Affairs, 1974. **Career:** Container Corp of Amer, personnel mgr, 1974-75; Gen Dynamics, employee relations dir, 1975-78; Wiley, Ette & Assoc, vice pres, 1978-79; Monsanto Co, director human resources, 1979-. **Orgs:** Chairman, Howard University Cluster Executive Council, Florida A&M; executive comm, St Louis Univ Billiken Club; board of directors, Franklin Neighborhood Assn; St Clair County Planning Commission. **Honors/Awds:** Inducted into the Illinois Basketball Hall of Fame, 1977; Metro Area Hall of Fame, 1987; St Louis University Hall of Fame, 1993. **Home Addr:** 13 Towne Hall Estates, Belleville, IL 62223. **Business Addr:** Director, Affirmative Action, Monsanto Co, 800 N Lindberg Blvd, St Louis, MO 63141.

WILEY, HERLEY WESLEY
Cleric (retired), consultant. **Personal:** Born Dec 16, 1914, Caswell County, NC; married Doris White; children: Howard Wesley, Dennis Wayne. **Educ:** BTh, 1944. **Career:** 1st Bapt Ch, pastor 1943-47; Friendship Bapt Ch, 1947-53; Forsyth County, mission dir 1953-55; Zion Bapt Ch, 1955, 1964-68; pastor until 1985; consultant to Baptist churches in metropolitn Washington, DC, currently. **Orgs:** Dir Coop Ministries So Bapt Home Mission Bd, So Bapt Conv 1968-; pastor Covenant Bapt Ch; Budget Com Progressive Nat Bapt Conv; exec bd Lott Carey Foreign Missionary Conv; Council Chs Greater Wash; mem Inter-Faith Com. **Business Addr:** 3845 S Capt St, Washington, DC 20032.

WILEY, JOHN D., JR.
Educator. **Personal:** Born Sep 24, 1938, Fodice, TX; married Clara. **Educ:** BS 1959; MS 1960; Univ of Houston, advanced study. **Career:** Dillard Univ, instructor, 1960-63; Inst Serv to Educ and Advncd Study, consultant 1967-70; Texas Southern University, assistant professor 1970-79, associate professor, 1980-, coordinator of developmental program, Department of Mathematics, 1989-. **Business Addr:** Dept of Mathematics, Texas Southern University, 3200 Cleburne Ave, Houston, TX 77004.

WILEY, KENNETH LEMOYNE
Physician. **Personal:** Born Jan 10, 1947, San Antonio, TX; son of Dolores Shields Wiley (deceased) and Elmer Wiley (deceased); married Linda Diane Nixon; children: Kenneth Jr, Brian. **Educ:** Trinity Univ, BS 1968; OK State Univ, MS 1970; Meharry Medical Coll, MD 1977. **Career:** Private Practice, internal medicine 1980-. **Orgs:** Mem Alpha Phi Alpha, Alpha Omega Alpha, Society of Sigma Xi. **Military Serv:** AUS capt 3 yrs; Bronze Star, Technical Service Medal. **Home Addr:** 6150 Eastover Dr, New Orleans, LA 70128. **Business Addr:** MD Care, Inc, 3840 St Bernard Ave, New Orleans, LA 70122, (504)283-4182.

WILEY, LEROY SHERMAN
Government official. **Personal:** Born Oct 30, 1936, Sparta, GA. **Educ:** Ft Valley State Coll, BS 1960; Clark Coll, 1968; Univ of GA, 1966-69; GA Coll, MS 1975-77. **Career:** Ft Valley State Coll, suprv maintenance dept 1958-60; Hancock Central HS, instr dept chmn 1960-61; Boddie HS, instr 1963-64; Hancock Central HS, instr, chmn of sci dept 1964-70; Upward Bound Study Ctr, dir 1973; Learning Ctr, couns asst field rep 1975; Hancock Cty Emergency Mgmt Agency, dir, coord 1984; Hancock Cty, clerk of superior ct 1970-. **Orgs:** Mem Kappa Alpha Psi, CB Radio Club Inc, Masonic Orders, Hancock Cty Dem Club, Hancock Cty Br NAACP, GA Assoc of Black Elected Officials, Veterans Assoc of GA Coll of Milledgeville, GA Ed Assoc, GA Farm Bur Assoc, Natl Assoc of Retarded Children, Cty Officials Assoc of GA; comm chmn BSA; post comdr Amer Legion #530 1984-85; mem, trustee bd St Mark AME Church. **Honors/Awds:** 1st black since reconstr & only black serving as clerk of Superior Court; Outstanding Contrib in Civil Rights Movement in Hancock Cty 1982. **Military Serv:** Army GA Natl Guard 2yrs. **Business Addr:** Clerk of Superior Court, Hancock County, PO Box 451, Sparta, GA 31087.

WILEY, MARCELLUS
Professional football player. **Personal:** Born Nov 30, 1974. **Educ:** Columbia. **Career:** Buffalo Bills, defensive end, 1997-. **Business Addr:** Professional Football Player, Buffalo Bills, One Bills Dr, Orchard Park, NY 14127, (716)648-1800.

WILEY, MARGARET Z. RICHARDSON
Business executive. **Personal:** Born Jun 27, 1934, Jackson, NC; married Sampson; children: Brian, Judith. **Educ:** City Coll of NY, 1955-56; Scott's Coll of Cosmetology, 1963-65; IN U, 1967-69. **Career:** Nat Minority Supplier Devel Council, exec dir/chf oper ofcr 1978-; Devco Local Devel Corp, pres 1973-78; Natl Devel Council, exec dir 1972-78; Summit Labs Indpls, educ & mrktng dir 1965-72; Americana Salon, owner 1974-. **Orgs:** Adv bd Enterprising Women 1978-; mem Revenue Plng Bd of Montclair NJ 1978; mem NAACP 1980. **Honors/Awds:** Recipient Outst Sales & Outst Mgmt/Sales Awrds Summit Labs Indianapolis 1969-70; Distng Achvmnt/Serv Awrd The Links Inc Seattle 1976; Mayor Citation City of Baltimore 1979; recipient Woman's Outst Award in Bus NAACP NY 1980; recipient Woman of the Year Awrd Serv/Devel of Minority Bus Natl Assn of Black Manufactrs Wash DC 1980. **Business Addr:** Broker, J H Rudd Real Estate Agency, 312 Orange Rd, Montclair, NJ 07042.

WILEY, MAURICE
Administrative assistant. **Personal:** Born Jan 13, 1941, Pine Bluff, AR; son of Mr and Mrs Hosie Wiley. **Educ:** Univ of AR-Pine Bluff, BS 1963; CA State Univ Los Angeles, MA 1972. **Career:** Pasadena Unified School Dist, math teacher 1966-69; Inglewood Unified School Dist, math teacher 1969-72, guidance counselor 1972-82, coordinated coll prep programs 1982-88, admin asst to the supt, l989-. **Orgs:** Consultant College Preparatory Programs & H S Counseling; mem Inglewood Chamber of Commerce Educ Comm; mem Phi Delta Kappa Educ Frat 1974-; pres Inglewood Counseling & Psychology Assoc 1986; participant NAFEO Conf Nations Black Colls 1986; participant UCLA Counselors Inst Univ of CA 1986; mem Inglewood Mgmt Assoc, Inglewood/Centinela Valley Youth Counseling Adv Comm. **Honors/Awds:** Outstanding Young Men in Amer Pasadena Chamber of Commerce 1970; Most Eligible Bachelor Ebony Magazine 1971; Counselor/Teacher of the Yr Inglewood High School 1980; Awd of Excellence Inglewood Sch Dist 1984; Comm Unity Commendation City of Inglewood CA 1986; Inglewood Chamber of Commerce Commendation 1989; Young Black Scholars Role Model of the Year 1992; California Lottery Millionaires Club 1989-. **Military Serv:** AUS staff sgt 1963-65; Outstanding Achievement Awd 1965.

WILEY, MORLON DAVID
Professional basketball player. **Personal:** Born Sep 24, 1966, New Orleans, LA. **Educ:** California State Univ at Long Beach, Long Beach, CA, 1984-88. **Career:** Dallas Mavericks, 1988-89; Orlando Magic, 1989-93; Dallas Mavericks, 1993-. **Business Addr:** Professional Basketball Player, Dallas Mavericks, Reunion Arena, 777 Sports St, Dallas, TX 75207.

WILEY, RALPH
Author, satirist, lecturer, screenwriter. **Personal:** Born Apr 12, 1952, Memphis, TN; son of Dorothy & Ralph; married Holly A Cypress (divorced); children: Colen Cypress Wiley. **Educ:** Knoxville Coll, BS, bus management, 1975. **Career:** Oakland Tribune, 1975-82; Sports Illustrated, sr writer, 1982-89; HIP, Inc, chairman, 1987-. **Business Addr:** Chairman, Heygood Images Productions, Inc, 4120 2nd St, SW, Washington, DC 20032.

WILEY, RENA DELORIS
Social service. **Personal:** Born Jul 29, 1953, Effingham County, GA; daughter of Rena Elizabeth Canady and Rev J B Canady; divorced; children: Hawa Shahlette, Sherri Latrice, Elizabeth Renae, Omega Lynn. **Educ:** GA Southwestern Coll, BS Psych 1976; Augusta Coll, MS Clinical Psych 1977. **Career:** Sumter Cty Taylor Cty Mental Retard Ctr, behavior spec 1977-78; Taylor Cty Mental Retard Ctr, acting dir 1978; Middle Flint Behavioral Healthcare, equal employment oppty rep, dir of child & adolescent outpatient svcs, 1978-, part time employment with area PhD Psychologist; behavior spec child & adolescent prog 1978-. **Orgs:** City Zoning Appeals Bd, 1996-; Habitat For Humanity, family selection committee; mem Delta Sigma Theta 1973-; school bd mem Amer City Bd of Ed 1980-93; provider of area workshops, Child Sexual Abuse/Child Abuse, other children's issues; sec Early Bird Civitan Club 1983-84; jr hs group facilitator Taylor Cty Pregnancy Prevention Prog 1984-; pres Sumter Cty Mental Health Assoc 1984-85; bd of dir GA Mental Health Assoc 1984-85; group facilitator Arrive Alive GA 1985; pres elect Early Bird Civitan Club 1985, pres 1986-; District 8 Infant Mortality Task Force 1986-; Sumter 2000 Committee; consultant to area agencies and schools; vice chairman, Americus City Board of Ed 1980-93; pres, Visions for Sumter, 1995-96, bd mem, 1984-. **Honors/Awds:** Blue Key Natl Honor Frat GA Southwestern Coll 1981; Outstanding Serv Awd Sumter Cty Mental Health Assoc 1982; C&A Program, Employee of the Year, 1997; Outstanding Svc to African-American Drum Majors, Americus/Sumter Cty, 1997; author of children's coloring books/stories. **Home Addr:** 212 Barnum Dr, Americus, GA 31709. **Business Addr:** Behavior Specialist, Sr., Americus Area Mental Health, 415 W Forsyth, Americus, GA 31709, (912)931-2504.

WILEY, WILLIAM R.
Research scientist. **Personal:** Born Sep 3, 1931, Oxford, MS; son of Edna Alberta Threlkeld Wiley and William Russel Wiley; married Myrtle Louise Smith; children: Johari. **Educ:** Tougaloo Coll, BS, chemistry, 1954; Univ of Illinois, MS, microbiology, 1960; Washington State Univ, PhD, bacteriology, 1965. **Career:** Battelle Pacific NW Labs, rsch scientist 1965-69, mgr cellular & molecular biology sect 1969-72, coord life sci prog 1972-74, mgr biology dept 1974-79, dir of rsch 1979-84; Washington State Univ Pullman WA, adj assoc prof of bacteriology 1969-; Battelle Meml Inst, Pacific NW Div, senior vice president and director, 1984-94, Science and Technology Policy, senior vice president, 1995-. **Orgs:** Mem Amer Soc of Biological Chemists, Amer Soc of Microbiology, Amer Assoc for the Advancement of Sci, Soc for Experimental Biol & Med; lecturer Black Exec Exchange Prog 1969-; adj assoc prof microbiol WA State Univ 1968-; mem WA Tech Ctr Sci Adv Panel 1984-; mem bd dir WA MESA Prog Univ of WA Seattle 1984-90, WA Tech Ctr 1984-88, United Way of Benton & Franklin Counties 1984-; Tri-City Indust Devel Council 1984-; Forward Washington 1984-; mem WA Council for Tech Advancement 1984-85; mem bd dir The Northwest Coll & Univ Assoc for Sci 1985-; mem Tri-City Univ Center Citizens Adv Council 1985-; mem Gov Gardner's Higher Educ Coord Bd 1986-89; mem bd trust Carver Tsch Found of Tuskegee Univ 1986-; mem bd trustees WA State Univ Found 1986-89; Washington State Governor's Economic Development and Environmental Enhancement Task Force; Off of Technology Assessment's Advisory Panel on Arctic Impacts; Natl Foreign Language Ctr, advisory bd; Council of the Government-Univ-Industry Research Roundtable; Fred Hutchinson Cancer Research Center, bd of trustees; Whitman Coll Bd of Overseers; Oregon Graduate Inst of Science and Technology, bd of trustees; Southern Univ En-

gineeering Exec Commitee; SAFECO Corp; bd of dir; Northwest Natural Gas, bd of dirs; Federal Reserve Bank of San Francisco, Seattle Branch, bd of dirs. **Honors/Awds:** Author and coauthor of 22 journal publs, co-author of one book; Alumni Achievement Award, Washington State University, 1986; Honorary Doctor of Laws Degree, Gonzaga University, 1988; Honorary Doctor of Science Degree, Whitman College, 1990; US Black Engineer Magazine, Black Engineer of the Year Award, 1994; US Dept of Energy, Distinguished Associate Award, 1994. **Military Serv:** US Army corpl 1954-56. **Business Addr:** Senior Vice Pres, Battelle Memorial Inst, Scince and Technology Policy, PO Box 999, Richland, WA 99352.

WILEY-PICKETT, GLORIA
Government official (retired). **Personal:** Born Jul 5, 1937, Detroit, MI; daughter of Fannie Smith Wiley and Elmer Wiley; divorced; children: Michele Joy Pickett-Wells. **Educ:** Attended, Detroit Inst of Tech 1954-56, Wayne State Univ 1980-82. **Career:** US Dept of Defense, accounting tech, federal womens prog coord 1971-73, supervisory procurement asst 1973-75; US Dept of Labor/ESA/OFCCP, equal opportunity specialist 1975-81, supervisory equal opportunity specialist, asst district dir, retired 1995. **Orgs:** Mem, sub comm, SE Michigan March of Dimes Fashion Extravaganza 1971-, Natl Assoc of Human Rights Workers 1981-; elected to board of directors, Michigan Chapter NAHRW, 1989; Natl Assoc of Female Execs Inc 1983-; treasurer, DGL Inc 1984-86; chairperson, prog comm, Amer Business Women's Assoc Spirit of Detroit Chap 1985-; mem, Founder's Soc, Detroit Inst of Arts; mem, Natl Assn of Human Rights Workers; mem, Natl Assn of Female Executives Inc; mem, NAACP. **Honors/Awds:** Letter of Commendation for Performance DOD DLA DCASR; Special Achievement Awd for Outstanding Contributions to the EEO Prog Dept of Defense DLA DCASR.

WILFONG, HENRY T., JR.
Accountant. **Personal:** Born Feb 22, 1933, Ingals, AR; married Aline Jane Guidry; children: Bernetta, Brian. **Educ:** UCLA, BA 1958, MBA 1960. **Career:** Wilfong & Co, sr prtnr; Nat Assn Minority CPA Firms, pres 1971. **Orgs:** Elected city councilman 1973; apptd CA Council Criminal Justice 1974; bd dir Nat Bus League & Ca Soc CPA'S. **Honors/Awds:** Fred D Patterson Awrd 1974; 10 Top Minority Bus Yr Awrd 1972. **Military Serv:** AUS sgt 1954-56. **Business Addr:** Associate Administrator, Minority Small Business Admin, Small Business Administration, 1441 L St NW, Washington, DC 20416.

WILFORD, HAROLD C.
Editor. **Personal:** Born Sep 18, 1924, St Louis, MO; married Dorothy; children: Jacquelyn. **Career:** Studebaker Auto Mfg, machinist 1946; Smart Cleaners, owner 1947; US Post Office, clerk 1951; East St Louis Nightclub, owner 1953-60; Grace Durocher Dress Design, clk 1962; Slays Restaurant, chef 1966; Argus Newspaper, ad mgr 1967, entertainment editor 1967; Entertainment Artists, personnel business mgr. **Orgs:** Mem Amvets; pres & dir Jazzville USA 1970-72; press agent Regal Sports Promotions Inc; Ebony Fashion Fair; consult Sonic Soul Enterprises 1973; hon judge pr Miss Black Am Pagent MO 1970-73; PR Congressman Wm Clay 1968-74; mem Police Youth Corp; Ardell Film Intl Prod Co; pr dir United Black Comm Fund; St Louis Expo; Black Packing House Workers Pres. **Honors/Awds:** Citation Armed Svcs; Good Conduct Medal; Distinguished Serv Awrd Amvets 1972; Certificate Serv 1969. **Military Serv:** AUS corpl 1943-46. **Business Addr:** 4595 Martin Luther King Blvd, St Louis, MO 63140.

WILFORK, ANDREW LOUIS
County official. **Personal:** Born Apr 27, 1947, Quitman, GA; married Viola Irene Godwin (divorced); children: Jermaine, Whitney; married Yolanda Yvette Hallmon. **Educ:** FL Intl Univ, BS Soc Work 1974. **Career:** Metro-Dade County Waste Dept, service rep 1971-72, enforcement officer to coordinator 1972-74, area supr 1974-78; Metro-Dade Cty Public Works Dept, transfer station 1978-80, supr transfer station admin 1980-86; superintendent 1986-, dir dept of solid waste collection. **Honors/Awds:** Certificate of Recognition, Peabody Solid Waste Management, 1979; Certificate for Valuable and Distinguished Service to the State of Florida. **Military Serv:** AUS sergeant 3 yrs. **Business Addr:** Dir, Dept of Solid Waste, Metro Dade County, 8675 NW 53rd St, Suite 201, Miami, FL 33166-4598.

WILHOIT, CARL H.
Registered professional engineer. **Personal:** Born Aug 15, 1935, Vandalia, MO; married Daisy Glascoe; children: Raquel, Marcus. **Educ:** Lincoln U, 1958-60; Howard U, BS 1962; Catholic U, M 1973. **Career:** New Town Devel DC Dept of Housing & Comm Devel, engrng coord; DC Dept of Hwys & Traffic, civil engr 1962-67; Dept of Civil Engrng Fed City & Coll Washington DC, lctr 1975-76. **Orgs:** Mem ASCE; Nat Assn of Housing & Redevelopment Officials 1971; mem Nat Soc of Professional Engrs (NSPE) 1977. **Military Serv:** USAF a/1c 1955-58. **Business Addr:** 1325 G St NW, Washington, DC 20005.

WILKENS, LEONARD R.
Professional basketball coach. **Personal:** Born Oct 28, 1937, Brooklyn, NY; son of Henrietta Cross Wilkens and Leonard R Wilkens; married Marilyn J. Reed, Jul 28, 1962; children: Leesha, Randy, Jamee. **Educ:** Providence College, BA, economics, 1960. **Career:** St Louis Hawks, player, 1960-68; Seattle SuperSonics, player-coach, 1968-72; Cleveland Cavaliers, player, 1972-74; Portland Trail Blazers, player-coach, 1974-75, coach, 1975-76; Seattle SuperSonics, head coach, 1977-85, general manager, 1985-86; Cleveland Cavaliers, head coach, 1986-93; Atlanta Hawks, head coach, 1993-. **Orgs:** Honorary chairman, Marymount-Cavs RP Golf Classic, 1987—; chair, Make-a-Wish Golf Tournament, 1988; Boys and Girls Clubs of Greater Cleveland; Catholic Diocese of Cleveland; Rainbow Babies; Children's Hospital; Kidney Foundation; NBA Players Assn, vp, 1961-69; NBA Coaches Assn, pres. **Honors/Awds:** National Invitation Tournament, Most Valuable Player, 1960; Rhode Island Heritage Hall of Fame, 1961; NBA All-Star Game, Most Valuable Player, 1971, representative, 1973; coached Seattle Super Sonics to NBA Championship, 1979; City of Hope Sportsman of the Year, Congressional Black Caucus Coach of the Year, CBS Coach of the Year, Black Publisher of America Coach of the Year, 1979; honorary doctor of humanities, Providence College, 1980; Urban League-Witney Young Outstanding Citizen Award, 1980; Golden Shoe Award, Shoes for Kids, 1988; Digital NBA Coach of the Month, December, 1988; enshrined in the Naismith Memorial Basketball Hall of Fame, 1990; coached four NBA All-Star teams; Basetball Weekly, Coach of the Year; City of Hope/Sport Magazine, Victor Award, 1994; IBM/NBA Coach of the Year, 1994; Most Outstanding Player in the New England Area, 1960, 1961; NIT-NIKE Hall of Fame; NYC Basketball Hall of Fame; Brooklyn Hall of Fame; US Olympic Basketball Team, Atlanta, head coach, 1996. **Special Achievements:** United States Olympic Men's Basketball Team, asst, 1992, coach, 1996; Winningest coach in NBA history; participated in more games as player and/or head coach than anyone else in league history; winningest coach in Cleveland history, 1992-93. **Military Serv:** US Army, Quartermaster Corps, 2nd Lieutenant, 1961-62. **Business Addr:** Head Coach, Atlanta Hawks, 1 CNN Center NW S Tower, Suite 405, Atlanta, GA 30335, (404)827-3800.

WILKERSON, BRUCE ALAN
Professional football player. **Personal:** Born Jul 28, 1964, Loudon, TN; married Antionette; children: Starkicia, Jeremy. **Educ:** Tennessee. **Career:** Los Angeles Raiders, tackle, 1987-94; Jacksonville Jaguars, 1995; Green Bay Packers, 1996-. **Business Addr:** Professional Football Player, Green Bay Packers, 1265 Lombardi Ave, Green Bay, WI 54304, (414)494-2351.

WILKERSON, DANA
Professional basketball player. **Personal:** Born Feb 27, 1969. **Educ:** Long Beach State Univ. **Career:** Long Beach Stingrays, guard, 1997-. **Business Addr:** Professional Basketball Player, Long Beach Stingrays, One World Trade Center, Ste 202, Long Beach, CA 90831-0202, (562)951-7297.

WILKERSON, DIANNE
State representative. **Career:** State of Massachusetts, senate seat, currently. **Special Achievements:** First African-American female to hold senate seat for Massachusetts. **Business Addr:** State Representative, Massachusetts State House, Senate State House, Boston, MA 02133, (617)722-2000.

WILKERSON, MARGARET BUFORD
Educator. **Personal:** Born Apr 3, 1938, Los Angeles, CA; daughter of Gladys Buford and George Buford; married Stanley; children: Darren, Cullen, Gladys-Mari. **Educ:** Univ of Redlands, BA History (magna cum laude) 1959; UCLA, Teachers Cred 1960-61; Univ Of CA Berkeley, MA Dramatic Art 1967, PhD Dramatic Art 1972. **Career:** YWCA Youngstown OH, adlt pgm dir 1959-60; YWCA Los Angeles, adlt pgm dir 1960-62; Jordan HS LA CA, drama/engl tchr 1962-66; English Dept Dramatic Art Dept, lctr 1968-74; Dept Afro-Am Studies UC Berkeley, lctr 1976-83; Ctr for Study Ed & Adv of Women, dir 1975-83; Univ of CA Berkeley African American Studies Dept, prof and chair, 1988-. **Orgs:** V pres/adm Am Theatre Asso 1983-85; chair Black Theatre Prog/Am Theatre Asso 1979-83; adv bd Bus & Prof Womens Fndtn 1983-; consult Am Cncl on Ed Natl Identification Prog for Womdn Adms 1980-; panelist Natl Rsrch Cncl/Lhumanitgies Doct Comm 1983-; consult CA Arts Cncl 1984-; mem Natl Cncl of Negro Women; mem Univ of CA Berkeley Black Alumni Club; mem NAACP; founder/dir Kumoja Players 1971-75; bd of trustees, San Francisco Theological Seminary, 1987-. **Honors/Awds:** Hon dr/Humane Letters Univ of Redlands 1980; humanities flwshp Rockefeller Fndtn 1982-83; sr postdoctoral flwshp Natl Rsrch Cncl/Ford Found 1983-84; Ford Flwshp/Dissertation Ford Fndtn 1970; otstndng black alumna Univ of CA Berkeley Black Alumni Club 1976; Kellogg Lecturer Am Cncl on Ed 1980; co-editor Black Scholar theatre issue & other publs; author of "9 Plays by Black Women" New Amer Library 1986; Honoree, Equal Rights Advocates, 1989; College of Fellows of the American Theatre/JF Kennedy Ctr for Performing Arts, 1990; Award for Exemplary Educational Leadersip/Black Caucus of American Assn of Higher Education, 1990; Profile of Excellence, KGO-TV, San Francisco, 1990; Association of American Theatre, Career Achievement Award for Outstanding Educator, 1996. **Business Addr:** Professor, Chair, University of California-Berkeley, Dept of Dramatic Art, 101, 3335 Dwinelle Annex, Berkeley, CA 94720.

WILKES, JAMAAL (KEITH)
Sports/financial business consultant, professional basketball player (retired). **Personal:** Born May 2, 1953, Berkeley, CA. **Educ:** UCLA, 1974; Professional Designation, Investment Real Estate; Award in General Business Studies; California Real Estate Broker; California Insurance Agent/Broker; Series 7 & 63 Securities Licenses. **Career:** Golden State Warriors, 1975-77, Los Angeles Lakers, 1978-85, Los Angeles Clippers, 1985. **Orgs:** Los Angeles Urban League, bd of dirs, former mem; Western Region United Way, bd of dirs; UCLA Foundation, bd of trustees; Los Angeles Athletic Club, bd of governors, former mem. **Honors/Awds:** All Star Team 1976, 1981, 1983; 4 time NBA World Champion; 2 time NCAA Basketball & Scholastic All-American; UCLA Athletic Hall of Fame; GTE Academic Hall of Fame, inductee, 1990; Boys & Girls Club of America, Natl Hall of Fame, Inducted. **Business Addr:** Jamaal Wilkes Enterprises, 433 N Camden Dr, Ste 600, Beverly Hills, CA 90210.

WILKES, REGGIE WAYMAN
Professional football player (retired). **Personal:** Born May 27, 1956, Pine Bluff, AR. **Educ:** GA Tech, BS Biology 1978; attending Morehouse School of Med, Univ of PA Med School exchange prog. **Career:** Linebacker: Philadelphia Eagles, 1978-86; Atlanta Falcons, 1987.

WILKES, SHELBY R.
Ophthalmologist. **Personal:** Born Jun 30, 1950, Crystal Springs, MS; married Jettie M Burnett MD; children: Martin, Andrew. **Educ:** Alcorn State Univ, BS (Summa Cum Laude) 1971; Johns Hopkins Univ Sch of Medicine, MD 1975. **Career:** Univ of Rochester Sch of med Dept of Surgery, intern-resident 1975-76; Mayo Clinic, resident 1977-79; MA Eye & Ear Infirmary, fellow retina serv 1980-81; Univ of IL Eye & Ear Infirmary, rsch fellow 1976; Harvard Univ Sch of Medicine, clinical asst in ophthalmology 1982-83; Emory Univ Sch of Medicine, asst prof of ophthalmology; Morehouse School of Med Atlanta GA, asst clinical prof dept of surgery; vitreoretinal surgeon, ophthalmologist; Atlanta Eye Consultants, pres. **Orgs:** Mem Alpha Phi Alpha, NAACP, Atlanta Med Assoc, GA State Med Assoc, Assoc for Rsch in Vision & Ophthalmology 1978-, Amer Med Assoc 1978-; fellow AmerAcad of Ophthalmology 1981-; mem Natl Medical Assn 1981-; mem bd of dir Amer Diabetes Assoc GA Affiliate Inc 1985. **Honors/Awds:** Honors Soc Alcorn State Univ 1970-71; Ophthalmic Alumni Awd Mayo Clinic 1980; Disting Alumni Citation selected by Natl Assn for Equal Oppor in Higher Educ 1985; papers, with E S Gragoudas, "Regression patterns of uveal melanomas after proton beam irradiation" Ophthalmology 1982 89,7 p840; with M Beard, D M Robertson & L Kurland "Incidence of retinal detachment" Rochester MN Amer Journal of Ophthalmology 1982. **Business Addr:** President, Atlanta Eye Consultants, 615 Peachtree St NE, Ste 815, Atlanta, GA 30308.

WILKES, WILLIAM R.
Clergyman. **Personal:** Born Apr 10, 1902, Eatonton, GA; married Nettie Julia; children: William, Alfred. **Educ:** Morris Brown Coll, AB; Garret Theol Sem; Northwestern U; Morris Brown, hon DD; other hon DD & LLD. **Career:** 13th Episcopal Dist (KY & TN) of AME Ch, bishop 1972-; 3rd Dist, bishop; also presided over 16th, 12th & 6th dist. **Business Addr:** 1002 Kirkwood Ave, Nashville, TN 37204.

WILKIE, EARL AUGUSTUS T.
Counselor, educational administrator, artist. **Personal:** Born Mar 15, 1930, Philadelphia; son of Evelyn Wilkie and Roland Wilkie. **Educ:** Cheyney University, BS, education, 1961; Temple University, education media, 1975; University of Pennsylvania, MFA, 1978; Philadelphia College of the Arts, sculpture workshop, 1978-79; Fleisher Memorial, ceramics, 1982; Westminster Theological Seminary, religious study, 1985. **Career:** Elwyn Inc, director of vocational training, 1962-65, director of adult education programs, 1965-69, Junior and Senior High School Work Study Program, 1964-75, programs and residential services, coordinator, 1977-80, American Institute, executive director, 1981-84; Horizon House, director of vocational rehabilitation, 1985; United Rehabilitation Services, director of operation, 1986, Out-Patient Dept, Child Guidance Dept, director, 1987; Child Stabilization Center, director, 1990; Pennsylvania Institute of Technology, counselor/administrator, currently; consultant. **Orgs:** Philadelphia Council of the Arts, City of Philadelphia, committee chairman Roland Ayers, sponsor, 1988-89; ALAC Center for the Visual and Performing Arts, executive director, 1989; National Conference of Artists, Executive Committee, 1982. **Honors/Awds:** Consultant, Jerusalem Elwyn Institute, Millie Shiam Center, Swedish Village, Jerusalem, Israel, 1991; publications: Guidelines for Developing Individual Habilitation Plan, designer; "Something Is Wrong," Trends Journal of Resources, United Presbyterian, 1970, recorded by Geneva Recording Co, 1970; exhibitor, Bacchanal Gallery, Philadelphia, PA, 1988-89, Afro-American Art Museum, 1986,

Stockton State College, 1987-88; assisted in establishment of DuBois Gallery, University of Pennsylvania, 1975; Fulbright Fellowship Grant, for study in Tanzania, (unable to accept because of US State Dept travel restrictions); first prize, sculpture, Afro-American Museum, Philadelphia, 1980; Certificate of Appreciation, Exchange Club, Vineland, NJ, 1982; appreciation award, United Rehabilitation Services, 1985. **Military Serv:** USAF 1951-55. **Business Addr:** Counselor, Administrator, Pennsylvania Institute of Technology, 800 Manchester Ave, Media, PA 19063.

WILKINS, ALLEN HENRY

Educator. **Personal:** Born May 23, 1934, Elberton, GA; son of Mattie Lue Allen Wilkins and William Henry Wilkins; married Jean E (divorced). **Educ:** Tuskegee Inst, BS 1957; Catholic Univ, MS 1973. **Career:** Washington DC Govt, Dept of Highways, horticulture inspector 1961-69; Navy Facilities Engineers, landscape architect, general engineer 1969-73; Univ District of Columbia, prof of horticulture/landscape design, 1973-. **Orgs:** Licensed landscape architect State of MD 1973-86; mem Amer Soc Landscape Architects 1973-86; vice pres Washington DC NEA 1982-84; mem Amer Horticulture Scientists 1986; mem Alpha Psi Alpha; deacon choir mem Washington DC Congregational Church. **Honors/Awds:** First Black horticultural inspector for Washington DC Govt; Public Service Award, Washington DC Govt 1960; Citation for Public Service, Mayor City of Greenbelt MD 1985; Devel of master plans for several Dept of Defense projects; Landscape-urban design plans for several parks, two schools. **Business Addr:** Prof Horticulture/Landscaping, Univ of the District of Columbia, 4200 Conn Ave NW, B644 Rm 2036, Washington, DC 20008.

WILKINS, BETTY

Founder/journalist. **Personal:** Born Mar 31, 1922, Braddock, PA; married; children: Gloria, Raymond, Robert Jr, Donald, Margaret, Patricia. **Educ:** Denver Opportunity Sch Journalism, Grad 1957. **Career:** KFML Radio, 2 hr gospel show; KC Call, Denver editor; KDKO Radio, soc columnist with Honey Bee's show; Denver Weekly News, editor. **Orgs:** Pres Sophisticates & Soc & Civ Club; vice pres Astro Jets; sec Pond Lily; mem Jane Jefferson Dem Club; Mayors council human relations; mem Bronze Dau Am; State Assn Colored Wmns Clubs; Council Negro Wmn; CO Spress Wmns Club; black del for Geo McGovern from Denver to Miami 1972; committeewoman in E Denverfor 20 yrs; res Delta Mothers Club; Zion Circle Seven; The Denver Beauty Guild; life mem & pub rel chmn NAACP. **Honors/Awds:** Syl Morgan Smith Comm Aw Trophy 1976; Publ Relat Aw Astro Jets 1977; Originator of "Ten Best Dressed Blk Women" Denver; Miss Bronze Dau Awrd 1958; Robert L Vaden Aw 1972; Harriet Tubman Dist Serv Aw 1973; Wmn Yr 1972; Com Awrd Metro Club 1979; Hall of Fame Aw May D & F 1980.

WILKINS, CHARLES O.

Management consultant. **Personal:** Born Jun 18, 1938, Louisville, KY; married Diane Blodgett Wilkins, Jun 19, 1975; children: Nicole, Jennifer. **Educ:** Central State University, Wilberforce, Ohio, BA, 1961; University of California Graduate School, Los Angeles, CA, 1961-63. **Career:** Johnson & Johnson, Raritan, NJ, supervisor, employment, 1965-72; The Singer Company, New York, NY, manager, world headquarters personnel, 1972-80; NYS Urban Development Corporation, New York, NY, vice president, human resources, 1980-84; Performance Plus Management Consulting, East Brunswick, NJ, president, 1984-. **Orgs:** Alpha Phi Alpha, 1958-; Sigma Pi Phi (Boule), 1987-; American Society for Personnel Administration, 1991-; Urban League BEEP; vice pres, human resources, YMCA of Greater New York, 1991-; board member, Health Watch. **Military Serv:** US Army, 1st Lt, 1963-65. **Business Addr:** President/Senior Consultant, Performance Plus Management Consulting, 11 Pilgrim Run, East Brunswick, NJ 08816.

WILKINS, DAVID BRIAN

Educator. **Educ:** Harvard University; Harvard Law School, JD. **Career:** US Supreme Court Justice Thurgood Marshall, clerk; Harvard Law School, professor, currently. **Special Achievements:** Fourth African-American tenured professor at Harvard University. **Business Addr:** Professor, Harvard School of Law, Langdell Hall, Rm 360, 1545 Massachusetts Ave, Cambridge, MA 02138, (617)495-5000.

WILKINS, DOMINIQUE (JACQUES)

Professional basketball player. **Personal:** Born Jan 12, 1960, Paris, France; married Nicole Berry. **Educ:** Attended, Georgia 1983. **Career:** Atlanta Hawks, professional basketball player, 1983-94; LA Clippers, 1994; Boston Celtics, 1994-95; Panathinaikos Athens (Greece), 1995-96; San Antonio Spurs, 1996-97; Team-System Bologna (Italy), 1997-. **Honors/Awds:** MVP 1981 SEC Tournament; NBA All-Rookie team 1982-83; NBA Player of the Week Awds in each of last two seasons; NBA Scoring title 1985-86; winner NBA Slam Dunktitle 1985, 1990, runner up 1986; NBA Player of the Month January 1986; has led Hawks in scoring in 136 of last 159 games; All-NBA first team, 1986; All-NBA second team, 1987-88, 1991, 1993; All-NBA third team, 1989, 1994. **Special Achievements:** NBA Draft, First round pick, #3, 1982; NBA, All-Star game, 1986-94. **Business Addr:** Professional Basketball Player, San Antonio Spurs, 600 Market St, Ste 102, San Antonio, TX 78205, (512)224-4611.

WILKINS, ERVIN W.

Attorney. **Personal:** Born Mar 29, 1919, Asheville, NC; son of Ruth D Wilkins (deceased) and Cornelius F Wilkins (deceased); married Eppsyline Tucker; children: Sharee, Ervin Jr, La Verne. **Educ:** Livingstone Coll, AB, 1940; Northwestern Univ, Grad Work, History, 1941; Howard Univ, AM, 1946; Ohio State Univ, Law, 1947-50; Western Reserve Univ, Law, 1959-60; Cleveland Marshall Law School, JD, 1960, Grad Law, 1965; Western Reserve Univ, Grad School Law, Law Medicine, 1967. **Career:** Post Office, postal clerk, acting foreman 14 yrs; Cleveland School System, hs teacher, 11 yrs; real estate salesman, 6 years; gen practice, 1960-66, 1969-72; State Ohio, spl counsel atty-gen, 1970-72; US Atty, VA, atty, 1972-82; private practice, atty. **Orgs:** Ohio Bar Assn; Natl Bar Assn; Civic League Greater Cleveland; NAACP; elected trustee, Livingstone Coll, North Carolina, 1976; mem, trustee, co-chmn, Men's Plng Comm, St Paul AME Zion Church, Cleveland; dist trustee, Ohio, Ann Conf AME Zion Church; trust Srs of Ohio, 1978-82; mem, Screening Comm Civic League of Greater Cleveland, 1982-85; successor to Congressman Louis Stokes as atty for St Paul AME Zion Church; trustee, Livingstone Coll, Salisbury, NC, 1976-. **Honors/Awds:** Magna Cum Laude; salutatorian, class 1940; Livingstone Coll; mem, Zeta Sigma Pi; completed 4 year coll course in 3 1/2 years A average, grad school, history, Howard Univ; winner treatises, Lawyers Co-operative Pub Co, highest average law sales law damages Cleveland Marshall Law School; scored 3245 state bar exam; awarded meritorious achievement award, Cleveland Bar Assn; Fed Outstanding Comm Serv Award, 1976; outstanding legal serv, Cleveland, 1971; citation, Alumni Meritorious Serv Award, Livingston Coll, 1975; Author of "33 Years in Hell", 1987. **Special Achievements:** Author, "Elizabeth Duncan Koontz, Women's Great Champion" 1919-1989.

WILKINS, GABRIEL NICHOLAS

Professional football player. **Personal:** Born Sep 1, 1971, Cowpens, SC; children: Gabrielle Nicole, Alexis, Chemoya. **Educ:** Gardner-Webb, attended. **Career:** Green Bay Packers, defensive end, 1994-. **Business Addr:** Professional Football Player, Green Bay Packers, 1265 Lombardi Ave, Green Bay, WI 54304, (414)494-2351.

WILKINS, GERALD BERNARD

Professional basketball player. **Personal:** Born Sep 11, 1963, Atlanta, GA; married Vita; children: Jasmyn Alexandria, Holli Dai. **Educ:** Moberly Area Junior College, Moberly, MO, 1981-82; Univ of Tennessee-Chattanooga, Chattanooga, TN, 1982-85. **Career:** New York Knicks, guard, 1985-92, Cleveland Cavaliers, 1992-95; Vancouver Grizzlies, 1995-96; Orlando Magic, 1996-. **Business Addr:** Professional Basketball Player, Orlando Magic, One Magic Pl, Orlando, FL 32801, (407)649-3200.

WILKINS, HENRY, III

Government official, educator. **Personal:** Born Jan 4, 1930, Pine Bluff, AR; son of Minnie B Jones-Wilkins and Henry Wilkins Jr; married Josetta Edwards, Oct 30, 1954; children: Henry IV, Felecia, Mark, Angela. **Educ:** Univ of Arkansas at Pine Bluff (AM&N) BA 1957; Atlanta Univ, MA 1963. **Career:** AR Dist 54, state rep, currently; Univ of Arkansas at Pine Bluff, assoc prof, history/political Sci 1959-89. **Orgs:** Mem AR Delegation Dem Natl Conv 1972; mem Am Assn Coll & Univ Prof; Am Political Sci Assn; So Political Sci Assn; Am Alumni Council; mem Elks Lodge; American Political Science Assn, Arkansas Political Science Assn; Interested Citizens for Voter Education and Registration; Chamber of Commerce. **Honors/Awds:** NAACP Political Achvmnt Award Negro Youth Org 1960; AR State Dem Party Exec Committe; Merrill Fellows grant; Korean Commendations Medals; Some Aspects of the Cold War 1945-1950, Brown Book Company 1963. **Military Serv:** AUS sgt 1954. **Home Addr:** 303 N Maple St, Pine Bluff, AR 71601.

WILKINS, HERBERT PRIESTLY, SR.

Business executive. **Personal:** Born Jan 9, 1942, Boston, MA; son of Katherine Wilkins and William Wilkins; married Sheran R Morris; children: Herbert Jr, Monique, Michelle. **Educ:** Boston Univ, BS 1965; Harvard Univ Grad School of Business Admin, MBA 1970. **Career:** Lucas, Tucker & Co, principal 1969-73; Urban Natl Corp, senior vice pres 1973-75; Wilkins & Co, consultant 1975-77; Syndicated Communications Inc, Washington, DC, president, 1977-89; Syndicated Communications Venture Partners II (syncom), L P, Washington, DC, managing general partner, 1990-; Syncom Management Co. Inc, president, 1990-. **Orgs:** Mem bd of overseers Harvard Comm Health Plan Boston 1973-83; former chmn of bd Amer Assoc of Minority SBC's 1979-83; pres Stellar Comm Corp 1981-89; dir Natl Assoc of Minorities in Cable TV 1983-90; pres OFC, Inc 1984-89; dir, Freedom Natl Bank, 1987-90; dir, Black Entertainment Television, 1984-; dir, Chicago Cable Television, 1985; mem, mgmt, Comm District Cablevision, L.P., 1983. **Honors/Awds:** Service Awds Natl Cable TV Assoc 1983, Federal Communications Comm Adv Committee on Minority Ownership 1984, Natl Assn of Investment Co Natl Cable Television Assn. **Business Addr:** Managing General Ptr, Syncom Fund, 8401 Colesville Rd, Ste 300, Silver Spring, MD 20910.

WILKINS, JOSETTA EDWARDS

Educator. **Personal:** Born Jul 17, 1932, Little Rock, AR; daughter of Laura Bridgette Freeman Edwards and James Wesley Edwards; married Henry Wilkins III, Oct 30, 1954 (deceased); children: Calvin Tyrone, Henry IV, Cassandra Felecia, Mark Reginald, Angela Juanita. **Educ:** AM&N College, BSE, 1961; University of Arkansas, MEd, 1967; Oklahoma State University, EdD, 1987. **Career:** Arkansas Council/Farmer Workers, deputy director, man-power training, 1967-73; University of Arkansas, Pine Bluff, assistant director and coordinator, cooperative education, 1973-76, director, cooperative education, 1977-87, intermin director of univ relations and development, 1987-88, professor, currently. **Orgs:** Jefferson County Juvenile Detention Commission; United Methodist Church, Episcopacy Committee; Martin Luther King, Jr, Holiday Commission, chair political activities committee; American Association for Counseling and Development; American Association for Adult and Continuing Education; Arkansas Personnel and Guidance Association; Literacy Council Advisory Board; Joint Education Committee. **Honors/Awds:** Phi Beta Sigma, Outstanding Service Award, 1992; Arkansas Democratic Black Caucus, Recognition Award, 1992; Blacks in Government, Central Arkansas Chapter, Outstanding Service Award, 1992; Phi Beta Lambda, Appreciation Award, 1992; Cooperative Education Program, Outstanding Service Award, 1992. **Home Addr:** 303 N Maple, Pine Bluff, AR 71601, (501)534-5852.

WILKINS, KENNETH C.

County government official. **Personal:** Born Sep 20, 1952, New York, NY; son of June I (Whitehead) Wilkins and James A Wilkins. **Educ:** Shaw Univ, Raleigh NC, BA 1974; Bowling Green State Univ, Bowling Green OH, MA 1975; Univ of Kentucky, Lexington, JD 1978; NC Inst of Politics, fellow, 1989. **Career:** NC Dept of Correction, Raleigh, legal staff, 1978-79; Shaw Univ, Raleigh NC, asst to exec vice pres, 1979-83; County of Wake, Raleigh NC, register of deeds, 1983-. **Orgs:** Bd mem, Mediation Services of Wake County, 1982-; exec comm, NC Leadership Forum, 1985-; bd mem, Haven House, 1986-; bd mem, Garner Road Family YMCA, 1986-; chair, United Negro Coll Fund Campaign, Raleigh, 1988-; Natl Assn of Counties; NC Assn of Registers of Deeds. **Honors/Awds:** Distinguished Alumni Public Service Award, Shaw Univ, 1984; Heart & Soul Award, WAUG-AM, 1988; plaque, Garner Road YMCA, 1988; fellow, NC Inst of Politics, 1989. **Business Addr:** Register of Deeds, County of Wake, PO Box 1897, Wake County Courthouse, Room 814, Raleigh, NC 27602.

WILKINS, LEONA B.

Music educator. **Personal:** Born Feb 9, 1922, Winston-Salem, NC; daughter of Lottie Gibson Wilkins and Estridge H Wilkins. **Educ:** NC Central Univ, BA 1941; Univ MI, MMus 1944, PhD 1971; Sorbonne Univ Paris, France, cert 1968. **Career:** Raleigh NC, teacher 1942-44; St Louis, teacher 1952-55; Detroit, teacher 1955-64; Bluefield State, 1944-45; Hampton Inst, 1945-48; TN State Univ, 1948-52; E MI Univ 1964-68; Temple Univ, 1968-72; Northwestern Univ, assoc prof 1972-; Northwestern Univ, assoc prof emeritus, 1988-; Trinity Episcopal Church, Chicago, IL, dir, children's music educ, 1990-. **Orgs:** Mem Music Educ Conf; Intl Soc of Music Educators; Amer Assn of Univ Profs, Am Orff-Schulwerk Assn; Coll Music Soc; Alpha Kappa Alpha; mem Bicentennial Commn for MENC 1974-76; Comn for Revision of Natl Tchrs Exam for Music Educ 1974-75; consult IL State Arts Plan; Comn for Revision of Music Objectives for Natl Assessment of Educ Progress Task Force; Role of the Arts Comm USOE; MENC; consult Evanston Public School Dist 65. **Honors/Awds:** Consult Silver Burdett Music Series 1970-71. **Business Addr:** Associate Professor, Northwestern Univ, Sch of Music, Evanston, IL 60201.

WILKINS, RILLASTINE ROBERTA

Systems analyst (retired). **Personal:** Born Jul 24, 1932, Taft, OK; daughter of Willie and Canzaty Smith; married Clarence E Wilkins; children: Nathlyn Barksdale, Clarence Henry. **Educ:** Muskegon Comm Coll; Muskegon Business Coll; Tech Instr Inst; Univ of WI Eau Claire. **Career:** General Telephone Co of MI, telephone oper 1957-62, serv rep 1962-67, div comm instr 1967-71, contact records suprv of bus accts 1973-79, phone mart mgr 1979-81, customer serv mgr 1981-83, analyst customer relations 1983-88. **Orgs:** Chairperson, Human Resources Commn, Muskegon Couty; chairperson, Comm Devel Commn, bd mem, Econ Devel Commn, City of Muskegon Heights; bd mem, Muskegon Area Transcript Syst, Muskegon County; chairperson, Zoning Bd of Appeals City of Muskegon Heights; chairperson, Community Serv Commn, Muskegon County; past pres Urban League Bd of dir; life mem NAACP; past pres Every Woman's Place; past pres Tri-City Woman's Club; past pres Urban League Guild of Greater Muskegon; bd mem Heritage Hosp; bd mem Greater Muskegon Chamber of Comm; bd mem Black Women's Political Caucus of Greater Muskegon; St Bd Podiatric Med; pres Women in Municipal Govt State of MI 1979; co-chairperson, Allocations & Review Comm United Way 1980-81; bd mem, sec Greater Musk Seaway Fest 1980-82; vice pres Mondale Task Force Youth Employment 1980; vice-chmn, Reg Planning Comm, Muskegon County, 1981; Chairperson, Community Emer Clrghs, 1983; reg convenor, Natl Urban League, 1983-84; Natl Black Caucus of Local Elected Officials, 1976-, president, 1988-90; Jr Achievement Advisor, 1972; past president, NBC/LEO, (Nat'l Black Caucus of Local Elected Officials). **Honors/Awds:** Jr Achievement Advisor 1972; 1st Woman Post Advisor for Explorers Career Devel 1973; Speakers Bureau Gen Telephone of MI 1973; Citizens Awd from Residents of Muskegon & Muskegon Hts 1974; Women's Ed Resource Comm 1979; Cert of Commendation Muskegon Comm Coll 1979; Boss of the Day WZZR Grand Rapids MI 1980; Cert of Merit St Josephs Christian Comm Ctr 1980; Pace Awd Muskegon Comm Coll, 1980; Plaque of Congratulations Black Women's Political Caucus 1980; Chosen Woman of the Year by the Black Women's Political Caucus, 1983; served 3 consecutive terms as mayor pro-tem of the City of Muskegon Heights, MI (a first for male/female).

WILKINS, ROGER L.
Scientist (retired). **Personal:** Born Dec 14, 1928, Newport News, VA; married Nasira Ledbetter (deceased); children: Yvonne Diane, Roger (dec'd). **Educ:** Hampton Inst, BS 1951; Howard Univ, MS 1952; Univ So CA, PhD 1967. **Career:** Lewis Flight Propulsion Lab, aeronautical rsch scientist 1952-55; Rocketdyne, sr tech spl 1955-60; Aerospace Corp, sr staff scientist 1960-91. **Orgs:** Mem Combustion Inst; Amer Inst Aeronautics & Astronautics; Gen Alumni Assn Univ So CA; pres 1972-92, 1979-81 So CA Natl Hampton Alumni Assn treas 1974-75. **Honors/Awds:** Urban League Vocation Awd 1965; Serv Awd Natl Sor Phi Delta Kappa Beta 1969; Aerospace Corp Advanced Study Grant 1965-66; Hon Chemical Soc.

WILKINS, ROGER WOOD
Educator. **Personal:** Born Mar 25, 1932, Kansas City, MO; son of Helen Natalie Jackson Clayton and Earl W Wilkins; married Patricia A King, Feb 21, 1981; children: Amy T, David E, Elizabeth W C. **Educ:** Univ of Michigan, Ann Arbor MI, AB 1953, LLB 1956. **Career:** Attorney, NY, NY, 1956-62; State Dept, foreign aid dir, special asst, 1962-66; US Dept of Justice, Washington DC, asst attorney general of US, 1966-69; Ford Foundation, New York NY, program dir & asst to pres, 1969-72; Washington Post, Washington DC, mem of editorial bd, 1972-74; New York Times, New York NY, mem of editorial bd & columnist, 1974-79; Washington Star, Washington DC, assoc ed, 1980-81; Inst for Policy Studies, Washington DC, senior fellow, 1982-; George Mason Univ, Fairfax VA, Clarence J Robinson Prof of History & Amer Culture, 1987-; CBS, New York, NY, radio commentator, 1982-85; Mutual Broadcasting, Alexandria, VA, radio commentator, 1985-87; Natl Public Radio, Washington, DC, radio commentator, 1990-. **Orgs:** Bd mem, NAACP Legal Defense Fund 1970-, Pulitzer Prize Bd 1980-89, Fund for Investigative Journ 1980-, Villers Foundation 1987-, Natl Constitution Center 1988-, PEN/Faulkner Foundation 1989-, Univ of District of Columbia 1989-; vice chair of bd, African-Amer Inst, 1982-; mem of Comm for Racial Justice Policy, Joint Center for Pol Studies, 1982-; mem of comm of overseers, Harvard Univ Afro-Amer Studies, 1984-; mem of steering comm, Free South Africa Movement, 1984-. **Honors/Awds:** Coordinated Nelson Mendela's 1990 Visit to the US; Shared Pulitzer Prize for reports on Watergate, 1973; Chairman, Pulitzer Prize Bd, 1987-88; hon LLD from Central MI Univ 1975, Wilberforce Univ 1984, Union of Experimenting Universities 1986; author of A Man's Life, Simon & Schuster, 1982; regents lecturer, Univ of Calif, Santa Cruz, 1985; Woodrow Wilson School lecturer, Princeton Univ, 1987; Roger Baldwin Civil Liberties Award, New York Civil Liberties Union, 1987; author, Quiet Riots, ed with Fred R Harris, Pantheon, 1989; wrote & narrated front line documentaries broadcast on PBS, "Keeping the Faith," 1987, "Throwaway People," 1990. **Business Addr:** Professor, History, George Mason University, MSN ID6/Attn: Roger Wilkins, 4400 University Dr., Fairfax, VA 22030-4444.

WILKINS, THOMAS A.
Government executive. **Personal:** Born Feb 1, 1930, Lawrenceville, VA; married A Delores Bohannon; children: Lisa Delores, Thomas Alan, Mark Anderson. **Educ:** NO VA Univ dpa 1976, mpa 1975; fed exec inst 1971; NYU, ma 1957; st pauls coll, bs 1951. **Career:** DC Dept of Manpower, dir 1972-; US Dept of Labor, Manpower admin 1965-72; Voc Rehab Serv Glenn Dale Hosp DC Dept Pub Hlth, chief 1959-65; Voc Serv Dept of Corr NYC, asst dir 1957-59; Dept of Corr NYC, prin instr 1955-57. **Orgs:** Mem Am Soc of Pub Admin; bd dir Interstate Conf of Emplymnt Sec Agency Inc; Fed Bus Assn; Am Personnel & Guid Assn; Nat Voc Guid Assn; charter mem Natl Rehab Counselisng Assn; Nat Rehab Assn; Mayor's Cabinet DC; Mayor's Adv Com on Narcotics Addiction DC; mem Metro Washington DC Bd Trade (Businessman's Adv Com); DC Bicentennial Commn; Fed Adv Bd DC Sch System; Fed Review Team, Coord Comm Child Care DC; layman Episcopal Ch; Omega Psi Phi; DAV & mem Reston Homeowners Assn; Hunters Woods Village Council, Reston VA; mem bd trustees St Paul's Coll; past mem bd exec comm ACLU; past bd mem Fair Housing Inc; mem Mayor's Overall Econ Devel Com; mem Mayor's Com on hndcpd; bd trustees Davis Meml Goodwill Industries. **Honors/ Awds:** Sustained Superior Perf Awrd US Dept Labor 1974; So Historcl Preservations of Am 1976-77; Distng Trustee Awrd St Pauls Coll 1972; Outst Perf Awrd Manpower Admin 1969; Vocational Rehab Admin Intern & Flwshp 1960.

WILKINS, THOMAS ALPHONSO
Educator/orchestra conductor. **Personal:** Born Sep 10, 1956, Norfolk, VA; son of Wallace Y Wilkins, Sr.; married Sheri-Lee, Jun 14, 1985. **Educ:** Shenandoah Conserva of Music, BME 1978; New England Conserva of Music, MM 1982. **Career:** Shenandoah Conservatory Symphony, asst conductor 1976-78; Busch Entertainment Corp, music dir 1971-82; New England Conservatory Repetory Orches, asst conductor 1981-82; North Park Coll Orchestra, music dir; director orchestral studies Univ of Tennessee, Chattanooga. 1987-89. **Orgs:** Active mem Phi Mu Alpha Frat 1976-; conductor Northwest IN Youth Orchestra 1983-; asst conductor Northwest IN Symphony Orchestra 1983-.

WILKINSON, BRENDA
Poet and writer for children. **Personal:** Born Jan 1, 1946, Moultrie, GA; daughter of Ethel Anderson Scott and Malcolm Scott; married; children: Kim, Lori. **Educ:** Hunter College of the City University of New York. **Career:** Poet and author of books for children. **Orgs:** Mem, Authors Guild; mem, Authors League of America. **Honors/Awds:** National Book Award nomination, 1976, for Ludell; Ludell and Willie was named one of the outstanding children's books of the year by New York Times and a best book for young adults by American Library Assn, both 1977. **Business Addr:** Board of Global Ministries, 475 Riverside Dr, New York, NY 10115.

WILKINSON, DAN
Professional football player. **Personal:** Born Mar 13, 1973, Dayton, OH. **Educ:** Ohio State. **Career:** Cincinnati Bengals, defensive end, 1994-. **Special Achievements:** Selected by Cincinnati Bengals as first pick overall in first round of NFL draft, 1994. **Business Addr:** Professional Football Player, Cincinnati Bengals, One Bengals Dr, Cincinnati, OH 45202, (513)621-3550.

WILKINSON, DONALD CHARLES
Educator. **Personal:** Born Feb 12, 1936, Madison, FL; divorced; children: Donald Clark. **Educ:** Wilbur Wright Tech, 1960-64; Detroit Inst of Tech, 1964-65; Univ of MI, BA 1969; Sonoma State Coll, MA 1972. **Career:** Sonoma State Coll, asst prof & counselor of Physiology 1971-; Educ Devel Center Newton MA, 1970-71; WJ Maxey Boys Training School, boys supr 1965-69; Detroit Courier, staff wsrither repoter 1961-62; Detroit Water Dept, engr 1956-61; sculptr in wood 1970. **Orgs:** Mem, Alpha Phi Alpha; mem Freelance Civil Rights Activist 1960-68; conslt Blk Tutorial Project 1965; advisor, Morgan Comm School, 1970-71; Ford Found Grant in Early Childhood Educ; rsch & teaching British Infant School Syst, Sherard Infant School Engineering. **Business Addr:** 1801 Cotati Ave, Rohnert Park, CA 94928.

WILKINSON, DORIS
Educator. **Personal:** Born in Lexington, KY; daughter of H T (deceased) and R L Wilkinson. **Educ:** Univ of Kentucky, BA, 1958; Case Western Univ, MA, 1960, PhD, 1968; Johns Hopkins Univ, MPH, 1985. **Career:** Macalester Coll, assoc/full, professor 1970-77; Amer Soc Assn, exec associate, 1977-80; Howard Univ, professor, 1980-84; Univ of Virginia, Charlottesville, VA, visiting professor, 1984-85; Univ of Kentucky, Lexington, KY, professor, 1985-94; Harvard Univ, Cambridge, MA, visiting scholar, 1989-90, visiting professor, summers 1992, 1993, 1994, 1997. **Orgs:** Eastern Sociological Soc, 1983-84; pres, District of Columbia Sociological Soc, 1982-83; bd of overseers, Case Western Reserve Univ, 1982-85; public educ, Comm Amer Cancer Soc, 1982-85; exec office budget comm, American Sociological Assn, 1985-88; pres, Soc for the Study of Social Problems, 1987-88; vice president, American Sociological Assn, vice pres, 1991-92, council, 1995-97; Kentucky Commission on Women, 1993-96; Kentucky African-American Commission, 1994-. **Honors/Awds:** Articles & books published, 1968-; NIH Fellow, 1963-66; Woodrow Wilson Fellow, 1959-61; NIE Grant, 1978-80; NCI, research contract, 1985-88; Dubois-Johnson-Frazier Award, Amer Sociological Assn, 1988; Omicron Delta Kappa Natl Leadership Hon, 1987; Grant from the Kentucky Humanities Commission for a project on Afro-Amer physicians, 1988-89; Women's History Month Award, Midway College, 1991; Public Humanities Award, Kentucky Humanities Council, 1990; Hall of Distinguished Alumni, Univ of Kentucky, 1989; Ford Fellow, Harvard Univ, 1989-90; Great Teacher Award, 1992; Distinguished Professorship, 1992; Distinguished Scholar, Assoc of Black Sociologists, 1993. **Business Addr:** Professor, Department of Sociology, University of Kentucky, Lexington, KY 40506.

WILKINSON, FREDERICK D., JR.
Business executive. **Personal:** Born Jan 25, 1921, Washington, DC; son of Margaret W and Frederick D Wilkinson Sr; married Jeane; children: Sharon, Dayna, Frederick III. **Educ:** Howard Univ, AB (magna cum laude), 1942; Army Univ Center of Oahu, certificate, business law, accounting, 1946; Harvard Univ, MBA (with distinction), 1947;. **Career:** Macy's, jr asst buyer, 1949-50, sr asst buyer 1950-52, buyer, mdse manager 1952-68, vice pres 1968-74; New York City Transit Auth, exec officer passenger serv, exec officer surface transit, 1974-76; American Express Co, vice pres travel 1977-79, vice pres consumer card 1979-85, sr vice pres 1985-93, consultant, currently. **Orgs:** Trustee, Natl Urban League, Natl Treasurer; bd of overseers, Cornell Univ Med Coll & Graduate School of Medical Sciences; director, UNC Ventures; MTA, Inspector General Advisory Bd, acting chmn, Citizen's Advisory Cmte, permanent; Brookdale Center of Hunter Coll, co-chair; Westchester Clubmen Foundation; Hofstra Univ Business School, dean's advisory bd. **Honors/Awds:** Good Scout of the Yr BSA; Alumni Achievement Awd Howard Univ; Wm H Moss Brotherhood. **Military Serv:** US Army, infantry capt, 4 yrs. **Business Addr:** Consultant, American Express Co, World Financial Center, 200 Vesey St, New York, NY 10285-5100.

WILKINSON, JAMES WELLINGTON
Physician. **Personal:** Born Dec 8, 1935, Hampton, VA; married Cormay; children: Yolanda. **Educ:** Wesleyan Univ Hampton Inst, BA 1962; Hampton Inst, MA 1965; Med Coll of VA, MD 1970. **Career:** Hampton Publ School, teacher 1962-65; Hampton Inst, teacher 1965-69; Private practice, physician, family med 1971-. **Orgs:** Chmn Med Records Comm Whittaker Mem Hosp; mem PSRU, Peninsular Med Soc, Old Dominion Med Soc, Natl Med Assoc; bd of dir YWCA; mem Wesleyan UnivAlumni Assoc, Hampton Inst Alumni Assoc, Med Coll VA Alumni Assoc. **Honors/Awds:** Cert Adv Study AMA, VA Med Soc; Fellow Amer Acad of Family Physicians 1982, The Amer Soc of Contemporary Med & Surgery 1983, The Acad of Psychosomatic Med 1984. **Business Addr:** Physician, 534 Elizabeth Lake Dr, Hampton, VA 23669-1724.

WILKINSON, MARIE L.
Company executive. **Personal:** Born May 6, 1910, New Orleans, LA; daughter of Charles and Maude La Beau; married Charles; children: Donald, Sheila Scott. **Educ:** New Orleans U, Bus 1921; Straight Coll (now known as Dillard U). **Career:** P & W Truck Parts & Equip Inc, owner, pres; Aura Human Rels Commn, pres 26 yrs; Marie Wilkinson Child Devel Ctr, pres 20 yrs; Aurora Feed the Hungry Inc, pres 20 yrs. **Honors/Awds:** Cath Woman of Year Diocese of Rockford 1956; Beautiful People Awrd Chicago Urban League 1970; Citizenshp Citation Awrd No IL Dist Optmist 1968; fndng pres emeritus Aurora Urban League 1978; Honorary Doctor of Laws Honoris Causal, Aurora Univ, 1990; Key to the City, Aurora, IL, 1988. **Business Addr:** Owner, P&W Truck Parts & Equip Inc, 648 N View St, Aurora, IL 60506.

WILKINSON, RAYMOND M., JR.
Automobile dealer. **Personal:** Born Oct 28, 1943, St Louis, MO; son of Elizabeth Wilkinson and Raymond M Wilkinson Sr; married Betty J Taylor, Nov 6, 1965; children: William, Ray III, Heather. **Educ:** General Motors Inst, Flint MI, dealer-operator degree, 1981. **Career:** US Postal Service, St Louis MO, carrier, 1961-75; Don Darr Pontiac, St Louis MO, salesperson 1975-80, manager 1981-83; Ray Wilkinson Buick-Cadillac Inc, pres & gen mgr, currently. **Orgs:** Mem, NAACP-Racine 1984-, UNCF-Racine 1985-; bd mem, Racine Wed Optimists 1984-, West Racine Businessmen 1985-, Racine Sickle Cell 1986-. **Honors/Awds:** Best Buick Dealer in Class, Buick Motor, 1986-88, 1990, 1992-94; Minority Small Business Award, Racine NAACP, 1989; B E's 100, Black Enterprise Magazine, 1992, 1994, 1995, Board of Directors, 1996, 1997; Firstar Bank of Racine, Board of Directors, Racine Youth Leadership Academy, 1994-96. **Business Addr:** President & General Manager, Ray Wilkinson Buick-Cadillac Inc, 6001 Washington Ave, PO Box 085150, Racine, WI 53408.

WILKINSON, ROBERT SHAW, JR.
Physician. **Personal:** Born Jul 11, 1928, Brooklyn, NY; son of Melissa Ruth Royster Wilkinson (deceased) and Robert Shaw Wilkinson (deceased); married Carolyn Elizabeth Cobb, Jun 24, 1951; children: Amy Elizabeth, Karin Lynn, Robert Montague. **Educ:** Dartmouth Coll, BA 1950; NY Univ, MD 1955. **Career:** George Washington Univ, assoc clinical prof med; Amer Bd Intl Medicine, diplomate; Group Health Assn Inc, staff physician 1962-68; George Washington Univ Hosp, attending phys 1962-; private practice, physician 1968-96; medical advisor, Inter-Amer Devel Bank 1976-; Georgetown Medical Faculty Associates, 1996-; Georgetown Univ, Division of General Medicine, asst prof of medicine, 1996-; Georgetown Univ Hosp, attending physician, 1996-. **Orgs:** Med Soc DC, AMA, fellow, Amer Coll of Physicians; Acad Medicine DC; Sigma Pi Phi Faternity, Espilon Boule, 1971-. **Honors/Awds:** The Dartmouth Alumni Award, Dartmouth Coll, 1987. **Military Serv:** AUS MC capt 1956-58. **Business Addr:** Physician, 2141 K St NW, Ste 401, Washington, DC 20037, (202)872-1973.

WILKINSON, SHEPPARD FIELD
Business executive. **Personal:** Born in Jefferson, TX; son of Millie Elizabeth Wilkinson and Rev. John Seaborn Wilkinson (deceased). **Educ:** Butler Jr Coll, Grad; Prairie View A&M U; Tyler Jr Coll. **Career:** Tyler Leader, owner fndr; Dallas Star Post, advertising mgr; Tyler Tribune, advertising mgr; Port Arthur Edition Houston Informer, editor advertising mgr; Prairie View A&M U, pub rels publicity ofcr; Jarvis Christina Coll; Wiley Coll. **Orgs:** Mem Tyler Orgn Men; Tyler, Smith Co Voters League; NAACP; Bethlehem Bapt Ch. **Honors/Awds:** Recpt Best Publ Awrd TX Coll; recg Outsdng Serv USN; Cert Awrd Delta Sigma Theta Sor; spl awrd for Serv BSA; N Tyler Br YMCA.

WILKS, GERTRUDE
Educational administrator. **Personal:** Born Mar 9, 1927, Lisbon, LA; married Otis; children: Otis Jr, Danny, Patricia. **Career:** Mothers for Equal Educ, dir 1965; Nairobi Day & High School, dir 1966; Orignator for "Sneak-Out Prgm" 1965. **Orgs:** Fndr MEE 1955; fndr Recherch Corp 1965; fndr Sat Tutorial Day Sch 1966; org Annette Latorre Nursery & Sch 1967; fndr Mothers Homemkng Ind 1968; org black & white conf; org MEE Educ Day Care 1970; org MEE Extended Day Care 1976; org one parent fam grp; consult HEW; consult Ravenswood Elem Dist; consult Stanford Tchr Trng; consult San Jose Sch Dist; consult Palo Alto Sch Dist; consult Coll of San Mateo; consult Foothill Coll; consult Wright Inst Coun; mem EPA Munic coun; mayor 1976; mem United Way Plng; chmn bd of trustees Great Friendship Bapt Ch; commr & vchm Redevel E Palo Alto; chrtr mem Nairobi Coll Bd1963-72; comm coun Ravenswood Elem Dist; bd dir EPA Neigh Hlth Ctr; commr San Mateo Co Econ Oppty Commin; ex-of mem Comm Action Counc; pres Missionary Bapt Soc. **Honors/Awds:** Outst comm serv OICW 1966; St Sen Rules Resol 1973; Black Child Devel Inst Awrd 1973; Phoebe Hearst Awd 1974; Resol of Commend EPA Muni Coun 1974; citizen awd Kiwanis Club 1976; commend CA Lt Gov 1976; bicen awd Trinity Bapt Ch 1976; proclam Palo Alto & EPA Muni Coun 1976; serv to mankind awd Los Altos Sertoma Club 1977; "Black Strength & Black Survival" 1968; "What is the Problem" 1969; "Nairobi Sch Syst" 1969. **Business Addr:** 1194 Saratoga Ave, East Palo Alto, CA 94303.

WILKS, JAMES LEE
Organization financial officer. **Personal:** Born Feb 5, 1951, Chester, SC; son of Ivry Wilks and James A Wilks; married LaVon Wilks, May 10, 1991; children: Lega, Louia, Jordan. **Educ:** Bernard M Barnett, BBA, 1973. **Career:** American Express, asst dir of Intl Services, 1980-85; ACD/Head Start, fiscal coordinator, 1985-95, vice pres, finance, 1995-. **Orgs:** Father's Rights Metro, president, 1990-. **Honors/Awds:** Fathers Rights Metro, Father of the Year, 1994. **Home Addr:** 384 Greene Ave, Brooklyn, NY 11216-1108.

WILLACY, HAZEL M.
Attorney. **Personal:** Born Apr 20, 1946, Mississippi; daughter of Willie Barnes Martin and Julious Martin; married Aubrey B; children: Austin Keith, Louis Samuel. **Educ:** Smith Clg, BA 1967; Case Western Reserve U, JD 1976. **Career:** Bureau of Labor Stats, lbr ecnmst 1967-72; Baker Hostetter, atty 1976-80; Sherwin Williams, labor rel atty 1980-82, asst dir labor relations, 1983-87, dir Labor Relations, 1987-93; dir, Empl Policies/Labor Relations, 1993-. **Orgs:** Mem ABA OH St Bar Asso 1976-; president, board of directors, Northeast Chapter, Industrial Relations Research Assn 1995-97; mem, bd of trustees, Meridia Physician Network, 1995-; community advisors, Cleveland Music School Settlement, 1994-. **Honors/Awds:** Order of Coif 1976; articles publ 1970, 76, 80. **Home Addr:** 3145 Laurel Rd, Cleveland, OH 44120. **Business Addr:** Director, Employment Policies & Labor Relations, Sherwin Williams Co., 12 Midland Bldg, 101 Prospect Ave, Cleveland, OH 44115.

WILLIAM, THOMPSON E.
City government official. **Personal:** Born Dec 26, 1924, New York, NY; married Elaine Allen; children: 2. **Educ:** Brooklyn Coll, BA; LLB. **Career:** NY State Senate, mem 1964-66; New York City Council, mem. **Orgs:** Mem Am Bar Assn; Bedford Stuyvesant Lawyers Assn; mem exec bd regional dir chmn legal redress com Brooklyn Br. **Honors/Awds:** Dem Recipient Purple Heart Combat Infantrymen's Badge. **Military Serv:** AUS WW II. **Business Addr:** 768 Putnam Ave, Brooklyn, NY 11221.

WILLIAMS, A. CECIL
Clergyman. **Personal:** Born Sep 22, 1929, San Angelo, TX; married Janice Mirikitani; children: Kim, Albert. **Educ:** Huston-Tillotson Coll, BA 1952; Perkins School of Theol, BD 1955; Pacific School Religon, Grad Work. **Career:** St Paul Meth Church, asst minister 1954; Meth Church, minister 1955; Houston-Tillotson Coll, chaplain & teacher 1956-59; St James Meth Church, minister 1961-64; Glide Mem United Meth Church, minister 1964-. **Orgs:** Instr Ch Soc Crisis; bd mem Martin Luther King Ctr Soc Change; host KPIX-TV Vibrations for a New People; interviewed Angela Davis in prison, Sammy Davis Jr, Coretta Scott King. **Honors/Awds:** Have been publ in many mags; created Glide Celebrations; Emmy Awd San Francisco Natl Acad TV Arts & Sci 1972; Man of the Year Sun Reporter 1967; featured in PBS-TV special hosted by Maya Angelou 1992. **Business Addr:** Minister, Glide Memorial United Meth Ch, 330 Ellis St, San Francisco, CA 94102.

WILLIAMS, AARON
Professional basketball player. **Personal:** Born Jan 2, 1971; married Heather, 1997. **Educ:** Xavier (OH). **Career:** Utah Jazz, forward, 1993-94; Milwaukee Bucks, 1994-95; Vancouver Grizzlies, 1996-97; Seattle Supersonics, 1997-. **Business Addr:** Professional Basketball Player, Seattle Supersonics, PO Box 900911, Seattle, WA 98109, (206)281-5850.

WILLIAMS, ADA L.
Educational Administrator. **Personal:** Born Aug 22, 1933, Waxahachie, TX; daughter of Lueada Gregory Gipson Lewis and Henry Lee Gipson; married Clyde L Williams, Jun 8, 1957; children: Adrian Dwight Williams. **Educ:** Huston-Tillotson Coll, BA, 1955; North TX Sate Univ, MA, 1968. **Career:** Dallas Independent School Dist, specialist, counselor, employee relations, 1955-present. **Orgs:** Life mem, NEA; TEA evaluation team, 1975; NE Univ Eval Team 1975; mem TX Assn of Parlimentarians, Natl Assn of Parlimentarians; pres Classroom Tchrs of Dallas 1975-79; mem coord bd Natl Council of Accreditation for Teacher Educ; mem St Paul AME Church; mem NAACP; appointed by Governor to 6 yr term as one of the commrs on the Credit Union Commn for the State; mem Dallas Teachers Credit Union Bd, chairman, 1979-; mem Delta Sigma Theta Sor Inc; mem Delta Kappa Gamma Soc Inc; mem Oak Cliff B & PW Club Inc; mem Natl Cncl of Accreditation for Teacher Educ; visiting team Univ of North Florida , Eastern New Mexico Univ, and OK Christian Univ; parliamentarian for TX PTA 1984-86; mem Appeals Bd NEA/NCATE 1985-. **Honors/Awds:** Teacher of the Year, 1969-71; nominee 1984 TX's Gov's Women Hall of Fame; 1984 Obudswoman Awd South Dallas B&PW Club; Outstanding Educator TX Legislation 1983-85; Honored by Delta Kappa Gamma Soc Inc, numerous years beginning 1984-; Achievement Awd Natl Women of Achievement Orgs 1987; Honored w/the TX Honorary Life Membership, 1987; Achievement Award Delta Kappa Gamma Soc, 1981-89; Trailblazer Award, South Dallas B&PW Club Inc, 1976, TV presentation on Parlimentary Procedures, 1989; Have written many parliamentary opinions; many educational, civic, religious, and club awards; Honored by Credit Union Executive Society Board Members, Director of the Year, 1996; Professional Parliamentarian, 1978; Board of Directors, Health Access Providing Services for People with AIDS. **Business Addr:** Specialist: Governmental/Internal Relations, Dallas Independent Sch Dist, 3700 Ross Ave, Dallas, TX 75204.

WILLIAMS, AENEAS DEMETRIUS
Professional football player. **Personal:** Born Jan 29, 1968, New Orleans, LA; married Tracy; children: Saenea. **Educ:** Southern Univ, bachelor's degree in accounting. **Career:** Phoenix Cardinals, defensive back, 1991-93; Arizona Cardinals, 1994-. **Honors/Awds:** NFL Players Assn, NFC Defensive Rookie of the Year; Pro Bowl, 1994, 1995, 1996. **Business Addr:** Professional Football Player, Arizona Cardinals, 8701 S Hardy, Tempe, AZ 85284, (602)379-0101.

WILLIAMS, ALEXANDER, JR.
Judge. **Educ:** Howard Univ School of Law. **Career:** Howard Univ School of Law, professor; Prince Georges County, state attorney, 1987; US District Court, District of Maryland, federal judge, 1994. **Business Addr:** Federal Judge, US District Court, 6500 Cherrywood Ln, Greenbelt, MD 20770, (301)344-0637.

WILLIAMS, ALFRED HAMILTON
Professional football player. **Personal:** Born Nov 6, 1968, Houston, TX; married Lena; children: Dominique, Justin, Christopher Alfred. **Educ:** Univ of Colorado, attended. **Career:** Cincinnati Bengals, defensive end, 1991-94; San Francisco 49ers, 1995; Denver Broncos, 1996-. **Honors/Awds:** Pro Bowl, 1996. **Business Addr:** Professional Football Player, Denver Broncos, 13655 Broncos Pkwy, Englewood, CO 80112, (303)649-9000.

WILLIAMS, ALMA MINTON
Utility company executive. **Personal:** Born Apr 28, 1937, Little Rock, AR; daughter of Thelma Yancy Minton and Paul L Minton; children: K Andre Sr, Judith E. **Educ:** Talladega College, BA, 1958; Utah State University, 1963; Central Connecticut State University, 1964; University of Arkansas, Fayetteville, 1965-66; Winona State College, 1969; Huston-Tillotson College, 1970; Bemis Lawrence School of Real Estate, broker's license, 1973; University of Arkansas at Little Rock School of Law, JD, 1977. **Career:** Little Rock Public School District, teacher, 1960-77; Supreme Court of Arkansas, law clerk, 1977-78; Jones and Tiller Law Firm, law clerk, 1978-79; Arkansas Power and Light Company, procedures anyalyst, 1979-81, manager, community relations, 1981-, special assistant to the President of Entergy Corp, 1985-. **Orgs:** Board chairman, Southwest Educational Development Laboratory, 1994-95; Southeastern Electric Educational Services Cmte, 1981-, past chmn; Greater Little Rock Public Education Cmte, Chamber of Commerce, 1982-, past chmn; president, Arkansas Chapter, American Association of Blacks in Energy, 1988-92; past chmn, Edison Electric Institute Educational Services Cmte, 1991-92; National Energy and Economics Cmte, NAACP; Energy Source Advisory Cncl; National Association of Partners in Education; Alpha Kappa Alpha Sorority; Ballet Arkansas Inc, bd of dirs; Arkansas Business and Education Alliance, steering cmte; Leadership Roundtable; SCAN, bd of directors. **Honors/Awds:** Honorary Citizens Award, City of Little Rock, 1985; Prism Award in Education, Arkansas Chapter, Public Relations Society of America, 1989; Common Goals Award for Outstanding Electric Utility Consumer Program, Edison Electric Institute, 1989; Friend of Education Award, Arkansas Education Association, 1989; Chairman's Award for Satisfying Internal and External Constituents, Energy Corp, 1990; Omega Psi Phi Fraternity, Citizen of the Year Award, 1991. **Business Addr:** Manager, Community Relations, Corporate Communications, Arkansas Power and Light, PO Box 551, Little Rock, AR 72203.

WILLIAMS, ALPHONZA
City official. **Personal:** Born Sep 10, 1933, Marshall, TX; son of Arvee Williams and Telas Williams; divorced; children: Anthony Kirk. **Educ:** Wiley Coll Marshall TX, BS 1961; Prairie View Coll, 18 sem hrs 1961, 1973; Elba School of Ins Denver CO, Cert 1968; East TX Police Acad, Police Ct 1968; Kilgore Coll TX, 90 hrs Real Estate 1971-72; TSU School of Law Houston, JD 1976; Southwest TX State Univ St Marcus, 1983. **Career:** Marshall, TX, police officer 1958-73; Dallas ISD Dallas, TX, tchr 1962-63; GC Stephens Real Estate, salesman 1969-73; Milburn Real Estate, Salesman 1974-76; Ave C Apts, mgr 1975-76; Oleus Williams Real Estate, salesman 1977; Williams Asphalt, pres; William & Hicks Constr Co, co-owner; Rosehill Garden, vp/asst treas/corp mgr; Marshall-Harrison Cty, judge, 1983-. **Orgs:** Member, The Kiwanis Club of America; executive board of directors, North East Texas Economic Development District, ARK-TX Regional Development Company; vice president, Williams & Williams. **Honors/Awds:** Phi Beta Sigma Bus Awd 1971; Cert of Achievement Galilee Sr Matrons 1983; Disting Citizenship Awd Alpha Kappa Alpha 1984; Cert of Honor The Links Intl 1984; Prof License to Practice Law Enforcement; 1st black police officer & sgt in Marshall TX; 1st black Appeal Referee in Eastern TX; 1st black Justice of the Peace in Eastern TX; Certificate for Meritorious Service, City of Marshall; Certificate of Appreciation, East Texas Human Development Corporation; Certificate of Honor, The Links Inc; Certificate of Award, Nu Omega Chapter, Alpha Kappa Alpha Sorority, Inc. **Military Serv:** USAF a/1c 4 yrs; USAF Reserves 2 yrs. **Home Addr:** 2207 South St, Marshall, TX 75670.

WILLIAMS, ALVIN
Professional basketball player. **Personal:** Born Aug 6, 1974; son of Alvin Williams Sr. and Alfreda Williams. **Educ:** Villanova. **Career:** Portland TrailBlazers, guard, 1997-98; Toronto Raptors, 1998-. **Business Addr:** Professional Basketball Player, Toronto Raptors, 150 York St, Ste 110, Toronto, ON, Canada M5H 3S5, (416)214-2255.

WILLIAMS, ALYSON
Entertainer. **Personal:** Born May 11, 1961, New York, NY; daughter of Shirley M Williams and Robert Lee Booker. **Educ:** City Coll of New York; Marymount Manhattan College. **Career:** Singer, actress; albums: Raw, 1989, Alyson Williams, 1992; plays: Wicked Way, I Need A Man. **Special Achievements:** First guest vocalist to perform with Branford Marsalis and the Tonight Show Band, 1992. **Business Addr:** Recording Artist, Def Jam Recordings, 652 Broadway, 3rd Fl, New York, NY 10012, (212)979-2610.

WILLIAMS, ANITA SPENCER
Educator. **Personal:** Born in Philadelphia, PA; daughter of Julia Walker Spencer and Thomas Spencer; married Willie G Williams, Jun 7, 1958; children: Diane, Stephen, Karen. **Educ:** Cheyney Univ, Cheyney PA, BS (cum laude), 1967; Temple Univ, Philadelphia PA, EdM 1971, EdD 1988. **Career:** School District of Philadelphia, PA, teacher, 1967-71, reading specialist, 1971-85, auxiliary vice principal, 1985-86, teacher trainer, 1986-87, administrative asst, 1987-. **Orgs:** Mem, Alpha Phi Sigma Natl Honor Soc, 1966-; mem, Intl Reading Assn, 1972-; consultant, Progress Educational Program, 1977-80; mem, Black Women's Educational Alliance, 1980-82; educational dir, Waters Community Center, 1980-88; mem, Phi Delta Kappa Educational Fraternity, 1985-. **Honors/Awds:** First Scholar of the Year, Cheyney Univ, 1966. **Business Addr:** Administrative Assistant, Office for Senior High Schools, School District of Philadelphia, 21st Street & the Parkway, Room 501, Philadelphia, PA 19103.

WILLIAMS, ANN CLAIRE
Judge. **Personal:** Born Aug 16, 1949, Detroit, MI; daughter of Dorothy E Garrett Williams and Joshua Marcus Williams; married David J Stewart, Aug 25, 1979; children: one son, one daughter. **Educ:** Wayne State Univ, Detroit MI, BA, Education, 1970; Univ of Michigan, Ann Arbor MI, MA, Guidance/ Counseling, 1972; Univ of Notre Dame Law School, Notre Dame IN, JD, 1975. **Career:** Judge Robert A Sprecher, law clerk, 1975-76; US Attorney's Office, Assistant United States attorney, 1976-83; US Attorney's Office, Organized Crime Drug Enforcement Task Force for North Central Region, chief, 1983-85; Judicial Conference of the US, chair of court administration & case management committee, 1993-97, committee mem, 1990-93; Just the Beginning Foundation, chair; Federal Judges Association, president-elect; National Institute for Trial Advocacy, board of trustees, faculty member, 1979-; US District Court, judge, 1985-. **Orgs:** Univ of Chicago Laboratory School Bd of Trustees, 1988-, Univ of Notre Dame Bd of Trustees 1988-; Museum of Science & Industry Bd of Trustees, 1991-97. **Honors/Awds:** Edith S Sampson Memorial Award, Illinois Judicial Council, 1986; Thurgood Marshall Award, Chicago Kent College of Law, 1986; Headliner Award, Women of Wayne State Univ Alumni, 1987; Honorary JD, Lake Forest College, 1987; Honorary Doctor of Public Service, University of Portland, 1993; Honorary JD, Univ of Notre Dame, 1997. **Business Addr:** Judge, United States District Court, 219 S Dearborn St, Rm 1988, Chicago, IL 60604.

WILLIAMS, ANN E. A.
Educational adminstrator. **Personal:** Born Sep 21, 1946, Jacksonville, FL; divorced. **Educ:** FL A&M U, BS 1968. **Career:** Duval Co Bd of Public Instruction, instr, asst principal, currently; Duval Co Juvenile Court, coun 1969; A Philliph Randoph Inst, exec counc; FL Jr Coll Jax FL Adult Educ, instructor; Minority Affairs Com of Duval Teachers United. **Orgs:** Jacksonville Jaycees; HOPE Chapel Christian Assembly Inc, Cub Scout Den Ldr; pres Dem Women's of FL Inc; Dem Exec Com; Nat Coun of Negro Women Inc; exec com NAACP Leag of Women Voters; Coun of Soc Studies; vice pres Duval Tchrs United; memshp com YWCA; United Meth Women; Jacksonville Inc, NABSE, volunteer. **Business Addr:** Asst Principal of Community Education, Duval County Board of Public Instruction, 3800 Crown Point Rd, Jacksonville, FL 32257.

WILLIAMS, ANNALISA STUBBS
Business executive. **Personal:** Born Sep 23, 1956, Youngstown, OH; daughter of Eula Grace Harris Stubbs and Julius Saffold Stubbs; married Michael D Williams, Sep 7, 1985; children: Michael James (dec), Alexandria Katherine-Grace Williams, James Robert II. **Educ:** Kent State Univ, BA 1977; Univ of Akron, MA 1979; Univ of Akron Law Sch, JD 1984. **Career:** Kent State Univ, pre-law adv 1976-77, orientation instr 1976-77, resident staff adv 1976-77; OH Civil Rights Comm, investigator/intake spec 1977-79; Metro Regional Transit Auth, personnel equal employment minor bus dir 1979-84, employee relations officer 1984-85; City of Akron, asst law dir 1985-89; Roadway Services Inc Akron OH, manager, 1989-. **Orgs:** Mem Delta Sigma Theta 1980-; Urban Leagues Youth Committee; bd of dirs Information Line; bd of trustees, Prep Ohio; mem Delta Sigma Theta Sor Inc; mem Akron Barristers Club; mem Akron Bar Association; mem Akron Urban League; mem West Side Neighbors; treas Comm to Re-elect Councilman Michael D Williams; trustee, Ohio Ballet, 1988-. **Honors/Awds:** Superior Scholarship Alpha Lambda Delta Kent State 1977; Disting Scholarship Pi Sigma Alpha Kent State 1977; Outstanding Black Student Black United Students Kent State 1977; 1st place Akron Law Sch Client Counseling Competition 1983. **Home Addr:** 584 Avalon Ave, Akron, OH 44320.

WILLIAMS, ARMON
Professional football player. **Personal:** Born Aug 13, 1973. **Educ:** Univ of Arizona, attended. **Career:** Houston Oilers, defensive back, 1997-. **Business Addr:** Professional Football Player, Tennessee Oilers, c/o Baptist Sports Park, 7640 H 70-5, Nashville, TN 37221.

WILLIAMS, ARMSTRONG
Public relations executive, columnist. **Personal:** Born Feb 5, 1960, Marion, SC. **Educ:** SC State Coll, BS (Honors) 1981. **Career:** Senator Strom Thurmond, legislative aide 1980; Congressmen Carroll Campbell, legislative aide 1981; Congressmen Floyd Spence, legislative aide 1981; US Dept of Ag, legislative analyst 1981-83; US Equal Employment Opport Comm, confidential asst to chmn; Graham Williams Group, CEO, currently; syndicated columnist, currently. **Orgs:** Bd advisors Dupree Constr 1981-; bd of dir Comptex Assoc 1982-; advisory bd Child-Help USA 1982-; consult marketer Smooth as Silk Enterprises James Wilkes Pres 1984-; chmn bd of dir Travis Winkey Fashion Mag 1982-. **Honors/Awds:** Bicentennial Public Speaking Award 1976; ROTC Sojourner Awd 1978; Youth of the Year Congressional Black Caucus 1982-83; Falcons Public Serv The Falcons 1983-84; Public Serv Phi Beta Sigma 1982-83; Liberal Arts Howard Univ School of Liberal Arts 1983-84; One of 30 most influential young Blacks in Amer under 30 March, 1985 Ebony Mag; appeared on Phil Donahue Show Feb 25 "America's Top Black Conservatives". **Home Addr:** 201 Masschusetts Ave NE, #217-A, Washington, DC 20002.

WILLIAMS, ARNETTE L.
Educator. **Personal:** Born Sep 3, Logan, WV; married Clarence L Williams; children: Cheryl, Reginald. **Educ:** BS 1943. **Career:** Marion Co WV, former teacher. **Orgs:** Former vol work Girl Scouts Boy Scouts Little League PTA Grey Lady ARC Military Hosps Overseas; chairwoman of bd co-founder Reston Sect Nat'l Council Negro Women 1973; mem Reston Planned Parenthood Comm Established Community Clinic 1974; aptd mem Planned Parenthood Council No VA; mem Wolf Trap Asso forPerforming Arts; FISH; United Fund; Int'l Womens Org 1975; mem Social Club "Sagarities" Serv Oriented; Lions Aux Maternal Grandmother Grandfather Were Among First Black Tchrs in Henry Co VA.

WILLIAMS, ARTHUR G., JR.
Judge (retired). **Personal:** Born Feb 11, 1919, New Haven, CT; son of Maude Williams and Arthur Williams; married Carolyn Downs; children: Arthur G III. **Educ:** Howard U, AB 1943; Columbia Law Sch, LLB 1948. **Career:** Ct of Common Pleas St of CT, ret judge 1965-76; Ct of Common Pleas CT, judge 1966-76; Circ Ct CT 1961-75; Madison CT, corp couns 1953-60. **Orgs:** Dir Union Tr Co. **Business Addr:** P O Box 351, Madison, CT 06443.

WILLIAMS, ARTHUR K.
Business executive. **Personal:** Born Sep 25, 1945, Albany, GA. **Educ:** Monroe Area Voc-Tech School, Cert 1965; Albany Jr Coll, 1975; Albany Area Voc Tech School, Continuing Ed 1979-; Nationwide Ins Training School, Independent Agent 1979. **Career:** Al Rankim Shriners, bookkeeper 1973; Albany State Coll, accountant 1965-79; City of Albany Ward 3, commiss 1982-86; Arthur Williams Ins Agency, agent 1979-. **Orgs:** Corp mem Boys Club of Albany 1979-85; treas NAACP 1980-85; mem GA Municipal Assoc 1982-85; reg coord Rainbow Coalition 1984; mem Nationwide Ins Independent Cont Assoc 1984; Boys & Girls Clubs of America, dir of regional training. **Military Serv:** AUS Reserve sfc E-7 16 yrs; US Commendation, Viet Service 1969. **Home Addr:** 518 Holloway Ave, Albany, GA 31701.

WILLIAMS, ARTHUR LOVE
Physician. **Personal:** Born Jun 4, 1940, Priscilla, MS; married Patricia; children: Terri, Toni, Tara. **Educ:** Jackson State Coll, BS 1962; Meharry Med Coll, MD 1966; Hubbard Hosp, Intern 1966-67; Hubbard Hosp, Resd 1970-73. **Career:** Pvt Prac, physician 1974; Med Prgm Baylor Coll Med, tchr comm 1974-; Hubbard Hosp Dept Internal Med, instr asst prof chf resd 1972-74; Univ TX Med Educ Prgm, tchg staff 1976-; St Elizabeth Hosp, chf staff pres med 1977-. **Orgs:** Mem Houston Med Forum; Harris Co Med Soc; Nat Med Assn; AMA; bd mem CCEMS 1976-77; sec Houston Med Forum 1977; chmn Educ Com 1975-77; ann GPA-Forde Meml Lectr & Banq 1975-77; bd cert Internal Med 1973; chairman, PPO Board, St Joseph Hosp, 1994-95, member governing board, 1994-96, chairman, Department of Medicine, 1992-94. **Honors/Awds:** Air Medal Commendation 1969-70; Flight Surgeon 1967-70. **Military Serv:** USAF capt 1966-70. **Business Addr:** Mullins & Williams, 4315 Lockwood, Houston, TX 77026.

WILLIAMS, AUBIN BERNARD
Construction company executive. **Personal:** Born Mar 27, 1964, Detroit, MI; son of Sadie J Francis Williams and Eddie C Williams Sr. **Educ:** Wayne State Univ, Detroit, MI, BS, 1987. **Career:** Williams & Gilliard, Detroit, MI, field supt, 1978-82; A & S Construction, Detroit, MI, marketing rep, 1982-85; Williams & Richardson Co, Inc, Detroit, MI, pres; The Williams Corporation, chairman, currently. **Orgs:** mem, mkting comm, Associated General Contracts of Amer, 1988-; mem, Detroit Economic Club, 1988-; sec, Assn of Black General Contractors, 1989-; mem, Natl Assn of African American Business, 1991-. **Honors/Awds:** Construction Co of the Year, Dept of Commerce, 1989; Co of the Year, Natl Assn of Black MBA's, 1989. **Business Addr:** Chairman, The Williams Corp, 220 W Congress, Ste 200, Detroit, MI 48226.

WILLIAMS, BARBARA ANN
Air traffic control specialist. **Personal:** Born Jun 12, 1945, Cleveland, OH; daughter of Beatrice Williams Hill (deceased) and Edward Jordan; married Howard Louis Williams, Jan 6, 1973; children: Nicole Yvonne. **Educ:** Cuyahoga Community Coll, Cleve, OH, 1963-65; Federal Aviation Admin, air traffic controller, mgmt training programs; Embry-Riddle Aeronautical Univ, Daytona Beach, FL, currently. **Career:** Federal Aviation Admin, Cleveland, OH, journeyman air traffic controller, 1970-77, training specialist, 1977-84; Federal Aviation Admin, Des Plaines, IL, quality assurance specialist, 1984; Federal Aviation Admin, Cleveland, OH, area supervisor, 1984-88, sr mgr/area mgr, 1988-. **Orgs:** Pres, Negro Business & Professional Women, Cleveland Club, 1985-89; mem, Links, Inc, 1988-; mem, Cleveland Chapter, Jack & Jill of America, 1986-, treas, 1989-91; natl treas, Professional Women Controllers, 1978-81; general chair, Ebony Fashion Fair, Negro Business & Professional Women, Cleveland Club, 1986-; mem, Federal Mgrs Assn, 1986-. **Honors/Awds:** Admin Award of Excellence, Federal Aviation Admin, 1988; Professional of the Year, Negro Business & Professional Women, 1987; Tribute, Congressman Louis Stokes, 1986; Federal Woman of Achievement Award, Cleveland Federal Exec Bd, 1984, 1986; Professional Award, 1988. **Home Addr:** 25510 S Woodland Rd, Beachwood, OH 44122. **Business Addr:** Area Manager, Air Traffic, Federal Aviation Administration-Cleveland ARTCC, 326 East Lorain St-ZOB13, Oberlin, OH 44074.

WILLIAMS, BARRY LAWSON
Company executive. **Personal:** Born Jul 21, 1944, Manhattan, NY; son of Otis & Ilza Williams; divorced; children: Barry, Jaime, Andrew. **Educ:** Harvard Coll, BA, 1966; Harvard Bus School, MB, 1971; Harvard Law School, JD, 1971. **Career:** Mckinsey & Co, senior consultant, 1971-78; Bechtel Group, mgr principal, 1978-87; Williams Pacific Ventures Inc, pres, 1987-. **Orgs:** Amer Pres Co, dir, 1984-; Northwestern Mutual Life, dir, 1986-; Pacific Gas & Elec, dir, 1992; Lucas Arts, dir, 1992; Tenera LP, dir, 1993; Simpson Manufacturing, dir, 1994; Harvard Alumni Assn, pres, 1994-95; USA Group, dir, 1995. **Honors/Awds:** Silver Spur Award; Allston Burr Award; Corning Fellowship. **Business Addr:** President, Williams Pacific Ventures Inc, 100 First St, Ste 2350, San Francisco, CA 94105, (415)896-2311.

WILLIAMS, BENJAMIN VERNON
Journalist (retired), freelance writer. **Personal:** Born Jan 25, 1927, StLouis, MO; married Vivian Hickman; children: Benjamin Jr, Gregory, Alan. **Educ:** San Francisco State Univ, BA 1961. **Career:** San Francisco Sun-Reporter, news reporter 1963-66; San Francisco Examiner, newspaper reporter 1963-66; San Francisco State Univ, lecturer 1968-; KPIX-TV Ch 5, news reporter 1966-91. **Orgs:** Mem Oakland Athletic Club 1975-; bd of dir Oakland Boys Club 1975-; bd of dir Oakland YMCA 1977-; bd of dirs Amer Red Cross Oakland Branch; mem Amer Heart Assoc Alameda Chapt. **Honors/Awds:** Jane Harrah Awd in Journalism San Francisco Lawyers Club 1965; San Francisco Press Club Awd (2) San Francisco Press Club (tv & radio news) 1966 & 1971; McQuade Awd Disting Programming Assn of Catholic Newsmen 1974; Broadcast Media Awd for Single Accomplishment & Highest Standards in TV-News San Francisco State Univ 1976; Emmy Awd for TV News No CA Emmy 1976. **Military Serv:** AUS sgt 1945-47.

WILLIAMS, BERNIE (BERNABE FIGUEROA)
Professional baseball player. **Personal:** Born Sep 13, 1968, San Juan, PR. **Career:** New York Yankees, outfielder, 1991-. **Business Addr:** Professional Baseball Player, New York Yankees, 161st St and River Ave, Yankee Stadium, Bronx, NY 10451, (718)293-4300.

WILLIAMS, BERTHA MAE
Educator, psychologist. **Personal:** Born Jul 10, 1927, Brighton, TN; divorced; children: Kenneth M. **Educ:** AZ State U, BA 1964; AZ State U, MA 1966; AZ State U, PhD 1973. **Career:** Univ of CA Los Angeles, counseling psychologist 1976-; Univ of TN Knoxville, asst prof/psychologist 1973-76; AZ State Univ Tempe, couns 1971-73; Luke Elem School Luke AFB, couns 1967-71; Luke Elem School Luke AFB, teacher 1963-67. **Orgs:** Bd of dirs Desert Sch Fed Credit Union 1968-71; Sch Bd Louisville KY, consult 1975; bd of mgmt YWCA 1977-80; vice pres bd of mgmt YWCA 1980-. **Honors/Awds:** Outstanding Achievement in Educ Univ of TN 1974; "Trust & Self-Disclosure Among Black Coll Students" Journal of Counseling Psychology 1974; "Black Women, Assertiveness vs Agressiveness" Journal of Afro-Am Issues 1974; "Assertion Traing" The Orientation Review 1978. **Business Addr:** UCLA, 4223 Math Science, Los Angeles, CA 90024.

WILLIAMS, BERYL E. W.
Education administrator (retired). **Personal:** Born May 23, 1913, Bangor, ME; daughter of Elizabeth A Jackson Warner (deceased) and James H Warner (deceased); married Roger Kenton Williams, Jun 8, 1942 (deceased); children: Scott Warner. **Educ:** Univ of ME, AB 1935; Univ of ME, MA 1940; Univ of ME, DPed 1972; courses & workshops at, Univ of Chicago, MI State Univ, Johns Hopkins Univ, Univ of MD, Morgan State University. **Career:** Gilbert Acad, teacher 1936-37; Claflin Coll, teacher 1937-40; A&T Coll, teacher 1946-48; Morgan State Univ, teacher 1948-63; Ctr for Continuing Educ Morgan State Univ, dean 1963-81, dean Emeritus Continuing Studies, 1981-. **Orgs:** Pres MD League of Women's Clubs 1957-59; comm orgnzr troop ldr Central MD Girl Scout Council 1959-63; trust US Assn of Evening Students 1966-; bd Greater Baltimore YWCA 1967-70; vice pres Baltimore City Bd of School Commissioners 1974-84; lay speaker United Methodist Church 1975-; bd mem Advance Fed Savings & Loan Assoc 1978-; chmn adv bd MEOC 1981-; dir Baltimore Women's Fair 1982,83; vice pres bd mem Park Heights St Acad 1982-; bd mem Women's Civic League of Baltimore 1985-; golden life mem NAACP; life mem Coll Language Assn; mem N Amer Assn of Summer Sessions; chmn Intl Div, NCNW of Greater Baltimore, historian, Morgan State Univ Women, Natl Caucus on Black Aged (Morgan Chapter); advisor Baltimore Sister Cities, Liberia. **Honors/Awds:** Woman of the Year; Vol of The Yr; Conselling Adults; Pubs "How to Take Tests"; listed in "Twenty Black Women" F Beckles; Community Serv Award; Sojourner Truth Award, Natl Assoc of Negro Business & Professional Women's Clubs; Humanitarian Award Howard Cornish Alumni Assoc Morgan State; Mother's Day Peace Award.

WILLIAMS, BETTY SMITH
Nurse, educator. **Personal:** Born Jul 22, 1929, South Bend, IN; daughter of Nellie Mae Lindsay Smith and John Wesley Smith; married Harold Louis Williams, Jul 10, 1954. **Educ:** Howard Univ, BS; Western Reserve Univ, MN; School of Nursing, UCLA, MS; School of Public Health UCLA, Dr PH. **Career:** Visiting Nurse Assn Cleveland, staff nurse 1954-55; LA City Health Dept, staff nurse 1955-66; Mt St Mary's Coll LA, asst prof 1956-69; Charles Drew Post Graduate Medical School LA, public health nurse consultant 1970-71; UCLA School of Nursing, asst prof 1969-, asst dean student affairs 1974-75; asst dean acad affairs 1975-76; School of Nursing Univ of CO Health Science Center Denver, dean & prof 1979-84; Kaiser Permanente, consultant; Delta Sigma Theta Center for Life Develop, exec dir; prof, California State Univ Long Beach, 1988-. **Orgs:** Founder 1968, pres 1969-74 Council of Black Nurses Inc LA; mem Natl Caucus of Black Health Workers APHA; founding charter member, 1971, bd dirs, exec comm, pres, Natl Black Nurses Assn Washington DC, Pres, 1995-; affirmative action task force Amer Nurses Assn; mem CA Nurses Assn; bd dir Blue Cross of Southern CA 1976-80; pres DST Telecomm Inc

1975-79, natl treasurer 1971-75; Delta Sigma Theta Inc Public Serv Org; Op Womanpower Inc; Watts Towers Art Center; Com for Simon Rodia's Towers In Watts; Charles Drew Post-Graduate Med School Continuing Educ for Nurses' Task Force; pres, LA Alumnae Chapter Delta Sigma Theta Inc; life mem NAACP; dir, board of directors, Blue Cross of California 1986-95. **Honors/Awds:** Nurse Traineeship Grant Graduate Study US Public Health Serv 1965-66; Fellow Amer Public Health Assn 1969; Natl Sojourner Truth Award Natl Business & Professional Womens Clubs Inc 1972; Fellow Amer Acad of Nursing; Hon mem Chi Eta Phi; establishes, Betty Smith Williams Scholarship, University of California, Los Angeles, School of Public Health, 1989, National Honorary Member Iota Phi Lamda Sorority, 1997-. **Business Addr:** Professor Emeritus, Department of Nursing, California State University Long Beach, 1250 Bellflower Rd, Long Beach, CA 90840.

WILLIAMS, BEVERLY
Professional basketball player. **Personal:** Born Nov 9, 1965. **Educ:** Univ of Texas, BA, 1991. **Career:** Long Beach Stingrays, guard, 1997-. **Business Addr:** Professional Basketball Player, Long Beach Stingrays, One World Trade Center, Ste 202, Long Beach, CA 90831-0202, (562)951-7297.

WILLIAMS, BILLY DEE
Actor. **Personal:** Born Apr 6, 1937, New York, NY; married Teruko Nakagami Williams; children: Corey, Miyako, Hanako. **Educ:** Natl Acad Fine Arts & Design, attended. **Career:** Films: The Cool World, A Taste of Honey, Hallelujah Baby, Firebrand of Florence, Lady Sings the Blues, Mahogany, Scott Joplin, The Last Angry Man, 1959, I Have a Dream, 1976, The Empire Strikes Back, The Return of the Jedi, Night Hawks, Marvin & Tige, Fear City, Deadly Illusion, 1987, Batman, 1989; TV films: Carter's Army, Brian's Song, The Glass House, The Hostage Tower, Children of Divorce, Shooting Stars, Chiefs, Christmas Lilies of the Field, Scott Joplin, Time Bomb; television appearances: The Jeffersons, The Interns, The FBI, Mission Impossible, Mod Squad, Police Woman, Dynasty; Broadway and off-Broadway appearances: Hallelujah Baby, Ceremonies in Dark Old Men, Fences. **Orgs:** Mem Actors Workshop in Harlem. **Honors/Awds:** Emmy nomination for Brian's Song. **Home Addr:** 605 N Oakhurst Dr, Beverly Hills, CA 90210.

WILLIAMS, BILLY LEO
Professional baseball coach. **Personal:** Born Jun 15, 1938, Whistler, AL; married Shirley Williams; children: Valarie, Nina, Julia, Sandra. **Career:** Chicago Cubs, outfielder, 1961-74; Oakland Athletics, outfielder, 1974-76; Chicago Cubs, minor league hitting instructor, 1978-79, hitting instructor, 1980-82; Oakland Athletics, coach, 1983-85; Chicago Cubs, coach, 1986-87, 1992-; Cleveland Indians, coaching asst. **Honors/Awds:** Baseball Writers Assn of America, Rookie of the Year, 1961; Player of the Year, National League 1972; The Sporting News, Major League Player of the Year 1972; Played in the All Star Game six times; Holds the National League record for most consecutive games played (1,117); Tied major league records for most home runs in two consec games (5) 1968; hit 3 home runs in one game 1968; tied major league record for most consecutive doubles in one game (4) 1969; inducted into Chicago Sports Hall of Fame 1982; elected to Baseball Hall of Fame 1987; had jersey #26 retired by the Chicago Cubs, 1987. **Business Addr:** Dugout Coach, Chicago Cubs, 1060 W Addison St, Chicago, IL 60613, (773)404-2827.

WILLIAMS, BILLY MYLES
Laboratory director. **Personal:** Born Sep 6, 1950, Kings Mountain, NC; son of Mattie Ashley Williams and Willis Frank Williams; married Rosemarie Delores Wesson. **Educ:** Univ of NC Chapel Hill, BS 1972; Central MI Univ, MS 1980. **Career:** Martin Marietta Chemicals, 1972-74; Dow Chemical Co, 1974-, laboratory dir, currently. **Orgs:** Mem Sigma Xi 1982-, Sigma Iota Epsilon 1984-, AAAS 1985-, Big Brothers; chmn Midland Sect Amer Chemical Soc 1988-89. **Home Addr:** 615 Woodstone Dr, Baton Rouge, LA 70808-5163.

WILLIAMS, BISMARCK S.
Educator. **Personal:** Born Sep 8, 1928, Mobile, AL; married Avery W; children: Bismarck Jr, Rhonda. **Educ:** Morehouse Coll, AB 1947; Atlanta U, MBA 1950. **Career:** Roosevelt Univ, associate dean; Walter E Heller Coll, dir; Advanced Mgmt Rsch, lectr 1967-; Roosevelt Univ, prof 1957; Roosevelt Univ, lectr 1955-57; AM&N Coll, purch agent/instr 1952-54. **Orgs:** Fin Mgmt Assn; Midwest Fin Assn. **Business Addr:** 430 S Michigan Ave, Chicago, IL 60605.

WILLIAMS, BOOKER T.
Business executive. **Personal:** Born Apr 28, 1920, Corapeake, NC; married Jeanne LeBlanc; children: 9. **Educ:** Univ of Michigan Law School, LLB 1955. **Career:** MI Indep Press Inc, business mgr 1976-; Pherc Inc Elec Installation Co, business mgr 1970-76; Washtenaw Co MI, asst prosecuting atty 1964-70; private practice 1956-64; Willow Run Branch NAACP, legal counsel 1957-68; Washtenaw Co Black Economic Devel League, legal counsel 1970-73. **Orgs:** Mem Alpha Phi Alpha and several other civic organizations. **Honors/Awds:** Certificate of Merit, Natl Police Officers Assn of Amer, 1970; Certificate of Appreciation, Washtenaw Co Sheriff Dept Jr Deps, 1968; Freedom Award Certificate, NAACP. **Military Serv:** AUS 1st lt 1942-47. **Business Addr:** 124 E Washington St, Ann Arbor, MI 48104.

WILLIAMS, BRAINARD
Automobile dealer. **Career:** Hayward Pontiac-Buick-GMC Truck, pres, currently. **Special Achievements:** Company is ranked #95 on Black Enterprise magazine's 1997 list of Top 100 Black businesses. **Business Addr:** President, Hayward Pontiac-Buick-GMC Truck, 21994 Mission Blvd, Hayward, CA 94541, (510)582-4436.

WILLIAMS, BRIAN
Professional football player. **Personal:** Born Dec 17, 1972, Dallas, TX. **Educ:** USC, bachelor's degree in public administration, 1996. **Career:** Green Bay Packers, linebacker, 1995-. **Business Addr:** Professional Football Player, Green Bay Packers, 1265 Lombardi Ave, Green Bay, WI 54304, (414)494-2351.

WILLIAMS, BRIAN CARSON
Professional basketball player. **Personal:** Born Apr 6, 1969, Fresno, CA; son of Patricia A. Phillips and Tony. **Educ:** Maryland; Arizona. **Career:** Orlando Magic, forward/center, 1991-93; Denver Nuggets, 1993-95; Los Angeles Clippers, 1995-96; Chicago Bulls, 1996-97; Detroit Pistons, 1997-. **Special Achievements:** NBA Draft, First round pick, #10, 1991; NBA Championship, Chicago Bulls, 1997. **Business Addr:** Professional Basketball Player, Detroit Pistons, 2 Championship Dr, Auburn Hills, MI 48326, (248)377-0100.

WILLIAMS, BRIAN O'NEAL
Professional baseball player. **Personal:** Born Feb 15, 1969, Lancaster, SC. **Educ:** South Carolina. **Career:** Houston Astros, pitcher, 1991-94; San Diego Padres, 1995; Detroit Tigers, 1996; Baltimore Orioles, 1997-. **Business Addr:** Professional Baseball Player, Baltimore Orioles, 333 W Camden St, Baltimore, MD 21201, (410)685-9800.

WILLIAMS, BRUCE E.
Business executive. **Personal:** Born Sep 2, 1931, St Paul, MN; married Wilma Allen; children: Deborah Lynn, Lisa Marie. **Educ:** Mankato State Coll, BS 1956; MS 1970; Union Grad Sch, PhD 1977. **Career:** Rockefeller Found, asst director; 1972-; Minneapolis Schs, asst supt 1971-72; Minneapolis Schs, prin 1968-71; Minneapolis Schs, tchr 1962-68; Summer Staff Devel Prog Minneapolis Pub Schs, dir 1966; Juv Detention Group, supvr 1960-61; Registered Basketball & Football, official. **Orgs:** Mem Am Assn Sch Adminstr; Assn Supervision & Curriculum Dev Nat Alliance Black Sch Educators; Mankato State Coll Alumni Assn; YMCA; vice pres Afro-Am Educators Assn (Mpls); Hall of Fame Mankato State U; Rockefeller Found Fellow; trustee Macalester Coll St Paul; pres gen educ bd NY School Bd System; mem NY State Human Rights Advisory Council; mem Educ Adv Comm Natl Urban League; mem NY Gov's Adv Comm of Black Affairs. **Military Serv:** AUS sp 4th class 1957-59.

WILLIAMS, BUCK (CHARLES LINWOOD)
Professional basketball player. **Personal:** Born Mar 8, 1960, Rocky Mount, NC; married Mimi; children: Julien, Malek. **Educ:** Univ of MD, College Park MD, attended. **Career:** New Jersey Nets, forward, 1982-89, Portland Trail Blazers, 1990-96; New York Knicks, 1996-. **Orgs:** NBA Players Assn, pres, currently. **Honors/Awds:** Mem US Olympic Team 1980; NBA All-Rookie Team 1982; NBA Rookie of the Year 1982; Named to All-NBA Second Team 1983; NBA, All-Defensive first team, 1990, 1991; NBA, All-Defensive second team, 1988, 1992; NBA All-Star, 1982, 1983, 1986. **Business Addr:** Professional Basketball Player, New York Knicks, 2 Pennsylvania Plaza, New York, NY 10121, (212)465-5867.

WILLIAMS, CALVIN JOHN, JR.
Professional football player. **Personal:** Born Mar 3, 1967, Baltimore, MD. **Educ:** Purdue University, bachelor's degree, hotel/restaurant management. **Career:** Philadelphia Eagles, wide receiver, 1990-. **Business Addr:** Professional Football Player, Philadelphia Eagles, 3501 S Broad St, Philadelphia, PA 19148, (215)463-2500.

WILLIAMS, CAMILLA
Operatic soprano. **Personal:** Born Oct 18, Danville, VA; married Charles T Beavers. **Educ:** VA State Univ, BS 1941. **Career:** Created role of Madame Butterfly as 1st black contract singer at New York City Ctr 1946; created 1st Aida at New York City Ctr 1948; 1st NY perf of Mozart's "Idomeneo" w/ Little Orch Soc 1950; 1st tour of Alaska 1950; 1st European tour 1954; 1st Viennese perf of Menotti's "Saint of Bleecker St" 1955; Amer Fest in Belgium 1955; 1st African tour for US State Dept 1958-59; 1st tour of Israel 1959; guest of Pres Eisenhower-concert for Crown Prince of Japan 1960; tours in Europe, Asia & Australia 1962; NY perf of Handel's "Orlando"; 1st tour of Poland 1974; Bronx Coll, prof of voice 1970; Brooklyn Coll, prof of voice 1970-73; Queens Coll, prof of voice 1974-; IN Univ, 1st black prof of voice 1977-. **Orgs:** Mem Natl Soc of Arts & Letters 1981. **Honors/Awds:** Honored by the Gov of VA Linwood Holton as Distinguished Virginian 1971; listed in Danville VA Museum of Fine Arts & History Hall of Fame 1974; Camilla Williams Park designatd in Danville VA 1974; honored by IN Univ Sch of Music Black Music Students Orgn for Outstanding Achievements in the field of music 1979; honored by Gov Julian M Carroll of KY as a "Kentucky Colonel" 1979; Hon mem Sigma Alpha Iota 1980; Natl Soc of Arts & Letters, mem 1981; honored guest of the NY Philharmonic 10,000th Concert Celebration 1982; honored by Philadelphia Pro Arte Soc 1982; first black prof of voice to teach at Central Conservatory of Music BeijingPeople's Republic of China 1983; Disting Awd of Ctr for Leadership & Develop 1983; included in first ed of Most Important Women of the Twentieth Century, new of Grove's Dictionary of Music & Musicians 1984; Taylor-Williams student residence hall is named at VA State Univ in honor of Billy Taylor & Camilla Williams; Virginia St Univ at Petersburg, Honorary Doctor of Music, 1985; Arts and Humanities Award, Virginia State University, 1989. **Home Addr:** 2610 E 2nd St, Bloomington, IN 47401. **Business Addr:** Professor of Voice, Indiana Univ, School of Music, Bloomington, IN 47401.

WILLIAMS, CARLETTA CELESTE
Nurse. **Personal:** Born Mar 5, 1956, Steubenville, OH; daughter of Catherine B Scruggs Platt and Franklin T Platt Sr; married Calvin C Williams Jr; children: Charles, PJ, Cecilia. **Educ:** WV Northern Comm Coll, AD of Nursing 1977; West Liberty State Coll, BS Nursing 1986; Duquesne Univ, MSN, nursing administration, 1992. **Career:** OH Valley Hosp, dietary aide 1972-77; Weirton Medical Ctr, registered nurse 1977-79; Johns-Hopkins Hosp, registered nurse CCU 1979-80; Weirton Medical Ctr registered nurse CCU 1980-; Weirton Medical Center, Weirton, WV, head nurse, critical care unit, 1986-. **Orgs:** AACN 1986-; BPW 1986-; church nurse Second Baptist Church 1987; member, Golden Star Chorus, Second Baptist Church, 1988. **Honors/Awds:** Woman of the Year in Health Care, Cameo-The Women's Center, Steubenville, OH, 1990; Sigma Theta Tau, 1992; CCRN, 1983-. **Home Addr:** 522 Maxwell Ave, Steubenville, OH 43952. **Business Addr:** Head Nurse CCU, Weirton Medical Center, 601 Colliers Way, Weirton, WV 26062.

WILLIAMS, CARLTON RAY, JR.
Educational administrator. **Personal:** Born Sep 6, 1957, New York City, NY; married Deborah Whitten. **Educ:** Radford Univ, BS General Psych 1979, MS Industrial/Organ Psych 1984. **Career:** Radford Univ, residential life dir 1980-82, asst dir of admissions 1982-84; Roanoke Coll, asst dean of admissions 1984-. **Orgs:** Co-founder Radford Univ Chap of Amer Soc of Personnel Admin 1980; mem VA Assn of Student Personnel Admins 1982-; mem VA Assoc of Collegiate Registrars & Admiss Counselors 1982-; co-founder parliamentarian VA Admissions Council on Black Concerns 1983-; mem Amer Soc of Personnel Adminis 1984-; mem Personnel Assoc of Roanoke Valley 1985-. **Honors/Awds:** Co-authored grant Summer Transition Program for Minority Students Peer Counseling Network Prog for Minority Students 1983; panelist/presenter VA Assoc of Coll Registrars Conf 1983, 1984; mem State Accessibility Task Force for Blacks in Higher Educ VA Admiss Coun on Black Concerns & VA State Council on Higher Educ 1984. **Business Addr:** Assistant Dean of Admissions, Roanoke College, Salem, VA 24153.

WILLIAMS, CAROLYN CHANDLER
Educator. **Personal:** Born Jan 13, 1947, Maben, MS; daughter of L A Chandler and Norris Dean & Irene Dean; married LT Williams; children: Lori Tysandra, Letonya. **Educ:** MS Valley State Univ, BA 1968; MS State Univ, MEd 1973, PhD 1975. **Career:** Aberdeen Pub Schs, eng teach 1968-70; Oktibbeha Co Schs, eng teach 1970-71; Mary Holmes Coll, inst 1971-73; MS State Univ, inst 1974-75, asst prof 1975-78; assoc prof 1978-82; prof 1982-; Mississippi State Univ, Starkville, MS, administrative intern 1987. **Orgs:** Bd of dirs Mid South Educ Rsch Assn 1982-; pres, Midsouth Educational Research Assn, 1988-89; pres, Mississippi Reading Assn, 1990-91. **Honors/Awds:** Outstanding Univ Prof Assn of Univ Prof 1977; Outstanding Young Woman State Jaycees MS 1981; Outstanding Young Woman Starkville Jaycees local 1981; Outstanding Young Educator Phi Delta Kappa local 1982; Starkville Area Hall of Fame, Starkville Area Chamber of Commerce, 1990. **Business Addr:** Prof of Instruction, Mississippi State Univ, PO Box 6331, Mississippi State, MS 39762.

WILLIAMS, CAROLYN H.
Judge. **Career:** MI Circuit Court, Family Div, probate judge, currently. **Orgs:** MI Probate Judges Assn, immed past pres. **Business Addr:** Probate Judge, Family Division of Circuit Court, 1400 Gull Rd, Kalamazoo, MI 49001, (616)385-6001.

WILLIAMS, CAROLYN RUTH ARMSTRONG
Educator, scholar, educational administrator, consultant. **Personal:** Born Feb 17, 1944, Birmingham, AL; daughter of Lois Adel America Merriweather and Lonnie Armstrong; married James Alvin Williams Jr, Mar 16, 1968. **Educ:** TN State Univ, BS 1966; HI Univ, Cert in Asian Studies 1970; Northwestern

Univ, MA 1972; Cornell Univ, MA 1978, PhD 1978; Fellow Harvard Univ, postdoctorate 1981-83; Exeter Univ England, selected to particip in course seminar ''Educational Admin, The Management of Change'' 1985; Chinese University of Hong Kong, seminar on Hong Kong, 1992; MIT Course Management Strategies for the Multi-cultural, 1993; MIT Course on Literary Dialogues for Managers & Executives, 1990. **Career:** Barringer HS, history tchr 1967-69; Thomas Jefferson HS, history teacher 1969-70; Union Coll, instr dept of history 1970-73; Tompkins Cty Comm Coll,adj prof 1973-76; SUNY Cortland, lecturer/instructor, dept history 1973-76; Cornell Univ Career Ctr, assoc dir 1976-82; Harvard Univ, head proctor 1983; US Senator Paul Tsongas, spec proj asst 1983; NC Central Univ, asst to the vice chancellor for univ relations 1983-87; Vanderbilt Univ, asst dean for Minority Affairs & Women Engineering Programs & assoc prof 1987-; Biomedical Coordinator, 1993-; Adjunct Professor of History, Tenn State University, currently. **Orgs:** Exec bd mem admin counselors NAWDAC 1980-82; mem Comm Blacks in Higher Ed & Black Coll & Univ 1980-81; ed consult LeMoyne Coll Higher Ed Preparation Prog 1981-; ed consult & co-founder Youth Data Inc 1981-; exec bd mem Phi Delta Kappa, Natl Assoc for Women Deans; mem Delta Sigma Theta Inc; appointed to Natl Assoc for Women Admin, counselors journal board 1986-88; proposal reader for US Dept of Educ 1989-; NSF Site Reviewer for Gateway Coalition, 1994-; NAMEPA Rgn bd chair, 1992-96, exec bd of dirs, 1992-; executive regional bd Natl Society of Black Engineers 1987-; Rotary Intl; Technical Coordinator for Natl Society of Women Engineers 1989-91; NIH, national advisory committee, biomedical research support, 1993-; member, Committee for Natl Institutes of Environment, advisory bd, 1993-; Women in Science, national secretary, 1992-94; NAMEPA Region B, treasurer, 1996-98. **Honors/Awds:** Woodrow Wilson Admin Fellow 1983-86; Thycydidean Honor Soc Awd YWCA Women of Achievement Awd; Phi Delta Kappa, Sigma Rho Sigma Honor Soc Awd Phi Alpha Theta Awd; Doctoral Dissertation Funded by Rockefeller Found, Fellowship/Scholarship Cornell Univ, Northwestern Univ; YMCA Women of Achievement Awd 1984-85 & 86-87; Burton Lecturer for Harvard Univ Ed School Colloquaim Bd 1983; Natl Society of Black Engineers Community Leadership Award, 1987; 1st Black Dean in Engineering School; 1st women's dean in engineering school; National Society of Black Engineers Charles E Tunstall Award for Best Minority Engineering Program in US 1990-91; NAMPERA Ryn B Award, 1992; Vanderbilt Univ, Affirmative Action Award, September 1989-90; NAMEPA Region B Award, 1993-96; NAMEPA Region B Chain Awd, 1996; National Society of Black Engineers, National Appreciation Award, 1997. **Home Addr:** 36 Morningside Dr, Cortland, NY 13045. **Business Addr:** Vanderbilt Univ, School of Engineering, PO Box 6006, Station B, Nashville, TN 37235.

WILLIAMS, CARROLL BURNS, JR.
Scientist, educator. **Personal:** Born Sep 24, 1929, St Louis, MO; son of Maxine Henderson Williams and Carroll Burns Williams; children: Robyn Claire, Margaret ''Maya'', Carroll Blake. **Educ:** Univ MI, BS 1955, MS 1957, PhD 1963. **Career:** US Forest Service, rsch forester 1961-65, rsch entomologist 1965-68, proj leader 1968-72; Yale Sch of Forestry, lectr 1969-72; US Forest Svc, forest insect ecologist 1972-75, pioneer sci 1975-84; proj leader 1984-88; adjunct prof Univ CA, Berkeley 1988-. **Orgs:** Consult Ecology & Ecosystems NSF 1971-74; tech consult USFS Insecticide Field Tests 1973-; registered professional forester CA; Entomol Soc of Amer; Soc of Amer Foresters; dir Berkeley Sch Bd Berkeley Unified Sch Dist 1977-84; vis prof Black Exchange Prog Natl Urban League 1975-84; board of directors, Berkeley-Albany YMCA, 1979-; board of directors, Berkeley Rotary, 1990-94; board of trustees, New Perspectives Inc, Alcohol & Drug Counseling, 1985-87; East Bay Regional Park District, Ward 1, director, 1991-92; board of directors, Berkeley Public Education Foundation, 1993-95. **Military Serv:** US Marine Corps staff sgt 1951-53. **Business Addr:** Adjunct Professor, Dept of Environmental Seience, Policy & Mgmt, University of California - Berkeley, 145 Mulford Hall, Berkeley, CA 94720.

WILLIAMS, CASSANDRA FAYE
Exploration palaeontologist. **Personal:** Born Aug 16, 1948, Sherrill, AR; daughter of Millye L. Dickerson-Beatty and Lewis Williams; children: Kyra Erica. **Educ:** Northeastern Illinois State University, 1966-67; University of Arkansas, Pine Bluff, AR, BS, 1970; Kent State University, South Dakota School of Mines, 1978; Tulane University, New Orleans, LA, MS, 1979. **Career:** University of Chicago Hospitals and Clinics, Chicago, IL, clinical biochemist, 1970-71; Orleans Parish School Board, New Orleans, LA, biology teacher, 1971-72; Chevron USA, New Orleans, LA, exploration palaeontologist, 1972—. **Orgs:** American Association of Stratigraphic Palynologists; Gulf Coast section, Society of Economic Palaeontologists and Mineralogists; International Commission for Palynology; American Association of Blacks in Energy; Tau Iota Mu; national convention delegate, 1984-88, president, New Orleans club, 1985-86, national convention co-chair, 1986, National Association of Negro Business and Professional Women's Clubs; Delta Sigma Theta. **Honors/Awds:** Voluntary service awards, NAACP, 1984, Chevron USA, 1984; outstanding achievement awards, National Association of Negro Business and Professional Women's Clubs, 1984, 1986; outstanding service award, New Orleans chapter, National Business League, 1987; World Service Award, and Volunteer Service Award, Girl Scouts of America, 1988. **Home Addr:** 7601 Briarwood Dr, New Orleans, LA 70128.

WILLIAMS, CATHERINE G.
Appointed government official. **Personal:** Born Nov 21, 1914, Des Moines, IA; married Richard Jr. **Educ:** Cortez Bus Coll, grad 1948; Soc Work Univ of IA MA 1965; Drake U, grad soc/psy. **Career:** IA Dept of Social Serv, dep commr 1975-; Div of Comm Serv IA Dept of SS, dir 1973-75; Bureau of Family & Adult Serv IA Dept of Asso, dir; Bureau of Family & Adult Serv ID of SS, assoc Dir; IA Dept of Social Serv, child welfare staff dev; Polk Co IA Dept of Social Serv Com, child welfare supr. **Orgs:** Mem NAACP Scholarship; commr Planning & Zoning Commn Des Moines 1980-; bd mem Willkie Hosue Inc. **Honors/Awds:** Social Worker of the Year NASW IA Chap 1980; IA Hall of Fame for Women Women's Hall of Fame 1980; Black Women of Achievement Cultural Devel Com 1980; MarkHall Lectr Univ of IA Sch of Social Work 1980. **Business Addr:** Iowa Dept of Social Services, 5th Floor Hoover Bldg, Des Moines, IA 50319.

WILLIAMS, CHARLENE J.
News reporter. **Personal:** Born Jul 13, 1949, Atlantic City, NJ. **Educ:** Columbia U, MS 1972; Cum Laude Boston U, BS 1967-71. **Career:** WTOP Radio Post Newsweek Stas Inc Wash DC, radio news editor 1972-; Westinghouse Broadcasting Co NY, part-time rewriter; Columbia U, adminstr asst 1971-72; WBUR Boston Univ FM Radio Sta, disc-jockey editorl writer prod dir; Boston Univ Year Book Hub, gen assignment editor; WCRB Waltham Am Fed TV & Radio Artists. **Orgs:** Communications Assn Inc; Sigma Delta Chi; writer for Columbian Comm Newsletter; Adams Morgan Orgn; vol Heart Fund; ARC; DC Black Repetory; CRI Inst; pres Student Body Boston Univ 1970-71; pres Student Body Columbia Univ 1971-72. **Honors/Awds:** Scarlet Key Honor Soc Boston Univ 1971; Nat Honor Soc Atlantic City HS 1967.

WILLIAMS, CHARLES C.
Real estate developer, county official. **Personal:** Born Oct 10, 1939, Pontiac, MI; children: Charles C III, Cassandra, Veronica. **Educ:** FL A&M Univ, Po Sci 1958-62; NC Central Univ Law School, 1962-63. **Career:** Atlanta Reg Commission, dir of commun 1974-78; GA Power Co, manpower resources coord 1978-80; Amertelco Inc, exec vice pres 1980-84; Air Atlanta, spec consto chair of bd 1984-; Fulton Cty Bd of Commiss, commissioner, currently. **Orgs:** Bd mem West End Med Center 1980-83; bd of managers, mem Assn of Cty Commiss of GA 1978-; vice pres Natl Assn of Counties 1985-88; exec comm mem Natl Dem Cty Officials 1985-; district mem at large Boy Scouts of Amer 1985-86; bd mem Neighborhood Justice Ctr 1985-86; mem Coalition of 100 Black Men; GABEO; NAACP; Kappa Alpha Phi; Natl Assn of Black Cnty Officials; West End Neighborhood Developemnt, Inc. **Honors/Awds:** Plaque YMCA Butler St Century Club 1973-; Atlanta Southside Comm Hlth Center Comm Serv Awd; West End Med Center Cert of Appreciation; plaque from Atlanta Medical Assn 1980-; Atlanta Business League Torch Bearer Awd 1985; plaque Concerned Citizens of Atlanta; plaque Jomandi Prod 1986-; Mem United Negro Coll und; mem Neighborhood Arts Center; Metro Atlanta SCLC Comm Serv Awd; Hearts and Hands Fdn for Hanicapped, Inc. **Home Addr:** 731 Lawton St SW, Atlanta, GA 30310.

WILLIAMS, CHARLES E., III
Attorney. **Personal:** Born May 10, 1946, New York City, NY. **Educ:** Franklin & Marshall Coll, AB 1966; Columbia Univ School of Law, JD 1969. **Career:** Marshall Bratter Greene Allison & Tucker NYC, assoc 1970-72; NAACP Legal Defense & Ed Fund Inc, asst counsel; Bureau of Labor Serv City of NY, dir 1978-79; Dep Sec of State NY State Dept, gen counsel 1979-82; State of NY, acting sec of state 1982; New York City Housing Authority, gen counsel 1983-. **Orgs:** Mem New York City Bar Assoc, NBA, Natl Conf Black Lawyers. **Military Serv:** USAR spl 4/c 1969-. **Business Addr:** General Counsel, New York City Housing Auth, 250 Broadway, Room 620, New York, NY 10007.

WILLIAMS, CHARLES EARL
Fire marshal. **Personal:** Born Jul 29, 1955, Memphis, TN; son of Ardelia & Perry Williams. **Educ:** University of MI, Fire Academy, beginning & advanced, firefighting; Tustin Mich School for arson investigators. **Career:** River Rouge Fire Dept, sgt, 1987, lt engineer and line lt, 1991, capt engineer, 1994, fire marshal, 1994-. **Orgs:** Downriver Mutual Aid Fire investigators, 1994-; International Assn of Fire Investigators, 1994-; President, Union Local 517, River Rouge Firefighters Assn, 1994-; Demolition Committee and Renovation, City of River Rouge, 1994-. **Special Achievements:** First African-American Fire Marshal City of River Rouge, MI; City-wide Education in Fire Prevention. **Business Addr:** Fire Marshal, City of River Rouge Fire Dept, 10600 W Jefferson, River Rouge, MI 48218, (313)842-1718.

WILLIAMS, CHARLES J., SR.
Institutional clergyman. **Personal:** Born Apr 1, 1942, Wayne Co, NC; married Linda Oates; children: Valerie, Charles, Jr, Antraun. **Educ:** Christian Inst 1966; Shaw U, AB 1973; M Div, 1975; Ibis, DMin 1975. **Career:** Cherry Hosp, Clinical I Chaplain, mental health tech 1960-74; Western Assembly Disciples of Christ Churches, bishop. **Orgs:** Chmn Western Disciples Chs of Christ Council Bd 1969-72; pastor White Oak Disciples Ch 1968-; chmn of Evangelism Com of Wester Assy NC Assn of Chplns1972-74; mem Disciples Chs of Christ Council; bd mem Afro-ministers Alliance; Masons Founder Western Assembly Disciples of Christ Ushers Conv 1970; Bishop1977. **Business Addr:** Bishop, Western Assembly Disciples of, Christ Churches, PO Box 133, Goldsboro, NC 27530.

WILLIAMS, CHARLES MASON, JR.
Educational administrator. **Personal:** Born Nov 25, 1960, Newark, NJ; son of Genetta Williams and Charlie Williams; married Maritza Farnum-Sharp, Aug 6, 1988 (divorced); children: Aleida Mercedes. **Educ:** Rider College, BA, 1984; Rutgers University, MPA, 1989. **Career:** Essex County College, EOF officer, 1984-86; Rider College, assistant director, admissions, 1986-87; Trenton State College, EOF academic advisor, 1989-. **Orgs:** New Jersey Educational Opportunity Fund Professional Association, 1984-, corresponding secretary, 1984-86, sector representative, 1993; Committee on Undergraduate Programs, Practices, and Standards, 1992-; Rider College Inter-Cultural Alumni Association, 1990-. **Honors/Awds:** NJEOFPA, Service Award, 1986; Trenton State College, College Union Board, Outstanding Minority Staff Award, 1990. **Home Addr:** 81 Lanning St, Trenton, NJ 08618.

WILLIAMS, CHARLES RICHARD
Black exposition executive. **Personal:** Born Jan 11, 1948, Indianapolis, IN; divorced; children: Maisha, Charles Jr, Robert, Ramone. **Educ:** Black Hawk Coll. **Career:** Comm Serv Div Indianapolis, asst to dir 1974-76; Gov Comm Serv Studeis 1974; NAACP Nat Conv, exec coord 1972-73; Alaska Barge & Transport, purchasing agt 1968-72; City of Indianapolis, special asst to the Mayor 1976-83; pres, Indiana Black Expo, Inc. 1983-. **Orgs:** V ward chmn Center Township Wards; precinct com Pike Township; v chmn Rep Nghbrhd Fin Com; mem Screening Com 11th Dist; chmn So Dist IN State Black Rep Cncl; exec mem Marion Co Rep Club; mem Pike Township Rep Club; Marion Co Young Rep Club; personnel chmn Inspls Pre-schl; mem Market Pl; vice pres IN Black Expo; mem Big Bros; NAACP; rep Mayor on Bd Goodwill Ind; bd Heritage Place Sr Citizens; bd Indianapolis Clean City Com; bd Fallcreek YMCA; mem Afro-care. **Honors/Awds:** Achvmt award Rep Central Com; outsdng serv award Rep Nghbrhd Fin Com; comm serv award Butler Tarkington; jefferson award Indinapolis Star IN 1979; freedom award IN Prince Hail Masons 1978; serv & award Tech 300 Prgm; cert recog outsdng ldrshp; award; Office of Human Resources City Indlps; The Educ Assoc Human Rights Awd. **Military Serv:** USN 1965-68. **Business Addr:** 3145 N. Meridian St., Indianapolis, IN 46208.

WILLIAMS, CHARLES THOMAS
Company executive. **Personal:** Born May 4, 1941, Charleston, MO; son of Mary Williams and Melvin Williams; married Janet E McLaughlin; children: Robin, Tracey, Justin, Drew, Douglass. **Educ:** Lake Michigan Coll, AA 1962; Western MI Univ, BS 1965; Univ of MI, MA 1970, PhD 1971. **Career:** Detroit Schools, teacher 1965-69; MI Educ Assn, educ consult 1971-73, educ adminstr, assoc exec dir 1973-84; Nat Educ Assn, dir human & civil rights 1984-. **Orgs:** Mem Natl Alliance of Black Sch Educators, Amer Soc for Curriculum Develop, Phi Delta Kappa, Black Roundtable, Martin Luther King Jr Ctr for Nonviolent Social Change; bd mem Center for Democratic Renewal. **Business Addr:** Dir Human & Civil Rights, Natl Educ Assn, 1201 Sixteenth St NW, Washington, DC 20036.

WILLIAMS, CHARLIE
Professional football player. **Personal:** Born Feb 2, 1972, Detroit, MI. **Educ:** Bowling Green State, attended. **Career:** Dallas Cowboys, defensive back, 1995-. **Business Addr:** Professional Football Player, Dallas Cowboys, One Cowboys Pkwy, Irving, TX 75063, (214)556-9900.

WILLIAMS, CHARLIE J.
Association executive. **Personal:** Born Jun 22, 1947, Camphill, AL; son of Cora M & Jimmy D Williams; divorced; children: Renell, Darnella. **Educ:** Wayne State Univ, BS, recreation leadership, 1970, additional studies towards MPA, 1970-75; WSU School of Law, JD, 1980; Walsh Inst Taxation Program, masters, 1982. **Career:** City of Detroit, deputy dir, Public Works Dept, 1978-79; dir of housing, 1979-80, exec asst to the mayor, 1980-82, dir, personnel, 1982-83, chief exec asst & chief of staff, Mayor's Office, 1992-93, dir, Water & Sewerage Dept, 1993-94; New Detroit, Inc, pres, 1994-96. **Orgs:** Private Industry Council, 1994-; MI Cancer Foundation, bd mem, 1994-; Jr League, bd mem, 1994-; Howard Baker Foundation, pres, 1993-; State Bar of MI, 1981-; Wolverine Bar Assn, 1994-; Booker T Washington Bus Assn, 1994-; Comprehensive Health Services of Detroit, bd mem, 1982-. **Honors/Awds:** President of the US, President's Volunteer Action Award, 1994; MI United Thoroughbred Breeders & Owners Assn, MI Horseman of

the Year, 1991. **Special Achievements:** Served as the chairperson of the City of Detroit's Devil's Night Task Force, which led to the reduction in arson and related problems-over 35,000 people were mobilized in this process and the fires were reduced to that of an average night, these efforts resulted in public recognition through the media and the Detroit City Council by way of a resolution, The anti-arson program also received national recognition and was replicated in Camden, New Jersey, 1985-94. **Business Addr:** President, New Detroit Inc, 645 Griswold, Ste 2900, Detroit, MI 48226, (313)496-2000.

WILLIAMS, CHARLOTTE LEOLA
Health service assistant. **Personal:** Born May 28, 1928, Flint, MI; married Charles Clifford Williams Sr; children: Charlita Walker, Charles C Williams Jr, Cathryn Sanders. **Educ:** Flint Sch of Practical Nursing, Cert/License 1961. **Career:** St Joseph Hosp Flint, rcvry rm nrs 1961-65; Flint Bd of Ed, hm-sh cnslr 1965-68; Genesee Co Govt, elected ofcl 1965-84; Flint Osteo Hosp, asst to the pres 1980-83; Beecher Ballenger Hlth Sys, asst to the pres 1983-. **Orgs:** Pres Natl Assn of Counties 1st Black Female 1979-80; co comm Genesee Co Bd of Comm 1st Female Elected 1965-80; chair Genesee Co Bd of Hlth Genesee Co Hlth Dept 1968-85; officer/Mem Quinn Chapel AME Ch Lifetime; aging comm MI Office of Services to the Aging 1983-; bd mem YWCA of Greater Flint 1980-; bd mem United Way of Genesee & Lapeer Counties 1985. **Honors/Awds:** Downtown merchants awd Flint Downtown Merchants 1976; pol achvmnt Negro Bus & Prof Womens Club 1975; AME Church Missionary Awd African Meth Episcopal Ch Missionary Women 1983; law day awd '84 Genesee Co Bar Asso 1984; pub serv awd Natl Assn of Counties 1980. **Home Addr:** 2030 Barks St, Flint, MI 48503. **Business Addr:** Assistant to the President, Beecher Ballenger Health Sys, 3921 Beecher Rd, Flint, MI 48502.

WILLIAMS, CHERYL L.
Electrical services executive. **Personal:** Born Dec 31, 1954, San Diego, CA; daughter of Edna Payne Peavy and Joseph Peavy; married Peavy Williams, Dec 18, 1976; children: Derryl Jr, Cheryl. **Educ:** San Jose State University, BS, psychology, 1973-77; San Diego State University, summer program, 1978; UCSD, PPS, credential program, 1979-81. **Career:** San Diego City School, hearing & placement, 1978-83; National Circuits, marketing, 1983-84; San Diego Circuit Board Service, president, 1984-. **Orgs:** Webster Community Council, 1986-; Delta Sigma Theta Sorority, 1976-. **Honors/Awds:** United States Small Business, Minority Small Business Person of the Year, 1989. **Special Achievements:** Small Business Outlook, General Dynamics Convair Division, 1989; News Brief, San Diego Minority Business Development Center, 1989; Minority Business Entrepreneur, 1989. **Business Addr:** President/Chief Executive Officer, San Diego Circuit Board Service, 4645 Ruffner St, Ste 204, San Diego, CA 92111, (619)279-6518.

WILLIAMS, CHESTER ARTHUR
Clergyman. **Personal:** Born in Valls Creek, WV. **Educ:** Moody Bible Inst Chicago, gen bible 1964; Greenville Coll IL, BA 1966; New Sch for Soc Research NYC, MA 1968; Rutgers Univ New Brunswick NJ, PhD 1977. **Career:** New Brunswick Comm Church NJ, minister; Douglass Coll Rutgers State Univ New Brunswick, asst prof 1973-; Family Day & Care Brooklyn, dir 1970; Comm Progress Ctr Brooklyn, health & welfare specialist 1969; Brooklyn Coll, lectr 1968; Comm Action Council Akron, soc worker 1966; Afro-spanish Consumer Coop Brooklyn, dir 1970; Save the Youth/Children Orgn Brooklyn, founder & dir 1973. **Orgs:** Founder & bd chmn Parents Coop Nursery Sch 1974; chief organizer & consult Nat Black Quadracentennial 1976; Alpha Kappa Sigma Greenville Coll 1966; Comm Serv Family Day Care Careers Program 1970. **Honors/Awds:** Founded & directed "St Olympics" Brooklyn & New Brunswick 1974; black & Puerto Rican faculty & staff award Douglass Coll Rutgers 1978; comm serv award Martin Luther King Jr Players; New Brunswick & high sch model students; neighborhood girls' club 1978-80; first Am black to receive PhD in sociology Rutgers Univ New Brunswick NJ 1977. **Business Addr:** Douglass Coll, Rutgers State Univ, New Brunswick, NJ 08901.

WILLIAMS, CHESTER LEE
Educator, businessman. **Personal:** Born Jul 24, 1944, Durham, NC; married Lauren B Sapp; children: Corey T, Christopher J, Cheston J. **Educ:** North Carolina Central Univ, Durham, NC, BA 1967; Univ of Michigan, Ann Arbor, MI, MFA 1971. **Career:** Wright Re-Educ Sch, instr 1964-68; Fiberglass Unltd Co, fiberglass techn 1965-69; St Thomas Moore's Sch, instr 1966; Sch of Design, instr creative woodwork & furn design 1968; Duke Univ Women's Club, instr water color techn 1968-69; Natl Air Pollution Contr Cntr, illustrator 1969; Voorhees Coll, asst prof of art apprec & arts & crafts 1971-74; FL A&M Univ, assoc prof of art, sculpture; NC Central Univ, assoc prof of sculpture dept art; Williams Foundry, Durham, NC, pres. **Orgs:** Mem Coll Art Assn; Natl Conf of Artists; So Assn of Sculptors Inc; mem Faculty Senatre FL A&M Univ 1980; pres cabinet FL A&M Univ 1984; dir FAMU Art Gallery FL A&M Univ 1974-78 & 1983-84; adv to Esquire Soc Club Voorhees Coll 1971-74; parliamentarian comm on faculty Voorhees Coll 1973-74; Fine Arts Council of FL Div of Cultural Affairs; mem Visual Arts Adv Panel 1977 & 1983; Tallahassee City Comm app to Arts Selection Comm 1977-79; bd mem LeMoyne Art Found Tallahassee, FL 1979-84; visiting artist, Duke Univ Women's Club 1969; Univ of TX at Odessa 1973; Allpalachian State Univ 1975; Leon Dist Schools &the Tallahassee Arts Cncl 1976-78; Broward Comm Coll Pompano Beach, FL 1977; Elizabeth City State Univ 1984. **Honors/Awds:** Recipient Sculpture Award 17th Ann Major FL Artists Show 1980; Grant Fine Arts Council of FL 1977-78; Pres Disting Serv Award Voorhees Coll 1973-74; particip in many art shows & exhibitions incl NC Mus of Art, Downtown Art Gallery, numerous others; researching a bibliography of materials by and about the Blacks of the Fine Arts; writing basic textbook on the fundamentals of beginning sculpture; writing and illust a book on the Black protest art of the 1960's; numerous other articles and reviews including, Joy McLlwain "Sculptor with a Message of Hope" Tallahassee 1984 p 15; A L Nyerges "The Black Artist as Artist" EPOCH Feb 1983 p 14-16.

WILLIAMS, CHRISTOPHER J.
Financial executive. **Career:** The Williams Capital Group, LP, CEO, 1993-. **Special Achievements:** Company is ranked #11 on Black Enterprise magazine's 1997 list of 15 Top Black investment companies. **Business Addr:** CEO, The Williams Capital Group, LP, 919 3rd, New York, NY 10022, (212)688-6237.

WILLIAMS, CLARENCE
Consultant. **Personal:** Born Oct 1, 1945, Shreveport, LA; son of Hearlean Willis Williams and Leonard Williams Sr; children: Kevin M, Makala O, Maleah R. **Educ:** Southern Univ; Seattle Comm Coll. **Career:** Seattle Black Fire Fighter Assoc, pres 1970; Intl Assoc of Black Professional Fire Fighters, nw reg dir 1975, exec vice pres & a/a officer 1980; Seattle Fire Dept, lt 1981; Barden Cablevision of Seattle, dir of oper 1982; IABPFF, pres 1984-88; Pryor, McClendon & Counts Investment Bankers, consultant, 1993-. **Orgs:** Pres Bd of Dir for CACC 1975; bd mem NW Conf Black Public Officials 1980; co chmn Sea Urban League Scholarship Fund Raising 1981; trustee Mt Zion Baptist Church 1981; chmn of publicity Girls Club of Puget Sound 1984; bd mem Seattle Urban League; rep Nat'l Black Leadership Roundtable; mem WA State MLK Jr Commission; Alumni Leadership Tomorrow Prog/Seattle Chamber of Comm; mem Southern Univ Alumni of Seattle WA; registrated lobbyist, State of WA, 1993. **Honors/Awds:** Hon fire fighter Shreveport LA Fire Dept 1976; Most Outstanding Young Man of Amer The US JayCees 1978, 1981; Furthering the Cause of Human Rights United Nations Assn 1979; Affirmative Action Awd Seattle Urban League 1982; Comm Serv Black Law Enforcement Officers Assoc 1984; Men of Achievement, 1996. **Military Serv:** WA State NG spec 4th class 6 years. **Business Addr:** Past President, Intl Assn Black Professional Firefighters, PO Box 22005, Seattle, WA 98122.

WILLIAMS, CLARENCE EARL, JR.
Clergyman. **Personal:** Born May 10, 1950, Tuscaloosa, AL. **Educ:** St Joseph Coll Rensselaer IN, BA Sociology & French 1973; Cath Theol Union Chicago, MDiv & MA 1974-80. **Career:** Natl Black Seminarians Assn, bd chmn 1970; Acad of the Afro-World Comm, founder & pres 1977; St Anthony RC Ch, pastor 1978; The Black Catholic Televangelization Network, pres 1986; Soc of the Precious Blood, clergyman 1978-. **Orgs:** Exec dir of This Far by Faith, The Black Catholic Chapel of the Air a natl radio evangel prog; created in 1983 the "Come and Go" evangelization training prog of cassettes & filmstrips; participant intl "Mass for Shut-Ins"TV prog from Detroit 1982-; producer of documentary series onTV "Search for a Black Christian Heritage"; producer and host of syndicatedTV series "Black and Catholic" 1986; Madonna University, bd of trustees, 1997-. **Honors/Awds:** 1st producer & dir of Black vocations filmstrips 1978; 1st black priest ordained in Diocese of Cleveland 1978; author of numerous articles and pamphlets on the Black Catholic experience; Natl Black Catholic Seminarians Assn named its annual achievement awd "The Fr Clarence Williams Awd" 1984. **Business Addr:** Pastor, Soc of the Precious Blood, 5247 Sheridan, Detroit, MI 48213.

WILLIAMS, CLARENCE G.
Educator. **Personal:** Born Dec 23, 1938, Goldsboro, NC; married Mildred Cogdell; children: Clarence Jr, Alton. **Educ:** NC Central, BS 1961; Hampton Univ, MS 1967; Univ of CT, PhD 1972; Cornell Univ, graduate study 1965; Harvard Univ, postdoctoral study 1975. **Career:** Williamsburg Public Schools VA, teacher 1961-64; Hampton Univ, asst dean of men, instructor, 1964-68; Univ of CT, professional counselor 1968-72; MIT, asst dean of graduate school 1972-74, special asst to pres 1974-, acting director of the office of minority education, 1980-82, equal opportunity officer, 1984-94, professor of urban studies & planning, 1993-. **Orgs:** Amer Personnel & Guidance Ass n; Assn of Non-White Concerns; Coll Student Personnel Assn; Phi Delta Kappan; Black Citizens of Newton; NC CU Alumni Assn, Hampton Inst Alumni Assn, Univ of CT Alumni Assn, Alpha Phi Alpha; former president of the board and member, MA Pre-Engineering Program; founder, co-chmn Black Admin Conf on Issues Facing Black Admin at Predominantly White Inst 1982-84; consultant, founder, Greater Boston Interuniversity Council 1984-; bd dir Buckingham Browne & Nichols School 1985-91; bd dir Freedom House 1986-; consultant, Bank of New England 1986-92. **Honors/Awds:** Recipient Hampton Inst Summer Study Fellowship; certificate, Harvard Univ Inst for Educ Mgmt 1975; Ford Found Fellowship for Admin; YMCA Black Achievers 1979; The 100 Listing - Black Influentials in Boston, 1987-91; Excellence in Leadership, minority education, MIT, 1990; Freedom House Award, 1986; "Muchas Gracias" Award, Hispanic Community at MIT, 1990; publication, "Proceedings First Natl Conf on Issues Facing Black Admin at Predominantly White Colleges & Univs", "Black Students on White Campuses During a Period of Retrenchment"; " Role Models and Mentors for Blacks at Predominantly White Campuses,"; Editor, Reflections of the Dream, 1975-94: Twenty Years of Celebrating the Life of Dr Martin Luther King at MIT, 1995. **Business Addr:** Special Assistant to the President, Adjunct Professor, Urban Studies & Planning, Massachusetts Institute OF Technology, 77 Mass Ave, 3-221, Cambridge, MA 02139.

WILLIAMS, CLARICE LEONA
District school superintendent. **Personal:** Born Dec 26, 1936, Los Angeles, CA; married Jarrod B Williams; children: Jarrod Barrett II, Courtni Clarice. **Educ:** CA State Univ Los Angeles, BA 1966; CA State Polytechnic Univ, MA 1974; Univ of NE-Lincoln, PhD 1978. **Career:** Los Angeles Unified School Dist, teacher 1965-66; Ontario-Montclair School Dist Ontario CA, teacher 1966-72; Fr Flanagan's Boys Town School System NE, reading specialist, reading coord, asst principal, curriculum coord 1972-79; Riverside Unified School Dist, principal Monroe Elem, principal Central Middle School, dist dir of special educ 1979-82; Lucerne Valley Union School Dist CA, dist superintendent 1982-. **Orgs:** Mem Phi Delta Kappa, Assoc of CA Sch Administrators, Assoc for Supervision and Curriculum Develop, Lucerne Valley Chamber of Commerce. **Honors/Awds:** US Congressional Awd 1984; Honors Masters Program. **Business Addr:** School District Superintendent, Lucerne Valley Union Sch Dist, LVSR Box 900, Lucerne Valley, CA 92356.

WILLIAMS, CLAYTON RICHARD
Associate judge (retired). **Personal:** Born Dec 2, 1920, St Louis, MO; son of Margaret Williams and Richard Williams; married Virginia Tyler; children: Shari. **Educ:** Attended Shurtleff Coll 1946-48; Lincoln Univ Sch of Law, LLB 1954. **Career:** Private Practice, attorney 1955-65; Madison Co IL, asst public defender 1966-67; Madison Co Legal Serv Soc, dir 1967-71; Madison Co IL, asst states atty 1972-73; Third Judicial Circuit Edwardsville IL, assoc judge, retired 1987. **Orgs:** Vice pres & pres Alton Wood River Bar Assn 1968-70; pres Alton Br NAACP. **Honors/Awds:** Whitney Young Awd Madison St Clair City Urgan League 1975; Outstanding Black Judge Cook Co Bar Assn 1975; Brotherhood Awd Campbell Chapel AME Church 1976. **Military Serv:** AUS t/5 1942-45.

WILLIAMS, CLYDE
Attorney. **Personal:** Born Feb 23, 1939, South Carolina; married; children: 2. **Educ:** JD, BA 1960-65. **Career:** Williams, DeLaney & Simkin, former atty. **Orgs:** Mem Gen Counsel Ofc Staff of Fed Hsng Adminstrn DC; mem Wayne Twp Board Richmond; elected pub ofcl mem Rep Party of IN; vice pres Hoosier State Bar Assn; ABA Assn; Nat Bar Assn. **Business Addr:** 48 S 7 St, Richmond, IN 47374.

WILLIAMS, CODY
City councilman. **Career:** Former coordinator for minority and women-owned business programs in Phoenix; Phoenix City Council, councilman, 1994-. **Special Achievements:** Only the third African American ever elected to the Phoenix City Council. **Business Addr:** Councilmember, Phoenix City Council, 200 W. Washington, 11th Fl., Phoenix, AZ 85003, (602)262-7493.

WILLIAMS, DANIEL
Professional football player. **Personal:** Born Dec 15, 1969, Ypsilanti, MI. **Educ:** Toledo. **Career:** Denver Broncos, defensive end, 1993-96; Kansas City Chiefs, 1997-. **Business Addr:** Professional Football Player, Kansas City Chiefs, One Arrowhead Dr, Kansas City, MO 64129, (816)924-9300.

WILLIAMS, DANIEL EDWIN
Clinical psychologist. **Personal:** Born Nov 24, 1933, Mobile, AL; son of Demaris Lewis Brown and Robert Williams; married Mildred E Olney, Jun 15, 1957; children: Denise, Michele, Melanie. **Educ:** Seton Hall US, Orange, NJ, BA, 1962; St Johns Univ, New York, MS, 1963, PhD, 1968. **Career:** Mt Carmel Guild, Newark, NJ, psych, 1963-65; East Orange, NJ, Public Schools, school psych, 1965-68; Daniel E Williams, PhD, PA, clinical psychologist, 1974-; Montclair State Coll, assoc professor of psych. **Orgs:** Pres, Natl Assn of Black Psychologists, 1980-81; pres, New Jersey chapter Assn of Black Psychologists, 1973-75 & 1981-83; bd mem, Psychological Examiners, State of New Jersey, 1973-75; mem, bd of educ, Plainfield, NJ, 1972-74. **Honors/Awds:** ABPP diplomate in clinical psychology, Amer Bd of Prof Psych, Amer Psychological Assn, 1977. **Military Serv:** USAF, staff/sargent, 1951-55. **Business Addr:** Assoc Professor of Psych, Montclair State College, Montclair, NJ 07043.

WILLIAMS, DANIEL LOUIS
Contractor. **Personal:** Born Aug 15, 1926, Hardeeville, SC; son of Mattie Freeman Williams and Adbell Williams Sr; married Pauline Cave; children: Sharon, Daniel Jr, Brenda, Derrick, Devon, Dewitt. **Educ:** Savannah State Coll, 1946-48. **Career:** Masons (Prince Hall), sr warden, 1950; Shriners, Illinois potentate, 1968-70; St Phillips Baptist Church, decon, 1968; Beaufort-Jasper Career Educ Center, vice-chmn, 1974; Career Educ Center, chmn, 1986; Jasper County; school bd mem. **Military Serv:** USN, stm 1st class, Victory award, 1944-45. **Home Addr:** PO Box 417, Hardeeville, SC 29927.

WILLIAMS, DANIEL SALU
Educator. **Personal:** Born Feb 14, 1942, Brooklyn, NY; son of Loriene H Williams and David D Williams; married Sheila; children: Peter, Megan. **Educ:** Brooklyn Coll, BA Art 1965; Univ of OR, MA Jrnlsm 1969. **Career:** Ohio Univ, assoc prof of art 1969-88, chmn Photography 1980-81, 1989-91, special asst provost 1987-, prof of art 1988-, director, Minority Graduate Student Recruitment, 1994-; chair, photography dept, 1995-, asst vice pres, for minority graduate affairs, 1997-. **Orgs:** Natl Conf of Artists 1972-; Soc for Photographic Ed 1970-; advisory bd mem, Images Gallery, Cincinnati, OH 1987-91. **Honors/Awds:** OH University Research Grant 1982, 1984-; teaching asst University of OR 1967-69; Langston Hughes Visiting Professor of African and African-American Studies, University of KS, 1992; Individual Artist Fellowship, Ohio Arts Council, 1983-85, 1988, 1990; The National African-American Museum & Cultural Center, Wilberforce, OH. **Special Achievements:** Commission: photo-montage wall murals (12 panels), 22' high x 25' wide each and three simultaneous slide show projections depicting Afro-American life in the 1950's era, "African-American Life from WW II to the Civil Rights Act of 1965," completed 1988; Artwork in Permanent Collections: Studio Museum in Harlem, NY; Museum of Modern Art, NY; Natl Museum of American Art, Smithsonian Institution, Wash DC; U of Kansas; Princeton University; Haverford College, Haverford, PA. **Home Addr:** 42 Sunnyside Dr, Athens, OH 45701. **Business Addr:** Asst Provost, Prof of Art, Ohio University, 307 Cutler Hall, Athens, OH 45701.

WILLIAMS, DARRYL EDWIN
Professional football player. **Personal:** Born Jan 7, 1970, Miami, FL; married Marlina; children: Darryl Jr. **Educ:** Miami (Fla.). **Career:** Cincinnati Bengals, defensive back, 1992-95; Seattle Seahawks, 1996-. **Business Addr:** Professional Football Player, Seattle Seahawks, 11220 NE 53rd St, Kirkland, WA 98033, (206)827-9777.

WILLIAMS, DAVID GEORGE
Physician. **Personal:** Born Jan 5, 1939, Chicago, IL; married Judith; children: Sheryl, John, Jacqueline. **Educ:** Provident Hosp Chicago, RN 1961; Trenton State Coll, BA 1972; Hahne Mannmedical Coll Philadelphia, MD 1976. **Career:** Physician, private practice, cons, prison furlough bd. **Orgs:** Pres Bell-Williams & Med Assn PA 1979-; dir med NJ Prison System 1977; resident Univ of PA 1976-79; mem AMA; vice pres Medical Class 1972. **Honors/Awds:** Nat Defense Serv Medal; Vietnam Serv Medal 1965; Republic of Vietnam Campaign Medal w/Device; hon soc Trenton State Coll 1972. **Military Serv:** AUS 1960; AUS Capt 1963-68. **Business Addr:** Trenton State Prison, Physician, 3rd & Fed Sts, Trenton, NJ 08625.

WILLIAMS, DAVID W.
Judge. **Personal:** Born Mar 20, 1910, Atlanta, GA; son of Maude Lee and William Williams; married Ouida M White, Jun 11, 1939; children: David Jr, Vaughn Charles. **Educ:** Los Angeles City Coll; UCLA, AB, 1934; USC Law Sch, LLB, 1937. **Career:** Law practice, 1937-55; Los Angeles Municipal Ct, judge, 1956-62; Los Angeles Superior Court, judge, 1963-69; Santa Monica branch court, presiding judge, 1966-68; Central District of California, US district judge, 1969-. **Orgs:** Amer Bar Assn; Amer Law Inst; Langston Bar Assn; Amer Judicature Soc; NAACP;Sigma Pi Phi Fraternity; Kappa Alpha Psi Fraternity; bd of councilors, USC Law School. **Honors/Awds:** Professional Achievement Award, UCLA Alumni, 1966; Professional Achievement Award, USC Alumni, 1973; Lifetime Achievement Award, Langston Bar Assn, 1988. **Business Addr:** US District Judge, Roybal Federal Building, Suite 7100, 255 East Temple Street, Los Angeles, CA 90012.

WILLIAMS, DEBORAH ANN
Education specialist. **Personal:** Born Nov 28, 1951, Washington, DC; daughter of Marguerite Stewart Hamilton and Harold Williams. **Educ:** Ripon College, BA 1973. **Career:** Overlook Elem/Prince George's MD, teacher; C&P Telephone Co, service rep; Natl Inst of Educ, corres coord, admin officer; Dept of Education/Office of Rsch, staff asst; program analyst US Dept of Educ; US Department of Education, ed program specialist. **Orgs:** Sec Ever Ready Chorus & Club Corinthian Baptist Church 1972-; Northern Virginia Choral Guild. **Honors/Awds:** Dir's Superior Serv Awd Natl Inst of Education 1979. **Business Addr:** Education Program Specialist, US Dept of Education, 555 New Jersey Ave NW, Washington, DC 20208, (202)219-2204.

WILLIAMS, DEBORAH BROWN
Clergywoman. **Personal:** Born Dec 15, 1957, Detroit, MI; daughter of Gloria Cole Brown and Ellis Brown; married Gregory Williams, Jun 11, 1983; children: Gregory C II, Gianna Charise. **Educ:** Wayne State University, Detroit, MI, BS, Education, 1980; Garrett-Evangelical Theology Seminary, Evanston, IL, Masters, Divinity, 1983. **Career:** Ebenezer AME Church, Detroit, MI, staff minister, 1977-80; Trinity AME Church, Waukegan, IL, student minister, 1982; Emmanuel Temple AME Church, Chicago, IL, supply pastor, 1983; St Paul AME Church, Glencoe, IL, senior pastor, 1983-. **Orgs:** Fourth district coordinator, African Methodist Episcopal Connectional Women in Ministry, 1988-92; board of directors, chairman, minority task force, Illinois Prairie Girl Scout Council, 1989-; Chicago Ministerial Alliance, 1983-; secretary, Chicago Annual Conference, 1989-; national minority recruiter, 12th National Workshop on Christians & Jews, 1989. **Honors/Awds:** Mediation Moments in African Methodist, contributor, AME Publishing, 1986.

WILLIAMS, DEBRA D.
Computer services executive. **Personal:** Born Aug 20, 1959, Philadelphia, PA; daughter of John Luther and Dorothy Gertrude. **Educ:** Penn State Univ, BA, social welfare, 1979; American Univ, MS, telecommunications mgmt, 1985; Univ of MD, MS, telecommunications mgmt, 1995. **Career:** Bureau of the Census, computer sys programmer, 1980-87, analyst, 1987-90, computer specialist, 1990-97, computer services div chief, 1998-. **Orgs:** Delta Sigma Theta Sor. **Special Achievements:** First female computer services dision chief at the Census Bureau. **Business Addr:** Computer Services Division Chief, Bureau of the Census, 17101 Melford Blvd, Bowie, MD 20715, (301)457-1770.

WILLIAMS, DENIECE
Vocalist, songwriter. **Personal:** Born 1951; divorced; children (previous marriage): Kenderick, Kevin; children: Forrest. **Educ:** Purdue University, nursing. **Career:** Former member of Wonderlove, back-up singers for Stevie Wonder; back-up singer for Earth Wind and Fire; solo artist, albums include: This Is Niecy, 1976; My Melody, 1981; Niecy, 1982; I'm So Proud, 1983; Hot On the Trail; My Melody; Special Love; Let's Hear It for the Boy, 1984; So Glad I Know, 1986; Water Under the Bridge, 1987; I Can't Wait, 1988; As Good As It Gets, 1989; "Too Much, Too Little, Too Late," duet with Johnny Mathis, 1978; Christian Production Company, founder. **Honors/Awds:** "It's Gonna Take a Miracle," Grammy Award nomination, 1983; So Glad I Know, Grammy Award, 1986. **Home Addr:** Vocalist, c/o Agency for Preferred Artists, 9000 Sunset Blvd, 12th Fl, Los Angeles, CA 90069, (310)273-0744. **Business Addr:** Vocalist, Water Under the Bridge, c/o William Morris, 10100 Santa Monica Blvd, 16th Fl, Los Angeles, CA 90067, (310)556-2727.

WILLIAMS, DENNIS
Military officer. **Personal:** Born Nov 12, 1957, Los Angeles, CA; son of Earnestine Wright Williams and Joseph Williams (deceased); married Roberta M Clair, Mar 8, 1980; children: Nikolas D, Derrik M. **Educ:** Univ of Southern CA, BA 1980; USAF Lowry AFB, Munitions Maintenance School, attended 1980-81; Webster Univ, MA 1982; Compton Community Coll, AA, 1977. **Career:** USAF McConnell AFB, munitions maintenance officer 1981-84; Univ of Akron, asst prof aerospace studies 1984-87; Kadena AB, aircraft maintenance officer 1987-. **Orgs:** Mem Univ of Akron Black Alumni Assn 1984-86; adviser Univ of Akron Arnold Air Soc 1984-87, Univ of Akron Angel Flight 1984-87; adviser, Univ of Akron, Natl Soc of Black Engineers 1986-87. **Honors/Awds:** Mem Omicron Delta Kappa 1985-87. **Military Serv:** USAF, capt, 1980-; Air Force Commendation Medal, Outstanding Unit Awd, Longevity, Training, Marksmanship Ribbons 1980-87.

WILLIAMS, DICK ANTHONY
Actor. **Personal:** Born Aug 9, 1938, Chicago, IL; married Gloria Edwards. **Educ:** Malcolm X College; Kennedy King College. **Career:** New Federal Theatre, co-founder; playwright of numerous pieces including: One, Black and Beautiful, A Big of Black, also directed and produced numerous plays; film appearances include: Uptight, 1968; The Last Man, 1969; Who Killed Mary What's 'Er Name?, 1971; The Anderson Tapes, 1971; The Mack, 1973; Five on the Black Hand Side, 1973; Slaughter's Big Rip-Off, 1973; Dog Day Afternoon, 1975; The Long Night, 1976; Deadly Hero, 1976; The Deep, 1977; An Almost Perfect Affair, 1979; The Jerk, 1979; The Star Chamber, 1983; Summer Rental, 1985; Mo' Better Blues, 1990; television appearances include: Something So Right, 1982; Keeping On, 1984; Cagney & Lacey, 1984; For Us the Living: The Medgar Evers Story, 1984; Trauma Center, 1984; Hart to Hart, 1984; Trapper John MD, 1984; Stingray, 1986; Theeting, 1989; Homefront, 1991-. **Honors/Awds:** Drama Desk Award, Tony nomination, AUDELCO Theatre Award, all for What Winesellers Buy, 1974; Tor Award, Tony nomination, both for Black Picture Show, 1975; AUDELCO Award Black Theatre Recognition Award, 1975. **Business Addr:** Actor, Intl Creative Management, 8899 Beverly Blvd, Los Angeles, CA 90048, (310)550-4000.

WILLIAMS, DONALD
Graphics company executive. **Personal:** son Of Jean and Elmer Williams (deceased). **Career:** Williams Graphics, CEO, currently. **Business Addr:** CEO, Williams Graphics, 5423 Penn Ave, Pittsburgh, PA 15206, (412)363-2429.

WILLIAMS, DONALD EUGENE
Business executive, clergyman. **Personal:** Born Jan 4, 1929, DeLand, FL; son of Willie Bertha Kenner-Williams and John Kenner-Williams; married Leah Keturah Pollard-Williams, Sep 11, 1955; children: Donald, Jr, Celeste, Michele A Williams. **Educ:** Kane Bus School, 1951-52; Shelton Coll, 1952-54; Wayne Coll, 1970-72. **Career:** Church of God, pastor 1962-76; Church of God World Svc, dir minority min 1976-81; Church of God Missionary Bd, assoc exec sec 1981-87; Church of God World Service, Associate Director, 1987-. **Orgs:** Pres Ministerial Assoc 1964-69; vice pres Literacy Council 1964-69; cty jail chaplain Wayne Cty MI 1972-76; dir Rotary Intl 1983-; police chaplain Detroit Police Dept 1972-76; mem Commiss on Human Rights 1983-89; Indiana State Police Chaplain, 1990-97; life mem NAACP. **Honors/Awds:** Dedicated Serv Girls Clubs of Amer 1969, Boys Clubs of Metro Detroit 1975, Detroit Police Dept 1976; Outstanding Service Award, Church of God Missionary Board, 1987. **Business Addr:** Associate Executive Secretary, Church of God Missionary Bd, 1303 E 5th St, Anderson, IN 46018.

WILLIAMS, DONALD H.
Educator. **Personal:** Born Oct 29, 1936, Chicago, IL; son of Theresa P. Williams and Herbert G. Williams; married Sharon Rebecca Hobbs, Jun 18, 1983; children: David, Jonathan, Rebecca. **Educ:** Univ of IL, BA 1957, MD 1962; Univ of IL Rsch & Educ Hosp, internship 1962-63, residency 1964-67. **Career:** Conn. Mental Health Cntr, chief inpatient serv 1971-73; Yale Univ, asst prof 1971-77; Conn. Mental Health Cntr, head Med Eval Unit 1973-78, chief Comm Supp Serv 1973-79; Yale Univ, assoc prof of psych 1977-84; Conn. Mental Health Center, asst chief for clin aff 1979-84; MI State Univ, prof/chairperson of Psychiatry 1984-89. **Orgs:** Amer Publ Health Assn 1968; Amer Orthopsychiatric Assn 1968; consult Natl Inst of Mental Health 1971-81; consult West Haven Veterans Admin Hosp 1971-80; Fellow Amer Psychiatric Assn 1974; treas Black Psychiatrists of Amer 1978-80. **Honors/Awds:** IL Psychiatric Soc Resch Award Referee 1968; Archieves of Gen Psychiatry; Amer Journl of Psychiatry; Social Psychiatry; 17 articles and numerous professional presentations. **Military Serv:** AUS Reserves Psychiatrist 801 Gen Hosp 1968-69; Cpt Medical Corps 1963-68. **Business Addr:** Professor, Department of Psychiatry, East Fee Hall, Michigan State University, East Lansing, MI 48824, (517)353-3888.

WILLIAMS, DOROTHY DANIEL
Educator. **Personal:** Born Aug 22, 1938, Kinston, NC; daughter of Willie Mae Wingate Daniel (deceased) and Fonie Daniel (deceased); divorced; children: William Daniel. **Educ:** Hampton Inst, BSN, 1960; New York Univ, Grad Courses, 1965; East Carolina Univ, MS, HEC, 1977, MSN, 1980. **Career:** New York City & Los Angeles, CA, staff nurse, 1960-66; Einstein Hospital, Bronx, NY, head nurse, 1966-69; Baltimore City Schools, Vocational Div, teacher, 1969-73; Lenoir Mem Hospital, School of Nursing, instructor, 1973-74; East Carolina Univ, School of Nursing, asst professor of maternal-child nursing, 1974-. **Orgs:** By law comm mem, North Carolina Nurse Assn, 1983-85; sec convention delegate Dist 32, NCNA, 1983-85; vice pres, Delta Rho Zeta Chapter, Zeta Phi Beta Sor Inc, 1983-85; lecturer, State Bd of Nursing Review Courses, AHEC; mem, 1980-, chmn, 1981-82, 1985, 1997-, School of Nursing Curriculum Comm; developer, Leadership Seminar; panelist, consultant, developer, Adolescent Pregnancy/Parenting Seminar; by laws comm, Assn of Black Nursing Faculty in Higher Educ, 1986-; board of review, ABNF Journal, 1991-; task force mbr, Infant Mortality and AIDS, Community Task Force on Community Relations; appointed to ECU Pre Med, Pre Dental Advisory Council, 1992-; bd mem, Community Health Center. **Honors/Awds:** Natl Nurse Honor Soc, Beta Chapter, Sigma Theta Tau, 1978; ECU Lambda Mu Chap Zeta Phi Beta, advisor, 1983-; Selected to participate in the minority health leadership workshop, Chapel Hill, NC, 1985; ECU Greek Affairs Advisor Comm, appointed, 1984; HERA, for Outstanding Sorority Advisor, Panhellenic Council of ECU, 1986; appointment to Research Bd of Advisors, Amer Biographical Inst, Inc, 1987; Zeta of the Year, Delta Rho Zeta Chapter, Zeta Phi Beta Sorority, 1988, 1993. **Business Addr:** Asst Professor of Nursing, East Carolina University, Nursing Bldg, Greenville, NC 27834.

WILLIAMS, DOROTHY P.
Educational administrator. **Personal:** Born Nov 24, 1938, Tallahassee, FL; divorced; children: Gerald Herbert, Debra Michelle. **Educ:** FL A&M Univ, BS 1960; Syracuse Univ, MSLS 1967; Univ of North FL, 1974-75. **Career:** Lincoln Memorial HS, librarian 1960-61; JW Johnson Jr HS, head librarian 1962-68; Raines HS, head librarian 1968-71; Univ of North FL, asst dir libs 1971-82; FL A&M Univ, dir of publications, beginning 1983, interim vp of univ relations, currently. **Orgs:** EEO/AA coord Univ of North FL 1976-82; staff coord State Bd of Educ Adv Comm on the Educ of Blacks in FL 1984-; bd mem Jacksonville Comm Economic DevCouncil 1981-83; past pres Jack-

sonville Natl Council of Negro Women 1978-81; past pres Jacksonville Chapter of Links Inc 1985-87; past pres Friends of FAMU Black Archives 1985-88; FAMU Foundation, bd of dirs, secretary, 1993-. **Honors/Awds:** Teacher of the Year James Weldon Johnson Jr HS 1966; Service Award Alpha Kappa Alpha Sorority 1978; Community Serv Award Grant Meml AME Church 1979, 1988, 1990; Rattler Pride Award; Distinguished Alumni Award (NAFEO), 1993; Florida A&M Univ, Gallery of Distinction, College of Arts and Sciences, 1987. **Home Addr:** 748 E 9th Ave, Tallahassee, FL 32303. **Business Addr:** Interim VP, Univ Relations, Florida A & M Univ, Martin Luther King Jr Blvd, Tallahassee, FL 32307, (904)599-3491.

WILLIAMS, DOUG LEE
Football coach. **Personal:** Born Aug 9, 1955, Zachary, LA. **Educ:** Grambling State Univ, BS, education, 1978. **Career:** Quarterback: Tampa Bay Buccaneers, 1978-82; Oklahoma Outlaws (USFL), 1984; Arizona Wranglers (USFL), 1985; Washington Redskins, 1986-89; Pointe Coupee Central, athletic dir; Jacksonville Jaguars, college scout; Morehouse College, head coach, 1997; Grambling State Univ, head coach, 1998-. **Special Achievements:** First team All-American; Led the Washington Redskins to victory in Super Bowl XXII. **Business Addr:** Head Football Coach, Morehouse College, 830 Westview Dr SW, Atlanta, GA 30314.

WILLIAMS, E. THOMAS, JR.
Investor, banking executive. **Personal:** Born Oct 14, 1937, New York, NY; son of Elnora Bing Williams and Edgar T "Ned" Williams; married Auldlyn Higgins; children: Brooke Higgins Bing Williams; Eden Bradford Bing Williams. **Educ:** Brooklyn College, BA, economics, 1960. **Career:** Chase Manhattan Bank, Vice Pres & Sr Loan Officer for Int'l Private Banking 1972-83; Fordham Hill Owners Corp, president 1983-89, chairman, 1990-92; Elnora, Inc, president/CEO, 1993-. **Orgs:** Trustee Boys Harbor Inc; trustee Central Park Conservancy Bd; trustee Atlanta Univ Ctr; bd mem NAACP Legal Defense Fund; mem Sigma Pi Phi; 100 Black Men, Inc; Thomas Franklin Bing Trust; Nehemiah Housing Trust; Fiduciary Trust Co. International, director and chair of audit committee; trustee Vestry of Trinity Church Wall St; trustee Cathedral Church St John the Divine Treasurer; The Schomburg Ctr for Rsch in Black Culture; chmn Schomberg Soc; trustee, Grace Mansion Conservancy; trustee, Brooklyn Museum; trustee, The Museum of Modern Art; University Club of New York, River Club of New York; Omega Psi Phi. **Honors/Awds:** Black Enterprise cover story, April, 1986; New York Magazine cover story, January 19, 1987; Patron of the Arts Award, Studio Museum, Harlem, 1987. **Military Serv:** Peace Corps, Ethiopia I 1962-63. **Home Addr:** 145 East 74 Street, New York, NY 10021. **Business Addr:** President/CEO, Elnora, Inc., 82 Hempstead Street, Sag Harbor, NY 11963.

WILLIAMS, EARL
Musician. **Personal:** Born Oct 8, 1938, Detroit, MI; son of Evelyn Webb Williams and Paul Williams; married Ronda G Snowden MD, Dec 21, 1985; children: Earl Jr, Kevin, Damon, Lauren, Brandon. **Educ:** Detroit Conserv of Music, attended 1949-51; Detroit Inst of Musical Arts, attended 1951-53; Borough of Manhattan Comm Coll, attended 1973-75; Empire State Coll, New York, NY BA 1986-88. **Career:** Paul "Hucklebuck" Williams Orchestra, musician (drummer) 1957-59; Eddie Heywood Trio, musician 1959-61; Recording/TV/Radio, studio drummer 1961-73; Sam "The Man" Taylor Japan Tour, drummer 1964-65 & 1972; Music Matrix Publ Co, musician/pres; State University at Old Westbury, Old Westbury, NY, adjunct instructor, 1991-; Five Towns College, Dix Hills, NY, adjunct instructor, 1991-94; Long Island University, adjunct instructor, CW Post Campus, Brookville, NY, 1994-; Valerie Capers Trio. **Orgs:** Mem NARAS (Natl Acad of Recording Artists Arts and Scis) 1979; lectures/demonstrations/concerts in various univs and cultural inst 1968-85; mem Broadcast Music Inc BMI, 1960. **Honors/Awds:** Drummer with, Diahann Carroll-Cannes Film Festival 1965; WNET-TV "Soul Show" 1968-69; NBC-TV "Someone New Show" 1969-72; ABC-TV "Jack Parr Show" 1973-74; Lena Horne 1973-74; A Chorus Line (Broadway) 1975-79; Alvin Ailey Dance Co 1979; Jean-Pierre Rampal 1980-81; JVC Jazz Festival, Nice, France, 1989; North Sea Jazz Festival, The Hague, The Netherland, 1993; Mary Lou Williams, Women in Jazz Festival Kennedy Center, 1997.

WILLIAMS, EARL, JR.
Educational administrator, city official, clergyman. **Personal:** Born Mar 27, 1935, Thomasville, GA; son of Flossie Adams Williams and Earl Williams Sr; married Faye Harris Williams, Dec 10, 1958; children: Earl III, Jennifer, Angela, Thomas, Jeffrey. **Educ:** Fort Valley State College, Fort Valley, GA, BA, 1963; Valdosta State College, Valdosta, GA, MA, 1975. **Career:** Professional Baseball, 1956, 1957, 1962; United State Marine Corps, 1958-61; City of Thomasville, GA, mayor, 1985-89; Thomas County Board of Education, Thomasville, GA, principal, 1963-91; City of Thomasville, GA, city council, 1980-91; Pastor 2nd Presbyterian Church, Thomasville, GA, 1980-. **Orgs:** Kappa Alpha Psi Fraternity, Mason SP Jones #118 NAACP, Georgia Association of Educators; NEA board of directors, Thomasville Community Bank; board of directors, Salvation Army; member of Flint River Presbytery, Black Mayor Assn of Georgia. **Honors/Awds:** 1st Black City Council Person in Thomasville, GA, 1981-; 1st Black Mayor City of Thomasville, GA, 1985-89; Elected to the Hall of Fame, Fort Valley State College, 1985; 1985 Honorary Dr of Law From Faith College, Birmingham, AL, 1986. **Military Serv:** USMC, E-4, 1958-61; Most Valuable Player USMC 1959-61; All Marine Team 1959, 1960, 1961. **Business Addr:** Principal, Central Middle School, Thomas County Board of Educations, E Pinetree Blvd, Thomasville, GA 31792.

WILLIAMS, EARL WEST
City official. **Personal:** Born Jul 20, 1928, Montgomery, AL; married Frances Jenkins; children: Earl Jr, Reginald, Eric. **Educ:** Morehouse Coll, attended 1947; Alabama State Univ, BS 1950; Cleveland State Univ, attended 1973. **Career:** Cleveland Bd of Educ, teacher 1953-55; Beneficial Finance Co, asst mgr 1956-62; City of Cleveland Comm Devel, citizen participation adv 1962-64, project dir 1964-70; Community Relations Bd, executive dir. **Orgs:** Pres elect 1986-87, mem Natl Assoc of Human Rights Workers; trustee Greater Cleveland Interchurch Cncl, Office of School Monitoring and Comm Relations, St James AME Church; mem Leadership Cleveland, Omega Psi Phi Frat Inc, Beta Rho Boule-Sigma Psi Phi Frat. **Honors/Awds:** US Congressional Certificate of Achievement US Congress 1982; Disting Awd Cleveland Comm Relations Bd 1986; Outstanding Citizen Omega Psi Phi Frat 1986; President's Certificate of Appreciation Natl Assoc of Human Rights Workers 1986. **Military Serv:** AUS t/sgt 2 yrs. **Business Addr:** Consultant, 18219 Van Aken Blvd, Shaker Heights, OH 44122.

WILLIAMS, EDDIE NATHAN
Research executive. **Personal:** Born Aug 18, 1932, Memphis, TN; son of Georgia Lee Barr Williams and Ed Williams; married Jearline F Reddick, Jul 18, 1981; children: Traci (Halima), Edward L Williams, Terence Reddick. **Educ:** Univ of Illinois, Urbana, BS, 1954; Atlanta Univ, Atlanta GA, postgraduate study, 1957; Howard Univ, Washington DC, postgraduate study, 1958. **Career:** Atlanta Daily World Newspaper, Atlanta GA, reporter, 1957-58; US Senate Comm on Foreign Relations, Washington DC, staff asst, 1959-60; US Dept of State, Washington DC, foreign service res officer, 1961-68; Univ of Chicago IL, vice pres, 1968-72; Joint Center for Political and Economic Studies, Washington DC, pres, 1972-. **Orgs:** Natl Coalition on Black Voter Participation, bd of dirs; Blue Cross/Blue Shield of the National Capital Area; YMCA of Metro Washington; Harrah's Entertainment Corp; Black Leadership Forum; Council on Foreign Relations, Omega Psi Phi; Garnd Sire Archon-Elect, Sigma Pi Phi. **Honors/Awds:** Hon DHL, Chicago State University, 1994; Hon LLD, Univ of the District of Columbia, 1986; Hon DHL, Bowie State Univ, 1980; Congressional Black Caucus Adam Clayton Powell Award, 1981; Keynote Address Award, Natl Conf of Black Political Scientists, 1988; Achievement Award, Black Alumni Assn, Univ of IL, 1988; MacArthur Foundation Prize Fellows Award, 1988; Washingtonian Magazine, Washingtonian of the Year Award, 1991; National Black Caucus of State Legislators, Nation Builder Award, 1992; Ebony Magazine "100 Most Influential Organization Leaders," 1997; author of numerous newspaper, magazine, journal, and book articles, 1963-. **Military Serv:** US Army, first lieutenant, 1955-57. **Business Addr:** President, Joint Center for Political and Economic Studies, 1090 Vermont Ave NW, Suite 1100, Washington, DC 20005.

WILLIAMS, EDDIE R., JR.
Educational administrator. **Personal:** Born Jan 6, 1945, Chicago, IL; son of Anna Maude Jones Williams (deceased) and E R Williams (deceased); married Shirley King Williams, May 31, 1969; children: Karen Lynn, Craig DeWitt, Evan Jonathan. **Educ:** Ottawa University, Ottawa, Kansas, BA (highest honors), mathematics, 1966; Columbia University, PhD, mathematics, 1971. **Career:** Northern Illinois University, associate professor of mathematics, 1970-91, associate director, operating budgets, 1978-83, budget and planning, deputy director, 1983, director, 1983-85, assistant vice pres, administrative affairs, vice pres, division of finance and planning, 1985-96; senior vice president, finance & facilities, 1996-. **Orgs:** South Park Baptist Church, assistant pastor, director, youth activities, 1970-, senior pastor, 1997-; University Resource Advisory Committee; Presidential Commission on Status of Minorities; University Affirmative Action Committee, 1974-; American Mathematical Society. **Military Serv:** US Navy, Capt, 1981-; Navy Commendation Medal for Meritorious Achievement, 1990; Campus Liaison Officer of the Year, 1991. **Home Addr:** 175 Buena Vista, De Kalb, IL 60115. **Business Addr:** Sr. Vice President, Finance and Facilities, Northern Illinois University, Lowden Hall, Rm 109, De Kalb, IL 60115.

WILLIAMS, EDNA C.
Educator, musician. **Personal:** Born Oct 22, 1933, Chicago, IL. **Educ:** Roosevelt Univ, Mus B 1957, Mus M 1959. **Career:** Joliet Conservatory of Mus, instr 1962-64; Northern IL Univ, assoc prof. **Orgs:** Mem IL Assn for Supvsn and Curriculum Devel 1974; mem Natl Assn of Tchr of Singing Inc 1965; bd mem Natl Assn of Negro Musicians 1976. **Honors/Awds:** Sue Cowan Hintz Voice Award 1955; Oliver Ditson Voice Scholarship 1956; John Hay Whitney Fellowhsip 1959; Kenwood Male Chorus Award 1959. **Business Addr:** Associate Professor, Northern Illinois University, Dept of Music, De Kalb, IL 60115.

WILLIAMS, EDWARD ELLIS
Business executive. **Personal:** Born Jun 23, 1938, Hazelhurst, MS; married Sarah Robertson; children: Karen, Edward Jr. **Educ:** Univ of IL Coll of Pharmacy, B 1963. **Career:** Walgreen, pharmacist 1964, store mgr 1965, dist mgr 1967, dist mgr 1979, regional vp, currently. **Orgs:** Mem Chicago South End Jaycees 1966; mem Chicago Pharmacist Assn 1967; dir of events MS State Traveling Club 1976. **Honors/Awds:** Outstanding Young Man of the Yr Chicago S End Jaycees 1966; Spl Achiever Chicago YMCA 1978; Humanitarian Awd MS State Traveling Club 1979. **Business Addr:** Regional VP, Walgreen Co, 200 Wilmot Rd, Deerfield, IL 60015.

WILLIAMS, EDWARD JOSEPH
Banking executive. **Personal:** Born May 5, 1942, Chicago, IL; son of Joseph and Lillian; married Ana Ortiz; children: Elaine, Paul. **Educ:** Roosevelt Univ, BBA, 1973. **Career:** Mut Home Delivery, Chicago, owner, 1961-63; Harris Trust & Savings Bank, Chicago, sr vice pres, 1964-. **Orgs:** Trust Adler Planetarium, 1982; mem, Consumer Adv Council, Washington, 1986-; chmn, Provident Medical Center, 1986; mem, Natl Bankers Assn, Urban Bankers Forum, The Economic Club of Chicago; pres, Neighborhood Housing Services, 1990-; dir, Chicago Capital Fund; dir, Low Income Housing Trust Fund, 1989-; dir, Chapin-May Foundation, 1988-; trustee, treas, Adler Planetarium; advisory comm chr, Art Inst of Chicago; dir, Chapin-May Foundation; dir, Chicago Botanic Garden; dir, Chicago Capital Fund; dir, v/chr, Chicago Coun on Urban Affairs; trustee, treas, Chicago Low Income Housing Trust Fund; dir, Leadership Coun, Metro Open Communities; dir, former pres, Neighborhood Housing Svcs of Chicago; trustee, former chmn, Provident Med Ctr; trustee, Roosevelt Univ. **Honors/Awds:** Distinguished Alumni Award, Clark Coll, Atlanta, 1985; Pioneer Award, Urban Bankers Forum, 1986. **Business Addr:** Exec VP, Harris Bank, 111 W Monroe, Chicago, IL 60603.

WILLIAMS, EDWARD M.
Oral surgeon. **Personal:** Born Dec 10, 1933, Augusta, GA; married Davide Bradley (divorced); children: Brent, Kurt, Scott. **Educ:** Morehouse Coll, BS 1954; Atlanta Univ, MS 1963; Howard Univ, DDS 1968, cert oral surgy 1971. **Career:** Atlanta Pub Sch Sys, tchr 1958-63; Priv Prac, oral surgeon. **Orgs:** Mem Am Dent Assn GA Dent Assn; Am Soc Oral Surg; GA Soc Oral Surg; Internal Assn Oral Surg; Fellow Am Dent Soc of Anethesiology; mem NAACP; Am Cancer Soc; YMCA; Alpha Phi Alpha; Beta Kappa Chi. **Honors/Awds:** Award in Anesthesiology Howard Univ 1968; Award in Periodontics Howard Univ 1968. **Military Serv:** AUS 1956-58. **Business Addr:** 75 Piedmont Ave NE, Ste 440, Atlanta, GA 30303.

WILLIAMS, ELLIS
Cleric, law enforcement officer (retired). **Personal:** Born Oct 27, 1931, Raymond, MS; son of Elise Morrison McDowell and Currie Williams; married Priscilla Norman, Jan 9, 1954; children: Debra Lucas, Rita Singleton, Claude, Lathan, Glenn, Zelia. **Educ:** Loyola Univ, BA, 1972, MEd, 1974, MCJ, 1981. **Career:** New Orleans Police Dept, police officer, 1965, fingerprint tech, 1968, polygraphist, 1974; Jefferson Vocational & Tech School, lecturer, 1981-; New Orleans Police Dept, police commander, retired; Historic Second Baptist Church, New Orleans, LA, assoc minister, currently. **Orgs:** Historian Kappa Delta Pi, 1973-74; vice chmn, Louisiana Polygraph Bd, 1981-82; mem, Louisiana & Intl Assn of Ident, Freedmens Missionary Baptist Assoc of Louisiana, Natl Baptist Training Union, Sunday School Congress; Natl Org of Black Law Enforcement Exec; member, Imperial Council, Prince Hall Affiliation; member, Eureka Consistory #7 Prince Hall Affiliation; member, United Supreme Council, Prince Hall Affiliation. **Home Addr:** 3108 Metropolitan St, New Orleans, LA 70126.

WILLIAMS, ELYNOR A.
Food company executive. **Personal:** Born Oct 27, 1946, Baton Rouge, LA; daughter of Naomi Theresa Douglas Williams and Albert Berry Williams. **Educ:** Spelman Coll, BS Home Economics 1966; Cornell Univ, MPS Communication Arts 1973. **Career:** Eugene Butler Jr-Sr High school, home economics teacher 1966-68; Genl Foods Corp, publicist package editor copy editor 1968-71; Cornell Univ, COSEP tutor 1972-73; NC Agricultural Extension Svc, comm specialist 1973-77; Western Elec, sr public relations specialist 1977-83; Hanes Group Winston-Salem, dir of corp affairs, 1983-86; Sara Lee Corp, dir of public affairs, 1986-90, vice pres, public responsibility, 1990-. **Orgs:** Bd of dirs Univ of NC at Greensboro 1981-91; bd of dirs YWCA 1984-86; adv bd NC Women's Network 1985; Natl Tech Adv Comm OICs of Amer Inc 1985-92; Exec Comm Natl Women's Economic Alliance 1985; vice pres public affairs & comm bd of dirs Gr Winston-Salem Chamber of Commerce 1985-86; mem Business Policy Review Council, 1988-; Women's Institute, 1988-; bd of dirs Cosmopolitan Chamber of Commerce, Chicago, IL, 1988-91; National Hispanic Corporate Council; natl corporate adv bd Natl Org for Women; corporate adv bd Natl Women's Political Caucus; League of Women Voters; Intl Assn of Business Comm; Public Relations Society of Amer; Natl Assn of Female Execs; bd of dirs Exec Leadership Council; board of directors, National Coalition of 100 Black Women, 1991-. **Honors/Awds:** Dist Alumnae of the Yr Natl Assn for Equal Oppor in Higher Educ 1983; Bus & Entrepre-

neurship Awd Natl Alumnae Assn of Spelman Coll 1984; Hon Doc of Humane Letters Clincon Jr Coll SC 1984; Acad of Achievers YWCA NY 1984; Boss of the Yr Winston-Salem Chap Prof Secretaries Intl 1984-85; Outstanding Contribution in Business Winston-Salem Chap Natl Council of Negro Women 1985; Kizzy Award, Black Women's Hall of Fame, 1987; Outstanding Service Award, National Council of Negro Women, Midwest chapter, 1988; Black & Hispanic Achievers Industry Award, YMCA, 1988; Vanguard Award, Women in Communications Inc, 1988; Spectra Award of Excellence, Intl Assoc of Business Communicators, Chicago, IL, 1988; Racial Justice Award, YWCA, 1988; Trio award, University of Illinois, 1989; Silver Trumpet, PubliciClub of Chicago, 1990; selected as one of 100 ''Best and Brightest Black Women in Corporate America''; Leadership America Participant, Ebony 1990. **Home Addr:** 222 E Chestnut St, Apt 9B, Chicago, IL 60611-2351. **Business Addr:** Vice President, Public Responsibility, Sara Lee Corporation, 3 First National Plaza, Chicago, IL 60602.

WILLIAMS, ENOCH H.
City official (retired). **Personal:** Born Jun 21, 1927, Wilmington, NC; son of Pauline Williams and Howell Williams; married Elizabeth Peterson (divorced); children: Dr Kamau Kokoyi, Charrise Williams Adamson; married Marian. **Educ:** New York School for Social Research, 1958; New York University, Real Estate Institute, 1967; Long Island University, BS, 1967. **Career:** The Stuyvord Action Council, founder & former vice pres, 1964-66; School Dist No 11, Bronx, admin officer, 1967; Youth-in-Action Inc, comm org specialist, 1967-69; Brooklyn Local Economic Devel Corp, pres, 1967-73; Enoch Williams & Assocs Inc, pres, 1967-77; Commerce Labor Indus corp of Kings, vice chmn, bd of dirs, 1968-77; Housing Devel Corp Council of Churches, exec dir, 1969-78; Columbia Univ, Fed Annual Housing Specialist Program, lecturer, 1970-72; Housing Devel & Mgmt Training Seminars, dir, coord & lecturer, 1970-76; New York City Council, city councilman, 1978-97. **Orgs:** Vice pres, Unity Democratic Club, 1961-73; chmn, Businessmen Advisory Bd, 1966-67; Urban League; NAACP; Interfaith Housing Strategy Comm of New York; Citizens Housing & Planning Council; duty training officer, New York City Selective Serv; youth serv comm chmn, New York City Council; committeeman, New York State 55th AD; state dir, New York City Selective Serv; American Institute of Housing Consultants; Community Service Society. **Honors/Awds:** Several military & civic awards. **Special Achievements:** Delegate Natl Democratic Convention, 1968, 1972; Elected to New York City Council, 1977, 1982, 1985, 1989, 1991; Elected District Leader, 55th Assembly District, 1986, 1988, 1990, 1992. **Military Serv:** New York Army National Guard, brigadier general, retired, appointed rank of major general, 1990.

WILLIAMS, ERIC C.
Professional basketball player. **Personal:** Born Jul 17, 1972, Newark, NJ. **Educ:** Providence. **Career:** Boston Celtics, forward, 1995-97; Denver Nuggets, 1997-. **Special Achievements:** NBA, First Round Draft Pick, #14 Pick, 1995. **Business Addr:** Professional Basketball Player, Denver Nuggets, 1635 Clay St, Denver, CO 80204-1743, (303)893-6700.

WILLIAMS, ERIK GEORGE
Professional football player. **Personal:** Born Sep 7, 1968, Philadelphia, PA; children: Shay. **Educ:** Central State (Ohio), attended. **Career:** Dallas Cowboys, tackle, 1991-. **Honors/Awds:** Pro Bowl, 1993, 1996. **Business Addr:** Professional Football Player, Dallas Cowboys, One Cowboys Pkwy, Irving, TX 75063, (214)556-9900.

WILLIAMS, ERNEST Y.
Educator, physician. **Personal:** Born Feb 24, 1900, Nevis, WI; married Matilda; children: Ernest Y, Shirley Y, Joan C. **Educ:** Howard Univ Med Sch, BSMD. **Career:** Howard Univ Med School, Prof Emeritus dept neurology & psychiatry, head of NP serv 32 yrs. **Orgs:** Chmn 13 yrs, past consult Crownsville State Hosp; VA Hosp; NIMH Consult St ElizHosp; MS Soc of DC; co-founder DC Orgn for Alcoholsim; Child Psychiatric Clinic. **Honors/Awds:** Recipient plaque from NMA for Med Leadership; plaque in Recgntn 30 yrs serv NMA; Outstanding Tchr Howard Univ 1948. **Business Addr:** Howard Univ Hosp, Ga Ave & W Sts NW, Washington, DC.

WILLIAMS, ETHEL JEAN
Educator (retired). **Personal:** Born May 7, 1922, Paterson, NJ; daughter of Ethel Jean Hopper Williams and George Williams. **Educ:** New Jersey State Teachers' College, Paterson, NJ, BS, education, 1944; Columbia University, grad studies, 1945-48. **Career:** Paterson Board of Education, Paterson, NJ, elementary teacher, 1948-70; Paterson Board of Education, Paterson, NJ, guidance counselor, 1970-80; St Joseph Hospital, Paterson, NJ, counselor, WIC program, 1980-82; The Catholic Community Center, Paterson, NJ, currently; The Ethel J Williams Scholarship Fund, chairperson of the bd. **Orgs:** Administrator, Catholic Communtiy Center, 1965-; pres, BLACK, 1980-; past vice pres, Commission for Black Catholic Ministries, 1988-90; member, Coalition for Public Accountability, Diocese of Paterson, 1980-85; member, NAACP, 1960-; member, NOW (Natl & Local). **Honors/Awds:** Pro Ecclesia Et Pontifice, Papal Honor, John Paul II, 1981; Lumen Christi, Catholic Church Extension Society, 1986; President's Volunteer Action Award, Citation, Ronald Reagan, 1988; Humanitarian Award, Head Start (Natl), National Head Start Assn, 1990; NAACP Community Service Award, 1980; Distinguished Service Award, Paterson Interfaith Organizations Commissions, 1980; MLK Award, Religious Leadership, 100 Black Women, 1986. **Home Addr:** 325 Ellison St, Paterson, NJ 07501. **Business Addr:** Ethel J Williams Scholarship Fund, c/o Tri-County Scholarship Fund, 100 Hamilton Plaza, Ste 520, Paterson, NJ 07505.

WILLIAMS, ETHEL LANGLEY
Librarian (retired). **Personal:** Born in Baltimore, MD; daughter of Carrie A. and William H.; married Louis J Williams (deceased); children: Carole J Jones. **Educ:** Howard Univ, AB 1930; Columbia Univ NYC, BS 1933; Howard Univ, MA 1947-50. **Career:** Bd of Public Welfare Wash DC, caseworker 1933-35; Library of Congress, process filer & order searcher 1936-40; Moorland Spingarn Collection, supr project 271 & 328, works progress adminstrn 1939; Howard U, reference librarian cataloger 1941-47; Howard Univ Sch of Religion Library, retired librarian 1946-75; Writings, A Catalogue of Books in the Moorland Found 1939, Afro-Am Newspaper 1945-46, Negro History Bulletin 110-16 1945, Journal of Negro Educ 1945-46, Handbook of Instr in the Use of the Sch of Rel Library 1955, Revised 1968; Editor, Biographical Dir of Negro Ministers 1965, 1970, 1975. **Orgs:** Co-editor, Afro-Am Rel Studies A Comprehensive Bibliography with Locations in Am Libraries 1970, Howard Univ Bibliography & African & Afro-Am Relig Studies 1977. **Home Addr:** 1625 Primrose Rd, NW, Washington, DC 20012.

WILLIAMS, EUGENE
Professional football player. **Personal:** Born Oct 14, 1968, Blair, NE. **Educ:** Iowa State, attended. **Career:** Miami Dolphins, guard, 1991-92; Cleveland Browns, 1993-94; Atlanta Falcons, 1995-. **Orgs:** Big Brothers/Big Sisters. **Honors/Awds:** Cleveland Browns Touchdown Club, Doug Dieken Humanitarian Award, 1994. **Business Addr:** Professional Football Player, Atlanta Falcons, Two Falcon Place, Suwanee, GA 30174, (404)945-1111.

WILLIAMS, EUPHEMIA G.
Educator. **Personal:** Born Oct 17, 1938, Bagwell, TX; daughter of Blanche M Pouge Goodlow and Otis J Goodlow; married James A Williams (divorced 1987); children: Caren, Christopher, Curt, Catherine. **Educ:** University of Oklahoma, Norman, OK, BS, 1961; University of Colorado, Boulder, CO, MS, 1973, PhD, 1981. **Career:** Okla City-Co Health, Okla City, OK, public health nurse, 1966-1970; Univ of Colo, Boulder, CO, campus nurse, 1973-1974; Univ of Colo, Denver, CO, assist prof, instructor, 1974-1981; Cameron Univ, Lawton, OK, assoc prof & chair, nursing, 1981-1982; Metropolitan St Coll, Denver, CO, dept chair & prof, assoc prof-nursing, 1982-1988; Southwest MO St Univ, Springfield, MO, professor & dept head, nursing, 1988-. **Orgs:** Mem, American Nurses Association; mem, American Public Health Association; faculty counselor, Alpha Kappa Chap, Sigma Theta Tau, International Honor Society of Nursing, 1976-78; mem, Human Rights Commission, Colorado Nurses Assoc, 1984-88; chairperson, Council of Deans/ Directors of Nursing Programs in Colorado, 1886-87. **Honors/ Awds:** Nurse Educator of the Year, SW MO Nursing Educ Consort, 1990; Leadership Springfield, Springfield Chamber of Commerce, 1989-90. **Business Addr:** Department Head, Southwest Missouri State University, Department of Nursing, 901 South National, Springfield, MO 65804.

WILLIAMS, EVERETT BELVIN
Association executive. **Personal:** Born Oct 26, 1932, Hennessey, OK; married Marianne Hansson; children: Karin Cecelia, Barbro Susanne. **Educ:** Denver Univ, BA 1955; Columbia Univ, MA 1957, PhD 1962, MS 1970. **Career:** Various NY & NJ VA Hosps, trainee 1957-60; Hunter Coll, lectr, counselor 1960-62; Columbia Univ, Teachers College, research assoc, 1961-62; Barnard Coll, lectr 1962-63; Columbia Coll, counselor 1963-64; Columbia Univ Computer Center, dir 1964-71; Columbia Univ, assoc prof 1970-71, assoc dean 1970-71, adj prof 1971-75, vice pres operations 1972-75, vice pres coll bd prog 1975-77; Educ Testing Serv, sr vice pres prog areas 1982; Williams & Weisbrodt, partner/private consultant; Turrell Fund, executive director, 1989-. **Orgs:** Certified Psychologist NY 1964; mem Amer Psychol Assn, Amer Assn for the Advancement of Sci, NY State Psychol Assn, Philosophy of Sci Assn, Amer Acad for Polit & Soc Sci, Assn for Educ Data Sys, Assn for Computing Machinery, Assn for Symbolic Logic, Phi Delta Kappa, Kappa Delta Pi; bd dir Lisle Fellowship 1964-67; adv com Response of NYSPA to Social Issues; Inst of Elec & Electronic Engrs; mem NY State Comm for Children 1971-74; bd trustees Dalton Schs 1967-74; Harvard Bd of Overseers 1973-74; dir Index Fund of Amer Inc 1974; sr consul Belmar Computer Serv Inc; chmn Assn of Black Psychol; field assessment officer field selection officer Peace Corps; field selection officer Tchrs Corps; consult psychol SEEK Prog; consult Metro Mental Health Clinic; consult FreshAir Fund; consult Natl Ur League; chmn Review Com on Testing of Minorities; mem Intercoll Knights; mem Natl Sci Found; mem Omicron Delta Kappa, Psi Chi, Phi Beta Kappa, Danforth Fellowship, Danforth Teaching; fellow Sigma Xi; rsch fellow Conf on Learning & Educ Process 1965. **Honors/Awds:** Author, Deductive Reasoning in Schizophrenia 1964, Intro to Psychology 1963, Assn Between Smoking & Accidents 1966, Driving & Connotative Meanings 1970.

WILLIAMS, FELTON CARL
Educational administrator. **Personal:** Born Mar 30, 1946, Los Angeles, CA; son of Abraham Williams; married Mary Etta Baldwin; children: Sonia Yvette, Felton Jr. **Educ:** Los Angeles Harbor Community Coll, AA, 1970; California State Univ, Long Beach, BA, 1972, MBA, 1975; Claremont Grad School, PhD, 1985. **Career:** CSU, Long Beach, junior staff analyst, 1972-73, admin asst, 1972-73, supvr, 1974-79; CSU, Dominguez Hills, affirmative action officer, asst to president, 1985-86, assoc dir learning assistance center, director student programs, 1991-. **Orgs:** Pres, San Pedtro-Wilmington NAACP 1976-, Region I NAACP 1979-80; bd mem, Selective Serv System, Region IV, 1981, Employee Readiness Support Center, 1986-87; CSULB Alumni Board, 1991. **Honors/Awds:** Resolution Outstanding Community Contr California Legislature, 1980; Certificate of Appreciation Chamber of Commerce/ Community Devel, 1980; Outstanding Alumnus, Los Angeles Harbor College, 1989. **Military Serv:** AUS, specialist, 5 E-5, 2 years. **Business Addr:** Assoc Dir, Learning Assistance Ctr, California State Univ, Dominguez Hills, 1000 E Victoria St, Carson, CA 90747.

WILLIAMS, FITZROY E.
Computer services executive. **Personal:** Born Nov 6, 1953, St James, Jamaica; son of Lester & Lurena Williams; married Yvonne, Aug 20, 1977; children: Jhamel, Joshua. **Educ:** College of Arts Science & Technology, asst electronic engineering, 1977. **Career:** Jamaica Intl Telecommunication, senior tech, 1972-81; Scientific Atlanta, senior engineer, 1982-95; Democratic Natl Convention, dir of technology, 1995-96; Tri-Millennium Technologies, pres, 1996-. **Business Addr:** President, Tri-Millennium Technologies Inc, 225 W Washington St, Ste 2200, Chicago, IL 60606.

WILLIAMS, FRANK J.
Real estate broker. **Personal:** Born Aug 29, 1938, Arkansas; son of Ada Frye Jones and Seldon Williams; married Joanne; children: Michael, Craig, Renee, Jannie. **Educ:** Attended Bogan Jr Coll; Kennedy-King Coll; Real Est Inst at Central YMCA Comm Coll. **Career:** US Post Ofc, mail carrier 1961-66; Midwest Realty, salesman 1966-68, sales mgr 1968-70; EW Realty Co, prof 1970-71; Licensed Real Estate Broker 1969-; F J Williams Realty Co, founder/pres 1971-. **Orgs:** Mem Councl of Local Bd; pres Natl Assn of Real Estate Brokers; mem Licensed Real Estate/License Law Officials Liaison Com; mem natl Assn of Realtors-Area Prop; Mgmt Broker for VA Admin; instr Real Est Sales & Brokerage Real Est Inst of Cent YMCA Comm Coll; instr Real Est Trans Course Chicago Real Est Bd/Hall Inst Univ of Chicago; chmn NAACP Housing Com; asst chmn adv com Utilization of Subsidies to Increase Black Adoptions; past chmn SE Section Luth Athletic Assn; mem Urban Homestead Coalition; mem Chicago Real Est Bd Admis Com; mem Timothy Luth Ch; mem Community Devel Adv Committee (appointed by Mayor Harold Washington); pres NAACP Chicago Southside Branch 1978-85; chmn Chicago Real Est Bd's Equal Opportunity Comm; chmn New Horizons Task Force apptd by Gov James RThompson; mem Recreanal Task Force apptd by Gov James R Thompson; adv bd mem Black on Black Love; bd mem Black Historic Checagou Dusable Fort Dearborn Historical Commn Inc; mem Cancer Prevention Soc; sec Chicago Bd of Realtors 1987; bd mem Ada S. McKinley Service 1989; bd mem Neighborhood Housing Service 1989; pres elect Chicago Bd of Realtor 1989, president, 1989-90; bd mem Community Investment Corp 1988. **Honors/Awds:** Recipient of Educ Devel Award Dearborn Real Estate Bd; Educ Cert of Appreciation Phi Beta Lambda; Award of Achievement CA Assn of Real Estate Brokers Inc; Black Businessman of the Month Award Chicago South End Jaycees; Award of Recogn Chicago Real Est Bd 1973; Elmore Baker Award from Dearborn Real Est Bd; Appreciation Awd Realtors Real Estate School; Outstanding Service Awd Natl Caucus and Ctr for the Black Aged Inc; Certified Real Estate Brokerage Manager-CRB; Certified Residential Specialist-CRS. **Business Addr:** Real Estate Broker-Appraiser, F J Williams Realty, 7825 South Western Ave, Chicago, IL 60620.

WILLIAMS, FRANK JAMES
Artist, educator. **Personal:** Born Feb 17, 1959, Chicago, IL; son of Barbara J Williams & Arthur Green; married Rebecca P Williams, Apr 15, 1992. **Educ:** St Edward's University, painting & design, 1978-80; Univ of Oklahoma, BFA, painting & drawing, printmaking & design, 1984; University of California, UCLA, MFA, painting & drawing, 1988; Skowhegan School of Art, 1989. **Career:** UCLA, teaching assoc, 1987-88; Daniel Weinberg Gallery, preparator, 1988-89; St Monica Coll, art instructor, 1990-91; Los Angeles County Museum of Arts, preparator, 1992; Bishop Mora Salesian High School, art chairperson, art teacher, 1992-94; Barnsdall Art Ctr, art instructor, 1997-; UCLA, extension, art instructor, 1998-. **Honors/Awds:** California Afro American Museum, Artist in Residence, 1995; Skowhegan School of Painting & Sculpture, Skowhegan Art Fellowship, 1989; UCLA, Hortense Fishbaugh Memorial Scholarship, 1988, Sydney A Temple Scholarship, 1988, Grad-

uate Opportunity Fellowship, 1985. **Special Achievements:** Many exhibitions including: "New Expression," California Afro American Museum, 1990, "Frozen Moments," 1995; "The Art of Frank Williams," Santa Monica Coll, 1989; "Los Angeles Art Festival," Long Beach Art Association Gallery, 1990; "New Works," Frederick Wight Art Gallery, UCLA, 1988. **Home Addr:** 1709 Monte Vista St, Pasadena, CA 91106.

WILLIAMS, FRED C.
Educator, ophthalmologist (retired). **Personal:** Born Jun 8, 1922, Phoenix, AZ; son of Emily Crump Williams and Fred Vernon Williams; married Kathryn Davenport Williams, May 13, 1953; children: Fred C Jr, Andrew Sydney. **Educ:** Arizona State University, Tempe, AZ, AB, 1943; Meharry Medical College, Nashville, TN, MD, 1946. **Career:** University of California Medical School, clinical professor, 1967-90. **Orgs:** President, Military Ophthalmological Society, 1965-67; chairman, Ophthalmology Section, San Francisco Medical Society, 1985-90. **Honors/Awds:** Arizona Greater Builder's Award in Medicine. **Military Serv:** US Army Medical Corps, Lt Col, 1946-67; Bronze Star, 1958, Legion of Merit, 1967.

WILLIAMS, FREDDYE HARPER
State official. **Personal:** Born Jan 9, 1917, Bay Springs, MS; daughter of Mittie Harper and Fredrick Harper; married Calvin Williams, Feb 2, 1933 (deceased); children: John Frederick, James Altrice, Candy Calvina. **Educ:** Oklahoma Univ Extension School; USAF Inst of Tech. **Career:** Tinker AFB, management analyst 1943-73; OK City Bd of Education, pres-member 1973-79; State of OK, state representative 1980-. **Orgs:** Bd mem Urban League, YWCA; mem League of Women Voters; mem Zeta Phi Beta Sorority; Natl Black Caucus of State Legislators; Natl Conf State Legislators; Federation of Colored Women's Clubs. **Honors/Awds:** Finer Womanhood Award Zeta Phi Beta Sorority; Black History Award Langston Univ 1984-85; 1985 Citizen of the Year Omega Psi Phi Fraternity 1985; Outstanding Humanitarian Award 1985; YWCA Leadership Award 1989; YMCA Special Achievement Award 1989. **Business Addr:** State Representative, State of Oklahoma, State Capitol Bldg-Rm 435A, Oklahoma City, OK 73105.

WILLIAMS, FREDERICK BOYD
Cleric. **Personal:** Born Apr 23, 1939, Chattanooga, TN; son of Matlyn Goodman Williams and Walter Howard Williams. **Educ:** Morehouse College, BA, 1959; Howard University, 1959-60; General Theological Seminary, STB, 1963; Colgate-Rochester Div School, DMin, 1975. **Career:** NASA, research mathematician, 1959-60; St Luke's Episcopal Church, curate, 1963-65; St Clement's Episcopal Church, rector, 1966-72; Diocese of Botswana, Africa, honorary canon, 1979-; Church of the Intercession, rector, 1972-. **Orgs:** Harlem Congregations Community Improvement, Inc, chairman, 1991-; NYC Black Leadership Commission on AIDS, commissioner, 1991-; Anglican Representative to UN, advisory board, 1992-; World Conference on Afro-Anglicanism, founder/treasurer, 1984-; Boys Choir of Harlem, chairman of board, 1975-85; Cathedral of St John, trustee, 1979-81; Opera Ebony, chairman of the board, 1976-86; HIV Curriculum Committee, New York Board of Education, committee member, 1991-93; Intl Voluntary Services, Inc, Washington DC, mem, bd of dirs, 1997-; General Theological Seminary, NYC, mem, bd of trustees, 1998-; Amistad Research Ctr, New Orleans, LA, mem, bd of dirs, 1997-; The Balm in Glead, Inc, chair, natl clergy advisory comm, 1993-. **Honors/Awds:** Ford Foundation, Scholarship, 1955-59; Howard University, Fellowship, 1959-60; Colgate-Rochester Div School, Martin Luther King Jr, Fellowship, 1971-75; Harvard University, Merrill Fellow, 1984; King Chapel, Morehouse College, Board of Preachers, 1988; The Commonwealth Univ, D C L (hon), 1993; Univ of North Carolina at Winston-Salem, gray lecturer, 1994. **Special Achievements:** Author, articles in Nashotah Review, 1972, St Luke's Journal of Theology, 1979, Lenten Booklet, Cocu, 1984, Journal of Religious Thought, 1987; Anglican Theological Review, 1995. **Business Addr:** Rector, Intercession Episcopal Church, 550 W 155th St, New York, NY 10032, (212)283-6200.

WILLIAMS, FREDERICK DANIEL CRAWFORD
Govt official, pharmaceuticals salesman, med lab technologist. **Personal:** Born Dec 13, 1943, Marysville, OH; married Vivian Roe Andrews (divorced); children: Sharonne, Tawanna, Duane. **Educ:** Villanova Univ, AB Humanities w/Sci Conc 1969, 36 graduate hours Social & Political Philosophy 1972. **Career:** Hosp of the Univ of Penna, medical lab technologist 1968-75; American Red Cross, medical lab technologist 1975-77; The Upjohn Co, pharmaceutical sales rep 1977-81; Warner-Lambert Techn AO Scientific Instruments Div, sales rep 1981-82; MDS Health Grp Inc, acct rep 1982-84; Borough of Lawnside, vice pres of council; Atlantic City Health Dept, field representative for disease control & intervention. **Orgs:** New Jersey Black Issues Convention, secretary; Natl Assn of Local Elected Officials; Natl Black Leadership Roundtable; Omega Psi Phi, life member; Natl Rifle Assn. **Military Serv:** AUS E-3 hon discharge 1961-64.

WILLIAMS, GARY C.
Educator. **Personal:** Born Jan 7, 1952, Santa Monica, CA; son of Eva & James Williams; married Melanie Reeves Williams, Jun 28, 1980; children: Jennifer, Sara. **Educ:** UCLA, BA, 1973; Stanford Law School, JD, 1976. **Career:** California Agricultural Labor Relations Board, staff attorney; ACLU Foundation of Southern California, asst legal dir, staff attorney; Loyola University School of Law, professor, currently. **Orgs:** Southern Christian Leadership Conference/LA, bd of dir; ACLU of Southern California, bd of dir; Mount Hebron Baptist Church, chairman; Stanford Law School Board of Visitors. **Special Achievements:** Hastings Constitutional Law Quarterly, "The Wrong Side of the Tracks," p 845, 1992; Southwestern University Law Review, "Can Government Limit Tenant Blacklisting?," vol 24, p 1077, 1995. **Business Addr:** Professor, Loyola University School of Law, 1441 W. Olympic Blvd., Los Angeles, CA 90043, (213)736-1090.

WILLIAMS, GAYLE TERESE TAYLOR
Journalist. **Personal:** Born Apr 5, 1964, Bronx, NY; daughter of Mararuth Taylor and Arthur James Taylor; married Terry Desmond Williams, Apr 15, 1989. **Educ:** Fordham University, Bronx, NY, BA, 1984; Columbia University, New York, NY, MSJ, 1986. **Career:** Newsday, Long Island, NY, reporter intern, summer, 1984; New York Newsday, New York, NY, editorial asst, 1984-85; New Haven Register, New Haven, CT, reporter, intern, summer, 1985; Worcester Telegram & Gazette, Worcester, MA, reporter, 1986-89; New Haven Register, New Haven, CT, reporter, 1990-91; Gannett Suburban Newspapers, reporter, 1991-94, reader services editor; United Way of Westchester & Putnam, vice pres for communications, currently. **Orgs:** Member, National Assn of Black Journalists, 1986-; board member, Connecticut Assn of Black Journalists, 1990-91; Westchester Black Journalists Association, founding president, 1991; Westchester Black Journalists Association, vice pres, 1992-. **Honors/Awds:** Volunteer Award, Bentley Gardens Nursing Home, 1990; Reporting Award, "Best of Gannett," 1992. **Home Addr:** 333 Hillside Ave, White Plains, NY 10603-2807. **Business Phone:** (914)997-6700.

WILLIAMS, GENEVA J.
Association executive. **Personal:** married Otha; children: Monique, Otha, Devon. **Career:** United Way Community Services, president/chief executive officer, executive vice pres/COO, currently. **Orgs:** Greater Detroit Volunteer Leadership Coalition, member. **Business Addr:** Executive Vice Pres/COO, United Way Community Services, 1212 Griswold, Detroit, MI 48226, (313)226-9444.

WILLIAMS, GEORGE
Sports coach. **Career:** St Augustine's College, men's track coach; US Olympics, track and field coach, 1996. **Special Achievements:** NCAA, Division II men's track and field title, 1990-96; CIAA, Conference title, 1982-96. **Business Addr:** Coach, Men's Track, St Augustine College, 1315 Oakwood, Raleigh, NC 27610, (919)516-4236.

WILLIAMS, GEORGE ARTHUR
Dentist. **Personal:** Born Feb 9, 1925, Huntsville, AL; son of Ola Grace Hicks Williams (deceased) and Alexander Samuel Williams (deceased); married Mary Ann Brown; children: George A Jr, Chappelle Miles, Valeria Tomme, Gina Ann Reid, Michael Alexander (dec), Grayson Andrew, George Ransom Reid Jr. **Educ:** Attended, Gary Jr Coll, Clark Coll, Meharry Med Coll Sch of Dentistry 1948. **Career:** Private Practice, dentist 1948-. **Orgs:** Pres Ewell Neil Dent Hon Soc Meharry Med Coll 1946; mem Implant Denture Acad 1953; mem Bd Dirs United Fund 1959; mem TrusteeBd Allen Univ 1960; pres Inter-co Med Dental & Pharm Assn 1961; served Florence Comm Relations Comm 1962-65; mem SC Del to White House Conf on Youth and Children Wash DC 1960; mem Gen Conf Los Angeles 1960; mem Aiken Found Rehab Com 1962; mem Genl Conf Cincinnati 1964; personal dedication chmn bd of dirs Boys Club of Florence 1965-; mem Genl Conf Philadelphia 1968; pres NC SC Area Council Boys Clubs Amer 1968-70; mem Chicago Dental Soc 1968-73; mem bd of Gr Florence Cof C 1970; mem bd of dirs Citizens of So Nat Bank 1977-; mem NAACP; mem Local State and Natl Dental Orgns; chmn bd of dirs Mt Zion AME Housing Projects; apptd by Gov John CWest as commr Florence DarliTech Educ 1971-84; general chrm United Negro Coll Fund, Fl Area 1984. **Honors/Awds:** Doctor of the Yr Inter-Co Med Dental and Pharm Assn 1961; Outstanding Serv Awd Boys Club of Florence 1966; Man and Boy Awd Boys Club of Florence 1968, 1977; Outstanding Comm Serv Zeta Phi Beta Sor Inc 1972-73; Citizen of the Yr Sta WYNN 1977; Professional and Humanitarian Awd Alpha Phi Alpha Frat 1978; 25 Yrs of Serv to Mankind Meharry Med Coll 1948-73; Fellow Royal Soc of Health London Eng 1973-; "This is Your Life" in recognition of 35 years of Dental Service 1983; elected chrm bd of dir C & S Bank 1985; chm bd of dir Florence-Darlington Tech Coll 1985; honorary chm "Florence Salute to Harry Carson" 1987; Boy's Club of America-Bronze Keystone & Serv Bar for 21 years of devoted serv 1985. **Military Serv:** AUS Army Denatl Corp. **Business Addr:** 350 N Dargan St, Florence, SC 29501.

WILLIAMS, GEORGE L., SR.
Educational administrator. **Personal:** Born Aug 6, 1929, Florence, SC; married Jean McKiever; children: Sandra, George Jr, Karen, Charles. **Educ:** SC State Coll, AB Pre-Law Major 1953, Masters Educ & Public Sch Admin 1961; Catholic Univ. **Career:** Pilgrim Ins, dist mgr 1953-55; Chestnut High School, govt/econ teacher, 1956; Whittemore High School, govt/econ teacher, 1960; Conway High School, history/geography teacher, 1968, asst principal, 1969; Coastal Carolina Coll, evening prof 1969-74; North Myrtle Beach High School, principal 1974-86 (retired). **Orgs:** Mem, Natl Assn of Secondary School Principals; mem, State Assn of Secondary School Principals; mem, Horry County Assn of School Admin, Omega Fraternity Inc; adv delegate, Natl Student Council Convention, 1965; pres, Horry County Assn of School Admin, 1974; delegate, Natl Educ Convention, 1974 & 1975; pres, Horry County Educ Assn, 1975; chmn, Conway Housing Authority, 1979; discussion chmn, Natl Assn of Secondary School Principals, 1982; appointed by Pres Ronald Reagan to Local Selective Serv Bd; chairman of bd, McKiever's Funeral Home Inc; bd of trustees, First Citizen Bank; bd of trustees, Conway Hosp Inc. **Honors/Awds:** Omega Man of the Year, Beta Tau Chap, 1975; chmn bd of trustees, Horry Georgetown Technical Coll, 1977-84. **Business Addr:** Retired Principal, North Myrtle Beach High School, Route 1 Box 27, North Myrtle Beach, SC 29582.

WILLIAMS, GEORGE W., III
Educator. **Personal:** Born Dec 27, 1946, Chattanooga, TN; married A Virginia Davis; children: Darius. **Educ:** Lane Coll Jackson TN, BS 1968. **Career:** WI Educ Assn Council, organizer 1973-; Beloit Mem High School Beloit WI, math teacher 1968-73; Vice Pres 1971; Beloit Educ Assn, pres 1973; Rock Valley United Teachers, bd dirs 1972-73. **Orgs:** Mem WI Council Math Tchrs 1968-73; WI Educ Assn 1968-74; Official Black Caucus 1971-73; Greater Beloit Kiwanis Club; Alpha Phi Alpha; bd dirs Black Resource Personnel; del to rep assembly WI Educ Assn 1969-73; del Nat'l Educ Assn Conv 1971-73; del & chmn Resolutions Com 1971-73; bd dirs Beloit Teen Cntr 1971-73; chmn Martin Luther King Scholarship Fund. **Honors/Awds:** Beloit Corp Scholarship Awd 1972; Outstanding Tchr of Beloit 1972. **Business Addr:** WI Educ Assn, 10201 W Lincoln Ave, Milwaukee, WI.

WILLIAMS, GEORGIANNA M.
Educator. **Personal:** Born Sep 23, 1938, Kansas City, KS; daughter of Marguerite Buford Carter and Walter George Carter Sr; married Wilbert B Williams Sr; children: Candace R Cheatem, W Ben Williams, II. **Educ:** Univ of MO in Kansas City, BA 1972; UMKC, MPA 1973; Ford Fellowship Program, MPA 1973; Drake Univ, Ed Adm 1986; Iowa State University, Danforth Program 1992. **Career:** Kansas City, MO School District, Language devt specialist, 1972-77; Des Moines School Dist, 20th century rdg lab specialist 1977-81, reading teacher 1981-86, gifted/talented consultant 1986-; Drake Univ, Des Moines, IA, instructor, 1987-89. **Orgs:** Iowa Women in Educational Leadership 1987-; mem Alpha Kappa Alpha; bd of dirs Young Women's Resource Ctr 1985-; mem International Reading Assn; mem Drake Univ Grad Adv Cncl; mem Assoc of Supervision & Curriculum Develop, Iowa Women in Educ Leadership, Natl Assoc of Gifted Children, Iowa Talented & Gifted Assoc, Des Moines Talented & Gifted Cncl, Des Moines Public Schools Staff Devel Adv Cncl, Professional Growth Adv Commn, Natl Alliance of Black School Educators; member, Houghton Mifflin Teacher Advisory Council, 1989-; member, Young Women's Resource, 1985-90; member, State Historical Society of Iowa, 1990-; board of directors Edco Credit Union 1992-; Delta Kappa Gamma Society International 1992-; National Middle School Association 1991-. **Honors/Awds:** Ford Fellowship grant 1973; Connie Belin Fellowship Univ of IA Gifted Educ 1982; Thatcher Awd Nat'l Daughters of the American Revolution 1986; mem Pi Lambda Theta Hon Frat, Phi Theta Kappa Honor Frat; Phi Delta Kappa, 1989-. **Home Addr:** 4809 80th Pl, Des Moines, IA 50322-7344. **Business Addr:** Gifted/Talented Consultant, Des Moines Indep School Dist, 1800 Grand Ave, Des Moines, IA 50307.

WILLIAMS, GERALD
Professional football player. **Personal:** Born Sep 8, 1963, Waycross, GA. **Educ:** Auburn Univ, attended; Duquesne University, elementary education, attending. **Career:** Pittsburgh Steelers, nose tackle, 1986-92; Carolina Panthers, 1995-. **Orgs:** Active with charitable organizations. **Honors/Awds:** Chief Award, 1991. **Business Addr:** Professional Football Player, Carolina Panthers, 227 N. Washington Rd., Charlotte, NC 28202.

WILLIAMS, GERALD FLOYD
Professional baseball player. **Personal:** Born Aug 10, 1966, New Orleans, LA. **Educ:** Grambling State. **Career:** New York Yankees, outfielder, 1992-96; Milwaukee Brewers, 1996-97; Atlanta Braves, 1998-. **Business Addr:** Professional Baseball Player, Atlanta Braves, 521 Capitol Ave SW, Atlanta, GA 30312, (404)522-7630.

WILLIAMS, GEROME
Professional football player. **Personal:** Born Jul 9, 1973. **Educ:** Univ of Houston. **Career:** San Diego Chargers, defensive back, 1997-. **Business Addr:** Professional Football Player, San Diego Chargers, 9449 Friars Rd, Qualcomm Stadium, San Diego, CA 92108, (619)280-2111.

WILLIAMS, GREGORY HOWARD
Educator, educational administrator. **Personal:** Born Nov 12, 1943, Muncie, IN; son of James A Williams; married Sara C; children: Natalia, Zachary, Carlos, Anthony. **Educ:** Ball St U, BA 1966; Univ of MD, MA 1969; George Washington U, JD 1971, MPhil 1977, PhD 1982. **Career:** Delaware Co, IN, deputy sheriff 1963-66; US Senate, legal aide 1971-73; GW Washington Project Washington DC, coord 1973-77; Univ of IA, assoc dean law prof 1977-87, professor of law, 1987-93; Ohio State University, College of Law, dean, 1993-. **Orgs:** Consultant Foreign Lawyer Training Prog Wash DC 1975-77; consultant Natl Inst (Minority Mental Health Prog) 1975; mem IA Adv Comm US Civil Rights Commn 1978-88; mem IA Law Enforcement Academy Council 1979-85. **Honors/Awds:** Book, Law and Politics of Police Discretion 1984; article ''Police Rulemaking Revisited'' Journal Laws & Cont Problems 1984; article ''Police Discretion'' IA Law Review 1983; book The Iowa Guide to Search & Seizure 1986; Author, Life on the Color Line, The True Story of a White Boy Who Discovered He Was Black, 1995. **Business Addr:** Dean, Ohio State University, College of Law, 55 W 12th Avenue, Columbus, OH 43210.

WILLIAMS, GREGORY M.
Chief executive automotive dealership. **Career:** Sentry Buick Inc, Omaha NB, chief executive, 1988; Executive Pontiac-GMC Truck Inc, Tustin CA, chief executive, 1989. **Business Addr:** Executive Pontiac-GMC Truck Inc, PO Box 5016, Thousand Oaks, CA 91359-5016.

WILLIAMS, GUS
Professional basketball player. **Personal:** Born Oct 10, 1953, Mount Vernon, NY. **Educ:** Southern CA, Deg Commun 1975. **Career:** Golden State Warriors, 1976-77, Seattle SuperSonics, 1978-80, 1982-84, Washington Bullets, 1985-86, Atlanta Hawks, 1987. **Honors/Awds:** Made 2 All-Star Game appearances; 2nd team All-NBA performer following the 1980 season & chosen to 1st team in 1982; League's Comeback Player of the Year 1982;NBA All-Rookie team in 1976; All-PAC-8 selection jr & sr yrs So CA; All-Amer Honors following sr season.

WILLIAMS, HAL
Actor, business executive. **Personal:** Born Dec 14, Columbus, OH; son of Mr and Mrs Kenneth M Hairston; children: Halroy Jr, Terri. **Educ:** Attended acting classes at Theatre 40, Theatre West, and Ralph Nichols workshops; Ohio State Univ, Columbus, OH; Columbus School of Art and Design, Columbus, OH. **Career:** Television series regular on: On the Rocks, Sanford & Son, Sanford, That Girl, 227, Private Benjamin, The Waltons, Harry O, The Sinbad Show; television guest appearances on: Knots Landing, The White Shadow, Nobody's Perfect, Off the Wall, The Jeffersons, Caribe, SWAT, Gunsmoke, Kung-Fu, Good Times, Police Woman, The Magician, Cannon, numerous others; TV movies include: The 10 Commandments, The Young Landlords, All the Money in the World, Police Story, Skin Game, Roots II-The Next Generation, The Celebrity and the Arcade Kid; Cherokee Kid; Westside Waltz; appearances include: film, Private Benjamin, Hard Core, On the Nickel, Cool Breeze, Escape Artist; The Rookie; theater appearnces: 227, Los Angeles productions; Halmarter Enterprises, Inc, Los Angeles, CA, owner, currently. **Orgs:** Bd mem LA Actors Theatre 1976-; involved w/Watts Health Foundation, Natl Brotherhood of Skiers Western Region Orgn; Natl Brotherhood of Skiers; United States Ski Assn, Four Seasons West; board member, Challengers Boys/Girls Club, Los Angeles, CA, 1975-; Screen Actors Guild; Actors Equity; American Federation of TV & Radio Artists, 1971-. **Honors/Awds:** Keys to City of San Bernardino for participation as Grand Marshal in Annual Black History Parade 1980, 1981; Drum Major Award, Southern Christian Leadership Conference, 1987; Image Award, NAACP, 1986; awards for participation & other activities from San Bernadino, CA, & Riverside, CA. **Business Addr:** Owner, Halmarter Enterprises Inc, PO Box 90460, Los Angeles, CA 90009-0460.

WILLIAMS, HARDY
State government official, attorney. **Personal:** Born Apr 14, 1931, Philadelphia, PA; married Carole; children: Lisa, Anthony Hardy, Clifford Kelly, Lanna Amia. **Educ:** Pennsylvania State University, grad; University of Pennsylvania, LLD. **Career:** Community Legal Services, bd mbr, practicing attorney; Pennsylvania General Assembly, representative, 1970-82, state senator, 1983-. **Orgs:** Black Family Services Inc; Blacks Networking for Progress Inc; Delaware Valley Ecumenical Council; African American Delaware Valley Port Corp. **Honors/Awds:** Black Law School Assn, Univ of Pennsylvania, Hardy Williams Award for Excellence, first recipient; Big Brother's Recognition Award; Brotherhood Jaycees, Outstanding Citizen Award; Chiropractic Fellowship of PA, Senator of the Year, 1990; Buffalo Soldiers Award. **Business Addr:** State Senator, Pennsylvania General Assembly, 3801 Market St, Ste 200, Philadelphia, PA 19104.

WILLIAMS, HAROLD DAVID
Utility company executive. **Personal:** Born Jun 3, 1944, Fayetteville, NC; son of Willie Raymond Williams & Willie Ann Williams; married Sharon A Williams, Dec 19, 1974; children: Markeith, Carmen, DeNai. **Educ:** Coppin State College, MS, 1978; The Johns Hopkins Univ, MAS, 1987; State Univ of NJ, management certification, 1994. **Career:** Amtrak, buyer, 1980-82; Baltimore Gas & Elec, buyer, 1982-87, procurement admin, 1987-89, dir procurement opportunity program, 1989-. **Orgs:** Jim Rouse Entrepreneurial Fund, Inc, bd of dirs, 1997; Alliance, Inc, bd of dirs, 1997; MD/DC Minority Supplier Development Council, chair, 1995-96, vice-chair, 1996-; American Association of Blacks in Energy, 1994-; Department of Energy Natural Gas Minority Business Development Roundtable, 1996-; Minority Business Development of the Edison Electric Institute, chair, 1993-96, mem, currently; Purchasing Management Assn of Maryland; Omega Psi Phi Fraternity. **Honors/Awds:** National Association for Equal Opportunity in Higher Education, Distinguished Alumni Award, 1997; Recognized by Sen Paul Sarbanes & the Fullwood Foundation for Outstanding Community Service, 1997; Maryland Minority Contractors Assn, J William Parker Award, 1996; Governor's Citation & Mayors Citation, 1996; Natl Eagle Leadership Institute, Eagle Award, 1994; Black Achievers Award, 1994; US Dept of Commerce & Small Business Administration, Distinguished Corporate Award, 1994; Parren J Mitchell Award, 1993; Rotary Foundation, Paul Harris Fellow Award, 1997. **Business Addr:** Director, Baltimore Gas & Electric Co, 2900 Lord Baltimore Dr, Rutherford Business Ctr, Purchasing & Material Management, Baltimore, MD 21244, (410)597-6873.

WILLIAMS, HAROLD EDWARD
City alderman. **Personal:** Born Oct 12, 1949, Starkville, MS; married Ozzie Ann Hill; children: Tonya, Tracey. **Educ:** MS State Univ. **Career:** Brookville Garden Apts, aptmt mngr 1978-; City of Starkville, alderman 1977-. **Orgs:** Mem NAACP 1969-; mem MS Mncpl Assoc 1977-; vice chrmn of board Prairie Oppty Inc 1979-; mem Rising Star Lodge #31 1979-; scoutmaster BSA 1980-; accred resident mngr Inst of Real Estate Mgt 1984. **Home Addr:** 14 Eutaw St, Starkville, MS 39759. **Business Addr:** Alderman Ward 6, City of Starkville, PO Box 629, Starkville, MS 39759.

WILLIAMS, HAROLD L., JR.
Consumer research analyst. **Personal:** Born Jul 19, 1958, Louisville, KY; son of Harold & Frances; children: Harold III. **Educ:** Univ of Louisville, BS, accounting, 1981. **Career:** Brown & Williamson Tobacco Corp, consumer research analyst, currently. **Orgs:** Amer Institute of CPA's; KY Soc of CPA's. **Special Achievements:** CPA. **Business Addr:** Consumer Research Analyst, Brown & Williamson Tobacco Corp, PO Box 35090, Louisville, KY 40232, (502)568-8039.

WILLIAMS, HAROLD LOUIS
Architect. **Personal:** Born Aug 4, 1924, Cincinnati, OH; son of Geneva C Timberlake Williams and Leonard H Williams; married Betty L Smith. **Educ:** Wilberforce Univ Acad, graduate 1943; Talladega Coll 1946-47; Miami Univ OH BArch 1952; Univ of Southern CA 1976. **Career:** Harold L Williams Assoc Archt & Urban Planners, owner 1960-; Paul R Williams FAIA, proj arch 1955-60; Fulton Krinsky & DelaMonte, arch draftsman, 1952-55. **Orgs:** Mem, AIA; founding mem, Natl Org of Minority Arch; vice pres, NOMA, 1976-77; mem, Soc of Am Registered Arch; mem Constr Specs Inst; fdg mem 1st pres Minority Arch & Planners; mem, Univ of So CA Arch Guild; LA C of C; LA Gen Plan Task Force, 1977; mem, LA Town Hall Forum; chmn, Comm for Simon Rodia's Towers in Watts 1966-70; vice pres bd of dir Avalon Carver Comm Ctr 1964; mem Western Reg Urban League; mem NAACP. **Honors/Awds:** Achvmt Award Comm Simon Rodia's Towers in Watts 1970; Award for Design Excell Compton City Hall; Award Design Excel LA Child Dev Cntr; Society Am Reg Arch 1973; Onyx Award NOMA 1975; Design Excellence, State Office Building, Van Nuys, CA, NOMA, 1985; Design Excellance, Compton Civic Center, NOMA, 1984; Advancement to College of Fellows, AIA, 1994; Advancement to Membership NOMA Counsel, 1993. **Military Serv:** USNR radioman 1st class 1943-46. **Home Addr:** 5630 Arch Crest Dr, Los Angeles, CA 90043. **Business Addr:** Architect, Harold Williams Associates, 3250 Wilshire Blvd, Ste 1305, Los Angeles, CA 90010.

WILLIAMS, HARRIETTE F.
Educational administrator (retired), educational consultant. **Personal:** Born Jul 18, 1930, Los Angeles, CA; daughter of Virginia C Flowers and Orlando Flowers; married Irvin F Williams; children: Lorin, Lori. **Educ:** UCLA, BA 1952; CA State Univ at LA, M Secondary Admin 1956, Genl Pupil Personnel Serv Credentials; UCLA, Genl Administration Credential, Comm Coll Adminstrn Credentials, Genl Elem Tchng Credential 1973, Doctorate Urban Educ Policy & Planning 1973. **Career:** Ramona HS, head counselor & acting prin 1960-63; Drew Jr HS, head counselor 1963-66; Div of Secondary Educ, proj coord & asst admin coord 1966-68; Hollenbeck Jr HS, vice prin 1968; Bethune Jr HS, vice prin 1968-70; UCLA, fellow & asst dir 1970-73; Pepperdine Univ, asst prof 1975-80; Palisades HS, asst principal 1973-76; Foshay Jr HS, principal 1976-80; Manual Arts HS Principal 1980-82; Sr HS Div, dir of instruction 1982-85, admin opers 1985-91; educational consultant, currently. **Orgs:** Natl Assn of Second Sch Principals; adv bd Honor Societies; Jr High Vice Principals Exec Comm; Sr High Asst Principals Exec Comm; Women in Educ Leadership; Statewide Assn of California Sch Administrators; state chair, Urban Affairs; Region 16; pres, ACSA Region XVI 1989-90; resource person Liaison Citizen Prog; chairperson Accreditation Teams for Western Assn of Schs & Colls; citywide chmn Girls' Week; sponsor for Student Week 1984-91; sponsor for Girls' Week 1981-84; exec bd mem UCLA Doctoral Alumni Assn; vp Cncl of Black Administrator, exec bd, 1982-84; Ralph Bunche Scholarship Comm, UCLA Alumni Assn, bd of dirs, 1982-84, vp, 1992-94; bd of dirs UCLA Gold Shield; UCLA Educ Assn; California State Univ, LA Educ Support Group; treasurer Inglewood Pacific Chapter, Links Inc, 1987-89; president, Lullaby Guild, 1987-89; Wilfandel Club, 1970-, pres, 1994-97; Los Angeles County Commissioner, Children and Families, 1996-. **Honors/Awds:** Pi Lambda Theta 1952; Kappa Delta Pi 1972; Delta Kappa Gamma 1977; LA Mayor's Golden Apple Award for Excellence in Educ Spring 1980; PTA Hon Life Membership 1975, 1981, 1990; Sojourner Truth Award LA Chap of the Natl Assn of Business & Professional Women's Clubs; Minerva Award; Delta Sigma Theta Inc; Sentinel Comm Award; Affiliated Tchrs of LA Serv Award. **Home Addr:** 6003 Wrightcrest Dr, Culver City, CA 90232.

WILLIAMS, HARVEY JOSEPH
Orthodontist. **Personal:** Born Sep 4, 1941, Houston, TX; married Beverly; children: Nichole, Natasha, Nitalya, Steven. **Educ:** San Fernando Valley State Coll, BA 1964; UCLA, 1964-65; Howard Univ Coll Dentistry, DDS 1969; Howard Univ Coll Dentistry, Cert Ortho 1969-71. **Career:** General practice, 1969-71; Natl Med Assn, asst regional dir, proj 75 1971-74; Univ of California, clinical prof 1972-84; Martin Luther King Jr County Hospital, staff orthodontist 1972-80; private practice, orthodontist 1972-; Private Dental Practice, expanded, 1983, renamed The Tooth Spa Group Practice; Records and Angel City Productions, CEO & owner; Williams Enterprises, CEO & owner; County of Los Angeles, Contraction For Private Dental Services; H Claude Hudson Comprehensive Health Ctr, 1989-92; Hubert H Humphrey Comprehensive Health Ctr, 1990-; Edward R Royal Comprehensive Health Ctr, 1995-. **Orgs:** Mem Western Dental Soc, Natl Dental Soc, Amer Assn Ortho, Pacific Coast Soc Ortho, Amer Dental Assn, Angel City Dental Soc, Channels; mayor City of LA; comm Ind & Commerce San Fernando Valley; comm econ devel NE San Fernando Valley; bd of trustees Western Dental Soc; adv bd LA Mission Coll. **Honors/Awds:** Certificate of Appreciation Pacific Coast Soc Ortho; City of Inglewood, Commendation Los Angeles County. **Business Addr:** 8615 Crenshaw Blvd, Inglewood, CA 90305.

WILLIAMS, HARVEY LAVANCE
Professional football player. **Personal:** Born Apr 22, 1967, Hempstead, TX. **Educ:** Louisiana State University. **Career:** Kansas City Chiefs, running back, 1991-93; Oakland Raiders, 1994-. **Business Addr:** Professional Football Player, Oakland Raiders, 1220 Harbor Bay Pky, Alameda, CA 94502, (510)615-1875.

WILLIAMS, HAYWARD J.
Dentist. **Personal:** Born Jun 27, 1944, Port Arthur, TX; married Haslett J; children: Hoyt, Jason. **Educ:** LA Southwest Coll, predental major 1967; Univ of So CA, DDS 1976. **Career:** Dublin GA, dentist private practice 1976-; Bibb Co Health, dentist 1976. **Orgs:** Bd of dir NAACP 1980; vice pres Optimist Club Laurens Dublin 1980. **Honors/Awds:** AFDH Scholarship 1976; Most Inspiring Minority Student Univ of So CA 1976. **Business Addr:** 112 C Rowe St, Dublin, GA 31021.

WILLIAMS, HELEN B.
Educator. **Personal:** Born Mar 29, 1916, Dewmoine, IL; widowed. **Educ:** So IL U, BEd 1942; NC Coll, MSPH 1952; SIU Carbondale, MA 1962. **Career:** Purdue Univ, asst prof & counselor 1968-; Tougallo Coll, asst prof 1964-67; Benedict Coll Columbia SC, asst prof french 1957-62. **Orgs:** Mem IN Interreligious Commn Human Resources; Am Assn Univ Women; NAACP OEO. **Honors/Awds:** Award Urban Serv 1968; Dist Educator Award Alpha Phi Alpha 1973; Lane Bryant Vol Citation 1968; Harambee Black Student Award 1975; Purdue Leather Medal Award1972; Purdue Helen Schleiman Award 1975. **Business Addr:** HSSE PURDUE Univ, West Lafayette, IN 47906.

WILLIAMS, HELEN ELIZABETH
Educator. **Personal:** Born Dec 13, 1933, Timmonsville, SC; daughter of Hattie Pearl Sanders Baker and Eugene Weldon Williams; children: Broderick Kevin, Terrence Meredith. **Educ:** Morris College, BA 1954; Phoenix College, Certificate 1959; Atlanta Univ, MSLS 1960; Queens College, Certificate 1966; Univ of IL-Urbana, CAS 1969; Univ of WI-Madison, PhD 1983. **Career:** Williams Memorial High School, St George, SC, teacher/librarian 1955-57; Carver High School, Spindale, NC, teacher/librarian 1957-58; Percy Julian Elem Sch, librarian 1959-60; Brooklyn Public Library, librarian 1960-62; Mt Vernon Public Library, librarian 1963-64; Jenkins Hill High School,librarian/teacher 1964-66; Westchester Co Library System, librarian 1966; White Plains City Public Schools, librarian 1966-68, 1969-73; Bro-Dart Inc, library consultant 1976-81; Univ of MD, College Park, MD, lecturer 1981-83, professor 1983-. **Orgs:** Mem Library Adminis and Managerial Assoc 1977-80; mem Black Caucus of the Amer Library Assoc 1977-; mem MD Educ Media Organization 1981-; mem Amer

Library Assoc 1977-; mem Amer Assoc of School Librarians; mem Young Adults Serv Div; mem Assoc of Library Services to Children; member National Council of Negro Women, Inc 1990-. **Honors/Awds:** Beta Phi Mu Intl Library Sci Honor Frat 1960-; Fellow Higher Education Act 1966; Fellow Natl Defense Educ Act 1967-68; Fellow Comm on Institutional Cooperation 1973-76; Book Reviewer School Library Journal 1981-; Disting Alumnus Awd Morris Coll 1985; Disting Alumni of the Year Citation Natl Assoc for Equal Oppor in Higher Educ 1986; Fulbright Professorship, University of the South Pacific, Suva, FIJI 1988-89; editor "The High/Low Consensus," Bro-Dart Publishing Co 1980; editor "Independent Reading, K-3" Bro-Dart Publishing Co 1980; editor Books By African American Authros and Illustrators for Children and Young Adults, American Library Assn. **Home Addr:** 1921 Lyttonsville Rd, Silver Spring, MD 20910-2245. **Business Addr:** Professor of Librarianship, Univ of Maryland, College of Library & Info, Hornbake Bldg Rm 4105, College Park, MD 20742.

WILLIAMS, HENRY

Construction company executive. **Personal:** Born Nov 7, 1923, St Louis, MO; son of Aljay Williams, Sr; married Nellie S Williams; children: Soammes F. **Educ:** Attended Iowa Univ, Iowa City IA; Lincoln Univ, Jefferson City MO; Heidelberg Univ, Heidelberg, Germany; and American Univ, Ft Benning GA. **Career:** Hanknell Construction Co, proprietor. **Orgs:** Past Supreme Grand Master of Modern Free & Accepted Masons of the World, Inc. **Military Serv:** US Army, sergeant major. **Business Addr:** Past Supreme Grand Master, Modern Free & Accepted Masons of the World, Inc, PO Box 1072, Columbus, GA 31901.

WILLIAMS, HENRY P.

Educator. **Personal:** Born Sep 3, 1941, Birmingham, AL; son of Carrie Clanton and Charles Williams; married Joyce Williams, Sep 28, 1968; children: Gavin Charles, Courtney Joy. **Educ:** State Univ of North Carolina, Fayetteville, NC, BS, 1967; SUNY Coll at Brockport, EdM, 1973; SUNY at Buffalo, Buffalo, NY, EdD, 1983. **Career:** Wilson Magnet School, Rochester, NY, principal, 1980-85; Roanoke City Publi c Schools, Roanoke, VA, dept supt, 1986-88; Virginia Polytechnic Inst, Dept of Educ Admin, lecturer, 1985-86; SUNY-Oswego, Oswego, NY, lecturer, visiting prof, 1989-90; Syracuse Univ, Syracuse, NY, lecturer, 1989-90; Syracuse City School Dist, Syracuse, NY, supt, 1989-. **Orgs:** Board of dirs, United Way of Central NY, 1989-; advisory bd, Syracuse Area Salvation Army, 1990-; bd of dirs, Onondaga Savings Bank, 1989-; committee mem, congressman James Walsh's Human Advisory Comm, 1989-; exec bd, Hiawatha Council of the Boy Scouts of America, 1989-. **Honors/Awds:** Distinguished Alumni Award, State Univ of North Carolina at Fayetteville, 1988; Educational Leadership Award, Magnet Schools, Rochester, NY, 1985; Dedicated Educator Award, Eta Rho Lambda, Alpha Phi Alpha, 1985; Educator of the Year, Phi Delta Kappa, 1983; Prism Award, 1990.

WILLIAMS, HENRY R.

Oral surgeon. **Personal:** Born Nov 3, 1937, Birmingham; married Juanita; children: Leslie Alison, Mark, Matthew. **Educ:** Univ Cincinnati, BS 1959; Meharry Med Coll, DDS 1967; Univ MD, resident oral surg 1970. **Career:** Albert B Sabin, research asst 1959-61; Leon H Schmidt, research asst 1961-63; Christ Hosp, inst med rearch 1963-67; Provident Hosp, intern 1968-70. **Orgs:** Mem Natl Dental Assoc; MC Dental Soc treas; bd Oral Surg; Middle Atlantic Soc & Baltimore Soc Oral Surgs; 1st Black Oral Surg Resident Univ MD. **Honors/Awds:** Winner Natl Elks oratorical contest 1954. **Business Addr:** 2523 Liberty Hgts, Baltimore, MD 21215.

WILLIAMS, HENRY S.

Physician. **Personal:** Born Aug 26, 1929, New York City, NY; son of Margaret and Hiram; married Frances S; children: Mark, Paul, Bart. **Educ:** NY City Coll, BS 1950; Howard Univ, MD 1955; Brooke Army Hosp, intern 1956; Letterman Army Hosp, resd 1957-60. **Career:** LA Co Sheriff's Dept, radiologist; Charles R Drew Med Sch LA, clinical assoc prof of radiology; Charles Drew Univ, interim pres of medicine and science, 1989-91; private practice, radiologist, currently. **Orgs:** Mem CA Bd of Med Quality Assurance; diplomate Natl Bd of Med Examiners; diplomate Amer Bd of Radiology; fellow Amer Coll of Radiology; fellow Amer Coll of Angiology; mem LA Radiological Soc; mem CA Radiological Soc; mem Natl Med Assn, Golden State Med Assn; mem Charles R Drew Medical Soc; mem Amer Medical Assn; mem CA Med Assn; mem LA Co Medical Assn; past mem CA Physicians Service; past mem The Harvard Sch; past mem Joint Commn Accreditation of Hosps; past chmn Urban Health Comm CA Med Assn; past counselor CA Med Assn. **Military Serv:** AUS Med Corps maj. **Business Addr:** Radiologist, 3756 Santa Rosalia, Ste #203, Los Angeles, CA 90008.

WILLIAMS, HERB E.

College basketball coach. **Personal:** Born Jun 26, 1946, Chicago, IL; son of Mary Poole and Austin Williams; married Marilyn O'Neal, Jul 22, 1965; children: Allen, Mikki, Douglas, Mary. **Educ:** University of Evansville, Evansville, IN, BA, 1968; Chicago State University, Chicago, IL, MA, 1982. **Career:** Centralia High School, Centralia, IL, asst basketball coach, 1970-72; Rich South High School, Richton Pk, IL, head track/asst basketball coach, 1972-74; Hillcrest High School, Country Club Hill, IL, head basketball coach, 1974-75; Evanston High School, Evanston, IL, head basketball coach, 1975-84; Michigan State University, East Lansing, MI, asst basketball coach, 1984-90; Idaho State University, Pocatello, ID, head basketball coach, 1990-. **Orgs:** National Assn Basketball Coaches, 1983-; mem, Rotary Club, 1990-; sec, Chessman Club, 1980-84; IL Basketball Coaches Assn, 1970-86; Idaho Coaches Assn, 1990. **Honors/Awds:** IL Basketball Hall of Fame, 1974; Evansville University Hall of Fame, 1980; Centralia IL Sports Hall of Fame, 1990; IL Basketball Northern Dist Coach of the Year, 1984, Kiwanis Club Man of the Year, Evanston, IL, 1984; Big Sky Conference, coach of year, 1994. **Business Addr:** Head Basketball Coach, Idaho State University, Holt Arena, Box 8173, Pocatello, ID 83209.

WILLIAMS, HERB L.

Professional basketball player. **Personal:** Born Feb 16, 1958, Columbus, OH; married Deborah; children: Erica, Jabriele. **Educ:** Ohio State, 1981. **Career:** Indiana Pacers, forward-center, 1982-89, Dallas Mavericks, 1989-92; New York Knicks, 1992-. **Orgs:** Holds bsktbl camp each summer in hometown; active in Boys and Girls Clubs. **Honors/Awds:** Twice has rejected nine shots in a single game most by a Pacer in an NBA game; 3 time honorable mentn All-Am selection; fnshd career as Ohio State's all-time leading scorer (2011); named Ohio's Class AAA Player of Year. **Business Addr:** Professional Basketball Player, New York Knicks, 2 Pennsylvania Plaza, New York, NY 10121, (212)465-5867.

WILLIAMS, HERBERT C.

Agency director. **Personal:** Born Jan 17, 1930, Redbird, OK; married Ruthie M; children: 5. **Career:** Am Woodmens Life Ins Co, agency dir 19620. **Orgs:** Mem Nat Assn of Life Underwriters; vP Millionaires Club Nat Inst Assn; bd mem Underwriters Assn; life mem NAACP 1972-; Elks Lodge 1959; Ch Educ Com Elks 1974; mem New Breed Repub Club 1964 Pres 1974; adv bd mem KWKI Radio 1972; YMCA; Friendship Bapt Ch. **Honors/Awds:** Awared Certificate Science of Personal Achievement 1963; Life Ins Agency Mngmt Assn 1972; Nat Ins Assn Certificate of Achievmens 1964. **Business Addr:** 845 Minnesota Ave, Kansas City, KS 66101.

WILLIAMS, HERBERT LEE

Physician. **Personal:** Born Dec 23, 1932, Citronelle, AL; divorced; children: Lezli, Candace. **Educ:** Talladega Coll, BA 1952; Atlanta U, MS 1954; Meharry Med Coll, MD 1958. **Career:** Surgeon pvt prac 1965-. **Orgs:** Pres Herbert Williams MD Inc; mem Alpha Omega Alpha Hon Med Soc; diplomate Am Bd Surgery; flw Am Coll Surgeons; Intl Coll Surgeons; Am SocAbdominal Surgeons Chf sug serv Williams AFB Hosp 1963-65. **Military Serv:** USAF maj. **Business Addr:** 323 N Prairie Avenue #425, Inglewood, CA 90301.

WILLIAMS, HERMAN

Elected official. **Personal:** Born Dec 7, 1943, Washington; children: Herman III, Daniel, James. **Educ:** Academy of Health Sciences, 1973; Baylor Univ, 1975; Montgomery College, 1980. **Career:** Upper Maple Ave Citizens Assn, liaison 1980; Commission on Landlord Tenant Affairs, commissioner 1980-82; Metropolitan Washington Planning & Housing Assn, bd member 1980-82; Metropolitan Council of Governments, committee member 1983-. **Orgs:** Bd of directors United Planning Assn 1964-65; founder Winchester Tenants Assn 1978; vice pres Parkview Towers Tenant Assn 1980; city-county liaison Upper Maple Ave Citizens Assn 1981; organizer Takoma Parks Ceremony in honor of Martin Luther King, Jr 1982-; instrumental in redistricting Takoma Park voting policy 1982; establishing Dept of Housing 1983; organized Takoma Park Youth Day. **Honors/Awds:** Elizabeth Skou Achievement Awd Winchester Tenants Assn 1978; 2nd Black elected official in Takoma Park, MD since 1890; only Black elected official in Mongtomery County, MD; selected for Honorary Dinner Committee NAACP 1984-85. **Military Serv:** AUS specialist 5 1974-77; Letter of Commendation Good Conduct Natl Defense 1974-77; Expert Field Medical Badge 1976. **Business Addr:** City Councilman, City of Takoma Park, 7500 Maple Ave, Takoma Park, MD 20912.

WILLIAMS, HERMAN MICHAEL

Branch bank manager. **Personal:** Born Oct 2, 1965, Birmingham, AL; son of Edythe Joyce Williams and Herman Williams; married Martha B Williams Bozeman, Sep 1, 1990. **Educ:** University of Albama at Birmingham, Birmingham, AL, BS, finance, 1983-88. **Career:** South Central Bell, Birmingham, AL, comptroller, 1984; US Postal Service, Birmingham, AL, casual, 1987; Lister Hill Medical Library, Birmingham, AL, Library Asst I, 1984-88; University Credit Union, Birmingham, AL, member services, 1987-88; Altus Bank, Birmingham, AL, branch supervisor, 1988-90; First Alabama Bank, Birmingham, AL, branch manager, 1990-. **Orgs:** Member, Alabama Young Banker, 1991; member, Birmingham Jaycees, 1991; member, Alabama Assn of Bankers, 1990-91; member/promotion comm, Financial Management Assn, 1987-89; member, Free and Associated Masons. **Honors/Awds:** Sales Associate for the Month, First Alabama Bank, 1991; Million Dollar Sales Award, Branch, First Alabama Bank, 1990; Selling Naturally Certificate of Accomplishment, First Alabama Bank, Kaset Program, 1990; Supervision Series Certificate of Accomplishment, First Alabama Bank, Omega Program, 1991; Certificate of Accomplishment, Altus Bank, Selling Skills for Bankers, Altus Bank, 1989.

WILLIAMS, HILDA YVONNE

Record company executive. **Personal:** Born Aug 17, 1946, Washington, NC; daughter of Martha Jane Blount and Willie Joseph Williams. **Educ:** Hunter Coll, New York, NY, 1978-80. **Career:** Teachers Coll, exec sec 1964-67; Bus Careers, exec 1967-69; Esquire Mag, admin asst 1969-73; RCA Corp, admin asst 1973-75, reg promotion mgr 1975-87; Polygram Records, regional promotion, 1987-89; Capitol Records, New York, NY, regional promotion, 1989-90; Warner Bros Records, New York, NY, co-national director, black music promoter, 1990-. **Orgs:** Mem Frat of Rec Exec 1976-; mem NAACP 1976; co-producer 5th Annual Superstar Celebrity Games 1980; president, 1983-88, member, 1973-, Black Music Assn, New York Chapter; member, board of directors, National Black Music Assn, 1986-88. **Honors/Awds:** Black Achiever in Industry, YMCA of Greater New York, 1982; Jack the Rapper Black Music Award, 1990. **Business Addr:** Co-National Director, Black Music Promotion, Warner Bros Records, 75 Rockefeller Plaza, New York, NY 10019.

WILLIAMS, HOMER LAVAUGHAN

Physician. **Personal:** Born Dec 10, 1925, Kalamazoo, MI; married Ruth; children: Aaron, Valerie, Andre. **Educ:** OH Coll Chiropody, DSC 1954; Western MI U, BS 1962; Howard Univ Sch Med, MD 1966; Adron Gen Hosp, Dr ortho surg 1971. **Career:** Orthopaedist, self. **Orgs:** Mem Charles Drew Soc; LA Co Med Assn; AMA; Nat Med Assn Chmn orthopaedic & bd Morningside Hosp. **Honors/Awds:** W Adams Hosp Pub "Intraosseous Vertebral Venography in Comparison with Myelograph in Diagnosing Disc Disease" 1969. **Military Serv:** AUS cp 1944-46. **Business Addr:** 336 E Hillcrest Blvd, Inglewood, CA 90301.

WILLIAMS, HOSEA L.

Civil rights activist. **Personal:** Born Jan 5, 1926, Attapulgus, GA; married Juanita Terry; children: Barbara Jean, Elizabeth LaCenia, Hosea Lorenzo II, Andre Jerome, Yolanda Felicia. **Educ:** Morris Brown Coll, BA, chemistry; Atlanta Univ, MS. **Career:** Crusader Newspaper, publisher 1961-; SCLC, natl prog dir 1967-69, natl exec dir 1969-71, 1977-79, reg vice pres 1970-71, organizer & pres Metro Atlanta 1972-; Poor Peoples Union of Amer; organizer & pres 1973-; Martin Luther King Jr People's Church of Love Inc, pastor 1972-; GA State Rep 54th House Dist, rep beginning 1974; Kingwell Chem Corp, pres 1975-76; SE Chem Mfg & Distrib Corp, fndr CEO 1976-; Pres Reagan, advisor 1980-; Voice of the Crusader TV Show 1982-; Black Promoters Survival Council 1983; Afro-Amer Japanese Intl Econ Inst Inc 1984; City of Atlanta GA, city councilman; Dekalb County, commissioner. **Orgs:** Mem Phi Beta Sigma Inc, Natl Order of Elks & Free & Accepted Masons, Southern Christian Leadership Conf, NAACP, Disabled Amer Veterans, Veterans of Foreign Wars, Amer Legion, Natural Sci Soc, Black Image Theatre, Metro Summit, GA's Voter League, Amer Chem Soc, Natl Black Leaders for Pres Reagan, Natl Black Coalition, Natl Comm of Black Churchmen, Natl Democratic Party. **Honors/Awds:** Comm Serv Awd Delta Sigma Theta Sor Inc 1963; Cause of Freedom in the Tradition of True Democracy GA State 1963; Unselfish Public Serv in the Field of Race Relations Awd Coastal Empire Emancipation Assn 1962; Ten Yrs of Satisfactory Serv Awd US Dept of Agriculture 1961; Civic Achievement Awd US Dept of Agriculture Marketing Serv 1956; Chapter of the Yr Awd Atlanta Chap SCLC 1973; Afro-Amer Patrolmen's League Comm Serv Awd 1975; Civic Achievement Awd Comm & Race Relations Natl Alumni Assn of Morris Brown Coll; Citizen of the Yr Awd Eta Omega Frat Inc 1975; Business of the Yr Awd Bronner Bros 1975; Civil Rights Leader of the Yr Awd Black Media Inc Black Publishers of Amer 1975; Most Courageous Leadership in the Freedom Movement Awd NAACP 1960-61;SCLC National Affiliate of the Yr Awd Natluthern Christian Leadership Conf 1963; Comm Action Agency Awd Tuskegee AL 1976; Antler Guard Awd IBPOE of W of the Grand Exalter Ruler of the Elks 1954; Civil Rights Demonstrator of the Decade. **Special Achievements:** First African American to be arrested protesting South Africa's system of apartheid; first African American research scientist hired by the federal government south of the Mason-Dixon Line. **Military Serv:** US Army, SSgt, 1944-46. **Home Addr:** PO Box 170188, Atlanta, GA 30317.

WILLIAMS, HOWARD COPELAND

Economist (retired). **Personal:** Born May 29, 1921, Quitman, GA; son of Janie Williams and Edward Williams; married Blanche; children: Stephanie, Howard. **Educ:** BS, MS, PhD 1953. **Career:** A&T State Univ, assoc prof 1947-51; OH State Univ, assoc prof 1953-61; Nommensen Univ Medan Indonesia, visiting prof 1961-63; Africa Regional Study by the Big Ten Univ's to evaluate AID Univ Contracts Worldwide, home campus liaison 1965-67; OH State Univ, prof 1964-71; Office of Specl Trade Rep Exec Office of the Pres, sr agr advisor 1973-75; ASCS Office of Admin, dir analysis staff 1976-81; ASCS, dir commodity analysis div 1981-87. **Honors/Awds:** Social Sci Res Council Post-Doc Fellowship NC State Univ 1956; Soc Sci Council Travel Grant to attend Intl Conf of Agr Economists 1964; Mershon Natl Security Prog Grant for Study of European Economic Comm. **Military Serv:** AUS pfc 1942-46. **Home Addr:** 12621 Prestwick Dr, Fort Washington, MD 20744.

WILLIAMS, HUBERT
Police director. **Personal:** Born Aug 19, 1939, Savannah, GA; married Annette; children: Alexis, Susan, Hubert Carl. **Educ:** Elec Engr Tech, Cert 1962; John Jay Coll of Criminal Justice, AS 1968, BS 1970; Harvard Law Sch, Fellow 1970-71; Rutgers Univ Sch of Law, jD 1974; FBI Acad Nat Exec Inst, 1977. **Career:** City of Newark Police Dept, police dir 1974-; Newark High-impact Anti-crime Prgm, exec dir 1973-74; Newark Police Dept, police offcr 1962-73; Rutgers Sch of Criminal Justice, adjunct prof. **Orgs:** Intl Assn of Chiefs of Police; Am Soc of Criminology; adv com Nat Inst; pres Nat Orgn of Black Law Enforcement Offcrs; adv bd Police Found Exec Training Sem 1976; selection com mem City of Stanford CT Pol Ice Chief 1977; FBI Acad Nat Exec Inst 1977; New Scotland Yard Eng 1977; selection com mem City of LA Police Chief 1978; pres Nat Assn of Police Com Relations Ofcrs 1971-73; Mayors Educ Task Force 1971-76; bd of of dir Nat Assn of Urban Criminal Justice Planners 1972-74; Intl Assn of Chiefs of Police 1973-; turstee Tw Hundred Club 1973-; bd of dir Police Exec & Research Forum 1975-; camp mgmt com UMCA 1975-78; Am Bar Assn 1976-; fdng pres Nat Orgn of Black Law Enforcement Exec 1976-79; NJ Bar Assn 1976-; Fed Bar Assn 1977-; St & Com Educ Task Force 1977-;adv bd Esex Co Coll Crim Justi-Prgm 1978-; consult to pub safety com Nat League of Cities 1978-; edit adv bd mem John Jay Coll Jour of Am Acad of Professional Law Enforcement 1978-; mem 74th Dist Rotary Intl. **Honors/Awds:** Research Fellow Harvard Law Sch for Criminal Justice; Bronze Shields & Merit Awds 1965; honored Com for Incentive for Human Achvmt 1967; Humanitarian Awd Newark Businessmens Assn 1968; Appcrt Awd S Ward Little League 1970; ldrshp Awd Nat Assn of Police Comm Relations Ofcr 1973; achvmt Awd Police AcadAssn 1974; Man of Yr Awd 4H 1974; Apprct Awd Spcl Police Assn 1975; Achvmt Awd Bronze Shields Orgn 1975; Comm Serv Awd Speedy Olympics 1975; Recog of Excel Awd Dr King Comm Ctr 1976; spcl Crime Recog Awd NJ Voice Newspaper 1977; spcl Narcotic Enforcement Awd Drug Enforcement Adminstrn 1977; Apprct Awd Newark Intl Airports 50th Anniv 1978; publ articles various magazines 1978-79. **Business Addr:** President, Police Foundation, 1001 22nd St NW, Washington, DC 20008.

WILLIAMS, HUGH HERMES
Physician, educator. **Personal:** Born Nov 11, 1945, Port of Spain, Trinidad and Tobago; son of Norma D Balcon Baird and Hugh Lionel Williams; married Leandra M, Jul 8, 1977; children: Kelly Victoria, Janelle Victoria. **Educ:** Attended Univ of West Indies, Kingston, Jamaica 1965-72, Howard Univ, Washington DC 1974-76, McMaster Univ, Hamilton, Ontario, Canada 1976-78, Cleveland Clinic Foundation, Cleveland, OH 1978-80; received BSC and MD. **Career:** Univ of Tennessee, Memphis, instructor 1980-81, asst prof of medicine 1981-90, assoc prof 1990-91, clinical associate professor, 1991-. **Orgs:** Member of Amer Society of Nephrology, Natl Kidney Foundation, Intl Society of Nephrology, Amer Society of Internal Medicine, Amer Heart Assn; Fellow of Amer College of Physicians. **Honors/Awds:** Author of "Reversible Nephrotic Range Proteinuria and Renal Failure in Athero Embolic Renal Disease," 1989, and "Altered Sensitivity of Osmotically Stimulated Vasopressin Release in Quadriplegic Subjects," 1989. **Home Addr:** 9469 Inglewood Cove, Germantown, TN 38139. **Business Addr:** 220 South Claybrook, #206, Memphis, TN 38104.

WILLIAMS, IRA JOSEPH
Clergyman. **Personal:** Born Aug 5, 1926, Elizabeth City, NC; son of Mr & Mrs Moses Williams; married Elsie Moore; children: Pamela, Anthony, Angela. **Educ:** Store Coll; Kingsley Sch of Rel, BTh 1952, BD 1954; Am Bible Coll, DD; Union Chris Bible Inst, AB 1972; Howard U; Shaw U, Cert in Social Studies & Bapt Doctrine; Univ of NC; Pacific Coll, M 1974. **Career:** Antioch Bapt Church, Norfolk VA, minister, currently. **Orgs:** mem Civil Rights Coord Team Nashville; executive board member, Old Eastern Bapt Assn of North Carolina; Nat Pres United Chris Front for Brotherhood; moderator Old Dominion Missionary Bapt Assn; exec bd of VA Bapt St Conv; Mayors Adv Com; Atlantic Nat Bank Adv Bd; exec bd Norfolk Com for Improvement of Education; life member, NAACP; member, Hampton Ministers Conference. **Honors/Awds:** Citation of Honor, Womens Aux of Norfolk Comm Hosp; comm Leaders & Noteworthy Am 1976-77; Humanitarian Plaque, SE Tidewater Oppor Proj; Man of the Year, WRAP Radio Station Tidewater VA 1979; Mason 32 Deg; author of several pamphlets; Excellence Award, NAACP, 1990; Award, City of Norfolk, VA, 1990. **Military Serv:** USN WWII, Korean War. **Business Addr:** President, People Pleasing Products Inc, Box 476, Norfolk, VA 23501.

WILLIAMS, IRA LEE
Union official. **Personal:** Born Jul 30, 1930, Benson, NC; son of Carrie Williams and Sam Williams; children: Sharon. **Educ:** North Carolina Central Univ, BA, 1961; North Carolina Central Law School, JD, 1964. **Career:** New York, NY, Bd of Educ, teacher, 1964-68; Marion Gaines Hill, PC, clerk, 1970-72; New York, NY, legal staff, 1972-79; Bronze Amer Sports Network, Inc, chmn of the bd, 1973-86; SSEU Local 371, vice pres, 1983-86; video tape productions, entertainment agent, producer, sports promoter, 1983-86. **Orgs:** Pres, United Neighbors Civic Assn, 1964-68; personnel dir, Baisley Park Coalition, 1970-78; mem, Natl Bar Assn, 1970-86; natl pres, Natl Org for Athletic Devel, Inc. **Military Serv:** AUS, corpl, 1948-53. **Home Addr:** 140-17-160 St, Jamaica, NY 11434. **Business Addr:** Vice Pres, SSEU Local 371, 817 Broadway, New York, NY 10003.

WILLIAMS, JAMEL
Professional football player. **Personal:** Born Dec 22, 1973. **Educ:** Univ of Nebraska, attended. **Career:** Washington Redskins, defensive back, 1997-. **Business Addr:** Professional Football Player, Washington Redskins, 13832 Redskin Dr, Herndon, VA 22071, (703)471-9100.

WILLIAMS, JAMES
Public utilities administrator. **Personal:** Born Dec 15, 1934, Huntsville, AL; son of Ovenia Smith and William Clemons; divorced; children: James E Jr, Gwendolyn A Iley, Regina L. **Educ:** Franklin University, associates degree, business administration, 1978; Southern Illinois University, BS, occupational education, 1978; Michigan State University, MBA program, 1983. **Career:** PUCO, utilities examiner II, 1975-83, utilities examiner III, 1983-85, supervisor, 1985-86, public utilities administrator, 1986-. **Orgs:** American Cancer Society, co-chairperson advisory board, 1993-; NAACP (Columbus Branch), veteran's committee chairman, 1988-92; York Rite Masons, national grand secretary, 1990-. **Honors/Awds:** Columbus Dispatch, Community Service Award, 1992; American Cancer Society, Outstanding Service Award, 1991-92; Ohio House of Representatives, special recognition, CALP Graduate, 1986. **Military Serv:** US Air Force, tech sergeant, 1954-75; outstanding noncomission officer, 1969; Commendation Medal, 1975. **Business Addr:** Public Utilities Administrator, Public Utilities Commission of Ohio, 180 E Broad St, 6th Fl, Columbus, OH 43215-3793, (614)466-4687.

WILLIAMS, JAMES ARTHUR
Educator. **Personal:** Born May 9, 1939, Columbia, SC; married; children: Angela, Melody, James II. **Educ:** Allen U, BA music ed 1960; Univ IL, MS 1964. **Career:** Stillman Coll, chmn Dept of Music choral dir; CA Johnson HS SC, educator 1960-69; Morris Coll, 1965 & 68; Univ IL, Allen Univ, Columbia, SC Public School; Sidney Pk CME Church SC, choir dir; Bethlehem Baptist Church SC. **Orgs:** Guest cond All City HS Chorus SC; Columbia SC All City HS Chorus; Univ AL Tuscaloosa AL; Tuscaloosa Comm Singers AL; adjudicator Univ AL 1972; Tuscaloosa Co Jr Miss Pageant 1972; past pres Palmetto St Music Tchrs Assn; mem Am Choral Dir Assn; Music Educators Nat Conf; Alpha Phi Alpha Frat Inc; bd dir Columbia SC Choral Soc 1967-69; steering com Mus Arts Dr; bd dir Tuscaloosa Comm Singers; Music Com Tuscaloosa Arts & Humanities Council.

WILLIAMS, JAMES DEBOIS
Communications director. **Personal:** Born Nov 5, 1926, Baltimore, MD. **Educ:** Temple Univ, BA 1948. **Career:** Philadelphia Tribune, reporter 1950-51; The Carolinian, city editor 1951-53; Afro-Am, city editor 1953-57; Baltimore Afro-Amer, mng editor 1959-64; Morgan St Coll, visiting prof 1961-63; Washington Afro-Am, editor-mgr 1964-67; Office of Econ Oppor, dir pub affairs for comm act prog 1967-68, deputy dir 1968-69; US Comm on Civ Rights, dir off of info & publ 1970-72; Natl Urban League, commun dir 1972-86; NAACP, national director of public relations, 1986-94, public relations consultant, 1994-. **Orgs:** Mem Howard Univ, PA Newspaper Publ Assn, Towson St Tchr Coll; MD-DE Press Assn; mem Natl Newspaper Publ Assn; DC Police Dept; consult Census Bur& Pres Comm on Rural Pov; mem US Inter-Agcy Task Force on Inner-City Comm; mem Exec Comm Natl Commun Coun of Health & Welfare Agcy; v chpsn AdvCounc of Nat Org to Corp for Pub Broad; mem Pub Rel Soc of Amer; mem Adv Bd REBOP TV Prog. **Honors/Awds:** Merit Awd Balt Branch NAACP 1961; Best Feature story of the yr MD-DE Press Assn 1963; Best Editorial of the Yr MD-DE Press Assn 1964; 2nd Prize Best Edit of the Yr Publ Assn 1965; Best Feature Story of the yr Natl Newspaper Publ Assn 1965; Newsman of the Yr Capital Press Club; Awd for Serv Off of Econ Oppor 1968; Excell in Commun Howard Univ 1973; author "The Black Press & The First Amendment"; editor "The State of Black America".

WILLIAMS, JAMES E., JR.
Human resources generalist. **Personal:** Born Aug 28, 1936, Philadelphia, PA; son of Gladys G Vincent; married Lois Collins; children: Karl, Robert, Renee. **Educ:** West Chester Univ, PA, BS 1959; Siena Coll, MS 1968. **Career:** American Bar Association, director, human resources 1989-93; Montgomery Ward & Co Inc, field personnel mgr 1984-86, hq personnel mgr 1986-89; Dept of Military Sci Howard U, chmn/prof 1976-79; Honolulu Dist Recruiting Command Honolulu, comdg officer 1974-76; Armed Forces Examining Entrance Station Honolulu, commanding ofcr 1973; CORDS Adv Team MACV Vietnam, operation adviser 1972; 3d Bn 26 Artillery, exec ofcr 1970-71; 101st Airborne Div Vietnam, insp gen 1968-69; Mil Sci Siena Coll, asst prof 1965-68; Btry A 2d Bn 73d Arty Germany, commanding ofcr 1964; Btry A 2d Rocket/Howitzer Bn 73 Artillery Germany, commanding ofcr 1963; Hershey Medical Ctr, manager, employment, 1994-. **Orgs:** Life mem Alpha Phi Alpha; life mem NAACP; West Chester University Alumni Assn; Alpha Phi Alpha; The Retired Officers Assoc; Aircraft Owners & Pilots Assoc; international board of directors, US-TOO, International, Inc. **Honors/Awds:** Anne Hines Allen Human Rights Awd The Main Line Branch NAACP 1979; Disting Alumni Awd West Chester Univ Alumni Assoc 1978. **Military Serv:** 5th Training Battalion Ft Sill OK commanding ofcr 1979-81; AUS Field Artillery Training Ctr Ft Sill OK exec ofcr 1981, dep commander 1982; HQ US Army Depot System Command Chambersburg PA, dir security plans & operations 1983-84 retired col 1984; Legion of Merit; Combat Infantry Badge; (3) Bronze Star Medal 1968, 1969, 1972; (3) Air Medals Vietnam Cross of Gallantry w/Bronze Star 1968, 1972. **Home Addr:** 1089 Country Club Dr, Camp Hill, PA 17011-1049. **Business Addr:** Mgr, Employment, Penn State University Milton S Hershey Medical Ctr, 500 Univ Dr, Hershey, PA 17033, (717)531-3947.

WILLIAMS, JAMES EDWARD
Service company executive. **Personal:** Born Apr 29, 1943, Berkeley, CA; son of Ruth E Williams and J Oscar Williams Sr; divorced; children: Erin, Landin. **Educ:** San Francisco State University, BA, 1969; Golden Gate University, MBA, 1974. **Career:** ITEL Corp., international CFO, 1971-81; Tektronix Corp., international controller, 1982-84; Syntex Corp., treasurer, vice pres, 1984-86; Masstor Systems, CFO, 1987-89; Tegal Corp., CFO, 1990-92; LePro Corp., president, 1992-. **Orgs:** National Assn of Corporate Treasurers, board of directors, 1985-, past president, past chmn; Financial Officers of Northern California; Treasurers Club of San Francisco; Hubert Hoover Boys & Girls Club of Menlo Park, board of directors. **Special Achievements:** Guest speaker: Euromency Conference on Treasury Management, London, 1986; Santa Clara and San Jose State Universities, 1989; International Finance Seminar, Portland State University, 1983.

WILLIAMS, JAMES EDWARD
Attorney. **Personal:** Born Jan 2, 1955, Alexandria, LA; married Sharon Valencia; children: Tenisha Nicole, Jahron E. **Educ:** New Mexico State Univ, BA 1976, MA 1977; Georgetown Univ Law Ctr JD 1980; Columbia Univ Law Sch/Parker Sch of Foreign & Comparative Law, attended 1986. **Career:** Honeywell Inc, contract mgmt 1980-81, corporate atty 1981-. **Orgs:** Mem Delta Theta Phi Law Frat 1979; mem EEO Adv Council Honeywell 1980; mem United Way Solicitation Comm 1980-81; mem Amer Bar Assn 1981; mem MN Bar Assn 1981; mem MN Minority Lawyers Assn 1981; vice pres FOCUS 1981; adv United Way Allocations Comm 1981-82; advisor Junior Achievement 1981-83; bd mem African American Cultural Ctr 1981-84; mem City of Golden Valley Human Rights Comm 1982-; prog chmn West Suburban Black History Month Comm 1982-; prog chmn Rotary Intl 1984-; mem Govs Art's Task Force 1985; member, American Chamber of Commerce, 1991-; member, International Rotary, 1991-. **Honors/Awds:** Omega Psi Phi Dist Scholar; Natl Soc of Sons of the Amer Revolution Medal, Ribbon of Excellence, Academic Cluster, Arnold Air Soc; Phi Kappa Phi; Rhodes Scholar Nominee 1976. **Business Addr:** Asia Pacific Group Counsel & Corporate Secretary, Honeywell Inc/Honeywell Asis Pacific Inc, 1 Harbour Rd, Office Tower, Convention Plaza, Suite 3001, Stanley, Hong Kong.

WILLIAMS, JAMES EDWARD
Professional football player. **Personal:** Born Oct 10, 1968, Natchez, MS. **Educ:** Mississippi State. **Career:** New Orleans Saints, linebacker, 1990-94; Jacksonville Jaguars, 1995; San Francisco 49ers, 1997-. **Business Addr:** Professional Football Player, San Francisco 49ers, 4949 Centennial Blvd, Santa Clara, CA 95054, (415)562-4949.

WILLIAMS, JAMES H., JR.
Educator. **Personal:** Born Apr 4, 1941, Newport News, VA; son of Margaret L. Mitchell and James H. Williams; children: James H III, Sky M M. **Educ:** Newport News Shipyard Apprentice School, Mech Designer 1965; MA Inst Tech, SB 1967, SM 1968; Trinity Coll, Cambridge Univ PhD 1970. **Career:** Newport News Shipbuilding & Dry Dock Co, apprentice-sr design engr 1960-70; Intl Consultant, 1970-87; MIT, prof of mech engrg 1970-. **Orgs:** Mem NTA 1975-, ASME 1978-, ASNT 1978-; fellow I Diag Eng 1983-; advisor Natl Science Foundation 1985-87. **Honors/Awds:** Charles F Bailey Bronze, Silver & Gold Medals 1961-63; Ferguson Scholar MIT 1963-67; So Fellowship Fund Fellow Cambridge Univ 1968-70; Ralph Teetor Awd SAE 1974; Everett Moore Baker Awd, Outstanding Undergrad Tech MIT 1973; Grant NSF Faculty Partic 1974; duPont professorship; Edgerton professorship; Den Hartog Disting Ed Awd 1981; School of Engineering, Professor of Teaching Excellence 1991; Charles F Hopewell Faculty Fellow, 1993. **Business Addr:** Prof of Mechanical Engrg, Massachusetts Inst of Technology, 77 Massachusetts Ave Rm 3-360, Cambridge, MA 02139.

WILLIAMS, JAMES HIAWATHA
Educational administrator. **Personal:** Born Sep 10, 1945, Montgomery, AL; son of Johnnie Mae Robinson-Strother and James Hiawatha Williams; married Jann A Fleming, Feb 13, 1994; children: James M, John V (deceased), Kasha G, Jameelah I. **Educ:** Los Angeles City Coll, Los Angeles CA, AA, 1967; California State Univ, Los Angeles CA, BA, 1973; Pepperdine Univ, Los Angeles Ca, MS, 1974; Washington State Univ, Pullman WA, PhD, 1983. **Career:** California State Polytechnic Univ, Pomona CA, asst prof 1977-81, assoc dean & assoc prof 1980-85, dean of Coll of Arts & full prof 1988-; Spokane Community College, pres, currently. **Orgs:** Mem, Phi Delta Kappa, 1977-; pres, Pomona Valley NAACP, 1984-86; mem, Phi Beta Delta, 1988-; National Association for Ethnic Studies, executive board member, 1988-, president, 1992-; Phi Kappa Phi, 1989-; pres-elect, Council of Colleges of Arts & Sciences, 1994. **Honors/Awds:** Prism of Excellence Award, Jerry Voorhis Claremont Democratic Club, 1986; Martin Luther King Jr Humanitarian Award, Pomona Valley NAACP, 1987; Services to Youth, Claremont Area Chapter Links Inc, 1988. **Business Addr:** President, Spokane Community College, 1810 N Greene St, MS 2150, Spokane, WA 99207-5399.

WILLIAMS, JAMES OTIS
Professional football player. **Personal:** Born Mar 29, 1968, Pittsburgh, PA. **Educ:** Cheyney, attended. **Career:** Chicago Bears, tackle, 1991-. **Business Addr:** Professional Football Player, Chicago Bears, 1000 Football Dr, Halas Hall at Conway Park, Lake Forest, IL 60045-4829, (847)295-6600.

WILLIAMS, JAMES R.
Attorney, judge. **Personal:** Born Sep 16, 1933, Lowndes Co, MS; married Catherine; children: Michael, Jacqueline. **Educ:** Univ of Akron, BA, JD 1965. **Career:** Northern Dist of OH, US Atty 1978-82; Parms Purnell, Stubbs & Williams, former partner 1969-78; City of Akron, former councilman-at-large 1970-78. **Orgs:** Former treas Akron Bar Assn; former pres Summit Co Legal Aid Soc; natl pres Alpha Phi Alpha Frat Inc. **Honors/Awds:** Outstanding Achievement Awd Alpha Phi Alpha 1973; Liberian Humane Order of African Redemption Citation, Dr William R Tolbert Jr, Pres of Rep of Liberian 1973; Top Hat Awd, Pittsburgh Courier 1977; Ebony's 100 Most Influential Black Americans 1980; Alpha Phi Alpha Fraternity's National Award of Merit. **Military Serv:** US Army, 1953-55. **Home Addr:** 1733 Brookwood Dr, Akron, OH 44313.

WILLIAMS, JAMES THOMAS
Physician, educator. **Personal:** Born Nov 10, 1933, Martinsville, VA; son of Ruth E Thomas Williams and Harry P Williams; married Jacqueline; children: Lawrence, Laurie. **Educ:** Howard Univ, BS 1954, MD 1958. **Career:** Philadelphia Gen Hosp, intern 1958-59; DC Gen & Freedmens Hosp, resd 1959-62, 1964-65; Howard Univ Coll Med, fellow endocrinology 1965-67; DC Gen Hosp, physician 1967-; Howard Univ Hosp, physician 1967-; Howard Univ Coll of Med, asst prof 1967-74, assoc prof 1974-85, professor 1985-. **Orgs:** Mem Amer Bd Internal Med, diplomate, 1967-, recertified Oct 1974, Oct 1980; Amer Diabetes Assoc; Home Care Prog, DC Government, med officer, 1968-89; Medico-Chirurgical Soc of DC; Natl Med Assoc; Med Soc of DC; Endocrine Soc; Amer Coll Physicians, fellow; Am Brd Endocrinology & Metabolism, diplomate, 1972; Alpha Omega Alpha Honor Medical Society; Sigma Pi Phi Fraternity. **Military Serv:** US Army, MC capt 1962-64. **Business Addr:** Professor of Medicine, Howard Univ Coll of Med, 2041 Georgia Ave NW, Washington, DC 20060.

WILLIAMS, JAMYE COLEMAN
Editor (retired). **Personal:** Born Dec 15, 1918, Louisville, KY; daughter of Jamye Harris Coleman and Frederick Douglass Coleman Sr; married McDonald Williams, Dec 28, 1943; children: Donna Williams Selby. **Educ:** Wilberforce Univ, BA 1938; Fisk Univ, MA 1939; Ohio State Univ, PhD 1959. **Career:** Edward Waters Coll, Jacksonville FL, educator 1939-40; Shorter Coll Little Rock, 1940-42; Wilberforce Univ OH, 1942-56; Morris Brown Coll, 1956-58; Tennessee State Univ, 1959-87, dept head of communications, 1973-87; The AME Church Review, editor, 1984-92. **Orgs:** Exec comm Nashville Branch NAACP 1960-; mem bd of governors Natl Council of Ch 1976-; member, Theta Alpha Phi; member, Pi Kappa Delta; member, Kappa Delta Pi; bd dir John W Work III Found; mem Links Inc; member, Delta Sigma Theta; golden heritage life member, NAACP; member, World Methodist Council, 1981-91; board of directors, Nashville Community Foundation, 1991-; The National Conference (NCCJ), 1988-; Registry of Election Finance of Tennessee, 1990-96. **Honors/Awds:** Outstanding Teacher Award 1976; Teacher of the Year, TN State Univ 1968; Woman of the Year, Nashville Davidson & Co Business & Professional Women's Club 1978; Citizen of the Year, Nashville Alumnae Chapter Delta Sigma Theta 1979; co-editor "The Negro Speaks: The Rhetoric of Contemporary Black Leaders"; Salute to Black Women Award, Howard Univ, 1986; Distinguished Service Award, Tennessee State Univ, 1988; Lifetime Achievement Award, Kappa Alpha Psi Fraternity, 1990; Recipient with McDonald Williams, Human Relations Award, The Natl conf of Christians and Jews, 1992. **Home Addr:** 2011 Jordan Dr, Nashville, TN 37218.

WILLIAMS, JANE E.
City official. **Personal:** Born Jul 19, 1947, Paterson, NJ; daughter of Mae J Jenkins Williams and John D Williams. **Educ:** Passaic County Community Coll; Paterson State Coll; Seton Hall Univ; Rutgers Univ, Municipal clerk certification, intl municipal clerk certification. **Career:** City of Paterson, City Clerk's Office, various secretarial titles, 1966-78; Paterson Planning Board, commissioner, 1971-72; City of Paterson, deputy city clerk, 1978-89, municipal clerk, 1990-. **Orgs:** Municipal Clerks Assn of Passaic County, recording sec; New Jersey State Municipal Clerk's Assn; Intl Clerk's Assn; Passaic County Mental Health Assn, vice chairperson; Municpal Clerk's Assn, treasurer; New AME Zion Church, numerous positions; Natl Council of Negro Women; NAACP; St Joseph Hosp & Med Ctr, bd of trustees; Fidelity Chapter 16 Order of Easter Star. **Honors/Awds:** New AME Zion Church, Pastor's Aide Club, Special Award, Women's Gospel Chorus, certificate, Christian Seminar Award, 1985; Congress Award, 1989; Assembly Award, 1989; Senate Award, 1989; Conference Workers Club; New Jersey General Assembly, honored. **Business Addr:** Municipal Clerk, City of Paterson, 155 Market St, Paterson, NJ 07505.

WILLIAMS, JANICE L.
Manager. **Personal:** Born Aug 23, 1938, Allentown, PA; daughter of Cora L Merritt and William E Merritt; children: Lisa, Jerome. **Educ:** Muhlenberg Coll, BA, 1970; Lehigh Univ, MEd, 1974. **Career:** Muhlenberg Coll, asst dir admissions, 1970-74; Pennsylvania Power & Light Co, various positions to mgr placement & EEO programs, 1974-. **Orgs:** Mem, Muhlenberg Coll, Council for Continuing Educ, 1976; bd mem, YWCA, 1975-77; pres, Negro Cultural Center, 1975-77; bd mem, Head Start of Lehigh Valley, 1975-77; educ comm, Pennsylvania Chamber of Commerce, 1976-77; bd mem, Allentown Police Civil Serv, 1979-, United Way of Lehigh Cty, 1981-88; bd, friends comm, Muhlenerg Coll Corp, 1987-89; mem, Muhlenberg Coll Bd of Assocs, 1987-89; pres, Lehigh Valley Personnel Assoc, 1989-90; dir, Allentown School Bd of Educ, 1987-. **Honors/Awds:** Woman of the Year, Allentown NAACP, 1987.

WILLIAMS, JARVIS ERIC
Professional football player. **Personal:** Born May 16, 1965, Palatka, FL. **Educ:** Univ of Florida, attended. **Career:** Miami Dolphins, safety, 1988-. **Business Addr:** Professional Football Player, Miami Dolphins, 2269 NW 199th St, Miami, FL 33056-2600.

WILLIAMS, JASON HAROLD
Government official. **Personal:** Born Nov 11, 1944, Baltimore, MD; son of Mary Boyd Williams and James Edward Williams. **Educ:** Univ of Maryland, College Park, MD, BS, 1966; UCLA, Los Angeles, CA, 1971-73. **Career:** Building Services, Los Angeles, CA, executive assistant, 1971-73, deputy director, 1973-75, chief deputy director, 1975-82, director, 1982-85; Facilities Management, Los Angeles, CA, assistant director, 1985-87; Los Angeles County Dept of Health Services, Los Angeles, CA, senior assistant, hospitals admin, 1987-. **Orgs:** Treasurer, Southern California Chapter, National Forum for Black Public Administrators, 1990-91; finance chair, Forum '91 Planning Committee, 1990-91; member allocations committee, United Way of Los Angeles, 1975-; member United Way Board, United Way of Los Angeles, 1983-85; chairman special task force, United Way of Los Angeles, 1988-. **Honors/Awds:** Award of Appreciation, Los Angeles Olympic Org Committee, 1984; Award of Recognition, Los Angeles Olympic Org Committee, 1984; Distinguished Leadership, United Negro College Fund, 1986; Outstanding Leadership, Brotherhood Crusade, 1980-82, 1985-87; Silver & Gold Leadership, United Way, 1979-82, 1984-89; USC Black Alumni Association, Ebonics Support Group, Award of Appreciation, 1990. **Military Serv:** US Air Force Res, 2nd Lt, 1962-66. **Business Addr:** Sr Asst, Hospitals Admin, County of Los Angeles, Dept of Health Services, 313 N Figueroa St, Suite 803, Los Angeles, CA 90012, (213)240-8372.

WILLIAMS, JAY OMAR
Professional football player. **Personal:** Born Oct 13, 1971, Washington, DC; married Erica; children: Jamye, Jai. **Educ:** Wake Forest, attended. **Career:** St Louis Rams, defensive end, 1995-. **Business Addr:** Professional Football Player, St Louis Rams, One Rams Way, St Louis, MO 63045, (314)982-7267.

WILLIAMS, JAYSON
Professional basketball player. **Personal:** Born Feb 22, 1968, Ritter, SC; children: Monique, Ejay. **Educ:** St John's University. **Career:** Philadelphia 76ers, forward, 1990-92, New Jersey Nets, 1992-. **Business Addr:** Professional Basketball Player, New Jersey Nets, Brendan Byrne Ave, 405 Murray Hill Pkwy, East Rutherford, NJ 07073, (201)935-8888.

WILLIAMS, JEAN CAROLYN
Educator. **Personal:** Born Aug 30, 1956, Mullins, SC; daughter of Remel Graves Gause and Fred Gause, Jr; married Vaugn McDonald Williams Jr, Jul 21, 1979. **Educ:** Spelman Coll, Atlanta, GA, BA 1978; Universidad Iberoamericana, Mexico City, Mexico, certificate 1983; University of Georgia, Athens, certificate 1987; Georgia State University, Atlanta, MAT, 1983. **Career:** Douglas County Schools System, Douglasville, GA, Spanish teacher beginning 1978, teacher of English as a second language 1982-86, 1990-92, arts and languages dept, head, currently; ambassador, speaker, consultant for Georgia Dept of Education, 1988; Governor's Task Force on Teacher's Pay for Performance, 1991. **Orgs:** Mem of Steering Comm, Academic Alliances, 1986-; mem of Staff Devel Council, Douglas County Schools, 1986-; head of Instructional & Professional Devel Comm, Douglas County Assn of Educators, 1987-88 & 1989-90; chair of Challenge, Douglas County High School, 1989-92; member of Foreign Language Assn of Georgia, GA Athletic Coaches Assn, Advisory Bd of the Southern Conf on Language Teaching, Amer Assn of GA, Phi Delta Kappa, Alpha Kappa Alpha, Delta Kappa Gamma, National Educators Assn's Congressional Contact Team, Professional Negotiation Task Force; Professional League of Schools, Leadership Team; Performance Learning System, Inc, instructor of Project TEACH and Teaching through learning channels. **Honors/Awds:** Editor of Albricias!, Spanish Today, and The Beacon, 1980-89; grant to attend seminar on Afro-Hispanic literature, GA Endowment for the Humanities, 1984; assoc editor of Afro Hispanic Review; Douglas County Teacher of the Year (Christa McAuliffe Award), Douglas County Schools, 1987-88; AATSP-GA Teacher of the Year, GA chapter of Amer Assn of Teachers of Spanish and Portuguese, 1987-88; GA Teacher of the Year award from Encyclopaedia Brittanica, Good Housekeeping, and Council of Chief State School Officers, 1987-88; Certificate of Excellence, Foreign Lang Assn of GA, 1988; Excellence in Education award from NASSP, Burger King, and CCSSO, 1988; Milken Family Foundation, National Educator, 1990; nominee for National Teachers Hall of Fame and Walt Disney Teachers' Hall of Fame. **Home Addr:** 6703 Sutton Place, Douglasville, GA 30135. **Business Addr:** Head, Department of Arts and Languages, Douglas County Comprehensive High School, Douglas County Schools, 8705 Campbellton St, Douglasville, GA 30134.

WILLIAMS, JEAN PERKINS
Personnel director. **Personal:** Born Sep 21, 1951, Mt Olive, NC; daughter of Mr & Mrs Willie R Perkins; divorced; children: Sonja. **Educ:** Cornell Univ School of Industrial Rel, Cert EEO Spec 1976; Pace Univ White Plains NY, BS Liberal Studies 1981; North Carolina A&T State University, Greensboro, NC, Masters, adult education, 1989. **Career:** Ciba-Geigy Corp NY, corp eeo coord 1975-76, sr personnel admin 1976-78; Amer Cyanamid Lederle Labs, equal oppty affairs mgr 1978-80; Amer Home Products Corp, personnel manager 1980-83; Goodyear Tire & Rubber Co, employment manager; Guilford Technical Community College, dir of personnel, 1990-. **Orgs:** Mem Amer Bus Womens Assoc 1982-, Corp Womens Network 1976-80; bd of dir Union Child Day Care Ctr White Plains NY 1976-77; bd mem Central NC School for Deaf 1980-83; task force mem Equal Employment Oppty Commiss WA 1975-76, NAACP 1977-79; search committee member for Executive Dir of YWCA-Greensboro 1986; committee of 100, Personnel Managers Assn, Greensboro, NC.. **Honors/Awds:** Keynote speaker Amer Mgmt Assoc 1979; speaker Natl Bus & Professional Womens Club 1979. **Home Addr:** 3210 Oliver Dr., Greensboro, NC 27406-9289. **Business Addr:** Director of Personnel, Guilford Technical Community College, PO Box 309, Jamestown, NC 27282.

WILLIAMS, JEANETTE MARIE
Educational administrator. **Personal:** Born Jul 11, 1942, Shaw, MS; daughter of Mary Roach and Lonnie Roach; married (widowed); children: Renee L Burwell, Howard S Jr, Karen A, Sharon A Gober. **Educ:** Wilson Jr Coll, 1968; Chicago State Univ, BS, Biology, 1969; Chicago State Univ, MS, Biology, 1977; Northern Illinois Univ, education specialist degree, 1995. **Career:** Haven Middle School, teacher, 1971-72; Chicago Public Schools, teacher, 1972-74; Malcolm X Coll, curriculum spec, 1974-77; Kennedy-King Coll, asst prof of biology, 1977-, Title III, dir, 1983-86, assistant dean of student services, currently. **Orgs:** Mem, Natl Assn of Biology Teachers, 1978-; Assn for Supvr & Curriculum Devel, 1980; president, Assn for the Study of African-American Life & History, 1982-; consultant, Educ Mgmt Assn, 1982-83; advisor, Phi Theta Kappa, 1982-, president Chicago Branch; bd dir, Black Women's Hall of Fame, 1983-; bd of dir, Kennedy-King Coll, Natl Youth Sports Program, 1987-; American Association of University Women, 1989-; American Association of Women in Community & Junior Colleges; Natl Council of Negro Women Inc; Alpha Kappa Alpha International Sorority, Xi Nu Omega Chapter. **Honors/Awds:** Scholarship Chicago Chemical Co, 1971; Advisor's Hall of Honor Illinois, Phi Theta Kappa, 1984; Distinguished Teacher Award Local 1600, Kennedy King Chapter, 1984; Advisor's Hall of Honor IL Phi Theta Kappa 1985; IL Phi Theta Kappa Most Disting Advisor 1985; Outstanding Illinois Advisor, Phi Theta Kappa, 1989; Illinois Advisors Hall of Honor, Phi Theta Kappa, 1989, 1991; Women on the Move in the City Colleges, City Colleges of Chicago, 1990. **Business Addr:** Associate Professor of Biology, Chicago City Coll, Kennedy-King Coll, 6800 S Wentworth Ave, #3E18, Chicago, IL 60621-3798, (312)602-5159.

WILLIAMS, JEFFREY LEN
Journalist. **Personal:** Born Sep 21, 1959, Delhi, NY; son of Diane & Odell Williams Sr; children: Alia. **Educ:** SUNY at New Paltz, BA, 1981; Univ of Maryland, MA, 1985. **Career:** Frederick News-Post, copy editor, 1986; Lexington Herald-Leader, copy editor, 1987-88; Hartford Courant, copy editor, 1988-91; Chicago Tribune, asst metro copy editor, metro copy editor. **Orgs:** Natl Assn of Black Journalists, 1987-. **Honors/ Awds:** SUNY, Chancellor's Award, 1981; SUNY at New Paltz, Minority Recruitment Award, 1981, Dean's List Award, 1980-81. **Business Addr:** Assistant Metro Copy Editor, Chicago Tribune, 435 N Michigan Ave, 4th Fl, Chicago, IL 60611.

WILLIAMS, JEROME
Professional basketball player. **Personal:** Born May 10, 1973, Washington, DC. **Educ:** Montgomery College; Georgetown Univ, BA in sociology. **Career:** Detroit Pistons, forward, 1996-. **Orgs:** Phoebe Foundation; MADD; Optimist Club of Southfield; Jerome Williams Rookie Camp and Mentor Program, found. **Business Addr:** Professional Basketball Player, Detroit Pistons, 2 Championship Dr, Auburn Hills, MI 48326, (248)377-0100.

WILLIAMS, JEROME D.
Educator. **Personal:** Born Jan 11, 1947, Philadelphia, PA; son of Gloria Williams and Jerome Williams; married Lillian Harrison Williams, Jun 21, 1969; children: Denean, Derek, Daniel, Dante, Dachia. **Educ:** Univ of Pennsylvania, Philadelphia, PA, BA, 1969; Union College, Schenectady, NY, MS, 1975; Univ of Colorado, Boulder, CO, PhD, 1986. **Career:** General Electric Company, Schenectady, NY, senior publicist, 1969-78; Solar Energy Research Institute, Golden CO, manager, public information, 1978-81; Penn State Univ, University Park, PA, assoc professor, 1987-. **Orgs:** Member of executive board, Society for Consumer Psychology, 1989-; member, Assn for Consumer Research, 1982-; member, Amer Marketing Assn, 1980-; member, Amer Psych Assn, 1986-; member, Academy of Marketing Science, 1984-. **Business Addr:** Associate Professor of Marketing, 707C Business Administration Building, Pennsylvania State University, University Park, PA 16802.

WILLIAMS, JESSE
Elected official. **Personal:** Born Jul 18, 1922, Sylvania, GA; son of Ethel Prescott Williams and Evenezer Williams; married Edna Williams, Oct 27, 1967; children: Ethel M Cooper, Jesse Jr, Walter A, Pamerla J Ellis, Josie P, Thmas H, Pancia Oliver, Mary A, Keith L, Tami L Singleton, Danny R, Janice R Prescott, A; children: Alda M Burgest, Angela F Bassett. **Career:** Lovell Hill Baptist Church, chmn of bd 1948; Frank Cooper Baptist Assn, treas 1970-96; Frank Cooper Sunday School Convention, supt 1972-96; City of Hilltonia, city council; mayor, 1988-96. **Orgs:** Mem Mason Lodge No 433; mem Lemar Carter Conser of 32nd; S & B Decon & Brother Hood Union, president. **Home Addr:** 191 C Street, Sylvania, GA 30467.

WILLIAMS, JESTER C.
Educator, clergyman. **Personal:** Born Oct 27, 1924, Greenwood, MS; son of Maggie Ellington Williams and J. W. Williams; married Sina Flowers, May 22, 1950 (divorced); children: Jester C Jr, India Ruth, James Carter. **Educ:** Alcorn A&M Univ, BS, 1950; MS Valley State Univ, Delta State Univ, MS State Univ, Gammon Theol Sem, attended; Laural School of Medical & Dental Assistants, graduated 1989; Liberty University Home Bible Institute, Lynchburg, VA, diploma, 1990. **Career:** Oak Park HS Laurel MS, 1949-50; Brooks HS Drew MS, principal 1951-56; Walnut Grove, Pleasant Valley United Church, 1960-61; Belzoni-Inverness Charges, 1961-63; Greenville, Revels United MC, 1963-64; Providence, Jones Chapel, Buford Chapel United Meth Church, Epworth United Meth Church 1964-66; Decel United Meth Church 1967-68; Hopson Bayou, teacher, 1964-68; Marshall HS, N Carrollton MS, 1968-72; Rasberry United Meth Ch 1969; Revels United Meth Ch 1970-71; Vaiden Circuit MS 1971-72; Greenwood City School, sub teacher 1973-77, 1985; Corinth, 1974; St Paul United Meth Ch, Lindsey Chapel, Jones Chapel, West Point MS 1975-77; Pickens Circuit, Union Mem United Meth Ch, Franklin United Meth Ch, 1977-80; Barurick UM Church & Tillman Chapel UMC, pastor, 1992-93, 1995-96. **Orgs:** American Legion; AARP. **Military Serv:** USAF Sgt 1943-46; Good Conduct Medal, WW II; Victory Medal; American Service Medal; Asiatic-Pacific Service Medal.

WILLIAMS, JEWEL L.
Elected official (retired). **Personal:** Born Feb 11, 1937, Canton, MS; married Frank Williams (divorced); children: Anthony, Frank, Kerry, Debra Whitehead, Darcy Donaldson. **Educ:** Mary Holmes Jr Coll, Bus; Jackson State Univ, Soc 1969-71. **Career:** Head Start, comm organizer 1966-73; Canton Public Schools, social worker 1974-84; Universal Life Ins Co, sales rep 1984-86; City of Canton, alderman 1979-94; WMGO Radio Station, dir of public affairs. **Orgs:** Asst sec, Woman for Progress; sec, bd of dir MYL Family Health Ctr 1973-79; bd mem Central Miss Legal Serv 1976-83; bd mem NAACP 1979-; pres MadisonCty Women for Progress 1980-82; exec comm MS Democratic Party; pres, Lucy C Jefferson Federated Club Inc; board of directors, Rainbow Literacy; board of directors, Canton Chambers of Commerce; board of directors, Save the Children of Madison Co; mem Madison Cty Historical Society. **Honors/ Awds:** Outstanding Service Project Unity Inc 1979; Outstanding in Community Women for Progress 1983; Outstanding Sales Service Universal Life Ins Co 1985; Outstanding Award, Jackson Links Inc. **Home Addr:** 513 Cauthen St, Canton, MS 39046.

WILLIAMS, JOANNE LOUISE
Journalist. **Personal:** Born Apr 10, 1949, Milwaukee, WI; daughter of Vida Eugenia Smith Williams and John J Williams; married LaMont Nicholson; children: John Brooks Nicholson. **Educ:** Northwestern University, Evanston, IL, BS, 1971. **Career:** WTMJ-TV & Radio, Milwaukee, WI, anchor, reporter, producer, 1971-76; WGN-TV & Radio, Chicago, IL, reporter, producer, writer, 1976-79; WITI-TV, Milwaukee, WI, anchor, medical reporter, 1979-. **Orgs:** Natl Assn of Black Journalists, 1983-, president, currently; president, Milwaukee Press Club, 1982; member, Milwaukee Forum, 1982-87; Future Milwaukee graduate, 1982; Wisconsin Black Media Association, president. **Honors/Awds:** First Television Fellowship in Medical Reporting, Case Western Reserve School of Medicine, 1987; Woman of Color Award, Milwaukee Black Women's Network, 1983. **Business Addr:** President, Milwaukee Chatper - National, Association of Black Journalists/Wisconsin, Black Media Association, WITI-TV, 9001 N Green Bay Rd, Milwaukee, WI 53217.

WILLIAMS, JOE
Entertainer. **Personal:** Born 1918, Cordele, GA; married Jillean. **Career:** Singer, composer, actor, 1935-; Count Basie Orchestra, singer, 1954-61; soloist, 1961-, began touring in 1969; recordings: "Everyday I Have The Blues"; "All Right, Okay, You Win"; "Smack Dab In The Middle"; "Teach Me Tonight"; "A Man Ain't Suppose to Cry;" "Everynight"; "A Child Is Born"; "Did I Ever Really Live"; "Yesterday, Today and Tomorrow"; "Here's To Life". **Orgs:** NARAS; Society of Singers; AFTRA; ACTRA; SAG; NAACP; Musicians Union Local 47. **Honors/Awds:** Honorary Doctorate of Music, Berklee School of Music, 1988; Honorary Doctorate of Music, Hamilton College, 1991; Playboy Jazz Readers and Critics Award; Hollywood Walk of Fame star, 1983; Governor's Award, National Academy of Recording Arts and Sciences, 1983, Black Legend Award; Grammy Award, Best Jazz Vocal, 1985; For the Love of Joe, Society of Singers Tribute, 1991; Image Award, NAACP, 1985; Georgia Music Hall of Fame, 1988; Intl Jazz Hall of Fame, 1997; Jazz Vocalist Award, Los Angeles Jazz Society, 1997. **Business Addr:** c/o John Levy Enterprises Inc, 2820 W Charleston Blvd #C-22, Las Vegas, NV 89102.

WILLIAMS, JOE H.
City official. **Personal:** Born Oct 7, 1937, Tuskegee, AL; married Marilyn Bryant Hainesworth; children: Melani, Mario. **Educ:** Republic Indus Educ Inst, Elect Maint 1970-78. **Career:** General Motors Corp, electrician 1965-; Williams Electric Co, owner 1973-; Seventh Ward Warren OH, councilman 1977-; Precinct D Warren OH, precinct comm head 1984-; Warren 7th Ward, councilman, pres, currently. **Orgs:** Bd mem NAACP 1968-; pres West Warren Improvement Council 1968-; bd mem Warren Electrician Bd 1980-; elected pres, Warren City Council, 1990-; mem, Natl Steering Committee of Clinton/Gore 1996 Campaign. **Honors/Awds:** Honorary Mayor of Tuskegee AL 1977; Gen Motors Awd for Excellence General Motors Lordstown 1984; Outstanding Community Serv NAACP 1984; Award from Natl Assn of Negro Business & Professional Women's Club for Distinguished Serv as a Black Elected Official for the City of Warren, OH 1985; Joe H Williams Day April 14, 1985 for Outstanding Comm Serv from Mayor Daniel J Sferra Warren, OH; Governor's Special Recognition from Richard Celeste 1985; Hon Auditor of State from Thomas E Ferguson 1985; City Council Citation from Jerry Crispino; NY Assembly Citation from Larry Seebrook, 1991. **Home Addr:** 2855 Peerless SW, Warren, OH 44485. **Business Addr:** Councilman, Warren 7th Ward, 2855 Peerless SW, Warren, OH 44485.

WILLIAMS, JOHN (HOT ROD)
Professional basketball player. **Personal:** Born Aug 9, 1962, Sorrento, LA; married Karen; children: John Jr, Johnfrancis, Johnpaul, Johnna. **Educ:** Tulane Univ, 1981-85. **Career:** Cleveland Cavaliers, forward-center, 1986-95; Phoenix Suns, 1995-. **Honors/Awds:** NBA All-Rookie Team, 1987. **Business Addr:** Professional Basketball Player, Phoenix Suns, PO Box 515, Phoenix, AZ 85001, (602)379-7867.

WILLIAMS, JOHN ALFRED
Author, educator, journalist. **Personal:** Born Dec 5, 1925, Jackson, MS; son of Ola Mae Jones Williams and John Henry Williams; married Lorrain Isaac, Oct 5, 1965; children: Gregory D, Dennis A, Adam J. **Educ:** Syracuse Univ, BA 1950, Grad Sch, 1950-51. **Career:** Coll of the Virgin Islands, lecturer black lit 1968; CUNY, lecturer creative writing 1968-69; Sarah Lawrence Coll, guest writer 1972-73; Univ of CA Santa Barbara, regents lecturer 1973; CUNY LaGuardia Comm Coll, disting prof 1973-78; Univ of HI, vstg prof 1974; Boston Univ, vstg prof 1978-79; Exxon vstg prf New York Univ 1986-87; Rutgers Univ, prof of Engl 1979-93, Paul Robeson Prof of English, 1990-93; Bard Ctr, fellow, 1994-95. **Orgs:** Columnist, stringer, spec assignment, staff The Natl Leader, Progressive Herald, Assoc Negro Press, The Age, The Defender, Post-Standard, The Tribune, The Courier; Holiday Magazine Europe 1965-66; corresp Newsweek Africa 1964-65; dir of info Amer Comm on Africa 1957, spec events WOV NY 1957; corresp Ebony-Jet Spain 1958-59; WNET-TV writer, narrator on location Nigeria, Spain, 1964-65; bd of dir Coord Council Literary Mags 1983-85; bd of dir Jrnl of African Civilizations 1980-;contrib ed Politicks 1977, Amer Jnrl 1972-74; ed bd Audience Mag 1970-72; contrib ed Herald-Tribune Book Week 1963-65; asst to publ Abelard Schuman 1957-58; editor & publ Negro Mkt Newsletter 1956-57. **Honors/Awds:** Novels: The Berhama Account, 1985; Mothersill and the Foxes, 1975; The Man Who Cried I Am, 1967; Click Song, 1982; Junior Bachelor Soc, 1975; Jacob's Ladder, 1987; non-fiction books incl: If I Shop I'll Die: The Comedy and Tragedy of Richard Pryor, 1991; The McGraw-Hill Intro to Lit, 1st ed, 1984, 2nd ed, 1994; Flashbacks: A 20-Year Diary of Article Writing, 1973; The King God Didn't Save: Martin Luther King, Jr, 1970; The Most Native of Sons: Richard Wright, 1970; Amistad 1, 1970, Amistad 2, 1971; This is My Country, Too, 1965; Syracuse Univ, DLih, 1995; Univ Mass, Dartmouth, DLiH, 1978; Natl Inst of Arts and Letters, 1962; Syracuse Univ, Centenial Medal, Outstanding Achievement, 1970; Natl Endownment for the Arts, 1977; US Observer, 23rd Premio Casa Awd, 1985; Disting Writer Awd, Middle Atlantic Writers, 1987; NJ Lit Hall of Fame, Michael Awd, 1987; Africa, Her History, Lands & People, 1963; Drama: Last Flight from Ambo Ber, 1981; August Forty-Five, 1991; Vangui (libretto), 1996; Safari West, 1998. **Military Serv:** USNR, Pharm Mate 3/c, 1943-46.

WILLIAMS, JOHN EARL
Mortician, elected official. **Personal:** Born Aug 7, 1948, Raleigh, NC; son of Lucy Johnson Williams and Thaddeus Williams; married Karen A Brown-Williams, Apr 17, 1987. **Educ:** NC Central Univ, BS Commerce 1967; Fayetteville Tech Inst, AAS Funeral Serv Ed 1977. **Career:** Scarborough & Hargett Funeral Home Inc, staff mem, admin asst 1967-72; Durham Cty Hosp Corp, dir, admin asst 1972-73; Beaunit Corp Rsch Triangle Park, vice pres of fin 1973-74; Scarborough & Hargett Funeral Home Inc, bus mgr 1977-78; Haywood Funeral Home Inc, mortician 1978-79; NC Dept of Commerce, Natural Resources & Commun Devel, auditor 1979-86; owner and operator, Weaver & Williams Funeral Service, Inc, 1986-. **Orgs:** Mem Durham City Cncl 1983; Hayti Development Corp; bd dir Durham C of C; Highways and Streets Comm; NC & Natl Funeral Directors & Morticians Assns; NC Museum of Life and Science; bd dir Triangle "J" Cncl of Govt; mem Advisory Cncl on Employment NAACP Durham Chapter; Durham Comm on Affairs of Black People; Durham Alumni Chapter of Kappa Alpha Psi Fraternity. **Home Addr:** PO Box 57, Haw River, NC 27258. **Business Addr:** Bynum Weaver-Williams Funeral Service, Inc., 110 N. Merritt Mill Road, Chapel Hill, NC 27516.

WILLIAMS, JOHN HENRY
Clergyman. **Personal:** Born Feb 24, 1948, Venice, IL; married Emma Jean Johnson; children: Reginold, Dean, John Jr, Shelonda, Nicole, Milton. **Educ:** Southern IL Univ Edwardville, 1976-78; State Comm Coll E St Louis, 1981. **Career:** Venice Independent Baseball League, pres 1970-81; Madison Branch of NAACP, pres 1976-80; Venice Citizen Comm Devel, chmn 1977-78; People Org to Benefit Children in Venice, pres 1981-83; Venice Local Utilities Bd, vice chmn 1983-; Venice Neighborhood Crime Watch Prog, mem 1984; New Salem MB Church, pastor 1982-; CITY of Venice ILL, alderman, 1989-. **Orgs:** Mem Intl Union of Operating Engrs 1971-, Free & Accepted Ancient York Rite Mason 1972-; former pres Venice Park Bd of Commiss 1982-83; mem Venice Park Bd of Commiss 1987; River Bluff Girl Scouts Council, 1992. **Honors/ Awds:** Million Dollar Club Madallion 71st Annual NAACP Convention 1980; Two Local Awards Madison Branch NAACP 1980; Citation for Community Serv Tri-Cities Area United Way 1982; Pastor of the Year Awd Spot Light Review 1983; Comm Serv Madison Progressive Women Org 1984; State of Arkansas Governor Bill Clinton, Arkansas Travel Certificate Award, 1986; Bethel AME Church, Achievement Award, 1986; Project Cleanup Drugs and Alcohol Community Award, 1990; Kool Achiever Awards, nominee, 1992; Venice Public Schools, Junior Beta Club, Martin Luther King Jr Community Award, 1992; State of Illinois Governor Jim Edgar, Council of Aging Board of Directors Appointee, 1991. **Home Addr:** 619 Washington, Venice, IL 62090. **Business Addr:** Pastor, New Salem MB Church, 1349 Klein St, Venice, IL 62090.

WILLIAMS, JOHN L.
Cleric, dentist, business executive. **Personal:** Born Dec 31, 1937, Lubbock, TX; son of Mary Williams and Rev Nathaniel Williams; married Annie L Emmanuel; children: LeCretria, Stephanie, John John, Nandilyn, John Mark, LaShunda, Samuel John, John Luther Jr. **Educ:** TX Southern U, BChem 1960; Howard Dental Sch, DDS 1965. **Career:** Faith Tabernacle COGIC, gen prctnr/pastor, currently; Williams & Sons Funeral Home, owner, director, currently; DDS, currently. **Orgs:** Charles H George Dental Soc, 1965; Academy of General Dentistry; Am Chem Soc; supt So Houston Dist 1983; TX Dental Assn Houston Dist Dental Soc, 1989, American Dental Assn. **Honors/Awds:** Alpha Phi Alpha Frat 1960; Sal Dunbar Sr Hi Lubbock, TX 1956; Academy of General Dentistry, 1976. **Home Addr:** 4436 So MacGregor Way, Houston, TX 77021.

Business Addr: Pastor, Faith Tabernacle COGIC, 11800 Cullen Blvd, Houston, TX 77047.

WILLIAMS, JOHN L.
Professional football player. **Personal:** Born Nov 23, 1964, Palatka, FL. **Educ:** Univ of Florida, attended. **Career:** Seattle Seahawks, fullback, 1986-. **Business Addr:** Professional Football Player, Seattle Seahawks, 11220 NE 53rd St, Kirkland, WA 98033-7595.

WILLIAMS, JOHN R.
Optometrist. **Personal:** Born Mar 14, 1937, Richmond; married Sandra; children: 3 Sons. **Educ:** Virginia Union U, BS 1959; IL Coll Optometry, OD 1963. **Career:** Optometrist, self emp mem VA. **Orgs:** Am Optometric Assn 1960-; Nat Optometric Assn 1968-; Metro Dev Corp 1972-; Asso Investors 1972-73; Mem Capitala Reg Park Auth 1968-71; bd mem Salvation Army Boys Club 1965-74; bd mem Friends Assn; bd mem Big Bro Am Inc 1968-74; bd mem v chmn Church Hill Multi-serv Ctr Inc; v chmn Richmond, IN Auth 1973-74. **Business Addr:** 1122 N 25 St, Ste D, Richmond, VA 23223.

WILLIAMS, JOHN WALDO
Cleric. **Personal:** Born Mar 15, 1911, Como, TX; married Susie Marguerite Green; children: Clara L Woods, Nona R Fisher, Anita J Gates. **Educ:** Butler Coll, BA, 1935, DD 1939. **Career:** Cypress Baptist Assoc, moderator 1960-; BM&E Convention of TX, vice pres 1961-; Natl Bapt Con USA Inc, bd of dir 1982-. **Orgs:** Pastor Ebenezer Baptist Church 1941-. **Honors/Awds:** 30 Yrs Loyal Serv Ebenezer Bapt Church Youth 1941-71; Invaluable Serv Cypress Baptist Assn 1961-71; Meritorious Serv Cypress Congress of Christian Ed 1943-81. **Home Addr:** PO Box 253, Como, TX 75431.

WILLIAMS, JOHNNY WAYNE
Educational administrator. **Personal:** Born Dec 18, 1946, Lewisburg, TN; son of Essie M Williams and James A Williams; married Coralee Henry Williams, Jun 23, 1968; children: Kimberly M. **Educ:** Tennessee State Univ, BS, 1968; Univ of Northern Colorado, MA, 1974; Troy State Univ, EdS, 1981; Univ of Sarasota, EdD, 1993. **Career:** US Air Force, officer positions, 1968-88; North Carolina A & T State Univ, chair, Dept of Aerospace Studies, 1985-88; Columbia State Community Coll, exec dir of job training programs, 1988-90, dean of student services, 1990-94, vice pres student svcs, 1994-. **Orgs:** Maury County Federal Credit Union, dir, 1991-; Maury County Literacy Council, 1993-; Maury County Vocational Program, 1991-; Job Trainings Private Industry Council, 1992-. **Special Achievements:** Dissertation, The Swinging Door, Dropout Characteristics at a Small Rural Community College, 1993; Dissertation, Air Force ROTC, Cadet Attitudes Toward Field Training, 1981. **Military Serv:** US Air Force, lt col, 1968-88; Commendation Medal; 3rd Oak Leaf Cluster; Meritorious Service Medal, 2nd Oak Leaf Cluster. **Home Addr:** 324 Alden Cove Dr, Smyrna, TN 37167.

WILLIAMS, JOSEPH B.
Judge. **Personal:** Born Jul 12, 1921, Annapolis; married Eva; children: Joseph Jr, John. **Educ:** New York Univ, LlB, LlM 1949-52; Hampton Inst, BS 1942; US Merchant Marine Acad 1944. **Career:** Law Offices, 1949-66; NY, judge 1966-70; New York City Model Cities Administr, 1970-73; Family Ct, judge 1973-; New York City Admin Judge Family Div, dep 1974 senate of NY, justice sup ct 1977. **Orgs:** Former chmn bd trustees Cornerstone Bapt Ch; former chmn bd Bedrford Styvesant Rest Corp; trustee Nat Counc of Juv & Fam Ct Judges; trustee New Sch for Soc Rsrch; mem Brooklyn Museum; mem Brooklyn Inst Arts & Sc; past v chmn Hampton Inst Bd Trustees; NY Co Lawyers Assn; Am Bar Assn; Kings Co Criminal Bar Assn; Vera Inst Justice; Wiltwyck Sch Boys. **Military Serv:** UNS 1944-46 lt 1950-52. **Business Addr:** Supreme Court of Kings County, 360 Adams St, Brooklyn, NY 11201.

WILLIAMS, JOSEPH BARBOUR
Insurance company executive. **Personal:** Born Aug 20, 1945, New York, NY; son of Mary Alice Porter Williams and Joseph Pins Barbour Jr; married Felicia Ann Thomas Williams, Jun 7, 1972; children: Christie Dawn. **Educ:** Talladega College, Talladega, AL, BA, 1967. **Career:** Central Life Ins of Florida, Tampa FL, pres/CEO, 1972; Central Life Employees Credit Union, Tampa, FL, pres, 1987-. **Orgs:** Assistant treasurer, Greater Tampa Urban League, 1984-; member, NAACP, Tampa Chapter, 1990-; member, Hillsborough Board of Consumer Affairs, 1986-90. **Honors/Awds:** Blount Trophy For Agency Offices, Exceptional Performance, National Insurance Assn, 1985; Certificate of Merit, Outstanding performance in insurance bureau, National Insurance Association, 1982, 1976; Service Award, Advisor For, Omega Psi Phi Fraternity, University South Florida, 1974. **Military Serv:** US Navy, Lt, 1968-72; National Defense Service Medal, 1968. **Business Addr:** President, CEO, Central Life Insurance Company of Florida, PO Box 110, Tallahassee, FL 32302-0100.

WILLIAMS, JOSEPH HENRY
Physician. **Personal:** Born Jun 15, 1931, Columbia, SC; son of Ruby Catherine Winthrop Williams and Carter Edmund Williams; married C Patricia; children: Joseph Jr. **Educ:** Howard U, BS 1950, MD 1954; NYU, diploma 1960. **Career:** Park City Hosp, attdng surgeon 1962-. **Orgs:** Am Bd Surgery 1967; mem Fairfield Co Med Soc; CT St Med Soc. **Honors/Awds:** Flw Am Soc Abdominal Surgeons 1963; Fellow American Coll of Surgeons, 1982. **Military Serv:** AUS 1956-58. **Business Addr:** 6901 Old York Rd, Philadelphia, PA 19126-2234.

WILLIAMS, JOSEPH LEE, JR.
Business executive. **Personal:** Born Mar 25, 1945, Madison, WV; son of Loretta M Lawson Williams and Joseph Lee Williams Sr; married Shirley Ann Johnson; children: Yvette, Yvonne, Mary, Joseph. **Educ:** Marshall Univ, BBA Finance 1978; Mayors' Leadership Inst 1984. **Career:** Ebony Golf Classic, founder/dir 1971-87; City of Huntington, mem city council 1981, asst mayor 1983-84, mayor 1984-85; Basic Supply Co, president, CEO, 1977-; First Sentry Bank, director, 1996-. **Orgs:** Comm Huntington Urban Renewal Authority 1983-85; mem Huntington Rotary Club 1983-; bd of dirs Huntington Area Chamber of Commerce 1984-; bd of trustees Cabell-Huntington Hosp 1984-85; bd of dirs United Way of the River Cities 1984-; mem City of Huntington Interim Loan Comm 1985; life mem NAACP; Huntington Area Chamber of Commerce, West Virginia Partnership for Progress Council, 1989-; bd of directors, Huntington Industrial Corp; exec bd member of the United Way of the River Cities Foundation; Unlimited Future Inc, chairperson, 1991-96; Marshall University College of Business, advisory bd, 1994-. **Honors/Awds:** Outstanding Black Alumni Marshall Univ 1984; Outstanding Citizen Awd Huntington WV Negro Business & Professional Women's Clubs 1985; Subcontractor of The Year, West Virginia SBA, 1987; Minority Business Person of the Year, West Virginia SBA, 1988; featured in Union-Carbide Corp's Natl News magazine, 1989; featured in E I duPont de Nemours & Co's TEMPO Natl Newsletter, 1989; Huntington, VA, Medical Center's Black History Month Award, 1990-; Ernst & Young Inc, Merrill Lynch Entrepreneur of the Year, regional finalist, 1991. **Business Addr:** President, CEO, Basic Supply Co, Inc, 628 8th Ave, PO Box 936, Huntington, WV 25712-0936.

WILLIAMS, JOSEPH R.
Clergyman. **Personal:** Born Oct 22, 1918, St Joseph, LA; son of Ellen Brown Williams and Abram Williams Sr; married Georgia Lee Van; children: Josephine W White, Robert C Williams, Linda W McLemore, Ronald J Williams, Yvonne W Shropshire, Kevin R Williams. **Educ:** Leland Coll, AB 1954; UASFI, AM 1963; CCRI, DD 1983. **Career:** Pastor, Little Zion 1943-47; pastor, Evergreen 1944-50, 1952-64; pastor, Straight Life 1957-59; pastor, Mt Olivet 1946-48; pastor, Mt Pilgrim 1956-59; pastor, Elm Grove Baptist Church 1952-; pastor, New Sunlight Baptist Church 1958-; Semi Extn Dean 1958. **Orgs:** Aff HMB Southern Baptist Convention; Bible Exp; Org EPIC mem advisory bd Comm Advancement Inc (CAI); vpres E Baton Rouge Min. **Honors/Awds:** Honarary Mayor, Baton Rouge, LA, 1977; Adjutant General, State of LA, 1978; Honorary Colonel State of LA, 1985; Honorary DA, EBR Parish, 1983; 25 yrs Pastors Award, Elm Grove Baptist Church, 1977; 25 yrs Pin Award Home Mission Bd Southern Baptist, 1983; Minister of the Year, Baton Rouge, Laymen, 1987; Deaconiate Instruction Award, 1987; 50yrs Gospel Preacher Award, State of LA Dept of Chr Educ, 1986. **Military Serv:** AUS 1948-51; Fourregre (fr.) 1949; SEATO; Asiatic Combat Ribbon, Good Conduct Ribbon, 1951.

WILLIAMS, JUNIUS W.
Attorney. **Personal:** Born Dec 23, 1943, Suffolk, VA; son of Bernyce White Williams and Maurice Lanxton Williams; children: Camille, Junea. **Educ:** Amherst Coll, BA 1965; Yale Law Sch, JD 1968; Inst of Pol Kennedy Sch of Gov Harvard Univ, fellow 1980. **Career:** Newark Comm Devel Admin & Model Cities Prog, dir 1970-73; Essex Newark Legal Svcs, exec dir 1983-85; City of Newark, candidate for mayor 1982; Private Practice, attorney 1973-83, 1985-; "Return to the Source," New Jersey, business manager, vocalist, instrumentalist, 1985-; real estate developer, Newark, NJ, 1987-; Town of Irvington, Irvington, NJ, legislative counsel, 1990-94, town attorney, 1994-. **Orgs:** 3rd vice pres Natl Bar Assn; 2nd vice pres 1976; pres Natl Bar Assn 1978-79; mem bd of dirs Agricultural Missions Inc; mem Natl, Amer, NJ, Essex Co Bar Assn; mem Critical Minorities Problems Comm; Natl Assn Housing & Redevel Officials; mem Equal Oppor Fund Bd 1980; Essex Co Ethics Comm 1980; fndr & dir Newark Area Planning Assn 1967-70; co-chmn Comm Negotiating Team NJ Coll Med & Dentistry Controversey 1967; guest spkr/lecturer Yale Univ, Harvard Law Sch, Rutgers Univ, Cornell Univ, Univ NC; pres Yale Law Sch Assoc of NJ 1981-82; fndr/pres Leadership Development Group 1980-; consultant Council of Higher Educ in Newark; bd of trustees Essex Co Coll 1980-84; mem & former sec Newark Collaboration Group; founder/first chmn Ad Hoc Comm of Univ Heights 1984-86; UniversityHeights Neighborhood Development Corp., consultant, developer, 1986-93. **Honors/Awds:** Distinguished Service Awd Newark Jaycees 1974; Concerned Citizens Awd Bd of Concerned Citizens Coll of Med & Dentistry of NJ; Fellow MARC 1967-68, 1973. **Special Achievements:** Youngest person to be elected president of the National Bar Association. **Business Addr:** Attorney, 132 Harper Ave, Irvington, NJ 07111, (201)373-0100.

WILLIAMS, KAREN ELAINE
Airline executive. **Personal:** Born Apr 5, 1956, Louisa, VA; daughter of Marion Buckner and Curtis Jasper; married; children: Cossia, Yvette. **Educ:** Renton Vocational Institution, certificate, 1976; Lake Washington Vocational Tech, certificate, 1977; Griffin Business College, BA, 1980. **Career:** Ideal Realty Co, secretary/receptionist, 1984-86; Deloitte Haskins & Sells, administrative support, 1986-87; Boeing Co, data base controller, 1987-88, scheduler/planner, 1988-92, employee dev specialist, 1992-. **Orgs:** Electronettes Drill Team, treasurer; AIO Charter Association. **Honors/Awds:** Certificate of Training for Proficiency, 1988; Certificate of Training for Scheduler Briefing, 1989; Pride in Excellence Award, 1987, 1990. **Business Addr:** Employee Dev Specialist, Boeing Corporation, PO Box 3707, M/S 98-39, Seattle, WA 98108.

WILLIAMS, KAREN HASTIE
Attorney. **Personal:** Born Sep 30, 1944, Washington, DC; daughter of Beryl Lockhart Hastie and William H Hastie; married Wesley S Williams Jr; children: Amanda Pedersen, Wesley Hastie, Bailey Lockhart. **Educ:** Univ of Neuchatel Switzerland, Cert 1965; Bates Coll, BA 1966; Fletcher School of Law & Diplomacy Tufts Univ, MA 1967; Columbus Law School Catholic Univ of Amer, JD 1973. **Career:** Fried Frank Harris Shriver & Kampelman, assoc atty 1975-77; US Senate Comm on Budget, chief counsel 1977-80; Office of Fed Procurement Policy Office of Mgmt & Budget, admin 1980-81; Crowell & Moring, of counsel 1982, sr partner. **Orgs:** Past chmn, Amer Bar Assoc Publ Contract Law Sect; bd of dir Crestar Bank Washington DC; Lawyers Comm for Civil Rights Under Law; board of directors Federal National Mortgage Association; board of directors Washington Gas Light Co; chair Black Student Fund; bd of dir exec comm DC Chap Amer Red Cross; chair, bd of dir Greater Washington Rsch Ctr; bd of dir NAACP Legal Defense Fund; former mem Trilateral Commission; Continental Airlines Inc, bd of directors; bd of directors, Sun America Inc. **Honors/Awds:** Director's Choice Award, 1993; National Women's Economic Alliance; Breast Cancer Awareness Award, Columbia Hospital for Women, 1994; Judge Learned Hand Award, 1995, American Jewish Committee. **Business Addr:** Senior Partner/Attorney, Crowell and Moring, 1001 Pennsylvania Ave, NW, Washington, DC 20004.

WILLIAMS, KAREN RENEE
Physician. **Personal:** Born Jan 27, 1954, Baton Rouge, LA; daughter of Eva Castain Williams and Alvin C Williams; married Cornelius A Lewis, Jul 30, 1983; children: Geoffrey P Lewis, Brittany E Lewis. **Educ:** Xavier Univ, BS 1975; Howard Univ Coll of Medicine, MD 1978; Tulane Univ, Pediatric Residency Program 1978-81. **Career:** LA State Univ Sch of Medicine/Earl K Long Hosp, instructor/dir pediatric emergency room 1981-87, asst prof of pediatrics, 1987-; head of pediatric infectious diseases, pediatric dept, 1985-. **Orgs:** Mem East Baton Rouge Parish Medical Assoc 1981-87, East Baton Rouge Parish Medical Soc 1985-87; Alpha Omega Alpha Medical Honor Society. **Business Addr:** Assistant Professor of Pediatrics, Louisiana State University School of Medicine, Earl K Long Hospital, 5825 Airline Highway, Baton Rouge, LA 70808.

WILLIAMS, KARL
Professional football player. **Personal:** Born Apr 10, 1971, Rowlett, TX. **Educ:** Texas A&M-Kingsville, attended. **Career:** Tampa Bay Buccaneers, wide receiver, 1996-. **Business Addr:** Professional Football Player, Tampa Bay Buccaneers, One Buccaneer Place, Tampa, FL 33607, (813)870-2700.

WILLIAMS, KATHERINE
Educational consultant. **Personal:** Born Sep 7, 1941; daughter of Norma D Williams Baird and Hugh L Williams; divorced; children: Garvin J. **Educ:** Harvard Univ, MEduc 1984, EdD 1987. **Career:** Workers Bank of Trinidad & Tobago, operations officer/acting chief accountant 1971-75; Matouk Intl, import officer 1976; Caribbean segment of Festival of Amer Folklife Smithsonian Inst, coord 1979-80; Festivals Mag, editor/publisher 1979-83; Smithsonian Inst, consul rsch inst on immigration & ethnic studies 1979-83; Dept of State Washington DC, consultant writer and software evaluator 1985-86; New York State Dept of Social Serv, project dir, 1987-90; Instructional Systems, Inc, Hackensack, NJ, dir of project planning and implementations, 1990-94; educational planning consultant, 1994-. **Orgs:** Harvard Club at the National Press Club. **Honors/Awds:** Author, "Computers, Our Road to the Future" used as text Washington DC Public Sch System 1982-; author "Where Else But America?"; named Women of Achievement in Montgomery Co 1977; Fellowship grant DC Comm on the Arts & Humanities 1981; photographic exhibit Museum of Modern Art of Latin America OAS Washington DC 1981; Sumner Museum & Archives, Washington DC, In the Cosmos (exhibition), 1998. **Home Addr:** 1440 N St NW, Ste 616, Washington, DC 20005.

WILLIAMS, KEITH DAVID. See DAVID, KEITH.

WILLIAMS, KELVIN EDWIN
Educator. **Personal:** Born Aug 16, 1964, Detroit, MI; son of Mary Williams; married Latrese Williams, Nov 17, 1990; children: Kyrah. **Educ:** Florida Memorial College, BS. **Career:** Miami Dade Public Schools, learning disabilities teacher, 1987-; Institute of Black Family Life, executive dir, 1993-; Natl Federation Interscholastic Official Assn, referee, 1994-. **Orgs:** Kappa Alpha Psi Fraternity, 1983-; 500 Role Model of Excellence Program, 1995-; Miami-Dade Law Enforcement Task Force & Intergroup Relations, 1993; Miami-Dade Sports, recreation, environmental cbo advisory bd, 1997; Miami Alliance of Black School Educators, 1994-; Arabian Nights Foundation, bd mem, 1997-; Office of Commissioner Barbara Carey, volunteer, 1996-. **Honors/Awds:** 500 Role Model of Excellence Program, Role Model Award, 1995; Department of Juvenile Justice, Honorary Juvenile Justice Deputy, 1995; Mount Olive Primitive Baptist Church, Black Role Model, 1994-95. **Home Addr:** 5001 SW 150th Terrace, Miramar, FL 33027. **Business Phone:** (305)688-4605.

WILLIAMS, KEN
Sports administrator. **Career:** Professional baseball player, retired 1992; Chicago White Sox, director of minor league operations/special asst to chmn, vp, player devel, currently. **Special Achievements:** One of the youngest people to hold a high position in pro baseball. **Business Addr:** Vice Pres, Player Development, Chicago White Sox, 333 W 35th St, Chicago, IL 60616, (312)924-1000.

WILLIAMS, KENNETH HERBERT
Attorney & elected official (retired). **Personal:** Born Feb 15, 1945, Orange, NJ; married Susan Marie Griffin; children: Kenneth H, Meryl E. **Educ:** Howard Univ Liberal Arts, BA 1967; Howard Univ School of Law, JD 1970. **Career:** US Capitol Police, patrolman 1969-70; Newark Urban Coalition, asst to dir 1970; City of East Orange, judge municipal 1977-82, asst city counsel 1972-75; Ernst & Ernst CPA Firm, tax attorney 1970-71; City of East Orange, city councilman 1984-85. **Orgs:** Mem NAACP 1970-, Amer Bar Assn 1971; counsel East Orange Jaycees 1972; chmn City of East Orange Juvenile Conf Com 1973-75; mem Natl Bar Assn; Judicial Comm 1977-82, Amer Judges Assn 1978. **Honors/Awds:** Outstanding Black Attorney Black Women Lawyers of NJ 1979; White House Fellow Nomination 1981; Outstanding Citizenship NJ Fed of Colored Women's Clubs Inc 1984; Cert of Appreciation Seton Hall Univ 1985. **Military Serv:** ROTC 1963-65.

WILLIAMS, KENNY RAY
Professional basketball player. **Personal:** Born Jun 9, 1969, Elizabeth City, NJ. **Educ:** Barton County Community College; Elizabeth City State. **Career:** Indiana Pacers, forward, 1990-. **Business Addr:** Professional Basketball Player, Indiana Pacers, 300 E Market St, Indianapolis, IN 46204, (317)263-2100.

WILLIAMS, KEVIN A.
Pizza company executive. **Personal:** Born Sep 17, 1956, Ypsilanti, MI; son of Jean LeBlanc Williams and Booker Williams. **Educ:** Cleary College of Business, Ypsilanti, MI; Eastern Michigan University, Ypsilanti, MI. **Career:** Washtenaw Co, MI, executive lieut, 1983; Domino's Pizza, Ann Arbor, MI, national director of protective service, 1985; Domino's Pizza, Atlanta, GA, assistant area vice president, 1986; Domino's Pizza, Baltimore, MD, regional director, 1987-89; Domino's Pizza, Sacramento, CA, area vice president, 1989; Domino's Pizza, Ann Arbor, MI, vice president field administrator, 1989-90, vice pres, operations, 1990-. **Orgs:** Board of directors, Huron Services for Youth; board of directors, Metropolitan Commerce Corp; board of directors, Harriet St Commerce Center. **Honors/Awds:** Various awards for meritorious service from Washtenaw County Sheriff's Office, Washtenaw Co, MI. **Business Addr:** Vice President for Operations, Domino's Pizza Inc, 30 Frank Lloyd Wright Dr, Ann Arbor, MI 48103.

WILLIAMS, KEVIN RAY
Professional football player. **Personal:** Born Jan 25, 1971, Dallas, TX. **Educ:** Miami (Fla.), attended. **Career:** Dallas Cowboys, wide receiver, 1993-96; Arizona Cardinals, 1997-. **Business Addr:** Professional Football Player, Arizona Cardinals, 8701 S Hardy, Tempe, AZ 85284, (602)379-0101.

WILLIAMS, KIM
Professional basketball player. **Personal:** Born Oct 14, 1974. **Educ:** DePaul Univ, attended. **Career:** Utah Starzz, guard, 1997-. **Honors/Awds:** Conference USA Player of the Year, 1997. **Business Addr:** Professional Basketball Player, Utah Starzz, 301 West South Temple, Salt Lake City, UT 84101, (801)355-3865.

WILLIAMS, KIMMIKA L. H.
Author, journalist, playwright. **Personal:** Born Jan 7, 1959, Philadelphia, PA; daughter of Lillian Yvonne Curry Hawes and Samuel S Hawes Jr; children: Essence, Tenasha. **Educ:** Howard University, Washington, DC, BA, journalism, 1980; Temple Univ, MFA, Playwriting; Future Faculty Fellow, Anthropology Dept, Temple University. **Career:** Philadelphia Tribune, Philadelphia, PA, reporter/columnist, 1984-86; Pennsylvania Prison Society, Philadelphia, PA, instructor, 1985-89; Bob Lott Production, Philadelphia, PA, scriptwriter, 1986-89; WXPN-FM, Philadelphia, PA, arts host/producer, 1989-90; Village Arts Center, Philadelphia, PA, instructor, 1990-; Walnut St Theatre, Philadelphia, PA, outreach instructor/actress, 1990-; Temple Univ, post graduate teaching fellow in the theatre dept; Theatre Dept, Temple University, adjunct, 1996-. **Orgs:** Member, International Women's League for Peace and Freedom, 1988-; member, National Black Authors Tour, 1989-; member, National Black Storytellers, 1988-; Theater Association of Pennsylvania, 1994; Philadelphia Dramatist Center, 1993. **Honors/Awds:** American Poetry Center Grant, Teacher's Fellowship, 1990; Playwright's Fellowship, Theatre Assn of Pennsylvania, 1990-91; Artist Grant, Philadelphia Neighborhood Arts Project, 1990; Published Books, Negro Kinship, The Pack, Halley's Comet, It Ain't Easy To Be Different, God Made Men Brown, Selrahc Publication, 1982-90; Minneapolis Playwrights Center Exchange Grant, 1993; Writing Partnership Teachers Grant, 1995; Pew Charitable Trust Exchange Playwright with the Minneapolis Playwrights Center, 1996; Lila Wallace Creative Arts Fellow, American Antiquarian Society, 1995-96; Future Faculty Fellowship-Anthropology, 1996; American Antiquarian Society Research Grant/Lila Wallace Creative Artists Grant, 1996-97; Pew Charitable Trust Exchange Grant Penumbra Theatre, Minneapolis, MN, 1996. **Special Achievements:** Published books: Negro Kinship to the Park; Halley's Comet; It Ain't Easy to be Different; God Made Men Brown, Selrahc Publication, 1982-90; Published Books: Envisioning a Sea of Dry Bones, 1994; Epic Memory: Places and Spaces I've Been, 1995. **Business Addr:** Temple University, Theater Department, 13th & Norris St, Philadelphia, PA 19122, (215)204-7341.

WILLIAMS, KNEELY
Clergyman. **Personal:** married Dorothy M. **Educ:** Central Baptist Seminar, 1948; Bethel Baptist Coll, 1979. **Career:** New Hope Baptist Church, pastor. **Orgs:** Pastor New Hope Baptist Church 1985; bd mem NAACP 1985, St Paul OIC 1985, Urban League 1985. **Honors/Awds:** Serv MN State Human Rights 1970, St Paul Human Rights 1975, MN State Council of Churches 1977, MN State Bapt Convention 1980. **Business Addr:** Pastor, New Hope Baptist Church, 1115 Dayton Ave, St Paul, MN 55104.

WILLIAMS, LAFAYETTE W.
Dentist. **Personal:** Born Dec 17, 1937. **Educ:** Morehouse Coll, BS 1960; Meharry Med Coll, DDS 1968. **Career:** Central St Hosp Milledgeville GA, mem staff 1968-69; Pvt Practice Valdosta, dentistry 1969-; Valdosta Nursing Home Intl Nursing Care Center, mem staff. **Orgs:** Mem Valdosta Black Comm Action Group; Beta Kappa Chi; Alpha Phi Alpha; Mason Shriner, 32 Deg; Elk mem; Fedn Dentaire Internatiolnale; trustee Lowndes Co Prog Voters League; mem Nat Assn of Realtors; Am Profnl Practice Assn; Puritan Intl Dental Soc; Am Soc for Preventive Dentirstry; Chicago Soc; Acadeny of Gen Dentistry; Nat Dental Assn; Am Dental Assn; GA; SW Ldist Dental Socs; owner Reasonable Rentals Valdosta-lowndes Co; C of C; NAACP. **Business Addr:** 415 S Ashley St, Valdosta, GA 31601.

WILLIAMS, LARRY
Educator. **Personal:** Born Nov 27, 1965, Washington, DC; son of Sallie E Williams & Eddie N Williams; divorced. **Educ:** Attended Pennsylvania Univ, music, 1983-85; Peabody Conservatory of Music, BA, music, 1988, graduate performance diploma, 1990. **Career:** The New World Symphony Orchestra, 1990-92; Florida International Univ, brass dept, chair, prof of horn, 1990-92; Miami Brass Consort, hornist, 1992-94; Univ of Maryland, Baltimore County; Peabody Institute Preparatory, Brass/Wind Dept, chair, horn instr, 1994-. **Orgs:** The Arts for Talented Youth Program, advisor, 1994-97; The Herald Brass Program, dir, 1994-. **Honors/Awds:** Yale Gordon Trust, Second Prize, Concerto Competition, 1990; Peabody Conservatory, Soloist, Graduation Ceremony, 1990; Peabody Institute, Career Development Grant, 1996-98. **Special Achievements:** CD-The Morpheus Trio, 1998; Ebony Magazine, "Fifty Leaders of Tomorrow," 1995; Peabody News, "Heralding A New Program," 1994; Tours: Japan, Europe, US, 1994-. **Home Addr:** 1101 N Calvert St, Apt 709, Baltimore, MD 21202. **Business Phone:** (410)783-8577.

WILLIAMS, LARRY C.
Attorney. **Personal:** Born May 17, 1931, Seneca, SC; married Theresa; children: Margo, Larry Jr, Edward, John, David Lauren, Joseph. **Educ:** Howard Univ, BA 1954, LLB 1959. **Career:** Houston, Waddy, Bryant & Gardner; Variable Annuity Life Insurance Co.; Corp Counsel Office of DC, asst corp counsel; Larry C Wiliams & ASC, attorney, currently. **Orgs:** Regional Counsel US & Brewers Assn; former gen cnsl Nat Bus League; Nat Funeral Dir & Morticians Assn; United Way of Nat Capitol Area; mem past pres DC C of C; Metro WA Bd Trade; bd Metro YMCA; former bd mem Nat Cncl Christians & Jews; life mem Alpha Phi Alpha Frat Inc; mem 32nd Deg Mason; Shriner; Mecca Temple #10; Mem Transition Commn to Devel Orgn of First City Cncl under Home Rule. **Business Addr:** Attorney, Larry C Williams & Associates, 666 11th St NW, Ste 1050, Washington, DC 20001.

WILLIAMS, LASHINA BRIGETTE
Computer company executive. **Personal:** Born Oct 22, 1957, Houston, TX; daughter of Myrtle Morrow and Chauncey K Morrow Jr; divorced. **Educ:** Prairie View A&M Univ, BS, Mechanical Engineering, 1980; Atlanta Univ, MBA, 1984. **Career:** Phillips Petroleum, mechanical engineer, 1980-82; Digital Equipment,intern, 1983; IBM, Gaithersburg, MD, product planning/program mgmt, 1985-. **Orgs:** Mem, Natl Black MBA Assn, 1983-, Delta Sigma Theta Sor. **Honors/Awds:** IBM Appreciation Award, 1992, 1994; MBA, Forum Speaker, Natl Black MBA Assn, 1986. **Home Addr:** 3819 Ridgeview, Missouri City, TX 77489.

WILLIAMS, LEA E.
Educator, association administrator. **Personal:** Born Dec 21, 1947, Paducah, KY; daughter of Mae Frances Terrell Williams and Nathanial H Williams. **Educ:** Kentucky State Univ, Frankfort KY, BA (with distinction), 1969; Univ of Wisconsin, Milwaukee WI, MS, 1973, Teachers Coll, Columbia Univ, New York NY, MA 1977, EdD 1978. **Career:** Milwaukee Public Schools, WI, sixth grade teacher, 1969-73; Milwaukee Area Tech Coll, WI, ABE instructor, 1973-74; United Negro College Fund, New York NY, program evaluator 1978-80, proposal writer 1980-81, CAI research dir 1981-82, asst dir of Educ Services 1982-86, dir of Educ Services 1982-86, vice pres of Educ Services 1988-89; National Action Council for Minorities in Engineering, exec vice pres 1989-. **Orgs:** Editorial board, Thrust employment journal, 1980-85; panelist, Natl Endowment for the Humanities, 1983-85; Natl Leadership Forum, Amer Council on Educ, 1986; mem, Amer Educ Research Assn, 1986-; consulting editor, NY State Governor's Advisory Comm on Black Affairs, 1987-88; pres, Assn of Black Women in Higher Educ, 1987-89; advisory comm, Assn of Amer Colleges, 1988; commissioner, Natl Assn of Independent Colleges and Univs, 1988-91; exec bd, Amer Assn of Higher Educ, 1989-91; division chair, Natl Assn for Women in Education, 1989-91, editorial board, Initiatives, 1989-; board of governors, Amer Assn of Engineering Societies, 1989-95; board of directors, Triangle Coalition for Science & Technology Educ, 1991-95, vp board of directors, 1993-95; Family Dynamics Inc, board of trustees, 1993-; Advisory Council, Harlem Branch YWCA, 1995-. **Honors/Awds:** Alpha Kappa Mu Honor Society, 1969; Phi Delta Kappa, 1975; author of "The United Negro College Fund in Retrospect" 1980, "The Plight of Junior Faculty at Black Private Colleges" 1985, "Missing, Presumed Lost: Minority Teachers in the Nation's Classroom" 1989; Unity Award in Media for Education Reporting 1990 Awarded by Lincoln Univ in Missouri; Paducah Black Historian Achievement Award in Education, 1991; Kentucky State University, Distinguished Service Award, 1994. **Business Addr:** Exec Vice President, National Action Council for Minorities in Engineering, 350 5th Ave, Ste 2212, New York, NY 10118-2299.

WILLIAMS, LEON LAWSON
Elected official. **Personal:** Born Jul 21, 1922, Weeletka, OK; son of Elvira E Lott Williams and Lloyd R Williams; children: Karen E, Leon L Jr, Susan P Rogers, Penny, Jeffery, Alisa O. **Educ:** San Diego State Univ, BA 1950; Univ of San Diego School of Law, 1961; Natl Univ, Doctorate 1985. **Career:** San Diego County Sheriff Dept, admin officer 1957-66; Neighborhood Youth Corps, dir 1966-70; San Diego Urban League, exec dir 1968; City of San Diego, councilman 1969-82; Federal Mart Corp, consultant, 1972-76; County of San Diego, supervisor, 1983-. **Orgs:** County of San Diego, Bd of Supervisors, chairman, 1985, 1990; dir San Diego Coll of Retailing 1986; life mem NAACP; dir Metro Transit Develop Bd, Natl Assn of Counties; California State Association of Counties, president; dir San Diego Region Water Reclamation Bd; chmn Service Authority for Freeway Emergencies; Alpha Pi Boule of Sigma Pi Phi Fraternity, 1976-91. **Honors/Awds:** Distinguished Serv to Community Black Federation of San Diego County, Greater San Diego Business Assoc, Metro Transit Develop Bd, Natl Cultural Foundation; Outstanding Contribution 1978, Distinguished Serv Awd 1985 NAACP; Black Achievement Awd 1981, Freedom Awd 1981 Action Enterprises; Recognition for being First Black Chairman of the Bd of Supervisors County of San Diego Black Leadership Council 1985. **Business Addr:** County Supervisor, County of San Diego, 1600 Pacific Highway (A500), San Diego, CA 92101.

WILLIAMS, LEONARD, SR.
Director of corrections. **Personal:** Born Sep 7, 1945, Youngstown, OH; son of Arvella Church and Willie (deceased); divorced; children: Leonard Jr, Lucy Arvella, McKenzie Michael. **Educ:** Youngstown State Univ, Youngstown OH, AAS 1973, BS 1975, MS 1979. **Career:** Commercial Shearing, Youngstown OH, draftsman, 1969-70; Youngstown Police Dept, OH, patrolman 1970-77, sergeant 1977-81, lieutenant 1981-85; Youngstown Bd of Education, part-time security officer, 1973-85; Eastern Ohio Forensic Lab, part-time polygraph examiner, 1976-78; Tri-State Lab, part-time polygraph examiner, 1978-85; consultant, East Cleveland OH Civil Service Commn; Cuyahoga County Jail, Cleveland OH, administrator, 1985-87; Univ of Akron OH, prof, 1987-92; Ohio Department of Rehab & Correction, Bureau of Adult Detention, jail inspector, 1992-96; Maitoning County Justice Ctr, director of corrections, currently. **Orgs:** Bd mem, Natl Black Police Assn, 1981-90; co-founder & bd mem, United Humanitarian Fund, 1982-; chair, Eastern

Region NBPA, 1983-87; chair, Natl Black Police Assn, 1986-88; mem, Ohio Court of Claims Public Awareness Advisory Council, 1988-89. **Honors/Awds:** Police Officer of the Year, Bd of Realtors, 1970; Mem of Year, Black Knight Police Assn, 1976; Man of Year, Natl Assn of Negro Bus & Prof Women, 1983; Mem of Year, Eastern Region NBPA, 1984; Renault Robinson Award, NBPA, 1987; author of "Peace Keeping and the Community: A Minority Perspective," 1988, and "Use of Excessive Force in the Minority Community," 1989. **Military Serv:** US Air Force, E-3, 1963-67. **Home Addr:** 223 Greeley Lane, Youngstown, OH 44505.

WILLIAMS, LEROY JOSEPH
Auditor. **Personal:** Born Apr 13, 1937, New Orleans, LA; married Verna M Lewis; children: Linda M Thomes, Gregory C Lewis, Sandra Lewis. **Educ:** Olympic Coll, AA 1969; Univ WA, BA 1972; Univ Puget Sound, grad work 1973-74. **Career:** City of Seattle, City Council Legislative Auditor; Seattle Model City Prgm, fiscal consult 1972-73; The Boeing Co, cost accounting 1972-73, material controller1961-72; USN Exchange Bremerton, buyer 1960-61; Municipality of Metropolitan Seattle, audit manager, 1972-. **Orgs:** Mem Bremerton Sch Bd 1971-77; mem WA St Educ TV Commn 1974-77; mem WA St Ferry Adv Com 1973-77; Williams Pvt Tax Consult 1972-; legislative rep WA St Sch Dir 1974-; mem Hamma Hamma #35 Masonic Lodge Prince Hall Grand Lodge WA Jurisdiction 1965-; mem Cascadian Consistory PHA AASR 1970-; mem Supreme Counsel 33 Deg Mason 1977; mem Sinclair Bapt Ch 1960-; ch sch Supt 1965-70; mem trustee bd 1965-; chtr mem Cr Union Audit Com 1972-73; Worshipful Master Hamma Hamma Lodge #35; mem Olympic Coll Assn of Higher Educ 1973-; mem Aldephil Inst 1975-; African American Affairs Commission, appted by Gov Mike Lowery, 1995. **Military Serv:** USN 3rd class yoeman 1955-59. **Business Addr:** Audit manager, Municipality of Metropolitan Seattle, Municipal Bldg, 600 4th Ave, Seattle, WA 98104.

WILLIAMS, LESLIE J.
Health service administrator. **Personal:** Born Aug 18, 1947, New Orleans, LA; children: Kimberly, Kevin. **Educ:** Southern Univ BR, BS Pre-Med 1967; Southern Univ NO, BS Bus Admin 1975, AA Real Estate 1978. **Career:** VD/Tuberculosis Clinic New Orleans Health Dept, adm dir 1979-83; City Health Dept, deputy dir. **Orgs:** Mem Urban League of Greater New Orleans; mem Natl Assn of Real Estate Brokers; mem Amer Public Health Assn; 32 Degree Mason Ancient & Accepted Scotch Rite of Free Masonry 1980-85; instructor Southern Univ New Orleans 1983-85. **Honors/Awds:** Licensed Real Estate Salesperson LA; Licensed Sanitarian State of LA; Cert of Participation Amer Med Assn 1981. **Military Serv:** AUS commissioned warrant officer 2-11 yrs; Army Achievement Medal; Natl Defense Ribbon. **Business Addr:** Deputy Dir, City Health Department, 1300 Perdido St Rm 8E73, New Orleans, LA 70112.

WILLIAMS, LISA R.
Educator. **Personal:** Born Feb 11, 1964, Toledo, OH; daughter of Mr & Mrs Williams. **Educ:** Wright State Univ, BS, business, 1986, MBA, 1988; Ohio State Univ, MA, 1992, PhD, 1992. **Career:** Dayton Power & Light, market analyst, 1984-87; General Motors, market analyst, 1987; Central State Univ, asst prof of bus, 1988-89; Penn State Univ, asst prof of bus logistics, 1992-. **Orgs:** Council of Logistics Management, 1990-; Amer Society of Transport & Logistics, 1992-; Alpha Kappa Alpha Sorority, 1990-; African Amer Women Investment Group, treasurer, 1993-. **Honors/Awds:** Penn state Univ, Teaching Excellence Award, 1997; Council of Logistics Management, Logistics Fellow, 1991; Wright State Univ, Four Year Academic Scholarship, 1982-86; Ohio State Univ, Univ Graduate Fellow, 1989-90; Penn State Univ, Faculty Research Grant, 1992-94; Wright State Univ, Dean's List, 1983-84. **Special Achievements:** First African-Amer Woman to Graduate with PhD in Bus from Ohio State, 1992; Book: Evolution Status & Future of the Corp Transportation Function, 1991; "Understanding Distribution Channels: Interorganizational Study of EDI," 1994; "Moving Toward LIS Theory Dev: A Framework of Adoption," 1995; "Shipper, Carrier & Consultant Perspectives of EDI," 1995. **Business Addr:** Asst Prof, Business Logistics, Penn State University, College of Business Administration, 509K Business Administration Bldg, University Park, PA 16802, (814)863-3563.

WILLIAMS, LLOYD L.
Legislator. **Personal:** Born Jul 26, 1944, St Thomas, Virgin Islands of the United States; married Irene Creque; children: Lisa Marie, Taya Ayanna. **Educ:** Moravian College, BA 1966; New York Univ, MA Cert Orthodics & Presthetics; VA Commonwealth Univ, MA Cert; Am Univ Wash DC, Master's, political science. **Career:** Youth Club in Action, adv tut; Wayhne Aspinall JHS, teacher, Dept of Social Welfare, vocational rehab counselor; VI Legislature, special asst to legislator, 1972; VI 10th, 11th, 12th & 13th Legislatures, majority leader, 1976-78; VI 14th Legislature, senator; Public Safety Commission, chair. **Orgs:** Mem Task Force Criminal Code Rev Proj; mem Board Tri-Island Eco Devel Council; mem Bd VI Montessori Sch Delegate to Constl Conv.

WILLIAMS, LOIS STOVALL
Educational administrator. **Personal:** marrIed Dr Anderson J Williams Jr; children: Eight. **Educ:** Morgan State Univ, bachelor's degree, natural sciences; Loyola College, master's degree, psychology; Univ of Connecticut, doctorate degree, higher education administration; Harvard Univ, Inst for Educational Mgmt, certificate. **Career:** Norfolk State Univ, prof of psychology, 14 years; Hampton Univ, Center for Teaching Excellence, director; American Testing Services, sr vp of administration; Passaic County Community College, dean of instruction; Knoxville College, president, 1995-. **Special Achievements:** First female president of Knoxville College, 1995. **Business Addr:** President, Knoxville College, 901 College St, Knoxville, TN 37921, (615)524-6500.

WILLIAMS, LONDELL
Government official. **Personal:** Born Apr 23, 1939, Texarkana, AR; married Mary. **Educ:** Los Angeles St Coll, BA 1958; Los Angeles Bible Inst, dD 1960; Univ AR 1953-55. **Career:** Ave Bapt Ch, pastor 1969-; Dept HEW Soc Security Admn, claims Develr 1969-; AUS, personnel specl 1964-68; US Treas Dept Bur Customs, acctg tech 1958-59; AUS Corps Engr, contract specl 1955-58. **Orgs:** City Bd Dir Texarkana AR 1977-; mem Texarkana AR & Texarkana TX C of C 1976-; jury commr Miller, Hempstead, Lafayette, Howard 1975-76; bd mem Texarkana Human Devel Ctr 1977; grand mastger Master Mason AF & AM Bronzeville Lodge 83 1974-77; Texarkana Ministerial Alliance 1971-77. **Honors/Awds:** Bert Lambert Awd 1974-75; Otsdng Integrity & Character Displayed in City 1973; high quality Increase Awd HEW 1976; Sharp Shooter Awd; Good Conduct Medal . **Military Serv:** AUS Lambert Awd 1974-75; Otsdng Integrity & Character Displayed in City 1959-61. **Business Addr:** Po BOX 1214, State Line, Texarkana, TX 75501.

WILLIAMS, LONNIE RAY
Educational administrator. **Personal:** Born Jan 21, 1954, Stephens, AR; son of Rosie M Williams and Lonnie Williams; married Mary Woods, Apr 10, 1987; children: Landra, Kevin, Keaton. **Educ:** Univ of AR, Fayetteville, BSBA, 1977, MEd, 1983, EdS, 1991. **Career:** Univ of Arkansas-Fayetteville, police patrolman, 1976-78, night mgr, student union, 1978-84, dir minority engineering, 1983-86, asst dean of students, 1986-91, assistant vice chancellor for student services, 1991-. **Orgs:** Region V, adv bd mem, Natl Soc of Black Engineers, 1984-87; Region B, chairperson elect, NAMEPA 1985-86; chairperson, Arkansas Assn for Multicultural Counselling, 1986-87; mem, Arkansas Assn for Counseling Guidance & Devel, 1986-; mem, Omega Psi Phi Fraternity; bd mem, Washington County Equal Opportunity Agency, 1988-91; mem, North Arkansas Girl Scouts of America Board of Directors; Arkansas Association for Multicultural Counseling & Development, president-elect, 1993-95, president, 1995-97; Arkansas College Personnel Association, executive board member, 1992-96; Arkansas Counseling Assn, executive board member, 1994-97; American Counseling Assn, member, 1995-; American College Personnel Assn, member, 1995-; National Assn of Student Personnel Administrators, member, 1997. **Honors/Awds:** Outstanding Serv, Univ of Arkansas Chapter, NSBE, 1983-86; Co-Outstanding Adv Bd Mem, Region V Adv Bd, NSBE, 1985; Outstanding Faculty/Staff Mem Black Student Association, 1987; Employee of the Year, Professional Non-faculty, Univ of Arkansas, 1991; Advisor of the Year, Arkansas Black Students Assn, 1993. **Home Addr:** 13162 Reed Rd, Fayetteville, AR 72701-9778.

WILLIAMS, LORECE P.
Educator. **Personal:** Born Jan 22, 1927, Luling, TX; married Nathan H; children: Nicholas, Natalie. **Educ:** Huston Tillotson Coll, BS 1947; Our Lady Lake Coll, MSW 1962; Tulane Univ New Orleans, further study. **Career:** ARC Brooke Army Med Ctr, dir 1969-; Our Lady Lake Coll, prof social work 1965-69; Incarnate Word Coll San Antonio, diagnostician 1969, lectr, cons, group ldr - San Antonio Jr League at Incarnate Word College, Trinity University, Texas University, church groups, social work agencies, schs, natl assn Social Workers; Council Social Work Edn. **Orgs:** Faculty Welfare Council; Admissions & Schlrshp; Alpha Kappa Alpha Sorority; Race & Rel Commn; Sex & Religion; Status Women; Governors Commn Crime & Prevention; Cath Family & Child bd dir; Child Serv Bureau bd dir. **Honors/Awds:** Excellence in Writing Awds; Theta Sigma Phi, Growing Up - Texas, pub 1972; co-author Bientennial Book, Folklore Texas Cultures. **Business Addr:** 411 SW 24 St, San Antonio, TX 78285.

WILLIAMS, LORENZO
Professional basketball player. **Personal:** Born Jul 15, 1969, Ocala, FL. **Educ:** Polk Community Coll; Stetson. **Career:** Charlotte Hornets, center, 1992; Orlando Magic, 1992; Boston Celtics, 1993; Orlando Magic, 1993; Charlotte Hornets, 1994; Dallas Mavericks, 1994-96; Washington Wizards, 1996-. **Business Addr:** Professional Basketball Player, Washington Wizards, MCI Center, 601 F St NW, Washington, DC 20071, (301)622-3865.

WILLIAMS, LOTTIE MAE
Government official. **Personal:** Born Sep 2, 1931, Kinloch, MO; daughter of Ora Pearl Townsend Cherry and John B Hughes; married Ronald D Williams, Jun 25, 1977; children: Oranda Celastine Burns, Lenora Goolsby. **Educ:** Florissant Valley Junior Coll, St Louis MO, degree in accounting, 1972; St Louis Univ, St Louis MO, liberal arts degree 1980, urban affairs degree 1982. **Career:** General Amer Insurance, St Louis MO, claims examiner, 1966-67; Bozada Drayage, St Louis MO, office mgr, 1967-71; City of St Louis MO, asst accountant, 1971-73; State Arts Council, St Louis MO, fiscal/budget officer, 1973-76; City of St Louis MO, Child Nutrition Dept, food monitor/budget officer, 1977-80; City of Velda Village MO, mayor, 1981-83 & 1987-97. **Orgs:** Mem 1969-, deaconess 1982-, Christ Pilgrim Rest MB Church; project dir, Cultural & Recreation Center, 1976-78; mem 1978-, bd of dir 1979-87, Lupus Foundation of MO; mem, League of Women Voters, 1979-; sec 1981-83, mem 1987-, treas 1988-, MO Chapter of Black Mayors; mem, St Louis County Municipal League, 1981-83 & 1987-; mem 1981-83, city rep 1987-, MO Municipal League; co-chair, Citizens for County Progress, 1985-; chair, Task Force to Monitor the Metropolitan Sewer District, 1986-; bd of dir, Health Care Is a Human Right, 1986-; bd of dir, Coalition for the Environment, 1986-; bd of dir, Municipal Radio Systems, 1987-; co-host, radio talk show on KIRL, 1987-; mem, Task Force Comm for County Reorganization, St Louis County Municipal League, 1988; mem, Natl Conf of Black Mayors, 1988-; vice chair, Black Elected Officials for Balanced Govt, 1989, second vice president, 1993-95. **Honors/Awds:** Women in Management Award, Univ of Kansas, 1974; Governmental Acct Award, US Civil Service Commn, 1976; Electronic Data Processing award, MO State In-Service Training, 1976; Back to School Award, MO Natl Educ Assn, 1981; Certificate of Appreciation, Amer Cablevision, 1982; Certificate of Appreciation, MO House of Reps, 1982; Certificate of Appreciation, Natl League of Cities' Women in Municipal Govt, 1983; Certificate of Recognition, Campaign for Human Dignity, 1985; Certificate of Appreciation, Bethel African Methodist Episcopal Church, 1987; Certificate of Appreciation, St Louis County Municipal League, 1988. **Special Achievements:** Drew Map to reorganize St Louis Co. Council to enable African Americans to be elected; first African American female mayor elected in Missouri, 1981. **Home Addr:** 7100 Lexington, Velda Village, MO 63121.

WILLIAMS, LOUIS NATHANIEL
Educator. **Personal:** Born Dec 27, 1929, Atlanta, GA; son of Natalie Crawford Williams and Phillip James Williams; married Charlotte Howard (divorced 1986). **Educ:** Tennessee State Univ, Nashville, TN, BS, 1950; Howard Univ, Washington, Dc, MS, 1952; Univ of Washington, Seattle, WA, PhD, 1959. **Career:** Florida Normal College, St Augustine, FL, prof of psychology, 1960-61; Shaw Univ, Raleigh, NC, assistant professor of psychology, 1967-69; Univ of the District of Columbia, Washington, DC, professor of psychology, 1969-87. **Orgs:** Nominated as pres-elect, Association of Black Psychologists, 1989. **Honors/Awds:** President, Sigma Rho Sigma Honor Society, Tennessee State Univ, 1950; Fellowship, Howard University, MS degree, 1950. **Military Serv:** Army, SP2, 1954-56; Most Outstanding Soldier in Basic Training. **Home Addr:** 1994 Pine Cone Dr, SW, Atlanta, GA 30331.

WILLIAMS, LOUISE BERNICE
City official. **Personal:** Born May 30, 1937, Abinton, PA; daughter of Mary Grasty Duncan and Richard S. Duncan; divorced; children: Cynthia Whitfield, Robert Whetts, Brian Whetts, Kimberly Williams. **Educ:** Lancaster School of Business, exec sec 1964; Lincoln Univ attended; Shippenburg State Coll, Cert for Dist Justices 1973. **Career:** Dist Justice Office, admin clerk 1970-73; City of Lancaster 3rd & 7th Ward, dist justice 1973-85; Consolidated Dist Justice Offices City of Lancaster, admin dist justice 1983-85. **Orgs:** Mem Planned Parenthood of Lancaster 1978-81, Urban League of Lancaster 1979-84; pres Girls Serv of Lancaster Inc 1975-81, NAACP 1980-82; mem Lancaster County District Justice Assn; bd mem Planned Parenthood of Lancaster County 1988-; mem Commn of Cultural Diversity Millersville Univ. **Honors/Awds:** Boss of the Year Amer Business Women's Assoc 1976; Outstanding Citizen City of Lancaster 1981; Past Pres Awd Girls Serv of Lancaster Inc 1981. **Home Addr:** 331 S Franklin St, Lancaster, PA 17602. **Business Addr:** 308 E King St, Lancaster, PA 17602.

WILLIAMS, LUCRETIA MURPHY
Educational administrator. **Personal:** Born Aug 16, 1941, Springfield, OH; daughter of Lenore Dorsey Smith and Wilbur Otho Murphy; children: David Walter Bentley, Robin Lenore. **Educ:** Central State Univ, BS, Elementary Educ, 1965, MEd, Guidance & Counseling, 1969; Ohio State Dept of Educ, gen aptitude test battery training, vocational guidance training certification, 1974; Xavier University, admin certification elementary & secondary, 1976. **Career:** Onondago Co Welfare, social worker, 1966-67; AT&T Technologies, personnel counselor, summer, 1970; Columbus Public Schools, guidance counselor, 1969-77, asst principal, 1977-78; Neptune Township Public Schools, principal, 1978-79; Columbus Public Schools, admin, 1979-. **Orgs:** Life mem, Natl Alliance of Black School Employees; mem, Natl Assn of Secondary School Principals, Ohio Alliance of Black School Educ, Columbus Alliance of Black School Educ, Columbus Admin Assn, Columbus Central Office Admin Assn; Delta Sigma Theta; mem, Circle-Lets, Inc; mem, Mayor's Council on Youth. **Honors/Awds:** A Comparative Study of Faculty Knowledge of Guidance Serv in the High Schools of

Springfield, OH, Master Thesis, Central State Univ, 1969; Columbus Area Leadership Program, 1989; Commendation Ohio House of Reps, 1988, 1992; Commendation Ohio Senate, 1992. **Special Achievements:** Author of "Columbus Schools, Police Unite for Zero Tolerance," School Safety Update, Nov 1996. **Business Addr:** Columbus Public Schools, 270 E State St, Columbus, OH 43215.

WILLIAMS, MACEO MERTON
Educational administrator, cleric. **Personal:** Born Oct 27, 1939, Baltimore, MD; married Margaret D Moon. **Educ:** Morgan State Univ, AB 1966; Univ of Baltimore, MPA program, 1975-76; Wesley Theological Seminary, M Div Prog 1985; Howard Univ, MDiv 1986; Howard Univ Divinity Sch, DMin 1991. **Career:** State of MD, probation agent 1965-66; Dept of Housing, area coord 1966-71; Concentrated Employ Program US Dept Labor, coord 1971-74; MD Parole Comm, parole comm appointed by Gov Harry Hughes 1983-88; Bay Coll of MD, dean of students 1974-79; Centreville-Cordova Charge United Methodist Church, pastor 1986-90; Simpson United Methodist Church, pastor, 1991-95; Martin Luther King Jr Memorial United Methodist Church, pastor, 1995-. **Orgs:** Mem NAACP 1962-; bd mem Dept of Housing & Comm Devel United Meth Ch 1970-; pres Five in Five Dem Club 1974; Charter Revision Commn 1974-76; bd of trustees Keswick Nursing Home 1973-76; mem Prince Hall Grand Lodge F&AM of MD Zion Lodge #4; mem Natl Assn of Student Svcs; mem Natl Assn of Coll Couns; Morgan state Univ Alumni; Howard Univ Alumni; life mem, Black methodists for Church Renewal; life mem, NAACP; Baltimore City Coll, Hall of Fame, 1997. **Special Achievements:** Maryland Parole Comm, parole comm appointed by Gov Harry Hughes, 1983-88, appointed by Gov William Donald Schaefer, 1989-93, 1994-99. **Business Addr:** Pastor, Martin Luther King Jr Memorial United Methodist Church, 5114 Windsor Mill Rd, Baltimore, MD 21207.

WILLIAMS, MALCOLM DEMOSTHENES. See Obituaries section.

WILLIAMS, MALVIN A.
Educator. **Personal:** Born Apr 20, 1942, Mayersville, MS; son of Catherine Williams and Oscar Williams; married Delores G; children: Angela, Katrina, Tiffany, Malvin Jr. **Educ:** Alcorn State Univ, BS 1962; AZ State Univ, MNS 1966; Univ of Southwestern LA, PhD 1971-75. **Career:** Greenville Public Schools, instructor 1962-65; Alcorn State Univ, instructor 1966-71, registrar & asst dean 1975-76, vp of academic affairs 1976-. **Orgs:** Bd dirs Watson Chapel AME Church 1975-; mem planning/steering comm Mgmt Info System Jackson MS 1979-; bd dirs Claiborne Co Chamber of Comm 1982-; chmn Council of Chief Academic Officers 1984-86. **Honors/Awds:** Sci Faculty Fellowship Awd NSF 1971-72; ASU Ed Office Personnel Assoc Boss of the Year 1982. **Business Addr:** Vice Pres of Academic Affairs, Alcorn State University, 1000 ASU Drive #869, Lorman, MS 39096.

WILLIAMS, MARCUS DOYLE
Judge, lecturer. **Personal:** Born Oct 24, 1952, Nashville, TN; son of Pansy D Williams and John F Williams; married Carmen Myrie Williams MD; children: Aaron Doyle, Adam Myrie. **Educ:** Fisk Univ, BA, 1973 (university honors); Catholic Univ of Amer, School of Law, JD, 1977. **Career:** Office of the Commonwealth Atty, asst commonwealth atty, 1978-80; George Mason Univ, lecturer in business legal studies, 1980-95; Office of the County Atty, asst county atty, 1980-87; Gen Dist Court, judge, 1987-90; Circuit Court, judge, 1990-; National Judicial College, faculty, 1992. **Orgs:** Bd mem, Fairfax-Falls Church, Criminal Justice Adv Bd, 1980-81; freelance writer and reviewer, 1981-; mem, Amer Business Law Assn, 1984-; bd of assocs, St Paul's Coll, 1986-87; vice chmn, Continuing Legal Educ Comm, Fairfax Bar Assn, 1986-87; Virginia delegate, National Conference of Special Court Judges, 1990; Omega Psi Phi Fraternity, 1971. **Honors/Awds:** Beta Kappa Chi, Scientific Honor Soc, Fisk Univ Chapter, 1973; Distinguished Youth Award, Office of the Army, Judge Advocate Gen, 1976; Thomas J Watson Fellow, 1977-78; Fairfax County Bd of Supvr, Serv Commendation, 1987; Serv Appreciation Award, Burke-Fairfax Jack & Jill, 1989; Service Appreciation Award, Black Law Students Assn of Catholic University, 1990; Otis Smith Alumnus Award, 1997; American Participant Program Lectures, Liberia, Zambia, Botswana, sponsored by USIA, 1990; articles: "Arbitration of Intl Commercial Contracts: Securities and Antitrust Claims," Virginia Lawyer, 1989, "European Antitrust Law and its Application to Amer Corp," Whittier Law Review, 1987, "Judicial Review: The Guardian of Civil Liberties and Civil Rights," George Mason University Civil Rights Law Journ 1991, "Lawyer, Judge, Solicitor, General Education: A Tribute to Wade H McCree, Jr," National Black Law Journal, 1990. **Business Addr:** Judge, Circuit Court, 4110 Chain Bridge Rd, Fairfax, VA 22030.

WILLIAMS, MARGARET ANN
Government official. **Personal:** Born Dec 25, 1954, Kansas City, MO. **Educ:** Trinity College; The Annenberg School of Communications, Univ of PA. **Career:** The White House, Office of Hilary Clinton, asst to the pres & chief of staff to the first lady, currently. **Business Phone:** (202)456-6266.

WILLIAMS, MARGO E.
Journalist. **Personal:** Born Dec 30, 1947, St Louis, MS; daughter of Bertha Williams and James R Williams. **Educ:** Harris Teachers Coll, BA, 1970; St Louis Univ, MA, 1972; Southern Illinois Univ, BA, 1975; St Louis Univ, Post Grad. **Career:** St Louis Bd of Educ, teacher/counselor, 1970-75; KMOX-TV, CBS, St Louis, TV teacher, 1973-75; Southern Illinois Univ, acad advisor, 1975-76; WMAR-TV, Baltimore, MD, host/producer, 1976-77; WKBN-TV, CBS, Youngstown, OH, minority affairs dir, 1977-82; TV & radio producer/host, WKBN-TV, CBS, Youngstown, OH, 1982-88; News reporter/writer WKBD TV, Detroit, MI, producer/host "For The Record," Black History segments, society freelance writer, Detroit News, Detroit, MI; president/CEO, Margo E Williams & Associates, Inc, Public Relations Firm, Detroit, MI, 1990; Barden Cablevision, senior producer, 1989-92; The Crisis, Black Enterprise, freelance writer. **Orgs:** Mem, Alpha Kappa Alpha, NAACP, Urban League, Soc of Professional Journalists; vice pres, Amer Business Women's Assoc, 1983-87; chmn, Ways & Means Comm, 1984, Altrusa Club Intl; media-workshop coord, Natl Assn of Black Journalist, 1983-84; coord, Women's Career Workshops; vice pres, Natl Assn of Black Journalists, Jim Dandy Ski Club; hosted, United Negro Coll Telethon, ABC, Youngstown, OH; co-coord, Afro-Amer Festival, Youngstown, OH; pres, Consumer Credit Advisory Bd, Youngstown, OH; pres, Natl Assn of Black Journalists, Detroit Chapter; Your Heritage House Writers; Women's Economic Club; Natl Assn of Women Business Owners; bd mem, Booker T Washington Business Assn; bd mem, Family Services of Detroit & Wayne County, 1995-. **Honors/Awds:** Received 15 Community Serv Awards, 1977-84; Outstanding Black Woman in the Media; Ohio Media Award, Honored for Community Serv with a special resolution & plaque from Youngstown City Council; Appeared in Glamour Magazine Career Section; Woman of the Year Award, 1982; appeared in Ebony Magazine, Broadcasting Magazine, Millimeter Magazine & RCA Today Magazine; Guest Speaker, Special Programs, Black History Month, Youngstown State Univ;Motivational Speaker, Women's Conf of Concerns, Detroit, MI, 1989; Black Professionals In Film and Video Award, 1991. **Home Addr:** 615 Griswold, #820, Detroit, MI 48226.

WILLIAMS, MARTHA S.
Educator. **Personal:** Born Nov 30, 1921, Philadelphia, PA; divorced. **Educ:** State Coll, BS 1949; Wayne St U, MSLS 1971. **Career:** Foch School, arts teacher 1974-; Detroit Schools, librarian 1964-74; teacher, owner of nursery school 1949-64; Phil Tribune, newspaper exper 1942-44; Gary Neigh House, dir of nursery prog; Bristol England, exchange teacher 1977. **Orgs:** Mem Am Lib Assn; Asso Sch Libr; Mich Assn Media Edn; Active in Rep Party 1952-; prec del Gary IN 1952-; v chmn Gary City Rep Comm; del StateConv 1954-; del Rep Nat Conv 1976; Mich Rep State Comm Nat Black Rep Counc; mem 5th Pct Police Comm Coun; mem Grtr Christ Bapt Ch; mem Sch Comm Coun Apptd by Pres Ford to Adv Comm to Nat Comm on Lib & Inform Serv 1977; mem Delta Sigma Theta Sor. **Home Addr:** 18840 Orleans, Detroit, MI 48203.

WILLIAMS, MATTHEW ALBERT
Physician. **Personal:** Born Jun 24, 1929, Atlanta, GA; son of Alberta Hendricks Williams and Charles R Williams; married Vira E Kennedy; children: Linda M Lucas, Nanci J Newell, Pamela L Steele. **Educ:** Morehouse Clg Atlanta, Ga, BS 1950; Howard Univ Washington DC, MD 1955; Harbor Gen Hosp Torrance, CA, Int Med 1961. **Career:** Paradise Vly Med Staff, pres 1975-77; Matthew A Williams MD Med Corp, pres, currently. **Orgs:** Mem Am Clg of Physicians; Am Soc of Int Med; Alpha Pi Boule; Alpha Omega Alpha; Hnr Med Soc; mem executive committee, Paradise Valley Hosp; past mem cncl San Diego Med Soc 1977; past mem cncl San Diego Soc of Int Med 1977; mem Bd of Overseers Univ of CA at San Diego 1984; mem Alpha Phi Alpha Frat. **Honors/Awds:** Elder Untd Pres Ch. **Military Serv:** USN lt comm med 1955-58. **Home Addr:** 5740 Daffodil Ln, San Diego, CA 92120. **Business Addr:** President, Matthew A Williams MD, 502 Euclid Ave, Ste 201, National City, CA 91950.

WILLIAMS, MAXINE BROYLES
Social worker. **Personal:** Born Aug 6, Pittsburgh, PA; widowed. **Educ:** Wilberforce U, BS; Univ of M, Adv Social Admn; WSU, Ldrshp Training & Pub; WCSW, In-Training Pgm Cert Ed Soc Serv. **Career:** Wayne Co Mental & Estates Div 1966-73; Wayne Co Dept Soc Welfare 1949-66; Wane Co Probate Ct Med Div 1940-45. **Orgs:** Dir Publicity & Pub Rel Communication Commn; St Matthew's & St Joseph's Epis Ch; exec bd mem African Art Gallery Com, vestry-woman St Matthew's & St Joseph's Epis Ch; pub relat chrwmn AAGC; fdrs Soc Detroit Inst of Arts; consult Santa Rosa Comm Grp; mem Women's ComUnited Negro Clg Fund; Cathedral Ch of St Paul Chpt; coord Cncl on Human Relat; Ch Women United; League of Women Voters; Detroit Assc of Women's Clbs; Detroit Hist Soc; Intrntl Inst; Metro YWCA; NW Voters Regis Grp; Alpha Kappa Alpha Sor; Alpha Rho Omega Detroit; NAACP; Detroit Friends of Pub Libr Inc; Detroit Urban League; Soc Wrkrs Clb of Detroit; fdrs Soc Detroit Inst of Art; exec bd mem Women's Council United Negro Coll fund; chmn Annual Banquet UNGF; exec bd Amer Assoc Univ Women; pres ParishCouncil St Matthew's & St Jos Episcopal Church. **Honors/Awds:** Humanitarian Awd Wo-He-Lo Literary Soc; 15 yr Serv Pin Detroit Urban League 1953-68; 30 Yr Serv Medallion Alpha Kappa Alpha Sor 1946-77; num awrds for Vol Work & Comm Partic; Spirit of Detroit Awd in Recognition of Exceptional Achievement Outstanding Leadership and Dedication to Improving the Quality of Life; Awd of Merit of many years of serv to Friends of African Art Founders Soc Detroit Inst of Arts; Community Awd Volunteer Work Detroit Receiving Hosp; Nation-Wide Net Work Participant Boston MA Convention, Amer Assn Univ of Women; Citation Detroit Church Woman United; Induction Prestigious Quarter Century Club Natl Urban league; Annual meeting Los Angeles CA Detroit Citation AAUW 25 Yr Serv Pin Detroit Urban League; Gen Chairperson & Coord Anniv Celebrations StMattew's St Jospeh's Ecopal Church; 1941-86. **Home Addr:** 9000 E Jefferson F4, Apt 7, Detroit, MI 48214.

WILLIAMS, MCCULLOUGH, JR.
Mortician. **Personal:** Born Nov 27, 1927, Youngstown, OH; son of Marcielette Boisseau Williams and McCullough Williams; married Juanita Fleming, Dec 2, 1951; children: McCullough III, Crystal A Costa, Sterling A. **Educ:** Cleveland College of Mortuary Science, mortuary science, 1950. **Career:** McCullough Williams Funeral Home, owner, 1951; president, 1977-; Williams Publishing Co, chairman, 1983-92. **Orgs:** Youngstown Bd of Educ, mem, 1970-76, pres, 1973-76; Board of Funeral Directors and Embalmers of Ohio, president, 1987-92; Butler Institute of American Art, board of trustees, 1986-; Northeastern Ohio Educational Television, board of trustees, 1988-92; Youngstown/Mahoning County Visitors Bureau, executive board, 1989-; Belmont Ave Revitalization Project, chairman, 1992-; 50/50 Role Models, past president, 1992; Roberts Deliberating Club, president, 1952-92; Youngstown State University Committee 2000, 1992-. **Honors/Awds:** Youngstown Area Chamber of Commerce, Youngstowner Award Community Service, 1992; Roberts Deliberating Club, Human Relations Award, 1958; Links, High Lites in Blacks, 1974; City of Youngstown, Education for Civic Responsibility, 1987; US Small Business Administration, Ohio Minority Advocate of the Year, 1988; Interdenominational Women Clergy, Family Man of the Year, 1989; Ohio Black Expo, Black Businessman of the Year, 1990; Ohio State Univ, 50/50 Role Model, Community Service Honoree, 1994; Curbstone Coaches Athletics Hall of Fame, 1995. **Special Achievements:** Youngstown, third ward councilman, 1957-61. **Business Addr:** President, Sterling-McCullough Williams Funeral Home, 632 Belmont Ave, Youngstown, OH 44502.

WILLIAMS, MCDONALD
Educator, editor (retired). **Personal:** Born Nov 13, 1917, Pittsburgh; son of Margaaret Bailey Williams and Alexander McDonald Williams; married Jamye Harris Coleman Williams, Dec 28, 1943; children: Donna Williams Selby. **Educ:** Univ Pittsburgh, BA 1939, LittM 1942; OH State Univ, PhD 1954. **Career:** Wilberforce Univ OH, educator 1942-56; Tuskegee Inst, visiting prof, Eng, 1955; Morris Brown Coll GA, educator 1956-58; Atlanta Univ, 1957; TN State Univ, educator, honors program dir 1958-88; AME Church Review, Nashville, TN, associate editor, 1984-92. **Orgs:** Modern Language Assn; mem NW Nashville Civitan Club; exec com Northwest YMCA Center; exec com Nashville Br NAACP 1968-; Alpha Phi Alpha, Sigma Pi Phi, Golden Key. **Honors/Awds:** Teacher of the Year, TN State Univ 1979; Corp sec NW Nashville Civitan Clb; coeditor "The Negro Speaks: The Rhetoric of Contempory Black Leaders"; Outstanding Service Award, Tennessee State University, 1988; Wellness Ctr at Northwest YMCA renamed McDonald Williams Wellness Ctr; Honors Ctr at Tennessee State University, renamed McDonald Williams Honors Ctr, 1995.

WILLIAMS, MELVIN
University administrator. **Personal:** Born Jun 17, 1944, Kansas City, MO; son of Naomi Long; married Beate Charlotte Farran; children: Amy, Micah, Jonah. **Educ:** Pittsburg State Univ, BS Ind Tech 1967, MS Sociology 1973. **Career:** Peace Corps, volunteer 1967-69; Southeast KS Comm Act Program, dir social serv 1970-76; Vista Prog, dir, 1974-76; City of Parsons, Comm Development & Affirmative Action, asst dir, 1976-78; Univ of KS, Med Ctr, Affirmative Action, dir, 1978-, asst hospital admini, 1981-84; NIH Biomedical Research Apprenticeship Program, dir, 1981-84; Health Careers Pathways Program, Post Baccalaureate Program, dir, 1986-. **Orgs:** SDOP Mid-America Synod, pres, 1971-90; Greater KC Assn for Affirmative Action, mem, 1978-83, pres, 1981-82; American Assn for Affirmative Action, mem, 1981-; Natl Ass of Minority Med Educ, mem, 1985-; Children's Ctr for the Visually Impaired, 1979-87, treas, 1984-86; Lollipop Foundation, founding mem, 1984-87; Leadership 2000, charter bd mem, 1985-87; City of Mission, KS, councilman, 1985-; KUMC Credit Union, bd of dirs, 1985-89; Planned Parenthood of Greater Kansas City, mem, bd of dirs, 1994-; Kansas League of Municipalities, bd of dirs, 1994; United Comm Services, bd of dirs, 1995-. **Honors/Awds:** KC's 50 Most Influential Black Americans, 1983; Black Achiever Kansas City, MO, SCLS, 1986; Grant Health Careers Pathways Program, Div of Disadvantaged Assistance 1986-; Post Baccalaureate Program, 1990-; Minority Apprenticeship Program, NIH, 1981-94; Edward V Williams, MD Awardee, 1991. **Business Addr:** Dir, Univ of KS Medical Center, 39th & Rainbow Blvd, Kansas City, KS 66160.

WILLIAMS, MELVIN D.
Educational administrator. **Personal:** Born Feb 3, 1933, Pittsburgh, PA; son of Gladys and Aaron; married Faye W Strawder; children: Aaron E, Steven R, Craig H. **Educ:** Univ of Pittsburgh, AB Econ (Honors), 1955; Univ of Pittsburgh, MA Anthropology, 1969, PhD Anthropology, 1973; Carlow Coll, Natl Certificate in Secondary Educ, 1973. **Career:** Wholesale periodical Distr Co, owner-oper, 1955-66; Johnson Publishing Co, field representive, 1958-61; NDEA Title IV, fellow anthropology, 1966-69; Carlow Coll, faculty instr, asst prof, dept of sociology & anthropology, 1969-75; Colgate Univ, Olive B O'Connor, chair, 1976-77; Univ of Pittsburgh, faculty, assoc prof, anthropology, 1976-79; Intl Journal of Cultural & Social Anthropology, assoc editor of ethnology, 1976-79; Univ of Pittsburgh, adj research prof, anthropology, 1979-82; Purdue Univ, faculty, prof of anthropology, dept of sociology & anthropology, 1979-83; Univ of Maryland Coll Park, affil prof, urban studies, 1984-88, faculty prof of anthropology, 1983-88; Univ of Michigan, faculty, prof of anthropology, 1988-, dir, Comprehensive Studies Program, 1988-91. **Orgs:** 24 acad committees including chmn minority affairs comm, Colgate Univ, affirm action comm, Colgate Univ; deans grad review bd, Faculty of Arts & Sci, Univ of Pittsburgh, rep faculty assembly Univ of Pittsburgh; Univ senate, Purdue Univ; chancellors commiss on ethnic minority issues Univ of Maryland, campus senate to represent anthropology & Afro-Amer studies, Univ of Maryland, pres, Black Faculty Staff assoc, Univ of Maryland; Ombudsman, 1991-93, senate assembly, 1993-96, University of Michigan; 24 mem incl fellow vstg lecturer Amer Anthropological Assoc, Amer Assoc of Univ Prof, Anthropological Soc of Washington, Phi Delta Kappa, pres, org NAACP, Sigma XI, Soc of Ethnic & Special Studies, NYAS, fellow Soc of Applied Anthropology, Deans Council, Univ of Michigan. **Honors/Awds:** 53 publications incl "Observations in Pittsburgh Ghetto Schools" Anthrop Educ Quarterly 1981; "On the St Where I Lived" Holt Rinehart & Winston 1981; "Notes from a Black Ghetto in Pittsburgh" Critical Perspective of Third World Amer Race Class Culture in Amer 1983; "Community in a Black Pentecostal Church"; 51 honors & awards incl Black Achiever Award by Talk Mag, Hon Reception in Recognition of Scholarly Achievements by Dept of Anthrop Univ of Pittsburgh 1975; MC, The Presidents Dinner for Graduating Seniors, Carlow Coll 1975; Bishops Serv Award, Catholic Diocese of Pittsburgh 1975; Hadley Cantril Memorial Award 1976; received highest teaching evaluations in the history of the univ 1976; keynote speaker, Afro-Amer Family Conf, Purdue Univ; invitedspeaker, Martin Luther King Program, 1. **Military Serv:** AUS, PA Natl Guard. **Business Addr:** Prof, Dept of Anthropology, Univ of Michigan, 1054 LS&A Bldg, Ann Arbor, MI 48109.

WILLIAMS, MELVIN WALKER
Physician. **Personal:** Born Jan 28, 1939, New York, NY; son of Wilhelmina Curtis Williams and Shirley C Williams; married Marilyann Thomas; children: Jennifer, Martin. **Educ:** Fordham Univ, BS 1960; Howard Univ, MD 1967; Harvard University School of Public Health, MPH 1973. **Career:** US Public Health Serv Hosp, internship 1967-68; US Public Health Serv, commd ofcr 1967-77, 1980-; St Elizabeth's Hosp, 1968-70; MA Gen Hosp Boston, residency 1970-73; NIMH-Staff Coll, assoc dir 1973-77; Job Corp Hlth Office, US Dept of Labor, consult 1973-; NIMH, teacher 1973-; private practice, psychiatry 1973-; Howard Univ, tchr dept of psychiatry 1974-75; Amer Bd of Psychiatry & Neurology, certified 1976; Howard University, assistant clinical professor, department of psychiatry 1976-; Amer Bd of Psychiatry & Neurology, examiner 1977-; Dist of Columbia, interim commissioner of Mental Health, 1992-93. **Orgs:** Black Psychiatrists of Amer; Natl Med Assn; Alliance for Psychiatric Prog; Amer Psychiatric Assn; Amer Med Assn; Commd Ofcrs Assn of US Pub Hlth Serv; WA Psychiatric Soc Chi Delta Mu Frat; Kappa Alpha Psi Frat; assoc, NIMH Mental Hlth Career Devel Prog 1970-75; fellow Harvard Med Sch Dept of Psychiatry 1970-73; co-author Black Parent's Handbook 1975; Commissioned Officers Association of the US Pub Hlth Serv 1967-. **Military Serv:** U.S. Public Health Service, captain, 1967-77, 1980-92. **Business Addr:** Physician, 1616 18th St NW, Suite 101, Washington, DC 20009.

WILLIAMS, MICHAEL DOUGLAS
Professional basketball player. **Personal:** Born Jul 23, 1966, Dallas, TX. **Educ:** Baylor University. **Career:** Detroit Pistons, guard, 1988-89; Phoenix Suns, 1989-90, Charlotte Hornets, 1989-90; Indiana Pacers, point guard, 1990-92; Minnesota Timberwolves, guard, 1992-. **Business Addr:** Professional Basketball Player, Minnesota Timberwolves, 600 1st Ave N, Minneapolis, MN 55403, (612)375-7444.

WILLIAMS, MILTON. See EL-KATI, MAHHMOUD.

WILLIAMS, MILTON LAWRENCE
Judge. **Personal:** Born Nov 14, 1932, Augusta, GA; son of Helen Reilly Williams and William Richard Williams; married Rose King Williams, Oct 22, 1960; children: Milton Jr, Darrie T. **Educ:** New York Univ, BS, 1960; New York Law School, LLB, 1963. **Career:** Allstate Insurance Co, staff attorney; Small Business Administration, regional counsel; Hunts Point Legal Services, general counsel & dir; Knapp Commission, assoc general counsel; McKay Commission on Attica, exec dir; NYC Civil Service Commission, special prosecutor; Criminal Court of the City of New York, judge, 1977-78; New York County Criminal Court, supervising judge, acting justice of the Supreme Court 1978-83; NY Supreme Court, admin judge of the first judicial dist, 1983-85; NY State Supreme Court, justice, deputy chief admin judge, 1985-93, associate justice, Appellate Div, First Dept, 1994-. **Orgs:** Assn of the Bar of the City of New York; numerous past memberships. **Honors/Awds:** Honorary Doctorate of Laws, New York Law School; Charles Carroll Award, The Guild of Catholic Lawyers; Harlan Fiske Stone Award, NY State Trial Lawyers Assn; Humanitarian Award, NY County Lawyers Assn; Outstanding Achievement Award, Bronx Black Bar Assn; Judge Capozolli Award, NY County Lawyers Assn; Golda Meir Award, Jewish Lawyers Guild; Metropolitan Black Bar Assn Award. **Military Serv:** US Navy, 2nd class petty officer, 1951-55. **Business Addr:** Associate Justice, Appellate Division, First Dept, New York State Supreme Court, 27 Madison Avenue, New York, NY 10010.

WILLIAMS, MOE
Professional football player. **Personal:** Born Jul 26, 1974, Columbus, GA; son of Marethia Williams. **Educ:** Univ of Kentucky, attended. **Career:** Minnesota Vikings, running back, 1996-. **Business Addr:** Professional Football Player, Minnesota Vikings, 9520 Vikings Dr, Eden Prairie, MN 55344, (612)828-6500.

WILLIAMS, MONTEL
Talk show host. **Personal:** Born in Baltimore, MD; married Grace; children: 3 daughters, 1 son. **Educ:** Naval Academy Prep School, beginning 1975; United States Naval Academy, BS, 1980; Defense Language Inst, degree in Russian, 1982-83. **Career:** US Marine Corps, officer, beginning 1974; motivational speaker; administrator of nonprofit association; "The Montel Williams Show," host, executive producer, 1991-; CBS, Matt Waters, actor, 1996. **Honors/Awds:** US Chamber of Commerce, Special Services Award, 1988; Esquire Magazine, Man of the Year, 1988; proclamations from mayors of East St Louis and St Louis, 1991; commendation from city of Los Angeles Mayor Tom Bradley, 1991; Omaha Public Schools, Award for Meritous Work With Youth, Omaha Public Schools, 1991; NATAS Emmy Award, 1995-96; Silver Satellite Award, Recipient, 1996; American Women in Radio & Television, Silver Satellite Award, 1996; Crystal Apple Award, 1996; numerous other plaques, proclamations, and awards. **Special Achievements:** First African-American male talk-show host on daytime television; filmed introduction to motion picture Glory; first African American enlisted marine selected to attend the Naval Academy Prep School; hosted a community affairs program in Denver entitled "The Fourth R: Kids Rap About Racism," for which he won a local Emmy; Author: Mountain Get Out of My Way, 1996; numerous others. **Military Serv:** US Marine Corps, officer, beginning 1974; military awards include: Armed Forces Expeditionary Medal; Humanitarian Service Medal; two Navy Expeditionary Medals; Navy Achievement Medal; two Navy Commendation Medals; two Meritorious Service Awards. **Business Addr:** Talk Show Host, Montel Williams Show, c/o Viacom International, 433 W 53rd St, New York, NY 10019, (212)830-0300.

WILLIAMS, MONTY (TAVARES MONTGOMERY)
Professional basketball player. **Personal:** Born Oct 8, 1971, Fredericksburg, VA. **Educ:** Notre Dame, bachelor's degree in communications. **Career:** New York Knicks, forward, 1994-96; San Antonio Spurs, 1996-. **Business Addr:** Professional Basketball Player, San Antonio Spurs, 600 E Market St, San Antonio, TX 78205, (210)554-7773.

WILLIAMS, MORRIS
Business executive. **Personal:** Born Oct 20, Texarkana, AR; son of Izora Williams and Edward Williams; married Geraldine Copeland; children: Shawn Copeland, PhD. **Educ:** Wayne State Univ, BS BA 1940; Univ of Detroit, grad studies. **Career:** Detroit Housing Commission, jr acct 1941-47; Morris O Williams & Co, owner, pres, 1948-. **Orgs:** Mem Nat'l Society Public Accts; mem (past state treasurer) Ind Accts Assoc Mich; brd of dirs YMCA, Fisher Branch; mem Omega Psi Phi Fraternity; mem African Methodist Episcopal Church; life mem NAACP; mem Detroit Idlewilders, Inc; National Supreme Council, A&ASR Masons; National Association of Enrolled Agents. **Special Achievements:** Founded the Under Graduate Chap, Nu Sigma of the Omega Psi Phi Fraternity, Wayne State University; First African-American in State of Michigan to qualify as an enrolled agent for the US Treasury Department. **Military Serv:** Infantry Volunteer Officer Candidate 1943. **Business Addr:** President, Morris Williams & Co, 2101 W Grand Blvd, Detroit, MI 48208-1195.

WILLIAMS, MOSES, SR.
Policeman (retired), parish official. **Personal:** Born Aug 15, 1932, Franklin Parish; married Matra; children: Rhonda, Matra, Lula, Otha, Brenda, James, Jessie, Moses Jr, Robert, Allen, Betty. **Career:** Tallulah Police Dept, 23 years. **Orgs:** Pres Steering Comm 1967-77; vice pres Madison Vote League Inc 1964-84; pres Delta Comm Action Colo Gov Treen Staff 1979-83; bd of dir Devel Block Grant Washington DC; elected to state HH Way from the 5th Regional 1980-; pres vice pres bd dirs Delta Comm Action 1965-76; pres Madison Parish Bd of Econ Devel Loan Bd 1971-77; Madison Parish Police Jury, vice pres, 1972-77, serving 5th term, currently; HEW Police Jury Assn; Municipal Police Off Assn; 5th Dist Black Caucus Comm; commr Madison Parish Port; adv coun bd Title IV Sch Bd; NAACP; RDA Rural Devel Assn; Magnolia St Peace Off Assn; BSA; McCall Sr High PTA; Marquis Who's Who Publ Bd 1976-77; 5th Dist LA Educ Assn 1972; Evening Star Lodge No 113 1972; Louisiana Police Officer Assn; City of Tallulah, auxiliary police officer; Criminal and Juvenile Justice Committee; Appointed to NACO Steering Committee, Justice & Public Safety Steering Committee, Washington, DC; Appointed to Drainage Public Works and Water Resources Committee; Elected president, 5th Region District Police Jury Assn, Louisiana; Elected, finance chairman, Madison Parish Police Jury; Elected, chairman, All Black Election officerial of Madison Parish. **Honors/Awds:** Colone Gov Staff 1973, 1979-83; Reg VII Drug Training & Resource Ctr. **Special Achievements:** Only Black in the state of Louisiana who was a Police officer and an Elected Police Juror at the same time. **Home Addr:** 601 W Green, Tallulah, LA 71282.

WILLIAMS, NANCY ELLEN WEBB
Government official. **Personal:** Born Aug 1, Quincy, IL; daughter of Garnet Davis Webb and Charles Webb; married Jesse B Williams, Apr 11, 1959 (deceased); children: Cynthia, Troy, Peter, Wendy. **Educ:** Quincy Coll, BA 1957; Tennessee A&I Univ, 1961; Univ of Nevada, MPA 1977. **Career:** Shelby City Training School, teacher 1957-61; State of Nevada, sr dep prob ofcr 1961-74; Clark Co NV, dir probation serv 1974-80, dir child protect serv, currently; exec dir Cultural Alliance Found, publishing firm 1985-; freelance writer, Las Vegas, NV 1985-. **Orgs:** Mem NV Crime Commn 1970-; NV So Reg Dist Allocation Comm 1970-; adv bd NV Juv Delinquency 1974; mem NV Peace Officers Standards Comm 1975-; chmn Juv Task Force So NV 1974-; Task Force Corrections So NV 1970-74; field faculty Intl Coll 1977; dir Child Haven 1981-84; bd mem Univ of Humanistic Studies Las Vegas NV, Faculty of UHS 1984. **Honors/Awds:** Doctor of Humane Leters, Univ of Humanistic Studies 1986; Distinguished Woman Award, Soroptomist Intl 1986; Nevada Art Council, mini-grant, 1992. **Special Achievements:** Writer, When We Were Colored, publication/poetry volume, 1986; Dinah's Pain and other poems of The Black Life Experience, 1988; Them Gospel Songs, 1990. **Business Addr:** Dir, Child Protective Services, Clark County, 3342 S Sandhill Rd, #129, Las Vegas, NV 89121.

WILLIAMS, NAOMI B.
Educator, educational administrator. **Personal:** Born Dec 4, 1942, New Smyrna, FL; married Mac James Williams Sr; children: Pam, Mac Jr, Essie, Brenda Yolanda, Roderick, Wendell. **Educ:** Bethune-Cookman Coll, BS 1963; Florida A&M Univ, MEd 1973; Stetson Univ, Certificate Counseling 1974; Rollins Coll, Specialist in Educ 1976; Nova Univ, EdD 1980; International Bible Institute & Seminary, associate of religious education, Bible teacher/ministers diploma. **Career:** Volusia Co Public Schools, teacher 1963-67, dean of girls/counselor 1967-73, asst high school principal 1973-74; Daytona Beach Jr Coll, dir of admissions/recruiting 1974-78; St Petersburg Jr Coll, college registrar 1978-, campus registar/dir of admissions, 1986; Volusia Co Public Schools, math/science teacher recruiter, currently. **Orgs:** Mem Amer Assoc of Collegiate Registrars and Admission Officers, FL Assoc of Collegiate Registrars and Admission Officers, FL Assoc of Comm Colls, Southern Assoc of Collegiate Registrars and Admissions Officers; past bd of dirs United Way; mem Bethune-Cookman Coll Alumni Assoc; past bd of dirs "Spirit"; education director Mt Carmel Baptist Church; Sunday school teacher Mt Carmel Baptist Church; mem Grad Chap Kappa Delta Pi; Grad Chap Delta Sigma Theta Sor; Urban League; adult advisor Clearwater Youth Council NAACP; dir of adult sunday sch dept Mt Carmel Baptist Church; Top of the World Kiwanis Club. **Honors/Awds:** First Black Female Asst Principal in a Sr High School Volusia Co Schs Daytona Beach FL; First Black Dir of Admissions Daytona Beach Comm Coll Daytona Beach FL; First Black Registrar St Petersburg Jr Coll; graduation speaker Trinity Arts and Technical Acad The Philippines; Teacher of the Year Awd Campbell Sr High School Daytona Beach; Mother of the Year from Ben and Mary's Kindergarten Daytona Beach; founders day speaker Delta Sigma Theta Sor Clearwater Branch; Gulfcoast Business Women Association, Community Volunteer Certificate; St Petersburg Jr College, Women on the Way Challenge Center Certificate; Mainland Senior High School, Counselor of the Year Award. **Home Addr:** 1300 Ridge Avenue, Clearwater, FL 34615. **Business Addr:** Registar, St. Petersburg Junior College, 2465 Drew Street, Clearwater, FL 34625.

WILLIAMS, NAPOLEON
Business executive, elected official. **Personal:** Born Nov 24, 1919, Vienna, GA; married Joyce Henry; children: Gail L, Sonya. **Educ:** Ft Valley State Coll, BS Soc Studies, Natural Sci; Atlanta Univ, MA Admin; Atlanta School of Mortuary Sci. **Career:** Vienna High & Indus School, principal 1952-70; Vienna HS, principal 1970-76; GA Southwestern Coll, instructor, 1977-78; JW Williams Funeral Home, pres, currently. **Orgs:** Mem Dooly Cty Bi-Racial Comm, 32 Degree Mason, Noble of the Mystic Shrine of Amer; chmn Dooly Cty Bd of Health; mem

NAACP; mem bd of dir West Central GA Comm Action Council; pres GMA 3rd Dist 1984-85. **Honors/Awds:** Hon Doctor of Law Degrees; Co-author Dooly Cty School Bldg named in honor of N Williams Health & Phys Ed Bldg; Gtea for Meritorious Serv to the Cause of Ed; Intl Personnel Rsch Creativity Awd Creative & Successful Personalities 1972; Distinguished Serv Awd Recipient Ft Valley State Coll 1981; Distinguished Serv Awd Recipient City of Vienna 1976. **Military Serv:** WWII Vet; Awarded, WWII Vict Medal, Amer Serv Medal, European/African/Middle East Serv Medal, Good Cond Medal AR 600-68 Philippine Liber Serv Ribbon. **Business Addr:** President, JW Williams Funeral Home, 407 17th Ave West, Cordele, GA 31015.

WILLIAMS, NATALIE
Professional basketball player. **Personal:** Born Nov 30, 1970; daughter of Nate Williams and Robyn Barker. **Educ:** UCLA, bachelor's degree in sociology. **Career:** Portland Power, center, 1996-. **Honors/Awds:** Pac-10 Athlete of the Year, 1996; Utah's Woman Athlete of the Century, 1996. **Business Addr:** Professional Basketball Player, Portland Power, 439 N Broadway, Portland, OR 97227, (503)249-1130.

WILLIAMS, NORRIS GERALD
Educational administrator, journalist. **Personal:** Born May 12, 1948, Oklahoma City, OK; son of Mattye Williams and Norris Williams; married Carolyn Ann Moch, Aug 28, 1970; children: Diarra Koro, Ayanna Kai, Jawanza Jamaal, Norris Emanuel. **Educ:** Wiley Coll TX, BS (Honor Student) 1970; Central State Univ OK, MS 1977. **Career:** Douglass HS, OK City, all conf pitcher 1966; Images KFGL & KAEZ, radio talk show host 1977-78; R&B Prod, Jam Prod, Feyline Prod, C&F Prod, promotional consultant, 1979-82; OK City Publ Schools, coach 1970-75, teacher 1970-77; Park & Rec Dept OK City, mgr 1970-82; Black Dispatch Publ Co, sports ed 1979-82; Univ of OK black student services, coord 1977-, minority student services, dir 1988-. **Orgs:** Sec, treas Kappa Alpha Psi 1968-70; pres KAZI Comm Serv 1972-73; pres Images Comm Serv 1976-78; pres Assoc of Black Personnel Univ of OK 1979-80; Pres Assoc of Black personnel 1982-83; mem OKABSE 1984-85; commiss OK Black Historical Soc 1984-85; mem Alpha Chi Chap Kappa Alpha Psi; polemarch Norman Alumni Chapter, Kappa Alpha Psi 1986-88. **Honors/Awds:** Outstanding Student Kappa Alpha Psi Alpha Chi Wiley Coll 1969; Baseball Coach of the Year Capitol Conf OK City 1975; Staff Person of the Year Black Peoples Union Univ of OK 1977-79; Comm Serv Awd 1983; Univ of OK Outstanding Achievement Awd 1984; Commissioner Higher Educ for OK Assoc of Black School Educators 1985. **Business Addr:** Dir, Minority Student Services, Univ of Oklahoma, 731 Elm, Hester 220, Norman, OK 73019.

WILLIAMS, NOVELLA STEWART
Association executive. **Personal:** Born Jul 13, 1927, Johnston Co, NC; daughter of Cassie Stewart and Charlie Stewart; married Thomas Williams, Oct 5, 1944; children: Charles, Frank, Willis, Thomas, Kim, Michelle, Pam. **Educ:** Rutgers Univ, 1971; Univ of Pennsylvania Wharton School, 1974. **Career:** Citizens for Prog, fndr pres 1974-. **Orgs:** Chmn bd dir W Philadelphia Comm Free Sch 1969-; dir Philadelphia Anti Poverty Commin 1970-; pres Peoples Hlth Serv 1973-; prtnr & consult Ed Mgmt Assc 1973-; sec bd dir Hlth Sys Agcy of SE PA 1976-; consult US Consumer Prod Safety Commin 1975-76; v chmn YMCA 1970; bd dir RCHPC; bd dir SE PA Am Red Cross 1976; bd dir Philadelphia Urban Coalitiion 1977; mem By Laws; person & consumer aff Com Philadelphia Hlth Mgmt Corp 1976-; del Dem Natl Conv 1976; mem dem Crdntl Com 1976; mem Dem Rules Com 1976; Dem Del Whip 1976; coord 513 Women's Com Carter-Mondale Camp; White House Conf on Hunger 1970; Red Book 1970; prin Natl Ed Assc 1972; Seven Sch 1971; Harcourt-Brace-World-Measurement & Conf 1969; House Foreign AffSub-comCongrssnl Rec 1970; co-chairperson, The Philadelphia Urban Coalition, 1989-oard of trustees, Lincoln University, 1977; trustee, United Way, 1981. **Honors/Awds:** Human Rights Award, Philadelphia Commission on Human Relations, 1968; Comm Organization Award, OIC, 1970; Outstanding Service Award, White House Conference on Small Business, 1980. **Business Addr:** Founder/President, Citizens for Progress, Inc, 5236 Market St, Philadelphia, PA 19139.

WILLIAMS, ORA
Educator (retired). **Personal:** Born Feb 18, 1926, Lakewood, NJ; daughter of Ida Bolles Roach Williams and Charles Williams. **Educ:** Virginia Union University, Richmond, VA, AB, 1950; Howard University, Washington, DC, MA, 1953; University of California, Irvine, CA, PhD, 1974. **Career:** Southern University, Baton Rouge, LA, instructor, 1953-55; Tuskegee Institute, Tuskegee, AL, instructor, 1955-57; Morgan State University, Baltimore, MD, instructor, 1957-65; Camp Fire Girls, Inc, New York, NY, program advisor, 1965-68; California State University, Long Beach, CA, professor, 1968-88, professor emerita, 1988-; Virginia Union University, visiting professor, 1990-91. **Orgs:** College Language Association; BEEM-Black Experience as Expressed in Music, board of directors, 1982; NAACP; Afro-American Youth Association, 1984; Delta Sigma Theta Sorority:. **Honors/Awds:** Co-author of article ''Johnny Doesn't/Didn't Hear,'' Journal of Negro History, spring, 1964; author, American Black Women in the Arts and Social Sciences: A Bibliographical Survey, Scarecrow Press, 1973, 1978, 1994; Author: Just Like Meteor: A Bio-Bibliography of the Life and Works of Charles William Williams; Second Annual Achievement Award in Humanities and Performing Arts Research, Virginia Union University Alumni Association of Southern California, 1983; Pillar of the Community Award, Long Beach Community Improvement League, 1988; Outstanding Service Award, Mayor of Long Beach, 1988; Consortium of Doctors, Savannah, GA, 1993. **Business Addr:** Professor Emerita, California State University, Dept of English, 1250 Bellflower Blvd, Humanities Office Bldg, Long Beach, CA 90840.

WILLIAMS, ORA P. See THOMAS, ORA P.

WILLIAMS, PAT
Professional football player. **Personal:** Born Oct 24, 1972. **Educ:** Texas A&M. **Career:** Buffalo Bills, defensive tackle, 1997-. **Business Addr:** Professional Football Player, Buffalo Bills, One Bills Dr, Orchard Park, NY 14127, (716)648-1800.

WILLIAMS, PATRICIA ANNE
Justice. **Personal:** Born Dec 16, 1943, New York, NY; daughter of Kathleen Valerie Carrington Williams and David Charles Williams Jr. **Educ:** Cornell U, BA 1965; Cert of African Inst Columbia U, MA 1967; Yale Univ Law Sch, JD 1972. **Career:** Criminal Court of the City of New York, acting justice, currently; SDNY, asst us atty 1977-86; Willkie Farr & Gallagher, assc atty 1972-76; New Haven Legal Asst Assc, legal clk 1971-72; New York City Crim Justice Coord Council, law clerk summer 1970; Phelps-Stokes Fund NYC, sec admin asst 1967-69. **Orgs:** Assn of the Bar of the City of New York; Federal Bar Council; American Judges Assn; Judicial Friends; NY County Lawyers Assn. **Honors/Awds:** Scroll of Achievement North Shore Chapter of Natl Assn of Negro Business and Professional Women's Clubs Inc 1985, 1987; East Elmhurst Corona Civic Assn, Inc, 1991; Criminal Justice Section of the New York County Lawyers, Recognition Awd, 1996. **Business Addr:** Acting Justice of the Supreme Court, State of New York, 851 Grand Concourse, Bronx, NY 10451.

WILLIAMS, PATRICIA HILL
Educational administrator. **Personal:** Born May 3, 1939, Richmond, VA; daughter of Virginia Hill and Marshall Hill; divorced; children: Tory Therese. **Educ:** State Univ of New York, Old Westbury, BA, 1976; New York Inst of Tech, MA, Communications Art, 1981; Kellogg Fellow in International Development (1984-86); State University of New York, Stony Brook, MA, liberal studies, 1991; Harvard Graduate School of Education, Graduate Education Certificate, management development, 1992. **Career:** Babylon Beacon Newspaper, assoc editor, 1971-79; New York Amsterdam News, columnist, 1972-84; Amer Cancer Soc, public information officer, 1977-80; State Univ of New York at Farmingdale, asst to the pres; Suffolk County Human Rights Commissioner, 1990-; President Bush's Board of Advisors on Historically Black Colleges & Universities, 1991; Partners of the Americas, Inter American ex bd, 1992-94; African Development Foundation Board of Advisors, 1993; Inter-American Foundation, bd of dirs, currently. **Orgs:** Past pres Partners of the Americas, Long Island/St Vincent; mem, Alpha Kappa Alpha Theta Iota Omega, pres, 100 Black Women of Long Island, 1995; former bd mem, State Univ Confederation of Alumni Assoc, 1983-, State Univ of New York, Council for Univ Advancement, 1985; former commr, Babylon Historic Comm; President Reagan's appointee, Natl Advisory Council on Women's Educ Programs, 1987-90; northeast region chairperson Natl Black Republic Council; LI center for Business & Professional Women, NAACP, NCNW; founding board, Episcopal Charities of Long Island, 1992; Pres Clinton's appointee to the Inter-American Foundation, 1995-2000; representative to 4th world, Conference on Women, 1995. **Honors/Awds:** Woman of the Year Media Award, Bethel AME Church, 1980; PR Award of Excellence, LI Flower Show, 1983; Comm Serv in Public Relations & Comm 100 Black Men of LI, 1983; Fellow Intl Devel WK Kellogg Found, 1984-86; Woman of the Year, New York State Council of Black Republicans, 1986, 1987, 1988; Outstanding Alumna of the Year, Suny/Coll of Old Westbury, 1988; 1990 Newsday Community Service Award; Honoree in Education, LI Center for Business and Professional Women, 1992; Woman of the Year, Zonta of Suffolk; Victims Info Bureau Domestic Violence, Jr League of LI, 1996. **Business Addr:** Assistant to the President, State University of New York-Farmingdale, Administration Bldg, Farmingdale, NY 11735.

WILLIAMS, PATRICK NEHEMIAH
Construction company executive. **Personal:** Born Sep 28, 1928, St Croix, Virgin Islands of the United States; son of Ingerborg Cassimeer and Norman P. A. Williams; married Inez Byron, Dec 21, 1951; children: Glenice, Sharon, Lindel, Wayne, Patrice, Denise, Donna, Patrick M, Raymond, Aisha. **Educ:** Pace Univ, BPS 1976. **Career:** Dist of St Croix, senator 1963-65; Legislature of VI, consult 1965-70, exec dir 1970-81; The Chase Manhattan Bank, asst mgr 1981-82; VI Dept of Ag, commississioner; Zeon Construction Corp, asst to the pres, currently. **Orgs:** State chmn Dem Party of the VI 1964-72; sec, treas, NASBE 1976-78; chmn VI Bd of Ed 1978-80; commiss VI Dept of Agriculture 1983-87; chairman, board of directors, WTJX-Channel 12, Virgin Islands Public Television System; chairman, bd of trustees, University of The Virgin Islands; Board of Education; chairman, State Board of Education, currently. **Honors/Awds:** Author ''Virgin Islands 1917-Present'' Pace Univ 1976; Legislative Resolution l988. **Military Serv:** USMS lance corp 8 yrs. **Business Addr:** Assistant to President, Zenon Construction Corp, PO Box 5440, Sunny Isle, St Croix, Virgin Islands of the United States 00823-5440.

WILLIAMS, PAUL
Federal government official. **Personal:** Born Aug 6, 1929, Jacksonville, IL; son of Bernice Wheeler Williams and Russell Williams; married Ora Mosby; children: Reva. **Educ:** Illinois College, BA, 1956; Federal Executive Inst, 1971; Brookings Inst, 1975; Harvard University, Kennedy School of Govt, 1980; Pacific Inst, certificate, Facilitator Investment in Excellence, 1988; American University, certificate, Executive Development Seminar, 1984. **Career:** City of Chicago, director of finance, 1956-63; Department of State, intl admin officer, 1963-68; United Planning Organization, associate director finance and administration, 1964; HUD, director, Office of Mgt Hsg, FHA commr, director, 1968-90, gen deputy asst/secr, Fair Hsg, 1993-94, deputy asst/secr, Mgt & Opor Fair Hsg, 1994-96, retired, 1997. **Orgs:** HUD Chapter Senior Executive Association, treasurer, 1989, president, 1991-93. **Honors/Awds:** HUD, Certificate of Merit, 1974,Superior Service Award, 1975, nominee, Presidential Award for Outstanding Civilian Service, 1973; Certificate of Special Achievement, 1984; US Secretary of State, citation recipient; US Commn Pacific, commendation, 1967; Illinois College, Distinguished Citizens Award, 1976, honorary degree, 1979; Outstanding Performance Rating 1982, 1983; Sr Executive Service Performance Award, 1983; Comm on Fraud Waste & Mismanagement, Certificate of Special Achievement, 1984; Outstanding Performance Rating, 1993-96; Senior Executive Performance Review Board, 1991-96; HUD Sec, Distinguished Service Award, 1996; Maryland Governor's Citation for Outstanding Government Service, 1963-96. **Military Serv:** US Army, 1948-52.

WILLIAMS, PELHAM C.
Business executive. **Personal:** marrIed Mary Ellen Williams; children: Tyrone C, Pelham L III, Pamela L. **Career:** Williams-Russell and Johnson, Inc, senior executive officer, currently. **Orgs:** Metro Atlanta Chamber of Commerce; Metro Atlanta Regional Leadership Foundation. **Special Achievements:** Listed as #95 of 100 top industrial service companies, Black Enterprise, 1992. **Business Addr:** Chief Executive Officer, Williams-Russell and Johnson, Inc, 771 Spring St NW, Atlanta, GA 30308, (404)853-6800.

WILLIAMS, PEYTON, JR.
Educational administrator. **Personal:** Born Apr 10, 1942, Cochran, GA; married Sandra E Pryor; children: Rachelle Lenore, Tara Alyce. **Educ:** Ft Valley State Coll, BS; Tuskegee Inst, MA; Univ GA, EDS. **Career:** State Schools & Special Activities GA Dept of Educ, asso state supt 1977-; Cen Middle School, prin 1970-77; Cen Elementary School, prin 1967-70; Cen HS, prin vice-prin 1964-67. **Orgs:** Chmn First Dist Professional Devel Commn; mem GA Tchr Educ Council 1974-77; mem GA Assn of Educators Gov Task Force; sec GA Middle Sch Prins Assn 1973; mem Adv Com Gov Conf on Educ 1977; mem bd dir Screen-Jenkins Regional Library 1973-77; bd dir Screven Co Dept of Family & Children Svcs; mem Citizens Adv Coun Area 24 Mental Health/Mental Retardation; bd dir CSRA Office of Econ Opportunity 1971-77; mem Bd dir Screven Co C of C 1974; mem Screven-Sylvania Arts Coun; mem adv bd Screven Co Assn for Retarded Children; mem Omega Psi Phi Frat; Selective Serv Local Bd #128; mem Policy Com CSRA OEO; scoutmaster Boy Scout Troop 348; organist choir dir St Paul Bapt Church; Natl Dropout Prevention Network, chmn of the exec bd, 1992-. **Honors/Awds:** Educator of the Year Screven-Sylvania Optimist Club 1976; Distinguished Serv Award Screven Co Bd of Edn; Most Valuable Mem Trophy GA Council of Deliberation 32 Degree Masons PHA; Outstanding Serv Award Screven Co Chap NAACP; Plaque of Appreciation Screven Co Chap Am Cancer Soc; Meritorious Serv Award St Paul Bapt Ch; Adminstr of Yr Award Phi Delt Kappa 1980. **Business Addr:** Ste 231, State Office Bldg, Atlanta, GA 30334.

WILLIAMS, PHILIP B.
Attorney. **Personal:** Born Dec 30, 1922, Gonzales, TX; married Frances A. **Educ:** Roosevelt U, BSC 1952; DePaul U, LIB 1963, JD 1969. **Career:** Self Employed Atty, 1966-; Chgo, po clk 1947-52; IRS, collection ofcr & revenue agent 1952-64; Serv Fed Savings & Loan Assc, mgr 1964-66. **Orgs:** Bd mem cncl Park Grove Real Est Inc 1967-; bd mem cncl Crestway Maint Corp 1970-; mem Cook Cty IL State & Am Bar Assc; mem Tech Asst Adv Bd; United Bldrs Assc of Chgo; mem Comm Adv Cncl; chgo Bapt Isnt. **Military Serv:** AUS sgt 1943-45. **Business Addr:** 8032 S Cottage Grove Ave, Chicago, IL.

WILLIAMS, PRESTON N.
Educator. **Personal:** Born May 23, 1926, Alcolu, SC; son of Bertha Bell McRae Williams and Anderson James Williams; married Constance Marie Willard; children: Mark Gordon, David Bruce. **Educ:** Washington & Jefferson Coll, AB 1947, MA 1948; Johnson C Smith Univ, BD 1950; Yale Univ, STM 1954; Harvard Univ, PhD 1967. **Career:** Boston Univ School Theol, Martin Luther King Jr prof social ethics 1970-71; Harvard Div School, acting dean 1974-75, Houghton prof theol & contemporary change 1971-. **Orgs:** Acting dir WEB DuBois Inst 1975-77; editor-at-large Christian Century 1972-; mem, pres Amer Acad Religion 1975-; dir, pres Amer Soc Christian Ethics 1974-75; mem Phi Beta Kappa. **Honors/Awds:** Contrib articles to professional jrnls; ordained to ministry Presb Church 1950. **Business Addr:** Houghton Professor of Theology and Comtemporary Change, Harvard Divinity School, 45 Francis Ave, Cambridge, MA 02138.

WILLIAMS, RALEIGH R.
Real estate broker, tax service. **Personal:** marrIed Vernell Johnson; children: Rudolph, Karen, Kevin, Kenneth. **Educ:** Economis Univ Omaha, Bge. **Career:** Retired Serviceman; Raleigh A Williams Realty Construction & Income Tax Serv, re broker, income tax cons, gen contractor & mgmt cons. **Orgs:** Pres Dulleton Ct NAACP; Boy Scout Master; mgr Little League Baseball; coach Little League Football; mem Am Inst Industrial Eng; pres Young Men Bus Assc; tres OEO; NCO of Qtr; Perrin AFB 1967. **Honors/Awds:** Baseball Champion Colorado Springs 1965; spec recognition for political work NAACP Chpt. **Military Serv:** USAF 1952-72. **Business Addr:** 611 A Padgett Loop, Walterboro, SC 29488.

WILLIAMS, RALPH O.
Health services company executive. **Career:** ROW Sciences Inc, chief executive officer, currently. **Special Achievements:** Company is ranked #49 on Black Enterprise's list of top 100 industrial/service companies, 1994. **Business Addr:** CEO, ROW Sciences Inc., 1700 Research Blvd. #400, Rockville, MD 20850, (301)294-5400.

WILLIAMS, RANDOLPH
Attorney. **Personal:** Born Mar 29, 1944, Montgomery, AL; children: Randall. **Educ:** Bowie State Coll, BA 1969; Georgetown Univ Law School, JD 1973. **Career:** District Attorney's Office, deputy dist attny, currently. **Orgs:** Mem Natl Conf of Black Laywers, Natl Bar Assoc, Amer Bar Assoc, Natl Dist Attny Assoc; PA Bar Assn; District of Columbia Bar Assn. **Military Serv:** USAF airman 1st class 1962-65. **Business Addr:** Deputy District Attorney, District Attorneys Office, 1421 Arch St, Philadelphia, PA 19102.

WILLIAMS, REGGIE
Professional basketball player. **Personal:** Born Mar 5, 1964, Baltimore, MD. **Educ:** Georgetown Univ, Washington, DC, 1983-87. **Career:** Los Angeles Clippers, 1987-90; Cleveland Cavaliers, 1990; San Antonio Spurs, 1990; Denver Nuggets, 1991-96; New Jersey Nets, 1996-. **Special Achievements:** NBA Draft, First round pick, #4, 1987. **Business Addr:** Professional Basketball Player, New Jersey Nets, Brendan Byrne Arena, East Rutherford, NJ 07073, (201)935-8888.

WILLIAMS, REGINA VLOYN-KINCHEN
City official. **Personal:** Born Nov 15, 1947, Detroit, MI; daughter of Mary Lee & Nathaniel Kinchen (both deceased); married Drew B Williams; children: Traci A, Kristin L, Drew Michael. **Educ:** Eastern MI Univ, BS 1971; Virginia Commonwealth Univ, MPA 1987. **Career:** City of Ypsilanti, dir of personnel & labor relations 1972-79; City of Richmond, dir of personnel 1979-82; Commonwealth of VA, state dir of personnel & training 1982-85; J Sargeant Reynolds Comm Coll, adjunct prof 1982-; City of Richmond, VA, asst city manager, 1985-89; Natl Fire Training Academy, adjunct faculty, 1989-; City of San Jose, San Jose, CA, asst city manager, 1989-94, city manager, 1994-; San Jose State Univ, San Jose, CA, adjunct faculty member, 1991-. **Orgs:** Former president, Natl Forum for Black Public Administrators; former vice pres, Intl City Management Assn, National Academy Public Administration, co-founder past pres Richmond Chap Conf of Minority Public Administrators; workshop leader, guest lecturer at natl professional conferences; adjunct faculty mem J Sargeant Reynolds Comm Coll; mem Alpha Kappa Alpha Sor Inc; founding mem and vice pres South Bay Chapter of 100 Black Women. **Honors/Awds:** Contributor to Virginia Govt textbook "By the Good People of Virginia", by C Fleming, Serwa Award, Virginia Chapter, Natl Coalition of 100 Black Women, 1989; Public Service Award, Mercury Newspaper & Women's Fund, 1994. **Business Addr:** City Manager, City of San Jose, 801 N First St, Rm 436, San Jose, CA 95110.

WILLIAMS, REGINALD CLARK
Government administrator, cleric. **Personal:** Born Aug 22, 1950, DeLand, FL; son of Geraldine L Merrick; married Ella Mae Ashford; children: Deirdre LaFay, Andre Terrell. **Educ:** Seminole Jr Coll, AA Gen Studies 1975-77; Univ of Central FL, BS Bus Admin 1977-80. **Career:** East Central FL Reg Planning Co, rsch analyst 1971-77; Cty of Volusia Planning Dept, program coord 1977-80, comm devel admin asst 1980-81, acting dir 1985-86, comm devel dir 1981-86, community services director 1986-. **Orgs:** Coach West Volusia Pop Warner Football Assoc 1976-84; mem Natl Assoc of Hsg & Redevel Off 1977-; sponsor Electrifying Gents 1982-84; bd mem FL Comm Devel Assoc 1983-, chairman 1987, Comm Hsg Res Bd 1984-88; member national Forum for Black Public Administrator, chairman West Volusia Martin Luther King Planning Committee; bd mem Alcohol, Drug Mental Health Planning Council, chairman 1992; mem Stewart Treatment Center Advisory Bd; Mt Calvary Free Will Baptist Church, deacon, 1988-92, minister, 1992-. **Honors/Awds:** Cert of Recogn West Volusia YMCA 1981; Cert of Apprec Youth of St Annis Prim Baptist Church 1982; Cert of Apprec Electra Lytes Charity Club 1983; Coachof Year West Volusia Pop Warner Parents Assoc 1983; Cert of Recogn Electra Lyles Charity Club 1985; Recognition Volusia County Constituency for Children 1988, Cert of Apprec. United Way, 1990, Cert. Appreciation Cocaine Babies Junior Service League 1989, Community Service Award Stewart Treatment Center 1990. **Business Addr:** Dir Community Services Department, County of Volusia, 123 W Indiana Ave, DeLand, FL 32720-4611.

WILLIAMS, REGINALD T.
Company executive. **Personal:** Born May 14, 1945, Newark, NJ; married Dorothy; children: Remington, Sunshine. **Educ:** Essex Cty Coll, AAS 1970; Rutgers Univ New Brunswick NJ, BA 1972; Temple Univ Philadelphia, MA 1975. **Career:** Essex Cty Urban League, dir of econ devel & employment 1969-72; City of Newark NJ, dir of consumer affairs 1970-72; Bucks Cty Comm Action Agency, asst exec dir 1973-74; Various Corps & US Govt, consult minority affairs, various corps 1973-; United Way of Central MD, dir of affirmative action 1976-79; Urban-League of Lancaster Cty PA, exec dir. **Orgs:** Sec Eastern Reg Council of Urban League; dept host Evening Mag WJZ-TV Baltimore. **Honors/Awds:** "Guide to Minority Bus in Newark" Barton Press 1970; Consumer Protection Awd US Fed Trade Comm 1971; Howard Cty Human Relations Awd Howard Cty MD 1976; Outstanding Young Columbian Awd Columbia Jaycees 1979; "A Buyers Guide to Doing Business with Minority vendors," TPC Printing Ctr HRMC Publisher 1985.

WILLIAMS, RICHARD, JR.
Elected official. **Personal:** Born Feb 10, 1933, Alcoa, TN; son of Gertrude Williams and Richard Williams; married Evelyn Robinson; children: Vivien Williams. **Educ:** Ft Gordon Military Acad of Leadership, Certificate 1953; US DOE Courier Training Serv Albuquerque NM, 1973. **Career:** Greyhound Bus Lines, baggage & matl handler 1963-73; US DOE Courier Serv Oak Ridge TN, courier 1973-79; Sears Roebuck & Co, catalog sales; Blount County Dist 1, commissioner. **Orgs:** Past worshipful master Granite Lodge #289 1977; commiss Blount Cty TN 1984-; mem Blount Cty Exec Comm of the Republican Party 1984-; serves as Minority-at-Large Rep of 16-County East Tennessee Devel Dist; 33rd Degree Mason; illustrious potentate Almas Temple #71; deacon & Sunday School tchr St John Baptist Church Alcoa, TN; mem Committee on Committees, Cable Authority Comm, Highway Comm, Airport Hazard Comm, Community Action Comm; alt delegate to 1984 Natl Republican Conv; past commander-in-chief of Alcoa Consistory No 175; mem Homecoming '86 Comm; mem Martin Luther King State Holiday Comm; commander in chief Alcoa Consistory #175; past pontentate Almas Temple #71; sheriff comm Blount County Beer Bd; chairman, Blount County Historical Record's Committee, 1990; Appointed Colonel, Camp dido. **Honors/Awds:** Mason of the Year East Tennessee Chap 1977; Shriners Outstanding Leadership Awd Alcoa TN 1979; Devoted Serv Awd Shriners East TN; Colonel Aide De Camp presented by Governor Lamar Alexander 1984; 3 Performance Awards for Professionalism from US Dept Energy; numerous church awards for Christian Leadership. **Military Serv:** AUS, US Corp of Military Police corpl 1953-55; Grad with top honors from Ft Gordon Military Acad Ft Gordon GA. **Home Addr:** 167 McMillan St, Alcoa, TN 37701.

WILLIAMS, RICHARD E., JR.
State official. **Personal:** Born Jun 8, 1962, Richmond, VA; son of Gloria Bowman Williams and Richard Williams Sr. **Educ:** University of Virginia, Charlottesville, VA, BA, American Government, 1984. **Career:** Virginia House of Delegates, Richmond, VA, records asst, 1985-86; Democratic Party of Virginia, Richmond, VA, party organizations coordinator, 1987-88; University of Virginia, Charlottesville, VA, dir of alumni affair, 1988-89; Office of the Attorney General, Richmond, VA, asst dir of constituent affairs, 1990-. **Orgs:** Member, Science Museum of Virginia, 1989-; member, New Kent Civic League, 1987-; member, NAACP, 1980-; member, University of Virginia Alumni Association, 1984-; member, Jaycees, 1988-. **Honors/Awds:** University of Virginia Alumni Award, Outstanding Service, University of Virginia, 1984; 50 Leaders of America, Ebony Magazine, 1990.

WILLIAMS, RICHARD LEE
Public relations executive. **Personal:** Born Sep 11, 1959, Edenton, NC; son of Annie M & Luther L Williams, Sr. **Educ:** North Carolina A&T State Univ, BS, 1984; Wake Forest Univ, MBA, 1998. **Career:** Raleigh Times, reporter, 1984-87; Gannett Suburban Newspapers, asst city editor, 1987-92; Winston-Salem Chronicle, exec editor, 1993-94; RJ Reynolds Tobacco Co, public relations rep, 1994-. **Orgs:** Winston-Salem Urban League, steering comm chmn, 1996-; vice chmn, 1997-; Best Choice Center, mktg/public relations comm chmn, 1996-; Piedmont Opera, former bd mem, 1993. **Honors/Awds:** National Newspapers Publishers Association, Merit Award, 1994. **Home Addr:** 1676 Quillmark Rd, Winston-Salem, NC 27127.

WILLIAMS, RICHARD LEE, II
Journalist. **Personal:** Born Sep 11, 1959, Edenton, NC; son of Annie Smallwood Williams and Luther Lee Williams Sr. **Educ:** North Carolina A & T State Univ, Greensboro, NC, BS, 1984. **Career:** Chowan Herald, Edenton, NC reporter, 1982; Mid-Atlantic Communications, Greensboro, NC, talk show host; 1982-83; Winston Salem Chronicle, Winston-Salem, NC, reporter, 1983; WNAA-FM Radio, Greensboro, NC, sports dir, 1983-84; News & Observer Pub Co, Raleigh, NC, reporter, 1984-87; Gannett Westchester Newspapers, White Plains, NY, editor, 1987-. **Orgs:** Natl Assn of Black Journalists; NAACP; Urban League; United Way; Omega Psi Phi Fraternity, Inc. **Honors/Awds:** General News Category 1st Place, NABJ, 1989.

WILLIAMS, RICHARD LENWOOD
Dentist. **Personal:** Born Mar 11, 1931, Schenectady, NY; married Martha E; children: Brian Lenwood, Kevin Allyn, Darren Wayne, Lori Elaine. **Educ:** Fisk U, BA 1953; Howard U, DDS 1957. **Career:** Queens Gen Hosp 1958-73; Self Employed Dent 1977. **Orgs:** Mem Dent Assc Queens Clinc Soc; fin sec Queens Clin Soc; record & sec Queens Clin Soc 1977; mem Alpha Phi Alpha Frat; chmn Les Amis of Queens 1970; tres Les Amis of Queens 1977. **Business Addr:** 120-27 New York Blvd, Jamaica, NY 11434.

WILLIAMS, ROBERT B.
Attorney. **Personal:** Born Aug 10, 1943, Washington, DC; married. **Educ:** University of Maryland, BA, 1966, School of Law, JD, 1972. **Career:** Self-employed, private practice, attorney, currently. **Orgs:** Howard Cty Bar Assn; American Bar Assn; Ellicott City, Rotary Club-MD, pres; Sigma Phi Epsilon; Baltimore Rubgy Football Club. **Honors/Awds:** University of Maryland, dean's list. **Military Serv:** US Army, spec 4, 1967-69; Army Commendation Medal. **Business Addr:** Partner, Attorney, 8386 Court Ave, Ellicott City, MD 21043.

WILLIAMS, ROBERT H.
Physician, educator. **Personal:** Born Dec 1, 1938, Washington, DC; married Judy R Williams. **Educ:** Howard U, BS 1959, MS 1960; Howard Univ Clg of Med, MD 1964. **Career:** Family Practice Howard Univ Coll of Med, asst prof; Comm Group Health Found Inc, med dir; Walter Reed Army Hosp & Med Officer, intern 1965-67; DeWitt Army & Hospital, chief med clinics 1968-69 15th inf div vietnam, med officer 1967-68; Howard Univ Coll of med, fellow 1970-71. **Orgs:** Mem Natl Med Assc; mem Med Soc of DC; chmn Fmly Prac Scientific Pgm; Natl Med Assc 1971. **Honors/Awds:** Recipient Milton K Francis Schlrshp Awrd 1961; bronze star Army Commendation Medal 1968; combat medic badge 1968. **Military Serv:** AUSMC capt/mjr 1964-69. **Business Addr:** Howard Univ Coll of Med, 2400 Sixth St NW, Washington, DC 20059.

WILLIAMS, ROBERT L.
Government official. **Educ:** Jackson State Univ, degree. **Career:** Jackson Metropolitan Crime Commission; Jackson, MS, councilman, 1997-. **Special Achievements:** Youngest councilmember ever elected in Jackson, MS. **Business Addr:** Councilman, City of Jackson, City Hall, 219 S President St, Jackson, MS 39205, (601)960-1091.

WILLIAMS, ROBERT L.
Educator. **Personal:** Born Feb 20, 1930, Biscoe, AR; married Ava L; children: Robbie, Julius, Yvonne, Larry, Reva, Dorothy, Robert A Michael. **Educ:** Philadner Smith Coll, BA 1953; Wayne St Univ, MEd 1955; Washington Univ, PhD 1961. **Career:** AR St Hosp, asst psychologist 1955-57; VA Hosp, psychology trainee 1957-61, St Louis asst chief psychology serv 1961-66; Spokane WA, exec dir hospital improvement 1966-68; NIMH, 9th region mental health consultant psychology 1968-69; VA Hosp, chief psychology serv 1969-70; Washington Univ, assoc prof psychology 1969-70, prof of psychology dir black studies prog 1970-74; Robert L Williams Assoc Inc, founder/pres 1973-; Washington Univ, prof psychology 1970-. **Orgs:** Bds & comms NIMH 1970-72; past natl chmn Assoc Black Psychologists; Amer Personel & Guidance Assn; chmn bd of dir Inst of Black Studies Inc Cognitive Styles of Black People, Identity Issues, Personality Development Tsts Black People; dir Comprehensive Trtmt Unit & Psychological Consult at Lindell Hospital St Louis MO; many articles published. **Honors/Awds:** Citizen of the Yr 8th Dist Meeting KC MO 1983; Yes I Can Awd 1984. **Business Addr:** Prof of Psychology, Washington Univ, Box 1109, St Louis, MO 63130.

WILLIAMS, ROBERT LEE
Educational administrator (retired). **Personal:** Born Jul 19, 1933, Lorman, MS; married Wilma McGee; children: Schelia,

Robert, Philvester, Dennis, Meshell. **Career:** Board of Education, Jefferson County Public School, Fayette, Mississippi, 1966-90. **Honors/Awds:** NAACP Award 1969; honor citizen Kenner, Louisiana 1969; Mississippi State Convention, NAACP 1969. **Home Addr:** Rt 2 Box 132, Lorman, MS 39096.

WILLIAMS, ROBERT LEE
Educational administrator. **Personal:** Born Jun 3, 1936, Shreveport, LA; son of Thelma and M C; married Dorothy Young; children: Janis, Jennifer, Ginetta, Tara. **Educ:** Grambling State Univ, BS 1959; Xavier Univ, Further Study 1960; LA Tech Ruston, Further Study 1970; Southern Univ Baton Rouge, MEd 1970. **Career:** Southern Univ at Shreveport, dir upward bound 1978, chmn speech dept 1979-, dir of evening div. **Orgs:** Owner Private Employment Agency 1964, Product Co 1968, Dixie Janitorial Serv 1970-85, Restaurant 1972; bd mem Caddo Par School Bd 1975-84; mem bd of dir Caddo Comm Action Agency 1975-84. **Honors/Awds:** Grant in cont ed Southern Univ New Orleans 1972; Received approx 50 awards. **Home Addr:** 1538 Martha Ave, Shreveport, LA 71101. **Business Addr:** Chm of Speech Dept, Southern Univ, 3050 Dr Martin L King Dr, Shreveport, LA 71107.

WILLIAMS, ROBERT LEE, JR.
Physician, public health consultant. **Personal:** Born May 16, 1955, Dayton, OH; son of Loretta Delores Thomas Williams and Robert Lee Williams Sr; married Dawn Manning, Jul 11, 1987; children: Camille Monique. **Educ:** Morgan State Univ, BS, 1977; Meharry Medical Coll, MD, 1986; Hahnemann Univ Hospital, 1986-90; Emory University, MPH 1996. **Career:** US Army Chemical Corps, military instructor, 1977-79; Third Armored Div Europe, chem staff officer, 1979-82; Meharry Medical Coll, medical student, 1982-86; Hahnemann Univ Hospital, ob/gyn resident, 1986-90, chief resident, 1989-90; Morehouse School of Medicine, Dept of Ob/Gyn, clinical instructor, 1990-91, asst prof, 1991-; Southwest Hosp, board of directors, 1995-97. **Orgs:** Life mem, Kappa Alpha Psi Fraternity, 1976-; mem, Amer Medical Assn, 1982-; Natl Alumni Assn of Morgan State Univ, 1984-; Natl Alumni Assoc of Meharry Medical Coll, 1986-; mem, NAACP, 1986-; junior fellow, Amer Coll of Ob/Gyn, 1986-; mem, Natl Assn of Doctors, 1987-; mem Natl Medical Assn, 1986-; mem, Atlanta Medical Assn, 1991-; mem, GA State Obstetrical Soc, 1991-; board of directors, Obnet Women's Healthcare Network, LLC, Atlanta 1996; Southwest Hosp, president, medical staff, 1995-97; Public Health & Epidemiology, Atlanta GA, consultant, 1996-; American Public Health Association, 1996-. **Honors/Awds:** Upjohn Achievement Award in Obstetrics and Gynecology, 1986; Promethean Kappa Tau Honor Society, MSU, 1974; Beta Kappa Chi, Science Org, MSU, 1975-77; author, "A Retrospective Study of Pregnancy Complicated with Infection by Treponema Pallidum," Hahnemann Hospital, 1988, "Cocaine Use in a High-Risk Obstetrical Population: How Serious Is the Problem," Hahnemann Hospital, 1989; Administrative Chief Resident of the Year, Hahnemann Hosp, 1990; Active Candidate for Certification, American Bd of Ob/Gyn, 1990; ROTC Distinguished Military Cadet/Graduate, Morgan State Univ, 1975-77; coauthor "Cocaine Use at the Time of Admission to a Labor & Delivery Unit.". **Military Serv:** AUS capt 5 yrs; Army Achievement Medal 1982. **Business Addr:** 505 Fariburn Rd, Ste 200, Atlanta, GA 30301.

WILLIAMS, ROBERT W. See Obituaries section.

WILLIAMS, RODNEY ELLIOTT
Chief of police (retired). **Personal:** Born Nov 14, 1928, San Francisco, CA; son of Ruby Williams and Nelson Williams; married Joyce Gray; children: Rodney II, Brian, Vivian. **Educ:** San Francisco City Coll, AA 1956; San Francisco State Univ, BA 1972; Golden Gate Univ, MA 1973. **Career:** San Francisco Police Dept, dir 1969-77; City & Cnty of San Francisco, insp of police retired July 1983; Peralta Comm College Dist, chief of police 1983-88; 9th Circuit United States Court of Appeals, special deputy US marshal, 1989-. **Orgs:** Bd of dir Westside Mental Health 1971-75; Reality House W 1972-76; bd of dir Comm Streetwork Ctr 1972-76; guest lecturer Golden Gate Univ 1973; Life tchng credential State of CA Comm Coll Dist in Pub Adm. **Honors/Awds:** Commendation State of CA Assembly 1968, 1977; Cert of Hon Bd of Supr 1968; Liberty Bell Award SF Bar Assn 1974; commendation, CA State Asembly 1983; commendation, CA State Senate 1983. **Military Serv:** AUS 1951-53.

WILLIAMS, ROGER
Education administrator. **Educ:** Morehead Clg, BA 1965; Atlanta U, MA 1972. **Career:** Paine Coll, asst to dean 1977-; French Paine Coll, dir instr 1976-77; Wonder World Child Devel Center Inc 1971-74; Twilight Sewing Plant, bookkeeper 1968; W Side High School, French instructor 1966-68. **Orgs:** Mem Assn Overseas Educators; NAACP; sec Twilight Improvement Assn, financial officer Amer Legion Post 597; Fulbright Assistantship 1965-66; French Govt. **Honors/Awds:** Fellowship Lycee Marcel Pagnol, Marseilles France, 1965-66. **Military Serv:** Military Serv 1968-70. **Business Addr:** Rt 2 Box 230 D, Lincolnton, GA 30817.

WILLIAMS, ROGER L.
Automobile dealer. **Career:** Southwest Ford Sales Inc, chief executive officer, currently. **Special Achievements:** Company is ranked #68 on Black Enterprise's list of top 100 auto dealers, 1994. **Business Addr:** CEO, Southwest Ford Sales Inc., 59th Pennsylvan, Oklahoma City, OK 73119, (405)681-6651.

WILLIAMS, RON ROBERT
Assistant basketball coach. **Personal:** Born Sep 24, 1944, Weirton, WV; son of Blanche and Raymond; married Faye; children: Eric, Raynia. **Educ:** West Virginia Univ, BS 1968. **Career:** San Francisco Warriors, professional basketball player 1968-73; NBA Milwaukee Bucks Retired Sphix, professional basketball plyr 1968; Univ of California, Berkeley CA, assistant basketball coach 1981-84; Iona Coll, New Rochelle, NY assistant basketball coach 1984-. **Orgs:** First basketball player to Play So Conf All-Amer 1967-68; All Conf So & Conf 1965-68. **Honors/Awds:** Athlete of year 1968; All Dist All-Amer NBA Team; Upper Ohio Valley Hall of Fame 1985; West Virginia Sport Hall of Fame 1987.

WILLIAMS, RONALD
Mayor. **Career:** Tuskegee Institute High School, principal; former aide; City of Tuskegee, mayor, currently. **Orgs:** Greenwood Bapt Church; National Business League; Elks, Optimist International; Masons; Shriners; Alpha Phi Alpha Fraternity; Tuskegee University, Board of Trustees. **Honors/Awds:** Optimist Club, International Service Award; Tiger Cubs Pack 170, Service Award; Tuskegee Institute Middle School, Distinguished Service Award. **Business Addr:** Mayor, City of Tuskegee, Tuskegee Municipal Complex, P O Box 830687, Tuskegee, AL 36083, (334)727-0065.

WILLIAMS, RONALD CHARLES
Attorney. **Personal:** Born Jun 19, 1948, Corsicana, TX; divorced; children: Steven, Anita. **Educ:** CO Sch of Mines, BS 1971; Univ of Utah, MBA 1978; Univ of CO, JD 1979. **Career:** US Dept of the Interior, patent counsel 1979-82; Storage Tech Corp, corp & patent counsel 1982-85; private practice, attorney-at-law. **Orgs:** Pres Tapestry Films Inc; bd of dirs Cadric Drug Rehab Org. **Military Serv:** AUS capt 4 1/2 yrs. **Business Addr:** Attorney-at-Law, 2413 Washington #250, Denver, CO 80205.

WILLIAMS, RONALD LEE
Elected official. **Personal:** Born Aug 31, 1949, Washington, DC; married Fern M; children: Ron Williams II, Nateshia, Natia M. **Educ:** Univ of the Dist of Columbia, Soc 1977. **Career:** Shaw UM Food & Clothing Bank, vice chmn 1981-; SE Vicarate Cluster of Churches, chmn of the bd 1984-85; Advisory Neighborhood Commiss, chairperson 1984-; Camp Simms Citizen Adv Task Force, chmn 1984-; Christian Social Concerns, dir. **Orgs:** Mil personnel tech Sec of the Army/Army Discharge Review Bds 1973-; bd mem Concerned Citizens on Alcohol/Drug Abuse 1982-, Comm Action Involvement 1983-; United Way 1983; UBF 1983-; chairperson, Hands Across the Community, United Methodist Church, 1990-93; coordinator, Summer Tent Ministry, 1990-92; Black Community Developer Program, Inc, exec dir. **Honors/Awds:** Letters Appreciation/Commendations and Plaques from Community Org, Mayor, City Council 1980. **Military Serv:** AUS 124th Signal Battalion 3 yrs. **Business Addr:** Dir, Church & Soc Christians for Social Concerns, 2525 12th Pl SE, Washington, DC 20020.

WILLIAMS, RONALD WESLEY
Airline customer service manager. **Personal:** Born Nov 16, 1946, Chicago, IL; son of Odessa Shelton Williams and Richard G Williams; married Doris; children: Donna, Michele. **Educ:** Chapman Coll, BA, 1974. **Career:** United Airlines, asst to vice pres, 1976-79, passenger serv mgr, 1979-80, city mgr, 1980-83, customer serv mgr, 1983-84, general mgr customer serv. **Orgs:** Treasurer North Merced California Rotary Club, 1974; vice pres, Lions Club, 1979; mem, Toledo Sales & Mktg, 1980; bd mem, WGTE TV Comm Adv Bd, 1980; comm mem, Bowling Green Univ, Aerotech Advisory Comm, 1980; volunteer, United Way Corp Rep, 1981; mem, Skal Club, 1976; mem, Madison, WI, Public Safety Review Bd, 1989-; bd of dir, Wexford Village Home Owners Assn, 1989-. **Honors/Awds:** Award of Merit, United Airlines, 1988; private pilot, 1976-. **Military Serv:** IL Army Natl Guard 1966-67. **Business Addr:** General Manager, Customer Service, United Airlines, Minneapolis-St Paul Intl Airport, St Paul, MN 55111.

WILLIAMS, ROSA B.
Public relations manager. **Personal:** Born Sep 29, 1933, Starke, FL. **Educ:** Santa Fe Comm Coll, AA 1976. **Career:** Comm Action Agency, super of Outreach workers 1965-70; Bell Nursery, supervising cook 1965-70; Comm Action Agency, super 1971-72; Alachua Co Coord Child Care, eligibility worker 1972; Sunland Ctr Dept of HRS, activities coord 1983-. **Orgs:** Mem of the following organs Elk 33 Degree; chmn Concerned Citizen for Juvenile Justice; League of Women Voters; chmn Alachua Co Democratic Club; Alachua Co Democratic Exec Comm; chmn Debonaire Social Club; bd of dirs Shands Hosp; chmn bd of dirs United Gainesville Comm Develop Corp; Comm on the Status of Women; Sickle Cell Organ of Alachua Co; Alachua Co Girls Club of Amer; NW 5th Ave Neighborhood Crime Prevention Prog; adv council Displaced Homemaker Prog; 1st vice chmn Alachua Co NAACP; dir United Way; Alachua Co Coord Child Care; Alachua Co Economic Develop; Comm Policy Adv Comm; chairperson, Black on Black Task Force. **Honors/Awds:** Recognition of Contribution Cultural Arts Coalition; Gainesville Sun's 6th Most Influential Citizen Recognition; Comm Serv Awd NAACP 1968; Very Important Citizen Recognition City of Gainesville 1974; Leadership & Achievement Awd Alpha Phi Alpha Frat 1974; dir United Way 1968-71, 1975-80; Outstanding Serv to Comm Awd Gainesville Review of Issues & Trends 1978; Comm Serv Awd Alpha Phi Alpha 1979; Disting Serv to the Comm in Field of Educ Lodge 1218 IBPOE Elks 1983; Disting Serv Awd Alachua Co Educ Assn 1983; Citizen Against Criminal Environment Gainesville Police Dept 1984; Springhill Baptist Church contribution to Black Comm 1984. **Business Addr:** Public Relations Manager, Sunland Training Ctr, PO Box 1150, Gainesville, FL 32602.

WILLIAMS, RUBY MAI
Association executive. **Personal:** Born Aug 30, 1904, Topeka, KS; married Melvin Williams. **Educ:** KS State Tchrs Clge, tchng credential 1931. **Career:** Pasadena NAACP 1966-; real estate sales; natl Youth Work Com 1962-69; Golden State Life Ins Co, cashier & clk 1936-43; CA State Employment, cnslng & Placement 1932-36. **Orgs:** Pres Pasadena Dem Womens Club 1967-68; pres Interracial Womens Club 1969-70; org & pres NW Citizens of Pasadena 1978; chmn Pasadena Recreation Commn 1971-72; adv Com Citizens Urban Renewal Pasadena 1977; mayors com City of Pasadena 1979-; adv com Kid Space-Mus for Children 1979-. **Honors/Awds:** Citizen of Year Pasadena Human Relations 1975; listed in Pasadena 100 Yrs of History 1975; Woman of Year Knights of Pythians LA CA 1976; Citizens Award PTA 1977; YWCA Woman of Year Pasadena YWCA 1977; Youth Work Award Natl Youth Work Com NY 1977; 1st Black Kindergarten Tchr Topeka.

WILLIAMS, RUDY V.
Educational administrator. **Personal:** Born in Waxahachie, TX; married Ora Ruth Pitts; children: Keith W, Derwin B, Cedric L, Risha V. **Educ:** Huston-Tillotson Clge Austin TX, bS Bus Admin; Univ of AZ Tucson, MEd 1964; FL Atlantic Univ Boca Raton FL, edS 1975. **Career:** Miami-Dade Comm Coll, assc dean 1970-, admin asst 1969-70; Comm Action Agency EOPI Miami FL, prog admin 1966-69; Sears Roebuck & Co, salesman 1967-69; Tucson Public School, teacher 1963-66; Bureau of Indian Affairs, prin teacher 1956-63; Southern Assn of Coll & School, consult 1972-; FL Intl Univ Miami, adj prof 1975-. **Orgs:** Mem Phi Beta Sigma Frat 1952-; vice pres St Albans Day Nursery 1970-; mem Phi Delta Kappa 1972-. **Honors/Awds:** "Unemployment Waste Away" FL Voc Jour 1978; "FL Comm Clge Occupational Deans & Dir Competencies" unpub 1979; "Viable Guidance for the Minority Student"Minority Educ 1979. **Military Serv:** AUS sgt 1954-56. **Business Addr:** Miami-Dade Comm Coll, 1101 SW 104 St, Miami, FL 33176.

WILLIAMS, RUNETTE FLOWERS. See FLOWERS, RUNETTE.

WILLIAMS, RUSSELL, II
Production sound mixer. **Personal:** Born Oct 14, 1952, Washington, DC; children: Myles Candace, Khemet Ellison. **Educ:** The American University, BA, film production, literature, 1974; University of Sound Arts, electronics certificate, 1979. **Career:** WRC/NBC Television, video tape, audio engineer, 1973, 1977; WMAL/ABC Radio, engineer, editor, 1978-79; Sound Is Ready, motion picture sound recording owner; Intersound Studios, studio engineer, 1981; University of California, School of Radio, Television, and Film, associate professor, 1990; American University, Columbia University, Howard University, UCLA, and others, masters class lecturer, 1990-; Irv Schechter Agency. **Orgs:** Academy of Motion Picture Arts and Sciences, Sound Branch; Academy of Television Arts and Sciences, Sound Branch; Alliance of Black Entertainment Technicians; Cinema Audio Society; International Alliance of Theatrical Stage Employes, Local 695. **Honors/Awds:** Nominee, BAFTA Craft Awards, Best Sound, 1992; Best Achievement in Sound "Oscar" for Dances with Wolves, AMPAS, 1990; Best Achievement in Sound "Oscar" for Glory, AMPAS, 1989; Outstanding Achievement in Sound "Emmy" for Terrorist on Trial (CBS), ATAS, 1988. **Business Phone:** (310)278-8070.

WILLIAMS, RUTHANN EVEGE
Business executive. **Personal:** Born May 13, 1945, Buffalo, NY; divorced; children: Nichole Suzanne. **Educ:** SUNY Buffalo, BS Secondary Ed 1962-66, MS History Ed 1971, PhD Higher Ed Admin 1981. **Career:** Buffalo Public Schools, teacher 1966-71; Erie Comm Coll, asst to prof 1971-75; SUNY Buffalo, dir of urban planning 1975-76; Northern VA Comm Coll, asstto pres 1976-77; Burroughs Corp, dir public affairs 1982-86; Equitable Life Assurance Soc of the US, dir of corporate support 1986-, exec asst to the chairman. **Orgs:** Bd of dir Children's Hosp, Detroit Historical Soc; mem bd of control Lake Superior Coll; mem, bd of dir Gifts in Kind Natl United Way; mem Public Relations Soc of Amer, Detroit Chap of Links Inc; bd of dir Health Watch. **Honors/Awds:** Article CASE Currents

1981; Women in Educational Fundraising. **Home Addr:** 200 E 71st St Apt 15G, New York, NY 10021. **Business Addr:** Exec Asst to Chrmn of Board, Equitable Life Assurance Soc, of the US, 787 7th Avenue, New York, NY 10019.

WILLIAMS, SAMM-ART (SAMUEL ARTHUR)
Actor, director, playwright. **Personal:** Born Jan 20, 1946, Burgaw, NC; son of Valdosia Williams and Samuel Williams. **Educ:** Morgan State College, BA, political science/psychology, 1968. **Career:** Theater appearances include: Nowhere to Run, Nowhere to Hide, 1974; Liberty Call, 1975; Waiting for Mongo, 1975; The First Breeze of Summer, 1975; Eden, 1976; The Brownsville Raid, 1976-77; Night Shift, 1977; Black Body Blues, 1978; Nevis Mountain Dew, 1978-79; Old Phantoms, 1979; Home, 1982-83; film appearances include: The Wanderers, 1979; Dressed to Kill, 1980; Blood Simple, 1984; Hot Resort, 1985; Night of the Juggler, 1980; television appearances include: numerous stories on American Playhouse, 1985-86; 227, 1987; Frank's Place, story editor/actor, 1987; All My Children; Search for Tomorrow; related career: Freedom Theatre, company member, 1968-73; Negro Ensemble Company, 1973-78; actor in tv commercials; writings include: Welcome to Black River, 1975; The Coming, 1976; Do Unto Ots, 1976; A Love Play, 1976; The Last Caravan, 1977; Brass Birds Don't Sing, 1978; Home, 1979-80; Sophisticated Ladies, contributor, 1981; Friends, 1983; Eyes of the American, 1985; Cork, 1986; numerous television shows and unproduced plays, 1975-; Fresh Prince of Bel-Air, writer/producer, currently. **Orgs:** Omega Psi Phi Frat, 1967-; Screen Actors Guild; Writers Guild of America; Dramatists Guild. **Honors/Awds:** Tony Award nomination, Home, 1980; Outer Critics Circle, John Gassner Playwriting Award, Home, 1980; Guggenheim Fellowship for playwriting, 1981; North Carolina Governor's Award, 1981; Natl Endowment Fellowship for playwriting, 1984; Audelco Recognition Award, Home, 1980; Antoinette Perry Award, nomination, Best Play, Home, 1980.

WILLIAMS, SANDRA K.
Attorney. **Personal:** Born Mar 17, 1954, Houston, TX; daughter of Claretha Bradley Williams and Joe Williams; children: Katherine A. **Educ:** Smith Coll, Northampton MA, AB, 1975; Univ of Michigan, Ann Arbor MI, JD, 1978. **Career:** Natl Labor Relations Bd, Washington DC, staff atty, 1978-81, Los Angeles CA, field atty, 1981-82; CBS Inc, Los Angeles CA, labor atty, 1982-89, broadcast counsel, 1989-90, deputy west coast counsel, 1990-95, asst gen counsel, 1995-. **Orgs:** State Bars of: Texas, Washington, DC, California, 1978-; LA County Bar Assn, 1983-; Black Women Lawyers Association of Los Angeles, 1985-; California Assn of Black Lawyers, 1986-. **Business Addr:** Assistant General Counsel, CBS Inc, 7800 Beverly Blvd, Los Angeles, CA 90036.

WILLIAMS, SANDRA ROBERTS
Educator. **Personal:** Born Nov 2, 1940, Houston, TX; daughter of Thelma Roberts and Brownie Roberts; children: David, Michele. **Educ:** Texas Southern Univ-Houston, BM, Educ, 1961; Univ of New Mexico-Albuquerque, MA, 1980. **Career:** Houston Independent School, music & classroom teacher, 1962-64; Albuquerque Public Schools, classroom teacher, 1964-70; Univ of New Mexico, academic advisor/counselor, 1973-81; Univ of Texas, Medical Branch, program coord, 1982-, director of recruitment, currently. **Orgs:** Consultant, analytical reading, test taking skills, note taking skills, time management skills; admin, Saturday Biomedical Sciences Forum, 1983-; mem, Natl Assn of Medical Minority Educ, Science Inc, School Health Programs, Advisory Comm, Delta Sigma Theta Inc, Galveston Alumni, Natl Tech Assn. **Special Achievements:** Publications, "Medical School Familiarization Program, Health Careers Network," Vol III, No 2, November, 1983; "Academic Support Services presents, Learning Strategies Workshop, Featuring Test Taking and Reading Skills," w/JE Spurlin, UTMB Publication, March, 1983. **Home Addr:** 10201 Schaper Dr, Galveston, TX 77554. **Business Addr:** Director of Recruitment, University of Texas Medical Branch, G210 Ashbel Smith, Galveston, TX 77550.

WILLIAMS, SCOTT CHRISTOPHER
Professional basketball player. **Personal:** Born Mar 21, 1968, Hacienda Heights, CA; married Lisa. **Educ:** Univ of North Carolina. **Career:** Chicago Bulls, center-forward, 1990-94; Philadelphia 76ers, 1994-. **Business Addr:** Professional Basketball Player, Philadelphia 76ers, One Corestates Complex, Philadelphia, PA 19148, (215)339-7676.

WILLIAMS, SCOTT W.
Educator. **Personal:** Born Apr 22, 1943, Staten Island, NY. **Educ:** Morgan State Clge, BS 1964; Lehigh Univ, MS 1967, PhD 1969. **Career:** PA State Univ Allentown Center, instr 1968-69; Morgan State Coll, instr 1969; PA State Univ Univ Park, reseach assc 1969-71; State Univ of NY at Buffalo, asst prof 1971-; SUNY, assc prof math 1977-; Rochester Folk Art Guild, instr 1975-; Amer Math Soc Notices, editor 1975-. **Orgs:** Mem Amer Math Soc; mem Rochester Folk Art Guild 1972-; chmn Balck Uhuru Soc 1967-69.

WILLIAMS, SERENA
Professional tennis player. **Career:** Tennis player, currently. **Special Achievements:** Competed against sister Venus in the Australian Open, the first time two African American sisters competed against each other in a pro event.

WILLIAMS, SHERLEY ANNE
Educator, author. **Personal:** Born Aug 25, 1944, Bakersfield, CA; daughter of Lelia Maria (Siler) Williams and Jessee Winson Williams; children: John Malcolm. **Educ:** Fresno State Coll (now California State Univ, Fresno), BA, 1966; Howard Univ, graduate study, 1966-67; Brown Univ, MA, 1972. **Career:** Fresno State Coll (now California State Univ, Fresno), co-dir of tutorial program, 1965-66, lecturer in ethnic studies, 1969-70; Miles Coll, Atlanta, GA, admin internal asst to pres, 1967-68; affiliated with Systems Devel Corp, Santa Monica, CA, 1968-69; Federal City Coll, Washington, DC, consultant in curriculum devel and community educator, 1970-72; California State Univ, Fresno, assoc prof of English, 1972-73; Univ of California, San Diego, La Jolla, asst prof, 1973-76, assoc prof, 1976-82, prof of Afro-Amer literature, 1982—, dept chrpsn, 1976-82. **Orgs:** Mem, Poetry Soc of Amer; mem, Modern Language Assoc. **Honors/Awds:** Author of Give Birth To Brightness: A Thematic Study in Neo-Black Literature, Dial, 1972, The Peacock Poems, Wesleyan Univ Press, 1975, Some One Sweet Angel Chile (poems), Morrow, 1982, and Dessa Rose, Morrow, 1986; Natl Book Award nomination, 1976, for The Peacock Poems; Fulbright lecturer, Univ of Ghana, 1984; Dessa Rose was named a notable book in 1986 by the New York Times.

WILLIAMS, SHERMAN
Photo editor. **Personal:** Born Jan 1, 1961, Fort Benning, GA; son of Addie Williams and Thomas Williams. **Educ:** OH State Univ, Columbus, OH, BA, 1983. **Career:** Public Opinion, Chambersburg, PA, staff photographer, 1984-85; Standard-Examiner, Ogden, UT, staff photographer, 1985-87; The Hartford Courant, Hartford, CT, staff photographer, 1987-, picture editor, 1990-91; The Philadelphia Inquirer, picture editor, 1991-. **Orgs:** Vice pres, CT Assn of Black Communicators, 1987-; co-program dir, bd or dir, Greater Hartford Minority Jour Program, 1990-91; student clip contest chair, Natl Press Photographers Assn, 1990-91; Historians Double Diamonds Ski Club, 1989-90; mem, Natl Press Photographer Assn, 1985-; mem, Natl Assn of Black Journalists, 1986-. **Honors/Awds:** CT New Photographer of the Year, 1988; Honorable Mention, Natl Assn of Black Journalists Photo Contest, 1989; 1st & 3rd Place Photo Awards, CT News Photogs, 1991; 4th Region 1, NPPA Contest, 1988; 1st Place News Photo, Northern Short Course.

WILLIAMS, SHERMAN
Professional football player. **Personal:** Born Aug 13, 1973, Mobile, AL. **Educ:** University of Alabama, attended. **Career:** Dallas Cowboys, running back, 1995-. **Special Achievements:** Selected in the 2nd round/47th overall pick in the 1995 NFL Draft. **Business Addr:** Professional Football Player, Dallas Cowboys, 1 Cowboys Pkwy, Irving, TX 75063, (214)556-9900.

WILLIAMS, SHIRLEY YVONNE
Physician. **Personal:** Born in Washington, DC. **Educ:** Howard Univ, 1955, 1959; NY Med Ctr, resd 1962. **Career:** Outpatient Ambulatory Svc, dir. **Orgs:** Mem State Bd of Mental Health; State Cncl of Alcohol & Drugs; chmn Assc of CT Outpatient Clinics; Assc of Nervous & Mental Disease; Amer Psych Assc; Amer Acad of Sci; Natl Med Assc; AMA; Fairfield Co Assc; life mem NAACP; chmn Keystone House; mem bd Carver Fnd Father Looney 1977. **Honors/Awds:** Fellow Amer Psychiat Assc. **Business Addr:** 24 Stevens St, Norwalk, CT 06856.

WILLIAMS, SIDNEY B., JR.
Attorney. **Personal:** Born Dec 31, 1935, Little Rock, AR; son of Eloise Gay Cole and Sidney B Williams Sr; married Carolyn. **Educ:** Univ WI, BS 1961; George Washington Univ Law Sch, JD 1967. **Career:** Upjohn Co, patent atty, currently; US Patent Office, patent exmr; Gen Am Transp Corp, rsrch devel engr; Montreal Alouettes, professional ftbl player. **Orgs:** Mem MI DC Bar Assn; Kalamazoo Co MI Am Nat Patent Law Assn Bd; tsts Borgess Hosp bd dir Douglas Comm Assn All Am Ftbl Team Chem & Engring; News 1957-58; mem Iron Cross Hon Soc 1958. **Military Serv:** USMCR. **Business Addr:** Attorney, 301 Henrietta, Kalamazoo, MI 49001.

WILLIAMS, SNOWDEN J.
Instructor. **Personal:** Born Jul 19, 1959, Detroit, MI; son of Claudette and Snowden. **Educ:** Guilford Coll, BS 1981; IESA Caracas Venezuela, MBA 1982; Univ NC-Chapel Hill, MBA 1983. **Career:** IBM, public sector consultant 1983-85, acct mktg rep 1986-90, advisory instructor, marketing education, 1991-. **Orgs:** Consultant NBMBA Assn 1986-. **Honors/Awds:** Consortium Fellowship for Grad Study in Mgmt 1981-83.

WILLIAMS, STANLEY KING
Government official. **Personal:** Born Jan 25, 1948, Columbus, GA; son of Lucille Willis Williams and Robert Williams; married Judy Chichester Williams, Apr 5, 1986; children: Lanita L, Malik K. **Educ:** Shaw Univ, Raleigh, NC, BA 1970. **Career:** Shaw University, student counselor, 1967-70; COPE Newark, youth job development specialist, 1968-69; North Carolina Dept of Corrections, classification specialist, 1970; US Army Germany, neuropsychiatric tech/drug counseling, 1970-72; Programs Gales Maternity Clinic, coordinator, 1972-74; Department of Manpower, job development specialist, 1972; Veterans Employment DC Dept of Labor/Veterans Admin Regional Office, supervisor & coordinator, 1976-86; DC Dept of Employment Service, supervisor, 1986-89, operations manager, NE Employment Center, 1989-94; South Capital Employment Ctr, operations manager, 1994-95; US Department of Labor, director of veterans employment & training, 1995-. **Orgs:** Chmn Mt Pleasant Advisory Neighborhood Commn 1976-80; Dept of Human Resources, consultant sex educ program 1973; DC Govt establishment of ANC Citizens Neighborhood Council Coordinating Comr, advisor 1975; pres King Enterprises Inc; mem Amer Legion WA Alliance for Neighborhood Govts; chmn Mt Pleasant Advisory Neighborood Comm; del DC Black Assembly; mem Shaw Univ Alumni Assn; mem Bancroft PTA; student of Economics & Political Trends; com S African Self-determination; Smithsonian Fellow Smithsonian Inst; asst in estab 1st Army drug program in Germany 1971; coordinator & supvr Veterans Employment Center VA Regional Office 1976; pres, King Enterprises, 1976; sr deacon, Shiloh Baptist Church, Washington, DC, 1987; American Legion, Carter G Woodson Chapter, Association for the Study of African-American Life & History; 1st vice chairman, Brotherhood of Shiloh Men, Shiloh Baptist Church. **Honors/Awds:** Appreciation Award ANC 70 1977; Congressional Appreciation Award Congressman Fountroy 1978; Outstanding Srv Award Mt Pleasant Advisory Neighborhood Commn 1978; Meritorious & Distinguished Serv Award VFW 1978; Commend Award Vietnam Veteran Civic Council 1978; Comm Serv Award Natl Black Veteran Org 1979; drafted adopted signed the org Neighborhood Bill of Responsibilities & Rights Independence Square Philadelphia 1976; promoter/sponsor, promoted largest gospel convention given in Washington, DC, 1983; Community Service Award, DC City Council, 1982. **Military Serv:** AUS sergeant E-5 1970-72. **Home Addr:** 1806 Lawrence St, NE, Washington, DC 20018. **Business Phone:** (202)724-7004.

WILLIAMS, STARKS J.
Physician. **Personal:** Born Feb 16, 1921, Orangeburg, SC; son of Daisy Gaither Williams and Willie White Williams; married Elizabeth McWilliamson, Mar 17, 1990; children: Michael, Sara, Mary, Candace, Cantis. **Educ:** SC State Clge Orangeburg, BS 1942; Meharry Med Coll Nashville, MD 1945. **Career:** Doctors Clinic, sec/assc 1954-; Richard Cabot Clinic Prog City Proj Mercy Hospital KC MO, chief pediatrician 1965-70. **Orgs:** Reg VII med consult Head Start Consultation Proj HEW 1977-; med consult State of MO Sickle Cell Prog 1974-; bd mem Visiting Nurse Assn KC MO 1972-78; com mem Site-Selection & Establishment Met Jr Clge KC MO 1969; med dir Niles Home for Children 1965-; bd mem/treas Comm Dev Corp; pres bd dir Lincoln Redevelopment Corp; bd mem/treas Alpha Plastic Corp; chmn bd dir Third World Trading Corp; pres TNW Intl; mem Natl Med; assc mem KC Med Soc; mem Jackson Co Med Soc; mem Mid Westerners Club; mem Omega Psi Phi Frat; diplomate Amer Bd of Pediatrics 1951; fellow Amer Acad of Pediatrics; clinical assc prof Univ of MO Sch of Med. **Military Serv:** AUS capt med corp & reserve 1952-54. **Business Addr:** Physician, 2525 E Meyer Blvd, Kansas City, MO 64132.

WILLIAMS, STEPFRET
Professional football player. **Personal:** Born Jun 14, 1973, Minden, LA. **Educ:** Northeast Louisiana, attended. **Career:** Dallas Cowboys, wide receiver, 1996-. **Business Addr:** Professional Football Player, Dallas Cowboys, One Cowboys Pkwy, Irving, TX 75063, (214)556-9900.

WILLIAMS, STERLING B., JR.
Physician. **Personal:** Born Apr 3, 1941, Little Rock, AR; divorced; children: Angela, Spencer, Sterling III. **Educ:** Univ of IL, BS 1963; Northern IL Univ, MS 1966; Univ of AR Med Center, MD 1973; Univ AR Med Center, PhD. **Career:** IL Inst of Tech Rsch Inst, rsch asst 1963; School of Nursing Univ AR Med Center, instr 1971; Private practice, physician 1976-; Univ of KS Med Ctr, assoc prof 1979-; Columbia Univ Coll of Physicians & Surgeons, prof 1987-; Harlem Hospital Center; dir of dept of Ob/Gyn, 1987-. **Orgs:** Mem, Natl Coalition on Health; general council, KC Union Presbyterian; coord Minority Student Admissions Adv Comm; mem Univ KS Med Center, KC Civic Chorus, Alpha Phi Alpha Soc Frat, Sigma Xi Rsch Hon soc, NIH Predoctoral Fellow Univ of AR 1966-69; solo singing pref KC Symphony Orchestra; vice chmn Presbyterian Council on Theology & Culture; mem Kaw Valley Med Soc, Sigma Pi Phi Frat. **Honors/Awds:** Phi Eta Sigma Scholastic Honorary. **Business Addr:** Professor, Columbia Univ/Harlem Hosp, 506 Lenox Ave, Dept of Ob & Gyn, New York, NY 10037.

WILLIAMS, SYLVIA J.
Educator. **Personal:** Born Jul 11, 1939, Washington, DC; daughter of Mary Coghill Burnett and Wallace Burnett; children: Deborah Bushrod, Rodney Williams. **Educ:** Bowie State Coll, BS 1964, MA, 1970; attended Univ Maryland. **Career:** Prince Georges Co Bd of Educ, teacher 27 yrs. **Orgs:** Mem

NAACP; chmn Educ Com Local Branch; past sec King George Citizens Assn 1973-74; past counseling & testing coord Sickle Cell Assn; sec Vikingettes Social Club; mem Dial a Ride; coord Local Rainbow Coalition, Wilder for Lt Governor, Host and Hostesses for Mayor Marion Barry's Inagural Reception; mem NAACP; coord Health and Social Serv of Natl Capitol Baptist Convention; bd mem Rappohonack Assoc; Citizens Advisory Comm to the District of Columbia, mem of exec bd; 4th vice pres, Washington, DC, branch, NAACP, 1991; national co-chairperson Region 7, Women in NAACP, 1987-; redistricting committee member, King George County, VA, 1991; vice pres, Project Shares. **Honors/Awds:** Charlotte B Hunter Citizenship Awd 1962; Mayors Youth Council Awd 1963; Citizen of the Yr Omega Psi Phi 1974; Sickle Cell Assn Awd 1971-83; Amer Citizenery Awd 1983; Instructor of the Year Mt Bethel Bapt Assoc 1983; Outstanding Serv Awd by Life Membership Div of Natl Office NAACP 1983; Rainbow Coalition Awd of Merit 1984; American Humanitarian Awd 1984; Volunteer of the Year AT&T; Unsung Heroine Awd NAACP; Presidential Award, Washington DC, branch, NAACP, 1990; Merit Award, National Women in NAACP; NAACP, Keeper of the Flame Award, 1992.

WILLIAMS, T. JOYCE
Educator (retired). **Personal:** Born Jan 24, 1930, Muskogee Co; married Paul Williams Jr; children: Cheryl Elizabeth Jackson, Jacquelyn Elaine. **Educ:** Wichita State Univ, BA 1965, EdM 1974. **Career:** Bd of Educ USD 259, teacher 1965-85. **Orgs:** Trainer Local Bldg Dir Ldrshp Acad K NEA 1975-76; co-org Ethnic Minority Caucus NEA Wichita 1975-76; chmn Pub Affairs TV Prog NEA Wichita 1975; elected mem PR&R Com NEA Wichita 1979; delegate Local State Natl Rep Assemblies NEA 1974, 75, 79, 80; adv 1980, historian pub rel 1976-78 Sigma Gamma Rho Sorority; life mem NAACP; Political Action Com 1979; mem Holy Savior Cath Ch Wichita; Vol God's Food Pantry-Holy Savior Church, 1986-88; Elected Human Resources Bd, City of WI, 1989-; Elected city official Department of Human Services, 1990-93; Elected 4 yr term CPO, NE Wichita, 1994-; Nominated mem Intl Society of Poets, 1996-97; Life mem, Intl Society of Poets, pen name ''Mama'' Williams, 1996-. **Honors/Awds:** Wichita's Tchr of Year 1975; recipt mini-grant Prog, Teaching with Interest Centers 1975; Chair Small Grp Session KS Conf on Language Arts Studies 1978; article to editor Wichita Eagle-Beacon 1979; Letter of Appreciation from CPO Coordinator, Offic of City Mgr, 1995; Elected to Intl Poetry Hall of Fame, 1997. **Special Achievements:** Speaker-rep to address House of Reps, Topeka, KS, 1995-; Poem, Entry ''Through the Hourglass My Vision,'' Mama Joyce Williams, national lib of poetry, 1996-; poems published in ''Best Poems of 1997,'' and ''Best Poems of 1998;'' exhibit on the WWW at http://www.poets.com. **Home Addr:** 4025 Christy, Wichita, KS 67220.

WILLIAMS, TARA
Professional basketball player. **Personal:** Born Jul 23, 1974. **Educ:** Auburn. **Career:** Phoenix Mercury, forward, 1997; Detroit Shock, 1998-. **Business Addr:** Professional Basketball Player, Detroit Shock, The Palace of Auburn Hills, 2 Championship Dr, Auburn Hills, MI 48326, (248)377-0100.

WILLIAMS, TERRI L.
Educational administrator. **Personal:** Born May 18, 1958, Bridgeton, NJ. **Educ:** Howard Univ, BS 1981, MEd 1984. **Career:** The Wash Alcohol Counseling Ctr, admin asst 1980-82; Howard Student Special Svcs, educ specialist 1984-85; Howard Upward Bound, sr counselor 1985-86; St Lawrence Univ, asst dir of admissions 1986-. **Orgs:** Mem Delta Sigma Theta Inc 1978-; public relations coord BOF Howard Univ Alumnae 1983-; volunteer DC Mayor's Re-election Comm 1986; exhibitors coord Mid-Eastern Assoc of Educ Oppor Prog Personnel 1986. **Honors/Awds:** Outstanding Young Women of Amer 1982,85; MEAEOPP Conf Serv Awd 1986; Mayor's Summer Youth Emp Program Contribution Awd. **Home Addr:** RD 2 Russell Rd, Box 166, Canton, NY 13617. **Business Addr:** Asst Dir of Admissions, St Lawrence University, Admissions Office, Canton, NY 13617.

WILLIAMS, TERRIE MICHELLE
Corporate public relations consultant. **Personal:** Born May 12, 1954, Mt Vernon, NY; daughter of Marie and Charles. **Educ:** Brandeis Univ, BA (Cum Laude) 1975; Columbia Univ NY, MA 1977. **Career:** New York Hosp, medical social worker 1977-80; The Black Filmmaker Foundation, prog admin 1980-81; The Black Owned Comm Alliance, exec dir 1981-82; The World Inst of Black Communications, exec dir 1982; Essence Communications Inc, vp/dir of corporate communication 1982-87; pres the Terrie Williams Agency, 1988-. **Orgs:** Mem-at-large Brandeis Univ Alumni Assoc; mem Natl Corporate Adv Bd; mem communications comm Amer Heart Assoc; mem Women in Communications. **Honors/Awds:** DParke Gibson Awd for PR Public Relations Soc of Amer 1981; Building Brick Awd New York Urban League 1987; Women in Communications, Matrix Award in Public Relations, 1991. **Special Achievements:** Co-author with Joe Cooney, The Personal Touch, Warner Books, 1994. **Business Addr:** President, The Terrie Williams Agency, 1500 Broadway, New York, NY 10036.

WILLIAMS, TERRY
Publisher. **Personal:** Born Jun 1952, Aberdeen, MS; daughter of Julia Bowen Williams and Earl Williams; married Dwight K Deans, Jan 1985; children: Julia Rosa, Mariah Teresa, Kramer Montgomery. **Educ:** Spelman College, BA, 1974. **Career:** Young Horizons Indigo, publisher, currently. **Special Achievements:** Author: Black Sanity; Author: African-American Children's Party Planning Guide; Black, Family City Prop; African-American Children Day Book; African-American Parents Resource Guide; African-American Family City Profile; African-American Children's Religious Sourcebook. **Business Addr:** Publisher, Young Horizons Indigo, PO Box 371595, Decatur, GA 30037-1595, (404)241-5003.

WILLIAMS, THEARTRICE
Consultant. **Personal:** Born May 16, 1934, Indianolia, MS; son of Ollie Gray Williams and Fred Mack Williams; married Mary Louise Sales, May 19, 1962; children: Christopher, Jeffrey, Laurie. **Educ:** Univ of IL BA 1956; U of PA, MSW 1962; Northwestern U, 1971. **Career:** Phyllis Wheatley Comm Ctr Mpls, MN, exec dir 1965-72; State of MN, ombudsman for corrections 1972-83; Minneapolis Comm Dev Agcy, dir public hsng 1983-85; Humphrey Inst of Public Affairs Univ of MN, senior fellow, 1985-91; Rainbow Research, senior project associate, 1991-. **Orgs:** Trustee Minneapolis Fndtn 1974-83; 1st vice pres Natl Assn of Social Wrkrs 1981-83; dir The Citizens League 1980-83; chm Minority Schlrshp & Grants Prog Am Luth Ch 1970-87; president of the board, Operation De Novo; commr Minnesota Sentencing Guidelines Commn 1986-. **Honors/Awds:** Ldrshp flw Bush Fndtn Mpls, Mn 1970; dist Serv NASW Mn Chptr 1977, Natl Chptr 1983; otstandng achvmnt Natl Assn Blacks in Criminal Justice 1978; Polemarch, St. Paul-Minneapolis Alumni Chapter, Kappa Alpha Psi Fraternity 1988-; Achievement Award North Central Province, Kappa Alpha Psi Fraternity; Venture Capital and Job Development Strategies for The Black Community, Special Report; Humphrey Inst of Public Affairs, 1987; The Church as Partner in Community Economic Development, special report; Humphrey Inst of Public Affairs, 1990. **Military Serv:** US Army, sp4 1958-60. **Business Addr:** Sr Project Associate, Rainbow Research, 621 W Lake St, Minneapolis, MN 55408.

WILLIAMS, THEODORE, JR.
Automobile dealer. **Personal:** Born Jul 6, 1951, Chicago, IL; son of Theodore & Shirley Williams Sr; married Olivia, Jun 12, 1976; children: Theodore III, Brandon N. **Educ:** Trinadad State College, 1971-73. **Career:** Bob Neal Pontiac, Toyota, sales mgr, 1972-84; Jarrell Pontiac, Toyota, sales mgr, 1984-85; Bonnie Brook Ford, Ford Motor Co, 1985-88; Shamrock Lincoln-Mercury, president, 1988-. **Orgs:** Rotary Club of South Bend, 1989-; NAACP, life mem, 1992-; Lincoln-Mercury Dealer Assn, 1993-; Nissan Dealer, advisory council, 1992-; Minority Bus Dev Council, 1992-; St Joseph Chamber of Commerce, 1992-; Michiana Comm Hosp, 1992-; Crime Stoppers, bd mem, 1989-92. **Honors/Awds:** Black Enterprise, Top 100 Auto Dealer, 1991; Minority Bus Dev Council, Entrepreneur of the Year, 1993. **Business Addr:** President, Shamrock Lincoln-Mercury Nissan Saab, 120 West McKinley Ave, Mishawaka, IN 46545, (219)256-0211.

WILLIAMS, THEODORE R.
Educator. **Personal:** Born Jan 17, 1931, Palestine, TX; married Louise M Pogue; children: Wayne R, Darrell R, Brian K, Marica L, Thea Elaine. **Educ:** TX Southern Univ, BS 1952, MS 1954; Attended, OR State Univ, St Lawrence Univ, Univ of Washington, AZ State Univ; Univ of IA, PhD 1972. **Career:** St Philip's College, chmn biology dept 1954-75, asst/assoc dean 1972-82, acting pres 1982, vice pres of acad affairs emeritus 1986-. **Orgs:** Mem Phi Beta Sigma Frat 1951; mem bd trustees San Antonio Museum Assoc 1973-82; adv bd mem United Colls of San Antonio 1973-; dir Bexar Co Anemia Assoc 1978-80; appraisal review bd mem Bexar Appraisal Dist 1985-; dir Guardianship Adv Bd 1985-; member, Sigma Pi Phi Fraternity, 1988; program officer, Texas Higher Education Cooridnating Board 1991-. **Honors/Awds:** Natl Medical Fellowship Grant 1959-60; Summer Grant Natl Sci Foundation 1959, 1961, 1963, 1967; Fellowship Southern Fellowship Found 1969-71; mem Beta Kappa Chi Scientific Hon Soc; Vice Pres Academic Affairs Emeritus St Philip's Coll 1986. **Military Serv:** AUS pfc 2 yrs. **Home Addr:** 1315 Virginia Blvd, San Antonio, TX 78203.

WILLIAMS, THOMAS ALLEN
Government official. **Personal:** Born Mar 23, 1959, New York, NY; son of Minnie Johnson Williams and Jessie Williams. **Career:** Matt's Handi Mart, Buena Vista GA, mgr; ET's Arcade, Buena Vista GA, owner; T-N-T Restaurant, Buena Vista GA, owner; City of Buena Vista GA, mayor, currently. **Orgs:** Vice pres, GA Conf of Mayors; chair, 3rd District Gabeo; mem, Area Planning & Development, Marion County Bd of Health, Advisory Bd of Community Service, Sen Citizens Meals on Wheels Program. **Honors/Awds:** Black Business Award, Columbus Times Newspaper; Mayor's Motorcade, West Central Regional Hosp, 1986, 1987 & 1988; 30 Leaders of the Future, Ebony magazine, 1988.

WILLIAMS, THOMAS PEDWORTH. See Obituaries section.

WILLIAMS, TYRONE
Professional football player. **Personal:** Born Oct 22, 1972. **Educ:** Wyoming, attended. **Career:** Chicago Bears, defensive end, 1997-. **Business Addr:** Professional Football Player, Chicago Bears, 1000 Football Dr, Halas Hall at Conway Park, Lake Forest, IL 60045-4829, (847)295-6600.

WILLIAMS, TYRONE
Professional football player. **Personal:** Born May 31, 1973, Bradenton, FL; married Shantel; children: Cameron. **Educ:** Nebraska, attended. **Career:** Green Bay Packers, defensive back, 1996-. **Business Addr:** Professional Football Player, Green Bay Packers, 1265 Lombardi Ave, Green Bay, WI 54304, (414)494-2351.

WILLIAMS, ULYSSES JEAN
Educator, counselor. **Personal:** Born Sep 15, 1947, Memphis, TN; daughter of Ann Moton Warren and Ulysses Warren; married Foster Williams Sr; children: Tasha A, Foster, LaQuentin D, AnQuentin T. **Educ:** Philander Smith College, 1964-67; Univ of Central Ark, BSE 1969, MSE 1973; Ark State Univ, Cert Behavior Disorders 1980, Gifted and Talented Certification 1985; AR State Univ, Elementary Principalship Certification 1987, Counselor Education Certification, 1992. **Career:** Cotton Plant Elem School, secretary, 1969-70; Helena-West Helena Public Schools, 1970-78, 1988-89; East Ark Regional Mental Health Center, educational specialist 1978-81; Lucilia Wood Elem School, educator, 1982-88; Holly Grove Public Schools, 1989-; MSE, counselor education, 1993-. **Orgs:** Ark Ed Assn 1970-; Natl Ed Assn 1970-; PTA 1970-; Arkansas Counselors Association, 1989-; Arkansas Multicultural Association, 1989-; Arkansas Vocational Association, 1989-; pres Theta Gamma Zeta; Theta Gamma Zeta, founding president, 4 years; advisor to Amicae; regional & state coordinator South Central Region; chairman Operation Big Vote; NAACP; Second Baptist Church; chairman Christian Board of Ed; secretary Matrons; dir church choir; Gifted and Talented, advisory committee; Helena-West Helena Bd of Education 1980-86; state dir AR Zeta Phi Beta Sor Inc 1987-92; Elaine Six Year Plan Comm; comm mem Governor's Rural Devel Action Program, 1987-88; Laubach Board Member, tutor, 1988-. **Honors/Awds:** Outstanding Elem Teacher of Amer 1975; developed the Educational Component of the Adolescent Residential Facility 1978-81; Outstanding Serv as Ed Specialist 1980; Dedicated Serv as Therapeutic Foster Parents 1981-84; Zeta of the Year 1982; Outstanding Serv in the Community and Church 1983; AR Zeta of the Yr Award 1985; Outstanding Serv to South Central Region of Zeta Phi Beta Sor Inc; Zeta Phi Beta, Outstanding Service as State Director, Education Board Appointee. **Special Achievements:** Organizer: Archonette, teenage girl organization; Theta Gamma Zeta Branch of Zeta Phi Beta Sorority Inc; Young Adult Choir and Church Scholarship Fund; Parenting University, conduct parenting class and other workshops of interest; African-American Male Mentor Group, part of the Holly Grove Schools; designed report card and daily independent worksheet for emotionally disturbed youth. **Home Addr:** 239 Desota Street, West Helena, AR 72390.

WILLIAMS, VANESSA L.
Actress, singer. **Personal:** Born Mar 18, 1963, New York, NY; daughter of Milton and Helen Williams; married Ramon Hervey II, Jan 2, 1987 (divorced 1997); children: three. **Career:** Former Miss America; movie debut in The Pick Up Artist, appeared in movies Under the Gun, Eraser, Hoodlum, Soul Food; Albums: The Right Stuff, 1988; Comfort Zone, 1992; The Sweetest Days, 1994; Next, 1997; Hostess, Showtime At The Apollo; appearances on Soul Train, Live!, Dick Clark Presents, Club MTV, BET 'S Video Soul, and Live at the Improv; Television: Stompin at the Savoy, The Odyssey; Theater: broadway musical, Kiss of the Spider Woman, 1994. **Honors/Awds:** NAACP, Best New Female Recording Artist, 1988; Grammy Award nominations (3), The Right Stuff, 1993; Two Gold Records; NAACP Image Awards, Outstanding Actress, 1998.

WILLIAMS, VENUS EBONE STARR
Professional tennis player. **Personal:** Born Jun 1980; daughter of Richard and Brandee Williams. **Career:** Professional tennis player, currently. **Special Achievements:** Signed a multi-year sponsorship agreement with Reebok, 1995. **Business Addr:** Professional Tennis Player, c/o Reebok Intl Ltd, 100 Technology Center Dr, Stoughton, MA 02072.

WILLIAMS, VERNICE LOUISE
Telephone company manager (retired). **Personal:** Born Aug 13, 1934, Indianapolis, IN; daughter of Laura Chubbs Guthrie and Herman S Whitelaw Sr; married Andrew I Williams, Aug 26, 1950; children: Crystal B Thomas, Andrea J, Marlon I, Sherman A, Dewayne M, Karen R. **Educ:** Attended Indiana Univ-Purdue Univ at Indianapolis, 1970-72. **Career:** Army Finance C&R, Ft Benjamin, Harrison IN, auditor, 1952-67; Indiana Bell, Indianapolis IN, manager, 1974-92. **Orgs:** Bd mem & vice chair, Indiana Black Expo, 1974-; mem of steering comm, United Negro Coll Fund, 1982-; bd mem, Dialogue Today, 1985-; bd mem, Police Chief Advisory Council, 1987-; chair, IBE Youth Corp, 1988-. **Honors/Awds:** Minorities Engineering, Indiana Bell, 1984; Leadership Award, Chamber of Commerce, 1986; Outstanding Volunteerism, United Way, 1988; Mt Summitt award,

Indiana Bell, 1989; Presidents Club award, Indiana Bell, 1989; 200 Most Influential Blacks In Indiana, Outstanding Women In Indiana. **Home Addr:** 6136 N Meridian W Dr, Indianapolis, IN 46208.

WILLIAMS, VERNON R.
Automobile dealer. **Career:** Greenville Ford Lincoln-Mercury Inc, pres, currently. **Special Achievements:** Company is ranked #97 on Black Enterprise magazine's 1997 list of Top 100 Black businesses. **Business Addr:** President, Greenville Ford Lincoln-Mercury Inc, PO Box 1927, Greenville, TX 75403, (903)455-7222.

WILLIAMS, VESTA
Singer. **Career:** A&M Records, singer, currently. **Business Addr:** Singer, c/o A & M Records, 1416 N La Brea Ave, Los Angeles, CA 90028.

WILLIAMS, VIRGINIA WALKER
Journalist. **Personal:** Born in Alabama; divorced; children: Mamie W. **Educ:** AL State Univ, BS; Marquette Univ, Masters Journalism. **Career:** Milwaukee Publ Schools, reading specialist; Milwaukee Publ Schools, journalist editor; Milwaukee Fire & Police Comm, journalist. **Orgs:** Mem Soc of Prof Journalist, Women in Communication, Pi Lambda Theta, Phi Delta Kappa NAACP; asst journalist Zonta Club of Milw; edit staff West Side News; publ Echo Magazine; freelance writer published in five anthologies. **Honors/Awds:** Headliner Award Women in Communications; Good Citizens City of Milw; ach Black Women's Network; srv award Milwaukee Public Schl; Women Against the Odds WI Humanities Soc; Poet Honored by Zonta Club of Milwaukee for poetry published in Zonta newsletter monthly. **Home Addr:** PO Box 2107, Milwaukee, WI 53201.

WILLIAMS, W. BILL, JR.
Company sales executive. **Personal:** Born Aug 19, 1939, Chicago, IL; son of Ellen Brassfield Williams and William Williams Sr; married Syleste Tillman Williams, Aug 29, 1965; children: Karen, Kevin, Keyth. **Educ:** Chicago State University, Chicago, IL, BS, business management; Loading Supervisor's Course, London, England, British Airways Corp. **Career:** United Airlines, Chicago, IL, operation supervisor, 1960-63; Butler Aviation, Chicago, IL, operation supervisor, 1963-70; Sullair Corp, Michigan City, IN, sales engineer, 1970-75; Chicago Convention & Tourism Bureau, Chicago, IL, director of sales, 1975-89; K & J Shine Parlors, Chicago, IL, owner, 1985-; Chicago Convention & Tourism Bureau, Chicago, IL, associate vice president, 1989-. **Orgs:** Marketing director, IBPOEW, 1985-; intl vice pres/convention chairman, Rat Pack International, 1985-; sovereign grand inspector gen, United Sureme Council, PHA, 1987-; life member, Kappa Alpha Psi Fraternity, 1982-; board member, National Coalition of Black Meeting Planners, 1985-89; vice pres, Society of Government Meeting Planners. **Honors/Awds:** Outstanding Achievement Award, Urban Programs West, YMCA, 1985-; Man of the Year, Norman La Harry Scholarship Foundation, 1985; Black Innovator Award, 1982; Outstanding Service Award, Chicago State University, 1979. **Military Serv:** USMC, CPL, 1957-60, Good conduct medal. **Business Addr:** Associate Vice President, Sales, Chicago Convention and Tourism Bureau, McCormick Place on the Lake, Lower Level 7, Chicago, IL 60616.

WILLIAMS, W. CLYDE
Educational administrator. **Personal:** Born in Cordele, GA; married Elaine; children: Joyce, Clyde, John, Gregory. **Educ:** Holsey Cobb Inst 1951; Paine Clge, AB 1955; Howard Univ, BD 1959; Interdenom Theol Ctr, MRE 1961; Atlanta Univ, MA 1969; Paine Clge, DD 1972; Univ of AL, Hon PhD 1976. **Career:** Miles Coll, pres 1971-; Consult on Church & Union, assc gen sec 1969-71; Assc for Christ Train & Svc, staff assc 1969-; Interdenom Theol Ctr, regist & dir of admin 1967-69, dir 1963-67; Christ Meth Epis Church, dir of youth work & adult educ 1960-63; Howard Univ, asst dir of stud act 1959-; NY St Coun of Church, chaplain 1957-58. **Orgs:** Dir boys work Bethlehem Ctr 1954-56; adv com US Dept of St; stud fin aid coun US Dept of HEW; res adv panel US Ofc of Educ Sch Monitor & Consum Prot Proj; Sickle Cell Dis adv com NIH; co-chmn Comm Aff Com of Oper New Birmingham; v chmn AL Comm for Human & Pub Policy; bd dir UnitNegro Clge Fund; bd dir Birmingham Cable Comm; bd dir Birmingham Urban Leag; bd dir Natl Com of Black Chmen; bd dir Amer Natl Red Cross; bd trustee Birmingham Symphony Assc; exec bd BSA; exec com Jefferson Co Child Dev Counc; Cit Adv Counc Jefferson Co; Birmingham Manpower Area Plan Coun; Lay Adv Coun St Vincent's Hosp; AL Assc for Adv of Private Clge ch commn on scout; NAACP; YMCA; Alpha Phi Alpha Frat Educ Hon Soc Kappa DeltaPi 1975. **Honors/Awds:** Man of Year Omega Psi Phi Frat; Alumni Achiev Award Paine Clge 1971; Outst Educ So Beauty Cong 1972; Outst Educ Fed of So Coop 1975; Cit Award Lawson St Comm Clge 1974; City of Birmingham Mayor's Cit 1974; Outst Achiev in Spt of Police Athlet Birmingham Police Athlet Team 1975. **Business Addr:** Miles Coll, P O Box 3800, Birmingham, AL 35208.

WILLIAMS, W. DONALD
Physician. **Personal:** Born Mar 5, 1936, Winter Park, FL; son of Emma Austin Williams and Eldridge L Williams, Sr; divorced; children: Susan A, Jordan H. **Educ:** San Francisco State Coll, AB 1967; Stanford Univ School of Med, MD 1974. **Career:** NYC, rsch chem 1958-59; San Francisco, med tech 1964-69; Dept of Lab Med, chief res 1975-77; Univ CA San Francisco, MD 1974-; Univ of Chicago, asst prof pathology; LAC-USC Med Ctr, chief clinical hematology, pediatrics. **Orgs:** Org mem Black Students Union San Francisco State Coll 1966; Beta Nu Chapter Alpha Phi Alpha 1954; co-founder Black Man's Free Clinic San Francisco 1968; founder dir Mid-Peninsula Sickle Cell Anemia Fnd 1971; mem UCSF Med School Admissions Comm 1976-77; CA State Advisory Commn for Sickle Cell Anemia 1972-75; mem Sci Adv Commn Natl Assn for Sickle Cell Disease 1972-75; mem Amer Soc Hematology; fellow Amer Soc Clinical Pathology; fellow, Amer Academy Pediatrics. **Military Serv:** AUS sgt 1959-65; AUS maj 1978-79; USAR ltc 1982-97. **Business Addr:** Ontario Health & Medical Center, 1341 E. 4th Street, Ste. B, Ontario, CA 91764.

WILLIAMS, WALKER RICHARD, JR.
Equal employment opportunity officer. **Personal:** Born Jul 11, 1928, Dayton, OH; son of Addie Mary Smith Williams and Walker Richard Williams Sr; married Emma Jean Griffin; children: Yvette, Timothy, Walker III. **Educ:** Attended, Univ of Dayton. **Career:** Supervisor-supply cataloger 1961-66; USAF 2750 ABW, WPAFB, personnel mgmt spec 1966-69, employee relations specialist 1969-70, equal employment oppor officer 1971-88, chief eeo & affirm action prog; Youth Service USA-Dayton, Dayton, OH, dir, 1988-89; self-employed, EEO investigator, grievance examiner as a contractor for defense logistics agency, Army and Air Natl Guard, instructor, Office of Personnel Management, 1989-. **Orgs:** Bd mem & past pres, Jefferson Township Bd of Educ; Dayton Bd of Educ Guidance Adv Comm for Project VEET, City Wide Vocational Educ Adv Comm; advisory comm, Radcliff Elem Sch Intervention; bd of dirs Dayton Opportunities Industrialization Ctr; bd of dirs Domestic Action Programs of Wright-Patterson AFB Inc; Governor's Commn to Preserve the Statue of Liberty; OH Bureau of Employment Serv Job Serv Employees Commn; Greene Vocational Sch Business Adv Comm; mem & past pres Dayton Selectmen; bd of dirs and 3 times past pres Wright-Patterson Quarter Century Club; mem Urban League, Blacks in Govt; business adv comm United Negro Coll Fund; mem Natl Black Caucus of Local Elected Officials, Natl Black Caucus of Black School Bd Members; Black Elected Democrats of Ohio; historian and past chmn Dayton Intergovt EqualEmployment Oppor Cncl; NAACP; Miami Valley Personnel Assn; Intl Personnel t Assn; Air Force Assn; Miami Valley Military Affairs Council; Retired Officers Assn. **Honors/Awds:** James W Cisco Awd Dayton Intergovt EEO Cncl; EEO Employee of the Year Awds Dayton Chamber of Commerce, Dayton Intl Personnel Mgmt Assn; Special Awd Dayton Chap Jack & Jill Inc; President's Awd Blacks in Govt; Certificate of Recognition Accomplishment in Humanities St Margaret's Episcopal Church; Certificate of Recognition for Outstanding Service and Dedication to Humanity Dayton NAACP; Certificate of Awd for Outstanding Accomplishments in Comm Serv Dayton Urban League; Certificate for Outstanding Serv to Youth Girl Scouts of Amer; Walker Williams Day in Dayton, by Mayor R Clay Dixon, 1987-89; Special Awd United Negro Coll Fund; Russell Lyle Service Award, Wright Patterson Quarter Century Club; numerous Air Force Awds for Performance, including Air Force Civilian Serv Awd; Special Award, Wilberforce Univ; Supervisor of the Year Award, Miami Valley Chap of Federally Employed Women; Hispanic Heritage Comm Award; OH State Dept of Educ Voc-Ed Award; Community Service Award, Dayton Bd of Educ; Special Award, Blacks in Govt; Service Award, 2750 ABW; Community Service Award, Dayton Veterans Administration Ctr. **Military Serv:** AUS Natl Guard capt 20 yrs. **Home Addr:** 5050 Fortman Drive, Dayton, OH 45418.

WILLIAMS, WALLACE C.
Business executive. **Personal:** Born in North Carolina; divorced; children: Wallace Jr, Joyce. **Educ:** Boro-Hall Acad NY, 1946; Pace College NY, 1948; Columbia Univ, 1950; Detroit Inst of Tech, BS, 1958; Wayne State Univ, Business Technology, 1970; Univ of Detroit. **Career:** NY State Employ Svc, interviewer, 1947-53; US Bur of Prisons, correctional aid prison fiscal officer, 1953-58; MI Employment Securities Commn, interviewer, 1958-65, employment sec exec, 1965-69; MI Dept of Commerce, econ devel exec, 1969-; CCAC-ICBIF, director, 1979; MI Dept of Labor, coordinator of Manpower Program; J L Dumas Construction Co, business devel mgr & consultant; State of Michigan, Office of Minority Business Enterprises, director; Detroit Economic Growth Corp, director for City of Detroit; METCO Engineering Services Inc, vice pres of business development; Royal Oak Township Planning Commission, chairman; Univ of MI, School of Business, dir, 1986-96. **Orgs:** Trustee, mem, Exec Coun Trade Union Ldrshp Council; past president, Booker T Washington Bus Assn; exec bd, Inner City Bus Improvement Forum; chmn, Minority Bus Oppor Com; ed & publ, Minority Bus Newsletter; bd mem, HOPE Inc; mem, New Detroit Minority Adv Com; Wayne Co Bd of Commr Minority Adv Co; serv ofcr, VFW TF Burns Post 5793; bd mem, Lewis Bus College; bd dir, People's Comm Civic League; mem, Bus Adv Com Detroit Chamber of Comm; mem, Tr Bd Orchestra Hall Fnd; golden heritage, NAACP; coord, Christian Prison Flwshp Prog; asst reg vice pres, Natl Bus League; vice chmn, Highland Park YMCA; mem, Adv Planning Council Wayne Co; dir, Minority Business Services, U of M, Ann Arbor. **Honors/Awds:** Community Service Award, Booker T Washington Business Assn; Businessman of the Year Awards, Wayne County Bd of Commissioners & Gamma Phi Delta, 1984; Outstanding Public Service Award, Michigan Lupus Foundation; Outstanding Service Award, State of Michigan; Spirit of Detroit Award, City of Detroit; Appreciation Award, US Dept of Commerce; City of Flint, MI Proclaimations from Mayor Woodrow Stanley; City Council, Mayor Coleman Young, City of Detroit; City Council, Royal Oak Township, Appreciation Award; Bethel AME Church Missionary Society. **Military Serv:** AUS sgt 1942-46. **Business Addr:** University of Michigan Business School, 506 E Liberty St, Ann Arbor, MI 48104.

WILLIAMS, WALLY JAMES, JR.
Professional football player. **Personal:** Born Feb 19, 1971, Tallahassee, FL; children: Bronson. **Educ:** Florida A&M, attended. **Career:** Cleveland Browns, center, 1993-95; Baltimore Ravens, 1996-. **Business Addr:** Professional Football Player, Baltimore Ravens, 11001 Owings Mills Blvd, Owings Mills, MD 21117, (410)654-6200.

WILLIAMS, WALTER
Attorney, judge. **Personal:** Born Jun 13, 1939, Yazoo City, MS; son of Mary Lee Knight and Walter Williams, Sr; married Helen M Hudson, Jul 4, 1964; children: Toni Marshea. **Educ:** Univ of WI, Cert 1961; John Marshall Law Sch, JSD 1970; Jackson State Univ Jackson MS 1958-62. **Career:** Williams, Slaughter & Williams, partner; Malcolm X Coll, tchr; Circuit Court of Cook County, juvenile div, associate judge, currently. **Orgs:** Amer Bar Assc; Chicago Bar Assc; pres Cook Co Bar Assc; IL St Bar Assc; Natl Bar Assc; Alpha Phi Alpha Frat; Jackson St Univ Alumni; John Marshall Law Sch Alumni; IL Judicial Council; IL Judges Assn; American Judges Assn. **Honors/Awds:** Cook County Bar Assn Leadership Award 1964; Jr Coun Award Cook Co Bar Assc 1975; Outstanding Yazoo Citizen Award 1975; Outstanding Achievement Award Yazoo Brothers Club 1987; Jackson State University, Appreciation Award, 1993; Cook County Bar Association, Kenneth E Wilson Award, 1993; Illinois Council of Juvenile and Family Court Judges, Distinguished Service Award, 1994. **Military Serv:** DOS spec e-5 1966. **Home Addr:** 5555 S Everett, Chicago, IL 60637. **Business Phone:** (312)373-8881.

WILLIAMS, WALTER ANDER
Professional basketball player. **Personal:** Born Apr 16, 1970, Washington, DC. **Educ:** Univ of Maryland, bachelor's degree in management and consumer studies. **Career:** Sacramento Kings, guard-forward, 1992-96; Miami Heat, 1996; Toronto Raptors, 1996-98; Portland TrailBlazers, 1998-. **Honors/Awds:** NBA All-Rookie Second Team, 1993. **Special Achievements:** NBA Draft, First round pick, #7, 1992; appeared in the film ''Eddie'', 1996. **Business Addr:** Professional Basketball Player, Portland TrailBlazers, 1 Center Court, Ste 200, Portland, OR 97227, (503)234-9291.

WILLIAMS, WAYNE ALLAN
Research consultant. **Personal:** Born Oct 8, 1964, Brooklyn, NY; son of Rose Williams and Isreal Williams. **Educ:** Davidson College, BA, classical studies, 1989; Boston College, MEd, educational research, evaluation & measurement, 1991. Harvard Univ, EdD, student, human devt, & psychology, currently. **Career:** Philadelphia Public Schools Testing Reform, statistical consultant, 1990-91 ; Boston College, Development Office, research asst, 1990-91; Education Develop ment Center, research intern, 1991; Boston College, Career Center, statistical consultant, 1991-94; Boston College, Center for the Study of Testing, Evaluatio n, & Educational Policy, faculty research asst, 1991-93; Basic Plus Mathematics Project Evaluation, co-evaluator, 1992-93; Lesley College, Algebra Project Eva luation, statistical consultant, 1993-95; Harvard Graduate School of Education Career Center, statistical consultant, 1993-95; Harvard University Divinity Sch ool, statistical research associate, 1995-. **Orgs:** American Educational Research Assn, 1991-; Benjamin Banneker Charter School , initial board of trustees, 1994-96; Phi Delta Kappa, 1992-. **Honors/Awds:** National Honor Society, 1992; Cumberland County Medical Society Award, 1983 ; Fayetteville Chapter of Links Honoree, 1983; Davidson College, Eumenean Liter ary Society Certificate, 1987; AME Zion Church, North Charlotte District Outsta nding Service Award, 1987; Davidson College, Academic Awareness Certificate for Academic Achievement, 1989; Harvard University, Baker Fellow, 1993-95. **Special Achievements:** Author: ''Developing a Multi-tiered Database for Measuring Systemic School R eform,'' 1995. **Home Addr:** 22 Peabody Terrace, #11, Cambridge, MA 02138.

WILLIAMS, WESLEY S., JR.
Attorney. **Personal:** Born Nov 13, 1942, Philadelphia; married Karen Roberta Hastie; children: Amanda, Wesley, Bailey. **Educ:** Harvard U, Magna Cum Laude 1963; Woodrow Wilosn Fellow Fletcher Sch of Law & Dipl, MA 1964; Harvard U, JD 1967; Columbia U, LLM 1969. **Career:** Covington & Burling,

partner 1975-, asso 1970-75; Georgetown U, adj prof law 1971-73; US Sen Com on DC, couns 1969-70; Columbia U, assoc-in-law 1968-69; DC City Cncl, couns 1967-69. **Orgs:** Mem US Circuit Judge Nominating Commn 1977-; mem Com on Legislation Bar 1973-; mem Exec Ecom Wash Lawyers' Com for Civil Rights Under Law 1972-; mem Circuit Judicial Conf 1971-; pres Bd Trustees Family & Child Serv Wash 1974-; mem Bd Dir Nat Symphony Orch Assn 1972-; pres bd trustees Nat Child Rsrch Ctr 1980-; life mem Wash Urban League. **Business Addr:** Covington & Burling, 1201 Pennsylvania Ave NW, Washington, DC 20044.

WILLIAMS, WILBERT
Labor official (retired). **Personal:** Born Mar 30, 1924, Crockett, TX; married Theresa; children: Gentry, Raschelle, Keola, Lewis, Kimberly. **Educ:** Phillis Wheatley HS, diploma 1942; TX Southern Univ, BS 1947-52. **Career:** Intl Assn Machinist #2007, pres 1957-61; AFL-CIO, field rep 1964-74; AFL-CIO Dept of Org & Field Svcs, asst to dir 1974-83; AFL-CIO Region IV, admin 1983-86, dir, 1986-90. **Orgs:** Pres AME Church TX Conf Laymen 1972-73; life subscriber NAACP 1974-; Natl Bd A Philip Randolph Institute 1974-. **Honors/Awds:** Outstanding Laymen TX Conf Laymen 1983; William E Pollard TX State A Philip Randolph Inst 1985. **Military Serv:** USN BM 2/C 1943-45.

WILLIAMS, WILBERT EDD
Computer software engineer. **Personal:** Born Sep 13, 1948, Fayetteville, NC; son of Mary Moore Williams and Edd Williams; married Yolanda Faye DeBerry; children: Danica Michelle, Donata Merie. **Educ:** Fayetteville State Univ, BS (Summa Cum Laude) 1977; Univ of MI-Ann Arbor, MS 1978; Duke Univ, MBA 1986. **Career:** US Navy, digital display tech 1967-74; Bell Labs, mem of tech staff 1977-79; ABB T&D Co, systems & software engr 1979-86, mgr product software 1986-. **Orgs:** Mem Amer Soc of Naval Engrs 1978-, Jack & Jill of Amer 1982-; corporate minority spokesperson Westinghouse 1983-; comm ambassador Westinghouse Electric 1983-; mem St Matthew Budget & Finance Comm 1984-; vice pres St Matthew Scholarship Comm 1986-87. **Honors/Awds:** Fellowship to Univ of MI Bell Laboratories 1977-78; Distinguished Corporate Alumni NAFEO 1983; Tuition Support for Duke MBA Westinghouse Electric 1984-86. Corporate Community Service, Westinghouse Electric, 1988. **Military Serv:** USNR lt commander 23 yrs; Armed Forces Reserve Medal 1986.

WILLIAMS, WILBERT LEE
Clergyman, educator. **Personal:** Born Aug 25, 1938, Corsicana, TX; son of Mr & Mrs Calvin Williams, Sr; married Catherine L Lemons, Dec 30, 1961; children: Sheila, Stuart, Cynthia. **Educ:** Prairie View A&M Coll, BS 1960; Howard Univ School of Law, JD 1971; Inst for New Govt Attys 1971; Howard Univ School of Divinity, 1987-90 M Div. **Career:** US Dept of Agr, farm mgmt supr 1965-68; United Planning Org Wash DC, exec ofcr 1968-71; US Dept of Agr Office of Gen Counsel Wash DC, atty 1971-84; US Dept of Agr, equal opportunity officer; pastor, The First New Horizon Baptist Church, currently. **Orgs:** Past vice pres & founding mem CHASE Inc; former mem DC Neighborhood Reinvestment Commission; past mem bd dir Neighborhood Legal Serv Program Washington DC; past mem bd trustee United Planning Org Washington DC. **Honors/Awds:** Recip 1st Annual Achievement Award OEO Natl Advisory Comm for Legal Serv Program 1968. **Special Achievements:** President and founder, The First New Horizon Community Development Corp. **Military Serv:** US Army 1961-64. **Business Addr:** Pastor, The First New Horizon Baptist Church, PO Box 176, Clinton, MD 20735.

WILLIAMS, WILLIAM J.
Educator. **Personal:** Born Dec 25, 1935, Montgomery, AL; son of Celestine Reynolds and Eugene W Phillips; children: Morgan Lynn, Paige Whitney. **Educ:** Morehouse Coll, bachelor's degree, 1952; NY Univ, master's degree, 1954; Univ of So CA, PhD, 1966. **Career:** NY State Com/Govtl Operations NY City, admin adv 1959-60; Bldg Serv Union, rsch dir joint council #8 1960-61; CA State Legislature, consult 1961-62; US Congressman Augustus F Hawkins, congressional field dir 1962-66; US Equal Employment Oppor Comm, dep staff dir 1966-67; US Commn on Civil Rights, dir western progs 1967-68; LA Co/LA City, employee relations bd mediator 1974; Univ So CA, prof, currently. **Orgs:** Exec dir Negro Polit Action Assn CA 1964-66; dem candidate Sec of State of CA 1966; pres, USC Chapter, Amer Assn Univ Profs, 1974-75; Pres, Inst for Applied Epistemics; Dir, Educ Consulting & Counseling Serv; Pres, Diversified Servs. **Honors/Awds:** Teaching Excellence Award, School of Public Admin, USC, 1978; Man of the Year, Alpha Phi Omega; Distinguished Prof Award, USC Graduate Student Assn, 1989. **Special Achievements:** Publications: ''The Miracle of Abduction,'' Epistemics Institute Press, 1985; ''Semantic Behavior & Decision Making,'' Monograph Publishing Series, A subsidiary of Univ Microfilms Intl, 1978; ''Epistemics: Personalizing the Process of Change,'' Univ Publishers, 1975; ''Selections from Semantic Behavior & Decision Making,'' 1975; ''Uncommon Sense & Dimensional Awareness,'' Univ Publishers, 1973; ''General Semantics & the Social Sciences,'' Philosophical Library, 1972. **Military Serv:** USAF sgt 1952-54. **Business Addr:** Professor, Univ of Southern California, University Park, Los Angeles, CA 90007, (213)740-0370.

WILLIAMS, WILLIAM THOMAS
Educator. **Personal:** Born Jul 17, 1942, Cross Creek, NC; son of Hazel Davis Williams and William T Williams; married Patricia A DeWeese; children: Nila, Aaron. **Educ:** City Univ of NY/New York City Comm Coll, AAS 1962; Pratt Inst, BFA 1966; Skowhegan Schl of Painting and Sculpture, 1965; Yale Univ, MFA 1968. **Career:** Pratt Inst, painting fac 1970; Schl of Visual Arts, painting fac 1970; CUNY Brooklyn Coll, prof of art 1971-; Skowhegan Schl of Painting & Sculpture, res painting fac 1971, 1974, 1978; VA Commonwealth Univ, distinguished visiting commonwealth prof of art 1984. **Orgs:** Govenor Skowhegan Schl of Painting & Sculpture 1972-90; artistic bd Cinque Gallery 1978-90; bd trustees Grace Church Schl 1984-87. **Honors/Awds:** Individual Artist Award Painting Natl Endowment for the Arts and Humanities 1965, 1970; painting Creative Arts Public Serv Grant 1975, 1981; Faculty Research Award City Univ of NY 1973, 1984, 1987; John Simon Guggenheim Fellowship/John Simon Guggenheim Memorial Foundation 1987; Mid-Atlantic Foundation Fellowship, 1994; Studio Museum in Harlem/Annual Award for Lifetime Achievement, 1992. **Business Addr:** Professor of Art, CUNY, Brooklyn Coll, Brooklyn, NY 11210.

WILLIAMS, WILLIE, JR.
Business executive. **Personal:** marrIed Nellie Redmond. **Educ:** Benedict Coll, BA; Rutgers U, grad study; MI State U; SC State Coll; Univ of SC. **Career:** Willie Williams Real Estate Inc, pres & Founder; Richland Co, inst pub schs; Upward Bound Univ of SC, couns; Midland Tech Ctr; Benedict Coll, placement dir; SC Chap NAREB, pres; chmn bd Palmetto Home Counseling Inc & Success Investment Co. **Orgs:** Mem Columbia Bd of Realtors; State Mfgrs Housing Commn; Richland Co Planning Commn Bd Dir Columbia Urban League; adv bd Columbia Opportunities Industrialization Ctr of SC; bd trustees Benedict Coll; Friendship Jr Coll; life mem NAACP; Omicron Phi Chap of Omega Psi Phi; city chmn 1974 UNCF Campaign. **Business Addr:** Willie Williams Real Est Inc, 6023 Two Notch Rd, Columbia, SC.

WILLIAMS, WILLIE ELBERT
Educator, mathematician. **Personal:** Born Jun 6, 1927, Jacksonville, TX; married Doris Lee Matlock; children: Lois E, Willys E, Donald A, Linda W, Dorwyl L. **Educ:** Huston Tillotson Clge Austin TX, BS Math cum laude 1952; TX So Univ Houston, MS Math 1953; MI State Univ, PhD Math 1972. **Career:** Lufkin Independent School Dist, teacher 1953-59; Cleveland Bd of Educ, chmn of dept math 1960-73; Case-Western Reserve Univ, adj prof of math 1964-68; Deep Accellerated Math Prog, dir 1973-78; Florida Intl Univ, assoc prof. **Orgs:** Consult Natl Follow Through Prog 1974-75; deacon 2nd Bapt Ch 1975-80; state rep Omega Psi Phi Frat State of FL 1979-80; pres Concerned Black Educ in Higher Educ in FL 1980-81; evaluator of College Title III Programs; vice pres, chair anticrime comm PULSE; pres Black Faculty FL Intl Univ; lecturer BAM; recruiter Black Faculty and Black Students. **Honors/Awds:** Outstanding Teacher Awd Univ of CO 1954; Master Tchr Award Martha Holden Jennings Fnd 1973. **Military Serv:** AUS corpl 1945-49; Occupation Good Conduct Medal. **Business Addr:** Associate Professor Retired, Florida International Univ, Miami, FL 33199.

WILLIAMS, WILLIE J.
Educator. **Personal:** Born Jan 8, 1949, Chester Co, SC; married Louvenia Brooks. **Educ:** Voorhees Clge, BS. **Career:** Industrial Educ Devel Corp Proj Dir Jobs 70 Prog 1970-73; Atlanta GA Custom Packagers & Processors Inc, personnel dir 1973-74; Colquitt Co Bd of Educ Moultries GA, teacher 1974-. **Orgs:** Mem Amateur Softball Assc Umpires 1975-; mem Free Accepted Masons 1973-; Omega Psi Phi Frat 1968-; Natl State & Local Educ Assc 1974-75; Steering Com Quarter Sys for Colquitt Co Sch 1974-75; mem Colquitt Co Civil Defense Rescue Team 1973-; registered Emer Med Tech State of GA; mem State of GA Dept of Defense Rescue Workers; Honor Soc Finley Sr High Sch 1964-66. **Honors/Awds:** Dale Carnegie Cert of Appreciation for Grad Asst 1973. **Business Addr:** Norman Pk High Sch, Norman Park, GA.

WILLIAMS, WILLIE JAMES
Educator, track and field coach. **Personal:** Born Sep 12, 1931, Gary, IN; son of Orrie (deceased) & Elnora Williams; married Barbara, Dec 31, 1955; children: Darla, Margot. **Educ:** Univ of IL, BS, 1955; IN Univ, MS, 1971. **Career:** School City of Gary Indiana, teacher-coach, 1958-82; Univ of IL, sprint coach, 1982-;. **Orgs:** NCAA Track & Field Assn, 1982-. **Honors/Awds:** International Track & Field Federation, set world record in 100 meter dash, 1956; Inducted into Indiana High School Coaches Track & Field Hall of Fame, 1980; Pan Amer Games, gold medal, 4 X 100 relay, Mexico City 1955. **Special Achievements:** Published Track Article on Sprinting, The Coaching Clinic, Prentice Hall, Feb 1980. **Military Serv:** US Army, spec-1, 1955-57; International Military Sports, sprint champion, 100 meter dash, 1956. **Home Addr:** 1607 Trails Dr, Urbana, IL 61801, (217)337-6616. **Business Addr:** Assistant Men's Track Coach, University of Illinois - Champaign, 505 E. Armory Dr, Armory Bldg, Rm235-F, Champaign, IL 61820, (217)333-7969.

WILLIAMS, WILLIE JAMES, JR.
Professional football player. **Personal:** Born Dec 26, 1970, Columbia, SC; married Melissa; children: Dominique. **Educ:** Western Carolina. **Career:** Pittsburgh Steelers, defensive back, 1993-96; Seattle Seahawks, 1997-. **Business Addr:** Professional Football Player, Seattle Seahawks, 11220 NE 53rd St, Kirkland, WA 98033, (206)827-9777.

WILLIAMS, WILLIE JR.
Educator. **Personal:** Born Mar 24, 1947, Independence, LA; son of Leanner Anner Booker Williams and Willie Williams Sr; married Deborah A Broady; children: Willie III. **Educ:** Southern Univ, BS, 1970; IA State Univ, MS, 1972, PhD, 1974. **Career:** Lincoln Univ, assoc prof, physics 1979-84, Lincoln Univ, prof, physics, 1984-; Dept of Defense, physical scientist 1980-82; Lincoln Univ, chmn Science Math div, prof & chmn of physics, 1978-80; Lincoln Advanced Science & Engineering Reinforcement Program (Laser) 1981-96. **Orgs:** Consultant, Mobil Oil Co 1977; physical scientist, Natl Bureau of Standards, 1979; NASA Fellow NASA 1979; ONR Fellow Naval Research Lab 1980; chrmn Cheyney Lincoln Temple Cluster 1978-80; mem PRIME Bd of Dir 1977-, AAUP NY Acad Of Sciences, Sigma Xi; Dir, Lincoln Advance Science & Engineering Reinforcement Program, 1981-; mem, Oxford Rotary, 1986-89; American Physical Society; Mathematical Association of America; American Association of Physics Teachers; American Association for the Advancement of Science; New York Academy of Sciences; Philadelphia based Comprehensive Regional Center for Minorities Steering Committee; Sigma Pi Sigma; Philadelphia based LASER Program, pre-college effort, director. **Honors/Awds:** Lindback Award, Lincoln Univ, 1976; CLT Award, Cheyney Lincoln Temple Cluster, 1974-78; Excellence in Science & Technology; White House Initiative on HBCU's, 1988; Participaton in Science Symposium, Physics Dept, Southern Univ, 1991; Participation in African-American History Month, US Navy Intl Logistics Control Office, 1991. **Business Addr:** Professor, Lincoln Univ, Physics Dept, Lincoln University, PA 19352.

WILLIAMS, WILLIE L.
Law enforcement official. **Personal:** Born Oct 1, 1943, Philadelphia, PA; son of Helen S Williams and Willie L Williams Sr; married Oct 22, 1966; children: Lisa, Willie L Jr, Eric. **Educ:** Northwestern University, certificate, police administration, 1978; Philadelphia College of Textiles & Science, ABA, 1982; Public Safety Media Institute, 1986; Center for Creative Leadership, Eckerd College, senior leadership, 1986; Harvard University, Police Executive Research Forum, certificate, 1987; FBI National Executive Institute, 1989; St Joseph University, master's degree candidate, 1991. **Career:** Fairmont Park Guards, police officer, 1964-72; City of Philadelphia, police detective, 1972-74, police sergeant, 1974-76, Juvenile Aid Division, police lieutenant, 1976-84, 22nd and 23rd Police District, police captain, commander, 1984-86, Training Bureau, Civil Affairs Division, North Police Division, police inspector, head, 1986, deputy commissioner of administration, 1988, police commissioner, 1988-92; Temple University, University of Pennsylvania, University of Delaware, lecturer, instructor, currently; City of Los Angeles, Police Dept, chief of police, 1992-97. **Orgs:** National Organization of Black Law Enforcement Executives, immediate past national president; International Association of Chiefs of Police; Alpha Signian Lambda National Honors Society; Pennsylvania Juvenile Officers Association; Southeastern Pennsylvania Chiefs of Police; Los Angeles County Chiefs Association; Janes Memorial Methodist Church, West Oak Lane Youth Association; Boy Scouts of America, former scout master. **Honors/Awds:** Recipient of ten police department commendations and numerous civic awards; Attorney General of the US, William French Smith Award. **Business Addr:** Chief of Police, Los Angeles Police Department, 150 N Los Angeles St, Parker Center, Rm 615, Los Angeles, CA 90012.

WILLIAMS, WILLIE LAVERN
Educator. **Personal:** Born Dec 24, 1940, Little Rock, AR; married Margaret Jean Lee; children: Gregory, Kristy, Karen, Stephen. **Educ:** San Jose State Clge, BA 1962; CA State Univ Long Beach, Tchng Cert 1963; Univ of AZ, MEd 1977. **Career:** Univ of AZ, adj assc prof & coach 1969-; Compton HS, educ & coach 1964-69; CA State Univ Long Beach, coach 1963-64. **Orgs:** Mem intl competition com The Athletics Congress 1977-; chmn US Olympic Com 1977-; mem coaches com Track & Field/USA 1979-; mem NAACP 1969-; mem Natl Urban League 1972-; regl chmn The Athletics Congress 1974-; reg VII rep US Track Coaches Assc 1976-80; regl dir Track & Field USA 1978-. **Honors/Awds:** CA Interscholastic Federation Coach of Year CIF 1969; NCAA Region VII Coach of Year NCAA 1972; NCAA Region VII Coach of Year NCAA 1973-; Assist US Olympic Team Coach US Olympic Com 1980.

WILLIAMS, WILLIE S.
Psychologist. **Personal:** Born May 8, 1932, Prattville, AL; married Marva R Flowers; children: Kevin, Keith, Karla. **Educ:** Wichita State Univ, AB, Chem & Math, 1958; Xavier OH, MEd, Admin & Personnel Serv 1960; MI State Univ, PhD Counseling Psychology 1970. **Career:** Case Western Reserve

Univ School of Med, assoc dean for student affairs; NIMH Min Ctr, asst chief for Psychology Rsch & Training Program; Univ of Cincinnati, sr counselor & asst prof of psychology, Cincinnati Police Dept, psychology conselor; Willie S Williams PhD Inc, pres. **Orgs:** Pres, Phi Delta Kappa ANWC; Amer Personnel & Guild Assn; treasurer, Assn, Black Psychologists; Amer Psychology Assn; Kappa Alpha Psi. **Military Serv:** AUS 1953-55. **Business Addr:** President, Willie S Williams PhD Inc, 20310 Chagrin Blvd, Shaker Heights, OH 44122.

WILLIAMS, WYATT CLIFFORD

Federal employee organizer. **Personal:** Born May 29, 1921, Pittsburgh, PA; married Dorothy Mae Jones; children: Angelica Angell, Valeria, Marva. **Educ:** Duquesne University, attended, 1939; University of Pittsburgh, 1952-54; Penn State University; American University. **Career:** Natl Alliance of Postal & Federal Employees, pres local 510 Pgh 1959-65, natl 1st vice pres 1965-70, presidential aide 1970-71, natl 2nd vice pres 1979-. **Orgs:** Amvets; Klan Watch-NOW; Common Cause; NAACP; League of Women Voters. **Military Serv:** US Army, acting platoon staff sgt, 1943-46. **Home Addr:** 7403 St Ranahan St, Pittsburgh, PA 15206. **Business Addr:** 2nd Natl Vice President, NAPFE, 1628 11th St NW, Washington, DC 20001.

WILLIAMS, YARBOROUGH, JR.

Elected official. **Personal:** Born Mar 24, 1950, Warrenton, NC; married Carolyn M; children: Consherto V, Yarborough, Juroid C. **Educ:** NC State Univ, voc; Vance Granvillco Coll, drafting. **Career:** Franklinton City Schools, teacher 17 yrs; Warren Co Pub Sch Dist, sch bd mem. **Orgs:** Mem NAACP; pres Warren Co Political Action Council; pres Boys Club; mem School Bd; Warren Co Bd of Election; Warren Co Democratic Party; mem NCSBA; mem NCEA. **Honors/Awds:** Teacher of the Year Assoc of General Contractors of Amer 1986. **Home Addr:** Rt 4, Box 513, Warrenton, NC 27589. **Business Addr:** School Board Member, Warren Co Pub Sch Dist, P O Box 397, Franklinton, NC 27525.

WILLIAMS, YARBOROUGH BURWELL, JR.

Business executive. **Personal:** Born Mar 4, 1928, Raleigh, NC; son of Mattie Williams and Yarborough Williams Sr; married Shirley; children: Dennis, Craig, Yarvette. **Educ:** VA Union U, BA 1954; Univ of VA, MEd 1966. **Career:** Comm Affairs Newport News Shipbuilding A Tenneco Co, vice pres 1985; Newport News Shipbuilding, pres staff 1970-73; John Marshall HS, asst prin; HS of Richmond Lynchburg VA, soc studies tchr. **Orgs:** Mem City Council 1973-74; pres Richmond Educ Assn 1967-69; mem State Bd Comm Colls 1969-; bd mem Peninsula Un Way; bd of trustees VA Union U; Nat Urban Affairs Council; Peninsula Drug Abuse Council; Peninsula Human Resources Council. **Honors/Awds:** Recip Pres Citation Peninsula Family Serv 1975; Distin Serv Awards City of Hampton 1974; Comm Serv Honor Metro Mag Tidewater VA 1974. **Military Serv:** AUS 1950-52. **Business Addr:** 4101 Washington Ave, Newport News, VA 23607.

WILLIAMS, YVONNE CARTER

Educator. **Personal:** Born Feb 12, 1932, Philadelphia, PA; daughter of Evelyn Lightner Carter (deceased) and Patterson H. Carter (deceased); married Dr Theodore Williams, Jul 3, 1954; children: Lynora A, Alison P, Meredith J, Lesley Y. **Educ:** PA State Univ, BA (cum laude) 1953; Harvard Law Sch, 1953-54; Univ of CT, MA (honors) 1955; Case Western Reserve Univ, PhD 1981. **Career:** Dept of Educ Univ of CT, admin Asst; Ashland Wayne Comm Action Comm, dir of rsch 1964-66; Wayne Co Headstart, social worker 1967-68; Wooster Public Schools, visiting teacher 1968-69; OH State Univ, lecturer 1971-72; College of Wooster, asst to the dean, asst prof of pol sci, dir of black studies 1973-74, assoc prof, prof of pol sci/black studies, dir of black studies 1983-, dean of faculty 1989-95; consultant/evaluator, Lilly Endowment, NEH, Middle States and N Central Assocs. **Orgs:** Alpha Kappa Alpha; Wayne Co Bd of Mental Health & Retardation 1969-76; Wooster City Charter Comm 1971-72; League of Women Voters delegate to Natl Convention 1972; Head Start Parents' Adv Council 1970-73; Mayor's Alternate to NEFCO 1974-75; bd of dirs College Hills Retirement Village 1973-; Wooster City Charter Review Comm 1980; City of Wooster Human Relations Council 1978-; bd of governors Wooster Comm Hosp 1981-; bd of trustees Health Trustee Inst 1986-1988; Advisory Bd, Wayne County Adult Basic Educ, 1987-89; Ohio Humanities Council, 1989-96. **Honors/Awds:** John Hay Whitney Fellowship; AHS Fellowship Case Western Reserve Univ; Alumni Fellowship Case Western Reserve Univ; Jessie Smith Noyes Found Scholarship; Faculty Develop Grant, Morris Fund Coll of Wooster. **Home Addr:** 659 College Ave, Wooster, OH 44691. **Business Addr:** Director of Blk Studies, College of Wooster, Wooster, OH 44691, (216)263-2416.

WILLIAMS, YVONNE LAVERNE

Attorney, educational administrator. **Personal:** Born Jan 7, 1938, Washington, DC; daughter of Verna L Rapley Williams and Smallwood E Williams (deceased). **Educ:** Barnard Coll, BA, 1959; Boston Univ, MA, 1961; Georgetown Univ, JD, 1977. **Career:** US Info Agency, foreign serv officer, 1961-65; African-Amer Inst New York, dir womens Africa comm, 1966-68; Benedict Coll, Columbia, SC, assc prof African American studies, 1968-70; US Congress Washington, DC, press sec Hon Walter Fauntroy, 1970-72; African-Amer Scholars Council Washington, DC, dir 1972-73; Leva Hawes Symington Martin, Washington, DC, assoc atty, 1977-79; Brimmer & Co Washington, DC, asst vice pres, 1980-82; Tuskegee University, vice pres for Fed & Intl Rel & Legal Counsel 1983-1996; Academy for Educational Development Public Policy & Intl Affairs Fellowship Program, natl dir, 1996-. **Orgs:** Mem Oper Crossroads Africa, 1960-, Barnard-in-Washington, 1960-; mem Amer Bar Assoc, 1980-, Natl Bar Assoc, 1980-, Dist of Columbia Bar, 1980-; alumnae trustee, Barnard Coll, New York, NY, 1988-92; mem, Overseas Devel Council, Washington, DC, 1988-; bd of dir, Golden Rule Apartments, Inc, Washington, DC, 1986-. **Honors/Awds:** Boston University, African Research & Studies Program Fellowship, 1959-60. **Special Achievements:** Author, "William Monroe Trotter, (1872-1934)"; in Reid "The Black Prism," New York, 1969. **Business Addr:** National Director, Public Policy and International Affairs Fellowship Program, Academy for Educational Development, 1875 Conn Ave, NW, Washington, DC 20009.

WILLIAMS BOYD, SHEILA ANNE

Oil company credit manager. **Personal:** Born Apr 11, 1951, Chicago, IL; daughter of Kathryn Naomi Walker Boyd; divorced; children: Christine Williams, Kelly Boyd, Jamie Boyd, Michael Blakley. **Educ:** Olive Harvey Jr college, Chicago, IL, associate arts, accounting high honors, 1975; Roosevelt University, Chicago, IL, BSBA, accounting with honors, 1977; University of Chicago, Chicago, IL, executive MBA program, 1992. **Career:** Ernst & Young, Chicago, IL, senior auditor, 1977-79; Amoco Corporation, Chicago, IL, manager, professional audit practices, 1979-92, manager, banking coordination and development, 1993, manager, Credit Coordination, 1994-. **Orgs:** Board, University of Chicago Executive Program Club, 1993-; member of board of governors, Institute of Internal Auditors, Chicago Chapter, 1989-92; treasurer, National Black MBA Association, Chicago, Chapter, 1990. **Honors/Awds:** 100 of the Most Promising Black Women in Corporate America, Ebony Magazine, 1991; Dollars and Sense Magazine, Outstanding Business & Professional Award, 1991; Member of the Year, 1990, Institute of Internal Auditors, 1990; Movitator of Youths, Black Achievers of Industry Recognition, YWCA of Metropolitan Chicago, 1978; CPA, Illinois, 1979, Certified Internal Auditor, 1983. **Business Addr:** Manager, Credit Coordination, Amoco Corp Financial Operation, 200 E Randolph Dr, Chicago, IL 60601.

WILLIAMS-BRIDGERS, JACQUELYN L.

Government official. **Personal:** marrIed Daniel Bridgers; children: Two. **Educ:** Syracuse University, bachelor's degree, master's degree. **Career:** General Accounting Office, management analyst, associate director for housing and community development, numerous other positions; US State Department, inspector general, 1995-. **Orgs:** Chair, Board of External Auditors, Organization of American States. **Honors/Awds:** Arthur S Flemming Award; Meritorious Service Citation; three "Top Bonus" awards; four Outstanding Achievement Awards; Doctor of Humane Letters, Southeastern University, Washington, DC, 1996. **Special Achievements:** First African American and the first woman inspector general of the US State Department, 1995. **Business Addr:** Inspector General, US State Department, 2201 C St, Rm 6817, Washington, DC 20520-6817, (202)647-9450.

WILLIAMS DAVIS, EDITH G.

Geophysicist. **Personal:** Born Apr 8, 1958, Passaic, NJ; daughter of Ester Jean Rudolph Williams and James E Williams & Sam American; married Warren C Davis Jr, May 25, 1984. **Educ:** Univ of Miami, BS Geology 1981, geological expedition Guatemala C Amer 1978; Stanford Univ, MS Geophysics 1982, geophysical field expedition Nevada 1982; Univ of TX, Austin, MBA, 1991. **Career:** Oxygen Isotopic Lab, coord 1977, asst to Dr Cesare Emiliani 1977-78; US Geological Survey, geological field asst 1980; Marathon Oil Co, geophysical asst 1981; US Geological Survey, exploration geophysicist 1981-82; Mobil Oil Inc, exploration geophysicist 1983-86; Continental Airlines, Houston, TX, general sales reservation, 1987; Univ TX Grad School of Business Dean office, Austin, minority student affairs coordinator, 1987-89; 3M Headquarters, St Paul, MN, marketing intern, 1988; Prime Network, Houston, TX, director of business development, 1990; The Household of Faith, Texas Reservists Trust Fund, Houston, TX, administrator of trust fund, beginning 1991; ABBA Marketing Exchange, president, cofounder; Texas Natural Resource Conservation Commission, program administrator, currently. **Orgs:** Mem Miami Geological Soc 1976-78; pres United Black Students Organ 1978-79; sci coord Upward Bound Prog 1979; mem Delta Sigma Theta Sor 1979; mem AGU 1981-82; mem AAPG 1982-84; mem Amer Assn of Exploration Geophysics 1982-84; vice pres, MBA Women's Assn; National Black MBA Association, recording secretary, 1987-. **Honors/Awds:** John F Kennedy/Martin Luther King Scholarship Grant 1977-80; President's List 1978; United Black Students President's Awd 1978; Univ of Miami Honors Scholarship 1978; Shell Oil Scholarship Grant 1978-80; Amer Geologic Union Awd 1981-82; US Geologic Survey Fellowship 1981-82; Amer Geological Inst Fellowship 1981-82; National Black MBA Fellowship, 1987; Consortium for Graduate Study in Management Fellowship, 1988. **Business Addr:** PO Box 141753, Austin, TX 78714.

WILLIAMS-DIAL, E. FAYE

State official. **Personal:** Born Dec 20, 1941, Melrose, LA; daughter of Frances Lacour Williams and Vernon Williams. **Educ:** Grambling State Univ, BS (magna cum laude) 1962; Univ of Southern CA, MPA public admin 1971; George Washington Univ DC, Educ Policy Fellow 1981; Howard Univ School of Law JD (cum laude) 1985; City Univ of Los Angeles, PhD, 1993. **Career:** Trans International Group Inc, pres and ceo, currently; The Dail Marketing Group, vp/gen counsel; Los Angeles City Schools, teacher/dept chairperson 1964-71; Natl Ed Assn, dir Atlanta assoc of ed 1971-73, dir overseas ed assoc 1973-75; MI Ed Assoc/NEA, dir org & public relations 1975-81; MI Ed Assoc/NEA, dir prof devel & human rights 1981-82; Dist of Columbia Committee, Congress fellow judiciary & ed; Office of General Counsel of Natl Football League Players Assoc in Sports Law, intern; Larvadain & Scott Law Offices, atty-at-law, prof of law, Southern Univ Law Center, Baton Rouge, Louisiana. **Orgs:** Mem Alpha Kappa Mu Natl Hon Soc 1959-; life mem Delta Sigma Theta 1959-; natl pres Grambling State Univ Alumni Assoc 1981-; bd of dir, Partners for Peace; bd of dir, Council for the Natl Interest; Women for Mutual Security; bd dir Grambling Univ Athletic Found; treas, Straight Talk Economic Roundtable; chairperson, National Black Fair; candidate for US Congress won 49.3% of vote after winning the Dem Nom; US House of Representatives, Washington, DC, staff counsel, 1990-. **Honors/Awds:** Outstanding Alumnus of Historically Black Coll NAFEO 1981; Joan of Arc Awd LA Women in Politics; mem Hall of Fame of Black Women Attorneys 1986; Martin Luther King, Jr Commemorative Award, 1988; They Dare to Speak Out Peace Award, 1993; Delta Legacy Award, 1994; Blessed Are the Peacemakers Award, 1995. **Home Phone:** (202)554-0159. **Business Addr:** President, CEO, Trans International Group, 6495 New Hampshire Ave, Hyattsville, MD 20783, (301)891-3341.

WILLIAMS-DOVI, JOANNA

Educational administrator. **Personal:** Born Apr 16, 1953, Harrisburg, PA; daughter of Bertha Manervia Brown Williams and Thomas Edison Williams Sr; married Sewar M Dovi (divorced 1983). **Educ:** Cheyney University, Cheyney, PA, BA, 1977; Penn State University, Middletown, PA, currently. **Career:** Penn State University, Middletown, PA, admin asst, EET Program, 1984-88, admissions counselor of minority recruitment, 1988-. **Orgs:** Member, PA Assn of College Admission Counselor, 1987-; member, American Assn of Collegiate Registrars & Adm Office, 1987-; member, National Assn of College Admin Counselor, 1987-; leader, Girl Scouts Council of America, 1979-83; member, Delta Sigma Theta Sorority, Inc, 1990-; member, PA College Personnel Assn, 1990-. **Business Addr:** Admissions Counselor for Minority Recruitment, Admissions Office, Pennsylvania State University, 777 W Harrisburg Pike, Middletown, PA 17057-4898.

WILLIAMS-GARNER, DEBRA

Association executive, writer, consultant. **Personal:** Born Feb 9, 1957, Washington, DC; daughter of Sadie Williams Lark and Ernest E Williams Sr (deceased); married David Garner, Oct 2, 1982; children: Brooke N Garner, Evan D Garner. **Educ:** University of Bridgeport, Bridgeport, CT, BA, 1979. **Career:** Washington Star Newspaper, Washington, DC, freelance writer, 1979-81; Library of Congress, Washington, DC, editor/writer, 1981-85; Environmental Defense Fund, Washington, DC, media specialist, 1985-89; Providence Hospital, Washington, DC, public relations specialist, 1987-89; American Heart Association, Washington, DC, director of communications, 1989-92; freelance writer/promotion consultant, 1993-. **Orgs:** Journalist/chair of publicity committee, Delta Sigma Theta, Federal City Alumnae Chapter, 1990-92; African-American Writers Guild, 1989-; Capital Press Club, 1990-; Amer Academy of Poets, 1994-. **Honors/Awds:** Isiah Robinson Media Award, University of Bridgeport, 1979; 2nd Place Winner, "Words on the Wall", Poetry Contest, PA Writers Conference, 1994. **Special Achievements:** Author, Pipedreams, Ernest Hampton Press, 1988. **Home Addr:** 6606 Lansdale Street, District Heights, MD 20747.

WILLIAMS-GREEN, JOYCE F.

Educational administrator. **Personal:** Born Sep 6, 1948, Sanford, NC; daughter of Joseph A Williams; married Edward W Green, Sep 1, 1984. **Educ:** North Carolina Central Univ, BS, 1970; Herbert H Lehman Coll, MS, 1976; Virginia Polytechnic Inst & State Univ, EdD, 1984. **Career:** New York City Public School, teacher, 1971-76; Livingstone Coll, dir of learning center, 1976-80; Virginia Polytechnic Inst and State Univ, asst to the provost, 1987, assistant provost, 1987-. **Orgs:** Consultant, Janus Learning Center, 1986, North Carolina A&T, 1986; citizen representative, Blacksburg in the 80's, 1984-86; mem, cochair, Phi Kappa Phi, 1986-87; mem research comm, NACADA, 1986; bd mem, New River Community Sentencing Inc; member, Governor's Monitoring Committee, 1990-; bd mem, Warm Hearth Fdn, 1986-. **Honors/Awds:** Cunningham Research Fellowship, Virginia Tech, 1983; "The Effect of the Computer on Natl Educ," Computing Conf proceedings, 1983; Natl Certificate of Merit, NACADA, 1986. **Business Addr:** Asst Provost, Virginia Polytechnic Inst & State Univ, 201 Burruss Hall, Blacksburg, VA 24061.

WILLIAMS-HARRIS, DIANE BEATRICE
Educational administrator. **Personal:** Born Feb 1, 1949, Newark, NJ; divorced; children: Karl, Elayne. **Educ:** Boston Univ, BA 1971; Rutgers Univ Grad Sch of Educ, MEd 1977. **Career:** Prudential Ins Co, pension administrator 1971-73; Rutgers Univ Office of Undergrad Admissions, asst to the dir 1973-76, asst dir 1976-78, dir, 1978-82, assoc dir 1982-. **Orgs:** Mem Natl Assoc of College Admissions Counselors, Delta Sigma Theta, 100 Black Women. **Honors/Awds:** Sponsored participant in Women in Higher Educ 1977; Rutgers Univ Merit Awd 1986, 1993. **Business Addr:** Associate Dir/Undergraduate Admissions, Rutgers University, PO Box 2101, New Brunswick, NJ 08903.

WILLIAMS-MYERS, ALBERT J.
Educator. **Personal:** Born Mar 10, 1939, Edison, GA; son of Bessie Irene Williams and C Kilmer Myers; married Janice Diane Redmond, Oct 11, 1962; children: M Maluwa, Plaisimwana Renee. **Educ:** Wagner College, BA, 1962; UCLA, lifetime teaching certificate, 1969, MA, 1971, PhD, 1978. **Career:** Mobilization for Youth, work group leader, 1962-63; All Saints Parish School, teacher, 8th thru 11th grade, 1963-64; College of the Virgin Islands, head resident, director of activities, 1964-65; New York City Youth Board, street club worker, 1965-66; US Peace Corps, Malawi, Africa, volunteer, 1966-68; Carleton College, professor, 1976-79; SUNY Albany African-American Institute, executive director, 1990-91; SUNY College at New Paltz, professor, currently. **Orgs:** African Studies Association, 1971-80; New York African Studies Association, president, 1985-88; NAACP, Ellenville, Chapter, 1985-. **Honors/Awds:** Ford Foundation, Research in Africa & the Middle East Graduate Fellowship, 1973-74; Historic Hudson Valley, Distinguished African-American Researcher Award, 1992. **Special Achievements:** Writer, ''Slavery, Rebellion and Revolution in The Americas: A Historiographical Scenario on the Theses of Genovese and Others,'' Journal of Black Studies 26, 4 March 1996; Making The Invisible Visible: African-Americans in New York History, 1994; ''A Portrait of Eve: History of Black Women in Hudson Valley,'' 1987; Books Published: ''Long Hammering: Essays on the forging of an African American Presence in the Hudson River Valley to the Early Twentieth Century,'' Africa World Press, 1994; ''Destructive Impulses: An Examination of An American Secret in Race Relations: White Violence,'' University Press of America, 1995; NY City, African Americans and Selective Memory: An Historiographical Assessment of a Black Presence Before 1877; Journal of Afro-Americans in New York Life and History, July 1997. **Business Addr:** Professor, State University of New York, College at New Paltz, College Hall F-106, New Paltz, NY 12561, (914)257-2760.

WILLIAMSON, CARL VANCE
Government/private agency. **Personal:** Born Oct 3, 1955, Portsmouth, VA; son of Carolyn Williamson and Shelton Williamson. **Educ:** Virginia Commonwealth Univ, BS 1977; Univ of South FL, MBA 1984. **Career:** Group W Cable Inc, financial analyst 1983-85; MCI Telecommunications, sup-acctg & analysis 1985-86; Hampton Redevelopment/Housing Auth, housing mgmt sup 1986-. **Orgs:** Mem Omega Psi Phi Frat Inc 1974-, Amer Assoc of MBA Exec 1984-, Natl Black MBA Assoc 1985-; mem NAACP. **Home Addr:** 475 Water St, Apt 206, Portsmouth, VA 23704. **Business Addr:** Housing Mgmt Supervisor, Hampton Redevel/Hsg Authority, PO Box 280, Hampton, VA 23669.

WILLIAMSON, CARLTON
Professional football player (retired). **Personal:** Born Jun 12, 1958, Atlanta, GA; married Donna; children: Kevin Carlton. **Educ:** Univ of Pittsburgh, BS, 1981. **Career:** San Francisco 49ers, safety, 1981-87. **Honors/Awds:** All Rookie 1981; named Coll and Pro Football Weekly second team All-Pro and AP honorable mention ALl-Pro 1985; played in Pro Bowl, 1984, 1985.

WILLIAMSON, CORLISS MONDARI
Professional basketball player. **Personal:** Born Dec 4, 1973, Russellville, AR. **Educ:** Arkansas. **Career:** Sacramento Kings, forward, 1995-. **Special Achievements:** NBA, First Round Draft Pick, #13 Pick, 1995. **Business Addr:** Professional Basketball Player, Sacramento Kings, One Sports Pkwy, Sacramento, CA 95834, (916)928-6900.

WILLIAMSON, COY COLBERT, JR.
Nursing home owner/manager. **Personal:** Born Mar 27, 1936, Commerce, GA; married Betty Brown; children: Coylitia, Bettrena. **Educ:** Stillman Coll, BA Business 1962. **Career:** Atlanta Life Insurance Co, debit mgr 1963-64; Teachers Agency of GA, claims mgr 1964-66; ACTION Inc, fiscal officer 1966-70; Atlanta Mortgage Co, asst vice pres 1970; Univ of GA, asst mgr of loans and receivables 1970-71; Athens Model Cities, fiscal coord 1972-73; State of GA, fiscal mgmt spclst 1973-74; Grandview Care Ctr Inc, mgr 1974-83; We Care Enterprises Inc, mgmt specialist/consultant, owner 1983-. **Orgs:** Founder Athens Business and Professional Org 1978-82; mem Classic City Toastmasters 1980-81; sec & mem at large GA Health Care Assoc 1980-; fellow Amer Coll of Long-Term Administrators 1982-; mem Metro Atlanta Cncl of Nursing Home Adminis; life mem and polemarch Kappa Alpha Psi Frat; deacon and sunday sch supt Hill First Bapt Church; mem Athens Area Chamber of Commerce. **Honors/Awds:** Achievement & Leadership Awd Kappa Alpha Psi Frat; President's Golden/Dist List Stillman Coll 1983-; First black apptd by Gov to serve on GA Public Safety Bd 1984-. **Military Serv:** USAF a/1c 1954-58; US Peace Corps 1962-63. **Home Addr:** 1125 Whit Davis Rd, Athens, GA 30605. **Business Addr:** Owner/Manager, We Care Enterprises Inc, PO Box 146, Athens, GA 30603.

WILLIAMSON, ETHEL W.
Museum administrator, educator. **Personal:** Born Nov 28, 1947, Hallandale, FL; daughter of Essie L Washington and Harvey Washington; married Daniel A Williamson, Jun 20, 1970; children: Jason D. **Educ:** Central State University, BS, English, 1969; Teachers College, Columbia University, MA, MEd, guidance, 1973; Rutgers-The State University of New Jersey, museum studies certificate, 1992. **Career:** Huntington National Bank, training assistant, 1969-71; New Jersey Institute of Technology, assistant director, 1973-79, director, educational opportunity program, 1978-79; Douglass College, Rutgers University, assistant dean of students, 1979-81; Union County College, counselor generalist, 1986-90; Cooper-Hewitt, National Museum of Design, Smithsonian Institute, project coordinator, African-American design archive, 1991-. **Orgs:** African-American Museums Association, 1991-; Delta Sigma Theta Sorority, 1968-; Sisters United of New Jersey, 1992-; North Jersey Chapter of Jack and Jill of America, historian, 1985-91; New Jersey Chapter of Central State University Alumni Association, program committee chair, 1992-; Union County Cultural & Historical Commission, City of Plainfield historian, 1986-89. **Honors/Awds:** Smithsonian Institution, Office of Museum Programs, Academic Internship Award, 1991; Teachers College, Columbia University, minority graduate fellowship, 1971, 1972. **Special Achievements:** Co-curator of first individual exhibition by an African-American designer at the Cooper-Hewitt Museum; established a National African-American design archive at Cooper-Hewitt; ''Engineering Opportunity Program: A Concept and a Commitment,'' National Technical Association Journal, February 1976. **Home Addr:** 901 Grant Ave, Plainfield, NJ 07060, (908)561-4088. **Business Addr:** Project Coordinator, African-American Design Archive, Cooper-Hewitt, Smithsonian National Museum of Design, Department of Decorative Arts, 2 E 91st St, New York, NY 10128, (212)860-6960.

WILLIAMSON, HANDY, JR.
Educational administrator, international consultant. **Personal:** Born Oct 24, 1945, Louin, MS; son of Lilla M Nobles Williamson and Handy Williamson Sr; married Barbara Jean Herndon, Dec 28, 1968; children: Lilla-Marie Juliana. **Educ:** Pineywood Jr Coll, Pineywood MS, AA, 1965; Alcorn State Univ, Lorman MS, BS, 1967; Tennessee State Univ, Nashville TN, MS, 1969; Univ of Missouri, Columbia MO, MS 1971, PhD 1974. **Career:** Tennessee State Univ, Nashville TN, res asst, 1967-69; Univ of Missouri, Columbia MO, grad res asst, 1969-74; Tuskegee Univ, Tuskegee AL, assoc dir of res, 1974-77; Tennessee State Univ, Nashville TN, res dir, 1977-85; USAID, Washington DC, director/AD-15, 1985-88; Univ of Tennessee, Knoxville TN, dept head & prof, 1988-. **Orgs:** Mem, Gamma Sigma Delta, 1971; bd mem, Black Culture Ctr, Univ of MO, 1972-73, section chair, comm chair, 1974-, nominations comm, 1996-; AAEA; Title V Committee on Rural Development, 1975-77; pres, Phi Beta Sigma, Tuskegee chapter, 1975-77; charter mem, Optimist Club of Tuskegee, 1975-77; Task Force on Energy, 1976-77; Southern Region's Small Farm Functional Network, 1976-77; United Methodist Men, 1977; mem, chmn, TN Council of Agr Deans, 1977-85; consultant, Tennessee Valley Authority, 1979-80; consultant, Bd for Intl Food & Agric Devel, 1981-85; mem, legislative subcomm, ESCOP, 1981-84; mem, Paster Parish Comm, Clark UMC Church, 1981-85; mem, US Joint Council on Food & Agric, 1982-83; bd mem, Assn of Intl Prog Dirs, 1984-88; bd of dirs, Assnof State Univ, Dirs of Intl Agril Dev programs, 1984-88; NASULGC; White House Comm liaison, USAID, 1985-88; dir, Virginia Business Devel Center, 1987-; chairman AAEA Committee on Status of Blacks, 1991-93; vice chairman, Southern Agric Econ Department Heads Assn, 1991-92; member, SAEA Honorary Life Membership Committee, 1990-93; BOD United Methodist Found, 1994-; mentor, Black Achievers Assn, Knoxville TN, 1995-; charter mem, pres-elect, Sigma Pi Phi, 1996; TN State Univ Agribusiness Council, 1996-; TN Assn of Coll Teachers in Agr; Urban League. **Honors/Awds:** Gamma Sigma Delta, Univ of MO, 1971; Outstanding Young Man of America, Univ of MO, 1973; spearheaded establishment of Optimist Club of Tuskegee, 1975; internatl devel consultant, 1975-; author of articles on Black universities, 1977-89; testimony before US House & Senate subcomms, 1981-85; co-author of book on small farms in Tennessee, 1985; Presidential Plaques, TN State Univ, 1985 & 1987; Outstanding Service, USAID/Washington DC, 1986; Distinguished Alumni, Alcorn State Univ, 1987; mem of Pres Club, Univ of TN, 1988; Outstanding Black Agricultural Economist, American Agric Econ Assn, 1990; Prof Recognition Awd, University of Georgia, Collaborative Research Support Program, 1996; Leadership Development Training Awd, Univ of Puerto Rico-Mayaguez, 1996; Prof Recognition Awd, Univ of TN, Ronald McNair Postbaccalurate Achievement Program, 1996; Black Achiever's Awd, YMCA, Univ of TN, 1995; Distinguished Alumni Awd, Univ of Missouri, Columbia, 1993; ACE Exec Fellow Awd, Univ of CA, 1997-98; Amer Men and Women of Science, 1993; Men of Achievement, 1992; Institute for Leadership Effectiveness, Univ of TN, 1989; Presidential Awd, TN State Univ, 1993; numerous others. **Home Addr:** 12108 East Ashton Ct, Knoxville, TN 37922.

WILLIAMSON, HENRY M.
Cleric, association executive. **Career:** Operation PUSH, national president, CEO, 1991-92; Carter Temple, Reverend, currently. **Business Addr:** The Reverend, Carter Temple, 7841 S Wabash, Chicago, IL 60619, (312)874-0175.

WILLIAMSON, KAREN ELIZABETH
Marketing administrator. **Personal:** Born Dec 20, 1947, St Louis, MO; daughter of Elizabeth R Giddings Williamson and Irving A Williamson; divorced; children: Stephanie Elizabeth. **Educ:** Wellesley Coll MA, BA 1965-69; Univ of Chicago Grad Schl Bus, MBA 1969-71. **Career:** Philip Morris Inc NYC, asst brand mgr 1971-73; Avon Prod Inc NYC, prod couns 1973-76; HUD Washington, spl asst 1977-78; The White House, dep spl asst 1978-81; Satellite Business Systems, acct rep 1981-86; MCI, sr mgr natl accts 1986, 1988-89; Intl Ctr for Information Tech Washington, dir external relations 1987-88; Managed Healthcare Systems, vice president, marketing. **Orgs:** Bd of dir Nat Black MBA Assn 1972-75; mem Natl Black MBA Assoc 1986-, Coalition of 100 Black Women of DC, Washington Wellesley Club, Univ of Chicago Women's Business Group; Leadership Washington. **Honors/Awds:** Black Achievers Awd Harlem YMCA 1975.

WILLIAMSON, SAMUEL P.
Government administrator. **Personal:** Born Mar 5, 1949, Somerville, TN; son of Izoula Smith Williamson and Julius Williamson, Jr; married Brenda Joyce Lee Williamson, Sep 15, 1970; children: Keith Ramon Williamson, Yulanda Marie Williamson. **Educ:** Tennessee State University, Nashville, TN, BS, Math/Physics, 1971; North Carolina State University, Raleigh, NC, BS, Meteorology, 1972; Webster University, St Louis, MO, MA, Management, 1976. **Career:** Atomic Energy Commission, Oak Ridge, TN, research student, 1969; USAF, Charleston AFB, SC, weather detactment commander, 1972-77; Department of Commerce, NOAA, National Weather Service, Silver Spring, MD, dir, NEXRAD, 1977-. **Orgs:** Member, International Electrical/Electronics Engineers Society, 1989-, American Meteorological Society, 1980-, American Management Association, 1989-, Senior Executives Service Association, 1988-, National Guard Association, 1980-; officer, board of trustees & finance, Mt Calvary Baptist Church, 1986-. **Honors/Awds:** Superior Performance Achievement Award, 1978-90. **Military Serv:** US Air Force, Lt Col, 1971-91; received Air Force Commendation Medal, DCANG, Air Force Achievement Medal, DCANG. **Home Addr:** 19121 Barksdale Ct, Germantown, MD 20874.

WILLIAMSON, SAMUEL R.
Attorney. **Personal:** Born Nov 22, 1943, Ellaville, GA; son of Mittie M Williamson and Joseph S Williamson; married Barbara Ann Elliott; children: Patricia, Michael. **Educ:** Hampton Univ, BS 1965; Seton Hall Univ, JD 1975; Army Command & General Staff Coll, graduated, 1982. **Career:** AT&T Bell Lab, elec engr 1968-75, senior patent atty 1976-95; Lucent Technologies, Inc, corporate counsel, 1995-. **Orgs:** Mem Assn of Black Lab Employees 1970-85, Garden State Bar Assn 1976-, Natl Bar Assn 1976-, New York Urban League Inc 1982-; bd mem Natl Patent Law Assn 1988-89, pres, 1989-91; mem New Jersey Wing Civil Air Patrol 1983-; BEEP lecturer; mem NAI Inc, The Alliance Inc, AUSA, Amer Legion, YMCA, Phi Alpha Delta, Scabbard & Blade, Explorers; Prince Hall Mason. **Honors/Awds:** Electronics Assoc Honor Awd for Miliary Leadership; Awd for Unselfish Devotion to ABLE Inc. **Military Serv:** AUSR lt col 1965-93; Armed Forces Commendation. **Business Addr:** Corporate Counsel, Lucent Technologies Inc, 150 Allen Rd, Liberty Corner, NJ 07938, (908)903-6444.

WILLIAMSON-IGE, DOROTHY KAY
Educator. **Personal:** Born Apr 18, 1950, Parma, MO; daughter of Florida B Madden Williamson and Rufus A Williamson; married Adewole A Ige; children: Olufolajimi Wm. **Educ:** Southeast Missouri State Univ, BS, Speech, 1971; Central Missouri State Univ, MA, Speech Comm, 1973; Ohio State Univ, PhD, Speech, 1980. **Career:** Webster Grove Schools, speech & drama teacher, 1971-77; DOD Dependents Schools, drama teacher, 1977-78; Bowling Green State Univ, faculty & field exper coord, 1980-84; Indiana Univ NW, faculty, 1985-. **Orgs:** Public adv bd, Bowling Green State Univ, 1980-83; assoc, Ohio State Univ Black Alumni, 1980-; Phi Delta Kappa, 1980-; speech comm, assoc black caucus pres, legislative council, Black Oppor Task Force, 1981-87; State of Ohio Bd Redesign of Educ Programs, 1982; pres, Women Investing Together & program chairperson, Human Relations Comm, Bowling Green State Univ, 1984; TV radio newspaper interviews, keynote speeches, papers & consultantships in Midwest USA, Africa, Caribbean & Europe. **Honors/Awds:** Academic Scholarship Certificate Southeast Missouri State Univ, 1970; (Civilian) Intl Talent Search Judge, US Military, Ramstein, Germany, Air Force Base, 1978; TV, radio, newspaper interviews and keynote speeches, papers, consultantships in Midwest US, Africa, Caribbean & Europe, 1978-; published over 20 articles & book

chapters on communication education for minorities, the handicapped and women, 1981-87; Third World Peoples Award, Bowling Green State Univ, 1984; Department Head, Community WPA; Acting Department Head, Minority Studies. **Business Addr:** Professor, Indiana Univ NW, Communications Dept, 3400 Broadway, Gary, IN 46408.

WILLIAMS-STANTON, SONYA DENISE
Educator. **Personal:** Born May 31, 1963, Birmingham, AL; daughter of Carolyn W Williams and Sam L Williams; married Tom Stanton. **Educ:** Brown Univ, BA (honors) 1984; The Univ of MI Business School, MBA (honors) 1986, PhD, 1994. **Career:** Irving Trust Co, account rep 1986-88; Assistant Professor of Finance, Ohio State University, 1993-. **Orgs:** Pres Brown Univ Chapter Alpha Kappa Alpha 1982-83; mem Natl Black MBA Assoc, Financial Mgmt Assoc; vice pres University of Michigan Black Business Students Association; American Finance Association; National Economic Association; St Philips Episcopal Church. **Honors/Awds:** Fellowship Consortium for Graduate Study in Mgmt 1984-86; Scholarship Natl Black MBA Assoc 1985; Honor Soc Financial Mgmt Assoc 1985-87; Unisys Corporation Doctoral Fellowship, 1989-92; Michigan Merit Fellow, 1991-94. **Home Addr:** 383 Walhalla Rd, Columbus, OH 43202-1469.

WILLIAMS-TAITT, PATRICIA ANN
Educational administrator. **Personal:** Born Jul 3, 1947, Toledo, OH; daughter of Nettie & Charles Matthews; married Arthur R Taitt, Apr 12, 1992; children: Jason C. **Educ:** Wayne State Univ, BS, elementory education, 1969, educ admini; Dale Carnegie Inst, effective speaking; Ctr for Corp & Comm Relations, 1985; Leadership Detroit XII, 1990-91; IBM Leadership Development, 1993. **Career:** Det Public School Systems, 2nd grade teacher, 1969-70; Singer Career Systems, Detroit Job Corps, dir of educ, 1972-86; Mercy Health Systems, dir of community relations, 1986-89; Public Relations Consultant, 1986-; Greater Detroit Chamber of Commerce, Detroit Compact, deputy dir, 1989-. **Orgs:** Amer Red Cross, exec bd, 1994-; Booker T Washington, assoc publicity chairperson, 1984-90; Friends of Southwest, exec bd, 1990-; Partners Tabloid, editorial committee, 1986-89; Winship Community Council, vp, 1986-89; Amer Cancer Society, vp public information, 1988-89; Black Family Development Inc, co-chair, publicity chair, 1987-88. **Honors/Awds:** WWJ Radio, Citizen of the Week Award, 1994; Booker T Washington, Honor Sor Chairperson of Principal & Educators Luncheon; Bus Assn, Amer Cancer Society Services Plaque, 1989; Booker T Washington, 1992-94; City Council, Spirit of Detroit Award, 1988; Business Women of the Month, NW Area Business Assn, 1987. **Home Addr:** 18284 Murray Hill, Detroit, MI 48235, (313)273-5944. **Business Addr:** Dir of Community Relations and Public Policy, United Way Community Services, 1212 Griswold, Detroit, MI 48226, (313)226-9200.

WILLIE, CHARLES VERT
Educator. **Personal:** Born Oct 8, 1927, Dallas, TX; son of Carrie S Willie and Louis J Willie; married Mary Sue Conklin; children: Sarah S, Martin C, James T. **Educ:** Morehouse Coll, BA 1948; Atlanta Univ, MA 1949; Syracuse Univ, PhD 1957. **Career:** Syracuse Univ, inst, asst prof, assoc prof, prof of sociology 1952-74, chm, 1967-71, vp, 1972-74; Upstate Med Center Syracuse, NY Dept Preventive med, instructor 1955-60; Pres Comm on Delinquency Wash DC Project, research dir 1962-64; Dept of Psychiatry Harvard Med School, visiting lecturer 1966-67; Episcopal Divinity School, Cambridge, visiting lecturer, 1966-67; Harvard Univ, prof educ & urban studies, 1974-. **Orgs:** Tech Adv Comm Falk Fund 1968-; ind mem UNCF 1983-86; court appointed master expert witness/consultant school desegration cases in Brockton, Boston, Cambridge, Denver, Dallas, Houston, Little Rock, St Louis, Kansas City MO, Seattle, North Carolina, San Jose, Milwaukee, Lee County and St Lucie, FL 1974-; pres Eastern Sociological Soc 1974-75; American Sociological Association, council member, 1979-82, 1995-97, vice president, 1996-97; board member Soc Sci Rsch Council 1969-76; trustee Episcopal Div School 1969-; former vp, House of Deputies, General Convention of Episcopal Church in USA 1970-74; sr warden Christ Episcopal Church, Cambridge 1984-86; board member, former chair, Dana McLean Greeley Foundation for Peace and Justice, 1986-; former mem, President's Commn on Mental Health, USA, 1978; mem, Association of Black Sociologists; American Educational Research Association; Sociologists for Women in Society; Society for the Study of Social Problems. **Honors/Awds:** Phi Beta Kappa, 1972; Ms Magazine 10th Anniversary Issue, Male Hero, 1982; Maxwell School of Syracuse University, Distinguished Alumnus Award, 1974; National Association for Equal Opportunity in Higher Education Award, 1979; Society for the Study of Social Problems, Lee-Founders Award, 1986; Committee on the Role and Status of Minorities of the American Educational Research Association, Distinguished Career Contribution Award, 1990; International Institute for Interracial Interaction of Minneapolis, MN, Family of the Year Award, 1992; John LaFarge Award, Fairfield Univ, 1995; The Spirit of Public Service Award, Maxwell School of Syracuse Univ, 1994; The Dubois-Johnson-Frazier Award, Amer Sociological Assn, 1994; THe Robin Williams Distinguished Lecturership Award, Eastern Sociological Society, 1994; Morehouse College, Benjamin Mays Service Award, 1994; Myer Center Outstanding Book in Human Rights Award for co-editing Mental Health, Racism and Sexism, 1996; Assoc of Black Sociologists, Distinguished Career Award; Honorary Degrees: Berkeley Divinity School at Yale, DHL, 1972; Episcopal General Seminar of NY, DD, 1974; Harvard University, MA, 1974; Morehouse College, DHL, 1983; Rhode Island College, DHL, 1985; Syracuse University, DHL, 1992; Framingham State College, DL, 1992; Franklin Pierce Coll, DHL, 1996; Wentworth Inst of Technology, Det, 1996. **Special Achievements:** Author: Black Students at White Colleges, 1972; Racism and Mental Health, 1973; Race Mixing in the Public Schools, 1973; Black Colleges in America, 1978; Oreo, 1975; The Ivory and Ebony Towers, 1981; A New Look at Black Families, 4th edition, 1991; Race, Ethnicity and Socio-economic Status, 1983; School Desegregation Plans that Work, 1984; Black and White Families, 1985; Five Black Scholars, 1986; Metropolitan School Desegregation, 1986; Effective Education, 1987; Social Goals and Educational Reform, 1988; The Caste and Class Controversy on Race and Poverty, 1989; African-Americans and the Doctoral Experience, 1991; The Education of African-Americans, 1991; Theories of Human Social Action, 1994; Mental Health, Racism and Sexism, 1995; Controlled Choice, 1996; Black Power/White Power in Public Education, 1998; publication summary: over 20 books, over 100 articles or chapters in books. **Business Addr:** Professor of Education & Urban Studies, Graduate School of Education, Harvard University, Cambridge, MA 02138, (617)495-4678.

WILLIE, LOUIS J.
Business executive (retired). **Personal:** Born Aug 22, 1923, Fort Worth; son of Carrie Sykes Willie and Louis J Sr Willie; married Yvonne Kirkpatrick; children: Louis J III. **Educ:** Wiley Coll, BA 1943; Univ Michigan, MBA 1947; Amer Coll Lf Underwr, CLU. **Career:** Tennessee State Univ, instructor 1947; McKissack Bro Nashville; office manager 1950; Booker T Washington Ins Co B'Ham, exec vice pres 1952-; Citzens Fed Saving & Loan, vice pres sec treas 1956-; Booker T Washington Ins Co, pres, 1986-94. **Orgs:** Former director Birmingham Branch Fed Reserve Bank of Atlanta; bd dir Assn of Life Ins Cos; Natl Ins Assn; chrt Life Undrwrtrs; adv bd Salvation Army; bd dir A G Gaston Boys Club; emeritus board AmSouth Bancorporation; dir Alabama Power Co, until 1994; mem Newcomen Soc North America; board of directors United Way Central Alabama; NAACP; Univ of Michigan Alumni Club; president's council Univ of Alabama in Birmingham; mem Natl Black MBA Association; board of directors Birmingham Area Chamber of Commerce; bd of trustees Alabama Trust Fund; board of directors Meyer Found; board of directors Alabama Management Management Improvement Assn. **Honors/Awds:** Outstanding Ctzns Award Miles Coll 1972; Distinguished Ser Award; Comm Ser Council 1972-73; 1985 Brotherhood Awd Natl Conference of Christians and Jews; inducted into AL Acad of Honor 1986; University of Alabama at Birmingham, Honorary LLD; Greater Birmingham Manager of the Year, 1991; Birmingham Southern College, Honorary LLD; Greater Birmingham Area Community Service Award, 1993; National Black MBA Association, H Naylor Fitzhugh Award of Excellence, 1992. **Military Serv:** WW II veteran.

WILLIFORD, CYNTHIA W.
Educator (retired). **Personal:** Born Mar 14, 1917, Seneca, SC; married Preston. **Educ:** SC St Clg, BHE 1939; MI St U, MHE 1963. **Career:** HS Home Economics, teacher 1939-44; Clemson Coop Ext Serv, home economist 1974. **Orgs:** Sch bd mem Anderson Dist #5 1980-; v chm Anderson Dist #5 Sch Bd 1985-. **Home Addr:** 222 Hillcrest Circle, Anderson, SC 29624.

WILLIFORD, STANLEY O.
Editor, journalist, publisher. **Personal:** Born Jan 3, 1942, Little Rock, AR; son of Mary Esther Williford and Claude Theophilus Williford; married Corliss M; children: Steven D Woods, Nicole O Woods, Brian M, Brandon A. **Educ:** CA State Univ, B 1968. **Career:** Newsweek mag Detroit, trainee summer 1968; LA Times, reporter 1969-72; LA Sentinel, reporter 1972-74; LA Herald Examiner, copy editor 1975-76; Travel & Art Mag, co-publ 1977-78; Ichthus Records/Productions; LA Times, copy editor 1976-93; Crenshaw Christian Ctr, director of publications, 1993-94; Vision Publishing, president/founder, 1996-. **Orgs:** Sigma Delta Chi, 1968; board member, Crenshaw Christian Center, 1991-95. **Honors/Awds:** Fellowship, Washington Jrnl Ctr 1968; writer freelance articles in numerous natlly known mags in US; Natl Assn of Media Women Awd, 1974; Michele Clark Found, Awd for General Excellence in Reporting, Columbia Univ 1974; 1st black to edit CA State LA Univ newspaper 1967. **Military Serv:** AUS sp-4 1964-66; Soldier of the Month Award. **Business Addr:** Founder/President, Vision Publishing, PO Box 11166, Carson, CA 90746-1166.

WILLINGHAM, JAMES EDWARD
Association executive. **Personal:** Born Jun 15, 1948, Philadelphia, PA; son of Rubin and Ruth; married Dawn M. Willingham, Dec 31, 1995; children: Lynette Wesley, Lynore, Andrea, Tiffany. **Educ:** Philadelphia Community College, AA, 1974; Temple University, studied Urban Affairs, 1975; Empire State College of New York University, BA, 1980. **Career:** Boy Scouts of America, scout executive/CEO, currently. **Orgs:** Community Health Services, Inc, past president, board of directors, 1994-97; St. Francis Hospital & Medical Center, board of directors, 1995-; Capital Community College, advisory bd, 1995-; Kappa Alpha Psi Fraternity, Youth Programs, chair, 1990-; Sigma Pi Phi Fraternity, 1994-; Greater Hartford Chamber of Commerce, 1993-; Newpath, Inc., bd mem, 1997; Greater Hartford Urban League, 1993-. **Honors/Awds:** Bright Hope Baptist Church, William H. Gray's Outstanding Man of the Year Award, 1971; Four Chaplains Legion of Honor, Outstanding Service to All People Award, 1972; New York Urban League, Community Service to Youth Award, 1988; Kappa Alpha Psi Frat, Inc, Achievement Award, 1991; AME Zion Church, Role Model for African American Males, 1992. **Home Addr:** 16 Cliffmont Drive, Bloomfield, CT 06002, (860)242-7945. **Business Addr:** Scout Executive/CEO, Connecticut Rivers Council, Boy Scouts of America, PO Box 280098, 60 Darlin Street, East Hartford, CT 06128-0098, (860)289-6669.

WILLINGHAM, TYRONE
Football coach. **Career:** Minnesota Vikings, asst coach; Stanford Univ, head football coach, currently. **Business Addr:** Football Coach, Stanford University, Arrillag Familt Ctr, Stanford, CA 94305-6510.

WILLINGHAM, VONCILE
Government manager. **Personal:** Born Nov 9, 1935, Opp, AL; daughter of Ida Lee Liggins Lee and L K Lee; married Anderson Willingham Jr; children: Donna Marie, Doretta Monique. **Educ:** AL State Univ, BS Educ 1957; Univ of District of Columbia, MS Bus Educ 1977; The Amer Univ, MS Personnel and Human Resources Mgmt 1987. **Career:** Greene Co Bd of Educ, business educ instr 1957-58; UA Agency for Intl Develop, exec asst 1961-69, employee dev specialist 1970-77, equal employ mgr 1978-. **Orgs:** Mem Delta Sigma Theta Sor 1955-; mem Sargent Memorial Presbyter Chancel Choir 1975-; mem Southern MD Choral Soc 1983-; mem bd dirs Foreign Affairs Recreation Assoc 1985-; mem bd dirs Univ District of Columbia Sch of Business Educ; mem US AID Administrator's Adv Comm on Women; mem interagency comm Martin Luther King Federal Holiday Comm 1986. **Honors/Awds:** Fellowship Beta Eta Chap Delta Sigma Theta 1957; Equal Employment Oppor Awd US AGency for Intl Dev 1977; Certificates for Community Outreach to DC Public Schools 1979-84; Superior Honor Awd US Agency for Intl Dev 1981. **Business Addr:** EEO Manager, US Agency for Intl Develop, 21st St & Va Avenue NW, Washington, DC 20523.

WILLIS, ANDREW
Executive director. **Personal:** Born Oct 5, 1938, Jamesville, NC; married Shirley; children: LaShirl, Anqileena. **Educ:** NC A&T State U, BS 1964; Kent State U, MA 1967; Univ of NY at Buffalo, Atnd. **Career:** Urban League of Onondaga Co, exec dir 1973-; Erie Comm Coll, asst prof 1972-73; Buffalo Urban League Feb-Aug, acting exec dir 1972; Buffalo Urban League, dep dir 1968-72; State Univ Coll at Buffalo, pt instr 1969-72; Health & Welfare Buffalo Urban League, asso dir 1967-68; State Univ of NY at Buffalo, tchng asst 1964-67; Kent State U, grad asst 1964-67; Pub Welfare Dept Norfolk VA, caseworker Summer 1964. **Orgs:** Mem bd dirs PEACE Inc; mem NY State Health Planning Adv Council; bd dirs Intl Cntr of Syracuse; adv Council on Equal Opp; Manpower Adv Planning Council; EOP Com Educ Opp Cntr; exec Councils Nat Eastern Regional State; mem Com to Reactivate Local NAACP Chpt. **Honors/Awds:** USAF a1/c 1956-60. **Business Addr:** 100 New St, Syracuse, NY 13202.

WILLIS, CECIL B.
Chief executive automotive dealership. **Career:** Peninsula Pontiac, Inc, Torrance CA, chief executive, 1988. **Business Addr:** Peninsula Pontiac, Inc, 2909 Pacific Coast Highway, Torrance, CA 90505.

WILLIS, CHARLES L.
Judge. **Personal:** Born Sep 11, 1926, New York, NY; married Judith Lounsbury; children: Lisa, Michael Elliott, Susan Elliott, Christopher, John Elliott. **Educ:** NY Univ, 1947-51; CCNY, 1950-51; St John Univ School of Law, LLB 1955. **Career:** Monroe County District Attorney Office, asst district attorney, 1967-68; Monroe County, public defender, 1968-70; City of Rochester, corp counsel 1970-71, city court judge 1971-72; McKay Comm, 1st dep counsel 1972; State of NY, Family Court, supervising judge 1980-88, Supreme Court Justice, 1989-; 7th Judicial District, Administrative Judge, 1991. **Orgs:** Trustee, Monroe County Bar Assn, 1970-72; Advisor, 4th Judicial Dept, NY Advisory common Law Guardians; mem, Assn of Family Court Judges; dir, Urban League, Rochester Children's Convalescent Hospital, 1980-83, SPCC 1981-83, Center for Govt Rsch 1981-84. **Military Serv:** USN seaman 1st class 2 yrs. **Business Addr:** Justice, New York State Supreme Court, 7th Judicial District, Hall of Justice Exchange St, Rochester, NY 14614.

WILLIS, FRANK B.
Elected government official, publisher. **Personal:** Born Mar 13, 1947, Cleveland, MS; married Bobbie M Henderson; children: Oji-Camara Khari. **Educ:** Rochester Bus Inst, AA 1968; Dyke Coll, BS 1971. **Career:** City Urban Renewal Dept, family relocation aide 1972-74; Okang Commun Corp, pres 1973-; Cty

Dept of Soc Svcs, eligibility examiner 1974; Communicade Newspaper, publisher/editor 1981-; Rochester City School Dist, commiss. **Orgs:** Legislative intern Rapic Comm network Judicial Process Commiss 1977-78; mem Coalition of Chap I Parents 1978-; editor/writer Horambee Parents Newsletter Chap I Program 1979-80; mem Natl Alliance of Black School Educators 1980-, Caucus of Black School Bd Mems 1983-. **Honors/Awds:** Outstanding Personality Afro-Amer Soc Dyke Coll 1971; Serv Awd Greater Rochester Tougaloo Coll Alumni Assoc Inc 1983; Outstanding Serv Rochester City Schools Dist Advisory Council to Chap I 1983; Serv Urban League of Rochester 1984. **Home Addr:** 67 Elba St, Rochester, NY 14608.

WILLIS, FREDERIC L.
Legal educator. **Personal:** Born May 14, 1937, Handley, WV; divorced. **Educ:** LA Cty Coll, AA 1961; CA State U, BS 1970; UCLA, grad study 1971; Pepperdine Univ 1973. **Career:** LA dist atty, community affairs rep, investigator, 1967-71; LA Sheriff, deputy sheriff 1964-67, communications expert 1960-64; W LA Coll Admin of Justice, instructor, 1972-; SW LA Coll Admin of Justice Dept, coordinator, 1973-; LA District Attorney, supv inv/lieutenant, 1971-93; CSAN/Nevada, Child Support Assistance Network, director, 1993-. **Orgs:** Chmn LA Brotherhood Crusade Campaign 1971; chmn Sons of Watts OR Prog Adv Coun 1972; mem Men of Tomorrow; NAACP; New Frontier Dem Club. **Military Serv:** USAF airman 1st class 1956-59. **Business Addr:** 4254 Valley Spruce Way, North Las Vegas, NV 89030.

WILLIS, GLADYS JANUARY
Educator, chaplain. **Personal:** Born Feb 29, 1944, Jackson, MS; daughter of Emily Young January and John January (deceased); married A H Willis Jr; children: Juliet Christina, Michael Lamont. **Educ:** Jackson State Univ, BA 1965; Bryn Mawr Coll, Independent Study 1966; Michigan State Univ, MA 1967; Princeton Univ, PhD 1973; Lutheran Theological Seminary, Philadelphia PA, MDiv 1996. **Career:** Cheyney State Univ, instructor, English, 1967-68; Rider Coll, instructor, English, 1968-70; City University of New York, asst prof, English 1973-76; Pennsylvania Human Relations Commn, educ representative 1976-77; Lincoln Univ, assoc prof, chair 1977-84, prof, dept chair 1977-. **Orgs:** Founder, dir Coll Preparatory Tutorial 1974; mem, bd of dir Philadelphia Christian Academy 1977-, Natl Council of Teachers of English; reviewer Middle States Assn. **Honors/Awds:** Woodrow Wilson Natl Fellowship, Woodrow Wilson Natl Fellowship Found 1966-67; Princeton Univ Fellow, Princeton Univ 1970-73; The Penalty of Eve, John Milton and Divorce New York, Peter Lang 1984; Ordained Chaplain 1988; Outstanding Young Women of America, 1978; Lindback Distinguished Teachers Award, Lincoln Univ, 1984; Service Award, Lincoln Univ, 1992. **Home Addr:** 4722 Larchwood Ave, Philadelphia, PA 19143. **Business Addr:** Professor of English, Lincoln University, English Dept, Lincoln University, PA 19352.

WILLIS, ISAAC
Educator. **Personal:** Born Jul 13, 1940, Albany, GA; son of Susie M Willis (deceased) and R L Willis (deceased); married Alliene Horne Willis; children: two. **Educ:** Morehouse Coll, BS 1961; Howard Univ Coll of Med, MD 1965; Philadelphia Gen Hosp, Internship 1965-66; Howard Univ, Sepc Training Derm Resident, Post-Doctoral Rsch Fellow 1966-67; Univ of PA, Derm Resident, Post-Doctoral Rsch Fellow 1967-69. **Career:** Univ of PA, assoc of dermatology 1969-70; Univ of CA Med Ctr, attending physician 1970-72; Johns Hopkins Univ School of Med, asst prof of med dermatology 1972-73; Johns Hopkins Hosp, Baltimore City Hosps, Good Samaritan Hosp, attending physician 1972-73; Howard Univ Coll of Med, consult asst prof dermatology 1972-75; Emory Univ Sch of Med, asst prof of med 1973-75, assoc prof of med 1975-82; VA Hosp Atlanta GA, chief of dermatology 1973-80, acting chief of dermatology 1980-81; Morehouse Sch of Med, prof dept of med 1982-; Heritage Bank, bd of dirs 7 audit committee, 1985-88; Commercial Bank of Georgia, bd of dirs & chm audit comm, 1988-; Governor's Commission, GA, commissioner, 1991-; Natl Advisory Bd, NIH Institute, bd mem, 1991-. **Orgs:** Amer Dermatological Assn, Soc for Investigative Dermatology, Amer Soc for Photobiology, Amer Acad of Dermatology, Dermatology Found, Philadelphia Dermatological Soc, Natl Med Assn, Amer Med Assn, Natl Prog for Derm, Amer Fed for Clinical Res, Intl Soc of Tropical Derm, So Med Assn, Atlanta Derm Assn, GA Med Assn; bd of med dir Atlanta Lupus Erythematosus Found; bd of spec GA Dept of Human Resources Vocational Rehab; Dermatology Found Med & Scientific Comm, comm Dermatological med Devices of the Council on Govt Liaison of the Amer Acad of Dermatology; photobiology task force Natl Prog for Dermatology; self assessment comm Continuing Med Ed Amer Acad of Derm; Skin Cancer Found. **Honors/Awds:** Avalon Found Awd in Med; Morehouse Coll Alumni Achievement Awd 1983; Frontiers Intl Med Annual Awd 1983; several grants incl NIH, Hoescht Pharm, VA Projects, US EPA; guest prof, vstg prof, guest lecturer speaker at several coll & confs; 104 publs, books & abstracts incl Treatment of Resistant Psoriasis, A Combined Methaxsalen-Antralen Regimen 1973, Effects of Varying Doses of UV Radiation of Mammalian Skin, Simulation of Decreasing Stratospheric Ozone, 1983, Photoaugmentation of UBV Effects by UVA by 1984, Photochem, A New Promising Chem Dirivative 1982, Ultraviolet Light & Skin Cancer 1983, Polymorphous Light Eruptions, 1985; Doctorate of Science Degree, Morehouse Coll/Atlanta Univ, 1990. **Military Serv:** Letterman Army Inst of Rsch, maj 1970-82; 3297th USA Hosp col 1982-. **Business Addr:** Northwest Medical Center, 3280 Howell Mill Rd NW, Ste 342, Atlanta, GA 30327.

WILLIS, JAMES EDWARD, II
Professional football player. **Personal:** Born Sep 2, 1972, Huntsville, AL; children: Jade Elise. **Educ:** Auburn, attended. **Career:** Green Bay Packers, linebacker, 1993-94; Philadelphia Eagles, 1995-. **Business Addr:** Professional Football Player, Philadelphia Eagles, 3501 S Broad St, Philadelphia, PA 19148, (215)463-2500.

WILLIS, JILL MICHELLE
Lawyer. **Personal:** Born Jan 4, 1952, Atlanta, GA; daughter of Annette James Strickland and Louis Bell Willis Sr; married Paul Hugh Brown, May 28, 1988; children: Bryant Alexander Brown. **Educ:** Wellesley Coll, BA 1973; Columbia Univ Sch of Social Work, MS 1975; Rsch Scholar Natl Women's Educ Centre Saitama Japan 1979-80; Univ of Chicago LawSch, JD 1984. **Career:** United Charities of Chicago Family Serv Bureau, caseworker III 1975-79; Chapman & Cutler, assoc 1984-86; Allstate Insurance Co, asst counsel 1986-. **Orgs:** Adv bd Thresholds S 1977-78; mem bd of dirs Howe Developmental Ctr 1984-86; member American Bar Assn 1984-; member Chicago Bar Assn 1984-; Cook County Bar Assn 1984-. **Honors/Awds:** Waddell Fellowship Wellesley Coll Study E Africa 1972; Henry R Luce Scholar Asia Internship 1979-80; Chairman's Award Allstate Insurance Company 1988.

WILLIS, KATHI GRANT
Attorney. **Personal:** Born Dec 2, 1959, Knoxville, TN; daughter of Henrietta Arnold Grant and Lorenzo D Grant; married Henry W Willis, Oct 19, 1985; children: Elizabeth Danielle. **Educ:** Univ of VA, BA 1981; Univ of TN Coll of Law, JD 1984. **Career:** Provident Life and Accident Insurance Co, Chattanooga, TN, mgr, contracts & claims, 1986-88, attorney, 1988-89, asst counsel, 1989-, associate counsel, 1992-95; Healthsource, Inc, Chattanooga, TN, counsel, 1995-. **Orgs:** Alpha Kappa Alpha Sorority Inc; Chattonooga Chapter of Links, Inc; Junior League of Chattanooga. **Honors/Awds:** Recipient of Graduate Prof Opportunities Program Fellowship 1981-84. **Business Addr:** Law Department, Healthsource, 2 Fountain Square, Chattanooga, TN 37402.

WILLIS, KEVIN ALVIN
Professional basketball player. **Personal:** Born Sep 6, 1962, Los Angeles, CA. **Educ:** Jackson Community College, Jackson, MI, 1980-81; Michigan State Univ, East Lansing, MI, 1981-84. **Career:** Atlanta Hawks, forward/center, 1984-94; Miami Heat, 1994-96; Golden State Warriors, 1996; Houston Rockets, 1996-. **Special Achievements:** NBA Draft, First round pick, #11, 1984. **Business Addr:** Professional Basketball Player, Houston Rockets, 10 Greenway Plaza, Houston, TX 77046, (713)627-0600.

WILLIS, LEVY E.
Chief executive of bank. **Career:** Atlantic National Bank, Norfolk VA, chief executive, 1988. **Business Addr:** WPCE, 645 Church St, Suite 400, Norfolk, VA 23510.

WILLIS, MIECHELLE ORCHID
Athletic administrator. **Personal:** Born Feb 12, 1954, Lakewood, NJ; daughter of M Agnes Garland Willis and Vernon Willis. **Educ:** Grambling State University, Grambling, LA, BS, 1976, MS, 1978. **Career:** Montclair State College, Upper Montclair, NJ, head women's track coach, 1978-87; Temple University, Philadelphia, PA, associate dir of athletics, 1987-. **Orgs:** Member, Council of College Womens Athletic Administrators, 1990-; chair, Field Hockey Committee, Atlantic 10 Conference, 1988-; member, Delta Sigma Theta Sorority, Inc, 1975-78; member, Delta Psi Kappa Fraternity, 1976-78. **Military Serv:** US Air Force Reserves, staff sgt, 1983-89. **Business Addr:** Associate Director of Athletics, Intercollegiate Athletics, Temple University, 1900 N Board St, Philadelphia, PA 19122-2595.

WILLIS, ROSE W.
Cosmetologist and photographer. **Personal:** Born Jan 2, 1939, Columbus, GA; daughter of Christine Wright and Leonard Wright; divorced; children: Gwendolyn D Hunt, Sherry Ancrum. **Educ:** Natl Inst of Cosmetology, BA 1971, MA 1974, PhD 1978. **Career:** Lovely Lady Beauty Salon, Hollywood, FL, manager, owner, 1967-; Orange Blossom Cosmetologists Assoc, local pres unit 24 1969-78, parade state chmn 1970-80, state photographer 1980; Natl Beauty Culturists League, chmn of finance and registrar 1984-; Dillard High Comm School, Ft Lauderdale, sail program, 1992-94; Columbus Times News Paper, freelance photographer, currently. **Orgs:** Pres, 1978-94, Florida State of the National Beauty Culturists' League, North Miami beach, FL; member, National Council of Negro Women, 1979-94; treasurer, Theta Nu Sigma, Mu chapter, 1983-92; financial secretary, South Florida Business Assoc, 1988-93; member, Dade County School Board of Cosmetology, 1988-94; co-chairman, Dade County School of Cosmetology Advisory Committee; vp, Antioch Baptist Church Choir #1; mem, Nazareth Baptist Church. **Honors/Awds:** Woman of the Year Theta Nu Sigma Sor 1984; Outstanding Service Award, Bahamian Cosmetologists Association, 1989; Revlon, Leadership Award, 1991; NBCL, Cordelia G Johnson Pioneer Award, 1991; Antioch Baptist Church & Choir, No 1 for Thirty-Six Years, Outstanding Service & Dedication, Miami; FL Council, Thela Nu Sigma, Mu-Chapter & Natl Beauty Culturist's, Outstanding Service, Miami. **Business Addr:** Freelance Photographer, Columbus Times Newspaper, PO Box 2845, Columbus, GA 31902-2845.

WILLOCK, MARCELLE MONICA
Physician. **Personal:** Born Mar 30, 1938, Georgetown, Guyana. **Educ:** College of New Rochelle, BA 1958; Howard Univ, MD 1962; Columbia Univ, MA 1982; Boston Univ, MBA 1989. **Career:** NY Univ Sch of Medicine, asst prof 1965-74; Columbia Univ Coll of Physicians and Surgeons, asst prof 1978-82; Boston Univ Medical Ctr, chief of anesthesiology 1982-; Boston Univ Sch of Medicine, professor and chairman 1982-. **Orgs:** Pres Louis & Marthe Deveaux Foundation 1965-; pres Amer Medical Womens Assocof Massachusetts 1985-86; pres MA Soc of Anesthesiologists 1986-87, 1987-89; delegate Amer Soc of Anesthesiologists 1986-, dir, 1994-97; mem Assoc of Univ Anesthetists; sec/treasurer Society of Academic Anesthesia Chairmen 1989-91; Soc of Academic Anesthesiology Chairs, pres, 1994-96; The Medical Foundation, Boston, MA, secretary bd of dirs, 1992-94; College of New Rochelle, trustee, 1978-82; American Society of Anesthesiologists, board of directors, 1995-. **Honors/Awds:** Commencement Speaker Howard Univ Sch of Medicine 1982; member, Alpha Omega Alpha; College of New Rochelle, Medal. **Business Addr:** Professor and Chairman, Boston Univ Sch of Medicine, Dept of Anesthesiology, 88 E Newton St, Boston, MA 02118.

WILLOUGHBY, CLARICE E.
Business executive. **Personal:** Born Aug 6, 1934, Aliquippa, PA; married Paul. **Educ:** Central State U, BS 1958; Univ of Pittsburgh, MEd 1968; PA State Univ & MI St U, certificate for mgmt devel program 1973. **Career:** Marketing Researc H J Heinz Co, sr research asso, 1985; Univ of Pittsburgh, research asst 1964-68; Singer Lab Allegheny Gen Hosp Pittsburgh, research asst 1958-64. **Orgs:** Mem Am Marketing Asso Pittsburgh & NY Chpts; former student Affiliate of Am Chem Soc; matron Ermae Chap OES; treas Greater Pittsburgh Chap Central State Alumni Assn; past recording sec adv to Mu Chap at Univ of Pittsburgh; vice pres pres Pittsburgh Alumni Chap Delta Sigma Theta Inc; mem Youth Motivation Task Force.

WILLOUGHBY, SUSAN MELITA
Educational administrator. **Personal:** Born Nov 25, 1925; married Ralph M McNaughton; children: Gerald M, Juliette M. **Educ:** Atlantic Union Coll So Lancaster MA, BA Chemistry 1956; Clark Univ Worcester MA, MA Educ 1969; Harvard Univ Cambridge, EdD Admin 1972; Boston Univ Sch of Social Work, MA, MSW 1984; Boston Univ Sch of Medicine, MPH 1985. **Career:** Worcester Found for Experimental Biol, sr rsch chemist 1961-68; Center for Urban Studies Harvard Univ, dir counseling serv 1970-72; MA Consumer Council, Gov Sargent, gubernatorial appointee 1973-75; MA Public Health Council, Gov Dukakis, gubernatorial appointee 1975-79; Atlantic Union Coll, prof educ & behavioral sci 1972-, tenured prof & chmn dept of sociology and social work 1983-; Accreditation site visitor: New England Assn of Schools & Colleges, Council on Social Work Educ. **Orgs:** Mem Phi Delta Kappa/Pi Lambda Theta/AAUP 1972-; chmn Health Task Force MA State Consumer Council 1974-75; chmn Centennial Commn Atlantic Union Coll S Lancaster MA 1978-82; mem bd of trustees Atlantic Union Coll 1986-. **Honors/Awds:** Scholar Clark Univ, Harvard Univ 1968,71; several articles published Atlantic Union Gleaner (local) 1974-78, Atlantic Union Coll Accent Nat 1976-, Journal of Review & Herald (Intl) 1978; author "The Go-Getter" Pacific Press Publishing Assoc Boise ID 1985. **Home Addr:** 1029 George Hill Rd, PO Box 482, South Lancaster, MA 01561, (617)365-9782. **Business Phone:** (508)368-2191.

WILLOUGHBY, WINSTON CHURCHILL
Dentist. **Personal:** Born Jul 21, 1907, Port-of-Spain, Trinidad and Tobago; married Anselee Ellen Daniels; children: Ann Michelle, Gina Marie. **Educ:** Howard Univ Dntl Coll, 1933. **Career:** DC Hlth Dept Sch Clinic, staff 1938-44; Sci Session, chaired 4 sprks 1967-75; Table Clinics, svcd as judge. **Orgs:** Chmn Ticket Com; co-chmn Lunch & Learn; Pblcty Com; chmn Chldrns Com; chmn Tellers Com; chmn Necrology Com; chmn Attendance Com; spec asst genchmn Spring Postgrad Mtg 1976; chmn Pub Rels; chmn Dinner-Dance; mem DC Dntl Soc; Am Dntl Assn; Intl Assn of Anestheologists; intl Acad of Orthodontists; Fed Dentaire Intl; Chi Lambda Kappa Honor Dntl Soc; St Georges Episcopal Ch; Alpha Phi Alpha; Intl Platform Assn; The Smithsonian Inst Hearst Sch PTA; Am Assn for Advncmnt of Sci; WA Performing Arts Soc; Kiwanis Intl NW Club; adv bd Ward 3 Educ Fnd; Journalist Club in Sydney Australia; S Freemantle Pro Ftbl Club; bd mem WETA; mem bd govs Natl Grad Univ Fellow Intl Coll of Dntsts; fellow Royal Soc of Hlth London, England; Comm Leader of Am 1968. **Honors/Awds:** Outst Personal Assistance to Dev Nations of the

World, Dict of Intl Biography 1968; cert for rendering Salk Vaccine Oper Sugar Cube; Dentist of Year NEW 1975; num letters of appreciation comendations certs of appreciation. **Business Addr:** 1616 18th St NW, Washington, DC 20009.

WILLRICH, EMZY JAMES
Sales executive. **Personal:** Born Sep 16, 1959, Dallas, TX; son of Margie Crew-Willrich and Rev Theodis Willrich, Sr. **Educ:** Univ of Texas at Arlington, BBA, marketing, 1983; Texas Wesleyan University School of Law, JD, 1994. **Career:** Harte-Hanks Direct Marketing, sales consultant, 1986-87; Advanced Telemarketing Corp, marketing agent, 1987; United Advertising, data management supervisor, 1987-88; Consolidated Freightways, Inc, account manager, 1988-. **Orgs:** Amer Marketing Assoc 1982-87; Charter Mem Metroplex Egyptian History Soc; UTA Alumni Assoc Phonathon 1985; Hands Across America 1986; Black Enterprise Professional Network Exchange 1987; Grand Prairie NAACP, 1989; Dallas Urban League, 1989; African-American Men an Endangered Species, Inc; Natl Bar Assn, 1990; Delta Theta Phi International Law Fraternity; Texas Wesleyan University Student Bar Association; National Bar Assn. **Honors/Awds:** UTA Academic Achievement Awd 1981, 1982; UTA Alumni Leadership Scholarship for Academic Excellence and Campus Involvement 1982; Jesse Jackson Delegate to State Convention, 1988; West's Law & Tech Essay Winner, 1993. **Home Addr:** 705 Manning Road, Grand Prairie, TX 75051, (972)660-6951. **Business Addr:** Sales Executive, Consolidated Freightways Corp., 8505 Freeport Pkwy, Ste 500, Irving, TX 75063, (972)929-1202.

WILLS, CORNELIA
Educational administrator. **Personal:** Born Jun 22, 1953, Eastaboga, AL; daughter of Rosa Lee Elston Wills and Willie Wills Jr. **Educ:** Austin Peay State University, Clarksville, TN, BS, 1974; Tennessee State University, Nashville, TN, MEd, 1992; TN State Univ, EdD, 1997. **Career:** Tennessee State Univ, Nashville, TN, administrative secretary, 1974-77, 1979-81; Fisk University, Nashville, TN, office mgr, 1981-84; Meharry Medical College, Nashville, gift accounting coor, 1984-88; Tennessee Board of Regents, Nashville, TN, research analyst, 1988-89; Middle Tennessee State University, Murfreesboro, TN, dir of institutional research, 1989-. **Orgs:** Southern Assn for Institutional Research, 1996-; Association for Institutional Research, 1990-; Delta Sigma Theta Sorority, Inc, 1973-; consultant, Faculty Research Committee, 1989-; consultant, University Planning Committee, 1989-; Status of Women in Academe, 1991-; Tennessee Association for Institutional Research, 1989; Women in Higher Education in Tennessee, 1990-; Executive Committee on Institutional Effectiveness, 1992-; Task Force on Performance Funding, 1991-. **Honors/Awds:** Outstanding Student Teacher Award, Austin Peay State University Ambassador, Austin Peay State University, 1978; National Beta Club, 1970. **Business Addr:** Director, Institutional Research, Middle Tennessee State University, 153 Jones Hall, PO Box 140, Murfreesboro, TN 37132.

WILLS, JAMES WILLARD
Physician. **Personal:** Born Jan 23, 1933, Aquasco, MD; son of Clara Wright Wills and Rossie H. Wills; married Waltine; children: Phyllis, John, Cecil. **Educ:** Morgan State Coll, BS 1954; Howard Univ, MD 1961. **Career:** Glenn Dale Hosp, exec dir 1973-77; Glenn Dale Hosp, chief, med svc; Private practice, physician 1975-; chief medical officer, Area "C" Chest Clinic (Washington D.C.) 198l-. **Orgs:** Mem Alpha Phi Alpha, Medico-Chirurgical Soc DC, Natl Med Assoc. **Honors/Awds:** AUS 1st lt 1954-56. **Business Addr:** 14310 Old Marlboro Pike, Upper Marlboro, MD 20772.

WILMORE, GAYRAUD STEPHEN
Educator, editor (retired). **Personal:** Born Dec 20, 1921, Philadelphia, PA; married Lee Wilson; children: Stephen, Jacques, Roberta Wilmore-Hurley, David. **Educ:** Lincoln Univ, BA 1947; Lincoln Univ Theol Sem, BD 1950; Temple Univ School of Religion, stm 1952; Drew Theol Sem, doctoral studies 1960-63. **Career:** 2nd Presbyterian Church West Chester, pastor 1950-53; Mid-Atlantic Student Christian Movement, reg sec 1953-56; Pittsburgh Theol Sem, prof of soc ethics 1960-63; United Presbyterian Council on Church & Race, exec dir 1963-72; Boston Univ School of Theol, prof soc ethics 1972-74; Colgate Rochester Div School, ML King Jr prof beginning 1974; Interdenominational Theological Center, disting vstg scholar 1986-87; New York Theol Sem, MDIV Prog, dean, prof of Afro-Amer Religious Studies 1983-88; ITC, professor of church history 1988-90. **Orgs:** Amer Soc of Christian Ethics 1961-78; bd mem Faith & Order Commiss World Council of Church 1973-89; prof Black Church Studies Colgate Rochester Div School 1974-83; mem Ecum Assoc of Third World Theol 1976-; bd dir Black Theology Project Inc 1977-; consult Eli Lilly Endowment 1979-80; pres Soc for the Study of Black Religion 1979-80; contrib ed Christianity and Crisis 1986-; editor Journal of the ITC 1989-. **Honors/Awds:** Hon DD Lincoln Coll & Tusculum Coll 1965, 1972, Trinity Theol Sem 1989; Bruce Klunder Awd Presbyterian Interracial Council 1968; DD General Theol Sem, 1989; Hon LHD Lincoln Univ 1972; Payne Theological Seminary 1986, 1991. **Military Serv:** US Army, sgt 1943-46.

WILMOT, DAVID WINSTON
Attorney, educator. **Personal:** Born Apr 26, 1944, Panama; son of Bertha Wi;mot and David Wilmot; married Mary Elizabeth Mercer; children: Michele, Kristy, David II. **Educ:** Univ of AR, BA 1970; Georgetown Univ Law Ctr, JD 1973. **Career:** Little Rock, asst city mgr 1968-70; Dolphin Branton Stafford & Webber, legal asst 1970-72; Georgetown Univ Law Ctr, rsch asst; OEO Legal Svcs, intern; DC Proj on Comm Legal Asst, dep dir 1972-73; DC Convention Ctr Bd of Dirs, general counsel; Hotel Assoc Washington DC, general counsel; Georgetown Univ, asst dean, dir 1973-92; Harmon & Wilmot, partner, 1992-. **Orgs:** Pres Stud for Equality 1967-68; vice pres GULC Legal Aid Soc 1972-73; pres Black Amer Law Stud Assoc 1972-73; adv bd DC Bds & Comms Adv Bd Georgetown Today 1973-76; mem DC Bar, PA Bar;, US Supreme Court of Appeals, DC Ct of Appeals, Supreme Ct of PA, Assoc of Amer Law Schools, Law School Admin Council, Amer Bar Assoc, Trial Lawyers Assoc, Natl Bar Assoc, Natl Conf of Black Lawyers, Alpha Kappa Psi, Lawyers Study Group, Potomac Fiscal Soc; public employees relations bd Wash DC; mem Firemens & Policement Retirement Bd; mem bd of dirs Federal City Natl Bank, Washington Waterfront Restaurant Corp; mem bd of governors Georgetown Univ Alumni Assoc; mem bd of dirs District Cablevision Inc. **Honors/Awds:** Dean's List 1967-70; Dean's Counselor Awd Univ of AR 1969; Outstanding Serv Awd Georgetown Univ Stud Bar Assoc 1971; Cert of Merit DC Citz for Better Ed 1972; Jeffrey Crandall Awd 1972; WA Law Reptr Prize 1973; Robert D L'Heureux Scholorship. **Military Serv:** USAF E/5 1963-67. **Business Addr:** Partner, Harmon & Wilmot, LLP, 1010 Vermont Avenue, NW, Washington, DC 20005.

WILSON, ALVA L.
Cleric. **Personal:** Born Nov 21, 1922, Lake City, SC; son of Hattie Mayes Wilson and Malichi Wilson; married Carrie Williams; children: Allesia Muldrow, Charles K, Benita F. **Educ:** Allen Univ, AB, 1949; Gammon Theological Seminary, 1961. **Career:** Owner/Farmer, 1950; freelance horticulturist/landscaper, 1979-; UMSC Conf, clergyman. **Orgs:** Barber Shaw AFB, 1949-75; vice chmn, Health Education & Welfare Minister, 1972-78; Florence County District #3 School Bd, secretary, trustee bd, 1974-91. **Honors/Awds:** Leadership Training Inst Awd, SC Sch Bd Assn, 1975. **Military Serv:** US Army, pfc, 3 yrs. **Home Addr:** 330 West Thomas St, Lake City, SC 29560.

WILSON, ANGELA BROWN
Government official. **Personal:** Born Mar 31, 1961, Detroit, MI; daughter of Lillie M Brown & Bunnie Brown, Sr (deceased); married Errol S Wilson, Feb 25, 1995. **Educ:** Wayne State Univ, BSW, 1984; MSW, 1988. **Career:** Warren/Conner Dev Coalition, program dir, 1985-87; deputy dir, 1987-94; City of Detroit, exec asst to the mayor, 1994-. **Orgs:** Amer Friends Service Committee, bd mem & committee chair, 1980-; Dominican High School Bd of Assoc, 1994-; president, Det Catholic Pastoral Alliance, 1992-; Sacred Heart Church Sr Transportation, driver, 1990-; Save Our Spirit Coalition, spokesperson, 1986-93; Sacred Heart Church, minister of faith, 1982-; Natl Community Relations Div Amer Friends Service Committee, chairperson, 1981-95; NAACP; Wayne State Univ Alumni Assn; Knight & Ladies, St Peter Claver; Natl Organization of Community Dev Practitioners, Dev Leadership Network. **Business Addr:** Exec Asst to the Mayor, City of Detroit, 1126 City-County Building, Detroit, MI 48226, (313)224-1544.

WILSON, AUGUST
Playwright. **Personal:** Born 1945, Pittsburgh, PA; son of Daisy Wilson and David Bedford (stepfather); married Judy Oliver, 1981 (divorced). **Career:** Black Horizons Theatre Co, St Paul, MN, founder, 1968; plays: Ma Rainey's Black Bottom, 1985, Fences, 1986, The Piano Lesson, 1987, Joe Turner's Come and Gone, 1988; Two Trains Running, 1992; Seven Guitars. **Honors/Awds:** New York Drama Critic's Circle Awd; Tony nomination for Best Drama of the Season for Ma Rainey's Black Bottom; Pulitzer Prize for "Fences", 1987; Tony Awd for "Fences", 1987; Pulitzer Prize for "The Piano Lesson," 1990; Clarence Muse Award, 1992; Tony nominations for Seven Guitars. **Business Addr:** 600 First Avenue, Ste 301, Seattle, WA 98104.

WILSON, BARBARA JEAN
Business executive. **Personal:** Born Jun 5, 1940, Dallas, TX; married Porterfield (deceased); children: Porterfield Christopher. **Educ:** Prairie View A&M Coll, BS 1960-64; Gen Motors Inst Flint MI, 1975; Hadley Dealer Accounting School Royal Oak MI, 1975; Reynolds & Reynolds Computer School Dayton OH, 1980. **Career:** TC Hassell School Dallas TX, exec sec 1964-73; Chrysler Corp Mound Rd Engine Detroit, bookkeeper 1965-73; Porterfield Wilson Pontiac GMC Truck Mazda-Honda, exec sec 1973-79; Mazda Honda, pres oper 1979-84; Ferndale Honda, pres 1984-; Porterfield's Marina Village, Detroit, MI, president, 1989-. **Orgs:** Past pres Carats Inc Detroit Chap Natl Club 1969-; mem women's Econ Club 1975-; life mem NAACP 1975; mem Palmer Woods Assoc 1976, Amer Imported Auto Dealers 1979-, Detroit Auto Dealers Assn 1979-, Negro Bus & Prof Women 1979; mem Coalition of 100 Black Women of Detroit 1980. **Honors/Awds:** Spec Recog Awd Carats Inc Detroit Chap 1979; Candice Award of Business; Woman of the Year, 1987; Crain's Detroit Business, Michigan's Top 50 Business Owned & Operated by Women. **Business Addr:** President, Ferndale Honda, 21350 Woodward Ave, Ferndale, MI 48220.

WILSON, BERNARD
Professional football player. **Personal:** Born Aug 17, 1970, Nashville, TN; married Roslyn. **Educ:** Tennessee State, attended. **Career:** Tampa Bay Buccaneers, defensive tackle, 1993-94; Arizona Cardinals, 1994-. **Business Addr:** Professional Football Player, Arizona Cardinals, 8701 S Hardy, Tempe, AZ 85284, (602)379-0101.

WILSON, BLENDA J.
Educational administrator. **Personal:** Born Jan 28, 1941, Perth Amboy, NJ; daughter of Margaret Brogsdale Wilson and Horace Lawrence Wilson; married Dr Louis Fair Jr. **Educ:** Cedar Crest Coll, AB 1962; Seton Hall Univ, AM 1965; Boston Coll, PhD 1979. **Career:** Middlesex County Economic Opportunities Corp, New Brunswick, NJ, exec dir, 1968-69; Rutgers Univ, New Brunswick, NJ, asst to the provost, 1969-70, exec asst to the pres, 1969-72, asst provost, 1970-71; Harvard Grad School of Educ, Cambridge, MA, assoc dean for admin, 1972-75, lecturer on educ, 1976-82, sr assoc dean, 1972-82; Independent Sector, Washington, DC, vp, 1982-84; Colorado Commission on High Educ, Denver, CO, exec dir, 1984-88; Univ of Michigan-Dearborn, MI, chancellor, 1988-92; California State University, Northridge, president, 1992-. **Orgs:** Chair, Amer Assn for Higher Educ, 1990-; bd of dirs, The Alpha Center, 1988-91; adv comm Intl Foundation for Educ & Self-Help 1986-; bd of trustees, Boston Coll; the Foundation Center; bd of trustees, Sammy Davis Jr Natl Liver Inst, 1989; exec bd Detroit Area Boy Scouts of Amer; Detroit Chapter Natl Coalition of 100 Black Women; Dearborn Rotary; Assn of Governing Boards; mem, United Way for SE Mich, 1989; mem, Women's Econ Club of Detroit, 1989; bd of dirs, the Commonwealth Fund, 1981-; director, James Irvine Foundation; trustee, J Paul Getty Trust; dir, Children's TV Workshop. **Honors/Awds:** One of 100 Emerging Leaders in Amer, Higher Educ Change magazine, 1978; honorary degrees: Eastern Mich Univ, Doctor of Educ, 1990, Rutgers Univ, Doctor of Laws, 1989, Univ of Detroit, Doctor of Humane Letters, 1989, various others; Ebony Excellence "Women on the Move Award," Renaissance Chapter of Links, 1989; Michigan Bell Living Dream Award, Michigan Bell, 1989; 90 for the 90's, Crain's Detroit Business Magazine, 1990; Distinguished Leader, Washtenaw Community College, 1990; various others. **Business Addr:** President, California State University-Northridge, 18111 Nordhoff St, Northridge, CA 91330.

WILSON, BOBBY L.
Educator. **Personal:** Born Sep 30, 1942, Columbus, MS; son of Lillie Coleman Wilson and Johnnie B Wilson; married Mary, Dec 22, 1966; children: Anthony, Melanie, Malissa, Melinda. **Educ:** Alabama State College, BS 1966; Southern Univ, MS 1972; MI State Univ, PhD 1976. **Career:** Booker T Washington HS, instructor, 1966-70; Jefferson Davis HS, instructor, 1970-71; Michigan State Univ, grad asst, 1971-76; TX Southern Univ, asst prof, 1976-80, assoc prof, 1980-82; Exxon Rsch & Engineering, visiting prof, 1982-83; TX Southern Univ, assoc prof, 1983-85, prof, 1985-, Coll of Arts & Sciences, associate dean, 1986-87, dept head, 1987-89, interim dean of arts & sciences, 1989-90, vice pres of academic affairs, 1990-92, provost, 1992-94, professor, 1994-. **Orgs:** ACS; Beta Kappa Chi Honor Soc; Kappa Alpha Psi Frat; NAACP; Natl Geographic Soc; Natl Organization for the Professional Advancement of Black Chemists & Chemical Engineers; Natl Urban League; Smithsonian Inst; TX Academy of Science; TX Assn of College Teachers; Tri-County Civic Assn; TX Faculty Assn; The Forum Club of Houston; Sigma Xi; TX Inst of Chemists; American Institute of Chemists, student awards committee, 1988; Scientific Rsch Society, 1988; Bylaws Comm, 1988; president, Childrn Against Drugs & Drinking Inc. **Honors/Awds:** The Briargate Community, Audrey Logan Citizenship Award, 1988, Citizen of the Year Award, 1980; White House Initiative Faculty Award for Excellence in Sci & Tech, 1988; Kappa Alpha Psi, Southwest Province, Graduate Brother of the Year Award, 1988, Service Award, 1988, Houston Alumni Chapter, Spotlight Award, 1984; TX Southern Univ, Researcher of the Year, 1988, College of Arts & Sciences, Outstanding Teacher of the Year Award, 1989, Program Council, Showcase of Black Talent Award, 1989; McCleary Teacher of the Year Award, 1989; Fellow, The Amer Inst of Chemists, 1988; Albert Einstein World Award of Science Diploma, 1987; ROTC Gold Citation, 1967; Alpha Kappa Alpha Sorority, Community Serv Award, 1983; Natl Organization of Black Chemists & Chemical Engineers, Appreciation Award, 1984, Outstanding Teacher Award, 1985. **Special Achievements:** Author, over thirty scholarly manuscripts in national and international journals; co-author: General Chemistry Laboratory I Manual, Ginn Press, 1988; General Chemistry Laboratory II Manual, Ginn Press, 1989; two patents. **Business Addr:** Prof, Dept of Chem, Texas Southern University, 3100 Cleburne, Houston, TX 77004.

WILSON, CALVIN T.
Judge. **Personal:** Born Feb 25, 1928, Philadelphia, PA; son of Beatrice Culbreath Wilson and Ernest Wilson; married Yvonne

Garnett; children: Captain Calvin T. Wilson, II, M.D. **Educ:** Lincoln U, BA 1949; Howard U, Juris LLD 1952. **Career:** Sec Bd of Judges, asst atty gen 1961; PA Mun Court, court admin 1971; Court of Common Pleas, judge 1971-. **Orgs:** Mem Bd of City Trusts; mem Bd of Taxes & Rev; mem Comm of Mun Crt; mem Barristers Club of Philadelphia Bar Assn; mem The Pres Comm for Civ Rights UnderLaw; mem Met Hosp bd of dir 1976; mem trustee Mt Zion Bapt Ch; mem Boy Scouts of Am; Boystown; Stenton Neighbors Comm; PA Guardsmen Inc; pres Southeastern Pa. Area Chptr. of Muscular Dystrophy Assn l989; a national vice pres Muscular Dystrophy Assn l989. **Honors/Awds:** Chapel of the Four Chaplains Awrd 1977; NAACP Awrd; Awrd of the Puerto Rican Cit Comm; Black Pol Beauty Pagent Awrd; various comm awrds; Cert of Achvmnt Philadelphia Bar Assn 1968; Judge of the Year Natl Assn of Black Lawyers 1981; Sec Bd of Judges of Phila. **Business Addr:** Judge, Commonwealth of PA, Court of Common Pleas, 1st Judicial Dist, Philadelphia, PA 19107.

WILSON, CARL L.
Architect, clergyman. **Personal:** Born Dec 24, 1921, Warren, OH; son of Georgia Russell Crawford Wilson and Michael Robert Wilson, Sr; married Doris Hazel Bass; children: 1 son. **Educ:** OH State Univ, BS 1951. **Career:** Wright-Patterson Area Ofc Dayton, proj engr 1951-62; US Corps of Engrs, architect; USACE Asmara, Ethiopia, asst rsch eng 1962-66; Munsan-ni Korea 2nd Inf Div, install plng officer 1966-67; US Fed Bldg Canton, rsch eng 1968-69; IRS Add Covington KY, 1969-70; Baltimore Post Office, 1970-72; Cincinnati Bulk Mail Ctr, suprvsng staff of seventeen 1972-75; OH Area Office Dayton, asst area engr 1975-80; Montgomery Cty OH Bldg Reg Dept, dir 1980-83; Mt Olive Baptist Church, Dayton, Ohio, assoc minister, 1987-. **Orgs:** Reg arch State of OH 1958-; imp officer AEA Order Nobles Mystic Shrine 1968-86; past master progress Lodge 85; past commander in chief LD Easton Consistory 21; companion Johnson Chap 3 Columbus OH; past patron Lily of the Valley 55 Middletown OH; companion Solomon Johnson Council 4; Sir Knight Boone Commandery 27; mem US Supreme Council AASR North Jurisdiction; former natl dir Student Aid for Boys of Prince Hall Shriners; mem NAACP, Dayton Urban League; sec genl USC AASR (PHA) NJ 1975-83; imp potentate AEAONMS 1984-86; archon, Sigma Bowle, Sigma Pi Phi Fraternity, 1986-; coordinator, Minority Contractors Assistance Program, Dayton, Ohio 1989-. **Honors/Awds:** Only African American grad OSU School of Architecture 1919-1951; highest rank black fld official US Corps of Engrs; resident contracting officer on over 90 million dollars of US Gov Constrn Contracts; US Council's Gold Medal Achievement Award for Meritorious Service, Sovereign Grand Commanders Awd for Excellence; first black to serve as deputy dir Dept of Public Works State of OH 1983-84; cited in Ebony Magazine as one of 100 Most Influential Blacks in Amer 1985-86. **Military Serv:** AUS Sig Corps & Army Air Corps, WWII 1942-46. **Business Addr:** Box 382, Mid City Station, Dayton, OH 45402.

WILSON, CARROLL LLOYD
Educator. **Personal:** Born Jul 9, 1937, Jamaica; married Barbara Ellen Jones; children: Mark Lloyd, Eric Theodore, Ellen Clarice. **Educ:** Univ of ME at Orono, BA 1962; Kean Clge NJ, MA 1969; Rutgers Univ, Grad Studies. **Career:** Publ Health Educ State of ME, asst to dir 1962-63; Plainfield Publ Schl Plainfeild NJ, tchr & asst track coach 1963-69; Job Corps at Camp Kilmer NJ, recr spec 1966-67; Somerset Co Clge & Annandale Youth Corr Inst Annandale NJ, coord sp prog 1973-74. **Orgs:** Mem NJ Assc of Dev Educ 1980-; Cub Master Pack 1776 Boy Scouts of Amer 1982-85; mem Natl Council on Black Amer Affairs 1983-; bd dir Somerset Co Mental Health Assc 1978-81; bd trustees Corr Inst for Women Clinton NJ 1978-82; coach Hillsborough NJ Recreation Soccer 1981-; evulator, Middle States Assn of Colleges & Universities, l986-. **Honors/Awds:** Special Faculty Srv Award Somerset Co Coll 1975, Special Faculty Serv & Admin Award 1976, Black Student Union Adv Serv Award 1975-76. **Business Addr:** Professor of English, Raritan Valley Community Coll, PO Box 3300, Somerville, NJ 08876-1265.

WILSON, CASSANDRA
Vocalist. **Personal:** Born 1955, Jackson, MS; daughter of Herman B. Fowlkes and Mary Fowlkes; divorced; children: Jeris. **Career:** Vocalist; albums: Blue Light 'Til Dawn, New Moon Daughter; Rendezvous.

WILSON, CHARLES LEE, SR.
Company executive. **Personal:** Born Oct 25, 1941, Atlanta, GA; son of Ethel Wilson and William Fred Wilson Sr; divorced; children: Charles Lee Jr, Angela Y. **Educ:** Bethune Cookman College, BS, psychology; Temple University, MS, counseling guidance & administration; Rutgers University, education administration. **Career:** Camden NJ School System, teacher, guidance counselor; Philadelphia College of Art, registrar; Howard University, director of admission; U.S. Department of Education, consultant; Enterprises for New Directions Inc, ceo, president. **Orgs:** District of Columbia Multicultural Tourism Committee; State of Maryland Minority Advisory Committee. **Special Achievements:** Panelist, National Association of State Development Agencies National Conference on Tourism and Economic Development, Great New Orleans Multicultural Tourism Summit, Kansas City Minority Tourism Network; author of numerous reports and publications. **Business Phone:** (301)469-3301.

WILSON, CHARLES STANLEY, JR.
Funeral director. **Personal:** Born Aug 8, 1952, St Louis, MO; son of Vora Thompson Wilson and Charles S Wilson Sr. **Educ:** Boston U, BS 1974; Forest Park Sch of Mortuary Sci, 1976. **Career:** A L Beal Funeral Homes Inc, pres, currently; McDonnell Douglas Corp, rep 1979-80; Maritz Travel, travel dir 1976-79. **Orgs:** Mem Kappa Alpha Psi 1970-87; mem Caution Lodge No 23 Masons 1975-; mem Urban League of St Louis 1976-80; mem Danforth Found Leadership Program 1979-80; mem Camp Wyman Bd of Dir 1979-80; trustee bd Central Bapt Ch 1975-87; mem Black United Fund of St Louis 1974-80; pub rel chmn St Louis Undertakers Assn 1979-80; mem 1985-90, chairman 1989-90, MO State Bd of Embalmers & Funeral Dirs 1985-90; appointed by MO Govt Ashcroft 2nd vp, bd of dir Annie Malone Children's Home 1985-; mem MO Funeral Dirs Assn, St Louis Gateway Funeral Dirs Assn, Natl Funeral Dirs & Morticians Assn, Natl Funeral Dirs Assn 1985-; charter mem, 100 Black Men, 1987-91; mem, Corinthian Chapter Eastern Star, 1977-91; bd of dirs, Blacks Assisting Blacks Against Aids. **Honors/Awds:** Trustee Schlrshp Awd Sch of Educ Boston Univ 1972-73; Undergrad Achvmnt Awd; Northeastern Province Kappa Alpha Psi 1973-74; Outstanding Achievement Award, Central Baptist Church, 1990. **Business Addr:** President, A L Beal Funeral Homes Inc, 4746 W Florissant Pl, St Louis, MO 63115, (314)389-9675.

WILSON, CHARLES Z., JR.
Educator. **Personal:** Born Apr 21, 1929, Greenville, MS; widowed; children: Charles Zachary, III, Joyce Lynne, Joanne Catherine, Gary Thomas. **Educ:** Univ Of IL, BS 1952, PhD 1956; Carnegie Mellon U, post grad work 1959-61. **Career:** UCLA, vice chancellor Academic Prog , Prof Educ 1970-; Educ Planning Programs, special asst to adminstrv vice chancellor 1968-70; St Univ of NY, asso prof economics 1959-67; DePaul Univ, asst prof economics 1957-59. **Orgs:** Mem nominating com Am Assn for Advancement of Sci; bd trustees Tchrs Ins & Annuity Assn Coll Retirement Equities Fund 1971-; pres adv council on Minority Bus Enterprise 1972-76; UNA Panel for Advancement of US Japan Relations 1972-; consult Nat Inst of Educ Dept of HEW 1973- mem Adv Bd on Educ &Human Resources, The Rand Corp 1972-; chmn Bd Trustees The Joint Cntgr for Comm Studies 19702; mem bd dirs LA Co Museum of Art 1971-; bd dirs Black Economic Res Cntr New York City 1970-; mem Am Educ Res Assn; Inst of Mgmt Sci; Am Economics Assn; Am Assn of Univ Profs. **Honors/Awds:** Am Men of Sci Recip, Am Council on Educ Fellow 1967-68; Visiting Res Asso, Carnegie-mellon Univ 1961-62; Jr C of C Outstanding Young Man of Yr 1965, Binghamton NY; author "Orgnl Decision-making" 1967. **Business Addr:** UCLA 2127 Murphy Hall, 405 Hilgard Ave, Los Angeles, CA 90024.

WILSON, CHRISTOPHER A.
Journalist. **Personal:** Born Mar 22, 1961, Shelby, NC; married Gwendolyn Wilson, Aug 10, 1985; children: Evan, Grant. **Educ:** Winston Salem State University, business administration, 1983. **Career:** Central NC Investors Council, pres; Wall Streetwise, editor, currently. **Orgs:** Central NC Investors Council, reg pres. **Honors/Awds:** NAIC, Growth Stock of Year Winner, 1992; New Freedom Inv Group, Investor of the Year, 1991. **Special Achievements:** Publisher of 20 Most Commonly Asked Questions For Investment Clubs. **Business Addr:** Editor, Wall Streetwise, PO Box 12451, Durham, NC 27709.

WILSON, CLARENCE A.
Financial executive. **Personal:** Born Aug 27, 1943, Talladega, AL; son of Lara Montgomery Pruitt (deceased) and Philip Monroe Wilson (deceased); married Sue Carol Cottman Wilson, Jan 28, 1967; children: Brian, Eric. **Educ:** Indiana University, Bloomington, IN, BS, 1967, MBA, 1981. **Career:** Marathon Oil Co, Findlay, OH, senior planner, 1967-69; Du Pont Co, Wilmington, DE, business director, nylon staples, 1981-. **Orgs:** Member, Kappa Alpha Psi Fraternity, 1965-; member, Financial Executive Institute, 1989-; member, Dean of Business School Advisory Board, Indiana Univ, 1990-; member, Board of Directors, Neighborhood House, 1990-. **Home Addr:** 10 Alders Ln, Greenville, DE 19807.

WILSON, CLARENCE NORTHON
Dentist. **Personal:** Born Jun 6, 1920, Pittsburgh, PA; married Dorothy; children: Michelle, Candace. **Educ:** VA State Coll, BS 1942; Howard Univ Dental Sch, 1947. **Career:** Jersey City Med Ctr, intern 1949; North Side Forces, head of community center dental clinic, 1972-81; Dental Health Clinic, dir 1974-; Self-employed, dentist. **Orgs:** Pres Essex Co Dental Soc 1973-77; treas Commonwealth Dental Soc; Essex County Dental Society, treasurer, 1936. **Honors/Awds:** East Orange, NJ, Community Award. **Special Achievements:** First lieutenant in the Army Dental Corp, 1951, captain, 1952. **Business Addr:** 576 Central Ave, East Orange, NJ 07019.

WILSON, CLARENCE S., JR.
Attorney, educator. **Personal:** Born Oct 22, 1945, Brooklyn, NY; married Helena Chapellin Iribarren, Jan 26, 1972. **Educ:** Williams College, BA, 1967; Foreign Service Institute of the United States, 1969; Northwestern University, School of Law, JD, 1974. **Career:** US Department of State, Caracas, Venezuela, third secretary, vice counsel, 1969-71; Friedman and Koven, associate attorney, 1974-76; United States Gypsum Company, legal department, 1976-79; sole practitioner, 1979-81; Law Offices of Jewel S Lafontant, partner, 1981-83; Chicago-Kent College of Law, adjunct professor, 1981-94; Boodell, Sears, Sugrue, Giambalvo and Crowley, associate attorney, 1983-84; sole practitioner and counsel, 1984-; Columbia College, adjunct professor, 1996-. **Orgs:** Trustee, Chicago Symphony Orchestra, 1987-; Art Institute of Chicago, bd mbr, Cmte on Twentieth Century Painting, Sculpture, Development, 1989-, trustee, 1990-; director, 1974-83, advisory board member, 1983-, Citizens Information Service of Illinois; bd mbr, The Harold Washington Foundation, 1989-92; bd mbr, Implementation Cmsn of The Lawyers Trust Fund of Illinois, 1983-85; bd mbr, Northwestern Univ School of Law Alumni Assn, 1979-84; project manager, Dept of Justice Task Force, The President's Private Sector Survey on Cost Control in the Federal Government, "The Grace Commission," 1982-84; governing bd, Illinois Arts Cncl, 1984-89; Illinois representative, Arts Midwest, 1985-89; Chicago and Cook County Bar Associations; trustee, Merit Music Program, 1991-96; Chicago Department of Cultural Affairs, Mayor's Advsry Bd, 1988-97; School of the Art Institute of Chicago, mem bd of governors, 1994-; Dept of Music at the Univ of Chicago, visiting committee mem, 1992-; Ministry of Culture, Republic of Venezuela, special counsel, 1989-90; DuSable Museum of African American History Inc, outside counsel, 1988-95; Jazz Museum of Chicago, vice chair, 1994-97. **Special Achievements:** Author, "Visual Arts and the Law," in Law and the Arts—Art and the Law, 1979; author of several copyright/art law articles. **Business Addr:** Attorney at Law, 25 E Washington St, Ste 1500, Chicago, IL 60602, (312)984-0399.

WILSON, CLEO FRANCINE
Foundation administrator. **Personal:** Born May 7, 1943, Chicago, IL; daughter of Frances Page Watson and Cleo Chancey (deceased); children: David Patrice Silbar, SuLyn Silbar. **Educ:** Univ of IL-Chicago, BA 1976. **Career:** Playboy Enterprises Inc, supervisor 1980-82, grants mgr 1982-84, exec dir 1984, dir, Public Affairs, 1989-. **Orgs:** Vp Donors Forum of Chicago 1986-88; sec Chicago Women in Philanthrophy 1986-87, task force IL Interdisciplinary AIDS Adv Council 1986-87; pres Emergency Loan Fund 1987-89; chmn, Chicago Funders Concerned with AIDS, l989; Advisory Council, Chicago Dept of Cultural Affairs, l988-90; pres, AIDS Foundation of Chicago; Amer Civil Liberties Union of Illinois, 1996-, vp, 1997-. **Honors/Awds:** Distinction in English, Univ of Illinois, 1976; Kizzy Image Awd Black Woman Hall of Fame 1984; Chicago's Up & Coming (Black Business & Professional Women) Dollars & Sense Magazine 1985; Phenomenal Woman Awd, Expo for Today's Black Woman, 1997. **Business Addr:** Director, Public Affairs, Playboy Enterprises, Inc, 680 North Lake Shore Dr, Chicago, IL 60611, (312)751-8000.

WILSON, DANTON THOMAS
Newspaper executive editor. **Personal:** Born Dec 21, 1958, Houston, TX; son of Ann Elizabeth Briscoe Wilson and Thomas Henry Wilson; married Janis Richard Wilson, May 17, 1981; children: SeKou J Wilson, Khari T Wilson, Ayanna I Wilson. **Educ:** Grambling State University, Grambling, LA, bachelor of arts, 1981; Wayne State University, Detroit, MI, juris doctorate, 1989. **Career:** Detroit Free Press, Detroit, MI, reporter, 1981; Michigan Chronicle, Detroit, MI, reporter, 1982-86; City of Detroit Public Info, Detroit, MI, publicist, 1986-87; Michigan Chronicle, Detroit, MI, executive editor, 1987-. **Orgs:** Chairman, Orchard's Children's Service Media Assn, 1990-; member, Board of "Be the Best You Can Be" Organization, 1990-; member, Board of Rosa Parks Scholarship Fund, 1990-; member, Black United Fund Annual Dinner Committee, 1989-90; member, Black Law Students Association, 1985-90. **Honors/Awds:** James Wadsworth Community Service Award, Fellowship Chapel United Church, 1987; 1st place Community Service Award, 1986, 2nd place news story for series on drugs, 1983, National Newspaper Publishers Assn; Valedictorian, 1981, student government president, 1980-81, Grambling State University. **Business Addr:** Executive Editor, Editorial Dept, Michigan Chronicle, 479 Ledyard, Detroit, MI 48201.

WILSON, DANYELL ELAINE
Army official. **Personal:** Born Jul 16, 1974, Montgomery, AL; daughter of Shirley Wilson Rucks. **Educ:** Northern Virginia CC, attending. **Career:** US Army, military police officer/sgt, 1993-. **Special Achievements:** First African American female to receive the "Tomb Guard Identification Badge," its the second most least awarded military badge, 1997; first African American female guard at the Tomb of the Unknown Soldier. **Military Serv:** US Army, sgt, 1993-; Army Achievement Medal, 1996; Tomb Guard Badge, 1997. **Business Addr:** Sgt, US Army, 3rd US Infantry Regiment (TOG), Bldg 242, Fort Myer, VA 22211, (703)696-3149.

WILSON, DAVID
Educator. **Personal:** Born Nov 2, 1954, Thomaston, AL; son of Minnie Wilson and Henry Wilson. **Educ:** Tuskegee University, Tuskegee, AL, BS, 1977, MS, 1979; Harvard University, Cambridge, MA, EdM, 1984, PhD, 1987. **Career:** Research & Development Institute of Philadelphia, Philadelphia, PA, project dir, 1979-82; Kentucky State University, Frankfurt, KY, exec asst to vice pres for business affairs, 1984-85; Woodrow Wilson National Fellowship Foundation, Princeton, NJ, 1985-88; Rutgers University, Camden, NJ, assoc provost, 1988-94; Auburn Univ, vp for univ outreach, assoc provost, currently. **Orgs:** Member, board of directors, Afro-American Historical & Cultural Museum, Philadelphia, PA, 1988-, Walt Whitman Association, Camden, NJ, 1988-, Princeton Ballet, 1988-, Optimist Club of Lower Bucks, Bensalem, PA, 1986-91; member, Alpha Phi Alpha Fraternity, Inc, 1975-. **Honors/Awds:** Kellogg Fellow, WK Kellogg Foundation, 1988-92; Woodrow Wilson Fellow, Woodrow Wilson Natl Fellowship Foundation, 1984-85; One of America's Best and Brightest Young Business and Professional Men, Dollars and Sense Magazine, 1987; Certificate of Appreciation, Governor of Alabama, 1987; Certificate of Appreciation, Governor of Tennessee, 1988. **Home Addr:** 2521 Old Creek Trail, Auburn, AL 36830. **Business Addr:** VP for Univ Outreach, Auburn University, Auburn, AL 36849.

WILSON, DEMOND
Evangelist. **Personal:** Born in Valdosta, GA. **Educ:** Hunter Coll, attended. **Career:** Sanford & Son, actor 1972-77; Demond Wilson Ministries, evangelist.

WILSON, DONALD
Educational administrator. **Career:** Univ of Maryland, School of Medicine, dean. **Business Addr:** Dean, Sch of Medicine, University of Maryland, 655 W Baltimore St, Rm 14-029, Baltimore, MD 21201-1559, (410)706-7410.

WILSON, DONALD P.
Association executive. **Career:** Improved Benevolent Protective Order of Elks of the World, grand exalted ruler. **Business Addr:** Grand Exalted Ruler, Improved Benevolent Protective Order of Elks of the Wor, PO Box 159, Winton, NC 27986.

WILSON, DONELLA JOYCE
Educator. **Personal:** Born Jul 28, 1951, Milwaukee, WI; daughter of Emily Frenchie Bailey-Wilson and Paul Lawrence Wilson. **Educ:** Johnston Coll Redlands Univ, BA 1973; TX Southern Univ, MS 1977; Purdue Univ, MS 1979, PhD 1981. **Career:** Washington Univ, rsch assoc 1981; Harvard Sch Dental Medicine, assoc of oral pathology 1981-83; Whitehead Inst & MIT, Radcliffe Coll Bunting fellow 1983-85; Meharry Medical Coll, asst prof 1985-91; associate professor 1991-. **Orgs:** Mem Amer Assoc Adv Sci 1982-; vstg prof Univ of MA Boston 1983-84; mem Harvard Health Professions Admissions Comm 1985; FASEB vstg scientist Fed Amer Soc Biol 1986-; mem NSF Grant Review Panel Cell and Mol Biol 1987; St Henry's Choir; mem Beta Kappa Chi, Beta Beta Beta; mem, Amer Society for Cell Biology, 1983-. **Honors/Awds:** Recipient NSF and NIH First Awd 1986,87; Woman of the Year Compton CA 1987; "Future Makers," Ebony Magazine, Aug 1985; Outstanding Women of the World, 1989; Invited to speak on genetic engineering, British Broadcasting, 1990. **Home Addr:** 300 Cross Timbers Dr, Nashville, TN 37221. **Business Addr:** Associate Professor, Meharry Medical College, Div Biomedical Sciences, 1005 DB Todd Blvd, Nashville, TN 37208.

WILSON, EARL LAWRENCE
Prison administrator, corrections consultant. **Personal:** Born Jul 16, 1923, Philadelphia, PA; son of Helen J. Wilson and James R. Wilson. **Educ:** Villanova Univ, criminal justice courses, 1969-73; PA State Univ, certificate 1970; St Joseph Univ, seminars on labor relations. **Career:** Philadelphia Prison System, corrections officer, sergeant, lieutenant, captain, deputy warden, prison security coordinator, 1951-78, warden 1978-. **Orgs:** Examiner, PA Civil Serv Commn, 1974-; mem, PA Warden's Assn, 1978-; mem, Amer Correctional Assn, 1978-; consultant/adviser, Criminal Justice System; mem, Amer Correctional Assn; PA Prison Wardens Assn; past president, member, board of directors, The Therapeutic Center at Fox Chase (The Bridge); American Jail Association. **Honors/Awds:** Article on crime published in Ebony Magazine 1979; Lifetime Achievement Award presented, PA Prison Wardens Association, 1993. **Military Serv:** USAF, SSgt, 1944-46; Good Conduct Medal; Asiatic Pacific Ribbon. **Home Addr:** 301 Steeple Chase Drive, Exton, PA 19341-3121.

WILSON, EDITH N.
Educator. **Personal:** Born Apr 20, 1938, Columbia, SC; daughter of Ruth Sulton Friday and John Friday; married James E Wilson, Jan 3, 1980 (deceased); children: Michael J Harrison. **Educ:** Benedict Coll, BA 1961; Univ of OR, MA 1971. **Career:** Roosevelt HS, principal 1976; Univ of OR, coord Dir Asst Dir, 1970-76; Tongue Point Job Corp, teacher corp dir 1968-69; Portland Public Schools, art tchr 1968-70; Albina Art Center, cons; Stanford Ctr for Rsch & Devel; Western Tchr Corp Recruitment Ctr; Univ of NE Urban Educ Ctr; Natl Tchr Corp; CMTI, assoc Dir; Natl League of Cities, rep; State Dept Disadvantaged & Handicapped Commr Metro Arts Commn, cons; Gov Commn on Youth; principal, Tulsman Middle School 1979-80; dir of instruction 1982-. **Orgs:** Mem Natl Alliance of Black School Educators; Natl Cncl of Admin Women; Delta Sigma Theta Sor; ASCD Art Intrnshp Grant Univ of OR 1967; devel Afro-Amer Art Curriculum; Portland Public School; 1969; Course Goals for State Art Program 1970; exh Maryhurst Coll 1968-69; Devel Minority Career Educ Prgm; Career Educ Assessmnt Model 1973; bd of dir Childrens Museum 1987-88; Portland City Club 1987-. **Home Addr:** 19818 S W Statford Rd, West Linn, OR 97068.

WILSON, ERNEST
Manager. **Personal:** Born Nov 4, 1936, New York, NY; son of Bessie and Ernest; married; children: Ernest Jr, Steven, Patricia. **Educ:** New York Univ, BA; Certificate, mediation/conflict resolution, 1997; Super Center, computer training, 1997. **Career:** Freight Liner Corp, personnel mgr 1966-71; MBM Corp, personnel dir 1971-72; TRW Corp, personnel admin 1972-74; Commutronx Corp, personnel dir 1974-75; City of San Bernardino, dir affirmative act and comm affairs 1975-85, dir of safety, comm affairs 1985-88; California State Legislature, field representative, 1989-90; City of San Bernardino, CA, dir affirmative action, 1991-. **Orgs:** Vol leg adv to assemblyman 67th Dist State of CA 1979-80; mem Kiwanis Intl, Mexican/Amer Personnel Assn, Urban League, NAACP, Amer Soc for Training & Develop; mem Kiwanis Club San Bernardino; bd mem Black History Found; Economic Round Tabel, Westside Action Group; California Association of Affirmative Action Officers; American Association for Affirmative Action; vice pres, Easter Seal Society. **Honors/Awds:** Outstanding Achievement OSC Comm Orgn 1975; Outstanding Achievement Just X Club 1976; Cert of Outstanding Participation & Contributions CA Poly Univ 1979; Cert of Outstanding Achievement Mexican/Amer Mgmt Assn 1978; Cert of Appreciation Dr Martin Luther King Meml & Scholarship Fund Inc 1980; Citation for Comm Serv San Bernardino Light House of the Blind 1982; Scroll of Honor Omega Psi Phi Frat 1983; Cert of Achievement San Bernardino Black History 1983; Good Will Ambassador City of San Bernardino 1982; We Serve Awd Highland Dist Lions Club; Resolution by Mayor & Council City of San Bernardino Commending Leadership of the Affirmative Action Prog; Commendation Dept of Fair Employment & Housing State of CA; Cert of Achievement Equal Employment Oppty Comm; Certificate of Recognition, Civilrgency Management, 34th Senate Dist State of CA, 1990; Ruben S Ayala California State Senator, Certificate of Recognition, 1990; Provisional Accelerated Learning Center, Certificate of Award, 1991; San Bernidino National Forest, Certificate of Appreciation, 1992; American Heart Association, Certificate of Appreciation, 1992; San Bernidino Chamber of Commerce, Certificate of Recognition, 1992; Community Service Award, 1994; NAACP, Certificate of Recognition, 1996. **Military Serv:** US Army, staff sgt 1954-57. **Business Addr:** Dir, Affirmative Action, City of San Bernardino, 300 North D St, San Bernardino, CA 92418.

WILSON, F. LEON
Social-political writer. **Personal:** Born Sep 20, 1953, Akron, OH. **Educ:** Ohio State University, BS 1975, MBA 1983. **Career:** Central Control Systems, publisher/principal writer; The Black Agenda, Regional coordinator, 1983-; Code One Communications, principle agent, 1990-, sr proj manager, currently. **Orgs:** Chairman, Americans Against Apartheid 1985-87; Natl Black Wholistic Society, 1989-. **Honors/Awds:** Publications: The Black Agenda, Educating Blacks for Social, Political and Economic Development, Dorran Press 1983; Black Unity, Definition and Direction, CCS Press 1985; The Black Woman, Center of the Black Economy, CCS Press 1986; Emancipatory Psychology, CCS Press 1990. **Special Achievements:** :Author, Dream and Wings, CCS Press, 1994, White Supremacy: Sources & Uses, CCS Press, 1995. **Business Addr:** Regional Coordinator, Code One Communications, PO Box 09726, Columbus, OH 43209, (614)338-8383.

WILSON, FLIP (CLEROW)
Comedian, actor. **Personal:** Born Dec 8, 1933, Jersey City, NJ; divorced; children: four. **Career:** Television appearances include: The Flip Wilson Show, 1970-74; People Are Funny, 1984; Charlie & Co, 1985-86; That's Life, 1969; The Big Show, guest host, 1980; appeared in his own specials, 1974-76; Pinocchio, 1976; film appearances include: Uptown Saturday Night, 1974; Skatetown, USA, 1979; The Fish That Saved Pittsburgh, 1979; comedy albums include: Cowboys and Colored People, 1967; Flippin', 1968; Flip Wilson, You Devil You, 1968. **Honors/Awds:** Grammy Award, Best Comedy Record, 1971; Emmy Award, The Flip Wilson Show, Outstanding Writing Achievement in Variety or Music, 1971; numerous other awards. **Military Serv:** US Air Force, 1950-54.

WILSON, FLOYD EDWARD, JR.
Councilman. **Personal:** Born Nov 22, 1935, Lake Charles, LA; son of Leada R Wilson and Floyd Edward Wilson Sr; married Dorothy Lyons, Apr 9, 1988; children: J Keith, Tanya R Derryck M. **Educ:** Dillard Univ, BA 1959. **Career:** Eastern HS, tchr 1962-72; Hallmark Acad Children Ctr, owner admin 1968-78; Glenarden MD, councilman vice mayor 1969-74; Prince George's County Council, councilman 1974-. **Orgs:** Mem PG Bd Dir Social Srvs 1976-; vice chrmn NACO Criminal Justice Comm 1983-; chrmn COG Air Quality Comm 1984; First Black Elected to PG Cty Council 1974-; mem Alpha Phi Alpha Frat; Life Mem NAACP. **Business Addr:** County Councilman, Prince George's County Govt, County Admin Bldg, Upper Marlboro, MD 20772.

WILSON, FRANK EDWARD
Organization executive. **Personal:** Born Dec 5, 1940, Houston, TX; son of Samanther Gibbs Wilson and Wilson James; married Barbara Dedmon (died 1966); children: Tracey, Frank, Launi, Fawn, Christy. **Educ:** Southern University, Baton Rouge, LA, 1959-60; Fuller Graduate School of Theology, 1978-81. **Career:** Specolite Music, Inc, self-employed; Black Americans Response to the African Community, president, 1984-. **Orgs:** Fellowship West Inc, president, 1977-; Destiny Inc, secretary, board of directors; United Gospel Industry Council, board chairman. **Honors/Awds:** US Congress Award; Great Seal of the United States of America, 1986; RIAA, Song Writer/Record Producer Awards, 20 gold and platinum; NARAS, three Grammy awards; several awards for work with youth and development in Third World countries.

WILSON, FRANK FREDRICK, III
Physician. **Personal:** Born Jun 14, 1936, Oklahoma City, OK; son of Thelma Boyd Wilson and Frank F Wilson III; married Jacquelyn; children: Frank IV, Nathan, Yolanda, Coreen. **Educ:** Fisk Univ, BA 1956; attended Univ OK; Howard Univ Sch Med, BA 1961; Univ MO, intern spec educ Gen Hosp & Med Ctr 1961-65. **Career:** Physician Ob-Gyn; Univ of OK School of Med, clinical assoc prof, currently. **Orgs:** Dir Bd Park Commr 1971-74; Eastside YMCA 1972-73; Collins Garden Housing Corp 1972-74; OK City Ob-Gyn Soc sec treas 1973-74, exec bd 1974-77, pres 1975-76, vice pres 1976-77, pres 1977-; Touchstone Montessori Sch 1973-74; mem OK Co Med Soc, OK State Med Assn, AMA, Natl Med Assn; diplomate Natl Bd Med Exmnrs; Amer Fertility Soc; Amer Bd Ob-Gyn; fellow Amer Coll Ob-Gyn; Central Assn Ob-Gyn; chmn, admission bd, Univ of OK School of Med. **Military Serv:** AUS MC capt 1965-67. **Business Addr:** 700 NE 37th St, Oklahoma City, OK 73105.

WILSON, FREDERICK A.
Business executive. **Personal:** Born Aug 6, 1946, Brooklyn, NY; son of Annie Wood Wilson and Frederick Wilson; married Patricia B Bridges; children: Jacqueline, Deidre, Felicia. **Educ:** Johnson C Smith U, BA Psych 1969. **Career:** NY Life Ins Co, asst sales mgr; Bay Ridge Gen Office, asst mgr 1974, field underwriter 1971-74; GT Sound & Security Service, currently; PFW Distributors, CEO, currently. **Orgs:** Mem Nat Assn of Securities Dealers; mem 100 Black Men; mem Omega Psi Phi; mem NY Jaycees; US Jaycees; pastor, Humble Heart Christian Church. **Honors/Awds:** Black Achievers in Industry Award YMCA NY 1977.

WILSON, GERALD STANLEY
Composer, arranger, trumpeter. **Personal:** Born Sep 4, 1918, Shelby, MS; married Josefina Villasenor; children: Geraldine, Lillian, Nancy Jo, Anthony. **Career:** Composer, Royal Ste 1948, Josefina 1950, Blues for Yna Yna 1962, Viva Tirado 1963, Paco 1964, El Viti 1965, Carlos 1966, Teotihuacan Ste 1966, Collage 1968, Debut, Los Angeles Philharmonic Orch; trumpeter, arranger, composer for orchs Jimmie Lunceford 1939-42, Count Basie 1947-49, Duke Ellington 1947-66 ; mus performed at Carnegie Hall 1948, 1966, Mus Ctr Los Angeles 1968, Hollywood Bowl 1967; San Fernando Valley State Coll, mus dept 1969; CA State Univ Northridge; Univ of CA, Los Angeles, faculty, currently. **Orgs:** Condr own orch; participant Kongsberg Jazz Festival Norway 1973; arranged & orchestrated for Nancy Wilson/Ray Charles/Al Hibbler/Bobby Darin/Julie London/Al Hirt; music dir many TV shows; contributed orchestrations to Library of Ella Fitzgerald; faculty Music Dept San Fernando Valley State Coll 1969. **Honors/Awds:** Recipient awards Downbeat Mag 1963-64; nominations Nat Acad Rec Arts & Scis 1963-64; Paul Robeson Award; William Grant Still Award; Los Angeles CA, Jazz Society, Jazz Educators Award, 1990; Los Angeles Jazz Society, Jazz Arrangers Award, 1992, National Endowment for the Arts-American Jazz Masters Fellowship Grant, 1990. **Special Achievements:** The Gerald Wilson Collection, a collection of his compositions, arrangements, orchestrations and other papers concerning his career will be housed at the Library of Congress; travels, Verona Jazz Festival, Verona, Italy, 1986; London England to the North Sea Jazz Festival at Den Haag, the Netherlands, 1990.

WILSON, GRANT PAUL, JR.
Medical technologist. **Personal:** Born Mar 21, 1943, Harrodsburg, KY; son of Lorene Clarke Wilson and Grant P. Wilson Sr; married Elaine Adams Wilson, May 27, 1973; children: David, Jonathon, Nicholas. **Educ:** Tennessee State Univ, Nashville, TN, BS; St Joseph School of Medical Technology, Lexington, KY, MT(ASCP). **Career:** Humana Hospital Lake Cumberland, Somerset, KY, laboratory manager, 1979-93; City Council, Somerset, KY, councilman, 1981-; Somerset Housing Authority, 1994-96. **Orgs:** Omega Psi Phi Fraternity; Masonic Lodge; Chamber of Commerce. **Military Serv:** Army, Sergeant, 1968-70. **Home Addr:** 205 W Limestone, Somerset, KY 42501.

WILSON, GREER DAWSON
College administrator. **Personal:** Born Jan 5, 1943, Richmond, VA; divorced; children: Sarita M, Samia J. **Educ:** Indiana Univ, BME 1964; Hampton Inst, MA Counseling 1976; College of William & Mary, EdD 1984. **Career:** ACU-I, chmn comm on minority progs 1979-81, educ commn mem 1984-87, intl conf chairperson 1987; State Bd Mental Health & Mental Retardation, vice chmn 1985-; Hampton Univ, coord student activities & dir of student union. **Orgs:** Bd mem Peninsula Family Serv Travelers Aid 1984-; bd mem Alternatives Substance Abuse Prog 1985-; mem Assoc for Counseling & Develop; organist Bethel AME Church; mem Delta Sigma Theta Sor, Hampton HS Guidance Comm. **Honors/Awds:** Mem Kappa Delta Phi Honor Soc, Tau Beta Sigma Music Honor Soc; concert pianist; consultant on Leadership Develop & Racism for ACU-I. **Business Addr:** Coord Student Activities, Hampton University, Box 6224, Hampton, VA 23668.

WILSON, HARRISON B.
Educator. **Personal:** Born Apr 21, 1928, Amstead, NY; married Lucy; children: Benjamin, Harrison, John, Richard, Jennifer, Marquarite. **Educ:** KY State U, BS IN U, MS, DHS. **Career:** Norfolk State Coll, pres 1975-; Fisk Univ, exec asst pres; TN State Univ, dir coop educ; Jackson State Coll, chmn dept health physical educ 1960-67, head basketball coach 1951-60. **Orgs:** Mem bd dir VA Nat Bank; mem lay adv bd DePaul Hosp; mem VA State Adv Cncl on Vocational Edn; mem bd dir Hlth Welfare Rec Plng Cncl; Alpha Kappa Mu. **Business Addr:** President, Norfolk State University, 2401 Corprew Ave, Norfolk, VA 23504.

WILSON, HAZEL FORROW SIMMONS
Educator (retired). **Personal:** Born Jun 21, 1927, Houston, TX; daughter of Summie Lee Whittington Forrow and Sam W Forrow; married Jerrimiah Simmons (deceased); children: David Jerome, James (deceased). **Educ:** Attended Prairie View A&M Coll 1945-46; TX So Univ, BA 1954, MA 1974. **Career:** BH Grimes Elem School, teacher 1954-59; J R Reynolds Elem School, teacher 1959-68; Camp Fire Girls, field dir 1960-68; Fort Worth Independ Public School, Maude I Logan Elem, first Black coordinator reading improvement center 1972-; Ft Worth Public School, teacher 1968-72; Springdale Elementary School, Chapter I resource teacher, retired. **Orgs:** So reg dir Amicae 1960-64; charter mem Houston League Negro Bus & Prof Women's Club 1962-68; exec sec Houston Classroom Teachers Assn 1964-66; dir so region Zeta Phi Beta 1965-72; natl trust Zeta Phi Beta 1972-76; chairperson Zeta Phi Beta So Reg Exec Bd 1972-78; charter & 1st vice pres Gr Ft Worth Area Negro Bus & Prof Women's Club 1975-81; natl dir Stork's Nest Proj Zeta Phi Beta 1976-82; pres Kappa Silhouettes 1976-80; life mem NEA TX State Teachers Assn, TX Classroom Teacher's Assn, Ft Worth Classroom Teachers Assn; mem YWCA, YMCA; life mem Zeta Phi Beta; reg chairperson March of Dimes, Muscular Dystrophy, Leukemia So of Amer; ruling elder St Peter Presb Church 1980-87; pres Psi Zeta Chap Zeta Phi Beta Sor 1981-; pres Greater Fort Worth Area Negro Business & Professional Women, 1981-84; sponsor Zeta Amicae, 1981-; St Mark Cumberland Presbyterian Church, 1986-; pres Zeta Chapter, 1981-93. **Honors/Awds:** Outstanding Serv Awd TX So Univ 1962, 1963; Zeta of Yr 1964; 5 yr Serv Awd Zeta Amicae 1965; Outstanding Serv as dir Zeta Phi Beta 1965-72; So Reg Zeta of Yr 1974; So Reg 2nd place Undergrad sponsors 1975; March of Dimes Vol Serv Awd 1974-75; Ombudswoman S Cent Negro Bus & Prof Women 1976; 1st Natl Zeta Phi Beta Legacy Awd 1976; Lambda Zeta Sevice Award, 1984; Phi Beta Sigma Zeta of the Year, 1986; Psi Zeta's Zeta of the Year Awd 1987; Southern Region 25 Yr Regional Amicae Initiator, 1988; Phi Beta Sigma/Zeta Phi Beta Graduate Leadership Awad, 1988; Omega Psi Phi, Citizen of the Year, 1996. **Home Addr:** 2801 Sarah Jane Ln, Fort Worth, TX 76119.

WILSON, HELEN TOLSON
Business executive (retired). **Personal:** Born Feb 22, New Franklin, MO; daughter of Rev A A Tolson; married Jesse Wilson (deceased). **Educ:** Kansas City Conservatory of Music, attended 4 yrs; Dale Carnegie Inst of Charm & Voice, grad med tech; Attended Wayne State Univ, Tacome Warren, MI Univ; Wayne State Univ, BA Humanities 1957; Urban Bible Coll, DH Detroit MI 1984. **Career:** KC Young Matrons, pres, founder 1939; Detroit Soc Charm Sch, dir 1973-; US Govt, accounting tech retired 26 yrs; DSACE Coords Council for the Arts, pres, founder, currently. **Orgs:** Founder ZONTA Bus & Professional Women's Club 1944; mem, presidency elder, ME Medical Conference, Kansas City district, Kansas City, MO, 1954-; chmn Cinerama in Fashions Ford's Auditorium, 1957; gen chrmn dir organizer Alpha Theta Chap, 1960; gen chrmn Detroit Urban League 4th Annual Gala Dinner Ball, 1968; chrmn Natl Founders Day Gamma Phi Delta Sor 1969-; founder, pres, dance coordinator Council for the Arts, 1972-85; pres, founder Youth Assembly of Detroit Urban League, 1973-78; bd trustees Gamma Phi Delta Sor; gen chrmn & dir Gamma Phi Delta Sor's Exec Staff; gen chrmn dir of publicity N Region Gamma Phi Delta Sr Inc; natl boule chmn Gamma Phi Delta Sor Inc; mem Wheatley Provident Hosp Aux; dir Civic Fashion Show; supr KC MO HS Press; founder Youth Assemblyof the Detroit Urban Leag. **Honors/Awds:** Rose Pin Awd Gamma Phi Delta Sor Inc 1971; The Gov Awd (2) token 27 yrs; 25 yr pin Detroit Urban League Guild; Highest Awd The Detroit Zonta Club 1939-46; DHL, Wayne State Univ Detroit MI 1983; Picture Honor Roll Natl Urban League Inc 1986; Honored at 1986 Urban League & Guild Annual Gala.

WILSON, HENRY, JR.
Business executive. **Personal:** Born Nov 10, 1938, Taylor, TX; married Carrie L Twyman; children: Peggy Annette, Pamela Ann. **Educ:** Univ of Cincinnati, AS Engr 1968. **Career:** Cincinnati Water Work, engr tech 1957-64; Kaizer Engrs, engr 1964-68; Turner Constr Co, engr 1968-71; Wilson & Assc Arch & Engrs, pres 1971-. **Orgs:** Mem Natl Soc of Professional Engrs 1968-; dir Hamilton County State Bank 1980-; trustee Univ Cincinnati Fnd 1981- secr zoning bd appeals silverton oH 1980-; pastor cornerstone missionary Baptist Church 1984-; instr Cornerstone Bible Inst 1985; trustee Greater Cincinnati C of C 1985-88. **Honors/Awds:** Min Small Bus; Person of the Year US Small Bus Admin 1984. **Home Addr:** 6737 Elwynne Dr, Cincinnati, OH 45236. **Business Addr:** President, Wilson & Assc Inc, 4439 Reading Rd, Cincinnati, OH 45229.

WILSON, HUGH A.
Educator. **Personal:** Born Jun 20, 1940, Kingston, Jamaica; son of Ola Wilson and John Wilson. **Educ:** Howard U, BA 1963; Fordham Univ Sch of Social Svc, MSW 1967; Adelphi Univ, DSW, 1995. **Career:** Adelphi Univ NY, assoc prof; Inst for Suburban Studies, dir, 1975-85. **Orgs:** Dir Welfare Tenants Coord Com Mineola NY 1968-70; comm organizer Comm Coord Coun Long Beach, NY 1966-67; consult Westchester Urban League 1973; Yonkers Comm Action Prgrm 1971-72; Addiction Serv Agency of NY 1973; co-fndr & sec Alliance of Minority Group Ldrs in Nassau-Suffolk 1970. **Honors/Awds:** Awarded $45,000 by N Shore Unitarian Ch to set up Inst for Suburban Studies at Adelphi Univ 1973. **Business Addr:** Associate Professor, Department of Political Science, Adelphi University, Blodgett 202, Garden City, NY 11530.

WILSON, HUGHLYNE PERKINS
Educator. **Personal:** Born Jul 12, 1931, Louisville, KY; married Charles A Wilson; children: Stuart K. **Educ:** Howard Univ, BA 1951; Univ Louisville, MEd 1964. **Career:** Louisville Public Schools, teacher 1956-68; Univ KY, coord 1968-70; Louisville Public Schools, asst dir div certificated personnel 1970-72, dir 1972-74; KY School Dist, asst supr dept empl personnel serv. **Orgs:** Mem NEA, KY Assn Sch Admin, Amer Assn Sch Personnel, Amer KY Louisville Assns Childhood Educ; mem Urban League, Delta Sigma Theta Sor; mem Phi Delta Kappa; mem KY Assn of Sch Supts; mem bd of regents Western KY Univ Bowling Green. **Honors/Awds:** First woman asst supt Louisville Pub Schs. **Business Addr:** Asst Supr Dept Emp Personnel, KY Sch Dist, 3332 Newburg Rd, Louisville, KY 40218.

WILSON, J. RAY
Employee relations executive. **Personal:** Born Apr 16, 1937, Leesville, LA; son of Florence Wilson and Emmitt Wilson; married Dorothy Ellison Wilson, Jun 4, 1965; children: Taleia Appral, Marcus Ray. **Educ:** Texas Southern University, Houston, TX, BBA, 1965. **Career:** United California Bank, Los Angeles, CA, operations officer, 1965-67; Conoco Inc, Houston, TX, manager, employee relations, 1967-93. **Orgs:** Vice president, Chase Wood Civic Club, 1980-82; board member, Houston Area Urban League, 1979-86; advisor, The Network Group, 1982-; member, Amigo De Ser, 1979-. **Military Serv:** US Navy, Petty Officer, 1956-60; Good Conduct Medal, Honor Recruit.

WILSON, JACI LAVERNE
Government Official. **Personal:** Born Dec 9, 1961, Houston, TX; daughter of Mae Ola McKinley-Dogan. **Educ:** Texas Southern Univ, BA. **Career:** United States Senate, Carol Moseley-Braun; United States Trade Rep, EOP; Clinton-Gore campaign, democratic national convention, 1996; United States Department of State, secretary Albright; Democratic National Convention Comm, dep dir of convention housing, currently.

WILSON, JAMES DAVIS
Business executive. **Personal:** Born Jun 30, 1937, Kingstree, SC; married Lorraine Louise Poret; children: Angele, Tanya, Arianne. **Educ:** Morehouse Coll; Xavier Univ Coll of Pharmacy New Orleans; TX So U, BS 1963. **Career:** Wilson's Surgical Supplies, pres, currently; Walgreens Drug Store, phrmcst &mgr 1963-69. **Orgs:** New Orleans Prog Phrmcsts Assn; LA Pharm Assn; mem bd dir Natl Pharm Assn; Am Pharm Assn; LA State bd of Phrmcy; Nat Assn of Retail Druggists; Pharm Reference Agent; NAACP; Urban League of Grtr New Orleans; pres Univ Meth Men Assn; 3rd degree Mason; Chi Delta Mu Med Frat; Kappa Alpha Psi; bd mem YMCA; consult State C A P Agys; rep High Blood Pressure Symposium 1975; fndr & Co-Dir Boys City Res Camp 1964-67; mem bd dir Multi Media Ctr; cons Headstart Prog. **Honors/Awds:** Perceptor for Pharm Interns Awrd 1st black owner of surgical supplies co; ICBO Distinguished Achvmnt Awrd 1974; 1st black appt LA Bd of Pharm 1976. **Business Addr:** Pharmacist, 2019 Louisiana Ave, New Orleans, LA 70115.

WILSON, JEFFREY R.
Professor. **Personal:** chilDren: Rhonda, Roxanne, Rochelle. **Educ:** University of West Indies, St Augustine, W.I., BA, Mathematics, 1977; Iowa State University, Ames, IA, MS, Statistics 1980, PhD, Statistics, 1984. **Career:** Iowa State University, Ames, IA, graduate research assistant, 1980-83; Oklahoma State University, Stillwater, OK, visiting asst prof of statistics, 1983-84; Arizona State University, Tempe, AZ, asst professor of statistics, 1985-91, associate professor of statistics, director of interdisciplinary program in statistics, professor of economics, currently. **Orgs:** American Statistical Association, 1980; Royal Statistical Society, 1985. **Honors/Awds:** Teaching Award, Golden Key Honor Society, Arizona State University; Faculty Research Development Award, College of Business, AZ, 1990; Outstanding Graduate Teaching Award, College of Business, AZ, 1986; Distinguished Service Award, Minority Student Affairs, Ames, IA, Iowa State Univ, 1983, Final Year Book Prize, Math & Econ, Univ of West Indies, 1977; Mathematics Scholarship, Univ of West Indies, 1974-77; George Washington Carver Achievement Award, Iowa State Alumni Assn, 1995. **Business Addr:** Professor of Economics, Arizona State University, College of Business, Tempe, AZ 85287-3806.

WILSON, JERRY
Professional football player. **Personal:** Born Jul 17, 1973; children: Trittney, Tanner, Jerry III. **Educ:** Southern Univ, BS in rehabilitation counseling. **Career:** Miami Dolphins, defensive back, 1996-. **Business Addr:** Professional Football Player, Miami Dolphins, 2269 NW 199th St, Miami, FL 33056, (305)620-5000.

WILSON, JIMMIE L.
State representative. **Career:** State of Arkansas, representative, currently. **Business Addr:** State Representative, State of Arkansas, House of Representatives, State Capitol, Little Rock, AR 72201.

WILSON, JIMMY L.
Law enforcement official. **Educ:** American University, bachelor's degree, administration of justice. **Career:** District of Columbia Police Dept, member of force, 24 years, deputy chief of police, 5 years; City of Jackson, police chief, currently. **Business Addr:** Police Chief, City of Jackson Police Dept, PO Box 17, Jackson, MS 39205, (601)960-1217.

WILSON, JOHN
Artist, educator. **Personal:** Born Apr 14, 1922, Boston, MA; married Julia Kowitch; children: Rebecca, Roy, Erica. **Educ:** Museum Fine Arts School, grad 1944; Tufts Univ, BS 1947; Fernand Leger's Sch Paris 1949; Inst Politecnico Esmeralda School Art Mexico City 1952; Escuela de las Artes del Libro Mexico City 1954-55. **Career:** NY Bd of Educ, 1959-64; Boston Univ, prof art 1964-86, prof emeritus. **Honors/Awds:** Prizes natl exhibits 1951-69; purchase prize Hunterdon Art Ctr Annual Print Exhibit NJ 1958; num awds & citations; exhibits colls, univs, galleries, NY Metro Mus Art, France; illustrations in books, art pubns; created Dr Martin Luther King Jr Monument Buffalo NY 1983; created Dr Martin Luther King Jr Commemorative Statue US Capitol Washington DC. **Special Achievements:** Created monument: "Eternal Presence," Museum of the National Center of Afro-American Artists, Boston, MS, 1987. **Business Addr:** Professor Emeritus, Boston Univ Sch Visual Arts, 855 Commonwealth Ave, Boston, MA 02215.

WILSON, JOHN E.
Business executive, accountant. **Personal:** Born Dec 9, 1932, Chicago, IL; son of Carrie Wilson and Leroy Wilson; married Velma J Brown; children: Ginger, Kelly. **Educ:** BS 1954; CPA 1965. **Career:** Arthur J Wilson CPA, acct 1957-63; IL Commerce Comm, auditor 1963; Bowey's Inc, general acct 1964; Capitol Food Industries Inc, treasurer 1969-; Bates Packaging Co, controller 1969; John E Wilson Ltd, pres; Public Building Commission, Chicago IL, asst treasurer. **Orgs:** Mem Amer Inst of CPA's; IL Soc of CPA's; Natl Assn of Minority CPA's; mem Kappa Alpha Psi; Sigma Pi Phi; mem, Trinity United Church of Christ. **Honors/Awds:** Alumni Natl Award, 1996. **Special Achievements:** First African American to graduate from Northwestern Univ School of Commerce. **Military Serv:** USN 1955-57. **Business Addr:** President, John E Wilson, Ltd, 53 West Jackson Blvd, Chicago, IL 60604.

WILSON, JOHN T., JR.
Educator, occupational & environmental medicine, educational administrator. **Personal:** Born Jun 2, 1924, Birmingham, AL; son of Rosalie Rush Wilson and John T Wilson; married Artee F Young, Jun 21, 1980. **Educ:** Howard Univ, (cum laude) BS 1946; Columbia Univ, MD 1950; Univ of Cincinnati, ScD 1956. **Career:** Prof emeritus, 1992; Univ of Washington, chmn & prof Dept of Environmental Health 1974-80; NW Ctr for OCC Health & Safety, dir, 1977-87; OCC Medicine Residency Prog, dir, 1977-87; Howard Univ, prof & chmn Dept of Comm Health Practice 1971-74; Stanford Univ, asst prof Dept of Comm & Prevent Med 1969-71; Lockheed A/C Corp CA, life scis adv 1961-69; Bur of Occupational Health Santa Clara Co Health Dept CA, chief 1957-61. **Orgs:** Mem Armed Forces Epidemiology Bd 1977-; dir NW Occupational Safety & Health

Educ Resource Center 1977-87; dir Amer Acad of Occupational Med 1979-81; spec inoccupatonal med, Amer Bd of Preventive Med 1960; mem Washington Assn of Black Health Care Providers; life mem NAACP; dir Emerald City Bank, Seattle 1988-92. **Honors/Awds:** Natl Scholarship Awd, Howard Univ Alumni Assn 1965. **Business Addr:** Prof, Dept of Environmental Health, Univ of Washington, Seattle, WA 98195.

WILSON, JOHN W.
Administrator, educator. **Personal:** Born Jun 10, 1928, St Marys, GA; son of Ora and Albert; divorced; children: John Jr, Larry, Dwaughn. **Educ:** Albany St Coll, BS, Elementary Educ, 1951; Univ of Akron, MA, Educ Admin, 1970, EdD, 1983. **Career:** Albany State Coll, employee,1951; USAF, educ specialist, 1951-55; Cleveland Public Schools, elementary teacher, 1957-69; Univ of Akron, dir, Black Cultural Center & Afro-Amer Studies. **Orgs:** Pres, Natl Black Alliance Grad Educ, 1972-; overseas ext teacher, Univ of Wisconsin, (English), Korea, 1952; Higher Educ Comm, Natl Alliance of Black School Educ, 1984-; mem, Phi Delta Kappa, 1970-; NAACP, Omega Psi Phi, 1947-. **Honors/Awds:** Certificate & plaque, Martha Holden Jennings Scholar, 1966-67; certificate, Regional Council of Intl Educ, 1970-71, Ivory Coast and Lome, West Africa Workshop & Tour of Lagos, Dakar, Benin, 1980. **Military Serv:** USAF, Educ Spec, 1951-55. **Home Addr:** 11511 Martin Luther King Jr Dr, Cleveland, OH 44105. **Business Addr:** Director, Black Cultural Cntr, University of Akron, East Hall #202, Akron, OH 44325.

WILSON, JOHNNY LEAVERNE
Educator. **Personal:** Born Sep 17, 1954, Wilmington, NC; son of Mary Wilson and William E Wilson; children: Lynnezy Alorida Smith Wilson, Johnny Allen Smith Wilson. **Educ:** Winston Salem State University, BA, 1976; Central Missouri State Univ, MA, 1979; Atlanta University, Atlanta, GA, PhD, 1988. **Career:** Central Missouri, State University, Warrensburg, MO, work study assistant, 1976-78; Operation PUSH, Kansas City, MO, associate director international affairs commission, 1978-80; Atlanta University, Atlanta, GA, work study assistant, 1980-84; Morehouse School of Medicine, Atlanta, GA, circulation assistant, 1984-88; Atlanta Board of Education, supply teacher, 1984-88; Clark Atlanta Univ, Atlanta, Ga, assistant professor, 1988-. **Orgs:** President, JW Management and Associates, 1988-; member, National Conference Black Political Scientist, 1980-; board of directors, Mental Health Assn of Metro Atlanta Inc, 1989-90; member, Atlanta Employer Comm of Atlanta Fields Service Office, 1990-91; director of internship program, Clark Atlanta Univ, Dept of Political Science. **Honors/Awds:** Nominated for the Governor's Awards in the Humanities, 1991; PEW Memorial Trust and Sears Faculty Excellence Awards for Outstanding Undergraduate Teaching; Escalation of Tensions in Persian Gulf, Atlanta Voice, Sept 24, 1990; Black Politics in Atlanta: The Defeat of Andy Young, Atlanta Voice, Aug 1990; Going to War in the Gulf, Wilmington Journal, 1990; Book/Manuscript Reviewer for Urban Affairs and Waveland Press, 1990; PEW Mini Grant Clark Atlanta University, Research on black elderly mixing alcohol with prescription drugs to cure their physical ailments. **Business Addr:** Assistant Professor, Clark Atlanta University, Political Science Department, 240 James P Brawley Dr, SW, Atlanta, GA 30311.

WILSON, JON
Account executive. **Personal:** Born Sep 29, 1955, Canton, OH. **Educ:** OH Sch of Broadcast Technique Cleveland 1974. **Career:** WKNT Radio Kent OH, asst news dir 1974; WHBC Radio, combo announcer/engr 1974-76; United Companies Life Ins Baton Rouge, regional dir 1976-77; WHBC Radio,production specl 1976-77, Black music dir 1977-84; WHBC AM & FM, account exec 1984-; WHBC AM & FM, research dir/ co-op coord. **Orgs:** Mem Soc of Broadcast Engrs 1975; mem Black Music Assn 1979; mem bd of dir Canton Black United Fund Pub Relations Div 1979; mem bd of dirs Stark Co NAACP 1980, 1983; bd mem Metropoliatian Office Canton; youth committee YMCA; dir Presenters Bureau Commerce Div for The United Way; youth coach YMCA. **Honors/Awds:** Outstanding Teenagers of Amer Inc 1973; spec comm Stark Co NAACP 1979; Serv Awd E Central OH Easter Seals 1979; Outstanding Young Man of Amer Awd US Jaycees 1980; Spec Commendation Stark Co NAACP 1982; Spec Serv Awd Canton Area Big Bros/Big Sisters 1984-85; Ford Motor Marketing Inst Certification ''Satisfying Customer Needs''. **Business Addr:** Account Executive, WHBC AM & FM, 550 Market Ave South, Canton, OH 44701.

WILSON, JONATHAN CHARLES, JR.
Educator, artist. **Personal:** Born Nov 4, 1949, Buffalo, NY; son of Jean Jimison and Jonathan C Wilson Sr; married Nan Withers-Wilson, Jun 24, 1978. **Educ:** Rosary Hill College, BFA, 1971; University of Cincinnati, MA, 1972; University of Wisconsin, Madison, ABD, 1976; Northwestern University, MFA, 1983. **Career:** Loyola University, Chicago, associate professor, 1976-; actor, plays include: Fraternity, The Death of Bessie Smith, Union Boys, Burning Bright; director, plays include: Fraternity, From the Mississippi Delta, A Raisin in the Sun, Jump for Joy. **Orgs:** Playwright's Center, Chicago, chairman, board of directors, 1980-; Association for Theatre in Higher Education, 1981-; Society of Stage Directors and Choreographers, 1991-; Illinois Theatre Association, 1985-; Court Theater, Chicago, associate artist. **Honors/Awds:** Buffalo Common Council, Citation for work in professional theatre, 1992; Chicago Tribune's, Chicagoan in the Arts Award, 1991; Helen Hayes Association, Best Director, for From the Mississippi Delta, 1991; Jeff nomination, Best Director, Fraternity, Chicago, 1990. **Special Achievements:** Directed 3 educational video's for Loyola University, Chicago, 1990-91; production of Dr Endesha Holland's, From the Mississippi Delta, taped for the New York Public Library Archives, 1991; production of Duke Ellington's, Jump for Joy, received national & international press coverage, 1991. **Home Addr:** 923 Wesley Ave, Evanston, IL 60202. **Business Phone:** (312)508-3838.

WILSON, JOSEPH F.
Educator. **Personal:** Born Dec 2, 1951, Chicago, IL; son of Ida Wilson and Charles Wilson; married Maria Vazquez Wilson, May 6, 1984; children: Leslie. **Educ:** Columbia College, New York, NY, BA, 1973; Columbia University, New York, NY, MA, 1975, MPh, 1978, PhD, 1980. **Career:** Rutgers University, New Brunswick, NJ, assistant professor, 1980-86; Brooklyn College, Brooklyn, NY, associate professor, 1986-94, prof, 1994-; Brooklyn Coll Center for Diversity and Multicultural Education, currently. **Orgs:** Director, Brooklyn College Multicultural Center, 1990-95; appoints committee, Political Sceince Dept, 1989-95; executive committee, Black Faculty & Staff Association, 1987-95. **Honors/Awds:** Author, Tearing Down the Color Bar, Columbia University Press, 1989, The Reeducation of The American Working Class, Greenwood Press, 1990, Black Labor in America, Greenwood Press, 1986; Distinguished Tow Professor of Political Science, 1993-95. **Home Addr:** 215 W 91st, New York, NY 10024.

WILSON, JOSEPH HENRY, JR.
Dentist. **Personal:** Born Jan 29, 1966, Washington, DC; son of Frankie Jones Wilson and Joseph Henry Wilson Sr. **Educ:** St Louis University, BA, biology, 1987; University of Maryland, Baltimore College of Dental Surgery, DDS, 1991. **Career:** St Elizabeth's Hospital, dental resident, 1991-92; Hamilton Health Center, dentist, 1992-; Community Dental Associates PC, dentist, secretary, partner, 1992-. **Orgs:** American Dental Association, 1992-; Pennsylvania Dental Association, 1992-; Harrisburg Dental Society, 1992-. **Home Addr:** 4905 Janelle Dr, Harrisburg, PA 17112-2141, (717)232-8099. **Business Addr:** Partner, Secretary, Community Dental Associates, PC, 2451 N Third St, Harrisburg, PA 17110, (717)238-8163.

WILSON, JOY JOHNSON
Health policy commission staff member. **Personal:** Born Jul 12, 1954, Charleston, SC; daughter of Martha L Johnson and Everett W Johnson; married Ronald E Wilson; children: Devon, Trevon. **Educ:** Keene State College NH, BS 1976; Univ of NC at Chapel Hill, MRP 1978. **Career:** Natl Conf of State Leg, rsch assoc 1978-79, staff assoc 1979-82, sr staff assoc 1982-83, staff dir 1983-89; US Bipartisan Commission on Comprehensive Health Care, professional staff member, 1989-90; Natl Conference of State Legislatures, senior committee director, health, 1990-96; Federal Affairs Counsel & Director, Natl Conf of State Leg, health comm, 1996-. **Orgs:** Adv Neighborhood Commission 1981-84, treas of commission 1982-83; treas, Women and Health Roundtable 1986-87; member, Women in Government Relations, 1986-; member, American League of Lobbyists, 1987-89. **Business Addr:** Director, Federation Affairs Counsel, Health Committee, National Conference of State Legislatures, 444 North Capitol St, NW, Suite 500, Washington, DC 20001.

WILSON, KEN
Record company executive. **Career:** MCA Records, pres, black music, 1996-; Columbia Records, vp, black music promotion, until 1996. **Business Addr:** President, Black Music, MCA Records, 70 Universal City Plz, Universal City, CA 91608-1011, (818)777-4500.

WILSON, KIM ADAIR
Attorney. **Personal:** Born Sep 4, 1956, New York, NY; daughter of Walter Wilson (deceased) & Rosa J Wilson. **Educ:** Boston College, BA cum laude, 1978; Hofstra University School of Law, JD, 1982. **Career:** New York City Department of Investigation, investigative attorney, 1986-89; New York State Supreme Court, court attorney, 1989-. **Orgs:** National Bar Association, bd of governors, 1995-; New York State Bar Association, house of delegates, 1994-; Metropolitan Black Bar Association, president, 1994-96; NY State Bar Assoc, house of delegates, 1994-97. **Honors/Awds:** New York Association of Black Psychologists, The Nelson Mandela International Citizen of the Year Award, 1994; National Bar Association, Outstanding Bar Association Affiliate Chapter Award, 1995; The Judicial Friends, The Jane Matilda Bolin Award, 1996; Consortium of Doctors, Inductee, 1998. **Special Achievements:** Co-author: ''Affirmative Action Can Help Create Tradition of Excellence,'' New York Law Journal, May 1995; ''US Constitution and its Meaning to the African-American Community,'' National Bar Association Magazine, Volume 10, No 4, pp 3 & 30; Author of book review, Affirmative Action, Race & American Values, published my book review, New York Law Journal, Jan 10, 1997. **Business Addr:** Attorney, New York State Supreme Court, Bronx County, Civil Law Department, 851 Grand Concourse, Ste 217, Bronx, NY 10451, (718)590-3956.

WILSON, LANCE HENRY
Attorney, investment banker. **Personal:** Born Jul 5, 1948, New York, NY; son of Ruth Thomas Wilson and William H. Wilson; married Deirdre Jean Jenkins; children: Jennifer Lee. **Educ:** Hunter College, AB 1969; Univ of PA Law Sch, JD 1972. **Career:** Mudge Rose Guthrie & Alexander, attorney 1972-77; Equitable Life Assurance Soc of the US, assoc counsel 1977-81; US Dept of Housing & Urban Develop, exec asst to the sec 1981-84; New York City Housing Develop Corp, pres 1984-86; first vice pres, Paine Webber Inc, 1986-91; Private Business Ventures & Practice of Law, 1991-95; Greystone & Co., 1995-. **Orgs:** Mem NY State Bar Assn; Finance Committee of NYS Republican Party; vice pres NY Co Republican Comm, 1984-90; public mem Admin Conf of the US 1984-86; dir Visiting Nurse Service of NY 1984-90; trustee St Luke's/Roosevelt Hosp Center 1984-90; Dir Nat'l Housing Conf 1986-93; mem Federal Natl Mortgage Assn Advisory Council l986-88. **Honors/Awds:** Legal Writing Teaching Fellowship Univ of PA Law School 1971; Outstanding Leadership Awd IL Council of Black Republicans 1982; Outstanding Leadership Awd NY-State Council of Black Republicans 1982; Secty's Awd for Excellence US Dept of Housing & Urban Develop 1984; Outstanding Public Serv Awd Natl Assoc of Home Builders 1984; Exemplary Leadership Awd Natl Black Republican Council 1984; Housing Man of the Year, Nat'l & NY Housing Conf 1985; Humanitarian Awd, Southern Brooklyn Comm Org 1985; Private Sector Initiative Commendation, The White House 1986. **Military Serv:** US Army capt 3 months duty 6 yrs reserves. **Home Addr:** 530 E 76th St, New York, NY 10021.

WILSON, LAVAL S.
Former educational administrator. **Personal:** Born Nov 15, 1935, Jackson, TN; married Constance Ann; children: Laval Jr, Holly, Shawn, Nicole. **Educ:** Chicago Teachers Coll, BEd 1958; Univ of Chicago, MA 1962; Northwestern Univ, PhD 1967. **Career:** Chicago Schools, teacher/counselor 1958-64; Northwestern Univ Inst, asst dir 1965 & 1966; Evanston, IL, asst prin 1966-67, dir integration inst & follow-up prog 1967-70; Central School Evanston, IL, prin 1967-70; Philadelphia & Detroit Schools, supt's intern prog 1970-71; Hempstead, NY, asst supt curric & instr 1971-72 & 1973-74, acting supt of schools 1972-73; Berkeley, CA, supt of schools 1974-80; Rochester, NY, supt of schools 1980-85; Boston, MA, supt of schools 1985-90. **Orgs:** Amer Assn of Sch Admin, Assn for Supvsn & Curric Develop, Kappa Alpha Psi Frat, NAACP, Phi Delta Kappa, New York Cncl of Sch Dist Admin, League of Women Voters; Adv Bd of Girl Scouts of Genesee Valley 1984-; bd dirs Rochester Area Found 1984-; bd dirs Center for Govt Res Inc 1984-; bd dirs Buffalo Br of Fed Reserve Bank of NY 1984-; bd dirs Junior Achieve of Rochester 1983-; Otetiana Cncl Exec Bd Boy Scouts of Amer 1981-; bd trustees Rochester Museum & Sci Center 1981-; Rochester Rotary 1981-; editorial consult to Phi Delta Kappan publn of Phi Delta Kappa 1974-78;consultant to NY Univ, Common of PA Act 101 Western Reg, Amer Assn of Sch Admin, Race Deseg Inst Univ of Pittsburgh, Natl Inst of Educ, Natl Schl Boards Assn, Office of Educ, Far West Lab, Los Angeles Co Sch Dist, San Francisctate Univ, Wyandanch, NY Sch Dist, New York City Sch Dist 12, Encyclopedia Brittanica. **Honors/Awds:** Cert of Recogn for contributions to Rochester community by United Church Ministry 1985; Leadership Award, Rochester Chapter of Phi Delta Kappa 1985; Top Executive Educator Award Executive Educator 1984; Cert of Apprec, Mason Eureka Lodge No 36 1984; Commitment Plaque, Hospitality Charity Club 1984; Apprec Award, Grad Sch of Educ and Human Dev Univ of Rochester 1984; Community Serv Award, Rochester Assn of Black Communicators 1983; Special Serv Award, Rochester WEB DuBois Acad 1983; Apprec Plaque, Dist Adv Council to Chap 1 1982; Community Serv Plaque, Rochester Alumni Chap of Kappa Alpha Psi 1982; Apprec Plaque, Natl Conf on Parent Involvement 1981; City Proclamation of Apprec by Mayor ''Gus'' Newport and City Council members ofBerkeley 1980; Congressional Award, Congr Ronald Dellums 198Legislative Resolution of Spec Publ Recogn and Commend, CA Assemblyman Tom Bates, Assemblyman Elihu Harris & Sen Nicholas Petris 1980; Resolution of Apprec, Berkeley Bd of Educ 1980; Recogn Plaque, Berkeley Black principals 1980; Apprec Plaque, Phi Delta Kappa 1978.

WILSON, LAWRENCE C.
Business executive, city official (retired). **Personal:** Born May 16, 1932, Kansas City, KS; son of Alfretta and John R; divorced; children: Stacey Marie. **Educ:** LA Coll; KC Metro Jr Coll; Certified Public Housing Manager, 1983. **Career:** General machinist, 1955-68; Greater KC Council on Religion & Race, proj director 1969-71; Human Resources Corp KC MO, area coordinator 1963-69, director, 1971-72; Shawnee County Community Assistance and Action Inc, Topeka, Kansas, executive director, 1972-80; National Center for Community Action Inc, executive director, 1980-82; Topeka Housing Authority, deputy director, 1982-95. **Orgs:** Mem Topeka Opt Club; Natl Assn Comm Develop; Lawrence C Wilson Assoc; chmn KS Comm on Civil Rights; advr KS Sec of Social Rehabilitation Series; Topeka-Shawnee Co Metro Plng Comm; League of KS Municipalities Human Resources Comm; NAACP; Black Econ Union; KS Assn of Comm Action; dir OEO; exec comm & bd of dirs, Shawnee County Comm Assistance & Action Inc, Shawnee County Council Advocacy on Aging. **Honors/Awds:** Urban

Serv Award; Alliance of Businessmen Jobs Award; Appreciation Award Black Economic Union. **Military Serv:** USN 1949-53.

WILSON, LEON E., JR.
Bank executive. **Personal:** Born Mar 12, 1945, Maine; son of Ollie H Taylor Wilson and Leon E Wilson Sr; married Sharon Clements Wilson, Jun 1970; children: Erika, Erin. **Educ:** Boston University, Boston, MA, BS, 1975; Williams College, Williamstown, MA, 1975; University of Virginia, Charlottesville, VA, 1978; Harvard Business School, Cambridge, MA, PMD, 1986. **Career:** Shawmut Bank, Boston, MA, vice pres, 1966-83; Bank of Boston, Boston, MA, senior vice president, 1983; Fleet Financial Group, senior vice president, 1992-. **Orgs:** Advisory board, Boston University, 1990-; chairman, Roxbury Comm College Foundation, 1990-; member, Comm of Mass Employee Inv & Ownership Comm, 1990-; president, American Institute of Banking, 1982-83; commissioner, Plymouth Redevelopment, 1984; Harvard Univ task force, 1985; Boston Ballet, board member, 1994; Urban League of Eastern MA; United Negro Coll Fund. **Honors/Awds:** Black Achievement Award, YMCA, Professional Achievement Award, Boston Urban Bankers. **Military Serv:** Army Reserve, E4, 1966-72. **Business Addr:** Senior Vice President, Fleet Financial Group, Not for Profit Investment Management Group, 75 State St MABO-FO7B, Boston, MA 02109-1810.

WILSON, LEONARD D.
State program officer. **Personal:** Born Dec 6, 1933, Raleigh, NC; married Cynthia T; children: Edwin G, Anita V. **Educ:** BS 1970. **Career:** Raleigh-Wake Co Civil Def Agy, supr prsnl actng distrib & inspection of Geiger Counters 1966; Am Optical Co Raleigh, NC, messenger 1966-67; Wake CoOpport Inc Raleigh, 1969-71; Manpower, dir; Chavis Heights Comm Action Ctr, dir; NC Council of Ch Migrant Project, 1971-72; Emergency Food & Med Serv Guidlines, tech asst; Durham Co Hosp Inc, Lincoln Hosp, Durham, NC, employment coord 1975-73; Action Domestic Program, state prgm ofcr; US Govt Additional Training, Mid-Level Mgmt Trng, Bettsy Jeff Penn 4-H Cntr Winston-Salem 1969, Mid-Level Mgmt Follow-up Training 1970. **Orgs:** Pub prsnl mgmt disadvantaged training Univ of NC 1969; Low Income Housing Devel Tng, Low Income Housing Devel Corp, Durham NC 1969; Manpower Training Conf, Coastal Plains Regnl Commn Univ of GA Ctr for Continuing Educ Athens GA 1970; Audio-Visual Tng, Bettsy Jeff Penn 4-H Ctr 1970; Audio-Visual Training NC Cntrl Univ 1969; Auto Mech Tng, Ligon HS; Underwriter for NC Mutual Ins Co Raleigh 1964; Survival Training USN San Diego 1963; commissioned notary public 1970-75. **Honors/Awds:** Comm Orgns letter of appreciation Wayne Action Group for Econ Solvency Goldsboro, NC; Certificate of Membership NC Hosp Personnel Assn; US Naval Air Facility China Lake CA. **Military Serv:** AUS paratrooper 1953-56; USN 1960-64; USNR 3 yrs active. **Business Addr:** Action Domestic Programs, Federal Bldg Plaza, Louisville, KY 40201.

WILSON, LEROY, JR.
Attorney. **Personal:** Born Jun 16, 1939, Savannah, GA; son of Mary Louise (Frazier) Wilson and Leroy Wilson, Sr; married Helen Odum (divorced); children: Andrea; children: Jason, Christopher. **Educ:** Univ of Vienna Austria, 1959-60; Morehouse Coll, BS 1962; Univ of CA Berkeley, MS, JD 1965, 1968. **Career:** IBM, attny 1968-72; Covington Grant Howard, attny 1972; IBM, attny 1972-74; Private practice, attny 1974; Union Carbide Corp, attny 1974-82; Private practice, attny 1982-. **Orgs:** Dir The Assoc of Black Lawyers of Westchester Co Inc 1978-; gov mem exec comm Natl Bar Assoc 1979-1980; mem, Amer Bar Assoc; vice pres Natl Bar Assoc; public mem NY State Banking Bd 1983-87; chmn Assoc of Black Lawyers of Westchester Co Inc 1987-. **Honors/Awds:** Hon Woodrow Wilson Fellow 1962; Thayer Awd Civil Counsel to Sickle Cell Anemia Benefit US Mil Acad; Personal Counsel to His Excellency Godfrey Lukongwa Binaisa Fifth Pres of the Republic of Uganda. **Business Addr:** Attorney, 149 Grand St, White Plains, NY 10601.

WILSON, LEROY, III. See Obituaries section.

WILSON, LIONEL J. See Obituaries section.

WILSON, LUCY R.
Educational administrator. **Personal:** Born Sep 23, 1930, Hartsville, SC; married Harrison; children: April, Jennifer, Richard, John, Harrison, Benjamin. **Educ:** SC St Coll Orangeburg, (cum laude), BS 1951; IN Univ Bloomington, MS Guidance & Counseling 1954, EdD Guidance & Counseling 1960. **Career:** Darden School of Educ Old Dominion Univ, assoc dean 1975-; TN Mental Health Dept Nashville, dir adult serv 1967-75; Southern Univ Baton Rouge, prof psychology 1964-67; Educ Testing Serv Princeton, asst prog dir guidance serv 1962-67; Claflin Coll Orangeburg, dean of students 1956-62; Albany St Coll GA, dean of women 1954-56; Educ Testing Serv Princeton, consult 1971; HEW, consult 1974-78; Portsmouth Public School VA, consult 1974-80. **Orgs:** Area fol dir Nat March of Dimes 1975-77; chprsn Human Sexuality Task Force 1978-; bd of dir Planning Council of Tidewater 1978-. **Honors/Awds:** Scholar, Danforth Found 1958-59; 12 publs juried jours. **Business Addr:** Hampton Blvd, Norfolk, VA 23508.

WILSON, MADELAINE MAJETTE
Educator (retired). **Personal:** Born Aug 23, 1920, Suffolk, VA; daughter of Lula O Majette and Junnie E Majette; married John A Wilson, Oct 28, 1961 (deceased); children: John H Bellamy, Madelaine B Johnson, James Allen (deceased). **Educ:** Elizabeth City State University, BS, 1940; Virginia State University, MS, 1962. **Career:** Camden County Schools, primary teacher, 1941-42; Southampton County Public Schools, teacher, 1942-46; numerous teaching and educational administrative positions, 1946-90; City of Suffolk, Department of Parks and Recreation, senior citizens coordinator, 1990-. **Orgs:** St Mark's PE Church, eucharistic minister, choir member, trustee, 1975-93; Pinochle Bugs Inc, Suffolk Chapter, former senior warden, chaplain, former president; Alpha Kappa Alpha, Zeta Epsilon Omega Chapter, former basileus; Chums Club of Suffolk, charter member, 1st president, chaplain, reporter, 1937-93; Nansemond Chapter II 31 OES, PHA, past worthy matron, treasurer; Tri-County Trust for Retarded Citizens, board president, 1990-93; AARP, Widowed Persons Service, volunteer trainer, secretary-treasurer, 1992-93; Golden Olympics, steering committee, 1993. **Honors/Awds:** Department of Parks and Recreation;, Outstanding Senior Citizen of the Year, 1985; American Association of University Women, Woman of the Year; NAACP, Community Service Plaque, 1992; Virginia Cooperative Extension Department, Certificate of Service, 1993. **Home Addr:** 1115 Custis Rd, Suffolk, VA 23434.

WILSON, MANNIE L.
Clergyman. **Personal:** Born in O'Brien, FL; married Bettie; children: Ruth C. **Educ:** Roger Williams U; Am Bapt Theol Sem; Benedict Coll, (Hon DD). **Career:** Covent Ave Bapt Ch NYC, pastor. **Orgs:** Chmn of bd of council of Chs of City of NY; mem gbd trustees Union Theol Sem; pres bd tlrustees Knickerbocker Hosp; mem esec com So Christian Leadership Conf; preached sermon at White House at request of Pres Richard M Nixon Feb 1, 1970. **Honors/Awds:** Recipient of many honors including Silver Beaver Awd of BSA; Man of Yr Harlem Br YMCA. **Business Addr:** 420 W 145 St, New York, NY 10031.

WILSON, MARGARET BUSH
Attorney. **Personal:** Born Jan 30, 1919, St Louis, MO; daughter of M Berenice Casey Bush and James T Bush Sr; divorced; children: Robert Edmund III. **Educ:** Talladega Coll, (cum laude) BA 1940; Lincoln Univ Sch of Law, LLB 1943. **Career:** St Louis Lawyers for Housing, asst dir 1969-72; Acting Dir St Louis, Model City Prog, dep dir 1968-69; MO Comm Serv & Continuing Educ adminstr 1967-68, Legal Sv Cs Spl MO 1965-67; Asst Atty Gen MO, 1961-62; pvt practice St Louis, 1947-65; Rural Electrification Admin Dept Agr St Louis, legal atty 1943-45; Council on Legal Educ Oppor Inst St Louis Univ Sch of Law, instr Civil Procedure 1973; Wilson & Associates, sr partner. **Orgs:** V chmn Land Reutilization Aluth St Louis 1975-77; mem MO Council on Criminal Justice 1972-77; treas NAACP Nat Housing Corp; mem Arts & Educ Council, St Louis; Lawyers Assn; ABA; NBA; MO Bar Assn; Mound City Bar Assn; St Louis Bar Assn; Alpha Kappa Alpha; former dir Monsanto Co; trust Mutual Life Ins Co of NY; chmn natl Bd NAACP 1975-84; chmn bd trust St Augustine's Coll 1986-88; chmn bd dir The Intergroup Corp 1986-87; chmn bd of trustees, Talladega Coll 1988-91. **Honors/Awds:** Recipient Bishops Awd Episcopal Diocese MO 1963; Juliette Derricotte Fellow 1939-40; Honorary Degrees: Boston Univ, Washington Univ, Alabama State Univ, St Paul's College, Kenyon College, Smith College, Talladega College; Pioneer Award, 1995; Dr Martin Luther King Jr State (MO), Celebration Commission of Missouri, 1995. **Business Addr:** Senior Partner, Wilson & Associates, 4054 Lindell Blvd Ste 100, St Louis, MO 63108.

WILSON, MARGARET F.
Librarian. **Personal:** Born Aug 8, 1932, Monroeville, AL; daughter of Carrie Fountain and Leo Fountain; married Willie C Wilson; children: Monica R Shular, Veronica E McCarthy, Danita Y Wooten, Constance K Harris, Willie C II. **Educ:** AL State Coll, BS 1953; FL A&M Univ, MEd 1969; FL State Univ, MSLS 1972, AMD 1979. **Career:** Rosenwald High School, secretary/teacher 1953-55; FL A&M Univ, librarian 1963-. **Orgs:** Mem FL Library Assn 1972-, Special Libraries Assn 1972-, Heroines, Eastern Stars, 1979-, NAACP 1980-, Beta Phi Mu 1980-, Urban League 1980-, Amer Library Assoc 1983-, Amer Coll & Research Library 1983. **Honors/Awds:** Article "Zora Neale Hurston, Author & Folklorist," Negro History Bulletin 1982; "School Media Specialist Undergraduate Library Science Program," Journal Educ Media & Library Science 1986; "Selected Speeches of Florida A&M Univ, pres, l987," unpublished. **Business Addr:** University Librarian, Florida A&M University, Box 164, BB Tech Center, Tallahassee, FL 32307.

WILSON, MARKLY
Administrator. **Personal:** Born Mar 30, 1947, Bridgetown, Barbados; married Gonul Mehmet; children: 2. **Educ:** St Clair Coll Ontario Canada, attended; Adelphi Univ NY, attended. **Career:** Barbados Bd of Tourism, recept/clerk 1967-74; Skinner Sec School, bus English teacher 1967-74; Ministry of Civil Aviation, clerical officer 1967; Barbados Bd of Tourism, publ rel officer 1974, sales rep 1974-78, mgr 1978-. **Orgs:** Mem Photographic Soc Lindfield School 1959-62; pres Christ Church HS Debating Soc 1963; sec Christ Church HS Old Scholars Assoc 1967; mem Toastmasters Intl Bridgetown Chap 1968; mem Graybar Toastmasters Club 1974-; mem bd of dir CTA 1981-82; chmn Assembly of Natl Tourist Office Rep NY 1982,83 memNY Skal Club; dir Travel & Tourism Rsch Assoc; mem bd of adv Tourism Dept New School for Social Rsch. **Honors/Awds:** Awarded Cup for Most Outstanding Athlete of the Year Lindfield School; Victor Ludorum in Athletics Christ Church HS; Tourism Dir of the Year NY Based World Tourism Comm 1984; Awarded Tourist Dir of the Year by the World Travel Awd Comm 1984. **Business Addr:** US Manager, Barbados Board of Tourism, 800 Second Ave, New York, NY 10017.

WILSON, MICHAEL (WILD THING)
Professional basketball player. **Personal:** Born Jul 22, 1972. **Educ:** Univ of Memphis, Tennessee. **Career:** Harlem Globetrotters, forward, currently. **Special Achievements:** Established a new Guiness Book of World Record for a slam dunk, 1996. **Business Addr:** Professional Basketball Player, Harlem Globetrotters, 400 E Van Buren, Ste 300, Phoenix, AZ 85004, 800-641-4667.

WILSON, MILTON
Educational administrator. **Personal:** Born Jul 20, 1915, Paducah, KY; son of Shea Ray Wilson and Jess Wilson; married Zelda Summers; children: Zelda C Jefferson, Milton James Jr, Rhea Ann Farley. **Educ:** West Virginia State Coll, BS, Business, 1937; Indiana Univ, MCS, Business, 1945, DBA, Business, 1951; Univ of Chicago, attended, 1959-60. **Career:** St Phillips Jr Coll, head of business dept, business mgr, 1940-41; Samuel Plato Genl Contractor, chief accountant, 1941-43; Office For Emergency Mgmt, chief cost accountant, 1943-44; Hampton Inst, head of dept of acct, 1944-46; Dillard Univ, head of business dept, 1946-49; Texas Southern Univ, dean school of business, 1949-70; Harvard Univ, visiting professor of business, 1957-58; Private Practice, Houston, cpa, 1952-56; Wilson & Cooke, consultant in field, 1952-, sr partner, 1957-; Gen Acct Office, consultant, 1971-; Howard Univ, dean school of business & public admin, 1970-. **Orgs:** Consultant, City of Houston, TX, 1952-; mem, Dist of Columbia Inst of CPA; mem bd dirs, Amer Assembly of Collegiate Schools of Business; mem, Govt Relations Comm AACSB; chmn, advisor bd of dirs, United Natl Bank; mem, Comm on Minorities of the Amer Acct Assn; consult, Gen Acct, 1971-; mem, Dean's Advisory Council, Indiana Univ, 1979-; pres, Intl Assn of Black Business Educ, 1980; chmn, Deans Comm on Faculty Eval; mem, univ wide advisory comm on Student Recruitment & Articulation; mem steering comm, Center for the Study of Handicapped Children & Youth; mem minority recruitment & equal opportunity comm, Amer Inst of CPA's; memm Beta Gamma Sigma, Minority Doctoral Fellows Comm AICPA; mem bd of dirs, Inst for Amer Business, Howard Health Plan Inc; memconsult panel, Proctor & Gamble BusinesCurriculum Devel Program United Negro Coll Fund Inc; mem, The Campaign for Indiana, Indiana Univ Found, 1985; sec/treas, Beta Gamma Sigma, 1984; mem, Commn on Educ for the Business Profession; mem bd of dir, Howard Health Plan Inc, Great Western Financial Corp, Great Western Savings & Loan Assn; advisor to Select Comm on small business; mem, Initial Accreditation Comm; mem, deans's advidory council, Indiana Univ. **Honors/Awds:** Mem, Mu Chap Delta Mu Delta Natl Honor Soc in Business, Theta Chap Beta Gamma Sigma Hon Business Fraternity, Beta Alpha Psi Hon Acct Fraternity; Achievement Award Natl Assn of Black Accountants Inc, 1974; mem, Acad of Alumni Fellows School of Business Alumni Assn, Indiana Univ, 1978; Dow Jones Award AACSB, 1979; Award from Deans and Dirs Academic Affairs Area Howard Univ, 1980; Medal of Excellence Golden State Minority Found, 1981; recipient of medal of Excellence by the Golden State Minority Found, 1981; The undergrad baccalaureate programs of the School of Business & Public Admin at Howard Univ were accredited 1976 by the AACSB; The grad programs were accredited 1980 by AACSB. **Home Addr:** 14124 Northgate Dr, Silver Spring, MD 20906. **Business Addr:** Dean, Howard University, 2600 Sixth St NW Ste 571, Washington, DC 20059.

WILSON, MOOKIE (WILLIAM HAYWARD)
Professional baseball player. **Personal:** Born Feb 9, 1956, Bamberg, SC. **Educ:** Spartanburg Methodist College, Spartanburg, SC, attended; Univ of South Carolina, Columbia, SC, attended. **Career:** New York Mets, outfielder, 1980-89; Toronto Blue Jays, outfielder, 1989; New York Mets, community liaison, minor league asst, 1994-. **Business Addr:** Community Liaison, Minor League Asst, New York Mets, Shea Stadium, Flushing, NY 11368.

WILSON, NANCY
Singer, performer. **Personal:** Born Feb 20, 1937, Chillicothe, OH; married Rev Wiley Burton; children: Samanthia, Sheryl, Kenneth C. **Career:** Began career as singer with local groups then joined Rusty Bryant Band, singer 1956; Midwest & Canada, singing tour 1958; singing independently 1959-; Capitol Records, EMI Records Japan, Nippon Columbia Japan, Interface Japan, Epic Sony/CBS, recording artist; I'll Be A Song, Just To Keep You Satisfied, Forbidden Lover, singer; US, Japan, Europe, Indonea, intl concert tours; Police Story, Hawaii Five-O,

FBI, Room 222, performer; TV series Nancy Wilson Show, hostess 1974-75; The Big Score, performed. **Orgs:** Proj Equality, Black Caucus, Pres Council for Min Bus Enterprises, NAACP, SCLC; chmn Oper PUSH, United Negro Coll fund; mem Comm for the KennedyCtr of Performing Arts; contrib performances to many fund raising projs. **Honors/Awds:** Recorded over 50 record albums some of which brought her Grammy Awds; Paul Robeson Awd Urban League; Ruby Ring Awd Johnson & Johnson Co; 2 Emmy Awds; Black Book Awd; Best Female Vocalist Awd Playboy, Downbeat Jazz Polls; Grammy for Best Rhythm & Blues Recording 1964; Emmy for The Nancy Wilson Show.

WILSON, NATARSHA JULIET
Sales representative. **Personal:** Born Oct 22, 1961, Atlanta, GA. **Educ:** Berry Coll, BS 1982. **Career:** Continental Distributors, sales consultant; Soft Sheen Products Inc, territorial sales merchandiser; Redken Laboratories Inc, district sales mgr. **Home Addr:** 2795 Dodson Lee Dr, East Point, GA 30344.

WILSON, NORMA JUNE. See DAVIS, N. JUNE.

WILSON, OLLY W.
Composer, educator. **Personal:** Born Sep 7, 1937, St Louis, MO; son of Alma Grace Peoples Wilson and Olly W Wilson Sr; married Elouise Dolores Woods, Jun 27, 1959; children: Dawn Lynn, Kent Alan. **Educ:** Washington U, BM 1959; Univ of IL, MM (Honors) 1960; Univ of IA, PhD 1964. **Career:** Univ of CA Berkeley, prof of music; musician with local jazz groups in St Louis; played bass violin with St Louis Philharmonic Orch, St Louis Summer Chambers Players & Cedar Rapids Symphony Orch; educator FL A&M U; educator Oberlin Conservatory of Music Univ of CA Berkeley; author of compositions including chamber works, orchestral works & works for electronic media; conducted num concerts of contemporary music; orchestral compositions performed by major orchestras include Boston, Cleveland, San Francisco, St Louis, Houston, Oakland, Detroit Symphony Orchestras; Univ of CA Berkeley, prof of music, asst chancellor intl affairs. **Orgs:** Consult Natl Endowment for the Arts, Natl Endowment for the Humanities; bd dir Meet the Composer; mem Univ of CA Bekreley Young Musicians Prog; bd of overseers vstg comm Harvard Dept of Music; mem ASCAP, NAACP, Natl Urban League, Alpha Phi Alpha, Sigma Pi Phi; World Affairs Council, Institute of International Education. **Honors/Awds:** Recipient Dartmouth Arts Council Prize 1968; awarded Commission, Boston Symphony, Orchestra & Fromm Foundation 1970; awarded Guggenheim Flwslhp 1972-77; commission Oakland Symphony Orch 1973; award Otstandng Achvmnt in Music Composition Am Acad of Arts & Letters & Nat Inst of Arts & Letters 1974; natl Assoc of negro Musicians Awd 1974; Vstg Artist at Amer Acad in Rome 1978; Natl Endowment for Arts Commissions for Composition 1976; Koussevitsky Found Commission 1984; Houston Symphony Fanfare Commission 1986. **Business Addr:** Professor, Asst Chancellor, Univ of CA Berkeley, 126 California Hall, Berkeley, CA 94701.

WILSON, ORA BROWN
Educational administrator. **Personal:** Born Jul 13, 1937, Austin, TX; children: Evelyn J Jones. **Educ:** Huston-Tillotson Coll, BA 1960; Prairie View A&M Univ, MEd 1979. **Career:** Public Schools, teacher 1964-67; Austin Comm Coll, part-time instructor 1977-79; Huston-Tillotson Coll, teacher/adm asst 1967-79, title III coord 1979-. **Orgs:** Mem Austin-Travis Co MH-MR Adv Comm 1981-86; licensed Professional Counselor State of TX 1983; volunteer Austin Hospice 1983-; mem bd dirs Family EldeCare Inc 1986; mem Alpha Kappa Alpha Sor. **Honors/Awds:** Professional Proposal Developer Huston-Tillotson Coll 1979-; Special Service Awd Huston-Tillotson Coll 1981. **Home Addr:** 1801 Loreto Dr, Austin, TX 78721. **Business Addr:** Title III Coordinator/Planning Assoc to President, Huston-Tillotson College, 900 Chicon, Austin, TX 78702.

WILSON, PATRICIA A.
Educator. **Personal:** Born Feb 1, 1948, Conway, SC. **Educ:** Univ of MI BA, MA, PhDd candidate. **Career:** Univ of MI, asst dir of undergraduate addmissions. **Orgs:** Mem Black Faculty & Staff Univ of MI. **Business Addr:** 1220 SAB Univ of MI, Ann Arbor, MI 48104.

WILSON, PATRICIA I.
Educator. **Personal:** Born Jun 7, 1940, Belmont, NC; daughter of Blondine Henderson Isles and Hiawatha Isles; married Robert Erwin Wilson, Jun 17, 1961; children: Geoffrey Keith, Gary Stephen. **Educ:** North Carolina A&T State University, Greensboro, NC, BS, 1961; University of Kentucky, Lexington, KY, MA, 1979, EdD, 1984. **Career:** Morris Township Junior High, Morristown, NJ, teacher, 1963-65; Roxbury High, Succasunna, NJ, teacher, 1965-67; Morris Hills Regional High, Rockaway, NJ, teacher, 1968-71; Central High, Joliet, IL, teacher, 1972-73; Davenport West High School, Davenport, IA, teacher, 1974-77; University of Kentucky, Lexington, KY, instructor, 1979-81; Eastern Kentucky Univ, Richmond, KY, assistant professor, 1981-85; University of Kentucky, Lexington, KY, assistant professor, 1985-92; Alabama A&M University, associate professor, 1992-. **Orgs:** President, Delta Pi Epsilon, 1988-90; president, Association of Records Managers Administrators, 1988-89; secretary/treasurer, Phi Delta Kappa, 1990-91, membership vice pres, 1991-92; secretary, Alabama Business Ed Assn, 1994-, pres elect, 1996-97; treasurer, Gamma Nu chapter, Delta Pi Epsilon, 1997-; president, Alabama Business Educator Assoc, 1998-. **Honors/Awds:** President's Award, ARMA, 1986-87; Outstanding Researcher Award, A & M School of Business, 1994. **Home Addr:** 105 McNaron Dr, Madison, WI 35758-8182. **Business Phone:** (205)851-5081.

WILSON, RALPH L.
Clergyman, educator (retired). **Personal:** Born Mar 30, 1934, Tallahassee, FL; son of Mamie Roberts Wilson and Perman Wilson; married Joyce Ann Wright; children: Louis James Arnold, Sonja Libre, Kimberly Lefay, Ralph Larry II. **Educ:** FL A&M Univ, BS 1971; Univ of IL, graduate study; FL A&M, graduate study; FL Conf School Religion Tallahassee, certificate 1969. **Career:** FAUM, asst prof acct, retired, 1985; Vocational Tech Inst III FAMU, 1966-69; Lincoln High School, business mgr 1965-66; FAMU, messenger 1955-65; AME Church, conf sec 1965-78; FAMU Religious Activities, pastor 1973-77; AME Church Dist, presiding elder; FL Conf School of Religion, dean. **Orgs:** Mem Mason; mem 4-H leadership 1952; FL Conf Bd of Examiners; Co-advisor NAACP FAMU Chapter 1967-70; mem United Methodist Church work area on Campus Ministry 1971-78; dir FAMU religous activities 1973-77; Organizer & Chmn Chan Supervisory Com 1976-79; treasurer FL Conf AME Churches Fed Cred Union; mem Ministers Blacks Higher Educ; mem United Campus Ministry; life member, Nu Eta Lambda Chapter, Alpha Phi Alpha Fraternity, Inc; board of trustees, chairman, Committee on Academic Affairs, Edward Waters College; member, Big Bend Transit, Inc; chaplain, executive committee member, The Florida A&M University National Alumni Assn. **Honors/Awds:** Outstanding Young Minister FAMU 1970; Outstanding Religious Leader FAMU 1973; Outstanding Leadership, Taylor County Leadership Council, 1986.

WILSON, RAY F.
Educator. **Personal:** Born Feb 20, 1926, Giddings, TX; son of Fred Wilson; married Faye; children: Ray, Jr, Freddie, Roy, Mercedes. **Educ:** Huston Tillotson, BS 1950; TX So U, MS 1951; Univ TX, PhD 1953; TX So U, JD Law 1973. **Career:** Univ TX Austin, res scientist II 1951-53; TX Southern Univ, prof chem 1972-; Houston Comm Coll, part time instr chem 1972-; TX Southern Univ, grad & res adv presently. **Orgs:** Dir SE TX Sect Am Chem Soc L1967-68, 1969-70; counselor SE TX Section Am Soc 1968-69; Phi Alpha Delta Law Frat; Phi Beta Sigma Frat; vice pres 1955 SW Regional Meeting Am Chem Soc; Legislative Couns to US Congresswoman; Supt Pilgram Congregational Ch present; Comm Consult & Adv underprivilege on real estate; hs lect; president of TSU-TACT Chapter, president of PUC Credit Union. **Honors/Awds:** Awd Huston-Tillotson Coll acad achievement 1953; Beta Kappa Chi Achievement Awds TSU 1965; Faculty Forum Achievement Awd 1969; Faculty Forum Post Doctoral Cert of Achievement TSU 1970; Huston-Tillotson Alumni Assn Sci Achievement 1971; Human Resource of the US 1974. **Military Serv:** USN; petty officer 1944-46.

WILSON, REINARD
Professional football player. **Personal:** Born Dec 12, 1973. **Educ:** Florida State. **Career:** Cincinnati Bengals, linebacker, 1997-. **Special Achievements:** NFL Draft, First round pick, #14, 1997. **Business Addr:** Professional Football Player, Cincinnati Bengals, One Bengals Dr, Cincinnati, OH 45202, (513)621-3550.

WILSON, RITA P.
Telecommunications company executive. **Personal:** Born Oct 4, 1946, Philadelphia, PA; daughter of Julia Phoenix Parker (deceased) and Leroy Parker (deceased); married Harold Wilson, May 9, 1970; children: Marc Wilson. **Educ:** St Paul College, Lawrenceville, VA, BS, education, 1968; Temple University, Philadelphia, PA. **Career:** Children's Service Inc, Philadelphia, PA, social worker, 1968-70; Dept of Defense, Misawa, Japan, elem school teacher, 1971-73; Allstate Insurance Co, Northbrook, IL, senior vice president, 1974-94; Ameritech, Chicago, senior vice pres of corp communications, 1994-. **Orgs:** Trustee, National Center of Neighborhood Enterprise, 1991-; trustee, Foundation for American Communications, 1990-; public relations committee, Nat'l Assn of Independent Insurers, 1990-; board of directors, LeaderShape Inc, 1990-; board of executive advisors, College of Business, Northern Illinois University, 1988-. **Honors/Awds:** Dr Martin Luther King Jr Legacy Award, Boys & Girls Clubs, 1990; Twin Award, National YWCA, 1984; Top 100 Black Business & Professional Women, Dollars & Sense Magazine, 1985. **Business Addr:** Senior Vice President, Corp Communications, Ameritech, 30 S Wacker Dr., Chicago, IL 60606.

WILSON, ROBERT H.
Labor union official. **Personal:** Born in Columbia, SC; son of Marian M Wilson and Alex Wilson; married Elizabeth Wilson. **Educ:** Benedict College. **Career:** Butchers Union of Greater New York & New Jersey Local 174, pres. **Orgs:** Bd trustees Benedict Coll; exec bd Coalition of Black Trade Unionist 1972; adv bd Voc Ed New York City 1969; chmn Politics, Civil Politics & Civil Rights Comm Tst, Calvary Baptist Church; NAACP; exec cncl A Philip Randolph Ldrs of Tomorrow Schlshp Fund Inc; adv council Benedict Coll Alum Assn Inc No Jersey Chpt; ex bd New York St Coalition of Black Trade Unionist; bd of educ New York City Youth Empl & Training Program; bd of trustees Myopia Intl Rsrch Found Inc; life mem NAACP; chmn bd of trustees UFCW Local 174 Health and Pension Funds; chmn bd of trustees Commercial Health and Pension Funds; chmn bd of Trustees Local 174 Retail Health and Pension Funds. **Honors/Awds:** Deborah Hosp Found Award 1978; Easter Seal Soc Awd 1981; State of Israel Bonds Awd 1984; ACRMD Humanitarian Awd 1985; Commissioner of Plainfield Housing Authority, New Jersey; United Way Award, 1990; Consumer Assembly Award, 1990; Proclamation, City of New York, 1990; Proclamation, City of Newark. **Business Addr:** President, UFCW Local 174, 540 W 48th St, New York, NY 10036.

WILSON, ROBERT L.
Architect. **Personal:** Born Oct 17, 1934, Tampa, FL; married Mary; children: Kevin, Brian, Bret. **Educ:** Columbia U, BArch 1963, MArch 1969, M Urban Design 1971. **Career:** Private Practice, architect 1966-; Charles Luckman Asso Arch, proj arch 1963-66; Emery Roth & Sons, Arch, proj arch 1959-63; Voorhees, Walker, Smith & Haynes, arch designer 1957-59; Robt J Reilly, Arch, arch draftsman 1956-57. **Orgs:** Mem Amer Inst of Arch 1966-; pres CT Soc of Arch 1975; co-founder, dir Natl Organ of Minority Arch 1971-; dir Am Inst of Arch 1975; natl vice pres Am Inst of Arch 1976-77; consult Natl Acad of Scis; consult Natl Endowment for the Arts; lectr Yale U/ Hampton Inst/Tuskegee Inst/ Southern U/U of KS/U of TX; Dir City of Stamford Family & Children Serv 1974-75. **Honors/Awds:** Recip Design Awd CT Soc of Arch 1973.

WILSON, ROBERT LEE MILES
Personnel administrator. **Personal:** Born Mar 29, 1930, Jackson, AL; married Autrey Dickerson; children: Dianne Rhodes, Dan P. **Educ:** Our Lady of the Lake Univ San Antonio TX, BA Pol Sci 1971, MEd 1975; Nova Univ Ft Lauderdale FL, candidate for EdD. **Career:** UA Columbia Cablevision of TX Inc, dir personnel & comm relations 1979-; St Philips Coll San Antonio TX, dir student activities 1977-79, instr bus mgmt 1975-77; Manpower Programs City of San Antonio, asst dir 1971-75; AUS Intelligence Command Baltimore MD, counter intelligence officer 1957-70. **Orgs:** Dir adult bus prog Nat Alliance of Bus San Antonio 1979-; mem com San Antonio Personnel & Mgmt Assn 1979-; bd of dirs Jr Coll Student Personnel Assn of TX 1979-; pres United Meth Men St Paul Ch 1960-65; life mem Delta Rho Lambda Chap Alpha Phi Alpha Frat 1976-; pres St Philips Col Chap Am Asn of Univ Profs 1977-79; pres San Antonio Chap Nat Pan Hellenic Council 1978-. **Honors/Awds:** Recipient of Meritorious Serv Meda AUS 1970; Man of Yr St Paul United Meth Ch 1977-78. **Military Serv:** AUS; chief warrant officer; 1947-70.

WILSON, ROBERT STANLEY
Physician. **Personal:** Born Dec 16, 1923, Bessemer, AL; son of Katie Wilson and Derry Wilson; married Velma Jones. **Educ:** Howard Univ, BS (cum laude) 1950; Howard Univ Coll of Medicine, MD 1955; Fed Interagency Inst, Cert Adv Hosp 1967; Cornell Univ, Develop Prog HADP Hosp Admin/Health Admin 1968. **Career:** Wilkes Barre Gen Hosp, intern-gen rotating 1955-56; Vet Admin Hosp, resident internal med 1956-57; Vet Admin Rsch Hosp Chicago, resident rehab med 1958-61; Vet Admin Hosp, chief rehab med 1961-64; VA Central Office Washington DC, chief policy & prog develop 1965; Vet Admin Hosp Tuskegee, chief of staff 1965-69; Vet Admin Hosp, hosp dir 1969-72; Baylor Coll of Med, asso prof 1969-75; WAB Birmingham, clinic asso prof rehab med 1976-; private practice, physician 1969-. **Orgs:** Bd certified Natl Bd Med Examiners 1958; bd certified Amer Bd Phys Med Rehab 1963; Cert Hosp Admin VA Inter Agency Inst 1967; bd dirs exec com Birmingham Regional Health Systems Agency 1978-; mem AMA-NMA Jefferson Co Med Soc. **Military Serv:** AUS pfc 1943-46; Combat Infantry Badge 1945. **Business Addr:** Physician, 2930 9th Ave, Bessemer, AL 35020.

WILSON, RONALD M.
Association executive. **Personal:** Born Feb 19, 1949, Norfolk, VA; son of Wilhelmena Luster Wilson and Guy Wilson; married Katherine Stewart, Aug 30, 1986. **Educ:** Evergreen State Coll, Olympia WA, BA 1984; Baruch College of City Univ of NY, MPA 1985. **Career:** Metro Devel Council, Tacoma WA, program mgr, 1975-81; House of Reps, Olympia WA, legislative asst, 1981-84; Natl League of Cities, Washington DC, special asst to exec dir, 1984-85; Commonwealth of Pennsylvania, Harrisburg PA, exec policy specialist, starting 1985; United Way of Pennsylvania, director of public policy, 1992-. **Orgs:** Past local pres, Omega Psi Phi 1969-; mem, Natl Forum for Black Public Administrators 1984-, Intl City Mgmt Assn 1985-88, Amer Soc for Public Admn 1986-88; vp for public policy, Amer Society of Assn Execs. **Honors/Awds:** Future Leader Award, NW Conf of Black Public Officials, 1982; masters fellowship, Natl Urban Fellows, 1984; author of poetry collection Reflections of Spring, 1987; author of monthly column "Status Quotes," 1989. **Military Serv:** US Army, E-6, 1970-75; high-

est ranking leadership graduate. **Business Addr:** VP for Public Policy, United Way of Pennsylvania, 17 S Market Square, Harrisburg, PA 17101, (717)238-7365.

WILSON, RONALD RAY
Attorney. **Personal:** Born Sep 24, 1953, Galveston, TX; son of Carrie Wilson and Henry Wilson; married Treina Wilson; children: Erik, Colby. **Educ:** Univ TX Plan II Prog, BS 1977; Univ TX Law Sch, JD l988. **Career:** Comm on State Pension Sys, vice chmn; Subcomm on Energy Resources, chmn; Calendars Energy Resources & Finance Inst, com 1976; House of Rep 65th Session, state rep 1976-77, 66th session 1978-80, 67th session 1980-81; chmn Liquor Regulation 70th, 7lst, 72nd Sessions; Fisher Gallagher & Lewis. **Orgs:** Mem Harris Co Council of Organ 1976-80; liaison com Commissioning of Battleship USS TX 1976; chmn Select Comm on Jr Coll Funding 1980. **Honors/Awds:** The Prairie View A&M Univ Centennial Distinguished Pub Serv Awd Prairie View Business Indus Cluster Grp 1978; Cert of Appreciation Jerusalem Youth & Young Adults 1978; 50 Future Leaders of America, Ebony Magazine. **Business Addr:** State Representative, House of Representatives, PO Box 2910, Austin, TX 78768-2910.

WILSON, RUDOLPH GEORGE
Educator. **Personal:** Born Jun 17, 1935, River Rouge, MI; married Sandra Lavernn; children: Trent Duron, James Aaron, Dana Nicole, Amy Lynette. **Educ:** Los Angeles City Coll, AA, BA 1962, MA 1964; Washington Univ, PhD Candidate. **Career:** Southern Illinois Univ, assoc prof 1975-; Second Educ, lecturer 1969-72; Claremont High School, English teacher dept chmn 1964-69, master English teacher 1967-69; Juv Hall Couns 1961-63; Consult Affect Educ Drug Use & Abuse, Moral Educ, Val Educ, Ald Psychology, Methods of Teaching, Adult Educ, Flex Schedule, Humanistic Educ, Motiv of Reluctant Learner, English Educ, Supvr of Student Teachers, Teaching Learn Ctrs, Disc in the Sec Schools, Parent Effect Train, Transact Analy, Devel Teacher Compet; Southern IL Univ, dept chairperson curriculum instructor/prof, currently. **Orgs:** Mem Kappa Alpha Psi; funder, pres Southern IL Adoptive Parents Assn; bd mem Sr Citizens Inc; bd mem SW IL Area Agency on Aging; mem Edwardsville Dist 7 Bd of Educ 1972-; past pres Natl Assn for African Educ 1970-71; pres Faculty Sen, Southern IL Univ 1975-76; elected mem Pres Search Com, SIUE; vice pres Business Affairs Search Com; chmn Search Com for vice pres for student affairs. **Honors/Awds:** Teaching Excellence Award 1971; art pub Harcourt-Brace 1971; "Inner City Teaching Training Program" Office of Educ Journal 1972; Great Teacher Award 1974; Danforth Leadership Award; Danforth Fellow; Kimmel Leadership Award; Martin Luther King Award; St Louis American Outstanding Educator Award. **Military Serv:** USNA, ASA spec four 1957-60. **Business Addr:** Professor, Southern Illinois University, Box 1122, Edwardsville, IL 62026.

WILSON, SANDRA E.
Educator. **Personal:** Born Jun 13, 1944, Abington, PA; daughter of Frances Walton and James O Walton; married John H Wilson Jr; children: John III, Shawn. **Educ:** Cheyney Univ, BS Educ 1962-66; Montclair State Coll, MS Soc Science 1971; Beaver Coll, MA Humanities w/a concentration in Fine Arts 1984; Temple Univ, doctoral candidate, Urban Ed, 1993-. **Career:** Abington School Dist, teacher, 1966-67, 1969-80; teacher, mentally gifted program, 1981-86; Endicott School Dist, teacher 1967-68; Abinton School Dist, teacher, 1986-. **Orgs:** Mem Cheyney Alumni, NAACP, Abington Educ Assn, Natl Conf of Artists, Alpha Kappa Alpha, program dir Comm Oppor Council 1982-84; region rep PSEA Minority Affairs Comm 1984; pres, Montgomery County Chapter, Black Women's Educ Alliance 1981-85; PA Assn for Gifted Children; state rep PSEA, NEA Natl Rep Assembly 1986; vice pres Natl Chapter, Black Women's Educ Alliance, 1986; Coordinator youth council NAACP, Willow Grove Branch; sec Amer Assn for Univ Women, 1986; teacher testing comm PSEA/Educ Testing Serv 1987; Pres-elect, Natl Chapter, Black Women's Educ Alliance, 1988-; organist for the youth choir, Bethlehem Baptist Church; President Black Women's Educational Alliance National, 1991; NAACP Youth Director Eastern PA; NAACP, exec board, WG Chapter; director of Sandra Wilson Dramatic Ensemble, 1995. **Honors/Awds:** Phi Delta Scholarship 1962; Richard Humphrey's Scholarship 1962-66; Student Teacher of the Year Cheyney Univ 1966; Art Award Jenkintown Festival of the Arts 1980; vol serv NAACP Youth Job Conf 1983; Outstanding Serv Dedication Awd Citizen for Progress 1983; Distinctive Serv Award Black Women's Educ Alliance 1985; Black Women's Educ Alliance Leadership, 1986; NAACP Serv to Youth Award, 1988; Optomist of Amer Youth Serv Award, 1989; poem published in Poetic Voices of Amer, 1990; Nominated for Pennsylvania Teacher of the Year, 1995; BWEA Pres Award, 1993, BWEA, Mong Chapter, Newsletter Editor, 1993-. **Special Achievements:** Play We Are published in the International Journal of Black Drama, 1995; editor, Antioch Baptist, News From the Pews. **Home Addr:** 3106 Ori Place, Dresher, PA 19025.

WILSON, SHANICE
Vocalist. **Personal:** Born 1973, Pittsburgh, PA; daughter of Crystal Wilson. **Career:** Performed in national commercials for: Duncan Hines products, Colgate toothpaste, Kentucky Fried Chicken; solo artist, recordings include: Discovery, A&M Records, 1987; I Love Your Smile, Motown Records, 1991; 21 Ways .. to Grow, 1994. **Honors/Awds:** Star Search, vocal category, winner, 1985. **Business Addr:** Singer, c/o Motown Record Corp, 5750 Wilshire Blvd, Ste 300, Los Angeles, CA 90036-3697, (213)468-3500.

WILSON, SHERMAN ARTHUR
Educational administrator. **Personal:** Born Nov 2, 1931, Crowley, LA; married Cozette Givens; children: Sherman Jr, Sherod Andrew. **Educ:** Leland Clge, BS 1952; Tuskegee Inst, MSEd 1964; Univ of Southwestern LA, Masters, 1966. **Career:** Veteran Night School, teacher 1955-57; Carver HS, teacher 1956-65; Ross HS, princ 1965-70; Acadia Parish School Bd, supr sec educ 1970-84, admin of fed prog 1984-. **Orgs:** Pres St Martin Parish Educ Assn 1960-61, LIALO Dist III 1969-70, LA Assn of Supr & Consult 1976-79, Acadia Admin Assn 1980-81; chmn Acadia Parish Computer Steering Comm 1983-; treas PA Fed Credit Union 1970-; alderman City of Crowley Ward 3 Div B 1982. **Honors/Awds:** 32nd Degree Mason CF Ladd Lodge 48 1982; hnry Farmer of Year Crowley High Future Farmers 1974. **Military Serv:** AUS pvt 1st class 1952-54. **Home Addr:** 515 Ross Ave, Crowley, LA 70526. **Business Addr:** Administrator of Federal Programs, Acadia Parish School Board, PO Drawer 309, Crowley, LA 70527.

WILSON, SIDNEY, JR.
Automobile dealer. **Career:** Wilson Buick-Pontiac-GMC Truck Inc, CEO, president, currently. **Special Achievements:** Co. is ranked #67 on Black Enterprise magazine's list of top 100 auto dealers, 1992. **Business Addr:** CEO, President, Wilson Buick-Pontiac-GMC, Inc, 1639 US Highway 45 Byp, Jackson, TN 38305-4413, (901)422-3426.

WILSON, SODONIA MAE
Educator. **Personal:** Born Feb 25, Galveston, TX; daughter of Willie Mae Reed Moore and Rev Jasper Moore; married James Wilson, Mar 24, 1957; children: Demetrius D. **Educ:** French Hosp Sch of Nrsng, RN 1957; San Francisco City Clge, AS 1961; San Francisco State U, BA 1963, MA 1965; CA Schl of Prof Psycholgy, PhD 1973. **Career:** French Hosp SF CA, RN 1956-57; Ft Miley VA Hosp SF CA, RN 1957-60; SF Youth Guidance Ctr, cnslr 1966, probation ofc 1967; Office of Economic Opport, head start analyst 1968; SF Redvlpmnt Agcy, soc srv rep 1969; Sequoia Union HS Dist, cnslng coord 1969-72; Contra Costa Clge San Pablo CA, cnslr 1972-73, dir spec prog 1973-83, dir spec prog & serv fin aid officer 1983-85, mgr of instr & tech support serv 1985-86, dir spec progs & serv 1986-. **Orgs:** Pres CA Comm Clge Admin 1977-78; SF Unified Schl Dist 1982-; Commsr CA Student Aid Comm 1982-1985; vice pres SF Bd of Educ 1982-; Natl Women's Pol Caucus 1981-86, Black Women of Pol Action 1979-, Bay Area Black Women United 1982-84, SF Business & Prof Women's Club 1978-, Women in Higher Educ Assc 1980-84; pres SF Bd of Educ 1986-88; student aid commn 1982-85; vice pres SF Bd of Educ 1982-84; pres Contra Costa Community College District Management Council Executive Board, 1992. **Honors/Awds:** Evaluation of Coll Counseling Prog publ in ERIC 1972-; Merit of Honor Ernest Kay Hnr General Editor of Intl Biography 1973-; Schlrshp upon grad from HS; Resolution for Disting Serv to Student Aid Commiss 1985; Cert of Merit form CA Community Colls EOPS Assoc 1985; Cert of Apprec for Outstanding Dedicated Serv 1985; Cert of Awd from Marina Middle Schools 1985; Cert of Apprec for Support of Mathematics Engrg & Sci Acheivement 1986; Educational Acad Achievement Awd 1987; Cert of Commendation Natl Assn of Negro Bus & Professional Women's Clubs Inc 1987; Certificate of Award for Exceptional Achievement 1989; Woman of the Year Award 1989; Education Award for Development of Community Based Education Centers 1989; Certificate for Distinguished Services to the San Francisco Board of Education,SFrancisco Unified School District Board of Education, 1982-90; Certificate for Outstanding Services to San Francisco Board of Education, San Francisco African American Historical and Cultural Society, Inc, 1982-90; Certificate for Outstanding Services Rendered to the San Francisco Board of Education, San Francisco Alliance of Black School Educators, 1982-90; Alpha Kappa Alpha Plaque, Outstanding Service on the San Francisco Board of Education. **Home Addr:** 116 St Elmo Way, San Francisco, CA 94127.

WILSON, SONALI BUSTAMANTE (Z. SONALI BUSTAMANTE)
Attorney. **Personal:** Born May 31, 1958, Cleveland, OH; daughter of F Joy Simmons Bustamante and John H Bustamante; married N Stephen Wilson II, Apr 12, 1991; children: Martine Celeste. **Educ:** Boston University, Boston, MA, BA, 1980; Harvard University, Boston, MA, ALM, 1983; Georgetown University Law Ctr, Washington, DC, JD, 1986. **Career:** Office of Chief of Compliance, District of Columbia, Department of Consumer and Regulatory Affairs, law clerk, 1984-86; Supreme Court of Ohio, clerk, 1987; Arter & Hadden, Cleveland, OH, associate, 1986, litigation, 1988-. **Orgs:** American Bar Association, Pre-Law Counseling Committee, Young Lawyers Division; Cleveland Bar Association, Young Lawyer's Exec Council, 1988-; corresponding secretary, Links Inc of Cleveland; co-chair, National Trends, 1988-; Girlfriends of Cleveland, 1990-; board of trustees, Womenspace, 1988-91; United Way, Government Relations Committee, 1991-; Citizen's League of Greater Cleveland, 1990-. **Honors/Awds:** Citation for Achievement in Organization and Leadership from Massachusetts House of Representatives, 1979; Citation in Recognition of Service in Recruiting Young Adults for Boston NAACP from Gov King of Massachusetts, 1979. **Business Addr:** Associate, Arter and Hadden, 1100 Huntington Bldg, Cleveland, OH 44115.

WILSON, STANLEY CHARLES
Educator. **Personal:** Born Feb 2, 1947, Los Angeles, CA; son of Eleanor Mae Reid Wilson and Ernest Charles Wilson; married Jacquelyn Patricia Bellard; children: Jendayi Asabi. **Educ:** Chouinard Art School, 1965; California State Polytechnic Univ, Pomona, 1966; California State Univ, Los Angeles, CA, 1967; Otis Art Inst, Los Angeles, CA, BFA 1969, MFA, 1971;. **Career:** Jr Art Center, Los Angeles, CA, instructor, 1969-72; Southwestern Coll, Chula Vista, CA, asst professor, 1972-73; Otis Art Inst, Parsons Watts Towers, instructor, 1981; California State Polytechnic Univ, Pomona, CA, prof Visual Art, 1984-, Univ Art Gallery, dir, 1988-. **Orgs:** Gallery curator dir, California State Polytechnic Univ, Pomona, CA, 1975-85; planning & dir, Los Angeles Weave, Los Angeles Olympic Exhibit, 1984 planning bd west coast black artist Exhib, 1976; Brand Art Center, Glendale, CA; bd advisors, Watts Towers Art Center, Los Angeles, CA, 1977-79; bd artists, Brockman Gallery Productions, Los Angeles, CA, 1980-85; bd advisors, Africa Quarter, California State Polytechnic Univ, 1984-85; awards panelist, New Genre Fellowships, Gal Arts Council, Sacramento, CA, 1989; bd of advisors, Latin Amer Quarter, California Polytechnic Univ, Pomona, CA, 1989; award panelist, sculpture, California Arts Council, Sacramento, CA, 1990; awards panelist, sculpture, Colorado Council of Arts and Humanities, 1991; board of advisors, gallery committee, Armony Art Cen, Pasadena, CA, 1990-91; Illinois Arts Council, Fellowship Awards Panelist, 1991-; chmn, City of Pasadena, Arts Comm, 1997; natl develop comm, studio art, advanced placement, Princeton, NJ. **Honors/Awds:** Works published in Black Artist on Art, Vol #2, Lewis & Waddy 1971, Afro-Amer Artist, Boston Public Library 1973; Nominated Fulbright Fellowship West & East Africa, 1984-85; Intl Reg of Profiles, Cambridge, England, 1981; visiting artist in residence Aberdeen, SD, 1975; Art works in permanent collection of Atlanta Life Insurance Co & Prairie Coll, Texas A&M & Univ Union, California Polytechnic Univ, 1984, 1981, 1977; awarded artist fellowship; Natl Endowment of Art; artist in residence studio museum in Harlem, NY, 1986-87; awarded meritorious & professional promise award by California Polytechnic Univ, Pomona, CA, 1986; catalog, 6 African Amer Artist, California State Univ, Dominquez Hills, CA, 1989; California Art Review, 2nd edition, Chicago, Il,1989; California Art Review, 3rd editi Chicago, IL, 1991; 2 Man Exhibition, Sparc Gallery, Venice, CA, 1990; 1 Man Exhibition, San Antonio Art Institute, San Antonio, TX, 1992; visiting artist, University of Nevada-Las Vegas, 1990; LACTC, Metro Rail Commission, 1991; Pasadena Arts Commission, City of Pasadena, Visual Art Fellowship, 1991; California Polytechnic University, Pomona, Outstanding Professor, 1991; Served on Fellowship Award Panel, California Arts Council, Sacramento, California; Served on AP Review Panel Trenton, New Jersey; Curated/selected art works for Bakerfield College's Exhibition, Initational, Space Gallery, Los Angeles, CA, 1995; Appointed Arts Commission, City of Pasadena, California. **Home Addr:** 2704 W Ave 34, Los Angeles, CA 90065. **Business Phone:** (909)869-3508.

WILSON, STEPHANIE Y.
Economist. **Personal:** Born Feb 16, 1952, Pittsburgh, PA. **Educ:** Goddard Coll, BA 1973; State Univ of New York at Stonybrook, MA 1975, PhD 1978. **Career:** Abt Associates, Washington DC, vice pres & area mgr 1985-86, managing vice pres 1987-92, group vice pres, 1992-. **Orgs:** Past pres Natl Economic Assn, 1989-91; mem American Economic Assn; Professional Services Coun; US-Africa Business Coun; Society for International Development, past board member; US-South Africa Business Coun; US-Russian Business Coun; Corp. Coun on Africa; Association for Women in Development. **Business Addr:** Group Vice Pres, Abt Associates Inc, 4800 Montgomery Ln, Bethesda, MD 20814.

WILSON, THOMAS A., JR.
Banker. **Personal:** Born Sep 25, 1951, Baltimore, MD; son of Margaret R Stokes and Thomas A Wilson Sr; married Diane P Freeman, May 31, 1986; children: Cedric T, Dexter N. **Educ:** Morgan State University, BS, 1973. **Career:** Industrial Bank of Washington, comptroller of the currency, bank examiner, 1974-86, vice pres/loan review officer, 1986-88, senior vp/controller, 1988-. **Business Addr:** Senior VP/Controller, Industrial Bank of Washington, 4812 Georgia Ave NW, Washington, DC 20011-4500, (202)722-2000.

WILSON, TREVOR
Professional basketball player. **Personal:** Born Mar 16, 1968, Los Angeles, CA. **Educ:** Univ of California at Los Angeles, Los Angeles, CA, 1986-90. **Career:** Atlanta Hawks, 1990-. **Business Addr:** Professional Basketball Player, Atlanta Hawks, 1 CNN Center NW S Tower, Suite 405, Atlanta, GA 30335-0001.

WILSON, VELMA J.
Events planner. **Personal:** Born Aug 28, 1934, Chicago, IL; daughter of Joseph C Brown & Rubye Therkeld Brown; married John E Wilson, Jul 24, 1960; children: Ginger Renee, Kelly JoAnne. **Educ:** Chicago Teachers College of Chicago State University, bechelors degree, education, 1958, masters degree, education, 1963. **Career:** Board of Education, Chicago, primary teacher, 1958-68; Woodlawn Organization, director of family focus, 1977; Chicago Urban League, consultant young parents program, 1979-83; Harold Washington for Mayor, scheduler, 1982-83; City of Chicago, director of tourism, 1984-89; The Wilson Group, president, 1989-. **Orgs:** Operation Push, board member, 1976-; Women's Board Chicago Urban League, president, 1985-87; University of Chicago Lying In Hospital, sustaining mem, 1979-; Dusable Museum Bd, board member, 1977-85; ETA Board, mem, treasurer, secretary, 1978-83; Delta Sigma Theta, 1958-; Links Inc, Windy City, chair, national trends committee, 1995-; Jesse Owens Foundation, friend committee chair, 1991-92. **Honors/Awds:** Operation Push, Salute to Excellence, Women's Delegation To Lebanon, 1979, Community Consciousness, 1977; Chicago Urban League, Outstanding Service, 1985; Norman LaHarry Scholarship Foundation, Woman of the Year, 1987; City of Chicago, Outstanding Service, 1989. **Home Addr:** 1031 E Hyde Park, 2nd Fl, Chicago, IL 60615, (773)752-6680.

WILSON, WALTER JAMES
Professional football player. **Personal:** Born Oct 6, 1966, Baltimore, MD. **Educ:** East Carolina Univ, criminal justice major. **Career:** San Diego Chargers, wide receiver, 1990-. **Honors/Awds:** Set East Carolina Univ record with 91 receptions for 1,670 yards and 16 touchdowns; honorable mention all-America, Sporting News. **Business Addr:** Professional Football Player, San Diego Chargers, Jack Murphy Stadium, 9449 Friars Rd, San Diego, CA 92108.

WILSON, WESLEY CAMPBELL
Management consultant. **Personal:** Born Nov 29, 1931, Philadelphia, PA; son of Emily Wilson and Wesley Wilson; married Elaine Epps; children: Carl B, Wayne K, Michael K, Eric W. **Educ:** Morgan St U, BS 1954; The Coll of Wm & Mary, MEd 1974, adv cert educ 1978; Ed.D l986. **Career:** The Coll of Wm & Mary in VA, asst to the pres 1976-; C & W Asso Inc vice pres 1976-; The Coll of Wm & Mary, asst to the pres 1974-76. **Orgs:** Chmn Gov's commn Adv Gov of VA on EEO 1975-79; chmn sch bd Newport News VA Pub Sch 1977-; bd of trustees Peninsula United Way 1979-; mem Newport News Dem Com 1974-; exec bd 1st Dist Black Caucus 1975-; pres Alpha Alpha Chap Omega Psi Phi 1975-76. **Honors/Awds:** Citizen of Yr, Omega Psi Phi Newport News VA 1977 & 78; Man of Yr, Peninsula Negro Bus & Prof Women 1979; Educ & Politics Strange Bedfellows, Reading in VA 1979. **Military Serv:** AUS lt col 1954-74; Legion of Merit, Vietnamese Croos, Bronze Star, Dist Flying Cross all 1964-65. **Business Addr:** C & W Associates Inc, 825 Diligence Dr, Newport News, VA 23606.

WILSON, WILLIAM E.
Dentist, educator. **Personal:** Born Apr 12, 1937, Lebanon, OH; son of Mary Helen and Joseph Fredrick; married Doris Ashworth; children: William, Edwina, Edward II, Chester. **Educ:** Tennessee St Univ, BS 1951; Meharry Dental Coll, DDS 1955. **Career:** Malone College, educator; Sociol Inst Malone Coll, educator; Ohio Mobile Dental, dentist/pres, 1982-94; Bridgeworld Dental Health Education Corp, vice pres, 1995-; Canton Community Health Clinic, dental director, 1996. **Orgs:** Pres Canton Health Admin Comm, 1962-63; Canton City School Steering Comm, 1968-69; vice pres, Canton Dental Soc; SCDS; ASPDC; Charter Commr, City of Canton 1967; pres, Canton Black Coalition; US Civil Rights Comm of OH, 1969-80; Canton Welfare Fed Exc Com; mem NAACP; Kiwanian; United Fund Budget Comm, 1960-75; vice pres, Tri Co March of Dimes 1979-80; pres Buckeye St Dental Soc 1977-80; chmn Canton United Negro Coll Fund; chmn Campaign for Canton Black United Fund 1978-79; pres Urban League; bd Red Cross; tst Nat Dental Assn; tst OH Dental Assn; pres Children Dental Assn; Amer Dental; Assn Educator of Am Kiwanis; pres Tri Co March of Dimes 1976-77, 1977-; co-chmn, US Gov Urban Project; chmn, Educ Com of US CRC for OH Comm Planning Com City Of Canton Human Relations; Alpha Phi Alpha Franity; City of Canton, Health Planning Committee, 1991-92; Canton Health Community, bd of dirs; HM Club, Northeast Community, board. **Honors/Awds:** Citizen of the Year, 1968; JC of the Year, 1963; Human Relation Award City of Canton, 1968; Martin Luther King Humanitarian, Award State of Ohio, 1992. **Military Serv:** US Army Captain dental corp, 1955-57.

WILSON, WILLIAM JULIUS
Sociologist, educator. **Personal:** Born Dec 20, 1935, Derry Township, PA; son of Pauline Bracy Wilson and Esco Wilson (deceased); married Beverly Huebner; children: Colleen, Lisa, Carter, Paula. **Educ:** Wilberforce Univ, BA 1958; Bowling Green State Univ, MA 1961; Washington State Univ, PhD 1966. **Career:** Univ of MA, Amherst, asst prof of sociology 1965-69, assoc prof of sociology 1969-71; French-American Foundation, visiting professor of American studies, Ecole des Hautes Etudes en Sciences Sociales, Paris, 1989-90; College de France, Paris, lecturer, social science, 1990; Univ of Chicago, asso prof of sociology 1972-75, prof of sociology 1975-80, chmn, Sociology Dept 1978-81, 1984-87, Lucy Flower disting serv prof, sociology 1984-90, Lucy Flower Univ prof of sociology and public policy, 1990-96; Harvard Univ, Malcolm Wiener prof of social policy, prof of Afro-American studies, 1996-. **Orgs:** Chmn, rsch adv com Chicago Urban League, 1976-85; bd of dirs Social Sci Rsch Counc 1979-85; natl bd A Philip Randolph Inst 1981-; bd of dirs Chicago Urban League 1983-97; natl bd Inst for Rsch on Poverty, 1983-87; Spencer Foundation, 1987-96; George M Pullman Found, 1986-93; Carnegie Council on Adoloscent Devel, 1986-95; William T Grant Foundation's Commn on Youth and America's Future, 1986-88;bd of dirs Center for Advanced Study in the Behavioral Sciences 1989-95; bd of dirs Russell Sage Found 1989-; bd of trustees Spelman College 1989-; elected member American Philosophical Society 1990; elected member National Academy of Sciences 1991; Jerome Levy Economics Institute; Bard College, board of trustees, 1992-; Twentieth Century Fund, trustee, 1992-; Center on Budget and Policy Priorities, 1987-; Kennedy School of Government, Harvard University, Center for Public Policy,88-; Next AME Foundation, 1989-; National Humanities Center, 1990-; The Aspen Institute, Domestic Strategy Group, 1992-; Consortium of Social Science Assns, 1991-95; board of directors, Manpower Demonstration Research Corporation (New York), 1993-; President's Commission on White House Fellowships, 1994-; board of directors, Public/Private Ventures (Philadelphia), 1994-; President's Committee on the Natl Medal of Science, National Science Foundation, 1994-; Ctr for Public Integrity, advisory bd, 1995-; Wilberforce Univ, bd of trustees, 1995-; National Urban League, bd of dir, 1995-; National Academy of Science, Committee on Science, Engineering & Public Policy, 1995-98; Frederick D Patterson Research Institute (United Negro College Fund), bd of advisors, 1996-99. **Honors/Awds:** MacArthur Prize Fellow, The John D and Catherine T MacArthur Found, 1987-92; Fellow Amer Acad of Arts and Sciences, 1988; Fellow Amer Assn for the Advancement of Science 1988; The Godkin Lecturer, Harvard Univ 1988; Dr of Humane Letters Honoris Causa: Depaul Univ, 1989, Santa Clara Univ, 1988, Long Island Univ, 1986, Loyola Coll of Maryland, 1988, Columbia Coll in Chicago, 1988; Dr of Laws Honoris Causa, Mt Holyoke Coll, 1989, Marquette Univ, 1989; Distinguished Alumnus Award, Washington State Univ, 1988; C Wright Mills Award for the truly disadvantaged, Society for the Study of Social Problems, 1988; North Central Sociological Associations Scholarly Achievement Award, 1988; Washington-Monthly's Annual Book Award, 1988; American Sociological Association, Dubois, Johnson, Frazier Award, 1990; Tulane University, Bard College, John Jay College of Criminal Justice, Doctor of Humane Letters Honoris Causa, 1992; University of Pennsylvania, Southern Illinois University at Edwardsville, 1993; Bowling Green State University, State University of New York Binghampton, Princeton University, 1994; Doctor of Laws Honoris Causa, Northwestern University, 1993, Haverford Coll, 1995, Columbia Univ, 1995, Rutgers Univ, 1995, Morehouse Coll, 1996, Johns Hopkins Univ, 1996, Barat Coll, 1997, Niagra Univ, 1997, Dartmouth Coll, 1997, Univ of Amsterdam, 1998; Rhodes College, Memphis TN, Frank E Seidman Distinguished Award in Political Economy, 1994; American Academy of Political and Social Sciences, fellow, 1997; Time Magazine, One of 25 Most Influential Americans, 1996; Book When Work Disappears selected by NY Times Book Review as one of the notable books of 1996, and selected for the Sidney Hillman Foundation Award; American Academy of Achievement's 1997 Salute to Excellence guest of honor. **Special Achievements:** Author: Through Different Eyes, NY Oxford Press, 1973; The Declining Significance of Race, Univ of Chicago Press, 1978; The Truly Disadvantaged, Univ of Chicago Press, 1987. **Military Serv:** US Army, spec 4 class, 1958-60; Meritorious Serv Awd 1960. **Business Addr:** Professor, Afro-American Studies Dept, Harvard University, JF Kennedy School of Government, 79 JF Kennedy St, Cambridge, MA 02138.

WILSON, WILLIE FREDERICK (KWADWO I. BOAFO)
Cleric, educator. **Personal:** Born Mar 8, 1944, Newport News, VA; son of Samuel B & Lovey E Wilson; married Mary Lewis Wilson, Sep 29, 1973; children: Anika, Kalilia, Bashiri, Hamani. **Educ:** Ohio Univ, BS, 1966; Howard Univ, Divinity School, MDiv, 1969; Doctoral Studies, 1969-71. **Career:** Union Temple Baptist Church, pastor, 1973-. **Special Achievements:** Publication, ''The African American Wedding Manual''.

WILSON, WILLIE JAMES
Professional baseball player. **Personal:** Born Jul 9, 1955, Montgomery, AL. **Career:** Outfielder: Kansas City Royals, 1976-90, Oakland A's, 1991-92, Chicago Cubs, 1992-. **Special Achievements:** Sporting News, AL Silver Slugger team, 1980; Rawlings Sporting Goods Company, Sporting News, AL Gold Glove, outfielder, 1980. **Business Addr:** Professional Baseball Player, Chicago Cubs, Wrigley Field, 1060 W Addison St, Chicago, IL 60613, (312)404-2827.

WILSON, WILLIE MAE
Community service executive. **Personal:** Born Mar 18, 1942, Birmingham, AL; married William L; children: Bertrand LaMarr, Pelina. **Educ:** Knoxville College, BA; Univ of MN, MA. **Career:** St Paul Urban Leag, president, CEO, 1974-, chief executive officer, 1972-74, adminstr dep; Twin Cities Met Cncl, 1971; St Paul Urban Coal, housing & coord 1969-; Urban Leag, housing dir 1967-69; Econ Dev & Employ St Paul Urban Leag, acting dir 1967; Urban Leag Comm, organizer proj 1966-67; St Paul Bpu Lib, asst librar 1965-66; MN St Comm against Discrim, research clerk 1964. **Orgs:** Chpsn bd of comm St Paul Housing & Redev Auth & Comm 1972-76; chpsn Unit Way Cncl of Agcy Dir; vice pres St Paul Ramsey Counc of Agcy Dir; bd of dirs 1st Nat Bank of St Paul; Cit Leag; bd of dirs Comm Dev Corp; Oper 85 Planning Comm; MN Met Org for Displaced Women; Cncl of Executive Director Nat Urban Leag, president, 1980-82; tri-chmn, St Paul Publ Sch Sec Educ Adv Comm on Desegrat; Delta Sigma Theta Sor; Iota Phi Lambda Bus & Prof Womens Sor; Am Soc of Planning Off; Am Soc for Pub Administrn; St Paul Urban Leag; NAACP; vice pres Urban N Non-prof Housing Corp 1973; del St Paul Dem Farm Labor 1974; co-chmn Summit Univ Coalition apptd Joint Planning & Coord Act for Ramsey Co by St Paul Mayor Lawrence Cohen 1973. **Honors/Awds:** Apptd Chair, St Paul Housing Authority, St Paul Mayor George Latimer 1976; Schlrshp Cup, Birmingham Exch Club 1960; Samuel Ullman Schlrshp Awd 1960; Deans List, Knoxville Coll 1960-64; Woodrow Wilson Enrichment Schlrshp, Col Univ 1964; US Dept Housing & Urban Dev Urban Studies; Grad Work Flwshp, Univ of MN; grad 1st out of 116 stud Ullman HS 1960; grad 5th out of 95 stud Knoxville 1964. **Business Addr:** President, CEO, St Paul Urban League, 401 Shelby Ave, St Paul, MN 55102.

WILSON, WILSON W.
Military officer (retired). **Personal:** Born May 31, 1942, Quachita Parish, LA; son of Christel Jones Wilson and Phillip Wilson; married Georgia Crawford Wilson, Mar 1963; children: Suzzon E, Ellen M, Warren M, Gladys C. **Educ:** Southern Univ, BA 1964; McNeese State Univ, Roosevelt Univ, Univ KY, graduate study; Western KY Univ, M Public Admin 1975; further studies completed at Northeast State Univ. **Career:** AUS, min army off procurement; rep of Vietnam joint US staff for military assistance 1969-70, supply part officer 2nd infantry div Fort Polk LA 1978, 5th AUS headquarters staff off deputy chief of staff for ROTC, equal opportunity officer 5th infantry div Ft Polk LA, deputy comm commander Wertheim Military comm Wertheim Germany; Monroe City School System, science teacher, 1989-91; self employed, Monroe, LA, real estate broker, 1988-. **Orgs:** Office holder Hardin Co KY Branch NAACP 1973-75; Assn of AUS 1965-73; Minority Business Assn Alpha Phi Alpha Fraternity 1963; YMCA 1963; Prince Hall Masonic 1967; member, Monroe NAACP, Ouachita Branch, 1988-. **Honors/Awds:** Numerous military decor; rec'd numerous commend for part in educ seminars MW U's; part in lecture series at these same MW Univs; numerous TV appearances disc the role of black soldier in AUS & black military hist; Legion of Merit Award, US Army, 1989. **Military Serv:** AUS lt col 1964-89; numerous military awards. **Business Addr:** PO Box 265, Monroe, LA 71210.

WILSON-GEORGE, SYBIL
Sports franchise executive. **Career:** Miami Heat, Miami, FL, director of corporate education, special assistant to the executive vice pres, currently. **Honors/Awds:** Dade County Public School's Exemplary Partnership Award. **Business Addr:** Special Assistant to the Executive Vice Pres, Miami Heat, 1 SE 3rd Ave, Miami, FL 33131.

WILSON-SMITH, WILLIE ARRIE
Educator (retired). **Personal:** Born Jan 12, 1929, Charlotte, NC; daughter of Katie A Wilson Vance and Booker T Wilson (deceased); married Jack, Aug 27, 1949. **Educ:** Johnson C Smith Univ, BA 1956; Western Reserve Univ, MEd 1962. **Career:** Charlotte Mecklenburg School System, tchr 1957-80 retired; JB Iveys Millinery Shoe Repairing, 1951-54; Belks Shoe Repairing, 1954-57. **Orgs:** Life mem NEA; life mem NCAE; life mem NCACT; mem Alpha Kappa Alpha Sor Inc; Mecklenburg County Dem Womens Club; deputy dir 9th Dist Dem Women 1977-79; democratic candidate Charlotte City Council Dist 1, 1977; NC Dem Exec Comm; Womens Forum of NC; Charlotte BPC; past mem Charlotte CRC 1974-82; life mem New Emmanuel Congregational United Church of Christ; past mem Charlotte Mecklenburg NCCJ; PTA; Girl Scout Adv; Appt Study Comm on Relation Between Professional Employee Assn & Schl Bd 1973-75; apptd NC Adv Comm On Tchr Educ 1974-76; soror of yr AKA 1965; only black elected Mecklenburg Co Dem of Yr 1977; bd of trustees Central Piedmont Comm Coll 1979-87; volunteer office helper Charlotte Business League 1986, 1987; treasurer New Emannuel Congl UCC, 1989; chair of 12th US Congressional District-NC, 1997-99; Governor appointee to NC College Foundation bd of trustees, 1997-; NC High School volunteer 1997-. **Honors/Awds:** Grad Adv Award 1967; Oper Cir 1966; Apprec Award Gamma Delta 1965-74; Apprec Award Alpha Lambda Omega 1965-74; Service/Plaque New Emmanuel Congregational UCC 1987; Service/Plaque Central Piedmont Community Coll 1987. **Home Addr:** 1822 Grier Ave, Charlotte, NC 28216-5043.

WILTZ, CHARLES J.
Dentist. **Personal:** Born Oct 18, 1934, New Orleans, LA; married Vivianne Carey (deceased); children: Charles Jr, Cary E.

Educ: Xavier Univ, BS 1956; Howard Univ Sch of Dentistry, DDS 1967. **Career:** MA Genl Hosp, asst hematlgst 1959-61; Amer Polymer & Chem Corp, jr orgnc chmst 1962-63; Westside VA Hosp, staff dent 1968-69; Mile Sq Hlth Ctr, Chicago staff dentist 1970-71; Private Practice, dentist 1970-. **Orgs:** Consult IL Dental Serv; mem Academy Gen Dentistry, Chicago Dental Soc, IL State Dental Soc, Amer Dental Assn, Natl Dental Assn; Chi Delta Mu; bus mgr 1973 memshp chmn 1974 Lincoln Dental Soc; bd mem Billiken Wrld of Arts & Scis; mem Alpha Phi Alpha. **Honors/Awds:** Awds city & state hs basketball LA 1952; Outstanding Merit of Achvmt VA Hosp 1968; Ten Best Dressed Blk Men 1974-75-76 Chicago. **Military Serv:** AUS sp 4 1957-59 1961-62. **Business Addr:** 8701 S Racine Ave, Chicago, IL 60620.

WILTZ, PHILIP G., JR.
Physician. **Personal:** Born Jun 5, 1930, New Orleans, LA; married Barbara Allen; children: Teresa, Phyllis, Yvette. **Educ:** Savannah State Coll, BS 1952; NY Univ, MA 1956; Howard Univ, MD 1968. **Career:** NY Public Schs, teacher 1957-60; Washington DC Public Schs, teacher 1961-64; US Public Health Svcs, internship 1968-69, resident orthopedic surgery 1969-73; Private Practice, physician orthopedic surgery. **Orgs:** Mem Alpha Phi Alpha Frat. **Honors/Awds:** Phi Delta Kappa Hon Soc NY Univ 1957; Sigma Phi Frat. **Military Serv:** AUS corpl 1952-54; USPHS lt comdr 1968-73. **Business Addr:** 75 Piedmont Ave NE, #504, Atlanta, GA 30303.

WIMBERLY, EDWARD P.
Educator, clergyman. **Personal:** Born Oct 22, 1943, Philadelphia, PA; son of Evelyn P Wimberly and Edgar V Wimberly; married Anne Streaty, Jun 4, 1966; children: Michael Haynie. **Educ:** Univ of Arizona, BA, 1965; Boston Univ, School of Theology, STB, 1968, STM, 1971; Boston Univ Graduate School, PhD, 1976. **Career:** Emmanuel Church, pastor, 1966-68; St Andrews United Methodist Church, pastor, 1968-74; Worcester Council of Churches, urban minister, 1969-72; Solomon Carter Fuller Mental Health Center, pastoral consultant, 1973-75; Interdenominational Theological Center, Atlanta, assoc professor, 1975-83; Oral Roberts Univ, School of Theology, Tulsa, assoc professor, assoc dean, doctoral studies, 1983-85; Garrett Evangelical Theological Seminary, Evanston, IL, assoc professor, pastoral care, 1985-. **Orgs:** Bd of dirs, United Methodist Children's Home, 1977-83, Interdenominational Theological Center, 1982-83; mem, Amer Assn of Pastoral Counselors, 1976-, Amer Assn of Marriage & Family Therapists, 1976-, Friends of Wesley Comm Center, 1983-; mem & bd of dirs, Destination Discovery, 1983-. **Honors/Awds:** Serv award, United Methodist Children's Home, 1983; published, "Pastoral Counseling and Spiritual Values," 1982; co-author with Anne Wimberly, "Liberation and Human Wholeness," 1986; co-author with wife, "One House One Hope," 1989. **Business Addr:** Assoc Prof, Pastoral Counseling/Psych, 2121 Sheridan Rd Garrett Evangel Theological Seminary, Evanston, IL 60201.

WIMBERLY, MARCUS
Professional football player. **Personal:** Born Jul 8, 1974. **Educ:** Miami (Fla.). **Career:** Atlanta Falcons, defensive back, 1997-. **Business Addr:** Professional Football Player, Atlanta Falcons, Two Falcon Place, Suwanee, GA 30174, (404)945-1111.

WIMBISH, C. BETTE
Attorney. **Personal:** Born Mar 24, 1924, Perry, FL; daughter of Ola Mae Howard Davis and Tom Davis; married Ralph Melvin Wimbish, Nov 12, 1944 (deceased); children: Barbara Griffin, Ralph, Terence. **Educ:** FL Agr & Mech U, BS 1944, JD 1967. **Career:** FL Dept of Commerce, dep sec 1973-; City of St Petersburg, vice-mayor 1971-73, city cncl 1969-71; St Petersburg, gen law prac 1968-73; Pub Sch Sys, Hillsborough Co, instr, 1947-52; FL Mem Coll, instr 1945-46. **Orgs:** Mem Leag of Women Voters; mem Am Arbitration Assn; pres Caribe Export Mgmt Co; legal adv Delta Sigma Theta Sor; Nat Cncl of Negro Women; bd dirs Am Civil Libs Union; NAACP; bd mem S Reg Cncl, Task Forces on Sthrn Rural Dev & Ec Dev; FL Bar Assn; FL Gov Bar Assn; vice pres selec com Dem NatCom; consult CRS, Support Serv for US Dept of Justice & Ofc of Contract Compliance Support Serv of US Dept of Labor; guest lectr Univ of S FL; ABA; NBA; past mem Factory-Built Hsng, Adv Cncl; mem Commn on Ed Outreach & Svc; FL Dept of Commerce & Employer-employee Rels Adv Cncl; bd trustees The S Ctr for Intrntl Studies; committeewoman at large Dem Nat Com; FL A&M Univ Cncl of Advs; arbitrator, Labor Panel of Federal Medication and Conciliation Service, 1980-. **Honors/Awds:** Outstndng Woman in Gov Award, Orlando FL, Chap of Delta Sigma Theta Sor 1975; FL Women of Dist 1974. **Home Addr:** 7200 34th St S, St Petersburg, FL 33711-4932.

WIMBUSH, F. BLAIR
Attorney. **Personal:** Born Jul 24, 1955, Halifax County, VA; son of Sue Carol Lovelace Wimbush and Freddie B Wimbush; married Jane Seay Wimbush, Aug 1981. **Educ:** Univ of Rochester, BA 1977; Univ of Virginia, JD 1980; Duke Univ, Fuqua School of Business, Norfolk Southern Management Dev Program, 1996. **Career:** Norfolk & Western Railway Co, attorney 1980-83; Norfolk Southern Corp, solicitor 1983-85, asst general solicitor 1985-89, general attorney 1989-96, general solicitor, 1996-. **Orgs:** Mem Amer, Natl, VA, Old Dominion and Norfolk-Portsmouth Bar Assns; mem Assn of Transportation Practitioners, VA State Bar; mem Roanoke Museum of Fine Arts 1981-, secty 1982-84, vice pres 1984-86, pres 1986-87; mem Legal Aid Soc of Roanoke Valley 1982-86; mem United Way Special Study of Agencies 1983; mem Roanoke Co Transportation Safety Commn 1984-85; mem Roanoke City Arts Commn 1984-87; mem VA Commn for the Arts Area III Adv Panel 1985-87, Area VI Adv Panel 1988-90; mem natl bd dirs Big Brothers/Big Sisters of Amer 1986-92; mem Western VA Foundation for the Arts and Sciences 1986-87; American Red Cross, Tidewater 1990-93; American Heart Assn, Tidewater 1990-92; Virginia Commission on Women and Minorities in the Legal System, president, 1992-93; Virginia Law Foundation, board of directors & vp, 1994-95, pres, 1996-97; VA Symphony Orchestra, bd of dirs; Univ of VA Law School Alumni Council; Univ of VA Law School Business Advisory Council; Virginia State Bar Professionalism Course Faculty; VA State Bar, bd of governors, section on education. **Honors/Awds:** Roanoke Valley Chamber of Commerce Leadership Roanoke Valley 1984-85. **Business Addr:** General Solicitor, Norfolk Southern Corporation, 3 Commercial Place, Norfolk, VA 23510-2191, (757)629-2656.

WIMBUSH, GARY LYNN
College administrator. **Personal:** Born Oct 13, 1953, Warren, OH; married Aundra Diana Lewis; children: Brennan Jevon, Kyle Jameson. **Educ:** Oakwood Coll, BA 1975; Andrews Univ, MDiv 1977; Western State Univ Sch of Law, JD 1984. **Career:** Allegheny West Conference of SDA, sr clergymen 1975-80; Southeastern CA Conf of SDA, sr Clergyman 1980-84; Oakwood College, dir of admissions & recruitment1984-. **Orgs:** Chaplain (volunteer) Orange County Hospital System 1982-84; business mgr Viewpoint, A Theological Journal 1983-85. **Honors/Awds:** Pastor of the Year Awd Allegheny West Conference of SDA 1979; Outstanding Young Men of Amer 1986. **Business Addr:** Dir of Admissions/Recruitment, Oakwood College, Oakwood Road, Huntsville, AL 35896.

WIMP, EDWARD LAWSON
Owner. **Personal:** Born Feb 12, 1942, Chicago, IL. **Educ:** Roosevelt U, BS, BA 1966. **Career:** King Terco McDonald's Franchises, owner-operator 1969-; DEW Rlty, vp, broker 1961-69. **Orgs:** Pres Black McDonald's Operator's Assn 1985; bd mem Chicagoland McDonald's Operators Assn 1985; exec bd mem Nat Black McDonald's Operators Assn; bd, chmn Wabash YMCA 1985; bd of Mgrs Met YMCA'S 1985; mem Sigma Pi Phi Frat 1985. **Honors/Awds:** Nat Champion & World Speed Record Hldr, Am Hot Rod Assn 1963; Philanthropic World Community of Islam 1978; Outstndng Young Am US 1979; James H Tilehman Award, YMCA 1979. **Military Serv:** USNG Res 1965-71. **Business Addr:** 449 E 31st St, Chicago, IL 60616.

WINANS, BEBE (BENJAMIN)
Gospel vocalist. **Personal:** Born in Detroit, MI; son of David Winans Sr and Delores Winans; married Debra Denise; children: Miya Destiny. **Career:** Gospel duo with sister CeCe Winans beginning at Mount Zion Church of God and Christ, Detroit, MI; PTL Club, duo, 1982; Capitol Records, duo, currently; albums include: BeBe and CeCe Winans, 1987, Heaven, 1988, Different Lifestyles, 1991; Relationships, 1994; BeBe Winans, 1997; television appearance on "Ebony/Jet Showcase," 1991. **Special Achievements:** Stage appearances included Whitney Houston joining the duo to sing "Love Said Not So," 1989; 34th Grammy Awards, Best Contemporary Soul Gospel Album, 1992. **Business Addr:** Gospel Singer, c/o Sparrow Records, EMI Christian Music Group, PO Box 5085, 101 Winners Circle, Brentwood, TN 37024-5085.

WINANS, CECE (PRISCILLA WINANS LOVE)
Gospel vocalist. **Personal:** daugHter of David Winans Sr and Delores Winans; married Alvin Love; children: Alvin Love III, Ashley Love. **Career:** People That Love Club, gospel singer, 1982-85; gospel singe with brother BeBe Winans, albums include: BeBe and CeCe Winans, 1987; Heaven, 1988; Different Lifestyles, 1991; Relationships, 1994; beauty parlor, co-owner. **Honors/Awds:** Grammy Award, Best Contemporary Soul Gospel Album, Different Lifestyles, 1992. **Business Addr:** Gospel Singer, Relationships, c/o Sparrow Records, EMI Christian Music Group, PO Box 5085, 101 Winners Circle, Brentwood, TN 37024-5085.

WINANS, MARVIN L.
Cleric, vocalist. **Personal:** Born Mar 5, 1958, Detroit, Mi; son of David and Delores Winans; children: Mario, Marvin Jr, Josiah. **Career:** Member of the gospel group The Winans; albums include: Let My People Go, 1986; Decisions, 1988; Return, 1990; Introducing Perfect Praise, solo, 1992; Heart & Soul, 1995; Perfecting Church, pastor, currently; Marvin L Winans Academy of Performing Arts, president of the school board, currently. **Orgs:** I Care International. **Honors/Awds:** Gospel Music Association, Dove Award, 3 times; Stellar Award, Best Gospel Group, 8 times; 6 Grammy Awards. **Special Achievements:** Starred in Don't Get God Started, play, New York City, 1987; Author, Marvin Winans: Image is Everything, 1996; Foreword Writer, Who's Who among African Americans, 9th edition, 1996. **Business Addr:** Pastor, Perfecting Church, 7616 E Nevada St, Detroit, MI 48234-3131, (313)365-3787.

WINBUSH, CLARENCE, JR.
Freelance photographer. **Personal:** Born Nov 6, 1948, Chicago, IL; son of Velva Mae Winbush and Clarence Winbush; married Alice Barnett Winbush (divorced 1982); children: Clarence Chris, David Lionel. **Educ:** Attended Olive Harvey, Chicago, IL, 1980-81; Roosevelt Univ, Chicago, IL, 1990-. **Career:** System technician, AT&T, 1969-91; freelance photographer, currently. **Orgs:** Chairperson, Alliance of Black Telecommunications Employees, 1987-89; comm relations vice pres, Chicago Southend Jaycee's, 1982-85; Scoutmaster, St John Baptist Church, 1981-86. **Honors/Awds:** Award of Merit, Southend Jaycee's, 1984; Award of Merit, Chicago Council, BSA, 1985; Fellowship Award, St John Church-Baptiste, 1986; Award of Merit, honorable mention, Museum of Science and Industry, 1985-91. **Business Addr:** Freelance photographer, PO Box 06-7734, Chicago, IL 60661-7734.

WINBUSH, RAYMOND ARNOLD
Educator. **Personal:** Born Mar 31, 1948, Pittsburgh, PA; son of Harold & Dorothy Winbush; divorced; children: Omari, Sharifa, Farati. **Educ:** Oakwood College, BA, 1970; University of Chicago, AM, 1973, PhD, 1976. **Career:** Oakwood College, asst prof, chair behavioral sciences, 1973-77; Alabama A&M University, assoc prof, psychology, 1977-80; Vanderbilt Univ, asst prof, human devel counseling, 1980-84; United Press Intl, vp corporate research, 1984-86; Vanderbilt Univ, asst provost, 1986-94, assoc prof, human devel and dir Johnson Black Cultural Center, 1991-. **Orgs:** Natl Council for Black Studies, treasurer, 1992-; Assn of Black Psychologists, 1992-; American Psychological Assn, 1993-; Girl Scouts of America, 1993-. **Honors/Awds:** Cleveland SCLC, 1990 MLK Award, 1990; Ebony Magazine, Leader of Information Highway Technology. **Special Achievements:** Anxiety & Afrocentricity, Black Issues in Higher Educ, 1994. **Business Addr:** Professor, The Bishop Joseph Johnson Black Cultural Center, Vanderbilt University, Box 1666, Station B, Nashville, TN 37235.

WINCHESTER, KENNARD
Professional basketball player. **Career:** Houston Rockets, currently. **Business Addr:** Professional Basketball Player, Houston Rockets, The Summit, 10 Greenway Plaza, Houston, TX 77046-1099.

WINDER, ALFRED M.
Business executive. **Educ:** Allan Hancock Jr Coll, AA 1966; Rockhurst Coll, BS Indust Rel 1969. **Career:** KS City Area Transp Authority, mgr equal employment/minority bus enterprise 1978-80; Saudi Public Transit Co, mgr admin/personnel 1980-83; Bi-State Devel Agency, dep gen mgr admin 1983-84; Suburban Bus/West Towns, gen mgr; Gary Public Transp Corp, pres, gen mgr. **Orgs:** Mem COMTO 1983-85; exec bd IN Transp Assoc; policy comm mem Northern IN Reg Plng Commiss; mem Gary IN C of C; exec, v,o, COMTO Natl 1986-; Anderson Boys Club bd mem 1986-. **Honors/Awds:** AAU All Amer Basketball San Francisco CA 1962-63; Jr Coll All Amer Basketball Allan Hancock Coll CA 1975-66; Natl Assoc Intercollegiate Athletics All Amer Basketball MO 1968-69; Outstanding Citizen's Awd Black United Appeal MO 1978; Contractor of the Year Awd MO-KS Contractors Assoc 1978; Volunteer of the Year Boys Clubs of Greater Kansas City 1977-79; Volunteer of the Year Awardee St Louis MO School Dist 1984; Prestigous Presidents Awd 1986. **Military Serv:** AUS Canine Corp pfc 1962-64; Presidio of San Francisco. **Business Addr:** President, General Manager, Gary Public Transporation Corp, 100 West 4th Avenue, Gary, IN 46402.

WINDER, SAMMY
Professional football player. **Personal:** Born Jul 15, 1959, Madison, MS. **Educ:** Univ of Southern Mississippi, attended. **Career:** Denver Broncos, running back, 1982-. **Orgs:** Lions Club, Ambassadors of Madison County. **Honors/Awds:** Post-season play: AFC Championship Game, 1986, 1987, 1989, NFL Championship Game, 1986, 1987, 1989, Pro Bowl, 1984, 1986. **Business Addr:** Professional Football Player, Denver Broncos, 13655 Broncos Pkwy, Englewood, CO 80112-4151.

WINDHAM, REVISH
Human rights specialist. **Personal:** Born May 31, 1940, Panola, AL; son of Lillie Windham and Ike Windham, Sr; married Janice Bowman, Sep 22, 1985. **Educ:** Morris Brown Coll, BA 1958-66; Old Dominion Coll, 1967; New York City Coll, 1963; GROW NYC; New York Univ, New York, NY, MPA, 1989. **Career:** New York City Dept Soc Srv, caseworker 1968-70; NYS Div for Youth, youth counselor 1970-83; Black Forum Magazine, editor in chief 1978-80; NYS Div for Youth, youth empl voc spec 1984-90; NYS Div of Human Rights, human rights specialist 1990-. **Orgs:** Poetry editor Black Forum Magazine 1975-77; bd mem Black Caucus of DFY Employees Inc 1974-90; pres Morris Brown Coll Alumni 1978-82; charter mem MLK, Jr Ctr for Soc Change NY 1978-, Support Grp Minorities in Criminal Justice 1978; Amer Correctional Assn, Natl Criminal Justice Assn, 369th Veteran's Assn, Inc., Phi Beta Sigma Fratenity, Inc; advisory board member, Tip Program, 1990-. **Honors/Awds:** Poet of Year J Marks Press 1972; award of Appreciation Black Caucus of DFY Empl Inc 1984, 1987, Morris Brown Coll Alumni Assn of NY, 1981, Phi Beta Sigma Fraternity, 1987, Natl Library of Poetry, Editor's Choice Award,

1989. **Military Serv:** USN petty ofc 3rd class 1964-68. **Business Addr:** Human Rights Specialist II, NYS Div for Human Rights, 270 Broadway, New York, NY 10007.

WINDHAM, RHONDA
Sports administrator. **Career:** Los Angeles Sparks, WNBA, general mgr. **Business Addr:** General Manager, Los Angeles Sparks, 3900 W. Manchester Blvd., Inglewood, CA 90306, (310)330-2434.

WINE, DONALD GARY
Automobile company executive. **Personal:** Born Aug 16, 1951, Benton, AR; son of James (deceased) & Margaret Wine; married Dorothy, Jun 1, 1974; children: Donald II, Steven Gary. **Educ:** Wayne State Univ, Liberal Arts, 1984; Central MI Univ, Master in Administration, 1986. **Career:** GM Corp, various positions, production mgr, 1991-92, acting plant mgr, 1992-94, plant mgr, 1994-95, plant mgr for Cadillac/luxury car div, 1995-. **Orgs:** Longhorn Counsel, Boy Scouts of Amer, bd of dir, 1994-; City of Arlington TX Chamber of Commerce, bd of dir, 1994-; City of Ypsilanti MI Chamber of Commerce, bd of dir, 1992-93; Arlington Ind Schools, bd of dir, 1994-. **Business Addr:** Plant Manager, GM Corp Cadillac (CLCD) Plant, 2500 East General Motor Blvd, Detroit, MI 48202, (313)972-6000.

WINEGLASS, HENRY
Pharmacist. **Personal:** Born Sep 11, 1938, Georgetown, SC; son of Albertha Drayton Hasbin (deceased) and Johnnie Wineglass (deceased); married Josephine Arkwright, May 28, 1965; children: Vincent Antonio (deceased), Sheri LaDonna. **Educ:** Howard Univ, Washington DC, BS, 1962. **Career:** Fantle's Drugstore (formerly Dart Drug Corp), Landover MD, pharmacist, 1965-90; Safeway Pharmacy, pharmacist, 1990-. **Orgs:** Amer Pharmaceutical Assn, 1965-; Natl Pharmaceutical Assn, 1965-; DC Pharmaceutical Assn, 1965-; sec, Lambda Chapter, Chi Delta Mu, 1976-94; sec/meeting planner, Chi Delta Mu Inc Grand Chapter, 1981-92; Maryland Pharmacists Assn, 1982-; Natl Coalition of Black Meeting Planners, 1986-89; sergeant-at-arms, Howard Univ Alumni Club, 1988-89; Chi Delta Mu, Grand Chapter, president elect, 1992-94; Chi Delta Mu Fraternity, grand president elect, 1992-94, grand president, 1994-96. **Honors/Awds:** Certif of Appreciation, Lambda Chapter, Chi Delta Mu, 1973 & 1985; Citation of Appreciation, Dart Drug Prof Services Dept, 1980; Certif of Appreciation, Langdon School PTA, 1981; Doctor of Pharmacy, Maryland Pharmacists Assn, 1982; Man of the Year, Lambda Chapter, Chi Delta Mu, 1986; Certif of Appreciation, Howard Univ Coll of Pharmacy & Pharmacal Sciences, 1987; Grand President's Award, Chi Delta Mu Grand Chapter, 1988; Man of the Year, Plymouth Congregational UCC Men's Club, 1988. **Military Serv:** US Army, SP-5, 1961-64; honorable discharge, 1967. **Home Addr:** 1509 Evarts St NE, Washington, DC 20018-2017.

WINFIELD, ARNOLD F.
Corporate secretary. **Personal:** Born Sep 29, 1926, Chicago, IL; married Florence Frye; children: Michael A, Donna Winfield-Terry. **Educ:** Howard Univ, BS 1949; Wayne State Univ, Grad Study Biochem 1949-51. **Career:** Ordinance Corp, chemist, 1952-59, biochemist, 1969-71; Abbott Labs, reg prod mgr, 1953-71, mgr, regional affairs, Admin Consumer Division, 1971-83; 2nd Ward Evanston, alderman 1963-; Winfield & Assoc, consult 1983-; Colfield Foods Inc, corp sec 1983-. **Orgs:** Mem NAACP, Urban League, ACS, Reg Affairs Prof Soc, ASQC, Alpha Phi Alpha, Evanston Neighbors at Work; bd mem, Victory Gardens Theater, 1979-. **Honors/Awds:** Recip Youth Alliance Scholarship 1943; Jr Chamber of Commerce Man of the Year 1964; Serv Award Ebenezer Church 1966. **Military Serv:** US Army, PFC, 1945-46; WWII Victory Medal. **Business Addr:** President, Winfield & Associates, 1840 Delany, Gurnee, IL 60031.

WINFIELD, DAVID MARK
Professional baseball player (retired). **Personal:** Born Oct 3, 1951, St Paul, MN; married Tonya; children: Arielle Arline, David Mark II. **Educ:** Univ of MN, Pol Sci. **Career:** Outfielder: San Diego Padres, 1973-80; New York Yankees, 1981-88, 1990; California Angels, 1990-91; Toronto Blue Jays, 1992; Minnesota Twins, 1993-94; Cleveland Indians, 1994-96; FOX-TV, analyst for show "Baseball On FOX," 1996-. **Orgs:** Sponsor, founder David M Winfield Found to Aid Underprivileged Youth in Var Comm; mem Oxford Rec Ctr. **Honors/Awds:** Outstanding Coll Athlete, Attucks Brooks American Legion 1972; Outstanding Community Service, American Legion; National League All-Star Team, 1977-80; American League All-Star Team 1981-88; seven Golden Glove Awds; six Silver Slugger Awds. **Special Achievements:** Has played in 2 Championship Series and 2 World Series. **Business Addr:** Retired Professional Baseball Player, Minnesota Twins, Metrodome, 501 Chicago Ave S, Minneapolis, MN 55415.

WINFIELD, ELAYNE HUNT
Counselor. **Personal:** Born Feb 9, 1925, Waco, TX; married Walter Lee; children: Daryl Lynn, Kevin Ren. **Educ:** Paul Quinn Coll, BS 1954; Univ of TX, MA 1975; Cert in Educ Adm 1977. **Career:** Ector Co Public Schools, elementary counselor 1977, testing & measurement director 1984-; Special Educ Dept, Odessa TX, elementary counselor; Odessa TX, L/LD res teacher, teacher; Big Springs TX, teacher 1957-58; Midland TX, teacher 1955-56. **Orgs:** Mem, bd of dir NEA 1976-79; TX St Tchr Assn, Hum Rel Com 1974-78; TX Ed Agency Eval Team 1976; adj instr Univ of TX Permian Basin 1975; mem Alpha Kappa Alpha Sor; Am Assn of Univ Women; Delta Kappa Gamma Soc; 1st vice pres Qepa Kappa Chap 1976-79; Phi Delta Kappa Frat. **Honors/Awds:** Outst Elem Tchrs of Am 1973; Odessa Clsrm Tchrs HR Award 1974; TSTA Hum Rel Award 1974; Child Dev Profl. **Business Addr:** Director, Testing & Measurement, Ector County Independent School District, PO Box 3912, Odessa, TX 79762.

WINFIELD, FLORENCE F.
Physician (retired). **Personal:** Born Sep 21, 1926, Danville, KY; daughter of Margaret Allan Frye and John G Frye; married Arnold F Winfield; children: Michael A, Donna E Terry. **Educ:** Univ of WI, BA 1948; Woman's Medical Coll of PA, MD 1952; Residency: Children's Memorial Hosp, Evanston Hosp, Provident Hosp, bd certifield pediatrics, 1969. **Career:** Near North Children's Center, asst med dir 1969-71, med dir 1971-82; Winfield-Moody Health Clinic, acting med dir 1987-89. **Orgs:** Admissions Comm Northwestern Med School 1970-76; Med Consultant Evanston HS 1972-80; school bd Dist 65; bd Shore Schooll 1974-80, Family Focus 1978-91; Mental Health Bd of Evanston 1989-. **Honors/Awds:** Appreciation Award North Shore Assn for Retarded 1980; Appreciation Award Family Focus 1985. **Special Achievements:** Near North Health Center renamed Winfield Moody Health Ctr, in honor of Alma Moody & Dr Florence Winfield, 1989. **Home Addr:** 862 Forest Ave, Evanston, IL 60202.

WINFIELD, GEORGE LEE
City official. **Personal:** Born Jul 6, 1943, Petersburg, VA; son of Bessie Mae Jones Winfield and Robert Lee Winfield; married Ruby Rosenia Judd Winfield, Aug 26, 1967; children: G. Talawn, Tamory Berek, Takirra Amber. **Educ:** Howard University, Washington, DC, BSCE, 1972, MS, 1975. **Career:** Department of Public Works, Baltimore, MD, public works engineer, 1973-84, chief, 1984-86, acting bureau head, 1986-87, bureau head, 1987-88, deputy director, 1988—. **Orgs:** American Public Works Association; Governmental Refuse Collection and Disposal Association; board member, Managerial and Professional Society; American National Standards Committee; US Representative, International Solid Waste Association; American Planning Association; Board of Estimates; Planning Commission; Consultants Evaluation Board; chairman, Change Order Review Committee; EPA Peer Review Task Group; Risk Insurance Committee; president, Lida Lee Tall PTA, 1983-84; board member, Lida Lee Tall Governing Board, 1983-84. **Honors/Awds:** Black Engineer of Year, Career Communications/Mobile, 1989; Afro-American Pacesetter, African-American Heritage Society, 1989. **Military Serv:** US Air Force, 1964-68. **Business Addr:** Baltimore City Department of Public Works, 600 Abel Wolman Municipal Building, Baltimore, MD 21202.

WINFIELD, JAMES EROS
Attorney. **Personal:** Born Mar 20, 1944, Port Gibson, MS; son of Gertrude Moran Green and Elias Winfield Jr; married Linda H Evans, Jun 9, 1968; children: James Jr, Paul, Michael. **Educ:** Morris Brown Coll, BA, 1967; Univ of Mississippi, JD, 1972. **Career:** Vicksburg, MS, city prosecutor, 1977-81; Vicksburg-Warren School Dist, atty, 1986-; Wilkinson County School Dist, atty, 1991-. **Orgs:** Mem, Mississippi State Bar Assn, 1972-; pres, Morris Brown Coll Natl Alumni Assn, 1977-84; trustee, Morris Brown Coll, 1977-84; sec, treasurer, Warren County Park Commn, 1984-89; bd of Governors, Mississippi Trial Lawyers Assn, 1988-; chmn, Vicksburg-Warren Community Health Center, 1987-91; member, Magnolia Bar Assn, 1972-; member, Warren County Bar Assn, 1974-. **Honors/Awds:** Alumnus of the Year, Morris Brown Coll, 1977; Seminar speaker, Miss Trial Lawyers Assn, 1989, 1995. **Home Addr:** 2280 Freetown Rd, Vicksburg, MS 39180. **Business Addr:** Attorney, PO Box 1448, Vicksburg, MS 39181, (601)638-3911.

WINFIELD, LINDA FITZGERALD
Educational psychologist. **Personal:** Born Dec 9, 1948, Wilmington, DE; daughter of Bertha Mason Fitzgerald (deceased) and William L Fitzgerald; divorced; children: Kenneth Jr, David. **Educ:** Univ of Delaware, BA (with honors) 1975, MA 1981, PhD 1982. **Career:** New Castle County School Dist Consortium, supervisor rsch 1982-85; Educ Testing Servs, NAEP visiting scholar 1985-86; Temple Univ, asst prof of educ 1986-89; Temple & Johns Hopkins Univs, Baltimore MD, Center for Study of Effective Schooling for Disadvantaged Students; UCLA Graduate School of Education, visiting prof, 1989-92. **Orgs:** Mem Amer Educ Rsch Assoc 1977-; National Council on Measurement in Education; Phi Delta Kapp; Amer Psychological Assn. **Honors/Awds:** Woman of the Year in Rsch, Natl Assn of Univ Women 1984; Distinguished Alumni Gallery, Univ of Delaware 1984; AERA Palmer O Johnson Memorial Award, 1992; "Teachers' Beliefs Towards At-Risk Students in Inner Urban Schools," The Urban Review 1987; "Teachers' Estimates of Content Covered and First Grade Reading Achievement," Elementary School Journal 1987; Rockefeller Foundation Minority Research Fellowship 1987; Congressionally mandated federal contract on special strategies for educating disadvantaged students, co-director. **Business Addr:** Visiting Professor, UCLA Graduate School of Education, 405 Hilgard Ave, Los Angeles, CA 90024.

WINFIELD, PAUL EDWARD
Actor. **Personal:** Born May 22, 1941, Los Angeles, CA; son of Lois Beatrice Edwards Winfield and Clarence Winfield. **Educ:** University of Portland, 1957-59; Stanford University, Palo Alto, CA, 1959; Los Angeles City College, 1959-63; University of California at Los Angeles, 1962-64. **Career:** Stanford University, Palo Alto, CA, artist-in-residence, 1964-65; University of Hawaii, artist-in-residence, 1965; University of California at Santa Barbara, artist-in-resident, 1970-71; actor; films include Guess Who's Minding the Mint, 1969; Sounder, 1972; Gordon's War, 1973; Huckleberry Finn, 1974; Conrack, 1974; Hustle, 1975; Twilights Last Gleaming, 1976; A Hero Ain't Nothing But a Sandwich, 1978; Carbon Copy, 1981; White Dog, 1981; Star Trek II, The Wrath of Khan, 1982; Mike's Murder, 1982; On the Run, 1982; Damnation Alley, 1983; The Terminator, 1984; The Serpent and the Rainbow, 1988; Presumed Innocent, 1990; television appearances include Green Eyes, 1976; All Deliberate Speed, 1976; King, 1978; Under Seige, 1985;Delayed Justice: The Lenel Geter Story, 1986; The Charmings, 198Women of Brewster Place, 1988; Wiseguy, 1989; 227, 1989; LA Law, 1990; 83 Hours Till Dawn, 1990; Family Matters, 1991; has guest starred on numerous other television programs; theatre work includes Ceremonies in Old Dark Men; Enemy of the People; A Lesson from Aloes; Othello; Love Letters; Built to Last, sitcom star, 1997. **Orgs:** Screen Actors Guild; American Federation of Televison and Radio Artists. **Honors/Awds:** Academy Award Nomination for Sounder, 1973; Emmy Award Nomination for King, 1978, Roots II; Distinguished Citizen Award, California Federation of Black Leadership; Image Award, NAACP; Black Filmmakers Hall of Fame, NAACP; numerous others.

WINFIELD, SUSAN REBECCA HOLMES
Judge. **Personal:** Born Jun 13, 1948, East Orange, NJ; daughter of Mildred L Holmes and Thomas S Holmes; children: Jessica L, Heather B. **Educ:** Univ of Pennsylvania, BA, Math 1970; Boston Coll Law School, JD, 1976. **Career:** Law Office of Salim R Shakur, assoc atty 1976-78; Dept of Justice Criminal Div, staff atty 1978-79; Office of the US Attorney, asst US atty 1979-84; District of Columbia Superior Court, assoc judge 1984-90, appointed deputy presiding judge, family division 1990-. **Orgs:** mem, Asst US Attorney's Assn, 1979-, Shiloh Bapt Church, 1982-, The Barker Found, 1982-, Natl Assn of Women Judges, 1984-, Amer Judges Assn, 1984-, Women's Bar Assn of DC, 1984-, Black Adoptive Parents, Barker Found, 1983-present; DC Bar, 1978, Massachusetts Bar, 1976. **Honors/Awds:** Special Achievement Award, Office of US Attorney 1983-84. **Business Addr:** District of Columbia Courts, 500 Indiana Ave NW, Room 3510, Washington, DC 20001, (202)879-1272.

WINFIELD, THALIA BEATRICE
Business executive (retired). **Personal:** Born Oct 17, 1924, Surry, VA. **Educ:** VA State Univ, BS 1947. **Career:** Storer Coll Harpers Ferry, sec to pres 1947-49; Morehouse Coll Atlanta, sec to bursar 1949-54; Columbia Svgs & Loan Assn, pres. **Orgs:** Dir Carter Child Devel Ctr 1976-; trustee Citizens for Govtl Rsch Bur 1977-; Christ Presb Church elder 1978-, treas 1984; trustee Presbytery of Milwaukee 1984.

WINFIELD, WILLIAM T.
Manager. **Personal:** Born Oct 24, 1944, Baton Rouge; married Rita Gurney; children: William Gurney, Darlene Teresa. **Educ:** Southern Univ, attend. **Career:** Homestead Maint & Supplies, gen mgr 1985, entrepreneur, consultant, currently; Metropolitan Council, serving 3rd term. **Orgs:** Mem Eden Pk Act Com; exec bd First Ward Voters Leag; Mason; State Commission, Inter-Governmental Relations; chmn, Parish Democratic Exec Comm; chmn, Metro Council Finance & Exec Comm, 1998; exec comm, Louisiana Democratic Committee; pres, State Police Jury Assn Black Caucus; scoutmaster, Istrouma Area Boy Scout Council; deputy grand master, St Andrews Grand Lodge; bd mem, Boys and Girls Club of Winborne Ave, Baton Rouge; EBR Industrial Dev Bd; exec bd, Louisiana Municipal Black Caucus; dir-at-large, NABCO. **Honors/Awds:** Hon Dist Atty 1973. **Special Achievements:** First Baton Rougean to participate in a cooperative program with Marshall Space Flight Center, Southern Univ; first African American employed in engineering in the industrial complexes of Baton Rouge; trail blazer in the design, procurement, coordination and installation of Bridges on the Interstate Hwy System. **Business Addr:** 1331 N 39 St, Baton Rouge, LA 70802.

WINFREY, AUDREY THERESA
Nurse specialist. **Personal:** Born May 21, Houston, TX; daughter of E Agatha McIntyre and Arthur W Winfrey; divorced; children: Jennifer Holland. **Educ:** Grant Hosp, Diploma 1962; DePaul Univ, BSN 1969, MSN 1973; Univ of IL School of PH, MPH 1976. **Career:** Public health nurse, 1 Chicago Health Dept, 1963-66; nurse adv, USAID Vietnam Bureau, 1966-68; public health nurse, 1 Mile Square Health Center, 1968-70; Michael Reese Med Ctr School of Nursing, instr 1970-73; Univ of

IL Coll of Nursing, instr 1973-74; Chicago City Coll, asst prof 1974-77; US Postal Service, Chicago, Il, industrial nurse, 1988-90; University of Illinois, College of Nursing, Chicago, IL, med surg HTN researcher, 1988-90; Halsted Terrace, Nursing Home, Chicago, IL, supervisor, 1988-90; VA Westside Med Ctr, coord adm amb care nursing 1977-; Veterans Admin Chicago, IL nurse specialist hospital base home care 1987-90; Amb Care Clinics, primary nurse for surgical service, 1990-. **Orgs:** Zeta Phi Beta, Amer Nursing Assn, Natl League for Nurs, Amer Publ Health Assn, DePaul Univ, Univ of IL Alumni Assn; Women of Achievement membership committee 1987-; Plano Child Development Center bd member, VIP 1978-; Planning Board of VIA, St James Catholic Church 1986-; Variety Club Children Charities, 1980-. **Honors/Awds:** Civilian Govt Award; Medal of Achievement; Recog Award; Volunteer Service Award Plano Child Development Center 1983; CAHMCP Recognition Award Illinois Inst of Technology 1982; published article: "Maximum Amount of Medication: How Much Is Too Much Injected into One Site" Nursing, July 1985; Published article w/ Dr Eva D Smith of U of I, College of Nursing' "Church Based Hypertension Education Prgram," 1990. **Military Serv:** US Army Nurse Corp, Reserve, bird colonel, 1973-, chief nurse of the 395th CSH (HUS). **Business Addr:** Nurse Specialist, Hospital Base Home Care, VA Westside Medical Center, 820 S. Damen, #1, Chicago, IL 60612.

WINFREY, CHARLES EVERETT
Clergyman, educator. **Personal:** Born Mar 6, 1935, Brighton, TN; married Ernestine. **Educ:** Lane Coll, BA 1961; Vanderbilt U, MDiv 1964; Univ of TN, MS 1974. **Career:** Metro Public School Nashville, english teacher 1966-; CME Church Nashville, minister Capers Mem 1965-; Phillips Chapel CME Church Nashville, minister 1964-65; W Jackson Circuit CME, 1961-64; Graham Chapel CME Church Savannah, 1958-61. **Orgs:** Mem Ad Hoc Com; Kappa Alpha Psi; life mem NEA; mem Met Act Commn; TE MNEA; dean of ldrshp training Nashville-Clarksville Dist CME Ch. **Honors/Awds:** Rel Man of Yr, Kappa Alpha Psi 1971; Good Conduct Award, USMC 1954; chaplain St Sen 1973; Hon Sgt-at-Arms, St Leg 1974. **Military Serv:** USMC sgt 1950-54. **Business Addr:** 319 15 Ave N, Nashville, TN.

WINFREY, OPRAH
Talk show hostess, actress, producer, entrepreneur. **Personal:** Born Jan 29, 1954, Kosciusko, MS; daughter of Vernita Lee and Vernon. **Educ:** Tennessee State University, BA, speech, drama. **Career:** WVOL Radio Station, news reporter, 1971-72; WTVF-TV, reporter, news anchorperson, 1973-76; WJZ-TV, news anchorperson, 1976-78, host of morning talk show "People Are Talking" 1978-83; WLS-TV, host of talk show "AM Chicago," 1984; The Oprah Winfrey Show, host, 1985-, national syndication, 1986-; Harpo Productions, owner, producer, 1986-; films: The Color Purple, 1985; Native Son, 1986; ABC-TV mini-series, producer, actress, The Women of Brewster Place, 1989, series, "Brewster Place," 1990; ABC-TV Movie of the Week, executive producer, Overexposed, 1992; producer, actress, "Oprah Winfrey Presents: Before They Had Wings", 1997; producer, "The Wedding," ABC, 1998; host, supervising producer: series of celebrity interview specials, including: "Oprah: Behind the Scenes," 1992; ABC Afterschool Specials, 1991-93; host, executive producer: "Michael Jackson Talks To Oprah, 90 Prime-Time Minutes With The King of Pop," 1993; The Eccentric Restaurant, owner, currently; co-author, "You Make The Connection", 1997; "You Make The Connection", home video, prod, host, 1997. **Honors/Awds:** NOW, Woman of Achievement Award, 1986; Emmy Award, Best Daytime Talk Show Host, 1987, 1991, 1992; America's Hope Award, 1990; Broadcast Promotion Marketing Executives/Broadcast Design Association, Industry Achievement Award, 1991; International Radio and Television Society, Broadcaster of the Year, 1988; NAACP, Image Awards, 1989-92; NAACP, Entertainer of the Year Award, 1989; CEBA Awards, 1989-91; Academy Award and Golden Globe Award nominee, The Color Purple, 1985; inducted into Television Academy Hall of Fame; numerous others. **Business Addr:** Owner/Producer, Harpo Productions, 110 N Carpenter St, Chicago, IL 60607-2101, (312)633-1000.

WING, ADRIEN KATHERINE
Educator. **Personal:** Born Aug 7, 1956, Oceanside, CA; daughter of Dr John E (deceased) & Katherine P Wing; divorced; children: Che-Cabral R W Melson, Nolan Felipe J W Melson. **Educ:** Newark Academy, HS, 1974; Princeton, AB, 1978; UCLA, MA, 1979; Stanford Law School, JD, 1982. **Career:** Upward Bound, UCLA, teacher/counselor, 1979; Rosenfeld, Meyer & Susman, law clerk, 1980; United Nations, intern, 1981; Curtis, Mallet, et al, lawyer, 1982-86; Rabinowitz, Boudin, et al, lawyer, 1986-87; University of Iowa Law School, professor of law, 1987-. **Orgs:** National Conference of Black Lawyers, international chair, 1985-95; Transafrica Forum Scholars Council, 1993-; Association of Black Princeton Alumni Bd, 1982-87; Stanford Law School , bd of visitors, 1993-96; American Society of International Law, Southern Africa interest group chair, 1994-95; Transafrica Forum Journal, Bd of Editors, 1993-; Council on Foreign Relations, life member, 1993-; National Black Law Students Assn, bd of directors, 1981-82. **Honors/Awds:** Haywood Burns-Shanara Gilbert Award, 1997; National Conference of Black Lawyers, Hope Stevens Award, 1988; numerous others. **Special Achievements:** Over 40 publications including: Democracy, Constitutionalism & Future State of Palestine, Jerusalem, 1994; "Rape, Ethnicity, Culture", Critical Race Theory Reader, Temple Univ, 1995; "Weep Not Little Ones", in African Americans & the Living Constitution, Smithsonian, 1995; Editor of Critical Race Feminism: A Reader, NYU, 1997; Languages: French, Swahili, Portuguese. **Business Addr:** Professor, University of Iowa Law School, Iowa City, IA 52242, (319)335-9129.

WING, THEODORE W., II
Company executive. **Personal:** Born Jul 12, 1948, Philadelphia, PA; son of Mardie Phillip Wing and Theodore W Wing; married Denise; children: Hillary Allen Theodore. **Educ:** Howard University, Washington, DC, BA, 1970; Syracuse University, Syracuse, NY, MS, 1972; Temple University, Philadelphia, PA, REL, 1978-81; George Washington University, Washington, DC, MCPM, 1989-91; St Joseph's Univ, MS, 1997. **Career:** White House, special asst to the vice pres, 1970-71; Howard Univ, Washington, DC, special asst to the pres, 1971-72; Commonwealth of Pennsylvania, Harrisburg, PA, principle, 1972-74; City of Philadelphia, Philadelphia, PA, dir of federal funding and youth programs, 1974-78; AT &T Federal Systems, 1978-91; City of Philadelphia, deputy commissioner, 1991-92; Ray Communications, vice president, 1993-. **Orgs:** President, Howard University Alumni Club, 1978-81; chairman, Boys & Girls Clubs, Philadelphia, 1989-91; director, Downtown Industrial School, 1981-83; president, Philadelphia School System, Day Care Center, 1979-81; director, Tender Care, Inc, Philadelphia, 1989-91; founder, Syracuse Challenger Newspaper; educational honor society, Kappa Delta Pi; founder, Media Charter School for K-7 grades. **Honors/Awds:** Trustee Award, Bennet College, 1988; President's Award, University of Maryland, 1990; Outstanding Youth, John Wanamaker, 1970; Ben Franklin Award, Philadelphia Free Library, 1987; Alumni Award, Howard University, 1986. **Special Achievements:** Author, "Urban Education from the Bedlands to the Classroom,"; Winner of numerous awards and fellowships, public speaker, involved with several movie and tv productions and author of many scholarly papers. **Business Addr:** Vice President, Ray Communications, 3 Bala Plaza, East No 101, Bala Cynwyd, PA 19004.

WINGATE, DAVID GROVER STACEY, JR.
Professional basketball player. **Personal:** Born Dec 15, 1963, Baltimore, MD. **Educ:** Georgetown. **Career:** Philadelphia 76ers, guard-forward, 1986-89; San Antonio Spurs, 1989-91; Washington Bullets, 1991; Charlotte Hornets, 1992-95; Seattle Supersonics, 1995-. **Business Addr:** Professional Basketball Player, Seattle Supersonics, PO Box 900911, Seattle, WA 98109, (206)281-5850.

WINGATE, MAURICE FRANCIS
Placement agency executive. **Personal:** Born Oct 3, 1957, New York, NY; son of Ernest & Gertrude Wingate; married Rose Ann Wingate, May 21, 1988; children: Nigel Francis. **Career:** Best Domestic Services Agency Inc, president/CEO, 1993-. **Orgs:** One Hundred Black Men Inc, board of directors/vice chair. **Business Phone:** (212)685-0351.

WINGATE, ROSALEE MARTIN
Educator. **Personal:** Born Mar 10, 1944, New York, NY; daughter of Lucille Martin; children: Deshon, Tishana, Yvette. **Educ:** Univ of TX El Paso, BA 1967; Univ of TX Austin, MSSW, 1970, PhD 1979. **Career:** Meridell Achievement Ctr, social worker/administrator 1969-73; Mental Health-Mental Retardation, caseworker 1981-88; Huston-Tillotson Coll, head social sci div 1973-; Outreach Director for Project Reach (AIDS Project,) l988-; private therapist, l987-. **Orgs:** Social work certification State of TX 1983-; licensed professional counselor TX Bd of Examiner 1983-; vice pres Black Arts Alliance 1985-; mem, Natl Sorority of Phi Delta Kappa; teacher, Vocation Bible School in Belize, Central Amer, l985, l986, l988-89. **Honors/Awds:** Leadership Austin Chamber of Commerce 1981; Black Author's Award, l984, Rishon Lodge #l Community Serv Award, l988; H-TC President's Faculty Achievement Award, l989; John Seabrook Professorship in Social Science, l989-; author of book "I Like Myself" (children's book,) l977; article, "Feeling Secure in A Single Parent Home," l986; article, "Empowering Black Youths: AIDS Prevention," l989. **Home Addr:** 2105 Teakwood Dr, Austin, TX 78758. **Business Addr:** Dept of Soc Sci, Huston-Tillotson Coll, 900 Chicon St, Austin, TX 78702-2753.

WINGFIELD, DONTONIO
Professional basketball player. **Personal:** Born Jun 23, 1974, Albany, GA. **Educ:** Cincinnati. **Career:** Seattle SuperSonics, 1994-95; Portland TrailBlazers, 1995-. **Business Addr:** Professional Basketball Player, Portland TrailBlazers, 1 Center Court, Ste 200, Portland, OR 97227, (503)234-9291.

WINGFIELD, HAROLD LLOYD
Educator. **Personal:** Born Sep 22, 1942, Danville, VA. **Educ:** Fisk Univ, BA, 1970; Univ of Oregon, MA, 1973, PhD, 1982. **Career:** Sonoma State Univ, visiting asst professor, 1976-77; Tennessee State Univ, visiting asst professor, 1977-78; Arizona State Univ, visiting instructor, 1979-80; Univ of Rhode Island, visiting asst professor, 1980-84; Kennesaw State Univ, asst professor, 1985-90, assoc prof, 1990-. **Orgs:** Mem, Amer Political Science Assn, Western Political Science Assn, Southern Political Science Assn, Natl Conf of Black Political Scientists, NAACP, Amer Civil Liberties Union, Common Cause, People for the Amer Way; mem, Georgia State Democratic Comm; elected mem, Polk School District Bd of Educ. **Honors/Awds:** Author with W Jones and A Nelson, "Black Ministers, Roles, Behavior, and Congregation Expectations," Western Journal of Black Studies, 1979; author, "The Historical and Changing Role of the Black Church: The Social and Political Implication," Western Journal of Black Studies, 1988. **Military Serv:** US Army, 1967-69. **Business Addr:** Assoc Professor, Kennesaw State University, 1000 Chastain Rd, Kennesaw, GA 30144-5591.

WINGO, A. GEORGE
Government administrator. **Personal:** Born Dec 24, 1929, Detroit, MI; married Helen B Glassco; children: Alicia, Scott Andre. **Educ:** OH State Univ, 1954-57; Oakland Univ, 1970-71; Dept of Defense Schools. **Career:** Defense Construction Supply Ctr, commodity mgr, 1960-64; Tank Automotive MI, systems analyst 1966-74; Wright Patterson AFB OH, country mgr 1974-75; Eglin AFB OH, foreign military sales mgr 1976; USAF, program mgr; Systems Engineering & Management Co, support equipment mgr, 1989-. **Orgs:** Announcer Mid OH Assn; mem Citizens Council 1968-72. **Honors/Awds:** Father of the Year New Haven Schools 1973. **Military Serv:** AUS corpl 1951-54. **Business Addr:** Program Manager, Wright-Patterson AFB, ALXS, Dayton, OH 45433.

WINLEY, DIANE LACEY
Interior designer, hospital administrator, cleric. **Personal:** Born in New York, NY; daughter of Esther Jackson Lacey and William Lacey; married Ronald Winley. **Educ:** Univ of CT, Storrs, CT, BA, 1960; New York Theological Seminary; NY Theological Seminary, MDIV, 1994. **Career:** Spirit Landscapes and Interiors, pres, currently; Radio Station WWRL AM, dir pub affairs 1978-; Sydenham Hosp, dir patient relations & vol serv 1977-78; New York City Health Hosp Corp, asst to pres 1974-76; John Hay Whitney Ford Found, grantee 1971-73; City of New York, spl asst to mayor 1970-71; Hunts Point Multi-Serv Compre Health Cntr, dir 1968-70; Spring Valley United Church, assoc pastor, 1994-; United Church of Spring Valley, associate pastor. **Orgs:** Founding mem, Assn of Black Social Workers; organizer, 1st Natl Conf on Drug Abuse Policy for Minority Leaders 1972; candidate, State Leg; New York City project director, I Have a Dream Foundation; New York City exec director, Physicians for Social Responsibility, 1986-; member, board of directors, New York City Health Hospital Corp, 1982-. **Honors/Awds:** Twice Elected Dem Dist Leader; Ford Foundation Fellow, Ford Foundation, 1972-73; Fellow, John Hay Whitney, 1973-74; fellow, Revson foundation, 1981-82; Ellen Lurie Distinguished Service, Community Service Society, 1988. **Business Addr:** President, Spirit Landscapes & Interiors, PO Box 445, New York, NY 10037.

WINN, CAROL DENISE
Producer/director. **Personal:** Born Mar 18, 1962, San Francisco, CA; daughter of Mae Willie Baskins Winn and Edward Winn Jr. **Educ:** SF State University, San Francisco, CA, 1980-83; Howard University, Washington, DC, BA, 1987. **Career:** WJLA TV Ch 7, Washington, DC, news assistant, 1986-87; KBHK TV, San Francisco, CA, admn asst to pres/insurance claims admn, 1987-88, associate producer/director, 1988-89, producer/director, 1989-. **Orgs:** Recording secretary, Bay Area Black Journalists Association, 1989-90, scholarship chair, 1990-91, program chair, 1991-92. **Business Addr:** Producer/Director, KBHK-TV, 650 California St, 6th fl, San Francisco, CA 94108.

WINN, JOAN T.
Attorney/real estate broker. **Personal:** Born Apr 11, 1942, Dallas; divorced; children: Elbert Ikoyi. **Educ:** Dillard U, BA 1962; S Meth U, JD 1968. **Career:** Durham & Winn Dallas, atty 1968-70; US Dept of Labor & Off of Solicitor Dallas, trial atty 1970-73; Fed Appeals Auth US Civil Srv Commn, asst appeals ofcr 1973-75; Danas Co Ct at Law No 2, judge 1975-78; 191st St Judicial Dist Ct, judge 1978-80; Honeymill & Gunn Realty Co Inc, pres. **Orgs:** Mem St Bar of TX, Am Bar Assn, Dallas Bar Assn, JL Turner Leg Soc, Delta Sigma Theta, The Links Inc Dallas Chapt. **Honors/Awds:** Woman of the Year Zeta Phi Beta 1978; Women Helping Women Awd 1980; Women in Business Iota Phi Lambda 1986.

WINNINGHAM, HERMAN S., JR.
Professional baseball player. **Personal:** Born Dec 1, 1961, Orangeburg, SC; son of Lucille Brizz Winningham and Rev Herman S Winningham Sr; married Jane Moorman Winningham, Jan 20, 1990. **Educ:** South Community College. **Career:** Outfielder: New York Mets, 1984, Montreal Expos, 1984-88, Cincinnati Reds, 1988-92, Boston Red Sox, 1992-. **Honors/Awds:** Collected first big-league hit in second game of doubleheader against Padres with an RBI double against Eric Show; finished the 1984 season going 5 for 10 500 in a three-game series vs the Expos at Olympic Stadium; voted Jr Coll Player of the Yr at DeKalb (GA) South Comm Coll. **Home Addr:** 1542 Belleville Rd, Orangeburg, SC 29115.

WINSLOW, ALFRED A.
Regional director (retired). **Personal:** Born Jun 16, 1923, Gary, IN; son of Lenora and Harry; married Maude E Franklin (deceased). **Educ:** Northwestern Univ, BBA 1969; Wilson Jr Coll, AA 1964; Univ of Chicago, 1957-60. **Career:** Manpower Devel, various positions 1947-66, Chicago Reg Office, dir personnel div 1966-71, Central Reg, mgr 1971-73; US Postal Serv Office of Employee Relations, reg dir 1973-83 retired; Univ Park Condominium Assn, vice pres bd of dirs, 1986-88; vice pres, Afro-American Pub Co, 1985-. **Orgs:** Indus Relations Assn of Chicago; past chmn Post Ofc Bd of US Civic Serv Examiners in IL & MI; Field Museum of Natural Hist, Art Inst of Chicago, Chicago Ed TV Assn; past pres Cheryl Condominium, Evans-Langley Neighborhood Club; former capt, mem drive comm, exec bd, life mem NAACP; Amer Legion; life mem Northwestern Alumni Assoc; Soc of Personnel Admin. **Honors/Awds:** Pres Citation Pres Comm on Employment of Handicapped 1966; Outstanding Achievement Award Chicago Assoc of Comm & Indust 1968-70; WGRT Great Guy Award Comm Activities 1969; Delta Mu Delta Hon Soc; 1st Black Officer in Coast Guard Air Corps. **Military Serv:** USCGAF 1943-46. **Home Addr:** 1401 East 55th St, Chicago, IL 60615.

WINSLOW, CLETA MERIS
City official. **Personal:** Born Jul 18, 1952, Rockford, IL. **Educ:** TN State Univ, BS Social Work (w/Honors) 1973; Atlanta Univ Sch of Social Work, M 1975. **Career:** Vanderbilt Univ Rsch Ctr, psychotherapist social worker's aide 1972-73; Atlanta Univ Sch of Social Work, rsch asst 1974; Morehouse Coll Public Relations, sec 1975-76; Carrie Steele Pitts Children's Home, chief social worker 1976-79; Fulton County Bd of Commissioners, admin asst; City of Atlanta, Neighborhood Planning Unit, coordinator, currently. **Orgs:** Chair/mem West End Neighborhood Dev Inc 1977-; mem 1979-, natl treas 1985-, Natl Assoc of Neighborhoods; bd mem Christian Council of Church 1983-, West End Parents in Action Youth Anti-Drug 1985-, Joel Chandler Harris Assoc 1986-; mem Brown HS PTSA Magnet Prog and Voc Adv Cncl 1986-; Black Women's Coalition 1987-; Delta Sigma Theta; bd mem Boatrock Family Serv Center; bd Mental Hlth/Mental Retardation 1985. **Honors/Awds:** Outstanding Young Women of Amer 1981,83; Citywide Neighborhood Serv Awd Urban Life Assoc 1983; Movers and Shakers of Atlanta The Atlanta Constitution Newspaper 1984; APPLE Corps Honor for Outstanding Volunteer Serv in Educ; Awd for Volunteer Serv with Brown HS PTSA 1986; Cert of Appreciation from Fulton Cnty Employees Assn. **Home Addr:** 1123 Oglethorpe Ave, SW, Atlanta, GA 30310. **Business Addr:** Coordinator, Neighborhood Planning Unit, City of Atlanta, 68 Mitchell St Ste 1415, Atlanta, GA 30335.

WINSLOW, EUGENE
Business executive (retired). **Personal:** Born Nov 17, 1919, Dayton, OH; son of Lenora and Harry; married Bernice Vital; children: Kenneth, Michele Goree, Elesa Commerse. **Educ:** Dillard Univ, BA (cum laude) 1943; Art Inst of Chicago, Post Grad 1946; Inst of Design (IIT), Post Grad 1950. **Career:** Impac Inc, creative dir 1959-67; Barickman & Selders, art dir 1967-68; E Winslow & Assc, owner/consult beginning 1968; Afro-Amer Inc, CEO mkgt, 1963-93, pres, 1981-93. **Orgs:** Mem DuSable Museum, Southside Comm Art Ctr, Assc for the Study of Afro-Amer Life & History. **Honors/Awds:** Author, illustrator, Afro-Americans 76, 1975; Study Prints and other Educ Materials, 1964-84; illustrator, designer, Great Negroes Past and Present, 1964. **Military Serv:** USAAF 1st lt 1943-45. **Business Addr:** E Winslow & Assoc, 8201 S State, Chicago, IL 60619.

WINSLOW, KELLEN BOSWELL
Professional football player (retired). **Personal:** Born Nov 5, 1957, St Louis, MO; married Katrina McKnight. **Educ:** Univ of Missouri, attended. **Career:** San Diego Chargers, tight end, 1979-87. **Orgs:** Commissioner Kellen Winslow Flag Football League 1982; mem San Diego Police Dept reserve prog. **Honors/Awds:** All-American; played in Liberty Bowl, East-West Shrine Game, and Senior Bowl, 1979; led NFL in receptions, 1980-81; first team All-Pro, 1980, 1981, 1982; most catches by NFL receiver since 1981; set Chargers record for most points in game with 30, 1981; played in Pro Bowl, 1981-83, 1987; Offensive Player of the Game, Pro Bowl, 1981.

WINSLOW, KENNETH PAUL
Investment banker. **Personal:** Born Jul 22, 1949, Chicago, IL; son of Rose Rieras Winslow and Eugene Winslow. **Educ:** University of Illinois, BA, 1971; Harvard University, MBA, 1976; New York University, Advanced Professional Certificates, 1987. **Career:** Federal Deposit Insurance Corp., assistant examiner, 1972-74; Harvard University, research assistant, 1976-77; Chemical Bank, vice president, 1978-87; Benefit Capital Southwest Inc, president, 1988-. **Orgs:** ESOP Association, 1985-; National Center for Employee Ownership, 1985-. **Business Addr:** President, Benefit Capital Southwest Inc, 14800 Quorum Dr, Ste 200, Dallas, TX 75240, (214)991-3767.

WINSLOW, REYNOLDS BAKER
Educational administrator. **Personal:** Born Jul 25, 1933, Auburn, NY; son of Mary Baker Winslow and George M Winslow; married Ovetra Russ; children: Reynolds, Danielle Winslow Stamey, Christopher, Ericka. **Educ:** Syracuse Univ, BID 1961. **Career:** Thomas L Faul Assoc, Skaneateles NY, industrial designer, 1962-63; Crouse Hinds Co, industrial designer 1963-69; General Elec Co, industrial designer 1969-75; Syracuse Univ, minority engrg program coord 1976-83; Univ MA Coll of Engrg, dir Minority Engineering Program 1983-. **Orgs:** Allocation panel United Way of Central NY 1980-82; bd dirs Univ MA Comm for Collegiate Educ of Blacks & Minorities 1983-; bd dirs MA Pre-Engrg Program 1984-; regional chair Natl Assoc of Minority Engrg Prog Administrators 1985-86; natl treas Natl Assoc of Minority Engrg Program Admin 1986-89; vice pres, NAACP, 1989-91, pres, 1991-; Western MA Council, Girl Scouts of America, nomin comm, bd mem, 1994-; Roots International, Univ MA, bd mem, 1993-; Amherst Area Educ Alliance, bd mem, 1994. **Honors/Awds:** Achievement Recognition Award United Way of Central NY 1980; Silver Beaver Award Boy Scouts of Amer 1980; Serv to Youth Award YMCA 1980; Syracuse Univ Advocacy Award Office of Minority Affairs 1981; Dean's Award 1987. **Military Serv:** AUS Artillery sgt 2 yrs; Natl Defense Medal. **Business Addr:** Dir, Minority Engineering Program, University of Massachusetts, Coll of Engineering, Amherst, MA 01003, (413)545-2030.

WINSTEAD, VERNON A., SR.
Business executive, attorney, social worker. **Personal:** Born Sep 15, 1937, Roxboro, NC; married Claudette McFarland; children: Vernon Jr, Claudette. **Educ:** NC Central Univ, BS & BA Sociology & Health Educ, LLB 1962; attended John Marshall Law Sch; Univ of IL, MSW 1969, AM 1971, PhD 1972. **Career:** NC Dept of Public Aid, social worker 1962-63; NC Redevelopment Comm, relocation & contract spec 1963-65; US Labor Dept of Manpower Admins, manpower devel specialist 1965; VAW Indus Inc, labor rel specialist; consultant; arbitrator; Winstead Rest & Convalescent Homes, Durham NC, co-owner. **Orgs:** Member: NAACP, Natl Educ Assn, Natl Conf Black Lawyers, Natl Bar Assn, SE Kiwanis Businessmen's Organization, South Shore Ministerial Assn, Bravo Chapter Chicago Lyric Opera, Male Affiliate Natl Council of Negro Women (life member), Alpha Phi Alpha (life member); board mem: South Shore Comm, Joint Negro Appeal, St Philip Neri Parish School Board (chair); president: SE Area Kiwanis Intl, South Shore Comm, South Shore Econ Devel Comm; founder & exec co-dir: A Connecting Link, McFarland-Winstead Conf Center; founder & co-pastor, Interdenominational God First Church & Society; ordained Christian Life Interdenominational Minister, Univ Life Church; asst editor, Chicago South Shore Scene Newspaper. **Honors/Awds:** Outstanding Leadership Awd, Danforth Found; Monarch Awd for public service, Alpha Kappa Alpha, 1991. **Business Addr:** Labor Relations Specialist, VAW Industries Inc, 7426 So Constance, Chicago, IL 60605.

WINSTON, BONNIE VERONICA
Journalist. **Personal:** Born Mar 13, 1957, Richmond, VA. **Educ:** Northwestern Univ, BSJ 1978. **Career:** The Southern Illinoisan, reporting intern 1976; The Richmond VA Times-Dispatch, reporting intern 1977; The Huntington WV Advertiser, reporting intern 1978; TheRichmond VA Times-Dispatch, reporter 1979-86; The Boston MA Globe, state house bureau reporter 1986-. **Orgs:** Minority journalist-in-residence Tougaloo Coll Amer Soc of Newspaper Editors 1980; bd of dir VA Press Women of the Natl Fed of Press Women 1982-86; stringer The NY Times, 1983-86; bd of dir Richmond Chap Sigma Delta Chi, Soc of Professional Journalists 1983-86; plnng comm, staff mem Urban Journalism Workshop 1984-85; mem Natl Assoc of Black Journalists 1985-; free-lance writer Black Engr Mag 1986-. **Honors/Awds:** Natl Achievement Awd Northwestern Univ 1974; Alpha Lambda Delta Hon Soc Northwestern Univ 1975; Outstanding Young Women in Amer Awd 1982; Achievement Awd Miles W Conner Chap VA Union Univ Alumni Assoc 1982; 1st Place VA Press Assoc Writing Contest VPA 1983; United Press Intl Best Writing Awd UPI Virginia 1983. **Business Addr:** State House Bureau Reporter, The Boston Globe, 135 Morrissey Blvd, Boston, MA 02107.

WINSTON, DENNIS RAY
Educator. **Personal:** Born Feb 28, 1946, Hanover County, VA; son of Evelyn C. McDaniel Winston and James L. Winston; married Karen D Douglas; children: Kendra, Dennis. **Educ:** Norfolk State Coll, BA (Magna Cum Laude) 1969; Univ of Richmond, M 1979; Virginia Commonwealth Univ 1975-1979. **Career:** East End Middle School, art teacher 1971-75; Professional Artist, 1975-; Henderson Middle School, art teacher 1975-86; Richmond Public Schools Humanities Ctr, arts resource teacher 1986-; Studio Faculty Virginia Museum of Fine Arts 1988-. **Orgs:** Mem Smithsonian Assocs, VA Museum of Fine Arts, NAACP, Norfolk State Univ Alumni Assoc, Natl Conference of Artists, Xi Delta Lambda Chap Alpha Phi Alpha-Frat Inc; treas Central Region VA Art Educ Assoc 1985-87; mem political action comm Richmond Educ Assoc 1985; mem Phi Delta Kappa; bd of dirs Hand Workshop Crafts Museum; bd of dirs Printmaking Workshop - Richmond, VA; Natl Art Education Assn. **Honors/Awds:** Teacher of the Yr Richmond Public Schools 1984-85; Teacher of the Yr Henderson Middle School 1984-85; Middle School Art Teacher of the Yr 1985, Secondary Art Teacher of the Yr 1985 VA Art Educ Assoc; Purchase Awd African-Amer Museum Dallas 1985; Fitz Turner Comm Awd for Human Rights VA Educ Assoc 1985; Disting Alumni Citation of the Yr Awd Norfolk State Univ 1985; Recognition of Outstanding Achievements in Art Museum of Sci and Industry Chicago 1986; Disting Alumni Citation Natl Assoc for Equal Oppor in Higher Educ 1986; Man of the Yr 1986 VA Chapts of Alpha Phi Alpha Frat Inc, Eastern Region Alpha Phi Alpha Frat Inc; 1986 7th Annual Natl Art Exhibition & Competition Atlanta Life Insurance Co; Award of Honor, Ghent Arts Festival, Norfolk, VA1987; Educator of the Year, Phi Delta Kappa (Chapter) 1988; Citation of Service, Wilberforce Univ Nat Alumni Assn 1987; selected Virginia Museum's Artists in Education Program 1988; Educator of Year Virginia Commonwelth Univ Phi Delta Kappa 1988; Selected National Commercial Spot as Outstanding Education, blue Cross-Blue Shield of Virginia, 1990; Selected Illustrated Survey of Leading Contemporary Artists, American Artists Publications, 1990. **Military Serv:** USAR CW3.

WINSTON, GEORGE B., III
Computer company executive. **Personal:** Born Feb 16, 1943, Richmond, VA; son of Gertrude B Winston and George B Winston Jr. **Educ:** Hampton Institute, BS, 1965; Univ of Delaware, MBA, 1972. **Career:** Wilmington Trust Co, 1968-72; GBW Inc, 1972-73; Delaware State Banking Commission, 1973-75; Bank America Commercial Corp, vp, 1975-82; GBW International Computer Products, owner, 1983-. **Orgs:** Wilmington Chapter Hampton Alumni, president, 1987-; Monday Club, sec, 1991-; Better Business Bureau, board member 1993-. **Honors/Awds:** Delaware Minority Business, MBE Service Award, 1985; Nu Upsilon Chapter of Omega Psi Phi, Entrepreneurship Award, 1987. **Business Addr:** Owner, GBW International Computer Products, PO Box 888, Wilmington, DE 19899, (302)658-1315.

WINSTON, HENRY
Administrator. **Personal:** Born Apr 2, 1911, Hattisburg, MS; married Mary Fern Pierce. **Educ:** Honoris Causa Acad of Science of the USSR, 1976. **Career:** Unemployed Councils Natl, organizer 1931-33; S Negro Youth Congress, fnd & Org 1937-42; Young Communist League, natl admin sec 1938-42; Communist PartyUSA, natl org secr 1947-56, natl vice chrmn 1962-66, natl chrmn 1966-. **Orgs:** Mem Natl Council Amer Soviet Friendship 1970-, Natl Alliance Against Racist & Pol Repression 1972-, Natl Anti-Imperialist Movement in Solidarity with African Liberation 1973-. **Honors/Awds:** Medal Order of the October Revolution USSR 1976, Order of Seku-Bator Mongolia 1981, Order Frndshp of the Peoples USSR 1981, Order of Karl Marx German Democratic Rep 1982; title George Dimitrov Laureate Bulgaria 1982; "Strategy For A Black Agenda" Intl Publ Co Inc 1973; "Class, Race and Blk Lbrtn" Intl Publ Co Inc 1977. **Military Serv:** AUS sp-5 1942-45; Cert of Merit AUS 1944. **Business Addr:** Natl Chairman, Communist Party USA, 235 W 23rd St, New York, NY 10029.

WINSTON, HUBERT
Chemical engineer, educational administrator. **Personal:** Born May 29, 1948, Washington, DC; son of Helen Simmons Vincent and Hubert Winston. **Educ:** NC State Univ, BS 1970, MS 1973, PhD Chem Engineering 1975. **Career:** NC State Univ, asst prof dept of chem engrg 1975-77; Exxon Prod Rsch Co, rsch spec 1977-83; NC State Univ, assoc prof, undergrad admin dept of chem engrg 1983-86; NC State Univ, assistant dean of acad affairs college of engrg 1986-. **Orgs:** Mem Amer Inst of Chem Engrs, Natl Org for the Professional Advancement of Black Chemists & Chem Engrs, Engineer-in-Training with State of NC. **Military Serv:** USAR captain, fin 1974. **Business Addr:** Coordinator of Advising, North Carolina State Univ, Chemical Engineering, Box 7905, Raleigh, NC 27695.

WINSTON, JANET E.
Commissioner. **Personal:** Born Feb 7, 1937, Morristown, NJ; married Shurney Winston II; children: Shurney III. **Career:** Ernestine McClendon Agency NY, professional model, 1960-65; Belafonte Enterprises NY, sec/recpt, 1960-61; Music Corp of Amer NY, sec to vice pres, 1961-62; Johnson Publicity Co, Ebony fashion fair model, 1963-64; Janet Winston School of Charm NJ, owner-dir, 1966-70; Winston's Taxi Service NJ, owner, 1970-72; Winston's Family Tree Bar Club, owner, 1972-; Morristown Housing Authority, commissioner, 1972-91. **Orgs:** Pres, Morris Co Urban League Guild NJ, 1967-68; bd of dir, Morristown Neighborhood House NJ, 1972-; volunteer, Morristown Memorial Hospital, 1975-76. **Home Addr:** 8 Hazel St, Morristown, NJ 07960.

WINSTON, JEANNE WORLEY
Educational administrator. **Personal:** Born May 27, 1941, Washington, DC; daughter of Rosetta Curry Worley and Gordon Worley Sr; married Reuben Benjamin Winston; children: Kimberly L, Kandace J, Kia L, Reuben B II. **Educ:** District of Columbia Teachers College, BS, in elementary educ, 1963; George Washington Univ, MA, in elementary admin, 1967; Univ of Washington, DC, and Maryland Univ, admin post masters, 1967-78. **Career:** District of Columbia Alliance of Black School Educ, research comm mem, 1984-; District of Columbia Public Schools, teacher, 1963-67, grade chairperson, 1965-, supervising instructor, 1967-69, teacher, 1969-76, acting asst principal, 1976-77, staff devel coord, 1977-86, competence based curriculum comm chairperson, 1977, teacher, 1977-88,

teacher's convention building coord, 1984, AIMS coord, 1985, residential supervisory support program, 1985, math, science and minorities program, 1985, mentors program, 1986; District of Columbia Public Schools, Brightwood Elementary, Washington, DC, asst principal, 1988-. **Orgs:** Delta Sigma Theta, 1960-; PTA, 1963-; mem, Gethsemane Baptist Church, 1966-; NAACP, 1969-; Geo Washington Alumni Assoc, 1970-; Washington Teachers Union, 1970-; Urban League, 1975-; volunteer, Annual Toy Drive at Brookland School, 1980-; Natl Council of Negro Women, 1980; mem, Dist of Columbia Assn for Retarded Citizens, 1980-; District of Columbia Govt Employees Recreation Assn, 1985-; congributor and walk-a-thon participant, March of Dimes, 1985-; volunteer, Dist of Columbia Village, 1986-, District of Columbia Homeless Shelters, 1986-; member, Dist of Columbia Assn for Supervision and Curriculum Development, 1986-. **Honors/Awds:** Outstanding Teacher, Truesdell Elementary School, 1975; Outstanding Teacher, Research Club of Washington, DC, 1975; Exemplary Service, Region B, District of Columbia Public Schools, 1988. **Home Addr:** 1930 Kearney St NE, Washington, DC 20018. **Business Addr:** Assistant Principal, Brightwood Elementary School, District of Columbia Public Schools, 13th and Nicholson Sts, NW, Washington, DC 20011.

WINSTON, JOHN H., JR.
Physician. **Personal:** Born Aug 7, 1928, Montgomery, AL; married Bertha Moore; children: Georgette, Joni Winston Canty, Diva Dotson, Terri. **Educ:** Alabama State University, BS 1949; Columbia University, MA 1951; Meharry Medical College, MD 1956. **Career:** Physician, currently. **Orgs:** American College of Surgeons; American Medical Assn; Natl Medical Assn; bd mem, YMCA; Montogmery County Board of Education; Red Cross. **Military Serv:** US Air Force, one year. **Home Addr:** 1521 Robert Hatch Dr, Montgomery, AL 36106. **Business Addr:** Physician, 1156 Oak St, Montgomery, AL 36108.

WINSTON, LAMONTE
Sports administrator. **Personal:** Born Apr 10, 1959, Oakland, CA; son of Henry C & Georgia R Winston; married Claire L Winston, May 7, 1994; children: Cameron L. **Educ:** Merritt Jr Coll, 1977; Westminster Coll, 1978; Long Beach City Coll, AA, 1980; San Francisco State Univ, BA, 1986. **Career:** Kaiser Engineers, fitness trainer, 1982-85; Merritt Jr College, asst football coach, 1982-84; San Francisco State Univ, asst football coach, 1985-90; Univ of Nevada, asst football coach, 1990-93; Kansas City Chiefs, dir of player development, currently. **Orgs:** The Youth Ftd, bd of dirs, 1996-; NFL Player Programs, advisory comm, 1996-; Genesis School, special advisor, 1996-. **Honors/Awds:** San Francisco St Univ, SF St Football Hall of Fame, 1998. **Business Addr:** Director of Player Development, Kansas City Chiefs, 1 Arrowhead Dr, Kansas City, MO 64129, (816)924-9300.

WINSTON, LILLIE CAROLYN
Retired educator. **Personal:** Born Sep 26, 1906, Goodman, MS; daughter of Mattie Morgan and John Morgan; married Julises Winston; children: Lillie Howard, Sandra L Young, Juilses, Johnny Walker. **Educ:** Rust Coll, BS 1958; Univ of KY, Training Program 1966. **Career:** Bd of Ed, teacher, retired 1935-71; Bd of Ed, vp; principal Tallahassee Charleston, MS. **Orgs:** Teacher Headstart Program 1966, Art 1968; sub teacher Goodman Elem 1972; coord Holmes Cty Dem Party 1984; pres PTA, Cemetary Club, Goodman Missionary Baptist Church; Retired Teacher's Assn; mem Bd of Education 1980-. **Honors/Awds:** Council of Aging MS Virtute Armis 1980; Outstanding Grandparent Goodman Elem 1981. **Home Addr:** PO Box 224, Goodman, MS 39079.

WINSTON, MICHAEL R.
Educator. **Personal:** Born May 26, 1941, New York, NY; son of Jocelyn Anita Prem Das Winston and Charles Russell Winston; married Judith Marianno; children: Lisa M, Cynthia A. **Educ:** Howard Univ, BA 1962; Univ CA, MA 1964, PhD 1974. **Career:** Howard Univ, instr 1964-66; Inst Serv Edn, exec asst & assoc dir 1965-66; Educ Asso Inc, educ consult 1966-68; Langston Univ, devel consult 1966-68; Howard Univ, asst dean liberal arts 1968-69, dir res hist dept 1972-73; Moorland-Spingarn Res Ctr, dir 1973-83; Howard Univ, vice pres academic affairs 1983-90, Alfred Harcourt Foundation, vice president, 1992-93, president, 1993-. **Orgs:** Mem Amer Historical Assn, Assn Study Afro-Amer Life & Hist; co-author "Negro in the US"; co-editor "Dict Amer Negro Biography"; co-editor, Historical Judgements Reconsidered, 1988. **Honors/Awds:** Fellow Woodrow Wilson Intl Ctr for Scholars-Smithsonian Inst 1979-80. **Business Addr:** President, Aflred Harcourt Foundation, 8401 Colesville Rd, Ste 503, Silver Spring, MD 20910.

WINSTON, SHERRY E.
Musician, international negotiator, broker. **Personal:** Born Feb 15, 1947, New York, NY. **Educ:** Howard Univ, BMus 1968. **Career:** Flutist with own jazz band; Performed with: Ramsey Lewis, Grover Washington, Peabo Bryson, Regina Belle; Rotating Host: BET-TV'S "Jazz Central" with Lou Rawls; Albums: Do It For Love, 1986; Love Madness; Love Is, 1991; corp performances, Pepsi Cola, Coca Cola, Anheuser Busch, NAACP LDI, AT&T; Sherry Winston Enterprises, owner. **Orgs:** Natl Assn Market Developers, Black MBA's. **Honors/Awds:** Howard Univ Alumni Awd 1984; Grammy Nominee, 1991; Sally Award, 1991; Serwa Award 100 Black Women, 1993. **Business Addr:** Owner, Sherry Winston Enterprises, 518 E 80th St, New York, NY 10021.

WINT, ARTHUR VALENTINE NORIS
Educational administrator, professor. **Personal:** Born Oct 26, 1950, Kingston, Jamaica; son of Gwendolyn Nelson Wint and Noris Wint; married Carlotta Jo Bradley Wint, Apr 3, 1971; children: Tsenia, Jhason, Llarehn, Khirrah. **Educ:** Washington State University, Pullman, WA, BA, 1973; University of Washington School of Law, Seattle, WA, JD, 1976; Harvard University, Institute for Educational Management, 1993. **Career:** Evergreen Legal Services, Seattle, WA, legal asst, 1976-77; City of Seattle, Seattle, WA, eo investigator, 1977-79; Washington State University, Pullman, WA, dir of aff action, 1979-86; California State University, Fresno, Fresno, CA, asst to the president, dir of affirmative action, 1986-92; California State University, Fresno, executive assistant to president, 1992-; assoc prof of criminology, 1991-. **Orgs:** Academy of Criminal Justice Sciences, American Association for Affirmative Action, director Region IX, 1990-91; Public Info Committee, 1988-90, director Region X, 1985-86; California Association of AA Officers, 1986-; board member, Golden Valley Girl Scouts, 1987-90; NAACP, 1976-; Church of Christ, 1975-; Central California Employment, round table, 1989-. **Honors/Awds:** Teaching Leadership Award, NAACP, Fresno, 1989; Pew Teaching Award, University of Washington, 1989; Senate Intern, Washington State Senate, 1972. **Business Addr:** Exec Asst to the Pres/Dir, Human Resources, California State University, Fresno, 5150 N Maple Avenue, Fresno, CA 93740-0041, (209)278-2364.

WINTER, DARIA PORTRAY
Educator, city official. **Personal:** Born Sep 7, 1949, Washington, DC; daughter of Susie Lillian Alston Portray and James Michael Portray Jr; married Reginald Carroll Winter, Oct 6, 1973; children: Michael Alan Winter. **Educ:** Hampton Inst, BS, English educ, 1972; Univ of Virginia, MA, English, 1973; George Washington Univ, PhD program, 1988-89. **Career:** DC Office of Bicentennial Programs, asst to exec dir 1975-76; UDC Coop Extension Program, education specialist 1976-77; Univ of the District of Columbia, instructor of English 1977-97, asst prof of English, 1995-; Mayor of District of Columbia, general assistant, 1992-95; Southeastern Univ, asst prof of English; Lorton Coll Prison Program, faculty, 1998. **Orgs:** Alternate natl committeewoman DC Dem State Comm 1980-92; NEA Standing Comm on Higher Educ 1981-87; vice chair DC Democratic State Comm 1984-92; Democratic Natl Comm 1984-92; delegate to Democratic Convention 1984, 1988, 1992; Modern Language Assn, Coll Language Assn; NCTE; editor, Newsletter Natl Educ Assn Black Caucus 1987-89; Public Defender Service Bd of Trustees, 1988-92, commissioner, 1987-; District Statehood Commn, 1979-92; vice chair, DNC Eastern Region Caucus, 1988-92; bd mem, DC Juvenile Justice Advisory Group; bd mem, United Planning Organization; mem appointed by Pres Wm Clinton, Presidential Rank Commssion, 1994; chairperson, Univ of the District of Columbia Advocacy Committee, 1996. **Honors/Awds:** Appreciation Award, University of District of Columbia Student NEA, 1984; Appreciation Award in Support of Public Education, from superintendent, Floretta McKenzie, 1983; Outstanding Service Award; Distinguished Public Service Award, 1994; Univ of the District of Columbia, College of Liberal and Fine Arts, Image Award, 1996; Steering Committee of DC, Reclaim Our Youth Award, 1996. **Home Addr:** 1355 Underwood St, NW, Washington, DC 20012, (202)882-5178.

WINTERS, JACQUELINE F.
Government official, business executive. **Personal:** Born Apr 15, 1936, Topeka, KS; daughter of Catherine L Green Jackson and Forrest V Jackson; married Marc P; children: Anthony, Marlon, William, Brian Mc Clain. **Career:** Jackie's Ribs, pres; St of OR, asst to gov 1979-, prog exec 1971-79, field mgr 1969-70; Pacific NW Bell, srv adv 1968-69; Portland Model Cities, vol coord 1967-68. **Orgs:** Bd of dir OR Coll of Ed Found Bd of Trustees; mem st exec srv dir Marion-Polk United Way 1975; vp, pres Salem Br NAACP 1975-78; vice pres Salem Hum Rights Commn 1975; board member, Goodwill Industries of Oregon, 1991-; campaign chairperson 1981-82, pres 1982-83, United Way. **Honors/Awds:** Distinguished Srv, City of Salem 1976-77; Presidential Award, Salem NAACP 1977; Outstndng Comm Srv, United Way 1979; Outstndng Ldrshp, OR Woman of Color 1979; Martin Luther King, Jr Community Services, Willamette University, 1990. **Business Addr:** President, Jackie's Ribs Inc., 3404 Commercial S.E., Salem, OR 97302.

WINTERS, JAMES ROBERT
Elected government official. **Personal:** Born Aug 26, 1937, Pittsburgh, PA; married Diane Herndon; children: Angela, Richard, Lisa, Ryan. **Educ:** Fayetteville State Univ, BS 1965; Univ of Pgh, grad work sch of social work 1972. **Career:** YMCA Prog Ctr Pgh, caseworker 1966-67, prog dir 1967-70, exec dir 1970-72; Old Fort & Kiwanis YMCA Fort Wayne IN, urban dir 1972-78; Wayne Township Trustee's Office, trustee 1978-90. **Orgs:** Adv comm Univ Pgh Learn Leisure Prog 1967-70; organized Grambling-Morgan State Football Game (proceeds for Pgh YMCA) 1970; organized Pgh Pirate Baseball-Wives Benefit for Pgh YMCA Capital Campaign Fund Dr 1971; bd mem IN Criminal Justice Planning 1980; bd mem IN State Black Assembly 1980. **Honors/Awds:** Cert of Commendation Mayor's Office 1979; Hon Commander of the Garrison 1979. **Military Serv:** USN radarman 2nd class 1956-60; Good Conduct Medal. **Business Addr:** Chemical Waste Management of Indiana, Inc, 4636 Adams Center Rd, Fort Wayne, IN 46806.

WINTERS, KENNETH E.
Investment portfolio manager. **Personal:** Born Oct 22, 1959, Gonzales, TX; married Wendy C Gordon. **Educ:** St Mary's Univ, BBA 1985. **Career:** United Serv Automobile Assoc, financial reporting analyst 1979-83; USAA Real Estate Co, real estate analyst 1983; real estate asset manager 1983-87; Real Estate Acquisitions 1987-. **Orgs:** Mem Natl Assoc of Business Economists, Amer Finance Assoc; tutor English/Reading San Antonio Literacy Council. **Home Addr:** 1924 Middlefield Rd, Redwood City, CA 94063-2241. **Business Addr:** Real Estate Acquisition Rep, USAA Real Estate Company, USAA Bldg, San Antonio, TX 78288.

WINTERS, WENDY GLASGOW
Educational executive. **Educ:** Central CT State Coll, BS (Hon) Elem Ed 1952; Columbia Univ, MS Psych Social Work 1954; Yale Univ, PhD Sociology 1975. **Career:** Herrick House Bartlett IL, dir girls unit 1954; Comm Serv Soc NY, family caseworker, intake admin 1954-65; Norwalk Bd of Ed, social worker 1965-68; Univof CT School of Social Work, field instr 1967-80; Atlanta Univ School of Social Work, field instr 1970-71; Yale Univ Child Study Ctr, chief soc worker 1968-75, instr 1968-71, asst prof social work 1971, rsch assoc 1975-82; Univ of CT School of Social Work, assoc prof, asst dean for acad affairs 1975-78; Smith Coll Northampton, adj assoc prof social work, assoc prof sociology & anthropology, dean 1979-84. **Orgs:** Mem Amer Assoc of Univ Women, Amer Orthopsychiatric Assoc, Amer Sociological Assoc, Black Analysis Inc, Natl Assoc of Social Workers, New England Deans Assoc, New England Minority Women Admins; bd of corps Northampton Inst For Savings 1979-; bd dir 1977-80, exec comm 1977-79 Amer Orthopsychiatric Assoc; reg adv council 1975-78; chmn eval sub-comm 1977-78; CT State Dept of Children & Youth Svcs; sub-comm on commun serv grants of adv comm Commiss for Higher Ed 1976-77; bd of dir Leila Day Nurseries 1975-78, Gr New Haven Urban League 1969-71, Norwalk-Wilton Ed Proj 1967-68; juv justice adv comm CT Justice Commiss 1977; ed cultural adv comm Yale Office for Comm Affairs Devel 1974-75; adv comm Norwalk Comm Coll Ed Vocational Resource Ctr 1967-68; adv bd ProjectUpward Bound Cherry Lawn Schoo966-68. **Honors/Awds:** Univ Fellowship Yale Univ 1971-72,73-74; Ethel B Morgan Fellowship 1972-73; Commun Serv Soc Fellowship 1952-54; Univ of CT Rsch Found Grant 1976-78; New England Learning Resource System Fed Reg Resource Ctr Grant 1975-76; CT State Dept of Ed Grant BB103 1972-74; num guest lecturers & consult incl, NY, CT,GA, MA, ME, DC, VA, New Orleand, Toronto; LA State Bd of Ed & Natl Assoc of Social Workers "The Practice of Social Work in Schools" workshop Baton Rouge 1984; taped film on "Excellence" for Gen Elect Corp 1983; Bryn Mawr/Haverford Coll Evaluating team regarding diversity 1983. **Business Addr:** Dean of Arts and Sciences, Howard University, 2400 Sixth St NW, Washington, DC 20059.

WISE, C. ROGERS
Physician. **Personal:** Born Apr 8, 1930, Ft Worth, TX; married Margaret. **Educ:** Fisk U, BA ; Univ de Lausanne, MD, PhD. **Career:** Self-Employed, physician 1985; Meml Hosp, chf, dept anesth 1972-74; DePaul Hosp, 1971-75. **Orgs:** Mem Intrntl Anesth Rsrch Soc; Am Soc Anthes; mem, bd tst Laramie Co Comm Coll 1968; chmn, bd1974; v chmn 1973-77. **Business Addr:** PO Box 1144, Cheyenne, WY.

WISE, FRANK P.
Government official. **Personal:** Born Oct 28, 1942, Norfolk, VA; son of Marian C Williams and Frank P Wise Sr (deceased); divorced; children: Terri Lynn, Dawne Shenette. **Educ:** BBA 1965; MUA 1972. **Career:** US Nat Std Assn, research asst 1966-67; Eastern Airlines, coord 1967-68; Prince Geo Co, admin asst 1970-72; City of Cincinnati, mgmt analyst 1972; asst to the city mgr 1973-74; City of Savannah, asst city mgr 1975-78; City of East Cleveland, city manager 1979-83; City of Dallas, administration/finance, assistant director 1984-87, director, park and recreation, 1987-. **Orgs:** Intl City Mgmt Assn; chmn, Minority Coalition 1972-73; Fin Com, Conf Planning Com 1973, 1975, VP at-large 1975-76; vice pres at-large, Am Soc for Pub Admin, Conf of Minority Pub Adminstrs Sect on Hum Res Admin 1978-79; Natl Dev Dir Assn; National Recreation and Park Association 1984-; Texas Recreation and Park Society, 1984-; board member, Western Revenue Sources Management School, 1990-. **Honors/Awds:** Citations YMCA 1973; Mayoral Proclamation 1974; ICMA Urban Fellow 1970; article "What Role for Minority Assistance? The Second Dilemma," Pub Mgmt Mag 1972; "The Art of Serving Two Masters," Pub Mgmt Mag 1975; "Toward Equity of Results Achieved One Approach," Pub Mgmt Mag 1976; award of merit, OH Pks &

Rec Assn. **Military Serv:** US Army, capt, 1968-72; Cross of Gallantry 1970, Bronze Star 1970, Staff Medal 1970, Commendation Medal 1969. **Business Addr:** Assist Dir-Fin/Admin, City of Dallas, 1500 Marilla St #6FN, Dallas, TX 75201.

WISE, HENRY A., JR.
Physician. **Personal:** Born May 26, 1920, Cheriton, VA; married Roberta Morse; children: Henry II, Keith Evan. **Educ:** VA Union Coll, BS; Howard Univ, MS 1949, MD 1954. **Career:** Howard Univ, prof 1949-50; Bowie University, Bowie, MD; director of health services, 1957-90, coll physician 1957-; private practice, physician, currently. **Orgs:** Trustee Prince George Coll MD 1963-65; bd dir Dr's Hosp MD; mem Comprehensive Health Planning Adv Council Dr's Hosp; mem Alpha Phi Alpha Frat, Natl Med Assn, Assn Former, Interns, & Residents Howard Univ, Howard Univ Med Alumni Assn, American Professional Practice Assn, Amer Acad of Family Practice; Med Chi-of-State of MD; mem Prince George's Co Med Assn; Peer Review Comm Prince George's Genl Hosp sponsor MD Debutantes; mem Glenwood Park Civic Assn; mem Plymouth Congregational Church; Sigma Pi Phi Fraternity, Tuskegee Airmen Assn, Med Chi, Washington, DC. **Honors/Awds:** Outstanding Medical Serv to the Communities MD Debutantes; recipient awds from various civic groups for work with the MD Debutantes; recipient of many awards for outstanding community service. **Military Serv:** USAF 1st lt WWII. **Business Addr:** Physician, 8901 George Palmer Hwy, Lanham, MD 20706.

WISE, HERBERT ASHBY
Consultant. **Personal:** Born Feb 5, 1918, Philadelphia, PA. **Educ:** Franklin Univ Philadelphia, B of Bus Mgmt 1977; NJ Coll of Commerce, bus Admin, Acct 1949. **Career:** Housing Auth & Urban Redev Agy; pub housing mgr; Housing Auth & Urban Redev Agy, control clrk, sr acct clrk, mgmt aide, asst housing mgr, sr housing mgr,; Conf Wide Young Adult Flwshp Conf, Methodist Ch, pres Salem United Methodist Ch, asst pastor; tchr, ch sch, HS, jr HS, retired after 40 years; Public Housing Management, consultant, currently. **Orgs:** 1st black chaplain Dept of NJ VFW; cmdr 16th Dist VFW; cmdr Atlantic-Cumberland Co Cncl VFW; adjutant-qtrmstr Dist Co VFW; past post Cmndr, adjutant-qtrmstr Bruce Gibson Post 6594; intrntl treas Frontiers Intrntl; exec sec Atlantic City Frontiers Intrntl. **Honors/Awds:** Medal of Merit NJNG; Two Medals for Faithful Srv NGNG; Medal of Armed Forces Res NJNG; Medal of Asiatic Pacific Campaign; Medal Am Campaign; Medal WW II; Good Conduct Medal; Bronze Stars; plaque Outstndng Military Person NJNG 1962; Outstndng Qrtrmstr Award, 16th Dist 1955-76; Outstndng Adjutant Award 16th Dist 1955-76; citation Mbrshp Dr, Srvs Rendered as St Historian & St Guard in the Dept of NJ VFW 1943-46. **Military Serv:** US Natl Guard, sgt major, 1953-72.

WISE, WARREN C.
Construction Company Executive. **Personal:** Born Jun 4, 1948. **Career:** Wise Construction Co Inc, Dayton OH, chief executive, 1983-. **Orgs:** Dayton Rotary; NAMC; AGC. **Honors/Awds:** Businessman of the Year Award. **Business Addr:** Owner, Wise Construction Co Inc, 1705 Guenther Rd, Dayton, OH 45427.

WISE, WILLIAM CLINTON, SR.
Corporate manager. **Personal:** Born Jan 14, 1941, Steubenville, OH; son of Vivian Doggett Wise and Robert Clinton Wise; married Linda Rayam Wise (divorced 1988); children: Shawn, Sharon, Sandra, William Jr. **Educ:** Eastern Michigan University, labor law; United States Armed Forces Institute, business administration; Washtenaw Community College, psychology; University of Michigan Labor School. **Career:** City of Ann Arbor, Ann Arbor, MI, personnel dir, 1973-77; Ford Motor Co, Dearborn, MI, special program coord, 1977-84; Martin Marietta Corp, Bethesda, MD, mgr, management training, 1984-. **Orgs:** Exec advisor, National Technological Univ, 1991; member, American Society for Training & Development, 1984-. **Military Serv:** US Air Force, E-1, 1957-61. **Business Addr:** Corporate Manager, Martin Marietta Corporation, Training & Instructional Technology, 6801 Rockledge Dr, Bethesda, MD 20817.

WISE-LOVE, KAREN A. See LOVE, KAREN ALLYCE.

WISHAM, CLAYBRON O.
Development manager. **Personal:** Born Dec 28, 1932, Newport, AR; son of Willie Wisham and Charlie Wisham; married Evelyn Bailey, Sep 4, 1964; children: Deshay Appling, Lorna, Karen. **Educ:** Philander Smith Coll, BA, 1954; Univ of AR, MEd, 1963. **Career:** Centerior Energy Corp, mgr, training & devt, 1990-; Cleveland Elec Illuminating Co, general mgr, Operations, 1983-90, personnel admin, 1974-83; Cleveland State Univ, affirmative action officer, 1972-74; Union Commerce Bank, asst, vice pres personnel, 1970-72; Jones High School, guidance counselor, 1959-61; E End Boy's Club, exec dir 1957-59; AR Bapt Coll, dir of athletics, 1956-59. **Orgs:** Alpha Phi Alpha, 1952-; Urban League of Cleveland; Blacks in Mgmt, 1970-; NAACP; Greater Cleveland Growth Assn; Amer Assn of Blacks in Energy (charter mem); sr arbitrator, Cleveland Better Business Bureau; trustee Bd, Center for Rehabilitation Servs, Miles Ahead Inc; Marymount Hospital Civic Advisory Board; United Way Services Allocations Panel. **Honors/Awds:** 1st Black Personnel Recruiter in Corp Position, City of Cleveland, OH, 1965-; 1st Black Asst VP, Union Commerce Bank Personnel Dept, 1970; 1st Black Conf Chmn of EEO, Natl Sem for Edison Elec Inst, 1979; 1st Black Operations Mgr at Cleveland Elec Illuminating Co. **Military Serv:** AUS pfc 1954-56. **Business Addr:** Manager, Training & Development, Centerior Energy Corp, 2423 Payne Ave, Cleveland, OH 44114.

WITHERS, ERNEST
Photojournalist. **Personal:** Born 1922. **Career:** Photojournalist, currently. **Honors/Awds:** National News Assn, Best Photograph of the Year, 1968. **Special Achievements:** Photographs appeared in Time, Newsweek, Ebony, Jet, The New York Times, Washington Post, the Chicago Defender, and the PBS documentary "Eyes on the Prize."; Exhibitions: "Let Us March On," The Univ of Mississippi, 1987. **Business Addr:** Photojournalist, 333 Beale St, Memphis, TN 38103, (901)527-7476.

WITHERSPOON, ANNIE C.
Educator (retired). **Personal:** Born Oct 29, 1928, Bessemer, AL; daughter of Ethel Jones Cross and Ed Cross; married Willie George, Aug 17, 1959; children: Carole Lejuene, Yvas Lenese. **Educ:** WV St Coll, AB Ed 1951; Univ of AL, MA Elem Ed 1968. **Career:** Jefferson County School System Birmingham, teacher social studies, until retirement; ,guidance counselor 1956-70; Tuscaloosa, teacher 1952-56. **Orgs:** AL Ed Assn; Nat Ed Assn; Jefferson Co Ed Assn; NEA Minority Involvement Prog; coord Dist VI, Jefferson Co Area Wrkshp for Tchrs; ofcr Jefferson Co Voice of Tchrs for Ed; chairperson/deaconess, 1984-, New Pilgrim Baptist Church; chairperson, constitution committee, Dunbar/Abram Alumni, 1986-, Volunteer Tutorial Program, dir, 1992-; New Pilgrim Baptist Church Projects, past vice pres. **Honors/Awds:** Tchr of Yr 1968; AL Soc Studies Fair Dist & St Tchr Recog Awards 1972-74; first African-American pres of Jefferson Co Assn of Classroom Tchrs; Retirement Plaque, Outstanding Service to Children of Green Valley Elementary School for 15 Years, Green Valley PTA, 1985; Outstanding Service Award, Center Street School, 1986-87; Service Award, Blue and White Banquet, Dunbar/Abrams Alumni, 1987; West Virginia State Clg, Plaque in Honor of 35th Anniversary, 1990, Plaque in Honor of 40th Anniversary, 1991; New Pilgrim Baptist Church Educational Fund, Plaque in Honor of 20 Years Dedicated and Loyal Service.

WITHERSPOON, AUDREY GOODWIN
Educational administrator. **Personal:** Born Aug 19, 1949, Greenwood, SC; daughter of Essie Lue Chenault Goodwin and Hudson Goodwin; children: Jacintha Dyan, Andre LaVern. **Educ:** Lander University, BA, sociology, 1971; Clemson University, MEd, administration and supervision, 1975; Vanderbilt University, graduate study, educational leadership, 1982-83. **Career:** McCormick Co School District, teacher, 1971-72; GLEAMNS Head Start Program, social worker, parent coordinator, 1972-74, education director, 1974-75; GLEAMNS Human Resource Comm, child development, founder/director 1975-. **Orgs:** Lander University Class Agent 1988-96; reg vice chairperson, Gov Task Force 1979-82; vice chairperson, bd trustees, Greenwood Sch Dist 50, 1977-93; Natl Assn for Ed of Young Children, 1975-93; treas, Greenwood Br, NAACP 1979-96; chart mem, SC Child Develop Providers Inc, president, 1987, bd mem, 1978-96; Negro Business & Professional Womens Club, 1981-87; proj coord, region V, SC Voices for Children 1984-85; Gov Riley's Ed Transition Team, 1983-84; planning comm, Effective Schools SC, 1985; Mt Moriah Baptist Church; State Advisory Comm, Day Care Regulations, 1987-89; South Carolina Public Private Child Care Council, 1990; Early Childhood Education, Interagency Advisory Committee, 1990-91; Natl Council of Negro Women, 1989-93; SC School Boards Assn, 1990, 1992. **Honors/Awds:** Female Citizen of the Year, 1982; various state and natl community awards, 1982-92; Distinguished Alumni Award, Lander University, 1989; Distinguished Service Award, Greenwood Rotary Intl, 1993. **Home Addr:** 101 Stafford Dr, Greenwood, SC 29649-8922.

WITHERSPOON, JAMES. See Obituaries section.

WITHERSPOON, JOHN
Actor, comedian. **Career:** William Morris Agency, actor, currently. **Special Achievements:** Movies include: Vampire in Brooklyn; Fatal Instinct; Boomerang; Meteor Man; The Five Heartbeats; House Party; Bird; Hollywood Shuffle; Rat Boy; The Jazz Singer; Hot Rock; Hospital; Kidnapped; I'm Gonna Get You Sucka; television appearances include: "The Wayans Brothers," "Brother 2 Brother," "Townsend Television," "Late Night With Letterman," "Amen," "227," "You Again," "WKRP," "What's Happening Now," "Good Times," "The Richard Pryor Show," "The Redd Foxx Show," "The Comedy Store 15th Class Reunion," " Frank's Place," "Hill Street Blues," "Barnaby Jones," "The Incredible Hulk," opening comedy act for: The Commodores, Tom Jones, Chaka Khan, George Benson, Roberta Flack, Richard Pryor, Ashford and Simpson. **Business Addr:** Actor, c/o Agent, Jenny Delaney William Morris Agency, Inc, 151 El Camino Dr, Beverly Hills, CA 90212, (310)859-4000.

WITHERSPOON, R. CAROLYN
Corporate executive (retired). **Personal:** Born Oct 2, Detroit, MI; married William C Witherspoon; children: W Roger, L Courtney, David J. **Educ:** City Coll NY, BS 1951, MS 1956. **Career:** Town Hall NY, accountant 1945-48; Foreign Relations Library, treas; Council of Foreign Rel Inc, asst treas/comptroller 1952-87, retired. **Orgs:** Natl financial sec Natl Assn of Negro Business & Professional Women's Clubs Inc; mem Comm Rel Bd; adjustment com Teaneck; mem Kappa Delta Pi, Beta Alpha Psi.

WITHERSPOON, SOPHIA
Professional basketball player. **Personal:** Born Jul 6, 1969. **Educ:** Florida, BA in recreation. **Career:** New York Liberty, guard, 1997-. **Business Addr:** Professional Basketball Player, New York Liberty, Two Penn Plaza, New York, NY 10121, (212)564-9622.

WITHERSPOON, WILLIAM ROGER
Journalist. **Personal:** Born Mar 3, 1949, New York, NY; son of Ruth C. Witherspoon and William C. Witherspoon; married Cynthia O Bedford; children: Kir, Brie. **Educ:** Univ of MI Ann Arbor, 1966-67; Rider Coll Trenton NJ, 1973; Rutgers Univ, Livingstone Coll, New Brunswick NJ, 1975; Fairleigh-Dickinson Univ (Edward Williams Coll) Hackensack NJ, Liberal Arts 1976. **Career:** Star-Ledger Newark NJ, investment reporter, columnist, op-ed page, st house corr, columnist senate, assembly, banking, transportation & agriculture, general; assignment reporter 1970-75; NY Daily News, Sunday assignment editor NJ, health & environmental reporter Pasaic Cty reporter, New York City editor gen assignment reporter 1975-79; The Atlanta Constitution, columnist, health & science writer 1979-82; Time Magazine, SE Bur, Cable News Network, writer/producer; Black Enterprise Magazine, Newsweek, GQ Magazine, Fortune, Essence Magazine, Natl Leader, freelance writer 1982-85; Dallas Times Herald, editorial bd 1985-. **Orgs:** Mem, Atlanta African Film Soc, Natl Assn Black Journalists, Black Perspective 1970-73; contributing editor Essence Magazine; editorial advisory bd NAACP Crisis Magazine 1979-80; Dallas-Fort Worth Assn of Black Communicators. **Honors/Awds:** Special Citation, Reporting Awards Ed Writers Assn, 1982; 1st place Reg 5 Natl Assoc of Black Journalists 1982; Natl Headliners Club Award for Consistently Outstanding Special/Feature Column Writing 1981; Journalism Acolade Award GA Conf on Social Welfare 1981; 1st place energy series Media Award for Economic Understanding Series Amos Tuck School of Business Admin Dartmouth Coll 1980; 1st place outstanding news feature Atlanta Assn of Black Journalists 1980; UPI GA Newspaper Awds, 2nd place column writing, 3rd place spot news coverage of Three Mile Island 1979; author "Martin Luther King Jr To The Mountaintop" Doubleday & Co1985; Katie Award Best Editorial Press Club of Dallas 1986; First Place Editorial Writing TX Assoc Press Managing Editors 1987. **Business Addr:** Editorial Writer, Dallas Times Herald, 1101 Pacific Ave, Dallas, TX 75202.

WOLFE, DEBORAH CANNON PARTRIDGE
Educator, cleric. **Personal:** Born Dec 22, Cranford, NJ; daughter of Gertrude Moody Cannon Morris and David W Cannon Sr; divorced; children: H Roy Partridge Jr. **Educ:** Columbia Univ, EdD, MA; Jersey City State Coll, BS; Postdoctoral Study, Vassar Coll, Union Theological Seminary, Jewish Theological Seminary of Amer. **Career:** Tuskegee Univ, prof & dir grad work 1938-50; Queens College of CUNY, prof of education, 1950-86; vstg prof, NY Univ 1951-54, Univ of MI 1952, Fordham Univ 1952-53, Columbia Univ 1953-54, TX Coll 1955, Univ of IL 1956-57, Wayne State Univ 1961, Grambling Univ; US House of Reps, ed chief comm on ed & labor 1962-65; Macmillan Publ Co, ed consult 1964; NSF, consult 1967-70; City Univ Ctr for African & Afro-Amer Studies and African Study Abroad, dir 1968-77; Natl Leadership Training Inst US Ofc of Ed, cons, vocational & tech ed 1968-71; First Baptist Church Cranford NJ, assoc minister, 1975; Queens Coll, prof ed 1950-86; New Jersey State Board of Education, 1963-93. **Orgs:** Chair NJ State Bd of Higher Educ 1988-93; chmn admiss comm Queens Coll CUNY, UN Rep for Ch Women United 1971-; chmn AAUW Legis Prog Comm 1973-77; Commn on Fed Rel Amer Council on Ed 1972-77; trustee bd science serv AAAS; mem trustee bd Seton Hall Univ; adv comm Bd of Educ Cranford NJ; grand basileus, Zeta Phi Beta Sorority, 1954-65, chair, 1975-, Zeta Pi Beta Educ Found; sec Kappa Delta Pi Educ Foundation; vice pres, Natl Council of Negro Women; bd of dirs, Home Mission Council, Progressive Natl Baptist Convention; Resolutions Comm, Natl Assn of State Boards of Education; board of trustees: Science Service; Education Development Center; former pres, National Alliance of Black School Educators; chair, Monroe Human Relations Commission; pres, Rossmoor Interfaith Council. **Honors/Awds:** Bldgs named in honor of Deborah Wolfe: Trenton State Coll 1970, Macon County, AL ; Award Hon Mem, Natl Soc for Prevention of Juvenile Delinquency; Women of Courage Radcliffe Coll; Special Honors Natl Alliance of Black School Educators, Northeastern Region Natl Assn of Colored Women's Clubs, Shrewsbury AME Zion Church; Citizen of the Year B'nai B'rith 1986; Citation Serv Omega Psi Phi Fraternity; Sojourner Truth Award Natl Ann of Business & Professional Women; Top Ladies of Distinction Hon Mem, 1986; Medal for Comm Serv Queens Coll of CUNY, 1986; Distinguished Service Award, Univ of

Medicine & Dentistry of New Jersey and Seton Hall Univ; Honorary Doctorates: Stockton State Coll, Kean Coll of New Jersey, Jersey City State Coll Monmouth Coll, Centenary Coll, Bloomfield Coll, William Pater Coll, and numerous other educational institutions, 26 in all; Medal of Honor, Daughters of American Revolution; Women of Achievement, National YMCA; visiting scholar, Princeton Theological Seminary. **Business Addr:** First Baptist Church, 20 W State St, Cranford, NJ 07016, (908)276-2760.

WOLFE, ESTEMORE A.
Educator, business executive. **Personal:** Born Dec 29, 1919, Crystal Springs, MS; divorced. **Educ:** Jackson State Univ, BS 1947; Wayne State Univ, MEd; NY Univ, DFA; Boston Univ, D Ed. **Career:** Ins exec 30 yrs; writer lecturer teacher 39 yrs; Wright Mutual Ins Co, vice pres sec 1968-. **Orgs:** Couns consult tech organizer fdr pres Detroit Chap Friends of AMISTAD; mem Amer Fed Teachers, Detroit Fed Teachers, Acad Soc & Polit Sci, Amer Reading Assn; mem NAACP, Amer Assn Higher Educ, Natl Assn Intergroup Relat Officials; 1977 Centennial Plng Comm Jackson State Univ; Smithsonian Inst Assn; Cntrl United Methodist Ch; life mem Amer Museum Natl History; natl pres Friends of AMISTAD & bd chmn Brooklyn; natl chmn Urban Planning Comm; Natl Ins Assn; trustee Jackson State Devel Found Jackson MS, Boston Univ, Alumni of MI; past bd chmn Detroit Met Symphony Orch; notary pub with seal 32 yrs; organized voter registration & gathered more than 500 witnesses to US Senate Hearing of late Sen Theo G Bilbo Jackson MS proving intimidation of Negroes & other min causing the Senator to lose his Sen Seat in WA 1946-47; educ soc Wayne St Univ & Purdue U. **Honors/Awds:** Centennial Medallion & cit Jackson State U; Kiwanis Intl Brass Ruby-Studded Pin, Bronze Plaque, Test Banquet 1976; Estemore A Wolfe Day plaque & cit Boston Univ Alumni Assn; Bronze Plaque Wharton Sch Univ of PA 1977; Col on Gov Cliff Finch's Staff MS 1977; Bronze Pla/Citation Estemore A Wolfe Day Detroit 1978; Case II Awd Coun for the Adv & Support to Higher Ed 1979; Century Aw & Sch Dev Fnd of Jackson St U 1979;Pres Citation NAFEO Awd Wash DC Pres Carter as guest spkr 1979; 1st Century Pres Plaque 1980; Spirit of Detroit Plaque City Council & Mayor Coleman A Young 1980; Disting Leadership Awd State Senate of MI 1983; Gold "J" w/diamonds President's Club Jackson State Univ 1984; Hon LLD Syracuse Univ; Hon LHD Wilberforce Univ. **Military Serv:** AUS t/sgt 1942-46. **Business Addr:** Division Vice Pres, Wright Mutual Ins, 2995 E Grand Blvd, Detroit, MI 48202.

WOLFE, GEORGE C.
Writer, director, producer. **Personal:** Born in Frankfort, KY. **Educ:** Pomona College, BA, directing, 1976; New York University, MFA, playwrighting, musical theatre, 1983. **Career:** Queenie Pie, musical, writer, 1985; The Colored Museum, writer, 1986; Hunger Chic, writer: Trying Times/PBS, 1989; Spunk, writer/director, 1990; The Caucasian Chalk Circle, director, 1990; New York Shakespeare Festival, president, director, 1990-92; Minimun Wage, writer, 1991; The Colored Museum, writer, co-director, Great Performances, 1991; Moving Beyond the Madness, curator, 1991-92; Jelly's Last Jam, Broadway Musical, writer/director, 1991-93; Bring In Da Noise, Bring In Da Funk. **Orgs:** Dramatist Guild, executive council, 1992-93; Young Playwrights Festival, board of directors, 1992-93; New York Shakespeare Festival, artistic associate, 1991-93. **Honors/Awds:** Dorothy Chandler Award, 1992; Obie Award, 1990; 2 Tony Award Nominations, 1992; Drama Desk Award, 1992; Hull-Warriner Award, 1986; 2 Audelco Awards for Theatre, The George Oppenheimer; Newsday Award; The CBS/FDG New Play Award; The New York University Distinguished Alumni Award; The HBO/USA Playwrights Award; 9 Tony Award Nominations for Bring In Da Noise, Bring In Da Funk, 1996. **Special Achievements:** Publications: Jelly's Last Jam, Theatre Communications Group, 1993; Spunk, TCG, 1991; Two By Wolfe, Fireside Theatre, Inc, 1991; The Colored Museum, Grove Press, Inc, 1988. **Business Addr:** Director, Jelly's Last Jam, c/o Wiley Hausam, Agent, International Creative Management, Inc, 40 W 57th St, New York, NY 10019.

WOLFE, JOHN THOMAS
Educational administrator. **Personal:** Born Feb 22, 1942, Jackson, MS; son of Jeanette Wolfe and John Wolfe; children: Wyatt, John T, David A. **Educ:** Chicago State Univ, BEd 1964; Purdue Univ, MS 1972, PhD 1976. **Career:** Purdue Univ, mgr employee relations 1975-77; Fayetteville State Univ, English dept chair 1977-79, div head humanities & fine arts 1979-83, academic dean 1983-85; Bowie State Univ, provost and vice pres for academic affairs; Kentucky State Univ, Frankfort, KY, president, currently. **Orgs:** Pres Black Caucus Natl Council Teacher of English 1982-88; bd of dirs Bowie New Town Ctr Minority Adv Bd 1985-; steering comm Prince George's Co MD Univ High School 1985-87; standing comm of teacher preparation Natl Council of Teachers of English 1984-87; chair, advisory bd Prince George's County, MD Entrepreneurial Develop Program. **Honors/Awds:** Kappa Delta Pi Educ Honor Soc 1972; Hon Mem Alpha Kappa Mu Honor Soc 1983; Fellowship Amer Council on Educ 1982-83. **Business Addr:** President, Kentucky State University, East Main St, Frankfort, KY 40601.

WOLFE, WILLIAM K.
Company executive. **Personal:** Born Feb 9, 1926; son of Margaret Langston Wolfe Burrell and Carl L Wolfe; married Virginia King Wolfe, Jun 16, 1956 (divorced); children: Jane, Betty, Jonathan. **Educ:** Springfield Coll, 1951; Adelphi U, MS 1960. **Career:** YMCA Dayton OH, sec 1951-53; Stuyvesant Residence Club, children's supr 1953-54; New York City Housing Auth, housing coord 1954-58; Stuyvesant Comm Ctr, exec dir 1959-63; Urban League, Whitesplain, NY, CEO, 1963-67, Cleveland, OH, CEO, 1972-85; Urban League of Westchester Co Inc, exec dir; United Comm Corp,exec dir 1966-67; Ft Greene Comm Corp, exec dir 1968-69; Hunter Coll School of Soc Work, lecturer 1970-; Urban League of Gr Cleveland, exec; CEOGC, dep exec dir1985-87, interim exec dir 1987-. **Orgs:** Vol pres OH Wilberforce Conf 1978-; mem Natl Assn of Soc Workers; Natl Assn of Inter-Grp Relations Officers; mem Alpha Phi Alpha Fraternity; Rotary Club; Area Councils Assn; Businessmen Interracial Com; Cleveland Area Manpower Council; NAACP; City Club; bd trustees Metro Cleveland Jobs Council; Afro-Amer Cultural & Historical Soc; Natl Assn of Soc Welfare; instructor, Hunter School, SW New York, l967-72; CEO, Urban League of Bridgeport, l989; pres & bd mem, Ohio Welfare Coucil, l979-84; bd mem, N.A.B.SW., l968. **Honors/Awds:** Co-author "Reaching Out a Puerto Rican dialogue"; author, ed of many articles & papers; Founder Award, BPA, 1987, Award of Appreciation, Operation of Big Vote, l981; Column Call-Post, l982; Publication for urban League, l978-84. **Military Serv:** Army Air Force, Master Sergeant, l944-46.

WOLFMAN, BRUNETTA REID
Educational administrator. **Personal:** Born Sep 4, Clarksdale, MS; married Burton I Wolfman; children: Andrea C, Jeffrey Allen. **Educ:** Univ of CA Berkeley, BA 1957, MA 1968, PhD 1971; Boston Univ, DHL 1983; Northeastern Univ, DPed 1983; Regis College, DLaws 1984; Suffolk Univ, DHL 1985, Stonehill College 1985. **Career:** Univ of CA Berkeley, teaching fellow 1969-71; Dartmouth Coll, CA coord 1971-72, asst dean of faculty/asst prof 1972-74; Univ of MA, asst vice pres 1974-76; Wheelock Coll Boston, academic dean 1976-78; MA Dept of Educ, exec planner 1978-82; Roxbury Comm Coll, president 1983-. **Orgs:** Program dir YWCA Oakland & Berkeley CA 1959-63; exec dir Camp Fire Girls Berkeley 1963-67; consult Arthur D Little Inc 1977-78; pres New England Minority Women Admins 1977-78; bd dir Natl Ctr for Higher Educ Mgmt Systems 1978-; bd dir Boston Fenway Prog1979-; two articles in black separtism & social reality Pergamon Press 1977; overseer Boston Symphony Orchestra 1984; Museum of Fine Arts 1984; overseer Stone Ctr Wellesley Coll; bd Natl Conf of Christians &Jews; bd United States Trust Bank; bd Boston Private Indus Council; bd Amer Council on Education; councilor Council on Education for Public Health; urban commission AACJC. **Honors/Awds:** Paper presented & pub OECD Paris 1978; Natl Inst of Educ grant Superwomen Study 1978-79; papers presented annual meeting Amer Educ Rsch Assn 1980; "Roles" Westminster Press 1983. **Business Addr:** President, Roxbury Community College, 1234 Columbus Ave, Boston, MA 02119.

WOMACK, BOBBY DWAYNE
Singer. **Personal:** Born Mar 4, 1944, Cleveland, OH; son of Naomi Womack and Friendly Womack; married Regina K B Banks, Dec 31, 1975; children: Vincent, Bobby Truth, GinaRe. **Career:** Truth Records Inc recording artist. **Honors/Awds:** Provided schlrshp through Harry Womack Scholarship Fund; Youth Inspirational Awd 1975; Appreciation Awd Walter Reed Army Med Ctr; several gold records.

WOMACK, CARTER DEVON
Advertising executive. **Personal:** Born Jun 21, 1951, Greenville, AL; son of Jessie Payne Womack and Matthew Womack. **Educ:** Alabama A&M Univ, Normal, AL, BS, Chemistry, 1973. **Career:** Goodyear Tires Rubber Co, Akron, OH, corp mgr of EEO, 1973-87; Ryder System Inc, Miami, Fl, mgr of EEO programs, 1987-89; Ryder Truck Rental Inc, Miami, Fl, director employee relations, 1989-91; The Black Collegian Magazine, senior vice pres, 1991-. **Honors/Awds:** Sigma Man of the Year, Phi Beta Sigma, 1987; March of Dimes Service, March of Dimes, 1989; Outstanding Young Man of America, Jaycees, 1986-89; Top Business Professional, Dollars & Sense, 1990. .

WOMACK, CHRISTOPHER CLARENCE
Utility company executive. **Personal:** Born Feb 26, 1958, Greenville, AL; son of Ruby Womack; married Sabrina Shannon; children: Shannon Ashley, Christopher Michael. **Educ:** Western Michigan Univ, BS, public admin, 1979; American Univ, MPA, 1985. **Career:** US House of Representatives, legislative aide to Rep Leon E Panetta, 1979-84; Subcommittee on Personnel and Police, Comm on House Administration, staff dir, 1984-87; Alabama Power Co, governmental affairs rep, 1988-89, asst to the vp of public affairs, 1989-91, dir of comm relations, 1991-93; vp of public relations, 1993-95, sr vp of public relations & corp services, 1995-. **Orgs:** Alabama Ballet; Alabama Business Charitable Trust Fund, exec dir; Alpha Phi Alpha Education Foundation, chair; Birmingham Culture & Heritage Foundation, City Stages, trea; Birmingham Comm on Olympic Football; Bd of Deacons, Sixth Ave Baptist Church. **Honors/Awds:** Silver Knight of Management Award, 1994; Top 40 Under 40 Designation, Birmingham Business Journal, 1993; Leadership Birmingham, 1990. **Business Addr:** Senior VP, Alabama Power Co, 600 N 18th St, PO Box 2641, Birmingham, AL 35291, (205)250-2607.

WOMACK, HENRY CORNELIUS
Educator. **Personal:** Born Feb 18, 1938, Grapeland, MS. **Educ:** Alcorn St U, BS (summa cum laude) 1961; Wayne St U, MS 1965, PhD 1974. **Career:** Harper School of Nursing, dir basic science, 1965-69; Ball State University, associate professor, physiology and health, 1969-, teaching professor, 1990-. **Orgs:** Fed of Am Scientists 1974-; IN Acad of Sci 1974-; Human Biology Council 1974-; ACLU 1974-; AAAS 1974-; AAUP 1974-. **Honors/Awds:** Scholar of Yr, Omega Psi Phi Frat Inc 1961; fellow NDEA 1970-74. **Military Serv:** USAF au/c 1954-58. **Business Addr:** Associate Professor, Department of Physiology and Health Sciences, Ball State University, Muncie, IN 47306.

WOMACK, JOE NEAL, JR.
Insurance company representative. **Personal:** Born Oct 5, 1950, Mobile, AL; son of Annie Laura Brown Pressley and Joe N Womack, Sr.; married Juliette F Womack (divorced 1986); children: Joe Neal Womack, III; married Mary B Womack, Dec 1991. **Educ:** St Paul's College, Lawrenceville, VA, BS, Business, 1972. **Career:** Metropolitan Life, Mobile, AL, sales rep, 1972; Shell Chemical/DuPont, Mobile, AL, financial analyst, 1973-90; The Prudential, Mobile, AL, sales rep, 1990-. **Orgs:** Chairman, African-American Summit Steering Committee, 1989-; membership comm chair, Mobile Area Mardi Gras Association, 1987-; member, Alpha Phi Alpha Fraternity, 1972; member, Mardi Gras Maskers, 1988-. **Military Serv:** Marine Corps, major, 1973-. **Home Addr:** 2816 Westmoor Ct, Mobile, AL 36695.

WOMACK, JOHN H.
Janitorial company executive. **Personal:** Born Jul 8, 1944, Virginia; son of Elnora Womack and George Womack; married Bertha Womack; children: Tonya, John Jr, Monica. **Educ:** Fisher Junior College; Gordon-Conwell Theological Seminary, master of religious education, 1990. **Career:** McGarrahan Steel Erection, iron worker, 1970-77; Salem Fire Department, Salem, MA, firefighter, 1977-80; JJS Services/Peabody Paper, Peabody, MA, president/CEO, 1977-. **Orgs:** President, Black Corporate Presidents of New England; board of directors, Building Service Contractors Association International, 1986; board member, Job for Youth, 1990-. **Honors/Awds:** Minority Advocate of the Year, US Small Business Administration, 1984; Outstanding Services to Small Businesses, Boston Urban Bankers Forum James Ingram, 1984; Minority Small Business Person of the Year, US Small Business Administration. **Military Serv:** US Navy, E-4, 1963-67. **Business Addr:** President, JJS Services Inc, 197 Washington St, Peabody, MA 01960.

WOMACK, ROBERT W., SR. See Obituaries section.

WOMACK, STANLEY H.
Architect. **Personal:** Born Jul 8, 1930, Pittsburgh, PA; married Winona; children: S Mathew, Deborah, Scott. **Educ:** Howard Univ, BArch 1954. **Career:** Bellante & Clauss Arch & Engrs St Thomas VI, asst office mgr 1964-66; Edmund G Good & Partners Arch, job capt 1964-66; Lawrie & Green Arch, arch 1966-72; Murray/Womack Arch, partner 1972-76; Bender Royal Ebaugh Womack Inc Arch Engrs, principal 1976-78; Stanley H Womack Assoc Arch, owner. **Orgs:** Mem Amer Ins of Arch, PA Soc of Arch; life mem Omega Psi Phi; basileus Kappa Omega Chap Harrisburg PA; bd of dir Tri-Cty OIC; bd dir Police Athletic League; life mem NAACP; mem Urban league, St Paul Bapt Church; past comm chmn Cub Pack 21; bd dir Tri Cty Area YMCA; bd dir Tri-Cty United Way; track & cross country team Howard Univ; mem Harrisburg Tennis Team, Riverside Optimist Club, Harrisburg Rotary, Jaycees; bd dir Natl Jr Tennis League; pres Harrisburg Frontiers; mem Omega Psi Phi, Kappa Omega. **Honors/Awds:** 1975 Omega Man of the Year; Comm Leaders of Amer Awd; Achievement Awd Jaycees Intl; Sports Achievement Awd Pittsburgh Centennial. **Military Serv:** USAF 1st lt. **Business Addr:** Stanley H Womack Assoc Arch, Payne-Shoemaker Ste 301, Harrisburg, PA 17101.

WOMACK, TONY (ANTHONY DARRELL)
Professional baseball player. **Personal:** Born Sep 25, 1969, Danville, VA. **Educ:** Guilford College. **Career:** Pittsburgh Pirates, infielder, 1993-. **Business Addr:** Professional Baseball Player, Pittsburgh Pirates, PO Box 7000, Pittsburgh, PA 15212, (412)323-5000.

WOMBLE, JEFFERY MAURICE
Journalist. **Personal:** Born Apr 4, 1964, Fayetteville, NC; son of Corine McLean Womble (deceased) and Charles Leo Womble, Sr (deceased). **Educ:** Fayetteville State University, Fayetteville, NC, BA, English, 1986. **Career:** Fayetteville Observer, Fayetteville, NC, reporter, editor, 1982-. **Orgs:** Editor of

Sphinx, Alpha Phi Alpha Fraternity, 1990-; National Association Black Journalists, 1988-; Big Brothers Program, 1990-; Community Advisory Board of Junior League of Fayetteville; Alpha Phi Alpha Fraternity, Inc; Find-A-Friend, advisory board; Upward Bound, advisory bd, FSU; Women's Center of Fayetteville, teen advisory bd. **Honors/Awds:** Media Award, VFW Post 6018, 1987; Outstanding African-American Male Award from Alpha Kappa Alpha Sorority; Community Resource Specialist of Cumberland County Schools; Outstanding Journalist Award from Omar Ibyn Syiid; Cumberland County Minority AIDS Speaker's Bureau, Community Service Award; NC Working Press, 1st place, Profiles; Teen Advisory Board, Women's Center of Fayetteville, North Carolina Working Press, 1st place Profiles, 2nd place Fashion Writing. **Home Addr:** 629 Deep Creek Rd, Fayetteville, NC 28301. **Business Addr:** Reporter/Editor, Features Dept, Fayetteville Publishing Co, Whitfield St, PO Box 849, Fayetteville, NC 28302.

WOMBLE, LARRY W.
Educational administrator (retired), State representative. **Personal:** Born Jun 6, 1941, Winston-Salem, NC; son of Dorothy Gwyn Womble and Luchion Womble; married Lonnie Hamilton (divorced 1967). **Educ:** Winston-Salem State University, Winston-Salem, NC, BS, 1963; University of North Carolina at Chapel Hill, NC, certificate, 1967-68; University of North Carolina-Greensboro, Greensboro, NC, degree, 1975; Appalachian State University, Boone, NC, degree, 1977. **Career:** Winston-Salem/Forsyth County School, Diggs Intermediate, Winston-Salem, NC, dept chairman, instructor, 1971-74; Wake Forest University, Winston-Salem, NC, supervisor, dir, 1974-75; Winston-Salem/Forsyth County School, Old Town School, Winston-Salem, NC, asst principal, 1975-86, Mineral Springs, Winston-Salem, WI, asst principal, 1986-89, Cook Middle School, asst principal, 1989-90, Kennedy Middle School, Winston-Salem, NC, asst principal, 1990-91; Paisley Middle School, Winston-Salem, NC, asst prin, 1992-93; North Carolina House of Representatives, state representative, currently. **Orgs:** Life member, NAACP; Natl Black Caucus of Local Elected Officials, 1987-; Human Dev Policy Committee, 1989-; chm, Community Dev Housing/Gen Govt Committee, 1989-; Public Works Committee, 1989-; pres, NC Black Elected Municipal Officials, 1985-90. **Honors/Awds:** Young Educator of the Year, 1964-65; R J Reynolds Scholarship, various projects and ideas, R J Reynolds, 1971-72; Asst Principal of the Year, 1980-81; served as Ambassadors of Friendship Force to Europe and Kenya; Man of the Year Award, Winston-Salem Chronicle Newspaper, 1985. **Home Addr:** 1294 Salem Lake Rd, Winston-Salem, NC 27107, (910)784-9373. **Business Phone:** (910)733-5751.

WONDER, STEVIE (STEVLAND JUDKINS MORRIS)
Singer, songwriter. **Personal:** Born May 13, 1950, Saginaw, MI; son of Lula Mae Morris; married Syreeta Wright, 1971 (divorced 1972); children: Aisha, Keita Sawandi, Mumtaz Ekow. **Educ:** Michigan School for Blind, grad 1968. **Career:** Performances in England, Europe, Japan, Okinawa, Nigeria; appeared in motion pictures; guest appearances on TV including, Ed Sullivan, Mike Douglas, Tom Jones, American Bandstand, and Dinah Shore; Black Bull Music, founder/pres, 1970-; Wondirection Records, founder/pres, 1972-; singer/songwriter/pianist, currently; recordings include: "Tribute to Uncle Ray," 1963; "Uptight," 1966; "My Cherie Amour," 1970; "Signed, Sealed, Delivered," 1970; "Songs in the Key of Life," 1976; "I Just Called to Say I Love You," 1984; "Characters,", 1988; "Jungle Fever," 1991; numerous others. **Honors/Awds:** Won more than 15 Grammy Awards, including awards for best male vocalist in both pop & rhythm & blues categories, best pop song and best album. Inducted into Songwriters Hall of Fame, 1982; Academy Award for Best Original Song "I Just Called to Say I Love You" from The Lady in Red, 1984. **Special Achievements:** Participant in numerous social projects, including the creation of Martin Luther King Day National Holiday, AIDS awareness, anti-Apartheid demonstrations, and campaigns against drunk driving. **Business Addr:** Singer, c/o Theresa Cropper, Esq, 4616 Magnolia Blvd, Burbank, CA 91505.

WOOD, ANDREW W.
Clergyman, convention executive. **Personal:** Born Oct 13, 1919, Clinton, SC; son of Annie Lee Duckett Wood and General Wilson Wood; married Gertrude M Burton, Sep 29, 19 ; children: Verna M Wood Adams, Jesse Leon. **Educ:** Christian Bible Coll & Seminary; Bachelor of Teheology; MDiv. **Career:** Kilrny Temple Baptist Church, pastor 1947-54; Plgrm Rest Bapt Church, 1947-51; Mt Zion Baptist Church, 1951-60; First Bapt Church 1954-60; Missionary to Kenya EA 1981; Bethany Baptist Church 1960-. **Orgs:** Pres Windng Gulf Dist Sun Sch Conv 1949-51; Nr Nth Side Fellowship of Chs sec 1962, pres 1964; cor sec Cong Christian Ed 1962-71; spksman Civ Rights Org of Columbus 1966-69; exec sec OH Baptist Gen Conv; sec WV Bd Evnglsm; sec Coal River Dist Assn; mem exec bd WV Baptist St Conv; pres Baptist Pstrs Conf Columbus, 1970-78; asst dean Estn Union Dist Assn; judctry Metro Area Ch Bd of Columbus; mem Bapt Minstrl All of Columbus; mem Interdenom Minstrl All; Nat Bapt Conv USA Inc; mem NAACP, CLASP, Inst 1st Dist Women's Conv, 30 years; bursar EU Bible School; coord Columbus Baptist Simultaneous Revival, 1963-88; board of trustees, Ohio Council of Churches, 1990. **Honors/Awds:** OH Leadership Conf Plaque; OH Bapt Gen Conv for Outstanding Leadership & Achievements; Spec Recog & Hons because of work done in Bush country of Kenya in 200 Baptist Churches; Baptist Pastors Conf, pres, 1992-. **Home Addr:** 2864 Ivanhoe Dr, Columbus, OH 43209. **Business Addr:** Pastor, Bethany Baptist Church, 959 Bulen Ave, Columbus, OH 43206.

WOOD, ANTON VERNON
Business executive. **Personal:** Born Jun 7, 1949, Washington, DC. **Educ:** Shepherd Clge, BS 1971; Montgomery Clge, AA 1969. **Career:** DC Office of Consumer Prot, comm educ spec, serv area mgr; DC Power Inc, pub affairs dir; Wash Ecology Cen, prog dir; Wash Area Military & Draft Law Panel, couns. **Orgs:** Consult numerous elections in Wash; chmn Neighborhood Commn 6a 1975-; publ mem DC Nghbrhd Reinvestment Commn; chair com on Employment prac 1976-; bd dir Metro Wash Planning & Housing Assc; past chmn DC Statehood Party. **Business Addr:** 509 C St NE, Washington, DC 20002.

WOOD, BRENDA BLACKMON
TV news anchor/reporter. **Personal:** Born Sep 8, 1955, Washington, DC; daughter of Alma Montgomery Blackmon and Henry Blackmon Jr; married Keith Anthony Wood, Nov 25, 1978; children: Kristen Brooke, Kandis Brittany. **Educ:** Oakwood College, Huntsville, AL, 1973-75; Loma Linda Univ, Riverside CA, BA, 1977. **Career:** WAAY-TV, Huntsville AL, news reporter, 1977-80; WMC-TV, Memphis, TN, news anchor/reporter, 1980-88; WAGA-TV, Atlanta, GA, news anchor/reporter, 1988-. **Orgs:** Member, Natl Academy of Television Arts and Science, 1989-; president, Southern Society of Adventist Communicators, 1990-; member, Natl Association of Black Journalists, 1986-; Atlanta Association of Black Journalists; The Atlanta Press Club; American Women in Film. **Honors/Awds:** Gabriel Award of Merit (for TV Documentary "Ramses the Great"), The Catholic Denomination, 1986; Ace of Diamond Award, Women in Communication, GA, Chapter, 1990; Two Southern Regional Emmys, Best News Anchor; Four-Time Emmy Winner, Prime Time Specials; Emmy, Series Reporting; Emmy, News Team Coverage; Georgia Association of Broadcasters, News Personality of the Year, 1996; Atlanta Association of Bloack Journalist Award, Documentary & Special Reporting; Best Show Award, AABJ. **Business Addr:** News Anchor, WAGA-TV, 1551 Briarcliff Rd, NE, Atlanta, GA 30302.

WOOD, CURTIS A.
Attorney. **Personal:** Born Jul 31, 1942, Memphis, TN; son of Lou Lee and Curtis; married Claire O. **Educ:** Columbia Clge, BA 1964; Columbia Law Sch, LLB 1967. **Career:** Bedford Stuyvesant Restoration Corp, pres 1977-82, gen counsel 1972-77; Wood, Williams, Rafalsky & Harris, managing partner 1982-. **Orgs:** Mem NY Bar Assc; IL Bar Assc.

WOOD, DAISY M. (DEE)
Human resources executive. **Career:** General Electric Co, Global diversity and recruiting manager, currently. **Orgs:** National Pan-Hellenic Council, pres. **Home Addr:** 7904 Montero Drive, Prospect, KY 40059.

WOOD, GARLAND E.
Investment banker. **Personal:** Born Dec 29, 1943, New York, NY; children: Michelle, Cynthia, Scott. **Educ:** Columbia Coll, AB 1965; Columbia Business School, MBA 1972. **Career:** Goldman Sachs & Co, partner 1972-. **Business Addr:** Partner, Goldman, Sachs & Co, 85 Broad St, New York, NY 10004.

WOOD, HAROLD LEROY
Judge (retired). **Personal:** Born Dec 6, 1919, Bridgeport, CT; married Thelma Anne Cheatham; children: Gregory Lance, Laverne Jill Wertz. **Educ:** Lincoln Univ, AB 1942; Cornell Univ Law Sch, JD 1948; New York Univ Law Sch, LLM 1952. **Career:** Westchester Co Bd of Supers, super 1957-67; NY State Senate Albany, leg asst 1964; Mt Vernon City Common Council, alderman 1968-69; Westchester Co, family court judge 1969-71; Westchester Co, co court judge 1971-74; Supreme Court NY, justice of the supreme court 1974-95. **Orgs:** Local pres NAACP Mt Vernon NY; bd of dirs Mt Vernon Hosp; bd of dirs Urban League White Plains NY. **Military Serv:** USAF 2d lieut 1942-46. **Business Addr:** Kent, Hazzard, Wilson Greer & Fay, 50 Main St, White Plains, NY 10601.

WOOD, JEROME H., JR.
Educator. **Personal:** Born Mar 22, 1941, Washington, DC; son of Aramenta Alston Wood and Jerome H Wood, Sr. **Educ:** Howard Univ, BA (summa cum laude) 1962; Brown Univ, PhD 1969. **Career:** Temple Univ, instructor history 1966-69, asst prof history 1969-70; Haverford Coll, visiting asst prof history 1969-70; Swarthmore Coll, prof history, 1970-, assoc provost, 1986-89. **Orgs:** Assoc dir Afro-Amer Historical & Cultural Museum Philadelphia 1975-76; bd mem Media Fellowship Hse PA 1975-81; mem Historical Soc of PA, PA Abolition Soc, Amer Historical Assn, Latin Amer Studies Assn; several publications including "The Negro in Early PA" Eugene Genovese "Plantation Town & Co" 1974; "Conestoga Crossroads Lancaster PA 1730-1790" Harrisburg 1979; mem Phi Beta Kappa, Phi Alpha Theta; bd mem of Historian, Lansdowne PA Symphony Orchestra. **Honors/Awds:** Fulbright Research Scholar (Uruguay, Brazil, Venezuela) 1980; Fulbright Lecturer in US History Nankai Univ People's Republic of China 1983-84; Woodrow Wilson Dissertation Fellow, 1965-66; Honorary Woodrow Wilson Fellow, 1962-63; fluent in Spanish, Portuguese Languages. **Business Addr:** Professor, Dept of History, Swarthmore College, Swarthmore, PA 19081.

WOOD, JUANITA WALLACE
Director. **Personal:** Born Jun 30, 1928, Waycross, GA; divorced. **Educ:** Cntrl State Univ, BA; Northeastern IL Univ, MA Inner City Studies; John Marshall Sch of Law, atnd; Loyola Grad Schl Soc Work. **Career:** Dept of Human Resources Div Corrections on Youth Svcs, comm unit dir corrections soc work 1969-; counseling youths & families involved in Correctional Sys; neighborhood worker commn on youth welfare; caseworker childrens div 1958-64; Cook Co Juvenile Ct, probation ofcr 1953-58; Cook Co Pub Aid, caseworker 1952-53. **Orgs:** Mem NASW Law Sor 1958-61; Sensitivity Training Sessions & Seminars; mngrl training with present agcy US Civil Serv Commn; Cook Co Com on Crim Justice. **Honors/Awds:** Recip Award from Devel Grp Progs to deal with Youths & Families involved in Juvenile Justice Sys. **Business Addr:** Control Office, 640 N La Salle St, Chicago, IL.

WOOD, LAWRENCE ALVIN
Ophthalmologist. **Personal:** Born Jan 5, 1949, New York, NY; son of Lillian Miller Wood and Lawrence Wood; married Yvette Marie Binns, Feb 5, 1983; children: Lawrence A. **Educ:** Hunter Coll, BS 1972; Meharry Medical Coll, MD 1979; Naval Hospital, San Diego, CA, ophthamology residency, 1985-88. **Career:** Harlem Hosp, physical therapist 1972-75; Howard Univ Hosp, intern 1979-80; Public Health Svcs, general practitioner 1980-82; US Navy, flight surgeon 1982-85; dept head, ophthalmology, Millington Naval Hospital; Naval Hospital, Long Beach, CA, staff ophthalmologist. **Orgs:** Mem Acad of Ophthalmology 1985, Amer Medical Assoc 1986, Dramatist's Guild 1986. **Honors/Awds:** Flight Surgeon of the Year 1984; production of play "No Marks, Just Memories" 1986. **Military Serv:** USN, 9 yrs, Commander, 1991-; Navy Commendation Medal, 1983, 1991, Combat Action Ribbon, 1983, National Defense Ribbon, 1991.

WOOD, LEIGH C.
Telecommunications company executive. **Career:** Cellular One, chief executive officer, 1993-; Cellular Communications, vice president of operations, currently. **Business Addr:** CEO, Cellular One, 350 E. Wilson Bridge Rd., Worthington, OH 43085, (614)436-4331.

WOOD, LEON
Professional sports official. **Career:** NBA, referee, currently. **Business Addr:** NBA Official, National Basketball Association, 645 5th Ave, 15th Fl, New York, NY 10022-5986.

WOOD, MARGARET BEATRICE
City official. **Personal:** Born in Charleston, WV; daughter of Ivory B Morris and John D Morris; married Alvin B Wood; children: Alvin B Jr, Irene B, Llewellyn. **Educ:** Howard Univ, BA (Cum Laude) 1934; Central Connecticut State Univ, Elemementary Educ 30 hrs 1949; Univ of Hartford, MEd 30 hrs 1964; Bank State Coll NY, NDEA Inst 1969. **Career:** Hartford Public Schools, teacher 1948-60, reading consultant 1960-66, asst supvr reading & dir of IRIT 1966-75, coord of reading & communiction arts 1975-80; Town of Bloomfield, Bloomfield, CT, town treasurer, 1987-90. **Orgs:** Dir Summer School 1974; devel of Language Arts Generalist 1972; pres Comm Assoc of Reading Research 1976; adjunct prof Univ of Hartford Seminar St Croix & St Thomas 1978; councilman Town of Bloomfield CT 1969-75, deputy mayor 1974-75. **Honors/Awds:** Sojourner Truth Award, Natl Council of Negro Women 1972; Distinguished Serv Award, Hartford Chapter Delta Sigma Theta 1981. **Home Addr:** 131 Wadhams Rd, Bloomfield, CT 06002.

WOOD, MICHAEL H.
Physician, surgeon. **Personal:** Born Mar 28, 1942, Dayton, OH; married Florentina Serquina; children: Mark, Anthony, Michael Jr. **Educ:** IN Inst Tech, BS 1968; Meharry Medical Coll, MD 1972. **Career:** Westland Medical Ctr, chief dept surgery 1984-; WSU Sch of Medicine Dept Surgery, instructor 1977-78, clinical asst prof 1978-88, clinical assoc prof, 1988-; Detroit Riverview Hospital, chief, dept of surgery, 1990-; Cain-Wood Surgical Associates, physician, currently. **Orgs:** Chmn of bd Detroit Medical Group 1985-86. **Honors/Awds:** Biomedical Rsch Grant 1979-80, Rsch Awd Program 1980-81, Biomedical Rsch Support Grant 1981-82 Wayne State Univ; sponsor Frederick Coller Awd Amer Coll of Surgeons MI Chap 1980; Theodore McGraw Clinical Faculty Teaching Award, Wayne State University Dept of Surgery, 1990. **Military Serv:** USAF A2/c 4 yrs. **Business Addr:** Physician, Cain-Wood Surgical Associates, PC, 4160 John R Ste-805, Detroit, MI 48201.

WOOD, TOMMIE
Professional sports official. **Career:** NBA, referee, currently. **Orgs:** National Basketball Referees Association; NAACP. **Business Addr:** NBA Official, National Basketball Association, 645 5th Ave, 15th Fl, New York, NY 10022-5986.

WOOD, VIVIAN FRANCES
Academic librarian. **Personal:** Born Jan 28, 1945, Plainfield, NJ; daughter of Sarah Frances Wood and L Cassell Wood Sr (deceased). **Educ:** Howard Univ, BA, 1967; Catholic Univ, MA, 1969; Rutgers Univ, MLS, 1974. **Career:** DC Public Schools, teacher, 1969-71; Prince Georges County, Maryland, Public Library, asst librarian, 1971-73; Rutgers Univ, reference librarian/asst prof, 1974-81; Hofstra Univ, collection development librarian/asst prof of library services, 1981-. **Orgs:** Nassau County Library Assn, Academic and Special Libraries Div, pres, 1994; Nassau City Library Assn, Academic and Special Libraries Div, vp, 1993; Nassau County Economic Opportunity Commission, board member, 1985-92; New Jersey Library Assn, Academic Libraries Div, vp, 1979-80; Assn of Black Women in Higher Education, Nassau/Suffolk Chapter, Sec, exec bd mem, 1994-97. **Special Achievements:** Conference Paper, ''Bibliographic Overview of the Harlem Renaissance,'' Natl Endowment for the Humanities & Hofstra Univ; ''Iceland'' Read More About It, vol 3 of An Encyclopedia of Information Sources on Historical Figures & Events, Pierian Press, 1989; Conference Paper ''Collection Development for Africana Studies,'' Assoc of College & Research Libraries, 1993; United Nations Fourth World Conference on Women/NGO Forum in Beijing, China, delegate, 1995; Panelist: Race, Gender & Academe, United Nations Fourth World Conference on Women NGO Forum, Beijing, China, 1995; delegate, Research Librarians Delegation to South Africa, 1997. **Home Addr:** 726 Center Drive, Baldwin, NY 11510. **Business Addr:** Professor, Hofstra Univ, Axinn Library, 123 Hofstra, Hempstead, NY 11550, (516)463-6431.

WOOD, WILLIAM L., JR.
Attorney. **Personal:** Born Dec 4, 1940, Cleveland, OH; married Patricia Mixon; children: Robin, Melissa. **Educ:** Brown U, BA 1962; Yale Law Sch, JD 1965. **Career:** Untd Ch of Christ, 1964; Mandell & Wright Houston TX, assoc 1965-68; Intl Nickel Co N Y & Pfizer Inc NY atty 1968-71; Union Carbide Corp NY atty 1971-74; City of N Y, gen cnsl & controller 1974-79; NY S Atty Gen, chief ed bureau 1979-81; NY St Office of Prof Disc, exec dir 1981-85; Wood & Scher, Attys, partner 1985-. **Orgs:** Contributing editor, Discipline, natl journla covering prof discipline, 1982-84; Information Please Almanac, editor, 1981-82; NY St Dental Journal, What Every Dentist Should know about Prof Misconduct, June/July 1982 (vol 48 no 6 pp 378-380); NY St Dental Journal, an interview on prof dicipline Oct 1982 (vol 48 no 8 p 538); NY St Pharmacist, recent changes in prof dicipline (vol 57 no 1, Fall 1982, p v); NY St Dental Journal, Record retentiona professional responsibility even after the patient has gone, Feb 1984 (vol 50, no 2, p 98); NY St Pharmacist, To the new Supvr Pharmacist Congratulations & a word of Warning, summer 1983, vol 57, no 4; NY St Pharmacist, The violations comm vol 58, no 3, Spring 1984; Veterinary News, Legal Remedies for Unpaid Fees, May 1984; admtd to TX 1965, NY Bar 1969; NY St Bar Asso, Am Arbitration Asso, One Hundred Black Men Inc, Am Pub Hlth Asso, Natl Clearinghouse on Licensure, Enfrcmnt & Regulation. **Honors/Awds:** Black Achvrs in Industry Awd 1974 (Nom by Union Carbine Corp). **Home Addr:** 39 Sunset Dr, Croton On Hudson, NY 10520. **Business Addr:** Attorney, Wood & Scher Attys at Law, One Chase Rd, Scarsdale, NY 10583.

WOOD, WILLIAM S.
Attorney, judge. **Personal:** Born Dec 3, 1926, Chicago, IL; children: William Jr, Eugene T. **Educ:** Univ of Iowa, BA, 1947, LLD, 1950. **Career:** State Atty Office, asst atty, 1956-60; Private practice, 1960-83; Cook County Courts, assoc judge. **Orgs:** Mem, Def Lawyer Assn, Cook County Bar, Chicago Bar. **Military Serv:** USA 1950-53. **Business Addr:** Associate Judge, Cook County Court, Richard J Daley Center, Chicago, IL 60602.

WOOD, WILLIAM VERNELL, SR.
Business executive. **Personal:** Born Dec 23, 1936, Washington, DC; son of Amanda Wood and John Wood; married Sheila Peters; children: LaJuane, Andre, William Jr. **Educ:** Coalinga Jr Coll, 1956; Univ of So CA, BS 1957-60. **Career:** Green Bay Packers NFL, free safety, 1960-71; Philadelphia Bell WFL, head coach 1976-77; Toronto Argonauts Football Team, asst coach 1979-80, head coach 1980-82; Willie Wood Mech Sys Inc, pres 1983-. **Orgs:** Bd of dir Police Police Boys & Girls Club 1984-. **Honors/Awds:** All-Pro 6 Yrs NFL 1960-71; Pro-Bowl 8 yrs NFL 1960-71; 5 World Championship Team Green Bay Packers 1961-62, 1965-67; 1st two Superbowl Championship Teams 1966-67; All 25 yrs Team NFL 1982; NFL Hall of Fame 1989 Silver Anniversary Super Bowl All-Star Team. **Home Addr:** 7941-16th St NW, Washington, DC 20012.

WOODALL, ELLIS O., SR.
Educational administrator. **Personal:** Born Aug 18, 1927, Lithonia, GA; married Annie L; children: Diana A, Ellis Jr, Cynthia F, Melanie K. **Educ:** Morris Brown Coll, AB, BS; Atlanta Univ & Univ GA, grad work. **Career:** HS teacher 20 yrs; Pub Housing Comm; Rural Health Comm State of GA, past mem; City of Lithonia, city councilman; DeKalb Co, training officer. **Orgs:** Master Boy Scouts; past pres Lithonia Civic Club; mem Credit Union Fdrs Club; vice pres Lithonia Fed Credit Union; deacon clk Union Baptist Church; chmn City Finan. **Honors/Awds:** Com Tchr of Yr; Citizen of Yr Awd Lithonia Civic Club; Area Boy Scout Master Awd of Yr. **Military Serv:** WW II Victory Medal; Occupation of Japan Awd; PTO Metal Citation for Serv on War Crimes Trials.

WOODALL, JOHN WESLEY
Physician. **Personal:** Born May 24, 1941, Cedartown, GA; son of Estherlena Harris Woodall and Japheus P Woodall; married Janet Carol Nunn; children: John Wesley Jr, Japheus Clay, Janita Carol. **Educ:** Ball State Univ, BS Med Tech 1959-64; St Johns Med Ctr, Internship Med Tech 1964-65; IN Univ School of Med, MD 1965-69; Whishard Memorial Hospital, Rotating Internship 1969-70. **Career:** St Johns Hosp, chief Ob-Gyn 1974, chief family practice 1977; Bridges-Campbell-Woodall Med Corp, physician, owner. **Orgs:** Mem, diplomate Amer Acad of Family Practice; mem Fellow of Amer Acad of Family Practice, Aesculapian Med Soc, Amer Med Dir Assn, The Amer Geriatric Soc, Natl Med Assn, Urban League, Friendship Baptist Church; life mem NAACP. **Military Serv:** USAF capt 1970-72. **Business Addr:** Physician/Owner, Bridges Campbell Woodhal Med, 1302 Madison Ave, Anderson, IN 46016.

WOODALL, LEE ARTIS
Professional football player. **Personal:** Born Oct 31, 1969, Carlisle, PA; children: Lee Artis Jr. **Educ:** West Chester. **Career:** San Francisco 49ers, linebacker, 1994-. **Honors/Awds:** Pro Bowl, 1995. **Business Addr:** Professional Football Player, San Francisco 49ers, 4949 Centennial Blvd, Santa Clara, CA 95054, (415)562-4949.

WOODARD, A. NEWTON
Physician. **Personal:** Born Aug 3, 1936, Selma, AL; married Bettye Davillier. **Educ:** Xavier Univ New Orleans, BS 1956; Meharry Med Clge Nashville, MD 1960. **Career:** Central Med Ctr Los Angeles, co-owner & co-dir 1970-; Kate Bitting Reynolds Mem Hosp Winston-Salem, intern 1960-61; Charlotte Comm Hosp, resident 1961-62; Kate Bitting Reynolds Mem Hosp, 1962-66; Portsmouth Naval Hosp, 1966-68; Dr Bassett Brown, ptnrshp 1968-. **Military Serv:** USN lt com 1966-68. **Business Addr:** 2707 S Central Ave, Los Angeles, CA 90011.

WOODARD, ALFRE
Actress. **Personal:** Born in Tulsa, OK; daughter of Constance Woodard and M H Woodard; married Roderick Spencer. **Educ:** Boston Univ, BFA (cum laude). **Career:** Actress; films include: Crooklyn; Passion Fish; Rich in Love; Bopha; Blue Chips; Hearts & Souls; Extremities; Mandela; Cross Creek; Health; Miss Firecracker; Pretty Hattie's Baby; Grand Canyon; Remember My Name; television appearances include: The Piano Lesson; LA Law; St Elsewhere; Homicide; Unnatural Causes; Sara; Words by Heart; Fairie Tale Theatre; For Love of a Soldier; Go Tell It on the Mountain; The Killing Floor; Ambush Murders; Colored Girls; Sophisticated; Freedom Road; Trail of the Moke; Games Before We Forget; The Good Witch of Laurel Canyon; Hill St Blues; Palmerstown; Enos; White Shadow; Two by South; theatre appearances: Split Second; For Colored Girls; Bugs Guns; Leander Stillwell; Me and Bessie; Horatio; Vlast; A Christmas Carol; Map of the World; A Winter's Tale; How to Make an American Quilt; Star Trek First Contact; Primal Fear; Gullivers Travels; Miss Evers' Boys; The Member of the Wedding, Statistically Speaking; Down In The Delta. **Honors/Awds:** Miss KAY Chi Chap Boston Univ 1974; Academy Award Nominee Best Supporting Actress 1984; Emmy Award Winner Best Supporting Actress 1984; Golden Apple Award Best newcomer 1984; NAACP Image Award Best Actress 1984; Emmy Nominee 1985, 1986, 1989; Boston Univ Alumni Award for Excellence in the Profession, 1989; Emmy Nomination: A Mother's Courage: The Mary Thomas Story, 1990; ACE Award, Mandela; Golden Globe Awards, Best Actress, Miniseries or Movie Made For Television, 1997. **Business Addr:** Block-Korenbrat, Actress, 8271 Melrose, #115, Los Angeles, CA 90046.

WOODARD, CHARLES JAMES
Educational administrator. **Personal:** Born Jun 9, 1945, Laurel, MS; divorced; children: Andrea, Craig, Ashley, Adeena. **Educ:** Edinboro Univ of PA, BS 1968; Wayne State Univ, MA 1972; Univ of MI, PhD 1975. **Career:** Univ of MI Flint, asst/asst dean for special proj 1973-75; Allegheny Coll, assoc dean of students 1975-82; Coppin State Coll, dean of student services 1982-85; IN Univ Northwest, dean for student services 1985-87; Savannah State College, Student Affairs, vice president, dean, 1987-90; Cheyney University, Student Affairs, vice pres, appointed as loaned executive, 1992; Kutztown University of Pennsylvania, Student Affairs, vice president, dean, 1990-. **Orgs:** Natl Assoc Financial Aids for Minority Students, mem 1972-75; Amer Personnel & Guidance Assoc, mem 1975-; Non-White Concerns in Guidance, mem 1975-; Unity Inst for Human Devel, board mem 1976-80; Boy Scouts of America, board mem 1977-82; PA State Educ Assoc, race relations consultant 1978-81; American Higher Educ Assoc, mem 1985-; Salvation Army, board mem 1986. **Honors/Awds:** Kappa Delta Pi 1968; Publication, ''The Challenge of Your Life - A guide to help prepare students to get screened into higher education'' 1974; co-author, paper, ''A Comparative Study on Some Variables Related to Academic Success as perceived By Both Black and White Students'' 1977; co-author, paper, ''Enhancing the College Adjustment of Young Culturally Different Gifted Students'' 1986; Black Achievers Award, presented by Black Opinion Magazine, 1991; Phi Kappa Phi Honor Society, Faculty/Staff inductee, Kutztown Univ, 1997. **Business Addr:** VP, Student Affairs, Kutztown University, Kutztown, PA 19530.

WOODARD, FREDRICK
Educational administrator. **Personal:** Born Jan 29, 1939, Kingfisher, OK; son of Rosetta Reed Bishop and Ralph Woodard; married Barbara (died 1989); children: Jon, Jarilyn. **Educ:** Iowa Wesleyan College, Mt. Pleasant, IA, BA, 1961; University of Iowa, Iowa City, IA, MA, 1972, PhD, 1976. **Career:** West High School, Davenport, IA, teacher, 1961-66; Black Hawk Community College, Moline, IL, instructor, 1967-69; Cornell College, Mt. Vernon, IA, instructor, 1972-76; University of Iowa, Iowa City, IA, instructor, 1973-76, assistant professor, 1976-79, associate professor, 1979-80, acting associate dean of the Faculties, Office of Academic Affairs, 1981-83, associate dean of the Faculties, Office of the Vice President for Academic Affairs, 1983-90, associate vice president for Academic Affairs, 1990-, Museum of Art, interim director, 1990-92; University of California at San Diego, visiting associate professor, 1980. **Orgs:** Chair of session, Council on College Composition, 1975, 1977, 1981, 1983, 1985; chair of session, Midwest Modern Language Association, 1970, 1972, 1973, 1977-79, 1981-83; chair of session, National Council of the Teachers of English, 1985; member, American Library Association, 1980-; member, Modern Language Association, 1980-; committee member, Big 10 Academic Personnel Officers, 1985; committee member, Professional and Organizational Development Network in Higher Education, 1985-. **Business Addr:** Associate Vice President, Office of Academic Affairs, University of Iowa, 111 Jessup Hall, Iowa City, IA 52242.

WOODARD, KENNETH EMIL
Professional football player. **Personal:** Born Jan 22, 1960, Detroit, MI. **Educ:** Tuskegee Institute, attended. **Career:** Denver Nuggets, 1982-86; Pittsburgh Steelers, 1987; San Diego Chargers, linebacker, 1988-. **Honors/Awds:** Post-season play, 1986: AFC Championship Game, NFL Championship Game. **Business Addr:** Professional Football Player, San Diego Chargers, Jack Murphy Stadium, 9449 Friars Rd, San Diego, CA 92108.

WOODARD, LOIS MARIE
Systems analyst. **Personal:** Born in Porter, TX; married Laverne; children: Alesia Brewer, Erica Brewer, Cheryl Brewer. **Educ:** Los Angeles Trade Tech Coll, AA 1970; Cal Poly State Univ San Luis Obispo, BS 1975. **Career:** Cal Poly San Luis Obispo CA, data processor 1972-76; Burroughs Corp, programmer 1976-77; Long Beach Coll of Business, instructor 1977-80; Natl Auto & Casualty Ins, system analyst 1980-. **Orgs:** Business woman Esquire Cleaners 1979-87; pres Stewardess Bd #2 1st AME Ch 1980-82; natl auto co coord Youth Motivation Task Force 1984-87; conductress Order of Eastern Stars 1985-86; corresponding sec Zeta Phi Beta Sor 1986; mem NAACP 1986-87. **Honors/Awds:** Appreciation Awd 1st AME Church Pasedena CA 1981. **Home Addr:** 804 W Figueroa Dr, Altadena, CA 91001.

WOODARD, LYNETTE
Professional basketball player. **Personal:** Born Aug 12, 1959. **Educ:** Kansas. **Career:** Cleveland Rockers, guard, 1997-98; Detroit Shock, 1998-. **Honors/Awds:** Wade Trophy, 1981; Broderick Cup; NCAA Top Five Award; GTE Academic Hall of Fame, 1992. **Special Achievements:** First woman selected for the NCAA Top Five Award. **Business Addr:** Professional Basketball Player, Detroit Shock, The Palace of Auburn Hills, 2 Championship Dr, Auburn Hills, MI 48326, (248)377-0100.

WOODARD, SAMUEL L.
Educator. **Personal:** Born May 26, 1930, Fairmont, WV; married Linda Waples; children: Mary Ellen, Charlene, Gail, Dana. **Educ:** Mansfield State, BS 1953; Canisius Clge, MS 1959; State Univ of NY Buffalo, EdD. **Career:** Howard Univ, prof of educ admin; IL State Univ, assc prof of educ admin 1970-73; Philadelphia School Dist, dir prog impl 1968-70; Temple Univ, asst prof of educ 1967-68; Genesee-Humboldt Jr High Buffalo, vice prin 1966-67; Buffalo & LA, teacher 1954-66. **Orgs:** Intl Assc Appl Soc Scient; Intl Transactional Analysis Assc; Phi Delta Kappa; Natl All of Black Sch Educ; life mem NAACP; life mem Alpha Phi Alpha. **Honors/Awds:** 1st Black to rec Phoenician Trophy as outst Schlr-Athlete HS 1948; 1st Black to rec Doc in Educ Admin at State Univ of NY Buffalo 1966; 1st Black toteach on Educ TV in NY State Buffalo WNED-TV 1961-62. **Business Addr:** Prof of Educ Admin, Howard University, School of Education, Washington, DC 20059.

WOODBECK, FRANK RAYMOND
Radio executive. **Personal:** Born Feb 2, 1947, Buffalo, NY; son of Avil Woodbeck and George Woodbeck; married Virginia

Ann Carter; children: Harrison, Terry, Frank Raymond II. **Educ:** State Univ of NY at Buffalo, BS 1973. **Career:** Capital Cities Comm WKBW Radio, gen sales mgr 1977-80, pres and gen mgr 1980-84; Capital Cities Cable Inc, vice pres advertising 1985-86; Post-Newsweek Cable Inc, advertising vice pres 1986-91; ABC Radio Networks, vice pres affiliate marketing, west region 1992-. **Orgs:** Mem Omega Psi Phi Frat 1976-; ticket chmn Dunlop Pro Am Awds Dinner 1979-84; vice chmn/chairman Humboldt Branch YMCA 1979-84; mem Sigma Pi Phi Frat 1981-; treas ABC Radio Dir Affil Bd 1983-84; pres Buffalo Radio Assoc 1983-84. **Military Serv:** USAF staff sgt 1964-68; Air Force Commendation Medal, Natl Defense Medal, Vietnam Service Medal. **Home Addr:** 5161 W Plano Parkway, Plano, TX 75093-5006. **Business Addr:** VP, Affiliate Marketing, West Region, ABC Radio Networks, 13725 Montfort Drive, Dallas, TX 75240, (972)991-9200.

WOODBURY, DAVID HENRY
Scientist. **Personal:** Born Mar 29, 1930, Camden, SC; son of Arline and David; married Margaret Jane Claytor; children: Arline E, Brenda L, Laura R, Kathryn L, Larry D, David H. **Educ:** Johnson C Smith Univ, BS (cum laude) 1951; VA State Coll, MS (With Disc) 1952; Univ of MI, MD 1961. **Career:** Atomic Energy Comm, biologist 1955-57; Westland Med Center, dir nuclear med 1968-; Univ of MI, asst prof internal med 1968-; USPHS, dir Nuclear med 1967-68; Westland Med Center dir nuclear medicine. **Orgs:** Consultant FDA Radiopharmaceuticals Advisor 1978-82, NRC Advisory Comm 1979-; bd regents Amer Coll of Nuclear Physicians 1980-; chief med staff Wayne County Hosp 1974-75; vice pres Johnson C Smith Alumni Assn 1978; pres club Johnson C Smith Univ 1984; pres American Coll of Nuclear Physicians 1987. **Honors/Awds:** Robert C Word Scholar Johnson C Smith Univ 1950; fellow Amer Clge Nuclear Physicians 1982. **Military Serv:** AUS cpl; USPHS lt col 1961-68. **Business Addr:** Dir Nuclear Medicine, Westland Medical Ctr, Michigan At Merriman Rd, Westland, MI 48185.

WOODBURY, MARGARET CLAYTOR
Physician. **Personal:** Born Oct 30, 1937, Roanoke, VA; daughter of Roberta Morris Woodfin Claytor (deceased) and John Bunyan Claytor Sr (deceased); married David Henry Woodbury Jr; children: Laura Ruth, Lawrence DeWitt Jr, David Henry III, Arline Elizabeth, Brenda, Kathryn. **Educ:** Mount Holyoke Coll, AB Cum Laude 1958; Albany Medical Coll, Trustee Bio-Chem Award 1960; Meharry Med Coll, MD Pediatric Prize 1962. **Career:** US Pub Health Serv Hosp, Staten Island NY, asst chief med/endo 1967-68; US Pub Health Serv Hosp, Detroit MI, chief outpatient clinic 1968-69; US Pub Health Serv Outpatient Clinic, Detroit MI, med officer in charge 1969-71; Univ of Michigan Med School, instr med endo 1969-80, asst prof 1980-, HCOP proj dir 1984-, asst dean student & minority affairs 1983-90. **Orgs:** Admissions comm, Univ of Michigan Med Sch, 1978-83; mem chmn, ACAAP Univ of Michigan Med School, 1983-91; chair steering comm MLKCHC Series, 1984-85; nominating comm, bd alumnae 1981-85, trustee 1985-97, Mount Holyoke College; pres, Alumnae Assn of Mount Holyoke Coll, 1994-97; co-chair precinct, Ann Arbor Democratic Party, 1972-73; parent rep, Engrg Indust Support Program, 1978-82; founding mem, Ann Arbor Alliance of Achievement, 1981-89; volunteer various health related committees. **Honors/Awds:** Elected to membership, Alpha Omega Alpha Honor Medical Soc, Meharry Med Coll, 1962; Alumnae Medal of Honor, Mount Holyoke Coll, 1983; diplomate, Amer Bd of Internal Med, 1969; Dean's List, Albany & Meharry Med Coll 1959-62; 1st Biochemistry Award, Albany Med Coll, 1959; Pediatric Prize, Meharry Med Coll, 1961; cited as Outstanding Young Woman of Amer, 1967; elected Hon Mem, Sigma Gamma Rho Sor Inc, Outstanding Woman for the 21st Century, 1986; has published numerous articles in field of endocrinology, including "Quantitative Determination of Cysteine in Salivary Amylase," Mt Holyoke Coll, 1958; "Hypopituitarism in Current Therapy," WB Saunders Co, 1967; "Cushing's Syndrome in Infancy, A Case Complicated by Monilial Endocarditis," Am J Dis Child, 1971; "Three Generations of Familial Turner Syndrome," Annals of Int Med 1978; "Virilizing Syndrome Associated With Adrenocortical Adenoma Secreting Predominantly Testosterone," Am J Med 1979; "Hormones in Your Life From Childbearing (Or Not) to Menopause," Mt Holyoke Alumnae Quarterly 1980; "Scintigraphic Localization of Ovarian Dysfunction," J Nuc Med, 1988. **Special Achievements:** Co-author: Virginia Kaleidoscope: The Claytor Family of Roanoke & Some of its Kinships, from First Families of Virginia and Their Former Slaves, 1995. **Military Serv:** US Public Health Serv Senior Surgeon 1961-71.

WOODEN, RALPH L.
Educator. **Personal:** Born Mar 29, 1915, Columbus, OH; son of Lozanie Wooden and Isaiah Wooden; married Rosalie McLeod; children: Mari, Ralph L, Jr. **Educ:** North Carolina A&T State Univ, BS, 1938; US Air Force Tech Training Command School, Chanute Field IL, professional certificate, 1942; Ohio State Univ, MA, 1946; Ohio State Univ, PhD, 1956; Virginia State Coll, Post-Doctoral Study, 1954-58, 1969; Michigan State Univ, Post-Doctoral Study, 1967-68. **Career:** North Carolina A&T State Univ, professor emeritus of educ, dir educ, media center; No State High School, Hagerstown, MD, teacher, 1938-39; Univ North Carolina, Greensboro, NC, tech, 1939-40; Dudley High School, teacher, 1940-41; USAF, OUHD, school instructor, 1941-45; Univ of Wisconsin, Madison, WI, visiting professor in audiovisual educ, 1971; National Certification for Teacher Education, 1976. **Orgs:** Mem, Sigma Chapter, Phi Delta Kappa, 1950, Edit advisory bd, Audiovisual Ins Assn for Educ Comm & tech, 1974; mem, Natl Assn for Educ Comm & Tech; past pres & chmn bd dir North Carolina Assn for Educ Comm & Tech, 1973; mem, Natl Conv Plan Comm Assn for Educ Comm & Educ Tech Detroit, 1970, Minneapolis 1972; off delegate, Assn for Educ Comm & Tech Las Vegas, 1973; delegate, Univ North Carolina, Fac Assmbl, 1972-77; Leadership Conf, Lake Okoboj, IA, 1974; past chmn, Grad School Public Comm; mem Fac Ath Comm, adv grad stu in educ & media fac rep, Grad County, NC, A&T State Univ; advisory & consult to num schools in North Carolina; Gamma Tau Chapter, Alpha Kappa Mu Natl Hon Soc, 1936; Beta Chap Beta Kappa Chi Natl Science Hon Soc, 1947; Alpha Chapter, Epsilon Pi Tau Intl Hon Soc in Educ, 19 Theta Chap Kappa Delta Pi Int Hon Soc, 1961. **Honors/Awds:** Merrick Medal for Excellence in Tech Science, North Carolina A&T State Univ, 1938; Citizen of Year; Greensboro Citizens' Assn, 1965; North Carolina Outstanding Audio-Visual Educ, SE Businessmen's Assn, Minneapolis, 1972; Outstanding Alum in School of Educ, Natl Alum Assn of North Carolina A&T State Univ, 1973; Student, NEA, North Carolina A&T State Univ, Outstanding Achievement Award, 1973; United States Selective Services Presidential Awards, 1971. **Military Serv:** USAF. **Business Addr:** Prof Emeritus of Education, North Carolina A&T State Univ, Greensboro, NC 27411.

WOODEN, SHAWN
Professional football player. **Personal:** Born Oct 23, 1973, Willow Grove, PA. **Educ:** Univ of Notre Dame, BS in computer science. **Career:** Miami Dolphins, defensive back, 1996-. **Business Addr:** Professional Football Player, Miami Dolphins, 2269 NW 199th St, Miami, FL 33056, (305)620-5000.

WOODEN, TERRENCE TYLON
Professional football player. **Personal:** Born Jan 14, 1967, Hartford, CT; married Cindy. **Educ:** Syracuse, degree in sociology. **Career:** Seattle Seahawks, linebacker, 1990-96; Kansas City Chiefs, 1997-. **Honors/Awds:** Football Digest, All-Rookie Team, 1990; Ed Block Courage Award, 1992; Steve Largent Award, 1995. **Business Addr:** Professional Football Player, Kansas City Chiefs, One Arrowhead Dr, Kansas City, MO 64129, (816)924-9300.

WOODFOLK, JOSEPH O.
Educator. **Personal:** Born Mar 4, 1933, St Thomas, Virgin Islands of the United States; divorced. **Educ:** Morgan State Coll, AB; NM Highlands Univ, ME 1955; Morgan State Coll, MA; Indian Culture Univ Mysore India, cert grad studies 1973. **Career:** Baltimore Co Bd Educ, chmn Social studies dept 1969-; Baltimore Co Public Schools, teacher 1955-; State Univ NJ, teacher "Blacks in Amer Soc", "The Black Family"; NJ; DE; Johns Hopkins Univ. **Orgs:** Dev curriculum K-12 soc stud prog Balti Co 1969-; dir Fulbright Alumni India summer stud prog; mem Tchr Assc Balt Co; MD State Tchr Assc; Natl Educ Assc; Phi Alpha Theta; Gamma Theta Upsilon; Amer Hist Soc; MD Hist Soc; Org Amer Historians; Soc Hist Educ; NAACP; Friends of Kenya; Assc Foreign Students; Alumni Assc; NM Highlands Univ; mem Phi Delta Kappa John Hopkins Univ; Eastern reg dir of publ Phi Beta Sigma Frat; mem Amer Heart Assc Minority Comm Affairs; Phi Beta Sigma. **Honors/Awds:** Fulbright Flwshp 1973; spec recog award Eta Omega chap Phi Alpha Theta. **Business Addr:** Woodlawn Sr High Sch, 1801 Woodlawn Dr, Baltimore, MD 21207.

WOODFORD, HACKLEY ELBRIDGE
Physician (retired). **Personal:** Born Jul 2, 1914, Kalamazoo, MI; son of Bessie Agnes Hackley Woodford and Thomas Elbridge Woodford; married Mary Imogene Steele Woodford, Jun 7, 1940; children: Peggy Woodford-Forbes, Bremond John Niles, Joan Mary Abu Bakir, Barbara Ellen Tolbert. **Educ:** Western Michigan Univ, AB, 1936; Howard Medical School, MD, 1940; Post Grad School: Chicago, New York Univ, Tufts, Northwestern Univ, Harvard, Allegemeines Krakenhaus, Vienna, Austria; Univ of Michigan Medical School; UCLA and USC. **Career:** Provident Hospital, intern, 1940-41, resident, 1941-42; Private Practice, Benton Harbor, MI, 1945-70; Memorial Hospital, St Joseph, Michigan, chief of staff, 1964-69; Southern California Permanente Medical Group, physician 1970-84. **Orgs:** Certified Amer Bd Family Practice, 1970, recertified, 1976, 1982; fellow Amer Acad Family Physicians; Intl Soc Internal Medicine; fellow Amer Geriatric Soc; mem, N Shore School Bd, Benton Harbor, MI; life mem, NAACP; bd dir, Pasadena Foothill Urban League, Alpha Phi Alpha Fraternity, Alpha Pi Boule Sigma Pi Phi; scholarship donor, Howard Univ Medical School; contributing editor, US Black Business Recognition Award, AMA; life mem, Amer Medical Soc of Vienna, Austria, Amer Acad of Family Physicians; president, sire Archon, Xi Boule Sigma Pi Phi Fraternity, Los Angeles, CA 1980. **Honors/Awds:** Recognition Award, AMA; Kappa Rho Sigma, Scientific Honor Society, Western Michigan Univ, 1935-; Western Michigan University, Distinguished Alumnus, 1991. **Military Serv:** US Air Force, Captain, Tuskegee Airman, 1942-45. **Home Addr:** 16071 Avenida Lamego, San Diego, CA 92128, (619)451-1358.

WOODFORD, JOHN NILES
Journalist. **Personal:** Born Sep 24, 1941, Chicago, IL; married Elizabeth Duffy; children: Duffy, Maize, Will. **Educ:** Harvard Univ, BA (high honors), English literature, 1964, MA 1968. **Career:** Ebony Magazine, asst editor 1967-68; Muhammad Speaks Newspaper, editor in chief 1968-72; Chicago Sun Times, copy editor 1972-74; New York Times, copy editor natl desk 1974-77; Ford Motor Co, sr editor Ford Times 1977-80; Univ of MI, exec editor 1981-. **Orgs:** Univ of MI Assn of Black Professionals, Administrators, Faculty & Staff; Black Scholar Journal, essayist & reviewer. **Honors/Awds:** 3 Gold Medals and other Awds Council for Advancement and Support of Educ 1984-86. **Special Achievements:** Author: "A Journey to Afghanistan," Freedomways, 1985; "Messaging the Blackman," Voices From the Underground, Mica Press, 1992. **Home Addr:** 1922 Lorraine Pl, Ann Arbor, MI 48104. **Business Addr:** Executive Editor, Univ of Michigan, 412 Maynard, Ann Arbor, MI 48109.

WOODHOUSE, ENOCH O'DELL, II
Attorney. **Personal:** Born Jan 14, 1927, Boston. **Educ:** Yale Univ, atnd 1952; Univ of Paris France, jr yr 1951; Yale Law Sch; Boston Univ Law Sch, LLB 1955; Acad of Intl Law Peace Palace Hague Netherlands, 1960. **Career:** Pvt prac atty; US State Dept, diplomatic courier; City of Boston, asst corp coun; Intl French & German, pvt prac law; trial couns corp law. **Orgs:** Intl Bar Assc; mem Boston Bar Assc; Mass Trial Lawyers Assc exec com; Yale Club of Boston; Reserve Ofcrs Assc; amer Trial Lawyers Assc elected bd of Govs Yale 1975; aptd Liaison Ofcr for AF Acad; Judge Adv Gen. **Military Serv:** Srvd WW II, lt col AF Res. **Business Addr:** US Trust Bldg, 40 Court St, Boston, MA 02108.

WOODHOUSE, JOHNNY BOYD
Clergyman. **Personal:** Born Nov 9, 1945, Elizabeth City, NC; son of Helen Woodhouse and Charles Woodhouse; married Darlyn Blakeney; children: Yolanda, Johnny Jr, Fletcher, Touray. **Educ:** Elizabeth City State, BS 1967; Shaw Divinity, MD 1973; Virginia Seminary, DD 1983. **Career:** PW Moore HS, teacher 1970; NC Dept of Corrections, instr 1977; Johnston Tech Coll, instr 1978; Red Oak Grove Baptist Church, sr minister, 1980; Johnston Tech Coll, dir of human resources develop. **Orgs:** Mem NAACP; mem MIZPAH Temple #66 Goldsboro NC; instructor Women Correctional Cntr Raleigh NC; Master Mason Prince Hall; Natl Bapt Conv Inc; treas Smithfield Ministerial Conf; chmn bd NC Child & Day Care Ctr; vice pres Smithfield Minister's Conf 1975; vice moderator Tar River Missionary Bapt Assn 1980-; Tar River Association, moderator, 1988. **Honors/Awds:** NAACP Awd 1970; Pastor of Yr 1972; Martin Luther King Jr Award, 1991. **Home Addr:** PO Box 2103, Smithfield, NC 27577.

WOODHOUSE, ROSSALIND YVONNE
Human services agency executive. **Personal:** Born Jun 7, 1940, Detroit, MI; daughter of Pereditha Venable and Allen Venable; married Donald; children: Joycelyn, Justin. **Educ:** Univ of WA, BA sociology 1963; Univ of WA, MSW 1970; Univ of WA, PhD, 1983. **Career:** Custom Fit Productions, pres, 1998-; Urban League of Metropolitan Seattle WA, president/CEO, 1984-98; Rainier Bancorp, vice pres employee relations, 1981-84; WA State Dept of Licensing Olympia, dir 1977-81; Edmonds Comm Coll Lynnwood, instr coord 1973-77; Cntrl Area Motiv Prgm Seattle, exec dir 1971-73; Seattle Hsg Auth, comm orgn splst 1969-70; New Careers Proj Seattle, prog coord guide consult 1968. **Orgs:** Pres, Seattle Women's Commn 1971-72, 1975-76; mem, Alpha Kappa Alpha Sor, 1980-; board member, Seattle Private Industry Council, 1986-98; board of trustees, Central Washington University 1986-98; charter member, board of directors, National Association of Minority Trusteeship in Higher Education, 1990-. **Honors/Awds:** First female Motor Vehicle Dir in US or Canada; only black woman to direct a Cabinet Level Agency in WA State; Woman of Achievement, Women in Communications, 1991; Natalie Skells Award, 1989; Alumni Legend, Univ of Washington, 1987. **Business Addr:** President, Custom Fit Productions, 8204 S 124th St, Seattle, WA 98178, (206)772-5903.

WOODIE, HENRY L.
Engineer, clergyman. **Personal:** Born Oct 24, 1940, Tallahassee, FL; son of Willie Mae Simmons Stephens and Albert Woodie; married Kathey Curry Jones-Woodie, Oct 20, 1990; children: Henry LaSean, Dorian Small, Aaron Jones, Travis Jones. **Educ:** FL A&M Univ, BS 1963; Stetson Univ, BBA 1974; Rollins College, MSM 1979. **Career:** Brevard County Sch Sys FL, tchr; RCA Patrick AFB FL, mathematician; Auditor Gen Office FL, auditor; Daytona Beach Comm Coll, internal auditor; Bell South, engr mgr; African Methodist Episcopal Church, minister, 1991-. **Orgs:** Keeper of peace, Omega Psi Phi Fraternity, 1990-91. **Home Addr:** 10 Hardee Circle N, Rockledge, FL 32955.

WOODING, DAVID JOSHUA
Physician. **Personal:** Born Apr 10, 1959, Cleveland, OH; married Karen Aline Rogers; children: Joshua David. **Educ:** Oakwood College, BA 1981; Meharry Medical College, MD 1986. **Career:** Physician, currently. **Business Addr:** Physician, 11549 Honey Hollow, Moreno Valley, CA 92557.

WOODLAND, CALVIN EMMANUEL
Educator. **Personal:** Born Nov 3, 1943, LaPlata, MD; son of Mildred Woodland (deceased) and Philip H. Woodland (deceased). **Educ:** Morgan State Univ, BS 1965; Howard Univ, MA 1970; Rutgers Univ, EdD 1975; Southern California for Professional Studies, Psy D, 1997. **Career:** MD Dept of Health & Mental Hygiene, music & rehab therapist 1966-70; Essex Co Coll, counselor/dir of educ advisement 1970-74; Morgan State Univ Sch of Educ, dir of teacher corps, assoc prof of educ asst dean 1974-81; Coppin State Coll, dir of spec svcs, acting dean of students 1981-82; Charles County Comm Coll, dean 1982-86; Northern Virginia Comm Coll, dean beginning 1986-; vp of student dev, currently. **Orgs:** Evaluator Middle States Assoc of Colleges & Schools 1979-; Amer Psychological Assoc, Amer Assoc for Counseling Dev, Amer Assoc of Rehab Therapists, Natl Commission for African-American Education; Health & Human Services Board for Volusia/Flagler Counties, children & family's service committee; Volusia/Flagler Counties, juvenile justice board. **Honors/Awds:** HEW Fellow US Dept of Health, Educ Welfare 1976; ERIC Publications on Data Base as a Tool for Recruitment of Minority Students 1979, 85; Innovations in Counseling Psychology Book Review Journal of Contemporary Psychology 1979; Outstanding Achievement and Comm Serv Southern MD Chain Chap of Links 1986. **Home Addr:** 37 Parkview Lane, Ormond Beach, FL 32174.

WOODLEY, ARTO, JR.
Educational administrator. **Personal:** Born Aug 12, 1965, Tacoma, WA; son of Arto & Patricia E Woodley; married Yvette A Woodley, Nov 30, 1991. **Educ:** Bowling Green Univ, BS, 1988, MA, 1990. **Career:** Bowling Green State Univ, grad asst, 1988-90, asst to the vp for Univ relations, 1990-92; Wright State Univ, assoc dir of corp fundation relation, 1992-94; dir of advancement, School of Medicine, 1994-. **Orgs:** Boy Scouts of America, district commissioner, 1994-95; Mentoring Coalition, co-chair, 1994-95; Parity 2000, 1994-; Redeeming the Time Newsletter, editor, currently, Visions Newsletter, editor, 1990. **Honors/Awds:** Bowling Green State Univ, Presidential Service Award, 1988, 1990. **Special Achievements:** Speech: Dr King & the Civil Rights Movement: Was it Just A Dream?, 1994; Speech: Dr Carter G Woodson, the Father of Black History, 1990. **Business Addr:** Dir of Advancement, School of Medicine, Wright State Univ, 115K Medical Sci Bldg, Dayton, OH 45435, (513)873-2972.

WOODRIDGE, WILSON JACK, JR.
Architect. **Personal:** Born Aug 29, 1950, East Orange, NJ; divorced. **Educ:** Essex Cty Coll, AAS 1970; Cornell Univ Coll or Arch, BA 1975. **Career:** Bernard Johnson Inc, designer 1976-77; Skidmore Owings & Merrill, designer 1977-80; Welton Becket Assoc, project designer 1981; The Grad Partnership, project architect 1981-85; Essex County College, dir of Architecture Programs 1983-; Woodridge & Ray Architects 1985-. **Orgs:** Official interviewer Cornell Univ Alumni Secondary Comm 1975; chmn proj comm Houston Comm Design Ctr 1978-80; chmn fin comm Essex Cty Coll Alumni Assoc 1982-84; sec exec comm Houston Urban Bunch 1979-80. **Honors/Awds:** Outstanding Alumni Awd Essex Cty Coll 1984; East Orange Merchants Awd 1987. **Home Addr:** 305 South Burnet St, East Orange, NJ 07018. **Business Addr:** Dir of Architecture Prog, Essex County College, 303 University Ave, Newark, NJ 07102.

WOODRUFF, CHERYL
Editor. **Personal:** daugHter of Phy Stephens. **Career:** Fawcett Books; Ballantine Publishing Group, several positions including associate editor, founding editor, 1991-94, vice president/executive editor, 1994-. **Business Addr:** VP/Exec Editor, One World, Ballantine Books, 201 E. 50th St., 9th Fl., New York, NY 10022, (212)751-2600.

WOODRUFF, JAMES W.
Automobile dealership executive. **Career:** Woodruff Oldsmobile Inc, Detroit MI, chief executive, 1988; Pochelon Lincoln-Mercury Inc, chief executive, 1988-. **Business Addr:** Chief Executive, Pochelon Lincoln-Mercury, Inc, 5815 Bay Road, Saginaw, MI 48604.

WOODRUFF, JEFFREY ROBERT
Computer company executive, educator. **Personal:** Born Jul 13, 1943, Pittsburgh, PA; son of Alyce Bailey Woodruff and Robert Woodruff; married Vickie Hamlin Woodruff, Mar 21, 1970; children: Jennifer Ryan. **Educ:** Springfield Coll, BS 1966; New York Inst of Tech, MBA 1978. **Career:** KQV Radio Inc, dir rsch & devel 1968-70; WLS Radio Inc, dir rsch 1970-72; Elmhurst Coll Mgmt Program, faculty; Knoxville Coll Sem Program, vis prof; ABC AM Radio Stas, dir rsch & devel 1972-77, dir sales & rsch 1977-79; WDAI Radio, natl sales mgr 1979-80; North Central College, assistant professor, 1979-; IL Bell Telephone Co, acct exec indus consul 1980-83, mgr promos marketing staff 1983-91, area manager channel operations, 1991-93, staff manager, customer communications operations, 1993-; Ameritech Sales Promotion, dir, 1993-94; Computer Learning Ctr, lead instructor, 1994; DeVey Inst of Tech, instructor, 1994. **Orgs:** Mem Radio TV Rsch Cncl; Amer Marketing Assn; Delta Mu Delta; Radio Advertising Bur; GOALS Com; mem Black Exec Exchange Prog; Natl Urban League Inc; Youth Motivation Task Force; adjunct faculty New York Inst of Technology; consult Network Programming Concepts Inc; industry advisor Arbitron Adv Council Mensa Ltd; College of DuPage, Instructional Alternative Learning, visiting faculty; Aurora Univ, adjunct prof, 1995. **Honors/Awds:** Natl Alliance of Bus Innovator Awd Amer Rsch Bur 1972; Black Achievers in Ind Awd Harlem YMCA 1972; Ameritech Fellow, Northwestern Univ, Inst of Learning Services, 1990. **Military Serv:** USMC corpl 1966-68. **Home Addr:** 4559 Normandy Dr, Lisle, IL 60532.

WOODS, ALLIE, JR.
Actor, stage director, educator, writer, lecturer. **Personal:** Born Sep 28, Houston, TX; son of Georgia Stewart Woods and Allie Woods Sr; married Beverly (divorced); children: Allyson Beverly, Stewart Jordan. **Educ:** TX Southern Univ, BA; TN State Univ, MS; New School, producing for television; NY Univ, film production/writing for film/television; Ctr for the Media Arts, TV production. **Career:** Founding Member, Tony Award-winning Negro Ensemble Co; Chelsea Theatre Ctr Brooklyn Acad of Music, actor/dir; Lincoln Center Theatre Co, NY; The Actors Studio; Center Stage/Pittsburgh Public Theatre/Actors Theatre of Louisville/George Street Playhouse/Syracuse Stage/Cincinnati Playhouse in the Park, actor; LaMama Experimental Theatre Club NYC, dir-in-residence; John Jay Coll, Rutgers Univ, Univ of MO-Kansas City, Univ of Ibadan, Univ of Wash, Brooklyn Coll, teacher and/or guest artist; guest dir, Sunday Series NY Shakesphere Fest Pub Theatre; New Fed Theatre NYC, dir; State Univ of NY Old Westbury, asst prof; Coll of New Rochelle, lecturer speech comm; Bergen Comm Coll, Paramus, NJ, lecturer comm/theatre; Houston Public Schools, teacher; New York Shakespeare Festival/ New York City, actor; staging consultant Tony Brown's Journal's ''Malcolm and Elijah'', PBS-TV; visiting dir, Michigan State Univ; artistin-residence Texas Southern Univ; producer/director/commentary writer, ''Divestment'' video sponsored by the Center for the Media Arts; guest director Univ of Connecticut; Acting/Dir credits: Day of Absence, In White America, Song of the Lusitanian Bogey, The Gentleman Caller, Ceremonies in Dark Old Men, No Place to be Somebody, One Flew Over the Cuckoo's Nest, A Conflict of Interest, Tiger at the Gates, The Black Terror, Cotillion, When the Chickens Came Home to Roost, Dreams Deferred, No Place to be Somebody, Fences, Trains, Driving Miss Daisy, Mule Bone, The Brownsville Raid, The Forbidden City, Zora and Langston, Miss Evers' Boys; Two Trains Running, Mr Rickey Calls a Meeting; The Piano Lesson; To Kill a Mockingbird; Directed readings/workshop productions: Open Admissions, Scenes from God's Trombones and Short Eyes, Cage Bird, Alias, Othello; Ladybugs; Fortunes of the Moon. **Orgs:** Actors Equity Assn; Screen Actors Guild; Black Filmmaker Foundation; The Dramatists Guild; American Federation of Television and Radio Artists. **Honors/Awds:** Theatre Production Grant, Office of Economic Opportunity, Houston; Ford Found Fellowship Grant, Univ of Ibadan Nigeria; Non-fiction Literature Fellowship, New York Foundation for the Arts; Best Dir Drama AUDELCO Awds Comm; Filmmaker Grant American Film Inst; actor, Intl Theatre Fest London and Rome; actor/dir, Intl Theatre Fest Venice and Milan; actor, Intl Theatre Fest Perth and Adelaide, Australia; Honoree, Natl Black Arts Festival (North Carolina).

WOODS, ALMITA
Administrator. **Personal:** Born Jul 6, 1914, Eastover, SC; married Willie Michael; children: Robert, Leonard Michael. **Educ:** Benedict Coll, BA 1937; Atlanta Univ Sch of Work, 1938-40; Univ TX, 1950&54; Atlanta Univ Sch of Soc Work, MSW 1960. **Career:** Sickle Cell Syndrome Prgm NC Dept of Human Resources, Cons; Comm & Svcs, comm 1973; adoptions spec 1970-73; Tri-city Comm Action Prgm, dir 1969-70; psychiatric consult 1968-69; Nat OEO, consult 1967-70; Comm Serv Agency, 1960-66. **Orgs:** Pr Dir Jarvis Christian Coll 1957-60; dir Quaker's Merit Employment 1951-56; dir YMCA Br Austin 1950-51; mgr Robinson Const Co 1944-49; exec sec Negro Welfare Council 1941-44; interim dir Atlanta Urban League 1940-41; tchr 1935-38; fdr Ft Worth Urban League 1943; Woodlawn Comm Serv Council 1961; orgnrOnslow Co Sickle Cell Anemia Assn 1971; Nat Ladies Aux & Camp Lejeune Chpt; Montford Point Marine Assn 1974; NC Black Womens Polit Caucus 1977; columnist weekly newspapers; columnist Atlanta & Jour; initiated prgm weekly commentator The Negro Hour; mem adv com Chicago Human Relation Commn; adv com Woodlanw Urban Prog Ctr; mem Mayor's Com for Urban Renewal; chmn Onslow Co Sickle Cell Anemia Assn; past pres Ladies Aux Montford Point Marine Assn;MemMidville Bapt Ch; Nat Assn of Soc Works; Acad Cert Soc Workers; Sigma Gamma Rho Sor; Alpha Gamma Pi Sor; Staff NCO Wives Club; NAACP; Nat Assn of Black Soc Workers; various local orgns. **Honors/Awds:** Spec commendation MINUTE Am Friends Serv Com; 1 of 12 most Outstanding Women in Chicago; Alpha Gamma Pi Sor 1964; outstanding serv to Woodlawn Comm Services Agency, American Friendship Club 1966; spl letter of commendation Mayor Richard J Dailey 1966; Marine Wife of the Year Tri-command Camp Lejeune NC; finalist Mil Wife of the Year; appointed Gov Holshouser Gov Hunt States Council on Sickle Cell Syndrome; natl register of prominent Americans; Governor James G Martin, Order of the Long Leaf Pine, North Carolina's highest award, 1988. **Home Addr:** 122 Melody Ln, Jacksonville, NC 28540.

WOODS, ANDRE VINCENT
Company executive. **Personal:** Born Feb 21, 1947, Charleston, SC; son of Thelma Ruth Woods and Delbert Leon Woods; married Karen Lewis; children: Charity, Andre II, Meridith. **Educ:** Saint Augustine's College, BA, 1975. **Career:** South Carolina State Ports Authority, administrative analyst, 1975-80; Handyman Network, president, owner, 1981-. **Orgs:** Neighborhood Legal Services Corp, vice pres, 1977-; Eastside Business Association, vice pres, 1989-; Trident Chamber of Commerce, vice pres, 1991-92; Charleston Southern University, board of visitors, 1991-; Medical University, IRB board, 1990-; Junior Achievement, board of directors, 1990-; Trident 1000, 1990-91; Sigma Pi Phi, Grand Boule, 1990-. **Honors/Awds:** National Council for Negro Women, Outstanding Service Award, 1985; US Small Business Administration, Minority Entrepreneur of the Year, 1988; NAACP, Outstanding Freedom Fighter Award, 1973; US Small Business Administration, runner up to Small Business Person Award, 1988; Alpha Phi Alpha, Business Achievement Award, 1992. **Home Addr:** 236 Ashley Ave, Charleston, SC 29403. **Business Phone:** (803)577-9918.

WOODS, ARLEIGH MADDOX
Judge. **Personal:** Born Aug 31, 1929, Los Angeles, CA; daughter of Ida L Maddox and Benjamin Maddox; married William T. **Educ:** Chapman Coll, BS 1949; Southwestern Univ, LLB 1952; Univ of VA, LLM 1983; Univ of West Los Angeles, DDL 1984. **Career:** Levy Koszdin & Woods, atty 18 yrs, vice pres; CA Court of Appeal, presiding justice; State Commission on Judicial Performance, chair. **Orgs:** Vice pres Constitutional Rights Foundation 1980-; bd of dir Cancer Research Foundation 1983-; chmn of the bd of trustees, Southwestern Univ Schl of Law 1986; Various bar associations. **Honors/Awds:** Justice of the Year (CA) 1983; Woman of the Year Business & Professional Women 1982, YWCA 1984; Alumna of the Year Southwestern Univ 1994; Justice of the Year Los Angeles Trial Lawyers, 1989. **Business Addr:** Presiding Justice, CA Court of Appeal, 300 S Spring St, Los Angeles, CA 90013.

WOODS, BARBARA MCALPIN
Educational administrator. **Personal:** Born Dec 9, 1945, Nashville, TN; daughter of Ruth DuVall McAlpin and Dr Neal McAlpin Sr; married James F Woods; children: Trieste, Travis, Tamara. **Educ:** Univ of Kansas, BS 1967; St Louis Univ, MA 1982. **Career:** St Louis City Schools, teacher secondary English 1967-70; St Louis Univ, asst dir special academic programs 1972-77, acting dir Afro-American studies 1977-80, dir Afro-Amer stud/center-interdis studies 1980-. **Orgs:** Moderator/producer ''Black Issues Forum'' KADI radio-FM 1978-86; vice pres 84-85 & bd of dir Conference on Educ 1979-85; educ committee Urban League of Metro St Louis 1980-; charter member & chair Missouri Council for Black Studies 1982-84; bd of dirs Girl Scout Council 1981-85; task force Educ Prof Missouri, comm chair & steering comm 1984-87; bd of dir Kiwanis Camp Wyman St Louis 1984-87; moderator/producer ''Postscript'' KETC-TV; mem President's Advisory Council of Greater St Louis Girl Scout Council; natl advisory bd HERstory in Silhouette Project of the St Louis Public Schools; founder/convener Cross Cultural Conf on Women (bi-annual conf); founder, chair, bd of dirs, Youth Leadership St Louis Inc 1987-88; mem, bd of dirs, YWCA of Metropolitan St Louis1988-90; mem, bd of trustees, St is Art Museum 1989-91. **Honors/Awds:** Fellowship Multicultural Women's Inst, Univ of Illinois Chicago 1983; Top Ladies of Distinction Award, St Louis Chapter Top Ladies of Distinction 1984; Fellow, Leadership St Louis, Leadership St Louis Inc 1987-88; established/coordinated devel of Youth Leadership St Louis initially as a class project for the Ledership St Louis Fellows 1987-88, this high school leadership project is now an institionalized program. **Business Addr:** Dir, St Louis University, Afro-American Studies & Center, 221 N Grand Blvd, St Louis, MO 63103.

WOODS, BERNICE
Nurse, elected official. **Personal:** Born Sep 27, 1924, Port Arthur, TX; married Melvin J Woods; children: Melvin J Jr, Mary Jane, Jule Norman, Pernilla, Lewis, Kenneth Dale, Paulette, Dwight Clayton, Muriel Gale, Gregory Wayne. **Educ:** Attended East Los Angeles Jr Coll; CA School & Nursing, BS 1948; Univ of CA Los Angeles, BS Behavioral Sci 1965; CA State Univ Long Beach, MEd 1968. **Career:** Los Angeles Cty Gen Hosp, nurse retired after 28 yrs service; Compton Unified School Dist, bd of trustees mem. **Orgs:** Mem Queen of Sheba Grand Chap OES 1964; representation Delegate Assembly CA School Bd Assoc 1975-83; mem bd of trustees Compton Unified School Dist 1975-; mem Union Baptist Church, Democratic Club of Compton; pres Ladies Aux POP Warner Football; grand pres of Matron's Council OES; pres of Compton Union Council; PTA Parent Teacher Assn; mem Willowbrook State Park; pres/1st vp/2nd vice pres Natl Council of Negro Women; juvenile protect chmn 33rd Dist PTA; mem Southeast Mental Health Liaison Comm; mem NAACP Compton Chpt. **Honors/Awds:** Numerous awards incl, life mem Natl Council Negro Women 1974; Co-author Book ''I Am a Black Woman Who'' 1976; Helping All Children Natl School Bd Assoc 1978; 50 Year Serv Awd Parent Teacher Assoc 1978; Natl PTA Award 1984; Woman of the Year 1970 & 1975; mem Task Force to Secure Funds for Compton Unified Sch Dist 1974-75; Alternate Del to Dem Natl Conv NY 1976; Inner City Challange; Natl Council of Negro Women Achievers Award (4 times); Youth Athletic

Assn Award; Comm Award Block Clubs; Fraternal Award Order of the Eastern Star; Help All Agencies Dedicated Serv Award; Bethune Outstand Achieve Award; OutstandingChurch Serv Award; Outstanding Serv Award Lt Gov Mervyn Dymally; Bronze Medal Award Achievers Wash, DC; C of C Christmas Award. **Home Addr:** 1515 W 166th St, Compton, CA 90220. **Business Addr:** Board of Trustees, Compton Unified Sch Dist, 604 S Tamarind Ave, Compton, CA 90220.

WOODS, DARNELL
Human resources supervisor. **Personal:** Born Feb 13, 1961, Tucson, AZ. **Educ:** Dartmouth College, Hanover, NH, BA, 1983. **Career:** Pacific Gas & Electric, San Francisco, CA, supervisor college relations, 1985-; Dale Seymour Publications, Palo Alto CA, marketing mgr, 1983-85. **Orgs:** Member, College Placement Council, 1989-; member, National Assn of Minority Engineering Program Administrators, 1989-; member, American Management Assn NAMEPA, 1986-.

WOODS, ELISA R.
Information specialist. **Personal:** Born Apr 8, 1959, Chicago, IL; daughter of Mary L Bradley Woods and Marvell Woods. **Educ:** Clark College, Atlanta, GA, BA, 1981; Atlanta University, Atlanta, GA, MLS, 1983. **Career:** Lawrence Livermore Labs, Livermore, CA, technical information specialist, 1982; University of Colorado-Boulder, Boulder, CO, reference librarian, 1984-87; Booz Allen and Hamilton, Chicago, IL, research analyst, 1987-89; Grant Thornton, Chicago, IL, dir, information center, 1989-. **Orgs:** Member, ASIS, 1986-; chair, SLA, 1987-; member, AALL.

WOODS, GENEVA HOLLOWAY
Registered nurse anesthetist (retired). **Personal:** Born Sep 16, 1930, Saluda, SC; daughter of Mattie Dozier Holloway and Zonnie Holloway; married Sylvania Webb Sr; children: Sylvania Jr, Sebrena. **Educ:** Grady Hosp Sch of Nursing Atlanta, diploma 1949; Dillard Univ Sch of Anesthesia New Orleans LA, cert 1957; Real Estate Certificate - P.G. Comm. Coll Largo, MD 1983. **Career:** DC Gen Hosp Wash DC, staff nurse anesthetist 1979-85; St Elizabeth Hosp Wash DC, chief nurse anesthetist 1976-79; Providence Hosp Wash DC, chief nurse anesthetist 1971-76; DC Gen, staff nurse anesthetist 1960-70; Freedmen Hosp Howard Univ Wash DC, staff nurse 1955-57; Grady Meml Hosp Atlanta, asst head nurse 1952-54; Grady Meml Hosp Atlanta, prvt duty polio nurse 1950-52; DC ANaA, pres 1968-70; DC Lawyers Wives, parliamentarian 1974-76; PG Co Lawyers Wives, parliamentarian; certified real estate salesperson; registered nurse Providence Hosp. D.C. Substance Abuse. **Orgs:** Mem Upper Room Bapt Ch Wash DC 1961-; parliamentarian & charter mem Jack & Jills of PG Co Chap 1973-75; chmn Glenarden Inaugural Ball 1979; Chairman Saluda Rosen Wald/Riverside School Alumni Assn/Grady Nurses Alumni Assn D.C. Md. Va. Chapter. mem, bd of ethics, PG Co. **Honors/Awds:** Recipient mother of the yr award BSA Troop 1017 1966; cert parliamentarian parliamentarian Parliamentary Procecures Chicago IL 1970; continued professional excellence award Am Assn Nurse Chicago 1975&78; outstanding performance award St Elizabeth Hosp Wash DC 1978. **Home Addr:** 7816 Fiske Ave, Glenarden, MD 20706.

WOODS, GEORGE WASHINGTON
Chief executive officer. **Personal:** Born Mar 18, 1916, Colt, AR; son of Eliza and James; married Ophelia Henry; children: Dr George W, Michael F. **Educ:** AM&N Coll Pine Bluff AR, BA 1946; So IL U, attended 1968. **Career:** State Equal Oppor Office, dir; insurance estimator several insurance cos 1945-80; Office of Neighborhood Devel & Improvement, comm relations adv 1968-; City of Omaha NE, dir rehab 1968-71; Mechanic Drafting OIC Inc, instr 1970-; Woods Gen Home Improvement Co, owner 1951-68; OIC, drafting G instr 1971-; City of Omaha, land appraiser 1972-80; Woods Timber and Ranch Inc, operator; Woods Gen Home Improvement Co, owner 1951-68, dir. **Orgs:** Mem NACP 1935-80; Urban League 1950-56; minority rep Dem Party & Gov 1970-80; mem Omega Psi Phi Frat Inc, NAACP Inc; mem Allen Chapel AME Ch; mem Nat SEOO Exec Com; mem Kellom Comm Council; mem State System Com oranized United Contractor Assn of NE/COMM Serv Agt/ Infant Devel EncouragementProgram; chmn 11th Legislative Dist of Democratic Party 1987; chmn Urban League Legislative Comm; mem Catfish Farmers of Amer, Kellom Library Bd, South Omaha Neighborhood Assoc. **Honors/Awds:** Man Of The Year Kellom Community Council 1973; Leadership Award Kellom Community Council 1974; Service Awd Comm Action Assoc of NE 1985; Harry S Truman Awd 1986; numerous other awards. **Business Addr:** Dir, Woods General Home, 3327 Ruggles St, Omaha, NE 68111.

WOODS, GERALDINE PITTMAN
Scientist (retired). **Personal:** Born in W Palm Beach, FL; married Dr Robert I Woods Sr; children: D Jan, Jerri S Robert I Jr. **Educ:** Talladega Clg, 1938-40; Howard U, BS 1942; Radcliffe & Harvard U, MS 1943, PhD 1945; Benedict Clg, DSc 1977; Talladega Clg, DSc 1980. **Career:** NIH, special consultant, 1969-87. **Orgs:** Charles R Drew University, board of directors, 1991-; chm bd of trustees Howard Univ 1975-88; natl bd Girl Scts of USA 1975-78; chr of Ed Policy Comm Atlanta U; 1974-86; Inst of Med, Natl Academy of Sciences 1974-; board of directors Natl Comm for Cert of Phys Assts 1974-81; board of directors Robert Wood Johnson Hlth Pol Flwshp IOM NAS 1973-78; vice pres CA Post Secondary Ed Comm 1974-78; bd of trustees CA Museum Foundation, CA Museum of Sci & Ind 1971-79; chm Defense Adv Comm on Women in Services 1968; natl pres Delta Sigma Theta Sor 1963-67; NAACP, life mem; Natl Council of Negro Women, life mem; Urban League; AAAS; Federation of Am Scientists; Natl Inst of Sci; Delta Rsrch of Educational Foundation, president, 1983-88; pres Howard Univ Foundation. **Honors/Awds:** Phi Beta Kappa, Golden Key Society, Honorary Member; recipient of many awds & citation by org & govt; NMA, "Scroll of Merit," highest awd of LA Alumnae Chapter of Delta Sigma Theta; Merit Awd, highest awd of the Natl Org; Mary Chutch Terrell Awd; many awds from Howard U; selected as one of 20 famous African-American scientists; one of "Black Women Achieving Against the Odds," an exhibit by the Smithsonian Inst; Honorary Degrees: Meharry Medical College, DHL, 1988; Howard University, LHD, 1989; Fisk University, DSc, 1991. **Special Achievements:** Placed ground work and assisted development of Minority Access to Research Careers & Minority Biomedical Research Support Programs.

WOODS, HENRY, JR.
Manufacturing company executive. **Personal:** Born May 10, 1954, Clarksdale, MS; son of Estella Marie Woods and Henry Neal Woods; children: John M Hite. **Educ:** Utica Junior College, AA, 1974; Mississippi Valley State University, BA, 1976. **Career:** United California Bank, loan officer, 1977-79; Community Bank, business development officer, 1979-81; Crocker National Bank, business development officer, 1981-83; Golden State Financial, general partner, 1983-84; Woods and Associates/CERS Group, 1984; Thermo Brique West, senior vp, partner, 1991-. **Orgs:** Challenger Boys & Girls Club, board of directors, 1984-; Crossroad Arts Academy, board of trustee, 1989-; Technical Health Career School, board of directors, 1992-; Beacon of Hope Foundation, steering committee member, 1992-; Horace Mann School, One to One Team Mentoring Program, 1993. **Honors/Awds:** Mayor Tom Bradley, Commendation Award, 1992; Lieutenant Governor Leo McCarthy, Recognition Award, 1992; State Senator Diane Watson, Recognition Award, 1992. **Home Addr:** 600 W 9th St, #1013, Los Angeles, CA 90015.

WOODS, HORTENSE E.
Librarian. **Personal:** Born Mar 17, 1926, Malvern, AR; married Walter F; children: Marcia Laureen. **Educ:** AR AM & N Coll Pine Bluff, bA 1950; Cath Univ Washington, lS; UCLA & pepperdine U, study; Univ of Southern CA, grad. **Career:** Vernon Br Sr Lib, pub lib; Pine Bluff Pub Lib Bran Lib, 1954-59; Wilmington Br LA Pub Lib 1st Black Lib, 1961-65; Enterprise Sch Dist LA Co, org lib 1966-69; Lincoln HS Camden AR Sch Lib, 1950-51. **Orgs:** Dir All Cty Emp Asn LA 1973-; sec Cent C of C LA 1973-; mem Am Film Inst; bd mem Cntr for Women Dvel Long Beach CA; editorial consult Saturday Mag 1979; mem Staff Assn LA Pub Lib 1970-; mem Grant AME Ch Women's Day Nat Coun Negro Women. **Honors/Awds:** Edtr "Fav Delta Recipes" pub by Bev-ron Publ 1974; mem natl hon soc. **Business Addr:** Branch Librarian, Vernon Branch Library, 4504 S Central Ave, Los Angeles, CA 90011.

WOODS, JACQUELINE EDWARDS
Educator. **Personal:** Born Oct 10, 1947, Detroit, MI; children: John E Kemp. **Educ:** MI State Univ, BA 1969; Wayne State Univ, MEd 1970. **Career:** Various Educ Assocs/Colls, speech path/prof 1971-74; Long Beach Comm Coll District, dean resource develop energy prog dir 1975-79; Amer Assoc of Comm/Jr Colls, dir prog develop 1979-83; Amer Coll Testing Program, dir Washington DC office 1983-; Washington DC office, American College Testing Program, director, 1983-88; Association of Governing Boards of Universities & Colleges, vp, programs & public policy, 1988-90; for Institutional Advancement, Community College of Philadelphia, vp. 1991-. **Orgs:** Teaching asst consultant/trainer Jr Community College Inst 1979-; mem bd dirs United Way/United Black Fund Mgmt Serv 1982-84; mem DC bd dirs MI State Univ Black Alumni 1983-; chmn steering comm Women Administrators in Higher Educ 1984-; mem adv bd Natl Consortium for Educ Access 1985-; mem bd dirs Amer Assoc Higher Educ Black Caucus 1986-; convocation speaker Livingstone Coll 1986; NE Region, National Council on Black American Affairs, executive board; Executive Board of the AAHE Black Caucus, chair elect. **Honors/Awds:** Woman of the Yr Amer Business Women's Assoc Port City Chap 1973; Outstanding Young Women of Amer 1975; Appreciation Awd Natl Council Resource Dev (AACJC) 1983; Appreciation Awd League of United Lation Amer Citizens 1986; Outstanding Serv Awd AAHE Black Caucus (Nat) 1986. **Business Addr:** VP for Institutional Advancement, Community College of Philadelphia, 1700 Spring Garden St, Philadelphia, PA 19130.

WOODS, JANE GAMBLE
Publisher. **Personal:** Born Aug 26, 1928, St Louis, MO; widowed; children: JoAnn Austin, Judy W Williams, Patricia W May, Gail W McDuffie. **Educ:** Attended, Stowe Jr Coll, Lincoln Univ Jefferson City MO. **Career:** St Louis Sentinel Newspaper, publisher. **Orgs:** Past bd mem Natl Assn of Media Women; past bd mem St Louis Chap United Nations of Amer; past bd mem St Louis Chap ICBO; bd mem Natl Newspaper Pub Assn; bd mem Amalgamated Pub Inc; bd mem OIC St Louis Ch; pst bd mem KETC Ch 9 St Louis Regional Ed & Pub TV; pst trustee Deaconess Hosp;past bd mem Northside YMCA; mem adv bd Salvation Army; past mem adv bd Small Bus Adminstrn; past bd mem Com on Adminstrn Phyllis Wheatley YWCA; bd mem Jr Kindergarten; past bd mem MO Assn for Social Welfare; commr MO Housing Development Comm; bd mem Urban League of Metro St Louis; 2nd vice pres Natl Newspaper Publishers Assn. **Business Addr:** Publisher, St Louis Sentinel Newspaper, 3338 Olive St Ste 206, St Louis, MO 63103.

WOODS, JEROME
Professional football player. **Personal:** Born Mar 17, 1973, Memphis, TN. **Educ:** Memphis. **Career:** Kansas City Chiefs, defensive back, 1996-. **Special Achievements:** NFL Draft, First round pick, #28, 1996. **Business Addr:** Professional Football Player, Kansas City Chiefs, 1 Arrowhead Dr, Kansas City, MO 64129, (816)924-9300.

WOODS, JESSIE ANDERSON
Arts administrator. **Personal:** Born Apr 8, 1914, Chicago, IL; daughter of Mamie McGwin Anderson and Vance J Anderson; married James H Woods, Sep 9, 1939 (deceased); children: Victoria W Burgoyne, James A. **Educ:** Univ of Chicago, attended 1931-32; Univ of IL, attended 1932-33; Univ of Chicago, attended 1937-38; Harvard Univ, fellowship & certificate Arts Admin 1972. **Career:** Graham Artist Bureau, agent 1935-37; Univ of Chicago, research asst 1937-39; Woods Brothers Inc, office mgr 1941-53; Task Force/Alt Educ Natl Endowment for the Arts, consultant/co-chmn 1976; Urban Gateways, exec dir 1965-81; Reading Is Fundamental In Chicago, exec dir 1985-87. **Orgs:** Mem Alpha Gamma Pi 1975-; mem exec com Chicago Council on Fine Arts, mem Dusable Museum of African-Amer Histoty; Presidential appointment Natl Council on the Arts, 1978-84; appointed chmn advisory board, Chicago Dept of Cultural Affairs, 1983-; mem Bd of Overseers for Campus Life, Illinois Inst of Technology; Visiting Comm, School of Social Serv Admin, Univ of Chicago 1985-. **Honors/Awds:** Governor's Award/Contribution to Arts State of IL 1978; Chicago Comm on Human Relations Award Chicago 1978; Honorary Doctorate of Humane Letters Columbia Coll Chicago 1979; Honorary Doctor Fine Arts, Univ of IL. **Home Addr:** 5530 S Shore Dr, Chicago, IL 60637.

WOODS, MADELYNE I.
News anchor. **Personal:** Born Oct 10, 1965, Washington, DC; daughter of Mary Kittrell Woods and Lloyd Woods; married Jeffrey Williams, Nov 29, 1990. **Educ:** Howard University, Washington, DC, MA, mass communication, 1987; University of Maryland, College Park, MD, BS, broadcast journalism, 1986. **Career:** WHMM TV 32, Washington, DC, host, 1987-88; WJWJ TV 16, Beaufort, SC, news reporter, 1988-89; WCIV News 4, Charleston, SC, news reporter, 1989-90; Black Entertainment Television, Washington, DC, news anchor, 1990. **Orgs:** Member, National Assn of Black Journalists, 1987-; member, Washington Assn of Black Journalists, 1987-; member, National Academy of Arts and Sciences, 1987-88. **Business Addr:** News Anchor, Black Entertainment Television, 1899 9th St NE, Washington, DC 20018.

WOODS, MANUEL T.
Educator. **Personal:** Born May 10, 1939, Kansas City, KS; son of Mable Woods; married Wanda Emanuel; children: Susan, Daniel. **Educ:** Univ of MN, AA 1968, BA 1970, PhD 1978; Univ of Hartford, MEd 1973. **Career:** Univ of MN, new careers prog counselor 1967-70, office of admissions/reg asst dir 1970-85, office of student affairs asst to vice pres 1985-86, educ student affairs office dir 1986-92; Turning Point, Inc, vice pres for programs, 1992-. **Orgs:** Pres MN Counselors & Dirs of Minority Programs Assoc; pres Univ Assoc of Black Employees; program chairperson Upper Midwest Assoc of Collegiate Registrars and Admissions Officers; program convenor MN Counselors and Directors of Minority Programs, Counseling the Disadvantaged Student; comm mem Minneapolis Comm Coll Adv Bd. **Honors/Awds:** Bush Fellowship Awd, Bush Foundation, 1973; Outstanding Alumnus, Minneapolis Comm Coll, 1986. **Home Addr:** 5841 73rd Ave N, Apt 153, Brooklyn Park, MN 55429. **Business Addr:** VP for Programs, Turning Point, Inc, 1500 Golden Valley Rd, Minneapolis, MN 55411-3139.

WOODS, MELVIN LEROY
Business executive. **Personal:** Born May 10, 1938, Lexington, KY; married Elnora; children: Gregory, Alyssa. **Educ:** Jackson State U, BS 1962; VA Hosp, cert 1962; Univ IL, MS 1967; IUPUI, 1973-75. **Career:** Eli Lilly & Co, comm rel asso, mgr of public affairs, currently; Lilly Endowment Inc, prgm ofcr, 1973-77; Marion Co Asn Retarded Citz, dior adult serv 1970-73; So WI Colony & Union Cp Training Sch, supr therapist 1966-70; WI Parks & Recreation &3 Univ WI consult 1967; St Lukes Hosp, 1969-70; So IN Retardation Serv 972-73. **Orgs:** Mem WI Parks & Rec Assn 1966-73; IN Assn Rehab Facilities; bd mem Intl Assn Rehab Facilities 1972-73; Nat Assn Retarded Citz 1970-75; Am Assn Mental Deficiency 1973-77; mem Kappa Alpha Psi; Alpha Kappa Mu 1962. **Honors/Awds:** Distd

Hoosier citation IN Gov Office 1972; flwsp grant Univ I 1965; publ, The Devel of a Pay for Recreation Procedure in a Token Economy System; Mental Retardation 1971. **Military Serv:** AUS sp 4 1962-65. **Business Addr:** 1201 K St, Ste 760, Sacramento, CA 95814.

WOODS, PHILIP WELLS
Musician, composer. **Personal:** Born Nov 2, 1931, Springfield, MA; son of Clara Markley and Stanley; married Jill Goodwin; children: Kim Parker, Baird Parker, Garth, Aimee, Allisen Trotter, Tracey Trotter. **Educ:** Saxophone w/Harvey LaRose; attended, Juilliard Conservatory 1948-52. **Career:** Played with Dizzy Gillespie Band US Overseas 1965; played with Quincy Jones Band on European tours 1959-61; played with Benny Goodman Band touring USSR 1962 & Monterey Jazz Festival 1962; rec artist; Phil Woods Quintet, leader; European Rhythm Machine based in Paris, 1968-73; Phil Woods Quartet (Now Quintet), 1974-; Phil Woods' Little Big Band 1987-. **Orgs:** National Association of Jazz Educators; American Federation of Musicians; Composer "Rights of Swing" 1960; Sonata for Alto & Piano; Three Improvisions; I Remember; Deer Head Sketches. **Honors/Awds:** Winner on Alto Saxophone Down Beat Critics' Polls, 1975-90, 1992-1997; Reader's Polls, 1975-95; Grammy Awards Best Instrumental Jazz Performance Group, 1977, 1982, 1983; Honorary Doctorate, East Stroudsburg University, 1994. **Business Addr:** Box 278, Delaware Water Gap, PA 18327.

WOODS, ROBERT LOUIS
Dentist. **Personal:** Born Oct 24, 1947, Charlotte, NC; son of Effie E. Woods and Clifton Woods, Jr.; married Cynthia Dianne Hawkins; children: Sonja Nicole, Cheryl Lynnette. **Educ:** NC Central Univ, BS Biol 1969, MS Biol 1971; Univ of NC School of Dentistry, DDS 1977. **Career:** Duke Univ Med Ctr, rsch tech 1969; NC Agricultural & Tech Univ, instr of biol 1971-73; pvt practice, 1977-90; Univ of NC School of Dentistry, clinicalinstr 1979-81; Orange Chatham Comprehensive Health Svcs, lead staff dentist 1982-89. **Orgs:** Mem Amer Dental Assoc 1977-, NC Dental Soc 1977-, Old North State Dental Soc 1977-; bd dir fin comm chair Person Family Med Ctr 1979-81; bd dir facility comm chair Person Family Med Ctr 1979-81; mem, bd dir Parents for the Adv of Gifted Educ 1982-83. **Business Addr:** Polk Youth Institution, P.O. Box 2500, 1001 Veazey Rd., Butner, NC 27509.

WOODS, ROOSEVELT, JR.
Painter. **Personal:** Born Aug 15, 1933, Idabel, OK; son of Nannie Wharry Woods and Roosevelt Woods, Sr.; married Wanda; children: Dwynette, Senina. **Educ:** AZ State Univ, BS, MAE 1958. **Career:** AZ State Univ, prof; CO Clge Fine Art, prof of painting, emeritus; Phoenix Dist HS, tchr 1958; artist painter/printmaker. **Orgs:** One man & group shows 1955; works rep pvt & Pub collections throughout country.

WOODS, SANFORD L.
Automobile dealer. **Career:** Brandon Dodge Inc, chief executive officer, currently. **Special Achievements:** Company is ranked #25 on Black Enterprise's list of top 100 auto dealers, 1994. **Business Addr:** CEO, Brandon Dodge Inc., PO Box 76037, Tampa, FL 33675-1037, (813)620-4300.

WOODS, SYLVANIA WEBB, SR. See Obituaries section.

WOODS, SYLVIA
Restauranteur. **Personal:** Born Feb 2, 1926, Hemingway, SC; daughter of Van & Julia Pressley; married Herbert K Woods, Jan 18, 1944; children: Van, Bedelia, Kenneth, Crizette. **Educ:** La Robert Cosmetology School. **Career:** Sylvia's Restaurant, owner, currently. **Orgs:** Share Our Strength; City Meals on Wheels; Women's Roundtable. **Honors/Awds:** Women's Day Award, Cert of Appreciation, 1988; The Riverside Club, Business Award, 1991; African American Award, Business Award, 1990; The New York State Dept of Economic Devt, Business Award, 1994; Mayor of New York City, Certificate of Appreciation, 1992. **Special Achievements:** US Air Force, Cert of Appreciation, 1989; US Army, Cert of Appreciation, 1991; State of New York, Governor, Exec Chamber, 1992; NY Metro Roundtable, Lifetime Achievement Award, 1993; NAACP, Woman of the Year Award, 1978; Owned restaurant for the past 33 years. **Business Addr:** Owner, President, Sylvia's Restaurant, 328 Lenox Ave, New York, NY 10027, (212)996-0660.

WOODS, TIGER (ELDRICK)
Professional golfer. **Personal:** Born Dec 30, 1975, Long Beach, CA; son of Kultida Woods and Earl D Woods. **Career:** Professional golfer; All Star Cafe, partner. **Honors/Awds:** American Jr Golf Association, Player of the Year, 1991-92; Rolex, First Team All-American, 1991-92; Golfweek/Titleist, Jr Golfer of the Year, 1991; United States Golf Association, National Junior Amateur Champion, 1991-92; Insurance Youth Golf Classic Champion, 1992; US Amateur Golf Championship, 1994; US Masters Golf Tournament, champion, 1997; PGA, Player of the Year, 1997; Associated Press, Male Athlete of the Year, 1997; Johnnie Walker Classic, champion, 1998. **Special Achievements:** First African American to win US Amateur Golf Championship; Youngest person and first African American to win the US Masters Golf Tournament.

WOODS, TIMOTHY L.
Automobile dealership executive. **Career:** Chino Hills Ford, Inc, Chino CA, chief executive, 1988; Queen City Ford, chief executive, currently.

WOODS, WILBOURNE F.
Association executive. **Personal:** Born May 7, 1935, Magee, MS; divorced. **Educ:** Roosevelt University, BA, 1972. **Career:** City of Chicago, peace officer, currently. **Orgs:** Chairman, Midwest Region, Natl Black Police Assn. **Honors/Awds:** Member of the Year, Midwest Region, Natl Black Police Assn, 1986; Member of the Year, African-American Police League, 1991. **Home Addr:** 8155 South State Street, Chicago, IL 60619-4719.

WOODS, WILLIE
Company executive. **Career:** Digital Systems Research Inc, CEO, currently. **Special Achievements:** Company is ranked #54 on Black Enterprise's list of Top 100 Industrial/Service Companies, 1994. **Business Addr:** CEO, Digital Systems Research Inc, 4301 N Fairfax Dr, Ste 725, Arlington, VA 22203, (703)522-6067.

WOODS, WILLIE G.
Educational administrator. **Personal:** Born Nov 3, Yazoo City, MS; daughter of Jessie Turner Woods and Rev. John Wesley Woods. **Educ:** Shaw Univ Raleigh NC, BA Ed 1965; Duke Univ Durham NC, MEd 1968; Temple Univ PA, PA State Univ, NY Univ, attended; Indiana University of Pennsylvania, Indiana, PA, PhD English, 1995. **Career:** Berry O'Kelly School, language arts teacher 1965-67; Preston School, 5th grade teacher 1967-69, adult ed teacher 1968-69; Harrisburg Area Comm Coll, prof english/ed 1969-, dir acad found prog, 1983-87, asst dean of Academic Foundations and Basic Education Division, 1987-89, asst dean of Social Science, Public Services, and Basic Education Division, 1989-92. **Orgs:** Bd of mgrs Camp Curtin Branch of Harrisburg YMCA 1971-79; rep council 1972-, sec 1977-79, assoc ed 1981-, PA Black Conf on Higher Ed; exec bd 1978-, council chairperson 1981-82, Western Reg Act 101 Dir Council; bd of dir Alternative Rehab Comm Inc 1978-; bd of dir 1979-, charter mem sec 1981-82, treas 1982-83, PA Assoc of Devel Ed; bd of dir 1981-, sec 1984-85, Dauphin Residences Inc; bd of advisors 1981-, chairperson, acting chairperson, bd sec Youth Urban Serv Harrisburg YMCA; inst rep Natl Council on Black Amer Affairs of the Amer Assoc of Comm & Jr Coll 1983-. **Honors/Awds:** Cert of Merit for Community Serv Harrisburg 1971; Meritorious Faculty Contrib Harrisburg 1977; Outstanding Serv Awd PA Black Conf on Higher Ed 1980; Central Reg Awd for Serv PA Black Conf on Higher Ed 1982; Alpha Kappa Alpha Sor Outstanding Comm Serv Awd Harrisburg 1983; YMCA Youth Urban Serv Volunteer of the Year Awd 1983; Alpha Kappa Alpha Sor Basileus' Awd for Excellence as Comm Chair 1985; Administrative Staff Merit Award, Harrisburg Area Comm College, 1986; Outstanding Service Award, Black StudentUnion at Harrisburg Area Comm College, 1989; tribute for outstanding contributions to Harrisburg Area Comm College and to comm-at-large, HACC Minority Caucus, 1989; Alpha Kappa Mu Natl Hon Soc; Brooks Dickens Mem Award in Education. **Business Addr:** Acting Vice President, Faculty and Instruction, Harrisburg Area Community College, One HACC Drive, Harrisburg, PA 17110-2999.

WOODS-BURWELL, CHARLOTTE ANN
Elected official (retired). **Personal:** Born Jan 7, 1932, Ft Wayne, IN; daughter of Josephine Gaines Williams and Beauford Williams; married Lawrence Cornelius Burwell Sr, Jan 15, 1994; children: Beauford K, Brenda K Coleman, Parnell L Jr, Jeffry C. **Career:** Peg Leg Bates Country Club, ba mgr 1976, asst mgr 1980-86 off mgr 1987; Allen County Board of Voters Registration, Fort Wayne, IN, chief deputy, 1988-. **Orgs:** Bd mem Bd of Ethics Kerhonkson 1969-73, Ulster Cty Mental Health Assn 1970-76; chmn Tower of Rochester Dem Club 1970-; Rondout Valley School Board, 1983-87; New York State School Board Legislative Network, 1985-87; Prevention Connection Comm Drug & Alcohol Abuse; vice chairman, Allen County Democratic Party, 1987-; secretary, Lillian Jones Brown Club, 1988-; Ultra Art Club, 1988-. **Special Achievements:** Elected to Wayne Township Advisory Board, Mar 1992. **Home Addr:** 31 Northgate Dr, Albany, NY 12203.

WOODSON, AILEEN R.
Educational administrator (retired). **Personal:** Born Nov 27, 1927, East Chicago, IN; daughter of Gussie Smith Russell and Jenese R Woodson; married Edgar H Woodson, Jul 10, 1947; children: Adele H, Brett Denise. **Career:** Dublin Avenue Magnet Elementary School, principal, 1976-85; Los Angeles Unified School District, human resources division, interviewer, 1986-. **Orgs:** Invited member, Black Jewish Coalition, 1984; bd mem, PUSH, 1974-76; Council of Black Administrators, founder/chmn, 1971-79; Delta Sigma Theta Sorority, 1953-; pres, The Women Inc, 1962-64; mem, Holman Methodist Church, 1952-; life mem, NAACP; mem, Urban League; mem, SCLC; YMCA; Council of Black Administrators of Los Angeles; commissioner, Los Angeles Social Service Commission, 1984-; commissioner, Los Angeles Commission of Transportation, 1979-84; Los Angeles City Commission of Utilities & Transportation, 1972-79. **Honors/Awds:** Official Olympic Hostess, 1984 Olympics Games, Los Angeles, CA; Apple Award, 1981; Ambassador of Good Will Award, 1977; Recognition of Unselfishness & Outstanding Award, Dublin School Parents, 1980; Tribute to Parents Ward, Mayor Thomas Bradley, 1980; Honorary PTA Service Award, Dublin Ave School PTA, 1980; Proclamation for Unusual Service & Contributions, City of Huntington Park, 1976; Commendation Resolution, California State Assemblyman-Julian Dixon, 1973; Invitation to President's Committee on Employment of the Handicapped in Washington, DC; Freedom Foundation Award, 1970; Dedicated Service Pen Set, 95th Street School Staff; Award of Merit, Black Parents of Watts, 1970; PTA Sterling Pin Award, 112th Street School PTA, Watts, 1969; LA Sentinel Newspaper Award, 1963; Nominee for Sojoer Truth Award, Assn of Negro Business & Professional Women, 1963; Red Cross Five Year Pin, 1960; Minerva Award, Delta Sigma Theta, 1977. **Home Addr:** 4561 Don Felipe Drive, Los Angeles, CA 90008.

WOODSON, ALFRED F.
Banking executive. **Personal:** Born Feb 18, 1952, Georgetown, SC; son of Zelda J Woodson and Alfred F Woodson Sr; married Linda Washington Woodson, Dec 22, 1979. **Educ:** Princeton University, Princeton, NJ, BA, 1974. **Career:** Fidelity Bank, Philadelphia, PA, loan officer, 1974-78; First City, Texas, Houston, TX, vice pres, 1978-89; First American Metro Corp, McClean, VA, sr vice pres, 1989-. **Business Addr:** Executive Vice President, First American Metro Corp, 1751 Pinnacle Dr, Mc Lean, VA 22102-3834.

WOODSON, CHARLES R.
Health services officer. **Personal:** Born Feb 22, 1942, Louisville, KY; married. **Educ:** Univ of Lsvl, MSSW 1969; Lincoln Univ MO, BS 1963. **Career:** DHHS Pub Hlth Svc, proj dir 1979-; Assn of Colls of Ostpthc Med, dir ofc of spl opp 1974-79; Univ of Lsvll, dir ofc of blk afrs 1971-74; ActnCommn, dir nghbrhd orgn comm 1970-71; Sthflds Trtmnt Ctr, supt 1969-70. **Orgs:** Mem Am Pub Hlth Assn 1974-; mem Am Assn for Hghr Educ 1973-; mem Nat Assn of Blk Soc Wrkrs 1972-; mem Kappa Alpha Psi. **Honors/Awds:** PHS, Unit Commendation, PHS Citation. **Business Addr:** 4350 East-West Hwys, 9th Fl, Bethesda, MD 20814.

WOODSON, CLEVELAND COLEMAN, III
Petroleum company executive. **Personal:** Born Sep 5, 1946, Richmond, VA; son of Naomi Wilder Woodson and Cleveland C Woodson, Jr; married Jannifer Eileen Vaughan, Oct 26, 1968; children: Cleveland C IV, Camille C. **Educ:** Virginia Union Univ, BS Acct 1970; Case Western Reserve Univ, MBA. **Career:** Ernst & Whinney, sr auditor 1970-76; Marathon Oil Co, advanced auditor 1976-78, task force mem 1978, advanced acct analyst 1979, sr acct analyst 1979-80, supvr 1980-83; Marathon Petroleum Co, mgr 1983-86; Marathon Oil Co, mgr, 1987-. **Orgs:** Bd of dir Natl Assn of Black Accts 1971-73; mem Amer Inst of CPA's 1973-; chairperson acct personnel comm Cleveland Chapter OH Soc of CPA's 1975; treas/auditor Cleveland Jaycees 1975-76; Children Services Advisory Board, 1975-76; treasurer Wilson Vance Parent Teacher Org 1981-83, Central JH Parent Teacher Org 1983-84; mem Amer Assn of Blacks in Energy 1983-; treasurer, Findlay High Citizens Advisory Comm, 1984-89; mem, Hampton Univ Industry Advisory Cluster, 1982-; board of trustees, Hancock County Chapter of American Red Cross; Multicultural Advisory Committee, The University of Findlay. **Honors/Awds:** CPA State of OH 1973. **Home Addr:** 516 Bright Rd, Findlay, OH 45840.

WOODSON, DARREN RAY
Professional football player. **Personal:** Born Apr 25, 1969, Phoenix, AZ. **Educ:** Arizona State, bachelor's degree in criminal justice. **Career:** Dallas Cowboys, defensive back, 1992-. **Honors/Awds:** Pro Bowl, 1994, 1995, 1996. **Business Addr:** Professional Football Player, Dallas Cowboys, One Cowboys Pkwy, Irving, TX 75063, (214)556-9900.

WOODSON, JACQUELINE
Novelist. **Personal:** Born Feb 12, 1963, Columbus, OH; daughter of Mary Ann & Jack Woodson. **Educ:**. **Career:** Goddard College, MFA Program, associate faculty, 1993-95; Eugene Lang College, associate faculty, 1994; Vermont College, MFA Program, assoc fac, 1996. **Orgs:** Alpha Kappa Alpha. **Honors/Awds:** Granta, Fifty Best American Authors Under 40 Award, 1996; Kenyon Review Award, Literary Excellence in Fiction, 1995; Coretta Scott King, Honor Book Award, 1995, 1996; Jane Addams Children's Book Award, 1995, 1996; Publisher's Weekly, Best Book Award, 1994; Booklist, Editor's Choice Award; American Library Association, Best Book Award; American Film Institute Award. **Special Achievements:** Author: Last Summer With Maizon, 1990; The Dear One, 1991; Maizon At Blue Hill, 1992; Between Madison & Palmetto, 1993; The Book Chase, 1993; I Hadn't Meant To Tell You This, 1995; From The Notebooks of Malanin Sun, 1995; Autobiography of A Family Photo, 1995; A Way Out of No Way, 1996; The House You Pass On the Way, 1997. **Business Addr:** c/o Charlotte Sheedy Literary Agency, 65 Bleecker St, 12th Fl, New York, NY 10012.

WOODSON, JEFFREY ANTHONY
City official. **Personal:** Born May 21, 1955, Baltimore, MD; son of Evelyn Trent Woodson and Alfred C Woodson; married Paula Mason; children: Jeffrey Jr, Devon. **Educ:** Virginia State Univ, BA, 1976; Virginia Commonwealth Univ, MPA, 1983. **Career:** Southside Virginia Training Center, social worker, 1976-78, asst program mgr, 1978-83; City of Richmond, budget & mgmt analyst, 1983-85, senior budget analyst, 1985-91, strategic planning and budget director, 1991-. **Orgs:** Mem, Omega Psi Phi, 1973; chmn, membership comm, Amer Soc for Public Admin, 1983-; mem, Conf of Minority Public Admin, 1983-; Natl Forum for Black Public Admin, 1983-; chapter council, Amer Soc for Public Admin, 1985-87. **Honors/Awds:** Natl Jr Honor Soc, 1968; Outstanding Aced Frmn Award, Virginia State University, 1972; Outstanding Young Man of Amer, Jaycees, 1983; Productivity Analysis, Virginia Town & City Magazine (VA Municipal League), 1984. **Home Addr:** 10211 Duryea Dr, Richmond, VA 23235. **Business Addr:** Budget and Strategic Planning Director, City of Richmond, 900 E Broad St Rm 311, Richmond, VA 23219.

WOODSON, MIKE
Professional basketball player. **Personal:** Born Mar 24, 1958, Indianapolis, IN; married Terri Waters. **Educ:** IN Univ, 1980. **Career:** New York Knicks, 1981, New Jersey Nets, 1982, Kansas City Kings, 1982-85, Sacramento Kings, 1986, Los Angeles Clippers, 1987-88, Houston Rockets, 1989-. **Orgs:** Kings hon capt of Spec Olym team. **Honors/Awds:** Co-captain of US team which won a gold medal in 1979 Pan Amer Games; was named MVP in 79 IN Classic; won all-tourney honors 3 straight years; also won all-tourney honors in the Far West Classic and the Gator Bowl. **Business Addr:** Professional Basketball Player, Houston Rockets, 10 Greenway Plaza, Houston, TX 77046-1099.

WOODSON, ROBERT L.
Business executive. **Personal:** Born Apr 8, 1937, Philadelphia, PA; married Ellen Hylton Woodson; children: Robert L Jr, Ralph L, Jamal J. **Educ:** Cheyney State Coll, BS 1962; Univ of PA, MSW 1965; Univ of MA, doctoral prog. **Career:** Natl Urban League, dir; AEI Neighborhood Revitalization Proj, dir, resd fellow; Amer Enterprise Inst for Public Policy Rsch, adj fellow; Council for aBlack Economic Agenda, chmn; Natl Ctr for Neighborhood Enterprise, pres. **Orgs:** Consult US House of Rep Subcom on Crime-Judiciary Com 1978-79; dir Admin of Justice Div Natl Urban League 1972-78; mem Pres Commun on Mental Health 1978; fellow Natl Endowment for the Humanities 1977; bd dir Natl Ctr on Insts & Alternatives; bd of dir Ctr for Commun Change; bd dir Corp for Enterprise Devel; adv Natl Black Police Assoc, The Grassroots Network; pres adv council Private Sector Initiatives; lecturer at colls & univs in US & Europe; appeared on numTV & radio talk shows. **Honors/Awds:** Commun Serv Awd Martin Luther King Comm Ctr Houston 1976; Disting Serv Awd Natl Black Police Assoc 1980; publs incl, "Day Care" 1984, "Youth Crime Policies" 1983, "Investing in People, A Strategy to Combat, Not Preserve Poverty" 1983, "Helping the Poor Help Themselves" 1982, "The Importance of Neighborhood Organizations in Meeting Human Needs", "Youth Crime Prevention, An Alternative Approach", "Child Welfare Policy" 1982, "A Summons to Life, Mediating Structures & the Prevention of Youth Crime," 1981; editor "Youth Crime & Urban Policy, A View From the Inner City" 1981, "Mediating Structures Can Control Youth Crime" 1980, "The Justice Depts Fight Against Youth Crime, A Review of the Office of Juvenile Justice & Delinquency Prevention of LEAA"1978, "Predatory Crime & Black Youth" 1978; arles in Washington Post, Washington Star, NY times; editor Black Perspectives on Crime & the Criminal Justice System 1976. **Business Addr:** President, Ntl Cntr for Neighborhood Ent, 1367 Connecticut Avenue, NW, Washington, DC 20036.

WOODSON, RODERIC L.
Attorney. **Personal:** Born Aug 23, 1947, Philadelphia, PA; married Karen Smith; children: Roderic L. **Educ:** PA St U, BA 1969; Hwrd U, JD 1973. **Career:** Wdsn & Wdsn Attys & Cnsl at Law, prtnr; SEC, spl cnslr frdm of info ofcr 1976-79, atty advr corp fin 1973-75. **Orgs:** Mem PA Bar Assn 1973; mem St Bar Assn of GA 1974; mem DC Bar Assn 1979; mem Nat Bar Assn; mem Am Bar Assn; mem Fed Bar Assn; wash Bar Assn; mem Philadelphia Brstr's Assn; mem Gate City Bar Assn; corr sec Wash Bar Assn 1977-79, rec sec 1979-, bd of dir 1977-; Delta Theta Phi Lgl Frat; Kappa Alpha Psi Frat; Skull & Bns Soc. **Honors/Awds:** Am Jrsprdnc Awd 1972; outst almn awd Hayes Snt Delta Theta Phi Lgl Frat 1974; Outst Yng of Am 1980. **Business Addr:** Ste 220 806 15th St NW, Washington, DC 20005.

WOODSON, RODERICK KEVIN
Professional football player. **Personal:** Born Mar 10, 1965, Fort Wayne, IN; married Nikki; children: Marikah, Demitrius, Tia Rochelle. **Educ:** Purdue University, bachelor's degree in criminal justice. **Career:** Pittsburgh Steelers, cornerback, 1987-96; San Francisco 49ers, 1997; Baltimore Ravens, 1998-. **Honors/Awds:** First round draft pick, 1987; Pro Bowl, 1989, 1990, 1991, 1992, 1993, 1994, 1996; Associated Press, NFL Defensive Player of the Year, 1993; UPI, AFC Defensive Player of the Year, 1993; NFLPA, AFC Defensive Player of the Year, 1993, 1994; Ed Block Courage Award, 1994. **Business Addr:** Professional Football Player, Baltimore Ravens, 11001 Owings Mills Blvd, Owings Mills, MD 21117, (410)654-6200.

WOODSON, SHIRLEY A.
Artist, art educator, consultant. **Personal:** Born Mar 3, 1936, Pulaski, TN; daughter of Claude E Woodson and Celia Trotter Woodson; married Edsel Reid; children: Khari, Senghor. **Educ:** Wayne State Univ, BFA 1958; Art Inst of Chicago, grad study 1960; Wayne State Univ, MA 1965. **Career:** Detroit Public Schools, art supervisor; Exhibitions, Childe Hassam Found NY 1968, Arts Exended Gallery Detroit 1969, 2nd World Festival of African Culture Lagos Nigeria 1977, Howard Univ 1975; Forever Free Art by African Amer Women 1962-1980; Joslyn Museum Omaha NE 1981; Your Heritage House Museum 1984; "Share the Memories", Detroit Institute of Arts, 1987; Focus/Black Artists '88, Contemporary Art Center, Cincinnati, Ohio; Connecticut Gallery, Marlborogh, CT, 1989; Sherry Washington Gallery, 1989; "Coast to Coast: Nat'l Women of Color", Artists Books, Radford University, Radford, VA, 1990; "Walter O Evans Collection", King Tisdell Museum, Savannah, GA, 1991; Hughley Gallery, 1992; Exhibition: "I Remember 30 Years Civil Rights Movement," Corcoran Gallery of Art, Washington, DC, 1993. **Orgs:** Arts Extended Group 1958-72; Natl Conf of Artists 1975-. **Honors/Awds:** MacDowell Colony Felowship 1966; Purchase Award, Toledo Art Commission, Toledo, OH, 1984; Creative Artists Grant, Michigan Council for Arts, 1983, 1987; Creative Artists Grant, Detroit Council of Arts, 1987; Visual Arts Award, Michigan Women's Foundation, 1988; Arts Achievement Award, Wayne State University, Detroit, 1995. **Business Addr:** Artist, 5656 Oakman Blvd, Detroit, MI 48204.

WOODSON, THELMA L.
Educator (retired). **Personal:** Born Sep 1, 1920, Rutherford County, TN; daughter of Della Mae Jackson Pate (deceased) and Johnny Evans Pate Sr (deceased); married Theodore B Woodson, Nov 12, 1955 (deceased); children: Kevan B Woodson. **Educ:** Wayne State Univ, Detroit MI, BS Ed 1955, MEd 1960; educational specialist at University of Michigan, Ann Arbor MI, Michigan State Univ, Lansing MI, & Wayne State Univ, Detroit MI. **Career:** City of Nashville TN, recreation leader, 1941-43; Federal Govt, Detroit MI, statistical clerk, 1943-44; City of Detroit MI, recreation leader, 1944-55; Board of Educ, Detroit MI, teacher 1955-66, administrative intern 1966-68, asst principal 1968-72, principal 1972-86; T&T Industries Inc, corp dir 1964-74, corp pres 1974-79. **Orgs:** Mem, pres, Rho Sigma Chapter, Sigma Gamma Rho, 1954-; mem, Wayne Univ Alumni, 1955-; mem, bd chair, pres, Amer Bridge Assn, 1966-; mem, Amer Assn of Univ Women, 1968-86; mem, Natl Assn of Elementary School Principals, 1972-; mem, Urban Program in Health, 1977-81; mem, bd chair, Kirwood Mental Health Center, 1979-; mem, president, Rho Sigma Chapter Sigma Gamma Rho Sorority, 1954-89; mem, president, Wolverine Bridge Club, 1962-91. **Honors/Awds:** Citations from Detroit Bd of Educ 1963, National Education 1984, State of MI 1985, City of Detroit 1985, City of Nashville 1989. **Home Addr:** 2016 Glynn Ct, Detroit, MI 48206.

WOODSON, TRACY TODD
Engineer. **Personal:** Born Mar 15, 1960, Newark, NJ; son of An Young (deceased) and Harrison Marcellus Woodson (deceased); married Deanna Washington (divorced); children: Vernon Anthony. **Educ:** NJ Inst of Tech, BS 1984; Univ of Pennsylvania, Philidelphia, graduate management, 1990-. **Career:** ITT Defense communicationas, Cufton, NJ, quality assurance administrator, 1984-86; GE Reentry Systems, Philadelphia PA, Philadelphia, PA, contracts amdinistrator, 1990; GE Astro Space Division, Princeton, NJ, contracts admistrator, 1990-. **Orgs:** Associate member, American Management Association, 1989-; associate member, National Contract Management Association, 1990-; associate member, Society for International Affairs, 1990-. **Military Serv:** AUS E-3 1 yr; US Army Military Academy Preparatory, E-4, 1979-80.

WOODSON, WILLIAM D.
Consultant. **Personal:** Born Sep 9, 1929, Baltimore. **Educ:** Morgan State University, BA 1952; Howard University, LL B, 1957, JD 1958. **Career:** Command and Gerneral Staff, National Security Management; Logistics Executive Development, Dept of the Treasury. **Orgs:** NBA; ACLU; NAACP; ILR; OASIS; AARP; YMCA; ROA; TROA; NARF; HALT; USTA; Smithsonian. **Home Addr:** 20510 Falcons Landing Circle, No 1307, Sterling, VA 20165-7502.

WOODWARD, AARON ALPHONSO, III
Executive. **Personal:** marrIed Joan J; children: Aaron A IV, Allen A, Kelvin, Darnell. **Career:** Citibank 1970-73 Operations management; CUNY or Edgar Evers College Seek Program Fin Aid & Budget Officer; Various Insurance Cos, licensed insurance broker 1975-83; Count Basie Enterprises, business mgr 1983-84, secretary/treas 1983-84, mgr Count Basie Orchestra 1983-, co-trustee Diane Basie Trust 1983-, chief executive officer & co-executor 1983-87; co-guardian Diane Basie; record producer, Musicians Union Contractor, Entertainment Management, currently. **Orgs:** Chmn trustee bd Christ Baptist Church Coram NY; life mem NAACP; past pres Central State Univ Metro Alumni Chapt; mem Omega Psi Phi Frat Nu Omicron Chapt; mem Local 802 Musicians Union; mem Natl Alliance of Business Youth Motivation Task Force; consultant & chairperson Amer Mgmt Assoc; 100 Blackmen of New York YCM-SDG; chairman deacon board, member NARAS, voting member, bd of directors, International Jazz Hall of Fame, National Jazz Service Organization. **Honors/Awds:** Harlem YMCA Black Achiever in Industry; US Presidential Commendation for Service to Others; various Sales Achievement Awds for Insurance Sales; Natl Allianceof Business Youth Motivation Task Force Chairperson Awds; 1984 Grammy for "88 Basie Street" Natl TV; Presidential Medal of Freedom from President Reagan; Basie Awd Gov Kane of NJ; various other awds worldwide. **Business Addr:** Chief Executive Officer, Count Basie Enterprises, Inc, 200 W 57th St, Suite 601, New York, NY 10019.

WOODWARD, ISAIAH ALFONSO
Physician. **Personal:** Born Mar 6, 1912, Washington, DC; married Louise. **Educ:** Blfld Tchr Coll, BS 1936; Atl U, MA 1936; WV U, PhD 1969. **Career:** Morgan St U, asst prof prof chmn 1947-; Wash DC Census Dept, supr 1940-43. **Orgs:** Mem Phi Alpha Theta Hon Soc; Pi Gamma Mu Nat Soc; Sci Hon Soc; MD Bcntnnl Commn. **Military Serv:** USN 1943-47. **Business Addr:** 105 Morgan State Univ, Cold Spring Ln, Baltimore, MD 21239.

WOODY, JACQUELINE BROWN
Government official. **Personal:** Born Oct 13, 1949, Nansemond County, VA; daughter of Ernestine Cowling Brown and William Brown; married Curtis Woody, Sep 1974; children: Jonathan. **Educ:** Virginia Union University, Richmond, VA, BA, 1971; Rutgers University, New Brunswick, NJ, MLS, 1972. **Career:** Charles Taylor Public Library, Hampton, VA, librarian, 1972-75; Prince George's County Memorial Library, Maryland, branch mgr, 1975-89; Prince George's County Government, Maryland, Office of the County Executive, sister county relations coordinator, 1989-90, Commission for Children and Youth, education coordinator, 1990-92, Department of Family Services, program developer, 1992-94; Prince George's County Council, legislative assistant to councilmember, Dorothy Bailey, District 7, sr staff advisor, currently. **Orgs:** Board of directors, young adults services dir, American Library Association, 1983-86; member at large, Alpha Kappa Alpha Sorority, Iota Gamma Omega Chapter, 1988-; board member, Big Sisters, Washington Metro Area, 1978-79; member, academy selection board, appointed by US Congressmen Steny Hoyer, 1985-; trustee, Greater Mount Nebo AME Church, 1991-; Bonnie Johns Children's Fund, board of directors, 1992-. **Honors/Awds:** Outstanding Educator, Black Democratic Council, 1989; Proclamation, Outstanding Library Service to Community, Prince George's County Council, 1987; Prince George's County Department of Family Services Director's Award, 1994; Bonnie Johns Children's Fund, Cornerstone Award, 1994. **Home Addr:** 11323 Kettering Terrace, Upper Marlboro, MD 20772.

WOOLCOCK, OZEIL FRYER
Editor, journalist (retired). **Personal:** Born Nov 25, 1910, Atlanta, GA; daughter of Carrie Moreland Fryer (deceased) and John Perry Fryer (deceased). **Educ:** Clark Coll, AB; Atlanta Univ, Graduate Studies. **Career:** Atlanta Daily World Newspaper, Women's Interest editor/columnist 1985 (retired); Atlanta Public Schools, teacher (retired). **Orgs:** Mem Natl Assoc Media Women; Delta Sigma Theta Sor; Amer Busn Women, Soc of Professional Jrnlsts; Clark Coll Alumni Assoc. **Honors/Awds:** Tchr of Yr Atlanta Publ Schl 1966-6; serv award Delta Sigma Theta Inc 1969; excel in journ Sigma Gamma Pho Inc (nat) 1970; Comm Serv, C&S- comm 1972; excellency in Journ, Clark Coll Alumni Assn 1975; Media Women of Yr Natl Assn of Media 1980; comm serv High Museum of Art 1984; Natl Cncl of Black Mayors 1984; Certificate, Alumni, Clark Atl Univ, 1985; Women in Achievement; Meritorious Service Award, The Natl Assn of Negro Bus & Prof Women's Club Inc, 1992; featured in "Going Against the Wind," A Pictorial History of African Americans in Atlanta, 1992. **Home Addr:** 175 Florida Ave SW, Atlanta, GA 30310.

WOOLDRIDGE, DAVID
Business executive. **Personal:** Born Dec 6, 1931, Chicago, IL; married Juana Natalie Hampton; children: David Juan, Samuel William, Gregg Wayne. **Educ:** Rsvlt Univ Chgo, BS Physics 1961; MA Inst of Tech, MS Mgmt Sci 1973. **Career:** Motorola Inc, vice pres st & lcl sls commun & elctrncs 1978-, prod mgr 1976-78, prog mgr 1974-76; Hughes Arcrft Co, prog mgr 1973-74, mgr GED prog 1968-72, design engr 1961-68; LA City Coll, instr 1968-74. **Orgs:** Mem com to Mtvt Min Stud to Prs Engrng & Sci Crrs City Coll of NY 1980. **Honors/Awds:** Otstndng cntrbtn Yth Mtvtn Task Frc 1969; comm serv awd Alpha Kappa Alpha Sor 1971; otstndng serv & cntrbtn Prairie View A&M Coll 1971; Alfred P Sloan Fellow Hughes Arcrft Co. **Military Serv:** USAF a/1c 1949-52. **Business Addr:** 1303 E Algonquin Rd, Schaumburg, IL 60196.

WOOLFOLK, E. OSCAR
Retired educator. **Personal:** Born Mar 9, 1912, Tupelo, MS; son of Rev. & Mrs E. O. Woolfolk; married Norma B; children: David, Dennis. **Educ:** Talladega Coll, BA 1934; OH State Univ, MS 1939; Univ of Pgh, PhD 1949. **Career:** Claflin Coll, chem 1940-42; Scioto Ordnance Plant War Dept, chem 1942-43; US Bureau of Mines Pgh, rs chem 1943-49; Central States Univ, prof & chmnchem dept 1949-68; Central State Univ, dir div of natu sci & math 1955-57, dean coll arts & sci 1967-68, vice pres academic affairs 1968-71; Urbana Coll, visiting lecturer 1967-68; Fisk Univ, retired dean of univ 1973-78. **Orgs:** Exec sec Beta Kappa Chi 1954-62; pres Beta Kappa Chi 1963-64; fellow Amer Chem Soc; fellow 1966-67 Amer Assn for Adv of Sci; fellow/pres OH Acad ofSci; fellow Amer Inst of Chem; mem Amer Assn of Univ Prof, Natl Educ Assn, Amer Assn for Higher Educ, Phi Lambda Upsilon, Sigma Xi.

WOOLFORD, DONNELL
Professional football player. **Personal:** Born Jan 6, 1966, Baltimore, MD; married Carla; children: Cara, Ashley, Chad, Johnathan. **Educ:** Clemson Univ, attended. **Career:** Chicago Bears, defensive back, 1989-96; Pittsburgh Steelers, 1997-. **Business Addr:** Professional Football Player, Pittsburgh Steelers, Three Rivers Stadium, 300 Stadium Circle, Pittsburgh, PA 15212, (412)323-1200.

WOOLRIDGE, ORLANDO VERNADA
Professional basketball player. **Personal:** Born Dec 16, 1959, Mansfield, LA. **Educ:** Notre Dame, 1977-81. **Career:** Chicago Bulls, 1981-86, New Jersey Nets, 1987-88, Los Angeles Lakers, 1989-90, Denver Nuggets, 1990-91, Detroit Pistons, 1991-93; Milwaukee Bucks, 1993; Philadelphia 76ers, 1993-. **Honors/Awds:** Led Bulls in scoring avgng 193 pts per game; ranked 2nd in fld goal percentage hitting on 525 from field; mem of NBA Slam Dunk Team; was Bulls number one pick in 1981 coming out of Notre Dame. **Business Addr:** Professional Basketball Player, Philadelphia 76ers, PO Box 25040, Philadelphia, PA 19147.

WOOTEN, CARL KENNETH
Newspaper executive. **Personal:** Born Oct 14, 1947, Chester, PA; son of Hortensee E Washington Wooten and Adam D Wooten; married Barbra J Daniely; children: Tracy, Darryl. **Educ:** Univ of Pittsburgh, BA, History, 1969, MAT, 1971; Fairleigh Dickinson, MBA, 1981. **Career:** The Wall St Journal, advertising sales representative, 1971-74, sr sales representative, 1975-83, dist sales mgr, 1984-90, southeast sales mgr, 1990-95; Atlanta Business Chronicle, assoc publisher, 1995-. **Orgs:** Sec Toast Masters Fairleigh Dickinson, 1980; Business/Prof AA, 1981-83; Washington Ad Club; Youth Motivational Task Force, Xavier University, 1992; Atlanta Ad Club, board of directors; Big Brother/Big Sister, Metro Atlanta, bd of dirs, 1995-; American Cancer Society, Atlanta Unit, bd of dirs, 1995-; Red Cross Diaster Relief Cabinet, 1996; Georgia Council on Economic Education, bd of dirs, 1995; Omegas Psi Phi Fraternity, 1967; Community Foundation of Metro Atlanta, bd of dirs, 1997-. **Honors/Awds:** Atlantans Who Made a Difference, 1992; Leadership Atlanta Class of 1997; 100 Black Men, Atlanta, 1997. **Business Addr:** Associate Publisher, Atlanta Business Chronicle, 1801 Peachtree St, #150, Atlanta, GA 30309.

WOOTEN, JOHN
Sports personnel administrator. **Personal:** marrIed Beverly. **Educ:** University of Colorado. **Career:** Cleveland Browns, guard, 1959-68; Washington Redskins, guard, 1968-69; worked sixteen years for the Dallas Cowboys as scout, contract negotiator, and director of pro personnel; Pro Sports Advisors, player agent; National Football League, director of player programs, 1991-92; Philadelphia Eagles, scout, 1992-94, vice president/director of player personnel operations, 1994-. **Honors/Awds:** All-American lineman at the University of Colorado; two trips to the Pro Bowl; named to Cleveland Browns All-Time team, 1979. **Special Achievements:** One of the NFL's highest ranking African American officials at the front-office level. **Business Addr:** VP, Dir, Player Personnel Operations, Philadelphia Eagles, Veterans Stadium, 3501 S Broad St, Philadelphia, PA 19148, (215)463-2500.

WOOTEN, PRISCILLA A.
Association executive. **Personal:** Born Mar 31, 1936, Aiken, SC; married Joseph; children: Deborah M, Diana B, Donald T. **Educ:** NY U. **Career:** Family Wrkr, 1958-66; Hd Strt Prog, fmly asst 1966; Untd Prnts Assn, prnt educ trnr 1967; Brooklyn, educ asst 1967-68, hlth ntrtnst 1968, educ asst aux trnr 1968-69; Comm Liaison Wrkr, 1969-71; Ofc of Educ & Info Svc, prin nghbrhd sch wrkr1971-; Chnclr's Actn Cntr, pub rels dir 1971-. **Orgs:** Mem Evltng Team Dist 19 1969; Chrlt Plng Prog 1969-70; vice pres New York City Sch Bd Assn 1972, 1973, 1975, treas 1973-75; comm sch bd mem of Dist 19k 1967-; bd tst mem Luth Hosp of Brklyn; prog chrldy E NY Br NAACP; 1st vice pres M S Douglas Soc; Bd of Educ Empl; educ rep Grace Bapt Ch; mem Plng Bd5 Brklyn NY 1973-; 1st vice pres Dem Club 40th Ass Dist 1972-73; vice pres Dist 19 Comm Sch Bd 1973-; E NY Brwnsvl Com 1973-; vice pres New York City Sch Bd Assn1973-74,treas 1974-; mem bd dir of Frnds & Mus Jr HS Stud NYC; chmn Luth Hosp of Brklyn Ambul Clnc 1974-; rep Cntrl Bd Educ 1973-; mem Mnstr Grp NAACP 1974-; pres E Brklyn Civic Assn 1973-; mem Untd Polit Club 1974-. **Honors/Awds:** PTA Awd; Block Assn Awd 1973-75; Comm Sch Bd Awd 1973-75; Ch Awd Grace Bapt Ch Comm Wrk 1972-74; Lcl Sch Bd Awd Dist 19k 1968-70; Prscll Wtn Educ Soc Educ Awd 1974.

WOOTEN, TITO
Professional football player. **Personal:** Born Dec 12, 1971, Goldsboro, NC. **Educ:** Northeast Louisiana, attended. **Career:** New York Giants, defensive back, 1994-. **Business Addr:** Professional Football Player, New York Giants, Giants Stadium, East Rutherford, NJ 07073, (201)935-8111.

WORD, FLETCHER HENRY, JR.
Community service activist. **Personal:** Born May 25, 1919, Petersburg, VA; son of Adelaide Penister Word and Fletcher H Word Sr; married Virginia Brown; children: Fletcher H III, Sharman Word Dennis. **Educ:** VA State Coll, BS 1940, MS 1966; St John's Univ Law, 1 yr 1945; Univ of MD, study 1960. **Career:** Eastern Sr HS, teacher & counselor 1960-66; Public Sch Washington DC, counselor 1966-68; Hine Jr High, admin 1968-71; Kramer Jr HS, admin/assistant principal 1971-78; Johnson Jr HS, admin 1978-79; Birney Sch, admin 1979-83;. **Orgs:** Treas DC Assn Secondary Sch Principals 1979-82; Omega Psi Phi Frat 1937-; pres DC Assn of Secondary Sch Principals 1982-84; volunteer Natl Museum of Natural History; mem Ft Stevens Lions Club; mem St Gabriel Roman Catholic Church, 1960-. **Honors/Awds:** Catholic Serv to Youth 1964; Cert of Appreciation Boy Scouts of Amer 1965; Service Cert DC Public Schools 1970; 3 plaques from schools served 1981-84; Master Tchr Award 1985. **Home Addr:** 53 Underwood Place NW, Washington, DC 20012.

WORD, PARKER HOWELL
Physician. **Personal:** Born Jun 24, 1921, Petersburg, VA; children: Leslie, Parker, Lindsey. **Educ:** VA State Coll, BS 1941; Howard Univ Med Sch, attended 1944. **Career:** Human Develop Corp, med dir 1964-66; Staff Member, Deaconess Hosp, Homer G Phillips, Christian Hosp; Private Practice, physician. **Orgs:** Life mem NAACP; mem Urban League Local; Frontiers Inc. **Honors/Awds:** Mayor's Civic Awd 1969. **Military Serv:** AUSMC capt 1952-54. **Business Addr:** 3737 N Kingshighway, St Louis, MO 63115.

WORDLAW, CLARENCE, JR.
Elected official. **Personal:** Born Jan 28, 1937, Little Rock, AR; son of Thedora Shivers Wordlaw and Clarence Wordlaw Sr; married Pearlene Stegall; children: Zager, Derrick, Nicole, Thaddeus. **Educ:** Univ of IA, BS Liberal Arts 1959. **Career:** Beacon Neighborhood House, group work supervisor 1959-66; Circuit Ct of Cook Co, casework super 1966-68; Chicago Urban League, dir west side office 1969-70; IL Bell Telephone Co, public/personnel mgr, 1971-92, retired. **Orgs:** Bd of dirs Malcolm X Coll Mid-Mgmt Intern Prog; bd of mgrs Dr Martin Luther King Jr Unit Chicago Boys & Girls Clubs; mem Chicago Urban Affairs Council; bd of dirs Midwest Comm Council; mem NAACP; adv bd Career Training Inst of the Woodlawn Organ of Chicago; comm develop bd Office of Special Progs Univ of Chicago; mem SCLC; mem Kappa Alpha Psi Frat Inc; mem Police-Comm Relations Comm Maywood Human Relations Comm; bd of dirs Proviso East HS Booster Club, Maywood Chamber of Commerce; bd mem Austin Career Educ Ctr, board of directors, St Joseph HS; Operation PUSH; mem, bd of dirs, Foundation for Student Athletes, 1990-; Cook Co Sch Dist 89, school bd mem, 1983-. **Honors/Awds:** Outstanding Grad of Crane HS Class of 1955; All-Big Ten & Honorable Mention All-Amer Basketball selection in college 1958-59; Black Achievers of Indus Awd Metro Chicago YMCA, Chicago Sports Found Hall of Fame 1982; Community Oscar Awd Midwest Community Council; Archbishop Lykes, OFM, African American Male Image Award, 1995. **Military Serv:** AUS 1st lt 1959-68. **Business Addr:** School Board Member, Cook Co Sch Dist 89, 1133 S 8th Ave, Maywood, IL 60153.

WORFORD, CAROLYN KENNEDY
TV broadcaster. **Personal:** Born Apr 6, 1949, Kansas City, MO; daughter of Sarah Kennedy and Lester Kennedy; married Thomas Worford Jr, Jan 28, 1984; children: Roger, Ashleigh. **Educ:** Metropolitan Jr College, Kansas City, MO, 1967. **Career:** Southwestern Bell, Kansas City, MO, long distance operator, 1967; Hallmark Cards, Kansas City, MO, code analyst, 1968-74; KMBC-TV, Kansas City, MO, promotion asst, 1974-77; Allis-Chalmers, Kansas City, MO, personnel record clerk, 1977; KSHB-TV, Kansas City, MO, program dir, 1977-84; WJBK-TV, Southfield, MI, program mgr, 1984, dir of operations, 1995, dir of programming & audience devt, 1989-93, dir of programming and audience devt, 1993, station mgr, vp, program devt, 1995-. **Orgs:** NATPE, bd mem, 1989-, chp, 1995; corporate leader, Boys & Girls Club SE Michigan, 1885-; alumni mem, Leadership Detroit, 1988-; lifetime mem, NAACP, 1988-; mem, BUF, 1986-; BART. **Honors/Awds:** Leadership Detroit, Detroit Chamber of Commerce, 1987; Certificate of Appreciation, UNCF, 1987; Certificate of Appreciation, Detroit Public Schools, 1988; Outstanding Woman in Television, Top Management Award, Detroit Chapter of American Women in Radio and Television. **Special Achievements:** First African-American woman to head the NATPE. **Business Addr:** Station Manager/Vice Pres, Program Devt, WJBK-TV, Fox 2, PO Box 2000, Southfield, MI 48037-2000.

WORKMAN, AURORA FELICE ANTONETTE
Educator, business executive. **Personal:** Born May 24, 1962, New York, NY; daughter of Earthalee LaBoard Layne and Rawle Workman (deceased); children: Chykia Holliman, Cyer Layne (adopted nieces). **Educ:** Nassau Community College, Garden City, NY, AA, 1983; C.W. Post/Long Island University, Greenvale, NY, BS (honors), 1987. **Career:** New York Newsday, Melville, NY, editorial asst, 1980-; Roosevelt Junior/Senior High School, English teacher, 1984-90; Here Comes the Dawn, Hempstead, NY, pres, 1981-; Spec Projects, Human Resources, Labor Relations of Nassau Community College, admin off; Title I Program, educator, lecturer, academic enrichment & computer tutor; Life Skills Application Program, prevention specialist youth and young adults; 21st Century Communications Media, pres; The DAWN, publisher, editor. **Orgs:** Vice chairperson, Black Unity Day, New York, 1990, 1991; Tabernacle of One Accord Deliverance Ctr, Inc, administrator of exec concerns; Harambee Ctr, educational dir; Domestic Violence, and Children's & Youth, victims rights advocate; Incarcerated Men & Women, transitional counsler; Million Man March, Local Organizing Committee for Long Island, exec admin. **Honors/Awds:** Jack Berland Award, Nassau Community Federation of Teachers, 1983; Entreprenuer of the Year Award, 1991-92; The NLA Award of Long Island, Community Service, 1994, 1995, 1996; Builder's Award, Million Women Foundation, 1998. **Home Addr:** 840 Northgate Dr, Uniondale, NY 11553-3020.

WORKMAN, HAYWOODE WILVON
Professional basketball player. **Personal:** Born Jan 23, 1966, Charlotte, NC; son of Priscilla Funderburk Workman and Charles Workman. **Educ:** Winston-Salem State Univ, Winston-Salem, NC, 1984-85; Oral Roberts Univ, Tulsa, OK, 1985-89. **Career:** Topeka Sizzlers (CBA), guard, 1989-90; Atlanta Hawks, 1990; Illinois Express (CBA), 1990; Washington Bullets, 1990-91; Scavolini Pesaro (Italy), 1991-93; Indiana Pacers, 1993-. **Orgs:** Big Brothers; 100 Black Men of Indianapolis. **Honors/Awds:** CBA All-Rookie Team, 1990. **Business Addr:** Professional Basketball Player, Indiana Pacers, 300 E Market St, Indianapolis, IN 46204, (317)263-2100.

WORMLEY, CYNTHIA L.
Educator. **Personal:** Born Jan 15, 1953, Philadelphia. **Educ:** Hartt Coll of Mus, BM in Mus , BM in Mus Edn. **Career:** Philadelphia Bd of Public Educ, music teacher; Univ of Hartford Spiritual Choir, soloist; Hartt Coll Chamber Singers & Mdrgl Singers, soloist 1970-74. **Orgs:** Pres Epsilon Upsilon Chap Delta Sigma Theta Sor 1973-74; cmpny mem Opera Ebony/Phila; del Delta & Conv Atl GA 1973; mem Delta Sigma Theta Sor; NatCncl of Negro Wmn. **Honors/Awds:** 1st blk chld slst with Philadelphia Orchstr Age 9; num awds for comm serv in fld of Mus; Miss Ebony PA 1974; Schol Recip for Study in Opera Dept of Cnsrvtry of Mus Hchschl f r Musik Munich Germany 1979.

WORMLEY, DIANE-LOUISE LAMBERT
Business executive. **Personal:** Born Apr 28, 1948, Hartford, CT; divorced. **Educ:** William Smith Coll, BA 1970; Summer Institute for Women in Higher Education, Bryn Mawr College, attended 1989. **Career:** Mary Washington Coll, admissions couns 1970-71; Wheaton Coll, asst dir admissions 1971-73; Simmons Coll, asst dir admissions 1973-74; Stanford Univ, asst dir liberal arts 1974-76, dir 1976-78; Fisk Univ, dir career planning 1978-81; Atlanta Univ, dir corporate associates 1981-84; Univ of PA, asst dir The Penn Plann 1984-88, director product development and marketing 1988-94, director process management, division of finance, 1992-94, assoc treasurer, 1994-; Administrative Management Inst, Cornell Univ, instructor, 1993-95. **Orgs:** Assoc mem Natl Black MBA Assoc 1982-84; mem Southern College Placement Assoc 1978-84; Volunteers in Public Service 1991; pres, Alumnae Assn, Southern Smith Coll, 1994-95. **Honors/Awds:** Individual Achievement Natl Black MBA Atlanta 1983; Alumnae Assn, Citation, 1989. **Home Addr:** 4805 Regent St, Philadelphia, PA 19143. **Business Addr:** Assoc Treasurer, Univ of PA, 3451 Walnut St, Philadelphia, PA 19104.

WORRELL, AUDREY MARTINY
Physician. **Personal:** Born Aug 12, 1935, Philadelphia, PA; daughter of Dorothy Rawley Martiny and Francis A Martiny; married Richard V; children: Philip, Amy. **Educ:** Meharry Medical Coll, MD 1960; Fisk Univ, 1955; Whittier Coll, 1956; State Univ of NY at Buffalo Affld Hosp, Residency Training in Psychiatry 1964 . **Career:** Haverford State Hosp, chief of serv 1965-68; Univ of PA, Sch of Med, asst prof 1967; Erie County Mental Health Unit IV, Buffalo Psychiatric Ctr, chief 1970-74; VA Medical Ctr, Newington, CT, chief of psychiatry 1980-81; Univ of CT Sch of Med, asst prof of psychiatry, 1974-81, dir of div 1980-81, clinical prof of psychiatry, 1984-86; State of CT, commnsr of Mental Health 81-86; Vista Sandia Hosp, CEO & medical dir 1986-87; Lovelace Medical Center, dir geriatric psychiatry, 1986-93; Univ of New Mexico, assoc prof, 1986-; St Joseph Medical Center, director geriatric ser-

vices, 1993-. **Orgs:** Mem Amer Psychiatric Assn 1963-, CT State Psychiatric Assn 1967-87; Natl Assn of Mental Health Prgms Dir 1981; mem Amer Public Health Assn 1983-; Amer College of Psychiatry 1985. **Honors/Awds:** Diplomate Amer Brd of Psychiatry & Neurology 1970; certified as Mental Health Admnstr, Assn of Mental Health Admnstrs 1983; certified as Mental Health Admnstr, Amer Psychiatric Assn 1983. **Business Addr:** Director Geriatric Services Charter Corp, St Joseph Medical Center, 101 Hospital Loop NE, Ste 215, Albuquerque, NM 87109.

WORRELL, KAYE SYDNELL

Nurse. **Personal:** Born Aug 18, 1952, Axton, VA; married Cleveland D Worrell. **Educ:** Petersburg Gen Hosp Sch of Nursing, diploma 1973; Hampton Inst, BS Nursing 1975. **Career:** Petersburg Genl Hosp Sch of Nursing, instructor 1975-78; Southside Comm Coll, part-time nursing instructor 1983; Poplar Springs Hosp, unit coord RN. **Orgs:** Mem Waverly Improvement Assoc 1974-; sec Sussex Co Red Cross 1982-83; mem Petersburg Genl Hosp Sch of Nursing Alumnae 1984-85; mem & elected WaverlyTown Council 1978-86. **Honors/Awds:** Weekly health column Sussex-Surry Dispatch Newspaper Wakefield VA 1980-82; "Senior Citizen Hypertension Prog" paper published by MCV-VCU Allied Health Scis Div co-author of paper 1980. **Home Addr:** 8154 Beaverdam Rd, Waverly, VA 23890. **Business Addr:** Unit Coord RN, Poplar Springs Hospital, 350 Wagner Rd, Petersburg, VA 23805.

WORRELL, RICHARD VERNON

Physician, educator. **Personal:** Born Jun 4, 1931, Brooklyn, NY; son of Elaine Worrell and Elmer Worrell; married Audrey M; children: Philip, Amy. **Educ:** NY Univ, BA 1952; Meharry Med Coll, MD 1958; State Univ of NY at Buffalo Affltd Hosp, Residency Training in Orthopaedic Surgery, 1964. **Career:** Univ of PA, instr in Orthopedic Surgery 1968; Univ of CT Schl of Med, asst profsr of Orthopedic Surgery, 1968-77; Univ of CT Schl of Med, assoc profsr of Orthopedic Surgery, 1977-83; Univ of CT Schl of Med, asst Dean for Student Affrs, 1980-83; State Univ of NY, prof of Clinical Surgery, 1983-86; Univ of NM Medical Ctr, prof of orthopaedics, 1986-. **Orgs:** Fellow, American Acadmy of Orthopaedic Surgeons, 1970-; fellow, American College of Surgeons, 1970-; Royal Society of Medicine, London, affiliate, 1973-, member, 1992-; fellow, Intl Coll of Surgeons, 1981-; dir, Dept of Orthopaedic Surgery, Brookdale Hosp Medcl Cntr; profsr, Clinical Surgery, SUNY, Downstate Medcl Cntr, 1983-86; Academic Orthopaedic Society, 1991-; American Orthopaedic Assn, 1990-. **Honors/Awds:** Alpha Omega Alpha Hnr Medical Soc, Gamma of TN Chptr Meharry Mdcl Coll; Sickle Cell Disease Advsry Comm of the Natl Inst of Health, 1982-86. **Military Serv:** AUSR, capt, 1962-69. **Business Addr:** Professor of Orthopaedics, University of New Mexico Health Sciences Center Department of Orthopaedics, Albuquerque, NM 87131, (505)277-4107.

WORRILL, CONRAD W.

Educator. **Personal:** Born Aug 15, 1941, Pasadena, CA; son of Mr and Mrs Walter Worrill; married Talibah Collymore; children: Michelle, Femi, Sobenna, Aisha. **Educ:** George Williams Coll, BS 1968; Univ of Chicago, MA 1971; Univ of WI, PhD 1973. **Career:** Northeastern IL Univ Ctr for Inner City Studies, dept chair. **Orgs:** Weekly columnist Chicago Defender 1983-, and other black newspapers in Chicago and around the country; chmn Natl Black United Front 1985-; bd mem IL Black United Fund 1985-; mem Woodlawn Preservation Investment Corp 1987-; mem Chicago Housing Authority 1987-; talk show host WVON-AM, 1988-; Assn for Study of Classical African Civilizations. **Honors/Awds:** Received numerous awds for community involvement; AKA Monarch Awards; Worrill's World Book of Newspaper columns/articles have appeared in numerous African Amer publications. **Military Serv:** AUS splst 4th class 1962-64. **Business Addr:** Department Chair, Northeastern Illinois University, Ctr for Inner City Studies, 700 E George H. Clements Blvd., Chicago, IL 60653.

WORSHAIM, KEITH EUGENE

Law enforcement. **Personal:** Born Apr 17, 1960, Louisville, KY; son of John Henry Worsham, Jr & Mary Lou Worshaim; married Linda J Miller Worshaim, Feb 11, 1984; children: Bradford D, John W J. **Educ:** Kentucky State Univ, 1978-79. **Career:** Mississippi Univ for Women, campus security officer, 1982-83; Columbus Police Department, patrolman, 1983-88, narcotic agent, 1986-87, patrol corporal, 1988-92, patrol sergeant, 1992-95, patrol lt, 1995-98, comm oriented policing enforcement commander, 1998-. **Orgs:** Natl Organization of Black Law Enforcement Executives, 1998; Natl Black Police Officers Assn, 1998; Amer Law Enforcement Trainers Assn, advisory bd mem, 1995; World Police & Fire Games, state rep for state of MS, 1991; Big Brothers/Big Sisters of Columbus, MS, past bd mem, volunteer, 1983-87; Alabama/MS Peace Officers's Assn, founding mem, 1989-; Columbus Police Martial Arts, founder, 1991-95; Columbus Police Dept Athletics, founder, 1996-. **Honors/Awds:** House of Representatives State of MS, House Resolution #52 Commending in Efforts in Comm Relations, 1996. **Special Achievements:** MidSouth Regional Police & Fire Games Medalist, Pistol & Martial Arts, 1995, 1996; Intl Law Enforcement Games Medalist, Judo, Karate, and Tae Kwon Do, 1992, 1994; World Police & Fire Games Medalist, Karate, 1991, 1993. **Military Serv:** Army Natl Guard, KY & AL, private first class, 1979-82. **Home Addr:** PO Box 984, Columbus, MS 39703-0984. **Business Addr:** Shift Lieutenant, Columbus Police Department, PO Box 1408, Columbus, MS 39703-1408, (601)328-7561.

WORSHAM, JAMES E.

Union official. **Personal:** Born Jan 31, 1932, Chicago, IL; son of Minnie L Smith Worsham and Adolphus E Worsham; married Corrine Kelly Worsham, Jun 14, 1953 (died 1990); children: Valerie L, Vance E, Adrienne R. **Career:** US Postal Service, Chicago, IL, letter carrier, 1963-90, union steward, 1964-76, chief steward, 1976-78, US Postal Service, Washington, DC, national trustee, 1980-94; National Association of Letter Carriers, Chicago Branch #11, president, 1978-95, director of retired members, currently. **Orgs:** Member, Amalgamated Bank Labor Council, 1988-; chairman, Chicago Post Office Credit Union, 1986-; noble, Shriners, 1982-; Mason 32 degree, F&AM (Masonic), 1982-; Mason 3rd degree, F&AM (Masonic), 1959-; mem, official board, Emmanuel Baptist Church. **Honors/Awds:** Union bldg named in honor of James E Worsham. **Military Serv:** US Air Force, S/Sgt, 1949-53; received several medals, 1952, Korean War. **Business Addr:** Director of Retired Members, National Association of Letter Carriers, 100 Indiana Avenue, Washington, DC 20001.

WORSLEY, GEORGE IRA, JR.

Business executive. **Personal:** Born Apr 3, 1927, Baltimore, MD; married Gloria M Morris; children: Mary Elizabeth Cunningham, Gayll Annette. **Educ:** Howard Univ, BSME 1949. **Career:** George Ira Worsley Jr & Assocs, owner, 1964-; Dollar Bltz Assocs, engineer, 1959-64; General Engineering Assn, engr, 1949-59. **Orgs:** Adv bd Untd Comm Nat Bank; CEC; MW; ASHRAE; NTA; BOCA; WBA; NFPA. **Honors/Awds:** Elected Tau Beta Pi, Howard Univ, Alpha 1959. **Military Serv:** USNR smn 3rd cls 1945-46, sgt 1951-53. **Business Addr:** 7705 Georgia Ave NW, Washington, DC 20011.

WORTH, CHARLES JOSEPH

County official. **Personal:** Born Jun 6, 1948, Raleigh, NC; son of Rosa M Worth (deceased) and James H Worth; married Laurie Gray; children: Kellye N, Kimberlye N, Kourtnye N. **Educ:** NC A&T State Univ, BS Acctg 1970; NC Central Univ, MPA 1987. **Career:** Coopers & Lybrand, sr auditor 1970-74; Gen Signal Corp, sr internal auditor 1974-76; Bausch & Lomb, sr internal auditor 1976-79; The Soul City Co, dir of finance 1979-80; Charles J Worth & Assoc Inc, pres 1980-; Warren Cty, county mgr 1984-. **Orgs:** Mem Amer Soc for Public Admin, Natl Forum of Black Public Admin, Natl Assoc of Black County Officials, Conf of Minority Public Admin; bd mem NC City/Cty Mgmt Assoc, Natl Assoc of Cty Admin; life mem Omega Psi Phi Frat; former pres Vance-Warren Chap of SCLC; chmn Kerr-Tar Private Industry Council; mem Kerr Lake Bd of Realtors; treas Second Congressional Dist Black Caucus; mem Warren County Political Action Council, NC A&T State Univ Alumni Assoc, Intl City Mgmt Assoc, NC Assoc of Minority Business Inc, NAACP, Soul City Rural Volunteer Fire Dept; mem, Int City Mgmt Assn. **Honors/Awds:** 1st Black Appointed Mgr in State of NC 1984; Certificate of Appreciation Boy's Clubs of Amer 1978-79; Omega Man of the Year Zeta Alpha Chap Omega Psi Phi 1983; Cty Mgr Warren Cty NC 1984; Leadership Award, Kerr-Tar PIC, 1990; Distinguished Service Award, NABCO, 1990. **Home Addr:** 24 Macon Circle, PO Box 411, Manson, NC 27553. **Business Addr:** County Manager, Warren County, PO Box 619, Warrenton, NC 27589.

WORTH, JANICE LORRAINE

Registered nurse, business owner. **Personal:** Born Apr 2, 1938, St Louis, MO; daughter of Beatrice Farrar and Oscar Eugene Farrar (deceased); married J Quentin Worth, May 4, 1963; children: Quentin E, Sean Shannon, Jason Evan. **Educ:** St Mary's Hospital School of Nursing, nursing diploma, 1962; Forest Park Community College, AA, 1973; Washington University, 1990-. **Career:** Prestige Products Co, secretary/treasurer, 1982-; St Mary's Health Center, registered nurse/supervisor, 1991-. **Orgs:** St Louis Minority Business Development Center, 1983; MENA, 1985; Black Nurses Assn. **Honors/Awds:** Mideast Agency on Aging, Volunteer of the Year, 1994. **Business Addr:** Secretary/Treasurer, Prestige Products Co Inc, PO Box 3310, St Louis, MO 63130, (314)381-3030.

WORTH, STEFANIE PATRICE

Journalist. **Personal:** Born Nov 8, 1962, St Louis, MO; daughter of Patrice Ann Dandridge Worth and Calvert Lee Worth; married Kevin Rene Gibbs, Nov 28, 1988 (divorced 1989); children: Denmark Sebastian Gibbs. **Educ:** University of Missouri, Columbia, MO, BA, 1985. **Career:** KBIA Radio, Columbia, MO, reporter, anchor, 1983-84; KOMU-TV, Columbia, MO, reporter, anchor, 1985; WJLB-FM Radio, Detroit, MI, reporter, anchor, 1985-86; Michigan Chronicle, Detroit, MI, staff writer, 1987; Office of Detroit City Councilman John Peoples, Detroit, MI, special projects consultant, 1987-89; Wayne County Neighborhood Legal Services Detroit Street, Detroit, MI, law project administrative consultant, 1990; Michigan Chronicle, Detroit, MI, staff writer, 1990-. **Business Addr:** Staff Writer, Michigan Chronicle, 479 Ledyard, Detroit, MI 48201.

WORTHAM, BARRON WINFRED

Professional football player. **Personal:** Born Nov 1, 1969, Fort Worth, TX; married Caledra, Feb 22, 1997. **Educ:** Texas El-Paso, attended. **Career:** Houston Oilers, linebacker, 1994-96; Tennessee Oilers, 1997-. **Honors/Awds:** Ed Block Courage Award, 1995. **Business Addr:** Professional Football Player, Tennessee Oilers, c/o Baptist Sports Park, 7640 H 70-5, Nashville, TN 37221.

WORTHEY, RICHARD E.

Research analyst (retired). **Personal:** Born Aug 11, 1934, Greensboro, NC; married Peggie J McTier. **Educ:** A&T St U, BSEE 1960; AF Inst of Tech, MSSE 1964; OH St U, PhD 1969. **Career:** USAF Arntcl Sys Div, operat res ana; ASD Wrght-Pttrsn AFB, elec engr 1966-70, elec engr SEG 1960-66; Supervisory Operations, research analyst, 1970-80; Operations Research Div, chief, 1980-86; Advanced Systems Analysis, dir, 1986-89. **Orgs:** Mem Inst of Elec Engrs 1964-; chrprsn ASD Incntv Awds Com 1972-78; mem AF Smltr Adv Grp 1975-78; past pres mem Frwy Golf Club 1973-; mem Dayton Area Chap A&T St Univ Almn Assn 1971-; mem Masnc Ldg Cnsstry Shriners 1966-; mem AIAA 1976; mem Am Mngt Assn 1975; mem DOD/NASA Wrkng Grp on Smltr Tech 1976-78; 1 yr exec devel assgnm Ofc of Under Sec of Def for Rsrch & Engr 1979-80. **Honors/Awds:** Cert Pin 20 Yrs Serv 1976; Otstndng Perf Awds 1968, 1971, 1972, 1973, 1976; Letter of Commend Perf 1978; author more than 25 tech rprts & publ; nom Outstanding Dayton Area Engr 1972; Outstanding Performance Awards, 1981-84, 1986-88; Meritorious Civilian Service Award, 1986; Outstanding Civilian Career Service Award, 1989. **Military Serv:** USN rd1 1953-57. **Business Addr:** Aeronautical Sys Div ASD/XROM, Wright Patterson AFB, Dayton, OH 45433.

WORTHY, BARBARA ANN

Educator. **Personal:** Born Nov 1, 1942, Thomaston, GA; daughter of Laura Bell Jones Worthy and S T Worthy. **Educ:** Morris Brown Coll, Atlanta GA, BA, 1964; Atlanta Univ, Atlanta GA, MA, 1970; Tulane Univ, New Orleans LA, PhD, 1983. **Career:** Camilla High School, Camilla GA, social science teacher, 1964-69; Southern Univ at New Orleans LA, history teacher, 1970-, social sciences dept chair, currently. **Orgs:** Mem, Southern Historical Assn, 1983-; mem, Assn for Study of Afro-Amer Life & History, 1984-85; mem, Friends of Amistad, 1986-; bd of dir, Soc for the Study of Afro-LA & History, 1988-; mem, New Orleans League of Women Voters, 1988-; mem, Delta Sigma Theta. **Honors/Awds:** Overdyke History Award, North Louisiana Historical Assn, 1981; one of 14 participants selected from six institutions of higher educ in Louisiana to participate in six-week Intl Curriculum Seminar in Kenya & Tanzania, East Africa, summer, 1985. **Business Addr:** Chair, Social Sciences Dept, Southern University at New Orleans, 6400 Press Drive, History Department, New Orleans, LA 70126.

WORTHY, KYM

Judge. **Personal:** Born 1956; children: one. **Educ:** Univ of Michigan, political science and economics; Univ of Notre Dame Law School, JD, 1984. **Career:** Wayne County, MI, assistant prosecutor, 1984-94; Recorder's Court, judge, 1994-. **Special Achievements:** Successfully prosecuted the two Detroit police officers who were convicted of beating to death motorist, Malice Green, 1993. **Business Addr:** Judge, Recorder's Court, 1441 St. Antoine, Detroit, MI 48226.

WORTHY, LARRY ELLIOTT (LARRY DOC ELLIOTT)

Radio announcer. **Personal:** Born Aug 18, 1953, Koziousko, MS; son of Allie B Carter Worthy and Saul T Worthy; children: Larry Jr, Sincerely. **Educ:** Career Academy of Broadcasting, Milwaukee, WI, 3rd Class FCC License, 1972. **Career:** WAWA, Milwaukee, WI, announcer, public serv dir, music dir, 1972-81; WOAK, Atlanta, GA, announcer, 1981-82; WVEE, Atlanta, GA, announcer, 1982-83; WJLB, Detroit, MI, announcer, music dir, 1983-88; WHYT, Detroit, MI, announcer, 1988-89; WJZZ, Detroit, MI, announcer, promotion dir, 1989-. **Honors/Awds:** Radio Announcer of the Year, Metro Area Artists & Songwriters Assn, 1991; Big Mac Award, Best Announcer, Detroit News, 1986-88, 1990; Certificate of Merit, State of MI, 1987; 1st Honor Award, Best Radio Personality, MI Lottery Black Music Month, 1986; Testimonial Resolution, Detroit City Council, 1984.

WORTHY, WILLIAM, JR.

Journalist, educator. **Personal:** Born Jul 7, 1921, Boston, MA; son of Mabel R Posey (deceased) and William Worthy. **Educ:** Bates Coll, BA 1942; Harvard Univ, Nieman Fellow in Journalism 1956-57. **Career:** Howard University, Washington, DC, distinguished visiting professor, 1990-; University of Massachusetts, Boston, MA, journalist-in-residence, 1985-90; Boston University, Boston, MA, visiting professor, 1974-79; Journalism & Afro-Amer Studies, Boston Univ, prof, 1974-79; The Baltimore Afro-Amer, foreign correspondent & columnist, 1953-80. **Orgs:** Society of Nieman Fellows; American Civil Liberties Union. **Honors/Awds:** Right-to-know & freedom info awards Boston Press Club, Capital Press Club Lincoln Univ MO; author "The Rape of Our Neighborhoods" 1976; Journalism Award of the MA Legislative Black Caucus, 1988; Travelled to 58 countries, specializing in coverage of Third World revolutionary and neo-colonial issues, 1951-89. **Business Addr:** Educator, Journalist, 37 Haviland St, Boston, MA 02115.

WRAY, WENDELL LEONARD
Educator, librarian (retired). **Personal:** Born Jan 30, 1926, Pittsburgh, PA; son of Mary L Wray and Arthur J Wray. **Educ:** Bates Coll, AB (magna cum laude) 1950; Carnegie Inst of Tech, MSLS 1952; Mexico City Coll, Cert 1957; Columbia Univ, Cert 1973. **Career:** Carnegie Library of Pittsburgh, librarian 1952-59; NY Publ Library, adult group specialist 1959-64, dir North Manhattan Proj 1965-73; Univ of Pittsburgh Sch of Libr and Info Sci, prof 1973-81; Schomburg Center for Research in Black Culture, chief 1981-83; Univ of Pittsburgh Sch of Libr and Info Sci, prof, 1983-88. **Orgs:** Mem Amer Libr Assn 1973-; mem Oral Hist Assn 1973-; juror Educ Film Libr Assn 1968-; juror Notable Books Council-ALA 1978-82; juror Amer Book Awards1981, 1983; consult PA Black Hist Adv Comm 1983; consult Kinte Libr Foundation 1973-75; mem Assn for the Study of Afro-Amer Life and Hist 1973-; NAACP 1973-; Urban League 1986-; Holy Cross PE Church; Black Caucus of ALA; Historical Society of Western PA. **Honors/Awds:** Phi Beta Kappa 1950; Phi Sigma Iota 1948; Beta Phi Mu 1973, Award Schl of Libr and Information Sci 1973; Disting Alumnus Univ of Pittsburgh; "Pictorial Report of The North Manhattan Project 1965-1972". **Military Serv:** US Army Engineer Battalion Sgt Maj 1944-46. **Home Addr:** 1425 Lakeside Dr, Apt 201, Oakland, CA 94612-4339. **Business Addr:** Professor Emeritus, University of Pittsburgh, SLIS Building #631, 135 North Bellefied Ave, Pittsburgh, PA 15260.

WRENN, THOMAS H., III
Dentist. **Personal:** Born Oct 11, 1942, Mineola, TX; married Joel J Porter. **Educ:** Univ of MO at KC, DDS 1967; Univ of KC. **Career:** Dentist, pvt prac. **Orgs:** Mem past pres Heart of Am Dental Soc 1974; Am Dental Soc 1970; Nat Dental Soc 1967; Soc Action Com Univ of MO at KC Dental Sch 1974; mem NAACP 1973; Sthrn Chris Ldrshp Conf; Alpha Phi Alpha Frat; Jaycees of KC 1975. **Business Addr:** 5046 Prospect, Kansas City, MO 64130.

WRICE, DAVID
Police officer. **Personal:** Born May 31, 1937, Lorain, OH; son of Savannah Wilson Wrice and Johnnie Wrice; divorced; children: Sharon Wrice Moore, Leonard Church, Barbara J. Wrice, Daniel, David. **Educ:** Lorain County Community College, Lorain, OH, associate in police science, 1972; Heidelburg College, Tiffin, OH, bachelor's degree in psychology, 1974. **Career:** American Shipyard, Lorain, OH, foreman, 1963-66; Lorain County Community College, instructor; Lorain Police Department, Lorain, OH, 1966-, jail warden, 1985-; Lorain Metropolitan Housing Authority, resident asst watch coord, currently. **Orgs:** Delegate, National Black Police Association, 1986-; president, Lorain Minority Police Association, 1986-; commander, Herman Daniels VFW Post 8226, 1988-; moderator, Concerned Citizens of Lorain, 1989-; Buckeye Masonic Lodge; Al Lalim Temple. **Honors/Awds:** Appreciation Award, Second Baptist Church, 1970; Appreciation Award, Herman Daniels VFW Post 8226, 1974; Buddy PoPPV Award, Lorain County Veterans Council, 1975; Member of Year, Lorain County Minority Law Enforcement Association, 1986; Outstanding Community Service, Shilow Baptist Church, 1986; Century Club Award, National Black Police Association, 1986; Community Service Award, State of Ohio Auditor's Office, 1986. **Military Serv:** US Army, Spc 3rd class, 1954-57; received Good Conduct Medal, German Occupation Medal, Marksman Ribbon. **Home Addr:** 209 East 23rd St, Lorain, OH 44055.

WRICE, VINCENT J.
Business owner, educator, computer program analyst. **Personal:** Born Feb 20, 1963, Paterson, NJ; married Jun 29, 1991. **Educ:** Florida A&M University, BS, technology, 1986. **Career:** New Jersey Transit, systems analyst, 1986-88; Union County College, senior programmer analyst, adjunct instructor, 1990-; Proper Gander, president, currently. **Orgs:** National Society of Black Engineers; Kappa Alpha Psi; National Black Data Processing Association; Black Filmmaker Foundation. **Home Phone:** (201)433-1378. **Business Addr:** President, Proper Gander, 489 Jersey Ave, Jersey City, NJ 07302.

WRIGHT, ALBERT WALTER, JR.
Educator. **Personal:** Born May 8, 1925, San Antonio, TX; married Betty Jean. **Educ:** Huston-Tillotson Coll, BS 1949; TX Southern U, MS 1955; UCLA, PhD 1965. **Career:** CA State Univ Northridge, prof of accouting; UCA, teacher fellow 1961-65; TX Southern Univ, instr of business 1957-61; TL Pink HS, teacher athletic coach 1950-57. **Orgs:** Mem Amer Inst of Cert Pbl Acc 1962-; Amer Acctg Assn 1962-; Natl Assn of Acc 1965-; Nat Assn of Blk Acc 1975-; Beta Gamma Sigma Honor Soc 1964-; mem Beta Alpa Psi 1979; past mem Alpha Phi Alpha Frat 1947; mem Masonic Ldg 1946-. **Honors/Awds:** Educ Achvmt Awd Nat Assn of Blk Acc 1975; articles "Earnings Per Share" in mgmt acctng Natl Assn of Acc 1971; "Maintaining Balance in Financial Position" mngmt acctg Natl Assn of Acc 1969; "Net Income & Extra Charges & Credits" Natl Assn of Acc 1966; "The Blk Minority and the Acctg Prfn" UCLA 1969; cert of merit Natl Assn of Acc. **Military Serv:** USMC sgt 1943-46. **Business Addr:** Professor of Accounting, California State University, 18111 Nordhoff St, Northridge, CA 91330.

WRIGHT, ALEX
Professional football player. **Personal:** Born Jul 19, 1967. **Educ:** Auburn Univ, earned adult education degree. **Career:** Dallas Cowboys, wide receiver, 1990-. **Honors/Awds:** Track titles, 55-meter and 200-meter dash, Southeastern Conference, 1988. **Business Addr:** Professional Football Player, Dallas Cowboys, One Cowboys Pkwy, Irving, TX 75063-4999.

WRIGHT, ALONZO GORDON
Business executive. **Personal:** Born Jul 19, 1930, Cleveland, OH; married Patronella Ross; children: Cheryl, Joyce, Gordy. **Educ:** Hiram Coll, BA 1948; Western Reserve Univ Cleveland, LLB 1956. **Career:** Wright Dev Co, pres 1975-; Cleveland, atty 1957-58; Univ Euclid Urban Renewal Proj, dir 1963-65; Midwest Area Econ Devel Adm, dir 1965-67. **Orgs:** Pres Econ Resrcs Corp 1973-; pres Bay Dist Motor Car Dealers 1974-; vice pres Venice C of C 1974-; dir Santa Monica NCCJ; Economic Resources Corp, chairman. **Military Serv:** USN 1948-55. **Business Addr:** 9638 High Ridge Dr, Beverly Hills, CA 90210.

WRIGHT, BENJAMIN HICKMAN
Association executive. **Personal:** Born Aug 5, 1923, Shreveport, LA; son of Parthenia Hickman Wright and Nathan Wright; married Jeanne Jason. **Educ:** Univ of Cincinnati, BA 1950, MA 1951. **Career:** US Dept of State, econ & polit reporting officer 1952-53; Johnson Publishing Co, sales promotion & merchandising mgr 1952-66; Clairol Inc, mgr Urban Affairs & Ethnic Devel 1966-74; Johnson Pub Co, sr vice pres dir 1974; Black Media Inc, pres. **Orgs:** Business con Natl Comm of Black Churchmen; bd chmn pres NAMD NY Chap 1967-71; chmn Action Com for Self-Determination 1969-69; bd chmn NY Unit Black Econ Union 1970-71; mem Group for Advertising Progress 1970-71; bd mem John F Kennedy Meml Library for Minorities 1970-74; Nat ICBO 1971-; bd editors Jour of Black Econ & Bus Morehouse Coll; bd mem Sales Promo Exec Assn 1971-72; executive dir Natl Assault on Illiteracy Program (AOIP) 1980-. **Honors/Awds:** Alpha Phi Alpha Equitable Oppor Awd 1969; Media Workshop Awd of Excellence 1968; Outstanding Black Businessman of Yr Black Africa Promotions 1973; publ "A Voyage of Awareness"; Distinguished Service in Education, Phi Beta Sigma Fraternity, 1987; Baton for Progress Award for Distinguished Leadership, National Pan-Hellenic Council Inc, 1989; Honorary LHD, Univ of Cincinnati, 1971. **Military Serv:** USN 1943-46. **Business Addr:** Executive Director, AOIP, 231 W 29th St, Ste 1205, New York, NY 10001.

WRIGHT, BRUCE MCM.
Judge. **Personal:** Born Dec 19, 1918, Princeton, NJ; son of A Louise Thigpen and Bruce Alleyne Summers Wright; married Patricia Fonville, Dec 26, 1986; children: Geoffrey D S, Keith L T, Alexis, Bruce C T, Patrick, Tiffany. **Educ:** Lincoln Univ, BA 1942; NY Law Schl, LLB 1950. **Career:** Human Resources Admin, NYC, gen consl 1967-70; Criminal Court, NYC, judge 1970-79; Civil Court of NYC, judge 1980-82; Supreme Court of NY, justice; The Cooper Union for the Advancement of Science and Art, visiting professor, 1994-. **Orgs:** Brd mem Urban League of Greater NY 1952-56; advsry brd Fortune Soc 1971-; brd mem Inner City Round Table for Youth 1976-; co-founder, National Conference of Black Lawyers; Assn of the Bar of the City of New York; Youth Education Through Sports. **Honors/Awds:** Author From The Shaken Tower (Poetry) England 1944, Lincoln Univ Poets, edited with Langston Hughes 1954, Repetitions (Poetry) 1980; law review articles, critical reviews, etc; author Black Robes, White Justice, Racism in the Judicial System, published by Lyle Stuart, 1987; A Black Justice in a Ahite World, pub by Barricode Books, 1996; Honorary Degree, LLD, Lincoln University, 1973; Judge of the Year, National Bar Assn, 1975. **Military Serv:** AUS priv of inftry, 26th infantry reg, first inf division, 1942-46; Purple Heart with Oak Leaf Cluster; Bronze Star with Oak Leaf Cluster; Conspicuous Service Cross, others. **Home Addr:** 409 Edgecombe Ave, New York, NY 10032. **Business Addr:** Visiting Professor, The Cooper Union for the Advancement of Science & Art, Cooper Sq, New York, NY 10003.

WRIGHT, C. T. ENUS
Educator. **Personal:** Born Oct 4, 1942, Social Circle, GA; married Mary Stevens. **Educ:** Ft Wayne State Univ, BS 1964; Atlanta Univ, MA 1967; Boston Univ, PhD 1977. **Career:** GA Public Schools Social Circle, teacher 1965-67; Morris Brown Coll, mem faculty 1967-73, div chmn 1973-77; Eastern WA Univ, prog dir asst provost 1977-81; Cheyney Univ, pres 1982-86; FL Memorial Coll, vice pres academic affairs 1986-. **Orgs:** Dean of pledgees Phi Beta Sigma Ft Valley State 1963-64; pres Madison Bapt Sunday Sch & Training Union Congress 1967-78; worshipful master & 1st lt com Prince Hall Masons F & AM 1973-75; del Natl Dem Conv 1980; mem Pub Broadcasting Commn of State of WA 1980-; vice pres Cheney Lions Club 1980-; exec comm Boy Scouts of Amer Philadelphia 1982-; mem Natl Assn Equal Oppor in Higher Educ 1982-; mem Amer Hist Assn 1970-; mem Amer Baptist Club. **Honors/Awds:** Human Relations Scholar Boston Univ 1969-71; Phi Alpha Theta Hist Hon Soc Boston Univ 1971; Omicron Delta Kappa Leadership Soc Morris Brown Coll 1977; "A History of Black & Educ in Atlanta", "Atlanta Hist Bull" 1977; pub "Black History Week, A Time to Reflect" Eastern Wash Univ 1979.

WRIGHT, CARL JEFFREY
Publishing company executive, attorney. **Personal:** Born Nov 18, 1954; son of Lottie Mae Thomas Wright and Alvin Wright Sr; married Carole Gilmore Wright, May 28, 1983 (divorced); children: Stephen, Amanda, Natalie. **Educ:** Fisk University, Nashville, TN, BA, 1975; Georgetown University, Washington, DC, JD, 1979; Columbia University, New York, NY, MBA, 1982. **Career:** TransWorld Airlines, intl tariff's analyst, 1976-80; Johnson & Johnson, intl business development, 1982-84; Bristol-Myers Squibb, senior director of planning & administration, Corporate Devt Dept, Consumer Health & Personal Care Groups, vp of corp devt, 1984-94; Urban Ministries Inc, president & chief operating officer, currently. **Orgs:** Trustee, American Red Cross, SW Indiana Chapter, 1988-90; adjunct professor, University of Evansville Grad School, 1986-89; trustee, Black Student Fund, 1976-80; trustee, Circle Y Ranch, Bangor, MI; mem, American Bar Association; admitted, Pennsylvania Bar. **Honors/Awds:** Johnson & Johnson Leadership Award, Johnson & Johnson Co, 1980; One of America's Best and Brightest Business and Professional Men, Dollars & Sense Magazine, 1989. **Business Addr:** President & COO, Urban Ministries, Inc, PO Box 436987, Chicago, IL 60643-6987.

WRIGHT, CAROLYN ELAINE
Educator. **Personal:** Born Apr 22, 1951, Dayton, OH. **Educ:** Wright State Univ, BS 1973; MBA 1978. **Career:** Bolinga Black Cultural Resources Ctr, asst dir 1973-77, dir 1977-81. **Orgs:** Vice pres Day-Mont West Community Mental Health Ctr 1984-85; 1st vice pres Mary Scott Nursing Ctr 1984-85; chairperson Citizen's Advisory Council 1984-85. **Honors/Awds:** Professional internship Cleveland Scholarship Foundation 1983; graduate Black Leadership Program Dayton Urban League 1983-84. **Home Addr:** 1946 Haverhill Drive, Dayton, OH 45406. **Business Addr:** Asst Prof of Finance, Central State University, 167 Smith Hall, Wilberforce, OH 45384.

WRIGHT, CHARLES
Attorney. **Personal:** Born Oct 3, 1918, New Orleans, LA; married Alethia. **Educ:** Temple Univ, BS, LLB. **Career:** Atty, private practice; Commonwealth PA, deputy atty general. **Orgs:** Bd test Henry Luce Found. **Honors/Awds:** Scholars; Temple Univ; Princeton Seminary; Univ PA Presbyterian Med Center. **Military Serv:** USAF. **Business Addr:** 505 City Hall, Philadelphia, PA 19107.

WRIGHT, CHARLES E.
Airline company executive. **Personal:** Born Mar 1, 1946, Washington, DC; married Barbara H; children: Charles Wright Jr, Phillip. **Educ:** Howard Univ, 1964-69; workshops & seminars Xerox Prof Selling Skills; Negotiating Skills Seminar; Interpersonal Communications; Stress Mgmt; Effective Presentations. **Career:** Eastern Air Lines Inc, ticket agent 1969-76, sales rep 1976-80, mgr market develop 1980-83, mgr market develop & campus rep admin, beginning 1983; Leon County Tourist Development Council, exec dir, currently; Tallahassee Area Convention and Visitors Bureau, pres/CEO, currently. **Orgs:** Supervised Sr Citizens Passport Staff; monitored Fulfillment House Strategic Marketing Systems; mem bd of dirs Miami Dade Trade & Tourism Comm; adv bd World Inst of Black Communications; mem Natl Assn of Market Developers; bd mem Inner City Dance Troupe; host & producer of contemporary talk show Black Kaleidoscope on WCIX-TV Channel 6 Miami FL. **Honors/Awds:** US Army Outstanding Soldier of the 1st Basic Combat Training Brigade 1970. **Military Serv:** DC Natl Guard 1969-75; AUS. **Business Addr:** Executive Director, Leon County Tourist Devt Council, 200 West College Ave, Tallahassee, FL 32301.

WRIGHT, CHARLES H.
Physician (retired). **Personal:** Born Sep 20, 1918, Dothan, AL; married Louise Lovett; children: Stephanie, Carla. **Educ:** AL State Coll, BS 1939; Meharry, MD 1943. **Career:** Wayne State Univ Med Sch, asst clinical prof ob/gyn; Private Practice, medical doctor, until 1986. **Orgs:** Founder/pres African Med Educ Fund; founder/chmn of bd Afro-Amer Museum of Detroit; mem Univ of Detroit WTVS Channel 56; mem NAACP; published 20 med articles in natl & local med journals; wrote-produced musical drama Were You There?; legitimate stage & TV; author Roseson Labor's Forgotten Champion 1975. **Honors/Awds:** Physician of Yr Detroit Med Soc 1965; Omega Man of Yr 1965; Physician of Yr MI State Med Soc 1968.

WRIGHT, CHARLES STEVENSON
Writer. **Personal:** Born Jun 4, 1932, New Franklin, MO; son of Dorothy Hughes Wright and Stevenson Wright. **Educ:** Studied writing at Lowney Handy's Writers Colony, Marshall, IL. **Career:** Free-lance writer, beginning with regular column in weekly Kansas City Call; columnist, Village Voice. **Special Achievements:** Author of The Messinger, Farrar Straus, 1963,

The Wig, Farrar Straus and Giroux, 1966, Absolutely Nothing to Get Alarmed About, Farrar Straus, 1973. **Military Serv:** US Army in Korea, private, 1952-54. **Home Addr:** 308 E 8th St, # 7I, New York, NY 10009.

WRIGHT, CLINTON L. A.
Attorney. **Personal:** Born Oct 24, 1951, Kingston, Jamaica; son of Jemima Webster and Clinton Wright; married Antoinette Green Wright, Aug 24, 1974; children: Nia, Challa, Calvin. **Career:** State of Connecticut, assistant public defender, 1977-79; CIGNA Corp, Kennedy and Sullivan, sr litigation counsel, 1979-83; City of New Haven, Connecticut, assistant corp counsel, 1981-84, corporation counsel, 1990-91; James, Turner and Wright, law partner, 1983-89; Cooper, Liebowitz, Royster, Wright, law partner, 1990-91. **Orgs:** George Crawford Law Society, 1976-91; American Cancer Society, board of directors, 1988-91; American Red Cross, board of directors, 1989-91; United Way of Greater New Haven, board of directors, 1989-91; Connecticut Bar Association Committee for Minority Participation, chair, 1989-91; New Haven County Bar Association, executive committee, 1989-91.

WRIGHT, CRYSTAL ANDREA
Talent agency owner, publisher. **Personal:** Born Jan 13, 1958, Los Angeles, CA; daughter of Sharon Lewis & Ray Morrow; married Michael Stradford, Mar 10, 1990. **Educ:** Seattle Univ, 1976-78; Fashion Institute of Design & Merchandising, 1978-79; Univ of Washington, 1979-81. **Career:** Xerox Corp, acct exec, 1982-85; Bobby Holland Photography, artist rep, 1985-86; The Crystal Agency Inc, pres, 1986-; Set The Pace Publishing Group, owner, 1994-. **Orgs:** Womens Economic Development Corp, (WEDC), 1994-; Natl Assn of Women Business Owners, (NAWBO), 1996-; Women, Inc, 1996-. **Honors/Awds:** Womens Econ Dev Corp, Entrepreneur in Action, 1998. **Special Achievements:** The Hair Makeup & Styling Career Guide, 1995, 1997; First Hold Magazine for freelance hair, makeup and fashion stylists, 1997-. **Business Addr:** President, Crystal Agency Inc, 4237 Los Nietos Dr, Los Angeles, CA 90027-2911, (213)913-0700.

WRIGHT, DAWIN LYRON
Manager. **Personal:** Born Nov 24, 1951, Little Rock, AR; son of Ruby L Wright and Adell Wright; married Carolyn M Boone, Oct 30, 1970; children: Dedra L, Denita L. **Educ:** Kennedy-King College, AAS, automotive, 1970; Chicago State University, BS, industrial education, 1973, MS, occupational education, 1976. **Career:** Kennedy-King College, assistant professor, 1971-76; GM Corp., Chevrolet Motor Division, area service manager, 1976-78, personnel coordinator, 1978-80, assistant service manager, 1981-85, zone service manager, 1986-88, account manager, 1988-90, branch marketing manager, 1990-93, zone manager, 1993-94, assistant regional manager, 1994-. **Orgs:** Black Executive Forum, 1991-; 4 Us Investment, president, 1980-. **Business Addr:** Asst Reg'l Mgr, General Motors Corp Chevrolet Motor Division, 3031 W Grand Blvd, Detroit, MI 48202, (313)974-1607.

WRIGHT, DMITRI
Educational Administrator. **Personal:** Born Oct 17, 1948, Newark, NJ; son of Ruth and John Wright; married Karen Shields; children: Odin. **Educ:** Newark School of Fine Arts, valedictorian, 1970; Cooper Union, 1971-73; NYACK College, BS, organizational management, 1993. **Career:** Newark School of Fine and Industrial Arts, fine arts instructor, 1971-81; Brooklyn Museum Arts School, arts educator, 1972-82; Dmitri's Renaissance Workshops, principal master fine artist and instructor, 1983-; Connecticut Institute of Art, fine master art instructor, dean, dir of educ, fine and applied art, dir of spec programs. **Orgs:** Artist for Christ, founder; Connecticut Inst of Art, High Touch & High Tech Pigments to Pixels Programs, creative director. **Special Achievements:** Permanent collections: ATT Corp Collection; Brooklyn Museum Prints & Drawings; The Fine Arts Museum of Long Island, Mural Project; Newark Museum Contemporary Paintings; Newark Library; Urban Life Center Columbia MD; selected exhibitions: NYC; Adam L Gimbel Gallery Saks 5th Ave NYC; Westbeth Alumni; The Hudson Guild; Lever House Group Show Park Ave NYC; Rutgers Univ; Farleigh Dickenson Univ; 18th Natl Print Exhibition Brooklyn Museum; CA Palace of Legion of Honor San Francisco; Bridgewater State Coll Gallery MA 1987; one man show Images Gallery 1987; Sidney Rothman Gallery NJ 1987; Sound Shore Gallery NY 1986-87; Northeast Open 1986; Grove St Gallery MA, winter exhibit 1986-87; articles in various issues of: Art Today; Art Speaks; New Art Examiner; The New York Art Review (3rd edition); US Art; Greenwich's Newspaper and Greenwich News Newspaper, 1992-96; American Encyclopedia of Living Artist, 5th edition. **Home Phone:** (203)661-0105. **Business Addr:** Owner & Master Instructor, Dmitri's Renaissance Workshop, 106 Hunting Ridge Rd, Greenwich, CT 06830, (203)661-0680.

WRIGHT, EARL LEE
Educational administrator. **Personal:** Born Jul 5, 1941, Sinton, TX; son of Nola Beatrice Vaughn Wright and Earilee Wright; divorced; children (previous marriage): Arlene, Darius, Adrian, Laura. **Educ:** St Mary's Univ, BA 1965, MA 1970; Univ of TX at Austin, PhD 1975. **Career:** San Antonio Independent Sch Dist, teacher 1965-68; Swift and Company, management 1968-70; San Antonio Coll, prof and dean 1970-82, vice pres 1982-. **Orgs:** Mem Antioch Baptist Church 1951-; visiting prof Prairie View A&M Univ 1973-75; volunteer serv Northwest YMCA 1973-78; natl consultant Nova Univ 1978-90; bd dir San Antonio Boys Club of Amer 1981-82; mem United Way Comm Adv Bd 1981; consultant Kelly AFT Mgmt Org 1982; mem JCSPAT 1982-86, TACUSPA; mem Federal Exec Awds Panel 1984-85; hon mem Mayor's Martin Luther King Memorial Commn 1986; NAACP; speaker at state and natl conferences and conventions. **Honors/Awds:** Honorarium New York Univ 1982; Doctoral fellowship Univ of TX at Austin 1973-75; mem Phi Delta Kappa; numerous publications in the area of educational administration. **Home Addr:** 100 Bikeway Ln, San Antonio, TX 78231-1401. **Business Addr:** Vice President, San Antonio College, 1300 San Pedro Ave, San Antonio, TX 78212.

WRIGHT, EDWARD LUCIUS
Consulting company executive. **Personal:** Born Mar 9, 1925, Birmingham, AL; son of Julia Runnells Wright and Melchi Wright; married Mary Thomas Wright, Nov 7, 1944; children: Edwina, Julia, William, Michael. **Educ:** Howard University, Washington, DC, BSME, magna cum laude, 1952. **Career:** Esso/Humble Oil Bayway Refinery, Linden, NJ, senior eng, 1954-62; Comsip Inc, Linden, NJ, vice pres, 1962-76; Exxon Research & Engineering CO, Florham Park, NJ, eng associate, 1976-83; Xertex, Santa Fe Springs, CA, sales mgr, 1983-84; Comsip Inc, Linden, NJ, product mgr, 1984-89; H F Henderson Ind, West Caldwell, NJ, product mgr, beginning 1989; Edward L Wright & Associates, president, currently. **Orgs:** Mem, Instrument Society of America, 1954-; pres, Urban League of Eastern Union County NJ, 1956; pres, Rahway, NJ Public Library Bd of Dir, 1954; vice pres, Rahway, NJ Bd of Education, 1958-62; pres, Bayway Community Center Advisory Bd, 1962. **Honors/Awds:** NJ Section Award, Instrument Soc of America, 1987; Outstanding Achievement Award, NY Chapter Howard Univ Alumni, 1957; Charter Mem of Howard Univ, Chapter of Tau Beta Pi, 1952; ISA Fellow, 1990. **Military Serv:** US Army Air Corps, Aviation Cadet/PFC, 1941-44. **Business Addr:** President, Edward L Wright & Associates, Inc, 2 Bowers Dr, Mendham, NJ 07945.

WRIGHT, FALISHA
Professional basketball player. **Personal:** Born Jan 28, 1973; daughter of Brady Wright. **Educ:** San Diego State Univ, bachelor's degree in public administration, 1995. **Career:** Portland Power, guard, 1996-. **Business Addr:** Professional Basketball Player, Portland Power, 439 N Broadway, Portland, OR 97227, (503)249-1130.

WRIGHT, FLONZIE B.
Consulting company executive. **Personal:** Born Aug 12, 1942, Farmhaven, MS; daughter of Littie P Dawson-Brown and Frank Brown Sr; married William Russell Wright, Dec 17, 1989; children: Cynthia Verneatta Goodloe-Palmer, Edward Goodloe Jr, Lloyd Darrell Goodloe. **Educ:** Tougaloo College. **Career:** NAACP, branch dir, 1964-66; State Equal Employment Opportunity Officer and Training Coordinator, recruiter, 1966-73; US Equal Employment Opportunity Commission, 1974-89; The Wright Source, co-owner, currently. **Orgs:** Natl Council of Negro Women; NAACP; SCLC; Natl Caucus and Ctr for the Black Aged, board pres; Women for Progress, founding mem and pres; Bethune Day Care Center, charter mem; Vernon Dahmer Singers for Freedom, founder; AFGE Local 3599 AFL-CIO, pres; numerous others. **Honors/Awds:** Wyche Fowler Congressional Citation; Hollingsworth Realty, Salesperson of the Year; Lamoyne Coll, Honorary Degree; Tougaloo Coll, Fain Fellowship; EEOC, Chairman's Special Commendation; recipient of over 400 community awards and commendations. **Special Achievements:** The Songs That Brought Us Over; Martin, As I Knew Him; Author of, Looking Back To Move Ahead; established The Flonzie B Wright Scholarship Fund; Wrote 2nd Publication: "Its Prayer Time," for her senior friend, Mrs Mamie Clemons, 1997. **Home Addr:** 11942 Moses Rd, Germantown, OH 45327.

WRIGHT, FREDERICK DOUGLASS
Assistant dean/director. **Personal:** Born Aug 26, 1946, Columbia, GA; son of Mr & Mrs James Wright. **Educ:** Roosevelt Univ, BGS 1972, MA 1974; Princeton Univ, MA 1982, PhD 1982. **Career:** Univ of Notre Dame, asst prof 1978-, dir black studies program 1983-, asst dean 1986-. **Orgs:** Evaluator NJ Dept of Higher Educ 1985, 86; asst dir Natl Endowment for the Humanities Inst in Afro-Amer Culture 1987; mem The Amer Political Sci Assoc, The Western Social Science Assoc, The Southern Political Science Assoc, The Southwest Political Science Assoc, The Natl Conf of Black Political Scientists, The Assoc for the Study of Afro-Amer Life and History, The Natl Assoc of Black Studies Prog, The Indiana Assoc of Historians. **Honors/Awds:** R R McCormick Fellowship Princeton Univ 1977-78; Frazier Thompson Faculty-Staff Awd 1984; NDEA Fellowship Roosevelt Univ; invited participant NEH-Supported Summer Institute "Afro-American Religious Studies for College Teachers," 1984; published scholarly articles on Black Politics in the American South. **Business Addr:** Asst Dean/Dir, Univ of Notre Dame, Black Studies Program, 345 O'Shaughnessy Hall, Notre Dame, IN 46556.

WRIGHT, GEOFFREY
Judge. **Career:** Attorney; New York City Civil Court-Tenth District, judge, currently. **Business Addr:** Judge, New York Civil Court-Tenth District, 141 Livingston St, Rm 610, Brooklyn, NY 11201, (718)643-2866.

WRIGHT, GEORGE C., JR.
Former mayor. **Personal:** Born Mar 9, 1932, Chesapeake City, MD; son of Alice Brooks Wright and George C Wright; married Mary Guy, Jul 21, 1953; children: Terun Palmer, George C III, Sharon, Lisa. **Educ:** Maryland State Coll, Princess Anne MD, BS, 1953. **Career:** Dover A&B, Dover DE, chief of staffing, 1956-89 (retired); Town of Smyrna DE, mayor, 1984-95; ED League of Local Govt, executive director, 1989-. **Orgs:** Mem, Council on Police Training, DE, 1986-; bd mem, Kent Sussex Industries, 1987-; pres, DE League of Local Govt, 1990-92; vice pres, steward bd, Bethel AME Church, 1987-; worshipful master, St John's Lodge #7; 33rd Degree Mason. **Honors/Awds:** Received DAPA Award, Distinguished Public Administration, St of DE, 1994. **Military Serv:** US Army, E-5, 1952-54. **Home Addr:** 31 Locust St, Smyrna, DE 19977.

WRIGHT, GROVER CLEVELAND
Public relations manager. **Personal:** Born Apr 18, 1916, Marengo County, AL; married Irma Serena Palmer; children: Grover Edward, Gail Elaine. **Educ:** Psycho Corp, cert selection interviewing training 1973. **Career:** Pullman Co, sleeping car porter 1942-65, porter in charge 1965-68; Bd of Amer Missions, parish worker 1968-72; Div for Mission in N Amer, lay asso 1972;Luth Ch in Am Div for Prof Leadership, asso dir 1972-. **Orgs:** Pres N Philadelphia Improvement Council of Blocks 1960-; Boy and Cub Scoutmaster Boy Scouts of Amer 1960-72; bd chmn Assn of Comm Orgn for Reform Now ACORN 1978-80. **Honors/Awds:** Disting Serv Awd Boy Scouts of Amer 1965; Humanitarian Chapel of Four Chaplains 1966; Silver Beaver Awd Boy Scouts of Amer 1967; Serv Beyond Call of Duty Plaque Conf of Black Luth 1979. **Business Addr:** Associate Dir, Lutheran Church in Amer, 2900 Queen Lane, Philadelphia, PA 19129.

WRIGHT, HARRIETTE SIMON
Educator. **Personal:** Born Oct 3, 1915, Wadesboro, NC; widowed; children: Ernest, Franklin. **Educ:** Bluefield State Coll, BS elem ed 1951; IN U, MSW 1963. **Career:** Concord Coll, prof social work 1974-; Dept of Mental Health, comm mental health consult 1968-74; Vocational Rehab, chief social worker 1966-68; Dept of Welfare, supr child welfare 1955-66; Aplmer Mem Inst, dean of girls 1954-55; Lakin State Hospital, psych aide supr 1951-54; McDowell Cnty Bd of Educ, elem school teacher 1937-38. **Orgs:** Anti-Grammateus Alpha Kappa Alpha Sor 1951-80; chmn Mercer Co Comm on Aging 1979-; charter-bd mem Windy Mountain Learning Cntr 1974-; life mem NAACP. **Honors/Awds:** West Virginia, Social Worker of the Year, 1992; Mercer County, NAACP, Citizen of the Year, 1993; 1994 Citizens Award from Pastor Dr Lawrence L Beale, Mount Zion Baptist Church, Bluefield, WV.

WRIGHT, HOWARD
Professional basketball player. **Career:** Atlanta Hawks; Orlando Magic, 1993-.

WRIGHT, J. R.
City official (retired). **Personal:** Born Feb 28, 1921, Atlanta, GA; married Mildred Ann Baskin; children: Vincent, Marvin, Edwin. **Educ:** Claflin Coll, BS 1948; NY Univ, MA Admin 1954; King Mem Coll, LLD 1977. **Career:** School Dist 17, teacher 1948-57, elementary principal 1957-62; Hendersonville City Schools NC, high school principal 1962-64; Spartanburg SC, high school principal 1964-80; Bethlehem Ctr, exec dir 1982-86; City of Spartanburg SC, supervisor for special census 1987; Public Works Commission, commissioner, 1991-93. **Orgs:** Mem Urban Renewal Commiss 1965-69; consultant Southern Assoc of Secondary Schools 1970-80; pres S Spartanburg Sertoma Club 1980-81; Civil Serv Commn 1988-89, chmn 1981-90; County Affirmative Action Comm-Spartanburg County, 1988-; chmn of NAACP Educ Comm; SC Conference Methodist Church Council on Ministeries, 1984-92; SC Methodist Conference Board of Education 1988-92; SC Conference Methodist Home Board, 1992-94; SC Conference United Methodist Men, vice president, 1992; Appointed Probate Court Representative, 1994; Silverhill United Methodist Church's Methodist Men, pres; Upstate UNCF Campaign Fund, committee chairman. chairman. **Honors/Awds:** Teacher of the Year Rotary Club 1979-80; Plaque SC Assoc of Sec School Principals 1980; Service Award SC House of Representatives 1980; Service Award SC Secondary Schools Principals Assoc 1980; Comm Service Award Sertoma Intl 1981; Service Award Progressive Men 1987; Proclamation Award, City of Spartanburg, SC, 1991. **Military Serv:** AUS sgt 1942-46; Good Conduct, Arms Expert, ATA Serv Ribbon 1943-46. **Home Addr:** 203 Collins Ave, Spartanburg, SC 29306-4726.

WRIGHT, JACKSON THOMAS, JR.
Educator, physician. **Personal:** Born Apr 28, 1944, Pittsburgh, PA; son of Lillian Doak Wright and Jackson T Wright, Sr.; married Mollie L Richardson, Sep 2, 1967; children: Adina. **Educ:**

Ohio Wesleyan University, Delaware, OH, BA, 1967; University of Pittsburgh, Pittsburgh, PA, MD, 1976, PhD, 1977. **Career:** University of Michigan, Ann Arbor, MI, residency in internal medicine, 1977-80; Medical College of Virginia/Virginia Commonwealth University, Richmond, VA, assistant professor, 1980-86, associate professor of medicine and pharmacology, 1986-90; Case Western Reserve University, dir of clinical hypertension program, 1990-, prof of medicine, 1995-. **Orgs:** Chairman, Virginia state affiliate hypertension subcommittee, American Heart Association, 1984-86; vice chairman, hypertension scientific subsection, American Society for Clinical Pharmacology and Therapeutics, 1985-87; American Federation for Clinical Research; American College of Physicians; chair, internal medicine section, National Medical Association; member, executive committee, Old Dominion State Medical Society; vice president, Richmond Medical Society, 1985-87; member, executive committee, Association of Black Cardiologists; president, Black Education Association. **Honors/Awds:** Woodrow Wilson, Martin Luther King Fellow, 1971-73; University of Pittsburgh Equalization of Higher Education Fund Award, 1972-77; Student National Medical Association, MCV chapter, Certificate of Appreciation, 1982, 1984, 1985, 1986; American Heart Association, Program Service Award, 1986; Ame of Physicians Fellow, 1987. **Military Serv:** US Air Force, captain, 1967-71. **Business Addr:** Prof of Medicine, Clinical Hypertension Program, Case Western Reserve University, Division of Hypertension, School of Medicine, Rm W-165, Cleveland, OH 44106-4982.

WRIGHT, JAMES A.
Government official (retired). **Personal:** Born Nov 25, 1937, New Orleans, LA; son of Ethel M James Wright and Ernest Wright Sr; married Wilma J Kelly Wright, Oct 10, 1960; children: Gene N, Keith J, David J. **Educ:** Southern University, New Orleans LA, BS, 1973. **Career:** LA State Dept of Educ, New Orleans LA, supervisor, 1975-83; City of New Orleans LA, deputy dir, 1983-, deputy dir Department of Sanitation. **Orgs:** Alpha Phi Alpha Inc, 1972-; pres, Zulu Social Aid & Pleasure Club, 1976-; 4 Degree Knights of Peter Claver, 1984-; 3rd Degree Mason, 1985-; Natl Assn of Private Industry Councils, 1985-; Natl Job Training Partnership, 1986-; Natl Forum of Black Administrators, 1986-; co-chair, Telebank United Negro College Fund, 1989-; bd mem, US Selective Service System, currently; commissioner United States Department of Interior Jazz Preservation Study 1991-92; Zulu Social Aid and Pleasure Club Inc, recording secretary, 1996-. **Honors/Awds:** Pre-Medical Science degree, Southern Univ in New Orleans, 1973; various plaques from organizations and committees. **Military Serv:** US Army, PFC, 1956-58. **Home Addr:** 7320 Willowbrae Dr, New Orleans, LA 70127.

WRIGHT, JAMES CHRISTOPHER
Educator. **Personal:** Born Dec 25, 1918, Mecklenburg Co; married Annie B Smith. **Educ:** St Pauls Coll, BS 1953; VA State Coll, MS Indust Educ 1976. **Career:** Mecklenburg Co Sch, masonry tchr. **Orgs:** Bd mem Alpha Phi Alpha Frat; RC Yance Lodge #284 AF & AM; NAACP; SCLC; mem bd of dir Chase City Med Clinic; Mecklenburg Educ Assn; Am Vocatnl Assn; Nat Educ Assn mem town cncl; mayor Chase City, VA. **Military Serv:** AUS WW Ii 3 yrs.

WRIGHT, JAMES R.
Librarian, clergyman. **Personal:** Born May 12, 1941, Fayette, AL; son of Corine Henry and Elvertis Wright; married Mary A Law; children: James, Jr, Coretta, Jason. **Educ:** Alabama State Univ, BS 1962; State Univ NY Geneseo, MLS 1970; Cincinnati, OH, PhD Union Institute. **Career:** Rochester Public Library, dir, Phillis Wheatley Library, l969-88; St Jude's Educ Inst, Mont, AL, teacher, librarian, l962-66; Gary Public Library, Gary, IN, l966-68; AL A&M Univ, Huntsville asst to librarian, l968-69; published in Focus on in library, l968; Library Journal, l969; Coll & Rsch librarian, l979; Wilson Library Bulletin, l971; Youth Advisory Commn, Rochester Urban League, lecturer & speaker on problems in librarianship; Progressive Church of God in Christ, pastor, 1981-. **Orgs:** Bd dir Mont Neighborhood Cent; Black Res Inf Cent; Black-O-Media; chmn Black Caucus of Amer Library Assn 1973-74. **Business Addr:** Minister, Progressive Church of God in Christ, 270 Cumberland St, PO Box 9l4, Rochester, NY 14603.

WRIGHT, JAMES W.
Banker. **Career:** First Tuskegee Bank, CEO, currently. **Special Achievements:** Bank is listed #24 on Black Enterprise's list of top financial companies, 1994. **Business Addr:** President & Chief Executive Officer, First Tuskegee Bank, 301 N Elm St, Tuskegee, AL 36083, (205)727-2560.

WRIGHT, JANE C.
Surgeon, educator. **Personal:** Born Nov 30, 1919, NYC; married David D Jones; children: Jane, Alison. **Educ:** Smith Coll, AB 1942; NY Med Coll, MD 1945. **Career:** Visiting phys consultant, numerous hospital clinic, etc; NY Med Coll, assoc dean prof surgery. **Orgs:** Mem various offcs coms Manhattan Counc State Commn for Human Rights; Nat Med Assn; Manhattan Central Med Soc; Am Assn for Cancer Rsrch; NY Acad Scis; NY County Med Soc; NY Cancer Soc; African Rsrch Found; Am Cancer Soc; Am Assn for the Advcmnt of Sci; Sigma Xi; Medico-CARE; Am Soc Clin Oncology; Pres's Commn on Heart Disease; Alumni Assn of Women's Med Coll of PA; NY Acad Med; Phys Manpower; Med Soc of Cnty of NY; NY State Woman's Counc NY State Dept Commerce; Smith Coll Bd Trust; Am Assn for Cancer Rsrch; Nat Inst Hlth Med Sci Tng; Nat Inst of Gen Med Scis; Alpha Kappa Alpha. **Honors/Awds:** Num publs in field; num awds, hon, spl achvmts, recog. **Business Addr:** Professor of Surgery, New York Medical College, Elmwood Hall, Valhalla, NY 10595.

WRIGHT, JEANNE JASON (JEANNE JASON)
Editor. **Personal:** Born Jun 24, 1934, Washington, DC; daughter of Elizabeth Gaddis Jason and Robert S Jason Sr; married Benjamin Hickman Wright, Oct 30, 1965; children: Benjamin Jr, Deborah, David, Patricia. **Educ:** Radcliffe Coll, BA 1956; Univ of Chicago, MA 1958. **Career:** Psychiat social worker various mental health facilities 1958-70; Black Media Inc, gen mgr 1970-74, pres 1974-75; Natl Black Monitor, exec editor 1975-76, publisher, 1977-; Black Resources Inc, pres 1975-. **Orgs:** Mem Natl Assn of Media Women; mem Newswoman's Club of NY, Natl Assn of Social Workers Inc; mem Alpha Kappa Alpha Sor, Radcliffe Club of NY, Harvard Club of N.Y. **Honors/Awds:** Natl Assn of Black Women Attys Awd 1977; Second Annual Freedom's Jour Awd Journalism Students & Faculty Univ of DC 1979; Metro NY Chap Natl Assn of Media Women Media Woman of the Yr Awd 1984; Natl Media Woman of the Yr Awd Natl Assn of Media Women 1984; Communications Award, American Red Cross, Harlem Chapter, 1988. **Business Addr:** President, Black Resources Inc, 231 West 29th St, Ste 1205, New York, NY 10001-5209.

WRIGHT, JEFFERSON W.
Clergyman. **Personal:** Born Jul 24, 1935, Bluefield, WV. **Educ:** Attended VA State Coll; Marshall Univ, AB 1959; WV Univ Law Sch, grad; attended WV Univ So CA; Boston Univ Sch of Theo, STB 1963; Boston Univ Sch of Theo, MDiv 1973. **Career:** Hebrew Childrens Home, youth counselor 1959; Calvary Bapt Ch, student pastor 1959-60; LA Public Sch System, sch teacher 1960-61; Tremont St Ch, asst student minister 1961; Sheldon St Ch, pastor 1961-64; PA State Univ, part-time fac 1969-73; Second Baptist Ch Harrisburg, pastor 1964-. **Orgs:** Co-founder OIC of Harrisburg; mem Natl Bapt Amer Bapt Conv; mem Harrisburg Uptown Neighbors Together; adv comm of PA Dept of Health & Welfare; Urban Strat Com of Council of Christ; Natl Bd of Black Churchmen; founder First Black Sr Citizens Organ in Central PA; bd mem NAACP; moderator WITF-TV prog ATime to Act; mem Urban Coalition & Black Coalition of Harrisburg; past mem Mayors Cits; adv com chmn of subcom on Housing; bd dirs of Family & Childrens Svcs; Tri-Co Planned Parenthood Assn; mem adv bd Harrisburg Sch Dist. **Military Serv:** USAF.

WRIGHT, JEREMIAH A., JR.
Minister. **Personal:** Born Sep 22, 1941, Philadelphia, PA; children: Janet Marie, Jeri Lynne. **Educ:** Howard Univ, BA 1968, MA 1969; Univ of Chicago Sch of Divinity, MA 1975. **Career:** Zion Church, interim pastor 1968-69; Beth Eden Church, asst pastor 1969-71; Amer Assn of Theol Schools, researcher 1970-72; Trinity Church, pastor 1972-; Chicago Center for Black Religious Studies, exec dir 1974-75; Chicago Cluster of Theol Schools, lectr 1975-77; Seminary Consortium for Pastoral Educ, adjunct prof 1981-. **Orgs:** Bd dir Malcolm X Coll Sch of Nursing; bd dir Office for Church in Society (UCC); commr Commn for Racial Justice (UCC); IL Conf of Chs; Urban League Ministerial Alliance; Ecumenical Strategy Comm; IL Conf United Ch of Christ; Great Lakes Regional Task Force on Churches in Transitional Comm; bd dir Ctrs for New Horizons 1976-; Omega Psi Phi Frat 1960-77; Doric Lodge #77 F & AM (Masonic) 1976-; Western Consistory #28 1983-; Blk Clergy Caucus United Ch ofChrist 1972-; United Black Christians (Blk Caucus Lay & Clergy UCC) 1972-. **Honors/Awds:** Alpha Kappa Mu Honor Soc; Dean's list VA Union Univ; Dean's List Howard Univ 1968; Tching Asst Fellowship Howard Univ; Rockefeller Fellowship 1970, 1972;3 Presidential Commendations LB Johnson; songs publ "God Will Answer Prayer", "Jesus is His Name"; article publ "Urban Black Church Renewal" found in the "Signs of the Kingdom in the Secular City" edited by Helen Ujvarosy Chicago Covenant Press 1984. **Military Serv:** USMC pfc 1961-63; USN hm3 1963-67. **Business Addr:** Adjunct Professor, Sem Consort for Pastoral Educ, 532 W 95th St, Chicago, IL 60620.

WRIGHT, JOHN AARON
Educator. **Personal:** Born May 22, 1939, St Louis, MO; married Sylvia Henley; children: John Jr, David, Curtis. **Educ:** Harris Tchrs Coll, AB 1962; St Louis U, MmEd 1968, PhD 1978; Atlatnat U; MO U; Tchrs Coll Columbia U. **Career:** Ferguson-Florissant School Dist, asst supt pup serv & fed prog 1979-; St Louis Citizens Educ Task Force, exec dir 1977-79; Ferguson-Florissant School Dist, asst supt comm relations 1975-79; Kinloch School Dist, supt 1973-75; Steger Jr HS, asst prin 1970-73; John Griscom School, prin 1965-70. **Orgs:** Sch Bd Assn; Phi Delta Kappa; Nat Alliance of Blck Sch Educators; pres Grtr St Louis Alliance of Blck Sch Educators; Nat Sch Pub Relations Assn;Kiwanis; Anniversary Club; Grace Meth Ch; NAACP Sal Army del Intl Corps Cadet Conf in London 1956. **Honors/Awds:** Man of the Yr Omega Psi Phi Frat 1959, 67; ptcpnt Supt Work Conf Columbia Univ 1986; pres Univ City Sch Bd 1976; Danforth Ldrshp Flw 1977; MO Gov Adv Counc on Voctnl Educ 1977. **Special Achievements:** Author, Discovering African-American St Louis: A Guide to Historic Sites, Missouri Historical Society Press, 1994. **Business Addr:** 665 January, Ferguson, MO 63135.

WRIGHT, JOSEPH, JR. (JOBY)
College basketball coach. **Personal:** Born Sep 5, 1950, Savannah, GA; married Cathy Wright; children: Shay, Jenay, Cara, Joby III, Jesse. **Educ:** BS, physical education, 1980; MS, athletic counseling/recreation sports programming, 1990. **Career:** Indiana Univ, asst basketball coach, 1980-90; Miami Univ, head basketball coach, 1990-93; Univ of Wyoming, head basketball coach, 1993-. **Orgs:** USA Basketball, select team committee, 1993-96. **Honors/Awds:** Mid-America Conference, Coach of the Year, 1992-93. **Business Addr:** Head Basketball Coach, Univ of Wyoming, Box 3414, Laramie, WY 82071, (307)766-5114.

WRIGHT, JOSEPH H., JR.
Entertainment services. **Personal:** Born Feb 1, 1954, Chicago, IL; married Ronda R Preacely; children: Nahum, Gabriel, Nina. **Educ:** Kendall Coll, AA Music 1974; Millikin Univ, BA Music 1977; Attending, North Eastern IL Univ Grad Sch. **Career:** Body Sounder Inc, pres 1982-87; East Bank Club, fitness instructor 1982-; Soft Sheen Prods Inc, creative consultant 1983-87; Motivation Industry Inc, pres 1987-; JoRon Music Publishing Co, 1986-. **Orgs:** Musician/producer Amer Federation of Musicians 1972-; volunteer Chicago Bd of Education 1982-86; annual vocalist/conductor of Chicago Economic Develop Corp1984-87; songwriter/publisher ASCAP 1984-; annual guest speaker Hugh O'brian Youth Foundation 1986-87. **Honors/Awds:** Outstanding Young Men of Amer 1984; Chicago Assoc of Tech Societies 1986; Certificate of Thanks and Appreciation Chicago Public Schools; published "The Art of Body Sounding" book and tape. **Business Addr:** President/Producer, JoRon Music/Publishing Co, PO Box 4985, Chicago, IL 60680.

WRIGHT, JOSEPH MALCOLM
Educational administrator, court official. **Personal:** Born Sep 27, 1944, Toomsboro, GA; son of May O Dixon-Wright and Ed Wright; married Sheilah Delores Broome; children: Joseph Oliver, Tiffany Michele, Jennifer Nicole. **Educ:** Eastern Michigan University, BS 1969; Wayne State University, JD 1974; Harvard University, ed mgmt diploma 1983; Columbia State Univ, PhD, 1997. **Career:** GM-Buick, stat control asst 1965-67; GM-Chev, sr acct 1967-69; Univ of MI, suprv of payroll 1969-70; Univ of MI Coll of Arts Sci & Letters, admin mgr 1970-72; Univ of MI Dearborn, dean of student affairs 1973-88; Detroit Coll of Bus, adj prof 1975-77; Univ of MI, chmn minority affaris 1975-77; United Motors Corp, pres 1983-88; Wayne State Univ, adjunct prof, 1996; 36th District Court, associate judicial attorney/chief deputy court administrator 1988-. **Orgs:** Bd of dir, Washtenaw Cty Black Contr & Tradesmen Association 1967-72; citizen rep, Oak Pk Urban Renewal Council 1969-74; pres, JM Wright & Association Detroit 1972-; pres, dir, Association for Urban Legal Ed 1973-76; board of directors, Barrino Entertainment Corp 1973-79; adj prof, Wayne Cty Comm Coll 1975-; board of directors, Metamorphosis Inc NY 1975-79; New Detroit Inc Minority Bus Devel Comm 1978-80; Amer Arbitration Association 1979-; bd dir, Pink Ltd Allen Park MI 1979-85; Amer Bar Association, Natl Bar Assn, Wolverine Bar Association; board of directors, Inner-City Bus Improvement, Southeastern MI Bus Devel Ctr; NAACP; board of directors, Western Wayne/Oakland Cty Comm Housing Resource Bd, Fair Housing Ctr Detroit 1985-88; board of directors, Worldwide Entertainment, Ltd 1991-; board of directors, East-West Airlines, Inc 1990-; Pontchartrain Hotel Group, LLC, partner; Central City Investment Corp, board of directors. **Military Serv:** US Air Force Reserves, 1966-70. **Business Addr:** Chief Deputy Court Administrator, 36th District Court, 421 Madison Ave, Ste 5028, Detroit, MI 48226.

WRIGHT, JOYCE C.
Librarian, educator. **Personal:** Born Dec 17, 1951, Charleston, SC; daughter of Rhunette G Crawford and William Crawford; divorced. **Educ:** Voorhees College, Denmark, SC, BA, 1973; University of Michigan, Ann Arbor, MI, AMLS, 1974; University of Illinois at Urbana, Urbana, IL, CAS, 1986. **Career:** Trident Technical College, Charleston, SC, reference/documents librarian, 1974-76; Hampton Public Library, Hampton, VA, outreach librarian, 1976-78; Memphis Public Library, Memphis, TN, head of reference, 1978-80; Voorhees College, Denmark, SC, adminstrative librarian, 1980-85; University of Illinois, Urbana, IL, head of undergraduate library, associate professor of library administration, 1985-. **Orgs:** American Library Association; Illinois Library Association; Association of College & Research Libraries; American Association of University Professors; American Association of University Women; Alpha Kappa Alpha Sorority Inc. **Honors/Awds:** Undergraduate Instructional Award for Outstanding Undergraduate Teaching, University of Illinois, Urbana, 1987. **Business Addr:** Assoc Prof, Library Administration/Head, Undergrad Library, University of Illinois at Urbana, 1402 W Gregory Dr, Urbana, IL 61801.

WRIGHT, KATIE HARPER
Educator, journalist. **Personal:** Born Oct 5, 1923, Crawfordsville, AR; daughter of Connie Mary Locke Washington and James Hale Harper; married Marvin Wright, Mar 21, 1952; children: Virginia Jordan. **Educ:** Univ of Illinois, AB 1944, MEd 1959; St Louis Univ, EdD 1979. **Career:** East St Louis Public Schools, elem tchr 1944-57, spec educ tchr 1957-65, media dir 1966-71, spec educ dir 1971-78, asst supt of spec programs 1978-79; St Louis Argus Newspaper, columnist, 1979-84, 1986-; Harris-Stowe State Coll, assoc prof, 1980-; St Louis American Newspaper, columnist, 1984-85; St Louis Univ, learning specialist, 1989-; ILOD Crown Journal, natl editor, 1991-95. **Orgs:** E St Louis Election Bd, secty, 1978-88; assoc dir Magna Bank of Edgemont 1981-; Illinois Cmsn on Children 1973-, past v chmn; v chmn River Bluffs Girl Scout Council 1979-; Girl Scout Natl Bd 1981-84; bd mbr Mental Health; bd mbr Urban League; bd mbr United Way; E St Louis Library Bd 1964-81, past pres; charter mem Gateway Chapter of The Links Inc 1987-; pres St Clair County Mental Health Bd 1987-; Amer Library Trustees Assn, regional vice pres, 1992-; exec cmte, Urban League and United Way of St Louis; MENSA, proctor 1973-, past vice pres; Delta Sigma Theta Sorority, 1949-, past pres; Phi Delta Kappa, 1976-, past pres; Pi Lambda Theta Honor Society, 1978-, past pres; Kappa Delta Pi Honor Society, 1968-, past pres; Amer Institute of Parliamentarians, East St Louis Chapter, organizer, 1992-. **Honors/Awds:** Woman of Achievement St Louis Globe Democrat Newspaper 1974; Outstanding YWCA Alumnae Univ of IL 1984; Girl Scout Thanks Badge River Bluffs Girl Scout Council 1982; 1st Place Prize (for Author of Chapter History) Delta Sigma Theta Sorority 1979; Fellowship for Study in Peoples Republic of China 1983; Top ladies of Distinction Inc, Natl Branch, Natl Top Lady of Distinction, 1988-, Media Award, 1992; St Clair County YWCA, Woman of the Year, 1987, Leadership Award, 1991; Natl Honorary Mbr, Iota Phi Lambda Sorority Inc 1983-; Pres Bd of Trustees, First United Presbyterian Church, 1988-; World of Difference Award, World of Difference Organization, 1990; Vaskon High School Hall of Fame, Vashon High Sch-St Louis, 1989; Phenomenal Woman Award, Spelman College Alumni-St Louis, 1990; Kimmel Award, 1991; St Cr County Mental Hlth Center Award, 1992; ESL Business and Professional Women's Award, 1992; Distinguished Alumnus, Univ of Illinois, 1996; Illinois Senior Hall of Fame, 1997. **Home Addr:** 733 N 40 St, East St Louis, IL 62205. **Business Phone:** (314)340-3366.

WRIGHT, KEITH DEREK, SR.
Assistant manager computer operations. **Personal:** Born Jun 2, 1953, Orange, NJ; son of Lola Hunt Wright and Clarence Samuel Williams; divorced; children: Keisha, Keith, Khalid. **Educ:** Rutgers Univ, BA 1979, MLA in progress; Amer Mgmt Assoc, Cert. **Career:** System Develop Corp, sr computer operator 1972-74; Nabisco Brands Inc, computer shift supervisor 1975-69; Hoffman-LaRoche, sr supervisor 1979-86; Port Authority of NY & NJ, asst mgr computer opers 1986-. **Orgs:** Chairperson BDPA Newsletter 1983-85; past pres Black Data Processing Assoc 1984-86; chmn Parking Authority East Orange 1984-; counselor YMCA Linkage Prog 1985; bd of dirs Economic Develop East Orange 1986-; chairperson Public Relations BDPA 1987; chairman East Orange Economic Development 1988-; director Tri-City Citizens for Progress 1988-. **Honors/Awds:** YMCA Black Achievers Awd 1984; Scholastic Achievement Awd Essex League of Volunteer Workers 1971; publication ''History of Jazz in Newark NJ 1938-1970'', 1981. **Business Addr:** Asst Mgr Computer Operations, Port Authority of NY & NJ, One World Trade Center, New York, NY 10048.

WRIGHT, LARRY L.
Educator. **Personal:** Born Jun 20, 1954, Florida; son of Gertrude Robinson Wright and Dennis Wright. **Educ:** Chipola Junior College, Marianna, FL, AA, 1974; Florida State University, Tallahassee, FL, BS, 1976, MS, 1978, PhD, 1980. **Career:** Florida House of Representatives, Tallahassee, FL, research assistant, 1976; Florida State University, Tallahassee, FL, research assistant, 1977-78, teaching assistant, 1978-80; Center for Public Affairs & Governmental Services, Tallahasse, FL, consultant, 1982-84; Florida A&M University, Tallahassee, FL, associate professor, 1988-. **Orgs:** Membership, Florida Political Science Association, The American Society for Public Administration, The Georgia Political Science Association, The Southern Political Science Association, Association of Social and Behavior, Pi Sigma Alpha, NAACP, Scholarly Publication Committee, University Faculty Senate. **Honors/Awds:** Andrew W Mellon, Fellowship, 1996. **Business Addr:** Associate Professor of Political Science, Florida A&M University, 410 Tucker Hall, Tallahassee, FL 32307, (850)561-2067.

WRIGHT, LINWOOD CLINTON
Aeronautical engineer (retired). **Personal:** Born Mar 24, 1919, Augusta, GA; son of Maria Wright and Leon Wright; married Ernestine Louise McIver; children: Linda Wright Moore, Linwood Jr. **Educ:** Wayne State Univ, BS Aero Engr 1944; Univ of Cincinnati, MS Aero Engr 1960. **Career:** Natl Adv Comm for Aeronautics, aeronautical rsch scientist 1943-56; General Elec Aircraft Engine Bus Gr, mgr adv compressor rsch 1956-66, mgr adv tech mktg 1974-83; Garrett Ai Research Mfg Co LA, chief of aerodynamics 1966-72; Pratt & Whitney Aircraft Co, asst gas turbine mgr 1972-74; NASA, act dir propulsion power & energy 1983-85. **Orgs:** Mem Amer Inst of Aeronautics & Astronautics 1941-; part-time security salesman Putnam Financial 1971-72; mem Tech Mktg Soc of Amer 1975; mem past chap pres Sigma Pi Phi Prof Frat Cincinnati 1978-; mem Mayor's Task Force on Zoning Forest Park OH 1986; mem Economic Develop Comm Forest Park OH 1986-. **Honors/Awds:** Disting Alumni Awd Wayne State Univ 1958; guest lecturer Univ of TN Space Institute 1974; Disting Alumni Awd Univ of Cincinnati 1984; author or co-author of 21 published tech papers 1946-72. **Military Serv:** AAC enlisted reserve 1945-46. **Home Addr:** 11136 Embassy Dr, Forest Park, OH 45240.

WRIGHT, LORENZEN VERN-GAGNE
Professional basketball player. **Personal:** Born Nov 4, 1975, Memphis, TN; children: Lorenzen Jr. **Educ:** Memphis. **Career:** Los Angeles Clippers, center/forward, 1996-. **Special Achievements:** NBA Draft, First round pick, #7, 1996. **Business Addr:** Professional Basketball Player, Los Angeles Clippers, 3939 S Figueroa St, Los Angeles Sports Arena, Los Angeles, CA 90037, (213)748-8000.

WRIGHT, LOUIS DONNEL
Business executive, professional athlete (retired). **Personal:** Born Jan 31, 1953, Gilmer, TX; son of Verbena Wright and Glover Wright; married Vicki; children: Summer Marie, Kyla Lynn, Evan Louis. **Educ:** San Jose State U, Bus Mgt. **Career:** Denver Broncos, cornerback 1975-87; L Wright Enterprises, sec/tres, 1990-. **Orgs:** Conference champ Track Team 1973-74. **Honors/Awds:** Pro Bowl 1977-79, 1983, 1985; NEA All-Pro Team; Coll All-Star Game 1975; East-West Shrine Game 1975; All-Coast Football Selection 1975; Denver Broncos Team Captin 1985-86; named All NFL by Sporting News and Pro Football Weekly; mem 1986 NFL Pro Football team. **Business Addr:** Former Cornerback, Denver Broncos, 13655 Broncos Pkwy, Englewood, CO 80112-4151.

WRIGHT, LOYCE PIERCE
Government official. **Personal:** Born Dec 24, 1943, New Orleans, LA; daughter of Victoria Martin Pierce and Frank Pierce; married Louis Clifton Wright Jr, Feb 14, 1976; children: Kiana Tamika Wright. **Educ:** Southern Univ, Baton Rouge LA, BS 1965; Univ of New Orleans, LA, MEd 1976. **Career:** Orleans Parish School Bd, New Orleans LA, French/Spanish teacher, 1965-76; New Orleans Sickle Cell Anemia Foundation, assoc dir, 1976-81; Communirep Inc, New Orleans LA, mgmt consultant, 1980-86; Mayor's Office, City of New Orleans LA, dir, 1986-92; Excelth, Inc, dir of human resources, 1992-97; Southern Univ at New Orleans, asst vice chancellor for Academic Affairs, 1997. **Orgs:** Past pres/founding mem, New Orleans Sickle Cell Anemia Foundation, 1972-76; campaign coord for state, local & presidential candidates, 1981-88; consultant & marketing dir, educational journal SENGA; coordinator, Martin Luther King Jr Federal Holiday Comm, New Orleans LA, 1987-; vice pres, bd of dir, Mental Health Assn, New Orleans LA, 1988; mem, nominating comm, YWCA-USA, 1988-91; pres, bd of dir, YWCA of New Orleans, 1989-; mem, planning comm, Agency Relations Committee; Admission/Growth Committee Committee; United Way of New Orleans, 1989-; member, Delta Sigma Theta Sorority Inc, New Orleans Alumnae Chapter; founder, Phenomenal Women. **Honors/Awds:** Award for outstanding service, Governor of Louisiana, 1986; Second Mile Award, Natl Assn of Neighborhoods, 1987; Certificate of Merit, Mayor of New Orleans, 1988; Role Model Award, YWCA of New Orleans, 1989. **Home Addr:** 3945 Virgil Blvd, New Orleans, LA 70122.

WRIGHT, MARK ADRIAN
Plastic company executive. **Personal:** Born Jan 29, 1957, Philadelphia, PA; son of Richard Wright & Vera Lennon; married Sheela, Feb 12, 1983; children: Kyle, Adrian. **Educ:** Drexel University, BSME, 1979; Washington University, MBA, 1990. **Career:** Monsanto, sales rep, 1979-83, ford motor dev manager, 1983-86, world wide mkt manager, 1986-87, regional sales manager, 1987-90; AES, auto mktg manager Europe, 1990-93, sales manager Germany, 1993-94, director automotive, 1994-. **Orgs:** Society of Automotive Engineers, 1983-; Society of Plastic Engineers, board of directors, 1994-95. **Special Achievements:** Language Skills, French & German; Published in numerous plastic & engineering books; Presentations to SPE, SAE & Trade GroupS. **Business Addr:** Director Automotive, Americas, AES, 2401 Walton Blvd, PO Box 215137, Auburn Hills, MI 48321-5137, (810)377-6211.

WRIGHT, MARVIN
Educator (retired). **Personal:** Born May 20, 1917, Fulton, AL; son of Almeda Falconer Wright and Marvin Wright; married Katie Harper; children: Virginia Jordan. **Educ:** Xavier Univ, PhB 1947; Univ of Illinois, EdM 1962. **Career:** Professional musician, drummer 1940-50; E St Louis Public School, elem teacher 1948-65; School Dist 1984 E St Louis 1965-79; Atty General's Office E St Louis, admin investigator 1980-84. **Orgs:** Pres E St Louis Principals Org; mem Phi Delta Kappa Ed, IL Principal's Assoc, Natl Elem Prncipal's Assoc 1974-76; trustee VFW #3480; chmn bd of trustees State Comm Coll 1977-84; alternate dele 1976 Rep Natl Conv; trustee Belleville Men's Rep Club; comm man Boy Scout Troop; mem Illini Sr Citiznes Bd 1983; mem Civil Rights Comm E St Louis 1971-75; mrm 4-H Youth Committeeman 1971-; school memberhsip chmn E St Louis Branch NAACP; mem IL Div United Way Bd 1984-; city chmn Amer Cancer Soc St Clair Cty Unit 1976-77; mem Southern IL Black Republican Council; commander Veterans of Foreign Wars Post 3480, 1987-88; quartermaster Veterans of Foreign Wars Post 3480, 1988-. **Honors/Awds:** Meritorious Serv Awd Amer Cancer Soc 1976; Outstanding Serv Awd St Paul Church 1976; Outstanding Serv Awd E St Louis PTA 1976; Bd Mem of the Year Awd United Way 1983; East St Louis Criminal Justice Awd 1980; all state commander, Veterans Foreign Wars 1987. **Military Serv:** AUS staff sgt 1942-45; Overseas Serv Bar; Sivler Battle Star; Good Conduct Medal; WW II Victory Medal.

WRIGHT, MARY H.
Educator (retired). **Personal:** Born May 26, 1916, Suffolk, VA; daughter of Mamie Hamlett Henderson and Hamilton Martin Henderson; married Jeremiah A Wright Sr, Jun 8, 1938; children: Mary LaVerne Wright Miner, Jeremiah A Wright Jr. **Educ:** Virginia Union Univ, AB (Magna Cum Laude), 1935; Univ of Pennsylvania, MA, 1949, MS, 1959, DEd, 1971. **Career:** Surry Co Virginia Public School System, teacher, 1932-33; Worcester Co Maryland Public School System, teacher, 1935-39; Philadelphia, PA, Public School System, teacher, 1944-68, admin, 1968-78. **Orgs:** Research asst, 1965-66, master teacher, 1966-68, School of Educ, Univ of Pennsylvania; bd mem, Northwest Philadelphia Branch; life mem, NAACP. **Honors/Awds:** Natl Science Found Fellowship, Univ of Pennsylvania, 1958-59; Outstanding Community Serv Award, NAACP, 1975; Distinguished Serv to Youth Award, Miller Memorial Church, 1978; President's Award, Intl Assn of Ministers Wives, 1986.

WRIGHT, MICHAEL
Actor. **Personal:** son Of Alberta Wright. **Educ:** Lee Strasberg Theater. **Career:** Films: ''The Laundromat''; ''Bedtime Eyes''; ''The Wanderers''; ''The Principal''; ''The Five Heartbeats''; ''Sugar Hill''; role in television series ''V''. **Business Addr:** Actor, Sugar Hill, Artist Agency, 10000 Santa Monica Blvd., Ste. 305, Los Angeles, CA 90067, (310)277-7779.

WRIGHT, N'BUSHE
Actress. **Career:** Actress, currently. **Special Achievements:** Movies: Zebrahead, Dead Presidents, Blade. **Business Addr:** Actress, Lee Daniel Management, 151 W 74th St, New York, NY 10023, (212)721-1403.

WRIGHT, RALPH EDWARD
Business executive. **Personal:** Born Dec 29, 1950, Newark, NJ; married Sallie Riggins Williams; children: Galen, Garnel. **Career:** New York Stock Exchange, reporter, 1969-77; Carl H Pforzheimer and Co, clerk, stockbroker, 1977-89; Drexel Burnham, stockbroker, 1989-90; JJC Specialist Corp, stockbroker, 1990-95, Doley sec, vp 1995-96; W&P Securities, Inc., chair, CEO, 1996-. **Orgs:** George Junior Republic, board member; The Clearpool Camps, board member; Brokers United for Youth Scholarship Fund, board member; South Africa Chamber of Commerce. **Honors/Awds:** Tau Gamma Delta Sorority, Plaque, 1991; Community Leader of the Year as presented by Wheelchair Charities of New York, 1995. **Special Achievements:** First African-American Specialist New York Stock Exchange, 1981; featured in commercial, Black Entertainment Television: ''Profiles in Accomplishment,'' sponsored by Coca-Cola Co, 1984; one of the first recipients: Bull and Bear Statue given by the CNL on Minority Affairs, 1984; Profiled in College textbook Introduction to Business, Bio appears after chapter 19, 1987; also in Business in a Changing World, 1991; One of the main subjects in Pictorial Songs of My People, A Life Magazine Publication, p 34, Feb 1992; First African-American and American dealer at the Johannesburg Stock Exchange in South Africa, 1995. **Home Addr:** 9 Knob Hill Rd, Morganville, NJ 07751-9508. **Business Addr:** Exeter & Co, Members NYSE, 115 Broadway, New York, NY 10005.

WRIGHT, RAYMOND LEROY, JR.
Dentist. **Personal:** Born May 7, 1950, Fort Dix, NJ; children: Raymond III. **Educ:** Univ of IL, 1968-70; Univ of IL Coll of Dentistry, DDS 1970-74, Cert of Periodontics 1974-76. **Career:** Cermack Mem Hosp, staff dentist 1975-84; Chicago Bd of Health, dentist 1976-77; Dr Clarence McNair, dentist-periodontist 1976-77; Dr Roger Berkley, dentist-periodontist 1977-80; McHarry Medical Coll, asst prof 1978-83; Univ of IL Coll of Dentistry, asst prof 1977-85; Self-employed, 1980-. **Orgs:** Program chmn Lincoln Dental Soc 1980-81-82-84; scholarship chmn Natl Dental Assn 1982; parliamentarian Lincoln Dental Soc 1984-85; treas Lincoln Dental Society 1985-86; treas FEPA (Forum for the Evolution of the Progressive Arts); sec Lincoln Dental Soc 1986-87; program chmn Kenwood Hyde Park Branch Chicago Dental Soc 1986-87. **Honors/Awds:** Nomination Outstanding Young Men of America 1980; Service Awd Lincoln Dental Soc 1982; Service Awd Natl Dental Soc 1982.

WRIGHT, RAYMOND STANFORD
Beer wholesaler. **Personal:** Born Jan 13, 1949, Chicago, IL; son of Early R. Wright and William R. Wright; married Patricia Wright, Apr 30, 1988; children: Raymond Jr, Antoine. **Career:** Miller Brewing Co, area mgr, gen mgr, br mgr 1971-79; On Target Inc, pres 1980-83; Thomas Distributing Co, gen mgr 1983-85; IL Beverage Inc, pres,owner 1985-. **Orgs:** Mem bd dir DuSable Museum 1987-90; mem adv bd Chicago Alcoholic Treatment Ctr 1987; bd mem Goodwill Industries of America 1989-1990; Univ Michigan Alumni Assoc. **Business Addr:** President, Illinois Beverage Co, 441 N Kilbourn, Chicago, IL 60624.

WRIGHT, RICKEY
General surgery resident. **Personal:** Born Dec 8, 1958, Fayette, AL; son of Maxine Wright; children: Demetric D Fleming. **Educ:** TN State Univ, BS 1981; Meharry Medical Coll, MD 1986. **Career:** Western Reserve Care System, surgical resident; USAF, captain, Dyes AFB, Abiliance, TX, captain medical corp, currently. **Orgs:** Mem Masonic Lodge 1980-; pres Meharry Chapter Amer Medical Student Assoc 1984-85; mem Medical Student Council 1985-86; polemarch Kappa Alpha Psi Fraternity 1985-86; liason comm Amer Med Assoc, Student Natl Medical Assoc, Natl Medical Assn 1985-86; chmn membership comm NAACP 1985-86; mem Meharry Co Medical Assoc. **Honors/Awds:** Meharry Scholarship 1985. **Military Serv:** AFROTC; captain, USAF, 1989.

WRIGHT, ROBERT A.
Attorney, judge. **Personal:** Born Dec 8, 1919, Chester, PA; son of Anne Davis Wright and E Courtlandt Wright; married Mary Maloney; children: Robert C. **Educ:** Lincoln U, BA 1941; Temple Univ Sch of Law, LLB 1950. **Career:** Chester, PA, atty 1951-70; Delaware County, Media, PA, asst dist atty 1964-70, 32nd Judicial Dist of PA, judge, 1970-89, senior judge (part-time), 1989-. **Orgs:** Delaware County, Pennsylvania & American Bar Associations; Lawyers Club of Delaware County; PA Conf St Trial Judges; Amer Judicature Soc; PA Counc Juv Crt Judges; past mem Jud Inquiry & Review Bd; Crime Comm of Phi; Temple Law Alumni; NAACP; IBPOE of W, past exaulted ruler; Amer Leg; VFW; Cent Rest Rec Club; past bd of mgrs W Branch YMCA; hon mem Meth Men; Frat Ord of Police; Wm Penn Lodge 19; Chester Yth League; Mag Assn Delaware County Hon Awds; adv bd Delaware County Campus PA State U; Bunting Friendship Freedom House; Chester School Fund. **Honors/Awds:** First ann Achieve Awd Deputies Club of Elks IBPOE of W; American Spirit Preservation Award, Delaware County, PA, 1989; Donald J Orlowsky Memorial Award, Delaware County Bar Assn, 1989. **Military Serv:** US Army, 1st sgt 1943-46. **Business Addr:** Judge, Delaware County Court House, Media, PA 19063.

WRIGHT, ROBERT COURTLANDT
Elected official, judge. **Personal:** Born Nov 5, 1944, Chester, PA; son of Mary Wright and Robert Wright; married Florence Fletcher; children: Josie, Robert Jr. **Educ:** George Washington Univ, BA political sci 1966; Villanova Univ, Law Degree 1969. **Career:** Self employed, attorney 1970-91; PA Legislature, state rep 1981-91; Court of Common Pleas of Delaware County, judge 1992-. **Orgs:** Mem Tau Epsilon Phi Soc Frat 1963-; pres Republican Council of DE Cty 1977-91; exec bd Chester Branch NAACP 1978-91; exec bd Natl Black Caucus of State Leg 1981-84, PA Minority Business Devel Auth 1981-86; mem PA Legislative Black Caucus 1981-91; treas PA Legislative Black Caucus Foundation 1982-91. **Honors/Awds:** Community Serv Awd Chester Housing Authority PA 1981; Republican Cncl of Delaware County Outstanding Comm Serv Awd 1981; Southeast Delaware Co Family YMCA Awd 1982; Humanitarian Awd Chester Black Expo PA 1982; Mary Thomas Freedom Awd, NAACP Chester Branch 1983; Man of the Year Chester Scholarship Fund PA 1982,84; Outstanding Community Serv Awd Jeffrey Manor Civic Assn 1985; Outstanding Accomplishment in Field of Law Natl Sorority of Phi Delta Kappa Xi Chap 1987; Community Service Award, Operation PUSH of Delaware County 1990; Man of the Year Award, Chester Scholarship CCA 1988; Victim-Witness Rights Award, Domestic Abuse Project of Delaware County. **Home Addr:** 34 Rose Lane, Glen Mills, PA 19342.

WRIGHT, ROBERT L.
Association executive (retired). **Personal:** Born Sep 23, 1917, Malvern, PA; married Beulah C; children: Robert L Jr. **Educ:** Lincoln Univ, BA 1942; Temple Univ Law Sch. **Career:** Social Security Admin, benefit authorizer, until retirement. **Orgs:** Sec Malvern PTA Assn Malvern Pub Schs 1957-59; sec Troop Com #7 Boy Scouts of Amer 1960-61; sec Gr Valley High Gridiron Club 1962-63; vice pres CommAct Bd of Chester co West Chester 1968-71; vice pres UPAC 1968-; asst sec Malvern Mun Authority 1975-76; sec Mun Auth 1977-79; vice pres Mal Mun Authority 1980; life mem NAACP Golden Heritage; pres Main Line Branch NAACP 1964-89; past mem Main Line Youth for Christ Com; PA State Conference Executive Bd, 1980-. **Honors/Awds:** Legion of Merit Chapel of Four Chaplain Awd; Main Line Br NAACP, Isabelle Strickland Awd Main Line, 1981, Past President Award, 1989, Founders Awd; Cmnty Serv Awd Main Line Bus & Prof Women 1982; Silver Key for Volunteer Work; Chester County Cmsn, Proclamation in Recognition of Lifetime of Cmnty Service and Generosity, 1992. **Military Serv:** US military 1942-45.

WRIGHT, ROBERTA V. HUGHES
Attorney, educator. **Personal:** Born in Detroit, MI; daughter of Dr & Mrs Robert Greenidge; married Charles H Wright, Aug 19, 1989; children: Barbara, Wilbur B. **Educ:** Univ of MI, PhD 1973; Wayne State Univ Law Sch, JD; Wayne State U, MEd. **Career:** Detroit Pub Sch, past sch social worker; Detroit Comm on Children & Youth, past dir; Shaw Coll, past vice pres for Academic Affairs; County Public Admin, practicing lawyer Michigan Courts & admitted to practice bar, District of Columbia and Supreme Court of USA; Lawrence, former prof; First Independence Nat Bank, inst organizer & dir; Charro Book Co, Inc, vice pres, currently. **Orgs:** Mem Am Bar Assn; mem MI Bar Assn; past mem Am & MI Trial Lawyers Assn; mem Oakland Co Bar Assn; mem Detroit Bar Assn; Wayne State Univ Law Alumni; Univ of MI Alumni Assn; AKA Sorority; life mem NAACP; mem Renaissance Club; million dollar mem Museum of African American History. **Honors/Awds:** Recipient NAACP Freedom Award; MI Chronicle Newspaper Cit of Yr; Harriet Tubman Award; Alpha Kappa Alpha Sorority Recognition Award; Quality Quintet Award Detroit Skyliner Mag. **Business Addr:** Vice President, Charro Book Co Inc, 29777 Telegraph Rd #2500, Southfield, MI 48034.

WRIGHT, ROOSEVELT R., JR.
Educator. **Personal:** Born Jul 24, 1943, Elizabeth City, NC; son of Lillie Mae Garrett Wright and Roosevelt R Wright Sr. **Educ:** Elizabeth City State Univ, BS 1964; North Carolina Central Univ, MA 1969; Virginia State University, CGS, 1970; Syracuse Univ, PhD 1992. **Career:** SI Newhouse School of Comm, assoc prof, radio/TV, 1975-; NBC Radio Div WRC/WKYS Washington, acc exec 1974-75; Howard Univ Washington, DC, adj prof radio TV 1974-75; WTNJ Radio Trenton, NJ, gen manager 1973-74; North Carolina Central Univ, asst prof ed media 1972-73; WDNC-AM/FM Durham, NC, announcer radio engr 1972-73; Elizabeth City State Univ, asso dir ed media 1968-69; DC State Coll Dover, dir ed media 1969-70; WNDR Radio Syracuse, announcer radio engr 1970-72; WLLE Radio Raleigh, NC, program dir 1973-74; WOLF Radio Syracuse, NY, chief engineer 1980-84. **Orgs:** Historian Chi Pi Chap Omega Psi Phi Frat 1975-95; radio com mem Natl Assn of Educ Broadcasters 1976-80; adv Natl Acad of TV Arts & Scis Syracuse Chpt 1976-80; public affairs officer natl naval Officers Assoc 1983-85; chmn communications comm Amer Heart Assoc New York 1985-87; CEO WJPZ-FM Syracuse NY; US naval liaison officer, Syracuse Univ, 1981-; steward AME Zion Church; public affairs officer, US Navy, Great Lakes Cruise 1985-; mem communications comm, United Way of Onondaga County 1988-; bd mem Hiawatha Council Boy Scout of America, 1992-. **Honors/Awds:** Soldier of the Quarter 32AADC AUS 1967; Doctoral Flwsp Syracuse Univ 1970-72; Men's Day Awd Mt Lebanon AMEZ Ch Eliz City 1974, 1997; Upward Bound Prog Awd LeMoyne Coll Syracuse 1977; Ed Media & Speaker Awd NC Ed Media Assn 1977; Natl Council of Negro Women Communications Awd 1984, 1994; Syracuse Univ Pan Hellenic Council Awd 1986, 1987, 1989, 1990; Outstanding Mass Media Teacher Awd 1987-91; Naval Achievement Medal 1987, 1997; Keynote Speaker Awd, NAACP Jefferson Co Chapter, Watertown, NY 1989; Comm Serv Awd, Syracuse Univ 1988; consulting editor, "Cobblestone Magazine, History of Radio", 1988; Naval Commendation Medal, 1992, 1993, 1995; US Navy Campus Liaison Officer of the Year, 1992. **Military Serv:** US Army, sp/5, 1966-72; US Naval Reserves, captain, 1992-. **Home Addr:** 310 W Matson Ave, Syracuse, NY 13205. **Business Addr:** Schl of Publ Comms, Syracuse University, Syracuse, NY 13244-0003, (315)443-9244.

WRIGHT, SAMUEL LAMAR
Educational administrator. **Personal:** Born Jul 7, 1953, Boynton Beach, FL; son of Rovina Victoria Deal Wright and Samuel Louis Wright; children: Samuel Lamar Jr, Samaria Elizabeth. **Educ:** Univ of FL, BA 1974, MEd 1975; FL Atlantic Univ, postgrad courses, pub admin 1980-81; Univ of South FL, postgrad studies, educ leadership 1988-, doctoral program, spec ed, currently. **Career:** PBC Bd of Co Commissioners/Action Com, emp & personnel mgr 1975-76, dir Delray Bch TAC 1976-77, adm asst/planner 1977-79, asst dir 1979-84, head start dir 1984-85; Boynton Beach FL, city councilman 1981-85; Univ of South FL, Minority Student Organizations, advisor 1985-86; Greater Tampa Urban League, Clerical/Word Processing Training Program, center mgr 1986-87; Univ of South FL, Multicultural Admissions, assistant director, 1987-. **Orgs:** Bd of dirs Natl Black Caucus of Local Elected Officials 1982-84; mem State of FL Comm Serv Block Grant Adv Comm 1982-84; mem Kappa Alpha Psi Frat Inc 1972-; chmn Intergov Rel Comm 1984-85; mem FL Assn for Comm Action 1975-85; mem FAMU Alumni Assn of PBC 1979-85; mem Univ of FL Alumni Assn 1979-; mem City of Boynton Beach Black Awareness Comm 1981-85; mem FL Assoc of Comm Rel Profs 1982-84; bd of dirs So Cty Drug Abuse Found 1982-84; bd dir Dem Black Caucus of FL 1982-84; Boynton Beach Kiwanis Sunrisers 1982-85; bd mem Selective Serv Syst 1983-85; 1st vice pres FL Black Caucus of Local Elected Officials 1983-85; vice pres Comm Affairs Suncoast C of C 1983-85; mem Gr Boynton Beach C of C 1983-85; mem Natl Assoc of Black Social Workers Inc 1983-85; mem FL Head Start Assoc1984-85; chmn Legmm Boynton/Ocean Ridge Bd of Realtors 1984-85; elected to Dem Exec Comm Palm Beach 1983-85; Tampa Male Club 1989-; 100 Black Men of Tampa Inc 1988-89; Concerned Voters Coalition, 1991-; ambassador, Center of Excellence, Inc, 1988-; Revealing Truth Ministries; Hillsborough Alliance of Black School Educators, 1993-; Hillsborough County Children's Service Advisory Board, 1993-. **Honors/Awds:** Outstanding & Dedicated Serv Awd Concerned Citizens Voter's League of Boynton Beach 1981; Citizen of the Yr Omega Psi Phi Frat 1982; Outstanding Civic Leadership Awd Westboro Bus & Prof Women's Club of the Palm Beaches 1983; participant Leadership Palm Beach Co 1984-85; Martin Luther King Jr Award for Outstanding Leadership 1989; Community Service Award 1989; Kappa Alpha Psi Frat Polemarch's Award 1988-90; Outstanding Service Award in Religion 1988; USF Outstanding Service Award (Academic Affairs) 1988; State of Florida Notary Public. **Home Addr:** 3402-03 Park Square South, Tampa, FL 33613. **Business Addr:** Asst Dir, Multicultural Admissions, University of South Florida, 4202 East Fowler Ave SVC 1036, Tampa, FL 33620-6900.

WRIGHT, SARAH E.
Writer. **Personal:** Born Dec 9, 1928, Wetipquin, MD; daughter of Mary Amelia Moore Wright and Willis Charles Wright; married Joseph G Kaye; children: Michael, Shelley. **Educ:** Howard Univ, Washington DC, 1945-49; Cheyney State Teachers College, 1950-52; New York State University, Regents College, Albany, NY, BA, 1979; New School for Social Research, New York, various courses in writing; Long Island University, C W Post College. **Career:** Worked as teacher, bookkeeper, and office manager; writer; certified Poetry Therapist, 1986-; YMCA, The Writer's Voice, New York, NY, teach fiction writing, currently. **Orgs:** Mem, International PEN and Pen American Center; mem, Authors Guild; mem, Authors League of America; mem, Harlem Writers Guild; member, International Women's Writing Guild; member, National Association for Poetry Therapy, member, Pen & Brush Inc. **Honors/Awds:** Baltimore Sun Readability Award, 1969, for This Child's Gonna Live; McDowell Colony fellowships, 1972 and 1973; New York State Creative Artists Public Service Award for Fiction, and Novelist-Poet Award from Howard University's Institute for the Arts and Humanities' Second National Conference of Afro-American Writers, both 1976; published, A Philip Randolph: Integration in the Work Place, 1990, Silver Burdett Press/Simon & Schuster; The Distinguished Writer Award, Middle Atlantic Writers Assn, 1988; Zora Neale Hurston Award, The Zora Neale Hurston Society, Morgan State University, 1990; Salisbury State Univ, Distinguished Contribution to Literature; Award renamed Sarah E Wright Graduate Paper Award. **Home Addr:** 780 West End Ave, Apt 1-D, New York, NY 10025.

WRIGHT, SHARONE ADDARYL
Professional basketball player. **Personal:** Born Jan 30, 1973, Macon, GA. **Educ:** Clemson Univ. **Career:** Philadelphia 76ers, center-forward, 1994-96; Toronto Raptors, 1996-. **Honors/Awds:** NBA All-Rookie Second Team, 1995. **Special Achievements:** NBA Draft, First round pick, #6, 1994. **Business Addr:** Professional Basketball Player, Toronto Raptors, 150 York St, Ste 110, Toronto, ON, Canada M5H 3S5, (416)214-2255.

WRIGHT, SORAYA M.
Insurance executive. **Personal:** Born Dec 24, 1961, Oakland, CA; married Karl Wright, Jun 4, 1983; children: Dania, Deidre. **Educ:** Holy Names College, BA, 1985. **Career:** CNA Insurance Co.; Alexsis Risk Management, claim supervisor; The Clorox Co., claim manager, corporate risk manager, currently. **Orgs:** Risk & Insurance Management Society; East Oakland Youth Development Foundation, trustee; East Oakland Youth Development Ctr; Assumption School Board. **Honors/Awds:** Dollar & Sense, Outstanding Business & Professional Leader, 1993. **Business Addr:** Corporate Risk Manager, The Clorox Company, 1221 Broadway St, Oakland, CA 94612, (510)271-7000.

WRIGHT, STANLEY V.
Educator, coach. **Personal:** Born Aug 11, 1921, Englewood, NJ; married Hazel; children: Stanley, Toni, Sandra, Tyran. **Educ:** Springfield Coll, BS 1949; Columbia U, MA 1950; Univ TX, grad study 1956; IN U, 1968. **Career:** CA State Univ, prof phys educ & head track coach; Mexico City Olympic Games, asst track coach was responsible for athletes who won 6 gold medals set five world records & tying 1 in 6 events; US Olympic Track & Field Com, appointed for second time; US Olympic bd of Dir for next quadrennial; Munich Olympic Games, sprint coach 1972; dir of athleteics 1975; Natl Collegiate Ath Assn Recruit Com, 1977; Intl Olympic Acad USOC Com, 1977. **Honors/Awds:** Reciev many hon & awds; articles such as "Techniques Related to Spring Racing" have appeared in ldg athletic jours; part in over 200 hs & coll clinics.

WRIGHT, STEPHEN CALDWELL
Educator. **Personal:** Born Nov 11, 1946, Sanford, FL; son of Joseph Caldwell & Bernice I Wright. **Educ:** St Petersbury Jr Coll, AA, 1967; FL Atlantic Univ, BA, 1969; Atlanta Univ, MA, 1972; Indiana Univ of Pennslyvania, PhD, 1983. **Career:** Seminole County School Bd, teacher, 1969-70; Seminole Comm Coll, professor, 1972-. **Orgs:** Zora Festival of Arts & Humanities, national planning comm, 1989-99; Boys & Girls Club, chair, advisory council, 1993-96; Gwendolyn Brooks Writers Assn of FL, founder & pres, 1987-; Revelry Poetry

Journal, editor, 1987-; Florida Div of Cultural Affairs Literary Organizations Panel, panelist, 1996-98. **Honors/Awds:** Morgan State Univ, Distinguished Authors Series Award, 1998; Illinois Poet Laureate, Illinois Salutes Award, 1992; Gwendolyn Brooks Poetry Prize, 1984; Univ of South FL, First Superior Poet Award, 1969. **Special Achievements:** First Statement, poetry collection, 1983; Poems In Movement, poetry collection, 1984; Making Symphony: New & Selected Poems, 1987; ''Pearl,'' New Visions: Fiction by Florida Writers, 1989; Inheritance, poetry collection, 1992; Editor ''On Gwendolyn Brooks: Reliant Contemplation,'' 1995. **Home Addr:** 127 Langston Dr, Sanford, FL 32771, (407)323-7184. **Business Addr:** Prof, English Dept, Seminole Community Coll, 100 Weldon Blvd, Sanford, FL 32773, (407)328-2063.

WRIGHT, SYLVESTER M.
Clergyman. **Personal:** Born Feb 7, 1927, Dallas, TX; son of Rev & Mrs C W Wright; married Debra Diane Williams; children: Sylvester M II, Calvin Wesley, Moses. **Educ:** Butler Coll, AA 1945; Bishop Coll, BA 1949, MA 1954; TX Coll, DD 1982; Bishop Coll, DD. **Career:** Peoples Bapt Church, pastor 1954-; Interdenominational Ministries Alliance, pres 1964-; Peoples Baptist Church, pastor. **Orgs:** Moderator Fellowship Dist Assn; pres Missionary Baptist Gen Conv of TX; bd mem Dallas Black C of C; exec bd mem Dallas Br NAACP; trustee Bishop Coll Dallas; bd mem, Children Medical Ctr; vice pres, bd, Natl Missionary Baptist Conf. **Honors/Awds:** Serv Awd Dallas Urban League 1975; Ministries Awd Prairie View Ministering Conf 1976; Alumni Awd Lincoln HS 1979; Alumni Awd Bishop Coll. **Military Serv:** USAF pfc 1945-47. **Business Addr:** Pastor, Peoples Baptist Church, 3119 Pine St, Dallas, TX 75215.

WRIGHT, TOBY LIN
Professional football player. **Personal:** Born Nov 19, 1970, Phoenix, AZ. **Educ:** University of Nebraska, attended. **Career:** St Louis Rams, defensive back, 1995-. **Business Addr:** Professional Football Player, St Louis Rams, One Rams Way, St Louis, MO 63045, (314)982-7267.

WRIGHT, VERLYN LAGLEN
Journalist. **Personal:** Born Aug 2, 1963, Saginaw, MI; daughter of Leeunice Calloway Wright and Louis Wright. **Educ:** Southern University, Baton Rouge, LA, BA, 1983; University of Missouri, Columbia, MO, MA, 1986. **Career:** Dallas Times Herald, Dallas, TX, reporter, 1987-88; Patriot Ledger, Quincy, MA, copy editor, 1988-. **Orgs:** Member, National Assn of Black Journalists, 1986-; member, Boston Assn of Black Journalists, 1988-. **Business Addr:** Copy Editor, The Patriot Ledger, 400 Crown Colony, Quincy, MA 02169.

WRIGHT, WILL J.
Television station executive. **Personal:** Born Sep 9, 1950, Brooklyn, NY; son of Mildred & Gerard Wright; married Patricia Ann, Feb 27, 1981; children: Patricia Antoinette. **Educ:** Fordham University, BA, communications, 1972; Columbia University, Graduate School of Journalism, Michele Clark Fellowship, 1974. **Career:** CBS Network News, editor, writer, producer, 1972-1980; Cable News Network, sr producer, 1980-84; KYW-TV, assistant news director, 1984-87; KRIV Fox TV News, vp/news dir, 1987-92; WWOR-TV, news dir, 1992-. **Orgs:** Radio-Television News Director's Association, bd of dirs, 1993-98; Fordham University, bd of trustees, 1995-98. **Honors/Awds:** NATA/Houston, Miami, Emmy Awards Best Documentary, 1989, 1990, Best Spot News, 1991; NATA/NY Emmy Awards, Best Newscast, 1995, 1997, Best News Set, 1996; National Congress of Racial Equality Harmony Award, 1997. **Special Achievements:** Art Exhibits: New York Art Expo, 1995; Ward Nasse Gallery, Soho, NY, 1994, 1996; ''Because We Care,'' Art Exhibit, Morristown, NJ. **Business Addr:** News Director, WWOR - UPN 9 News, 9 Broadcast Plz, Secaucus, NJ 07096, (201)330-2220.

WRIGHT, WILLIAM A.
Automobile dealer. **Personal:** Born Apr 4, 1936, Kansas City, MO; son of Madeline S Wright and Robert B Wright; married Ceta D Wright, Jul 21, 1961. **Educ:** Western Washington State, Bellingham WA, BEd, 1961. **Career:** Los Angeles School District, teacher, 1961-68; Pro Golf Tour, professional golfer, 1964-77; Pasadena Lincoln-Mercury, Pasadena CA, owner, currently. **Orgs:** Mem, Black Ford Lincoln Mercury Dealers, 1978-; mem, NAACP, Pasadena Branch. **Honors/Awds:** Man of Year, State of WA, 1959; Golf Champ, Natl Public Links, 1959; Natl Intercollegiate Champ, 1960; Man of Year, Seattle WA, 1960. **Military Serv:** Army Natl Guard, private, 1960-66.

WRIGHT, WILLIAM GAILLARD
Educator. **Personal:** Born Jun 5, 1933, South Carolina; married Clara Baker. **Educ:** City Coll of NY, BA 1966; Middlebury Coll Madrid Spain, MA 1967. **Career:** City Coll of NY, lectr Spanish 1969-; Hopewell Vally Regional School Sys, teacher 1967-69; US PO, letter carrier-clerk 1958-66; NY City, Newark, NJ, educ com 1970-. **Orgs:** Chmn of bd Nghbrdh Housing Serv Newark 1977-78. **Honors/Awds:** The Newman Meml Schlshp The City Coll of NY 1966; 125th Anniver Awd Medal The City Coll of NY 1972; 4 jours fieldwork studies City Coll Students for Cultural Exch 1972-73 74-77; Brotherhood Awd Newark Human Rights Commn 1978. **Military Serv:** AUS pfc 1953-56. **Business Addr:** 138th St at Convent Ave, New York, NY 10031.

WRIGHT, WILSON, JR.
Educator. **Personal:** Born Apr 27, 1948, Prattville, AL; son of Mary Debardelabon Wright and Wilson Wright; married Malera Traylor Wright, Aug 4, 1990; children: Ursula, Karla, Tray. **Educ:** Alabama State University, Montgomery, AL, BA, 1969; Birmingham Southern College, Birmingham, AL, 1970; University of Alabama, Birmingham, DMD, 1974; Army Command General Staff College, 1989. **Career:** Fisk University, Nashville, TN, Biology, 1969-70; University of Alabama, School of Denistry, Birmingham, AL, instructor, 1974-77, asst professor, 1977-87, assoc denistry professor, 1987-93, professor, 1993-; 650th Med Det, commander, 1995. **Orgs:** Alabama Dental Society, 1975-; National Dental Association, 1975-; University of Alabama School of Denistry Alumni Association, 1974-; International Association for Dental Research, 1982-; member, Phi Phi Chapter, Omicron Kappa Upsilon, National Dental Honor Society, 1985-; Academy of General Dentistry, 1994-. **Honors/Awds:** Miles College Community Award, Miles College, 1979; awarded second place in competition, AADS meeting, Production of Dental Anatomy Videotape, 1983; recipient, International College of Denist Award, 1974. **Military Serv:** US Army, COL, 1977-; received medal of Achievement Accommodation, 1990; Army Accommodation Medal, 1996. **Business Addr:** Professor, Restorative Denistry, University of Alabama, School of Denistry, 1919 7th Ave S, Birmingham, AL 35294.

WRIGHT-BOTCHWEY, ROBERTA YVONNE
Attorney, educator. **Personal:** Born Oct 9, 1946, York, SC. **Educ:** Fisk U, BA 1967; Yale U, ISSP cert 1966; Univ MI Sch of Andrew Iii, JD. **Career:** Private Practice; NC Central Univ School of Law, asst prof corp counsel Tanzania Legal Corp Dar es Salaam Tanzania; Zambia Ltd Lusaka Zambia, sr legal asst rural devel corp. **Orgs:** Mem NC Assn of Blck Lawyers; Nat Bar Assn; Nat Conf of Black Lawyers; SC & DC Bar Assn; hon mem Delta Theta Phi; consult EPA 1976; lectr Sci Jury Sel & Evidence Workshop; legal adv Zambian Corp Del to Tel Aviv, Israel 1971; Atty Gen of Zambia Select Com to Investigate Railways 1972; Delta Sigma Theta Sor; consult Women's Prison Group 1975; consult EPA Environmental Litigation Workshop 1976; NCBL Commn to Invest Discrim Prac in Law Schs 1977; dir Councon Legal Educ Oppor Summer Inst 1977; Phi Beta Kappa 1967. **Honors/Awds:** Outstdg Young Women of Am 1976; Sydney P Raymond lectr Jackson State Univ 1977. **Business Addr:** PO Box 10646, 339 E Main, Rock Hill, SC 29730.

WRIGHTEN, JOHN H., III. **See Obituaries section.**

WYATT, ADDIE L.
Union executive, cleric, government official. **Personal:** Born Mar 8, 1924, Brookhaven, MS; daughter of Maggie Cameron and Ambrose Cameron; married Rev Claude S Wyatt Jr; children: Renaldo, Claude III. **Career:** Amalgamated Meat Cutters & Butcher Workmen of N Amer AFL-CIO, intl vp, dir womens affairs dept 1941-54; intl rep Amalgamated Meat Cutters 1968-74, dir women's affairs dept 1974-78, dir human reights dept 1978-, intl vice pres 1976-; intl vice pres UFCW-AFL-CIO 1979-84; personnel bd Chicago 1986-88; R.T.A. dir, exec vice pres Emerita CLUW, 1988. **Orgs:** Intl Adv Council of Amalgamated Meat Cutters & Butcher Workmen of N Amer AFL-CIO Union Women; co-pastor & minister of mus Vernon Park Church of God Chicago; former social ctr inst Chicago Bd of Ed; appointed to serve Protective Labor Legislative Comm of Pres Kennedy's Comm on Status of Women; former youth leader in Chicago; labor adv, co-worker Dr Martin Luther King Jr, Dr Ralph D Abernathy, Rev Jesse L Jackson; Jewish Labor Com Prog; adv & labor instr Labor Ed Roosevelt Univ; IL State AFL-CIO COPE Org; adv Citizen for Day Care; natl adv Womens Org Church of God; Coalition of Black Trade Unionists; League of Black Women; Natl Council of Negro Women; Chicago Urban League; Chicago NAACP; volunteer Youth & Comm Serv Chicago Housing Auth; Delta Sigma Theta; co-chair CBTA Woman; bd mem PUSH. **Honors/Awds:** Distinguished Labor Leaders Awd League of Black Women Woodlawn Org 1975; One of Twelve Outstanding Women of Year Time Magazine 1975; Ebony Magazine Citation 1977,80; Dr Martin Luther King Jr Labor Awd 1981; Outstanding Woman in Western Region Iota Phi Lambda; Urban Ministries Inc Awd; One of 100 Most Outstanding Black Amer Ebony Magazine 1981-84; Outstanding Woman Ladies Home Journal; Keeper of the Dream, Dr Martin Luther King Jr Center. **Business Addr:** Vernon Park Church of God, 9011 S Stony Island, Chicago, IL 60617.

WYATT, BEATRICE E.
Educator. **Personal:** Born May 23, Pittsburgh, PA; widowed. **Educ:** Virginia Union Univ, AB; Boston State Coll, MED; Michigan State Univ; New York Univ; Univ of Pittsburgh. **Career:** Lewis Middle School Boston Public Schools, admin asst principal; North Hampton County VA, teacher, guidance counseling; Dearborn Jr High School Boston, teacher, guidance advisor; Julia Ward Howe School Roxbury, teacher asst principal. **Orgs:** Charter mem Ft Hill Mental Health Assn; bd mem appointed by Gov Sargent to Boston Univ Area Mental Health Bd; pres Boston Alumni Chap Delta Sigma Theta Inc; mem Black Educ Assn of MA; past chairwoman Social Studies Coun of Boston, MA; regional coord Eastern Region Conf of Delta Sigma Theta 1974; mem Natl Coun of Negro Women 1972-74; organizer NCNW of Boston; mem Boston Guidance Counseling & MA Guidance Assn 1969; adv Coll & Univ Women of Iota Chap Delta Sigma Theta Sor 1969-72; mem First Baptist Church Boston; church school teacher, deaconess; chairwoman bd Christian Educ; mem Bicentennial Comm; past pres, present treas Woman's Soc First Baptist Church; mem Boston Children's Council. **Honors/Awds:** Neighborhood Awd Natl Coun for Christians & Jews 1972; bronze plaque for dedicated serv Iota Chap 1972; plaque Eastern Region Delta Sigma Theta outstanding leadership during Regional Conf 1974. **Business Addr:** Lewis Middle School, 131 Walnut Ave, Roxbury, MA 02119.

WYATT, CLAUDE STELL, JR.
Clergyman. **Personal:** Born Nov 14, 1921, Dallas, TX; married Addie Lorraine Cameron; children: Renaldo, Claude L. **Educ:** Attended, Wilson Coll 1955, Chicago Tchrs Coll 1956, Chicago Bapt Inst 1957; Urban Training Ctr for Christion Mission, cert 1960; Roosevelt Univ Labor Dept, cert 1974. **Career:** US PO, clerk 1947-65; Vernon Park Ch of God, reverend. **Orgs:** Consult Urban Ministries Anderson Coll IN 1978; consult for Ch Growth Com Anderson Coll 1979; bd mem Natl com of Black Churchmen 1975; bd mem Operation PUSH. **Honors/Awds:** Outstanding Leadership in REligion Operation PUSH Chicago 1973; Outstanding Bus & Professional Persons Blackbook Pubs Chicago 1978; Hon DD Degree Monrovia Univ1984. **Business Addr:** Vernon Park Church of God, 7653 S Maryland Ave, Chicago, IL 60619.

WYATT, LANCE EVERETT
Surgery resident. **Personal:** Born Jan 19, 1967, Nashville, TN; son of Drs Lewis & Gail Wyatt. **Educ:** Howard Univ, BS, 1984-88; Univ of CA, Los Angeles School of Med, MD, 1988-92; UCLA Medical Ctr, Div of General Surgery, Resident, 1992-; UCLA Div Plastic & Reconstructive Surgery, Research Fellowship, 1994-97. **Career:** Natl Inst of Health, summer research fellow, 1989; UCLA Med Ctr, internship, 1992-93, div of general surg, jr resident, 1993-94, Plastic & Reconstr Surg, sr research fellow, 1994-97, sr resident, 1997-98. **Orgs:** Surgical Resident Forum, co-founder, 1995; Amer Coll of Surgeons, participant in the candidate group; William P Longmire Surgical Soc; Soc of Black Academic Surgeons; Natl Med Assn, Morestin Soc; Amer Med Assn; The New Leaders, youth empowerment comm; Amer Soc for Bone & Mineral Research. **Honors/Awds:** UCLA Div Plastic & Reconstr Surgery, Best Basic Science Research, 1996; UCLA Div of Geriatric Med, Ralph Goldman Basic Research Award, 1996; Plastic Surg Educational Foundation, Lyndon Peer Fellow, 1996; Ebony Magazine, 50 Leaders of Tomorrow, 1995; Natl Inst of Health, Individual Natl Res Svc Award, 1995-97. **Special Achievements:** Plastic Surgery Educational Foundation Research Grant, 1995, 1997; book chap ''Lymphedema'' in Grabb & Smith's Plastic Surgery, 1997; book chap ''Lymphedema & Tumors of the Lymphatics,'' 1997; Vascular Surgery: A Comprehensive Review, Natl Presentations and Peer Reviewed publication; mentor, Angel City Links, 1990, 1995-98; KACE-Radio, Sunday Morning Live, ''Teen Sexuality,'' 1995. **Business Addr:** Senior Resident, Div of General Surgery, UCLA Medical Ctr, 10833 Le Conte Ave, Housestaff Mail Rm 16-155, Los Angeles, CA 90095, (310)825-6301.

WYATT, RONALD MICHAEL
Physican, health administrator. **Personal:** Born Mar 6, 1954, Selma, AL; son of Gladys & James Wyatt; married Pamela, Jul 28, 1984; children: Michael, Scott, Christopher. **Educ:** Univ of Alabama, Birmingham, BS, 1976, MD, 1985. **Career:** St Louis Univ School of Medicine, chief resident, 1987-88; St Louis VA Med Ctr, dir of ER, 1988-89; Peoples Health Ctr, medical dir, 1989-93; Central N Alabama Health Services, dir clinical services, 1993-; University of Alabama Birmingham School of Medicine, assistant dean. **Orgs:** National Assn of Community Health Ctrs, chair health policy comm, 1993-94; US Public Health Services, assoc recruitor, 1990-; Natl Coordinating Committee for Clinical Prevention Services, advisor, 1992-. **Honors/Awds:** US Public Health Services, Special Recognition Award, 1992; US National Health Services Corp, Exemplary Service, 1992. **Military Serv:** US Army, captain, 1989-; Army Commendation, Desert Storm. **Business Addr:** Huntsville Internal Medicine Associates, 250-220 Chateau Dr, Huntsville, AL 35801.

WYATT, S. MARTIN, III (JAMAL ABDUL-KABIR)
Journalist. **Personal:** Born Jul 31, 1941, Memphis, TN; son of Nadine Bragg Poindexter and S Martin Wyatt II; married Joyce Hanson, Aug 17, 1990; children: Marcus, Sabriya, Jamila, Aisha. **Educ:** Vallejo Junior College, Vallejo, CA, 1956-60; Univ of Washington, Seattle, WA, 1960-62. **Career:** KYAC Radio, Seattle, WA, sales mgr, 1966-72; KING-TV, Seattle, WA, sports anchor/writer, 1972-76; WRC-TV, Washington, DC, sports anchor/writer, 1976-80; KGO-TV, San Francisco, CA, sports anchor/writer, 1980-85; WMAR-TV, Baltimore MD, sports anchor/writer, 1986-88; Black Entertainment TV, Washington, DC, producer/anchor/writer, 1986-89; KGO-TV, San Francisco, CA, sports anchor/writer, 1989-. **Orgs:** Mem, Natl Assn Black Journalists, 1986-; mem, Bay Area Black Jour-

nalists, 18981-. **Honors/Awds:** Emmy Award, ''Bill Russell: A Man Alone,'' 1976; Access Award Finalist, ''Voyage of Courage,'' 1987; Sigma Delta Chi Winner for Series, ''Thoroughbred Breeding in MD,'' 1987; Martin Wyatt Day Declared in Seattle, WA, King County, May 27, 1976; 100 Black Men, Leaders in Action Awd, 1994; Delta Sigma Theta Sorority, Image Awd for Journalism 1995; Omega Boys & Girls Club, Annual Street Soldier Awd Winner, 1996; Vallejo Junior College, Solano College Athletic Hall of Fame, 1996. **Military Serv:** US Army, corporal, Special Commendation for Service in Vietnam, 1964-66. **Business Addr:** Sports Director, KGO-TV, Channel 7, 900 Front St, San Francisco, CA 94111.

WYATT, WILLIAM N. (BILL)
Agency director. **Personal:** Born Oct 21, 1953, Canton, OH; son of Helen Hood-Wyatt and Calvin W Wyatt; divorced; children: Chancelor, Shellie. **Educ:** Kent State University, business administration, 1967-72. **Career:** A-WY Entertainment, president/chief executive officer, currently; Dick Clark Agency, Urban Contemporary Division, director, currently. **Orgs:** Elks; Negro Oldtimers Baseball Hall of Fame. **Home Addr:** 6619 W Leland Way, #212, Hollywood, CA 90028. **Business Phone:** (310)288-5716.

WYATT CUMMINGS MOORE, THELMA LAVERNE
Judge. **Personal:** Born Jul 6, 1945, Amarillo, TX; daughter of Annie Lavernia Lott Wyatt (deceased) and James Odis Wyatt Sr (deceased); married Luke C Moore (deceased); children: Khari Sekou Cummings, Ayanna Rashida Cummings. **Educ:** Univ of California, BA 1965; Illinois Inst of Tech Fellowship in Psychodynamics 1966; Emory University Sch of Law, JD (with distinction) 1968-71. **Career:** Bd of Educ City of Chicago, tchr 1965-67; Atlanta Urban League, field rep 1967-69; Thelma Wyatt, atty 1971-74; Ward & Wyatt, atty 1974-77; Municipal Ct of Atlanta, judge 1977-80; City Ct of Atlanta, judge 1980-, State Court of Fulton County, judge, 1985-90; Superior Court of Fulton County, GA, judge, 1990-. **Orgs:** Georgia State Bar Assn, 1971-; American Bar Assn; National Bar Assn; past chairman, National Judicial Council; historian, Gate City Bar Assn, 1990-; Georgia Assn of Black Women Attorneys; Atlanta Bar Assn; American Judicature Society; American Judges Assn; Phi Alpha Delta; Alpha Kappa Alpha; life member, NAACP; Emory University, board of trustees; National Ctr for State Courts, board of directors. **Honors/Awds:** Emory Medal, 1992; WSB Living Legend Award, 1992; Thurgood Marshall Award, 1991; Gate City Bar Association President's Award, 1990; Government Award, Atlanta Business League, 1990; Outstanding Public Serv Award, Georgia Coalition of Black Women Inc, 1984; Outstanding Jurist Award, Gate City Bar Assn, 1983; Distinguished Serv, Natl Judicial Council, 1982, 1983, 1986, 1988; Essence Award for Outstanding Contributions, Essence magazine, 1982; Order of the Coif, Bryan Soc, Pi Delta Phi, Appellate Advocacy, Amer Jurisprudence Awds in Comm Law, Mortgages and Admin Law, John Hay Whitney Fellow, State of Illinois Fellow, Natl Urban League Fellow; 1st Distinguished Alumni Award, Emory BLSA, 1986; Emory Law School, Distinguished Alumni Awd, 1996; numerous other awards. **Business Addr:** Judge, Superior Court of Fulton County, 185 Central Avenue, SW, Suite T-4905, Atlanta, GA 30303.

WYCHE, LENNON DOUGLAS, JR.
Physician. **Personal:** Born Jul 13, 1946, Washington, DC; married Judith. **Educ:** Howard U, 1966; George Wash U, BS 1969; Meharry Med Sch, MD 1973. **Career:** Resd diagnostic radiology 1976-; USPHS Clinic, gen med ofcr 1974-46; USPHS, intern 1973-74. **Orgs:** Mem Alpha Phi Alpha Frat; Am Coll Radiology; NMA; jr mem Am Roentgen Ray Soc. **Honors/Awds:** Personal Serv Awd USPHS. **Military Serv:** USPHS lt comdr 1973-76. **Business Addr:** Dept Radiology Hermann Hosp, Houston, TX 77030.

WYCHE, PAUL H., JR.
Business Executive. **Personal:** Born Oct 16, 1946, Miami, FL; son of Gracie Thompson Wyche and Paul Howard Wyche; married Louise Everett, Dec 11, 1971; children: Shaina Nicole, Kimberly Elise. **Educ:** Miami-Dade Jr Coll; Univ Miami; Southeastern Univ, BS, public admin; Univ of Southern California & Southeastern Univ, graduate study business & pub. **Career:** Safety-Kleen Corp, 1993-, vp, corporate public affairs and governmental relations, 1991-93, dir, community relations and governmental affairs; E I du Pont de Nemours Co, public affairs rep 1980-82, public affairs consultant, 1982-88, public affairs manager, 1988-91; Natl Black News Serv Inc, pres dir 1972-84; US Environmental Protection Agency, assoc public affairs dir 1978-80, constituent devel & coordinator 1977-78, exec asst pub affairs dir 1975-77; US Rep Moakley, sr legislative asst 1973-75; US Rep Pepper (Dem-FL), legislative asst 1971-73; FL Memorial Coll, public relations dir 1970-71; The Miami Times, assoc editor 1970-71; Economic Opportunity Program Miami, dir public affairs 1968-70; WPLG-TV Miami, program moderator 1970-71; reporter, Miami News, 1965-68. **Orgs:** Life mem, NAACP; bd mem, Mt Vernon-Lee Enter Inc; Natl Urban League; PUSH; Sigma Delta Chi, 1968-; Natl Capital Press Clubs; Natl Young Demo Clubs; bd mem, Cncl Catholic Laity; pres, Good Shepherd Parish Cncl; Cong Staff Club; Admin Asst Assn; bd mem, S FL Econ Oppor Cncl; Dade Co Drug Abuse Advisory Bd; Jaycees; founding pres, chairman of the board, NW Miami Jaycees; vice pres, United Blck Fedn Dade Co; pres, FL Public Affairs Dirs; bd mem, Black Chamber of Commerce; pres, Caths for Shared Responsibility; pres, Good Shepherd Coun of the Laity; dir, Amer Heart Assn, 1982-85; trustee, West End City Day Care Nursery, 1983-85; chmn, Brandywine Professional Assn, 1984-91; dir, Delaware Alliance of Professional Women, 1984-86; pres, Civic Assn of Surrey Park, 1985-86; dir, Boy Scouts of America, 1985-90; pres, Opportunity ter Inc, 1986-90; vice chairman Govt Relations, bd of dirs, United Way of DE, 1987-90, chmn Govt Relations, United Way, 1987-89; dir, Mental Health Assn, 1988-90; dir, Layton Home for the Aged, 1988-90; trustee, Medical Center of Delaware Foundation, 1988-93; executive cmte, Human Services Partnership, 1989-91; dir, Delaware Community Investment Corporation, 1989-91; bd of dirs, Natl Assn of Chemical Recyclers, 1994-, vp, 1995-; Natl Assn of Manufacturers, Natl Public Affairs Steering Committee, 1994-; pres, bd of dir National Association of Chemical Recyclers, 1996-; bd of dir, Public Affairs Council, 1997-; mem, Conference Boards Corporate Strategies Council, 1997-; State Government Relations Council, 1995-. **Honors/Awds:** Awards reporting & broadcasting 1964, 1967, 1968; Silver Knight Award 1964; Superior Performance, US EPA, 1978; Outstanding Professionalism, Omega Psi Phi Fraternity, 1988; Outstanding Black Achiever in Business & Industry, YMCA, 1989; Outstanding Community Service, United Way of Delaware, 1990. **Business Addr:** VP, Corp Public Aff & Governmental Rel, Safety-Kleen Corp, 1000 N Randall Rd, Elgin, IL 60123-7857.

WYCHE, VERA ROWENA
Educational administrator (retired). **Personal:** Born Feb 2, 1923, Rowus Run, PA; married Julian C Wyche (deceased); children: Evangeline. **Educ:** Cheyney State, BS 1944; Howard Univ, MA 1945; Univ of MI, PhD 1974. **Career:** Detroit Public Schools, teacher 1949-63, admin principal 1963-71; Univ of MI, lecturer ed admin 1971-74; Eastern MI Univ, adjunct prof, School Housing, admin assoc to supt 1976-87. **Orgs:** Bd mem, Bilalian Child Devlpmnt Cntr, 1977-82; bd mem, Univ of MI Women, Detroit Chptr 1, 1976-84; mem, Natl Health & Safety Task Force, 1980-84; mem, Internatl Platform Assoc, 1980-; chr ed dev com, Nat'l Assn of Negro Bus & Prof Woman, 1981-83; mem, Detroit Woman's Forum, 1982-; mem, Congressional Advisory Comm, 1983-. **Honors/Awds:** Excell in Ldrshp BUF 1980; Woman of Excell NANBPW 1982. **Home Addr:** 16 Foxwood Dr, #BB, Morris Plains, NJ 07950-2650.

WYCLIFF, NOEL DON
Journalist. **Personal:** Born Dec 17, 1946, Liberty, TX; son of Wilbert A & Emily A Wycliff; married Catherine A Wycliff, Sep 25, 1982; children: Matthew William, Grant Erdmann. **Educ:** University of Notre Dame, BA, 1969; University of Chicago, 1969-70. **Career:** Chicago Sun-Times, reporter; The New York Times, editorial writer, 1985-90; Chicago Tribune, deputy editorial page editor, 1990-91, editorial page editor, 1991-. **Orgs:** National Association of Minority Media Executives, 1991-; American Society of Newspaper Editors, 1991-; National Association of Black Journalists; ASNE Writing Awds Committee, 1995-97; University of Notre Dame, College of Arts & Letters, advisory council, 1989-. **Honors/Awds:** ASNE Distinguished Writing Award for Editorials, 1997; Pulitzer Prize juror Finalist for the Pulitzer Prize for Editorial Writing, 1996; Chicago Journalism Hall of Fame, Inductee, 1996. **Special Achievements:** Occasional Contributor to Commonweal Magazaine, 1990-. **Business Addr:** Editorial Page Editor, Chicago Tribune, 435 N Michigan Ave, Chicago, IL 60611, (312)222-3431.

WYKE, JOSEPH HENRY
Executive director. **Personal:** Born Jan 9, 1928, New York, NY; married Margaret Elaine Whiteman. **Educ:** City Coll NYC, BSaS 1949; NY U, MA 1958, doctorate cand. **Career:** Westchester Coalition Inc, exec dir 1976-; Coll of M Ed Dentistry NJ, asst admintr 1975-76; Urban Coalition of Met Wilmington, DE, exec vice pres 1970-75; Urban League of Grtr New Brunswick, exec dir 1966-70. **Orgs:** Bd mem Afro-Am Cultural Found 1977-; chmn bd dirs Aspire Industr Inc 1978-; bd mem Westchester Comm Serv Councı 1979-; mem ''Edges'' 1978-; mem Julius A Thomas Soc 1978-. **Honors/Awds:** Recip Apprec for Serv Paul Robeson awd Urban League Grtr New Brunswick 1980; Martin Luther King Jr Awd Greenburgh Comm Cntr 1980. **Business Addr:** Westchester Coalition Inc, 235 Main St, White Plains, NY 10601.

WYKLE, MAY LOUISE HINTON
Educator, educational administrator. **Personal:** Born Feb 11, 1934, Martins Ferry, OH; daughter of Florence A Randall Hinton and John R Hinton; married William Lenard; children: Andra Sims, Caron. **Educ:** Ruth Brant School of Nursing, Diploma RN 1956; Western Reserve Coll Cleveland OH BSN 1962; Case Western Reserve Univ, MSN Psych Nursing 1969, PhD Ed 1981. **Career:** Cleveland Psychiatric Inst, staff nurse, head nurse, suprv 1956-64, dir nursing ed 1964; Univ Hospitals of Cleveland, admin assoc; Center on Aging & Health, director, associate dean for community affairs; Research Psychiatric Inst, MD Self-Style-compliance, NIA, black & white caregiver intervention, NIH; Case Western Reserve Univ, asst prof psych nursing, 1975, prof chair person, dir psych nursing, administrator assoc, gerontological nursing, 1989-. **Orgs:** Clinical nurse spec Fairhill Mental Health Ctr 1970; nursing consult VA Med Ctr 1980-85; bd mem Eliz Bryant Nursing Home 1983; proj dir Robert Wood Johnson Teaching Nursing Home; Research-Self Care among The Elderly; chairperson research committee Margaret Hagner House Nursing Home; Professional Advisory Brd-ARDA Org Cleveland OH; board of directors, Judson Retirement Center, 1989-; board member, Golden Age Center, Cleveland, OH, 1991; editorial board, Generations Magazine, 1991; National Panel on Alzheimers Disease, 1992. **Honors/Awds:** Alumni Awd Martins Ferry 1956; Sigma Theta Tau Nursing Hon Soc 1966; Disting Teaching Awd FPB School of Nursing 1975; Merit Awd Cleveland Council of Black Nurses 1983; Geriatric Mental Health Academic Award, 1983-86, Cleveland Pacesetter Award, 1986; Distinguished Alumni Award- Frances Payne Bolton School of Nursing, CWRU, 1986; Florence Cellar Professorship Gerontological Nursing F.P.B. School of Nursing CWRU 1989; John S. Diekoff Teaching Excellence Award (graduate) CWRU 1989; Wykle, M. & Dunkle R. Decision Making in Long Term Care 1988; fellow, Gerontological Society of America, 1991-; Distinguished Nurse Scholar, Lecturer, National Center for Nursing Research, 1991; Belle Sherwin Distinguished Nurse Award, 1992; fellow, American Academy of Nursing. **Special Achievements:** Co-author, Stress and Health among the Elderly, 1992. **Home Addr:** 34552 Summerset Rd, Cleveland, OH 44139-5635. **Business Addr:** Florence Cellar Professor, Gerontological Nursing, Case Western Reserve Univ, Frances Payne Bolton School of Nursing, 2121 Abington Rd, Cleveland, OH 44106.

WYMAN, DEVIN
Professional football player. **Personal:** Born Aug 29, 1973, East Palo Alto, CA. **Educ:** Kentucky State, attended. **Career:** New England Patriots, defensive tackle, 1996-. **Business Addr:** Professional Football Player, New England Patriots, 60 Washington St, Foxboro Stadium, Foxboro, MA 02035, (508)543-7911.

WYNN, ALBERT
Congressman. **Personal:** Born Sep 10, 1951. **Educ:** Georgetown Univ, JD. **Career:** Attorney; Maryland State Senate, 1987-92; US House of Representatives, congressman, 1992-. **Business Addr:** Congressman, US House of Representatives, 423 Cannon HOB, Washington, DC 20515-2004, (202)225-8699.

WYNN, CORDELL
College president. **Personal:** Born Feb 3, 1927, Eatonton, GA. **Career:** Stillman College, Tuscaloosa AL, president, 1981-97. **Orgs:** West Alabama Chamber of Commerce, chairman.

WYNN, DANIEL WEBSTER
Educator. **Personal:** Born Mar 19, 1919, Wewoka, OK; married Lillian Robinson; children: Marian Danita, Patricia Ann. **Educ:** Langston U, AB 1944, BD 1944; Howard U, MA 1945; Boston U, PhD 1954. **Career:** The United Meth Church, dir office of coll support bd of high educ ministry 1965-; Tuskegee Inst, chaplain prof of phil & relig 1955-65; Langston Univ, dean of stud 1954-55; Tuskegee Inst, acting chaplain asso prof of phil relig 1953-54; Bishop Coll, asst prof dean school of religion 1946-53; Kentucky St Coll, acting chaplain instr of social econ 1945-46; Natl Assn of Coll & Univ Chaplains & Directors of Religios Life Newletter, editor 1960-63; Directory of Amer Scholors Vol Iv 1964 69 74; Contemporary Authors Vols 25 28 1971; The Writers Directory, 1972. **Orgs:** Life mem Tuskegee Civic Assn; life mem NAACP; life mem Kappa Alpha Psi Frat. **Honors/Awds:** Author 5 books; contributor one encyclopedia 1 book & many jours; hon DD Eden Theol Sem 1959; hon LHD UT State Univ 1975; distngsd Alumnus Awd Langston Univ 1963; Man of the Yr Muskogee Serv League 1964; Rust Coll Shield for Ldrshp in Religion & Soc Devel 1974; serv plaque Wiley Coll 1973; cert of recog for Rsrch in Educ Phi Delta Kappa 1979. **Business Addr:** PO Box 871, Corner Grand Ave & 19th St, Nashville, TN 37202.

WYNN, GLADYS W.
Educator (retired). **Personal:** Born Apr 6, 1923, Suffolk, VA; daughter of Roxanna W Whitney and Edgar A Whitney; married Robert D Wynn, Jul 20, 1985. **Educ:** Johnson C Smith University, BA, 1944; Howard University, attended, 1947; University of Michigan, MA, 1956, art/lettering courses, 1957-66. **Career:** Sussex County School Board, principal, teacher, 1944-45; Southampton County School Board, principal, teacher, 1945-46; Louisa Public School, English, French, teacher, 1946-47; Port Deposit Public School, fourth grade teacher, 1947-48; Somerset School Board, English teacher, 1948-53; Suffolk City School Board, teacher of English and volunteer teacher of art after school hours, 1953-60; Norfolk Public School Board, teacher of English and art, 1960-88; teacher of In-School Suspension, 1985-88. **Orgs:** Councilof English Teachers, beginning 1953; Norfolk Education Association, life mem; First Bapt Ch, Scholarship Comm, Suffolk, VA; Missionary Circle, Helping Hand Club; Lily of the Valley; Suffolk Alumnae Chap, Delta Sigma Theta Sor; volunteered as a motivational correspondent for At Risk Students in the Norfolk Public Schools, 1997. **Honors/Awds:** Greenwood High School, Miss Greenwood High School, 1951, Teacher of the Year, 1952; Norview

Junior High, Teacher of the Year, 1968; Campostella Junior High, A-Team Trophy, 1985; Norfolk Public Schools, All-City Teaching Team, 1986, Teacher of the Year. **Special Achievements:** Headed first committee to carry group of students from Booker T Washington High School of Suffolk, VA, to New York City for educational tour; selected as discipline specialist by principal of school, circa 1980; honoree, volunteer for over 400 hours, 1989; received citation from superintendent of Norfolk Public Schools, 1988. **Home Addr:** 844 Ingleside Rd, Norfolk, VA 23502, (804)466-8057.

WYNN, LAMETTA K.
City official. **Personal:** married Thomas H. Wynn (deceased) (deceased); children: ten. **Career:** City of Clinton IA, mayor, currently. **Orgs:** Rotary International; bd of trustees, Mt Clare College; NAACP; Bethel AME Church (Steward); American Nurses Assn; Iowa Nurses Assn; served on Clinton Community School Board for twelve years, three years as pres; past chair, Iowa Commission on the Status of African Americans. **Honors/Awds:** Woman of Action, YWCA; Liberty Bell Award, Clinton County Bar Assn; honorary doctorate degree, Teikyo-Marycrest University; Outstanding Citizen Award, Iowa Gov Branstad; Named by Newsweek Magazine as one of 25 Most Dynamic Mayors in America. **Special Achievements:** First African-American to be elected mayor of Clinton (IA); first African-American woman to be elected mayor in Iowa. **Business Addr:** Mayor, City of Clinton, P O Box 2958, Clinton, IA 52733, (319)242-2144.

WYNN, MALCOLM
Police officer (retired). **Personal:** Born May 31, 1940, Greenville, MS; son of Roberta Hillard and Harry Wynn; married Billie Jean Moore, Feb 18, 1957; children: Caroline Ann, Anthony, Geraldine, Malcolm, Patrick Fitzgerald. **Educ:** MS Law Enforcement Training Academy, certificate, 1969; LSU Law Enforcement Institute, certificate, 1972; Delta State Univ, Cleveland, MS, 1972-74; FBI Natl Academy, Quantico, VA, certificate, 1977. **Career:** US Gypsum, Greenville, MS, finishing dept, 1965-68; Greenville Police Dept, Greenville, MS, police officer; chief of police, 1986-89; Greenville Public Schools, Greenville, MS, student activities supervisor. **Orgs:** Mem, Washington Boys Club, 1974-1980; mem, Greenville Chamber of Commerce, 1987-89. **Honors/Awds:** Outstanding Service, Elks Serene Lodge #567, 1978; Outstanding Service, Washington County Youth Court, 1975; Safety Award for Loyal & Devoted Service, Les Bonhur De Femmes, 1988; Civic Award, Kappa Tau Theta Sorority, 1988; Community Service Award, WDDT Radio Station, 1987; Public Service Award, Star Bethlehem Church, 1988.

WYNN, PRATHIA HALL
Minister. **Personal:** Born Jul 29, 1940, Philadelphia, PA; married Ralph; children: Simone, Dubois. **Educ:** Temple U, BA 1965; Princeton Theol Sem, MDiv 1981. **Career:** Mt Sharon Baptist Church Phila, PA, pastor 1978-; Solar Energy Com Resources Center of Hempstead Com Adiction Prog, cons. **Orgs:** Dir H Empstead Comm Action Prog; dir Nat Counc of Negro Women Training Inst 1971-72; prgm spclst 1969-71; asst dir Proj Womanpower 1967-68; NE FieldRep Proj Womanpower 1966-67; SNCC 1962-66; Admissions consult Coll for Human Servs; prgm as so Am Friends Serv Com; youth employ coord asst Philadelphia Counc for Comm Advncmt Sch bd trustee 1971-77; pres Bd of Educ Union Free Sch Dist #8 1973-77. **Business Addr:** Mt Sharon Bapt Church, 1609 W Girard Ave, Philadelphia, PA.

WYNN, RENALDO
Professional football player. **Personal:** Born Sep 3, 1974. **Educ:** Notre Dame. **Career:** Jacksonville Jaguars, defensive tackle, 1997-. **Special Achievements:** NFL Draft, First round pick, #21, 1997. **Business Addr:** Professional Football Player, Jacksonville Jaguars, 1 Stadium Pl, Jacksonville, FL 32202, (904)633-6000.

WYNN, ROBERT L., JR.
Business executive. **Personal:** Born Jan 25, 1929, Atlanta, GA; married Ethel Crawford; children: Teresa, Richard, Judith. **Educ:** Clark Coll, BA 1953; State Univ of IA, MS 1960. **Career:** Mainstream Computer Inc Memphis, pres 1968-72; Data Mgmt Sci Corp Memphis, pres; Universal Life Ins Co, vp. **Orgs:** Bd of dir Mutual Fed Savings & Loan Assoc 1970-72; life mem NAACP, Kappa Alpha Psi; mem Beta Kappa Chi, Alpha Upsilon Omega, YMCA, Shelby Cty Health & Ed Fac Bd; bd of dir Jr Achievement of Memphis, Natl Ins Assoc, Natl Bus League, Natl Mathematical Soc. **Military Serv:** AUS 1st lt 1955. **Business Addr:** Vice President, Actuary, Universal Life Insurance Co, 480 Linden Ave, Memphis, TN 38126.

WYNN, SYLVIA J.
Vice president/marketing & sales. **Personal:** Born Sep 30, 1941, New York, NY; daughter of Lucinda Townes Wynn and Frank Wynn. **Educ:** Hunter Coll CUNY, attended 1966-70; Simmons Middle Mgmt Prog, Certificate 1979. **Career:** The Gillette Co, product mgr 1978-81; Intl Playtex Inc, product mgr 1981-83; Johnson Products Co Inc, group prod mgr 1983-85, dir of mktg 1985-86, vice pres mktg & sales 1986-87; SJW Enterprises Chicago, IL pres. **Orgs:** Mem AMA; tutor Boston Half-Way House 1978-81; founding mem & chairperson Target Advertising Professionals. **Honors/Awds:** Boston Black Achiever Awd 1979. **Business Addr:** Pres, SJW Enterprises, 333 E Ontario St, Suite 1302B, Chicago, IL 60611.

WYNN, THOMAS HAROLD, SR.
Association administration, publisher. **Personal:** Born Jan 1, 1931, Brooklyn, NY; son of Clara Wynn and Thomas Scott Wynn; married Lauri Johnson Wynn, Feb 6, 1953; children: Cynthia, Thomas Jr, Spencer, Hillary, W Aaron. **Educ:** Virginia Union Univ, Richmond, VA, BS, 1952, Roosevelt Univ, Chicago, IL, 1957. **Career:** National Assn for Black Veterans, director of organization development, publisher, Eclipse newspaper, 1972-; Social Development Commission, director of veterans coordination, 1973-. **Orgs:** Service to Military Families Committee, Greater Milwaukee Chapter American Red Cross, 1970-; Council on Veteran Programs, WI Dept of Veterans Affairs, 1970-; 1st vice president, USO, 1990-; midwest rep, National Council of Churches, Vietnam Generation Ministries, 1973-85; Milwaukee County Veterans Commission, chairman, 1991-; Center for Veterans Issues Ltd, president, chief executive officer, 1991-. **Honors/Awds:** Community Development, 1990 Veterans Braintrust, US House of Representatives; Commendation Outstanding Achievement, WI Dept of Veterans Affairs, 1990; Community Service, Federal Employees, 1988; Cut the Red Tape, Rutgers Univ, 1984; Outstanding Service to Veterans of America, National Veteran Administration, 1972; Veterans Roundtable Participant, Presidential Transition Team, Little Rock, Dec 18, 1992. **Military Serv:** Army, Corporal, 1952-54; Good Conduct Medal, 1954. **Business Addr:** Director, Organization Development, National Assn for Black Veterans Inc, PO Box 11432, Milwaukee, WI 53211-0432.

WYNN, VALREE FLETCHER
Educator. **Personal:** Born May 9, 1922, Rockwall, TX; daughter of Alice Fletcher and Will Fletcher; widowed; children: Phail Jr, Michael David. **Educ:** Langston University, BA, 1943; Oklahoma State University, MA, 1951, PhD, 1976. **Career:** Lawton Board of Education, elementary and high school teacher, 1944-48, 1960-66; Cameron University, assistant professor, associate professor, professor, 1966-85, professor emeritus, 1985-. **Orgs:** Alpha Kappa Alpha, 1942-, past chapter basileus, international constitution committee, 1978-82, international honorary members/awards committee, 1990-93; Phi Kappa Phi Honor Society, 1985-; Phi Delta Kappa Honor Society, 1973-; board of directors: Lawton Public Schools Foundation, 1992-, US Senator David Boren's Foundation for Excellence, 1985-, Hospice, 1985-; State Martin Luther King Jr Holiday Commission, 1992-; Board of Regents of Oklahoma Colleges, mem & past president, 1985-93. **Honors/Awds:** Lawton Chamber of Commerce, Professor of the Year, 1985; St John's Baptist Church, Woman of the Year, 1992; Delta Sigma Theta, Outstanding Educator, 1985; Cameron University, Outstanding Service Award, 1993, Valree F Wynn Scholarship, 1985-; Oklahoma State University, Graduate Excellence Award, 1970-73; NAFEO, Distinguished Alumnus, 1990; Outstanding Woman of Comanche County, 1995; Cameron University Faculty Hall of Fame, 1996; Oklahoma Women's Hall of Fame, 1996; numerous others. **Home Addr:** 6901 Sprucewood Dr, Lawton, OK 73505.

WYNN, WILLIAM AUSTIN, JR.
Association executive. **Personal:** Born Nov 6, 1937, Sanford, FL; married Evelyn M Harris. **Educ:** Bethune Cookman Coll, BS 1961. **Career:** Urban Ventures SBIC, pres; Inner City Dev Found, pres; Untd Way Am, vp; Un Way of Dade Co, budget dir; Gr Miami Coalition Inc, exec vp; Econ Opps Prog Inc, asso dir. **Orgs:** Mem State Manpower Commn; State Human Rel Commn; dir Nat Ind Bank Pres Urban Ventures Inc; mem Fam Hlth Cntr; Tacolcy Youth Cntr; OIC. **Honors/Awds:** Nom Man of Yr 1974. **Business Addr:** Honorary Consul, Hon Consulate of Barbados, 741 NW 62nd St, Miami, FL 33150.

WYNNE, DANA
Professional basketball player. **Personal:** Born Feb 2, 1975. **Educ:** Seton Hall Univ. **Career:** Colorado Xplosion, forward, 1997-. **Business Addr:** Professional Basketball Player, Colorado Xplosion, 800 Grant St, Ste 410, Denver, CO 80203, (303)832-2225.

WYNNE, MARVELL
Professional baseball player. **Personal:** Born Dec 17, 1959, Chicago, IL. **Career:** Pittsburgh Pirates, outfielder, 1983-85; San Diego Padres, outfielder, 1986-89; Chicago Cubs, outfielder, 1989-90; Hanshin Tigers, Japanese Baseball League, 1990-. **Business Addr:** Professional Baseball Player, Chicago Cubs, 1060 Addison St, W, Wrigley Field, Chicago, IL 60613-4397.

WYNNS, CORRIE (CORYLISS)
Journalist. **Personal:** Born Jan 17, 1958, St Louis, MO; daughter of Helen De Wanda Foree Wynns and Rufus Wynns (deceased). **Educ:** Indiana University, Bloomington, IN, BA, 1983. **Career:** WKXI-AM, Jackson, MS, chief reporter, 1982; AP radio network, Washington, DC, news clerk, 1984; KEEL-AM, Shreveport, LA, producer/reporter/anchor, 1984-85; KDKS-FM, Shreveport, LA, News Director, 1985; Sheridan Broadcasting Network, Pittsburgh, PA, freelance correspondent, 1985-87; WAWA-AM, Milwaukee, WI, news director, 1985-87; WMAQ-AM, outside reporter, 1988-90, inside reporter, writer, 1990-92, editor, 1992-. **Orgs:** Member, National Assn of Black Journalists, 1979-; co-founder, Indiana University Black Telecommunications Assn, 1980; 2nd vice president, Milwaukee Section National Council of Negro Women, 1988. **Honors/Awds:** Journalism Award, Radio Series, What About the Father, National Assn of Black Journalists, 1987; Image Award, Milwaukee, Wisconsin, Career Youth Development, 1986; International Radio and Television Society, College Conference, 1987; Natl Assn of Black Journalists, International Reporting, Radio Series, South Africa Referendum, 1992. **Business Addr:** Journalist, WMAQ/AM 670, 455 Cityfront Plaza, 6th Floor, NBC Tower, Chicago, IL 60611, (312)245-6000.

WYNTER, LEON E.
Journalist, writer. **Personal:** Born Aug 30, 1953, New York, NY; son of Sylvia Juredini Wynter and Rupert Wynter; divorced. **Educ:** Yale University, New Haven, CT, BA, Psychology, 1974; New York University, New York, NY, MBA, Economics, 1979; New York University, New York, NY, Journalism, 1979-80. **Career:** Manufacturers Hanover Trust Corp, NY, lending officer corporate banking, 1974-79; Washington Post, Washington, DC, staff writer, 1980-84; Wall Street Journal, Dow Jones & Co, NY, staff reporter, 1984-; Baruch Coll, City Univ of New York, assoc prof of English/journalism, 1994-; Natl Public Radio, commentator "All Things Considered," 1993-. **Orgs:** 1989 Convention Committee, New York Assn of Black Journalists. **Honors/Awds:** Outstanding Communicator, Natl Black MBA Assn, 1992. **Business Addr:** Staff Reporter, The Wall Street Journal, 200 Liberty St, New York, NY 10281.

WYRE, STANLEY MARCEL
Educational administrator, educator. **Personal:** Born Mar 31, 1953, Detroit, MI; son of Mervell Wyre and Nathaniel Wyre; married Jerri Kailimai Wyre, 1988; children: Stanley III. **Educ:** Lawrence Institute of Technology, BS, 1976; Detroit College of Law, JD, 1984. **Career:** Walbridge Aldinger Co, project estimator, 1976-78; Palmer Smith Co., senior construction estimator/director, 1979-83; Charfoos, Christensen & Archer PC, attorney-at-law, 1984; Barton-Malow Co, construction manager, 1984-87; professional photographer; Detroit College of Law, adjunct professor, 1985-; Lawrence Institute of Technology, assistant professor, 1985-; Detroit Public Schools, assistant superintendent, 1992-. **Orgs:** American Arbitrator Association, arbitrator. **Business Addr:** Assistant Superintendent, Physical Plant, Detroit Public Schools, 5057 Woodward Ave, School Center Bldg, Ste 520, Detroit, MI 48202, (313)494-1770.

WYRICK, FLOYD I.
Educator. **Personal:** Born May 26, 1932, Chgo. **Educ:** Chicago State U, BE 1954; DePaul U, MA 1963; Univ of IL, PhD 1972; Phi Delta Kappa; Kappa Delta Pi. **Career:** Calumet HS Chicago Bd Educ, prin co-dir; Chicago Public School, teacher; Chicago City Coll; Northwestern Univ; Booz Allen & Hamilton, mgmt conselor; Adam & Assoc; Mitchell Watkins & Assoc. **Orgs:** Mem Nat Alli of Black Sch Educ; Am Assn of Sch Adminstrs; Nat Assn of Scndry Sch Prins; Samuel B Stratton Educ Assn; mem Am Civil Libs Union; People Unit to Save Human; Alpha Phi Alpha Frat; Comm Fund of Metro Chgo. **Military Serv:** AUS 1954-56. **Business Addr:** 8131 S May St, Chicago, IL 60620.

Y

YANCEY, ASA G., SR.
Hospital administrator, physician. **Personal:** Born in Atlanta, GA; son of Daisy L Sherard Yancey and Arthur H Yancey; married Carolyn E Dunbar Yancey, Dec 28, 1944; children: Arthur H II, MD, Carolyn L, MD, Caren L Yancey-Covinton, Asa G Jr, MD. **Educ:** Morehouse Coll, BS 1937; Univ MI, MD 1941. **Career:** Vet Admin Hosp Tuskegee AL, chief surg 1948-58; Hughes Spalding Hosp, chf surg 1958-72; Grady Mem Hosp, med dir 1972-89; Emory Univ Sch Med, assc dean 1972-89; Georgia Medical Care Foundation Inc, associate medical director, 1989-91; Emory Univ School of Medicine, prof of surgery emeritus; Morehouse School of Medicine, clinical prof of surgery. **Orgs:** Bd trustee GA Div Am Cancer Soc; fellow Am Coll Surgeons; diplomate Am Bd Surg; ed bd Jrnl of Natl Med Assn 1960-80; Am Surg Assn; Southern Surg Assn; Atlanta Bd of Ed 1967-77; life mem, golden heritage mem NAACP; Fulton-DeKalb Hospital Authority, the trustee body of Grady Memorial Hospital. **Honors/Awds:** Recip Distinguished Serv Morehouse Coll; Service Awd Atlanta Inquirer; Aven Cup; Hon Doctor of Science, Morehouse College; Hon Doctor of Science, Howard University. **Special Achievements:** Author, "A Modification of the Swenson Operation for Congenital Megacolon," Journal of the Natl Med Assn, Sep 1952, published 10 years prior to Soave's publication of the same operation. **Military Serv:** US Army 1st lt Medical Corp 1941. **Home Addr:** 2845 Engle Rd NW, Atlanta, GA 30318-7216.

YANCEY, CAROLYN LOIS
Pediatrician, pediatric rheumatologist. **Personal:** Born Sep 12, Tuskegee, AL; daughter of Dr and Mrs Asa G Yancey Sr. **Educ:** Spelman Coll/Atlanta Univ, BS 1968-72; Univ of Edinburgh Scotland UK, attended 1971-72; Howard Univ Coll of Medicine, MD 1976. **Career:** Univ of PA Childrens Hosp of Phila, resident 1976-79, fellow pediatric rheumatology 1979-81, instructor of pediatrics 1980-81, clinical asst prof of pediatrics 1981-82; Howard Univ Dept of Peds and Child Health, model practice coord 1982-83, clinical asst prof peds 1982-; Walter Reed Army Medical Ctr, clinical asst prof peds 1985-; George Washington Univ Sch of Medicine, asst clinical prof of child health & develop 1987-; Ped Rheum, Kaiser Permanente, Mid Atlantic, dir, 1983-94; CIGNA Health Care, Mid Atlantic, assoc med dir, 1994-. **Orgs:** Elected to Section of Rheumatology Amer Acad of Pediatrics 1983; diplomate and fellow Amer Acad of Pediatrics 1984; mem NMA and Amer Rheumatism Assoc 1979-; nominating comm Section of Rheumatology AAP 1987; medical advisory committee, Arthritis Foundation, Washington Metropolitan Chapter, 1990; executive committee, Section of Pediatric Rheumatology American Academy of Pediatrics, 1987-90; member, Junior League of Washington, DC, 1990-93. **Honors/Awds:** Dept Medical Awd Howard Univ Coll of Medicine 1976; Disting Alumni Citation of the Year Natl Assoc for Equal Oppor in Higher Educ 1985; Professional Excellence Award, Kaiser Permanente Medical Group 1991; elected chairperson, Section on Rheumatology, American Academy of Pediatrics 1991-94. **Business Addr:** Associate Medical Director, CIGNA Health Care, Mid-Atlantic, 9700 Patuxent Woods Drive, Columbia, MD 21046.

YANCEY, CHARLES CALVIN
City official. **Personal:** Born Dec 28, 1948, Boston, MA; son of Alice White Yancey (deceased) and Howell T Yancey Sr (deceased); married Marzetta Morrissette; children: Charles, Derrick, Sharif, Ashley. **Educ:** Tufts Univ, BA 1970; Harvard Univ, MPA 1991. **Career:** Commonwealth of MA, dir of admin 1977-79; Metro Area Planning Council, dir of finances 1979-82; CCY and Assoc, pres 1979-84; Legislative Branch of City Govt, city councillor 1984-. **Orgs:** Mem NAACP 1966-, Greater Roxbury Comm Devel Corp 1978-82, Transafrica 1979-, Codman Square Comm Devel Corp 1981-83; former pres Black Political Task Force 1982-83; mem Coastal Resources Advisory Bd 1983-; bd mem, Boston African-Amer Natl Historic Site, Taxpayers Equity Alliance of MA (TEAM), Roxbury YMCA, Boston Harbor Assoc; board member, American Lung Association, Boston, 1990-; board member, Americans for Democratic Action, 1991-. **Honors/Awds:** Elected vice pres North Amer Reg Action Against Apartheid Comm United Nations 1984; Citizen of the Year Omega Psi Phi 1984; Meritorious Comm Serv Kappa Alpha Psi 1984; Passage of Boston South Africa Divestment Legislation City Council 1984. **Business Addr:** City Councilman, Boston City Council, New City Hall, City Hall Square, Boston, MA 02201, (617)635-3131.

YANCEY, LAUREL GUILD
International broadcast attorney. **Personal:** Born Dec 12, 1953, Santa Rosa, CA; daughter of Helen E Branker Guild and George P Guild M D; married Arthur H Yancey II M D, Jun 19, 1988. **Educ:** Simmons Coll, BA 1975; Boston Coll Law School, JD 1978. **Career:** Federal Communications Commn, trial atty1981-82, general atty 1982-85, sr atty/advisor 1985-90; attorney/advisor (international) 1991-. **Orgs:** US Supreme Court Bar; DC and Massachusetts Bar Assns; mem Alpha Kappa Alpha Sorority Inc; board member Black Entertainment and Sports Lawyers Assn; mem Federal Communications Bar Assn 1989-; member, American Women in Radio and Television 1989-. **Honors/Awds:** Comm Serv Awd FCC 1979.

YANCEY, PRENTISS QUINCY
Attorney. **Personal:** Born Aug 20, 1944, Atlanta, GA; son of Prentiss Q Yancey; divorced; children: Prentiss III, Cristian, Schuyler. **Educ:** Villanova University, BA, 1966; Emory University, JD, 1969. **Career:** Smith, Gambrell & Russell, partner, 1969-. **Orgs:** Society of International Business Fellows, 1986-; Southern Center for International Studies, director; Clark Atlanta University, trustee, 1978-; Governor's Commission, education, criminal justice; Atlanta Charter Commission. **Military Serv:** US Army, lt, judge advocate general corps, 1969-76.

YANCY, DOROTHY COWSER
Educator, labor arbitrator, college president. **Personal:** Born Apr 18, 1944, Cherokee Cty, AL; daughter of Linnie Bell Covington Cowser and Howard Cowser; children: Yvonne. **Educ:** Johnson C Smith Univ, AB History 1964; Univ of MA Amherst, MA 1965; Atlanta Univ, PhD Polit 1978. **Career:** Albany State Coll Albany GA, instr history 1965-67; Hampton Inst Hampton VA, instr history 1967-69; Evanston Twp HS, teacher 1969-71; Barat Coll Lake Forest IL, dir black studies 1971-72; Georgia Inst of Tech, assistant professor, 1972-78, associate professor, 1978-88, professor, 1988-94; Johnson C. Smith Univ, prof, president, 1994-. **Orgs:** Mem: Assn for the Study of Afro-Amer Life & History, Industrial Relations Res Assn, Soc of Professionals in Dispute Resolutions; mem, labor panel Amer Arbitration Assn 1980; mem exec comm Assn of Soc & Behavioral Sci; mem So Pol Sci Assn; spec master, FL Public Employees Relations Commn; bd mem Assn for the Study of Afro-Amer Life & History; mem Labor Arbitration Panel Fed Mediation & Conciliation Serv; mediator, Mediation Res & Educ Proj, Northwestern Univ, 1988-; mem, Arbitration Panel, Bd of Regents State Univ System of FL & AFSCME, 1988-; chw, Woman Power Commission, The Links, Inc, 1990-94; Johnson C Smith Univ, board of trustees, 1991-94; bd, Charlotte Chamber of Commerce, Charlotte Urban League, Metro Charlotte YMCA. **Honors/Awds:** Fulbright-Hayes Scholar 1968; collaborating author, The Fed Gov Policy & Black Enterprise 1974; author, several scholarly articles & arbitration decisions; mem: Omicron Delta Kappa, Phi Kappa Phi Honor Soc, Leadership Atlanta Class, 1984; Distinguished Alumnus, Johnson C Smith Univ, 1981; Outstanding Teacher of the Year, Georgia Institute of Technology, 1985; mem, People to People Delegation of Labor Experts, to Soviet Union & Europe, 1988, to London, Berlin, & Moscow, 1990; The Academy of Political and Social Sciences of the Small Hural, Ulan Bator, Mongolia, Lecturer and Consultant, 1991. **Business Addr:** President, 100 Beatties Ford Rd, Johnson C Smith University, Charlotte, NC 28216.

YANCY, EARL J.
Business executive. **Career:** Yancy Minerals, CEO, currently. **Special Achievements:** Ranked 15 of 100 top industrial/service companies, Black Enterprise, 1992. **Business Phone:** (203)624-8067.

YANCY, PRESTON MARTIN
Educator. **Personal:** Born Oct 18, 1938, Sylvester, GA; son of Margaret Elizabeth Robinson Yancy and Preston Martin Yancy Sr (deceased); married Marilyn Leonard; children: Robert James, Grace Elizabeth. **Educ:** Morehouse Coll, BA 1959; Univ of Richmond, MH 1968; Syracuse Univ, MSS 1974, PhD 1979. **Career:** USAF, civilian supply clerk 1959-61; US Dept of Defense, civilian supply clerk 1961-69; VA Union Univ, professor 1969-, vice pres for academic affairs, 1994-; Richmond Free Press, columnist 1992-94, 1997-. **Orgs:** Columnist, Richmond Afro-Amer Newspaper 1967-71, 1974-82; Assoc for the Study of Afro Amer Life and History; member, Langston Hughes Society 1981-91; treasurer, Urban League of Greater Richmond, 1996-. **Honors/Awds:** Emory O Jackson Best Column Awards 1975-78, 1980; Doctoral Grants Ford Found 1973-75; Doctoral Grants United Negro Coll Fund 1978-79; Post Doctoral Grants United Negro Coll Fund 1981-84; book The Afro-Amer Short Story Greenwood Press 1986. **Home Addr:** PO Box 25583, Richmond, VA 23260. **Business Addr:** Professor, Communications, Virginia Union University, 1500 N Lombardy St, Richmond, VA 23220-1711, (804)257-5757.

YANCY, ROBERT JAMES
Educator. **Personal:** Born Mar 10, 1944, Tifton, GA; son of Margaret Elizabeth Robinson Yancy and Preston Martin Yancy; married Dorothy Cowser Yancy, Sep 8, 1967; children: Yvonne. **Educ:** Morehouse College, Atlanta, GA, BA, 1964; Atlanta University, Atlanta, GA, MBA, 1967; Northwestern University, Evanston, IL, PhD, 1973. **Career:** Hampton Institute, Hampton, VA, assistant professor, 1967-69; Atlanta University, Atlanta, GA, assistant professor/associate professor, 1971-82; Zebra Corporation, Atlanta, GA, president, 1972-1982; West Georgia College, Carrollton, GA, assistant professor, 1982; Southern Technical Institute, Marietta, GA, professor, 1983-86; Southern College of Technology, Marietta, GA, dean/management, 1986-. **Orgs:** Chair, University System of Georgia, Administrative Committee on Graduate Work, 1990-91; chair, University System of Georgia, Academic Review Committee on Business Administration, Fort Valley State College, 1989; advisory board, Hands, Fee, Mouth, Recipient of President Bush's Points of Light Award, 1988-91; member, Social Affairs Committee, 100 Black Men of Atlanta, 1989-90; chair, Annual Membership Campaign, Butler Street YMCA, 1977. **Honors/Awds:** Federal Government Policy and Black Business Enterprise-Ballinger, 1973; Black Georgian of The Year in Business, State Committee on History of Black Georgians, 1981; Living Legends In Black, Bi-Centennial Publication, Bailey Publishing Co. **Business Addr:** Dean, School of Management, Southern College of Technology, 1100 S Marietta Parkway, Marietta, GA 30060.

YARBORO, THEODORE LEON
Physician. **Personal:** Born Feb 16, 1932, Rocky Mount, NC; married Deanna Marie Rose; children: Theodore L Jr, Deanna R, Theresa L. **Educ:** NC Central Univ, BS 1954, MS 1956; Meharry Med Coll, MD 1963; Univ of Pgh Grad Sch of Pub Health, MPH 1979. **Career:** US Bureau of Mines, chemist/analytical & organic 1956-59; Shenango Valley Campus Penn State Univ, lecturer 1979-; Theodore L Yarboro MD Inc, family practitioner 1965-. **Orgs:** Mem Natl Med Assn 1965-; mem Amer Acad of Family Physicians 1965-; mem Amer Med Assn 1965-; mem/bd of dirs Mercer Co Branch NAACP 1965-; founder Shenango Valley Urban League 1968; bd dirs Shenango Valley Urban League 1968-78; founder/adv Dr Maceo E Patterson Future Physician Soc 1969-; charter diplomate Amer Bd of Family Prac 1970-; charter fellow Amer Acad of Fam Prac 1972-; mem bd trustees Natl Urban League 1973-78; mem Gov Adv Com on Multiple Health Screening 1975-76; mem Gov's Com on Health Educ in PA 1975-76; life mem NAACP 1976-; 3 publs Journal of Organic Chemistry, Journal of Chem, Engrg Data 1959-61. **Honors/Awds:** Disting Serv Awd Midwestern PA Chap Amer Heart Assn 1970 & 75; Disting Serv Awd Shenango Valley Urban League 1972; Man of the Yr Shenango Valley Jaycees 1972; Comm Serv Awd Mercer Co Branch NAACP 1976. **Military Serv:** USAF airman 1/c 1959. **Business Addr:** Family Practitioner, 755 Division St, Sharon, PA 16146.

YARBOROUGH, DOWD JULIUS, JR.
Physician. **Personal:** Born May 10, 1938, Winston-Salem, NC; married Merele; children: Danielle, Dowd III, Leyland. **Educ:** Morgan State Coll, 1963; Meharry Med Coll, 1967; Univ MI, 1974. **Career:** Houston TX, physic cardiol int med; Baylor Coll Med, tchr; Univ TX. **Orgs:** Mem AMA; NMA. **Honors/Awds:** Recog awd 1973. **Military Serv:** USN, LtCmdr, 1971-74. **Business Addr:** 2000 Crawford St, Houston, TX 77002.

YARBOROUGH, RICHARD A.
Educator, author. **Personal:** Born May 24, 1951, Philadelphia, PA; son of Yvonne K Newby Yarborough and John W Yarborough III; divorced. **Educ:** Mich State Univ, E Lansing MI, BA, 1973; Stanford Univ, Stanford CA, PhD, 1980. **Career:** Univ of California, Los Angeles CA, asst prof 1979-86, assoc prof 1986-. **Orgs:** Faculty res assoc, UCLA Center for African-Amer Studies, 1979-; mem 1987-92, chair 1989-90, exec comm of Div of Black Amer Literature & Culture, Modern Lang Assn; bd of editorial advisors, American Quarterly, 1987-91; mem, Natl Council, Amer Studies Assn, 1988-91; member, editorial board, African American Review, 1989-; California Council for the Humanities, 1992-96. **Honors/Awds:** US Presidential Scholar, 1969; Alumni Dist Scholar's Award, MI State Univ, 1969-73; Whiting Fellowship in Humanities, Stanford Univ, 1977-78; Natl Endowment for the Humanities fellowship, 1984-85; Dist Teaching Award, UCLA, 1987; Ford Foundation postdoctoral fellowship, 1988-89; general editor, "Library of Black Literature," Northeastern Univ Press, 1988-; coeditor, Norton Anthology of Afro-American Literature, 1996; author of scholarly essays in numerous journals & books; City of Los Angeles Commendation, 1990. **Special Achievements:** Assoc gen editor, The Heath Anthology of American Literature, 2nd ed, D C Heath, 1994, 3rd ed, Houghton Mifflin, 1998. **Business Addr:** Professor/Research/Writer, University of California, Los Angeles, Dept of English, 2225 Rolfe Hall, Box 951530, Los Angeles, CA 90095-1530.

YARBOROUGH, RYAN
Professional football player. **Personal:** Born Apr 26, 1971, Baltimore, MD. **Educ:** Wyoming. **Career:** New York Jets, wide receiver, 1994-95; Baltimore Ravens, 1997-. **Business Addr:** Professional Football Player, Baltimore Ravens, 11001 Owings Mills Blvd, Owings Mills, MD 21117, (410)654-6200.

YARBROUGH, DELANO
Educational administrator (retired). **Personal:** Born Sep 20, 1936, Thornton, AR; son of Sadie Yarbrough and Roy Yarbrough; married Samella O; children: Delano, Desiree, Darryl. **Educ:** Univ of AR Pine Bluff, BS; AZUSA Pacif Coll, MA 1971-73; Marquette; LeVerne; UCLA; Univ of SF, doct; Pepperdine Univ. **Career:** E HS Lilbourn, teacher 1961-63; US Navy, mathematician 1963-65; Pasadena Unified School District 1967-77, desegregation project dir; Del Yarbrough & Assocs, consultant; Eliot Middle School, principal 1981-94. **Orgs:** Mem ASCD, CSCD, APSA, Phi Delta Kappa; life mem, NAACP & UAPB Alumni Assn; Pasadena Educ Found; consultant Afro-Am Educ Cult Cntr; consultant Jet Propulsion Lab; v chmn ESAA; mem Natl Council Teacher Math; CA Math Council; CA State Math Framework Comm 1984-86; pres & mem, bd of dir, Diversified Educ Serv, Inc, 1981-. **Honors/Awds:** New Teacher of the Year Pasadena 1964; Commendation in educ for serv rendered in reducing racial isolation; Pasadena & Altadena Branches, NAACP, Community Service Awards; Tuskegee Univ, Natl Parents of the Year Award, 1988; Commendation from Pres Clinton, 1995. **Military Serv:** USAF airman 1/c 1954-58. **Business Addr:** Diversified Educational Services, Inc, 555 E Washington Blvd, Pasadena, CA 91104.

YARBROUGH, EARNEST
Magistrate. **Personal:** Born Mar 16, 1923, Buffalo; married Mary Holman. **Career:** MCAS, 1965-69; Ridgeland Clinic, supr trans 1970; Beaufort Jasper Compre Hlth Serv Inc, magis 1971-77. **Orgs:** Mem Elke Lodge; VFW Lodge. **Military Serv:** USN 1942-64.

YARBROUGH, MAMIE LUELLA
Elected official. **Personal:** Born Sep 19, 1941, Benton Harbor, MI; divorced; children: Dawn Delynne, Nyles Charles. **Educ:** Western MI Univ, 1959-60. **Career:** NBD F&M Bank, banking 1966-75; Berrien Homes Apts, housing mgr 1975-81; River Terrace Apts, housing mgr 1981-; Benton Harbor Area Sch Bd, vice pres. **Orgs:** Sec Benton Twp Citizens Adv Bd 1979; pres Benton Harbor Comm Arts Alliance 1980; mem Inst of Real Estate & Management 1981-; rep Berrien Co Intermediate Sch Dist 1984-. **Honors/Awds:** Certified Housing Mgr Natl Center for Housing Mgmt 1978; Accredited Resident Mgr Inst of Real Estate & Mgmt 1981. **Home Addr:** 1086 Monroe, Benton Harbor, MI 49022. **Business Addr:** School Board President, Benton Harbor Area Schl Dist, 300 River Terrace, Benton Harbor, MI 49022.

YARBROUGH, MARILYN VIRGINIA
Educator. **Personal:** Born Aug 31, 1945, Bowling Green, KY; daughter of Merca Lee Toole and William O Yarbrough (deceased); married David A Didion, Dec 31, 1987; children: Carmen Ainsworth, Carla Ainsworth. **Educ:** Virginia State Univ, BA 1966; UCLA, JD 1973. **Career:** IBM, systms eng 1966-68; Westinghouse, systms eng 1969-70; Catonsville Community College, instr data proc 1970; Boston College Law School, teaching fellow 1975-76; Duke Law School, visting prof 1983-84; Univ of Kansas, law prof, 1976-87 & assoc vice chancellor 1983-87; Univ of Tennessee-Knoxville, law dean 1987-91; University of North Carolina Law School, professor of law, 1992-. **Orgs:** Pres bd cmt wrk Law Sch Admsn Cncl 1976-89; bd mem Accrediting Cncl Ed Journalism Mass Communications 1976-83; chmn KS Crime Victims Reparations Bd, 1980-83; Lawrence Housing Auth 1984-86; council member Am Bar Assc Sect Legal Ed Admsn to the Bar 1984-85; pres United Way of Lawrence, KS, 1985; KS Commission on Civil Rights, 1986-; NCAA Conf on Infractions, 1986-88, chairman, 1986-87; Rotary International, 1988-90; Pulitzer Prize board, 1990-; Poynter Institute for Media Studies, board of directors, 1990-92; First American Bank of Knoxville, board of directors, 1987-; United Way of Knoxville, board of directors, 1990-91. **Honors/Awds:** Kansas Univ Women's Hall of Fame; Doctor of Laws, Univ of Puget Sound School of Law 1989; Frank D Reeves Award, Natl Conference of Black Lawyers 1988; Society of American Law Teachers Award, 1991; YWCA Tribute to Women Award for Education, 1989; Distinguished Alumni Award, Virginia State University, 1988; ABA, Women Lawyers of Achievement Award, 1991. **Business Addr:** Professor of Law, University of North Carolina Law School, Chapel Hill, NC 27599.

YARBROUGH, ROBERT ELZY
Attorney. **Personal:** Born Dec 16, 1929, Atlanta, GA. **Educ:** Boston Coll, BSBA 1951; Bstn Univ Law Sch, LlB 1958. **Career:** US Cust Serv Dept of Treas, sr impt splst 1975-; AUS & AUS Res, ret LTC FA 1949-77; US Cust Serv, impt splst 1963-; atty at law 1961-; US Post Ofc, clk 1954-61; AUS, ofcr 1951-54. **Orgs:** Bd of trust Bstn Latin Sch Alumni Asso 1980; mem Am Bar Assn MA Bar Assn; mem Prince Hall Grand Lodge F & AM of MA; mem Syria Temple #31 AEAONMS. **Honors/Awds:** Merit serv medal AUS 1977. **Military Serv:** Aus lt 1949-77. **Business Addr:** Custom House, Boston, MA 02109.

YARBROUGH, ROOSEVELT
Accountant. **Personal:** Born Jan 11, 1946, Pattison, MS. **Educ:** Chapman Coll, 1968; MS Valley State Univ, BS 1973; John Marshall Law School, 1981; Amer Mgmt Assoc Ctr for Mgmt Devel, 1982. **Career:** Ernst & Ernst, staff accountant 1975; Bailey Meter Co, budget analyst 1976; Southwest MS Legal Svcs, dir of admin 1982; First Entry Svcs, accountant; Claiborne Cty Schools, bd mem. **Orgs:** Directorship Claiborne Cty Bldg; mem Assoc for Suprv & Curriculum Devel, Black Ed & Econ Proj; pres NAACP, MS Cultural Arts Coalition, Claiborne CtyFamily Reunion. **Military Serv:** USMC cpr 3 yrs. **Home Addr:** PO Box 141, Pattison, MS 39144. **Business Addr:** School Board Member, Claiborne Co Dist 5, PO Box 337, Port Gibson, MS 39150.

YARDE, RICHARD FOSTER
Art professor, artist. **Personal:** Born Oct 29, 1939, Boston, MA; son of Enid Foster Yarde and Edgar St Clair Yarde; married Susan Donovan, Jul 8, 1967; children: Marcus, Owen. **Educ:** Boston Univ, BFA (cum laude) Painting 1962, MFA Painting 1964. **Career:** Boston Univ, asst prof of art 1965-71; Wellesley Coll, assoc prof of art 1971-76; Amherst Coll, visiting assoc prof 1976-77; MA Coll of Art, visiting artist, 1977-79; Mount Holyoke Coll, visiting assoc prof, Art, 1980-81; Univ of MA, Boston, prof of art, 1981-90; University of Massachusetts, Amherst, professor of art, currently. **Orgs:** Visual arts panelist MA Council Art & Humanities 1976-78; assoc mem Natl Acad of Design 1984-; board of overseers, Institute of Contemporary Art, Boston, MA, 1991-. **Honors/Awds:** Blanche E Colman Awd for Travel & Study in Nigeria 1970; Arcadia Found Awd for Painting NY 1975; Fellowship Grant in Painting Natl Endowment for the Arts 1976; Childe Hassam Purchase Amer Acad of Arts & Letters NY 1977; Henry W Ranger Fund Purchase Natl Acad of Design NY 1979; Childe Hassam Purchase Amer Acad of Arts & Letters NY 1982; Adolph & Clara Obrig Prize Natl Acad of Design 1983; Commn Art-in-Architecture Prog Genl Serv Admin Washington DC 1989; one person exhibit "Savoy" traveling to Studio Museum in Harlem, San Diego Museum, The Baltimore Museum, Studio Museum in Harlem, etc 1982-83; group exhibitions Metropolitan Museum of Art, Boston Museum of Fine Arts, Corcoran Gallery Washington DC; one person exhibts, Springfield Museum, 1987, Galerie Tension Paris, 1986, Utah Museum oine Arts, 1986; group exhibitions, Newport Art Museum, Newport, RI, 1990; Group, National Academy of Design, 1987; Massachusetts Artist's Fellowship (Painting), Mass Cultural Council, 1985; Alumni Award for Distinguished Contribution to the Arts, Boston University, 1987; The Chancellor's Award for Distinguished Scholarship, University of Massachusetts, Boston, 1984. **Business Addr:** Professor of Art, Univ of Massachusetts, Amherst, Fine Arts Center, Amherst, MA 01003.

YATES, ANTHONY J.
Basketball coach. **Personal:** Born Sep 15, 1937, Lawrenceburg, IN; married. **Educ:** Univ of Cincin, BS 1963. **Career:** Univ of IL, asst basktbl coach 1974-; Univ of Cincin, asst basktbl coach 1971-74; Cincin Royals Professional Basktbl Team, part time scout 1966-71; Fin Mgmt Corp, salesman 1968-71; Drake Mem Hosp, asst to admin & person & dir 1966-68; Shillitos Dept Store, asst employ mgr 1963-66. **Orgs:** Mem Nat Assn of Sec Deal; mem bd dir Nat AAU Basktbl League; mem bd dir Greater Cincin Jr Basktbl Assn; fmr mem Cincin Plan Parenthd; fmr mem Cincin Sch Found; fmr mem Baseball "Kid Gloves" game; fmr mem Cincin Met AAU; Tom Shell Tony Yates TV Basktbl Show WCPO TV 1964; color caster for WKRC radio broad of Univ of Cincin bsktbl games 1970-71; sports banquet spkr for Coca Cola Btlg Co 1963, 1964 1965. **Honors/Awds:** Mem Univ of Cincin Bsktbl Tm NCAA Bsktbl Champ 1961, 1962. **Military Serv:** USAF 1955-59.

YATES, ELLA GAINES
Librarian, consultant. **Personal:** Born Jun 14, 1927, Atlanta, GA; daughter of Laura Moore Gaines (deceased) and Fred D Gaines Sr (deceased); married Clayton R Yates II (deceased); children: Jerri Sydnor Lee. **Educ:** Spelman College, BA 1949; Atlanta Univ, MLS 1951; Rutgers Univ, sch lib cert 1956; Univ of GA, Inst for Training in Municipal Administration, cert for professional mgmt 1972, cert for advanced professional mgmt 1974; Morehouse Coll, HUD, cert mgmt for black administrators in state & municipal govt 1975; Atlanta Law Sch, JD 1979. **Career:** Orange Meml Hosp, part-time librarian 1964-66; Atlanta Univ Library, asst ref libn 1947-48; Brooklyn Public Lib, asst branch libn 1951-55; Orange Pub Lib, head of children's dept 1956-60; East Orange Public Lib, branch libn 1960-70; Montclair Pub Lib, asst dir 1970-72; Atlanta Univ, visiting prof grad lib sch 1972-73; Atlanta Fulton Pub Lib, asst dir 1972-76, dir 1976-81; Friendship Force, lib consult; VA State Lib & Archives, state libn & archivist 1986-90; library consultant, 1990-. **Orgs:** Consult: Seattle Oppors Industrialization Ctr 1982-84, Univ of WA 1982-83, US Commn on Civil Rights 1982, United Way Budget & Planning Adv Bd 1979-80, Martin Luther King Jr Archives 1977-81, Library Journal, US Office of Educ Bureau of Libs 1973-; Amer Lib Assn; exec comm Library of Congress "Center for the Book" 1979-; Assn of Coll & Res Libs 1981-; Natl Alumnae Bd of Spelman Coll 1984-; Wash Lib Assn Intellectual Freedom Comm 1981-84; Wash State Coalition Against Censorship 1983-84; Univ of WA Grad Lib Sch Visiting Comm 1982-84; Seattle Urban League Guild1982-84; Tuskegee Airmen Inc 1982-84; YMCA of Greater Atlanta Trustee Bd 1980-81; NJ Lib Assn; mem Atlanta Univ Natl Alumni Bd 1977-81; GA Public Broadcast Bd 1977-81; Friends of the Fulton Co Jail Bd; nominating comm Southeastern Lissn 1974; life mem, NAACP, Delta Sigma Theta. **Honors/Awds:** Phoenix Awd for Outstanding Employee Performance, City of Atlanta, 1980; Study Tour of Frankfurt Munich & West Berlin Germany 1980; Outstanding Alumna Spelman Coll 1977; Outstanding Alumna Atlanta Univ 1977; Outstanding Citizen of the Yr 1972; Professional Woman of the Yr 1964; publs "An Annotated Cumulative Index to the Journal of Negro History for the First 25 Years" Atlanta Univ 1951; "A Critical Evaluation of the Montclair NJ Grass Roots Summer Prog" NJ 1971; essay in What Black Librarians Are Saying, ed by EJ Josey, Scarecrow Press 1972; a paper in The Role of the Humanities in the Public Library, ed by Robt N Broadus, Amer Lib Assn 1979; "Sexism in the Library Profession" Library Journal Dec 15 1979 pp 2165-2619; Outstanding Librarian, Black Caucus of Amer Library Assn, 1989; Outsding in Govt & Educ, Richmond Chap of Coalition of 100 Black Women, 1989; Clark Atlanta University, Distinguished Service Award, 1991; Hall of Fame Award, Natl Alum Assn of Spelman College, 1995. **Home Addr:** 1171 Oriole Dr SW, Atlanta, GA 30311-2424.

YATES, LEROY LOUIS
Clergyman. **Personal:** Born Dec 8, 1929, Terry, MS; son of Mary Ella Summers (deceased) and Clarence Yates; married Beverly Joanne Pannell, Dec 26, 1951; children: Sara Doreen, Jonathan Allen, Joyce Ellen, Mary Francis Coultman, LeRoy Louis Jr. **Educ:** Moody Bible Inst Chgo, grad dipl 1956; Chicago State U, BA 1971; Chicago State U, MS 1979. **Career:** Westlawn Gospel Chapel, Chicago, IL, sr pastor, 1957-; Circle Y Ranch, Bangor, MI, exec dir, 1978-80; Chicago Medical School, microbiologist, 1968-79; Hektoen Inst Cook County Hosp, chief tech supvr, 1964-76. **Orgs:** Exec bd mem Leukemia Soc of Am 1961-80; exec bd sec PACE Inst Cook Co Jail Chicago 1969-80; mem of med adv bd Univ of IL Med Cntr 1978-80; exec bd mem Int Mag Pub 1967-80; draft bd mem Local Bd #58 1968-74; vol couns Westside Hol Fam Cntr 1978-80. **Honors/Awds:** Honorary Doctor of Humanities, Detroit Bible College, 1981. **Military Serv:** US Army, sgt, 20 months; Korean Service Medal with 3 Bronze Camp Stars, Med Co 9th regiment, 1951; Unit Natl Serv Medal, Med Co 9th regiment, 1951; Combat Medal Badge, IOS Serv Bar, Med Co 9th regiment, 1051; Merit Serv Award, IL selective Serv System, 1976. **Business Addr:** Senior Pastor, Westlawn Gospel Chapel, 2115 S St Louis, Chicago, IL 60623.

YATES, MARK
Banker. **Personal:** Born Sep 15, 1966, Memphis, TN; son of Andres N & Mary F Yates. **Educ:** Howard Univ, BA, 1988; Vanderbilt Univ, MBA, 1996. **Career:** Federal Express Corp, customer service agent, 1986-89; First Tennessee bank, vp com'l loan officer, 1989-. **Orgs:** Omega Psi Phi Fraternity, keeper of finance, 1993-94; Howard Univ Alumni Assn, 1988-; Boys Club, bd mem, 1993-. **Business Addr:** Vice President, First Tennessee Bank, 3885 South Perkins, Memphis, TN 38118, (901)366-3787.

YEARWOOD, AREM IRENE
Caterer (retired). **Personal:** Born in Americus, GA; married Randolph (died 1982). **Career:** Caterer, retired. **Orgs:** Mem Nat Coun of Negro Wom 1964-; pres New Sec NJ Life 1964-70; bd dir Westside Unit 1970-75; pres bd dirs 1972-73; mem Eta Phi Beta Sor 1966; treas Psi Chap 1969; Co Comm & Wom 20th Dist Westward Newark 1966-80; vol Vista Nat Immuniz Nat Med Assn; vol NCNW Prgm for Sr Cit Newark; aide to Assem 28th Dist Westward Essex Co 1974-76. **Honors/Awds:** 1st woman elected to Westside Unit; Boys Club Mother of the Year Award 1965; Boys Club Service Award 1966; Boys Club Outstanding Supp 1967; Woman of the Year Greyhound Afro-Amer 1969; NC NW Serv Awd 1971; Eta Phi Beta Comm Serv Awd 1972; Boys Club of Am Awd 1974; Bethune Achvmt Awd 1975; Bethune Bicent Awd 1976; Bethune Leg Awd 1976; Ch Wom Unit Awd 1975; NCNW Inc Life mem Guild In Serv Awd 1975; Wom of Yr Awd NCNW Inc 1976; Boys Club of New 10 yr Serv Awd 1978; NCNW Bethune Cent Awd 1975; Outst Wom of Yr of NJ NCNW 1979; elect to Natl Nom Com NCNW 1977-79; 15 yr Serv Awd; Boys Clubs of New 1980; Comm Serv Awd Nurses Assn; Martland Hosp Coll of Med & Dent of NJ 1977; Kenneth A Gibson Civic Association 5th Annual Brotherhood Award; NCNW Legacy Life Member Award 1981.

YEARWOOD, DAVID MONROE, JR.
Television executive. **Personal:** Born Nov 15, 1945; son of Una U Holder Yearwood and David M Yearwood; married Cristina Luisa Dale de Rollox; children: Edward, David III. **Educ:** Pace Univ, BBA 1978; Keller Grad Sch of Management, MBA Mgmt 1982, MBA Human Res 1983. **Career:** Natl Broadcasting Co NY, financial analyst 1970-75, mgr budgets 1975-77; Natl Broadcasting Co Chicago, mgr accounting 1977-80, dir finance & admin 1980-. **Orgs:** Chmn supervisory comm ABE Credit Union 1983-86; alumni council Keller Grad Sch 1984-; editorial bd WMAQ-TV 1982-; president, Illinois Broadcasters Assn, 1988-89. **Honors/Awds:** Cert of Merit Youth Motivation Comm 1979-80. **Military Serv:** USN Reserve petty officer 3rd 1966-70. **Business Addr:** Director, Fin & Admin, NBC, WMAQ-TV, 454 N Columbus Drive, Executive Office, Chicago, IL 60611.

YEARY, JAMES E., SR.
Educator. **Personal:** Born Jul 7, 1917, Harrogate, TN; married Kathelene Toney; children: Glenna, Aaron, James, Jr, Brenda. **Educ:** Morristown Jr Coll, 1941; TN State U, BS 1954; Tuskegee Inst, MSEd 1960. **Career:** Knoxville City Schools, teacher math dept chmn; Greenwood Annex Jr High Clarksville, prin; Knoxville Coll, asst prof consultant 1969-72; Edison HS Gary, teacher 1964-71; Burt HS Clarksville, teacher 1956-64; Elem School Teaching, 1941-46. **Orgs:** Mem St James Mason Lodge; Gen Elec fellowshp 1957; mem Nat Scl Found Austin Peay State Univ 1962-63; Fisk Univ 1959; TN State Univ 1960; IL Inst of Tech 1966; Univ IL 1968-69; min; life under; auth "War Inside"; colum INFO weekly 1968-69. **Honors/Awds:** Nat Sci Hon Soc Beta Kappa Chi; Nat Sci Acad Yr Inst 1959. **Military Serv:** AUS 1942-45. **Business Addr:** St Mary's Bapt Ch, 1038 Trenton St, Harriman, TN 37748.

YELDELL, JOSEPH P.
Government executive. **Personal:** Born Sep 9, 1932, Washington, DC; married Gladys Johnson; children: Gayle, Joi Lynn. **Educ:** DC Tchrs Coll, BS, mathematics, 1957; Univ of Pittsburgh, MEd, secondary administration, 1961. **Career:** Pgh Pub Sch, tchr 1958-61; DC Pub Sch, tchr 1961-62; Bureau Labor Stat, math stat 1962-64; IBM Corp, mktg rep 1964-70; DC City Cncl, councilman 1967-70, 1971; City of Washington DC, Dept of Hum Res, dir 1971-77, gen asst to mayor 1977-78, Automated Management Info Syst, special asst to city adm, 1979-83, Office of Emergency Preparedness, dir, 1983-90; JPY Associates Inc, pres, 1990-93; City of Washington DC, Human Resources Development, asst city adminstrator, 1993-94, Dept of Employment Services, act dir, 1993-. **Orgs:** Natl Forum for Black Public Administrators; Prince Hall Masons 330; Phi Beta Sigma Fraternity Inc; NAACP; Natl Urban League; DC Public Library, bd of trustees; Washington Ctr for Metropolitan Studies, bd of trustees; Reconstruction and Development Corp, bd of dirs; DC Commission on Academic Facilities; Washington Tech Inst, Science Advisory Committee; Howard Univ, President's Council; Federal City Coll, President's Council; Washington Urban Coaltion, bd of dirs; DC Public Schools, Title II Advisory Council; Bi-centennial Commission; DC Citizens for Better Public Education; DC Congress of PTAs, bd of managers; American Soc for Public Administrators; Natl Emergency Managers Assn; Natl Education Assn; American Academy of Political & Social Sciences. **Honors/Awds:** Outstndg com serv awd Dupont Pk Civic Assn 1972; outstndg cit awd Fed Civic Assn 1970; distin serv awd Wmns Dem Club 1970; civil serv of yr awd Nat AMVETS 1975; listed Fam Blacks Ebony mag; Natl Forum for Black Public Administrators, Pub-

lic Administrator of the Year, 1989. **Military Serv:** USAF a/1c 1954-58. **Business Addr:** Act Dir, DC Dept of Employment Services, 500 C St, NW, Ste 600, Washington, DC 20001.

YELDING, ERIC GIRARD
Professional baseball player. **Personal:** Born Feb 22, 1965, Montrose, AL. **Educ:** Chipola Junior College. **Career:** Shortstop: Houston Astros, 1989-92, Cincinnati Reds, 1992, Chicago Cubs, 1993-. **Business Addr:** Professional Baseball Player, Chicago Cubs, Wrigley Field, 1060 W Addison St, Chicago, IL 60613, (312)404-2827.

YELITY, STEPHEN C.
Chief executive. **Personal:** Born Oct 25, 1949, Littleton, NC; son of Martha Ella Pitchford Yelity and Stephen Jackson Yelity; married Matlyn Joyce Alston Yelity, Apr 22, 1973; children: Scott. **Educ:** Norfolk State Univ, Norfolk VA, BS, 1973. **Career:** Amer Cynamid, Wayne NJ, accountant, 1973-76; Johnson & Johnson, Chicapee & New Brunswick, sr accountant & financial analyst, 1976-79; Johnson & Johnson Baby Products, Skillman NJ, accounting mgr, 1979-84; Accurate Information Systems, S Plainfield NJ, pres & CEO, 1984-. **Orgs:** NY/NJ Minority Purchasing Council, 1986-; Black Data Processing Assn, 1987-; Intl Network of Unix System Uses, 1988-; Chamber of Commerce, 1988-; NJ Brain Trust, 1989-; Natl Urban League, 1989-; NAACP, 1989-. **Honors/Awds:** Minority Small Business Man of Year for NJ, Small Business Admin, 1987; Appreciation Award, Bell Communications Research, 1988; Appreciation Award, AT&T, 1988; Sponsor of Year, Black Date Processing Associates, 1988/1990; resentative of minority small business in NJ for Grand Jury testimony concerning public opinion of Public Law 99-661, 1988; nominee for SBA Region II Man of Year, 1989; among top 100 black businesspersons recognized, Black Enterprise, 1989 & 1990; featured in Time magazine article on black executives, "Doing It for Themselves," June 1989; Entrepreneur of the Year, YMCA, 1989.

YERGAN, ERIC
Stockbroker. **Personal:** Born in Long Island, NY. **Educ:** Marist College, Poughkeepsie, NY, BA; Harvard Business School. **Career:** A G Becker, salesman; Paine Webber Group Inc, first vice president, senior vice president, currently. **Special Achievements:** One of 25 "Hottest Blacks on Wall Street" listed in Black Enterprise, October, 1992. **Business Addr:** Senior Vice Pres, PaineWebber Group, Inc, 1285 Avenue of the Americas, New York, NY 10019, (212)713-2000.

YERGER, AMOS G.
Educator. **Personal:** Born Aug 6, 1914, Boynton, OK; married Willie C; children: Donald, Cardis, Carlotta. **Educ:** AB 1936; MS 1957. **Career:** Boynton, elem teacher 1932-57; prin instr 1957-73; Muskogee Cnty OK Educ Assn, retired vice pres; E Dist Music Teachers Assn, pres 1956; Boynton Comm Chorus, org dir 1950-54. **Orgs:** Mem Boynton City & Counc 1969-71; midwest reg dir Zeta Phi Beta Sor Inc 1970-74; sec Lee Cemet & Bur Co; state sec NAACP; v chmn Precint 50 Boynton; 4-H orgn ldr; chmn March of Dimes Boynton; ch clk Mt Zion Bapt. **Honors/Awds:** Dist soror awd 1969; comm serv awd 1969; disting wom 1971; outstndg tchr 1973; serv recog 1974; Zeta of yr 1975.

YERGER, BEN
Educational administrator. **Personal:** Born Dec 8, 1931, Hope, AK; married Charlene A; children: Valerie B, Benjamin Jr. **Educ:** Philander Smith Coll, BS 1951; San Fran U, MA 1969; Univ of CA, PhD 1975. **Career:** Vista Coll, dean stud serv 1978-; Merritt & Vista Coll, dir comm serv 1972-78; Grove St Coll, pres 1971; Merritt & Coll, admin asst to the pres 1968-71; Pub Sch Far West Educ Lab, sci educ resrch 1955-68. **Orgs:** Bd of dir Berkeley Area Comm Found 1980-; vice pres Resrch Devel Cntr for Soc Redes 1978-; chmn Yth Employ Counc Berkeley CA 1978-; chtr mem Assn of CA Comm Coll Admin 1975-; mem CCCCSA CCJCA NASPA AAHE AAER NCCSCE and others; Alpha Kappa Mu Hon Soc; Phil Smith Coll 1949-50; Beta Kappa Chi Sci Hon Soc Phil Smith Coll 1949-50; Alpha Phi Alpha & Cum Laude Phil Smith Coll 1949-50. **Honors/Awds:** Outstndg educat of Am in high educ awd 1971; Phi Delta Kappa Hon Soc Univ of CA 1973-; outstndg dissert awd Instit Rsrch Plan Com CA Assn of Comm & Jr Coll 1976-77. **Military Serv:** AUS non-com 1956. **Business Addr:** 2020 Milvia St, Berkeley, CA 94704.

YIZAR, JAMES HORACE, JR.
Educator, educational administrator. **Personal:** Born Aug 27, 1957, Los Angeles, CA; son of Mr & Mrs James H Yizar Sr. **Educ:** ID State Univ, BA 1983; Idaho State University, Master Counseling, 1990. **Career:** Campbell Comm Therapy Ctr, recreation coord 1981-82; Upward Bound, asst dir 1982-84; ID State Univ Student Support Services, coord 1984-90, counselor, learning specialist, asst trio director, 1990-94, trio dir, 1994-; Idaho State Special Olympics, game coordinator, 1992-93. **Orgs:** Mem Kappa Alpha Psi 1977-; advisor Epsilon Theta Chap 1984-; advisor Black Students Alliance, 1984-86; bd dirs Access For Idaho 1985-, bd president 1988-92; mem NAACP 1986-, local branch pres, 1994-98. **Honors/Awds:** Outstanding Volunteer Access for Idaho Program 1986; Outstanding Speaker Martin Luther King Day McCamon Sch Dist 1986. **Business Addr:** Director, Trio Programs, Idaho State Univ, Box 8345, Pocatello, ID 83209.

YOBA, MALIK (ABDUL-MALIK KASHIE YOBA)
Actor, singer, musician, youth activist-advocate. **Personal:** Born Sep 17, 1967, Bronx, NY; son of Mahmoudah Lanier and Abdullah Yoba. **Career:** CityKids Foundation, vice pres, 1988-93; Films: "Cool Runnings," 1993; "Smoke," upcoming; "Blue in the Face," upcoming; Copland, 1997; Ride, 1998; Television appearances: "Law & Order," "Where I Live"; Nature Boy Enterprises, pres/CEO, 1994-; Universal Television, actor, "New York Undercover," 1994-. **Orgs:** The CityKids Foundation, advisor, vice pres, 1993-; REACH, bd mem, 1992-; Hale House, committee member, 1995; Children's Peace Memorial, friend, 1994-. **Special Achievements:** Co-musical director, Emmy-Nominated television show, "CityKids," 1992; Co-star, "New York Undercover," first television dramatic series starring actors of color during prime-time, 1994; Noted as one of 30 young artists under 30 who will change American culture in the next 30 years, New York Times Magazine, 1994; Creator, youth self-esteem program, "Why are you on this Planet?" 1994. **Business Addr:** President/CEO, Nature-Boy Enterprises, 163 Third Ave, Ste 153, New York, NY 10003.

YOHANNES, DANIEL W.
Banking executive. **Personal:** Born in Ethiopia; married Saron; children: Tsedeye, Michael, Rebecca. **Educ:** Claremont McKenna College, BS, econ; Pepperdine University, MBA. **Career:** Colorado National Bank, CEO. **Business Addr:** CEO, Colorado National Bank, 918 17th St, Denver, CO 80202, (303)585-5000.

YORK, RUSSEL HAROLD
Physician. **Personal:** Born May 6, 1952, Chicago, IL; married Yvonne Taylor; children: Damion, Renee, Marucs. **Educ:** Kalamazoo Coll, BA 1974; Howard Univ, MD 1978. **Career:** Henry Ford Hospital, intern/resident 1978-81; Wayne State Univ, faculty mem/instructor 1984-86; Woodland Medical Group PC, private practice 1986-. **Orgs:** Mem Amer Rheumatism Assoc 1986-, MI Rheumatism Soc; assoc mem Amer Coll of Physicians. **Honors/Awds:** Diplomate Amer Bd of Internal Medicine 1982, Amer Bd of Rheumatology 1984; Minority Faculty Rsch Awd Wayne State Univ, 1984-85, 1985-86; Wayne State University, rheumatology fellowship, 1982-84.

YOUMAN, LILLIAN LINCOLN
Business executive. **Personal:** Born May 12, 1940, Ballsville, VA; daughter of Arnetha Hobson (deceased) and Willie Hobson; divorced; children: Darnetha, Tasha. **Educ:** Howard Univ, BA (Cum Laude) 1966; Harvard Univ, MBA 1969. **Career:** Sterling Inst, assoc 1969-72; Ferris & Co, stockbroker 1972-73; Bowie State University, instructor 1973-74; Unified Serv Inc, exec vice pres 1973-76; Centennial One, Inc, president 1976-. **Orgs:** Bd dirs Citizen Bank of MD; mem Md Small Business Financing Authority; bd dirs Natl Business League of So MD; bd Minority Business Legal Defense and Educ Fund; vice pres Building Service Contractors Assoc Intl; mem bd dirs Capitol Assoc of Building Serv Contractors; bd dirs Prince George's County Chamber of Commerce; chairperson Referral Aide Program United Way 1984; mem Anne ArundelCo and Prince George Co Minority Business Enterprise Task forces 1985. **Honors/Awds:** MD Small Business Person of the Yr 1981; US Dept of Commerce Cert of Appreciation 1981; MD Cert of Distinguished Citizenship 1981; Bigger and Better Business Awd Phi Beta Sigma Frat 1982; Business & Entrepreneurship Awd Spelman Coll 1983; Leadership in the Business Arena Awd Delta Sigma Theta Sor 1983; Minority Female Contractor of the Yr Dept of Commerce 1984; Harvard Business Sch Black Alumni Entrepreneurship Awd 1986; HUB Organization Entrepreneurship Awd 1986; Minority Business Directory Awd 1986; America's Top 100 Black Business and Professional Women Awd by Dollars & Sense magazine 1986; Outstanding Service Award, NIH, 1987; National Minority Entrepreneur of Year; MBDA 1988; Service Industry Award MBDA; 1988; Finalist, Entrepreneur of Year, Inc. Magazine 1989; Banking Pioneer Awa National Business League 1990; Salute to Blacks in Business Award, Howard Univ. 1991.

YOUNG, ALAN C.
Certified public accountant. **Personal:** Born Jan 16, 1953, Inkster, MI; son of Sarah Young and Anderson Young; married Colette Brooks, May 1, 1982; children: Aaron C, Adam C, Austen C. **Educ:** Michigan State University, BA, 1976; Walsh College, Masters of Tax, 1985. **Career:** Deloitte Haskins & Sells, senior, 1977-81; Keith Warlick & Co, manager, 1981-83; Alan C Young & Associates, president, CEO, managing director, 1983-. **Orgs:** National Association of Black Accountants, president; Booker T Washington Business Association, president, 1992-94, chairman of the board, 1995-; Detroit Chamber of Commerce, executive committee, treasurer, board of directors, 1992-; Detroit Economic Club, 1990-; Kappa Alpha Psi Fraternity, vice pres, alumni founder, 1972-; First Independence Bank, board of directors; Henry Ford Hospital, trustee brd. **Honors/Awds:** National Association of Black Accountants, Corporate Achievement Award, 1987. **Special Achievements:** Frequent interviewee on tax matters, WDIV-TV News, Detroit News. **Business Addr:** President, CEO, Managing Director, Alan C Young & Associates, PC, 2990 W Grand Blvd, Ste 310, Detroit, MI 48202, (313)873-7500.

YOUNG, ALAN JOHN
Automobile dealership owner. **Personal:** Born May 25, 1945, Chicago, IL; son of Marion E Bradley Campbell and John M Young; divorced; children: Jeffrey, Kimberly, Christopher. **Educ:** Univ of IL, BS Mktg 1968. **Career:** AY Shell Serv Station, owner 1969-77; GM Dealer Devel Acad, trainee 1977-79; Alan Young Buick, pres 1979-. **Orgs:** Bd mem NE Motor Vehicle Licensing bd, Lincoln Found, Univ of NE Found. **Honors/Awds:** In top 100 of Black Business Owners Black Enterprise Magazine 1981-97. **Business Addr:** President, Alan Young Buick-GMC Trucks Inc, 7724 NE Loop 820, Fort Worth, TX 76180.

YOUNG, ALBERT JAMES
Writer, publisher. **Personal:** Born May 31, 1939, Ocean Springs, MS; married Arlin. **Educ:** Univ of MI, 1957-61; Univ of CA, BA 1969. **Career:** Loveletter, founder, editor 1966-68; Stanford Univ, Edward H Jones lecturer creative writings 1969-76; Yardbird Publ Inc, editor 1970-76; Laser Films, screenwriter 1972; Stigwood Corp, screenwriter 1972; Yardbird Wing Editions, co-publ, co-editor 1975-; Verdon Prod, screenwriter 1976; First Artists prod, screenwriter 1976-77; Yardbird Lives, co-editor 1978; Quilt, co-editor 1980; Ask Me Now book, author 1980; Universal Studios, freelance writer, book publ, screenwriter 1979-. **Orgs:** Mem E Bay Negro Hist Soc, Authors Guild, Authors League, Writers Guild of Amer, San Francisco Press Club. **Honors/Awds:** Author "Dancing" 1969, "Snakes" Holt 1970, "The Song Turning Back Into Itself" Holt 1971, "Who Is Angelina?" 1975, "Geography of the Near Past" Holt 1976, "Sitting Pretty" Holt 1976; Joseph H Jackson Awd 1969; Wallace Stegner Writing Fellowship 1966; Natl Arts Council Awds 1968-69; Guggenheim Fellowship 1974; Natl Endowment Arts Fellowship Creative Writing 1974; Natl Endowment for Arts Spec Proj Grant to Create Dramatic Radio Series 1979. **Business Addr:** 514 Bryant St, Palo Alto, CA 94301.

YOUNG, ALFRED
Educator. **Personal:** Born Feb 21, 1946, New Orleans, LA; son of Mattie Rayno Young and Landry Young Sr; married Angela Marie Broussard; children: Tomara, Marcus, Malcolm, Miles Thurgood. **Educ:** Louisiana State Univ, New Orleans, LA, BA 1970; Syracuse Univ, MA 1972, PhD 1977. **Career:** History and African-American Studies, visiting professor, 1995-97; Syracuse Univ, lecturer Afro-Amer studies 1971, instr history 1971-72, asst prof history 1972-82, assoc prof history 1982-88; SUNY Oswego; Colgate Univ, Hamilton, NY, A Lindsay O'Connor Chair, 1988-89; Georgia Southern University, associate professor, 1989-94, professor of history, 1994-, director African and African-American studies program, 1991. **Orgs:** Keeper of finance, 1980-85, chapter historian, 1988-89, Omega Psi Phi Frat Inc Chi Pi chapter; adjunct prof history, Syracuse Univ/ Univ College Auburn Correctional Facility prog, 1981-89; consultant, faculty advisor, National Model OAU, Howard Univ, 1982—; bd mem, Friends of Syracuse Univ Alumni Organization, 1987-; board of directors, National Council for Black Studies, 1992-; Academic Council of the University Systems of Georgia Regents' Global Center, 1992-. **Honors/Awds:** Afro-Amer Fellowship Syracuse Univ 1970-72; Natl Fellowship Fund Fellow 1975-76 1976-77; Outstanding Young Men of Amer Award 1979; summer research grant NY State Afro-Amer Institute 1987; certificate of appreciation Howard Univ Model OAU, 1989; numerous publs including "The Historical Origin & Significance of the Afro-Amer History Month Observance" Negro History Bulletin 1982; selected papers presented including US Department of Education Title IV, Grant 1991-93; The National Council for Black Studies Inc, Certificate of Outstanding Service Award, 1994-96. **Special Achievements:** Contributor to Historical Dictionary of Civil Rights in the United States, 1992; Contributing Editor, African Homefront; "Internationalizing the Curriculum: Africa and the Caribbean," International Studies Association Conference, Acapulco, Mexico, 1993; "Dr, Carter G Woodson's Legacy of Academic Excellence & Social Responsibility," Morehouse College Black History Month Lecture, February 1, 1996; Booker T Washington's Ideas on Black Economic Development: the Tuskegee Experiment," Southern Conference on African-American Studies Inc, Baton Rouge, February 1995; "The African-American Response to Post-Reconstruction Conditions in the South, Birmingham, Alabama, February, 1993. **Military Serv:** USN yeoman 3rd class 1965-67. **Home Addr:** 104 Merman Dr, DeWitt, NY 13214. **Business Addr:** Professor of History, Georgia Southern University, PO Box 8054, Statesboro, GA 30460.

YOUNG, ALFRED F.
Professor. **Personal:** Born Apr 14, 1932, Clanton, AL; married; children: Quentin, Alfred. **Educ:** AL State U, BS 1957; AL State U, MS 1963; OK State U, EdD 1970. **Career:** E Highland HS Sylacauga AL, teacher 1957-58; GW Carver HS Montgomery, 1958-63; Benedict Coll, assoc prof 1967-68; OK State Univ, grad asst 1970; Benedict Coll, prof chem 1970-71; Ar-

gonne Natl Lab, faculty researcher 1971; Tel Aviv Univ Israel, intl studies 1973-74. **Orgs:** Mem Am Chemical Soc; Nat Science Tchrs Assn; Am Counc Edn; Am Assn Higher Educ Danforth Found; assoc Adv Counc Save Pub Edn; Head Start; OEO ;pres Columbia Assn Sickle Cell Anemia Found. **Honors/Awds:** Bausch & Lamb Scientific Awd. **Military Serv:** AUS sgt 1952-55. **Business Addr:** Dept of History, Northern Illinois University, De Kalb, IL 60115.

YOUNG, ANDREW
Association executive. **Personal:** Born Mar 12, 1932, New Orleans, LA; son of Daisy Fuller and Andrews J. Young; married Jean Childs, 1954 (died 1994); children: Andrea, Lisa, Paula, Andrew, III; married Carolyn Watson. **Educ:** Howard Univ, BS; Hartford Theological Seminary, BDiv. **Career:** United Church of Christ, pastor, 1955-57; National Council of Churches, associate director for youth work, 1957-61; United Church of Christ Christian Education Program, administrator, 1961-64; Southern Christian Leadership Conference, staff member, 1961-70; US House of Representatives, member, 1972-76; United Nations, US Ambassador, 1977-79; City of Atlanta, mayor, 1982-90; Metro Atlanta Chamber of Commerce, chm, 1996; Atlanta Committee for the Olympic Games, cochairman, currently; Law Intl, chmn, currently. **Orgs:** Freedom House, bd mem. **Honors/Awds:** First Black Congressman from Georgia since Jefferson Long; has received numerous honorary degrees; Pax-Christi Award, St John's Univ, 1970; Spingarn Medal; Medal of Freedom, 1980; played important role in the Civil Rights Movement in the 1960's; Alpha Kappa Alpha, Peace and Justice Award, 1991.

YOUNG, ANER RUTH
Educator. **Personal:** Born Feb 16, 1933, Perote, AL. **Educ:** AL State U, BS PE; San Francisco State, MA 1967. **Career:** Woodrow Wilson HS, dept head; middle school teacher, currently. **Orgs:** Mem Hall of Fame Am & CA Assn Hlth P Educ & Rec; CA Tchrs Assn; tchrs compet panel mem CA Tchrs Assn; sec San Francisco Classroom Tchrs Assn; State Coun; Bay Sec Coun; NEA; first chrpsn & co-fdr San Francisco Airport Police Ofcrs Assn; mem PTA; PE bd comp sports girls; sponsor schlrshp fund AL State; rare blood donor Irwin Meml Blood Bank; contrbtr support Sickle Cell Anemia; orig "SIT-INER" AL; mem So Poverty Law Ctr; vol Red Cross; splst Hlth & Fam Life Edn; fdr San Francisco Bay Area Chap AL State Alumni; dir ASU Nat Alum Assn Phi Delta Kappa Beta Nu Chpt; bd dir Nat Alumni Assn AL State; so sect spl serv for tchrs Cal-Te-A corp bds; mem NEA Nat Black Caucus; black liaison with Chicano & Asians Caucus; CA Tchrs Assn task force violence & vandal Sch; Lifemem NAACP; found SNCC. **Honors/Awds:** Coach of yr awd Woodrow Wilson Students 1975. **Business Addr:** 135 Van Ness Ave, San Francisco, CA 94102.

YOUNG, ANGELA LYNN
City official. **Personal:** Born Dec 1, 1968, Buffalo, NY; daughter of Charles & Carrie Phillips. **Educ:** Dillard University, BA, communications. **Career:** A Weight of Life, consultant, 1994-; City of New Orleans, communications/special event coord, 1994-. **Orgs:** Women of Excellence, coord of public relations, 1996-; Full Gospel Baptist church Fellowship, director of public relations, 1996-; French Quartee Festivals, 1995-; City of New Orleans Gumbo Holiday Committee, 1994-. **Honors/Awds:** Johnson Publishing Co, Future Leader of Tomorrow, 1995. **Business Addr:** Communications/Special Events Coordinator, City of New Orleans Mayor's Office of Communications, 1300 Perdido St, #2E10, New Orleans, LA 70112.

YOUNG, ARCHIE R., II
Research chemist. **Personal:** Born Jun 8, 1928, Camden, NJ; married Lena Hearo. **Educ:** Lincoln U, AB Chem 1949; Univ of PA, MS Chem 1950; Univ of PA, PhD Phys Chem 1955. **Career:** Exxon Res & Engineering Co, sr rsrch chem; Thiokol Chem Corp, res chem 1956-67; TN A&I State U, asso prof chem 1954-56; VA Union U, instr chem 1951-52; Ft Valley State Coll, instr chem 1950-51. **Orgs:** Mem Am Inst of Chemists; mem AAAS; Montclair Bd Educ 1965-70; Alpha Phi Alpha Frat. **Honors/Awds:** Recip Rohm & Haas Flwshp 1952-53; flw Am Inst Chemist; Sigma Xi 1954f Phi Lambda Upsion 1953. **Business Addr:** PO Box 8, Linden, NJ 07036.

YOUNG, ARLENE H.
Business executive. **Personal:** Born Dec 31, Orangeburg, SC; daughter of Nina Seaberry Hanton and Louis Hanton; married Eddie L Young, Dec 13, 1969; children: Eddie, Christopher, Patrick. **Educ:** Bennett College, BS, 1968; St Joseph's School of Medical Technology, MT Certificate, 1969; Oakland Community College, ARDMS, 1983; Central Michigan University, MSA, 1989. **Career:** Georgetown University Hospital, medical technologist, 1969; Walter Reed Army Medical Center, medical technologist, 1971; Midwest Medical Clinic, diagnostic medical sonographer, 1983; Hanton Industries, Inc, president, 1984-. **Orgs:** Delta Sigma Theta, 1968-; Arts and Letters Commission, 1992-94; Michigan State Council, Delta Sigma Theta, secretary, 1992-94; Southfield Alumnae Chapter, immediate past president, treasurer, 1990-94; Jack and Jill Oakland County Michigan Chapter, vice pres, 1992-93; National Council of Negro Women, 1986; National Association of Women Business Owners, 1987; National Association for Female Executives, 1992. **Honors/Awds:** State of Michigan, Top Forty Women Business Owners, 1989; Negro Business and Professional Women's Clubs, Inc, Successful Entrepreneurs, 1989; State of Michigan, Top Fifty Women Business Owners, 1988; Cub Scout Pack 1676, Cubmaster, 1986.

YOUNG, B. ASHLEY
Journalist. **Personal:** Born in Danville, IL; daughter of Annette Lewis Alexander and Will Roy Smith; married G Steven Young, Aug 6, 1978; children: Jessica M. **Educ:** Cincinnati Bible College and Seminary, working towards master's degree in theology; Kent State Univ, Kent, OH, BA, journalism, 1980. **Career:** Am Cong Gov Ind Hyg, Cincinnati, OH, copy editor, 1986-87; Cincinnati, OH, freelance, 1990-; Journal-News, Hamilton, OH, reporter/copy editor, 1988-. **Orgs:** Mem, Natl Assn of Black Journalists; mem, Ohio Newspaper Women's Assn; mem, Ohio Professional Writers. **Honors/Awds:** Journalism Award, Ohio Vet Med Assn, 1989. **Business Addr:** Journalist, Editorial, 228 Court Street, Hamilton, OH 45012.

YOUNG, BARBARA J.
Educational administrator. **Personal:** Born Nov 2, 1937, Muskogee, OK; daughter of Idessa Hammond Dossett and Major Alonzo Dossett; married Douglas Charles Young Jr; children: Crystal Marion Humphrey, Hammond George Bouldin, Daniel-le Humphrey. **Educ:** CSUS, BA, soc psychology, 1977, MS, counseling, 1981, EdD, admin, 1988. **Career:** Fresno State University, sec, 1967-69; California State University at Sacramento, exec asst pres, 1969-74, employment counselor, 1974-77, financial aid officer, 1977-83, student affairs officer, asst director, school relations, 1983-86; California State University, asst dean, 1986-90, associate dean, academic affairs, 1990-. **Orgs:** WASFA, 1977-; Black Professional Assn; SPAC; Delta Sigma Theta Sorority, Nu Lambda Chapter, 1977-; Sacramento Urban League, 1970-; PACROW; California Respiratory Care, bd mem, 1993; CAL-SOAP Advisory Board, bd mem, 1991-; Leadership CA, participatn, 1994; Lambda Kappa Mu Sorority, basileus, 1990; Pan African Doctoral Scholars, Inc, pres; United Way, Harbor City, bd mem; National Brd of Respiratory Care, board member, Leadership America, 1997. **Honors/Awds:** National Soror of the Year, Lambda Kappa Mu Sorority, 1996. **Home Addr:** 3707 Livingston Dr, Ste 301, Long Beach, CA 90803. **Business Addr:** Associate Dean, Academic Affairs Office, California State University, 400 Golden Shore Dr, Long Beach, CA 90802.

YOUNG, BRYANT COLBY
Professional football player. **Personal:** Born Jan 27, 1972, Chicago Heights, IL. **Educ:** University of Notre Dame, attended. **Career:** San Francisco 49ers, defensive tackle, 1994-. **Honors/Awds:** United Press International, NFL Defensive Rookie of the Year, 1994; Pro Bowl, 1996; Len Eshmont Award, 1996. **Business Addr:** Professional Football Player, San Francisco 49ers, 4949 Centennial Blvd, Santa Clara, CA 95054, (415)562-4949.

YOUNG, CARLENE HERB
Psychologist, educator (retired). **Personal:** Born in Selma, AL; divorced; children: Howard, Loren. **Educ:** Univ of Detroit, MA 1960; Wayne State Univ Detroit, EdD 1967; Wright Inst Berkeley CA, PhD 1976. **Career:** San Jose Police Department, Law Enforcement Psychological Services, psychologist, 1985-; San Jose State Univ, prof clinical psych 1969-92, professor emeritus, 1992; Univ of Detroit-Wayne State Univ, lectr ed psy/ed soc 1966-69; Oakland County Community College, dept chmn soc 1968; Title III Lincoln Child Development Center, proj dir 1967; Natl Teacher Corp, team leader 1966-67; Detroit Public School, teacher 1955-67. **Orgs:** Consult Dept of Def Race Rel Inst 1976-78; consult PMC 1978-79; consult Koba Asso Washington DC 1979; bd of dir Catholic Social Serv 1976-; vice pres CA Black Fac & Staff Assn 1977; exec sec/v Chmn/chair elect Nat Counc of Black Studies 1978 1980; consult Psych Assessment Law Enf Officers; adv comm CA State Personnel Bd Psych. **Honors/Awds:** Phi Kappa Phi Honor Society; Alpha Kappa Alpha Sorority Inc. **Special Achievements:** Editor: "Black Experience analysis & synthesis" Leswing Press, 1972; traveled: Africa (Cameroon, Senegal, Ivory Coast, Ghana, Mali, Somalia, Egypt); Europe; Mexico. **Business Addr:** Psychologist, 4950 Hamilton, Ste 105, San Jose, CA 95130.

YOUNG, CHARLES, JR.
Educational administrator. **Personal:** Born Aug 5, 1934, St Louis, MO; married Jessie Dolores Howell; children: Karen. **Educ:** Lincoln Univ MO, BS Ed 1957; Univ IL, Med 1962, EdD 1972. **Career:** St Louis Public School, teacher 1957-66, asst prin 1966-67, prin 1967-72; Urbana Comm School, prin 1972-1984; Joliet Public School, asst supt 1984-. **Orgs:** Mem Am Assc Sch Admn, Phi Delta Kappa 1964-, Kappa Alpha Psi 1952-, Rotary Intrntl 1985. **Honors/Awds:** Serv awrd Natl Assc Scndry Sch Prncpls 1966; ldrshp awrd Champaign Co Boys Clb 1978. **Military Serv:** AUSR capt. **Home Addr:** 2650 Black Rd, Joliet, IL 60435. **Business Addr:** Assistant Superintendent, Joliet Public Sch, 420 N Raynor, Joliet, IL 60435.

YOUNG, CHARLES ALEXANDER
Educator (retired), artist. **Personal:** Born Nov 17, 1930, New York, NY; son of Mary Rodgers Young and Charles A Young Sr; married Elizabeth Bell; children: Paula D. **Educ:** Hampton Univ, BS 1953; NY Univ, MA 1959; Catholic Univ, advance work in art 1964. **Career:** Dayton St Sch Newark, art tchr 1957-59; Fayetteville State Univ, art instr 1959-62; TN A&I State Univ, asst prof of art 1962-68; Federal City Coll, assoc prof of art, 1968-78; Univ of the Dist of Columbia, prof of art 1978-. **Orgs:** Chairperson of art Fed City Coll 1970-78; chairperson of art Univ of the Dist of Columbia 1978-84, 1989-; Coll Art Assn 1970-; Amer Artists Assn 1968-70; Natl Educ Assn 1975; Southeastern Art Assn 1965-66, 1968-77; Nashville Artist Guild 1964-68; Smith-Mason Gallery Washington 1970-; DC Commn on the Arts Visual Arts Panel 1973-79; Natl Conf of Artists, 1974-75, 1980-83; DC Commn of the Arts, 1980 design panel, 1981-82; Graphics Soc 1980; Natl Art Educ Assn 1980-91; DC Art Alliance of Greater Washington 1977; US Soc for Educ through Art 1978; College Art Assnc 1988-; Natl Conference of Artists 1986-91. **Honors/Awds:** Le Centre d'Art-Haiti 1982; Corcoran Gall of Art-DC 1982; UDC Faculty Art Exhibition-Alma Thomas Meml Art Gallery Shaw Jr HS Washington 1983, Marble Arch Gallery Regional Art Exhibition Charleston SC 1983; numerous publs & public collections including, paintings reproduced "Black Dimensions in Contemporary Art" compiled by Edward Atkinson; public collections, Fayetteville State Coll, Scottish Bank, Kennedy Inst; Black Art in Washington Washingtonian Mag 1973; published articles, Haitian Art Newsletter Vol 1 #6 Fall edition 1978 "African Odyssey;" Metro-Washington Mag March 1984 "Mainstream, A Place For Afro-AmerArtists?;" UDC Afro-Amer Art Catalog titled "Van Ness Campus Art Collection 1984" introduction; MLK Library-DC 1986; Afro-American Art Exhibition 1988; A Tribute To Washinhgton a Artists 1988; Black Image Exhibition Univ of District of Columbia Art Gallery, 1988; Painting reproduced in Art: African American, Samella Lewis 1987; One Man Exhibition Hampton Univ Museum, Hampton, VA, 1989-; Exhibition Museum of Modern Art, Gibellina, Italy, 1990; Exhibition Museum of Science and Industry (Black Creativity), Chicago, IL, 1991; State of the Art 93, Fine Arts Inst, Natl Exhibition of American Comtemporary Art, 1993; State Fine Arts Museum of Alma-Ata, Kazakstan, Russia, 1993; Fannie Mae Exhibition, 1996-97; Art Work Exhibited permanently in Coll, Hampton Univ Museum, 1997-. **Military Serv:** US Army, 1st lt, 1953-55; Overseas Decoration. **Home Addr:** 8104 W Beach Dr NW, Washington, DC 20012.

YOUNG, CHARLES LEMUEL, SR.
Business executive. **Personal:** Born Aug 27, 1931, Lauderdale County; married Doretha Connor (deceased); children: Charles L Jr, Deidre, Arthur, Veldora. **Educ:** TN A&I Univ, BS Business Admin 1948-51; Univ of Denver, Public Relations; Human Develop Inst. **Career:** Royal Oak Develop Co, pres; EF Young Jr Mfg, pres; MS Legislature, mem. **Orgs:** Exec comm & co-founder MS Action for Progress; past bd mem Inst of Politics; life mem NAACP; past dir Meridian Chamber of Commerce; past dir State Mutual Fed Savings & Loan. **Military Serv:** AUS sgt 1st class 2 yrs; Bronze Star; Good Conduct Medal; Korean Citation. **Home Addr:** 3120 15th St, Meridian, MS 39301. **Business Addr:** President, EF Young Jr Mfg Co, 425 26th Ave, Meridian, MS 39301.

YOUNG, CHARLIE, JR.
Elected city official. **Personal:** Born Apr 28, 1928, Leary, GA; married Kathryn Robinson; children: Gail Y Smith, Aaron Lee, Valerie Y Pittman. **Educ:** Leary School, 10th grade. **Career:** Presently City Councilman. **Home Addr:** PO Box 143, Leary, GA 31762.

YOUNG, CLARENCE, III
Production company executive. **Personal:** Born Apr 7, 1942, Dayton, OH; son of Louise McGee Young and Clarence Young Jr. **Educ:** Capital Univ, BA 1979. **Career:** Playwright Theatre W Dayton OH, dir 1968-82; Clarence Young III Production, independent producer, TV production 1982-; Ellison Sr Citizen Center, dir. **Orgs:** Independent TV producer, Clarence Young III 1982-; pres Clarence Young III Productions 1981-; pres-publisher Young Sound Music BMI 1981-; master mason Prince Hall Lodge Equity Lodge 121 1983. **Honors/Awds:** Outstanding Independent producer & TV editor, 1984 Access 30 Dayton, OH 1984; "I Am A Young Lady" Playwright Musical Dayton Art Inst 1981; Parity 2000's Ten Top African American Males, 1995. **Special Achievements:** Produced and wrote: The System, Black Love, Young Lady, Song of Memories Past, Bobby's Jacket, The Road to Brighton, Goobleg one; CD, Bow to the People. **Military Serv:** USAF a2c 1961-65. **Home Addr:** 840 N Broadway Street, Dayton, OH 45407.

YOUNG, COLEMAN A. **See Obituaries section.**

YOUNG, COLEMAN MILTON, III
Physician. **Personal:** Born Nov 13, 1930, Louisville, KY; son of Hortense Houston Young and C Milton Young Jr; married Waltraud Scheussler Young, Jul 4, 1987; children: C Milton IV, Lloyd M, Christopher H. **Educ:** Univ of Louisville, AB 1952; Meharry Med Coll, MD 1961. **Career:** Louisville Genl Hosp, intern 1961-62; St Joseph's Infirmary, resd 1962-65; Metha-

done Treatment Prog, fndr dir 1968-72; Private Practice, physician internal medicine, currently. **Orgs:** Chmn bd mem Park DuValle Neighborhood Health Center 1966-69; Gov Young Kentuckian's Adv Commn 1967-70; mem Louisville Jeffers on Co Air Pollution Control Bd 1968-77, chmn 1968-72; med Adv SSS 1968-73; mem Hon Order KY Col 1972; mem dir Drug Abuse Prog River Region Mental Health Bd 1972-73; med dir Comm Hospital 1972-75; consult drug prog River Region Mental Health Bd 1973-74; Gov Cncl Alcohol & Drug Abuse 1973; consult Senate Com Juv Prob 1973; mem Alpha Phi Alpha; AMA; life mem NAACP; editor bd chmn Black Scene Mag 1974-76; pres Falls City Med Soc 1982-85. **Honors/Awds:** Louisville Man Yr Awd WHAS TV 1970; natl adv Amer Assn Med Asst 1976-77; Disting Citizen Awd Key to City Mayor Harvey I Sloane 1977. **Special Achievements:** First African American undergraduate student at the University of Louisville, 1950; first African American medical intern at Louisville Gen Hospital, 1961; first African American medical resident trained at a priv institution in Kentucky, St. Joseph's Infirmary-Louisville, KY. **Military Serv:** AUS MC corpl 1952-54. **Business Addr:** Physician, 740 Zorn Ave Apt 4A, Louisville, KY 40206-1449.

YOUNG, DMITRI DELL
Professional baseball player. **Personal:** Born Oct 11, 1973, Vicksburg, MS. **Career:** St Louis Cardinals, infielder, 1996-. **Business Addr:** Professional Baseball Player, St Louis Cardinals, 250 Stadium Plaza, Busch Memorial Stadium, St Louis, MO 63102, (314)421-3060.

YOUNG, EDITH MAE
Educator. **Personal:** Born Oct 15, 1932, Denison, TX; daughter of Pinkie Rambo Franklin (deceased) and Joe C Young Sr (deceased). **Educ:** TX Coll, Certificate, Sec Sci 1951; Lincoln Univ MO, BSE 1961, MEd 1964; Univ of MO Columbia, EdD 1973. **Career:** Library, Lincoln U, MO, sec/admin asst 1951-66; Education & Center for Research in Social Behavior, Univ of MO Columbia, intern/voc tchr 1973; Center for Acad Devel UMSL, acting dir 1977-80; Educ Business Tchr Educ, instructor/asst prof 1966-70, 1973-77, 1980-, acting assoc dean, 1993-94; Univ of MO, St Louis, assoc prof of educ; University of Missouri St Louis, chair of educational studies department, 1995-. **Orgs:** Mem Delta Pi Epsilon 1970-; mem Kappa Delta Pi 1972-; mem Pi Lambda Theta 1973-; mem AAHE 1967-; mem AVA 1966-; mem NBEA 1962-; mem Alpha Kappa Alpha Sor 1967; educator examiner, National Accrediting Commission of Cosmetology Arts & Sciences 1985-; editorial advisory bd, Collegiate Press 1989-90; 1994-95. **Honors/Awds:** EPDA Doctoral Fellowship in Voc Educ 1971-73; ACE Fellow in Acad Admin 1979-80; Summer Faculty Research Fellowship UMSL 1975; Educator of the Year, Outstanding Leadership in Higher Educ, 1994. **Business Addr:** Chair, Educational Studies Department, University of Missouri, 8001 Natural Bridge Rd, St Louis, MO 63121.

YOUNG, EDWARD HIRAM, JR.
Meteorologist. **Personal:** Born Dec 10, 1950, Berkeley, CA; son of Grace Jean King Young (deceased) and Edward Hiram Young Sr; married Doris Kathleen Jackson, Nov 2, 1996. **Educ:** San Jose State Univ, BS Meteorology 1973; 2 yrs grad work in meteorology; N Harris Co Coll, courses in mgmt & business 1983-84; Delgado Community Coll, courses in computers 1987-88. **Career:** Natl Weather Svcs, meteorologist intern Portland, OR 1975-78; Riverside CA, agricultural meteorologist 1978-81; Ctr Weather Serv FAA Houston TX, aviation meteorologist 1981-84; Natl Weather Serv Southern Region, prog mgr 1981-87; Ft Worth TX S Region, spec serv met TX 1984-86; Natl Weather Svc, agri/forestry meteorologist 1986-, Pacific Region Headquarters, Honolulu HI, Technical Services Division, chief 1988-. **Orgs:** Mem bd dirs San Jose Chap Amer Red Cross 1970-72; mem Natl Coll Student Adv Council Amer Red Cross 1971-72; Black prog mgr Natl Weather Serv Wrn Reg 1978-81; mem bd of dirs Great Outdoors 1980-81; mem Amer Assn for the Advancement of Sci 1980; Black prog mgr Natl Weather Serv Srn Region 1981-; mem Amer Meteorological Soc 1970-; mem bd on Women & Minorities Amer Meteorological Soc 1985-87, chmn 1989-90; mem subcommittee Ft Worth United Way Allocations 1986; consultant SMART(Science, Mathematics, Aeronautics, Research, Technology & The Black Family) 1989; aux bd mem asst Baha'i Faith of Hawaiian Islands 1988, staff; chair, subcommittee Hawaii Martin Luther King Jr Interim Commission, 1990-95; US-China Peoples Friendship Assn 1995-; elected mem, National Spiritual Assembly of the Bahais of the Hawaiian Islands, 1997. **Honors/Awds:** Elks Leadership Awd Oakland CA Elks Club 1968; EEO Awd Natl Oceanic & Atmospheric Admin 1984; Dallas-Ft Worth Federal Exec Bd EEO Awd 1986; Presented a paper at SMART Conf, Howard Univ, Blacks in Meteorology 1989; nominated, Honolulu-Pacific Federal Exec Bd Outstanding Community Service Award, 1996; ''Doer of Good Deeds'' Award, Hawaii Chapter, B'Nai Brith 1995. **Home Addr:** 733 Bishop St, Suite 170-123, Honolulu, HI 96813. **Business Phone:** (808)532-6412.

YOUNG, ELIZABETH BELL
Consultant, lecturer, public speaker. **Personal:** Born Jul 2, 1929, Durham, NC; daughter of Mr & Mrs Joseph H Bell (deceased); married Charles A Jr. **Educ:** NC Central U, BA 1948, MA 1950; OH St U, PhD 1959. **Career:** Catholic Univ, graduate school prof 1966-79; Barber Scotia Coll NC; Talladega Coll AL; VA State Coll; OH State Univ; FL A&M Univ; Fayetteville State Univ NC; Howard Univ Wash DC; Univ of MD, Eastern Shore; Princess Anne, MD; Univ of the DC, Dept Speech Science (communications) & English, univ prof & chmn 1949-84; Natl & Intl Organizations & Universities, consultant & lecturer, 1981-; Congressional Staff Aide, 1980, 1987-91, Staff aide US House of Reps (Office of Congressman Walter E Fauntroy) 1980, 1987-91; Lecturer & Consultant US Govt (Office of Ed) 1981-87; field reader& team reviewer, US St Dept promotion panelist 1980-. **Orgs:** Mem of Bd (Public Mem Asso) 1979-; mem bd of dir Washington Ctr Music Thrpy Clinic; mem adv bd United Negro Clg Fund 1979-82; mem Congressional Adv B D on Educ 1979-82; mem Alpha Kappa Alpha Sor 1946-; bd mem Clinical Cert Am Speech-L & H Assn 1979-83; bd dir Handicapped Intervention Prog for High Risk Infants Wash DC 1978-87. **Honors/Awds:** Flw Am Speech, Lang, Hearing Asso 1980; Otstndng Alumni Awd OH St Univ 1976; publ Journal Articles in Field of Communications & Made Over 450 Speeches in US; Pioneer in field of speech Pathology & Audiology; 1st African-American to receive PRD in Speech Science; 1st African-American to obtain dual certification in Speech Pathology and Audiology; 1st African-American to obtain PhD from Ohio State Univ in communications and speech science, and started 1st certified speech & learning clinics in historically black colleges and universities. **Business Addr:** Consultant and Lecturer, Natl & Intrl Organ & Univ, 8104 W Beach Dr NW, Washington, DC 20012.

YOUNG, ELMER, JR.
Banker. **Personal:** Born Jul 4, 1924, Phila; married Thelma; children: Victor, Vincent. **Educ:** Temple U, BS 1952. **Career:** 1st PA Bank, sr vice pres 1970-; Dillingham Corp, proj mgr 1969-70; Progress Plaza Shopping Cntr , proj mgr cntr mgr 1968-69; Rev Dr Leon H Sullivan, asst 1965-69; IBM Corp, admin mgr 1957-65; broker real estate ins 1952-56. **Orgs:** Mem Philadelphia Urban League; Comm Devel Fund; v chmn United Fund 1976; Philadelphia Counc Comm Advance. **Honors/Awds:** Exemplor awrd NAACP 1975; publs Corporate Soc Accounting Praeger Pub 1973; Real Estate Today Nat Inst Real Estate Brokers 1971. **Military Serv:** AUS s/sgt 1946. **Business Addr:** Sr Vice Pres, First Pennsylvania Bank, 15 & Chestnut Sts, Philadelphia, PA 19101.

YOUNG, ELROY
Physician. **Personal:** Born Jan 7, 1923, RFD Olmsted, IL; son of Alice Calhoun and H G Young; married Mabel H Grant; children: Janice Lansey, Charles. **Educ:** Univ of Illinois, BS 1947; Meharry Medical College, MD 1951. **Career:** Self-employed medical doctor; Freedmen's Hospital, resident 1953-57; Lincoln Hospital, resident 1952-53; Lincoln Hospital, intern 1951-52. **Orgs:** Mem Baltimore City Medical Soc; Medical Chirugical Faculty of MD; Southern Medical Assn; Natl Medical Assn; Maryland Orthopaedic Soc; grand chaplin Chi Delta Mu Fraternity 1989-; treasurer Maryland Medical Assn 1989-; past president, Maryland Orthopaedic Soc; past member of bd, MOS; past member of bd, James Kerman Hospital, Baltimore, MD; elder, Madison Ave Presbyterian Church; mem, Southern Orthopaedic Assn. **Special Achievements:** First African-American Orthopaedic Surgeon in State of Maryland, 1957. **Military Serv:** AUS non-commissioned officer 1943-46. **Business Addr:** Medical Service Center, Inc., 1529 E North Ave, Baltimore, MD 21223.

YOUNG, ERIC ORLANDO
Professional baseball player. **Personal:** Born May 18, 1967, New Brunswick, NJ. **Educ:** Rutgers. **Career:** Los Angeles Dodgers, infielder, 1992, 1997-; Colorado Rockies, 1993-96. **Business Addr:** Professional Baseball Player, Los Angeles Dodgers, 1000 Elysian Park Ave, Los Angeles, CA 90012, (213)224-1530.

YOUNG, ERNEST WESLEY
Professional baseball player. **Personal:** Born Jul 8, 1969, Chicago, IL. **Educ:** Lewis College. **Career:** Oakland Athletics, outfielder, 1994-. **Business Addr:** Professional Baseball Player, Oakland Athletics, 7677 Oakport St, 2nd Fl, Oakland Coliseum Complex, Oakland, CA 94621, (510)638-4900.

YOUNG, F. CAMILLE
Dental director. **Personal:** Born Sep 3, 1928, Boston; married Dr Virgil J. **Educ:** Howard Univ, BS 1949; Howard Univ, DDS 1958; Univ of MI, MPH 1974. **Career:** Comm Group Hlth Found, chf of dental serv 1971-; Div of Dental Health Bureau of Hlth Resources Devel Dept of HEW, consultant, 1971-74; Comm Group Health Found, staff dentist 1969-71; DC Dept of Public Health, dental officer 1964-69; Private Practice, Washington DC, 1962-; Amer Fund for Dental Health, elected 5 yr term bd trsts 1972-; Howard Univ Coll of Dentistry, asst prof 1971-. **Orgs:** Vice pres, Robert T Freeman Dental Soc 1970-72; first woman to attain ofc mem Exec Bd 1966-72; chmn Speakers Bureau 1968-72; chmn Budget & Auditing Com 1968-70; chmn Social Com 1966-70; chmn Awards Com 1970; mem DC Dental Soc; chmn Table Clinic Com 1970; sec Dental Health Care Com 1968; mem Natl Dental Assn; pres, asst 1968-73; area dir Dentistry as a Career Prog Recruit Com 1968-73; chmn Protocol Com 1968, 1973; del Lse of Dels 1969-73; Nat Dental Assn Amer & Dental Assn Liaison Com 1968-73; chmn Travel Com 1970-73; mem Howard Univ Dental Alumni Assn; exec sec 1967-69; mem exec bd 1967-69; mem Am Dental Assn 1965-; Amer Public Health Assn 1972-; Natl Assn of Neighborhood Health Cntrs 1972-; Assn of Amer Women Dentists 1974-. **Honors/Awds:** Appeared on TV lectr & spkr at many schs & colls; recipient, Pres' Award Natl Dental Assn 1969; special award Natl Dental Assn 1973; represented Amer Dental Assn at First Black Women's Inst 1972 Hunger Convocation Amer Hotel NY; del White House Conf on Children 1970; co-authored article in Urban Health Dentistry in OEO Health Prog 1972. **Business Addr:** 3308 14 St NW, Washington, DC.

YOUNG, GEORGE, JR. (TOBY)
Radio station executive, state government coordinator. **Personal:** Born Oct 13, 1933, Gadsden, AL; children: Kathy Ann, Carrie Vernell Marie, Dorthy Louise. **Educ:** Lincoln Univ, MHS 1984. **Career:** From Where I Sit, True Gospel, WTPA TV, writer producer, MC; Harrisburg Glass Inc, affirm act coord 1952-68; Toby Young Show, Echos of Glory, Jazz Today WKBO Radio, staff announcer, hosted, producer 1965-71; Toby Young Enterprise, affirm act coord 1971-; TY Records, affirm act coord 1971-72; WCMB-WMIX Echoes of Glory; Toby Young Show, Party Line, Echoes of Glory, Project People WCMB Radio, comm rel spec 1971-; PN Civil Service Commission, affirmative action, PR contract compliance coordinator, currently. **Orgs:** Life mem NAACP; mem bd Camp Curtin YMCA, Harristown Comm Complex; bd mem Tri-County March of Dimes; chrpsn 1976 Edgemont Fire House; pres PA Chap Natl Assoc of Radio & TV Artists; bd mem Gaudinzia House; past co-chrpsn Congress of Affirm Action; past chmn, bd of mgrs, owners Soulville & Jay Walking Records; bd mem Natl Progressive Affirm Action Officers; mem Daughin Cty Exec Comm of Drug & Alcohol Inc, past master, dir of PR Central; Chosen Friend Lodge 43 F&AM Prince Hall Club 21 of Harrisburg PA. **Honors/Awds:** Winner of two Glow Awards; Gospel DJ of the Year; Meritorious Service Award. **Military Serv:** AUS 2 yrs USAR 4 1/2 yrs. **Business Addr:** Equal Opportunity/Contract Compliance Coordinator, PN Civil Serv Commission, Exec Offices, 320 Market Street, 4th Fl, PO Box 569, Harrisburg, PA 17108-0569.

YOUNG, IRA MASON
Attorney. **Personal:** Born Sep 20, 1929, St Louis, MO; son of Mamie Mason Young and Nathan B Young; married Lillie. **Educ:** Oberlin Coll, BA 1951; WA Univ, JD 1957. **Career:** Private Practice, attorney 1957-. **Orgs:** Mem MO State Bd of Law Examiners 1980-84; mem Natl Bar Assn; Amer Bar Assn; Amer Trial Lawyers Assn; Lawyers Assn St Louis; St Louis Metro Bar Assn; Mound City Bar Assn; bd dir Legal Aid Soc 1965-70; Family & Childrens Serv Greater St Louis; adv cncl Legal Serv Corp MO; bd dir Girl Scout Council St Louis. **Military Serv:** AUS 1951-53. **Business Addr:** Attorney, 509 Olive, Ste 1000, St Louis, MO 63101.

YOUNG, JAMES ARTHUR, III
Business executive. **Personal:** Born Jan 6, 1945, Augusta, GA; son of Pauline Elim Young and James A Young Jr; married Felisa Perez (divorced); children: Alvin Renato Young. **Educ:** Claflin Coll, BA 1967; Gable School of Art in Advertising, certificate, 1975. **Career:** Burke Co Bd of Educ Waynesboro, teacher 1967; Montgomery Co Bd of Educ Ailey GA, teacher 1967-68; CSRA Econ Oppor Auth Inc, task force leader 1970-71; Laney-Walker Mus Inc Augusta, exec dir 1976-. **Orgs:** Mem 2nd Shilo Baptist Church, Augusta 1957; mem Augusta Cultural Arts Assn 1977-80; mem Natl Trust for History Preservation 1979-80; mem Augusta-Richmond Co Music 1979-80; mem Greater Augusta Arts Council 1980; judge public school art contest Richmond Co Bd of Educ Augusta 1980; mem Seven-Thirty Breakfast Club Columbia, SC 1980. **Honors/Awds:** Founder/dir Laney-Walker Music Inc 1977; nominee Comm for major traveling exhbn Nation of Ghana & Nigeria 1980-81; panelist Leadership Augusta/Greater Augusta Chamber of Commerce. **Military Serv:** AUS E-2 1970-73; Hon Ret Disability. **Business Addr:** Executive Dir, Laney Walker Music Inc, 821 Laney Walker Blvd, Augusta, GA 30901.

YOUNG, JAMES E.
Banker. **Career:** City National Bank of New Jersey, senior vp of general administration and commercial loans; First Southern Bank, president/chief executive officer, 1993-. **Special Achievements:** Company is ranked #24 on Black Enterprise magazine's 1997 list of Top 100 Black businesses. **Business Addr:** Pres, CEO, First Southern Bank, PO Box 1019, Lithonia, GA 30058, (404)593-6360.

YOUNG, JAMES E.
Educator. **Personal:** Born Jan 18, 1926, Wheeling, WV; son of Edna (Thompson) Young and James E Young (deceased). **Educ:** Howard U, BS, MS 1949; MIT, MS, PhD 1953; Harvard Univ Div Med Sci, 1984-86. **Career:** Hampton Inst, instr physics 1946-49; Gen Atominics, consult 1957-58; Univ MN, vstg assoc prof 1964; Sir Rudy Peierls Oxford, rsch asst 1965-66; Harvard, vstg rsch sci 1978; Los Alamos Sci Lab, staff mem 1956-59; Tufts Univ Med Schools, rsch assoc neurosci dept

anatomy & cell biol 1986-; MIT, prof physics 1970-. **Orgs:** Mem Am Physiol Soc 1960-; Sigma Xi Hon Soc MIT 1953; post-doctoral fellow MIT Acoustics Lab 1953-55; Shell BP fellow Aeronautics Dept Southampton England 1956; NAS-NRC Ford fellow Niels Bohr Inst Copenhagen 1961-62; pres JEY Assoc; chief op officer MHT Ltd; tech dir CADEX; partner Escutcheon Inc. **Honors/Awds:** US Patent #4,564,798 Jan 1986. **Business Addr:** Professor Physics, MIT, 6-405/CTP, Cambridge, MA 02139.

YOUNG, JAMES E., JR.
Attorney. **Personal:** Born Jul 18, 1931, New Orleans, LA; married Eddie Mae Wilson; children: James, III, Adrienne, Darrin. **Educ:** So Univ Law Sch, JD 1960; So U, BA 1958. **Career:** Parish New Orelans, notary public 1962-; Private Practice, atty 1960-68; VA Reg Office, adjudicator 1966-68; NOLAC, neighborhood staff atty 1968-69; New Orleans Legal Ssst Corp, sr staff atty 1969-70, asst dir 1970-71; atty & notary public 1971-. **Orgs:** Mem LA State Bar Assn; Am Bar Assn; Am Judicature Soc; Louis A Martinet Legal Soc; spl consult & guest lectr So Univ in New Orleans Evening Div; Poverty & Consumer Law Panelist & Symposium partic Tulane U; gen cousel Cntrl Cty Econ Oppor Corp; past pres & charter mem Heritage Sq Devel Corp; past pres & mem Lake Area Pub Sch Improvement Assn; past pres & ofcr Edward Livingston Middle Sch; lifetime mem Nat Bar Assn; Kappa Alpha Psi Frat; mem & former ofcr Acad Pk Devel Assn; past pres New Orleans Pan-Hellenic Coun; former mem & exec com Cntrl Cty Econ Oppor Corp. **Honors/Awds:** Winner of 2 gold keys awards in natl art compet Nat Scholastic 1949 & 50; grad in top ten percent NCO Ldrshp & Motor Mechanics Sch USMC; contrbn & spl features editor coll newspaper; recip of Purple Heart. **Military Serv:** USMC 1951-54; Purple Heart Medal.

YOUNG, JAMES M., II
Marketing manager. **Personal:** Born Oct 29, 1946, Washington, DC; married Barbara Ann Johnson; children: Julie Elizabeth, Jason Michael. **Educ:** Fisk Univ Nashville, BA Biology 1968. **Career:** Serv Bur Co (Div Control Date Corp), mrktng mgr 1978-; F Serv Bur Co, proj adminstr educ 1977-78; Xerox Corp, mrktng rep 1971-74. **Orgs:** Mem Alpha Phi Alpha Frat 1965. **Honors/Awds:** Recip vietnam aviation medal AUS 1968-71. **Military Serv:** AUS cw2 1968-71. **Business Addr:** Service Bureau Co, 222 S Riverside Plaza Ste 23, Chicago, IL 60606.

YOUNG, JOHN W.
Budget analyst. **Personal:** Born Jun 18, 1927, Wash, DC; married; children: John, Dolores, Robert. **Educ:** Univ NE, BEd 1965; Univ TX, MA 1973. **Career:** Dept Planning & Rsrch Cty of El Paso, planning tech 1971-73; planner 1973; Pub Adminstrn Ofc Mgmt & Budget Cty of El Paso, budget analyst. **Orgs:** Mem Intl Cty Mgmt Assn; Municipal Finan Ofcrs Assn; Assn of US Army; Smithsonian Assos bd dirs El Paso Comm Action Prgm adminstr com ch; bd dirs Family Serv El Paso 2d vp; pub serv div chmn United Way of El Paso. **Honors/Awds:** US Army meritorious serv medal; bronze star medal; air medal; commend medal; sr parachutist badge. **Military Serv:** AUS lt col 1945-70. **Business Addr:** Office Management & Budget, City County, El Paso, TX 79901.

YOUNG, JONES. **See YOUNG, TERRI JONES.**

YOUNG, JOSEF A.
Psychotherapist. **Personal:** Born Mar 24, 1941, Memphis, TN; married Dr Joyce Lynom Young; children: Jorald (deceased). **Educ:** TSU,BS1962;MSU,Masters 1967; Univ of Tenn, Post Masters 1972;Southern Ill Univ at Carbondale, PhD 1981. **Career:** Mason, 1974- ; Alpha Phi Alpha, Vice Pres 1980; Center for Developmental Growth, Pres1980; Optimist Club International, Comm Chariman 1985. **Orgs:** Int'l Counseling Assn, Brd of Dir 1970; West Tenn Personnel and Guidance, Pres 1972-73; Black Psychologist Assn, 1983; Assoc of Black Psychologist, 1984- ;State Brd of Regents " How to teach the hard to learn student"; Tennessee Assoc of Counseling," Fetal Alcohol Syndrome and the Female Alcoholic" American Assocof Ethical Hypnosis. **Military Serv:** Air Force Reserve, 1958-60. **Home Addr:** 5131 Ravensworth Dr, Memphis, TN 38109. **Business Addr:** Senior Counselor, State Tech Inst at Memphis, 5983 Macon Cove, Memphis, TN 38134.

YOUNG, JOSEPH, JR.
Government official. **Career:** State of Michigan, Representative, currently. **Business Addr:** Representative, Michigan Legislature, House of Representatives, State Capitol, PO Box 30014, Lansing, MI 48909-7514, (517)373-1008.

YOUNG, JOYCE HOWELL
Physician. **Personal:** Born Mar 22, 1934, Cincinnati, OH; daughter of Addiebelle Foster Howell and Lloyd Marion Howell; married Coleman Milton Young III, Jun 25, 1960 (divorced); children: C Milton Young IV, Lloyd M Young, Christopher H Young. **Educ:** Fisk Univ, BA Zoology 1954; Womans Med Coll of PA, MD 1958; Miami Vly Hosp Dayton, OH, Cert Intrnshp 1959; Meharry Med Coll Hubbard Hosp, Cert Peds 1960, Cert Int Med 1961; Univ Louisville Chld Eval Ctr, Cert Grwth & Devel 1973. **Career:** Private Med Practice Lou KY, 1961-67; Univ Louisville Child Eval Ctr, ped devel spclst 1973-74; Park Duvalle Nghbrhd Hlth Ctr, med dir 1974-76; KY Dept of Human Resources, med cnsltnt 1984-. **Orgs:** Mem Alpha Kappa Alpha Sorority 1952-, Falls City Medical Soc 1961-, Jefferson Cnty Med Scty 1962-, KY Med Assn 1962-, Lou Links, Inc 1965-80; financial sec 1980-, mem 1973-, mem session 1988-, Shawnee Presbyterian Church; mem Lou Brd of Educ 1971-74, chrmn 1974; brd mem Lincoln Found 1974-; dir Continental Natl Bank of KY 1974-86; mem KY Human Rights Commn 1983-; mem American Medical Assoc; mem Syn Covenant Cabinet Ethnic Church Affairs 1983-86; treas KBPU 1983-; chmn Commn on Representation 1985-86; member, Executive Council Presbytery of Louisville, 1986-91; board member, Jefferson City Med Soc Business Bureau, 1990-. **Honors/Awds:** Apptmnt by governor KY Colonel 1962; Comm Serv Awrd Lou Links, Inc 1973-74, Alpha Kappa Alpha Sor 1974, Zeta Phi Beta 1975; series of articles on hlth Black Scene Mag 1975; diplomate, Amer Bd of Disability Consultants, 1989-. **Home Addr:** 739 S Western Pkwy, Louisville, KY 40211.

YOUNG, KEVIN CURTIS
Professional track athlete. **Personal:** Born Sep 16, 1966, Los Angeles, CA; son of Betty Champion and William Young. **Educ:** University of California, Los Angeles, BA, sociology, 1989. **Career:** Flavours Co Inc; Olympic track athlete, currently. **Orgs:** Alpha Phi Alpha Fraternity Inc, 1987-. **Honors/Awds:** International Amateur Athlete Foundation, Male Athlete of the Year, 1992; Track & Field News, Athlete of the Year, 1992; Harrison Dilliard Award, 1992; Jesse Owens Award, 1992; USOC Track & Field, Male Athlete of the Year, 1992; Olympic Games, Gold Medal, 400m Hurdles, 1992. **Business Addr:** Flavours Co Inc, 8860 Corbin Ave, #332, Northridge, CA 91324.

YOUNG, KEVIN STACEY
Professional baseball player. **Personal:** Born Jun 16, 1969, Alpena, MI. **Educ:** Southern Mississippi. **Career:** Pittsburgh Pirates, infielder, 1992-95; Kansas City Royals, 1996; Pittsburgh Pirates, 1997-. **Business Addr:** Professional Baseball Player, Pittsburgh Pirates, PO Box 7000, Pittsburgh, PA 15212, (412)323-5000.

YOUNG, LARRY
Government official. **Personal:** Born Nov 25, 1949, Baltimore, MD; son of Mable Payne. **Educ:** Univ of MD College Park, attended 1967-71. **Career:** Urban Environmental Affairs Natl Office Izaak Walton League of Amer, dir 1970-77; Young Beat Afro-Amer Newspaper, former columnist 1975-77; Ctr for Urban Environmental Studies, pres 1977-82; Natl Black Caucus of State Legislators, acting exec dir 1979-82; MD General Assembly 44th Legislative Dist, chmn house environmental matters comm 1975-; 1982-86; Executive Nominations Committee, chairman. **Orgs:** Chmn bd dirs Citizen's Democratic Action Orgn Inc; Baltimore Leadership Inc; chmn MD Health Convocation; chmn Health Roundtable; Isaak Walton League of Amer; co-chmn MD Conf on the Black Aged; legislative advisor Baltimore City Area Agency on Aging; New Shiloh Bapt Ch; Energy & Environmental Study Conf; bd dirs Univ of MD Systems; bd dirs/fndr Black Health Study Group. **Honors/Awds:** People to Watch in 1983 selected by Baltimore Magazine Ed Bd; Concerned Citizens Awd Amer Cancer Soc MD State Div 1980; Statesman Awd Bethel AME Ch 1980; MPHA Awd MD Public Hlth Assn For Your Support on Health Legislation 1980; Comm Serv Awd Gamma Chap Chi Eta Phi Sor Inc 1979; Comm Serv Awd We Need Prayer Headquarters; Legislator of the Yr 1978 MD Public Interest Rsch Group; Statesman Awd Baltimore Baptist Ministers' Conf 1977; Natl Assn for Environmental Educ Annual Awd 1976; Distinguished Citizenship Awd State of MD 1972; Afro-Amer Newspaper Honor Roll Awd 1971. **Home Addr:** 601 N Eutaw St, Ste 102, Baltimore, MD 21201.

YOUNG, LAWRENCE W., JR.
Educator. **Personal:** Born Dec 30, 1942, Cleveland, OH; son of Maggie Fuggs Young and Lawrence W Young Sr; married Eddye Pierce-Young (divorced 1989). **Educ:** Miami University, Oxford, OH, BA, 1965, Med, 1974. **Career:** Cleveland Board of Educaton, Cleveland, OH, teacher/English, 1965-69; Miami University, Oxford, OH, director/minority affairs, 1969-82; The Pennsylavnia State University, University Park, PA, director, Paul Robeson Cultural Center, 1982-. **Orgs:** Member, Alpha Phi Alpha, 1965; member, National Council of Black Studies, 1985; chair/steering committee, Assn of Black Cultural Centers, 1989; member, NAACP, 1969-. **Honors/Awds:** Omicron Delta Kappa, ODK, 1989; "Black Student Leadership on Campus" in Hand Book of Minority Student Services by Praxis Publications, 1990; Columnist, Centre Daily Times, 1990-; American Correspondent to "Afro Mart" Magazine, London, 1989-; Golden Key, 1992. **Special Achievements:** "The Minority Cultural Center on White Campus," Cultural Pluralismon Campus, American College Personnel Association, 1992. **Home Addr:** PO Box 251, State College, PA 16804. **Business Addr:** Director, Paul Robeson Cultural Center, The Pennsylvania State University, University Park, PA 16802.

YOUNG, LEE R.
Law enforcement official. **Personal:** Born Jan 8, 1947, Del Rio, TX; son of Abbylean A Ward Nunley and Leroy Young; married Mary Sanchez Young; children: Anthony Lee Young, Kristen Marie Young. **Educ:** St Edwards College, Austin, TX, 1973; Sam Houston State Univ, Huntsville, TX, 1973; Southwest TX Jr College, AA, 1973; Univ of TX, Austin, TX, BA, 1975. **Career:** Natl Park Service, Amistad Rec Area, Del Rio, TX, 1971-73; Texas Dept of Public Safety, Eagle Pass, TX, trooper TX hwy patrol, 1977-80; Texas Dept of Public Safety, Bryan, TX, trooper TX hwy patrol, 1975-77; Texas Dept of Public Safety, Del Rio, TX, trooper TX hwy patrol, 1980-88; Texas Dept of Public Safety, San Antonio, TX, criminal intelligence investigator, 1988; Texas Dept of Public Safety, Garland, TX, sgt TX ranger, 1988-. **Orgs:** Mem, Natl Police Officers Assn, 1988-; mem, Homocide Investigators of TX, 1990-; mem, TX Police Assn, 1988-; asst dir, Navy/Marine Corps Mars, 1980-; scoutmaster, Boy Scouts of America, 1990. **Honors/Awds:** Natl Honor Society, SW TX Jr College, 1972; Trail Blazer Award, So Dallas Business Women, 1989; Grand Marshal, Black History Parade, 1989. **Military Serv:** US Navy, petty officer, second class, 1966-70. **Business Addr:** Sergeant, Texas Ranger, Texas Dept of Public Safety, 4300 Community Blvd, Mc Kinney, TX 75070.

YOUNG, LEON
Business executive, city offical. **Personal:** Born Feb 10, 1924, Monroe, LA; son of Johnie Mae Elmo-Young and Pete Young; married Margaret M Dove, May 12, 1945; children: Denise Sharlene. **Career:** CO Springs, city council 1973, vice mayor 1980-; Young Janitorial Svcs, owner, 1955-. **Orgs:** Mem past pres Downtowners Civitan Intl Club; Minority Contractors of Region 8; Pioneer Mus Bd; Housing Authority Bd; Pikes Peak Regional Council of Govts; NAACP; CO Springs Utility Bd; chmn of Colorado Springs City Loan Comm; Minority Council of Arts; Old CO City Historical Soc; Negro Historical Assn of CO Springs. **Honors/Awds:** Several awds CO Springs work in newly renovated Shooks Run a lower income area in CO Springs. **Military Serv:** USN; Veteran Korean Conflict, WW II. **Business Addr:** President, Young Janitorial Serv, Ste #5, 415 S Weber, Colorado Springs, CO 80903.

YOUNG, LEON D.
State senator. **Career:** 16th Assembly District, Milwaukee, WI, state representative, currently. **Orgs:** Minority Male Forum on Corrections; Harambee Ombudsman Project. **Business Addr:** State Representative, Wisconsin House of Representatives, PO Box 8952, Madison, WI 53708.

YOUNG, LIAS CARL
Attorney (retired). **Personal:** Born Nov 21, 1940, Big Sandy, TX; son of Myrtle Davis Young and W L Young; married Rose Breaux Young, Sep 20, 1943; children: Victor, Kimberly, Phyllis. **Educ:** Tyler Jr Coll; TX Southern Univ; TX Southern Univ Law Sch, JD 1965. **Career:** Ofc of Regional Counsel US Dept HUD, atty advsr 1968-76; Fed Nat Mortgage Assn, associate regional counsel 1976-97. **Orgs:** Mem Fed Bar Assn; TX Bar Assn; past pres Ft Worth Chap Fed Bar Assn 1970-71; past sec 1966-68; National Bar Association. **Home Addr:** 4309 Star Dust Ln, Fort Worth, TX 76119. **Business Addr:** Associate Regional Counsel, Fannie Mae, 13455 Noel Rd, Galleria Tower II, Dallas, TX 75240.

YOUNG, LIONEL WESLEY
Radiologist. **Personal:** Born Mar 14, 1932, New Orleans, LA; son of Ethel Johnson Young (deceased) and Charles Henry Young (deceased); married Florence Inez Brown Young, Jun 24, 1957; children: Tina I, Lionel T, Owen C. **Educ:** Benedictine Coll, BS 1953; Howard Univ Coll of Medicine, MD 1957. **Career:** Univ of Rochester NY, radiology resident 1958-61; Children's Medical Ctr Akron, chmn of radiology; Northeastern Ohio Univ Coll of Medicine, chmn of radiology, 1986-91; Univ of Pittsburgh, Pittsburgh, PA, prof of radiology & pediatrics 1975-86; Loma Linda University Medical Center, director of pediatric radiology, currently. **Orgs:** Pres Soc for Pediatric Radiology 1984-85; pres Pittsburgh Roentgen Soc 1985-86; mem Sigma Pi Phi, mem Alpha Omega Alpha; pres, Akron Pediatric Radiologists, Inc 1986-91. **Honors/Awds:** Caffey Awd Soc for Pediatric Radiology 1970; Distinguished Service Award, Howard Univ Coll of Medicine 1987; Distinguished Alumnus Award, Howard Univ 1989. **Military Serv:** USN Med Corps lt comdr 1961-63. **Business Addr:** Director, Pediatric Radiology, Loma Linda University Medical Center, 11234 Anderson St, Loma Linda, CA 92354.

YOUNG, MARECHAL-NEIL ELLISON
Educational administrator. **Personal:** Born Sep 12, 1915, Palatka, FL; daughter of Ethel Urline Harrison Ellison and George F Ellison; married W Arthur Young, Dec 1939; children: Hitomi Matthews, Kwon Riley. **Educ:** Temple Univ, BSE 1935; Univ of PA, MA Sociology 1936, PhD Sociology 1944, MSW 1948, Post Grad Certificate (research) 1978. **Career:** William Penn HS Philadelphia School Dist, counselor 1942-45; Philadelphia Sch Dist, supr sec sch counseling 1945-51; Mayer Sulzberger JH Philadelphia Sch Dist, principal 1951-63; Philadelphia Sch Dist, aux dist supt 1963, dist supt1964-71, asso supt 1971-77; Moton Center for Independent Studies, fellow 1977-

78; Univ of PA, sr research assoc 1978-82; Synod of the Trinity of the Presbyterian Church Minority Student Recruitment Proj, founder, educ cons/indep research dir 1970-. **Orgs:** Educ sec Urban League of Pittsburgh 1938-42; youth counselor Nat Youth Admin 1935-38; lecturer/adjunct prof Univ of PA Sch of Social Work 1949-51; adjunct prof Prairie View A&M Coll 1949-70; adjunct prof Beaver Coll 1974-75; mem State Adv Comm on Mental Health Mental Retardation 1972-85; mem Philadelphia Cnty Bd Mental Health/Mental Retardation 1968-82; mem bd of trustees Drexel Univ 1969-; mem bd of trustees Beaver Coll 1971-; mem advisory bd Church Related Coll Presbyterian Church USA 1968-85; educ chrmn AAUW Philadelphia Branch 1978-88. **Honors/Awds:** A Distinguishd Daughter of PA appointed by Governor Shapp 1972; mem Pres Nat Advisory Council on Supplementary Ctrs & Serv appointed by Pres Nixon Washington, DC 1971-74; Hon Degree Doctorate of Letters from Drexel Univ Philadelphia 1979; apptd Commissioner Revision of Philadelphia City Charter 1987; Mainstreaming and Minority Children 1978; established the W Arthur Young Scholarship Foundation for Classical Instrumental Music Education, 1988-; Distinguished Service-Public Education Award, Philadelphia Educator's Roundtable, 1990. **Business Addr:** Director Synod Minority Student Recruitment Project, Synod of the Trinity, Pres Church, 5428 Haverford Ave, Philadelphia, PA 19139.

YOUNG, MARGARET BUCKNER
Author, educator. **Personal:** Born in Campbellsville, KY; daughter of Eva Buckner and Frank Buckner; widowed; children: Marcia Cantarella, Lauren Casteel. **Educ:** KY State Coll, BA English French 1942; Univ of MN, MA Educ Psychology 1945. **Career:** KY State Coll, teacher; Spelman Coll Atlanta Univ, educ psychology; written sev children's books, First Book of Amer Negroes, The Picture Life of Martin Luther King Jr, The Picture Life of Ralph Bunche, The Picture Life of Thurgood Marshall, Black Amer Ldrs Chmn, Whitney M Young Jr Memorial Foundation. **Orgs:** Aptd to 28th Gen Assembly of UN as Alt Rep of US 1973; Mar 1974 went to Nigeria & Ghana under cultural exchange prog of State Depts Bur of Educ & Cultural Affairs; visited Peoples Rep of China as mem of UNA-USA Nat Policy Panel on US-China Rela 1979; bd of visitors US Mil Acad 1979-81; mem Found Inc; elected to bd of dirs Philip Morris; NY Life Ins Co; Pub Policy Com of Advertising Council; dedicated USIS Whitney M Young Jr Library (meml to late husband); Director Emerita of Lincoln Center for the Performing Arts.

YOUNG, MARY E.
Educator. **Personal:** Born Jun 5, 1941, Harlan, KY. **Educ:** Detroit Bible Coll, BRE 1966; Eastern KY Univ, BA 1969; Eastern KY Univ, MA 1972; Univ of MI, ABD 1973-75. **Career:** Eastern KY Univ, counselor 1969-72; Univ of MI, counseling, lab practicum asst 1973-74, graduate teaching asst 1974-75; Washtenaw Comm Coll, counselor 1975-. **Orgs:** Mem Natl Ed Assoc 1975-, MI Ed Assoc 1975-, Washtenaw Comm Coll Ed Assoc 1975-; bd dir Circle Y Ranch Camp 1983-85; mem NAACP 1985-, Natl Black Child Inc 1985-86; Washtenaw Counselor's Association, 1992-93. **Honors/Awds:** Outstanding Faculty Awd Washtenaw Comm Coll 1984; Detroit Bible College, Alumni of the Year, 1978. **Special Achievements:** Natl Certified Career Counselor, 1985; Michigan Community College Counselor Academy, 1990-91; Licensed Professional Counselor, currently. **Business Addr:** Counselor, Washtenaw Comm Coll, PO Box D-1, Ann Arbor, MI 48106.

YOUNG, MICHAEL
Educator, researcher. **Personal:** Born Mar 28, 1950, Muskogee, OK; son of Betty Brady Young and Robert Young; married Tamera Whitely Young, Mar 16, 1991; children: Betsy, Brandon, Bethany, Ricky, Devin. **Educ:** Bacone College, Muskogee, OK, AA, 1970; Southwest Bapt Univ, Bolivar, MO, BA, 1972; Univ of Arkansas, Fayetteville, AR, MEd, 1974; Texas A & M, College Station, TX, PhD, 1975. **Career:** Campbellsville College, Campbellsville, KY, asst prof, 1975-78; Auburn Univ, Auburn, AL, asst prof, 1978-80; Univ of Arkansas, Fayetteville, AR, professor, 1980-; Health Education Projects Office, dir, currently. **Orgs:** Board of Directors, Soc for Scientific Study of Sexuality; founder, Amer Academy of Health Behavior; American School Health Association; American Alliance Health, Physical Education Recreation & Dance; American Public Health Association. **Honors/Awds:** University of Arkansas, College of Education, Teaching Award, 1990, Research Award, 1983, 1987; University of Arkansas Alumni Association, Distinguished Achievement in Research & Public Service Award; SW Baptist University, Distinguished Contributions to Education, 1990; Dept Alumni Award for Research & Scholarly Productivity, Texas A&M, HPE Dept, 1980; five US Department of Health & Human Services Awards, Outstanding Work in Community Health Promotion. **Business Addr:** Professor, Health Sciences, University of Arkansas, HP 308, Fayetteville, AR 72701.

YOUNG, N. LOUISE
Physician (retired). **Personal:** Born Jun 7, 1910, Baltimore, MD; married William Spencer. **Educ:** Howard U, BS 1927; Howard U, MD 1930; Freedman's Hosp, Intern 1930-31; Provident Hosp, Resd 1940-45. **Career:** OB-GYN Prac, retired phys; S Baltimore Gen Hosp, vis ob; General N Charles Union Meml, asso staff gyn 1950-52; Provident Hosp, act chf ob asst chf OB exec com vis staff & ob-gyn 1940-52; MD Training Sch Girls, staff phys 1933-40; Mcculloh Planned Parenthd Clinic, clinician 1935-42; Women Morgan State Coll, phys 1935-40; Douglas HS, 1936-69. **Orgs:** Chmn First Aid & Evacuation of Negro Women & Children Nat Emerg MD Cncl Def 1941-; med adv com MD Planned Parenthd & March of Dimes 1969-71; mem AMA; NMA; Med & Chirurgical Faculty MD; del Baltimore Cty Med Assn 1969-72; mem Monumental Med Soc; vice pres 1969-71; mem Am Fertility Soc; MD OB-GYN Soc; Med Com Human Rights; life mem NAACP; IBPOE of WAKA Sor; CORE; mem MD Com passage Abort Law; chmn com Prevent Passage Steriliz Law; Afro-Am Hon Roll 1947; Baltimore Howard Alumni 1930; Philamathions 1935f MD Hist Soc 1975; AKA Heritage Servis-Woman in Med 1971. **Home Addr:** 3239 Powhatan Ave, Baltimore, MD 21216-1934.

YOUNG, NANCY WILSON
Educator. **Personal:** Born May 1, 1943, Orangeburg, SC; married Dr R Paul Young; children: Ryan Paul. **Educ:** Clafin Coll, BS (cum laude) 1965; SC State Coll, 1966; George Peabody Coll, 1968; Univ of Miami, MEd 1970; Barry University, grad courses. **Career:** Wateree Elem School Lugoff SC, 3rd grade teacher, 1965-67; Miller School Waldoboro ME, teacher, summers, 1968-69; Univ of Miami, grad adv, 1969-70, asst dir of admiss, 1970-80; Interval International, personnel director, 1980-83; Miami-Dade Community College, employment administrator, 1983-91, faculty, 1991-. **Orgs:** Chmn TOEFL Rsch Comm ETS 1977-80; v chmn TOEFL Policy Council ETS 1977-80; exec comm TOEFL Policy Council ETS 1977-80; life mem Clafin Coll Alumni Assoc; consult CEEB Summer Inst The Coll Bd 1975-80; consult US State Dept for Visits to West Africa & Trinidad 1979; mem Univ of Miami Alumni Bd of Dir 1984-87; mem adv bd Epilepsy Found of S FL 1984-85; mem Comm on Total Employment Chamber of Commerce 1984-85; mem Dades Employ the Handicapped Comm 1984-; Dade County Chapter, Links; Jack & Jill of America; board of directors, 11th judicial nominating commission, 1991-94, New World Symphony 1992; Healthy People 2000, exec comm, 1995. **Honors/Awds:** Ford Found Fellowship, 1968-69; Alumni of the Year, Claflin College, 1991; Outstanding Alumnus of Claflin Coll, 1995. **Business Addr:** Faculty, Miami-Dade Community College, 11011 S W 104th St, Bldg 6319, Miami, FL 33176, (305)237-2178.

YOUNG, OLLIE L.
Human resources executive. **Personal:** Born Feb 8, 1948, Philadelphia, PA; daughter of Mary Huggins Jordan and Rev Samuel B Jordan Sr; married Reginald B Young; children: Stephanie D. **Educ:** Tarkio Coll, BA 1970; Temple Univ, MBA 1977. **Career:** Temple Univ Health Sci Ctr, asst personnel dir; Consolidated Rail Corp, personnel supervisor; Ducat Associates, consultant; The New York Times Regional, employee relations mgr; Gannett Co Inc, human resources dir; Rutgers University, asst dir, personnel services; Valic, financial planner, consultant; NPHS, hr, dir, currently. **Orgs:** Amer Mgmt Assn, 1984-; volunteer, New Geth Bapt Church Tutorial Prog 1985-; prog chmn, Newspaper Personnel Relations Assocs 1986-87; adv bd, Somerset YMCA 1986-; mgmt consultant Somerset United Way; ASPA 1987; CUPA, 1988-; Black MBA Assn. **Honors/Awds:** Frank Tripp Awd Gannett Co 1985; Tribute to Women in Industry Twin Somerset & Union 1986; People to People, Delegate, 1993. **Business Addr:** HR Director, NPHS, 8th & Girano Ave, Philadelphia, PA 19122, (215)787-2008.

YOUNG, PERRY H.
Pilot (retired). **Personal:** Born Mar 12, 1919, Orangeburg, SC; married Shakeh. **Educ:** Oberlin Coll; Howard U; Spartan Sch of Aeronautics; Am Flyers Ft Worth, TX. **Career:** Tuskegee Inst, flight instr 1941-45; Port Au Prince Haiti, fixed base operator 1946-48; SHADA Haiti, corp pilot 1949-53; PRWRA PR, corp pilot 1953-55; NY Airways Inc, pilot airline capt 1956-79; New York Helicopter, retired chief pilot; Island Helicopter, dir purchasing. **Orgs:** Mem Air Line Pilots Assn; founding mem Negro Airmen Internat; mem Am Helicopter Soc; mem Orgn of Black Airline Pilots. **Honors/Awds:** First black capt scheduled passenger Airline 1957; outst achvmt award Orgn of Black Airline Pilots 1979. **Military Serv:** USAAF flight instr. **Business Addr:** Dir Purchasing, Island Helicopter, North Ave, Garden City, NY 11530.

YOUNG, RAYMOND, JR.
Sales manager. **Personal:** Born Aug 22, 1960, Mobile, AL; son of Tenner Young and Raymond Young; married Lanie L Johnson. **Educ:** Alabama A&M Univ, BS Acctg 1982; Mt St Mary's Coll, MBA 1989. **Career:** JC Penney Co, mgmt trainee 1981; Superior Oil Co, junior accountant 1982; International Business Machine Corp, staff financial analyst 1982-87; Digital Equip corp, financial planning mgr, 1988-92, sales manager 1992-. **Orgs:** Sunday school instructor Mt Calvary Bapt Church 1983-; mem Montgomery Co Chap NAACP 1985-, Natl Black MBA Assoc 1987-; income tax advisor. **Honors/Awds:** Natl Deans List 1982; Delta Mu Delta Natl Honor Soc Business Admin 1982-; Outstanding Young Men of America, 1990. **Home Addr:** 11600 Whittier Road, Mitchellville, MD 20721.

YOUNG, REGINALD B.
Consultant, financial planner. **Personal:** Born Oct 17, 1947, Alexandria, LA; son of Willie Lee Gable Baty and Lloyd Baty; married Ollie L Jordan; children: Stephanie D. **Educ:** LaSalle Univ, MBA (hon) Mktg 1979-81; Tarkio Coll, BA Math 1968-71. **Career:** Frank B Hall & Co of PA Inc, account exec 1976-81; Waltington & Cooper Inc, vice pres marketing 1981-82; OR Assoc Inc, owner, pres 1982-83; Macy's NY, marketing systems support mgr 1983-86; OR Assoc Inc, owner, pres 1986-. **Orgs:** Founding mem, instr Omaha Chapter OIC 1967-68; insurance underwriter St Paul Co 1971-76; consultant New Gethsemane Baptist Church 1975-; consultant First PA Bank 1976-81; mem Natl Black MBA Assoc 1985-. **Honors/Awds:** Regional Representative Securities and Exchange Commission. **Home Addr:** 5703 Ravens Crest Dr, Plainsboro, NJ 08536. **Business Addr:** Owner, President, OR Assoc Inc, PO Box 7211, Princeton, NJ 08543.

YOUNG, RICHARD EDWARD, JR.
Business executive. **Personal:** Born Dec 30, 1941, Baltimore, MD; married Carol Emile Gette; children: Joyce Ann, Jeffrey Wendel. **Educ:** Univ MD, BA 1968-71; Rutgers U, MCRP 1971-73; Seton Hall U, JD 1978. **Career:** Econ Devel Planning, dir 1979; City of Newark, evltns chief 1974-79; United Way of Essex & W Hudson, Community Planning & Devel, assoc dir 1973-74; Fed Govt US Dept of HUD, urban planner 1972-73; NJ Dept of Community Affairs, 1971-72; Cty of Baltimore Dept Housing & Community Devel, housing inspector 1967-71. **Orgs:** Pres Centennial Communcations Inc; pres RE Young Assoc; pres ARTEP Inc; bd trustee, NJ Neuropsychiatric Inst 1977; bd trustee, vice pres Joint Connection Inc 1976; mem Amer Inst of Planners Assn 1970; 100 Black Men Inc 1974; Amer Soc Planning Officials 1970; NJ Soc of Professional Planners 1973; NJ Professional Planner License 1973. **Honors/Awds:** Outstanding Young Men of Amer 1976; NJ State Dept of Higher Educ Minority Scholarship 1974; Tri State Regional & Planning Comm, Fellowship in Urban Planning 1971-73. **Military Serv:** AUS maj 1964. **Business Addr:** c/o City of Newark, 920 Broad St, Newark, NJ.

YOUNG, RICKEY DARNELL
Car sales representative. **Personal:** Born Dec 7, 1953, Mobile, AL; son of Deloris Echols and Nathanial Young; married Gloria Waterhouse Young, Jun 23, 1984; children: Micah Cole, Colby Darnell. **Educ:** Jackson State Coll, BS 1975. **Career:** San Diego Chargers, running back 1975-78; MN Vikings, running back 1978-84; Edina Realty; sales rep Jeff Belzer's Todd Chevrolet; Forest Lake Ford-Jeep/Eagle, Forest Lake MN, sales representative; Eden Prairie Ford, sales representative; Courtesy Ford, vice pres/dealer, currently. **Orgs:** Chmn Heart/Lung Association 1981; chldrns fund Viking 1982. **Honors/Awds:** Pass Receiver Award, Viking's 1978. **Home Addr:** 148 Stacy Circle, Waconia, MN 55387.

YOUNG, RODNEY MENARD
Professional football player. **Personal:** Born Jan 25, 1973, Grambling, LA; son of Willie and Barbara Young. **Educ:** Louisiana State, attended. **Career:** New York Giants, defensive back, 1995-. **Business Addr:** Professional Football Player, New York Giants, Giants Stadium, East Rutherford, NJ 07073, (201)935-8111.

YOUNG, RONALD R.
Educational administrator. **Personal:** Born May 27, 1919, Nassau; married Marjorie L Saxton; children: Ronald S, Randall O, Rederic. **Educ:** AL State Coll Montgomery AL, BS 1947; AL State Coll Montgomery, AL, MEd 1958. **Career:** Miami-Dade Comm Coll S, EA EO coord S 1960-; AL State Tech Coll Montgomery, coach 1958-60; Montgomery Imrpovmnt Assn Montgomery, pres 1950; Amvets Post #16 Montgomery, comdr 1949; St Judes Educ Inst Montgomery, coach 1947-58. **Orgs:** Mem Counc of Black Am Affairs; chmn Dade Co Popul Task Force 1974; chmn Dade Co Planning & Adv Bd 1980; life mem Alpha Phi Alpha Frat; bd of dirsSt Albans Day Care 1973-79; bd of dirs Dade Co Youth Fair 1977-80. **Honors/Awds:** Recip outstng citzns awr Dade Co Planning Adv Bd 1980. **Military Serv:** AUS m sgt 1943-46. **Business Addr:** Miami-Dade Comm Coll S, 11011 SW 104th St, Miami, FL 33176.

YOUNG, RONALD R.
Petroleum company executive. **Personal:** Born Nov 13, 1948, Chester, SC; son of Alberta Murphy Young and John W Young; married Jacqueline Marie Jackson Young, Nov 2, 1985; children: Jenelle Renee, Nicole Christine, Whitney Marie. **Educ:** Hampton University, Hampton, VA, BS, Accounting, 1971, Syracuse University, Syracuse, NY, MBA, 1975. **Career:** Agway Inc (Agway Petroleum Corp), Syracuse, NY, vice pres, mkting, 1971-. **Orgs:** Board of directors, Grand Polemarch, Kappa Alpha Psi Fraternity, Inc.; board of trustees, 2nd V.P., WCNY, Public Broadcasting Syst. of Central New York, council member, State University of New York, Health Science Center at Syracuse, policy planning council, member, Leadership Greater Syracuse, advisory council, Syracuse University School of Social Work. **Honors/Awds:** Community Service Recognition, United Way of Central New York, 1988; Fraternity Service Awards, Kappa Alpha Psi Fraternity, Inc., 1979-86; Plaques, Certificates, Gifts, for speaking, Numerous Organiza-

tions, 1976-. **Business Addr:** Vice President, Marketing Department, Agway Petroleum Corporation, 333 Butternut Drive, DeWitt, NY 13214.

YOUNG, ROSE S.
Government official. **Personal:** Born Sep 18, 1943, Wadesboro, NC; daughter of Ethel R Sturdivant and Lester W Sturdivant (deceased); married Charles M Young, Sep 24, 1964; children: Robin, Charles M Jr. **Educ:** A&T University, 1960; Cortez Peters Business College, associates, 1961. **Career:** Walter Reed Medical Center, Army Medical Department, personnel specialist, 1976-85; US Court Administration Office, retirement specialist, personnel mgt specialist, 1985-86; Navy Recruitment Command, public affairs, management analyst, 1986-. **Orgs:** Federal Women, steering committee, 1982-85, Federal Women, program, 1987-; ITC, 1988; Sixth Church, deacon board member, ordained elder; NAACP; Delta Sigma Theta. **Honors/Awds:** Letter of Commendation, w/Silver Wreath, 1992, w/Plaque, 1993; Special Act Award, 1994; Civilian of the Year. **Business Addr:** Management Analyst, Public Affairs Office, Navy Recruiting Command, Marketing Communications Dept, 801 N Randolph St, Arlington, VA 22203-1991.

YOUNG, RUFUS KING
Clergyman (retired), educator. **Personal:** Born May 13, 1911, Dermott, AR; married Yvonne Smith Bruner; children: Essie Mae Laura Elizabeth, Rufus King, James Robert, Ellen Arneatha, Allena Ann. **Educ:** Shorter Coll, AB 1937; Payne Theol Sem Wilberforce U, BD 1940. **Career:** Bethel African Meth Epis Ch, pastor 1953-86; Jackson Theol Seminary Shorter Coll, dean 1967-68; Jackson Theol Seminary, dean 1983-87, prof, currently. **Orgs:** Trustee Shorter Coll 1951-; treas Shorter Coll 1954-; mem NAACP, AR Council of Human Rel, YMCA, Urban League, NLR Civic League, AR Dem Voters Assoc; bdmem Florence Crittendon Home, AR Serv Org, Central AR Human Serv Council, Health Oppors Provided for Everyone, PUSH; pres Glenview Improvement League 1970-; pres Christian Ministers Alliance of Greater Little Rock 1977-82. **Honors/Awds:** Delegate to the General Conf of the AME Church 1944, 1946, 1948, 1952, 1956, 1960, 1964, 1968, 1976, 1980, 1984; mem Methodist Bicentennial Tour of the historic places of Methodism 1984; Honorary DD Jackson Theological Seminary, Shorter College, 1953; Payne Theological Seminary, Wilberforce University, 1959; Doctor of Humane Letters, Morris Brown College, 1984. **Business Addr:** Professor, Jackson Theol Seminary, 604 N Locust St, North Little Rock, AR 72117.

YOUNG, RUTH L.
Government employee. **Personal:** Born Dec 19, 1943, Savannah. **Educ:** Bernard M Baruch Coll, Pub Bus Adminstrn 1970-71; York Coll Jamaica, 1974-; various short mnth courses from 1962-. **Career:** NY State US Dept of Labor Vets Employment Serv, asst vets employment rep 1974-; Summer Neighborhood Youth Corps of Educ Action & Youth Devel Progs OEO, exec sec supvr 1972-74; US Postal Serv, window clerk, clerk-typist 1965-73; Trans Urban Construction Co, girl friday 1965; James Weldon Johnson Community Center, typist-bookkeeper 1965; WAC, 1962-64; SH Kress Dept Store, salesgirl 1961. **Orgs:** Mem Fed Exec Bd NY Vets Affairs Com 1974-; Western NY Jobs for Bets Task Force 1974-; Am Legion 1975-; 369 Vets Assn Inc 1970-; Internatl Assn of Pers in Emplymnt Secrty 1974-; mem United De of Jamaica NY 1972-; OEO CAP Proj Econ Devel Cntr 1973-; asso mem Museum of Natural Hist 1974-. **Honors/Awds:** Recip serv awrd US Dept of Labor 10 rys Hon Svc; several letters of commend. **Business Addr:** US Dept of Labor, VES 303 W Old Country Rd, Hicksville, NY 11801.

YOUNG, SARAH DANIELS
Government official (retired). **Personal:** Born Sep 25, 1926, Wetumpka, AL; daughter of Novella Saxton Johnson (deceased) and Thomas Daniels II (deceased); married Anderson Crutcher (deceased); children: Saundrea Shillingford, Alan Cla. **Educ:** Detroit Inst of Commerce, Dipl Sec Sci 1946; Wayne State U, 1964-68. **Career:** Detroit Inst of Commerce Business Coll, sec to pres 1946-48; Fed Govt, med sec 1949-54; County of Wayne, admin sec ofc mgr labor rel analyst 1954-79. **Orgs:** Mem St Clement's Epis Ch 1948-; bd of canvassers' mem City of Inkster 1966-89; bd of dirs Chateau Cherry Hill Housing Corp 1973-89; commnr Public Housing Auth 1979-; mem chprsn "Friends of the Library" City of Inkster 1979-; bd of dirs natl editor in chief, natl tamias, trustee, Gamma Phi Delta Sor Inc; treas Diocese of MI ECW Exec Bd 1983; bd of dirs Northwest Guidance Clinic 1984-87; charter mem Top Ladies of Distinction Inc MI Metro Chap Exec Bd; mem Natl Council of Negro Women, YWCA, NAACP; mem, sec, Episcopal Diocese of Michigan Finance Committee 1987-. **Honors/Awds:** Pi Nu Tau Honor Award Detroit Inst of Commerce 1946; 1st black female analyst Wayne Co MI; Outstanding Serv Award as Natl Editor-in-chief Gamma Phi Delta Sor Inc 1978; Outstanding Adult Comm Serv Awd Alpha Kappa Alpha 1984; YWCA Service Award, 1991. **Home Addr:** 27164 Kitch Ave, Inkster, MI 48141.

YOUNG, TERRENCE ANTHONY
Banker. **Personal:** Born Feb 21, 1954, St Louis, MO; children: Terrence A Jr. **Educ:** Univ of IL Champaign, BA 1977, MBA 1979; State of IL, CPA 1980. **Career:** Inland Steel Co, finance 1979-83; The First Natl Bank of Chicago, vice pres 1983-92; Peal Development Co, pres, 1992-95; Fund for Community Redevelopment, development specialist, 1993-95; Chicago Partnership Office, Fannie May, dir, 1995-. **Orgs:** Mem Amer Inst of Certified Public Accountants, Alpha Phi Alpha Frat; bd pres, Covenant Development Corp; bd mem, Hispanic Housing Development Corp; bd mem, Black Pearl Gallery; Chicago Urban League, Metro Board; founding mem, Network of Real Estate Professionals; life mem, University of IL Alumni Assn. **Honors/Awds:** Outstanding Young Men of America 1985. **Home Addr:** 4119 S Drexel, Chicago, IL 60653. **Business Addr:** Director Chicago Partnership Office, Fannie Mae, 1 South Wacker Dr, Ste 1300, Chicago, IL 60606.

YOUNG, TERRI JONES (JONES YOUNG)
Educational administrator. **Personal:** Born May 11, 1957, Laurel, MS; daughter of Betty Jean Sanders Jones and Heywood Jones; married James Keith Young, Sep 6, 1986. **Educ:** Eastern Illinois University, Charleston, IL, BS, Business, 1979; Illinois Institute of Tech, Chicago, IL, MBA, 1989. **Career:** Illinois Institute of Tech, Chicago, Il, director, minority eng prog, 1980-87; Chicago State Univ, Chicago, IL, director, engineering studies, 1987-. **Orgs:** NAMEPA, national president, 1992-94; National Black MBA Assn, 1986-; Phi Gamma Nu, 1977-; NAACP, 1988-; NTA, 1989-. **Honors/Awds:** NAMEPA-National Leadership Award, 1995; NAMEPA-Region C Outstanding Program Administrator, 1990; Dr. Ronald McNair President's Recognition Award, NTA, 1986; Special Recognition Award, IIT Pre-University Programs, 1987; Special Recognition Award, Union of Concerned Black Students, 1986; Award of Appreciation, National Society of Black Engineers, 1988. **Business Addr:** Director, Engineering Studies Program, Chicago State Univ, 9501 S King Dr, Chicago, IL 60628-1598, (312)995-2358.

YOUNG, TOMMY SCOTT
Business executive. **Personal:** Born Dec 13, 1943, Blair, SC; son of Nancy Lee Thompson Young and John Robert Young; children: Tamu Toliver, Lee Thompson Young. **Educ:** CA State U, BA 1968; LA Cty Coll; Benedict Coll; CA State U, Post Grad. **Career:** Lord Baltimore Press printers asst; IBM Corp customer engineer, 1963-66; Meat & Theatre Inc, fndr/pres 1969-72; Watts Writers Workshop, instr 1969-71; SC Arts Commn, artist resd; Kitani Found Inc, exec dir/bd mem/fndr/chmn of bd 1974-84; The Equitable Life Assurance Soc of the US, financial planner 1984-; Raspberry Recordings, creative & performing artist 1965-. **Orgs:** GA Cncl for Arts; NC Cultural Arts Com 1973; dir Timia Enter 1974; chmn Educ Com Shel-Blair Fed Credit Union 1974-75; mem Governors Intl Yr of Child Com; mem Artistically Talented & Gifted Spcl Proj Adv Bd 1977-; mem Mann-Simons Adv Comm 1979-; mem SC Educ TV Adv Bd 1979-; mem Bro & Sisters Adv Bd 1979-; mem So Arts Fed Prgm Sel Com 1979-80; mem chmn SC Arts Commn 5 yr Planning Com for Richland Co 1979-80; mem SC Arts Commn Adn Adv Com; mem & treas SC Com Arts Agencies 1979-; mem Governor's Cultural Arts Com 1979-; mem Spoleto of Midlands Comm 1980; mem Governors Intl Yr of Child Com; consult Media Serv for Nat Endow for Arts 1979-; mem Columbia C of C; Nat Literary Soc; mem Natl Assn of Life Underwriters 1985-, Natl Assn for Preservation & Perpetuation of Storytelling1986-, Assn of Bl Storytelling 1987-, Toastmast ers International 1987-, Columbia Youth Collaborative 1989-, Southern Order of Storytellers, SC Storytellers Guild; chmn Christ Unity of Columbia 1988-, Youth Encouraged to Succeed 1989-. **Honors/Awds:** Dir prod "Angela is Happening" 1971-72; dir "Southern Fried" 1977; author "Black Blues & Shiny Songs" Red Clay Books 1977; recip "10 for the Future" Columbia Newspapers Inc 1978; Billings Educational Found Awd; Intl Platform Assoc; Gospel Music Workshop Amer; Natl Entertainment Conf; Natl Leaders Corps, The Equitable Financial Companies 1987; Distinguished Performance Citation, The Equitable Financial Companies 1988; author, Tommy Scott Young Spins Magical Tales, Raspberry Recordings 1985. **Military Serv:** USAF 1960-63.

YOUNG, WALLACE L.
Educator. **Personal:** Born Oct 5, 1931, New Orleans, LA; married Myra Narcisse. **Educ:** Attended, Loyola U, So U. **Career:** New Orleans Public Library, chmn of bd 1976-79; Senior Citizen Center, asst dir. **Orgs:** Pres bd mem NAACP; exec sec Knights of Peter Claver; past mem Dryades St YMCA; mem Free So Thtr; Nat Cath Conf for Interracial Justice; LA State Lib Devel Com; coord Cath Com Urban Ministry; mem Natl Office for Black Catholics, Natl Black Lay Catholic Caucus. **Honors/Awds:** TX Farmworker Awd Human Rights 1977; Human Relation Catholic Awd 1978; Black Catholic Man of Vision 1978; Dryades YMCA Man of the Yr Awd 1979; NOBC Outstanding Serv 1980; FST 1985. **Military Serv:** Ordanance Corps 1951-53. **Business Addr:** Assistant Dir, Senior Citizen Center, 219 Loyola Ave, New Orleans, LA 70112.

YOUNG, WALTER F.
Dentist, international consultant. **Personal:** Born Aug 18, 1934, New Orleans, LA; married Sonjia W; children: Tony Waller, Tonya Waller, Tammy, Nikki. **Educ:** BS DDS 1959; Howard Univ, Harvard School Bus, special prog 1976. **Career:** Iberville Parish, Comm Action, St Laudry Parish, S James Parish, St Helena Parish, dental dir; NV State Mental Hosp, dental dir 1969; NV State Penal Inst, 1964; Pvt Prac, dentist 1987; Young Int Dev Corp, pres 1975-. **Orgs:** Mem OIC; SCLC; former bd mem NAACP; bd mem Fulton Co Hospital Auth; bd trust GA Econ Task Force; mem GA Dental Assoc/Intl Fellows Prog Bd; Honorary Consul General to Liberia. **Military Serv:** USN 1959. **Business Addr:** President, Young Int Dev Corp, 2265 Cascade Rd SW, Atlanta, GA 30311.

YOUNG, WATSON A.
Physician (retired). **Personal:** Born Sep 27, 1915, Abbeville, SC; married Aundree Noretta Drisdale; children: Watson, Jr, Aundree, Jr, Ransom J, Leonard F, Anthony G. **Educ:** Univ MI, MD 1942. **Career:** Private Practice, Physician 1944-80. **Orgs:** Mem, Detroit Med Soc; Wolverine State Med Soc; Natl Med Assn; Wayne Cnty & MI State Med Socs; Amer Med Assn; Am Soc & Abdominal Surgeons; life mem NAACP; Alpha Phi Alpha Fraternity; Alpha Phi Alpha Fraternity, life mem. **Military Serv:** US Army Major 1954-56. **Home Addr:** 43691 I-94 S Service Drive, Belleville, MI 48111-2464.

YOUNGE, RICHARD G.
Attorney. **Personal:** Born Aug 27, 1924, Kirkwood, MO; married; children: Ruth, Torque, Margaret, Roland, Richard Jr. **Educ:** Univ of IL, BA 1947; Lincoln U, LLB 1953. **Career:** E St Louis IL, pract atty; Forward Hsing Corp, atty 20 yrs 1973; Citizens Devel Corp; Econ Devel So IL, engaged in promotion. **Orgs:** Pres Metro-East Bar Assn. **Honors/Awds:** Developed Housing & Bus Opportunities for Blacks in So IL; Mound City Bar Association & Metro-East Bar Association, Outstanding Legal Services to the Comm Award, 1982-84. **Military Serv:** AUS s sgt. **Business Addr:** 2000 State St, East Saint Louis, IL 62205.

YOUNGER, CELIA DAVIS
Educator. **Personal:** Born Aug 24, 1939, Gretna, VA; married James Arthur; children: Felicia A, Terri E. **Educ:** VA State Univ, BS 1970, MEd. **Career:** VA State Univ, prog coord student union 1971-73, asst dir financial aid 1973-75, business develop specialist and procurement officer 1974-78; J Sargeant Reynolds Comm Coll, adjunct faculty school of business 1974-75; Ocean County Coll, adjunct faculty school of business 1982-83; Georgian Court Coll, dir learning resource ctr 1978-83, dir educ oppor fund prog 1983-. **Orgs:** Mem Alpha Kappa Alpha Sor 1968-, EOF Professional Assoc 1978-; chairperson affirmative action comm workshop facilitator OC Adv Comm on Status of Women 1980-; exec bd mem Ocean County Girl Scouts 1983-; mem Amer Assoc of Univ Women, NJ Assoc of Develop Educ, NJ Assoc of Student Financial Aid Administrators Inc, Natl Assoc of Female Execs. **Honors/Awds:** Certificate of Appreciation Toms River Regional Bd of Educ 1984-85. **Business Addr:** Dir, Georgian Court College, Educational Oppor Fund Prog, Lakewood, NJ 08701.

YOUNGER, KENNETH C.
Auto dealer. **Personal:** Born in Missouri. **Career:** McDonnell Douglas Aircraft Corp CA, engr; Landmark Ford Fairfield OH, owner 1977-. **Orgs:** Founding mem Black Ford Lincoln-Mercury Dealers Assoc; pres Natl Assoc of Minority Automobile Dealers.

YOUNGER, LEWIS T., JR.
Highway patrol inspector. **Personal:** Born Sep 8, 1950, Eden, MS; son of Mary Gamble Younger and Lewis Younger Sr; married Robbie Kay Patrick Younger, Oct 15, 1984; children: Kristen Andrea, Lewis III. **Educ:** Jackson State Univ, Jackson, MS, 1968-72; Univ of VA, Charlottesville, VA, 1990. **Career:** Missisppi Highway Patrol, Jackson, MS, trooper, 1972-80, criminal investigator, 1980-82, master sergeant, 1982-86, captain, 1986-88, major, 1988-. **Orgs:** Mem, FBI Natl Academy Associates, 1990-; mem, Jackson/Hinds Emergency 911 Council, 1987-; mem, Andrew Wilson Lodge #712-A, !987-; mem, Central State Trooper's Coalition, 1986-; mem, bd of dir, Blacks in Law Enforcement, 1990-. **Honors/Awds:** Vernon Dahmer Award, MS State Conference NAACP, 1990; Silver Shield-Community Serve Award, J-COPS, 1988; Certificate of Appreciation, Drug Interdiction Program Federal Highway Administration, 1989. **Home Addr:** 712 Brandon Ave, Jackson, MS 39209.

YOUNGER, PAUL LAWRENCE (TANK)
Professional athlete, manager. **Personal:** Born Jun 25, 1928, Grambling, LA; married Lucille; children: Howard, Harriette, Lucy. **Educ:** Grambling Coll, BS 1949. **Career:** LA Rams, player 1949-57; Pittsburgh Steelers, player 1958; LA Rams, part-time personnel scout 1959-63, personnel scout 1963-75; San Diego Chargers FootballClub, asst gen mgr 1975-. **Military Serv:** AUS pvt 1951. **Business Addr:** Assistant General Manager, San Diego Chargers, PO Box 20666, San Diego, CA 92120.

YOUNGER, ROBERT D.
Electrical engineer. **Personal:** Born Jan 27, 1932, Grambling, LA; married Ann Dean Meadows; children: Cynthia, Louise, Carol, James. **Educ:** Purdue Univ Mankato State, Graduate Work (Cum Laude) 1957; Indiana Inst of Technology, BSEE; Harvard Univ Graduate School, 1976. **Career:** Magnavox Co, electrical engineer 1957-65; Control Data Corp, sr electrical engineer 1966-, dept mgr special test equipment 1966-. **Orgs:** Active Inner Comm work to interest & motivate young black students to seek careers in science & engineering; helped organize local org Minds for Progress Inc; mem NAACP, Urban League, Deacon; vice chmn City of Bloomington MN Comm on Human Rights; special advisor State Commn of Human Rights State of MN; mem Hon Frat. **Honors/Awds:** Award Coolidge Physics Prize; obtained patent in reactance measuring instrument; published paper Natl Tech Assoc Journal; featured in numerous newspaper articles. **Military Serv:** AUS sgt 1952-54. **Business Addr:** Sr Elect Engr, Dept Mgr, Control Data Corp, 7801 Computer Ave, Minneapolis, MN 55435.

YOUNG-SALL, HAJAR
Massage therapist. **Personal:** Born Jan 6, 1952, Asheville, NC; daughter of Curtis & Gladys Young; married El-Hadji Sall, May 21, 1995; children: Muhammad, Sulaiman, Khadijah. **Career:** Out of Africa, owner, 1990-92; International Massage Therapy Association, certified massage therapist, 1992-. **Orgs:** American Massage Therapy Association, vice pres, 1993-95; Sisters United Network, 1992-95; pres, Society Against Subtle Racist Acts. **Honors/Awds:** Healing Arts Honoree, Int'l Masseuse Fed. **Business Addr:** Certified Massage Therapist, International Massage Therapy Associates, Medical Arts Bldg, 1169 Eastern Pkwy, Ste 3450, Louisville, KY 40217, (502)458-7411.

YO YO (YOLANDA WHITAKER)
Rap singer. **Personal:** Born 1971, Los Angeles, CA. **Career:** Rap musician and recording artist, 1990-. **Orgs:** Intelligent Black Woman's Coalition, founder. **Special Achievements:** Albums: ''Make Way for the Motherlode,'' 1991; ''Black Pearl''; appeared in the films ''Boyz N the Hood,'' 1991 and ''Strapped,'' 1993. **Business Addr:** Rap Singer, c/o East West Records America, 75 Rockefeller Plaza, New York, NY 10019, (212)275-2500.

YUILL, ESSIE MCLEAN-HALL
Educator, (retired). **Personal:** Born Jan 31, 1923, Wise, NC; daughter of Lucy Hall and Edward Hall; married Lorenzo Yuill, Jun 12, 1965 (deceased); children: Lester Slade McLean. **Educ:** Shaw University, BA, 1946; Capital University, reading specialist certification, 1964; Ohio State University, MEd, 1970. **Career:** Johnsonville High School, English, 1950-55; Kent Elementary, 1961-67; Franklin Middle School, 1967-70; Barrett Middle, coordinator, supervisor of reading program, 1971-77; Berry Middle School, reading/communication, 1971-77; Briggs High School, reading/communication skills, 1977-79; Central High School, reading/communication skills, 1979-80; East High School, reading/communication skills, 1980-88. **Orgs:** Zeta Phi Beta; Quality of Sharing, charter member; King Performing Arts; Friends of Arts for Cultural Enrichment; University Women; Helen Jenkins Davis Scholarship Award Group; Columbus Symphony Orchestra, east unit; Child Devlopment Council, board member; MLK Breakfast, hostess; Quality of Sharing, charter member. **Honors/Awds:** Zeta Phi Beta, Distinguish Service Award, 1986-90; Quality of Sharing Recognition Award, 1981; Columbus Public School, Service Award, 1988; Teacher of the Year, 1986; Shiloh Baptist Church, Service Award, 1989; Miss Black Pageant, Les Ami Club, Judge, 1978. **Home Addr:** 354 Rhoads Ave, Columbus, OH 43205, (614)252-0190.

YUILLE, BRUCE
Dentist. **Career:** Dentist, currently. **Orgs:** Maryland Academy General Dentistry. **Honors/Awds:** Maryland Academy of General Dentistry, master dentist status, 1995. **Special Achievements:** First African American to receive master dentist status from MD Academy of General Dentistry. **Business Addr:** Dentist, 5310 Old Court Rd., Randallstown, MD 21133-5243, (410)521-1888.

Z

ZACHARY, HUBERT M.
Marketing executive. **Personal:** Born Nov 9, 1936, Hertford, NC; son of Arzalia Lightfoot Lyle and Hubert M. Zachary; married Brenda M. Fletcher; children: Hubert, Mia, Christian. **Educ:** Morgan State U, BS Chem 1966; WV U, MSIE 1969. **Career:** Western Electric Co, Baltimore, MD, industrial engineer, 1964-68, buyer, 1968-69, supvr product control, 1974-83, buyer, 1983-; Johns Hopkins Univ, instructor 1970-82; NY Tele Co, staff mgr 1983-84; NYNEX, New York, NY, staff director of marketing, 1986-90, marketing consultant, 1990. **Orgs:** Instructor Baltimore City Adult Educ 1966-78; pres Baltimore Cossocks Inc 1976. **Honors/Awds:** Pride Award for project management and evaluation, NYNEX, 1989.

ZACHARY, STEVEN W.
Government offical, educator. **Personal:** Born Apr 24, 1958, St Paul, MN; son of Martha A Zachary and Percy J Zachary; divorced; children: Steven Jr, James. **Educ:** Mankato State University, BS, 1981; University of Minnesota School of Law, JD, 1984. **Career:** City of St Paul, human rights specialist, 1984-92; William Mitchell College of Law, adjunct professor, 1989-92; State of Minnesota, diversity and equal opportunity director, 1992-97. **Orgs:** NAACP St Paul Branch, president, 1990-93; MCLU, board member, 1990-93; MN Minority Lawyer's Association, 1987-93; JRLC, criminal justice taskforce chairperson, 1991-92; St Peter Claver School, school board president, 1987-88. **Honors/Awds:** William Mitchell College of Law, Haines Distinguished Service Award, 1992. **Special Achievements:** What's In Store for Civil Rights in 1990. **Home Addr:** 18 Michael St, St Paul, MN 55119, (612)510-0926. **Business Addr:** Diversity & Equal Opportunity Director, State of Minnesota, Department of Employee Relations, 200 Centennial Office Bldg, 658 Cedar St, St Paul, MN 55155, (612)296-8272.

ZACHARY-PIKE, ANNIE R.
Farmer. **Personal:** Born May 12, 1931, Marvell, AR; daughter of Carrie Davidson (deceased) and Cedel Davidson (deceased); married Lester Pike, Apr 10, 1977. **Educ:** Homer G Phillips School of Nursing. **Career:** Farmer, owner & mgr 1,054 acres of farmland; Marvell School District, chapter I parent coordinator, 1990-91. **Orgs:** Mem, Eastern Star; NAACP; AR Assn Colored Women; Phillips Co Extnsn Hmmkrs Cncl; IPA; AR Cncl Hmn Rltns; AR Assn Crppld Inc; Wildlife Federation; EAME; Emergency Sch Asst Proj; Pta; 4-H; Farm Bureau; Farmers Home Admin; adv council FHA; USDA Civil Rights Commn; Council Aging; Fair Bd; Sm Bus Assn; Natl Council Christians & Jews; bd mem The Election Law Inst; Eastern Arkansas Mental Health; Delta Area Devel Inc; Workshop Inc; Rep, AR St Com Farm. **Honors/Awds:** Family Year Award 1959; 4-H Friendship 1959; Home Demonstration Woman Year 1965; Queens Womens Federated Club Inc 1969; Delg 1972 GOP Conv Wmn Yr, Alpha Kappa Alpha 1971; Hon PhD, CO St Christian Coll 1972.

ZAMBRANA, RAFAEL
Educator. **Personal:** Born May 26, 1931, Santa Isabel, Puerto Rico; married Laura E Alvarez; children: Gloria, Ralph, Aida, Magda, Wallace, Olga, Daphne. **Educ:** Catholic Univ of PR, BA Hist 1958; Attended, Columbia Univ courses in psychology 1965; Hunter College, 36 grad credits in secondary educ 1958-62; MSW 1974; City Univ of New York, PhD 1982. **Career:** Bd of Ed NY, jr hs teacher 1958-62; Rabbi Jacob Joseph HS, teacher 1962-65; Mobilization for Youth, soc worker 1965-67; PR Community Devel Proj, dir of training and block organization program, 1967-68; Lower East Side Manpower Neighborhood Serv Ctr, dir 1968-69; Williamsburg Community Corp, exec dir 1969-71; Community Devel Agency of NYC, Asst commiss 1971-74; Medgar Evers Coll of CUNY, prof of public admin 1974-; Medgar Evers Coll of CUNY, chairperson of soc sci div 1982-89; Medgor Evers College of CUNY, dean School of Business and Public Administration, 1990-93. **Orgs:** Consultant NYS Dept of Corrections 1976; consult Coney Island Com Corp 1969-78; bd mem Com Council of Greater NY 1969-76; advisory bd mem Mgmt Advisory Council, US Dept Labor Reg II 1980-82; past pres Council of PR and Hisp Org; pres MEC Faculty Org; institutional representative, Natl Assoc of Schools of PA; past local sch bd mem Dist 12 NYC. **Honors/Awds:** Meritorious Serv Awd Williamsburg Com Corp 1971; Devotion to Children Awd Supr Assoc New York City Local Sch Bd Dist #12 1977; $800,000 Manpower Ed Grant, US Dept of Labor 1979-83; Outstanding Ed Awd Student's Council Williamsburg Proj 1980; Articles publ in Teaching Publ Admin 1981-84, 1992-93. **Military Serv:** Honorable Discharge, 1950-55; Good Conduct Medal; Korean Serv Medal. **Home Addr:** 1125 Manor Ave, Bronx, NY 10472. **Business Addr:** School of Business & Public Administration, Medgar Evers College/CUNY, 1650 Bedford Ave, Brooklyn, NY 11225, (718)270-4958.

ZANDER, JESSIE MAE
Educational administrator. **Personal:** Born Jul 31, 1932, Inman, VA; married Johnny W Zander. **Educ:** Berea Coll, BA Elem Educ 1954; Univ of AZ, MA Elem Educ 1966; Univ of AZ, MA Cnslng Guid 1976. **Career:** Linweaver School Tucson Unified School Dist, prin 1980; Miles Exploratory Learning Center Tucson Unified School Dist, prin 1979-80; Tucson Unified School Dist, counselor 1976-79; Tucson Unified School Dist, teacher 1958-76; Tucson Indian Training School AZ, teacher jr high 1956-58; Benham Elem HS Benham KY, teacher 1954-58. **Orgs:** Consult Cltrl Awrns Admnstr Retreat 1975-76; coord poetry in schl AZ St Poetry Soc 1977-80; bd mem Pima Cncl on Chldrn Srvcs 1978-79; mem Educ DivAm Cancer Soc 1975; Tamiochus Alpha Kappa Alpha Sor Eta Epsilon Omega Chap 1976-81; vice pres AZ St Poetry Soc 1978; conf chrpsn AZ St Poetry Soc 1978-79. **Honors/Awds:** Otstndng Pres Cncl of Black Edctrs 1978-79 & 1979-80; Newspaper Article Open Educ Miles Exploratory Lrning Cntr 1980. **Business Addr:** Miles Expl Lrnng Ctr Tucson Un, 1010 E 10th St, Tucson, AZ 85717.

ZANDERS, ALTON WENDELL
Educational administrator. **Personal:** Born Sep 3, 1943, Amite, LA; married Gertrude Carral; children: Geleah Nicole, Anissa Monique. **Educ:** Southern Univ, BS 1965; Syracuse Univ, MS 1970, JD 1974. **Career:** New Orleans Public School System, teacher 1965-69; State Univ of New York, asst dir and dir of special programs 1970-79, affirmative action officer 1974-80; Univ of MO-Columbia, dir office of equal oppor 1981-. **Orgs:** Commissioner Human Rights Comm City of Columbia 1981-83; mem Amer Assoc for Affirmative Action 1985-; mem MO Black Leadership Assoc 1985-; bd dirs Multicultural Mgmt Program Sch of Journalism UMC 1985-; mem Minority Men's Network 1986-; bd dirs Kiwanis Club of Columbia 1986-; mem & State coord of HigherEduc Liaison Comm US Dept of Labor Office of Federal Contract Compliance Program (Midwest Region). **Honors/Awds:** NSF Dillar Univ 1969-70; NSF Syracuse Univ 1969; Administrative Internship State Univ of NY 1974; Public Trust Awd Coll of Law Syracuse Univ 1974; also 14 publications including ''Vita Banks for Minorities and Women, Do They Work?'' 1984 presented at the Amer Assoc for Affirmative Action 11th Annual Conf San francisco 1985.

ZEALEY, SHARON JANINE
Attorney. **Personal:** Born Aug 30, 1959, St Paul, MN; daughter of Freddie Ward Zealey and Marion Edward Zealey. **Educ:** Xavier University of Louisiana, BS, 1981; University of Cincinnati, JD, 1984. **Career:** Star Bank, corporate trust administrator, 1984-86; UAW Legal Services, attorney, 1986-88; Manley, Burke & Fisher, associate, 1988-1990; Ohio Attorney General, deputy attorney general, 1990-94; US Attorney, currently. **Orgs:** Bar Associations: American, National, Ohio, Cincinnati, Federal; Cincinnati Bar Association, board o trustees, 1990-94; Black Lawyer's Association of Cincinnati, president, 1989-91; Natl Bar Assn, board of governors, 1989-91; City of Cincinnati Equal Employment Opportunity Advisory Review Board, 1989-91; Legal Aid Society of Cincinnati, board of trustees, 1987-92, secretary, 1990-92; City of Cincinnati, Tall Stacks Commission, commissioner, 1991-96; Mayor's Commission on Children, commissioner, 1992-94; Greater Cincinnati Foundation Task Force on Affordable Home Ownership, 1992-93; US Sixth Circuit Court of Appeals, merit selection committee, 1992-93; Black Lawyers Assn of Cincinnati. **Honors/Awds:** Natl Bar Assn, Region VI, Member of the Year, 1990; Nicholas Longworth Award, Univ of Cincinnati Coll of Law, 1997. **Business Addr:** US Attorney, US Attorney's Office, 220 US Courthouse, 100 E 5th St, Cincinnati, OH 45202, (513)684-3711.

ZEITLIN, JIDE J.
Investment executive. **Personal:** Born in Ibaden, Nigeria; son of Arnold & Marian Zeitlin. **Educ:** Amherst College, AB, 1985; Harvard Univ, MBA, 1987. **Career:** Goldman Sachs, summer assoc, 1983-86, assoc, 1987-91, vp, 1991-96, partner and managing director, 1997-. **Orgs:** Amherst Coll, trustee, 1993-; Milton Academy, trustee, 1996-; Common Ground Community HDFC, dir, 1996-. **Business Addr:** Partner, Goldman, Sachs & Co, 85 Broad St, New York, NY 10004, (212)902-1000.

ZELIS, KAREN DEE
Attorney. **Personal:** Born Oct 21, 1953, Washington, DC; daughter of Jeanne Rivoire; divorced; children: Jason Christopher, Erika Nikole. **Educ:** University of California, BA, 1975; Armstrong Law School, JD, 1979. **Career:** Alameda County Family Court Services, secretary, 1982-83; Contra Costa District Attorney's Office, deputy district attorney, 1983-. **Orgs:** Charles Houston Bar Association, 1990-; American Bar Association, 1990-; Contra Costa Bar Association, 1990-; California State Bar Association, 1982-; California District Attorney's Association, 1983-. **Business Addr:** Deputy District Attorney, Contra Costa District Attorney's Office, 725 Court St, 4th Fl, Martinez, CA 94553, (415)646-4500.

ZELLARS, RAYMOND MARK
Professional football player. **Personal:** Born Mar 25, 1973, Pittsburgh, PA. **Educ:** Univ of Notre Dame, bachelor's degree in management. **Career:** New Orleans Saints, running back, 1995-. **Business Addr:** Professional Football Player, New Orleans Saints, 5800 Airline Hwy, Metairie, LA 70003, (504)733-0255.

ZENO, MELVIN COLLINS
Judge. **Personal:** Born Jul 14, 1945, Jonesboro, LA; son of Ruth Doyle Zeno and Nathaniel Zeno Sr (deceased); married Margie Loud, Dec 27, 1967; children: Monica Lureen, Micah Collins. **Educ:** Southern University, BS, 1967; Loyola University of the South, JD, 1974. **Career:** Red Ball Motor Freight Co, dock worker, 1966; Iberville Parish, speech & hearing therapist, 1968; Jefferson Parish, special education teacher, 1968-75; attorney at law, 1974-92; Xavier University, business law instructor, 1986-88; Jefferson Parish, assistant district attorney, 1975-92, 24th Judicial District Court, judge, division p, 1992-. **Orgs:** Louisiana State Special Olympics, director, 1969-; Hope Haven Madonna Manor Home for Boys, advisory board, 1984-; Martin L King Jr Task Force, co-founder, vice pres, board of directors, 1979-; Jefferson Parish Economic Development Commission, Business Development Expansion Advisory Committee, chairman; Jefferson Black Chamber of Commerce, Inc, co-founder, president, board of directors, 1989-92; March of Dimes Birth

Defects Foundation, board of directors, 1991; NAACP, life sustaining member; Omega Psi Phi Fraternity, internationl board of directors, 1983-90; American Bar Association; LA State Bar Association; Louis Martinet Legal Society; National Bar Association; American Judges Association; Louisiana Dist Judges Association; Fourth & Fifth Circuit Judges Association. **Honors/Awds:** Omega Psi Phi Fraternity, Inc, Man of the Year Award, 1980, 1981, 1984, 1991, 1992; Jefferson Black Chamber of Commerce, Inc, Outstanding Service Award, 1989-91; Martin Luther King Jr Task Force, Inc, Outstanding Service Award, 1991; Kenner Kiwanis Club, Outstanding Community Service Award, 1979. **Special Achievements:** Fourth National Conference on the Sexual Victimization of Children, lecturer; opened first African-American History Museum, Jefferson Parish, 1992; appointed Louisiana State Bar Association, attorney, arbitration board, 1991-92; elected international 1st vice grand basileus, Omega Psi Phi Fraternity, 1988; first black elected judge, 24th judicial district court, 1992. **Business Addr:** Judge, 24th Judicial Dist Court, Gretna Courthouse, Division P, Gretna, LA 70053, (504)364-3975.

ZENO, WILLIE D.
Business executive. **Personal:** Born Mar 28, 1942, Dallas, TX. **Educ:** Univ OK, MSEE 1972; Bus Bishop Coll, MBA 1968. **Career:** Hank Moore & Asso; Goodyear Aerospace, persnl dir; EOC US Dept Labor, dir; Engineering & Design Engineering Soc Am Leap, dir. **Orgs:** Urban Leg Nat Bsnsmn. **Honors/Awds:** Wk Design Eng Month (Goodyear). **Military Serv:** USN 1 lt.

ZIEGLER, DHYANA
Educator. **Personal:** Born May 5, 1949, New York, NY; daughter of Alberta A Guy Ziegler and Ernest Ziegler (deceased). **Educ:** Baruch Coll CUNY BA Program, BS (Cum Laude) 1981; Southern IL Univ-Carbondale, MA 1983, PhD 1985. **Career:** Essence Magazine, market researcher 1972-75; Rosenfeld Sirowitz & Lawson, copywriter & radio producer 1974-75; Patten and Guest Productions NY, regional mgr 1976-79; WNEW TV, internship desk asst & production asst; Seton Hall Univ, counselor for high school students 1979-81; Baruch Coll CUNY, English tutor & instructor for writing workshops 1979-81; Westside Newspaper, reporter 1980-; CBS TV Network, production intern 1980-81; Southern IL Univ Dept of Radio & Television, lab instructor 1981-83; Jackson State Univ Dept of Mass Comm, asst prof 1984-85; Univ of TN-Knoxville Dept of Broadcasting, asst prof of broadcasting 1985-90, assoc professor, 1990-. **Orgs:** Natl Political Congress of Black Women; Delta Sigma Theta Sor Inc; Phi Delta Kappa; grad fellow Post Doctoral Acad of Higher Educ; Speech Comm Assn; pres & founder Blacks in Communications Alliance; Natl Cncl of Negro Women Inc; legislative council Southern IL Univ Alumni Assn; panelist Metro Black Media Coalition Conference 1984, Southern IL Univ/Blacks in Communications Alliance 1985, Natl Black Media Coalition Conf 1985; speaker/consultant US Armed Forces Azores Portugal 1986; chmn/public relations, Kiwanis Club of Knoxville, 1988-; Southern Regional Devel Educ Project Coord, Delta Sigma Theta, 1988-; Women in Communications, Inc, vice pres of develop, pres-elect 1989, pres 1990-91;Society of Professional Journalists, 1988-. **Honors/Awds:** Seek Scholarship Awards for Academic & Service 1979-81 Baruch Coll; Rita Leeds Service Award 1981 Baruch Coll; Sheldon Memorial Award Baruch Coll 1981; Scrippt-Howard Award Baruch Coll 1981; United Press Intl Outstanding Achievement Radio Documentary 1982; Dept of Radio and TV SIUC Outstanding Radio Production Award 1982-83; Grad Dean's Doctoral Fellowship 1983-84; Paul Robinson's Roby Scholar Award Black Affairs Council 1984; Certificate of Merit Award Southern IL Univ Broadcasting Serv 1984; Ebony Bachelorette 1985; Seek Alumni Award Baruch Coll 1985; numerous publications and other professional works; Outstanding Faculty Member of the Year, Coll of Communications, UTK, 1987-88; Chancellor's Citation for Service, Univ of TN Knoxville, 1988, MaxRobinson, Jr, Turbulent Life of a Media phet, Journal of Black Studies, 1989, Challenging Racism in the Classrom: Paving the Road to the Future/Thoughts and Action-The Journal of the Natl Educ Assn, 1989; articles, "Women and Minorities on Network Television News," Journal of Broadcasting, Spring 1990, "Teaching Television News: A Classroom Newsroom Model," Feedback, Spring 1990; Faculty Research Award, 1992; Chancellor Citation for Extraordinary Service, 1992; State of Tennessee Governor's Award for Outstanding Achievement, 1991; Consortium of Doctors Award, 1991. **Special Achievements:** Co-author, Thunder and Silence: The Mass Media in Africa; several book chapters and journal articles. **Business Addr:** Associate Professor of Broadcasting, University of Tennessee, Dept of Broadcasting, 295 Communications Bldg, Knoxville, TN 37996.

ZIMMERMAN, EUGENE
Internist. **Personal:** Born Jul 7, 1947, Orangeburg, SC; married Sheila Beth Hughes; children: Brian, Monica. **Educ:** Jersey City State Coll, BA 1969; Howard Univ Medical Sch, MD 1973. **Career:** Harlem Hosp Ctr, intern 1973-74; Howard Univ Hosp, resident 1974-76; Student Health Serv of Gallanhet Coll, actg medical dir 1977-81; SENAB, medical dir 1979-84; Dept of Forensic Psychiatry, staff physician. **Orgs:** Mem Medical Soc of DC 1976-, NY Acad of Sciences 1984-. **Honors/Awds:** Bd Certified Internist Amer Bd of Internal Medicine 1985; "Staining Characteristics of Bone Marrow" w/Dr WD Sharpe 1968. **Home Addr:** 4621 Sargent Rd NE, Washington, DC 20017. **Business Addr:** Staff Physician, Dept of Forensic Psychiatry, 1905 E St SE Bldg 22, Washington, DC 20003.

ZIMMERMAN, LIZ. **See KEITT, L.**

ZIMMERMAN, MATTHEW AUGUSTUS, JR.
Military official, clergyman. **Personal:** Born Dec 9, 1941, Rock Hill, SC; son of Alberta Loretta Brown and Matthew Augustus; married Barbara Ann Boulware, Sep 5, 1964; children: Tina, Dana, Meredith. **Educ:** Benedict College, BS, 1962; Duke University, MDiv, 1965; Long Island University, MEd, 1975. **Career:** Headquarters, 3d Infantry Division, division staff chaplain, 1980-82; Training Doctrine Command, deputy staff chaplain, 1983-85; US Forces Command, command chaplain, 1985-89; US Army, deputy chief of chaplains, 1989-90, chief of chaplains, 1990-. **Orgs:** Military Chaplains Association; Association of US Army; USO Board of Governors; Kiwanis International; Omega Psi Phi Fraternity, Inc; Howard University School of Divinity, chairman, board of visitors. **Honors/Awds:** Benedict College, Doctor of Humane Letters, 1991; NAACP, Roy Wilkins Meritorious Service Award, 1990; Duke University Divinity School, Distinguished Alumni Award, 1991; South Carolina Black Hall of Fame, selectee, 1992. **Military Serv:** US Army, major general; Legion of Merit, Bronze Star, 3 Meritorious Service Medals, Army Commendation Medal, Vietnam Honor Medal. **Home Addr:** 5314 Echols Ave., Alexandria, VA 22311-1309, (703)522-5393. **Business Addr:** Chief of Chaplains, Department of the Army, Pentagon, Rm 1E416, Washington, DC 20310-2700, (202)695-1133.

ZIMMERMAN, SAMUEL LEE
Educational director. **Personal:** Born Apr 28, 1923, Anderson, SC; son of Corinne O Banks Zimmerman and William L Zimmerman; married Blanche Carole Williams Zimmerman, May 30, 1946; children: Samuel Lee Jr. **Educ:** Benedict College, AB Elemen Educ 1962; Graduate Study, Furman Univ 1965, 1968, Univ of Washington 1973, Glassboro State Coll 1974. **Career:** Greenville School Dist, elementary reading teacher 1961-70; The Greenville Piedmont, news reporter 1970-73; WFBC-TV, host for raparound 1976-77; WFBC Radio, host for raparound 1976-82; School Dist of Greenville Co, dir school/comm relations 1973-87; consultant, Partridge Assoc, 1988-. **Orgs:** Former vice pres at large Natl School Public Relations Assn 1979-81; SC Assn of School Admin; Comm to Study Educ in the State of SC; bd of dir SC Comm for the Blind; bd of dir Goodwill Indus of Upper SC; bd of trustees Springfield Baptist Church. **Honors/Awds:** AP Award Sampling Attitudes of Young Blacks 1969; William F Gaines Mem Award in Journalism 1971; Distinguished Serv Award City of Greenville 1974; Serv Certificate of Appreciation United Way of Greenville 1977; Natl School Public Relations Certificate of Appreciation 1976-77; Certificate of Award the Greenville Co Human Relations 1977-78; Whitney M Young, Jr Humaritarian Award, 1988; Outstanding Volunteer, United Negro Coll Fund, 1989. **Military Serv:** AUS T-5 2 yrs. **Home Addr:** 6 Allendale Lane, PO Box 6535, Greenville, SC 29606.

ZOLA, NKENGE (TERESA KRISTINE NKENGE ZOLA BEAMON)
Broadcast communicator. **Personal:** Born Apr 11, 1954, Detroit, MI; daughter of Maya Beamon-Dean and Henry Edward Moscow Beamon. **Educ:** University of Michigan, Ann Arbor, MI, 1975; Recording Institute of Det, East Detroit, MI, 1987; Wayne State University, Detroit, MI, 1976-77, 1989; Wayne County Community Coll. **Career:** Tribe Magazine, Detroit, MI, copy editor, 1976-77; WJLB AM/FM, Detroit, MI, continuity dir, 1977-78, news anchor, reporter, 1978-81; Christopher Pitts, Birmingham, MI, host, Jazzmasters: Keepers of the Flame, 1989-90; WDET-FM, Detroit, MI, producter, host, The Nkenge Zola Program, 1982-, news anchor, reporter, 1990-; Arts and Society, The Witness Magazine, editor, 1995. **Orgs:** Member, Project BAIT (Black Awareness in Television), 1976-; member, Afrikan Library Singers, 1989-; chair, Afrikan Child Enrichment Assn, 1989-; board member, Women's Justice Center, 1991-; board member, Creative Arts Collective, 1990-; forum coordinator, Creative Community Artist Support Group, 1990-; member, Advocators, National Org for an Amer Revolution, 1977-87; natl board member, Youth Council Pres, Detroit; cofounder, U of M Branch NAACP, 1970-76; James & Grace Lee Boggs Center to Nuture Community Development, 1996-; Casa de Unidad Cultural & Media Arts Center, board; Detroit Women's Coffee House, founding board, 1996-. **Honors/Awds:** Subject of tribute, "A Celebration of the Life of a Spiritual Warrior," Committee for Community Access to WDET, 1990; Exceptional Media Artist Award, Beatty & Assoc, 1990; Outstanding Supporter of Jazz Artists, Success Academy of Fine Arts, 1985; Spirit of Detroit Award, City of Detroit, 1985; editor, Loving Them to Life, New Life Publishers, 1987; Miss NAACP Detroit, NAACP, 1970; Michigan Association of Broadcasters First Place Award, Temple of Confessions, Detroit Press Club Award, 1995; Associated Press Award, 1992, 1995; Recipient Governor's Arts Award, 1995; Media Honor Roll, Arts Reporting; Recipient, Cultural Warrior Award, Societie of the Culturally Concerned. **Home Addr:** 91 E Philadelphia, Detroit, MI 48202. **Business Addr:** Producer/Host, Music & News Departments, Wayne State University/WDET-FM Public Radio, 6001 Cass, Detroit, MI 48202.

ZOLLAR, DORIS L.
Business executive. **Personal:** Born Dec 7, 1932, Little Rock, AR; married Lowell M; children: Nikki Michele, Lowell M Jr. **Educ:** Talladega Coll, BA 1951; UCLA Grad School, MA 1952; DePaul Univ, Post Grad 1952-54, 1958-59. **Career:** Chicago Publ School, teacher 1952-67; Childrens Haven Residential School for Multiple Handicapped Children, founder, org, school dir 1973-; The Independent Bulletin Newspaper, women's editor 1976-77; Triad Consulting Svcs, pres. **Orgs:** Comm leader Mid-West Conf of Pres Lyndon B Johnsons Comm on Equal Oppty 1964; mem Chicago Urban League 1965-, Lois R Lowe Womens Div UNCF 1966-, Jackson Park Highlands Assoc 1966-; vice pres Bravo Chap Lyric Opera of Chicago 1966; benefit chmn Ebony Fashion Fair 1968,69; corr sec IL Childrens Home & Aid Soc 198-70; publ rel fund raising consult Natl Med Assoc Project 75 1973-75; mem South Shore Comm 1974-; vice pres XXI bd Michael Reese Hosp 1974-76; Cook Cty Welfare Serv Comm 1975-; Chicago Publ School Art Soc of Chicago Art Inst 1975-; org & coord of 3 day conf wkshp Minority Constr Workers 1975; adv Midwest Assoc for Sickle Cell Anemia 1976-; adv The Black United Fund 1976-; mem Art in Public Places Bd 1976-, The Council of Foreign Affaris 1976;, IntlVisitors Ctr Bd 1976-; dir of fung devel The Woodlawn Org World Serv Council Natl YWCA 1976-. **Honors/Awds:** AKA Scholarship by competitive exam 1947; Exchange student from Talladega Coll to Cedar Crest Coll 1948-49; Florina Lasker Fellowship Awd 1951; Will RogersMeml Fellowship toward PhD in History 1952; "Ed Motivation of the Culturally Disadvantaged Youth" Chicago Bd of Ed 1958-60; Natl Med Assoc Awd Womens Aux 1966; The Pittsburgh Couriers Natl Ten Best Dressed 1972,73,74; Hon Librarian of the Chicago Publ Library City of Chicago 1974; the Commercial Breadbasket Assoc Awd 1975; Inst for Health Resources Devel Awd 1975; Oper PUSH Awd 1975,76; Person of the Day Awd Radio Stations WAIT, WBEE 1969,76; Beatrice CaffreyYouth Serv Inc Annual Merit Awd for Civic Achievement 1976; listed in Certain People 1977; Alpha Gamma Pi, Iota Phi Lambda Sor Bus & Professional Awd1977; dir IL International PoAuthority 1986-. **Business Addr:** President, Apex Construction Co Inc, 2100 S Indiana Ave, Chicago, IL 60616.

ZOLLAR, NIKKI MICHELE
Government official. **Personal:** Born Jun 18, 1956, Chicago, IL; daughter of Doris Lowe Zollar and Lowell M Zollar; married William A von Hoene Jr, Jun 18, 1983; children: William Lowell von Hoene, Branden Tracey. **Educ:** Johns Hopkins Univ, Baltimore MD, BA, 1977; Georgetown Univ Law Center, Washington DC, JD, 1980. **Career:** US District Court for Northern District of IL, judicial law clerk for Chief Judge James B Parsons, 1980-81; Lafontant, Wilkins, Jones & Ware, Chicago IL, associate, 1981-83; Kirkland & Ellis, Chicago IL, associate, 1983-85; Chicago Bd of Election Commissioners, chmn, 1987-90; Illinois Dept of Professional Regulation, director. **Orgs:** Chicago Heart Association, Women's Council; co-chair, telethon night event, UNCF, 1980-90; mem, Chicago Comm in Solidarity with Southern Africa, 1986-; mem, Community Outreach Comm, Field Museum of Natural History, 1987-90; mem, Georgetown Univ Law Center Alumni Bd, 1987-90; mem, Lois R Lowe Women's Bd, UNCF, 1987-; chair, educ comm, Chicago Architecture Foundation Board of Directors, 1987-90; mem, Alpha Gamma Pi, 1987-; co-chair, Law Exploring Comm, Young Lawyers Section of Chicago Bar Assn, 1988-90; mem, Woodland's Acad of the Sacred Heart bd of trustees, 1988-; mem, Chicago Urban League, 1988-; Community Youth Creative Learning Experience. **Honors/Awds:** Certificate of Outstanding Achievement, Illinois State Attorneys Appellate Service Comm, 1981; Service & Leadership Award, UNCF, 1983; Outstanding Young Professional, Chicago Urban Professionals, 1985; one of 100 Outstanding Black Business & Professional Women in US, Dollars & Sense, 1988; Martin Luther King Award, Boy Scouts of Amer, 1989; African-Amer Women's Achievement Award, Columbia Coll, 1989; Kizzy Award, Revlon/Kizzy Foundation, 1989; David C Hilliard Award, Chicago Bar Assn, 1989; Youth Service, Beatrice Caffrey, 1989; Achievement & Service to the Community Award, YMCA, 1991; Outstanding Achievement Award, YWCA. **Business Addr:** Director, Dept of Professional Regulation, State of Illinois, 100 W Randolph, Ste 9-300, Chicago, IL 60601.

ZU-BOLTON, AHMOS, II (DR. ZULU)
Writer, editor, folklorist, storyteller. **Personal:** Born Oct 21, 1935, Popularville, MS; son of Annie Lou McGee Zu-Bolton and Ahmos Zu-Bolton; married Kathy (divorced 1977); children: Bojavai, Sonoma, Amber Easter. **Career:** Howard University Afro-American Resource Center, Washington, DC, associate director; Hoo-Doo Magazine, Galveston, TX, editor, 1971-78; Georgia State Arts Commission, writer-in-residence, 1975; Texas Commission on the Arts, poet-in-residence, 1977-82; Galveston Arts Center, folklorist-in-residence, 1979; Northlake Arts Camp, writer-in-residence, 1984-85; Xavier University, professor of English, writer-in-residence, 1987-89; writer, editor, folklorist, storyteller, currently; Tulane University, professor of English, writer-in-residence, 1992-. **Orgs:** Board of directors, Association of Black Storytellers, 1989-. **Honors/Awds:** National Endowment for the Arts, Creative Writing Fellowship, 1979; Texas Commission on the Arts and Humanities, Critic's Fellowship, 1980; CCLM, Editor's Fellowship, 1981; Louisiana Division of the Arts, Creative Writing

Fellowship, 1987; Ford Foundation, Folklore Fellowship, 1989. **Special Achievements:** Books include: A Niggered Amen, 1975; Stumbling Thru: earth(ing)poems, 1980; Ain't No Spring Chicken, 1990; All My Lies Are True, 1990; plays include: The Widow Paris: A Folklore of Marie Laveau; The Funeral; Family Reunion: a one-woman drama; The Break-In; Louisiana Souvenir: a choreo-folkpoem; editor of: Energy West Poetry Journal, 1970-72; Griots' Works (anthology, co-edited with Kwa Tamani), 1971; The Last Cookie, 1972; Hoo-Doo Black Series, 1972-78; Synergy anthology, 1975; Black Box, 1974-77; producer and director of numerous plays and musicals; writings and poetry have appeared in many magazines and anthologies. **Military Serv:** US Army, Sp4, 1967-69; medic. **Business Addr:** Director, Copastetic Community Book Center, 1616 Marigny, New Orleans, LA 70117.

DR. ZULU. See ZU-BOLTON, AHMOS, II.

ZULU, ITIBARI M.
Librarian. **Personal:** Born Apr 24, 1953, Oakland, CA; married Simone N Koivogui Zulu, Aug 9, 1980; children: Akiba, Itibari Jr, Togba, Kadiatou. **Educ:** Merritt College, Oakland, CA, AA, 1974; California State University, Hayward, BA, 1976; San Jose State University, San Jose, CA, MLS, 1989; Amen-Ra Theological Seminary, Los Angeles, ThC, 1997. **Career:** Fresno Unified School District, Fresno, CA, teacher, 1981-89; California State University, Fresno, CA, lecturer, 1988-89; California State University, Fresno, CA, reference librarian, 1989-92; UCLA Ctr for African-American Studies, librarian, 1992-. **Orgs:** Chair-elect, chair, African-American Studies, Librarians Section of the Association of College & Research Libraries of the American Library Association, 1996-99; mem, Black Caucus of the American Library Association, mem, UCLA Black Faculty & Staff Association; chair, Antelope Valley Million Man March Commemorative Committee; mem, International Relations Committee Africa subcommittee of the American Library Association; mem, American Library Association; founding provost, Amen-Ra Community Assembly of California Inc; mem Association for the Study of Classical African Civilizations; mem, African Diaspora Conference; mem, African-American Library & Information Science Association. **Honors/Awds:** Jomo Kenyatta Dedication Award, African Student Union, California State Univ, Fresno, 1984; Adjunct Assistant Professor of Ethnic Studies, 1991; CA State Univ, Fresno, African American Organizations Council, Outstanding Support and Guidance Faculty Award, 1991; African American Library and Information Science Assn, founder, 1993; Multicultural Review, African and African American Studies, editor, 1993-; author, Ancient Kemetic Roots of Library and Information Science, 1996-; co-editor, Lexicon of African American Subject Headings, 1994; Contributing Editor: The Black Church Review, 1994-. **Business Addr:** UCLA Center for African American Studies, 160 Haines Hall, PO Box 951545, Los Angeles, CA 90095-1545.

Obituaries

ABERNATHY, JAMES R., II.
Attorney. **Personal:** Died Jul 14, 1996; married Claudia Mitchell; children: Kevin, Christopher, Tracey. **Educ:** Howard Univ, BA 1949, JD 1952; Univ of So CA, MPA 1975. **Career:** HEW, legal counsel on natl immun liab prog, legal consult black health providers task force on high blood pressure educ & control; NBA-NMA Health Law Comm, chmn; Black Congress on Health & Law; Amer Health Care Plan, atty & gen counsel; James R Abernathy II & Associates, San Francisco CA, attorney, currently. **Orgs:** Mem, St Bar of CA, Natl Bar Assn, Charles Houston Bar Assn, Natl Health Lawyers Assn, Natl Conf of Black Lawyers, San Francisco Lawyers Club, CA Trial Lawyers Assn, NAACP, Natl Lawyers Guild, Southern Pov Law Ctr, Minority Public Admin, Alpha Phi Alpha Frat; seminars on Health Law 1979-83 Natl Bar Assn Convention; lecturer at Univ of So CA, McGeorge School of Law; Dakarand Abidjan & Economics Conference in Africa, NBA Law, 1991; Society of Black Lawyers of England, NBA, 1991-92; Legal Education and International Law Committees. **Special Achievements:** Author of numerous publications including, "Legal Issues ConfrontingHealth Maint Orgs," "Evolution Strikes Blood Banking & Hospitals," "Sickle Cell Anemia, A Legal Conspectus.". **Business Addr:** Attorney, James R Abernathy II and Associates, 1309 Waller St, San Francisco, CA 94117.

ADAMS, QUINTON DOUGLAS.
Salesman. **Personal:** Born Apr 3, 1919, Etowah Co, AL; died Jun 19, 1997; married Ozella Oliver; children: Gwendolyn Delores, Roderick Douglas. **Career:** Adams Cleaners Gadsden AL, owner/oper 1940-66; Gadsden AL, bail bonder beginning 1960; John Thomas Ford Inc, sales rep. **Orgs:** Governing bd Headstart Inc 1974-97; bd mem Quality of Life & Health Ctr 1977-97; com mem State Bd of Educ Competency Testing 1978-97; master Lodge No 790 Masons 1945-97; pres Etowah Co Voters League 1952; chmn Polit Action Com NAACP 1970-97. **Honors/Awds:** Gold Star Serv Awd RSVP Retired Sr Vol Prog 1978; Plaque for Serv Recognition 40 yrs of Civil Religious & Polit Serv 1980; Law Commr State of AL 1980; Serv Awd Goodsell United Meth Ch 1980. **Business Addr:** Sales Rep, John Thomas Ford Inc, 205 Broad St, Gadsden, AL 35901.

ADKINS, RUTHERFORD.
Educational administrator. **Personal:** Born in Alexandria, VA; died Feb 6, 1998, Nashville, TN; married Nanci Pugh Adkins. **Educ:**Virginia State Univ; Howard Univ; Catholic Univ of America. **Career:** Knoxville College, professor of physics, pres; Fisk Univ, dir division of natural sciences and mathematics, interim pres, 1975-76, 1996-97, pres, 1997-98. **Business Addr:** President, Fisk University, 1000 17th Ave N, Nashville, TN 37208.

ALLISON, LUTHER.
Blues musician. **Personal:** Died Aug 12, 1997, Paris, WI; married Fannie Mae; children: Luther T, Bernard. **Career:** Musician, currently. **Honors/Awds:** BluesFoundation, W.C. Handy Blues Award, Blues Entertainer of the Year, 1996, 1997, Best Male Contemporary Blues Artist, Blues Band of the Year, Luther Allison & the James Solberg Band. **Special Achievements:** Released albums for Motown,first blues artist at record label; Alligator Records, albums include: Soul Fixin' Man, 1994; Blue Streak, 1995; Reckless, 1997. **Home Addr:** 007450.

ALSTON, HARRY L.
Association executive. **Personal:** Born Dec 12, 1914, Winston Salem, WV; died Jan 13, 1996; children: Harry Jr, Gloria, Douglas B. **Educ:** West Virginia State College, BS 1938; Atlanta University, MSW 1949. **Career:** Association executive. **Orgs:** Winston-Salem Urban League 1948-51, sec 1951-55, dir

1955-58; Indust Relations, So Field Div, Natl Urban League 1951-55; dir, prog dept, United Packinghouse Food & Allied Workers, AFL-CIO 1958-68; ed rep, Amalgamated Meat Cutters, AFL-CIO 1968-72; retired bd mem, Gary Urban League, Coaliton of Black Trade Unionists, NAACP, Natl Assn of Social Workers, American Academy of Social Workers, Alpha Phi Alpha; amalgamated meat cutters AFL-CIO, UFCW-AFL-CIO, dir civil rights, 1972-81. **Military Serv:** USCG 1942-46.

ANDERSON, HUBERT, JR.
Association executive. **Personal:** Born in Jackson, TN; died Nov 29, 1997. **Educ:** Gallaudet College, BA, history. **Career:** Indiana School for the Deaf, coach; American University, director of mail services, 1969-74; Gallaudet University, head basketball coach,intramural sports director, 1975-80; West Virginia Commission for the Deaf and Hard of Hearing, executive director. **Orgs:** National Association of the Deaf, 1972-97, board of directors, 1992-97, minorities outreach chairman; Washington, DC, municipal government committee, chairman; District of Columbia Association of Deaf Citizens, president, 1985-97; National Disabilities Coalition, Bush-Quayle Campaign, co-chairman, 1992; American Athletic Association, coach, publicity director, 1979-82, vp, 1982-84, president, 1984-86,; South East Athletic Assn of the Deaf, numerous positions including pres. **Honors/Awds:** Inducted into the South East Athletic Assn of the Deaf Hall of Fame, 1984; National Association of the Deaf 28th Biennial Convention, Knights of the Flying Fingers Service Award, 1988, first African-American honoree, Spirit of NAD Award, 1992; Silent World Magazine, Man of the Year, 1978; Gallaudet Univ, Delta Epsilon Sorority, Merit Man of the Year, 1978; World Games for the Deaf, gold medal, basketballcoach; Gallaudet University Community Relations Council, Annual Individual Achievement Award, 1986; Recognized for Outstanding Service to the Deaf Community, 1993; Teays Valley Baptist Church, Deaf Ministry; Outstanding Service as Executive Director, The West Virginia Commission for the Hearing Impaired, 1995. **Special Achievements:** Gallaudet University, first African-American basketball coach, 1975-80; Indiana School for the Deaf, second leading scorer with 1224 points; Indianapolis, city scoring champion, 1957-58; Miss Deaf America Pageant, 31st NAD Biennial Convention, judge at first pageant, 1972. **Business Addr:** Executive Director, West Virginia Commission for the Deaf and Hard of Hearing,4190 Washington St, W, Charleston, WV 25313.

ANDERSON, RUSSELL LLOYD.
Physician. **Personal:** Born Jan 12, 1907,Pittsburgh, PA; died Jun 4, 1991; son of Virginia and Sylvester; married Celeste Etta Johnson; children: Russell L Jr MD, Dorothy M Brickler, Dolores L Farr, Donald Louis. **Educ:** Univ of Pittsburgh, BS 1928, MS 1930, PhD 1933; Howard Univ MD 1946. **Career:** Johnson C Smith Univ, prof of Biology 1930-43;FL A&M Univ, prof of Biology 1946-50; Anderson-Brickler Medical Clinic, physician 1956-91. **Orgs:** Dir of student health serv FL A&M Univ 1950-67; mem Urban League; life & Heritage mem NAACP; bd com, Religion and Race, United Presb Church; mem NMA; mem Amer Medical Assn; mem AAAS. **Honors/Awds:** Elected to Board of Agricultural Stabilization and Conservation Committee of Leon County. **Military Serv:** US Army, 1st lieutenant 1943-47. **Business Addr:** Physician, Anderson-Brickler Med Clinic, 1705 S Adams St, Tallahassee, FL 32301.

ARBURTHA, LEODIES U.
Educational administrator. **Personal:** Born Dec 16, 1923, Warren, AR; died Sep 18, 1997; son of Ever Arburtha and Will Arburtha; married Mildred McGowan; children: Alexis, Louise, LeNardias, Leodies, Zillaway. **Educ:** Tuskegee Inst, BS 1948; Chicago State Univ, MS 1966; PhD program, Univ of Illinois. **Career:** Chicago Vocational HS, tchr graphic arts 1959-70, asst

prin 1968-97. **Orgs:** bd mem, South Shore and Metropolitan Chicago YMCA, 10 years; Intl Typographical Union; Phi Delta Kappa; reg dir IIEA Chicago, 8 years; dist dir, Phi Delta Kappa Intl 1976; natl rep NASSP Com on Asst Principalship 1974-78; chief exec officer Chicago Asst Principals Assn 1971-94; mem NEA, IEA, AVA, IVA, Kappa Alpha Psi; dir & dist 5 rep Phi Delta Kappa Intl; exec editor, Asst Principals Assn; editor and publisher, Chicago/Tuskegee Alumni monthly newsletter; team leader of 4-year project: "Teens Against Teen Pregnancy". **Honors/Awds:** AmerFed Tchrs Civic Awd, S Shore YMCA, 1974; special recognition plaque, Chicago HSAsst Principal's Assn, 1972, 1973; Merit Award, Tuskesee Univ, Natl Alumni Assn. **Home Addr:** 8732 S Calumet Ave, Chicago, IL 60619-6761.

BAILEY, LAWRENCE R., SR.
Attorney. **Personal:** Born Mar 31, 1918, Panama, CZ; died Apr 23, 1998, Queens, NY; son of Alma Small Bailey and Charles Wesley Bailey; married Norma Jean Thomas, May 20, 1961; children: Lawrence R Jr, Bruce, Lamont, Susan. **Educ:** Howard Univ, AB, 1939, JD, 1942. **Career:** Trial Lawyer, assistant counsel to City Council Pres, New York City, 1952-53; Vice Chmn, Metropolitan Transportation Authority, 1970-90. **Orgs:** Dir & Pres, Harlem Lawyer's Assn; Regional Dir, Natl Bar Assn; Chmn, Constitutional Revision Comm; Mem, Amer Bar Assn; New York Lawyer's Assn; Arbitrator, Amer Arbitration Assn; Legal Counsel, Jamaica Comm Corp; Queen'sCo Youth Athletic Center, Merrick Comm Center; Counsel & Mem of Bd, Queen's Urban League; Vice Chmn, Metropolitan Transportation Authority, New York State; Bd of Dir, Legal Aid Soc; NAACP; ACLU; Citizens Union Interview Panel; Greater Jamaica Development Corp, vice chairman; United Beach, Men of Queens. **Honors/Awds:** Queen's Urban League Dedication; Soc of Afro-Amer Transit Employees, Adam Clayton Powell Award; Adam Clayton Powell Memorial Award, 1972; Humanitarian Award, Kennedy King Democratic Club; Alumni Award, Howard Univ; Achievement Award, Old Timers Jamaica Inc, 1968; Achievement Award, Kappa Alpha Psi Fraternity, 1952. **Military Serv:** US Army, Chief Warrant Officer, Judge Advocate Dept, 1943-47; Bronze Star Medal, 93rd Inf Div. **Business Addr:** 199-10 Murdock Ave., Jamaica, NY 11412-2511.

BARTELLE, TALMADGE LOUIS.
Business executive. **Personal:** Born in Darlington, SC; died May 20, 1994; son of Dr & Mrs G F Bartelle; married Harriett Ruth Entzminger; children: Talmadge Jr, Barbara. **Educ:** SC State Coll, BS 1949, LLB1952; Amer Univ, MA 1965. **Career:** FAMU, asst prof of law 1952-54; Ft Ord CA, trial counsel 1955-58; France, asst staff judge adv 1959-62; Foreign Law & Status of Forces Br, chief 1965-67; Univ of MD, instr 1967-68; UN Command Korea, dep staff judge advocate 1967-68; JAGC Chf Tort Br Lit Div Dept of Army, lt col 1968-71; General Mills Inc, sr counsel 1971-90; Information Services Investigations, president, 1990-94. **Orgs:** Mem Supreme Court of SC; Supreme Ct of MN; US Dist Ct MN; Supreme Ct of the US; hearing examiner State of MN Dept of Human Rights 1976; mem Assn of Trial Lawyers of Amer; MN State Bar Assn; Hennepin Co Bar Assn; SC State Bar; Kappa Alpha Psi; bd dir Equal Employment Adv Council 1980; Northside Settlement Serv Inc 1976; allocations com United Way of Minneapolis Area 1975. **Honors/Awds:** US Law Week Awd & Lawyers Coop Prizes forSchlrsp 1952; Legion of Merit 1971; publ "Counterinsurgency & Civil War" 1964; 1st Black to receive direct commn in the Judge Advocate Gen Corps 1954. **Military Serv:** US Army, lt col 1971. **Business Addr:** President,Information Services Investigations, PO Box 27252, Minneapolis, MN 55427.

BATTEAST, MARGARET W.
Public relations director. **Personal:** Born May 26, 1904, Chicago, IL; died Dec 2, 1997; married Tracy W; children: Tracy B. Good PhD, Zelma. **Educ:** Northwestern Univ,BS 1937; DePaul Univ, grad work. **Career:** Shoop Elem Sch, tchr 1926; Public Sch, libr; Meliville W Fuller Sch, asst prin/acting prin; Chicago Bd of Edn, tchr; Sorority of Phi Delta Kappa, natl dir pub relations. **Orgs:** PastMatron Order of Eastern Star; first chmn Scholarship Com awarding first scholarship to needy student; past Basileus Mu Chap Chgo; pres Phidelka Found of Mu Chpt; mem Quinn Chapel AME Ch; delegate Chicago Annual Conf; deleg Gen Conf; sec Brotherhood of Quinn Chapel AME Ch; vice pres Paul Quinn Sr Missionary Soc; prom missionary educ chmn Chicago area Br Missionaries; supvr Young Adult Usher Bd of Quinn Chapel. **Honors/Awds:** Recip Award for Outstanding Serv in Comm from 1942-69 Mellville W Fuller Sch PTA upon retirement.

BAXTER, BELGIUM NATHAN.
Clergyman. **Personal:** Born Nov 3, 1921, Orangeburg, SC; died Aug 12, 1995; married Augusta Ruth Byrd; children: Nathan, Charles, Larry. **Educ:** Home Study Counseling 1970; State and District Church Schools and Seminars 1960-85. **Career:** United Council of Churches, exec bd 1970; Faith Chapel Outreach Center, exec dir 1971-73; Hbg Adult Educ, bd member 1972-75; Hbg Bethesda Mission, bd member 1974-80; Neighborhood Center of UMC, staff member-counsellor 1973-83; Faith Chapel Church of God in Christ, pastor. **Orgs:** Pastor Faith Chapel Church of God in Christ 1953-85;state sect'y PA Churches of God in Christ 1965-85; Hbg dist supt Churches of God in Christ 1968-85. **Honors/Awds:** Special achievement Office of Sec of Commonwealth 1971; special achievement Hbg Black Businessmen's Assn 1972; MartinLuther King Awd radio station WFEC 1980; Veteran's Acclaim Poet Laureate Gov Dick Thornburg 1980; special appreciation Pres Jimmy Carter 1980; special achievement PA House of Reps 1982; Publication of Pioneer Pastoral experience by Martin Luther King Fellows Press 1985. **Military Serv:** AUS cpl-company clerk 2 yrs; Good Conduct Medal Meritorious Svs Awd 1945. **Home Addr:** 2213 Clayton Ave, Harrisburg, PA 17109. **Business Addr:** Pastor, Faith Chapel Church, 1212 Edgemont Road, Harrisburg, PA 17109.

BEASLEY, ANNE VICKERS.
Public accountant. **Personal:** Born Sep 7, 1917, Orlando, FL; died Dec 8, 1997; married William Beasley. **Educ:** Manhattan Comm Coll, Associate Acctg 1965. **Career:** Union Theol Sem NYC, bookkeeping training teacher; notary public 30 yrs; real estate salesman 10 yrs; City of NY Housing Devel Admin, auditor 1973-74; St Nicholas Park Mgmt Corp, auditor, consult 1973; Bathgate Comm Housing Devel Corp, comptroller; Active VIP Bookkeeping Inc, owner-mgr. **Orgs:** Chmn Leadership Devel, Bd of Christian Ed, Convent Ave Bapt Church; staff instr Bapt Ed Ctr, Brooklyn & Long Island; mem NAACP, Natl Council Negro Women, Urban League, Carver Dem Club, YWCA, Church Women United, Womens Aux of the Army & Navy Union, Eastern Star, IBPOE of W, Leagueof Women Voters. **Honors/Awds:** Spec Leaderhip Awds in Church Order of Eastern Stars; IBPOE of W.

BELL, DENNIS PHILIP.
Journalist. **Personal:** Born Aug 29, 1948, Muskegon, MI; died Mar 14, 1995; son of Natalie VanArsdale Bell and Ezra Douglas Bell; married Jacqueline Nanette Bell, Sep 9, 1984; children: Tracey, Wesley, Cerise, Christopher. **Educ:** Univ of Michigan, 1 year; Hofstra Univ; summer training program, Berkeley, CA. **Career:** Newsday, Melville, NY, assistant L I editor, 1972-95, covered Nassau County and the courts. **Orgs:** Member, National Association of Black Journalists, 1980-95; member, National Alliance of Third World Journalists, 1989-95. **Honors/Awds:** Pulitzer Prize for International Reporting, 1984. **Military Serv:** Army, Sgt, E5, 1968-70. **Business Addr:** Journalist, Newsday, 235 Pinelawn Rd, Melville, NY 11747.

BELL, JAMES MILTON.
Psychiatrist. **Personal:** BornNov 5, 1921, Portsmouth, VA; died Mar 9, 1997; son of Lucy Henrietta Barnes andCharles Edward Bell Sr. **Educ:** NC Coll Durham NC, BS 1943; Meharry Med Coll Nashville TN, MD 1947; Karl Menninger School of Psychiatry Menninger Found Topeka KS, training gen psych 1953-56, child psych training 1957-58. **Career:** Harlem Hospital, intern rotating 1947-48; Winter Hosp Topeka, resident psych 1953-56; Community Mental Health Activity; Keller Army Hosp West Point, col ret consult extended duty; Parsons Child & Family Ctr Albany NY, psychiatrist-child & adolescent; Albany Med Coll of Union Univ, clinical prof psych; Berkshire Farm Ctr & Serv for Youth, clinical dir, psychiatrist, sr child and adolescent psychiatrist 1986-97. **Orgs:** Lite fellow Amer Orthopsychiatric Assoc; AmerColl of Psychiatry, former member, Committee on The Stanley Dean Award; chartermem Acad of Religion & Mental Health; Group for the Advancement of Psych; Council for the sections on Psych of Pan-Amer Med Assoc Inc; past president, NY Capital Dist Council on Child Psych; lite fellow Amer Soc for Adolescent Psych; Council for Exceptional Children; Amer Academy of Political & Soc Sci; Menninger Foundation; NY State Capitol Dist Br of the Amer Psych Association; National Med Association; Amer Med Association; Med Association National Association of Training-Schools & Juvenile Agencies; Association for Psych Treatment of Offenders; Association of the NY State Ed of the Emotionally Disturbed; NY State Soc for Med Rsch Inc; Rotary Club; life mem Reserve Officer Association of US; Amer Med Soc ofAlcoholism 1982-97; Association of Child Care Workers Inc; Alpha Omega Alpha; life fellow, Amer Psychiatric Association; former chairman, Committee on NationalAffairs; life fellow, Amer Academy of Child Psychiatry, former chairman, Committee on psychiatric Facilities for Children and Adolescents; fellow, Amer Coll ofPsychiatry; lite fellow, Amer Soc for Adolescent Psychiatry; life mem, AmericanLegion; life mem, Medical Society of the State of New York. **Honors/Awds:** Meharry National Alumni Association, Award for Outstanding Achievement in theArea of Medicine, 1980. **Military Serv:** US Army, col 1943-76; Army Commendation Medal, Meritorious Service Medal; Good Conduct Medal; World War II Victory Medal; Army of Occupation Medal; National Defense Service Medal. **Home Addr:** Hudsonview, Old Post Road North, Croton On Hudson, NY 10520. **Business Addr:** Senior Child/Adolescent Psych, Berkshire Farm Ctr/Serv Youth, Canaan, NY 12029.

BELL, WILLIAM AUGUSTUS, II.
Attorney. **Personal:** Born Aug 8, 1917, Augusta, GA; died Jul 1, 1996;son of Helen Caffey Bell and William A Bell; married Kathleen Coote, Jul 17, 1943; children: Jennifer K Bell McNeill, Millicent L Cleveland. **Educ:** Morehouse College, Atlanta, GA, AB, 1938; University of Michigan Law School, Ann Arbor, MI, JD, 1943. **Career:** Self-employed attorney, Detroit, MI, 1946-96. **Orgs:** Board member 1953-69, pres 1967-69, Detroit Urban League; chairman 1967-68, member, Michigan Family Committee. **Military Serv:** US Army,S/Sgt, 1942-45; 4 Battle Stars, Good Conduct Medal. **Business Addr:** Attorney, 1147 First National Bldg, Detroit, MI 48207.

BERNARD, JASON.
Actor. **Personal:** Died Oct 18, 1996, Burbank, CA. **Career:** Actor. **Honors/Awds:** Cable Ace Awards, nominated, Best Supporting Actor In A Movie or Miniseries, 1996. **Special Achievements:** Appeared in film and television including: "Wilma," 1977; "Cagney and Lacey," 1982-83; "High Performance," 1983; "The Meeting," PBS, 1989; "Herman's Head"; While You Were Sleeping, 1995; "Sophie and the Moonhanger," 1996.

BEXLEY, DONALD T.
Actor. **Personal:** Died Apr 15, 1997, Hampton, VA. **Career:** Actor; appeared in Sanford and Son as Bubba; made many guest appearances in TV and film.

BOATWRIGHT, CHRISTOPHER.
Dancer. **Personal:** Died 1997, San Francisco, CA; son of Mabel. **Educ:** Trained with Merce cunningham; American Ballet Theater; Alvin Ailey American Dance Center. **Career:** Stuttgart Ballet; Arizona Dance Theater; Lines Contemporary Ballet; San Francisco Ballet; teacher.

BOYD, BARBARA P.
Cleric. **Personal:** Died 1997, Jackson, MS. **Educ:** Campbell Coll, divinity degree. **Career:** AllenTemple AME Church, itinerant elder, begin 1961. **Special Achievements:** First woman ordained a minister in the AME denomination.

BRANSON, HERMAN RUSSELL.
Educator (retired), physicist, chemist. **Personal:** Born Aug 14, 1914, Pocahontas, VA; died Jun 7, 1995; son of Gertrude B and Harry C; married Corolynne Gray Branson; children: Corolynne Gertrude, Herman Edward. **Educ:** Univ of Pittsburgh, attended 1932-34; VA State Coll, BS (summa cum laude) 1936; Univ of Cincinnati, PhD physics 1939. **Career:** Dillard Univ, instructor in math & physics 1939-41; Howard Univ, prof & chm dept of physics 1941-68; Central State Univ, pres 1968-70; Lincoln Univ, pres 1970-85. **Orgs:** Mem Epsilon Boule Sigma Pi Phi Frat; mem Alpha Phi Alpha Frat Inc; fellow American Assn for the Advancement of Sci; mem Amer Assn of State Colls & Univs 1969-95; mem Amer Found for Negro Affairs 1973-95; mem Assn for the Study of Afro-Amer Life & History; mem Carver Rsch Found 1960-95; mem Egypt Exploration Soc 1971-95; mem MIT (corporation) 1979-95; mem Middle Atlantic Consortium for Energy Rsch 1980-95; mem Natl Acad of Scis; life mem NAACP; mem Natl Assn for Equal Oppor in Higher Educ 1969-95; mem Natl Assn of Independent Coll & Univ; mem Natl Inst of Independent Colls & Univs; mem Natl Medical Fellowships Inc 1971-95; life mem Natl Sci Tchrs Assn; mem NJ Marine Scis Consortium; mem Oxford Area C of C 1982-95; mem Philadelphia Bd of Public Educ; mem Rotary Club; mem Sea Grant Review Panel US Dept ofCerce 1980-95; mem Sigma Xi Soc; Hon mem Smithsonian Inst; mem US Dept of Energy; mem Univ City Sci Ctr 1972-95; mem Woodrow Wilson Natl Fellowship Found 1975-95. **Honors/Awds:** Sigma Pi Phi Scholarship Pgh 1933; Special Fellow in Physics 1936-37; Laws Fellow in Physics 1937-39 Univ of Cincinnati; ScD VA State 1967; ScD Univ of Cincinnati 1967; ScD Lincoln Univ 1969; LHD Brandeis Univ 1972; LLD Western MI Univ 1973; LHD ShawColl at Detroit 1978; Litt Drexel Univ 1982; ScD Northeastern Univ 1985; Sigma Pi Sigma; Pi Mu Epsilon; Rosenwald Fellow Univ Chicago 1940; Sr Fellow Natl RschCncl CA Inst of Tech 1948-49; Faculty Fellow Natl Sci Found Univ of Hamburg Germany & French Atomic Energy Comm (Saclay) 1962-63. **Home Addr:** 10906 Oakwood St, Silver Spring, MD 20901. **Business Addr:** Dir, Precollege Science and Math Research Program, Howard University, Washington, DC 20059.

BRISCOE, SIDNEY EDWARD, JR.
Business executive. **Personal:** Born Oct 5, 1929, Jennings, LA; died Jul 26, 1997; married Lana Pullman; children: Sidney III, Linda, Cora, Sheryl, Zannette, Darryl, Andrea, Maria, Bryan. **Educ:** Southern Univ, BS 1951. **Career:** Insurance Agency, owner; Consumer Finance Co, mgr 1969-72; Jefferson Davis Public School Bd, teacher 1954-72, principal 1953-54; Evangeline Parish School Bd, dir 1952-53.**Orgs:** Mem LA Oil & Gas Msm; mem Jefferson Davis Parish Police Jury; pres NAACP Jefferson Davis Chapter 1976-97; pres Local Comm Action Agency 1972-97;vice pres Holy Name Soc 1974-97; president, Jefferson Parish Government, 1994, 1995, 1st elected black to this body as president. **Honors/Awds:** Bishop honoree Cath Lafayette Diocese 1964; awrd ded serv to the Jeff Davis Parish 1975; cert Jeff Davis Com Action 1975. **Business Addr:** PO Box 497, Jennings,LA 70546.

BROOME, PERSHING.
Educator. **Personal:** Born Sep 15, 1921, Utica, MS; died Jan 11, 1995; son of PearlGibbs Broome and Cleveland Broome; married Annette E Chandler, Mar 2, 1968; children: Richard P, Robert P, Kimberly D, Michael E. **Educ:** TN A&I State Univ, BS Sci Ed 1957; Roosevelt Univ, MA Ed Admin & Suprv 1972, MA Guid & Couns 1977. **Career:** Bur HS, chmn sci dept, instr chem & physics 1957-59; Chicago Bd of Ed, instr chem & physics 1959-64; Thornridge HS, instr physics 1964-70,dean 1970-84, counselor 1984-95. **Orgs:** Treas Vlg of Phoenix 1967-75,80-95; mem bd of ed & sec, pres School Dist 151 1970-95; bd ed rep IL Assoc of School Bds 1975-95; chmn So Cook Cty Div IL Assoc of School Bds 1984-95; mem Faculty Assn Dist 205, IL Educ Assn, Natl Ed Assn, 1964-95; elect del NEA Conv 1976-77, IEA Conv 1978; mem Res Off Assn of US, Amer Assn of Physics Teachers, IL DeansAssn, ATO, APTO; dir, Illinois Assn of School Boards, 1990-95. **Military Serv:** AUS 1942-52; USAR 1952-73; retired AUS 1981; Good Conduct; WWII Victory Medals. **Home Addr:** 625 E 152nd St, Phoenix, IL 60426. **Business Addr:** Counselor, Thornridge High School, 15000 Cottage Grove, Dolton, IL 60419.

BROWN, ROGER.
Professional basketball player (retired). **Personal:** Died 1997; children: seven. **Educ:** Univ of Dayton, attended. **Career:** American Basketball Assn, Indiana Pacers, begin 1967. **Special Achievements:** Became ABA's first 10,000-point scorer; ABA Championship, Indiana Pacers, 1970-73.

BROWN, WILLIAM F.
Dentist. **Personal:** Born Jan 10, 1900, Lauderdale, MI; died Dec 2, 1989; married Mary Douge Freeland (deceased). **Educ:** Howard U, BS Lib Arts 1924, DDSColl of Dentistry 1929. **Career:** Priv Prac, dentist 1932-80 (retired). **Orgs:** Life mem Third Dist Dental Soc; State of NY Dental Soc; Am Dental Assn Mem, Alpha Phi Plpha Frat, Inc; Adv Com of Albany NY on Urban Rnwl; temporary & state commn on Cap City; 1st pres Albany NY branch NAACP 1932-34. **Honors/Awds:** Selec Serv Bd Recip, Omicron Kappa Upsilon Nat Dental Hon Soc, 1952; cit Albany Inter-Racial Council 1973; cit Plaque Cit of Yr, Omega Psi Phi Frat 1975; Albany NAACP recognition awd 1985.

BURGESS, JAMES R., JR.
Attorney. **Personal:** Born 1915, Putnam Co, TN; died Jun 22, 1997; married Doris Antoinette Murray. **Educ:** Univ of MD, BA 1961; Univ of IL, LLB 1965; Completed German Language Course in Oberammergau, Germany; Russian Language Course at ArmyLanguage Sch Presidio of Monterey, CA. **Career:** Army Officer 20 years; Champaign Co, state atty 1972-76, first asst state atty, supr atty; 1st black States Attorney in IL; 1st black US attorney Eastern/Southern Dist of IL 1977-82; private general law practice; Lawndale Legal Aid Office, inspector gen US Dept of Agriculture. **Orgs:** Pitched for semi-pro baseball Team; mem Pi Sigma Alpha Natl Honorary Soc; Phi Alpha Delta Law Frat; Urbana Rotary Club; First United Methodist Ch; various positions Boys' Club; bd mem Champaign Co Coun on Alcoholism; bd mem Champaign Co Children & Family Services; implemented Adult Diversion Prog as alternative to prosecution; introduced law-related education into Champaign Cty Public Schs; United Way, Champaign Cty, bd mem; visually impaired volunteer reader; mem, IL, Chicago & Federal Bar Assoc. **Honors/Awds:** Selected Artillery OCS Trng; dean's list for Scholastic achievement Univ of MD; citedby Los Angeles Area Coun & Far East Coun BSA; cited for outstanding service PhiAlpha Delta Law Frat. **Military Serv:** Army Officer 20 years, retired. **Business Addr:** Attorney, 811 West Springfield, Suite 3, Champaign, IL 61820.

BUTLER, BENJAMIN WILLARD.
Surgeon.**Personal:** Born Feb 27, 1933, Detroit, MI; died Apr 6, 1997; son of Millie L Butler and Marvin L Butler; married Ernestine Laverne Carter; children: Kenneth, Kevin, Karla. **Educ:** Univ MI, 1950-54; Meharry Med Coll, 1955-59.**Career:** Surgeon; VA Hosp, res; Childrens Hosp, 1964; Detroit Rec Hosp,intern 1959-60. **Orgs:** Cert Amer bd of Surgery; Amer Soc of Abdominal Surgery; fellow Am Coll of Surg; OH St Med Assn; past-pres Toledo Surgical Soc; Toledo Acad of Med; clinical assistant professor Med Coll of OH; Natl Med Assn, Society of Amer Gastrointestinal Endoscopic Surgeons. **Honors/Awds:** Localpres Sigma Pi Phi; past-pres Frontiers Interntl; Kappa Alpha Psi; elder Grace United Presby Ch; mem NAACP; published: ''Bilateral Congential Lumbar Hernia'' 1966-67; ''Successful Immediate Repair of a Traumatic Aorta-Inferior VenaCava Fistula'' 1974; ''Acute Gallstone Pancreatitis with Pseudocyst as a Complication,'' Journal of The National Medical Association, September 1981. **Military Serv:** US Navy, Lt Commander, 1960-62. **Business Addr:** Surgeon, 2052 Collingwood Blvd, Toledo, OH 43620.

BUTLER, HOMER L.
Educator, pharmacist (retired). **Personal:** Born Dec 23, 1932, Trenton, NJ; died Apr 1, 1997; son of Freda Sapp Belk Butler and Homer L Butler; married Andrea Reule; children: Paul, Jeremy. **Educ:** Temple Univ, BS 1958; Univ of IL at Springfield, MPA, 1994. **Career:** NJ State Hosp, psychiat tech 1951-52; sub postal clerk 1954-56; FMC Corps, lab tech1958-61; Sangamon State Univ, asst dean 1970-71, assoc dean student svcs 1971-73, dean students 1973-79, dean of student serv 1979-92, vice pres for student svcs, 1992-94; Univ of IL at Springfield, vice chancellor of student affairs, 1994-96. **Orgs:** Vol Peace Corps 1962-64; assoc dir Peace Corps Dakar 1964-66; dir Peace Corps Chad 1967-68; dep dir Peace Corps Ft Lamy Africa 1966-67; dir Div Specialized Recruiting Office of Vol Placement Peace Corps 1969-70; vice pres Sangamon Co United Way 1978-80; bd of dirs Girl Scouts 1980-86; Omega Psi Phi Frat; bd of dirs Red Cross 1987-96; bd of dirs Alzheimer's Assn 1990-96; CILCO, advisory board president, 1990-94; Junior League, advisory board, 1991-93; Red Cross State Service, council, 1995-97. **Honors/Awds:** Outstanding Alumni Awd Temple Univ 1967. **Military Serv:** USY sp-5 1956-58.

CARL, EARL LAWRENCE.
Educator. **Personal:** Born Mar 23, 1919, New Haven, CT; died Mar 30, 1996; married Iris Harris; children: Francine, Nina. **Educ:** Fisk U, AB 1942, JD 1948; Yale Law Sch, LLM 1960. **Career:** Thurgood Marshall School of Law, TX Southern Univ, dean, prof, dean of law 1958-59, prof of law 1960, assoc prof of law 1948. **Orgs:** Mem Nat Bar Assn Am Bar & Assn; vice pres in charge of legal affairs Phi Alpha Delta Parkwood Dr Civic Club; exec bd mem Houston Lighthouse for the Blind. **Honors/Awds:** Alpha Phi Alpha Named Dstng Prof Bd of Trustees TX So Univ 1974; named in Negroes & the Law Journal of Leg Educ 1965; publ articles, Negroes & the Law, Jrnl Leg Educ Vol 17 No 3 1965, The Shortage of Negro Lawyers, Jrn of Legal Educ Vol 20 No 1 1967; working on case book ''Cases and Materials on Minorities and the law''. **Business Addr:** TX So Law Sch, 3401 Wheeler, Houston, TX 77004.

CARPENTER, THELMA.
Singer. **Personal:** Born in Brooklyn, NY; died May 15, 1997, New York City, NY. **Career:** Singer; actress. **Special Achievements:** Sang with jazz greats Coleman Hawkins, Teddy Wilson, Count Basie; appeared in films, Hellzapoppin', 1941, The Wiz, 1978, The Cotton Club, 1984; appeared on Broadway in: Memphis Bound, 1944, Ankles Away, Bubblin' Brown Sugar, Hello Dolly!, standby for Pearl Bailey, 1968-69. **Home Addr:** 007450.

CASEY, EDMUND C.
Physician. **Personal:** Born in Marion, IN; died Mar 12, 1997; married Liliane Winkfield; children: Yvette, Yvonne, Amie. **Educ:** Attended Earlham Coll 1942-43, Univ of PA 1943; Meharry Med Coll, MD1948; City Hosp of Cleveland, internship 1948-49, residency pulmonary diseases 1949-50, internal medicine 1950-52; Post Grad Courses, Cook Co Hosp Grad Sch of Medicine 1958 1960 1961 1965, Amer Coll of Physicians 1965 1966. **Career:** Bethesda Hosp, admin tchng staff; Christ Hosp, assoc staff; Univ of Cincinnati, asst clinical prof of medicine; Private Practice, physician internal medicine 1954-97. **Orgs:** Mem Natl, Amer Medical Assns; mem former pres CincinnatiMed Assn; mem Acad of Medicine in Cincinnati; pres OH Thoracic Soc 1970-71; mem(various pos held) Natl Med Assn; co-dir of med 1969-71 co-dir of sect on internal med 1970-72 dir of coronary & intensive care units Bethesda Hosp; mem Dean'sComm on Admissions of Minority Students Univ of Cincinnati 1968-72; life mem Amer Radio Relay League, NAACP, Alpha Phi Alpha Frat; rep dir at large Amer Lung Assn 1972-97; mem of cncl on health manpower AMA 1971-74; mem (various positions held) Acad of Medicine; mem chmn Natl Adv Comm Sickle Cell Anemia Program of theNatl Inst of Health Dept of Health Educ & Welfare; pres SW OH Lung Assn 1977; mem bd trustees Central State Univ; mem bd trustees Mt Zion United Methodist Ch; chmnof comm on prog & get 1976-77 pres 1981-82 Amer Lung Assn; vice pres 1981, mem OH Lung Assn 1982-84; pres 1983, chmn 1982-84 Natl Commn on Certification of Physician's Assistants; chairman, Tuberculosis Committee for Tuberculosis Control, International Union Against Tuberculosis and Lung Disease. **Honors/Awds:** Hon DL Central State Univ 1983. **Business Addr:** 437 Melish, Cincinnati, OH 45229.

CHEATHAM, DOC. (ADOLPHUS ANTHONY)
Musician. **Personal:** Born 1905, Nashville, TN; died Jun 2, 1997. **Career:** Musician. **Honors/Awds:** Grammy, Award for Jazz Instrumental Solo, (posthumously) 1998. **Special Achievements:** Performed in New Orleans brass bands, bebop bands, Afro-Caribbean bands; performed with Cab Calloway, Billie Holiday, Benny Goodman; began singing, circa 1970s; began Sunday Brunch series at Sweet Basil, 1980-97. **Home Addr:** 007450.

CLARK, PATRICK.
Chef. **Personal:** Born 1956;died Feb 11, 1998, Princeton, NJ; son of Melvin (chef); married Lynette; children: Aleia, Ashley, Brooke, Preston, Cameron. **Career:** Odeon, chef, 1980;Cafe Luxembourg, chef; Metro's, owner, chef, 1988-90; Bice, chef, 1990; Hay-Adam Hotel, chef; Tavern on the Green, chef, 1995-98. **Business Addr:** Executive Chef, Tavern On The Green, Central Park West & 67th St, New York, NY 10023.

CLEAVER, ELDRIDGE.
Lecturer, author. **Personal:** Born Jun 5, 1935, Wabbeseka, AR; died May 1, 1998, Los Angeles, CA; married Kathleen Neal; children: Maceo, Toju. **Career:** Ramparts Magazine, editor and contributor; University of La Verne, diversity consultant, until 1998. **Orgs:** Co-founder/member, Black Panthers Party. **Honors/Awds:** Author, Soul on Ice 1968; Post Prison Writings and Speeches 1969; Eldridge Cleaver's Black Papers 1969; Soul on Fire 1978. **Home Addr:** 000900002600.

COLEMAN, WINSON.
Educator. **Personal:** Born Sep 10, 1905, Oskaloosa, LA; died Nov 25, 1984; married Theodora Dugas; children: Grace Mauvene (Edwards), Winson, Edwina Elaine (Clark). **Educ:** Penn Coll, BA 1928; Haverford Coll, MA 1929; Univ of Chicago, PhD 1950. **Career:** Johnson C Smith Univ, Charlotte NC, faculty mem 1929-84, philosophy prof, 1950-74, acad dean, 1962-69; Univ of CO, visiting lecturer 1960; Quarterly Review Higher Educ Among Negroes, editor 1963-84; Gen Educ Bd. **Orgs:** Mem Am Conf Acad Deans; Am Philos Assn; Mind Assn; Nat Educ Assn Presbyn.**Honors/Awds:** Fellow philosoph Univ Of Chicago 1947-49; Univ Fellow Philosophy 1949-50; Author of Article.

CROCKETT, GEORGE WILLIAM, JR.
Congressman (retired). **Personal:** Born Aug 10, 1909, Jacksonville, FL; died Sep 7, 1997, Washington, DC; son of Minnie A Jenkins Crockett and George William Crockett; married Ethelene Jones (deceased); children: Elizabeth Ann Hicks, George W III, Ethelene; married Harriette Clark, Aug 1980. **Educ:** Morehouse College, AB, 1931; Univ of Michigan School of Law, JD, 1934. **Career:** US Dept of Labor, attorney, 1939; Fair Labor Standards Act Administration, senior attorney; Fair Employment Practices Comm, hearing examiners, 1943; Intl United Auto Workers Fair Employment Practices Dept, founder and director, 1944; United Auto Workers, admin asst to intl sec/treas, gen counsel, 1946; Detroit Recorders Court, judge 1946-66, 1972-78, presiding judge,1974-78; Goodman Crockett Eden & Robb, senior partner; Michigan Court of Appeals, visiting judge; City of Detroit, acting corp counsel, 1980; US House of Representatives, member, 1980-91. **Orgs:** Phi Beta Kappa; mem Florida Bar Assn, West Virginia Bar Assn, US Supreme Court Bar, Michigan Bar Assn, Natl Lawyers Guild; founder and 1st chmn, Judicial Council of Natl Bar Assn; mem, NAACP, Kappa Alpha Psi, Natl Conf of Black Lawyers Friends & Founders Comm, Hartford Baptist Church. **Honors/Awds:** First Black lawyer in the US Dept of Labor; Honorary LLD Morehouse Coll 1972, Shaw Coll 1973; apptd by President Reagan as Public Delegate to United Nations 1987.

CUNNINGHAM, ARTHUR H.
Composer. **Personal:** Born Nov 11, 1928, Piermont, NY;died Mar 31, 1997, Nyack, NY; married Kate Davidson. **Educ:** Columbia Tch Coll, MA 1955-57; Fisk U, AB 1947-51; Juilliard Sch Music; Met Music Sch; studied with Riegger, Mennin, Work, Mehegan, & Teddy Wilson. **Career:** Composed; conducted; lectured; publ; perfromed; Cunningham Music Corp, owner. **Orgs:** Mem ACA; mem ASCAP; Am Music Center; recorded Desto Records; publ Theodore Presser Co; Actors Equity. **Honors/Awds:** ASCAP Awards for Composition 1972; Nat Endowment for The Arts Grant 1974; Distinguished Alumni Award, Teachers College, 1992; Goodwill Ambassador on behalf of America, Spanish Expo, Seville, Spain, 1992. **Special Achievements:** Performances by: New York Philharmonic, San Francisco Symphony, London Philharmonic, Seattle, Buffalo, and many European countries. **Military Serv:** AUS spl serv 1953-55. **Business Addr:** Box 614, Nyack, NY 10960.

CURRENT, GLOSTERBRYANT.
Clergyman (retired). **Personal:** Born Apr 26, 1913, Indianapolis, IN; died Jul 8, 1997, Queens, NY; son of Earsy P Current and John TCurrent; married Rebecca Busch; children: Angella, Gloster Jr, John. **Educ:** WV State, AB 1941; Wayne State Detroit, MI, MPA 1950; Rust Coll, Hon HHD 1977; Bethune Cookman Coll FL, Hon LLD 1977; attended Detroit Inst of Musical Art.**Career:** Detroit NAACP, exec sec 1941-46; New York NAACP, dir of branches 1946-77, administrator 1976-77; NAACP, dep to ex dir 1977-78; Westchester United Methodist Ch, pastor 1979-83; Brooklyn, NY NAACP, deputy exec dir 1983-84; retired administrator/retired minister; St. Paul United Methodist Church, organist, until 1995. **Orgs:** Life mem Kappa Alpha Psi Frat begin 1939; life memNAACP since 1957; Band Leader Gloster Current's Orchestra 1930-39; asst pastor St Paul United Methodist Ch 1953-78; bd mem NY State Minority Comm Aging begin 1984; bd mem Ft Schuyler House NY since 1984; bd mem Natl Caucus & Center on Black Aged begin 1983; bd mem & vice pres United Methodist City Soc NY 1975-97; pres, United Methodist City Society 1989-97; bd mem, General Bd of Discipleship, United Methodist Church 1984, 1988-97. **Honors/Awds:** Delegate Gen and Jurisdictional Conferences United Meth Ch 1972, 1976, 1984; Living Legacy Award from Natl Caucus Black Aged 1979; Natl Parliamentarian-NANM Natl Assn Negro Musicians1977-94. **Home Addr:** 100-30-203rd St, Hollis, NY 11423.

CURRIE, EDDIE L.
Business executive, clergyman. **Personal:** Born Sep 5, 1927, Brownsville, TN; died May 11, 1994; married Mildred. **Educ:** Lane Coll, BA 1954; San Francisco State; So Bapt Theol Sem, 1959; Memphis State U, BD 1974. **Career:** 1st Bapt Ch Brownsville; pastor 1957-67; Christ Missionary Bapt Ch; Soul Rands Inc, vice pres 1970-72; Lowensteins Dept Store, buyer, mgr 1972-73; Ed Currie & Assos. **Orgs:** Mem Memphis Bd Educ 1959-64; Memphis & Shelby County Neighborhood Youth Corps 1965-67; Nat Urban League 1967-69; Frontiers Intl Inc; Alpha Phi Alpha Frat; Nat Bus League; pres NAACP pres Haywood County Br 1960-65; Blk Econ Adv Com To Sml Bus Admst; Shelby County Dem Club; United Dem Com;W TN BM & E Assn; Memphis Educ Assn; TN Educ Assn; Nat Educ Assn mem Haywood County Civic & Welfare League 1959-67; Operation Freedom 1960-74. **Honors/Awds:** Acad Dean's Award 1954; Statue Liberty Annual Award, Women For Legisslative Action 1962; Humanitarian Award, Ministers Philadelphia & Vicinity 1964. **Military Serv:** AUS 1954-56. **Business Addr:** 347 N Main, Memphis, TN 38103.

CURRY, NORVELLE.
Physician. **Personal:** Born Apr 5, 1930, Memphis, TN; died Sep 24, 1996; son of Callie French Curry and Booker T Curry (deceased);married Eleanor Alice Barnes; children: Debra L Bowen, Norvelle M, Michael S, Michele R. **Educ:** LeMoyne Coll Memphis, BS 1951; NY Univ, MA 1954; Meharry Med Coll Nashville, MD 1955-59. **Career:** McKeesport Hosp PA, intern 1959-60; USN, gen med officer 1961-62; NAS N Island & Imperial Beach CA, naval flight surgeon 1962-66; NRMC San Diego, urology res 1966-70; NRMC Camp Pendelton CA, chief/dept of urology 1970-71; NRMC San Diego, asst chmn/dept of urology 1972-77; Naval Regional Med Ctr Camp Pendelton CA, chief dept of urology 1977-88. **Orgs:** Mem Soc of Govt Serv Urologists 1973; mem Assn Military Surgeons of US 1973; mem Amer Urology Assn 1973; diplomate Amer Bd of Urology 1973; fellow Amer Coll of Surgeons 1974. **Military Serv:** USN capt 1961-88; Natl Defense Medal. **Home Addr:** 3754 View Verde Ct, Bonita, CA 91902.

DANIEL, WALTER C.
Educator. **Personal:** BornMay 12, 1922, Macon, GA; died Mar 6, 1995; married LaUna Harris. **Educ:**Johson C Smith Univ, BA 1941, MA 1959; Bowling Green State Univ, PhD 1962; Lincoln Univ of MO, LHD (Hon) 1972; Harvard Univ Grad School of Bus, Post Doct. **Career:** LA City Schools, teacher; NC Central Univ, asst prof English; St Augustines Coll, prof & head of English; Div of Humanities, NC A&T State Univ, prof, head of English, chmn div of humanities; NC A&T, dir 13 coll curr devel proj;Lincoln Univ of MO, pres; Univ of MO Columbia, prof of English. **Orgs:** Mem Comm on Inst N Central Assoc of Coll & School; past pres MO Conf of Coll Pres; mem bd trustees MO School of Religion; mem Coll Lang Assoc, Rotary Intl; mem bd trustees Columbia Publ Library; vice pres admin Gr Rivers Council Boy Scouts of Amer; sec Capital Funds Comm Presbyterian Church US; comm Columbia MO HousingAuth; dir Natl Archetecture Accrediting Assoc; mem natl adv Council for Career Ed, Phi Delta Kappa, Phi Kappa Phi, Kappa Delta PiHon Scholastic Soc. **Honors/Awds:** Wisdom Awd of Honor Wisdom Soc 1970; Order of the Star of Africa Republic of Liberia 1972. **Business Addr:** Professor of English, Univ of Missouri, 210 A Arts & Science Building, Columbia, MO 65211.

DANIELS, JERRY FRANKLIN.
State excise police officer (retired). **Personal:** Born Dec 14, 1915, Indianapolis, IN; died Nov 7, 1995; sonof Anna Gleason Franklin Daniels (deceased) and Jerry R Daniels (deceased); married Jean M Watson, May 11, 1956; children: Charlotte Denise Huggins, Damon Anthony Daniels. **Educ:** Indiana Univ,

1950-52. **Career:** County Clerk, Indianapolis IN, deupty, 1946-48; Mac Arthur Conservatory of Music, Indianapolis IN, instructor, 1948-50; Sec of State, Indianapolis IN, deputy, 1950-54; State of Indiana, Indianapolis IN, excise police, 1958-86. **Honors/Awds:** Oneof the founding members of the Ink-Spots, 1930-36; author of a column for Indiana Harold, State Wide Newspaper on ''Making Mine Music''; Sagamore of Wabash, Governor Robert Orr, 1988. **Military Serv:** US Army, 43rd Seigneur Battalion, T/4, 1943-46, Line Chief, 5 Battle of Stars. **Home Addr:** 3632 NGuilford Ave, Indianapolis, IN 46205.

DARKINS, DUANE ADRIAN.

Clergyman. **Personal:** Born Oct 31, 1934; died 1993; married Betty Abbot; children: Duane Jr, Samuel. **Educ:** Trinity Coll, DD; Coll & Sem Pillar of Fire, DSS; PhD; Moody's Inst, MDiv; Univ of Pittsburgh; Fuller Normal Indsl Coll; Pittsburgh Theol Sem; Univ of Pittsburgh, LLD. **Career:** Faith Tabncl Ch of God in Christ, pastor; Eastern Jurisdiction of PA, consecrated asst bishop; Walk in Day Camp, fdr dir; Proj Serv Unlimited, exec-dir; Charles Harrison Mason Bible Coll, state vp; Commonwealth of PA, refree; Lichenstein & Bartiromo Law Firm, legal cons/adjunct; Controller Ofc City of Pittsburgh, chief auditor; Controller Ofc City of Pittsburgh, auditor; City of Pittsburgh, chief clerk; Nghbrhd Youth Corps, asst to coord. **Orgs:** Couns Outreach Approach Young Mens Christian Assn; chmn bd of dir; v chmn; treas; v sec; YMCA; chpln E End Jr Little League; chpln Silver Lake Comm Assn; chmn Citzns Of Polit Progress; preside City & Co Inauguration Afrs & Evenst; pres Psoriasis Found; chmn Mayor's Commn on Human Relat; past bd of dir mem NAACP; mem Homewood Brushton Renewal Council; trustee John J Kane Hosp; regstr Nat Ch of God in Christ; state vice pres Charles HarrisonBible Coll; regnl area dir Charles Harrison Mason Bible Coll; mem So Ldrshp Conf; pres Homewood Burshton Ministerian; bd of dir Race & Religion Council; pres fdr Penncostal Crusade Nationwide; fdr Outreach Radio Ministry Prgm; chpln Outreach Min Pennial Inst; pres Homewood Brushton Council of Chs; chpln mem Pittsburgh Hosp;chmn Ordination Bd of Nat FBinisters; chmn Invest Com Nat FBH Mins; supt Dist of & Ch of God in Christ; moderator EasternJurisdiction of PA; num political activities. **Honors/Awds:** Awards Hand& Hand; Talke Mag; Best Dress Man of Yr; Pittsburgh Courier; E Liberty Gafield Annual Awards; Martin Luther King Jr; consult panelist lectr numevents workshops. **Business Addr:** Chief Deputy Clerk of Courts, Allegheny County, 114 Court House, Pittsburgh, PA 15219.

DAVIS, EVELYN PAYNE.

Television executive, association founder. **Personal:** Born Dec 27, 1921, New Orleans, LA; died Jan 10, 1997, Manhattan, NY; married MynorPayne (died 1968); children: David; married Charles Davis; children: Liberty Davis Rashad. **Educ:** Attended Hunter College. **Career:** Worked in antipoverty programs, 1960s; Children's Television Workshop's Community EducationServices, vice pres, consultant, until 1992. **Orgs:** New York Coalition of 100 Black Women, founder, president; New York Urban League. **Special Achievements:** Led promotional campaign in inner city for ''Sesame Street'', 1969. **Home Addr:** 000900001600.

DAVIS, JAMES A.

Business executive. **Personal:** Born Nov 8, 1924, Philadelphia, PA; died Dec 18, 1995; married Lorraine J; children: Michael, Keith. **Educ:** Drexel U, BMech 1965; Howard U, Architecture 1953. **Career:** General Electric Co Urban Systems Program, program mgr; Philco-Ford Inc, project engr; Am Electronics Labs, sr engr; JaLords Inc, president; Sarah Potter Smith Com Devel Corp, consulting & mechanical & elec engr dir; licensed professional engr in Pennsylvania, Maryland, New York, New Jersey, Massachusetts, Delaware,Washington DC. **Orgs:** Mem IEEE; NSPG; ASHRAE; mem NAACP; on the beam club Concept Therapy. **Honors/Awds:** Achievement award Past Nat Pres Citation; scientific award Tech Design Philco Ford Inc; Invention Disclosure CryogenicStarter. **Military Serv:** USAF reserve captain 1952-65. **Business Addr:** JA Lords, 1080 N Delaware Ave, 5th Fl, Philadelphia, PA 19125.

DECLUE, ANITA.

Educator. **Personal:** DiedApr 11, 1998, St. Louis, MO; married Dr James; children: 2 Sons. **Educ:**WA U, BS 1974. **Career:** Gov Serv, 1942-69; St Louis Public Schools, substitute teacher begin 1970; Concordia Sem, delegate housing conf. **Orgs:**V chmn bd, mem League Women Voters; Human Resources.

DEWINDT, HAL.

Producer, director, actor. **Personal:** Bornin New York City, NY; died 1997, Los Angeles, CA; married Suzanne; children: Tracey, Drew. **Career:** Model; New York Shakespeare Festival, production stage manager; actor; ''The Angel Levine,'' asst producer; Loyola Marymount Univ, professor, acting, until 1997. **Orgs:** American Theatre of Harlem, found, artistic dir; Inner City Repertory Company, Los Angeles, artistic dir. **Special Achievements:** Ebony Fashion Fair, model, 1959-61; appeared in: ''Golden Boy,'' Broadway, ''Lost In The Stars,'' City Center, NYC. **Home Addr:** 002350003400001600.

DILLARD, SAMUEL DEWELL.

Business executive. **Personal:** Born Aug 12, 1913,Bolivar Co, MS; died Feb 6, 1997; married Geneva E Lambert; children: Allen C, Edsel B, James E, Wanda F, Kelly E, Wilma J. **Educ:** Tuskegee Inst, 1938;NC Central Univ Sch of Bus Administrn; Univ of NC Sch of Bus Adminstrn. **Career:** Dillard's & Sons Inc & Dillard's Bar-B-Q House , pres 1945-97. **Orgs:** Bd mem United Durham Inc; mem The Wildlife Assn; Doric Lodge #28; DurhamC of C; Durham Bus & Professional Chain; NAACP; Nat Bus League. **Honors/Awds:** Outstanding achievement in bus world Durham Bus & Professional Chain 1974. **Business Addr:** President, Sam Dillard & Sons, 4910 Barbee Rd, Durham,NC 27713-1604.

DIXON, BLANCHE V.

Educator. **Personal:** Born in Philadelphia, PA; died Sep 30, 1988; married Duvoille Dixon; children: Duvoille A, Carolyn, Douglas, Patricia, David, Charisse. **Career:** S Bronx Comm Progress Center, founder, bd mem 1964; Sch Dist 7,educ chmn 1965-70. **Orgs:** Mem Title I Com District 7; mem v chmn NY State Ruban & Com; mem former chmn Title Iii Com funded 3 million dollar South Bronx Supplementary educ cntr; past pres Parents Assn PS 29; JHS 38; IS145; first school bd re IS 151; founder bd mem Lucille Murray Child Devel Cntr NAACP; Urban League; mem Legislative Adv Council Assembleman Jose Serrano; founded United Black Educators. **Honors/Awds:** Recipient 10 Plaques Outstanding Comm Servicefor edn, humanitarinism, headership, civic participation; cited Urban League; honored testimonial dinner outstanding leadership comm relations; recipient special citation parent leadership JHS 145; recipient S Bronx Comm Corp Founder Plaque.

DOGGETT, BILL.

Musician. **Personal:** Died Nov 13, 1997, Manhattan, NY; married Angela. **Career:** Jazzpianist and organist; recording artist. **Special Achievements:** Worked with: the Lucky Millender Band, the Ink Spots, Helen Humes, Illinois Jacquet, Jimmy Rushing, Lucky Thompson and Louis Jordan; arranged ''Round Midnight'' for Cootie Williams; recorded singles, ''Big Dog,'' ''Honky Tonk''; recorded for King Records, Warner Brothers Records, Columbia and ABC Paramount. **Home Addr:** 007350007400.

DOTSON, WILLIAM S.

District manager (retired). **Personal:** Born Sep 29, 1911, Cave City, KY; died Oct 25, 1995; married Alice Duncan; children: 2 Adopted Daughters. **Educ:** KY State U, BS 1936. **Career:** Supreme Life Ins Co of Am, dist mgr. **Orgs:** Trustee Shiloh Bapt Ch; State treas NAACP 27 yrs; mem Omega Psi Phi Frat 40 yr man; past Nat pres KY State Univ Alumni Assn; life paying mem NAACP; mem Lexington Life Underwriters Assn; Gen Agents & Mgrs Assn; mem bd dir United Way of Bluegrass; sec Lexington KY Urban Renewal; vice pres Lexington GAMA; LUTC Grad. **Honors/Awds:** Recip Omega Man of Yr Psi Tau Chap 1975; 40 yr Plaque Omega Psi Phi Frat 1974.

DUNCAN, ROBERT TODD.

Concert singer, actor. **Personal:** Born Feb 12, 1903, Danville, KY; died Feb 28, 1998, Washington, DC; married Gladys; children: Charles C Duncan. **Educ:** Butler U, GA 1925; Columbia U, MA 1930; Howard U, Mus D 1930; OH Cent State U, Mus D; Valparaiso U, Doc of Humane Letters. **Career:** 2000 cncrt rctls in 56 countries 1940-65; Original Porgy in Geo Gershwins ''Porgy & Bess''; ''Cabin in the Sky'', performer 1940; ''The Sun Never Sets'', performer 1936; ''Lost in The Stars'', performer 1950; ''Synocopation'', performer 1940; ''Unchained'', performer 1955; ''Pagliacci'', performer; ''Carmen'', performer 1945; Louisville Municipal Coll, tchr English & Music 1925-30; Howard U, tchr 1931-35; prof of voice & head of dept of pub sch music 1930-45; presently voice instr & coach Wash. **Orgs:** Mem NAG White House Concert for Franklin D Roosevelt 1935. **Honors/Awds:** Medal of Honor Haiti 1945; Donaldson Awrd & NY Drama Critics Awrd for ''Lost in The Stars'' 1950; recorded ''Porgy & Bess''.**Business Addr:** 4130 16 St NW, Washington, DC 20011.

EDWARDS, G. FRANKLIN.

Educator. **Personal:** Born 1915; died Jan 13, 1998, Washington, DC; married Peggy Jervis Park Edwards; children: Donalee E. Wood. **Career:** Howard Univ, faculty, 1941-80, prof emeritus in sociology 1980-97, chmn of sociology dept; visiting sociology prof, Harvard Univ; visiting sociology prof, Washington Univ. **Orgs:** Ntl Capital Planning Commission, mem 1965-71, acting chmn 1969-70; mem, advisory bd, Ntl Capital Transportation Agency; mem, D.C. Home Rule Committee; mem, Washington Planning and Housing Assn; past pres, D.C. Sociological Society; advisory editor, American Jnl of Sociology, fellow, White House Historical Assn, 1979-97.

EVANS, WILLIAM C.

Cleric. **Personal:** Born Nov 3, 1899, Winchester, KY; died Apr 25, 1993; son of Anna and William; marriedEmma Lee Evans. **Educ:** Metro Bible Coll; VA Theological Seminary & Coll, DD. **Career:** South Hempstead Baptist Church, pastor 1940-93. **Orgs:** Chmn Evangelistic Bd E Baptist Assn; bd mem Empire State Conf; bd dir E Baptist Assn; bd mem Educ Center; mem Ministers Conf NY City; mem Natl Baptist Convention US Inc; bd mem Urban Renewal; mem Evangelistic Bd Natl Baptist Convention; life mem NAACP; New Home Lodge 1123 IBPOE Elks; street named in behalf; mem Republican Presidential Task Force 1981-93, United States Senatorial Club 1983-93. **Honors/Awds:** Commendation Gov NA Rockefeller; Unispan Awd Hofstra Univ; Commendation President Ronald Reagan; Commendation Governor M Coumo. **Business Addr:** Pastor, South Hempstead Baptist Church, 81 Maple Ave, Hempstead,NY 11550.

FIGURES, MICHAEL.

State legislator. **Personal:** Born Oct 13, 1947; died Sep 1996; married Vivian Davis; children: Akil, Davis. **Educ:** Degree from Stillman College; law degree from Univ of Alabama. **Career:** Alabama House of Representatives, Montgomery AL, state senator, District 33. **Honors/Awds:** Delegate to Democratic Natl Convention, 1980. **Business Addr:** House of Representatives, State Capitol, Montgomery, AL 36130.

FORD, CLAUDETTE FRANKLIN.

Equal employment specialist. **Personal:** Born May 5, 1942, Washington, GA; died Jan 15, 1996; married Louis Allan. **Educ:** Howard U, BA 1964; Am U, grad study 1967-69. **Career:** Office of Women's BusEnterprise-Small Bus Adminstrn, bus prog analyst 1979-96; Outreach Subcom of Pres Carter's Interaby Com on Women's Bus Enterprise, staff dir; exec ed proj dir a woman owned bus 5 yrs; Wash off of midwest based woman-owned mktg & pub rel firm, mgr early 60's; Delta Sigma ThetaNat Pub Serv Sor, asst; Am Savs & Loan LeagInc, information spl; Wash Off Kaiser Assn Advt, dir; EEOC; equal opp spl. **Orgs:** Fndr The Oracle Set Book Club; mem bd of dirs Nat Coor Coun on Drug Abuse Information; ass dir pub affairs & vol servs corp for pub broadcasting; natl 2nd vice pres Delta Sigma Theta Sor; mem Nat Bd YWCA; asst dir for comm affairs Corp for Pub Broadcastingf coor adv coun of 100 major natl orgns; vice pres Nat Capital Area YWCA; mem Nat Coun of Negro Women; mem NAACP; mem bd of dirs WashHalfway Home for Women. **Business Addr:** Small Business Administration, Washington, DC 20416.

FORD, ROBERT BENJAMIN, JR.

Librarian. **Personal:** Born Nov 27, 1935, Miami, FL; died Oct 18, 1993; son of Mary Ford Williams Mullins (deceased) and Robert B Ford Sr (deceased); married Seretta J Pertilla Ford, Aug 3, 1963; children: Lisa J, Maria F Bowles. **Educ:** Bethune-Cookman Coll, BA Speech Drama 1955; NY Univ Sch ofEduc NYC, MA 1958; Pratt Inst Lib Sch, MLS 1959; Rutgers Univ, PhD, 1988. **Career:** Bunche Park Elementary School, Opa Locka FL, teacher 1955-56; Dade County Public Schools Miami, librarian 1961-67; Engrg Socs Library NYC, monograph& serials cataloger 1967-68; Queensborough Community Coll Library NYC, serials & periodicals librarian 1968-70; Medgar Evers Coll Brooklyn, chief librarian 1970-85, adjunct assoc prof, speech 1979-83, assoc librarian, reader/info. **Orgs:** Tchr Adult Basic Educ Prog Dade Co Pub Schs 1965-67; refer librarian N Bellmore Pub Library N Bellmore NY 1969-72; sub tchr HS Equivalency Prog Urban CtrNY 1970-73; treas 1971-73, vice pres/pres elect 1988-93; Library Assn City Univof NY; sec Council of Chief Librarians City Univ of NY 1974-75; bd dir Coll & Univ Libraries Sect NY Library Assn 1979-81; treas/vp 1975-80, pres 1988-90; NY Black Librarians Caucus 1975-80; Medgar Evers College, Brooklyn, NY, chief librarian, 1970-85, adjunct assoc prof speech, 1979-83, assoc librarian, reader/info service, 1985-93. **Honors/Awds:** ''Title IIA-A Bargain at the Price, A Symposium'' Journ of Acad Librarianship 1979; ''Help for the Decision Maker, A Decision-Process Model'' The Bookmark 1979; president, Academic Libraries of Brooklyn, 1984-85; Y S Bennett, The Bookmark, Fall 1987. **Military Serv:** AUS pfc 1959-61. **Home Addr:** 119-33 235th St, Cambria Heights, NY 11411. **Business Addr:** Assoc Librarian, Reader, Info Services Library, Medgar Evers College Library, 1650 Bedford Ave, Brooklyn, NY 11225.

FORREST, LEON RICHARD.

Educator. **Personal:** Born Jan 8, 1937, Chicago, IL; died Nov 6, 1997; son of Adeline and Leon; married Marianne Duncan. **Educ:** Wilson Jr Coll, 1955-56; Roosevelt Univ, 1957-58; Univ of Chicago, 1958-60 1962-64. **Career:** Woodlawn Observer, managing editor 1967-69; Muhammed Speaks, assoc dir 1969-71, managing editor 1971-73; Northwestern Univ, prof Afro-Amer Studies 1973-97. **Orgs:** Mem The Authors Guild Inc 1974-97; awds pres Soc of Midland Authors 1981; pres Soc of Midland Authors 1981; lectr Yale-Rochester-Wesleyan 1974-89; librettist for opera commissioned IN Univ Sch of Music 1980. **Honors/Awds:** Sandburg Medallion Chicago Pub Library 1984; author of 3 novels & a play; Society of Midland Authors Award for Fiction; Friends of Literature; Du Sable Museum Award for Fiction; Mayor Harold Washington proclaims April 14, 1985 as ''Leon Forrest Day'' in Chicago. **Military Serv:** AUS spec 4 1960-62. **Business Addr:** Prof African-Amer Studies, Northwestern Univ, 633 Clark, Evanston, IL 60201.

FORSTER, CECIL R.

Psychologist. **Personal:** Born Apr 21, 1911, Brooklyn, NY; died Jan 11, 1996; son of Elvira Lord Forsterand Clarence Forster; married Evelyn P Lattimore; children: Cecil Jr, Sandra Preiss. **Educ:** NY U, BS 1936, MA 1938, PhD 1955. **Career:** VA Hosp,Brooklyn, chief counseling psychologist 1951-64; Neighborhood Youth Corps/US Dept Labor, regional dir 1965-66; Bureau of Work Pgms/US Dept of Labor, spec asst to admin 1966-67; Dept of Psychiatry/NY Med Coll, dir rehab serv 1967-69; Dept Psychiatry/NY Medical Coll, asst prof 1967; NY State Bd for Psychology, mem 1971-78; Psychology Dept Baruch Coll, adj asso prof 1971; New York City Plice Dept, New York, NY, sr psychological consultant, 1980-84; New York City Police Dept, srpsychological consult 1980-96; Private Practice. **Orgs:** Chrmn emeritus Committee for Public Higher Educ 1986-96; pres NY State Psychological Assn 1975-76. **Honors/Awds:** Distinguished Serv Award Assoc of Black Psychologists 1984; Honorary Surgeon, New York City Police Dept, 1981; Distinguished Serv Award NY Society of Clinical Psychologists 1979. **Military Serv:** USCGR chiefboatswain mate 1942-45. **Business Addr:** 862 E 21st St, Brooklyn, NY 11210.

FOSTER, FRANCES HELEN.
Actress, director. **Personal:** Born Jun 11, 1924, Yonkers, NY; died Jun 17, 1997, Fairfax, VA; married Robert Stansfield Foster, 1941 (died 1977); children: Terrell R, Bernette Ford, Lisa Yarboro, Russell M; married Morton Goldsen. **Educ:** Amer Theatre Wing, BA, 1952. **Career:** World Theatre Festival London, actress 1969; Munich Olympics play, actress 1972; Australia 1977; Negro Ensemble Co, actress, 1967-86. **Orgs:** Screen Actors Guild, 1952; Councillor, Actors Equity Assn 1953-67; founding mem, Negro Ensemble Co, 1967; artist-in-residence, City Coll of NY, 1973-77; Amer Fed of Radio & TV Artists; founding mem, Black Women in Theatre 1982. **Honors/Awds:** Audelco Best Actress, Do Lord Remember Me, 1978; Audelco Best Dir, Hospice, 1983; appeared in 25 NEC productions,more than 100 TV shows, films, soap operas; 1985 Obie for Sustained Excellence of Performance; NEC, Adolph Caesar Award, 1987. **Business Addr:** Actress-Director, 146 E 49th, #7B, New York, NY 10017.

FOX, EVERETT V.
Hospital executive. **Personal:** Born Jun 16, 1915, Richmond, VA; died Mar 3, 1997. **Educ:** Hampton Inst, BS, 1937; Univ ofChicago, MBA, 1960; Doctorate, pub admin, NYU, adv study, 1972; Grad Prog, hospadmin. **Career:** NYU Med Ctr, clinical asst prof, Preventive Medicine Hosp Admin; NYU Hosp, vp, admin, 1974-97; NYU Med Ctr, affiliation admin, 1965-74;Kate Bitting Reynolds Mem Hosp, med serv inves & admin, 1948-65; Winston Salem,accnt, priv prac, 1946-48; So Life Ins Co, supvr auditor, 1932-41. **Orgs:** First natl pres, Natl Assn of Health Serv, Execs; Com on Provision of Health Serv, Am Hosp Assn; pres, Univ of Chicago Alumni Assn; Am Coll of Hosp Admins; consult, Clinical Res Ctr, Com Natl Inst of Health, HEW; Natl Assn Health Serv Execs. **Honors/Awds:** CIAA Conf Basketball Champions, Hampton Inst, 1936; honor man, USN, 1941; award of honor, Am Hosp Assn, Spec Com on Provision of HlthServ, 1971; Clyde Reynolds Health Exec Award, Natl Assn of Health Serv Execs, 1975; Exec of Year, Natl Assn of Health Serv Execs; Health team on two week tour of Soviet Union observing health progs in four Soviet Union cities. **MilitaryServ:** USN, 1941-43. **Business Addr:** 550 1 Ave, New York, NY 10016.

FRANCIS, JOSEPH A.
Cleric. **Personal:** Born Sep 30, 1923, Lafayette, LA; died Sep 1, 1997. **Educ:** Catholic Univ Amer, BA, MA; Xavier Univ New Orleans, postgrad; Loyola Univ; Mt St Mary's Coll. **Career:** Ordained priest Roman Catholic Ch 1950; St Augustine's Sem, instr & asst dean of stdnts 1951-52; Holy Rosary Inst, asst dir 1952-60; Immaculate Heart of Mary Parish, adminstr 1960; Holy Cross Parish Austin, adminstr 1960-61; Pius X HS, instr 1961-62; Verbum Dei HS Watts CA, fdr & 1st prin 1962-67; Western Province of Soc of the Divine Word, provincial superior 1967-73; Sthrn Province of Soc of the Divine Word Bay St Louis, provicial superior 1973-97. **Orgs:** Pres bd mem Conf of Major Superiors of Men in the USA; bd mem Nat Cath Conf of Interracial Justice; Proj Equality; adv bd Nat Ofc for Blk Cath;bd trustees Divine Word Coll Epworth IA; Cath Theol Union Univ Chgo; mem Bd consult Diocese of Nathchez-Jackson; mem AD HOC Com NCCB on Priestly Ministry Formation; mem Blk Priests Caucus; trustee Immac Concept Sem Mahwah, NJ; bd overseers Harvard Div Sch. **Business Addr:** 139 Glenwood Ave, East Orange, NJ 07017.

FREEMAN, EVELYN.
Educator. **Personal:** Born Feb 16, 1940, Marksville, LA; died Nov 25, 1996. **Educ:** Western Washington, BA Educ 1962; Univ of WA, 5th yr; Seattle U; Univ of CA Los Angeles, MA 1973; Univ of Washington, PhD, 1986. **Career:** Issaquah Public School, prin 1974-79; Adams School, prin 1974; Long Beach, gifted program 1970-73; Leschi Seattle, established non-graded approach to reading & math 1966-70; Everett School District, dir of curriculum & instruction, 1988-95; Edmonds School District, assist sup of instruction, 1979-88. **Orgs:** Mem ESPA; NAACP; mem FIGHT Rochester, NY; foudn mem Nat Council of Negro Women Seattle; treas Seattle chap 1968f sec Los Angeles chpt. **Business Addr:** Everett School District #2, Everett, WA 98201.

GAINES, LESLIE DORAN. (BUBBA)
Performer. **Personal:** Born Feb 12, 1912, Waynesboro, GA; died Jun 30, 1997. **Career:** USO, entertainer AUS 1951-71; Three Dukes Internat, Aristocrats of Dancing, original mem 1932-41. **Orgs:** Mem NY Assn of Musicians; founding mem Copasetics 1950-80. **Honors/Awds:** Recip 5 Battle Stars. **Military Serv:** AUS corpl 1942-45.

GARLAND, PERCY A.
Photographer. **Personal:** Born Feb9, 1912, Versailles Boro, PA; died Jan 15, 1997, Pittsburgh, PA; married Hazel Hill Garland (died 1988); children: Phyllis. **Career:** Garland Enterprises. **Special Achievements:** One of first African americans in US to pursuecareer in industrial photography; designed and manufactured photographic and data recording equipment that has been used in a nuclear-powered aircraft carrier,nuclear submarine, an Apollo 12 reactor. **Home Addr:** 005700.

GARROTT, HOMER L.
Judge. **Personal:** BornApr 25, 1914, Los Angeles, CA; died Mar 14, 1998, CA; married Bertha Tabor; children: Diane. **Educ:** Southwestern Univ Sch of Law, LLB 1958. **Career:** Municipal Ct Compton Judicial Dist, judge 1973-84; Municipal Ct Los Angeles Judicial Dist, commr 1968-73; Juveniel Ct Los Angeles Co, referee 1967-68; LosAngeles Co, deputy pub defender 1964-67. **Orgs:** Bd of dir Southwestern Univ beginning 1978. **Military Serv:** US Army, spec, 1936-39. **Business Addr:** Compton Judicial District, 200 West Compton Blvd, Compton, CA 90220.

GATLIN, ELISSA L.
Educational administrator. **Personal:** Born Aug 10, 1948, Gary, IN; died Mar 1989. **Educ:** W MI Univ Kalamazoo, BS Speech Pathology 1970; MI State Univ E Lansing, MASpeech Pathology 1970, PhD Speech Pathology. **Career:** MI School for the-Blind Lansing, speech & language therapist & pre-school language consultant 1971-73; Provincial Hosp & Surgi-Clinic Lansing, paraprofessional, counselor 1973-76; MI State Univ E Lansing, teaching asst dept of audiology & speech science 1973-76; NE State Univ, Tahlequah OK, asst prof of special educ & clinic coord 1976-80; MI State Univ, adjunct asst prof dept of aud & speech science 1980-89; Collof Osteo Medicine, MI State Univ, dir of admissions 1980-85; Western Michigan Univ, dir Center for Human Services 1985. **Orgs:** Mem Amer Speech Hearing & Lang Assn; mem Amer Assn for Couns & Dev; mem Natl Assn of Med Min Educators, NAACP, Delta Sigma Theta Sor Inc, oral appraisal bd MI Dept of Civil Serv; bds dir Greater Kalamazoo YWCA, Kalamazoo Center for Independent Living, Red Cross; exec comm Southern Tier Chap of the March of Dimes; mem Kalamazoo County Childrenand Youth Servs Coordinating Council-Chair Adolescent Pregnancy and Parenthood Comm; mem Amer Pub Health Assn; mem Amer Soc of Allied Health Professions; mem Nat'l Soc of Allied Health Professions; mem Nat'l Rehabilitation Assn. **Honors/Awds:** Delta Kappa Gamma Hon Soc of Women Educators Tahlequah OK 1978. **Business Addr:** Director, Ctr for Human Servs, Western Michigan Univ, Henry Hall, Kalamazoo, MI 49008.

GLEASON, MAURICE FRANCIS.
Physician. **Personal:** Born Mar 7, 1909, Mobile, AL; died Apr 11, 1998; son of Minnie S Gleason and William R Gleason; married Eliza; children: Joy, Carew. **Educ:** John Carroll Univ, BS 1931; Meharry Med Coll, MD1940; Cleveland City Hosp, intern 1940-41; Provident Hosp, resident 1941-43. **Career:** State & 51st St Shopping Ctr, partner; Hyde Park Fed Savings & Loan Assn, former dir; private practice, physician. **Orgs:** Mem AMA, IL State Med Soc, Chicago Med Soc, Natl Med Assn, Prairie State Med Assn, Cook County Physicians Assn; fellow Amer Coll, Amer Soc Abdominal Surgeons, Intl Coll Surgeons, IL Soc Med Rsch; mem Amer Assn Maternal & Infant Health, Pan Amer Cytologican Soc, Intl Fertility Assn, Amer Soc Study Sterility, Amer Heart Assn, Hyde Park-Kenwood Neighborhood Redevel Corp, Hyde Park-Kenwood Comm Conservation Council,SE Chicago Comm Hyde Park-Kenwood Community Conf, Hyde Park Neighborhood Club, Urban League; life mem NAACP, Chicago Art Inst, Museum of Natural Hist, Planetarium soc, Cosmopolitan C of C, Ind Voters IL, League Women Voters, S Christ Leadership Conf PUSH, Amer Democratic Action, The Chicagoans, Royal Coterie Snakes, Original 40 Club Chgo; mem, Alpha Phi Alpha, Kappa Pi Hon Med School Soc, 1939. **Military Serv:** AUS maj 1943-46.

GOODEN, SAMUEL ELLSWORTH.
Clergyman, educator. **Personal:** Born Aug 25,1916; died Dec 18, 1993; married Elita Powell; children: Sharon, Rose. **Educ:** Union Coll, BA 1949; Columbia U, MA 1958. **Career:** S Atlantic Conf of Seventh Day Adventists, dir of youth activts, supt of school, dir Office ofPublic Affairs & Religious Liberty, dir public relations; GA Council on Moral &Civic Concerns, vice pres; Africa, coll prin; W Africa, missionary; vice prin, high school; NYC, prin elementary school. **Orgs:** Mem Phi Delta Kappa; Alpha Phi Alpha; AASA chmn W Manor Comm Action Group 1975. **Business Addr:** 235 Chicamauga Ave SW, Atlanta, GA 30314.

GREGORY, BERNARD VINCENT.
Telecommunications executive (retired), association administrator. **Personal:** Born Nov 5, 1926, New York, NY; died Dec 28,1997; son of Winnifred U Smith Gregory and Horace L Gregory; married Marion Arnetha Buck, Nov 16, 1946; children: Bernard II, Michele Verne Gregory Gee, RodneyGlenn. **Educ:** Wilberforce Univ, 1943-45; Central State Univ, BBA, 1948.**Career:** Beneficial Life, general manager, 1954-60; Supreme Life, associate brokerage supvr, asst agency dir, dir educ & training, 1960-72; Chicago Metro Mutual, ordinance agency mgr, 1972-75; Afro-American Life, vp/agency dir 1975-77; Prudential Insurance, assoc manager, advertising & sales promotion, 1977-79; Winston Mutual Life Ins Co, agency dir, 1979-81; Jacksonville Chamber of Commerce, minority youth empl dir, 1981; Southern Bell, acct exec, asst manager, telemarketing sales manager, 1981-97. **Orgs:** American Lung Association, Florida Chapter, president, 1993-97, American Lung Association Council, delegate-at-large, 1992; Jacksonville Community Foundation Board, chairman, resource development committee, 1992-97; National Conference of Christians and Jews, national board of trustees, 1993-97; Kappa Alpha Psi, life member; United Way of Northeast Florida, executive committee, board member, 1990-97, chairman, charter committee, 1991-97; United Negro College Fund, charter member, chairman, 1991-97. **Honors/Awds:** Outstanding Alumnus of the Year, Central State Univ, 1970; Rutledge H Pearson Memorial Award, Jacksonville Branch, NAACP, 1987; Outstanding Leadeship & Dedicated Serv, 1987, Jacksonville Urban League, bd of dirs, 1988; Outstanding Community Serv, Tots 'N' Teens Theatre Inc, 1989; Honorary Citizen, City of Houston, TX, 1975; Minority Youth Employment Program, 1981, Contribution to the Devel of Jacksonville, Bd of Govs, 1988, Volunteer of the Month, 1989, Jacksonville Chamber of Commerce; Exemplary Leadership, Northwest Council, 1988; Achievers' Club, Southern Bell, 1988-89; Outstanding Leadership, A. Philip Randolph Northside Skills Center, 1989; Certificate of Appreciation,Edward Waters Coll, 1987; Hornsby Trophy, Soc for the Advancement of Mgmt, Central State Univ, 1965; For Dedicatedrv, Community Economic Devel Council, 1987; Natl Certificate of Achievement, Amer Lung Assn, 1991; Community Service Award, Alpha Phi Alpha, 1989; Leadership/Community Service Award, El-Beth-El Divine Holiness Church, 1990; Keel Club, United Way of NE Florida, 1990, 1991, 1992; National Conference of Christians and Jews, Humanitarian Award, 1993; WTLV, Channel 12, Jacksonville, One of the ''12 Who Care,'' 1992; Florida Georgia Blood Alliance, Lifetime Award, for gift of life to community, 6-gallon donor, 1992; Jacksonville Chamber of Commerce, Northwest Council, Community Service Award, 1989, 1992; Mayor's Special Plaque for Support ofthe ''Jacksonville Together,'' Community-Based Series of Meetings, 1992; Florida Department of Labor and Employment Security, Florida Department of Elder Affairs, Volunteer Support of Florida's Older Worker Programs, 1992; Child Watch Partnership of Jacksonville, FL Inc, Participation in the Childwatch Leadership Training Institute, 1992. **Special Achievements:** First African-American agent with a African-American insurance co. to sell a $500,000 policy, Black Enterprise Magazine, 1969. **Military Serv:** US Navy Reserve, 1945-46. **Home Addr:** 8430 Sophist Circle E, Jacksonville, FL 32219. **Business Addr:** Board Member, Assistant Treasurer, American Lung Association of Florida, 5526 Arlington Rd, PO Box 8127, Jacksonville, FL 32239.

HAILE, RICHARD H.
Business executive. **Personal:** Born Aug 2, 1910, Camden, SC; died Dec 25, 1976; married Bessie E Pickett; children: Sylvia Nelson, Ralph H. **Educ:** Claflin Coll, BS 1932; Orangeburc SC; Gupton-Jones Coll of Mortuary Sct Nashville TN, 1933. **Career:** Hickman Elem Sch, prin 1934-43; Haile's Funeral Home, owner 1944-76. **Orgs:** Pres SC Morticians Assn Inc 1945-52; pres Nat Funeral Dir & MorticiansAssn Inc 1959-61; mem Exec Com Nat Funeral Dir & Morticians Assn Inc 1961-76; past basalus Omicron Phi Chpt; Omega Psi Phi Frat Columbia SC; basalus Chi Chi Chap Omega Psi Phi Frat Camden SC; past chmn Voter Educ Project Fifth Dist SC; past chmn Camden-Kershaw Co Br NAACP; mem, bd dir Office of Econ Opportunity Kershaw Co SC; past orshipful master Compostie Lodge #372 Masonic Order; past illustrous potentate AL Bar Temple Shriners; officer Trinity Unied Meth Ch. **BusinessAddr:** Rutledge at Ch St, Camden, SC 29020.

HAIRSTON, SAM.
Professional baseball player. **Personal:** Born in Crawford, MS; died Oct 31, 1997, Birmingham, AL; married Dora; children: John,Jerry, Sam Jr. **Career:** Negro League baseball, 1940s; signed with WhiteSox, 1950, played minor league team, Sacramento Sky Sox, 1951-63, played with Whit Sox, 1951; Birmingham Barons, coach, scout 1963-97. **Honors/Awds:** Western League Championship, Sacramento Sky Sox; Minor League MVP, 1953. **Special Achievements:** First African American on the Chicago White Sox, 1950. **Home Addr:** 009100.

HAMILTON, CHARLES S.
Clergyman. **Personal:** Born May 12, 1927, Cedartown, GA; died May25, 1997; married Lillie Mitchell; children: Ronald, Charletta, Rachael. **Educ:** Morehouse Coll, AB 1950; Morehouse Sch Rel, BD 1953, ITC STM 1964; Colgate Rochester Div Sch, DMin 1975. **Career:** Tabernacle Baptist Church, min-

ister. **Orgs:** Past pres Augusta Baptist Ministers Conf; GA Humane Relations Council; v moderator Walker Baptist Assn; mem City Council Augusta 1966-71;bd dir Morehouse Sch Rel 1969-75; Human Relations Comm 1971-74; mem ProgressiveNatl Baptist Conv; pres Comm Civil Rights; mem NAACP; Civil Serv Comm Augusta GA 1974-78; pres New Era Missionary Baptist Conv of GA; Augusta-Richmond Planning& Zoning Comm. **Honors/Awds:** Martin Luther King Jr Fellow 1972. **Military Serv:** AUS 1946-47. **Business Addr:** Minister, Tabernacle Baptist Church, 1223 Laney Walker Blvd, Augusta, GA 30901.

HARDY, JOHN LOUIS.
Educational administrator. **Personal:** Born Feb 22, 1937, Rayville, LA; died Jun 2, 1992; married Bernetta; children: Mike, David, John. **Educ:** Pasadena City Coll, AA 1958; CA State Poly UnivPomona, BS 1961; Azusa Pacific, MA 1970. **Career:** Azusa School Dist, teacher 1963; Pasadena City Coll, counselor 1970; Pasadena City Coll Extended Opportunity Program, dir. **Orgs:** Pres Sugar Ray Youth Found 1975; chmn Pasadena Comm Serv Comm 1976; pres, bd of ed Pasadena School Dist 1978-79. **Business Addr:** Dir, Pasadena City Coll, Extended Oppty Prog, 1570 E Colorado Blvd, Pasadena, CA 91106.

HASSELL, FRANCES M.
Business executive. **Personal:** Born Mar 26, 1925, Woodstock, TN; diedMar 12, 1996; divorced; children: Marian Hassell Whitson. **Educ:** Lane College, 1947; TN State Univ; Memphis State Univ; Baptist Christian Clg, BA; Trevecca Nazarene Univ, mgmt courses; Baptist Christian Univ, psychology, Christian counseling courses. **Career:** Adv Life Ins Unvrsl Life Ins Co, vice pres corp sec pub rltns 1980-96, asst vice pres pub rltns 1971-80, admin asst 1958-71, sec to vice pres 1950-58, br ofc clerk 1947. **Orgs:** Life Advtrs Assn; past mem LOMA Educ Com; life mem YWCA; NIA, HO Sect,vice pres, 1978-80, board ofdirectors, secretary; NAACP; Memphis Panel of Am Wmn; Memphis Chap PRSA; Mt Olive CME Ch; Junior Achievement of Greater Memphis, past board member; Memphis Area Chamber of Commerce; Lane Clg, trustee. **Honors/Awds:** LAA, Award of Excellence, 1973, 1974; An Outstndng Woman Who Work Memphis, 1973; Dillard Univ, New Orlns, Woman's Week Prin Spkr, 1964; Black Heritage, Honorary Chair and Honoree, 1996; Universal Life Ins Co, stockholders and brd honoree, 1996. **SpecialAchievements:** Author, researcher: Black History; Reflections of an African-American Kitchen, cookbook; African-American History Crossword Puzzle Book; compiled African-American History Booklet; textural artist. **Business Addr:** Vice President, Corp Secretary, Universal Life Insurance Co, 480 Linden Ave, Box 241, Memphis, TN 38101.

HAWKINS, THEODORE F.
Obstetrician, gynecologist. **Personal:** Born Apr 6, 1908, E Orange, NJ; died Oct 12, 1995; married Shirley R; children: Shirley C, Karen, Theodore Jr. **Educ:** Lincoln U, AB 1931; Meharry Med Coll, MD 1937; Grad Sch MedUniv PA, 1950. **Career:** Ob/Gyn, pvt pract. **Orgs:** Hosp affil Med Coll of PA & Hosp Miser Hosp; dip Am Bd Obs/Gyn; fellow Am Coll Obs/Gyn; fellow Am Coll Surg; mem Philadelphia Co Med Soc; Nat Med Soc; East PA Med Soc; bd YMCA; Wissahickon Boy's Club; Youth Serv; Plann Parenthood; Christian St Y'S Men'sClub; NAACP; Med Com Civil Rights. **Honors/Awds:** Dist alumnus Lincoln U; man of yr Chi Delta Mu; dist serv awd St Paul's Bapt Ch. **Home Phone:** (215)842-3310.

HAWKINS, WALTER LINCOLN.
Engineering consultant (retired). **Personal:** Born Mar 21, 1911, Washington, DC; died Aug 20, 1992; married Lilyan B Bobo; children: W Gordon, Philip L. **Educ:** Rensselaer Polytechnic Ins, ChE 1932; Howard U, MS 1934; McGillU, PhD 1938; Monclair State Clg & Kean Clg, LLD Hon 1975, 81; Stevens Inst of Tech, DEng Hon 1979; Howard U, DSci 1984. **Career:** McGill U, sessnl lctr 1938-41; Bell Lab, mem tech stf 1942-63, supr apld rsrch 1963-72, dept head apldrsrch 1972-74, asst dir chem rsrch lab 1974-76; Plastics Inst of Am, rsrch dir 1976-84; cnlsnt in matrl eng. **Orgs:** Frmr mem Bd of Trustees Montclair State 1963-74; mem Bd of Dir NACME 1980-92. **Honors/Awds:** Sigma Xi; hon scroll Am Inst of Chem 1970; Percy L Julian Awrd 1977; Intl Awrd Soc of Plastic Eng Inc 1984; President George Bush, Natl Medal of Technology, 1992.

HAYES, CHARLES A.
Congressman. **Personal:** Born Feb 17, 1918, Cairo, IL; died Apr 8, 1997, Hazel Crest, IL; married Edna J (deceased); children: Barbara Delaney, Charlene Smith. **Career:** Carpenters Local 1424, pres 1940-42; UPWA Grievance Comm, chmn 1943-49; UPWA, field rep 1949-54; Dist #1 UPWA, dist dir 1954-68; Amalgamated Meatcutters Union, dist dirand intl vice pres 1968-79; United Food & Commercial Workers Intl Union AFL-CIO& CLC, intl vice pres & dist dir region 12 1979-83; US House of Representatives, member, 1983-92. **Orgs:** Serves on Educ & Labor Commns, Small Business Commns; exec vice pres Coalition of Black Trade Unionists; vice pres Operation PUSH; exec bd mem ChicagoUrban League; IL St Commn on Labor Laws. **Business Addr:** Congressman, Chicago's 1st Dist, US House of Representatives, Washington, DC 20515.

HENDERSON, STEPHEN E.
Educator, educational administrator. **Personal:** Born Oct 13, 1925, Key West,FL; died Jan 7, 1997, Langley Park, MD; son of Leonora (Sands) Henderson and James Henderson; married Jeanne Holman, Jun 14, 1958; children: Stephen E Jr, Timothy A, Philip L, Alvin Malcolm. **Educ:** Morehouse Coll, A.B., 1949; Univ of Wisconsin, M.A., 1950, Ph.D., 1959. **Career:** Virginia Union Univ, Richmond, VA, teacher, 1950-62; Morehouse Coll, Atlanta, GA, prof of English and chmn of dept, 1962-71; Howard Univ, Washington, D.C., prof of Afro-Amer studies, 1971-97, dir of Inst for the Arts and the Humanities, 1973-97. **Orgs:** Natl Council of Teachers of English; Amer Assn of Univ Profs; Coll Languag e Assn; S Atlantic Modern Language Assn; Phi Beta Kappa. **Honors/Awds:** Danforth research grant; Southern Fellowships Fund grant; Amer Council of Learned Societies, General Educ Board grant; co-author of The Militant Black Writer in Africa and the United States, 1969; author of Understanding the New Black Poetry: Black Speech and Black Music as Poetic References, 1973. **Military Serv:** U.S. Army, 1944-45. **Home Addr:** 1703 Lebanon St., Langley Park, MD 20783. **Business Addr:** Director, Institute for the Arts and the Humanities, HowardUniversity, 2400 Sixth St NW, Washington, DC 20059.

HERBERT, JAMES BRUINEL. (JIMMY)
Track athlete. **Personal:**Born Jul 20, 1915, Manhattan, NY; died Oct 23, 1997, New Rochelle, NY; married Mary; children: James (deceased). **Educ:** New York Univ, BS, education, 1942, studied law and public administration. **Career:** Worked at post office; NYC Dept of Parks, recreation dir, 1952-56; NY Supreme court, Criminal Div, sr court officer captain, 1956-75; insurance salesman; real estate broker; trackmeet official. **Orgs:** NYU Track team, team captain; New York Exchange Track Team; Grand Street Boys Athletic Association; Democratic Party in Harlem and Washington Heights, dist leader; Democratic National Convention, delegate, 1968, 1988. **Honors/Awds:** Won many individual races, in high school and college; NY Knights of Columbus Games, first place, 1939; Amateur Athletic Union National Indoor Championships, first place, 1938, 1941; Mel Sheppard 600, first place, five times; Penn Relays. **Special Achievements:** Set records at: NewYork Knights of Columbus Games; Amateur Athletic Union National Indoor Championships; Univ of Chicago Relays; ran in Penn Relays as high school student and college student.

HERCULES, FRANK E. M.
Educator, author. **Personal:** Born Feb 12, 1911, Port of Spain, Trinidad and Tobago; died May 7, 1996; son of Millicent Dottin Hercules and Felix Eugene Michael Hercules; married Dellora C. Howard, 1946; children: John, Eric. **Educ:** Attended Univ Tutorial Coll, 1934-35, and Hon Soc of the Middle Temple of Inns of Court, 1935-39, 1950-51. **Career:** Loyola Univ, visiting professor; Xavier Univ, New Orleans, writer-in-residence. **Orgs:** Mem, final review panel, Natl Endowment for the Humanities. **Honors/Awds:** Author of novels: Where the Hummingbird Flies, Harcourt, 1961, I Want a Black Doll, Simon & Schuster, 1967, On Leaving Paradise, Harcourt, 1980; contributor to periodicals; Fletcher Pratt Memorial fellowship, Bread Loaf Writers Conf, 1961; Rockefeller fellowship for distinguished scholarship in the humanities, 1977; Contributor to anthology, Voices of Life, Praeger, 1975; American Society and Black Revolution,Harcourt Brace, Jovanovich, 1966. **Home Addr:** 531 Main St Apt 1308, Roosevelt Island, NY 10044.

HERNDON, LANCE H.
Information systems consultant/executive. **Personal:** Born Apr 4, 1955, New York, NY; died Aug 8, 1996; son of Jackie Herndon and Russell Herndon; married Jeannine Price Herndon, May 27, 1989. **Educ:** LaGuardia Community Coll, New York NY, BS Computer Science; City Univ, New York NY, BS Computer Science, 1978. **Career:** Generation Science, New York NY, consultant, 1973-78; Insurance Systems of Amer, New York NY, product consultant, 1978-80; ACCESS Inc, Atlanta GA, pres, 1980-96. **Orgs:** Mem, Atlanta Business League, Atlanta Chamber of Commerce, Black Data Processing Assn, Information Systems Consultant Assn, Natl Assn of 8 (a) Contractors; founding mem, Inc Council of Growing Companies; charter mem, Natl Civil Rights Museum and Hall of Fame; mem, Butler Street YMCA Century Club, Mothers Against Drunk Driving, NAACP, Operation PUSH, United Negro Coll Fund. **Honors/Awds:** Outstanding Business Achievements, Atlanta Minority Business Devel Center; Certificate of Appreciation, Amer Red Cross; Supplier of the Year, Atlanta Business League, 1987, 1988; 500 Fastest Growing Companies, INC magazine, 1988; articles: "Young Tycoons," Ebony Magazine, 1988, "Still Making It," Black Enterprise Magazine, 1988; Georgia Trend Magazine, 1988; Atlanta Tribune, 1988; National Minority Entrpreneur of the Year Award, 1993; National Service Firm of the Year, 1989; Entrepreneur of the Year, Atlanta Business League, 1990; Entrepreneur of the Year Award and Minority Small Business Person of the Year Award, Minority Enterprise Development Center Department of Commerce, 1991; Outstanding Atlantan, Outstanding Atlanta. **Business Addr:** President, ACCESS Inc, PO Drawer 566428, Atlanta, GA 31156-6428.

HOLLAND, WALLACE E.
Government official. **Personal:** Born Sep 18, 1926, Pontiac, MI; died Feb 28, 1998, MI; son of Ethel Genieva Baynard Holland and Thomas Charles Holland; married Exavier Evelyn Grandy Holland, 1948 (deceased); children: Patricia Williams, Lowry, Vincent, Gerard, Twyla (deceased), Diane. **Educ:** Oakland Community College, vocational courses; Oakland University, management courses. **Career:** General Motors Corp, Pontiac Division, mechanical supervisor, 1961-82; Pontiac City Council, member, 1970-82; City of Pontiac, appointed mayor, 1974-82, elected mayor, 1982-85, 1990. **Orgs:** Pontiac Area Urban League, board of directors;Citizens to Save our Schools, honorary co-chair, beginning 1990; Volunteers of America, adv bd, beginning 1990; Natl Conf of Black Mayors, Inc, beginning 1972;US Conference of Mayors, beginning 1972. **Honors/Awds:** General Motors, GM Excellence Award, 1975, 1977, 1978; Natl Assn of Negro & Professional Women, Man of the Year, 1981; Michigan Assn Osteopathic Physicians & Surgeons, Outstanding Leadership and Humanitarian Award, 1977; Certification of School Participation Award, 1990-91; Boy Scout of America, Century Member Award, 1979. **Military Serv:** US Air Force, tech 5, 1945-47. **Business Addr:** Mayor, City of Pontiac, 450 E Wide Track Dr, Pontiac, MI 48342.

HOWARD, GEORGE.
Musician. **Personal:** Born 1956; died Mar 22, 1998, Atlanta, GA. **Career:** Saxophonist, albums include: Asphalt Gardens, 1982; Steppin Out, 1984; Dancing in the Sun, 1985; Love and Understanding, 1991; Do I Cross Your Mind, 1992; When Summer Comes, 1993; A Home Far Away, 1994;Attitude Adjustment, 1996; The Very Best of George Howard, 1997; Midnight Mood,1998. **Business Addr:** Jazz Musician, c/o GRP Records Inc, 555 W 57th St, New York, NY 10019, (212)429-1000.

HOWARD BECKHAM, RUTH WINIFRED.
Psychologist. **Personal:** Died 1997, Washington, DC; married Dr. Albert Beckham (deceased). **Educ:** Earned doctorate,psychology. **Career:** Private practice. **Special Achievements:** First African American woman to earn a doctorate in psychology.

HUGHES, DANIEL WEBSTER.
Clergyman. **Personal:** Born Nov 25, 1926, St Louis; died Jan 30, 1990; married Ora Enochs; children: Hazel, Terease, Denise. **Educ:** Harris Tchr Coll, BA; Am Bapt Sem, BD; Webster Coll, MA; St Louis U, Grad Work. **Career:** Mt Zion Bapt Ch MO, pastor 1958-61; Nat Alumni Assn Am Bapt Sem, pres 1967-70; E Star Bapt Ch MO, pastor 1961-90; Missionary Bapt Educ Congress, pres 1973-90. **Orgs:** Mem Nat Bapt Conv; bd mem St Louis Branch NAACP; vice moderator Berean Dist Assn; bd trustee Am Bapt Sem & Western Bapt Coll; mem Urban League;Ministers Union St Louis. **Honors/Awds:** Minister Yr Berean Mem Nat Bapt Educ Congress; Pastors Div Nat-Bapt Inc Educ Congress Dist Assn 1970; 100 Club St Louis NAACP. **Military Serv:** USN 1943-46. **Business Addr:** 3121 St Louis Ave, St Louis, MO 63106.

HUNTER, WILLIAM L.
Educator. **Personal:** Born May 1, 1936, Spartenburg, SC; died Apr 4, 1996; married Patricia Jenkins; children: Kerri (deceased), Deidra (deceased). **Educ:** Central State Univ OH, BS (cum laude) 1959; Kent St Univ, MEd 1968. **Career:** Canton City school, teacher, coach 1959-67, guidance counselor, 1967-69, principal 1969-73, exec principal 1973-76, dir of human relations 1976-78, dir of personnel 1978-93, exec dir of human resources, 1993-96. **Orgs:** Treasurer, Canton Classroom Teachers Assn, 1965-66; chrmn mem Canton Civil Srvc Comm 1969-83;trustee Faith United Christian Church 1970-96; supreme council Omega Psi Phi Fraternity, Inc 1974-77; trustee Natl Urban League, Inc 1977-80; exec comm & vice pres United Way of Central Stark County 1980-90; chmn guidance advisory bd Ohio Dept of Educ 1980-81; American Assoc of School Personnel Administrators, exec bd, 1991-94; chmn, Pro Football Hall of Fame, Security Commission, 1986-89, Festival Security Comm 1986-89, Breakfast Comm, 1990-91, Festival Communications Comm,1991; Festival Volunteer Party Committee, chairman, 1994-95; Sigma Phi Boule; Sigma Pi Phi Fraternity. **Honors/Awds:** Omega Citizen of Yr Omega Psi Phi 4th Dist 1973; Omega Man of Yr Omega Psi Phi 4th Dist 1974; Educ of Yr Canton Black, Hist Comm 1978; Business Assoc of Yr Am Business Wmns Assoc Canton Chptr 1980; United Way Volunteer of the Year "Gold Key" Award 1985; Stark County-Community Action Agency Service Award, 1988; Dist Service Award, Amer Assoc of School Personnel Administration, 1994. **Business Addr:** Exec Dir of HumanResources, Canton City Schools, 617 McKinley Ave SW, Canton, OH 44707.

HUTSON, JEAN BLACKWELL.
Librarian (retired). **Personal:** Born Sep 7, 1914, Summerfield, FL; died Feb 4, 1998, New York, NY; daughter of Sarah Myers Blackwell and Paul Blackwell; married John Hutson, Jun 3, 1950 (deceased); children: Jean Frances (deceased). **Educ:** BarnardColl NY, BA 1935; Columbia Schl of Library Serv, BS 1936; King Mem Coll SC, LBD1976. **Career:** Schomburg Ctr for Rsrch in Blck Culture, curator & chief1948-80; City Coll of New York, adjunct prof 1960-72; Univ of Ghana West Africa,

asst librarian 1964-65; Research Libraries NY Public Library, asst dir collection management and development 1980-84. **Orgs:** Pres Harlem Cultural Council 1965-70 1984-, 1st vice pres 1971-83; mem Arts & Lttrs Comm Delta Sigma Theta Sor 1972-; mem bd of Dirs Martin Luther King Ctr 1973-; vice chairman, board of directors, Central Harlem Meals on Wheels, 1984-. **Honors/Awds:** Publications, Harlem Cultural Hist Metropolitan Museum 1969; Schomburg Ctr Encyclopedia of Library & Info Sci 1978. **Special Achievements:** Significant contributions to the establishment and growth of the Schomburg Center, New York Public Library, 1984; Distinguished Alumnae Barnard College, 1990. **Home Addr:** 2255 5th Ave #8F, New York, NY 10037.

JOHNSON, BEULAH C.
Educator (retired). **Personal:** Born Feb 25, 1909, Winston-Salem, NC; died Jul 7, 1995; daughter of Minnie Mary Feemster Crosby and Richard David Crosby; married James A Johnson, Sep 26, 1930 (deceased); children: Jacquelyne J Jackson, Jeanne J Penn, Viola E. **Educ:** Shaw Univ Raleigh, AB 1930; Tuskegee Inst Al, MEd 1957. **Career:** Tuskegee Inst AL, teacher 1938-65, 1968-74 retired. **Orgs:** Dir Macon Cty Comm Act Comm Inc 1964-68; pres Classroom Teachers Macon Cty, Macon Cty Ed Assoc 1971-73; treas ASTACT; mem Coalit for Imp Ed in AL; mem NEA, AEA; life mem, vice pres Tuskegee Civic Assoc; vice pres NAACP; sec AL State Chapt; chtr mem, sec AL Dem Conf Inc; sec, bd mem Stward Bd Wash Chpl AME Church; sec Lewis Adams Chap OES; chmn Pensions & Security Bd of Macon Cty 1974-95; mem Amer Assoc Univ Women, Kappa Sil, Phi Delta Kappa; bd dir Macon Cty Comm Act Comm Inc. **Honors/Awds:** Plaque for Contribs in Community Serv Tuskegee Chap Links 1981; Serv Awd for Unselfish Contribsto Comm at the 50th Southeast Reg Conf of Alpha Kappa Alpha 1982; Cert of Honorfor Outstanding Serv & Contribs to Comm Serv 1983; Citizens Awd in Recognition of the Acts of Public Serv to Humanity by Tuskegee Inst 1977; Cert of Merit & Appreciation for Meritorious & Faithful Serv to Your Comm County State & Nation byAL Dem Conf Inc 1977; Delta Sigma Theta Sorority Inc, Tuskegee Al, Certificate of Honor for Outstanding Service and Contribution to Community Service, 1983; Recognized by Zeta Phi Beta Inc, Alpha Xi Zeta Chapter; Recognized by Region IV for Service in Macon County, Al; Proclamation from City of Tuskegee, Johnny Ford, Mayor; Resolution from governing body of Tuskegee, Al, Honorey Tuskegee Civic Association in 1989 for more than 48 years of service to community and to the state of Alabama; Meritorius Award for Distinguished Achievement, Lewis Adams School, Lifus Johnson, principal, 1981.

JOHNSON, ED F.
Clergyman. **Personal:** Born Mar 8, 1937, Swansea, SC; died Nov20, 1997; son of Sallie Gray and O'Neal Johnson; married Wilma Williams; children: Juanzena, Edward Franklin Jr. **Educ:** Benedict Coll, AB 1965; ClemsonUniv, attended 1970-71; Univ of SC, attended 1971-72; Benedict Coll, Doctor of Divinity 1984. **Career:** Zion Hill Baptist Church, pastor 1962-66; Hall Hill Baptist Church, pastor 1963-66; Jerusalem Branch Baptist Church, pastor 1965; Bethlehem Baptist Church, pastor 1965-69; Morris Chapel Baptist Church, pastor1969-97; Greenwood-Ninety Six NAACP, pres 1971-76; Connie Maxwell Children's Home Greenwood, SC, social worker 1972-97; Baptist E&M Convention, vp. **Orgs:** Life mem Natl Assoc for the Advancement of Colored People; chmn Bd of Dir GLEAAMS HRC; teacher John G Richards School for Boys 1969, Saluda Cty School Dist High School 1966-71; social worker Connie Maxwell Children's Home 1972; bd of visitors Piedmont Technical Coll; bd mem of the Natl Baptist Conv of Amer; moderator of Little River Baptist Assn 6 years, pres Sunday School Congress 6 years, vice moderator 4 years; pres and vice pres, Baptist Edu and Missionary Convention of SC. **Honors/Awds:** Cert of Appreciation Med Univ of SC 1983; honorary doctorates from Benedict College, Columbia SC, and Morris College, Sumter SC. **Military Serv:** AUS spec 3 3 yrs. **Business Addr:** 1315 Bunche Ave,Greenwood, SC 29646.

JOHNSON, LYMAN T. (L.T)
Educator. **Personal:** Born in Columbia, TN; died Oct 3, 1997, Louisville, KY; married Juanita (deceased); children: Lyman Morrell. **Educ:**Virginia Union University, bachelors; University of Michigan, masters; University of Kentucky, 1949. **Career:** Central High School, teacher; Louisville Public Schools, principal; Jefferson County School Board. **Orgs:** NAACP, president, Louisville branch. **Special Achievements:** Helped integrate University of Kentucky, 1949.

JOHNSON, VAUGHN ARZAH.
Clergyman. **Personal:** Born Nov 22, 1951, Crisfield, MD; died Feb 5, 1994; son of Doris Jackson Johnson and Vaughn W Johnson; married Deborah Y Jarrett Johnson, Aug 18, 1973; children: Thomas, Kenneth, Jonathan. **Educ:** Univ of MD Eastern Shore, BA 1973; Gammon-Interdenominational Theol Center, MDiv 1976; NY Theol Sem, grad study. **Career:** Metro UMC, sr minister 1976-84; Ebenezer UMC, sr minister 1976-84; Univ of MD, campus minister 1976-84;Peninsula Conf United Methodist Church, associate council dir for ethnic minority minister beginning 1984; Wesley Temple United Methodist Church, pastor. **Orgs:** Pres of bd Headstart 1977-79; bd mem Shore Up 1980-82; founder & pres Black Ministerial Fellowship 1982-84. **Honors/Awds:** Crusade Scholar United Methodist Church 1973-75; Outstanding Achievement in Community Omega Psi Phi 1979; Chancellor's Awd Univ of MD 1980; Evangelism Awd Whatcoat UMC 1986; MartinLuther King Jr Award, Peninsula Conference United Methodist Church, 1990; Ministry 2000 Award. **Business Addr:** Minister, Wesley Temple United MethodistChurch, 1322 West Rd., Salisbury, MD 21801.

JOHNSON, WILLIAM HENRY.
Surgeon. **Personal:** Born Jul 8, 1926, Rosedale, KS; died Aug 23, 1995; son of Imogene Banks Johnson and William H Johnson;married Betty J Davis Johnson, 1970; children: nine. **Educ:** Kansas University, BS, zoology, 1949; Creighton Medical School, MD, 1955. **Career:** Private practice, general surgery & primary care, 1960-95. **Orgs:** American Board of Surgery, diplomate, 1962; American College of Surgery, fellow, 1968;Kappa Alpha Psi, 1947; Frontiers International, local club Omaha president, 7thdistrict director; Boys Club of America, board, 1976-95; Serra Club of Omaha, 1985; American Medical Assn; Nebr Medical Association, 1960-95; National Medical Association, 1960-95. **Military Serv:** US Army, m/sgt, 1945-47. **Business Addr:** General Surgeon, Johnson Medical Bldg, 2912 Manderson St, Omaha, NE 68111, (402)451-4510.

KENNARD, ROBERT ALEXANDER.
Architect. **Personal:** Born Sep 18, 1920, Los Angeles, CA; died Mar 24, 1995; son of Marie Louise Bryan and James Louis Kennard; married Helen Zellena King, Sep 4, 1949; children: Gail Marie, Lydia Helen, William Earl. **Educ:** Univ of Southern CA, Los Angeles, CA, BArch, 1949. **Career:** Richard Neutra/Robert Alexander, Los Angeles, CA, proj arch, 1949-51; Daniel Mann Johnson Mendenhall, Los Angeles, CA, proj mgr, 1952-54; Victor Gruen Assoc, Los Angeles, CA, proj mgr, 1954-57; Kennard Design Group, Los Angeles, CA, principal, 1957-95. **Orgs:** Bd mem, Central City Federation, 1966-78; bd mem, vp, Fraternity of Friends, Music Ctr, 1973-79; bd mem, American Red Cross, 1982-86; bd mem, Univ of Southern CA, Arch Guild, 1988-91; adv panel, Mayors Design Adv Panel, 1989-95. **Honors/Awds:** Whitney Young Citation, Amer Inst of Architects, 1991; Distinguished Alumnus, Univ of Southern CA, Architecture, 1991; College of Fellows, Amer Inst of Architects, 1986; Fellow, Inst for Advancement of Engineering, 1988; Act-So Award, NAACP, 1988. **Military Serv:** Corps of Engineers, 2nd Lt, 1942-46, 1950-51. **Business Addr:** Architect, Kennard Design Group, 3600 Wilshire Blvd, Ste 1820, Los Angeles, CA 90010.

KILGORE, THOMAS, JR.
Clergyman. **Personal:**Born Feb 20, 1913, Woodruff, SC; died Feb 4, 1998, Los Angeles, CA; married Jeanetta; children: Lynn Elda, Jini Medina. **Educ:** Morehouse Coll, AB 1935;Union Theol Sem, BD 1957. **Career:** Second Bapt Ch Los Angeles, sr pastor, retired 1985, pastor emeritus, 1985-98. **Orgs:** First black pres Am Bapt Conv 1971. **Honors/Awds:** Recipient honorary degrees from Shaw Univ 1956; & Morehouse Coll 1963; & Univ of So CA & VA Union Univ 1972. **Home Addr:** 1238 Westchester Place, Los Angeles, CA 90019.

KIMBROUGH, DAVID. (JUNIOR)
Musician. **Personal:** Born 1930; died Jan 17, 1998, Holly Springs, MS; children: Addie Boga, Patricia Hawthorne, Effie Gray, Shirley Richmond, Kent Malone, Robert Malone, Larry Washington, Rev. Larry Kimbrough. **Career:** Musician, first recorded in 1968 with the Philwood label; High Water Records; featured in documentary, Deep Blues, 1992; Recorded for the Fat Possum label, three albums. **Home Addr:** 007400.

LANDRY, LAWRENCE ALOYSIUS.
Research sociologist. **Personal:** Born Jun 21, 1935, Chicago, IL; died Jun 2, 1997; son of Evelyn M Martin Landry (deceased) and Oliver L Landry (deceased); married S Dolores Branche; children: Jennifer E, Michael H. **Educ:** Univ of Chicago, BA 1958, MA 1960. **Career:** ACT, chmn 1964-68; The BLK Group, vice pres 1969-71; Howard Univ, lecturer 1971-79; Associate Consultants Inc, pres 1971-97. **Orgs:** Co-chmn Chicago Friends of SNCC 1962-64; co-chmn Chicago Comm March on Washington 1963; chmn Chicago Sch Boycott Comm 1963-64; mem bd of dirs PUSH Intl Trade Bureau 1984-97; chairman, metropolitan area, Natl Rainbow Coalition1986 chairman, Wage-Hour Board, District of Columbia, 1989-91. **Honors/Awds:** Ford Foundation Fellow, The Univ of Chicago 1959-60; Outstanding Public Service Award, Black President's Roundtable, 1990; Reclaim Our Youth, Citizen Education Fund, Outstanding Public Service Award, 1996. **Home Addr:** 2936 Davenport St NW, Washington, DC 20008. **Business Addr:** President, AssociateConsultants, Inc, 1818 N Street NW Ste 405, Washington, DC 20036.

LARRIE, REGINALD REESE.
Educator, author. **Personal:** Born Sep 5, 1928, Detroit, MI; died Jun 21, 1997, Detroit, MI; son of Dora Rawlins Larrie and Robert Reese Larrie, Jr; married Margaret Price; children: Debra, Reginald, Jr, Raymond. **Educ:** Upper Iowa Univ, BA, 1979; Marygrove Coll, MEd, 1982, Pacific Western Univ, PhD, 1988. **Career:** Michigan Chronicle, auto writer, 1964-97; African Americans on Wheels, auto writer, 1996-97; Wayne County Community Coll, Detroit, MI, instructor, 1969-97; Black Sports Magazine, auto editor, 1973-75; Wayne State Univ, Detroit, MI, prof, 1976. **Orgs:** Comm mem 1969-97, New Detroit; mem 1969-97, Museum of African Amer History; mem 1970-97, Assoc for the Study of African Amer History; mem, 1975-97, Detroit Historical Soc; mem, Detroit Triumph Club. **Honors/Awds:** 15 years award, Commissioner, Boy Scouts of Amer, 1970; New Detroit Dedicated Service Award, 1971; City of Detroit Distinguished Service Award, 1976; Montgomery Ward Bicentennial Award, 1979; author of Corners of Black History, 1971, "Swing Low,Sweet Chariot," Black Experiences in Michigan History, 1975, Makin' Free, 1981; WXYZ-TV, February, 1973; WDIV-TV, 1990-92. **Business Addr:** Instructor, Wayne County Community College, 801 Fort St., Detroit, MI 48226.

LAWING, RAYMOND QUINTON.
Educator. **Personal:** Born Mar 3, 1910, Chesterfield Co, VA; died May 7, 1982; married Florence Jones; children: 6. **Educ:** VA State Coll, BS 1932; VSC & VPI Blacksburg VA, adavance study; Moody Bible Inst Chicago. **Career:** Appomattox Co, tchrof agriculture educ 1932-82; Appomattox VA, mnister of O local churches 1946-82. **Orgs:** Pres Appomattox Tchrs Assn 15 Yrs; pres E & W Bound SS Union; past moderator Hasadiah Bapt Assn; prs Appomattox Improvement Assn 1939-82; pres elect & pres Appomattox Educ 1971-72; mem Appomattox Educ Assn; mem VA Voc Assn;mem NVATA; mem NEA; mem NEA; pres Appomattox Assembly 1972; mem Appomatox Chap NAACP 1940-82; mem C of C 1970; mem Cancer Society; Hasadiah; Cornrstone Assn; PM Long Mt Lodge 204 F&A Masons; mem Phi Beta Sigma Frat. **Honors/Awds:** Recipient distinguished serv award Local Group 1948; 35-yr plaque VA Voc Agriculture Assn 1967; revere bowl Appomattox Educ Assn 1975.

LEE, HELEN JACKSON.
Social worker (retired). **Personal:** Born Jul 23, 1908, Richmond, VA; died Dec 3, 1997; widowed; children: Barbara Nan, Robert Edward Jr. **Educ:** VA State U, BA 1930. **Career:** NJ Dept of Human Svc, social worker 1971-73; NJ Dept of Human Svc, pub information asst 1967-71, asst supr stenog pool 1965-67, sec fire marshal 1962-65, sr clerk stenog 1947-62; Philadelphia Ed Chicago Defender, feature writer 1936-37; Philadelphia Ind, newspaper reporter 1937-38; Philadelphia Ed Pittsburgh Courier, newspaper reprtr 1938-40. **Orgs:** Historian Epsilon Upsilon Omega Alpha Kappa Alpha Soroity Inc 1985; charter mem Trenton Alumae Chap Epsilon Upsilon Omega; bd mem Central YWCA Trenton NJ; mem Trenton Mus Soc 1985; mem NJ Hist Soc Precious Pearl Award. **Honors/Awds:** Epsilon Upsilon Omega Chap Alpha Kappa Alpha Sorority Inc 1975; Citation for Literary Work Fire II Mag Trenton State Coll 1978; Comm Serv Award Metro Civic League & Bronzettes Inc 1978; Golden Sorority Cert; Alpha Kappa & Alpha Sorority Inc 1978; autobiography "Nigger in the Window" Doubleday & Co NY 1978; Comm Serv Award; Top Ladies of Distinction 1979; Meta A Griffith Service Award, Zonta Internation Club, 1986; cited in Past and Promise-Lives of New Jersey Women, Women's Project of New Jersey, Inc, 1990.

LEE, MICHAEL WARING.
Judge, educator. **Personal:** Born Jan 16, 1953, Baltimore, MD; died Oct 1, 1995; son of Frances Wilson Lee and Thomas M Lee. **Educ:** Johns Hopkins Univ, 1973; Macalester Coll, BA, 1975; Univ of Maryland, JD, 1978. **Career:** Univ of Maryland-School of Law, teaching & research asst, 1976-78, prof, 1987-95; Circuit Court for Baltimore City, law clerk baliff, 1978-79; Baltimore City Law Dept, asst solicitor, 1979-81; Mitchell Mitchell & Mitchell PA, managing atty, 1981-83; CoppinState Coll, asst prof of mgmt science, 1985; Univ of Baltimore School of Law, asst prof, 1985-87; University of Maryland School of Law, asst prof, 1987-95; Orphans Court of Baltimore City, chief judge. **Orgs:** Double bassist St PaulCivil Symphony Orchestra, 1971-75; bd mem, Univ of Maryland Law School Alumni Assoc, 1979-84; pres, Northwestern HS Alumni Assoc, 1980-84. **Honors/Awds:** Outstanding Young Man Jaycees, 1978; distinguished serv, Northwestern High School Alumni Assn, 1982; distinguished alumnus, Black Law Students Assn, Univ of Maryland Chapter, 1985; lecturer, Univ of Baltimore School of Law, 1986-87. **Business Addr:** Chief Judge, Orphans Court of Baltimore Cty, 311 Courthouse East, Baltimore, MD 21202.

LEONARD, WALTER FENNER. (BUCK)
Broker. **Personal:** Born Sep 8, 1907, Rocky Mount, NC;died Nov 27, 1997, Rocky Mount, NC. **Educ:** La Salle Extension U, real estate 1965. **Career:** Real estate broker; truant officer, asst in physical educ elem schs of Rocky Mount 1958-70; Professional baseball player, Negro Leagues, 17 years, Homestead (PA) Grays. **Orgs:** Natl Baseball Hall of Fame 1972-97; NC Sport Hall of Fame 1974-97; vice pres Rocky Mount Leafs Baseball team, Class A league; mem Comm Redevel Commn 1977; mem St James Bapt Ch of Rocky Mount, 32 degree Mason & Shriner. **Honors/Awds:** Baseball Hall of Fame 1972; honored by OIC Rocky Mount 1972; "Good Will" Ambassador of NC 1972; Boy Scouts Hall of Fame 1973; Tar Heel of the Week 1975; Referred to as the Black Lou Gehrig. **Business Addr:** 605 Atlantic Ave, Rocky Mount, NC 27801.

LEWIS, ANNE A.
Educator (retired). **Personal:** Born Apr 6, 1905, Cleveland, OH; died Feb 5, 1997; daughter of Birdie Evalina Boiseau and Arthur William Palmer; married Kenneth Lewis. **Educ:** Univ MI, AB 1930, grad study. **Career:** Juvenile Ct Detroit Pub Welfare US Employment Serv, social worker 1930-45; elem teacher, 1950-62; Detroit Urban League, adminstr asst dir rsch 1962-71 (retired). **Orgs:** Mem Tucson Chap Hospitality Intl; mem Detroit Urban League Guild; mem Univ of MI Alumni Assn;Tucson Art Ctr Leag & Tucson Museum of Art; AZ Sonora Desert Museum; Amer Assn Social Workers; Social Workers' Club of Detroit; mem Alpha Kappa Alpha Sor; YWCA; Original Willing Workers of Detroit; Amer Assn Retired Persons; speaker's bur United Found Torch Dr. **Honors/Awds:** Golden Soror 50 Year Mem Alpha Kappa Alpha.

LEWIS, JAMES EDWARD.
Artist, educator (retired). **Personal:** Born Aug 4, 1923, Phenix, VA; died Aug 6,1997; son of Pearlean Lewis and James T Lewis; married Jacqueline; children: James E Jr, Cathleen Susan. **Educ:** Philadelphia Coll of Art, BFAE 1949; Temple Univ, MFA 1950, Ford Foundation Faculty Fellow 1954; Syracuse Univ; Yale Univ, Ford Found Faculty Fellow 1955. **Career:** Morgan State Univ, dir gallery of art, Henry O Tanner prof of fine arts 1960-97. **Orgs:** Bd mem MD Artists Equity, Balto Council of Foreign Affairs, Orchard St Museum, School #33; pres Lillie Carroll Jackson Museum; chmn Baltimore City Comm for Hist & Archit Presvtn; bd mem Baltimore Counc on Intl visitors; alumni bd Philadelphia Coll of Art. **Honors/Awds:** Commiss Clarence M Mitchell Sculpture Courthouse BldgBalto MD 1985; Black Amer Serviceperson Bronze 9 1/2' Balto MD 1974; gallery renamed, James E Lewis Museum of Art, honor of forty-one years of contribution to the arts program, Morgan State University, 1990. **Military Serv:** USMC, Cpl, 3 yrs. **Home Addr:** 5011 Herring Run Dr, Baltimore, MD 21214.

LEWIS, SYLVIA AUSTIN.
Educational administrator (retired). **Personal:** Born Apr 8, 1921, Meredian, OK; died Mar 7, 1995; daughter of Viola Amanda Lewis Austin and Joseph H Austin; married Davis C Lewis Sr; children: David C Jr, Sanestelle. **Educ:** Langston Univ, BA 1942;Univ of Omaha, Grad Study 1954; Univ of OK, MEd 1959. **Career:** Ponca City, teacher 1942-51; Oklahoma City Schools, spec ed teacher 1954-67; OK City Schools, principal, curriculum spec 1954-67; Oppty Indust Ctrs, training adv 1967-74; Langston Univ, dean for student devel 1974-82; Dir Langston Univ Okla City Urban Ctr, 1982-85. **Orgs:** Vchmn State Conf Intl Womens Year Conf 1977; del-at-large Intl Womens Year Conf Houston 1977; mem ACLU State Bd OK Humanities Com 1979; consult Manpower Trng; mem NAACP, Urban League, United Nations Conf of Women 1979; 1986 Brd of Regents, Univ of Oklahoma; vice chairman, Univ of Oklahoma Board of Regents, 1991-92. **Honors/Awds:** Citation of Congratulations OK State Senate for Comm Serv 1971; Meritorious Awd YWCA 1979; 1986 Distinguished Zeta Awd; Natl office Zeta Phi Beta; Afro-American Hall of Fame, Oklahoma NTU Art Assn 1988. **Home Addr:** 2205 N Hood St, Oklahoma City, OK 73111.

LITTLETON, RALPH DOUGLASS.
Educational administrator (retired), government official. **Personal:** Born Nov 24, 1908,Bryan, TX; died Dec 3, 1995; son of Mabel Stubbs Littleton and R H Littleton; married Vergie Daizolu Hinton (deceased). **Educ:** Bishop Coll, BA 1930; Univ of No CO, MA 1948; Univ of CA, Post Grad 1960; Univ of USC, Post Grad 1964. **Career:** Brazos Cty Schools TX, principal 1934-43; John M Moore Elem School, principal 1943-48; Booker T Washington School, principal 1948-74; Governor'sPolicymaking board for the Aging, mem, 1991-95. **Orgs:** Pres Hobbs Teachers Assoc 1965; employment counselor NM State Employment Hobbs 1975-81; pres Chaporral Kiwanis Club 1978; lt gov Kiwanis Southwest Dist Div III 1985; vice pres Hobbs School Bd 1985. **Honors/Awds:** Hall of Fame Southeastern Ed Assoc of NM 1975; Hall of Fame Bishop Coll Dallas TX 1976. **Home Addr:** 703 S Jefferson St, Hobbs, NM 88240.

MANLEY, ALBERT EDWARD.
Former college president. **Personal:** Born Jan 3, 1908, SanPedro Sula, Honduras; died Mar 28, 1997, Montego Bay, Jamaica; married Audrey Elaine Forbes. **Educ:** Johnson C Smith Univ, BS 1930; Columbia Univ Teachers Coll, MA 1938; Univ Chicago, student 1942; Stanford Univ, EdD 1946; Johnson CSmith Univ, LLD 1966; Spelman Coll, LHD 1981. **Career:** Stephens-Lee High School Asheville NC, teacher 1931-34, principle 1935-41; Negro High Schools NC, supr 1941-45; Coll Arts & Sci, dean; NC Coll Durham, prof educ 1946-53; SchoolBus Mgmt Harvard Univ, guest lectr summers 1970-75, Univ WA 1976, Center Urban Educ Univ No IA 1980; Spelman Coll Atlanta, pres 1953-76, pres emeritus. **Orgs:** Mem NC Commn Interracial Coop 1941-49; mem GA Commn Interracial Coop; pres NC Coll Conf 1950; chmn council of pres Atlanta Univ Center, Univ Center in GA; mem natl adv comm on black higher educ Dept of Educ 1979-87; bd dir United Negro Coll Fund, Atlanta High Mus Art; bd dir, trustee MartinLuther King Jr CenterNon-Violent Social Change 1968-; trustee Atlanta Univ; chmn comm Disting Calloway Profs; mem NEA, Amer Teachers Assn, Intl Platform Assn, Phi Delta Kappa, Omega Psi Phi. **Honors/Awds:** Contrib articles to educ journals; Recipient Alumni Citation Johnson C Smith Univ 1950. **Home Addr:** 2807 18th St NW, Washington, DC 20009.

MAXEY, CARL.
Attorney. **Personal:** Born Jun 23, 1924, Tacoma, WA; died Jul 17, 1997, Spokane, WA; married Merrie Lou Douglas; children: William C, Bevan J. **Educ:** Univ of OR, BS 1948; Gonzaga Univ Spokane WA, LLB 1951. **Career:** Fredrickson Maxey Bell & Stiley PS, atty 1960; Domestic Rel Gonzaga Univ Sch of Law, tchr 1972-76; attorney. **Orgs:** Bar adm Wash & US Dist Ct 1951; chmn Pres Appointment Wash St Adv Com to US Commn on Civil Rights 1963-78; Speedy Trial ActPlanning Com US Dist Ct 1978; mem Spokane Co Bar Assn; past mem Judicial Selection Com; Judicial Liaison Com bar adm US Ct of Appeals; mem past chmn WA St Bar Assn; Criminal Law Sec Com; mem past sire archon Alpha Omicron Boul 1979; member, past president, NAACP Spokane WA Chapter 1991; Loren Miller Bar Association, 1988. **Honors/Awds:** Baynard Rustin Civil Rights Award, 1990; William O Douglas Bill of Rights Award, 1982; African-American Forum, Best Criminal Lawyer, 1990; Charles A Goldmark Award, 1988; Gonzaga Univ, School of Law, Law Medal, 1993; Keep the Dream Alive Award, Washington State Univ, 1993; Martindale-Hubbell,Bar Register of Preeminent Lawyers, 1993. **Business Addr:** W 1835 Broadway, Spokane, WA 99201.

MCCALL, LOUIS.
Musician. **Personal:** Born 1952?; died 1997, Stone Mountain, GA. **Career:** Musician. **Special Achievements:** Cofounder and drummer of group Con Funk Shun; singles include: ''Ffun'', 1971, ''Love Train'', 1982. **Home Addr:** 007450.

MCDANIELS, JOHN EDWARD, SR.
Educational administrator, military officer (retired). **Personal:** Born Feb 23, 1921, Monmouth, IL; died Apr 14, 1995; son of Helen Lucas McDaniels and John Martin McDaniels; married Margaret Currie; children: Charles Patterson, Erma Patterson, Sarah P Thomas, Jeffrey, John E Jr. **Educ:** Armed Forces Staff Coll, diploma 1968; Hampton Inst, BS History 1970; US Army-War Coll, diploma 1974; Central MI Univ, MA Admin 1976. **Career:** US Army, col 36 yrs; Fayetteville Tech Inst, admin asst to pres, vice pres for personnel. **Orgs:** Post commander Ft Lesley J McNair 1972-76; vice pres Joe BarrUnited Serv Organ 1978-79; mem Omega Psi Phi Frat Inc Beta Chi Chap 1980; SERTOMA International 1989. **Military Serv:** AUS col field artillery 36 yrs; Legion of Merit; Bronze Star; various combat and serv awds.

MCDOWELL, CLEVE.
Attorney, judge, city offical. **Personal:** Born Aug 6, 1941, Drew, MS; died Mar 13, 1997, Drew, MS; son of Ozett McDowell and Fudge McDowell. **Educ:** Jackson State Univ, 1963; Univ of Mississippi Law School, 1963; Texas Southern Univ Law School, JD. **Career:** Cook County Dept of Public Aid, staff consultant 1965-69; Coahoma Opportunity Inc, personnel dir 1969; Mississippi Head Start Training Coord Council, exec dir 1969-73; State of Mississippi, head start coord 1973-74; Mississippi Bar Legal Serv, assoc dir 1974-75; private practice, attny 1975-77; Clarksdale Office of Northern Mississippi Rural Legal Serv, managing atty 1977-79; Tunica County, judge; State Exec Field Dir of Mississippi NAACP 1985-87; Vice Mayor City of Drew MS 1986-97. **Orgs:** Mem NAACP; former pres Delta Phi Chap Alpha Phi Alpha; memMississippi State Penitentiary Bd of Dir 1971-76. **Business Addr:** Attorney-at-Law, Box 223, Drew, MS 38737.

MCKISSACK, WILLIAM DEBERRY.
Architect. **Personal:** Born Aug 29, 1925, Nashville, TN; died Feb 28, 1988; married Leatrice Harritt Buchanan; children: Andrea Franklin, Cheryl Joan, Deryl Kaye. **Educ:** Howard U, BArch 1951. **Career:** McKissack & McKissack Arch & Engrs Inc Nashivlle, 1951-88; McKissack & McKissack Arch & Engrs Inc, pres 1968-88; McKissack & McKissack Arch & Engrs chmn bd dir 1968-88; TN State Univ Nashville, instr gust lectr 1959-61. **Orgs:** Mem Nat Council of Registration Bds AIA; Nat Tech Assn; pres chmn bd dir Coll Hill Realty Co Nashville 1968-88; mem Frontiers of Am; Sigma Pi Phi; Omega Si Phi. **Military Serv:** USNR 1943-46. **Business Addr:** Morris MemlBldg, Nashville, TN 37201.

MILBURN, RODNEY.
Olympic athlete. **Personal:** Born May 18, 1950, Opelousas, LA; diedNov 11, 1997, Port Hudson, LA; married; children: three. **Career:** Trackand field athleted; Southern University, track coach until 1983; Georgia Pacific Paper Plant, loader, nine years. **Honors/Awds:** Olympic Gold Medalist, track and field, Munich, 1972.

MILLER, LUVENIA C.
Biological photographer. **Personal:** Born Sep 14, 1909, Eden,NC; died Sep 6, 1997. **Educ:** Hampton Inst, BS 1934; NY Isnt of Photog, Cert 1939; Army Air Field Photo Lab, Cert 1945; Progressive Sch of Photog, Cert 1949. **Career:** Army Forces Inst of Pathology Med Illustration, chief of gross photography 1951-75; H Ec Gram Sch Greensboro NC, instr 1934-42. **Orgs:** Mem Biolog Photog Assn Inc 1961-74, dir 1973-76; bd mem Vol Serv DC Gen Hosp 1970-74; mem Methodist Women 1950-74; mem NAACP 1950-74; Hampton Inst Alumni Assn 1945-74. **Honors/Awds:** Recip of 25 awards- Biolog Photog Assn Inc 1958-72; Am Mus of Nat Hist 1964; Defense Superior Perform 1965-72; Ladybird Johnson's Beautification Award ''Lawn Ranger'' Proj 1966; Chpn Beautification Com River Terr Wash DC 1967-70; Commend Vol Serv DC Gen Hosp 1972; 1st black woman in following- registered photog NC 1943; pub relations photog USAAF 1943-45; med photog Armed Forces Inst of Pathol Assn 1972; dir Biological Photog Assn Inc1973-76. **Home Addr:** 134 33 St NE, Washington, DC 20019.

MOORE, QUEEN MOTHER. (AUDLEY ELOISE)
Civil Rights activist. **Personal:** Born in New Iberia, LA; died May 2, 1997, Brooklyn, NY; married Frank Warner (died 1967); children: Thomas O. Warner. **Career:** Hair stylist. **Orgs:** Universal Negro Improvement Organization; National Coalition of Blacks for Reparations in America. **Honors/Awds:** Corcoran Gallery of Art, honoree, part of exhibit, I Dream A World, 1989. **Special Achievements:** Among black leaders of 1960s demanding reparations of US government; staged sit-in at Brooklyn Bd of Education meeting, 1966; National Coalition of Blacks For Reparations in America Conference, speaker, 1994.

MOORE, UNDINE SMITH.
Educator, composer, lecturer. **Personal:** Born Aug 25, 1904, Jarratt, VA; died Feb 6, 1989; married Dr James Arthur. **Educ:** Mus Sch Fisk U, AB 1st in class & honors 1926; Mus Tchr's Coll Columbia U, MA 1931; Howard Murphy, pvt study; Honoris Causa VA State Coll, MusD1972; Honoris Causa IN, U, MusD 1976. **Career:** VA State CollPetersburg, ret prof mus 1927-72; Richmond Comm Sch for Gifted, scholar in residence 1978; VA State Coll, artist in residence 1976; VA Unoin U, adj prof 1972-77; Coll of St Benedict St Joseph MN, vis prof 1973-75; Carleton Coll Northfield MN, vis prof 1972; Goldsboro NC, mus supr pub 1926. **Orgs:** Co-founder Black Mus Center VA State Coll 1968; mus consult Arts Educ State of VA 1978; sr adv Afro-Am Arts Inst of IN U; mem John Work Meml Found;mem ASCAP; mem women's comRichmond Symphony Orchestra 1978; mem Mus Educators Nat Conf; mem Alpha Kappa Alpha; mem Gillfield Bapt Ch. **Honors/Awds:** Recipient fine arts awards Fisk U, Atlanta U, VA Union U, VA State U, Norfolk State Coll, Nat Assn Negro Musicians, Huston-Tillotson, Morgan State U; cert of appreciation City of NY by Mayor John Lindsay; cert Mayor Arnold Petersburg VA; mus laureate VA 1977; lectr composer NY Philarmonic Celebration of Black Composers 1977; contributing author ''The Black Composer Speaks'' Scare Crow Press; pub ''Reflections on Afro-Am Mus'' Kent State Univ Press; recipient first Juilliard scholarship in piano Fisk U; choral compositions pub Warner Bros; Augsburg Mus Home; documentary IN Univ Black Artists Series. **Home Addr:** 800 St Olaf Ave, Northfield, MN55057.

MOSLEY, LAWRENCE EDWARD, SR.
Clergyman. **Personal:** Born Nov 7, 1953, Lynchburg, VA; died Jul 17, 1997;son of Grace T Mosley and Earl F Mosley Sr; married Tricia Mosley; children: Lawrence Jr, Tiffany. **Educ:** Lynchburg Coll, BA 1976; VA Union Univ, MDiv 1980. **Career:** Second Baptist Church, asst to pastor 1979-80; Rising Mt Zion Bapt Ch, pastor 1980-85; Westbrook Hosp, intake counselor 1983-85; LilydaleProgressive MB Church, pastor 1985-97. **Orgs:** Mem Chicago Chap VUU Alumni 1985-97, Greater New Era Dist Assn Chicago 1985-97, Baptist Genl State Convention of IL 1985-97, Natl Baptist Convention USA Inc 1985-97, Black on Black LoveInc 1986; bd mem 111th St YMCA Chicago 1986-97. **Honors/Awds:** Communityof Scholars VA Union Univ 1972; Scholarship Awd Blue Key Honor Frat; Outstanding Young Men of Amer Jaycees 1982. **Business Addr:** Pastor, Lilydale Progressive MB Church, 10706 S Michigan Ave, Chicago, IL 60628.

MOSS, CARLTON.
Filmmaker. **Personal:** Died Aug 15, 1997, Los Angeles, CA; widowed. **Educ:** Morgan State University, Baltimore.**Career:** Formed traveling troupe, ''Toward A Black Theater''; NBC, radio, writer; Works Projects Administration, Federal Theater; Lafayette Theater, chief asst; filmmaker; Fisk University, guest lecturer; Univ of CA-Irvine, professor. **Special Achievements:** Made many industrial movies, training films, schoolroom documentaries, including: ''Happy Teeth, Healthy Smile'',''The Negro Soldier'', 1943. **Home Addr:** 003400.

NABRIT, JAMES M., JR.
Educational administrator, attorney (retired). **Personal:** Born Sep 4, 1900, Atlanta, GA; died Dec 27, 1997, Washington, DC; married Norma Walton (deceased); children: James M Nabrit, III. **Educ:** Morehouse Coll, BA 1923; Northwestern U, JD 1927. **Career:** Leland Coll, instr 1925-28; AR State Coll, dean 1928-30; Howard Univ School of Law, faculty, 1936-60; Howard Univ, dean, administrative asst to the president, 1938-39, president, 1960-69, president emeritus; attorney, 1936-60.

Orgs: Apptd by Pres Johnson to US Dep Rep to UN 1965-67; mem numerous pub servcouncils & coms; mem bd Nat Center for Educ in Politics; Washington Ctr for MetStudies; adv council Nat Fund for Med Edn; mem Commn on Professional & Grad Study Assn of Am Colls; mem NEA; Legal Adv Com Nat Soc for Med Research; mem Am NatTX Bar Assns; Am Juridical Soc; Nat Lawyers Club; Nat Legal Com NAACP, Education Fund, dir emeritus NAACP Legal Defense & Education Fund, Inc. **Honors/Awds:** Numerous honorary degrees, other awards, & honors. **Home Addr:** 7211 16 St NW, Washington, DC 20012.

NEAL, JAMES P.,SR.
Cleric. **Personal:** Died 1997, Columbia, SC; married Geneva Outten Neal; children: James P III, Albert A. **Educ:** Morris Coll, Sumter, SC, 1930; Fisk Univ; South Carolina State Univ; Metaphysical Coll of Divinity, Indianapolis, IN, DDiv, 1957. **Career:** Teacher; principal; Antioch Baptist Church, pastor. **Orgs:** Baptist Educational and Missionary Convention of SC, affiliate minister. **Honors/Awds:** Morris College, Distinguished Alumnus Award, 1983. **Home Addr:** 002650.

NICHOLS, LEROY.
Association executive. **Personal:** Born Jan24, 1924, E Chicago, IN; died Oct 12, 1995; married Luella; children: Joanne, LeRoy, III, Gregory, Patty Sue, Cynthia, Kristopher, Michelle Denise. **Educ:** Baker Bus U, 1946; Mott Comm Coll, 1948-50; Univ MI, 1967; GM Inst, cert Estate Selling Methods, Real Estate Selling Methods 1970-71; Univ MI, Univ MI, Flint, cert Mgmt Mgrs 1972. **Career:** Buick Motor Div, prodn worker 1942-44; Chev Motor Div, machine operator 1946; Genesee Co Comm Action Agy, organizer/EOO1970; Genesee Co, bd supr 1964-68; Flint, MI, bd review 1968-69. **Orgs:**Flint Transp Authority 1969; Legal Aid Soc 1969; BSA bd dir 1970; mA Transp Authority chmn 1971; dist committeeman, Buick Motor 1944; chmn UAW, Civil Rights Comm 1955; chmn UAW Political Action Comm 1957; trustee Chev Local 659 1961; delegate UAW Conv CA 1966; delegate UAW Conv Detroit 1967; charter revision commr v chmn 1973; bd supr genesee co admin bldg, youth crime referral prog, bishop airport consol, new Mem McFarlen Park, Youth Summer Job Prog; Flint Youth Bureau; Urban League; Genesee Co Historical Soc; Comm Civic League; Bruin Club; YMCA Adv Comm; past Master John W StevensonLodge 56; F & AM Oman Temple No 72 Shriners, past potentate; NAACP; Mott Comm Coll Alumni; grand treas MWPH Grand Lodge MI; Imperial Auditor AEAONMS; Prince Hall Shriners, Mason 33 deg. **Military Serv:** AUS 1943-44. **Business Addr:** Executive Dir, Genesee County CAA, 601 S Saginaw St, Ste 301, Flint, MI 48505.

NORMAN, MAIDIE RUTH.
Actress, educator. **Personal:** Born Oct 16, 1912, Villa Rica, GA; died May 2, 1998, San Jose, CA; daughter of Lila Gamble and Louis Gamble; children: McHenry Norman III. **Educ:** Bennett Coll, BA 1934; Columbia Univ, MA 1937; Actors Lab Hollywood, 1946-49. **Career:** Actress in radio, TV, motion pictures & stage since 1946; TX State Coll Tyler, TX, instr summers 1955-56; Stanford Univ Palo Alto, CA, artist in residence 1968-69; Univ CA at LA, lecturer, dir, acting tchr 1970-77; retired tchr. **Orgs:** Mem StateBd CA Educ Theater Assn 1969-; mem So CA Educ Theater Assn; co-founder/bd mem ANTA West retired 1967-; mem Actors Equity Assn; AFTRA; mem Screen Actors Guild; mem League of Allied Arts; life mem Actors Fund; pres bd of Stevens House Coop UCLA retired; bd mem LA Contemp Dance Theater; mem Coord Comm 1984 Olympics Arts Festival; mem CA Cncl for the Arts Theater Div. **Honors/Awds:** Disting Serv CA Educ Theater Assn 1985; Black Filmmakers Hall of Fame Oakland, CA 1977; UCLA Chair of Honor upon retirement 1977; Black Student Faculty & Adm Award 1977; The Maidie Norman Award for Outstanding Research by an undergrad in Black Theater is given annually at UCLA; LA Sentinel Woman of the Yr Award 1963; Negro Authors Study Club Civic Serv Award 1957; Bennett Coll Achievement Award 1953; Cabrillo Award Acting Achievement 1952.

NORMENT, HANLEY.
Civil Rights activist. **Personal:** Born in Arkansas; died Jul 10, 1997, Silver Spring, MD; married Christa; children: Camille, Julian. **Educ:** Univ of Arkanasas, grad; Univ of MI, masters, political science. **Career:** US Commission on Civil Rights, civil rights officer, begin 1967; US Dept of Transportation, Office of Civil Rights, dir, until 1996. **Orgs:** NAACP, Montgomery Branch, begin 1960s, dir, 1980, vice pres, pres, 1990-92; NAACP, Maryland State Conference, 1994-, Black Leadership Summit, organizer, 1995-. **Home Addr:** 004000.

O'BRYANT, TILMON BUNCHE.
Law enforcement official. **Personal:** Born Aug 14, 1920, Edgefield, SC; died Jul 24, 1996; son of Annie O'Bryant and Lawrence O'Bryant; married Deidre. **Educ:** Amer Univ, 1967-70; FBI Natl Acad, graduate; Fed City Coll, MEd 1971. **Career:** Gen Acct Office, clerk 1954-57; Washington Technical Inst, teacher Police Admin, conducted promotional examination preparatory classes 1958-63, constructed entire promotional examination for Metropolitan Police Dept 1967; Metro Police Dept, plainclothes officer 1952-57, patrolman 1952-57, detective lieutenant 1960-62; detective captain 1966-68, uniformed captain1968, inspector 1968-69, dept chief of police in command of patrol div 1969, dept chief of police for personnel & training 1970-73, asst chief of police field operations 1973-74, asst chief of police 1974-96. **Orgs:** Chmn Friends for Help for Retarded Children 1962; US Senate Advisory Panel on Armed Violence inUrban Areas 1969; bd of dirs Police & Community Relations Commn, Natl Conf of Christians & Jews 1970; mem Pigskin & Kiwanis Clubs 1971-96; supvr, civic training, dir, bd of dirs Minority Recruiting in Law Enforcement 1974; pres bd of dirs 12th St YMCA; speaker Univ Pennsylvania, Mansfield Coll, Univ Wisconsin, Amer Univ, George Washington Univ, Univ of Miami; civic, business & serv orgs & chs on Modern Concept of Law Enforcement in Urban Soc. **Honors/Awds:** Police Dept Honorary Mention Award 1950; Protective Community Award by Washington Bd of Trade 1966; Washington DC Commr Oral Commendation for Outstanding Police Work 1968; Metropolitan Womens' Democratic Club Man of the Year Award 1971; over 100 letters of commendation from White House, business, religious & civic leaders. **Military Serv:** AUS 1943-45. **Home Addr:** 7948 Orchid St NW, Washington, DC 20012. **Business Addr:** Assistant Chief of Police, Metropolitan Police Dept, 300 Indiana Ave NW, Washington, DC 20001.

PAYTON, LAWRENCE.
Vocalist. **Personal:** Born in Detroit, MI;died Jun 20, 1997, Southfield, MI. **Career:** Vocalist, with group The Four Tops; songwriter. **Honors/Awds:** Rock and Roll Hall of Fame, inducted as Four Tops, 1990; Rhythm-and-Blues Foundation, Pioneer Award, 1997; Hollywood Walk of Fame, star as Four Tops, 1997. **Special Achievements:** Single with the Four Tops include: Baby, I Need Your Loving; I Can't Help Myself; It's TheSame Old Song; Reach Out, I'll Be There; Ain't No Woman Like The One I Got; I Believe In You and Me; solo single: One Woman Man.

PEACOCK, EULACE.
Track athlete, entrepreneur. **Personal:** Born Aug 27, 1914, Dothan, AL; died Dec 13, 1996, Yonkers, NY; married Betty, 1942 (died 1989); children: Linda DiGangi Freundlich, Eulace Clinton. **Educ:** Temple Univ. **Career:** Entrepreneur. **Special Achievements:** Majorrival of Jesse Owens; Amateur Athletic Union National Championship, 100 meter dash, first place, long jump, first place; won six national titles, 1933-45. **Military Serv:** Coast Guard, WWII. **Home Addr:** 008500.

PINSON, THOMAS J.
Educator, surgeon. **Personal:** Born Aug 1, 1927, Vicksburg, MS; died Oct 7, 1993; married Margo Dean; children: Tracey. **Educ:** Wilberforce Univ, BS 1948; Univ MI Coll Dent, MS 1957; Howard Univ Coll Dentistry, DDS 1953. **Career:** Freedman's Hosp Howard Univ Coll Dentistry, asst prof 1957-59, assoc prof 1959-60, prof & head dept oral surg 1960-65, dir clinics 1966-68, assoc dean hosp affairs & dir oral surg 1968-93. **Orgs:** Mem Natl, Amer Dental Assns; Robert T Freeman & DC Dent Socs; Amer Bd Oral Surg; Amer Cancer Soc; Intl Assn Dental Rsch; Amer Soc Oral Surg; mem NAACP, Urban League; Alumni Club Univ MI & Wilberforce Univ. **Honors/Awds:** Alumni Awd for Outstanding Contribution to Dental Educ and Admin 1973; Amer Cancer Soc In Grateful Acknowledgement of Outstanding Serv to the Cause of Cancer Control 1973; The Amer Cancer Society's Harold W Krogh Awd for Outstanding Work in the Control of Oral Cancer 1979; Faculty Recognition Awd for High Quality Instruction Scholarly Endeavors and Serv as Hallmarks of Excellence in Dental Educ 1986. **Business Addr:** Associate Dean Hospital Affair, Howard Univ Hospital, 2041 Georgia Ave NW, Washington, DC 20060.

POOLE, CECIL F.
Judge. **Personal:** Born in Birmingham, AL; died Nov 12, 1997, Kentfield, CA; son of Eva L Poole and William T Poole; married Charlotte Crump, Apr 3, 1942; children: Gayle, Patricia. **Educ:** Univ of MI, LLB; Harvard Univ, LLM 1939. **Career:** Practiced law in San Francisco; former asst dist atty for San Francisco; Gov Brown of CA, clemency sec 1959-61; N Dist of CA, US atty 1961-70; Univ of CA at Berkeley, regents prof of law 1970; Jacobs Sills & Coblents, counsel 1970-76; N Dist of CA, appointed US Dist Judge 1976; US Circuit Ct, circuit judge 9th circuit 1979-97. **Orgs:** Mem Adv Comm to Natl Comm for Reform of Federal Criminal Laws 1968-70; trustee Natl Urban League 1969-75; chmn Section of Individual Rights Amer Bar Assn 1971-72; mem House of Delegates ABA 1972-74; dir Levi Strauss & Co 1972-76; dir NAACP Legal Defense & Educ Fund 1973-76; mem ABA, San Francisco Bar Assn; Black Women Lawyers Assn; CA Assn of Black Lawyers; mem, United Way Agency Relations Council;chair, United Way Regional Admissions Committee; Amer Bar Assn; Langston Bar Assn; Los Angeles County Bar Assn; Los Angeles County Bar Assn Committee on the Status of Minorities in the Profession; Altrusa Club of Pasedena, CA, mem, Bd of Dir; Delta Sigma Theta Sorority; Licnoln Ave Baptist Church, Pasadena CA. **Military Serv:** USAF, Lt 1942-45. **Business Addr:** Judge, US Court of Appeals, PO Box 193939, San Francisco, CA 94119-3939.

POWELL, ROBERT E.
Association executive. **Personal:** Born Jan 31, 1919, Kansas City, KS; died Dec 25, 1995; son of Helen Powell and Manuel Powell; married Della Mae Weaver; children: Peggy Delores. **Educ:** HarvardUniv Bus Sch, 1960. **Career:** Laborers LU 1290, asst bus mgr 1956-59; Laborers' Intl Union of N Amer, 1st vice pres 1961; Mrs JW Jones Meml Chapel Inc; bd of dir pres, Douglass Bank (kck) bd of dir. **Orgs:** Helped set up first Labor Educ Cntr Columbus, OH; Civil Rights Act through Country; Urban League; SCLC; A Philip Randolph Ins Natl Consumers League; exec bd mem Indust Union DeptAFL-CIO. **Honors/Awds:** Disting Serv Award natl Urban League; Labor Affairs Prog in Recognition of 7 Years of Support & Devotion. **Military Serv:** USN Fireman 1st Class 1944-46.

PRATER-HARVEY, PEGGY.
Utility company executive. **Personal:** Born Oct 9, 1949,Memphis, TN; died Jul 2, 1997; daughter of Helen & Edwin Prater; married Perch H Harvey, Aug 18, 1973; children: Nicole Elizabeth. **Educ:** University ofTennessee, BS, 1971, MS, 1972; Johns Hopkins University, post graduate, 1975. **Career:** Cambridge School Department, educational psychologist; Memphis CIty Schools, educational psychologist, 1972-76; Booker T Washington Foundation &Mandex, Inc, consultant, 1976-78; Montgomery County Public Schools, educationalpsychologist, 1978-80; Memphis Light, Gas & Water Division, vice pres of human resources, 1987-97. **Orgs:** Memphis Arts Council, board of directors; Memphis Food Bank, board of directors; Memphis Rotary Club, board of directors; NAACP, board of directors, co-chair; National Civil Rights Museum, board of directors; Partners in Public Education, board of directors; Girls, Inc, board of directors, former chairperson; Leadership Memphis, board of directors, former chairperson. **Honors/Awds:** Dollars & Sense Magazine, America's Top Business & Professional Women, 1992. **Business Addr:** VP, Human Resources, Memphis Light, Gas & Water Division, 220 S Main St, Rm 510, Memphis, TN 38103, (901)528-4370.

PRIMO, QUINTIN E., JR.
Clergyman. **Personal:** Born Jul 1, 1913, Freedom Grove, GA; died Jan 15, 1998, Hockessin, DE; son of Alvira Wilhelmina Wellington (deceased) and Quintin E Primo Sr (deceased); married Winifred; children: Cynthia, Quintin III, Susan. **Educ:** Lincoln U, BA 1934; Lincoln U, STB 1937; VA Theological Sem, MDiv 1941, DD 1973; Seabury-Western Sem, DD 1972; General Theol Sem, STD 1973. **Career:** Ch in FL, NC, NY, DE, former pastor; Woodward Convoction of the MI Epis Diocese,dean; St Matthew's & St Joseph's Ch Detroit, former rector, pastor; Epis Diocese of Chgo, suffragan bishop 1972-84, interim bishop of DE, 1985-86. **Orgs:** Life trustee Rush-Presbyterian-St Luke's Med Center Chicago; trust PenninsulaUnited Methodist Home Inc Wilmington; trustee, St Augustine's College, Raleigh,NC; trustee, Lincoln University, PA. **Honors/Awds:** Fifth black ever elected as a bishop of the church; recip STD honor degrees from Gen Theol Sem of NY& VA Theol Sem; hon DD Seabury-Western Sem Evaston, IL; LHD honor degree St Augustine's Coll Raleigh; presidential citation, Natl Assn for Equal Opportunity inHigher Education, 1988.

PROCTOR, SAMUEL DEWITT.
Clergyman, educator. **Personal:** Born Jul 13, 1921, Norfolk, VA; died May 22, 1997, Cedar Rapids, IA; married Bessie Louise Tate; children: Herbert, Timothy, Samuel, Steven. **Educ:** VA Union Univ, AB 1942; Univ of PA, grad student 1944-45; Crozer Theol Sem, BD 1945; Yale Div Sch, student 1945-46; Boston Univ, ThD 1950. **Career:** Baptist Church, ordained to ministry 1943; Pond St Ch Providence, pastor 1945-59; VA Union Univ, prof religion & ethics 1949-50, dean sch of religion 1949-50, vice pres 1953-55, pres 1955-60; Agr &Tech Coll NC, pres 1960-64; Peace Corps, assoc dir 1963-64; Natl Council Chs, asso gen sec 1964-65; Office Econ Oppor, dir NE region spl asst to natl dir 1965-66; Inst for Serv to Educ, pres 1966-68; Univ WI Madison, univ dean spl projects1968-69; Rutgers Univ, prof educ grad sch 1969-84; Abyssinian Bapt Ch, minister1972-97. **Orgs:** Adjunct prof Union Theol Seminary New York City, Princeton Theol Seminary NJ; trustee Middlebury Coll; trustee Overseas Devel Cncl; trustee Christian Childrens Fund; United Negro Coll Fund; Crozer-Colgate Theol Sem;mem Kappa Alpha Psi, Sigma Pi Phi; life mem NAACP. **Honors/Awds:** Disting Serv Awd State Univ of NY at Plattsburgh 1966; Outstanding Alumnus Awd Boston Univ 1964; Hon Degrees, Bethune-Cookman Coll, Dillard Univ, UnivRI, Bloomfield Coll, Howard Univ, Bryant Coll, Bucknell Univ, Davidson Coll, Morehouse Coll, Ottawa Univ, Rider Coll, Stillman Coll, Atlanta Univ, Wilberforce Univ, VA Union Univ, Univ of MD, Coe Coll, St Peter's Coll, Fisk Univ, NC A&T State Univ, CentralMI Univ, Southeastern Mass Univ, VA State Univ, NC State Univ, Monmouth Coll, Boston Univ, Fairleigh-Dickenson Univ; wrote several books including: Sermons From The Black Pulpit, Preaching About Crises in the Community, The Substance of Things Hoped For: A Memoir of African American Faith, 1995.

PRYSOCK, ARTHUR.
Singer. **Personal:** Born in Spartanburg, SC; died 1997, Bermuda; married Jean; children: Jeanine, Jeanartta. **Career:** Singer,

jazz, R&B. **Honors/Awds:** Grammy Award, Best Jazz Performance by a Duo or Group for the Jazz Standard, Teach Me Tonight, with Betty Joplin, nominated, 1987, Best Jazz Vocal Performance, This Guy's In Love With You, nominated, 1988. **Special Achievements:** Recordings include: ''They All Say I'm The Biggest Fool,'' ''Because,'' ''I Wonder Where Our LoveHas Gone,'' all with the Buddy Johnson Band; ''I Worry About You,'' 1962; ''Teach Me Tonight,'' with Betty Joplin; ''This Guy's in Love With You.''.

QUIGLESS, MILTON DOUGLAS, SR.
Physician. **Personal:** Born Aug 16, 1904, Port Gibson, MS; died 1997, Tarboro, NC; son of John M & Agnes Quigless; married Helen Gordon Quigless, Sep 1, 1944; children: Helen, Milgon, Milton D Jr, Carol Marie. **Educ:** CraneCollege, AA, 1929; Meharry Medical College, MD, 1934. **Career:** Meharry Medical College, assoc prof, philosophy, phi physiology, 1935-36; self-employed physician, surgery, begin 1936. **Orgs:** Homer G Phillips Intern Assn, past pres; Old North State Medical Assn, past pres; Eastern Tarboro Citizens Assn, organizer and pres; Old North Site Medical Society, past pres, 1976. **Honors/Awds:** Heritage Hosp, Medical Practice & Svc Awd; The East Tarboro Citizens League Awd; Special Congressional Recognition; The Urban Club Awd; Rocky Mt Branch NAACP, Man of the Year Awd; FBLA Awd; Old North State Medical Society, Meritorious Service Awd; Meharry Medical College, President's Awd. **Special Achievements:** Organized East Tarboro Citizens Assn, 1947. **Business Addr:** Physician, The Quigless Clinic, 99 Main St, Tarboro, NC 27886.

RAGSDALE, LINCOLN JOHNSON.
Business executive. **Personal:** Born Jul 27, 1926, Muskogee, OK; died Jun 9, 1995; married Eleanor Dickey; children: Elizabeth, Gwendolyn Madrid, Lincoln J III, Emily. **Educ:**Tuskegee Inst, Instrument and Commercial Flying diploma; Lamson Business Coll Phoenix, Acctg and Mgmt diploma/certificate; CA Coll of Mortuary Science, diploma(Magna Cum Laude); Phoenix Coll, AA (w/Distinction); AZ State Univ, BS (w/ Distinction); Shorter College, LLD; Union Graduate School, PhD. **Career:** HomeRealty and Insurance Agency; partner; Natl Conf of Christians and Jews, mem bd of dirs 1957-95; Natl Business League Washington DC, bd of dirs; The AZ Club, bdof dirs; Rust Coll, bd of trustees; Sun State Savings and Loan Assoc, bd of dirs; Universal Memorial Ctr, Universal Sunset Chapel, chmn of bd of dirs; Intl Investment Co, owner/pres/ chmn of the bd of dirs; Valley Life & Casualty Ins, pres/chmn, bd of dirs. **Orgs:** Founder Intl Investment Co, Intl Construction Co, Valley Life and Casualty Insurance Group; co-founder Vesco Land Co, Home Security Finance Corp; licensed funeral dir and embalmer for State of AZ; licensed embalmer for State of OK; licensed real estate broker for the State of AZ; licensed general insurance agent for the State of AZ; licensed building contractor forthe State of AZ; past sec & mem of the bd of dirs Southwest Savings & Loan Assoc; mem Natl Urban League Bd of Trustees 1977-82; mem Memorial Hosp Foundation Bdof Trustees 1978-85; mem Iota Sigma Alpha Honor Soc, Omega Psi Phi Frat; mem American Legion Post #41, 33rd Degree Mason Masonic Lodge, Shriners; grand boule Sigma Pi Phi Frat. **Military Serv:** AUS Air Corps 2nd Lt, fighter pilot 1944-46; Honorable Discharge. **Business Addr:** Chairman of the Board, Valley Life & Casualty Ins, 1100 E Jefferson, Phoenix, AZ 85034.

RICHARDSON, DELROY M.
Attorney/utility executive/corporate secretary. **Personal:** Born Jun 26, 1938, Chicago, IL; died Aug 20, 1994;son of Roy Richardson; married Greta M; children: Gayle L, Monique N. **Educ:** UCLA, AB 1962; Univ of San Diego, JD 1969; Natl Univ, MBA 1975. **Career:** IRS, officer 1962-64; US Navy, legal officer 1964-67; Gen Dynamics, chieflabor relations 1968-71; San Diego Gas & Electric Co, atty 1971-83, asst corp sec 1983-86, corp sec 1986-94. **Orgs:** Mem Natl Bar, California State and San Diego County Bar Assns, NAACP, Navy League, Rotary Club, Black Atty Assn of San Diego County. **Honors/Awds:** Outstanding Young Man of the Year Finalist, Jr Chamber of Commerce 1973; Outstanding Alumnus of USD Law School l978. **Military Serv:** USN 1964-67; Captain USNR. **Business Addr:** Corporate Secretary, San Diego Gas & Elect Co, PO Box 1831 101 Ash St, San Diego, CA 92112.

RIDLEY, WALTER N.
Educational administrator, educator. **Personal:** Born in Newport News, VA; died Sep 26, 1997, West Chester, PA; married Henrietta; children: Yolanda Scheunemann, Don Leroy. **Educ:** Howard University, BA, MA; Ohio State; University of Minnesota; Univ of VA, PhD. **Career:** Virginia State College, teacher, administrator; St. Paul's College, academic dean; Elizabeth City College, president, 1958-68; West Chester Univeristy, professor. **Orgs:** US Commision on UNESCO; American Teachers Association, president, until 1966; National Education Association. **Special Achievements:** First African American to obtain a doctorate from a state-supported university in the South. **Home Addr:** 002750.

ROBINSON, HERBERT A.
Psychiatrist. **Personal:** Born Feb 19, 1927, Burkeville, VA; died Aug 11, 1997; divorced; children: Laura, Paul, Nancy, David. **Educ:** Syracuse U, BA 1950; Howard U, MD 1957; Orange Co Gen Hosp, intern; Metro State Hosp, Qpsychiatric resident. **Career:** Mental Health Servs Los Angeles Co Dept Health, psychiatrist, acting dir; Mental Health Servs LA Co, 1965; Camarillo State Hosp, dir aftercare clin1963-65; Day-Treatment Clinic Metro State Hosp, dir 1961-63. **Orgs:** Diplomate Am Bd Psychiatry & Neurology 1964; fellow Am Psychiatric Assn 1974; mem, com Task Force Poverty Manpower Com; mem Ins & Malpractice Review Com; Am Psychiatric Assn. **Honors/Awds:** Alumnus of Yr 1974. **Military Serv:** USAF. **Business Addr:** 1127 Wilshire Blvd, Los Angeles, CA 90017.

ROBINSON, JACQUELINE J.
Communications business executive (retired). **Personal:** Born Jun 18, Boston, MA; died Nov 8, 1997; daughter of Eugenia Johnson and Jack Johnson; married Alvin F; children: Alvin T II, Jacqueline. **Educ:** RN 1942; Assoc degree Spanish 1953; MEd 1975.**Career:** Radio WYCB, chmn of bd, 1982-88, retired; Jack & Jill Am Found, organization & first pres, 1968-75; Girl Friends Inc, natl pres 1972-76. **Orgs:** Mem Arlington Links; Minimum Wage Bd; past pres Faculty Wives Howard Univ 1954-56; dir Scholarship Bd Building Laborers 1965-97; sec Wash Community Broadcasting Sys 1965-97; organizer Wmn's Investment Group 1954-97; mem Delta Sigma Theta Inc; trustee Links Inc; Found annual scholarship in name of Jacqueline Robinson. **Honors/Awds:** Named Jacqueline Robinson Regional Competition Jack & Jill Am Found 1974; feature Black Enterprise Mag 1974, 1975; Key Cities KC MO 1970; St Louis 1974; Baltimore 1975.

ROBINSON,NATHANIEL.
Dentist. **Personal:** Born Jan 14, 1951, St Matthews, SC; died Jan 28, 1997; son of Anna Bartley Robinson and John Robinson; married Evelyn Caldwell (divorced). **Educ:** Claflin College, Orangeburg, SC, 1972; Temple University, Philadelphia, PA, DDS, 1977. **Career:** Self-employed, Washington, DC, dentist, 1977-97. **Orgs:** Member, Academy of General Dentistry, 1979-91. **Honors/Awds:** Top Dentists in Washington Area, Afro-American Newspaper, 1991, 1992; Award of Plaque for furthering patient education, Colgate Dental Health Advisory Board, 1989.

ROBINSON, NOAH, SR.
Railroad worker (retired). **Personal:** Born 1908, Piedmont, SC; died 1997, Greenville, SC; married Catherine; children: Jesse-Jackson, Noah Jr, George, John, Brooks, Archie, Maria. **Career:** Railroad worker; John J Ryan & Sons, cotton grader. **Honors/Awds:** Philadelphia Golden Gloves, boxing champion, 1926; Greenville City, resolution; Greenville County Council, resolution; South Carolina Senate, resolution.

ROWLAND, JAMES H.
Attorney. **Personal:** Born Jan 9, 1909, Adairsville, GA; died Jul 29, 1991; married Clara B Braswell; children: James H, William H II. **Educ:** Cheyney State Normal, 1929, BS Ed 1932, MEd 1934; OH State Univ; Howard Univ, LLB 1944; Howard Univ, JD 1954. **Career:** CCC, ed adv 1934-35; Bluefield State Coll WV, teacher, coach 1935-41; Howard Univ Washington, teacher, coach 1941-44; Bluefield State, 1944-45; Beckley WV,prac atty 1944-55; Harrisburg PA, atty 1955-91. **Orgs:** Mem State Bd of Ed WV 1953-55, State Bd of Ed PA 1963-79; pres Natl Assoc of State Bds of Ed 1970-71. **Honors/Awds:** James H Rowland Intermediate School (Harrisburg, PA)named in honor 1986. **Business Addr:** Attorney, 812 A N 17th St, Harrisburg, PA 17103.

RUSSELL, HARVEY CLARENCE.
Business executive (retired). **Personal:** Born Apr 14, 1918, Louisville, KY; died Feb 20, 1998, Bronx, NY; married Jacqueline Denison; children: Harvey, John, Denise Jones. **Educ:** KY State U, AB 1939; IN & MI U, 1939-41. **Career:** Pepsico Inc, vice pres, beginning 1965; Pespi-Cola Co, vice pres 1950-65; Rose-Meta Cosmetics, sls mgr 1948-50; WB Graham Assc 1946-48. **Orgs:** Mem NY State Bd Soc Welfare 1969-79; Afrcn Am & Inst 1968; US State Dept Adv Cncl on Afrcn Afrs 1967-69; OEO Adv Cncl 1967-69; US Dept LaborManpower Adv Com 1970-72; vice pres Natl Alliance Busmn 1969-70; mem Arden House Steering Com on Welfare 1967-69; UNA Com on S Africa 1970-72; co-chmn ICBO 1963-69; tst Tougaloo Clg 1966-70; mem NY Cncl Crime & Delinquency 1962-66; Yonkers Family Serv 1963-65; NY State Comm Aid 1964-; Natl Mun League 1969-; Bus Adv Cncl NAACP 1973-;Spl Contrib Fund Exec Commn 1975-; NAACP Legal Def Fund Bd & Exec Com 1974-; exec bd Natl Assc Study Afro-am Life & Hist 1975-; Kappa Alpha Psi; Alpha Kappa Delta; Sigma Pi Phi; natl pres Hudson River Mus Bd 1978-80; rep African-Am Dialogues Tunisia 1970, Lesotho 1975,The Sudan 1977. **Honors/Awds:** Achvmt awrd Alpha Kappa Alpha 1962; Natl Bus League 1963; KY state alumni awrd 1964; am jewish cong awrd 1965; Natl Assc Mkt Dev 1966; ICBO 1967; hon DHL Livingston Clg 1975. **Military Serv:** USCG lt 1942-46.

RUSSELL, MAURICE V.
Educator. **Personal:** Born May 7, 1923; died Feb 8, 1998, Rhinebeck, NY. **Educ:** Temple U, AB 1948; Columbia U, MSW 1950; Columbia U, edD 1964. **Career:** NY Univ Med Center, prof 1973-88; Social Serv Dept, dir 1973-88; Amer Public Health Assc, pres 1976-77; Einstein Med Center, prof 1970-73; Bronx Municipal Hospital Center, dir; Columbia Univ School of Public Health, assc prof 1965-70. **Orgs:** Vis prof Case Western Res 1971; lectr New Sch for Soc Rsrch 1974-75; chmn bd St Philips Comm Ctr; St Philips Day Care Ctr 1973-88; Am Cncl emigres in Profn 1970-88; Cancer Care & Am Cancer Found 1974-88; tres Robert Popper Found 1968-88; past pres Soc for Hosp Soc WorkDirs 1972; past chmn Columbia Univ Sch of Soc Work 1975; past chmn Training ComNatl Inst of Mental Hlth 1974; chmn Tech Advy Com New York City Hlth Dept 1968-73; flwshp Natl Inst of MentalHlth 1950. **Honors/Awds:** Outst comm serv awrd Natl Urban League 1965; outst soc worker Hlth Care in State of NY NY State Welfare Conf 1972; Ida M Cannon Awrd Am Hosp Assc 1973; Num Publ.

SCHATZMAN, DENNIS CLYDE.
Journalist. **Personal:** Born in Pittsburgh, PA; died Jul 16, 1997, Fullerton, CA; married Sandra Mancha Schatzman; children: Cicely. **Educ:** Univ of Pittsburgh, graduate; Dickinson School of Law, JD; Clemson Univ School of Business, attended. **Career:** Baltimore Afro American Newspaper, reporter; New Pittsburgh Courier, reporter; Winston-Salem Chronicle, reporter; Black Issues in Higher Education; CORE Times Magazine; Los Angeles Sentinel; District Court, judge; City of Pittsburgh, comptroller; California State Univ at Fullerton, journalism prof. **Orgs:**North Carolina State NAACP, exec dir; NABJ, exec dir. **Special Achievements:** Co-author, ''The Simpson Trial in Black and White,'' with Tom Elias.**Home Addr:** 004550003850.

SCOTT, LEONARDLAMAR.
Educator. **Personal:** Born Aug 9, 1924, Cherokee Cty, AL; died Apr 1989; married Velma J Turner; children: Patricia Ann Lee, Bernard Lewis, Brenda Louise Stallworth, Curtis Lamar. **Educ:** Tuskegee Inst, BS 1951; Univ of PA, 1963; UCLA, 1972; Northwestern, 1974; Tuskegee Inst Grad Study 28 hrs 1979. **Career:** High school coach: basketball, track, tennis, volleyball 1951-55; Little League, coach 1954-63; Scout Master, 1954-63; Natl Rehab Assoc, liaison officer; South East Chap Amer Corrective Therapy Assoc, pres 1974-75; Mt Olive Baptist Church, supt of sunday school 1976-89; vice chmn Deacon Bd; AFGE #110 pres 1964-89; VAMC Rehab Med, suprv clinical training, chief corrective therapy. **Orgs:** Registrar Civil Serv Reg & Voter's Act 1965; mem Tuskegee Civic Assoc 1966; rep VA Council 1980-83; sgt at arms AL State Council AFGE 1980-81; chaplain AFGE 5th Dist 1982-89; mem NAACP, KAY, Kappa Delta Pi; life mem DAV; mem Minuteman Society, Natl SS Society. **Honors/Awds:** Disting Serv Awd Scouting 1963; Professional Article publ by ACTA Jrnl ''Corrective Therapy as Profession'' 1975-76; Curriculum Unpubl for Maj in Phys Ed & Corrective Therapy; Compiled Clinical Training Handbook for VAMC Tuskegee AL Rehab Svc;pres AL Res Officers Minute Man Award recorded in the Res Officers Hall of FameState Capital Montgomery, AL 1977; Presenters Awd for Delivery of Speech to HS AL 1983; Stanley H Wertz Awd for Achievement in Corrective Therapy1986; Outstanding Performance Awd 1986. **Military Serv:** AUS tech sgt 2 1/2 yrs; USAF maj 21 yrs; Good Conduct Medal, Asiatic Campaign & Serv Medal, WWII Victory Medal, European Middle East Medal. **Home Addr:** 904 Howard Road, Tuskegee Institute, AL 36088. **Business Addr:** Clinical Trainee Superv VAMC, VAMC, Corrective Therapy Dept, Tuskegee, AL 36083.

SCOTT, RUTH PERRY.
Business partner, editor, teacher. **Personal:** Bornin Social Circle, GA; died 1997, Atlanta, GA; married Cornelius A. Scott; children: Jocely S. Walker, Portia A. **Educ:** Clark Univ, grad, magna cum laude, 1931; Atlanta Univ, grad work. **Career:** Teacher; Atlanta Daily World,bookkeeper, financial secretary, food editor. **Home Addr:** 008055.

SEARS, BERTRAM E.
Educator. **Personal:** Born Sep 28, 1930, Atlanta, GA; died Oct 4, 1996; son of Mattie and Ernest; married Frances; children: Sheryl, Kay, Bertram Jr. **Educ:** Morehouse Coll, BS 1951; Meharry Med Coll, MD, 1958; Hurley Hosp, internshp; Univ OK Hlth SciCtr, res 1959-61, 1963-64. **Career:** Univ of OK Hlth Sci Ctr, prof 1964-96; Cardiorespiratory Sci, prof schrm 1969-80; OK Children's Mem Hosp, chief of anthes 1964-84; Amer Bd of Anesth, dipl 1967; Amer Coll of Anesth, fellow 1967; Oklahoma Medical Center Respiratory Care Services, medical director, 1985-96. **Orgs:** Amer Med Assn 1967; Amer Assn of Univ Prof 1965; OK Co Med Soc 1961; Amer Acad of Pedia 1968; OK Soc of Anesth 1961; Am Assn for Respiratory Therapy 1969; OK Assn for Respir Ther 1969; YMCA; NAACP; Kappa Alpha Psi; trst Avery Chap AME Ch; Sigma Pi Phi. **Honors/Awds:** Pub, Compliations of Ketamine Anesth 32231, 1971; Exper with Ketamine Anesth, Journ of Natl Med Assn 6732 1975; Pneumothorax from an Obstructed Vent Port, anesthesiology 7311 1977. **Military Serv:** AUS med corps capt 1961-63. **Business Addr:** Department of Anesthesiology, University of Oklahoma, PO Box 26901, Oklahoma City, OK 73190.

SHABAZZ, BETTY.

Educational administrator, activist. **Personal:** Born May 28, 1936, Detroit, MI; died Jun 23, 1997, Bronx, NY; married Malcolm X (died 1965); children: Attallah, Qubilah, Ilyasah, Gamilah, Malikah, Malaak. **Educ:** Tuskegee Institute; Jersey City StateCollege, BA; Brooklyn State Hospital School of Nursing, RN; University of Massachusetts,MA, epublic health education, PhD, education administration. **Career:** Medgar Evers College, Communications and Public Relations, director. **Orgs:** The Links; Delta Sigma Theta Sorority; Jack and Jill of America. **Business Addr:** Director, Communications & Public Relations, Medgar Evers College, 1650 Bedford Ave, Brooklyn, NY 11225, (718)735-1948.

SHORES, ARTHUR D.

Attorney, civil rights activist. **Personal:** Died Dec 16, 1996, Birmingham, AL; married Theodora Warren; children:Helen Shores Lees, Barbara Shores Martin. **Educ:** Talladega College, bachelors, 1927; LaSalle Extension University, JD, 1935. **Career:** Attorney,until 1980s; Birmingham City Council, 1969-78; NAACP, staff attorney. **Special Achievements:** Involved in desegregating University of Alabama, 1950s, 1963. **Home Addr:** 001600003850.

SIMON, WALTER J.

Food company executive. **Personal:** Born Dec 1, 1941, New Orleans, LA; died Oct 10, 1997, Louisville, KY; son of Lola Simon and Henry Simon; married Margaret Peay; children: Christopher, Michael, Geanai. **Educ:** Benedict Coll, BS 1963; Hunter Coll, 1967. **Career:** Bronx State Hosp,chief therapist 1963-67; NY Nets ABA, pro basketball player 1967-70; Wise Planning of NY, reg rep, stockbroker 1969-70; KY Colonels ABA, pro basketball player 1970-75; KY Fried Chicken Corp, vice pres bus devel beginning 1975, vice pres offranchise devt. **Orgs:** Mem Intl Franchising Assoc 1976; bd mem, comm Jud Nominating Comm State of KY 1979; comm KY v comm on Human Rights 1980; Kentucky Derby Festival Committee; Louisville Urban League, chairman; Benedict College,bd of trustees, former mem; Univ of Louisville, bd of overseers. **Honors/Awds:** All Amer Coll Basketball NCAA-NAIA 1961; All Star All Pro NY Nets ABA Basketball 1968; Outstanding Young Man of KY Louisville Jaycees 1975; inducted in SC Athletic Hall of Fame, 1997. **Business Addr:** Vice President, Franchise Development, Kentucky Fried Chicken Corp, 1441 Gardiner Ln, Louisville, KY 40213.

SMITH, GRANVILLE N.

Clergyman. **Personal:** Born Jan 3, 1927, Tillatobia, MS; died May 28, 1997; married Hazel Brock. **Educ:** Midwestern Bible Coll, BRE 1968; Am Bapt Theo Sem, BA 1969; United Theo Sem, BTh 1973. **Career:** Mt Calvary Missionary Bapt Ch, pastor. **Orgs:** Chmn bd dirs Ops Industrialization Cntr 1973-75; first vice pres Gr Lakes Dist Congress of Religious Edn; vice pres Wolverine Bapt State Conv; Dir United Theo Sem Ext Cntr; instr Greek Homiletics New Testament Theo United Theo Sem Ext; instr Gr Lakes Dist Congress of Rel Edn; Wolverine St Congressof Rel Edn; Nat Sunday Sch & BTU Congress; mem Concerned Pastors for Social Action; CPSA; Fin Sec CPSA; sec-treas Chris Busnessmen's Assn; pres Great Lakes District Baptist Leadership & Educational Congress; chmn oratorical commission NatlBaptist Convention, USA, Inc; trea Natl Baptist Congress of Christian Education/Georgia Jackson Scholarship Commission; sec, board of directors, Foss Avenue Christian School of Elementary and Secondary Education; div chairperson, churches and clergy, United Negro College Fund, Flint MI; chmn development comm, AmericanBaptist College of American Baptist Theological Seminary; trustee bd, American Baptist Coll of ABTS; bd of trustees United Way of Genesee and Lapeer Counties; bd mem Flint Human Relations Commission. **Honors/Awds:** Recip hon doc united theo sem 1973; lectr World Bapt Youth Alliance 1974; rated fourth among natlbapt conv chs in foreign mission contrib Mt Calvary Bapt Ch 1973. **Military Serv:** USN steward 2 class 1944-46. **Business Addr:** 4805 N Saginaw St, Flint, MI 48505.

SMITH, HENRY R., JR.

Judge. **Personal:** Born Feb 6, 1917, Philadelphia, PA; died Jul 1995; son of Julia Black Smith and Henry R Smith; married Margaret Marshall Smith, Nov 28, 1941; children: Leslie R, Daryl H, Camille E. **Educ:** Pennsylvania State Coll, BA, 1939; Duquesne Univ Law School, LLB, 1949. **Career:** Pennsylvania State Employment Service, investigator, 1943-44; Housing Authority of theCity of Pittsburgh, PA, asst mgr, mgr, 1944-51, asst gen counsel, 1951-53; Allegheny County PA, asst dist atty, 1951-52; private practice of law; Allegheny County Planning Commn, planning analyst, 1964; Allegheny County Office of Economic Opportunity, director, 1964-69; elected judge of Ct of Common Pleas, 1969, served two ten-yr terms; consultant to Imo State, Nigeria, on implementation of constitutional govt, 1981. **Orgs:** Mem, Pennsylvania Bar Assn, Allegheny Bar Assn, Amer Judicature Soc, Pennsylvania State Trial Judges, Homer S. Brown Law Assn. **Honors/Awds:** Pittsburgh Courier Civil Rights Award, 1962; Pennsylvania NAACP Human Rights Award, 1969; New Pittsburgh Courier Top Hat Award, 1981; Distinguished Alumnus, Pennsylvania State Univ, 1984. **Home Addr:** 220 N Dithridge St, Apt 603, Pittsburgh, PA 15213. **Business Addr:** Senior Judge, Court of Common Pleas of Allegheny County, 535 Court House, Pittsburgh, PA 15219.

SNELL, JIMMY GREGORY.

Insurance company executive (retired), councilman. **Personal:** Born Jan 17, 1927, Waco, TX; died Oct 26, 1996; married Joanna Verdun; children: James, Jerald, Joseph, Juliette. **Educ:** Wiley Coll, BS, 1951. **Career:** Port Arthur Sch Dist, 1954-56; City of Austin, councilman 1975-96; Co Commissioner, precinct 11981-84, 1985-88; Atlanta Life Ins Co, gen mgr beginning 1952. **Orgs:** Mem NAACP, Urban League, Natl Bus League; bd mem Child Guidance; bd of comm council; Anderson Jr HS Human Relations Bd; St Austin's Church Finance Bd; chmn of bdChild Inc; scoutmaster campaign mgr Rev Martin Griffen state rep Wilhelmina Delco. **Honors/Awds:** Arthur DeWitty Awd NAACP 1974; Man of Yr Awd Omega PsiPhi 1976. **Military Serv:** USAF sgt 1945-47.

SPRIGGS, G. MAX.

Educator. **Personal:** Born Apr 24, 1925, Des Moines, IA; died Oct 6, 1997; married Phyllis Joan Leadon; children: James Max, Lyna Ruth Spriggs-Hasenjager, Daniel Edward. **Educ:** Drake Univ Des Moines IA, 1947-49; Univ of MN, BS 1950; St Cloud State U, MS 1967; Univ of MN, EdD 1972. **Career:** Moorehead State Univ, asso prof of special educ 1978-97; Univ of IL Urbana IL, chmn dept of special educ 1972-74; Roseville Area School St Paul MN, dir of special educ 1969-70; Highline School Dist Seattle WA, dir of special educ 1968-69; Minneapolis Public School, coordinator of MR program 1965-66. **Honors/Awds:** Ideal tchr Univ of MN 1950; Ski-U-Mah service to Univ Univ of MN 1950. **Military Serv:** NG capt 23 yrs. **Business Addr:** Moorhead State Univ, Moorhead, MN 56560.

SPRIGGS, RAY V.

Management consultant. **Personal:** Born Oct 5, 1937, West Chester, PA; died Mar 28, 1996; son of Anna Irons Spriggs and Harry Spriggs; married Velva; children: Vashon. **Educ:** Lincoln U, AB 1960; Univ of PA, Grad Sch of Education 1961; Univ of CA, Certif 1961; Univ of Ghana, Certif 1961. **Career:** Philadelphia, PA, teacher 1960; Damans & Associates, assocdir; Robert F Kennedy, proj coord 1977; Spriggs Assn, pres 1970; A L Nellum Assn Inc, trainer 1974; Unicorn Inc, consult 1974; Control Systems; First World Arts 'n' Crafts, pres, owner. **Orgs:** Inter Res Assoc, 1972; lctr, "Black Am/Black African Rel" Univ of OK, 1972; exec dir, Comm Action Bd 1967; asst exec dir Cleveland NAACP 1965; elected adv Neigh Commn 1976; pres Tenant Coun 1976; foun DC Tenants' Cong 1977; pres Oper Enlightenment Intl 1972; US Congressional Luncheon Speaker for Peace Corps 25th Anniv 1986. **Honors/Awds:** Walter White Schol IBPOEW oratorical winner; Webster Meredith awd in oratory; UnivPA fellow; publ poetry; first African American Peace Corps Volunteer, Ghana, 1961. **Business Addr:** Owner, First World Arts 'n' Crafts, 3649 New Hampshire Ave NW, Washington, DC 20010, (202)723-3350.

STARLING, JOHN CRAWFORD.

Physician. **Personal:** Born Nov 16, 1916, Charleston, WV; died Jan 25, 1983; married Anna; children: Nedra, Gayle, John. **Educ:** WV State Coll, 1938; Meharry Med Coll, 1942. **Career:** Private Practice, physician; Parkside Hospital, resident; Harlem Hosp, intern 1942-43. **Orgs:** Mem AMA; NMA; OH State Med Soc; Cleveland Med Soc; Amer SocAbdominal Surgeons; AAGP; Amer Geriatric & Soc; Catholic Physicians Guild; staff mem Huron Hospital; Polyclinic Hospital; Forest City Hospital All-Amer Football WV State Coll 1936; Kappa Alpha Psi Fraternity. **Honors/Awds:** Purple Heart, US Army. **Military Serv:** AUS major 1943-48; Purple Heart. **Business Addr:** 7916 Cedar Rd, Cleveland, OH 44103.

STEPHENS, JAMES ANTHONY.

City official. **Personal:** Born Jan2, 1914, McIntosh County, GA; died Dec 4, 1994; married Lillie Mae; children: Charles Richard, James Anthony Jr, Herbert Clark. **Educ:** Franklin Inst; Univ of GA, Cert Bnkng & Fin. **Career:** Brunswick Brnch Pstl Svc, ret pstlclrk 1940, ret equal opprtnty liason; Atlanta Life Ins, ret ins rep 1942-84; City of Brunswick, GA city cmmr 1978-94. **Orgs:** Chmn bd dir CAPDC 1980-81;chmn Glynn Co Boys Clbs of Am; mem Glynn Co Chmbr Comm Bd; Tuesday coord & mem Christian TV Mnstrs 1976-84; bd dir United Way of Glynn Co; bd dir Coastal Area Tourism; mem Gvnrs Adv Bd Area Plng & Dev Comm; pres Zion Bptst Asso. **Honors/Awds:** Ctzns Awrds GA Masonic Org; govnrs Adv Awrd State of GA 1984; PostalCmndtns Univ S Postal Svc; Serv awrd The Coastal Area Plng & Dev. **Home Addr:** 2417 Johnson St., Brunswick, GA 31520. **Business Addr:** Mayor Pro Tem, City of Brunswick, GA, P O Box 550, Brunswick, GA 31521.

STETH, RAYMOND.

Artist. **Personal:** Born 1917, Norfolk, VA; died Feb 6, 1997, Philadelphia, PA; children: two sons. **Educ:**Pennsylvania Museum School of Industrial Art, 1941-43; Barnes Foundation, 1942-44. **Career:** Sign Painter; vaudeville theatre company, member; Works Progress Administration, Graphic Arts div, artist, 1938; Philographic School of Art, cofounder, director, 1948-53; Pennsylvania Museum School of Industrial Art, instructor, 1949-51; Pennsylvania Academy of the Fine Arts, artist-in-residence; Philadelphia Print Club, guest curator, 1942-43. **Special Achievements:** Art exhibited at: Library of Congress, 1940; South Side Community Art Center, Chicago, 1941; Fort Huachuca, Arizona, 1943; Collections displayed at: Corcoran Gallery, Library of Congress, Metropolitan Museum of art, New York; Philadelphia Museum of Art. **Home Addr:** 000850.

STEWART,JERMAINE. (WILLIAM JERMAINE)

Singer. **Personal:** Died 1997, Oak Forest, IL. **Career:** Singer. **Special Achievements:** Songs include: "Word Is Out," "We Don't Have To Take Our Clothes Off.".

STEWART, MALCOLM M.

Business executive(retired). **Personal:** Born Apr 29, 1920, Salem, VA; died Mar 11, 1997; widowed; children: Michael, Paul, Malcolm. **Educ:** Attended NYU, RCA Inst, Queens Coll. **Career:** FL A&M Coll, instr radio shop & theory 1942-43;TV & appliance serv contracting 1946-52; Sperry Rand Corp, engr writer 1952-68, eeo admin 1968-70, admin mgr devel & training 1971-72, eeo admin Sperry Div, 1972until retirement. **Orgs:** Prog mgr Econ Devel Council of New York City 1970-71; experimental bus/edn partnership prog Bushwick HS; treas Natl Urban Affairs Council Inc; sr mem Soc for Teach Comm; mem adv council New York City Task Force on Youth Motivation; mem EDGES Group Inc. **Honors/Awds:** Natl Alliance of Businessmen Commendation Awds (4) 1971-75; Plans for Progress Certificate of Appreciation 1966; Bronze Plaque Econ Devel Council of NY. **Military Serv:** USAF 1943-46. **Home Addr:** 12615 Old Dorm Pl, Herndon, VA 22070.

STONE, MARCENIA LYLE. See STONE, TONI.

STONE, TONI. (MARCENIA LYLE STONE)

Professional baseball player. **Personal:** Died Nov 2, 1996, Alameda, CA; widowed. **Career:** San Francisco Sea Lions, baseball player; New Orleans Creoles, baseball player; Indianapolis Clowns, Negro League, 1953; Kansas City Monarchs. **Honors/Awds:** Women's Sports Foundation, International Women's Sports Hall of Fame, inductee, 1985. **Special Achievements:** First woman to play big-league baseball.

STUBBS, HAROLD K.

Attorney. **Personal:** Born Dec 8, 1940, FtLauderdale, FL; died May 10, 1989; married Sandra Kay; children: Michele, Lisa, Malaika, Nouvelle. **Educ:** Kent State Univ, BA 1963; Howard Law Sch, LLB 1966. **Career:** Parms Purnell Stubbs & Gilbert; atty; Criminal Div Summit Co, chief asst prosecutor; Akron Law Dept, asst prosecutor 1968-69; City of Akron, law director. **Orgs:** Bd mem East Akron Comm House; Akron Frontiers of Amer; mem Akron, OH, Amer Natl Bar Assns; pres Turf Builders Civic Group; bd mem Salvation Army; div chmn United Negro Coll Fund Dr 1973; West Akron YMCA 1973; chmn Akron Admin Com for the Akron Plan; bd trustees St Paul AME. **Honors/Awds:** Kappa Alpha Psi Akron Alumni Chap Blue Key Men's Honorary; Scabbard & Blade Military Hon. **Business Addr:** Law Dir, City of Akron, State Building, Akron, OH 44308.

STURDIVANT, JOHN NATHAN.

Administrator. **Personal:** Born Jun 30, 1938, Philadelphia, PA; died Oct 28, 1997, Falls Church, VA; children: Michelle T. **Educ:** Attended Lord Fairfax Comm Coll 1974-76; Antioch Univ, BA Labor Studies 1980; attended Univ of MD 1979-80. **Career:** Amer Fed of Govt Employees (AFL-CIO), Local 1754 sec 1962-64, vice pres 1965-67, pres1968-76; VA Council of Locals AFGE (AFL-CIO), vice pres 1970-73; VA Central Labor Council (AFL-CIO), mem exec bd 1973-97; Amer Fed of Govt Employees (AFL-CIO),admin asst to the exec vice pres 1980-84, exec vice pres 1984-97. **Orgs:** Labor appointee-chmn PR subcom No Valley Manpower Planning Council CETA 1973-76; bd of dirs NW Workshop for the Physically Handicapped 1974-77; Soc of Fed Labor Relations Prof 1974-97; mem Coalition of Black Trade Unionists 1975-97; 8th &10th Congress Dist Comm on Polit Educ COPE AFL-CIO 1976-97; Fairfax Co Demo ComVA Demo State Central Comm 1977-97. **Honors/Awds:** Cert of Achievement AUS Interagency Communications Agency 1969; Cert of Recognition Gtr Wash Central Labor Council. **Military Serv:** USAF A/2C 1956-60. **Business Addr:** Executive Vice President, AFL-CIO, 1325 Massachusetts Ave NW, Washington, DC 20005.

THOMAS, KENNETH ROGER.

Attorney at law, newspaper publisher. **Personal:** Born Jan 1, 1930, Cleveland, OH; died Nov 28, 1997, Los Angeles, CA; son of Augusta Dickerson & James Edward Thomas; married Jennifer Thomas, May 1983. **Educ:** Ohio Univ, BA, 1951, LLB, 1959, JD, 1967. **Career:** US Civil Service, Dept of Air Force Civilian; Japan Air Force Supply Depot, Tokyo, Japan, 1954-56; Management & Procedures Analyst; Attorney at Law, private practice, 1960-97; Probate Referee, 1974-97; Los Angeles Sentinel, chief exec officer, 1983-97. **Orgs:** State Bar of Ohio, 1959-; State Bar of CA, 1960-; Los Angeles County Bar Assn, 1962-; Langston Bar Association, 1960-; Los Angeles Trial Lawyers, 1965-; Natl Lawyers Guild, 1966-;Amer Arbitration Assoc, 1970-; Amer Bar Assn, 1963-; NAACP; Natl Newspaper Publishers Assn, 1983, board of directors, 1994; Natl Newspaper Publishers Assn, 1986-; CA Newspaper Publishers Assn, 1984-, board of directors, 1996-; Los Angeles Urban League, 1992-, board of directors, 1994-; numerous others. **Military Serv:** US Air Force, 1st Lt, 1951-53. **Business Addr:** CEO, Los AngelesSentinel, 3800 Crenshaw Blvd, Los Angeles, CA 90008, (213)299-3800.

THOMAS, MAXINE F.
Judge (retired). **Personal:** Born May 31, 1947, Los Angeles, CA; died Jan 16, 1998, Los Angeles, CA; daughter of Freddie Thompson Thomas and Mack Thomas. **Educ:** Los Angeles CityCollege, speech; California State College at Los Angeles, BA, speech, 1968; Univ of Iowa College of Law, JD 1971. **Career:** Western Center on Law and Poverty, 1969; Joseph Mayfield Realty Co., secretary, 1969; Los Angeles Neighborhood Legal Services, 1970-71; Meardon, Sueppel and Downer Law Firm, research assistant, 1970-71; Public Systems Research Institute, Watts Model Cities Program, community consultant, 1971-72; Atlantic Richfield Co., Legal Division, Corporate Finance Department, attorney, 1972-74; Pacific Lighting Corp., attorney, 1974-80; Los Angeles Municipal Court, judge, 1980-84, asst presiding judge, 1985, presiding judge, 1986-89. **Orgs:** American Bar Assn; Black Women Lawyers of California; California Association of Women Judges; California Elected Women; California Judges Assn; California Women Lawyers; California Assn of Black Lawyers; Delta Sigma Theta Sorority; John M Langston Bar Assn; NAACP; National Assn of Women Judges; Natl Bar Assn; National Conference of Black Lawyers; California Judicial Council, Advisory Cmte on Legal Forms, 1981; Pro Line Corp., board of directors, 1979. **Honors/Awds:** Los Angeles Sentinel, Woman of the Year, 1986; Natl Assn of Business & Professional Women, Honoree, 1986. **Special Achievements:** Founder: Night Small Claims Court, LA Municipal Court, 1982; co-founder: Night Civil Court, LA Municipal Court, 1984; Bar Admissions: Iowa, 1971; California, 1972. **Home Addr:** 849 S Highland Ave, Los Angeles, CA 90036.

THOMAS, STANLEY B., JR.
Communications company executive. **Personal:** Born Apr 28, 1942, New York, NY; died Apr 15,1995; son of Stanley & Marion Thomas. **Educ:** Yale Univ, BA political sci & history 1964. **Career:** Time Inc, exec trainee, asst to vice pres 1964-66, Ofc of Comm & Field Svcs, dept asst, sec 1969-73; assistant sec Human Development, HEW, 1973-77; ITT, exec for marketing strategy planning 1977-79; Home Box Office, Inc, asst to chmn & chief exec ofcr 1979-80, vice pres Nat Account Group 1981, sr vice pres Natl Account Group 1983, sr vice pres Affiliate Operations 1984-90; Time Warner Enterprises, senior vice pres, The Sega Channel, pres/CEO. **Orgs:** Board of directors, New York Urban Coalition; board of directors, YMCA of Greater New York; board of directors, Near East Foundation. **Honors/Awds:** Spl Citation Nominee Yale Univ Corp Sec's; Superior Serv Award HEW.

THURMAN, SUE BAILEY.
Activist, editor. **Personal:** Born in Pine Bluff, AR; died 1997, San Francisco, CA; married Howard Thurman (deceased); children: Anne, Olive Wong. **Educ:** SpelmanSeminary (College), attended; Oberlin Coll, graduated, 1926. **Career:** Afro-American Women's Journal, editor; activist. **Orgs:** National Council of Negro Women; Pilgrimage of Friendship; African Meeting Room, Museum of Afro-American History, founder; San Francisco Church for the Fellowship of All Peoples, co-found, 1944; first African American woman to meet with Mahatma Gandhi to discuss non violent resistance. **Home Addr:** 001600008055.

TOLBERT, EDWARD T.
County official. **Personal:**Born May 28, 1929, Toms River, NJ; died Nov 16, 1994; son of Bertha Dickson andEdward Tolbert; married Thelma Neal; children: Karen Paden. **Educ:** Toms-River HS, HS Diploma, 1949. **Career:** Berkeley Township Housing Auth, chmn mem 1965-70; Ocean Co Mental Health Bd, vp 1967-73; Ocean Co Emer Police, deputy chief 1971-73; Berkeley Township, township committeeman 1973-79, mayor 1974-75, co-committeeman; Ocean County, Toms River, NJ, housing officer, 1979-92. **Orgs:** Deputy chf pres Manitou Pk Vol Fire Co 1958-78; trustee Scnd Bapt Church Toms River 1962-69; trustee Homes for All Inc 1986, Natl Council on Alcoholism Ocean County 1986; board of directors, NAACP, 1988-94. **Military Serv:** AUS sgt 1950-53. **Home Addr:** 6 Fourth St, Toms River, NJ 08757. **Business Addr:** Co-Committeeman, Berkeley Township, Town Hall Berkeley Twp, Pinewald-Keswick Rd., Bayville, NJ 08721.

TUCKER, O. RUTH.
Broadcaster. **Personal:** Born Oct 15, Hemingway, SC; died Jun 30, 1997; daughter of Alberta Gilliard Davis (deceased) and Charlie Davis (deceased); married Erkskine Sr, Oct 27, 1956; children: Kelley A, Erskine R Jr, Allyson. **Educ:** Lincoln Hospital School of Nursing, Durham, NC, RN, 1953; University of Wisconsin, Milwaukee, Milwaukee, WI, BA, mass communication, 1978. **Career:** Hubbard Hospital, Nashville, TN, head nurse & assistant supervisor, 1953-56; Bronson Hospital, Kalamazoo, MI, asst head nurse, 1956-59; VA Hospital, Nashville, TN, staff nurse, 1959-1963; WTMJ Inc, Milwaukee, WI, assistant to manager/editorial affairs, 1978-88, assistant to manager/ person & edit affairs, 1988-90, assistant director media relations, 1990-97. **Orgs:** President, Milwaukee Links, 1989-97; chair, PR committee, African World Festival, 1987-97; general chairman, Community Arts Festival, 1978; general chairman, UNCFSpecial Event, 1983; board member, Milwaukee Society for Prof Journ, 1988-90; board member, University School Trustees, 1986-90; member, Alpha Kappa Alpha Sorority, Inc, 1981-97. **Honors/Awds:** Black Excellence Award, Milwaukee Times, 1986; Image Award, Career Youth Development, 1989, 1990; Soror of the Year Award, Alpha Kappa Alpha Sorority, 1991; Honorary Co-Chair, Interfaith Conference Friends, 1990. **Home Addr:** 1555 W Spruce Ct, River Hills, WI 53217. **Business Addr:** Asst Dir, Media Relations, WTMJ Inc, Community Affairs Dept,720 E Capitol Dr, PO Box 693, Milwaukee, WI 53201.

VAILS, DONALD.
Gospel vocalist, musician. **Personal:** Born in Atlanta, GA; died Sep 8, 1997, Clinton, MD. **Career:** Gospel vocalist; choir leader; musician; songwriter; New Light Baptist Church, minister of music.**Special Achievements:** Wrote or rearranged songs like: With a Made Up Mind; We've Come to Praise Him; worked with James Cleveland, Charles Nicks; performed with Aretha Franklin; formed group, Donald Vails Choraleers, 1968. **HomeAddr:** 007350007300007400.

WALKER-SHAW, PATRICIA.
Business executive. **Personal:** Born Jul 26, 1939, Little Rock, AR; died Jun 30, 1985; married Harold R Shaw Sr; children: Harold R Jr. **Educ:** Fisk Univ, BA (cum laude) 1961; TN State Univ, Teacher Cert 1962;Univ of TN Graduate School, social work 1966. **Career:** Tri-State Bank of Memphis, accounting trainee 1958-59; Universal Life Ins Co, underwriting clerk1961; IL State Dept of Public Aid, caseworker 1961-62; TN State Dept Public Welfare, caseworker children 1963-66; Universal Life Ins Co, keypunch oper exec vice pres 1966-82, pres chief exec officer 1983-85. **Orgs:** Pres Natl Ins Assn; bd of trustees Stillman Coll; bd of comm Memphis Light Gas & Water 1973-85; bd of dirs Memphis Branch Fed Reserve Bank of St Louis 1981-85. **Honors/Awds:** Outstanding Leadership Awd Coca-Cola & Dr Pepper Bottling Co of Memphis; Amer Black Achievement Awd Ebony Mag; Par Excellence Awd PUSH; Ten Outstanding Bus & Prof Dollars & Sense Mag 1983; JE Walker Minority Bus Person of the Year Memphis NBL 1983. **Business Addr:** President, Universal Life Ins Co, 480 Linden Ave, Memphis, TN 38101.

WALL, J. C.
Newspaper publisher. **Personal:** Born Apr 23, 1916, Carthage, TX; died Jul 10, 1997, Ecorse, MI; married Dorothy Braxton; children: Arlene Nolan. **Educ:** Bishop College. **Career:** worked in several war plants during WWII; the Telegram newspaper, publisher, 1945-97. **Orgs:** First Baptist Church; NAACP, life mem; National Newspaper Publishers Association; Michigan Minority Press Association; Southern Wayne County Chamber of Commerce. **Honors/Awds:** Numerous awards from civic, government and community organizations.

WALLACE, WILLIAM JAMES LORD.
College president emeritus. **Personal:** Born Jan 13, 1908, Salisbury, NC; died Apr 26, 1997; son of Lauretta Wallace and Thomas Wallace; married Louise Eleanor Taylor;children: Louise Eleanor. **Educ:** Univ of Pittsburgh, BS 1927; Columbia Univ, AM 1931; Cornell Univ, PhD 1937; Teachers Coll, attended 1947. **Career:** Livingstone Coll, instructor science 1927, chemistry 1928-32; Lincoln Univ, Jefferson City MO, prof chemistry 1932-33; West Virginia State Coll, instructor chemistry 1933-34, asst prof 1934-37, assoc prof 1937-43, prof 1943-97, actingadmin asst to pres 1944-45, admin asst 1945-50, acting pres 1952-53, pres 1953-73 retired; West Virginia State Coll, bd of advisors 1982-89. **Orgs:** Trustee 1939-97, presiding elder 1964-97, AME Zion Church West Virginia Dist 1964-88; trustee Herbert H Thomas Memorial Hospital Assn 1970-78; comm Kanawha Parks &Recreation Comm 1973-79; non-lawyer mem of Legal Ethics Comm of West Virginia State Bar 1980-86; chmn Kanawha County Library Bd 1958-61; chmn advisory comm to pres 1982-84, 1986-88, vice chmn 1984-86 West Virginia State Coll. **Honors/Awds:** Distinguished West Virginia Gov John D Rockefeller IV 1979; awarded third Washington-Carver Award for Outstanding Serv to the Citizens of West Virginia, West Virginia Dept of Culture & History 1986; Certificate & Plaque by West Virginia State Bar in recognition of Outstanding & Superb Contribution & Serv to the legal system & to justice 1986; presented Martin Luther King Jr ''Living the Dream'' Award for Scholarship 1987; Citations from Univ of Pittsburgh and West Virginia Univ; Livingstone Coll, LLD 1959; Concord Coll, LHD 1970; Alderson-Broaddus Coll, DSc 1971; West Virginia State Coll, Doctor of Letters 1981; Marshall Univ, Doctor of Pedagogy 1983. **Business Addr:** President Emeritus, West Virginia State College, PO Box 417, Institute, WV 25112-0417.

WATKINS, LEVI.
Educational administrator (retired). **Personal:** Born Jan 15, 1911, Montgomery, KY; died May 1993; son of Sallie Darden Watkins and Adam Watkins; married Lillian Bernice Varnado, Jun 8, 1940;children: Annie Marie Garroway, E Pearl McDonald, Levi Jr, Doristine Minott, Donald V, James A. **Educ:** TN St Univ, BS 1933; Northwestern Univ, MA 1940.**Career:** Burt HS, asst prin 1935-40; Parsons Jr Coll, Douglass Schools,asst dean supv prin 1940-53; AL St Univ, admissions & vet officer & adminstr asst topres 1948-53; founding pres, Owen College, 1953-59; Alabama State College, asst to pres, 1959-62; Alabama State Univ, pres, 1962-81; Bishop College, Dallas, TX, interim pres, 1986-88. **Orgs:** pres AL Assn Coll Adminstrs; st dir Am Assn St Colls & Univ; mem AL Educ Seminar; bd mem AL Adv Com Am Coll Testing Prog; Phi Delta Kappa; bd mem AL Citizens for Transp; Consumer Credit CounselingServ; sec Navys Adv Bd on Educ & Gng; Childrens Ctr of Montgomery Inc; AL St Safety Coor Com; Alpha Kappa Mu; Kappa Delta Pi; member, Montgomery Industrial Development Board, 1978-; member, Alabama Commission on Tax and Physical Policy Reform, 1990-91; member, Sigma Pi Phi Fraternity. **Honors/Awds:** Honorary degrees: Arkansas Baptist College, 1958, Alabama State Univ, 1974, Daniel Payne College, 1975, Selma Univ, 1980, Livingston Univ, 1983; Kentucky Colonel, 1981. **Home Addr:** 146 S Anton Dr, Montgomery, AL 36105.

WEAVER, ROBERT C.
Government administrator, educator (retired). **Personal:** Born Dec 29, 1907, Washington, DC; died Jul 17, 1997, Manhattan, NY; son of Florence Freeman Weaver and Mortimer G Weaver; married Ella V Haith (died 1991); children: Robert C (dec). **Educ:** Harvard Coll, BS (CumLaude) 1929; Harvard Univ, MA 1931, PhD 1934. **Career:** Dept Int ConsultHousing Div, adv neg affrs 1933-38; US Housing Auth, spec asst 1938-40; Nat'l Def Adv Comm, admin asst 1940-42; Labor Div Office of Prod Mgmt & War Bond Bd 1942-43; War Manpower Comm 1943-44; Chicago Mayor's Comm on Race Relations, dir 1944-45; Am Council on Race Relations, dircomm services 1945-48; UNRRA Mission to the Ukraine kiev, reports officer and acting chief 1946; John Hay Whitney Found, dir Oper Fellowship 1949-54; Fulbright Fellowships, selection committee for 2 European areas 1952-54; NY Dept of Comm Housing 1954; NY State Rent Admin 1955-59;Ford Found, consult 1959-60; New York City Hsng & Redev Bd, vchmn 1960-61; US Housing & Fin Agency, admin 1961-66; US Dept of Housing & Urban Devel, sec 1966-68; Baruch Coll, pres1969-70; Hunter Coll NY, dist prof 1971- retired. **Orgs:** Bd of dir Metro Life Ins Co 1969-78, Municipal Asst Corp begin 1975; bd of trustees Bowery Savings Bank 1969-80, Mt Sinai Hosp & Med School 1970-; Lincoln Inst of Land Policy board; mem Const Panel US Controller General 1973-; New YorkCity Conciliation & Appeals Bd for rent stabilization 1973-84; Harvard Univ Schof Design, visiting com 1978-83; exec comm of bd of NAACP Legal Defense Fund since 1978; Am Acad of Arts & Sciences 1985; Publications, Negro Labor, A Natl Problem 1946,The Negro Ghetto 1948, The Urban Complex 1964, Dilemmas of Urban America 1985; 175 articles; chmn of Task Force on the Democratic Developments of New Towns Twentieth Century Fund, 1971-72; mem of Bd of Dir and Research Policy Comm, Economic Devel Comm for the 1970's; chmn of Bd of Dir, NAACP, 1960-61; pres, Natl Comm Agst Discrimination in Housing, 1973-87. **Honors/Awds:** SpingarnMedal NAACP 1962; Russworm Award 1963; delivered The Annual Godkin Lectures at Harvard, 1965; Albert Einstein Commemorative Award 1968; Merrick Moore SpauldingAchievement Award 1968; Award for Public Serv US Gen Acctg Office 1975; New York City Urban League Frederick Douglass Award 1977; Schomburg Collection Award 1978; Elected to Hall of Fame Nat'l Assoc of Home Builders 1982; M Justin Herman Award of the Nat'l Assoc of Hsng & Redevelopment Officials 1986; Equal Opportunity Day Award of Natl Urban League, 1987; recipient of some 30 honorary degrees from Amherst, Boston Coll, Columbia, Elmira Coll, Howard, Harvard, Morehouse, Rutgers, Univ of Illinois, Univ of Michigan, Univ of Pennsylvania and others; Award for Innovations in Buildings, Amer Buildings Magazine, 1965; written numerous articles and four books. **Home Addr:** 215 E 68th St, New York, NY 10021.

WELLS, JUNIOR. (AMOS BLACKMORE)
Musician. **Personal:** Born Dec 9, 1934, West Memphis, AR; died Jan 15, 1998, Chicago, IL. **Career:** Harmonica Player, recordings include: Hoodoo Man Blues, 1965; Messin With the Kid, Early in the Morning, Good Morning Little Schoolgirl; Come On in This House, 1997. **Honors/Awds:** WC Handy Blues Award, 1997; Grammy Award Nomination for Come on In This House, 1997.

WHITE, ED PEARSON.
City official (retired). **Personal:** Born Mar 16, 1911, Woofruff County, AR; died Mar 3, 1997; son of Peraline Simpson Pearson and Link Pearson; married Dorothy Mae Byes Hill, Oct 14, 1962; children: Robert. **Career:** American Synimite Bauxite Co, laborer 1939-46; Minnesota Mine, tank cleaner 1947-60; White's Grocery, owner 1960-83; White's Recreation Center, owner; City of Wrightsville, mayor 1983-86. **Orgs:** Member Wrightsville Chamber of Commerce; member NAACP; deacon Zion Hill Baptist Church; member Black Mayor's Assn; chmn Wrightsville Citizens In Action. **Honors/Awds:** Martin Luther King Award-Black Community Devel Program of Hoover UMC for struggle to incorporate the township of Wrightsville; Outstanding Leadership, The Univ of Arkansas at Pine Bluff 1986; Outstanding Leadership & Dedicated Serv, City of Wrightsville 1986. **Home Addr:** 13409 Asher Rd, Little Rock, AR 72206. **Business Addr:** PO Box 282, Sweet Home, AR 72164.

WHITE, VAN FREEMAN.
City official (retired). **Personal:** Born Aug 2, 1924, Minneapolis, MN; died Jul 13, 1993; son of WellerWhite and Van White;

married Javanese Verona Ewing; children: Perri Merle, Javoni Verona. **Educ:** Univ of MN, attended. **Career:** Dept of Public Works City of Mpls, construction 1956-68; Dept of Economic Security, interviewer/counselor 1968-79; City of Minneapolis, council member 5th Ward, 1980-90. **Orgs:** Chairperson Govt Operations Comm; mem Comm on Youth Employment; mem Comm Develop Comm; mem Public Health & Safety Comm; co-author First Source Agreement Economic Develop Linked with Job Oppor for Disadvantaged & Unemployed Minneapolis Residents; chmn Viking Council Hiawatha Dist Comm Task Force Boy Scouts of Amer; founder & past chairperson Willard-Homewood Organ; 1st coord City Crime Prevention Prog; established Women/Minority Business Enterprise Set-Aside Prog Minority Women's Economic Task Force; mem Licenses & Consumer Services Comm. **Honors/Awds:** Political Achievement Awd NAACP 1980; Outstanding Civic Serv AwdMinneapolis Urban League 1981; article published in Essence magazine ''Pornography & Pride'' 1984; Outstanding Serv to Comm Phyllis Wheatley Comm Ctr 1984; Cert of Recognition USAF Acad Outstanding Contribution through USAF Academy &AFROTC Commissioning Progs; Outstanding Awareness Awd Minneapolis City Adv Common People with Disabilities; awd Natl Alliance of Business Jobs; Leader for Excellence Award, Natl Assn of Minority Contractors 1988; Outstanding Leadership Award from Twin Cities O.I.C. 1988; Commendation Award, City Council for Workable Program; Van Freeman White bust placed in City Hall. **Home Addr:** 800 Washburn Ave N, Minneapolis, MN 55411. **Business Addr:** Former Councilmember, City of Minneapolis, 307 City Hall, Minneapolis, MN 55415.

WHITEMAN, HERBERT WELLS, JR.
Bank executive. **Personal:** Born Sep 11, 1936, New York, NY; died Oct 18, 1997, Brooklyn, NY; son of Catherine Caton Whiteman and Herbert W Whiteman Sr; married Nola Lancaster; children: Cheryl Alyse Whiteman Brooks. **Educ:** Columbia Univ, BS Engrg 1964; NY Univ, MS Civil Engrg 1973; Harvard Univ Grad Bus Admin, Adv Mgmt Prog 1985. **Career:** IBM Corp, system engr 1965-70, mktg rep 1970-73, industry mktg rep 1973-74, sys engrg mgr 1974-75, intl mktg mgr 1975-77; Fed Reserve Bank, vicepres 1977-84, group vice pres 1984-96, vice pres bank supervision group. **Orgs:** Grammateus 1982-90, sire archon 1991-92, Sigma Pi Phi Boule, chairman of Audit and Budget of Grand Boule, 1991-94, Regional Sire Archon-Elect 1993-95; Regional Sire Archon, 1995-97; vice pres Colony South Brooklyn Settlement House 1985-97; pres, Urban Bankers Coalition 1989-91; regional vp, Natl Assn of Urban Bankers, 1990-97; Member of NY Clearinghouse; Member of the American Bankers Assoc Information Systems Security Committee; former member, American Bankers Assn Committee X9 on Financial Services of the American National Standards Institute;chairman of the board, York College Foundation; president, Amboy Neighborhood Center; vice chairman, Bedford Stuyvesant Restoration Corp, board member, treasury, Odyssey Home Foundation, board member, Transit Museum of NYC Board. **Honors/Awds:** Meritorious Service Award, National Assn of Urban Bankers, 1993, 1994; Banker of the Year Urban Bankers Coaliton 1980; Golden Circle IBM; Systems Symposium IBM; Presidents Awd Fed Reserve Bank 1983; Systems Engineer of the year, New York Banking IBM, 1968. **Business Addr:** Vice Pres, Bank Supervision Group, Federal Reserve Bank of NY, 33 Liberty St, New York, NY 10045, (212)720-6186.

WILLIAMS, MALCOLM DEMOSTHENES.
Educational administrator (retired). **Personal:** Born Sep 26, 1909, Warsaw, NC; died Nov 8, 1991; son of Martha Eliza Williams and Holly Williams; marriedRosa Lee Kittrell, Jun 30, 1930 (deceased); children: Frances Eliza. **Educ:** Fayetteville State Tchrs Coll, diploma (w/honors) 1934; Hampton Inst, BS (w/honors) 1938; Columbia Tchrs Coll, MA 1944, EdD 1951; diploma (with honors) Fayette State University, Fayetteville, N.C. 1928-1934; BS (with honors) Hampton Univ, Hampton, VA 1934-38. **Career:** NC, tchr prin supr pub sch 1928-52; Columbia Univ Teachers Coll, asst to the prof 1947; teacher Hampton Inst summer 1949; Shaw Univ, prof/dir Audio-visual aids 1952-55; TX So Univ, teacher summer school 1954-55; TN State Univ Nashville, faculty 1955-75. **Orgs:** Life mem NEA; mem Religious Heritage of Amer; past pres Frontiers Intl Inc; Phi Delta Kappa; Kappa Delta Pi UNA/USA; mem Omega Psi Phi Frat, Natl Soc for the Study of Educ. **Honors/Awds:** Silver Beaver Awd BSA; Disting Educator Religious Heritage of Amer; Nashville Urban League's Equal Oppor Day Awd. **Home Addr:** 630 Nocturne Dr, Nashville, TN 37207.

WILLIAMS, ROBERT W.
Business executive. **Personal:** Born Sep 21, 1922, Ottumwa, IA; died Sep 8, 1997, Pasadena, CA; son of Bertha E. Williams and Henry H. Williams; married Joan R Moore; children: Angela, Robin, Robert W II. **Educ:** Temple Univ, attended; UCLA, attended. **Career:** Bohemian Dist Co,salesman 1952-55; Falstaff Brewing Co, mgr 1957-65; Somerset Importers Ltd, mgr; Norton simon Co, marketing and communications specialist, untl 1984; Hunt Wesson, retired pres; True Image Prod, pres. **Orgs:** Mem LA African Sister City Comm, Natl Assoc Market Devel, Screen Actors Guild, Amer Fed TV Artists, Urban Coalition, Amer Friends Serv Comm, Brookside Mens Golf Club, NAACP, PTA; pres Devel Bd CA State Univ LA; mem Black Bus Assoc, Tuskegee Airmen Inc; commr, Utility Commn of Pasadena; President's Advisory Bd, California State Univ, Los Angeles; mem, Found Bd, California State Univ, Los Angeles. **Honors/Awds:** ''The Ottumwa Kid'', creat, prod & hosted human relatTV shows; 1st natl to host black talk show 1962; author ''Redtails at Ramitelli''. **Special Achievements:** Author & Co-Executive Producer of the highly acclaimed movie made for HBO ''The Tuskegee Airmen'' which won the prestigious ''Peabody Awd,'' NAACP ''Image Awd,'' three of nine nominations for ''Emmy Awards,'' one of seven ''Cable Ace,'' Awd nominations; Proclamations from Congress, State of California, County of Los Angeles, City of Los Angeles, City of Pasadena, The Urban League, many churches and schools. **Military Serv:** :USAF capt 1942-47; Disting Flying Cross; Air Medal w/6 OLC; Pres Unit Cit; mem,Tuskegee Airmen, 100th Squadron, 332nd Fighter Group. **Business Addr:** President, True Image Prod, 1220 N. Arroyo Blvd, Pasadena, CA 91103.

WILLIAMS, THOMAS PEDWORTH.
Government official. **Personal:** Born Oct 17, 1910, Brunswick, GA; died Oct 31, 1991; married Birdie Palmer. **Educ:** Clark Clge Atlanta GA, BA 1933; NY Univ NYC, MA 1956.**Career:** City of Brunswick GA, mayor pro tem 1978-80; McIntosh Co Acad Darien GA, asst prin 1970-79; Eulonia Elem Sch Eulonia GA, prin 1954-70; Folkston HS Folkston GA, asst prin 1951-54. **Orgs:** Elected to city commn S WardBrunswick GA 1976; bd dir Chamber of Comm City of Brunswick 1978-80; mem Chamber of Comm Tourist & Conv Council 1978-80; adv council mem Job Corp Glynco GA 1978-80; mem Brunswick-St Simons Causeway Com 1978-80; bd dir CAPDC Coastal Area Planning & Devel Commn 1978-80. **Honors/Awds:** Hnr mem GA Peace Officers Assc Brunswick GA 1977-81; Manifold Contrib to Mankind Prince Hall Grand Lodge 1979; serv rendered to Admin Fac Staff & Students Darien 1979; distg serv to Tourism Chamber of Comm Brunswick GA 1980; Travel Rep City of Brunswick to Taiwan China (Sisters City Prog) 1978; & Olinda Brazil (GA's Partners Prog) 1980. **Business Addr:** City of Brunswick, Gloucester St PO Box550, Brunswick, GA 31520.

WILSON, LEROY, III.
Educational administrator. **Personal:** Born Oct 11, 1951, Clearwater, FL; died Oct 31, 1995;married Alpha Marie Allen; children: Jobyna Nadirah; Sisina Eudora. **Educ:** East Side High School Newark NJ, HS Diploma 1969; Seton Hall Univ, South Orange NJ, (Political Science) BA 1973, (Asian Studies) MA 1977, (Public Admin) MPA1988. **Career:** Newark Star, Leger, newsreporter 1969-73; NY Stock Exchange, stock investigator 1973-75; Seton Hall Univ, Upward Bound, assoc dir, 1975-79, dir 1979-95. **Orgs:** Assn for Equality & Excellence in Educ, chmn, bdof dirs 1977-95; East Orange NJ Branch-Kiwanis Intl, vice pres 1981; East Orange, NJ YMCA, vice chmn, bd of mgmt 1981; Eta Pi Chapter-Omega Psi Phi Fraternity,basileus 1987-88; Abyssinia Temple No 1, potentate, 1986-87; Amer Mgmt Assn, 1985-95; Amer Soc for Public Admin, 1985-95. **Honors/Awds:** Mayor's Medal for Outstanding Student Leadership-City of Newark, NJ 1969; Omega Man of the Year-Kappa Eta Chapter-Omega Psi Phi Fraternity 1982; Distinquished Alumnus-New Jersey Educational Opportunity Fund 1986. **Business Addr:** Dir, Seton Hall University, 400 South Orange Ave, South Orange, NJ 07079.

WILSON, LIONEL J.
Attorney, former city official. **Personal:** Born Mar 14, 1915, New Orleans, LA; died Jan 23, 1998, Oakland, CA; married Dorothy P; children: Lionel B, Robin, Steven. **Educ:** Univ of CA Berkeley, BA 1939; Hastings Coll of Law, JD 1949. **Career:** Private practice, attny 1950-60; Oakland Piedmont, municipal court judge 1960-64; Alameda Cty, superior ct judge 1964-76; Criminal Div Alameda Superior Court, presiding judge; Appellate Dept of Alameda Cty Superior Court, presiding judge; City of Oakland, mayor 1977-90. **Orgs:** Chmn Presiding Judges of CA & Superior Courts; mem CETA; past pres, founding mem, bd of dir New Oakland Comm; adv com Alameda Cty Council on Alcoholism, Alameda Cty Mental Health Assoc; consult Far West School; chmn, pres Oakland Econ Devel Council Inc, Oakland Men of Tomorrow, Charles Houston Law Club; bd dir Oakland & Berkeley Br NAACP; chmn Oakland Anti-Poverty Bd; former chmn Legal Redress Com of Alameda Cty & Berkeley Br NAACP. **Honors/Awds:** 1st black judge in Alameda Cty; West Coast Reg Merit Awd NAACP; Awd for Outstanding Professional Serv No CA Med Dental & Pharmaceutical Assoc; The Oak CtrInc Awd, A Judge for All Seasons; Man of the Year Oakland Lodge 252 B'Nai Brith1977-78; 1st black mayor of Oakland CA 1977; Leadership Awd Chinese Amer Citizens Alliance 1979; Marcus-Foster Inst Awd; Outstanding Alumnus of the Oakland Publ School for Law & Govt 1979; appointed State Comprehensive Employment Training Act Bd Gov Edmund G Brown Jr; appointed by Pres Jimmy Carter to US Com on Selection of Fed Judicial Officers for US Court of Patents & Appeals. **Military Serv:** AUS 1st sgt 1941-45.

WITHERSPOON, JAMES. (SPOON)
Singer. **Personal:** Born Aug 8, 1923, Gurdon, AR; died Sep 18, 1997, Los Angeles, CA; married Diana; children: Angela Witherspoon-Ballard, Regina Witherspoon-Welch, James Witherspoon Jr. **Career:** Jay McShaun, singer 1940's; rhythm & blues singer 1950's; toured US, Europe 1960's; appearances incl Monterey Jazz Festival 1959. **Honors/Awds:** Downbeat Magazine, Critic's Poll New Star Award, 1961; inductee: Hollywood Palace Hall of Fame, 1993; Grammy awards, best traditional album, nominated, 1995. **Special Achievements:** Recordings include, ''Evolution of the Blues Song'', ''At the Renaissance'' 1960, ''Baby, Baby, Baby'' 1964, ''Best Blue Soon'' 1965, ''Blues Around Clock'' 1964, ''Blues for Easy Livers'' 1967, ''Blues Singer'', ''Evening Blues'', ''How'', ''Song of My Best Friends'' 1965, ''Spoon in London'' 1966, ''Love Is A Five Letter Word'' with Robben Ford, 1975; recorded with Ford album, ''Live At The Mint'', circa 1990. **Business Addr:** c/o Abby Hoffer Enterprises, 223 1/2 E 48th St, New York, NY 10017.

WOMACK, ROBERT W., SR.
Columnist, professional musician. **Personal:** Born Jul 10, 1916, Jackson, TN; died Dec 23, 1984; married Mary L Moore; children: Bobby. **Educ:** Univ of IL, attended 1930's; McArthur & Jordan Consult of Music 1940's. **Career:** Indianapolis Recorder Newspaper, assoc theatrical editorial columnist; BobCats TV All-Stars, bandleader 1939-67; Ferguson Bros Theatrical Agency, founder/prof of music 1940-50; Recorder Newspaper, assoc theatrical editor. **Orgs:** Began first interracial large band 1943; helped pass State Record Piracy Ban Bill in state leg 1974; mem Indianapolis NAACP; pol rep Elks Lodge 709; pres Womack Enterprises; mem Marion Co Sheriff's & Police Press Clubs 10 yrs, recorder 20 yrs; prof musician incl sideman 30 yrs; plays part-timedrummer; one of first blacks of AFM Loc 3. **Honors/Awds:** Started Musi-Entertainers' Club 1970; Writer of Yr by loc mus 1974. **Business Addr:** Assoc Theatrical Ed, Recorder Newspaper, 2901 N Tacoma Ave, Indianapolis, IN 46218.

WOODS, SYLVANIA WEBB, SR.
Judge (retired). **Personal:** Born Aug 4, 1927, Fort Gaines, GA; died Jun 21, 1997; married Geneva Holloway; children: Sylvania Jr, Sebrena. **Educ:** Morris Brown College, BA, 1949; Atlanta Univ, 1951; Washington College of Law, LLB, 1960.**Career:** Circuit Court of Maryland, judge, 1990-97; District Court of Maryland, judge, 1976-90; private practice, attorney, 1960-76; US Postal Aerv, clerk, 1955-60; DC Plc Dept, police officer, 1954-55. **Orgs:** DC Bar Assn, 1961; Natl Bar Assn; MD Bar Assn, 1969; Amer Bar Assn; J Davis Cnsstry 32nd Degree Masons; Flx Lodge No 3 Free and Accepted Masons; Upper Room Baptist Church, Deacon Bd; American Legion; YMCA; NAACP. **Honors/Awds:** Purple Heart, Erpn& Pcfc Thtrs, USN 1943-45. **Military Serv:** USN stewart's mate first class, 1943-45.

WRIGHTEN, JOHN H., III.
Attorney. **Personal:** Born in Edisto Island, SC; died Oct 2, 1996, Sumter,SC; married Dorothy Lillian Richardson; children: Doris Powell, Dr. Gwendolyn Montgomery, Jerushai Kelly, Jarma Tolbert,John H. 4th, James, Dwight, Michael, David, Quintus, Lyndon, Vonshurii. **Educ:** South Carolina State College LawSchool, JD. **Career:** Attorney, private practice, begin 1959. **Special Achievements:** Lawsuit against Univ of SC Law School in 1946 led to SC State College Law School for African American students.

YOUNG, COLEMAN A.
Educator, mayor (retired). **Personal:** Born May 24, 1918, Tuscaloosa, AL; died Nov 29, 1997, Detroit, MI; children: Coleman, Jr. **Educ:** Hon Doctorates, Univ of MI, Stillman Coll, Univ of Detroit, Wayne State Univ, Central State Univ. **Career:** MI Constitutional Conv, del 1961-62; State of MI, senator 1964-73; former ins executive; Chain of DryCleaners, mgr; City of Detroit, mayor 1974-93; Wayne State Univ, prof of urban affairs. **Orgs:** Involved in early organizing battles of UAW; took a leadership role in the Wayne Co CIO & combined civil rights & labor activities as exec sec Natl Negro Labor Council; vice chmn Democratic Natl Comm 1977-81; pres USConf of Mayors 1982-83. **Honors/Awds:** First African-American to serve on Democratic Natl Comm 1968; Jefferson Awd from the Amer Inst for Public Serv for the Greatest Public Serv performed by an elected or apptd official 1979; NAACPSpingarn Medal for Distinguished Achievement as an Afro-Amer 1981; 1982 Adam Clayton Powell Awd for Outstanding Political Leadership from Congressional Black Caucus. **Military Serv:** USAC commissioned officer WW II.

Geographic Index

ALABAMA

Alberta
Pettway, Jo Celeste

Alexander City
Powers, Runas, Jr.

Aliceville
King, Ceola

Andalusia
Carpenter, Lewis
Henderson, Lloyd D.

Anniston
Banks, Manley E.
Nettles, John Spratt
Owens, Nathaniel Davis
Trammell, William Rivers

Athens
Higgins, Bennett Edward

Atmore
Grissett, Willie James
McBride, Ullysses
Shuford, Humphrey Lewis

Auburn
Ferguson, Andrew L.
Hendricks, Constance Smith
Wilson, David

Bay Minette
Allen, Walter R.

Bayou La Batre
Benjamin, Regina M.

Beatrice
Brown, George Houston

Bessemer
Alexander, Lydia Lewis
Kidd, Herbert, Jr.
McDowell, Benjamin A.
Miller, Wilbur J.
Mitchell, Quitman J.
Patterson, Clinton David
Rogers, Freddie Clyde
Wilson, Robert Stanley

Birmingham
Adams, Oscar W., Jr.
Alexander, Lydia Lewis
Alexander, Wardine Towers
Anthony, Emory
Arrington, Richard, Jr.
Baker, Beverly Poole
Baldwin, Mitchell Cardell
Balton, Kirkwood R.
Baskin, Yvonne E.
Bell, William A.
Billingsley, Orzell, Jr.
Blankenship, Eddie L.
Blankenship, Glenn Rayford
Bonner, Bester Davis
Boykin, Joel S.

Brown, John Andrew
Burgess, Dwight A.
Calhoun, Eric A.
Campbell, Arthur Ree
Carter, Lemorie, Jr.
Chambers, Harry, Jr.
Champion, Jesse
Clemon, U. W.
Cunningham, Malena Ann
Dale, Louis
Davis, J. Mason, Jr.
Dickson, Charlie Jones
Dixon, Joseph N.
Eddleman, William Thomas
Edwards, Ronald Wayne
Evans, Leon, Jr.
Faush, Erskine R.
Flakes, Larry Joseph
Flood, Shearlene Davis
Gaston, Minnie L.
Graham, James C., Jr.
Griffin, Lula Bernice
Hammonds, Cleveland, Jr.
Harris, Paul E.
Hilliard, Earl Frederick
Ivory, Carolyn Kay
James, Frank Samuel, III
Jenkins, Shirley Lymons
Johnson, Leroy
Johnson, Sarah Yvonne
Jones, Clyde Eugene
Kennon, Daniel, Jr.
King, Lewis Henry
Knight, Toni
Lewis, James E.
Lewis, Jesse J.
Mack, Roderick O'Neal
Manney, William A.
Martin-Ogunsola, Dellita Lillian
Matchett, Johnson, Jr.
McCain, Ella Byrd
McNair, Chris
McTier, Roselyn Jones
McWhorter, Grace Agee
Milner, Michael Edwin
Mitchell, Ossie Ware
Morgan, Juanita Kennedy
Murray, Anna Martin
Nelson, Artie Cortez
Nelson, Debra J.
Newton, Demetrius C.
Newton, Robert
Nixon, John William
Owens, Kenneth, Jr.
Patrick, Jennie R.
Pitt, Clifford Sinclair
Priest, Marlon L.
Reese, Milous J.
Ricks, Albert William
Rivers, Valerie L.
Scales, Jerome C.
Shepherd, Elmira
Shipp, Melvin Douglas
Sloan, Albert J. H., II
Smith, Sundra Shealey
Smitherman, Rodger M.
Solomon, Donald L.
Spencer, Sharon A.
Spratt, Lewis G.
Stewart, Shelley
Stokes, Bunny, Jr.

Streeter, Debra Brister
Syler, M. Rene
Taylor, Albert, Jr.
Taylor, Andre Jerome
Thomas, Louphenia
Timmons-Toney, Deborah Denise
Turner, Yvonne Williams
Vaughn, Audrey Smith
Ward, Perry W.
Wells, Bobby Ray
White, Christine Larkin
Williams, W. Clyde
Womack, Christopher Clarence
Wright, Wilson, Jr.

Brewton
Jones, Sherman J.
Thomas, Robert Lewis

Brighton
Lewis, Richard U.
Thomas, Jewel M.

Camden
Johnson, Bobby JoJo
Pettway, Jo Celeste
Thomas, James L.

Catherine
Hayes, Charles

Chatom
Dixon, Willie

Clanton
Agee, Bobby L.

Daphne
Wickware, Damon

Decatur
Gilliam, Joel
Jacobs, Larry Ben
Ragland, Wylheme Harold

Demopolis
Lankster, Barrown Douglas

Dothan
Greenfield, William Russell, Jr.
Lawson-Thomas, Althea Shannon

Enterprise
James, Peggi C.

Eutaw
Isaac, Earlean
Kirksey, Peter J.
Means, Donald Fitzgerald

Fairfield
Lloyd, Barbara Ann
Scott, Carstella H.

Florence
Brown, Alyce Doss
Davis, Ernestine Bady
Hardy, Dorothy C.
Liner, Lamont

Robinson, Thelma Maniece

Forkland
Branch, William McKinley

Fort Deposit
Means, Elbert Lee

Gadsden
Adams, Quinton Douglas
Lowe, Jack, Jr.
Presley, Lawrence
Sandridge, John Solomon
Thomas, Spencer
Turman, Robert L., Sr.

Greenville
Cook, James E.

Grove Hill
Hansan, Samuel L.

Harvest
Lacy, Hugh Gale

Hayneville
Jackson, John
Means, Elbert Lee

Helena
Baker, Beverly Poole

Hueytown
Grayson, Elsie Michelle

Huntsville
Batts, Huntley
Bradley, Jessie Mary
Briggins, Charles E.
Buck, Judith Brooks
Campbell, Carlos, Sr.
Caples, Virginia
Crutcher, Buford
Germany, Sylvia Marie Armstrong
Grayson, George Welton
Henry-Fairhurst, Ellenae L.
Hereford, Sonnie Wellington, III
Heyward, James Oliver
Lacy, Hugh Gale
Lacy, Walter
McCray, Roy Howard
Mitchell, Dolphus Burl
Montgomery, Oscar Lee
Moseley, Calvin Edwin, Jr.
Rainey, Timothy Mark
Reaves, Benjamin Franklin
Reynolds, James W.
Richard, Floyd Anthony
Stanmore, Roger Dale
Wimbush, Gary Lynn
Wyatt, Ronald Michael

Hurtsboro
Stovall-Tapley, Mary Kate

Jacksonville
Foster, Portia L.
Fox, Theodore B.
Watts, Roberta Ogletree

Jasper
Underwood, Frankye Harper

Jemison
Reed, Eddie

Lafayette
Vester, Terry Y.

Letohatchee
Smith, Charles

Lisman
Edwards, Luther Howard

Livingston
Jackson, Claude
Jackson, Tommy L.

Lower Peach Tree
Smith, Frank

Madison
Reynolds, James W.
Richard, Floyd Anthony

Maxwell AFB
Calhoun, Dorothy Eunice
Cochran, Donnie L.

Midfield
Frazier, Jordan

Midway
Thomas, Wilbon

Mobile
Boyd, Marvin
Brown, D. Joan
Buskey, James E.
Chapman, Diana Cecelia
Dapremont, Delmont, Jr.
Day, Eric Therander
Figures, Thomas H.
Guyton, Sister Patsy
Hazzard, Terry Louis
Holloway, Joaquin Miller, Jr.
James, Lee A., Jr.
Johnson, Clinton Lee, Sr.
Kennedy, Cain James
Kennedy, James E.
Kennedy, Yvonne
Lamar, Cleveland James
McKinnis, Clifton T.
Mitchell, Joseph Christopher
Norvel, William Leonard
Patterson, Ronald E.
Porter, Charles William
Roberson, Earl
Smith, Elaine Marie
Smith, William Milton
Thrower, Julius B.
Ware, Irene Johnson
Womack, Joe Neal, Jr.

Montgomery
Baker, C. C.
Bell, Katie Roberson
Bibb, T. Clifford

Boggs, Nathaniel
Boyd, Delores Rosetta
Bryson, Ralph J.
Buskey, John
Calhoun, Dorothy Eunice
Calhoun, Gregory Bernard
Conley, Charles S.
Cook, Ralph D.
Davis, Norman Emanuel
DeShields, Harrison F., Jr.
Farrow, Willie Lewis
Figures, Michael
Gaines, Mary E.
Harris, Willa Bing
Harris, William H.
Holmes, Alvin Adolf
Hornbuckle, Dorethea
Howard, Leon
Johnson, Paul Edwin
Knight, John F., Jr.
Langford, Charles D.
Larkin, Byrdie A.
Lawson, William Daniel
Long, Gerald Bernard
Markham, Houston, Jr.
McClammy, Thad C.
McDuffie, Hinfred
McPherson, Vanzetta Penn
Mitchell, Kelly Karnale
Moore, Archie Bradford, Jr.
Moore, Nathan
Myers, Jacqualine Desmona
Norman, Georgette M.
Osby, Parico Green
Perdue, George
Powell, William J.
Price, Charles
Pryor, Calvin Caffey
Pryor, Julius, Jr.
Reed, Joe Louis
Robinson, Carrie C.
Sanders, Isaac Warren
Smiley, Emmett L.
Spears, Henry Albert, Sr.
Stanley, Curtis E.
Stanley, Kathryn Velma
Stevenson, Bryan
Thomas, Ora P.
Thompson, Myron H.
Vaughn, Percy Joseph, Jr.
Watkins, Levi
Weiss, Joyce Lacey
Winston, John H., Jr.

Normal
Byrd, Taylor
Covington, H. Douglas
Frazier, Leon
Gibson, John Thomas
Gurley, Dorothy J.
Henson, David Bernard
Heyward, James Oliver
Marbury, Carl Harris
Morrison, Richard David
Pearson, Clifton

Northport
Culpepper, Lucy Nell
Davis, Joseph Solomon
Thomas, Frankie Taylor

Opelika
Agee, Thomas Lee

Ozark
Jarmon, James Henry, Jr.

Pell City
McGowan, Elsie Henderson

Pine Hill
Johnson, Bobby JoJo
Mahan-Powell, Lena

Prattville
Larkin, Byrdie A.

Prichard
Boyd, Gwendolyn Viola, Dr.
Clark, William
Crenshaw, Reginald Anthony
Johnson, Viteria Copeland
Langham, John M.

Ridgeville
Adair, Charles, Jr.

Roanoke
Terry, Roy

Selma
Brown, Julius Ray
Dawson, B. W.
Garcia, William Burres
Hendricks, Constance Smith
Hunter, John Davidson
Jackson, Michael W.
Jenkins, Julius
Reese, Frederick D.
Sanders, Hank
Tate, Earnest L.

Sylacauga
McElrath, Wanda Faith
McIntyre, John Henry, Sr.

Talladega
Franklin, Harold A.
Johnson, Joseph B.
Mohr, Paul B.

Tuscaloosa
Appleton, Clevette Wilma
Culpepper, Lucy Nell
Delaney, John Paul
Fredd, Chester Arthur
Gray, Myrtle Edwards
Hall, Ethel Harris
Hubbard, Amos B.
Johnson, Rhoda E.
Lockett, James D.
Mallisham, Joseph W.
McCrackin, Olympia F.
Melton, Bryant
Owens, Charles Edward
Prewitt, Lena Voncille Burrell
Smith, Bettie M.
Stinson, Constance Robinson
Whittaker, Sharon Elaine

Tuscumbia
Bailey, Bob Carl
Smith, Otis Benton, Jr.

Tuskegee
Allman, Marian Isabel
Baker, Willie J.
Carter, Billy L.
Davis, Milton C.
Davis, Norman Emanuel
Ford, Johnny
Gray, Fred David
Hardy, Charlie Edward
Harvey, Richard R.
Henson, William Francis
Holland, Major Leonard
Holmes, Lee
Johnson, James A.
Lee, Detroit
Payton, Benjamin Franklin
Peterson, William T.
Robinson, Wilbur R.
Scott, Leonard Lamar
Smith, Jock Michael
Williams, Ronald
Wright, James W.

Tuskegee Institute
Adams, Eugene William
Baldwin, Wilhelmina F.
Biswas, Prosanto K.
Bowie, Walter C.
Carter, Herbert E.
Carter, Howard Payne
Childs, Theodore Francis
Dawson, William Levi
Goodwin, Robert T., Sr.
Henderson, James H. M.
Hodge, William Anthony
Huffman, Rufus C.
Louis, Suchet Lesperance
Payton, Benjamin Franklin
Price, John Elwood
Reed, Thomas J.
Robinson, Ella S.
St. Omer, Vincent V. E.
Scott, Leonard Lamar
Thompson, Charles H.
Washington, Linda Phaire
Whatley, Booker Tillman
Williams, Althea Bulls

Union Springs
Hodge, William Anthony
Lewis, Meharry Hubbard

Uniontown
May, James F.
Moore, David Bernard, II

Valley
Crawley, Oscar Lewis

York
Black, Lucius, Sr.
Nixon, Felix Nathaniel

ALASKA

Anchorage
Bailey-Thomas, Sheryl K.
Card, Larry D.
Davis, Bettye J.
Davis, Etheldra S.
Douglas, Nicholas
Greene, William
Jackson, Charles Ellis
Lyons, William B.
Neal, Sylvester
Patterson, Alonzo B.
Pendergraft, Michele M.
Smith, Carol Barlow
Taylor, Sterling R.

Eagle River
Greene, William

Fairbanks
Dunlap King, Virgie M.
Smith, Robert London

Juneau
Henderson, Remond
McSmith, Blanche Preston

North Pole
Hunter, James Nathaniel, II

Palmer
Simton, Chester

ARIZONA

Chandler
Fowler, Reggie

Coolidge
Colbert, George Clifford

Cottonwood
Bange, Monroe

Douglas
Cain, Johnnie M.
Sims, Deborah

Eloy
Beasley, Edward, III

Flagstaff
Hannah, Melvin James
Johnson, Theodore L.
Locket, Arnold, Jr.
Ross, Anthony Roger

Fort Huachuca
Allen, George Mitchell

Glendale
Barnwell, Henry Lee

Laveen
Minor, Willie

Mesa
Fuller, Dr. Harold David

Paradise Valley
Parker, Vernon B.

Phoenix
Ambers, Monique
Avent, Jacques Myron
Barnwell, Henry Lee
Beachem, Constance
Black, Joseph
Blackmon, Anthony Wayne
Blanton, Ricky

Brown, Tony
Bryant, Mark
Chapman, Samuel Milton
Cooper, Duane
Culver, Rhonda
Davis, Ben Jerome
Davis, Major
Dudley, Amos H.
Dumas, Richard
Foster, Toni
Gaines, Corey Yasuto
Gillom, Jennifer
Goode, Calvin C.
Grigsby, Jefferson Eugene, Jr.
Hall, Christine C. Iijima
Hamilton, Art
Henry, Herman
Jackson, Mannie L.
Jackson, Tia
Johnson, Gus, Jr.
Johnson, Kevin Maurice
Johnson, Ray
Jones, Chris
Kidd, Jason Fredrick
Knight, Tom
Kunes, Ken R.
Logan, George, III
Lowery, Carolyn T.
Mackey, Malcolm
Manning, Daniel Ricardo
McCloud, George Aaron
McDyess, Antonio Keithflen
Merchant, John F.
Meridith, Denise P.
Miller, Cheryl De Ann
Montague, Lee
Nelson, Doeg M.
Patterson, Cecil Booker, Jr.
Pearson, Stanley E.
Pettis, Bridget
Pitts, John Martin
Pulliam, Harvey Jerome, Jr.
Ragsdale, Lincoln Johnson
Robinson, Clifford Ralph
Scott, Dennis Eugene
Seneca, Arlena E.
Smith, Charles James, III
Stewart, Warren Hampton, Sr.
Tisdale, Waymon Lawrence
Walker, Carolyn
Watson, Genevieve
Webb, Umeki
White, Devon Markes
Wilber, Ida Belinda
Williams, Cody
Williams, John
Wilson, Michael

Scottsdale
Jackson, Karen Denise
Moore, Sam
Reid, F. Theodore, Jr.

Sun City West
Gaines, Thurston Lenwood, Jr.

Tempe
Alexander, Brent
Anderson, Steve
Bankston, Michael
Bennett, Tommy
Brouhard, Deborah Taliaferro
Brown, Lomas, Jr.
Bryant, Leon Serle
Caldwell, Mike Isiah
Campbell, Mark
Carter, Pat
Centers, Larry
Cobbins, Lyron
Culver, Rhonda
Darby, Matthew Lamont
Davis, Thomas Joseph
Douglas, Bobby Eddie
Edwards, Anthony
Edwards, John L.
Frazier, Herman Ronald
Guynes, Thomas
Hardaway, Jerry David
Harris, Rubie J.
Harris, Walter, Jr.
Harrison, Mernoy Edward, Jr.
Hill, Eric
Hollin, Kenneth Ronald
Howard, Ty
Irving, Terry Duane
Johnson, LeShon Eugene
Knight, Thomas
Lassiter, Kwamie
McCleskey, J.J.

McCombs, Tony
McElroy, Leeland
Miller, Jamir Malik
Minor, Willie
Montgomery, Toni-Marie
Moore, Derrick
Moore, Rob
Moore, Ronald
Redmon, Anthony
Rice, Simeon
Sanders, Frank Vondel
Smith, A. Wade
Smith, Cedric Delon
Stokes, Sheila Woods
Swann, Eric Jerrod
Swinger, Rashod
Ward, Arnette S.
Warren, Morrison Fulbright
Williams, Aeneas Demetrius
Williams, Kevin Ray
Wilson, Bernard
Wilson, Jeffrey R.

Tucson
Clarke, Raymond
Davis, Richard
Fluellen, Velda Spaulding
Goodwin, Felix L.
Hall, Albert
Harrell, Ernest James
Hernandez, Mary N.
Holsey, William Fleming, Jr.
Hopkins, Gayle P.
Johnson, Albert James
Lander, Cressworth Caleb
Lockett, Bradford R.
Meade-Tollin, Linda C.
Snowden, Fredrick
Thompson, Floyd
Todd, Charles O.
Walker, Maurice Edward
Whaley, Joseph S.
Zander, Jessie Mae

Yuma
Jefferson, James E.

ARKANSAS

Alexander
Dillard, Jackie Smith

Arkadelphia
Smith, Virginia M.
Thomas, Eula Wiley

Bentonville
Peterson, Coleman Hollis

Camden
Smith, Judy Seriale

Cherokee Village
Hollingsworth, John Alexander

Conway
Jones, Theodore

Cotton Plant
Babbs, Junious C., Sr.
Conley, Emmitt Jerome

Earle
Smith, Sherman

Edmondson
Croft, Ira T.

El Dorado
Barnes, Daniel B.
Gibson, Wayne Carlton
Sims, Pete, Jr.
Van Hook, George Ellis, Jr.

Fayetteville
Hoover, Theressa
Morgan, Gordon D.
Richardson, Nolan
Williams, Lonnie Ray
Young, Michael

Forrest City
Wilburn, Isaac Earphette

Coalinga
Russell, Beverly A.

Colton
Baker, Delbert Wayne
McKinney, Jesse Doyle

Compton
Andrews, Joseph Henry
Beauchamp, Patrick L.
Cade, Lionel C.
Clegg, Legrand H., II
Cobbs, David E.
Cooper, Lois Louise
Davis, Charles
Davis, Doris Ann
Dymally, Lynn V.
Filer, Kelvin Dean
Garrott, Homer L.
Goins, Mary G.
Hart, Emily
Henson, Charles A.
Hill, Betty J.
Hunn, Dorothy Fegan
Hunn, Myron Vernon
McKenna, George J., III
Patrick, Charles Namon, Jr.
Perdue, Franklin Roosevelt
Robinson, Jesse Lee
Sanders, Wesley, Jr.
Shah, Khalid Ibn
Wauls, Inez La Mar
White, Jerry
Woods, Bernice

Corona
Jackson, Vera Ruth
Tillman, Joseph Nathaniel

Corona Del Mar
Davis, Arthur D.

Cotati
Hill, Ray Allen

Covina
Allen, Charles E.
Walker, Arman Kennis

Culver City
Fanaka, Jamaa
Jackson, Giles B.
Lang, Charles J.
Lockley, Clyde William
Snowden, Raymond C.
Solomon, Barbara J.
Stevens, John Theodore, Sr.
Walden, Barbara
Washington, Rudy
Wilborn, Letta Grace Smith
Williams, Harriette F.

Cupertino
Bogus, SDiane Adamz
Clayton, Laura Ancelina

Cypress
Calhoun, Fred Steverson

Daly City
Ellis, Marilyn Pope
Lovelace, Onzalo Robert

Danville
Merritt, Anthony Lewis

Davis
Kondwani, Kofi Anum
Major, Clarence
Ramey, Melvin R.
Stewart, John Othneil

Diamond Bar
Davis, Brenda Lightsey-Hendricks
Hollingsworth, Alfred Delano

Downey
Grooms, Henry Randall

Dublin
Taylor, William Glenn

East Palo Alto
Satterwhite, Frank Joseph
Wilks, Gertrude

El Cajon
Riggs, Elizabeth A.

El Segundo
Doty, Romeo A.
Henderson, Charles
McPherson, William H.
Perkins, Louvenia Black
Powe, Joseph S.
Ray, Austin H.

Emeryville
Bragg, Robert Henry
Brown, Richard Earl
Harrold, Lawrence A.
Roach, Deloris

Encinitas
Alexander, Edward Cleve
Fisher, Edith Maureen

Encino
Maxwell Reid, Daphne Etta
McKnight, Brian
Mills, Donald
Mills, John
Milton, LeRoy
Najee
Warren, Michael
Washington, Keith

Fairfield
Robinson, Carol Evonne
Via, Thomas Henry

Folsom
Wells, Linda Ivy

Foster City
Pitts, Vera L.

Fremont
Jones, Vida Yvonne

Fresno
Aldredge, James Earl
Avery, Jeromye Lee
Burns, Felton
Curry, Andy
Ethridge, John E.
Ford, Richard D.
Fowlkes, Nelson J.
Francis, Charles S. L.
Goodwin, Hugh Wesley
Harvey, Raymond
Hunt, Samuel D.
Johnson, Frank J., Sr.
Jones, Ida M.
Kelley, Jack Albert
Kimber, Lesly H.
Parker, Stafford W.
Parks, James Edward
Pierce, Walter J.
Small, Lily B.
Smith, William James
White, Paul Christopher
Williams, Harold McNeal
Wint, Arthur Valentine Noris

Fullerton
Cobb, Jewel Plummer
Hagan, Willie James
Hargrove, John E.
McFerrin, Sara Elizabeth Copper
Nayman, Robbie L.
Smith, Jesse Owens
Stokes, Julie Elena

Gardena
Campbell, Everett O.
Florence, Jerry DeWayne
Hale, Gene
Johnson, Arthur L.
Lathen, Deborah Ann
Matthews, Leonard Louis
Parnell, Arnold W.
Sendaba, S. M.

Glendale
Ashford, L. Jerome
Carrington, Terri Lyne
Chavis, Omega Rochelle
Farrell, Cheryl Layne
Taylor, Edgar R.
White, Charles R.

Granada Hills
Mance, John J.
McCraven, Carl Clarke

Harbor City
Hardin, Eugene
Richardson, Alfred Lloyd

Hawthorne
Peele, John E., Jr.
Pualani, Gloria

Hayward
Adams, Cecil Ray
Ambeau, Karen M.
Andrews, Malachi
Ballard, Myrtle Ethel
Bassard, Yvonne Brooks
Bowser, Benjamin Paul
Carmichael, Benjamin G.
Chuks-Orji, Austin
Franklin, Allen D.
Kitchen, Wayne Leroy
Lovett, Mack, Jr.
Payne, Jerry Oscar
Pitts, Vera L.
White, Bryan
Williams, Brainard

Hollywood
Beverly, Frankie
Cole, Natalie
Fann, Al Louis
Goodson, James Abner, Jr.
Hammer, M. C.
Jackson, Freddie
Jordan, Stanley
King, Brett
McFerrin, Bobby
Moore, Melba
Morgan, Meli'sa
Neville, Aaron
Osborne, Jeffrey Linton
Peniston, CeCe
Ramsey, David P.
Shaw, Curtis Mitchell
Spencer, Tracie
Wyatt, William N.

Inglewood
Abdul-Jabbar, Kareem
Anderson, Henry L. N.
Barnes, William L.
Benjamin, Rose Mary
Bennett, Mario Marcell
Blount, Corie Kasoun
Bryant, Kobe B.
Campbell, Elden
Carson, Willis E.
Charles, Daedra
Colleton, Katrina
Davis, Willie D.
Dixon, Tamecka
Dorn, Roosevelt F.
Drew, Larry Donelle
Dymally, Mervyn M.
Fisher, Derek Lamar
Fox, Rick
Franklin, Kirk
Gant, Travesa
Hankins, Hesterly G., III
Horry, Robert Keith
James, Charles Leslie
Johnson, Earvin, Jr.
Jones, Eddie Charles
Kimble, Bettye Dorris
Matthews, Leonard Louis
Matthews, Mallory Louis
McBeth-Reynolds, Sandra Kay
McGee, Pamela
Moseley, James Orville B.
O'Neal, Shaquille Rashaun
Ormsby, William M.
Phillips, Frank Edward
Reid, Benjamin F.
Richardson, Nola Mae
Rooks, Sean Lester
Scott, Timothy Van
Seals, Shea
Simmons, Emmett Bryson, III
Simpson, Gregory Louis
Slade, Karen E.
Solomon, Joseph
Tatum, Ricky
Toler, Penny
Tucker, Curtis R.
Van Exel, Nick
Vincent, Edward
White, Artis Andre

Wideman, Jamila
Williams, Harvey Joseph
Williams, Herbert Lee
Williams, Homer LaVaughan
Windham, Rhonda

Irvine
Addy, Tralance Obuama
Jordan, William Alfred, III
Kelley, Will Gene
McKayle, Donald Cohen
Mitchell, Horace
Porter, John T.
Timm, Marion Eleanor
Williams, Harvey

Kensington
Major, Benjamin

Kenwood
Cray, Robert

La Crescenta
Hayes, Donna E.
Jackson, Stephanie A.

La Jolla
Bradley, David Henry, Jr.
Gaffney, Floyd
Heineback, Barbara Taylor
Hoston, Germaine A.
James, Luther
Penn, Nolan E.
Reynolds, Edward
Watson, Joseph W.
Wooten, Wilma J.

La Mesa
Powell, Richard Maurice

La Mirada
Land, Chester LaSalle

Laguna Hills
France, Frederick Doug, Jr.

Lake View Terrace
McCraven, Carl Clarke
Smith, William Fred

Lakeport
Arthur, Maynard

Lakewood
Morrison, Ronald E.

Lancaster
Clark, Beverly Gail
Hedgley, David Rice, Jr.

Larkspur
Banks, Joyce P.

Lockheed Corp
Holley, Vance Maitland

Loma Linda
Baker, Delbert Wayne
Davis, William R.
Young, Lionel Wesley

Lompoc
Matthews, Robbin
Rogers, Charles Leonard

Long Beach
Avery, Herbert B.
Blaylock, Enid V.
Clayton, James Henry
Davis-Wrightsil, Clarissa
Dunn, George William
Edwards, Oscar Lee
Griffith, Yolanda
Hartsfield, Arnett L., Jr.
LaCaille, Rupert Andrew
Lacy, Venus
Naphier, Joe L.
Person, Dawn Renee
Phillips, H. R.
Rains, Horace
Robinson, Jim C.
Stafford, Trisha
Stetson, Jeffrey P.
Taylor, Jesse Elliott, Jr.
Tillman, Talmadge Calvin, Jr.
Tucker, Marcus O., Jr.
Tunsil, Necole

Wilkerson, Dana
Williams, Betty Smith
Williams, Beverly
Williams, Ora
Wilson, James H.
Young, Barbara J.

Los Alamitos
Johnson, Joseph David
Peters, Samuel A.

Los Altos
Burroughs, Hugh Charles
Vaughters-Johnson, Cecilie A.

Los Angeles
Airall, Angela Maureen
Alexander, James W.
Alexander, Joseph Lee
Alexander, Josephine
Alexander, Theodore Thomas, Jr.
Alford, Thomas Earl
Alice, Mary
Alston, Kathy Diane
Anderson, Bernadine M.
Anderson, Marva Jean
Andrews, Adelia Smith
Arnold, Alton A., Jr.
Atkins, Brenda J.
Atkins, Pervis
Austin, Isaac Edward
Austin, Patti
Austin, Wanda M.
Backstrom, Don
Bailey, Arthur
Bailey, Lee
Bain, Josie Gray
Baker, Althea
Baki
Bankhead, Patricia Ann
Barclay, David Ronald
Barnes, John B., Sr.
Barnes, Willie R.
Barrett, Ronald Keith
Bath, Patricia E.
Batiste, Mary Virginia
Baylor, Elgin
Beal Bagneris, Michele Christine
Beasley, Arlene A.
Beasley, Jesse C.
Beaubien, George H.
Beavers, George A.
Becker, Adolph Eric
Becker-Slaton, Nellie Frances
Bell, Darryl
Bell, Melvyn Clarence
Benson, George
Benton, Nelkane O.
Berry, Gordon L.
Berry, Halle M.
Berry, LeRoy
Beverly, William C., Jr.
Biggers, Samuel Loring, Jr.
Billings, Earl William
Billingslea, Monroe L.
Black, James Tillman
Black, Keith
Blanding, Mary Rhonella
Boags, Charles D.
Bobbitt, Leroy
Boddie, Lewis F., Sr.
Borden, Harold F., Jr.
Boston, Archie, Jr.
Bowdoin, Robert E.
Bradley, Tom
Branton, Leo, Jr.
Brass, Reginald Stephen
Brenson, Verdel Lee
Brewer, Gregory Alan
Brooks, Theodore Roosevelt, Jr.
Broussard, Vernon
Brown, Chris
Brown, Deloris A.
Brown, Ewart F., Jr.
Brown, Jurutha
Brown, Leroy Thomas
Brown, Mary
Brown, Vernon E.
Buckhalter, Emerson R.
Bunkley, Lonnie R.
Burke, William Arthur
Burke, Yvonne Watson Brathwaite
Burton, Iola Brantley
Burton, Levar
Busby, Jheryl
Butts, Carlyle A.
Callender, Ralph A.
Calloway, Vanessa Bell
Calomee, Annie E.

Newark
McSwain, Berah D.

Newbury Park
Arties, Walter Eugene, III
Bland, Robert Arthur

North Hollywood
Cargill, Sandra Morris
Jones, Donna L.
Khan, Chaka
McMullins, Tommy
Morris, Dolores N.
Peters, Charles L., Jr.

Northridge
Anderson, Ronald Edward, Sr.
Burwell, William David, Jr.
Daniels, Jean E.
Moseka, Aminata
Obinna, Eleazu S.
Ratcliffe, Alfonso F.
Thomas, Nathaniel
Wilson, Blenda J.
Wright, Albert Walter, Jr.
Young, Kevin Curtis

Novato
King, William Frank
Nelson, Eileen F.

Oakland
Allen, Carol Ward
Allen, Robert L.
Anderson, John C., Jr.
Arbuckle, Pamela Susan
Armstrong, Sandra Brown
Bailey, Didi Giselle, MD
Bankston, Donald R.
Baranco, Gordon S.
Barber, Hargrow Dexter
Barber, Janice Denise
Bazile, Leo
Benton, Calvin B.
Berkley, Thomas Lucius
Bethea, Larry
Bobino, Rita Florencia
Broach, S. Elizabeth Johnson
Broussard, Cheryl Denise
Brown, Fannie E. Garrett
Brown, Oral Lee
Burris, John L.
Caffey, Jason Andre
Campbell, Gertrude M.
Cannon, Aleta
Cannon, Barbara E. M.
Carter, Geoffrey Norton
Cartwright, Joan S.
Cherry, Lee Otis
Clark, Claude Lockhart
Clift, Joseph William
Coaston, Shirley Ann Dumas
Coffey, Oscar J., Jr.
Coles, Bimbo
Cooper, Josephine H.
Crisman, Robert
Dampier, Erick Trevez
Davis, Cal Deleanor
Davis, Lester E.
Dwyer-Carpenter, Aleta
Easter, Wilfred Otis, Jr.
Ferrell, Duane
Ford, Judith Donna
Foster, Robert Davis
Foyle, Adonal
Freeman, Kenneth Donald
Gardner, Henry L.
Gilmore, Carter C.
Godbold, Donald Horace
Golden, Samuel Lewis
Goodman, Harold
Harbin-Forte, Brenda F.
Hargrave, Benjamin
Harkless-Webb, Mildred
Head, Laura Dean
Hebert, Stanley Paul
Herring, Bernard Duane
Herzfeld, Will Lawrence
Hewlett, Antoinette Payne
Hopkins, Donald Ray
Hopper, Cornelius Lenard
Jackson, Jim
Jackson, Mabel I.
James, Frederick John
James, Gillette Oriel
Jenkins, Bobby G.
Johnson, Gene C.
Johnson, Walter Louis, Sr.
Johnson, Wayne J.

Jones, Clara Stanton
Joseph-McIntyre, Mary
Kitchen, Wayne Leroy
Lampley, Edward Charles
League, Cheryl Perry
Lennon, Patrick Orlando
Lovelace, Onzalo Robert
Mack, Shane Lee
Mann, Marcus Lashaun
Marshall, Donyell Lamar
Matthews, James Vernon, II
McCullum, Donald Pitts
McDonald, Jason Adam
McGhee, Walter Brownie
McGowan, Thomas Randolph
McMorris, Samuel Carter
Metoyer, Carl B.
Mitchell, Charles, Jr.
Moore, Howard, Jr.
Moore, Jane Bond
Nash, Thomas
Nichols, Roy Calvin
Norman, Bobby Don
Owes, Ray
Parham, Alfred O., Sr.
Patterson, Charles Jerry
Patterson, Clarence J.
Patterson, William Benjamin
Payne, Jesse James
Pendergrass, Emma H.
Richard, James L.
Ross, William Alexander Jackson
Russell, Darrell
Sampson, James S.
Seidenberg, Mark
Simmons, Kenneth H.
Smith, J. Alfred, Sr.
Spears, Stephanie
Spencer, Felton LaFrance
Sprewell, Latrell
Staggers, Frank Eugene
Steele, Percy H., Jr.
Sterling, H. Dwight, Sr.
Sweet, Clifford C.
Sylvester, Odell Howard, Jr.
Taylor, Sister Marie de Porres
Taylor, Martha
Taylor, Michael
Tennant, Melvin, II
Terrell, Reginald V.
Thomas, Robert C.
Thurmond, Nate
Travis, Benjamin
Ward, Carole Geneva
Washington, Carl Douglas
Watkins, Ira Donnell
Weatherspoon, Clarence
Webster, William H.
White, Donald R.
Wray, Wendell Leonard
Wright, Soraya M.
Young, Ernest Wesley

Occidental
Snyder, George W.

Oceanside
Hoye, Walter B., II

Ontario
Sims, Adrienne
Williams, W. Donald

Orange
Caines, Ken
Moore, Evan Gregory
West, John Raymond

Orinda
Stokes, Carolyn Ashe
Swann, Eugene Merwyn

Oxnard
Johnson, Patricia Duren
Jones, Joyce
Pinkard, Bedford L.
Rimm, Byron Newton

Pacific Palisades
McBroom, F. Pearl

Pacoima
Barclay, David Ronald
Marshall, William Horace

Palm Desert
Brown, William McKinley, Jr.

Palm Springs
Beaver, Joseph T., Jr.

Palo Alto
Fleming, June H.
Green, William Ernest
Henderson, Robert Dwight
Jackson, Kennell A., Jr.
Smith, Roulette William
Thrower, Charles S.
Young, Albert James

Pasadena
Alston, Gilbert C.
Barthe, Richmond
Browne, Lee F.
Clark, Mario Sean
Cox, Sandra Hicks
Crayton, James Edward
Dobbs, Guy H.
Driver, Johnie M.
Gooden, Winston Earl
Hampton, Opal Jewell
Hardy, John Louis
Johnson, Charles Beverly
King, James, Jr.
Knight, Lynnon Jacob
Meeks, Willis Gene
Pannell, William E.
Reid, Joel Otto
Ridley, Charles Robert
Sandoz, John H.
Tyson, Bertrand Oliver
Wagner, Vallerie Denise
Williams, Frank James
Williams, Robert W.
Yarbrough, Delano

Perris
Gordon, Charles Franklin
Ingram, William B.

Pico Rivera
Lawson, Anthony Eugene, Sr.

Piedmont
Widener, Warren Hamilton

Pittsburg
Doss, LaRoy Samuel
Foster, Robert Davis
Harrold, Lawrence A.

Pleasanton
Blue, Vida, Jr.
Stickland, Eric L.

Pomona
Benson, James Russell
Daniels, David Herbert, Jr.
Dual, Peter A.
Ferguson, Lloyd N.
Miller, Loren, Jr.
Parker, G. John, Sr.
Speiginer, Gertha
Walton, Edward D.

Port Hueneme
Walker, Russell Dewitt

Portola Valley
Jackson, Oliver L.

Poway
Templeton, Garry Lewis

Rancho Palos Verdes
Savage, Edward W., Jr.

Rancho Santa Margarita
Jackson, Reggie Martinez

Red Bluff
Price, Phillip G.

Redding
Taylor, Arthur Duane

Redondo Beach
Fortune-Maginley, Lois J.

Redwood City
Brown, Reuben D.
Winters, Kenneth E.

Represa
Fonville, Danny D.

Richmond
Allen, William Duncan
Barnes, Matthew Molena, Jr.
Baskette, Ernest E., Jr.
Bates, Nathaniel Rubin
Farlough, H. Eugene, Jr.
King, William Frank
Nelson, Ronald J.
Nelson, William W.
Tramiel, Kenneth Ray, Sr.
Williams, Guthrie J.

Riverside
Anderson, Kathleen Wiley
Carson, Lois Montgomery
Davis, Brenda Lightsey-Hendricks
Holder, Philip
Jackson, Maurice
James, Etta
Livingston, L. Benjamin
Pace-Hinton, Lanita
Sanders, Glenn Carlos
Stinson, Donald R.
Teer, Wardeen

Rohnert Park
Webster, Niambi Dyanne
Wilkinson, Donald Charles

Rosemead
Hines, Kingsley B.

Sacramento
Abdelnaby, Alaa
Abdul-Rauf, Mahmoud
Abdul-Wahad, Tariq
Adair, Gwen
Alexis, Doris Virginia
Armistead, Milton
Ayers-Johnson, Darlene
Bailey, Agnes Jackson
Banks, Loubertha May
Bannerman-Richter, Gabriel
Bolton-Holifield, Ruthie
Bond, James G.
Brooks, Suzanne R.
Brown, Leroy Bradford
Burgess, Linda
Burrell, Garland
Byears, Latasha
Byrd, Albert Alexander
Canson, Fannie Joanna
Carter, Joseph, Jr.
Chappell, Ruth Rax
Clark, Fred Allen
Clark-Thomas, Eleanor M.
Clifford, Charles H.
Cooper, Joseph
Covin, David L.
Cullers, Samuel James
Dehere, Terry
Denmark, Robert Richard
Dodd, James C.
Foster, Raunell H.
Fulgham, Roietta Goodwin
Funderburke, Lawrence Damon
Gamble, Kevin Douglas
Gates, Thomas Michael
Gordon, Bridgette
Graves, Denique
Grayer, Jeffrey
Griffin, Ples Andrew
Gunn, Alex M., Jr.
Hall, Kathryn Louise
Henry, Marcelett Campbell
Hights, William E.
Hollis, Mary Lee
Hurdle, Hortense O. McNeil
Jackson, Fred James, Sr.
Johnson, Anthony
Johnson, Raymond L.
Jones, Asbury Paul
Jordan, Eddie
Kennedy, Callas Faye
LaMotte, Jean Moore
Lawrence, Paul Frederic
Lawson, Herman A.
Lee, William H.
Leflores, George O., Jr.
Long, James L.
Lytle, Alice A.
Marks, Rose M.
McGee, Adolphus Stewart
Moore, Jellether Marie
Netters, Tyrone Homer
Owens, Billy Eugene
Penn, Mindell Lewis
Peters, Kenneth Darryl, Sr.
Phillips, Edward Alexander

Pile, Michael David Mc Kenzie
Pogue, Lester Clarence
Polynice, Olden
Radden, Thelma Gibson
Ramey, Felicenne H.
Ransom, Gary Elliott
Raye, Vance Wallace
Riggins, Lester
Riles, Wilson Camanza
Robinson, Chris
Robinson, Muriel F. Cox
Robinson, Robert Love, Jr.
Rutland, William G.
Scott, Otis L.
Scott, Windie Olivia
Shaw, Ferdinand
Simmons, Joseph
Simmons, Lionel J.
Smith, Heman Bernard
Smith, Rufus Burnett, Jr.
Somerville, Addison Wimbs
Stewart, Michael
Strozier, Yvonne Iglehart
Tate, Lenore Artie
Tremitiere, Chantel
Walker, Jerry Euclid
Washington, Josie B.
Wayne, George Howard, Sr.
Webber, Chris
White, Ralph
Williamson, Corliss Mondari
Woods, Melvin LeRoy

Salinas
Holt, Fred D.

San Anselmo
Simmons, Stephen Lloyd

San Bernardino
Bailey, Joseph Alexander, II
Frazier, Dan E., Sr.
Henry, Mildred M. Dalton
Hobbs, John Daniel
Levister, Ernest Clayton, Jr.
Martin, Carolyn Ann
McVay, Charles
Motley, Ronald Clark
Newell, William
Patterson, Pola Noah
Shelton, Jewell Vennerrie (Elvoid)
Townsend, Arthur P.
Wilson, Ernest

San Bruno
Brooks, Harry W., Jr.
Ellis, Marilyn Pope

San Diego
Alexander, Edward Cleve
Bailey, Eugene Ridgeway
Barnes, Johnnie
Bartley, Talmadge O.
Bronner, James Arthur
Brooks, Sidney Joseph
Brown, Gary Leroy
Brownlee, Jack M.
Bush, Lewis Fitzgerald
Callender, Lucinda R.
Carey, Howard H.
Coleman, Marco Darnell
Craver, Aaron LeRenze
Crittenden, Ray
Crossley, Charles R., II
Daniels, Richard Bernard
Davis, Leonard Harry
Davis, Reuben Cordell
DeWitt, Rufus B.
Dumas, Michael Dion
Durden, Earnel
Fletcher, Terrell
Forde, James Albert
Fuller, William Henry, Jr.
Geiger, David Nathaniel
Gilliam, Earl B.
Graves, Clifford W.
Green, Ruth A.
Griffin, Lloyd
Griffith, John H.
Gwynn, Tony
Hales, Edward Everette
Hand, Norman
Harper, Dwayne Anthony
Harrison, Rodney Scott
Hayes, Floyd Windom, III
Haynes, Steven V.
Holmes, Richard Bernard
Houston, Bobby
Hoye, Walter B.

Dawson, Matthew H.
Ealey, Mark E.
Johnson, Stafford Quincy
McGowan, Thomas Randolph
Toney, Cornelius C.

Venice
Johnson, Charles H.

Visalia
Perry, Kenneth

Walnut
Ashford, Evelyn

Walnut Creek
Anderson, Joe Lewis, Sr.
Bancroft, Richard Anderson
White, Garland Anthony

West Covina
Harrison, Boyd G., Jr.

West Hills
McClure, Bryton Eric

West Hollywood
Barnes, Ernie, Jr.
Benson, Lillian
Cumber, Victoria Lillian
Herring, Leonard, Jr.
Jones, Robert G.
Martin Chase, Debra
Perry, Felton
Simone, Nina

Westlake Village
Graham, Odell
Jones, Gregory Wayne
White, Major C.

Whittier
Haynes, Ora Lee
Mendez, Hugh B.
Morris, Clifton

Wilmington
Carter, Ruth Durley
Edney, Steve

Woodland Hills
Coltrane, Alice Turiya
Graham, Odell
Horne, Lena
Nicholas, Fayard Antonio
Nichols, Nichelle

COLORADO

Aurora
Barrington, Hugh
Bryant, Russell Philip, Jr.
Faison, Derek E.
Faison, Sharon Gail
Love, James Ralph
Mosley, Edna Wilson
Plummer, Ora B.
Reed, Wilbur R.
Underwood, Arthur C.

Boulder
Brutus, Dennis Vincent
Clarke, Joy Adele Long
Davenport, Christian A.
Dodson, Jualynne E.
Flowers, William Harold, Jr.
Hall, Nancy M.
Nilon, Charles Hampton
Patton, Ricardo
Person, Waverly J.
Taylor, Kenneth Doyle
Washington, Warren Morton

Broomfield
Taylor, Kenneth Doyle

Castle Rock
Powell, Judson B., Jr.

Colorado Springs
Bowen, Clotilde Dent
Bradshaw, Gerald Haywood
Burnley, Kenneth
Burrell, Leroy
Campbell, Christopher Lundy

Conley, Mike
Conway, Wallace Xavier, Sr.
Cottingham, Robert T., Jr.
Devers, Gail
Exum, Wade F.
Fittz, Senga Nengudi
Guy, Mildred Dorothy
Hall, Darnell
Hendrix, Deborah Lynne
Jackson, Kevin
Jett, James
Johnson, Michael
Kingdom, Roger
Lowman, Carl D.
Mitchell, Dennis A.
Okino, Elizabeth Anna
Shipp, Pamela Louise
Simpson, Norvell J.
Smith, Rodney
Stewart, James
Torrence, Gwen
Young, Leon

Denver
Alexander, Cory Lynn
Allen, Esther Louisa
Allen, Ty W.
Anderson, Keisha
Barefield, Ollie Delores
Battie, Tony
Battle, Charles E.
Baylor, Don Edward
Bembry, Lawrence
Bolden, Charles E.
Borom, Lawrence H.
Brewer, Gregory Alan
Bruton, Bertram A.
Buckley, Victoria
Burks, Ellis Rena
Burras, Alisa
Campbell, Edna
Chambers, Olivia Marie
Clark, Morris Shandell
Daniel, Wiley Young
Davis, Walter Paul
Dennis, Evie Garrett
Diallo
Egins, Paul Carter, III
Ellis, LaPhonso Darnell
Fortson, Danny
Gardner, Ava Maria
Garner, Velvia M.
Garrett, Dean
Gibson, Roger Allan
Gill, Samuel A.
Gipson, Bernard Franklin, Sr.
Glenn, Cecil E.
Goldwire, Anthony
Goodwin, Curtis LaMar
Greer, Robert O., Jr.
Groff, Regis F.
Grove, Daniel
Harding, Vincent
Harkey, Michael Anthony
Harris, Freeman Cosmo
Harris, Rosalind Juanita
Hawley, Edward H.
Hickman, Thomas Carlyle
Holliman, David L.
Hollins, Leroy
Jackson, Anna Mae
Jackson, Bobby
Jackson, Franklin D. B.
Jackson, Gary Monroe
Jackson, Robert, Jr.
Jacques, Cornell
James, Kevin Porter
Johnson, Collis, Jr.
Johnson, Jerry L.
Jones, Bobby M.
Jones, Raymond Dean
Jordan, Claudia J.
Kennedy, Floyd C.
Lauderdale, Priest
Levy, Neil
Littles, Gene
Livingston, Rudolph
Lyle, Percy H., Jr.
Lyle, Ron
Malone, Herman
McElroy, Charles Dwayne
Moland, Willie C.
Moore, Lewis Calvin
Mosley, John William
Naves, Larry J.
Newman, John Sylvester, Jr.
Patterson, Robert L.
Phillips, Acen L.
Phillips, Earl W.

Phillips, Tari Lynn
Posey, Bruce Keith
Potts, L. Jennie
Rabouin, E. Michelle
Ray-Goins, Jeanette
Reed, Wilbur R.
Reynolds, James F.
Rhodes, Paula R.
Rison, Faye
Robertson, Alvin Cyrrale
Robertson, Charles E., Jr.
Robinson, Crystal
Rollins, Ethel Eugenia
Saunders, Kenneth Paul
Simpson, Darla
Simpson, Diane Jeannette
Smith, Charles Lamont
Smith, Harold Gregory
Smith, Priscilla A.
Smith, William French, II
Sprout, Francis Allen
Stewart, Paul Wilbur
Stith, Bryant Lamonica
Tanner, Gloria Travis
Tappan, Major William
Tate, Valencia Faye
Taylor, Paul David
Washington, Eric
Webb, Wellington E.
Webb, Wilma J.
Williams, Eric C.
Williams, Ronald Charles
Wynne, Dana
Yohannes, Daniel W.

Englewood
Adams, Eula L.
Atwater, Stephen Dennis
Braxton, Tyrone Scott
Brown, Jamie
Burns, Keith Bernard
Carswell, Dwayne
Chamberlain, Byron
Chavous, Barney Lewis
Clark, Morris Shandell
Crockett, Ray
Davis, Terrell
Dodge, Dedrick Allen
Durant, Celeste Millicent
Geathers, Jumpy
Gordon, Darrien X. Jamal
Green, Willie Aaron
Griffith, Howard Thomas
Hasselbach, Harald
Hilliard, Randy
James, Tory
Johnson, Darrius
Jones, Ernest Lee
Jones, Tony Edward
Lee, Charlie
Loville, Derek Kevin
Lynn, Anthony Ray
McKyer, Timothy Bernard
Mobley, John Ulysses
Pryce, Trevor
Sewell, Steven Edward
Sharpe, Shannon
Smith, Detron Negil
Smith, Neil
Smith, Rod
Traylor, Keith
Williams, Alfred Hamilton
Winder, Sammy
Wright, Louis Donnel

Fairplay
Evans, Ada B.

Fort Collins
Hiatt, Dana Sims

Golden
Brailsford, Marvin D.
Brewer, Moses
Brown, L. Don
Morgan-Smith, Sylvia
Oliver, Everett Ahmad

Greeley
George, Hermon, Jr.

Greenwood Village
Clayton, Robert L.

Highlands Ranch
Kaiser, James Gordon

La Junta
Miles, Larry Dave

Lakewood
Barrow, Joe Louis, Jr.
Roy, Joe Eddie, Sr.

Littleton
Morris, Bernard Alexander

Longmont
McCleave, Mildred Atwood
Poston

Morrison
Griffith, Gary Alan

Pueblo
Abebe, Teshome
Poole, James F.
Wells, Elmer Eugene

Sedalia
Cornell, Bob

Westminster
Daniels, Terry L.

CONNECTICUT

Ansonia
Smoot, Albertha Pearl
Walker, Lula Aquillia

Berlin
Springer, George Chelston

Bloomfield
Bennett, Bessye Warren
Cassis, Glenn Albert
Coleman, Eric Dean
Henderson, Carl L., Jr.
Long, Jerry Wayne
Martin, Ionis Bracy
Thompson-Clemmons, Olga Unita
Willingham, James Edward
Wood, Margaret Beatrice

Bridgeport
Cheek, Robert Benjamin, III
Eady, Mary E.
Fewell, Richard
Heyward, Don H.
Hunter, Patrick J.
Prestwidge-Bellinger, Barbara
 Elizabeth
Spear, E. Eugene

Bristol
Jackson, Tom
Morgan, Joe
Oliver, Pam
Roberts, Robin
Saunders, John P.
Stewart, Bernard

Cheshire
Bush, Evelyn
Ferguson, Shellie Alvin

Danbury
Furman, James B.
Gellineau, Victor Marcel, Jr.
Rountree, Ella Jackson
Stewart, Albert C.
Torian, Edward Torrence
Wilds, Constance T.

East Hampton
States, Robert Arthur

East Hartford
Crawford, David
Willingham, James Edward

East Lyme
Butts, Janie Pressley

Fairfield
Braden, Stanton Connell
Cross, Dolores E.
Johnson, Alvin Roscoe
Mazon, Larri Wayne
Merchant, John F.

Farmington
LaMarr, Catherine Elizabeth

Gales Ferry
Waterman, Thelma M.

Glastonbury
Edmonds, Norman Douglas

Greenwich
Brown, Nancy Cofield
Cureton, John Porter
Wright, Dmitri

Groton
Hamilton, Aubrey J.

Hamden
Cherry, Edward Earl, Sr.
Garner, Charles
Hallums, Benjamin F.
Highsmith, Carlton L.
Mazon, Larri Wayne
Potts, Harold E.
Turner, Diane Young

Hartford
Arnold, Rudolph P.
Banks, Arthur C., Jr.
Bennett, Collin B.
Bibby, Deirdre L.
Billington, Clyde, Jr.
Booker, Carl Granger, Sr.
Borges, Lynne MacFarlane
Crawford, Jayne Suzanne
Daniel, Alfred Irwin
Davis, Tara
Dennis, James Carlos
Dixon, Benjamin
Dyson, William Riley
Gaines, Edythe J.
Geyer, Edward B., Jr.
Green, Arthur L.
Hales, William Roy
Harris, James G., Jr.
Hickmon, Ned
Hill, E.C.
Hodges, Dale
Hodgson-Brooks, Gloria J.
Hogan, James Carroll, Jr.
Howard, Milton L.
Hoyt, Thomas L., Jr.
Hubbard, Hylan T., III
Joell, Pamela S.
Jones, Carolyn
King, Gayle
King, Richard Devoid
Long, Steffan
Martin, Russell F.
McFarlin, Kernaa D'Offert, Jr.
Miller, James Arthur
Milner, Thirman L.
Morgan-Welch, Beverly Ann
Mosley, Maurice B.
Parker, Henry Ellsworth
Perry, Carrie Saxon
Peterson, Gerard M.
Rawlins, Sedrick John
Robinson, John E.
Roland, Jannon
Simmons, John Emmett
Smalley, Paul
Smith, Frank Junius
Smith, Jennifer C.
Stephens, Elsie Marie
Stewart, John B., Jr.
Strong, Marilyn Terry
Tate, Deanna
Thompson, Winston Edna
Warren, Annika Laurin
Whaley, Charles H., IV

Madison
Williams, Arthur G., Jr.

Manchester
Freeman, Diane S.
Mingo, Pauline Hylton

Mansfield
Molette, Barbara J.

Marlborough
States, Robert Arthur

Meriden
Gooley, Charles E.

Middletown
Biassey, Earle Lambert
Thornton, Clifford E.

Milford
Alexander, Sidney H., Jr.

New Britain
Baskerville, Charles Alexander
Collins, Constance Renee Wilson
Jones, Charles, Jr.
Robinson, John E.
Savage, Archie Bernard, Jr.
Springer, George Chelston
Wallace, Claudette J.

New Haven
Barber, James W.
Blassingame, John W.
Carby, Hazel V.
Comer, James Pierpont
Daniels, John C.
Days, Drew Saunders, III
Griffith, Ezra
Hedgspeth, Adrienne Cassandra
Holley, Sandra Cavanaugh
Holly, Ella Louise
Holmes, Willie A.
Ince, Harold S.
Jackson, William E.
Jaynes, Gerald David
Jones, Emma Pettway
Jones, Ernest
Jones, William
Patton, Curtis Leverne
Pitts, William Henry
Robinson, Ann Garrett
Robinson, Charles E.
Robinson, Joseph, Jr.
Rogers, Victor Alvin
Shearin, Kimberly Maria
Slie, Samuel N.
Stepto, Robert Burns
Thomas, Gerald Eustis
Thompson, Robert Farris
Thorpe, Wesley Lee
Wearing, Melvin

New London
Gillis, Shirley J. Barfield
Hendricks, Barkley L.
Jennings, Bennie Alfred
Waller, Eunice McLean

Newington
Scott, R. Lee

North Haven
Hogan, James Carroll, Jr.

Norwalk
Coshburn, Henry S., Jr.
Fearing, John T.
Foster, Pearl D.
Maultsby, Sylvester
Sanderson, Randy Chris
Self, Frank Wesley
Walker, Vernon David
Wharton, Ferdinand D., Jr.
Williams, Shirley Yvonne
Wilson, Earl, Jr.

Norwich
Price, Paul Sanford

Orange
Fisher, Rubin Ivan

Plainville
Trotter, Lloyd G.

Rocky Hill
Maule, Albert R.

South Norwalk
Burgess, Robert E., Sr.

South Windsor
Lewis, Robert Alvin, Jr.

Stamford
Christophe, Cleveland A.
Gipson, Hayward R., Jr.
Gudger, Robert Harvey
Johnson, Charles Edward
Johnson, Donna Alligood
Jones, John L.

Lewis, George Ralph
Miles, Albert Benjamin, Jr.
Murray, J. Ralph
Nixon, James I., Jr.
Rand, A. Barry
Rozier, Gilbert Donald
Simmons, Ron

Storrs
Adams, Frederick G.
Lane, Eleanor Tyson
Molette, Carlton Woodard, II
Peters, James Sedalia, II
Spivey, Donald
Taylor, Ronald Lewis

Storrs Mansfield
Bagley, Peter B. E.
Cazenave, Noel Anthony
Terry, Angela Owen

Stratford
Cromwell, Margaret M.
Elliott, Frank George

Torrington
Lyons, A. Bates

Trumbull
McDaniel, Robert Anthony

Uncasville
White, Quitman, Jr.

Vernon
Alexander, Errol D.
Lane, Eleanor Tyson

Vernon-Rockville
Johnson, Arthur Lyman
Johnson, Marie Love

Waterbury
Brown, Otha N., Jr.
Glass, Robert Davis
Jordan, Jacquelyn D.
Thomas, Nina M.

Waterford
Kimmons, Carl Eugene

West Hartford
Martin, Arnold Lee, Jr.
McLean, John Lenwood
Payne, Cecilia

West Haven
Slie, Samuel N.

Weston
Lauderback, Brenda Joyce

Westport
Allen, Winston Earle
Clarke, Kenton

Willimantic
Carter, David G., Sr.
Jackson, Arthur Roszell
Molette, Barbara J.
Peagler, Owen F.

Wilton
Halliburton, Warren J.
Parker, George Anthony

Windham
Terry, Angela Owen

Windsor
Cave, Perstein Ronald
Echols, Ivor Tatum
Freeman, Walter Eugene
Johnson, Wayne Lee
Thornton-Anderson, Marion

Windsor Locks
Thaxton, Judy Evette

Woodbridge
Anderson, Bryan N.
Cherry, Edward Earl, Sr.

DELAWARE

Dover
Adams, Eva W.
Ball, Drexel Bernard
Bradberry, Richard Paul
Caldwell, M. Milford
Coleman, Rudolph W.
DeLauder, William B.
Ford, Nancy Howard
Hardcastle, James C.
Harris, Winifred Clarke
Henderson, Romeo Clanton
Johnson, Marguerite M.
Jones, Geraldine J.
Laws, Ruth M.
McPhail, Irving P.
Mishoe, Luna I.
Wardlaw, McKinley, Jr.

Georgetown
Jones, Albert J.

Greenville
Wilson, Clarence A.

Laurel
Selby, Cora Norwood

Milford
Fountain, William Stanley

Milton
Batten, Grace Ruth

New Castle
Petersen, Frank Emmanuel, Jr.
Rudd, James M.

Newark
Jones, James McCoy
Newton, James E.
Pinkney, Jerry
Sanders, Gwendolyn W.
Seams, Francine Swann
Whittaker, Terry McKinley

Seaford
Johnson, William Smith

Selbyville
Stamps, Herman Franklin

Smyrna
Wright, George C., Jr.

Wilmington
Alford, Haile Lorraine
Baber, Lucky Larry
Beckett, Sydney A.
Benefield, Michael Maurice, Jr.
Brown, Atlanta Thomas
Brown, Rodney W.
Cannon, Eugene Nathaniel
Carey, Claire Lamar
Carey, Harmon Roderick
Ford, Evern D.
Gilliam, James H., Jr.
Gilliam, James H., Sr.
Guyton, Alicia V.
Haskins, James W., Jr.
Holloway, Herman M., Sr.
Johnson, Joseph Edward
Mack, Sylvia Jenkins
Martin, Joshua Wesley, III
McMillian, Frank L.
Mitchell, Charles E.
Mobley, Joan Thompson
Mobley, Stacey J.
Nix, Theophilus Richard
Peters, Pamela Joan
Redding, Louis L.
Revelle, Robert, Sr.
Roberts, Harlan William, III
Savage, Dennis James
Sleet, Gregory M.
Smith, Janet K.
Wiggins, Leslie
Winston, George B., III

DISTRICT OF COLUMBIA

Bolling AFB
Edmonds, Albert Joseph
Harris, Maurice A.

Washington
Abney, Robert
Adair, Alvis V.
Adams, Alice Omega
Adams, Russell Lee
Addison, James David
Ademiluyi, Mozella Perry
Adeniyi-Jones, Katherine
Adeyiga, Olanrewaju Muniru
Alexander, Clifford L., Jr.
Alexander, John Wesley, Jr.
Alexander, Lenora Cole
Alexander, Richard C.
Alexander, Robin
Alexander-Whiting, Harriett
Alexis, Carlton Peter
Alfonso, Pedro
Allen, Benjamin P., III
Allen, Bernestine
Allen, Stanley M.
Allen, Willie B.
Amos, Kent B.
Ampy, Franklin R.
Anderson, Arnett Artis
Anderson, Bernard E.
Anderson, Carl Edwin
Anderson, Carol Byrd
Anderson, David Turpeau
Anderson, Donald L.
Anderson, Mary Elizabeth
Anderson, William A.
Archer, Juanita A.
Archibald, B. Milele
Argrett, Loretta Collins
Arnez, Nancy L.
Arnold, Wallace C.
Arties, Lucy Elvira Yvonne
Ashford, Laplois
Ashton, Vivian Christina R.
Atkins, Robert L.
Atkinson, Lewis K.
Attaway, John David
Audain, Linz
Auld, Albert Michael
Ausbrooks, Beth Nelson
Avery, Byllye Y.
Awkard, Linda Nanline
Babb, Valerie M.
Bailey, William H.
Baker, Willie L., Jr.
Banks, Priscilla Sneed
Banks, Sharon P.
Banks, Tazewell
Banks, Terry Michael
Banks, William Jasper, Jr.
Banner, William Augustus
Barber, Jesse B., Jr.
Barlow, William B.
Barnes, Boisey O.
Barnes, Iraline G.
Barrett, Andrew
Barrett, Matthew Anderson
Barry, Marion Shepilov, Jr.
Battle, Thomas Cornell
Beal, Lisa Suzanne
Beard, Lillian McLean
Beasley, Eula Daniel
Bell, Alexander F.
Bell, Harold Kevin
Bellamy, Everett
Belton, Howard G.
Benjamin, Donald S.
Benjamin, Tritobia Hayes
Bennett, Bobby
Bennett, Joyce Annette
Bennett, Marian C.
Bennett, Maybelle Taylor
Bernard, Nesta Hyacinth
Berry, Paul Lawrence
Berryman, Matilene S.
Bessent, Hattie
Besson, Paul Smith
Bishop, David Rudolph
Bishop, Sanford D., Jr.
Black, Charlie J.
Black, Frederick Harrison
Black, Rosa Walston
Blackwell, Lucien E.
Blakely, Allison
Blakely, Ronald Eugene
Blakey, William A.

Boghassian, Skunder
Bolden, Betty A.
Bolton, Linda Burnes
Bond, Julian
Booker, Johnnie Brooks
Booker, Simeon S.
Bothuel, Ethel C. S.
Bowden, Marion A.
Bowe, Riddick
Bowles, Howard Roosevelt
Bowron, Eljay B.
Boyd, George Arthur
Boykin, A. Wade, Jr.
Boze, U. Lawrence
Bradford, Arvine M.
Bradford, Charles Edward
Bradley, Melissa Lynn
Brady, Charles A.
Braithwaite, Gordon L.
Brangman, H. Alan
Branson, Herman Russell
Branton, Wiley Austin
Bremer, Charles E.
Brewington, Rudolph W.
Bridges, Lucille W.
Bridgewater, Albert Louis
Brieve-Martin, Ila Corrinna
Brimmer, Andrew F.
Brittain, Bradley Bernard, Jr.
Broadnax, Walter Doyce
Brockington, Donella P.
Brockington, Eugene Alfonzo
Brooke, Edward William
Brooks, Bernard W.
Brooks, Bette
Brooks, Charlotte Kendrick
Brooks, Leo Austin
Brooks, Sheila Dean
Brown, A. Sue
Brown, Barbara Ann
Brown, Brenda L.
Brown, Carolyn Thompson
Brown, Corrine
Brown, Costello L.
Brown, Cyril H.
Brown, Herman
Brown, Inez M.
Brown, Jesse
Brown, John Scott
Brown, Linda Jenkins
Brown, Robert J., III
Brown, Ronald H.
Brown, Warren Aloysius
Brown, Warren Henry, Jr.
Brown, Wesley Anthony
Brown, William, Jr.
Brown, Zora Kramer
Browne, Vincent J.
Bryant, Andrew Daniel
Bryant, Cunningham C.
Bryant, Donnie L.
Bryant, Robert Edward
Bryant, William Benson
Bullock, J. Jerome
Bullock, William Horace
Bundles, A'Lelia Perry
Bunton, Henry Clay
Burke, Brian
Burnett, Arthur Louis, Sr.
Burnett, David Lawrence
Burnett, Luther C.
Burroughs, John Andrew, Jr.
Burrus, William Henry
Burse, Luther
Bush, Mary K.
Bush, Nathaniel
Butcher, Goler Teal
Byrd, Jerry Stewart
Cafritz, Peggy Cooper
Cain, Simon Lawrence
Calbert, William Edward, Sr.
Caldwell, Marion Milford, Jr.
Calhoun, Cecelia C.
Calhoun, John
Calhoun, Noah Robert
Calhoun, Thomas
Callender, Clive Orville
Cambosos, Bruce Michael
Campbell, Bobby Lamar
Campbell, Leroy Miller
Cannon, Joseph Nevel
Caraway, Yolanda H.
Carnell, Lougenia Littlejohn
Carpenter, Barbara Anne
Carpenter, William Arthur, II
Carrington, Christine H.
Carroll, Beverly A.
Carroll, Raoul Lord
Carruthers, George Robert

Carson, Julia M.
Carson, Regina E. Edwards
Carter, Chester C.
Carter, Deborah
Carter, Norman L.
Carter, Vincent G.
Carter, William Beverly, III
Carter, Yvonne P.
Cashin, Sheryll
Chambers, John Curry, Jr.
Chapman, George Wallace, Jr.
Cheaney, Calbert N.
Cheatham, Betty L.
Childs, Winston
Chisholm, Joseph Carrel, Jr.
Chisholm, Reginald Constantine
Chism, Harolyn B.
Chivis, Martin Lewis
Christian-Green, Donna-Marie
Clark, LaWanna Gibbs
Clark, Savanna M. Vaughn
Clarke, Priscilla
Clay, William L.
Clayton, Eva
Clayton, Lloyd E.
Clements, George H.
Clemons, John Gregory
Clipper, Milton Clifton, Jr.
Clodius, Robert L.
Clyburn, James E.
Clyburn, John B.
Coffey, Gilbert Haven, Jr.
Cohen, Vincent H.
Cole, Arthur
Cole, Joseph H.
Cole Carey, Wilhemina, PhD
Coleman, Rodney Albert
Coleman, William T., III
Coleman, William T., Jr.
Collie, Kelsey E.
Collinet, Georges Andre
Collins, Barbara-Rose
Collins, Cardiss
Collins, LaVerne Vines
Collins, Paul L.
Collins, William Keelan, Sr.
Colvin, Alex, II
Conley, Herbert A.
Connor, Ulysses J., Jr.
Conyers, John, Jr.
Cook, Frank Robert, Jr.
Cook, Joyce Mitchell
Cooke, Nellie
Cooper, Barbara J.
Cooper, Clement Theodore
Cooper, Ernest, Jr.
Cooper, Jerome Gary
Cooper, Kenneth Joseph
Cooper, Maudine R.
Corbett, Doris R.
Corley-Saunders, Angela Rose
Courtney, Cassandra Hill
Cox, DuBois V.
Cox, Georgetta Manning
Cox, Otha P.
Crawford, Betty Marilyn
Crawford, Charles L.
Crawford, H. R.
Crawford, Vanella Alise
Crew, Spencer R.
Crocker, Cyril L.
Crockett, Edward D., Jr.
Cropp, Dwight Sheffery
Cruise, Warren Michael
Crusto, Mitchell Ferdinand
Cruz, Iluminado Angeles
Culpepper, Betty M.
Cummings, Elijah E.
Cunningham, William Michael
Currie, Betty
Curry, Sadye Beatryce
Dabney, David Hodges
Dalley, George Albert
Dames, Sabrina A.
Darden, Orlando William
Dash, Leon DeCosta, Jr.
Dates, Jannette Lake
Davenport, Lawrence Franklin
Davis, Arthur Paul
Davis, George Nelson, Jr.
Davis, Howard C.
Davis, Howlie R.
Davis, John Wesley
Davis, Johnetta Garner
Davis, Lisa R.
Davis, Marilynn A.
Davis, Michael DeMond
Davis, Preston Augustus
Davis, Terry Raymond

Davis, Thurman M., Sr.
Davis, Tyrone Theophulus
Davis, Walter G.
Davison, Frederic E.
Dawkins, Tammy C.
Dawson, Horace Greeley, Jr.
Deane, Robert Armistead
Dedmon, Jesse Oscar, Jr.
DeGraffenreidt, James H., Jr.
Delaney, Duane B.
Delaney, Harold
Delaney, Willi
DeMesme, Ruby B.
Dendy, Tometta Moore
Derryck, Vivian Lowery
Dessaso-Gordon, Janice Marie
De Veaux, Stuart Samuel
Devrouax, Paul S., Jr.
Diane, Mamadi
Diaw, Rosemary K.
Dickens, Doris Lee
Dickerson, Bette Jeanne
Dillard, Martin Gregory
Dillon, Owen C.
Dilworth, Mary Elizabeth
Dixon, Arrington Liggins
Dixon, Julian C.
Dixon, Margaret A.
Dixon, Yvonne T.
Donaldson, Jeff Richardson
Donegan, Charles Edward
Dowdy, James H.
Downing, John William, Jr.
Driver, Elwood T.
Druitt, Beverly F.
Duckenfield, Thomas Adams
Dudley, Godfrey D.
Dudley-Smith, Carolyn J.
Duke, Leslie Dowling, Sr.
Dukes, Ofield
Duncan, Louis Davidson, Jr.
Duncan, Robert Todd
Dunlap, Estelle Cecilia Diggs
Dupree, David H.
Durham, William R.
Duvall, Henry F., Jr.
Eaglin, Ruth
Early, James Counts
Eaton, David Hilliard
Eaton, Patricia Frances
Edelman, Marian Wright
Edmonds, Terry
Edwards, Cecile Hoover
Edwards, Harry T.
Edwards, Jerry
Edwards, Sylvia
Elmore, Ernest Eric
English, Richard A.
Enoch, Hollace J.
Epps, Charles Harry, Jr.
Epps, Roselyn Payne
Espy, Michael
Estep, Roger D.
Ethridge, Samuel B.
Eubanks, W. Ralph
Evans, Dorsey
Evanzz, Karl Anderson
Everett, Ralph B.
Ewing, Samuel Daniel, Jr.
Fagin, Darryl Hall
Fairley, Richard L.
Farmer, Sharon
Fattah, Chaka
Fauntleroy, John Douglass, Sr.
Fauntroy, Walter E.
Felder, Cain Hope
Feliciana, Jerrye Brown
Ferguson, Johnnie Nathaniel
Fernandes, Julie A.
Finlayson, Arnold Robert
Finney, Karen
Fisher, Edward G.
Fisher, Miles Mark, IV
Fitzgerald, William B.
Flake, Nancy Aline
Fleming, Patricia Stubbs
Fletcher, Arthur Allen
Fletcher, Patricia Louise
Flowers, Sally A.
Fomufod, Antoine Kofi
Ford, Antoinette
Ford, Claudette Franklin
Ford, Debra Holly
Ford, Harold Eugene, Sr.
Ford, Harold Eugene, Jr.
Ford, James W.
Ford, Kenneth A.
Foster, Jylla Moore
Fowler, William E., Jr.

Fox, Charles Washington, III
Fox, Richard K., Jr.
Francis, Henry Minton
Franklin, Dolores Mercedes
Franklin, Hardy R.
Franks, Everlee Gordon
Franks, Gary A.
Frazer, Victor O.
Freeman, Albert Cornelius, Jr.
Freeman, Preston Garrison
Freeman, Robert Turner, Jr.
Freeman, Warren L.
French, MaryAnn
Frizzell, Aretha S.
Fry, Louis Edwin, Jr.
Frye, Robert Edward, Sr.
Fudge, Marcia L.
Fuller, Gloria A.
Fulwood, Sam, III
Futrell, Mary Hatwood
Gaffney, Mary Louise
Gaillard, Bernard
Gaither, Dorothy B.
Garibaldi, Antoine Michael
Gary, Lawrence Edward
Gaskins, Henry Jesse
Gaskins, Mary Ann
Gatewood, Lucian B.
Gatling, Joseph Theodore
Gauger, Tom
Gayle, Lucille Jordan
Gee, William Rowland, Jr.
George, Alma Rose
George, Luvenia A.
George, Theodore Roosevelt, Jr.
Gerald, Melvin Douglas, Sr.
Geraldo, Manuel Robert
Gibson, Johnnie M. M.
Gibson, Reginald Walker
Gidney, Calvin L.
Gilliam, Arleen Fann
Gilliam, Dorothy Butler
Gilliam, Sam, Jr.
Gilmore, Al Tony
Gladden, Brenda Winckler
Gladden, Major P.
Glasgow, Douglas G.
Glaude, Stephen A.
Glen, Ulysses, Jr.
Gloster, John Gaines
Goff, Wilhelmina Delores
Golden, Donald Leon
Golden, Joyce Marie
Golden, Myron
Goldson, Alfred Lloyd
Goldson, Amy Robertson
Goodson, Annie Jean
Goodwin, Maria Rose
Goodwin, Robert Kerr
Gordon, Edwin Jason
Graham, Michael Angelo
Grant, Harvey
Grant, Nathaniel
Grantley, Robert Clark
Graves, Allene
Graves, Curtis M.
Gray, Donnee L.
Gray, Edward Wesley, Jr.
Gray, Karen G.
Gray, Wilfred Douglas
Grayson, Byron J., Sr.
Greaux, Cheryl Prejean
Green, Ernest G.
Green, Georgia Mae
Green, Sterling
Greene, Grace Randolph
Greene, Horace F.
Greene, Jerry Louis
Greenfield, Eloise
Greenfield, Robert Thomas, Jr.
Gregory, Frederick Drew
Gregory, Henry C., III
Gregory, Robert Alphonso
Griffin, Bobby L.
Griffith, Reginald Wilbert
Grigsby, Margaret Elizabeth
Hager, Joseph C.
Hailes, Edward A.
Hairston, Eddison R., Jr.
Hairston, Joseph Henry
Haley, George Williford Boyce
Hall, Elliott Sawyer
Hall, Kim Felicia
Halyard, Michele Yvette
Ham, Darvin
Ham, Debra Newman
Hamilton, Edwin
Hamilton, Eugene Nolan
Hammond, Kenneth T.

Hammond, Ulysses Bernard
Hampton, Cheryl Imelda
Hampton, Delon
Hampton, Ronald Everett
Hardman-Cromwell, Youtha Cordella
Hardy, Willie J.
Hargrave, Charles William
Hargrave, Thomas Burkhardt, Jr.
Harkins, Rosemary Knighton
Harper, Bernice Catherine
Harper, Mary Starke
Harps, William S.
Harris, Bryant G.
Harris, Caspa L., Jr.
Harris, Charles F.
Harris, Charles Wesley
Harris, DeLong
Harris, Gary Lynn
Harris, Gleason Ray
Harris, James A.
Harris, Marcelite J.
Harris, Norman W., Jr.
Harris, Robert F.
Harris, William H., Jr.
Harris, William J.
Hart, Christopher Alvin
Hart, Harold Rudoff
Harvey, Louis-Charles
Hastings, Alcee Lamar
Hawkins, John Russell, III
Hawkins, Steven Wayne
Hayden, John Carleton
Hayes, Charles A.
Hayes, Edward, Jr.
Hayward, Jacqueline C.
Haywood, Hiram H., Jr.
Haywood, Margaret A.
Hazel, Janis D.
Henderson, Eddie L.
Henderson, Elmer W.
Henderson, Stephen E.
Hendricks, Beatrice E.
Henry, Brent Lee
Henry, Walter Lester, Jr.
Henry, Warren Elliott
Hensley, Willie L.
Herman, Alexis M.
Herndon, Craig Garris
Hicks, H. Beecher
Hicks, Sherman G.
Higgins, Chester A., Sr.
Hill, Arthur James
Hill, Caesar G.
Hill, Cynthia D.
Hill, Michael Edward
Hill, Sylvia Ione-Bennett
Hill, Wendell T., Jr.
Hillman, Gracia
Hilton, Tanya
Hobbs, Alma Cobb
Hobson, Robert R.
Holder, Eric H., Jr.
Holland, Ethel M.
Holliday, Bertha Garrett
Holman, M. Carl
Holmes, Dorothy E.
Holt, Maude R.
Hope, John, II
Hope, Richard Oliver
Hopkins, Ernest Loyd
Horad, Sewell D., Sr.
Horton, James T.
Horton, Joann
Hosten, Adrian
Howard, Dalton J., Jr.
Howard, Juwan Antonio
Howard, Tanya Millicent
Hoyte, Arthur Hamilton
Hubbard, Stanley, Sr.
Hudson, Robert L.
Hudson, William Thomas
Hughes, Catherine Liggins
Hughes, Harvey L.
Hull, Everson Warren
Hunt, Darrold Victor
Hunt, Isaac Cosby, Jr.
Hunter, Frances S.
Hunter, Gertrude T.
Hunter, Jerry L.
Hunter-Gault, Charlayne
Hurt, Louis T., Jr.
Hussein, Carlessia Amanda
Hutchins, Joshua I., Jr.
Hutchins, Lawrence G., Sr.
Hutchinson, Louise Daniel
Hutton, Marilyn Adele
Hyde, William R.
Irving, Clarence Larry, Jr.

Isaacs, Stephen D.
Isom, Eddie
Israel, Mae H.
Ivery, James A.
Jackson, Dorothy R., J.D.
Jackson, Edgar Newton, Jr.
Jackson, Frederick
Jackson, James Talmadge
Jackson, Jesse L., Jr.
Jackson, Leroy Anthony, Jr.
Jackson, Marvin Alexander
Jackson, Norlishia A.
Jackson, Raymond T.
Jackson, Ronald G., Sr.
Jackson, Sandra Stevens
Jackson, Tammy
Jackson-Lee, Sheila
James, Clarence L., Jr.
Jefferson, Karen L.
Jefferson, William J.
Jefferson-Moss, Carolyn
Jenkins, Melvin E., Jr.
Jenkins, Ozella
Jenkins, Robert Kenneth, Jr.
Jenkins, Thomas O.
Jessup, Gayle Louise
Jeter, Clifton B., Jr.
Jeter, Thomas Elliott
Johnson, Ben
Johnson, Derrick Gibbs
Johnson, Eddie Bernice
Johnson, Edward M.
Johnson, F. J., Jr.
Johnson, James Walter, Jr.
Johnson, Johnnie L., Jr.
Johnson, Lloyd A.
Johnson, Lorraine Jefferson
Johnson, Mal
Johnson, Mitchell A.
Johnson, Norma Holloway
Johnson, R. Benjamin
Johnson, Robert
Johnson, Robert L.
Johnson, Ronald Cornelius
Johnson, Roosevelt Young
Johnson, William Paul, Jr.
Johnson, Wyneva
Johnson-Crockett, Mary Alice
Jones, Alexander R.
Jones, Clifton Ralph
Jones, Elaine R.
Jones, George Williams
Jones, Gerald Winfield
Jones, Jacqueline Valarie
Jones, James C.
Jones, Kelsey A.
Jones, Leonade Diane
Jones, Lois Mailou
Jones, Meredith J.
Jones, Nolan E.
Jones, Roscoe T., Jr.
Jones, Roy Junios
Jones, Sidney Alexander
Jones, Thomas L.
Jones, William Bowdoin
Jones-Wilson, Faustine Clarisse
Jordan, Carolyn D.
Jordan, Emma Coleman
Jordan, Ralph
Jordan, Vernon E., Jr.
Jordan-Harris, Katherine
Joseph, James Alfred
Joy, James Bernard, Jr.
Kaiser-Dark, Phyllis E.
Kea, Arleas Upton
Kearse, Gregory Sashi
Keith, Doris T.
Kelly, Sharon Pratt
Kendall, Robert, Jr.
Kendrix, Moss H., Sr.
Kennard, William Earl
Kennedy, Henry H., Jr.
Kerr, Hortense R.
Kilpatrick, Carolyn Cheeks
Kilpatrick, Robert Paul
King, Colbert I.
King, Frederick L., Jr.
King, Patricia Ann
King, William Charles
Kirkland-Briscoe, Gail Alicia
Knight, Athelia Wilhelmenia
Knight, Robert S.
Labner, Joyce A.
Lacey, Marc Steven
Lacey, Wilbert, Jr.
Ladner, Joyce A.
Lambert, Rollins Edward
Landers, Renee M.
Landry, Dolores Branche

Landry, Lawrence Aloysius
Lane, Lois A.
Langhart, Janet
Lang-Jeter, Lula L.
Latcholia, Kenneth Edward
Latham, Weldon Hurd
Lawson, William R.
Lawyer, Cyrus J., III
Layton, William W.
Leace, Donal Richard
Leak, Lee Virn
Ledbetter, Ruth Pope
Lee, Bernard Scott
Lee, Bertram M.
Lee, Debra Louise
Lee, Norvel L. R.
Lee, Sheila Jackson
Leffall, LaSalle Doheny, Jr.
Leftwich, Norma Bogues
Leftwich, Willie L.
Leigh, Fredric H.
Leland, Joyce F.
Leland, Mickey
LeMelle, Tilden J.
Lemmons, Herbert Michael
Lewis, Colston A.
Lewis, Delano Eugene
Lewis, Green Pryor, Jr.
Lewis, John Robert
Lewis, Peggy
Lewis, Reta Jo
Lewis, Tom
Lewis, Vincent V.
Lewis, William A., Jr.
Lightfoot, Jean Drew
Lightfoote, William Edward, II
Lindsey, Jerome W.
Lloyd, Raymond Anthony
Lockhart-Moss, Eunice Jean
Lofton, Kevin Eugene
Lovelace, Gloria Elaine
Loving, James Leslie, Jr.
Lowe, Richard Bryant, III
Lucas, C. Payne
Lucy, William
Lyle, James M.
Mack, Gladys Walker
Mack, John L.
Mack, Julia Cooper
Mack, Voyce J.
Mahone, Charlie Edward, Jr.
Majors, Edith Sara
Malcom, Shirley Mahaley
Maldon, Alphonso
Malveaux, Floyd
Manager, Vada O'Hara
Manley, Albert Edward
Mann, Marion
Marbury, Donald Lee
Marion, Phillip Jordan
Marks, Kenneth Hicks, Jr.
Marsh, Pearl-Alice
Marshall, Charles H.
Marshall, Etta Marie-Imes
Marshall, Thurgood
Marshall, Thurgood, Jr.
Martin, Bertha M.
Martin, Charles Howard
Martin, Curtis Jerome
Martin, Ernest Douglass
Martin, John Thomas
Martin, Sylvia Cooke
Mason, DaCosta V.
Mason, Donna S.
Mason, Hilda Howland M.
Matthews, Claude Lankford, Jr.
Matthews, Cynthia Clark
Maultsby, Dorothy M., Esq.
Mauney, Donald Wallace, Jr.
Mayes, McKinley
Mazique, Edward C.
Mazique, Frances Margurite
McAdoo, Harriette P.
McAllister, Singleton Beryl
McAlpine, Robert
McCants, Coolidge N.
McCloud, Thomas Henry
McCollough, Walter
McCray, Maceo E.
McCray, Nikki
McDonald, Herbert G.
McElroy, Lee A., Jr.
McGee, James Madison
McGinty, Doris Evans
McHenry, Donald F.
McIntosh, Simeon Charles
McKelpin, Joseph P.
McKenzie, Floretta D.
McKinney, Cynthia Ann

McKinney, Roseline
McLaren, Douglas Earl
McLaughlin, David
McLaughlin, Joseph C.
McLaughlin, Katye H.
McMorris, Jacqueline Williams
McQueen, Kevin Paige
McWilliams, James D.
McZier, Arthur
Meek, Carrie P.
Mehreteab, Ghebre-Selassie
Mensah, E. Kwaku
Mickle, Andrea Denise
Miles, Carlotta G.
Millender-McDonald, Juanita M.
Miller, E. Ethelbert
Miller, George Carroll, Jr.
Miller, Jeanne-Marie A.
Miller, Lawrence Edward
Miller, Luvenia C.
Miller, Russell L., Jr.
Miller, Tedd
Mills, Cheryl
Mims, Beverly Carol
Mims, Oscar Lugrie
Miner, William Gerard
Mitchell, Benson Doyle, Sr.
Mitchell, Corinne Howard
Mitchell, Melvin Lester
Mitchell, Robert C.
Mitchell, William Grayson
Mitchell, Zinora M.
Mitchem, Arnold Levy
Mohr, Diane Louise
Montgomery, Edward B.
Montgomery, Evangeline Juliet
Moore, Evelyn K.
Moore, Jerry A., Jr.
Moore, Penny
Moose, George E.
Moragne, Lenora, Ph.D.
Morgan, Alice Johnson Parham
Morris, Archie, III
Morris, Calvin S.
Morris, Mary Helen
Morrison, James W., Jr.
Morrison, Trudi Michelle
Mortimer, Delores M.
Mosee, Jean C.
Moseley Braun, Carol Elizabeth
Moses, Alice J.
Muhammad, Askia
Murdock, Nathaniel H.
Murphy, Frances L., II
Murphy, George B., Jr.
Murphy, Laura W.
Murray, James Hamilton
Murray, Tracy Lamonte
Mutcherson, James Albertus, Jr.
Myers, Ernest Ray
Myers, Frances Althea
Myers, Samuel L.
Myers, Stephanie E.
Nabrit, James M., Jr.
Nash, Bob J.
Nash, Curtis
Nash, Eva L.
Neely, Henry Mason
Nellum, Albert L.
Neloms, Henry
Nelson, Charles J.
Nelson, Richard Y., Jr.
Neufville, Mortimer H.
Newman, Constance Berry
Newman, Theodore Roosevelt, Jr.
Newsome, Clarence Geno
Newsome, Steven Cameron
Newton, Robert B.
Newton, Robin Caprice
Nichols, Edwin J.
Nichols, Sylvia A.
Niles, Lyndrey Arnaud
Nimmons, Julius F., Jr.
Norman, William S.
Norrell-Thomas, Sondra
Northern, Robert A.
Norton, Edward Worthington
Norton, Eleanor Holmes
Nutall, James Edward
Oates, Wanda Anita
Obera, Marion L.
O'Bryant, Beverly J.
O'Bryant, Constance Taylor
O'Bryant, Tilmon Bunche
O'Leary, Hazel
Oliver-Simon, Gloria Craig
Ollison, Ruth Allen
Onyejekwe, Chike Onyekachi
Orr, Janice

Ottley, Neville
Owens, Brigman
Owens, David Kenneth
Owens, Joan Murrell
Owens, Major R.
Owens, Robert Leon, III
Oyewole, Saundra Herndon
Page, Clarence
Page, John Sheridan, Jr.
Palmer, Darlene Tolbert
Palmer, Ronald DeWayne
Parker, Averette Mhoon
Parker, Barrington D.
Parker, Charles McCrae
Parker, E. Charmaine Roberts
Parrott-Fonseca, Joan
Patrick, Deval L.
Patterson, Barbara Ann
Patterson, Elizabeth Hayes
Payne, Donald M.
Payne, Ethel Lois
Payne, N. Joyce
Payton, Carolyn Robertson
Peacock, Nicole
Peagler, Frederick Douglass
Peery, Benjamin Franklin, Jr.
Pendleton, Florence Howard
Penn, John Garrett
Perry, June Carter
Perry, Moses L., Jr.
Perry, Robert Cephas
Perry, Shirley
Peterson, Audrey Clinton
Peterson, Sushila Jane-Clinton
Pettus-Bellamy, Brenda Karen
Petty, Bruce Anthony
Petty, Rachel Monteith
Phillips, Frederick Brian
Phillips, Ralph Leonard
Pierce, Reuben G.
Pinckney, Theodore R.
Pinkett, Harold Thomas
Pinson, Margo Dean
Pinson, Thomas J.
Pinson, Valerie F.
Pointer, Richard H.
Pollard, Emily Frances
Ponder, Eunice Wilson
Ponder, Henry
Pope, Henry
Pope, James M.
Posey, Ada
Poussaint, Renee Francine
Powell, Georgette Seabrooke
Powell, Michael K.
Press, Harry Cody, Jr.
Price, Andrea R.
Pride, John L.
Proctor, Sonya T.
Pruitt, Anne Smith
Purnell, Marshall E.
Quander, Rohulamin
Quarles, Herbert DuBois
Quarrelles, James Ivan
Queen, Evelyn E. Crawford
Quincy, Ronald Lee
Quinn, Diane C.
Quinton, Barbara A.
Quivers, Eric Stanley
Raines, Franklin D.
Ramsey, Henry, Jr.
Randolph, Laura B.
Rangel, Charles B.
Rankin, Edward Anthony
Rankin, Michael L.
Rashad, Johari Mahasin
Raspberry, William J.
Ray, David Bruce
Ray, William Benjamin
Reagon, Bernice Johnson
Reed, Kathleen Rand
Reed, Vincent Emory
Reed-Miller, Rosemary E.
Reid, Leslie Bancroft
Reid, Ronda Eunese
Reinhardt, John Edward
Reynolds, Mel
Rhoden, Richard Allan
Ricanek, Carolyn Wright
Rice, David Eugene, Jr.
Rice, Emmett J.
Rice, Lois Dickson
Richardson, Bernard L.
Richardson, Robert Eugene
Richmond, Mitch
Richmond, Rodney Welch
Rier, John Paul, Jr.
Risher, John R., Jr.
Roach, Hildred Elizabeth

Roane, Philip Ransom, Jr.
Roberts, James E.
Roberts, Talmadge
Robinson, Aubrey Eugene, Jr.
Robinson, Eugene Harold
Robinson, Gloria
Robinson, Harry G., III
Robinson, Leonard Harrison, Jr.
Robinson, Peter Lee, Jr.
Robinson, Sandra Hawkins
Robinson, Sharon Porter
Roddey, Bertha M.
Rogers, Elijah Baby
Rogers, Judith W.
Rogers, Michael Charles
Rolle, Albert Eustace
Roscoe, Wilma J.
Ross, Frank Kenneth
Rosser, Samuel Blanton
Roundtree, Dovey
Roux, Vincent J.
Rowan, Carl Thomas
Ruffin, Paulette Francine
Rush, Bobby
Russell, Ernest
Saffel, E. Frank
Samara, Noah Azmi
Sample, Herbert Allan
Sampson, Calvin Coolidge
Sanders, Rober LaFayette
Satcher, David
Saunders, Edward Howard
Saunders, John Edward, III
Saunders, Mauderie Hancock
Saunders, William Joseph
Savage, James Edward, Jr.
Scales, Patricia Bowles
Sconoover, Brenda Brown
Scott, Aundrea Arthur
Scott, Helen Madison Marie
   Pawne Kinard
Scott, Kenneth Richard
Scott, Nigel L.
Scott, Robert Cortez
Scott, Roland B.
Scott-Clayton, Patricia Ann
Scruggs-Leftwich, Yvonne
Secundy, Marian Gray
Segre, Greta Eubank
Sewell, Isiah Obediah
Shackelford, Lottie H.
Shakoor, Waheedah Aqueelah
Shammgod, God
Shaw, Bernard
Shaw, Talbert Oscall
Shayen, Hubert S.
Shell, Theodore A.
Shippy, John D.
Shiver, Jube, Jr.
Shopshire, James Maynard
Showell, Hazel Jarmon
Shuman, Jerome
Siler, Brenda Claire
Silva, Omega C. Logan
Simmons, Althea T. L.
Simmons, Belva Tereshia
Simmons, Joseph Jacob, III
Simmons, Samuel J.
Simms, Margaret Constance
Simpkins, William Joseph
Simpson, Carole
Sims, Diane Marie
Sindler, Michael H.
Singleton, Harry M.
Slater, Rodney E.
Sloan, Edith Barksdale
Smalls, Jacquelyn Elaine
Smith, Alfred J., Jr.
Smith, Anne Street
Smith, Carol J.
Smith, Chester B.
Smith, Cleveland Emanuel
Smith, Conrad P.
Smith, Debbie A.
Smith, Eddie Glenn, Jr.
Smith, Edith B.
Smith, Edward Nathaniel, Jr.
Smith, Frank, Jr.
Smith, Gregory Robeson, Sr.
Smith, J. Clay, Jr.
Smith, Janice Evon
Smith, John Raye
Smith, Joseph F.
Smith, Judith Moore
Smith, Lafayette Kenneth
Smith, Marietta Culbreath
Smith, Patricia G.
Smith, Vida J.
Smith, Wallace Charles

Smith, Wayne Franklin
Smythe-Haith, Mabel Murphy
Snowden, Sylvia Frances
Sockwell, Oliver R., Jr.
Solomon, Wilbert F.
Spaulding, Aaron Lowery
Spaulding, William Ridley
Spearman, Leonard Hall
   O'Connell, Sr.
Speight, Eva B.
Speights, Nathaniel H.
Spencer, Michael Gregg
Spriggs, Ray V.
Spriggs, William
Spurlock, Jeanne
Stalling, Ronald Eugene
Standard, Raymond Linwood
Stanton, Robert G.
Starr, J. J.
Stebbins, Dana Brewington
Stent, Michelle Dorene
Stephenson, Allan Anthony
Sterling, Jeffrey Emery
Stevens, Lisa Maria
Stewart, Bennett McVey
Stewart, Imagene Bigham
Stewart, Pearl
Stewart, Ruth Ann
Stockton, Barbara Marshall
Stokes, Gerald Virgil
Stokes, Louis
Strait, George Alfred, Jr.
Streets, Fran A.
Strickland, Rodney
Strudwick, Warren James, Sr.
Sturdivant, John Nathan
Sullivan, Emmet G.
Sulton, John Dennis
Suneja, Sidney Kumar
Sutton, Dianne Floyd
Swygert, H. Patrick
Syphax, Burke
Tang, Deborah Canada
Tarver, Elking, Jr.
Tate, Eula Booker
Tatem, Patricia Ann
Taylor, Arnold H.
Taylor, Charles Edward
Taylor, Charley R.
Taylor, Estelle Wormley
Taylor, Helen Hollingshed
Taylor, Mildred E. Crosby
Taylor, Orlando L.
Taylor, William L.
Tearney, Russell James
Temple, Donald Melvin
Terrell, Mary Ann
Thaxton, June E.
Thomas, Arthur Lafayette, III
Thomas, Clarence
Thomas, Edith Peete
Thomas, Eunice S.
Thomas, Fred
Thomas, James O., Jr.
Thomas, Janis P.
Thomas, Joan McHenry Bates
Thomas, Juanita Ware
Thomas, Ralph Charles, III
Thomas-Bowlding, Harold Clifton
Thompson, Bennie G.
Thompson, Daniel Joseph
Thompson, Jeffrey Earl
Thompson, John Robert, Jr.
Thompson, Linda Jo
Thompson, Mozelle W.
Thompson, Portia Wilson
Thornell, Richard Paul
Thornton, Tracey
Thornton, Wayne T.
Thorpe, Earl Howard
Thorpe, Otis Henry
Tidwell, Billy Joe
Tilghman, Cyprian O.
Touchstone, John E.
Towns, Edolphus
Towns, Eva Rose
Townsend, Wardell C., Jr.
Trapp-Dukes, Rosa Lee
Traylor, Eleanor W.
Trescott, Jacqueline Elaine
Trowell-Harris, Irene
Tucker, Karen
Tucker, Walter Rayford, III
Turner, Carmen Elizabeth
Turner, Joseph Ellis
Turner, Leslie Marie
Turner, Margery
Turner, Marvin Wentz
Turner, Willie

Turner, Winston E.
Tutt, Lia S.
Tutt, Walter Cornelius
Upshaw, Gene
Valentine, J. T.
Valien, Preston
Vanderpool, Eustace Arthur
Van Hook, Warren Kenneth
Vaughn, William Samuel, III
Waddell, Theodore R.
Wagner, Annice
Walker, Angelina
Walker, Ann
Walker, Betty Stevens
Walker, James
Walker, John T.
Walker, Kenneth R.
Walker, Lucius
Walker, M. Lucius, Jr.
Walker, Roslyn Adele
Walker, William Paul, Jr.
Wallace, Ben
Wallace, C. Everett
Wallace, Paul Starett, Jr.
Walters, Curla Sybil
Walton, Flavia Batteau
Walton, Tracy Marshall, Jr., M.D.
Ware, Omego John Clinton, Jr.
Warfield-Coppock, Nsenga
Washington, Adrienne Terrell
Washington, Bennetta B.
Washington, Consuela M.
Washington, Robert Benjamin, Jr.
Washington, Robert E.
Washington, Walter E.
Waters, Maxine
Waters, Neville R., III
Watkins, Mozelle Ellis
Watkins, Shirley R.
Watlington, Janet Berecia
Watson, Theresa Lawhorn
Watson, Thomas S., Jr.
Watson, Tony J.
Watt, Melvin L.
Watts, J. C., Jr.
Weaver, Frank Cornell
Weaver, Reginald Lee
Webber, Paul R., III
Webster, Charles
Welsing, Frances Cress
Wesley, Charles H.
Wesley, Nathaniel, Jr.
West, Togo Dennis, Jr.
Wharton Boyd, Linda F.
Wheat, Alan
Whipps, Mary N.
Whisenton, Andre C.
White, Ida Margaret
White, Jack E.
White, John Clinton
White, Robert L.
Whitfield, Vantile E.
Whiting, Barbara E.
Whitney, Christopher Antoine
Whitten, Jamie L.
Wiese, Ronald
Wiggins, Lillian Cooper
Wilcher, Shirley J.
Wilcox, Janice Horde
Wiles, Spencer H.
Wiley, Herley Wesley
Wiley, Ralph
Wilfong, Henry T., Jr.
Wilhoit, Carl H.
Wilkins, Allen Henry
Wilkinson, Robert Shaw, Jr.
Williams, Anthony
Williams, Armstrong
Williams, Charles Thomas
Williams, Deborah Ann
Williams, Eddie Nathan
Williams, Ernest Y.
Williams, Ethel Langley
Williams, Hubert
Williams, James Thomas
Williams, Karen Hastie
Williams, Katherine
Williams, Larry C.
Williams, Lorenzo
Williams, Melvin Walker
Williams, Paul R.
Williams, Robert H.
Williams, Ronald Lee
Williams, Stanley King
Williams, Wesley S., Jr.
Williams, Wyatt Clifford
Williams, Yvonne LaVerne
Williams-Bridgers, Jacquelyn L.
Willingham, Voncile

Willoughby, Winston Churchill
Wilmot, David Winston
Wilson, John A.
Wilson, Joy Johnson
Wilson, Milton
Wilson, Richard Melbourne, Sr.
Wilson, Thomas A., Jr.
Wineglass, Henry
Winfield, Susan Rebecca Holmes
Winston, Jeanne Worley
Winter, Daria Portray
Winters, Wendy Glasgow
Wood, Anton Vernon
Wood, William Vernell, Sr.
Woodard, Samuel L.
Woodfork, Carolyn Amelia
Woods, Madelyne I.
Woodson, Robert L.
Woodson, Roderic L.
Word, Fletcher Henry, Jr.
Worsham, James E.
Worsley, George Ira, Jr.
Wynn, Albert
Yeldell, Joseph P.
Young, Charles Alexander
Young, Elizabeth Bell
Young, F. Camille
Zimmerman, Eugene
Zimmerman, Matthew Augustus, Jr.

FLORIDA

Apopka
Harvey, Gerald

Archer
Harris, Oscar L., Jr.

Avon Park
Cox, Arthur James, Sr.
Dennard, Willie James A., II

Belle Glade
Atkinson, Regina Elizabeth
Grear, Effie C.
Grear, William A.

Boca Raton
Barton, Wayne Darrell
Weatherspoon, Jimmy Lee

Boynton Beach
Ceasar, Sherita Therese

Bushnell
Coney, Loraine Chapell

Cantonment
Seabrook, Bradley Maurice

Cape Coral
Sawyer, William Gregory

Clearwater
Cleary, Louise I.
Hatchett, Paul Andrew
Ladson, Louis Fitzgerald
Reynolds, Clarence
Russell, Leon W.
Williams, Naomi B.

Cocoa
Murphy, Beatrice M.

Coconut Creek
Crawford, Carl M.
Miller, Dorsey Columbus, Jr.

Coral Gables
Dunn, Marvin
Rose, Alvin W.
Smith, Marzell

Coral Springs
Ruffin, John Walter, Jr.

Crestview
Daggs, Leon, Jr.

Dania
Nearn, Arnold Dorsey, Jr.

Davie
Liverpool, Herman Oswald

Daytona Beach
Bronson, Oswald P., Sr.
Burney, Harry L., Jr.
Crosslin, Evelyn Stocking
Dunn, William L.
Frink, John Spencer
Hamlin, Ernest Lee
Higgins, Cleo Surry
Miller, Jake C.
Moore, Richard V.
Moses, Harold Webster
Primus-Cotton, Bobbie J.
Pyles, J. A.
Rembert, Emma White
Taylor, Joseph H.
Waters, Wimbley, Jr.
Watson, Odest Jefferson, Sr.

DeLand
Williams, Reginald Clark

Delray Beach
Alexander, Preston Paul, Jr.
Daniels, Earl Hodges
Newsome, Elisa C.
Paris, Calvin Rudolph
Pompey, Charles Spencer

Eatonville
Vereen, Nathaniel

Eglin A F B
Sanders, George L.

Eustis
Jackson, Alvin B., Jr.
Matthews, Irving J.
Napper, James Wilbur

Florida City
Smith, Juanita Smith

Fort Lauderdale
Allen, W. George
Bass, Leonard Channing
Battle, Gloria Jean
Black, Malcolm Mazique
Carroll, Vinnette Justine
Clarke, Everee Jimerson
Cole, James O.
Crutchfield-Baker, Verdenia
Davis, Julia H.
Ferguson, Wilkie Demeritte, Jr.
Gainey, Leonard Dennis, II
Hansberry-Moore, Virginia T.
Henry, Bobby, Jr.
Hill, James O.
Hudson, Ronald
Johnson, David, III
Morrison, Samuel F.
Pinson, Vada Edward, Jr.
Rawls, Raleigh Richard
Reddick, Thomas J., Jr.
Shirley, Calvin Hylton
Taylor, Daisy Curry
Taylor, Norman Eugene
Taylor, Theodore D.
Whitmore, Darrell

Fort Myers
Ackord, Marie Mallory
Pitts, Lee H.
Shoemaker, Veronica Sapp
Weaver, Charles P.

Fort Pierce
Flowers, Ralph L.
Hawkins, Andre
Newbold, Simeon Eugene, Sr.

Fort Walton Beach
Smith, Nathaniel, Jr.

Gainesville
Alexander, Laurence Benedict
Ayers, George Waldon, Jr.
Carter, James L.
Cole, Thomas Winston, Sr.
DuPree, Sherry Sherrod
Green, Aaron Alphonso
Harris, Oscar L., Jr.
Hart, Jacqueline D.
Haskins, James S.
Hill-Lubin, Mildred Anderson
Phillip, Michael John
Reynolds, Ida Manning
Smith, Walter L.
Williams, Rosa B.

Green Cove Springs
Love, Joe W.

Havana
Davis, Marva Alexis

Heathrow
Weston, M. Moran, II, Ph.D.

Hialeah
Coatie, Robert Mason

Hollywood
Mack, Wilhelmena

Homestead
Armstrong, William

Homosassa
Irvin, Monford Merrill

Homosassa Springs
Hall, Hirold C.

Immokalee
Cochran, James David, Jr.

Jacksonville
Adams, Afesa M.
Aikens, Chester Alfronza
Barlow, Reggie Devon
Beasley, Aaron Bruce
Belton, C. Ronald
Best, Jennings H.
Brackens, Tony
Brown, Derek Vernon
Burns, Jesse L.
Carswell, Gloria Nadine Sherman
Cherry, Deron
Cobbin, W. Frank, Jr.
Coleman, Benjamin Leon
Cone, Cecil Wayne
Cone, Juanita Fletcher
Davis, Travis Horace
Evans, Donna Browder
Figures, Deon Juniel
Foster, James H.
Freeland, Shawn Ericka
Gallon, Dennis P.
Glover, Nat
Gregory, Bernard Vincent
Hall, Dana Eric
Hampton, Frank, Sr.
Hardy, Kevin
Hightower, J. Howard
Holmes, Wendell P., Jr.
Hudson, Christopher Resherd
Hurst, Rodney Lawrence
Huyghue, Michael
Jackson, Norman A.
Jackson, Willie Bernard, Jr.
Jones, Damon
Jordan, Randy Loment
Lea, Jeanne Evans
Lucas, Willie Lee
Marshall, Reese
Mathis, Sallye Brooks
McGill, Michele Nicole Johnson
Means, Natrone Jermaine
Metcalf, DaVinci Carver
Mitchell, Orrin Dwight
Mitchell, Robert L.
Moore, Will H.
Owens, Debbie A.
Powell, Leola P.
Pritchett, Kelvin Bratodd
Robinson, Eddie Joseph, Jr.
Rodgers, Anthony Recarido, Sr.
Ruth, James
Sams, James
Searcy, Leon, Jr.
Shelton, Daimon
Simmons, Clyde, Jr.
Simpson, Mary W.
Smith, Jimmy Lee, Jr.
Smith, Joseph Edward
Stewart, James Ottis, III
Thomas, Dave G.
Threats, Jabbar
Tillman, Cedric
Watson, Cletus Claude
Williams, Ann E. A.
Williams, Isiah J., III
Wynn, Renaldo

Key West
Chandler, Theodore Alan

Kissimmee
Booth, William H.

Lake Buena Vista
Carter, Warrick L.
Rivers, Johnny
Thomas, Mitchell, Jr.

Lake City
Anders, Richard H.

Lake Park
Holland, William Meredith

Lake Wales
Austin, James P.

Lakeland
Blake, Wendell Owen
Ivey, Mark, III

Lauderdale Lakes
Paige, Windell

Lauderhill
Benson, Hayward J., Jr.
Miller, Dorsey Columbus, Jr.

Longwood
Neal, Frederic Douglas

Mac Dill AFB
Hubbard, Josephine Brodie

Maitland
Ham-Ying, J. Michael

Mary Esther
Rasheed, Howard S.

Miami
Abdul-Jabbar, Karim
Ali, Grace L.
Allen, Jane Elizabeth
Anderson, Willie Lloyd
Askins, Keith Bernard
Atkins, C. Clyde
Barnes, Diane
Beamon, Robert A.
Bellamy, Angela Robinson
Bigby Young, Betty
Bonilla, Bobby
Bowens, Tim
Brewster, Luther George
Bridges, James Wilson
Bridges, Rochelle Marie
Brigance, O.J.
Brown, James Lamont
Brown, John Ollis
Brown, LeRoy Ronald
Brown, P. J.
Bryant, Castell Vaughn
Buckley, Terrell
Carter, Anthony Jerome
Carter, Judy Sharon
Causwell, Duane
Champion, James A.
Clark, Leon Henry
Clark, Roslyn M.
Coatie, Robert Mason
Conner, Laban Calvin
Cryer, Linkston T.
Cunningham, Courtney
Curry, Victor Tyrone
Day, Todd Fitzgerald
Demeritte, Edwin T.
Drayton, Troy Anthony
Duper, Mark Super
Dyer, Bernard Joel
Elligan, Irvin, Jr.
Ellis, George Washington
Everett, Cynthia A.
Fair, Talmadge Willard
Ferguson, Terri Lynette
Fitzpatrick, Albert E.
Floyd, Cliff
Foster, Rosebud Lightbourn
Frazier, Eufaula Smith
Gardener, Daryl
Gilbert, Shedrick Edward
Gilford, Vera E.
Golden, Willie L.
Green, Hugh
Green, Walter
Green, Yatil
Greene, Joe
Greer, Tee S., Jr.
Hadley, Howard Alva, Jr.

O'Neal, Malinda King
Osborne, William Reginald, Jr.
Palmer, James D.
Parker, Thomas Edwin, III
Parks, Bernard
Patrick, Vincent Jerome
Patterson, Curtis Ray
Pattillo, Roland A.
Payne, Jacqueline LaVerne
Pender, Mel
Pendleton, Terry Lee
Peoples, Dottie
Perdue, Wiley A.
Perry-Holston, Waltina D.
Persons, W. Ray
Phillips, Bertha
Pickens, Ernestine W. McCoy
Pickens, William Garfield
Pinado, Alan E., Sr.
Pledger, Verline S.
Poe, Booker
Pope, Derrick Alexander
Porter, Mia Lachone
Powell, C. Clayton
Price, Charles Eugene
Price, James Rogers
Pride, Curtis John
Prothro, Johnnie Watts
Pugh, Thomas Jefferson
Rates, Norman M.
Recasner, Eldridge David
Reed, James W.
Reed, Lambert S., II
Reese, Mamie Bynes
Reeves, Alexis Scott
Render, William H.
Renford, Edward
Richardson, Timothy L.
Richmond, Myrian Patricia
Roberts, Trish
Robie, Clarence W.
Robinson, Angela Yvonne
Robinson, Edsel F.
Robinson, Jontyle Theresa
Robinson, Joseph William, Sr.
Robinson, Michael David
Robinson, Robert G.
Ross, Catherine Laverne
Ross, Kevin Arnold
Roundtree, Saudia
Rounsaville, Lucious Brown, Jr.
Rouse, Jacqueline Anne
Royster, Don M., Sr.
Ruffin, John H., Jr.
Rush, Eddie F.
Russell, Herman Jerome
Russell, Jerome
Samples, Jared Lanier
Sampson, Thomas Gatewood
Saunders, Barbara Ann
Scott, Albert J.
Scott, Cornelius Adolphus
Scott, Linzy, Jr.
Scott, Mary Shy
Scott, Portia Alexandria
Scott, Rachel Loraine
Sears, Leah Jeanette
Sheftall, Willis B., Jr.
Shelton, Bryan
Shelton, Lee Raymond
Shockley, Grant S.
Simmons, Eric O.
Simmons, Isaac Tyrone
Sinclair, Clayton, Jr.
Skinner, Robert L., Jr.
Slaughter, Vernon L.
Smith, Beverly Evans
Smith, C. Miles, Jr.
Smith, Gregory Allen
Smith, Herman Brunell, Jr.
Smith, John B.
Smith, LaSalle, Sr.
Smith, Luther Edward, Jr.
Smith, Robert Edward
Smith, Steven Delano
Smith-Epps, E. Paulette
Smothers, Ronald Eric
Stanley, LaNett
Stargell, Willie
Steele, Michael W.
Stephens, E. Delores B.
Strong, Otis Reginald, III
Styles, Julian English
Sullivan, Louis Wade
Sutton, Ozell
Tate, Horace Edward
Taylor, Anderson
Teamer, Charles C.
Thomas, Franklin Whitaker

Thomas-Samuel, Kalin Normoet
Thompson, Edwin A.
Thompson, Joseph Earl, Sr.
Thompson, Larry D.
Threatt, Robert
Todd, William S.
Tomlinson, Robert
Tottress, Richard Edward
Triche, Arthur, Jr.
Tucker, Cynthia Anne
Tucker, Michael Anthony
Tucker, Samuel Joseph
Tunstall, Lucille Hawkins
Turk, Alfred J., II
Turner, Joseph Ellis
Turner, Kim Smith
Tusan, Gail S.
Usher
Vause, Gary, II
Vivian, Cordy Tindell
Wade, Lyndon Anthony
Wade-Gayles, Gloria Jean
Walker, Charles W.
Walker, Larry M.
Walker, Maria Latanya
Walker, Mark Lamont
Waller, Robert Lee
Walton, Harriett J.
Walton, Mildred Lee
Ward, Horace T.
Ware, J. Lowell
Ware, Janis L.
Ware, R. David
Ware, William
Warren, Nagueyalti
Warren, Rueben Clifton
Waters, John W.
Watkins, Lottie Heywood
Watson, Aaron
Watts, Anne Wimbush
Webb, Melvin Richard
Webb, Spud
Webster, Isabel Gates
Whalum, Wendell P.
White, Claude Esley
White, Richard H.
White, Wendell F.
White, William T., III
Whitfield, Alphonso
Whitfield, Willie, Jr.
Whitlow, Barbara Wheeler
Whitney, W. Monty
Wilkens, Leonard R.
Wilkes, Shelby R.
Williams, Charles C.
Williams, Doug Lee
Williams, Edward M.
Williams, Gerald Floyd
Williams, Hosea L.
Williams, Lillian C.
Williams, Louis Nathaniel
Williams, Pelham C.
Williams, Peyton, Jr.
Williams, Robert Lee, Jr.
Willis, Isaac
Wilson, Johnny Leaverne
Wilson, Trevor
Wiltz, Philip G., Jr.
Winslow, Cleta Meris
Wood, Brenda Blackmon
Woolcock, Ozeil Fryer
Wooten, Carl Kenneth
Wyatt Cummings Moore, Thelma LaVerne
Yancey, Asa G., Sr.
Yates, Ella Gaines
Young, Michael M.
Young, Walter F.

Augusta
Beard, Laronce D.
Booth, Le-Quita
Brigham, Henry
Brown, James
Carter, James Edward, Jr.
Carter, Judy L.
Gordon, Barbara A.
Hamilton, Charles S.
Herrington, Perry Lee
Hobbs, Joseph
Hollis, Clarence O.
Howard, Henry L.
Hunt, Eugene
Hunter, William Andrew
Jagnandan, Wilfred Lilpersaud
Jefferson, Patricia Ann
Kellar, Arthur H.
Kelly, Thomas, Jr.
Lawrence, James T.

Lewis, Shirley A. R.
Mays, Carrie J.
Millender, Mallory Kimerling
Neal, Alimam Butler
Paschall, Evita Arneda
Powell, Addie Scott
Rice, Louise Allen
Robertson, Quincy L.
Scott, Hubert R.
Stallings, James Raiford
Walker, Solomon W., II
Washington, Isaiah Edward
Young, James Arthur, III

Austell
Perdue, John F.

Avondale Estates
Britton, Theodore R.
Harris, William Joseph, II

Berkley Lake
Hammond, W. Rodney

Blackshear
Taylor, Reginald Redall, Jr.

Bogart
Locklin, James R.

Brunswick
Stephens, James Anthony
Williams, Thomas Pedworth

Buford
Bell, Robert Wesley

Byron
Burton-Junior, Eva Westbrook
Junior, Ester James, Jr.

Carrollton
Morgan, Harry

Cartersville
Wheeler, Susie Weems

Cave Spring
Chubb, Louise B.

Clarkston
McIntosh, Frankie L.

College Park
Armour, Christopher E.
Blackwell, Willie
Blanchet, Waldo Willie E.
Davis, Marilyn Ann Cherry
Harmon, James F., Sr.
Hightower, Anthony
McCall, Emmanuel Lemuel, Sr.
Moore, Richard Earle
Whitest, Beverly Joyce

Columbus
Baskin, Clarence L.
Battle, Jacqueline
Belcher, Margaret L.
Booth, Le-Quita
Brown, James O.
Bryant, Jerome Benjamin
Buckner, Mary Alice
Cook, Henry Lee, Sr.
Davis, Gregory A.
DeVore, Ophelia
Ford, George Washington, III
Fortson, Walter Lewis
Mitchell, Ophelia D.
Smyre, Calvin
Turner, Geneva
Turner, Mikoel
Williams, Henry
Willis, Rose W.

Commerce
Mayfield, JoAnn H.O.

Conyers
Aikens-Young, Linda Lee

Cordele
Rivers, Alfred J.
Williams, Napoleon

Covington
Cobb, Harold
Lawhorn, John B.

Culloden
Campbell, Margie

Decatur
Adams, Gregory Albert
Baranco, Gregory T.
Belcher, Jacqueline
Brown, Thomas Edison, Jr.
Burroughs, Robert A.
Bush, T. W.
Epps, John S.
Ferguson, Elliott LaRoy, II
Fields, Richard A.
Gilmore, C. Tyrone, Sr.
Hale, Cynthia Lynnette
Harris, Archie Jerome
Hunt, Maurice
Kimbro, Dennis Paul
Lewis, Charles McArthur
Lewis, Polly Meriwether
Matlock, Kent
McBride, Cornell, Sr.
McKenzie, Eli, Jr.
Merritt, Wendy
Moore, Harold Earl, Jr.
Moss, Wayne B.
Norman, Moses C.
Nunnally, David H., Sr.
Perrimon, Vivian Spence
Pope, Derrick Alexander
Smith, Leo Grant
Smith, Paul
Thacker, Sandra J.
Vaughan, Gerald R.
White, Raymond Rodney, Sr.
White, William T., III
Williams, Terry

Douglasville
Beasley, Victor Mario
McMillan, Regina Ellis
Williams, Jean Carolyn

Dublin
Broomes, Lloyd Rudy
Williams, Hayward J.

East Point
Brown, Frank Lewis
Godfrey, William R.
Harris, Archie Jerome
Hilliard, Patsy Jo
Paige, Ralph
Williams, Valencia
Wilson, Natarsha Juliet

Ellaville
Goodwin, William Pierce, Jr.

Ellenwood
Edmonds, Bevelyn
Odoms, Willie O.
Parks, Alfred G., Jr.

Evans
Karangu, David

Fairburn
Cofer, Michael Lynn
Hall, James Reginald
Ward, Sandra L.

Fayetteville
Jones, Michael Andrea
Minor, Emma Lucille

Forest Park
Hodge, Ernest M.

Fort Benning
Burton, Charles Howard, Jr.
Gaines, Oscar Cornell

Fort Gordon
Gray, Robert E.

Fort Valley
Church, Robert T., Sr.
Edwards, Claybon Jerome
Fletcher, Tyrone P.
Horton, Dollie Bea Dixon
Junior, Ester James, Jr.
Langston-Jackson, Wilmetta Ann Smith
Prater, Oscar L.
Simmons, Julius Caesar, Sr.
Walker, Melvin E., Jr.

Georgetown
Kendrick, Tommy L.

Gray
Green, Clyde Octavious

Griffin
Head, Raymond, Jr.
Reeves, Alan M.

Hapeville
Lucas, William S.

Hephzibah
Brown, Bettye Jean
Godbee, Thomasina D.

Hiram
Fitzgerald, Roy Lee

Junction City
Carter, Christopher Anthony

Kennesaw
Davis, Frank Allen
Wingfield, Harold Lloyd

La Grange
Lewis, Frank Ross
Miley, Debra Charlet

Lawrenceville
Lawrence, Theresa A. B.
Truvillion, Wendy

Leary
Young, Charlie, Jr.

Lincolnton
Freeman, Denise
Williams, Roger

Lithia Springs
Collier, Millard James, Jr., M.D.

Lithonia
Clemons, James Albert, III
Collier-Bridgeforth, Barbara
Daniels, Frederick L., Jr.
Lewis, Willard C.
Shakespeare, Easton Geoffrey
Sulton, Jacqueline Rhoda
Warren, Nagueyalti
Young, James E.

Macon
Braswell, Palmira
Brunson, Pierce B.
Byas, Ulysses
Ewing, James Melvin
Jones, James B.
McGee, Sylvia Williams
Smith, Eddie D., Sr.
Swain, Hamp
Vinson, Julius Ceasar
Walton, DeWitt T., Jr.
Williams, Melvyn J.
Wimberly, James Hudson

Madison
Charis, Sister

Marietta
Armour, Christopher E.
Baskett, Kenneth Gerald
Brown, Raymond Madison
Burton, Charles Howard, Jr.
Dean, Daniel R.
James, Dorothy Marie
Jordan, George Washington, Jr.
Koger, Michael Pigott, Jr.
McWilliams, Alfred E., Jr.
Moon, Walter D.
Payne, Jacqueline LaVerne
Powell, Clarence Dean, Jr.
See, Letha A.
Thomas, Pamella D.
Tuggle, Dorie C.
Yancy, Robert James

Martin
Hughes, Ernelle Combs

Martinez
Johnson, George, Jr.
Paschall, Evita Arneda

Mayfield
Hunt, James, Jr.

McDonough
Jones, Emanuel Davie

Metter
Hodges, Cother L.
Robinson, Catherine
Whitaker, Mical Rozier

Midway
Clancy, Magalene Aldoshia

Milledgeville
Cook, Mary Murray
Monroe, Annie Lucky
Taylor, Willie Marvin

Morrow
Ryan-White, Jewell

Nahunta
Rainge, Nathaniel

Newnan
Ashmore, Andrea Lynn
Bostic, James Edward, Jr.

Norcross
Patterson, Gerald William

Norman Park
Williams, Willie J.

Oliver
Brown, Justine Thomas

Peachtree City
Ivey Yarn, Barbara Lynne

Riceboro
McIver, John Douglas

Riverdale
Granger, Edwina C.

Rockmart
Billingslea, Edgar D.

Rome
Askew, Bonny Lamar

Roswell
Lottier, Patricia

Savannah
Adams, Eugene Bruce
Adams, Floyd, Jr.
Alls, Howard E.
Bell, Joseph N.
Booker, Walter M.
Brantley, Daniel
Brock, Annette
Bynes, Frank Howard, Jr.
Cooper, Curtis V.
Eke, Kenoye Kelvin
Ford, Bowles C.
Freeman, Nelson R.
Gadsden, Eugene Hinson
Gardener, William E., Jr.
Garrison, Esther F.
Gay, Benjamin
Harris, Lolita Pazant
Hicks, Doris Morrison
Honeycutt, Andrew E.
Jackson, Suzanne Fitzallen
Jamerson, John William, Jr.
James, Robert Earl
James, Shirley B.
Johnson, Otis Samuel
Jordan, Abbie H.
Jordan, Anne Knight
Keith, Leroy
Martin, Clarence L.
Martin, Shedrick M., Jr.
Mathis, Frank
McDew, Stephen Maxwell, Jr.
Milledge, Luetta Upshur
Mitchell, Bennie Robert, Jr.
Moore, Henry J.
Morse, John E., Jr.
Muley, Miriam
Pelote, Dorothy B.
Polite, Marie Ann
Reynolds, Viola J.
Silver, Joseph Howard, Sr.

Stevens, Reatha J.
Thomas, Priscilla D.
Walton, Hanes, Jr.
Whitaker, Von Frances
Wiggins, Clifton Allen, Sr.

Smithville
Mitchell, Douglas

Smyrna
Smith, Quentin T.
Thornton, Jackie C.

Sparta
Dixon, Jimmy
Ingram, Edith J.
Wiley, Leroy Sherman

Statesboro
Grant, Wilmer, Jr.
Newson, Roosevelt, Jr.
Whitaker, Mical Rozier
Young, Alfred

Stone Mountain
Brewer, Alvin L.
Brown, John Baker, Jr.
Liverpool, Charles Eric
Marsh, Ben Franklin
Persons, W. Ray
Scales, Erwin Carlvet
Shackelford, William G., Jr.
Smith, Philip Gene
Sumler-Edmond, Janice L.

Suwanee
Archambeau, Lester Milward, III
Bennett, Cornelius O'landa
Bolden, Juran
Booker, Michael
Brandon, David Sherrod
Buchanan, Raymond Louis
Bush, Devin
Davis, Antone Eugene
Downs, Gary McClinton
Emanuel, Bert Tyrone
Fountaine, Jamal
Hamilton, Ruffin
Hayes, Mercury
Haynes, Michael David
Mathis, Terance
McGill, Lenny
Miller, Nate
Norman, Wallace
Pleasant, Anthony Devon
Sanders, Ricky Wayne
Smith, Charles Henry, III
Tuggle, Jessie Lloyd
West, Edward Lee, III
White, William Eugene
Whitfield, Robert
Williams, Eugene
Wimberly, Marcus

Sylvania
Badger, Lloyd, Jr.
Williams, Jesse

Thomasville
Fortson, Henry David, Jr.
McIver, Margaret Hill
Morris, Ella Lucille
Williams, Earl, Jr.

Thomson
Greene, Joseph David

Tifton
Graydon, Wasdon, Jr.

Tyrone
Bellamy, Ivory Gandy

Union City
Brown, Michael L.
Ivey, Rebecca

Valdosta
Brown, Ola M.
Hall, Eugene Curtis
Richardson, Mary Margaret
Roberts, Edgar
Williams, Lafayette W.

Villa Rica
Morgan, Harry

Wadley
Charles, Lewis
Johnson, B. A.

Warner Robins
Moore, Jesse
Pogue, Richard James
Trainer, James E.

Waycross
Bonner, Theophulis W.
Gaines, Oscar Cornell

Waynesboro
Griggs, James C.
Lodge, Herman

Whitesburg
Gamble, Robert Lewis

Winterville
Clifton, Ivery Dwight

Woodbine
Brown, Willis, Jr.

Woodstock
Daniel, James L.

HAWAII

Aiea
Richards, Leon

Honolulu
Ball, Richard Erwin
Campbell, Charles M.
Carroll, Annie Haywood
Edwards, John W., Jr.
Richards, Leon
Smith, Richard Alfred
Young, Edward Hiram, Jr.

Lihue
King, LeRoy J.

Mililani
James, Arminta Susan

IDAHO

Boise
Brown, Booker T.
Mercy, Leland, Jr.

Eagle
Spigner, Marcus E.

Mountain Home
Montgomery, Robert E.

Pocatello
Williams, Herb E.
Yizar, James Horace, Jr.

ILLINOIS

AMF OHare
Norwood, William R.

AMF Ohare
Fraser, Thomas Edwards

Abbott Park
Carey, Wayne E.

Alsip
Rayon, Paul E., III

Alton
Green, Robert L.

Argo
Taylor, William Henry, Sr.

Argonne
Gay, Eddie C.
Robinson, Jack, Jr.
Smith, Aubrey Carl, Jr.

Arlington Heights
Martin, Gwendolyn Rose
Phillips, W. Thomas

Aurora
McMillan, Robert Frank, Jr.
Whitaker, Pernell
Wilkinson, Marie L.

Barrington
Carpenter, Clarence E., Jr.
Moore, Shirley L.

Bedford Park
Buford, William M., III

Belleville
Chalmers, Thelma Faye
Gregory, Wilton D.
LeCompte, Peggy Lewis
McCaskill, Earle
Otis-Lewis, Alexis D.
Steele, Ruby L.
Wiley, Gerald Edward

Bellwood
Bailey, Ronald W.

Bloomington
Jones, Eva
Mosley, Roosevelt Charles, Jr.

Blue Island
Olawumi, Bertha Ann

Broadview
Johnson, Patricia Dumas

Buffalo Grove
Dukes, Ronald

Cairo
Nelson, Harold E.

Calumet City
Muhammad, Wallace D.
Rucker, Alston Louis

Carbondale
Bryson, Seymour L.
Guthrie, Robert V.
Hayes, Richard C.
Jones, Jennie Y.
Robinson, Walter G.
Stalls, M.
Welch, Harvey, Jr.

Centralia
Tinsley, Donald P.
Walker, William Harold

Champaign
Barkstall, Vernon L.
Burgess, James R., Jr.
Caroline, J. C.
Clay, Ernest H., III
Copeland, Robert M.
Cowan, Larine Yvonne
Davidson, U. S., Jr.
Griggs, Mildred Barnes
Harris, Zelema M.
Norman, P. Roosevelt
Pirtle, J. W.
Underwood, James
Whitmore, Charles
Williams, Willie James

Charleston
Coker, Adeniyi Adetokunbo
Colvin, William E.
Ibelema, Minabere
Lane, Johnny Lee
Ridgeway, Bill Tom

Chicago
Abdullah, Larry Burley
Adair, Andrew A.
Adams, Billie Morris Wright
Adams, Carol Laurence
Adams, Sheila Mary
Akin, Ewen M., Jr.
Albert, Charles Gregory
Alexander, Alison Harris
Alexander, James Arthur
Alexander, Louis G., Sr.
Allen, Mark
Amaker, Norman Carey

Amaro, Ruben
Anderson, George A.
Anderson, Howard D.
Anderson, Monroe
Anthony-Perez, Bobbie M.
Apea, Joseph Bennet Kyeremateng
Arburtha, Leodies U.
Armster-Worrill, Cynthia Denise
Artope, William
Askew, James R.
Austin, Carrie
Bacon, Gloria Jackson
Bailey, Adrienne Yvonne
Bailey, Donn Fritz
Bailey, Duwain
Baldwin, James
Ball, William Batten
Ball-Reed, Patrice M.
Banks, Charlie
Banks, Jerry L.
Barnett, Alfreda W. Duster
Barnett, Etta Moten
Barnett, William
Barney, Willie J.
Barrow, Willie T.
Baskins, Lewis C.
Bateman, Paul E.
Bates, Barbara Ann
Bates, Louise Rebecca
Beal, Jacqueline Jean
Beck, Angel Carter
Bell, Carl Compton
Bell, George Antonio
Bell, William Jerry
Belle, Albert Jojuan
Belliny, Daniel S.
Bennett, Deborah Minor
Bennett, Lerone, Jr.
Benson, Sharon Marie
Berry, Edwin C.
Berry, Leonidas H.
Biblo, Mary
Black, Leona R.
Black, Walter Kerrigan
Blair, Chester Laughton Ellison
Bland, Heyward
Blanks, Wilhelmina E.
Blouin, Rose Louise
Booth, Keith
Boswell, Paul P.
Bowles, Barbara Landers
Bowman, James E., Jr.
Boyd, William Stewart
Braden, Everette Arnold
Branch, Dorothy L.
Brazil, Robert D.
Bristow, Lonnie R.
Bromery, Keith Marcel
Brooks, Delores Jean
Brooks, Frank B.
Brooks, Gwendolyn
Brown, Buck
Brown, Clarice Ernestine
Brown, Constance Charlene
Brown, Emmett Earl
Brown, Floyd A.
Brown, Geoffrey Franklin
Brown, Joan P.
Brown, Joseph Clifton
Brown, Milbert Orlando
Brown, Milton F.
Brown, Randy
Brown, Reginald
Brown, Rose Denise
Brown, Stephen H.
Brownlee, Geraldine Daniels
Brownlee, Lester Harrison-Pierce
  MacDougall
Brownridge, J. Paul
Bryant, Clarence
Bryant, Preston
Bryant, Robert E.
Bryson, Cheryl Blackwell
Buckner, James L.
Buckney, Edward L.
Burns, Diann
Burns, Willie Miles
Burrell, Barbara
Burrell, Scott David
Burrell, Thomas J.
Burroughs, Leonard
Burroughs, Sarah G.
Burrus, Clark
Bush, Ernest
Butler, Jerome M.
Butler, Jerry
Bynoe, Peter C. B.
Cage, Patrick B.
Caldwell, James E.

Sanders, Victoria Lynn
Saunders, Vincent E., III
Sawyer, Roderick Terrence
Scott, Alice H.
Scott, Ruby Dianne
Scott-Heron, Gil
Scrutchions, Benjamin
Seabrook, Lemuel, III
Seals, Connie C.
Sengstacke, Fred D.
Sengstacke, John H.
Sessoms, Furmin Douglas
Shackelford, George Franklin
Sharrieff, Osman Ibn
Shaw, Martini
Sheares, Reuben A., II
Sherrell, Charles Ronald, II
Shirley, James M.
Simmons, Geraldine Crossley
Simmons, James Richard
Simmons, Willie, Jr.
Simpkins, Dickey
Sims-Davis, Edith R.
Sizemore, Barbara A.
Skinner, Clementine Anna
  McConico
Smith, Allen Joseph, Sr.
Smith, Ann Elizabeth
Smith, Daniel H., Jr.
Smith, Elmer G., Jr.
Smith, Kenneth Bryant
Smith, Lemuel T.
Smith, Paul Bernard
Smith, Renetta
Smith, Thelma J.
Somerville, Dora B.
Sosa, Samuel
South, Leslie Elaine
Spann, Melody
Speights, John D.
Speller, Eugene Thurley
Spurlock, Oliver M.
Starks, Robert Terry
Statham, Carl
Steele, Bobbie L.
Stepto, Robert Charles
Stevens, Michelle
Stevenson, James Earl
Stewart, Charles J.
Stewart, William O.
Stratton-Morris, Madeline
  Robinson Morgan
Strawn, Aimee Williams
Strayhorn, Earl E.
Stricklin, James
Stringer, Nelson Howard, Jr.
Stroger, John Herman, Jr.
Sumner, Thomas Robert
Sutton, Sterling E.
Sykes, Weathers Y.
Taylor, Bernard C.
Taylor, Cora
Taylor, James
Taylor, William Henry, Sr.
Temple, Herbert
Temple, Ronald J.
Terrell, Mable Jean
Terrell, Melvin C.
Thatcher, Harold W.
Thomas, Frank Edward
Thomas, Mary Maxwell
Thomas, Terra Leatherberry
Thompson, Hobson, Jr.
Thompson, Lowell Dennis
Thompson, Mark Randolph
Thompson, Richard Ellis
Thornton, John C.
Thurman, Cedric Douglas
Thurston, William A.
Tillman, Paula Sellars
Todd, Thomas N.
Tolliver, Joel
Tolliver, Richard Lamar
Townsel, Ronald
Travis, Dempsey J.
Truitt, Kevin
Tucker, Robert L.
Vance, Lawrence N.
Vance, William J., Sr.
Vertreace, Martha Modena
Walker, Albertina
Walker, Allene Marsha
Walker, Lee H.
Waller, Larry
Ward, Calvin
Ware, Dyahanne
Warren, Charles P.
Washington, Albert
Washington, Bernie

Washington, Eli H.
Washington, Elmer L.
Washington, Harold
Watkins, Judge Charles, Jr.
Watson, Clyniece Lois
Watt, Garland Wedderick
Weaver, Audrey Turner
Wedgeworth, Robert, Jr.
West, Christopher O.
West, Donda C.
Wheaton, Thelma Kirkpatrick
Wheeler, Lloyd G.
White, Deidre R.
White, Jesse C., Jr.
White, Lois Jean
Whiting, Leroy
Whiting, Willie
Whitmal, Nathaniel
Whyte, Garrett
Williams, Ann Claire
Williams, Billy Leo
Williams, Bismarck S.
Williams, David S., Jr.
Williams, Edward Joseph
Williams, Elynor A.
Williams, Fitzroy E.
Williams, Frank J.
Williams, Jeanette Marie
Williams, Jeffrey Len
Williams, Ken
Williams, Philip B.
Williams, W. Bill, Jr.
Williams, Walter
Williams Boyd, Sheila Anne
Williamson, Henry M.
Wilson, Clarence S., Jr.
Wilson, Cleo Francine
Wilson, John E.
Wilson, Rita P.
Wilson, Velma J.
Wilson, Willie James
Wiltz, Charles J.
Wimp, Edward Lawson
Winbush, Clarence, Jr.
Winfrey, Audrey Theresa
Winfrey, Oprah
Winslow, Alfred A.
Winslow, Eugene
Winstead, Vernon A., Sr.
Wood, Juanita Wallace
Wood, William S.
Woods, Jessie Anderson
Woods, Wilbourne H.
Worrill, Conrad W.
Wright, Carl Jeffrey
Wright, Jeremiah A., Jr.
Wright, Joseph H., Jr.
Wright, Raymond Stanford
Wyatt, Addie L.
Wyatt, Claude Stell, Jr.
Wycliff, Noel Don
Wynn, Sylvia J.
Wynne, Marvell
Wynns, Corrie
Wyrick, Floyd I.
Yates, LeRoy Louis
Yearwood, David Monroe, Jr.
Yelding, Eric Girard
Young, James M., II
Young, Terrence Anthony
Young, Terri Jones
Zollar, Doris L.
Zollar, Nikki Michele

Chicago Heights
Beck, Saul L.
Gavin, L. Katherine
Hammond, Clyde
Martin, Lorenzo E.
McIntosh, Rhodina Covington
Paul, Alvin, III

Crete
Parker, Jacquelyn Heath

Creve Coeur
Vincent, Marjorie Judith

Danville
Blanden, Lee Ernest
Foster Foulks, Ivadale Marie
McDonald, G. Michael
McDonald, Michael G.

De Kalb
Daniel, Phillip T. K.
Moore, Juliette R.
Thurman, Alfonzo
Williams, Eddie R., Jr.

Williams, Edna C.
Young, Alfred F.

Decatur
Beddingfield, Edward C.
Dobbins, Alphondus Milton
Ford, Deborah Lee
Livingston, Horace
Stockard, Betsy

Deerfield
Cade, Henry
Cobb, Cynthia Joan
Harrold, Jeffery Deland
Walsh, Deborah Snow
Williams, Edward Ellis

Des Plaines
Brooks, Clyde Henry
Franklin, Garrome P.
Shoffner, James Priest

Dolton
Broome, Pershing
Whitehurst, Steven Laroy

Downers Grove
McKinzie, Barbara A.

East Moline
Edwards, Kenneth J.

East Peoria
Upah, Dennis

East Saint Louis
Younge, Richard G.

East St Louis
Allen, Edna Rowery
Bush, Gordon
Clayborne, Oneal
Davis, Dupree Daniel
Dennis, Philip H.
Dunham, Katherine
Gentry, LaMar Duane
Haynes, Eugene, Jr.
Jackson, Arthur Mells, II
Jackson, Willis Randell, II
Jordan, Anne E.
Lawson, Charles H., III
Mason, William E.
McGaughy, Will
Murphy, Della Mary
Redmond, Eugene B.
Thompson, Lloyd Earl
Wharton, Milton S.
Wright, Katie Harper

Edwardsville
Bell, Doris E.
Grist, Arthur L., Sr.
Hampton, Phillip Jewel
Pyke, Willie Oranda
Smith, Joseph Edward
Wilson, Rudolph George

Elgin
Edwards, Marvin E.
Liautaud, James
Vessup, Aaron Anthony
Wyche, Paul H., Jr.

Elmhurst
Harris, Carol R.
Sutton, Wilma Jean

Evanston
Alexis, Marcus
Bethel, Kathleen Evonne
Binford, Henry C.
Bransford, William L.
Brownlee, Lester Harrison-Pierce
  MacDougall
Byrdsong, Ricky
Carter, Robert Thompson
Cheeks, Carl L.
Cherry, Warren W.
Forrest, Leon Richard
Harley, Philip A.
Harris, Robert Allen
Helms, David Alonzo
Jordan, Thurman
Lowe, Eugene Yerby, Jr.
McMillan, Lemmon Columbus, II
Morton, Lorraine H.
Norwood, John F.
Osborne, Gwendolyn Eunice

Phillips, Bertrand D.
Phillips, Daniel P.
Reynolds, Bruce Howard
Slaughter-Defoe, Diana T.
Sorey, Hilmon S., Jr.
Spurlock-Evans, Karla Jeanne
Stickney, Janice L.
Summers, Edna White
Taylor, Hycel B.
Wilkins, Leona B.
Wilson, Jonathan Charles, Jr.
Wimberly, Edward P.
Winfield, Florence F.

Evergreen Park
Bernoudy, Monique Rochelle
Salter, Roger Franklin

Flossmoor
Marsh, McAfee

Forsyth
Moorehead, Thomas

Freeport
Parker, James L.

Galesburg
Hord, Frederick Lee

Glendale Heights
Burke, Kirkland R.

Glenview
Edwards, Rondle E.
Roebuck-Hayden, Marcia

Glenwood
Fentress, Shirley B.
Howard, Billie Jean
Rockett, Damon Emerson

Gurnee
Winfield, Arnold F.

Hanover Park
Harrison, Delbert Eugene

Harvey
Brown-Nash, JoAhn Weaver
Demonbreun, Thelma M.
Farley, Carl David
Taylor, Gloria Jean

Hazel Crest
Nichols, Alfred Glen
Robertson, Alan D.

Herrin
Carthen, John, Jr.

Highland Park
McCallum, Walter Edward

Hinsdale
Hopson, Melvin Clarence

Hoffman Estates
Hill, Marvin Lewis
Moran, Joyce E.
Payton, Walter Jerry

Homewood
Banks, Ronald
Richmond, Delores Ruth
Sagers, Rudolph, Jr.

Hopkins Park
Runnels, Bernice

Itasca
Richardson, Johnny L.

Jacksonville
Ferrell, Rachelle

Joliet
Bolden, Raymond A.
Dukes, Carl R.
Gavin, Mary Ann
Hinch, Andrew Lewis, Sr.
Nichols, Walter LaPlora
Singleton, Isaac, Sr.
Young, Charles, Jr.

Kankakee
McCuiston, Stonewall, Jr.

Lake Forest
Allen, Tremayne
Autry, Darnell
Bell, Ricky
Bownes, Fabien
Carter, Marty LaVincent
Carter, Thomas
Carter, Tony
Conway, Curtis LaMont
Cox, Bryan Keith
Cox, Ronald
Dulaney, Michael
Engram, Bobby
Forbes, Marlon
Graves, Roderick Lawrence
Harris, Raymont LeShawn
Harris, Sean Eugene
Harris, Walter Lee
Hicks, Michael
Hughes, Tyrone Christopher
Hutchison, Peyton S.
Lowery, Michael
Minter, Barry Antoine
Penn, Christopher Anthony
Reeves, Carl
Robinson, Marcus
Salaam, Rashaan
Simpson, Carl Wilhelm
Spellman, Alonzo Robert
Stargell, Tony
Thierry, John Fitzgerald
Williams, James Otis
Williams, Tyrone

Lisle
Allen, S. Monique Nicole
Mass, Edna Elaine
Nichols, Alfred Glen
Robinson, Johnathan Prather
Tucker-Allen, Sallie
Woodruff, Jeffrey Robert

Lockport
Blade-Tiggens, Denise Patricia

Lombard
Spooner, John C.

Lovejoy
Matthews, Dorothy

Macomb
Bracey, Willie Earl
Bradley, William B.

Makanda
Shepherd, Benjamin A.

Markham
Carroll, Lawrence W.
Demonbreun, Thelma M.
McIlvaine, Donald

Matteson
Johnson, Eric G.
Kirkland, Gwendolyn Vickye
Warmack, Kevin Lavon

Maywood
Brown, Joseph Davidson, Sr.
King, John G.
Pratt, Melvin Lemar
Reid, Harold Sherman
Rodez, Andrew LaMarr
Rose, Bessie L.
Sharpp, Nancy Charlene
Smith, Dolores J.
Wordlaw, Clarence, Jr.

Melrose Park
McNelty, Harry

Midlothian
Branch, Otis Linwood

Moline
Collins, James H.
Earl, Acie Boyd, II

Morton Grove
Croft, Norman F.

Mount Prospect
Sayers, Gale E.

Jones, William Edward
Journey, Lula Mae
Joyner, John Erwin
Keglar, Shelvy Haywood
Kennedy, Frank D. R.
Kimbrew, Joseph D.
King, Joseph Prather
King, Warren Earl
Lee, Nathaniel
Leek, Sandra D.
Lewis, Cleveland Arthur
Little, Chester H.
Little, Leone Bryson
Little, Monroe Henry
Lowe, Aubrey F.
Lyons, Lloyd Carson
Martin, Steven Albert
Mathis, Dedric
Mays, William G.
McCoy, Anthony Bernard
McDaniel, Emmanuel
McElroy, Raymond Edward
McKey, Derrick Wayne
Mickey, Gordon Eugene
Miller, Reginald Wayne
Montgomery, Delmonico
Moore, Cleotha Franklin
Myers, Woodrow Augustus, Jr.
Newton, Pynkerton Dion
Owsley, Betty Joan
Paddio, Gerald
Parker-Sawyers, Paula
Pierce, Raymond O., Jr.
Pollard, Marcus LaJuan
Powell, Carl
Powers, Clyde J.
Price, Joseph L.
Ramey, Adele Marie
Ransom, Willard Blystone
Rawls, George H.
Rhea, Michael
Rice, Fredrick LeRoy
Richmond, Norris L.
Robinson, Donald Lee
Robinson, Sherman
Rodman, Michael Worthington
Rose, Jalen
Ross, Edward
Rucker, Robert D., Jr.
Rudolph, Wilma Glodean
Sanders, Michael Anthony
Scott, Brent
Scott, Leonard Stephen
Scott, Marvin Bailey
Selby, Myra C.
Sellers, Walter G.
Shello, Kendel
Shields, Landrum Eugene
Slash, Joseph A.
Smith, John Arthur
Spearman, Larna Kaye
Stephens, Charles Richard
Stevenson, Lillian
Stokes, Lillian Gatlin
Strong, Amanda L.
Summers, Joseph W.
Talley, John Stephen
Tandy, Mary B.
Tate, David
Taylor, Gilbert Leon
Taylor, Henry Marshall
Thomas, Edward P.
Thompson, LaSalle, III
Townsend, Mamie Lee Harrington
Tribble, Huerta Cassius
Vickers, Kipp E.
Walker-Smith, Angelique Keturah
Ward, John Preston
Warren, Lamont
Watkins, Joseph Philip
Watts, Damon Shanel
Waugh, Judith Ritchie
Wells, Payton R.
West, Mark Andre
White, Woodie W.
Whittington, Bernard M.
Williams, Charles Richard
Williams, Kenny Ray
Williams, Vernice Louise
Womack, Robert W., Sr.
Workman, Haywoode Wilvon

Kokomo
Artis, Myrle Everett
Clarke, Theodore Henson

Marion
Pettiford, Quentin H.

Merrillville
Dawkins, Wayne J.
Roman, Migual

Michigan City
Jones, King Solomon
Meriweather, Melvin, Jr.

Mishawaka
Williams, Theodore, Jr.

Muncie
Dowery, Mary
Goodall, Hurley Charles, Sr.
Greenwood, Charles H.
Greenwood, Theresa M. Winfrey
Kelley, Daniel, Jr.
Kumbula, Tendayi Sengerwe
McIntosh, Alice T.
Payne, June Evelyn
Plummer, William H., Jr.
Womack, Henry Cornelius

Munster
Senegal, Charles

New Albany
Craft, E. Carrie

New Castle
Walker, William B.

New Haven
Sharpe, Audrey Howell

Noblesville
Hansen, Wendell Jay

Notre Dame
Adams, Howard Glen
Cleveland, Granville E.
Outlaw, Warren Gregory
Peters, Erskine Alvin
Wright, Frederick Douglass

Richmond
Dansby, Jesse L., Jr.
Patterson, Paul A.
Sawyer, George Edward
Williams, Clyde
Williams, Marion J.

Shelbyville
Garrett, James Edward, Jr.

South Bend
Batteast, Robert V.
Calvin, Virginia Brown
Gilkey, William C.
Giloth-David, King R.
Hughes, Hollis Eugene, Jr.
Joyner, Lemuel Martin
Martin, Charles Edward, Sr.
Outlaw, Warren Gregory

St Meinrad
Davis, Cyprian

Terre Haute
Conyers, James E.
Hill, John C.
Howell, Laurence A.
Lyda, Wesley John
Martin, Mary E. Howell
Muyumba, Francois R.
Simpson-Taylor, Dorothy Marie
Swindell, Warren C.

Valparaiso
Bernoudy, Monique Rochelle
Hatcher, Richard Gordon
Neal, William J.

Vincennes
Summitt, Gazella Ann
Waddles, George Wesley, Sr.

West Lafayette
Bell, Clara Ellen
Blalock, Marion W.
Francisco, Joseph Salvadore, Jr.
Mobley, Emily Ruth
Peck, Carolyn
Skinner, Ewart C.
Turner, Robert, Jr.
Williams, Helen B.

Zionsville
Ross, N. Rodney

IOWA

Ames
Graham, Frederick Mitchell
Smith, Eugene DuBois

Anamosa
Grant, Kingsley B.

Ankeny
Gilbert, Fred D., Jr.
Howard, Glen

Cedar Falls
Kirkland-Holmes, Gloria
Monteiro, Marilyn D.S.

Cedar Rapids
Harris, Percy G., M.D.
Lawrence, Montague Schiele
Lipscomb, Darryl L.

Clinton
Wynn, LaMetta K.

Davenport
Drew-Peeples, Brenda
Johnson, Geraldine Ross
Johnson, John Thomas
Mumford, Jeffrey Carlton
Pollard, Freeman Wallace
Walker Williams, Hope Denise

Des Moines
Cason, Udell, Jr.
Colston, Monroe James
Crawford, James Maurice
Daniels, Preston
Davis, Evelyn K.
Easley, Jacqueline Ruth
Estes, John M., Jr.
Gentry, Nolden I.
Glanton, Luther Thomas, Jr.
Higgs, Mary Ann Spicer
Houston, Marsh S.
Maxwell, Roger Allan
Morris, Robert V., Sr.
Nickerson, Don Carlos
Strickland, Frederick William, Jr.
Williams, Catherine G.
Williams, Georgianna M.

Dubuque
Jaycox, Mary Irine

Epworth
Simon, Joseph Donald

Fort Dodge
Burleson, Jane Geneva
McGrath, Clarice Hobgood

Indianola
Nichols, Dimaggio

Iowa City
Chezik, John
Davis, Leodis
Davis, N. June
Dungy, Claibourne I.
Dungy, Madgetta Thornton
Harris, Michael Wesley
Hawkins, Benny F., Sr.
Henry, Joseph King
Jones, Phillip Erskine
Knight, W. H., Jr.
Mask, Susan L.
McPherson, James Alan
Monagan, Alfrieta Parks
Rodgers, Vincent G.
Turner, Darwin T.
Wheeler, Theodore Stanley
Wing, Adrien Katherine
Woodard, Fredrick

Keokuk
Weldon, Ramon N.

Mason City
Hiatt, Dietrah

Newton
Ward, Lloyd David

Sioux City
Bluford, Grady L.
Silva, Arthur P.

Waterloo
Abebe, Ruby
Anderson, Ruth Bluford
Cribbs, Williams Charles
Scott, Melvina Brooks
Weems, Vernon Eugene, Jr.

West Des Moines
Crawford, James Maurice
Greene, Franklin D.
Saunders, Meredith Roy

KANSAS

Bonner Springs
Sanders, Archie, Jr.

Emporia
Bonner, Mary Winstead

Hutchinson
Crable, Dallas Eugene

Junction City
Dozier, Morris, Sr.
Early, Paul David

Kansas City
Caldwell Swisher, Rozella Kathrine
Collins, Bernice Elaine
Criswell, Arthurine Denton
Davis, James Parker
Franklin, Benjamin Edward
Freeman, Edward Anderson
Jackson, Elmer Carter, Jr.
Jackson-Sirls, Mary Louise
Jenkins, Melvin L.
Jerome, Norge Winifred
Johnson, Ralph C.
Jones, Herman Harvey, Jr.
Jones, Sherman Jarvis
Justice, Norman E.
Littlejohn, John B., Jr.
Meeks, Cordell David, Jr.
Miller, Dennis Weldon
Pinkard, Deloris Elaine
Simmons, Harold Lee
Smith, Edward Charles
Smith, Garland M., Jr.
Washington, Alonzo Lavert
Washington, Nancy Ann
White, Luther D.
Williams, Herbert C.
Williams, Melvin

Lawrence
Adams, Samuel Levi, Sr.
Bremby, Roderick LeMar
Gardner, Cedric Boyer
Sanders, Robert B.
Vannaman, Madi T.
Washington, Marian

Leavenworth
Moore-Stovall, Joyce
Phelps, Constance Kay

Manhattan
Boyer, James B.
Switzer, Veryl A.
Taylor-Archer, Mordean

Mission
Criswell, Arthurine Denton

Newton
Rogers, George, III

North Newton
Rogers, George, III

Olathe
Brogden, Robert, Jr.

Overland Park
Claiborne, Lloyd R.
Rakestraw, Kyle Damon

Pittsburg
Hill, Dennis Odell

Salina
Parker, Maryland Mike

Shawnee
Jerome, Norge Winifred

Shawnee Mission
Boggan, Daniel, Jr.
Mitchell, Dean Lamont
Mitchell, Emmitt W.
Rakestraw, Kyle Damon

Topeka
Alexander, F. S. Jack
Barker, Pauline J.
Bolden, James Lee
Bugg, Robert
Cavens, Sharon Sue
Douglas, Joe, Jr.
Gardner, Cedric Boyer
Griffin, Ronald Charles
Henderson, Frank S., Jr.
Hendricks, Steven Aaron
Lewis, Wendell J.
Littlejohn, John B., Jr.
Love, Clarence C.
Otudeko, Adebisi Olusoga
Parks, Gilbert R.
Parks, Sherman A.
Rainbow-Earhart, Kathryn Adeline
Richards, William Earl
Thompson, Joseph Allan

Wichita
Anderson, Eugene
Cranford, Sharon Hill
Cribbs, Theo, Jr.
Garrett, Leonard P.
Harris, Richard, Jr.
Hayes, Graham Edmondson
Hutcherson, Bernice B. R.
Johnson, Thomas H.
King, Clarence Maurice, Jr.
McAfee, Charles Francis
McCray, Billy Quincy
Mitchell, Jacob Bill
Preston, Richard Clark
Pyles, John E.
Wesley, Clarence E.
Williams, T. Joyce
Williams-Bell, Elois

Winfield
Brooks, William P.

KENTUCKY

Adairville
Washington, Edward, Jr.

Ashland
Fryson, Sim E.

Barbourville
Daniels, Anthony Hawthorne

Berea
Baskin, Andrew Lewis
Olinger, David Y., Jr.

Bowling Green
Ardrey, Saundra Curry
Carr, Kipley DeAne
Esters, George Edward
Hardin, John Arthur
Jackson, Earl J.
Long, John Edward
Martin, Carnelius A.
Moxley, Frank O.
Starks, Rick

Clinton
Dillard, Howard Lee

Covington
Hall, Howard Ralph

Earlington
Johnson, Arthur T.

Elizabethtown
Green, Larry W.

Fort Knox
McGriggs-Jamison, Imogene

Frankfort
Banks, Ronald Trenton
Brooks, A. Russell
Evans, William Clayton
Fletcher, Winona Lee
Gibson, Betty M.
Graham, Delores Metcalf
Hill, Carl M.
Lambert, Charles H.
Lyons, Donald Wallace
McDaniel, Karen Cotton
Nichols, George, III
Ridgel, Gus Tolver
Smith, Andrew W.
Smith, Carson Eugene
Smith, Mary Levi
Troupe, Marilyn Kay
UmBayemake Joachim, Linda
Williams, Robert D., Sr.
Wolfe, John Thomas

Georgetown
Mason, Luther Roscoe

Glasgow
Watts, Wilsonya Richardson

Harlan
Fluker, Philip A.

Highland Heights
Bell, Sheila Trice
Washington, Michael Harlan

Lexington
Bramwell, Fitzgerald Burton
Brown, Gary W.
Fakhrid-Deen, Nashid Abdullah
Finn, Robert Green
Fleming, Juanita W.
Gaines, Victor Pryor
Harris, Joseph John, III
Jackson, Lee Arthur
Jefferson, Robert R.
Locke-Mattox, Bernadette
Peltier, Arma Martin
Reed, Sheila A.
Smith, Carson Eugene
Smith, John Thomas
Smith, Tubby
Steele, Harold L.
Stephens, Herman Alvin
Stout, Louis
Wilkinson, Doris

Louisville
Amos, Larry C.
Anderson, Carey Laine, Jr.
Anderson, Jay Rosamond
Aubespin, Mervin R.
Bateman, Michael Allen
Bather, Paul Charles
Bingham, Rebecca Josephine
Bishop, Ronald L.
Blye, Cecil A., Sr.
Brazley, Michael Duwain
Brummer, Chauncey Eugene
Burks, Juanita Pauline
Burns, Tommie, Jr.
Burse, Raymond Malcolm
Carter, Kenneth Gregory
Chatmon, Linda Carol
Chestnut, Edwin, Sr.
Clayborn, Wilma W.
Clingman, Kevin Loren
Coleman, James William
Cooper, Ronald Louis
Cruz, Virgil
Davidson, Rudolph Douglas
Foree, Jack Clifford
Goodwin, Martin David
Graham, Tecumseh Xavier
Hackett, Wilbur L., Jr.
Hart, Brenda G.
Hodge, W. J.
Holmes, Robert Kathrone, Jr.
Hudson, James Blaine, III
Huff, William
Hutchinson, Jerome
Jackson, Thelma Conley
James, Grace M.
Jeffries, Fran M.
Jones, Chester
Jones, Yvonne Vivian
Lanier, Shelby, Jr.

Love, Eleanor Young
Lyles, Leonard E.
Martin, Janice R.
McDonald, Larry Marvin
McMillan, Joseph H.
Meeks, Reginald Kline
Moragne, Maurice S.
Mudd, Louis L.
Payne, Mitchell Howard
Powers, Georgia M.
Richardson, Rhonda Karen
Roberts, Charles L.
Roberts, Ella S.
Robinson, Jonathan N.
Robinson, Samuel
Sharp, Charles Louis
Simon, Walter J.
Simpson, Frank B.
Smith, Robert W.
Smith, Tommie M.
Spicer, Carmelita
Stephenson, Carolyn L.
Street-Kidd, Mae
Summers, William E., IV
Thomas, Patrick Arnold
Turner, M. Annette
Upshaw, Sam, Jr.
Walker, Cynthia Bush
Wallace, John Howard
Walls, Fredric T.
Washington, Patrice Clarke
Watts, Beverly L.
Williams, Harold L., Jr.
Wilson, Hughlyne Perkins
Wilson, Leonard D.
Yeager, Thomas Stephen
Young, Coleman Milton, III
Young, Herman A.
Young, Joyce Howell
Young-Sall, Hajar

Midway
Bradley, Walter Thomas, Jr.

Morehead
Strider, Maurice William

Muldraugh
Shaw, Henry

Newport
O'Donnell, Lorena Mae

Paducah
Coleman, Robert A.
Harvey, Wardelle G.

Princeton
Moore, Allyn D.

Prospect
Burse, Raymond Malcolm
Wood, Daisy M.

Radcliff
Richard, Henri-Claude

Russellville
Hampton, Willie L.

Shelbyville
Nichols, George, III

Somerset
Wilson, Grant Paul, Jr.

LOUISIANA

Abbeville
Myles, Herbert John

Alexandria
Hines, J. Edward, Jr.
Larvadain, Edward, Jr.
Metoyer, Rosia G.
Patrick, Julius, Jr.

Angie
Ross, Emma Jean

Angola
Rideau, Wibert

Bastrop
Cotton, Henry
Hamlin, Arthur Henry
Loche, Lee Edward
Montgomery, Payne

Baton Rouge
Alexander, Ronald Algernon
Baucom, Joyce
Boddie, Gwendolyn M.
Brown, Georgia W.
Brown, Reginald Royce, Sr.
Burchell, Charles R.
Caillier, James Allen
Calloway, Curtis A.
Cobb, Thelma M.
Collier, Clarence Marie
Collins, Warren Eugene
Cummings, Roberta Spikes
Davidson, Kerry
Dickens, Samuel
Doomes, Earl
Durant, Thomas James, Jr.
Ellois, Edward R., Jr.
Evans, Mattie
Fields, Cleo
Green, Brenda Kay
Hall, David Anthony, Jr.
Hall, Robert Joseph
Hardy, Timothy W.
Haynes, John K.
Haynes, Leonard L., Jr.
Hayward, Olga Loretta Hines
Holden, Melvin Lee
Horton, Matt
Hubbard, Jean P.
Isadore, Harold W.
Jeffers, Ben L.
Jemison, Theodore Judson
Johnson, Ernest L.
Johnson, Jon D.
Johnson-Blount, Theresa
Jones, Johnnie Anderson
Lane, Pinkie Gordon
LaVergne, Luke Aldon
Lee, Allen Francis, Jr.
London, Gloria D.
Martin, Julia M.
Mayfield, William S.
Mays, David
McNairy, Sidney A.
Mencer, Ernest James
Moch, Lawrence E.
Moncrieff, Peter
Montgomery, Trent
Nelson, Otha Curtis, Sr.
Nesbitt, Robin Anthony
Oliver, Robert Lee
Patin, Joseph Patrick
Peoples, VerJanis Andrews
Perkins, Huel D.
Perry, Emma Bradford
Prestage, James J.
Prestage, Jewel Limar
Raby, Clyde T.
Richardson, Rupert Florence
Ridley, Harry Joseph
Robinson, Edward Ashton
Sheeler, Homer J., Sr.
Smith, Thielen
Stamper, Henry J.
Steptoe, Roosevelt
Stone, Jesse Nealand, Jr.
Tarver, Leon R., II
Wells, Roderick Arthur
Weston, Sharon
Williams, Billy Myles
Williams, Karen Renee
Winfield, William T.

Belle Rose
Melancon, Norman

Bogalusa
Jenkins, Gayle Expose
Mims, Raymond Everett, Sr.

Boyce
Lewis, Gus Edward

Breaux Bridge
Edgar, Jacqueline L.

Bunkie
Sheppard, Stevenson Royrayson

Crowley
Julian, John Tyrone
Wilson, Sherman Arthur

Cullen
Underwood, Maude Esther

Duson
Chargois, Jenelle M.

Eunice
Fields, Savoynne Morgan
Sergeant, Carra Susan
Thomas, Marvette Jeraldine

Ferriday
Davis, Sammy, Jr.

Franklinton
Martin, Rayfus
Tate, Matthew

Grambling
Bibbs, Patricia
Days, Rosetta Hill
Emmanuel, Tsegai
Ford, Luther L.
Gallot, Richard Joseph
Garrett, Louis Henry
Githiga, John Gatungu
Hicks, Raymond A.
Lee, Pauline W.
Lundy, Harold W.
Mansfield, Andrew K.
Robinson, Eddie
Sanders, William Mac
Smith, Arthur D.

Greensburg
Paddio-Johnson, Eunice Alice

Gretna
Snowden, Phillip Ray
Zeno, Melvin Collins

Harahan
Harding, Robert

Harvey
Eziemefe, Godslove Ajenavi
Guidry, David

Houma
Butler, Michael Keith

Jennings
Briscoe, Sidney Edward, Jr.

Jonesboro
Bradford, James Edward

Kenner
Ellis, Zachary L.
Riley, Emile Edward

Killona
Packer, Daniel Fredric, Jr.

Lafayette
Baranco, Raphael Alvin
Gaines, Ernest J.
Garrett, Aline M.
Handy, Horatio
Hegger, Wilber L.
Jackson, Joshua
McKnight, Albert J.
McZeal, Alfred, Sr.
Prudhomme, Nellie Rose
Taylor, Vanessa Gail
Thompson, Hilton Lond

Lake Charles
Blackwell, Faye Brown
Cole, Charles Zhivaga
Prudhomme, Nellie Rose
St. Mary, Joseph Jerome
Shelton, Harold Tillman

Lake Providence
Closure, Vanilla Threats
Frazier, Ray Jerrell

Lebeau
Labrie, Harrington

Lutcher
Jones, Nathaniel, Sr.

Mandeville
Ward, Keith Lamont

Mansfield
Patterson, Dessie Lee

Maringouin
Hollins, Joseph Edward

Marrero
Gumms, Emmanuel George, Sr.

Melville
Haynes, Willie C., III

Metairie
Allen, Eric Andre
Bates, Mario Doniel
Brown, Derek Darnell
Cherry, Je'Rod
Coaxum, Henry L., Jr.
Davis, Don
Davis, Isaac
Davis, Troy
Dixon, Ernest
Dowdell, Marcus L.
Fields, Mark Lee
Glover, La'Roi Damon
Guliford, Eric Andre
Harper, Alvin Craig
Harvey, Richard Clemont, Jr.
Hastings, Andre Orlando
Hill, Randal Thrill
Hills, Keno
Jenkins, Trezelle Samuel
Johnson, Joseph
Jones, Brian Keith
Jones, Clarence
Knight, Sammy
Martin, Wayne
McCrary, Fred Demetrius
Mickell, Darren
Mitchell, Keith
Molden, Alex
Naeole, Chris
Newman, Anthony
Roaf, William Layton
Robbins, Austin Dion
Siglar, Ricky Allan
Smith, Irvin Martin
Tubbs, Winfred O'Neal
Washington, Mickey Lynn
Zellars, Raymond Mark

Minden
Reeder, Willie R., Jr.

Monroe
Garrett, Louis Henry
James, Elridge M.
Jones, Charles D.
Miller, Joseph Herman
Newman, Kenneth J.
Pierce, Abe, III
Turner, Ervin
Wilson, Wilson W.

Natchitoches
Johnson, Ben D.

New Iberia
Carrier, Clara L. DeGay
Henderson, James Henry, Sr.
Small, Stanley Joseph

New Orleans
Amos, Ethel S.
Aramburo, Sophie Watts
Augustus, Franklin J. P.
Barney, Clarence Lyle
Barthelemy, Sidney John
Bashful, Emmett W.
Bates, Lionel Ray, Sr.
Bell, Warren A.
Bonnot, Madelyn
Borders, Florence Edwards
Braden, Henry E., IV
Brazile, Penny
Breda, Malcolm J.
Broussard, Arnold Anthony
Brown, Debria M.
Brown, Joan Rhodes
Bruno, Michael B.
Burns, Leonard L.
Burrell, Morris

Butler, Max R.
Butler, Michael Keith
Bynum, Horace Charles, Sr.
Byrd, Joseph Keys
Carey, Addison, Jr.
Carter, James P.
Carter, Oscar Earl, Jr.
Carter, Troy A.
Charbonnet, Louis, III
Chigbu, Gibson Chuks
Clanton, Lemuel Jacque
Colbert, Ernest, Sr.
Connor, George C., Jr.
Cook, Samuel DuBois
Copelin, Sherman Nathaniel, Jr.
Craft, Sally-Ann Roberts
Dalferes, Edward R., Jr.
Davis, Jacklean Andrea
Dejoie, C. C., Jr.
Dent, Thomas Covington
Doley, Harold E., Jr.
Dorsey, John L.
Duncan, Sandra Rhodes
Edwards, Preston Joseph
Epps, Anna Cherrie
Feltus, James, Jr.
Ferdinand, Keith C.
Foster, Janice Martin
Francis, Norman C.
Gates, Audrey Castine
Gayle, Irving Charles
Gibson, Antonio Marice
Goins, Richard Anthony
Grace, Marcellus
Gray, James Austin, II
Green, Hydia Lutrice
Guillaume, Alfred Joseph, Jr.
Hampton, Edwin Harrell
Harvey, Jacqueline V.
Haydel, James V., Sr.
Hutchinson, James J., Jr.
Jackson, Johnny, Jr.
James, Felix
Javery, Michael
Jefferson, Andrea Green
Johnson, Bernette Joshua
Jolly, Mary B.
Jones, Albert Allen
Jordan, Eddie J., Jr.
Jordan, Eddie Jack, Sr.
Kazi, Abdul-Khaliq Kuumba
Keeler, Vernes
Kelly, Marion Greenup
LaCour, Nathaniel Hawthorne
LeDoux, Jerome G.
Lee, Silas, III
Leonard, Catherine W.
Levell, Edward, Jr.
Lipps, Louis Adam
Lomax, Michael L.
Loving, Rose
Lundy, Larry
Marchand, Melanie Annette
Mayfield, Curtis
McDaniels, Warren E.
Misshore, Joseph O., Jr.
Montgomery, Willie Henry
Moore, Hazel Stamps
Morial, Marc
Morial, Sybil Haydel
Mosley, Carolyn W.
Ortique, Revius Oliver, Jr.
Osakwe, Christopher
Patnett, John Henry
Peeler, Diane Faustina
Pennington, Richard
Peoples, Gerald
Perkins, Thomas P.
Perry, Harold Robert
Pinkett, Allen Jerome
Pittman, Keith B.
Porter, Blanche Troullier
Powell, Bettye Boone
Raphael, Paul W.
Richard, Alvin J.
Roberts, Cecilia
Robinson, Carl Dayton
Robinson, Sandra Lawson
Roussell, Norman
Saulny, Cyril
Scott, John T.
Setlow, Valerie Petit
Shorty, Vernon James
Sigur, Wanda Anne Alexander
Singleton, James Milton
Smith, Norman Raymond
Stampley, Gilbert Elvin
Taylor, Herman Daniel
Thomas, Joseph W.

Towns, Sanna Nimtz
Verrett, Joyce M.
Ward, James Dale
Washington, Betty Lois
Washington, Robert Orlanda
Weather, Leonard, Jr.
Webb, Schuyler Cleveland
Wells, Barbara Jones
Wiley, Kenneth LeMoyne
Williams, Cassandra Faye
Williams, Ellis
Williams, Leslie J.
Wilson, James Davis
Worthy, Barbara Ann
Wright, James A.
Wright, Loyce Pierce
Young, Angela Lynn
Young, Wallace L.
Zu-Bolton, Ahmos, II

Opelousas
Climmons, Willie Mathew
Dauphin, Borel C.
Hamilton, Joseph Willard
Harris, Alonzo
Loeb, Charles P., Jr.
Richard, Arlene Castain
Terrence, August C.

Pineville
Cadoria, Sherian Grace
Coleman, Lemon, Jr.

Plaquemine
Dawkins, Michael James
Dawson, Peter Edward
Johnson, Charles E.

Pleasant Hill
Shannon, George A.

Port Allen
Morgan, Haywood, Sr.

Rayne
Senegal, Nolton Joseph, Sr.

Ruston
Emmanuel, Tsegai
Haynes, Leonard L., III

Shreveport
Abdul-Rahman, Tahira Sadiqa
Allen, Elbert E.
Aytch, Donald Melvin
Bennett, Lonnie M.
Buggs, James
Christopher, John A.
Collier, Louis Malcolm
Dixon, Tom L.
Dyas, Patricia Ann
Epps, Dolzie C. B.
Farr, Herman
Green, Jerome
Hardy, Eursla Dickerson
Hayes, Albertine Brannum
Holt, Dorothy L.
Holt, Edwin J.
Holt, Essie W.
Holt, James Stokes, III
Huckaby, Hilry, III
Jacobs, Bunyan
Kinchen, Dennis Ray
Patton, Joyce Bradford
Pennywell, Phillip, Jr.
Peoples, Joyce P.
Phillips, June M. J.
Redden, Camille J.
Sanders, Larry Kyle
Simpkins, Cuthbert O.
Smith, Granville L.
Smith, Robert H.
Stewart, Carl E.
Tarver, Gregory W.
Williams, Robert Lee

Slidell
Campbell, Otis Levy

St Gabriel
Thomas, Alvin

Tallulah
Anthony, Leander Aldrich
Williams, Moses, Sr.

Varnado
Ross, Emma Jean

West Monroe
Brown, Philip Rayfield, III

Zachary
Jackson, Audrey Nabors

MAINE

Auburn
Rogers, Bernard Rousseau

Augusta
Burney, William D., Jr.
Skinner, Byron R.

Lewiston
Jenkins, John

Old Orchard Beach
Cummings, E. Emerson

Old Town
Varner, James, Sr.

Orono
Varner, James, Sr.

Portland
Ramsey, Jerome Capistrano
Talbot, Gerald Edgerton

Wells
Davis, Luther Charles

MARYLAND

Aberdeen
Bruce, Carol Pitt

Aberdeen Proving Ground
Cannon, Paul L., Jr.
Monroe, James W.

Adelphi
Butler, Loretta M.
Giles-Gee, Helen Foster

Annapolis
Allen, Aris Tee
Duncan, Charles Tignor
Gerald, William
Hoyle, Classie
Lawlah, Gloria Gary
Massie, Samuel Proctor
Mosley, Elwood A.
Murphy, Margaret Humphries
Powell, Robert Meaker
Raymond, Henry James, II
Trotter, Decatur Wayne

Arnold
Ballard, James M., Jr.
Fisher, E. Carleton
Hynson, Carroll Henry, Jr.

Ashton
Evanzz, Karl Anderson

Baltimore
Adams, Curtis N.
Adams, Gregory Keith
Adams, Victorine Quille
Alexander, A. Melvin
Alexander, Marcellus Winston, Jr.
Allen, Karen
Alomar, Roberto
Amprey, Walter G.
Anderson-Tanner, Frederick T., Jr.
Armstrong, Ernest W., Sr.
Arnold, Haskell N., Jr.
Avent, Edwin Vernon
Aziz, Kareem A.
Baines, Harold Douglas
Baines, Henry T.
Bando, Thelma Preyer
Banks, Saundra Elizabeth
Barnes, Paul Douglas
Battle, Mark G.
Bell, James Edward
Bell, Lawrence A., III
Bell, Robert Mack
Boonieh, Obi Anthony

Boulware, Peter
Brailey, Troy
Bramble, Peter W. D.
Bridges, Leon
Brooks, Dunbar
Brown, Benjamin Leonard
Brown, Eddie C.
Brown, Linda Jenkins
Brown, Marsha J.
Brunson, Dorothy Edwards
Brunt, Samuel Jay
Bryant, William Arnett, Jr.
Bryson, W. O., Jr.
Buckson, Toni Yvonne
Bundy, James Lomax
Burke, Gary Lamont
Burnett, Calvin W.
Burnett, Sidney Obed
Burns, Clarence Du
Cameron, Ulysses
Carson, Benjamin Solomon, Sr.
Carter, Charles Edward
Carter, Joseph Chris
Chambers, Donald C.
Chapman, Nathan A.
Chester, Joseph A., Sr.
Chissell, John T.
Cline, Eileen Tate
Cole, Harry A.
Collier, Eugenia W.
Collins, Clifford Jacob, III
Colvin, Ernest J.
Conaway, Mary Ward Pindle
Cooper, Gary T.
Cordery, Sara Brown
Crew, John L., Sr.
Crosse, St. George Idris Bryon
Curry, Michael Bruce
Daley, Guilbert Alfred
Daniel, Colene Yvonne
Daniels, Sidney
David, George F., III
Davidson, Charles Robert
Davis, Andre Maurice
Davis, Clarence
Davis, Eric Keith
Davis, John Alexander
Davis, Samuel C.
DeLoatch, Eugene
Dickson, Onias D., Jr.
Diggs, Irene
Dixon, Ardena S.
Dixon, Richard Nathaniel
Dockery, Richard L.
Donaldson, Leon Matthew
Dorsey, Denise
Douglass, Robert Lee
Draper, Edgar Daniel
Draper, Frances Murphy
Dupree, Edward A.
Durant, Naomi C.
Durham, Joseph Thomas
Emeagwali, Dale Brown
Emeagwali, Philip
Evers-Williams, Myrlie
Faulcon, Clarence Augustus, II
Faw, Barbara Ann
Ferguson, Derek Talmar
Ferguson, Sherlon Lee
Fitts, Leroy
Fleming, Ellis T.
Ford, Hilda Eileen
Francois, Emmanuel Saturnin
Franklin, Renty Benjamin
Fraser, Thomas Petigru
Frazier-Ellison, Vicki L.
Frisby, H. Russell, Jr.
Froe, Otis David
Gaddy, Beatrice
Gardner, Bettye J.
Gill, Roberta L.
Graham, Richard A.
Gray, C. Vernon
Green, Lester L.
Grier, Johnny
Hall, Reginald Lawrence
Hammonds, Jeffrey Bryan
Hampton, Thomas Earle
Hardnett, Carolyn Judy
Hargrove, John R.
Hargrove, Milton Beverly
Harris, Melvin
Harris, Noah Alan, Sr.
Harris, Thomas Waters, Jr.
Harris, Vander E.
Harrison, Daphne Duval
Harrison, Hattie N.
Hartsfield, Howard C.
Haskins, Joseph, Jr.

Hawthorne, Lucia Shelia
Hayden, Carla Diane
Hayman, Warren C.
Haynes, James H.
Haysbert, Raymond Victor, Sr.
Hendricks, Elrod Jerome
Henson, Daniel Phillip, III
Higginbotham, Eve Juliet
Hill, Robert Bernard
Hill, Thelma W.
Hoff, Nathaniel Hawthorne
Hollis, Meldon S., Jr.
Holloway, Arthur D.
Holt, John J.
Hooks, Frances Dancy
Howard, Ellen D.
Howard, Joseph Clemens
Howard, Leslie Carl
Hrabowski, Freeman Alphonsa, III
Hughes, Essie Meade
Hunt, Edward
Hunter, Richard C.
Hynson, Carroll Henry, Jr.
Ike, Alice Denise
Jackson, Harold Jerome
James, Richard L.
Johnson, Carroll Randolph, Jr.
Johnson, Edna DeCoursey
Johnson, John J.
Johnson, Kenneth Lavon
Johnson, Loretta
Johnson, Shirley
Jones, Clifton Ralph
Jones, Grover William, Jr.
Jones, Susan Sutton
Josey, Leronia Arnetta
Jowers, Johnnie Edward, Sr.
Kelley, Delores G.
King, George W., Jr.
King, Ora Sterling
King-Hammond, Leslie
Knight, Franklin W.
Lansey, Yvonne F.
LaVeist, Thomas Alexis
Lawson, Quentin Roosevelt
Leacock, Ferdinand S.
Lee, Lena S. King
Lee, Michael Waring
Lewis, James Edward
Lewis, Viola Gambrill
Ligon, Claude M.
Lindsay, Gwendolyn Ann Burns
Lokeman, Joseph R.
London, Denise
Lopes, Davey
Madison, Stanley D.
Marriott, Salima Siler
Martin, Elmer P.
Martin, Joanne Mitchell
Massey, Jacquelene Sharp
Mathews, Keith E.
Mathis, William Lawrence
May, Lee Andrew
McConnell, Catherine Allen
McConnell, Roland C.
McDonald, George
McFadden, Nathaniel James
McKenzie, Vashti
McLaughlin, Eurphan
Mfume, Kweisi
Miller, Thomas Patton
Mills, Alan Bernard
Minion, Mia
Moore, Christine James
Moore, James L.
Moore, Lenny Edward
Morris, Frank Lorenzo, Sr.
Morton, Cynthia Neverdon
Morton, James A.
Murphy, Arthur G.
Murphy, John H., III
Newsome, Ozzie
Nwanna, Gladson I. N.
Oden, Gloria
Oliver, John J., Jr.
Oliver, Kenneth Nathaniel
Outlaw, Patricia Anne
Owens, Ronald C.
Parker, Claude A.
Parker, James Thomas
Parker, Jeff, Sr.
Parks, Henry Green, Jr.
Payne, Osborne Allen
Petersen, Arthur Everett, Jr.
Phillips, Eugenie Elvira
Phillips, Glenn Owen
Pollard, William E.
Pope, Addison W.
Pratt, Joan M.

Pratt, Ruth Jones
Proctor, William H.
Pryor, Bernard Bruce
Quaynor, Thomas Addo
Quivers, William Wyatt, Sr.
Rayford, Floyd Kinnard
Raymond, Henry James, II
Reid, Sina M.
Rhodes, Arthur Lee, Jr.
Rice, Pamela Ann
Richardson, Earl Stanford
Richardson, Frank
Robertson, Karen A.
Robinson, Anthony W.
Rogers, Dianna
Roulhac, Edgar Edwin
Roy, Americus Melvin
Sands, Rosetta F.
Saunders, Elijah
Sawyer, Broadus Eugene
Schmoke, Kurt Lidell
Scribner, Arthur Gerald, Jr.
Sheffey, Ruthe G.
Shinhoster, Earl
Simmons, Charles William
Simms, Stuart Oswald
Simon, Elaine
Sinkler, George
Sloan, David E.
Smith, Benjamin Franklin
Smith, Lee Arthur
Smith, Lonnie
Smith, Mary Carter
Smith, Oscar A., Jr.
Smith, William M., Jr.
Solomon, James Daniel
Stanley, Eugene
Stanley, Hilbert Dennis
Stansbury, Clayton Cresvell
Starks, Doris Nearror
Styles, Kathleen Ann
Sweeney, John Albert
Taylor, Edward Walter
Taylor, Jeffery Charles
Taylor, Julius H.
Terborg-Penn, Rosalyn M.
Theodore, Yvonne M.
Thomas, Jacqueline Marie
Thomas-Carter, Jean Cooper
Thompson, Garland Lee
Tildon, Charles G., Jr.
Waddy, Walter James
Wade, Bruce L.
Walden, Emerson Coleman
Walker, Ernestine
Warren, Otis, Jr.
Waters, Kathryn
Watkins, Levi, Jr.
Weaver, Garland Rapheal, Jr.
Webster, Lenny
Whitten, Benjamin C.
Williams, Brian O'Neal
Williams, Harold David
Williams, Henry R.
Williams, Larry
Williams, Maceo Merton
Williams, Roger Kenton
Wilson, Donald
Winfield, George Lee
Woodfolk, Joseph O.
Woodward, Isaiah Alfonso
Young, Elroy
Young, Larry
Young, N. Louise

Beltsville
Battle, Mark G.
Blake, Peggy Jones
Hammond, James Matthew
Subryan, Carmen

Bethesda
Ballard, Kathryn W.
Barham, Wilbur Stectson
Branche, William C., Jr.
Counts, George W.
Davenport, Chester C.
Elmore Archer, Joyce A.
Epps, Roselyn Payne
Floyd, Jeremiah
Gaston, Marilyn Hughes
Gilmore, Al Tony
Gray, Brian Anton
Hoyle, Classie
Jackson, Charles N., II
Johnson, David Freeman
Johnson, Wayne Alan
Jones, Cheryl Arleen
May, James Shelby

McKee, Adam E., Jr.
McKinney, Rufus William
Miller, Herbert J.
Parham, Deborah L.
Phillips, Leo Augustus
Powell, Juan Herschel
Press, Harry Cody, Jr.
Rodgers, Johnathan A.
Sarreals, E. Don
Singleton, Kathryn T.
Wamble, Carl DeEllis
Wilson, Stephanie Y.
Wise, William Clinton, Sr.
Woodson, Charles R.

Bowie
Anderson, Leon H.
Arrington, Pamela Gray
Bolles, A. Lynn
Boone, Zola Ernest
Britton, John H., Jr.
Chew, Bettye L.
Clark, Vernon L.
Davis, Russell Andre
Funn, Courtney Harris
Hall, Willie Green, Jr.
Johnson, G. R. Hovey
Neal, Charlie
Newhouse, Quentin, Jr.
Palmer, Edgar Bernard
Smith, Perry Anderson, III
Tipton, Elizabeth Howse
Turner, Evelyn Evon
Williams, Debra D.

Brentwood
Hall, Raymond A.
Kashif, Ghayth Nur
Parkinson, Nigel Morgan
Smith, Perry Anderson, III

Bryans Rd
Davis, Donald Gene

Burtonsville
Covington, M. Stanley
Toussaint, Rose-Marie

California
Lancaster, John Graham

Camp Springs
Jackson, Ronald G., Sr.
Perrin, David Thomas Perry
Pinkney, John Edward
Reynolds, Barbara A.
Roscoe, Wilma J.

Capital Heights
Doyle, Erie R.

Capitol Heights
Beard, Montgomery, Jr.
Blackburn, Charles Miligan, II
Cousins, James R., Jr.
Dodson, Vivian M.
Rogers, Norman
Tarver, Elking, Jr.

Catonsville
Fullwood, Harlow, Jr.
Koram, M. Jamal

Centreville
Perine, James L.

Chevy Chase
Carter, William Beverly, III
Gavin, James Raphael, III
Hudson, Anthony Webster
Pinson, Margo Dean
Streeter, Denise Williams
Todman, Terence A.
Wilburn, Victor H.

Clinton
Feliciana, Jerrye Brown
Gant, Wanda Adele
Johnson, Jacob Edwards, III
Love, Lynnette Alicia
Saint-Louis, Rudolph Anthony
Williams, Wilbert Lee

College Park
Anderson, Amel
Billingsley, Andrew
Bolles, A. Lynn
Carroll, Charles H.

Cunningham, William Dean
Dill, Bonnie Thornton
Driskell, David C.
Fletcher, Howard R.
Fries, Sharon Lavonne
Glover, Denise M.
Hampton, Robert L.
Holman, Benjamin F.
Humphrey, Margo
Johnson, Martin Leroy
Johnson, Raymond Lewis
Landry, L. Bartholomew
Lomax, Dervey A.
Moss, Alfred A., Jr.
Scott, Marvin Wayne
Senbet, Lemma W.
Shelton, Harvey William
Walters, Ronald
Williams, Helen Elizabeth

Columbia
Atkinson, Gladys Whitted
Brown, George Philip
Brown, Shirley Ann Vining
Bruce, Preston, Jr.
Fleming, David Aaron
Hamilton, John Mark, Jr.
Harris, Marion Hopkins
Hoff, Nathaniel Hawthorne
Iglehart, Lloyd D.
James, David Phillip
King, Ora Sterling
Lawes, Verna
Ligon, Doris Hillian
Logan, Frenise A.
Martin, Sylvia Cooke
McDonald, R. Timothy
Newsome, Clarence Geno
Rotan, Constance S.
Seriki, Olusola Oluyemisi
Starks, Doris Nearror
Ware, Charles Jerome
Washington, Dante Deneen
West, Herbert Lee, Jr.
Whiting, Albert Nathaniel
Wilds, Jetie Boston, Jr.
Yancey, Carolyn Lois

Cumberland
Peck, Leontyne Clay
Powell, Darrell Lee

Delmar
Harleston, Robert Alonzo

District Heights
Williams-Garner, Debra

Dundalk
Brooks, Dunbar
Buckson, Toni Yvonne

Ellicott City
Brown, William T.
Henderson, Lenneal Joseph, Jr.
Hightower, Herma J.
Price, Suzanne Davis
Wiles, Joseph St. Clair
Williams, Robert B.

Emmitsburg
Brown, Carrye Burley

Fairmont Heights
Gray, Robert R.

Forestville
Crockett, Gwendolyn B.
Doxie, Marvin Leon, Sr.
Johnson, Aaron LaVoie
Reid, Ronda Eunese
Turner, Evelyn Evon

Fort Meade
Scribner, Arthur Gerald, Jr.

Fort Washington
Boardley, Curtestine May
Dickerson, Harvey G., Jr.
Ford, Florida Mae
Gray, Donnee L.
Hunigan, Earl
Kirton, Edwin Eggleston
Lucas, Gerald Robert
Mathis, Sharon Bell
Pointer, Richard H.
Williams, Howard Copeland

Frederick
Lockwood, James Clinton

Gaithersburg
Jackson, David Samuel
Quivers, Eric Stanley
Rodman, John
Sydnor, E. George

Germantown
Grayson, Byron J., Sr.
Grayson, Jennifer A.
Hackey, George Edward, Jr.
Williamson, Samuel P.

Glen Burnie
Doles, Maurice DeWitt

Glenarden
Brown, Stanley Donovan
Fletcher, James C., Jr.
James, Henry Nathaniel
Woods, Geneva Holloway

Glenn Dale
Miller, M. Sammye
Pounds, Augustine Wright

Greenbelt
Day, John H., Jr.
Powell, Darlene Wright
Simpson, Donnie
Whitlock, Fred Henry
Williams, Alexander, Jr.

Hagerstown
Hardy, Michael Leander
Hill, Lawrence Thorne

Hillcrest Heights
Lawlah, Gloria Gary

Hyattsville
Broadwater, Tommie, Jr.
Flanagan, T. Earl, Jr.
Gaskin, Leroy
Robinson, Daniel Lee
Williams-Dial, E. Faye

Kensington
Cannon, Calvin Curtis
Jenkins, Elaine B.
Layton, Benjamin Thomas

Landover
Amaya, Ashraf
Bacon, Albert S.
Bickerstaff, Bernard Tyrone, Sr.
Bridgeman, Donald Earl
Brown, William H.
Callender, Valerie Dawn
Davidson, Alphonzo Lowell
English, Albert J.
Hall, Alton Jerome
Irvin, Byron Edward
Johnson, Buck
Pemberton, Hilda Ramona
Turpin, Mel Harrison
Unseld, Wes
Walker, Kenneth

Langley Park
Henderson, Stephen E.

Lanham
Jones-Smith, Jacqueline
Mickle, Andrea Denise
Murray, Gary S.
Noel, Patrick Adolphus
Raiford, Roger Lee
Stephens, Wallace O'Leary
White, Sylvia Kay
Wise, Henry A., Jr.

Largo
Bridgeman, Donald Earl
Cloud, W. Eric
James, David Phillip

Laurel
Alexander, John Wesley, Jr.
Hewitt, Basil
Hunter, Edwina Earle
Smith, Lafayette Kenneth

Laytonsville
Prather, Jeffrey Lynn

Leonardtown
Dillard, June White
Lancaster, John Graham

Lexington Park
Herndon, Harold Thomas, Sr.

Lutherville
Clark-Gates, Brenda

Mitchellville
Adams, Yolanda
Arrington, Lloyd M., Jr.
Barham, Wilbur Stectson
Day, John H., Jr.
Finney, Essex Eugene, Jr.
Hall, Alton Jerome
Hall, Willie Green, Jr.
Leeke, John F.
Lowe, Hazel Marie
Perrin, David Thomas Perry
Quarles, Benjamin A.
Quarles, Ruth Brett
Scales, Patricia Bowles
Streeter, Denise Williams
Young, Raymond, Jr.

New Carrollton
Dorse, Bernice Perry

North Bethesda
Morrison, James W., Jr.

North Potomac
Hunt, Betty Syble

Olney
Holmes, Arthur, Jr.
Holmes, Wilma K.
Johnson, Leonard W., Jr.

Owings Mills
Alexander, Derrick Scott
Blackshear, Jeffery
Brady, Donny
Brown, Cornell Desmond
Brown, Orlando Claude
Burnett, Robert Barry
Byner, Earnest Alexander
Cotton, Kenyon
Daniel, Eugene
Ethridge, Raymond Arthur, Jr.
Gatewood, Wallace Lavell
Green, Eric
Holmes, Priest Anthony
Hugley, Betty Jean
Jackson, Michael Dwayne
Jenkins, DeRon Charles
Jones, James Alfie
Jones, Rondell Tony
Keyes, Alan L.
Langham, Antonio
Lewis, Jermaine Edward
Lewis, Ray Anthony
Marshburn, Everett Lee
McCloud, Tyrus Kamall
Morris, Byron "Bam"
Newsome, Vincent Karl
Ogden, Jonathan Phillip
Rhett, Erric Undra
Richardson, Wallace Herman, Jr.
Roe, James Edward, II
Singleton, Nate
Thompson, Bennie
Vinson, Anthony
Webster, Larry Melvin, Jr.
Williams, Wally James, Jr.
Woodson, Roderick Kevin
Yarborough, Ryan

Oxon Hill
Blunt, Roger Reckling
Gaskin, Leroy
Mitchell, B. Doyle, Jr.
Nash, Daniel Alphonza, Jr.
Nash, Robert Johnson

Pittsville
Franklin, Herman

Port Deposit
Fraser, Rhonda Beverly

Potomac
Bowles, Joyce Germaine
Davis, Jean M.
Kuykendall, Crystal Arlene
Singh, Rajendra P.

Taylor, Charles Edward

Princess Anne
Brooks, Carolyn Branch
Brooks, Henry Marcellus
Childs, Oliver Bernard, Sr.
Copeland, Leon L.
Ellis, Edward V.
Franklin, Herman
Hedgepeth, Chester Melvin, Jr.
Hytche, William P.
Johnson, Leon
Marion, Claud Collier
Mitchell, JudyLynn
Moore, Jean E.
Spikes, Delores R.
Whittington, Harrison DeWayne

Randallstown
Crosse, St. George Idris Bryon
Moore, Lenny Edward
Murray, Mabel Lake
Oliver, Kenneth Nathaniel
Yuille, Bruce

Riverside
Olivera, Herbert Ernest

Rock Hall
Thompson, Ryan Orlando

Rockville
Avery, Waddell
Belton, Edward DeVaughn
Carter, Enrique Delano
Clark, Harry W.
Dandy, Roscoe Greer
Davis, Thurman M., Sr.
Dines, George B.
Earley, Keith H.
Greenfield, Roy Alonzo
Hall, Evelyn Alice
Hardy-Hill, Edna Mae
Herndon, Gloria E.
Holmes, Wilma K.
Jackson, Shirley Ann
Johnson, Elaine McDowell
Key, Addie J.
Lavizzo-Mourey, Risa Juanita
Marbury, Donald Lee
Martin, William R.
Moone, James Clark
Moore, Roscoe Michael, Jr.
Moore, Susie M.
Morris, John P., III
Moseley-Davis, Barbara M.
Obayuwana, Alphonsus Osarobo
Parron, Delores L.
Pounds, Moses B.
Powell, William O., Jr.
Reed, Theresa Greene
Robinson, William Andrew
Sanders, Rober LaFayette
Williams, Ralph O.

Salisbury
Brooks, Henry Marcellus
Hedgepeth, Chester Melvin, Jr.
Hopkins, Thomas Franklin
Hudson, Jerome William
Johnson, Vaughn Arzah
Johnson, William Smith
Lide, William Ernest
Maddox, Elton Preston, Jr.
Mitchell, JudyLynn
Talbot, Alfred Kenneth, Jr.

Seabrook
Jennings, Margaret Elaine
Johnson, Raymond Lewis
Jones, Hardi Liddell
Sewell, Isiah Obediah

Seat Pleasant
Theodore, Keith Felix

Silver Spring
Alexander, Benjamin Harold
Alexander, Dawn
Alford, Brenda
Barfield, Rufus L.
Battle, Maurice Tazwell
Beckham, Barry Earl
Bell, Sheila Trice
Bellamy, Everett
Blakely, Allison
Booker, Johnnie Brooks
Branson, Herman Russell

Brown, Lillie Richard
Burrell, Emma P.
Butler, Broadus Nathaniel
Coles, Anna Bailey
Colyer, Sheryl Lynn
Corbin, Angela Lenore
Countee, Thomas Hilaire, Jr.
Davenport, Ernest H.
Davis, Frank Derocher
Day, Daniel Edgar
Delaney, Harold
Dorman, Hattie L.
Durham, Joseph Thomas
Elmore, Ernest Eric
Gartrell, Bernadette A.
Gist, Lewis Alexander, Jr.
Grant, Nathaniel
Hairston, Abbey Gail
Hamilton, Samuel Cartenius
Hawkins, John Russell, III
Hill, Robert Lewis
Holman, Karriem Malik
Holmes, Arthur, Jr.
Howze, Karen Aileen
Hudson, Merry C.
Hull, Bernard S.
Hymes, William Henry
Jackson, Raymond T.
Johnson, Wayne Alan
Jones, Lawrence N.
King, William Charles
Madison, Eddie L., Jr.
Mayberry, Claude A., Jr.
McAlpine, Robert
Means, Craig R.
Moore, Johnnie Adolph
Morse, Mildred S.
Morse, Oliver
Nix, Roscoe Russa
Northern, Christina Ann
Pollard, Alfonso McInham
Porter, Carol Denise
Ray, Rosalind Rosemary
Ray, Walter I., Jr.
Reed, Beatrice M.
Rosser, Pearl Lockhart
Sabin, Glenn
Samara, Noah Azmi
Sarreals, E. Don
Scott, Kenneth Richard
Seabrooks-Edwards, Marilyn S.
Shannon, Odessa M.
Shepard, Gregory
Stuart, Reginald A.
Theodore, Keith Felix
Thomas, Roderick
Thompson, Cecil, Sr.
Valmon, Andrew Orlando
Viltz, Edward Gerald
Walker, James
Wallace, Richard Warner
Watkins, Shirley R.
Watts, Carl Augustus
White, Ronald P.
Wilcox, Janice Horde
Wilkins, Herbert Priestly, Sr.
Williams, Helen Elizabeth
Wilson, Milton
Winston, Michael R.

St Marys City
Clifton, Lucille

Suitland
Pinkney, John Edward
Thompson, Deborah Maria, M.D.

Takoma Park
Hammond, James Matthew
Johnson, Lloyd A.
Porter, Clarence A.
Williams, Herman

Temple Hills
Harris, Peter J.
Jones, Christine Miller
Joyner, Claude C.

Towson
Clay, Camille Alfreda
Daley, Thelma Thomas
Gissendanner, John M.
Josey, Leronia Arnetta
Lee, LaVerne C.
Olivera, Herbert Ernest
Savage, Vernon Thomas
Torain, Tony William

Upper Marlboro
Brown, John Mitchell, Sr.
Caldwell, Sandra Ishmael
Ford, Kenneth A.
Johnson, G. R. Hovey
Loving, James Leslie, Jr.
McCloud, Thomas Henry
Napper, Hyacinthe T.
Rogers-Grundy, Ethel W.
Turner, Marvin Wentz
Wills, James Willard
Wilson, Floyd Edward, Jr.
Woody, Jacqueline Brown

Waldorf
Scott, Hattie Bell
Sherrod, Ezra Cornell

Wheaton
Jupiter, Clyde Peter
Quick, R. Edward

MASSACHUSETTS

Amherst
Boyer, Horace Clarence
Bracey, John Henry, Jr.
Bromery, Randolph Wilson
Darity, Evangeline Royall
Darity, William A.
Delany, Samuel Ray
Du Bois, David Graham
Frye, Charles Anthony
Gentry, Atron A.
Harris, William M.
Lateef, Yusef
Love, Barbara
Nnaji, Bartholomew O.
Tillis, Frederick C.
Wideman, John Edgar
Winslow, Reynolds Baker
Yarde, Richard Foster

Andover
Eubanks, John Bunyan

Arlington
Greenidge, James Ernest
Morrison, Garfield E., Jr.

Ashley Falls
Jamal, Ahmad

Bedford
Hopkins, Perea M.

Belchertown
Lester, Julius

Beverly
Thompson, William L.

Boston
Aikens, Alexander E., III
Alexander, Joyce London
Allen, Zuline Gray
Amiji, Hatim M.
Amory, Reginald L.
Anderson, Kenny
Anderson, Michael Wayne
Arkhurst, Joyce Cooper
Bailey, Gary
Barros, Dana Bruce
Batson, Ruth Marion
Beard, Charles Julian
Birchette-Pierce, Cheryl L.
Bispham, Frank L.
Bocage, Ronald J.
Bowen, Bruce
Bowman, Jacquelynne Jeanette
Brookes, Bernard L.
Brown, Rodger L., Jr.
Budd, Wayne Anthony
Buford, Damon Jackson
Bullins, Ed
Bunte, Doris
Burnham, Margaret Ann
Burton, Ronald E.
Byrd, George Edward
Carr, M. L.
Cash, James Ireland, Jr.
Chandler, Dana C., Jr.
Collins, Tessil John
Crawford, James Wesley
Daniel, Jessica Henderson
Davis, Arthur, Jr.

Davis, Willie J.
Dawson, Andre Nolan
Dilday, Judith Nelson
Dugger, Edward, III
Edelin, Kenneth C.
Edney, Tyus Dwayne
Edwards, Wilbur Patterson, Jr.
Ellison, Pervis
Eure, Dexter D., Sr.
Fitch, Harrison Arnold
Fonvielle, William Harold
Foster Nash, Bernadine
Gaither, Barry
Garner, Grayce Scott
Garrity, Monique P.
Gates, Otis A., III
Gordon, Thomas
Griffin, Judith Berry
Grimes, Calvin M., Jr.
Grimes, Darlene M. C.
Grooms, Karen Victoria Morton
Hall, David
Hamer, Steve
Hampton, Henry Eugene, Jr.
Handy, Delores
Harris, Barbara Clemente
Harris, David Ellsworth
Harris, John Everett
Harrison-Jones, Lois
Hatcher, William Augustus
Hawkins, Michael
Hayden, Robert C., Jr.
Haygood, Wil
Haynes, Michael E.
Heard, Marian L.
Henry, Joseph Louis
Hilliard, Alicia Victoria
Ireland, Roderick Louis
Jacks, Ulysses
Jackson, Derrick Zane
Jackson, Ellen Swepson
Jackson, Reginald Leo
Jefferson, Reggie
Jobe, Shirley A.
Johnson, Wendell Norman, Sr.
Jones, Clarence J., Jr.
Jones, Dontae' Antijuaine
Jones, Gayl
Jones, Popeye
Jones, Victoria C.
Knight, Muriel Bernice
Knowles, Em Claire
Lanier, Anthony Wayne
Laymon, Heather R.
Lee, M. David, Jr.
Leoney, Antoinette E. M.
Lewis, Elma I.
Lewis, Maurice
Long, Juanita Outlaw
Loury, Glenn Cartman
Lowery, Donald Elliott
Maith, Sheila Francine
Martin, Ralph C., II
Martin, Richard Cornish
Matory, Yvedt L.
Mbere, Aggrey Mxolisi
McCarty, Walter Lee
McClain, James W.
McIntyre, Mildred J.
Mercer, Ronald
Miles, June C.
Miller, Melvin B.
Millett, Ricardo A.
Minor, Greg Magado
Montgomery, Keesler H.
Moseley, Frances Kenney
Murphy, Michael McKay
Nelson, David S.
Nelson, Leon T.
Norris, Donna M.
Norris, Lonnie H.
O'Bryant, John D.
O'Leary, Troy Franklin
Overbea, Luix Virgil
Owens-Hicks, Shirley
Palmer, Laura Olivia
Parks, Paul
Peebles-Wilkins, Wilma Cecelia
Pena, Tony
Peoples, Florence W.
Petty-Edwards, Lula Evelyn
Pierce, Rudolph F.
Pinckney, Stanley
Portis, Kattie Harmon
Poussaint, Alvin Francis
Prelow, Arleigh
Prothrow-Stith, Deborah Boutin
Prunty, Howard Edward
Putnam, Glendora M.

Reynolds, Pamela Terese
Rice, Jim
Roberts, Wesley A.
Robinson, Jack E.
Rushing, Byron D.
Russell, George A.
Scott, Deborah Ann
Settles, Darryl Stephen
Sherwood, Wallace Walter
Smith, Warren
Snowden, Gail
Soden, Richard Allan
Spicer, Kenneth, Sr.
Spruill, James Arthur
Stamps, Leon Preist
Stith, Charles Richard
Stull, Donald L.
Swan, Edward McCallan, Jr.
Tarpley, Natasha Anastasia
Thomas, David Anthony
Thompson, Benjamin Franklin
Vaughn, Mo
Veney, Marguerite C.
Venson, John E.
Walker, Antoine Devon
Walker, Eugene Kevin
Walters, Hubert Everett
Warren, Joseph David
Washington, Mary Helen
Watkins, Michael Thomas
Watson, Georgette
Weddington, Elaine
Wesley, David
White, Augustus A., III
White, Richard C.
Whiteside, Larry
Wiggs, Jonathan Louis
Wiley, Fletcher Houston
Wilkerson, Dianne
Willock, Marcelle Monica
Wilson, John
Wilson, Leon E., Jr.
Winston, Bennie Veronica
Wolfman, Brunetta Reid
Woodhouse, Enoch O'Dell, II
Worthy, William, Jr.
Yancey, Charles Calvin
Yarbrough, Robert Elzy

Bridgewater
Johnson, Addie Collins
Santos, Henry J.

Brockton
Thomas, John

Brookline
Birchette-Pierce, Cheryl L.
Christian, John L.
Cromwell, Adelaide M.
Daniel, Jessica Henderson
Fortune, Alvin V.
Pilot, Ann Hobson
Potter, Judith Diggs

Brookline Village
Cofield, James E., Jr.

Burlington
Hurd, Joseph Kindall, Jr.

Cambridge
Adams, Carol Laurence
Anderson, Perry L.
Bailey, James W.
Barnett, Evelyn Brooks
Bennett, Robert A.
Brown, Jeffrey LeMonte
Bush, Patricia
Carey, Jennifer Davis
Castle, Keith L.
Crite, Allan Rohan
Curwood, Stephen Thomas
Daniels, Alfred Claude Wynder
Dansby, Robert
Davis, William E., Sr.
Dike, Kenneth Onwuka
Dixon, John M.
Fleurant, Gerdes
Gates, Henry Louis, Jr.
Gomes, Peter John
Graham, Saundra M.
Guinier, Ewart
Hardeman, James Anthony
Harrington, Philip Leroy
Hawkins, James C.
Higginbotham, A. Leon, Jr.
Hopkins, Esther Arvilla
Huggins, Nathan Irvin

MICHIGAN

Mallebay-Vacqueur Dem, Jean
   Pascal
McKinney, Billy
Nelson, Rex
O'Bannon, Charles
Reid, Don
Robinson, Will
Sealy, Malik
Stackhouse, Jerry Darnell
Sutton, James Carter
Trueblood, Vera J.
Walker, Tracy A.
Williams, Brian Carson
Williams, Jerome
Williams, Tara
Woodard, Lynette
Wright, Mark Adrian

Baldwin
Williams, Robert Franklin

Battle Creek
Baines, Tyrone Randolph
Bullock, Clifton Vernice
Hicks, Veronica Abena
McKinney, James Ray
Overton-Adkins, Betty Jean
Petett, Freddye Webb
Stewart, Joseph M.
Taylor, Charles Avon

Bay City
Baker, Oscar Wilson
Selby, Ralph Irving

Belleville
Cothorn, Marguerite Esters
Crawford, Margaret Ward
Young, Watson A.

Benton Harbor
Cooke, Wilce L.
Ealy, Mary Newcomb
Madison, Shannon L.
McKeller, Thomas Lee
Miller, Charles D., Jr.
Yarbrough, Mamie Luella

Berrien Springs
Miles, Norman Kenneth
Warren, Joseph W.

Beverly Hills
Brooks, Arkles Clarence, Jr.

Big Rapids
Gant, Raymond Leroy
Unaeze, Felix Eme

Bingham Farms
Day, Cheryl D.
Franklin, Ronald E.
Harps, Cheryl L.
Jones, William Barnard

Birmingham
Jackson, James E., Sr.
N'Namdi, George Richard
Richie, Leroy C.
Theus, Lucius

Bloomfield Hills
Butler, John Donald
Cooley, Keith Winston
Douglas, Walter Edmond, Sr.
Eagan, Catherine B.
Foster, Bellandra Benefield
Parker, H. Wallace

Brighton
Davis, H. Bernard

Brohman
Freeman, McKinley Howard, Sr.

Cassopolis
Danzy, LeRoy Henry
Underwood, Joseph M., Jr.

Chelsea
Goodwin, Donald Edward

Chesterfield
Hill, George Calvin

Clarkston
Newton, Eric Christopher

Clinton
Shamberger, Jeffery L.

Clio
Hatter, Henry

Dearborn
Armstrong, Walter
Bray, Leroy, Sr.
Chappell, Michael James
Clarke, Benjamin Louis
Davie, Damon Jonathon
Dixon, Louis Tennyson
Ellis, Michael G.
Givens, Lawrence
Howard, Norman
Jemison, Aj D.
Jones, Cloyzelle Karrelle
Jones, Mable Veneida
Lartigue, Roland E.
Lee, Aubrey Walter, Jr.
Lee, Dorothy A. H.
Madison, Ronald L.
Miller, Jean Carolyn Wilder
Munson, Robert H.
Procter, Harvey T.
Procter, Harvey Thornton, Jr.
Renick, James C.
Turner, Allen H.
Washington, Floyd, Jr.

Detroit
Adams, Charles Gilchrist
Adams, Katherine
Adams, Thomas J.
Ahmad, Jadwaa
Alexander, DeAngelo Heath
Alexander, Larry
Allen, Alex James, Jr.
Allen, Charles Edward
Allison, Vivian
Anderson, Barbara Stewart Jenkins
Anderson, Eloise B. McMorris
Anderson, Moses B.
Anderson, Nicholas Charles
Anderson, Oddie
Anthony, Wendell
Archer, Dennis Wayne
Archer, Trudy DunCombe
Arrington, Harold Mitchell
Arrington, Robyn James, Jr.
Atchison, Leon H.
Aubert, Alvin Bernard
Austin, Richard H.
Ayala, Reginald P.
Bailer, Kermit Gamaliel
Bailey, Carol A.
Baldwin, Olivia McNair
Bandy, Riley Thomas, Sr.
Banks, Beatrice
Banks, William Venoid
Baranco, Beverly Victor, Jr.
Barden, Don H.
Barnett, Lester
Barrow, Thomas Joe
Bartee, Kimera Anotchi
Barthwell, Jack Clinton, III
Bass, Robert
Batchelor-Farmer, Karen
Bates, Alonzo W.
Baxter, Wendy Marie
Baylor, Emmett Robert, Jr.
Baylor, Margaret
Beatty, Robert L.
Bell, Edna Talbert
Bell, Edward F.
Bell, Karl I.
Bell, Mary L.
Bell, William Augustus, II
Benbow, Lillian Pierce
Bennett, George P.
Beverly, Creigs C.
Bing, Dave
Bishop, James, Jr.
Black, Bill
Blackwell, Arthur Brendhal, III
Blackwell-Hatcher, June E.
Bobo, Roscoe Lemual
Boddie, Arthur Walker
Boggs, James
Bond, Alan D.
Bonner, Ellis
Bowens, Gregory John
Boyce, Charles N.
Bozeman, Catherine E.
Bradfield, Clarence McKinley
Bradfield, Horace Ferguson
Bradley, Roosevelt, Jr.
Bradley, Vanesa Jones

Bradley, Wayne W.
Bray, Hiawatha
Brewer, James A., Sr.
Bridgeforth, Arthur Mac, Jr.
Bridgewater, Paul
Briscoe, Thomas F.
Brock, Gerald
Broughton, Christopher Leon
Brown, Clifford Anthony
Brown, Gates
Brown, Georgia R.
Brown, H. Franklin
Brown, Helen E.
Brown, Jesse
Brown, Morse L.
Browne, Ernest O., Jr.
Bryant, Kathryn Ann
Burden, Pennie L.
Burkeen, Ernest Wisdom, Jr.
Burks, Darrell
Butler, Charles W.
Byrd, Frederick E.
Cain, Waldo
Caison, Thelma Jann
Camp, Kimberly
Cargill, Gilbert Allen
Carr, Virgil H.
Carter, Arthur Michael
Carter, Harriet LaShun
Carter, Lewis Winston
Carter, Ora Williams
Carter, Robert Louis, Jr.
Catchings, Yvonne Parks
Cauthen, Richard L.
Chapman, Melvin
Chastang, Jeffry
Chenevert-Bragg, Irma J.
Chestang, Leon Wilbert
Chillis, Natalie A.
Clark, Irma
Clark, Tony
Clay, Eric Lee
Cleage, Albert B., Jr.
Cleaver, Johnny
Clements, Walter H.
Clermont, Volna
Cleveland, Clyde
Cobbin, Gloria Constance
Cockerham, Haven Earl
Coffee, Lawrence Winston
Coleman, April Howard
Coleman, Dennis
Coleman, Everod A.
Coleman, Helen
Coleman, Trevor W.
Collins, Jeffrey
Colson, Lewis Arnold
Combs, Julius V., M. D.
Conner, Gail Patricia
Conyers, Nathan G.
Cook, Julian Abele, Jr.
Cooley, Wendy
Cooper, Evelyn Kaye
Cooper, Robert N.
Cortada, Rafael Leon
Costa, Annie Bell Harris
Cotman, Ivan Louis
Cox, James L.
Cozart, John
Craig, Rhonda Patricia
Crawford, Brenita
Crews, William Hunter
Crisp, Robert Carl, Jr.
Crockett, George W., III
Croft, Wardell C.
Cross, Haman, Jr.
Currie, Jackie L.
Curtis, Austin W.
Curtis, Ivery
Curtis, Jean Trawick
Cushingberry, George, Jr.
Cuyler, Milton
Dade, Malcolm G., Jr.
Daggs, LeRoy W.
Daniels, Jesse
Darden, Anthony Kojo
Darity, Janiki Evangelia
Darnell, Edward Buddy
Davenport, C. Dennis
Davidson, Arthur B.
Davis, Denice Faye
Davis, Donald
Davis, Edward
Davis, Erellon Ben
Davis, Marion Harris
Davis, Mary Agnes Miller
Davis Anthony, Vernice
Day, Burnis Calvin
Dennard, Brazeal Wayne

Dent, Gary Kever
DeRamus, Betty
DeSantis, Maggie
Dismuke, Mary Eunice
Dixon, Leonard Bill
Dodd, Geralda
Dortch, Heyward
Doss, Lawrence Paul
Doss, Theresa
Dotson, Norma Y.
Dowdell, Dennis, Jr.
Dowell, Clyde Donald
Downer, Willie
Drain, Gershwin A.
Dudley, Herman T.
Dulin, Robert O., Jr.
Dumas, Karen Marie
Dunbar, Joseph C.
DunCombe, C. Beth
Dunmore, Albert J.
Dunmore, Gregory Charles
Dunner, Leslie B.
Duplessis, Harry Y.
Dykes, Marie Draper
Eagan, Emma Louise
Easley, Damion
Edmonds, Curtis
Edwards, Abiyah, Jr.
Edwards, Carl Ray, II
Edwards, Esther Gordy
Edwards, Prentis
Edwards, Rupert L.
Elliott, John
Evans, Deborah Ann
Evans, Elinor Elizabeth
Evans, Thomas
Evans, Warren Cleage
Everett, Kay
Fair, Darwin
Farmer, Karen Batchelor
Farmer, Nancy
Farrell-Donaldson, Marie D.
Feaster, Bruce Sullivan
Feemster, John Arthur
Ferrebee, Thomas G.
Fields, M. Joan
Fields, Stanley
Fitzpatrick, Julia C.
Fobbs, Kevin
Fontayne, K. Nicole
Ford, Geraldine Bledsoe
Ford, William L., Jr.
Forte, Linda Diane
Franklin, Eugene T., Jr.
Franklin, Lance Stonestreet
Frohman, Roland H.
Gardner, Loman Ronald
Gardner, Samuel C.
Gartin, Claudia L.
Gaskin, Jeanine
Gay, Saundra
Gibson, Cheryl Dianne
Gibson, JoAnn
Gibson, Sarah L.
Giles, Joe L.
Givens, Leonard David
Givhan, Robin Deneen
Goldsberry, Ronald Eugene
Goodwin, Della McGraw
Goodwin, Jesse Francis
Gordon, Aaron Z.
Gragg, Lauren Andrea
Graham, Charlene
Graves, Irene Amelia
Graves, Leslie Theresa
Graves, Ray Reynolds
Green, Charles A.
Green, Eddie L.
Green, Elizabeth Lee
Green, Forrest F.
Green, John M.
Green, Verna S.
Grier, John L.
Griffith, Vera Victoria
Gunn, Arthur Clinton
Hackett, Harry G.
Hale, Janice Ellen, Ph.D.
Hall, Perry Alonzo
Hall-Keith, Jacqueline Yvonne
Hamilton, Rainy, Jr.
Hammons, Mary
Haney, Don Lee
Hankins, Andrew Jay, Jr.
Hannah, Beverly K.
Harlan, Carmen
Harper, Laydell Wood
Harpole, Mildred
Harrington, Gerald E.
Harris, Harcourt Glenties

Harris, Joseph Benjamin
Harris, Joseph Preston
Harris, Marjorie Elizabeth
Harris, William Anthony
Harrison, Ernest Alexander
Hatcher, Lillian
Hathaway, Cynthia Gray
Haugabook, Terrence Randall
Hayden, Frank
Hayes-Giles, Joyce V.
Heath, Comer, III
Henderson, Angelo B.
Herndon, Larry Lee
Hewitt, Ronald Jerome
Hill, George Hiram
Hilliard, William Alexander
Hines, Rosetta
Hinkle, Jackson Herbert
Hobson, Donald Lewis
Hodges, Harold Earl
Holbert, JoAnne
Holley, Jim
Hollowell, Kenneth Lawrence
Holman, Forest H.
Holsey, Steve
Hood, Denise Page
Hood, Elizabeth F.
Hood, Harold
Hood, Morris, Jr.
Hood, Nicholas
Horne, Kimmi
Howell, Rachel
Howze, Dorothy J.
Hubbard, Marilyn French
Hudson, Lester Darnell
Hughes, Carl D.
Humphries, James Nathan
Humphries, Paula G.
Hunt, Jeffrey C.
Hunter, Brian Lee
Hunter, Teola P.
Hutchison, Harry Greene, IV
Ice, Anne-Mare
Ingram, James William, Jr.
Jackson, Charles E., Sr.
Jackson, Dorothea E.
Jackson, George K.
Jackson, Hiram
Jackson, Pamela J.
Jackson, Tomi L.
James, John
Jefferson, Arthur
Jefferson, Horace Lee
Jenkins, Marilyn Joyce
Jensen, Marcus C.
Johnson, Arthur J.
Johnson, Cynthia L. M.
Johnson, Francis Edward, Jr.
Johnson, John
Johnson, Mildred H.
Johnson, Robert
Johnson, Tommie Ulmer
Johnson, Vinnie
Johnson, Zodie Anderson
Jones, Carol Joyce
Jones, David L.
Jones, Dorinda A.
Jones, Irma Renae
Jones, K. Maurices
Jones, Robert Bernard, Sr.
Jones, Vera Massey
Jordan, Robert L.
Keemer, Edgar B.
Keith, Damon Jerome
Keith, Luther
Kelley, Wilbourne Anderson, III
Kelly, Ida B.
Kendall, Michelle Katrina
Kennedy-Scott, Patricia
Kiah, Ruth Josephine
Kimmons, Willie James
King, Emery C.
King, John L.
King, John Thomas
Kispert, Dorothy Lee
Kornegay, Francis A.
Lane, Richard
Lang, Winston E.
Larrie, Reginald Reese, Ph.D.
Lawson, William Emmett
Leatherwood, Robert P.
Leber, Mariann C.
Lee, Aubrey Walter, Sr.
Lee, Consella Almetter
Lee, Otis K.
Lemon, Michael Wayne, Sr.
Lewis, Alonzo Todd
Lewis, Billie Jean
Lewis, Charles Henry

Lewis, David Baker
Lewis, Lyn Etta
Lewis, Walton A.
Lewis-Langston, Deborah
Lipscomb, Curtis Alexander
Little, Ronald Eugene
Littlejohn, Edward J.
Lloyd, Leona Loretta
Lloyd, Leonia Jannetta
Lofton, Ernest
Love, Karen Allyce
Lowery-Jeter, Renecia Yvonne
Lucas, Stephanie
Lucas, William
Maben, Hayward C., Jr.
Mabrey, Marsha Eve
Mack, Cleveland J., Sr.
Maddox, Jack H.
Madgett, Naomi Long
Major, Henrymae M.
Makupson, Walter H.
Mallett, Conrad L., Sr.
Mallett, Conrad L., Jr.
Malone, Rosemary C.
Manlove, Benson
Marshall-Walker, Denise Elizabeth
Martin, Kimberly Lynette
Mason, Howard Keith
Mason, John
Massey, Selma Redd
Mathews, George
Mathis, Gregory
Mausi, Shahida Andrea
Mays, William O.
McClelland, Marguerite Marie
McCloud, Aaron C.
McFarland, Ollie Franklin
McGee, Sherry
McGregor, Edna M.
McGruder, Robert G.
McHenry, James O'Neal
McKinnon, Isaiah
McKinnon, Patrice
McLemore, Andrew G.
McMurry, Walter M., Jr.
McPhail, Sharon M.
Mickens, Maxine
Miller, Cylenthia LaToye
Miller, Doris Jean
Miller, Jacqueline B.
Miller-Reid, Dora Alma
Minter, Eloise Devada
Mitchell, Augustus William, M.D.
Mitchell, Lilyann Jackson
Moore, Alfred
Moore, Warfield, Jr.
Moran, George H.
Morcom, Claudia House
Morgan, Monica Alise
Morris, William H.
Morrison, Jacqueline
Morton, Charles E.
Moten, Emmett S., Jr.
Munday, Reuben A.
Murphy, Charles A.
Murphy, Raymond M.
Napoleon, Benny Nelson
Napoleon, Harry Nelson
Neale, Chinyere
Nelson, Nathaniel W.
Newell, Kathleen W.
Nicco-Annan, Lionel
N'Namdi, Carmen Ann
Nolan, Robert L.
O'Banner-Owens, Jeanette
O'Neale, Sondra
Owens, Keith Alan
Pailen, Donald
Parker, Bernard F., Jr.
Parker, Darwin Carey
Parker, Jean L.
Parnell, William Cornellus, Jr.
Parrish, Maurice Drue
Patrick, Lawrence Clarence, Jr.
Patterson, Joan Lethia
Patterson, Michael Duane
Pattman, Virgil Thomas, Sr.
Paul, John F.
Pearson, Ramona Henderson
Penn-Atkins, Barbara A.
Peoples, L. Kimberly
Perkins, James Connelle
Perkins, Myla Levy
Perkins, Robert E. L.
Perry, Gary W.
Perry, Joseph James
Perry, Lowell W.
Perry-Mason, Gail F.
Phelps, William Anthony

Phillips, Robert Hansbury
Phillips, Wilburn R.
Pickett, Dovie T.
Pitts, Cornelius
Pitts, Jack Nelson Evangelista
Price, Brenda G.
Price, Glenda Delores
Pride, J. Thomas
Pulliam, Betty E.
Quinn, Longworth D.
Randall, Dudley Felker
Rayford, Brenda L.
Reed, Gregory J.
Reed, Kimberley Del Rio
Reid, Irvin D.
Reide, Jerome L.
Revely, William
Richardson, Ralph H.
Richmond, Cassius
Riley, Dorothy Winbush
Rivers, Jessie
Robbins, Robert J.
Roberson, Dalton Anthony
Roberson, Lawrence R.
Roberts, Bip
Roberts, Roy S.
Robinson, Jane Alexander
Robinson, Milton J.
Ross, Mary Olivia
Roulhac, Roy L.
Rowe, Nansi Irene
Ruffin, Ronald R.
Sailor, Elroy
Sanders, Delbert
Scafe, Judith Arlene
Scott, Brenda M.
Scott, Joseph M.
Scott, Robert Jerome
Seabrooks, Nettie Harris
Shade, George H., Jr.
Shakoor, Adam Adib
Shamborguer, Naima
Shannon, Robert F.
Sharp, James Alfred
Shavers, Catherine
Shaw, Carl Bernard
Shealey, Richard W.
Sheard, John H.
Sheffield, Horace L., Jr.
Shelton, Joseph B.
Shipley, Anthony J.
Shoulders, Ramon Henkia
Shurney, Dexter Wayne
Simmons, Janice
Simpkins, J. Edward
Simpson, Harry L.
Slaughter, Jewell L.
Slaughter, Peter
Smith, Gerald Wayne
Smith, Loretta Gary
Smith, Robert, Jr.
Smith-Gray, Cassandra Elaine
Snead, David Lowell
Snowden, Gilda
Softley, Donald
Sowell, Myzell
Spann, Paul Ronald
Spight, Benita L.
Stallworth, Thomas Fontaine, III
Stearns Miller, Camille Louise
Stephens, Cynthia Diane
Stepp, Marc
Stevenson, Jerome Pritchard, Sr.
Steward, Emanuel
Stewart, Darneau V.
Stewart, Kenneth C.
Stotts, Valmon D.
Stovall, Audrean
Strong, Craig Stephen
Strong, Douglas Donald
Strong, Helen Francine
Swan, George W., III
Swan, Lionel F.
Swanson, O'Neil D.
Swift, Linda Denise
Tabor, Lillie Montague
Talbert, Ted
Tappes, Shelton
Taylor, Anna Diggs
Taylor, Benjamin Garland
Taylor, Cledie Collins
Taylor, Pauline J.
Teasley, Marie R.
Telfair, Brian Kraig
Thomas, Edward S.
Thomas, Reginald Maurice
Thomas, Rodolfo Rudy
Thomas, Sheryl Ann Benning
Thompson, Gayle Ann-Spencer

Thurman, Gary Montez, Jr.
Tinsley-Williams, Alberta
Townsend, Leonard
Travis, Myron
Trent, Jay Lester
Tucker, Paul, Jr.
Turman, Kevin
Turner, David
Turner, Melvin E.
Turner, Reginald M., Jr.
Turner, Richard M., III
Turner, Tom
Varner, Harold R.
Varner, Nellie M.
Venable, Abraham S.
Vernon-Chesley, Michele Joanne
Vest, Donald Seymour, Sr.
Vest, Hilda Freeman
Vincent, Charles
Wahls, Myron Hastings
Walker, Willie Leroy
Walton, Anthony Scott
Ward, Velma Lewis
Ware, Jewel C.
Warren, James Kenneth
Wash, Glenn Edward
Washington, Luisa
Washington, Sherry Ann
Waterman, Homer D.
Waters, Mary D.
Watkins, Aretha La Anna
Watkins, Harold D., Sr.
Watkins, Rolanda Rowe
Watson, Anne
Watson, Clifford D.
Watson, Milton H.
Watson, Perry
Watson, Susan
Watters, Linda A.
Watts, Lucile
Ways, Marcus
Whitaker, Louis Rodman
White, Donald F.
White, Richard Thomas
White-Hunt, Debra Jean
Whitney, Rosalyn L.
Whitten, Charles F.
Williams, Aubin Bernard
Williams, Charlie J.
Williams, Clarence Earl, Jr.
Williams, Geneva J.
Williams, Margo E.
Williams, Martha S.
Williams, Maxine Broyles
Williams, Morris
Williams, Patricia R.
Williams, Randy
Williams-Taitt, Patricia Ann
Wilson, Angela Brown
Wilson, Danton Thomas
Wilson, Porterfield
Winans, Marvin L.
Wine, Donald Gary
Wisdom, David Watts
Wolfe, Estemore A.
Wood, Michael H.
Woodson, Shirley A.
Woodson, Thelma L.
Worth, Stefanie Patrice
Worthy, Kym
Wright, Dawin Lyron
Wright, Joseph Malcolm
Wyre, Stanley Marcel
Young, Alan C.
Zola, Nkenge

Dexter
Sutton, Sharon Egretta

Durand
Johnson, Michael

East Lansing
Allen, William Barclay
Bonham, Vence L., Jr.
Bouknight, Reynard Ronald
Coleman, Don Edwin
Coleman, Herman W.
Gunnings, Thomas S.
Hine, Darlene Clark
Holloway, Albert Curtis
Jackson, Julius Hamilton
Jones, Arthur L.
Lang, Marvel
Lipscomb, Wanda Dean
Maddox, Julius A.
Martin, Blanche
Mays, William, Jr.
Norvell, Merritt J., Jr.

Pierre, Percy Anthony
Pipes, William H.
Radcliffe, Aubrey
Scarborough, Charles S.
Smitherman, Geneva
Stockman, Ida J.
Tate, James A.
Thornton, Dozier W.
Turner, Moses
Vance, Irvin E.
Weil, Robert L.
Williams, Donald H.

Eastpointe
Hall, Jeffrey Maurice

Erie
Horton, Willie Wattison

Farmington
Jones, Mable Veneida

Farmington Hills
Bernard, Sharon Elaine
Jensen, Renaldo Mario
Jones, David L.
Munday, Cheryl Casselberry

Ferndale
Farrow, Harold Frank
Giles, Joe L.
Jones, Jesse J., Jr.
Jones, Theresa C.
Majors, Mattie Carolyn
McRipley, G. Whitney
Smith, H. Russell
Wilson, Barbara Jean

Flat Rock
Harrell, Charles H.

Flint
Aldridge, Karen Beth
Baker, Darryl Brent, Sr.
Beard, Martin Luther
Bivins, Ollie B., Jr.
Boyd, Melba Joyce
Bullard, Edward A., Jr.
Callaway, Dwight W.
Conyers, Jean L.
Dach, Michael E.
DeMille, Darcy
Diggs, Roy Dalton, Jr.
Dismuke, Leroy
Duncan, Verdell
Epps, A. Glenn
Griffin, Michael D.
Gunn, Willie Cosdena Thomas
Harris, Helen B.
High, Claude, Jr.
Howard, Mamie R.
Kennedy, James E.
Kimbrough, Clarence B.
King, Richard L.
Kornegay, William F.
Loving, Pamela Yvonne
Makokha, James A. N.
Marable, Herman, Jr.
McGuire, Cyril A.
McVay, Michael
Montgomery, James C.
Moran, George H.
Mullens, Delbert W.
Newman, Paul Dean
Nichols, LeRoy
Patterson-Townsend, Margaret M.
Petross, Precious Doris
Piper, W. Archibald
Pirtle, Ronald M.
Price, William S., III
Reed, Joann
Robertson, John Gilbert
Sanders, Rhonda Sheree
Scruggs, Cleorah J.
Sevillian, Clarence Marvin
Smith, Granville N.
Stanley, Woodrow
Thompson, Jesse M.
Twigg, Lewis Harold
Washington, Valdemar Luther
Williams, Charlotte Leola

Frankenmuth
Shelton, John W.

Fremont
Davis, Theodis C.

Garden City
Settles, Rosetta Hayes

Gobles
Daniel, Griselda

Grand Blanc
Bennett, Al
Jackson, Garnet Nelson

Grand Rapids
Brooks, Rodney Norman
Collins, Paul
Culpepper, Richard
Drew, Stephen Richard
Franks, Julius, Jr.
Gibson, Benjamin F.
Hair, John
Holliman, Argie H.
Hoskins Clark, Tempy M.
Logan, Benjamin Henry, II
Mathis, Walter Lee, Sr.
McDonald, Jon Franklin
McGhee, Georgia Mae
Small, Isadore, III
Smith, Bruce L.
Snead, John D.
Suggs, Robert Chinelo
Turner, George Timothy

Grosse Pointe Farms
Smith, Zachary

Grosse Pointe Park
Watters, Linda A.

Hart
Nalley, Ruth
Waters, Nancy

Highland Park
Blackwell, Robert B.
Bledsoe, William
Downes, Dwight
Harrison, Ernest Alexander
Hope, Julius Caesar
Lewis, James O.
Lewis-Kemp, Jacqueline
McClung, Willie David
Porter, Linsey

Holland
Smith, Fronse Wayne, Sr.

Houghton
Gill, Glenda Eloise
McCoy, Walter D.

Howell
Livingston-Wilson, Karen
Tupper, Leon

Idlewild
Bullett, Audrey Kathryn
Winburn, B. J.

Inkster
Bradford, Equilla Forrest
Cox, Wendell
Ezell, William Alexander
James, Naomi Ellen
Johnson, Cynthia
Johnson, Willie
LeCesne, Terrel M.
Warren, Gertrude Francois
Young, Sarah Daniels

Jackson
Breeding, Carl L.
Clay, Nathaniel, Jr.
Love, J. Gregory
Pryor, Cecil, Jr.
Thompson, James W.
Turner, George Cordell, II

Kalamazoo
Baskerville, Pearl
Brinn, Chauncey J.
Daniel, Griselda
Davis, Charles Alexander
Dube, Thomas M. T.
Floyd, Elson
Gammon, Reginald Adolphus
Gatlin, Elissa L.
Hodge, Charles Mason
Hudson, Roy Davage
Jerrard, Paul

Jones, Leander Corbin
Lacey, Bernardine M.
Moore, Beverly
Payne, Vernon
Pettiford, Steven Douglas
Phillips, Romeo Eldridge
Smith, Isabelle R.
Spradling, Mary Elizabeth Mace
Walker, Lewis
Walker, Moses L.
Washington, Arthur, Jr.
Washington, Earl Melvin
Washington, Von Hugo, Sr.
White, Damon J.
Williams, Carolyn H.
Williams, Sidney B., Jr.

Lansing
Brown, Robert, Jr.
Canady, Hortense Golden
Cason, David, Jr.
Costa, Annie Bell Harris
Drake, Lawrence M., II
Dunnings, Stuart, II
Evans, Eva L.
Ferguson, Joel
Gillum, Ronald M.
Glass, James
Guthrie, Carlton Lyons
Guthrie, Michael J.
Hall, Jack L.
Holmes, David S., Jr.
Hood, Raymond W.
Jackson, Darnell
James, Stephen Elisha
Jeff, Gloria Jean
Jones, Lewis Arnold, Jr.
Leatherwood, Larry Lee
Lett, Gerald William
Lipscomb, Wanda Dean
McNeely, Matthew
Metcalf, Andrew Lee, Jr.
Murphy, Raymond M.
Nichols, Ronald Augustus
O'Neal, Connie Murry
Porter, Grady J.
Price, Hubert, Jr.
Reynolds, Nanette Lee
Richardson, Gilda Faye
Rodgers, Shirley Marie
Scott, Martha
Smith, Gloria R.
Smith, Virgil Clark, Jr.
Stallworth, Alma G.
Stallworth, Oscar B.
Sykes, Abel B., Jr.
Thomas, Claude Roderick
Thomas, Samuel
Vaughn, Ed
Vaughn, Jackie, III
Verbal, Claude A.
Wallick, Ernest Herron
Young, Joseph, Jr.
Young, Joseph Floyd, Sr.

Lathrup Village
Abraham, Sharon L.
Beckles, Benita Harris
Holliday, Prince E.
Thompson, Karen Ann

Madison Heights
Chapman, Gilbert Bryant, II

Marquette
Rauch, Doreen E.

Marshall
Gray, Marcus J.

Mount Clemens
Burns, Sarah Ann
Clark, Louis James
Hill, Bobby
Rickman, Lewis Daniel, Sr.

Mount Morris
Jackson, Gregory

Mount Pleasant
Baugh, Joyce A.
Brown, Paula Evie
Drake, Leonard
Hill, James L.
Sykes, William Richard, Jr.
Toms-Robinson, Dolores C.

Muskegon
Coleman, Elizabeth Sheppard
Pressley, Stephen, Jr.
Williams, John H.

Muskegon Heights
Howell, Willie R.
Jones, Patricia Yvonne
Terrell, John L.

New Haven
Stone, Dolores June

Niles
Hamilton, Arthur Lee, Jr.

Northville
Sanders, Wendell Rowan

Novi
Davis, Diane Lynn
Richardson, Andra Virginia

Oak Park
Farr, Melvin, Sr.
Hines, Frances Nero
Johnson, Clarissa
Miller-Holmes, Cheryl

Okemos
Barron, Wendell
Gillum, Ronald M.

Plymouth
Parker, Walter Gee

Pontiac
Abrams, Kevin
Aldridge, Allen Ray
Anderson, Gary Wayne
Bailey, Robert Martin Luther
Brown, Christopher C.
Canty, Otis Andrew
Carrier, Mark Anthony
Carter, Anthony
Chambers, Pamela S.
Colon, Harry
Conley, James Sylvester, Jr.
Elliss, Luther
Harrison, Charlie J., Jr.
Harrison, Chris
Hatchett, Elbert
Hempstead, Hessley
Holland, Wallace E.
Jamison, George R., Jr.
Jefferies, Greg Lamont
Johnson, Andre
Jones, Victor Tyrone
Kendall, Michelle Katrina
Langford-Morris, Denise
Lee, Larry Dwayne
Lynch, Eric
Mahone, Barbara J.
Malone, Van Buren
Matthews, Billie Watson
McCorvey, Kez
McCree, Edward L.
McLemore, Thomas
Milburn, Glyn Curt
Moore, Herman Joseph
Moore, Walter Louis
Morgan, Richard H., Jr.
Morton, Johnnie James
Porcher, Robert, III
Preston, Franklin DeJuanette
Rice, Ronald
Riggs, Harry L.
Rivers, Ronald Leroy
Roberts, Ray
Sanders, Barry
Scroggins, Tracy
Stewart, Ryan
Tharpe, Larry
Tripp, Lucius Charles
Waldroup, Kerwin
Ware, Albert M.
Washington, Jacquelin Edwards
Westbrook, Bryant
Westbrook, Scott C., III

Port Huron
Lang, Isaac, Jr.

Portage
Phillips, Romeo Eldridge

Redford
Butler, Keith Andre
Lewis, Carmen Cortez

River Rouge
Hylton, Kenneth N.
Johnson, William
Milton, Samuel Byron
Williams, Charles Earl

Rochester
Atlas, John Wesley
Davis, Joseph
Dykes, DeWitt S., Jr.
Gardiner, George L.
Harrison, Algea Othella
Henry, Egbert Winston
Kilpatrick, Richardo Ivan
Minor, Billy Joe

Rochester Hills
Sutton, James Carter

Romulus
Henderson, William Avery
Martin, Lee

Roseville
Latimer, Frank Edward
Pickard, William Frank

Royal Oak
Morgan, Joseph C.
Shelby, Khadejah E.

Saginaw
Barnes, Vivian Leigh
Clark, Leon Stanley
Colvin, Alonza James
Crawford, Lawrence Douglas
Daniels, Ruben
Ferrell, Rosie E.
Finney, Michael Anthony
Galloway-Briggs, Lula
Gamble, Kenneth L.
Hall, David McKenzie
Leek, Everett Paul
McKandes, Darnell Damon
McKandes, Dorothy Dell
McWright, Carter C.
Nix, Rick
Perry, LaVal
Poston, Carl C., Jr.
Scott-Johnson, Roberta Virginia
Thorns, Odail, Jr.
Wilson, James Paris
Woodruff, James W.

Saline
Hall, Eddie

Southfield
Adams, Don L.
Addison, Caroline Elizabeth
Allen, Lecester L.
Allen, Van
Allen, Zalonya
Anderson, William Gilchrist
Badger, Brenda Joyce
Ball, Brenda Louise
Benford, Edward A.
Berry, Charles F., Jr.
Berry, Jay
Brooks, Robert
Brown, Richard Osborne
Burdette, LaVere Elaine
Burgette, James M.
Chapman, Gilbert Bryant, II
Coleman, Donald Alvin
Davidson-Harger, Joan Carole
Dortch, Heyward
Doss, Juanita King
Douglas, Walter Edmond, Sr.
Dudley, Calmeze Henike, Jr.
Ferguson, Patricia A.
Fields, Dexter L.
Gardner, LaMaurice Holbrook
Givens, Donovahn Heston
Glass, Herman J., Sr.
Grandberry, Nikki
Gray, E. Delbert
Gregory, Karl Dwight
Harris, Terea Donnelle
Harvey, Linda Joy
Hill, Robert A.
Hollowell, Melvin L.
Hurst, Cleveland, III
Isaacs, Patricia

Jackson, James E., Sr.
Jefferson-Ford, Charmain
Johnson, Davis
Johnson, Gage
Johnson, Roy Lee
Johnson, Sandra Virginia
Jones, Gus
Kaigler-Reese, Marie Madeleine
Lawrence, Brenda
Love, Jon
Masse, Donald D.
McArthur, Barbara Jean
McKinney, Olivia Davene Ross
McNorriell, Mozell M.
Norman, Clifford P.
Orr, Marlett Jennifer
Perry, Gary W.
Perry, Lowell Wesley, Jr.
Perry, Marc Aubrey
Posey, Deborah
Prince, Carol
Pryde, Arthur Edward
Reeves, John E.
Reeves, Julius Lee
Rodgers, Horace J.
Rogers, David William
Shelton, Roy Cresswell, Jr.
Smith, Denver Lester
Spears, Sandra Calvette
Stewart, Loretta A.
Strong, Peter E.
Taylor, Carol Ann
Thomas, Joseph Edward, Jr.
Turner, Linda Darnell
Vaughn, Clarence B.
Warden, George W.
White, Gary Leon
Worford, Carolyn Kennedy
Wright, Roberta V. Hughes

Southgate
Spears, Mary

St Clair Shores
Featherstone, Karl Ramon

St Joseph
Hawkins, Mary L.

Sterling Heights
Hines, Jimmie
Newton, Eric Christopher
Taylor, Herbert Charles

Thompsonville
Perry, Margaret

Three Rivers
Murray, Edna McClain

Troy
Biagas, Edward D.
Brooks, William C.
Bryant, N. Z., Jr.
Edwards, Verba L.
George, Pauline L.
Irby, Mary
Jackson, Cornelia Pinkney
Robbins, Kevin F.
VanEtten, Lorraine

University Center
Goodson, Martin L., Jr.
Thompson, Willie Edward

Utica
Gothard, Barbara Wheatley

Vicksburg
Long, Monti M.

Warren
Bridgforth, Walter, Jr.
Farmer, Forest J.
Glenn, Edward C., Jr.
Hill, Kenneth Randal
Hughes, Wilbur B.
Lowe, Sylvia Oneice
Lowe, Walter Edward, Jr.
McNeill, Cerves Todd
O'Neal, Rodney
Pattman, Virgil Thomas, Sr.
Pryde, Arthur Edward
Riley, Rosetta Margueritte
Sanders, Barbara A.
Turner, Harry Glenn
Welburn, Edward Thomas, Jr.

Washington
Gothard, Donald L.

Wayne
Mallett, Rosa Elizabeth

West Bloomfield
Jackson, William Alvin
Livingston-White, Deborah J. H.
Reed, Derryl L.
Trent, James E.

Westland
Bluford, James F.
Coleman, Hurley J., Jr.
Woodbury, David Henry

Ypsilanti
Armstrong, Walter
Beatty, Charles Eugene, Sr.
Brown, Ronald Edward
Clarke, Velma Greene
Collins-Eaglin, Jan Theresa
Dill, Gregory
Edwards, Gerald Douglas
Hamilton, Theophilus Elliott
Holloway, Nathaniel Overton, Jr.
Horne-McGee, Patricia J.
Jolley, Edward B., Jr.
Jones, Richard
Martin, Sherman Theodore
McKanders, Kenneth Andre
Peoples, Gregory Allan
Perry, Robert Lee
Porter, John W.
Rhodes, Robert Shaw
Robinson, Albert Arnold

MINNESOTA

Arden Hills
Laroche, Gerard A.

Bloomington
English, William E.
Raphael, Bernard Joseph

Brooklyn Center
Watson, Perry, III

Brooklyn Park
Francis, Delma J.
Woods, Manuel T.

Burnsville
Posey, Edward W.
Robinson, John G.

Collegeville
McCall, Aidan M.

Cottage Grove
Parham, Frederick Russell
Sergent, Ernest, Jr.

Eden Prairie
Alexander, Derrick
Ball, Jerry Lee
Banks, Antonio Dontral
Bobo, Orlando
Carter, Cris
Chapman, Sharon Jeanette
Clemons, Duane
Cunningham, Randall
Daniels, LeShun
Edwards, Dixon Voldean, III
Evans, Chuck
Fuller, Corey
George, Ronald
Gilliam, Frank Delano
Glapion, Michael J.
Glover, Andrew Lee
Gray, Torrian
Green, Dennis
Green, Robert David
Griffith, Robert Otis
Harris, Jean Louise
Henderson, Keith Pernell
Hoard, Leroy
Jordan, Steve Russell
Lee, Carl, III
Lewis, Leo E., III
McDaniel, Edward
McDaniel, Randall Cornell
Merriweather, Michael Lamar

Palmer, David
Prior, Anthony
Randle, John
Reed, Jake
Rice, Allen Troy
Rudd, Dwayne
Sherman, Ray
Smith, Fernando Dewitt
Smith, Robert Scott
Stringer, Korey
Thomas, Orlando
Walker, Jay
Washington, Dewayne Neron
Wheeler, Leonard Tyrone
Williams, Moe

Edina
Jam, Jimmy
Law, M. Eprevel
Lewis, Terry
McKerson, Effie M.

Forest Lake
Kemp, Leroy Percy, Jr.

Golden Valley
Marsh, Donald Gene
Thomas, William Christopher

Lakeville
Kelly, Murry

Mankato
Ellison, David Lee

Minneapolis
Alexander, Pamela Gayle
Bailey, Thurl Lee
Baker, Robert N.
Bartelle, Talmadge Louis
Belton, Sharon Sayles
Belton, Y. Marc
Boone, Robert Franklin
Boston, McKinley, Jr.
Bowman, Earl W., Jr.
Brewer, Rose Marie
Brooks, Roy Lavon
Brown, Jarvis Ardel
Brown, Michael
Burroughs, Tim
Carr, Chris Dean
Carson, Emmett D.
Chapman, Sharon Jeanette
Coffey, Richard
Coleman, Melvin D.
Copeland, Richard Allen
Davis, Brian
Davis, Michael James
Davis, Van
Edwards, Ronald Alfred
Eller, Carl L.
Fowler, James Daniel, Jr.
Francis, Delma J.
Frank, Tellis Joseph, Jr.
Garnett, Kevin
Glass, Gerald Damon
Glover, Gleason
Green, Richard R.
Hall, Hansel Crimiel
Harrison, Jeanette LaVerne
Haskins, Clem Smith
Hawkins, LaTroy
Henry, Daniel Joseph
Hogan, William E., II
Hyter, Micheal C.
Jackson, Stanley Leon
James, Ronald
Johnson, Charles W.
Johnson, Cyrus Edwin
Jordan, Reggie
Kennon, Rozmond H.
King, Reatha Clark
King, Stacey
Lange, LaJune Thomas
Latham, Chris
Lawrence, Thomas R., Jr.
Lawton, Matthew, III
Lloyd, Marcea Bland
Mack, Rudy Eugene, Sr.
Marbury, Stephon
Maxey, Marlon Lee
Minor, David M.
Mitchell, Samuel E., Jr.
Moore, Cornell Leverette
Moore, Wenda Weekes
Myers, Samuel L., Jr.
Nixon, Otis Junior
Oliva, Pedro, Jr.
Otieno-Ayim, Larban Allan

Porter, Terry
Posey, Edward W.
Posten, William S.
Powell, Robert John
Prince, Cheryl Patrice
Propes, Victor Lee
Puckett, Kirby
Richardson, Joseph
Roberts, Brett
Roberts, Stanley Corvet
Rochester, Geof
Roxie Mi, John B Reggans Jr
Rozier, Clifford Glen, II
Shackleford, Charles
Sims, Carl W.
Smith, Chris G.
Smith, Henry Thomas
Snowden, Frank Walter
Southall, Geneva H.
Taborn, John Marvin
Taylor, David Vassar
Terrill, W. H. Tyrone, Jr.
Warder, John Morgan
Washington, Thomas
Watkins, Izear Carl
Wheat, DeJuan Shontez
White, Van Freeman
Wilderson, Frank B., Jr.
Williams, Michael Douglas
Williams, Theartrice
Winfield, David Mark
Woods, Manuel T.
Younger, Robert D.

Minnetonka
Morgan, Robert Lee
Powell, Wayne Hugh

Moorhead
Spriggs, G. Max

Northfield
Miller, Robert Laverne
Moore, Undine Smith

St Cloud
Tripp, Luke Samuel

St Paul
Caldwell, George Theron, Sr.
Canty, George
Cooper-Lewter, Nicholas Charles
El-Kati, Mahhmoud
England, Rodney Wayne
Garner, John W.
Griffin, James Stafford
Howell, Sharon Marie
Lambert, LeClair Grier
Lewis, Jeffrey Mark
Lewis, Virginia Hill
Nicholson, Jessie R.
Page, Alan Cedric
Sergent, Ernest, Jr.
Troup, Elliott Vanbrugh
Waynewood, Freeman Lee
White, William O.
Wilderson, Thad
Williams, Kneely
Williams, Ronald Wesley
Wilson, Willie Mae
Zachary, Steven W.

Waconia
Young, Rickey Darnell

White Bear Lake
Owens, Jerry Sue

MISSISSIPPI

Arcola
Harris, Clifton L.

Batesville
Herring, Larry Windell

Belzoni
Reed, Clara Taylor

Biloxi
Howze, Joseph Lawson
Mason, Gilbert Rutledge
Palmer, Terry Wayne
Rhodeman, Clare M.
Stallworth, William Fred

Brandon
Jones, Chester Ray

Byhalia
Taylor, John L.

Canton
Blackmon, Barbara Anita
Blackmon, Edward, Jr.
Esco, Fred, Jr.
Simmons, Shirley Davis
Williams, Jewel L.

Clarksdale
Espy, Henry
Henry, Aaron E.

Cleveland
Evans, Ruthana Wilson
Smith, Daniel Morris, Sr.
Tolliver, Ned, Jr.
Washington, David Warren

Columbia
Irvin, Regina Lynette
James, Sidney J.
Porter, Richard Sylvester

Columbus
Brooks, Leroy
Elzy, Amanda Belle
Penson, Charles
Rogers, Peggy J.
Shamwell, Joe
Turner, Bennie
Worshaim, Keith Eugene

Crawford
Hill, Sam

Crystal Springs
Newsome, Burnell

Diamondhead
Labat, Eric Martin

Drew
Gough, Walter C.
McDowell, Cleve
Tolliver, Ned, Jr.

Edwards
Lee, Aaron
Pritchard, Daron

Ellisville
Jones, Joni Lou

Fayette
Bingham, Arthur E.
Evers, James Charles
Gales, James
Guice, Leroy
Harris, Burnell
Hayes, Marion LeRoy

Friars Point
Washington, James Lee

Gautier
Davis, John Wesley, Sr.

Glendora
Thomas, Johnny B.

Goodman
Winston, Lillie Carolyn

Greenville
Cartlidge, Arthur J.
Goliday, Willie V.
Hall, Harold L.
Phillips, Earmia Jean
Pollard, Muriel Ransom

Greenwood
Cornwall, Shirley M.
Jordan, David Lee

Gulfport
Abston, Nathaniel, Jr.
Kelly, John Russell

Hattiesburg
Floyd, Vernon Clinton
Green, James

LeFlore, Larry
Owens, Charlene B.

Hazlehurst
Hill, Annette Tillman

Holly Springs
Beckley, David Lenard
Bell, Felix C.
Jones, Gwendolyn J.
Lampley, Paul Clarence
Malone, Amanda Ella
McMillan, William Asbury, Sr.
Reaves, Ginevera N.
Smith, Nellie J.
Totten, Bernice E.

Indianola
Matthews, David
Pollard, Muriel Ransom
Randle, Carver A.

Itta Bena
Brinkley, Norman, Jr.
Henderson, Robbye R.
Smith Nelson, Dorothy J.
Sutton, William Wallace
Ware, William L.

Jackson
Ayers-Elliott, Cindy
Ballard, Billy Ray
Banks, Fred L., Jr.
Bell, Jimmy
Bell, Leon
Bennett, Patricia W.
Bills, Johnny Bernard
Bland, Bobby Blue
Britton, Albert B., Jr.
Brocks-Shedd, Virgia Lee
Brown, R. Jess, Sr.
Byrd, Isaac, Jr.
Cameron, John E.
Cameron, Joseph A.
Cameron, Mary Evelyn
Catchings, Howard Douglas
Clark, Dave
Clay, Henry Carroll, Jr.
Cox, Warren E.
Dorsey, L. C.
Ellis, Tellis B., III
Foster, E. C.
Gates, Jimmie Earl
Gibbs, Robert Lewis
Hackett, Obra V.
Harris, William McKinley, Sr.
Harvey, Clarie Collins
Haynes, Worth Edward
Johnson, David E.
Johnson, James R.
Johnson, Linda Dianne
Johnson-Carson, Linda D.
Jones, Chester Ray
Jones, Mavis N.
Jones, Theodore Cornelius
Kyles, Sharron Faye
Luckett, Barbara J.
Lyons, James E., Sr.
Mack, Ally Faye
Macklin, Anderson D.
Magee, Sadie E.
Mayes, Clinton, Jr.
McLemore, Leslie Burl
Middleton, Richard Temple, III
Miller, Melvin Allen
Moreland-Young, Curtina
Myers, Lena Wright
Owens, George A.
Pennington, Jesse C.
Perkins, John M.
Polk, Richard A.
Presley, Oscar Glen
Rigsby, Esther Martin
Rundles, James Isaiah
Sanders, Lou Helen
Shepherd, Malcolm Thomas
Simon, Kenneth Bernard
Smith, George S.
Smith, Katrina Marita
Smith, Otrie
Smith, Robert
Smith, Robert L. T., Sr.
Stewart, James A., III
Stringfellow, Eric DeVaughn
Teeuwissen, Pieter
Thompson, Rosie L.
Thompson-Moore, Ann
Tingle, Lawrence May
Trottman, Charles Henry

Walker, Jimmie
Walker, Margaret Abigail
Washington, Earlene
Wheeler, Primus, Jr.
White, Frankie Walton
Williams, Robert L.
Wilson, Jimmy L.
Younger, Lewis T., Jr.

Jonestown
Shanks, James A.

Knoxville
Michael, Charlene Belton

Lamar
Allen, James Trinton

Laurel
Walker, Jimmy L.

Lexington
Bills, Johnny Bernard
Brown, Annie Gibson
Clark, Robert G.

Lorman
Bristow, Clinton, Jr.
Shepphard, Charles Bernard
Walker-Gibbs, Shirley Ann
Williams, Malvin A.
Williams, Robert Lee

Macon
Brooks, Richard Leonard

Mayersville
Blackwell, Unita

McComb
Ahllock, Theodore

Mendenhall
Weary, Dolphus

Meridian
Darden, Charles R.
Kornegay, Hobert
Little, Reuben N.
McMurtry-Reed, Lillie Eloise
Thompson, Imogene A.
Young, Charles Lemuel, Sr.

Metcalfe
Lindsey, S. L.

Mississippi State
Person, William Alfred
Williams, Carolyn Chandler

Morton
Johnson, Gloria Dean

Moss Point
Ellerby, William Mitchell, Sr.

Mound Bayou
Johnson, Hermon M., Sr.
Lucas, Earl S.
Moore, Thomas H.

Natchez
Edney, Norris Allen, I
Gray, James E.
Lewis, Charles Bady
West, George Ferdinand, Jr.

Oakland
Jones, Franklin D.

Oxford
Buchanan, Calvin D.
Chambliss, Alvin Odell, Jr.
Evans, Robert Oran
Jackson, Ava Nicola

Pattison
Yarbrough, Roosevelt

Pickens
Clarke, Henry Louis

Port Gibson
Brandon, Carl Ray
Davis, Frank
Doss, Evan, Jr.

McNeil, Ryan Darrell
Miller, Fred
Mitchell, Eugene
Mitchell, Martha Mallard
Montgomery, George Louis, Jr.
Moore, Jerald
Morrow, Jesse
Morrow, Laverne
Nicholson, Lawrence E.
Noble, John Pritchard
Norwood, Kimberly Jade
Nutt, Maurice Joseph
O'Hara, Leon P.
O'Neal, Leslie Cornelius
Orr, Clyde Hugh
Pace, Orlando
Peay, Isaac Charles, Sr.
Perine, Martha Levingston
Perry, Gerald
Phifer, Roman Zubinsky
Polk, George Douglas
Prather, Thomas L., Jr.
Price, David B., Jr.
Prophete, Beaumanoir
Randolph, Bernard Clyde
Reeves, Louise
Ricketts, David William
Riley, Eve Montgomery
Roberts, Michael V.
Russell, William P.
Sanford, Mark
Saulsberry, Charles R.
Scurlock, Michael
Shaw, Booker Thomas
Shaw, Charles A.
Shelton, O. L.
Shelton, Reuben Anderson
Small, Torrance
Smiley, William L.
Smith, Fredrick E.
Smith, Ozzie
Smith, Vernice Carlton
Smith, Wayman F., III
Smith, William Xavier
Stamps, Lynman A., Sr.
Steib, James T.
Stevens, Sharon A.
Stodghill, Ronald
Stodghill, William
Styles, Lorenzo
Taylor, Eugene Donaldson
Taylor, Theodore Roosevelt
Thomas, Benjamin
Thomas, J.T.
Thomas, Lillie
Tillman, Mary A. T.
Todd, Cynthia Jean
Toliver, Virginia F. Dowsing
Trottman, Alphonso
Troupe-Frye, Betty Jean
Ukabam, Innocent O.
Valley, Thomas James
Vaughn, William Smith
Vickers, Eric Erfan
Walker-Thoth, Daphne LaVera
Walton, Elbert Arthur, Jr.
Washington, Emery, Sr.
Watson, Robert C.
Wheeler, Betty McNeal
White, Gloria Waters
White, Nan E.
Whiten, Mark Anthony
Wigfall, Samuel E.
Wiley, Gerald Edward
Wilford, Harold C.
Williams, Brenda Paulette
Williams, Jay Omar
Williams, Robert L.
Wilson, Charles Stanley, Jr.
Wilson, Margaret Bush
Witherspoon, Fredda
Woods, Barbara McAlpin
Woods, Jane Gamble
Word, Parker Howell
Worth, Janice Lorraine
Wright, Frederick Bennie
Wright, Toby Lin
Young, Dmitri Dell
Young, Edith Mae
Young, Ira Mason

Velda Village
Williams, Lottie Mae

Warrensburg
Dunson, Carrie Lee

Wentzville
Berry, Chuck

MONTANA

Billings
Stone, Keith

Emigrant
Morsell, Frederick Albert

Helena
Duncan, Joan A.

NEBRASKA

Bellevue
Butts, Craig E.
Shoffner, Garnett Walter

Lincoln
Bowman, William Alton
Branker, Julian Michael
Crump, Arthel Eugene
Henderson, Gerald Eugene
Hodges, Clarence Eugene
McGee, Gloria Kesselle
McGee, Waddell
Newkirk, Gwendolyn
Parker, Keith Dwight
Peterson, Harry W.
Wallace, Ritchie Ray

Omaha
Atkins, Edna R.
Baker, Dave E.
Barnett, Alva P.
Belgrave, Oran
Cain, Herman
Coffey, Barbara J.
Crawford, Samuel D.
Foxall, Martha Jean
Gaines, Ray D.
Jackson, Denise
Johnson, William Henry
Lafontant, Julien J.
Lintz, Frank D. E.
Maye-Bryan, Mamie
Okhamafe, Imafedia
Pearson, Herman B.
Person, Earle G.
Robinson, Alcurtis
Ross, Martha Erwin
Secret, Philip E.
Shumpert, Terrance Darnell
Smith, Alonzo Nelson
Steans, Edith Elizabeth
Stewart, Freddie Mardrell
Thomas, Jim
Thompson, John Andrew
Wead, Rodney Sam
Welch, Ashton Wesley
Woods, George Washington

NEVADA

Carson City
Arberry, Morse, Jr.
Vance, Tommie Rowan

Henderson
Jackson, Kenya Love

Las Vegas
Bennett, Marion D.
Brigham, Freddie M.
Clarke, Angela Webb
Crawford, Cranford L., Jr.
Daniel, Simmie Childrey
Dennis, Karen
Fitzgerald, Roosevelt
Futch, Edward
Gates, Yvonne Atkinson
Guy, Addeliar Dell, III
Hatcher, Lizzie R.
Ita, Lawrence Eyo
Jarman, Patricia Morse
Jay, James M.
Kinnaird, Michael Leon
Knight, Gladys Maria
Langston, Esther J.
Lockette, Agnes Louise
McCarrell, Clark Gabriel, Jr.
McDaniels, Alfred F.
McMillan, James Bates
Miller, Norma Adele

Muhammad, M. Akbar
Newton, Jacqueline L.
Overstreet, Everett Louis
Pate, John W., Sr.
Patterson, Lloyd
Perry, Harold
Rayford, Lee Edward
Troutman, Porter Lee, Jr.
Williams, Joe
Williams, Nancy Ellen Webb

North Las Vegas
Rhodes, John K.
Robinson, William Earl
Tillmon, Joey
Willis, Frederic L.

Reno
Berry, Ondra Lamon
Harper, Harry Dandridge
Holloway, Jerry
Mack, Luther W., Jr.
Manning, Jane A.
Seals, R. Grant

Sparks
Hall, Jesse J.

NEW HAMPSHIRE

Barrington
Curwood, Sarah T.

Concord
Burkette, Tyrone

Hanover
Breeden, James Pleasant
Cook, William Wilburt
Hill, Errol Gaston
Lahr, Charles Dwight
Lewis, H. Ralph

Manchester
Towns, Maxine Yvonne

Portsmouth
Hilson, Arthur Lee

NEW JERSEY

Absecon
Andrews, Adolphus

Asbury Park
Harris, Lorenzo W.

Atco
Gault, Marian Holness
Matthew, Clifton, Jr.

Atlantic City
Alleyne, Edward D.
Clayton, Willie Burke, Jr.
Darkes, Leroy William
Griffin, Jean Thomas
LaSane, Joanna Emma
Milligan, Hugh D.
Norrell-Nance, Rosalind Elizabeth
Shabazz, Kaleem
Smith, Roger Leroy
Stewart, W. Douglas

Avenel
Greenleaf, Louis E.

Basking Ridge
Jackson, Georgina
Rhinehart, N. Pete

Bayonne
Cannon, Davita Louise Burgess
Hamill, Margaret Hudgens

Bayville
Tolbert, Edward T.

Bellmawr
Mosley, Elwood A.

Belmar
Roper, Grace Trott

Bergenfield
Welch, John L.

Berkeley Heights
Crawford, Curtis J.

Beverly
Kinniebrew, Robert Lee

Blackwood
McLaughlin, Jacquelyn Snow

Bloomfield
DeGeneste, Henry Irving

Brick
Owens, Judith Myoli

Bridgeton
Hursey, James Samuel

Bridgewater
Harris, Nathaniel C., Jr.

Budd Lake
Cornish, Jeannette Carter

Burlington
Akins, Allen Clinton
Arnold, David

Caldwell
Hill, Dianne

Camden
Bryant, Wayne R.
Catlin, Robert A.
Cogdell, D. Parthenia
Cottrol, Robert James
Dixon, Ruth F.
Edgerton, Brenda Evans
Fitzgerald, Carrie Eugenia
Freeman, Ronald J.
Gilliams, Tyrone
Horton, Stella Jean
Jones, Betty Harris
King, William L.
Mathes, James R.
Matthews, Jessie L.
Montgomery, Gregory B.
Poe, Alfred
Sabree, Clarice Salaam
Steptoe, Lamont Brown
Thompson, Aaron A.
Venable, Robert Charles

Chatham
Richardson, Charles Ronald

Cherry Hill
Austin, Ernest Augustus
Butler, Rebecca Batts
Foard, Frederick Carter
Grist, Ronald
Thornton, Otis
Vann, Gregory Alvin
Walker, Manuel Lorenzo
Waters, William David

Chesilhurst
Alwan, Mansour

Clementon
Sturdivant, Ralph A.

Cliffside Park
Gordon-Dillard, Joan Yvonne

Cliffwood
Drake, Pauline Lilie

Collingswood
Brimm, Charles Edwin

Cranbury
Caliman, Wayman Gazaway, Jr.

Cranford
Austin, Mary Jane
Mohamed, Gerald R., Jr.
Wolfe, Deborah Cannon Partridge

Dayton
Maynor, Vernon Perry

Deepwater
Cooper, John R.

Delran
Williams, Wilbur

East Brunswick
Johnson, Edward Elemuel
Wilkins, Charles O.

East Orange
Anderson, William A.
Bowser, Hamilton Victor, Sr.
Bowser, Robert Louis
Burr, Lawrence C.
Butler, Neil A.
Chastang, Mark J.
Clark, James N.
Cooke, Thomas H., Jr.
Cooper, Cardell
Craig, Claude Burgess
Daniels, Joseph
Edmonson, Bernie L.
Forbes, Calvin
Foster, Delores Jackson
Foster, James Hadlei
Francis, Joseph A.
Gibson, Althea
Giles, Althea B.
Giles, William R.
James, Henry Grady, III
Jarrett, Gerald I., Jr.
Jennings, Everett Joseph
Lambert, Joseph C.
Lapeyrolerie, Frank M.
Lewis, Aubrey C.
Peterson, Michelle Monica
Queen, Robert Calvin
Rasheed, Fred
Roberts, Paquita Hudson
Scott, Donnell
Thorburn, Carolyn Coles
Washington, James Edward
Wilson, Clarence Northon
Woodridge, Wilson Jack, Jr.

East Rutherford
Agnew, Raymond Mitchell, Jr.
Armstead, Jessie
Barber, Tiki
Brown, Roosevelt H., Jr.
Buckley, Marcus Wayne
Cage, Michael Jerome
Calloway, Christopher Fitzpatrick
Cassell, Samuel James
Cheeks, Maurice Edward
Crennel, Romeo A.
Cross, Howard
Douglas, Omar
Douglass, Maurice Gerrard
Ellsworth, Percy
Gatling, Chris Raymond
Gill, Kendall Cedric
Hamilton, Keith Lamarr
Hampton, Rodney
Harris, Lucious H., Jr.
Harris, Robert Lee
Hilliard, Ike
Holsey, Bernard
Jones, Cedric
Kittles, Kerry
Lee, Kurk
Levington, Clifford Eugene
Lewis, Thomas
Massey, Robert Lee
McDaniel, Xavier Maurice
Miller, Corey
Oben, Roman
Pegram, Erric Demont
Pierce, Aaron
Randolph, Thomas
Reed, Willis
Rivers, Len
Sparks, Phillippi Dwaine
Stone, Ronald
Strahan, Michael Anthony
Taylor, Lawrence Julius
Theus, Reggie
Toomer, Amani
Vaughn, David, III
Way, Charles Christopher
Wheatley, Tyrone
Williams, Jayson
Williams, Reggie
Wooten, Tito
Young, Rodney Menard

Edison
Avery, James S.
McGuire, Paul M., Jr.
Robinson, Walker Lee

Elizabeth
Coleman, Rudy B.
Ismial, Salaam Ibn
Walker, Tanya Rosetta

Englewood
Brown, Arnold E.
Drakeford, Jack
Emeka, Mauris L. P.
English, Whittie
Gallagher, Abisola Helen
Horne, Edwin Clay
Jenkins, Augustus G., Jr.
Mendes, Donna M.
Mosley, James Earl, Sr.
Polk, Gene-Ann
Taylor, Walter Scott
Treadwell, Fay Rene Lavern

Englewood Cliffs
Barrow, Denise
Draper, Everett T., Jr.
Moorhead, John Leslie

Ewing
Mays, Alfred Thomas
Tolliver, Lennie-Marie P.

Fairton
Gray, Keith A., Jr.

Farmingdale
Oates, Caleb E.

Flemington
Gonzalez, Cambell

Fort Lee
Gibbs, Karen Patricia

Fort Monmouth
Somerville, Patricia Dawn

Franklin Lakes
Haley, Earl Albert

Franklin Park
Phillips, Edward Martin

Freehold
Gumbs, Philip N.
Hughes, George Vincent

Glassboro
Clark, Douglas L.
Ellis, Calvin H., III
Harris, Dolores M.
James, Herman Delano
Moore, Oscar William, Jr.
Robinson, Randall S.
Sills, Marvin G.

Glen Ridge
Griffith, Mark Richard

Greendell
Fletcher, Sylvester James

Guttenberg
Johnson, Verdia Earline

Hackensack
Coleman, Chrisena Anne
Fournier, Collette V.
Givens, Joshua Edmond
Lavergneau, Rene L.

Haddonfield
Bruner, Van B., Jr.

Highland Park
Collier, Albert, III
Luckey, Irene

Hightstown
Quince, Kevin

Hoboken
Gomez, Daniel J.

Holmdel
Johnson, Anthony Michael

Irvington
Bost, Fred M.
Foreman, Lucille Elizabeth
Stanley, Craig A.
Williams, Junius W.

Iselin
Miles, Frank J. W.

Jersey City
Curson, Theodore
Foster, Delores Jackson
Gallagher, Abisola Helen
Harrold, Austin Leroy
Jackson, Bobby L.
Jones, Ben F.
Kafele, Baruti Kwame
Littlejohn, Joseph Phillip
McGhee, Samuel T.
Mitchell, Judson, Jr.
Myers, Walter Dean
Neals, Huerta C.
Patterson, Grace Limerick
Peoples, Sesser R.
Perkins, William O., Jr.
Queen Latifah
Slade, Phoebe J.
Tayari, Kabili
Tolentino, Shirley A.
Watson, Herman Doc
Watson, John Clifton
Wrice, Vincent J.

Kenilworth
Peterson, Michelle Monica

Lakewood
Brown, Clarence William
Younger, Celia Davis

Lawnside
Bryant, James W.
Cotton, Garner
Foote, Yvonne
Moore, Hilliard T., Sr.
Smith, Morris Leslie

Lawrenceville
Baskerville, Penelope Anne
Brooks, Carol Lorraine
Haqq, Khalida Ismail
Moorman, Holsey Alexander
Turner, Shirley

Liberty Corner
Williamson, Samuel R.

Lincroft
Jones, Floresta Deloris
Scott, Hosie L.

Linden
Young, Archie R., II

Little Silver
Davis, Susan D.

Madison
Richardson, Charles Ronald

Mahwah
Blackwell, Noble Virgil
Johnson, Joe

Maple Shade
Drew, James Brown

Maplewood
Anderson, Carlton Leon
Boyd, Robert Nathaniel, III
Boyer, Marcus Aurelius
Brooks, Rosemary Bittings
Campbell, Rogers Edward, III
Cooper, Daneen Ravenell
Holmes, Herbert
Phillips, Eric McLaren, Jr.
Robbins, Leonard
Roper, Richard Walter
Slaton, Gwendolyn C.
Spraggins, Stewart
Stone, Reese J., Jr.

Marlton
Lewis, W. Arthur
Thomas, Linda

Mays Landing
Andrews, Adolphus

Mendham
Wright, Edward Lucius

Middletown
Heath, Bertha Clara
James, Alexander, Jr.

Millburn
Weng, Peter A.

Monmouth Junction
Cherry, Theodore W.

Montclair
Allen-Noble, Rosie Elizabeth
Bolden, Theodore E.
Connor, Herman P.
Duncan, Stephan W.
Ewing, William James
Foreman, Lucille Elizabeth
Frye, William Sinclair
Griffith, John A.
Hamilton, John Joslyn, Jr.
McRae, Thomas W.
Newman, Geoffrey W.
Reid, Malissie Laverne
Sharp, Jean Marie
Walker, George T.
Wiley, Margaret Z. Richardson
Williams, Daniel Edwin

Moorestown
Armstead, Wilbert Edward, Jr.
Green, Joseph, Jr.
Waynes, Kathleen Yanes

Morganville
Wright, Ralph Edward

Morris Plains
Lawson, Bruce B.
Wyche, Vera Rowena

Morristown
Anderson, Ivy I.
Crump, Wilbert S.
Johnson, Juliana Cornish
Montgomery, Ethel Constance
Sandidge, Kanita Durice
Scavella, Michael Duane
Winston, Janet E.

Mount Holly
Matlock, Thomas, Jr.

Mount Laurel
Anderson, Kenneth Richard

Murray Hill
Mitchell, James Winfield

New Brunswick
Bethel, Leonard Leslie
Bolden, Frank Augustus
Carman, Edwin G.
Charles, Bernard L.
Davis, George B.
Epps, C. Roy
Gary, Melvin L.
Gibson, Donald B.
Giles, Waldron H.
Hammond, Debra Lauren
Hinds, Lennox S.
Hollar, Milton Conover
Khan, Ricardo M.
Lambert, Benjamin Franklin
Lane, Nancy L.
Lewis, David Levering
Luckey, Irene
Nelson, Gilbert L.
Nurse, Richard A.
Richardson, Wayne Michael
Rooks, Charles Shelby
Scott, Harold Russell, Jr.
Stevens, Maxwell McDew
Strickland, Dorothy S.
Stringer, C. Vivian
Williams, Chester Arthur
Williams-Harris, Diane Beatrice

New Providence
Coram, Willie Mae

New Rochelle
McCormack, Edward G.

Newark
Arbuckle, Ronald Lee, Sr.
Banks, Cecil J.
Bateman, Celeste
Baugh, Edna Y.
Beatty, Pearl
Bell, S. Aaron
Bettis, Anne Katherine
Branch, George
Brown, Simon F.
Brown, William H.
Clark, Joe Louis
Coleman, Claude M.
Contee, Carolyn Ann
Coram, Willie Mae
Cowan, James R.
Cuyjet, Aloysius Baxter
Daniels, A. Raiford
Davis, Adrianne
Davis, Harold Matthew
Davis, Matilda Laverne
Dean, Clara Russell
Evans, Gwendolyn
Felton, James Edward, Jr.
Flagg, E. Alma W.
Fraser, Rodger Alvin
Gibson, Kenneth Allen
Gilmore, Edwin
Gona, Ophelia Delaine
Grauer, Gladys Barker
Graves, Carole A.
Gunthorpe, Uriel Derrick
Hall, Lawrence H.
Hamilton, John Joslyn, Jr.
Harris, Earl
Harrison, James, Jr.
Hazelwood, Harry, Jr.
Hill, Mary Alice
Holloway, Harris M.
Hurt, Patricia
James, Sharpe
Jessie, Waymon Thomas
Johnson, Golden Elizabeth
Johnson, Joshua
Johnson, Robert L.
Johnson, Theodore Thomas
King, Marcellus, Jr.
Lenix-Hooker, Catherine Jeanette
Lester, Betty J.
Lewis, Henry
Lewis, Samuel, Jr.
Lister, David Alfred
Marius, Kenneth Anthony
Marshall, Carter Lee
Matthews, Vincent
Maynor, Kevin Elliott
Merritt, William T.
Mesa, Mayra L.
Muldrow, Catherine
Neizer, Meredith Ann
Owens, Ronald
Payne, William D.
Perry, John B.
Plummer, Milton
Porter, Ellis Nathaniel
Prezeau, Louis E.
Raines, Colden Douglas
Robinson, Alfreda P.
Robinson, Jeannette
Scott, Harold Russell, Jr.
Slaton, Gwendolyn C.
Stalks, Larrie W.
Stancell, Dolores Wilson Pegram
Story, Otis L, Sr.
Tate, Herbert H.
Tate, Herbert Holmes, Jr.
Taylor, Iris
Terrell, Stanley E.
Thomas, Janice Morrell
Thomas, Philip S.
Thurman, Marjorie Ellen
Tucker, Donald
Weeks, Renee Jones
White, Ella Flowers
Woodridge, Wilson Jack, Jr.
Woodruff, Constance Oneida
Young, Richard Edward, Jr.

Newton
Fletcher, Sylvester James

North Bergen
Mayo, Harry D., III

North Brunswick
Chapman, Alice Mariah
Sims, Harold Rudolph
Thomas, Ralph Albert

Nutley
Gaither, Richard A.

Ocean City
MacClane, Edward James
Taylor, Prince Albert, Jr.

Oceanport
Carter, Charles Michael

Orange
Brown, Robert Lee
Handwerk, Jana D.
Perkins, Lewis Bryant, Jr.

Palisade
McLeon, Nathaniel W.

Palmyra
Flournoy, Valerie Rose

Paramus
Hadden, Eddie Raynord

Park Ridge
Gaffney, Leslie Gale
Hawkins, Tramaine

Parsippany
Powell, Gayle Lett

Passaic
Samuels, Olive Constance

Paterson
Baker, Henry W., Sr.
Barnes, Martin G.
Benson, Gilbert
Brown, Chauncey I., Jr.
Collins, Elliott
Epps, Naomi Newby
Frazier, Shirley George
Garner, Mary E.
Gist, Jessie M. Gilbert
Harrington, Elaine Carolyn
Harris, Thomas C.
Hemby, Dorothy Jean
Hicks, William H.
Irving, Henry E., II
Kline, William M.
LaGarde, Frederick H.
Nickerson, Willie Curtis
Richardson, Louis M.
Rowe, Albert P.
Williams, Ethel Jean
Williams, Jane E.

Pennington
Khatib, Syed Malik

Penns Grove
Pope, Courtney A.
Williams, L. Colene

Piscataway
Essien, Francine
Gordon-Dillard, Joan Yvonne
Jessup, Marsha Edwina
Johnson, Edward Elemuel
Mohamed, Gerald R., Jr.
Nelson, Jonathan P.
Phillips, Edward Martin
Richardson, Otis Alexander
Wainwright, Oliver O'Connell

Plainfield
Bethel, Leonard Leslie
Bright, Herbert L., Sr.
Brown, Marshall Carson
Ganey, James Hobson
Harris, Jerome C., Jr.
Hillman, Brenda L.
Lattimore, Everett Carrigan
Satchell, Elizabeth
Smith, Stanley G.
White, Ella Flowers
Williamson, Ethel W.

Plainsboro
Young, Reginald B.

Ferguson, Derek Talmar
Galiber, Joseph L.
Gamble, Oscar Charles
Gates, Paul Edward
Gidron, Richard D.
Graham, Jo-Ann Clara
Grant, Claude DeWitt
Greene, Aurelia
Greene, Jerome Alexander
Harris, Robert Eugene Peyton
Haynes, George Edmund, Jr.
Hewlett, Dial, Jr.
Hicks, Edith A.
Hill, Marnesba D.
Humphrey, Sonnie
Jackson, Karl Don
James, Gregory Creed
Jeter, Derek
Johnson, Charles Ronald, Sr.
Johnson, Patricia L.
Johnson, Robert T.
Jordan, Marilyn E.
Lacey, Archie L.
Lambert, Samuel Fredrick
Lee, Mildred Kimble
Levister, Wendell P.
Lewis, William Sylvester
Lloyd, George Lussington
Mariel, Serafin
Maynard, Edward Samuel
McGee, Hansel Leslie
Minter, Thomas Kendall
Morgan-Cato, Charlotte Theresa
Moses, Johnnie, Jr.
Palmer, Edward
Payne, Lisa R.
Pugh, Clementine A.
Raines, Timothy
Randolph, Willie Larry, Jr.
Reid, Desiree Charese
Reid, Roberto Elliott
Richardson, Anthony W.
Robinson, William James
Ross, Regina D.
Samuels, Leslie Eugene
Shepherd, Saundra Dianne
Simpson, Samuel G.
Small, Kenneth Lester
Springer, Lloyd Livingstone
Strawberry, Darryl
Taylor, Sandra Elaine
Terrell, Francis D'Arcy
Thompson, Sister Francesca
Thompson, Oswald
Valdes, Laura
Vick, Harold E.
Warner, Ivan
Watson, Robert Jose
White, William H.
Williams, Bernie
Williams, Patricia Anne
Wilson, Kim Adair
Wood, Courtney B.
Zambrana, Rafael

Bronxville
Kenan, Randall G.

Brooklyn
Abdul-Malik, Ahmed H.
Abdul-Malik, Ibrahim
Abrahams, Andrew Wordsworth
Addei, Arthella Harris
al-Hafeez, Humza
Allen, Percy, II
Anderson, Madeline
Anthony, Jeffrey Conrad
Atkins, Thomas Irving
Ausby, Ellsworth Augustus
Banks, Ellen
Barnett, Lorna
Barnett, Teddy
Battle, Turner Charles, III
Behrmann, Serge T.
Bell, Travers J., Sr.
Benjamin, Monica G.
Bical, Sam
Biddle, Stanton F.
Bloomfield, Randall D.
Blow, Sarah Parsons
Bostic, Dorothy
Bowman, Joseph E., Jr.
Boyce, John G.
Braithwaite, Mark Winston
Bramwell, Henry
Brown, Lawrence S., Jr.
Bryant-Mitchell, Ruth Harriet
Callender, Wilfred A.
Carter, Betty

Carter, Zachary Warren
Cave, Claude Bertrand
Cave, Vernal G.
Champion, Tempii Bridgene
Chisholm, Clarence Edward
Corbie, Leo A.
Coward, Onida Lavoneia
Crew, Rudolph F.
Criner, Clyde
Daughtry, Herbert Daniel
Davidson, Arthur Turner
Dennis, Rodney Howard
Douglass, Lewis Lloyd
Dummett, Jocelyn Angela
Eastmond, Joan Marcella
Edmond, Alfred Adam, Jr.
Edwards, Audrey Marie
Edwards, Bessie Regina
Edwards, Thomas Oliver
Esposito, Giancarlo
Evans-Tranumn, Shelia
Faulkner, Carolyn D.
Faulkner, Geanie
Fierce, Milfred C.
Flateau, John
Ford, Robert Benjamin, Jr.
Forster, Cecil R.
Francois, Theodore Victor
French, Joseph Henry
Gabriel, Benjamin Moses
Galamison, Milton A.
Gall, Lenore Rosalie
Galvin, Emma Corinne
Gardner, Jackie Randolph
Glee, George, Jr.
Goode, James Edward
Goodwin, Norma J.
Greaves, McLean
Green, Thomas L., Sr.
Greene, Charles Rodgers
Greene, Clifton S.
Hall, L. Priscilla
Hicks, Daisy C.
Hicks, Willie Lee
Higgins, Chester Archer, Jr.
Hill, Richard Nathaniel
Hobson, Charles Blagrove
Holden, Dorothy M.
Howard, Vera Gouke
Howell, Amaziah, III
Inniss, Charles Evans
Isaac, Brian Wayne
Jackson, Emory Napoleon
Jackson, Randolph
JeanBaptiste, Carl S.
John, Daymond
Johnson, Luther Mason, Jr.
Johnson, Michael Anthony
Johnson, Miriam B.
Johnson, Norman B.
Johnson, Rita Falkener
Johnson, Robert H.
Johnson, Sterling
Johnson, Vincent L.
Jones, Hortense
Jones, Louis Clayton
Jones, Thomas Russell
Jones, Vann Kinckle
Jones, William A., Jr.
Kernisant, Lesly
King, Ruth Allen
King, Shaka C.
Lawrence, Charles B.
Lee, Joie
Lee, William James Edwards, III
Leon, Tania J.
Lewis, Woodrow
Lindo, J. Trevor
Mahoney, Keith Weston
Majete, Clayton Aaron
Marshall, Calvin Bromley, III
Marshall, Warren
Martin, George Alexander, Jr.
Maxwell, Marcella J.
McFadden, Frederick C., Jr.
McLaughlin, Andree Nicola
McMichael, Earlene Clarisse
Meade, William F.
Mercer, Valerie June
Merideth, Charles Waymond
Miles, Frederick Augustus
Millett, Knolly E.
Mister, Melvin Anthony
Mitchell, Roderick Bernard
Monteiro, Thomas
Monteverdi, Mark Victor
Moore, Colin A.
Moore, Jacob
Morancie, Horace L.

Morris, Celeste
Naylor, Gloria
Nelson-Holgate, Gail Evangelyn
Nor, Genghis
Omolade, Barbara
Owens, Victor Allen
Page, Willie F.
Perry, Richard
Persaud, Inder
Phillips, Dilcia R.
Pierre-Louis, Constant
Primm, Beny Jene
Pugh, Robert William, Sr.
Ramirez, Gilbert
Ratcliff, Wesley D.
Reid-McQueen, Lynne Marguerite
Rivers, Louis
Robinson, Clarence G.
Robinson, Maude Eloise
Seymore, Stanley
Shabazz, Betty
Shannon, Sylvester Lorenzo
Simmons, Esmeralda
Slade, Walter R., Jr.
Smith, Louis
Smith Freeman, Patricia M.
Sneed, Gregory J.
Spradley, Frank Sanford
Stanislaus, Gregory K.
Stephens, Brooke Marilyn
Steptoe, John Lewis
Sterling, Charles A.
Stroud, Milton
Swiggett, Ernest L.
Thomas, Lloyd A.
Thomas, Lucille Cole
Thompson, Leroy B.
Thompson, Mavis Sarah
Thompson, Theodis
Thompson, William Coleridge
Traylor, Rudolph A.
Trent, Richard Darrell
Umolu, Mary Harden
Vernon, Francine M.
Wilks, James Lee
William, Thompson E.
Williams, Joseph B.
Williams, William Thomas
Wright, Geoffrey
Zambrana, Rafael

Buffalo
Acker, Daniel R.
Adams-Dudley, Lilly Annette
Amin, Karima
Arthur, George Kenneth
Baugh, Florence Ellen
Bennett, William Donald
Brooks, Tilford Uthratese
Brown, Byron William
Charles, Roderick Edward
Cochran, S. Thomas
Coles, Robert Traynham
Curtin, John T.
Davis, Twilus
De Veaux, Alexis
Diji, Augustine Ebun
Durand, Henry J., Jr.
Easley, Brenda Vietta
Echols, David Lorimer
Eve, Arthur O.
Fleming, Carolyn
Fordham, Monroe
Glover, Diana M.
Granger, Carl Victor
Grant Bishop, Ellen Elizabeth
Harrison, Carol L.
Holley, Sharon Yvonne
Humes, Emanuel I., Sr.
Hunter, Archie Louis
Jones, Leeland Newton, Jr.
Kendrick, Joy A.
Kenyatta, Mary
Kenyatta, Muhammad Isaiah
Key, Jesse
Kirkland, Theodore
Lawrence, Edward
Lawson, Cassell Avon
Lewis, Ora Lee
McDaniel, James Berkley, Jr.
McGrier, Jerry, Sr.
McRae, Ronald Edward
Merritt, Joseph, Jr.
Neal, Brenda Jean
Nickson, Sheila Joan
Noles, Eva M.
Palmer, Robert L., II
Peterson, Lorna Ingrid
Price, Alfred Douglas

Randolph, Toni Regina
Robinson, Barry Lane
Robinson, Edith
Sarmiento, Shirley Jean
Scales-Trent, Judy
Sconiers, Rose H.
Scott, Hugh B.
Sims, Barbara M.
Sims, William
Smith, Bennett W., Sr.
Taylor, Henry Louis, Jr.
Tisdale, Celes
Williams, Lenore

Cambria Heights
Baniteau, Joseph
Benjamin, Arthur, Jr.
Boyd-Foy, Mary Louise
Ford, Robert Benjamin, Jr.
Reide, Saint Clair Eugene, Jr.
Southern, Eileen Jackson
Southern, Joseph
Waldon, Alton Ronald, Jr.

Canaan
Bell, James Milton

Canton
Williams, Terri L.

Carle Place
Mitchell, Carlton S.

Carthage
Jordan, John Wesley

Central Islip
Fillyaw, Leonard David
McCalla, Erwin Stanley

Chappaqua
Sobers, Waynett A., Jr.

Chazy
Madison, Jacqueline Edwina

Clifton Park
Ballard, Allen Butler, Jr.
Bedell, Frederick Delano

Clinton
Johnson, C. Christine

Cooperstown
Bell, Cool Papa
Wharton, Dolores D.

Copiague
Hibbert, Dorothy Lasalle

Coram
Byers, Marianne
Green, Mildred A.

Corning
Baity, Gail Owens
Derbigny, Rhoda L.
Watkins, Robert Charles
Wheat, James Weldon, Jr.

Cortland
Newkirk, Thomas H.
Smith, Keith Dryden, Jr.
Williams, Carolyn Ruth Armstrong

Cortlandt Manor
Carter, George E.
Jones, Yvonne Harris

Coxsockie
McDowell, Samuel E.

Croton On Hudson
Bell, James Milton
Van Liew, Donald H.
Wood, William L., Jr.

Croton on Hudson
Harris, Michele Roles

DeWitt
Young, Alfred
Young, Ronald R.

Delmar
Thornton, Maurice

Dix Hills
Cave, Alfred Earl
Walker, Wesley Darcel

Dobbs Ferry
Ephraim, Charlesworth W.
Tarter, Roger Powell, M.D.

Douglaston
Jenkins, Herman Lee

East Elmhurst
Archer, Eva P.
Booth, William H.
Holloman, John L. S., Jr.
Jackson, Andrew Preston
Kaiser, Ernest Daniel
Lopez, Mary Gardner
Preston, Edward Lee

East Greenbush
Brown, Lester J.

East Hampton
Daly, Marie Maynard

East Meadow
Jonas, Ernesto A.

East Patchogue
Washington, Herman A., Jr.

Elmhurst
Kelly, Ernece Beverly

Elmira
McGee, JoAnn
Washington, Edith May Faulkner

Elmont
Chrichlow, Livingston L.
Chrichlow, Mary L.
Cobbs, Winston H. B., Jr.
Mereday, Richard F.

Elmsford
Dodds, R. Harcourt
Jones, Yvonne De Marr
King, Charles Abraham
Ross, Winston A.

Fairport
Hannah, Mosie R.
Jackson, Fred H., Jr.
Lechebo, Semie

Far Rockaway
Maple, Goldie M.

Farmingdale
Bellinger, Harold
Blake, Carlton Hugh
Palmer, Noel
Williams, Patricia Hill

Floral Park
Argrette, Joseph
Callender, Carl O.

Flushing
Andrews, Benny
Banks, Haywood Elliott
Burns, W. Haywood
Byam, Milton S.
Gilkey, Bernard
Huskey, Butch
Jenkins, Herman Lee
McCraw, Tom
McRae, Brian Wesley
Thompson, Ryan Orlando
Wilson, Mookie

Franklin Square
Blackwell, Milford

Freeport
Alers, Rochelle
Jenkins, Elizabeth Ameta
Lee, Stratton Creighton
Smith, Hale
Watson, Denton L.
Wilder, Mary A. H.

Fresh Meadows
Starke, Catherine Juanita

Garden City
Campbell, Emmett Earle
Dawson, Lumell Herbert
Harrison, Beverly E.
James, Marquita L.
Jenkins, Kenneth Vincent
Lewis, Lloyd Alexander, Jr.
Mills, Hughie E.
Roberson, Gloria Grant
Wilson, Hugh A.
Young, Perry H.

Geneva
Wade, George A.

Germantown
Rollins, Walter Theodore

Glen Cove
Carroll, Robert F.

Glens Falls
Thomas, Roy L.

Great Neck
Brown, Roy Hershel
Guilmenot, Richard Arthur, III

Griffiss A F B
Thorpe, Herbert Clifton

Hamilton
Bryce-Laporte, Roy Simon

Hartsdale
Early, Robert S.
Frelow, Robert Dean
Jackson, Luther Porter, Jr.
Jackson, Warren Garrison
Jacob, John Edward

Hastings On Hudson
Adams, Alger LeRoy

Hauppauge
Miller, Lawrence A., Jr.

Helmuth
DuBois, Asa Stephen

Hempstead
Adams, Robert Hugo
Anderson, Richard Darnoll
Andrews, Phillip
Austin, Raymond
Bagley, Gregory P.
Baxter, Frederick Denard
Bonaparte, Lois Ann
Boone, Clinton Caldwell
Brown, Corwin Alan
Brown, Denise Sharon
Brown, Joyce
Burns, Lamont
Coleman, Marcus
Cross, Betty Jean
Day, Terry
Douglas, Hugh
Evans, Donald Lee
Evans, William C.
Farrior, James
Ferguson, Jason
Foskey, Carnell T.
Glenn, Aaron DeVon
Gordon, Dwayne
Graham, Jeff Todd
Green, Victor Bernard
Hagood, Jay
Hamilton, Bobby
Harris, James
Hayes, Chris
Haynes, Ulric St. Clair, Jr.
Henderson, Jerome Virgil
Hunter, Deanna Lorraine
Johnson, Keyshawn
Johnson, Leon
Johnson, Pepper
Jones, Marvin Maurice
Lewis, Lloyd Alexander, Jr.
Lewis, Mo
Logan, Ernest Edward
Lott, Ronnie
Marshall, Anthony Dewayne
Marshall, Calvin Bromley, III
Marshall, Leonard
McNeil, Freeman
Mickens, Ray
Murrell, Adrian Bryan
Myers, L. Leonard

Neal, Lorenzo LaVon
Phears, William D.
Rainsford, Greta M.
Roberts, William Harold
Robinson, Beverly Jean
Samuel, Lois S.
Smith, Otis
Sowell, Jerald
Swinney, T. Lewis
Terry, Rick
Thomas, Blair
Thomas, Eric Jason
Thompson, Eugene Edward
Van Dyke, Alex
Ward, Dedric
White, William J.
Wood, Vivian Frances

Henrietta
Byas, Thomas Haywood

Hicksville
Isaac, Brian Wayne
Lee, Chandler Bancroft
Young, Ruth L.

Hollis
Current, Gloster Bryant

Hopewell Junction
Johnson, Andrew

Huntington
Howard, Susan E.

Huntington Station
Boozer, Emerson, Jr.

Hyde Park
Sims, Constance Arlette

Islip Terrace
Jerome, Joseph D.

Ithaca
Dalton, Raymond Andrew
Harris, Robert L., Jr.
Hart, Edward E.
Hill, Sandra Patricia
Lorthridge, James E.
McClane, Kenneth Anderson, Jr.
Miller, Richard Charles
Smith, Keith Dryden, Jr.
Sogah, Dotsevi Y.
Weissinger, Thomas, Sr.

Jamaica
Aiken, William
Allen, Gloria Marie
Bailey, Lawrence R., Sr.
Bell, Maud Melinda
Bernard, Canute Clive
Brown, Sherman L.
Bryan, David Everett, Jr.
Burgie, Irving Louis
Claytor, Charles E.
Cook, Ladda Banks
Copeland, Ray
Cormier, Lawrence J.
Couche, Ruby S.
Cright, Lotess Priestley
Dockett, Alfred B.
Douglass, Melvin Isadore
Dye, Luther V.
Edwards, Thomas Oliver
Ellis, Ernest W.
Faust, Naomi Flowe
Flake, Floyd H.
Flatts, Barbara Ann
Fox, Thomas E., Jr.
Frazier, Adolphus Cornelious
Gaskin, Leonard O.
Graham, Helen W.
Greene, Beverly A.
Haynes, Eleanor Louise
Hill, Arthur Burit
Holder, Reuben D.
Holmes, Carl
Jenkins, Cynthia
Johnson, Taylor Herbert
Kelly, Florida L.
Kelly, James Clement
Kidd, Charles C., Sr.
Ledee, Robert
Lucas-Edwards, Florence V.
Marshall, Lewis West, Jr.
McCarthy, Fred
Meacham, Henry W.

Mitchell, Loften
Moore, Emanuel A.
Moore, Jacob
Moore, Richard
Naphtali, Ashirah Sholomis
Norris, Charles L., Sr.
Pierce, Cynthia Straker
Ramsey, Walter S.
Ray, Jacqueline Walker
Reid, Edith C.
Reide, Saint Clair Eugene, Jr.
Richardson, Ernest A.
Riley, Beryl Elise
Rowe, Richard L.
Satterfield, Patricia Polson
Shields, Del Pierce
Spradley, Frank Sanford
Taylor, Janice A.
Thompson, Frank L.
Whitehead, James T., Jr.
Williams, Ira Lee
Williams, Richard Lenwood

Jamestown
McDonald, Anita Dunlop
Peterson, Clarence Josephus
Taylor, Vivian A.
Thompson, Geraldine

Jeffersonville
Graham, Mariah

Jericho
Fonrose, Harold Anthony

Johnson City
Porter, Michael Anthony

Kew Gardens
Lewis, Daniel

Kings Point
Jenkins, Emmanuel Lee

Kingston
Ione, Carole
Marquez, Camilo Raoul
Smith-Taylor, Donna Lyn

Latham
Burke, Rosetta

Lawrence
Davis, Brownie W.

Long Island City
Anderson, Avis Olivia
Bludson-Francis, Vernett Michelle
Bowen, Raymond C.
Fax, Elton C.
Harris, J. Robert, II
Holmes, Cloyd James
Hood, Robert E.
Washington, Herman A., Jr.

Lynbrook
Slater, Phyllis Hill

Manhasset
Dreyfuss, Joel P.

Melville
Bell, Dennis Philip
Haynes, Ulric St. Clair, Jr.
Howard, Susan E.
Jackson, Earl C.
Payne, Leslie
Watkins, Mary Frances
Weston, Martin V.

Merrick
Miller, Anthony Glenn

Middletown
Best, William Andrew
Sands, Mary Alice

Mineola
Robbins, Alfred S.
Service, Russell Newton

Mohegan Lake
Jones, Yvonne Harris

Monroe
Maynard, Edward Samuel

Monticello
Rea, Joseph

Mount Kisco
Quinn, Adrian

Mount Vernon
Bell, S. Aaron
Bozeman, Bruce L.
Cleveland, Hattye M.
Dungie, Ruth Spigner
George, Constance P.
Holliday-Hayes, Wilhelmina Evelyn
Moses, MacDonald
Robinson, Carol W.
Robinson, Melvin P.
Scott, Jean Sampson
Tarter, James H., Sr.
Wright, Cecil

Mt Vernon
Brown, Beatrice S.

Nanuet
Love, Darlene

New City
Duffoo, Frantz Michel

New Hampton
Sands, George M.

New Hyde Park
Skeene, Linell De-Silva

New Paltz
Grant, James
Williams-Myers, Albert J.

New Rochelle
Boddie, Daniel W.
Boyce, William M.
Branch, William Blackwell
Brooks, Norman Leon
Davis, Ossie
Edley, Christopher F., Sr.
Edwards, Theodore Unaldo
Goulbourne, Donald Samuel, Jr.
Hite, Nancy Ursula
Quash, Rhonda

New York
Aaliyah
Abbott, Gregory
Abdul, Raoul
Abdus-Salaam, Sheila
Adair, Robert A.
Adams, Bennie
Adams, Clarence Lancelot, Jr.
Adams, Edward Robert
Adams, Marie Elizabeth
Adams, Oleta
Addams, Robert David
Adderley, Nathaniel
Addison, Adele
Adolph, Gerald Stephen
Ailey, Alvin
Alexander, Estella Conwill
Ali, Rashied
Allen, Alexander J.
Allen, Betty
Allen, Clyde Cecil
Allen, Marcus
Allen, William Oscar
Alligood, Douglass Lacy
Alston, Casco, Jr.
Alston, James L.
Alveranga, Glanvin L.
Anderson, Amelia Veronica
Anderson, Harold A.
Anderson, Helen Louise
Andrews, Raymond
Applewhaite, Leon B.
Armstrong, Robb
Ashhurst, Carmen
Austin, Joyce Phillips
Avant, Clarence
Axtell, Roger E.
Ayers, Roy
Backus, Bradley
Badu, Erykah
Bailey, Adrienne Yvonne
Bailey, Pearl
Bain, Linda Valerie
Baker, Gwendolyn Calvert
Baldwin, George R.
Baldwin, James

Ballard, Bruce Laine
Ballard, Harold Stanley
Balmer, Horace Dalton, Sr.
Banks, Carlton Luther
Banks, Jeffrey
Bankston, Archie M.
Baraka, Ras
Barboza, Anthony
Bargonetti, Jill
Barnes, Joseph Nathan
Barnes, N. Kurt
Barr, LeRoy
Barragan, Ricardo M.
Barzey, Raymond Clifford, II
Bassett, Angela
Batten, Tony
Battle, Kathleen
Beal, Bernard
Beckford, Tyson
Beckham, Edgar Frederick
Bell, Derrick Albert, Jr.
Bell, Raleigh Berton
Bell, Travers J., Jr.
Bell, Yvonne Lola
Bellamy, Bill
Benjamin, Ronald
Bennett, Courtney Ajaye
Bennett, Debra Quinette
Benoit, Edith B.
Berry, Philip Alfonso
Billingsley, Ray C.
Billops, Camille J.
Bisamunyu, Jeanette
Blackman, Rolando Antonio
Blair, George Ellis, Jr.
Blakey, Art
Blaylock, Ronald
Blayton-Taylor, Betty
Bogle, Donald
Bolden, J. Taber, III
Bolling, Deborah A.
Bond, George Clement
Bond, James Max, Jr.
Bone, Winston S.
Bonner, Anthony
Booker, James E.
Boston, Gretha
Boulware, Fay D.
Bowen, Emma L.
Bowman, Joseph E., Jr.
Boyce, Joseph Nelson
Boyd-Foy, Mary Louise
Bracey, William Rubin
Bradford, Benona Hamlin
Bradford, Gary C.
Bradford, Martina Lewis
Bradley, Edward R.
Bradley, Jeffrey
Bragg, Joseph L.
Bramwell, Patricia Ann
Brandy
Braugher, Andre
Braxton, Toni
Bray, Rosemary
Bridgewater, Dee Dee
Brisbane, Samuel Chester
Brokaw, Carol Ann
Brothers, Tony
Brown, A. David
Brown, Bertrand James
Brown, Brian A.
Brown, Carolyn
Brown, Clifton George
Brown, Courtney Coleridge
Brown, Foxy
Brown, Harriett Baltimore
Brown, James
Brown, Lloyd Louis
Brown, Renee
Brown, Roscoe C., Jr.
Brown, Tony
Bryan, Flize A.
Bryant, Franklyn
Bryant-Reid, Johanne
Buckley, Gail Lumet
Bulger, Lucille O.
Burley, Dale S.
Burns, Jeff, Jr.
Burns, Khephra
Busby, Everett C.
Busta Rhymes
Butler, Melba
Butler, Michael E.
Butts, Calvin Otis, III
Butts, Hugh F.
Byrd, Janell
Byrd, Joan Eda
Cadogan, Marjorie A.
Caldwell, Benjamin

Callender, Leroy R.
Cameron, Randolph W.
Campbell, Bebe Moore
Campbell, Dick C.
Campbell, George, Jr.
Campbell, Mary Schmidt
Campbell, Thomas W.
Camper, Diane G.
Cannon, George Dows
Cantarella, Marcia Y.
Capers, Eliza Virginia
Capers, James
Carey, Mariah
Carey, Patricia M.
Carlton, Pamela Gean
Carmichael, Stokely
Carreker, William, Jr.
Carroll, Edward Major
Carroll, Harry Milton
Carroll, Robert F.
Carter, Nanette Carolyn
Carter, Robert Lee
Cartey, Wilfred G. O.
Cartwright, Marguerite Dorsey
Cary, Lorene
Casey, Frank Leslie
Cave, Herbert G.
Champion, Tempii Bridgene
Chapman, Alice Mariah
Charity, Lawrence Everett
Chenault, Kenneth
Cherot, Nicholas Maurice
Chideya, Farai Nduu
Childress, Alice
Childs, Chris
Childs, Faith
Chisholm, June Faye
Chisholm, Samuel Jackson
Christian, Spencer
Chuck D
Chunn, Jay Carrington, II
Clark, James Irving, Jr.
Clark, Mamie Phipps
Clark, Patricia Ann
Clark, Patrick
Clark, Rosalind K.
Clark, Shirley Lorraine
Clark, Vincent W.
Clarke, John Henrik
Clarke, Richard V.
Clarke, Thomas P.
Clash, Kevin
Clemendor, Anthony Arnold
Clements, Emmett
Clemons, Alois Ricardo
Cobb, Charles E.
Cogsville, Donald J.
Coleman, Columbus E., Jr.
Coleman, George Edward
Coleman, Leonard
Coleman, Ornette
Coleman Morris, Valerie
  Dickerson
Collins, Theodicia Deborah
Combs, Sean J.
Cone, James H.
Conwill, Kinshasha
Cook, Beverly L.
Coolio
Coombs, Orde
Cooper, J. California
Cooper, Merrill Pittman
Cooper, Winston Lawrence
Cooper-Farrow, Valerie
Cooper-Gilstrap, Jocelyn
Corbin, Sean
Cornwell, W. Don
Cornwell, William David
Corrin, Malcolm L.
Cortez, Jayne
Cortor, Eldzier
Cose, Ellis
Counts, Allen
Cousin, Philip R.
Cowell, Catherine
Coye, Dena E.
Craig-Rudd, Joan
Crawford, Dan
Crider, Edward S., III
Cross, June Victoria
Cummings, Aeon L.
Cummings, Pat
Curry, William Thomas
Curtis, James L.
Curvin, Robert
Dailey, Thelma
Dais, Larry
Dale, Clamma Churita
Daniels, Ron D.

Dauway, Lois McCullough
Davis, Clarence A.
Davis, Darwin N.
Davis, Earl S.
Davis, Gene A.
Davis, James Edgar
Davis, John Aubrey
Davis, Lance Roosevelt
Davis, Lisa E.
Davis, Preston A., Jr.
Davis, Ronald R.
Davis, Sammy, Jr.
Davis, Willie James
Dawkins, Stan Barrington Bancroft
Day, William Charles, Jr.
Dean, Diane D.
De Fossett, William K.
DeGeneste, Henry Irving
de Jongh, James Laurence
deMille, Valerie Cecilia
Dennis, Walter Decoster
Derricotte, C. Bruce
DeSouza, Ronald Kent
Dickens, Lloyd Everett
Dickerson, Ralph
Dinkins, David N.
Disher, Spencer C., III
Dixon, John Frederick
Dixon-Brown, Totlee
Doby, Lawrence Eugene, Sr.
Dodson, Howard, Jr.
Donegan, Dorothy
Dorsey, Herman Sherwood, Jr.
Dottin, Robert Philip
Dowdell, Kevin Crawford
Downing, Will
Du Bois, Nelson S. D'Andrea, Jr.
Ducksworth, Marilyn Jacoby
Dudley, Edward R.
Dukes, Hazel Nell
Dukes, Walter L.
Dumpson, James R.
Durant, Karen
Durant-Paige, Beverly
Dutton, Marie
Dyson, Ronnie
Eagle, Arnold Elliott
Eastman, Eleanor Corinna
Easton, Richard James
Eccles, Peter Wilson
Eckstine, Ed
Eddings, Cynthia
Edmond, Alfred Adam, Jr.
Edmonds, Kenneth
Edwards, David H., Jr.
Edwards, Delores A.
Edwards, Dennis, Jr.
Edwards, George R.
Edwards, Leo Derek
Eikerenkoetter, Frederick J., II
Elliott, Joy
Ellison, Ralph Waldo
Emanuel, James Andrew
English, Alex
Erskine, Kenneth F.
Esposito, Giancarlo
Essoka, Gloria Corzen
Estes, Simon Lamont
Evans, Albert
Evans, Charlotte A.
Evans, Faith
Evans, Hugh
Evans-Tranumn, Shelia
Ewing, Patrick Aloysius
Faison, Frankie
Farr, Llewellyn Goldstone
Farrell, Samuel D.
Farrow, Sallie A.
Faulkner, Geanie
Fay, Toni G.
Ferguson, Renee
Finley, Ewell W.
Fischer, Lisa
Fischer, William S.
Flack, Roberta
Flatts, Barbara Ann
Fleming, Alicia DeLaMothe
Flemming, Charles Stephen
Fletcher, Robert E.
Flood, Eugene, Jr.
Ford, Conrad A.
Ford, Kisha
Ford, Wallace L., II
Forde, Fraser Philip, Jr.
Fornay, Alfred R., Jr.
Foster, Frances Helen
Foster, Gloria
Fox, Everett V.
Fox, Thomas E., Jr.

Fraser, Jean Ethel
Frazier, Audrey Lee
Frazier, Ramona Yancey
Frazier, Walt
Freeman, Harold P.
French, Howard W.
Fugett, Jean S., Jr.
Fuller, Charles
Fuller, Curtis D.
Fuller, Jack Lewis
Fulton, Robert Henry
Gaither, James W., Jr.
Gardner, Warren E., Jr.
Garland, Phyllis T.
Garner, Melvin C.
Garner, Nathan Warren
Garnett, Ronald Leon
Garrett, Melvin Alboy
Gaston, Arnett W.
Gates, Clifford E., Jr.
Gates, Jacquelyn Burch
Gatling, Patricia Lynn
Gayle, Addison, Jr.
Gayle-Thompson, Delores J.
Gee, Al
Ghent, Henri Hermann
Gibbes, Emily V.
Gibson, Nell Braxton
Gibson, Robert
Giles, Nancy
Gill, Jacqueline A.
Gill, Johnny
Gillespie, Dizzy
Gillespie, Marcia A.
Glenn, Wynola
Glover, Kenneth Elijah
Goines, Leonard
Golden, Marita
Gomez, Jewelle L.
Goode, Victor M.
Goodwin, Stephen Robert
Gordon, Bruce S.
Gordon, Carl Rufus
Gordon, Helen A.
Gordone, Charles Edward
Gourdine, Simon Peter
Govan, Reginald C.
Grant, Darlene Camille
Grantham, Charles
Graves, Barbara E.
Graves, Earl G.
Graves, Earl G., Jr.
Graves, Johnny
Graves, Valerie Jo
Gray, Ronald A.
Gray-Morgan, LaRuth H.
Grayson, Stanley Edward
Greaves, William
Green, Dennis O.
Greene, Gabrielle Elise
Greene, Gregory A.
Greene, John Sullivan
Greene, Richard T.
Greer, Baunita
Gregg, Eric
Grier, Rosey
Griffith, Mark Richard
Griffiths, Errol D.
Grigsby, David P.
Grillo, Luis
Guillebeaux, Tamara Elise
Guitano, Anton W.
Gumbel, Bryant Charles
Gumbel, Greg
Guy, Jasmine
Guy, Rosa Cuthbert
Habersham-Parnell, Jeanne
Hackney, L. Camille
Haddon, James Francis
Hadnott, Bennie L.
Haizlip, Ellis Benjamin
Hale, Clara McBride
Hale, Lorraine
Hall, Arsenio
Halliburton, Christopher
Hamilton, Charles Vernon
Hampton, Kym
Handwerk, Jana D.
Hankin, Noel Newton
Hanna, Roland
Hardison, Ruth Inge
Hardy, Michael A.
Harper, Conrad Kenneth
Harrell, Andre
Harris, Francis C.
Harris, John Clifton
Harris, Joseph R.
Harris, Margaret R.
Harrison, Shirley Dindy

Harty, Belford Donald, Jr.
Harvey, Steve
Harvey-Salaam, Dyane Michelle
Harvin, Alvin
Haskins, James S.
Hatcher, Jeffrey F.
Hawkins, Edwin
Haye, Clifford S.
Haywood, Spencer
Haywoode, M. Douglas
Headley, Shari
Heard, Nathan Cliff
Heavy D
Hegwood, William Lewis
Henderson, Butler Thomas
Hendricks, Jon
Hermanuz, Ghislaine
Hewett, Howard
Hewitt, John H., Jr.
Hewitt, Vivian Davidson
Hicks, Daisy C.
Hicks, John J.
Higgins, Chester Archer, Jr.
Higginsen, Vy
Hill, Lauryn
Hill, Velma Murphy
Hines, Laura M.
Hinton, Warren Miles
Hodges, David Julian
Holder, Geoffrey
Holder, Idalia
Holland, J. Archibald
Hollins, Hue
Holloman, John L. S., Jr.
Holmes, Carlton
Hopkins, John Orville
Horne, June C.
Horton, Carl E., Sr.
House, Michael A.
Houston, Allan Wade
Houston, Cissy
Houston, W. Eugene
Houston, Whitney
Howard, George
Howard, M. W., Jr.
Howard, Norman Leroy
Howell, Robert J., Jr.
Hoyte, Lenon Holder
Hudlin, Reginald Alan
Hudlin, Warrington
Hudson, Frederick Bernard
Hudson, Frederick Douglass
Huntley, Lynn Jones
Hurd, David James, Jr.
Hutson, Jean Blackwell
Hyman, Phyllis
Ibrahim, Abdullah
Imbriano, Robert J.
Ingrum, Adrienne G.
Innis, Roy Emile Alfredo
Irvin, Milton M.
Isaac, Yvonne Renee
Jackson, Alfred Thomas
Jackson, Beverly Anne
Jackson, Beverly Joyce
Jackson, Charles Richard, Jr.
Jackson, Esther Cooper
Jackson, George
Jackson, Hal
Jackson, Janine Michele
Jackson, Paul, Jr.
Jackson, Pazel
Jacobs, Thomas Linwood
James, Alexander, Jr.
James, Charles Ford
James, Juanita T.
Jamison, Judith
Jarrett, Hobart Sidney
Jeffers, Jack
Jefferson, Margo
Jeffries, Leonard
Jemmott, Hensley B.
Jenkins, Adelbert Howard
Jenkins, Carol Ann
Jenkins, George E., III
Johnson, Barbara C.
Johnson, Bernard
Johnson, Edward A.
Johnson, Herschel Lee
Johnson, Joe
Johnson, John W.
Johnson, Larry Demetric
Johnson, Marie Elizabeth
Johnson, Marjorie Lynn
Johnson, Patrice Doreen
Johnson, Roy Steven
Johnson, Vickie
Johnson, Virginia Alma Fairfax
Johnson, William L.

Johnson, William Thomas
Johnson Cook, Suzan Denise
Jones, Benjamin E.
Jones, Billy Emanuel
Jones, Caroline Robinson
Jones, Cedric Decorrus
Jones, Charisse Monsio
Jones, David R.
Jones, Delmos J.
Jones, Duane L.
Jones, Furman Madison, Jr.
Jones, Harold M.
Jones, James A.
Jones, James P.
Jones, Quincy Delight, Jr.
Jones, Robert Wesley
Jones, Sidney Eugene
Jones, Thomas W.
Jordan, Montell
Jordan, Patricia Carter
Jordan, Vincent Andre
Joseph, Raymond Alcide
Kappner, Augusta Souza
Karpeh, Enid Juah Hildegard
Kearse, Amalya Lyle
Kelley, William Melvin
Kelly, Patrick
Kelly, R.
Kemp, Emmerlyne Jane
Kendrick, Carol Yvonne
Killens, John Oliver
King, Anita
King, B. B.
King, Cecilia D.
King, Woodie, Jr.
Kinsey, Jim
Kirkland, Theodore
Kirwan, Roberta Claire
Kitt, Eartha Mae
Kluge, Pamela Hollie
Knight, Perry Vertrum
Knox, George L., III
Knuckles, Kenneth J.
Kotto, Yaphet
Kravitz, Lenny
Lane, Charles
Latimer, David Christopher
Lawrence, Charles Radford, II
Lawrence, Merlisa Evelyn
Lawrence, Prestonia D.
Lawrence, Sandra
Lazard, Betty
Lee, Andrea
Lee, Dorothea
Lee, Felicia R.
Lee, Margaret S.
Lee, Mildred Kimble
Lee, Ritten Edward
Lee, Spike
Lee, William Thomas
Lee Sang, Sharon Nolan
LeFlore, Lyah
Leggett, Renee
LeMelle, Wilbert John
Lemon, Ann
Lenoir, Henry
LeNoire, Rosetta
LeVert, Gerald
Levy, Valerie Lowe
Lewis, Ananda
Lewis, Edward T.
Lewis, Emmanuel
Lewis, Hylan Garnet
Lewis, Ida Elizabeth
Lewis, Loida Nicolas
Lewis, Reginald F.
Lewis, William M., Jr.
Lewis, William Sylvester
Lippman, Lois H.
Little, Cleavon Jake
L L Cool J
Lofton, Michael
Logue-Kinder, Joan
London, Clement B. G.
Louard, Agnes A.
Love, Mildred L.
Love, Thomas Clifford
Lowe, Jackie
Lowery, Mark
Lynch, Hollis R.
Mac, Bernie
Mack, Phyllis Green
Maitland, Tracey
Majete, Clayton Aaron
Mangum, Robert J.
Mann, Philip Melvin
Mapp, Edward C.
Mardenborough, Leslie A.
Marsalis, Ellis

Olean
Howard, Keith L.

Oneonta
Morris, Stanley E., Jr.

Orangeburg
Boschulte, Alfred F.
Holland, Laurence H.

Orchard Park
Brown, Reuben
Burris, Jeffrey Lamar
Covington, Damien
Dubenion, Elbert
Early, Quinn Remar
Holmes, Darick
Irvin, Ken
Jackson, Raymond DeWayne
James, Rick
Johnson, Lonnie
Jones, Henry
Kerner, Marlon
Kinnebrew, Larry D.
Louchiey, Corey
Maddox, Mark Anthony
Martin, Emanuel
Moulds, Eric Shannon
Nails, Jamie
Northern, Gabriel O'Kara
Odomes, Nathaniel Bernard
Perry, Marlo
Reed, Andre Darnell
Rogers, Sammy Lee
Smedley, Eric
Smith, Antowain
Smith, Bruce Bernard
Smith, Leonard Phillip
Smith, Thomas Lee, Jr.
Spriggs, Marcus
Talley, Darryl Victor
Thomas, Thurman Lee
Washington, Ted
Wiley, Marcellus
Williams, Pat

Otisville
Owens, Grady D., Sr.

Owego
Wells, James A.

Ozone Park
Veal, Yvonnecris Smith

Patchogue
Harris, Lester L.

Pearl River
Holland, Laurence H.

Pittsford
Harvey, Beverly Ann
Osborne, Clayton Henriquez
Rodgers, William M., Jr.

Plattsburgh
Judson, Horace Augustus

Pleasantville
Edwards, Claudia L.
Grimes, John J.

Pomona
Davis, Clarence
Gordon, Edmund W.
Lawrence, Margaret Morgan

Port Chester
Bailey, Doris Jones
Reavis, John William, Jr.

Port Jefferson Station
Shockley, Alonzo Hilton, Jr.

Potsdam
Mitchell, Julius P.

Poughkeepsie
Berkley, Constance E. Gresham
Peterson, Lloyd, Jr.
Stanley, Columbus Landon, Sr.
Tarver, Marie Nero
Thompson, Sherwood

Purchase
Burton, Ronald J.
Harrison, Ronald E.
Howard, John Robert

Queens Village
DeHart, Panzy H.
Goslee, Leonard Thomas
Somerville, Robert Alston

Rego Park
Archie, James Lee
Cox, Robert L.

Rensselaer
Brown, Lester J.
Dugger, Clinton George

Riverdale
Carrion, Odessa
Downie, Winsome Angela
Johnson, Carl Thomas
Price, Judith
Stent, Madelon Delany

Riverhead
Anderson, Leslie Blake
Floyd, Marquette L.
Manning, Randolph H.

Rochdale Village
Craig-Rudd, Joan

Rochester
Aklilu, Tesfaye
Allen, Shirley Jeanne
Anderson, David Atlas
Augustine, Matthew
Banks, Perry L.
Brown, Joseph Samuel
Brown, Maxine J. Childress
Burgett, Paul Joseph
Byas, Thomas Haywood
Campbell, Alma Porter
Carson, Loftus C.
Cooper, Walter
Daniels, William James
Davis, Reuben K.
Dickson, Daryl M.
Dobson, Dorothy Ann
Everett, J. Richard
Fagbayi, Mutiu Olutoyin
Flores, Joseph R.
Fowler, John D.
Graves, Raymond Lee
Hannah, Mosie R.
Harrison, Robert Walker, III
Henry, William Arthur, II
Horne, Marvin L. R., Jr.
Hubbard, Calvin L.
Hunter, Clarence Henry
James, Timothy Arcee
Jefferson, Fredrick Carl, Jr.
Johnson, Robert
Johnson, William A., Jr.
Jones, Marsha Regina
Langston, Andrew A.
Lechebo, Semie
Lomax-Smith, Janet E.
McAndrew, Anne E. Battle
McCree, Samuel W.
McCuller, James
McDaniel, Sharon A.
Mitchell, Nelli L.
Moore, Carol Louise
Norman, James H.
O'Connor, Rodney Earl
Parris, Alvin, III
Paul, Beatrice
Ray, Andrew
Redon, Leonard Eugene
Rhodes, Jacob A.
Scott, Ruth
Stevens, Patricia Ann
Walker, Mary Alice
Willis, Charles L.
Willis, Frank B.
Wright, James R.

Rockville Centre
Davis, William M., Jr.
Jackson, Earline
Jenkins, Elizabeth Ameta
London, Roberta Levy
Mitchell, Billy M.

Rome
Harper, Neville W.

Roosevelt
Blake, Carlton Hugh
Francis, Livingston S.
Goodson, Frances Elizabeth
Johnson, Michele
Scott-Ware, Barbara Ann

Roosevelt Island
Hercules, Frank E. M.

Roslyn
Addei, Arthella Harris

Roslyn Heights
Jordan, Patricia

Rye
Redd, Orial Anne

Sag Harbor
Carter, JoAnne Williams
Demby, William E., Jr.
Whitehead, Arch S., III
Williams, E. Thomas, Jr.

Saratoga Springs
Trammer, Monte Irvin

Scarsdale
Bruce, Kenneth E.
Foster, Frank B., III
Harper, Elizabeth
Wood, William L., Jr.

Schenectady
Starkey, Frank David

Selden
Byers, Marianne
Green, Mildred A.
Jefferson, Marcia D.
Stevenson, Russell A.

Smithtown
Drew, Thelma Lucille
Johnston, Henry Bruce

Somers
Hearon, Dennis James
McCarley, Phyllis

South Ozone Park
Thomas, Terence

South Salem
Heacock, Don Roland

Spring Valley
Marrs, Stella

Springfield Gardens
Driggriss, Daphne Bernice
Sutherland

Staten Island
Betty, Warren Randall
Davis, Agnes Maria
Graves, Jerrod Franklin
Lacy-Pendleton, Stevie A.
Lyles, William K.
Pipkins, Robert Erik
Thomas, Charles Columbus
Trapp, Ellen Simpson
Troupe, Quincy Thomas, Jr.
Vogel, Roberta Burrage

Stone Ridge
Reynolds, Milton L.
Staats, Florence Joan

Stony Brook
Anderson, Edgar L.
Baraka, Imamu Amiri
Kennedy, Theodore Reginald
McKay, Karen Nimmons
McWorter, Gerald A.
Pindell, Howardena D.
Short, Kenneth L.
Turner, W. Burghardt
Walker, Annie Mae

Suffern
Wilder, Cora White

Syracuse
Beard, Melvin Charles
Boyd, Thomas
Brown, Glenn Willard
Dowdell, Dennis, Sr.
Felton, Ann Shirley
Fitchue, M. Anthony
Freeman, Marianna
Ivey, Horace Spencer
Lee, Kermit J., Jr.
McMillan, Douglas James
Pollard, William Lawrence
Rasberry, Robert Eugene
Scruggs, Otey Matthew
Timberlake, Constance Hector
Townes, Sandra L
Turner, Eugene
Wells-Merrick, Lorraine Roberta
Willis, Andrew
Wright, Roosevelt R., Jr.

Tarrytown
Whitely, Donald Harrison

Troy
Dukes, Jerome Erwin
Hammett, Willie Anderson
Knowles, Eddie
Miller, Frederick A.

Tupper Lake
Francis, Richard L.

Uniondale
Risbrook, Arthur Timothy
Workman, Aurora Felice Antonette

Utica
Mathis, David
Taylor, Kimberly Hayes

Valhalla
Whitely, Donald Harrison
Wright, Jane C.

Valley Cottage
Marr, Carmel Carrington

Valley Stream
Burwell, Bryan Ellis

Wappingers Falls
Johnson, Jeh Vincent

Watertown
Fletcher, Glen Edward

Webster
Denson, Fred L.
Holmes, Aldo R.
Howard, Darnley William

West Babylon
Adkins, William

West Hempstead
Mims, George L.

West Hurley
Newman, David, Jr.

West Islip
Carter, Darline Louretha

West Nyack
Dunbar, Harry B.

West Point
Bazil, Ronald
Gorden, Fred A.

Westbury
Evans, Alicia
Palmer, Noel
Risbrook, Arthur Timothy

White Plains
Beane, Robert Hubert
Bronz, Lois Gougis Taplin
Carney, Alfonso Linwood, Jr.
Clark, Vincent W.
Cooke, Lloyd M.
Cox, Jesse L.
English, Marion S.
Fowlkes, Nancy P.
Frelow, Robert Dean
Fudge, Ann Marie

Grant, Claude DeWitt
Harris, Robert Eugene Peyton
Jackson, Joseph T.
Johnson, Jesse J.
Johnson, Wendy Robin
Jordan, Wesley Lee
King, Charles Abraham
King, Lawrence C.
Lawrence, James Franklin
Lloyd, Wanda
Montgomery, Harry J.
Moody, William Dennis
Moss, Anni R.
Parker, Barrington D., Jr.
Parnell, John V., III
Prince, Ernest S.
Redd, M. Paul, Sr.
Reynolds, Grant
Riggs, Enrique A.
Robeson, Paul, Jr.
Rutledge, Jennifer M.
Simpson, Walter
Singletary, Inez M.
Spaulding, Lynette Victoria
Stephens, Doreen Y.
Sudderth, William H.
Swiggett, Ernest L.
Turnbull, Horace Hollins
West, Joseph King
Williams, Gayle Terese Taylor
Wilson, Leroy, Jr.
Wood, Harold Leroy
Wyke, Joseph Henry

Whitesboro
Wertz, Andrew Walter, Sr.

Woodside
Castleberry, Edward J.
Gaines, Adriane Theresa
Sanders, Vincent

Yonkers
Beane, Robert Hubert
Harper, Leonard Alfred
McLeod, Georgianna R.
Miller, Jacqueline Elizabeth
Odom, Stonewall, II
Phillips, Dilcia R.
Tolbert, Bruce Edward

Yorktown Heights
Ross, Winston A.

Yorkville
Norris, William E.

NORTH CAROLINA

Ahoskie
Weaver, Joseph D.

Apex
Cunningham, Robert Shannon, Jr.

Asheville
Bacoate, Matthew, Jr.
Bowman, Janet Wilson
Harrell, Robert L.
Locke, Don C.
Thomas, Wade Hamilton, Sr.

Ayden
Brown, Julius J.

Bayboro
Bell, Kenneth M.
Jones, Ammia W.

Bear Creek
Thompson, Carl Eugene

Belmont
Logan, Juan Leon

Bolton
Greene, Edith L.

Burlington
Shanks, William Colemon, Jr.
Styles, Richard Wayne
Wade, Eugene Henry-Peter

Mebane
Cain, Frank

Morehead City
Tate, Eleanora Elaine

Mount Olive
Jones, Leora

Murfreesboro
Hunter, Howard Jacque, Jr.

Nashville
Moore, Arvelle, Sr.

Navassa
Brown, Louis Sylvester

New Bern
Frazier, Reginald Lee
Godette, Franklin Delano
 Roosevelt
Harmon, John H.
Raynor, Robert G., Jr.

Oxford
McKissick, Floyd B.

Pfafftown
Floyd, Vircher B.

Pinebluff
Capel, Felton Jeffrey

Polkton
Kersey, Elizabeth T.

Powellsville
Coley, Donald Lee

Raeford
McPherson, Roosevelt
Morrisey, Jimmy

Raleigh
Allen, Brenda Foster
Allen, Jacob Benjamin, III
Andrews, James Edward
Arrington, Warren H., Jr.
Ball, Richard E.
Beatty, Ozell Kakaskus
Blue, Daniel Terry, Jr.
Burton, Leroy Melvin, Jr.
Carter, James Harvey
Carter, Wilmoth Annette
Clark, Edward Depriest, Sr.
Clark, Lawrence M., Sr.
Clarke, James Alexander
Cofield, Elizabeth Bias
Cook, Charles A.
Dandy, Clarence L.
Dempsey, Joseph P.
Edwards, John Wilson
Fisher, Judith Danelle
Fitch, Milton F., Sr.
Franklin, Bernard W.
Frye, Henry E.
Garner, Edward, Jr.
Gill, Rosa Underwood
Groffrey, Frank Eden
Hager, Roscoe Franklin
Hairston, Raleigh Daniel
Harris, Cynthia Julian
Hinton, Christopher Jerome
Horton, Larnie G.
Ishman, Sybil R.
Jones, Anthony Ward
Larkins, John Rodman
Lightner, Clarence E.
Lovelady, Rueben Leon
Lumpkin, Adrienne Kelly
Luten, Thomas Dee
Merritt, Bishetta Dionne
Miller, John H.
Moore, Albert
Moore, Lenard Duane
Palmer, Elliott B., Sr.
Peebles, Allie Muse
Pettis, Joyce Owens
Pickett, Henry B., Jr.
Pope, Mary Maude
Quigless, Milton Douglas, Jr.
Reed, Addison W.
Robinson, Prezell Russell
Silvey, Edward
Sims, Genevieve Constance
Smith, Carl William

Smith, James Almer, III
Spencer, Joan Moore
Strachan, Lloyd Calvin, Jr.
Sutton, Gloria W.
Wade, Beryl Elaine
Ward, Everett Blair
Watford-McKinney, Yvonne V.
Webb, Harold H.
Wilkins, Kenneth C.
Williams, George
Winston, Hubert

Reidsville
Gordon, Ronald Eugene
Griggs, Harry Kindell, Sr.

Research Triangle Park
Adkins, Rodney C.
Gatewood, Algie C.

Roaring River
Gilreath, Coot, Jr.

Rockingham
Hutton, William

Rocky MOunt
Brooks, Eric

Rocky Mount
Cooke, Michael
Deloatch, Myrna Spencer
Gay, Helen Parker
Grimes, William Thomas, Sr.
Jones, Ruth Braswell
Leonard, Walter Fenner
Morgan, Hazel C. Brown

Rose Hill
Monk, Edd Dudley

Salisbury
Bailey, Ricardo
Koontz, Elizabeth Duncan
Massey, Reginald Harold
Rountree, Louise M.

Sanford
Fisher, Judith Danelle
McPherson, James R.
Morgan, Joseph L.

Shannon
McRae, Emmett N.

Sharpsburg
Beasley, Annie Ruth

Shelby
Ford, Aileen W.
Jones, Martha E.

Smithfield
Woodhouse, Johnny Boyd

Soul City
Crump, Janice Renae
McKissick, Evelyn Williams

South Mills
Skimmer, Aluster Carl

Southern Pines
Thompson, Herman G.
Wade, Kim Mache

Southport
Adams, Nelson Eddy

Tar Heel
Andrews, James F.

Tarboro
Deloatch, Myrna Spencer
Quigless, Milton Douglas, Sr.
Ray, Moses Alexander

Thomasville
Lewis, Matthew, Jr.

Tillery
Grant, Gary Rudolph

Tryon
Carson, Warren Jason, Jr.
Massey, Carrie Lee

Wadesboro
Little, Herman Kernel

Warrenton
Ballance, Frank Winston, Jr.
Henderson, Nannette S.
Williams, Yarborough, Jr.
Worth, Charles Joseph

Washington
Randolph, Louis T.

Weldon
Shoffner, Clarence L.

Whiteville
Jones, H. Thomas, II
Sellars, Harold Gerard

Wilkesboro
Gilreath, Coot, Jr.

Wilmington
Berry, Lisbon C., Jr.
Blanks, Delilah B.
Bryant, Ezzia
Gore, Ethel P.
Jervay, Thomas Clarence, Sr.
Moore, Katherine Bell
Newkirk, Inez Doris
Sidbury, Harold David
Waddell, Ruchadina LaDesiree

Wilson
Coleman, Avant Patrick
Felton, James A.
Ward, Thomas

Windsor
Cherry, Andrew Jackson
Coley, Donald Lee

Winston-Salem
Angelou, Maya
Bass, Marshall Brent
Bell, Winston Alonzo
Black, Veronica Correll
Bradshaw, Lucy Hyman
Brown, Clark S.
Brown, Hazel Evelyn
Brown, Jasper C., Jr.
Burke, Vivian H.
Butler, J. Ray
Caldwell, James L.
Caldwell, Lisa Jeffries
Chenault, Myron Maurice
Cobb, Harold James, Jr.
Crews, William Sylvester
Duren, Emma Thompson
Easley, Eddie V.
Erwin, Richard C.
Eure, Herman Edward
Evans, Mutter D.
Gaillard, Ralph C., Sr.
Gaines, Clarence E., Sr.
Goodwin, Kelly Oliver Perry
Hauser, Charlie Brady
Hayes, Roland Harris
Hedgley, David R.
Herrell, Astor Yeary
Hutton, Ronald I.
Hymes, Jesse
Jackson, Felix W.
Johnson, Sheila Monroe
Lewis, Henry S., Jr.
Malloy, H. Rembert
McEachern, D. Hector
Miller, Ward Beecher
Mitchell, Carol Greene
Murphy, Daniel Howard
Newell, Virginia K.
Noisette, Ruffin N.
Oubre, Hayward Louis
Parker, Karen Lynn
Pierre, Jennifer Casey
Pollard, Alton Brooks, III
Ruffin, Benjamin S.
Sadler, Kenneth Marvin
Sadler, Wilbert L., Jr.
Scales, Manderline Elizabeth
Schexnider, Alvin J.
Sprinkle-Hamlin, Sylvia Yvonne
Tate, David Kirk
Thompson, Cleon Franklyn, Jr.
Turner, Vivian Love
Turner, William Hobert
Wagner, David H.
Walls, Willie J.

Williams, Kenneth Raynor
Williams, Richard Lee
Womble, Larry W.

Winton
Wilson, Donald P.

Zebulon
Vereen, Michael L.

NORTH DAKOTA

Grand Forks
Henderson-Nocho, Audrey J.

OHIO

Akron
Arnold, Helen E.
Ashburn, Vivian Diane
Branham, George, III
Brown, Ronald Paul
Chapman, Martin Odes
Crutchfield, James N.
Curtis-Rivers, Susan Yvonne
Dominic, Irwing
Evege, Walter L., Jr.
Ferguson, Idell
Fort, William H.
Foye-Eberhardt, Ladye Antionette
Greene, Charles Lavant
Harris, Robert D.
Jones, Delores
Kennard, Patricia A.
King, Lawrence Patrick
McClain, Andrew Bradley
McClain, Shirla R.
Morgan, Dolores Parker
Morgan, Eldridge Gates
Payne, James Edward
Payne, Margaret Ralston
Peake, Edward James, Jr.
Robinson, Luther H., Jr.
Roulhac, Joseph D.
Scruggs, Sylvia Ann
Silas-Butler, Jacqueline Ann
Stewart, Gregory
Stubbs, Harold K.
Sykes, Vernon Lee
Williams, Annalisa Stubbs
Williams, James R.
Wilson, John W.

Alliance
Davison, Edward L.
Walton, James Edward

Ashland
Pulley, Clyde Wilson

Ashtabula
Brown, Ronald Paul
Shelby, Reginald W.

Athens
Alsbrook, James Eldridge
Childs, Francine C.
Perdreau, Cornelia Whitener
Ross-Lee, Barbara
Williams, Daniel Salu

Austintown
Robinson, R. David

Barberton
Berry, Archie Paul

Batavia
Doddy, Reginald Nathaniel
Warren, Clarence F.

Beachwood
Fufuka, Tika N.Y.
Holt, Donald H.
Leggon, Herman W.
Williams, Barbara Ann

Beavercreek
Vivians, Nathaniel Roosevelt

Bedford Heights
Ackerman, Patricia A.

Berea
Banks, Carl
Powell, Craig
Pruitt, James Boubias

Bowling Green
Moss, Crayton L.
Ribeau, Sidney
Scott, John Sherman
Taylor, Jack Alvin, Jr.

Brook Park
Bluford, Guion Stewart, Jr.

Brunswick
Temple, Oney D.

Canton
Ball, John Calvin, Sr.
Bell, Yolanda Maria
Calhoun, Jack Johnson, Jr.
Fisher, Robert F.
Gravely, Melvin J.
Herring, William F.
Houston, Kenneth Ray
Hunter, William L.
Kyle, Odes J., Jr.
McIlwain, Albert Hood
Moore, Charles D.
Murphy, Vanessa
Nwa, Willia L. Deadwyler
Pressley, DeLores
Wilson, Jon

Centerville
Ross, Robert P.
Warren, Lee Alden

Chillicothe
McLaughlin, Benjamin Wayne

Cincinnati
Abercrumbie, Paul Eric
Ambrose, Ashley Avery
Anderson, Willie Aaron
Bates-Parker, Linda
Bennett, Delora
Berry, Theodore M.
Bieniemy, Eric
Blake, Jeff
Bolden, Veronica Marie
Bond, Howard H.
Booth, Lavaughn Venchael
Bowen, William F.
Brasey, Henry L.
Bronson, Fred James
Brown, Anthony
Brown, Herbert R.
Bryant, Napoleon Adebola, Jr.
Burgest, David Raymond
Burlew, Ann Kathleen
Caldwell, Esly Samuel, II
Cargile, William, III
Carter, Ki-Jana
Casey, Edmund C.
Castenell, Louis Anthony, Jr.
Chapman, David Anthony
Chenault, John
Chess, Robert Hubert
Clarke, Ray E.
Clinton, Thomas R.
Collins, Andre Pierre
Collins, Patricia Hill
Cooper, Constance Marie
Cooper, Emmett E., Jr.
Copeland, John
Cornelison, Carole Jane
Cross, William Howard
Cureton, Michael
Deane, Morgan R.
Dixon, Gerald Scott
Doddy, Reginald Nathaniel
Dunbar, Thomas Jerome
Dunn, David
Edwards, Arthur James
Edwards, Ruth McCalla
Elliott, Lori Karen
Eubanks, Dayna C.
Fleming, Vernon Cornelius
Fowler, Barbara Ann
Francis, James
Fuller, Dewey C.
Garner, Thomas L.
Goodloe, Celestine Wilson
Gordon, Lois Jackson
Graham, Scottie
Grant, Cheryl Dayne
Greene, Willie Louis

Hall, Joseph A.
Harris, Charles Cornelius
Harris, Lenny
Hawkins, Lawrence C.
Henderson, Theresa Crittenden
Hicks, Eleanor
Hinton, Milton
Holmes, E. Selean
Hooker, Odessa Walker
Hord, Noel Edward
Jackson, Damian Jacques
Jenkins, Roger J.
Johnson, Fran
Johnson, Joseph Harvey
Jones, James Wesley
Jones, Nathaniel R.
Jones, Roderick Wayne
Jones, William Lawless
Jones, Winton Dennis, Jr.
Jordan, Marjorie W.
Keels, Paul C.
King, W. James
Langford, Jevon
Larkin, Barry Louis
Lawson, Lawyer
Logan-Tooson, Linda Ann
Mack, Tremain
Marshall, H. Jean
McClain, William Andrew
McDonald, Ricardo Milton
McGee, Tony
McGoodwin, Roland C.
McIntyre, Linda
McLean, Marquita Sheila McLarty
Meacham, Robert B.
Merchant, John Cruse
Merenivitch, Jarrow
Merriweather, Robert Eugene
Morris, Elizabeth Louise
Morton, William Stanley
Nelson, Ramona M.
Newberry, Cedric Charles
Norton, Aurelia Evangeline
Nunnally, Jonathan Keith
Oates, Louis S.
Oxley, Lucy Orintha
Parham, Marjorie B.
Parker, E. Gerald
Paul, Tito
Payne, Rod
Person, Leslie Robin
Pickens, Carl McNally
Pleasant, Albert E., III
Pryor, Chester Cornelius, II
Purvis, Andrew
Reed, Allene Wallace
Reese, Pokey
Rijo, Jose Antonio
Rivers, Clarence Joseph
Sanders, Reginald Laverne
Sawyer, Corey
Scott, Darnay
Sells, Mamie Earl
Shade, Sam
Shamblee, Charles Y., Jr.
Shuttlesworth, Fred L.
Sierra, Ruben Angel
Smiley-Robertson, Carolyn
Smith, Calvert H.
Smith, Paul M., Jr.
Southern, Charles O.
Spencer, James Arthur, Jr.
Spencer, Marian Alexander
Stallings, Ramondo Antonio
Stewart, Ronald Patrick
Stone, Harold Anthony
Thomas, John Henderson, III
Thompson, Sylvia Moore
Tillery, Dwight
Timmons, Ozzie
Tovar, Steven Eric
Turner, Mark Anthony
Walter, John C.
West, John Andrew
Wilbekin, Harvey E.
Wilkinson, Dan
Wilson, Henry, Jr.
Wilson, Reinard
Wilson, Sheila J.
Zealey, Sharon Janine

Cleveland
Adams, Leslie
Adrine, Ronald Bruce
Alexander, Gary
Alomar, Sandy
Alomar, Sandy, Jr.
Anderson, Derek
Andrews, William Henry

Arnold, Ethel N.
Atkins, Russell
Banks, Marguerita C.
Barnes, Ronald Lewis
Barrett, James A.
Battle, John Sidney
Batts, Terry Milburn
Bell, James H.
Bell, Rouzeberry
Benn, Ishmael
Bennett, William Ronald
Bernstein, Margaret Esther
Billue, Zana
Boone, Alexandria
Boyd, Evelyn Shipps
Braxton, Janice Lawrence
Brisker, Lawrence
Brown, Bernice H.
Brown, Rushia
Brown, Virgil E., Jr.
Brownlee, Wyatt China
Burke, Lillian W.
Burnett, Bescye P.
Burns, Dargan J.
Burose, Renee
Bustamante, J. W. Andre
Butler, Annette Garner
Butler, Mitchell Leon
Carter, Kevin Antony
Caviness, E. Theophilus
Chandler, Everett A.
Chandler, Mittie Olion
Chapman, Robert L., Sr.
Chatman, Anna Lee
Clark, Sanza Barbara
Clay, Cliff
Clouden, LaVerne C.
Cochran, Herschel J.
Collins, Daisy G.
Connally, C. Ellen
Crosby, Fred McClellen
Cross, Jack
Crouther, Betty M.
Crutcher, Betty Neal
Crutcher, Ronald Andrew
Davidson, Lurlean G.
Davis, Robert E.
Douglas, Janice Green
Douglas, Sherman
Drake, Daniel D.
Dumas, Tony
Duncan, Geneva
Dunnigan, Jerry
Earls, Julian Manly
Eatman, Janice A.
Edwards, Michelle
Edwards, Robert Valentino
Ellis, J. Delano, II
Fleming, Charles Walter
Flewellen, Icabod
Floyd, Mark S.
Fonville, Chad Everette
Forbes, George L.
Franco, Julio Cesar
Franklin, Grant L.
Franklin, Milton B., Jr.
Fraser, George C.
Freeman, Claire E.
Gaines, Clarence L.
Gallager, Mike John
Gilbert, Albert C.
Gilliam, Robert M., Jr.
Gooden, Dwight Eugene
Graham, Donald
Graham, Gregory Lawrence
Greer, Thomas H.
Guffey, Edith A.
Hall, Brian Edward
Harper, Sara J.
Harris, Leodis
Hawthorne, Nathaniel
Head, Edith
Henderson, Cedric
Higgins, Roderick Dwayne
Hill, Alfred
Huggins, Clarence L.
Hunter, David
Jackson, Michael Ray
James, Henry Charles
James, Ronald J.
Johnson, Adrienne
Johnson, Andrew L., Jr.
Johnson, Mattiedna
Jones, Merlakia
Jones, Stephanie Tubbs
Justice, David Christopher
Kemp, Shawn T.
Kerr, Walter L.
Knight, Brevin

Lairet, Dolores Person
Lane, Jerome
Lang, Antonio
Lee, Oliver B.
Lee, Shirley Freeman
Lockhart, Barbara H.
Lofton, Kenneth
Lowe, Sidney Rochell
Mackel, Audley Maurice, III
Madkins, Gerald
Malone, Eugene William
Marshall, Donny
Maxwell, Anita
McClain, Jerome Gerald
McCollum, Anita LaVerne
McDowell, Elvin
McNeil, Lori Michelle
Meaux, Ronald
Miller, Maposure T.
Minter, Steven Alan
Mixon, Clarence W.
Morris, Milton Curtis
Moss, Otis, Jr.
Murphy, Donald Richard
Murray, J-Glenn
Murray, Sylvester
Nance, Larry Donell
Nicholson, Tina
Ozanne, Dominic L.
Ozanne, Leroy
Payden, Henry J., Sr.
Peoples, Earl F., Sr.
Person, Wesley Lavon
Phillips, F. Allison
Phillips, James Lawrence
Phills, Bobby Ray, II
Pinkney, Arnold R.
Polley, William Emory
Poole, Dillard M.
Pottinger, Albert A.
Powell, Bernice Jackson
Powell-Jackson, Bernice
Prout, Patrick M.
Ribbins, Gertrude
Rice, Robert C.
Rice, Susie Leon
Roberts, John B.
Roberts, Narlie
Romans, Ann
Rosemond, Manning Wyllard, Jr.
Rowan, Albert T.
Saffold, Oscar E.
Saffold, Shirley Strickland
Samuels, Marcia L.
Scott, Shawnelle
Seymour, Robert F.
Sharpe, Calvin William
Shaw, Alvia A.
Shumate, Glen
Starling, John Crawford
Stewart, Mae E.
Stokes, Carl Burton
Thomas, William L.
Tipton-Martin, Toni
Tolliver, Stanley Eugene, Sr.
Tukufu, Darryl S.
Tyree, Patricia Grey
Tzomes, Chancellor Alfonso
Valentine, Darnell
Webb, James Eugene
White, Frederic Paul, Jr.
White, George W.
Whitehead, David William
Whitley, R. Joyce
Willacy, Hazel M.
Wilson, John W.
Wilson, Sonali Bustamante
Wisham, Claybron O.
Womack, Andrew A.
Wright, Jackson Thomas, Jr.
Wykle, May Louise Hinton

Cleveland Heights
Madison, Leatrice Branch
Madison, Robert P.
McLendon, John B., Jr.
Russell, Leonard Alonzo
Seaton, Shirley Smith

Clyde
Lloyd, Phil Andrew

Columbus
Alexander, Dorothy Dexter
Allen, Jerry Ormes, Sr.
Anglen, Reginald Charles
Ayers, Randy
Barnes, Yolanda L.
Beatty, Otto, Jr.

Bell, Tom, Jr.
Blackwell, J. Kenneth
Bland, Arthur H.
Blount, Wilbur Clanton
Booth, Charles E.
Boyd, Terry A.
Brown, Ralph H.
Brunson, Frank
Butler, Darraugh Clay
Carter, Percy A., Jr.
Cole, Ransey Guy, Jr.
Coleman, Frankie Lynn
Coleman, Michael Bennett
Coleman, Ronald K.
Cook, Elizabeth G.
Craig, Elson L.
Crews, Victoria Wilder
Davis, William J.
Day, Donald K.
Dodson, William Alfred, Jr.
Duncan, Robert M.
Evans, Helen W.
Evans, James L.
Evans, Liz
Fields, Brenda Joyce
Fisher, David Andrew
Flint, Mary Frances
Foster-Grear, Pamela
Frasier, Ralph Kennedy
Frazier, Frances Curtis
Freeman, Shirley Walker
Garraway, Michael Oliver
Garrison, Jewell K.
Gibbs, Jack Gilbert, Jr.
Gillespie, Avon E.
Goldston, Ralph Peter
Gramby, Shirley Ann
Greer, Robert O.
Gregory, Michael Samuel
Gresham, Donald
Griffin, Ann White
Griffin, Archie
Haddock, Mable J.
Hairston, Rowena L.
Hale, Phale D.
Hamlar, David Duffield, Sr.
Hardin, Marie D.
Harper, Eugene, Jr.
Harris, Jack
Hart, Phyllis D.
Heflin, Marrion
Hendricks, Leta
Hickman, Garrison M.
Hicks, Clayton Nathaniel
Hicks, William James
Hill, Billy
Hogan, Edwin B.
Holland, Robin W.
Holloway, Ardith E.
Hoover, Felix A.
Hope, Marie E.
Hughes, Donna Lundin
Humphrey, Howard John
Jackson, James Garfield
Jackson, Janet E.
James, Troy Lee
Johnson, William Theolious
Jones, Michelle
Jones, Peter Lawson
Kirksey, M. Janette
La Cour, Louis Bernard
Larkin, Michael Todd
Link, Joyce Battle
Love, Lamar Vincent
Luckey, Evelyn F.
Lyman, Webster S.
Maddox, Margaret Johnnetta Simms
Maddox, Odinga Lawrence
Mallory, William L.
Marshall, Carl Leroy
McCall, Patricia
McDaniel, William T., Jr.
McGee, Rose N.
McLin, C. J., Jr.
Merchant, James S., Jr.
Merritt-Cummings, Annette
Miller, Ray, Jr.
Moore, Cynthia M.
Moore, Floreese Naomi
Morris, Leibert Wayne
Moss, James Edward
Myles, William
Nelson, William Edward, Jr.
Newsome, Ronald Wright
Noel, Gerald T., Sr.
Nowlin, Frankie L.
Owens, Arley E., Jr.
Parks, Edward Y.

Patterson, Cheryl Ann
Pearson, James A.
Pettigrew, Grady L., Jr.
Preston, Eugene Anthony
Ransier, Frederick L., III
Reece, Guy L., II
Reed, Clarence Hammit, III
Revish, Jerry
Rhett, Michael L.
Roberts, Margaret Mills
Robinson, S. Yolanda
Rogers, Gwendolyn H.
Rudd, Charlotte Johnson
Ruffin, Richard D.
Saunders, Jerry
Scott, Artie A.
Smallwood, Osborn Tucker
Smith, Herald Leonydus
Smith, Janet Maria
Smith, Toni Colette
Spencer, Larry Lee
Stevenson, Unice Teen
Stewart, Mac A.
Stull, Robert J.
Stull, Virginia Elizabeth
Sullivan, Edward James
Sullivan, Ernest Lee
Sykes, Vernon Lee
Taylor, Arlene M. J.
Thompson, Isaiah
Thrower, Julius A.
Tinsley, Dwane L.
Tolbert, Herman Andre
Tolbert, Lawrence J.
Trout, Nelson W.
Turner-Forte, Diana
Wade, Jacqueline E.
Wade, William Carl
Walker, Charles H.
Walker, Watson Herchael
Watkins-Cannon, Gloria Ann
Weddington, Wilburn Harold, Sr.
West, Pheoris
White, David D.
White, Ernest G.
White, Janice G.
White, Kenneth Eugene, Sr.
Williams, Gregory Howard
Williams, James
Williams, Lucretia Murphy
Williams, Mary Ann Sheridan
Williams-Stanton, Sonya Denise
Wilson, F. Leon
Wilson, Nevia Aneice
Wood, Andrew W.
Yuill, Essie McLean-Hall

Dayton
Adams, Lucinda Williams
Adams, Martha E. W.
Adegbile, Gideon Sunday Adebisi
Anthony, Brenda Tucker
Bailey-Worthy, Carletta
Benyard, William B., Jr.
Black, Don Gene
Blunden, Jeraldyne K.
Brown, Charles Sumner
Brown, Emma Jean Mitchell
Coates, Janice E.
Cunningham, John F.
Dixon, Richard Clay
Earley, Stanley Armstead, Jr.
Ferguson, Edward A., Jr.
Flack, Harley Eugene
Ford, Robert Blackman
Fowler, Barbara Ann
Francis, James L.
Frazier, Jimmy Leon
Gilmore, Marshall
Green, Richard Carter
Grooms-Curington, Talbert Lawrence, Sr.
Gunn, Gladys
Hall, Charles Harold
Hall, Fred, III
Harrison, William Edgar
Haskins, Clemette
Howard, Lillie Pearl
Johnson, Lillian Mann
Jones, Robert Earl
Leaphart, Eldridge
Leigh, William A.
Lemmie, Valerie
Lewis, Lloyd E., Jr.
Littlejohn, Bill C.
Lovelace, Dean Alan
Lucas, Leo Alexander
Martin, Cornelius A.
Martin-Cross, Denise L.

Mason, Billy Josephine
Mays, Dewey Ordric, Jr.
McCollum, Alice Odessa
McIlwain, Nadine Williams
Melrose, Thomas S.
Neal, Edna D.
Nixon, Harold L.
Nutt, Ambrose Benjamin
O'Neal, Raymond W., Sr.
Patmon, Claude
Powell, David L.
Railey-Worthy, Carletta
Smith, Alphonso Lehman
Smith, Frederick Ellis
Taylor, Robert Earlington, Jr.
Taylor, Sinthy E.
Taylor, Vivian Lorraine
Vickers, Jim, Jr.
Walker, Willie F.
Ward, Daryl
Washington, John William
Williams, Terry
Williams, Walker Richard, Jr.
Wilson, Carl L.
Wingo, A. George
Wise, Warren C.
Woodley, Arto, Jr.
Worthey, Richard E.
Wright, Carolyn Elaine
Young, Clarence, III

Delaware
King, Thomas Lawrence
Small, Vernon
Stewart, Mac A.
Tynes, Richard H.

Dublin
Corbin, Stampp W.
Davis, Latina
Edwards, Tonya
Ford, Stacey
Harrison, Lisa Darlene
Johnson, Shannon
Jones, Ronald Lyman
Still, Valerie
Tate, Sonja
Taylor, Arlene M. J.

East Canton
Powell, William

East Cleveland
Harris, MaryAnn
Hart, Mildred
Head, Edith
Johnson, Almeta Ann
Keenon, Una H. R.
Pittman, Darryl E.
Reese, Gregory Lamarr
Thomas-Richardson, Valerie Jean

Elyria
Haney, Darnel L.

Enon
Smithers, Oral Lester, Jr.
Smithers, Priscilla Jane

Evendale
Lowry, James E.

Fairborn
Roberts, Willie

Fairfield
Robertson, Oscar Palmer

Findlay
Woodson, Cleveland Coleman, III

Forest Park
Wright, Linwood Clinton

Gahanna
Brunson, Frank
Gore, John Michel
Newsome, Ronald Wright
Rhett, Michael L.

Galloway
Vaughn, Eugenia Marchelle
  Washington

Garfield Heights
Couch, Ludie

Genoa
Grady, Glenn G.

Germantown
Wright, Flonzie B.

Granville
Lyles, Dewayne
Rawlings, Martha

Grove City
Vaughn, Eugenia Marchelle
  Washington

Hamilton
Young, B. Ashley

Highland Heights
Neavon, Joseph Roy

Hillsboro
Warner, Melvin

Hiram
Hemphill, Frank
Thompson, Eric R.

Holland
Clark, Mildred E.

Huron
Lawyer, Vivian

Kent
Chambers, Doris Foster
Chambers, Fredrick
Crosby, Edward Warren
Ekechi, Felix K.
McMillan, Jacqueline Marie
Meadows, Ferguson Booker, Jr.
Meier, August
Payne, Margaret Ralston
Stevens, George Edward, Jr.
Turner, Doris J.
Van Dyke, Henry
Waters, Gary

Lima
Pruitt, Michael

London
Scurry, Fred L.

Lorain
Wrice, David

Mansfield
Dorsey, Harold Aaron
McCaulley, James Alan, III
Payton, Jeff
Washington, Henry L.

Marion
Henderson, Randy

Massillon
Beane, Patricia Jean

Maumee
Alderson, Kenith

Middletown
Ewers, James Benjamin, Jr.
Kimbrough, Thomas J.
Robinson, Roosevelt, III
Sampson, Marva W.

Mount Gilead
Best, Sheila Diane

New Albany
Tinsley, Dwane L.

Newark
Thorne, Cecil Michael

Oakwood Village
Wainwright, Gloria Bessie

Oberlin
Hernton, Calvin Coolidge
Peek, Booker C.
Walker, Frances
White, Clovis Leland
Williams, Barbara Ann

Oxford
Hargraves, William Frederick, II
Jackson, W. Sherman
Musgrave, Marian Elizabeth
Patton, Rosezelia L.
Powell, Myrtis H.
Tidwell, John Edgar

Painesville
Walker, Wendell P.

Paulding
Miles, Vera M.

Pickerington
Heflin, Marrion

Reynoldsburg
Chenault, William J.
Gregory, Michael Samuel
Owens, Arley E., Jr.

Rio Grande
Keels, James Dewey

Salem
Alexander, Cornelia

Sandusky
Seavers, Clarence W.

Shaker Heights
Benning, Emma Bowman
Brown, Malcolm McCleod
Butler, Annette Garner
Crawford, Muriel C.
Freeman, Lelabelle Christine
Groves, Delores Ellis
Jackson, Gerald Milton
Jackson, Kenneth William
Jacobs, Gregory Alexander
Johnson, Henderson A., III
Jones, Lisa Payne
Jones, Peter Lawson
Mackel, Audley Maurice, III
Murphy, Donald Richard
Richie, Winston Henry
Samuels, Marcia L.
Smith, Herbert C.
Whitley, William N.
Williams, Earl West
Williams, Willie S.

Sidney
Humphrey, James Philip

Solon
Anderson, Warren E.

Spring Valley
Phillips, Lloyd Garrison, Jr.

Springfield
Ayers, Timothy F.
Beavers, Nathan Howard, Jr.
Brice, Eugene Clay
Chatman, Jacob L.
Cherry, Robert Lee
Garrett Harshaw, Karla
Goodson, Leroy Beverly
Henry, Robert Clayton
Jenkins, Carl Scarborough
Nesbitt, Charles E.
Reed, Maurice L.
Smithers, Priscilla Jane
Swain, Michael B.

Steubenville
Palmer, Dennis, III
Williams, Carletta Celeste

Stow
Dominic, Irwing

Toledo
Butler, Benjamin Willard
Carlisle, James Edward, Jr.
Cholmondeley, Paula H. J.
Cook, Levi, Jr.
Copeland, Terrilyn Denise
Dowell, Ollie Willette
Edgerton, Art Joseph
Franklin, Robert Vernon, Jr.
Gandy, Roland A., Jr.
Gray, Joseph William
Hannah, Johnnie, Jr.
Hubbard, Paul Leonard

Jones, Casey C.
McDaniel, Charles William
Newsome, Emanuel T.
Phifer, B. Janelle Butler
Porter, Scott E.
Sheppard, Ronald John
Sommerville, Joseph C.
Taylor, David Richard, III
Thompson, Lancelot C. A.
Turner, Eddie William
Walden, Robert Edison
Washington, Edith Stubblefield

Troy
Bell, Trenton Grandville

Twinsburg
Bryant, William Henry, Jr.

University Heights
Bagley, Stanley B.
Seaton, Shirley Smith

Urbancrest
Craig-Jones, Ellen Walker

Van Wert
Connor, James Russell

Warren
Breckenridge, John L.
Logan, Joseph Leroy
Pegues, Robert L., Jr.
Perkins, Marion V.
Robinson, Learthon Steven, Sr.
Williams, Joe H.

Warrensville Heights
Ashley, Corlanders
Bugg, Mayme Carol
Kelley, Robert William
Walker, Dorothea Bernice

West Chester
Harris, Charles Cornelius

Westerville
Luckey, Evelyn F.
Smith, Toni Colette

Wickliffe
Hunter, Frederick Douglas

Wilberforce
Ball, Jane Lee
Davis, Willis H. "Bing"
Fleming, John Emory
Garland, John William
Hargraves, William Frederick, II
Henderson, John L.
Hudgeons, Louise Taylor
Jackson, Samuel S., Jr.
Mayo, Blanche Irene
McStallworth, Paul
Onwudiwe, Ebere
Padgett, James A.
Pinkney, Betty Kathryn
Thomas, Arthur E.
Wright, Carolyn Elaine

Woodlawn
Smiley, James Walker, Sr.

Wooster
Jefferson, Alphine Wade
Williams, Yvonne Carter

Worthington
Wood, Leigh C.

Wright Patterson AFB
Vivians, Nathaniel Roosevelt

Xenia
Dansby, Jesse L., Jr.
Hall, Fred, III

Yellow Springs
Amos, Oris Elizabeth Carter
Graham, Precious Jewel
Rice, Edward A.

Youngstown
Alexander, Roland
Atkinson, Eugenia Calwise
Bacon, Barbara Crumpler
Black, Willa

Bright, Alfred Lee
Carter, Raymond Gene, Sr.
Carter, Romelia Mae
Cooper, Syretha C.
Coston, Bessie Ruth
Echols, Mary Ann
Frost, Hugh A.
Halface, Frank Edward
Hughes, Jimmy Franklin, Sr.
Huntley, Richard Frank
James, Dava Paulette
Johnson, Andrew L., Sr.
McCroom, Eddie Winther
Pruitt, Fred Roderic
Shipmon, Luther June
Spencer, Brenda L.
Walker, Cindy Lee
Williams, Leonard, Sr.
Williams, McCullough, Jr.

Zanesville
Gilbert, Richard Lannear
Watiker, Albert David, Jr.

OKLAHOMA

Ardmore
McKerson, Mazola

Boley
Lee, Forrest A., Sr.
Matthews, Mary Joan
Spann, Theresa Tieuel
Walker, Ronald Plezz

Chouteau
Ray, Johnny

Claremore
Gladney, Marcellious

Edmond
Lehman, Paul Robert

Fort Sill
Joy, James Bernard, Jr.

Frederick
Evaige, Wanda Jo

Guthrie
Owens, Wallace, Jr.

Hartshorne
Webber, William Stuart

Langston
Carey, Phillip
Fisher, Ada L. Spivel
Green, Theodis Guy
Hall, Calvin
Holloway, Ernest Leon
Jones, Viola
King, Ruby Ryan
Manning, Jean Bell
Manning, Reuben D.
Morgan, Booker T.
Prewitt, Al Bert
Rogers, George

Lawton
Barfield, Leila Millford
Barfield, Quay F.
Davenport, J. Lee
Dean, Felton
Owens, Charles Clinton
Wynn, Valree Fletcher

McAlester
Brown, James Marion
Newman, Miller Maurice

Muskogee
Beasley, Cora Thomas
Richardson, DeRutha Gardner
Simmons, Donald M.
Thomas, Erma Lee Lyons

Norman
Blake, John
Henderson, George
Hill, Anita Faye
Kamoche, Jidlaph Gitau
Perkins, Edward Joseph
Williams, Norris Gerald

Oklahoma City
Atkins, Hannah Diggs
Barclay, Carl Archie
Bedford, William
Benton, Leonard D.
Brown-Francisco, Teresa Elaine
Byrd, Camolia Alcorn
Cox, James Alphonso
Cox, Kevin C.
Darrell, Lewis E.
Davis, Denyvetta
Gigger, Helen C.
Gigger, Nathaniel Jay
Grigsby, Troy L., Sr.
Hall, Melvin Curtis
Hardeman, Carole Hall
Henderson, Joyce Ann
Humphrey, Marian J.
Jackson, Mattie Lee
Jackson, Walter K.
Kirk, Leroy W.
Lee, Theodosia L. Crawford
Lewis, Sylvia Austin
McLeod, Michael Preston
McMurry, Kermit Roosevelt, Jr.
Miles-LaGrange, Vicki
Murrell, Sylvia Marilyn
Nelson, Debra Ponder
Parks, Thelma Reece
Porter, E. Melvin
Rogers, George
Rucker, Frank L., Jr.
Sartin, Johnny Nelson, Jr.
Sears, Bertram E.
Swain, Alice M.
Tipton, Danell
Todd, Melvin R.
Tollett, Charles Albert, Sr.
Varner, Jewell C.
Williams, Freddye Harper
Williams, Roger L.
Wilson, Frank Fredrick, III

Pryor
Lewis, Clarence K.

Redbird
Billups, Mattie Lou

Spencer
Sloss, Minerva A.

Stillwater
Arnold, Lionel A.
Combs, Willa R.
Cunningham, Calvin Malcolm
Hamilton, Leonard
Mitchell, Earl Douglass, Jr.
Shipp, Howard J., Jr.
Simmons, Bob

Taft
Davis, Lelia Kasenia

Tulsa
Anderson, Chester R.
Anderson, Elizabeth M.
Brown, John, Jr.
Bryant, Hubert Hale
Bryant-Ellis, Paula D.
Butler, Roy
Cannon, Chapman Roosevelt, Jr.
Cannon, Donnie E.
Chappelle, Thomas Oscar, Sr.
Clark, Major
Evans, Leon Edward, Jr.
Hayes, Alvin, Jr.
Hill, Fannie E.
Hill, LaVerne
House, Millard L.
Hudson, Andrew Harold
Jeffrey, Charles James, Jr.
Johnson, Paul L.
Lacy, Edward J.
Lewis, Charles H.
Pegues, Wennette West
Ragsdale, Charles Lea Chester
Robbins, Herman C.
Samuels, Everett Paul
Sanders, Hobart C.
Staten, Mark Eugene
Taylor, Thad, Jr.
Williams, Art S.

OREGON

Beaverton
Chriss, Henry Thomas
Jones, Esther B.
Lewellen, Michael Elliott
Ryan, Marsha Ann
Smith, Wilson Washington, III
Ussery, Terdema Lamar, II

Corvallis
Branch, Harrison
Gamble, Wilbert
Seals, Gerald

Eugene
Brown-Wright, Marjorie
Campbell, Gary Lloyd
Carter, Lawrence Robert
Coleman, Edwin Leon, II
Cooke, Leonard
Gainer, John F.
Hill, Pearl M.
Taylor, Quintard, Jr.
Wade, Joseph Downey

Gresham
Boyland, Dorian Scott
Parker, Clarence E.
Stokes, Johnnie Mae

Milwaukie
Martinez, Ralph

Portland
Augmon, Stacey Orlando
Benton, Phyllis Clora
Bernstine, Daniel O.
Black, Gail
Booker, Venerable Francis
Borum, Regina A.
Britton, Elizabeth
Brooks, James O'Neil
Brown, Webster Clay
Cato, Kelvin
Christian, Geraldine Ashley
    McConnell
Crawley, Sylvia
Dark, Lawrence Jerome
Dark, Okianer Christian
Deiz, Mercedes F.
DePreist, James Anderson
Flipper, Carl Frederick, III
Grant, Brian Wade
Guy, George V.
Harrington, Denise Marion
Hartzog, Ernest E.
Heflin, John F.
Henry, Samuel Dudley
Higgins, Sean Marielle
Irby, Galven
Jackson, Frederick Leon
Jackson, John H.
Johnson, Dave
Leonard, Carolyn Marie
Lister, Alton Lavelle
McCoy, Gladys
Milton, DeLisha
Morris, Laticia
Nunn, Bobbie B.
O'Neal, Jermaine
Plummer-Talley, Olga Ann
Pool, Vera C.
Powell, Elaine
Rider, Isaiah, Jr.
Rogers, Carlos Deon
St. John, Primus
Slater, Reggie
Spicer, Osker, Jr.
Stoudmaire, Damon
Taylor, Michael Loeb
Thompson, Kevin
Walker, James Zell, II
Wallace, Rasheed Abdul
Williams, Natalie
Williams, Walter Ander
Wingfield, Dontonio
Wright, Falisha

Salem
Carter, Margaret Louise
McCoy, William
Toran, Kay Dean
Winters, Jacqueline F.

Troutdale
Henry, Samuel Dudley

West Linn
St. John, Primus
Wilson, Edith N.

PENNSYLVANIA

Aliquippa
Meade, Melvin C.
Smith, Eugene
Wallace, Ronald Wilfred

Allentown
Battle, Turner Charles, III
Bell, Ngozi O.
Edwards, Lewis
Outten, Willie
Williams, Robert Carroll

Allison Park
Sessoms, Frank Eugene

Aston
Jones, James R., III

Bala Cynwyd
Anderson, Kernie L.
Bishop, Alfred A.
Durham, C. Shelby
Dyer-Goode, Pamela Theresa
Hutchins, Francis L., Jr.
Patterson, James
Wing, Theodore W., II

Bloomsburg
Bryan, Jesse A.

Braddock
Essiet, Evaleen Johnson

Breinigsville
Asom, Moses T.

Bristol
Reed, Jerrildine

Bryn Mawr
Allen, Blair Sidney
Kirby, Nancy J.
Mayden, Ruth Wyatt

California
Graham, Albertha L.

Camp Hill
Williams, James E., Jr.

Chadds Ford
Braxton, John Ledger

Chalfont
Clifford, Maurice C.
Murray, Nevada

Chester
Bohannan-Sheppard, Barbara
Cavin, Alonzo C.
Holmes, Leo S.
Leake, Willie Mae James
Nails, John Walker
Riley, William Scott

Cheyney
Cade, Valarie Swain
McCummings, LeVerne
Mullett, Donald L.
Wilson, Wade

Claysville
Blount, Melvin Cornell

Coatesville
Brickus, John W.
Johnson, Paul Lawrence
Lee, Daniel
Middleton, Rose Nixon
Washington, John Calvin, III

Connellsville
Farmer, Robert Clarence

Conshohocken
Dent, Anthony L.

Darby
Moore, Charlie W.
Tyler, Robert James, Sr.

Delaware Water Gap
Woods, Philip Wells

Doylestown
Ali-Jackson, Kamil
Hill, Bennett David
Potter, Myrtle Stephens

Dresher
Wilson, Sandra E.

East Stroudsburg
Graham, Patricia
Holmes, Everlena M.

Easton
Holmes, Larry
Houston, William DeBoise
Jones, Alfredean

Edinboro
Dillon, Aubrey
Robinson, Curtis
Stewart, Elizabeth Pierce

Erie
Summers, David Stewart
Trice, William B.

Exton
Wilson, Earl Lawrence

Farrell
Sanders-West, Selma D.
Simon, Lonnie A.

Fort Washington
Davis, Ronald

Gettysburg
Matthews, Harry Bradshaw

Glen Mills
Redding, Louis L.
Wright, Robert Courtlandt

Glenside
Reed, Jerrildine

Greensburg
Harvell, Valeria Gomez

Harrisburg
Ash, Richard Larry
Barnett, Ethel S.
Baxter, Belgium Nathan
Bradley, Andrew Thomas, Sr.
Braxton, Harriet E.
Cannon, Paul L., Jr.
Chambers, Clarice Lorraine
Clark, Donald Lewis
Cox, James Alexander
Cummings, Cary, III
Daniels, LeGree Sylvia
Davis, Michael DeMond
Foggs-Wilcox, Iris
Fuget, Charles Robert
Gadsden, Nathaniel J., Jr.
Gilmore, Charles Arthur
Gordon, Derek E.
Gordon, Fannetta Nelson
Hankins, Freeman
Hargrove, Trent
Hughes, Vincent
Johnson, Benjamin Washington
Love, George Hayward
Madison, Richard
Mitchell, Brenda K.
Mitchell, Stanley Henryk
Montgomery, William R.
Morrison, Clarence Christopher
Noonan, Allan S.
Peguese, Charles R.
Preston, Joseph, Jr.
Prioleau, Sara Nelliene
Richards, Winston Ashton
Robinson, Rosalyn Karen
Roebuck, James Randolph, Jr.
Rowland, James H.
Sharpe, Ronald M.
Smalls, Charley Mae
Spigner, Donald Wayne
Street, T. Milton

Utley, Richard Henry
White, Scott A., Sr.
Wilson, Joseph Henry, Jr.
Wilson, Ronald M.
Womack, Stanley H.
Woods, Willie G.
Young, George, Jr.

Hazleton
Harris, Arthur Leonard, III

Hershey
Bradley, Andrew Thomas, Sr.
Harvey, Harold A.
Mortel, Rodrigue
Washington, Leonard, Jr.
Williams, James E., Jr.

Horsham
Hill, Jeffrey Ronald
Jordan, J. St. Girard
Miller, C. Conrad, Jr.

Imperial
Outlaw, Sitnotra

Indiana
Anderson, James Alan

Jenkintown
Smith, Robert Johnson

King of Prussia
Smith, G. Elaine
Thomas, Edward Arthur

Kutztown
Morgan, Robert W., II
Scott, Basil Y.
Westmoreland, Samuel Douglas
Woodard, Charles James

Lafayette Hill
Loris, Joseph James
Samuels, Charlotte

Lamberton
Crawford, Clinton Wayne

Lancaster
Bondurant, Milton J.
Williams, Louise Bernice

Lansdowne
Waiters, Ann Gillis
White, Haskel

Levittown
Jordan, Josephine E. C.

Lincoln University
Johnson, William T. M.
Mayes, Doris Miriam
Pettaway, Charles, Jr.
Rodgers, Joseph James, Jr.
Sudarkasa, Niara
Williams, Willie Jr.
Willis, Gladys January

Lock Haven
Lynch, Robert D.

Mc Keesport
Hart, Barbara McCollum
Mason, Major Albert, III
Richardson, Lacy Franklin

Media
Wilkie, Earl Augustus T.
Wright, Robert A.

Middletown
Gilpin, Clemmie Edward
Mallette, Carol L.
Richards, Winston Ashton
Williams-Dovi, Joanna

Mill Hall
Lynch, Robert D.

Millersville
Hopkins, Leroy Taft, Jr.

Monroeville
Mikell, Charles Donald
Wheeler, Shirley Y.

Moon Twp
Bullard, Keith

Norristown
Booker, Thurman D.
Davenport, Horace Alexander
Jones, Ervin Edward

North Wales
Bass, Herbert H.

Palmerton
Brantley, Kenneth

Petrolia
Lee, John C., III

Philadelphia
Ackridge, Florence Gateward
Adom, Edwin Nii Amalai
Aldridge, Markita
Alexandre, Journel
Ali, Shahrazad
Allen, Terrell Allison, III
Alston, Derrick Samuel
Alston, Floyd William
Anderson, Cody
Anderson, J. Morris
Anderson, Ronald Gene
Anderson, Sarah A.
Archie, Shirley Franklin
Asante, Kariamu Welsh
Asante, Molefi Kete
Bailey, Curtis Darnell
Bailey, Harry A., Jr.
Baker, Floyd Edward
Baker, Houston A., Jr.
Bambara, Toni Cade
Barnett, Fred Lee, Jr.
Batiste, Kim
Beckett, Charles Campbell
Beckles, Ian Harold
Bell, Lawrence F.
Bell, Thom R.
Benson, Rubin Author
Benton, George A.
Berry, Mary Frances
Biggs, Cynthia DeMari
Blockson, Charles L.
Bogle, Robert W.
Bol, Manute
Bond, Cecil Walton, Jr.
Bond, Gladys B.
Bostic, Viola W.
Bouie, Simon Pinckney
Bradtke, Mark
Brantley, Clifford
Brazington, Andrew Paul
Brooker, Moe Albert
Brooks, Barrett
Brown, Jamie Earl S., Jr.
Brown, William H., III
Bullock, Samuel Carey
Bullock, Thurman Ruthe
Bunyon, Ronald S.
Burrell, George Reed, Jr.
Burton-Lyles, Blanche
Caldwell, Adrian Bernard
Campbell, Michele
Cannon, Elton Molock
Cannon, Katie Geneva
Carr, Leonard G.
Carter, Fred
Case, Arthur M.
Chamberlain, Wesley Polk
Chandler, Allen Eugene
Chapman, Lee Manuel
Chappell, Emma Carolyn
Clark, Augusta Alexander
Clark, Jesse B., III
Clark, Willie Calvin
Clarke, Eugene F., Jr.
Clarke, Leon Edison
Clayton, Constance Elaine
Clayton, Matthew D.
Coleman, Derrick D.
Coleman, Joseph E.
Collier-Thomas, Bettye
Collins, Sylvia Durnell
Conner, Darion
Cooper, Edward Sawyer
Copeland, Russell
Cousins, Althea L.
Crawley, A. Bruce
Crudup, Gwendolyn M.
Cummings, Midre Almeric
Darling, James
Davis, James A.
Davis, Jean E.

Davis, Johnny Reginald
Davis, Mark Anthony
Dawkins, Brian
Days, Michael Irvin
Dennis, Andre L.
Dennis, Edward S. G., Jr.
Dickens, Helen Octavia
Dickerson, Ron
Dimry, Charles Louis, III
Dixon, Valena Alice
Dobson, Regina Louise
Dowkings, Wendy Lanell
Driver, Richard Sonny, Jr.
Drummond, David L., Sr.
Du Bose, Robert Earl, Jr.
Dunn, Jason
Echols, Alvin E.
Elcock, Claudius Adolphus Rufus
Ellis, Benjamin F., Jr.
Ellis, Leander Theodore, Jr.
Embrey, Sherry
Emmons, Rayford E.
Evans, Dwight
Evans, Samuel London
Evans, Therman E.
Farmer, Clarence
Farmer, Ray
Fattah, Falaka
Ferere, Gerard Alphonse
Ferguson, Sherman E.
Fields, Ewaugh Finney
Finn, Joseph
Fisher, Joseph
Fontaine, John M.
Fordham, Cynthia Williams
Forster, Cecil R., Jr.
French, George Wesley
Frett, La Keshia
Frink Reed, Caroliese Ingrid
Fryar, Irving Dale
Gaines, Sedalia Mitchell
Gamble, Kenneth
Garner, Charlie
Giles, James T.
Gilmore, Richard G.
Glanville, Douglas Metunwa
Gomes, Wayne M.
Goode, W. Wilson
Goodson, Adrienne M.
Gordon, Levan
Gordon, Robert L.
Goss, Linda
Granger, Shelton B.
Grant, John H., Sr.
Graves, Jackie
Graves, Mary Louise
Gray, Mel
Green, Clifford Scott
Green, Franklin D.
Green, Liller
Green, Rickey
Guinier, Carol Lani
Gundy, Roy Nathaniel, Jr.
Hagins, Ogbonna
Hairston, Harold B.
Hall, Daniel A.
Hall, Julia Glover
Hamm, Barbara Lawanda
Hammond, Benjamin Franklin
Hancock, Gwendolyn Carter
Hansbury, Vivien H.
Hardin, Herbert G.
Hareld, Gail B.
Harmon, Sherman Allen
Harper, Ronald J.
Harris, Al Carl
Harris, DeWitt O.
Harris, Jeanette G.
Harris, Jon
Harris, Reggie
Harvey, William James, III
Haskins, Michael Kevin
Hawes, Bernadine Tinner
Hawkins, Gene
Hayre, Ruth Wright
Herrod, Jeff Sylvester
Hickman, Jerry A.
Hill, Kenneth D.
Hill, William Randolph, Jr.
Hinderas, Natalie
Hobbs, Wilbur E.
Holloway, Hiliary H.
Holmes, William B.
Holton, Priscilla Browne
Hopkins, Wes
Hopson, Harold Theodore, II
Howard, Humbert Lincoln
Huff, Leon Alexander
Hunt, Portia L.

Hunter, Kristin
Hunter, Robert J.
Hunter, Tracey Joel
Hunter-Lattany, Kristin Eggleston
Hyman, Mark J.
Inyamah, Nathaniel Ginikanwa N.
Iverson, Allen
Jackson, Burnett Lamar, Jr.
Jackson, Ricardo
Jangdharrie, Wycliffe K.
Jasper, Edward Videl
Jefferson, Greg
Jenkins, Andrew
Jenkins, Lozelle DeLuz
Jeter, Joseph C., Jr.
Johnson, Elmore W.
Johnson, Jimmie
Johnson, Ron
Johnson, Ronald
Johnson, Walton Richard
Johnson, Willie F.
Jolly, Elton
Jones, Chris Todd
Jones, Ernest Edward
Jones, G. Daniel
Jones, Jimmie Simms
Jones, Ozro T., Jr.
Kalu, Ndukwe Dike
Kamau, Mosi
Kelsey, Gary Matthew
Kennedy, William Thomas, Jr.
Kernodle, Obra Servesta, III
Kidd, Warren Lynn
King, Gwendolyn Stewart
King, Julian F.
King, Robert Samuel
King, William Moses
Langston, Josephine Davidnell
Lee, Edward S.
Leonard, Curtis Allen
Lewis, Samuel, Jr.
Lightfoot, William P.
Linton, Gordon J.
Linton, Sheila Lorraine
Lomax, Walter P.
Lucas, John
Lynch, Rufus Sylvester
Maddox, Garry Lee
Magee, Wendell Errol
Malone, Jeff Nigel
Manning, Eddie James
Mansfield, Carl Major
Mapp, Robert P.
Mapp, Yolanda I.
Marsh, Tamra Gwendolyn
Martin, I. Maximillian
Mathis, Thaddeus P.
Mayberry, Jermane
McCoy, James F.
McGill, Thomas L., Jr.
McKee, Theodore A.
McKie, Aaron Fitzgerald
McMillon, Billy
McQueen, Anjetta
McWilliams, Taj
Melvin, Harold James
Merriweather, Barbara Christine
Miller, Bubba
Miller, Horatio C.
Minyard, Handsel B.
Mitchell, Joann
Mitchell, Sadie Stridiron
Moore, Acel
Moore, Richard Baxter
Moore, Robert Andrew
Mott, Stokes E., Jr.
Murray, Thomas W., Jr.
Myrick, Howard A., Jr.
Neal, Richard
Newman, LeGrand
Nicholson, Alfred
Nixon, Gladys
Odom, Vernon Lane, Jr.
Okore, Cynthia Ann
Oliver, Frank Louis
Oliver, Ronald Daniel
Overton, Douglas M.
Owens, LaMonte
Padulo, Louis
Palmer, Edward
Parker, Anthony
Parks, Donald B.
Paul, Wanda D.
Peete, Rodney
Perry, William E.
Pittman, Audrey Bullock
Poindexter, Charles L. L.
Poindexter, Malcolm P.
Portlock, Carver A.

Powell, Thomas Francis A.
Pratt, A. Michael
Prattis, Lawrence
Pryor, Malcolm D.
Quick, Mike
Ratliff, Theo Curtis
Reed, Jasper Percell
Reed, Michael H.
Rhodes, Jeanne
Rhodes, Ray
Richardson, Henry J., III
Riscoe, Romona A.
Ritter, Thomas J.
Roach, Lee
Robinson, Charles
Robinson, Charlotte L.
Robinson, Denauvo M.
Robinson, Gary O.
Robinson, Jason Guy
Rogers-Lomax, Alice Faye
Roulhac, Nellie Gordon
Rouse, Donald E.
Russell, Keith Bradley
Sanchez, Sonia Benita
Sanders, Steven LeRoy
Sanford, Mallory
Seale, Bobby
Seay, Dawn Christine
Shamwell, Ronald L.
Shaw, Brian K.
Shelton, Ulysses
Sigler, I. Garland
Simmons, Howard L.
Simmons, Maurice Clyde
Simpson, Stephen Whittington
Singletary, Reggie
Smith, Andre Raphel
Smith, Ben
Smith, Darrin Andrew
Smith, Marie Evans
Snow, Eric
Solomon, Freddie
Speller, J. Finton
Spencer, Margaret Beale
Staley, Dawn
Staley, Duce
Staley, Kenneth Bernard
Staten, Everett R.
Stewart, Kebu
Stewart, Ronald L.
Stone, Daniel M.
Stout, Juanita Kidd
Stovall, Stanley V.
Stubbs, George Winston
Sullivan, Leon Howard
Tann, Daniel J.
Tasco, Marian B.
Taylor, Bobby
Taylor, Susan Charlene
Thomas, Carl Alan
Thomas, Harry Lee
Thomas, Hollis
Thomas, Tim
Thomas, W. Curtis
Thomas, William Harrison, Jr.
Thompas, George Henry, Jr.
Thompson, Gloria Crawford
Thompson, Milt
Timmons, Bonita Terry
Timpson, Michael Dwain
Toney, Anthony
Tucker, C. DeLores
Tucker, Michael Kevin
Tucker, Wilbur Carey
Turner, George R.
Tyler, B. J.
Tyree-Walker, Ida May
Valentine, John
Vargus, Ione D.
Vaughn, Alvin
Vincent, Troy
Voorhees, John Henry
Waites-Howard, Shirley Jean
Walker, Charles E.
Walker, Manuel Lorenzo
Walker, Valaida Smith
Wallace, Robert Eugene, Jr.
Waller, Juanita Ann
Wansel, Dexter Gilman
Ware, Gilbert
Washington, Jacquelyn M.
Washington, Paul M.
Waters, Andre
Watson, Bernard C.
Watters, Richard James
Weddington, Wayne P., Jr.
Weiner, Charles R.
Wells, Ira J. K., Jr.
White, Clayton Cecil

Whiting, Emanuel
Williams, Anita Spencer
Williams, Calvin John, Jr.
Williams, Hardy
Williams, Joseph Henry
Williams, Kimmika L. H.
Williams, Novella Stewart
Williams, Randolph
Williams, Scott Christopher
Willis, Gladys January
Willis, James Edward, II
Willis, Miechelle Orchid
Wilson, Calvin T.
Woods, Jacqueline Edwards
Woolridge, Orlando Vernada
Wooten, John
Wormley, Diane-Louise Lambert
Wright, Charles
Wright, Grover Cleveland
Wynn, Prathia Hall
Young, Elmer, Jr.
Young, Marechal-Neil Ellison
Young, Ollie L.

Pittsburgh
Allen, Philip C.
Allensworth, Jermaine LaMont
Anise, Ladun Oladunjoye E.
Arnold, Jahine
Bailey, Henry
Baldwin, Cynthia A.
Barksdale Hall, Roland C.
Bell, Myron Corey
Bell, Paul, Jr.
Bettis, Jerome Abram
Biggs, Shirley Ann
Bobonis, Regis Darrow, Jr.
Brown, Adrian Demond
Brown, Byrd R.
Brown, Emil Quincy
Brown, J.B.
Brown, John C., Jr.
Burley, Jack L., Sr.
Cain, Lester James, Jr.
Campbell, George Lynn
Charlton, George N., Jr.
Clark, John Joseph
Coleman, Andre Clintonian
Collier, Louis Keith
Conley, John A.
Conley, Martha Richards
Conley, Steven
Copeland, Kevon
Craig, Cheryl Allen
Crawford, Clinton Wayne
Curry, Clarence F., Jr.
Daniel, Jack L.
Darkins, Duane Adrian
Davis, Nathan T.
Dawson, Dermontti Farra
Dunmore, Charlotte J.
Effort, Edmund D.
Emmons, Carlos
Epperson, David E.
Eskridge, John Clarence
Faison, Helen Smith
Fernandez, John Peter
Finley, Skip
Flowers, Lethon
Foggie, Charles H.
Ford, Vernon N.
Fortson, Elnora Agnes
Frye, Nadine Grace
Fuget, Henry Eugene
Fuller, Randy Lamar
Garland, Hazel Barbara
Gibson, Oliver Donnovan
Gildon, Jason Larue
Gist, Karen Wingfield
Gordon, Alexander H., II
Griggs, Judith Ralph
Hamlin, David W.
Harris, Eugene Edward
Harris, Franco
Harris, George Dea
Harrison, Nolan
Hawkins, Alexander A.
Hawkins, Courtney Tyrone, Jr.
Hayes, J. Harold, Jr.
Henry, Kevin Lerell
Holliday, Corey Lamont
Holmes, Earl
Howard, Elizabeth Fitzgerald
Howard, Lawrence Cabot
Howard, Leon W., Jr.
Howell, Chester Thomas
Hunter, Brian Ronald
Irvis, K. Leroy
Jackson, John

Nichols, Elaine
Owens, Mercy P.
Patterson, Kay
Peay, Samuel
Pinckney, Clementa
Pride, Hemphill P., II
Prioleau, Peter Sylvester
Richardson, Leo
Robinson, Eunice Primus
Rodgers, Augustus
Rowe, Marilyn Johnson
Russell, Edwin R.
Salmond, Jasper
Scott, Juanita Simons
Scott, Robert L.
Shannon, David Thomas, Sr.
Smalls, O'Neal
Spain, Hiram, Jr.
Swinton, David Holmes
Swinton, Sylvia P.
Waldo, Carol Dunn
Williams, Willie, Jr.

Conway
DeWitt, Franklin Roosevelt
Frink, Samuel H.
Lee, James E.
Stevens, Cleveland

Denmark
Bryan, Curtis
Carpenter, Carl Anthony
Chapman, Julius
Dawson, Lawrence E.
Dawson, Leonard Ervin
Henry, John Wesley, Jr.

Eastover
Scott, Lewis Nathanel

Effingham
Canty, Ralph Waldo

Florence
Adams, Lillian Louise T.
Beck, Roswell Nathaniel
Diggs, William P.
Gaines, John A., Sr.
Harley, Legrand
Williams, George Arthur

Frogmore
Grosvenor, Verta Mae

Gaffney
Foster, Mildred Thomas
Reid, Duane L.
Rosemond, Lemuel Menefield
Sanders, James William

Georgetown
Kennedy, Karel R.

Graniteville
Kellar, Arthur H.

Great Falls
Hall, John Robert

Greenville
Beverly, Benjamin Franklin
Channell, Eula L.
Cooper, Ethel Thomas
Corbitt, John H.
Crosby, Willis Herman, Jr.
Cureton, Stewart Cleveland
Flemming, Lillian Brock
Kirby-Davis, Montanges
Mitchell, Theo W.
Peden, S. T., Jr.
Reid, Janie Ellen
Robinson, Myron Frederick
Talley, Michael Frank, Sr.
Walker, J. Wilbur
Zimmerman, Samuel Lee

Greenwood
Caldwell, John Edward
Johnson, Ed F.
Witherspoon, Audrey Goodwin

Greer
Golden, Louie

Hardeeville
Williams, Daniel Louis

Hilton Head Island
Butler, Marjorie Johnson
Campbell, Emory Shaw
Driessen, Henry, Jr.

Holly Hill
Morant, Mack Bernard

Hollywood
Holmes, Mary Brown

Johnsonville
Tanner, James W., Jr.

Lake City
Wilson, Alva L.

Lancaster
Jeter, Delores DeAnn

Laurens
Carter, John R.
Coleman, Marian M.
Rhodes, Audrey B.

Loris
Watson, Fred D.

Lynchburg
Jefferson, Clifton

Mc Cormick
Gilchrist, Robertson

McBee
Mack, Levorn

McClellanville
Smalls, Marcella E.
Weathers, J. Leroy

Moncks Corner
Butler, Clary Kent
Middleton, Vertelle D.
Mitchum, Dorothy M.

Moore
Brooks, Bernard E.

Mount Pleasant
Brown, Angela Yvette

Mullins
Reaves, Franklin Carlwell

Newberry
Caldwell, John Edward

North Charleston
Brown, William Melvin, Jr.

North Myrtle Beach
Montgomery, Joe Elliott
Williams, George L., Sr.

Orangeburg
Abraham, Sinclair Reginald
Brunson, Debora Bradley
Caldwell, Rossie Juanita Brower
Evans, Arthur L.
Glover, Agnes W.
Gore, Blinzy L.
Harris, Gil W.
Hickson, William F., Jr.
James, Carrie Houser
Jenkins, Barbara Williams
Johnson, Carl Lee
Johnson, Doris Elayne
Johnson, Vermelle Jamison
Jones, Marcus Earl
Keitt, L.
Lee, George
Mack, Fred Clarence
Mack, Oscar
Manning, Hubert Vernon
Martin, Frank C., II
McFadden, James L.
Michaux, Henry G.
Middleton, Bernice Bryant
Mosely, Kenneth
Nance, M. Maceo, Jr.
Reuben, Lucy Jeanette
Rogers, Oscar Allan, Jr.
Smith, Albert E.
Stewart, Adelle Wright
Tisdale, Henry Nehemiah
Twiggs, Leo Franklin

Washington, Sarah M.
Winningham, Herman S., Jr.

Parksville
Gilchrist, Robertson

Pawleys Island
Manigault, Walter William

Pelzer
Reid, Janie Ellen

Pendleton
Morse, Annie Ruth W.

Port Royal
Morgan-Washington, Barbara
Robinson, Henry

Rains
Johnson, Robert B.

Rembert
Brooks, W. Webster

Ridgeland
Hicks, Doris Morrison

Ridgeville
Holmes, Mary Brown

Rock Hill
Bethea, Mollie Ann
Copeland, Elaine Johnson
Douglas, John Daniel
Ervin, Deborah Green
Evans, Spofford L.
Goggins, Horace
Moreland, Sallie V.
Sebhatu, Mesgun
Wright-Botchwey, Roberta Yvonne

Seabrook
Kline, Joseph N.

Sellers
Jones, Frank

Seneca
Martin, Amon Achilles, Jr.

Simpsonville
Floyd, James T.

Spartanburg
Allen, Ottis Eugene, Jr.
Carson, Warren Jason, Jr.
Porter, John Henry
Talley, James Edward
Wiles, Leon E.
Wright, J. R.

Springfield
Abraham, Sinclair Reginald

St Stephen
Ransom, Norman

Summerville
Johnson, T. J.
Ross, Charles
Singleton, Benjamin, Sr.
Washington, Arnic J.

Sumter
Finney, Ernest A., Jr.
Gray, Ruben L.
Hardin, Henry E.
Johnson, Wilbur Eugene
Mellette, David C.
Millican, Arthenia J. Bates
Richardson, Luns C.
Sampson, Dorothy Vermelle
Thomas, Latta R., Sr.
Vereen-Gordon, Mary Alice
Weston, Larry Carlton

Walterboro
Manigo, George F., Jr.
Thompson, Johnnie
Williams, Raleigh R.

SOUTH DAKOTA

Brookings
Butler, Eugene Thaddeus, Jr.

Roslyn
Diggs, Lawrence J

TENNESSEE

Alcoa
Williams, Richard, Jr.

Athens
Cheek, James Edward

Bolivar
Hicks, Delphus Van, Jr.
Lake, Alfreeda Elizabeth
Shaw, Johnny
Shaw, Opal

Brentwood
Brown, Alvin Montero
Chance, Kenneth Bernard
Crenshaw, Waverly David, Jr.
Jackson, Ada Jean Work
Story, Charles Irvin
White, Katie Kinnard
Winans, BeBe
Winans, CeCe

Brighton
Rose, Shelvie

Brownsville
Rawls, William D., Sr.
Rawls Bond, Charles Cynthia
Smith, James Russell

Charleston
Parker, Charles Thomas

Chattanooga
Allen, Minnie Louise
Bell, James L., Jr.
Brown, Tommie Florence
Edwards, John Loyd, III
Jackson, Horace
Jackson, Luke
Jones, Carolyn G.
Jones, William O.
McCants, Jesse Lee, Sr.
McClure, Fredrick H. L.
McDaniel, Paul Anderson
Miller, James
Page, Jerome W.
Peoples, Erskine L.
Provost, Marsha Parks
Robinson, Clarence B.
Roddy, Howard W.
Scruggs, Booker T., II
Stewart, William H.
Thomas, Sirr Daniel
Willis, Kathi Grant

Clarksville
Gachette, Louise Foston
Joyce, Donald Franklin
Mock, James E.

Collierville
Smith, A. Z.

Columbia
Hines, Morgan B.

Covington
Bommer, Minnie L.

Dyersburg
Biggs, Richard Lee
Jaycox, Mary Irine
Mitchell, George L.
Seibert-McCauley, Mary F.

Franklin
Mills, Mary Elizabeth

Gallatin
Malone, J. Deotha
Nance, Jesse J., Jr.
Sherrill, Vanita Lytle

Gates
Nance, Booker Joe, Sr.
Nance, Jesse J., Jr.

Germantown
Dotson, Philip Randolph
Williams, Hugh Hermes

Goodlettsville
Boone, Carol Marie

Harriman
Barnes, Delorise Creecy
Yeary, James E., Sr.

Henderson
Saunders, Elizabeth A.

Humboldt
Carr, Lenford
Coleman, Andrew Lee
Smith, James Russell

Jackson
Boone, Clarence Donald
Chambers, Alex A.
Coleman, Veronica F.
David, Arthur LaCurtiss
Hudson, Don R.
Kirkendoll, Chester Arthur, II
McClure, Wesley Cornelious
McCure, Wesley C.
Savage, Horace Christopher
Shaw, Willie G.
Wilson, Sidney, Jr.
Wolf, James

Jonesborough
McKinney, Ernest Lee, Sr.

Knoxville
Booker, Robert Joseph
Bourne, Beal Vernon, II
Brown, Mark
Byas, William Herbert
Creswell, Isaiah T., Jr.
Davidson, Elvyn Verone
Felder-Hoehne, Felicia Harris
Franklin, Clarence Frederick
Gillespie, Bonita
Greene, Sarah Moore
Hardy, Walter S. E.
Hatton, Barbara R., PhD.
Hodges, Carolyn Richardson
Hodges, John O.
Houston, Wade
Hunt, Barbara Ann
Kindall, Luther Martin
Lucas, Wilmer Francis, Jr.
Moore, Thomas L.
Owens, Jefferson Pleas
Peek, Marvin E.
Redmond, Jane Smith
Rollins, Avon William, Sr.
Russell, John Peterson, Jr.
Smith, Rufus Herman
Turner, John Barrimore
Tyson, John C.
Welch, Olga Michele
Whaley, Mary H.
Williams, Lois Stovall
Williamson, Handy, Jr.
Ziegler, Dhyana

Lebanon
Burton-Shannon, Clarinda

Lexington
Reese, Viola Kathryn

Martin
Black, Frank S.
Parker, Henry H.

Maryville
Mosley, Tracey Ray

Mc Minnville
Campbell, Otis, Jr.

Memphis
Bailey, D'Army
Bates, Willie Earl
Bennett, Arthur T.
Berhe, Annette Toney
Blackmon, Joyce McAnulty
Bledsoe, Melvin

Bolton, Julian Taylor
Bond, Wilbert, Sr.
Brooks, Todd Frederick
Brown, Claudell, Jr.
Brown, Edward Lynn
Brown, George Henry, Jr.
Brown, Robin R.
Bryant, Anxious E.
Bufford, Edward Eugene
Burgess, Melvin Thomas, Sr.
Burns, Calvin Louis
Busby, V. Eugene
Byas, James Spencer, Sr.
Caffey, Rick
Carter, Patrick Henry, Jr.
Chambliss, Prince C., Jr.
Clark, LeRoy D.
Coleman, Harry Theodore
Coleman, Wisdom F.
Cox, Dianne Fitzgerald
Currie, Eddie L.
Davis, Bunny Coleman
Davis, Edward
DeCosta-Willis, Miriam
Delk, Fannie M.
DeVaughn-Tidline, Donna
  Michelle
Dickerson, Warner Lee
Dixon, Roscoe
Duckett, Gregory Morris
Ford, Fred, Jr.
Ford, James W.
Ford, John Newton
Ford, Lisa Denise
Garrett, Cheryl Ann
Gholson, General James, Jr.
Gholson, Robert L.
Gilliam, Herman Arthur, Jr.
Gipson, Lovelace Preston, II
Green, Al
Green, Reuben H.
Haralson, Larry L.
Harrell, H. Steve
Harris, John H.
Haskins, Morice Lee, Jr.
Hassell, Frances M.
Herenton, Willie W.
Hill, Clara Grant
Hollowell, Johnny Laveral
Hooks, Michael Anthony
Hooks, Mose Yvonne Brooks
Horton, Odell
House, N. Gerry
Howard, Aubrey J.
Howard, Osbie L., Jr.
Howell, Gerald T.
Hurd, William Charles
Jackson, Henry Ralph
Jackson, John, III
Jackson-Teal, Rita F.
Jamerson, Jerome Donnell
Jenkins, Charles E., Sr.
Johnican, Minerva Jane
Johnson, Betty Jo
Johnson, Cato, II
Johnson, Clinisson Anthony
Johnson, Fred D.
Johnson, Jerry Calvin
Joiner, Burnett
Jones, Lorean Electa
Jones, Velma Lois
Jordan, John Edward
Lawston, Marjorie Gray
Marshall, Tom, Sr.
Martin, Cortez Hezekiah
McWilliams, Alfred Edeard
Melancon, Donald
Miles, Rachel Jean
Miller, Andrea Lewis
Montgomery, Dwight Ray
Moore, Jossie A.
Morris, Herman, Jr.
Northcross, Deborah Ametra
Owens, Chandler D.
Parham, Brenda Joyce
Perry, Lee Charles, Jr.
Prater-Harvey, Peggy
Primous, Emma M.
Robinson, George L.
Rodgers, Charles
Roy, John Willie
Royal, James E.
Rudd, Willie Lesslie
Sengstacke, Whittier Alexander,
  Sr.
Sessoms, Glenn D.
Seymour, Laurence Darryl, M. D.
Sharpe, V. Renee
Shaw, Frederick B.

Shotwell, Ada Christena
Smith, Lila
Smith, Maxine Atkins
Smith, Vasco A.
Stansbury, Markhum L.
Stevens, Rochelle
Stockton, Clifford, Sr.
Strickland, Herman William, Jr.
Suggs, William Albert
Talley, Curtiss J.
Taylor, Harold Leon
Thomas, N. Charles
Thompson, Harold Fong
Tieuel, Robert C. D.
Tolbert, Odie Henderson, Jr.
Turner, Jesse H., Jr.
Turner, Johnnie Rodgers
Venson, Clyde R.
Walker, A. Maceo, Sr.
Walker, Felix Carr, Jr.
Walker, George Edward
Walker, Walter Lorenzo
Walker-Shaw, Patricia
Waller, Robert Lee
Ward, Daniel
Warren, Lee Alden
Watson, Ben
Watts, Victor Lewis
Westbrook, Joseph W., III
Whalum, Kenneth Twigg
Wharton, A. C., Jr.
Wilks, Carl S.
Williams, Hugh Hermes
Withers, Ernest
Wynn, Robert L., Jr.
Yates, Mark
Young, Josef A.

Murfreesboro
Clark, Bertha Smith
Glanton, Lydia Jackson
Hare, Linda Paskett
Hughes, Bernice Ann
McAdoo, Henry Allen
Pleas, John Roland
Rucker, Nannie George
Wills, Cornelia

Nashville
Abernathy, Ronald Lee
Adkins, Cecelia Nabrit
Adkins, Rutherford
Allen, Harriette Louise
Archer, Susie Coleman
Ashley Harris, Dolores B.
Atchison, Calvin O.
Babb, Michael
Babb, Morgan
Bacon, William Louis
Bailey, William R.
Baldwin, Lewis V.
Bell, Wendolyn Yvonne
Belton, Robert
Benson, Wanda Miller
Bernard, Harold O.
Bernard, Louis Joseph
Birch, Adolpho A., Jr.
Bishop, Blaine Elwood
Boone, Carol Marie
Bowden, Joseph Tarrod
Boyd, Theophilus B., III
Braddock, Marilyn Eugenia
Bradley, J. Robert
Brinkley, Charles H., Sr.
Brooks, Marcellus
Brown, Dorothy Lavania
Brown, James Harvey
Burton, Kendrick
Byrd, Isaac
Calhoun, Calvin Lee
Campbell, Otis, Jr.
Chance, Kenneth Bernard
Chatterjee, Lois Jordan
Childress, Jay
Cobbs, Susie Ann
Conley, James Monroe
Cook, Anthony Andrew
Crouch, Andrae
Crowell, Bernard G.
Davidson, Rick Bernard
Davis, James W.
Davis, Willie Clark
DeBerry, Lois Marie
DeBerry, Vickie Miller
Dent, Carl Ashley
DeShields, Harrison F., Jr.
Dixon, Roscoe
Dooley, Wallace Troy
Dorsett, Anthony Drew, Jr.

Douglas, Mansfield, III
Driver, Rogers W.
Dudley, Charles Edward
Easley, Billy Harley
Edwards, Eunice L.
Elam, Lloyd C.
Elliott, Derek Wesley
Elliott, Irvin Wesley
England, Eric Jevon
Evans, Josh
Fancher, Evelyn Pitts
Felix, Dudley E.
Fielder, Fred Charles
Ford, Henry
Fort, Jane
Foster, Henry Wendell
Fuller, Vivian L.
George, Eddie
Giles, Henrietta
Gray, Sterling Perkins, Jr.
Guess, Francis S.
Hall, Lemanski
Hamberg, Marcelle R.
Hamby, Roscoe Jerome
Handy, William Talbot, Jr.
Harper, Thelma Marie
Hayes, Melvin Anthony
Haynes, William J., Jr.
Hefner, James A.
Henderson, Cheri Kaye
Hill, George C.
Hill, Henry, Jr.
Hodge, Cynthia Elois
Holmes, Kenny
Holmes, Robert L., Jr.
Hooks, Benjamin Lawson
Hopkins, Bradley D.
Horton, Carrell Peterson
Howard, Samuel H.
Hull, George, Jr.
Isibor, Edward Iroguehi
Jackson, Andrew
Jackson, Arthur James
Jackson, Clinton
Jackson, Steven Wayne
Johnson, Charles William
Johnson, Ernest Kaye, III
Johnson, Ezra Ray
Jones, Enoch
Jones, Lenoy
Jones, Roger Carver
Jordan, Harold Willoughby
Junior, Samella E.
Kelley, Robert W.
Kilcrease, Irvin Hugh, Jr.
Killens, Terry Deleon
Kimbrough, Charles Edward
Lafayette, Bernard, Jr.
Lee, Andre L.
Lemeh, Dorotha Hill
Lewis, Daryll Lamont
Lewis, Helen Middleton
Lewis, Roderick Albert
Lillard, Kwame Leo
Logan, Bertie Hawthorne
Long, Ophelia
Lownes, Millicent Gray
Luis, William
Lytle, Marilyn Mercedes
Mallette, John M.
Marshall, Betty J.
Martin, James Larence
Martin, Ruby Julene Wheeler
Marts, Lonnie
Maupin, John E., Jr.
McGruder, Charles E.
McKissack, Leatrice Buchanan
McKissack, William Deberry
McNair, Steve
McReynolds, Elaine A.
Mitchell, Edwin H., Sr.
Mix, Bryant Lee
Mobley, Eugenia L.
Moore, Robert F.
Moses, Henry A.
Murray, Albert R.
Murrell, Barbara Curry
Nicholson, Aleathia Dolores
Nightingale, Jesse Phillip
Patton, Princess E.
Perry, Frank Anthony
Peterman, Leotis
Peters, Sheila Renee
Poellnitz, Fred Douglas
Powell, John Lewis
Ramsey, Freeman, Jr.
Redd, George N.
Richardson, Elisha R.
Robertson, Marcus Aaron

Robinson, Martha Dolores
Roby, Reginald Henry
Rogers, Decatur Braxton
Russell, Derek Dwayne
Sanders, Chris
Scott, Veronica J.
Shockley, Ann Allen
Shockley, Thomas Edward
Smith, Jessie Carney
Stewart, Rayna Cottrell
Stinson, Joseph McLester
Straight, Cathy A.
Strong, Blondell McDonald
Temple, Edward Stanley
Thomas, Rodney Dejuane
Traughber, Charles M.
Walker, Denard
Walker, Gary Lamar
Washington, Sandra Beatrice
Watson, Vernaline
White, Sharon Brown
Wiggins, Charles A.
Wilkes, William R.
Williams, Armon
Williams, Avon Nyanza, Jr.
Williams, Carolyn Ruth Armstrong
Williams, Jamye Coleman
Williams, Malcolm Demosthenes
Wilson, Donella Joyce
Winbush, Raymond Arnold
Winfrey, Charles Everett
Wortham, Barron Winfred
Wynn, Daniel Webster

Oak Ridge
Colston, Freddie C.
Lewis, Kenneth Dwight
Minter, Wilbert Douglas, Sr.
Porter, Patrick A.
Revis, Nathaniel W.
Shipe, Jamesetta Denise Holmes
Smith, Lila
Smith, Rufus Herman
Upton, E. H.

Old Hickory
Finch, Janet M.

Pulaski
Brown, James Monroe

Smyrna
Williams, Johnny Wayne

South Pittsburg
Moore, Hiram Beene

Spring Hill
Fletcher, Milton Eric

Tullahoma
Duncan, Lynda J.

Whiteville
Robertson, Evelyn Crawford, Jr.

TEXAS

Addison
Pearson, Drew
Shead, Ken

Arlington
Anderson, Alfred Anthony
Browne, Jerry
Connor, Dolores Lillie
DeSassure, Charles
Foster, Deborah Valrie
Goodwin, Thomas Jones
Hester, Arthur C.
LeGrand, Bob
McLemore, Mark Tremell
Oliver, Darren Christopher
Redus, Gary Eugene
Smith-Croxton, Terri
Taylor, Dalmas A.

Austin
Adams, Edward B.
Anderson, Marcellus J., Sr.
Baker, Kimberley Renee
Baye, Lawrence James J.
Belle, John Otis
Brewington, Donald Eugene
Brown, Rubye Golsby
Bryant, Andrea Pair

Burton, Barbara Ann
Butler, John Sibley
Chargois, James M.
Delco, Wilhelmina R.
Edwards, Matthew D.
Evans, Akwasi Rozelle
Evans, Roxanne J.
Francis, Patrick John
Hanson, John L.
Haugstad, May Katheryn
Higginbotham-Brooks, Renee
Hill, James L.
James, Daniel, III
Jordan, Barbara Charline
Kennedy, Brenda Picola
Kerr, Stanley Munger
King, John Q. Taylor, Sr.
Larry, Jerald Henry
Mann, Thomas J., Jr.
Marsh, Alphonso Howard
McDaniel, Reuben R.
McMillan, Joseph Turner, Jr.
McRoy, Ruth Gail
Means, Bertha E.
Nelson, Wanda Lee
Nesby, Donald Ray, Sr.
Oliver, Jesse Dean
Overstreet, Morris L
Overton, Volma Robert
Parker, Joseph Caiaphas, Jr.
Powell, Philip Melancthon, Jr.
Scott, Richard Eley
Sikes, Melvin Patterson
Smith, Starita Ann
Tucker, Geraldine Jenkins
Urdy, Charles E.
Vernon, Alexander
Walker, Sheila Suzanne
Ward, Nolan F.
White, Barbara Williams
Williams Davis, Edith G.
Wilson, Ora Brown
Wilson, Ronald Ray
Wingate, Rosalee Martin

Bastrop
Navarro, Wilfred, III

Baytown
Hadnot, Thomas Edward
Piper, Elwood A.
Steele, Joyce Yvonne

Beaumont
Jones, Kirkland C.

Bedford
Merton, Joseph Lee

Bryan
Kern-Foxworth, Marilyn L.
Marshall, Pluria W., Sr.

Carrollton
Cox-Crooks, Tobi
Daniels, Curtis A.

Carthage
Beck, Hershell P.

Cedar Park
Johnson, Andrew
Morrison, Paul-David

China
Prejean, Ruby D.

Cleveland
Hayes, Elvin E., Sr.
Turner, Carl

College Station
Carreathers, Kevin R.
Kern-Foxworth, Marilyn L.
Majors, Anthony Y.
Rice, Mitchell F.
Watkins, Melvin

Commerce
Talbot, David Arlington Roberts,
  Sr.

Como
Williams, John Waldo

Conroe
Irvin, Charles Leslie

Corpus Christi
Carline, William Ralph
Gray, Valerie Hamilton
Gurley, Helen Ruth
Sanders, Woodrow Mac

Corsicana
Waters, Sylvia Ann

Crosby
Mitchell, Tex Dwayne

Cypress
Berry, Benjamin Donaldson

Dallas
Alexander, Drew W.
Allen, Billy R.
Allen, Warren H.
Baraka, Larry
Bardwell, Rufus B., III
Beard, Butch
Beck, Arthello, Jr.
Bell, H. B.
Berry, Gemeral E., Jr.
Bogus, Houston, Jr.
Brashear, Berland Leander
Brossette, Alvin, Jr.
Brown, Ellen Rochelle
Bryant, John Richard
Buckner, Quinn
Cambridge, Dexter
Campbell, Mary Delois
Campbell, Tony
Carter, Kelly Elizabeth
Carter, Kenneth Wayne
Ceballos, Cedric Z.
Clark, Caesar A. W.
Cleamons, James Mitchell
Colston Barge, Gayle S.
Cooper, Larry B.
Cornelius, Ulysses S., Sr.
Cottrell, Comer J.
Cunningham, E. Brice
Custis, Ace
Darby, Castilla A., Jr.
Davis, Hubert Ira, Jr.
Dawson, Jesse R.
Dick, George Albert
Edwards O'Bannon, Donna M.
Eichorst, Fran
Emory, Emerson
Espree, Allen James
Esquivel, Argelia Velez
Evans, Vernon D.
Ewell, Yvonne Amaryllis
Fagan, Harold Leonard
Farris, Deborah Ellison
Finley, Michael H.
Ford, David Leon, Jr.
Ford, Janice T.
Foreman, Joyce Blacknall
Foutz, Samuel Theodore
Frazier, William James
Gaines, Ava Candace
Gaston, Patricia Elaine
Glover, Clarence Ernest, Jr.
Gray, Carol Coleman
Gray, James Howard
Green, A. C., Jr.
Hammond, Ulysses S., Jr.
Hankins, Anthony Mark
Harden, Robert James
Harper, T. Errol
Hayes, Curtiss Leo
Hayes-Jordan, Margaret
Henderson, Ruth Faynella
Hendricks, Richard D.
Hill, Hattie
Hill, Vonciel Jones
Hilliard, Delories
Hodge, Donald Jerome
Holmes, Zan W., Jr.
Howard, Brian
Hudson, Charles Lynn
Hunter, Charles A.
Hunter, Irby B.
Jackson, Brenda
Jackson, David M.
Jackson, Lurline Bradley
Johnson, Charles B.
Johnson, Iola Vivian
Johnson, Marion T.
Johnson, Patricia Anita
Jones, Lester C.
Kidd, Foster
Kirk, Ron
Kirven, Mythe Yuvette
Knight, Richard, Jr.

Lacy, Versia Lindsay
Laday, Kerney
Lander, C. Victor
Lander, Fred Leonard, III
Lane, Eddie Burgyone
Larry, Jerald Henry
Lassiter, Wright Lowenstein, Jr.
Lee, Anthony Owen
Lee, Fred D., Jr.
Lever, Lafayette
Malone, Sandra Dorsey
Mason, Edward James
McCaa, John K.
McClane, Don
McClure, Frederick Donald
McFall, Mary
Mercer, Dave
Mitchell-Brooks, Beverly
Montgomery, Mildren M.
Morris, Wayne Lee
Newhouse, Robert F.
Nobles, Patricia Joyce
O'Bannon, Donna Edwards
O'Bannon, Edward Charles, Jr.
Orr, Ray
Ortiz, Victor
Pack, Robert John, Jr.
Pailin, David
Parker, Charlie
Parker, Fred Lee Cecil
Phelps-Patterson, Lucy
Powell, Dudley Vincent
Powell, John
Pride, Charley
Ragsdale, Paul B.
Ray, Francis
Reeves, Khalid
Respert, Shawn Christopher
Richards-Alexander, Billie J.
Roberts, Alfred Lloyd, Sr.
Robertson, Gertrude
Robertson, Lynn E.
Robinson, Harry, Jr.
Rollins, Richard Albert
Rowe, Jasper C.
Ruffin, Herbert
Sanders, Patricia Roper
Sharpton, Denise
Shine, Theodis
Smith, Doug
Smith, Stevin
Stahnke, William E.
Steele, Cleophas R., Jr.
Stewart, Edward L.
Strickland, Erick
Sulieman, Jamil
Sullivan, Allen R.
Sweets, Ellen Adrienne
Taylor, Eartha Lynn
Taylor, Gayland Wayne
Thomas, Deon
Thomas, Kurt Vincent
Thompson, Frank William
Tinsley, Fred Leland, Jr.
Wade, Norma Adams
Walker, Samaki Ijuma
Ware, John
Washington, James A.
Wattley, Thomas Jefferson
West, Royce Barry
White, Mabel Meshach
White, Randy
Wiley, Morlon David
Williams, Ada L.
Winslow, Kenneth Paul
Wise, Frank P.
Witherspoon, William Roger
Woodbeck, Frank Raymond
Wright, Sylvester M.
Young, Lias Carl

DeSoto
Giddings, Helen
Saulter, Gilbert John

Del Rio
McAlister, Joe Michael

Denison
Turner, Larry V.

Denton
Hildreth, Gladys Johnson
Jackson, Governor Eugene, Jr.
Simon, Matt
Smith, Edward
Sparks, Clifton Tinsley
Terrell, Francis
Thibodeaux, Mary Shepherd

Totten, Herman Lavon
Wallace, Milton De'Nard
Washington, Roosevelt, Jr.
Wesley III, Herman Eugene

Desoto
Saddler, William E.

Dickinson
Hearne, Earl
Johnson, Wayne Wright, III

El Paso
Greer, Edward
Ramsey, Donna Elaine
Shuffer, George Macon, Jr.
Washington, Johnnie M.
Young, John W.

Ennis
Coleman, Raymond Cato

Euless
Stripling, Luther

Farmers Branch
Bumphus, Walter Gayle

Forest Hill
Badgett, Edward

Fort Worth
Bowman-Webb, Loetta
Briscoe, Leonard E.
Brooks, Marion Jackson
Cary, Reby
Clark, Randolph A.
Davis, L. Clifford
DuBose, Isaac, Jr.
English, Robert James
Fretwell, Carl Quention, II
Hardeman, Strotha E., Jr.
Hegmon, Oliver Louis
Heiskell, Michael Porter
Hicks, Maryellen
Jennings, Devoyd
Johnson, Erma Chansler
Johnson, Mervil V.
Johnson, Phyllis Campbell
Johnson, Wilhelmina Lashaun
Johnson, William Lee, Jr.
Knox-Benton, Shirley
Lewis, Erma
Lister, Willa M.
McEwing, Mitchell Dalton
Mitchell, Huey P.
Sims, Theophlous Aron, Sr.
Standifer, Ben H.
Standifer, Lonnie Nathaniel
Staples, Gracie Bonds
Stewart, Dorothy Nell
Terrell, Robert E.
Wilson, Hazel Forrow Simmons
Young, Alan John
Young, Lias Carl

Galveston
Brooks, Don Locellus
Hearne, Earl
Norris, Walter, Jr.
Robertson, Paul Francis
Simmons, Annie Marie
Stanton, Janice D.
Williams, Sandra Roberts

Garland
Thornton, Willie James, Jr.
Ward, Anna Elizabeth

Grand Prairie
Howard, Calvin Johnson
Willrich, Emzy James

Grapevine
Bell, Rosalind Nanette

Greenville
Williams, Vernon R.

Hawkins
Acrey, Autry
Hall, Delilah Ridley
Hawkins, Dorisula Wooten
Holmes, Lorene B.
Lanier, Dorothy Copeland

Hearne
McDaniel, Billy Ray

Helotes
Banks, Laura N.

Hempstead
Carter, Gwendolyn Burns
Singleton, Leroy, Sr.

Henderson
Stevenson, Leon

Houston
Adams, Elaine Parker
Adams, Samuel Clifford, Jr.
Alexander, Alma Duncan
Allen, Andrew A.
Anderson, Doris J.
Andrews, Rawle
Andrews, William Phillip
Bacon, Robert John, Jr.
Baker, Kimberley Renee
Banfield, Edison H.
Baptiste, Hansom Prentice, Jr.
Barkley, Charles Wade
Barnett, Carl L., Sr.
Barnett, Marguerite Ross
Barrows, Bryan H., III
Bass, Kevin Charles
Beard, James William, Jr.
Belcher, Leon H.
Bell, Derek Nathaniel
Bell, Robert L.
Berry, Weldon H.
Bickham, L. B.
Bishop, Verissa Rene
Blair, Curtis
Boney, J. Don
Bonner, Alice A.
Boyd, Barbara Jean
Bradley, Jack Carter
Branch, Eldridge Stanley
Bransford, Paris
Bright, Willie S.
Brooks, Hunter O.
Brooks, Sylvia
Brown, Abner Bertrand
Brown, Freddiemae Eugenia
Brown, Lee Patrick
Brown-Guillory, Elizabeth
Bryant, Faye B.
Buckner, William Pat, Jr.
Buggage, Cynthia Marie
Bullock, James
Butler, Eula M.
Bynam, Sawyer Lee, III
Cabell, Enos M., Jr.
Caggins, Ruth Porter
Carl, Earl Lawrence
Carter, Joye
Carter, Lenora
Chandler, Effie L.
Chapman, Dorothy Hilton
Chase, John S.
Clark, Clarence Bendenson, Jr.
Clark, David Earl
Claye, Charlene Marette
Claye, Clifton Maurice
Cooley, Archie Lee, Jr.
Cooper, Cynthia
Cooper, Gordon R., II
Cooper, Matthew N.
Copeland, Barry Bernard
Cormier, Rufus, Jr.
Covington, James Arthur
Cox, Corine
Craven, Judith
Cunningham, James J.
Cunningham, Richard T.
Curbeam, Robert L.
Cureton, Earl
Davis, Algenita Scott
Davis, Emanual
Dickerson, Thomas L., Jr.
Dillard, Melvin Rubin
Dixon, Brenda Joyce
Dixon, James Wallace Edwin, II
Dodson, Selma L.
Dotson, Betty Lou
Douglas, Aubry Carter
Douglas, James Matthew
Drexler, Clyde
Edwards, Al E.
Edwards, Horace Burton
Elie, Mario Antoine
Ellis, Rodney
Eugere, Edward J.
Everett, Carl Edward

Everett, David Leon, II
Ewing, Mamie Hans
Fadulu, Sunday O.
Fain, Constance Frisby
Ford, Marion George, Jr.
Foreman, George Edward
Foreman, Peggy E.
Franklin, Martha Lois
Frazier, Charles Douglas
Frelow, Robert Lee, Jr.
Garrison-Jackson, Zina Lynna
Gathe, Joseph C.
Gilmore, Robert McKinley, Sr.
Gite, Lloyd Anthony
Gloster, Jesse E.
Glover, Robert G.
Gooden, Cherry Ross
Graham, Ladell
Grate, Isaac, Jr.
Grays, Mattelia Bennett
Green, Al
Green, Pha M.
Gregg, Harrison M., Jr.
Guyton, Wanda
Hall, Anthony W., Jr.
Hall, Benjamin Lewis, III
Hall, Horathel
Hammond, Melvin Alan Ray, Jr.
Hannah, Mack H., Jr.
Harding, Michael S.
Harrington, Othella
Harris, Bernard A., Jr.
Harris, Fran
Harris, Vera D.
Haynes, George E., Jr.
Henry, Forest T., Jr.
Hervey, Billy T.
Higgins, Clarence R., Jr.
Hodge, Norris
Honore, Stephan LeRoy
Hopkins, Albert E., Jr.
Huckaby, Henry Lafayette
Hunter, Oliver Clifford, Jr.
Ingram, LaVerne Dorothy
Jackson, Harold Leonard
Jackson, Roy Joseph, Jr.
James, Betty Nowlin
Jefferson, Andrew L., Jr.
Jefferson, Joseph L.
Jefferson, Overton C.
Jemison, Mae C.
Johnson, Caliph
Johnson, Edward Arnet
Johnson, Lectoy Tarlington
Johnson, Rudolphus
Jones, Barbara Ann Posey
Jones, Charles
Jones, Edith Irby
Jones, Gaynelle Griffin
Jones, Howard James
Jones, Joseph
Jones, Zoia L.
Kennedy, Nathelyne Archie
Kleven, Thomas
Lattimore, Oliver Louis, Sr.
Lede, Naomi W.
Lee, Robert Emile
Lewis, Carl
Lewis, Frederick Carlton
Lloyd, Lewis Kevin
Lomas, Ronald Leroy
Mabrie, Herman James, III
Malbroue, Joseph, Jr.
Marshall, Julyette Matthews
McAfee, Carrie R.
McDonald, Curtis W.
McDonald, Mark T.
McDonald, Willie Ruth Davis
McElroy, George A.
McLaurin, Daniel Washington
McMillan, Mae F.
McNeil, Alvin J.
Mease, Quentin R.
Miles, Ruby A. Branch
Miller, Theodore H.
Mitchell, Tex Dwayne
Moore, Lois Jean
Moore, Milton Donald, Jr.
Moore, Yolanda
Moorehead, Bobbie Wooten
Mooring, Kittye D.
Morgan, Robert, Jr.
Morgan-Price, Veronica Elizabeth
Morris, Lewis R.
Mothershed, Spaesio W.
Mouton, James Raleigh
Mwamba, Zuberi I.
Nicks, William James, Sr.
Olajuwon, Hakeem Abdul

Paige, Roderick
Pearson, Michael Novel
Peavy, John W., Jr.
Perrot, Kim
Plummer, Matthew W., Sr.
Poindexter, Zeb F.
Poston, Carl
Poston, Kevin
Prophet, Richard L., Jr.
Ramirez, Richard M.
Randle, Berdine Caronell
Randle, Lucious A.
Ratliff, Joe Samuel
Reid, Goldie Hartshorn
Reynolds, Harry G.
Rhodes, Rodrick
Richards, LaVerne W.
Riley, Wayne Joseph
Robinson, Frank J.
Robinson, Jayne G.
Robinson, Larry
Routt, Thomas H.
Scott, Charles E.
Seals, Maxine
Seymour, Barbara H.
Shange, Ntozake
Shields, Varee, Jr.
Smith, Al Fredrick
Smith, George V.
Smith, Roland Blair, Jr.
Speller, Charles K.
Spurlock, Racquel
Stamps, Joe, Jr.
Stephens, Joseph, Jr.
Stickney, William Homer, Jr.
Stone, John S.
Swoopes, Sheryl
Taylor-Thompson, Betty E.
Terry, Robert James
Thomas, Earl
Thomas, Gloria V.
Thomas, Sherri Booker
Thompson, Clarissa J.
Thompson, Tina
Threatt, Sedale Eugene
Thurston, Paul E.
Tryman, Mfanya Donald
Turner, Elmyra G.
Wadley, Bernice
Walker, Carl, Jr.
Walker, May
Walker, Stanley M.
Wardlaw, Alvia Jean
Wardlaw, Alvin Holmes
Washington, Craig A.
Webster, Winston Roosevelt
Wells, Patrick Roland
White, Dezra
Wickliff, Aloysius M., Sr.
Wiley, John D., Jr.
Williams, Arthur Love
Williams, John L.
Willis, Kevin Alvin
Wilson, Bobby L.
Winchester, Kennard
Woodson, Mike
Wyche, Lennon Douglas, Jr.
Yarborough, Dowd Julius, Jr.

Humble
Teague, Gladys Peters

Irving
Alexander, Hubbard Lindsay
Allen, Larry Christopher
Anderson, Antonio
Benson, Darren
Briggs, Greg
Brooks, Macey
Carver, Shante
Coakley, Dexter
Davis, Wendell
Davis, William Augusta, III
Deramus, Bill R.
English, Deborah
Galbraith, Scott
Godfrey, Randall Euralentris
Haley, Charles Lewis
Hegamin, George
Hill, Calvin
Horton, Raymond Anthony
Irvin, Michael Jerome
Jeffcoat, James Wilson, Jr.
Laday, Kerney
Lavan, Alton
Lee, Anthony Owen
Lett, Leon
Little, Helen R.
Mathis, Kevin

McCormack, Hurvin
Merritt, Thomas Mack
Miller, Anthony
Mobley, Singor
Morris, Frank Lorenzo, Sr.
Newton, Nate
Pittman, Kavika
Sanders, Deion Luwynn
Scott, Werner Ferdinand
Simpson-Watson, Ora Lee
Smith, Emmitt J., III
Smith, Kevin Rey
Smith, Vinson Robert
Stoutmire, Omar
Strickland, Fredrick William, Jr.
Stubblefield, Raymond M.
Thomas, Broderick
Tolbert, Tony Lewis
Townsell, Jackie Mae
Tucker, Sheilah L. Wheeler
Walker, Herschel
Wheaton, Kenny
Williams, Charlie
Williams, Erik George
Williams, Sherman
Williams, Stepfret
Willrich, Emzy James
Woodson, Darren Ray
Wright, Alex

Jacksonville
Johnson, Margie N.

Jasper
Milligan, Unav Opal Wade

Katy
Bostick, Laurence Herbert

Kilgore
Garrett, Cain, Jr.
Tolbert, Jacquelyn C.

Killeen
Grace, Horace R.

Kingwood
Early, Ezzard Dale

La Marque
Pratt, Mable

La Porte
Hills, James Bricky

Lancaster
Simmons, Frank
Stafford, Don

Livingston
Smith, Irvin L.

Longview
Bailey, Clarence Walter
Harper, Robert Lee
Probasco, Jeanetta
Tolbert, Jacquelyn C.

Lubbock
Henry, Charles E.
Richardson, Eddie Price, Jr.
Snell, Joan Yvonne Ervin

Lufkin
Henderson, I. D., Jr.
Meyer, Alton J.
Pierre, Dallas

Marlin
Dorsey, Leon D., Sr.
Douglas, Arthur E.
Lynn, James Elvis

Marshall
Anderson, S. A.
Carter, Lamore Joseph
Hayes, Robert E., Sr.
Houston, Lillian S.
Johnson-Helton, Karen
Lamothe, Isidore J., Jr.
Miller, Telly Hugh
Sanders, Larry Kyle
Shaw, Warren
Stallworth, Jeremiah T.
Williams, Alphonza

Mc Kinney
Young, Lee R.

Mesquite
Mills, Glenn B., Jr.

Missouri City
Miles, Ruby A. Branch
Williams, LaShina Brigette

Nacogdoches
Allen, George
Prince, Andrew Lee

New Waverly
Straughter, Edgar, Sr.

Odessa
Winfield, Elayne Hunt

Orange
Jeter, Velma Marjorie Dreyfus
Robertson, Andre Levett

Palestine
Hunt, O'Neal

Paris
Key, June Roe

Pearland
Mullett, Donald L.
Odom, Darryl Eugene

Plano
Bogus, Houston, Jr.
Powell, Julie
White, Alvin, Jr.
Woodbeck, Frank Raymond

Port Arthur
Evans, Amos James
Freeman, Ruby E.
Guidry, Arreader Pleanna
Myles, Herbert John

Prairie View
Barrows, Bryan H., III
Berry, Benjamin Donaldson
Carter, Gwendolyn Burns
Clemons, Earlie, Jr.
Hines, Charles A.
Jacket, Barbara Jean
Jackson, Frank Donald
Jones, Barbara Ann Posey
Martin, Edward Williford
Prestage, Jewel Limar
Shine, Theodis
Talley, Clarence, Sr.
Woolfolk, George Ruble

Randolph A F B
Beason, Kenneth Garrett
Newton, Lloyd W.

Richardson
Ford, David Leon, Jr.
Jenifer, Franklyn Green
Jones, Alphonzo James
Lockhart, Eugene, Jr.
McNary, Oscar Lee

Riviera
Scott, Gloria Dean Randle

Round Rock
Miller, Frank Lee, Jr.

San Antonio
Andrews, Charles Clifton, Jr.
Briscoe, Hattie Ruth Elam
Byrd, Sherman Clifton
Coggs, Granville Coleridge
Crawford, Deborah Collins
Creft, Brenda K.
Cummings, Terry
Daniels, Lloyd
Derricotte, Eugene Andrew
Donahue, William T.
Duncan, Tim
Elliott, Sean Michael
Floyd, Eric Augustus
Foster, Lloyd L.
Gaffney, Thomas Daniel
Geary, Reggie
Greenwood, David
Haywood, Norcell D.

Herrera, Carl Victor
Hilliard, Robert Lee Moore
Hudspeth, Gregory Charles, Sr.
Jackson, Earl, Jr.
Jackson, Jaren
James, Hamice R., Jr.
Johnson, Avery
Johnson, Timothy Julius, Jr.
Knight, Negele Oscar
Lawrence, Leonard E.
Maxwell, Vernon
May, Dickey R.
McClure, Donald Leon, Sr.
Nance, Herbert Charles, Sr.
Nelson, Ivory Vance
Person, Chuck Connors
Pressey, Paul Matthew
Pulley, Clyde Wilson
Reed, Florine
Reid, J. R.
Robinson, David Maurice
Rose, Malik Jabari
Slaughter, John Etta
Smith, Charles Daniel, Jr.
Stewart, Bess
Thurston, Charles Sparks
Walker, Mary L.
Warrick, Alan Everett
Watson, Leonidas
Webb, Joe
Wilkins, Dominique
Williams, Lorece P.
Williams, Monty
Williams, Theodore R.
Winters, Kenneth E.
Wright, Earl Lee

San Augustine
Garner, Lon L.

San Marcos
Smith, Joanne Hamlin

Seabrook
Bastine, Lillian Beatrice

Simonton
Cockrell, Mechera Ann

Spring
Ingram, LaVerne Dorothy
James, Advergus Dell, Jr.

Sugar Land
Lee, Robert Emile

Temple
Harrison, Roscoe Conklin, Jr.
Hornsby, B. Kay
Kennedy, Jimmie Vernon
Peek, Gail Lenore

Terrell
Anderson, Abbie H.
Evans, Jack
Jackson, Seaton J.
Lee, Gerald E.

Texarkana
Burke, Denzer
Williams, Londell

Texas City
Carter, Thomas Floyd, Jr.
Johnson, Milton D.
Pratt, Alexander Thomas

The Woodlands
Lewis, Charles Michael

Thompsons
Morgan, Fletcher, Jr.

Trinidad
Newton, James Douglas, Jr.

Tyler
Butler, Pinkney L.
Clark, Jimmy E.
Early, Paul David
Hancock, Allen C.
Johnson, David Horace
Jones, John P.
Lanier, Marshall L.
Patton, Mitchell
Sanders, Sally Ruth
Smith, Gloria Dawn

Waits, Va Lita Francine

Universal City
Smith, Joanne Hamlin

Victoria
Cade, Harold Edward
Sanders, Laura Green

Waco
Allen, Van Sizar
Harrison, Emma Louise
Hooker, Eric H.
Johnson, Lawrence E., Sr.
Jones, Marilyn Elaine
King, Arthur Thomas
Leonard, Leon Lank, Sr.
Richards, DeLeon Marie
Talbot, Theodore A.

Wichita Falls
Boston, Horace Oscar
Stephens, David

Willis
Straughter, Edgar, Sr.

UTAH

Magna
Green, Darryl Lynn

Ogden
Oliver, Daily E.

Provo
Gill, Troy D.

Salt Lake City
Anderson, Shandon Rodriguez
Booker, Karen
Bush, Lenoris
Carr, Antoine Labotte
Coleman, Ronald Gerald
Cope, Donald Lloyd
Cunningham, William L.
Davis, France Albert
Eisley, Howard Jonathan
Foster, Gregory Clinton
Gill, Troy D.
Griffith, Darrell Steven
Guillory, William A.
Hardmon, Lady
Head, Dena
Henry, Alberta
Hicks, Jessie
Jones, Curley C.
Malone, Karl
Morris, Christopher Vernard
Palmer, Wendy
Russell, Bryon Demetrise
Samuels, Wilfred D.
Vaughn, Jacque
Williams, Kim

VERMONT

Bennington
Dixon, William R.

Burlington
Clemmons, Jackson Joshua Walter
McCrorey, H. Lawrence

Charlotte
Clemmons, Jackson Joshua Walter

Middlebury
Beatty, Martin Clarke

Rutland
Wakefield, J. Alvin

VIRGINIA

Accomac
Cooper, Samuel H., Jr.

Alexandria
Andrews, Rosalyn McPherson
Barlow, William B.
Barrett, Matthew Anderson
Bell, Hubert Thomas, Jr.
Booker, Vaughan P. L.
Branche, Gilbert M.
Brown, Michael DeWayne
Burton, David Lloyd
Bussey, Charles David
Byrd, Melvin L.
Chapman, Audrey Bridgeforth
Conliffe, Carl
Cromartie, Eugene Rufus
DeSandies, Kenneth Andre
Foster, Luther H.
Francis, E. Aracelis
Gaines, Sylvester, Jr.
Gaither, Dorothy B.
Garrett, James F.
Handy, Lillian B.
Hardie, Robert L., Jr.
Harris, Lee Andrew, II
Hodges, Helene
Johnson, Mal
Lockett, Alice Faye
Mabrey, Ernest L., Jr.
Mathur, Krishan
McClenic, Patricia Dickson
McMillan, Wilton Vernon
Morgan, Alice Johnson Parham
Pemberton-Heard, Danielle Marie
Pierson, Kathryn A.
Prince, Richard Everett
Rackley, Lurma M.
Ramseur, Andre William
Roye, Monica R. Hargrove
Smith, James Charles
Thoms, Donald H.
Tyler, Shirley Neizer
Zimmerman, Matthew Augustus, Jr.

Annandale
Brown, Ruby Edmonia
Coates, Shelby L.
Murphy, Jeanne Claire Fuller

Arlington
Aggrey, O. Rudolph
Agurs, Donald Steele
Ashe, Arthur R., Jr.
Bell, William McKinley
Blount, Charlotte Renee
Bonner, Alice Carol
Brooks, Rodney Alan, Sr.
Brown, George L.
Brownlee, Dennis J.
Brownlee, Vivian Aplin
Davis, Ruth A.
Dual, J. Fred, Jr.
Gooden, C. Michael
Gorman, Bertha Gaffney
Green, Deborah Kennon
Hanford, Craig Bradley
Henderson, Crawford, Sr.
Holman, Kwame Kent Allan
Jackson, Kevin L.
Johnson, Charles Bernard
Jordan, Kenneth Ulys
Kearse, Barbara Stone
Lander, Cressworth Caleb
Lang-Jeter, Lula L.
Lawrence, Ollie, Jr.
Lindsay, Horace Augustin
Lister, Valerie Lynn
Mathis, Deborah F.
May, James Shelby
McCants, Odell
Moncure, Albert F.
Morton, Norman
Newman, William Thomas, Jr.
Parham, Dashton Daniel
Parker, Lutrelle Fleming
Rand, Cynthia
Scott, Samuel
Sinnette, Calvin Herman
Sinnette, Elinor DesVerney
Smith, Carolyn Lee
Smith, Chester B.
Smith, Douglas M.
Townsend, Ron
Tucker, Geraldine Coleman
Vereen, Dixie Diane
Wallace, Peggy Mason
Washington, MaliVai
Wickham, DeWayne
Woods, Willie
Young, Rose S.

Ashburn
Coleman, Monte
Elewonibi, Mohammed Thomas David
Kaufman, Mel

Bena
Evans, William E.

Blacksburg
Giovanni, Nikki
Warren, Herman Lecil
Williams-Green, Joyce F.

Boydton
McLaughlin, George W.

Burke
Sylvas, Lionel B.

Centreville
Brown, Charles Edward
Faulding, Juliette J.

Chantilly
Monk, Art

Charles City
Adkins, Iona W.
Jones, Lloyd O.

Charlottesville
Dove, Rita Frances
Garrett, Paul C.
McClain, Paula Denice
Scott, Charlotte Hanley
Scott, Nathan A., Jr.
Smith, Kevin L.
Washington, Joseph R., Jr.

Chatham
Merritt, Willette T.

Chesapeake
Barnard-Bailey, Wanda Arlene
Fears, Emery Lewis, Jr.
Johnson, William A.
Jordan, George Lee, Jr.
McCall, Barbara Collins
Owens, Hugo Armstrong, Sr.
Singleton, James LeRoy
Taylor, Donald Fulton, Sr.
Tucker, Billy J.
Walton, James Madison

Chester
Booker, Corliss Voncille

Chesterfield
Byrd, Arthur W.
Crawford, Vanessa Reese

Clifton
Haston, Raymond Curtiss, Jr.

Clifton Forge
Goode, George Ray

Colonial Heights
Thigpen, Calvin Herritage

Copper Hill
Stuart, Ivan I.

Culpeper
Hinton, Hortense Beck
Nelms, Michael

Dahlgren
Hughes, Isaac Sunny

Danville
Fitzgerald, Charlotte Diane
Jennings, Sylvesta Lee
Mason, Cheryl Annette

Dinwiddie
Knox, Wayne D. P.

Doswell
Tillman, Christine L.

Dumfries
Jones, Marcus Edmund
Stallworth, Eddie, Jr.

Eastville
Bell, Charles Smith

Emporia
Ward, Anna Elizabeth

Fairfax
Aklilu, Tesfaye
Allen, Benjamin P., III
Brittain, Bradley Bernard, Jr.
Butler, Douthard Roosevelt
Coleman, Gilbert Irving
DeCosta-Willis, Miriam
Dennis, Rutledge Melvin
Ecton, Virgil E.
English, Reginald
Faulding, Juliette J.
Gray, Clarence Cornelius, III
Gray, William H., III
Haynes, Farnese N.
Heard, Blanche Denise
Ingram, Earl Girardeau
Jackson, Darrell Duane
Lee, Kevin Brian
Miller, Marquis David
Price, David Lee, Sr.
Sims, Keith Eugene
Swain, Ronald L.
Whiting, Thomas J.
Wilkins, Roger Wood
Williams, Marcus Doyle
Williams, Walter E.

Fairfax Station
Ruffner, Ray P.

Falls Church
Bonner, Alice Carol
Chatman-Driver, Patricia Ann
Ellison, Pauline Allen
Greenlee, Peter Anthony
Hairston, William
Stansbury, Vernon Carver, Jr.

Farmville
Darnell, Rick
Miller, Erenest Eugene

Forest
Proctor, Earl D.

Fort Eustis
Godbolt, Ricky Charles

Fort Myer
Wilson, Danyell Elaine

Franklin
Harrison, A. B.

Fredericksburg
Birchette, William Ashby, III
Davies, Lawrence A.
Farmer, James

Glen Allen
Pierce, Gregory W.

Great Falls
Gee, William Rowland, Jr.

Hampton
Adeyiga, Adeyinka A.
Bontemps, Jacqueline Marie Fonvielle
Brown, William Crawford
Carter, Alphonse H.
Carter, Carolyn McCraw
Clark, Laron Jefferson, Jr.
Coles, John Edward
Darden, Christine Mann
Duncan, John C., Jr.
Gartrell, Luther R.
Gilliard, Joseph Wadus
Harvey, Norma Baker
Harvey, William R.
Henderson, James H.
Holloman, Thaddeus Bailey
Jamaludeen, Abdul Hamid
Jefferson, M. Ivory
Jenkins, Luther Neal
Jones, Bonnie Louise
Jones, Edward Norman
Jones, Michele Woods
Jones, Reginald L.
Lindsay, Beverly
Locke, Mamie Evelyn

McGhee, Nancy Bullock
Morris, Margaret Lindsay
Owens, Angle B., Jr.
Parham, James B.
Payne, Richelle Denise
Pleasant, Mae Barbee Boone
Porter, Michael LeRoy
Reynolds, Eleanor
Reynolds, Eric
Taylor, Wilford, Jr.
Ward, Albert M.
Watkins, James Darnell
Whitlow, Woodrow, Jr.
Wilkinson, James Wellington
Williamson, Carl Vance
Wilson, Greer Dawson
Wright, Stephen Junius, Jr.

Harrisonburg
Davis, Abraham, Jr.
Gabbin, Alexander Lee
Gabbin, Joanne Veal
Sampson, Ralph

Haymarket
Curry, Jerry Ralph
Gravely, Samuel L., Jr.

Herndon
Alexander, Patrise
Allen, Terry Thomas, Jr.
Ashmore, Darryl Allan
Boutte, Marc Anthony
Bowie, Larry
Campbell, Jesse
Davis, Stephen
Dishman, Cris Edward
Duff, Jamal Edwin
Ellard, Henry Austin
Evans, Leomont
Gaines, William Albert
Green, Darrell
Guilford, Diane Patton
Jenkins, James
Johnson, Tre
Lang, Kenard
Logan, Marc Anthony
McHenry, Emmit J.
Mims, Christopher Eddie
Mitchell, Brian Keith
Owens, Rich
Patton, Joseph
Patton, Marvcus Raymond
Pounds, Darryl
Rhodes, Edward Thomas, Sr.
Richard, Stanley Palmer
Shepherd, Leslie Glenard
Simmons, Edward
Sims, Keith
Stewart, Malcolm M.
Stubblefield, Dana William
Thomas, Chris Eric
Turner, Scott
Williams, Jamel

Hopewell
Edmonds, Campbell Ray

Keswick
Bates, George Albert

King George
Hughes, Isaac Sunny

King William
Reid, Miles Alvin

Lawrenceville
Adesuyi, Sunday Adeniji
Harrison, Harry Paul
Jenkins, Clara Barnes
Jones, Oris Pinckney
Law, Thomas Melvin
Rhoades, Samuel Thomas
Satcher, Robert Lee, Sr.
Thurman, Frances Ashton
Wilson, Connie Drake

Leesburg
Tolbert, John W., Jr.

Lexington
Lewis, J. B., Jr.
McCloud, Anece Faison
Parker, Michael Wayne

Locust Grove
Coleman, Gilbert Irving
Hinton, Hortense Beck

Lorton
Ruffner, Ray P.

Lynchburg
Anderson, Doreatha Madison
Hopkins, Vashti Edythe Johnson
Mangum, Charles M. L.
Mitchell, James H.
Wheelan, Belle Smith

Manassas
Archer, Chalmers, Jr.
Jackson, Elijah
Jones, Jimmie Dene
Polk, Anthony Joseph

Martinsville
Hobson, William D.
Muse, William Brown, Jr.

Mc Lean
Albright, William Dudley, Jr.
Alston, Kathy Diane
Blackmon, Mosetta Whitaker
Davis, Nathaniel Alonzo
Dorsey, Sandra
Lightfoote, William Edward, II
Lindsay, Horace Augustin
Malone, Claudine Berkeley
Metters, Samuel
Raullerson, Calvin Henry
Sechrest, Edward Amacker
Sudarkasa, Michael Eric Mabogunje
Thomas, Lydia Waters
Woodson, Alfred F.

Midlothian
Al-Mateen, K. Bakeer
Smith, Shirley LaVerne
Thompson, Brenda Smith

Newport News
Allen, Charles Claybourne
Banks, Dwayne Martin
Binns, Silas Odell
Harper, William Thomas, III
Kendall, Mark Acton Robertson
Mason, Felicia Lendonia
Miller, George N., Jr.
Pope, Mirian Artis
Price, Ray Anthony
Scott, C. Waldo
Williams, Yarborough Burwell, Jr.
Wilson, Wesley Campbell

Norfolk
Alexander, Otis Douglas
Alexander, Rosa M.
Allen, Maxine Bogues
Ashby, Reginald W.
Barnard-Bailey, Wanda Arlene
Barnes, Anne T.
Barrett, Walter Carlin, Jr.
Bempong, Maxwell A.
Bowser, James A.
Boyd, Joseph L.
Britt, L. D.
Brockett, Charles A.
Brooks, Phillip Daniel
Byrd, Helen P.
Carroll, William
Carter, Gene Raymond
Cauthen, Cheryl G.
Clemons, Michael L.
Crawley, George Claudius
Dandridge, Rita Bernice
Davis, Katie Campbell
Earl, Archie William, Sr.
Ellis, Benjamin F., Jr.
Freeman, James Jasper
Garnette, Booker Thomas
Gay, James F.
Hargrove, Andrew
Harris, Carl Gordon
Haynes, Alphonso Worden
Hoffler, Richard Winfred, Jr.
Hopkins, John David
Howard, Linwood E.
Isaac, Joseph William Alexander
Jeffries, Freddie L.
Lane, George S., Jr.
Lewis, Jesse Cornelius
Lowe, Scott Miller

Maddox, Marion Thelma
Madrey, Minnie Gregg
Mapp, David Kenneth, Jr.
Marshall, Herbert A.
Mason, William Thomas, Jr.
McCall, Barbara Collins
McLeod, Lorine Cole
Miller, James S.
Newsome, Moses, Jr.
Ozim, Francis Taiino
Parham, Thomas David, Jr.
Pope, Mirian Artis
Rawls, Dorothy
Reid, Milton A.
Rhodes, Lord Cecil
Riddick, Phillip L.
Robinson, William Peters, Jr.
Ryder, Georgia Atkins
Scott, Judith Sugg
Shepard, Beverly Renee
Spiva, Ulysses Van
Stith, Antoinette Freeman
Thomas, Earle Frederick
Tyler, Gerald DeForest
White-Parson, Willar F.
Williams, Ira Joseph
Willis, Levy E.
Wilson, Harrison B.
Wilson, Lucy R.
Wimbush, F. Blair
Wynn, Gladys W.

Oakton
Davis, Nathaniel Alonzo

Palmyra
Holland, Dorreen Antoinette

Petersburg
Bailey, Gracie Massenberg
Barnwell, Benjamin Burdee, Jr.
Berry, Lemuel, Jr.
Clayton, Robert Louis
Crawford, Vanessa Reese
Crocker, Wayne Marcus
Howard, Vivian Gordon
Johnson, Harry A.
Mackey, Andrew, Jr.
Moore, Eddie N., Jr.
Norris, Ethel Maureen
Powell, Grady Wilson
Ruff, Jamie Carless
Sabourin, Clemonce
Thigpen, Calvin Herritage
Toppin, Edgar Allan
Worrell, Kaye Sydnell

Portsmouth
Cooper, Iris N.
Daniels, Elizabeth
Hill, Robert J., Jr.
Holley, James W., III
Jenkins, Harry Lancaster
Jones, Helen Hampton
Moody, Eric Orlando
Morrison, Johnny Edward
Nixon, James Melvin
Smith, Rachel Norcom
Smith, Robert Lawrence, Sr.
Taylor, Almina
Wesley, Clemon Herbert, Jr.
Whitehurst, Charles Bernard, Sr.
Williamson, Carl Vance

Quantico
Carter, William Thomas, Jr.
Nunn, Robinson S.

Quinton
Green, Calvin Coolidge

Radford
Jones, Stanley Bernard

Reston
Ahart, Thomas I.
Brown, Charles Edward
Calbert, Roosevelt
Campbell, Carlos Cardozo
Cooke, William Branson
Doleman, Robert J.
Gill, Laverne McCain
Howard, Linda J.
Johnson, Johnnie L., Jr.
Lawson, William R.

Richmond
Adiele, Moses Nkwachukwu
Al-Mateen, Cheryl Singleton
Anderson, Pearl G.
Ballard, Janet Jones
Bell, Theron J.
Belle, Walton M.
Benton, James Wilbert, Jr.
Billings, Sister Cora Marie
Bledsoe, Carolyn E. Lewis
Boatwright, Joseph Weldon
Booker, Corliss Voncille
Boone, Elwood Bernard, Jr.
Bowser, McEva R.
Brown, Lucille M.
Cameron, Wilburn Macio, Sr.
Carter, Gilbert Lino
Carter, Wesley Byrd
Cheatham, Linda Moye
Christian, Mary T.
Clark, Walter H.
Conyers, Charles L.
Cook, Wallace Jeffery
Creighton-Zollar, Ann
Cummings, Charles Edward
Dance, Daryl Cumber
Dark, Okianer Christian
Davis, Esther Gregg
Davis, Melvin Lloyd
Davis, William Hayes, Sr.
Deese, Manuel
Dell, Willie J.
Dickerson, Tyrone Edward
Dixon, Leon Martin
Dungee, Margaret R.
Eggleston, Neverett A., Jr.
El-Amin, Sa'ad
Fowlkes, Doretha P.
Gibson, William M.
Gray, Earl Haddon
Gregory, Roger Lee
Gumbs, Oliver Sinclair
Harris, Gladys Bailey
Harris, Paul Clinton, Sr.
Haskins, William J.
Hassell, Leroy Rountree, Sr.
Henley, Vernard W.
Herbert, Douglas A.
Hill, Oliver W.
Jackson, Hermoine Prestine
James, Allix Bledsoe
James, Kay C.
Jamison, Birdie Hairston
Johnson, William Randolph
Jones, William C.
Kendall, Randolph C., Jr.
Kennedy, Joseph J., Jr.
Kenney, Walter T.
Laisure, Sharon Emily Goode
Lambert, Benjamin J., III
Lambert, Leonard W.
Lanier, Willie
Latney, Harvey, Jr.
Leary, James E.
Lewis, Ronald C.
Madu, Anthony Chisaraokwu
Marsh, Henry L., III
McClendon, Lloyd Glenn
Meadows, Richard H.
Miller, Laurel Milton
Miller, Yvonne Bond
Mitchell, Michelle Burton
Moore, Quincy L.
Mosby, Carolyn Lewis
Nichols, Paul
Oliver, Jerry Alton, Sr.
Owens, Lynda Gayle
Pickett, Donna A.
Pollard, Herbert
Reed, Daisy Frye
Roberts, Samuel Kelton
Robertson, Benjamin W.
Simmons, S. Dallas
Sims, Esau, Jr.
Smith, Voydee, Jr.
Southall, Herbert Howardton, Sr.
Spencer, James R.
Spurlock, James B., Jr.
Spurlock, LaVerne B.
Stallings, Gregory Ralph
Taylor, Valerie Charmayne
Teekah, George Anthony
Thomas, Jacquelyn Small
Thompson, Brenda Smith
Townes, Clarence Lee, Jr.
Tucker, James F.
Tucker, Samuel Wilbert
Tyson, John C.
Walker, Laneuville V.

Wallace, Helen Winfree-Peyton
Walston, Woodrow William
Weaver, John Arthur
Welch, Winfred Bruce
West, Valerie Y.
Wilder, Lawrence Douglas
Williams, John R.
Winfree, Murrell H.
Woodson, Jeffrey Anthony
Yancy, Preston Martin

Roanoke
Adams, Paul Brown
Bruce, Antoinette Johnson
Burks, James William, Jr.
Cason, Joseph L.
Stovall, Melody S.
Taylor, Noel C.
Whitworth, Claudia Alexander

Rocky Mount
Hamilton, McKinley John

Salem
Statum, Hayward S.
Williams, Carlton Ray, Jr.

Sandy Hook
Bowles, James Harold, Sr.

Smithfield
Britt, Paul D., Jr.
Gray, Charles Henry

South Hill
Scranage, Clarence, Jr.

Spotsylvania
Hatchett, William F.

Springfield
Adams, Theodore Adolphus, Jr.
Eley, Randall Robbi
Forte, Johnie, Jr.
McClenic, Patricia Dickson
Ruffin, Paulette Francine
Tucker, Geraldine Coleman

St Stephens Church
Pollard, Percy Edward, Sr.

Sterling
Woodson, William D.

Suffolk
Glover, Bernard E.
Harrell, William Edwin
Hart, Ronald O.
Wilson, Madelaine Majette

Surry
Poindexter, Gammiel Gray
Tunstall, June Rebecca

Tazewell
Garner, June Brown

Trevilians
McLaughlin, George W.

Vienna
Harris, Lee Andrew, II
Roane, Glenwood P.
Scott, Gilbert H.
Weaver, Gary W.

Virginia Beach
Banks, June Skinner
Dildy, Catherine Greene
Duke, Ruth White
Green, Barbara-Marie
Kinchlow, Harvey Ben
Miller, Ingrid Fran Watson
Moody, Fredreatha E.
Moore, Gregory B.
Reynolds, Charles McKinley, Jr.
Rice, Haynes
Smith, Alfonzo
Strayhorn, Earl Carlton
White-Parson, Willar F.
Wiggins, Joseph L.

Warsaw
Johns, Sonja Maria
Veney, Herbert Lee

Waverly
Worrell, Kaye Sydnell

West Point
Reid, Miles Alvin

Williamsburg
Bryce, Herrington J.
Charlton, Jack Fields
Gieseking, Hal
Honablue, Richard Riddick, M.D.
Matthews, Christy
Pinson, Hermine Dolorez
Stone, William T.

Wise
Dawson, Bobby H.

Woodbridge
Carter, William Thomas, Jr.
Sylvas, Lionel B.

Yorktown
Mason, Felicia Lendonia

WASHINGTON

Arlington
Taylor, Henry F.

Bellevue
Elliott, J. Russell
Jackson, Arthur D., Jr.
Mabrey, Marsha Eve

Bellingham
Shropshire, Harry W.

Chehalis
Pope, Isaac S.

Everett
Freeman, Evelyn

Federal Way
Little, Floyd

Fort Lewis
Briggs, Paul W.

Issaquah
Anderson, James R., Jr.

Kent
McGhee, James Leon

Kirkland
Adams, Sam Aaron
Atkins, James
Ballard, Howard Louis
Barber, Michael
Bellamy, Jay
Blades, Bennie
Blades, Brian Keith
Broussard, Steven
Brown, Chadwick Everett
Brown, Reggie
Bryant, Jeff Dwight
Cain, Joseph Harrison, Jr.
Crumpler, Carlester
Daniels, Phillip Bernard
Davis, Tyree
Edmunds, Ferrell, Jr.
Galloway, Joey
Glover, Kevin Bernard
Graham, Derrick
Hardy, Darryl Gerrod
Hobbs, Daryl Ray
Jones, Walter
Kennedy, Cortez
Lincoln, Jeremy Arlo
Logan, James
McKenzie, Reginald
McKnight, James
Moon, Warren
Moss, Winston
Parker, Riddick
Pritchard, Michael Robert
Seigler, Dexter
Sinclair, Michael Glenn
Smith, Lamar
Springs, Shawn
Strong, Mack
Thomas, Fred
Warren, Christopher Collins, Jr.

Williams, Darryl Edwin
Williams, John L.
Williams, Willie James, Jr.

Lynnwood
Brown, Marva Y.

Marysville
Odum, Milton D.

Mercer Island
Jones, Albert L.

Mill Creek
Donaldson, James Lee, III

Olympia
Bailey, Mona Humphries
Belcher, Lewis, Jr.
Fregia, Darrell Leon
Ingram, Winifred
Parson, Willie L.

Pullman
Purce, Thomas Les
Sampson, Kelvin

Renton
Fitzpatrick, B. Edward
Franklin, Benjamin
Franklin, Clyde
Haynes, Sue Blood
Jones, Leon C.
Sharp, J. Anthony

Richland
Wiley, William R.

Seattle
Abe, Benjamin Omara A.
Alex, Gregory K.
Alexander, Don H.
Anderson, Betty Keller
Anthony, Eric Todd
Anthony, Gregory C.
Aycock, Angela Lynnette
Baker, Vin
Banks, James Albert
Bennett, Daina T.
Bennette, Connie E.
Blake, J. Paul
Brooks, Fabienne
Brooks, Norward J.
Burton, Philip L.
Butler, Johnnella E.
Carmichael, Carole A.
Carter, Arlington W., Jr.
Cartwright, Bill
Chambliss, Ida Belle
Cotton, James
Debro, Julius
Easley, Kenny, Jr.
Eason, Oscar, Jr.
Ellis, Dale
Enis, Shalonda
Farris, Jerome
Fearn-Banks, Kathleen
Fleming, George
Frye, Reginald Stanley
Gayton, Gary D.
Griffey, Ken, Jr.
Griffey, Ken, Sr.
Gulley, Wilson
Gunter, Laurie
Hailey, Priscilla W.
Hawkins, Hersey R., Jr.
Hill, James A., Sr.
Houston, Alice V.
Howard, Stephen
Hubbard, Walter T.
Johnson, Charles Richard
Johnson, Charles V.
Johnson, Niesa
Jones, Edward Louis
Kennedy Franklin, Linda Cheryl
Kersey, Jerome
Kimbrough-Johnson, Donna L.
Langford, Victor C., III
Large, Jerry D.
Lawrence, Jacob A.
Lee, Vivian Booker
Lee, Vivian O.
Leigh, James W., Jr.
Leonard, Gloria Jean
Leonard, Jeff
Leslie, Marsha R.
Locke, Hubert G.
Lofton, Andrew James

Macklin, John W.
McCarthy, Gregory O'Neil
McConnell, Conrad
McCrimmon, Nicky
McElroy, Colleen J.
McGee, Henry W., Jr.
McKinney, Samuel Berry
McMillan, Nate
Miles, Edward Lancelot
Miller, Constance Joan
Miller, Earl Vonnidore
Mitchell, Windell T.
Morris, Ernest Roland
Mumford, Esther Hall
Newhouse, Millicent DeLaine
Ollee, Mildred W.
Osborne, Oliver Hilton
Pappillion, Glenda M.
Payton, Gary Dwayne
Peoples, John Derrick, Jr.
Perkins, Sam Bruce
Pounds, Kenneth Ray
Priester, Julian Anthony
Purnell, Carolyn J.
Reynolds, Andrew Buchanan
Rice, Constance Williams
Rice, Norman Blann
Scott, Joseph Walter
Shaw, Spencer Gilbert
Sims, Ronald Cordell
Slocumb, Heathcliff
Spigner, Clarence
Spratlen, Thaddeus H.
Stanford, John H.
Stephens, Herbert Malone
Stewart, Larry
Tabor, Langston
Thomas, Liz A.
Thompson, Alvin J.
Toliver, Paul Allen
Tyner, Regina Lisa
Ward, Ronald R.
Washington, James W., Jr.
Whiting, Val
Williams, Aaron
Williams, Clarence
Williams, Karen Elaine
Williams, Leroy Joseph
Wilson, August
Wilson, John T., Jr.
Wingate, David Grover Stacey, Jr.
Womack, William Martin
Woodhouse, Rossalind Yvonne

Spokane
Chase, James
Givens, Rocelious
Greene, Nathaniel D.
Maxey, Carl
Roseman, Jennifer Eileen
Smith, James, Jr.
Williams, James Hiawatha

Tacoma
Baugh, Lynnette
Boddie, Algernon Owens
Brown, Leo C., Jr.
Crawford, Ella Mae
Davis, Alfred C., Sr.
Gilven, Hezekiah
Hankerson, Elijah H.
Mimms, Maxine Buie
Smith, LeRoi Matthew-Pierre, III
Tanner, Jack E.
Wesley, Barbara Ann
Williams, Kirk A.

Vancouver
Nettles, Willard, Jr.

Vashon
McGehee, Nan E.

Walla Walla
King, Charles E.

WEST VIRGINIA

Beckley
Bradshaw, Doris Marion
Chambers, Madrith Bennett
Dobson, Helen Sutton
Martin, James Tyrone
Payne, Brown H.
Scott, Albert Nelson
Seay, Lorraine King

Bethany
Airall, Zoila Erlinda

Bluefield
Froe, Dreyfus Walter

Charleston
Anderson, Hubert, Jr.
Brown, Willard L.
Canady, Herman G., Jr.
Carter, Phyllis Harden
James, Betty Harris
James, Charles H., III
James, Charles Howell, II
Jenkins, Drewie Gutrimez
Marshall, Charlene Jennings
Matthews, Virgil E.
Mitchell-Bateman, Mildred
Shaw, Richard Gordon
Smoot, Carolyn Elizabeth

Clarksburg
Cox, Otis Graham, Jr.

Dunbar
Griffin, Ervin Verome
Lee, Ivin B.
Russell, James A., Jr.

Fairmont
Hinton, Gregory Tyrone

Harpers Ferry
Miller, Thelma Delmoor

Hedgesville
Johnson, Frederick Douglass

Huntington
Carter, Philip W., Jr.
Henderson, Herbert H.
Lawson, Robert L.
Redd, William L.
Williams, Joseph Lee, Jr.

Hurricane
Peters, Roscoe Hoffman, Jr.

Institute
Carper, Gloria G.
Carter, Hazo William, Jr.
Carter, Phyllis Harden
Garrett, Naomi M.
Giles, Charlotte Emma
Griffin, Ervin Verome
Smoot, Carolyn Elizabeth
Thompson, Litchfield O'Brien
Wallace, William James Lord

Keystone
Jackson, Aubrey N.

Martinsburg
Roberts, Cheryl Dornita Lynn

Morgantown
Belmear, Horace Edward
Brooks, Dana DeMarco
Cabbell, Edward Joseph
Gray, Kenneth D.
Gwynn, Florine Evayonne
Hughes, Johnnie Lee
Jackson, Ruth Moore
Louistall-Monroe, Victorine
    Augusta
Walker, Ernest L.
Wells, Leartha
White, Harold Rogers

Nitro
Anderson, Robert H.
Johnson, Carl Elliott

Oak Hill
Simms, Albert L.

Parkersburg
Jones, William W.

Philippi
Jones, Idus, Jr.
Redd, Thomasina A.

Shepherdstown
Roberts, Cheryl Dornita Lynn

Weirton
Jackson-Gillison, Helen L.
White, William J.
Williams, Carletta Celeste

Welch
Stephens, Booker T.

Wheeling
Lewis, Houston A.
Moore, John Wesley, Jr.

Williamson
Manuel, John N.

WISCONSIN

Beloit
Knight, Walter R.
Thompson, Joseph Isaac

Brookfield
Jones, Fredrick E.

Eau Claire
Taylor, Dale B.

Elkhorn
Waddell, Ruchadina LaDesiree

Green Bay
Bennett, Edgar
Berry, Latin
Brooks, Robert Darren
Brown, Gilbert Jesse
Butler, LeRoy
Cobb, Reginald John
Darkins, Christopher Oji
Davis, Tyrone
Dotson, Earl Christopher
Dotson, Santana
Evans, Douglas Edwards
Freeman, Antonio Michael
Galbreath, Harry Curtis
Harris, Bernardo Jamaine
Hayden, Aaron Chautezz
Henderson, William Terrelle
Holland, Darius
Hollinquest, Lamont
Hovell, Larry L.
Joyner, Seth
Lee, Mark Anthony
Levens, Dorsey
Lewis, Sherman
Mayes, Derrick
McKenzie, Keith
Mickens, Terry KaJuan
Mullen, Roderick
Newsome, Craig
Robinson, Eugene
Sharper, Darren
Smith, Jermaine
Taylor, Aaron Matthew
White, Reginald Howard
Wilkerson, Bruce Alan
Wilkins, Gabriel Nicholas
Williams, Brian
Williams, Tyrone

Kenosha
Duerson, David R.
Shade, Barbara J.
Smith, Eleanor Jane
Traha, Dennis

Kewaunee
Qamar, Nadi Abu

La Crosse
Mitchem, John Clifford

Madison
Ally, Akbar F.
Bonds, Kevin Gregg
Davis, Erroll B., Jr.
Davis, Luther Charles
Davis, Richard
Dejoie, Carolyn Barnes Milanes
Evans, Patricia P.
Franklin-Hammonds, Betty A.
George, Gary Raymond
Henderson, Hugh C.
Henderson, Virginia Ruth
    McKinney
High, Freida

Hopkins, Dianne McAfee
Jones, James Edward, Jr.
Julian, Percy L., Jr.
Lowery, Birl
Manuel, Edward
Marrett, Cora B.
Nunnery, Willie James
Peace, G. Earl, Jr.
Salter, Kwame S.
Sharp, Charles Louis
Shivers, S. Michael
Smith, Barbara Wheat
Thomas, Wilbur C.
Toon, Al Lee
Turner, Robert Lloyd
Ward, Walter L., Jr.
Wilson, Patricia I.
Young, Leon D.

Milwaukee
Allen, Ray
Aman, Mohammed M.
Artison, Richard E.
Barrett, Sherman L.
Beach, Walter G., II
Beard, Israel
Beauchamp, Louis
Bellegarde-Smith, Patrick
Bender, Barbara A.
Bones, Ricky
Bowie, Willette
Brandon, Terrell
Breaux, Timothy
Broussard, Leroy
Buckhanan, Dorothy Wilson
Calvin, Earl David
Calvin, Willie J.
Cameron, James
Carpenter, Joseph, II
Clevert, Charles N., Jr.
Colbert, Virgis W.
Conyers, Nathan
Coward, Jasper Earl
Curry, Michael
Evans, Phillip L.
Faucett, Barbara J.
Felder, Harvey
Finlayson, William E.
Ford, Sarah Ann
Gilliam, Armon Louis
Grissom, Marquis Dean
Halyard, Ardie Adlena
Hicks, Ingrid Diann
Hill, Tyrone
Holt, Kenneth Charles
Holt, Mikel
Honeycutt, Jerald
Jackson, Harold Baron, Jr.
Jamison, Lafayette
Johnson, Ben E.
Johnson, Ervin, Jr.
Johnson, Geneva B.
Johnson, Jared Modell
Johnson, Marlene E.
Johnson-Crosby, Deborah A.
Jones, James Bennett
Jones, Jerrel W.
Jones, Walter L.
Jordan, J. Paul
Kane, Eugene A.
Lang, Andrew Charles
Lockett, Sandra Bokamba
Lynch, M. Elizabeth
Matthis, James L., III
Maxwell, Hazel B.
McLean, Zarah Gean
Murrell, Peter C.
Nevels, Zebedee James
Newfield, Marc Alexander
O'Flynn-Thomas, Patricia
Oglivie, Benjamin A.
Olapo, Olaitan
Ologboni, Tejumola F.
Palmer, John A.
Parks, James Clinton, Jr.
Parrish, Clarence R.
Patterson, Jacqueline J.
Perry, Elliott
Perry, June Martin
Pollard, Diane S.
Prince, Joan Marie
Purnell, Mark W., CIMA
Rayford, Zula M.
Riley, Glenn Pleasants
Robinson, Glenn A.
Ross, Lee Elbert
Sealls, Alan Ray
Smith, Bubba
Smith, Symuel Harold

Spaights, Ernest
Spence, Joseph Samuel, Sr.
Swan, Monroe
Tate, Cornelius Astor
Thomas, Patricia O'Flynn
Torrence, Duane
Tucker, O. Ruth
Williams, George W., III
Williams, Joanne Louise
Williams, Virginia Walker
Wynn, Thomas Harold, Sr.

Racine
Buckhanan, Dorothy Wilson
Smith, Eleanor Jane
Swanson, Charles
Turner, Robert Lloyd
Wilkinson, Raymond M., Jr.

Rhinelander
Platteter, Marie

Ripon
Myrick, Randy

River Falls
Bailey, Robert B., III
Norwood, Tom

River Hills
Tucker, O. Ruth

Whitewater
Hewing, Pernell Hayes

WYOMING

Cheyenne
Byrd, James W.
Jeffrey, Ronnald James
Mercer, Arthur, Sr.
Wise, C. Rogers

Laramie
Wright, Joseph, Jr.

Rock Springs
Stevens, Althea Williams

BAHAMAS

Nassau
Brown, Theophile Waldorf
Poitier, Sidney

BERMUDA

Hamilton
Swan, John William David

ALBERTA

Calgary
Iginla, Jarome

Edmonton
Grier, Mike
Pless, Willie

BRITISH
COLUMBIA

Coquitlam
Brockenborough, Joseph Antonio

Vancouver
Abdur-Rahim, Shareef
Brashear, Donald
Brown, Marcus James
Daniels, Antonio
Edwards, Blue
Edwards, Douglas
Jackson, Stuart Wayne
Lynch, George DeWitt, III
Mack, Sam

Massenburg, Tony Arnel
Mayberry, Lee
Mobley, Eric
Moten, Lawrence Edward, III
Newbill, Ivano Miguel
Peeler, Anthony Eugene
Smith, Michael John
West, Doug

ONTARIO

Hamilton
Robinson, James Edward

Mississauga
James, Herbert I.
Peterson, Oscar Emmanuel

Thornhill
Foster, Cecil A.

Toronto
Billups, Chauncey
Brown, Dee
Camby, Marcus D.
Christie, Douglas Dale
Davis, Joseph M.
Denton, Herbert H., Jr.
Garner, Chris
Gaston, Cito
Guzman, Juan Andres Correa
Henderson, Rickey Henley
Hughes, Mark
King, Jimmy
Lewis, Martin
Long, John
Marshall, Paul M.
McGrady, Tracy
Miller, Oliver J.
Person, Robert Alan
Rogers, Roy, Jr.
Stewart, Shannon Harold
Thomas, Isiah Lord, III
Thomas, John
Trent, Gary Dajaun
Walker, Darrell
Wallace, John
Williams, Alvin
Wright, Sharone Addaryl

QUEBEC

Montreal
Harper, Tommy
May, Derrick Brant
Pringle, Mike
Tinsley, Lee Owen
White, Rondell Bernard

COSTA RICA

San Jose
Baltimore, Richard Lewis, III

DENMARK

Copenhagen
Burns, Ronald Melvin
Thigpen, Edmund Leonard

ENGLAND

London
Kellman, Denis Elliott
Marsalis, Wynton
Scott, Jacob Reginald

FRANCE

Paris
Sharpless, Mattie

GERMANY

Hamburg
Laing, Edward A.

Herforst
Gomez, Kevin Lawrence Johnson

GUAM

Brewer, David L., III

HONG KONG

Stanley
Williams, James Edward

HUNGARY

Budapest
Fearn, James E., Jr.

INDONESIA

Jakarta
Rogers-Reece, Shirley

ITALY

Assisi Santario
Kellogg, Reginald J.

Milan
Dantley, Adrian Delano

Roma
Donawa, Maria Elena

Rome
Donawa, Maria Elena
Walker, Howard Kent

JAMAICA

Bridge Port
Carter, Martin Joseph

Kingston
Nettleford, Rex Milton
Powell, Aston Wesley
Robinson, Maurice C.

JAPAN

Tokyo
Bruce, James C.
Moseby, Lloyd Anthony

Yokosuka
Baxter, Charles F., Jr.

KENYA

Nairobi
Gecau, Kimani J.

MEXICO

Cuernavaca
Catlett, Elizabeth

NETHERLANDS

Amsterdam
Scott, James Henry

The Hague
Duncan, Charles Tignor
McDonald, Gabrielle Kirk

NICARAGUA

Managua
Newell, Matthias Gregory

NIGERIA

Benin City
Thibodeaux, Sylvia Marie

Lagos
Ford, William R.

Owerri
Uzoigwe, Godfrey N.

Port Harcourt
Nnolim, Charles E.

PUERTO RICO

Old San Juan
Routte-Gomez, Eneid G.

REPUBLIC OF SOUTH AFRICA

Capetown
Ming, Donald George K.

SAUDI ARABIA

Dhahran
Kent, Ernest

VIRGIN ISLANDS OF THE UNITED STATES

Christiansted
Joseph, Antoine L.

Frederiksted
Abramson, John J., Jr.
Christian, Cora LeEthel

Kingshill
Abramson, John J., Jr.

Kingshill, St Croix
Garcia, Kwame N.

St Croix
Belardo de O'Neal, Lilliana
Bryan, Adelbert M.
Christian, Cora LeEthel
Garcia, Kwame N.
Hood, Charles McKinley, Jr.
King, Howard A. T.
Lorde, Audre Geraldine
McCoy, George H.
Petersen, Eileen Ramona
Rivera, Eddy
Sheen, Albert A.
Terrell, Catherine Milligan
Thomas, Maurice McKenzie
Thomas, Monica Maria Primus
Williams, Patrick Nehemiah

St Thomas
Ballentine, Krim Menelik
Berryman, Macon M.
Bourne, Judith Louise
Brady, Julio A.
Brown, William Rocky, III
Bryan, Clarice
Carroll, James S.
Christian, Almeric L.
Christian, Eric Oliver, Jr.
Claxton, Melvin L.
Dawson, Eric Emmanuel
Dennis, Hugo, Jr.
Evans, Melvin H.
Harding, John Edward
Heyward, Ilene Patricia
Hodge, Derek M.
Kean, Orville E.
Krigger, Marilyn Francis
Lyons, Laura Brown
Meyers, Ishmael Alexander
Millin, Henry Allan
Nibbs, Alphonse, Sr.
Sprauve, Gilbert A.
Stapleton, Marylyn A.
Thomas, Audria Acty
Todman, Jureen Francis
Turnbull, Charles Wesley
Watlington, Mario A.

St. Thomas
Brown, Walter E.

Occupation Index

Lee, Joie
Lemmons, Kasi
LeNoire, Rosetta
Lewis, Dawnn
Lewis, Emmanuel
Lindo, Delroy
Long, Nia
Love, Darlene
Love, Faizon
Lowe, Jackie
Lumbly, Carl
Mac, Bernie
MacLachlan, Janet A.
Marshall, Donald James
Marshall, William Horace
Martin, Christopher
Martin, D'Urville
Martin, Helen Dorothy
May, Charles W.
May, Floyd O'Lander
McDonald, Audra Ann
McElrath, Wanda Faith
McGill, Michele Nicole Johnson
McNair, Chris
McNeill, Cerves Todd
McQueen, Kevin Paige
Merkerson, S. Epatha
Method Man
Mills, Stephanie
Mitchell, Donald
Mitchell, Loften
Moore, Juanita
Moore, Melba
Moore, Shemar
Morgan, Debbi
Morris, Garrett
Morsell, Frederick Albert
Morton, Joe
Moseka, Aminata
Moss, Anni R.
Murphy, Eddie
Nelson, Novella C.
Nelson-Holgate, Gail Evangelyn
Nicholas, Denise
Nicholas, Fayard Antonio
Nichols, Nichelle
Norman, Maidie Ruth
Nunez, Miguel A.
Owens, Geoffrey
Page, Harrison Eugene
Parsons, Karyn
Patten, Edward Roy
Payne, Allen
Payton-Noble, JoMarie
Pearman, Raven-Symone Christina
Perry, Felton
Peters, Brock G.
Phifer, Mekhi
Pinkett, Jada
Pinkins, Tonya
Plummer, Glenn
Poitier, Sidney
Pounder, C. C. H.
Powell, Kevin
Pryor, Richard
Purdee, Nathan
Queen Latifah
Ralph, Sheryl Lee
Ramsey, David P.
Randle, Theresa
Rashad, Phylicia
Reese, Della
Reid, Tim
Rentie, Frieda
Reuben, Gloria
Reynolds, James Van
Rhames, Ving
Richards, Beah
Richards, DeLeon Marie
Richardson, Salli
Rippy, Rodney Allen
Robinson, Holly
Robinson, Jason Guy
Rochon, Lela
Rock, Chris
Rogers, Timmie
Rolle, Esther
Ross, Diana
Roundtree, Richard
Rowell, Victoria Lynn
Russ, Timothy Darrell
Russell, Nipsey
St. John, Kristoff
Sanford, Isabel G.
Scott, Larry B.
Sharp, Saundra
Short, Bobby
Simone, Nina
Simpson, O. J.

Sinbad
Smith, Toukie A.
Smith, Will
Snipes, Wesley
Stickney, Phyllis Yvonne
Sullivan, J. Christopher
Summer, Cree
Tate, Larenz
Taylor, Meshach
Tero, Lawrence
The Artist
Thigpen, Lynne
Thomas, Philip Michael
Todd, Beverly
Townsend, Robert
Tucker, Chris
Tunie, Tamara
Turman, Glynn
Tyson, Cicely
Uggams, Leslie
Underwood, Blair
Vance, Courtney
Vanity
Van Peebles, Mario
Van Peebles, Melvin
VelJohnson, Reginald
Vereen, Ben Augustus
Vincent, Irving H.
Walbey, Theodosia Emma Draher
Walker, Charles
Ward, Douglas Turner
Warfield, Marsha
Warner, Malcolm-Jamal
Warren, Michael
Washington, Denzel
Washington, Isaiah
Washington, Keith
Washington, Leroy
Washington, Von Hugo, Sr.
Wayans, Damon
Wayans, Keenen Ivory
Weathers, Carl
Whitaker, Forest
Whitaker, Mical Rozier
White, Jaleel
White, Michael Jai
Whitfield, Lynn
Williams, Alyson
Williams, Billy Dee
Williams, Dick Anthony
Williams, Hal
Williams, Joe
Williams, Montel
Williams, Samm-Art
Williams, Vanessa L.
Wilson, Demond
Wilson, Flip
Wilson, Jonathan Charles, Jr.
Wilson, Nancy
Winfield, Paul Edward
Winfrey, Oprah
Witherspoon, John
Woodard, Alfre
Woods, Allie, Jr.
Wright, Michael
Wright, N'Bushe
Yoba, Malik

Activism, Political/Civil/Social Rights

Abebe, Ruby
Al-Amin, Jamil Abdullah
Ali, Kamal Hassan
Ali, Rasheedah Ziyadah
Allen, George Mitchell
Allen, Mark
Allen, Wendell
Anthony, Wendell
Ardrey, Saundra Curry
Ashton, Vivian Christina R.
Bailey, Doris Jones
Barbee, Lloyd Augustus
Barfield, Clementine
Bates, Daisy
Beckett, Charles Campbell
Bell, George
Bell, Trenton Grandville
Bennett, Debra Quinette
Bennett, Delores
Bennett, Marion D.
Billingsley, Andrew
Bolton, Wanda E.
Bookert, Charles C.
Borges, Lynne MacFarlane
Bowman, Phillip Jess
Bradley, Melissa Lynn
Bradley, Melvin LeRoy
Breeden, James Pleasant

Breeding, Carl L.
Brown, Amos Cleophilus
Brown, Clarence William
Brown, Delores Elaine
Brown, Jim
Brown, Joseph Samuel
Brown, Zora Kramer
Bullett, Audrey Kathryn
Burgess, Robert E., Sr.
Butts, Calvin Otis, III
Cafritz, Peggy Cooper
Cameron, James
Carmichael, Stokely
Carr, Kipley DeAne
Castro, George A.
Chargois, Jenelle M.
Childs, Josie L.
Chisholm, Shirley
Clarke, Raymond
Coleman-Burns, Patricia Wendolyn
Collins, Clifford Jacob, III
Colson, Lewis Arnold
Cosby, Camille Olivia Hanks
Cox, John Wesley
Current, Gloster Bryant
Dabney, David Hodges
Daniels, Richard D.
Daniels, Ron D.
Daughtry, Herbert Daniel
Dauphin, Borel C.
Davenport, Christian A.
Davis, Andre Maurice
Dejoie, Michael C.
Dent, Thomas Covington
Dickson, Onias D., Jr.
Doxie, Marvin Leon, Sr.
Du Bois, David Graham
Dulin, Joseph
Dyer, Bernard Joel
Eason, Oscar, Jr.
Edelman, Marian Wright
Edwards, Abiyah, Jr.
English, William E.
Eure, Jerry Holton, Sr.
Evans, Akwasi Rozelle
Farmer, James
Flack, William Patrick
Flanagan, Robert B., Sr.
Fletcher, Louisa Adaline
Fletcher, Robert E.
Francis, Livingston S.
Frazier, Rick C.
Galloway-Briggs, Lula
Glanton, Sadye Lyerson
Graham, James C., Jr.
Greene, Sarah Moore
Gregory, Richard Claxton
Grier, Rosey
Groff, Regis F.
Guyton, Tyree
Hall, John Robert
Hall, Kathryn Louise
Hamilton, Aubrey J.
Hamilton, John Joslyn, Jr.
Hardy, Michael A.
Hare, Julia Reed
Harper, John Roy, II
Harris, Varno Arnello
Hashim, Mustafa
Head, Laura Dean
Henderson, Wade
Henderson-Nocho, Audrey J.
Hernandez, Aileen Clarke
Hill, Anita Faye
Hill, Cynthia D.
Hillman, Gracia
Hodges, Virgil Hall
Holloman, John L. S., Jr.
Holman, Karriem Malik
Holt, Aline G.
Hooks, Frances Dancy
Hope, Julius Caesar
Hoppes, Alice Faye
Hunter, Howard Jacque, Jr.
Innis, Roy Emile Alfredo
Irby, Galven
Irving-Gibbs, Fannye
Isaac, Telesforo Alexander
Jackson, Grandvel Andrew
Jackson, Jesse Louis
Jackson, Michael
Jackson, Ronald G., Sr.
Jennings, Bernard Waylon-Handel
Jessie, Waymon Thomas
Johnson, Arthur J.
Johnson, Georgianna
Johnson, Gregory Wayne
Jones, David R.
Jones, Hardi Liddell

Jones, Johnnie Anderson
Jones, Yvonne De Marr
Jordan, Bettye Davis
Jordan-Harris, Katherine
Joyner, Irving L.
Kee, Marsha Goodwin
Kelly, John Paul, Jr.
King, Coretta Scott
King, Earl B.
Lanier, Shelby, Jr.
Lee, Lena S. King
Lillard, Kwame Leo
Lipscomb, Darryl L.
Lowery, Carolyn T.
Luper, Clara M.
Mack, John W.
Mackey, John
Malone, Cleo
Marshall, Pluria W., Sr.
McCane, Charlotte Antoinette
McGinnis, James W.
Meeks, Reginald Kline
Mfume, Kweisi
Miller, Dennis Weldon
Mitchell, Robert Lee, Sr.
Moody, Anne
Moore, Queen Mother
Morrison, Jacqueline
Moss, James Edward
Muhammad, Valencia
Murphy, Laura W.
Nails, John Walker
Nettles, John Spratt
Newman, Miller Maurice
Nickson, Sheila Joan
Nix, Rick
Nix, Roscoe Russa
Norment, Hanley
Norrell-Nance, Rosalind Elizabeth
Odom, Stonewall, II
Orr, Janice
Owens, Hugo Armstrong, Sr.
Parks, Rosa
Pennick, Aurie Alma
Peoples, Earl F., Sr.
Perez, Altagracia
Powell, Addie Scott
Pritchard, Robert Starling, II
Ransby, Barbara
Richie, Winston Henry
Riley, William Scott
Roberts, Janice L.
Robinson, Anthony W.
Rollins, Avon William, Sr.
Romney, Edgar O.
Ross, Winston A.
Scruggs-Leftwich, Yvonne
Seale, Bobby
Shabazz, Betty
Shabazz, Kaleem
Shah, Khalid Ibn
Sharpton, Alfred Charles, Jr.
Shaw, Nancy H.
Shoemaker, Veronica Sapp
Simmons, Albert Bufort, Jr.
Simton, Chester
Smith, Judy Seriale
Smith, Maxine Atkins
Smith, Philip Gene
Smith, Tommie M.
Sowell, Thomas
Spencer, Marian Alexander
Spicer, Kenneth, Sr.
Stallings, George Augustus, Jr.
Stewart, Warren Hampton, Sr.
Swindell, Warren C.
Talbot, Gerald Edgerton
Tate, Eula Booker
Taylor, Jeffery Charles
Thurman, Sue Bailey
Todd, Thomas N.
Todman, Jureen Francis
Vaughn, Audrey Smith
Walker, J. Wilbur
Washington, Alonzo Lavert
Washington, Jacquelin Edwards
Watson, Dennis Rahiim
Wattleton, Alyce Faye
Weathersby, Joseph Brewster
Williams, Frederick Boyd
Williams, Hosea L.
Williamson-Ige, Dorothy Kay
Wilson, Angela Brown
Wilson, F. Leon
Wilson, Margaret Bush
Woodhouse, Rossalind Yvonne
Woods, Almita
Wright, Flonzie B.
Wyatt, Addie L.

Wynn, Thomas Harold, Sr.
Yoba, Malik

Actuarial Science
Mosley, Roosevelt Charles, Jr.
Parker, Herbert Gerald
Ross, Emma Jean

Advertising/Promotion
(See Also **Management/Administration—Advertising/Marketing/Public Relations**)
Allen, Clyde Cecil
Alligood, Douglass Lacy
Anderson, Bryan N.
Anderson, Harold A.
Anderson, Marjorie
Artope, William
Ashmore, Andrea Lynn
Bailey, Curtis Darnell
Baker, Gregory D.
Barrow, Lionel Ceon, Jr.
Barrows, Bryan H., III
Beatty, Robert L.
Bell, Raleigh Berton
Bishop, Sanford D., Jr.
Black, David Eugene, Sr.
Black, Willa
Blackshear, Julian W., Jr.
Block, Leslie S.
Bostic, Lee H.
Bradley, London M., Jr.
Brown, Brian A.
Brown, Tony
Burns, Dargan J.
Burrell, Barbara
Burrell, Thomas J.
Burroughs, Sarah G.
Butler, Michael E.
Calhoun, Lillian Scott
Carnegie, Randolph David
Carter, Kenneth Wayne
Chargois, Jenelle M.
Chisholm, Samuel Jackson
Clipper, Milton Clifton, Jr.
Coleman, Donald Alvin
Colston Barge, Gayle S.
Cook, Elizabeth G.
Cooper, Winston Lawrence
Cullers, Vincent T.
Curry, Charles H.
Dale, Louis
Dale, Robert J.
Davis, Lisa R.
Driver, Richard Sonny, Jr.
Duncan, Lynda J.
Early, Sybil Theresa
Edmonds, Terry
Edwards, John Loyd, III
Edwards, Oscar Lee
Evans, Alicia
Franklin, Percy
Freeland, Shawn Ericka
Frelow, Robert Lee, Jr.
Gallager, Mike John
Gant, Phillip M., III
Garrett, Ruby Grant
Giles, Althea B.
Giles, William R.
Giles-Alexander, Sharon
Givens, Joshua Edmond
Goodson, James Abner, Jr.
Graves, Valerie Jo
Gray, Andrew Jackson
Greenidge, James Ernest
Guy, Lygia Brown
Harper, Laydell Wood
Harris, David L.
Harris, Ray, Sr.
Haskins, Michael Kevin
Haynes, Eleanor Louise
Henderson-Nocho, Audrey J.
Herring, Leonard, Jr.
Heyward, Isaac
Hill, Kenneth D.
Hilliard, Amy S.
Hite, Nancy Ursula
Holland, J. Archibald
Holliman, Argie N.
Holloway, Ardith E.
House, Michael A.
Hoye, Walter B.
Hubbard, Marilyn French
Hudson, Keith
Humphrey, James Philip

Hampton, Phillip Jewel
Harden, Marvin
Hayes, Vertis
Hegwood, William Lewis
High, Freida
Hinton, Alfred Fontaine
Jackson, Oliver L.
Jackson, Suzanne Fitzallen
Johnson, Timothy Julius, Jr.
Jones, Calvin Bell
Jones, Lois Mailou
Lane, Julius Forbes
Lark, Raymond
Lawrence, Jacob A.
Lee-Smith, Hughie
Locke, Donald
Logan, Juan Leon
Martin, Ionis Bracy
McCants, Coolidge N.
McMillan, Douglas James
McMillan, James C.
Miller, Thomas Patton
Mitchell, Dean Lamont
Morrison, Keith Anthony
Nelson, Eileen F.
Norman, Bobby Don
Norwood, Tom
Onli, Turtel
Oubre, Hayward Louis
Owens, Wallace, Jr.
Padgett, James A.
Pannell, Patrick Weldon
Pindell, Howardena D.
Pitts, George Edward, Jr.
Purdee, Nathan
Reid, Robert Dennis
Rickson, Gary Ames
Ringgold, Faith
Roberts, Malkia
Robinson, Ella S.
Ryder, Mahler B.
Saint James, Synthia
Sandoval, Dolores S.
Sandridge, John Solomon
Searles, Charles R.
Shands, Franklin M., Sr.
Simms, Carroll Harris
Smith, James David
Smith, Vincent D.
Snowden, Gilda
Snowden, Sylvia Frances
Talley, Clarence, Sr.
Thomas, Matthew Manjusri, Jr.
Tomlinson, Robert
Walker, Larry M.
Washington, James W., Jr.
Watkins, Ira Donnell
West, Pheoris
Whyte, Garrett
Williams, Frank James
Williams, William Thomas
Wilson, John
Wilson, Sandra E.
Woods, Roosevelt, Jr.
Woodson, Shirley A.
Wright, Dmitri
Yarde, Richard Foster
Young, Charles Alexander

Art, Visual—Sculpting

Arkansaw, Tim
Billington, Clyde, Jr.
Birch, Willie
Boozer, Emerson, Jr.
Burroughs, Margaret Taylor
Carter, Allen D.
Catlett, Elizabeth
Chase-Riboud, Barbara DeWayne
Clark, Edward
Davidson, Donald Rae
Douglas, Elizabeth Asche
Fittz, Senga Nengudi
Foreman, Doyle
Gaskin, Leroy
Geran, Joseph, Jr.
Guyton, Tyree
Gwaltney, John L.
Hamilton, Edward N., Jr.
Hardison, Ruth Inge
Harris, William Joseph, II
Hayes, Vertis
Hodgson-Brooks, Gloria J.
Hubbard, Calvin L.
Hunt, Richard Howard
Jackson, Oliver L.
Jackson, Vera Ruth
Johnson, Stephanie Anne
Jolly, Marva Lee

Jordan, Eddie Jack, Sr.
Maynard, Valerie J.
McMillan, Douglas James
McMillan, James C.
Michaux, Henry M., Jr.
Miller, Thomas Patton
Montgomery, Evangeline Juliet
Neely, David E.
Oubre, Hayward Louis
Owens, Wallace, Jr.
Padgett, James A.
Paige, Alvin
Purifoy, Noah Sylvester
Sandridge, John Solomon
Searles, Charles R.
Simms, Carroll Harris
Snowden, Gilda
Talley, Clarence, Sr.
Taylor, Michael Loeb
Warmack, Gregory
Washington, James W., Jr.
Weil, Robert L.
Wilkie, Earl Augustus T.
Williams, Chester Lee
Williams, William Thomas
Wilson, John
Wilson, Stanley Charles

Art, Visual—Not Elsewhere Classified

Adams, John Oscar
Anderson, Amelia Veronica
Arnold, Ralph M.
Asma, Thomas M.
Ausby, Ellsworth Augustus
Bell, Ngozi O.
Benjamin, Tritobia Hayes
Billingsley, Orzell, Jr.
Billingsley, Ray C.
Billington, Clyde, Jr.
Boggs, Nathaniel
Bonner, Theophulis W.
Boozer, Emerson, Jr.
Brailsford, Marvin D.
Bright, Alfred Lee
Byrd, Joan Eda
Carter, Ora Williams
Carter, Yvonne P.
Catchings, Yvonne Parks
Catlett, Elizabeth
Claye, Charlene Marette
Cooley, Nathan J.
Cortor, Eldzier
Crouther, Betty Jean
Curtis-Rivers, Susan Yvonne
Dalton, Raymond Andrew
Day, Burnis Calvin
DeKnight, Avel
Driskell, David C.
Dunnigan, Jerry
Edmonds, Josephine E.
Epting, Marion
Fittz, Senga Nengudi
Gaskin, Leroy
Gilliam, Sam, Jr.
Gilliard, Joseph Wadus
Grauer, Gladys Barker
Grist, Raymond
Hardman, Della Brown Taylor
Harrison, Pearl Lewis
Hendricks, Barkley L.
Hogu, Barbara J. Jones
Huggins, Hazel Renfroe
Humphrey, Margo
Imhotep, Akbar
Ingram, Gregory Lamont
Irmagean
Jackson, Reginald Leo
Jessup, Marsha Edwina
Johnson, Benjamin Earl
Johnson, Clarissa
Johnson, Rita Falkener
Jones, Ben F.
Jones, Calvin Bell
Jones, Grace
Kamau, Mosi
King-Hammond, Leslie
Lawrence, Prestonia D.
Lewis, Elma I.
Ligon, Doris Hillian
Love, Edward A.
Maynard, Valerie J.
Mayo, Barry Alan
McCane, Charlotte Antoinette
McCray, Billy Quincy
McElrath, Wanda Faith
Mills, Joey Richard
Morgan-Welch, Beverly Ann

Morris, Earl Scott
Newton, James E.
Olugebefola, Ademola
Outterbridge, John Wilfred
Owens, Andi
Owens, Wallace, Jr.
Patterson, Curtis Ray
Pearson, Clifton
Peerman-Pledger, Vernese Dianne
Pinckney, Stanley
Pindell, Howardena D.
Piper, Adrian Margaret Smith
Powell, Georgette Seabrooke
Raab, Madeline Murphy
Richardson, Frank
Roberts, Malkia
Robinson, Anthony W.
Robinson, Jontyle Theresa
Saar, Betye I.
Sarmiento, Shirley Jean
Scott, John T.
Sills, Thomas Albert
Simon, Jewel Woodard
Simpson, Merton Daniel
Smith, Alfred J., Jr.
Smith, Vincent D.
Staats, Florence Joan
Steth, Raymond
Styles, Freddie L.
Taylor, Cledie Collins
Taylor, Michael Loeb
Temple, Herbert
Terrell, Mable Jean
Tessema, Tesfaye
Thompson, Lowell Dennis
Todd, Charles O.
Twigg, Lewis Harold
Walker, George Edward
Webb, Veronica Lynn
White, Clarence Dean
Williams, Daniel Salu
Wilson, Stanley Charles
Winston, Dennis Ray
Woods, Jessie Anderson
Woodson, Shirley A.
Young, Charles Alexander

Association Management

Ackridge, Florence Gateward
Adair, Andrew A.
Adams, Gregory Keith
Adams, Quinton Douglas
Adams, V. Toni
Addams, Robert David
Addison, Caroline Elizabeth
Alexander, Alma Duncan
Alexander, Harry Toussaint
Alexander, John Stanley
Alexander, Mervin Franklin
Alexander, Sidney H., Jr.
Alexander, Warren Dornell
Alford, Brenda
Allen, Alexander J.
Allen, Edna Rowery
Allen, James Trinton
Allen, Karen
Allen, Terrell Allison, III
Allen, Wendell
Alston, Harry L.
Ambrose, Ethel L.
Anderson, Donald L.
Anderson, Doreatha Madison
Anderson, Hubert, Jr.
Anderson, Mary Elizabeth
Anderson, Michael Wayne
Anderson, Nicholas Charles
Anderson, Perry L.
Andrews, Carl R.
Anthony, Wendell
Aramburo, Sophie Watts
Ashford, Laplois
Ashley, Lillard Governor
Asinor, Freddie Andrew
Bailey, Doris Jones
Baines, Tyrone Randolph
Banks, Waldo R., Sr.
Barefield, Ollie Delores
Barney, Clarence Lyle
Barrow, Willie T.
Bateman, Celeste
Bates, Clayton Wilson, Jr.
Batson, Ruth Marion
Batteast, Margaret W.
Battle, Mark G.
Battle, Maurice Tazwell
Baugh, Florence Ellen
Beal, Lisa Suzanne
Beasley, Arlene A.

Beckett, Justin F.
Beckham, Edgar Frederick
Bell, H. B.
Bell, Thom R.
Benjamin, Ronald
Bettis, Anne Katherine
Billups, Mattie Lou
Bingham, Rebecca Josephine
Bishop, Cecil
Black, Willa
Blanks, Wilhelmina E.
Blocker, Helen Powell
Bofill, Angela
Bogle, Robert W.
Bolden, Betty A.
Bolton, Julian Taylor
Bookert, Charles C.
Bostic, Viola W.
Boutte, Ernest John
Bradley, Jack Carter
Bradley, Roberta Palm
Bramble, Peter W. D.
Brantley, Daniel
Braxton, Harriet E.
Bridgewater, Paul
Briscoe, Sidney Edward, Jr.
Brown, Annie Gibson
Brown, Clarence William
Brown, Claudell, Jr.
Brown, Henry H.
Brown, James Monroe
Brown, Joan P.
Brown, Philip Rayfield, III
Brown, William J.
Brown, William McKinley, Jr.
Brown, Zora Kramer
Bruce, Antoinette Johnson
Bryant, Carl
Bryant, Franklyn
Bryant, Jesse A.
Bryant, R. Kelly, Jr.
Buford, James Henry
Bulger, Lucille O.
Bunte, Doris
Burgess, Dwight A.
Burney, Harry L., Jr.
Bush, Lenoris
Butler, Patrick Hampton
Callaway, Dwight W.
Campbell, James W.
Cannon, Edith H.
Canson, Virna M.
Carey, Audrey L.
Carey, Howard H.
Cargile, C. B., Jr.
Carpenter, Barbara West
Carroll, Sally G.
Carson, Emmett D.
Carter, George E.
Carter, Gilbert Lino
Carter, Jesse Lee, Sr.
Carter, Martin Joseph
Carter, Robert Thompson
Carter, Ruth Durley
Carter, Weptanomah Washington
Cassis, Glenn Albert
Chaney, Alphonse
Chapman, Julius
Chenault, Myron Maurice
Cherry, Lee Otis
Cherry, Robert Lee
Childs, Theodore Francis
Clark, Jesse B., III
Clark, Theodore Lee
Cleaver, Eldridge
Clemons, Linda K.
Clingman, Kevin Loren
Coachman, Winfred Charles
Colbert, Ernest, Sr.
Coleman, Herman W.
Coles, Joseph C.
Collins, Constance Renee Wilson
Collins, Rosecrain
Connor, Dolores Lillie
Cooke, Lloyd M.
Cooper, Augusta Mosley
Cooper, Merrill Pittman
Cooper, William B.
Corrin, Malcolm L.
Costen, James H.
Cox, Otha P.
Coyle, Mary Dee
Craig, Claude Burgess
Craven, Judith
Crawford, Charles L.
Crawford, James Wesley
Crawford, Jayne Suzanne
Cright, Lotess Priestley
Cromartie, Eugene Rufus

Crouther, Melvin S., Jr.
Cummings, James C., Jr.
Curvin, Robert
Dailey, Quintin
Dandy, Roscoe Greer
Daniel, Mary Reed
Daniels, William James
Davies, Lawrence A.
Davis, Evelyn Payne
Davis, Fred
Davis, John Albert
Davis, Luther Charles
Davis, Mary Agnes Miller
Davis, Milton C.
Davis, Norman Emanuel
Davis, Patricia C.
Davis, Preston Augustus
Davis, Ronald R.
Davis, Willie Floyd, Jr.
Dean, Diane D.
Dean, Willie B.
De Fossett, William K.
Delaney, Willi
Delpit, Lisa Denise
de Passe, Suzanne
DePriest, Darryl Lawrence
Dickerson, Ralph
Dismuke, Mary Eunice
Dobson, Helen Sutton
Dobynes, Elizabeth
Dockery, Richard L.
Dooley, Wallace Troy
Dorsey, Harold Aaron
Dorsey, Herman Sherwood, Jr.
Dorsey, Sandra
Douglas, Walter Edmond, Sr.
Drake, Pauline Lilie
Dreher, Lucille G.
Drew, Thelma Lucille
Driggriss, Daphne Bernice
  Sutherland
Duggins, George
Dukes, Walter L.
Duncan, Geneva
Easley, Brenda Vietta
Eaton, Patricia Frances
Ecton, Virgil E.
Edelman, Marian Wright
Edley, Christopher F., Sr.
Edwards, John Loyd, III
Edwards-Aschoff, Patricia Joann
Eichelberger, Brenda
Elcock, Claudius Adolphus Rufus
Elder, Almora Kennedy
Elliott, John
Ellis, P. J.
Emeka, Mauris L. P.
English, Alex
English, Henry L.
Epps, C. Roy
Epps, Dolzie C. B.
Ethridge, Samuel B.
Evans, Amos James
Evans, Samuel London
Evans, Webb
Fair, Darwin
Fair, Talmadge Willard
Farmer, Clarence
Fattah, Falaka
Fields, M. Joan
Fields, William I., Jr.
Finnie, Roger L., Sr.
Fisher, Shelley Marie
Flamer, John H., Jr.
Flateau, John
Fletcher, Patricia Louise
Floyd, Jeremiah
Fluker, Philip A.
Ford, Aileen W.
Ford, Kenneth A.
Ford, William L., Jr.
Foster, James H.
Foster, Jylla Moore
Fowler, Queen Dunlap
Foxx, Laura R.
Francis, Cheryl Margaret
Francis, Livingston S.
Francis, Patrick John
Franklin, Eugene T., Jr.
Franklin, Hardy E.
Frazier, Adolphus Cornelious
Frazier, Audrey Lee
Frazier, Eufaula Smith
Frazier, Rick C.
Freeman, Kerlin, Jr.
French, George Wesley
Frost, Hugh A.
Fudge, Marcia L.
Fudge, Marsha L.

Titus, LeRoy Robert
Todman, Terence A.
Tokley, Joanna Nutter
Traylor, Horace Jerome
Tripp, Luke Samuel
Tukufu, Darryl S.
Turner, Bennie
Turner, Ervin
Turner, Melvin Duval
Turner, Moses
Turner, Tina
Upton, E. H.
Veal, Howard Richard
Vinson, Julius Ceasar
Wade, Lyndon Anthony
Walker, Eugene Kevin
Walker, Lula Aquillia
Walker, Tanya Rosetta
Walker, William Sonny
Walsh, Everald J.
Walton, Flavia Batteau
Ward, Melvin Fitzgerald, Sr.
Ward, Zana Rogers
Ware, Charles Jerome
Washington, C. Clifford
Washington, Jacquelin Edwards
Washington, Josie B.
Washington, Rudy
Waterman, Thelma M.
Watkins, Mary Frances
Watkins, Robert Charles
Watson, Bernard C.
Watson, Carole M.
Watson, Dennis Rahiim
Watson, Joann Nichols
Watson, Theresa Lawhorn
Weathers, Margaret A.
Wesley, Clarence E.
Wharton, Dolores D.
Wheat, Alan
Whipps, Mary N.
White, Lois Jean
White, Robert L.
White, William T., III
Whitfield, Vantile E.
Wilber, Margie Robinson
Wilcox, Preston
Wiley, Margaret Z. Richardson
Williams, Ann E. A.
Williams, Charles Richard
Williams, Eddie Nathan
Williams, Geneva J.
Williams, Herman
Williams, James E., Jr.
Williams, Kenneth Herbert
Williams, Lea E.
Williams, Novella Stewart
Williams, Reginald T.
Williams, Ronald Lee
Williams, Ruby Mai
Williams, Wyatt Clifford
Williamson, Henry M.
Willis, Andrew
Wilson, Clarence Northon
Wilson, Cleo Francine
Wilson, Donald P.
Wilson, Frank Edward
Wilson, Ronald M.
Winston, Henry
Winters, James Robert
Wolfe, William K.
Woodson, Robert L.
Wooten, Priscilla A.
Wright, Grover Cleveland
Wright, Robert L.
Wyke, Joseph Henry
Wynn, William Austin, Jr.
Young, Margaret Buckner

Astronomy
See **Physics/Astronomy**

Athletics
See **Sports—Amateur;
Sports—Professional/
Semiprofessional; Sports—Not
Elsewhere Classified; Sports
Coaching/Training/ Managing/
Officiating**

Auditing
See **Accounting/Auditing**

Automobile Industry
See **Manufacturing—Motor
Vehicles; Retail Trade—Motor
Vehicles, Parts, and Services;
Wholesale Trade—Motor
Vehicles and Parts**

Aviation
See **Airline Industry**

Banking/Financial Services
Abdullah, Sharif
Adams, Cecil Ray
Aikens, Alexander E., III
Allen, Benjamin P., III
Anderson, Carol Byrd
Anderson, Leon H.
Anderson, Marcellus J., Sr.
Arbuckle, John Finley, Jr.
Arnold, Rudolph P.
Arrington, Lloyd M., Jr.
Ashburn, Vivian Diane
Avery-Blair, Lorraine
Backstrom, Don
Baker, Darryl Brent, Sr.
Ballard, Edward Hunter
Baltimore, Roslyn Lois
Baptista, Howard
Barkley, Mark E.
Baskette, Ernest E., Jr.
Bather, Paul Charles
Battle, Bernard J., Sr.
Battle, Charles E.
Battle, Jacqueline
Beal, Bernard
Beal, Jacqueline Jean
Becote, Fohliette W.
Bell, Charles A.
Bell, Joseph N.
Bell, Karl I.
Belmear, Horace Edward
Bennett, Joyce Annette
Benson, Sharon Marie
Bernard, Nesta Hyacinth
Biggins, J. Veronica
Black, Rosa Walston
Bland, Edward
Blow, Sarah Parsons
Booker, Simeon S.
Booker, Vaughan P. L.
Bowden, Marion A.
Bowie, Walter C.
Bowman, James E., Jr.
Boyd, Marvin
Bradberry, Richard Paul
Bradshaw, Lawrence A.
Bradshaw, Wayne-Kent
Brandford, Napoleon, III
Bridgeman, Donald Earl
Brigham, Freddie M.
Brimmer, Andrew F.
Brooks, Don Locellus
Broussard, Cheryl Denise
Brown, Eddie C.
Brown, John C., Jr.
Brown, John Mitchell, Sr.
Brown, Joyce
Brown, Reuben D.
Brown, Rose Denise
Brown, Yolanda
Brown-Harris, Ann
Bryant-Ellis, Paula D.
Bryant-Reid, Johanne
Burgin, Bruce L.
Burrus, Clark
Burton, Barbara Ann
Bush, Charles Vernon
Bush, Mary K.
Carlton, Pamela Gean
Carpenter, Lewis
Carr, Roderich Marion
Carroll, Raoul Lord
Carter, Kevin Antony
Cartwright, James Elgin
Chapman, Nathan A.
Chappell, Emma Carolyn
Chatterjee, Lois Jordan
Chavis, Omega Rochelle
Chivis, Martin Lewis
Christophe, Cleveland A.
Clark, Walter H.
Clark, Walter L.
Clay, Timothy Byron
Clayton, Kathleen R.
Cohen, Gwen A.
Coleman, Cecil R.

Coleman, Columbus E., Jr.
Coles, John Edward
Collins, Joanne Marcella
Cook, Keith Lynn
Cook, Rufus
Coombs, Fletcher
Cooper-Farrow, Valerie
Corley, Leslie M.
Cornwell, W. Don
Counts, Allen
Cowans, Alvin Jeffrey
Cox, DuBois V.
Cox, Robert L.
Crawley, A. Bruce
Crews, William Sylvester
Cummings, Aeon L.
Cunningham, William Michael
Curry, Levy Henry
Curtis-Bauer, M. Benay
Daniel, Alfred Irwin
Daniels, Anthony Hawthorne
Daniels, Frederick L., Jr.
Daniels, LeGree Sylvia
Daniels, Lemuel Lee
Davidson, Charles Robert
Davidson, Lurlean G.
Davis, Alfred C., Sr.
Davis, Diane Lynn
Davis, Jean M.
Davis, Milton
Davis, Nigel S.
Davis, Roland Hayes
Day, William Charles, Jr.
DeGeneste, Henry Irving
Derricotte, C. Bruce
Dickens, Jacoby
Dickson, Reginald D.
Disher, Spencer C., III
Dixon, Richard Nathaniel
Doig, Elmo H.
Dolby, Edward C.
Doley, Harold E., Jr.
Dudley, Eunice
Dugger, Edward, III
Dunmore, Lawrence A., Jr.
Duster, Benjamin C., IV
Eagan, Catherine B.
Easton, Richard James
Eccles, Peter Wilson
Edmonds, Norman Douglas
Eley, Randall Robbi
Ellis, Ernest W.
Ellis, Rodney
Elmore, Stephen A., Sr.
Evans, Charlotte A.
Evans, Cheryl Lynn
Evans, Leon Edward, Jr.
Ewing, Samuel Daniel, Jr.
Farmer, Hilda Wooten
Farrell, Cheryl Layne
Farrow, William McKnight, III
Feddoes, Sadie C.
Felder, Thomas E.
Felton, Otis Leverna
Ferguson, Johnnie Nathaniel
Fields, Samuel Bennie
Fierce, Hughlyn F.
Fisher, Ronald L.
Fitzgerald, William B.
Flood, Eugene, Jr.
Flores, Leo
Follmer, Paul L.
Forde, Fraser Philip, Jr.
Forte, Linda Diane
Foster, Deborah Valrie
Foster, William K.
Fowler, James Daniel, Jr.
Franklin, Oliver St. Clair, Jr.
Frasier, Ralph Kennedy
Fuget, Henry Eugene
Funderburg, I. Owen
Garrison-Corbin, Patricia Ann
Gary, Howard V.
Gibbs, William Lee
Givhan, Mercer A., Jr.
Glover, Hamilton
Glover, Kenneth Elijah
Goodwin, Stephen Robert
Grady, Walter E.
Graham, Donald
Graves, Clifford W.
Gray, Naomi T.
Gray, Ronald A.
Grayson, Stanley Edward
Green, Anita Lorraine
Green, Dennis O.
Green, Ernest E.
Green, Gloria J.
Green, Hydia Lutrice

Green-Campbell, Deardra Delores
Greene, Frank S., Jr.
Greene, Richard T.
Greer, Baunita
Gregg, Lucius Perry
Griffin, Lloyd
Grigsby, Calvin Burchard
Grigsby, David P.
Grisham, Arnold T.
Grist, Ronald
Haddon, James Francis
Hadnott, Grayling
Hamer, Judith Ann
Hamilton, John M.
Hammonds, Alfred
Hannah, Mack H., Jr.
Hannah, Mosie R.
Harrington, Gerald E.
Harris, Curtis Alexander
Harris, Jeanette G.
Harris, Nathaniel C., Jr.
Harris, Stanley Kenyon
Harrison, Booker David
Harrison, Delbert Eugene
Hart, Ronald O.
Harvey, Richard R.
Haskins, Joseph, Jr.
Haskins, Morice Lee, Jr.
Hatchett, Paul Andrew
Hayden, William Hughes
Haywood, George Weaver
Heard, Blanche Denise
Hedgepeth, Leonard
Henley, Vernard W.
Herndon, Phillip George
Hill, Henry, Jr.
Hobson, Mellody L.
Hodge, Norris
Holloman, Thaddeus Bailey
Holloway, Harris M.
Holloway, Hiliary H.
Holmes, Richard Bernard
Homer, Ronald A.
Houston, Seawadon Lee
Howard, Linwood E.
Howard, Osbie L., Jr.
Hudson, Elbert T.
Hudson, Paul C.
Hull, Everson Warren
Humphrey, Marian J.
Hunt, Eugene
Hurt, James E.
Hutchinson, James J., Jr.
Jackson, Charles E., Sr.
Jackson, Denise
Jackson, Eugene L.
Jackson, Pazel
James, Robert Earl
Jeffers, Grady Rommel
Jenkins, Carlton J.
Jenkins, Robert Kenneth, Jr.
Jennings, Sylvesta Lee
Johns, Stephen Arnold
Johnson, Alexander Hamilton, Jr.
Johnson, Cleveland, Jr.
Johnson, David E.
Johnson, Edward, Jr.
Johnson, Ernest L.
Johnson, Mitchell A.
Johnson, Pompie Louis, Jr.
Johnson, Stephen L.
Johnson, William
Johnson, William C.
Jones, David L.
Jones, Leora
Jones, Milton H., Jr.
Jones, Shalley A.
Jones, Thomas W.
Jordan, Carolyn D.
Jordan, Emma Coleman
Joseph-McIntyre, Mary
Kea, Arleas Upton
Kemp, C. Robert
Kinder, Randolph Samuel, Jr.
King, Colbert I.
King, George W., Jr.
Kirkland, Gwendolyn Vickye
Knight, W. H., Jr.
Lambert, Joseph C.
Lanier, Willie
Lansey, Yvonne F.
Lavelle, Robert R.
Laymon, Heather R.
Lazard, Betty
Lee, Aubrey Walter, Sr.
Lee, Aubrey Walter, Jr.
Lee, John M.
Lee, John Robert E.
Lemon, Ann

Lewis, Andre
Lewis, Thomas P.
Lewis, Willard C.
Linyard, Richard
London, Gloria D.
Loney, Carolyn Patricia
Long, Steffan
Lowe, Aubrey F.
Lowery, Donald Elliott
Lyons, Lamar
Lyons, Lloyd Carson
Mack, C.
Mack, Roderick O'Neal
Maitland, Tracey
Malloy, H. Rembert
Malone, Claudine Berkeley
Manley, Bill
March, Anthony
Mariel, Serafin
Marshall, Wilfred L.
Martin, Charles Howard
Martin, Herman Henry, Jr.
Martin, I. Maximillian
Matthews, Harry Bradshaw
Matthews, Westina Lomax
Matthis, James L., III
Maule, Albert R.
Mausi, Shahida Andrea
Mayes, Doris Miriam
Mayo, Harry D., III
McBride, Frances E.
McCants, Keith
McClain, Jerome Gerald
McClenic, David A.
McClinton, Suzanne Y.
McClure, Fredrick H. L.
McCrackin, Olympia F.
McDemmond, Marie V.
McDonald, Anita Dunlop
McEachern, D. Hector
McGuire, Rosalie J.
McKinney, Olivia Davene Ross
McLin, Lena Johnson
McMullins, Tommy
McMurry, Kermit Roosevelt, Jr.
McNair, Barbara J.
McQueen, Michael Anthony
McReynolds, Elaine A.
Miles, Frederick Augustus
Miller, George Carroll, Jr.
Miller, Helen S.
Miller, James
Miller, Ward Beecher
Milner, Michael Edwin
Minyard, Handsel B.
Mister, Melvin Anthony
Mitchell, B. Doyle, Jr.
Mitchell, Carlton S.
Montgomery, Fred O.
Montgomery, George Louis, Jr.
Moore, Brenda Carol
Moore, Cornell Leverette
Moore, John Wesley, Jr.
Moorehead, Justin Leslie
Morris, William H.
Moses, Edwin
Mosley, Christopher D.
Mosley, Edna Wilson
Mosley, Elwood A.
Motley, John H.
Mullings, Paul
Muse, William Brown, Jr.
Myles, Wilbert
Naphtali, Ashirah Sholomis
Neal, Mario Lanza
Newsome, Ronald Wright
Newton, Ernest E., II
Newton, James Douglas, Jr.
Njoroge, Mbugua J.
Nunn, John, Jr.
Oglesby, Tony B.
Oguniesi, Adebayo O.
Oliver, Kenneth Nathaniel
O'Neal, Stanley
Ourlicht, David E.
Owens, Mercy P.
Oxendine, John Edward
Oyalowo, Tunde O.
Palmer, Terry Wayne
Parker, George Anthony
Parker, Henry Ellsworth
Patterson, Clinton David
Patterson, Ronald E.
Pearce, Richard Allen
Pearson, Marilyn Ruth
Pearson, Michael Novel
Pease, Denise Louise
Pendergraft, Michele M.
Perine, Martha Levingston

Hargrave, Charles William
Harris, Betty Wright
Harris, James Andrew
Harris, Thomas C.
Herrell, Astor Yeary
Holland, Laurence H.
Innis, Roy Emile Alfredo
Jackson, Roy Joseph, Jr.
Johnson, William Randolph
Jones, Winton Dennis, Jr.
King, James, Jr.
King, William Frank
Kirklin, Perry William
Lee, Charlotte O.
Lester, William Alexander, Jr.
Lewis, Virginia Hill
Louis, Joseph
Low, Patricia Enid Rose
Macklin, John W.
Madison, Jacqueline Edwina
Matabane, Sebiletso Mokone
Matthews, Virgil E.
McBee, Vincent Clermont
McClendon, Raymond
McLean, John Lenwood
Mitchell, James Winfield
Morris, Marlene C.
Morrison, Harry L.
Neblett, Richard F.
Nelson, Ivory Vance
Onyejekwe, Chike Onyekachi
Payton, Albert Levern
Peace, G. Earl, Jr.
Price, David B., Jr.
Satcher, Robert Lee, Sr.
Schooler, James Morse, Jr.
Shoffner, James Priest
Smith, Fronse Wayne, Sr.
Smith, Joseph Edward
Smith, Morris Leslie
Sogah, Dotsevi Y.
Spurlock, Langley Augustine
Sudbury, Leslie G.
Tatem, Patricia Ann
Thompson, Lancelot C. A.
Thurston, Paul E.
Walters, Marc Anton
Weaver, John Arthur
Williams, Billy Myles
Wilson, Bobby L.
Young, Archie R., II

Chiropractic
Barnett, Lorna
Carpenter, Ann M.
Fair, Frank T.
Smith, Katrina Marita

Choreography
See **Dance/Choreography**

Civil Rights Activism
See **Activism, Political/Civil/ Social Rights**

Clergy—Catholic
Alex, Gregory K.
Allain, Leon Gregory
Alleyne, Edward D.
Anderson, Moses B.
Barrett, Walter Carlin, Jr.
Bigham, Reta Lacy
Braxton, Edward Kenneth
Carroll, Beverly A.
Carter, Martin Joseph
Charis, Sister
Clements, George H.
Cody, William L.
Conwill, Giles
Cross, William Howard
Curtis, Joseph F., Sr.
Davis, Agnes Maria
Davis, Martin
Delarue, Louis C.
Dupre, John Lionel
Ebo, Sister Antona
Emmons, Rayford E.
Fisher, David Andrew
Foster, Carl Oscar, Jr.
Francis, Joseph A.
Francois, Theodore Victor
Geyer, Edward B., Jr.
Gomez, Daniel J.
Goode, James Edward

Gregory, Wilton D.
Guyton, Sister Patsy
Harris, Hassel B.
Haywood, Hiram H., Jr.
Hegger, Wilber L.
Hill, Bennett David
Howell, Sharon Marie
Howze, Joseph Lawson
Joy, James Bernard, Jr.
Kellogg, Reginald J.
Lambert, Rollins Edward
LeDoux, Jerome G.
Marino, Eugene Antonio
Marshall, Paul M.
Mathis, Johnny
Matthews, Jessie L.
McMillan, Joseph H.
Mitchell, Henry B.
Moore, Emerson J.
Murray, J-Glenn
Neavon, Joseph Roy
Norvel, William Leonard
Nutt, Maurice Joseph
Phelps, Constance Kay
Pierce, Earl S.
Powell, Robert Meaker
Ricard, John H.
Richards, Sister Loretta Theresa
Rivers, Clarence Joseph
Robinson, Fisher J.
Rowe, Christa F.
Roy, Americus Melvin
Roy, Jasper K.
Shaw, Mario William
Shuffer, George Macon, Jr.
Smith, Paul Bernard
Stallings, George Augustus, Jr.
Steib, James T.
Stewart, Kenneth C.
Talley, Curtiss J.
Taylor, Sister Marie de Porres
Thompson, Sister Francesca
Towns, Maxine Yvonne
Vincent, Daniel Paul
Watson, Cletus Claude
Wells, Patrick Roland
Westray, Kenneth Maurice
Whitt, Dwight Reginald
Williams, Clarence Earl, Jr.

Clergy—Moslem/Muslim
Al-Amin, Jamil Abdullah
al-Hafeez, Humza
Fakhrid-Deen, Nashid Abdullah
Farrakhan, Louis
Kashif, Ghayth Nur
Muhammad, Abdul-Rasheed
Muhammad, Conrad
Muhammad, Wallace D.
Sharrieff, Osman Ibn

Clergy—Protestant
Adams, Charles Gilchrist
Adams, David, Jr.
Adams, John Hurst
Adkins, Cecelia Nabrit
Allen, Willie B.
Anderson, Patricia Hebert
Anderson, Vinton Randolph
Andrews, Frazier L.
Armstrong, Ernest W., Sr.
Austin, Joyce Phillips
Bagley, Stanley B.
Bailey, Randall Charles
Baker, Delbert Wayne
Baldwin, Lewis V.
Barksdale, Leonard N., III
Barnwell, Henry Lee
Barrow, Willie T.
Batten, Grace Ruth
Battle, Maurice Tazwell
Bayne, Henry G.
Beavers, Nathan Howard, Jr.
Bell, Leon
Bellinger, Luther Garic
Bellinger, Mary Anne
Bennett, Lerone J.
Bennett, Patricia W.
Best, Sheila Diane
Bethel, Kathleen Evonne
Bishop, Alfred A.
Blair, Lacy Gordon
Blake, Elias, Jr.
Blake, Wendell Owen
Blount, Larry Elisha
Blue, Vida, Jr.
Bond, Lloyd

Bone, Winston S.
Boone, Clarence Wayne
Boonieh, Obi Anthony
Booth, Charles E.
Booth, Lavaughn Venchael
Bouie, Preston L.
Bowman, Phillip Jess
Boyd, Barbara P.
Bradley, James Howard, Jr.
Branch, B. Lawrence
Branch, Dorothy L.
Branch, G. Murray
Branch, Geraldine Burton
Branch, William McKinley
Breckenridge, Franklin E.
Brenson, Verdel Lee
Brewington, Donald Eugene
Bright, Herbert L., Sr.
Bronson, Fred James
Brown, Amos Cleophilus
Brown, Andrew J.
Brown, Annie Carnelia
Brown, Charles Sumner
Brown, Delores Elaine
Brown, George Houston
Brown, Greggory Lee
Brown, Jeffrey LeMonte
Brown, Leo C., Jr.
Brown, Philip Rayfield, III
Brown, William Rocky, III
Bryant, John G.
Bryant, John Richard
Bunton, Henry Clay
Burns, Calvin Louis
Burrell, Emma P.
Burrell, Morris
Butler, Charles W.
Butler, Clary Kent
Butler, Ernest Daniel
Butler, J. Ray
Butler, Keith Andre
Butler, Max R.
Butts, Calvin Otis, III
Byrd, Sherman Clifton
Caesar, Shirley
Calbert, William Edward, Sr.
Callahan, Samuel P.
Cameron, John E.
Campbell, E. Alexander
Campbell, Gilbert Godfrey
Cannon, Katie Geneva
Canty, Ralph Waldo
Carr, Leonard G.
Carroll, Edward Gonzalez
Carter, Lawrence E., Sr.
Carter, Percy A., Jr.
Cary, William Sterling
Casey, Carey Walden, Sr.
Caviness, E. Theophilus
Chambers, Clarice Lorraine
Chandler, Harold R.
Chapman, Robert L., Sr.
Chappelle, Thomas Oscar, Sr.
Charis, Sister
Charlton, Charles Hayes
Cherry, Andrew Jackson
Childs, Francine C.
Clark, Caesar A. W.
Clay, Henry Carroll, Jr.
Clay, Julius C.
Clay, Willie B.
Cleage, Albert B., Jr.
Clemons, Earlie, Jr.
Clinkscales, John William, Jr.
Cobb, Harold
Cobb, Harold James, Jr.
Cole, Adolph
Coleman, Caesar David
Coleman, Rudolph W.
Coley, Donald Lee
Collins, Paul L.
Collins, Robert H.
Collins, William, Jr.
Cone, James H.
Cook, Haney Judaea
Cook, James E.
Cook, Wallace Jeffery
Cooley, James F.
Cooper-Lewter, Nicholas Charles
Corbitt, John H.
Cornelius, Ulysses S., Sr.
Cousin, Philip R.
Covington, James Arthur
Crawford, Nathaniel, Jr.
Crews, William Hunter
Cross, Haman, Jr.
Crosse, St. George Idris Bryon
Cruz, Virgil
Cuff, George Wayne

Cunningham, E. Brice
Cunningham, John F.
Cunningham, Richard T.
Cureton, Stewart Cleveland
Current, Gloster Bryant
Currie, Eddie L.
Curry, Michael Bruce
Curry, Mitchell L.
Curry, Victor Tyrone
Dabney, David Hodges
Dance, Daryl Cumber
Dancy, William F.
Dandridge, Rita Bernice
Daniels, Alfred Claude Wynder
Daniels, Rebecca Haywood
Daniels, Richard Bernard
Daniels, Ruben
Darkes, Leroy William
Daughtry, Herbert Daniel
David, Keith
Davidson-Harger, Joan Carole
Davis, Clarence A.
Davis, Evelyn K.
Davis, Frank Derocher
Davis, Gloria-Jeanne
Davis, John Wesley, Sr.
Davis, Ossie B.
Davis, Twilus
Davis, Tyrone Theophilus
Delk, Yvonne V.
Del Pino, Jerome King
Dempsey, Joseph P.
Dennis, Walter Decoster
Dickerson, Adolphus Sumner
Dickerson, Dennis Clark
Diggs, William P.
Dixon, Ernest Thomas, Jr.
Dixon, James Wallace Edwin, II
Dodson, William Alfred, Jr.
Doggett, John Nelson, Jr.
Dorn, Roosevelt E.
Dorsey, Clinton George
Douglass, Melvin Isadore
Downey, Aurelia Richie
Driver, Louie M., Jr.
Driver, Rogers W.
Drummond, David L., Sr.
Du Bose, Robert Earl, Jr.
Dudley, Charles Edward
Dudley, Crayton T.
Dugger, Clinton George
Dulin, Robert O., Jr.
Dumas, Floyd E.
Dunston, Alfred G.
Dykes, DeWitt Sanford, Sr.
Easley, Paul Howard, Sr.
Elligan, Irvin, Jr.
Ellis, Elward Dwayne
Erwin, James Otis
Erwin, Richard C.
Evans, Clay
Evans, Lorenzo J.
Evans, Thomas
Evans, William C.
Farr, Herman
Felder, Cain Hope
Felker, Joseph B.
Feltus, James, Jr.
Fields, Edward E.
Fitts, Leroy
Fleming, Thomas A.
Foggie, Charles H.
Foggs, Edward L.
Fontenot, Albert E., Jr.
Ford, Florida Mae
Foreman, George Edward
Foster, James Hadlei
Franklin, Robert Michael
Franklin, Wayne L.
Freeman, Edward Anderson
Freeman, Thomas F.
Freeman, William M.
Fuller, James J.
Gadsden, Nathaniel J., Jr.
Gainer, John F.
Gaines, Ava Candace
Garrett, Thaddeus, Jr.
Gaston, Joseph Alexander
Gay, Benjamin
Gaylord, Ellihue, Sr.
George, Carrie Leigh
George, Constance P.
Gerald, William
Gibbes, Emily V.
Gibson, Ernest Robinson
Gibson, John A.
Gibson, William M.
Gilbert, Eldridge H. E.
Gilbert, Shedrick Edward

Gilcreast, Conway, Sr.
Gill, Laverne McCain
Gillespie, William G.
Gilmore, Marshall
Gilmore, Robert McKinley, Sr.
Githiga, John Gatungu
Glover, Clarence Ernest, Jr.
Gomes, Peter John
Goodwin, Kelly Oliver Perry
Gordon, Alexander H., II
Graham, Tecumseh Xavier
Granberry, James Madison, Jr.
Grant, Debora Felita
Grant, Jacquelyn
Graves, Raymond Lee
Grayson, Byron J., Sr.
Green, Calvin Coolidge
Green, Clyde Octavious
Green, Reuben H.
Green, William Edward
Greene, Jerome Alexander
Greene, William
Grigsby, Marshall C.
Groce, Herbert Monroe, Jr.
Gumms, Emmanuel George, Sr.
Guyton, Booker T.
Hailes, Edward A.
Hairston, Otis L.
Hairston, Raleigh Daniel
Hale, Cynthia Lynnette
Hale, Phale D.
Hall, Addie June
Hall, Kirkwood Marshal
Hamilton, Charles S.
Hamilton, McKinley John
Hamlin, Ernest Lee
Hammond, James Matthew
Hammond, Kenneth Ray
Handon, Marshall R., Jr.
Handy, William Talbot, Jr.
Hansen, Wendell Jay
Hardin, Henry E.
Hardman-Cromwell, Youtha Cordella
Hargrove, Milton Beverly
Harris, Barbara Clemente
Harris, David, Jr.
Harris, Michael Neely
Harris, Wesley Young, Jr.
Harris, William R.
Harrold, Austin Leroy
Harvey, Louis-Charles
Harvey, Wardelle G.
Harvey, William James, III
Harvin, Durant Kevin, III
Hathaway, Anthony, Jr.
Hawkins, Calvin D.
Hawkins, Howard P.
Hawkins, Reginald A.
Hayden, John Carleton
Hayes, Curtiss Leo
Haynes, Leonard L., Jr.
Haynes, Michael E.
Haynes, Neal J.
Hedgley, David R.
Hegmon, Oliver Louis
Hemphill, Miley Mae
Henderson, Isaiah Hilkiah, Jr.
Henry, David Winston
Henson, Charles A.
Herron, Vernon M.
Herzfeld, Will Lawrence
Hewitt, Basil
Hicks, H. Beecher, Jr.
Hicks, Henry Beecher, Sr.
Hicks, Richard R.
Hicks, Sherman G.
Higginbotham, Kenneth Day, Sr.
Higgins, Sammie L.
Hights, William E.
Hildebrand, Richard Allen
Hill, Anita June
Hill, Rufus S.
Hill, Vonciel Jones
Hilliard, William Alexander
Hilson, Arthur Lee
Hinkle, Jackson Herbert
Holley, Jim
Holmes, James Arthur, Jr.
Holmes, Zan W., Jr.
Hooker, Eric H.
Hooks, Benjamin Lawson
Hope, Julius Caesar
Hopkins, Barry L.
Horton, Larnie G.
Houston, David R.
Houston, W. Eugene
Howard, M. W., Jr.
Howard, Raymond Monroe, Sr.

Clergy—Not Elsewhere Classified

Anthony, Wendell
Bagley, Stanley B.
Baxter, Belgium Nathan
Beason, Kenneth Garrett
Boyd, William Stewart
Bradford, Arvine M.
Bradford-Eaton, Zee
Bradley, Roosevelt, Jr.
Bullett, Audrey Kathryn
Carry, Helen Ward
Chambers, Alex A.
Chatman, Melvin E.
Cheek, Donald Kato
Cheeks, Darryl Lamont
Chrichlow, Livingston L.
Cobbs, Harvey, Jr.
Colemon, Johnnie
Conaway, Mary Ward Pindle
Current, Gloster Bryant
Davis, Willie Floyd, Jr.
Dudley, Charles Edward
Durant, Naomi C.
Edwards, Abiyah, Jr.
Eikerenkoetter, Frederick J., II
Ellis, J. Delano, II
Ford, Richard D.
Gerald, William
Gibson, Nell Braxton
Giloth-David, King R.
Gooden, Samuel Ellsworth
Goodwin, Hugh Wesley
Green, Sterling
Guyton, Sister Patsy
Harley, Philip A.
Heyward, Isaac
Hoover, Theressa
Hotchkiss, Wesley Akin
Jackson, Jesse Louis
Jackson, Wiley, Jr.
Jacobs, Gregory Alexander
Johnson, Carroll Randolph, Jr.
Jones, Frank Benson
Jones, Vernon A., Jr.
King, Barbara Lewis
Logan, Thomas W. S., Sr.
McFall, Mary
McKelpin, Joseph P.
McKinney, Norma J.
Mills, Larry Glenn
Mitchell, Ella Pearson
Moran, Robert E., Sr.
Owens, Lynda Gayle
Perry, Joseph James
Pope, Courtney A.
Reynolds, Barbara A.
Shannon, Sylvester Lorenzo
Sharpton, Alfred Charles, Jr.
Sherrod, Charles M.
Stewart, Imagene Bigham
Waddles, Charleszetta Lina
Warren, Annika Laurin
Watkins, Joseph Philip
Wesley III, Herman Eugene
Whatley, Ennis
White, Reginald Howard
Williams, Chester Arthur
Williams, Hosea L.
Williamson, Henry M.
Wood, Andrew W.
Wright, Jeremiah A., Jr.

Community Service

Addison, Terry Hunter, Jr.
Aiken, Kimberly Clarice
Alexander, Cornelia
Alexander, John Stanley
Ali, Rasheedah Ziyadah
Anderson, Hubert, Jr.
Anderson, Louise Payne
Anderson, Oddie
Anderson, Patricia Hebert
Andrews, Phillip
Austin, Joyce Phillips
Bacoate, Matthew, Jr.
Bacon, Charlotte Meade
Badger, Brenda Joyce
Bailey, Agnes Jackson
Bailey, Doris Jones
Bailey, Ronald W.
Baldwin, Mitchell Cardell
Banner, Melvin Edward
Barnes, Martin G.
Bell, Raleigh Berton
Bellamy, Verdelle B.
Belmear, Horace Edward
Bennett, Debra Quinette

Bennett, Marion D.
Bernard, Michelle Denise
Best, Willie Armster
Block, Leslie S.
Blow, Sarah Parsons
Bolton, Wanda E.
Bommer, Minnie L.
Borges, Lynne MacFarlane
Bradley, Melissa Lynn
Bradley, William B.
Bright, Herbert L., Sr.
Brooks, Suzanne R.
Brown, Bernice Baynes
Brown, Hazel Evelyn
Bullett, Audrey Kathryn
Burden, Pennie L.
Burgess, James R., Jr.
Burgess, Robert E., Sr.
Butler, Darraugh Clay
Byrd, Harriett Elizabeth
Cain, Lester James, Jr.
Campbell, Emory Shaw
Carroll, Annie Haywood
Castleman, Elise Marie
Childs, Josie L.
Clemons, Linda K.
Cole, Charles Zhivaga
Cole Carey, Wilhemina, PhD
Coleman, Frankie Lynn
Collins, Joanne Marcella
Colson, Lewis Arnold
Comer, Jonathan
Cooper, Earl, II
Couch, James W.
Couche, Ruby S.
Cox, James L.
Cox, John Wesley
Craig-Jones, Ellen Walker
Crawford, Betty Marilyn
Cromwell, Margaret M.
Crosby, Willis Herman, Jr.
Dailey, Thelma
Daniels, Richard D.
Davidson, Alphonzo Lowell
Davie, Damon Jonathon
Davis, Cal Deleanor
Davis, Evelyn Payne
Davis, Preston Augustus
DeWindt, Hal
Dixon, Margaret A.
Dixon, Valena Alice
Dobbins, Alphondus Milton
Doby, Allen E.
Dockery, Richard L.
Dorsey, Herman Sherwood, Jr.
Dowery, Mary
Duncan, Alice Geneva
Duster, Donald Leon
Early, Ida H.
Eatman, Janice A.
Evans, Liz
Fattah, Falaka
Ferguson, Terri Lynette
Ferrell, Rosie E.
Flack, William Patrick
Flippen, Frances Morton
Florence, Johnny C.
Fobbs, Kevin
Foushee, Geraldine George
Gaddy, Beatrice
Gaines, Edythe J.
Garrett, Cheryl Ann
Gates, Audrey Castine
Gates, Jacquelyn Burch
Gay, Helen Parker
Gibson, Cheryl Dianne
Gilbert, Richard Lannear
Gilbert, Shedrick Edward
Gillette, Frankie Jacobs
Greene, Grace Randolph
Greene, Robert Charles
Greene, William
Greenwood, John T.
Grier, Rosey
Hackey, George Edward, Jr.
Hager, Joseph C.
Hale, Lorraine
Hamilton, John Joslyn, Jr.
Hamlet, James Frank
Hamlin, Ernest Lee
Hare, Julia Reed
Harmon, Sherman Allen
Harrington, Philip Leroy
Harris, Archie Jerome
Harris, James G., Jr.
Harris, Oscar L., Jr.
Harris, Willa Bing
Hasson, Nicole Denise
Henderson, Cheri Kaye

Hill, Annette Tillman
Hoppes, Alice Faye
Horton, Dollie Bea Dixon
Hughes, Hollis Eugene, Jr.
Hunter, Robert J.
Hutchins, Jan Darwin
Irving-Gibbs, Fannye
James, William M.
Jeffrey, Ronnald James
Jenkins, Elaine B.
Jennings, Devoyd
Johnson, Alexander Hamilton, Jr.
Johnson, Beverley Ernestine
Johnson, Cynthia
Johnson, Lorna Karen
Johnson, Otis Samuel
Jones, Booker Tee, Sr.
Jones, Carol Joyce
Jones, Ernest Edward
Jones, Sidney Eugene
Jones-Grimes, Mable Christine
Keith, Doris T.
Kelley, Jack Albert
Kennedy, Callas Faye
Khadar, Mohamed A.
King, Earl B.
Knox, Wayne D. P.
Langston-Jackson, Wilmetta Ann Smith
League, Cheryl Perry
Lemon, Michael Wayne, Sr.
Lewis, Tom
Love, Karen Allyce
Loveless, Theresa E.
Maddox, Elton Preston, Jr.
Madison, Leatrice Branch
Marable, June Morehead
Marrs, Stella
Marsh, Ben Franklin
Marshall, Joseph Earl, Jr.
Martin, Kimberly Lynette
Massey, Hamilton W.
McCleave, Mansel Philip
McMillan, Horace James
Meadows, Lucile Smallwood
Metters, Samuel
Mickins, Andel W.
Miller, Anthony Glenn
Miller, Ethel Jackson
Miller, Lawrence A., Jr.
Miller, Lawrence Edward
Miller-Reid, Dora Alma
Mitchell, Roderick Bernard
Monagan, Alfrieta Parks
Moore, Cleotha Franklin
Moore, Lenny Edward
Morning, John
Morris, Fred H., Jr.
Morris, Gertrude Elaine
Morrison, Jacqueline
Murphy, Jeanne Claire Fuller
Myles, Ernestine
Nelson, Patricia Ann
Nelson, Rex
Newman, Miller Maurice
Nix, Rick
Nix, Roscoe Russa
Norris, Fred Arthur, Jr.
Odom, Stonewall, II
Owens, Lynda Gayle
Parker, Jacquelyn Heath
Peterson, Michelle Monica
Pittman, Audrey Bullock
Pitts, Dorothy Louise Waller
Pounds, Elaine
Redd, M. Paul, Sr.
Richardson, Harold Edward
Richardson, Timothy L.
Ritchie, Louise Reid
Robinson, Maude Eloise
Robinson, S. Yolanda
Robinson-Ford, Denise Renee
Rockett, Damon Emerson
Rogers, Freddie Clyde
Romans, Ann
Ross, Mary Olivia
Rouse, Gene Gordon, Sr.
Russell, Dorothy Delores
Saunders, Jerry
Saunders-Henderson, Martha M.
Scott, Carstella H.
Shaw, Ann
Shores, Arthur D.
Shropshire, John Sherwin
Simmons, James Richard
Slie, Samuel N.
Small, Kenneth Lester
Smith, Alonzo Nelson
Smith, Fronse Wayne, Sr.

Smith, Marvin Preston
Smith, Richard Alfred
Smith, William Fred
Smithers, Priscilla Jane
Smith-Gray, Cassandra Elaine
Soaries, DeForest Blake, Jr.
Spencer, Larry Lee
Spencer, Shanita Rene
Stalls, M.
Stanyard, Hermine P.
Stewart, Dorothy Nell
Stewart, Loretta A.
Stovall-Tapley, Mary Kate
Taylor, Richard L.
Tero, Lawrence
Thomas, Eunice S.
Thomas, Joan McHenry Bates
Thomas, Liz A.
Thomas, Reginald Maurice
Thompson, Geraldine
Thompson, Linda Jo
Thurman, Sue Bailey
Tokley, Joanna Nutter
Townsend, Mamie Lee Harrington
Turner, Vivian Love
Turner, Yvonne Williams
Tyler, Robert James, Sr.
Waddles, Charleszetta Lina
Walker-Thoth, Daphne LaVera
Warren, Gertrude Francois
Washington, Arthur, Jr.
Waterman, Thelma M.
Watkins, Mozelle Ellis
Watkins, Rolanda Rowe
Weary, Dolphus
Webb, Lucious Moses
Weldon, Onah Conway
Weldon, Ramon N.
Wells, Barbara Jones
White, Lois Jean
White, Ralph
Whitten, Eloise Culmer
Williams, Charlie J.
Williams, Ethel Jean
Williams, Geneva J.
Williams, Harriette F.
Williams, Jesse
Williams, John Henry
Williams, Joseph R.
Williams, Reginald Clark
Williams, Ronald Lee
Williams, Sylvia J.
Williams, T. Joyce
Williams, Theartrice
Willingham, James Edward
Wilson, Willie Mae
Woods, Almita
Woodson, Aileen R.
Word, Fletcher Henry, Jr.
Wordlaw, Clarence, Jr.
Workman, Aurora Felice Antonette
Wright, Benjamin Hickman
Wright, Keith Derek, Sr.
Wyatt, Addie L.
Yearwood, Arem Irene
Zambrana, Rafael

Computer Science— Programming/Software Development

Battle, Charles E.
Beaubien, George H.
Bell, Theodore Joshua, II
Benton, Nelkane O.
Boyd, Joseph L.
Brooks, Pauline C.
Burris, Chuck
Cameron, Krystol
Carter, Anthony Jerome
Chatman-Driver, Patricia Ann
Clarke, Kenton
Curtis, Harry S.
Dyer, Charles Austen
Emeagwali, Philip
Gibbons, Walter E.
Hanford, Craig Bradley
Harris, Carolyn Ann
Harvey, Maurice Reginald
Haynes, Sue Blood
Hedgley, David Rice, Jr.
Henderson, Robert Dwight
Herndon, Harold Thomas, Sr.
Herndon, Lance H.
Holmes, William
Houston, Johnny L.
Jackson, Karen Denise
James, Alexander, Jr.
Jenkins, George Arthur, Jr.

Jennings, Margaret Elaine
John, Anthony
Johnson, William Smith
Mabrey, Ernest L., Jr.
Martin, Sherman Theodore
Massaquoi, Hans J.
McAdoo, Henry Allen
McAfee, Carrie R.
Miller, Arthur J.
Mizzell, William Clarence
Moore, Jellether Marie
Morrison, Yvonne Florant
Moseley-Davis, Barbara M.
Murray, Spencer J., III
Newton, Eric Christopher
Odoms, Willie O.
Perkins, Gladys Patricia
Perry, Jerald Isaac, Sr.
Peterson, Michelle Monica
Porter, Mia Lachone
Powe, Joseph S.
Smith, James Charles
Stephens, Wallace O'Leary
Turner, Vivian Love
Vereen, Michael L.
Webster, John W., III
Williams, Ralph O.
Williams, Wilbert Edd

Computer Science— Systems Analysis/Design

Aklilu, Tesfaye
Allen, John Henry
Ashburn, Vivian Diane
Baldwin, Mitchell Cardell
Bowman, Janet Wilson
Brice, Eugene Clay
Carnell, Lougenia Littlejohn
Carter, Anthony Jerome
Carter, Mary Louise
Carter, Perry W.
Casterlow, Carolyn B.
Chatman-Driver, Patricia Ann
Clark, Jerald Dwayne
Crawford, Betty Marilyn
Davis, William W., Sr.
Denmark, Robert Richard
Dupree, David H.
Elizey, Chris William
English, Reginald
Farrington, Thomas Alex
Franklin, Martha Lois
Greene, Ronald Alexander
Gundy, Roy Nathaniel, Jr.
Hankins, Hesterly G., III
Hannah, Johnnie, Jr.
Haynes, Sue Blood
Henderson, Robert Dwight
Herndon, Harold Thomas, Sr.
Herndon, Lance H.
Howard, Tanya Millicent
Hughes, Isaac Sunny
James, Alexander, Jr.
Jenkins, Yolanda L.
Jennings, Margaret Elaine
Johnson, Arthur E.
Johnson, William Paul, Jr.
Jones, Frank Benson
Leggon, Herman W.
Martin, Sherman Theodore
McAdoo, Henry Allen
McAfee, Carrie R.
McHenry, James O'Neal
Miller, Arthur J.
Miller, George Carroll, Jr.
Minion, Mia
Mizzell, William Clarence
Moore, Jellether Marie
Morrison, Yvonne Florant
Morton, Norman
Murray, Gary S.
Nash, Henry Gary
Newton, Eric Christopher
Odoms, Willie O.
Prothro, Gerald Dennis
Robinson, Michael David
Rodgers, William M., Jr.
Sanders, Glenn Carlos
Seymore, Stanley
Shaw, Carl Bernard
Singleton, Kathryn T.
Smiley-Robertson, Carolyn
Smith, Roulette William
Stafford, Earl W.
Stephens, Wallace O'Leary
Swain, Michael B.
Taylor, Arlene M. J.
Timberlake, John Paul

Trent, Jay Lester
Washington, Herman A., Jr.
Weatherspoon, Jimmy Lee
Wells, James A.
Williams, LaShina Brigette
Williams, Ralph O.
Williams, Wilbert Edd
Woodard, Lois Marie
Wrice, Vincent J.

Computer Science—Not Elsewhere Classified

Butler, Washington Roosevelt, Jr.
Byrd, George Edward
Cooper, Daneen Ravenell
Davis, Denyvetta
Gravely, Samuel L., Jr.
Greaves, McLean
Green, Calvin Coolidge
Hannah, Johnnie, Jr.
Heard, Blanche Denise
Hubbard, Darrell
Johnson, David, III
Johnson, Patricia Dumas
Jones, Isaac, Jr.
Lahr, Charles Dwight
Lewis, Richard John, Sr.
Morris, Bernard Alexander
Ratcliffe, Alfonso F.
Robertson, Paul Francis
Scott, Kenneth Richard
Simmons, Isaac Tyrone
Stansbury, Vernon Carver, Jr.
Stephens, Wallace O'Leary
Thomas, Ronald F.
Walker, Willie M.
Williams, Cheryl L.
Wright, Keith Derek, Sr.

Computer Services (See Also Management/ Administration— Computer Systems/Data Processing)

Arbuckle, Ronald Lee, Sr.
Ashburn, Vivian Diane
Ball, Roger
Bright, Herbert L., Sr.
Brockington, Donella P.
Brown, Joseph Clifton
Byrd, Herbert Lawrence, Jr.
Cameron, Krystol
Carter, J. B., Jr.
Castle, Keith L.
Clark, Jerald Dwayne
Clarke, Kenton
Coates, Shelby L.
Cochran, Harold Lloyd, Jr.
Cooper, Irmgard M.
DeSassure, Charles
Edwards, Luther Howard
Elizey, Chris William
Farrington, Thomas Alex
Fuller, Gloria A.
Green, Darryl Lynn
Grier, John K.
Gundy, Roy Nathaniel, Jr.
Handy, Lillian B.
Harvey, Maurice Reginald
Hawes, Bernadine Tinner
Hearon, Dennis James
Ireland, Lynda
Johnson, Nathaniel J., Sr.
Joyner, Claude C.
Liautaud, James
London, Eddie
Long, Jerry Wayne
Mabrey, Ernest L., Jr.
Miles, Albert Benjamin, Jr.
Miller, Herbert J.
Morton, Norman
Perry, Lee Charles, Jr.
Peters, Charles L., Jr.
Porter, Mia Lachone
Ratcliff, Wesley D.
Reed, Clarence Hammit, III
Robinson, Robert Love, Jr.
Sheats, Marvin Anthony
Shepard, Gregory
Smith, Joshua Isaac
Swain, Michael B.
Taylor, Albert, Jr.
Terrell, Mable Jean
Thorpe, Earl Howard
Tuckett, LeRoy E.
Viltz, Edward Gerald

Walker, Vernon David
Whaley, Charles H., IV
White, Earl Harvey
Whitfield, Willie, Jr.
Williams, Debra D.
Williams, Fitzroy E.
Williams, Katherine
Williams-Green, Joyce F.
Wilson, F. Leon
Winston, George B., III
Yelity, Stephen C.
Young, Reginald B.

Construction

See **Building/Construction; Retail Trade—Building/ Construction Materials; Wholesale Trade—Building/ Construction Materials**

Consulting

Adams, Robert Thomas
Adams, Sheila Mary
Ahart, Thomas I.
Alexander, Cornelia
Alexander, Lenora Cole
Alexander, Preston Paul, Jr.
Alexander, Rosa M.
Alexander, Sidney H., Jr.
Alexander, Theodore Thomas, Jr.
Alfred, Rayfield
Allen, Robert L.
Allen, Wendell
Allston, Thomas Gray, III
Amin, Karima
Amos, Kent B.
Amos, Oris Elizabeth Carter
Anderson, Carl Edwin
Anthony, Jeffrey Conrad
Apea, Joseph Bennet Kyeremateng
Arbuckle, Pamela Susan
Ashby, Lucius Antoine
Atkins, Carl J.
Ayers-Elliott, Cindy
Babbs, Junious C., Sr.
Bacoate, Matthew, Jr.
Bailey, Bob Carl
Bailey, Curtis Darnell
Bailey, Ronald W.
Bain, Linda Valerie
Ballentine, Krim Menelik
Banks, Laura N.
Batiste, Mary Virginia
Baugh, Florence Ellen
Beamon, Robert A.
Beard, Lillian McLean
Beard, Montgomery, Jr.
Beck, Clark E.
Bell, Lawrence F.
Bell, William Charles
Bell, William Vaughn
Bennett, Daina T.
Black, Charles E.
Black, James Tillman
Blackwell, Robert B.
Blakely, Ronald Eugene
Block, Carolyn B.
Bradford-Eaton, Zee
Bradley, London M., Jr.
Brazier, William H.
Bridgewater, Herbert Jeremiah, Jr.
Brockington, Eugene Alfonzo
Brooks, Bernard E.
Brooks, Charlotte Kendrick
Broome, Pershing
Brown, Arnold E.
Brown, Bernice Baynes
Brown, Joeanna Hurston
Brown, Les
Brown, Robert, Jr.
Brown, Robert Joe
Brown, William H.
Bryant, Robert E.
Bullett, Audrey Kathryn
Burdette, LaVere Elaine
Burks, Darrell
Burleson, Helen L.
Burns, Dargan J.
Burton, Barbara Ann
Burton, Donald C.
Byas, Ulysses
Byrd, Manford, Jr.
Caines, Ken
Calhoun, Lillian Scott
Calomee, Annie E.
Cameron, Randolph W.

Cantarella, Marcia Y.
Carr, Kipley DeAne
Carroll, Edward Major
Carroll, Robert F.
Carter, Carolyn McCraw
Carter, Thomas Allen
Carver, Patricia Anne
Chambers, Harry, Jr.
Chandler, Mittie Olion
Charlton, Jack Fields
Christian, Eric Oliver, Jr.
Clark, Jerald Dwayne
Clark, Kenneth Bancroft
Clark, Sanza Barbara
Clayton, Lloyd E.
Clyne, John Rennel
Cole, John L., Jr.
Cole, Patricia A.
Cole Carey, Wilhemina, PhD
Coleman, Barbara Sims
Collins, Leroy Anthony, Jr.
Colston Barge, Gayle S.
Conway, Wallace Xavier, Sr.
Conwill, William Louis
Cook, Charles A.
Cook, Levi, Jr.
Cook, William Wilburt
Cooke, Lloyd M.
Cooke, Paul Phillips
Cooke, Thomas H., Jr.
Cooley, Keith Winston
Cooper, Earl, II
Cooper, Linda G.
Cooper-Lewter, Nicholas Charles
Cornell, Bob
Cornish, Betty W.
Countee, Thomas Hilaire, Jr.
Craft, Thomas J., Sr.
Crocker, Clinton C.
Cruzat, Gwendolyn S.
Curry, Jerry Ralph
Cuyjet, Aloysius Baxter
Davis, Arthur, III
Davis, Charles
Davis, Esther Gregg
Davis, Howlie R.
Davis, Major
Dawson Boyd, Candy
Dean, Diane D.
Dember, Jean Wilkins
Diane, Mamadi
Dixon, Arrington Liggins
Dixon, Diane L.
Donaldson, Richard T.
Donawa, Maria Elena
Dorsey, Ivory Jean
Doss, Lawrence Paul
Drennen, Gordon
Dukes, Ronald
Dunn, Bruce Eric
Eaves, A. Reginald
Eccles, Peter Wilson
Edwards, Monique Marie
Edwards, Oscar Lee
Ellington, Ida Karen
Eure, Jerry Holton, Sr.
Evans, Billy J.
Evans, Grover Milton, Sr.
Evans, Mattie
Evans, Milton L.
Evans, Ruthana Wilson
Evans, William E.
Ewell, Yvonne Amaryllis
Fauntroy, Walter E.
Ferguson, Robert Lee, Sr.
Ferrell, Rosie E.
Fisher, Edith Maureen
Flewellen, Icabod
Flipper, Carl Frederick, III
Flournoy, Valerie Rose
Fonvielle, William Harold
Ford, Florida Mae
Fox, William K., Sr.
Francis, Cheryl Margaret
Fraser, George C.
Frazier, Shirley George
Frost, Olivia Pleasants
Frye, Reginald Stanley
Gainer, Andrew A.
Gainer, John F.
Garrett, Thaddeus, Jr.
Gayles, Joseph Nathan Webster, Jr.
Gerald, Gilberto Ruben
Gibson, Elvis Edward
Gibson, JoAnn
Giles, Althea B.
Gillespie, Marcia A.
Gillette, Frankie Jacobs

Gilmore, Charles Arthur
Gilmore, Robert McKinley, Sr.
Gipson, Reve
Glass, Virginia M.
Glover, Denise M.
Godbold, Donald Horace
Gooden, Cherry Ross
Grace, Horace R.
Grant, Claude DeWitt
Gravenberg, Eric Von
Graves, Clifford W.
Gray-Little, Bernadette
Greaux, Cheryl Prejean
Green, Calvin Coolidge
Greene, Marvin L.
Gregory, Karl Dwight
Gregory, Michael Samuel
Griffin, Betty Sue
Grinstead, Amelia Ann
Guillory, Linda Semien
Gunter, Laurie
Hale, Janice Ellen, Ph.D.
Hampton, Delon
Hampton, Wanda Kay Baker
Handy, Lillian B.
Harrell, Oscar W., II
Harrington, Denise Marion
Harris, Archie Jerome
Harris, Bryant G.
Harris, Gladys Bailey
Harris, James G., Jr.
Harris, Margaret R.
Harris, Mary Styles
Harris, Vernon Joseph
Harris McKenzie, Ruth Bates
Hawkins, Mary L.
Head, Evelyn Harris Shields
Henderson, Lenneal Joseph, Jr.
Henry, Charles E.
Herbert, Benne S., Jr.
Herrington, Perry Lee
Hicks, Eleanor
High, Claude, Jr.
Hill, Hattie
Hogan, Edwin B.
Holman, Alvin T.
Holmes, Wilma K.
Holton, Priscilla Browne
Howze, Karen Aileen
Hudlin, Richard A.
Hunt, Portia L.
Hurst, Cleveland, III
Irons, Paulette
Jackson, Acy Lee
Jackson, Warren Garrison
Jefferson, Andrea Green
Jenkins, Elaine B.
Johnson, Benjamin, Jr.
Johnson, Brent E.
Johnson, Carl Earld
Johnson, Cleveland, Jr.
Johnson, F. J., Jr.
Johnson, Luther Mason, Jr.
Johnson, Mal
Johnson, Marie Love
Johnson, Samuel Harrison
Johnson, Stephanye
Johnson, Tommie Ulmer
Johnson, Wayne Lee
Johnson, William Paul, Jr.
Johnston, Wallace O.
Jones, Carolyn G.
Jones, Effie Hall
Jones, Harley M.
Jones, Isaac, Jr.
Jones, Jimmie Dene
Jones-Grimes, Mable Christine
Jordan, Casper LeRoy
Keglar, Shelvy Haywood
Kennedy, Callas Faye
King, Jeanne Faith
King, Lewis Henry
King, Reginald F.
Kirby-Davis, Montanges
Knott, Albert Paul, Jr.
Kondwani, Kofi Anum
Koram, M. Jamal
Kunjufu, Jawanza
Lambert, LeClair Grier
Landry, Lawrence Aloysius
Lapeyrolerie, Myra Evans
Larry, Charles Edward
LaSane, Joanna Emma
Lattimer, Robert L.
Lawrence, Paul Frederic
Leace, Donal Richard
Lee, Bertram M.
Leeke, John F.
Lewis, Arthur W.

Lewis, Vincent V.
Lewis, William M., Jr.
Livingston-White, Deborah J. H.
Locke, Don C.
Lokeman, Joseph R.
Lowry, James Hamilton
Lumpkin, Adrienne Kelly
Lynn, Louis B.
Lyons, A. Bates
Lyons, Laura Brown
Mabrey, Harold Leon
Majete, Clayton Aaron
Major, Benjamin
Mallett, Rosa Elizabeth
Malone, Claudine Berkeley
Mance, John J.
Marsh, McAfee
Marshall, Timothy H.
Matory, Deborah Love
Maxie, Peggy Joan
McClendon, Carol A.
McHenry, Douglas
McKenzie, Reginald
McLaughlin, Andree Nicola
McNeely, Charles E.
Mendez, Hugh B.
Meneweather, Earl W.
Merritt, Wendy
Miller, Arthur J.
Miller, Dennis Weldon
Miller, George Carroll, Jr.
Miller, George N., Jr.
Mills, Mary Lee
Minor, Jessica
Montgomery, Catherine Lewis
Moody, Fredreatha E.
Moone, Wanda Renee
Moore, Charlie W.
Moore, Lenny Edward
Morisey, Patricia Garland
Morris, Ella Lucille
Morris, Horace W.
Morrison, James W., Jr.
Morse, Mildred S.
Morse, Oliver
Moss, Robert C., Jr.
Moss, Tanya Jill
Murray, Thomas Azel, Sr.
Myers, Ernest Ray
Myers, Stephanie E.
Nellum, Albert L.
Nelson, Gilbert L.
Nelson, Ramona M.
Newhouse, Quentin, Jr.
Nicholas, Mary Burke
Nix, Rick
Noble, Jeffrey V.
Norman, Georgette M.
Olapo, Olaitan
Orticke, Leslie Ann
Overall, Manard
Owens, Hugo Armstrong, Sr.
Owens, Judith Myoli
Owens, Lynda Gayle
Paige, Windell
Parker, Darwin Carey
Parker, James L.
Parker, Lee
Parks, George B.
Parsons, Philip I.
Patterson, Lloyd
Patterson, Lydia R.
Pattillo, Joyce M.
Patton, Jean E.
Patton, Rosezelia L.
Pearson, Clifton
Penn, Robert Clarence
Pentecoste, Joseph C.
Perkins, Frances J.
Perkins, Huel D.
Perry, Benjamin L., Jr.
Perry, Leonard Douglas, Jr.
Perry-Mason, Gail F.
Phelps, C. Kermit
Phillips, Edward Martin
Pinkett, Harold Thomas
Pitts, Vera L.
Pleas, John Roland
Porter, Charles William
Porter, Ellis Nathaniel
Powell, Kenneth Alasandro
Prather, Jeffrey Lynn
Price, Wallace Walter
Ray, James R., III
Reed, Clarence Hammit, III
Rembert, Emma White
Reynolds, Andrew Buchanan
Rhodes, John K.
Rice, Mitchell F.

Riddick, Eugene E.
Riles, Wilson Camanza
Ritchie, Louise Reid
Roberts, Jacqueline Johnson
Roberts, Lillian
Robinson, Charlotte L.
Robinson, Leonard Harrison, Jr.
Robinson, Michael David
Robinson, Sherman
Robinson, Verneda
Robinson, Willie C.
Rodgers, Rod Audrian
Rohadfox, Ronald Otto
Rosser, Pearl Lockhart
Rudd, Amanda S.
Sampson, Ronald Alvin
Samuels, Leslie Eugene
Sanders, Glenn Carlos
Sanders, Patricia Roper
Sanders-West, Selma D.
Sandoval, Dolores S.
Sarkodie-Mensah, Kwasi
Saunders, Doris E.
Scaggs, Edward W.
Scott, Melvina Brooks
Scott, Ruth
Seneca, Arlena E.
Shackelford, William G., Jr.
Sharp, J. Anthony
Shaw, Spencer Gilbert
Shields-Jones, Esther L. M.
Shropshire, Thomas B.
Simms, Darrell Dean
Simms, Robert H.
Sims, Diane Marie
Sims, Harold Rudolph
Small, Kenneth Lester
Smith, Carolyn Lee
Smith, Conrad P.
Smith, Dolores J.
Smith, Edgar E.
Smith, Lafayette Kenneth
Smith, Paul M., Jr.
Smith, Symuel Harold
Smith, William Fred
Sobers, Waynett A., Jr.
Spivey, William Ree
Spriggs, Ray V.
Spurlock, Dorothy A.
States, Robert Arthur
Stewart, John B., Jr.
Stickney, Janice L.
Streeter, Denise Williams
Strong, Blondell McDonald
Sudarkasa, Michael Eric
    Mabogunje
Sulieman, Jamil
Swain, Michael B.
Swanigan, Jesse Calvin
Tatum, Carol Evora
Taulbert, Clifton LeMoure
Taylor, Charles Edward
Taylor, Welton Ivan
Terrill, W. H. Tyrone, Jr.
Thames, Uvena Woodruff
Thibodeaux, Mary Shepherd
Thomas, David Anthony
Thomas, Edward Arthur
Thomas, Franklin A.
Thomas, Lucille Cole
Thomas, Lydia Waters
Thomas, Roderick
Thomas, Wade Hamilton, Sr.
Thompson, French F., Jr.
Thompson, Geraldine
Times, Betty J.
Tobin, Patricia L.
Tramiel, Kenneth Ray, Sr.
Tucker, Dorothy M.
Turner, Bailey W.
Turner, Geneva
Turner, M. Annette
Turner, William Hobert
Turner-Forte, Diana
Turner-Givens, Ella Mae
Tyner, Regina Lisa
Waden, Fletcher Nathaniel, Jr.
Waiters, Gail Elenoria
Wakefield, J. Alvin
Walker, Willie M.
Walker Williams, Hope Denise
Wallace, Renee C.
Wallace, Ritchie Ray
Ware, Omego John Clinton, Jr.
Washington, Edith May Faulkner
Weaver, Frank Cornell
Webb, Harold, Sr.
Weston, Sharon
Wharton Boyd, Linda F.

White, James David
White, Jesse C., Jr.
White, Nan E.
White, Yolanda Simmons
Whiting, Thomas J.
Wiles, Joseph St. Clair
Wilkins, Charles O.
Wilkinson, Frederick D., Jr.
Williams, Barry Lawson
Williams, Betty Smith
Williams, Carolyn Ruth Armstrong
Williams, Charles C.
Williams, Robert Lee, Jr.
Williams, Wayne Allan
Williams-Garner, Debra
Williamson, Handy, Jr.
Wilson, Charles Lee, Sr.
Wilson, Hugh A.
Witherspoon, Audrey Goodwin
Woodson, Shirley A.
Woodson, William D.
Wright, Edward Lucius
Wright, Flonzie B.
Yancy, Robert James
Yarborough, Richard A.
Young, Angela Lynn
Young, Elizabeth Bell
Young, Reginald B.

Corrections
See **Criminology/Corrections**

Counseling—Career/ Placement
Armster-Worrill, Cynthia Denise
Baker, Sharon Smith
Banks, Ronald Trenton
Beard, Montgomery, Jr.
Blakely, Ronald Eugene
Bond, Gladys B.
Brandon, Barbara
Bright, Willie S.
Bruce, Carol Pitt
Bryant, Leon Serle
Chambers, Harry, Jr.
Charlton, Charles Hayes
Chatmon, Linda Carol
Coleman, Frankie Lynn
Congleton, William C.
Coston, Bessie Ruth
Fleming, Alicia DeLaMothe
Flewellen, Icabod
Foster, Lloyd L.
Freeman, Nelson R.
Gilliams, Tyrone
Granville, William, Jr.
Gregory, Michael Samuel
Hackett, Obra V.
Harris, Archie Jerome
Harris, Margaret R.
Harrison, Shirley Dindy
Hawkins, William Douglas
High, Claude, Jr.
Holley, Vance Maitland
Horton, Dollie Bea Dixon
Howard, Jules Joseph, Jr.
Jackson, Alfred Thomas
Jackson, Earl J.
Joell, Pamela S.
Johnson, Joseph David
Jones, Nancy Reed
Kelley, Robert W.
Logan, Alphonso
Massey, Ardrey Yvonne
Maxie, Peggy Joan
McGuire, Chester C., Jr.
Meeks, Willis Gene
Meshack, Sheryl Hodges
Nance, Herbert Charles, Sr.
Neely, David E.
Peck, Leontyne Clay
Robinson, John G.
Robinson, Maude Eloise
Ross, Emma Jean
Shanks, Wilhelmina Byrd
Shoffner, Garnett Walter
Stanton, Janice D.
Story, Charles Irvin
Sweet, Terrecia W.
Thomas, Patrick Arnold
Thompson, Gayle Ann-Spencer
Tuggle, Dorie C.
Walker, Cynthia Bush
Watson, Jackie
White, Sharon Brown
Williams, Carolyn Ruth Armstrong

Williams, James E., Jr.
Wingate, Maurice Francis
Young, Mary E.

Counseling—Marriage/ Family
Abston, Nathaniel, Jr.
Ali, Fatima
Baker, Sharon Smith
Bobino, Rita Florencia
Brass, Reginald Stephen
Chapman, Audrey Bridgeforth
Childs, Francine C.
Clark, Fred Allen
Cooper-Lewter, Nicholas Charles
Crawford, Vanella Alise
Dejoie, Carolyn Barnes Milanes
Dillard, June White
Easley, Paul Howard, Sr.
Erskine, Kenneth F.
Fresh, Edith McCullough
Hall, Christine C. Iijima
Harris-Pinkelton, Norma
Hunter, James Nathaniel, II
James, Gillette Oriel
King, Jeanne Faith
Lane, Eddie Burgyone
LeFlore, Larry
Lewis, Henry S., Jr.
Lloyd, George Lussington
McKeller, Thomas Lee
McKelpin, Joseph P.
McNeill-Huntley, Esther Mae
Millard, Thomas Lewis
Milledge, Luetta Upshur
Revely, William
Richardson, Lacy Franklin
Ross, Emma Jean
Sarmiento, Shirley Jean
Savage, James Edward, Jr.
Shoffner, Garnett Walter
Sullivan, Martha Adams
White, Nan E.
Woods, Almita

Counseling—Mental Health
Abston, Nathaniel, Jr.
Andrews, James E.
Anthony-Perez, Bobbie M.
Barber, William, Jr.
Bobbitt, Leroy
Bradford-Eaton, Zee
Brandon, Barbara
Brewington, Donald Eugene
Brown, James Marion
Brown, Robert J., III
Cissoko, Alioune Badara
Clay, Camille Alfreda
Coleman, Barbara Sims
Crawford, James Wesley
Crews, Victoria Wilder
Dejoie, Carolyn Barnes Milanes
Dember, Jean Wilkins
Doggett, John Nelson, Jr.
Draper, Frances Murphy
Echols, Mary Ann
Erskine, Kenneth F.
Feliciana, Jerrye Brown
Ferguson, Robert Lee, Sr.
Ford, Deborah Lee
Greene, Mitchell Amos
Hall, Kirkwood Marshal
Handon, Marshall R., Jr.
Harper, Walter Edward, Jr.
Hill, Paul Gordon
Hodgson-Brooks, Gloria J.
Horton, Dollie Bea Dixon
Jenkins, Adelbert Howard
Jenkins, Louis E.
King, Jeanne Faith
Lee, Shirley Freeman
Mahoney, Keith Weston
Manley, Audrey Forbes
Mayo, Julia A.
McFall, Mary
McGee, Gloria Kesselle
Mendes, Helen Althia
Mendez, Hugh B.
Morgan, Alice Johnson Parham
Muhammad, Abdul-Rasheed
Neighbors, Dolores Maria
Nelson, Wanda Lee
Perry, Robert Lee
Prather, Jeffrey Lynn
Ragland, Wylheme Harold

Richardson, Lacy Franklin
Richardson, Rupert Florence
Robertson, Evelyn Crawford, Jr.
Stokes, Julie Elena
Tucker, Samuel Joseph
Walker-Thoth, Daphne LaVera
White, Tommie Lee
Wilder, Mary A. H.
Wiley, Rena Deloris
Williams, Robert L.
Woods, Almita
Young, Mary E.

Counseling— Rehabilitation
Allen, Jacob Benjamin, III
Blackwell, Faye Brown
Brunson, David
Cheek, Donald Kato
Clendenon, Donn A.
Cleveland, Hattye M.
Crawford, James Wesley
Davis, Esther Gregg
Dennis, Philip H.
Gaddy, Beatrice
Harris, Archie Jerome
Hart, Tony
Hawkins, Mary L.
Jenkins, Elaine B.
Jones, Yvonne De Marr
Lewis, Ronald Stephen
Lewis, Wendell J.
Mack, Nate
Malone, Cleo
Maxie, Peggy Joan
McCroom, Eddie Winther
Meshack, Sheryl Hodges
Robinson, Vernon Edward
Shorty, Vernon James
Talley, William B.
Trotter, Decatur Wayne
UmBayemake Joachim, Linda
Wilber, Ida Belinda

Counseling—School/ Academic
Anderson, Doris J.
Armstrong, Ernest W., Sr.
Bailey, Agnes Jackson
Barnett, Samuel B.
Baskerville, Pearl
Bell, Kenneth M.
Blakey, William A.
Block, Leslie S.
Bowser, James A.
Bramwell, Henry
Branch Richards, Germaine Gail
Brooks, Janice Willena
Brooks, Patrick, Jr.
Brooks, Rosemary Bittings
Broome, Pershing
Brouhard, Deborah Taliaferro
Brown, Ronald Paul
Brunson, Debora Bradley
Bryant, Carl
Buck, Vernon Ashley, Jr.
Burns, Felton
Butler, Douthard Roosevelt
Carper, Gloria G.
Carter, Herbert E.
Clack, Floyd
Coatie, Robert Mason
Coleman, Rudolph W.
Cooke, Lloyd M.
Daley, Guilbert Alfred
Davis, Doris Ann
Dawson, Leonard Ervin
Days, Rosetta Hill
Demons, Leona Marie
Dillon, Gloria Ann
Driver, Louie M., Jr.
Dudley-Smith, Carolyn J.
Dunn-Barker, Lillian Joyce
Early Lambert, Violet Theresa
Eatman, Janice A.
Edmonds, Bevelyn
Edwards, Dorothy Wright
Evans, Ruthana Wilson
Faison, Helen Smith
Feliciana, Jerrye Brown
Flippen, Frances Morton
Franklin, Harold A.
Gallagher, Abisola Helen
George, Carrie Leigh
Gilbert, Jean P.
Gist, Jessie M. Gilbert

Glover, Arthur Lewis, Jr.
Graham, Chestie Marie
Graham, Patricia
Grayson, Barbara Ann
Guice, Gregory Charles
Guidry, Arreader Pleanna
Gunn, Willie Cosdena Thomas
Hallums, Benjamin F.
Haney, Darnel L.
Harper, Walter Edward, Jr.
Hiatt, Dietrah
Hill, Annette Tillman
Howard, Vera Gouke
James, Gregory Creed
Jones, Albert J.
Jones, Edward Norman
Jones, Hortense
Jones, Yvonne De Marr
Kendrick, Tommy L.
Lipscomb, Darryl L.
Lockerman, Geneva Lorene
    Reuben
Lockhart, Verdree, Sr.
Lucas, Linda Gail
Lynn, James Elvis
Major, Henrymae M.
McCloud, Anece Faison
McGee, JoAnn
McGregor, Oran B.
McGuffin, Dorothy Brown
McKanders, Julius A., II
McKinney, Jesse Doyle
Meade, William F.
Meeks, Reginald Kline
Meshack, Sheryl Hodges
Miller, Tedd
Mitchem, John Clifford
Moore, Lenny Edward
Moore, Quincy L.
Morrison, Juan LaRue, Sr.
Moxley, Frank O.
Napper, James Wilbur
Newton, Jacqueline L.
O'Bryant, Beverly J.
Palmer, Edgar Bernard
Patterson, Barbara Ann
Patterson, Joan Delores
Pierce, Walter J.
Poole, Rachel Irene
Pringle, Nell Rene
Quarles, Ruth Brett
Reece, Avalon B.
Riggins, Lester
Robinson, William Earl
Rogers, Dianna
Ross, Emma Jean
Sanders, Woodrow Mac
Scott-Johnson, Roberta Virginia
Sergeant, Carra Susan
Simmons, Julius Caesar, Sr.
Stephenson, Carolyn L.
Stewart, Gregory
Sullivan, Allen R.
Summers, Retha
Sweet, Terrecia W.
Thomas, Eula Wiley
Thompson, Beatrice R.
Tramiel, Kenneth Ray, Sr.
Trotman, Richard Edward
Washington, Josie B.
Washington, Sandra Beatrice
Webb, Georgia Houston
Wheeler, Julia M.
Wilkie, Earl Augustus T.
Williams, Bertha Mae
Williams, Carolyn Ruth Armstrong
Williams, Charles Mason, Jr.
Williams, Ulysses Jean
Williams-Dovi, Joanna
Winfield, Elayne Hunt
Workman, Aurora Felice Antonette
Yizar, James Horace, Jr.
Zachary-Pike, Annie R.

Counseling—Not Elsewhere Classified
Abdul-Malik, Ibrahim
Aziz, Samimah
Badger, Brenda Joyce
Bass, Herbert H.
Benson, George
Buckley, Victoria
Bullett, Audrey Kathryn
Carson, Irma
Cobbs, Harvey, Jr.
Coleman, Marian M.
Collins, Paul L.
Davis, Richard C.

Terry, Garland Benjamin
Theodore, Keith Felix
Thompson, Floyd
Thompson, James W.
Thompson, William Henry
Trice, William B.
Trimiar, J. Sinclair
Tutt, Lia S.
Vaughns, Fred L.
Walters, Warren W.
Walton, DeWitt T., Jr.
Wareham, Alton L.
Watkins, James Darnell
Waynewood, Freeman Lee
Weaver, Garland Rapheal, Jr.
Webb, Harvey, Jr.
Webster, Charles
Wells, Bobby Ray
White, Artis Andre
White, George
White, Kermit Earle
Whitworth, E. Leo, Jr.
Williams, Edward M.
Williams, George Arthur
Williams, Harvey Joseph
Williams, Hayward J.
Williams, Lafayette W.
Williams, Richard Lenwood
Wilson, Joseph Henry, Jr.
Wilson, William E.
Wiltz, Charles J.
Woods, Robert Louis
Wrenn, Thomas H., III
Wright, Raymond LeRoy, Jr.
Wright, Wilson, Jr.
Young, F. Camille
Young, Walter F.
Yuille, Bruce

Directing/Producing (Performing Arts)

Allen, Debbie
Anderson, J. Morris
Anderson, Madeline
Arties, Walter Eugene, III
Barnes, Karen Michelle
Batten, Tony
Billings, Sister Cora Marie
Billington, Clyde, Jr.
Bolling, Carol Nicholson
Bolling, Deborah A.
Boulware, Patricia A.
Bowser, Yvette Lee
Branch, William Blackwell
Brooks, Avery
Brown, Reginald DeWayne
Browne, Roscoe Lee
Burnett, Zaron Walter, Jr.
Cannon, Reuben
Carroll, Vinnette Justine
Cartwright, Carole B.
Chinn, John Clarence
Clay, Stanley Bennett
Coker, Adeniyi Adetokunbo
Coleman, Elizabeth Sheppard
Collie, Kelsey E.
Collins, Tessil John
Combs, Sean J.
Cook, Smalley Mike
Cosby, William Henry
Crawford, Deborah Collins
Curtis Hall, Vondie
Dash, Hugh M. H.
Davis, Ossie
de Passe, Suzanne
Destine, Jean-Leon
DeWindt, Hal
Dickerson, Ernest
Dixon, Ivan N.
Dunmore, Gregory Charles
Dutton, Charles S.
Ellington, Mercedes
Elliott, William David
Eskridge, John Clarence
Fales, Susan
Fanaka, Jamaa
Faulkner, Geanie
Flake, Nancy Aline
Fletcher, Winona Lee
Foster, Frances Helen
Gaffney, Floyd
Gainer, John F.
Gamble, Kenneth
Gates, Thomas Michael
Gramby, Shirley Ann
Greaves, William
Gregory, Sylver K.
Guillaume, Robert

Haddock, Mable J.
Hairston, William
Halliburton, Christopher
Hardison, Kadeem
Harris, Helen B.
Harris, Tom W.
Harrison, Paul Carter
Head, Helaine
Hendry, Gloria
Hicklin, Fannie
Higginsen, Vy
Hill, Errol Gaston
Hobson, Cekimber
Holder, Geoffrey
Horsford, Anna Maria
Howard, Leslie Carl
Hudlin, Reginald Alan
Hudlin, Warrington
Hudson, Dianne Atkinson
Hudson, Frederick Bernard
Hughes, Allen
Hurte, Leroy E.
Hutchins, Jan Darwin
Imhotep, Akbar
Ione, Carole
Jackson, George
Jackson, Jermaine Lajuane
Jam, Jimmy
James, Hawthorne
James, Luther
Jessup, Gayle Louise
Johnson, Chas Floyd
Johnson, Stephanie Anne
Joyner, Lemuel Martin
Khan, Ricardo M.
King, Woodie, Jr.
King, Yolanda D.
Klausner, Willette Murphy
Kotto, Yaphet
Laneuville, Eric Gerard
Lange, Ted W., III
LaSane, Joanna Emma
Lee, Spike
LeFlore, Lyah
Lemmons, Kasi
LeNoire, Rosetta
Lipscombe, Margaret Ann
Livingston-White, Deborah J. H.
Lucas, Wilmer Francis, Jr.
MacLachlan, Janet A.
Marshall, William Horace
Martin, Darnell
Martin, D'Urville
Martin, James Larence
Martin Chase, Debra
McDuffie, Dwayne Glenn
McHenry, Emmit J.
McKee, Adam E., Jr.
Meek, Russell Charles
Merritt, Wendy
Mitchell, Arthur
Morris, Dolores N.
Moseka, Aminata
Moss, Carlton
Nelson, Novella C.
Newman, Geoffrey W.
Nicholas, Denise
Page, Harrison Eugene
Palcy, Euzhan
Parker, William Hayes, Jr.
Parks, Gordon Roger Alexander Buchannan
Pawley, Thomas D., III
Peoples, Dottie
Peters, Brock G.
Pinkney, Rose Catherine
Poitier, Sidney
Porter, Henry Lee
Prelow, Arleigh
Reed-Humes, Robi
Reid, Tim
Rich, Matty
Richards, Lloyd G.
Riley, Teddy
Robinson, Ernest Preston, Sr.
Robinson, Jason Guy
Robinson, Matt
Rodgers, Nile
Rodgers, Rod Audrian
Russell, Charlie L.
Ryan-White, Jewell
Sanders-Oji, J. Qevin
Schultz, Michael A.
Scott, Harold Russell, Jr.
Sharp, Saundra
Shivers, P. Derrick
Simmons, Russell
Singleton, John
Springer, Ashton

Stewart, Horace W.
Talbert, Ted
Teer, Barbara Ann
The Artist
Thomas, Nathaniel
Thomas, Ora P.
Thomas, Philip S.
Tillman, George, Jr.
Todd, Beverly
Townsend, Robert
Van Peebles, Mario
Vaughn, Nora Belle
Vincent, Irving H.
Vinson, Chuck Rallen
Wade, Kim Mache
Wagoner, J. Robert
Walker, Ethel Pitts
Warren, Michael
Washington, Von Hugo, Sr.
Wayans, Keenen Ivory
West, Valerie Y.
Whitaker, Mical Rozier
Wilkerson, Margaret Buford
Williams, Dick Anthony
Williams, Robert W.
Wilson, Jonathan Charles, Jr.
Winfrey, Oprah
Wolfe, George C.
Woods, Allie, Jr.
Wyatt, William N.
Young, Clarence, III
Zu-Bolton, Ahmos, II

Ecology

Alexander, Benjamin Harold
Bond, Howard H.
Cullers, Samuel James
Green, Carolyn Louise
Hendricks, Leta
Hoyte, James Sterling
Lillard, Kwame Leo
Malcom, Shirley Mahaley
McLean, Mary Cannon
Mesiah, Raymond N.
Nelson, Edward O.
Williams, Howard Copeland

Economics

Adams, Robert Thomas
Anderson, Carol Byrd
Anise, Ladun Oladunjoye E.
Bell, Elmer A.
Blakely, Charles
Browne, Robert Span
Brown-Wright, Marjorie
Butler, John Gordon
Clifton, Ivery Dwight
Clingman, Kevin Loren
Coleman, Sinclair B.
Conrad, Cecilia Ann
Cullers, Samuel James
Davie, Damon Jonathon
Davis, Patricia Staunton
Duren, Emma Thompson
Edwards, Alfred L.
Flood, Eugene, Jr.
Foreman, S. Beatrice
Gloster, Jesse E.
Gregory, Karl Dwight
Harris, Donald J.
Jaynes, Gerald David
King, Arthur Thomas
Kirby, Money Alian
Lemuwa, Ike Emmanuel
Loury, Glenn Cartman
Marshall, Wilfred L.
McMurry, Walter M., Jr.
Myers, Samuel L., Jr.
O'Neal, Raymond W., Sr.
Onwudiwe, Ebere
Perry, Wayne D.
Perry-Holston, Waltina D.
Plinton, James O., Jr.
Ridgel, Gus Tolver
Senbet, Lemma W.
Simms, Margaret Constance
Smythe-Haith, Mabel Murphy
Spriggs, William
Stewart, James Benjamin
Swann, Eugene Merwyn
Sykes, Vernon Lee
Sylvester, Patrick Joseph
Thompson, Carol Belita
Warren, Joseph David
Weaver, Robert C.
Wilson, Ronald M.
Wilson, Stephanie Y.

Editing

See Writing/Editing—Fiction; Writing/Editing—Nonfiction; Writing/Editing—Plays, Screenplays, TV Scripts; Writing/Editing—Poetry; Writing/Editing—Not Elsewhere Classified

Education—Adult/ Vocational

Adams, Robert Eugene
Allen, Brenda Foster
Anderson, Chester R.
Arburtha, Leodies U.
Arnold, Alton A., Jr.
Banks, Lula F.
Batiste, Mary Virginia
Batten, Grace Ruth
Beasley, Cora Thomas
Bell, S. Aaron
Bell, Warren, Jr.
Bennett, Joyce Annette
Black, Frank S.
Block, Leslie S.
Brinkley, Charles H., Sr.
Brooks, Norward J.
Brunson, David
Bryant, Carl
Butler, Loretta M.
Carter, Allen D.
Clark-Hudson, Veronica L.
Colbert, George Clifford
Cole Carey, Wilhemina, PhD
Coleman, Avant Patrick
Collins, Tessil John
Colvin, Alex, II
Cunningham, Arthur H.
Davis, L. Clifford
Day, Burnis Calvin
Dean, Vyvyan Coleman
DeJarmon, Elva Pegues
Dorman, Hattie L.
Dyce, Barbara J.
Eastmond, Joan Marcella
Elam, Dorothy R.
Ellis, George Washington
Fisher, Edith Maureen
Flowers, Loma Kaye
Franklin, Clarence Frederick
Fulgham, Roietta Goodwin
Gallwey, Sydney H.
Gillum, Ronald M.
Goines, Leonard
Gurley, Dorothy J.
Hailes, Edward A.
Hall, Joseph A.
Hamilton, James G.
Harris-Ebohon, Altheria Thyra
Haynes, Worth Edward
Heidt, Ellen Sullivan
Hollingsworth, John Alexander
Holt, Dorothy L.
Horton, Dollie Bea Dixon
Hull, Akasha
Jackson, Darrell Duane
Jackson, Leo Edwin
Jackson-Sirls, Mary Louise
Jefferson, Hilda Hutchinson
Johnson, Carroll Jones
Johnson, Frederick E.
Jolly, Elton
King, Thomas Lawrence
Knight, Muriel Bernice
Lackey, Edgar F.
Mack, Gordon H.
Mack, Sylvia Jenkins
Majors, Edith Sara
Mallett, Rosa Elizabeth
Martin, Rayfus
McCloud, Anece Faison
McDonald, Larry Marvin
Middleton, Richard Temple, III
Miller, William O.
Mitchell, Henry Heywood
Moore, Annie Jewell
Moore, Hazel Stamps
Morris, Dolores Orinskia
Morse, Annie Ruth W.
Nelson, Patricia Ann
Newhouse, Millicent DeLaine
Patrick, Opal Lee Young
Patton, Jean E.
Pratt, J. C.
Price, Brenda G.
Price, Ray Anthony
Pulliam, Betty E.

Quarles, George R.
Rich, Wilbur C.
Riggins, Lester
Robinson, Milton Bernidine
Ryder, Mahler B.
Sands, George M.
Saunders, Robert Edward
Saunders-Henderson, Martha M.
Scruggs, Sylvia Ann
Seams, Francine Swann
Selby, Cora Norwood
Smith, James Almer, Jr.
Smith, Rachel Norcom
Spruill, Albert Westley
Stephens, E. Delores B.
Stewart, Bess
Taylor, Vivian Lorraine
Thames, Uvena Woodruff
Thomas, David Anthony
Thomas, Louphenia
Thompson, Priscilla Angelena
Thompson, Winston Edna
Turner-Forte, Diana
Vaughn, Alvin
Walker, Charles Douglas
Watson, Cletus Claude
White-Ware, Grace Elizabeth
Williams, Katherine
Willingham, Voncile
Wright, Dmitri
Wright, James Christopher
Yuill, Essie McLean-Hall

Education—College/ University

Abdullah, Larry Burley
Abe, Benjamin Omara A.
Abram, James Baker, Jr.
Adair, Alvis V.
Adair, James E.
Adams, Afesa M.
Adams, Carol Laurence
Adams, Clarence Lancelot, Jr.
Adams, Eva W.
Adams, Joseph Lee, Jr.
Adams, Robert Eugene
Adams, Russell Lee
Adams, Samuel Levi, Sr.
Addei, Arthella Harris
Adesuyi, Sunday Adeniji
Akbar, Na'im
Albam, Manny
Aldredge, James Earl
Aldridge, Delores Patricia
Alexander, Drew W.
Alexander, Edward Cleve
Alexander, Estella Conwill
Alexander, Harry Toussaint
Alexander, Joseph Lee
Alexander, Laurence Benedict
Alexander, Sidney H., Jr.
Alexander, Theodore Martin, Sr.
Alexander, Theodore Thomas, Jr.
Alexander-Whiting, Harriett
Alexis, Marcus
Alford, Haile Lorraine
Alfred, Dewitt C., Jr.
Ali, Kamal Hassan
Ali, Schavi Mali
Allen, Betty
Allen, Blair Sidney
Allen, Esther Louisa
Allen, Harriette Louise
Allen, Karen
Allen, Samuel Washington
Allen, Shirley Jeanne
Allen, Walter R.
Allen, William Barclay
Allen, William Duncan
Allen-Noble, Rosie Elizabeth
Alsbrook, James Eldridge
Amaker, Norman Carey
Aman, Mohammed M.
Amiji, Hatim M.
Amory, Reginald L.
Amos, Oris Elizabeth Carter
Anderson, Avis Olivia
Anderson, Bernard E.
Anderson, David Atlas
Anderson, James R., Jr.
Anderson, Ruth Bluford
Anderson, Talmadge
Anderson, Thomas Jefferson
Anderson, William A.
Anderson, William Gilchrist
Anderson Janniere, Iona Lucille
Anderson-Tanner, Frederick T., Jr.
Andrews, Benny

Haines, Charles Edward
Haines, Diana
Hair, John
Hairston, Eddison R., Jr.
Hale, Janice Ellen, Ph.D.
Haley, Johnetta Randolph
Hall, Addie June
Hall, Benjamin Lewis, III
Hall, David
Hall, David McKenzie
Hall, James Reginald
Hall, Joseph A.
Hall, Joseph Clemon
Hall, Julia Glover
Hall, Kim Felicia
Hamilton, Charles Vernon
Hamilton, Edwin
Hamilton, Eugene Nolan
Hamilton, Franklin D.
Hamilton, Paul L.
Hamlin, David W.
Hammond, Benjamin Franklin
Hammond, James Matthew
Hampton, Grace
Hampton, Phillip Jewel
Hampton, Robert L.
Ham-Ying, J. Michael
Haney, Darnel L.
Hankins, Hesterly G., III
Hanna, Cassandra H.
Hansbury, Vivien H.
Hardaway, Ernest, II
Hardeman, Carole Hall
Harden, Marvin
Hardin, Eugene
Hardin, John Arthur
Harding, Robert E., Jr.
Harding, Vincent
Hardman-Cromwell, Youtha Cordella
Hardwick, Clifford E., III
Hardy, John Louis
Hargraves, William Frederick, II
Hargrove, Andrew
Harleston, Robert Alonzo
Harley, Philip A.
Harper, Curtis
Harper, Earl
Harper, Michael Steven
Harper, Walter Edward, Jr.
Harper, William Thomas, III
Harrell, Oscar W., II
Harrington, Elaine Carolyn
Harris, Charles Somerville
Harris, Charles Wesley
Harris, Donald J.
Harris, Edward E.
Harris, Elbert L.
Harris, Geraldine E.
Harris, Gil W.
Harris, Harcourt Glenties
Harris, James E.
Harris, John Everett
Harris, John H.
Harris, Joseph John, III
Harris, Marion Hopkins
Harris, Michael Wesley
Harris, Narvie J.
Harris, Robert Allen
Harris, Robert L., Jr.
Harris, Ruth Coles
Harris, Sidney E.
Harris, Trudier
Harris, Vander E.
Harris, Walter, Jr.
Harris, Willa Bing
Harris, William Allen
Harris, William McKinley, Sr.
Harrison, Algea Othella
Harrison, Daphne Duval
Harrison, Emma Louise
Harrison, Faye Venetia
Harrison, Paul Carter
Harris-Pinkelton, Norma
Hart, Brenda G.
Hartman, Hermene Demaris
Hartsfield, Arnett L., Jr.
Harvey, Harold A.
Harvey, William M.
Harvey-Salaam, Dyane Michelle
Haskins, James S.
Hatcher, Ester L.
Hatcher, Kendra Denise
Hawkins, Benny F., Sr.
Hawkins, Dorisula Wooten
Hawthorne, Lucia Shelia
Hayden, John Carleton
Hayden, Robert C., Jr.
Hayes, Albertine Brannum

Hayes, Annamarie Gillespie
Hayes, Charles Leonard
Hayes, Floyd Windom, III
Hayes, Leola G.
Hayes, Vertis
Haynes, Barbara Asche
Haynes, Eugene, Jr.
Haynes, James H.
Haynes, John Kermit
Haynes, Leonard L., Jr.
Haynes, Leonard L., III
Haywood, L. Julian
Head, Laura Dean
Hearn, Rosemary
Heath, James E.
Hedgepeth, Chester Melvin, Jr.
Heflin, John F.
Hegeman, Charles Oxford
Hemmingway, Beulah S.
Henderson, George
Henderson, Lenneal Joseph, Jr.
Henderson, Nannette S.
Henderson, Stanley Lee
Henderson, Stephen E.
Hendricks, Barkley L.
Hendricks, Constance Smith
Henry, Egbert Winston
Henry, James T., Sr.
Henry, Mildred M. Dalton
Henry, Samuel Dudley
Henry, Walter Lester, Jr.
Henry, Warren Elliott
Hereford, Sonnie Wellington, III
Hermanuz, Ghislaine
Hernton, Calvin Coolidge
Herrell, Astor Yeary
Herron, Carolivia
Hewing, Pernell Hayes
Hewitt, Vivian Davidson
Heyward, James Oliver
Hicks, Arthur James
Hicks, Clayton Nathaniel
Hicks, Eleanor
Hicks, Ingrid Diann
Hicks, Leon Nathaniel
Higgins, Chester A., Sr.
High, Freida
Hightower, J. Howard
Hildreth, Gladys Johnson
Hill, Anita Faye
Hill, Bennett David
Hill, Errol Gaston
Hill, Esther P.
Hill, James Lee
Hill, Patricia Liggins
Hill, Paul Gordon
Hill, Ray Allen
Hill, Sylvia Ione-Bennett
Hilliard, Alicia Victoria
Hill-Lubin, Mildred Anderson
Hilson, Arthur Lee
Hinds, Lennox S.
Hine, Darlene Clark
Hines, Charles A.
Hines, Laura M.
Hinton, Alfred Fontaine
Hinton, Gregory Tyrone
Hinton, Hortense Beck
Hintzen, Percy Claude
Hoagland, Everett H., III
Hobbs, Joseph
Hodge, Charles Mason
Hodges, Carolyn Richardson
Hodges, David Julian
Hodges, John O.
Hogan, Beverly Wade
Hogu, Barbara J. Jones
Holbert, Raymond
Holland, Major Leonard
Holley, Sandra Cavanaugh
Holloway, Joaquin Miller, Jr.
Holman, Benjamin F.
Holmes, Herbert
Holmes, Lorene B.
Holmes, Louyco W.
Holmes, Robert A.
Holmes, Zan W., Jr.
Holsey, Lilla G.
Holt, Edwin J.
Holt, Grace S.
Holt, James Stokes, III
Hood, Harold
Hooks, Benjamin Lawson
Hooks, Mose Yvonne Brooks
Hooper, Gerald F.
Hope, Richard Oliver
Hopkins, Dianne McAfee
Hopkins, Leroy Taft, Jr.
Hopkins, Thomas Franklin

Hopkins, Vashti Edythe Johnson
Hord, Frederick Lee
Horn, Lawrence Charles
Hornburger, Jane M.
Horne, Aaron
Horne, Edwin Clay
Horne, Gerald Charles
Horne-McGee, Patricia J.
Hornsby, Alton, Jr.
Horton, Carrell Peterson
Hosten, Adrian
Hoston, Germaine A.
Houston, Johnny L.
Houston, Lillian S.
Howard, Elizabeth Fitzgerald
Howard, John Robert
Howard, Lawrence Cabot
Howard, Lillie Pearl
Howard, Lytia Ramani
Howard, Mamie R.
Howard, Shirley M.
Howard, Vivian Gordon
Howe, Ruth-Arlene W.
Howell, Malqueen
Howze, Karen Aileen
Hoyt, Thomas L., Jr.
Hoyte, Arthur Hamilton
Hrabowski, Freeman Alphonsa, III
Hubbard, Amos B.
Hudson, Frederick Douglass
Hudson, Herman C.
Hudson, James Blaine, III
Hudson-Weems, Clenora Frances
Hudspeth, Gregory Charles, Sr.
Huff, Louis Andrew
Huggins-Williams, Nedra
Hughes, Joyce A.
Hull, Akasha
Hull, George, Jr.
Humphrey, Kathryn Britt
Humphrey, Margo
Hunn, Dorothy Fegan
Hunt, Barbara Ann
Hunt, Maurice
Hunt, Portia L.
Hunter, Charles A.
Hunter, David Lee
Hunter, Kristin
Hunter, Lloyd Thomas
Hunter, Patrick J.
Hunter, William Andrew
Hunter-Lattany, Kristin Eggleston
Huntley, Richard Frank
Hurd, David James, Jr.
Hurd, James L. P.
Hutcherson, Bernice B. R.
Hutchins, Francis L., Jr.
Hutchinson, George
Hutson, Jean Blackwell
Ibekwe, Lawrence Anene
Ibelema, Minabere
Ingram, Robert B.
Irvine, Carolyn Lenette
Irvine, Freeman Raymond, Jr.
Isaac, Eugene Leonard
Ishman, Sybil R.
Ita, Lawrence Eyo
Ivey, Horace Spencer
Jacket, Barbara Jean
Jackson, Agnes Moreland
Jackson, Andrew
Jackson, Arthur James
Jackson, David Samuel
Jackson, Dorothea E.
Jackson, Duane Myron
Jackson, Edgar Newton, Jr.
Jackson, Edward R.
Jackson, Jacquelyne Johnson
Jackson, James Sidney
Jackson, James Talmadge
Jackson, Julius Hamilton
Jackson, Keith Hunter
Jackson, Kennell A., Jr.
Jackson, Luther Porter, Jr.
Jackson, Marvin Alexander
Jackson, Murray Earl
Jackson, Paul L.
Jackson, Prince Albert, Jr.
Jackson, Raymond T.
Jackson, Reginald Leo
Jackson, Rudolph Ellsworth
Jackson, Thelma Conley
Jackson, W. Sherman
Jacobs, Norma Morris
Jacobs, Sylvia Marie
Jamerson, Jerome Donnell
James, Carrie Houser
James, Charles L.
James, David Phillip

James, Elridge M.
James, Felix
James, Hamice R., Jr.
James, Luther
James, Marquita L.
James, Robert D.
James, William
Jarrett, Gerald I., Jr.
Jarrett, Hobart Sidney
Jarrett, Thomas D.
Jay, James M.
Jaynes, Gerald David
Jeffers, Jack
Jefferson, Alphine Wade
Jefferson, Joseph L.
Jeffries, Leonard
Jeffries, Rosalind R.
Jenkins, Adelbert Howard
Jenkins, Carl Scarborough
Jenkins, Clara Barnes
Jenkins, Edmond Thomas
Jenkins, Kenneth Vincent
Jenkins, Melvin E., Jr.
Jennings, Lillian Pegues
Jennings, Robert Ray
Jerome, Norge Winifred
Johnson, Addie Collins
Johnson, Alcee LaBranche
Johnson, Arthur Lyman
Johnson, Audreye Earle
Johnson, Betty Jo
Johnson, Beulah C.
Johnson, Cage Saul
Johnson, Caliph
Johnson, Charles
Johnson, Charles H.
Johnson, Charles Richard
Johnson, Dorothy Turner
Johnson, Douglas H.
Johnson, Edna DeCoursey
Johnson, Edward A.
Johnson, Edward Elemuel
Johnson, Frederick E.
Johnson, Georgia Anna Lewis
Johnson, Golden Elizabeth
Johnson, Harold R.
Johnson, Harry A.
Johnson, Ivory
Johnson, Jacob Edwards, III
Johnson, Jeh Vincent
Johnson, Jerry Calvin
Johnson, Joe
Johnson, John W.
Johnson, Johnny B.
Johnson, Lemuel A.
Johnson, Leroy Ronald
Johnson, Lorraine Jefferson
Johnson, Martin Leroy
Johnson, Norris Brock
Johnson, Patricia Dumas
Johnson, Raymond Lewis
Johnson, Rhoda E.
Johnson, Roosevelt Young
Johnson, Theodore L.
Johnson, Tobe
Johnson, Tommie Ulmer
Johnson, Vannette William
Johnson, Vermelle Jamison
Johnson, Waldo Emerson, Jr.
Johnson, Walter J.
Johnson, Walter Lee
Johnson, Willard Raymond
Johnson-Brown, Hazel Winfred
Johnson Cook, Suzan Denise
Johnson-Helton, Karen
Johnson-Odim, Cheryl
Joiner, Burnett
Jones, Ann R.
Jones, Barbara Ann Posey
Jones, Ben F.
Jones, Butler Alfonso
Jones, Clifton Ralph
Jones, Cloyzelle Karrelle
Jones, Delmos J.
Jones, Donald W.
Jones, Edward Louis
Jones, Ferdinand Taylor, Jr.
Jones, Floresta Deloris
Jones, George H.
Jones, George Williams
Jones, Gerald E.
Jones, Harold M.
Jones, Hortense
Jones, Howard James
Jones, Ida M.
Jones, Idus, Jr.
Jones, Irma Renae
Jones, James Edward, Jr.
Jones, James McCoy

Jones, Jennie Y.
Jones, Jesse W.
Jones, Lawrence N.
Jones, Leander Corbin
Jones, Leeland Newton, Jr.
Jones, Lois Mailou
Jones, Lucius
Jones, Marcus Earl
Jones, Nettie Pearl
Jones, Oliver, Jr.
Jones, Peter Lawson
Jones, Phillip Erskine
Jones, Reginald L.
Jones, Rena Talley
Jones, Roy Junios
Jones, Shirley Joan
Jones, Theodore Cornelius
Jones, Vann Kinckle
Jones, William Bowdoin
Jones, William W.
Jones, Woodrow Harold
Jones, Yvonne Vivian
Jones-Grimes, Mable Christine
Jones-Wilson, Faustine Clarisse
Jordan, Abbie H.
Jordan, Casper LeRoy
Jordan, Eddie Jack, Sr.
Jordan, Emma Coleman
Jordan, George Lee, Jr.
Jordan, Harold Willoughby
Jordan, Jacquelyn D.
Jordan, John Wesley
Jordan, June M.
Jordan, Kenneth Ulys
Jordan, Wesley Lee
Jordan, William Alfred, III
Joyce, Donald Franklin
Kadree, Margaret Antonia
Kaigler-Reese, Marie Madeleine
Kamau, Mosi
Kamoche, Jidlaph Gitau
Kebede, Ashenafi Amde
Keene, Paul F., Jr.
Kelley, Delores G.
Kelly, Earl Lee
Kelly, Ernece Beverly
Kenan, Randall G.
Kendall, Mae Armster
Kennedy, Adrienne Lita
Kennedy, Anne Gamble
Kennedy, Floyd C.
Kennedy, Joseph J., Jr.
Kennedy, Joyce S.
Kennedy, Karel R.
Kennedy, Matthew W.
Kennedy, Theodore Reginald
Kennedy, William Thomas, Jr.
Kenney, Virgil Cooper
Kenyatta, Mary
Kern-Foxworth, Marilyn L.
Kerr, Hortense R.
Keyser, George F.
Khatib, Syed Malik
Kiah, Ruth Josephine
Kilimanjaro, John Marshall
Kilson, Martin Luther, Jr.
Kimbro, Dennis Paul
Kimbrough, Marjorie L.
Kindall, Luther Martin
King, Arthur Thomas
King, Calvin E.
King, Charles E.
King, Hulas H.
King, Lewis M.
King, Mary Booker
King, Ora Sterling
King, Patricia Ann
King, Rosalyn Cain
King, Thomas Lawrence
King, William J.
King, Yolanda D.
King-Hammond, Leslie
Kirk, Sarah Virgo
Kirk-Duggan, Cheryl Ann
Kirkland, Jack A.
Kirkland, Theodore
Kirkland-Holmes, Gloria
Kirklin, Perry William
Kisner, Robert Garland
Kitchen, Wayne Leroy
Kleven, Thomas
Knight, Franklin W.
Knight, Robert S.
Knight, W. H., Jr.
Koger, Linwood Graves, III
Komunyakaa, Yusef
Krigger, Marilyn Francis
Kumanyika, Shiriki K.
Kumbula, Tendayi Sengerwe

Kyles, Josephine H.
Lacey, Wilbert, Jr.
Lacy, Versia Lindsay
Lafontant, Julien J.
Laguerre, Michel S.
Lahr, Charles Dwight
Laing, Edward A.
Lairet, Dolores Person
Lampley, Calvin D.
Landers, Renee M.
Landry, L. Bartholomew
Lane, Johnny Lee
Lane, Pinkie Gordon
Langston, Esther J.
Langston-Jackson, Wilmetta Ann Smith
Lanier, Dorothy Copeland
Lanier, Marshall L.
Larkin, Byrdie A.
Larosiliere, Jean Darly Martin
Larrie, Reginald Reese, Ph.D.
Latham, Weldon Hurd
LaVeist, Thomas Alexis
Law, Thomas Melvin
Lawrence, Annie L.
Lawrence, Jacob A.
Lawrence, William Wesley
Lawson-Thomas, Althea Shannon
Leacock, Stephen Jerome
Leak, Lee Virn
Lechebo, Semie
Lede, Naomi W.
LeDoux, Jerome G.
Lee, Allen Francis, Jr.
Lee, Charlotte W.
Lee, Clifton Valjean
Lee, Dorothy A. H.
Lee, Guy Milicon, Jr.
Lee, Helen Elaine
Lee, Kermit J., Jr.
Lee, Lena S. King
Lee, M. David, Jr.
Lee, Margaret Carol
Lee, Michael Waring
Lee, Mildred Kimble
Leffall, LaSalle Doheny, Jr.
LeFlore, Larry
LeFlore, William B.
Leggon, Herman W.
Lehman, Paul Robert
Lemeh, Dorotha Hill
LeMelle, Tilden J.
Leonard, Curtis Allen
Lester, Donald
Lester, Julius
Lester, William Alexander, Jr.
Lewis, Almera P.
Lewis, Cary B., Jr.
Lewis, Cleveland Arthur
Lewis, David Levering
Lewis, H. Ralph
Lewis, Harold T.
Lewis, Henry, III
Lewis, Hylan Garnet
Lewis, James Edward
Lewis, Lauretta Fields
Lewis, Leo E., III
Lewis, Lonzy James
Lewis, Margaret W.
Lewis, Meharry Hubbard
Lewis, Ramsey Emanuel, Jr.
Lewis, Samella
Lewis, Therthenia Williams
Lewis, Viola Gambril
Lewis, William Sylvester
Lightfoot, Sara Lawrence
Lightfoot, William P.
Lillie, Vernell A.
Lincoln, C. Eric
Lindsay, Beverly
Lindsey, Jerome W.
Lipscomb, Darryl L.
Lipscombe, Margaret Ann
Little, Monroe Henry
Little, Ronald Eugene
Little, Willie Howard
Littlejohn, Edward J.
Littlejohn, Walter L.
Livingston, Joyce
Lloyd, Barbara Ann
Lloyd, Raymond Anthony
Lockard, Jon Onye
Locke, Don C.
Locke, Donald
Locke, Hubert G.
Locke, Mamie Evelyn
Lockett, James D.
Lockette, Agnes Louise
Lockwood, James Clinton

Logan, Frenise A.
Lomas, Ronald Leroy
London, Clement B. G.
Long, Charles H.
Long, Earnesteen
Long, John Edward
Long, Juanita Outlaw
Long, Richard A.
Louard, Agnes A.
Louistall-Monroe, Victorine Augusta
Loury, Glenn Cartman
Love, Barbara
Love, Edward A.
Love, Eleanor Young
Love, Mabel R.
Love, Thomas Clifford
Low, Patricia Enid Rose
Lowe, Eugene Yerby, Jr.
Lowery, Birl
Lownes, Millicent Gray
Lucas, James L.
Lucas, Rubye
Lucas, Wilmer Francis, Jr.
Luckey, Evelyn F.
Luckey, Irene
Luis, William
Lyda, Wesley John
Lynch, Hollis R.
Lynch, Lillie Riddick
Lynch, Rufus Sylvester
Maben, Hayward C., Jr.
Mack, Ally Faye
Mack, Joan
Mack, Wilbur Ollio
Macklin, Anderson D.
Macklin, John W.
Madgett, Naomi Long
Madu, Anthony Chisaraokwu
Magee, Sadie E.
Mahone, Charlie Edward, Jr.
Majete, Clayton Aaron
Major, Clarence
Majors, Richard G., III
Makokha, James A. N.
Malone, Gloria S.
Malone, J. Deotha
Manley, Albert Edward
Mann, Marion
Manning, Blanche Marie
Manning, Jean Bell
Manning, Reuben D.
Mansfield, Carl Major
Mapp, Edward C.
Mapp, Frederick Everett
Mapp, Yolanda I.
Marable, June Morehead
Marion, Claud Collier
Marius, Kenneth Anthony
Marriott, Salima Siler
Marshall, Carl Leroy
Marshall, Carter Lee
Marshall, Edwin Cochran
Marshall, Herbert A.
Marshall, Paule Burke
Martin, Basil Douglas
Martin, Bertha M.
Martin, Carolyn Ann
Martin, Cortez Hezekiah
Martin, Curtis Jerome
Martin, Elmer P.
Martin, Ernest Douglass
Martin, Evelyn B.
Martin, Harold B.
Martin, Hoyle Henry
Martin, Joanne Mitchell
Martin, John W.
Martin, Ruby Julene Wheeler
Martin, Tony
Martin, Walter L.
Martin-Ogunsola, Dellita Lillian
Marve, Eugene Raymond
Massey, Reginald Harold
Massey, Walter Eugene
Matabane, Sebiletso Mokone
Mathis, Walter Lee, Sr.
Matlock, Kent
Matthews, Dolores Evelyn
Matthews, Hewitt W.
Matthews, Virgil E.
Matthews, Westina Lomax
Maultsby, Portia K.
Maultsby, Sylvester
Maxwell, Hazel B.
Mayes, Helen M.
Mays, Vickie M.
Mays, William, Jr.
McAdams, David
McAdoo, Henry Allen

McArthur, Barbara Jean
McBrier, Vivian Flagg
McBroom, F. Pearl
McClain, Jerome Gerald
McClain, Paula Denice
McClain, Shirla R.
McClain, William Andrew
McClaskey, William H.
McClean, Vernon E.
McClearn, Billie
McCleave, Mildred Atwood Poston
McClelland, Marguerite Marie
McCloud, Aaron C.
McClure, Donald Leon, Sr.
McCluskey, John A., Jr.
McCollum, Alice Odessa
McConnell, Roland C.
McCormick, Larry William
McCoy, James Nelson
McDaniel, Reuben R.
McDaniel, Robert Anthony
McDaniels, Alfred F.
McDaniels, Jeaneen J.
McDaniels, John Edward, Sr.
McDonald, Edmund Morris
McDonald, Larry Marvin
McDuffie, Joseph deLeon, Jr.
McElroy, Lee A., Jr.
McElvane, Pamela Anne
McFadden, Arthur B.
McFadden, Nathaniel James
McFarlin, Emma Daniels
McFerrin, Sara Elizabeth Copper
McGathon, Carrie M.
McGhee, Reginald D.
McGhee, Samuel T.
McGlothan, Ernest
McGregor, Edna M.
McGruder, Charles E.
McGuire, Cyril A.
McHenry, Douglas
McIntosh, Frankie L.
McIntosh, James E.
McIntosh, Walter Cordell
McIntyre, Dianne Ruth
McKanders, Kenneth Andre
McKandes, Dorothy Dell
McKayle, Donald Cohen
McKee, Adam E., Jr.
McKenna, George J., III
McKenzie, Eli, Jr.
McKenzie, Reginald
McKinney, Ernest Lee, Sr.
McKinney, George Dallas, Jr.
McKinney, Rufus William
McKoy, Clemencio Agustino
McLaughlin, Dolphy T.
McLaughlin, Jacquelyn Snow
McLaughlin, LaVerne Laney
McLaughlin, Megan E.
McLaurin, Freddie Lewis, Jr.
McLaurin, Jasper Etienne
McLean, John Lenwood
McLean, Mable Parker
McLeod, Georgianna R.
McMichael, Earlene Clarisse
McMillan, Douglas James
McMillan, William Asbury, Sr.
McMillian, Frank L.
McPhail, Sharon M.
McRae, Ronald Edward
McRae, Thomas W.
McReynolds, Elaine A.
McSmith, Blanche Preston
McStallworth, Paul
McSwain, Berah D.
McWhorter, Millard Henry, III
McWilliams, Alfred E., Jr.
McWilliams, Alfred Edeard
McWright, Carter C.
Meade-Tollin, Linda C.
Meadows, Cheryl R.
Meadows, Lucile Smallwood
Means, Craig R.
Means, Donald Fitzgerald
Means, Kevin Michael
Mease, Quentin R.
Melancon, Donald
Melton, Bryant
Mensah, E. Kwaku
Meridith, Denise P.
Meriwether, Roy Dennis
Meshack, Lula M.
Michael, Dale R.
Michaux, Henry M., Jr.
Mickens, Ronald Elbert
Middleton, Richard Temple, III
Milburn, Corinne M.

Miles, Carlotta G.
Miles, Frank J. W.
Miles, June C.
Miles, Rachel Jean
Millard, Thomas Lewis
Milledge, Luetta Upshur
Miller, Andrea Lewis
Miller, Anna M.
Miller, Bernice Johnson
Miller, Henry B., Jr.
Miller, Ingrid Fran Watson
Miller, James Arthur
Miller, Jeanne-Marie A.
Miller, John H.
Miller, Louise T.
Miller, M. Sammye
Miller, Ronald Baxter
Miller, Russell L., Jr.
Miller, Samuel O.
Miller, Tedd
Miller, Telly Hugh
Miller, Warren F., Jr.
Miller, Yvonne Bond
Miller-Jones, Dalton
Millican, Arthenia J. Bates
Mimms, Maxine Buie
Mims, Beverly Carol
Mims, George L.
Minor, Billy Joe
Mitchell, Earl Douglass, Jr.
Mitchell, Edwin H., Sr.
Mitchell, Ella Pearson
Mitchell, Henry Heywood
Mitchell, Loften
Mitchell-Kernan, Claudia Irene
Mitchem-Davis, Anne
Moaney, Eric R.
Mobley, Eugenia L.
Mobley, Sybil C.
Molette, Barbara J.
Molette, Carlton Woodard, II
Monagan, Alfrieta Parks
Monroe, Annie Lucky
Monroe, Lillie Mae
Monteiro, Thomas
Montgomery, Toni-Marie
Moody, Charles David, Sr.
Moo-Young, Louise L.
Moore, Alice Evelyn
Moore, Annie Jewell
Moore, Archie Bradford, Jr.
Moore, Jossie A.
Moore, Juliette R.
Moore, Larry Louis
Moore, Lenard Duane
Moore, Nathan
Moore, Oscar James, Jr.
Moore, Oscar William, Jr.
Moore, Quincy L.
Moore, Robert F.
Moore, Undine Smith
Moran, Robert E., Sr.
Morant, Mack Bernard
Moreland, Lois Baldwin
Moreland-Young, Curtina
Morgan, Booker T.
Morgan, Gordon D.
Morgan, Harry
Morgan, Hazel C. Brown
Morgan, Jane Hale
Morgan, Raleigh, Jr.
Morgan-Cato, Charlotte Theresa
Morisey, Patricia Garland
Morris, Bernard Alexander
Morris, Calvin S.
Morris, Clifton
Morris, Effie Lee
Morris, Kelso B.
Morris, Major
Morris, Margaret Lindsay
Morris, Stanley E., Jr.
Morris, William H.
Morris-Hale, Walter
Morrison, Juan LaRue, Sr.
Morrison, K. C.
Morrison, Keith Anthony
Morrison, Toni
Morrow, Jon Howard, Jr.
Morse, Oliver
Mortimer, Delores M.
Morton, Charles E.
Morton, Cynthia Neverdon
Mosee, Jean C.
Moseka, Aminata
Moseley, Calvin Edwin, Jr.
Mosely, Kenneth
Moses, Henry A.
Mosley, Carolyn W.
Mosley, Geraldine B.

Mosley, Marie Oleatha
Moss, Alfred A., Jr.
Moss, Robert C., Jr.
Moss, Simeon F.
Moten, Chauncey Donald
Moxley, Frank O.
Murray, Albert L.
Murray, Anna Martin
Murray, James Hamilton
Murray, Mabel Lake
Murray, Thomas W., Jr.
Musgrove, Margaret Wynkoop
Muwakkil, Salim
Muyumba, Francois N.
Mwamba, Zuberi I.
Myers, Ernest Ray
Myers, Jacqualine Desmona
Myers, Lena Wright
Myers, Samuel L., Jr.
Myrick, Howard A., Jr.
Myricks, Noel
Nagan, Winston Percival
Nance, Jesse J., Jr.
Neal, Green Belton
Neal, Homer Alfred
Neavon, Joseph Roy
Neely, David E.
Nelson, Wanda Lee
Nelson, William Edward, Jr.
Nelson-Holgate, Gail Evangelyn
Nettleford, Rex Milton
Newell, Virginia K.
Newhouse, Quentin, Jr.
Newkirk, Gwendolyn
Newman, Geoffrey W.
Newsome, Clarence Geno
Newson, Roosevelt, Jr.
Newton, Jacqueline L.
Newton, James E.
Newton, Oliver A., Jr.
Neyland, Leedell Wallace
Nichols, Charles Harold
Nichols, Owen D.
Nicholson, Lawrence E.
Niles, Lyndrey Arnaud
Nilon, Charles Hampton
Nnolim, Charles E.
Noble, John Charles
Noble, Ronald K.
Noguera, Pedro Antonio
Noles, Eva M.
Norman, Alex James
Norman, Georgette M.
Norman, Maidie Ruth
Norman, William H.
Norris, Arthur Mae
Norris, Donna M.
Norris, Ethel Maureen
Norris, Lonnie H.
Northcross, Wilson Hill, Jr.
Northern, Robert A.
Norton, Aurelia Evangeline
Norton, Eleanor Holmes
Norwood, Kimberly Jade
Nunnally, David H., Sr.
Nwanna, Gladson I. N.
Oates, Gisele Casanova
Obinna, Eleazu S.
Oden, Gloria
Oglesby, James Robert
Ogletree, Charles J., Jr.
O'Guinn, Jo Lynn
Okhamafe, Imafedia
Okunor, Shiame
Oliver, Daily E.
Oliver, Melvin L.
Olivera, Herbert Ernest
Olugebefola, Ademola
Omolade, Barbara
Osakwe, Christopher
Osborne, Alfred E., Jr.
Osborne, Oliver Hilton
Osby, Parico Green
Owens, Andi
Owens, Charles Edward
Owens, George A.
Owens, Joan Murrell
Owens, Wallace, Jr.
Oyewole, Saundra Herndon
Padgett, James A.
Padulo, Louis
Page, Willie F.
Paige, Alvin
Painter, Nell Irvin
Palmer, Edgar Bernard
Palmer, Robert L., II
Palmer, Ronald DeWayne
Pannell, William E.
Parham, Johnny Eugene, Jr.

Parker, Henry H.
Parker, Jacquelyn Heath
Parker, Keith Dwight
Parker, Kellis E.
Parker, Sidney Baynes
Parker, Stephen A.
Parks, Arnold Grant
Parks, George B.
Parks, James Dallas
Parson, Willie L.
Pasteur, Alfred Bernard
Patrick, Odessa R.
Patrick, Opal Lee Young
Patterson, Elizabeth Ann
Patterson, Elizabeth Hayes
Patterson, Evelynne
Patterson, Grace Limerick
Patterson, Lydia R.
Patterson, Orlando Horace
Patterson, Raymond R.
Patterson, Willis Charles
Pattillo, Roland A.
Patton, Curtis Leverne
Paul, Alvin, III
Payton, Albert Levern
Peace, G. Earl, Jr.
Peagler, Frederick Douglass
Pearson, Clifton
Peck, Leontyne Clay
Peebles, Allie Muse
Peebles-Wilkins, Wilma Cecelia
Peek, Booker C.
Peery, Benjamin Franklin, Jr.
Pemberton, Gayle R.
Pemberton, Priscilla Elizabeth
Penceal, Bernadette Whitley
Penny, Robert
Penny, Robert L.
Pennywell, Phillip, Jr.
Pentecoste, Joseph C.
Peoples, VerJanis Andrews
Perdreau, Cornelia Whitener
Pereira, Sarah Martin
Perkins, Edward Joseph
Perkins, Linda Marie
Perry, Aubrey M.
Perry, Brenda L.
Perry, Leonard Douglas, Jr.
Perry, Patsy Brewington
Perry, Richard
Perry, Robert Lee
Person, Dawn Renee
Person, William Alfred
Persons, W. Ray
Peterman, Peggy M.
Peters, Erskine Alvin
Peters, James Sedalia, II
Peters, Samuel A.
Peterson, Alphonse
Peterson, Lorna Ingrid
Petioni, Muriel M.
Pettis, Joyce Owens
Petty, Rachel Monteith
Petty-Edwards, Lula Evelyn
Phelps, C. Kermit
Phelps, Constance Kay
Phillip, Michael John
Phillips, Earl W.
Phillips, Edward Martin
Phillips, Glenn Owen
Phillips, James Lawrence
Phillips, June M. J.
Phillips, Romeo Eldridge
Pickens, Ernestine W. McCoy
Pickens, William Garfield
Pierce, Chester Middlebrook
Pierce, Cynthia Straker
Pierce, Raymond O., Jr.
Pierce, Reuben G.
Pierce, Walter J.
Pinado, Alan E., Sr.
Pindell, Howardena D.
Pinkney, Alphonso
Pinkney, Jerry
Pinn, Samuel J., Jr.
Pinson, Hermine Dolorez
Pinson, Thomas J.
Piper, Adrian Margaret Smith
Piper, W. Archibald
Pittman, Audrey Bullock
Pitts, Vera L.
Plummer, Michael Justin
Plummer, Ora B.
Plumpp, Sterling Dominic
Pogue, Frank G., Jr.
Pointer, Richard H.
Polk, Gene-Ann
Polk, William C.
Pollard, Alton Brooks, III

Pollard, Diane S.
Ponder, Eunice Wilson
Poole, Marion L.
Pope, Derrick Alexander
Porter, Clarence A.
Porter, Curtiss E.
Potts, Harold E.
Powell, Dudley Vincent
Powell, Patricia
Powell, Philip Melancthon, Jr.
Pratt, Louis Hill
Press, Harry Cody, Jr.
Prestage, Jewel Limar
Preston, George Nelson
Preston, Michael B.
Prettyman, Quandra
Prewitt, Lena Voncille Burrell
Price, Alfred Douglas
Price, Charles Eugene
Price, John Elwood
Price, Ramon B.
Priester, Julian Anthony
Proctor, William H.
Propes, Victor Lee
Prothro, Johnnie Watts
Prudhomme, Nellie Rose
Pruitt, Anne Smith
Pruitt, George Albert
Pugh, Clementine A.
Pugh, Roderick W.
Pullen-Brown, Stephanie D.
Pulley, Clyde Wilson
Pyke, Willie Oranda
Queen, Evelyn E. Crawford
Quinton, Barbara A.
Rabouin, E. Michelle
Radcliffe, Aubrey
Rainey, Bessye Coleman
Ramey, Felicenne H.
Ramey, Melvin R.
Rampersad, Arnold
Ramseur, Andre William
Randall, Ann Knight
Randolph, Robert Lee
Ransby, Barbara
Ransom, Preston L.
Rashford, John Harvey
Ravenell, Mildred
Ravenell, William Hudson
Rawlins, Elizabeth B.
Ray, Jacqueline Walker
Ray, Judith Diana
Ray, William Benjamin
Rayford, Phillip Leon
Reaves, Benjamin Franklin
Redd, Thomasina A.
Redmond, Eugene B.
Reed, Charlotte
Reed, Daisy Frye
Reed, James
Reed, James W.
Reed, Jasper Percell
Reed, Michael H.
Reed, Rodney J.
Reese, Mamie Bynes
Register, Jasper C.
Reid, Joel Otto
Reid, Leslie Bancroft
Reid, Robert Dennis
Reid, Roberto Elliott
Reid, Vernon H.
Reide, Jerome L.
Reid-Merritt, Patricia Ann
Rembert, Emma White
Renfroe, Earl W.
Reuben, Lucy Jeanette
Revis, Nathaniel W.
Reynolds, Edward
Reynolds, Grant
Reynolds, Mel
Reynolds, Viola J.
Rhines, Jesse Algeron
Rhodes, Paula R.
Rice, Horace Warren
Rice, Louise Allen
Rice, Mitchell F.
Rice, Pamela Ann
Rich, Wilbur C.
Richard, Alvin J.
Richards, Johnetta Gladys
Richards, Leon
Richards, Lloyd G.
Richards, Winston Ashton
Richardson, Charles Ronald
Richardson, Elisha R.
Richardson, Henry J., III
Richmond, Tyronza R.
Ridgeway, Bill Tom
Ridley, Alfred Denis

Ridley, Walter N.
Rier, John Paul, Jr.
Riley, Clayton
Ringgold, Faith
Rison, Faye
Ritchie, Joe
Rivers, Louis
Roach, Hildred Elizabeth
Roane, Philip Ransom, Jr.
Roberson, Gloria Grant
Roberts, Kay George
Roberts, Malkia
Roberts, Roy J.
Robertson, Alan D.
Robertson, Benjamin W.
Robertson, Paul Francis
Robertson, Quincy L.
Robinson, Andrew
Robinson, Ann Garrett
Robinson, Carrie C.
Robinson, Cecelia Ann
Robinson, Charles E.
Robinson, Curtis
Robinson, Edward A.
Robinson, Ella S.
Robinson, Eunice Primus
Robinson, Frank J.
Robinson, Genevieve
Robinson, Jayne G.
Robinson, Jim C.
Robinson, Jontyle Theresa
Robinson, Kitty
Robinson, Lawrence B.
Robinson, Luther D.
Robinson, Maude Eloise
Robinson, Milton J.
Robinson, Prezell Russell
Robinson, Walter G.
Robinson, William Henry
Rocha, Joseph Ramon, Jr.
Rockett, Damon Emerson
Rodgers, Augustus
Rodgers, Carolyn Marie
Rodgers, Joseph James, Jr.
Rodgers, Vincent G.
Rogers, Charles D.
Rogers, Norman
Rollins, Richard Albert
Rose, Alvin W.
Rose, Arthur
Ross, Catherine Laverne
Ross, Lee Elbert
Rosser, Samuel Blanton
Rotan, Constance S.
Rouse, Jacqueline Anne
Rouse, Terrie
Rowe, Audrey
Royster, Philip M.
Rucker, Nannie George
Rushing, Byron D.
Russell, Charlie L.
Russell, Ermea J.
Russell, George A.
Russell, James A., Jr.
Russell, Joseph D.
Rutledge, Essie Manuel
Rutledge, Philip J.
Ryder, Georgia Atkins
Sadler, Wilbert L., Jr.
Saffold, Oscar E.
St. John, Primus
St. Omer, Vincent V. E.
Salmon, Jaslin Uriah
Samuels, Olive Constance
Samuels, Wilfred D.
Sanchez, Sonia Benita
Sanders, Charles Lionel
Sanders, Larry Kyle
Sanders, Robert B.
Sanders, Woodrow Mac
Sandle, Floyd Leslie
Sandoval, Dolores S.
Sands, George M.
Sands, Mary Alice
Santos, Henry J.
Sapp, Lauren B.
Sarkodie-Mensah, Kwasi
Satchell, Elizabeth
Satchell, Ernest R.
Satcher, Robert Lee, Sr.
Saunders, Elijah
Saunders, Mary Alice
Saunders, Mauderie Hancock
Saunders-Henderson, Martha M.
Savage, Horace Christopher
Savage, Vernon Thomas
Sawyer, Broadus Eugene
Sawyer, William Gregory
Scales, Alice Marie

Scales, Jerome C.
Scales, Manderline Elizabeth
Scales-Trent, Judy
Scarborough, Charles S.
Schooler, James Morse, Jr.
Scott, Charlotte Hanley
Scott, Elsie L.
Scott, Harold Russell, Jr.
Scott, John Sherman
Scott, John T.
Scott, Joseph Walter
Scott, Juanita Simons
Scott, Levan Ralph
Scott, Marvin Wayne
Scott, Mona Vaughn
Scott, Nathan A., Jr.
Scott, Osborne E.
Scott, Otis L.
Scott, Portia Alexandria
Scott, Roland B.
Scott, Veronica J.
Scruggs, Allie W.
Scruggs, Otey Matthew
Seals, R. Grant
Sealy, Joan R.
Searles, Charles R.
Sears, Bertram E.
Seaton, Shirley Smith
Sebhatu, Mesgun
Secret, Philip E.
Secundy, Marian Gray
See, Letha A.
Seibert-McCauley, Mary F.
Senbet, Lemma W.
Settles, Rosetta Hayes
Shack, William A.
Shade, Barbara J.
Shakoor, Adam Adib
Sharp, Charles Louis
Sharp, J. Anthony
Sharpe, Calvin William
Shaw, Ann
Shaw, Ferdinand
Shaw, Spencer Gilbert
Shaw, Theodore Michael
Sheffey, Ruthe G.
Shelton, Roy Cresswell, Jr.
Shepherd, Benjamin A.
Sherwood, Wallace Walter
Shields, Clarence L., Jr.
Shine, Theodis
Shipp, Howard J., Jr.
Shipp, Melvin Douglas
Shockley, Ann Allen
Shockley, Thomas Edward
Shopshire, James Maynard
Short, Kenneth L.
Shorty, Vernon James
Shotwell, Ada Christena
Showell, Hazel Jarmon
Shropshire, John Sherwin
Shuford, Humphrey Lewis
Shuman, Jerome
Sikes, Melvin Patterson
Siler, Joyce B.
Sillah, Marion Rogers
Silver, Joseph Howard, Sr.
Simmons, Annie Marie
Simmons, James E.
Simmons, John Emmett
Simmons, Sylvia J.
Simon, Joseph Donald
Simpkins, J. Edward
Simpson-Taylor, Dorothy Marie
Sims, Genevieve Constance
Singh, Rajendra P.
Singleton, Leroy, Sr.
Sinkler, George
Sinnette, Elinor DesVerney
Sizemore, Barbara A.
Skinner, Clementine Anna
   McConico
Skinner, Elliott P.
Skinner, Ewart C.
Slade, Phoebe J.
Slaughter, John Etta
Slaughter-Defoe, Diana T.
Sloss, Minerva A.
Small, Lily B.
Smalls, O'Neal
Smallwood, Osborn Tucker
Smith, A. Wade
Smith, Alphonso Lehman
Smith, Andrew W.
Smith, Benjamin Franklin
Smith, Bettie M.
Smith, Carol J.
Smith, Charles Edison
Smith, Charles F., Jr.

Smith, Charlie Calvin
Smith, Dolores J.
Smith, Donald Hugh
Smith, Dorothy Louise White
Smith, Edgar E.
Smith, Edward Nathaniel, Jr.
Smith, Eleanor Jane
Smith, Fredrick E.
Smith, Gerald Wayne
Smith, Geraldine T.
Smith, Hale
Smith, Herald Leonydus
Smith, J. Clay, Jr.
Smith, James David
Smith, Jesse Owens
Smith, Joanne Hamlin
Smith, John Arthur
Smith, Joseph Edward
Smith, Joshua L.
Smith, Keith Dryden, Jr.
Smith, Luther Edward, Jr.
Smith, Mary Levi
Smith, Nellie J.
Smith, Paul
Smith, Paul Bernard
Smith, Paul M., Jr.
Smith, Pearlena W.
Smith, Philip Gene
Smith, Quentin T.
Smith, Robert Charles
Smith, Robert Lawrence, Sr.
Smith, Robert London
Smith, Robert P., Jr.
Smith, Roland Blair, Jr.
Smith, Roulette William
Smith, Susan L.
Smith, Vernon G.
Smith, Virginia M.
Smith, Walter L.
Smith, William Pernell, Jr.
Smitherman, Carole
Smitherman, Geneva
Smithey, Robert Arthur
Smith Freeman, Patricia M.
Smith Nelson, Dorothy J.
Smythe-Haith, Mabel Murphy
Snowden, Frank Walter
Snowden, Sylvia Frances
Sogah, Dotsevi Y.
Solomon, Barbara J.
Somerville, Addison Wimbs
Sommerville, Joseph C.
Southall, Geneva H.
Southerland, Ellease
Southern, Eileen Jackson
Southern, Joseph
Sowell, Thomas
Spaulding, Jean Gaillard
Spears, Henry Albert, Sr.
Spencer, Margaret Beale
Spencer, Michael Gregg
Spigner, Clarence
Spiva, Ulysses Van
Sprauve, Gilbert A.
Spriggs, G. Max
Sprout, Francis Allen
Spruill, Albert Westley
Spruill, James Arthur
Spurlock, Jeanne
Stalls, M.
Stamps, Spurgeon Martin David,
   Jr.
Stanback, Thurman W.
Stancell, Arnold Francis
Stanley, Carol Jones
Staples, Robert E.
Starke, Catherine Juanita
Starks, Robert Terry
Steele, Claude Mason
Steele, Ruby L.
Steele, Shelby
Stennis-Williams, Shirley
Stent, Madelon Delany
Stephens, E. Delores B.
Stephens, Lee B., Jr.
Stepto, Robert Burns
Stetson, Jeffrey P.
Stevens, Althea Williams
Stevens, George Edward, Jr.
Stevens, Thomas Lorenzo, Jr.
Stevenson, Russell A.
Stewart, Albert C.
Stewart, Bess
Stewart, Elizabeth Pierce
Stewart, James Benjamin
Stewart, John Othneil
Stewart, Mac A.
Stewart, Pearl
Stewart, William H.

Stinson, Joseph McLester
Stith, Melvin Thomas
Stockman, Ida J.
Stokes, Gerald Virgil
Stokes, Julie Elena
Stokes, Sheila Woods
Stone, Chuck
Stone, Kara Lynn
Strickland, Dorothy S.
Strickland, Frederick William, Jr.
Strider, Maurice William
Stripling, Luther
Stuart, Marjorie Mann
Stull, Virginia Elizabeth
Styles, Kathleen Ann
Subryan, Carmen
Suggs, Robert Chinelo
Sullivan, Allen R.
Sullivan, J. Christopher
Sullivan, Zola Jiles
Sumler-Edmond, Janice L.
Suneja, Sidney Kumar
Sutton, Dianne Floyd
Sutton, Sharon Egretta
Sutton, Walter L.
Sutton, William Wallace
Swan, George W., III
Swan, L. Alex
Sweeney, John Albert
Swindell, Warren C.
Swinton, Sylvia P.
Sykes, Vernon Lee
Sykes, William Richard, Jr.
Sylvas, Lionel B.
Sylvester, Melvin R.
Sylvester, Patrick Joseph
Syphax, Burke
Taborn, John Marvin
Talbot, Alfred Kenneth, Jr.
Talbot, David Arlington Roberts,
   Sr.
Talbot, Gerald Edgerton
Talbot, Theodore A.
Talley, Michael Frank, Sr.
Talley, William B.
Tanner, James W., Jr.
Tanter, Raymond
Tarter, Roger Powell, M.D.
Tarver, Leon R., II
Tate, Merze
Taylor, Arnold H.
Taylor, Charles Avon
Taylor, Dale B.
Taylor, Dalmas A.
Taylor, David Vassar
Taylor, Edward Walter
Taylor, Estelle Wormley
Taylor, Felicia Michelle
Taylor, Henry Louis, Jr.
Taylor, Howard F.
Taylor, Hycel B.
Taylor, Jerome
Taylor, Joseph T.
Taylor, Julius H.
Taylor, Michael Loeb
Taylor, Mildred D.
Taylor, Orlando L.
Taylor, Paul David
Taylor, Quintard, Jr.
Taylor, Robert, III
Taylor, Ronald Lewis
Taylor, Stuart A.
Taylor, Thad, Jr.
Taylor, William L.
Taylor-Thompson, Betty E.
Tearney, Russell James
Temple, Edward Stanley
Terborg-Penn, Rosalyn M.
Terrell, Francis
Terrell, Francis D'Arcy
Terrell, Mary Ann
Terrell, Melvin C.
Terrell, Robert L.
Thelwell, Michael M. Ekwueme
Thibodeaux, Mary Shepherd
Thomas, Carl Alan
Thomas, Charles Columbus
Thomas, Claude Roderick
Thomas, Eula Wiley
Thomas, Gerald Eustis
Thomas, Harry Lee
Thomas, Herman Edward
Thomas, James Samuel
Thomas, Joyce Carol
Thomas, Kendall
Thomas, Latta R., Sr.
Thomas, Louphenia
Thomas, Lucille Cole
Thomas, Mary A.

Thomas, Matthew Manjusri, Jr.
Thomas, Nathaniel
Thomas, Pamella D.
Thomas, Robert Lewis
Thomas, Rodolfo Rudy
Thompson, Sister Francesca
Thompson, Litchfield O'Brien
Thompson, Marcus Aurelius
Thompson, Regina
Thompson, Robert Farris
Thompson, Sidney
Thomson, Gerald Edmund
Thorburn, Carolyn Coles
Thornell, Richard Paul
Thornton, Clifford E.
Thrower, Julius A.
Thurman, Alfonzo
Thurston, Paul E.
Tidwell, John Edgar
Tildon, Charles G., Jr.
Tillman, Talmadge Calvin, Jr.
Timberlake, Constance Hector
Tipton, Dale Leo
Tisdale, Celes
Tobias, Randolf A.
Tolbert, Odie Henderson, Jr.
Tolliver, Lennie-Marie P.
Tolliver, Richard Lamar
Tomlinson, Robert
Toms-Robinson, Dolores C.
Toombs, Charles Phillip
Toppin, Edgar Allan
Tottress, Richard Edward
Towns, Sanna Nimtz
Trader, Harriet Peat
Traylor, Eleanor W.
Treadwell, David Merrill
Trent, Marcia M.
Trice, William B.
Trimiar, J. Sinclair
Tripp, Luke Samuel
Trottman, Charles Henry
Troupe, Marilyn Kay
Troupe, Quincy Thomas, Jr.
Troutman, Porter Lee, Jr.
Truitte, James F.
Tucker, Dorothy M.
Tucker, M. Belinda
Tucker, Norma Jean
Tucker, Wilbur Carey
Tunstall, Lucille Hawkins
Turnbull, Charles Wesley
Turner, Castellano Blanchet
Turner, Doris J.
Turner, Evelyn Evon
Turner, Geneva
Turner, Jean Taylor
Turner, John B.
Turner, John Barrimore
Turner, Wallace E.
Turner, William H.
Twigg, Lewis Harold
Tyler, Gerald DeForest
Tyson, Lorena E.
Umolu, Mary Harden
Unaeze, Felix Eme
Uzoigwe, Godfrey N.
Valdes, Pedro H.
Vance, Irvin E.
Vanderpool, Eustace Arthur
Van Dyke, Henry
Van Hook, Warren Kenneth
Vargus, Ione D.
Varner, James, Sr.
Varner, Nellie M.
Vernon, Alexander
Vertreace, Martha Modena
Vessup, Aaron Anthony
Via, Thomas Henry
Vick-Williams, Marian Lee
Violenus, Agnes A.
Visor, Julia N.
Vogel, Roberta Burrage
Wade, Achille Melvin
Wade, Jacqueline E.
Wade-Gayles, Gloria Jean
Wahls, Myron Hastings
Waiguchu, Muruku
Walden, Robert Edison
Walker, Annie Mae
Walker, Charles
Walker, Charles Ealy, Jr.
Walker, Cynthia Bush
Walker, Ernest L.
Walker, Ernestein
Walker, Ethel Pitts
Walker, Frances
Walker, George Edward
Walker, Kenneth R.

Walker, Larry M.
Walker, Lewis
Walker, Margaret Abigail
Walker, Sheila Suzanne
Walker, Stanley M.
Walker, Valaida Smith
Walker, Wilbur P.
Walls, George Hilton, Jr.
Walter, John C.
Walters, Curla Sybil
Walters, Hubert Everett
Walters, Ronald
Walton, Edward D.
Walton, Harriett J.
Walton, James Edward
Walton, R. Keith
Ward, Carole Geneva
Ward, Daniel
Ward, James Dale
Ward, Jerry Washington, Jr.
Ward, John Preston
Wardlaw, McKinley, Jr.
Ware, Gilbert
Ware, William L.
Warren, Herman Lecil
Warren, Joseph David
Warren, Joseph W.
Warren, Morrison Fulbright
Warren, Nagueyalti
Warren, Stanley
Washington, Earl Melvin
Washington, Gladys J.
Washington, Herman A., Jr.
Washington, James Lee
Washington, James Melvin
Washington, John William
Washington, Joseph R., Jr.
Washington, Linda Phaire
Washington, Mary Helen
Washington, Michael Harlan
Washington, Paul M.
Washington, Robert Orlanda
Washington, Sarah M.
Washington, Thomas
Washington, Von Hugo, Sr.
Waters, Henrietta E.
Waters, John W.
Watkins, Judge Charles, Jr.
Watson, Betty Collier
Watson, Dennis Rahiim
Watson, Eugenia Baskerville
Watson, Genevieve
Watson, John Clifton
Watson, Joseph W.
Watts, Anne Wimbush
Watts, Roberta Ogletree
Wead, Rodney Sam
Weaver, Garrett F.
Weaver, John Arthur
Weaver, Robert C.
Weaver, William Courtsworthy, II
Webb, Harold, Sr.
Webb, Harvey, Jr.
Webb, Melvin Richard
Weber, Shirley Nash
Webster, Niambi Dyanne
Weddington, Rachel Thomas
Weddington, Wilburn Harold, Sr.
Weil, Robert L.
Weiss, Joyce Lacey
Welburn, Ronald Garfield
Welch, Ashton Wesley
Welch, Harvey, Jr.
Welch, Olga Michele
Welch, Winfred Bruce
Wells, Patrick Roland
Welmon, Vernis M.
West, Cornel
West, Donda C.
West, George Ferdinand, Jr.
West, Harold Dadford
West, Herbert Lee, Jr.
West, John Raymond
West, Pheoris
West, Valerie Y.
West, William Lionel
Westmoreland, Samuel Douglas
Whaley, Mary H.
Wharton, A. C., Jr.
Wharton, Clifton R., Jr.
Wharton Boyd, Linda F.
Whatley, Booker Tillman
Wheeler, Shirley Y.
Whitaker, Mical Rozier
Whitaker, Von Frances
White, Augustus A., III
White, Barbara Williams
White, Booker Taliaferro
White, Clayton Cecil

White, Clovis Leland
White, Don Lee
White, Frederic Paul, Jr.
White, Harold Rogers
White, Howard A.
White, Katie Kinnard
White, Sandra LaVelle
White, Tommie Lee
Whitely, Donald Harrison
White-Parson, Willar F.
Whiting, Albert Nathaniel
Whitten, Charles F.
Whittington, Harrison DeWayne
Wideman, John Edgar
Wiggins, Joseph L.
Wiggins, William H., Jr.
Wilder, Cora White
Wilderson, Frank B., Jr.
Wiley, John D., Jr.
Wilkerson, Margaret Buford
Wilkins, Allen Henry
Wilkins, David Brian
Wilkins, Henry, III
Wilkins, Josetta Edwards
Wilkins, Leona B.
Wilkins, Roger Wood
Wilkinson, Donald Charles
Wilkinson, Doris
Wilkinson, Robert Shaw, Jr.
Williams, A. Cecil
Williams, Ann E. A.
Williams, Beryl E. W.
Williams, Betty Smith
Williams, Bismarck S.
Williams, Camilla
Williams, Carolyn Chandler
Williams, Carolyn Ruth Armstrong
Williams, Carroll Burns, Jr.
Williams, Chester Arthur
Williams, Daniel Edwin
Williams, Daniel Salu
Williams, Donald H.
Williams, Dorothy Daniel
Williams, Earl, Jr.
Williams, Edna C.
Williams, Ernest Y.
Williams, Euphemia G.
Williams, Fred C.
Williams, Gary C.
Williams, Gregory Howard
Williams, Helen B.
Williams, Helen Elizabeth
Williams, Hugh Hermes
Williams, James H., Jr.
Williams, James Hiawatha
Williams, James Thomas
Williams, Jamye Coleman
Williams, Jeanette Marie
Williams, Jerome D.
Williams, John Alfred
Williams, Kimmika L. H.
Williams, Larry
Williams, Lisa R.
Williams, Louis Nathaniel
Williams, Malcolm Demosthenes
Williams, Marcus Doyle
Williams, McDonald
Williams, Melvin D.
Williams, Naomi B.
Williams, Norris Gerald
Williams, Ora
Williams, Preston N.
Williams, Robert H.
Williams, Scott W.
Williams, Sherley Anne
Williams, Sterling B., Jr.
Williams, W. Clyde
Williams, Wilbert Lee
Williams, William J.
Williams, William Thomas
Williams, Willie Elbert
Williams, Willie Jr.
Williams, Willie L.
Williams, Willie LaVern
Williams, Yvonne Carter
Williams-Myers, Albert J.
Williamson-Ige, Dorothy Kay
Williams-Stanton, Sonya Denise
Willie, Charles Vert
Willis, Gladys January
Willock, Marcelle Monica
Willoughby, Susan Melita
Wilmore, Gayraud Stephen
Wilson, Blenda J.
Wilson, Bobby N.
Wilson, Carroll Lloyd
Wilson, Charles Z., Jr.
Wilson, Clarence S., Jr.
Wilson, David

Wilson, Donald
Wilson, Donella Joyce
Wilson, Greer Dawson
Wilson, Hugh A.
Wilson, Jeffrey R.
Wilson, John
Wilson, Jonathan Charles, Jr.
Wilson, Joseph F.
Wilson, Patricia I.
Wilson, Ralph L.
Wilson, Rudolph George
Wilson, Stanley Charles
Wilson, William E.
Wilson, William Julius
Wing, Adrien Katherine
Wingate, Rosalee Martin
Wingfield, Harold Lloyd
Winston, Hubert
Wint, Arthur Valentine Noris
Winter, Daria Portray
Winters, Wendy Glasgow
Wolfe, Deborah Cannon Partridge
Wolfe, William K.
Womack, Henry Cornelius
Wood, Michael H.
Woodard, Fredrick
Woodard, Samuel L.
Wooden, Ralph L.
Woodland, Calvin Emmanuel
Woods, Allie, Jr.
Woods, Roosevelt, Jr.
Woods, Willie G.
Woodward, Isaiah Alfonso
Woolfolk, E. Oscar
Worrell, Richard Vernon
Worrill, Conrad W.
Worthy, Barbara Ann
Worthy, William, Jr.
Wray, Wendell Leonard
Wrice, David
Wrice, Vincent J.
Wright, Albert Walter, Jr.
Wright, Dmitri
Wright, Harriette Simon
Wright, Jackson Thomas, Jr.
Wright, Jane C.
Wright, Katie Harper
Wright, Larry L.
Wright, Roosevelt R., Jr.
Wright, Stephen Caldwell
Wright-Botchwey, Roberta Yvonne
Wykle, May Louise Hinton
Wynn, Valree Fletcher
Wyre, Stanley Marcel
Wyrick, Floyd I.
Yancey, Carolyn Lois
Yancy, Dorothy Cowser
Yancy, Preston Martin
Yarborough, Dowd Julius, Jr.
Yarborough, Richard A.
Yarbrough, Marilyn Virginia
Yarde, Richard Foster
Yizar, James Horace, Jr.
Young, Alfred
Young, Alfred F.
Young, Carlene Herb
Young, Charles Alexander
Young, Coleman A.
Young, Edith Mae
Young, Elizabeth Bell
Young, F. Camille
Young, Lawrence W., Jr.
Young, Marechal-Neil Ellison
Young, Michael
Young, Nancy Wilson
Zachary, Steven W.
Zambrana, Rafael
Ziegler, Dhyana
Zu-Bolton, Ahmos, II
Zulu, Itibari M.

Education—Elementary/Secondary

Abney, Robert
Acklin, Pamela Lyn
Adams, Lillian Louise T.
Adams, M. Elizabeth
Aikens-Young, Linda Lee
Alexander, DeAngelo Heath
Alexander, Dorothy Dexter
Alexander, Theodore Thomas, Jr.
Allen, Walter R.
Alston, Betty Bruner
Amin, Karima
Anders, Richard H.
Anderson, Louise Payne
Anderson, S. A.
Arkhurst, Joyce Cooper

Arties, Lucy Elvira Yvonne
Atchison, Lillian Elizabeth
Bailey, Adrienne Yvonne
Baker, Henry W., Sr.
Baldwin, Wilhelmina F.
Banks, Dwayne Martin
Banks, June Skinner
Banner, Melvin Edward
Barefield, Morris
Barker, Timothy T.
Barnes, Diane
Barnes, Vivian Leigh
Basey, Ovetta T.
Beady, Charles H., Jr.
Bean, Bobby Gene
Bean, Walter Dempsey
Beasley, Annie Ruth
Becker-Slaton, Nellie Frances
Bell, Charles Smith
Bell, George
Bell, Kenneth M.
Benson, Lillian
Bing, Rubell M.
Bins, Milton
Birchette, William Ashby, III
Block, Leslie S.
Bond, Ollie P.
Bothuel, Ethel C. S.
Bowser, James A.
Bowser, Vivian Roy
Bradley, William B.
Breeding, Carl L.
Bronz, Lois Gougis Taplin
Brooks, James Taylor
Brooks, Norman Leon
Brooks, Richard Leonard
Brooks, Rosemary Bittings
Brown, Bernice Baynes
Brown, Conella Coulter
Brown, Effie Mayhan Jones
Brown, Emma Jean Mitchell
Brown, Hezekiah
Brown, James Marion
Brown, Justine Thomas
Brown, Malcolm McCleod
Brown, Michael DeWayne
Brown, Otha N., Jr.
Brown, Rubye Golsby
Bruce, Antoinette Johnson
Bryant, Jenkins, Jr.
Burns, Ollie Hamilton
Burroughs, Margaret Taylor
Burton, Iola Brantley
Burton, Lana Doreen
Buskey, James E.
Butler, Velma Sydney
Butts, Janie Pressley
Byas, Ulysses
Campbell, Alma Porter
Campbell, Mary Allison
Cargill, Gilbert Allen
Carlisle, James Edward, Jr.
Carpenter, Ann M.
Carter, Esther Young
Carter, Gwendolyn Burns
Carter, James
Carter, Ora Williams
Caswell, Catheryne Willis
Catchings, Yvonne Parks
Clark, Joe Louis
Clark, Mildred E.
Clarke, Joy Adele Long
Clayborn, Wilma W.
Cluse, Kenny Joseph
Coatie, Robert Mason
Colbert, Benjamin James
Coleman, Jean Ellen
Coleman, Lemon, Jr.
Collins, Gordon Geoffrey
Collins, Marva Delores Nettles
Combs, Sylvester Lawrence
Cook, Vernice Wilhelmina Barnes
Cooke, Nellie
Corprew, Charles Sumner, Jr.
Crouther, Betty M.
Daniels, Lincoln, Sr.
Daniels, Peter F.
Davidson, Tommy
Davis, Donald
Davis, Elaine Carsley
Davis, H. Bernard
Davis, Major
Dean, Vyvyan Coleman
Dennard, Brazeal Wayne
Didlick, Wells S.
Dildy, Catherine Greene
Dixon, Margaret A.
Dixon, Ruth F.
Douglas, Edna M.

Douglas, John Daniel
Douglas, Joseph Francis
Douglass, M. Lorayne
Dove, Pearlie C.
Draper, Sharon Mills
Dudley-Washington, Loise
Duke, Ruth White
Dunlap, Estelle Cecilia Diggs
Dunlap King, Virgie M.
Dunn, James Earl
Dunn-Barker, Lillian Joyce
Dyson, William Riley
Eastmond, Joan Marcella
Eaton, Patricia Frances
Echols, Doris Brown
Edwards, G. Franklin
Edwards, Jean Curtis
Edwards, Miles Stanley
Evaige, Wanda Jo
Evans, Mary Adetta
Evans, William E.
Farrell, Odessa Wright
Farrow, Willie Lewis
Fillyaw, Leonard David
Fisher, Shelley Marie
Flores, Joseph R.
Ford, Lisa Denise
Foree, Jack Clifford
Foster, Edward, Sr.
Frazier, Pauline Clarke
Freeman, Kerlin, Jr.
Freeman, William M.
Frink Reed, Caroliese Ingrid
Fuller, Dr. Harold David
Funn, Carlton A., Sr.
Fuse, Bobby LeAndrew, Jr.
Gaither, Magalene Dulin
Gallwey, Sydney H.
Gantt, Walter N.
Gaskin, Leroy
Gaskins, Henry Jesse
Gaskins, Louise Elizabeth
Gaskins, Mary Ann
Gayle, Lucille Jordan
Gayles-Felton, Anne Richardson
Gibbs, Alma G.
Gillis, Shirley J. Barfield
Gist, Karen Wingfield
Givens, Abe, Jr.
Gooden, Samuel Ellsworth
Goodrich, Harold Thomas
Gordon, Ethel M.
Gordon, Fannetta Nelson
Graham, Delores Metcalf
Graham, Helen W.
Gray, Joanne S.
Gray, Myrtle Edwards
Green, Brenda Kay
Green, Calvin Coolidge
Green, William Edward
Greene, John Sullivan
Greene, Marvin L.
Greenwood, Theresa M. Winfrey
Griffin, Edna Westberry
Grissett, Willie James
Groves, Delores Ellis
Gunn, Gladys
Guy, Mildred Dorothy
Gwynn, Florine Evayonne
Hager, Joseph C.
Hales, Mary Ann
Hall, Katie
Hamberlin, Emiel
Hamilton, Paul L.
Hamlin, Arthur Henry
Hampton, Opal Jewell
Hansberry-Moore, Virginia T.
Hansbury, Vivien H.
Hansen, Joyce Viola
Hardy, Eursla Dickerson
Harkless-Webb, Mildred
Harper, Geraldine
Harris, Burnell
Harris, Cornelia
Harris, Narvie J.
Harris-Ebohon, Altheria Thyra
Harrison, Emma Louise
Hayes, Curtiss Leo
Hayes, Marion LeRoy
Haynes, Neal J.
Henderson, Ruth Faynella
Henderson, Virginia Ruth
  McKinney
Hendrix, Martha Raye
Henry, David Winston
Higgins, Bennett Edward
Higgs, Mary Ann Spicer
Hill, Barbara Ann
Hill, Clara Grant

Hoff, Nathaniel Hawthorne
Holland, Dorreen Antoinette
Holland, Robin W.
Holman, Doris Ann
Holmes, Wilma K.
Holt, Deloris Lenette
Hooker, Odessa Walker
Hooks, James Byron, Jr.
Hope, Marie H.
Hopkins, Dianne McAfee
Hoskins Clark, Tempy M.
Houze, Jeneice Carmel Wong
Hoyte, Lenon Holder
Hubbard, Calvin L.
Hughes, Carl D.
Hughes, Essie Meade
Hunter, Cecil Thomas
Hunter, Edwina Earle
Hutton, David Lavon
Ingram, William B.
Irons, Sandra Jean
Isaac, Telesforo Alexander
Jackson, Cornelia Pinkney
Jackson, Fred James, Sr.
Jackson, Garnet Nelson
Jackson, Richard E., Jr.
Jackson, Vera Ruth
Jackson, Willis Randell, II
Jacobs, Thomas Linwood
James, Arminta Susan
Jenkins, Drewie Gutrimez
Jenkins, Shirley Lymons
Jeter, Velma Marjorie Dreyfus
Johnson, Addie Collins
Johnson, Joseph Edward
Johnson, Lorraine Jefferson
Johnson, Louise Mason
Johnson, Lyman T.
Johnson, Mertha Ruth
Johnson, Rebecca M.
Johnson, Wayne Leon
Jones, Betty Jean T.
Jones, Christine Miller
Jones, Ruth Braswell
Jones, Sherman J.
Jones, Velma Lois
Jones, Zoia L.
Jordan, David Lee
Jordan, John Wesley
Jordan, Mabel B.
Jordan, Patricia
Jordan, Robert A.
Julian, John Tyrone
Kafele, Baruti Kwame
Kendrick, Tommy L.
Kimble, Bettye Dorris
Kimmons, Carl Eugene
King, Lloyd
Knox-Benton, Shirley
Langston-Jackson, Wilmetta Ann
  Smith
Lawson, Quentin Roosevelt
Leace, Donal Richard
LeCompte, Peggy Lewis
Lee, Clara Marshall
Leggette, Violet Olevia Brown
LeGrand, Bob
Leonard, Catherine W.
Lewis, Anne A.
Lewis, Carmen Cortez
Linton, Sheila Lorraine
Little, Willie Howard
Littlejohn, Samuel Gleason
Logan, Alphonso
Long, John Bennie
Ludley, Richard
Lyles, Marie Clark
Lyons, Charles H. S., Jr.
Mack, Pearl Willie
Maddox, Julius A.
Madison, Leatrice Branch
Malone, J. Deotha
Malry, Lenton
Mangum, Ernestine Brewer
Marks, Lee Otis
Marshall, Etta Marie-Imes
Marshall-Walker, Denise Elizabeth
Martin, Rayfus
Mason, B. J.
Mason, Donna S.
Mathis, Thaddeus P.
Maxwell, Marcella J.
May, James Shelby
Mayberry, Claude A., Jr.
May-Pittman, Ineva
McBride, Shelia Ann
McCannon, Dindga Fatima
McClain, James W.
McClellan, Edward J.

McClelland, Marguerite Marie
McClendon, Carol A.
McClure, Donald Leon, Sr.
McConnell, Roland C.
McCoy, Frank Milton
McElrath, Wanda Faith
McGowan, Elsie Henderson
McGuirt, Milford W.
McIntosh, Alice T.
McKenzie, Edna B.
McMillan, Joseph H.
McMillan, Wilton Vernon
McPherson, Roosevelt
McPherson, Vanzetta Penn
McTyre, Robert Earl, Sr.
Meadows, Richard H.
Medearis, Victor L.
Merriweather, Michael Lamar
Micks, Deitra R. H.
Miles, Ruby A. Branch
Miller, Ethel Jackson
Miller, Thomas Patton
Miller, William O.
Miller-Reid, Dora Alma
Minor, Emma Lucille
Mobley, Charles Lamar
Montgomery, Joe Elliott
Montgomery, Payne
Moore, Helen D. S.
Moore, Lenny Edward
Moore, N. Webster
Moorehead, Bobbie Wooten
Morgan, Juanita Kennedy
Morgan, Mary H. Ethel
Morris, Margaret Lindsay
Morrison, Gwendolyn Christine
  Caldwell
Morse, Annie Ruth W.
Morston, Gary Scott
Moss, James Edward
Muhammad, Conrad
Murphy, Robert L.
Murray, Edna McClain
Murray, Mabel Lake
Musgrove, Margaret Wynkoop
Myers, Stephanie E.
Myles, Ernestine
Neal, James P., Sr.
Nelson, Cleopatra McClellan
Newberry, Trudell McClelland
N'Namdi, Carmen Ann
Nor, Genghis
Northern, Robert A.
Nunery, Gladys Cannon
Nunn, Bobbie B.
Nunnally, David H., Sr.
Nwa, Willia L. Deadwyler
Oates, Wanda Anita
O'Ferrall, Anne F.
O'Kain, Marie Jeanette
Orr, Marlett Jennifer
Owens, Isaiah H.
Owens, Jefferson Pleas
Owsley, Betty Joan
Oyeshiku, Patricia Delores Worthy
Palmer, Elliott B., Sr.
Palmer-Hildreth, Barbara Jean
Parker, Lee
Patrick, Opal Lee Young
Paul, Vera Maxine
Pelote, Dorothy B.
Perkins, William O., Jr.
Perrimon, Vivian Spence
Phillips, Acen L.
Phillips, Frances Caldwell
Phillips, Helen M.
Phillips, Rosemarye L.
Pierce, Reuben G.
Piper, Elwood A.
Pitts, Vera L.
Polite, Marie Ann
Porter, Blanche Troullier
Porter, Henry Lee
Pratt, Mable
Presley, Calvin Alonzo
Primous, Emma M.
Quarles, Herbert DuBois
Rambo, Bettye R.
Ready, Catherine Murray
Reddick, Alzo Jackson
Reddick, Linda H.
Reece, Avalon B.
Reed, Eddie
Reed, Joann
Reese, Frederick D.
Reese, Mamie Bynes
Reid, Maude K.
Reynolds, Audrey Lucile
Rhodeman, Clare M.

Richardson, DeRutha Gardner
Richardson, Odis Gene
Rigsby, Esther Martin
Roberts, Lorraine Marie
Roberts, Margaret Ward
Robertson, Gertrude
Robertson, Quindonell S.
Robinson, Carol W.
Robinson, Kenneth Eugene
Robinson, Norman T., Jr.
Rogers, Peggy J.
Romans, Ann
Ross, Emma Jean
Rudd, Charlotte Johnson
Russell, Dian Bishop
Samuels, Charlotte
Scott, Mary Shy
Scott-Johnson, Roberta Virginia
Scruggs, Cleorah J.
Seay, Lorraine King
See, Letha A.
Segre, Greta Eubank
Selby, Cora Norwood
Shannon, Marian L. H.
Sharpe, Audrey Howell
Sherow, Don Carl
Simpson, John
Simpson, Juanita H.
Sloss, Minerva A.
Small, Stanley Joseph
Smalls, Dorothy M.
Smith, Deborah P.
Smith, Frank
Smith, Juanita Smith
Smith, Mary Carter
Smith, Mildred B.
Smith, Pearlena W.
Smith, Quentin P.
Smith, Robert Johnson
Smith, Robert Lawrence, Sr.
Smoot, Carolyn Elizabeth
Smotherson, Melvin
Speight, Eva B.
Spradley, Frank Sanford
Springer, George Chelston
Stallings, Gregory Ralph
Stanislaus, Gregory K.
Stanley, Hilbert Dennis
Stanyard, Hermine P.
Stevenson, Jerome Pritchard, Sr.
Stewart, Loretta A.
Stratton-Morris, Madeline
  Robinson Morgan
Strong, Marilyn Terry
Suggs, William Albert
Swanson, Edith
Tate, Matthew
Taylor, Anderson
Taylor, John L.
Taylor, Mildred D.
Taylor, Octavia G.
Thomas, Erma Lee Lyons
Thomas, Juanita Ware
Thomas, Monica Maria Primus
Thompson, Clarissa J.
Thompson, Imogene A.
Thompson, John Andrew
Thompson, Lauretta Peterson
Thompson, Rosie L.
Thompson, Sylvia Moore
Thurman, Marjorie Ellen
Tingle, Lawrence May
Todd, Charles O.
Todman, Jureen Francis
Tolliver, Ned, Jr.
Turnbull, Walter J.
Turner, Johnnie Rodgers
Turner, Willie
Turner-Forte, Diana
Tyler, Shirley Neizer
Tyson, Lorena E.
Underwood, Frankye Harper
Usry, James LeRoy
Varner, Jewell C.
Vaughn, Alvin
Walker, Larry Vaughn
Walker, William Harold
Wallace, Milton De'Nard
Ward, Albert A.
Ward, Daniel
Warren, Gertrude Francois
Washington, Ada Catherine
Washington, Arna D.
Washington, Emery, Sr.
Washington, Mary Parks
Watkins, Charles Booker, Sr.
Watson, Roberta Conwell
Watts, Wilsonya Richardson
Wayne, Justine Washington

West, John Raymond
Westbrook, Joseph W., III
Wheaton, Thelma Kirkpatrick
Wheeler, Betty McNeal
White, Gregory Durr
White, Phillip, III
White-Hunt, Debra Jean
White-Ware, Grace Elizabeth
Whittington, Harrison DeWayne
Wilborn, Letta Grace Smith
Williams, Carolyn Ruth Armstrong
Williams, Ethel Jean
Williams, Georgianna M.
Williams, Jean Carolyn
Williams, Jester C.
Williams, Kelvin Edwin
Williams, Sylvia J.
Williams, Ulysses Jean
Wilson, Edith N.
Wilson, Floyd Edward, Jr.
Wilson, Hazel Forrow Simmons
Wilson, John W.
Wilson, Madelaine Majette
Wilson, Sandra E.
Wilson, Wilson W.
Wilson-Smith, Willie Arrie
Winfrey, Charles Everett
Winston, Dennis Ray
Winston, Lillie Carolyn
Witherspoon, Annie C.
Woods, Almita
Woolcock, Ozeil Fryer
Workman, Aurora Felice Antonette
Wright, Dmitri
Wright, Mary H.
Wynn, Gladys W.
Yuill, Essie McLean-Hall

Education—Not Elsewhere Classified

Alexander, Alma Duncan
Allen, Edna Rowery
Anderson, Barbara Stewart Jenkins
Anderson, Doris J.
Anderson, Gloria L.
Anderson, John C., Jr.
Anderson, Ruth Bluford
Auld, Albert Michael
Aziz, Samimah
Bachus, Marie Darsey
Balthrope, Jacqueline Morehead
Bankhead, Patricia Ann
Banks, Waldo R., Sr.
Barber, William, Jr.
Barrett, Sherman L.
Beane, Patricia Jean
Beckett, Sydney A.
Bellinger, Luther Garic
Belton, C. Ronald
Belton, Howard G.
Bennett, Bessye Warren
Bennett, Collin B.
Bills, Johnny Bernard
Binns, Silas Odell
Birchette, William Ashby, III
Block, Leslie S.
Blunden, Jeraldyne K.
Boone, Clinton Caldwell
Bothuel, Ethel C. S.
Bowser, Robert Louis
Boykin, A. Wade, Jr.
Boynton, Asa Terrell, Sr.
Bradley, James Monroe, Jr.
Bradley, Roosevelt, Jr.
Briggins, Charles E.
Broadnax, Melvin F.
Brooks, Charlotte Kendrick
Brooks, Daisy M. Anderson
Brown, Annie Carnelia
Brown, Willis, Jr.
Brunt, Samuel Jay
Bryant, Edward Joe, III
Bullett, Audrey Kathryn
Burford, Effie Lois
Butler, Eula M.
Butler, Rebecca Batts
Cafritz, Peggy Cooper
Cain, Johnnie M.
Calomee, Annie E.
Campbell, Margie
Carrier, Clara L. DeGay
Carson, Irma
Caviness, Lorraine F.
Channell, Eula L.
Cherry, Cassandra Brabble
Chissell, John T.
Clardy, William J.
Clark, Bertha Smith

Cole, Arthur
Coleman, Avant Patrick
Coleman, Winson
Collins, Elsie
Cooper, Ethel Thomas
Copeland, Emily America
Copeland, Ray
Coppedge, Arthur L.
Cowden, Michael E.
Cummings, E. Emerson
Dale, Robert J.
Daley, Guilbert Alfred
Darden, Christopher A.
Davis, Donald
Davis, Etheldra S.
Davis, Nathan W., Jr.
Davis, William Hayes, Sr.
Davis, Willie A.
Daye, Charles Edward
DeClue, Anita
Douglass, M. Lorayne
Dowd, Maria
Dungee, Margaret R.
Eaves, A. Reginald
Elligan, Irvin, Jr.
Ellington, Mercedes
Elliott, John
Ellis, O. Herbert
Erwin, Claude F., Sr.
Eubanks, John Bunyan
Eubanks, Rachel Amelia
Evans, Ada B.
Evans, Mattie
Faison, Helen Smith
Fann, Al Louis
Faust, Naomi Flowe
Fears, Emery Lewis, Jr.
Ferguson, Sherman E.
Finley, Betty M.
Fittz, Senga Nengudi
Flagg, E. Alma W.
Fleming, Thomas A.
Floyd, Jeremiah
Ford, Deborah Lee
Foreman, S. Beatrice
Fortune, Gwendoline Y.
Foster, Frank B., III
Foster, James H.
Fountain, William Stanley
French, George Wesley
Futrell, Mary Hatwood
Gaines, Ray D.
Gaskin, Leonard O.
Gates, Audrey Castine
George, Luvenia A.
Gholston, Betty J.
Gibbes, Emily V.
Gilbert, Eldridge H. E.
Gilmore, Al Tony
Givens, Sister Clementina M.
Goodwin, Norma J.
Gordon, Aaron Z.
Gordon, Fannetta Nelson
Graham, Albertha L.
Graham, Chestie Marie
Graham, Delores Metcalf
Grant, Jacquelyn
Green, Reuben H.
Griffin, James Stafford
Griffith, Vera Victoria
Gunn, Alex M., Jr.
Guyton, Sister Patsy
Hale, Janice Ellen, Ph.D.
Hall, Horathel
Hamill, Margaret Hudgens
Hardman-Cromwell, Youtha Cordella
Harkins, Rosemary Knighton
Harper, Walter Edward, Jr.
Harris, Narvie J.
Harris, Wesley Young, Jr.
Harrison, Carol L.
Harrison, Don K., Sr.
Harrison, Robert Walker, III
Hatcher, Ester L.
Hayes, Richard C.
Haynes, Farnese N.
Haynes, George E., Jr.
Hemphill, Miley Mae
Henderson, Australia Tarver
Hendrix, Deborah Lynne
Henry, Charles E.
Henry, Joseph King
Henry, Thomas
Higgins, Sammie L.
Hill, Hattie
Hill, Paul Gordon
Hilton, Tanya
Holland, Spencer H.

Holly, Ella Louise
Holmes, Barbara J.
Holmes, E. Selean
Hopkins, Edna J.
Houston, Marsh S.
Howard, Billie Jean
Howard, Gwendolyn Julius
Howze, Dorothy J.
Hudson, Winson
Hutton, David Lavon
Hutton, Gerald L.
Inyamah, Nathaniel Ginikanwa N.
Isaac, Ephraim
Izell, Booker T.
Jackson, Clarence H.
Jackson, Frank Donald
Jackson-Foy, Lucy Maye
James, Betty Harris
Jangdharrie, Wycliffe K.
Johnson, Lorretta
Johnson, Marie Elizabeth
Johnson, Michael Anthony
Johnson, Valrie E.
Jones, Brent M.
Jones, Geraldine J.
Jones, Idus, Jr.
Jones, Katherine Elizabeth Butler
Jones, Lawrence W.
Jones, Sondra Michelle
Joyner, Irving L.
Kelly, Florida L.
Kimbrough, Thomas J.
King, Ruby Ryan
Koram, M. Jamal
Laney, Robert Louis, Jr.
Lark, Raymond
Laroche, Gerard A.
Law, M. Eprevel
Lawing, Raymond Quinton
Lawrence, Prestonia D.
Laws, Ruth M.
Lawyer, Cyrus J., III
Lee, Aaron
Leonard, Carolyn Marie
Leonard, Walter J.
Lewis, Green Pryor, Jr.
Lightfoot, Jean Harvey
Lofton, Dorothy W.
Lovett, Leonard
Lyle, Roberta Branche Blacke
Lynn, James Elvis
Lyons, Laura Brown
Mack, Charles Richard
Manning, Blanche Marie
Martin, Ionis Bracy
Martin, Lawrence Raymond
Mason, Donna S.
Mason, Howard Keith
Mayfield, Curtis
Maynor, Kevin Elliott
McCants, Coolidge N.
McClure, Exal, Jr.
McDowell-Head, Lelia M.
McKerson, Mazola
McNelty, Harry
Miller, Robert, Jr.
Miller, Saundra Celia
Mims, Robert Bradford
Mitchell, Ella Pearson
Mitchell, Henry Heywood
Montague, Lee
Montgomery, William R.
Moore, Jane Bond
Morris, Elise L.
Morton, Norman
Morton, Patsy Jennings
Moss, Otis, Jr.
Muldrow, James Christopher
Murray, J-Glenn
Myers, Jacqualine Desmona
Nelson-Holgate, Gail Evangelyn
Nesbitt, Prexy-Rozell William
Nettles, Willard, Jr.
Newell, Matthias Gregory
Nichols, Walter LaPlora
Nicholson, Aleathia Dolores
Norman, William H.
Notice, Guy Symour
O'Neal, Eddie S.
Onli, Turtel
Page, Marguerite A.
Paige, Windell
Palmer, James E.
Patterson, Curtis Ray
Patton, Robert
Peace, Eula H.
Peeler, Diane Faustina
Perkins, Frances J.
Perry, Jean B.

Petty, Reginald E.
Phillips, Barbara
Player, Willa B.
Pledger, Verline S.
Pompey, Charles Spencer
Poole, Marion L.
Porter, Blanche Troullier
Potter, Judith Diggs
Pryor, Lillian W.
Puryear, Alvin N.
Radden, Thelma Gibson
Rayford, Zula M.
Reaves, E. Fredericka M.
Reaves, Franklin Carlwell
Reinhardt, John Edward
Ridgel, Gus Tolver
Roberts, Cheryl Dornita Lynn
Roberts, Lorraine Marie
Roberts, Samuel Kelton
Robinson, Adeline Black
Robinson, Catherine
Rogers-Lomax, Alice Faye
Rose, Shelvie
Rountree, Ella Jackson
Samkange, Tommie Marie
Schumacher, Brockman
Scott, Ruth Perry
Scruggs, Sylvia Ann
Scrutchions, Benjamin
Seabrook, Bradley Maurice
Sevillian, Clarence Marvin
Simmons, James E.
Simpson, Harry L.
Slaughter, Carole D.
Smith, Charles Daniel, Jr.
Smith, Marietta Culbreath
Smith, Reginald D.
Smith, Robert London
Smith, Wallace Charles
Soaries, DeForest Blake, Jr.
Springer, George Chelston
Stanyard, Hermine P.
Stull, Robert J.
Swain, Alice M.
Talley, James Edward
Talley, John Stephen
Tanner, James W., Jr.
Taylor, Almina
Thibodeaux, Sylvia Marie
Thomas, Gloria V.
Thomas, Jacquelyn Small
Thomas, Louphenia
Thomas, Ronald F.
Thompas, George Henry, Jr.
Tillman, Lillian G.
Toomer, Vann Alma Rosalee
Trim, John H.
Troupe, Marilyn Kay
Turner, Elmyra G.
Tyson, Lorena E.
Verrett, Joyce M.
Waiters, Ann Gillis
Walden, Robert Edison
Walker, Mary Alice
Walker, Wilbur P.
Wallace, Claudette J.
Walls, Melvin
Washington, Leroy
Washington, Thomas
Watley, Margaret Ann
Watson, Wilbur H.
Watts, Roberta Ogletree
Weaver, Reginald Lee
Whaley, Wayne Edward
Wheeler, Susie Weems
White, Clayton Cecil
White, Ella Flowers
White, Frederic Paul, Jr.
Whiteside, Ernestyne E.
Williams, Ann E. A.
Williams, Arnette L.
Williams, Donald H.
Williams, James Arthur
Williams, Lorece P.
Williams, Malcolm Demosthenes
Williams, Martha S.
Williams, T. Joyce
Williams, Willie J.
Williford, Cynthia W.
Wilson, Hughlyne Perkins
Wilson, Ray F.
Wimberly, Edward P.
Winfield, Linda Fitzgerald
Wolfe, Estemore A.
Woodall, Ellis O., Sr.
Woodfolk, Joseph O.
Wormley, Cynthia L.
Wright, Jeremiah A., Jr.
Wright, Stanley V.

Wright, William Gaillard
Wyatt, Beatrice E.
Wynn, Daniel Webster
Wynn, Malcolm
Yeary, James E., Sr.
Yerger, Amos G.
Zimmerman, Samuel Lee

Educational Administration

Abercrumbie, Paul Eric
Abraham, Sharon L.
Abraham, Sinclair Reginald
Ackerman, Patricia A.
Acrey, Autry
Adams, Afesa M.
Adams, Dolly Desselle
Adams, Elaine Parker
Adams, Eva W.
Adams, Frederick G.
Adams, Howard Glen
Adams, Kattie Johnson
Adams, Lucinda Williams
Adams, Richard Melvin, Jr.
Adams, Russell Lee
Adams, Verna May Shoecraft
Adams-Dudley, Lilly Annette
Addei, Arthella Harris
Adesuyi, Sunday Adeniji
Adeyiga, Adeyinka A.
Adkins, Rutherford
Aggrey, O. Rudolph
Aikens-Young, Linda Lee
Airall, Angela Maureen
Airall, Zoila Erlinda
Akin, Ewen M., Jr.
Albright, Robert, Jr.
Alexander, James Arthur
Alexander, John Wesley, Jr.
Alexander, Lydia Lewis
Alexander, Theodore Thomas, Jr.
Alexis, Carlton Peter
Ali, Fatima
Ali, Grace L.
Ali, Kamal Hassan
Allen, Betty
Allen, Brenda Foster
Allen, Carol Ward
Allen, George
Allen, Lecester L.
Allen, Maxine Bogues
Allen, Philip C.
Allen, Van Sizar
Allen-Noble, Rosie Elizabeth
Allston, Thomas Gray, III
Ally, Akbar F.
Alston, Floyd William
Amos, Ethel S.
Amprey, Walter G.
Anders, Richard H.
Anderson, Amel
Anderson, Carl Edwin
Anderson, David Atlas
Anderson, Del Marie
Anderson, Eloise B. McMorris
Anderson, Granville Scott
Anderson, Henry L. N.
Andrews, Adolphus
Andrews, James F.
Andrews, Maxine Ramseur
Andrews, William Pernell
Anthony-Perez, Bobbie M.
Appleby-Young, Sadye Pearl
Arburtha, Leodies U.
Archer, Chalmers, Jr.
Archer, Susie Coleman
Armster-Worrill, Cynthia Denise
Armstrong, J. Niel
Armstrong, Matthew Jordan, Jr.
Arnez, Nancy L.
Arnold, Alton A., Jr.
Arnold, Clarence Edward, Jr.
Arnold, Helen E.
Arrington, Richard, Jr.
Asbury, William W.
Atchison, Calvin O.
Atkins, Brenda J.
Austin, Bobby William
Austin, Mary Jane
Aziz, Kareem A.
Babbs, Junious C., Sr.
Baber, Lucky Larry
Bacon, Barbara Crumpler
Bagby, Rachel L
Bailey, Adrienne Yvonne
Bailey, Donn Fritz
Bailey, Eugene Ridgeway
Bailey, Gracie Massenberg

DeShields, Harrison F., Jr.
Deskins, Donald R., Jr.
DeSousa, D. Jason
DeSouza, Ronald Kent
DeWitt, Rufus B.
Dickens, Helen Octavia
Dickerson, Harvey G., Jr.
Dickerson, Janet Smith
Dickinson, Gloria Harper
Dickson, David W. D.
Dike, Kenneth Onwuka
Dillard, Martin Gregory
Dillenberger, R. Jean
Dillon, Aubrey
Dilworth, Mary Elizabeth
Dismuke, Leroy
Dixon, Ardena S.
Dixon, Benjamin
Dixon, Blanche V.
Dixon, Margaret A.
Dixon, Ruth F.
Dixon, Tom L.
Dobbs, John Wesley
Dodson, Jualynne E.
Donaldson, Jeff Richardson
Dotson, Philip Randolph
Douglas, Arthur E.
Douglas, Harry E., III
Douglas, Samuel Horace
Douglass, Melvin Isadore
Dove, Pearlie C.
Dowdy, Lewis C.
Downing, Stephen
Dozier, Richard K.
Draper, Edgar Daniel
Draper, Frederick Webster
Drewry, Cecelia Hodges
Drewry, Henry Nathaniel
Dual, Peter A.
DuBose, Otelia
Duke, Ruth White
Dukes, Jerome Erwin
Dulin, Joseph
Dumas, Rhetaugh Graves
Dummett, Clifton Orrin
Dunbar, Harry B.
Dungy, Claiborne I.
Dungy, Madgetta Thornton
Dunnigan, Jerry
Dunson, Carrie Lee
Durand, Henry J., Jr.
Durant, Charles E.
Durham, Joseph Thomas
Duster, Troy
Duvall, Henry F., Jr.
Dykes, Marie Draper
Eady, Mary E.
Early, Ida H.
Early Lambert, Violet Theresa
Easley, Charles F., Sr.
Easter, Rufus Benjamin, Jr.
Easter, Wilfred Otis, Jr.
Eaton, Minetta Gaylor
Eaton, Patricia Frances
Echols, Mary Ann
Edelin, Kenneth C.
Edgerton, Art Joseph
Edmonds, Thomas Nathaniel
Edney, Norris Allen, I
Edwards, Cecile Hoover
Edwards, Marvin E.
Edwards, Miles Stanley
Edwards, Robert
Edwards, Robert Valentino
Edwards, Rondle E.
Edwards, Thomas Oliver
Elam, Lloyd C.
Ellis, Calvin H., III
Ellis, Edward V.
Ellis, George Washington
Elzy, Amanda Belle
Emmanuel, Tsegai
English, Richard A.
Engs, Robert Francis
Epperson, David E.
Epps, Anna Cherrie
Epps, Charles Harry, Jr.
Epps, Dolzie C. B.
Ervin, Deborah Green
Esquivel, Argelia Velez
Estep, Roger D.
Esters, George Edward
Estes, Sidney Harrison
Ethridge, Robert Wylie
Ethridge, Samuel B.
Eubanks, Eugene E.
Evans, Arthur L.
Evans, Crecy Ann
Evans, David Lawrence

Evans, Donna Browder
Evans, Eva L.
Evans, Jack
Evans, Ruthana Wilson
Evans, William E.
Evans-Tranumn, Shelia
Eve, Christina M.
Evege, Walter L., Jr.
Ewell, Yvonne Amaryllis
Ewers, James Benjamin, Jr.
Fair, Frank T.
Faison, Helen Smith
Fakhrid-Deen, Nashid Abdullah
Farris, Vera King
Faulk, Estelle A.
Faulkner, Geanie
Faw, Barbara Ann
Feaster, Bruce Sullivan
Feaster, LaVerne Williams
Felder, Tyree Preston, II
Feliciana, Jerrye Brown
Ferguson, Joel
Ferguson, St. Julian
Fielder, Fred Charles
Fields, Brenda Joyce
Fields, Dexter L.
Fields, Ewaugh Finney
Fields, Savoynne Morgan
Finch, Janet M.
Finch, William H.
Finn, John William
Fisher, E. Carleton
Fitchue, M. Anthony
Flack, Harley Eugene
Flamer, John H., Jr.
Fleming, Bruce E.
Fleming, George
Fleming, Melvin J.
Fleming, Quince D., Sr.
Fletcher, Patricia Louise
Flood, Shearlene Davis
Floyd, Elson
Floyd, Jeremiah
Floyd, Samuel A., Jr.
Floyd, Vircher B.
Foggs, Joyce D.
Fomufod, Antoine Kofi
Foote, Yvonne
Ford, Aileen W.
Ford, Charles
Ford, Donald A.
Ford, Nancy Howard
Ford, Richard D.
Ford, Virginia
Fort, Edward B.
Fort, Jane
Forte, Johnie, Jr.
Foster, Delores Jackson
Foster, Henry Wendell
Foster, Mildred Thomas
Foster, Rosebud Lightbourn
Foster, William Patrick
Fowler, John D.
Fowler, Queen Dunlap
Fox, Jeanne Jones
Francis, Edith V.
Francis, Gilbert H.
Francis, Norman C.
Franklin, Allen D.
Franklin, Bernard W.
Franklin, Herman
Franklin, Robert Michael
Fraser, Leon Allison
Frazier, Leon
Fredd, Chester Arthur
Freeman, Albert Cornelius, Jr.
Freeman, Denise
Freeman, Diane S.
Freeman, Evelyn
Freeman, Nelson R.
Freeman, Preston Garrison
Freeman, Ruges R.
Frelow, Robert Dean
French, George Wesley
Fries, Sharon Lavonne
Froe, Otis David
Frost, Olivia Pleasants
Fuget, Charles Robert
Fuller, Dr. Harold David
Fuller, James J.
Funn, Carlton A., Sr.
Funn, Courtney Harris
Gabbin, Joanne Veal
Gadsden, Nathaniel J., Jr.
Gainer, Ruby Jackson
Gaines, Clarence E., Sr.
Gaines, Edythe J.
Gaines, Herschel Davis
Gaines, Paul Laurence, Sr.

Gaines, Sedalia Mitchell
Gaines, Victor Pryor
Gall, Lenore Rosalie
Gallon, Dennis P.
Gant, Raymond Leroy
Gardiner, George L.
Gardner, Bettye J.
Gardner, Frank W.
Gardner, Loman Ronald
Garibaldi, Antoine Michael
Garner, Charles
Garner, La Forrest Dean
Garvin, Mildred Barry
Gaskins, Henry Jesse
Gaskins, Louise Elizabeth
Gaskins, Mary Ann
Gaston, Joseph Alexander
Gaston, Minnie L.
Gates, Paul Edward
Gatewood, Algie C.
Gatewood, Wallace Lavell
Gatlin, Elissa L.
Gault, Marian Holness
Gavin, L. Katherine
Gayle, Lucille Jordan
Gayles, Joseph Nathan Webster,
  Jr.
Gaymon, Nicholas Edward
George, Claude C.
Gerald, Arthur Thomas, Jr.
Germany, Sylvia Marie Armstrong
Gibbs, Sandra E.
Gibson, Betty M.
Gibson, John Thomas
Gibson, Sarah L.
Gibson, William M.
Gilbert, Fred D., Jr.
Gilbert, Shirl E., II
Giles, Willie Anthony, Jr.
Giles-Gee, Helen Foster
Gilliam, Roosevelt Sandy, Jr.
Gilmore, Charles Arthur
Gilmore, John T.
Gilreath, Coot, Jr.
Gist, Jessie M. Gilbert
Givens, Henry, Jr.
Glanton, Lydia Jackson
Glasgow, Douglas G.
Glenn, Cecil E.
Glenn, Wynola
Gloster, Hugh Morris
Glover, Agnes W.
Glover, Clarence Ernest, Jr.
Godbold, Donald Horace
Goddard, Rosalind Kent
Goins, Mary G.
Golden, Louie
Goldsby, W. Dean, Sr.
Gooden, Samuel Ellsworth
Goodloe, Celestine Wilson
Goodman, James Arthur, Sr.
Goodson, Frances Elizabeth
Goodwin, Della McGraw
Goodwin, Mercedier Cassandra de
  Freitas
Gordon, Bertha Comer
Gordon, Charles Eugene
Gore, Joseph A.
Gothard, Barbara Wheatley
Grace, Marcellus
Graham, Jo-Ann Clara
Graham, Precious Jewel
Grant, Claude DeWitt
Grant, James
Grant, McNair
Grauer, Gladys Barker
Gravenberg, Eric Von
Graves, Irene Amelia
Gray, Earl Haddon
Gray, James E.
Gray, Myrtle Edwards
Gray, Pearl Spears
Graydon, Wasdon, Jr.
Gray-Morgan, LaRuth H.
Grays, Mattelia Bennett
Grayson, Harry L.
Grear, Effie C.
Green, Eddie L.
Green, Liller
Green, Robert L.
Green, William Edward
Greene, Charles Lavant
Greene, Charles Rodgers
Greene, John Sullivan
Greene, William Henry L'Vel
Greenfield, Roy Alonzo
Greenwood, Charles H.
Greer, Tee S., Jr.
Griffin, Betty Sue

Griffin, Ervin Verome
Griffith, John H.
Griggs, Harry Kindell, Sr.
Griggs, James Clifton, Jr.
Griggs, Judith Ralph
Grigsby, Jefferson Eugene, III
Grigsby, Marshall C.
Grimes, Voni B.
Grimsley, Ethelyne
Grissett, Willie James
Groffrey, Frank Eden
Groomes, Freddie Lang
Groves, Delores Ellis
Groves, Harry Edward
Guillaume, Alfred Joseph, Jr.
Guillory, William A.
Guiton Hill, Bonnie
Gumms, Emmanuel George, Sr.
Gunn, Gladys
Gurley, Helen Ruth
Guyton, Sister Patsy
Gwin, Wiliviginia Faszhianato
Gwynn, Florine Evayonne
Habersham-Parnell, Jeanne
Hackett, Obra V.
Hackley, Lloyd Vincent
Hagan, Willie James
Hair, John
Hairstone, Marcus A.
Haley, Johnetta Randolph
Hall, Addie June
Hall, Christine C. Iijima
Hall, David
Hall, Delilah Ridley
Hall, Dolores Brown
Hall, Ethel Harris
Hall, Jesse J.
Hall, Perry Alonzo
Hall, Robert Johnson
Hamilton, Theophilus Elliott
Hammett, Willie Anderson
Hammond, Benjamin Franklin
Hammond, Kenneth Ray
Hammonds, Cleveland, Jr.
Haney, Darnel L.
Haqq, Khalida Ismail
Hardcastle, James C.
Hardeman, Carole Hall
Hardin, Henry E.
Hardwick, Clifford E., III
Hardy, Dorothy C.
Hare, Linda Paskett
Hargrave, Benjamin
Harleston, Bernard Warren
Harmon, William Wesley
Harper, Eugene, Jr.
Harper, Joseph W., III
Harrigan, Rodney Emile
Harrington, Philip Leroy
Harris, Arthur Leonard, III
Harris, Calvin D.
Harris, Carl Gordon
Harris, Cynthia Julian
Harris, Dolores M.
Harris, James E.
Harris, Jasper William
Harris, Joseph John, III
Harris, Joseph R.
Harris, Marjorie Elizabeth
Harris, MaryAnn
Harris, Narvie J.
Harris, Robert L., Jr.
Harris, Ruth Coles
Harris, Sidney E.
Harris, Vander E.
Harris, Walter, Jr.
Harris, Wesley L.
Harris, William H.
Harris, William M.
Harris, Winifred Clarke
Harris, Zelema M.
Harrison, Beverly E.
Harrison, Emma Louise
Harrison, Ernest Alexander
Harrison, Mernoy Edward, Jr.
Harrison-Jones, Lois
Harris-Pinkelton, Norma
Hart, Barbara McCollum
Hart, Emily
Hart, Jacqueline D.
Hart, Noel A.
Hartman, Hermene Demaris
Hartzog, Ernest E.
Harvey, Louis-Charles
Harvey, William Henry L'Vel
Hatton, Barbara R., PhD.
Hauser, Charlie Brady
Hawk, Charles N., Jr.
Hawkins, Andre

Hawkins, Gene
Hawkins, James
Hawkins, Lawrence C.
Hawkins, Muriel A.
Hayden, John Carleton
Hayden, Robert C., Jr.
Hayes, Leola G.
Hayes, Marion LeRoy
Hayman, Warren C.
Haynes, Alphonso Worden
Haynes, Barbara Asche
Haynes, James H.
Haynes, John Kermit
Haynes, Sue Blood
Haynes, Ulric St. Clair, Jr.
Haynes, Willie C., III
Hayre, Ruth Wright
Hazzard, Terry Louis
Hazzard, Walter R.
Hearn, Rosemary
Heath, Comer, III
Hedgepeth, Chester Melvin, Jr.
Hedgespeth, George T., Jr.
Hefner, James A.
Heidt, Ellen Sullivan
Hemby, Dorothy Jean
Hemphill, Frank
Henderson, George
Henderson, James H.
Henderson, James H. M.
Henderson, John L.
Henderson, Joyce Ann
Henderson, Lloyd D.
Henderson, Romeo Clanton
Henderson, Stephen E.
Henderson, Theresa Crittenden
Henry, Charles E.
Henry, Forest T., Jr.
Henry, John Wesley, Jr.
Henry, Joseph King
Henry, Joseph Louis
Henry, Marcelett Campbell
Henry, Samuel Dudley
Henry, Warren Elliott
Henson, David Bernard
Henson, William L.
Herbert, Adam, Jr.
Herd, John E.
Herenton, Willie W.
Herrell, Astor Yeary
Heyward, James Oliver
Hiatt, Dana Sims
Hibbert, Dorothy Lasalle
Hicklin, Fannie
Hickman, Garrison M.
Hicks, Arthur James
Hicks, Daisy C.
Hicks, Doris Askew
Hicks, Edith A.
Hicks, Raymond A.
Higgins, Cleo Surry
Hightower, Herma J.
Hill, Dianne
Hill, George C.
Hill, John C.
Hill, Julia H.
Hill, Pearl M.
Hill, Richard Nathaniel
Hill, Robert Bernard
Hill, Rosalie A.
Hilliard, Asa Grant, III
Hilson, Arthur Lee
Hinton, Hortense Beck
Hixson, Judson Lemoine
Hodge, Charles Mason
Hodge, W. J.
Hoff, Nathaniel Hawthorne
Hogan, Fannie Burrell
Hogges, Ralph
Holbert, JoAnne
Hollar, Milton Conover
Holliday, Frances B.
Hollin, Kenneth Ronald
Hollins, Joseph Edward
Holloway, Ernest Leon
Holloway, Ernestine
Holloway, J. Mills
Holloway, Jerry
Holmes, Everlena M.
Holmes, Lorene B.
Holmes, Robert A.
Holmes, Zan W., Jr.
Holt, Dorothy L.
Holt, Essie W.
Holt, Grace S.
Holt, Kenneth Charles
Holton, Priscilla Browne
Honeycutt, Andrew E.
Hooker, Eric H.

Mikell, Charles Donald
Miles, Carlotta G.
Miles, E. W.
Miller, Andrea Lewis
Miller, Carroll Lee
Miller, Doris Jean
Miller, Dorsey Columbus, Jr.
Miller, Earl Vonnidore
Miller, Erenest Eugene
Miller, Jacqueline Elizabeth
Miller, John H.
Miller, M. Sammye
Miller, Margaret Greer
Miller, Marquis David
Miller, Mattie Sherryl
Miller, Melvin Allen
Miller, Richard Charles
Miller, Telly Hugh
Miller-Holmes, Cheryl
Mills, Mary Elizabeth
Milton, Octavia Washington
Mims, George L.
Minor, Emma Lucille
Minor, Willie
Minter, Eloise Devada
Minter, Thomas Kendall
Mitchell, Horace
Mitchell, Joann
Mitchell, Joseph Christopher
Mitchell, JudyLynn
Mitchell, Julius P.
Mitchell, Katherine Phillips
Mitchell, Marian Bartlett
Mitchell, Ossie Ware
Mitchell, Robert L.
Mitchell, Tex Dwayne
Mitchell-Kernan, Claudia Irene
Mitchem, Arnold Levy
Mitchem, John Clifford
Mobley, Sybil C.
Mohr, Paul B.
Moland, Willie C.
Monroe, Charles Edward
Monroe, Lillie Mae
Montague, Lee
Monteiro, Marilyn D.S.
Monteiro, Thomas
Montgomery, Oscar Lee
Montgomery, Trent
Moody, Charles David, Sr.
Moody, Harold L.
Moore, Albert
Moore, Alice Evelyn
Moore, Archie Bradford, Jr.
Moore, Beverly
Moore, Christine James
Moore, Eddie N., Jr.
Moore, Floreese Naomi
Moore, Gary E.
Moore, Helen D. S.
Moore, Jean E.
Moore, Juliette R.
Moore, Larry Louis
Moore, Nathan
Moore, Parlett Longworth
Moore, Richard Earle
Moore, Richard V.
Moore, Rodney Gregory
Mooring, Kittye D.
Morant, Mack Bernard
Moreland, Lois Baldwin
Moreland, Sallie V.
Moreland-Young, Curtina
Morgan, Joseph L.
Morgan, Robert W., II
Morial, Sybil Haydel
Morris, Charles Edward, Jr.
Morris, Dolores Orinskia
Morris, Ernest Roland
Morris, Frank Lorenzo, Sr.
Morris, Leibert Wayne
Morris, Lewis R.
Morris, Major
Morris, Stanley E., Jr.
Morrison, Gwendolyn Christine
   Caldwell
Morrison, Keith Anthony
Morrison, Richard David
Mortel, Rodrigue
Mortimer, Delores M.
Morton, Lorraine H.
Mosby, Carolyn Lewis
Moses, Henry A.
Moses, Yolanda T.
Moss, Simeon F.
Moss, Wilmar Burnett, Jr.
Mullett, Donald L.
Murdock, Patricia Green
Murphy, Margaret Humphries

Murray, Sylvester
Murray, Thomas Azel, Sr.
Murrell, Barbara Curry
Muse, Willie L.
Myers, Ernest Ray
Myles, Herbert John
Myrick, Howard A., Jr.
Nabrit, James M., Jr.
Nance, M. Maceo, Jr.
Nayman, Robbie L.
Neal, Edna D.
Neal, Ira Tinsley
Neely, David E.
Nellums, Michael Wayne
Nelson, Debra J.
Nelson, H. Viscount, Jr.
Nelson, Ivory Vance
Nelson, Wanda Lee
Netterville, George Leon, Jr.
Neufville, Mortimer H.
Newberry, Trudell McClelland
Newkirk, Gwendolyn
Newkirk, Thomas H.
Newlin, Rufus K.
Newsome, Emanuel T.
Newsome, Moses, Jr.
Newson, Roosevelt, Jr.
Newton, James E.
Neyland, Leedell Wallace
Nichols, Owen D.
Nicholson, Alfred
Nickson, Sheila Joan
Nimmons, Julius F., Jr.
Nixon, Harold L.
N'Namdi, Carmen Ann
Noble, John Charles
Norrell-Nance, Rosalind Elizabeth
Norrell-Thomas, Sondra
Norris, Lonnie H.
Northcross, Deborah Ametra
Norwood, Tom
Nunnally, David H., Sr.
Nurse, Richard A.
Nutt, Ambrose Benjamin
Nwagbaraocha, Joel O.
O'Bryant, Beverly J.
Oden, Walter Eugene
O'Donnell, Lorena Mae
Oglesby, James Robert
Okunor, Shiame
Oldham, Algie Sidney, Jr.
Ollee, Mildred W.
O'Neale, Sondra
Ortiz, Delia
Osborne, Alfred E., Jr.
Outlaw, Warren Gregory
Overton-Adkins, Betty Jean
Owens, Angle B., Jr.
Owens, Curtis
Owens, George A.
Owens, Jerry Sue
Owens, Robert Leon, III
Owens, Thomas C., Jr.
Paddio-Johnson, Eunice Alice
Padulo, Louis
Page, Marguerite A.
Paige, Roderick
Palmer, Dennis, III
Palmer, Elliott B., Sr.
Palmer, Noel
Parham, James B.
Parker, Fred Lee Cecil
Parker, Herbert Gerald
Parker, Jacquelyn Heath
Parker, Matthew
Parker, Paul E.
Parks, Arnold Grant
Parks, Thelma Reece
Paschal, Willie L.
Pates, Harold
Patrick, Julius, Jr.
Patrick, Opal Lee Young
Patterson, Cecil Lloyd
Patterson, Christine Ann
Patterson, Evelynne
Patterson, Joan Delores
Patterson, Joan Lethia
Patton, Gerald Wilson
Patton, Joyce Bradford
Payne, James Floyd
Payne, Jerry Oscar
Payne, Margaret Ralston
Payne, Mitchell Howard
Payne, N. Joyce
Payne, Richelle Denise
Payne, Vernon
Payton, Benjamin Franklin
Payton, Carolyn Robertson
Peagler, Owen F.

Pegues, Robert L., Jr.
Pegues, Wennette West
Peguese, Charles R.
Pendleton, Bertha Mae Ousley
Pendleton, Florence Howard
Penelton, Barbara Spencer
Penn, Nolan E.
Pennington, Leenette Morse
Pennywell, Phillip, Jr.
Peoples, Gerald
Peoples, Gregory Allan
Peoples, John Arthur, Jr.
Peoples, Joyce P.
Peoples, L. Kimberly
Peoples, Sesser R.
Peoples, VerJanis Andrews
Perdue, George
Perdue, John F.
Perdue, Wiley A.
Perine, James L.
Perkins, Myla Levy
Perry, Aubrey M.
Perry, Benjamin L., Jr.
Perry, Frank Anthony
Perry, Leonard Douglas, Jr.
Perry, Patsy Brewington
Perry, Robert Lee
Person, Dawn Renee
Peterman, Leotis
Peters, Fenton
Peterson, Lloyd, Jr.
Peterson, Marcella Tandy
Pettigrew, L. Eudora
Petty-Edwards, Lula Evelyn
Peyton, Jasper E.
Phelps, Constance Kay
Phelps, Donald Gayton
Phillip, Michael John
Phillips, Barbara
Phillips, Dilcia R.
Phillips, Frances Caldwell
Phillips, June M. J.
Phillips, Rosemarye L.
Pickett, Robert E.
Pierce, Reuben G.
Pierre, Percy Anthony
Pinkard, Deloris Elaine
Pinkney, Arnold R.
Pinkney, Betty Kathryn
Pinson, Margo Dean
Pitt, Clifford Sinclair
Pittman, Sample Noel
Pitts, Dorothy Louise Waller
Player, Willa B.
Pleasant, Albert E., III
Pleasant, Mae Barbee Boone
Pleasants, Charles Wrenn
Plummer-Talley, Olga Ann
Poellnitz, Fred Douglas
Pogue, Frank G., Jr.
Poindexter, Charles L. L.
Poindexter, Robert L.
Polite, Marie Ann
Polk, Lorna Marie
Polk, Robert L.
Pollard, Freeman Wallace
Pollard, Raymond J.
Pollard, William Lawrence
Ponder, Henry
Poole, Dillard M.
Poole, Rachel Irene
Porche-Burke, Lisa
Porter, Henry Lee
Porter, John W.
Porter, Otha L.
Portlock, Carver A.
Potts, Robert Lester
Potts, Sammie
Pounds, Augustine Wright
Pounds, Moses B.
Powell, Archie James
Powell, Leola P.
Powell, Myrtis H.
Prater, Oscar L.
Pratt, Alexander Thomas
Pratt, Mable
Prejean, Ruby D.
Prestage, James J.
Prestage, Jewel Limar
Prezeau, Maryse
Price, David Lee, Sr.
Price, Glenda Delores
Price, Paul Sanford
Price-Curtis, William
Primous, Emma M.
Primus-Cotton, Bobbie J.
Probasco, Jeanetta
Prothrow-Stith, Deborah Boutin
Provost, Marsha Parks

Pruitt, Anne Smith
Pruitt, George Albert
Pyke, Willie Oranda
Pyles, J. A.
Quarles, Ruth Brett
Quinn, Alfred Thomas
Raines, Walter R.
Rambo, Bettye R.
Ramsey, Henry, Jr.
Ramsey, James H.
Randall, Queen F.
Randle, Lucious A.
Randolph, Elizabeth
Randolph, James B.
Ransburg, Frank S.
Ransom, Lillie
Rao, Koduru V. S.
Raphael, Bernard Joseph
Rates, Norman M.
Rattley, Jessie M.
Rauch, Doreen E.
Rawlins, Elizabeth B.
Ray, Andrew
Rayburn, Wendell Gilbert
Ray-Goins, Jeanette
Reaves, Benjamin Franklin
Reaves, Ginevra N.
Reavis, John William, Jr.
Redd, Thomasina A.
Reddick, Alzo Jackson
Redmond, Jane Smith
Reed, Addison W.
Reed, Allene Wallace
Reed, Charlotte
Reed, James W.
Reed, Joann
Reed, Rodney J.
Reed, Vincent Emory
Reid, Benjamin F.
Reid, Irvin D.
Reid, Janie Ellen
Reid, Maude K.
Reid, Miles Alvin
Renick, James C.
Reynolds, Grant
Reynolds, Harry G.
Rhoades, Samuel Thomas
Ribeau, Sidney
Rice, Condoleezza
Rice, Constance Williams
Rice, Edward A.
Richard, R. Paul
Richards, Hilda
Richards, LaVerne W.
Richards, Leon
Richardson, Charles Ronald
Richardson, DeRutha Gardner
Richardson, Earl Stanford
Richardson, Leo
Richardson, Luns C.
Richardson, Mary Margaret
Richardson, Odis Gene
Richardson, Roger Gerald
Richmond, Tyronza R.
Ricks, George R.
Ridley, Harry Joseph
Ridley, May Alice
Ridley, Walter N.
Riggins, Lester
Rigsby, Esther Martin
Riley, Dorothy Winbush
Rinsland, Roland D.
Ritchey, Mercedes B.
Rivers, Robert Joseph, Jr.
Rivers, Vernon Frederick
Robbins, Herman C.
Roberson, Earl
Roberts, Alfred Lloyd, Sr.
Roberts, Bryndis Wynette
Roberts, Edward A.
Roberts, Grady H., Jr.
Roberts, Hermese E.
Roberts, Lorraine Marie
Roberts, Paquita Hudson
Roberts, Roy J.
Robertson, Evelyn Crawford, Jr.
Robertson, Quincy L.
Robertson, Quindonell S.
Robinson, Alfreda P.
Robinson, Andrew
Robinson, Charlotte L.
Robinson, Eunice Primus
Robinson, Harry G., III
Robinson, Jeannette
Robinson, Martha Dolores
Robinson, Prezell Russell
Robinson, S. Yolanda
Robinson, Samuel
Robinson, Thelma Maniece

Robinson, Walter G.
Robinson, Willie C.
Rodgers, Augustus
Rodgers, Joseph James, Jr.
Rodgers, Shirley Marie
Rogers, Decatur Braxton
Rogers, George, III
Rogers, Oscar Allan, Jr.
Rogers, Peggy J.
Rogers-Reece, Shirley
Rollins, Richard Albert
Roney, Raymond G.
Roper, Bobby L.
Roscoe, Wilma J.
Ross, Anthony Roger
Ross, Ralph M.
Ross-Audley, Cheryl Jvonne
Rosser, James M.
Ross-Lee, Barbara
Roulhac, Edgar Edwin
Roulhac, Nellie Gordon
Roussell, Norman
Rowe, Christa F.
Royster, Philip M.
Rudd, Charlotte Johnson
Ruffin, Paulette Francine
Runnels, Bernice
Russell, Dian Bishop
Russell, Ermea J.
Russell, James A., Jr.
Russell, John Peterson, Jr.
Russell, Joseph J.
Russell, Maurice V.
Russell, Milicent De'Ance
Rutherford, Harold Phillip, III
Rutledge, Philip J.
Ryder, Georgia Atkins
Salmond, Jasper
Samuels, Charlotte
Sanders, Gwendolyn W.
Sanders, Isaac Warren
Sanders, Lou Helen
Sanders, Robert B.
Sands, Mary Alice
Sands, Rosetta F.
Satcher, Robert Lee, Sr.
Saunders, Elizabeth A.
Saunders, Mary Alice
Saunders, William Joseph
Saunders-Henderson, Martha M.
Savage, Archie Bernard, Jr.
Savage, William Arthur
Sawyer, William Gregory
Schexnider, Alvin J.
Scott, Basil Y.
Scott, Gloria Dean Randle
Scott, Hosie L.
Scott, Hugh J.
Scott, Juanita Simons
Scott, Julius S., Jr.
Scott, Levan Ralph
Scott, Mona Vaughn
Scruggs, Allie W.
Scruggs, Booker T., II
Seals, Maxine
Seaton, Shirley Smith
Seay, Norman R.
Sellers, Thomas J.
Sellers, Walter G.
Seneca, Arlena E.
Sergeant, Carra Susan
Sessons, Allen Lee
Sevillian, Clarence Marvin
Shabazz, Betty
Shade, Barbara J.
Shakir, Adib Akmal
Shakoor, Waheedah Aqueelah
Shannon, David Thomas, Sr.
Shannon, Robert F.
Sharp, Jean Marie
Sharpe, Audrey Howell
Shaw, Mary Louise
Shaw, Talbert Oscall
Sheftall, Willis B., Jr.
Shelton, Jewell Vennerie (Elvoid)
Shepherd, Benjamin A.
Shepherd, Greta Dandridge
Sherrell, Charles Ronald, II
Sherrill, William Henry
Shipley, Anthony J.
Shropshire, John Sherwin
Shuford, Humphrey Lewis
Sills, Gregory D.
Silvey, Edward
Simmelkjaer, Robert T.
Simmons, Charles William
Simmons, Esmeralda
Simmons, Howard L.
Simmons, James E.

Yizar, James Horace, Jr.
Young, Aner Ruth
Young, Barbara J.
Young, Charles, Jr.
Young, Lawrence W., Jr.
Young, Marechal-Neil Ellison
Young, Nancy Wilson
Young, Ollie L.
Young, Rufus King
Young, Terri Jones
Younger, Celia Davis
Zambrana, Rafael
Zander, Jessie Mae
Zanders, Alton Wendell
Zimmerman, Samuel Lee
Zollar, Doris L.

Electronics

See **Computer Science—Programming/Software Development; Computer Science—Systems Analysis/Design; Computer Science—Not Elsewhere Classified; Engineering—Electrical/Electronics; Retail Trade—Electrical/Electronics Products; Wholesale Trade—Electrical/Electronics Products**

Engineering—Aerospace

Armstead, Wilbert Edward, Jr.
Austin, Wanda M.
Bailey, Antoinette M.
Bluford, Grady L.
Bluford, Guion Stewart, Jr.
Bolden, Charles E.
Bryant, William Henry, Jr.
Bynes, Glenn Kenneth
Carter, Arlington N.
Crossley, Frank Alphonso
Crump, Nathaniel L., Sr.
Curbeam, Robert L.
Darden, Christine Mann
Davenport, J. Lee
Day, John H., Jr.
Doty, Romeo A.
Dual, J. Fred, Jr.
Dunn, W. Paul
Ferguson, Robert Lee, Sr.
Freeman, Walter Eugene
Garrett, James F.
Gillispie, William Henry
Gorman, Bertha Gaffney
Graham, Odell
Grant, John H., Sr.
Greene, Lionel Oliver, Jr.
Grooms, Henry Randall
Hadden, Eddie Raynord
Hamlet, James Frank
Harris, Wesley L.
Hervey, Billy T.
Holley, Vance Maitland
Hornbuckle, Napoleon
House, James E.
Jackson, Earl C.
Jenkins, Luther Neal
Jensen, Renaldo Mario
Jones, Larry Wayne
Jordan, George Washington, Jr.
King, James, Jr.
Lang, Charles J.
Lawson, Anthony Eugene, Sr.
Lewis, James Earl
Lewis, Robert Alvin, Jr.
McCalla, Erwin Stanley
McLean, Dennis Ray
Meeks, Willis Gene
Mehlinger, Kermit Thorpe
Murphy, Alvin Hugh
Myers, Earl T.
Nutt, Ambrose Benjamin
Parker, James L.
Perkins, Gladys Patricia
Phillips, John Jason, II
Porter, Michael Anthony
Powe, Joseph S.
Pualani, Gloria
Ragsdale, Charles Lea Chester
Randolph, Bernard P.
Rogers, Charles Leonard
Rose, Raymond Edward
Rucks, Alfred J.
Samara, Noah Azmi
Sampson, Henry Thomas
Sheffey, Fred C.

Smithers, Oral Lester, Jr.
Taylor, Julius H.
Voldase, Iva Sneed
Wagner, Vallerie Denise
Walker, Willie M.
Weaver, Frank Cornell
Whitlow, Woodrow, Jr.
Wilkins, Roger L.
Wright, Linwood Clinton
Zeno, Willie D.

Engineering—Chemical

Adeyiga, Adeyinka A.
Bauldock, Gerald
Cannon, Joseph Nevel
Dawkins, Michael James
Edwards, Robert Valentino
Evans, Milton L.
Frazier, Julie A.
Herrell, Astor Yeary
Howard, Donald R.
Jacobs, Larry Ben
Levister, Ernest Clayton, Jr.
Lindsay, Eddie H. S.
Marchand, Melanie Annette
Parnell, Arnold W.
Patrick, Jennie R.
Stancell, Arnold Francis
Tufon, Chris
Wilson, Ray F.
Winston, Hubert
Wood, Jerome H., Jr.

Engineering—Civil

Amory, Reginald L.
Apea, Joseph Bennet Kyeremateng
Atkins, Richard
Bass, Joseph Frank
Bates, Valentino Travis
Bell, James L., Jr.
Blunt, Madelyne Bowen
Bowser, Benjamin Paul
Bowser, McEva R.
Cooper, Lois Louise
Cotton, Garner
Davis, James Edgar
Davis, Leonard Harry
Davis, Lester E.
DeHart, Henry R.
Emeagwali, Philip
Ewing, James Melvin
Flakes, Larry Joseph
Ford, Kenneth A.
Gray, Valerie Hamilton
Hadnot, Thomas Edward
Hampton, Delon
Harding, John Edward
Hicks, William L.
Humphrey, Howard John
Jackson, John, III
Jackson, Larry Eugene
Jeffries, Freddie L.
Jones, James Bennett
Jones, Raymond Morris
Jordan, Frederick E.
Kennedy, Nathelyne Archie
Kidd, Charles C., Sr.
Ligon, Claude M.
McGee, Waddell
Moore, Charlie W.
Olapo, Olaitan
Overstreet, Everett Louis
Patin, Jude W. P.
Powell, Juan Herschel
Powers, Mamon M., Jr.
Ramey, Melvin R.
Robinson, Curtis L.
Robinson, Hugh Granville
Rohadfox, Ronald Otto
Sinclair, Benito A.
Smith, William Howard
Staley, Kenneth Bernard
Taylor, Gayland Wayne
Thacker, Floyd Gary
Tucker, Paul, Jr.
Weaver, Herbert C.
White, Charles R.
White, Donald F.
Winfield, George Lee

Engineering—Electrical/Electronics

Adkins, Rodney C.
Alexander, Louis G., Sr.
Alwan, Mansour

Anderson, Kenneth Richard
Asom, Moses T.
Bagley, Gregory P.
Barrett, Richard O.
Bell, Ngozi O.
Blalock, Marion W.
Bray, Leroy, Sr.
Brewer, Gregory Alan
Brown, Roderick
Brunson, Frank
Bryant, Anthony
Burkett, Gale E.
Butts, Craig E.
Byrd, Herbert Lawrence, Jr.
Colson, Joseph S., Jr.
Cooper, Daneen Ravenell
Courtney, Stephen Alexander
Demby, James E.
Diamond, John R.
Doddy, Reginald Nathaniel
Douglas, Joseph Francis
Douglass, Robert Lee
Driver, Johnie M.
Ellis, Johnell A.
Ferguson, Sherlon Lee
Floyd, Vernon Clinton
Garrett, Cain, Jr.
Gaylor, Adolph Darnell
Graham, Odell
Gray, Maceo
Green, Joseph, Jr.
Green, Lester L.
Hardie, Robert L., Jr.
Hargrove, Andrew
Harper, Sarah Elizabeth Grubbs
Harris, Bryant G.
Harris, Gary Lynn
Harris, Larry Vordell, Jr.
Harris, Vernon Joseph
Herndon, Harold Thomas, Sr.
Hill, Raymond A.
Hornbuckle, Napoleon
Javery, Michael
Johnson, Earl
Johnson, Frederick E.
Jones, William J.
Jordan, George Washington, Jr.
Keyser, George F.
King, John G.
King, Reginald F.
Knight, Lynnon Jacob
Lawrence, Rodell
Leaphart, Eldridge
Lewis, James Earl
Mabson, Glenn T.
Madison, Ronald L.
Mallebay-Vacqueur Dem, Jean Pascal
Marius, Kenneth Anthony
Marsh, Alphonso Howard
McCraw, Tom
McDonald, William Emory
McLaurin, Jasper Etienne
Melrose, Thomas S.
Melton, Bryant
Miller, Theodore H.
Mitchell, Jacob Bill
Montague, Nelson C.
Monteith, Henry C.
Murray, Spencer J., III
Nash, Henry Gary
Nelson, Edward O.
Nibbs, Alphonse, Sr.
Nichols, Nick
Overall, Manard
Owens, David Kenneth
Padulo, Louis
Parham, Frederick Russell
Parker, Darwin Carey
Polk, George Douglas
Pollard, Muriel Ransom
Ransom, Preston L.
Rogers, Charles Leonard
Rose, Bessie L.
Rucks, Alfred J.
Russell, Wesley L.
Sanders, Rober LaFayette
Sechrest, Edward Amacker
Shelton, Roy Cresswell, Jr.
Sherman, Thomas Oscar, Jr.
Smith, Dennis Rae
Smith, Roger Leroy
Spencer, Michael Gregg
Stanley, Columbus Landon, Sr.
Stephens, Wallace O'Leary
Stewart, Malcolm M.
Strachan, Lloyd Calvin, Jr.
Stricklin, James
Taylor, Ellis Clarence, Sr.

Taylor, Kenneth Doyle
Terrell, Richard Warren
Thaxton, June E.
Thorpe, Herbert Clifton
Turner, Allen H.
Vereen, Michael L.
Vivians, Nathaniel Roosevelt
Waddell, Theodore R.
Walker, Ernest L.
Walker, Willie M.
Wallace, Richard Warner
Washington, Darryl McKenzie
Waters, William L.
Watkins, John M., Jr.
Wesley, Clemon Herbert, Jr.
White, William J.
Whitlow, Barbara Wheeler
Williams, Cheryl L.
Williamson, Samuel R.
Woodie, Henry L.
Worthey, Richard E.
Younger, Robert D.

Engineering—Industrial

Crumpton, Lesia
Elliott, J. Russell
Esogbue, Augustine O.
Hatter, Henry
Jenkins, Woodie R., Jr.
Jennings, Everett Joseph
King, Hulas H.
Lewis, Cleveland Arthur
Lillard, Kwame Leo
Lovelace, Onzalo Robert
Mills, Lois Terrell
Mitchell, Jacob Bill
Moody, Cameron Dennis
Nnaji, Bartholomew O.
Nutt, Ambrose Benjamin
Rakestraw, Kyle Damon
Richards, William Earl
Spencer, Brenda L.
Stith, Antoinette Freeman
Tynes, Richard H.
Umolu, Sheila Andrea
Ware, Albert M.
Washington, John Calvin, III
Winslow, Reynolds Baker

Engineering—Mechanical

Barnes, Matthew Molena, Jr.
Barton, Rhonda L.
Beck, Clark E.
Borum, Regina A.
Bryant, William Henry, Jr.
Butler, John O.
Charlton, Jack Fields
Colvin, Alex, II
Daniels, Jerry Franklin
Davis, James A.
Dorsey, Herman Sherwood, Jr.
Elliott, J. Russell
Fearing, John T.
Fleming, David Aaron
Franklin, Benjamin
Gee, William Rowland, Jr.
Godbolt, Ricky Charles
Harper, Sarah Elizabeth Grubbs
Hooker, Douglas Randolf
Hull, Bernard S.
Jackson, Earl C.
Jackson, Joseph T.
Johnson, Carl Elliott
Johnston, Wallace O.
Keyes, Andrew Jonathan, Sr.
King, Lawrence Patrick
Lartigue, Roland E.
Lewis, Cleveland Arthur
Lowe, Sylvia Oneice
Marshall, Donald James
McCuiston, Stonewall, Jr.
Murphy, Alvin Hugh
Neal, Eddie
Parker, Irvin
Parnell, Arnold W.
Pogue, Brent Daryl
Porter, Michael Anthony
Reed, Cordell
Reeves, Julius Lee
Riddick, Eugene E.
Rohr, Leonard Carl
Slater, Phyllis Hill
Taylor, Edward Walter
Trueblood, Vera J.
Tufon, Chris
Verbal, Claude A.
Walker, M. Lucius, Jr.

Ware, Albert M.
Watkins, Charles B., Jr.
Webster, Cecil Ray
Williams, James H., Jr.

Engineering—Metallurgical/Ceramic/Materials

Bragg, Joseph L.
Bragg, Robert Henry
Chapman, Gilbert Bryant, II
Charlton, Jack Fields
Crossley, Frank Alphonso
Dixon, Louis Tennyson
Evans, Billy J.
Freeman, Walter Eugene
Hawkins, Walter Lincoln
McClendon, Raymond
Mitchell, James Winfield
Phillips, Edward Martin
Sigur, Wanda Anne Alexander
Trent, John Spencer

Engineering—Mining (*See Also* **Mining/Quarrying**)

Hughes, Johnnie Lee

Engineering—Nuclear

Jupiter, Clyde Peter
Knox, Wayne Harrison
LeVert, Francis E.
Lewis, Kenneth Dwight
Marsh, Alphonso Howard
Miller, Warren F., Jr.
Pogue, Brent Daryl
Snowden, Phillip Ray
Trappier, Arthur Shives

Engineering—Petroleum

Avery, James S.
Coshburn, Henry S., Jr.
Granville, William, Jr.
Grimes, Darlene M. C.
Kirklin, Perry William
Landers, Naaman Garnett
Lee, Robert Emile
Riddick, Eugene E.
Shackelford, George Franklin

Engineering—Not Elsewhere Classified

Ambeau, Karen M.
Armstead, Wilbert Edward, Jr.
Behrmann, Serge T.
Bland, Heyward
Bowser, McEva R.
Brailey, Troy
Brooks, A. Russell
Brooks, John S.
Brown, Gary W.
Caines, Ken
Callender, Leroy R.
Carter, Troy A.
Cooley, Keith Winston
Davis, Leonard Harry
Davis, Nathaniel Alonzo
Dixon, Louis Tennyson
Donaldson, Richard T.
Eason, Oscar, Jr.
Esquerre, Jean Roland
Eziemefe, Godslove Ajenavi
Ferguson, Sherlon Lee
Finn, Robert Green
Gaither, James W., Jr.
Gartrell, Luther R.
Gay, Eddie C.
Goodwin, Donald Edward
Gothard, Donald L.
Graham, Frederick Mitchell
Griffin, Floyd Lee, Jr.
Griffin, Michael D.
Grooms, Henry Randall
Henderson, Charles
Hill, Robert J., Jr.
Hooker, Douglas Randolf
Howard, Tanya Millicent
Irons, Paulette
Jackson, Richard H.
Javery, Michael
Jenkins, Woodie R., Jr.
Johnson, Earl
Johnson, Frederick E.

Kennedy, Nathelyne Archie
Kidd, Charles C., Sr.
Lambert, Samuel Fredrick
Lue-Hing, Cecil
Mabrey, Ernest L., Jr.
Madison, Shannon L.
Martin, Montez Cornelius, Jr.
McCuiston, Frederick Douglass, Jr.
McDonald, Willie Ruth Davis
Morgan, Haywood, Sr.
Morgan, Robert, Jr.
Murphy, Alvin Hugh
Murray, Gary S.
Neal, Curtis Emerson, Jr.
Neal, Eddie
Pattman, Virgil Thomas, Sr.
Phillips, John Jason, II
Porter, John T.
Purce, Thomas Les
Ratcliffe, Alfonso F.
Ray, Judith Diana
Richardson, Alfred Lloyd
Rogers, Elijah Baby
Sanders, Barbara A.
Sanders, Woodrow Mac
Sawyer, Deborah M.
Scribner, Arthur Gerald, Jr.
Seabrook, Bradley Maurice
Sims, Diane Marie
Snell, Joan Yvonne Ervin
Stallworth, Oscar B.
Sutton, Mary A.
Taylor, Kenneth Doyle
Tucker, Paul, Jr.
Turner, Franklin James
Vanderburg, Craig Terrence
Via, Thomas Henry
Webster, Theodore
White, Quitman, Jr.
Wilhoit, Carl H.
Woodson, Tracy Todd

**Entertainment/
Recreation—Not
Elsewhere Classified**
(See Also **Acting; Dance/
Choreography;
Directing/Producing
(Performing Arts);
Music—Composing/
Songwriting; Music—
Conducting/Directing;
Music—Instrumental;
Music—Vocal; Music—
Not Elsewhere
Classified; Sports—
Amateur; Sports—
Professional/
Semiprofessional;
Sports—Not Elsewhere
Classified)**
Amin, Karima
Anderson, Bernadine M.
Anderson, Tony
Ashhurst, Carmen
Atkins, Pervis
Avant, Clarence
Baki
Barnes, Karen Michelle
Bateman, Celeste
Bell, Lawrence F.
Bell, S. Aaron
Bellamy, Bill
Blanc, Eric Anthony-Hawkins
Booth, William H.
Bowser, Yvette Lee
Boyd, Wilhemina Y.
Broughton, Christopher Leon
Brown, Debria M.
Brown, Joan P.
Brown, William T.
Burke, Kirkland R.
Carter, Daisy
Chamberlain, Wilt Norman
Clarke, Priscilla
Clash, Kevin
Clemons, Linda K.
Collins, Bernice Elaine
Cosby, Camille Olivia Hanks
Cosby, William Henry
Cumber, Victoria Lillian
Cummings, Terry
Dawson, Horace G., III
DeWindt, Hal
Douglas, Elizabeth Asche

Duke, Bill
Dupri, Jermaine
Durant-Paige, Beverly
Eckstine, Ed
Evans, Gregory James
Fay, Toni G.
Fearn-Banks, Kathleen
Folks, Leslie Scott
Goldberg, Whoopi
Gordon, Derek E.
Gray, F. Gary
Gregory, Richard Claxton
Griffey, Dick
Griffith, Gary Alan
Hagins, Ogbonna
Harris, Tricia R.
Harrison, Wendell Richard
Hart, Harold Rudoff
Haymon, Alan
Holden, Aaron Charles
Hollins, Leroy
Jackson, Eugene D.
Jackson, George
James, Toni-Leslie
Jeter, Clifton B., Jr.
Johnson, Chas Floyd
Johnson, Henry Wade
Johnson, Patricia L.
Jones, Donna L.
Jones, Gary
Joseph, Lloyd Leroi
Karpeh, Enid Juah Hildegard
Kilgore, Twanna Debbie
King, Gayle
Kountze, Vallery J.
Lawrence, Elliott
Lee, Debra Louise
Lewis, Charles Henry
Love, Darlene
Lythcott, Janice Logue
Mac, Bernie
MacLachlan, Janet A.
Martin Chase, Debra
Maxwell Reid, Daphne Etta
McElvane, Pamela Anne
McKayle, Donald Cohen
Mereday, Richard F.
Moore, Juliette R.
Morgan-Welch, Beverly Ann
Morris, Garrett
Moss, Carlton
Mumford, Thaddeus Quentin, Jr.
Murphy, Vanessa
Nellums, Michael Wayne
Okino, Elizabeth Anna
Parker, James L.
Parsons, Richard
Phelps, William Anthony
Pinkney, William D.
Pressley, DeLores
Richardson, Timothy L.
Riggins, Jean
Roberts, Virgil Patrick
Robinson, Ernest Preston, Sr.
Rolle, Janet
Ruffin, John Walter, Jr.
Russ, Timothy Darrell
Sabree, Clarice Salaam
Saunders, Theodore D.
Shaw, Spencer Gilbert
Simpson, Donnie
Smalls, Marva
Smith, Mary Carter
Sneed, Gregory J.
Stephens, Juanita K.
Stephney, Bill
Stewart, Horace W.
Sutton, Oliver Carter, II
Taylor, Almina
Taylor, Tyrone
Thompson, Oswald
Varner, Nellie M.
Walker, Tracy A.
Watson, Dennis Rahiim
Wheaton, Frank Kahlil
Williams, Russell, II
Wilson, Flip
Wilson, Madelaine Majette
Woodward, Aaron Alphonso, III
Young, Tommy Scott

Fashion Design
Adewumi, Jonathan
Banks, Jeffrey
Barkley, Rufus, Jr.
Bates, Barbara Ann
Dunmore, Gregory Charles
Fuller, Jack Lewis

Geran, Joseph, Jr.
Haggins, Jon
Hankins, Anthony Mark
Hilton, Stanley William, Jr.
Johnson, Marie Elizabeth
Kani, Karl
King, Shaka C.
Lockett, Bradford R.
May, Charles W.
McCants, Coolidge N.
McCray, Darryl K.
McGee, Benjamin Lelon
Miller-Lewis, S. Jill
Moore, Annie Jewell
Morgan, Rose
Perkins, Louvenia Black
Petterway, Jackie Willis
Ralph, Sheryl Lee
Saint James, Synthia
Smith, Dorothy O.
Williams, Ira Lee

Financial Services
See **Banking/Financial
Services; Management/
Administration—Accounting/
Financial**

**Fire Prevention and
Control**
Alfred, Rayfield
Blackshear, William
Bouie, Merceline
Brown, Carrye Burley
Brown, Thomas Edison, Jr.
Douglas, Joe, Jr.
Dyas, Patricia Ann
Edmonds, Curtis
Gladman, Charles R.
Golden, Samuel Lewis
Graham, Charlene
Hairston, Harold B.
Hart, Noel A.
Howard, Robert Berry, Jr.
Jackson, Frank Donald
Johnson, George, Jr.
Kimbrew, Joseph D.
Lewis, Ronald C.
Love, J. Gregory
Lowery, Robert O.
Math, John
McDonald, Alden J., Jr.
Neal, Sylvester
Nearn, Arnold Dorsey, Jr.
Parker, G. John, Sr.
Perry, Benjamin
Spaulding, Romeo Orlando
Stewart, Charles J.
Stewart, John B., Jr.
Sudderth, William H.
Tatem, Patricia Ann
Watkins, Harold D., Sr.
Wester, Richard Clark
Williams, Charles Earl

**Food and Beverage
Industry**
See **Manufacturing—Food/
Beverages; Restaurant/Food
Service Industry; Retail
Trade—Food and Beverages;
Wholesale Trade—Food and
Beverages**

Foreign Service
Adams, Samuel Clifford, Jr.
Baker, James E.
Boldridge, George
Brown, Warren Henry, Jr.
Burroughs, John Andrew, Jr.
Carter, George E.
Carter, William Beverly, III
Clyne, John Rennel
Cooper, LaMoyne Mason
Davis, Robert N.
Flemming, Charles Stephen
Fox, Richard K., Jr.
Golden, Myron
James, Charles Alexander
Jones, William Bowdoin
Kirby, Money Alian
LeMelle, Tilden J.
LeMelle, Wilbert John

Mack, John L.
McKenzie, Wilford Clifton
Moone, James Clark
Moose, George E.
Nelson, Charles J.
Palmer, Ronald DeWayne
Perkins, Edward Joseph
Perry, June Carter
Pinder, Frank E.
Reinhardt, John Edward
Render, Arlene
Shropshire, Harry W.
Skinner, Elliott P.
Spearman, Leonard Hall
O'Connell, Sr.
Todman, Terence A.
Walker, Howard Kent

Forestry/Forest Industries
Anderson, Russell Lloyd
Burse, Luther
Cartwright, Charles
Jackson, Charles N., II
Keene, Sharon C.
Wilds, Jetie Boston, Jr.
Williams, Carroll Burns, Jr.

Funeral Service
See **Mortuary Services**

**Gallery/Museum
Administration/
Education**
Baskin, Andrew Lewis
Batson, Ruth Marion
Beck, Arthello, Jr.
Benjamin, Rose Mary
Bibby, Deirdre L.
Booker, John, III
Booker, Robert Joseph
Brown, Joseph Clifton
Burroughs, Margaret Taylor
Camp, Kimberly
Campbell, Mary Schmidt
Clayton, Mayme Agnew
Conway, Wallace Xavier, Sr.
Conwill, Kinshasha
Crew, Spencer R.
Crossley, Charles R., II
Driskell, David C.
Eaton, James Nathaniel, Sr.
Felton, Zora Belle
Fleming, John Emory
Flewellen, Icabod
Gaither, Barry
Ghent, Henri Hermann
Gilliam, Sam, Jr.
Halfacre, Frank Edward
Harris, William Anthony
High, Freida
Hodges, David Julian
Holmes, E. Selean
Howard, Leslie Carl
Jackson, Earl, Jr.
Jeffries, Rosalind R.
Johnson, Patricia Anita
Kelley, Jack Albert
Lane, Julius Forbes
Lenix-Hooker, Catherine Jeanette
Lester, George Lawrence
Lewis, James Edward
Ligon, Doris Hillian
Martin, Frank C., II
McCray, Billy Quincy
Miller, Margaret Elizabeth Battle
Miller-Lewis, S. Jill
Montgomery, Evangeline Juliet
Moore, Marian J.
Newman, Constance Berry
Newsome, Steven Cameron
N'Namdi, George Richard
Parrish, Maurice Drue
Peerman-Pledger, Vernese Dianne
Pindell, Howardena D.
Porter, Michael LeRoy
Reagon, Bernice Johnson
Robbins, Warren
Robinson, Harry, Jr.
Rouse, Terrie
Sanders-Oji, J. Qevin
Saunders-Henderson, Martha M.
Shifflett, Lynne Carol
Sims, Lowery Stokes
Smythe, Victor N.
Stewart, Paul Wilbur

Stewart, Ruth Ann
Stovall, Melody S.
Taylor, Cledie Collins
Taylor, Gilbert Leon
Taylor, Pauline J.
Walker, Roslyn Adele
Washington, Sherry Ann
Williamson, Ethel W.

Geography
Hotchkiss, Wesley Akin
Jones, Marcus Earl
King, Thomas Lawrence
West, Herbert Lee, Jr.

Geology/Geophysics
Baskerville, Charles Alexander
Bromery, Randolph Wilson
Brown, Charles Edward
Norman, Bobby Don
Owens, Joan Murrell
Person, Waverly J.
Thomas, Sherri Booker
Underwood, Maude Esther
Williams, Cassandra Faye

Geophysics
See **Geology/Geophysics**

**Government Service
(Elected or Appointed)/
Government
Administration—City**
Adams, Floyd, Jr.
Adams, Joseph Lee, Jr.
Adams, T. Patton
Adams, Victorine Quille
Aldridge, Karen Beth
Alexander, Cornelia
Allen, Carol Ward
Allen, Charles Claybourne
Allen, Dozier T., Jr.
Allison, Vivian
Alwan, Mansour
Anderson, Pearl G.
Archer, Dennis Wayne
Arrington, Marvin
Arrington, Richard, Jr.
Arthur, George Kenneth
Ashton, Vivian Christina R.
Askew, Bonny Lamar
Atkins, Edmund E.
Atkins, Fredd
Austin, Carrie
Avent, Jacques Myron
Avery, Jeromye Lee
Ayers, Timothy F.
Bacon, Randall C.
Badger, Lloyd, Jr.
Badgett, Edward
Bailey, Duwain
Bailey, Harry A., Jr.
Baker, Sharon Smith
Baldwin, Olivia McNair
Bankett, William Daniel
Banks, Caroline Long
Banks, Garnie
Banks, Priscilla Sneed
Banks, Saundra Elizabeth
Barfield, Leila Millford
Barnes, Martin G.
Barnes, Thomas
Barnett, William
Barry, Marion Shepilov, Jr.
Barthelemy, Sidney John
Bass, Joseph Frank
Bateman, Celeste
Bates, Alonzo W.
Bather, Paul Charles
Battle, Joe Turner
Baylor, Emmett Robert, Jr.
Beal Bagneris, Michele Christine
Beasley, Annie Ruth
Beasley, Edward, III
Beatty, Charles Eugene, Sr.
Beatty, Pearl
Beck, Hershell P.
Beck, Saul L.
Beckham, William J., Jr.
Belardo de O'Neal, Lilliana
Bell, Elmer A.
Bell, George
Bell, Lawrence A., III

Bell, Wilhemenia
Bell, Winston Alonzo
Bell, Yvonne Lola
Belton, Sharon Sayles
Bennett, Arthur T.
Bennett, George P.
Bennett, Marion D.
Berry, Philip Alfonso
Bethea, Edwin Ayers
Bethea, Gregory Austin
Billups, Florence W.
Birru, Mulugetta
Blackshear, William
Blackwell, Faiger Megrea
Blackwell, Harvel E.
Blackwell, Robert B.
Blackwell-Hatcher, June E.
Blanford, Colvin
Bledsoe, Carolyn E. Lewis
Bolles, A. Lynn
Bolling, Deborah A.
Bolton, Wanda E.
Bonaparte, Lois Ann
Bonaparte, Norton Nathaniel, Jr.
Bond, Michael Julian
Boone, Clarence Wayne
Bosley, Thad
Bowens, Gregory John
Bowman, William McKinley, Sr.
Bowser, Vivian Roy
Boyd, Gwendolyn Viola, Dr.
Boykin, A. Wade, Jr.
Bradford, Steve
Bradley, Tom
Bremby, Roderick LeMar
Bronz, Lois Gougis Taplin
Brooks, Alvin Lee
Brooks, Christine D.
Brooks, Richard Leonard
Broussard, Arnold Anthony
Brown, Benjamin Leonard
Brown, Charlie
Brown, Chauncey I., Jr.
Brown, Constance Charlene
Brown, Evelyn
Brown, Evelyn Drewery
Brown, Hoyt C.
Brown, James Marion
Brown, Joseph Davidson, Sr.
Brown, Julius J.
Brown, Jurutha
Brown, Justine Thomas
Brown, LeRoy
Brown, Maxine J. Childress
Brown, Nancy Cofield
Brown, Otha N., Jr.
Brown, Stanley Donovan
Browne, Ernest C., Jr.
Brownridge, J. Paul
Bryant, Donnie L.
Bryant, Teresena Wise
Buggage, Cynthia Marie
Bullock, Thurman Ruthe
Burden, Pennie L.
Burke, Vivian H.
Burkeen, Ernest Wisdom, Jr.
Burleson, Jane Geneva
Burney, William D., Jr.
Burns, Clarence Du
Burrell, George Reed, Jr.
Burris, Chuck
Burts, Ezunial
Busby, V. Eugene
Bush, Gordon
Butler, Keith Andre
Butler, Pinkney L.
Byrd, Nellie J.
Cadogan, Marjorie A.
Caldwell, John Edward
Calhoun, Eric A.
Campbell, Mary Delois
Campbell, Mary Schmidt
Campbell, William
Campbell, William Earl
Cannon, Aleta
Carman, Edwin G.
Carpenter, Lewis
Carr, Lenford
Carter, Edward Earl
Carter, James
Carter, John R.
Carter, Judy Sharon
Carter, Mary Louise
Cates, Sidney Hayward, III
Cheatham, Betty L.
Cheatham, Linda Moye
Cherry, Theodore W.
Childs, Josie L.
Christian, John L.

Clancy, Magalene Aldoshia
Clark, Augusta Alexander
Clark, Leon Stanley
Clayborne, Oneal
Cleaver, Emanuel, II
Cleveland, Clyde
Clifford, Maurice C.
Cobb, Ethel Washington
Cobb, Harold
Cobbin, Gloria Constance
Cofer, James Henry
Cole, John L., Jr.
Cole, Joseph H.
Cole Carey, Wilhemina, PhD
Coleman, Avant Patrick
Coleman, Joseph E.
Coleman, Lemon, Jr.
Coleman, Michael Bennett
Coleman, Michael Victor
Coleman, Raymond Cato
Coleman, Robert A.
Colvin, Alonza James
Comer, Jonathan
Comer, Zeke
Conaway, Mary Ward Pindle
Conley, Emmitt Jerome
Conner, Marcia Lynne
Cooke, Wilce L.
Cooley, Nathan J.
Cooper, Cardell
Cooper, Maudine R.
Copeland, Kevon
Cousins, William, Jr.
Cox, Tyrone Y
Craig-Jones, Ellen Walker
Crawford, H. R.
Crawford, Lawrence Douglas
Crawley, Darline
Crawley, George Claudius
Crockett, George W., III
Croft, Ira T.
Cromartie, Ernest W., II
Cropp, Dwight Sheffery
Crow, Hiawatha Moore
Cunningham, Glenn Dale
Currie, Jackie
Daniels, Jesse
Daniels, John C.
Daniels, Preston
Dantley, Adrian Delano
Darkins, Duane Adrian
Darnell, Edward Buddy
Davenport, Lawrence Franklin
David, George F., III
Davidson, Alphonzo Lowell
Davidson, Robert C., Jr.
Davidson, Rudolph Douglas
Davidson-Harger, Joan Carole
Davis, Arthur, III
Davis, Carrie L. Filer
Davis, Harold
Davis, John W., III
Davis, L. Clifford
Dawkins, Miller J.
Deese, Manuel
DeHart, Henry R.
Dell, Willie J.
Demonbreun, Thelma M.
Denning, Joe William
Dennis, Shirley M.
Devereueawax, John L., III
Didlick, Wells S.
Dillard, Howard Lee
Dillard, Jackie Smith
Dixon, Ardena S.
Dixon, Lorraine L.
Dixon, Richard Clay
Dobbins, Albert Greene, III
Dobbins, Lucille R.
Doby, Allen E.
Dodson, Vivian M.
Donahue, William T.
Donegan, Charles Edward
Dotson-Williams, Henrietta
Douglass, Melvin Isadore
Dowell, Clyde Donald
Dowell-Cerasoli, Patricia R.
Downes, Dwight
Drake, Pauline Lilie
Drakeford, Jack
Drew-Peeples, Brenda
Driessen, Henry, Jr.
Duckett, Gregory Morris
Dudley, Herman T.
Dudley, Juanita C.
Dukes, Hazel Nell
Dumpson, James R.
Dupree, Edward A.
Echols, Alvin E.

Edwards, Luther Howard
Edwards, Shirley Heard
Edwards, Theodore Unaldo
Elder, Geraldine H.
Ellis, Rodney
Ellison, David Lee
English, Clarence R.
Esco, Fred, Jr.
Espy, Henry
Etheredge, James W.
Evaige, Wanda Jo
Evans, Elinor Elizabeth
Evans, Grover Milton, Sr.
Evans, Joe B.
Evans-McNeill, Elona Anita
Everett, Kay
Evers, James Charles
Ewing, James Melvin
Fairman, John Abbrey
Fisher, Robert F.
Fitzgerald, Howard David
Fitzgerald, Roy Lee
Fleming, June H.
Flemming, Lillian Brock
Fletcher, James C., Jr.
Flippins, Gregory L.
Fontayne, K. Nicole
Ford, Aileen W.
Ford, Johnny
Ford, Wallace L., II
Foster, E. C.
Fountain, William Stanley
Francis, James L.
Francisco, Anthony M.
Frazier, Dan E., Sr.
Frazier, Ray Jerrell
Frelow, Robert Lee, Jr.
Frost, William Henry
Frost, Wilson
Gaines, Paul Laurence, Sr.
Gallot, Richard Joseph
Gamble, Janet Helen
Gamble, Kenneth L.
Gamble, Robert Lewis
Gardner, Henry L.
Garner, Lon L.
Garner, Mary E.
Garrett, Joyce F.
Garrett, Paul C.
Gates, Audrey Castine
Gay, Helen Parker
Gayles, Franklin Johnson
Gayles, Lindsey, Jr.
Gentry, LaMar Duane
Gibson, James O.
Gibson, Kenneth Allen
Gibson, Paul, Jr.
Gilbert, Richard Lannear
Gilcreast, Conway, Sr.
Gilford, Rotea J.
Gilmore, Carter C.
Givens, E. Terrian
Givins, Abe, Jr.
Gonzaque, Ozie Bell
Goode, Calvin C.
Goodwin, Jesse Francis
Goodwin, Kelly Oliver Perry
Goodwin, Mercedier Cassandra de
   Freitas
Gordon, Charles D.
Gordon, Winfield James, Sr.
Goree, Janie Glymph
Graham, Catherine S.
Gray, Robert Dean
Gray, Robert R.
Gray, Valerie Hamilton
Green, Angelo Gray
Green, Darlene
Green, Forrest F.
Green, Larry W.
Green, Theodis Guy
Green, Thomas L., Sr.
Greene, Edith L.
Griffin, Ann White
Griffin, Percy Lee
Griffith, Vera Victoria
Hairston, Rowena L.
Hall, Anthony W., Jr.
Hall, Eugene Curtis
Hall, Katie
Hall, Raymond A.
Hall, Robert L.
Hamilton, Phanuel J.
Hamilton, Wilbur Wyatt
Hamilton-Rahi, Lynda Darlene
Hamlin, Arthur Henry
Hampton, Thomas Earle
Haney, Napoleon
Haralson, Larry L.

Hardin, Marie D.
Harmon, Clarence
Harrell, William Edwin
Harris, Clifton L.
Harris, Earl L.
Harris, Jerome C., Jr.
Harris, Joseph R.
Harris, Melvin
Harrold, Austin Leroy
Harvey, Gerald
Hatcher, Richard Gordon
Hayden, Frank
Hayes, Jim
Haymore, Tyrone
Head, Raymond, Jr.
Head, Samuel
Henderson, Erma L.
Henderson, Gerald Eugene
Henderson, Ronald
Herman, Kathleen Virgil
Hewitt, Ronald Jerome
Hewlett, Antoinette Payne
Hightower, Willar H., Jr.
Hill, Betty J.
Hill, Gilbert
Hill, James O.
Hill, Mary Alice
Hilliard, Delories
Hilliard, Patsy Jo
Hinch, Andrew Lewis, Sr.
Hines, Carl R., Sr.
Holden, Nate
Holder, Reuben D.
Holland, Loys Marie
Holland, Wallace E.
Holliday, Alfonso David
Holliday-Hayes, Wilhelmina
   Evelyn
Holmes, Gary Mayo
Holmes, Leo S.
Holmes, Litdell Melvin, Jr.
Hoover, Jesse
Horton, Dollie Bea Dixon
Howard, Osbie L., Jr.
Howard, Robert Berry, Jr.
Hubbard, Arnette Rhinehart
Hubbard, Paul Leonard
Huger, James E.
Hughes, Jimmy Franklin, Sr.
Hughes, Mamie F.
Hunt, Jeffrey C.
Hunter, Cecelia Corbin
Hutchins, Jan Darwin
Ingram, Robert B.
Isaac, Yvonne Renee
Jackson, Alvin B., Jr.
Jackson, Bobby L.
Jackson, Charles Ellis
Jackson, James Garfield
Jackson, John
Jackson, Leo Edwin
Jackson, Maynard Holbrook
Jackson, Pamela J.
Jackson, Richard E., Jr.
Jacobs, Hazel A.
James, Naomi Ellen
James, Sharpe
Jangdharrie, Wycliffe K.
Jarmon, James Henry, Jr.
Jarrett, Valerie B.
Jeffers, Ben L.
Jefferson, Clifton
Jefferson, Hilda Hutchinson
Jefferson, James E.
Jefferson, Robert R.
Jenkins, Andrew
Jenkins, John
Jenkins, Woodie R., Jr.
Johnson, Albert James
Johnson, Arthur T.
Johnson, B. A.
Johnson, Barbara C.
Johnson, Ben E.
Johnson, Beverley Ernestine
Johnson, Carroll Jones
Johnson, Clinton Lee, Sr.
Johnson, Harvey
Johnson, James A.
Johnson, James R.
Johnson, Joy J.
Johnson, Leon F.
Johnson, Marlene E.
Johnson, Phyllis Campbell
Johnson, R. Benjamin
Johnson, Sarah H.
Johnson, Walter Louis, Sr.
Johnson, Wendell L., Jr.
Johnson, Wilhelmina Lashaun
Johnson, William A., Jr.

Jones, Anthony, Jr.
Jones, Clarence J., Jr.
Jones, Cornell
Jones, Earl Frederick
Jones, Frank
Jones, Gerald E.
Jones, Irma Renae
Jones, Joni Lou
Jones, Lawrence W.
Jones, Leeland Newton, Jr.
Jones, Nathaniel, Sr.
Jones, Patricia Yvonne
Jones, Theresa Diane
Jones, Viola
Jones, William
Jordan, Marilyn E.
Jordan, Patricia Carter
Keels, James Dewey
Keith, Doris T.
Kelly, James Johnson
Kelly, Marion Greenup
Kelly, Sharon Pratt
Kenney, Walter T.
Kimber, Lesly H.
King, Cecilia D.
King, Ceola
King, John Thomas
Kirk, Ron
Kirven, Mythe Yuvette
Knight, Dewey W., Jr.
Knight, Walter R.
Knight, William Rogers
Knuckles, Kenneth J.
Laisure, Sharon Emily Goode
Lampkin, Cheryl Lyvette
Lander, Cressworth Caleb
Lane, Allan C.
Lang, Winston E.
Langham, John M.
Larkins, E. Pat
Lawson, Lawyer
Lawson, Quentin Roosevelt
Leake, Willie Mae James
LeCesne, Terrel M.
Lee, Aaron
Lee, Edward S.
Lee, Howard N.
Lee, Van Spencer
Leeke, Madelyn Cheryl
Leeper, Ronald James
Lemmie, Valerie
Lewis, Diane
Lewis, Diane Claire
Lewis, Richard U.
Lewis, Woodrow
Lindsey, S. L.
Lipscomb, Darryl L.
Lister, Willa M.
Locke, Henry Daniel, Jr.
Locke, Mamie Evelyn
Lofton, Andrew James
Lomax, Dervey A.
Lovelace, Dean Alan
Lucas, Earl S.
Lucas, Maurice F.
Ludley, Richard
Lyda, Wesley John
Lyle, Roberta Branche Blacke
Lyles, Marie Clark
Lynn, James Elvis
Mack, Gladys Walker
Mack, Levorn
Mahan-Powell, Lena
Makokha, James A. N.
Malone, Amanda Ella
Manager, Vada O'Hara
Mannie, William Edward
Mansfield, Andrew K.
Marsh, Henry L., III
Marshall, Etta Marie-Imes
Marshall, Wilfred L.
Martin, Hoyle Henry
Martin, Janice R.
Martin, Sylvia Cooke
Mason, Howard Keith
Mathis, Robert Lee
Mathis, Sallye Brooks
May, James Shelby
Mayfield, William S.
McCants, Odell
McClain, Earsalean J.
McClendon, Kellen
McCrackin, Olympia F.
McDaniel, Charles William
McEachern-Ulmer, Sylvia L.
McEachin, James
McFadden, Samuel Wilton
McGee, Adolphus Stewart
McGhee, Samuel T.

McGhee, Walter Brownie
McGlover, Stephen Ledell
McGuire, Paul M., Jr.
McIver, John Douglas
McIver, Margaret Hill
McKeller, Thomas Lee
McLean, John Alfred, Jr.
McLemore, Thomas
McMillan, James C.
McNeely, Matthew
McNeil, Frank William
McZeal, Alfred, Sr.
Meadows, Ferguson Booker, Jr.
Meeks, Reginald Kline
Meeks, Willis Gene
Middlebrooks, Felicia
Miles, Vera M.
Miles, Willie Leanna
Millender, Mallory Kimerling
Miller, Laurel Milton
Miller, Wilbur J.
Mitchell, Douglas
Mitchell, Parren James
Mitchell, Quitman J.
Montgomery, Joe Elliott
Montgomery, Payne
Moore, Beverly
Moore, Dwayne Harrison
Moore, Henry J.
Moore, Katherine Bell
Moore, Walter Louis
Morancie, Horace L.
Morgan, Joseph C.
Morial, Marc
Morrison, Robert B., Jr.
Morton, Lorraine H.
Moss, Estella Mae
Moss, Tanya Jill
Moss, Wayne B.
Murray, Sylvester
Murrell, Sylvia Marilyn
Myles, Herbert John
Neal, Richard
Nelson, Flora Sue
Nelson, Harold E.
Nelson, Ronald Duncan
Nesbitt, Prexy-Rozell William
Netters, Tyrone Homer
Nettles, Willard, Jr.
Newman, Kenneth J.
Newton, James Douglas, Jr.
Noah, Leroy Edward
Noble, John Pritchard
Norrell-Nance, Rosalind Elizabeth
Norris, Walter, Jr.
O'Connor, Thomas F., Jr.
Odom, Darryl Eugene
Officer, Carl Edward
O'Kain, Roosevelt
Oliver, Jerry Alton, Sr.
O'Neal, Fredrick William, Jr.
Osborne, Hugh Stancill
Palmer, Douglas Harold
Parker, Stafford W.
Parker-Sawyers, Paula
Parks, Thelma Reece
Parrish, John Henry
Parrish, Maurice Drue
Parsons, Richard
Patrick, Julius, Jr.
Patrick, Lawrence Clarence, Jr.
Patterson, Dessie Lee
Patterson, William Benjamin
Patton, Robert
Paul, John F.
Payne, James Edward
Pearson, Herman B.
Penn, Robert Clarence
Perry, Carrie Saxon
Perry, William Rodwell, III
Peterson, Gerard M.
Peterson, Rocky Lee
Pierce, Abe, III
Pierce, Frank Powell
Pinkard, Bedford L.
Pittman, Darryl E.
Pittman, Keith B.
Pitts, Dorothy Louise Waller
Porter, Linsey
Porter, Otha L.
Pounds, Elaine
Pratt, Joan M.
Prewitt, Al Bert
Pritchard, Daron
Quander, Rohulamin
Quarrelles, James Ivan
Quash, Rhonda
Quinn, Alfred Thomas
Quinn, Diane C.

Raab, Madeline Murphy
Ramseur, Isabelle R.
Rattley, Jessie M.
Ray, Mary E.
Reese, Frederick D.
Reeves, John E.
Revelle, Robert, Sr.
Rhodes, Anne L.
Ricanek, Carolyn Wright
Rice, Judith Carol
Rice, Robert C.
Rice, Susie Leon
Richardson, Gilda Faye
Richardson, Harold Edward
Richardson, Louis M.
Richardson, Rhonda Karen
Richmond, Myrian Patricia
Riley, Wayne Joseph
Riley, William Scott
Rivers, Valerie L.
Roberson, F. Alexis H.
Roberts, Charles L.
Robertson, Charles E., Jr.
Robinson, Clarence G.
Robinson, Henry
Robinson, Kenneth
Robinson, William
Robinson, William Earl
Rogers, Freddie Clyde
Rogers, Gwendolyn H.
Ruffin, Ronald R.
Rundles, James Isaiah
Samples, Jared Lanier
Sampson, Marva W.
Samuel, Frederick E.
Samuels, Annette Jacqueline
Samuels, Leslie Eugene
Sanders, Archie, Jr.
Sanders, Wesley, Jr.
Schatzman, Dennis Clyde
Schmoke, Kurt Lidell
Sconier-LaBoo, Andrea
Scott, Brenda M.
Scott, Carstella H.
Scott, Donald L.
Scott-Johnson, Roberta Virginia
Scruggs-Leftwich, Yvonne
Seabrooks, Nettie Harris
Seabrooks-Edwards, Marilyn S.
Seals, Gerald
Session, Johnny Frank
Sewell, Richard Huston
Shakoor, Adam Adib
Shakoor, Waheedah Aqueelah
Shanks, James A.
Shannon, George A.
Sharp, James Alfred
Sharpp, Nancy Charlene
Shelby, Khadejah E.
Shepherd, Veronika Y.
Sheppard, Stevenson Royrayson
Sherrod, Charles M.
Sherwood, O. Peter
Shivers, S. Michael
Shoemaker, Veronica Sapp
Shores, Arthur D.
Silva, Henry Andrew
Simms, James Edward
Sims, Lydia Theresa
Sinclair, Benito A.
Sindler, Michael H.
Singleton, James Milton
Singleton, Leroy, Sr.
Smallwood, William Lee
Smith, Carol Barlow
Smith, Dorothy O.
Smith, Edward Charles
Smith, Frank, Jr.
Smith, James, Jr.
Smith, Juanita Smith
Smith, Sam
Smith, Toni Colette
Smith, Vernel Hap
Snell, Jimmy Gregory
Southern, Charles O.
Spann, Noah Atterson, Jr.
Spaulding, William Ridley
Spellman, Oliver B., Jr.
Spencer, Marian Alexander
Spurlock, Dorothy A.
Stallworth, Ann P.
Stamps, Leon Preist
Stanley, Columbus Landon, Sr.
Stanley, Ellis M., Sr.
Stanley, Woodrow
Stapleton, Marylyn A.
Steans, Edith Elizabeth
Steger, C. Donald
Stent, Nicole M.

Stephens, James Anthony
Stewart, Charles J.
Stewart, Dorothy Nell
Stewart, John B., Jr.
Stewart, Mae E.
Stewart, W. Douglas
Stockard, Betsy
Stovall-Tapley, Mary Kate
Stubblefield, Jennye Washington
Summers, Edna White
Summers, William E., IV
Swinton, Lee Vertis
Tarver, Marie Nero
Tasco, Marian B.
Taylor, DeForrest Walker
Taylor, Sister Marie de Porres
Taylor, Noel C.
Taylor, Norman Eugene
Taylor, Reginald Redall, Jr.
Taylor, Richard L.
Teele, Arthur Earle, Jr.
Teer, Wardeen
Terrell, Robert E.
Terry, Frank W.
Thomas, Erma Lee Lyons
Thomas, Jewel M.
Thomas, Joseph Edward, Jr.
Thompson, Aaron A.
Thompson, Benjamin Franklin
Thompson, Betty Lou
Thompson, Bobby E.
Thompson, Jesse M.
Thompson, Johnnie
Thompson, Priscilla Angelena
Tillery, Dwight
Tinsley-Williams, Alberta
Todd, William S.
Todman, Jureen Francis
Tolbert, John W., Jr.
Tolliver, Thomas C., Jr.
Torian, Edward Torrence
Touchstone, John E.
Townsell, Jackie Mae
Trice, Juniper Yates
Troupe-Frye, Betty Jean
Truitt, Kevin
Tucker, Donald
Turner, Sharon V.
Turner, Winston E.
Tyson, Edward Charles
Usry, James LeRoy
Vaughn, Mary Kathryn
Vereen, Nathaniel
Vincent, Edward
Wade, Beryl Elaine
Wade, Casey, Jr.
Wainwright, Gloria Bessie
Waiters, Gail Elenoria
Walker, Ann B.
Walker, Willie Leroy
Waller, Eunice McLean
Walls, Melvin
Ward, Albert M.
Ward, Anna Elizabeth
Ware, John
Washington, Arnic J.
Washington, David Warren
Washington, Eli H.
Washington, Henry L.
Washington, Isaiah Edward
Washington, James Lee
Washington, Lester Renez
Washington, Walter E.
Watkins, Izear Carl
Watkins, Mozelle Ellis
Watson, Juanita
Watts, John E.
Way, Curtis J.
Webb, Joe
Webb, Wellington E.
Webster, Lonnie
Weeks, Deborah Redd
Welch, John L.
Wells, Billy Gene
Wesson, Cleo
West, Marcellus
Wester, Richard Clark
Weston, Sharon
Wharton Boyd, Linda F.
Whitaker, Willard H.
White, Billy Ray
White, Ed Pearson
White, Michael Reed
White, Van Freeman
Whiting, Leroy
Wiggins, Lillian Cooper
Wilbekin, Harvey E.
Wiley, Rena Deloris
Wilkins, Rillastine Roberta

William, Thompson E.
Williams, Cody
Williams, Earl, Jr.
Williams, Earl West
Williams, Enoch H.
Williams, Frederick Daniel
  Crawford
Williams, Harold Edward
Williams, Jane E.
Williams, Jesse
Williams, Jewel L.
Williams, Joe H.
Williams, Lottie Mae
Williams, Regina Vloyn-Kinchen
Williams, Reginald Clark
Williams, Robert L.
Williams, Rodney Elliott
Williams, Ronald
Williams, Thomas Allen
Williams, Wayne Allan
Williams, Willie L.
Wilson, Ernest
Wilson, Grant Paul, Jr.
Wilson, Lawrence C.
Wilson, Lionel J.
Winfield, George Lee
Winston, Janet E.
Winter, Daria Portray
Wise, Frank P.
Womble, Larry W.
Wood, Margaret Beatrice
Woods, Bernice
Woods, Jessie Anderson
Woods-Burwell, Charlotte Ann
Woodson, Jeffrey Anthony
Word, Fletcher Henry, Jr.
Wright, George C., Jr.
Wright, J. R.
Wright, James A.
Wright, Loyce Pierce
Wyatt, Addie L.
Wynn, LaMetta K.
Yancey, Charles Calvin
Yeldell, Joseph P.
Young, Charlie, Jr.
Young, Coleman A.
Young, John W.
Young, Leon
Young, Richard Edward, Jr.
Young, Sarah Daniels
Zachary, Steven W.
Zambrana, Rafael
Zollar, Nikki Michele

Government Service (Elected or Appointed)/ Government Administration—County

Adkins, Iona W.
Agee, Bobby L.
Ahllock, Theodore
Alers, Rochelle
Alexander, Ronald Algernon
Anderson, Carl Edward
Anderson, Marva Jean
Anderson, Ruth Bluford
Aytch, Donald Melvin
Baker, Willie J.
Baldwin, Cynthia A.
Banks, Lula F.
Battle, Gloria Jean
Beane, Robert Hubert
Beasley, Daniel L.
Bell, Charles Smith
Bell, Edna Talbert
Bell, William Vaughn
Benson, Gilbert
Bishop, David Rudolph
Bishop, James, Jr.
Black, Lee Roy
Blackwell, Robert B.
Bond, James Max, Jr.
Bonds, Kevin Gregg
Booth, William H.
Brooks, Leroy
Brown, Byron William
Brown, Carroll Elizabeth
Brown, Emmett Earl
Brown, George Houston
Brown, Joseph Samuel
Buggs, James
Butler, Jerry
Carrier, Clara L. DeGay
Carter, Arthur Michael
Carter, Joye
Chalmers, Thelma Faye
Chatman, Alex
Clark, Joe Louis

Clay, Rudolph
Clement, Josephine Dobbs
Cofield, Elizabeth Bias
Cole, Arthur
Coleman, Hurley J., Jr.
Coleman, John H.
Collins, Corene
Collins, Lenora W.
Cooper, Michael Gary
Cooper, Samuel H., Jr.
Cribb, Juanita Sanders
Crutchfield-Baker, Verdenia
Cushingberry, George, Jr.
Cutler, Donald
Daniel, Alfred Irwin
Davis, Abraham, Jr.
Davis, Angela Yvonne
Davis, Anita Louise
Davis, Harold
Davis, James Keet
Davis, Richard C.
Dawson, Lumell Herbert
Dillon, Vermon Lemar
Dixon, Leonard Bill
Dixon, Willie
Dobson, Dorothy Ann
Dodson, William Alfred, Jr.
Doss, Evan, Jr.
Douglas, John Daniel
Dozier, Morris, Sr.
DuBose, Otelia
Duncan, Joan A.
Dunn, James Earl
Easter, Hezekiah H.
Eaves, A. Reginald
Evans, Warren Cleage
Ewell, Raymond W.
Favors, Anita
Fletcher, James C., Jr.
Foster Foulks, Ivadale Marie
Foushee, Geraldine George
Freeland, Robert Lenward, Jr.
Freeman, McKinley Howard, Sr.
Froe, Dreyfus Walter
Fuller, Thomas S.
Gardner, Walter
Gates, Yvonne Atkinson
Gillis, Theresa McKinzy
Gilven, Hezekiah
Godfrey, William R.
Graham, George Washington, Jr.
Grant Bishop, Ellen Elizabeth
Graves, Clifford W.
Gray, C. Vernon
Gray, Marcus J.
Green, Raymond A.
Griffin, Percy Lee
Hadley, Sybil Carter
Hannah, Hubert H., Sr.
Harris, Burnell
Harris, Mary Lorraine
Harris, Sarah Elizabeth
Harris, Varno Arnello
Harris, Vera D.
Hathaway, Maggie Mae
Hayes, Charles
Henderson, I. D., Jr.
Hicks, Delphus Van, Jr.
Hightower, Michael
Hill, Bobby
Hill, Jacqueline R.
Holbert, JoAnne
Huff, Lula Lunsford
Hunt, Betty Syble
Hunter, John W.
Hunter, Teola P.
Isaac, Earlean
Jackson, Alvin B., Jr.
Jefferson, Robert R.
Johnson, Bobbie Gene
Johnson, Bobby JoJo
Johnson, Robert T.
Johnson, Vannette William
Johnson, Wayne Wright, III
Johnson, Willie F.
Jones, Ervin Edward
Jones, Lloyd O.
Jones, Nellie L.
Joyner, Gordon L.
Kelley, Wilbourne Anderson, III
Kennedy, Willie B.
Kerr, Stanley Munger
Kimbrough-Johnson, Donna L.
King, Lawrence Patrick
King, Martin Luther, III
Kithcart, Larry E.
Kline, Joseph N.
Labrie, Harrington
Lancaster, John Graham

Lawrence, Lonnie R.
Lewis, Polly Meriwether
Littleton, Ralph Douglass
Liverpool, Charles Eric
Lodge, Herman
Logan, Willie Frank, Jr.
Marable, Herman, Jr.
Martin, Carl E.
Martin, Montez Cornelius, Jr.
Martin, Ralph C., II
Mathis, Frank
Mathis, William Lawrence
McAdoo, Henry Allen
McBee, Vincent Clermont
McCray, Christopher Columbus
McCroom, Eddie Winther
McKinnon, Patrice
McNairy, Francine G.
Means, Elbert Lee
Means, Fred E.
Melton, Frank E.
Mereday, Richard F.
Middlebrooks, Felicia
Miller, Lawrence A., Jr.
Miller, Lawrence Edward
Milton, Israel Henry
Mitchell, Windell T.
Montague, Christina P.
Morcom, Claudia House
Morgan, Haywood, Sr.
Morse, Annie Ruth W.
Mosby, Nathaniel
Moseley Braun, Carol Elizabeth
Moss, Estella Mae
Newman, Nathaniel
Ortiz, Victor
Parker, Bernard F., Jr.
Patrick, James L.
Payne, Lisa R.
Payne, Samuel, Sr.
Pearson, Ramona Henderson
Pelote, Dorothy B.
Pemberton, Hilda Ramona
Pinckney, James
Porter, Grady J.
Preston, Eugene Anthony
Prince, Edgar Oliver
Pugh, G. Douglas
Redd, Orial Anne
Reynolds, Ida Manning
Rist, Susan E.
Robertson, Charles E., Jr.
Robertson, Evelyn Crawford, Jr.
Robinson, Barry Lane
Robinson, John G.
Roddy, Howard W.
Rose, Shelvie
Rumph, Annie Alridge
Russell, Leon W.
Ruth, James
Saunders, Robert William, Sr.
Scott, Otis, Sr.
Service, Russell Newton
Shannon, Odessa M.
Simmons, Joyce Hobson
Sims, Ronald Cordell
Singletary, Inez M.
Smith, Bobby Antonia
Smith, Charles
Smith, George S.
Smith, James Russell
Smith, Toni Colette
Smith, Vasco E.
Snead, John D.
Spears, Henry Albert, Sr.
Stalks, Larrie W.
Steele, Bobbie L.
Steppe, Cecil H.
Stevens, Patricia Ann
Tate, Herbert Holmes, Jr.
Tatum, Mildred Carthan
Taylor, David Richard, III
Taylor, Eric Charles
Taylor, Norman Eugene
Teague, Gladys Peters
Thomas, Liz A.
Thomas, Priscilla D.
Thomas, Wilbon
Thompson, Benjamin Franklin
Tibbs, Edward A.
Tillman, Paula Sellars
Times, Betty J.
Tolbert, Edward T.
Toliver, Paul Allen
Totten, Bernice E.
Trees, Candice D.
Tucker, Eric M.
Turman, Robert L., Sr.
Turner, Melvin E.

Turner, Sharon V.
Tusan, Gail S.
Tyler, Robert James, Sr.
Underwood, Joseph M., Jr.
Van Hook, George Ellis, Jr.
Vaughn, Eugenia Marchelle
    Washington
Waddell, Ruchadina LaDesiree
Ware, Jewel C.
Washington, David Warren
Washington, John Calvin, III
Webber, William Stuart
Webster, Karen Elaine
Weldon, Ramon N.
White, Donald R.
White, Jesse C., Jr.
White, Paul Christopher
White, Raymond Rodney, Sr.
White, William T., III
Wiley, Leroy Sherman
Wilfork, Andrew Louis
Wilkins, Kenneth C.
Williams, Charles C.
Williams, Harriette F.
Williams, Jason Harold
Williams, Leon Lawson
Williams, Moses, Sr.
Williams, Nancy Ellen Webb
Williams, Richard, Jr.
Wilson, Floyd Edward, Jr.
Winslow, Cleta Meris
Woods-Burwell, Charlotte Ann
Woody, Jacqueline Brown
Worth, Charles Joseph
Wright, Charles E.

**Government Service
(Elected or Appointed)/
Government
Administration—State**

Abebe, Ruby
Abernathy, Ralph David, III
Abramson, John J., Jr.
Adams, Edward Robert
Adams, Jean Tucker
Adiele, Moses Nkwachukwu
Alexander, F. S. Jack
Alexis, Doris Virginia
Allen, Bettie Jean
Allen, Harriette Louise
Anderson, Eugene
Andrews, Emanuel Carl
Applewhaite, Leon B.
Arberry, Morse, Jr.
Arlene, Herbert
Atkins, Hannah Diggs
Atkinson, Curtis L.
Austin, Richard H.
Ayers-Johnson, Darlene
Baker, Thurbert E.
Banks, J. B.
Barnett, Ethel S.
Barrows, Bryan H., III
Bates, Nathaniel Rubin
Beatty, Otto, Jr.
Beckett, Sydney A.
Bell, Theron J.
Bellinger, Mary Anne
Bennett, Maybelle Taylor
Billingsley, Ray C.
Bishop, James, Jr.
Black, Joseph
Black, Leona R.
Blackmon, Barbara Anita
Blackwell, J. Kenneth
Blanden, Lee Ernest
Block, Leslie S.
Blount, Charlotte Renee
Bludson-Francis, Vernett Michelle
Blue, Daniel Terry, Jr.
Bonds, Kevin Gregg
Boone, Alexandria
Boone, Carol Marie
Borders, Michael G.
Boschulte, Joseph Clement
Brady, Charles A.
Bragg, Robert Lloyd
Branch, William McKinley
Brent, David L.
Brooks, Carol Lorraine
Brooks, Christine D.
Brooks, Tyrone L.
Brown, Dwayne Marc
Brown, Joeanna Hurston
Brown, Lester J.
Brown, Mary Katherine
Brown, Reginald Royce, Sr.
Brown, Robert, Jr.

Brown, William Rocky, III
Brown, Willie B.
Brown-Francisco, Teresa Elaine
Bryant, Andrea Pair
Bryant, Clarence
Bryant, Jenkins, Jr.
Bryant, Wayne R.
Buckley, Victoria
Burney, William D., Jr.
Burris, Roland W.
Bush, Evelyn
Buskey, James E.
Buskey, John
Byrd, Harriett Elizabeth
Caldwell, Edwin L., Jr.
Calloway, DeVerne Lee
Canton, Douglas E.
Capehart, Johnnie Lawrence
Cargill, Gilbert Allen
Carter, Jandra D.
Carter, Margaret Louise
Carter, Pamela Lynn
Carter, Phyllis Harden
Carter, Troy A.
Cary, Reby
Casey, Clifton G.
Castro, George A.
Chambers, Madrith Bennett
Charbonnet, Louis, III
Chatman, Alex
Christian, Mary T.
Clack, Floyd
Clark, Leonard Weslorn, Jr.
Clark, Robert G.
Clark, William
Clarke, Alyce Griffin
Clarke, Henry Louis
Clark-Thomas, Eleanor M.
Clay, William Lacy, Jr.
Cogsville, Donald J.
Coleman, Andrew Lee
Coleman, Eric Dean
Collins, Barbara-Rose
Collins-Bondon, Carolyn R.
Collins-Grant, Earlean
Conley, Herbert A.
Connor, George C., Jr.
Conyers, John, Jr.
Copelin, Sherman Nathaniel, Jr.
Cotharn, Preston Sigmunde, Sr.
Cotman, Ivan Louis
Cox, Kevin C.
Crable, Dallas Eugene
Crawford, Odel
Crawford, William A.
Crews, Victoria Wilder
Cribbs, Theo, Sr.
Crouch, Robert Allen
Crump, Arthel Eugene
Cummings, Frances McArthur
Cummings, Theresa Faith
Cunningham, William L.
Curls, Phillip B.
Curry, Phyllis Joan
Custer-Chen, Johnnie M.
Dames, Kathy W.
Daniel, Alfred Irwin
Daniels, George Benjamin
Daniels, Joseph
DaValt, Dorothy B.
Davis, Bennie L.
Davis, Bettye J.
Davis, Clifton D.
Davis, John Aubrey
Davis, Monique Deon
Davis Anthony, Vernice
Dawson, Eric Emmanuel
Dean, James Edward
DeBerry, Lois Marie
Delco, Wilhelmina R.
Delpit, Joseph A.
Diggs, Estella B.
Dillard, Thelma Deloris
Dixon, Isaiah, Jr.
Dixon, Richard Nathaniel
Dixon, Roscoe
Dorsett, Katie Grays
Douglass, John W.
Drakes, Muriel B.
Durham, Eddie L., Sr.
Dyson, William Riley
Easter, Hezekiah H.
Edwards, Al E.
Edwards, Jean Curtis
Edwards, John Wilson
Ellerby, William Mitchell, Sr.
Epps, A. Glenn
Escott, Sundra Erma
Evans, Dwight

Eve, Arthur O.
Farr, Llewellyn Goldstone
Farrell, Herman Denny, Jr.
Ferguson, Rosetta
Fielding, Herbert Ulysses
Fields, Cleo
Figures, Michael
Figures, Vivian Davis
Fitch, Milton F., Jr.
Foggs-Wilcox, Iris
Ford, John Newton
Fordham, Cynthia Williams
Foster, Robert Davis
Frazier, Frances Curtis
Frazier, Wynetta Artricia
Frazier-Ellison, Vicki L.
Freeman, McKinley Howard, Sr.
Freeman-Wilson, Karen Marie
Fregia, Darrell Leon
Frisby, H. Russell, Jr.
Fuget, Charles Robert
Gadsden, Nathaniel J., Jr.
Gaines, Edythe J.
Galiber, Joseph L.
Gamble, Janet Helen
Gardner, Cedric Boyer
Garner, Velvia M.
Garrett, James Edward, Jr.
Gayles, Franklin Johnson
George, Gary Raymond
Giddings, Helen
Gilbert, Frank
Gillum, Ronald M.
Glass, Robert Davis
Goodall, Hurley Charles, Sr.
Goodman, George D.
Goodson, Annie Jean
Gordon, Derek E.
Gore, John Michel
Gorman, Bertha Gaffney
Goward, Russell A.
Graham, Saundra M.
Gramby, Shirley Ann
Grayson, George Welton
Greene, Aurelia
Greene, Charles Edward Clarence
Greenleaf, Louis E.
Griffin, Betty Sue
Griffin, Ples Andrew
Groff, Regis F.
Grove, Daniel
Guiton Hill, Bonnie
Gulley, Wilson
Gunn, Alex M., Jr.
Hale, Phale D.
Hall, Ethel Harris
Hall, Katie
Hall, Kenneth
Hamilton, Art
Hamilton, Aubrey J.
Hammock, Edward R.
Hammonds, Garfield, Jr.
Hampton, Thomas Earle
Harding, John Edward
Hargrave, Benjamin
Hargrett, James T., Jr.
Harley, Legrand
Harper, Ruth B.
Harper, Thelma Marie
Harrell, Oscar W., II
Harris, Melvin
Harris, Oscar L., Jr.
Harris, Paul Clinton, Sr.
Hart, Phyllis D.
Hauser, Charlie Brady
Haynes, Michael E.
Haynes, Worth Edward
Henderson, Frank S., Jr.
Henderson, Hugh C.
Henderson, Remond
Hendricks, Steven Aaron
Henry, Marcelett Campbell
Hicks, William H.
Higginbotham-Brooks, Renee
Hightower, Anthony
Hilliard, Earl Frederick
Hodge, Derek M.
Hodges, Virgil Hall
Hogan, Beverly Wade
Holden, Melvin Lee
Holloway, Herman M., Sr.
Holmes, Alvin Adolf
Holmes, Robert A.
Holt, John J.
Hood, Morris, Jr.
Hood, Raymond W.
Horton, Larnie G.
Houston, Agnes Wood
Hudson, Merry C.

Hughes, Vincent
Hunter, Howard Jacque, Jr.
Hunter, Teola P.
Hynson, Carroll Henry, Jr.
Ingram, William B.
Irons, Paulette
Irvis, K. Leroy
Jacks, Ulysses
Jackson, Alphonse, Jr.
Jackson, Darnell
Jackson, Johnny, Jr.
Jackson, Lee Arthur
Jacobs, Ennis Leon, Jr.
James, Kay C.
James, Troy Lee
Jeff, Gloria Jean
Jefferson-Moss, Carolyn
Jenkins, Andrew James
Jenkins, Cynthia
Jenkins, John
Jewell, Jerry Donal
Johnson, Benjamin Washington
Johnson, Clinton Lee, Sr.
Johnson, F. Raymond
Johnson, Glenn T.
Johnson, James R.
Johnson, Jon D.
Johnson, Julia L.
Johnson, Justin Morris
Johnson, Paul Edwin
Johnson, Phyllis Mercedes
Johnson, Wayne Wright, III
Jones, Casey C.
Jones, Charles D.
Jones, Chester
Jones, Chester Ray
Jones, Christine Miller
Jones, Daryl L.
Jones, Emil, Jr.
Jones, Marilyn Elaine
Jones, Peter Lawson
Jones, Sherman Jarvis
Jordan, Orchid I.
Josey, Leronia Arnetta
Kane, Jacqueline Anne
Kelley, Delores G.
Kennedy, Sandra Denise
Kennedy, Yvonne
Kindall, Luther Martin
Lambert, Benjamin J., III
Lambert, LeClair Grier
Langford, Arthur, Jr.
Langford, Charles D.
Larry, Jerald Henry
Lawlah, Gloria Gary
Lawrence, Archie
Lawson, Herman A.
Leatherwood, Larry Lee
Leek, Sandra D.
LeFlore, Larry
Lester, Jacqueline
Lewis, James B.
Lewis, W. Arthur
Ligon, Claude M.
Lima, George Silva
Linton, Gordon J.
Lloyd, Walter P.
Long, Gerald Bernard
Lopez, Mary Gardner
Love, Clarence V.
Lucas, David Eugene
Lyons, A. Bates
Mallory, William L.
Malry, Lenton
Mann, Thomas J., Jr.
Markette-Malone, Sharon
Marriott, Salima Siler
Marrow-Mooring, Barbara A.
Marshall, Charlene Jennings
Martin, Gwendolyn Rose
Maultsby, Dorothy M., Esq.
McCall, Marion G., Jr.
McCall, Patricia
McClain, Dorothy Mae
McCracken, Frank D.
McCrimon, Audrey L.
McGee, Timothy Dwayne
McKinney, Richard Ishmael
McLaughlin, George W.
McNeil, Alvin J.
McRipley, G. Whitney
Meadows, Richard H.
Meek, Carrie P.
Meek, Kendrick
Meeks, Perker L., Jr.
Meredith, James Howard
Michel, Harriet Richardson
Miles, Norman Kenneth
Miller, Lawrence A., Jr.

Jones, Lorean Electa
Jones, Meredith J.
Jones, Napoleon A., Jr.
Jones, Randy Kane
Jones-Smith, Jacqueline
Jordan, Carolyn D.
Jordan, Eddie J., Jr.
Josey, Leronia Arnetta
Joyner, Claude C.
Kaiser-Dark, Phyllis E.
Kea, Arleas Upton
Kennard, William Earl
Kilpatrick, Carolyn Cheeks
Kilpatrick, Robert Paul
Kimbrough, Kenneth R.
King, Clarence Maurice, Jr.
King, Frederick L., Jr.
King, Gwendolyn Stewart
King, Howard O.
King, William Charles
Knott, May
Labat, Eric Martin
Landers, Renee M.
Lang-Jeter, Lula L.
Langston-Jackson, Wilmetta Ann
    Smith
Latcholia, Kenneth Edward
Latimer, Allie B.
Lavizzo-Mourey, Risa Juanita
Layton, Benjamin Thomas
Lee, Sheila Jackson
Lee, Vivian Booker
Lee, Vivian O.
Leeper, Lucius Walter
LeFlore, Larry
Lewis, Arthur W.
Lewis, John Robert
Lewis, Peggy
Lightfoot, Jean Drew
Lima, George Silva
Lippman, Lois H.
Littlejohn, John B., Jr.
Lockett, Alice Faye
Lowe, Hazel Marie
Lucas, Gerald Robert
Lucas, William
Mack, John L.
Madison, Richard
Maldon, Alphonso
Manley, Audrey Forbes
Mansfield, W. Ed
Marbury, Martha G.
Marsh, Ben Franklin
Martin, Shedrick M., Jr.
Matory, Deborah Love
May, James F.
Mayes, Nathaniel H., Jr.
Mazon, Larri Wayne
McAfee, Flo
McAllister, Singleton Beryl
McCraven, Carl Clarke
McFarlin, Kernaa D'Offert, Jr.
McIntosh, James E.
McKinney-Johnson, Eloise
McMorris, Jacqueline Williams
McReynolds, Elaine A.
Means, Kevin Michael
Medford, Isabel
Meriweather, Melvin, Jr.
Michael, Charlene Belton
Millender-McDonald, Juanita M.
Miller, Lorraine
Miller, Norman L.
Mills, Cheryl
Mims, Oscar Lugrie
Miner, William Gerard
Mitchell, Parren James
Montgomery, Edward B.
Moon, Walter D.
Moore, Johnnie Adolph
Moore, Minyon
Moore, Roscoe Michael, Jr.
Moose, George E.
Morgan, Fletcher, Jr.
Morgan, Juanita Kennedy
Morris, Archie, III
Morrison, Trudi Michelle
Mosley, John William
Napper, Hyacinthe T.
Nash, Bob J.
Nash, Eva L.
Newman, Constance Berry
Nichols, Sylvia A.
Nixon, Harold L.
Norfleet, Janet
Norment, Hanley
Norris, LaVena M.
Norton, Edward Worthington
Norton, Eleanor Holmes

O'Bannon, Donna Edwards
O'Bryant, Constance Taylor
O'Leary, Hazel
Oliver-Simon, Gloria Craig
Osborne, Ernest L.
Owens, Major R.
Pappillion, Glenda M.
Parham, Deborah L.
Parron, Delores L.
Parrott-Fonseca, Joan
Patrick, Deval L.
Payne, Donald M.
Peacock, Nicole
Perry, June Carter
Perry, Robert Cephas
Peters, Aulana Louise
Peterson, Audrey Clinton
Phillips, Earl W.
Pinson, Valerie F.
Polk, Lorna Marie
Pope, James M.
Posey, Ada
Pounds, Moses B.
Powell, Michael K.
Raines, Franklin D.
Ramseur, Andre William
Rand, Cynthia
Rangel, Charles B.
Rashad, Johari Mahasin
Reed, Wilbur R.
Reeves, Willie Lloyd, Jr.
Reid, Clarice Wills
Render, Arlene
Reynolds, James W.
Rice, Emmett J.
Rice, Lewis, Jr.
Rice, William E.
Roberts, Louis Wright
Robinson, Gloria
Robinson, Sharon Porter
Robinson, Vernon Edward
Rogers, Ormer, Jr.
Rollins, Avon William, Sr.
Rudd, James M.
Rush, Bobby
Russell, Ernest
Saint-Louis, Rudolph Anthony
Satcher, David
Saulter, Gilbert John
Saunders, Robert William, Sr.
Savage, Augustus A.
Scoonover, Brenda Brown
Scott, Robert Cortez
Scott-Clayton, Patricia Ann
Scruggs, Sylvia Ann
Scruggs-Leftwich, Yvonne
Sewell, Isiah Obediah
Shannon, John William
Sharpless, Mattie
Shippy, John D.
Slade, Walter R., Jr.
Slater, Rodney E.
Sleet, Gregory M.
Smith, Charles Lebanon
Smith, Chester B.
Smith, Gregory Robeson, Sr.
Smith, Lila
Smith, Patricia G.
Smith, Renetta
Smith, Robert London
Smith, Rufus Herman
Smith, Shirley LaVerne
Smythe-Haith, Mabel Murphy
Solomon, David
Solomon, Wilbert F.
Spearman, Leonard Hall
    O'Connell, Sr.
Spigner, Marcus E.
Stanton, Robert G.
Starks, Rick
Stephenson, Allan Anthony
Stewart, Ruth Ann
Stiell, Phelicia D'Lois
Stokes, Louis
Strode, Velma McEwen
Sullivan, Louis Wade
Sutton, Ozell
Taylor, Daisy Curry
Taylor, Gayland Wayne
Taylor, Helen Hollingshed
Taylor, Patricia Tate
Teague, Gladys Peters
Terry, Frank W.
Thomas, Carol M.
Thomas, Clarence
Thomas, Edith Peete
Thomas, Eunice S.
Thomas, James O., Jr.
Thompas, George Henry, Jr.

Thompson, Bennie G.
Thompson, Mozelle W.
Thornton, Tracey
Todman, Terence A.
Towns, Edolphus
Townsend, Wardell C., Jr.
Tribble, Huerta Cassius
Tucker, Walter Rayford, III
Turner, Winston E.
Turner, Yvonne Williams
Tyler, Cheryl Lynnett
Valentine, Deborah Marie
Valien, Preston
Vaughn, William Smith
Vinson, Rosalind Rowena
Walker, Angelina
Walker, Ann
Walker, Melford Whitfield, Jr.
Wallace, C. Everett
Walton, Reggie Barnett
Warmly, Leon
Warren, Rueben Clifton
Washington, Consuela M.
Washington, Craig A.
Waters, Maxine
Watford-McKinney, Yvonne V.
Watkins, Shirley R.
Watlington, Janet Berecia
Watson, Karen Elizabeth
Watt, Melvin L.
Weaver, Robert C.
Webb, Wilma J.
Whisenton, Andre C.
White, Evelyn M.
White, Ida Margaret
Whitlow, Woodrow, Jr.
Whitmore, Charles
Whitten, Jamie L.
Wilber, Margie Robinson
Wilcher, Shirley J.
Wiley-Pickett, Gloria
Wilkins, Thomas A.
Williams, Ann Claire
Williams, Deborah Ann
Williams, Debra D.
Williams, Fred C.
Williams, Howard Copeland
Williams, Lloyd L.
Williams, Margaret Ann
Williams, Paul
Williams, Wyatt Clifford
Williams-Bridgers, Jacquelyn L.
Winslow, Alfred A.
Woodson, Charles R.
Wynn, Albert
Young, Leon D.
Young, Rose S.
Young, Ruth L.

Government Service (Elected or Appointed)/ Government Administration—Not Elsewhere Classified
(*See Also* **Judiciary**)

Abramson, John J., Jr.
Bembry, Lawrence
Booker, Johnnie Brooks
Broadnax, Walter Doyce
Burris, Chuck
Cain, Frank
Carthan, Eddie James
Chambers, Olivia Marie
Chatman, Anna Lee
Chatman, Jacob L.
Cherry, Theodore W.
Clarke, Anne-Marie
Coffey, Gilbert Haven, Jr.
Collins, Carter H.
Cope, Donald Lloyd
Darkins, Duane Adrian
Dymally, Lynn V.
Fernandes, Julie A.
Foster, Robert Leon
Francis, Charles S. L.
Giles, Althea B.
Giles, William R.
Gill, Roberta L.
Haines, Diana
Hardy, Willie J.
Hawkins, Walter L.
Haynes, Willie C., III
Jennings, Bernard Waylon-Handel
Johnson, Jared Modell
Johnson, Richard Howard
Jones, Lisa Payne
Jones, Willie

Lacy, Walter
Lane, Vincent
Lay, Clorius L.
Montague, Christina P.
Morgan, Fletcher, Jr.
Newman, Paul Dean
Reid, Ronda Eunese
Roper, Richard Walter
Sailor, Elroy
Scott, Beverly Angela
Simpson, Samuel G.
Smiley, James Walker, Sr.
Stanton, Janice D.
Sterling, H. Dwight, Sr.
Tayari, Kabili
Toran, Kay Dean
Van Lierop, Robert F.
Ward, James Dale
Ware, Jewel C.
Williams, John Earl
Williamson, Carl Vance
Wilson, Jaci Laverne
Windham, Revish

Graphic Design
See **Art, Visual—Commercial Art/Graphic Design**

Health Care—Not Elsewhere Classified
(*See Also* **Chiropractic; Dentistry; Health Services Administration; Medicine—specific categories, e.g. Medicine—Anesthesiology; Nursing; Nutrition; Optometry; Pharmacy; Podiatry**)

Abdul-Malik, Ibrahim
Ali-Jackson, Kamil
Anderson, Howard D.
Barclay, Robin Marie
Bellamy, Ivory Gandy
Benjamin, Donald S.
Beraki, Nailah G.
Bernard, Harold O.
Best, Jennings H.
Betts, Sheri Elaine
Blount, Wilbur Clanton
Bowen, William F.
Bracey, Willie Earl
Brown, Dorothy Lavania
Brown, Marsha J.
Brown, William McKinley, Jr.
Buckner, William Pat, Jr.
Burks, Juanita Pauline
Calhoun, Thomas
Carter, Carolyn McCraw
Cash, Bettye Joyce
Chandler, Harold R.
Chivers, Gwendolyn Ann
Collins, Sylvia Durnell
Cooper, Almeta E.
Cooper, Gary T.
Copeland, Betty Marable
Copeland, Terrilyn Denise
Copelin, Sherman Nathaniel, Jr.
Davis, Darwin N.
Davis, James Parker
Davis, James W.
Davis, Myrtle Hilliard
deMille, Valerie Cecilia
Dorsey, Joseph A.
Dual, Peter A.
Durham, C. Shelby
Evans-Dodd, Theora Anita
Fairman, John Abbrey
Fleming, Arthur Wallace
Fort, Jane
Fowler, Barbara Ann
Fowlkes, Nelson J.
Francois, Emmanuel Saturnin
Gaffney, Mary Louise
Glover, Arthur Lewis, Jr.
Gramby, Shirley Ann
Gray, Carol Coleman
Hall-Turner, Deborah
Hamberg, Marcelle R.
Harkins, Rosemary Knighton
Harris, Jean Louise
Harrison, Roscoe Conklin, Jr.
Hawkins, Muriel A.
Holland, Ethel M.

Hollingsworth, John Alexander
Horne, June Merideth
Hudson, Roy Davage
Hussein, Carlessia Amanda
Jackson, Lurline Bradley
Johnson, Cynthia L. M.
Johnson, Ernest Kaye, III
Johnson, Patricia Duren
Jones, Ervin Edward
Jones, Kenneth Leroy
Joyner, John Erwin
Kidd, Foster
Larrie, Reginald Reese, Ph.D.
Lindsay, Gwendolyn Ann Burns
Lockett, Harold James
Lucas, John
Marshall, Wilfred L.
Martin, Bertha M.
Mason, Terry
McArthur, Barbara Jean
McCutcheon, Lawrence
Miller, Lawrence A., Jr.
Miller, Lesley James, Jr.
Mims, Robert Bradford
Mosley, Marie Oleatha
Noble, John Pritchard
Norris, James Ellsworth Chiles
Parham, Brenda Joyce
Parker, Walter Gee
Peters, Pamela Joan
Petty, Bruce Anthony
Pinkney, Dove Savage
Powell, C. Clayton
Price, Glenda Delores
Prince, Joan Marie
Ragland, Wylheme Harold
Rann, Emery Louvelle
Reed, Theresa Greene
Remson, Anthony Terence
Rivers, Kenyatta O.
Roberts, Lillian
Rosemond, John H.
Roulhac, Edgar Edwin
Sands, Mary Alice
Scranage, Clarence, Jr.
Seams, Francine Swann
Shelton, Lee Raymond
Shields-Jones, Esther L. M.
Shirley, Edwin Samuel, Jr.
Shorty, Vernon James
Sims, Adrienne
Sinnette, Calvin Herman
Smalls, Jacquelyn Elaine
Smith, Conrad Warren
Smith, Karen Lynette
Smith, Symuel Harold
Smith, Tommie M.
Steele, Joyce Yvonne
Stevenson, Lillian
Stinson, Donald R.
Stovall-Tapley, Mary Kate
Street, Vivian Sue
Strong, Amanda L.
Sweatt, James L., III
Taylor, Dale B.
Taylor, Paul David
Teague, Robert
Theodore, Keith Felix
Thompson, Eugene Edward
Thompson, Sherwood
Timmons, Bonita Terry
Tokun, Ralph
Turner, Vivian Vanessa
Wade, Mildred Moncrief
Walker, Moses L.
Walters, Frank E.
Watson, Milton H.
Wattleton, Alyce Faye
Watts, Charles Dewitt
Wigfall, Samuel E.
Wiggins, Charles A.
Williams, Edward Ellis
Williams, Melvin Walker
Williams, Shirley Yvonne
Williamson, Coy Colbert, Jr.
Williamson, Karen Elizabeth
Wilson, Grant Paul, Jr.
Wilson, Joy Johnson
Wingate, Rosalee Martin
Winston, John H., Jr.
Young-Sall, Hajar

Health Services Administration
Adair, Robert A.
Adams, Ronald, Jr.
Adiele, Moses Nkwachukwu
Alexander, Paul Crayton

Alexander, Wardine Towers
Allen, Herbert J.
Allen, Percy, II
Allen, Van Sizar
Allen, Wendell
Allen, William Oscar
Allen, Zuline Gray
Alveranga, Glanvin L.
Andrews, William Henry
Arrington, Harold Mitchell
Ashford, L. Jerome
Atkinson, Gladys Whitted
Austin, Ernest Augustus
Avery, Byllye Y.
Ayala, Reginald P.
Bacon, Gloria Jackson
Ball, Clarence M., Jr.
Barclay, Robin Marie
Bartley, Talmadge O.
Bassard, Yvonne Brooks
Batiste, Edna E.
Bell, Rouzeberry
Bellamy, Ivory Gandy
Belton, C. Ronald
Benjamin, Donald S.
Berkley, Thomas Lucius
Billops, Camille J.
Blackwell, David Harold
Blount, Wilbur Clanton
Bonner, Della M.
Bowers, Mirion Perry
Branch, Eldridge Stanley
Branch, Geraldine Burton
Brannon, James R.
Braynon, Edward J., Jr.
Brookes, Bernard L.
Brooks, Phillip Daniel
Brooks, Todd Frederick
Brooks, William P.
Brown, A. Sue
Brown, Glenn Arthur
Brown, Walter E.
Brown, William McKinley, Jr.
Brown, Zora Kramer
Bryant, William Arnett, Jr.
Burrows, Clare
Butler, Michael Keith
Caison, Thelma Jann
Campbell, Charles Everett
Campbell, Emmett Earle
Camphor, Michael Gerard
Cantrell, Forrest Daniel
Capel, Wallace
Carson, Regina E. Edwards
Carter, Jandra D.
Carter, Oscar Earl, Jr.
Chapman, Charles F.
Chastang, Mark J.
Christian, Cora LeEthel
Christian, John L.
Clark, John Joseph
Clarke, Leon Edison
Clayton, Lloyd E.
Cleveland, Hattye M.
Cleveland, Tessie Anita Smith
Clifford, Maurice C.
Clifton, Rosalind Maria
Cochran, James David, Jr.
Combs, Julius V., M. D.
Cooper, Curtis V.
Corinaldi, Austin
Couch, James W.
Cowan, James R.
Craft, Thomas J., Sr.
Craig, Frederick A.
Crawford, Brenita
Croslan, John Arthur
Crutcher, Betty Neal
Culpepper, Lucy Nell
Daniel, Colene Yvonne
Daniels, Jordan, Jr.
Darity, Janiki Evangelia
Darke, Charles B.
Davis, Adrianne
Davis, Brownie W.
Davis, Gregory A.
Davis, Myrtle Hilliard
Davis Anthony, Vernice
Delphin, Jacques Mercier
DeVaughn-Tidline, Donna
  Michelle
Dorsey, L. C.
Downer, Luther Henry
Duckett, Gregory Morris
Dudley-Washington, Loise
Dumpson, James R.
Dunn, Marvin
Dunston, Walter T.
Earls, Julian Manly

Eddy, Edward A.
Edwards, Lonnie
Elders, M. Joycelyn
Eller, Carl L.
Ellis, O. Herbert
English, Perry T., Jr.
Epps, Charles Harry, Jr.
Erskine, Kenneth F.
Evans, Patricia E.
Evans, Therman E.
Fairman, John Abbrey
Fields, Richard A.
Forde, James Albert
Foster, Pearl D.
Fox, Everett V.
Franklin, Dolores Mercedes
Fraser, Alvardo M.
Frazier, Lee Rene
Frazier, Wynetta Artricia
Fregia, Darrell Leon
French, Joseph Henry
Furlough, Joyce Lynn
Garner, John W.
Garnes, William A.
Gaston, Marilyn Hughes
Gates, Paul Edward
Gatson, Wilina Ione
George, Alma Rose
Gilmore, Edwin
Gladney, Marcellious
Goodson, Leroy Beverly
Goodwin, Jesse Francis
Goodwin, Norma J.
Goulbourne, Donald Samuel, Jr.
Graham, Richard A.
Green, Ruth A.
Greene, Horace F.
Grist, Arthur L., Sr.
Guyton, Alicia V.
Hairstone, Marcus A.
Hall, Evelyn Alice
Hall, Kathryn Louise
Hamilton-Bennett, Maisha
Ham-Ying, J. Michael
Hannah, Hubert H., Sr.
Harper, Elizabeth
Harris, Hassel B.
Harris, Jean Louise
Harris, Ona C.
Harvey, Jacqueline V.
Hayes, Edward, Jr.
Heard, Georgina E.
Heineback, Barbara Taylor
Henry, Brent Lee
Herring, Marsha K. Church
Hickman, Jerry A.
Hogan, James Carroll, Jr.
Holland, Loys Marie
Holliday, Alfonso David
Holmes, Everlena M.
Holt, Maude R.
Hopper, Cornelius Lenard
Howard, Joseph H.
Howard, Osbie L., Jr.
Howard, Samuel H.
Howard, Shirley M.
Hoyle, Classie
Humphries, Charles, Jr.
Hunn, Dorothy Fegan
Hunter, Gertrude T.
Hussein, Carlessia Amanda
Ince, Harold S.
Ivory, Carolyn Kay
Jackson, Lurline Bradley
Jenkins-Scott, Jackie
Johnson, Cato, II
Johnson, Cleveland, Jr.
Johnson, Elaine McDowell
Johnson, Ernest Kaye, III
Johnson, James Kenneth
Johnson, Robert
Johnson, Taylor Herbert
Johnson-Brown, Hazel Winfred
Johnson-Scott, Jerodene Patrice
Jones, Billy Emanuel
Jones, James R., III
Jones, Sondra Michelle
Jordan, Thurman
Jordan, Wilbert Cornelious
Kelly, Thomas, Jr.
Kennedy-Scott, Patricia
King, Edgar Lee
King, John L.
King, Talmadge Everett, Jr.
Kirchhofer, Wilma Ardine
  Lyghtner
Land, Chester LaSalle
Lattimer, Agnes Dolores
Lavizzo-Mourey, Risa Juanita

Ledbetter, Ruth Pope
Lee, Andre L.
Lee, Rotan
Lee, Vivian Booker
Lee, Vivian O.
Lewis, Alonzo Todd
Lewis, Therthenia Williams
Lockhart, Barbara H.
Logan, Lloyd
Long, Ophelia
Lyles, Madeline Lolita
Lyles, William K.
Mack, Wilhelmena
Malone, Cleo
Manley, Audrey Forbes
Marion, Phillip Jordan
Marsh, Donald Gene
Marshall, Carter Lee
Marshall, Don A., Sr.
Martin, Lee
Mayberry-Stewart, Melodie Irene
McCaa, John K.
McCabe, Jewell Jackson
McCants, Odell
McClain, Andrew Bradley
McCoy, George H.
McCoy, Gladys
McCraven, Marcus R.
McDaniel, James Berkley, Jr.
McDonald, Mark T.
McGee, Gloria Kesselle
McGee, Hansel Leslie
McGregor, Edna M.
McLeod, James S.
McMillan, Jacqueline Marie
McMillan, James Bates
McWhorter, Rosalynd D.
Meeks, Perker L., Jr.
Menzies, Barbara A.
Metcalf, Zubie West, Jr.
Metoyer, Carl B.
Milbourne, Larry William
Mills, Mary Lee
Mitchell, Dwayne Oscar
Moone, James Clark
Moone, Wanda Renee
Moore, Alfred
Moore, Joseph L.
Moore, Lois Jean
Morgan, Alice Johnson Parham
Morgan, Eldridge Gates
Morgan, Rudolph Courtney
Murray, James Hamilton
Myers, Woodrow Augustus, Jr.
Odom, Darryl Eugene
Opoku, Evelyn
Osborne, William Reginald, Jr.
Parham, Deborah L.
Patterson-Townsend, Margaret M.
Paxton, Phyllis Ann
Payne, Jerry Oscar
Peoples, Florence W.
Persaud, Inder
Peters, Kenneth Darryl, Sr.
Pettiford, Reuben J., Jr.
Pile, Michael David Mc Kenzie
Pinckney, Lewis, Jr.
Pinkney, Dove Savage
Pinson, Thomas J.
Plummer, Ora B.
Poole, Rachel Irene
Porter, Lionel
Potts, Harold E.
Pounds, Moses B.
Powell, Charles P.
Price, Andrea R.
Price, Faye Hughes
Priest, Marlon L.
Primm, Beny Jene
Ralston, Edward J.
Reed, Clara Taylor
Renford, Edward
Richardson, Nola Mae
Richardson, Rupert Florence
Richie, Sharon Ivey
Rickman, Lewis Daniel, Sr.
Riley, Wayne Joseph
Risbrook, Arthur Timothy
Roberts, Cheryl Dornita Lynn
Roberts, Jonathan
Robertson, Evelyn Crawford, Jr.
Robinson, Maude Eloise
Robinson, Robert G.
Robinson, Thomas Donald
Roddy, Howard W.
Rosser, James M.
Rowan, Michael Terrance
Rutledge, William Lyman
Sadler, Kenneth Marvin

Sampson, Marva W.
Sanders, Augusta Swann
Sanders, Sally Ruth
Sanford, Mark
Sconier-LaBoo, Andrea
Setlow, Valerie Petit
Sewell, Richard Huston
Shelton, Lee Raymond
Shurney, Dexter Wayne
Simmons, Janice
Simpson, Dazelle Dean
Singletary, Inez M.
Sinnette, Calvin Herman
Sirmans, Meredith Franklin
Smith, Eddie Glenn, Jr.
Smith, Gloria Dawn
Smith, Gloria R.
Smith, Quentin T.
Smith, Richard Alfred
Smith, Sundra Shealey
Solomon, Denzil Kenneth
Sorey, Hilmon S., Jr.
Spears, Sandra Calvette
Standard, Raymond Linwood
Stent, Nicole M.
Story, Otis L, Sr.
Street, Vivian Sue
Strickland, Frederick William, Jr.
Strong, Amanda L.
Sullivan, Louis Wade
Tappan, Major William
Taylor, Paul David
Thomas, Edward S.
Thomas, Marla Renee
Thomas, Pamella D.
Thomas-Richardson, Valerie Jean
Thompson, Theodis
Thornton, Jackie C.
Tingle, Lawrence May
Toby, William, Jr.
Towns, Myron B., II
Trice, Jessie Collins
Turner, Jean Taylor
Walker, Allene Marsha
Walker, Dorothea Bernice
Walker, Grover Pulliam
Walston, Woodrow William
Wamble, Carl DeEllis
Warren, Rueben Clifton
Watson, Anne
Watson, Vernaline
Webb, Harvey, Jr.
Webb, Linnette
Welch, John L.
Wesley, Nathaniel, Jr.
Wheeler, Primus, Jr.
White, Paul Christopher
Whitest, Beverly Joyce
Wiggins, Charles A.
Williams, Jason Harold
Wilson, Robert Stanley
Woods, Almita
Woods, Geraldine Pittman
Worrell, Audrey Martiny
Worth, Janice Lorraine
Wyatt, Ronald Michael
Yancey, Asa G., Sr.
Yarbrough, Earnest
Young, Wallace L.

History

Anthony, David Henry, III
Ballard, Allen Butler, Jr.
Barksdale Hall, Roland C.
Billups, Myles E., Sr.
Blocker, Helen Powell
Bond, Julian
Bracey, Henry J.
Brooks, Rosemary Bittings
Brown, Courtney Coleridge
Brown, Jeffrey LeMonte
Brown, John Mitchell, Sr.
Cabbell, Edward Joseph
Callum, Agnes Kane
Calomee, Annie E.
Carey, Harmon Roderick
Carpenter, William Arthur, II
Clark, Major
Clarke, John Henrik
Claye, Charlene Marette
Coleman, Ronald Gerald
Connor, Dolores Lillie
Crew, Spencer R.
Crosby, Edward Warren
Crouchett, Lawrence Paul
David, Arthur LaCurtiss
Davis, Thomas Joseph
Dickerson, Dennis Clark

Drewry, Henry Nathaniel
DuPree, Sherry Sherrod
Eaton, James Nathaniel, Sr.
Edwards, John Loyd, III
Ekechi, Felix K.
Elliott, Derek Wesley
Ellis, Marilyn Pope
Flewellen, Icabod
Ford, Marcella Woods
Franklin, John Hope
Galloway-Briggs, Lula
Gill, Gerald Robert
Gilmore, Al Tony
Goodwin, Maria Rose
Green, John M.
Guy, Mildred Dorothy
Ham, Debra Newman
Hardin, John Arthur
Harding, Vincent
Harris, Elbert L.
Harris, Francis C.
Harris, Michael Wesley
Hayden, Robert C., Jr.
Hill, Bennett David
Holmes, E. Selean
Holmes, James Arthur, Jr.
Hudson, James Blaine, III
Hyman, Mark J.
Jackson, Kennell A., Jr.
Jacobs, Sylvia Marie
Jamerson, Jerome Donnell
James, Felix
Jefferson, Alphine Wade
Johnson, Leroy Ronald
Jones, Edward Louis
Jordan, Thomas Alton
King-Hammond, Leslie
Knight, Franklin W.
Layton, William W.
Lee, Clara Marshall
Ligon, Doris Hillian
Lockett, James D.
Marshall, Albert Prince
Matthews, Christy
Matthews, Vincent
McConnell, Catherine Allen
McConnell, Roland C.
Miller, M. Sammye
Mitchell, Loften
Moore, Marian J.
Morrow, John Howard, Jr.
Morse, Annie Ruth W.
Morton, Cynthia Neverdon
Moss, Alfred A., Jr.
Mumford, Esther Hall
Painter, Nell Irvin
Patton, Gerald Wilson
Peterman, Peggy M.
Phillips, Glenn Owen
Pinkett, Harold Thomas
Price, Suzanne Davis
Ransby, Barbara
Reagon, Bernice Johnson
Reynolds, Edward
Roberts, Wesley A.
Robinson, Genevieve
Rouse, Jacqueline Anne
Rushing, Byron D.
Saunders, Robert Edward
Scruggs, Otey Matthew
Sinkler, George
Smith, Charlie Calvin
Stratton-Morris, Madeline
  Robinson Morgan
Strickland, Arvarh E.
Sumler-Edmond, Janice L.
Tall, Booker T.
Tate, Merze
Taylor, Henry Louis, Jr.
Terborg-Penn, Rosalyn M.
Thomas, Robert Lewis
Troupe, Marilyn Kay
Turnbull, Charles Wesley
Turner, Wallace E.
Washington, Michael Harlan
Welch, Ashton Wesley
Williams, Carolyn Ruth Armstrong
Winston, Michael R.
Woodson, William D.
Young, Alfred

Horticulture
See **Landscape/Horticultural
Services**

Journalism— Photojournalism (See Also Photography)

Journalism—Print (See Also Writing/Editing— Nonfiction)

Jones, Nathaniel R.
Jones, Raymond Dean
Jones, Stephanie Tubbs
Jones, Thomas Russell
Jones, Vera Massey
Jordan, Claudia J.
Joy, Daniel Webster
Kearney, Jesse L.
Kearse, Amalya Lyle
Keenon, Una H. R.
Keith, Damon Jerome
Kennedy, Brenda Picola
Kennedy, Cain James
Kennedy, Henry H., Jr.
Kilcrease, Irvin Hugh, Jr.
King, Donald E.
Lancaster, Gary Lee
Lander, C. Victor
Lange, LaJune Thomas
Langford-Morris, Denise
Lankster, Barrown Douglas
LaVergne, Luke Aldon
Lay, Clorius L.
Lee, Michael Waring
Lee, Sheila Jackson
Leek, Sandra D.
Leighton, George Neves
Lester, Betty J.
Levister, Wendell P.
Lewis, Daniel
Lewis, Jannie
Lewis, William A., Jr.
Lewis-Langston, Deborah
Lloyd, Leona Loretta
Logan, Benjamin Henry, II
Long, James L.
Long, William H., Jr.
Lott, Gay Lloyd
Luke, Sherrill David
Lytle, Alice A.
Mack, Julia Cooper
Mallett, Conrad L., Jr.
Mangum, Robert J.
Manning, Blanche Marie
Mapp, Calvin R.
Marshall, Consuelo B.
Marshall, Thurgood, Jr.
Martin, Baron H.
Martin, Daniel Ezekiel, Jr.
Martin, Janice R.
Martin, Joshua Wesley, III
Mathews, Lawrence Talbert
Mathis, Gregory
Matthews, Aquilla E.
Maxwell, Stephen Lloyd
May, Lee Andrew
McBeth, Veronica Simmons
McBeth-Reynolds, Sandra Kay
McCaulley, James Alan, III
McCollum, Alice Odessa
McCollum, Anita LaVerne
McCummings, LeVerne
McDade, Joe Billy
McDonald, G. Michael
McDonald, Gabrielle Kirk
McFarland, Arthur C.
McKay, Patti Jo
McKee, Theodore A.
McMillian, Theodore
McNairy, Francine G.
McNeal, Don
McPherson, William H.
Meeks, Cordell David, Jr.
Miles, June C.
Miles-LaGrange, Vicki
Miller, E. Ethelbert
Miller, Edith
Miller, Isaac H., Jr.
Miller, Loren, Jr.
Mills, Billy G.
Mitchell, Zinora M.
Montgomery, Alpha LeVon, Sr.
Montgomery, Keesler H.
Moore, Thelma W. C.
Moore, Warfield, Jr.
Morcom, Claudia House
Morgan-Price, Veronica Elizabeth
Morris, Fred H., Jr.
Morrison, Clarence Christopher
Morrison, Johnny Edward
Morrow, Dion Griffith
Morse, John E., Jr.
Motley, Constance Baker, Sr.
Murphy, Harriet Louise M.
Myatt, Gordon J.
Naves, Larry J.
Neals, Felix
Nelson, David S.
Newman, Theodore Roosevelt, Jr.

Newman, William Thomas, Jr.
Niles, Alban I.
Nix, Robert N. C., Jr.
Nunn, Robinson S.
O'Banner-Owens, Jeanette
O'Bryant, Constance Taylor
Ortique, Revius Oliver, Jr.
Ortiz, Victor
Otis-Lewis, Alexis D.
Overstreet, Morris L.
Owens, Nathaniel Davis
Page, Alan Cedric
Parker, Barrington D., Jr.
Parks, Sherman A.
Parrish, Clarence R.
Patrick, Isadore W., Jr.
Patterson, Cecil Booker, Jr.
Patterson, Robert L.
Payne, Gary D.
Pearson, James A.
Peavy, John W., Jr.
Peay, Samuel
Penn, John Garrett
Penn, Shelton C.
Petersen, Eileen Ramona
Pettway, Jo Celeste
Pierce, Lawrence Warren
Pincham, R. Eugene, Sr.
Pitts, Donald Franklin
Poole, Cecil F.
Posten, William S.
Prattis, Lawrence
Price, Charles
Price, William S., III
Pyles, John E.
Queen, Evelyn E. Crawford
Ramirez, Gilbert
Ramseur, Donald E.
Rankin, Michael L.
Ransom, Gary Elliott
Raye, Vance Wallace
Reddick, Thomas J., Jr.
Redding, Louis L.
Reece, Guy L., II
Reid, Ellis Edmund, III
Richardson, Andra Virginia
Richardson, Scovel
Riggs, Elizabeth A.
Riley, Eve Montgomery
Rivers, Denovious Adolphus
Robbins, Alfred S.
Roberson, Dalton Anthony
Robinson, Aubrey Eugene, Jr.
Rodgers, Edward
Rogers, John W.
Rogers, Judith W.
Roulhac, Joseph D.
Roulhac, Roy L.
Rowe, Jasper C.
Rucker, Robert D., Jr.
Ruffin, John H., Jr.
Ruth, James
Saffold, Shirley Strickland
Salone, Marcus
Samples, Benjamin Norris
Sanderlin, James B.
Sandifer, Jawn A.
Sandoz, John H.
Satterfield, Patricia Polson
Schatzman, Dennis Clyde
Sconiers, Rose H.
Scott, Hugh B.
Scott, Richard Eley
Sears, Leah Jeanette
Selby, Myra C.
Shaw, Booker Thomas
Shaw, Charles A.
Shaw, Leander J., Jr.
Shields, Karen Bethea
Simmons, Paul A.
Sims, Barbara M.
Smith, George Bundy
Smith, Henry R., Jr.
Smith, Joscelyn E.
Smith, Renetta
Smitherman, Carole
South, Leslie Elaine
Spear, E. Eugene
Spencer, James R.
Spurlock, Oliver M.
Squire, Carole Renee Hutchins
Steele, Cleophas R., Jr.
Stephens, Cynthia Diane
Stephens, Herbert Malone
Stephens, William Haynes
Stewart, Carl E.
Stone, William T.
Stout, Juanita Kidd
Strayhorn, Earl E.

Stringer, Thomas Edward, Sr.
Strong, Craig Stephen
Sullivan, Emmet G.
Swan, John William David
Taliaferro, Viola J.
Tanner, Jack E.
Taylor, Anna Diggs
Taylor, Vernon Anthony
Taylor, Wilford, Jr.
Terrell, Mary Ann
Thomas, Clarence
Thomas, Claude Roderick
Thomas, Lucia Theodosia
Thomas, Mary Maxwell
Thomas, Maxine F.
Thompson, Anne Elise
Thompson, Myron H.
Thompson, Sandra Ann
Thompson, William Coleridge
Thompson, William S.
Tibbs, Edward A.
Tolentino, Shirley A.
Toles, Edward Bernard
Townsend, Leonard
Trumbo, George William
Tucker, Herbert E., Jr.
Tucker, Marcus O., Jr.
Tuffin, Paul Jonathan
Tusan, Gail S.
Van Hook, George Ellis, Jr.
Wagner, Annice
Wahls, Myron Hastings
Waits, Va Lita Francine
Walker, Carl, Jr.
Wallace, John E., Jr.
Ward, Horace T.
Ware, Charles Jerome
Warner, Ivan
Warren, Joyce Williams
Watson, J. Warren
Watson, James L.
Watt, Garland Wedderick
Watts, Lucile
Webber, Paul R., III
Weeks, Renee Jones
Weiner, Charles R.
West, Joseph King
Wharton, Milton S.
White, George W.
White, Ronnie L.
Whiting, Willie
Wilder, Kurt
Williams, Alexander, Jr.
Williams, Alphonza
Williams, Ann Claire
Williams, Arthur G., Jr.
Williams, Carolyn H.
Williams, Clayton Richard
Williams, David W.
Williams, Jewel L.
Williams, Joseph B.
Williams, Louise Bernice
Williams, Marcus Doyle
Williams, Milton Lawrence
Williams, Patricia Anne
Williams, Walter
Willis, Charles L.
Wilson, Calvin T.
Winfield, Susan Rebecca Holmes
Wood, Harold Leroy
Wood, William S.
Woods, Arleigh Maddox
Woods, Sylvania Webb, Sr.
Worthy, Kym
Wright, Bruce McM.
Wright, Geoffrey
Wright, Robert A.
Wright, Robert Courtlandt
Wrighten, John H., III
Wyatt Cummings Moore, Thelma LaVerne
Zeno, Melvin Collins

Labor Relations
See **Labor Union Administration; Management/ Administration—Personnel/ Training/Labor Relations**

Labor Union Administration
Adams, Nelson Eddy
Andrews, James Edward
Anthony, Leander Aldrich
Baker, Willie L., Jr.
Barrett, James A.

Bell, Tom, Jr.
Bishop, David Rudolph
Bolden, Betty A.
Breckenridge, Jackie B.
Bremer, Charles E.
Brokaw, Carol Ann
Brown, Emmett Earl
Brown, Louis Sylvester
Bryant, Connie L.
Burrus, William Henry
Burton, John H.
Carr, Sandra Jean Irons
Clark, LeRoy D.
Claytor, Charles E.
Corprew, Wilbert E.
Davis, Frank Derocher
Davis, George B.
Davis, Norman Emanuel
Davis, Shirley E.
Day, Donald K.
Dixon, Jimmy
Dixon, Yvonne T.
Downes, Dwight
Druitt, Beverly F.
Faulding, Charles
Fisher, Joseph
Francis, Ray William, Jr.
Fulton, Robert Henry
Gales, James
Gilliam, Arleen Fain
Glass, James
Goode, George Ray
Graves, Carole A.
Green, Oliver Winslow
Hargrove, John E.
Harris, Leon L.
Hester, Melvyn Francis
Hollowell, Kenneth Lawrence
Holmes, Cloyd James
Hubbard, Stanley, Sr.
Hutchins, Lawrence G., Sr.
Hutchinson, Chester R.
Irons, Sandra Jean
Jackson, Franklin D. B.
Jackson, Lee Arthur
Jackson, Mattie J.
Johnson, Georgianna
Johnson, James H.
Johnson, Lonnie L.
Lee, William Thomas
Lewis, Green Pryor, Jr.
Locket, Arnold, Jr.
Lofton, Ernest
Lorthridge, James E.
Lucy, William
Lynch, Leon
McCray, Joe Richard
McMillian, Josie
McNorton, Bruce Edward
Melton, Harry S.
Miller, Doris Jean
Montgomery, Oliver R.
Moore, Lewis Calvin
Murphy, Donald Richard
Naphier, Joe L.
Norris, Fred Arthur, Jr.
Ottley, Austin H.
Patterson, Joan Lethia
Peake, Edward James, Jr.
Peterson, Clarence Josephus
Pollard, Alfonso McInham
Porter, Grady J.
Pratt, Melvin Lemar
Rhett, Michael L.
Richmond, Rodney Welch
Roberts, Kim A.
Roberts, Lillian
Rocha, Joseph Ramon, Jr.
Romney, Edgar O.
Rudd, Willie Lesslie
St. Mary, Joseph Jerome
Springer, George Chelston
Stewart, William O.
Stodghill, William
Stone, Dolores June
Sturdivant, John Nathan
Tate, Eula Booker
Taylor, William Henry, Sr.
Thomas, Ralph Charles, III
Todman, Jureen Francis
Turner, Doris
Turner, Edward L.
Turner, Tina
Underwood, Frankye Harper
Upshaw, Gene
Waddy, Walter James
Walker, Joe
Watkins, Ted
Webb, Lucious Moses

Whipps, Mary N.
Williams, Wilbert
Williams, Wyatt Clifford
Wilson, Robert H.
Worsham, James E.
Wyatt, Addie L.

Landscape/Horticultural Services
Church, Robert T., Sr.
Grace, Horace R.
Lintz, Frank D. E.
Owens, Angle B., Jr.
Shoemaker, Veronica Sapp
Wilkins, Allen Henry

Law Enforcement
Adams, Paul Brown
Adkins, Leroy J.
Albert, Charles Gregory
Allen, Robert
Alveranga, Glanvin L.
Anderson, Carl Edward
Anderson, Leslie Blake
Anderson, Perry L.
Arbuckle, Ronald Lee, Sr.
Artison, Richard E.
Ball, John Calvin, Sr.
Balmer, Horace Dalton, Sr.
Barnes, Diane
Barnett, William
Barrett, Jacquelyn H.
Barton, Wayne Darrell
Beasley, Victor Mario
Bell, Eldrin A.
Bennett, Delores
Berry, Mary Frances
Billingsley, Andrew
Bishop, Sherre Whitney
Boyle, Jim
Bracey, John Henry, Jr.
Bradley, Walter Thomas, Jr.
Branch, William McKinley
Brooks, Clyde Henry
Brooks, Fabienne
Brooks, Israel, Jr.
Brown, Diana Johnson
Brown, Frank Lewis
Brown, Joseph Davidson, Sr.
Brown, Lee Patrick
Brown, Robert, Jr.
Brown, Thomas Edison, Jr.
Brown, Walter E.
Bryan, Adelbert M.
Buckley, Edward L.
Bullock, J. Jerome
Burgess, Melvin Thomas, Sr.
Burton, Donald C.
Bush, T. W.
Byrd, James W.
Cage, Patrick B.
Calhoun, Jack Johnson, Jr.
Callender, Carl O.
Cantrell, Forrest Daniel
Capehart, Johnnie Lawrence
Carpenter, Lewis
Carroll, James S.
Carter, Christopher Anthony
Casey, Clifton G.
Chambers, Pamela S.
Chapman, Diana Cecelia
Clark, Roslyn M.
Clarke, Priscilla
Clayton, Willie Burke, Jr.
Coleman, Claude M.
Coleman, Donald
Conner, Gail Patricia
Cooke, Leonard
Cooley, James F.
Cooper, Drucilla Hawkins
Cooper, Julius, Jr.
Cousins, Frank
Coy, John T.
Crouch, Robert Allen
Cunningham, Glenn Dale
Cureton, Michael
Darden, Orlando William
Davis, Esther Gregg
Davis, Francis D.
Davis, Goliath J., III
Davis, Harvey
Davis, Jacklean Andrea
Davis, Willie J.
Day, Eric Therander
DeGeneste, Henry Irving
Drake, Maggie W.

Drummond, Thornton B., Jr.
Edwards, Theodore Thomas
Ellis, J. Delano, II
Featherstone, Karl Ramon
Ferrebee, Thomas G.
Fillyaw, Leonard David
Fitzgerald, Herbert H.
Fonville, Danny D.
Foushee, Geraldine George
Frazier, Joseph Norris
Gatling, Patricia Lynn
Gibson, John A.
Gibson, Johnnie M. M.
Gilliam, Joel
Glover, Nat
Golden, Willie L.
Green, Lisa A.
Greenberg, Reuben M.
Griffin, James Stafford
Griffin, Ronald Charles
Guillory, Julius James
Hackett, Wilbur L., Jr.
Hackey, George Edward, Jr.
Hall, Jack L.
Hampton, Ronald Everett
Hargrove, Trent
Harvard, Beverly Bailey
Henderson, Carl L., Jr.
Herbert, Douglas A.
Hicks, Delphus Van, Jr.
Hill, Arthur Burit
Hill, Deirdre Hughes
Hillard, Terry
Holliday, Alfonso David
Holliday-Hayes, Wilhelmina
   Evelyn
Howard, Calvin Johnson
Howard, Paul Lawrence, Jr.
Howell, Willie R.
Hudson, John D.
Irvin, Regina Lynette
Isaacs, Stephen D.
Ivy, James E.
Jackson, Carlos
Jackson, Darnell
Jackson, George K.
Jackson, James Garfield
Jackson, Tommy L.
Jason, Henry Thomas
Jefferson-Ford, Charmain
Jenkins, Marilyn Joyce
Johnson, Cleveland, Jr.
Johnson, Leon F.
Johnson, Robert T.
Jones, Frank
Jones, Irma Renae
Jones, Sherman Jarvis
Kelley, Jack Albert
Kinchen, Dennis Ray
Knox, Dorothy Dean
Knox, Stanley
Kyles, Dwain Johann
Kyles, Sharron Faye
Lanier, Shelby, Jr.
Lankster, Barrown Douglas
Lay, Clorius L.
Lee, Ivin B.
Leland, Joyce F.
Lemon, Michael Wayne, Sr.
Lockley, Clyde William
Logan, Carolyn Green
Love, James O., Sr.
Lowe, Jack, Jr.
Malone, Rosemary C.
Mannie, William Edward
Mapp, David Kenneth, Jr.
Marsh, Sandra M.
Marshall, Tom, Sr.
Martin, Patricia Elizabeth
Martin, Ralph C., II
Matthews, Robert L.
McBee, Vincent Clermont
McGriff, Deborah M.
McHenry, Mary Williamson
McKelpin, Joseph P.
McKinnon, Isaiah
McKitt, Willie, Jr.
McKnight, Albert J.
Montgomery, Keesler H.
Morris, Carolyn G.
Morrison, Garfield E., Jr.
Morrison, Johnny Edward
Morrison, Trudi Michelle
Mosley, James Earl, Sr.
Moss, James Edward
Moss, Thomas Edward, Sr.
Murray, Albert R.
Napoleon, Benny Nelson
Neal, Richard

Nelson, Doeg M.
Nelson, Harold E.
Nelson, Ronald Duncan
Nesby, Donald Ray, Sr.
O'Bryant, Tilmon Bunche
Oliver, Everett Ahmad
Oliver, Jerry Alton, Sr.
Oliver, Ronald Daniel
Osborne, Hugh Stancill
Owens, Ronald
Parker, Charles Thomas
Parker, Vernon B.
Patterson, Lloyd
Pennick, Janet
Pennington, Richard
Perkins, Thomas P.
Peterson, Alan Herbert
Pierce, Samuel R., Jr.
Proctor, Sonya T.
Randolph, Leonard Washington,
   Jr.
Rhett, Michael L.
Rice, Fred
Rice, Lewis, Jr.
Rich, Stanley C.
Richards, Edward A.
Riley, William Scott
Robinson, Clarence G.
Rodez, Andrew LaMarr
Rodgers, Anthony Recarido, Sr.
Scott, Elsie L.
Shanks, James A.
Sharpe, Ronald M.
Simmons, Harold Lee
Singleton, Benjamin, Sr.
Smith, Janet K.
Smith, LaSalle, Sr.
Smith, Marvin Preston
Stafford, Don
Stalling, Ronald Eugene
Stephen, Joyce
Stroud, Milton
Swain, James H.
Sylvester, Odell Howard, Jr.
Tate, Earnest L.
Taylor, Benjamin Garland
Taylor, DeForrest Walker
Taylor, Vanessa Gail
Taylor, Vernon Anthony
Terry, Adeline Helen
Thomas, Joseph Edward, Jr.
Thomas, Nina M.
Thomas, Robert Lewis
Thomas, Rodolfo Rudy
Thompas, George Henry, Jr.
Thompson, Oswald
Tillmon, Joey
Travis, Myron
Tucker, Dorothy M.
Turner, Eddie William
Turner, Leslie Marie
Turner, Melvin E.
Underwood, Joseph M., Jr.
Vaughn, William Smith
Veals, Craig Elliott
Venson, Clyde R.
Wade, Casey, Jr.
Waith, Eldridge
Walker, May
Ward, Benjamin
Ward, Nolan F.
Washington, Leonard, Jr.
Watford-McKinney, Yvonne V.
Watson, Herman Doc
Watson, Jackie
Wearing, Melvin
Webb, Joseph G.
Weldon, Ramon N.
White, June Joyce
Williams, Ellis
Williams, Hubert
Williams, Leonard, Sr.
Williams, Moses, Sr.
Williams, Rodney Elliott
Williams, Willie L.
Wilson, Jimmy L.
Woods, Wilbourne F.
Worshaim, Keith Eugene
Wrice, David
Wynn, Malcolm
Young, Lee R.
Younger, Lewis T., Jr.

Law/Legal Services
Abernathy, James R., II
Adams, Edward Robert
Adams, Gregory Albert
Adams, John Oscar

Addams, Robert David
Ahmad, Jadwaa
Albert, Charles Gregory
Alexander, Clifford L., Jr.
Alexander, James, Jr.
Alexander, Robin
Alford, Haile Lorraine
al-Hafeez, Humza
Ali-Jackson, Kamil
Allen, George Mitchell
Allen, Jerry Ormes, Sr.
Allen, W. George
Alls, Howard E.
Al'Uqdah, William Mujahid
Amaker, Norman Carey
Aman, Mohammed M.
Anderson, Edwyna G.
Anderson, George Allen
Anderson, Leslie Blake
Anderson, Richard Charles
Andrews, Judis R.
Archibald, B. Milele
Armistead, Milton
Arnelle, Hugh Jesse
Arnold, Rudolph P.
Atkins, Edna R.
Atkins, Thomas Irving
Audain, Linz
Austin, Joyce Phillips
Awkard, Linda Nanline
Backus, Bradley
Bailer, Bonnie Lynn
Bailey, Jerry Dean
Bailey, Lawrence R., Sr.
Bain, Raymone Kaye
Baker, Althea
Baker, Beverly Poole
Baker, Oscar Wilson
Baker, Thurbert E.
Baker-Kelly, Beverly
Baldwin, Cynthia A.
Baldwin, George R.
Ball, Richard E.
Ball, William Batten
Ballance, Frank Winston, Jr.
Ball-Reed, Patrice M.
Banks, Cecil J.
Banks, Haywood Elliott
Banks, Patricia
Banks, Richard Edward
Banks, Richard L.
Banks, Sharon P.
Bankston, Archie M.
Barbee, Lloyd Augustus
Barksdale, Leonard N., III
Barnes, Joseph Nathan
Barnes, Stephen Darryl
Barnes, William L.
Barnes, Willie R.
Barnes, Yolanda L.
Bartelle, Talmadge Louis
Barzey, Raymond Clifford, II
Baskerville, Randolph
Bateman, Paul E.
Bates, Arthur Verdi
Bates, George Albert
Batine, Rafael
Bauduit, Harold S.
Baugh, Edna Y.
Beal Bagneris, Michele Christine
Beamon, Arthur Leon
Beane, Dorothea Annette
Beard, Charles Julian
Beard, James William, Jr.
Beasley, Ulysses Christian, Jr.
Beasley, Victor Mario
Beatty, Otto, Jr.
Beech, Harvey Elliott
Belcher, Nathaniel L.
Bell, Napoleon A.
Bell, Sheila Trice
Bell, William A.
Bell, William Augustus, II
Bell, William Jerry
Bellamy, Angela Robinson
Bellamy, Everett
Belton, Howard G.
Belton, Robert
Benefield, Michael Maurice, Jr.
Bennett, Arthur T.
Bennett, Bessye Warren
Bennett, Patricia A.
Benton, James Wilbert, Jr.
Berkley, Constance E. Gresham
Bernstine, Daniel O.
Berry, LeRoy
Berry, Theodore M.
Bessent, Hattie
Besson, Paul Smith

Beverly, Frankie
Black, Lee Roy
Blackmon, Anthony Wayne
Blackmon, Barbara Anita
Blades, Brian Keith
Blade-Tiggens, Denise Patricia
Blair, Charles Michael
Blakely, William H., Jr.
Blount, Clarence W.
Blount, Larry Elisha
Bludson-Francis, Vernett Michelle
Blue, Daniel Terry, Jr.
Blunt, Roger Reckling
Boatwright, Joseph Weldon
Bocage, Ronald J.
Boddie, Arthur Walker
Bolden, Dorothy Lee
Bolden, Frank Augustus
Boney, J. Don
Booker, James E.
Booth, Le-Quita
Bostic, James Edward, Jr.
Boulware, William H.
Bourne, Beal Vernon, II
Bourne, Judith Louise
Bowman, Jacquelynne Jeanette
Boyd, Charles Flynn
Boyd, Thomas
Boze, U. Lawrence
Bracey, William Rubin
Bracey, Willie Earl
Braden, Everette Arnold
Braden, Henry E., IV
Bradley, Edward R.
Branton, Leo, Jr.
Brashear, Berlaind Leander
Braxton, John Ledger
Brazil, Ernest L.
Breckenridge, Franklin E.
Breckenridge, John L.
Brewer, Curtis
Briscoe, Hattie Ruth Elam
Bristow, Clinton, Jr.
Brokaw, Carol Ann
Brooke, Edward William
Brooks, Rosemary Bittings
Brooks, Roy Lavon
Brown, Benjamin Leonard
Brown, Byrd R.
Brown, Deloris A.
Brown, Denise J.
Brown, Dwayne Marc
Brown, Edwin C., Jr.
Brown, Franchot A.
Brown, Irma Jean
Brown, Jamie Earl S., Jr.
Brown, Janice Rogers
Brown, Jasper C., Jr.
Brown, Lewis Frank
Brown, Ralph H.
Brown, Virgil E., Jr.
Brown, Willard L.
Brown, William H., III
Brownlee, Wyatt China
Brownridge, J. Paul
Bruce, Kenneth E.
Brummer, Chauncey Eugene
Bryan, David Everett, Jr.
Bryant, Andrea Pair
Bryant, Hubert Hale
Bryant, Regina Lynn
Bryant, Robert E.
Bryant, Wayne R.
Bryson, Cheryl Blackwell
Buchanan, Calvin D.
Buckner, Mary Alice
Budd, Wayne Anthony
Bugg, Mayme Carol
Bullock, James
Burgess, James R., Jr.
Burke, Yvonne Watson Brathwaite
Burnham, Margaret Ann
Burris, John L.
Burris, Roland W.
Burroughs, Robert A.
Burse, Raymond Malcolm
Bush, Nathaniel
Bussey, Reuben T.
Butcher, Goler Teal
Butler, Frederick Douglas
Butler, Jerome M.
Butler, Patrick Hampton
Bynoe, John Garvey
Byrd, Frederick E.
Byrd, Isaac, Jr.
Byrd, Jerry Stewart
Cadogan, Marjorie A.
Cage, Patrick B.
Cain, Frank Edward, Jr.

Cain, Robert R., Jr.
Cain, Simon Lawrence
Caldwell, James E.
Caldwell, Lisa Jeffries
Callender, Carl O.
Callender, Wilfred A.
Calvin, Michael Byron
Camp, Marva Jo
Campbell, Christopher Lundy
Cannon, H. LeRoy
Carlisle, James Edward, Jr.
Carney, Alfonso Linwood, Jr.
Carpenter, Raymond Prince
Carroll, James S.
Carroll, Raoul Lord
Carter, Billy L.
Carter, Charles Edward
Carter, Charles Michael
Carter, Theodore Ulysses
Carter, Zachary Warren
Cason, Marilynn Jean
Chambers, John Curry, Jr.
Chambers, Julius LeVonne
Chambliss, Alvin Odell, Jr.
Chambliss, Prince C., Jr.
Chancellor, Carl Eugene
Chandler, Everett A.
Chandler, James P.
Chapman, David Anthony
Charity, Ruth Harvey
Cheek, King Virgil, Jr.
Chenault, Kenneth
Cherot, Nicholas Maurice
Chess, Sammie, Jr.
Childs, Joy
Childs, Winston
Clark, Augusta Alexander
Clark, Leonard Weslorn, Jr.
Clark-Gates, Brenda
Clay, Eric Lee
Clay, William Lacy, Jr.
Clayton, Laura Ancelina
Clayton, Matthew D.
Clayton, Theaoseus T.
Clegg, Legrand H., II
Clements, Walter H.
Clendenon, Donn A.
Cloud, Sanford, Jr.
Cloud, W. Eric
Clyne, John Rennel
Cobb, John Hunter, Jr.
Cochran, Johnnie L., Jr.
Cohen, Vincent H.
Cole, James O.
Cole, Ransey Guy, Jr.
Coleman, April Howard
Coleman, Arthur H.
Coleman, Claude M.
Coleman, Eric Dean
Coleman, Michael Bennett
Coleman, Michael Victor
Coleman, William T., Jr.
Coleman, William T., III
Collins, Daisy G.
Collins, Kenneth L.
Collins, Robert Frederick
Collins, Theodicia Deborah
Colter, Cyrus J.
Conley, Charles S.
Conley, John A.
Conley, Martha Richards
Cook, Frank Robert, Jr.
Cook, Rufus
Cooper, Almeta E.
Cooper, Clarence
Cooper, Clement Theodore
Cooper, Gordon R., II
Cooper, Joseph
Corlette, Edith
Cormier, Rufus, Jr.
Cornish, Jeannette Carter
Cornwell, William David
Countee, Thomas Hilaire, Jr.
Cousins, William, Jr.
Covington, M. Stanley
Cox, Sandra Hicks
Cox, Warren E.
Crenshaw, Ronald Willis
Crenshaw, Waverly David, Jr.
Crockett, George William, Jr.
Crockett, Gwendolyn B.
Cromartie, Ernest W., II
Cruise, Warren Michael
Crump, Arthel Eugene
Crusto, Mitchell Ferdinand
Cunningham, Courtney
Cunningham, E. Brice
Cunningham, F. Malcolm
Cunningham, T. J.

Latham, Weldon Hurd
Lathen, Deborah Ann
Latimer, Allie B.
Latney, Harvey, Jr.
LaVergne, Luke Aldon
Lawrence, Archie
Lawrence, Lonnie R.
Lawson, John C., II
Lawson, Marjorie McKenzie
Leacock, Stephen Jerome
Lee, Debra Louise
Lee, Lena S. King
Lee, Michael Waring
Lee, Nathaniel
Leek, Everett Paul
Leek, Sandra D.
Lee Sang, Sharon Nolan
Leftwich, Norma Bogues
Leftwich, Willie L.
Leighton, George Neves
Lenoir, Kip
Leoney, Antoinette E. M.
Lester, Betty J.
Lester, Elton J.
Lewis, Cary B., Jr.
Lewis, Daniel
Lewis, David Baker
Lewis, Reta Jo
Lewis, William A., Jr.
Lewis-Langston, Deborah
Lindsay, Reginald C.
Lindsey, Terry Lamar
Link, Joyce Battle
Littlejohn, Bill C.
Littlejohn, Edward J.
Livingston-Wilson, Karen
Lloyd, Leona Loretta
Lloyd, Leonia Jannetta
Lloyd, Marcea Bland
Lockhart, James B.
Lofton, Mellanese S.
Logan, George, III
Long, James Alexander
Lucas, Sherrill David
Luke, Sherrill David
Lyle, Freddrenna M.
Lyman, Webster S.
Maith, Sheila Francine
Mallory, George L., Jr.
Malone, Charles A.
Mangum, Charles M. L.
Mann, George Levier
Mann, Thomas J., Jr.
Mannie, William Edward
Manning, Howard Nick, Jr.
Mapp, Calvin R.
Marable, Herman, Jr.
Marks, Kenneth Hicks, Jr.
Marr, Carmel Carrington
Marsh, Henry L., III
Marsh, Sandra M.
Marsh, William A., Jr.
Marsh, William Andrew, III
Marshall, Reese
Martin, Charles Howard
Martin, Clarence L.
Martin, Daniel E.
Martin, Daniel Ezekiel, Jr.
Martin, Joshua Wesley, III
Martin, Ralph C., II
Martin Chase, Debra
Martin-Cross, Denise L.
Mason, William Thomas, Jr.
Mass, Edna Elaine
Mathis, Gregory
Mathur, Krishan
Matthews, Cynthia Clark
Maultsby, Dorothy M., Esq.
Maxey, Marlon Lee
May, Lee Andrew
Mayberry, Patricia Marie
Mazique, Frances Margurite
McAlpine, Robert
McCants, Jesse Lee, Sr.
McCaulley, James Alan, III
McClain, Andrew Bradley
McClain, William L.
McClean, Vernon E.
McClenic, Patricia Dickson
McClure, Fredrick H. L.
McClure, Wesley Cornelious
McCoy, William
McCraven, Carl Clarke
McCroom, Eddie Winther
McCrorey, H. Lawrence
McDaniel, Paul Anderson
McDonald, Mike
McFarland, Arthur C.
McFarland, Claudette

McFarland, Ollie Franklin
McGee, Henry W., Jr.
McGee, James Madison
McGinnis, James W.
McGinty, Doris Evans
McGriff, Deborah M.
McGriggs-Jamison, Imogene
McIlwain, Nadine Williams
McIntosh, Rhodina Covington
McIntosh, Walter Cordell
McKanders, Kenneth Andre
McKandes, Darnell Damon
McKee, Lonette
McKinney, Samuel Berry
McKissick, Floyd B., Jr.
McLaren, Douglas Earl
McLaughlin, Andree Nicola
McLaughlin, Eurphan
McLin, Lena Johnson
McMillan, Robert Frank, Jr.
McNeil, Frank
McNeill, Susan Patricia
McNeill-Huntley, Esther Mae
McPherson, William H.
McQuay, James Phillip
McWorter, Gerald A.
Medina, Benny
Meeks, Reginald Kline
Merchant, John Cruse
Merchant, John F.
Mercy, Leland, Jr.
Metoyer, Rosia G.
Michaux, Eric Coates
Michaux, Henry G.
Michel, Harriet Richardson
Middlebrooks, Felicia
Miles, June C.
Miller, Cylenthia LaToye
Miller, Melvin B.
Millner, Dianne Maxine
Minor, Jessica
Minter, Kendall Arthur
Mitchell, Charles E.
Mitchell, Huey P.
Mitchell, Iverson O., III
Mitchell, Stanley Henryk
Mitchell, Theo W.
Mobley, Stacey J.
Montgomery, Gregory B.
Moody, Eric Orlando
Moore, Colin A.
Moore, Cornell Leverette
Moore, Elizabeth D.
Moore, Emanuel A.
Moore, Fred Henderson
Moore, Howard, Jr.
Moore, Jane Bond
Moore, Richard Baxter
Moore, Rodney Gregory
Moran, Joyce E.
Morgan, Richard H., Jr.
Morgan-Price, Veronica Elizabeth
Morial, Marc
Morris, Herman, Jr.
Morris, Melvin
Morrison, Robert B., Jr.
Morrow, Samuel P., Jr.
Morton, William Stanley
Moseley Braun, Carol Elizabeth
Mosley, Maurice B.
Mott, Stokes E., Jr.
Muckelroy, William Lawrence
Munday, Reuben A.
Murphy, Clyde Everett
Murphy, Donald Richard
Murphy, Ira H.
Murphy, Romallus O.
Murrain, Godfrey H.
Murray, Archibald R.
Myricks, Noel
Nabrit, James M., Jr.
Nabrit, James M., III
Nails, John Walker
Naphtali, Ashirah Sholomis
Napoleon, Benny Nelson
Nash, Curtis
Neal, Earl Langdon
Neal, Langdon D.
Neals, Felix
Neely, David E.
Neely, Henry Mason
Nelson, Gilbert L.
Nelson, Mary Elizabeth
Nelson, Otha Curtis, Sr.
Nesbitt, Robin Anthony
Neusom, Thomas G.
Newell, Kathleen W.
Newhouse, Millicent DeLaine
Newton, Andrew E., Jr.

Newton, Demetrius C.
Newton, Robert
Nichols, Edward K., Jr.
Nicholson, Jessie R.
Nickerson, Don Carlos
Nobles, Patricia Joyce
Northcross, Wilson Hill, Jr.
Northern, Christina Ann
Norwood, Kimberly Jade
Nunnery, Willie James
O'Bannon, Donna Edwards
Ogletree, Charles J., Jr.
Oguniesi, Adebayo O.
Olinger, David Y., Jr.
Oliver, Jesse Dean
Oliver, John J., Jr.
Oliver, Robert Lee
Oliver-Simon, Gloria Craig
O'Neal, Raymond W., Sr.
Orr, Janice
Orridge, Jeffrey Lyndon
Ortique, Revius Oliver, Jr.
Otis-Lewis, Alexis D.
Owens, Ronald C.
Ozanne, Dominic L.
Page, Rosemary Saxton
Pailen, Donald
Palmore, Roderick A.
Parker, H. Wallace
Parker, Jerry P.
Parker, Joseph Caiaphas, Jr.
Parker, Kellis E.
Parker, Vernon B.
Parks, Bernard
Parks, Edward Y.
Parks, George B.
Parks, James Edward
Parms, Edwin L.
Paschall, Evita Arneda
Paterson, Basil Alexander
Patrick, Deval L.
Patrick, Lawrence Clarence, Jr.
Patterson, Elizabeth Hayes
Patterson, Michael Duane
Payne, Jacqueline LaVerne
Payne, James Edward
Payton, Jeff
Payton, Nolan H.
Payton, Willis Conwell
Peek, Gail Lenore
Peele, John E., Jr.
Pemberton-Heard, Danielle Marie
Pendergrass, Emma H.
Pennick, Aurie Alma
Pennington, Jesse C.
Peoples, Veo, Jr.
Persons, W. Ray
Peters, Aulana Louise
Peters, Samuel A.
Peterson, Rocky Lee
Pettigrew, Grady L., Jr.
Phillips, Frank Edward
Pierce, Cynthia Straker
Pierce, Frank Powell
Pierce, Lawrence Warren
Pierce, Rudolph F.
Pierson, Kathryn A.
Pinkney, Betty Kathryn
Pittman, Darryl E.
Pitts, Cornelius
Pitts, Ronald James, Sr.
Plummer, Matthew W., Sr.
Poindexter, Gammiel Gray
Pope, Derrick Alexander
Porter, E. Melvin
Posey, Bruce Keith
Poston, Carl
Poston, Carl C., Jr.
Poston, Kevin
Pottinger, Albert A.
Powell, Darlene Wright
Pratt, A. Michael
Preiskel, Barbara Scott
Price, Charles Eugene
Pride, Hemphill P., II
Pride, Walter LaVon
Procter, Harvey Thornton, Jr.
Proctor, Timothy DeWitt
Pryor, Calvin Caffey
Purnell, Carolyn J.
Putnam, Glendora M.
Pyles, John E.
Quander, Rohulamin
Rabouin, E. Michelle
Ramey, Adele Martin
Ramsey, Jerome Capistrano
Randle, Carver A.
Randolph, Lonnie Marcus
Randolph-Jasmine, Carol Davis

Ransier, Frederick L., III
Rauch, Doreen E.
Ravenell, William Hudson
Rawls, Raleigh Richard
Ray, Greg Alan
Ray, Rosalind Rosemary
Raynor, Robert G., Jr.
Rearden, Sara B.
Redd, William L.
Reed, Alfonzo
Reed, Gregory J.
Reed, Jerrildine
Reed, Kimberley Del Rio
Reed, Michael H.
Reeves, Willie Lloyd, Jr.
Reid, Inez Smith
Reid, N. Neville
Reid, Selwyn Charles
Reide, Jerome L.
Reid-McQueen, Lynne Marguerite
Renfroe, Iona Antoinette
Reynolds, Grant
Rhinehart, June Acie
Rhinehart, Vernon Morel
Rhodes, Paula R.
Rice, David Eugene, Jr.
Rice, Fredrick LeRoy
Rice, Judith Carol
Richardson, Andra Virginia
Richardson, Delroy M.
Richardson, Ralph H.
Richardson, Rhonda Karen
Richardson, Robert Eugene
Richardson, Wayne Michael
Richie, Leroy C.
Risher, John R., Jr.
Rist, Susan E.
Rivera, Eddy
Rivers, Denovious Adolphus
Rivers, Valerie L.
Roane, Glenwood P.
Robbins, Kevin F.
Roberts, Bryndis Wynette
Robinson, Carl Cornell
Robinson, Edward Ashton
Robinson, Jack, Jr.
Robinson, Learthon Steven, Sr.
Robinson, Leonard Harrison, Jr.
Robinson, Maurice C.
Robinson, Rosalyn Karen
Robinson, Sandra Hawkins
Rolark, M. Wilhelmina
Ross, Kevin Arnold
Rotan, Constance S.
Roulhac, Roy L.
Roundtree, Dovey
Rowe, Nansi Irene
Rowland, James H.
Roye, Monica R. Hargrove
Russell, Ermea J.
Ryan, Agnes C.
Saint-Louis, Rudolph Anthony
Salone, Marcus
Sampson, Thomas Gatewood
Samuels, Ronald S.
Sanders, Hank
Sanders, Joseph Stanley
Saulsberry, Charles R.
Sawyer, George Edward
Sawyer, Roderick Terrence
Scales-Trent, Judy
Scavella, Michael Duane
Scott, Hugh B.
Scott, Judith Sugg
Scott, Lawrence William
Scott, Nigel L.
Scott, Windie Olivia
Scott-Clayton, Patricia Ann
Scurry, Fred L.
Selby, Ralph Irving
Senegal, Nolton Joseph, Sr.
Senegal, Phyllis J.
Seraile, Janette
Sessoms, Furmin Douglas
Seymour, Barbara H.
Shakoor, Adam Adib
Sharpe, Calvin William
Shaw, Curtis Mitchell
Shaw, Denise
Shaw, Theodore Michael
Sheen, Albert A.
Shelton, Reuben Anderson
Shepard, Huey Percy
Sherwood, O. Peter
Sherwood, Wallace Walter
Shields, Karen Bethea
Shores, Arthur D.
Shuman, Jerome
Silas-Butler, Jacqueline Ann

Simmelkjaer, Robert T.
Simmons, Esmeralda
Simmons, Geraldine Crossley
Simms, Stuart Oswald
Simpson, Stephen Whittington
Sims, Genevieve Constance
Sims, William
Sinclair, Clayton, Jr.
Singleton, Harry M.
Slaughter, Fred L.
Slaughter, Vernon L.
Sleet, Gregory M.
Sloan, David E.
Smalls, O'Neal
Smirni, Allan Desmond
Smith, Charles Edison
Smith, Charles Lamont
Smith, Conrad P.
Smith, Daniel H., Jr.
Smith, David R.
Smith, DeHaven L.
Smith, Frederick D.
Smith, H. Russell
Smith, Harold Teliaferro, Jr.
Smith, Heman Bernard
Smith, Herman Talliferrio
Smith, J. Clay, Jr.
Smith, Jeraldine Williams
Smith, Jock Michael
Smith, Rachel Norcom
Smith, Stanley G.
Smith, William James
Smitherman, Rodger M.
Soden, Richard Allan
Soliunas, Francine Stewart
Sowell, Myzell
Spain, Hiram, Jr.
Spaulding, Lynette Victoria
Spear, E. Eugene
Speights, Nathaniel H.
Spence, Joseph Samuel, Sr.
Spencer, Shanita Rene
Spottsville, Clifford M.
Springer, Eric Winston
Squire, Carole Renee Hutchins
Stampley, Gilbert Elvin
Stancell, Dolores Wilson Pegram
Stanley, Carol Jones
Stanley, Kathryn Velma
Staton, Donna Hill
Stearns Miller, Camille Louise
Stent, Michelle Dorene
Stent, Nicole M.
Stevens, Cleveland
Stewart, Carolyn House
Stewart, John O.
Stokes, Louis
Stone, William T.
Storey, Robert D.
Stroger, John Herman, Jr.
Strong, Helen Francine
Stubbs, Harold K.
Sudarkasa, Michael Eric
  Mabogunje
Sumler-Edmond, Janice L.
Sumner, Thomas Robert
Sutton, Norma J.
Sutton, Oliver Carter, II
Swain, James H.
Swann, Eugene Merwyn
Swanson, Charles
Sweet, Clifford C.
Swinton, Lee Vertis
Talley, Michael Frank, Sr.
Tann, Daniel J.
Tarter, Roger Powell, M.D.
Tate, David Kirk
Tate, Herbert Holmes, Jr.
Taylor, Carol Ann
Taylor, Charles Edward
Taylor, Clarence B.
Taylor, David Richard, III
Taylor, Eartha Lynn
Taylor, Eric Charles
Taylor, Janice A.
Taylor, Jeffery Charles
Taylor, Patricia E.
Taylor, William L.
Teele, Arthur Earle, Jr.
Teeuwissen, Pieter
Telfair, Brian Kraig
Temple, Donald Melvin
Terrell, Francis D'Arcy
Terrell, Mary Ann
Terrell, Reginald V.
Terrill, W. H. Tyrone, Jr.
Terry, Adeline Helen
Thigpen, Calvin Herritage
Thomas, Edward Arthur

Thomas, Franklin A.
Thomas, James O., Jr.
Thomas, Joseph W.
Thomas, Kendall
Thomas, Kenneth Roger
Thomas, Maxine Suzanne
Thomas, Samuel Haynes, Jr.
Thompson, Albert W., Sr.
Thompson, Almose Alphonse, II
Thompson, Daniel Joseph
Thompson, Herman G.
Thompson, Larry D.
Thompson, M. T., Jr.
Thompson, Marttie L.
Thompson, William L.
Thorpe, Josephine Horsley
Tillman, Paula Sellars
Tinsley, Dwane L.
Tinsley, Fred Leland, Jr.
Todd, Thomas N.
Tolliver, Stanley Eugene, Sr.
Toote, Gloria E. A.
Townsend, Murray Luke, Jr.
Townsend, P. A.
Travis, Benjamin
Tucker, Geraldine Jenkins
Tucker, Herbert E., Jr.
Tucker, Karen
Tucker, Michael Kevin
Tucker, Robert L.
Tudy Jackson, Janice
Tuffin, Paul Jonathan
Turner, Reginald M., Jr.
Twine, Edgar Hugh
Uku, Eustace Oris, Sr.
Underwood, Arthur C.
Valdes, Laura
Valentine, J. T.
Vance, Lawrence N.
Van Hook, George Ellis, Jr.
Van Lierop, Robert F.
Vaughters-Johnson, Cecilie A.
Veals, Craig Elliott
Venson, Clyde R.
Vertreace, Walter Charles
Vickers, Eric Erfan
Vinson, Rosalind Rowena
Waddell, Ruchadina LaDesiree
Wade, Beryl Elaine
Wagner, David H.
Waits, Va Lita Francine
Walker, Betty Stevens
Walker, Charles Douglas
Walker, Charles H.
Walker, Cora T.
Walker, Grover Pulliam
Walker, Melford Whitfield, Jr.
Walker, Stanley M.
Walker, Sterling Wilson
Walker, Tanya Rosetta
Walker, Woodson DuBois
Wallace, C. Everett
Wallace, Paul Starrett, Jr.
Wallace, Robert Eugene, Jr.
Walton, Elbert Arthur, Jr.
Walton, James Madison
Ward, John Preston
Ward, Keith Lamont
Ward, Nolan F.
Ward, Ronald R.
Ward, Sandra L.
Ware, Charles Jerome
Ware, Dyahanne
Ware, R. David
Warrick, Alan Everett
Washington, Consuela M.
Washington, Craig A.
Washington, Robert Benjamin, Jr.
Washington, Roosevelt, Jr.
Washington, Valdemar Luther
Washington, Walter E.
Waters, Martin Vincent
Watford-McKinney, Yvonne V.
Watson, Aaron
Watson, Mildred L.
Watson, Solomon B., IV
Watt, Garland Wedderick
Watts, Frederick, Jr.
Way, Gary Darryl
Weber, Daniel
Webster, Lesley Douglass
Webster, William H.
Webster, Winston Roosevelt
Weekes, Martin Edward
Weeks, Deborah Redd
Weems, Vernon Eugene, Jr.
Welch, Edward L.
Wells, Ira J. K., Jr.
West, George Ferdinand, Jr.

West, John Andrew
West, Royce Barry
West, Togo Dennis, Jr.
Weston, Larry Carlton
Wharton, A. C., Jr.
White, Claude Esley
White, D. Richard
White, Frankie Walton
White, Frederic Paul, Jr.
White, Howard A.
White, James S.
White, Janice G.
White, Javier A.
White, Richard Thomas
Whitehead, David William
Whiting, Barbara E.
Whiting, Thomas J.
Whiting, Willie
Whitted, Earl, Jr.
Wickliff, Aloysius M., Sr.
Wilbekin, Harvey E.
Wilbon, Joan Marie
Wilcher, Shirley J.
Wiley, Fletcher Houston
Wilkins, Ervin W.
Willacy, Hazel M.
Williams, Annalisa Stubbs
Williams, Arthur Q., Jr.
Williams, Charles E., III
Williams, Clayton Richard
Williams, Clyde
Williams, Gary C.
Williams, Gregory Howard
Williams, James R.
Williams, Junius W.
Williams, Karen Hastie
Williams, Larry C.
Williams, Philip B.
Williams, Randolph
Williams, Robert B.
Williams, Ronald Charles
Williams, Sandra K.
Williams, Sidney B., Jr.
Williams, Wesley S., Jr.
Williams, Yvonne LaVerne
Williams-Dial, E. Faye
Williamson, Samuel R.
Willis, Frederic L.
Willis, Jill Michelle
Willis, Kathi Grant
Wilmot, David Winston
Wilson, Clarence S., Jr.
Wilson, Kim Adair
Wilson, Lance Henry
Wilson, Margaret Bush
Wilson, Sonali Bustamante
Wimbush, F. Blair
Winfield, James Eros
Wing, Adrien Katherine
Winstead, Vernon A., Sr.
Wood, Curtis A.
Wood, William L., Jr.
Woodhouse, Enoch O'Dell, II
Worthy, Kym
Wright, Carl Jeffrey
Wright, Charles
Wright, Clinton L. A.
Wright, Joseph Malcolm
Wright, Robert A.
Wright, Roberta V. Hughes
Wright-Botchwey, Roberta Yvonne
Wyre, Stanley Marcel
Yancey, Laurel Guild
Yancey, Prentiss Quincy
Yarbrough, Marilyn Virginia
Yarbrough, Robert Elzy
Young, Ira Mason
Young, Lias Carl
Younge, Richard G.
Zachary, Steven W.
Zealey, Sharon Janine
Zelis, Karen Dee
Zollar, Nikki Michele

Library/Information Science

Adams, Elaine Parker
Alexander, Otis Douglas
Alford, Thomas Earl
Allen, Ottis Eugene, Jr.
Aman, Mohammed M.
Anderson, Barbara Louise
Anderson, Gladys Peppers
Arkhurst, Joyce Cooper
Armstrong, Evelyn Walker
Atchison, Lillian Elizabeth
Avery, Charles
Awkard, Julita Castro

Axam, John Arthur
Baldwin, Wilhelmina F.
Barnes, Fannie Burrell
Battle, Thomas Cornell
Beachem, Constance
Bean, Bobby Gene
Bell, Katie Roberson
Bethel, Jesse Moncell, Sr.
Bickham, L. B.
Birchette-Pierce, Cheryl L.
Blake, Peggy Jones
Bond, Louis Grant
Bond, Ollie P.
Bowens, Johnny Wesley
Boyce, William M.
Brown, Atlanta Thomas
Brown, Freddiemae Eugenia
Brown, Harriett Baltimore
Brown, Richard Earl
Burnett, Bescye P.
Burns, Ollie Hamilton
Byam, Milton S.
Byrd, Joan Eda
Caldwell, Rossie Juanita Brower
Calhoun, Dorothy Eunice
Cameron, Ulysses
Cannon, Tyrone Heath
Carter, Darline Louretha
Cash, Pamela J.
Chapman, Dorothy Hilton
Chisum, Gloria Twine
Chitty, Murela Elizabeth
Clack, Doris H.
Clark, Patricia Ann
Clarke, Joy Adele Long
Clayton, Mayme Agnew
Clayton, Minnie H.
Cleveland, Granville E.
Coaston, Shirley Ann Dumas
Coleman, Jean Ellen
Conner, Laban Calvin
Cooke, Anna L.
Copeland, Emily America
Craft, Guy Calvin
Crocker, Wayne Marcus
Cruzat, Gwendolyn S.
Culpepper, Betty M.
Cummings, Roberta Spikes
Cunningham, William Dean
Curtis, Jean Trawick
Davis, Denice Faye
Davis, Elaine Carsley
Davis, Herman E.
Davis, Sandra B.
Dennis, Gertrude Zelma Ford
Dupree, Sandra Kay
DuPree, Sherry Sherrod
Ellis, Elizabeth G.
Estes, Elaine Rose Graham
Evans, Deborah Ann
Fancher, Evelyn Pitts
Felder-Hoehne, Felicia Harris
Fisher, Alma M.
Fisher, Edith Maureen
Fitzhugh, Kathryn Corrothers
Ford, Robert Benjamin, Jr.
Franklin, Hardy R.
Freeman, Shirley Walker
Fuller, Gloria A.
Funn, Courtney Harris
Gardiner, George L.
Gay, Birdie Spivey
Gaymon, Nicholas Edward
Gill, Jacqueline A.
Gilton, Donna L.
Gleason, Eliza
Glover, Denise M.
Goddard, Rosalind Kent
Goss, Theresa Carter
Grant, George C.
Gray, Beverly A.
Gray, Donnee L.
Gray, Dorothy Peyton
Griffin, Richard George, Jr.
Guilford, Diane Patton
Gunn, Arthur Clinton
Hale, Kimberly Anice
Ham, Debra Newman
Hardnett, Carolyn Judy
Hardy, Eursla Dickerson
Hargrave, Charles William
Harris, Loretta K.
Harris, Tom W.
Hart, Mildred
Harvell, Sylvia Valeria Gomez
Hayden, Carla Diane
Hayward, Olga Loretta Hines
Henderson, Robbye R.
Hendricks, Leta

Hernandez, Mary N.
Hewitt, Vivian Davidson
Hicks, Doris Askew
Hill, Ellyn Askins
Hogan, Fannie Burrell
Holley, Sharon Yvonne
Hopkins, Dianne McAfee
Howard, Elizabeth Fitzgerald
Hunt, Charles Amoes
Hunter, Tracey Joel
Hutson, Jean Blackwell
Hylton, Andrea Lamarr
Irving, Ophelia McAlpin
Isadore, Harold W.
Ivey, Rebecca
Jackson, Andrew Preston
Jackson, Ruth Moore
James, Olive C. R.
James, Stephen Elisha
Jefferson, Karen L.
Jefferson, Marcia D.
Jenkins, Althea H.
Jenkins, Barbara Williams
Jenkins, Cynthia
Jenkins, George Arthur, Jr.
Jobe, Shirley A.
Johnson, Doris Elayne
Johnson, Dorothy Turner
Johnson, Gloria Dean
Johnson, Minnie Redmond
Johnson, Sheila Monroe
Johnson, Shirley
Johnson-Blount, Theresa
Jolivet, Linda Catherine
Jones, Clara Stanton
Jones, Clifton Patrick
Jones, Curley C.
Jones, Gwendolyn J.
Jones, Helen Hampton
Jones-Trent, Bernice R.
Jordan, Casper LeRoy
Josey, E. J.
Joyce, Donald Franklin
Kaiser, Ernest Daniel
Kendrick, Curtis L.
King, Thomas Lawrence
Knowles, Em Claire
Lambert, Jeanette H.
Lawrence, Eileen B.
Lawrence, Viola Poe
Lee, Pauline W.
Leonard, Gloria Jean
Lewis, Billie Jean
Lewis, Frank Ross
Livingston, Joyce
Lockett, Sandra Bokamba
Logan, Carolyn Alice
Louistall-Monroe, Victorine
    Augusta
Lucas, Willie Lee
Lyons, Donald Wallace
Mack, Phyllis Green
Madison, Jacqueline Edwina
Mangum, Ernestine Brewer
Marks, Rose M.
Marshall, Anita
Martin, Rosetta P.
Mason, Hilda Howland M.
Mathis, Thaddeus P.
Matthews, Leonard Louis
Matthews, Vincent
Maye, Richard
McCain, Ella Byrd
McCall, Barbara Collins
McCormick, Larry William
McCoy, James F.
McCoy, James Nelson
McCrary-Simmons, Shirley Denise
McCray, Melvin
McDaniel, Karen Cotton
McKeller, Thomas Lee
McKinney, Wade H., III
McKitt, Willie, Jr.
McLaughlin, Megan E.
McPherson, James Alan
McTyre, Robert Earl, Sr.
Metcalf, DaVinci Carver
Middleton, Ernest J.
Miles, Ruby A. Branch
Miller, Constance Joan
Miller, Erenest Eugene
Miller, Evelyn B.
Miller, Jake C.
Miller, Robert, Jr.
Miller, Sylvia Alberta Gregory
Miller-Holmes, Cheryl
Mobley, Emily Ruth
Mohr, Diane Louise
Moore, Hazel Stamps

Moore, M. Elizabeth Gibbs
Morgan, Jane Hale
Morris, Effie Lee
Morris, Ella Lucille
Morrison, Samuel F.
Mothershed, Spaesio W.
Muldrow, James Christopher
Murphy, Paula Christine
Newell, Matthias Gregory
Page, James Allen
Page, John Sheridan, Jr.
Paschal, Eloise Richardson
Patterson, Grace Limerick
Patterson, Pola Noah
Peguese, Charles R.
Pendergrass, Margaret E.
Perry, Emma Bradford
Peterson, Lorna Ingrid
Pinkett, Harold Thomas
Powell, Addie Scott
Price, Pamela Anita
Price, Paul Sanford
Ramsey, Donna Elaine
Randall, Ann Knight
Randall, Dudley Felker
Reason, Joseph Henry
Redden, Camille J.
Reed, Lola N.
Reese, Gregory Lamarr
Riley, Barbara P.
Roberson, Gloria Grant
Robertson, Karen A.
Robinson, Carol W.
Robinson, Carrie C.
Robinson-Walker, Mary P.
Roney, Raymond G.
Roper, Grace Trott
Rountree, Louise M.
Royster, Vivian Hall
Rudd, Amanda S.
Russell, Beverly A.
Sanders, Lou Helen
Sapp, Lauren B.
Sarkodie-Mensah, Kwasi
Scott, Alice H.
Shaw, Spencer Gilbert
Shockley, Ann Allen
Siler, Freddie Bush
Simton, Chester
Singley, Elijah
Sinnette, Elinor DesVerney
Slaton, Gwendolyn C.
Smith, Benjamin Franklin
Smith, Daniel H., Jr.
Smith, Jessie Carney
Smith, Juanita Jane
Smith-Epps, E. Paulette
Smith Freeman, Patricia M.
Smythe, Victor N.
Spencer, Joan Moore
Spradling, Mary Elizabeth Mace
Sprinkle-Hamlin, Sylvia Yvonne
Staley, Valeria Howard
Stallworth, Ann P.
Stephens, Brenda Wilson
Stephens, Elsie Marie
Stewart, Ruth Ann
Stinson, Linda
Strong, Blondell McDonald
Sutton, Gloria W.
Swift, Linda Denise
Sylvester, Melvin R.
Thomas, Frankie Taylor
Thomas, Lucille Cole
Thomas, Maurice McKenzie
Thompson, Bette Mae
Thompson, Hobson, Jr.
Tolbert, Odie Henderson, Jr.
Toliver, Virginia F. Dowsing
Toomer, Clarence
Totten, Herman Lavon
Towns, Rose Mary
Trent, Marcia M.
Turner, Marcellus
Twine, Edgar Hugh
Tyson, John C.
UmBayemake Joachim, Linda
Unaeze, Felix Eme
Venable, Andrew Alexander, Jr.
Walters, Mary Dawson
Weissinger, Thomas, Sr.
Whisenton, Andre C.
Whitner, Donna K.
Williams, Ethel Langley
Williams, Helen Elizabeth
Wilson, Margaret T.
Wood, Vivian Frances
Woods, Elisa R.
Woods, Hortense E.

Woody, Jacqueline Brown
Wray, Wendell Leonard
Wright, James R.
Wright, Joyce C.
Yates, Ella Gaines
Zulu, Itibari M.

Management/ Administration— Accounting/Financial
(See Also **Accounting/ Auditing)**

Adams, Don L.
Adams, Edward B.
Aiken, William
Ali, Grace L.
Anderson, Elizabeth M.
Anthony, Brenda Tucker
Armstrong, Kevin
Arnold, Haskell N., Jr.
Ashby, Lucius Antoine
Ashley, Corlanders
Austin, Richard H.
Ayers-Elliott, Cindy
Bailey, Jerry Dean
Baldwin, Carolyn H.
Ball, Brenda Louise
Barkley, Mark E.
Barnes, N. Kurt
Bassett, Dennis
Bell, Marilyn Lenora
Benham, Robert
Benjamin, Monica G.
Bennett, William Donald
Best, William Andrew
Bouknight, Reynard Ronald
Bryant, Regina Lynn
Bryant-Reid, Johanne
Burges, Melvin E.
Burke, Olga Pickering
Campbell, Carlos Cardozo
Carswell, Gloria Nadine Sherman
Carter, Norman L.
Cave, Perstein Ronald
Chambers, Harry, Jr.
Chism, Harolyn B.
Chivis, Martin Lewis
Clark, John Joseph
Clark, Walter L.
Clayton, Robert L.
Cohen, Gwen A.
Connell, Cameron
Cox, Taylor H., Sr.
Craig-Rudd, Joan
Crim, Rodney
Culbreath-Manly, Tongila M.
Cunningham, Erskine
Davenport, C. Dennis
Davenport, Ernest H.
Davis, Harold R.
Davis, Tyrone Theophilus
Dickerson, Harvey G., Jr.
Doss, Lawrence Paul
Durham, William R.
Ealy, Mary Newcomb
Edgerton, Brenda Evans
English, Deborah
Faulding, Juliette J.
Fentress, Shirley B.
Ferguson, Edward A., Jr.
Fletcher, James Andrew
Flippen, Frances Morton
Forde, Fraser Philip, Jr.
Francisco, Anthony M.
Frasier, Ralph Kennedy
Frazier-Ellison, Vicki L.
Gillespie, Bonita
Godfrey, William R.
Gonzalez, Cambell
Gordon, Alexander H., II
Green, Jarvis R.
Greene, Gabrielle Elise
Greene, Gregory A.
Guitano, Anton W.
Haile, Annette L.
Hall, David McKenzie
Hall, Ira D.
Haralson, Larry L.
Harris, Robert Eugene Peyton
Harvey, Richard R.
Hawes, Bernadine Tinner
Hawkins, Gene
Hearne, Earl
Henderson, James J., Sr.
Henderson, Remond
Howard, Osbie L., Jr.
Hudson, Paul C.

Huff, Lula Lunsford
Humphrey, Marian J.
Jackson, Harold Leonard, Jr.
James, Dorothy Marie
Johnson, Roy Lee
Johnson, Wallace Darnell
Jones, Leonade Diane
Jones, Shalley A.
Jordan, Marilyn E.
Jordan, Thurman
Junior, Ester James, Jr.
Kelley, William E.
King, Cecilia D.
King, Edgar Lee
King, Marcellus, Jr.
Kirkland, Gwendolyn Vickye
Lander, Cressworth Caleb
Latimer, Frank Edward
Law, M. Eprevel
LeGall, Terrence George
Lemon, Ann
Lemuwa, Ike Emmanuel
Lewis, Jeffrey Mark
Lewis, William M., Jr.
Liverpool, Charles Eric
Lovelace, Onzalo Robert
Lowman, Carl D.
Lucas, Leo Alexander
Mack, Fred Clarence
Mariel, Serafin
Mathis, David
May, Floyd O'Lander
McClomb, George E.
McDonald, Jeffrey Bernard
McKinzie, Barbara A.
McPhatter, Thomas H.
Micks, Deitra R. H.
Miller, George Carroll, Jr.
Miller, George N., Jr.
Moore, Charles W.
Mosley, Edna Wilson
Nanula, Richard D.
Naphtali, Ashirah Sholomis
Nelson, Ricky Lee
Newell, Kathleen W.
Norman, Patricia
Nunn, John, Jr.
Palmer, Dennis, III
Parnell, William Cornellus, Jr.
Patterson, Cheryl Ann
Paul, Wanda D.
Pearson, Jesse S.
Pearson, Ramona Henderson
Pirtle, Ronald M.
Posey, Deborah
Powell, Aston Wesley
Powell, Wayne Hugh
Price, Albert H.
Rasheed, Howard S.
Reed, Adolphus Redolph
Reed-Clark, Larita D.
Reid, Desiree Charese
Rentie, Frieda
Rhinehart, N. Pete
Riley, Avis Monica
Riley, Charles W., Sr.
Robinson, S. Benton
Rollins, Avon William, Sr.
Ross, Frank Kenneth
Sandidge, Kanita Durice
Saunders, Vincent E., III
Scales, Erwin Carlvet
Segree, E. Ramone
Sellers, Theresa Ann
Sendaba, S. M.
Shepherd, Malcolm Thomas
Shoemaker, Veronica Sapp
Shropshire, Harry W.
Singleton, Herbert
Sloan, Maceo Kennedy
Smith, Chester B.
Smith, Lawrence John, Jr.
Stahnke, William E.
Stamper, Henry J.
Stevenson, Unice Teen
Stokes, Sheila Woods
Streeter, Denise Williams
Swanston, Clarence Eugene
Tarter, Robert R., Jr.
Teamer, Charles C.
Thompson, Jeffrey Earl
Thompson, Karen Ann
Thompson, Sylvia Moore
Torian, Edward Torrence
Trapp, Donald W.
Tucker, Eric M.
Turner, Mark Anthony
Turner, Marvin Wentz
Turpin, Mel Harrison

Vance, Tommie Rowan
Varnado, Arthur
Vest, Donald Seymour, Sr.
Wade, William Carl
Walker, Willie Leroy
Wallace, Charles Leslie
Warfield, Robert N.
Watts, Carl Augustus
Wheat, James Weldon, Jr.
White, Clarence Dean
Williams, James
Williams, Ruthann Evege
Woodson, Cleveland Coleman, III
Woodson, Jeffrey Anthony
Wright, Ralph Edward
Wright, Soraya M.
Yearwood, David Monroe, Jr.
Young, Ollie L.

Management/ Administration— Advertising/Marketing/ Public Relations *(See Also* **Advertising/ Promotion)**

Acon, June Kay
Adams, Edward B.
Adams, Theodore Adolphus, Jr.
Alexander, Dawn
Allston, Thomas Gray, III
Anderson, Al H., Jr.
Anderson, Ivy I.
Andrews, Rosalyn McPherson
Arnold, Ethel N.
Ashburn, Vivian Diane
Ashmore, Andrea Lynn
Atchison, Leon H.
Atkins, Fredd
Austin, Janyth Yvonne
Avery, James S.
Ayers-Elliott, Cindy
Bailey, Myrtle Lucille
Baker, Gregory D.
Baker, Kimberley Renee
Ball, Drexel Bernard
Banfield, Anne L.
Banks, Beatrice
Barber Dickerson, Ornetta M.
Bates, Willie Earl
Beach, Walter G., II
Beckett, Evette Olga
Bell, Diana Lynne
Bell, Rosalind Nanette
Bennett, Ivy H.
Berry, Gemeral E., Jr.
Bisamunyu, Jeanette
Black, Don Gene
Blackwell, Milford
Blackwell, Patricia A.
Blake, J. Herman
Block, Leslie S.
Bontemps, Jacqueline Marie Fonvielle
Booker, Anne M.
Boon, Ina M.
Bostic, Viola W.
Boyce, Joseph Nelson
Boyce, Laura E.
Bradford, Martina Lewis
Britton, John H., Jr.
Brown, Priscilla
Brown, Robin R.
Brown, Sharon Marjorie Revels
Brown, Tony
Brown-Francisco, Teresa Elaine
Buckhanan, Dorothy Wilson
Burke, William Arthur
Burnett, Collie, Jr.
Burns, Jeff, Jr.
Burris, Bertram Ray
Bush, Patricia
Bussey, Charles David
Butler, Joyce M.
Caldwell, Marion Milford, Jr.
Calhoun, Lillian Scott
Cameron, Randolph W.
Campbell, Rogers Edward, III
Caraway, Yolanda H.
Carroll, Robert F.
Carter, Kenneth Gregory
Carter, Kenneth Wayne
Chapman, Sharon Jeanette
Chargois, Jenelle M.
Chess, Eva
Clarke, Everee Jimerson
Clayton, Robert L.
Clemons, Alois Ricardo

Clemons, John Gregory
Clowney, Audrey E.
Cobbin, W. Frank, Jr.
Cochran, Harold Lloyd, Jr.
Collins, Gordon Geoffrey
Collins, Tessil John
Cooper, Candace Lucretia
Cooper, Emmett E., Jr.
Coward, Jasper Earl
Cox, Dianne Fitzgerald
Crawford, Barbara Hopkins
Crombaugh, Hallie
Cross-McClam, Deloris Nmi
Cureton, John Porter
Curry, Charles E.
Davis, Charles
Davis, Luella B.
Davis, Walter Paul
Dejoie, Michael C.
Dennis, James Carlos
Derbigny, Rhoda L.
Dixon, John Frederick
Donald, Arnold Wayne
Dottin, Roger Allen
Dowd, Maria
Doxie, Marvin Leon, Sr.
Draper, Frances Murphy
Dukes, Ofield
Dumas, Karen Marie
Durant-Paige, Beverly
Duvall, Henry F., Jr.
Dyer, Joe, Jr.
Eades, Vincent W.
Eady, Lydia Davis
Easley, Eddie V.
Echols, James Albert
Edwards, Oscar Lee
Edwards, Ronald Wayne
Ellington, Brenda Andrea
Evans, Alicia
Evans, Liz
Farrow, William McKnight, III
Fay, Toni G.
Ferguson, Idell
Ferguson, Terri Lynette
Fernandez, John Peter
Florence, Jerry DeWayne
Flowers, D. Michelle
Fobbs, Kevin
Fontenot-Jamerson, Berlinda
Foreman, Lucille Elizabeth
Foushee, Prevost Vest
Frelow, Robert Lee, Jr.
Gaffney, Leslie Gale
Gaines, Adriane Theresa
Gamble, Eva M.
Gellineau, Victor Marcel, Jr.
George, Pauline L.
Giles, Althea B.
Giles, William R.
Gipson, Reve
Givens, Joshua Edmond
Glover, Sarah L.
Gordon, Bruce S.
Gordon, Edwin Jason
Graham, Stedman
Gregory, Robert Alphonso
Griffith, Gary Alan
Griffiths, Errol D.
Guilmenot, Richard Arthur, III
Hackney, L. Camille
Hall, Fred, III
Hankin, Noel Newton
Hanson, John L.
Harris, Douglas Allan
Harris, Lee Andrew, II
Harris, Michele Roles
Harrison, Ronald E.
Harrison, Roscoe Conklin, Jr.
Hatcher, Jeffrey F.
Hatcher, Kendra Denise
Hawkins, James C.
Herring, Leonard, Jr.
Herring, Marsha K. Church
Herring, William F.
Hill, Jeffrey Ronald
Hilliard, Amy S.
Holmes, Carlton
Holt, Veitya Eileene
Horton, Carl E., Sr.
Horton, Dollie Bea Dixon
House, James E.
Hudson, Frederick Bernard
Hughes, Donna Lundin
Hunter, Clarence Henry
Hutchins, Jan Darwin
Inniss, Charles Evans
Jackson, Gail P.
Jackson, Mary

Jackson, Reggie Martinez
Jackson, Rusty
Jackson, William Alvin
Jackson-Ransom, Bunnie
Jackson Robinson, Tracy Camille
Jaycox, Mary Irine
Jefferson, Andrea Green
Jemmott, Hensley B.
Jenkins, Bobby G.
Jenkins, John
Jenkins, Yolanda L.
Johnson, Cleveland, Jr.
Johnson, Donna Alligood
Johnson, Juliana Cornish
Johnson, Wayne Alan
Jones, Cedric Decorrus
Jones, Delores
Jones, DeVerges Booker
Jones, Marsha Regina
Jones, Robert G.
Jones, Victoria Gene
Killingsworth Finley, Sandra Jean
King, Gwendolyn Stewart
Knox, George L., III
Ladner, Terria Roushun
Larry, Charles Edward
Latimer, David Christopher
LaVelle, Avis
Lee, Ronald B.
Leggett, Renee
Leigh, Fredric H.
Lewis, Byron E.
Lewis, Charles Michael
Lewis, Robert Alvin, Jr.
Livingston-White, Deborah J. H.
Locklin, James R.
Logan, Harold James
Logue-Kinder, Joan
London, Denise
Love, Karen Allyce
Lucas, Victoria
Lyle, Percy H., Jr.
Majors, Mattie Carolyn
Makokha, James A. N.
Manley, Dexter
Manuel, Edward
Marshall, H. Jean
Marshall, Pluria William, Jr.
Martin, Franklin Farnarwance
Martin, Gertrude S.
Martin, Hosea L.
Massey, Ardrey Yvonne
Maule, Albert R.
McCullough, Frances Louise
McDonald, Herbert G.
McKenzie, Miranda Mack
McNeil, Robert Lawrence, Jr.
McPherson, James R.
McWhorter, Grace Agee
Merritt, Bishetta Dionne
Merriweather, Barbara Christine
Miller, C. Conrad, Jr.
Mills, Doreen C.
Mintz, Reginold Lee
Mitchal, Saundra Marie
Mitchell, Carol Greene
Mitchell, Lilyann Jackson
Mitchell, Martha Mallard
Mitchell, Robert P.
Monteverdi, Mark Victor
Moore, Anthony Louis
Moore, Johnnie Adolph
Morgan-Smith, Sylvia
Morton, Marilyn M.
Morton, Patsy Jennings
Mosby, Carolyn Elizabeth
Moss, Anni R.
Moss, Wayne B.
Moyo, Yvette Jackson
Mudd, Louis L.
Muhammad, M. Akbar
Muley, Miriam
Murdock, Patricia Green
Murphy, Daniel Howard
Murray, James P.
Nelson, Debra Ponder
Nelson, Mario
Newman, Paul Dean
Norman, Clifford P.
Palmer, Laura Olivia
Pandya, Harish C.
Parham, Marjorie B.
Parker, Kai J.
Parker, Thomas Edwin, III
Parker, William Hartley
Parks, James Clinton, Jr.
Parsons, Philip I.
Passmore, Juanita Carter
Pearson, Preston James

Penn, Mindell Lewis
Perez, Anna
Perry, Eugene Calvin, Jr.
Perry, Lowell Wesley, Jr.
Perry, Marc Aubrey
Phelps-Patterson, Lucy
Phillips, Colette Alice-Maude
Pickett, Donna A.
Pierre, Jennifer Casey
Pierson, Kathryn A.
Pounds, Elaine
Powell, Julie
Powell, Kenneth Alasandro
Powell-Jackson, Bernice
Price, George Baker
Proctor, Earl D.
Pualani, Gloria
Ray, Austin H.
Ray, Walter I., Jr.
Reece, Steven
Reed, Vincent Emory
Rhodes, C. Adrienne
Rhodes, Jeanne
Richardson, Valerie K.
Richardson, William J.
Robinson, Johnathan Prather
Robinson, Leonard Harrison, Jr.
Rochester, Geof
Rogers, Desiree Glapion
Rogers-Reece, Shirley
Roseman, Jennifer Eileen
Sagers, Rudolph, Jr.
Salmond, Jasper
Salter, Kwame S.
Sayers, Gale E.
Scott, Jacob Reginald
Scott, Werner Ferdinand
Scott-Jackson, Lisa Odessa
Seals, Connie C.
Sewell, Luther Joseph
Sharpton, Denise
Shaw, Ardyth M.
Shepard, Linda Irene
Shipe, Jamesetta Denise Holmes
Shropshire, Thomas B.
Shumate, Glen
Siler, Brenda Claire
Simmons, Maurice Clyde
Simmons-Edelstein, Dee
Simons, Renee V. H.
Slater, Helene Ford Southern
Smith, Charles James, III
Smith, Dawn C. F.
Smith, Gregory Robeson, Sr.
Smith, Oscar Samuel, Jr.
Smith, Ralph O'Hara
Smith-Gaston, Linda Ann
Spraggins, Stewart
Spratlen, Thaddeus H.
Spurlock, James B., Jr.
Staten, Everett R.
Steele, Michael W.
Stephens, Doreen Y.
Stevens, John Theodore, Sr.
Stevens, Rochelle
Stewart, Edward L.
Stewart, Joseph M.
Stith, Antoinette Freeman
Stone, Harold Anthony
Sutton, Charyn Diane
Sykes, William Richard, Jr.
Tassie, Robert V.
Tatum, Wilbert A.
Taylor, Edgar R.
Taylor, Tommie W.
Taylor, Valerie Charmayne
Tennant, Melvin, II
Thompson, Gloria Crawford
Thurmond, Nate
Triche, Arthur, Jr.
Tucker, Sheilah L. Wheeler
Tyner, Regina Lisa
Utley, Richard Henry
Wade, Brent James
Walker, Tracy A.
Warren, Gina Angelique
Warren, Lee Alden
Warrick-Crisman, Jeri Everett
Washington, Luisa
Waters, Paul Eugene, Jr.
Waugh, Judith Ritchie
Weaver, Frank Cornell
West, Togo Dennis, Jr.
Wharton, Ferdinand D., Jr.
Whitney, Rosalyn L.
Wilcox, Preston
Williams, Alma Minton
Williams, Armstrong
Williams, Elynor A.

Williams, Gayle Terese Taylor
Williams, Harold L., Jr.
Williams, Richard Lee
Williams, Rosa B.
Williams, Snowden J.
Williams, Terrie Michelle
Williams, Yarborough Burwell, Jr.
Williams Davis, Edith G.
Williamson, Karen Elizabeth
Williams-Taitt, Patricia Ann
Winley, Diane Lacey
Winslow, Alfred A.
Womack, Carter Devon
Womack, Christopher Clarence
Wood, Anton Vernon
Woodbeck, Frank Raymond
Woodruff, Jeffrey Robert
Wordlaw, Clarence, Jr.
Wright, Mark Adrian
Wyatt, William N.
Wyche, Paul H., Jr.
Young, Angela Lynn
Young, James M., II
Young, Ronald R.
Zachary, Hubert M.

Management/ Administration— Computer Systems/Data Processing

Adkins, Rodney C.
Ahart, Thomas I.
Andrews, Nelson Montgomery
Ball, Roger
Bell, Diana Lynne
Bell, Sandra Watson
Brasey, Henry L.
Brockington, Eugene Alfonzo
Bryant, Regina Lynn
Byrd, Percy L.
Cargill, Sandra Morris
Carter, Charles Michael
Casterlow, Carolyn B.
Coates, Shelby L.
Cooper, Daneen Ravenell
Cooper, William B.
Corbin, Stampp W.
Cunningham, Robert Shannon, Jr.
Davis, Denyvetta
DeSassure, Charles
Doty, Romeo A.
Doxie, Marvin Leon, Sr.
Ellis, Ladd, Jr.
English, William E.
Franklin, Martha Lois
Gragg, Lauren Andrea
Grant, Claude DeWitt
Gray, Christine
Greene, Jerry Louis
Hall, David McKenzie
Hammond, James A.
Handy, Lillian B.
Heard, Blanche Denise
Hughes, Isaac Sunny
Hylton, Taft H.
Ingram, Phillip M.
Isaacs, Doris C.
Jacobs, Patricia Dianne
Jacques, Cornell
John, Anthony
Johnson, Nathaniel J., Sr.
Jones, Isaac, Jr.
Jordan, George Washington, Jr.
Joyner, Claude C.
Kinsey, Bernard
Kline, Joseph N.
Lautenbach, Terry
Lawrence, Rodell
Lewis, Richard John, Sr.
Mayo, James Wellington
Miller, Arthur J.
Miller, George N., Jr.
Moran, George H.
Moseley-Davis, Barbara M.
Moss, Anni R.
O'Neal, Fredrick William, Jr.
Parker-Robinson, D. LaVerne
Perry, Jerald Isaac, Sr.
Perry, Lee Charles, Jr.
Powell, Kenneth Alasandro
Rice, Lois Dickson
Ridgeway, William C.
Roberts, Angela Dorrean
Rodman, John
Saunders, Vincent E., III
Sharpe, V. Renee
Sherrod, Ezra Cornell
Shipe, Jamesetta Denise Holmes

Smiley-Robertson, Carolyn
Smith, James Charles
Stroud, Lawrence Lowell
Swain, Michael B.
Taylor, Arlene M. J.
Terrell, Richard Warren
Turner, Yvonne Williams
Umolu, Sheila Andrea
Viltz, Edward Gerald
Wade, Brent James
Wallace, Peggy Mason
Wells, Linda Ivy

Management/ Administration— Consultation/Analysis (See Also Consulting)

Adams, Samuel Clifford, Jr.
Adolph, Gerald Stephen
Ahart, Thomas I.
Alexander, Benjamin Harold
Alexander, Clifford L., Jr.
Alexander, Errol D.
Alexander, Lenora Cole
Alfonso, Pedro
Allen, Billy R.
Allen, George Mitchell
Allen, Jane Elizabeth
Amos, Kent B.
Bain, Linda Valerie
Banks, Charlie
Barnes, Martin G.
Barnhill, Helen Iphigenia
Barrow, Lionel Ceon, Jr.
Baskin, Yvonne E.
Battle, Turner Charles, III
Bell, William Jerry
Bell, William McKinley
Best, Jennings H.
Black, Charles E.
Black, Charlie J.
Blackwell, Faye Brown
Blackwell, Randolph Talmadge
Blankenship, Eddie L.
Block, Leslie S.
Bolden, J. Taber, III
Bolden, John Henry
Bonaparte, Tony Hillary
Booker, James Avery, Jr.
Booker, Loretta Love
Bradford, Charles Edward
Brailsford, Marvin D.
Braxton, John Ledger
Brewer, Moses
Britton, Theodore R., Jr.
Brookes, Bernard L.
Brooks, Bernard E.
Brown, Arnold E.
Brown, Bernice Baynes
Brown, John Mitchell, Sr.
Brown, Sherman L.
Brown, Warren Henry, Jr.
Buck, Vernon Ashley, Jr.
Bullard, Edward A., Jr.
Bullock, J. Jerome
Bunyon, Ronald S.
Burris, Bertram Ray
Bussey, Charles David
Butler, John Gordon
Byam, Milton S.
Byrd, Arthur W.
Byrd, Percy L.
Cain, Gerry Ronald
Caines, Ken
Canty, Miriam Monroe
Carey, Carnice
Cargill, Sandra Morris
Chenault, William J.
Christian, John L.
Clanagan, Mazzetta Price
Clark, John Joseph
Cole, Patricia A.
Coleman, Everod A.
Cooper, Earl, II
Cooper, Walter
Cramer, Joe J., Jr.
Cross, Austin Devon
Cunningham, Randall
Cuyjet, Aloysius Baxter
Dalferes, Edward R., Jr.
Daniel, Jack L.
Daniels, A. Raiford
Davis, Clarence A.
Davis, Edward
Davis, Erroll B., Jr.
Davis, Frank Allen
Davis, Preston Augustus
Davis, Ronald P.

Debnam, Chadwick Basil
Dickson, Reginald D.
Dorman, Hattie L.
Dotson, Betty Lou
Douglas, Herbert P., Jr.
Dowdell, Kevin Crawford
Dukes, Ronald
Dupree, David H.
Durand, Winsley, Jr.
Dyer, Charles Austen
Eccles, Peter Wilson
Echols, James Albert
Ellison, Pauline Allen
Evans, Leon, Jr.
Evans-McNeill, Elona Anita
Faulkner, Carolyn D.
Fergerson, Miriam N.
Flipper, Carl Frederick, III
Fontayne, K. Nicole
Fonvielle, William Harold
Ford, Claudette Franklin
Ford, David Leon, Jr.
Foster, Deborah Valrie
Francis, Gilbert H.
Franklin, Allen D.
Franklin, Shirley Clarke
Franklin, William B.
Freeland, Russell L.
Freeman, Robert Turner, Jr.
Fregia, Darrell Leon
Frye, Robert Edward, Sr.
Gallagher, Abisola Helen
Gamble, Janet Helen
Garrison-Corbin, Patricia Ann
Gibson, Sarah L.
Gillespie, Rena Harrell
Gilliam, James H., Sr.
Gilliam, Reginald Earl, Jr.
Gillispie, William Henry
Goines, Leonard
Gooden, C. Michael
Gothard, Donald L.
Graham, Jo-Ann Clara
Gravenberg, Eric Von
Gray, Brian Anton
Grayson, Jennifer A.
Greene, Mitchell Amos
Greenwood, John T.
Griffin, Ples Andrew
Hager, Roscoe Franklin
Hall, Nancy M.
Hampton, Leon
Harris, Howard F.
Harris, J. Robert, II
Harris, Marion Hopkins
Hawkins, Lawrence C.
Hernandez, Aileen Clarke
Herndon, Lance H.
Herron, Vernon M.
Hicks, H. Beecher, Jr.
High, Claude, Jr.
Hill, Raymond A.
Hill, Rosalie A.
Hodges, Clarence Eugene
House, James E.
Houston, Marsh S.
Hubbard, Walter T.
Hudson, Frederick Bernard
Hutton, Gerald L.
Jackson, Horace
James, Clarence L., Jr.
Jamison, Leila Duncan
Jenkins, Drewie Gutrimez
Jenkins, Joseph Walter, Jr.
Jenkins, Woodie R., Jr.
Johnican, Minerva Jane
Johnson, Fred D.
Johnson, Frederick E.
Johnson, Joseph David
Johnson, Ronald Cornelius
Johnson, Stephanye
Jones, Carolyn G.
Jones, Hortense
Jones, Raymond Morris
Keels, James Dewey
Kelly, John Paul, Jr.
Kendrick, Joy A.
King, Howard O.
King, Warren Earl
Kirby-Davis, Montanges
Kline, Joseph N.
Larry, Jerald Henry
Leigh, Fredric H.
Lewis, Charles Henry
Lewis, Jeffrey Mark
Lewis, Richard John, Sr.
Lewis, William M., Jr.
Llewellyn-Travis, Chandra
Luis, William

Luten, Thomas Dee
Lynch, M. Elizabeth
Marriott, Salima Siler
Marsh, Ben Franklin
Matney, William C., Jr.
Mayfield, Curtis
Mayo, James Wellington
McClain, Jerome Gerald
McFarlin, Emma Daniels
McIntosh, Rhodina Covington
McLean, Mary Cannon
McMillan, Jacqueline Marie
McNeil, Freeman
Meeks, Reginald Kline
Mereday, Richard F.
Merriweather, Thomas L.
Micks, Deitra R. H.
Middleton, Vertelle D.
Miller, Arthur J.
Miller, Frederick A.
Miller, George Carroll, Jr.
Miller, Ray, Jr.
Moore, Wenda Weekes
Moran, George H.
Morancie, Horace L.
Morris, Charles Edward, Jr.
Morrison, James W., Jr.
Morrow, Laverne
Murrell, Sylvia Marilyn
Naphtali, Ashirah Sholomis
Neblett, Richard F.
Newton, Eric Christopher
Njoroge, Mbugua J.
Oliver-Simon, Gloria Craig
Patterson, William Benjamin
Peters, Charles L., Jr.
Petersen, Arthur Everett, Jr.
Peterson, Marcella Tandy
Petty, Bruce Anthony
Phillips, Leroy Daniel
Phillips, Ralph Leonard
Pitchford, Gerard Spencer
Pogue, Brent Daryl
Polite, Craig K.
Pollard, Percy Edward, Sr.
Porter, James H.
Powell, Aston Wesley
Reynolds, Andrew Buchanan
Rice, Constance Williams
Richards-Alexander, Billie J.
Richardson, Ernest A.
Robinson, Eric B.
Robinson, Ernest Preston, Sr.
Robinson, Verneda
Ruffin, John Walter, Jr.
Rutledge, Jennifer M.
Sample, William Amos
Sanders-West, Selma D.
Satterwhite, Frank Joseph
Scott, Benjamin
Scott, Ruth
Scribner, Arthur Gerald, Jr.
Seabrooks-Edwards, Marilyn S.
Shackelford, Lottie H.
Shepard, Linda Irene
Shepherd, Malcolm Thomas
Simms, Robert H.
Small, Kenneth Lester
Smith, Carolyn Lee
Smith, Fronse Wayne, Sr.
Smith, Walter L.
Smith-Whitaker, Audrey N.
Spradley, Mark Merritt
Stanley, Hilbert Dennis
Steptoe, Lamont Brown
Sterling, H. Dwight, Sr.
Stevens, Maxwell McDew
Stokes, Carolyn Ashe
Story, Charles Irvin
Stovall, Audrean
Strachan, Lloyd Calvin, Jr.
Strong, Blondell McDonald
Stroud, Louis Winston
Sutton, Dianne Floyd
Taylor, Michael
Taylor, Patricia Tate
Taylor, Robert Derek
Thomas, William Christopher
Tillman, Joseph Nathaniel
Todman, Terence A.
Townes, Clarence Lee, Jr.
Trapp, Donald W.
Turner, Marvin Wentz
Umolu, Sheila Andrea
Van Hook, Warren Kenneth
Ward, Haskell G.
Ware, Omego John Clinton, Jr.
Warmack, Kevin Lavon
Watkins, Mose

Watson, Thomas S., Jr.
Weaver, George Leon-Paul
White, Earl Harvey
Whitehurst, Charles Bernard, Sr.
Williams, Terrie Michelle
Wilson, Johnny Leaverne
Wilson, Wesley Campbell
Winters, James Robert
Woods, Geraldine Pittman
Woodson, Jeffrey Anthony
Wormley, Diane-Louise Lambert
Wynn, Sylvia J.
Wyrick, Floyd I.
Yarbrough, Delano
Yergan, Eric
Young, Ollie L.
Young, Reginald B.

Management/ Administration— General

Abramson, John J., Jr.
Adams, Eula L.
Addams, Robert David
Adderley, Herb Anthony
Addy, Tralance Obuama
Adkins, Rodney C.
Aklilu, Tesfaye
Alex, Gregory K.
Alexander, Kelly Miller, Jr.
Alexander, Theodore Martin, Sr.
Alexander, William M., Jr.
Alfonso, Pedro
Ali, Schavi Mali
Allen, Anita Ford
Allison, Ferdinand V., Jr.
Amos, Wally
Anderson, Carlton Leon
Anderson, Donald Edward
Anderson, George Allen
Anderson, Kernie L.
Anderson, Warren E.
Anthony, Clarence Edward
Archie, Shirley Franklin
Ashby, Lucius Antoine
Ashhurst, Carmen
Atkins, Pervis
Augustine, Matthew
Aziz, Samimah
Bacoate, Matthew, Jr.
Bacon, Randall C.
Badgett, Edward
Bailey, Gary
Bailey, William H.
Baines, Henry T.
Baker, Gwendolyn Calvert
Baldon, Janice C.
Baltimore, Roslyn Lois
Balton, Kirkwood R.
Banks, Caroline Long
Banks, Charlie
Banks, Manley E.
Banks, Waldo R., Sr.
Bankston, Charles E.
Barnes, Anne T.
Baskett, Kenneth Gerald
Bates, Barbara Ann
Battle, Turner Charles, III
Baylor, Emmett Robert, Jr.
Beavers, Robert M., Jr.
Becton, Rudolph
Bell, Theron J.
Belton, Y. Marc
Bigham, Reta Lacy
Binford, Henry C.
Birtha, Jessie M.
Blackburn, Benjamin Allan, II
Blackman, Rolando Antonio
Blalock, Marion W.
Blanks, Wilhelmina E.
Block, Leslie S.
Bolden, Charles Frank, Jr.
Bolden, Frank Augustus
Bolden, John Henry
Boldridge, George
Bond, Alan D.
Bond, Gladys B.
Bourgeois, Adam
Boutte, Alvin J.
Bowie, Walter C.
Bowles, Barbara Landers
Bowser, McEva R.
Bradshaw, Doris Marion
Bramble, Peter W. D.
Bridges, Leon
Brigham, Freddie M.
Brimmer, Andrew F.
Broadnax, Walter Doyce

Brock, Louis Clark
Brooks, Frank B.
Brooks, Harry W., Jr.
Brown, Carl Anthony
Brown, Denise J.
Brown, Raymond Madison
Brown, Walter E.
Brownlee, Dennis J.
Brunson, Dorothy Edwards
Buckner, James L.
Bullard, Keith
Bunyon, Ronald S.
Burges, Melvin E.
Burley, Jack L., Sr.
Burroughs, Hugh Charles
Busby, Jheryl
Butler, Pinkney L.
Byrd, Lumus, Jr.
Cain, Robert R., Jr.
Caines, Ken
Camp, Marva Jo
Campbell, George, Jr.
Cannon, Reuben
Carlo, Nelson
Carr, Virgil H.
Carroll, Charlene O.
Carter, Arlington W., Jr.
Cartwright, James Elgin
Cason, Joseph L.
Chargois, James M.
Charlton, George N., Jr.
Chennault, Madelyn
Childs, Winston
Chriss, Henry Thomas
Christian, John L.
Chuks-Orji, Austin
Clark, Mario Sean
Clarke, Raymond
Cole, John L., Jr.
Coleman, Frankie Lynn
Coleman, Robert L.
Connor, Dolores Lillie
Connor, Herman P.
Connor, James Russell
Conyers, Jean L.
Cooper, Barbara J.
Cooper, Michael Jerome
Corley, Eddie B.
Cormier, Lawrence J.
Cottrell, Comer J.
Cox, Otha P.
Crawford, Curtis J.
Cunningham, William
Curry, Charles H.
Dames, Sabrina A.
Daniels, Willie L.
Darden, Calvin
Dates, Jannette Lake
Davenport, Chester C.
Davis, Donald Gene
Davis, Etheldra S.
Davis, Julia H.
Davis, Melwood Leonard
Davis, Ronald P.
Davis, Ronald W.
Dent, Preston L.
Dickerson, Pamela Ann
Dixon, Arrington Liggins
Doig, Elmo H.
Dowdy, James H.
Drake, Lawrence M., II
Drakeford, Jack
Dual, J. Fred, Jr.
Dukes, Hazel Nell
Dukes, Ofield
Duncan, Sandra Rhodes
Dymally, Mervyn M.
Earls, Julian Manly
Easley, Kenny, Jr.
Eastmond, Leon
Eckstine, Ed
Edwards, George R.
Eggleston, Neverett A., Jr.
Eller, Carl L.
Ellis, Ladd, Jr.
Enders, Murvin S.
English, Henry L.
Evans, James L.
Ewing, James Melvin
Exum, Thurman McCoy
Faison, Derek E.
Fann, Al Louis
Farrell, Samuel D.
Farrington, Thomas Alex
Ferguson, Andrew L.
Fields, Brenda Joyce
Fitzpatrick, B. Edward
Fleming, Alicia DeLaMothe
Fleming, Ellis T.

Fleming, John Emory
Fletcher, Glen Edward
Floyd, Vernon Clinton
Folks, Leslie Scott
Ford, Antoinette
Foreman, Joyce Blacknall
Forte, Patrick
Fowler, Reggie
Francis, Gilbert H.
Francis, Livingston S.
Franklin, Clarence Frederick
Frazier, Audrey Lee
Frazier, Jordan
Frazier, Lee Rene
Frazier-Ellison, Vicki L.
Freisen, Gil
Fugett, Jean S., Jr.
Fuller, Doris J.
Fullwood, Harlow, Jr.
Gainer, Andrew A.
Gainey, Leonard Dennis, II
Gallot, Richard Joseph
Gardner, Edward G.
Garrett, Ruby Grant
Garrett, Thaddeus, Jr.
Gary, Willie E.
Gee, William Rowland, Jr.
Gellineau, Victor Marcel, Jr.
Gibson, James O.
Gidron, Richard D.
Giles, Joe L.
Gilliam, Herman Arthur, Jr.
Gipson, Hayward R., Jr.
Goldston, Nathaniel R., III
Goode, W. Wilson
Gooden, C. Michael
Goodman, Harold
Gordon, Darrell R.
Grady, Glenn G.
Graham, James C., Jr.
Grant, Charles Truman
Grant, Gary Rudolph
Grantham, Charles
Graves, Allene
Gray, George W., III
Gray, Moses W.
Greaves, William
Green, Carolyn Louise
Green, Hydia Lutrice
Green, Roland, Sr.
Green, Sterling
Greene, Clifton S.
Greene, Nathaniel D.
Griffey, Dick
Griffin, Bertha L.
Griffith, Gary Alan
Grigsby, Calvin Burchard
Grimes, Calvin M., Jr.
Groce, Herbert Monroe, Jr.
Groff, Regis F.
Gunnings, Thomas S.
Hadnott, Bennie L.
Hall, Alton Jerome
Hall, Brian Edward
Hall, Hansel Crimiel
Hamilton, Howard W.
Hammond, James A.
Hampton, Wanda Kay Baker
Handy, Lillian B.
Hankins, Anthony Mark
Harper, Earl
Harrell, Andre
Harris, Franco
Harris, Joseph Benjamin
Harris, Marcelite J.
Harris, Marion Rex
Harris, Rex
Harris, Thomas C.
Harris, Tricia R.
Harris-Ebohon, Altheria Thyra
Hartaway, Thomas N., Jr.
Hasty, Keith A.
Hawkins, James C.
Hawkins, La-Van
Hayes-Jordan, Margaret
Haysbert, Raymond Victor, Sr.
Head, Evelyn Harris Shields
Head, Helaine
Hebert, Zenebework Teshome
Henderson, LeMon
Henderson, William Avery
Herbert, John Travis, Jr.
Herrington, Perry Lee
Hester, Melvyn Francis
Highsmith, Carlton L.
Hightower, Dennis Fowler
Hill, Cynthia D.
Hill, George Hiram
Hill, Robert K.

Hipkins, Conrad
Hodge, Ernest M.
Hodges, Clarence Eugene
Hodges, Virgil Hall
Holland, Robert, Jr.
Holliday, Alfonso David
Holliday, Prince E.
Holliman, David L.
Holmes, Arthur, Jr.
Hooker, Douglas Randolf
Hooper, Michele J.
Hord, Noel Edward
Hovell, Larry L.
Howard, Agnes Marie
Howell, Amaziah, III
Hubbard, Darrell
Hubbard, Reginald T.
Hudson, Elbert T.
Hudson, Paul C.
Huggins, David W.
Hughes, Catherine Liggins
Hughes, George Vincent
Humphrey, Sonnie
Hunt, Edward
Hutt, Monroe L.
Hyler, Lora Lee
Ingram, Kevin
Ingram, Phillip M.
Ireland, Lynda
Irvin, Milton M.
Isaacs, Doris C.
Isler, Marshall A., III
Jackson, Beverly Anne
Jackson, Brenda
Jackson, Donald J.
Jackson, Emory Napoleon
Jackson, Gerald E.
Jackson, Horace
Jackson, Kenya Love
Jackson, Mannie L.
Jacob, John Edward
Jacques, Cornell
James, Charles H., III
James, Charles Howell, II
James, Clarence L., Jr.
James, John
James, Stephen Elisha
Jefferson, Clifton
Jemison, Aj D.
Johns, Michael Earl
John-Sandy, Rene Emanuel
Johnson, Barbara
Johnson, Cyrus Edwin
Johnson, Davis
Johnson, George Ellis
Johnson, Joan B.
Johnson, John H.
Johnson, Mark A.
Johnson, Robert L.
Johnson, T. J.
Johnson, William Randolph
Jones, Anthony Ward
Jones, Benjamin E.
Jones, David R.
Jones, Larry Wayne
Jones, Lester C.
Jones, Robert Wesley
Jones, Ruth Braswell
Jones, Yvonne Harris
Jordan, Carolyne Lamar
Jordan, Thurman
Kaiser, James Gordon
Kendrick, L. John, Sr.
Kilimanjaro, John Marshall
King, Clarence Maurice, Jr.
Kunes, Ken R.
Labat, Wendy L.
Labrie, Harrington
Laday, Kerney
Lamont, Barbara
Lander, Cressworth Caleb
Landry, Dolores Branche
Lang, Isaac, Jr.
Langford, Daria
Lanier, Jesse M., Sr.
Law, M. Eprevel
Lawes, Verna
Lawrence, Henry
Lawrence, Prestonia D.
Lawson, Anthony Eugene, Sr.
Lawson, Charles H., III
Lawson, Jennifer Karen
Lawson, William R.
Leavell, Dorothy R.
LeDay, John Austin
Lee, Andre L.
Lee, Bertram M.
Lee, Charles Gary, Sr.
Lee, Detroit

Lee, Gloria A.
Lee, Jefferi K.
Lee, Ronald B.
Lee, Stratton Creighton
Lee, William H.
Leigh, Fredric H.
Leonard, Sugar Ray
LeVert, Gerald
Lewis, Ora Lee
Lindsay, Horace Augustin
Lloyd, James
Locke, Henry Daniel, Jr.
Lockhart-Moss, Eunice Jean
Long, Steffan
Loveless, Theresa E.
Lucas, Victoria
Lucus, Emma Turner
Lundy, Gerald
Lundy, Larry
Luster, Jory
Lytle, Marilyn Mercedes
Mack, C.
Maitland, Tracey
Majors, Anthony Y.
Manlove, Benson
Martin, Elmer P.
Martin, Joanne Mitchell
Mathews, Keith E.
Maxwell, Bertha Lyons
Mays, W. Roy, III
McCain, Ella Byrd
McClain, Andrew Bradley
McClammy, Thad C.
McClenic, David A.
McDaniel, Elizabeth
McDonald, Herbert G.
McElvane, Pamela Anne
McFarland, Ollie Franklin
McHenry, James O'Neal
McIntosh, Rhodina Covington
McKenzie, Floretta D.
McKenzie, Wilford Clifton
McKinney, Samuel Berry
McKissack, Leatrice Buchanan
McLaughlin, Benjamin Wayne
McMillan, Enolia Pettigen
McZeal, Alfred, Sr.
McZier, Arthur
Meeks, Willis Gene
Merchant, John F.
Merenivitch, Jarrow
Merritt, Bishetta Dionne
Meyers, Ishmael Alexander
Michel, Harriet Richardson
Miller, Charles D., Jr.
Miller, Norman L.
Mills, John L.
Mitchell, Jacob Bill
Mitchell, Roderick Bernard
Moncrieff, Peter
Moore, Jerry A., Jr.
Moore, Joseph L.
Moragne, Lenora, Ph.D.
Morgan, Randall Collins, Sr.
Morgan, Rose
Morris, Horace W.
Morrow, Jesse
Morse, Oliver
Moses, Edwin
Moss, Tanya Jill
Motley, David Lynn
Mullens, Delbert W.
Murray, Gary S.
Myles, Wilbert
Neal, Earl Langdon
Nellums, Michael Wayne
Neloms, Henry
Nelson, A'Lelia
Nelson, Charles J.
Nelson, Otha Curtis, Sr.
Nelson, Ronald J.
Newberry, Cedric Charles
Newkirk, Thomas H.
Nicco-Annan, Lionel
Nixon, Felix Nathaniel
Nixon, James I., Jr.
Noble, John Pritchard
Norman, Bobby Don
Norris, William E.
Odom, Carolyn
O'Flynn-Thomas, Patricia
Orr, Ray
Ozanne, Leroy
Paddio-Johnson, Eunice Alice
Pailen, Donald
Pannell, Patrick Weldon
Parker, George Anthony
Parker, James Thomas
Parker, Jean L.

Parker, Matthew
Parker, Stafford W.
Parrish, James Nathaniel
Patrick, Charles Namon, Jr.
Patrick, Jennie R.
Patterson, John T., Jr.
Payne, Osborne Allen
Payne, Ronnie E.
Payton, Walter Jerry
Pearson, Drew
Perry, Eugene Calvin, Jr.
Perry, LaVal
Peters, Charles L., Jr.
Petterway, Jackie Willis
Petty, Bruce Anthony
Phelps-Patterson, Lucy
Phillips, Daniel P.
Pickard, William Frank
Pinckney, Andrew Morgan, Jr.
Plinton, James O., Jr.
Plunkett, Raphael Hildan
Poe, Alfred
Porter, E. Melvin
Porter, John W.
Powell, Adam Clayton, III
Powell-Jackson, Bernice
Price, Albert H.
Price, Phillip G.
Procope, John Levy
Pruitt, Michael
Pruitt, Mike
Pryor, Malcolm D.
Queen Latifah
Randall, Queen F.
Raullerson, Calvin Henry
Ray, Walter I., Jr.
Reid, Malissie Laverne
Reid, Sina M.
Reid, Vernon H.
Reid-McQueen, Lynne Marguerite
Rhodes, Edward Thomas, Sr.
Rhone, Sylvia M.
Rice, Linda Johnson
Richards, William Earl
Richards-Alexander, Billie J.
Richardson, Albert Dion
Richardson, Joseph
Richardson, Linda Waters
Riggs, Enrique A.
Riles, Wilson Camanza
Roberts, Janice L.
Robertson, Oscar Palmer
Robinson, John F.
Robinson, Melvin P.
Robinson, Myron Frederick
Robinson, Will
Rodman, John
Rodriguez, Ruben
Roebuck-Hayden, Marcia
Rogers, Ormer, Jr.
Roundtree, Eugene V. N.
Rowe, William Leon
Roy, John Willie
Ruffin, John H., Jr.
Ruffin, John Walter, Jr.
Samuels, James E.
Samuels, Leslie Eugene
Satterwhite, Frank Joseph
Scales, Patricia Bowles
Scott, Arthur Bishop
Scott, Becky Beckwith
Scott, Donnell
Scott, Gilbert H.
Scott, Helen Madison Marie Pawne Kinard
Scott, Judith Sugg
Scott, Larry B.
Scribner, Arthur Gerald, Jr.
Seals, Connie C.
Seavers, Clarence W.
Shanks, Wilhelmina Byrd
Shead, Ken
Shealey, Richard W.
Sheffey, Fred C.
Shepherd, Malcolm Thomas
Shepherd, Veronika Y.
Sherrell, Charles Ronald, II
Shields, Cydney Robin
Shivers, P. Derrick
Simmons, Albert Bufort, Jr.
Simmons, Donald M.
Simmons, Russell
Simmons, Willie, Jr.
Simms, Robert H.
Simon, Elaine
Simpson, Merton Daniel
Sims, Adrienne
Singleton, Benjamin, Sr.
Singleton, Ernie

Slash, Joseph A.
Sloan, Maceo Kennedy
Smith, Albert E.
Smith, Bruce L.
Smith, Darryl C.
Smith, G. Elaine
Smith, Gregory Kevin Prillerman
Smith, Guy Lincoln, IV
Smith, John Raye
Smith, Kevin L.
Smith, Lawrence John, Jr.
Smith, Nathaniel, Jr.
Smith, Oscar A., Jr.
Smith, Quentin Paige, Jr.
Smith-Croxton, Terri
Smithers, Priscilla Jane
Sneed, Gregory J.
Sneed, Paula A.
Sobers, Waynett A., Jr.
Sockwell, Oliver R., Jr.
South, Wesley W.
Spriggs, Ray V.
Staley, Kenneth Bernard
Stancell, Arnold Francis
Stebbins, Dana Brewington
Stephens, Charles Richard
Stephens, Juanita K.
Stephenson, Charles E., III
Sterling, Charles A.
Stewart, Freddie Mardrell
Sullivan, Leon Howard
Sutton, Nathaniel K.
Sutton, Percy E.
Swanston, Clarence Eugene
Sykes, Ray
Tabor, Langston
Tate, Lenore Artie
Taylor, Charles E.
Taylor, Henry F.
Taylor, Henry Marshall
Taylor, Michael
Taylor, Patricia Tate
Taylor, Robert Derek
Taylor, Sinthy E.
Temple, Oney D.
Terrell, Dorothy
Terry, Roy
Thermilus, Jacque E.
Thomas, Earl
Thomas, Joan McHenry Bates
Thomas, Linda
Thomas, Lydia Waters
Thomas, Stanley B., Jr.
Thomas, Terra Leatherberry
Thompson, Albert N.
Thompson, Frank L.
Thompson, Jesse
Tillman, Joseph Nathaniel
Todman, Terence A.
Trammer, Monte Irvin
Tresvant, John Bernard
Trotter, Lloyd G.
Tucker, C. DeLores
Tucker, Leota Marie
Turner, Bennie
Turner, Geneva
Turner, Harry Glenn
Turner, Jesse H., Jr.
Turner, M. Annette
Turner, Vivian Love
Tyrrell, James A.
Tyson, Edward Charles
Urquhart, James McCartha
Ussery, Terdema Lamar, II
Utendahl, John O.
Valdes, Pedro H.
Valentine, Herman E.
Vaughan, James Edward
Venable, Abraham S.
Waden, Fletcher Nathaniel, Jr.
Walker, Eugene Kevin
Walker, James
Walker, Willie F.
Wallace, Arnold D., Sr.
Wallace, Arthur, Jr.
Waller, Louis E.
Ware, Carl
Warfield, Robert N.
Warren, Clarence F.
Warren, Henry L.
Warren, Otis, Jr.
Washington, Carl Douglas
Washington, Earl S.
Watiker, Albert David, Jr.
Wattley, Thomas Jefferson
Webb, James Eugene
Webb, James O.
Webb, Joe
Weems, Vernon Eugene, Jr.

Wells, Roderick Arthur
Wesley, Clemon Herbert, Jr.
White, Gary Leon
White, James Louis, Jr.
White, Nathaniel B.
White, Wendell F.
White, William E.
White, William J.
Whiteman, Herbert Wells, Jr.
Whiting, Leroy
Whitmal, Nathaniel
Whitney, W. Monty
Whitney, William B.
Whitworth, Claudia Alexander
Wilds, Jetie Boston, Jr.
Wilkinson, Sheppard Field
Williams, Donald
Williams, Hal
Williams, Joseph Lee, Jr.
Williams, Paul
Williams, Pelham C.
Williams, Terrie Michelle
Williams, Wallace C.
Willie, Louis J.
Wilson, Barbara Jean
Wilson, Charles Stanley, Jr.
Wilson, Frederick A.
Winfield, Arnold F.
Wolfe, Estemore A.
Womack, John H.
Woodhouse, Rossalind Yvonne
Woods, Willie
Woodward, Aaron Alphonso, III
Wormley, Diane-Louise Lambert
Worsley, George Ira, Jr.
Wrice, Vincent J.
Wright, Alonzo Gordon
Wright, Joseph Malcolm
Wright, Louis Donnel
Yancy, Earl J.
Yelity, Stephen C.
Yergan, Eric
Youman, Lillian Lincoln
Young, James Arthur, III
Young, Leon
Zollar, Doris L.

Management/ Administration— Operations/Maintenance

Alexander, Robin
Banks, Charlie
Barber, William, Jr.
Barfield, John E.
Barnes, Matthew Molena, Jr.
Bates, William J.
Blake, J. Paul
Brailsford, Marvin D.
Brewster, Luther George
Brockington, Donella P.
Brown, Rose Denise
Burks, Juanita Pauline
Burnett, Luther C.
Bustamante, J. W. Andre
Campbell, Gertrude M.
Cannon, Tyrone Heath
Cargill, Sandra Morris
Ceasar, Sherita Therese
Chenault, Kenneth
Clark, Louis James
Coaxum, Henry L., Jr.
Cochran, Edward G.
Colbert, Virgis W.
Cooke, Thomas H., Jr.
Crawford, David
Daniels, Sidney
Dill, Gregory
Donald, Arnold Wayne
Donaldson, Richard T.
Dorsey, Herman Sherwood, Jr.
Dortch, Heyward
Elliott, J. Russell
Evans, Leon, Jr.
Gamble, Eva M.
Glen, Ulysses, Jr.
Griffin, Bertha L.
Griffin, Michael D.
Haile, Annette L.
Harding, Michael S.
Hardy, Michael Leander
Harrold, Lawrence A.
Havis, Jeffrey Oscar
Hayes-Giles, Joyce V.
Hobson, William D.
Hodges, Clarence Eugene
Holliman, David L.
Holmes, Litdell Melvin, Jr.
Holmes, Robert Kathrone, Jr.

Hunigan, Earl
Johnson, Andrew
Johnson, Charles Edward
Johnson, Fran
Johnson, Miriam B.
Leigh, Fredric H.
Levell, Edward, Jr.
Louis, Joseph
Lowry, James E.
Martin, George Alexander, Jr.
Martin, Walter L.
Martin, William R.
McDonald, Willie Ruth Davis
McLaurin, Freddie Lewis, Jr.
Meriwether, Louise
Miller, George Carroll, Jr.
Milligan, Unav Opal Wade
Moore, Alstork Edward
Mosley, Elwood A.
Neal, Brenda Jean
Nearn, Arnold Dorsey, Jr.
Neizer, Meredith Ann
Nicholas, Philip, Sr.
Parker, Irvin
Petersen, Frank Emmanuel, Jr.
Pitchford, Gerard Spencer
Redon, Leonard Eugene
Reed, Cordell
Reeves, Julius Lee
Rimm, Byron Newton
Rogers, Charles Leonard
Rogers-Reece, Shirley
Sanders, Laura Green
Sanderson, Randy Chris
Simmons, Willie, Jr.
Smith, Aubrey Carl, Jr.
Smith, Donald M.
Stallworth, Ann P.
Stephens, Wallace O'Leary
Stewart, Ronald L.
Taylor, Charles E.
Thomas, Samuel
Ukabam, Innocent O.
Vanderburg, Craig Terrence
Verbal, Claude A.
Wainwright, Oliver O'Connell
Walker, Russell Dewitt
Washington, Darryl McKenzie
Watkins, Price I.
Weissinger, Thomas, Sr.
Westbrook, Franklin Solomon
Williams, Barbara Ann
Williams, Edward Ellis
Williams, Stanley King
Woodson, Tracy Todd

Management/ Administration— Personnel/Training/ Labor Relations

Adams, Albert W., Jr.
Adderly, T. C., Jr.
Albright, William Dudley, Jr.
Alexander, Preston Paul, Jr.
Allen, Billy R.
Anderson, Elizabeth M.
Anderson, Joe Lewis, Sr.
Arnette, Dorothy Deanna
Arrington, Pamela Gray
Bailey, Antoinette M.
Bailey, Ronald W.
Baity, Gail Owens
Baldwin, Louis J.
Banks, Paula A.
Barclay, David Ronald
Barksdale, Mary Frances
Barnes, Diane
Barnhill, Helen Iphigenia
Barrett, Iris Louise Killian
Baskerville, Penelope Anne
Bates, George Albert
Bayless, Paul Clifton
Beasley, Dave, Jr.
Beckles, Benita Harris
Bell, Sandra Watson
Bellinger, Harold
Bender, Barbara A.
Berry, Paul Lawrence
Berry, Philip Alfonso
Bessent, Hattie
Biggs, Cynthia DeMari
Bivens, Shelia Reneea
Black, Rosa Walston
Black, Veronica Correll
Blackmon, Joyce McAnulty
Blackmon, Mosetta Whitaker
Blakely, Edward James
Blakely, Ronald Eugene

Blakely, William H., Jr.
Block, Leslie S.
Blue, Vida, Jr.
Boags, Charles D.
Bolden, Frank Augustus
Bolden, J. Taber, III
Bolden, John Henry
Bolden, Veronica Marie
Bolling, Bruce C.
Bond, Ollie P.
Boswell, Arthur W.
Boyd, Rozelle
Boyd, Theophilus B., III
Branch, Andre Jose
Bridgeman, Donald Earl
Brooks, Wadell, Sr.
Browder, Anne Elna
Brown, A. David
Brown, Booker T.
Brown, Clarence William
Brown, Joeanna Hurston
Brown, Jurutha
Bruce, Carol Pitt
Bryant-Mitchell, Ruth Harriet
Bryant-Reid, Johanne
Bugg, Robert
Burges, Melvin E.
Burns, Sarah Ann
Burrows Dost, Janice H.
Bussey, Charles David
Caines, Ken
Caldwell, George Theron, Sr.
Caldwell, John Edward
Caldwell, Lisa Jeffries
Cammack, Charles Lee, Jr.
Canty, Otis Andrew
Carey, Claire Lamar
Carey, Wayne E.
Carroll, Charles H.
Carter, Jandra D.
Carter, Judy Sharon
Carter, Patrick Henry, Jr.
Cason, Marilynn Jean
Cates, Sidney Hayward, III
Chalmers, Thelma Faye
Champion, James A.
Chandler, Effie L.
Chapman, Alice Mariah
Chapman, Charles F.
Chappell, Ruth Rax
Childs, Joy
Christian, Dolly Lewis
Cissoko, Alioune Badara
Clack, R. C.
Clark, James Irving, Jr.
Clarke, Benjamin Louis
Cobb, Cynthia Joan
Cockerham, Haven Earl
Collins, James H.
Colyer, Sheryl Lynn
Cooper, Barbara J.
Cooper, Irmgard M.
Cooper, Linda G.
Copes, Ronald Adrian
Cornell, Bob
Cornwell, William David
Cotton, Albert E.
Cox, M. Maurice
Crawley, Oscar Lewis
Cribb, Juanita Sanders
Cross, Austin Devon
Crosse, St. George Idris Bryon
Crump, Wilbert S.
Crusoe-Ingram, Charlene
Cureton, John Porter
Cujyet, Aloysius Baxter
Davis, Brownie W.
Davis, Gloria-Jeanne
Dean, James Edward
Deloatch, Myrna Spencer
Dent, Gary Kever
Dewberry-Williams, Madelina Denise
Dickson, Daryl M.
Doanes-Bergin, Sharyn F.
Dominic, Irwing
Dorman, Hattie L.
Dorsey, Herman Sherwood, Jr.
Dotson, Betty Lou
Douglas, Mae Alice
Douglas, Mansfield, III
Dowdell, Dennis, Jr.
Downes, Dwight
Dungie, Ruth Spigner
Dunn, Ross
Eagle, Arnold Elliott
Early, Robert S.
Edmond, Paul Edward
Edwards, Bessie Regina

Edwards, Verba L.
Enders, Murvin S.
English, Marion S.
Evans, Gwendolyn
Evans, Phillip L.
Faucett, Barbara J.
Felder, Tyree Preston, II
Ferrell, Rosie E.
Fisher, Rubin Ivan
Fitzpatrick, Albert E.
Fleming, Alicia DeLaMothe
Flemming, Lillian Brock
Fletcher, Milton Eric
Ford, Evern D.
Ford, Hilda Eileen
Foster, Jylla Moore
Foster, LaDoris J.
Francis, E. Aracelis
Franklin, Clarence Frederick
Frazier, Ramona Yancey
Gaskin, Jeanine
Gaston, Linda Saulsby
Gaston, Mack Charles
Gavin, Mary Ann
Gibson, JoAnn
Gilmore, Carter C.
Glover, Diana M.
Gomez, Dennis Craig
Goodwin, Evelyn Louise
Gordon-Dillard, Joan Yvonne
Gordon-Shelby, Lurdys Marie
Grant, Nathaniel
Graves, Allene
Gray, Brian Anton
Greaux, Cheryl Prejean
Gudger, Robert Harvey
Guillory, Linda Semien
Gurley, Helen Ruth
Haley, Earl Albert
Hall, Nancy M.
Hamer, Judith Ann
Hardeman, James Anthony
Hareld, Gail B.
Harmon, M. Larry
Harrington, Denise Marion
Harris, Eugene Edward
Harris, Robert D.
Harris, Robert Eugene Peyton
Harris McKenzie, Ruth Bates
Harrison, Shirley Dindy
Hatchett, William F.
Hawkins, Lawrence C.
Hawkins, William Douglas
Hawthorne, Kenneth L.
Hayes-Giles, Joyce V.
Heard, Georgina E.
Henderson, Larry W.
Hendon, Lea Alpha
Herbert, Benne S., Jr.
Higgins, Ora A.
High, Claude, Jr.
Hightower, Michael
Hill, Alfred
Hill, Deborah
Hill, James H.
Hill, Leo
Holder, Idalia
Hollon, Herbert Holstein
Holman, Forest H.
Holmes, Leo S.
Holt, Donald H.
Hopson, Melvin Clarence
Horton, Lemuel Leonard
Houston, Agnes Wood
Houston, Corinne P.
Hudson, Anthony Webster
Hudson, Jerome William
Hunigan, Earl
Hunter, William L.
Isaac, Brian Wayne
Jackson, Dwayne Adrian
Jackson, Yvonne Ruth
James, Herbert I.
James, Peggi C.
Jenkins, Joseph Walter, Jr.
Jenkins, Monica
Johnson, Alvin Roscoe
Johnson, Carl Earld
Johnson, Cleveland, Jr.
Johnson, Joseph David
Johnson, Milton D.
Johnson, Warren S.
Jolly, Mary B.
Jones, Dorinda A.
Jones, John L.
Jones, Lemuel B.
Jones, Ronald Lyman
Jones, Willie
Jordan, John Wesley

Kearse, Barbara Stone
Kee, Marsha Goodwin
Killion, Theo M.
Kimbrough-Johnson, Donna L.
King, John L.
Kirby-Davis, Montanges
Kornegay, William F.
Kyle, Odes J., Jr.
Lackey, Edgar F.
Lane, Nancy L.
Lawrence, Ollie, Jr.
Lawrence, Thomas R., Jr.
Lawson, Herman A.
LeBlanc, Michael J.
Lee, Kevin Brian
Leigh, Fredric H.
Leonard, Gloria Jean
Lewis, Aubrey C.
Lewis, Floyd Edward
Lewis, Henry S., Jr.
Lewis, Meharry Hubbard
Lister, David Alfred
Lister, Willa M.
Little, Brian Keith
Long, James, Jr.
Lovelace, Gloria Elaine
Lowery-Jeter, Renecia Yvonne
Lowry, William E., Jr.
Mahone, Barbara J.
Marbury, Martha G.
Mardenborough, Leslie A.
Marsh, Ben Franklin
Mason, William E.
Mathis, Frank
McAllister, Leroy Timothy, Sr.
McGuire, Raymond J.
McIntosh, Rhodina Covington
McKinney, Olivia Davene Ross
McLaughlin, David
McLean, Mary Cannon
McMillan, Elridge W.
Merideth, Charles Waymond
Merriweather, Thomas L.
Miller, Frederick A.
Miller, George Carroll, Jr.
Mills, Larry Glenn
Mims, Raymond Everett, Sr.
Montgomery, Earline Robertson
Moore, Cleotha Franklin
Moore, Robert Andrew
Moragne, Maurice S.
Morrow, Laverne
Mosley, Elwood A.
Moyler, Freeman William, Jr.
Naphier, Joe L.
Newman, Constance Berry
Nunn, John, Jr.
Nurse, Robert Earl
Oliver-Simon, Gloria Craig
Orr, Clyde Hugh
Osborne, Clayton Henriquez
Parker, Joyce Linda
Passmore, William A.
Pattillo, Joyce M.
Pearson, Marilyn Ruth
Peoples, Harrison Promis, Jr.
Perry, Alexis E.
Peterson, Coleman Hollis
Phillips, Robert Hansbury
Pickett, Donna A.
Pogue, D. Eric
Polk, Eugene Steven, Sr.
Pollard, Percy Edward, Sr.
Pope, Ruben Edward, III
Porter, Gloria Jean
Porter, John T.
Powell, Bettye Boone
Powell, Kenneth Alasandro
Powell, Robert John
Powers, Clyde J.
Procter, Harvey Thornton, Jr.
Ramseur, Andre William
Reynolds, Andrew Buchanan
Richardson, Joseph
Richardson, Ralph H.
Roberts, Ella S.
Roberts, Roy S.
Robinson, Jeannette
Robinson, John G.
Robinson, Ronnie W.
Rogers-Reece, Shirley
Rosenthal, Robert E.
Ross-Audley, Cheryl Jvonne
Rutledge, Jennifer M.
Salter, Kwame S.
Sandidge, Kanita Durice
Sands, George M.
Saunders, John Edward, III
Savage, James Edward, Jr.

Schenck, Frederick A.
Schutz, Andrea Louise
Scott, Helen Madison Marie
  Pawne Kinard
Sellers, Theresa Ann
Shawnee, Laura Ann
Shepard, Linda Irene
Simmons, Thelma M.
Simms, Robert H.
Smith, Dolores J.
Smith, James, Jr.
Smith, LeRoi Matthew-Pierre, III
Smith, Shirley LaVerne
Smith, William Fred
Somerville, Patricia Dawn
Spearman, Larna Kaye
Spencer, Brenda L.
Spencer, Gregory Randall
Spicer, Kenneth, Sr.
Spight, Benita L.
Spriggs, Ray V.
Stacia, Kevin Maurice
Starkey, Frank David
Steans, Edith Elizabeth
Steele, Warren Bell
Stewart, Malcolm M.
Story, Charles Irvin
Suggs, Robert Chinelo
Sutton, Dianne Floyd
Swain, James H.
Tate, Valencia Faye
Taylor, DeForrest Walker
Taylor, Mildred E. Crosby
Terrill, W. H. Tyrone, Jr.
Theodore, Yvonne M.
Thomas, Mitchell, Jr.
Thomas, Samuel
Thompson, Jesse M.
Thompson, Portia Wilson
Tillman, Paula Sellars
Toliver, Virginia F. Dowsing
Towns, Myron B., II
Tucker, Geraldine Jenkins
Tudy Jackson, Janice
Tuggle, Dorie C.
Turner, Diane Young
Turner, Linda Darnell
Turner, Vivian Love
Turnley, Richard Dick, Jr.
Turnquest, Sandra Close
Vance, Tommie Rowan
Vannaman, Madi T.
Vaughn, Audrey Smith
Vertreace, Walter Charles
Walker, Tracy A.
Walker, William Sonny
Ward, Lenwood E.
Warren, James Kenneth
Washington, Ava F.
Washington, Jacqueline Ann
Webb, Lucious Moses
Wells, Linda Ivy
Wells-Davis, Margie Elaine
White, Alvin, Jr.
Wilds, Jetie Boston, Jr.
Wilford, Harold C.
Wilkins, Charles O.
Willacy, Hazel M.
Williams, Annalisa Stubbs
Williams, Felton Carl
Williams, Harold David
Williams, James
Williams, James E., Jr.
Williams, Janice L.
Williams, Jean Perkins
Williams, Karen Elaine
Williams, Melvin
Williams, Stanley King
Willingham, Voncile
Wilson, J. Ray
Wilson, Wesley Campbell
Winstead, Vernon A., Sr.
Wint, Arthur Valentine Noris
Wise, William Clinton, Jr.
Wisham, Claybron O.
Woods, Andre Vincent
Wooten, John
Young, Nancy Wilson
Young, Ollie L.

Management/ Administration— Purchasing

Banks, Charlie
Banks, Lula F.
Butler, Darraugh Clay
Camphor, Michael Gerard
Carey, Carnice

Cargill, Sandra Morris
Connor, Dolores Lillie
Edwards, Lewis
Fleming, Vernon Cornelius
Gamble, William F.
Gibson, Wayne Carlton
Glenn, Dennis Eugene
Hamlin, David W.
Harris, Joseph Elliot, II
Hayes-Giles, Joyce V.
Hightower, Willar H., Jr.
Horne, June C.
Jackson, Audrey Nabors
Jackson, Mary
Johnson, Wendy Robin
Keitt, L.
Kirksey, M. Janette
Knott, May
London, Roberta Levy
Lowe, Walter Edward, Jr.
Merchant, James S., Jr.
Payne, Cynthia Paulette
Payne, Ronnie E.
Rakestraw, Kyle Damon
Reynolds, James W.
Rhodes, Edward Thomas, Sr.
Richardson, Johnny L.
Smith, Lafayette Kenneth
Strudwick, Lindsey H., Sr.
Sutton, James Carter
Washington, Earlene
Whitest, Beverly Joyce
Wiley, Gerald Edward
Zachary, Hubert M.

Management/ Administration—Sales

Adams, Quinton Douglas
Alexander, Kelly Miller, Jr.
Anderson, Marcellus J., Sr.
Baker, Gregory D.
Banks, Ronald
Barrett, Matthew Anderson
Benton, Phyllis Clora
Birtha, Jessie M.
Bisamunyu, Jeanette
Bolden, Wiley Speights
Brown, Gilbert David, III
Browne, Vincent Jefferson, Jr.
Bryant, Franklyn
Burton, Ronald J.
Butler, Oliver Richard
Carey, Pearl M.
Chapman, Rosyln C.
Clanagan, Mazzetta Price
Cochran, S. Thomas
Coshburn, Henry S., Jr.
Daniel, James L.
Daniels, Cecil Tyrone
Davis, Frank
Davis, H. Bernard
DeLeon, Priscilla
Derbigny, Rhoda L.
Dixon, Brenda Joyce
Dorsey, Ivory Jean
Evans, Elinor Elizabeth
Faison, Sharon Gail
Forde, Fraser Philip, Jr.
Fuller, Norvell Ricardo
Gaillard, Ralph C., Sr.
George, Pauline L.
Gordon, Alexander H., II
Gregory, Bernard Vincent
Griffith, Gary Alan
Griffiths, Errol D.
Hall, Alton Jerome
Harris, Larry Vordell, Jr.
Harris, Marion Rex
Harris, Stanley Eugene
Herron, Bruce Wayne
Holloway, Ardith E.
Jackson, Kevin L.
Jackson, William Alvin
Jackson, William Ed
Jamison, Lafayette
Johnson, Frank Scott
Johnson, Juliana Cornish
Johnson, Mark A.
Jones, William Barnard
King, Lawrence C.
Lawson, Bruce B.
Lewis, Robert Alvin, Jr.
Lewis, Stephen Christopher
Lloyd, Phil Andrew
Marshall, H. Jean
Marshall, Pluria William, Jr.
Maule, Albert R.
Monroe, Robert Alex

Moragne, Maurice S.
Morrow, W. Derrick
Mullins, Jarrett R.
Neal, Joseph C., Jr.
Norman, Clifford P.
Northover, Vernon Keith
Parker, William Hartley
Patnett, John Henry
Perry, Gary W.
Phillips, Basil Oliphant
Phillips, Constance Ann
Pierce, Aaronetta Hamilton
Pillow, Vanita J.
Pressey, Junius Batten, Jr.
Ray, Walter I., Jr.
Richmond, Delores Ruth
Robbins, Carl Gregory Cuyjet
Roberts, Blanche Elizabeth
Robinson, Patricia Jervis
Rogers, Desiree Glapion
Rogers-Grundy, Ethel W.
Roundtree, Nicholas John
Russell, Kay A.
Scott, Gilbert H.
Seay, Dawn Christine
Shelton, Charles E.
Simmons, Eric O.
Sims, Keith Eugene
Small, Isadore, III
Smith, Charles
Sterling, Charles A.
Stitt, E. Don
Stokes, Rueben Martine
Swan, Edward McCallan, Jr.
Tate, Adolphus, Jr.
Taylor, Cassandra W.
Temple, Oney D.
Thurman, Cedric Douglas
Walton, James Donald
Washington, Edward
Watts, Victor Lewis
West, Bruce Alan
White, James Louis, Jr.
White, Wendell F.
Whitfield, Willie, Jr.
Wiley, Forrest Parks
Wilkinson, Raymond M., Jr.
Williams, Edward Ellis
Williams, Everett Belvin
Willrich, Emzy James
Wilson, Barbara Jean
Woodbeck, Frank Raymond
Woodruff, Jeffrey Robert
Wooten, Carl Kenneth
Wynn, Sylvia J.
Young, Raymond, Jr.

Management/ Administration—Not Elsewhere Classified
(*See Also* **Association Management; Educational Administration; Health Services Administration; Labor Union Administration; Sports Coaching/Training/ Managing/Officiating**)

Adams, Marie Elizabeth
Allen, Winston Earle
Andrews, Adelia Smith
Arterberry, Vivian J.
Atchison, Calvin O.
Bacon, Charlotte Meade
Baker, Gregory D.
Baldwin, John H.
Ballard, Kathryn W.
Bartow, Jerome Edward
Bass, Marshall Brent
Beavers, Nathan Howard, Jr.
Bell, Joseph Curtis
Bell, William Vaughn
Bellamy, Walter
Bembry, Lawrence
Benton, Leonard D.
Bernard, Sharon Elaine
Berryman, Matilene S.
Blackwell, Patricia A.
Blake, Elias, Jr.
Bolden, Dorothy Lee
Borden, Harold F., Jr.
Bost, Fred M.
Bowles, Barbara Landers
Boyd-Clinkscales, Mary Elizabeth
Brewer, Moses

Connor, James Russell
Dade, Malcolm G., Jr.
Davidson, Ezra C., Jr., M.D.
Davis, Harold R.
Dawson, Matel, Jr.
Dent, Gary Kever
Dillard, Howard Lee
Dixon, Louis Tennyson
Donaldson, Richard T.
Edwards, Dennis L.
Edwards, Gerald Douglas
Edwards, Verba L.
Ellis, Michael G.
Embry, Wayne, Sr.
Enders, Murvin S.
Farmer, Forest J.
Fletcher, Milton Eric
Florence, Jerry DeWayne
Frost, William Henry
Goldsberry, Ronald Eugene
Goodwin, Donald Edward
Hall, Alfonzo Louis
Hall, Elliott Sawyer
Herring, William F.
Hunter, Clarence Henry
Irby, Mary
Jensen, Renaldo Mario
Jones, Emanuel Davie
Kelly, Thomas Maurice, III
Kent, Deborah Stewart
Kornegay, William F.
Lartigue, Roland E.
Latimer, Frank Edward
Lewis, W. Howard
Mallebay-Vacqueur Dem, Jean Pascal
McLaughlin, LaVerne Laney
Merchant, James S., Jr.
Moorehead, Thomas
Mullens, Delbert W.
Newman, Paul Dean
Nixon, James I., Jr.
O'Neal, Rodney
Perry, Gary W.
Peters, Roscoe Hoffman, Jr.
Pettiford, Steven Douglas
Polk, Eugene Steven, Sr.
Preston, Franklin DeJuanette
Proctor, Earl D.
Reeves, Julius Lee
Richie, Leroy C.
Riley, Rosetta Margueritte
Roberts, Roy S.
Sanders, Barbara A.
Seibert-McCauley, Mary F.
Sendaba, S. M.
Stevens, Warren Sherwood
Stitt, E. Don
Thorns, Odail, Jr.
Turner, Harry Glenn
Verbal, Claude A.
Ware, Albert M.
Washington, Floyd, Jr.
Welburn, Edward Thomas, Jr.
Wine, Donald Gary

Manufacturing—Paper and Allied Products
Broussard, Catherine Dianne
Bryant, Clarence W.
Burns, Tommie, Jr.
Croft, Norman F.
Foreman, Joyce Blacknall
Kendrick, L. John, Sr.
McIver, Margaret Hill
Nichols, Nick
Smith, Bob
Smith, H. Russell
Wallace, Arthur, Jr.

Manufacturing—Textile Mill Products
Crawley, Oscar Lewis
Mays, Carrie J.
Thornton, Cora Ann Barringer
Wilson, Clarence A.

Manufacturing—Not Elsewhere Classified
Addy, Tralance Obuama
Bates, Robert E., Jr.
Byrd, George Edward
Clyburn, John B.
Crutcher, Betty Neal
Fontenot, Albert E., Jr.

Gaillard, Ralph C., Sr.
Hall, Harold L.
Hill, Rufus S.
Hogan, William E., II
Hutt, Monroe L.
Jackson, Elijah
Kennedy, Howard E.
King, Hulas H.
King, William Frank
Knott, Albert Paul, Jr.
Knox, George L., III
Lewis, George Ralph
Long, James, Jr.
Lovelace, John C.
Marshall, Jonnie Clanton
McLaughlin, Benjamin Wayne
McLean, Dennis Ray
Melton, Frank E.
Nelson, Jonathan P.
Osborne, Clayton Henriquez
Pitts, Brenda S.
Reddrick, Mark A.
Richardson, Otis Alexander
Roberts, Bobby L.
Rush, Sonya C.
Smith, Guy Lincoln, IV
Smith, Wilson Washington, III
Stone, Reese J., Jr.
Thomas, Roy L.
Ward, Lloyd David
White, Quitman, Jr.
Woods, Andre Vincent
Woods, Henry, Jr.
Woodson, Cleveland Coleman, III
Young, Charles Lemuel, Sr.

Marketing
See Advertising/Promotion; Management/Administration—Advertising/Marketing/Public Relations

Mathematics
Carroll, Edward Major
Cash-Rhodes, Winifred E.
Dale, Clamma Churita
Draper, Everett T., Jr.
Dunlap, Estelle Cecilia Diggs
Earl, Archie William, Sr.
Emeagwali, Philip
Hedgley, David Rice, Jr.
Houston, Johnny L.
Howell, Amaziah, III
Hughes, Isaac Sunny
Johnson, Edward A.
Johnson, Martin Leroy
Johnson, Raymond Lewis
King, Calvin E.
King, John Q. Taylor, Sr.
Lahr, Charles Dwight
Lyons, Charles H. S., Jr.
Mabson, Glenn T.
McAdoo, Henry Allen
McLaurin, Jasper Etienne
Mickey, Gordon Eugene
Monteith, Henry C.
Morris, Charles Edward, Jr.
Morton, Norman
Porter, Henry Lee
Reed, Maurice L.
Richards, Winston Ashton
Svager, Thyrsa F.
Thomas, Ronald F.
Tisdale, Henry Nehemiah
Vance, Irvin E.
Wallace, Milton De'Nard
Waller, Eunice McLean
Walton, Harriett J.
Whitlock, Fred Henry
Williams, Willie Elbert

Medicine—Anesthesiology
Briscoe, Edward Gans
Clark, Morris Shandell
Ivey Yarn, Barbara Lynne
Lord, Clyde Ormond
Neal, Alimam Butler
Primm, Beny Jene
Sears, Bertram E.
Smith, Oswald Garrison
Swiner, Connie, III
Willock, Marcelle Monica

Medicine—Cardiology
Anderson, Arnett Artis
Banks, Tazewell
Barnes, Boisey O.
Batties, Paul Terry
Belton, C. Ronald
Charleston, Gomez, Jr.
Cooper, Edward Sawyer
Cutliff, John Wilson
Daniels, Curtis A.
Ellis, Tellis B., III
Ferdinand, Keith C.
Fontaine, John M.
Gibson, Harris, Jr.
Haywood, L. Julian
Hilliard, General E.
Jonas, Ernesto A.
Mays, Travis Cortez
McBroom, F. Pearl
Neals, Huerta C.
Oliver, Ronald
Parker, Jeff, Sr.
Pearson, Stanley E.
Quivers, Eric Stanley
Revis, Nathaniel W.
Ross, Edward
Sanders, George L.
Saunders, Elijah
Smith, Ernest Howard
Yarborough, Dowd Julius, Jr.

Medicine—Dermatology
Alexander, A. Melvin
Anderson, William A.
Boswell, Bennie, Jr.
Brown, Roy Hershel
Butler, John Donald
Callender, Valerie Dawn
Clarke, Greta Fields
Dilworth, Jacquelyn Brewer
Earles, Rene Martin
McDonald, Charles J.
McDonald, Curtis W.
Moore, Milton Donald, Jr.
Quigless, Milton Douglas, Sr.
Taylor, Susan Charlene
Willis, Isaac

Medicine—Family Practice
Adiele, Moses Nkwachukwu
Anderson, Benjamin Stratman, Jr.
Anderson, Russell Lloyd
Andrews, Rawle
Armour, Christopher E.
Artis, Myrle Everett
Audain, Linz
Barclay, Carl Archie
Benjamin, Regina M.
Boddie, Algernon Owens
Brimm, Charles Edwin
Briscoe, Edward Gans
Brown, Calvin Anderson, Jr.
Brown, Ewart F., Jr.
Brown, William, Jr.
Butler, Charles H.
Carney, Robert Matthew
Carson, Dwight Keith
Carter, James Earl, Jr.
Christian, Cora LeEthel
Clarke, Angela Webb
Collier, Millard James, Jr., M.D.
Cooper, Charles W.
Creary, Ludlow Barrington
Crump, Carolyn F.
Dapremont, Delmont, Jr.
Davis, Matilda Laverne
Dugas, Henry C.
Dyer-Goode, Pamela Theresa
Fisher, Edward G.
Floyd, Dean Allen
Frazier, Jimmy Leon
Gardner, Jackie Randolph
Garrison, Robert E., Jr.
Gerald, Melvin Douglas, Sr.
Goodson, Leroy Beverly
Goodwin, William Pierce, Jr.
Hadley, Howard Alva, Jr.
Hairston, Oscar Grogan
Hammel-Davis, Donna P.
Ham-Ying, J. Michael
Harris, Percy G., M.D.
Hereford, Sonnie Wellington, III
Hines, William E.
Johns, Sonja Maria
Johnson, Lucien Love
Jones, Alphonzo James

King, William Moses
Lee, Daniel
Little, Robert Benjamin
Logan, Joseph Leroy
Martin, James Tyrone
Mason, Herman, Jr.
Matthews, Merritt Stewart
McMillan, Horace James
McMillan, James Bates
Millett, Knolly E.
Mitchell, Joseph Rudolph
Moore, Harold Earl, Jr.
Murphy, Charles A.
Pierce, Gregory W.
Quigless, Milton Douglas, Sr.
Randolph, Bernard Clyde
Richard, Arlene Castain
Sessoms, Frank Eugene
Shields, Clarence L., Jr.
Shirley, Calvin Hylton
Slade, John Benjamin, Jr.
Spigner, Donald Wayne
Strickland, Frederick William, Jr.
Tarter, Roger Powell, M.D.
Thompson, Deborah Maria, M.D.
Veney, Herbert Lee
Wade, Eugene Henry-Peter
Walker, Manuel Lorenzo
Weddington, Wilburn Harold, Sr.
Whaley, Joseph S.
Wilkinson, James Wellington
Wise, Henry A., Jr.
Woodall, John Wesley
Woodford, Hackley Elbridge

Medicine—Internal Medicine
Archer, Juanita A.
Ballard, Harold Stanley
Banks, Tazewell
Baskerville, Samuel J., Jr.
Batties, Paul Terry
Berry, Lemuel, Jr.
Billingsly, Marilyn Maxwell, M.D.
Blair, James H.
Bogues, Tyrone
Bouie, Simon Pinckney
Bristow, Lonnie R.
Brown, Lawrence S., Jr.
Brown, Leroy Bradford
Brown, Marsha J.
Bryan, Flize A.
Bryant, T. J.
Buckhalter, Emerson R.
Burton, Leroy Melvin, Jr.
Bynes, Frank Howard, Jr.
Campbell, Otis, Jr.
Casey, Edmund C.
Chisholm, Joseph Carrel, Jr.
Clift, Joseph William
Cobbs, Winston H. B., Jr.
Cone, Juanita Fletcher
Cook, Charles A.
Cooper, Edward Sawyer
Corbin, Angela Lenore
Counts, George W.
Cruz, Iluminado Angeles
Cummings, Charles Edward
Cunningham, William E.
Curry, Sadye Beatryce
Dillard, Martin Gregory
Dixon, Leon Martin
Douglas, Janice Green
Dowling, Monroe Davis, Jr.
Duffoo, Frantz Michel
Dugas, A. Jeffrey Alan, Sr.
Edwards, Rupert L.
Ellis, Tellis B., III
Emory, Emerson
England, Rodney Wayne
Epps, Anna Cherrie
Ernst, Reginald H.
Ferdinand, Keith C.
Floyd, Winston Cordell
Fontaine, John M.
Foster, Pearl D.
Fraser, Leon Allison
Frazer, Eva Louise
Fredrick, Earl E., Jr.
Gavin, James Raphael, III
Grate, Isaac, Jr.
Greene, Charles Rodgers
Grigsby, Margaret Elizabeth
Hale, Edward Harned
Hamilton, Ross T.
Hardin, Eugene
Harris, Bernard A., Jr.
Harris, Jean Louise

Harris, Terea Donnelle
Harrison, Robert Walker, III
Haywood, L. Julian
Henry, Walter Lester, Jr.
Henson, William Francis
Herring, Bernard Duane
Hewlett, Dial, Jr.
Hoffler, Richard Winfred, Jr.
Holloman, John L. S., Jr.
Jackson, Benita Marie
Johnson, Cage Saul
Johnson, Charles
Johnson-Crockett, Mary Alice
Jonas, Ernesto A.
Jones, Edith Irby
Kadree, Margaret Antonia
Kennedy, Karel R.
Kilpatrick, George Roosevelt
King, Talmadge Everett, Jr.
Koger, Michael Pigott, Sr.
Lavizzo-Mourey, Risa Juanita
Levister, Ernest Clayton, Jr.
Malveaux, Floyd
Mapp, Yolanda I.
Marius, Kenneth Anthony
McBroom, F. Pearl
McFadden, Gregory L.
McFadden, James L.
McWhorter, Rosalynd D.
Meacham, Henry W.
Menzies, Barbara A.
Metcalf, Zubie West, Jr.
Miller, Russell L., Jr.
Mims, Robert Bradford
Moore, Oscar James, Jr.
Nash, Daniel Alphonza, Jr.
Natta, Clayton Lyle
Neal, Green Belton
Neals, Huerta C.
Newsome, Cola King
Onyejekwe, Chike Onyekachi
Osborne, William Reginald, Jr.
Palmer, Doreen P.
Palmer, James D.
Parker, Jeff, Sr.
Parks, Donald B.
Pearson, Stanley E.
Peebles-Meyers, Helen Marjorie
Powell, Charles P.
Powers, Runas, Jr.
Priest, Marlon L.
Pruitt, Fred Roderic
Reed, James W.
Render, William H.
Rhodes, Robert Shaw
Riley, Wayne Joseph
Risbrook, Arthur Timothy
Robinson, Clarence G.
Robinson, James Waymond
Sanders, George L.
Scott, Veronica J.
Shanks, William Colemon, Jr.
Shelton, Harold Tillman
Shervington, E. Walter
Silva, Omega C. Logan
Simmons, Ellamae
Smith, Elmer G., Jr.
Smith, Henry Thomas
Solomon, James Daniel
Standard, Raymond Linwood
Starling, John Crawford
Taliaferro, Nettie Howard
Teekah, George Anthony
Thomas, Pamella D.
Thompson, Alvin J.
Thompson, Eugene Edward
Titus-Dillon, Pauline Y.
Vaughn, William Samuel, III
Walker, Eugene Henry
Walker, Maria Latanya
Wiley, Kenneth LeMoyne
Williams, Ernest Y.
Williams, Hugh Hermes
Williams, James Thomas
Williams, Matthew Albert
Wills, James Willard
Woodbury, David Henry
Woodbury, Margaret Claytor
Wright, Jackson Thomas, Jr.
Wyatt, Ronald Michael
Yarborough, Dowd Julius, Jr.
Young, Coleman Milton, III
Young, Elroy

Medicine—Neurology
Adams, Alice Omega
Black, Keith
Blackwell, Lucien E.

Burnett, Calvin
Carson, Benjamin Solomon, Sr.
Chapman, William Talbert
Dennis, Philip H.
Hopper, Cornelius Lenard
Hudson, Roy Davage
Hyde, Deborah
Lightfoote, William Edward, II
McLawhorn, James Thomas, Jr.
Slade, Walter R., Jr.
Summers, David Stewart
Tripp, Lucius Charles
Wyche, Lennon Douglas, Jr.

Medicine—Obstetrics/ Gynecology

Aikins-Afful, Nathaniel Akumanyi
Arrington, Harold Mitchell
Avery, Herbert B.
Blockson, Charles L.
Bloomfield, Randall D.
Boddie, Gwendolyn M.
Boone, Clarence Donald
Boyce, Charles N.
Bridges, James Wilson
Brooks, Todd Frederick
Buffong, Eric Arnold
Burton, Juanita Sharon
Burton-Shannon, Clarinda
Campbell, Sylvan Lloyd
Carter, Dorval Ronald
Chatman, Donald Leveritt
Clay, Reuben Anderson, Jr.
Clemendor, Anthony Arnold
Combs, Julius V., M. D.
Comvalius, Nadia Hortense
Cooper, Gary T.
Crocker, Cyril L.
Davidson, Elvyn Verone
Deane, Robert Armistead
DeSandies, Kenneth Andre
Dickens, Helen Octavia
Dorsey, Taffy Anne, M. D.
Dyer-Goode, Pamela Theresa
Earley, Stanley Armstead, Jr.
Edelin, Kenneth C.
Finlayson, William E.
Foster, Henry Wendell
Fraser, Rodger Alvin
Freemont, James McKinley
Gaither, Dorothy B.
Garrett, E. Wyman
George, Theodore Roosevelt, Jr.
Gibson, Cheryl Dianne
Gillette, Lyra Stephanie
Gleason, Maurice Francis
Greenfield, Robert Thomas, Jr.
Hawkins, Theodore F.
Hayling, William H.
Hickmon, Ned
Hilliard, Robert Lee Moore
Holmes, Herbert
Hurd, Joseph Kindall, Jr.
Hutchins, Francis L., Jr.
Isaac, Joseph William Alexander
Ivey, Mark, III
Jackson, Leroy Anthony, Jr.
Johnson, Gage
Johnson, James S.
Jones, Sidney Alexander
Jones, William C.
Keemer, Edgar B.
Kernisant, Lesly
Lampley, Edward Charles
Lawrence, George Calvin
Lee, Clifton Valjean
Lowe, Scott Miller
Lucas, Dorothy J.
Major, Benjamin
Mason, Clifford L.
McDaniel, Myra Atwell
McGaughy, Will
McGruder, Charles E.
Miller, Dexter J., Jr.
Mitchell, Joseph Rudolph
Moorhead, Joseph H.
Mortel, Rodrigue
Nichols, Ronald Augustus
Obayuwana, Alphonsus Osarobo
Oshiyoye, Adekunle
Pattillo, Roland A.
Phillips, Eugenie Elvira
Pierre, Gerald P.
Powell, Dudley Vincent
Ragland, Michael Steven
Richard, Floyd Anthony
Sanders, Hobart C.
Scott, Lawrence William

Shade, George H., Jr.
Shirley, Calvin Hylton
Sirmans, Meredith Franklin
Smiley, William L.
Smith, Cleveland Emanuel
Smith, Gregory Allen
Stringer, Nelson Howard, Jr.
Taylor, Eugene Donaldson
Tucker, Wilbur Carey
Tweed, Andre R.
Tyson, Bertrand Oliver
Waite, Norma Lillia
Washington, John William
Weather, Leonard, Jr.
Williams, Robert Lee, Jr.
Wilson, Frank Fredrick, III
Wright, Charles H.
Young, N. Louise
Young, Watson A.

Medicine—Ophthalmology

Brewington, Thomas E., Jr.
Brown, John Ollis
Brown, Richard Osborne
Cauthen, Cheryl G.
Dawson, Robert Edward
Dockery, Robert Wyatt
Gray, James Howard
Green, James L.
Higginbotham, Eve Juliet
Manuel, Louis Calvin
Palmer, Edward
Pryor, Chester Cornelius, II
Saunders, Meredith Roy
Scott, Timothy Van
Smith, Joe Elliott
Stubbs, George Winston
Venable, Howard Phillip
Wicker, Henry Sindos
Wilkes, Shelby R.
Williams, Fred C.
Wood, Lawrence Alvin

Medicine—Pathology

Adams, Eugene William
Alexander, Wardine Towers
Anderson, Barbara Stewart Jenkins
Bowman, Jacquelynne Jeanette
Bowman, James E., Jr.
Carter, Joye
Champion, Tempii Bridgene
Clemmons, Jackson Joshua Walter
Donawa, Maria Elena
Evans, Patricia E.
Grant, Kingsley B.
Greer, Robert O., Jr.
Mann, Marion
Mobley, Joan Thompson
Sampson, Calvin Coolidge
Tarter, Roger Powell, M.D.
Towns, Myron B., II

Medicine—Pediatrics

Adams, Billie Morris Wright
Alexander, Drew W.
Allen, Gloria Marie
Al-Mateen, K. Bakeer
Beard, Lillian McLean
Betts, Sheri Elaine
Betty, Warren Randall
Billingsly, Marilyn Maxwell, M.D.
Booker, Carl Granger, Sr.
Bryant, William Arnett, Jr.
Caison, Thelma Jann
Carson, Benjamin Solomon, Sr.
Carter, James P.
Chandler, Allen Eugene
Chenevert, Phillip Joseph
Clark, Bettie I.
Clermont, Volna
Cochran, James David, Jr.
Cole, Maceola Louise
Culpepper, Lucy Nell
Cunningham, Verenessa Smalls-Brantley
Davis, James F.
DeLilly, Mayo Ralph, III
Dennard, Turner Harrison
Downing, John William, Jr.
Dummett, Jocelyn Angela
Dungy, Claibourne I.
Earley, Stanley Armstead, Jr.
Elam, Harry Penoy
Epps, Roselyn Payne
Evans, Patricia E.

Flowers, Runette
Fomufod, Antoine Kofi
Freeman, Lelabelle Christine
French, Joseph Henry
Gaspard, Patrice T.
Gaston, Marilyn Hughes
Gayle, Helene Doris
Gayle-Thompson, Delores J.
Gibson, Ralph Milton
Gough, Walter C.
Graham, LeRoy Maxwell, Jr.
Gray, Joseph William
Green, Frederick Chapman
Harden, Robert James
Higgins, Clarence R., Jr.
Hopkins, Donald Roswell
Hudson, Robert L.
Hyatt, Herman Wilbert, Sr.
Ice, Anne-Mare
Jackson, Rudolph Ellsworth
Jenkins, Melvin E., Jr.
Johnson, Robert L.
Lachman, Ralph Steven
Lewis, Vivian M.
Manley, Audrey Forbes
Martin, James Tyrone
Nash, Helen E.
Neal, Herman Joseph
Nelson, Artie Cortez
Opoku, Evelyn
Parker, Walter Gee
Payton, Victor Emmanuel
Penny, Robert
Pettus-Bellamy, Brenda Karen
Phillips, James Lawrence
Poe, Booker
Polk, Gene-Ann
Pope, Isaac S.
Quivers, Eric Stanley
Quivers, William Wyatt, Sr.
Rainsford, Greta M.
Reid, Clarice Wills
Robinson, Carl Dayton
Robinson, Sandra Lawson
Rogers-Lomax, Alice Faye
Rosser, Pearl Lockhart
Rosser, Samuel Blanton
Scott, Roland B.
Simpson, Gregory Louis
Sinnette, Calvin Herman
Smith, Conrad Warren
Smith, Ernest Howard
Smith, John Arthur
Sulton, Jacqueline Rhoda
Thomas, Lloyd A.
Tillman, Mary A. T.
Vaughn, William Samuel, III
Veal, Yvonnecris Smith
Watson, Clyniece Lois
Webb, Zadie Ozella
Wethers, Doris Louise, M.D.
Whitten, Charles F.
Williams, Donald H.
Williams, Karen Renee
Williams, Starks J.
Williams, W. Donald
Winfield, Florence F.
Yancey, Carolyn Lois
Young, Joyce Howell
Young, Lionel Wesley

Medicine—Psychiatry

Adom, Edwin Nii Amalai
Alfred, Dewitt C., Jr.
Al-Mateen, Cheryl Singleton
Bacon, Robert John, Jr.
Bailey, Didi Giselle, MD
Ballard, Bruce Laine
Bell, Carl Compton
Bell, James Milton
Biagas, Edward D.
Blackwell, Lucien E.
Blake, Carl LeRoy
Bowen, Clotilde Dent
Broomes, Lloyd Rudy
Brown, Ruby Edmonia
Butts, Hugh F.
Calhoun, Joshua Wesley
Cambosos, Bruce Michael
Carter, James Harvey
Carter, Wesley Byrd
Celestin, Toussaint A.
Charles, Roderick Edward
Clark, Harry W.
Cobbs, Price Mashaw
Comer, James Pierpont
Crum, Albert B.
Curtis, James L.

Dabbs, Henry Erven
Daniels, Jordan, Jr.
DeLeon-Jones, Frank A., Jr.
Dennis, Philip H.
Dennis, Rodney Howard
Dickens, Doris Lee
Diji, Augustine Ebun
Dillihay, Tanya Clarkson
Douglas, Florence M.
Dupre, John Lionel
Elam, Lloyd C.
Ellis, Leander Theodore, Jr.
Emory, Emerson
Exum, Wade F.
Fields, Dexter L.
Fisher, Judith Danelle
Flowers, Loma Kaye
Foster, Douglas Leroy
Francis, Richard L.
Franklin, Curtis U., Jr.
Fraser, Alvardo M.
Geary, Clarence Butler
Gill, Troy D.
Glanville, Cecil E.
Greene, Horace F.
Griffith, Ezra
Gullattee, Alyce C.
Heacock, Don Roland
Hollar, Milton Conover
Horne, June Merideth
Howard, Howell J., Jr.
Hueston, Oliver David
Hutchinson, Carell, Jr.
Jackson, Jacquelyne Johnson
Jefferson, Roland Spratlin, M.D.
Jones, Billy Emanuel
Jordan, Harold Willoughby
King, Joseph Prather
King, Richard Devoid
Lacey, Wilbert, Jr.
Lawrence, Leonard E.
Lawrence, Margaret Morgan
Lindo, J. Trevor
Lipscomb, Wendell R.
Lockett, Harold James
Marquez, Camilo Raoul
Mayo, Julia A.
McMillan, Mae F.
Mehreteab, Ghebre-Selassie
Millis, David Howard
Mitchell, Nelli L.
Mitchell-Bateman, Mildred
Moore, Evan Gregory
Nelson, Artie Cortez
Norris, Donna M.
Oxley, Leo Lionel
Parks, Gilbert R.
Parrish, Rufus H.
Pierce, Chester Middlebrook
Pinderhughes, Charles Alfred
Pope, Henry
Posey, Edward W.
Poussaint, Alvin Francis
Rainbow-Earhart, Kathryn Adeline
Reid, F. Theodore, Jr.
Robinson, Herbert A.
Robinson, Luther D.
Robinson, Muriel F. Cox
Ross, Phyllis Harrison
Sanders, Wendell Rowan
Sealy, Joan R.
Simpson, Willa Jean
Smith, James Almer, Jr.
Smith, Louis
Smith, Otrie
Smith, Quentin T.
Spaulding, Jean Gaillard
Spurlock, Jeanne
Stephens, Herman Alvin
Thomas, John Wesley
Tolbert, Herman Andre
Towns, Eva Rose
Tutt, Walter Cornelius
Walden, Robert Edison
Williams, Donald H.
Williams, Melvin Walker
Worrell, Audrey Martiny
Wright, Jane C.

Medicine—Radiology

Bell, James Edward
Collins, James Douglas
Farmer, Robert Clarence
Goldson, Alfred Lloyd
Hankins, Andrew Jay, Jr.
Ingram, LaVerne Dorothy
Jones, Lewis Arnold, Jr.
Lachman, Ralph Steven

Mansfield, Carl Major
Mitchell, Edwin H., Sr.
Moore-Stovall, Joyce
Patterson, Elizabeth Ann
Perry, Harold
Richard, Henri-Claude
Rogers, Bernard Rousseau
Smith, Edward Nathaniel, Jr.
Smith, John Arthur
Stent, Theodore R.
Suneja, Sidney Kumar
Thomas, Lillie
Tokun, Ralph
Weaver, John Arthur
West, William Lionel
Young, Lionel Wesley

Medicine—Surgery

Allison, W. Anthony
Anderson, William Gilchrist
Bacon, William Louis
Banks, William Jasper, Jr.
Barber, Jesse B., Jr.
Baxter, Charles F., Jr.
Bernard, Harold O.
Bernard, Louis Joseph
Boddie, Gwendolyn M.
Bowers, Mirion Perry
Britt, L. D.
Bryan, Flize A.
Butler, Benjamin Willard
Butler, Michael Keith
Cain, Waldo
Calhoun, Noah Robert
Calhoun, Thomas
Callender, Clive Orville
Canady, Alexa I.
Cave, Alfred Earl
Clarke, Leon Edison
Clarke, Theodore Henson
Cockburn, Alden G., Jr.
Cunningham, Paul Raymond Goldwyn
Curry, William Thomas
Davidson, Arthur B.
Davidson, Arthur Turner
Davidson, Earnest Jefferson
Debas, Haile T.
Dooley, Wallace Troy
Fisher, Edward G.
Fleming, Arthur Wallace
Ford, Debra Holly
Freeman, Harold P.
Funderburk, William Watson
Gaines, Ray D.
Gaines, Thurston Lenwood, Jr.
Garrison, Jordan Muhammad, Jr.
George, Alma Rose
Gipson, Bernard Franklin, Sr.
Gladden, Major P.
Gordon, Walter Carl, Jr.
Hall, Jeffrey Maurice
Hall, Reginald Lawrence
Hardaway, Ernest, II
Hegeman, Charles Oxford
Hill, George Calvin
Hill, Julius W.
Holmes, Herbert
Holsey, William Fleming, Jr.
Horton, Clarence Pennington
Huckaby, Henry Lafayette
Huggins, Clarence L.
Hyde, Maxine Deborrah
Hyde, William R.
Idewu, Olawale Olusoji
Jackson, Oscar Jerome
Johns, Sonja Maria
Johnson, William Henry
Jones, Herbert C.
Jordan, Carl Rankin
Kildare, Michel Walter Andre
King, Wesley A.
Koger, Linwood Graves, III
Lawrence, Montague Schiele
Leacock, Ferdinand S.
Leffall, LaSalle Doheny, Jr.
Lightfoot, William P.
Lowe, James Edward, Jr.
Maben, Hayward C., Jr.
Mackel, Audley Maurice, III
Maitland, Conrad Cuthbert
Martin, Paul W.
Mason, Gilbert Rutledge
Matory, William Earle, Jr.
Matory, Yvedt L.
Matson, Ollie Genoa
McLaughlin, Katye H.
Mendenhall, John Rufus

Mendes, Donna M.
Morgan, Eldridge Gates
Ofodile, Ferdinand Azikiwe
Patin, Joseph Patrick
Peterson, Carl M.
Phillips, Lloyd Garrison, Jr.
Pierce, Raymond O., Jr.
Pryor, Julius, Jr.
Quigless, Milton Douglas, Sr.
Quigless, Milton Douglas, Jr.
Rankin, Edward Anthony
Rawls, George H.
Richardson, Madison Franklin
Riley, Emile Edward
Rivers, Robert Joseph, Jr.
Robinson, Walker Lee
Rogers, Norman
Rolle, Albert Eustace
Ross, William Alexander Jackson
Sanders, Hobart C.
Scantlebury-White, Velma Patricia
Scott, Linzy, Jr.
Seymour, Laurence Darryl, M. D.
Shelton, Harold Tillman
Simon, Kenneth Bernard
Smith, Freddie Alphonso
Starling, John Crawford
Strudwick, Warren James, Sr.
Swan, Lionel F.
Syphax, Burke
Taylor, Harold Leon
Taylor, Paul David
Thomas, Harry Lee
Tipton, Dale Leo
Tollett, Charles Albert, Sr.
Toussaint, Rose-Marie
Tripp, Lucius Charles
Walker, Mark Lamont
Watkins, Michael Thomas
Watts, Charles Dewitt
Wiggins, Charles A.
Williams, Herbert Lee
Winfrey, Audrey Theresa
Wood, Michael H.
Worrell, Richard Vernon
Wyatt, Lance Everett, M.D.
Yancey, Asa G., Sr.

Medicine—Not Elsewhere Classified (*See Also* Pharmacy; Veterinary Medicine)

Abdullah, Tariq Husam
Abrahams, Andrew Wordsworth
Adair, Robert A.
Adegbile, Gideon Sunday Adebisi
Adeyiga, Olanrewaju Muniru
Aikins-Afful, Nathaniel Akumanyi
Alexander, Joseph Lee
Alexandre, Journel
Alston, Kathy Diane
Anderson, Arnett Artis
Anderson, Benjamin Stratman, Jr.
Anderson, William A.
Andrews, Rawle
Angell, Edgar O.
Armour, Christopher E.
Atkins, Sam Oillie
Atkinson, Lewis K.
Bailey, Joseph Alexander, II
Ballard, James M., Jr.
Banfield, Edison H.
Banks, Marshall D.
Barber, Hargrow Dexter
Baron, Neville A.
Bass, Leonard Channing
Bataille, Jacques Albert
Bath, Patricia E.
Beard, Martin Luther
Beck, Roswell Nathaniel
Bentley, Herbert Dean
Berry, Lemuel, Jr.
Best, Prince Albert, Jr.
Billops, Camille J.
Blair, James H.
Blake, Milton James
Blount, Melvin Cornell
Booker, Teresa Hillary Clarke
Booker, Venerable Francis
Boone, Clinton Caldwell
Boone, Elwood Bernard, Jr.
Boschulte, Alfred F.
Bowles, Howard Roosevelt
Bowman, Jacquelynne Jeanette
Bradfield, Clarence McKinley
Branch, Eldridge Stanley
Branch, Geraldine Burton
Bridges, Alvin Leroy

Brisbane, Samuel Chester
Brooks, Marion Jackson
Brooks, Theodore Roosevelt, Jr.
Brown, Alvin Montero
Brown, George Philip
Brown, John Ollis
Brown, Marsha J.
Brown, William McKinley, Jr.
Bryant, Henry C.
Bryant, Jerome Benjamin
Buffong, Eric Arnold
Bugg, George Wendell
Burch, Reynold Edward
Caldwell, Esly Samuel, II
Calhoun, Calvin Lee
Callender, Clive Orville
Campbell, Emmett Earle
Campbell, Everett O.
Campbell, Otis, Jr.
Cantwell, Kathleen Gordon
Capel, Wallace
Carney, Robert Matthew
Carson, Dwight Keith
Carter, James Earl, Jr.
Carter, James Edward, III
Carter, Oscar Earl, Jr.
Cave, Claude Bertrand
Cave, Herbert G.
Chambers, Donald C.
Chapman, George Wallace, Jr.
Chapman, Joseph Conrad, Jr.
Chisholm, Reginald Constantine
Chissell, John T.
Clanton, Lemuel Jacque
Clark, Charles Warfield
Clark, Granville E., Sr.
Clarke, Angela Webb
Clendeninn, Neil J.
Coffey, Gilbert Haven, Jr.
Coggs, Granville Coleridge
Coleman, Arthur H.
Collier, Torrence Junis
Combs, Julius V., M. D.
Conrad, Emmett J.
Corbin, Angela Lenore
Cornely, Paul B.
Cotman, Henry Earl
Covington, John Ryland
Cowell, Catherine
Craig, Elson L.
Crockett, Edward D., Jr.
Crump, Carolyn F.
Cruzat, Edward Pedro
Cummings, Cary, III
Curry, Norvelle
Cutliff, John Wilson
Cuyjet, Aloysius Baxter
Davidson, Charles Odell
Davis, Benjamin O., Jr.
Dawkins, Stephen A.
Dawson, Peter Edward
Delphin, Jacques Mercier
Dent, Carl Ashley
Diggs, Roy Dalton, Jr.
Dillon, Owen C.
Douglas, Aubry Carter
Dowling, Monroe Davis, Jr.
Downer, Luther Henry
Duffoo, Frantz Michel
Dugas, Henry C.
Duke, Leslie Dowling, Sr.
Duncan, Louis Davidson, Jr.
Dunmore, Lawrence A., Jr.
Edghill, John W.
Edwards, John W., Jr.
Elliott, Frank George
English, Perry T., Jr.
Ennix, Coyness Loyal, Jr.
Epps, Charles Harry, Jr.
Eugere, Edward J.
Exum, Wade F.
Feemster, John Arthur
Felix, Dudley E.
Fleming, Arthur Wallace
Floyd, Dean Allen
Folk, Frank Stewart
Fonrose, Harold Anthony
Foulks, Carl Alvin
Francois, Emmanuel Saturnin
Franklin, Grant L.
Franks, Everlee Gordon
Frazier, William James
Funderburk, William Watson
Gaines, Ray D.
Gathe, Joseph C.
Gayle, Helene Doris
Gibson, Edward Lewis
Gilmore, Edwin
Givens, Donovahn Heston

Gladney, Marcellious
Gordon, Charles Franklin
Granger, Carl Victor
Grant, Kingsley B.
Grate, Isaac, Jr.
Green, Clyde Octavious
Green, James L.
Greene, Charles Rodgers
Greene, Robert Charles
Greenfield, William Russell, Jr.
Gumbs, Oliver Sinclair
Hadley, Howard Alva, Jr.
Hakima, Mala'ika
Hall, Charles Harold
Hall, Daniel A.
Hall, Reginald Lawrence
Hall, Robert Joseph
Halyard, Michele Yvette
Hamberg, Marcelle R.
Hardin, Eugene
Hardy, Walter S. E.
Harris, Harcourt Glenties
Harris, Lorenzo W.
Harris, Noah Alan, Sr.
Harris, Norman W., Jr.
Harris, Percy G., M.D.
Harris, Thomas Waters, Jr.
Harrison, A. B.
Hart, Edward E.
Harvey, Harold A.
Hegeman, Charles Oxford
Hicks, Michael L.
Hicks, William James
Higginbotham, Peyton Randolph
Hill, George Calvin
Hill, Lawrence Thorne
Hill, XaCadene Averyllis
Hobbs, Joseph
Hoffler, Richard Winfred, Jr.
Hoffman, Joseph Irvine, Jr.
Hollowell, Melvin L.
Holmes, Herbert
Honablue, Richard Riddick, M.D.
Hopkins, Donald Roswell
Hopkins, John David
Hosten, Adrian
Howell, Rachel
Hoyte, Arthur Hamilton
Huggins, Clarence L.
Hunter, Oliver Clifford, Jr.
Hurd, William Charles
Hyde, William R.
Idewu, Olawale Olusoji
Jackson, Arthur James
Jackson, Marvin Alexander
Jackson, Seaton J.
JeanBaptiste, Carl S.
Jenkins, Carl Scarborough
Jessup, Marsha Edwina
Johnson, James Kenneth
Johnson, John Thomas
Johnson, Lectoy Tarlington
Johnson, Linda Dianne
Johnson, Melvin Russell
Johnson, Walton Richard
Jones, Furman Madison, Jr.
Jones, George Williams
Jones, Herbert C.
Jones, Miles James
Jones, Percy Elwood
Jones, Vann Kinckle
Kennon, Rozmond H.
King, Delutha Harold
Kirby, Jacqueline
Kisner, Robert Garland
Lachman, Ralph Steven
Lamothe, Isidore J., Jr.
Lawrence, Leonard E.
Lawrence, Margaret Morgan
Lee, Edwin Archibald
Leevy, Carroll M.
Little, General T.
Little, Robert Benjamin
Little, Ronald Eugene
Littles, James Frederick, Jr.
Lloyd, Raymond Anthony
Logan, Joseph Leroy
Lomax, Walter P.
Long, Irene
Lowman, Isom
Luck, Clyde Alexander, Jr.
Mabrie, Herman James, III
Magee, Robert Walter
Maloney, Charles Calvin
Mapp, John Robert
Marion, Phillip Jordan
Martin, Ernest Douglass
Matthews, Miriam
Mays, James A.

McBroom, F. Pearl
McCarrell, Clark Gabriel, Jr.
McCullers, Eugene
McFaddin, Theresa Garrison
McIntyre, Mildred J.
McKnight, Reginald
McSwain, Rodney
Meacham, Robert B.
Means, Kevin Michael
Meares, Paula G. Allen
Meeks, Stephen Abayomi
Miller, Dexter J., Jr.
Miller, Edith
Millis, David Howard
Mims, Robert Bradford
Mitchell, Augustus William, M.D.
Moore, Hiram Beene
Moore, Marcellus Harrison
Moragne, Rudolph
Mosee, Jean C.
Mosley, Edward R.
Motley, Ronald Clark
Mowatt, Oswald Victor
Murphy, Charles A.
Mutcherson, James Albertus, Jr.
Myers, Debra J.
Nash, Daniel Alphonza, Jr.
Natta, Clayton Lyle
Nelson, Artie Cortez
Nelson, Robert Wales, Sr.
Newborn, Odie Vernon, Jr.
Newton, Pynkerton Dion
Newton, Robin Caprice
Noel, Patrick Adolphus
Noonan, Allan S.
Norman, Calvin Haines
Norris, James Ellsworth Chiles
Northcross, David C.
Onyejekwe, Chike Onyekachi
Osibin, Willard S.
Ottley, Neville
Ozim, Francis Taiino
Parker, Averette Mhoon
Patton, Curtis Leverne
Penny, Robert
Perara, Mitchell Mebane
Perry, Frank Anthony
Perry, Harold
Petioni, Muriel M.
Phillips, Lloyd Garrison, Jr.
Pierce, Raymond O., Jr.
Pierre-Louis, Constant
Piper, Paul J.
Piper, W. Archibald
Pollard, Emily Frances
Powell, Thomas Francis A.
Powers, Runas, Jr.
Preston, Swanee H. T., Jr.
Prophete, Beaumanoir
Prothrow-Stith, Deborah Boutin
Pryor, Julius, Jr.
Quarles, Joseph James
Raiford, Roger Lee
Raine, Charles Herbert, III
Rains, Horace
Randolph, Bernard Clyde
Reed, Kathleen Rand
Reed, Theresa Greene
Reese, Milous J.
Reid, Edith C.
Reid, Roberto Elliott
Rhetta, Helen L.
Rhodes, Robert Shaw
Richard, Henri-Claude
Ridges-Horton, Lee Esther
Riley, Emile Edward
Roberts, James E.
Roberts, Margaret Mills
Robinson, Lawrence D.
Robinson, Luther D.
Robinson, William Andrew
Rogers, Bernard Rousseau
Rosemond, John H.
Rosemond, Lemuel Menefield
Rosser, Samuel Blanton
Ross-Lee, Barbara
Roux, Vincent J.
Ruffin, Richard D.
Saffold, Oscar E.
St. Omer, Vincent V. E.
Satcher, David
Saunders, Edward Howard
Savage, Edward W., Jr.
Scantlebury-White, Velma Patricia
Scipio, Laurence Harold
Scott, Deborah Ann
Scott, Leonard Lamar
Scott, Linzy, Jr.
Scott, Veronica J.

Seymour, Laurence Darryl, M. D.
Seymour, Robert F.
Shurney, Dexter Wayne
Silva, Omega C. Logan
Simmons, Earl Melvin
Simmons, Ellamae
Simpson, Dazelle Dean
Sims, Edward Hackney
Skeene, Linell De-Silva
Skerrett, Philip Vincent
Slade, John Benjamin, Jr.
Slaughter, Peter
Smith, Joe Elliott
Smith, Roulette William
Speller, Charles K.
Spencer, Sharon A.
Staggers, Frank Eugene
Stanmore, Roger Dale
Stephens, George Benjamin Davis
Sterling, Jeffrey Emery
Stinson, Joseph McLester
Strayhorn, Earl Carlton
Strickland, Frederick William, Jr.
Strong, Douglas Donald
Stubbs, George Winston
Stull, Virginia Elizabeth
Swan, Lionel F.
Swinney, T. Lewis
Taylor, Paul David
Taylor, Scott Morris
Taylor, Veronica C.
Thigpen, Calvin Herritage
Thomas, Audria Acty
Thomas, Edward P.
Thomas, Pamella D.
Thomas, Spencer
Thomas-Richards, Jose Rodolfo
Thompson, Deborah Maria, M.D.
Thompson, Frank William
Thompson, Lloyd Earl
Thompson, Mavis Sarah
Thomson, Gerald Edmund
Thorne, Cecil Michael
Thornhill, Herbert Louis
Tilley, Frank N.
Tipton, Dale Leo
Tollett, Charles Albert, Sr.
Toussaint, Rose-Marie
Tripp, Lucius Charles
Tucker, Anthony
Tucker, Billy J.
Tunstall, June Rebecca
Turk, Alfred J., II
Tyree-Walker, Ida May
Vaughn, Clarence B.
Vaughn, William Samuel, III
Veal, Yvonnecris Smith
Vester, Terry Y.
Wade, Eugene Henry-Peter
Waite, Norma Lillia
Walden, Emerson Coleman
Walker, G. Edward
Walker, William Paul, Jr.
Walters, Curla Sybil
Walton, Tracy Matthew, Jr., M.D.
Washington, Johnnie M.
Watkins, Judge Charles, Jr.
Watts, Charles Dewitt
Weaver, John Arthur
Weaver, Joseph D.
Webb, Zadie Ozella
Weddington, Wayne P., Jr.
Whaley, Joseph S.
White, Augustus A., III
White, Dezra
White, Garland Anthony
White, Sandra LaVelle
Wilkinson, Robert Shaw, Jr.
Williams, Arthur Love
Williams, David George
Williams, Henry R.
Williams, Henry S.
Williams, Homer LaVaughan
Williams, Joseph Henry
Williams, Sterling B., Jr.
Willock, Marcelle Monica
Willoughby, Winston Churchill
Wilson, James Davis
Wilson, John T., Jr.
Wilson, Robert Stanley
Wilson, William E.
Wiltz, Philip G., Jr.
Wise, C. Rogers
Woodall, John Wesley
Woodard, A. Newton
Woodbury, Margaret Claytor
Wooding, David Joshua
Word, Parker Howell
Worrell, Richard Vernon

Wright, Rickey
Yarboro, Theodore Leon
York, Russel Harold
Young, Elroy
Young, Joyce Howell
Young, Watson A.
Zimmerman, Eugene

Meteorology
Davis, Belva
Emeagwali, Philip
Huff, Janice Wages
Lewis, Lonzy James
Sarreals, E. Don
Sealls, Alan Ray
Wardlaw, McKinley, Jr.
Washington, Warren Morton
Williamson, Samuel P.
Young, Edward Hiram, Jr.

Microbiology
See **Biology/Microbiology**

Military—Air Force
Banton, William C., II
Bartley, William Raymond
Beckles, Benita Harris
Bluford, Grady L.
Bluford, Guion Stewart, Jr.
Bowman, William Alton
Coleman, Rodney Albert
Crawford, Nathaniel, Jr.
Creft, Brenda K.
Cushman, Vera F.
Davis, Donald Gene
DeMesme, Ruby B.
Duncan, John C., Jr.
Edmonds, Albert Joseph
Gomez, Kevin Lawrence Johnson
Goodwin, Evelyn Louise
Gregory, Frederick Drew
Hargraves, William Frederick, II
Harris, Marcelite J.
Jackson, Fred H., Jr.
Jones, Daryl L.
Kelly, James Johnson
Lawson, Herman A.
Lewis, Robert Louis
Martin, Curtis Jerome
McAllister, Leroy Timothy, Sr.
McNeill, Susan Patricia
McNeill-Huntley, Esther Mae
Mercer, Arthur, Sr.
Mercer, Valerie June
Miles, Edward Lancelot
Morgan, John Paul
Nance, Herbert Charles, Sr.
Newton, Lloyd W.
Patterson, Joan Delores
Person, Leslie Robin
Pogue, Richard James
Randolph, Bernard P.
Ray, Richard Rex
Richards, Edward A.
Rutland, William G.
Shippy, John D.
Showell, Milton W.
Smith, Robert London
Vaughn, Clarence B.
Vivians, Nathaniel Roosevelt
Voorhees, John Henry
Wertz, Andrew Walter, Sr.
Williams, Dennis
Williams, Walker Richard, Jr.
Wingo, A. George
Worthey, Richard E.
Wright, Rickey

Military—Army
Adiele, Moses Nkwachukwu
Allen, Esther Louisa
Armstrong, Ernest W., Sr.
Arnold, Wallace C.
Bailey, Lawrence R., Sr.
Barnes, Wilson Edward
Becton, Julius Wesley, Jr.
Brailey, Troy
Brown, Dallas C., Jr.
Brown, John Mitchell, Sr.
Brown, Stanley Donovan
Burton, Charles Howard, Jr.
Byrd, Melvin L.
Cadoria, Sherian Grace
Calbert, William Edward, Sr.

Caldwell, James E.
Clark, Major
Coleman, William T., III
Copes, Ronald Adrian
Cromartie, Eugene Rufus
Davis, Belva
Davison, Frederic E.
Day, Daniel Edgar
Dickerson, Harvey G., Jr.
Dozier, Morris, Sr.
Early, Paul David
Ellis, Benjamin F., Jr.
Fletcher, Tyrone P.
Forte, Johnie, Jr.
Freeman, Warren L.
Gaines, Oscar Cornell
Garrett, Louis Henry
Godbolt, Ricky Charles
Gorden, Fred A.
Graves, Jerrod Franklin
Gray, Kenneth D.
Gray, Robert E.
Greene, Jerry Louis
Hall, James Reginald
Hanford, Craig Bradley
Harleston, Robert Alonzo
Harrell, Ernest James
Hawkins, John Russell, III
Hawkins, Walter L.
Heflin, Marrion
Hensley, Willie L.
Heyward, James Oliver
Hines, Charles A.
Hogans, William Robertson, III
Holmes, James Arthur, Jr.
Jackson, David Samuel
Jacob, Willis Harvey
James, Frank Samuel, III
Johnson, Benjamin Washington
Johnson, Julius Frank
Johnson, Leon F.
Johnson, Leroy
Johnson, Theodore, Sr.
Johnson-Brown, Hazel Winfred
Jordan, John Wesley
Kennedy, Marvin James
Kirby, Money Alian
Lane, Julius Forbes
Layton, Benjamin Thomas
Leigh, Fredric H.
Lenhardt, Alfonso Emanuel
Long, John Bennie
Mabrey, Harold Leon
Mack, Faite
Martin, John Thomas
Mason, Luther Roscoe
McDaniels, Warren E.
McGrady, Eddie James
McGrath, Clarice Hobgood
McGriggs-Jamison, Imogene
McKinney, Gene C.
Monroe, James W.
Moore, Gary E.
Moorman, Holsey Alexander
Mosley, Marie Oleatha
Murphy, Charles William
Oxley, Leo Lionel
Paige, Emmett, Jr.
Patin, Jude W. P.
Polk, Anthony Joseph
Powell, Colin L.
Prather, Thomas L., Jr.
Rettig, Frannie M.
Richie, Sharon Ivey
Ruffin, Paulette Francine
Sanders, George L.
Settles, Carl E.
Shannon, John William
Shields-Jones, Esther L. M.
Smith, Elaine Marie
Spencer, Anthony Lawrence
Stanford, John Henry
Taylor, Clarence B.
Taylor, Wilford, Jr.
Turman, Robert L., Sr.
Turner, Joseph Ellis
Vernon, Alexander
Washington, Samuel, Jr.
Watkins, John M., Jr.
Webster, Cecil Ray
White, Kenneth Eugene, Sr.
White, Leo, Jr.
Williams, Fred C.
Williamson, Samuel R.
Wilson, Danyell Elaine
Wilson, Wilson W.
Zimmerman, Matthew Augustus, Jr.

Military—Coast Guard
Hollowell, Johnny Laveral

Military—Marine Corps
Beasley, Dave, Jr.
Bolden, Charles E.
Nunn, Robinson S.
Petersen, Frank Emmanuel, Jr.
Sims, William
Varner, Robert Lee, Sr.
Walls, George Hilton, Jr.
Watkins, Price I.
Womack, Joe Neal, Jr.

Military—National Guard
Alexander, Richard C.
Berry, Mary Frances
Brooks, James Taylor
Bryant, Cunningham C.
Bryant, William Henry, Jr.
Burke, Rosetta
Chandler, Allen Eugene
Dawson, Eric Emmanuel
Effort, Edmund D.
Folk, Frank Stewart
Freeman, Warren L.
Henderson, William Avery
Hood, Charles McKinley, Jr.
James, Daniel, III
Johns, Sonja Maria
Jones, Daryl L.
Langford, Victor C., III
Meeks, Larry Gillette
Moorman, Holsey Alexander
Nall, Alvin James, Jr.
Parker, G. John, Sr.
Santos, Mathies Joseph
Sherman, Thomas Oscar, Jr.
Spigner, Marcus E.
Trowell-Harris, Irene
Ward, Daniel
Williamson, Samuel P.

Military—Navy
Bailey, Eugene Ridgeway
Baxter, Charles F., Jr.
Braddock, Marilyn Eugenia
Brewer, David L., III
Brown, Clarence William
Brown, Wesley Anthony
Camphor, Michael Gerard
Carter, William Thomas, Jr.
Cochran, Donnie L.
Curbeam, Robert L.
Daniels, A. Raiford
Davis, Walter Jackson, Jr.
Ferguson, Robert Lee, Sr.
Garrett, Cain, Jr.
Gaston, Mack Charles
Goodman, Robert O., Jr.
Gravely, Samuel L., Jr.
Green, Consuella
Hacker, Benjamin Thurman
Ingram, LaVerne Dorothy
Johnson, B. A.
Johnson, Wendell Norman, Sr.
Kimmons, Carl Eugene
Lawhorn, Robert Martin
Lewis, Arthur W.
Lomax, Dervey A.
Matabane, Sebiletso Mokone
McCallum, Walter Edward
McCampbell, Ray Irvin
Morgan, Robert, Jr.
Norman, William S.
Saunders, Kenneth Paul
Shipp, Melvin Douglas
Simpkins, William Joseph
Smith, Millard, Jr.
Taylor, Ernest Norman, Jr.
Thomas, Gerald Eustis
Tzomes, Chancellor Alfonso
Wamble, Carl DeEllis
Watson, Tony J.
Webb, Schuyler Cleveland
Williams, Montel
Williams, Wilbert Edd
Wright, Roosevelt R., Jr.

Military—Not Elsewhere Classified
Brooks, Leo Austin
Chambers, Pamela S.

De Fossett, William K.
Duggins, George
Esquerre, Jean Roland
Hester, Arthur C.
Howard, Calvin Johnson
Jackson, Frank Donald
Jeffries, Freddie L.
Jordan, Anne Knight
Robinson, William
Stuart, Ivan I.
Turner, Joseph Ellis
Vernon, Alexander

Mining/Quarrying (See Also **Engineering—Mining**)
Graves, Sherman Teen
Harris, Rex
Lawrence, Philip Martin

Modeling
Banks, Tyra
Beckford, Tyson
Belafonte, Shari
Bridgewater, Herbert Jeremiah, Jr.
DeVore, Ophelia
Johnson, Beverly
Kilgore, Twanna Debbie
Leslie, Lisa
Moore, Annie Jewell
Moore, Kenya
Moss, Anni R.
Murphy, Vanessa
Plunkett, Raphael Hildan
Pressley, DeLores
Rentie, Frieda
Scott, Nelson
Simmons-Edelstein, Dee
Smith, Chelsi
Stewart, Brittanica
Turner, Yvonne Williams

Mortuary Services
Adams, Eugene Bruce
Agee, Bobby L.
Bourgeois, Adam
Brown, Clark S.
Brown, LeRoy
Charbonnet, Louis, III
Chase, Arnett C.
Cofer, James Henry
Colin, George H.
Dorsey, Leon D., Sr.
Duncan, Sandra Rhodes
Echols, Ruby Lois
Edwards, Claybon Jerome
Estes, John M., Jr.
Fielding, Herbert Ulysses
Ford, George Washington, III
Ford, Harold Eugene, Sr.
Freeman, David Calvin, Sr.
Fritz, Moses Kelly
Gachette, Louise Foston
Gaines, Ava Candace
Gaines, Samuel Stone
Garner, Lon L.
Greene, Charles Andre
Greene, Nelson E., Sr.
Grier, Arthur E., Jr.
Griffin, Floyd Lee, Jr.
Haile, Richard H.
Hampton, Willie L.
Harvey, Clarie Collins
Henry, Robert Clayton
Hickson, Eugene, Sr.
Higgins, Bennett Edward
Holmes, Wendell P., Jr.
Hornsby, B. Kay
Jefferson, Clifton
Jenkins, Augustus G., Jr.
Johnson, I. S. Leevy
Leake, Willie Mae James
Lewis, J. B., Jr.
Lightner, Clarence E.
Manigault, Walter William
Mays, David
McAdoo, Henry Allen
McEachern-Ulmer, Sylvia L.
McLeod, Michael Preston
Monk, Edd Dudley
Montgomery, Fred O.
Morton, James A.
Morton, Margaret E.
Patterson, Paul A.
Powell, Robert E.

Randolph, Louis T.
Sims, Pete, Jr.
Singleton, Leroy, Sr.
Smith, Frances C.
Stone, William T.
Stovall-Tapley, Mary Kate
Summers, Joseph W.
Swanson, O'Neil D.
Warner, Isaiah H.
Watts, Wilsonya Richardson
Williams, John Earl
Williams, McCullough, Jr.
Williams, Napoleon
Wilson, Charles Stanley, Jr.

Motor Vehicle Industry
See **Manufacturing—Motor Vehicles; Retail Trade—Motor Vehicles, Parts, and Services; Wholesale Trade—Motor Vehicles and Parts**

Moving Services
See **Transportation/Moving Services**

Museum Administration/ Education
See **Gallery/Museum Administration/Education**

Music—Composing/ Songwriting
Adams, Leslie
Adderley, Nathaniel
Albam, Manny
Albright, Gerald Anthony
Ali, Rashied
Arkansaw, Tim
Artis, Anthony Joel
Ashby, Dorothy J.
Ashford, Nicholas
Atkins, Russell
Atkins, Sam Oillie
Austin, Dallas
Ayers, Roy
Bagby, Rachel L
Baker, Anita
Baker, David Nathaniel, Jr.
Baker, Gregory D.
Beasley, Victor Mario
Bell, Thom R.
Benoit, Edith B.
Berry, Benjamin Donaldson
Biggers, Samuel Loring, Jr.
Bland, Bobby Blue
Brown, Tyrone W.
Bryson, Peabo
Burgie, Irving Louis
Butler, Jerry
Butler, Washington Roosevelt, Jr.
Carey, Mariah
Carrington, Terri Lyne
Carter, Betty
Carter, Warrick L.
Chapman, Tracy
Charles, Ray
Cherrelle
Christian, Eric Oliver, Jr.
Clarke, Stanley Marvin
Coleman, George Edward
Coleman, Ornette
Cowden, Michael E.
Criner, Clyde
Crouch, Andrae
Cummings, Terry
Cunningham, Arthur H.
Curson, Theodore
Curtis, Marvin Vernell
Davis, Nathan T.
Davis, Richard
Davis, Willie James
Day, Morris
DeBarge, El
Diddley, Bo
Dixon, William R.
Doggett, Bill
Domino, Fats
Donegan, Dorothy
Duke, George M.
Dupri, Jermaine
Edmonds, Kenneth
Edwards, Leo Derek

Elliot, Missy
Eubanks, Kevin
Eubanks, Rachel Amelia
Fischer, William S.
Flack, Roberta
Ford, Fred, Jr.
Foster, Frank B., III
Franklin, Kirk
Fuller, Curtis D.
Gainer, John F.
Garner, Charles
Gaskin, Leonard O.
Golightly, Lena Mills
Hairston, Jester
Hampton, Lionel Leo
Hancock, Herbert Jeffrey
Harris, Margaret R.
Harris, Robert Allen
Hayes, Isaac
Heavy D
Henderson, Ruth Faynella
Hendricks, Jon
Hill, Andrew William
Holmes, Robert L., Jr.
Howard, George
Huff, Leon Alexander
Ice Cube
Ice-T
Ighner, Benard T.
Ingram, James
Jackson, C. Bernard
Jackson, Freddie
Jackson, Jermaine Lajuane
Jackson, Michael
Jackson, Milton
Jacquet, Jean Baptiste Illinois
Jamal, Ahmad
Jarreau, Al
Jeffers, Jack
Johnson, Albert J.
Johnson, Willie
Jones, Glenn
Jones, Maxine
Jones, Quincy Delight, Jr.
Jordan, Stanley
Kebede, Ashenafi Amde
Kelly, R.
Kemp, Emmerlyne Jane
Kennedy, Joseph J., Jr.
Kimble, Bettye Dorris
Kirkland, Kenny David
Lasley, Phelbert Quincy, III
Lateef, Yusef
Lee, William James Edwards, III
Leon, Tania J.
LeVert, Gerald
Lewis, Dawnn
Lewis, Ramsey Emanuel, Jr.
Lincoln, C. Eric
Livingston-White, Deborah J. H.
L L Cool J
Lutcher, Nellie
Lyte, M. C.
Marsalis, Ellis
Martin, Christopher
May, Dickey R.
Mayfield, JoAnn H.O.
McFall, Mary
McFerrin, Robert
McGill, Michele Nicole Johnson
McKnight, Brian
McLean, John Lenwood
McLinn, Harry Marvin
McNeil, DeeDee
McNeil, Ernest Duke
McNeill, Cerves Todd
Moore, Carman Leroy
Moore, Undine Smith
Morgan, Meli'sa
Mumford, Jeffrey Carlton
Najee
Nicholas, Brenda L.
Nicholas, Philip, Sr.
Nor, Genghis
Osby, Gregory Thomas
Ousley, Harold Lomax
Owens, Jimmy
Parker, Ray, Jr.
Parris, Alvin, III
Pate, John W., Sr.
Porter, Roy Lee
Price, John Elwood
Priester, Julian Anthony
Qamar, Nadi Abu
Queen Latifah
Reagon, Bernice Johnson
Reeves, Dianne
Reid, Antonio
Richie, Lionel Brockman, Jr.

Riley, Teddy
Roach, Max
Robinson, Dawn
Rodgers, Nile
Rogers, Timmie
Rollins, Walter Theodore
Rudd-Moore, Dorothy
Rushen, Patrice
Russell, George A.
Sabree, Clarice Salaam
Santos, Henry J.
Scott-Heron, Gil
Shamborguer, Naima
Shepherd, Berisford
Simone, Nina
Simpson, Valerie
Smith, Hale
Smith, Howlett P.
Smith, Will
Sure, Al B.
Tate, Cornelius Astor
The Artist
Thomas, Robert Charles
Thomas, Terence
Tillis, Frederick C.
Tyner, McCoy
Vails, Donald
Vandross, Luther R.
Walden, Narada Michael
Walker, George T.
Wansel, Dexter Gilman
Washington, Grover, Jr.
Washington, Keith
White, Barry
White, Karyn
Williams, Deniece
Williams, Joe
Wilson, Frank Edward
Wilson, Gerald Stanley
Wilson, Olly W.
Wilson, Shanice
Winans, CeCe
Woods, Philip Wells

Music—Conducting/Directing

Abdul-Malik, Ahmed H.
Albam, Manny
Alexander, Otis Douglas
Anderson, Thomas Jefferson
Atkins, Carl J.
Bagley, Peter B. E.
Baker, David Nathaniel, Jr.
Black, Lucius, Sr.
Bland, Arthur H.
Brice, Percy A., Jr.
Brooks, Norman Leon
Burnim, Mellonee Victoria
Byard, John Arthur, Jr.
Christian, Eric Oliver, Jr.
Costen, Melva Wilson
Curtis, Marvin Vernell
Davis, Arrie W.
Davis, Lloyd
Davis, Louis Garland
Davis, Willie James
Dennard, Brazeal Wayne
DePreist, James Anderson
Dixon, William R.
Doggett, Bill
Downing, Alvin Joseph
Dunner, Leslie B.
Earl, Acie Boyd, II
Edmonds, Kenneth
Elliott, Anthony Daniel, III
Eubanks, Kevin
Fears, Emery Lewis, Jr.
Felder, Harvey
Fischer, William S.
Foster, William Patrick
Freeman, Paul D.
Gainer, John F.
Hairston, Jester
Hampton, Edwin Harrell
Hampton, Lionel Leo
Harris, Carl Gordon
Harris, Margaret R.
Harris, Robert Allen
Harris, Walter, Jr.
Harvey, Raymond
Hunt, Darrold Victor
Hurte, Leroy E.
Jackson, Isaiah Allen
Jeffers, Jack
Johnson, Randall Morris
Jones, Harold M.
Jones, Quincy Delight, Jr.
Kirby, Money Alian

Kirk-Duggan, Cheryl Ann
Kyle, Genghis
Lampley, Calvin D.
Lane, Johnny Lee
Leon, Tania J.
Mabrey, Marsha Eve
McGehee, Nan E.
Mobley, Charles Lamar
Moore, Carman Leroy
Moore, Kermit
Morgan, Michael
Ousley, Harold Lomax
Pate, John W., Sr.
Pollard, Alfonso McInham
Porter, Karl Hampton
Porter, Roy Lee
Roberts, Kay George
Rushen, Patrice
Smith, Andre Raphel
Smith, Wilson Washington, III
Stripling, Luther
Tate, Cornelius Astor
Treadwell, Fay Rene Lavern
Turnbull, Walter J.
Vails, Donald
Walden, Narada Michael
Walker, Charles E.
Ward, Calvin Edouard
Ward, Daniel
Washington, Grover, Jr.
White, Clayton Cecil
White, Don Lee
Wilkins, Thomas Alphonso
Womack, Robert W., Sr.

Music—Instrumental

Abdul-Malik, Ahmed H.
Adams, Armenta Estella
Adderley, Nathaniel
Albright, Gerald Anthony
Ali, Rashied
Allen, Sanford
Allen, William Duncan
Allison, Luther
Arties, Walter Eugene, III
Ashby, Dorothy J.
Ayers, Roy
Bates, Arthur Verdi
Benoit, Edith B.
Benson, Hayward J., Jr.
Berry, Chuck
Blake, Alphonso R.
Blake, Carl LeRoy
Bradley, Hilbert L.
Brice, Percy A., Jr.
Brown, Tyrone W.
Burrell, Kenneth Earl
Burton-Lyles, Blanche
Butterfield, Don
Campbell, Thomas W.
Carrington, Terri Lyne
Chapman, Tracy
Cheatham, Doc
Clarke, Stanley Marvin
Clouden, LaVerne C.
Coleman, George Edward
Coleman, Ornette
Coltrane, Alice Turiya
Cray, Robert
Crutcher, Ronald Andrew
Cunningham, Arthur H.
Curson, Theodore
Da Brat
Daniels, Jean E.
Dickerson, Lowell Dwight
Diddley, Bo
Dixon, William R.
Doggett, Bill
Donegan, Dorothy
Downing, Alvin Joseph
Duke, George M.
Elliott, Anthony Daniel, III
Ellis, Ernest W.
Eubanks, Kevin
Eubanks, Rachel Amelia
Ewing, John R.
Fears, Emery Lewis, Jr.
Ferguson, St. Julian
Ford, Fred, Jr.
Foster, Frank B., III
Foster, William Patrick
Fuller, Curtis D.
Gaines, Leslie Doran
Garner, Charles
Gaskin, Leonard O.
Gholson, General James, Jr.
Giles, Charlotte Emma
Gill, Samuel A.

Graham, Larry, Jr.
Hampton, Edwin Harrell
Hampton, Lionel Leo
Handy, John Richard, III
Hanna, Cassandra H.
Hanna, Roland
Harris, Margaret R.
Haynes, Eugene, Jr.
Heath, James E.
Hence, Marie J.
Hill, Andrew William
Hooker, John Lee
Horn, Lawrence Charles
Howard, George
Hunter, Edwina Earle
Hurd, David James, Jr.
Hurd, James L. P.
Hurst, Robert
Ibrahim, Abdullah
Jackson, Milton
Jacquet, Jean Baptiste Illinois
Jamal, Ahmad
Jeffers, Jack
Jones, Harold M.
Jones, Quincy Delight, Jr.
Jordan, Robert
Jordan, Robert A.
Jordan, Stanley
Kemp, Emmerlyne Jane
Kennedy, Anne Gamble
Kennedy, Joseph J., Jr.
Kennedy, Matthew W.
Kimbrough, David
King, B. B.
Kirby, Money Alian
Kirkland, Kenny David
Kyle, Genghis
Lane, Johnny Lee
Lasley, Phelbert Quincy, III
Lateef, Yusef
Lawrence, Azar Malcolm
Lee, William James Edwards, III
Lewis, Ramsey Emanuel, Jr.
Lutcher, Nellie
Marsalis, Branford
Marsalis, Ellis
Marsalis, Wynton
McCall, Louis
McCoy, Frank Milton
McElrath, Wanda Faith
McGill, Michele Nicole Johnson
McLean, John Lenwood
McLean, Mable Parker
McLean, Zarah Gean
McNeill, Cerves Todd
Mencer, Ernest James
Merritt, Anthony Lewis
Miller, Horatio C.
Mitchell, Billy M.
Montgomery, Toni-Marie
Moore, Kermit
Morgan, Clyde Alafiju
Najee
Newborn, Phineas Lajette, Jr.
Newson, Roosevelt, Jr.
Northern, Robert A.
Osby, Gregory Thomas
Ousley, Harold Lomax
Owens, Jimmy
Parham, Frederick Russell
Pate, John W., Sr.
Patterson, Willis Charles
Payton, Nicholas
Pettaway, Charles, Jr.
Pilot, Ann Hobson
Pollard, Alfonso McInham
Preston, Edward Lee
Priester, Julian Anthony
Qamar, Nadi Abu
Riley, Teddy
Roach, Max
Robinson, Melvin P.
Rollins, Walter Theodore
Rushen, Patrice
Sabree, Clarice Salaam
Sample, Joe
Santos, Henry J.
Saunders, Theodore D.
Shepherd, Berisford
Simmons, Clayton Lloyd
Smith, Howlett P.
Smith, James Oscar
Smith, John L., Jr.
Summer, Donna Andrea
Swindell, Warren C.
Tate, Grady B.
Taylor, William Edward
Terry, Saunders
Thigpen, Edmund Leonard

Thomas, Robert Charles
Thompson, Marcus Aurelius
Tolliver, Charles
Turner-Givens, Ella Mae
Tyner, McCoy
Vails, Donald
Wade, Bruce L.
Walden, Narada Michael
Walker, Frances
Walton, Ortiz Montaigne
Wansel, Dexter Gilman
Washington, Grover, Jr.
Washington, Oscar D.
Watts, Andre
Wells, Junior
White, Lois Jean
Wilkins, Leona B.
Williams, Earl
Williams, Junius W.
Williams, Larry
Wilson, Gerald Stanley
Winston, Sherry E.
Wonder, Stevie
Woods, Philip Wells

Music—Vocal

Aaliyah
Abdul, Raoul
Adams, Oleta
Adams, Yolanda
Addison, Adele
Albert, Donnie Ray
Alexander, Dorothy Dexter
Allen, Betty
Allison, Luther
Alston, Gerald
Arnold, David
Arroyo, Martina
Ashford, Nicholas
Austin, Patti
Badu, Erykah
Baker, Anita
Barnett, Etta Moten
Battle, Kathleen
Belafonte, Harry
Bell, Ricky
Belle, John Otis
Berry, Benjamin Donaldson
Beverly, Creigs C.
Bland, Bobby Blue
Bledsoe, William
Blige, Mary J.
Bodrick, Leonard Eugene
Bradley, Jessie Mary
Brandy
Braxton, Toni
Bridgewater, Dee Dee
Brown, Bobby
Brown, Debria M.
Brown, Foxy
Brown, Ruth
Bryson, Peabo
Busta Rhymes
Butler, Jerry
Cade, Walter, III
Caesar, Shirley
Campbell, Tevin
Campbell, Tisha
Capers, Eliza Virginia
Carey, Mariah
Carpenter, Thelma
Carrington, Terri Lyne
Carroll, Diahann
Carter, Betty
Carter, Nell
Chapman, Tracy
Charles, Ray
Cheatham, Doc
Checker, Chubby
Cherrelle
Christian, Eric Oliver, Jr.
Chuck D
Clark, Rosalind K.
Clouden, LaVerne C.
Cole, Natalie
Coolio
Costen, Melva Wilson
Crouch, Andrae
Cummings, Terry
Cunningham, Arthur H.
Da Brat
Dais, Larry
D'Angelo
Daniels, Jean E.
Darby, Castilla A., Jr.
Davis, Billy, Jr.
Davis, Clarence A.
Davis, Lloyd

Winbush, Raymond Arnold
Winfield, Linda Fitzgerald
Young, Carlene Herb
Young, Josef A.

Public Administration
See Government Service
(Elected or Appointed)/
Government Administration—
City; Government Service
(Elected or Appointed)/
Government Administration—
County; Government Service
(Elected or Appointed)/
Government Administration—
State; Government Service
(Elected or Appointed)/
Government Administration—
Federal; Government Service
(Elected or Appointed)/
Government Administration—
Not Elsewhere Classified

Public Utilities
Adderly, T. C., Jr.
Ambeau, Karen M.
Anderson, Edwyna G.
Anthony, Bernard Winston
Arnold, Haskell N., Jr.
Bankston, Archie M.
Barnes, Iraline G.
Barney, Lemuel Jackson
Baugh, Lynnette
Blackmon, Edward, Jr.
Boutte, Alvin J.
Bradley, Phil Poole
Brooks, Carl
Brown, Joseph Davidson, Sr.
Chancellor, Carl Eugene
Daniel, James L.
Daniels, Alfred Claude Wynder
Davis, Leodis
DeGraffenreidt, James H., Jr.
Delaney, Howard C.
Doby, Allen E.
Dorsey, Herman Sherwood, Jr.
Earley, Charity Edna
Edwards, Ronald Alfred
Enders, Murvin S.
English, Marion S.
Flint, Mary Frances
Fontenot-Jamerson, Berlinda
Franklin, Wayne L.
Gooley, Charles E.
Goss-Seeger, Debra A.
Grant, Howard P.
Grantley, Robert Clark
Griffith, John A.
Harrell, William Edwin
Harris, Robert L.
Hayes-Giles, Joyce V.
Horton, Dollie Bea Dixon
Hursey, James Samuel
Hyler, Lora Lee
Inniss, Charles Evans
Jackson, Brenda
Jenkins, Monica
Jennings, Devoyd
Jones, Delores
Jones, H. Thomas, II
Jones, Victoria Gene
King, Gwendolyn Stewart
Lewis, Lloyd E., Jr.
Loche, Lee Edward
Lofton, Andrew James
Loyd, Walter, Jr.
Manlove, Benson
McCraw, Tom
McKinney, Samuel Berry
McPherson, James R.
McZier, Arthur
Moore, Gregory B.
Morris, Herman, Jr.
Morrow, Charles G., III
Packer, Daniel Fredric, Jr.
Penn, Mindell Lewis
Phillips, Edward Alexander
Pinkney, Betty Kathryn
Pitts, James Donald, Jr.
Prater-Harvey, Peggy
Reeves, Michael S.
Richardson, Delroy M.
Richardson, Harold Edward
Richardson, Valerie K.
Rogers, Alfred R.

Roland, Benautrice, Jr.
Rollins, Lee Owen
Scott, R. Lee
Settles, Trudy Y.
Smith-Gaston, Linda Ann
Speights, Nathaniel H.
Stevenson, Unice Teen
Strachan, Lloyd Calvin, Jr.
Sykes, Robert A.
Tate, Sherman E.
Taylor, Andre Jerome
Taylor, S. Martin
Thaxton, June E.
Thomas, Samuel
Tufon, Chris
Turner, George Cordell, II
Urdy, Charles E.
Vaughn, Audrey Smith
Waiters, Lloyd Winferd, Jr.
Ware, Irene Johnson
Warren, Henry L.
Washington, Earlene
Washington, Nancy Ann
Watkins, William, Jr.
Watts, Patricia L.
Wells, Barbara Jones
Whitehead, David William
Williams, Alma Minton
Williams, James
Williams, Janice L.
Woods, Darnell

Publishing/Printing
Adams, Floyd, Jr.
Adams, Robert Hugo
al-Hafeez, Humza
Ali, Shahrazad
Allen, S. Monique Nicole
Anderson, Donald Edward
Andrews, Rosalyn McPherson
Bailey-Thomas, Sheryl K.
Ball, Jane Lee
Bates, Daisy
Bauldock, Gerald
Beaver, Joseph T., Jr.
Beckham, Barry Earl
Bell, Alberta Saffell
Benson, Wanda Miller
Black, David Eugene, Sr.
Blair, George Ellis, Jr.
Boghassian, Skunder
Bogus, Houston, Jr.
Boyd, Terry A.
Brazier, William H.
Bridgeman, Dexter Adrian
Bronner, Bernard
Brown, Barbara Ann
Bryant, Russell Philip, Jr.
Burns, Jeff, Jr.
Burns, Willie Miles
Burns-Cooper, Ann
Burton, Ronald J.
Cannon, Davita Louise Burgess
Carter, Lenora
Carter, Perry W.
Chandler, Alton H.
Checole, Kassahun
Cherry, Charles William
Cherry, Lee Otis
Collins, Daniel A.
Conyers, Nathan
Cooke, William Branson
Coombs, Orde
DeVore, Ophelia
Draper, Frances Murphy
Driver, David E.
Driver, Richard Sonny, Jr.
Ducksworth, Marilyn Jacoby
DuPree, Sherry Sherrod
Durham, Eddie L., Sr.
Dutton, Marie
Dyer, Bernard Joel
Eady, Lydia Davis
Easter, Eric Kevin
Edmonds, Tracey
Edwards, Audrey Marie
Edwards, Claudia L.
Edwards, Preston Joseph
Enoch, John D.
Eubanks, W. Ralph
Farrell, Robert C.
Fay, Toni G.
Felder, Loretta Kay
Fentress, Robert H.
Ferguson, Derek Talmar
Ferguson, Robert Lee, Sr.
Flagg, E. Alma W.
Foard, Frederick Carter

Foster, Frank B., III
French, James J.
Garner, Nathan Warren
Gilbert, Herman Cromwell
Glover, Robert G.
Gordon, Edwin Jason
Grant, George C.
Graves, Earl G.
Gray, Wilfred Douglas
Green, Barbara-Marie
Green, Pha M.
Grigsby, Lucy Clemmons
Grist, Raymond
Guy-Sheftall, Beverly
Hailey, Priscilla W.
Hales, William Roy
Hamilton, James G.
Hansford, Louise Todd
Harris, Charles F.
Harris, David, Jr.
Harris, Fred
Harris, Freeman Cosmo
Harris, Peter J.
Hartman, Hermene Demaris
Hill, Marvin Lewis
Holt, Deloris Lenette
House, Michael A.
Howard, Aubrey J.
Hudson, Cheryl Willis
Hunter, Norman L.
Hurte, Leroy E.
Ingrum, Adrienne G.
Jackson, Karen Denise
Jackson, Karl Don
James, Juanita T.
Jenkins, Frank Shockley
Jervay, Paul Reginald, Jr.
Jessup, Marsha Edwina
Jeter, Sheila Ann
John-Sandy, Rene Emanuel
Johnson, Eunice Walker
Johnson, Frank J., Sr.
Johnson, John H.
Johnson, R. Benjamin
Johnson, Verdia Earline
Jones, Leonade Diane
Joseph, Raymond Alcide
Kafele, Baruti Kwame
Kearse, Gregory Sashi
Kelly, John Russell
Kilimanjaro, John Marshall
Kimber, Lesly H.
Koram, M. Jamal
Latif, Naimah
Lawson Roby, Kimberla
Lee, Debra Louise
Lee, Ritten Edward
Lee, William H.
Leeke, Madelyn Cheryl
Lewis, Edward T.
Lewis, Ida Elizabeth
Lewis, James D.
Love, Ruth Burnett
Lovick, Calvin L.
Mack, Donald J.
Marr, Warren, II
Martin, Franklin Farnarwance
Masse, Donald D.
Maxwell, Roger Allan
McClure, Frederick Donald
McElroy, Lee A., Jr.
McKinney, James Ray
McPherson, Vanzetta Penn
McWright, Carter C.
Meyer, Alton J.
Miley, Debra Charlet
Minor, Tracey L.
Mixon, Veronica
Monroe, James H.
Moody, Fredreatha E.
Moragne, Lenora, Ph.D.
Morant, Mack Bernard
Morris, Celeste
Morse, Joseph Ervin
Morton, Patsy Jennings
Moyo, Yvette Jackson
Mumford, Esther Hall
Murphy, Frances L., II
Murphy, John H., III
Myers, Stephanie E.
Nelson, Leon T.
Nichols, Alfred Glen
Noble, Jeffrey V.
Odom, Carolyn
O'Flynn-Thomas, Patricia
O'Neal, Malinda King
Onli, Turtel
Osby, Simeon B., Jr.
Parker, E. Charmaine Roberts

Parker, Ted N., Jr.
Paschall, Evita Arneda
Pemberton-Heard, Danielle Marie
Perry, Rita Eggleton
Peters, William Alfred
Pettress, Andrew William
Petty, Reginald E.
Porter, Charles William
Poussaint-Hudson, Ann Ashmore
Procope, John Levy
Puckrein, Gary Alexander
Queen, Robert Calvin
Reid, Milton A.
Rhinehart, June Acie
Rhodes, Jeanne
Rice, Linda Johnson
Richardson, Eddie Price, Jr.
Robinson, Beverly Jean
Robinson, Nina
Roebuck-Hayden, Marcia
Roney, Raymond G.
Sales, Richard Owen
Samuel, Jasper H.
Sanders-Oji, J. Qevin
Scott, Cornelius Adolphus
Scott, Ruth Perry
Sewell, Luther Joseph
Shepard, Ray A.
Shepphard, Charles Bernard
Smith, Charles U.
Smith, Clarence O.
Smith, Herald Leonydus
Smith, Janet Maria
Smith, John B.
Smith, Joshua Isaac
Smith, Norman Raymond
Spight, Benita L.
Staats, Florence Joan
Steptoe, Lamont Brown
Sterling, H. Dwight, Sr.
Stewart, Ruth Ann
Swan, Lionel F.
Talbot, Gerald Edgerton
Tandy, Mary B.
Tatum, Elinor Ruth
Taylor, Sandra Elaine
Taylor, Susan L.
Thomas, Benjamin
Thompson, Charles H.
Thrower, Charles S.
Thurman, Sue Bailey
Tomlinson, Randolph R.
Trammer, Monte Irvin
Turner, Yvonne Williams
Vest, Donald Seymour, Sr.
Vest, Hilda Freeman
Wall, J. C.
Wallace, Arnold D., Sr.
Ware, Janis L.
Ware, William
Washington, James A.
Waterman, Homer D.
Waters, Wimbley, Jr.
Watkins, Sylvestre C., Sr.
Wells, Billy Gene
Wesley, Valerie Wilson
Wesley III, Herman Eugene
White, Nathaniel B.
Whitworth, Claudia Alexander
Williams, Booker T.
Williams, Terry
Williford, Stanley O.
Willis, Frank B.
Wilmore, Gayraud Stephen
Wilson, F. Leon
Winston, Michael R.
Woodruff, Cheryl
Woods, Jane Gamble
Wooten, Carl Kenneth
Worth, Janice Lorraine
Wright, Crystal Andrea
Wright, Joseph H., Jr.
Young, Albert James

Radio Broadcasting Industry
Anderson, Kernie L.
Andrews, Charles Clifton, Jr.
Arnold, John Russell, Jr.
Bailey, Bob Carl
Bailey, Lee
Beach, Walter G., II
Bell, Melvyn Clarence
Benham, Robert
Bishop, Sanford D., Jr.
Bolen, David B.
Brown, Floyd A.
Brown, James

Brown, Sharon Marjorie Revels
Brunson, Dorothy Edwards
Burley, Dale S.
Butler, Clary Kent
Carter, Robert T.
Chretien, Gladys M.
Cole, Lydia
Collinet, Georges Andre
Connell, Cameron
Cox, Wendell
Curry, Victor Tyrone
Davis, Willie D.
Dixon-Brown, Totlee
Dodson, Selma L.
Evans, Liz
Finley, Skip
Fletcher, Cliff
Freeland, Shawn Ericka
Gaines, Adriane Theresa
Gee, Al
Gilford, Vera E.
Gilliam, Herman Arthur, Jr.
Golightly, Lena Mills
Green, Verna S.
Hampton, Cheryl Imelda
Hansen, Wendell Jay
Harris, Daisy
Harris, Jack
Harvey, Linda Joy
Hickson, William F., Jr.
Hines, Rosetta
Hopson, Harold Theodore, II
Horton, Dollie Bea Dixon
Howard, Samuel H.
Jackson, Hal
Jarrett, Vernon D.
Johnson, Mal
Jones, Robert Bernard, Sr.
Langston, Andrew A.
Lee, Aubrey Walter, Jr.
Lee, Bertram M.
Lewis, Delano Eugene
Little, Helen R.
Manney, William A.
Mason, John
Mathews, Keith E.
Mayo, Blanche Irene
McGee, Rose N.
McKee, Lonette
Meek, Russell Charles
Moncrieff, Peter
Nightingale-Hawkins, Monica R.
Owens, Debbie A.
Parks, Alfred G., Jr.
Payne, Lisa R.
Peters, Roscoe Hoffman, Jr.
Robinson, Jacqueline J.
Robinson, James Edward
Roland, Johnny E.
Sainte-Johnn, Don
Shields, Del Pierce
Simpson, Donnie
Singleton, Kenneth Wayne
Smith, C. Miles, Jr.
Smith, Darryl C.
Smith, Edith B.
Smith, Judith Moore
South, Wesley W.
Spruill, Robert I.
Stamps, Herman Franklin
Stansbury, Markhum L.
Sutton, Percy E.
Sutton, Pierre Monte
Terry, Bob
Varner, James, Sr.
Ward, Sandra L.
Washington, Robert E.
Waters, Neville R., III
White, Deidre R.
Williams, Charlene J.
Wilson, Jon
Winley, Diane Lacey
Woodbeck, Frank Raymond
Worthy, Larry Elliott
Wynns, Corrie
Zola, Nkenge

Real Estate
Abdul-Rahman, Tahira Sadiqa
Allen, Charles Edward
Allen, James H.
Alston, James L.
Anderson, Marcellus J., Sr.
Arbuckle, Ronald Lee, Sr.
Armstrong, Ernest W., Sr.
Baker, LaVolia Ealy
Barden, Don H.
Barrow, Denise

Bates, William J.
Beard, Israel
Beard, Montgomery, Jr.
Bell, James H.
Bell, William Augustus, II
Billingsley, Ray C.
Bingham, Rebecca Josephine
Blanden, Lee Ernest
Bonaparte, Tony Hillary
Booker, Simeon S.
Boswell, Arnita J.
Bradshaw, Doris Marion
Brandt, Lillian B.
Brisco, Gayle
Briscoe, Leonard E.
Brooks, John S.
Brown, Arnold E.
Brown, Franchot A.
Brown, John Mitchell, Sr.
Brown, Julius J.
Brown, Oral Lee
Brown, Rodger L., Jr.
Brown, Willie B.
Browner, Ross
Bryant, Anxious E.
Bunkley, Lonnie R.
Burges, Melvin E.
Burleson, Helen L.
Burrell, Leroy
Bynoe, John Garvey
Campbell, Bobby Lamar
Carter, James
Carter, Lemorie, Jr.
Carter, Lewis Winston
Charlton, George N., Jr.
Chenault, William J.
Christian, John L.
Church, Robert T., Sr.
Clark, Douglas L.
Coelho, Peter J.
Cofield, James E., Jr.
Collins, Charles Miller
Collins, Rosecrain
Conley, Charles S.
Cooke, Thomas H., Jr.
Cooper, Joseph
Cornwall, Shirley M.
Crawford, H. R.
Crawley, Darline
Daniels, A. Raiford
Daniels, Anthony Hawthorne
DaValt, Dorothy B.
Davidson, Charles Robert
Davis, Thurman M., Sr.
Dickerson, Warner Lee
Dobbins, Albert Greene, III
Dowdy, James H.
Dunigan, Mayme O.
Dyer-Goode, Pamela Theresa
Edwards, Al E.
English, Whittie
Evans, Lillie R.
Ferguson, Idell
Ferguson, Joel
Ferguson, St. Julian
Fisher, Shelley Marie
Fletcher, Louisa Adaline
Fowlkes, Doretha P.
Franks, Gary A.
Frost, Olivia Pleasants
Garner, June Brown
Green, Walter
Greer, Edward
Hagood, Henry Barksdale
Harps, William S.
Harris, Clifton L.
Harris, Richard, Jr.
Helms, David Alonzo
Henson, Daniel Phillip, III
Hill, Alfred
Hilton, Stanley William, Jr.
Hines, Ralph Howard
Hodge, Norris
Holt, Veitya Eileene
Hooks, James Byron, Jr.
Hooks, Michael Anthony
Horton, Lemuel Leonard
Hymes, Jesse
Isaacs-Lowe, Arlene Elizabeth
Isler, Marshall A., III
Jackson, Emil A.
Jackson, Gerald Milton
Jackson, Nathaniel G.
Jackson, Ocie
Jarrett, Valerie B.
Jefferson, Patricia Ann
Jenkins, Robert Kenneth, Jr.
Johnson, Carl J.
Jones, Booker Tee, Sr.

Jones, Robert Wesley
Jones, Theresa Mitchell
Jordan, Bettye Davis
Kimbrough, Charles Edward
King, Richard L.
King, W. James
Kinniebrew, Robert Lee
Kirk, Leroy W.
Lane, Vincent
Lavelle, Robert R.
Law, M. Eprevel
Lee, Stratton Creighton
Leonard, Walter Fenner
Lively, Ira J.
Lloyd, James
London, Edward Charles
Maddox, Jack H.
Martin, Reddrick Linwood
McGhee, James Leon
McKissack, Leatrice Buchanan
McLaurin, Freddie Lewis, Jr.
McStallworth, Paul
Michel, Harriet Richardson
Miller, George Carroll, Jr.
Miller, William O.
Mingo, Pauline Hylton
Mintz, Reginold Lee
Minyard, Handsel B.
Mitchell, Roscoe E.
Montgomery, George Louis, Jr.
Morrow, Phillip Henry
Motley, David Lynn
Neal, Alimam Butler
Nelson, Ramona M.
Newhouse, Robert F.
Norris, LaVena M.
Norwood, Ronald Eugene
Packer, Lawrence Frank
Parker, William C., Jr.
Patterson, Michael Duane
Peer, Wilbur Tyrone
Peete, Calvin
Pena, Robert Bubba
Perry, Jerald Isaac, Sr.
Peters, Charles L., Jr.
Phillips, Daniel P.
Phillips, June M. J.
Pinado, Alan E., Sr.
Pounds, Kenneth Ray
Powell, Kenneth Alasandro
Ragland, Sherman Leon, II
Randle, Berdine Caronell
Rayon, Paul E., III
Reece, Steven
Reed, Beatrice M.
Reed, Gregory J.
Reed, Wilbur R.
Reid, Malissie Laverne
Reid, Rubin J.
Richie, Winston Henry
Richmond, Delores Ruth
Rivera, Eddy
Robinson, Edsel F.
Robinson, Floyd A.
Robinson, James L.
Robinson, Renault A.
Robinson, William
Ruffner, Ray P.
Samuels, Marcia L.
Satchell, Elizabeth
Scott, Charles E.
Scott, Hattie Bell
Seabrook, Juliette Theresa
Seriki, Olusola Oluyemisi
Shipp, Maurine Sarah
Sillah, Marion Rogers
Slaughter, Fred L.
Slaughter, Jewell L.
Smith, Daniel H., Jr.
Somerset, Leo L., Jr.
Spaulding, Daniel W.
Steward, Lowell C.
Stewart, W. Douglas
Stinson, Constance Robinson
Stith, Antoinette Freeman
Stone, Reese J., Jr.
Strong, Blondell McDonald
Sutton, Wilma Jean
Swan, John William David
Tanner, Gloria Travis
Terrell, Henry Matthew
Thomas, Samuel Haynes, II
Thomas, Wade Hamilton, Sr.
Thompson, Carl Eugene
Thornhill, Adrine Virginia
Thornton, Wayne T.
Toon, Al Lee, Jr.
Travis, Dempsey J.
Travis, Geraldine

Turner, Ervin
Turner, Lana
Tyler, Robert James, Sr.
Varner, Nellie M.
Wallace, Helen Winfree-Peyton
Ward, Lorene Howelton
Ware, Dyahanne
Warren, Otis, Jr.
Wash, Glenn Edward
Washington, Floyd, Jr.
Watkins, Lottie Heywood
Whisenton, Andre C.
White, Kenneth Eugene, Sr.
White, Luther D.
White, Ralph
Wilkins, Ervin W.
Williams, Enoch H.
Williams, Frank J.
Williams, Harold Edward
Williams, Leslie J.
Williams, Raleigh R.
Williamson, Carl Vance
Wilson, Grant Paul, Jr.
Winn, Joan T.
Winslow, Cleta Meris
Winters, Kenneth E.
Woods, Geneva Holloway
Woods, George Washington
Wright, Samuel Lamar
Yarbrough, Mamie Luella
Young, Terrence Anthony

Regional Planning
See **Urban/Regional Planning**

Religion
See **Clergy—Catholic;
Clergy—Moslem/Muslim;
Clergy—Protestant; Clergy—
Not Elsewhere Classified**

Restaurant/Food Service
Industry (*See Also* **Retail
Trade—Food and
Beverages**)
Ash, Richard Larry
Bailey, William H.
Beavers, Robert M., Jr.
Bell, Raleigh Berton
Bell, Yvonne Lola
Blackwell, Unita
Brown, Doris
Brown, Oral Lee
Burrell, Leroy
Cain, Herman
Clark, Patrick
Coaxum, Harry Lee
Coleman, Dennis
Dawson, Horace G., III
Dillard, Samuel Dewell
Duerson, David R.
Fletcher, Sylvester James
Fullwood, Harlow, Jr.
Garrett, Louis Henry
Gay, Helen Parker
Goldston, Nathaniel R., III
Griffin, Bertha L.
Hamilton, Aubrey J.
Harty, Belford Donald, Jr.
Hawkins, La-Van
Hill, Joseph Havord
Hollins, Leroy
Jackson, Yvonne Ruth
Jones, Wilbert
Kwaku-Dongo, Francois
Kyles, Dwain Johann
Lanier, Jesse M., Sr.
Lee, Otis K.
Lockhart, Eugene, Jr.
Lundy, Larry
Marshall, Betty J.
Mathis, Sallye Brooks
McTeer, George Calvin
Mines, Raymond C., Jr.
Mingo, Pauline Hylton
Moten, Emmett S., Jr.
Pickard, William Frank
Rogers-Reece, Shirley
Settles, Darryl Stephen
Shelton, John W.
Simmons, Stephen Lloyd
Sims, Esau, Jr.
Smith, Zachary
Smoot, Albertha Pearl

Smothers, Ronald
Stephenson, Charles E., III
Taylor, Frank Anthony
Thornton, John C.
Tolbert, John W., Jr.
Toon, Al Lee, Jr.
Turner, Melvin Duval
Valentine, Deborah Marie
Walker, Freeman, III
Watkins, Rolanda Rowe
White, Alvin, Jr.
Williams, Kevin A.
Williams, Thomas Allen
Winters, Jacqueline F.
Woods, Sylvia

Retail Trade—Apparel
and Accessories
Adewumi, Jonathan
Anderson, Helen Louise
Bates, Louise Rebecca
Brown-Harris, Ann
Burrell, Leroy
Colston Barge, Gayle S.
Crowell-Moustafa, Julia J.
Dixon, Brenda Joyce
Duncan, Joan A.
Eggleston, Neverett A., Jr.
Foster-Grear, Pamela
Franklin, David M.
Fufuka, Tika N.Y.
Gwynn, Florine Evayonne
Hankins, Anthony Mark
Harkness, Jerry
Horne, June C.
Howard, Edward T., III
Howard, Henry L.
Hudson, Jerome William
Hyter, Micheal C.
Jackson, Acy Lee
Jackson, Grant Dwight
Kendrick, Carol Yvonne
King, Shaka C.
Lauderback, Brenda Joyce
Lett, Gerald William
Marshall, Julyette Matthews
Maxwell Reid, Daphne Etta
May, Charles W.
McBride, Frances E.
McCray, Darryl K.
Moore, Annie Jewell
Owens, Thomas C., Jr.
Parker, Jean L.
Powell, Gayle Lett
Reed-Miller, Rosemary E.
Sanders, Glenn Carlos
Sherrod, Ezra Cornell
Stocks, Eleanor Louise
Taylor, Tommie W.
Watkins, Wynfred C.
White, Sylvia Kay

Retail Trade—Building/
Construction Materials
Coleman, James William
Cunningham, Randall
Ellis, Zachary L.
Hale, Gene
Knox, William Robert
Winfield, William T.

Retail Trade—Drugs and
Toiletries
Bronner, Bernard
Bynum, Horace Charles, Sr.
Caver, Carmen C. Murphy
Clarke, Joseph Lance
Gaskin, Frances Christian
Parham, Samuel Levenus
Potter, Myrtle Stephens
Pratt, Ruth Jones
Ruffin, John Walter, Jr.
Strickland, R. James

Retail Trade—Electrical/
Electronics Products
Brooks, Harry W., Jr.
Brown, Leander A.
Butts, Craig E.
Foreman, Joyce Blacknall
Harris, Carol R.
Horton, Larkin, Jr.
McGlover, Stephen Ledell

Parker, Percy Spurlark
Ramsey, Walter S.
Rand, A. Barry
Rawlings, Marilyn Manuela
Robie, Clarence W.
Tabor, Langston
Thompson, Taylor
Wilson, Frederick A.

Retail Trade—Food and
Beverages
Ahllock, Theodore
Anderson, Alfred Anthony
Anderson, Eugene
Bell, Raleigh Berton
Billue, Zana
Brooks, Frank B.
Calhoun, Gregory Bernard
Canady, Blanton Thandreus
Clarke, Priscilla
Dunham, Robert
Fluellen, Velda Spaulding
Frazier, Joe
Frazier, Ranta A.
Goss, Tom
Greene, Clifton S.
Harris, Earl L.
Heard, Lonear Windham
Hopson, Melvin Clarence
Hunt, Edward
Isaacs, Patricia
Jackson, Denise
Kelly, Ida B.
Mack, Luther W., Jr.
McGee, Buford Lamar
Milner, Thirman L.
Murray, Edna McClain
Nelson, Mario
Patterson, Gerald William
Peacock, Eulace
Reed, Lambert S., II
Ruffin, John Walter, Jr.
Shaw, Carl Bernard
Shoulders, Ramon Henkia
Simon, Walter J.
Smith, Oscar A., Jr.
Townsell, Jackie Mae
Wimp, Edward Lawson
Wright, Raymond Stanford
Yearwood, Arem Irene

Retail Trade—Furniture/
Home Furnishings
Castle, Keith L.
Clark, Robert G.
Crosby, Fred McClellen
Dean, Daniel R.
Foreman, Joyce Blacknall
France, Frederick Doug, Jr.
Grier, John K.
Johnson, Costello O.
Johnson, Eunita E.
Marshall, Julyette Matthews
McGoodwin, Roland C.
Merritt, Wendy

Retail Trade—General
Merchandise
Brown, A. David
Coleman, Robert L.
Hendricks, Richard D.
Killion, Theo M.
Lester, Nina Mack
Maynard, Edward Samuel
McGee, Sherry
McGhee, James Leon
Moran, Joyce E.
Patton, Rosezelia L.
Ruffin, John Walter, Jr.
Shanks, Wilhelmina Byrd
Watkins, Wynfred C.
White, Claude Esley

Retail Trade—Hardware
Pugh, Robert William, Jr.
Roundtree, Nicholas John
Sutton, Clyde A., Sr.

Retail Trade—Motor Vehicles, Parts, and Services

Armstrong, William
Bankston, Charles E.
Baranco, Gregory T.
Barnett, Carl L., Sr.
Barron, Reginald
Barron, Wendell
Beckford, Orville
Benjamin, Tritobia Hayes
Bennett, Lonnie M.
Beverly, Benjamin Franklin
Beyer, Troy
Boykins, Ernest A.
Boyland, Dorian Scott
Bradley, James George
Branham, George, III
Brown, John, Jr.
Brown, Larry T.
Bullard, Keith
Bunche, Curtis J.
Cabell, Enos M., Jr.
Cain, Nathaniel Z., Jr.
Callaway, Louis Marshall, Jr.
Campbell, William Earl
Carter, Will J.
Carthen, John, Jr.
Chargois, James M.
Chuks-Orji, Austin
Chukwueke, Gerald Ndudi
Clifford, Thomas E.
Cochran, Todd S.
Cockerham, Peggy
Conyers, Nathan G.
Corley, Eddie B.
Dade, Malcolm G., Jr.
Danzy, LeRoy Henry
Davis, Richard O.
Dawson, Bobby H.
Delk, James F., Jr.
Dillard, Howard Lee
Doss, LaRoy Samuel
Douglas, Walter Edmond, Sr.
Early, Ezzard Dale
Edgar, Jacqueline L.
Eggleston, Neverett A., Jr.
Falkner, Bobbie E.
Farr, Melvin, Sr.
Ferguson, Ralph
Fletcher, Glen Edward
Frazier, Jordan
Fregia, Ray
Frink, Samuel H.
Fryson, Sim E.
Gatewood, Algie C.
Gidron, Richard D.
Gordon, Darrell R.
Grace, Princeton
Greene, Franklin D.
Harper, Ball R.
Harper, T. Errol
Harrell, Charles H.
Harrell, H. Steve
Harrison, Boyd G., Jr.
Hatcher, Robert
Hayes, Elvin E., Sr.
Henry-Fairhurst, Ellenae L.
Hill, Robert A.
Hines, Jimmie
Hodge, Ernest M.
Holyfield, Evander
Hovell, Larry L.
Hughes, George Vincent
Hysaw, Guillermo Lark
Jackson, Clarence A.
Jackson, Gregory
Jackson, Nathaniel G.
Johnson, Albert William, Sr.
Johnson, Hester
Johnson, Robert
Johnson, Sam
Johnson, T. J.
Jones, Fredrick E.
Jones, James B.
Jones, James V.
Jones, Lester C.
Jones, Theresa C.
Karangu, David
Keels, Paul C.
Kemp, Leroy Percy, Jr.
Kindle, Archie
Lee, Chandler Bancroft
Lee, Fred D., Jr.
Lewis, Clarence K.
Littleton, Rupert, Jr.
Lloyd, Phil Andrew
Long, Monti M.
Majors, Anthony Y.

Mallisham, Joseph W.
March, Anthony
Martin, Cornelius A.
Martin, Russell F.
Martin, Wayne
Martinez, Ramon Jaime
Matthews, Irving J.
McClain, William L.
McClammy, Thad C.
McGregor, Edna M.
Merritt, Bishetta Dionne
Meyers, Ishmael Alexander
Mitchell, Emmitt W.
Mitchell, George L.
Mitchell, James H.
Moncrief, Sidney A.
Montgomery, Robert E.
Moore, Allyn D.
Moore, Jesse
Nelson, Ronald J.
Newberry, Cedric Charles
Nichols, Dimaggio
Norris, William E.
Oliver, James L.
Parker, Clarence E.
Parker, Michael Wayne
Perry, LaVal
Piper, Elwood A.
Preston, Leonard
Price, Phillip G.
Prophet, Richard L., Jr.
Pruitt, Michael
Reeves, Alan M.
Roberts, John Christopher
Rodgers, Pamela E.
Roy, John Willie
Rutledge, George
Shack, William Edward, Jr.
Shamberger, Jeffery L.
Shaw, Henry
Simmons, Frank
Smith, Charles Leon
Stitt, E. Don
Stokes, Sterling J.
Sutton, Nathaniel K.
Swain, Hamp
Sykes, Ray
Taylor, Henry F.
Temple, Oney D.
Thompson, Jesse
Thompson, Johnnie
Trainer, James E.
Turner, Bill
Turner, George Timothy
Walker, Jimmy L.
Walker, William B.
Warren, Clarence F.
Watkins, Jerry D.
Weiss, Ed, Jr.
Wells, Payton R.
White, Bryan
White, Ernest G.
White, Luther J.
Wickware, Damon
Wilkinson, Raymond M., Jr.
Williams, Brainard
Williams, Gregory M.
Williams, Roger L.
Williams, Theodore, Jr.
Williams, Vernon R.
Willis, Cecil B.
Wilson, Sidney, Jr.
Woodruff, James W.
Woods, Sanford L.
Woods, Timothy L.
Wright, William A.
Young, Alan John
Young, Rickey Darnell
Younger, Kenneth C.

Retail Trade—Service Industry

Andrews, Phillip
Barham, Wilbur Stectson
Bledsoe, Melvin
Fisher, Edith Maureen
Frazier, Shirley George
Herndon, Harold Thomas, Sr.
Jean, Kymberly
Johnson, Alfred
Lowery, Bobby G.
Mosley, Elwood A.
Murphy, Michael McKay
Phelps, William Anthony
Roper, Deidre
Saunders, Jerry
Steele, Joyce Yvonne
Warren, Fred Franklin

Winston, George B., III

Retail Trade—Not Elsewhere Classified

Alexander, Kelly Miller, Jr.
Banks, Manley E.
Banks, Ronald
Barfield, Quay F.
Barker, Pauline J.
Barney, Willie J.
Benton, Phyllis Clora
Boston, McKinley, Jr.
Brogden, Robert, Jr.
Brown, Robert Cephas, Sr.
Burns, Tommie, Jr.
Capel, Felton Jeffrey
Carter, Patrick Henry, Jr.
Castle, Keith L.
Coleman, Donald
Connor, Dolores Lillie
Custis, Clarence A.
Fluellen, Velda Spaulding
France, Frederick Doug, Jr.
French, Robert P.
Funn, Carlton A., Sr.
Grear, William A.
Hazel, Janis D.
Hilton, Stanley William, Jr.
Jackson, James E., Sr.
Jackson, Lurline Bradley
King, Frederick L., Jr.
Lawrence, Henry
Lawrence, Philip Martin
Layton, William W.
Mannie, William Edward
McGhee, Georgia Mae
McGoodwin, Roland C.
Morrison, Paul-David
Owens, Thomas C., Jr.
Paris, Calvin Rudolph
Patton, Jean E.
Peterson, Coleman Hollis
Phillips, Barbara
Pratt, Melvin Lemar
Robinson, Frank J.
Robinson-Ford, Denise Renee
Stewart, Brittanica
Walker, Lee H.
Warder, John Morgan
Warren, Fred Franklin
Westbrooks, Logan H.
Willis, Rose W.

Sales Management
See **Management/ Administration—Sales**

Science—Not Elsewhere Classified (*See Also* **Agricultural Science; Biology/Microbiology; Botany; Chemistry; Ecology; Oceanography; Physiology; Zoology**)

Basri, Gibor Broitman
Boyd, Evelyn Shipps
Bragg, Joseph L.
Bridgewater, Albert Louis
Brown, Shirley Ann Vining
Cameron, Joseph A.
Chicoye, Etzer
Collins, Limone C.
Cooper, Walter
Curbeam, Robert L.
Diggs, Lawrence J
Franklin, Lance Stonestreet
Franklin, Renty Benjamin
Gantt, Gloria
Garraway, Michael Oliver
Gavin, James Raphael, III
Graham, Rhea L.
Greene, Lionel Oliver, Jr.
Hannah, Marc Regis
Henderson, Nannette S.
Hendricks, Marvin B.
Hymes, William Henry
Ingram, Robert B.
Jackson, Duane Myron
James, Herbert I.
Jemison, Mae C.
Johnson, Michael Anthony
King, Lewis M.
Kornegay, Wade M.
Kumanyika, Shiriki K.

Malcom, Shirley Mahaley
Malone, Thomas Ellis
McDowell-Head, Lelia M.
McIntyre, Mildred J.
Mehlinger, Kermit Thorpe
Milton, LeRoy
Mitchell, Joseph Christopher
Moore, George Thomas
Mortimer, Delores M.
Nelson, Edward O.
Parnell, John V., III
Philander, S. George H.
Phillips, Leo Augustus
Phillips, Lloyd Garrison, Jr.
Pratt, Alexander Thomas
Rhoden, Richard Allan
Roane, Philip Ransom, Jr.
Rose, Raymond Edward
Smalls, Charley Mae
Smith, Robert London
Smith, Roulette William
Sogah, Dotsevi Y.
Standifer, Lonnie Nathaniel
Thomas, Mary A.
Trent, John Spencer
Turner, Vivian Vanessa
Urdy, Charles E.
Weaver, John Arthur
Wiley, William R.
Williams, Carolyn Ruth Armstrong
Williams, Ralph O.
Wilson, Donella Joyce

Social Rights Activism
See **Activism, Political/Civil/ Social Rights**

Social Work

Adair, Alvis V.
Adair, Andrew A.
Adams, Anne Currin
Aldredge, James Earl
Alexander, Robert I.
Allen, Alexander J.
Allen, Herbert J.
Allen, Zuline Gray
Anderson, James R., Jr.
Anderson, Marva Jean
Appleton, Clevette Wilma
Armstead, Chapelle M.
Armstead, Ron E.
Arnold, Helen E.
Atkinson, Eugenia Calwise
Atkinson, Regina Elizabeth
Bailey, Gary
Baker-Parks, Sharon L.
Ballard, Myrtle Ethel
Barnard-Bailey, Wanda Arlene
Battle, Mark G.
Baugh, Florence Ellen
Beckett, Charles Campbell
Benson, Rubin Author
Berry, Paul Lawrence
Berry, Philip Alfonso
Berry, Weldon H.
Blount, Larry Elisha
Bommer, Minnie L.
Bozeman, Maggie Simmons
Brabson, Howard V.
Bramwell, Henry
Brass, Reginald Stephen
Brooks, Rodney Norman
Brown, Denise Sharon
Brown, Joan P.
Brown, Tommie Florence
Brown-Wright, Marjorie
Bruce, Kenneth E.
Bugg, Mayme Carol
Burgest, David Raymond
Burlew, Ann Kathleen
Burns, Geraldine Hamilton
Busby, Everett C.
Butler, Melba
Carter, James L.
Carter, Romelia Mae
Castleman, Elise Marie
Chambers, Madrith Bennett
Chavis, Theodore R.
Clemmons, Clifford R.
Coleman, Barbara Sims
Collins, Constance Renee Wilson
Cooper, Syretha C.
Coston, Bessie Ruth
Cothorn, Marguerite Esters
Cox, Arthur James, Sr.
Crawford, Cranford L., Jr.

Crawford, Margaret Ward
Creditt, Thelma Cobb
Croslan, John Arthur
Dale, Robert J.
Daniel, David L.
Daniels, Ron D.
Darden, Anthony Kojo
Davis, Bettye J.
Davis, Dupree Daniel
Davis, Mary Agnes Miller
Davis-Williams, Phyllis A.
DeHart, Panzy H.
Dell, Willie J.
Deloatch, Myrna Spencer
Dismuke, Mary Eunice
Dobson, Dorothy Ann
Dorsey, L. C.
Douglas, Walter Edmond, Sr.
Dudley, Juanita C.
Dugger, Clinton George
Dunigan, Mayme O.
Dunmore, Charlotte J.
Dyer, Bernard Joel
Ealey, Mark E.
Eaton, Thelma Lucile
Echols, Ivor Tatum
English, Richard A.
Erskine, Kenneth F.
Evans-Dodd, Theora Anita
Faison, Helen Smith
Ferrell, Rosie E.
Fields, Alva Dotson
Fields, William I., Jr.
Floyd, Vircher B.
Forney, Mary Jane
Fowlkes, Nancy P.
Foye-Eberhardt, Ladye Antionette
Francis, E. Aracelis
Francis, Livingston S.
Fresh, Edith McCullough
Fuerst, Jean Stern
Garrison, Jewell K.
Gary, Lawrence Edward
Gomez, Kevin Lawrence Johnson
Goulbourne, Donald Samuel, Jr.
Graham, Precious Jewel
Grant, Timothy Jerome
Grant Bishop, Ellen Elizabeth
Gray, Keith A., Jr.
Grayson, Elsie Michelle
Green, Richard Carter
Hairston, Raleigh Daniel
Hall, Joseph A.
Hall, Yvonne Bonnie
Hardeman, James Anthony
Harris, Cornelia
Harris, Wesley Young, Jr.
Haynes, Alphonso Worden
Hemphill, Paul W.
Hill, Sandra Patricia
Hodge, Marguerite V.
Holt, Fred D.
Hubbard, Josephine Brodie
Hudson, Winson
Hunter, Patrick J.
Hunter, Robert J.
Ivey, Horace Spencer
Jenkins, Edmond Thomas
Johnson, Audreye Earle
Johnson, Ed F.
Johnson, Elaine McDowell
Johnson, Lloyd A.
Johnson, Otis Samuel
Johnson, Richard Howard
Johnson, Samuel Harrison
Johnson, Waldo Emerson, Jr.
Jones, Bertha Diggs
Jones, Richard Julius
Jones, Sam H., Sr.
Jones, Shirley Joan
Jordan, Thomas Alton
Journey, Lula Mae
Kent, Melvin Floyd
Key, Addie J.
Kirk, Sarah Virgo
Kirkland, Jack A.
Kispert, Dorothy Lee
Lang, Winston E.
Langston, Esther J.
Lee, Helen Jackson
Lee, Ritten Edward
Lee, Shirley Freeman
LeFlore, Larry
Leigh, James W., Jr.
Levy, Valerie Lowe
Lewis, Almera P.
Lewis, Colston A.
Lewis, Lyn Etta
Lewis, Martha S.

Bonner, Alice Carol
Booker, Karen
Booker, Michael
Booker, Vaughn Jamel
Boone, Robert Franklin
Bosley, Freeman Robertson, Jr.
Boston, Archie, Jr.
Bouie, Tony Vanderson
Boulware, Peter
Boutte, Marc Anthony
Bowden, Joseph Tarrod
Bowdoin, Robert E.
Bowen, Bruce
Bowens, Tim
Bowie, Larry
Bowie, Oliver Wendell
Bownes, Fabien
Boyd, Delores Rosetta
Brackens, Tony
Bradtke, Mark
Brady, Donny
Brandon, David Sherrod
Brandon, Terrell
Brashear, Donald
Braxton, Janice Lawrence
Braxton, Tyrone Scott
Breaux, Timothy
Bridgeman, Junior
Bridges, Bill
Brigance, O.J.
Briggs, Greg
Brisby, Vincent Cole
Brock, Louis Clark
Bronson, Zack
Brooks, Barrett
Brooks, Bucky
Brooks, Derrick
Brooks, James Robert
Brooks, Macey
Brooks, Robert Darren
Broussard, Steven
Brown, Adrian Demond
Brown, Anthony
Brown, Chadwick Everett
Brown, Chris
Brown, Chucky
Brown, Cindy
Brown, Cornell Desmond
Brown, Corwin Alan
Brown, Dee
Brown, Derek Darnell
Brown, Derek Vernon
Brown, Emil Quincy
Brown, Gary Leroy
Brown, Gilbert Jesse
Brown, J.B.
Brown, James Lamont
Brown, Jamie
Brown, Jarvis Ardel
Brown, Larry
Brown, Lomas, Jr.
Brown, Marcus James
Brown, Michael
Brown, Orlando Claude
Brown, P. J.
Brown, Randy
Brown, Ray, Jr.
Brown, Reggie
Brown, Reuben
Brown, Roger
Brown, Rushia
Brown, Timothy Donell
Browne, Jerry
Browner, Joey Matthew
Browner, Ross
Browning, John
Bruce, Aundray
Bruce, Isaac Isidore
Bryant, Jeff Dwight
Bryant, Junior
Bryant, Kobe B.
Bryant, Mark
Buchanan, Raymond Louis
Buckley, Curtis LaDonn
Buckley, Marcus Wayne
Buckley, Terrell
Buford, Damon Jackson
Bullett, Vicky
Burgess, Linda
Burks, Ellis Rena
Burnett, Robert Barry
Burns, Keith Bernard
Burns, Lamont
Burras, Alisa
Burrell, Scott David
Burris, Jeffrey Lamar
Burroughs, Sammie Lee
Burroughs, Tim

Burton, Kendrick
Bush, Devin
Bush, Lewis Fitzgerald
Butler, LeRoy
Butler, Mitchell Leon
Butts, Marion Stevenson, Jr.
Byars, Keith Allan
Byears, Latasha
Byner, Earnest Alexander
Byrd, Isaac
Caffey, Jason Andre
Cage, Michael Jerome
Cain, Joseph Harrison, Jr.
Caldwell, Adrian Bernard
Caldwell, Mike Isiah
Calloway, Christopher Fitzpatrick
Cambridge, Dexter
Camby, Marcus D.
Cameron, Michael Terrance
Campbell, Edna
Campbell, Elden
Campbell, Jesse
Campbell, Mark
Campbell, Michele
Campbell, Milton Gray
Campbell, Tony
Canty, Chris
Carew, Rodney Cline
Carr, Antoine Labotte
Carr, Chris Dean
Carr, Kenny
Carr, M. L.
Carr, William
Carrier, Mark
Carrier, Mark Anthony
Carroll, Joe Barry
Carruth, Rae
Carswell, Dwayne
Carter, Anthony
Carter, Cris
Carter, Dale Lavelle
Carter, Deborah
Carter, Joseph Chris
Carter, Kevin Louis
Carter, Ki-Jana
Carter, Marty LaVincent
Carter, Nigea
Carter, Pat
Carter, Perry Lynn
Carter, Thomas
Carter, Thomas, II
Carter, Tony
Cartwright, Bill
Carver, Shante
Cassell, Samuel James
Cato, Kelvin
Causwell, Duane
Ceballos, Cedric Z.
Cedeno, Cesar
Centers, Larry
Chamberlain, Byron
Chamberlain, Wesley Polk
Chamberlain, Wilt Norman
Chambliss, Chris
Chaney, Don
Charles, Daedra
Cheaney, Calbert N.
Cheeks, Maurice Edward
Cherry, Je'Rod
Childress, Randolph
Childs, Chris
Christie, Douglas Dale
Clark, David Earl
Clark, Gary C.
Clark, Rico
Clark, Tony
Clark, Willie Calvin
Clay, Willie James
Clayborn, Ray Dewayne
Clemons, Duane
Coakley, Dexter
Coates, Ben Terrence
Cobb, Reginald John
Cobbins, Lyron
Cofer, Michael Lynn
Coffey, Richard
Coleman, Andre Clintonian
Coleman, Benjamin Leon
Coleman, Derrick D.
Coleman, Marco Darnell
Coleman, Marcus
Coleman, Monte
Coles, Bimbo
Coles, Darnell
Colleton, Katrina
Collier, Louis Keith
Collins, Andre Pierre
Collins, James
Collons, Ferric Jason

Colon, Harry
Congreaves, Andrea
Conley, Steven
Conner, Darion
Conner, Lester Allen
Conway, Curtis LaMont
Cook, Anthony Andrew
Cook, Toi Fitzgerald
Cooper, Cecil
Cooper, Cynthia
Cooper, Duane
Cooper, Michael Jerome
Copeland, Horace Nathaniel
Copeland, John
Copeland, Russell
Corbin, Tyrone Kennedy
Coryatt, Quentin John
Cotton, James
Cotton, Kenyon
Covington, Damien
Cowens, Alfred Edward, Jr.
Cox, Bryan Keith
Cox, Ronald
Craver, Aaron LeRenze
Crawford, Keith
Crawford, Vernon
Crawley, Sylvia
Crittenden, Ray
Crockett, Ray
Crockett, Zack
Cross, Howard
Cross-Battle, Tara
Crumpler, Carlester
Cummings, Midre Almeric
Cummings, Terry
Cunningham, Randall
Cunningham, Rick
Cureton, Earl
Curry, Dell
Curry, Eric Felece
Curry, Michael
Custis, Ace
Cuyjet, Cynthia K.
Daggs, LeRoy W.
Dampier, Erick Trevez
Dandridge, Bob
Daniel, Eugene
Daniels, Antonio
Daniels, LeShun
Daniels, Lloyd
Daniels, Phillip Bernard
Darby, Matthew Lamont
Dar Dar, Kirby David
Dare, Yinka
Darkins, Christopher Oji
Darling, James
Davidson, Fletcher Vernon, Jr.
Davis, Alonzo J.
Davis, Anthony D.
Davis, Antone Eugene
Davis, Antonio Lee
Davis, Ben Jerome
Davis, Brian
Davis, Charles Alexander
Davis, Chili
Davis, Cyprian
Davis, Dale
Davis, Don
Davis, Emanual
Davis, Erellon Ben
Davis, Eric Keith
Davis, Eric Wayne
Davis, Hubert Ira, Jr.
Davis, Isaac
Davis, John
Davis, Latina
Davis, Mark Anthony
Davis, Reuben Cordell
Davis, Stephen
Davis, Tara
Davis, Terrell
Davis, Terry Raymond
Davis, Travis Horace
Davis, Troy
Davis, Tyrone
Davis, Walter Paul
Davis, Wendell
Davis, William Augusta, III
Davis, Willie Clark
Davison, Jerone
Davis-Wrightsil, Clarissa
Dawkins, Brian
Dawkins, Johnny
Dawkins, Sean Russell
Dawson, Andre Nolan
Dawson, Dermontti Farra
Dawson, Lake
Day, Terry
Day, Todd Fitzgerald

Deese, Derrick
Dehere, Terry
DeLeon, Jose
Delk, Tony Lorenzo
Denson, Damon
Dent, Richard Lamar
DeShields, Delino Lamont
Dickerson, Eric Demetric
Dimry, Charles Louis, III
Dishman, Cris Edward
Dixon, Diane L.
Dixon, Ernest
Dixon, Gerald Scott
Dixon, Tamecka
Doby, Lawrence Eugene, Sr.
Dodge, Dedrick Allen
Dogins, Kevin
Doleman, Christopher John
Donaldson, James Lee, III
Dorsett, Anthony Drew, Jr.
Dorsett, Tony Drew
Dotson, Earl Christopher
Dotson, Santana
Douglas, Hugh
Douglas, James
Douglas, Omar
Douglas, Sherman
Douglass, Maurice Gerrard
Dowdell, Marcus L.
Downing, Stephen
Downs, Gary McClinton
Drakeford, Tyronne James
Drayton, Troy Anthony
Drew, Larry Donelle
Drexler, Clyde
Driessen, Dan
Dubenion, Elbert
Dudley, Rickey
Duerson, David R.
Duff, Jamal Edwin
Dulaney, Michael
Dumars, Joe, III
Dumas, Tony
Dumas, Troy
Duncan, Tim
Dunn, David
Dunn, Jason
Dunn, Warrick
Dunston, Shawon Donnell
Duper, Mark Super
Durham, Leon
Durham, Ray
Dye, Ernest Thaddeus
Dye, Jermaine Terrell
Earl, Acie Boyd, II
Early, Quinn Remar
Easler, Michael Anthony
Easley, Damion
Easley, Kenny, Jr.
Edmunds, Ferrell, Jr.
Edney, Tyus Dwayne
Edwards, Anthony
Edwards, Blue
Edwards, Dixon Voldean, III
Edwards, Donald Lewis, Jr.
Edwards, Douglas
Edwards, James Franklin
Edwards, Kevin Durell
Edwards, Michelle
Edwards, Teresa
Edwards, Tonya
Egins, Paul Carter, III
Eisley, Howard Jonathan
Elder, Lee
Elewonibi, Mohammed Thomas David
Elie, Mario Antoine
Ellard, Henry Austin
Elliott, Sean Michael
Ellis, Dale
Ellis, LaPhonso Darnell
Ellis, LeRon Perry
Ellison, Jerry
Ellison, Pervis
Elliss, Luther
Ellsworth, Percy
Emanuel, Bert Tyrone
Embry, Wayne, Sr.
Emmons, Carlos
England, Eric Jevon
English, Albert J.
English, Stephen
Engram, Bobby
Enis, Shalonda
Epps, Phillip Earl
Erving, Julius Winfield
Espy, Cecil Edward
Ethridge, Raymond Arthur, Jr.
Evans, Chuck

Evans, Donald Lee
Evans, Douglas Edwards
Evans, Josh
Evans, Lee
Evans, Leomont
Everett, Carl Edward
Everett, Thomas Gregory
Ewing, Patrick Aloysius
Fann, Chad Fitzgerald
Farmer, Ray
Farr, D'Marco
Farrior, James
Faulk, Marshall William
Ferguson, Jason
Fernandez, Tony
Ferrell, Duane
Fielder, Cecil Grant
Fields, Kenneth
Fields, Mark Lee
Finley, Michael H.
Fisher, Derek Lamar
Fleming, Vern
Fletcher, Terrell
Flowers, Lethon
Floyd, Cliff
Floyd, Eric Augustus
Floyd, Malcolm
Floyd, William Ali
Folston, James Edward
Fontenot, Albert Paul
Fonville, Chad Everete
Forbes, Marlon
Ford, Henry
Ford, Kisha
Ford, Stacey
Foreman, George Edward
Fortson, Danny
Foster, George Arthur
Foster, Gregory Clinton
Foster, Kevin Christopher
Foster, Toni
Fountaine, Jamal
Fox, Rick
Foyle, Adonal
Francis, James
Franco, Julio Cesar
Frank, Tellis Joseph, Jr.
Frazier, Walt
Free, World B.
Freeman, Antonio Michael
Freeman, Lauretta
Frett, La Keshia
Fryar, Irving Dale
Fugett, Jean S., Jr.
Fuhr, Grant Scott
Fuller, Corey
Fuller, Randy Lamar
Fuller, William Henry, Jr.
Funderburke, Lawrence Damon
Gaines, Corey Yasuto
Gaines, William Albert
Gaither, Katryna
Galbraith, Scott
Galbreath, Harry Curtis
Galloway, Joey
Gamble, Kevin Douglas
Gamble, Oscar Charles
Gandy, Wayne Lamar
Gant, Ronald Edwin
Gant, Travesa
Garbey, Barbaro
Gardener, Daryl
Garner, Charlie
Garner, Chris
Garnett, Kevin
Garrett, Dean
Garrison-Jackson, Zina Lynna
Gash, Samuel Lee, Jr.
Gaskins, Percell
Gaston, Cito
Gatling, Chris Raymond
Gattison, Kenneth Clay
Gault, Willie James
Geary, Reggie
Geathers, Jumpy
George, Eddie
George, Ronald
George, Tate Claude
Gerald, Melvin Douglas, Sr.
Gervin, George
Gibson, Althea
Gibson, Antonio Marice
Gibson, Oliver Donnovan
Gibson, Robert
Gildon, Jason Larue
Gilkey, Bernard
Gill, Kendall Cedric
Gilliam, Armon Louis

Gilliam, Frank Delano
Gillom, Jennifer
Gilmore, Artis
Glanville, Douglas Metunwa
Glass, Gerald Damon
Glass, Virginia M.
Glenn, Aaron DeVon
Glenn, Tarik
Glenn, Terry
Glover, Andrew Lee
Glover, Kevin Bernard
Glover, La'Roi Damon
Godfrey, Randall Euralentris
Goldwire, Anthony
Gomes, Wayne M.
Gonzalez, Tony
Gooch, Jeff
Gooden, Dwight Eugene
Goodson, Adrienne M.
Goodwin, Curtis LaMar
Goodwin, Thomas Jones
Gordon, Bridgette
Gordon, Darrien X. Jamal
Gordon, Dwayne
Gordon, Lancaster
Gordon, Thomas
Graham, Derrick
Graham, Gregory Lawrence
Graham, Jeff Todd
Graham, Paul
Graham, Scottie
Grant, Brian Wade
Grant, Harvey
Grant, Horace Junior
Grant, Stephen Mitchell
Graves, Denique
Gray, Carlton Patrick
Gray, Derwin Lamont
Gray, Earnest
Gray, Ed
Gray, Jerry
Gray, Johnnie Lee
Gray, Mel
Gray, Torrian
Grayer, Jeffrey
Green, A. C., Jr.
Green, Darrell
Green, Eric
Green, Hugh
Green, Litterial
Green, Rickey
Green, Robert David
Green, Roy
Green, Sean Curtis
Green, Sidney
Green, Victor Bernard
Green, Willie Aaron
Green, Yatil
Greene, Joe
Greene, Willie Louis
Greenwood, David
Greer, Cherie
Greer, Hal
Grier, Marrio Darnell
Griffey, Ken, Jr.
Griffin, Leonard James, Jr.
Griffith, Darrell Steven
Griffith, Howard Thomas
Griffith, Robert Otis
Griffith, Yolanda
Grissom, Marquis Dean
Groce, Clifton Allen
Guliford, Eric Andre
Guynes, Thomas
Guyton, Wanda
Guzman, Juan Andres Correa
Gwynn, Tony
Hackett, Barry Dean
Hagler, Marvelous Marvin
Hagood, Jay
Hairston, Jerry Wayne
Hairston, Sam
Haley, Charles Lewis
Hall, Albert
Hall, Dana Eric
Hall, Lemanski
Hall, Timothy
Ham, Darvin
Hamer, Steve
Hamilton, Bobby
Hamilton, Darryl Quinn
Hamilton, Harry E.
Hamilton, Keith Lamarr
Hamilton, Ruffin
Hammonds, Jeffrey Bryan
Hampton, Kym
Hampton, Rodney
Hancock, Darrin
Hand, Jon Thomas

Hand, Norman
Hanks, Merton Edward
Hardaway, Anfernee Deon
Hardaway, Timothy Duane
Hardmon, Lady
Hardy, Darryl Gerrod
Hardy, Kevin
Harkey, Michael Anthony
Harper, Alvin Craig
Harper, Derek Ricardo
Harper, Dwayne Anthony
Harper, Ronald
Harper, Terry
Harper, Tommy
Harrington, Othella
Harris, Al Carl
Harris, Anthony
Harris, Bernardo Jamaine
Harris, Corey Lamont
Harris, Derrick
Harris, Fran
Harris, Jackie Bernard
Harris, James
Harris, Jon
Harris, Lenny
Harris, Leonard Anthony
Harris, Lucious H., Jr.
Harris, Pep
Harris, Raymont LeShawn
Harris, Reggie
Harris, Robert Lee
Harris, Sarah Elizabeth
Harris, Sean Eugene
Harris, Walter Lee
Harrison, Chris
Harrison, Lisa Darlene
Harrison, Marvin Daniel
Harrison, Nolan
Harrison, Rodney Scott
Harvey, Antonio
Harvey, Kenneth Ray
Harvey, Richard Clemont, Jr.
Hasselbach, Harald
Hastings, Andre Orlando
Hasty, James Edward
Hatcher, William Augustus
Hawkins, Courtney Tyrone, Jr.
Hawkins, Hersey R., Jr.
Hawkins, LaTroy
Hawkins, Michael
Hayden, Aaron Chautezz
Hayes, Charlie
Hayes, Chris
Hayes, Elvin E., Sr.
Hayes, Jonathan Michael
Hayes, Melvin Anthony
Hayes, Mercury
Haynes, Michael David
Haywood, Spencer
Head, Dena
Heard, Herman Willie, Jr.
Hearns, Thomas
Hearst, Garrison
Hegamin, George
Hempstead, Hessley
Henderson, Alan Lybrooks
Henderson, Cedric
Henderson, Gerald
Henderson, Jerome Virgil
Henderson, Keith Pernell
Henderson, Rickey Henley
Henderson, William Terrelle
Henry, Herman
Henry, Kevin Lerell
Herndon, Larry Lee
Herrera, Carl Victor
Herrod, Jeff Sylvester
Heyward, Craig William
Hicks, Jessie
Hicks, Michael
Higgins, Roderick Dwayne
Higgins, Sean Marielle
Highsmith, Alonzo Walter
Hill, Bruce Edward
Hill, Calvin
Hill, E.C.
Hill, Eric
Hill, Grant Henry
Hill, Gregory LaMonte
Hill, Kenneth Wade
Hill, Randal Thrill
Hill, Tyrone
Hilliard, Ike
Hilliard, Randy
Hills, Keno
Hinson, Roy Manus
Hitchcock, Jimmy Davis, Jr.
Hoard, Leroy
Hobbs, Daryl Ray

Hodge, Donald Jerome
Hodges, Craig Anthony
Hodges, Dale
Holland, Darius
Holland-Corn, Kedra
Holliday, Corey Lamont
Hollier, Dwight Leon
Hollinquest, Lamont
Holmes, Clayton Antwan
Holmes, Darick
Holmes, Earl
Holmes, Jerry
Holmes, Kenny
Holmes, Larry
Holmes, Lester
Holmes, Priest Anthony
Holsey, Bernard
Holt, Leroy
Holton, Michael David
Holyfield, Evander
Honeycutt, Jerald
Hopkins, Bradley D.
Hopkins, Wes
Horn, Joseph
Horry, Robert Keith
Horton, Raymond Anthony
Horton, Willie Wattison
Houston, Allan Wade
Houston, Bobby
Houston, Kenneth Ray
Howard, Brian
Howard, Desmond Kevin
Howard, Juwan Antonio
Howard, Stephen
Howard, Ty
Hubbard, Phil
Hubbard, Trent
Huckaby, Malcolm
Hudson, Charles Lynn
Hudson, Christopher Resherd
Hughes, Mark
Hughes, Robert Danan
Hughes, Tyrone Christopher
Humphrey, Bobby
Humphrey, Robert Charles
Humphries, Jay
Hunter, Brian Lee
Hunter, Brian Ronald
Hunter, Lindsey Benson, Jr.
Hunter, Tony Wayne
Huskey, Butch
Iginla, Jarome
Ingram, Garey
Ingram, Stephen
Irvin, Byron Edward
Irvin, Ken
Irvin, Michael Jerome
Irvin, Monford Merrill
Irving, Terry Duane
Ismail, Qadry Rahmadan
Ismail, Raghib Ramadian
Israel, Steven Douglas
Iverson, Allen
Ivery, Eddie Lee
Jackson, Bo
Jackson, Bobby
Jackson, Calvin Bernard
Jackson, Charles Richard, Jr.
Jackson, Damian Jacques
Jackson, Greg Allen
Jackson, Jaren
Jackson, Jim
Jackson, John
Jackson, Keith Jerome
Jackson, Mark A.
Jackson, Michael Dwayne
Jackson, Michael Ray
Jackson, Raymond DeWayne
Jackson, Reggie Martinez
Jackson, Rickey Anderson
Jackson, Roy Lee
Jackson, Stanley Leon
Jackson, Steven Wayne
Jackson, Tammy
Jackson, Tia
Jackson, Tyoka
Jackson, Waverly
Jackson, Willie Bernard, Jr.
Jacobs, Tim
Jacquet, Nate
James, Dion
James, Henry Charles
James, Kevin Porter
James, Tory
Jamison, George R., Jr.
Jasper, Edward Videl
Jeffcoat, James Wilson, Jr.
Jefferies, Greg Lamont
Jefferson, Greg

Jefferson, Reggie
Jefferson, Shawn
Jenkins, Billy
Jenkins, DeRon Charles
Jenkins, James
Jenkins, Melvin
Jenkins, Trezelle Samuel
Jensen, Marcus C.
Jeter, Derek
Jett, James
Johnson, Adrienne
Johnson, Andre
Johnson, Anthony
Johnson, Anthony Scott
Johnson, Avery
Johnson, Buck
Johnson, Charles Edward, Jr.
Johnson, Charles Everett
Johnson, Darrius
Johnson, Dave
Johnson, Earvin, Jr.
Johnson, Edward Arnet
Johnson, Ellis Bernard
Johnson, Ervin, Jr.
Johnson, Ezra Ray
Johnson, Jimmie
Johnson, Joseph
Johnson, Kelley Antonio
Johnson, Kenneth Lance
Johnson, Kevin Maurice
Johnson, Keyshawn
Johnson, Lance
Johnson, Larry Demetric
Johnson, Leon
Johnson, LeShon Eugene
Johnson, Lonnie
Johnson, Melvin Carlton, III
Johnson, Niesa
Johnson, Pepper
Johnson, Raylee Terrell
Johnson, Ron
Johnson, Roy Edward
Johnson, Shannon
Johnson, Tiffani
Johnson, Tre
Johnson, Troy Dwan
Johnson, Vance Edward
Johnson, Vickie
Johnson, Vinnie
Johnson, Wallace Darnell
Johnson, William Arthur
Johnson, William Edward
Johnstone, Lance
Joiner, Charles, Jr.
Jones, Aaron Delmas, II
Jones, Andruw Rudolf
Jones, Bobby M.
Jones, Brian Keith
Jones, Caldwell
Jones, Carolyn
Jones, Cedric
Jones, Charles
Jones, Charlie
Jones, Chris
Jones, Chris Todd
Jones, Clarence
Jones, Cobi N'Gai
Jones, Damon
Jones, Donta
Jones, Dontae' Antijuaine
Jones, Eddie Charles
Jones, Edward Lee
Jones, Ernest Lee
Jones, Gary DeWayne
Jones, Henry
Jones, James
Jones, James Alfie
Jones, Jimmie Simms
Jones, Lenoy
Jones, Marcus
Jones, Merlakia
Jones, Michael Anthony
Jones, Michael David
Jones, Popeye
Jones, Reggie
Jones, Robert Lee
Jones, Roderick Wayne
Jones, Roger Carver
Jones, Rondell Tony
Jones, Selwyn Aldridge
Jones, Tony Edward
Jones, Victor Tyrone
Jones, Walter
Jordan, Andrew
Jordan, Brian O'Neil
Jordan, Charles
Jordan, Darin Godfrey
Jordan, Eddie

Jordan, Michael
Jordan, Paul Scott
Jordan, Randy Loment
Jordan, Reggie
Jordan, Steve Russell
Joyner, Seth
Joyner-Kersee, Jackie
Judson, William Thadius
Junior, E. J., III
Justice, David Christopher
Kalu, Ndukwe Dike
Kaufman, Napoleon
Kazadi, Muadianvita Matt
Kelly, Joseph Winston
Kelly, Michael Raymond
Kemp, Shawn T.
Kennedy, Cortez
Kennedy, Lincoln
Kennison, Eddie Joseph, III
Kerner, Marlon
Kersey, Jerome
Keys, Randolph
Kidd, Jason Fredrick
Kidd, Warren Lynn
Killens, Terry Deleon
Kimble, Bo
King, Albert
King, Bernard
King, Shawn
King, Stacey
Kinnebrew, Larry D.
Kirby, Terry Gayle
Kirkland, Levon
Kittles, Kerry
Knight, Brevin
Knight, Negele Oscar
Knight, Sammy
Knight, Thomas
Knight, Tom
Knox, William Robert
Kroon, Marc Jason
Lacy, Venus
Lake, Carnell Augustino
Land, Daniel
Landreaux, Kenneth Francis
Landrum, Tito Lee
Lane, Jerome
Lane, Richard
Lang, Andrew Charles
Lang, Antonio
Lang, Kenard
Langford, Jevon
Langham, Antonio
Lanier, Willie
Lankford, Raymond Lewis
Larkin, Barry Louis
Lassiter, Kwamie
Latham, Chris
Lathon, Lamar Lavantha
Lauderdale, Priest
Lavan, Alton
Law, Ty
Lawrence, Henry
Lawson, Jason
Lawton, Matthew, III
Leavell, Allen
Lee, Amp
Lee, Carl, III
Lee, Derrek Leon
Lee, Mark Anthony
Lee, Shawn Swaboda
Legette, Tyrone
Lemon, Chester Earl
Lemon, Meadowlark
Lenard, Voshon Kelan
Lennon, Patrick Orlando
Leonard, Jeff
Leonard, Sugar Ray
Leslie, Lisa
Lester, George Lawrence
Lester, Tim Lee
Lett, Leon
Levens, Dorsey
Lever, Lafayette
Levingston, Clifford Eugene
Lewis, Albert Ray
Lewis, Carl
Lewis, Darren Joel
Lewis, Daryll Lamont
Lewis, Jermaine Edward
Lewis, Martin
Lewis, Mo
Lewis, Ray Anthony
Lewis, Roderick Albert
Lewis, Ronald Alexander
Lewis, Thomas
Lincoln, Jeremy Arlo
Lippett, Ronnie Leon
Lipps, Louis Adam

Robinson, Chris
Robinson, Clifford Ralph
Robinson, Crystal
Robinson, Damien
Robinson, David Maurice
Robinson, Eddie Joseph, Jr.
Robinson, Eugene
Robinson, Glenn A.
Robinson, James
Robinson, Larry
Robinson, Marcus
Robinson, R. David
Robinson, Rumeal James
Roby, Reginald Henry
Rodgers, Derrick
Rodman, Dennis Keith
Roe, James Edward, II
Rogers, Carlos Deon
Rogers, Rodney Ray, Jr.
Rogers, Roy, Jr.
Rogers, Sammy Lee
Roland, Jannon
Rollins, Tree
Romes, Charles Michael
Rooks, Sean Lester
Rose, Jalen
Rose, Malik Jabari
Roundfield, Danny Thomas
Roundtree, Saudia
Royal, Andre Tierre
Royal, Donald
Roye, Orpheus
Rozier, Clifford Glen, II
Rudd, Dwayne
Ruffin, John Walter, Jr.
Russell, Bryon Demetrise
Russell, Campy
Russell, Darrell
Salaam, Rashaan
Salley, John Thomas
Sam, Sheri
Sampson, Charles
Sampson, Ralph
Sanders, Barry
Sanders, Chris
Sanders, Deion Luwynn
Sanders, Frank Vondel
Sanders, Michael Anthony
Sanders, Reginald Laverne
Sanders, Ricky Wayne
Sapp, Warren
Sawyer, Corey
Sconiers, Daryl Anthony
Scott, Brent
Scott, Chad
Scott, Darnay
Scott, Dennis Eugene
Scott, Shawnelle
Scott, Todd Carlton
Scroggins, Tracy
Scurlock, Michael
Seale, Samuel Ricardo
Seals, Raymond Bernard
Seals, Shea
Sealy, Malik
Searcy, Leon, Jr.
Seigler, Dexter
Sewell, Steven Edward
Shackleford, Charles
Shade, Sam
Shammgod, God
Sharpe, Shannon
Sharper, Darren
Sharperson, Michael Tyrone
Shaw, Brian K.
Shaw, Sedrick
Shaw, Terrance
Shaw, Willie G.
Shedd, Kenny
Sheffield, Gary Antonian
Shello, Kendel
Shelton, Bryan
Shelton, Daimon
Shepherd, Leslie Glenard
Shields, Will Herthie
Shockley, Alonzo Hilton, Jr.
Shumpert, Terrance Darnell
Sierra, Ruben Angel
Sievers, Eric Scott
Sifford, Charlie
Siglar, Ricky Allan
Simien, Tracy Anthony
Simmons, Clyde, Jr.
Simmons, Edward
Simmons, Lionel J.
Simmons, Ron
Simmons, Wayne General
Simpkins, Dickey
Simpson, Carl Wilhelm

Simpson, Darla
Simpson, Ralph Derek
Sims, Keith
Sinclair, Michael Glenn
Singletary, Reggie
Singleton, Alshermond
Singleton, Chris
Singleton, Nate
Slade, Christopher Carroll
Slater, Jackie Ray
Slater, Reggie
Slocumb, Heathcliff
Small, Torrance
Smedley, Eric
Smith, Al Fredrick
Smith, Anthony
Smith, Antowain
Smith, Ben
Smith, Bruce Bernard
Smith, Bubba
Smith, Cedric Delon
Smith, Charles C.
Smith, Charles Daniel, Jr.
Smith, Charles Henry, III
Smith, Charlotte
Smith, Chris G.
Smith, Darrin Andrew
Smith, Dennis
Smith, Derek Ervin
Smith, Detron Negil
Smith, Doug
Smith, Emmitt J., III
Smith, Fernando Dewitt
Smith, Frankie L.
Smith, Irvin Martin
Smith, James Odell
Smith, Jermaine
Smith, Jimmy Lee, Jr.
Smith, Kevin Rey
Smith, Lamar
Smith, Lee Arthur
Smith, Leonard Phillip
Smith, Lonnie
Smith, Marquette
Smith, Michael John
Smith, Neil
Smith, Otis
Smith, Otis Fitzgerald
Smith, Ozzie
Smith, Robert Scott
Smith, Rod
Smith, Rodney Marc
Smith, Steven Delano
Smith, Stevin
Smith, Thomas Lee, Jr.
Smith, Tommie
Smith, Tony
Smith, Vernice Carlton
Smith, Vinson Robert
Snow, Eric
Snow, Percy Lee
Solomon, Freddie
Sosa, Samuel
Sowell, Jerald
Sparks, Phillippi Dwaine
Sparrow, Rory Darnell
Spears, Marcus
Spellman, Alonzo Robert
Spencer, Felton LaFrance
Spencer, James Arthur, Jr.
Spikes, Irving
Spinks, Michael
Sprewell, Latrell
Spriggs, Marcus
Springs, Shawn
Spurlock, Racquel
Stackhouse, Jerry Darnell
Stafford, Trisha
Staley, Dawn
Staley, Duce
Stallings, Ramondo Antonio
Stallworth, John Lee
Stargell, Tony
Starks, John Levell
Steed, Joel Edward
Stephens, Jamain
Stephens, Joseph, Jr.
Stephenson, Dwight Eugene
Steward, Kordell
Stewart, David Keith
Stewart, James Ottis, III
Stewart, Kebu
Stewart, Kordell
Stewart, Larry
Stewart, Michael
Stewart, Rayna Cottrell
Stewart, Ryan
Stewart, Shannon Harold
Still, Art Barry

Still, Bryan Andrei
Still, Valerie
Stinson, Andrea
Stith, Bryant Lamonica
Stokes, J. J.
Stone, Dwight
Stone, Ronald
Stone, Toni
Stoudmaire, Damon
Stoutmire, Omar
Strahan, Michael Anthony
Strawberry, Darryl
Strickland, Erick
Strickland, Fredrick William, Jr.
Strickland, Mark
Strickland, Rodney
Stringer, Korey
Strong, Derek Lamar
Strong, Mack
Stubblefield, Dana William
Stubbs, Daniel, II
Styles, Lorenzo
Suber, Tora
Swann, Eric Jerrod
Sweatt, James L., III
Swinger, Rashod
Swoopes, Sheryl
Talley, Darryl Victor
Tanner, Barron
Tarpley, Roy James, Jr.
Tate, David
Tate, Deanna
Tate, Sonja
Tatum, Kinnon
Taylor, Aaron Matthew
Taylor, Bobby
Taylor, Charley R.
Taylor, Jason
Taylor, Johnny
Taylor, Lawrence Julius
Taylor, Maurice De Shawn
Teagle, Terry Michael
Teague, George Theo
Templeton, Garry Lewis
Terry, Rick
Tharpe, Larry
Theus, Reggie
Thierry, John Fitzgerald
Thigpen, Yancey Dirk
Thomas, Blair
Thomas, Broderick
Thomas, Calvin Lewis
Thomas, Chris Eric
Thomas, Dave G.
Thomas, Debi
Thomas, Deon
Thomas, Derrick Vincent
Thomas, Eric Jason
Thomas, Frank Edward
Thomas, Fred
Thomas, Henry Lee, Jr.
Thomas, Hollis
Thomas, J.T.
Thomas, Jim
Thomas, John
Thomas, Kurt Vincent
Thomas, Lamar Nathaniel
Thomas, Orlando
Thomas, Rodney Dejuane
Thomas, Rodney Lamar
Thomas, Thurman Lee
Thomas, Tim
Thomas, William Harrison, Jr.
Thompson, Bennie
Thompson, Kevin
Thompson, LaSalle, III
Thompson, Milt
Thompson, Ryan Orlando
Thompson, Sharon
Thompson, Tina
Thornton, Andre
Thorpe, Otis Henry
Threatt, Sedale Eugene
Thurmond, Nate
Tidwell, Billy Joe
Tillman, Cedric
Timmons, Ozzie
Timpson, Michael Dwain
Tinsley, Lee Owen
Tipton, Danell
Tisdale, Waymon Lawrence
Tolbert, Tony Lewis
Toler, Penny
Toney, Anthony
Tongue, Reginald Clinton
Toomer, Amani
Tovar, Steven Eric
Townsend, Andre
Trapp, James

Traylor, Keith
Tremitiere, Chantel
Trent, Gary Dajaun
Trice, Trena
Truitt, Olanda
Tubbs, Winfred O'Neal
Tucker, Michael Anthony
Tuggle, Jessie Lloyd
Tunsil, Necole
Turnbull, Renaldo Antonio
Turner, Eric
Turner, Scott
Tyler, B. J.
Tyson, Mike
Tyus, Wyomia
Upshaw, Gene
Upshaw, Regan
Upshaw, Willie Clay
Uwaezuoke, Iheanyi
Valentine, Darnell
Van Dyke, Alex
Van Exel, Nick
Vanover, Tamarick
Vaughn, David, III
Vaughn, Gregory Lamont
Vaughn, Jacque
Vaughn, Mo
Vaught, Loy Stephon
Venable, Max
Vickers, Kipp E.
Vincent, Troy
Vinson, Anthony
Wade, Terrell
Waldroup, Kerwin
Walker, Antoine Devon
Walker, Bracey Wordell
Walker, Chester
Walker, Darnell Robert
Walker, Darrell
Walker, Denard
Walker, Derrick Norval
Walker, Gary Lamar
Walker, Herschel
Walker, Jay
Walker, Kenneth
Walker, Samaki Ijuma
Walker, Wayne
Walker, Wesley Darcel
Wallace, Aaron
Wallace, Ben
Wallace, John
Wallace, Rasheed Abdul
Wallace, Robert Eugene, Jr.
Wallace, Steve
Ward, Charlie, Jr.
Ward, Dedric
Ward, Gary Lamell
Ward, Melvin Fitzgerald, Sr.
Ward, Ronnie
Warren, Christopher Collins, Jr.
Warren, Lamont
Warrick, Bryan Anthony
Washington, Claudell
Washington, Dante Deneen
Washington, Dewayne Neron
Washington, Eric
Washington, Lionel
Washington, MaliVai
Washington, Marvin Andrew
Washington, Mickey Lynn
Washington, Ted
Waters, Andre
Watkins, Melvin
Watson, Robert Jose
Watters, Richard James
Watts, Damon Shanel
Way, Charles Christopher
Weatherspoon, Clarence
Weatherspoon, Teresa
Webb, Richmond Jewel
Webb, Spud
Webb, Umeki
Webber, Chris
Webster, Larry Melvin, Jr.
Webster, Lenny
Webster, Marvin Nathaniel
Wesley, David
West, Doug
West, Edward Lee, III
West, Mark Andre
Westbrook, Bryant
Westbrook, Michael
Whatley, Ennis
Wheat, DeJuan Shontez
Wheatley, Tyrone
Wheaton, Kenny
Wheeler, Leonard Tyrone
Wheeler, Mark Anthony
Whigham, Larry Jerome

Whitaker, Louis Rodman
Whitaker, Pernell
White, Devon Markes
White, Frank, Jr.
White, Jo Jo
White, Randy
White, Reginald Howard
White, Rondell Bernard
White, Rory Wilbur
White, Steven
White, William Eugene
Whiten, Mark Anthony
Whitfield, Robert
Whiting, Val
Whitmore, Darrell
Whitney, Christopher Antoine
Whittington, Bernard M.
Wideman, Jamila
Wiggins, Mitchell
Wiley, Marcellus
Wiley, Morlon David
Wilkerson, Bruce Alan
Wilkerson, Dana
Wilkes, Jamaal
Wilkes, Reggie Wayman
Wilkins, Dominique
Wilkins, Gabriel Nicholas
Wilkins, Gerald Bernard
Wilkinson, Dan
Williams, Aaron
Williams, Aeneas Demetrius
Williams, Alfred Hamilton
Williams, Alvin
Williams, Armon
Williams, Bernie
Williams, Beverly
Williams, Brian
Williams, Brian Carson
Williams, Brian O'Neal
Williams, Buck
Williams, Calvin John, Jr.
Williams, Charlie
Williams, Clarence
Williams, Daniel
Williams, Darryl Edwin
Williams, Eric C.
Williams, Erik George
Williams, Eugene
Williams, Gerald Floyd
Williams, Gerome
Williams, Gus
Williams, Harvey Lavance
Williams, Herb L.
Williams, Jamel
Williams, James Edward
Williams, James Otis
Williams, Jarvis Eric
Williams, Jay Omar
Williams, Jayson
Williams, Jerome
Williams, John
Williams, Karl
Williams, Kenny Ray
Williams, Kevin Ray
Williams, Kim
Williams, Lorenzo
Williams, Michael Douglas
Williams, Moe
Williams, Monty
Williams, Natalie
Williams, Pat
Williams, Reggie
Williams, Ron Robert
Williams, Scott Christopher
Williams, Serena
Williams, Sherman
Williams, Stepfret
Williams, Tara
Williams, Tyrone
Williams, Tyrone
Williams, Venus Ebone Starr
Williams, Wally James, Jr.
Williams, Walter Ander
Williams, Willie James, Jr.
Williamson, Carlton
Williamson, Corliss Mondari
Willis, James Edward, II
Willis, Kevin Alvin
Wilson, Bernard
Wilson, Jerry
Wilson, Michael
Wilson, Reinard
Wilson, Trevor
Wilson, Walter James
Wilson, Willie James
Wimberly, Marcus
Winchester, Kennard
Winder, Sammy
Winfield, David Mark

Fernandez, John Peter
Franklin, Wayne L.
Gates, Jacquelyn Burch
Gibbons, Walter E.
Grayson, Byron J., Sr.
Gregory, Bernard Vincent
Grier, Johnny
Heyward, Ilene Patricia
Hite, Nancy Ursula
Hodges, Patricia Ann
Honore, Stephan LeRoy
Hoppes, Alice Faye
Huggins, Linda Johnson
Jackson, Georgina
Jackson, Shirley Ann
James, Charles Ford
James, Ronald
Jeter, Joseph C., Jr.
Johnson, Jerry L.
Lawson, Bruce B.
Lewis, Charles McArthur
Logan, Harold James
Love, Jon
Mateen, Malik Abdul
Miller, Andrea Lewis
Montgomery, Ethel Constance
Morris, Bernard Alexander
Nobles, Patricia Joyce
Owens, Brigman
Owens, Victor Allen
Phillips, Eric McLaren, Jr.
Pickens, William Garfield
Pinkney, John Edward
Reed, Derryl L.
Rice, Cora Lee
Robinson, Jack E.
Rockett, Damon Emerson
Salaam, Abdul
Savage, James Edward, Jr.
Simmons, Thelma M.
Smith, Anthony Edward
Smith, Beverly Evans
Spradling, Mary Elizabeth Mace
Spurlock, James B., Jr.
Stevenson, Unice Teen
Stovall, Audrean
Summers, Retha
Travis, Alexander B.
Turner, Robert S., Jr.
Walker, Vernon David
Washington, William Montell
Wells, Robert Benjamin, Jr.
Wesley, Clemon Herbert, Jr.
Whaley, Charles H., IV
Williams, Vernice Louise
Winbush, Clarence, Jr.
Wing, Theodore W., II
Wood, Leigh C.
Woodie, Henry L.
Wordlaw, Clarence, Jr.

Television/Cable Broadcasting Industry

Abney, Robert
Allen, Marcus
Anderson, Bernadine M.
Arnold, John Russell, Jr.
Bailey, William H.
Baldwin, Louis J.
Barden, Don H.
Baxter, Albert James, II
Bell, Victory
Bellamy, Bill
Berry, Ondra Lamon
Blackwell, Faye Brown
Bolden, John Henry
Bond, John Percy, III
Boston, McKinley, Jr.
Boulware, Patricia A.
Bowser, Kyle D.
Brittain, Bradley Bernard, Jr.
Brooks, Sheila Dean
Brown, Ellen Rochelle
Brownlee, Jack M.
Bryant, Kathryn Ann
Bush, Charles Vernon
Cafritz, Peggy Cooper
Cannon, Reuben
Cartwright, Carole B.
Castro, George A.
Champion, Jesse
Cheatham, Henry Boles
Christian, Spencer
Clayton, Xernona
Cochran, S. Thomas
Cole, Lydia
Collinet, Georges Andre
Collins, Tessil John

Cooley, Wendy
Cornelius, Don
Cornwell, W. Don
Coward, Onida Lavoneia
Coye, Dena E.
Craft, Sally-Ann Roberts
Crippens, David L.
Crombaugh, Hallie
Crump, Janice Renae
Culbreath-Manly, Tongila M.
Davis, Evelyn Payne
Davis, Frederick D.
Davis, Preston A., Jr.
Dejoie, Michael C.
Denson, Fred L.
Dilday, William Horace, Jr.
Dixon, Valena Alice
Dorsey, Sandra
Dunn, Bruce Eric
Dyer, Joe, Jr.
Easter, Eric Kevin
Edwards, Delores A.
Edwards, George R.
Evans, Liz
Ferguson, Joel
Ferguson, Renee
Flake, Nancy Aline
Fortune-Maginley, Lois J.
Fox, Charles Washington, III
Gaines, Adriane Theresa
Gaines, Mary E.
George, Pauline L.
Gibbs, Karen Patricia
Giles, Henrietta
Gordon-Dillard, Joan Yvonne
Grandberry, Nikki
Greer, Karyn Lynette
Griffith, Mark Richard
Grinstead, Amelia Ann
Guitano, Anton W.
Hagan, Gwenael Stephane
Hall, Arsenio
Hamm, Barbara Lawanda
Hampton, Henry Eugene, Jr.
Haney, Don Lee
Hansen, Wendell Jay
Harrell, Andre
Hatcher, Jeffrey F.
Hawthorne, Angel L.
Hayward, Ann Stewart
Hayward, Jacqueline C.
Hazel, Janis D.
Henderson, Eddie L.
Herman, Kathleen Virgil
Hill, Mervin E., Jr.
Hobson, Charles Blagrove
Holden, Aaron Charles
Holloway, Douglas V.
Horton, Dollie Bea Dixon
Howard, Samuel H.
Hudson, Dianne Atkinson
Huff, Janice Wages
Isaacs McCoy, Leslie Ellen
Jackson, Beverly Anne
Jackson, Beverly Joyce
Jackson, Donald J.
Jackson, Eugene D.
Jaycox, Mary Irine
Jenkins, Carol Ann
Jessup, Gayle Louise
Johnson, Chas Floyd
Johnson, Dennis
Johnson, Henry Wade
Johnson, Iola Vivian
Johnson, Jay
Johnson, Mal
Jones, Cheryl Arleen
Jones, James Wesley
Jones, Leonade Diane
Jones, Marcus Edmund
Jones, Victoria C.
Joseph, Lloyd Leroi
Karpeh, Enid Juah Hildegard
Kennard, Patricia A.
Kinchlow, Harvey Ben
King, Brett
Klausner, Willette Murphy
Lamont, Barbara
LaMotte, Jean Moore
Langford, Debra Lynn
Lawson, Debra Ann
Lawson, Jennifer Karen
LeCompte, Peggy Lewis
Lee, Jefferi K.
LeFlore, Lyah
Levy, Victor Miles, Jr.
Lewis, Ananda
Lewis, Byron E.
Lewis, Maurice

Lewis, Ronald Stephen
Llewellyn, James Bruce
Love, Thomas Clifford
Lowry, William E., Jr.
Manley, Dexter
Marbury, Donald Lee
Marshall, Patricia Prescott
Martin, Carol
Matchett, Johnson, Jr.
Mathews, Keith E.
McCovey, Willie Lee
McCree, Edward L.
McEwen, Mark
McEwing, Mitchell Dalton
McGee, Henry Wadsworth, III
McGee, James H.
McKee, Clarence Vanzant, Jr.
McKee, Lonette
McNeal, Timothy Kyle
Melton, Frank LeRoy
Mercer, Arthur, Sr.
Miller, Lamar Perry
Minter, Kendall Arthur
Mohamed, Gerald R., Jr.
Moodie, Dahlia Maria
Moore, Cynthia M.
Moore, George Anthony
Moore, Gregory B.
Morris, Dolores N.
Morrison, Ronald E.
Morse, Mildred S.
Murray, James P.
Murray, John W.
Myles, Stan, Jr.
Myrick, Clarissa
Neal, Charlie
Nightingale-Hawkins, Monica R.
Ollison, Ruth Allen
Owens, Debbie A.
Palmer, Darlene Tolbert
Perry, Alexis E.
Perryman, Lavonia Lauren
Petty, Bob
Pinkney, Rose Catherine
Pool-Eckert, Marquita Jones
Posey, Deborah
Pounds, Elaine
Poussaint, Renee Francine
Powell, Adam Clayton, III
Powell, Kevin
Prelow, Arleigh
Price, Ray Anthony
Purvis, Archie C., Jr.
Ramsey, Jerome Capistrano
Rashad, Ahmad
Revish, Jerry
Rickman, Ray
Riley, Glenn Pleasants
Roberts, Kim A.
Roberts, Michael V.
Robinson, John L.
Robinson, Johnathan Prather
Robinson, Robin
Rodgers, Johnathan A.
Rogers, David William
Rolle, Janet
Ryan-White, Jewell
Scafe, Judith Arlene
Scott, Robert Jerome
Scott, Samuel
Simmons-Edelstein, Dee
Simpson, Donnie
Simpson, O. J.
Singleton, Kenneth Wayne
Small, Sydney L.
Smith, Barbara
Smith, Gerald Wayne
Smith, Joseph F.
Stewart, Bernard
Talbert, Ted
Tang, Deborah Canada
Taylor, Ellis Clarence, Sr.
Taylor, Miles Edward
Thomas, Arthur Lafayette, III
Thomas, Janis P.
Thomas-Samuel, Kalin Normoet
Thoms, Donald H.
Townsend, Ron
Tuller, John
Vaughan, James Edward
Vincent, Irving H.
Wallace, Arnold D., Sr.
Warfield, Robert N.
Washington, Carl Douglas
Waters, Brenda Joyce
Waters, Paul Eugene, Jr.
Watkins, Sylvestre C., Sr.
Watson, Ben
Watson, Karen Elizabeth

Watts, Rolanda
Waugh, Judith Ritchie
Webb, Clifton Alan
White, Winifred Viaria
Whitehead, Eddie L.
Wiegand-Moss, Richard Clifton, Jr.
Williams, Benjamin Vernon
Williams, Charlene J.
Williams, Joanne Louise
Williams, Montel
Wilson, Robert Lee Miles
Winfrey, Oprah
Winn, Carol Denise
Woodbeck, Frank Raymond
Worford, Carolyn Kennedy
Yancey, Laurel Guild
Yearwood, David Monroe, Jr.
Young, George, Jr.
Zola, Nkenge

Translation/Interpretation

Hodges, Patricia Ann
Jackson, William Ed

Transportation/Moving Services

Aiken, William
Allen, Bernestine
Allen, Stanley M.
Allen, Ty W.
Atkinson, Eugenia Calwise
Baker, Robert N.
Barnes, Ronald Lewis
Black, Billy Charleston
Black, Walter Kerrigan
Bledsoe, Melvin
Bond, Alan D.
Branker, Julian Michael
Brazil, Robert D.
Brown, Edward Lynn
Browne, Vincent Jefferson, Jr.
Buckson, Toni Yvonne
Burks, James William, Jr.
Burts, Ezunial
Butler, Roy
Carter, Will J.
Clark, Leon Henry
Claybourne, Edward P.
Cooke, Thomas H., Jr.
Copeland, Richard Allen
Cormier, Lawrence J.
Curry, Jerry Ralph
DeLibero, Shirley A.
Diane, Mamadi
Dottin, Roger Allen
Duncan, Sandra Rhodes
Edwards, Horace Burton
Ferguson, Elliott LaRoy, II
Ferguson, Sherlon Lee
Fisher, George Carver
Florence, Johnny C.
Frazier, Joe
Gabriel, Benjamin Moses
Garrett, Melvin Alboy
George, Edward
Green, Roland, Sr.
Griffith, John A.
Gulley, Wilson
Hall, Brian Edward
Hampton, Thomas Earle
Harris, Archie Jerome
Harris, David Ellsworth
Hart, Christopher Alvin
Henderson, Gerald
Henry, I. Patricia
Hicks, Henderson
Hill, Arthur Burit
Hogan, Carolyn Ann
Holloway, Albert Curtis
Hunter, John W.
Jackson, Fred H., Jr.
James, Charles H., III
James, John
Johnson, Albert James
Jones, Eva
Jones, Frank Benson
Jordan, Josephine E. C.
Kendrick, L. John, Sr.
Lee, John Robert E.
Lewis, Samuel, Jr.
Logan-Tooson, Linda Ann
Mansell, Buford H. L.
Martin, Angela M. Coker
Martin, Frank T.
McClellan, Frank Madison

Medford, Isabel
Merritt, Thomas Mack
Moore, Alstork Edward
Moore, David Bernard, II
Moore, Katherine Bell
Morris, John P., III
Neizer, Meredith Ann
Newhouse, Robert F.
Norwood, William R.
Patterson, Charles Jerry
Perry, John B.
Petersen, Arthur Everett, Jr.
Pitcher, Frederick M. A.
Price, James Rogers
Robinson, Albert Arnold
Robinson, Daniel Lee
Robinson, Kenneth
Rounsaville, Lucious Brown, Jr.
Scott, Beverly Angela
Sigler, I. Garland
Simmons, Eric O.
Simon, Rosalyn McCord
Smith, LeRoi Matthew-Pierre, III
Spencer, Rozelle Jeffery
Stewart, Ronald Patrick
Stokes, Rueben Martine
Taylor, Martha
Thomas, Charles W.
Tyree, Patricia Grey
Waters, Kathryn
Wedgeworth, Robert, Jr.
White, Gary Leon
Whitehead, James T., Jr.
Wilkinson, Marie L.
Williams, Bruce E.
Williams, Lisa R.
Winder, Alfred M.

Travel Industry

Bailey, Myrtle Lucille
Bridgewater, Herbert Jeremiah, Jr.
Bright, Kirk
Burns, Leonard L.
Campbell, Blanch
Campbell, Franklyn D.
Davis, Adrianne
Davis, Agnes Maria
DeMille, Darcy
Dildy, Catherine Greene
Gardner, Ava Maria
Grimsley, Ethelyne
Harris, David Ellsworth
Henderson, Freddye Scarborough
Henderson, Jacob R.
Jackson, Mary
James, Timothy Arcee
Johnson, Fran
Miller, Saundra Celia
Mingo, Pauline Hylton
Norman, William S.
Paul, Wanda D.
Pitcher, Frederick M. A.
Plinton, James O., Jr.
Quick, R. Edward
Rochester, Geof
Saunders, Barbara Ann
Sessoms, Glenn D.
Shumate, Glen
Skinner, Robert L., Jr.
Spears, Stephanie
Spencer, Brenda L.
Strong, Otis Reginald, III
Taylor, Cassandra W.
Taylor, Valerie Charmayne
Walker, Eugene Kevin
Williams, W. Bill, Jr.
Wilson, Charles Lee, Sr.
Wilson, Markly

Urban/Regional Planning

Allen, Charles Claybourne
Arbuckle, John Finley, Jr.
Armstead, Ron E.
Bennett, Maybelle Taylor
Best, Jennings H.
Black, Malcolm Mazique
Blayton-Taylor, Betty
Bridges, Leon
Brooks, Dunbar
Brown, John Scott
Brown, Norman E.
Burnett, Luther C.
Campbell, Wendell J.
Cason, David, Jr.
Catlin, Robert A.
Coleman, Hurley J., Jr.
Colston, Monroe James

Fanaka, Jamaa
Fisher, Edith Maureen
Fornay, Alfred R., Jr.
Foster, Cecil A.
Franklin, J. E.
Fraser, George C.
French, MaryAnn
Fulwood, Sam, III
Gates, Henry Louis, Jr.
Gibson, Donald B.
Giddings, Paula Jane
Gilbert, Herman Cromwell
Gill, Laverne McCain
Gill, Troy D.
Gillespie, Marcia A.
Gilmore, Al Tony
Green-Campbell, Deardra Delores
Greenwood, Theresa M. Winfrey
Grigsby, Lucy Clemmons
Grosvenor, Verta Mae
Guy, Rosa Cuthbert
Guy-Sheftall, Beverly
Hall, Addie June
Halliburton, Warren J.
Hamilton, Paul L.
Hamilton, Virginia
Harris, Eddy Louis
Harris, Francis C.
Harris, Trudier
Harris McKenzie, Ruth Bates
Haskins, James S.
Haskins, James W., Jr.
Hayden, Robert C., Jr.
Hewitt, John H., Jr.
Holland, J. Archibald
Holman, Benjamin F.
Holt, Deloris Lenette
Hoover, Felix A.
Howard, Janice Lynn
Howard, Joseph H.
Hudson, Theodore R.
Hutchinson, Earl Ofari
Hyman, Mark J.
Ingrum, Adrienne G.
Ione, Carole
Jackson, Garnet Nelson
Jackson, Harold Jerome
Jackson, Kennell A., Jr.
Jackson, LaToya
Jamison, Lafayette
Jarrett, Hobart Sidney
Jellerette deJongh, Monique
  Evadne
Johnson, Georgia Anna Lewis
Jones, Edward Louis
Jones-Wilson, Faustine Clarisse
Jordan, June M.
Kaiser, Ernest Daniel
Kashif, Ghayth Nur
Kelley, William Melvin
Keyes, Alan L.
Kimbro, Dennis Paul
Kimbrough, Marjorie L.
Kincaid, Jamaica
King, Anita
Kirby, Money Alian
Kotto, Yaphet
Kunjufu, Jawanza
Lamar, Jake
Larkin, Byrdie A.
Larrie, Reginald Reese, Ph.D.
Layton, William W.
Lee, Andrea
Lester, Julius
Lewis, David Levering
Liverpool, Charles Eric
London, Clement B. G.
Long, Richard A.
Madhubuti, Haki R.
Madison, Eddie L., Jr.
Mapp, Edward C.
Marcere, Norma Snipes
Marr, Warren, II
Marshall, Albert Prince
Mason, Brenda Diane
Mathabane, Mark Johannes
Mathes, James R.
McCall, Nathan
McConnell, Roland C.
McElroy, Colleen J.
McKee, Adam E., Jr.
McKissack, Fredrick Lem, Sr.
McKissack, Patricia Carwell
Meek, Russell Charles
Meriwether, Louise
Meriwether, Roy Dennis
Millican, Arthenia J. Bates
Mindolovich, Monica Harris
Moody, Anne

Moore, Lenard Duane
Moore, Shelley Lorraine
Moorehead, Eric K.
Morton, Cynthia Neverdon
Muhammad, Valencia
Mumford, Esther Hall
Murray, Albert L.
Murray, Virgie W.
Nelson, Jill
Nettleford, Rex Milton
Nivens, Beatryce Thomasinia
Noles, Eva M.
Norman, Bobby Don
Omolade, Barbara
Page, Clarence
Page, James Allen
Patton, Jean E.
Pawley, Thomas D., III
Pemberton, Gayle R.
Perkins, Myla Levy
Perry, Margaret
Pinkney, Alphonso
Pinson, Hermine Dolorez
Porter, Henry Lee
Porter, Michael LeRoy
Porter, Roy Lee
Pratt, J. C.
Prelow, Arleigh
Price, Suzanne Davis
Rackley, Lurma M.
Ralph, Sheryl Lee
Rampersad, Arnold
Ransby, Barbara
Redmond, Eugene B.
Richardson, Odis Gene
Riley, Dorothy Winbush
Roberts, Hermese E.
Roberts, Tara Lynette
Robeson, Paul, Jr.
Robinson, Ella S.
Robinson, William Henry
Rodney, Martin Hurtus
Russell, Sandra Anita
Saint James, Synthia
Sampson, Calvin Coolidge
Sandoval, Dolores S.
Saunders, Doris E.
Scruggs-Leftwich, Yvonne
Sharp, Saundra
Shields, Cydney Robin
Shockley, Ann Allen
Simms, Darrell Dean
Small, Kenneth Lester
Smith, Barbara
Smith, Charles U.
Smith, Jessie Carney
Smith, Robert L. T., Sr.
Smythe-Haith, Mabel Murphy
Sowell, Thomas
Steele, Shelby
Stephens, Brooke Marilyn
Stepto, Robert Burns
Stewart, John Othneil
Stratton-Morris, Madeline
  Robinson Morgan
Strayhorn, Lloyd
Tarry, Ellen
Tate, Merze
Taulbert, Clifton LeMoure
Thelwell, Michael M. Ekwueme
Thomas, Ron
Tollett, Charles Albert, Sr.
Travis, Dempsey J.
Tyehimba, Cheo Taylor
Van Peebles, Melvin
Walker, Alice Malsenior
Walker, Sheila Suzanne
Walter, Mildred Pitts
Washington, Rudy
Watkins, Sylvestre C., Sr.
Watson, Denton L.
Watson, Thomas S., Jr.
West, Cornel
White, Constance C. R.
White, Phillip, III
Whitehurst, Steven Laroy
Wiley, Ralph
Wilkins, Roger Wood
Williams, Ethel Langley
Williams, John Alfred
Williams, Sherley Anne
Wilson, Joseph F.
Witherspoon, William Roger
Woodhouse, Rossalind Yvonne
Wright, Charles Stevenson
Wynter, Leon E.
Young, B. Ashley
Young, Margaret Buckner

Writing/Editing—Plays, Screenplays, TV Scripts

Abney, Robert
Angelou, Maya
Baraka, Imamu Amiri
Beckham, Barry Earl
Benson, James Russell
Bolling, Carol Nicholson
Bradley, Andrew Thomas, Sr.
Bradley, David Henry, Jr.
Branch, Otis Linwood
Branch, William Blackwell
Brown, Reginald DeWayne
Brown-Guillory, Elizabeth
Bullins, Ed
Burns, Khephra
Caldwell, Benjamin
Clark, Fred Allen
Clay, Stanley Bennett
Cleage, Pearl Michelle
Coleman, Wanda
Coles, Kim
Colley, Nathaniel S.
Collie, Kelsey E.
Collins, Tessil John
Cooper, Barry Michael
Cooper, J. California
Cowden, Michael E.
Dash, Hugh M. H.
de Jongh, James Laurence
Dent, Thomas Covington
Dickey, Eric Jerome
Dunham, Katherine
Evans, Mari
Fales, Susan
Fax, Elton C.
Fewell, Richard
Franklin, J. E.
Fuller, Charles
Goss, Clayton
Greaves, William
Gregory, Sylver K.
Hairston, William
Hamilton, Arthur Lee, Jr.
Harris, Tom W.
Harris, William Anthony
Harrison, Paul Carter
Hobson, Charles Blagrove
Hudlin, Reginald Alan
Hudson, Frederick Douglass
Ione, Carole
James, Hawthorne
James, Luther
Jefferson, Roland Spratlin, M.D.
Kennedy, Adrienne Lita
Keymah, Crystal T'Keyah
King, Woodie, Jr.
Kotto, Yaphet
Lane, Charles
Lee, Spike
Lemmons, Kasi
Lucas, Wilmer Francis, Jr.
McElroy, Colleen J.
McNeill, Cerves Todd
Mitchell, Loften
Molette, Carlton Woodard, II
Moore, Lenard Duane
Moss, Winston
Mumford, Thaddeus Quentin, Jr.
Naylor, Gloria
Page, Harrison Eugene
Pawley, Thomas D., III
Penny, Robert L.
Perry, Felton
Powell, Kevin
Pryor, Richard
Reid, Tim
Rich, Matty
Richardson, Odis Gene
Robinson, Ella S.
Robinson, Matt
Russell, Charlie L.
Scott, John Sherman
Scott, Larry B.
Scott, Robert Jerome
Shange, Ntozake
Sharp, Saundra
Shelton, Millicent Beth
Singleton, John
Smith, Anna Deavere
Stetson, Jeffrey P.
Thomas, Joyce Carol
Tillman, George, Jr.
Townsend, Robert
Van Peebles, Mario
Van Peebles, Melvin
Vasquez, Joseph B.
Wade, Kim Mache
Wagoner, J. Robert

Ward, Douglas Turner
Wayans, Damon
Wesley, Richard Errol
West, Cheryl L.
Wiley, Ralph
Williams, Dick Anthony
Williams, John Alfred
Williams, Kimmika L. H.
Williams, Samm-Art
Wilson, August
Wilson, Sandra E.
Wolfe, George C.
Wood, Lawrence Alvin
Zu-Bolton, Ahmos, II

Writing/Editing—Poetry

Abdul, Raoul
Alexander, Estella Conwill
Allen, Samuel Washington
Angelou, Maya
Arnez, Nancy L.
Atkins, Russell
Aubert, Alvin Bernard
Bacon, Charlotte Meade
Baraka, Imamu Amiri
Bellinger, Mary Anne
Berhe, Annette Toney
Berkley, Constance E. Gresham
Boyd, Louise Yvonne
Brewton, Butler E.
Brooks, Gwendolyn
Brooks, Rosemary Bittings
Brown, Barbara Mahone
Brutus, Dennis Vincent
Bullett, Audrey Kathryn
Bunyon, Ronald S.
Butler, Washington Roosevelt, Jr.
Cain, Johnnie M.
Chase-Riboud, Barbara DeWayne
Chinn, John Clarence
Clarke, LeRoy P.
Clifton, Lucille
Coleman, Ronald K.
Coleman, Wanda
Cortez, Jayne
Cowden, Michael E.
Cox, Joseph Mason Andrew
Dejoie, Carolyn Barnes Milanes
Dent, Thomas Covington
Derricotte, Toi
Dove, Rita Frances
Evans, Mari
Faust, Naomi Flowe
Fortson, Elnora Agnes
Gilbert, Christopher
Giovanni, Nikki
Golightly, Lena Mills
Gomez, Jewelle L.
Green, Barbara-Marie
Greenlee, Sam
Grimes, Nikki
Grosvenor, Verta Mae
Hairston, William
Hardy, Dorothy C.
Harper, Michael Steven
Harris, Margaret R.
Henderson, David
Hogue, Leslie Denise
Hoppes, Alice Faye
Hord, Frederick Lee
Hull, Akasha
Jackson, Fred James, Sr.
Jackson, Garnet Nelson
Jackson, Suzanne Fitzallen
Jenkins, Frank Shockley
Johnson, Joe
Jones, Gayl
Jordan, June M.
Kirby, Money Alian
Komunyakaa, Yusef
Lacy, Walter
Lane, Pinkie Gordon
Lester, Julius
Liverpool, Charles Eric
London, Clement B. G.
Madgett, Naomi Long
Madhubuti, Haki R.
Madison, Jacqueline Edwina
Major, Clarence
Marbury, Donald Lee
McClaskey, William H.
McElroy, Colleen J.
McElroy, George A.
McNeil, DeeDee
Miller, Erenest Eugene
Miller, Frank Lee, Jr.
Moore, Lenard Duane
Patterson, Raymond R.

Penny, Robert L.
Porter, Henry Lee
Ramseur, Andre William
Randall, Dudley Felker
Richardson, Nola Mae
Rickson, Gary Ames
Riley, Dorothy Winbush
Robinson, Ella S.
Rodgers, Carolyn Marie
Saint James, Synthia
Scott-Heron, Gil
Scott-Ware, Barbara Ann
Shange, Ntozake
Sharp, Saundra
Simmons, Earl Melvin
Skinner, Ewart C.
Smith, Mary Carter
Smith, Robert L. T., Sr.
Southerland, Ellease
Spears-Jones, Patricia Kay
Steptoe, Lamont Brown
Subryan, Carmen
Tarpley, Natasha Anastasia
Thomas, Joyce Carol
Thompson, Cecil, Sr.
Tillis, Frederick C.
Tisdale, Celes
Troupe, Quincy Thomas, Jr.
Vertreace, Martha Modena
Wade-Gayles, Gloria Jean
Walker, Alice Malsenior
Walker, Margaret Abigail
Ward, Jerry Washington, Jr.
Warren, Nagueyalti
Washington, James W., Jr.
Washington, Oscar D.
Welburn, Ronald Garfield
Whitehurst, Steven Laroy
Wilkinson, Brenda
Williams, John Alfred
Williams, Kimmika L. H.
Williams, Nancy Ellen Webb
Williams, Sherley Anne
Williams, T. Joyce
Williams-Garner, Debra
Windham, Revish
Wright, Sarah E.
Wright, Stephen Caldwell
Zu-Bolton, Ahmos, II

Writing/Editing—Not Elsewhere Classified

Adams, Robert Hugo
Anderson, Betty Keller
Baker-Kelly, Beverly
Bembery, Chester Allen, Jr.
Berhe, Annette Toney
Blanton, Ricky
Brown, Roscoe C., Jr.
Cain, Gerry Ronald
Caines, Bruce Stuart
Ceasar, Sherita Therese
Chambers, John Curry, Jr.
Cleaver, Eldridge
Clifton, Lucille
Coleman, Winson
Costa, Annie Bell Harris
Crews, Donald
Crite, Allan Rohan
Dale, Walter R.
Downs, Crystal
Draper, Everett T., Jr.
Duvall, Henry F., Jr.
Eaton, Lela M. Z.
Edmonds, Terry
Ervin, Hazel Arnett
Evans, Mattie
Flagg, E. Alma W.
Fortune, Gwendoline Y.
Frelow, Robert Lee, Jr.
Golphin, Vincent F. A.
Greenfield, Eloise
Hernton, Calvin Coolidge
Hill, James H.
Hill, Michael Edward
Hill, Paul Gordon
Hogue, Leslie Denise
Holt, Mikel
Howard, Elizabeth Fitzgerald
Jackson, Norlishia A.
Johnson-Helton, Karen
Kazi, Abdul-Khaliq Kuumba
Kinchen, Arif S.
Lindsay, Gwendolyn Ann Burns
Llewellyn-Travis, Chandra
Lockman, Norman Alton
Lucas, James L.
Luis, William